THE WHOLE STORY

3000 years of
sequels and sequences

R

THE WHOLE STORY

3000 years of sequels and sequences

Compiled by
John E Simkin

THORPE

Published 1996 by D W Thorpe,
part of Reed Educational and Professional Publishing
18–22 Salmon Street
Port Melbourne, Victoria 3207
Australia

Reprinted 1997

Email: customer. service @ thorpe. com. au

A division of Reed International Books Pty Ltd ACN 001002357

A Reed Elsevier company

National Library of Australia Cataloguing-in-Publication data

The whole story: 3000 years of sequels and sequences

Includes index.
ISBN 1 875589 26 0

1. Sequels (Literature) – Bibliography. 2. Series (Publications) – Bibliography. 3. English literature – Bibliography

011.48

Typeset in Australia by Veronica Peek
Cover design by Cate Mills
Printed in Australia by McPherson's Printing Group, Maryborough

Availability
In Australia, Thorpe titles are available directly from the publisher. In New Zealand, orders should be placed with Thorpe in Wellington. In the UK and EC, contact Bowker-Saur in East Grinstead, Sussex. In the USA, contact R R Bowker in New Providence, NJ. Throughout Asia, contact Reed Academic in Singapore.

CONTENTS

INTRODUCTION

The appeal of sequels is in their ability to answer the questions: ‘What happened next? Is that the whole story? Did this character do anything else? How would this character act in another set of circumstances?’ It appears that the curiosity of the reading public is increasing if judged by the ever-increasing number of sequels which are being published including those to long-established works by Jane Austen, Emily Brontë, Margaret Mitchell, Daphne du Maurier and others.

There are several kinds of connections between books which qualify them for inclusion in this record of ‘sequels and sequences’. The largest number are those which follow the activities of one or two characters. By far the most numerous is the ‘Sexton Blake’ series. The 1615 titles listed here are certainly not the complete list. It still remains for some fan to publish the definitive bibliography in some accessible medium. Sexton Blake is followed by his American counterpart Nicholas Carter with 632 titles in the original series and 259 in his reincarnation as Nick Carter, a highly sexed spy.

There are also many examples of long sequences in Western fiction with the longest – the ‘Larry and Stretch’ series (428 titles) – by Marshall Grover, an Australian author. Of the science fiction series the longest and still growing, is ‘Doctor Who’ (166 titles) with the German ‘Perry Rhodan’ series of which 137 titles have been translated.

Characters in sequences are sometimes based on real people, such as Eleanor Roosevelt in the detective series by her son, Elliott, and King Edward VII in Peter Lovesey’s ‘Bertie’ series. Series can also be created from a secondary character in fiction. Notable examples are Harry Flashman, the school bully from *Tom Brown’s schooldays*, who has a sequence of his own and Inspector Sholto Lestrade, the detective who tagged along and took credit in some of Sherlock Holmes’ cases; his life is being documented by M J Trow.

Families, some covering generations and centuries, account for over 400 sequences. Some are fictional, eg the 18-volume ‘Sackett family’ series by Louis L’Amour and the growing number of family sequences by Virginia Andrews and her literary successors. Some are factual or based on fact, eg the ‘Norman’, ‘Plantagenet’, and ‘Stuart’ series by Jean Plaidy.

In some cases a place provides the common thread which links the titles in a sequence, as in J T Edson’s ‘Rockabye County’ series or the ‘South London’ series by Mary Jane Staples or, as in J R R Tolkien’s ‘History of Middle Earth’ series, the setting of the original sequence – the ‘Lord of the Rings’ trilogy – provides the background for other stories.

These same works and others by Tolkien exemplify the ‘fantasy history’ sequence. Robert Heinlein’s ‘Future history’ series is another example. These works are distinguished from true historical fiction in that the latter has identifiable events and/or characters. There are few historical events and periods which have not been made the subject of historical fiction sequences from ‘prehistoric’ times to the English, French, Russian and American revolutions and beyond.

My own interest in sequels began at the age of ten. There was an infantile paralysis epidemic in Australia which prevented my brothers and me from going to church and Sunday school so we spent the winter Sunday afternoons around the fire with our mother reading to us from the works of H V Morton. Soon after I was given the job of class librarian in my first year at high school. In sorting through the collection I had inherited I found a copy of *Alice through the looking glass*. I was intrigued by it and wasn’t satisfied until I had a copy of its prequel.

Work on this project began in 1975. At the time I was chief librarian of a public library service in Victoria. Part of my responsibility was management of a co-operative store on behalf of the public libraries of the state. The books deposited in the store were 20th-century literature with related critical and biographical works. About 90% of the contents were fiction. I did most of the cataloguing of books placed in the store in my own time. As I proceeded

I recorded sequels information where it applied. By the time I left the position in 1990 the collection had grown to 96,000 volumes and I had a very large file of sequels information.

Then I began a new career as a bibliographer and indexer. I presented a proposal to D W Thorpe, for whom I have compiled a number of works, that I expand the file to become a comprehensive list of sequels in English. The proposal was accepted and work began in earnest in 1993.

My original estimate was for approximately 58,000 titles. In the event the database on which the book is based has over 85,000 titles in sequences with a further 10,000 related works mentioned in notes. The database is continuing to grow as sequels are being published in what appears to be increasing numbers, especially in the fields of crime, science and fantasy fiction and, particularly in the United Kingdom, of children's fiction.

There are many books which list sequels, some listing sequels information incidental to other critical or bibliographical information. Of those designed primarily to record sequels the most comprehensive to date is the now two-volume work produced by the Association of Assistant Librarians, published originally in 1922. In its earlier editions this work aimed to be comprehensive. However in recent years it has been restricted generally to sequences published since 1950 and represents more or less those volumes which one might find in an English public library. All other lists have some specific focus either in recording sequels in a particular genre or using some criteria for selection related to their use.

In compiling this work I have followed leads from a large number of sources. This has involved a great deal of cross checking in bibliographic sources and in many cases with copies of the works. However, the nature of sequels is such that in some cases there is no definitively correct sequence. Sometimes this applies to the selection of works which actually belong in a particular sequence, in some cases to the order in which the works should be read, while in some cases the works are companion or parallel volumes rather than intended to be read in chronological sequence.

The Whole Story is divided into three sections. They are:

Section I: Sequels and Sequences

All titles, including variants, are listed and numbered, the original title first, with the date of first publication. In the case of titles translated from another language the date is generally that of the original edition; in these cases, where the original title is in a language which uses Roman script and is known, it is given in a note. In cases where series titles have not been supplied by the authors they have been created. Cross-references from all other variations have been provided. Notes supply information about omnibus volumes, volumes of selections and companion volumes; in some cases where one sequence has generated others, reference is made to bibliographic works which may be used to help readers find their way in some quite complicated interrelationships. An example of this kind of note can be found at the end of the 'Star trek' series. The original series has now developed into nine sequences.

Section II: Title Index

All titles, including those in notes, are listed with the sequence or sequences in which they appear.

Section III: Author Index

Includes all authors and, in the case of some picture book illustrators, are listed with (i) the titles of the sequences in which they have created one or more volumes, and (ii) the titles of books which are included in notes with the sequence name and number where they are listed.

Acknowledgments

In the early years of this project my good friend Marion Piper gave valuable help as a dedicated library cataloguer in setting the pattern which has been followed since. In the later stages John Nieuwenhuizen acted as a scout, passing on a large number of clues to new volumes and sequences. He and others gave moral support, apparently assuming that I had taken on a tedious task. In fact I have enjoyed every moment of the work. Nevertheless I thank them sincerely for their consideration and indulgence. Otherwise I thank my library colleagues who supported the co-operative store project which supplied me with this fascinating work.

The compilation of the database was carried out using Titan software from Knowledge Engineering, Melbourne. I have found this software eminently suitable for the compilation of large bibliographic works. Helen Wreford is responsible for the programming for transition from database to printed book.

John E Simkin

February 1996

SEQUELS AND SEQUENCES

A

A-American series
Drackett, Phil
1 *Fighting days, A-American* (1944)
2 *Come out fighting, A-American* (1944)

A B C Hawkes series
Ephesian
1 *A.B.C.'s test case* (1936)
2 *A.B.C. investigates* (1937)
Short stories
3 *A.B.C. solves five* (1937)
Short stories

A.D.C. series
Bradley, Shelland
1 *Adventures of an A.D.C.* (1910)
2 *More adventures of an A.D.C.* (1915)

A.I. Gang series
This sequence has two authors
Coville, Bruce
1 *Operation Sherlock* (1986)
Lawrence, Jim
2 *Cutlass clue* (1986)
Coville, Bruce
3 *Robot trouble* (1986)
4 *Forever begins tomorrow* (1986)

A J Raffles series
Hornung, Ernest William
see **Raffles series**

A.J.Wentworth series
Ellis, Humphry Francis
1 *Papers of A.J.Wentworth, B.A.* (1949)
Vexations of A.J.Wentworth, B.A.
2 *A.J.Wentworth, B.A., retd.* (1962)
Papers of A.J.Wentworth, B.A., retd.
3 *Swan song of A.J.Wentworth* (1982)

A Mazing Monster series
Slater, Jim
1 *Great gulper* (1979)
2 *Bignose* (1979)
3 *Tricky troggle* (1979)
4 *Dimmo* (1979)
5 *Webfoot* (1979)
6 *Greeneye* (1979)
7 *Winkybird* (1979)
8 *Wormball* (1979)
9 *Snuggly* (1980)
10 *Kleenum* (1980)
11 *Swiggo* (1980)
12 *Big Snowy* (1980)

A.P.E. series
Daniels, Norman A
see **Man from A.P.E. series**

A Pennyfeather series
Olsen, D B
see **Professor A Pennyfeather series**

A S Pennington series
Brandon, John Gordon
see **Arthur Stukeley Pennington series**

A series
Zukofsky, Louis
Poetry
1 *A 1-12* (1959)
Revised edition 1966
2 *A 13-21* (1969)
3 *A 22-23* (1975)
4 *A 24* (1972)
One volume edition entitled *A*, 1978

Aahz series
Asprin, Robert Lynn
see **Skeeve series**

Aann series
Foster, Alan Dean
see **Flinx of the Commonwealth series**

Aarn Munro series
Campbell, John Wood
1 *Mightiest machine* (1947)
2 *Incredible planet* (1949)

Aaron Eisenberg and William Kendall series
Chase, Philip
1 *Deadly crusade* (1976)
2 *Merchants of death* (1976)
3 *Betrayal in Eden* (1976)
4 *Defame and destroy* (1976)

Aaron series
Harris, Joel Chandler
1 *Story of Aaron, so called, the son of Ben Ali* (1896)
Told by his friends and acquaintances
2 *Aaron in the wildwoods* (1897)

Abaloc series
Curry, Jane Louise
1 *Beneath the hill* (1967)
2 *Change-child* (1969)
3 *Daybreakers* (1970)
4 *Over the sea's edge* (1971)
5 *Watchers* (1975)
6 *Birdstones* (1977)
7 *Wolves of Aam* (1981)
8 *Shadow dancers* (1983)

Abandoned farm series
Sanborn, Katherine Abbott
1 *Adopting an abandoned farm* (1891)
2 *Abandoning an adopted farm* (1894)

Abbe Coignard series
France, Anatole
1 *At the sign of the Reine Pedauque* (1893)
Original edition entitled *La rotisserie de la Reine Pedauque*
2 *Opinions of Jerome Coignard* (1893)
Original edition entitled *Les opinions de Jerome Coignard*
3 *Merrie tales of Jaques Tournebroche, and, Child life in town and country* (1908)
Original editions entitled *Les contes de Jacques Tournebroche, and Filles et garcons, nos enfants*

Abbe Pierre Fremont trilogy
Zola, Emile
Translated from the French
1 *Lourdes* (1894)
2 *Rome* (1896)
3 *Paris* (1898)

Abbe Pierre series
Hudson, Jay William
1 *Abbe Pierre* (1922)
2 *Abbe Pierre's people* (1928)

Abbey family series
De Voto, Bernard
1 *Crooked mile* (1924)
2 *House of Sun-Goes-Down* (1928)

Abbey girls first generation series
Oxenham, Elsie J
For an analysis of the relationship between the three series about the Abbey girls see *Junior bookshelf*, February 1966
1 *Girls of the Hamlet Club* (1914)
2 *Abbey girls* (1920)
3 *Girls of the Abbey School* (1921)
4 *Abbey girls go back to school* (1922)
5 *New Abbey girls* (1923)
6 *Abbey girls again* (1924)
7 *Abbey girls in town* (1926)
8 *Queen of the Abbey girls* (1926)
9 *Jen of the Abbey School* (1927)
10 *Abbey girls win through* (1928)
11 *Abbey School* (1928)
12 *Abbey girls at home* (1930)
13 *Abbey girls play up* (1930)
14 *Abbey girls on trial* (1931)
15 *Biddy's secret* (1932)
16 *Rosamund's victory* (1933)
17 *Maidlin to the rescue* (1934)
18 *Call of the Abbey School* (1934)
19 *Joy's new adventure* (1935)
20 *Rosamund's tuck-shop* (1937)
21 *Maidlin bears the torch* (1937)
22 *Rosamund's castle* (1938)

Abbey girls retrospective series
Oxenham, Elsie J
The time period of this sequence fits between *The girls of the Abbey School* and *The new Abbey girls* in the **Abbey girls first generation series**
1 *Schooldays at the Abbey* (1938)
2 *Secrets of the Abbey* (1939)
3 *Stowaways in the Abbey* (1940)
4 *Schoolgirl Jen at the Abbey* (1950)
5 *Strangers at the Abbey* (1951)
6 *Selma at the Abbey* (1952)
7 *Tomboys at the Abbey* (1957)

Abbey girls second generation series
Oxenham, Elsie J
1 *Jandy Mac comes back* (1941)
2 *Maid of the Abbey* (1943)
3 *Two Joans at the Abbey* (1945)
4 *Abbey champion* (1946)
5 *Robins in the Abbey* (1947)
6 *Fiddler for the Abbey* (1948)
7 *Guardians of the Abbey* (1950)
8 *Rachel in the Abbey* (1952)
9 *Dancer from the Abbey* (1953)
10 *Song of the Abbey* (1954)
11 *Two queens at the Abbey* (1959)

Abbey of Kilkhampton series
Croft, Herbert
Originally published anonymously
1 *Abbey of Kilkhampton* (1780)
Alternative title: Monumental records for the year 1980
2 *Second part of The Abbey of Kilkhampton* (1780)
3 *Wreck of Westminster Abbey* (1788)
Alias the year two thousand, alias the ordeal of sepulchral candour

Abbey School series
Oxenham, Elsie J
see **Abbey girls first generation series**

Abbey series
Leyland, Eric
1 *Abbey sees it through* (1956)
2 *Conspiracy at Abbey* (1957)
3 *Abbey on the warpath* (1958)
4 *Abbey turns the tables* (1959)
5 *Abbey makes the grade* (1960)
6 *Odd man out at Abbey* (1961)

Abbey series
Mulford, Philippa Greene
1 *World is my eggshell* (1986)
2 *Making room for Katherine* (1994)

Abbeyford trilogy
Dickinson, Margaret
1 *Sarah* (1981)
2 *Adeline* (1981)
3 *Carrie* (1981)

Abbie an' Slats series
Capp, Al
1 *Abbie an' Slats* (1983)
2 *Abbie an' Slats 2* (1984)

Abbie Deal series
Aldrich, Bess Streeter
1 *Lantern in her hand* (1928)
2 *White bird flying* (1931)

Abbie series
Chandos, Dane
1 *Abbie* (1947)
2 *Abbie and Arthur* (1961)

Abbot and Thorne series
Penn, John
see **Inspector George Thorne and Sergeant Bill Abbot series**

Abbot series
Whitaker, Beryl
see **John Abbot series**

Abbott series
Cody, Al
see **Montana series**
Crane, Frances
see **Pat and Jean Abbott series**
Langham, James R
see **Samuel G Abbott series**
Webster, Jean
see **Judy Abbott series**

Abby Jones series
Giff, Patricia Reilly
1 *Have you seen Hyacinth Macaw?* (1981)
2 *Tootsie Tanner, why don't you talk?* (1987)
3 *Loretta P Sweeny, where are you?* (1990)

Abdallah series
Dombrowski, Katrina
1 *Abdallah and the donkey* (1928)
A tale of woe and joy for children from eight to eighty years
2 *Fat camel of Bagdad* (1929)

Abe Larson series
Krasney, Samuel A
1 *Death dies in the street* (1955)
2 *Design for dying* (1956)
3 *Homicide west* (1961)
4 *Homicide call* (1962)

Abe Lieberman series
Kaminsky, Stuart Melvin
1 *Lieberman's folly* (1991)
2 *Lieberman's choice* (1993)
3 *Lieberman's day* (1994)

Abe Martin series
Hubbard, Kin
1 *Abe Martin of Brown County* (1906)
2 *Brown County almanack* (1910)
3 *Brown County folks* (1910)
4 *Short furrows* (1912)
5 *Abe Martin primer* (1914)
6 *Back country folks* (1914)
7 *Abe Martin's sayings and sketches* (1915)
8 *New sayings* (1916)
9 *Abe Martin's back country sayings* (1917)
10 *Abe Martin on the the War and other things* (1918)
11 *Abe Martin's home cured philosophy* (1919)
12 *Abe Martin, joker on facts* (1920)
13 *These days* (1922)
14 *Comments of Abe Martin and his neighbors* (1923)
15 *Fifty two weeks of Abe Martin* (1924)
16 *Abe Martin on things in general* (1925)
17 *Abe Martin, hoss sense and nonsense* (1926)
18 *Abe Martin's wise cracks* (1927)
Also contains *The Skunk Ridge papers*
19 *Abe Martin's barbed wire* (1928)
20 *Abe Martin's town pump* (1929)
21 *Abe martin's broadcast* (1930)
Companion volumes: *The Abe Martin almanack*, 1908, 1909, 1912, 1921

Abe Stroud series
Caine, Geoffrey
see **Abraham Stroud series**

Abel and Lilith series
Rayner, Claire
see **Performers series**

Abel Rosnovski and William Kane series
Archer, Jeffrey
see **William Kane and Abel Rosnovski series**

Abelard Voss series
Cameron, Donald Clough
1 *Murder's coming* (1939)
2 *Grave without grass* (1940)
3 *And so he had to die* (1941)

Abercrombie Lewker series
Styles, Showell
see **Sir Abercrombie Lewker series**

Abigail Patience Danforth series
Jackson, Marian J A
see **Miss Abigail Patience Danforth series**

Abigail Sanderson and Robert Forsythe series
Giroux, E X
see **Robert Forsythe and Abigail Sanderson series**

Abigail series
Cox, David
Music by Betty Beath
Musical plays
1 *Abigail and the bushranger* (1976)
2 *Abigail and the rainmaker* (1976)

Abigail series
Miller, Moira
1 *Oh, Abigail!* (1981)
2 *Just like Abigail* (1983)

Abigail Trent and Lone Eagle series
Bittner, F Rosanne
see **Savage destiny series**

Abigail trilogy
Corcoran, Barbara
1 *Abigail* (1981)
2 *Abbie in love* (1981)
3 *Husband for Gail* (1981)

Abilene series
Ladd, Justin
1 *Peacemaker* (1988)
2 *Sharpshooter* (1988)
3 *Pursuers* (1988)
4 *Night riders* (1988)
5 *Half breed* (1988)
6 *Hangman* (1989)
7 *Prizefighter* (1989)
8 *Whiskey runners* (1989)
9 *Tracker* (1989)
10 *General* (1989)
11 *Hellion* (1989)
12 *Cattle baron* (1990)
13 *Pistoleer* (1990)
14 *Lawman* (1990)
15 *Barlow brides* (1990)
16 *Deputy* (1990)

Abington series
Marshall, Archibald
1 *Abington Abbey* (1918)
2 *Graftons* (1919)

Able Team series
Stivers, Dick
This pseudonym is used by several authors, including Tom Arnett, G H Frost, Paul Hofrichter, Stephen Mertz, L R Payne, Larry Powell, Ron Renauld, Chuck Rogers, C J Shiao, Norman Winski whose authorship is indicated against those titles where it is known
1 *Tower of terror* (1982)
[Payne]
2 *Hostaged island* (1982)
[Payne; Winski]
3 *Texas showdown* (1982)
[Payne; Powell]
4 *Amazon slaughter* (1983)
[Shiao]
5 *Cairo countdown* (1983)
[Hofrichter]
6 *Warlord of Azatlan* (1983)
7 *Justice by fire* (1983)
[Frost]
8 *Army of devils* (1983)
[Frost]
9 *Kill school* (1983)
[Frost]
10 *Royal flush* (1984)
[Mertz]
11 *Five rings of fire* (1984)
[Arnett]
12 *Deathbites* (1984)
[Arnett]
13 *Scorched earth* (1984)
[Frost]
14 *Into the maze* (1984)
[Frost]
15 *They came to kill* (1984)
[Frost]
16 *Rain of doom* (1985)
[Frost]
17 *Fire and maneuver* (1985)
[Frost]
18 *Tech war* (1985)
[Frost]
19 *Ironman* (1985)
[Frost]
20 *Shot to hell* (1985)
[Rogers]
21 *Death strike* (1985)
[Frost]
22 *World War III game* (1986)
[Arnett]
23 *Fall back and kill* (1986)
[Rogers]
24 *Blood gambit* (1986)
[Arnett]
25 *Hard kill* (1986)
[Rogers]
26 *Iron god* (1986)
[Rogers]
27 *Cajun angel* (1986)
[Rogers]
28 *Miami crash* (1987)
[Rogers]
29 *Death ride* (1987)
[Arnett]
30 *Hit and run* (1987)
[Rogers]
31 *Ghost train* (1987)
[Rogers]
32 *Fire cross* (1987)
[Rogers]
33 *Cowboy's revenge* (1987)
[Renauld]
34 *Clear shot* (1988)
[Renauld]

Abner series
Capp, Al
see **Li'l Abner series**
Post, Melville Davisson
see **Uncle Abner series**

Abolitionist series
McPherson, James Munro
1 *Struggle for equality* (1964)
Abolitionists and the negro in the Civil War and Reconstruction
2 *Abolitionist legacy* (1976)
From Reconstruction to the NAACP

Abracadabra series
Becker, Eve
1 *Thirteen means magic* (1989)
2 *Love potion* (1989)
3 *Magic mix-up* (1989)
4 *Sneezing spell* (1990)
5 *Instant popularity* (1990)
6 *Too much magic* (1990)

Abraham Kozminski series
Downes, Quentin
see **Detective Inspector Abraham Kozminski series**

Abraham Lincoln series
Morrow, Honore Willsie
1 *Dearer than all* (1917)
2 *Benefits forgot* (1917)
A story of Lincoln and mother love
3 *Lost speech of Abraham Lincoln* (1925)
One volume edition entitled *The Lincoln stories of Honore Morrow*, 1934

Abraham Lincoln trilogy
Bacheller, Irving
1 *Boy for the ages* (1937)
2 *Man for the ages* (1919)
A story of the builders of democracy
3 *Father Abraham* (1925)
A tale of the last years of Abraham Lincoln

Abraham Lincoln trilogy
Morrow, Honore Willsie
see **Great Captain trilogy**

Abraham Stroud series
Caine, Geoffrey
1 *Curse of the vampire* (1991)
2 *Wake of the werewolf* (1991)
3 *Legion of the dead* (1992)

Abu Ali series
Van Woerkom, Dorothy
1 *Abu Ali* (1976)
Three tales of the Middle East
2 *Friends of Abu Ali* (1978)

Abyssinia Jackson series
Thomas, Joyce Carol
1 *Marked by fire* (1982)
2 *Bright shadow* (1983)

Acadia series
Roberts, Charles George Douglas
1 *Forge in the forest* (1896)
The narrative of the Acadian Ranger, Jean de Mer, Seigneur de Briart and how he crossed the Black Abbe and of his adventures in a strange fellowship
2 *Sister to Evangeline* (1898)
Lovers in Acadia
The story of Yvonne de Lamourie and how she went into exile with the villagers of Grand Pre

According to grandma series
Haines, Alice Calhoun
1 *When grandma was little* (1907)
2 *What grandma says* (1907)

Accursed kings series
Druon, Maurice
1 *Iron King* (1955)
Original edition entitled *Le Roi de Fer*; based on the life of Philip IV of France
2 *Strangled queen* (1955)
Original edition entitled *La reine etranglee*; based on the life of Louis X of France
3 *Poisoned crown* (1956)
Original edition entitled *Les poisons de la couronne*; based on the last months of Louis X of France
4 *Royal succession* (1957)
Original edition entitled *La loi des males*; based on the conflict following the death of Louis X leading to the coronation of Philip V
5 *She-Wolf of France* (1959)
Original edition entitled *La Louvre de France*; based on the life of Isabella, wife of Edward II of England
6 *Lily and the lion* (1960)
Original edition entitled *Le lis et le lion*; set during the early years of the reign of Edward III of England

Ace Chaney series
Garrison, Christian
1 *Snake doctor* (1980)
2 *Paragon man* (1981)

Ace of spies series
Lockhart, Robin Bruce
see **Reilly series**

Ace series
Horler, Sydney
1 *Enter the Ace* (1941)
2 *Hell's brew* (1952)
3 *Dark night* (1953)

Achille Peroni series
Holme, Timothy
see **Inspector Achille Peroni series**

Achilles series
Bates, Herbert Ernest
1 *Achilles the donkey* (1962)
2 *Achilles and Diana* (1963)
3 *Achilles and the twins* (1964)

Acquaintances series
Toynbee, Arnold Joseph
Autobiography
1 *Acquaintances* (1967)
2 *Experiences* (1969)

Act of God trilogy
Kotani, Eric
1 *Act of God* (1985)
2 *Island worlds* (1987)
3 *Between the stars* (1988)

Action Man series
Brogan, Mike
1 *Hold the bridge* (1977)
2 *Snow, ice and bullets* (1977)
3 *Taking of Monte Carrillo* (1977)
4 *Operation sky-drop* (1977)
5 *Counter-attack* (1977)
6 *Tough way out* (1977)
7 *Rand on Shuando* (1978)
8 *Spy trap* (1978)

Acton series
Bramhall, Marion
see **Kit Acton series**

Adam and Eve series
Twain, Mark
see **Diaries of Adam and Eve series**

Adam and Rosie series
Thwaites, Lyndsay
see **Super Adam and Rosie Wonder series**

Adam Breck series
Orvis, Kenneth
1 *Night without darkness* (1965)
2 *Doomsday list* (1974)

Adam Brodie series
Wylie, Ida Alexa Ross
1 *Towards morning* (1918)
2 *Brodie and the deep sea* (1920)

Adam Cyber and Jason Starr series
Heath, Peter
see **Jason Starr and Adam Cyber series**

Adam Dalgliesh series
James, Phyllis Dorothy
see **Commander Adam Dalgliesh series**

Adam Drew and Katherine Cornish series
Hanson, Virginia
1 *Death walks the post* (1938)
2 *Casual slaughters* (1939)
3 *Mystery for Mary* (1942)

Adam Flute series
Launay, Droo
1 *She modelled her coffin* (1961)
2 *New shining white murder* (1962)
3 *Corpse in camera* (1963)
4 *Death and still life* (1964)
5 *Two-way mirror* (1964)
6 *Scream* (1965)

Adam Gifford series
Lejeune, Anthony
1 *News of murder* (1961)
2 *Duel in the shadows* (1962)
3 *Dark trade* (1965)
Death of a pornographer

Adam Hood series
Rich, Nicholas
1 *Blane document* (1972)
2 *Spy now, pay later* (1972)
3 *Seajet spies* (1973)

Adam Horne series
Hill, Porter
see **Captain Adam Horne series**

Adam Hunter series
Conway, Norman
1 *Omega operation* (1974)
2 *Alpha Death* (1975)
Operation Alpha Death

Adam Joshua series
Smith, Janice Lea
1 *Monster in the third dresser drawer, and other stories about Adam Joshua* (1981)
2 *Kid next door, and other headaches* (1984)
3 *Show-and-tell war, and other stories about Adam Joshua* (1988)
4 *Pet day* (1989)
5 *It's not easy being George* (1989)
6 *Turkey's side of it* (1990)
A Thanksgiving story
7 *There's a ghost in the coatroom* (1991)
8 *Nelson in love* (1992)
A Valentine's Day story
9 *Serious science* (1993)

Adam Kane series
Bennett, William Robert
1 *Man from Checkmate* (1971)
2 *Dossier on a mantis* (1972)

Adam Larey series
Grey, Zane
1 *Wanderer of the wasteland* (1923)
2 *Stairs of sand* (1943)

Adam Link series
Binder, Eando
1 *Adam Link in the past* (1950)
2 *Adam Link, robot* (1965)

Adam Ludlow and Inspector Montero series
Nash, Simon
see **Inspector Montero and Adam Ludlow series**

Adam Macadam series
Duff, Douglas Valder
1 *Sea-Serpent Island* (1957)
2 *Ocean haul* (1957)
3 *Sea-bed treasure* (1957)
4 *San Matteo* (1957)
5 *Black ivory* (1958)
6 *Pale grey men* (1958)
7 *At close grips* (1959)
8 *Crusader's gold* (1959)
9 *Undersea oiltanker* (1959)
10 *Stolen aircraft carrier* (1959)
11 *King's rescue* (1960)
12 *Adam Macadam, naval cadet* (1961)
13 *Pirates aboard!* (1961)

Adam Quill series
Brahms, Caryl
see **Inspector Adam Quill series**

Adam Quirke series
Gridban, Volsted
1 *Master must die* (1953)
2 *Lonely astronomer* (1954)

Adam series
Cheney, Brainard
1 *This is Adam* (1958)
2 *Devil's Elbow* (1969)

Adam series
Simpson, Colin
1 *Adam in ochre* (1951)
Inside Aboriginal Australia
2 *Adam with arrows* (1953)
Inside New Guinea
3 *Adam in plumes* (1954)

Adam series
Wood, Christopher
see **John Adam series**

Adam Square series
Stewart, Marjorie
1 *Adam Square* (1932)
2 *Mysterious way* (1933)

Adam Steele series
Gilman, George G
1 *Violent peace* (1974)
Rebels and assassins die hard
2 *Bounty hunter* (1974)
3 *Hell's Junction* (1974)
4 *Valley of blood* (1975)
5 *Gun run* (1975)
6 *Killing art* (1975)
7 *Cross-fire* (1975)
8 *Comanche carnage* (1976)
9 *Badge in the dust* (1976)
10 *Losers* (1976)
11 *Lynch town* (1976)
12 *Death trail* (1977)
13 *Bloody border* (1977)
14 *Delta duel* (1977)
15 *River of death* (1977)
16 *Nightmare at noon* (1978)
17 *Satan's daughters* (1978)
18 *Hard way* (1978)
19 *Tarnished star* (1979)
20 *Wanted for murder* (1979)
21 *Wagons east* (1979)
22 *Big game* (1979)
23 *Fort Despair* (1979)
24 *Manhunt* (1980)
25 *Woman* (1980)
26 *Preacher* (1981)
27 *Storekeeper* (1981)
28 *Stranger* (1981)
29 *Big prize* (1981)
30 *Killer mountains* (1982)
31 *Cheaters* (1982)
32 *Wrong man* (1983)
33 *Valley of the shadow* (1983)
34 *Runaway* (1983)
35 *Stranger in a strange town* (1983)
36 *Hellraisers* (1984)
37 *Canyon of death* (1985)
38 *High stakes* (1985)
39 *Rough justice* (1985)
40 *Sunset ride* (1986)
41 *Killing strain* (1986)
42 *Big gunfight* (1987)
43 *Hunted* (1987)
44 *Code of the West* (1987)
45 *Outcasts* (1987)
46 *Return* (1988)
47 *Trouble in paradise* (1988)
48 *Going back* (1989)
49 *Long shadow* (1989)

Adam Steele's war series
Gilman, George G
see **Steele's war series**

Adam Swann series
Delderfield, Ronald Frederick
1 *God is an Englishman* (1970)
2 *Theirs was the kingdom* (1971)
3 *Give us this day* (1973)

Adam trilogy
Sibley, Kathleen
1 *Adam and the football* (1972)
2 *Adam and the F.A. Cup* (1975)
3 *Adam and the football mystery* (1979)

Adams and Collins series
Masters, M
see **Hawkeye Collins and Amy Adams series**

Adams series
Blackmon, Anita
see **Adelaide Adams series**
Brace, Timothy
see **Anthony Adams series**
Burrough, Reath J
see **Smiley Adams series**
Dean, Karen Strickler
see **Maggie Adams series**
Dekobra, Maurice
see **Bradley Adams series**
Hollingsworth, Leonard
see **Superintendent Adams series**
Palmer, Bernard
see **Lori Adams series**
Rinehart, Mary Roberts
see **Nurse Hilda Adams series**
Sage, Dana
see **Donald O'Keefe Adams series**
Saint James, Daniel
see **Brothers in blood series**
Storey, Alice
see **Samantha Adams series**

Addams family series
This sequence has three authors
Sharkey, Jack
1 *Addams family* (1965)
Miksch, William
2 *Addams family strikes back* (1965)
Faucher, Elizabeth
3 *Addams family* (1991)
Companion volumes: *The Addams family, a novelization*, by Stephanie Calmenson, 1991, *The Addams chronicles, everything you ever wanted to know about the Addams family*, by Stephen Cox, 1991, *Addams family revealed, an unauthorized look at America's spookiest family*, by James Van Hise, 1991

Addie series
Lawlor, Laurie
1 *Addie across the prairie* (1986)
2 *Addie's Dakota winter* (1989)

Addie series
Rock, Gail
1 *House without a Christmas tree* (1974)
2 *Thanksgiving treasure* (1974)
3 *Addie and the King of Hearts* (1976)
4 *Dream for Addie* (1986)

Addison Kent series
Moorhouse, Hopkins
1 *Gauntlet of Alceste* (1921)
2 *Golden scarab* (1926)

Addle of Eigg series
Dunn, Mary
see **Lady Addle of Eigg series**

Addy series
Porter, Connie
1 *Meet Addy, an American girl* (1993)
2 *Addy learns a lesson* (1993)
3 *Addy's surprise* (1993)

Adelaide Adams series
Blackmon, Anita
1 *Murder a la Richelieu* (1937)
Hotel Richelieu murders
2 *There is no return* (1938)
Riddle of the dead cats

Adelaide Peters series
Neels, Betty
1 *Sister Peters in Amsterdam* (1969)
2 *Blow hot, blow cold* (1969)
Surgeon from Holland

Adele Doring series
North, Grace May
1 *Adele Doring of the Sunnyside Club* (1919)
2 *Adele Doring on a ranch* (1920)
3 *Adela Doring at boarding-school* (1921)
4 *Adele Doring in camp* (1922)
5 *Adele Doring at Vineyard Valley* (1923)

Adept trilogy
Kurtz, Katherine
1 *Adept* (1991)
2 *Lodge of the lynx* (1992)
3 *Templar treasure* (1993)

Adjusters series
Winston, Peter
1 *Assignment to Bahrein* (1967)
2 *ABC affair* (1967)
3 *Glass cipher* (1968)
4 *Doomsday vendetta* (1968)
Sequence continued under the author's real name Jack Laflin
Laflin, Jack
5 *Temple at Ilumquh* (1970)

Adjutant Grijpstra and Sergeant De Gier series
Van de Wetering, Janwillem
see **De Gier and Grijpstra series**

Adkins series
Foxall, Raymond
see **Harry Adkins series**

Adler series
Douglas, Carole Nelson
see **Irene Adler series**
Silver, Victoria
see **Laura Adler series**

Admiral of the Fleet, Earl of Caraway series
Herbert, Alan Patrick
1 *Number nine* (1951)
2 *Made for man* (1958)

Admiral's granddaughter series
Gould, Elizabeth Lincoln
1 *Admiral's granddaughter* (1907)
2 *Admiral's little housekeeper* (1910)
3 *Admiral's little secretary* (1911)
4 *Admiral's little companion* (1912)

Adnam Pratt series
Grand, Sarah
1 *Adnam's orchard* (1912)
2 *Winged victory* (1916)

Adolph Grundt series
Williams, Valentine
see **Clubfoot series**

Adolphe series
Constant, Benjamin
1 *Adolphe* (1816)
An anecdote found among the papers of an unknown person; original edition entitled *Adolphe*
2 *Cecile* (1951)
Original edition entitled *Cecile*

Adonis trilogy
Lambert, William J
1 *Adonis* (1969)
2 *Adonis at Actum* (1970)
3 *Adonis at Bomasa* (1970)

Adrano series
Bradley, Michael
see **Johnny Adrano series**

Adrian Criddle series
Strong, Ben
see **Professor Adrian Criddle series**

Adrian Mole series
Townsend, Sue
1 *Secret diary of Adrian Mole, aged 13 3/4* (1982)
Companion volumes: *The secret diary of Adrian Mole, play*, 1985, *The secret diary of Adrian Mole songbook*, 1985
2 *Growing pains of Adrian Mole* (1984)
Numbers 1 and 2 also published in one volume entitled *Adrian Mole diaries*, 1985
3 *True confessions of Adrian Albert Mole* (1989)
4 *Adrian Mole from minor to major* (1991)
The Mole diaries, the first ten years
5 *Wilderness years* (1993)

Adrian series
Silverman, Marguerite Ruth
see **Inspector Christopher Adrian series**

Adrian Titterton series
Brown, Edward
see **Major Adrian Titterton series**

Adrien Zograffi series
Istrati, Panait
1 *Kyra Kyralina* (1924)
Kyra, my sister
Original edition entitled *Kyra Kyralina*
2 *Uncle Anghel* (1924)
Original edition entitled *Oncle Anghel*
3 *Bandits* (1926)
Originally published in two volumes entitled *Presentation des Haidones*, and *Domnitza de Snagov*; other volumes in this sequence not translated

Adrienne Bishop series
Ellery, Jan
1 *Last set* (1979)
2 *High strung* (1980)

Adrigoole series
O'Donnell, Peadar
1 *Adrigoole* (1929)
2 *Knife* (1930)
There will be fighting

Advanced dungeons and dragons adventure gamebook series
This sequence has twelve authors
Phillips, Terry
1 *Soulforge* (1985)
Smith, Curtis
2 *Test of the ninja* (1985)
Blashfield, Jean
3 *Master of Ravenloft* (1986)
Simon, Morris
4 *Sceptre of power* (1986)
Moore, Roger Elwood
5 *Nightmare realm of Baba Yaga* (1986)
Simon, Morris
6 *Sorcerer's crown* (1986)
Niles, Douglas
7 *Lords of doom* (1986)
Simon, Morris
8 *Clash of the sorcerers* (1986)
Martindale, T Chris
9 *Curse of the werewolf* (1987)
Phillips, Terry
10 *Gates of death* (1987)
Brumbaugh, James
11 *Trail sinister* (1987)
Varney, Allen
12 *Vanishing city* (1987)
Despain, Dezra
13 *Shadow of Nordmaar* (1988)
Perrin, Steve
14 *Spawn of dragonspear* (1988)
Martindale, T Chris
15 *Prince of thieves* (1988)
Companion volumes: *Oriental adventures*, by David Cook, Gary Gygax and Francois Marcela-Froideval, 1985, *Grehawk adventures, a compendium of Greyhawk ideas for the AD&D playing system*, by James Michael Ward, 1988

Advanced dungeons and dragons reference books series
Ward, James Michael
1 *Advanced dungeons and dragons deities and demigods cyclopedia* (1980)
Revised edition 1980
2 *Advanced dungeons and dragons legends and lore* (1984)

Advanced theology for very tiny persons series
Sanford, Doris
1 *Child of God* (1988)
2 *Friends of God* (1988)
3 *Names of God* (1988)
4 *World of God* (1988)

Adventure girls series
Blank, Clair
1 *Adventure girls at K Bar O* (1936)
2 *Adventure girls at Happiness House* (1936)
3 *Adventure girls in the air* (1936)

Adventure in history series
Barbary, James
1 *Fort in the forest* (1962)
Fort in the wilderness
2 *Engine and the gun series* (1963)
3 *Student buccaneer* (1963)
4 *Pike and the sword* (1963)
5 *Ten thousand heroes* (1963)
6 *Boy mutineer* (1966)
Young mutineer
7 *Which side are you on?* (1968)

Adventure Island story books
Howson, John Michael
1 *Flower Potts and the giant* (1969)
2 *Birthday party* (1969)
3 *Clown and the pirates* (1969)
4 *Frosty the snowman* (1969)

Adventure series
Bayley, Viola
1 *Paris adventure* (1954)
2 *Lebanon adventure* (1955)
3 *Kashmir adventure* (1956)
4 *Corsican adventure* (1957)
5 *Turkish adventure* (1957)
6 *Swedish adventure* (1959)
7 *London adventure* (1962)
8 *Italian adventure* (1964)
9 *Scottish adventure* (1965)
10 *Welsh adventure* (1966)
11 *Austrian adventure* (1968)
12 *Jersey adventure* (1969)
13 *Adriatic adventure* (1970)
14 *Caribbean adventure* (1971)
15 *Greek adventure* (1972)
Blyton, Enid
1 *Island of adventure* (1944)
Mystery island
2 *Castle of adventure* (1946)
3 *Valley of adventure* (1947)
4 *Sea of adventure* (1948)
5 *Mountain of adventure* (1949)
6 *Ship of adventure* (1950)
7 *Circus of adventure* (1952)
8 *River of adventure* (1955)
Ingram, James Henry
1 *I found adventure* (1951)
Travels in Arctic Russia, Finland, Scandinavia, Spitzbergen
2 *Land of mud castles* (1952)
Travel in Morocco
3 *Road to adventure* (1953)
Travels in Yugoslavia and Scandinavia

Adventure series
Johns, William Earl
see **Digger Driscoll series**
Price, Willard
see **Hal and Roger Hunt series**

Adventurer in chains series
Orsborne, Dod
Reminiscences
1 *Voyage of the Girl Pat* (1937)
2 *Danger is my destiny* (1955)
3 *Voyage of the Victory* (1956)
4 *Adventurer in chains* (1957)

Adventures around the compass series
Volumes in this sequence are published variously under the author's real name Stephen Daniel Frances and the pseudonyms Joe North and Bob West
North, Joe
1 *Adventures of a taxi driver* (1976)
West, Bob
2 *Adventures of a private eye* (1977)
Frances, Stephen Daniel
3 *Adventures of a plumber's mate* (1978)
Based on a screenplay written under the pseudonym Sid South

Adventures before fifty series
Baker, Denys Val
see **Cornish series**

Adventures in frontier America series
Chambers, Catherine E
1 *California gold rush* (1984)
Search for treasure
2 *Daniel Boon and the wilderness road* (1984)
3 *Flatboats on the Ohio, westward bound* (1984)
4 *Frontier dream* (1984)
Life on the Great Plains
5 *Frontier farmer* (1984)
Kansas adventures
6 *Frontier village* (1984)
A town is born
7 *Indiana days* (1984)
Life in a frontier town
8 *Log-cabin home* (1984)
Pioneers in the wilderness
9 *Texas roundup* (1984)
Life on the range
10 *Wagons west* (1984)
Off to Oregon

Adventures in history series
Barbary, James
see **Adventure in history series**

Adventures in Kroy series
Le Guin, Ursula Kroeber
1 *Adventure of Cobbler's Rune* (1982)
2 *Solomon Leviathan's nine hundred and thirty-first trip around the world* (1983)

Adventures in memory series
Service, Robert William
Autobiography
1 *Ploughman of the moon* (1945)
2 *Harper of Heaven* (1948)
A record of radiant living

Adventures in the time machine series
Faraday, Robert
1 *Anytime rings* (1963)
2 *Samax, the gladiator* (1964)

Adventures in the unknown series
Claudy, Carl Harry
1 *Mystery men of Mars* (1933)
2 *Thousand years a minute* (1933)
3 *Land of no shadow* (1933)
4 *Blue Grotto terror* (1934)

Adventures of Ali series
Voegeli, Max
1 *Wonderful lamp* (1955)
2 *Prince of Hindustan* (1960)

Adventures of Alyx series
Russ, Joanna
1 *Picnic on paradise* (1968)
2 *Alyx* (1976)

Adventures of Buster and Betty series
Dicks, Terrance
1 *New beginning* (1988)
2 *In trouble* (1988)
3 *River rats* (1989)

Adventures of Captain Hatteras series
Verne, Jules
1 *At the North Pole* (1866)
Journey to the North Pole
English at the North Pole
Original edition entitled *Les aventures du Capitaine Hatteras*, part 1
2 *Wilderness of ice* (1866)
Field of ice
Desert of ice
Ice desert
Original edition entitled *Les aventures du Capitaine Hatteras*, part 2
One volume edition entitled *The adventures of Captain Hatteras*, 1876

Adventures of Conrad Stargard series
Frankowski, Leo
1 *Cross-time engineer* (1986)
2 *High-tech knight* (1989)
3 *Radiant warrior* (1989)
4 *Flying warlord* (1989)
5 *Lord Conrad's lady* (1990)

Adventures of Cugel the Clever series
Vance, Jack
1 *Seventeen virgins* (1979)
2 *Bagful of dreams* (1979)
One volume edition 1979

Adventures of Dunlop series
Reeder, Colin
1 *Dunlop and the eggs* (1992)
2 *Dunlop catches cold* (1992)
3 *Dunlop gives chase* (1992)
4 *Dunlop goes to the rescue* (1992)

Adventures of Jo, Zette and Jocko series
Herge
1 *Valley of the cobras* (1986)
Original edition entitled *La vallee des cobras*
2 *Stratoship Twenty Two* (1986)
Destination New York
Mister Pump's legacy
Original edition entitled *Le testament de M. Pump*

Adventures of Sherlock Hound series
Sivers, Brenda
see **Sherlock Hound series**

Adventures of Skippy series
This sequence has two authors
Based on a television series
Odgers, Sally Farrell
1 *Skippy and the bird smugglers* (1992)
Boland, Jason
2 *Skippy goes bush* (1992)

Adventures of the Empire Princess series
Diamond, Graham
see **Stacy series**

Adventures of Wonk series
Levy, Muriel
see **Wonk series**

Adventures series
Grayson, David
1 *Adventures in contentment* (1906)
2 *Adventures in friendship* (1910)
3 *Friendly road* (1913)
4 *Hempfield* (1916)
5 *Great possessions* (1917)
6 *Adventures in understanding* (1925)
7 *Adventures in solitude* (1931)
8 *Countryman's year* (1936)

Adventurous Allens series
Grove, Harriet Pyne
1 *Adventurous Allens* (1932)
2 *Adventurous Allens afloat* (1932)
3 *Adventurous Allens find mystery* (1932)
4 *Adventurous Allens marooned* (1932)
5 *Adventurous Allens' treasure* (1933)

Adventurous Four series
Blyton, Enid
1 *Adventurous Four* (1941)
2 *Adventurous Four again* (1947)

Adventurous Nine series
Prime, Heather
1 *Adventurous Nine* (1949)
2 *Nine on the trail* (1951)
3 *Nine afloat* (1952)

Adversary series
Wilson, Francis Paul
1 *Keep* (1981)
2 *Reborn* (1990)
3 *Reprisal* (1991)
Reprisals
4 *Nightworld* (1992)
Companion volumes: *The tomb*, 1984, *The touch*, 1986

Advise and consent series
Drury, Allen
see **Washington series**

Aeriel trilogy
Pierce, Meredith Ann
1 *Darkangel* (1982)
2 *Gathering of gargoyles* (1984)
3 *Pearl of the soul of the world* (1990)
One volume edition entitled *The darkangel trilogy*, 1990

Aeroplane boys series
Ashton, Lamar
1 *In the clouds for Uncle Sam* (1910)
Alternative title: Morey Marshall of the Signal Corps
2 *Stolen aeroplane* (1910)
Alternative title: How Bud Wilson made good
3 *Aeroplane express* (1910)
Alternative title: The Boy Aeronaut's grit
4 *Boy Seronaut's Club* (1910)
Alternative title: Flying for fun
5 *Cruise in the sky* (1911)
Alternative title: The legend of the great pink pearl
6 *Battling the bighorns* (1911)
Alternative title: Aeroplane in the Rockies
7 *When scout meets scout* (1912)
Alternative title: The aeroplane spy
8 *On the edge of the Arctic* (1913)
Alternative title: An aeroplane in snowland

Aescendune trilogy
Crake, Augustus David
see **Chronicles of Aescendune trilogy**

Aesop in verse series
Paxton, Tom
1 *Aesop's fables retold in verse* (1988)
2 *Belling the cat, and other Aesop's fables* (1990)
3 *Androcles and the lion, and other Aesop's fables* (1991)

Aesthete series
Acton, Harold
Autobiography
1 *Memoirs of an aesthete* (1948)
2 *More memoirs of an aesthete* (1970)

Aeyrie trilogy
Marks, Laurie J
see **Children of Triad trilogy**

Affairs series
Armfelt, Roger
1 *Country affairs* (1945)
2 *Village affairs* (1946)
3 *Shapton affairs* (1948)

Africa series
Dinesen, Isak
1 *Out of Africa* (1937)
Originally published under the author's real name Baroness Karen Blixen
2 *Shadows on the grass* (1960)
Companion volume: *Letters from Africa, 1914-1931*, 1981

African dictatorship trilogy
Farah, Nuruddin
1 *Sweet and sour milk* (1979)
2 *Sardines* (1981)
3 *Close sesame* (1983)

African negro series
Baptist, R Hernekin
1 *Four handsome negresses* (1931)
2 *Wild deer* (1934)

African politics series
Sandbrook, Richard
1 *Politics of basic needs* (1982)
Urban aspects of assaulting poverty in Africa
2 *Politics of Africa's economic stagnation* (1985)
3 *Politics of Africa's economic recovery* (1993)

African rulers series
Gann, Lewis Henry
see **Rulers of Africa series**

African tales series
Greaves, Nick
1 *When hippo was hairy, and other tales from Africa* (1988)
2 *When lion could fly, and more tales from Africa* (1993)

African tales series
Harman, Humphrey
1 *Tales told near a crocodile* (1962)
Stories from Nyanza
2 *More tales told near a crocodile* (1973)
3 *Tales told to an African king* (1978)

African travels series
Perham, Margery
1 *African apprenticeship* (1974)
An autobiographical journey in southern Africa, 1929
2 *East African journey* (1976)
Kenya and Tanganyika, 1929-30
3 *West African passage* (1983)
A journey through Nigeria, Chad and Cameroons, 1931-1932

African trilogy
Achebe, Chinua
1 *Things fall apart* (1958)
2 *No longer at ease* (1960)
3 *Arrow of gold* (1964)

African wildlife series
Hart, Susanne
1 *Too short a day* (1966)
Tame and the wild
2 *Life with Daktari* (1969)
Two vets in East Africa
3 *Listen to the wild* (1972)

Afrikorps series
Dolan, Bill
1 *Afrikorps* (1991)
2 *Iron horse* (1991)
3 *White rhino* (1992)
4 *Sea stallion* (1992)
5 *Lion mountain* (1993)
6 *Cobra curse* (1993)

Afro-Bets series
Hudson, Wade
1 *Afro-Bets book of black heroes from A to Z* (1988)
Co-author: Valerie Wilson Wesley; an introduction to important black achievers
2 *Afro-Bets alphabet rap song* (1990)
3 *Afro-Bets kids* (1992)
Alternative title: I'm gonna be!

After midnight stories series
Myers, Amy
1 *After midnight stories* (1985)
2 *Second book of after midnight stories* (1986)
3 *Third book of after midnight stories* (1987)
4 *Fourth book of after midnight stories* (1988)
5 *Fifth book of after midnight stories* (1991)

After such knowledge series
Blish, James
1 *Doctor Mirabilis* (1964)
2 *Black Easter* (1968)
Alternative title: Faust Aleph-Null
3 *Day after judgment* (1971)
Numbers 2 and 3 also published in one volume entitled *The devil's day*, 1990
4 *Case of conscience* (1959)
One volume edition entitled *After such knowledge*, 1991

After the bomb series
Miklowitz, Gloria Dubov
1 *After the bomb* (1985)
2 *Week one* (1987)

After the spell wars series
Hale, F J
1 *Ogre castle* (1988)
2 *In the sea nymph's lair* (1989)

Aftermath series
Vigliante, Mary
1 *Land* (1979)
2 *Colony* (1979)

Afternoon light series
Menzies, Robert Gordon
1 *Afternoon light* (1967)
Memories of men and events
2 *Measure of the years* (1970)

Agatha Raisin series
Beaton, M C
1 *Agatha Raisin and the quiche of death* (1992)
2 *Agatha Raisin and the vicious vet* (1993)
3 *Agatha Raisin and the potted gardener* (1994)

Agatha Welch series
Johns, Veronica Parker
1 *Hush, Gabriel!* (1941)
2 *Shady doings* (1941)

Agaton Sax series
Franzen, Nils Olof
1 *[Agaton Sax, kipper till]* (1955)
No English edition
2 *Agaton Sax and the League of Silent Exploders* (1956)
Original edition entitled *Agaton Sax och den ljudloesa spraengaemnesligan*
3 *Agaton Sax and the haunted house* (1957)
Original edition entitled *Agaton Sax och vita moess-mysteriet*
4 *Agaton Sax and the diamond thieves* (1959)
Original edition entitled *Agaton Sax och de slipade diamantjuvarna*
5 *Agaton Sax and the Scotland Yard mystery* (1961)
Original edition entitled *Agaton Sax och det gamla pipskaegget*
6 *Agaton Sax and the criminal doubles* (1963)
Original edition entitled *Agaton Sax och Bykoepings gaestebud*
7 *Agaton Sax and the incredible Max brothers* (1965)
Agaton Sax and the Max brothers
Agaton Sax and the bank robbers
Original edition entitled *Agaton Sax och Broederna Max*
8 *Agaton Sax and the Colossus of Rhodes* (1966)
Original edition entitled *Agaton Sax och den bortkomne Mr Lispington*
9 *Agaton Sax and the big rig* (1967)
Original edition entitled *Agaton Sax och de okontanta miljardaererna*
10 *Agaton Sax and the London computer plot* (1967)
Original edition entitled *Agaton Sax och den svaellande rotmos-affaren*
11 *Agaton Sax and Lispington's grandfather clock* (1978)

Age of darkness series
Cook, Hugh
see **Chronicles of an age of darkness series**

Age of Elegance series
Veryan, Patricia
1 *Lord and the gypsy* (1978)
Debt of honour
2 *Love's duet* (1979)
Perfect match
3 *Nanette* (1981)
4 *Feather castles* (1982)
5 *Married past redemption* (1983)
6 *Noblest family* (1983)
7 *Sanguinet's crown* (1985)
8 *Give all to love* (1987)
Companion volume: *Some brief folly*, 1981

Age of magic trilogy
McGowen, Tom
1 *Magical fellowship* (1991)
2 *Trial of magic* (1992)
3 *Question of magic* (1993)

Age of Roosevelt series
Schlesinger, Arthur Meier
1 *Crisis of the old order, 1919-1933* (1957)
2 *Coming of the New Deal* (1959)
3 *Politics of upheaval* (1960)

Agency series
Moore, Melissa
1 *Susan* (1981)
2 *Kate* (1982)
3 *Jessica* (1983)

Agency trilogy
Meltzer, David
1 *Agency* (1968)
2 *Agent* (1968)
3 *How many blocks in the pile?* (1968)

Agent Brad Spear series
This sequence has two authors
Cunningham, Chet
1 *Cheyenne payoff* (1981)

2 *Silver mistress* (1981)
3 *Tucson temptress* (1981)
4 *Frisco lady* (1981)
5 *Painted women* (1981)
Calhoun, Chad
6 *Hidden princess* (1982)
Titles of numbers 7 and 8 not identified
9 *Wild dancer* (1982)
10 *Lady rustler* (1982)
11 *Mountain green* (1982)
12 *Gambler's woman* (1982)

Agent for Cominsec series
Hayes, Ralph Eugene
1 *Bloody Monday conspiracy* (1974)
2 *Doomsday conspiracy* (1974)
3 *Turkish mafia conspiracy* (1974)
4 *Hellfire conspiracy* (1974)
5 *Nightmare conspiracy* (1974)
6 *Death makers conspiracy* (1975)

Agent for secrets series
Sharmat, Marjorie Weinman
see **Olivia Sharp series**

Agent Nine series
Dean, Graham
1 *Agent Nine solves his first case* (1935)
2 *Agent Nine solves the jewel mystery* (1936)

Agent of personality quartet
Harris, Wilson
1 *Eye of the scarecrow* (1965)
2 *Waiting room* (1967)
3 *Tumatumari* (1968)
4 *Ascent to Omai* (1970)

Agent of T.E.R.R.A. series
Maddock, Larry
see **Hannibal Fortune and Webley series**

Agent series
Miller, Steve
1 *Agent of change* (1988)
2 *Carpe diem* (1989)

Agent thirteen series
Dille, Flint
1 *Invisible empire* (1986)
2 *Serpentine assassin* (1986)
3 *Acolytes of darkness* (1987)
4 *Iron fist, velvet glove* (1987)
Rendezvous with destiny

Agent triple zero eight series
Allison, Clyde
1 *Our man from SADISTO* (1965)
2 *Our girl from MEPHISTO* (1965)
3 *Nautipuss* (1965)
4 *Go-go SADISTO* (1966)
5 *Desdemona affair* (1966)
6 *Gamefinger* (1966)
7 *SADISTO royale* (1966)
8 *Triple zero eight meets Gnatman* (1966)
9 *For your sighs only* (1966)
10 *Lost bomb* (1966)
11 *Merciless mermaids* (1966)
12 *Mondo SADISTO* (1966)
13 *Triple zero eight meets Modesta Blaze* (1966)
14 *Sex-ray* (1966)
15 *Roburta the Conqueress* (1966)
16 *From rapture with love* (1966)
17 *Ice maiden* (1967)
18 *Sin funnel* (1967)
19 *Platypussy* (1968)
20 *Desert damsels* (1968)

Ages in chaos series
Velikovsky, Immanuel
1 *From the Exodus to King Akhnaton* (1952)
2 *Earth in upheaval* (1955)
3 *Oedipus and Akhnaton* (1960)
4 *People of the sea* (1977)
5 *Rameses II and his time* (1978)

Agnes Carmichael series
Cohen, Anthea
see **Nurse Agnes Carmichael series**

Agnes series
Leslie, Madeline
see **Little Agnes series**

Agutter series
Llewellyn, Sam
see **Charlie Agutter series**

Ah-choo series
Mayer, Mercer
1 *Ah-choo* (1976)
2 *Hiccup* (1976)
3 *Oops* (1977)

Ahmed ben Hassan series
Hull, Edith Maude
see **Sheik Ahmed ben Hassan series**

Aia series
Vivian, Evelyn Charles
1 *Fields of sleep* (1923)
2 *People of the darkness* (1924)
One volume edition entitled *Aia*, 1978

Aidensfield series
Rhea, Nicholas
1 *Constable on the hill* (1979)
2 *Constable on the prowl* (1980)
3 *Constable around the village* (1981)
4 *Constable across the moors* (1982)
5 *Constable in the dale* (1983)
6 *Constable by the sea* (1985)
7 *Constable along the lane* (1986)
8 *Constable through the meadow* (1988)
9 *Constable in disguise* (1989)
10 *Constable among the heather* (1990)
11 *Constable by the stream* (1991)
12 *Constable on call* (1992)
13 *Constable around the green* (1993)
14 *Constable beneath the trees* (1994)

Aiken family trilogy
Thompson, Mary Wolfe
1 *Two in the wilderness* (1967)
2 *Wilderness winter* (1968)
3 *Wilderness wedding* (1970)

Ainslie family series
Clydesdale, Abby
see **Alys Heavers series**

Ainslie series
Stahl, Hilda
see **Amber Ainslie series**

Ainsworth series
Underwood, Michael
see **Martin Ainsworth series**

Air combat series
This sequence has two authors
Burtis, Thomson
1 *Daredevils of the air* (1932)
2 *Four aces* (1932)
3 *Wind for Wing* (1932)
4 *Flying blackbirds* (1932)
Adams, Eustace
5 *Doomed demons* (1935)
6 *Wings of the navy* (1936)
7 *War wings* (1937)

Air-conditioned nightmare series
Miller, Henry
1 *Air-conditioned nightmare* (1945)
2 *Remember to remember* (1947)

Air detective series
Jackson, Basil
1 *Crooked flight* (1984)
2 *Spy's flight* (1986)
3 *Terror flight* (1988)

Air Force series
Moura, Joni
1 *Tender loving care* (1972)
2 *If it moves, kiss it!* (1973)

Air hostesses series
Baker, Trudy
see **Coffee, tea or me girls series**

Air mail series
Theiss, Lewis Edwin
1 *Piloting the U.S. mail* (1927)
Alternative title: Flying for Uncle Sam
2 *Search for the lost mail plane* (1928)
3 *Trailing the air mail bandit* (1929)
4 *Flying reporter* (1930)
5 *Pursuit of the flying smugglers* (1931)
6 *Wings of the Coast Guard* (1932)

Air mystery series
Powell, Van
1 *Mystery crash* (1932)
2 *Haunted hangar* (1932)
3 *Vanishing airliner* (1932)

Air Patrol series
Buddee, Paul
1 *Air Patrol and the hijackers* (1973)
2 *Air Patrol and the saboteurs* (1973)
3 *Air Patrol and the secret intruders* (1973)
4 *Air Patrol and the underwater spies* (1973)

Air pilot series
Scott, Sheila
Memoirs of a woman air pilot
1 *I must fly* (1968)
2 *On top of the world* (1973)
Barefoot in the sky
Wright, Philip Lee
1 *East bound air mail* (1930)
Alternative title: Fighting fog, storm and hard luck
2 *Air express holdup* (1930)
Alternative title: How pilot George Selkirk carried thru
3 *Mail pilot's hunch* (1930)
Alternative title: A crash in Death Valley

Air service boys series
Beach, Charles Amory
1 *Air service boys flying for France* (1918)
Alternative title: The young heroes of the Lafayette Escadrille
2 *Air service boys over the enemy's lines* (1918)
Alternative title: The German spy's secret
3 *Air service boys over the Rhine* (1918)
Alternative title: Fighting above the clouds
4 *Air service boys in the big battle* (1919)
Alternative title: Silencing the big guns
5 *Air service boys flying for victory* (1919)
Alternative title: Bombing the last German stronghold
6 *Air service boys over the Atlantic* (1920)
Alternative title: The longest flight on record

Air war series
Whitehouse, Arch
1 *Fighters in the sky* (1959)
2 *Bombers in the sky* (1960)
3 *Combat in the sky* (1961)
4 *Adventure in the sky* (1961)
5 *Action in the sky* (1962)

Airfield series
Prince, Alison
1 *Sinister airfield* (1982)
2 *Night landings* (1983)
3 *Scramble!* (1984)

Airline series
Greatorex, Wilfred
1 *Take off* (1981)
2 *Ruskin's Berlin* (1982)

Airman series
Charlwood, Don
Autobiography
1 *Marching as to war* (1990)
2 *Journey into night* (1991)

Airman's odyssey trilogy
Saint-Exupery, Antoine de
1 *Night flight* (1931)
Original edition entitled *Vol de nuit*
2 *Wind, sand and stars* (1939)
Original edition entitled *Terre des hommes*
3 *Flight to Arras* (1941)
Night flight to Arras
Original edition entitled *Pilote de guerre*

Airplane Boys series
Craine, Edith Janice
1 *Airplane Boys on the border line* (1930)
2 *Airplane Boys at Cap Rock* (1930)
3 *Airplane Boys discover the secrets of Cuzco* (1930)
4 *Airplane Boys flying to Amy-Ran Fastness* (1930)
Flying to Amy-Ran Fastness
5 *Airplane Boys at Platinum River* (1931)
At Platinum River
6 *Airplane Boys with the revolutionists in Bolivia* (1931)
With the revolutionists in Bolivia
7 *Airplane Boys in the Black Woods* (1932)
8 *Airplane Boys at Belize* (1932)

Airport series
This sequence has two authors
Hailey, Arthur
1 *Airport* (1968)
Stewart, Kerry
2 *Airport '80* (1979)

Airship Boys series
This sequence has two authors
Sayler, Harry Lincoln
1 *Airship Boys* (1909)
Alternative title: The quest of the Aztec treasure
2 *Airship Boys adrift* (1909)
Alternative title: Saved by an aeroplane
3 *Airship Boys due north* (1910)
Alternative title: By balloon to the Pole
4 *Airship Boys in the barren lands* (1910)
Alternative title: The secret of the white Eskimos
5 *Airship Boys in finance* (1911)
Alternative title: The flight of the flying cow
6 *Airship Boys' ocean flyer* (1911)
Alternative title: New York to London in twelve hours
7 *Airship Boys as detectives* (1913)
Alternative title: On secret service in cloudland
Cass, Delysle F
8 *Airship Boys in the Great War* (1913)
Alternative title: The rescue of Bob Russell

Ajax series
Patchett, Mary Elwyn
1 *Ajax the warrior* (1953)

Ajax, golden dog of the Australian bush
2 *Tam the untamed* (1954)
3 *Treasure of the Reef* (1955)
Great Barrier Reef
4 *Return to the Reef* (1956)
5 *Outback adventure* (1957)
6 *Call of the bush* (1959)
7 *End of the outlaws* (1961)
8 *Golden wolf* (1962)
9 *Ajax and the haunted mountain* (1963)
10 *Ajax and the drovers* (1964)

Akhenaten series
Drury, Allen
1 *God against the gods* (1976)
2 *Return to Thebes* (1977)

Akimbo series
McCall Smith, Alexander
1 *Akimbo and the elephants* (1990)
2 *Akimbo and the lions* (1992)
3 *Akimbo and the crocodile man* (1993)

Al Barney series
Chase, James Hadley
1 *Ear to the ground* (1968)
2 *You're dead without money* (1972)

Al Bronson series
Koehler, Robert Portner
1 *Steps to murder* (1943)
2 *Murder expert* (1945)
3 *Tread gently* (1945)

Al Capsella series
Clarke, Judith
1 *Heroic life of Al Capsella* (1988)
2 *Al Capsella and the watchdogs* (1990)
3 *Al Capsella on holidays* (1992)
Al Capsella takes a vacation

Al Colby series
Dodge, David
1 *Long escape* (1948)
2 *Plunder of the sun* (1949)
3 *Red tassel* (1950)

Al Delaney series
Black, Thomas B
1 *Whitebird murders* (1946)
2 *Three-thirteen murders* (1946)
3 *Pinball murders* (1947)
4 *Four dead mice* (1954)
Million dollar murder

Al Glenne series
Braun, Maurice-Gilles
Translated from the French
1 *Apostles of violence* (1962)
Original edition entitled *Apotres de la violence*
2 *Operation Jealousy* (1965)
Original edition entitled *Plan Jalousie*
3 *Operation Atlantis* (1966)
4 *That girl from Istanbul* (1966)

Al Jaffee gags series
Jaffee, Al
1 *Al Jaffee gags* (1974)
2 *Al Jaffee gags again* (1975)

Al Krug and Casey Kellog series
Weston, Carolyn
see **Casey Kellog and Al Krug series**

Al Mundy series
Brewer, Gil
Based on a television series entitled It takes a thief
1 *Devil in Davos* (1969)
2 *Mediterranean caper* (1969)
3 *Appointment in Cairo* (1970)

Al Murphy series
Paulsen, Gary
1 *Murphy* (1987)
2 *Murphy's gold* (1988)
3 *Murphy's herd* (1989)
4 *Murphy's war* (1990)
5 *Murphy's stand* (1993)

Al series
Greene, Constance Clarke
1 *Girl called Al* (1969)
2 *I know you, Al* (1975)
3 *Your old pal, Al* (1979)
4 *Alexandra the great* (1982)
5 *Just plain Al* (1986)
6 *Al's blind date* (1989)

Al Wheeler series
Brown, Carter
see **Lieutenant Al Wheeler series**

Al White series
Holden, Genevieve
see **Lieutenant Al White series**

Al Zimmerman series
George, Theodore
see **Lieutenant Al Zimmerman series**

Alacrity FitzHugh trilogy
Daley, Brian
1 *Requiem for a ruler of worlds* (1985)
2 *Jinx on a Terran inheritance* (1985)
3 *Fall of the white ship Avatar* (1987)

Alamo Bowie series
Martin, Charles Morris
1 *Law for Tombstone* (1937)
2 *Gun law* (1938)

Alamo series
Moore, Arthur
1 *Man called Alamo* (1975)
2 *Night riders* (1978)

Alamut series
Tarr, Judith
1 *Alamut* (1989)
2 *Dagger and the cross* (1991)
A novel of the Crusades

Alan Banks series
Robinson, Peter
see **Chief Inspector Alan Banks series**

Alan Bernhardt series
Wilcox, Collin
1 *Bernhardt's Edge* (1988)
2 *Silent witness* (1990)
3 *Except for the bones* (1991)

Alan Brett series
Garrett, Robert
1 *Run down* (1970)
2 *Spiral* (1971)

Alan Carr series
Westerman, Percy Francis
1 *His unfinished voyage* (1937)
2 *Cadet Alan Carr* (1938)
3 *Alan Carr in the Near East* (1942)
4 *Alan Carr in the Arctic* (1943)
5 *Alan Carr in command* (1945)

Alan Craig series
Gray, Malcolm
1 *Look back on murder* (1985)
2 *Matter of record* (1987)
3 *Unwelcome presence* (1989)

Alan Ford series
Wells, Carolyn
1 *Bride of a moment* (1916)
2 *Faulkner's folly* (1917)
3 *Room with the tassels* (1918)
4 *Murder will in* (1942)

Alan Fraser series
Desmond, Hugh
1 *Suicide pact* (1942)
2 *Hand of vengeance* (1945)
3 *Viper's sting* (1946)
4 *Death walks in scarlet* (1948)
5 *Clear case of murder* (1950)
6 *Calling Alan Fraser* (1951)
7 *Pact with the Devil* (1952)
8 *Deliver us from evil* (1953)
9 *Night of the crime* (1953)
10 *Death parade* (1954)
11 *Destination, death* (1955)
12 *She met murder* (1956)
13 *Appointment at eight* (1957)
14 *Lady, where are you?* (1957)
15 *Poison pen* (1958)
16 *Doorway to death* (1959)
17 *In fear of the night* (1960)
18 *Case of the blue orchid* (1961)
19 *Fanfare for murder* (1961)
20 *Stay of execution* (1962)
21 *Bodies in a cupboard* (1963)
22 *Silent witness* (1963)
23 *Slight case of murder* (1963)
24 *Condemned* (1964)
25 *Hostage to death* (1964)
26 *Someday I'll kill you* (1964)
27 *Dark shadow* (1965)
28 *Murder strikes at dawn* (1965)
29 *Not guilty, My Lord* (1965)
30 *Lady has claws* (1966)
31 *Horror at the moated mill* (1967)
32 *Murder on the moor* (1967)
33 *Mask of terror* (1968)
34 *We walk with death* (1968)

Alan French series
Gollin, James
see **Philomel Foundation series**

Alan Grant series
Tey, Josephine
see **Inspector Alan Grant series**

Alan Grofield series
Stark, Richard
1 *Score* (1964)
Killtown
2 *Handle* (1966)
Run lethal
3 *Damsel* (1967)
4 *Dame* (1969)
5 *Blackbird* (1969)
6 *Lemons never lie* (1971)
7 *Butcher's moon* (1974)

Alan Kelton series
Alexander, Martin
1 *Death is too good for you* (1969)
2 *Dream before dying* (1970)

Alan Lewrie series
Lambdin, Dewey
A story of a sailor in the British Navy in the 18th century
1 *King's coat* (1989)
2 *French admiral* (1990)
3 *King's commission* (1991)
4 *King's privateer* (1992)
5 *Gun ketch* (1993)

Alan Markby and Meredith Mitchell series
Granger, Ann
see **Meredith Mitchell and Chief Inspector Alan Markby series**

Alan Metcalfe series
Finkel, George
see **Group Captain Alan Metcalfe series**

Alan Miller series
Hunt, Peter
1 *Murders at Scandal House* (1933)
2 *Murder for breakfast* (1934)
3 *Murder among the nudists* (1934)

Alan Morgan series
Fox, Gardner Francis
1 *Warrior of Llarn* (1964)
2 *Thief of Llarn* (1966)

Alan, Roslin and James series
Lyon, Elinor
see **James, Alan and Roslin series**

Alan Russell series
Fitzgerald, Nigel
1 *Midsummer malice* (1953)
2 *Rosy pastor* (1954)
3 *Candles are all out* (1960)
4 *Ghost in the making* (1960)

Alan Saxton series
Miles, Keith
1 *Bullet hole* (1986)
2 *Double eagle* (1987)
3 *Green murders* (1990)
4 *Flagstick* (1991)

Alan Sebrill trilogy
Upward, Edward
1 *In the thirties* (1962)
2 *Rotten elements* (1969)
3 *No home but the struggle* (1977)
Also includes *The rotten elements*

Alan Steel series
Robertson, Colin
1 *Clash of Steel* (1965)
2 *Judas spies* (1966)
3 *Project X* (1968)

Alanbrooke diaries series
Bryant, Arthur
see **Second World War series**

Alard family trilogy
Kaye-Smith, Sheila
1 *Superstitition Corner* (1934)
2 *Gallybird* (1934)
3 *End of the House of Alard* (1923)

Alaric the Minstrel series
Eisenstein, Phyllis
1 *Born to exile* (1978)
2 *In the Red Lord's reach* (1989)

Alasdair and Lachlann Ban series
McLean, Allan Campbell
1 *Ribbon of fire* (1962)
2 *Sound of trumpets* (1966)

Alaska series
Martin, Martha
Reminiscences of life in Alaska
1 *O rugged land of gold* (1953)
2 *Home in the bear's domain* (1954)

Alaskan trapper series
Radau, Hans
see **Little Fox series**

Alastair and Sarah series
Willson, Robina Beckles
see **Sarah and Alastair series**

Alastair, Elizabeth and Peter Robin series
Fitzgerald, Hilary
1 *Home farm* (1952)
2 *Far Away Farm* (1957)

Alastair Granby series
Beeding, Francis
see **Colonel Alastair Granby series**

Alastair Macalastair series
Dick, Alexandra
1 *And only man* (1944)
2 *Old-fashioned Christmas* (1944)
3 *Curate's crime* (1945)
American edition published under the author's real name, Sibyl Erikson
4 *Macalastair looks on* (1947)
5 *Cross purposes* (1950)

Alastor trilogy
Vance, Jack
1 *Trullion* (1973)
Alastor 2262

Alastor trilogy

2 *Marune* (1975)
Alastor 933
3 *Wyst* (1978)
Alastor 1716

Alban de Bricoule trilogy
Montherlant, Henry de
1 *Matador* (1926)
2 *Boys* (1969)
3 *Dream* (1922)

Albany series
Godey, John
see **Jack Albany series**

Albany series
Kennedy, William
1 *Ink truck* (1969)
2 *Legs* (1975)
3 *Billy Phelan's greatest game* (1978)
4 *Quinn's book* (1988)
Set in the period before the American Civil War
Companion volume: *O Albany, an urban tapestry*, 1983

Albatross series
Cross, John Keir
1 *Angry planet* (1945)
An authentic first-hand account of a journey to Mars in the spaceship Albatross, compiled from notes and records by various members of the expedition
2 *S O S from Mars* (1954)
Red journey
A first-hand account of the second and third Martian expeditions by the space-ships Albatross and Comet compiled from notes and records by various members of the exploring parties

Albemarle series
Fletcher, Inglis
see **Carolina series**

Albemarle trilogy
Coulter, Catherine
see **Victoria Albemarle trilogy**

Alberg series
Wright, Laurali R
see **Sergeant Karl Alberg series**

Alberic the dragon series
Greaves, Margaret
1 *Charlie, Emma and Alberic* (1980)
2 *Charlie, Emma and the dragon family* (1982)
3 *Charlie, Emma and the school dragon* (1984)
4 *Charlie, Emma and dragons to the rescue* (1986)

Albert and the lion series
Edgar, Marriott
Based on monologues first performed by Stanley Holloway
1 *Lion and Albert* (1977)
2 *Albert comes back* (1980)

Albert and Willow series
Miller, Margaret Jessy
see **Willow and Albert series**

Albert and Witherspoon series
Smith, Doris Buchanan
see **Lloyd Albert and Ancil Witherspoon series**

Albert Argyle series
Story, Jack Trevor
1 *Live now, pay later* (1963)
2 *Something for nothing* (1963)
3 *Urban district lover* (1964)

Albert Campion series
This sequence has two authors
Allingham, Margery
1 *Crime at Black Dudley* (1929)
Black Dudley murder
2 *Mystery mile* (1929)
Revised edition 1968
3 *Look to the lady* (1931)
Gyrth chalice mystery
4 *Police at the funeral* (1931)
5 *Sweet danger* (1933)
Kingdom of death
Fear sign
6 *Death of a ghost* (1934)
7 *Flowers for the judge* (1936)
Legacy in blood
8 *Case of the late pig* (1937)
Published in the USA in *Mister Campion, criminologist*, 1937
9 *Dancers in mourning* (1937)
Who killed Chloe?
10 *Fashion in shrouds* (1938)
Revised edition 1965
11 *Mister Campion and others* (1939)
Editions differ in content and partly overlap *Mister Campion, criminologist*, 1937, and *The case book of Mister Campion*, 1947
12 *Black plumes* (1940)
13 *Traitor's purse* (1941)
Sabotage murder mystery
14 *Coroner's pidgin* (1945)
Pearls before swine
15 *More work for the undertaker* (1948)
Revised edition 1968
16 *Tiger in the smoke* (1952)
17 *Beckoning lady* (1955)
Estate of the beckoning lady
18 *Hide my eyes* (1958)
Tether's end
Ten were missing
19 *China governess* (1962)
20 *Mind readers* (1965)
21 *Cargo of eagles* (1968)
Completed by the author's husband, Philip Youngman Carter
Carter, Philip Youngman
22 *Mister Campion's farthing* (1969)
23 *Mister Campion's falcon* (1970)
Mister Campion's quarry
Also stories featuring Campion in *The Allingham case-book*, 1969, and, *The Allingham minibus*, 1973, by Margery Allingham

Albert Divine series
John, Stephen
1 *I like it that way* (1969)
2 *How about this way?* (1970)
3 *Any way you like* (1972)
4 *This way, please!* (1973)
5 *Coming my way?* (1974)
6 *Have it your own way* (1975)

Albert Finn and Billy Boyo series
Niall, Ian
see **Billy Boyo and Albert Finn series**

Albert Grope series
Mann, Francis Oscar
1 *Albert Grope* (1931)
2 *Grope carries on* (1932)
3 *Three, the drive* (1933)

Albert Henry Hawkins series
Dickens, Frank
1 *Albert Henry Hawkins, the naughtiest boy in the world* (1971)
2 *Albert Henry Hawkins, the naughtiest boy in the world and the space rocket* (1978)
3 *Albert Henry Hawkins, the naughtiest boy in the world and the Olympic Games* (1980)

Albert John series
Silcock, Ruth
1 *Albert John out hunting* (1980)
2 *Albert John in disgrace* (1981)

Albert, Prince of Wales series
Lovesey, Peter
see **Bertie series**

Albert Samson series
Lewin, Michael Zinn
1 *Ask the right question* (1971)
2 *Way we die now* (1973)
3 *Enemies within* (1974)
4 *Night cover* (1976)
Albert Samson is a minor character in this title
5 *Silent salesman* (1978)
6 *Missing woman* (1981)
7 *Hard line* (1982)
8 *Out of season* (1984)
Out of time
9 *Late payments* (1986)
10 *Child proof* (198)

Albert series
Jezard, Alison
1 *Albert* (1968)
2 *Albert in Scotland* (1969)
3 *Albert and Henry* (1970)
4 *Albert's Christmas* (1970)
5 *Albert up the river* (1971)
6 *Albert and Digger* (1972)
7 *Albert and Tum Tum* (1973)
8 *Albert goes to sea* (1973)
9 *Albert, police bear* (1975)
10 *Albert goes trekking* (1976)
11 *Albert's circus* (1977)
12 *Albert goes treasure-hunting* (1978)
13 *Albert on the farm* (1979)

Albert series
Levy, Elizabeth
see **Fat Albert series**
Stannard, Russell
see **Uncle Albert series**

Albert the dragon series
Weir, Rosemary
1 *Albert the dragon* (1961)
2 *Further adventures of Albert the dragon* (1964)
3 *Albert the dragon and the centaur* (1968)
4 *Albert and the dragonettes* (1977)
5 *Albert's world tour* (1978)

Alberta series
Sandel, Cora
1 *Alberta and Jacob* (1926)
2 *Alberta and freedom* (1931)
3 *Alberta alone* (1939)

Albie Harris series
Dean, Amber
1 *Dead man's float* (1944)
2 *Chanticleer's muffled crow* (1945)
3 *Call me Pandora* (1946)
Blonde is dead
4 *Wrap it up* (1946)
5 *No traveler returns* (1948)
6 *Snipe hunt* (1949)
7 *August incident* (1951)
8 *Devil threw twice* (1954)

Albigensian trilogy
Closs, Hannah
1 *High are the mountains* (1946)
2 *And sombre the valleys* (1949)
3 *Silent tarn* (1955)

Albin series
Lofgren, Ulf
1 *Albin is never afraid* (1975)
Original edition entitled *Albin ar aldrig radd*
2 *Albin lends a hand* (1975)
Original edition entitled *Albin hjalpar till*
3 *Albin and the crazy bicycle* (1977)
Original edition entitled *Albin och den snuffige cyceln*
4 *Albin and the strange umbrella* (1977)
Original edition entitled *Albin och det markvardiga paraplet*
5 *Albin and his friend Ali Baba* (1983)
6 *Albin and the magic wand* (1983)
7 *Albin and the parrot* (1983)
8 *Albin and the rainbow* (1983)

Albine series
Allen, Hervey
see **Disinherited series**

Albion trilogy
Lawhead, Stephen
see **Song of Albion trilogy**

Albion trilogy
Sinclair, Andrew
1 *Gog* (1967)
2 *Magog* (1972)
3 *King Ludd* (1988)

Albright family series
Johnston, Norma
see **Sterling family series**

Alcibiades series
Brun, Vincenz
1 *Alcibiades, beloved of gods and men* (1935)
2 *Alcibiades, forsaken by gods and men* (1936)

Aldair series
Barrett, Neal
1 *Aldair in Albion* (1976)
2 *Aldair, master of ships* (1977)
3 *Aldair, across the misty sea* (1980)
4 *Legion of beasts* (1982)

Alden All Stars series
Hallowell, Tommy
1 *Duel on the diamond* (1990)
2 *Jester in the back cover* (1990)
3 *Shot from midfield* (1990)
4 *Last chance quarterback* (1990)

Alden family series
Warner, Gertrude Chandler
see **Boxcar children series**

Alderley series
Garner, Alan
1 *Weirdstone of Brisingamen* (1960)
Weirdstone
2 *Moon of Gomrath* (1963)

Alderley series
Stanley, Maria Josepha
Edited by Nancy Mitford
1 *Ladies of Alderley* (1938)
1841-1850
2 *Stanleys of Alderley* (1939)
1851-1865

Alderly series
Robards, Karen
see **Lady Catherine Alderly series**

Aldgate series
Finn, Ralph Leslie
Reminiscences of an East End Jewish family
1 *No tears in Aldgate* (1963)
Time remembered
2 *Spring in Aldgate* (1968)
Grief forgotten

Aldington series
Holland, Isabelle
see **Claire Aldington series**

Aldo Sossi series
Hurwitz, Johanna
1 *Much ado about Aldo* (1978)
2 *Aldo Applesauce* (1979)
3 *Aldo Ice Cream* (1981)
4 *Aldo Peanut Butter* (1990)
Companion volumes: *Tough-Luck Karen*, 1982, *Hurricane Elaine*, 1986

Aldric Talvarin series
Morwood, Peter
see **Book of years series**

Aldrich series
McDonnell, Jinny
see **Kim Aldrich series**

Alec Bowden series
Leeson, Robert
1 *Third class genie* (1975)
2 *Genie on the loose* (1983)
3 *Last genie* (1993)

Alec Cavender series
Tokson, Elliot
1 *Desert captive* (1977)
2 *Cavender's Balkan quest* (1977)

Alec Haig series
Haig, Alec
1 *Sign on for Tokyo* (1968)
2 *Peruvian printout* (1970)
3 *Flight from Montego Bay* (1972)

Alec Sinclair series
Macarthur, David Wilson
1 *Mystery of the David M* (1932)
2 *Landfall* (1933)

Aleese series
Miner, Jane Claypool
see **Ellynne Aleese series**

Alelia trilogy
Dixelius, Hildur
see **Sara Alelia trilogy**

Aleria Farrell series
Comstock, Jarrod
see **These lawless worlds series**

Alert series
Lampton, Christopher
1 *Blizzard alert!* (1991)
2 *Earthquake alert!* (1991)
3 *Forest fire alert!* (1991)
4 *Hurricane alert!* (1991)
5 *Tornado alert!* (1991)
6 *Volcano alert!* (1991)

Alerting kids to the danger zones series
Berry, Joy
1 *Alerting kids to the danger of kidnapping* (1984)
2 *Alerting kids to the danger of sexual abuse* (1984)
3 *Alerting kids to the danger of abuse and neglect* (1984)
Companion volume: *A parent's guide to the danger zones*, by Joy Berry and Kathy McBride, 1985

Aleshine and Lecks series
Stockton, Frank Richard
see **Mrs Lecks and Mrs Aleshine series**

Alessandra series
Kaplow, Robert
1 *Alessandra in love* (1989)
2 *Alessandra between* (1992)

Alessandro di Ganzarello, Coleridge Tucker and Jennifer Norrington series
Drummond, Ivor
see **Lady Jennifer, Sandro and Colly series**

Alex and Beryl series
Oliver, Marjorie Mary
1 *Menace on the moor* (1960)
2 *Riddle of the tired pony* (1964)

Alex and Maddy Phillips series
Zimmerman, R D
see **Maddy and Alex Phillips series**

Alex and Merrill trilogy
Main, Carol
see **Fraser family trilogy**

Alex Balfour series
Appel, Allen
1 *Time after time* (1985)
2 *Twice upon a time* (1988)
3 *Till the end of time* (1990)

Alex Dartanian series
Rainey, Rich
1 *Venus underground* (1982)
2 *Porn tapes* (1983)
3 *Hit parade* (1983)
4 *Cult point forty five* (1984)
5 *Nightmare network* (1984)
6 *Dragon slaying* (1985)

Alex Delaware series
Kellerman, Jonathan
1 *When the bough breaks* (1985)
Shrunken heads
2 *Blood test* (1986)
3 *Over the edge* (1987)
4 *Silent partner* (1989)
5 *Time bomb* (1990)
6 *Private eyes* (1992)
7 *Devil's waltz* (1993)
8 *Daddy, daddy* (1994)
9 *Self-defense* (1995)

Alex in Wonderland series
King, Alexander
see **Mine enemy grows older series**

Alex Jason series
Sugar, Andrew
see **Enforcer series**

Alex Kane series
Preston, John
see **Mission of Alex Kane series**

Alex Mackenzie and Sarah Deane series
Borthwick, J S
see **Sarah Deane and Alex Mackenzie series**

Alex series
Dickinson, Mary
1 *Alex's bed* (1980)
2 *Alex and Roy* (1981)
Best friends
3 *Alex and the baby* (1982)
4 *Alex's outing* (1983)
5 *New clothes for Alex* (1984)

Alex series
Duder, Tessa
1 *Alex* (1987)
2 *Alex in winter* (1989)
3 *Alessandra* (1991)
Alex in Rome
4 *Songs for Alex* (1992)
One volume edition entitled *The Alex quartet*, 1992

Alex Smith and Tony Bevan series
Forster, Peter
1 *Play the ball* (1967)
2 *Play the man* (1970)
3 *Disinherited* (1971)

Alex Tanner series
Donald, Anabel
1 *Uncommon murder* (1993)
2 *In at the deep end* (1994)

Alex Werner series
Weinberg, Robert
1 *Devil's auction* (1988)
2 *Armageddon box* (1991)

Alexander and Bunch series
Wood, Andrew
see **Bunch and Alexander series**

Alexander Botts series
Upson, William Hazlett
1 *Alexander Botts, earthworm tractors* (1929)
Alexander the greatest
2 *Earthworms in Europe* (1931)
Alexander Botts makes the old world tractor-conscious
3 *Keep 'em crawling* (1943)
Earthworms at war
4 *Botts in war, Botts in peace* (1944)
Earthworms can take anything
5 *Earthworms through the ages* (1947)
The wisdom of Anexander Botts
6 *Hello, Mister Henderson* (1949)
7 *No rest for Botts* (1951)
Selections: *The best of Botts*, 1961; companion volume: *Original letters of Alexander Botts*, 1963

Alexander Bunyip series
Salmon, Michael
1 *Monster that ate Canberra* (1972)
A book for the younger generations of Canberra
2 *Son of the monster* (1973)
A story of Canberra in the year 2022
3 *Travels with the monster* (1974)
A story of Alexander's adventures overseas
4 *Monster in space* (1977)
Alexander's adventures on the planet of Kronos
5 *Alexander Bunyip* (1980)
6 *Alexander Bunyip and the swagman* (1980)
7 *Bush fire* (1981)
8 *Brother Bert comes to stay* (1981)
9 *Birthday party* (1981)
10 *Cousin Emma and the green jungle* (1981)
11 *Monster who ate Australia* (1986)
12 *New monster that ate Canberra* (1990)
Companion volume: *The little monster cook book*, by Jan and Michael Salmon, 1986

Alexander Caspian series
Burke, John Frederick
see **Doctor Alexander Caspian series**

Alexander Chane and Vladimer Karlov series
Hayes, Ralph Eugene
see **Check Force series**

Alexander Columbus Banyana series
Elliott, Janice
1 *Birthday unicorn* (1970)
2 *Alexander in the land of Mog* (1973)

Alexander Cornell series
Michel, Milton Scott
see **Doctor Alexander Cornell series**

Alexander Hero series
Gallico, Paul
1 *Too many ghosts* (1959)
2 *Hand of Mary Constable* (1964)

Alexander Magnus and Norma Gold series
Resnicow, Herbert
1 *Gold solution* (1983)
2 *Gold deadline* (1984)
3 *Gold frame* (1984)
4 *Gold curse* (1986)
5 *Gold gamble* (1988)

Alexander Scott and Kelly Robinson series
Tiger, John
see **I spy series**

Alexander series
Herrman, Frank
see **Giant Alexander series**

Alexander series
Viorst, Judith
Illustrated by Ray Cruz
1 *Alexander and the terrible, horrible, no good, very bad day* (1972)
2 *Alexander, who used to be rich last Sunday* (1978)

Alexander Sheridan series
Stuart, Vivian
see **Captain Alexander Sheridan series**

Alexander the Great series
Renault, Mary
1 *Fire from heaven* (1969)
2 *Persian boy* (1972)
3 *Funeral games* (1981)
One volume edition entitled *The Alexander trilogy*, 1984; companion volume: *The nature of Alexander*, 1975

Alexander trilogy
Kirkman, Marshall Monroe
1 *Romance of Alexander the prince* (1909)
2 *Romance of Alexander the king* (1909)
3 *Romance of Alexander and Roxana* (1909)

Alexandra series
Greene, Constance Clarke
see **Al series**

Alexandria quartet
Durrell, Lawrence
1 *Justine* (1957)
2 *Balthazar* (1958)
3 *Mountolive* (1958)
4 *Clea* (1960)

Alexandria Thaine and Rane Falconer trilogy
De Blasis, Celeste
see **Wild Swan trilogy**

Alexei Hamilton series
Plowman, Stephanie
1 *Three lives for the Czar* (1969)
2 *My kingdom for a grave* (1970)

Alf Gorilla series
Grater, Michael
1 *Alf Gorilla* (1986)
2 *Alf Gorilla adrift* (1988)

Alf Higgins series
Darlington, William Aubrey
1 *Alf's button* (1919)
2 *Alf's carpet* (1928)
3 *Alf's new button* (1940)

Alfar series
Boyer, Elizabeth H
see **World of the Alfar series**

Alfie Atkins series
Bergstrom, Gunilla
1 *Alfie and his secret friend* (1977)
Original edition entitled *Alfons och odjuret*
2 *Who'll save Alfie Atkins?* (1977)
Original edition entitled *Vem raddar Alfons Aberg?*
3 *You're a sly one, Alfie Atkins!* (1977)
Original edition entitled *Listigt, Alfons Aberg!*
4 *Alfie and the monster* (1978)
Original edition entitled *Alfons och hemlige Mallgan*
5 *Who's scaring Alfie Atkins?* (1982)
Original edition entitled *Ar du feg, Alfons Aberg?*
6 *You have a girl friend, Alfie Atkins?* (1983)
Original edition entitled *Var ar bus-Alfons?*
7 *Is that a monster, Alfie Atkins?* (1984)
Original edition entitled *Vem spokar, Alfons Aberg?*

Alfie Rose series
Hughes, Shirley
1 *Alfie gets in first* (1982)

Alfie Rose series

2 *Alfie's feet* (1984)
3 *Alfie gives a hand* (1984)
4 *Evening at Alfie's* (1984)
Companion volumes: *The big Alfie and Annie Rose storybook*, 1988, *The big Alfie out-of-doors storybook*, 1992

Alfie series
Naughton, Bill
1 *Alfie* (1966)
2 *Alfie darling* (1970)

Alfred and Lester series
Slepian, Jan
1 *Alfred summer* (1980)
2 *Lester's turn* (1981)

Alfred Baum series
Kartun, Derek
1 *Beaver to fox* (1983)
2 *Flittermouse* (1984)
3 *Megiddo* (1987)

Alfred Brooks trilogy
Lipsyte, Roger
see **Contender trilogy**

Alfred Hagart series
Smith, Alexander
1 *Alfred Hagart's household* (1865)
2 *Miss Oona McQuarrie* (1866)

Alfred Hitchcock and the Three Investigators series
Arthur, Robert
see **Three Investigators series**

Alfred Rawson series
Dorrance, Ethel Smith
see **Sergeant Alfred Rawson series**

Alfred series
Hodges, Cyril Walter
see **King Alfred series**

Alfred Stanley Rosher series
Scott, Jack S
see **Detective Inspector Alfred Stanley Rosher series**

Algerian series
Larteguy, Jean
1 *Centurions* (1960)
2 *Praetorians* (1961)

Algernon Alexander Gunning Hendry series
Berkley, Tom
1 *We keep a pub* (1955)
2 *I go on the films* (1957)
3 *We cope with the kids* (1958)

Algy, Peter and Jeremy series
Scott, Philip
1 *Galleon's Bay* (1953)
2 *Negro's ring* (1954)
3 *River adventure* (1955)

Ali and Dizzy series
Shaw, Jane
1 *Anything can happen* (1964)
2 *Nothing happened after all* (1965)

Ali Baba Bernstein series
Hurwitz, Johanna
1 *Adventures of Ali Baba Bernstein* (1985)
2 *Hurray for Ali Baba Bernstein* (1989)
3 *Ali Baba Bernstein, lost and found* (1992)

Ali series
Voegeli, Max
see **Adventures of Ali series**

Alias Smith and Jones series
Fox, Brian
1 *Outlaw trail* (1969)
2 *Unholy angel* (1969)
3 *Dead ringer* (1971)
4 *Apache gold* (1971)
5 *Dragooned by Fox* (1971)
6 *Trick shot* (1976)
Companion volume: *Alias Smith and Jones*, 1976

Alice and Emily series
Starling, Jill
1 *Alice in reflection* (1987)
2 *Emily in waiting* (1988)

Alice and me series
Rogers, Paul
see **Me and Alice series**

Alice Greenwood series
Barr, Pat
1 *Chinese Alice* (1981)
2 *Uncut jade* (1983)
One volume edition entitled *Jade*, 1982

Alice in Bibleland series
Davidson, Alice Joyce
1 *Story of creation* (1984)
2 *Story of Noah* (1984)
3 *Story of Jonah* (1984)
4 *Psalms and Proverbs for you* (1984)
5 *Story of David and Goliath* (1985)
6 *Story of baby Moses* (1985)
7 *Story of baby Jesus* (1985)
8 *Story of the loaves and the fishes* (1985)
9 *Prayers and graces* (1986)
10 *Story of Daniel and the lions* (1986)
11 *Story of Easter* (1988)
12 *Twenty-third Psalm* (1988)
13 *Prodigal son* (1989)
14 *Story of Exodus* (1989)
15 *Story of Joshua* (1989)
16 *Story of Esther* (1989)
17 *Story of Isaac's wife* (1989)
18 *Story of Paul* (1989)
19 *Story of the good Samaritan* (1989)
20 *Story of Ruth and Naomi* (1989)
21 *Story of Jesus and his disciples* (1989)
22 *Story of the lost sheep* (1989)
23 *Story of the Tower of Babel* (1989)
24 *Lord's prayer* (1989)

Alice in Wonderland parodies series
This sequence, by several authors whose works have been inspired by Lewis Carroll's stories, are listed in chronological order of publication
Lewis, Caroline
This pseudonym is used by M H Temple, James Stafford Ransome and Harold Begbie in collaboration
1 *Clara in Blunderland* (1902)
2 *Lost in Blunderland* (1903)
Bangs, John Kendrick
3 *Alice in Blunderland* (1907)
An irridescent dream
Evarts, Richard Conover
4 *Alice's adventures in Cambridge* (1913)
Wyatt, Horace
5 *Malice in Kulturland* (1914)
Otterbourg, Edwin Max
6 *Alice in Rankbustland* (1923)
Hope, Edward
7 *Alice in the Delighted States* (1928)
Short, Jackson
8 *Blue Alice* (1972)
Anderson, Jack
9 *Alice in Blunderland* (1983)
Companion volume: *Alicia in Blunderland*, edited by Peter Schuyler Miller, 1983

Alice in Wonderland sequels series
This sequence, by several authors whose works have been inspired by Lewis Carroll's stories, are listed in chronological order of publication
Carryl, Charles Edward
1 *Davy and the goblin* (1885)
Alternative title: What followed reading Alice's adventures in Wonderland
Richards, Anna Matlock
2 *New Alice in the old Wonderland* (1895)
La Prade, Ernest
3 *Alice in Orchestralia* (1925)
Alice in Orchestra Land
Alice in Music Land
The third title is a revised edition
4 *Marching notes* (1929)
Wilson, Yates
5 *More Alice* (1959)
Adair, Gilbert
6 *Alice through the needle's eye* (1984)
Amadio, Nadine
7 *New adventures of Alice in Rainforest Land* (1988)

Alice in Wonderland series
Carroll, Lewis
1 *Alice's adventures in Wonderland* (1865)
Alice's adventures under-ground
Alice in Wonderland
2 *Through the looking glass and what Alice found there* (1871)
Alice through the looking glass
One volume edition entitled *The annotated Alice*, 1960; sequels to this sequence are listed under **Alice in Wonderland sequels series**, and parodies under **Alice in Wonderland parodies series**

Alice Nestleton series
Adamson, Lydia
1 *Cat in the manger* (1990)
2 *Cat in wolf's clothing* (1991)
3 *Cat of a different color* (1992)
4 *Cat by any other name* (1992)
5 *Cat in the wings* (1992)
6 *Cat with a fiddle* (1993)
7 *Cat in the glass house* (1993)

Alice Penny series
Bliss, Adam
1 *Murder upstairs* (1934)
2 *Four times a widower* (1936)

Alice series
Edmondson, Garry Cotton
1 *Ship that sailed the time stream* (1965)
Expanded edition 1978
2 *To sail the century sea* (1981)

Alice series
Naylor, Phyllis Reynolds
1 *Agony of Alice* (1985)
2 *Alice in rapture* (1989)
3 *Reluctant Alice* (1991)
4 *All but Alice* (1992)
5 *Alice in April* (1993)

Alicia series
Brown, Sandra
1 *Breakfast in bed* (1983)
2 *Send no flowers* (1984)

Alicia von Helsing series
Mathewson, Joseph
1 *Alicia's trump* (1980)
2 *Death turns right* (1982)

Alien Island series
Sherred, Thomas L
1 *Alien Island* (1970)
2 *Alien main* (1985)
Co-author: Lloyd Biggle

Alien series
Foster, Alan Dean
1 *Alien* (1979)
2 *Aliens* (1986)

Alien speedway series
Wylde, Thomas
see **Roger Zelazny's Alien speedway series**

Alien stars series
Mitchell, Elizabeth
1 *Alien stars* (1985)
2 *After the flames* (1985)
3 *Under the wheel* (1987)
4 *Free lancers* (1987)

Alien trace series
Major, H M
1 *Alien trace* (1984)
2 *Time twister* (1984)

Aliens and robots series
Leigh, Stephen
see **Robots and aliens series**

Aliens series
Etra, Jonathan
1 *Aliens for breakfast* (1988)
2 *Aliens for lunch* (1991)

Aliens series
Perry, Steve
1 *Earth hive* (1992)
2 *Nightmare asylum* (1993)
3 *Female war* (1993)
Co-author: Stephani Perry

Alisha series
Taylor, Janelle
see **Sioux series**

Alison and John series
Daniell, David Scott
1 *Flight one, Australia* (1958)
2 *Flight two, Canada* (1959)
3 *Flight three, United States of America* (1959)
4 *Flight four, India* (1960)
5 *Flight five, Africa* (1961)
6 *Flight six, the Holy Land* (1962)

Alison Gordon series
Wager, Walter
1 *Blue leader* (1979)
2 *Blue moon* (1980)
3 *Blue murder* (1981)

Alison Hope and Inspector Nick Trevellyan series
Kelly, Susan
1 *Hope against hope* (1991)
2 *Time of hope* (1992)
3 *Hope will answer* (1993)

Alison Plantaine trilogy
Mosco, Maisie
see **Between two worlds trilogy**

Alison series
Stuart, Sheila
1 *Alison's Highland holiday* (1945)
2 *More adventures of Alison* (1947)
3 *Alison's Christmas adventure* (1948)
4 *Well done, Alison* (1949)
5 *Alison's Easter adventure* (1950)
6 *Alison's poaching adventure* (1951)
7 *Alison's kidnapping adventure* (1952)
8 *Alison's pony adventure* (1953)
9 *Alison's island adventure* (1954)
10 *Alison's spy adventure* (1955)
11 *Alison and the witch's cave* (1956)
12 *Alison's yacht adventure* (1957)
13 *Alison's riding adventure* (1958)
14 *Alison's cliff adventure* (1959)
15 *Alison's caravan adventure* (1960)

Alison Vernon series
Knight, Brigid
see **Ashenden series**

Alison Young series
Campbell, Alice
1 *Door closed softly* (1939)
2 *They hunted a fox* (1940)

Alistair Duncan series
Ross, Cameron
1 *Case for compensation* (1980)
2 *Villa plot, counterplot* (1981)
3 *Scaffold* (1981)

Alister Woodhead series
Clements, Eileen Helen
1 *Let him die* (1939)
2 *Cherry harvest* (1943)
3 *Berry green* (1945)
4 *Weathercock* (1949)
5 *Chair-lift* (1955)
6 *Discord in the air* (1955)
7 *Other island* (1956)
8 *Back in daylight* (1957)
9 *Uncommon cold* (1958)
10 *High tension* (1959)
11 *Honey for the marshal* (1960)
12 *Note of enchantment* (1961)
13 *Let or hindrance* (1963)

All aboard series
Rand, Edward Augustus
1 *All aboard for sunrise lands* (1881)
A trip through California, across the Pacific to Japan, China and Australia
2 *All aboard for the lakes and mountains* (1883)
A trip to picturesque localities in the United States

All creatures great and small series
Herriot, James
see **Vet series**

All is but a beginning series
Neihardt, John Gneisenau
Autobiography
1 *All is but a beginning* (1972)
Youth remembered, 1881-1901
2 *Patterns and coincidences* (1978)

All-Jewish cartoon series
Gerberg, Mort
1 *All-Jewish cartoon collection* (1986)
2 *More all-Jewish cartoons, yet* (1987)

All men are islands trilogy
Duncan, Ronald
Autobiography
1 *All men are islands* (1964)
2 *How to make enemies* (1968)
3 *Obsessed* (1977)

All nations series
Toer, Pramoedya Ananta
1 *This earth of mankind* (1975)
Original edition entitled *Bumi manusia*
2 *Child of all nations* (1980)
Original edition entitled *Anak semua bangsa*

All-of-a-kind family series
Taylor, Sydney
1 *All-of-a-kind family* (1951)
2 *More all-of-a-kind family* (1954)
3 *All-of-a-kind family uptown* (1958)
4 *All-of-a-kind family downtown* (1972)
5 *Ella of all-of-a-kind family* (1978)

All-over-the-world series
Optic, Oliver
1 *Missing million* (1891)
Alternative title: The adventures of Louis Belgrave
2 *Millionaire at sixteen* (1892)
Alternative title: The cruise of the Guardian-Mother
3 *Young knight-errant* (1893)
Alternative title: Cruising in the West Indies
4 *Strange sights abroad* (1893)
Alternative title: A voyage in European waters
5 *American boys afloat* (1893)
Alternative title: Cruising in the Orient
6 *Young navigators* (1893)
Alternative title: The foreign cruise of the Maud
7 *Up and down the Nile* (1894)
Alternative title: Young adventurers in Africa
8 *Asiatic breezes* (1895)
Alternative title: Students on the wing
9 *Across India* (1895)
Alternative title: Live boys in the Far East
10 *Half round the world* (1895)
Alternative title: Among the uncivilized
11 *Four young explorers* (1896)
12 *Pacific shores* (1898)
Alternative title: Adventures in Eastern seas

All-Star Meatballs series
Mooser, Stephen
1 *Babe Ruth and the home run Derby* (1992)
2 *Terrible tickler* (1992)
3 *Scary scraped up skaters* (1992)
4 *Headless snowman* (1992)
5 *Snow bowl* (1992)
6 *Muscle mania* (1993)
7 *Amazing stories* (1993)
8 *April fools* (1993)

All that series
Sellar, Walter Carruthers
1 *Ten sixty six and all that* (1930)
2 *And now all this* (1932)
3 *Horse nonsense* (1933)
4 *Garden rubbish, and other country bumps* (1936)

All the rivers run trilogy
Cato, Nancy
see **Australian trilogy**

All upon series
George, Jean Craighead
1 *All upon a stone* (1971)
2 *All upon a sidewalk* (1974)

Allain and Stevens series
Graeme, Bruce
see **Superintendent William Stevens and Inspector Pierre Allain series**

Allan Cameron series
Connor, Ralph
see **North-West Mounted Police series**

Allan Dice series
Hill, Peter
see **Commander Allan Dice series**

Allan Quatermain series
Haggard, Henry Rider
1 *Marie* (1912)
2 *Allan's wife* (1887)
3 *Child of storm* (1913)
4 *Tale of three lions* (1887)
Numbers 2 and 4 also published in one volume entitled *Allan's wife, and other tales*, 1889, which also includes *Long odds*, which forms a bridge between 6 and 7
5 *Maiwa's revenge* (1888)
6 *Allan the hunter* (1898)
Also includes *A tale of three lions*, 1887; originally published as Hunter Quatermain's story in *Allan's wife, and other tales*, 1889
7 *Holy flower* (1915)
Allan and the holy flower
8 *Heu-Heu* (1924)
Alternative title: The monster
9 *She and Allan* (1921)
10 *Treasure of the lake* (1926)
11 *Ivory child* (1916)
12 *Finished* (1917)
Magepa the buck, published in *Smith and the pharaohs, and other tales*, 1920 forms a bridge between numbers 12 and 13
13 *King Solomon's mines* (1885)
Adaptated version from the film, by Jean Francis Webb, 1950; parodies: *King Solomon's treasures*, by John De Morgan, 1887, *King Solomon's wives*, by John De Morgan, 1887, *King Solomon's wives*, by Hyder Ragged, 1887
14 *Ancient Allan* (1920)
15 *Allan and the ice gods* (1927)
16 *Allan Quatermain* (1887)
Allan Quatermain and the lost city of gold
The second title is an edition abridged by Sarah Litvinoff, 1986

Allan series
Beardmore, George
see **Lesley Allan series**
Rath, Virginia
see **Rocky Allan series**
West, Joyce
see **Gabrielle Allan series**

Allan Stewart series
Van Siller, Hilda
1 *Complete stranger* (1965)
2 *Mood for murder* (1966)
3 *Biltmore call* (1967)

Allard series
Barclay, Bill
see **Nick Allard series**

Allard trilogy
Joyce, Cyril
see **Greg Allard trilogy**

Allardyce series
Bennett, Dorothy
1 *Chaos makers* (1968)
2 *Operation chaos* (1969)

Alldera series
Charnas, Suzy McKee
1 *Walk to the end of the world* (1974)
2 *Motherlines* (1978)
Numbers 1 and 2 also published in one volume 1989
3 *Furies* (1994)

Allen Cheyney series
Cosgrave, Patrick
see **Colonel Allen Cheyney series**

Allen family series
Lamplugh, Lois
1 *Pigeongram family* (1955)
2 *Nine bright shiners* (1955)
3 *Vagabond's castle* (1957)
4 *Rockets in the dunes* (1958)
5 *Sixpenny runner* (1960)
6 *Midsummer mountains* (1961)

Allen series
Anson, Lindsay
see **Peter Allen series**
Bancroft, Edith
see **Jane Allen series**
Dunning, Hal
see **Jim-Twin Allen series**
Forbes, Graham B
see **Frank Allen series**
Greene, Joseph
see **Dig Allen series**
Holley, Marietta
see **Samantha and Josiah Allen series**

Allens series
Grove, Harriet Pyne
see **Adventurous Allens series**

Alley Jaggers series
West, Paul
see **Jaggers family series**

Alleyn series
Marsh, Ngaio
see **Inspector Roderick Alleyn series**

Alliance-Union series
Cherryh, Carolyn Janice
1 *Heavy time* (1991)
2 *Hellburner* (1992)
3 *Downbelow Station* (1981)
4 *Forty thousand in Gehenna* (1983)
5 *Merchanter's luck* (1982)
6 *Rimrunners* (1989)
7 *Pride of Chanur* (1982)
8 *Chanur's venture* (1984)
9 *Kif strikes back* (1985)
10 *Chanur's homecoming* (1986)
11 *Cyteen* (1988)
11.1 *Betrayal* (1988)
11.2 *Rebirth* (1988)
11.3 *Vindication* (1988)
12 *Cuckoo's egg* (1985)
13 *Serpent's reach* (1980)
14 *Kesrith* (1978)
15 *Shon'jir* (1978)
16 *Kutath* (1979)
Numbers 14-16 also published in one volume entitled *The faded sun trilogy*, 1987
17 *Brothers of earth* (1976)
18 *Hunter of worlds* (1977)

Alligator case series
Pene du Bois, William
1 *Alligator case* (1965)
2 *Horse in the camel suit* (1967)

Allington trilogy
Wiat, Philippa
1 *Heir of Allington* (1973)
2 *Knight of Allington* (1974)
3 *Rebel of Allington* (1974)

Allison series
Fisher, Clay
see **Ben Allison series**
Meade, Richard
see **John Allison series**

Allotment Lane School series
Joy, Margaret
1 *Tales from Allotment Lane School* (1985)
2 *Allotment Lane School again* (1985)
3 *Hild at Allotment Lane School* (1987)

Allport series
Everton, Francis
see **Detective Inspector Allport series**

Allsorts series
Fletcher, Audrey
Illustrated by Beryl Sanders
1 *Joseph and his jointed camel* (1986)
2 *Abrar's holiday* (1986)
3 *Wedding* (1986)
Numbers 1-3 also published in one volume entitled *Allsorts*, 1987
4 *Rubbish dumpers* (1986)
5 *Foggy Christmas* (1986)
6 *Wet dinner-time* (1986)
Numbers 4-6 also published in one volume entitled *More allsorts*, 1987

Allways trilogy
Nichols, Beverley
1 *Down the garden path* (1932)
2 *Thatched roof* (1933)
3 *Village in a valley* (1934)

Ally and Mike series
Elfman, Blossom
see **Mike and Ally series**

Alma series
Breitenbach, Louise Marks
1 *Alma at Hadley Hall* (1912)
2 *Alma's sophomore year* (1913)

3 *Alma's junior year* (1914)
4 *Alma's senior year* (1915)

Almonds and raisins trilogy
Mosco, Maisie
1 *Almonds and raisins* (1979)
2 *Scattered seed* (1980)
3 *Children's children* (1981)

Almost sisters series
Makris, Kathryn
1 *Sisters scheme* (1991)
2 *Sisters war* (1991)
3 *Sisters team* (1992)

Alms for oblivion series
Raven, Simon
1 *Rich pay late* (1964)
2 *Friends in low places* (1965)
3 *Sabre Squadron* (1966)
4 *Fielding Gray* (1967)
5 *Judas boy* (1968)
6 *Places where they sing* (1970)
7 *Sound the retreat* (1971)
8 *Come like shadows* (1972)
9 *Bring forth the body* (1974)
10 *Survivors* (1976)

Alney series
Coxhead, Elizabeth
1 *Play toward* (1952)
2 *Midlanders* (1953)

Alo Nudger series
Lutz, John
1 *Buyer beware* (1976)
2 *Nightlines* (1985)
3 *Right to sing the blues* (1986)
4 *Ride the lightning* (1987)
5 *Dancer's debt* (1988)
6 *Time exposure* (1989)
7 *Diamond eyes* (1990)
8 *Dancing with the dead* (1992)
9 *Thicker than blood* (1993)

Aloha series
Keene, Day
see **Johnny Aloha series**

Along my line series
Harding, Gilbert
Autobiography
1 *Along my line* (1953)
2 *Master of none* (1958)

Alonzo Mactavish series
Cheyney, Peter
1 *Adventures of Alonzo Mactavish* (1943)
2 *Alonzo Mactavish again* (1943)
3 *Murder of Alonzo* (1943)
4 *He walked in her sleep, and other stories* (1946)
Mactavish
5 *Lady in green, and other stories* (1947)

Alorie series
Salsitz, R A V
1 *Unicorn dancer* (1986)
2 *Daughter of destiny* (1988)

Alot series
Watson, Jean
1 *Fred Fear-Alot* (1980)
2 *Humphrey Hope-Alot* (1980)
3 *Magnus Think-Alot* (1980)
4 *Martha Do-Alot* (1980)
5 *Grant Grab-Alot* (1980)
6 *Desmond Dither-Alot* (1980)
7 *Harriet Help-Alot* (1980)
8 *Lucy Laugh-Alot* (1980)
9 *Kitty Cry-Alot* (1980)
10 *Lottie Lie-Alot* (1980)

Aloysius Kelly series
Worsley-Gough, Barbara
1 *Alibi innings* (1954)
2 *Lantern Hill* (1957)

Aloysius Kennedy series
O'Duffy, Eimar
1 *Spacious adventures of the man in the street* (1928)
2 *Asses in clover* (1933)

Alpaca series
Billam, Rosemary
1 *Alpaca* (1982)
Fuzzy Rabbit
2 *Alpaca in the park* (1985)
Fuzzy Rabbit in the park
3 *Come on Alpaca* (1988)
Fuzzy Rabbit and the little brother problem
4 *Alpaca saves Christmas* (1991)
Fuzzy Rabbit saves Christmas

Alphabet series
Baum, Lyman Frank
1 *Army alphabet* (1900)
2 *Navy alphabet* (1900)

Alphabet series
Gorey, Edward
1 *Fatal lozenge* (1960)
2 *Hapless child* (1961)
3 *Sinking spell* (1965)
4 *Chinese obelisks* (1970)
5 *Glorious nosebleed* (1974)
Companion volume: *Utter zoo alphabet*, 1967

Alphabet series
Grafton, Sue
see **Kensey Millhone series**

Alscott experiment series
Stanley, Bennett
1 *Alscott experiment* (1954)
2 *Sea to Eden* (1954)

Alt series
Harrison, Harry
see **Jason Din Alt series**

Altair series
Lane, Carl Daniel
1 *Treasure cave* (1953)
2 *Black tide* (1954)

Alternate series
Greenberg, Martin Harry
see **What might have been series**

Alternate world series
Anderson, Poul
1 *Three hearts and three lions* (1961)
2 *Midsummer tempest* (1974)

Altruria series
Howells, William Dean
1 *Traveller from Altruria* (1894)
2 *Through the eye of the needle* (1907)

Alun Barry series
O'Hara, Kenneth
1 *View to a death* (1958)
2 *Sleeping dogs lying* (1960)

Alvarez series
Jeffries, Roderic Graeme
see **Inspector Enrique Alvarez series**

Alvear family trilogy
Gironella, Jose Maria
Translated from the Spanish
1 *Cypresses believe in God* (1953)
2 *One million dead* (1961)
3 *Peace after war* (1966)

Alvin Dustine Fog series
Edson, John Thomas
see **Cap Fog series**

Alvin Fernald series
Hicks, Clifford Byron
1 *Marvelous inventions of Alvin Fernald* (1960)
2 *Alvin's secret code* (1963)
3 *Alvin Fernald, foreign trader* (1966)
4 *Alvin Fernald, mayor for a day* (1970)
5 *Alvin Fernald, superweasel* (1974)
6 *Alvin's swap shop* (1976)
7 *Alvin Fernald, TV anchorman* (1980)
8 *Wacky world of Alvin Fernald* (1981)
9 *Alvin Fernald, master of a thousand disguises* (1986)

Alvin Maker series
Card, Orson Scott
1 *Seventh son* (1987)
2 *Red prophet* (1988)
3 *Prentice Alvin* (1989)
One volume edition entitled *Hatrack River, the tales of Alvin Maker, part one*, 1989

Alys Heavers series
Clydesdale, Abby
1 *Sign of the witch* (1977)
2 *Witch's curse* (1978)

Alys series
Macdonald, Una
1 *Alys-all-alone* (1911)
2 *Alys in Happyland* (1913)

Alysa series
Taylor, Janelle
see **Princess Alysa series**

Alyx series
Russ, Joanna
see **Adventures of Alyx series**

Am and Ed Hunter series
Brown, Fredric
see **Ed and Am Hunter series**

Amabel series
Prior, Natalie Jane
1 *Amazing adventures of Amabel* (1990)
2 *Amabel abroad* (1991)

Amanda and April series
Pryor, Bonnie
1 *Amanda and April* (1986)
2 *Merry Christmas, Amanda and April* (1990)

Amanda and Lutie Beagle series
Chanslor, Torrey
see **Lutie and Amanda Beagle series**

Amanda Curzon and Oscar Sallis series
Usher, Frank
1 *Man from Moscow* (1965)
2 *No flowers in Braslov* (1968)
3 *Boston crab* (1970)

Amanda Nightingale series
Revelli, George
1 *Commander Amanda Nightingale* (1968)
2 *Resort to war* (1970)
3 *Amanda's castle* (1972)
4 *Amanda in Spain* (1976)
5 *Amanda in Berlin* (1978)

Amanda Pepper series
Roberts, Gillian
1 *Caught dead in Philadelphia* (1987)
2 *Philly stakes* (1989)
3 *I'd rather be in Philadelphia* (1992)
4 *With friends like these* (1993)
5 *How I spent my summer vacation* (1994)

Amanda series
Colbert, Anthony
1 *Amanda has a surprise* (1971)
2 *Amanda goes dancing* (1972)

Amanda series
Himmelman, John
1 *Amanda and the witch switch* (1985)
2 *Amanda and the magic garden* (1987)

Amanda Valentine series
Beecham, Rose
1 *Introducing Amanda Valentine* (1992)
2 *Second guess* (1994)

Amarilly series
Maniates, Belle Kanaris
1 *Amarilly of Clothes-Line Alley* (1915)
2 *Amarilly in love* (1917)

Amartus series
Cradock, Phyllis
see **Atlantis series**

Amateur Cracksman series
Hornung, Ernest William
see **Raffles series**

Amazing adventures of Morph series
Dowling, Patrick
Based on characters created by David Sproxton and Peter Lord
1 *Swimming pool* (1980)
3 *Birthday party* (1981)
4 *Poor old Morph!* (1981)
Numbers 3 and 4 also published in one volume 1981

Amazing Koalas series
Campbell, Peter
1 *Koala party* (1972)
2 *Koalas' spring clean* (1972)
3 *Amazing koalas* (1978)
This volume includes numbers 1 and 2 as well as *Eucalyptus pie*, and *The amazing Wiley*

Amazing Spiderman series
This sequence has four authors
Wein, Len
1 *Mayhem in Manhattan* (1978)
Kupperberg, Paul
2 *Crime campaign*(1979)
3 *Murdermoon* (1979)
David, Peter
4 *As the world burns* (1987)

Amazing stories series
This sequence has four authors
Emery, Clayton
1 *Four-D funhouse* (1985)
Simon, Morris
2 *Jaguar!* (1985)
Kirchoff, Mary Lynn
3 *Portrait in blood* (1985)

Amazon warrior series
Green, Sharon
see **Jalav series**

Amazons and Swallows series
Ransome, Arthur
see **Swallows and Amazons series**

Amazons series
Salmonson, Jessica Amanda
1 *Amazons!* (1979)
2 *Amazons II* (1982)

Amber Ainslie series
Stahl, Hilda
1 *Deadline* (1990)
2 *Abducted* (1990)
3 *Undercover* (1991)
4 *Blackmail* (1991)

Amber series
Zelazny, Roger
see **Kingdom of Amber series**

Amber trilogy
Barbieri, Elaine
1 *Amber fire* (1981)
2 *Amber treasure* (1983)
3 *Amber passion* (1985)

Amberdon and Argee series
Schmitz, James Henry
see **Telzey Amberdon and Trigger Argee series**

Ambers series
Saint Clair, Elizabeth
see **Marilyn Ambers series**

Amberwood series
Rundle, Anne
1 *Amberwood* (1972)
2 *Heronbrook* (1975)
3 *Judith Lammeter* (1976)

Ambo series
Warriner, Thurman
see **Mister Scotter series**

Ambridge series
Webb, Geoffrey
see **Archers of Ambridge series**

Ambrose and Dominique Frayne series
McIntosh, J T
1 *Take a pair of private eyes* (1968)
Based on a play by Peter O'Donnell
2 *Coat of blackmail* (1970)

Ambrose Chitterwick series
Berkeley, Anthony
1 *Poisoned chocolates case* (1929)
2 *Piccadilly murder* (1929)
3 *Trial and error* (1937)

Ambrose Kangaroo series
Macintyre, Elisabeth
1 *Ambrose Kangaroo* (1941)
2 *Ambrose Kangaroo has a busy day* (1944)
3 *Ambrose Kangaroo goes to town* (1964)
4 *Ambrose Kangaroo delivers the goods* (1978)

Ambrose Low series
Cecil, Henry
1 *No bail for the judge* (1952)
2 *According to the evidence* (1954)

Ambrose Mahon series
Courtier, Sidney Hobson
1 *Glass spear* (1950)
2 *One cried murder* (1956)
3 *Come back to murder* (1957)
4 *Shroud for Unlac* (1958)
5 *Let the man die* (1961)
6 *Corpse won't sing* (1964)
7 *Mimic a murderer* (1964)
8 *Corpse at least* (1966)

Ambrose Usher series
Davey, Jocelyn
1 *Undoubted deed* (1956)
Capitol offence
2 *Naked villainy* (1958)
3 *Touch of stagefright* (1960)
4 *Killing in hats* (1965)
5 *Treasury alarm* (1976)
6 *Murder in paradise* (1982)
7 *Dangerous liaison* (1988)

Ambrose West series
Levene, Philip
1 *Ambrose in London* (1959)
2 *Ambrose in Paris* (1960)

Amelia Bedelia series
Parish, Peggy
1 *Amelia Bedelia* (1963)
2 *Thank you, Amelia Bedelia* (1964)
3 *Amelia Bedelia and the surprise shower* (1966)
4 *Come back, Amelia Bedelia* (1971)
5 *Play ball, Amelia Bedelia* (1972)
6 *Good work, Amelia Bedelia* (1976)
7 *Teach us, Amelia Bedelia* (1977)
8 *Amelia Bedelia helps out* (1979)
9 *Amelia Bedelia and the baby* (1981)
10 *Amelia Bedelia goes camping* (1985)
11 *Merry Christmas, Amelia Bedelia* (1986)
12 *Amelia Bedelia's family album* (1988)

Amelia Butterworth series
Green, Anna Katharine
1 *Affair next door* (1897)
2 *Lost man's lane* (1898)
3 *Circular study* (1900)
4 *One of my sons* (1901)
5 *Initials only* (1911)
6 *Mystery of the hasty arrow* (1917)

Amelia Jane series
Blyton, Enid
1 *Naughty Amelia Jane!* (1939)
2 *Amelia Jane again* (1946)
3 *More about Amelia Jane* (1954)

Amelia Peabody Emerson series
Peters, Elizabeth
1 *Crocodile on the sandbank* (1975)
2 *Curse of the pharaohs* (1981)
3 *Mummy case* (1985)
4 *Lion in the valley* (1986)
5 *Deeds of the disturber* (1988)
6 *Last camel died at noon* (1991)
7 *Snake, the crocodile and the dog* (1992)

Amelia series
Hooper, Muriel
1 *Amelia and the angels* (1960)
2 *Amelia and the robber rats* (1962)

Amelia Underwood and Jherek Carnelian series
Moorcock, Michael
see **Jherek Carnelian and Amelia Underwood series**

Ameliaranne series
This sequence has eight authors
Heward, Constance
1 *Ameliaranne and the green umbrella* (1920)
2 *Ameliaranne keeps shop* (1928)
3 *Ameliaranne, cinema star* (1929)
Ameliaranne and the monkey
Joan, Natalie
4 *Ameliaranne in town* (1930)
Gilmour, Margaret
5 *Ameliaranne at the circus* (1931)
Joan, Natalie
6 *Ameliaranne and the big treasure* (1932)
Farjeon, Eleanor
7 *Ameliaranne's prize packet* (1933)
Ameliaranne and the magic ring
8 *Ameliaranne's washing day* (1934)
Gilmour, Margaret
9 *Ameliaranne at the seaside* (1935)
Thompson, K L
10 *Ameliaranne at the zoo* (1936)
Heward, Constance
11 *Ameliaranne at the farm* (1937)
12 *Ameliaranne gives a Christmas party* (1938)
13 *Ameliaranne camps out* (1939)
14 *Ameliaranne keeps school* (1940)
15 *Ameliaranne goes touring* (1941)
Osborne, Eileen
16 *Ameliaranne and the jumble sale* (1943)
Gilmour, Margaret
17 *Ameliaranne gives a concert* (1945)
Morris, Ethelberta
18 *Ameliaranne, bridesmaid* (1946)
Wood, Lorna
19 *Ameliaranne goes digging* (1948)
Morris, Ethelberta
20 *Ameliaranne's moving day* (1950)

America-Africa-Asia trilogy
Baumann, Hans
1 *Son of Columbus* (1957)
2 *Sons of the Steppe* (1957)
3 *Barque of the brothers* (1958)

America and England series
Bailey, Anthony
Autobiography
1 *America lost and found* (1980)
2 *England first and last* (1985)

America series
Herzog, Arthur
1 *Make us happy* (1978)
2 *Glad to be here* (1979)

America series
White, Ted
see **Captain America series**

America two thousand and forty series
Innes, Evan
1 *America two thousand and forty* (1986)
2 *Golden world* (1986)
3 *City in the mist* (1987)
4 *Return* (1988)
5 *Star explorer* (1988)

American adventure series
Doyle, Arthur Conan
1 *Our American adventure* (1923)
2 *Our second American adventure* (1924)
Roddy, Lee
1 *Overland escape* (1989)
2 *Desperate search* (1989)
3 *Danger on Thunder Mountain* (1989)
4 *Secret of the Howling Cave* (1990)
5 *Flaming trap* (1990)
6 *Terror in the sky* (1991)
7 *Mystery of the phantom gold* (1991)
8 *Gold train bandits* (1992)
9 *High country ambush* (1992)

American adventures series
Coatsworth, Elizabeth
see **Once-upon-a-time-in-America series**

American Avenger series
Emmett, Robert
1 *Beat a distant drum* (1981)
2 *Ride the tiger* (1982)
3 *Devil's finger* (1982)
4 *King, bishop, knight* (1982)
5 *Trojan horses* (1982)

American bicentennial series
Jakes, John
see **Kent family series**

American Civil War battles series
Cozzens, Peter
1 *No better place to die* (1990)
The battle of Stones River
2 *This terrible sword* (1992)
The battle of Chickamauga

American Civil War episodes series
Crane, Stephen
1 *Red badge of courage* (1895)
An episode of the American Civil War
2 *Little regiment, and other episodes of the American Civil War* (1896)
Pictures of war

American Civil War, naval series
Mason, Francis Van Wyck
1 *Proud new flags* (1951)
2 *Blue hurricane* (1954)
3 *Our valiant few* (1956)
To whom be the glory

American Civil War series
Benson, Blackwood Ketcham
1 *Who goes there?* (1900)
2 *Friend with the countersign* (1901)

American Civil War series
Edson, John Thomas
1 *Comanche* (1967)
2 *You're in command now, Mr Fog* (1973)
Rebel vengeance
3 *Big gun* (1973)
4 *Under the stars and bars* (1970)
5 *Fastest gun in Texas* (1963)
6 *Matter of honour* (1981)
7 *Kill Dusty Fog!* (1970)
8 *Devil gun* (1966)
9 *Colt and the sabre* (1966)
10 *Rebel spy* (1968)
11 *Bloody border* (1969)
12 *Back to the bloody border* (1970)

American Civil War series
Ray, Delia
1 *Nation torn* (1990)
The story of how the Civil War began
2 *Behind the blue and gray* (1991)
The soldier's life in the Civil War

American Civil War series
Sinclair, Harold
1 *Horse soldiers* (1956)
2 *Cavalryman* (1958)

American Civil War series
Slaughter, Frank Gill
1 *In a dark garden* (1946)
2 *Stubborn heart* (1950)

American Civil War series
Verne, Jules
see **North against South series**

American Civil War trilogy
Graham, Heather
see **Civil War trilogy**

American Civil War trilogy
Johnston, Mary
1 *Long roll* (1911)
2 *Cease firing* (1912)
3 *Michael Forth* (1919)

American colonial series
Swanson, Neil Harman
1 *Judas tree* (1933)
2 *First rebel* (1937)
3 *Forbidden ground* (1938)
4 *Silent drum* (1940)
5 *Unconquered* (1947)
A novel of the Pontiac conspiracy

American dynasty series
Bronte, Louisa
1 *Vallette heritage* (1978)
2 *Van Rhyne heritage* (1979)
3 *Gunther heritage heritage* (1981)

American emperor series
Tracy, Louis
see **Vansittart series**

American experiment series
Burns, James Macgregor
1 *Vineyard of liberty* (1982)
2 *Workshop of democracy* (1985)
3 *Crosswinds of freedom* (1989)

American football series
James, Laurence
1 *Running back* (1988)
2 *End zone* (1989)

American freedom trilogy
Smith, George
see **Glencannon family trilogy**

American girl series
Bradley, Shelland
1 *American girl in India* (1907)
2 *American girl at the Durbar* (1912)

American girls collection, Felicity series
Tripp, Valerie
see **Felicity series**

American girls collection, Molly series
Tripp, Valerie
see **Molly series**

American girls collection, Samantha series
Tripp, Valerie
see **Samantha series**

American history series
McGovern, Ann
1 *If you sailed on the Mayflower* (1969)
2 *If you lived in colonial times* (1964)
3 *If you lived with the Sioux Indians* (1974)
4 *If you grew up with Abraham Lincoln* (1966)
5 *If you lived with the circus* (1971)

American history trilogy
Scott, Evelyn
1 *Migrations* (1927)
An arabesque in histories; set in the gold rush of 1849
2 *Wave* (1929)
Set during the American Civil War
3 *Calendar of sin* (1931)
American melodramas; originally published in two volumes

American history trilogy
Stacton, David
1 *Signal victory* (1960)
2 *Judges of the secret court* (1961)
3 *Tom Fool* (1962)

American in London series
Hanff, Helene
Reminiscences of an American in London
1 *Eighty four Charing Cross Road* (1970)
2 *Duchess of Bloomsbury Street* (1973)
3 *Q's legacy* (1985)

American Indian chiefs series
This sequence has two authors
Tomlinson, Everett Titsworth
1 *Trail of Black Hawk* (1915)
2 *Trail of the Mohawk* (1916)
Tomlinson, Paul Greene
3 *Trail of Tecumseh* (1917)

American Indian series
Lange, Dietrich
1 *On the trail of the Sioux* (1912)
2 *Silver island of the Chippewa* (1913)
3 *Lost in the fur country* (1914)
4 *In the great wild north* (1915)
5 *Lure of the black hills* (1916)
6 *Lure of the Mississippi* (1917)
7 *Silver cache of the Pawnees* (1918)
8 *Shawnee's warning* (1919)
9 *Threat of Sitting Bull* (1920)
10 *Raid of the Ottawa* (1921)
11 *Mohawk ranger* (1922)
12 *Iroquois scout* (1923)
13 *Sioux runner* (1924)
14 *Gold rock of the Chippewa* (1925)
15 *Boast of the Seminole* (1930)
16 *On the fur trail* (1931)

American Indian series
Wolfson, Evelyn
1 *American Indian habitats* (1978)
How to make dwellings and shelters with natural materials
2 *American Indian utensils* (1979)
How to make baskets, pottery and woodenware with natural materials
3 *American Indian tools and ornaments* (1981)
How to make implements and jewelry using bone and shell

American Jewry series
Birmingham, Stephen
1 *Our crowd* (1967)
The great Jewish families of new York
2 *Rest of us* (1984)
The rise of America's Eastern European Jews

American life series
Sedges, John
1 *Long love* (1949)
2 *Townsman* (1945)
3 *Voices in the house* (1953)
One volume edition entitled *American triptych*, 1958

American national development series
Churchill, Winston
1 *Richard Carvel* (1899)
2 *Crossing* (1904)
3 *Crisis* (1901)
4 *Coniston* (1906)
5 *Mister Crewe's career* (1908)
6 *Far country* (1915)

American Navy series
Fowler, William Morgan
1 *Rebels under sail* (1976)
The American Navy during the Revolution
2 *Jack Tars and commodores* (1984)
The American Navy, 1783-1815

American novel series
Geismar, Maxwell
1 *Rebels and ancestors* (1953)
1890-1915
2 *Last of the provincials* (1947)
1915-1925
3 *Writers in crisis* (1942)
1925-1940

American painting series
Flexner, James Thomas
see **History of American painting series**

American palace series
Rhodes, Evan Harold
1 *Bless this house* (1982)
2 *Forged in fury* (1982)
3 *Valiant hearts* (1983)
4 *Distant dream* (1984)

American patriot series
Elliot, Douglass
1 *New breed* (1981)
2 *Great deception* (1982)

American pioneer trilogy
Richter, Conrad
1 *Trees* (1940)
2 *Fields* (1946)
3 *Town* (1950)
One volume edition entitled *The awakening land*, 1966

American Reconstruction series
Dixon, Thomas
1 *Leopard's spots* (1902)
A romance of the white man's burdern
2 *Clansman* (1904)
An historical romance of the Ku Klux Klan; numbers 1 and 2 dramatized as *The Clansman*, 1905
3 *Traitor* (1907)
A story of the fall of the invisible empire

American Revolution series
Carter, Alden Richardson
1 *Colonies in revolt* (1988)
2 *Darkest hours* (1988)
3 *At the forge of liberty* (1988)
4 *Birth of the republic* (1988)

American Revolution series
Fritz, Jean
1 *George Washington's breakfast* (1969)
2 *And then what happened, Paul Revere?* (1973)
3 *Why don't you get a horse, Sam Adams?* (1974)
4 *Where was Patrick Henry on the twenty ninth of May?* (1975)
5 *Will you sign here, John Hancock?* (1976)
6 *What's the big idea, Ben Franklin?* (1976)
Companion volumes: *The secret diary of Jeb and Abigail, growing up in America, 1776-1783*, 1976, *Can't you make them behave, King George*, 1977, *Traitor, the case of Benedict Arnold*, 1981, *Shh, we're writing the Constitution*, 1987

American Revolution series
Simms, William Gilmore
1 *Partisan* (1835)
2 *Mellichampe* (1836)
A legend of the Santee
3 *Scout* (1841)
Kinsman
Alternative title: The black riders of Congaree
4 *Katherine Walton* (1851)
Alternative title: The rebel of Dorchester
5 *Sword and the distaff* (1853)
Woodcraft
Alternative titles: Fair, fat and forty, and Hawks about the dovecote
6 *Forayers* (1855)
Alternative title: The raid of the dog-days
7 *Eutaw* (1856)

American Revolution series
Van de Water, Frederic Franklin
1 *Reluctant rebel* (1948)
2 *Wings of the morning* (1955)
3 *Day of battle* (1958)
4 *Catch a falling star* (1949)

American Revolution trilogy
Chambers, Robert William
1 *Cardigan* (1901)
2 *Maid-at-arms* (1902)
3 *Reckoning* (1905)

American scouting series
Tomlinson, Everett Titsworth
1 *Pursuit of the Apache chief* (1920)
2 *Scouting on the border* (1920)
3 *Mysterious rifleman* (1921)
4 *Scouting with Mad Anthony* (1922)
5 *Scouting on the old frontier* (1923)
6 *Scouting in the wilderness* (1924)
7 *Pioneer scouts of the Ohio* (1924)
8 *Scouting on Lake Champlain* (1925)
9 *Scouting on the Mohawk* (1925)
10 *Washington's young scouts* (1926)
11 *Scouting in the desert* (1927)
12 *Spy of Saratoga* (1928)
13 *Scouting with Daniel Boone* (1931)
14 *Scouting with Kit Carson* (1931)

American society series
Lewis, Sinclair
1 *Babbitt* (1922)
2 *Man who knew Coolidge* (1928)

American tail series
Teitelbaum, Michael
see **Fievel series**

American tourist series
Cotes, Sarah Jeanette
1 *American girl in London* (1891)
2 *Voyage of consolation* (1898)

American War of Independence series
Mason, Francis Van Wyck
1 *Three harbours* (1938)
2 *Stars on the sea* (1940)
3 *Rivers of glory* (1942)
4 *Eagle in the sky* (1948)

American West series
Guthrie, Alfred Bertram
see **Settlement of the American West series**

American West trilogy
De Voto, Bernard
1 *Year of decision, 1846* (1943)
Set during the war with Mexico, 1845-48
2 *Across the wide Missouri* (1947)
3 *Course of empire* (1952)
Westward the course of empire

American years trilogy
Sinclair, Harold
1 *American years* (1938)
2 *Years of growth, 1861-1893* (1940)
3 *Years of illusion* (1941)

Americana series
Willoughby, Lee Davis
1 *Cincinnati* (1990)
2 *Baton Rouge* (1990)
3 *Portland* (1991)
4 *Omaha* (1991)

Amerindian prehistory series
Mayhar, Ardath
1 *People of the mesa* (1992)
2 *Island in the swamp* (1993)

Ames and Quarrel series
Krentz, Jayne Ann
see **Verity Ames and Jonas Quarrel series**

Ames series
Eichler, Alfred
see **Martin Ames series**
Farca, Marie C
see **Andrew Ames series**
Freeman, Lucy
see **Doctor William Ames series**
Grey, Zane
see **Arizona Ames series**
Roden, Henry Wisdom
see **Sid Ames series**
Wells, Helen
see **Cherry Ames series**

Amiss series
Edwards, Ruth Dudley
see **Robert Amiss series**

Amityville horror series
This sequence has four authors
Anson, Jay
1 *Amityville horror* (1977)
Holzer, Hans
2 *Murder in Amityville* (1979)
3 *Amityville curse* (1981)
Jones, John G
4 *Amityville horror 2* (1982)
5 *Amityville horror 3* (1984)
Final chapter
McGill, Gordon
6 *Amityville three-D* (1984)
Jones, John G
7 *Amityville, the untold story* (1985)
Holzer, Hans
8 *Secret of Amityville* (1985)
Jones, John G
9 *Evil escapes* (1988)
10 *Horror returns* (1989)

Among the animals series
Pierson, Clara Dillingham
1 *Among the meadow people* (1897)
2 *Among the forest people* (1898)

3 *Among the farmyard people* (1899)
4 *Among the pond people* (1901)
5 *Among the night people* (1902)
6 *Among the garden people* (1904)

Among the Sioux series
Hanson, Joseph Mills
1 *With Sully into the Sioux Land* (1910)
2 *With Carrington on the Bozeman Trail* (1912)

Amorous cheat series
Creighton, Basil
1 *Amorous cheat* (1920)
2 *Old Eve* (1922)

Amory series
Du Soe, Robert C
see **Jonathan Amory series**

Amos Clackworthy series
Booth, Christopher B
Short stories
1 *Mister Clackworthy* (1925)
2 *Mister Clackworthy, con man* (1927)

Amos Crowle series
Hanson, Victor Joseph
1 *Black Heart Crowle* (1978)
2 *Bells in an empty town* (1979)
3 *Guns of Black Heart* (1980)
4 *Hands of Amos Crowle* (1981)
5 *Amos Crowle, widow-maker* (1981)
6 *Black Heart's bunch* (1982)
7 *Hardneck and Amos* (1982)
8 *Call him Amos* (1982)
9 *Greenhorn days* (1983)
10 *Black Amos* (1983)
11 *Black Amos, lawbringer* (1984)
12 *Law of Amos C* (1985)
13 *Amos lives* (1990)
14 *Shroud for Amos* (1990)
15 *Legend of Amos* (1991)

Amos Flagg series
Randall, Clay
1 *Amos Flagg, lawman* (1964)
2 *Amos Flagg, high gun* (1965)
3 *Amos Flagg rides out* (1966)
4 *Amos Flagg, bushwacked* (1967)
Bushwacked
5 *Amos Flagg has his day* (1968)
6 *Amos Flagg, showdown* (1970)

Amos Hatcher series
Banks, Oliver
1 *Rembrandt panel* (1980)
Rembrandt file
2 *Caravaggio obsession* (1984)

Amos Lee Mappin series
Footner, Hulbert
1 *Mystery of the folded paper* (1930)
Folded paper mystery
2 *Death of a celebrity* (1938)
3 *Murder that had everything* (1939)
4 *Nation's missing guest* (1939)
5 *Murderer's vanity* (1940)
6 *Who killed the husband?* (1941)
7 *House with the blue door* (1942)
8 *Death of a saboteur* (1943)
9 *Unneutral murder* (1944)
10 *Orchids to murder* (1945)

Amos McGuffin series
Upton, Robert
1 *Who'd want to kill old George?* (1977)
2 *Fade out* (1984)

Amos Petrie series
Turner, John Victor
1 *Death must gave laughed* (1932)
First round murder
2 *Who spoke last?* (1932)
3 *Amos Petrie's puzzle* (1933)
4 *Murder, nine and out* (1934)
5 *Death joins the party* (1935)
6 *Homicide haven* (1936)
7 *Below the clock* (1936)

Amos Walker series
Estleman, Loren D
1 *Motor City blue* (1980)
2 *Angel Eyes* (1981)
3 *Midnight man* (1982)
4 *Glass highway* (1983)
5 *Sugartown* (1984)
6 *Every brilliant eye* (1986)
7 *Lady yesterday* (1987)
8 *Downriver* (1988)
9 *General murders* (1988)
Ten Amos Walker mysteries
10 *Silent thunder* (1989)
11 *Sweet women lie* (1990)

Amphibians series
Wright, Sydney Fowler
1 *Amphibians* (1925)
A romance of 500,000 years hence
2 *World below* (1951)
Dwellers
One volume edition entitled *The world below*, 1929

Amsterdam Cop series
Van de Wetering, Janwillem
see **De Gier and Grijpstra series**

Amsterdam series
Lawrence, Michael
see **Johnny Amsterdam series**

Amtrak wars series
Tilley, Patrick
1 *Cloud warrior* (1983)
2 *First family* (1985)
3 *Iron master* (1987)
4 *Blood river* (1988)
5 *Death bringer* (1989)
6 *Earth-thunder* (1990)
Companion volume: *Dark visions, an illustrated guide to the Amtrak wars*, by Patrick Tilley and Fernando Fernandez, 1988

Amusement trilogy
Delderfield, Ronald Frederick
1 *Nobody shouted author* (1951)
2 *For my own amusement* (1968)
3 *Overture for beginners* (1970)

Amy Adams and Hawkeye Collins series
Masters, M
see **Hawkeye Collins and Amy Adams series**

Amy and Emily series
Vail, Amanda
see **Emily and Amy series**

Amy and Laura series
Sachs, Marilyn
1 *Amy moves in* (1964)
2 *Laura's luck* (1965)
3 *Amy and Laura* (1966)
This sequence is followed by the **Veronica Ganz series**

Amy Brewster series
Merwin, Samuel Kimball
1 *Knife in my back* (1945)
2 *Message from a corpse* (1945)
3 *Matter of policy* (1946)

Amy Parry series
Humphreys, Emyr
1 *Flesh and blood* (1974)
2 *Best of friends* (1978)
3 *Salt of the earth* (1985)
4 *Absolute hero* (1986)
5 *Open secrets* (1988)

Amy Prescott series
Hendricksen, Louise
see **Doctor Amy Prescott series**

Amy Randolph trilogy
Wells, Marian
1 *Silver highway* (1989)
2 *Colorado gold* (1988)
3 *Out of the crucible* (1988)

Amy Tupper series
Bell, Josephine
1 *Wolf, wolf!* (1979)
2 *Question of inheritance* (1980)

Amyard series
Lister, Stephen
see **Kilakura series**

Amyot family series
Nicole, Christopher
1 *Amyot's Cay* (1964)
2 *Blood Amyot* (1964)
3 *Amyot crime* (1965)

Anansi series
Makhanlall, David Paschal
1 *Best of Brer Anansi* (1973)
2 *Invincible Brer Anansi* (1974)
3 *Brer Anansi strikes again* (1976)
4 *Brer Anansi's bag of tricks* (1978)
5 *Long live Brer Anansi* (1979)
6 *Further adventures of Brer Anansi* (1980)

Anastasia Jugedinska series
Swan, Phyllis
see **Anna J series**

Anastasia Krupnik series
Lowry, Lois
1 *Anastasia Krupnik* (1979)
2 *Anastasia again!* (1981)
3 *Anastasia at your service* (1982)
4 *Anastasia, ask your analyst* (1984)
5 *Anastasia on her own* (1985)
6 *Anastasia has the answers* (1986)
7 *Anastasia's chosen career* (1987)
8 *Anastasia at this address* (1991)

Anatole Flique series
Booth, Charles Gordon
1 *Murder at high tide* (1930)
2 *Cat and the clock* (1935)

Anatole series
Titus, Eve
1 *Anatole* (1956)
2 *Anatole and the cat* (1957)
3 *Anatole and the robot* (1960)
4 *Anatole over Paris* (1961)
5 *Anatole and the poodle* (1965)
6 *Anatole and the piano* (1966)
7 *Anatole and the thirty thieves* (1969)
8 *Anatole and the toyshop* (1970)
9 *Anatole in Italy* (1973)
10 *Anatole and the Pied Piper* (1979)

Anatole series
Willard, Nancy
1 *Sailing to Cythera, and other Anatole stories* (1974)
2 *Island of the grass king* (1979)
3 *Uncle Terrible* (1982)

Anatolian trilogy
Kazan, Elia
see **Stavros the Anatolian trilogy**

Ancestors series
Lucas, Edward Verrall
1 *Reading, writing and remembering* (1932)
2 *Old contemporaries* (1935)

Ancestral voices series
Lees-Milne, James
Diaries
1 *Ancestral voices* (1975)
1942-43
2 *Prophesying peace* (1977)
1944-45
3 *Caves of ice* (1983)
1946-47
4 *Midway on the waves* (1985)
1948-49
Companion volume: *Another self*, 1970

Ancient Egypt series
Roberts, Irene
1 *Throne pharaohs* (1974)
2 *Hatshepsut* (1976)
3 *Kingdom of the Sun* (1987)
4 *Song of the Nile* (1987)

Ancient history series
Swann, Thomas Burnett
1 *Minikins of Yam* (1976)
2 *Cry silver bells* (1977)
3 *Forest of forever* (1971)
4 *Day of the minotaur* (1966)
5 *Queens walk in the dusk* (1977)
6 *Green phoenix* (1972)
7 *Lady of the bees* (1976)
8 *Wolfwinter* (1972)
9 *Weirwoods* (1967)
10 *Gods abide* (1976)
11 *Tournament of thorns* (1976)
12 *Will-o-the-wisp* (1976)
13 *Not-world* (1975)
14 *Goat without horns* (1971)

Ancient Japan series
Manley, Ruth
1 *Plum rain scroll* (1978)
2 *Dragon stone* (1982)
3 *Peony lantern* (1987)

Ancient mariner trilogy
Willis, William
Autobiography
1 *Seven little sisters* (1955)
Gods were kind
A 6,700-mile voyage alone across the Pacific
2 *Angel on each shoulder* (1966)
Whom the sea has taken
3 *Hundred lives of the ancient mariner* (1967)

Ancient science series
Tomas, Andrew
1 *We are not the first* (1971)
2 *On the shores of endless worlds* (1974)
The search for cosmic life

Ancient sunlight series
Williamson, Henry
see **Chronicles of ancient sunlight series**

Ancil Witherspoon and Lloyd Albert series
Smith, Doris Buchanan
see **Lloyd Albert and Ancil Witherspoon series**

And so series
Roberts, Cecil
1 *And so to Bath* (1940)
2 *And so to America* (1946)
3 *And so to Rome* (1950)

Anders series
Allbeury, Ted
see **Tad Anders series**
Jobson, Hamilton
see **Inspector Anders series**
Nicole, Christopher
see **Jonathan Anders series**

Anders series
Unnerstad, Edith
1 *Spettecake holiday* (1957)
2 *Grandmother's journey* (1960)
3 *Journey to England* (1961)

Anders series
York, Andrew
see **Jonathan Anders series**

Andersen series
Mace, Merlda
see **Christine Andersen series**

Anderson Crow series
McCutcheon, George Barr
1 *Daughter of Anderson Crow* (1907)
2 *Anderson Crow, detective* (1920)
Short stories

Anderson family series
Anderson, Verily
1 *Spam tomorrow* (1956)

Anderson family series

2 *Our square* (1957)
3 *Beware of children* (1958)
4 *Daughters of divinity* (1960)
5 *Flo affair* (1963)
6 *Northrepp grandchildren* (1968)
7 *Scrambled egg for Christmas* (1970)

Anderson series
Buckley, Eunice
see **Rex Anderson series**
Clifton, Lucille
see **Everett Anderson series**
Compton, David Guy
see **Ben Anderson series**
Murray, William Buckley
see **Lou Anderson series**
Sadler, Jeff
see **Marshal Andrew Anderson series**
Simon, Seymour
see **Einstein Anderson series**
Southworth, Louis
see **Inspector Tom Anderson series**
Trevor, Leslie
see **Policewoman series**

Andie and the boys series
Harrell, Janice
1 *Andie and the boys* (1990)
2 *Dooley Mackenzie is totally weird* (1991)
3 *Brace yourself* (1991)

Andrakis trilogy
Shillitoe, Tony
1 *Guardians* (1992)
2 *Kingmaker* (1993)
3 *Dragon Lords* (1993)

Andrea Perkins series
Coker, Carolyn
1 *Other David* (1985)
2 *Vines of Ferrara* (1986)
3 *Hand of the lion* (1988)

Andrea Quill series
Morgan, Damian
1 *Playing for keeps* (1989)
2 *Played out* (1993)

Andrea Reid and David Ramsay series
Matschat, Cecile Hulse
1 *Murder in Okefenokee* (1941)
2 *Murder at the Black Crook* (1943)

Andreas and Tamara Valeshoff series
Ambler, Eric
1 *Uncommon danger* (1937)
Background to danger
2 *Cause for alarm* (1938)

Andreas Hofer series
Westall, William
1 *With the Red Eagle* (1897)
2 *Red bridal* (1899)

Andrew Ames series
Farca, Marie C
1 *Earth* (1972)
2 *Complex man* (1973)

Andrew and Becky series
Wells, Marian
see **Wedding dress series**

Andrew and Pip series
Wilson, Keane
see **Pip and Andrew series**

Andrew Anderson series
Sadler, Jeff
see **Marshal Andrew Anderson series**

Andrew Ash series
Grierson, Francis Durham
see **Superintendent Andrew Ash series**

Andrew Basnett series
Ferrars, Elizabeth
American editions are published under the name E X Ferrars
1 *Something wicked* (1983)
2 *Root of all evil* (1984)
3 *Crime and the crystal* (1985)
4 *Other devil's name* (1986)
5 *Murder too many* (1988)
6 *Smoke without fire* (1990)

Andrew Blake series
Gunn, John
1 *Humpy in the hills* (1960)
2 *Goodbye Island* (1963)

Andrew Broom series
McInerny, Ralph
1 *Cause and effect* (1987)
2 *Body and soul* (1989)
3 *Frigor mortis* (1989)
4 *Savings and loans* (1990)

Andrew Connington series
Irwin, Grace
1 *Least of all saints* (1957)
2 *Andrew Connington* (1958)

Andrew Dalziel and Sergeant Pascoe series
Hill, Reginald
see **Superintendent Andrew Dalziel and Sergeant Pascoe series**

Andrew Frampton series
Plummer, Thomas Arthur
see **Detective Inspector Andrew Frampton series**

Andrew Laird series
Macleod, Robert
American edition of this sequence published under the pseudonym Michael Kirk
1 *All other perils* (1974)
2 *Dragonship* (1976)
3 *Salvage job* (1978)
4 *Cargo risk* (1980)
5 *Mayday from Malaga* (1983)
6 *Cut in diamonds* (1985)
7 *Witchline* (1988)

Andrew McCall series
Carrel, Mark
1 *Blood-pit* (1967)
2 *Shadow of a hawk* (1967)
3 *Tears of blood* (1967)
4 *Sword of silk* (1967)
5 *Dark age of violence* (1967)

Andrew McMurdo series
Morland, Nigel
see **Chief Inspector Andrew McMurdo series**

Andrew Pearson series
Shepherd, Eric
see **Superintendent Andrew Pearson series**

Andrew Quentin and Jane Winfield series
Peterson, Audrey
see **Jane Winfield and Andrew Quentin series**

Andrew Ryder series
Weston, Cole
1 *Buffalo Gal* (1987)
2 *Longhorn sisters* (1987)
3 *Ryder's army* (1987)
4 *Tong war* (1987)
5 *Flaming arrows* (1987)
6 *Badlands blood* (1987)
7 *Showdown* (1987)
8 *Blood vengeance* (1987)
9 *Range war* (1987)
10 *Blood on the staked plains* (1987)
11 *Yellow Lotus Tong* (1987)

Andrew Salmond series
Dundas, Lawrence
1 *Spider at the Elvira* (1949)
2 *He liked them murderous* (1964)
3 *Strange smell of murder* (1965)

Andrew Thornyold series
Almedingen, Edith Martha
1 *Fair haven* (1956)
2 *Dark splendour* (1961)

Andrew Torrent series
Cores, Lucy
see **Captain Andrew Torrent series**

Andrews series
Rodgers, Mary
see **Annabel Andrews series**

Android Tanner series
White, Ted
1 *Android avenger* (1965)
2 *Spawn of the death machine* (1968)

Andromeda series
Hoyle, Fred
1 *A for Andromeda* (1962)
A novel of tomorrow
2 *Andromeda breakthrough* (1964)
A novel of tomorrow's universe

Andy and Arab Blake series
Powell, Richard
see **Arab and Andy Blake series**

Andy and Panuck series
Machetanz, Frederick
1 *Panuck* (1939)
2 *On Arctic ice* (1940)

Andy and Sue McVeigh series
Macveigh, Sue
see **Captain Andy and Sue McVeigh series**

Andy Bastian series
Wormser, Richard
see **Lieutenant Andy Bastian series**

Andy Burnett series
White, Stewart Edward
1 *Long rifle* (1932)
2 *Ranchero* (1933)
3 *Folded hills* (1934)
Numbers 1-3 also published in one volume entitled *The saga of Andy Burnett*, 1947
4 *Stampede* (1942)
Companion volume: *Walt Disney's Andy Burnett*, by Charles Spain Verral, 1958

Andy Kane series
Brown, Carter
1 *Hong Kong caper* (1962)
Rewritten from *Blonde, bad and beautiful*, 1957
2 *Bird in a guilt-edged cage* (1962)
Guilt-edged cage
Rewritten from *That's piracy, my pet*, 1957

Andy Lane series
Adams, Eustace Lane
1 *Fifteen days in the air* (1928)
2 *Over the Polar ice* (1928)
3 *Racing around the world* (1928)
4 *Runaway airship* (1929)
5 *Pirates of the air* (1929)
6 *On the wings of flame* (1929)
7 *Mysterious monoplane* (1930)
8 *Flying windmill* (1930)
9 *Plane without a pilot* (1930)
10 *Wings of adventure* (1931)
11 *Across the top of the world* (1931)
12 *Prisoners of the clouds* (1932)
13 *Doomed demons* (1935)
14 *Wings of the Navy* (1936)
15 *War wings* (1937)

Andy McMurdo series
Morland, Nigel
see **Chief Inspector Andrew McMurdo series**

Andy Pandy series
Bird, Maria
1 *Andy Pandy's garden* (1952)
2 *Andy Pandy's little house* (1952)
3 *Playing with Andy Pandy* (1952)
4 *Andy Pandy and his hobby horse* (1953)
5 *Andy Pandy and the gingerbread man* (1953)
6 *Andy Pandy's washing day* (1953)
7 *Andy Pandy's nursery rhymes* (1954)
8 *Andy Pandy and the ducklings* (1954)
9 *Andy Pandy's tea-party* (1954)
10 *Andy Pandy's jump-up book* (1954)
11 *Andy Pandy, Teddy and Looby Loo* (1954)
12 *Andy Pandy in the country* (1955)
13 *Andy Pandy's jack-in-the-box* (1955)
14 *Andy Pandy's shop* (1955)
15 *Andy Pandy and Teddy at the zoo* (1956)
16 *Andy Pandy and the white kitten* (1956)
17 *Andy Pandy and the willow tree* (1956)
18 *Andy Pandy builds a house for Looby Loo* (1956)
19 *Andy Pandy's kite* (1957)
20 *Andy Pandy paints his house* (1958)
21 *Andy Pandy's shopping bag* (1958)
22 *Andy Pandy and the hedgehog* (1959)
23 *Andy Pandy's puppy* (1959)
24 *Andy Pandy and the woolly lamb* (1959)
25 *Andy Pandy and the teddy dog* (1960)
26 *Andy Pandy's dovecot* (1960)
27 *Andy Pandy and the baby pigs* (1961)
28 *Andy Pandy's little goat* (1961)
29 *Andy Pandy and the patchwork cat* (1962)
30 *Andy Pandy and the snowman* (1962)
31 *Andy Pandy's new pet* (1963)
32 *Andy Pandy's weather house* (1963)
33 *Andy Pandy plays lions and tigers* (1964)
34 *Andy Pandy's playhouse* (1964)
35 *Andy Pandy and the badger* (1965)
36 *Andy Pandy and the green puppy* (1965)
37 *Andy Pandy and the scarecrow* (1966)
38 *Andy Pandy's red motor car* (1967)
39 *Andy Pandy and the yellow dog* (1968)
40 *Andy Pandy and the spotted cow* (1971)
41 *Andy Pandy and the baby monkey* (1972)
42 *Andy Pandy and the tiny piglet* (1972)
Companion volumes: *Andy Pandy, the baby clown*, by Freda Lingstrom and Maria Bird, 1953, *Andy Pandy's busy friends*, anonymous, 1973; omnibus volume: *Andy Pandy's adventures*, 1959

Andy series
Hurt, Freda Mary
1 *Andy in trouble* (1953)
2 *Andy keeps a secret* (1954)
3 *Andy takes the lead* (1955)
4 *Andy gets the blame* (1956)
5 *Andy in danger* (1957)
6 *Andy finds a way* (1959)
7 *Andy goes abroad* (1960)
8 *Andy wins the prize* (1961)
9 *Andy and her twin* (1963)
10 *Andy meets a hero* (1964)
11 *Andy looks for gold* (1965)

Andy series
Miller, Moira
1 *What size is Andy?* (1984)
2 *Where does go Andy go?* (1985)

Andy series
Taylor, Reginald
1 *Andy and the mascots* (1957)
2 *Andy and the water crossing* (1958)
3 *Andy and the display team* (1959)
4 *Andy and the sharpshooters* (1959)
5 *Andy and the secret papers* (1961)
6 *Andy and the miniature war* (1962)
7 *Andy and the royal review* (1963)
8 *Andy and his last parade* (1965)

Angel Brown series
Montrose, Graham
1 *Angel of no mercy* (1968)
2 *Angel of death* (1968)
3 *Where Angel treads* (1969)
4 *Angel abroad* (1969)
5 *Matter of motive* (1969)
6 *Angel of vengeance* (1970)
7 *Angel in Paradise* (1970)
8 *Send for Angel* (1970)
9 *Ask for angel* (1970)
10 *Angel and the Nero* (1971)
11 *Fanfare for Angel* (1971)
12 *Angel at arms* (1971)
13 *Angel and the red admiral* (1972)

Angel Eyes series
Longley, W B
1 *Miracle of revenge* (1985)
2 *Death's Angel* (1985)
3 *Wolf Pass* (1985)
4 *Chinatown justice* (1985)
5 *Logan's army* (1986)
6 *Bullets and bad times* (1986)
7 *Six Gun Angel* (1986)
8 *Avenging Angel* (1986)
9 *Angel for hire* (1987)

Angel Graham series
Russell, Richard
1 *Reunion* (1979)
2 *Point of reference* (1979)
3 *Paperbag* (1979)

Angel Park All-Stars series
Hughes, Dean
1 *Making the team* (1990)
2 *Big base hit* (1990)
3 *Winning streak* (1990)
4 *What a catch!* (1990)
5 *Rookie star* (1990)
6 *Pressure play* (1990)
7 *Line drive* (1990)
8 *Championship game* (1990)
9 *Superstar team* (1991)
10 *Stroke of luck* (1991)
11 *Safe at first* (1991)
12 *Up to bat* (1991)
13 *Play-off* (1991)
14 *All together now* (1991)

Angel Park Hoop Stars series
Hughes, Dean
1 *Nothing but net* (1992)
2 *Lucky's tricks* (1992)
3 *Go to the hoop!* (1993)
4 *On the line* (1993)

Angel Park Soccer Stars series
Hughes, Dean
1 *Kickoff time* (1991)
2 *Defense!* (1991)
3 *Victory goal* (1992)
4 *Psyched!* (1992)
5 *Backup goalie* (1992)
6 *Total soccer* (1992)
7 *Shake up* (1993)
8 *Quick moves* (1993)

Angel series
Christian, Frederick H
see **Frank Angel series**

Angel series
Delton, Judy
1 *Backyard Angel* (1983)
2 *Angel in charge* (1985)
3 *Angel's mother's boyfriend* (1986)
4 *Angel's mother's wedding* (1987)
5 *Angel's mother's baby* (1989)

Angel series
Kilworth, Garry
1 *Angel* (1993)
2 *Archangel* (1994)

Angel series
Ryder, Thom
see **Avenging Angel series**

Angela and Ian Kendall series
Baxter, Gillian
1 *Pantomime ponies* (1969)
2 *Save the ponies!* (1971)
3 *Ponies by the sea* (1974)
4 *Ponies in harness* (1977)

Angela Carlyle series
Du Barry, Michele
1 *Into passion's dawn* (1981)
2 *Across captive seas* (1981)
3 *Toward love's horizon* (1981)

Angela Harpe series
Lawrence, James D
1 *Dream girl* (1975)
2 *Emerald oil caper* (1975)
3 *Gilded snatch caper* (1975)
4 *Godmother caper* (1975)

Angela Mitchell and Charlie Ellis series
Lavelle, Sheila
see **Charlie Ellis and Angela Mitchell series**

Angela trilogy
Robinson, Nancy Konheim
1 *Oh honestly, Angela!* (1985)
2 *Angela, private citizen* (1989)
3 *Angela and the broken heart* (1991)

Angele series
Catalan, Henri
see **Soeur Angele series**

Angelina Ballerina series
Holabird, Katharine
1 *Angelina Ballerina* (1983)
2 *Angelina and the princess* (1984)
3 *Angelina at the fair* (1985)
4 *Angelina's Christmas* (1985)
5 *Angelina on stage* (1986)
6 *Angelina and Alice* (1987)
7 *Angelina and the dragon* (1988)
8 *Angelina's birthday surprise* (1989)
9 *Angelina's baby sister* (1991)
10 *Chrismas with Angelina* (1992)
11 *Angelina dances* (1992)
12 *Angelina ice-skates* (1993)
Companion volumes: *Angelina's birthday and address book*, 1986, *Angelina's book and doll package*, 1989

Angeline Tredennick series
Sanborn, Ruth Burr
1 *Murder by jury* (1932)
2 *Murder on the Aphrodite* (1935)

Angelique series
Golon, Sergeanne
Translated from the French
1 *Angelique* (1957)
1.1 *Marquise of the Angels* (1957)
1.2 *Road to Versailles* (1957)
2 *Angelique and the king* (1959)
3 *Angelique and the Sultan* (1960)
Angelique in Barbary
4 *Angelique in revolt* (1961)
5 *Angelique in love* (1961)
6 *Countess Angelique* (1967)
6.1 *In the land of the Redskins* (1967)
6.2 *Prisoner of the mountains* (1967)
7 *Temptation of Angelique* (1969)
7.1 *Jesuit trap* (1969)
7.2 *Gold Beard's downfall* (1969)
8 *Angelique and the demon* (1972)
9 *Angelique and the ghosts* (1976)

Angelo DiStefano trilogy
Janifer, Laurence Mark
1 *Target, Terra* (1968)
2 *High hex* (1969)
3 *Wagered world* (1969)

Angelo series
Lieberman, Rosalie
see **Brother Angelo series**

Angelo series
Giono, Jean
1 *Angelo* (1958)
Original edition entitled *Angelo, introduction aux infortunes du hussard*
2 *Hussar on the roof* (1951)
Horseman on the roof
Original edition entitled *Le hussard sur le toit*
3 *Man of straw* (1957)
Straw man
Original edition entitled *Le bonheur fou*

Angels in the snow series
Lambert, Derek
1 *Angels in the snow* (1969)
2 *Red house* (1972)

Angel's luck series
Faust, Joe Clifford
1 *Desperate measures* (1989)
2 *Precious cargo* (1990)
3 *Essence of evil* (1990)

Angels series
Norman, Mick
see **Gerry Vinson series**

Angels series
This sequence has two authors
Milne, Paula
1 *Angels* (1975)
2 *Flight of Angels* (1976)
3 *New Angels* (1978)
Georgeson, Valerie
4 *Duty calls* (1979)

Angeltown Keeps and Doc Hennessy series
Bancroft, Tex
1 *Gold Horse Canyon* (1952)
2 *Prairie Dusters* (1953)

Angelwalk series
Elwood, Roger
1 *Angelwalk* (1988)
A modern fable
2 *Fallen angel* (1990)

Anglesea series
Milner, George
see **Ronald Anglesea series**

Anglo-Irish relations series
O'Riordan, Conal
1 *Soldier born* (1927)
A story of youth
2 *Soldier of Waterloo* (1928)
Napoleon passes
A story of manhood
Numbers 1 and 2 also published in one volume entitled *Yet do not grieve*, 1928
3 *Soldier's wife* (1935)
4 *Soldier's end* (1938)
5 *Judith Quinn* (1939)
6 *Judith's love* (1940)
7 *Adam of Dublin* (1920)
A romance of to-day
8 *Adam and Caroline* (1921)
9 *In London* (1922)
The story of Adam and marriage
10 *Married life* (1924)

Angria series
Bronte, Charlotte
1 *Twelve adventurers, and other stories* (1925)
2 *Legends of Angria* (1933)

Angry young man series
Paul, Leslie
1 *Boy down Kitchener Street* (1957)
2 *Angry young man* (1951)
3 *Living hedge* (1946)

Angstrom series
Updike, John
see **Rabbit Angstrom series**

Anguish series
Wolfe, Humbert
Autobiography
1 *Now a stranger* (1933)
2 *Upward anguish* (1938)

Angus Fane and Kiss Darling series
Yardley, James
see **Kiss Darling and Angus Fane series**

Angus Macwhorter series
Keeler, Harry Stephen
1 *Vanishing gold truck* (1941)
2 *Case of the jeweled ragpicker* (1948)
Ace of Spades murder
The second title is the English edition and is longer than the American edition
3 *Stand by, London calling* (1953)

Angus Mott and Mike Yeadings series
Curzon, Clare
see **Superintendent Mike Yeardings and Sergeant Angus Mott series**

Angus series
Flack, Marjorie
1 *Angus and the ducks* (1930)
2 *Angus and the cat* (1931)
3 *Angus lost* (1932)
4 *Wag-Tail Bess* (1933)
Angus and Wag-Tail Bess
5 *Topsy and Angus and the cat* (1935)
6 *Topsy* (1935)
Angus and Topsy

Animal adventure series
Darby, Joan
1 *Pudgy, the beaver* (1963)
2 *Skippy, the skunk* (1963)
3 *Squeaky, the squirrel* (1963)
4 *Becky, the rabbit* (1964)
5 *Sally, the screech owl* (1964)
6 *Sandy, the swallow* (1964)
7 *Gomar, the gosling* (1969)
8 *Kate, the cat* (1969)
9 *Doc, the dog* (1970)
10 *Hamilton, the hamster* (1970)
11 *horace, the horse* (1970)
12 *Pat, the parakeet* (1970)

Animal antics series
Salmon, Michael
1 *Bears go exploring* (1990)
2 *Monsters on the move* (1990)
3 *Dinosaurs on holiday* (1990)
4 *Elephants at work* (1990)

Animal behavior series
Freedman, Russell
1 *Animal instincts* (1970)
Co-author: James E Morriss
2 *Animal architects* (1971)
3 *Animal fathers* (1976)
4 *Animal games* (1976)
5 *Tooth and claw* (1980)
A look at animal weapons
6 *Animal superstars* (1981)
Biggest, strongest, fastest, smartest

Animal fun series
Brown, Mik
1 *Animal fun ABC* (1982)
2 *Animal fun 123* (1982)

Animal hotel series
Cooper, Diana Davis
Experiences in running boarding kennels
1 *Animal hotel* (1979)
2 *Up to scratch* (1981)
3 *Mere folly* (1982)

Animal Inn series
Vail, Virginia
1 *Pets are for keeps* (1986)
2 *Kid's best friend* (1986)
3 *Monkey business* (1987)
4 *Scaredy cat* (1987)
5 *Adopt-a-pet* (1987)
6 *All the way home* (1987)
7 *Pet makeover* (1990)
8 *Petnapped!* (1990)
9 *One dog too many* (1990)
10 *Parrot fever* (1990)
11 *Oh dear!* (1990)
12 *Gift horse* (1991)

Animal is born series
White, William
1 *Frog is born* (1972)
2 *Turtle is born* (1973)
3 *Earthworm is born* (1975)
4 *Mosquito is born* (1981)

Animal library series
Mayne, William
1 *Come, come to my corner* (1986)
2 *Corbie* (1986)
3 *Tibber* (1986)
4 *Barnabas walks* (1986)
5 *Lamb Shenkin* (1987)
6 *House in town* (1987)
7 *Leapfrog* (1987)
8 *Mousewing* (1987)

Animal life stories series
Torgersen, Don Arthur
1 *Ziggy the elephant* (1977)
2 *Polar bears and the seals* (1977)
3 *Mountain gorilla* (1977)
4 *Golden eagles* (1977)
5 *Great tigers of India* (1977)
6 *Wolves of Isle Royale* (1977)
7 *Big gator of the Everglades* (1977)
8 *Porpoises and the sailor* (1977)
9 *Prairie Town dog* (1977)
10 *Wild ostrich of the Kalahari* (1977)
11 *Cheetahs of the Serengeti Plain* (1977)
12 *Blue shark* (1977)

Animal lore and disorder series
Riddell, James
Divided books
1 *Animal lore and disorder* (1947)
2 *Hit or myth* (1949)
3 *Up and down on the farm* (1980)

Animal Rescue Farm series
Hart, Sharon M
1 *Stolen horse* (1988)
2 *Animal orphan* (1988)

Animal safari nature series
Torgersen, Don Arthur
1 *Elephant herds and rhino horns* (1982)
2 *Lion prides and tiger tracks* (1982)
3 *Giraffe hooves and antelope horns* (1982)
4 *Killer shales and dolphin play* (1982)
5 *Bear claws and furry tails* (1983)
6 *Wolf fangs and fox dns* (1983)
7 *Turtles, snakes and alligator jaws* (1983)
8 *Great apes and monkey tails* (1983)

Animal series
Lilly, Kenneth
Board books
1 *Animal jumpers* (1984)
2 *Animal climbers* (1984)
3 *Animal swimmers* (1984)
4 *Animal runners* (1984)
5 *Animal builders* (1984)

Animal shape series
McCue, Dick
Board books
1 *Froggie's treasure* (1983)
2 *Kitty's colors* (1983)
3 *Teddy dresses* (1983)
4 *Ducky's seasons* (1983)
5 *Bunny's numbers* (1984)
6 *Puppy's day school* (1984)
7 *Panda's playtime* (1985)
8 *Kitten's Christmas* (1985)
9 *Baby Elephant's bedtime* (1985)
10 *Raccoon's hide and seek* (1985)

Animal stories series
Burgess, Thornton Waldo
1 *Bobby Coon's mistake* (1940)
Bobby Coon's surprise
2 *Three little bears* (1940)
Bear scare
3 *Peter Rabbit proves a friend* (1940)
Peter Rabbit goes scouting
4 *Reddy Fox's sudden engagement* (1940)
Reddy Fox leaves in a hurry
5 *Paddy's surprise visitor* (1940)
Paddy the Beaver's visitor
6 *Merry coasting party* (1940)
Fun at the queer trail
7 *Young Flash, the deer* (1940)
Flash the young deer
8 *Robber meets his match* (1940)
Robber the rat loses out

Animal story-books
Burgess, Thornton Waldo
see **Bedtime story-books series**

Animal twins series
Tompkins, Jane
1 *Polar bear twins* (1937)
2 *Penguin twins* (1939)
3 *Beaver twins* (1940)
4 *Snowshoe twins* (1941)
5 *Raccoon twins* (1942)
6 *Red squirrel twins* (1950)
7 *Black bear twins* (1952)
8 *Porcupine twins* (1955)
9 *Otter twins* (1957)
10 *Reindeer twins* (1957)

Animals and their ecosystems series
Taylor, Dave
1 *Lion and the savannah* (1990)
2 *Elephant and the scrub forest* (1990)
3 *Bison and the Great Plains* (1990)
4 *Alligator and the Everglades* (1990)

Animals and their women series
Cohen, Barbara
1 *Dogs and their women* (1989)
2 *Cats and their women* (1992)
3 *Horses and their women* (1993)

Animals of course series
Bailey, Jill
1 *Noses* (1984)
2 *Mouths* (1984)
3 *Feet* (1984)
4 *Eyes* (1984)

Animals series
Bowring, Mary
1 *Animals come first* (1976)
2 *Animals before breakfast* (1978)
3 *Animals round the clock* (1981)

Animals series
Rosenberg, Amye
1 *Animals naughty and nice* (1986)
2 *Animals wild and wooly* (1987)

Animals you'd like to meet series
Drescher, Henrik
1 *Whose scaly tale?* (1987)
African animals
2 *Whose furry nose?* (1987)
Australian animals

Animiles series
Reeves, James
1 *Prefabulous animiles* (1957)
2 *More prefabulous animiles* (1975)

Anjani series
Titan, Earl
1 *Gold of Akada* (1951)
2 *Anjani the Mighty* (1951)

Ann and Eve series
Sharber, Kate Trimble
1 *Annals of Ann* (1910)
2 *At the age of Eve* (1911)

Ann and Jim Henderson series
Peel, Hazel Mary
1 *Fury, son of the wilds* (1959)
2 *Pilot, the hunter* (1962)
3 *Pilot, the chaser* (1964)
4 *Easter, the show jumper* (1965)
Show jumper
5 *Jago* (1966)
6 *Night Storm, the flat racer* (1966)
7 *Dido and Rogue* (1967)
8 *Gay Darius* (1968)
9 *Untamed!* (1969)

Ann and John Davies series
Styles, Showell
1 *Journey with a secret* (1968)
2 *Tent on top* (1971)

Ann and Paul series
Marokvia, Mireille
1 *Jannot* (1959)
2 *Nanette* (1960)
3 *Grococo* (1961)
4 *Belle Arabelle* (1962)

Ann and Peter series
Someren, Liesje van
see **Kennedys abroad series**

Ann and Susan series
Wahlstedt, Viola
1 *Present for granny* (1965)
2 *Ann and Susie keep shop* (1965)
3 *Granny's secret attic* (1967)
4 *Ann and Susie pick berries* (1968)
5 *Goodbye, Ann and Susie* (1970)

Ann Bartlett series
Johnson, Martha
1 *Ann Bartlett, navy nurse* (1941)
2 *Ann Bartlett in Bataan* (1943)
3 *Ann Bartlett in the South Pacific* (1944)
4 *Ann Bartlett returns to the Philippines* (1945)
5 *Ann Bartlett on stateside duty* (1946)

Ann Fielding series
Ingate, Mary
1 *Sound of the weir* (1974)
Remembrance of Miranda
2 *This water laps gently* (1977)

Ann Hales series
Ingate, Mary
see **Ann Fielding series**

Ann Jackman series
Pinkerton, Kathrene
1 *Adventure north* (1940)
2 *Fox Island* (1942)
3 *Farther north* (1944)

Ann, Mike and Belinda series
Blyton, Enid
see **Mike, Belinda and Ann series**

Ann of Cambray trilogy
Lide, Mary
1 *Ann of Cambray* (1984)
2 *Gifts of the queen* (1985)
3 *Royal quest* (1987)
Hawks of Sedgemont

Ann Rankin series
Buddee, Paul
1 *Ann Rankin and the lost valley* (1973)
2 *Ann Rankin and the great flood* (1973)
3 *Ann Rankin and the boy who painted horses* (1973)
4 *Ann Rankin and the house on Coolabah Hill* (1973)

Ann Sheldon series
Smyth, John George
1 *Paradise Island* (1958)
2 *Trouble in Paradise* (1959)
3 *Ann goes hunting* (1960)

Ann Sterling series
Grove, Harriet Pyne
1 *Ann Sterling* (1926)
2 *Ann and the Jolly Six* (1926)
3 *Ann crosses a secret trail* (1926)
4 *Ann's search rewarded* (1926)
5 *Courage of Ann* (1926)
6 *Ann's ambitions* (1927)
7 *Ann's sterling heart* (1928)

Anna and Carl series
Frank, Leonhard
see **Carl and Anna series**

Anna and Elspeth Patterson trilogy
Stirling, Jessica
see **Elspeth and Anna Patterson trilogy**

Anna and James series
Boden, Hilda
1 *Wonderful penny stamp* (1969)
2 *Canal House* (1969)

Anna and Jean series
Lyon, Elinor
see **Jean and Anna series**

Anna and Johan de Villiers series
Muller, Mary
1 *Green peaches ripen* (1968)
2 *Cloud across the moon* (1970)
3 *Stones of Africa* (1972)

Anna and Steve series
Hardcastle, Michael
see **Steve and Anna series**

Anna and Tim series
Ball, Duncan
1 *Case of the graveyard ghost* (1994)
2 *Case of the walkabout clock* (1994)

Anna Friedman series
Plain, Belva
1 *Evergreen* (1978)
2 *Golden cup* (1986)
3 *Tapestry* (1988)

Anna Hudson series
Gilchrist, Ellen
1 *Anna papers* (1988)
2 *I cannot get you close enough* (1990)
Three novellas, each one dealing with a character from *The Anna papers*
This sequence is preceded by the short story, Anna, part I, published in *Drunk and love*, 1988

Anna J series
Swan, Phyllis
1 *Find Sherri* (1979)
2 *Trigger lady* (1979)
3 *Death inheritance* (1980)
4 *You've had it girl* (1980)

Anna Lavinia series
Brown, Helen Dawes
1 *Little Miss Phoebe Gay* (1895)
2 *Her sixteenth year* (1901)
3 *How Phoebe found herself* (1912)

Anna Lavinia series
Brown, Palmer
1 *Beyond the pawpaw trees* (1954)
2 *Silver nutmeg* (1956)

Anna Lee series
Cody, Liza
1 *Dupe* (1980)
2 *Bad company* (1982)
3 *Stalker* (1984)
4 *Head case* (1985)
5 *Under contract* (1987)
6 *Backhand* (1991)

Anna, Paul and Tommycat series
Girard, Nicole
Translated from the French
1 *Anna, Paul and Tommycat say hello* (1987)
2 *Looking for Tommycat* (1987)
3 *Where is Tommycat?* (1988)
4 *Letter from the moon* (1988)
5 *Tommycat comes back at last* (1988)
6 *Tommycat is gone again* (1988)

Anna Peters series
Law, Janice
1 *Big payoff* (1976)
2 *Gemini trip* (1977)
3 *Under Orion* (1978)
4 *Shadow of the palms* (1980)
5 *Death under par* (1981)

Anna series
Frow, Marion
see **Intelligence Corps series**

Anna series
Fynn
1 *Mister God, this is Anna* (1974)
2 *Anna's book* (1986)
3 *Anna and the black knight* (1990)

Anna series
Kenward, Jean
see **Ragdolly Anna series**

Anna series
Kerr, Judith
1 *When Hitler stole Pink Rabbit* (1971)
2 *Other way round* (1975)
3 *Small person far away* (1978)

Anna series
Little, Jean
1 *From Anna* (1972)
2 *Listen for the singing* (1977)

Anna series
Sandberg, Inger
Illustrated by Lasse Sandberg
1 *Anna and the magic hat* (1965)
Little Anna and the magic hat
Original edition entitled *Lilla Anna och trollerihatten*
2 *What Anna saw* (1965)
Oriinal edition entitled *Vad Anna fick se*
3 *What Anna saved* (1965)
What Little Anna saved
Original edition entitled *Vad lilla Anna sparade paa*
4 *Anna's mother has a birthday* (1966)
Little Anna's mother has a birthday
Original edition entitled *Lilla Annas mammafyller aar*
5 *When Anna had a cold* (1966)
When Little Anna had a cold
Original edition entitled *Naer lilla Anna var foerkyld*
6 *Little Anna and the tall uncle* (1971)
Original edition entitled *Lilla Anna och lange Farbrorn pa havet*
7 *Where is little Anna's dog?* (1972)
Original edition entitles *Var ar lilla Annas hund*
This sequence is followed by the **Kate series**

Anna series
Sandwall-Bergstrom, Martha
1 *Anna all alone* (1946)
Original edition entitled *Kulla-Gulla*
1 *Anna at Bloom Farm* (1946)
Original edition entitled *Kulla-Gulla pa blomgarden*
3 *Anna keeps her promise* (1946)
Original edition entitled *Kulla-Gulla haller satt lofte*
4 *Anna wins through* (1946)
Original edition entitled *Kulla-Gulla vinner en seger*
5 *Anna at the manor house* (1947)
Original edition entitled *Kulla-Gulla pa herrgarden*
6 *Anna solves the mystery* (1947)
Original edition entitled *Kulla-Gulla loser en gata*

Anna Southwood series
Bedford, Jean
1 *Worse than death* (1991)
Co-author: Tom Kelly
2 *To make a killing* (1992)

Anna Truly series
Drummond, Violet Hilda
see **Miss Anna Truly series**

Anna Zordan series
Eastwood, James
1 *Chinese visitor* (1965)
2 *Little dragon from Peking* (1967)
Seduce and destroy
3 *Diamonds are deadly* (1969)
Come die with me

Annabel Andrews series
Rodgers, Mary
1 *Freaky Friday* (1972)
2 *Billion for Boris* (1974)
3 *Summer switch* (1982)

Annabel Fidelity Bunce series
Davidson, Alan
1 *Friend like Annabel* (1982)
2 *Just like Annabel* (1983)
3 *Even more like Annabel* (1985)
4 *New, thinking Annabel* (1985)
5 *Little yearnings of Annabel* (1986)

Annabella series
Fitt, Mary
1 *Annabella at the lighthouse* (1955)
2 *Annabella takes a plunge* (1955)
3 *Annabella to the rescue* (1955)
4 *Annabella and the smugglers* (1957)

Annabelle series
O'Farrell, Kathleen
see **Lattimer children series**

Annals series
Deveraux, Jude
see **Montgomery annals series**

Annapolis alphabet series
Stevens, William Oliver
Pictures and limericks
1 *Annapolis alphabet* (1906)
2 *Another Annapolis alphabet* (1907)

Anne and David Layton series
Roberts, Marion
1 *Red greed* (1934)
2 *Mask for crime* (1935)

Anne and Francis Woodward series
Lowndes, Joan Selby
see **Francis and Anne Woodward series**

Anne and Jeffrey McNeill series
Du Bois, Theodora
1 *Armed with a new terror* (1936)
2 *Death weras a white coat* (1938)
3 *Death dines out* (1939)
4 *Death tears a comic strip* (1939)
5 *Death comes to tea* (1940)
6 *Death is late to lunch* (1941)
7 *McNeills chase a ghost* (1941)
8 *Body goes round and round* (1942)
9 *Wild duck murders* (1943)
10 *Case of the perfumed mouse* (1944)
11 *Death sails in a high wind* (1945)
12 *Murder strikes an atomic unit* (1946)
13 *Footsteps* (1947)
14 *Face of hate* (1948)
15 *Devil and destiny* (1948)
16 *It's raining violence* (1949)
Money, murder and the McNeills
17 *Fowl play* (1951)
18 *Cavalier's corpse* (1952)
19 *Seeing red* (1954)

Anne and John Webb series
Presnell, Frank G
see **John and Anne Webb series**

Anne Boleyn series
Reeve, Linda Dawn
1 *Early years* (1980)
2 *Royal suitor* (1981)

Anne Clarke series
Martin, Nancy
1 *Call the nurse* (1966)
2 *Call the courier* (1967)

Anne Davenport McLean series
Yates, Margaret Tayler
1 *Hush-hush murders* (1937)
2 *Death sends a cable* (1938)
3 *Midway to murder* (1941)
4 *Murder by the yard* (1942)

Anne Neville series
Irwin, Frances
1 *White pawn* (1972)
2 *White queen* (1974)

Anne Shirley series
Montgomery, Lucy Maud
see **Avonlea series**

Anne Thornton series
Anthony, Lotta Rowe
1 *Anne Thornton, Wetamoo* (1922)
2 *Anne Thornton, junior guide* (1924)
3 *Anne Thornton* (1925)

Anne Thorpe series
Martin, Nancy
see **Anne Clarke series**

Anne Wylde series
Hughes, Glyn
1 *Hawthorn goddess* (1984)
2 *Rape of the rose* (1987)

Annegret series
Benary, Margot
1 *Blue mystery* (1951)
2 *Shooting star* (1953)
3 *Time to love* (1953)

Annerley Junction series
Lunn, Hugh
see **Lunns of Annerley Junction series**

Annesley series
Everton, Francis
see **Inspector George Annesley series**

Annette Dancy series
Hill, Lorna
1 *Dancing Peel* (1954)
2 *Dancer's luck* (1955)
3 *Little dancer* (1956)
4 *Dancer in the wings* (1958)
5 *Dancer in danger* (1960)
6 *Dancer on holiday* (1962)

Annette series
Cheyne, Irene
1 *Annette of River Bend* (1941)
2 *Annette and Company* (1942)

Annette series
Schroeder, Doris
see **Walt Disney's Annette series**

Annetze de Steur series
Morrison, Margaret
1 *Flying high* (1940)
2 *Wider horizons* (1952)

Annie Besant series
Nethercot, Arthur Hobart
1 *First five lives of Annie Besant* (1961)
2 *Last four lives of Annie Besant* (1963)

Annie Brennan series
Raine, Norman Reilly
see **Tugboat Annie series**

Annie Jordan series
Post, Mary Brinker
1 *Annie Jordan* (1954)
2 *Matt Regan's woman* (1955)

Annie Kilburn series
Howells, William Dean
1 *Annie Kilburn* (1888)
2 *Quality of mercy* (1892)

Annie Laurance and Max Darling series
Hart, Carolyn Gimpel
1 *Death on Demand* (1987)
2 *Design for murder* (1988)
3 *Something wicked* (1988)
4 *Honeymoon with murder* (1989)
5 *Little class on murder* (1989)
6 *Deadly valentine* (1990)
7 *Christie caper* (1991)
8 *Southern ghost* (1992)

Annie Marble series
Forester, Cecil Scott
1 *Voyage of the Annie Marble* (1929)
2 *Annie Marble in Germany* (1930)

Annie Oakley series
Schroeder, Doris
Based on a television series
1 *Danger at Diablo* (1955)
2 *Ghost town secret* (1956)

Annie Parsons trilogy
Shears, Sarah
1 *Annie Parsons* (1979)
2 *Annie's boys* (1979)
3 *Annie's kingdom* (1980)

Annie series
Ehrlich, Amy
1 *Annie* (1982)
The storybook based on the movie
2 *Annie finds a home* (1982)
3 *Annie and the kidnappers* (1982)

Annie series
Hollan, Linda
1 *All the right moves* (1991)
2 *Class act* (1992)

Annie series
Lait, Jack
see **Polack Annie series**

Annie series
Louhi, Kristiina
1 *Annie's day* (1986)
Original edition entitled *Ainon Kanssa*
2 *Annie's year* (1986)
Original edition entitled *Ainon vuosi*

3 *Annie is almost three* (1987)
Original edition entitled *Aino pikkuinen tytto*
4 *Annie and the new baby* (1987)
Original edition entitled *Aino ja pakkasen poika*

Annie series
Manushkin, Fran
1 *Annie finds Sandy* (1981)
2 *Annie goes to the jungle* (1981)
3 *Annie and the desert treasure* (1981)
4 *Annie and the party thieves* (1982)

Annie series
Tuite, Hugh
see **Helpless Annie series**

Annie Sugden series
Mackenzie, Lee
1 *Annie Sugden's country diary* (1978)
2 *Early days at Emmerdale Farm* (1979)

Annie Tyson-Tyree and Whit Pynchon series
Pedneau, Dave
see **Whit Pynchon and Annie Tyson-Tyree series**

Anno's journey series
Anno, Mitsumasa
Translated from the Japanese
1 *My journey* (1977)
Anno's journey
2 *My journey II* (1978)
Anno's Italy
3 *Anno's journey III* (1981)
Anno's Britain
4 *Anno's USA* (1983)

Annwn series
Smith, George Henry
1 *Scourge of the blood cult* (1961)
2 *Kar Kaballa* (1969)
3 *Witch Queen of Lochlann* (1969)
4 *Second war of the worlds* (1976)
5 *Island snatchers* (1978)

Another day series
O'Donnell, Peadar
Autobiography
1 *Gates flew open* (1932)
Account of a jail term in 1923-24
2 *Salud!* (1937)
An Irishman in Spain
3 *There will be another day* (1963)

Another world series
Myrdal, Jan
Translated from the Swedish; autobiographical novels
1 *Childhood* (1991)
2 *Another world* (1993)

Anson family series
Ripley, Alexandra
see **Charleston series**

Anstruther series
Nicholas, Jerome
see **Bill Anstruther series**
Plain, Josephine
see **Colin Anstruther series**

Answer series
Wright, Harry Norman
1 *Answer to worry and anxiety* (1976)
2 *Answer to depression* (1976)
3 *Answer to the fulfilled marriage* (1976)
4 *Answer to discipline* (1976)
5 *Answer to family communication* (1977)
6 *Answer to frustration and anger* (1977)
7 *Answer to divorce* (1977)
8 *Answer to in-law relationships* (1977)
9 *Answer to building your self-image* (1977)
10 *Answer to parent-teen relationships* (1977)
11 *Answer to loneliness* (1977)
12 *Answer to submission and decision making* (1977)

Ant and Bee series
Banner, Angela
1 *Ant and Bee* (1950)
An alphabetical story for tiny tots
2 *More Ant and Bee* (1956)
3 *One, two, three with Ant and Bee* (1958)
4 *Around the world with Ant and Bee* (1958)
5 *More and more Ant and Bee* (1961)
Another alphabetical story
6 *Ant and Bee and the rainbow* (1962)
A story about colours
7 *Ant and Bee and Kind Dog* (1963)
8 *Happy birthday with Ant and Bee* (1964)
9 *Ant and Bee and the ABC* (1966)
10 *Ant and Bee time* (1969)
11 *Ant and Bee and the secret* (1970)
12 *Ant and Bee and the doctor* (1971)
13 *Ant and Bee big buy bag* (1971)
14 *Ant and Bee go shopping* (1972)

Antarctic series
McLaughlin, William Raffan Davidson
1 *Antarctic raider* (1960)
2 *So thin the line* (1963)

Antarctic Utopia series
Sweven, Godfrey
1 *Riallaro, the archipelago of exiles* (1901)
2 *Limanora, the island of progress* (1903)

Antares series
McCollum, Michael
1 *Antares dawn* (1986)
2 *Antares passage* (1987)

Antelope Company trilogy
Hall, Willis
1 *Return of the Antelope Company* (1985)
2 *Antelope Company ashore* (1986)
3 *Antelope Company at large* (1987)

Ante-room series
Dickson, Lovat
Autobiography
1 *Ante-room* (1959)
2 *House of words* (1963)

Anthea and Justin Rutherford series
Ley, Alice Chetwynd
see **Justin Rutherford and Anthea series**

Anthem series
Reno, James
see **Texas Anthem series**

Anthi series
Blakeney, Jay D
1 *Children of Anthi* (1985)
2 *Requiem for Anthi* (1990)

Anthony Adams series
Brace, Timothy
English editions published under the author's real name Theodore Pratt
1 *Murder goes fishing* (1936)
2 *Murder goes in a trailer* (1937)
3 *Murder goes to the dogs* (1938)
4 *Murder goes to the World's Fair* (1939)

Anthony Bathurst series
Flynn, Brian
1 *Billiard-room mystery* (1927)
2 *Case of the black twenty-two* (1928)
3 *Mystery of the peacock's eye* (1928)
4 *Murders near Mapleton* (1929)
5 *Invisible death* (1929)
6 *Five red fingers* (1929)
7 *Creeping Jenny mystery* (1930)
Crime at the Crossways
8 *Murder en route* (1930)
9 *Orange axe* (1931)
10 *Triple bite* (1931)
11 *Padded door* (1932)
12 *Edge of terror* (1932)
13 *Spiked lion* (1933)
14 *League of Matthias* (1934)
15 *Horn* (1934)
16 *Case of the purple calf* (1934)
Ladder of death
17 *Sussex cuckoo* (1935)
18 *Fortescue candle* (1936)
19 *Fear and trembling* (1936)
Somerset murder case
20 *Tread softly* (1937)
21 *Cold evil* (1938)
22 *Ebony stag* (1938)
23 *Black edged* (1939)
24 *Case of the faithful heart* (1939)
25 *Case of the painted ladies* (1940)
26 *They never came back* (1940)
27 *Such bright disguises* (1941)
28 *Glittering prizes* (1942)
29 *Reverse the charges* (1943)
30 *Grim maiden* (1944)
31 *Case of Elymas the sorcerer* (1945)
32 *Conspiracy at Angel* (1947)
33 *Sharp quillet* (1947)
34 *Exit Sir John* (1947)
35 *Swinging death* (1948)
36 *Men for pieces* (1949)
37 *Black agent* (1950)
38 *Where there was smoke* (1950)
39 *And cauldron bubble* (1951)
40 *Ring of Innocent* (1952)
41 *Seventh sign* (1952)
42 *Running nun* (1952)
43 *Out of the dusk* (1953)
44 *Feet of death* (1954)
45 *Doll's done dancing* (1954)
46 *Shaking spear* (1955)
47 *Mirador collection* (1955)
48 *Dice are dark* (1956)
49 *Toy lamb* (1956)
50 *Wife who disappeared* (1957)
51 *Hands of justice* (1957)
52 *Nine cuts* (1958)
53 *Saints are sinister* (1958)

Anthony Brandon series
Peters, Bryan
see **Brandon and Lundstrom series**

Anthony Daintrey series
Knight, Peter
1 *Bramble Fortress* (1961)
2 *Boreas adventure* (1963)

Anthony Dare series
Marshall, Archibald
1 *Anthony Dare* (1923)
2 *Education of Anthony Dare* (1924)
3 *Anthony Dare's progress* (1925)

Anthony England series
Elliott, William James
1 *Silk* (1942)
2 *Shot-silk* (1943)
3 *Sheer silk* (1946)
4 *Spun silk* (1947)

Anthony Ferrara series
Rohmer, Sax
1 *Tales of secret Egypt* (1918)
2 *Brood of the witch-queen* (1918)

Anthony Hamilton series
Frost, Frederick
see **Secret service series**

Anthony Howard series
McCutcheon, Hugh
1 *Angel of light* (1951)
Murder at the Angel
2 *Cover her face* (1954)

Anthony Lyveden series
Yates, Dornford
1 *Anthony Lyveden* (1921)
2 *Valerie French* (1923)

Anthony Mallory series
Lindsey, Johanna
1 *Love only once* (1985)
2 *Tender rebel* (1988)

Anthony Martin series
Francis, William
1 *Rough on rats* (1942)
I.O.U. murder
2 *Bury me not* (1943)

Anthony Monday series
Bellairs, John
1 *Treasure of Alpheus Winterborn* (1978)
2 *Dark secret of Weatherend* (1984)
3 *Lamp from the warlock's tomb* (1988)

Anthony Mornington, George Hawkins and Tommy Malins series
Dix, Maurice Buxton
see **Tommy Malins, Anthony Mornington and George Hawkins series**

Anthony Nicholas Twin series
Masters, Doug
see **TNT series**

Anthony Post series
Irving, Alexander
see **Doctor Anthony Post series**

Anthony Ravenhill series
Foster, Reginald Francis
1 *Missing gates* (1924)
2 *Lift murder* (1924)
Body in the shaft
3 *Anthony Ravenhill, crime merchant* (1926)
4 *Music gallery murder* (1927)
5 *Moat house mystery* (1928)
6 *Murder from beyond* (1930)
7 *Something wrong at Chillery* (1931)
Mystery at Chillery
Something wrong at Chillery

Anthony Read series
Toye, Stanley
1 *Cyanide!* (1940)
2 *Sinners in clover* (1945)
3 *Prelude to peril* (1946)

Anthony Rillington series
Orde-Powlett, Nigel
1 *Cast of death* (1932)
2 *Driven death* (1933)

Anthony Rogers series
Nowlan, Philip Francis
see **Buck Rogers series**

Anthony Rome series
Rome, Anthony
see **Tony Rome series**

Anthony Ruthven Gethryn series
Macdonald, Philip
see **Colonel Anthony Ruthven Gethryn series**

Anthony series
Heath, Eric
see **Wade Anthony series**

Anthony Slade series
Gribble, Leonard Reginald
see **Superintendent Anthony Slade series**

Anthony Trant series
Downing, John Hyatt
1 *Sioux City* (1940)
2 *Anthony Trant* (1941)

Anthony Trent series
Martyn, Wyndham
1 *Anthony Trent, master criminal* (1918)
2 *Secret of the silver car* (1920)
3 *Mysterious Mister Garland* (1922)
4 *Return of Anthony Trent* (1923)
5 *Recluse of Fifth Avenue* (1925)
6 *Trent of the lone hand* (1927)
7 *Triumphant prodigal* (1928)
8 *Anthony Trent, avenger* (1928)
9 *Murder island* (1928)
10 *Death fear* (1929)
11 *Trent trail* (1930)
12 *Social storming* (1930)
13 *Scarlett murder* (1931)
14 *Great Ling plot* (1933)
15 *Death by the lake* (1934)
16 *Nightmare Castle* (1935)
17 *Criminals all* (1935)
18 *House of secrets* (1936)
19 *Old manor crime* (1937)
20 *Blue Ridge crime* (1937)
21 *Murder walks the deck* (1938)
22 *Trent fights again* (1939)
23 *Ghost city killers* (1940)
24 *Headland House affair* (1941)
25 *Men without faces* (1943)
26 *Last scourge* (1946)
27 *Stones of enchantment* (1948)
28 *Manhunt in murder* (1950)

Anthony Vereker series
Forsythe, Robin
1 *Missing or murdered* (1929)
2 *Hounds of justice* (1930)
3 *Polo ground mystery* (1932)
4 *Pleasure cruise mystery* (1933)
5 *Ginger cat mystery* (1935)
Murder at Marston Manor
6 *Spirit murder mystery* (1936)

Anthony Verrell
Graeme, Bruce
see **Lord Blackshirt series**

Anthony Villiers series
Panshin, Alexei
1 *Star well* (1968)
2 *Thurb revolution* (1968)
3 *Masque world* (1969)

Anthony Ware series
Wells, Susan
1 *Murder is not enough* (1939)
2 *Footsteps in the air* (1940)
3 *Death is my name* (1942)
4 *Witches' pond* (1947)

Anthropol Detective Agency series
Trimble, Louis
1 *Anthropol* (1968)
2 *Noblest experiment in the galaxy* (1970)

Anthropos series
White, John
see **Archives of Anthropos series**

Anti-coloring book series
Striker, Susan
1 *Anti-coloring book of exploring space on earth* (1980)
2 *Anti-coloring book of red letter days* (1981)
3 *Anti-coloring book of masterpieces* (1982)
4 *Anti-coloring book for adults only* (1983)
5 *Build a better mouse trap* (1983)
6 *Superpowers anti-coloring book* (1984)
7 *Young at art* (1985)
An anti-coloring book for pre-schoolers
8 *Mystery anti-coloring book* (1991)
9 *Newspaper anti-coloring book* (1992)
Companion volume: *The anti-coloring calendar*, 1983

Anti-coloring series
Striker, Susan
1 *Anti-coloring book* (1978)
Co-author: Edward Kimmel
2 *Second anti-coloring book* (1979)
Co-author: Edward Kimmel
3 *Third anti-coloring book* (1980)
Co-author: Edward Kimmel
4 *Fourth anti-coloring book* (1981)
5 *Fifth anti-coloring book* (1983)
6 *Sixth anti-coloring book* (1984)

Antigeos trilogy
Capon, Paul
1 *Other side of the sun* (1950)
2 *Other half of the planet* (1952)
3 *Down to earth* (1954)

Antigua Players series
Gollin, James
1 *Philomel Foundation* (1980)
2 *Eliza's galiardo* (1983)
3 *Verona passamezzo* (1985)

Antique dealer series
Bremond d'Ars, Yvonne de
see **Journal of an antique dealer series**

Antoine Cirret series
Hely, Elizabeth
1 *Dominant third* (1959)
I'll be judge, I'll be jury
2 *Mark of displeasure* (1960)

Anton Drakov series
Winters, Jon
1 *Drakov memoranda* (1979)
2 *Catenary exchange* (1983)
3 *Berlin fugue* (1985)

Anton Dymek series
Riley, Frank
see **Father Anton Dymek series**

Anton Stryker series
Nighbert, David Franklin
1 *Timelapse* (1988)
2 *Clouds of Magellan* (1991)

Antonio Cervantes series
Cook, Bruce
1 *Mexican standoff* (1988)
2 *Rough cut* (1990)
3 *Death as a career move* (1992)
4 *Sidewalk Hilton* (1994)

Antonio series
Marston, John
Verse plays
1 *Antonio and Mellida* (1599)
2 *Antonio's revenge* (1599)
One volume edition 1902

Antony Havilland series
Gielgud, Val
1 *Gravelhanger* (1934)
Ruse of the vanished women
2 *Outrage in Manchukuo* (1937)
3 *Fall of a sparrow* (1949)
Stalking horse
4 *Special delivery* (1950)

Antony Maitland and Sir Nicholas Harding series
Woods, Sara
see **Sir Nicholas Harding and Antony Maitland series**

Antony series
Curzon, Colin
see **Mark Antony series**

Antrian series
Wisler, Gary Clifton
1 *Antrian messenger* (1986)
2 *Seer* (1988)
3 *Mind trap* (1990)

Antrobus series
Durrell, Lawrence
1 *Esprit de corps* (1957)
2 *Stiff upper lip* (1958)
3 *Sauve qui peut* (1966)
Omnibus volumes: *The best of Antrobus*, 1974, *Antrobus complete*, 1985

Anzac series
Hogue, Oliver
1 *Love letters of an Anzac* (1916)
2 *Trooper Bluegum at the Dardanelles* (1916)
Descriptive narrative of the more desperate engagements on the Gallipoli Peninsula
3 *Cameliers* (1919)

Apache Anderson series
Sadler, Jeff
see **Marshal Andrew Anderson series**

Apache series
Burroughs, Edgar Rice
1 *War chief* (1927)
2 *Apache devil* (1933)

Apache series
James, William M
This pseudonym is used by Terry Harknett, John Barton Harvey and Laurence James as indicated against each title
1 *First death* (1974) [Harknett]
2 *Knife in the night* (1974) [James]
3 *Duel to the death* (1974) [Harknett]
4 *Death train* (1975) [James]
5 *Fort Treachery* (1975) [Harknett]
6 *Sonora slaughter* (1976) [Harknett]
7 *Blood line* (1976) [James]
8 *Blood on the tracks* (1977) [Harknett]
9 *Naked and the savage* (1977) [James]
10 *All blood is red* (1977) [Harknett]
11 *Cruel trail* (1978) [James]
12 *Fool's gold* (1978) [James]
13 *Best man* (1979) [Harknett]
14 *Born to die* (1979) [James]
15 *Blood rising* (1979) [Harvey]
16 *Texas killing* (1980) [James]
17 *Blood brother* (1980) [Harvey]
18 *Slow dying* (1980) [James]
19 *Fast living* (1981) [James]
20 *Death dragon* (1981) [Harvey]
21 *Blood wedding* (1981) [James]
22 *Border killing* (1982) [James]
23 *Death Valley* (1983) [James]
24 *Death ride* (1983) [Harvey]
25 *Times past* (1983) [James]
26 *Hanging* (1983) [Harvey]
27 *Debt of blood* (1984) [James]

Apafi series
Jokai, Mor
see **Michael Apafi series**

Ape Man series
Garron, Marco
see **Azan series**

Ape Swain series
Da Cruz, Daniel
1 *Landfall finesse* (1975)
2 *Pipe dream finesse* (1975)
3 *Captive city* (1976)

Aphrodite series
Durrell, Lawrence
see **Revolt of Aphrodite series**

Apology for the life of Jean Robertson series
Sandison, Janet
1 *Jean in the morning* (1969)
2 *Jean at noon* (1971)
3 *Jean in the twilight* (1972)
4 *Jean towards another day* (1975)

Apostle Peter series
Douglas, Lloyd Cassel
1 *Robe* (1942)
2 *Big Fisherman* (1948)

Appalachee Red series
Andrews, Raymond
1 *Appalachee Red* (1978)
2 *Rosiebelle Lee Wildcat Tennessee* (1979)
3 *Baby Sweet's* (1983)

Appeasement series
Gilbert, Martin
1 *Roots of appeasement* (1966)
2 *Appeasers* (1963)
Revised edition 1967

Apple Lock series
Curry, Jane Louise
1 *Daybreakers* (1970)
2 *Birdstones* (1977)

Apple Market Street series
Hill, Mabel Betsy
see **Judy Jo series**

Apple Porter series
Lovell, Marc
see **Appleton Porter series**

Apple tree series
Pearce, Mary Emily
1 *Apple tree lean down* (1973)
2 *Jack Mercybright* (1974)
3 *Sorrowing wind* (1975)
Numbers 1-3 also published in one volume entitled *Apple tree saga*, 1976
4 *Land endures* (1978)
5 *Seedtime and harvest* (1980)

Applebury tales series
Bradbury, Catherine
1 *Badger Wood* (1986)
2 *Willow Pool* (1986)
3 *Cowslip Meadow* (1987)
4 *Holly Lane* (1987)

Appleby series
Innes, Michael
see **Sir John Appleby series**
Koehler, Robert Portner
see **Pecos Appleby series**
Trease, Geoffrey
see **Mark Appleby series**

Apples Carstairs series
Myles, Simon
1 *Big black* (1974)
2 *Big needle* (1974)
Big apple
3 *Big hit* (1975)

Appleton Porter series
Lovell, Marc
1 *Spy game* (1980)

Appleton Porter series

2 *Spy with his head in the clouds* (1982)
3 *Spy on the run* (1982)
4 *Apple spy in the sky* (1983)
5 *Apple to the core* (1983)
6 *How green was my Apple* (1984)
7 *Only good Apple in a barrel of spies* (1984)
8 *Spy who got his feet wet* (1985)
9 *Spy who barked in the night* (1986)
10 *Good spies don't grow on trees* (1986)
11 *Spy who fell off the back of a bus* (1988)
12 *That great big trenchcoat in the sky* (1988)

Appleyard family series
Kent, Louise Andrews
1 *Mrs Appleyard's year* (1942)
2 *Mrs Appleyard's kitchen* (1942)
3 *With kitchen privileges* (1953)
4 *Summer kitchen, Mrs Appleyard's of course* (1956)
Mrs Appleyard's summer kitchen
5 *Winter kitchen, Mrs Appleyard's of course* (1963)
Mrs Appleyard's winter kitchen
6 *Mrs Appleyard and I* (1968)
Companion volume: *Mrs Appleyard's family kitchen, a treasury of Vermont country recipes*, 1977, second edition 1984

Appleyards series
Edwards, David
1 *Appleyards* (1955)
2 *Appleyards again* (1956)

Apprentice adept series
Anthony, Piers
1 *Split infinity* (1980)
2 *Blue adept* (1981)
3 *Juxtaposition* (1982)
Numbers 1-3 also published in one volume entitled *Double exposure*, 1982
4 *Out of phaze* (1987)
5 *Robot adept* (1988)
6 *Unicorn point* (1989)
7 *Phaze doubt* (1990)

Apprentices series
Garfield, Leon
1 *Lamplighter's funeral* (1976)
2 *Mirror, mirror* (1976)
3 *Cloak* (1976)
4 *Moss and Blister* (1976)
5 *Labour in vain* (1976)
6 *Valentine* (1977)
7 *Fool* (1977)
8 *Rosy Starling* (1977)
9 *Dumb cake* (1977)
10 *Tom Titmarsh's devil* (1977)
11 *Filthy beast* (1978)
12 *Enemy* (1978)
One volume edition entitled *The apprentices*, 1978

April and Amanda series
Pryor, Bonnie
see **Amanda and April series**

April Dancer series
Avallone, Michael
see **Girl from U.N.C.L.E.series**

April Panhasard series
Hine, Muriel
1 *Half in earnest* (1910)
2 *April Panhasard* (1913)

April series
Roscoe, Mike
see **Johnny April series**

Aprilioth trilogy
Kernaghan, Eileen
1 *Journey to Aprilioth* (1980)
2 *Songs from the drowned lands* (1983)
3 *Sarsen witch* (1989)

Aqualung twins series
Falkner, Frederick
1 *Aqualung twins find Chinese treasure* (1956)
2 *Aqualung twins and the vanishing people* (1957)
3 *Aqualung twins and the Iron Crab* (1959)

Aquanauts series
Stanton, Ken
1 *Cold blue death* (1970)
2 *Ten seconds to zero* (1970)
3 *Seek, strike and destroy* (1971)
4 *Sargasso secret* (1971)
5 *Stalkers of the sea* (1972)
6 *Whirlwind beneath the sea* (1972)
7 *Operation Deep Six* (1972)
8 *Operation Steelfish* (1972)
9 *Evil cargo* (1973)
10 *Operation Sea Monster* (1974)
11 *Operation Mermaid* (1974)

Aquiliad trilogy
Sucharitkul, Somtow
1 *Aquiliad* (1988)
Also published as *Aquila in the new world* under the pseudonym S P Somtow; sequence continued under the pseudonym S P Somtow
Somtow, S P
2 *Aquila and the iron horse* (1988)
3 *Aquila and the sphinx* (1988)

Aquilon, Cal and Veg series
Anthony, Piers
see **Of man and mantra trilogy**

Arab and Andy Blake series
Powell, Richard
1 *Don't catch me* (1943)
Case of the curious chair
2 *All over but the shooting* (1944)
Death talks out of turn
The second title is an abridged edition
3 *Lay that pistol down* (1945)
4 *Shoot if you must* (1946)
5 *And hope to die* (1947)

Arab history series
Glubb, John Bagot
1 *Great Arab conquests* (1963)
630-680AD
2 *Empire of the Arabs* (1963)
680-860AD
3 *Course of empire* (1965)
The Arabs and their successors, 860-1156

Arabel and Mortimer series
Aiken, Joan
1 *Arabel's raven* (1972)
2 *Escaped black mamba* (1973)
Arabel and the escaped black mamba
3 *Bread bin* (1974)
Numbers 1-3 also published in one volume editions entitled *Tales of Arabel's raven*, 1974, and *Arabel's raven*
4 *Mortimer's tie* (1976)
5 *Spiral stair* (1979)
6 *Mortimer and the sword Excalibur* (1979)
Numbers 4-6 also published in one volume entitled *Arabel and Mortimer*, 1980
7 *Mystery of Mister Jones's disappearing taxi* (1982)
8 *Mortimer's portrait on glass* (1982)
Numbers 7 and 8 also published in one volume entitled *Mortimer's cross*, 1983
9 *Mortimer says nothing, and other stories* (1985)

Arabella Braithwaite series
Spence, Eleanor
1 *Switherby pilgrims* (1967)
2 *Jamberoo Road* (1969)

Arabella Frant series
Fearon, Diana
1 *Death before breakfast* (1959)
2 *Murder-on-Thames* (1960)

Arabian Nights trilogy
Gardner, Craig Shaw
1 *Other Sinbad* (1991)
2 *Bad night for Ali Baba* (1991)
3 *Last Arabian Nights* (1993)
Companion volume: *Sinbad, the thirteenth voyage*, by Raphael Aloysius Lafferty, 1989

Arabian travel series
Philby, Harry St John Bridger
1 *Heart of Arabia* (1922)
A record of travel and exploration in two volumes
2 *Sheba's daughter* (1939)
A record of travel in southern Arabia
3 *Pilgrim in Arabia* (1943)
4 *Arabian days* (1948)
5 *Forty years in the wilderness* (1957)

Arafel's saga series
Cherryh, Carolyn Janice
see **Ealdwood series**

Aragon series
Millar, Margaret
see **Tom Aragon series**

Ara-Karn series
Corby, Adam
see **Doom-quest of Ara-Karn series**

Arbat trilogy
Rybakov, Anatoli
Translated from the Russian
1 *Children of the Arbat* (1987)
2 *Fear* (1989)
The third volume of the trilogy is not yet translated

Arbuckle series
Smyth, Gwenda
see **Mrs Arbuckle series**

Arbuthnot series
Croy, Catherine
see **Julia Arbuthnot series**
Temple-Ellis, N A
see **Montrose Arbuthnot series**

Arc One series
Hughes, Monica
1 *Devil on my back* (1984)
2 *Dream catcher* (1986)

Arcade explorers series
McEvoy, Seth
1 *Save the Venturians!* (1985)
2 *Revenge of the Raster Gang* (1985)
3 *Electronic hurricane* (1985)
4 *Magnetic ghost of Shadow Island* (1985)

Arcadia series
Coney, Michael Greatrex
1 *Mirror image* (1972)
2 *Syzygy* (1973)
3 *Brontomek!* (1976)

Arcadia series
Lowndes, Marie Belloc
1 *I too, have lived in Arcadia* (1941)
A record of love and of childhood
2 *Where love and friendship dwelt* (1943)
3 *Merry wives of Westminster* (1946)
4 *Passing world* (1948)

Arcadia trilogy
Hardy, Lyndon
1 *Master of the five magics* (1980)
2 *Secret of the sixth magic* (1984)
3 *Riddle of the seven realms* (1988)

Arcadian trilogy
Eaton, Evelyn
1 *Quietly my captain waits* (1940)
2 *Restless are the sails* (1941)
3 *Sea is so wide* (1943)

Arcady series
Sutcliffe, Halliwell
1 *Episode in Arcady* (1898)
2 *Bachelor in Arcady* (1904)
3 *Benedick in Arcady* (1906)

Arceval series
Madariaga, Salvador de
see **Julio Arceval series**

Archaeology series
Fidler, Kathleen
1 *Treasure of Ebba* (1968)
2 *Gold of Fast Castle* (1970)

Archaeology series
Pond, Roy
1 *Pyramid voyagers* (1991)
Rescue mission to the tombs abd treasures of Egypt's past
2 *Tomb travellers* (1991)
Beyond the gateways and guardians of Egypt's underworld

Archdeacon and Mister Scotter series
Warriner, Thurman
see **Mister Scotter series**

Archdeacon series
Alington, Cyril Augustine
1 *Archdeacons afloat* (1946)
2 *Archdeacons ashore* (1947)
3 *Blackmail in Blankshire* (1949)
4 *Gold and gaiters* (1950)

Archer series
Carr, Joseph Baker
see **Oceola Archer series**
Clevely, Hugh
see **Maxwell Archer series**
Conford, Ellen
see **Jenny Archer series**
Gibbs, Anthony
see **John Archer series**
Henry, Clay
see **Matt Archer series**
Longley, W B
see **Angel Eyes series**
Macdonald, Ross
see **Lew Archer series**

Archers of Ambridge series
This sequnce has four authors
Webb, Geoffrey
1 *Archers of Ambridge* (1954)
2 *Archers intervene* (1956)
Miles, Keith
3 *Ambridge summer* (1975)
Hayles, Brian
4 *Spring at Brookfield* (1975)
Gallagher, Jock
5 *To the victor the spoils* (1988)
6 *Return to Ambridge* (1988)
7 *Borchester echoes* (1988)
Companion volumes: *Doris Archer's Ambridge diary*, 1972, *Twenty-five years of the Archers, a who's who of Ambridge*, 1975

Arches of the years series
Sutherland, Halliday
1 *Arches of the years* (1933)
2 *Time to keep* (1934)
3 *In my path* (1936)

Archibald Beldrum and Nigel Blair series
Hay, Lindsay Fitzgerald
1 *It wasn't a nightmare* (1937)
2 *Terrible hand* (1937)
3 *No mean tartar* (1938)

Archibald McGillicuddy series
Bateman, Robert
1 *Archie, young detective* (1961)
2 *Mystery for Archie* (1963)
3 *Archie abroad* (1964)
4 *Archie and the missing stamps* (1965)
5 *Archie's Italian adventure* (1966)
6 *Strange case for Archie* (1967)
7 *Archie on the trail* (1968)

Archibald Penny series
Jackson, Wallace
1 *Zadda Street affair* (1934)
2 *Extraordinary case of Mister Bell* (1935)

Archie Burford series
Macclure, Victor
see **Inspector Archie Burford series**

Archie Goodwin and Nero Wolfe series
Stout, Rex
see **Nero Wolfe and Archie Goodwin series**

Archie Lumsden series
Saltmarsh, Max
1 *Highly inflammable* (1936)
2 *Clouded moon* (1937)
3 *Indigo death* (1938)

Archie series
Bateman, Robert
see **Archibald McGillicuddy series**

Archives of Anthropos series
White, John
1 *Tower of Geburah* (1978)
2 *Iron sceptre* (1981)
3 *Sword bearer* (1986)
4 *Gaal the conqueror* (1989)

Archy and Mehitabel series
Marquis, Don
1 *Archy and Mehitabel* (1930)
2 *Archy's life of Mehitabel* (1933)

Archy Buller series
Hough, Richard Alexander
1 *Buller's guns* (1981)
2 *Buller's Dreadnought* (1982)
3 *Buller's victory* (1984)

Archy McNally series
Sanders, Lawrence
1 *McNally's secret* (1992)
2 *McNally's luck* (1992)
3 *McNally's risk* (1993)

Arcot, Morey and Wade series
Campbell, John Wood
1 *Black star passes* (1953)
2 *Islands of space* (1956)
3 *Invaders from the infinite* (1961)
One volume edition entitled *John W Campbell anthology*, 1973

Arctic series
Helmericks, Bud
see **Bob Hamilton series**

Arctic world series
Kalman, Bobbie
1 *Arctic animals* (1988)
2 *Arctic community* (1988)
3 *Arctic land* (1988)
4 *Arctic whales and whaling* (1988)

Ardan series
Verne, Jules
see **From the earth to the moon series**

Ardel series
Jensen, Kris
1 *FreeMaster* (1990)
2 *Mentor* (1991)

Arden Blake series
Garis, Cleo Fausta
1 *Missing at Marshlands* (1934)
2 *Mystery of Jockey Hollow* (1934)
3 *Orchard secret* (1934)

Arden Gifford series
Newton, Suzanne
1 *End to perfect* (1984)
2 *Place between* (1986)

Arden series
Chalmers, Margaret Piper
see **Sylvia Arden series**

Arden series
Nesbit, Edith
1 *House of Arden* (1908)
2 *Harding's luck* (1909)

Ardencester series
Davis, Oswald Harcourt
1 *Soft goods* (1923)
2 *Smite the rock!* (1924)
3 *Home brewed* (1932)
4 *This great city* (1967)

Ardfalloch series
Stevenson, Dorothy Emily
1 *Smouldering fire* (1935)
2 *Katherine Wentworth* (1964)
3 *Katherine's marriage* (1965)
Marriage of Katherine

Ardito Piccardi series
Coccioli, Carlo
1 *Heaven and earth* (1950)
Original edition entitled *Il cielo e la terra*
2 *White stone* (1958)
Original edition entitled *Le caillou blanc*

Ardleigh family series
Knight, Brigid
1 *Sword between* (1968)
2 *Prisoner of the past* (1972)

Areia Darenga trilogy
Mezo, Francine
1 *Fall of worlds* (1980)
2 *Unless she burn* (1981)
3 *No earthly shore* (1981)

Argand series
Rathbone, Julian
see **Jan Argand series**

Argee and Amberdon series
Schmitz, James Henry
see **Telzey Amberdon and Trigger Argee series**

Argle series
Pardoe, Margot
see **Macalister series**

Argonia series
Scarborough, Elizabeth Ann
1 *Song of sorcery* (1982)
2 *Unicorn creed* (1983)
Numbers 1 and 2 also published in one volume entitled *Songs from the Seashell archives*, volume 1, 1987
3 *Bronwyn's bane* (1983)
4 *Christening quest* (1985)
Numbers 3 and 4 also published in one volume entitled *Songs from the Seashell archives*, volume 2, 1988

Argos mythos series
Lafferty, Raphael Aloysius
1 *Devil is dead* (1971)
2 *Archipelago* (1979)
3 *More than Melchisedech* (1983)
4 *Promontory goats* (1988)
5 *How many miles to Babylon* (1989)
6 *Dotty* (1990)
7 *Episodes of the Argo* (1990)

Argus series
Erdrich, Louise
1 *Love medicine* (1984)
Revised edition 1993
2 *Beet queen* (1986)
3 *Tracks* (1988)
4 *Bingo palace* (1994)

Argus series
Sernine, Daniel
1 *Argus steps in* (1990)
Original edition entitled *Argus intervient*
2 *Those who watch over earth* (1990)
Original edition entitled *Organisation Argus*

Argus Steele series
Lee, Babs
1 *Model is murdered* (1942)
2 *Passport to oblivion* (1943)
3 *Measured for murder* (1944)
Co-author: Clare Castler Saunders

Argyle series
Story, Jack Trevor
see **Albert Argyle series**

Ariadne Oliver series
Christie, Agatha
see **Mrs Ariadne Oliver series**

Aristo Autos series
Leasor, James
1 *They don't make them like that anymore* (1969)
2 *Never had a spanner on her* (1970)
3 *Host of extras* (1973)

Aristocrats series
Saint-Pierre, Michel de
1 *Aristocrats* (1954)
Original edition entitled *Les aristocrates*
2 *New aristocrats* (1960)
Original edition entitled *Les nouveaux aristocrates*

Arizona Ames series
This sequence has two authors
Grey, Zane
1 *Arizona Ames* (1932)
Grey, Romer Zane
2 *Other side of the canyon* (1970)
3 *Showdown at Lone Tree* (1970)
4 *Gun trouble in Tonto Basin* (1971)
5 *King of the outlaw horde* (1982)
6 *Marauders of Gallows Valley* (1982)
7 *Danger rides the dollar wagon* (1982)
Numbers 5, 6 and 7 were published in one volume entitled *King of the outlaw horde*, 1982

Arizona saga series
Brown, Joseph Paul Summers
1 *Blooded stock* (1990)
2 *Horseman* (1991)
3 *Ladino* (1991)

Arizona trilogy
Ellis, Edward Sylvester
1 *Off the reservation* (1908)
Alternative title: Caught in an Apache raid
2 *Trailing Geronimo* (1908)
Alternative title: Campaigning with Crook
3 *Round-up* (1908)
Alternative title: Geronimo's last raid

Arizona trilogy
Williams, Jeanne
1 *Valiant women* (1980)
2 *Harvest of fury* (1981)
3 *Mating of hawks* (1982)

Arjuna's family series
Bonnici, Peter
1 *First rains* (1984)
2 *Festival* (1984)

Ark series
Hoch, Edward Dentinger
see **Simon Ark series**

Arkady Renko series
Smith, Martin Cruz
1 *Gorky Park* (1981)
2 *Polar Star* (1989)
3 *Red Square* (1992)

Arkell series
Wood, Ellen
see **Mildred Arkell series**

Arkmae series
Cutt, William Towrie
1 *Message from Arkmae* (1972)
2 *Seven for the sea* (1972)

Arlette Van der Valk series
Freeling, Nicolas
Continuation of the **Van der Valk series** from the death of Inspector Piet Van der Valk
1 *Long silence* (1972)
Aupres de ma blonde
2 *Widow* (1979)
3 *One damn thing after another* (1981)
Arlette

Arlington Street trilogy
Leslie, Henrietta
1 *Emily in Arlington Street* (1942)
2 *Martha Plover* (1944)
3 *Young Sam* (1946)

Arly Hanks series
Hess, Joan
1 *Malice in Maggody* (1987)
2 *Mischief in Maggody* (1988)
3 *Much ado in Maggody* (1989)
4 *Madness in Maggody* (1990)
5 *Mortal remains in Maggody* (1991)
6 *Maggody in Manhattan* (1992)
7 *O little town of Maggody* (1993)
8 *Martians in Maggody* (1994)

Arly series
Peck, Robert Newton
1 *Arly* (1989)
2 *Arly's run* (1991)

Armageddon trilogy
Rankin, Robert
1 *Armageddon* (1990)
The musical
2 *They came and ate us* (1991)
The B-movie
3 *Suburban book of the dead* (1992)
The remake

Armata series
Erskine, Thomas
1 *Armata* (1817)
A fragment
2 *Second part of Armata* (1817)
One volume edition entitled *Armata*, 1817

Armenian girl series
Kherdian, David
Based on the life of the author's mother
1 *Road from home* (1979)
2 *Finding home* (1981)
Companion volume: *Root River run*, 1984

Armiston series
Anderson, Frederick Irving
see **Oliver Armiston series**

Armitage family series
Chesney, Marion
see **Six sisters series**

Armitage family series
Aiken, Joan
1 *All you've ever wanted, and other stories* (1953)
2 *More than you bargained for, and other stories* (1955)
3 *Armitage, Armitage, fly away home* (1968)

Armitage series
Cobb, Belton
see **Bryan Armitage series; Kitty Armitage series**
McLeave, Hugh
see **Doctor Stephen Armitage series**

Armitage trilogy
Kelsey, Franklyn
see **James Armitage trilogy**

Armstrong Custer series
Johnston, Terry Conrad
see **General Armstrong Custer series**

Armstrong series
White, Alan
see **Inspector Armstrong series**

Army Air Corps series
Rosenbaum, Ray
1 *Falcons* (1993)
2 *Hawks* (1994)

Army and navy series
Optic, Oliver
1 *Soldier boy* (1863)
Alternative title: Tom Somers in the Army
2 *Sailor boy* (1863)
Alternative title: Jack Somers in the Navy
3 *Young lieutenant* (1865)
Alternative title: The adventures of an army officer
4 *Yankee middy* (1865)
Alternative title: The adventures of a naval officer
5 *Fighting Joe* (1865)
Alternative title: The fortunes of a staff officer
6 *Brave Old Salt* (1865)
Alternative title: A story of the great rebellion

Army boy series
Kilboure, Charles Evans
1 *Army boy in Pekin* (1912)
2 *Army boy in the Philippines* (1913)
3 *Army boy in Mexico* (1914)
4 *Army boy in Alaska* (1915)

Army boys series
Randall, Homer
1 *Army boys in France* (1919)
Alternative title: From training camp to trenches
2 *Army boys in the French trenches* (1919)
Alternative title: Hand to hand fights with the enemy
3 *Army boys on the firing line* (1919)
Alternative title: Holding back the German drive
4 *Army boys in the big drive* (1919)
Alternative title: Smashing forward to victory
5 *Army boys marching into Germany* (1919)
Alternative title: Over the Rhine with the Stars and Stripes
6 *Army boys on German soil* (1920)
Alternative title: Our doughboys quelling the mobs

Arnhem Land series
Wells, Ann Elizabeth
1 *Tales from Arnhem Land* (1959)
2 *Rain in Arnhem Land* (1961)

Arnholt series
Latta, Gordon
1 *Arnholt makes his bow* (1931)
Toni diamonds
2 *Re-enter Arnholt* (1932)
3 *Exit Arnholt* (1935)

Arnie series
Carlson, Nancy
1 *Arnie and the stolen markers* (1987)
2 *Arnie goes to camp* (1988)
3 *Arnie and the new kid* (1990)

Arnison series
Thompson, Edward
1 *Introducing the Arnisons* (1935)
2 *John Arnison* (1939)

Arnold and Merrion series
Burton, Miles
see **Inspector Arnold and Desmond Merrion series**

Arnold and Webster series
Roche, Patricia K
see **Webster and Arnold series**

Arnold Keene and Bernard Young series
Wood, Eric
1 *Death in the mews* (1937)
2 *Hands of death* (1937)
3 *Death of an oddfellow* (1938)

Arnold Landon series
Lewis, Royston
1 *Gathering of ghosts* (1982)
2 *Most cunning workmen* (1984)
3 *Trout in the milk* (1986)
4 *Men of subtle craft* (1987)

Arnold series
Knipe, Emilie Benson
see **Benedict Arnold series**

Arnold Wragge series
Capon, Paul
1 *Hosts of Midian* (1946)
2 *Dead man's chest* (1947)
3 *Image of a murder* (1949)

Arrest and trial series
Daniels, Norman A
Based on a television series
1 *Arrest and trial* (1963)
2 *Missing witness* (1964)

'Arris series
Poultney, Clifford Blake
see **Mrs 'Arris series**

Arrow and Peacock series
Mantell, Laurie
see **Sergeant Steve Arrow and Chief Inspector Peacock series**

Arrow and saber series
Carrington, G A
see **Marcus Cavanaugh series**

Arrow in the blue series
Koestler, Arthur
Autobiography
1 *Arrow in the blue* (1952)
2 *Invisible writing* (1954)
3 *Stranger in the square* (1983)
Written in collaboration with his wife Cynthia prior to their joint suicide in 1983

Arrow series
Deptula, Walter
see **Frank Arrow series**

Arrow series
Myers, Walter Dean
1 *Adventure in Granada* (1985)
2 *Hidden shrine* (1985)
3 *Duel in the desert* (1986)
4 *Ambush in the Amazon* (1986)

Arrows trilogy
Lackey, Mercedes
see **Heralds of Valdemar trilogy**

Arsene Lupin series
Leblanc, Maurice
1 *Exploits of Arsene Lupin* (1907)
Seven of hearts
Extraordinary adventures of Arsene Lupin
Arsene Lupin, gentleman burglar
Original edition entitled *Arsene Lupin, gentleman-cambrioleur*
2 *Arsene Lupin versus Holmlock Shears* (1908)
Blonde lady
Arsene Lupin versus Herlock Sholmes
Arrest of Arsene Lupin
Original edition entitled *Arsene Lupin contre Herlock Sholmes*; also published as *Sherlock Holmes versus Arsene Lupin*, and as *The fair-haired lady*; alternative title: The case of the golden blonde
3 *Hollow needle* (1909)
Original edition entitled *L'aiguille creuse*
4 *Eight hundred and thirteen* (1910)
Original edition entitled *813*
5 *Crystal stopper* (1912)
Original edition entitled *Le bouchon de cristal*
6 *Confessions of Arsene Lupin* (1913)
Original edition entitled *Les confidences d'Arsene Lupin*
7 *Teeth of the tiger* (1914)
Original edition entitled *Les dents du tigre*
8 *Golden triangle* (1917)
Original edition entitled *La triangle d'or*
9 *Coffin Island* (1920)
Secret of Sarek
Original edition entitled *L'Ile aux Trents Cercuils*
10 *Eight strokes of the clock* (1922)
Original edition entitled *Les huits coups de l'horlege*
11 *Candlestick with seven branches* (1924)
Memoirs of Arsene Lupin
Original edition entitled *La Comtesse de Cagliostro*
12 *Girl with the Green eyes* (1927)
Arsene Lupin, super-sleuth
Original edition entitled *La demoiselle aux yeux verts*
13 *Jim Barnett intervenes* (1928)
Arsene Lupin intervenes
Original edition entitled *L'Agence Barnett et Cie.*
14 *Melamare mystery* (1929)
Original edition entitled *La demeure mysterieuse*
15 *Double smile* (1933)
Woman with two smiles
Original edition entitled *La femme aux deux sourires*
16 *Return of Arsene Lupin* (1933)
Original edition entitled *Victor, de la Brigade Mondaine*
Companion volume: *Arsene Lupin*, by Edgar Jepson and Maurice Leblanc, based on the play by Maurice Leblanc and Francis De Croiset, 1909

Arslan series
Rathbone, Julian
see **Colonel Nur Bey series**

Art and Hector series
Gunn, Neil Miller
see **Young Art and old Hector series**

Art school series
Kitchen, Paddy
see **Vanessa Talisend series**

Art trilogy
Cary, Joyce
1 *Herself surprised* (1941)
2 *To be pilgrim* (1942)
3 *Horse's mouth* (1944)

Artful Bodger series
Winton, John
see **Navy series**

Arthur Abdel Simpson series
Ambler, Eric
1 *Light of day* (1962)
Topkapi
2 *Dirty story* (1967)

Arthur and Ben series
Billam, Rosemary
see **Ben and Arthur series**

Arthur and Emma series
Hoban, Russell
1 *Dinner at Alberta's* (1975)
2 *Arthur's new power* (1978)

Arthur and Gawain trilogy
Bradshaw, Gillian
1 *Hawk of May* (1980)
2 *Kingdom of summer* (1981)
3 *In winter's shadow* (1982)
One volume edition entitled *Down the long wind, the magical trilogy of Arthurian Britain*, 1984

Arthur and Merlin series
Stewart, Mary
see **Merlin and Arthur series**

Arthur and Paul series
Rockwell, Anne Foote
see **Paul and Arthur series**

Arthur C Clarke's Venus prime series
Preuss, Paul
see **Venus prime series**

Arthur Crook series
Gilbert, Anthony
1 *Murder by experts* (1936)
2 *Man who wasn't there* (1937)
3 *Murder has no tongue* (1937)
4 *Treason in my breast* (1938)
5 *Clock in the hatbox* (1939)
6 *Bell of death* (1939)
Spy for Mister Crook
7 *Dear dead woman* (1940)
Death takes a redhead
8 *Vanishing corpse* (1941)
She vanished in the dawn
9 *Woman in red* (1941)
Mystery of the woman in red
10 *Something nasty in the woodshed* (1942)
Mystery in the woodshed
11 *Case of the tea-cosy's aunt* (1942)
Death in the blackout
12 *Mouse who wouldn't play ball* (1943)
Thirty days to live
13 *He came by night* (1944)
Death at the door
14 *Scarlet button* (1944)
Murder is cheap
15 *Don't open the door* (1945)
Death lifts the latch
16 *Black stage* (1945)
Murder cheats the bride
17 *Spinster's secret* (1946)
By hook or by Crook
18 *Death in the wrong room* (1947)
19 *Die in the dark* (1947)
Missing widow

20 *Lift up the lid* (1948)
Innocent bottle
21 *Death knocks three times* (1949)
22 *Murder comes home* (1950)
23 *Nice cup of tea* (1950)
Wrong body
24 *Lady-killer* (1951)
25 *Miss Pinnegar disappears* (1952)
Case for Mister Crook
26 *Footsteps behind me* (1953)
Black death
Dark death
27 *Snake in the grass* (1954)
Death won't wait
28 *Is she dead too?* (1955)
Question of murder
29 *And death came too* (1956)
30 *Riddle of a lady* (1956)
31 *Give death a name* (1957)
32 *Death against the clock* (1958)
33 *Third crime lucky* (1959)
Prelude to murder
34 *Death takes a wife* (1959)
Death casts a long shadow
35 *Out for the kill* (1960)
36 *She shall die* (1961)
After the verdict
37 *Uncertain death* (1961)
38 *No dust in the attic* (1962)
39 *Ring for a noose* (1963)
40 *Fingerprint* (1964)
41 *Knock, knock who's there?* (1964)
Voice
42 *Passenger to nowhere* (1965)
43 *Looking glass murder* (1966)
44 *Visitor* (1967)
45 *Night encounter* (1968)
Murder anonymous
46 *Missing from her home* (1969)
47 *Death wears a mask* (1970)
Mister Crook lifts the mask
48 *Tenant for the tomb* (1971)
49 *Murder's a waiting game* (1972)
50 *Nice little killing* (1974)

Arthur Dent series
Adams, Douglas Noel
1 *Hitch-hiker's guide to the galaxy* (1979)
Based on a radio play of the same name broadcast in 1978
2 *Restaurant at the end of the universe* (1980)
3 *Life, the universe and everything* (1982)
Numbers 1-3 also published in one volume entitled The hitch-hiker's trilogy, 1984
4 *So long, and thanks for all the fish* (1984)
Numbers 1-4 also published in one volume entitled *The hitch-hiker's quartet*, 1986 and *The more than complete hitch-hiker's guide*, 1990, including *Zaphod plays it safe*
5 *Mostly harmless* (1992)
Companion volumes: *Hitch-hiker's companion, the original galaxy radio scripts*, 1985, *Don't panic, the official Hitch-hiker's guide to the galaxy handbook*, by Neil Gaiman, 1988

Arthur Gordon Pym series
This sequence has two authors
Poe, Edgar Allan
1 *Narrative of Arthur Gordon Pym of Nantucket* (1838)
Arthur Gordon Pym
Wonderful adventures of Arthur Gordon Pym
Alternative title: Shipwreck, mutiny and famine
Verne, Jules
2 *Antarctic mystery* (1897)
Original edition entitled *Le sphinx des glaces*
One volume edition 1960; companion volume: *A strange discovery*, by Charles Romyn Dake, 1899

Arthur Halstead series
Hayes, William Edward
1 *Black doll* (1936)
2 *Before the cock crowed* (1937)
3 *Black chronicle* (1937)

Arthur Helmuth series
Ellis, Edward Sylvester
1 *Arthur Helmuth* (1891)
2 *Check two one three four* (1891)

Arthur James Wentworth series
Ellis, Humphry Francis
see **A.J.Wentworth series**

Arthur Jeffrey series
Webster, Henry Kitchell
1 *Whispering man* (1908)
2 *Ghost girl* (1913)

Arthur Martinson series
Fitzsimmons, Cortland
1 *Bainbridge murder* (1930)
2 *Manville murders* (1930)

Arthur Milton series
Henderson, Laurence
see **Sergeant Arthur Milton series**

Arthur Pendennis series
Thackeray, William Makepeace
1 *History of Pendennis* (1850)
Pendennis
His fortunes and misfortunes, his friends and his greatest enemy
2 *Newcomes* (1855)
Memoirs of a most respectable family, edited by Arthur Pendennis, Esq
3 *Adventures of Philip on his way through the world* (1862)
Philip
Showing who robbed him, who helped him and who passed him by

Arthur Raneleigh series
Luther, Mark Lee
1 *Card thirteen* (1930)
2 *Saranoff murder* (1930)

Arthur Salisbury and Frank Shearer series
Crawford, Robert
1 *Cockleburr* (1969)
Pay as you die
2 *Kiss the boss goodbye* (1970)
Also published under the author's real name Hugh Crauford Rae
3 *Badger's daughter* (1971)
Also published under the author's real name Hugh Crauford Rae

Arthur series
Ashe, Geoffrey
see **King Arthur series**

Arthur series
Brown, Marc
1 *Arthur's nose* (1976)
2 *Arthur's eyes* (1979)
3 *Arthur's valentine* (1980)
4 *Arthur goes to camp* (1982)
5 *Arthur's Halloween* (1982)
6 *Arthur's April fool* (1983)
7 *Arthur's Thanksgiving* (1983)
8 *Arthur's Christmas* (1984)
9 *Arthur's tooth* (1985)
10 *Arthur's teacher trouble* (1986)
11 *Arthur's baby* (1987)
12 *Arthur's birthday wish* (1988)
13 *Arthur's pet business* (1990)
14 *Arthur meets the President* (1991)

Arthur series
Coren, Alan
1 *Buffalo Arthur* (1976)
2 *Arthur the Kid* (1976)
3 *Lone Arthur* (1976)
4 *Railroad Arthur* (1977)
5 *Klondike Arthur* (1977)
6 *Arthur's last stand* (1977)
7 *Arthur and the great detective* (1979)
8 *Arthur and the bellybutton diamond* (1979)
9 *Arthur and the purple panic* (1981)
10 *Arthur versus the rest* (1982)

Arthur series
Hanratty, Peter
1 *Last knight of Albion* (1986)
2 *Book of Mordred* (1988)

Arthur series
Hoban, Lillian
1 *Arthur's Christmas cookies* (1972)
2 *Arthur's honey bear* (1974)
3 *Arthur's pen pal* (1976)
4 *Arthur's prize reader* (1978)
5 *Arthur's funny money* (1981)
6 *Arthur's Halloween* (1984)
7 *Arthur's loose tooth* (1985)
8 *Arthur's great big valentine* (1991)
9 *Arthur's camp-out* (1992)

Arthur series
Jones, Courtway
see **King Arthur series**
Kennealy, Patricia
see **Tales of Arthur series**

Arthur series
Wright, Kit
Illustrated by Eileen Browne
1 *Arthur's granny* (1978)
2 *Arthur's sister* (1978)
3 *Arthur's father* (1978)
4 *Arthur's uncle* (1978)

Arthur Sinclair series
Masterman, Walter Sidney
see **Sir Arthur Sinclair series**

Arthur Stukeley Pennington series
This sequence has two authors
Brandon, John Gordon
1 *West End* (1933)
2 *Murder in Mayfair* (1934)
3 *One-minute murder* (1934)
4 *Riverside mystery* (1935)
5 *Pawnshop murder* (1936)
6 *Snatch game* (1936)
7 *Death tolls the gong* (1936)
8 *Bond Street murder* (1937)
9 *Death in Downing Street* (1937)
10 *Regent Street raid* (1938)
11 *Cork Street crime* (1938)
12 *Mister Pennington comes through* (1939)
13 *Death in the ditch* (1940)
14 *Mister Pennington goes nap* (1940)
15 *Mister Pennington barges in* (1941)
16 *Mister Pennington sees red* (1942)
17 *Death in Jermyn Street* (1942)
18 *Death in D Division* (1943)
19 *Case of the would-be widow* (1950)
20 *Corpse rode on* (1951)
21 *Murderer's stand-in* (1953)
22 *Call-girl murders* (1954)
23 *Death of a Greek* (1955)
24 *Murder on the beam* (1956)
25 *Death of a socialite* (1957)
26 *Murder in Pimlico* (1958)
27 *Corpse from the City* (1958)
28 *Death stalks in Soho* (1959)
Brandon, Gordon
29 *Murder comes smiling* (1959)
30 *Death of a mermaid* (1960)

Arthur trilogy
Graham, Amanda
Illustrated by Donna Gynell
1 *Arthur* (1984)
Who wants Arthur?
2 *Educating Arthur* (1987)
3 *Always Arthur* (1990)

Arthurian cycle series
Monaco, Richard
see **Parsival series**

Arthurian cycle trilogy
Godwin, Parke
1 *Firelord* (1980)
2 *Beloved exile* (1984)
3 *Last rainbow* (1985)
Companion volume: *Invitation to Camelot, an Arthurian anthology of short stories*, 1988

Arthurian knights trilogy
Sutcliff, Rosemary
1 *Light beyond the forest* (1979)
The quest for the Holy Grail
2 *Sword and the circle* (1981)
King Arthur and the Knights of the Round Table
3 *Road to Camlann* (1981)
The death of king Arthur

Arthurian legends series
Pyle, Howard
1 *Story of King Arthur and his knights* (1903)
Book of King Arthur
2 *Story of the champions of the Round Table* (1905)
3 *Story of Sir Launcelot and his companions* (1907)
4 *Story of the Grail and the passing of Arthur* (1910)

Arthurian series
Roberts, Dorothy James
1 *Launcelot, my brother* (1956)
2 *Kinsmen of the Grail* (1963)

Arthurian trilogy
Canning, Victor
see **Crimson chalice trilogy**
Newman, Robert
see **Tertius trilogy**

Arthur's aunt series
East, Helen
1 *Cat for a noisy day* (1984)
2 *Caterpillar at breakfast* (1984)
3 *Tortoise for bedtime* (1984)
4 *Crocodile out shopping* (1984)

Artie Wu and Quincy Durant series
Thomas, Ross
1 *Chinaman's chance* (1978)
2 *Out on the rim* (1987)

Artist's life trilogy
Munnings, Alfred
Autobiography
1 *Artist's life* (1950)
2 *Second burst* (1951)
3 *Finish* (1952)

Artless series
Jones, Joanna
1 *Artless flat-hunter* (1963)
2 *Artless commuter* (1965)

Artor series
Capon, Paul
1 *Warrior's moon* (1960)
2 *Kingdom of the bulls* (1961)
3 *Lord of the chariots* (1962)
4 *Golden cloak* (1963)

Arturo Bandini series
Fante, John
1 *Wait until spring, Bandini* (1938)
2 *Ask the dust* (1939)
3 *Dreams from Bunker Hill* (1981)

Arundel series
Mallory, Clare
see **Merry Arundel series**
Roberts, Kenneth Lewis
see **Chronicles of Arundel series**

Arvada Jones series
Wayne, Les
1 *West of Omaha* (1981)

Arvada Jones series

2 *Cheyenne manhunt* (1981)
3 *Warpaint* (1982)
4 *Arvada Jones and the orphans of the trail* (1982)

Arvo Laurila series
Low, Ona
1 *To his just deserts* (1986)
A story of Finland
2 *Murky shadows* (1987)
A story of the Venetian lagoon

Arvon series
Norton, Andre
1 *Crystal gryphon* (1972)
2 *Jargoon pard* (1974)

Arwen series
Bradley, Marion Zimmer
Inspired by the **Lord of the Rings trilogy**, by John Ronald Reuel Tolkien
1 *Jewel of Arwen* (1974)
Short stories
2 *Parting of Arwen* (1974)
Short stories

Arzor series
Norton, Andre
1 *Beast master* (1959)
2 *Catseye* (1961)
3 *Lord of thunder* (1962)

As I please series
Lyttleton, Humphrey
The memoirs of an old Etonian trumpeter
1 *I play as I please* (1954)
2 *Second chorus* (1958)
3 *Take it from the top* (1975)
An autobiographical scrapbook

Asaf Khan series
Afghan
1 *Explots of Asaf Khan* (1922)
Short stories
2 *Wanderings of Asaf* (1923)

Asaph Clume series
Goldman, Raymond Leslie
1 *Murder of Harvey Blake* (1931)
2 *Murder without motive* (1938)
3 *Death plays solitaire* (1939)
4 *Snatch* (1940)
5 *Murder behind the mike* (1942)
6 *Purple shell* (1947)

Asbjorn Krag series
Elvestad, Sven
see **Osborne Crag series**

Asch series
Kirst, Hans Hellmut
see **Gunner Asch series**
Lyons, Arthur
see **Jacob Asch series**

Asey Mayo series
Taylor, Phoebe Atwood
1 *Cape Cod mystery* (1931)
2 *Death lights a candle* (1932)
3 *Mystery of the Cape Cod players* (1933)
4 *Mystery of the Cape Cod tavern* (1934)
5 *Sandbar sinister* (1934)
6 *Tinkling symbol* (1935)
7 *Deathblow Hill* (1935)
8 *Crimson patch* (1936)
9 *Out of order* (1936)
10 *Figure away* (1937)
11 *Octagon House* (1937)
12 *Annulet of gilt* (1938)
13 *Banbury Bog* (1938)
14 *Spring harrowing* (1939)
15 *Criminal C.O.D.* (1940)
16 *Deadly sunshade* (1940)
17 *Perennial boarder* (1941)
18 *Six iron spiders* (1942)
19 *Three plots for Asey Mayo* (1942)
Asye Mayo trio
Three novelettes entitled *The wander bird plot, The Headacre plot, The swan-boat plot*
20 *Going, going, gone* (1943)
21 *Proof of the pudding* (1945)
22 *Asey Mayo trio* (1946)
Three novelettes entitled *The third murderer, Murder rides the gale, The stars spell death*
23 *Punch with care* (1946)
24 *Diplomatic corpse* (1951)

Asgard series
Stableford, Brian Michael
1 *Journey to the center* (1982)
Journey to the centre
The second title is a revised edition
2 *Invaders from the centre* (1990)
3 *Centre cannot hold* (1990)

Ash Burlefoot series
Mykle, Agnar
1 *Lasso round the moon* (1954)
Original edition entitled *Lasso rundt fra luna*
2 *Song of the red ruby* (1958)
Original edition entitled *Sangen om den rode rubin*

Ash series
Grierson, Francis Durham
see **Superintendent Andrew Ash series**

Ash staff trilogy
Fisher, Paul R
1 *Ash staff* (1979)
2 *Hawks of Fellheath* (1980)
3 *Princess and the thorn* (1980)
4 *Mont Cant gold* (1984)

Ash Tallman series
Braun, Matt
1 *Highbinders* (1984)
2 *Crossfire* (1984)
3 *Wages of sin* (1984)

Ashanti series
Appiah, Peggy
1 *Tales of an Ashanti father* (1967)
2 *Pineapple child, and other tales from Ashanti* (1969)
3 *Why the hyena does not care for fish, and other tales from the Ashanti* (1977)

Ashbel Field series
Allis, Marguerite
1 *Now we are free* (1952)
2 *To keep us free* (1953)
3 *Brave pursuit* (1954)
4 *Rising storm* (1955)
5 *Free soil* (1958)

Ashdown Forest series
Willard, Barbara
see **Mantlemass series**

Ashe series
Ashe, Saxon
see **Saxon Ashe series**
Howard, James Arch
see **Steve Ashe series**
Kersh, Cyril
see **Minnie Ashe series**
Langoulant, Allan
see **Captain Ashe series**

Ashenden series
Knight, Brigid
1 *Walking the whirlwind* (1940)
2 *Piping on the wind* (1940)

Asher Bockhorn series
Cohen, Barry
1 *Taking of Satcon Station* (1982)
Co-author: Jim Baen
2 *Blood on the moon* (1984)

Asher Lev series
Potok, Chaim
1 *My name is Asher Lev* (1972)
2 *Gift of Asher Lev* (1990)

Asher series
Hultman, Helen Joan
see **Tim Asher series**

Ashes series
Johnstone, William Wallace
1 *Out of the ashes* (1983)
2 *Fire in the ashes* (1984)
3 *Anarchy in the ashes* (1984)
4 *Blood in the ashes* (1985)
5 *Alone in the ashes* (1985)
6 *Wind in the ashes* (1986)
7 *Smoke from the ashes* (1987)
8 *Danger in the ashes* (1988)
9 *Valor in the ashes* (1988)
10 *Trapped in the ashes* (1989)
11 *Death in the ashes* (1990)
12 *Survival in the ashes* (1990)
13 *Fury in the ashes* (1991)
14 *Courage in the ashes* (1991)
15 *Terror in the ashes* (1992)
16 *Vengeance in the ashes* (1993)
17 *Battle in the ashes* (1993)
18 *Flames from the ashes* (1993)
19 *Treason in the ashes* (1994)

Ashley series
Steele, Chester K
see **Colonel Robert Lee Ashley series**

Ashley Tempest series
Fox-Davies, Arthur Charles
1 *Dangerville inheritance* (1906)
2 *Average man* (1907)
3 *Mauleverer murders* (1907)
4 *Duplicate death* (1910)
5 *Ultimate conculsion* (1912)

Ashlu cycle series
Baker, Scott
1 *Nightchild* (1979)
Revised edition 1983
2 *Firedance* (1986)
3 *Drink the fire from the flames* (1987)

Ashton and Bourke series
McNab, Claire
see **Inspector Carol Ashton and Sergeant Mark Bourke series**

Ashton and Brown series
Stuart, Becky
see **Kellogg Brown and Carey Ashton series**

Ashton family series
This sequence has three authors
Baker, Kathleen
1 *Family at war* (1970)
Powell, Jonathan
2 *To the turn of the tide* (1971)
Russell, Ray
3 *Towards victory* (1972)

Ashton Ford series
Pendleton, Don
1 *Ashes to ashes* (1986)
2 *Eye to eye* (1986)
3 *Mind to mind* (1987)
4 *Life to life* (1987)
5 *Heart to heart* (1987)
6 *Time to time* (1988)

Ashton-Kirk series
McIntyre, John Thomas
1 *Ashton-Kirk, investigator* (1910)
2 *Ashton-Kirk, secret agent* (1912)
Secret agent, Ashton-Kirk
3 *Ashton-Kirk, special detective* (1912)
Special detective, Ashton-Kirk
4 *Ashton-Kirk, criminologist* (1918)

Ashton series
Antill, Elizabeth
see **Inspector Simon Ashton series**
Egleton, Clive
see **Peter Ashton series**

Ashwin trilogy
Sidgwick, Ethel
1 *Lady of leisure* (1914)
2 *Duke Jones* (1915)
3 *Accolade* (1915)

Asia in turmoil series
Harvester, Simon
1 *Bamboo screen* (1955)
2 *Tiger in the north* (1955)
3 *Dragon road* (1956)
4 *Paradise men* (1956)
5 *Golden fear* (1957)
6 *Copper butterfly* (1957)
7 *Yesterday walkers* (1958)
8 *Hour before zero* (1959)
9 *Chinese hammer* (1960)
10 *Unsung road* (1960)
11 *Moonstone jungle* (1961)
12 *Silk road* (1962)
13 *Troika* (1962)
Flying horse
14 *Red road* (1963)
15 *Flight in darkness* (1964)
16 *Assassins road* (1965)
17 *Shadows in a hidden land* (1966)
18 *Treacherous road* (1966)
19 *Battle road* (1967)
20 *Zion road* (1968)
21 *Nameless road* (1969)
22 *Moscow road* (1970)
23 *Sahara road* (1972)
24 *Corner of the playground* (1973)
25 *Forgotten road* (1974)
26 *Siberian road* (1976)

Asian missionary trilogy
Patterson, George Neilson
Memoirs of a missionary in Tibet
1 *Tibetan journey* (1954)
2 *God's fool* (1956)
3 *Up and down Asia* (1958)

Asian series
Clavell, James
A sequence of novels based on the clash of Western and Eastern cultures - China, Japan, Iran
1 *Shogun* (1975)
2 *Tai-pan* (1966)
3 *King Rat* (1962)
4 *Noble house* (1981)
5 *Whirlwind* (1986)

Ask Oliver series
Dicks, Terrance
1 *Mystery of the missing diamond* (1982)
2 *Mystery of the haunted hospital* (1982)
3 *Mystery of the smugglers' treasure* (1983)
4 *Mystery of the missing train* (1984)
5 *Fireworks mystery* (1984)
6 *Gupta's Christmas* (1985)
7 *Vicky's victory* (1986)

Asked out series
Hunt, Gary
1 *Now that you've asked her out* (1989)
2 *Now that he's asked you out* (1989)

Askham family series
Thorne, Nicola
1 *Never such innocence* (1985)
2 *Yesterday's promises* (1986)
3 *Bright morning* (1986)
4 *Place in the sun* (1987)

Asmun Hill series
Hawton, Hector
1 *Murder at H.Q.* (1945)

2 *Murder most foul* (1946)
3 *Unnatural causes* (1947)
4 *Deadly nightcap* (1949)
5 *Nine singing apes* (1950)
7 *Rope for the judge* (1954)

Aspen series
Hirschfeld, Burt
1 *Aspen* (1976)
2 *Aspen affair* (1990)

Assam series
Bower, Ursula Graham
Reminiscences of travel in Assam
1 *Naga path* (1950)
2 *Hidden land* (1953)

Assassin series
Revere, John D
see **Justin Perry series**

Assassins series
McCurtin, Peter
1 *Manhattan massacre* (1973)
2 *New Orleans holocaust* (1973)
3 *Boston bust* (1973)

Assault series
Caillou, Alan
see **Cabot Cain series**

Assault series
This sequence has two authors
Flynn, J J
1 *Raid on Reichswald Fortress* (1974)
Floyd, C J
2 *Taking of Kommand Group 8* (1975)
3 *Sands run red* (1976)

Assault troop series
Harding, Ian
1 *Bloodbeach* (1983)
2 *Death in the forest* (1983)
3 *Clash on the Rhine* (1984)
4 *End run* (1984)

Assignment series
Aarons, Edward Sidney
see **Sam Durell series**

Assignment to catastrophe series
Spears, Edward
1 *Prelude to Dunkirk, July 1939-May 1940* (1954)
2 *Fall of France, June 1940* (1954)

Assistant District Attorney Bernie Simmons series
This sequence has two authors
Lockridge, Frances
1 *And left for dead* (1962)
2 *Devious ones* (1964)
English edition entitled *Four hours to fear*, published under the pseudonym Francis Richard
Lockridge, Richard
3 *Squire of death* (1965)
English edition published under the pseudonym Francis Richards
4 *Plate of red herrings* (1968)
English edition published under the pseudonym Francis Richards
5 *Twice retired* (1970)
6 *Something up a sleeve* (1972)
7 *Death on the hour* (1974)

Assistant District Attorney Butch Karp series
Tanenbaum, Robert K
1 *No lesser plea* (1987)
2 *Depraved indifference* (1989)
3 *Immoral certainty* (1991)
4 *Reversable error* (1992)
5 *Material witness* (1993)
6 *Justice denied* (1994)

Associated shades series
Bangs, John Kendrick
1 *House-boat on the Styx* (1896)
2 *Pursuit of the house-boat* (1897)
3 *Enchanted typewriter* (1899)

Asterix push-out series
Bell, Anthea
Based on the series by Rene Goscinny and Albert Uderzo; illustrated by John Grace
1 *Asterix and the Roman camp* (1978)
2 *Asterix and his village* (1978)
3 *Asterix in ancient Egypt* (1978)
4 *Asterix and the circis of Rome* (1978)
5 *Asterix and the pirates* (1978)
6 *Asterix and the twelve tasks* (1978)

Asterix series
Goscinny, Rene
1 *Asterix, the Gaul* (1961)
Original edition entitled *Asterix le gaulois*
2 *Asterix and the golden sickle* (1962)
Original edition entitled *La serpe d'or*
3 *Asterix and the Goths* (1963)
Original edition entitled *Asterix et les goths*
4 *Asterix, the gladiator* (1964)
Original edition entitled *Asterix gladiateur*
5 *Asterix and Cleopatra* (1965)
Original edition entitled *Asterix et Cleopatre*
6 *Asterix and the banquet* (1965)
Original edition entitled *Le Tour de gaule d'Asterix*
7 *Asterix and the Normans* (1966)
Original edition entitled *Asterix et les normands*
8 *Asterix in Britain* (1966)
Original edition entitled *Asterix chez les bretons*
9 *Asterix and the big fight* (1966)
Original edition entitled *Le combat des chefs*
10 *Asterix, the legionary* (1967)
Original edition entitled *Asterix legionnaire*
11 *Asterix at the Olympic Games* (1968)
Original edition entitled *Asterix aux jeux olympiques*
12 *Asterix and the chieftain's shield* (1968)
Original edition entitled *Le bouclier arverne*
13 *Asterix and the cauldron* (1969)
Original edition entitled *Asterix et le chaudron*
14 *Asterix in Spain* (1969)
Original edition entitled *Asterix en Hispanie*
15 *Asterix in Switzerland* (1970)
Original edition entitled *Asterix chez les helvetes*
16 *Asterix and the Roman agent* (1970)
Original edition entitled *La Zizanie*
17 *Mansions of the gods* (1971)
Original edition entitled *Les maisons des dieux*
18 *Asterix and the soothsayer* (1972)
Original edition entitled *Le devin*
19 *Asterix and the laurel wreath* (1972)
Original edition entitled *Les lauriers de Cesar*
20 *Asterix in Corsica* (1973)
Original edition entitled *Asterix en Corse*
21 *Asterix and Caesar's gift* (1974)
Original edition entitled *Le cadeau de Cesar*
22 *Asterix and the great crossing* (1975)
Original edition entitled *La Grande Traversee*
23 *Obelix and Company* (1976)
Original edition entitled *Obelix et compagnie*
24 *Rene Goscinny and Albert Uderzo present the twelve tasks of Asterix* (1976)
Twelve tasks of Asterix
Original edition entitled *Rene Gosciny et Albert Uderzo presentent les douze travaux d'Asterix;* contains 12 stories also published separately
25 *Asterix in Belgium* (1980)
Original edition entitled *Asterix chez les belges;* numbers 1 8, 25 also published in one volume entitled *Three adventures of Asterix*, 1979; sequence continued by Albert Uzerzo
Uderzo, Albert
26 *Asterix and the great divide* (1981)
27 *Asterix and the black gold* (1982)
28 *Asterix and Son* (1983)
29 *Asterix versus Caesar* (1986)
Based on *Asterix, the gladiator*, 1964, and *Asterix, the legionary*, by Rene Goscinny and Albert Uderzo, 1967
30 *Asterix and the magic carpet* (1988)
Companion volume: *Operation Getafix*, 1990, based on a film of the same name

Aston and Flo series
Benjamin, Floella
see **Flo and Aston series**

Astonishing adventures of Captain Ketchup series
Stern, Simon
1 *Neptune's treasure* (1972)
2 *Moon trip* (1973)
3 *Jungle journey* (1974)

Astorbilt series
Lazare, Lewis
see **Ernie Astorbilt series**

Astra series
Norton, Andre
1 *Stars are ours* (1954)
2 *Star born* (1957)

Astride the times series
Maass, Joachim
1 *Magic year* (1944)
2 *Weeping and the laughter* (1939)
Originally announced as a trilogy

Astride two worlds series
Brata, Sasthi
Autobiography
1 *My god died young* (1968)
2 *Traitor to India* (1976)
Astride two worlds
Search for home

Astromance series
Fitzgerald, Julia
1 *Flame of the East* (1986)
2 *Daughter of the gods* (1986)
3 *Pasadoble* (1986)
4 *Kiss from Aphrodite* (1987)
5 *Castle of the enchantress* (1987)
6 *Jade moon* (1988)
7 *Devil in my arms* (1989)
8 *Temple of butterflies* (1989)
9 *Glade of jewels* (1989)
10 *Bridge of rainbows* (1989)
11 *Pagan blossoms* (1989)

Astronomers series
Banville, John
1 *Doctor Copernicus* (1976)
2 *Kepler* (1981)
3 *Newton letter* (1982)
4 *Mefisto* (1986)

Aswell series
Brown, Wenzell
see **Peter Aswell series**

At bat series
Gutman, Bill
1 *At bat* (1973)
2 *Cedeno, Rose, Bonds and Fish* (1974)

Atalanta and Pansy series
Symons, Geraldine
1 *Rose window* (1964)
2 *Quarantine child* (1966)
3 *Workhouse child* (1969)
4 *Miss Rivers and Miss Bridges* (1971)
5 *Mademoiselle* (1973)

Atchafalaya series
Edler, Timothy J
see **Tales from the Atchafalaya series**

A-Team series
Heath, Charles
1 *A-Team* (1983)
2 *Small but deadly wars* (1984)
3 *When you comin' back, Range Rider* (1984)
4 *Old scores to settle* (1984)
5 *Ten percent of trouble* (1984)
6 *Operation Desert Son* (1984)
Sequence continued under the author's real name Ron Renauld
Renauld, Ron
7 *Bullets, bikinis and bells* (1985)

Atha series
Heppenstall, Rayner
see **Harold Atha series**

Athalie series
Chambers, Robert William
1 *Quick action* (1914)
2 *Athalie* (1915)

Athelson family series
Kettle, Jocelyn
1 *Athelsons* (1972)
2 *Gift of onyx* (1974)

Athelstan Digby series
Harvey, William Fryer
1 *Misadventures of Athelstan Digby* (1920)
Short stories
2 *Mysterious Mister Badman* (1934)

Athelstan King series
Mundy, Talbot
1 *King, of the Khybers* (1916)
King of the Khyber Rifles
2 *Nine unknown* (1924)
3 *Caves of terror* (1932)

Atherley series
Ashton, Charles
see **Jack Atherley series**
Bridge, Ann
see **Hetta Atherley series**

Atkins series
Bergstrom, Gunilla
see **Alfie Atkins series**
Davies, Andrew
see **Marmalade Atkins series**
Kelland, Clarence Budington
see **Catty Atkins series**

Atkinson family series
Hardwick, Mollie
1 *Atkinson heritage* (1978)
2 *Sisters in love* (1979)
3 *Dove's nest* (1980)
One volume edition entitled *The Atkinson century*, 1980

Atlan saga series
Gaskell, Jane
1 *Serpent* (1963)
1.1 *Serpent* (1963)
1.2 *Dragon* (1963)
2 *Atlan* (1965)
3 *City* (1966)
4 *Some summer lands* (1977)

Atlan series
This sequence has four authors
Vlcek, Ernst
1 *Spider desert* (1977)

Atlan series
Darlton, Clark
2 *Flight from Tarkihl* (1977)
Kneifel, Hans
3 *Pale country pursuit* (1977)
Scheer, Karl Herbert
4 *Crystal Prince* (1977)
Darlton, Clark
5 *War of the ghosts* (1977)

Atlantean Earth series
Hancock, Niel
see **Circle of light series**

Atlantean saga series
Bradley, Marion Zimmer
1 *Web of light* (1982)
2 *Web of darkness* (1983)
One volume edition entitled *The fall of Atlantis*, 1987

Atlanteans series
Tucci, Niccolo
see **Those of the lost continent series**

Atlantic series
Alger, Horatio
1 *Young circus rider* (1883)
2 *Do and dare* (1884)
3 *Hector's inheritance* (1885)
4 *Helping himself* (1886)

Atlantis series
Cradock, Phyllis
1 *Gateway to remembrance* (1949)
2 *Eternal echo* (1950)

Atlantis trilogy
Timlett, Peter Valentine
1 *Seedbearers* (1974)
2 *Power of the serpent* (1976)
3 *Twilight of the serpent* (1977)

Atom Chasers series
Macvicar, Angus
1 *Atom Chasers* (1956)
2 *Atom Chasers in Tibet* (1957)

Aton series
This sequence has two authors
Anthony, Piers
1 *Chthon* (1967)
2 *Phthor* (1975)
Platt, Charles
3 *Plasm* (1987)
4 *Soma* (1989)

Atreides trilogy
Herbert, Frank
see **Paul Atreides trilogy**

Atta Olivia Clemens trilogy
Yarbro, Chelsea Quinn
1 *Flame in Byzantium* (1987)
2 *Crusader's torch* (1988)
3 *Candle for D'Artagnan* (1989)

Attack force series
Hunter, Joe
1 *French assignment* (1976)
2 *Mission to the gods* (1976)
3 *Roman holiday* (1976)
4 *Vampire mission* (1977)

Attar the Merman series
Graham, Robert
1 *Attar's revenge* (1975)
2 *War of nerves* (1975)

Attitudes towards history series
Burke, Kenneth
1 *Acceptance and rejection* (1937)
The curve of history
2 *Analysis of symbolic structure* (1937)
One volume second edition entitled *Attitudes towards history*, 1959; third edition 1984

Attwell series
Underwood, Michael
see **Sergeant Nick Attwell series**

Aubrey and Maturin series
O'Brian, Patrick
see **Jack Aubrey and Stephen Maturin series**

Aubrey family trilogy
West, Rebecca
1 *Fountain overflows* (1956)
2 *This real night* (1984)
3 *Cousin Rosamund* (1986)

Aubrey Nash series
Davis, Tech
1 *Terror on Compass Lake* (1935)
2 *Full fare for a corpse* (1937)
3 *Murder on Alternative* (1938)

Aubrey Saint John Major series
Greene, L Patrick
1 *Major, diamond buyer* (1924)
2 *Devil's kloof* (1928)
3 *Major adventures* (1928)
4 *Red idol* (1928)
5 *Major, knight errant* (1929)
6 *White man's stride* (1929)
Short stories
7 *Major exploits* (1930)
8 *Major developments* (1931)
9 *Major occasions* (1931)
10 *Major hazards* (1932)
11 *Forbidden valley* (1932)
12 *Just vengeance* (1934)
13 *Point of a thousand spears* (1934)
14 *Splendid exile* (1935)
15 *Lake of the dead* (1935)
16 *Black tie rising* (1936)
17 *Drums call the Major* (1938)
18 *Escape from liberty* (1939)
19 *Face value* (1939)

Aubrey series
O'Brien, Patrick
see **Captain Jack Aubrey series**
Thomas, Craig
see **Kenneth Aubrey series**

Aubry series
Travers, Hugh
see **Madame Dominique Aubry series**

Auckland series
Chrystie, Edward M
see **Leathers Auckland series**

Audley and Butler series
Price, Anthony
see **Doctor David Audley and Jack Butler series**

Audran series
Effinger, George Alec
see **Marid Audran series**

Audrey Rose series
De Felitta, Frank
1 *Audrey Rose* (1975)
2 *For love of Audrey Rose* (1982)

Audrey series
Nash, Frances Olivia Hartopp
1 *How Audrey became a guide* (1922)
2 *Audrey in camp* (1923)
Numbers 1-2 also published in one volume 1923
3 *Audrey at school* (1925)
4 *Audrey, the sea ranger* (1931)
One volume edition entitled *The Audrey books*, 1933

Audunsson series
Undset, Sigrid
see **Master of Hestviken series**

Augherim series
Foyle, Kathleen
1 *Doctor's lady* (1949)
2 *Whither thou goest* (1951)
3 *Other people's shoes* (1954)

August and Edevart series
Hamsun, Knut
see **Edevart and August series**

August series
Abbott, Jacob
1 *August and Elire* (1871)
2 *Hunter and Tom* (1871)
3 *Schooner Mary Ann* (1872)
4 *Granville Valley* (1872)

Augusta Hortense Carey series
Hoult, Norah
1 *Smilin' on the vine* (1941)
2 *Augusta steps out* (1942)

Auguste Didier series
Myers, Amy
1 *Murder in Pug's Parlour* (1986)
2 *Murder in the limelight* (1987)
3 *Murder at Plum's* (1989)
4 *Murder at the masque* (1991)
5 *Murder makes an entree* (1992)
6 *Murder under the kissing bough* (1992)
7 *Murder in the smokehouse* (1994)

Auguste Jantry series
Graeme, Bruce
see **Inspector Albert Jantry series**

Auguste Maller series
Gregoire, Jean Albert
1 *Twenty-four hours at Le Mans* (1955)
2 *Money masters* (1956)

Augustine series
Hughes, Richard Arthur Warren
see **Human predicament series**

Augustus Champnell series
Marsh, Richard
1 *Beetle* (1897)
2 *Seen and the unseen* (1900)
Also four stories featuring Champnell in *An aristocratic detective*, 1900

Augustus Maltravers series
Richardson, Robert
1 *Latimer mercy* (1985)
2 *Bellringer Street* (1988)

Augustus Mandrell series
McAuliffe, Frank
Each volume includes 4 novelettes
1 *Of all the bloody cheek* (1965)
2 *Rather a vicious gentleman* (1968)
3 *For murder I charge more* (1971)

Augustus S F X Van Dusen series
Futrelle, Jacques
see **Professor Augustus S F X Van Dusen series**

Augustus series
Epstein, June
Illustrated by Alison Lester
1 *Augustus* (1984)
2 *Augustus conducts the band* (1984)
3 *Augustus teaches the children* (1984)
4 *Augustus flies a plane* (1984)
5 *Augustus works in a factory* (1984)
6 *Augustus plays football* (1984)
7 *Augustus the painter* (1984)
8 *Augustus the king* (1984)

Augustus series
Henderson, Le Grand
1 *Augustus and the river* (1939)
2 *Augustus goes south* (1940)
3 *Augustus and the mountain* (1941)
4 *Augustus helps the Navy* (1942)
5 *Augustus helps the Army* (1943)
6 *Augustus helps the Marines* (1943)
7 *Augustus drives a jeep* (1944)
8 *Augustus flies* (1944)
9 *Augustus saves a ship* (1945)
10 *Augustus hits the road* (1946)
11 *Augustus rides the border* (1947)
12 *Augustus and the desert* (1948)

Auld Reekie series
Macgregor, Alasdair Alpin
Autobiography
1 *Goat-wife* (1939)
Portrait of a village; revised edition 1951
2 *Vanished waters* (1942)
Portrait of a Highland childhood
3 *Auld Reekie* (1943)
Portrait of a Lowland childhood
4 *Turbulent years* (1945)
Portrait of youth in Auld Reekie

Aunt and Uncle series
McCardell, Roy Larcom
1 *My Aunt Angie* (1930)
2 *Book of my Uncle Oswald* (1931)

Aunt Jane series
Hall, Eliza Calvert
1 *Aunt Jane of Kentucky* (1907)
Selections entitled *Sally Ann's experience*, 1907
2 *Land of long ago* (1909)
3 *Clover and blue grass* (1916)

Aunt Jane's nieces series
Van Dyne, Edith
1 *Aunt Jane's nieces* (1906)
2 *Aunt Jane's nieces abroad* (1907)
3 *Aunt Jane's nieces at Millville* (1908)
4 *Aunt Jane's nieces at work* (1909)
5 *Aunt Jane's nieces in society* (1910)
6 *Aunt Jane's nieces and Uncle John* (1911)
7 *Aunt Jane's nieces on vacation* (1912)
8 *Aunt Jane's nieces on the ranch* (1913)
9 *Aunt Jane's nieces out west* (1914)
10 *Aunt Jane's nieces in the Red Cross* (1915)

Aunt Joan and Noreen series
Dawson, Helen
see **Noreen and Aunt Joan series**

Aunt Jo's scrap-bag series
Alcott, Louisa May
1 *My boys* (1872)
2 *Shawl-straps* (1872)
3 *Cupid and Chow-Chow* (1874)
4 *My girls* (1878)
5 *Jimmy's cruise in the Pinafore* (1879)
6 *Old-fashioned Thanksgiving* (1882)

Aunt Martine and Pascalet series
Bosco, Henri
see **Pascalet and Aunt Martine series**

Aunt Nina series
Brandenberg, Franz
1 *Aunt Nina and her nephews and nieces* (1984)
2 *Aunt Nina's visit* (1984)
3 *Aunt Nina, good night!* (1989)

Auntie Mame series
Dennis, Patrick
1 *Auntie Mame* (1955)
2 *Around the world with Auntie Mame* (1958)

Auntie series
De Manio, Jack
Autobiography
1 *To auntie, with love* (1967)
2 *Life begins too early* (1970)

Aurelian and Zenobia series
Ware, William
see **Zenobia and Aurelian series**

Aurelio Zen series
Dibdin, Michael
1 *Ratking* (1988)
2 *Vendetta* (1989)
3 *Cabal* (1992)
4 *Dead lagoon* (1994)

Aurelius Smith series
Scott, Reginald Thomas Maitland
1 *Secret Service Smith* (1923)
2 *Black magician* (1925)
3 *Ann's crime* (1926)
Smith of the Secret Service
The second title was published anonymously
4 *Aurelius Smith, detective* (1927)
Short stories
5 *Murder stalks the mayor* (1935)
6 *Agony column murders* (1946)
7 *Nameless ones* (1947)

Aurora Greenway series
McMurtry, Larry
1 *Terms of endearment* (1975)
2 *Evening star* (1992)

Aurora series
Hester, Randolph Thompson
Study for community development of a town in North Carolina
1 *Goals for Aurora* (1975)
2 *This book is about Aurora* (1976)
3 *Aurora land use plan* (1976)

Aurora series
Vestly, Anna Catharina
1 *Hallo, Aurora!* (1966)
Hello, Aurora!
Original edition entitled *Aurora i blokk z*
2 *[Aurora og pappa]* (1967)
No English edition
3 *Aurora and the little blue car* (1968)
Original edition entitled *Aurora og den vesla blaa bilen*
4 *Aurora and Socrates* (1969)
Original edition entitled *Aurora og Sokrates*
5 *Aurora in Holland* (1970)
Original edition entitled *Aurora i Holland*
6 *[Aurora paa burtigruten]* (1971)
No English edition
7 *[Aurora fra Fabelvik]* (1972)
No English edition

Aurora Teagarden series
Harris, Charlaine
1 *Bone to pick* (1992)
2 *Three bedrooms, one corpse* (1994)

Auschwitz series
Levi, Primo
see **Survival in Auschwitz series**

Austen series
Hocking, Anne
see **Inspector William Austen series**

Austin Clapp series
Miller, Wade
see **Lieutenant Austin Clapp series**

Austin family series
L'Engle, Madeleine
1 *Meet the Austins* (1960)
2 *Moon by night* (1963)
3 *Twenty-four days before Christmas* (1964)
4 *Young unicorns* (1968)
5 *Ring of endless light* (1980)

Austin series
Caidin, Martin
see **Six Million Dollar Man series**
Sheehan, Patrick Augustine
see **Geoffrey Austin series**

Australian Army in World War II series
Lambert, Eric
1 *Twenty thousand thieves* (1952)
2 *Veterans* (1954)

Australian children series
Lester, Alison
1 *Clive eats alligators* (1985)
2 *Rosie sips spiders* (1988)
3 *Tessa snaps snakes* (1990)

Australian destiny series
Dengler, Sandy
1 *Power of Pinjarra* (1988)
2 *Taste of victory* (1989)
3 *East of outback* (1990)

Australian guerilla series
Idriess, Ion Llewellyn
1 *Shoot to kill* (1942)
2 *Sniping* (1942)
3 *Guerilla tactics* (1942)
4 *Trapping the Jap* (1942)
5 *Scout* (1943)

Australian houses series
Cuffley, Peter
1 *Australian houses of the twenties and thirties* (1993)
2 *Australian houses of the forties and fifties* (1993)

Australian nature tales series
This sequence has two authors and three illustrators
Rees, Leslie
1 *Story of Shy the platypus* (1944)
Illustrated by Walter Cunningham
2 *Story of Karrawingi the emu* (1946)
Illustrated by Walter Cunningham
Watson, Ina
3 *Silvertail* (1946)
The story of a lyrebird; illustrated by Walter Cunningham
Rees, Leslie
4 *Story of Sarli the Barrier Reef turtle* (1947)
Illustrated by Walter Cunningham
5 *Story of Shadow the rock wallaby* (1948)
Illustrated by Walter Cunningham
6 *Story of Kurri Kurri the kookaburra* (1950)
Illustrated by Margaret Senior
7 *Story of Aroora the red kangaroo* (1952)
Illustrated by John Singleton; numbers 1, 4, 7 also published in one volume entitled *Australian nature tales*, 1958
8 *Two-thumbs* (1953)
Story of Two-thumbs the koala
Illustrated by Margaret Senior; numbers 1, 2, 4, 7, 8 also published in one volume entitled *Treasury of Australian nature stories*, 1974
9 *Story of Koonaworra the black swan* (1957)
Illustrated by Margaret Senior
10 *Story of Wy-Lah the cockatoo* (1959)
Illustrated by Walter Cunningham
Watson, Ina
11 *Larry* (1961)
The story of an Australian seagull; illustrated by Margaret Senior
Rees, Leslie
12 *Story of Russ the Australian tree kangaroo* (1964)
Illustrated by Walter Cunningham
Companion volumes: *Gecko, the lizard who lost his tail*, 1944, *Mokee, the white possum*, 1973, *Billa, the wombat who had a bad dream*, 1988

Australian saga series
This sequence has two authors
Timms, Edward Vivian
1 *Forever to remain* (1948)
2 *Pathway to the sun* (1949)
3 *Beckoning shore* (1950)
4 *Valleys beyond* (1951)
5 *Challenge* (1952)
6 *Scarlet frontier* (1953)
7 *Fury* (1954)
8 *They came from the sea* (1955)
9 *Shining harvest* (1956)
10 *Robina* (1958)
11 *Big country* (1962)
Timms, Alma
12 *Time and change* (1971)

Australian soldier series
Pinney, Peter
1 *Barbarians* (1988)
A soldier's New Guinea diary
2 *Glass cannon* (1990)
Bougainville diary, 1944-45
3 *Devil's garden* (1992)
Solomon Islands war diary, 1945

Australian story series
Casey, Maie
1 *Australian story, 1837-1907* (1962)
History of the author's family
2 *Tides and eddies* (1966)
Autobiography

Australian trilogy
Bridges, Roy
1 *And all that beauty* (1929)
2 *Negrohead* (1930)
3 *Trinity* (1931)

Australian trilogy
Cato, Nancy
1 *All the rivers ran* (1958)
2 *Time, flow softly* (1959)
3 *But still the stream* (1962)
One volume edition entitled *All the rivers run*, 1978

Australian wife series
Bouras, Gillian
Memoirs
1 *Foreign wife* (1988)
2 *Fair exchange* (1991)

Australians series
Bonner, Terry Nelsen
see **New South Wales series**

Australians series
Long, William Stuart
1 *Exiles* (1979)
2 *Settlers* (1980)
3 *Traitors* (1981)
4 *Explorers* (1983)
5 *Adventurers* (1983)
6 *Colonists* (1984)
7 *Goldseekers* (1985)
8 *Patriots* (1986)
Gallant
9 *Empire builders* (1987)
10 *Seafarers* (1988)
11 *Nationalists* (1989)
12 *Imperialists* (1989)

Author series
Allan, Mabel Esther
Autobiography
1 *To be an author* (1982)
2 *More about being an author* (1985)

Auto boys series
Braden, James Andrew
1 *Auto boys* (1908)
2 *Auto boys' outing* (1909)
3 *Auto boys' quest* (1910)
4 *Auto boys' camp* (1911)

Autobiography of a corpse series
Masefield, John
1 *Dead Ned* (1938)
2 *Live and kicking Ned* (1939)

Automobile girls series
Crane, Laura Dent
1 *Automobile girls at Newport* (1910)
Alternative title: Watching the summer parade
2 *Automobile girls in the Berkshires* (1910)
Alternative title: The ghost of Lost Man's Trail
3 *Automobile girls along the Hudson* (1910)
Alternative title: Fighting fire in Sleepy Hollow
4 *Automobile girls at Chicago* (1912)
Alternative title: Winning out against heavy odds
5 *Automobile girls at Palm Beach* (1912)
Alternative title: Proving their mettle under southern skies
6 *Automobile girls at Washington* (1913)
Alternative title: Checkmating the plots of foreign spies

Automobile series
Ellis, Edward Sylvester
1 *From low to high gear* (1906)
2 *Lost Dragon* (1907)

Autry series
Hamilton, Bob
see **Gene Autry series**

Autumn angels trilogy
Cover, Arthur Byron
1 *Autumn angels* (1975)
2 *Platypus of doom, and other nihilists* (1976)
3 *East wind rising* (1979)

Autumn series
Macneice, Louis
1 *Autumn journal* (1939)
2 *Autumn sequel* (1954)

Autumn world series
Gravel, Geary
1 *Alchemists* (1984)
2 *Pathfinders* (1986)

Avaryan Rising trilogy
Tarr, Judith
1 *Hall of the Mountain King* (1986)
2 *Lady of Han-Gilden* (1987)
3 *Fall of princes* (1988)
One volume edition entitled *Avaryan Rising*, 1988

Avatar trilogy
Awlinson, Richard
This pseudonym is used by Scott Ciencin, Troy Denning and Janice Lowder as indicated against each title
1 *Shadowdale* (1989)
[Ciensin]
2 *Tantras* (1989)
[Ciensin; Lowder]
3 *Waterdeep* (1989)
[Denning]
Companion volumes: *Pool of radiance*, by Jane Cooper Hong and James Michael Ward, 1989, *The Forgotten Realms atlas*, by Karen Wynn Fonstad, 1990, *Elminster, the making of a mage*, by Ed Greenwood, 1994

Avenger series
Cunningham, Chet
see **Matt Hawke series**

Avenger series
Robeson, Kenneth
This pseudonym is used by Paul Ernst – numbers 1-24 – and Ron Goulart – numbers 25-36
1 *Justice, Inc.* (1972)
2 *Yellow hoard* (1972)
3 *Sky walker* (1972)
4 *Devil's horns* (1972)
5 *Frosted death* (1972)
6 *Blood ring* (1972)
7 *Stockholders in death* (1972)
8 *Glass mountain* (1973)
9 *Tuned for murder* (1973)
10 *Smiling dogs* (1973)
11 *River of ice* (1973)
12 *Flame breathers* (1973)
13 *Murder on wheels* (1973)

14 *Three gold crowns* (1973)
15 *House of death* (1973)
16 *Hate master* (1973)
17 *Nevlo* (1973)
18 *Death in slow motion* (1973)
19 *Pictures of death* (1973)
20 *Green killer* (1974)
21 *Happy killers* (1974)
22 *Black death* (1974)
23 *Wilder curse* (1974)
24 *Midnight murder* (1974)
25 *Man from Atlantis* (1974)
26 *Red moon* (1974)
27 *Purple zombie* (1974)
28 *Doctor Time* (1974)
29 *Nightwitch devil* (1974)
30 *Black chariots* (1974)
31 *Cartoon crimes* (1974)
32 *Death machine* (1975)
33 *Blood countess* (1975)
34 *Glass man* (1975)
35 *Iron Skull* (1975)
36 *Demon Island* (1975)

Avengers series
This sequence has four authors
Macnee, Patrick
1 *Deadline* (1965)
2 *Dead duck* (1966)
Garforth, John
3 *Floating game* (1967)
4 *Laugh was on Lazarus* (1967)
5 *Passing of Gloria Munday* (1967)
6 *Heil Harris!* (1967)
Laumer, Keith
7 *Afrit affair* (1968)
8 *Drowned queen* (1968)
9 *Gold bomb* (1968)
Daniels, Norman A
10 *Magnetic man* (1968)
11 *Moon express* (1969)

Avengers superheroes series
This sequence has two authors
Binder, Otto
1 *Avengers battle the earth-wrecker* (1967)
Michelinie, David
2 *Man who stole tomorrow* (1979)

Avenging Angel series
Ryder, Thom
1 *Avenging Angel* (1975)
2 *Angel alone* (1975)
Sequence continued under the author's real name John Barton Harvey
Harvey, John Barton
3 *Junkyard Angel* (1977)

Avenging Twins series
McCulley, Johnston
1 *Avenging Twins* (1927)
2 *Avenging Twins collect* (1927)

Avenue series
Delderfield, Ronald Frederick
1 *Dreaming suburb* (1958)
2 *Avenue goes to war* (1958)
One volume editions entitled *The Avenue story*, 1964, and *The avenue*, 1969

Average series
Heymann, Tom
1 *On an average day* (1989)
2 *On an average day in the Soviet Union* (1990)
3 *In an average lifetime* (1992)
4 *On an average day in Japan* (1992)

Averidan series
Clough, Brenda Wang
1 *Crystal crown* (1984)
2 *Dragon of Mishbil* (1985)
3 *Realm beneath* (1986)
4 *Name of the sun* (1988)

Averill trilogy
Meyers, Roy
see **Dolphins trilogy**

Avery and Pearl series
Mackenzie, Compton
see **Jenny Pearl and Maurice Avery series**

Avery Gregg and Tony Ellis series
Koehler, Robert Portner
1 *Road house murders* (1946)
2 *Hooded vulture murders* (1947)
3 *Blue parakeet murders* (1948)

Aveyard series
Fraser, James
see **Inspector Bill Aveyard series**

Aviation series
Langley, John Prentice
1 *Trail blazers of the skies* (1927)
Alternative title: Across to Paris and back
2 *Spanning the Pacific* (1927)
Alternative title: A non-stop hop to Japan
3 *Masters of the airlanes* (1928)
Alternative title: Around the world in fourteen days
4 *Pathfinder's great flight* (1928)
Alternative title: Cloud chasers over the Amazon jungle
5 *Air voyagers of the Arctic* (1929)
Alternative title: Sky pilots' dash across the Pole
6 *Desert hawks on the wing* (1929)
Alternative title: Heading south, Algiers to Capetown
7 *Chasing the setting sun* (1930)
Alternative title: A hop, skip and jump to Australia
8 *Bridging the seven seas* (1930)
Alternative title: On the airlane to Singapore
9 *Staircase of the wind* (1931)
Alternative title: Over the Himalayas to Calcutta

Aviator series
Cobb, Frank
1 *Battling the clouds* (1921)
2 *Aviator's luck* (1921)
3 *Dangerous deeds* (1921)

Avignon quintet
Durrell, Lawrence
1 *Livia* (1978)
Alternative title: Buried alive
2 *Monsieur* (1974)
Alternative title: The Prince of Darkness
3 *Constance* (1982)
Alternative title: Solitary practices
4 *Sebastian* (1983)
Alternative title: Ruling passions
5 *Quinx* (1985)
Alternative title: The Ripper's tale

Avillion series
Craik, Dinah Maria
1 *Romantic tales* (1859)
2 *Domestic stories* (1860)
Originally published in one volume entitled *Avillion, and other tales*, 1853

Avis series
Phillpotts, Eden
see **Book of Avis series**

Avon family series
Heyer, Georgette
1 *These old shades* (1926)
2 *Devil's Cub* (1932)
3 *Infamous army* (1937)

Avonlea series
Montgomery, Lucy Maud
1 *Anne of Green Gables* (1908)
2 *Anne of Avonlea* (1909)
3 *Chronicles of Avonlea* (1912)
4 *Anne of the island* (1915)
5 *Anne of Windy Poplars* (1936)
Anne of Windy Willows
6 *Anne's house of dreams* (1917)
7 *Anne of Ingleside* (1939)
8 *Rainbow Valley* (1919)
9 *Rilla of Ingleside* (1921)
10 *Further chronicles of Avonlea* (1920)
Short stories
11 *Road to yesterday* (1974)
Companion volume: *The Anne of Green Gables cookbook*, by Kate Macdonald, 1985

Avons series
Wallace, Edgar
see **Black Avons series**

Awakeners series
Tepper, Sheri S
1 *Northshore* (1987)
2 *Southshore* (1987)
One volume edition entitled *The awakeners*, 1987

Awakening land trilogy
Richter, Conrad
see **American pioneer trilogy**

Awakening series
Macnamara, Rachel Swete
1 *Awakening* (1914)
2 *Marriage has been arranged* (1917)

Awol series
Shurtleff, Bertrand Leslie
1 *Awol, K9 commando* (1944)
2 *Short leash* (1945)
3 *Awol musters out* (1946)
Awol at large
4 *Long leah* (1947)

Axa series
Avenell, Donne
Based on a comic strip series
1 *Chosen* (1981)
Axa, the beginning
2 *Desired* (1982)
3 *Brave* (1983)
Also includes *The gambler*
4 *Earthbound* (1983)
Also includes *The tempted*
5 *Eager* (1984)
Also includes *The carefree*
6 *Dwarfed* (1984)
Also includes *The untamed*
7 *Mobile* (1985)
Also includes *The unmasked*
8 *Castaway* (1986)
Also includes *The seeker*
9 *Escapist* (1988)
Also includes *The starstruck*, and *The betrayers*
Companion volume: *Axa in color*, 1987

Axbrewder series
Stephens, Reed
see **Mick Axbrewder series**

Ayesthorpe trilogy
Blake, M Glaiser
1 *Peterloo weaver* (1980)
2 *Peterloo inheritance* (1981)
3 *Bitter legacy* (1982)

Ayla series
Auel, Jean Marie
see **Earth's children series**

Aylett series
Meik, Vivian
see **Geoffrey Aylett series**

Aylsham series
Heaven, Constance
see **Oliver Aylsham series**

Aylwin series
Curry, Avon
see **Jerome Aylwin series**

Aylwin series
Watts-Dunton, Theodore
1 *Aylwin* (1898)
2 *Coming of love* (1898)
This poem is based on the theme of love at war with death developed in the novel Aylwin, 1898

Ayres and his Battle Birds series
Bowen, Robert Sidney
see **Dusty Ayres and his Battle Birds series**

Ayrton family series
Stevenson, Dorothy Emily
1 *Amberwell* (1955)
2 *Summerhills* (1956)

Aysgill family trilogy
White, Alan
1 *Homeward tide* (1981)
2 *Vanishing land* (1982)
3 *Years of change* (1983)

Azan series
Garron, Marco
1 *Missing safari* (1950)
2 *Lost city* (1950)
3 *Jungle fever* (1950)
4 *White fangs* (1951)
5 *Tribal war* (1951)
6 *King hunters* (1951)

Azaro series
Okri, Ben
1 *Famished road* (1991)
2 *Songs of enchantment* (1993)

Aziyade series
Loti, Pierre
1 *Constantinople* (1879)
Original edition entitled *Aziyade*
2 *Phantom from the east* (1892)
Original edition entitled *Fantome d'orient*

Azor series
Crowley, Maude
1 *Azor* (1948)
2 *Azor and the haddock* (1949)
3 *Azor and the blue-eyed cow* (1951)
4 *Tor and Azor* (1955)

B

B F Cage series
Israel, Peter
1 *Hush money* (1974)
2 *French kiss* (1976)
3 *Stiff upper lip* (1978)

B.O.W.C. series
De Mille, James
see **Brethren of the White Cross series**

B series
Saro-Wiwa, Ken
see **Mister B series**

Baabee series III
Khalsa, Dayal Kaur
1 *Bon voyage Baabee* (1984)
2 *Happy birthday Baabee* (1984)
3 *Merry Christmas Baabee* (1984)
4 *Welcome twins* (1984)

Babar series
This sequence has two authors
Brunhoff, Jean de
1 *Story of Babar, the little elephant* (1931)
Original edition entitled *Histoire de Babar, le petit elephant*
2 *Travels of Babar* (1932)

Babar's travels
Original edition entitled *Le voyage de Babar*
3 *Babar the king* (1933)
Original edition entitled *Le roi Babar*
4 *A B C of Babar* (1934)
Babar's A B C
Original edition entitled *A B C de Babar*
5 *Zephir's holiday* (1934)
Babar's friend Zephir
Babar and Zephir
Original edition entitled *Les vacances de Zephir*
6 *Babar and his children* (1938)
Babar at home
Original edition entitled *Babar en famille*
7 *Babar and Father Christmas* (1940)
Original edition entitled *Babar et le Pere Noel*
Brunhoff, Laurent de
8 *Babar's cousin, that rascal Arthur* (1947)
Babar and that rascal Arthur
Original edition entitled *Babar et ce coquin d'Arthur*
9 *Babar's picnic* (1949)
Original edition entitled *Pique-nique chez Babar*
10 *Babar's visit to Bird Island* (1952)
Original edition entitled *Babar dans l'Isle Oiseaux*
11 *Babar's fair will be opened next Sunday* (1954)
Original edition entitled *La fete de Celesteville sera ouverte dimanche prochain*
12 *Babar and the professor* (1956)
Original edition entitled *Babar et le Professeur Grifaton*
13 *Babar's castle* (1961)
Original edition entitled *Le chateau de Babar*
14 *Babar comes to America* (1965)
Original edition entitled *Babar en Amerique*
15 *Babar loses his crown* (1966)
Original edition entitled *Babar a New York*
16 *Babar goes skiing* (1967)
Babar in the snow
Original edition entitled *Babar fait du ski*
17 *Babar the gardener* (1967)
Original edition entitled *Babar jardinier*
18 *Babar goes on a picnic* (1967)
Babar's day out
Original edition entitled *Babar en promenade*
19 *Babar's games* (1968)
20 *Babar at the seashore* (1969)
Babar at the seaside
Original edition entitled *Babar a la mer*; numbers 16, 17, 18, 20 also published in one volume entitled *Babar's trunk*, 1969
21 *Babar and the doctor* (1969)
Original edition entitled *Babar et le docteur*
22 *Babar learns to drive* (1969)
Original edition entitled *Babar aux sports d'hiver*
23 *Babar goes visiting* (1969)
24 *Babar's moon trip* (1969)
25 *Babar's birthday surprise* (1970)
Original edition entitled *L'Anniversaire de Babar*
26 *Babar keeps fit* (1969)
Babar the athlete
Original edition entitled *Babar fait du sport*
27 *Babar the artist* (1969)
Babar the painter
Original edition entitled *Babar artiste peintre*
28 *Babar the camper* (1969)
Babar goes camping
Original edition entitled *Babar campeur*
29 *Babar visits another planet* (1972)
Babar on the secret planet
Original edition entitled *Babar sur la planete molle*
30 *Meet Babar and his family* (1973)
31 *Babar the pilot* (1970)
Babar to the rescue
Original edition entitled *Babar aviateur*
32 *Babar's bookmobile* (1974)
33 *Babar the cook* (1970)
Babar bakes a cake
Original edition entitled *Babar patissier*
34 *Babar and the Wully-Wully* (1975)
Original edition entitled *Babar et le Wouly Wouly*
35 *Babar saves the day* (1976)

Babcary series
Goldsmith, John
see **Mrs Babcary series**

Babel series
Haycraft, John
1 *Babel in Spain* (1958)
2 *Babel in London* (1966)

Babenberg series
Cost, March
see **Princess Victorian Babenberg series**

Babs and Jackie series
Berrisford, Judith Mary
see **Jackie and Babs series**

Babs series
Avery, Elizabeth
1 *Margaret days* (1959)
2 *Marigold summer* (1960)

Babs series
Colver, Alice Ross
1 *Babs* (1917)
2 *Babs at Birchwood* (1919)
3 *Babs at college* (1920)
4 *Babs at home* (1921)

Babushka series
Polacco, Patricia
1 *Babushka's doll* (1990)
2 *Babushka Baba Yaga* (1993)

Baby and Penny series
Mazzetti, Lorenza
see **Penny and Baby series**

Baby animal love series
McCue, Lisa
1 *Kittens love* (1990)
2 *Puppies love* (1990)
3 *Bunnies love* (1991)
4 *Ducklings love* (1991)

Baby animal series
James, Robin
Board books
1 *Baby farm animals* (1983)
2 *Baby zoo animals* (1983)
3 *Baby forest animals* (1983)
4 *Baby pets* (1983)

Baby Bear series
Hill, Eric
1 *At home* (1983)
2 *My pets* (1983)
3 *Park* (1983)
4 *Up there* (1983)
5 *Baby Bear's bedtime* (1984)
6 *Good morning, Baby Bear* (1984)

Baby board books series
Oxenbury, Helen
1 *Holidays* (1982)
2 *Shopping* (1982)
3 *Animals* (1982)
4 *Helping* (1982)
5 *Bedtime* (1982)
6 *Friends* (1985)
7 *Playing* (1985)
8 *Dressing* (1985)
9 *Working* (1985)
10 *Family* (1985)

Baby books, new series
Ormerod, Jan
see **New baby books series**

Baby books series
Ormerod, Jan
1 *Dad's book* (1985)
2 *Reading* (1985)
3 *Sleeping* (1985)
4 *Messy baby* (1985)

Baby Bunny series
Cosgrove, Stephen Edward
1 *Bunny's playtime* (1984)
2 *Sleeping time Bunny* (1984)
3 *Bunny's busy day* (1984)
4 *Bunny goes to market* (1984)
5 *Bunny bakes a cake* (1986)

Baby doll board books series
Dolce, Janet Ellen
1 *Smiling Sandy* (1989)
2 *Cuddly Casey* (1989)
3 *Toddling Terry* (1989)
4 *Patty Cake* (1989)

Baby doll series
Williams, Tennessee
1 *Baby doll* (1955)
The script for the film
2 *Milk train does'nt stop here anymore* (1962)
A play in one act

Baby don't series
Storm, Michael
1 *Baby don't love hoodlums* (1953)
2 *Baby don't say goodbye* (1953)

Baby Elephant series
Joslin, Sesyle
1 *Brave Baby Elephant* (1960)
2 *Baby Elephant's trunk* (1961)
3 *Senor Baby Elephant* (1962)
4 *Baby Elephant and the secret wishes* (1962)
5 *Baby Elephant goes to China* (1963)
6 *Baby Elephant's baby book* (1964)

Baby Jay series
VerDorn, Bethea
Board books
1 *Daytime and Baby Jay* (1987)
2 *Playtime and Baby Jay* (1987)
3 *Naptime and Baby Jay* (1987)
4 *Rhymetime and Baby Jay* (1987)

Baby Rabbit series
Manushkin, Fran
1 *Little Rabbit's baby brother* (1986)
2 *Be brave, Baby Rabbit* (1990)
Co-author: Lucy Bate

Baby series
Kilroy, Sally
Board books
1 *Baby colours* (1983)
2 *Babies' bodies* (1983)
3 *Noisy homes* (1983)
4 *Babies' homes* (1984)
5 *Babies' outings* (1984)
6 *Busy babies* (1984)
7 *Babies' zoo* (1984)

Baby series
Matterson, Neil
1 *It's a baby* (1982)
2 *It's another baby* (1982)
3 *More babies* (1983)
Companion volume: *Is he biting again*, 1983

Baby series
Miranda, Anne
Illustrated by Dorothy Stott
1 *Baby talk* (1987)
2 *Baby walk* (1988)

Baby-sitter series
Stine, Robert Lawrence
1 *Baby-sitter* (1989)
2 *Baby-sitter II* (1991)

Baby-Sitters Club mystery series
Martin, Ann Matthews
1 *Stacey and the missing ring* (1991)
2 *Beware Dawn!* (1991)
3 *Mallory and the ghost cat* (1992)
4 *Kristy and the missing child* (1992)
5 *Mary Anne and the secret in the attic* (1992)
6 *Mystery at Claudia's house* (1992)
7 *Dawn and the disappearing dogs* (1992)
8 *Jessi and the jewel thieves* (1993)
9 *Kristy and the haunted mansion* (1993)
10 *Stacey and the mystery money* (1993)
Number 11 not identified
12 *Dawn and the surfer ghost* (1993)
13 *Mary Anne and the library mystery* (1994)
14 *Stacey and the mystery at the mall* (1994)
15 *Kristy and the vampires* (1994)
16 *Claudia and the clue in the photograph* (1994)

Baby-Sitters Club readers special request series
Martin, Ann Matthews
1 *Logan's story* (1992)
2 *Logan Bruno, boy baby-sitter* (1993)

Baby-Sitters Club series
Martin, Ann Matthews
1 *Kristy's great idea* (1986)
2 *Claudia and the phantom phone calls* (1986)
3 *Truth about Stacey* (1986)
4 *Mary Anne saves the day* (1987)
5 *Dawn and the impossible three* (1987)
6 *Kristy's big day* (1987)
7 *Claudia and Mean Janine!* (1987)
8 *Boy-crazy Stacey* (1987)
9 *Ghost at Dawn's house* (1988)
10 *Logan likes Mary Ann!* (1988)
11 *Kristy and the snobs* (1988)
12 *Claudia and the new girl* (1988)
13 *Good-bye Stacey, good-bye* (1988)
14 *Hello, Mallory* (1988)
15 *Little Miss Stoneybrook, and Dawn* (1988)
16 *Jessi's secret language* (1988)
17 *Mary Ann's bad-luck mystery* (1988)
18 *Stacey's mistake* (1988)
19 *Claudia and the bad joke* (1988)
20 *Kristy and the walking disaster* (1989)
21 *Mallory and the trouble with the twins* (1989)
22 *Jessi Ramsey, pet-sitter* (1989)
23 *Dawn on the Coast* (1989)
24 *Kristy and the Mother's Day surprise* (1989)
25 *Mary Anne and the search for Tigger* (1989)
26 *Claudia and the sad good-bye* (1989)
27 *Jessi and the Superbrat* (1989)
28 *Welcome back, Stacey!* (1989)
29 *Mallory and the secret diary* (1989)
30 *Mary Anne and the great romance* (1990)
31 *Dawn's wicked stepsister* (1990)
32 *Kristy and the secret of Susan* (1990)
33 *Claudia and the great search* (1990)
34 *Mary Anne and too many boys* (1990)
35 *Stacey and the mystery of Stoneybrook* (1990)

36 *Jessi's baby sister* (1990)
37 *Dawn and the older boy* (1990)
38 *Kristy's mystery admirer* (1990)
39 *Poor Mallory* (1990)
40 *Claudia and Middle School* (1991)
41 *Mary Anne versus Logan* (1991)
42 *Jessi and the dance school phantom* (1991)
43 *Stacey's emergency* (1991)
44 *Dawn and the big sleepover* (1991)
45 *Kristy and the baby parade* (1991)
46 *Mary Anne misses Logan* (1991)
47 *Mallory on strike* (1991)
48 *Jessi's wish* (1991)
49 *Claudia, the genius of Elm Street* (1991)
50 *Dawn's big date* (1992)
51 *Stacey's ex-best friend* (1992)
52 *Mary Anne and too many babies* (1992)
53 *Kristy for president* (1992)
54 *Mallory's dream horse* (1992)
55 *Jessi's gold medal* (1992)
56 *Keep out, Claudia!* (1992)
57 *Dawn saves the planet* (1992)
58 *Stacey's choice* (1992)
59 *Mallory hates boys, and gym* (1992)
60 *Mary Anne's makeover* (1993)
61 *Jessi and the awful secret* (1993)
62 *Kristy and the worst kid ever* (1993)
63 *Claudia's freind friend* (1993)
64 *Dawn's family feud* (1993)
65 *Stacey's big crush* (1993)
66 *Maid Mary Anne* (1993)
67 *Dawn's big move* (1993)
68 *Jessi and the bad baby-sitter* (1993)
69 *Get well soon, Mallory* (1993)
70 *Stacey and the cheerleaders* (1993)
71 *Claudia and the perfect boy* (1994)
72 *Dawn and the We Kids Club* (1994)
73 *Mary Anne and Miss priss* (1994)
74 *Kristy and the copycat* (1994)
75 *Jessi's horrible prank* (1994)
76 *Stacey's lie* (1994)
77 *Dawn and Whitney, friends forever* (1994)
78 *Secret Santa* (1994)

Companion volumes: *Baby-Sitters Club postcard book*, 1991, *Baby-Sitters Club guide to baby-sitting*, 1993, *Baby-Sitters Club notebook*, by Sonia Black and Pat Brigandi, 1991, *Baby-Sitters Club trivia and puzzle fun book*, by Kara Adamo, 1992

Baby-Sitters Club super specials series
Martin, Ann Matthews
1 *Baby-Sitters on board!* (1988)
2 *Baby-Sitters summer vacation* (1989)
3 *Baby-Sitters winter carnival* (1989)
4 *Baby-Sitters island adventure* (1990)
5 *California girls!* (1990)
6 *New York, New York* (1991)
7 *Snowbound* (1991)
8 *Baby-Sitters at Shadow Lake* (1992)
9 *Starring the Baby-Sitters Club* (1992)
10 *Sea City, here we come!* (1993)
11 *Baby-SDitters remember* (1994)

Baby-Sitters little sister series
Martin, Ann Matthews
1 *Karen's witch* (1988)
2 *Karen's roller skates* (1988)
3 *Karen's worst day* (1989)
4 *Karen's Kittycat Club* (1989)
5 *Karen's school picture* (1989)
6 *Karen's little sister* (1989)
7 *Karen's birthday* (1990)
8 *Karen's haircut* (1990)
9 *Karen's sleepover* (1990)
10 *Karen's grandmother* (1990)
11 *Karen's prize* (1990)
12 *Karen's ghost* (1990)
13 *Karen's surprise* (1990)
14 *Karen's New Year* (1991)
15 *Karen's in love* (1991)
16 *Karen's goldfish* (1991)
17 *Karen's brothers* (1991)
18 *Karen's home run* (1991)
19 *Karen's good-bye* (1991)
20 *Karen's carnival* (1991)
21 *Karen's new teacher* (1991)
22 *Karen's little witch* (1991)
23 *Karen's doll* (1991)
24 *Karen's school trip* (1992)
25 *Karen's pen pal* (1992)
26 *Karen's ducklings* (1992)
27 *Karen's big joke* (1992)
28 *Karen's tea party* (1992)
29 *Karen's cartwheel* (1992)
30 *Karen's kittens* (1992)
31 *Karen's bully* (1992)
32 *Karen's pumpkin patch* (1992)
33 *Karen's secret* (1992)
34 *Karen's snowy day* (1993)
35 *Karen's doll house* (1993)
36 *Karen's new friend* (1993)
37 *Karen's tuba* (1993)
38 *Karen's big lie* (1993)
39 *Karen's wedding* (1993)
40 *Karen's newspaper* (1993)
41 *Karen's school* (1993)
42 *Karen's pizza party* (1993)
43 *Karen's toothache* (1993)
44 *Karen's big weekend* (1993)
45 *Karen's twin* (1994)
46 *Karen's baby-sitter* (1994)
47 *Karen's kite* (1994)
48 *Karen's two families* (1994)
49 *Karen's stepmother* (1994)
50 *Karen's lucky penny* (1994)
51 *Karen's big top* (1994)
52 *Karen's mermaid* (1994)

Companion volumes: *Baby-Sisters little sister, secret diary*, 1991, *Baby-Sitters little sister, school scrapbook*, 1993

Baby-Sitters little sister super specials series
Martin, Ann Matthews
1 *Karen's wish* (1990)
2 *Karen's plane trip* (1991)
3 *Karen's mystery* (1991)
4 *Karen, Hannie and Nancy, the three musketeers* (1992)
5 *Karen's baby* (1992)
6 *Karen's campout* (1993)

Baby unicorn series
Marzollo, Jean
1 *Baby unicorn* (1987)
2 *Baby unicorn and baby dragon* (1989)

Babydays series
Jessel, Camilla
1 *Baby's day* (1985)
2 *Baby's toys* (1985)
3 *Baby's bedtime* (1985)
4 *Baby's clothes* (1985)
5 *Baby's food* (1986)

Babyland series
Jesse, Louie
1 *Babyland abroad* (1913)
2 *Babyland in history* (1914)

Companion volume: *Songs and games of Babyland abroad*, 1916

Baby's day series
Metcalfe, Penny
1 *Morning* (1987)
2 *Afternoon* (1987)
3 *Evening* (1987)
4 *Night* (1987)

Bachelor maid series
Thurston, Ida Treadwell
1 *Bachelor maid and her brother* (1898)
2 *Village contest* (1899)
Alternative title: No surrender

Back to the future trilogy
This sequence has two authors; based on screenplays
Gipe, George
1 *Back to the future* (1985)
Companion volume: *Back to the future*, by Robert Loren Fleming, 1985
Gardner, Craig Shaw
2 *Back to the future, part two* (1989)
3 *Back to the future, part three* (1990)

Companion volume: *Back to the future, the official book of the complete movie trilogy*, by Sally Hibbin and Michael Klastorin, 1990

Back to the soil series
Todd, Burbank L
1 *Hiram, the young farmer* (1914)
Alternative title: Making the soil pay
2 *Hiram in the Middle West* (1915)
Alternative title: A young farmer's upward struggle

Backblocks doctor series
Gordon, Doris
Reminiscences
1 *Backblocks baby doctor* (1955)
2 *Doctor down under* (1958)

Background and foreground series
Swinnerton, Frank
1 *Background with chorus* (1956)
English literary fashion between 1901 and 1917
2 *Figures in the foreground* (1963)
Literary reminiscences, 1917-1940

Backstreets series
Brooke, Jonathan
1 *Slackness* (1994)
2 *Big up!* (1994)

Bad babies series
Bradman, Tony
1 *Bad Babies' counting book* (1985)
2 *Bad Babies' book of colours* (1986)
3 *Bad babies' book of months* (1987)

Bad Boris series
Jenkin-Pearce, Susie
1 *Bad Boris and the new kitten* (1986)
2 *Bad Boris and the birthday* (1987)

Bad boy series
This sequence has two authors
Gray, Walter T
1 *Bad boy's diary* (1880)
2 *Bad boy abroad* (1883)
The funniest book of the age
3 *Bad boy at home and his experiences in trying to become an editor* (1885)
Golden Rod
4 *Bad boy in the country* (1892)
Selections: *Bad boy's adventures*, by Little Georgie, 1904

Companion volume: *A naughty girl's diary*, by Walter T Gray, 1884, *A good boy's diary*, 1905

Bad boy series
Peck, George Wilbur
see **Peck's bad boy series**

Bad girls series
Rhodes, Susan
1 *Now you'll think I'm awful* (1967)
2 *And when she was bad she was popular* (1968)

Bad News Bunny series
Saunders, Susan
1 *Third-prize surprise* (1987)
2 *Back to nature* (1987)
3 *Stop the presses* (1987)
4 *Who's got a secret?* (1987)
5 *Caught in the act* (1987)
6 *Narrow escape* (1987)

Baddies series
Impey, Rose
1 *Baked bean queen* (1986)
2 *Demon Kevin* (1986)
3 *Tough Teddy* (1986)
4 *Bedtime beast* (1987)
5 *Little smasher* (1987)
6 *Toothbrush monster* (1987)

Bader series
Reynolds, Mack
see **Rex Bader series**

Badge of honor series
Griffin, W E B
1 *Men in blue* (1988)
2 *Special operations* (1989)
3 *Victim* (1991)
4 *Witness* (1992)
5 *Assassin* (1992)
6 *Murderer* (1995)

Badge series
Reno, Bill
1 *Sundance* (1987)
2 *Faceless man* (1987)
3 *Black coffin* (1987)
4 *Powder River* (1987)
5 *London's revenge* (1988)
6 *Showdown* (1988)
7 *Imposter* (1988)
8 *Stranger* (1988)
9 *Backlash* (1989)
10 *Blood trail* (1989)
11 *Dark canyon* (1989)
12 *Death list* (1989)
13 *Outcast* (1989)
14 *Gallows* (1989)
15 *Farrell's war* (1990)
16 *Cannon's grave* (1990)
17 *Vulture* (1990)
18 *Cougar* (1990)
19 *Gunhawk* (1990)
20 *Widow Valley* (1991)
21 *Deadlock* (1991)
22 *Gun trap* (1991)
23 *Death badge* (1991)
24 *Hunted* (1991)

Badger Brock series
Bingham, John
see **Superintendent Badger Brock series**

Badger Coe and Blizzard Wilson series
Cameron, Caddo
see **Private Badger Coe and Sergeant Blizzard Wilson series**

Badger series
B B
see **Bill Badger series**
Winton, John
see **Navy series**

Badger's Bend series
Rhodes, John
see **Tim and Betsy series**

Badman series
Borg, Jack
see **Thady Corey series**

Badshah series
Casserly, Gordon
see **Jungle series**

Badwater series
Nelson, Al P
1 *Cowpunchers of Badwater* (1936)
2 *Bullets for Badwater* (1936)

Baeier series
Slovo, Gillian
see **Kate Baeier series**

Baer series
Resnicow, Herbert
see **Ed and Warren Baer series**

Baer triplets series
Moore, Bertha B
see **Triplets series**

Baggable tales series
Treloar, Bruce
1 *Beware, take care* (1988)
2 *Only me from over the sea* (1988)

Bagley series
Pochocki, Ethel
see **Grandma Bagley series**

Bagpuss beginners series
Postgate, Oliver
Illustrated by Peter Firmin
1 *Mister Rumbletum's gumboot* (1974)
2 *Song of Pongo* (1974)
3 *Silly old Uncle Feedle* (1974)

Bagpuss series
Postgate, Oliver
Illustrated by Peter Firmin
1 *Bagpuss in the sun* (1974)
2 *Bagpuss on a rainy day* (1974)

Bagshaw series
Wilson, Bob
see **Stanley Bagshaw series**

Bagshot series
Telscombe, Anne
see **Miss Bagshot series**

Bagthorpes series
Cresswell, Helen
1 *Ordinary Jack* (1977)
2 *Absolute zero* (1978)
3 *Bagthorpes unlimited* (1978)
4 *Bagthorpes versus the world* (1979)
5 *Bagthorpes abroad* (1984)
6 *Bagthorpes haunted* (1985)
7 *Bagthorpes liberated* (1985)
8 *Bagthorpe triangle* (1992)

Bailey-Martin series
White, Percy
see **Mister Bailey-Martin series**

Bailey series
Bailey, Hilea
see **Hilea Bailey and Hilary Dunsany Bailey series**
Borg, Jack
see **Hogleg Bailey series**
Carter, Bruce
see **Nick Bailey series**
Cookson, Catherine
see **Bill Bailey series**
Dobson, Margaret
see **Jane Bailey series**
Huggins, Roy
see **Stuart Bailey series**

Bain series
Vance, John Holbrook
see **Sheriff Joe Bain series**

Bain trilogy
Mackenzie, J Alexander
see **Canaan trilogy**

Baines family series
Miles, Patricia Mary
1 *Sweet peril* (1987)
2 *Beloved enemy* (1987)

Baines series
James, Leigh Franklin
see **John Cooper Baines series**
Saville, Malcolm
see **Marston Baines series**

Baird family series
Edwin, Maribel
1 *Bridge under the water* (1957)
2 *Snowbound bus* (1960)
3 *Hidden house* (1963)

Baird family series
Pinkerton, Kathrene
1 *Hidden harbor* (1951)
Hidden harbour
2 *Second meeting* (1956)
3 *Year of enchantment* (1957)
Secret river

Baird series
Kauffman, Reginald Wright
see **Frances Baird series**

Baird trilogy
Weikel, Anna Hamline
see **Betty Baird trilogy**

Baja California series
Gardner, Erle Stanley
1 *Hovering over Baja* (1961)
2 *Hidden heart of Baja* (1962)
3 *Off the beaten track in Baja* (1967)

Baker series
Brown, Carter
see **Larry Baker series**
Huston, Howard Chauncey
see **Detective Charles A Baker series**
L'Amour, Louis
see **Cullen Baker series**
Mills, Osmington
see **Superintendent William Baker series**
Norman, Barry
see **Paul Baker series**

Baker Street Irregulars series
Dicks, Terrance
Based on characters from the Sherlock Holmes stories by Sir Arthur Conan Doyle
1 *Case of the missing masterpiece* (1978)
Missing masterpiece
2 *Case of the Fagin file* (1978)
Fagin file
3 *Case of the blackmail boys* (1979)
4 *Case of the cinema swindle* (1980)
5 *Case of the ghost grabbers* (1980)
6 *Case of the cop catchers* (1981)
7 *Case of the disappearing diplomat* (1986)
8 *Case of the comic crooks* (1986)
9 *Case of the haunted holiday* (1987)
Haunted holiday
10 *Case of the criminal computer* (1987)
Criminal computer

Baker Street series
Haughey, Thomas Brace
see **Geoffrey Weston series**

Baker Street Sports Club and Dallas O'Neil series
Jenkins, Jerry Bruce
see **Dallas O'Neil and the Baker Street Sports Club series**

Balcombe Hall series
Martyn, Harriet
1 *Jenny and the syndicate* (1982)
Revised edition 1984
2 *Jenny and the sphinx* (1983)
3 *Jenny and the new headmistress* (1984)
4 *Jenny and the new girls* (1985)

Baldwin Hamey series
Keevil, John Joyce
Biographies of the Baldwin Hameys, father and son
1 *Hamey the stranger* (1952)
2 *Stranger's son* (1953)

Baldwin series
Ocork, Shannon
see **T T Baldwin series**

Baley series
Asimov, Isaac
see **Elijah Baley series**

Balfour series
Appel, Allen
see **Alex Balfour series**
Stevenson, Robert Louis
see **David Balfour series**

Balkan series
Grier, Sydney Carlyon
1 *Uncrowned king* (1896)
A romance of high politics
2 *Crowned queen* (1898)
The romance of a ministry of state
3 *Kings of the East* (1900)
A romance of the near future
4 *Prince of the captivity* (1902)
Epilogue to a romance

Balkan trilogy
Grier, Sydney Carlyon
1 *Heir* (1906)
2 *Heritage* (1908)
3 *Prize* (1910)

Ballad of Wuntvor trilogy
Gardner, Craig Shaw
1 *Difficulty with dwarves* (1987)
2 *Excess of enchantments* (1988)
3 *Disagreement with death* (1989)
One volume edition entitled *The wanderings of Wuntvor*, 1989

Ballantyne series
Smith, Wilbur Addison
see **Zouga Ballantyne series**

Ballard series
Sinclair, Dennis
see **Greg Ballard series**

Ballet family series
Allan, Mabel Esther
see **Garland family series**

Ballet memoirs series
De Mille, Agnes
Autobiography
1 *Dance to the piper* (1951)
2 *And promenade home* (1958)

Ballet One series
Asher, Sandra Fenichel
1 *Best friends get better* (1989)
2 *Mary-in-the-Middle* (1990)
3 *Pat's promise* (1990)
4 *Can David do it!* (1991)

Ballet school series
White, Constance Mary
1 *Ballet school mystery* (1951)
2 *Dancer's daughter* (1955)
3 *New girl at ballet school* (1957)
4 *Ballet school rivals* (1958)

Ballou family series
McCarthy, Gary
1 *Horsemen* (1992)
2 *Cherokee Lighthorse* (1992)
3 *Texas Mustangers* (1993)
4 *Blue bullet* (1993)
5 *Stallion Valley* (1994)

Ballpoint bananas series
Keller, Charles
1 *Ballpoint bananas, and other jokes for kids* (1973)
2 *More ballpoint bananas* (1977)
Companion volume: *Star-spangled bananas, and other revolutionary riddles*, 1974

Ballygullion series
Doyle, Lynn
1 *Ballygullion* (1908)
2 *Dear Ducks, and other Ballygullion stories* (1925)

Ballyreagh Jumping Team series
Brims, Bernagh
1 *Runaway riders* (1963)
2 *Red rosette* (1965)

Balon series
Johnstone, William Wallace
see **Beasts series**

Balsamo series
Dumas, Alexandre
see **Memoirs of a physician series**

Balzan of the cat people trilogy
Moore, Wallace
1 *Blood stones* (1975)
2 *Caves of madness* (1975)
3 *Lights of Zetar* (1976)

Balzic series
Constantine, K C
see **Mario Balzic series**

Bambi series
Salten, Felix
1 *Bambi* (1926)
Original edition entitled *Bambi*
2 *Bambi's children* (1939)
Original edition entitled *Bambis Kinder*

Bamsan Kiet series
Alexander, Gary
see **Superintendent Bamsan Kiet series**

Ban series
McLean, Allan Campbell
see **Alasdair and Lachlann Ban series**

Banana republic trilogy
Asturias, Miguel Angel
see **Guatemala trilogy**

Banana series
Heide, Florence Parry
1 *Banana twist* (1978)
2 *Banana blitz* (1983)

Bananas series
Keller, Charles
see **Going bananas series**

Bandinangi series
Odgers, Sally Farrell
1 *Five easy lessons* (1989)
2 *Kayak!* (1992)
3 *Three missing days* (1993)

Bandini series
Fante, John
see **Arturo Bandini series**

Bandy papers series
Jack, Donald
see **Journals of Bartholomew Bandy series**

Bang to rights series
Norman, Frank
Autobiography
1 *Banana boy* (1969)
2 *Bang to rights* (1958)
An account of prison life
3 *Stand on me* (1960)
4 *Guntz* (1962)

Banion series
Finnegan, Robert
see **Dan Banion series**

Bank Vale United series
Hardcastle, Michael
1 *In the net* (1971)
2 *United!* (1973)
3 *Away from home* (1974)
4 *Free kick* (1974)

Banks series
Robinson, Peter
see **Chief Inspector Alan Banks series**

Banner series
Chapman, Robert
see **Rex Banner series**

Bannerman series
Flynn, Jay
see **Jim Bannerman series**

Bannerman series
Maxim, John R
1 *Bannerman solution* (1989)
2 *Bannerman effect* (1989)
3 *Bannerman's law* (1991)

Bannermere series
Trease, Geoffrey
1 *No boats on Bannermere* (1949)
2 *Under Black Banner* (1951)
3 *Black Banner players* (1952)
4 *Black Banner abroad* (1954)
5 *Gates of Bannerdale* (1956)

Banning series
Easton, Nat
see **Bill Banning series**

Bannion series
Norman, Earl
see **Burns Bannion series**

Bannister series
Crossley, Maude
see **Guy Bannister series**
Newton, Dwight Bennett
see **Jim Bannister series**

Bantan series
Gardner, Maurice Benjamin
1 *Bantan, god-like islander* (1936)
Bantan of the islands
The second title is a revised edition
2 *Son of the wilderness* (1939)
3 *Bantan and the island goddess* (1942)
4 *Bantan defiant* (1955)
5 *Bantan valiant* (1957)
6 *Bantan incredible* (1960)
7 *Bantan primeval* (1961)
8 *Bantan fearless* (1963)
9 *Bantan and the mermaids* (1970)
10 *Bantan's quest* (1974)
11 *Ancestors of Bantan* (1976)
12 *New adventures of Bantan* (1977)

Bantu series
Jabavu, Noni
1 *Drawn in colour* (1960)
2 *Ochre people* (1963)

Banyana series
Elliott, Janice
see **Alexander Columbus Banyana series**

Baphomet series
Barbet, Pierre
1 *Baphomet's meteor* (1972)
Original edition entitled *L'empire du Baphomet*
2 *Cosmic crusade* (1980)
Original edition entitled *Croisade stellaire*
One volume edition entitled *Cosmic crusaders*, 1980

Bar B boys series
Sabin, Edward Legrand
1 *Bar B boys* (1909)
Alternative title: The young cowpunchers
2 *Range and trail* (1910)
Alternative title: The Bar B's great drive
3 *Circle K* (1911)
Alternative title: Fighting for the flock
4 *Old Four-Toes* (1912)
Alternative title: The hunters of the peaks
5 *Treasure mountain* (1913)
Alternative title: The young prospectors
6 *Scarface Ranch* (1914)
Alternative title: Young homesteaders

Bara quartet
Parry, Anne Spencer
1 *Land behind the world* (1976)
2 *Lost souls of the twilight* (1977)
3 *Crown of darkness* (1979)
4 *Crown of light* (1980)

Barbapapa first book series
Tison, Annette
1 *Barbapapa's theatre* (1978)
2 *Colour and Barbapapa* (1978)
3 *Counting and Barbapapa* (1978)
4 *Shape and Barbapapa* (1978)

Barbapapa series
Tison, Annette
1 *Barbapapa* (1970)
2 *Barbapapa's voyage* (1971)
3 *Barbapapa's new house* (1972)
4 *Barbapapa's ark* (1974)
5 *Barbapapa's school* (1976)
6 *Barbapapa's winter* (1982)

Barbara Baum series
Colver, Anne
1 *Bread-and-Butter Indian* (1964)
2 *Bread-and-Butter journey* (1970)

Barbara Dering series
Rives, Amelie
1 *Quick and the dead* (1889)
2 *Barbara Dering* (1893)

Barbara Hale series
Garis, Lilian C
1 *Barbara Hale, a doctor's daughter* (1926)
2 *Barbara Hale and Cozette* (1926)

Barbara Havers and Thomas Lynley series
George, Elizabeth
see **Inspector Thomas Lynley and Sergeant Barbara Havers series**

Barbara Holloway series
Wilhelm, Kate
1 *Death qualified* (1991)
2 *Best defense* (1994)

Barbara series
Wright, Mabel Osgood
see **Commuter's wife series**

Barbara Winthrop series
Broughall, Helen Katherine
1 *Barbara Winthrop at boarding school* (1925)
2 *Barbara Winthrop at camp* (1926)
3 *Barbara Winthrop, graduate* (1927)
4 *Barbara Winthrop abroad* (1929)

Barbarians series
Adams, Robert
1 *Barbarians* (1986)
Co-authors: Martin Harry Greenberg and Charles Gordon Waugh
2 *Barbarians II* (1988)
Co-authors: Pamela Crippen Adams and Martin Harry Greenberg

Barbary Lane series
Maupin, Armistead
see **Tales of the city series**

Barber trilogy
Reid, Forrest
see **Tom Barber trilogy**

Barbie France series
Stevenson, Dorothy Emily
1 *Five windows* (1953)
2 *Tall stranger* (1957)

Barbie series
Lawrence, Cynthia
Based on the doll character
1 *Barbie's New York summer* (1962)
2 *Here's Barbie* (1962)
Co-author: Bette Lou Maybee
3 *Barbie and Ken* (1963)
Co-author: Bette Lou Maybee
4 *Barbie solves a mystery* (1963)
5 *Barbie, Midge and Ken* (1964)

Barbour family trilogy
Caldwell, Taylor
see **Bouchard family trilogy**

Barcello series
Ransome, Stephen
see **Lieutenant Lee Barcello series**

Barclay series
Elder, Michael
1 *Nowhere on earth* (1973)
2 *Perfumed planet* (1973)
Flight to terror
3 *Down to earth* (1973)
4 *Seeds of frenzy* (1974)
5 *Island of the dead* (1975)

Barclay series
Paul, Ernest
see **George Barclay series**

Bard series
Taylor, Keith
1 *Bard* (1981)
2 *Voyage of Ormungandr* (1984)
Bard II
First longship
3 *Wild sea* (1986)
4 *Ravens' gathering* (1987)
5 *Felimid's homecoming* (1991)

Bard trilogy
Scott, Michael
see **Tales of the bard trilogy**

Barden series
Manley-Tucker, Audrie
see **Julie Barden series**

Bardic voices series
Lackey, Mercedes
1 *Lark and the wren* (1992)
2 *Robin and the kestrel* (1993)
3 *Eagle and the nightingale* (1995)

Bare bear series
Alborough, Jez
1 *Bare bear* (1984)
2 *Running bear* (1985)

Barefoot series
Felicity, *Sister*
Autobiography
1 *Barefoot journey* (1961)
2 *Spring comes barefoot* (1965)

Bare-Head series
Lambourne, John
see **Jim Burnett series**

Barely there series
Cosgrove, Stephen Edward
1 *Fiddler* (1988)
2 *Shadow chaser* (1988)
3 *Gossamer* (1988)
4 *Derby Downs* (1988)

Barfield series
Jones, Olive
Illustrated by Leslie Wood
1 *Jenny's one and only cat* (1966)
2 *Jenny and the bantam hen* (1966)
3 *Foal* (1966)
4 *Rat hunt* (1966)
5 *Simon's rabbits* (1966)
Numbers 3-5 also published in one volume entitled *Pets in Barfield*, 1971
6 *Pigeons* (1968)
7 *Pigs in the kitchen* (1968)
8 *Hedgehogs in the cellar* (1968)
Numbers 6-8 also published in one volume entitled *Adventures in Barfield*, 1971
9 *Pip and seagull* (1968)
10 *Newts in the pond* (1968)
11 *Shetland ponies* (1968)
Numbers 9-11 also published in one volume entitled *Summer in Barfield*, 1971
12 *Peacock* (1969)
Numbers 1, 2 and 12 also published in one volume entitled *Jenny lives in Barfield*, 1971

Barforth trilogy
Jagger, Brenda
1 *Clouded hills* (1980)
2 *Flint and roses* (1981)
3 *Sleeping sword* (1982)

Barker family series
Phipson, Joan
1 *Family conspiracy* (1962)
2 *Threat to the Barkers* (1963)

Barkham Street trilogy
Stolz, Mary
1 *Dog on Barkham Street* (1960)
2 *Bully of Barkham Street* (1963)
3 *Explorer of Barkham Street* (1985)
One volume edition entitled *Barkham Street trilogy*, 1989

Barlach series
Durrenmatt, Friedrich
see **Kommissar Hans Barlach series**

Barley series
Palmer, Juliette
1 *Barley sow, barley grow* (1978)
2 *Barley ripe, barley reap* (1979)

Barlow series
Carter, Robert A
see **Nicholas Barlow series**
Martin, Troy Kennedy
see **Chief Inspector Barlow series**

Barlowe series
Smith, C I D
see **Inspector Barlowe series**

Barly fields series
Nathan, Robert
1 *Fiddler in barly* (1926)
2 *Woodcutter's house* (1927)
3 *Bishop's wife* (1928)
4 *Orchid* (1931)
5 *There is another heaven* (1929)
One volume edition entitled *The barly fields*, 1939

Barmy Jeffers series
Brennan, James Herbert
1 *Barmy Jeffers and the Quasimodo walk* (1988)
2 *Return of Barmy Jeffers and the Quasimodo walk* (1988)
3 *Barmy Jeffers and the shrinking potion* (1989)

Barnabas Collins series
Ross, Marilyn
1 *Dark shadows* (1966)
2 *Victoria Winters* (1967)
3 *Strangers at Collins House* (1967)
4 *Mystery of Collinwood* (1967)
5 *Curse of Collinwood* (1968)
6 *Barnabas Collins* (1968)
7 *Demon of Barnabas Collins* (1969)
8 *Foe of Barnabas Collins* (1969)
9 *Phantom of Barnabas Collins* (1969)
10 *Barnabas Collins versus the warlock* (1969)
11 *Secret of Barnabas Collins* (1969)
12 *Peril of Barnabas Collins* (1969)

13 *Barnabas Collins and the mysterious ghost* (1970)
14 *Barnabas Collins and Quentin's demon* (1970)
15 *Barnabas Collins and the gypsy wish* (1970)
16 *House of dark shadows* (1970)
17 *Barnabas, Quentin and the mummy's curse* (1970)
18 *Barnabas, Quentin and the avenging ghost* (1970)
19 *Barnabas, Quentin and the nightmare assassin* (1970)
20 *Barnabas, Quentin and the crystal coffin* (1970)
21 *Barnabas, Quentin and the haunted cave* (1970)
22 *Barnabas, Quentin and the frightened bride* (1970)
23 *Barnabas, Quentin and the Scorpio curse* (1970)
24 *Barnabas, Quentin and the serpent* (1970)
25 *Barnabas, Quentin and the witch's curse* (1970)
26 *Barnabas, Quentin and the magic potion* (1971)
27 *Barnabas, Quentin and the body snatchers* (1971)
28 *Barnabas, Quentin and Doctor Jekyll's son* (1971)
29 *Barnabas, Quentin and the grave robbers* (1971)
30 *Barnabas, Quentin and the sea ghost* (1971)
31 *Barnabas, Quentin and the mad magician* (1971)
32 *Barnabas, Quentin and the hidden tomb* (1971)
33 *Barnabas, Quentin and the vampire beauty* (1972)

Barnabas Jones series
Stokes, Manning Lee
1 *Wolf howls murder* (1945)
2 *Green for a grave* (1946)

Barnaby and Bell series
Oldfield, Pamela
1 *Barnaby and Bell and the birthday cake* (1985)
2 *Barnaby and Bell and the lost button* (1985)

Barnaby and Miles series
Chan, Melissa
see **Inspector Joe Barnaby and Francesca Miles series**

Barnaby Frost series
Lee, Laurel
1 *Barnaby Frost* (1979)
2 *Barnaby Frost plants a seed* (1980)

Barnaby Grayle series
Sayer, Walter William
1 *Sellers of death* (1940)
2 *Nemesis Club* (1946)
3 *Mine sinister hunt* (1948)

Barnaby series
Helps, Racey
1 *Upside-down medicine* (1946)
2 *Barnaby camps out* (1947)
3 *Barnaby in search of a house* (1948)
4 *Barnaby and the scarecrow* (1953)
5 *Barnaby's spring clean* (1956)

Barnaby series
Johnson, Crockett
1 *Barnaby* (1943)
2 *Barnaby and Mrs O'Malley* (1944)

Barnaby series
Pender, Lydia
1 *Barnaby and the horses* (1961)
Revised edition 1980
2 *Barnaby and the rocket* (1972)

Barnaby series
Shaw, Howard
see **Inspector Barnaby series**
White, Leslie Turner
see **Captain Barnaby series**

Barnaby Shrew series
Augarde, Steve
1 *Barnaby Shrew goes to sea* (1978)
2 *Barnaby Shrew, Black Dan and the mighty Wedgwood* (1979)

Barnaby Skye series
Wheeler, Richard Seabrook
see **Skye's West series**

Barnaby trilogy
Trollope, Frances
see **Widow Barnaby trilogy**

Barnard series
Jacobs, Thomas Curtis Hicks
see **Chief Inspector Barnard series**

Barnavaux series
Mille, Pierre
1 *Under the Tricolor* (1908)
Original edition entitled *Barnavaux et quelques femmes*
2 *Louise and Barnavaux* (1912)
Original edition entitled *Louise et Barnavaux*

Barncraig series
Setoun, Gabriel
1 *Barncraig* (1893)
Episodes in the life of a Scottish village
2 *Sunshine and Haar* (1895)

Barne series
Cousins, Edmund George
see **Colonel Richard Barne series**

Barnery series
Chardonne, Jacques
see **House of Barnery series**

Barnes and Howe series
Franklin, Eugene
see **Berkeley Barnes and Larry Howe series**

Barnes series
Barton, George
see **Bromley Barnes series**
Bowen, Robert Sidney
see **Gerry Barnes series**
Bradley, Marion Zimmer
see **Leslie Barnes series**
Cunliffe, John Arthur
see **Farmer Barnes series**
Gunter, Archibald Clavering
see **Mister Barnes series**
Hilary, Richard
see **Ezell Barnes series**
Nott, Loraine
see **Ceb Barnes series**
Ottolengui, Rodrigues
see **John Barnes series**
Runyan, John
see **Tom Barnes series**

Barnett series
Miller, Ben E
see **Cory Barnett series**

Barney Custer series
Burroughs, Edgar Rice
1 *Eternal lover* (1925)
2 *Mad king* (1926)

Barney Forge and Doctor Saint George Peachy series
Starnes, Richard
1 *Another mug for the bier* (1950)
2 *And when she was bad she was murdered* (1950)
3 *Other body in Grant's Tomb* (1951)

Barney Gantt series
Strange, John Stephen
1 *Bell in the fog* (1936)
2 *Silent witnesses* (1938)
Corpse and the lady
3 *Rope enough* (1938)
Ballot box murders
4 *Picture of the victim* (1940)
5 *Look your last* (1943)
6 *Make my bed soon* (1948)
7 *Deadly beloved* (1952)
8 *House on Ninth Street* (1976)

Barney Hyde series
Brent, Nigel
1 *Scarlet lily* (1953)
2 *Motive for murder* (1954)
3 *Blood in the bank* (1954)
4 *Dig the grave deep* (1955)
5 *Murder swings high* (1956)
6 *Leopard died too* (1957)
7 *Golden angel* (1958)
8 *Badger in the dusk* (1959)
9 *No space for murder* (1960)
10 *Spider in the web* (1960)

Barney series
Blyton, Enid
1 *Rockingdown mystery* (1949)
2 *Rilloby Fair mystery* (1950)
3 *Ring o'Bells mystery* (1951)
4 *Rubadub mystery* (1952)
5 *Rat-a-tat mystery* (1956)
6 *Ragamuffin mystery* (1959)

Barney series
Butler, Dorothy
1 *My brown bear Barney* (1989)
2 *My brown bear Barney in trouble* (1993)

Barney series
Casserley, Anne
1 *About Barney* (1957)
2 *Barney the donkey* (1960)

Barney series
Chase, James Hadley
see **Al Barney series**
Weir, Rosemary
see **Uncle Barney series**

Barnum series
Goulart, Ron
1 *Fire-eater* (1970)
2 *Death cell* (1971)
3 *Plunder* (1972)
4 *Shaggy planet* (1972)
5 *Whiff of madness* (1976)
6 *Wicked cyborg* (1978)
7 *Empire 99* (1980)
8 *Cyborg king* (1981)
9 *Daredevils, Ltd.* (1987)
Companion volume: *Spacehawk, Inc.*, 1974

Barnwell Brownie Guide Pack series
Sykes, Pamela
1 *Air day for the Brownies* (1968)
2 *Brownies at the zoo* (1969)
3 *Brownies and the fire* (1970)
4 *Brownies on television* (1972)
5 *Brownies in hospital* (1974)
6 *Brownies throw a party* (1976)
7 *Brownies and the flood* (1987)

Baron Munchausen series
This sequence has four authors
Raspe, Rudolf Erich
1 *Baron Munchausen's narrative of his marvellous travels and campaigns* (1785)
Many other editions including additional stories all published as by Raspe
Numbers 2-7 written by various authors using the pseudonym Rudolf Erich Raspe include further adventures with some overlapping text
2 *Sequel to the adventures of Baron Munchausen* (1792)
Humbly dedicated to Mr Bruce the Abyssinian traveller, as the Baron conceives it may be of some service to him making another expedition in Abyssinia
3 *Travels by sea and land of the renowned Baron Munchausen* (1803)
Including a tour through the United States in the year 1803
4 *Munchausen at Walcheron* (1811)
Exploits at Walcheron, the Dardanelles, Talavera, Cintra, etc.
5 *Gulliver revived* (1813)
Including a tour of the United States of America in 1803 and the first two chapters of a second tour in 1810
6 *Surprising travels and adventures of Baron Munchausen* (1819)
To which is added a sequel containing his expedition into Africa
7 *Munchausen at the Pole* (1819)
Together with a correct list of the curiosities brought home and deposited in the Museum and Tower of London
Bangs, John Kendrick
8 *Mister Munchausen* (1901)
A true account of some of the recent adventures beyond the Styx
Worfel, W G
9 *Munchausen XX* (1904)
The wondrous but veracious happenings which befell my ancestors
Brandeis, Julian Walter
10 *Extraordinary exploits and experiences of Munchausen, M.D.* (1924)

Baron series
Brett, John Michael
see **Hugo Baron series**
Daniels, Norman A
see **Bruce Baron series**

Baron series
Morton, Anthony
1 *Meet the Baron* (1937)
Man in the blue mask
2 *Baron returns* (1937)
Return of Blue Mask
3 *Baron at bay* (1938)
Blue Mask at bay
4 *Baron again* (1938)
Salute Blue Mask!
5 *Alias the Baron* (1939)
Alias Blue Mask
6 *Baron at large* (1939)
Challenge Blue Mask!
7 *Versus the Baron* (1940)
Blue Mask strikes again
8 *Call for the Baron* (1940)
Blue Mask victorious
9 *Baron comes back* (1943)
10 *Case for the Baron* (1945)
11 *Reward for the Baron* (1945)
12 *Career for the Baron* (1946)
13 *Baron and the beggar* (1947)
14 *Rope for the Baron* (1948)
15 *Blame the Baron* (1949)
16 *Books for the Baron* (1949)
17 *Cry for the Baron* (1950)
18 *Trap the Baron* (1950)
19 *Shadow the Baron* (1951)
20 *Attack the Baron* (1951)
21 *Warn the Baron* (1952)
22 *Baron goes east* (1953)
23 *Danger for the Baron* (1953)
24 *Baron in France* (1953)
25 *Baron goes fast* (1954)
26 *Nest egg for the Baron* (1954)
Deaf, dumb and blonde
27 *Help from the Baron* (1955)
28 *Hide the Baron* (1956)
29 *Frame the Baron* (1957)
Double frame
30 *Red-Eye for the Baron* (1958)
Blood red
31 *Black for the Baron* (1959)
If anything happened to Hester

32 *Salute for the Baron* (1960)
33 *Branch for the Baron* (1961)
Baron branches out
34 *Bad for the Baron* (1962)
Baron and the stolen legacy
35 *Sword for the Baron* (1963)
Baron and the Mogul sword
36 *Baron on board* (1964)
37 *Baron and the Chinese puzzle* (1965)
38 *Sport for the Baron* (1966)
39 *Affair for the Baron* (1967)
40 *Baron and the missing old masters* (1968)
41 *Baron and the unfinished portrait* (1969)
42 *Last laugh for the Baron* (1970)
43 *Baron goes a-buying* (1971)
44 *Baron and the arrogant artist* (1972)
45 *Burgle the Baron* (1973)
46 *Baron, king-maker* (1975)
47 *Love for the Baron* (1979)

Baron Trump series
Lockwood, Ingersoll
1 *Travels and adventures of Little Baron Trump and his wonderful dog Bulger* (1890)
2 *Baron Trump's marvellous underground journey* (1893)

Baron Veseloffsky series
Horler, Sydney
1 *False-face* (1926)
2 *Miss Mystery* (1928)

Baron Von Kaz series
Teilhet, Darwin Le Ora
1 *Ticking terrors murders* (1935)
2 *Feather cloak murders* (1936)
Co-author: Hildegarde Tolman Teilhet
3 *Crimson hair murders* (1936)
Co-author: Hildegarde Tolman Teilhet
4 *Broken face murders* (1940)
Co-author: Hildegarde Tolman Teilhet

Baroness Penelope Saint-John Orsini series
Kenyon, Paul
1 *Ecstasy connection* (1974)
2 *Diamonds are for dying* (1974)
3 *Death is a ruby light* (1974)
4 *Hard-core murder* (1974)
5 *Operation Doomsday* (1974)
6 *Sonic slave* (1974)
7 *Flicker of doom* (1974)
8 *Black gold* (1975)

Barr Breed series
Ballinger, Bill Sanborn
1 *Body in the bed* (1948)
2 *Body beautiful* (1949)

Barr series
Wells, Helen
see **Vicki Barr series**

Barradine series
Jepson, Edgar
see **Lord Barradine series**

Barrett Lake series
Singer, Shelley
1 *Following Jane* (1993)
2 *Picture of David* (1993)
3 *Searching for Sara* (1994)

Barrett series
Percy, Walker
see **Will Barrett series**

Barrie series
Reynolds, Adrian
see **Professor Dennis Barrie series**

Barrin series
Lane, Gret
see **John Barrin series**

Barrington Hewes-Bradford series
Hamilton, Adam
see **Peacemaker series**

Barron series
Darby, Ruth
see **Peter and Janet Barron series**
Jones, Raymond F
see **Ron Barron series**

Barrow brothers series
Bechdolt, Jack
1 *Hidden waters* (1931)
2 *Frozen treasure* (1931)
3 *Race of the rails* (1931)
4 *Jungle diamonds* (1931)
5 *Lost Vikings* (1931)

Barrow family series
Clark, Joan
1 *Wild man of the woods* (1985)
2 *Moons of Madeleine* (1987)

Barrow series
Quarry, Nick
see **Jake Barrow series**

Barrows series
Eades, Maud L
see **Winston Barrows series**

Barry College of Technology series
Lewis, Catherine
see **Lisa Thomas series**

Barry Donovan series
Wright, Steve
1 *Love, Avalon* (1990)
2 *Drop in the ocean* (1991)
3 *Break in the traffic* (1992)

Barry Kegan series
Vinter, Michael
1 *Place of execution* (1969)
2 *Rat in a trap* (1971)
3 *Wounds of treason* (1972)

Barry Link series
Vigilant
1 *Lynx, V.C.* (1936)
2 *Lynx, spyflyer* (1936)
3 *Lynx, counterspy* (1937)
4 *Lynx, V.C., flies again* (1944)

Barry Lyndon series
This sequence has two authors
Thackeray, William Makepeace
1 *Memoirs of Barry Lyndon, Esq.* (1844)
Barry Lyndon
Luck of Barry Lyndon
Wood, Christopher
2 *Further adventures of Barry Lyndon by himself* (1976)

Barry McKenzie series
Humphries, Barry
Cartoon stories reprinted from *Private Eye*
1 *Wonderful world of Barry McKenzie* (1968)
2 *Bazza pulls it off* (1971)
3 *Barry McKenzie holds his own* (1974)

Barry O'Dell series
Chipperfield, Robert Orr
1 *Unseen hands* (1920)
2 *Man in the jury box* (1921)

Barry Parker series
Mogridge, Stephen
1 *Barry and the Hurricane Squadron* (1960)
2 *Barry and the Circus raids* (1961)
3 *Barry and the V weapons* (1963)

Barry series
Brand, Max
see **Dan Barry series**
O'Hara, Kenneth
see **Alun Barry series**
Rowe, Anne
see **Inspector Barry series**

Barry series
Tring, A Stephen
1 *Barry's exciting year* (1951)
2 *Barry gets his wish* (1952)
3 *Barry's great day* (1954)

Barrytown trilogy
Doyle, Roddy
1 *Commitments* (1988)
2 *Snapper* (1990)
3 *Van* (1991)

Barsac mission series
Verne, Jules
1 *Into the Niger Bend* (1919)
Original edition entitled *L'etonnante aventure de la Mission Barsac*, part 1
2 *City in the Sahara* (1919)
Original edition entitled *L'etonnante aventure de la Mission Barsac*, part 2

Barsetshire series
Thirkell, Angela
1 *High Rising* (1933)
2 *Wild strawberries* (1934)
3 *Demon in the house* (1934)
4 *August folly* (1936)
5 *Summer half* (1937)
6 *Pomfret Towers* (1938)
7 *Brandons* (1939)
8 *Before lunch* (1939)
9 *Cheerfulness breaks in* (1940)
10 *Northbridge Rectory* (1941)
11 *Marling Hall* (1942)
12 *Growing up* (1943)
13 *Headmistress* (1944)
14 *Miss Bunting* (1945)
15 *Peace breaks out* (1946)
16 *Private enterprise* (1947)
17 *Love among the ruins* (1948)
18 *Old Bank House* (1949)
19 *County chronicle* (1950)
20 *Duke's daughter* (1951)
21 *Happy returns* (1952)
22 *Jutland Cottage* (1953)
23 *What did it mean?* (1954)
24 *Enter Sir Robert* (1955)
25 *Never too late* (1956)
26 *Double affair* (1957)
27 *Close quarters* (1958)
28 *Love at all ages* (1959)
29 *Three score and ten* (1961)
Completed by Caroline Alice Lejeune after the author's death

Barsetshire series
Trollope, Anthony
see **Chronicles of Barsetshire series**

Barstow series
Montgomery, Rutherford George
see **Kent Barstow series**

Bart Challis series
Nolan, William Francis
1 *Death is for losers* (1968)
2 *White cad cross-up* (1969)

Bart Condor series
Wright, Wade
1 *Suddenly you're dead* (1964)
2 *Blood in the ashes* (1964)
3 *Hearse waiting* (1965)
4 *Until she dies* (1965)
5 *Blonde target* (1966)
6 *Two faces of death* (1970)

Bart Gould series
Milton, Joseph
1 *President's agent* (1963)
Title page has the author's name as Joseph Hilton
2 *Assignment assassination* (1964)
Running spy
3 *Worldbreaker* (1964)
4 *Big blue death* (1965)
5 *Baron Sinister* (1965)
6 *Death makers* (1966)
7 *Man who bombed the world* (1966)
8 *Operation, World War Three* (1966)

Bart Hardin series
Alexander, David
1 *Terror on Broadway* (1954)
2 *Paint the town black* (1954)
3 *Shoot a sitting duck* (1955)
4 *Murder of Whistler's brother* (1956)
5 *Die, little goose* (1956)
6 *Death of Humpty Dumpty* (1957)
7 *Hush-a-bye murder* (1957)
8 *Dead, man, dead* (1959)

Barth series
Howe, James
see **Sebastian Barth series**
Schier, Norma
see **Kay Barth series**

Bartholomew Bandy series
Jack, Donald
see **Journals of Bartholomew Bandy series**

Bartholomew Dane series
Dark, Rex
1 *Ming vase mystery* (1936)
2 *Wardour Street mystery* (1936)
3 *Dead men tell* (1937)
4 *Channing affair* (1937)
5 *Invisible hand* (1937)
6 *Uranian jewel case* (1939)
7 *Spy two hundred and twenty two* (1940)

Bartholomew series
Carroll, John Richard
see **Don Bartholomew series**
Gunning, Sally
see **Peter Bartholomew series**
Richards, Kel
see **Ben Bartholomew series**

Bartlett series
Elias, David
see **Nell Bartlett series**
Johnson, Martha
see **Ann Bartlett series**

Bartley series
Dutton, Charles Judson
see **John Bartley series**

Barton and Best series
Pearson, Parry
see **Jeremy Barton and Samuel Best series**

Barton family series
Sykes, Pamela
1 *Flying summer* (1966)
2 *Flight to an island* (1970)

Barton series
Boylston, Helen Dore
see **Sue Barton series**
Jones, Elwyn
see **Dick Barton series**

Barton trilogy
Busby, Francis Marion
see **Demu trilogy**
Gibbs, Philip
see **John Barton trilogy**

Barty Dale series
Smith, Cicely Fox
1 *Ship aground* (1940)
2 *Painted ports* (1948)

Baseball history series
Seymour, Harold
1 *Early years* (1960)
2 *Golden age* (1971)
3 *People's game* (1990)

Baseball Joe series
Chadwick, Lester
1 *Baseball Joe of the Silver Stars* (1912)
Alternative title: The rivals of Riverside
2 *Baseball Joe on the school nine* (1912)
Alternative title: Pitching for the blue banner
3 *Baseball Joe at Yale* (1913)
Alternative title: Pitching for the college championship
4 *Baseball Joe in the Central League* (1914)
Alternative title: Making good as a professional pitcher
5 *Baseball Joe in the Big League* (1915)
Alternative title: A young pitcher's hardest struggles
6 *Baseball Joe on the Giants* (1916)
Alternative title: Making good as a twirler in the metropolis
7 *Baseball Joe in the World Series* (1917)
Alternative title: Pitching for the championship
8 *Baseball Joe around the world* (1918)
Alternative title: Pitching on a grand tour
9 *Baseball Joe, home run king* (1922)
Alternative title: The greatest pitcher and batter on record
10 *Baseball Joe saving the League* (1923)
Alternative title: Breaking up a great conspiracy
11 *Baseball Joe, captain of the team* (1924)
Alternative title: Bittle struggles on the diamond
12 *Baseball Joe, champion of the League* (1925)
Alternative title: The record that was worth while
13 *Baseball Joe, club owner* (1926)
Alternative title: Putting the home town on the map
14 *Baseball Joe, pitching wizard* (1928)
Alternative title: Triumphs on and off the diamond

Baseball series
James, Laurence
1 *Grand slam* (1988)
2 *Home run* (1988)

Baseball series
Witwer, Harry Charles
1 *From baseball to Boches* (1918)
2 *Smile a minute* (1919)

Basi series
Saro-Wiwa, Ken
see **Mister B series**

Basic Black series
Black, Arthur
Humorous pieces by a Canadian television show host
1 *Basic Black* (1981)
2 *Back to Black* (1986)
3 *That old Black magic* (1989)
4 *Arthur, Arthur* (1991)

Basil Brush series
Firmin, Peter
1 *Basil Brush goes boating* (1969)
2 *Basil Brush goes flying* (1969)
Numbers 1 and 2 also published in one volume entitled *Two tales of Basil Brush*, 1982
3 *Basil Brush in the jungle* (1970)
Numbers 1-3 also published in one volume entitled *Three tales of Basil Brush*, volume 1, 1979
4 *Basil Brush at the seaside* (1970)
Basil Brush at the beach
Numbers 3 and 4 also published in one volume entitled *Basil Brush takes off*, 1983
5 *Basil Brush finds treasure* (1971)
6 *Basil Brush and the dragon* (1971)
Basil Brush and a dragon
7 *Basil Brush gets a medal* (1973)
8 *Basil Brush builds a house* (1973)
Numbers 6-8 also published in one volume entitled *Three tales of Basil Brush*, volume 2, 1979
9 *Basil Brush on the trail* (1979)
10 *Basil Brush and the windmills* (1979)

Basil Chimpy series
Judah, Aaron
1 *Basil Chimpy isn't bright* (1959)
2 *Basil Chimpy's comic right* (1960)

Basil of Baker Street series
Titus, Eve
1 *Basil of Baker Street* (1958)
2 *Basil and the lost colony* (1964)
3 *Basil and the pygmy cats* (1971)
4 *Basil in Mexico* (1976)
5 *Basil in the Wild West* (1981)

Basil Seal series
Waugh, Evelyn
1 *Black mischief* (1932)
2 *Put out more flags* (1942)

Basil series
Hobson, Polly
see **Inspector Basil series**

Basil Willing series
McCloy, Helen
1 *Dance of death* (1938)
Design for dying
2 *Man in the moonlight* (1940)
3 *Deadly truth* (1941)
4 *Who's calling* (1942)
5 *Cue for murder* (1942)
6 *Goblin market* (1943)
7 *One that got away* (1945)
8 *Through a glass darkly* (1950)
9 *Alias Basil Willing* (1951)
10 *Long body* (1955)
11 *Two-thirds of a ghost* (1956)
12 *Mister Splitfoot* (1968)
13 *Burn this* (1980)
Also two stories featuring Basil Willing in *Singing diamonds*, 1965, also published as *Surprise, surprise*

Basnett series
Ferrars, Elizabeth
see **Andrew Basnett series**

Basque trilogy
Laxalt, Robert
1 *Sweet promised land* (1986)
2 *Basque hotel* (1989)
3 *Governor's mansion* (1994)
Companion volume: *In a hundred graves, a Basque portrait*, 1972

Bass series
Anthony, David
see **Stanley Bass series**
Cameron, Eleanor
see **Tyco Bass series**
Johnston, Terry Conrad
see **Titus Bass series**
Truss, Seldon
see **Inspector Bass series**

Bassett and Gregory series
Stratton, Roy
see **Scott Gregory and Justin Bassett series**

Bassett series
Cooper, Gordon
see **Kate Bassett series**
Ryland, Clive
see **Chief Inspector George Bassett series**

Bastable family series
Nesbit, Edith
1 *Story of the Treasure Seekers* (1899)
Treasure Seekers
2 *Wouldbegoods* (1901)
3 *New Treasure Seekers* (1904)
Numbers 1-3 also published in one volume entitled *The Bastable children*, 1928
4 *Oswald Bastable and others* (1905)

Bastable series
Moorcock, Michael
see **Oswald Bastable series**

Bastard series
Newman, Gordon F
see **Terry Sneed series**

Bastian series
Wormser, Richard
see **Lieutenant Andy Bastian series**

Bastion series
Harrison, Richard
see **Chief Inspector William Bastion series**
Holt, Gavin
see **Professor Luther Bastion series**

Bat Hardin series
Reynolds, Mack
1 *Commune 2000A.D.* (1974)
2 *Towers of Utopia* (1975)
3 *Rolltown* (1976)
4 *Police patrol, 2000A.D.* (1977)

Bat Masterson series
This sequence has two authors; based on a television series
O'Connor, Richard
1 *Bat Masterson* (1958)
Lee, Wayne
2 *Bat Masterson* (1960)

Batarde series
Leduc, Violette
1 *Batarde* (1964)
Original edition entitled *La batarde*
2 *Mad in pursuit* (1970)
Original edition entitled *La folie en tete*

Batchelor series
Keyes, Frances Parkinson
1 *Steamboat Gothic* (1952)
2 *Larry Vincent* (1953)
One volume edition entitled *Steamboat Gothic*, 1952

Bateman family series
Masters, John
1 *Ravi Lancers* (1972)
2 *Himalayan concerto* (1976)

Bates and Jones series
Floren, Lee
see **Judge Lemanuel Bates and Tobacco Jones series**

Bates series
Bloch, Robert
see **Psycho series**
Cresswell, Helen
see **Posy Bates series**
Shreve, Susan Richards
see **Joshua T Bates series**

Bathurst series
Flynn, Brian
see **Anthony Bathurst series**
Lynch, Lawrence L
see **Neil Bathurst series**

Batman series
This sequence has six authors
Lyon, Winston
1 *Batman versus the fearsome foursome* (1966)
Based on a screenplay
2 *Batman versus the three villains of doom* (1966)
Based on a television series
Wenk, Richard
3 *Doomsday prophecy* (1986)
Gardner, Craig Shaw
4 *Batman* (1989)
Based on a moving picture
5 *Batman murders* (1990)
Greenberg, Martin Harry
6 *Further adventures of Batman* (1990)
Short stories
7 *Further adventures of the Joker* (1990)
Short stories
Lansdale, Joe Richard
8 *Captured by the engines* (1991)
Hawke, Simon
9 *To stalk a specter* (1991)
Based on a moving picture
Gardner, Craig Shaw
10 *Batman returns* (1992)
Based on a moving picture
Companion volumes: *Batman*, by Hal Schuster, 1986, *The official Batman handbook*, by Joel Eisner, 1986, *Batman official souvenir magazine*, by Gary Gerani, 1989, *Batmania, plus the story of the incredible Batman television revival*, by James Van Hise, 1989, *The serial adventures of Batman*, by James Van Hise, 1989, *Tales of the dark knight, Batman's first fifty years, 1939-1989*, by Mark Vaz, 1989

Battle Birds and Dusty Ayres series
Bowen, Robert Sidney
see **Dusty Ayres and his Battle Birds series**

Battle circle trilogy
Anthony, Piers
1 *Sos the rope* (1968)
2 *Var the stick* (1972)
3 *Neq the sword* (1975)
One volume edition entitled Battle circle, 1978

Battle series
Christie, Agatha
see **Superintendent Battle series**

Battleship boys series
Patchin, Frank Gee
1 *Battleship boys at sea* (1910)
Alternative title: Two apprentices in Uncle Sam's Navy
2 *Battleship boys' first step upward* (1911)
Alternative title: Winning their grades as petty officers
3 *Battleship boys in foreign service* (1911)
Alternative title: Earning new ratings in European seas
4 *Battleship boys in the tropics* (1912)
Alternative title: Upholding the American flag in a Honduras revolution
5 *Battleship boys under fire* (1916)
Alternative title: The dash for the besieged Kam Shan Mission
6 *Battleship boys in the wardroom* (1918)
Alternative title: Winning their commissions as line officers
7 *Battleship boys with the Adriatic chasers* (1918)
Alternative title: Blocking the path of the undersea raiders
8 *Battleship boys on sky patrol* (1918)
Alternative title: Fighting the Hun from above the clouds

Battlesquad 1942 series
Bradley, Jack
1 *Alamein attack* (1982)
2 *Slaughter on Sicily* (1983)
3 *Killer winter* (1984)
4 *Bloody bridgehead* (1984)

Battlestar Galactica series
Larson, Glen A
1 *Battlestar Galactica* (1978)
Co-author: Robert Thurston
2 *Cyclon death machine* (1979)
Co-author: Robert Thurston
3 *Tombs of Kobol* (1979)
Co-author: Robert Thurston
4 *Young warriors* (1980)
Co-author: Robert Thurston
5 *Galactica discovers earth* (1980)
Co-author: Mike Resnick
6 *Living legend* (1982)
Co-author: Nicholas Yermakov
7 *War of the gods* (1982)
Co-author: Robert Thurston
8 *Greetings from earth* (1983)
Co-author: Ron Goulart
9 *Experiment in Terra* (1984)
Co-author: Ron Goulart
10 *Long patrol* (1984)
Co-author: Ron Goulart
11 *Nightmare machine* (1985)
Co-author: Robert Thurston
12 *Die, Chameleon!* (1986)
Co-author: Robert Thurston
13 *Apollo's war* (1987)
Co-author: Robert Thurston
14 *Surrender the Galactica!* (1988)
Co-author: Robert Thurston
Companion volumes: *Battlestar Galactica*, by James A Lely, 1979, *The Battlestar Galactica storybook*, by Charles Edward Mercer, 1979, *Encyclopedia Galactica, from the fleet library aboard the Battlestar Galactica*, by Bruce R Kraus, 1979

BattleTech series
This sequence has three authors
Keith, William Henry
1 *Decision at Thunder Rift* (1986)
2 *Mercenary's star* (1987)
3 *Price of glory* (1987)
Mayhar, Ardath
4 *Sword and the dagger* (1987)
Charrette, Robert N
5 *Heir to the dragon* (1989)
6 *Wolves on the border* (1989)

Battletech series: Blood of Kerensky trilogy
Stackpole, Michael
see **Blood of Kerensky trilogy**

Battletech series: Warrior trilogy
Stackpole, Michael
see **Warrior trilogy**

Battling Mendez series
Marshall, William Leonard
1 *Manila Bay* (1986)
2 *Whisper* (1988)

Batts series
Dewey, Thomas Blanchard
see **Singer Batts series**
Gleitzman, Morris
see **Rowena Batts series**

Batwing Jones trilogy
Madison, Holt
1 *Brush country killers* (1952)
2 *Lawless marshal* (1955)
3 *Killers' round-up* (1958)

Baum series
Colver, Anne
see **Barbara Baum series**
Kartun, Derek
see **Alfred Baum series**

Bawtrey series
Enefer, Douglas
see **Sam Bawtrey series**

Bax series
Collinson, Roger
see **Bobby Bax series**

Baxter series
Blair, Marcia
see **Tory Baxter series**
Edwards, Sylvia
see **Sally Baxter series**

Baxter series
Forsyth, Anne
1 *Baxter the travelling cat* (1981)
2 *Baxter and the golden pavements* (1984)
3 *Baxter by the sea* (1987)

Bayard series
Seifert, Elizabeth
1 *Substitute doctor* (1957)
2 *New doctor* (1958)
Doctor Jamie
3 *Doctor on trial* (1959)
4 *Honor of Doctor Shelton* (1962)
Honour of Doctor Shelton
5 *Doctor comes to Bayard* (1964)
6 *Doctor with a mission* (1967)
7 *Doctor in judgment* (1971)
8 *Doctor's destiny* (1972)
9 *Four doctors, four wives* (1975)
10 *Doctor's desperate hour* (1976)

Bayles series
Arnold, Margot
see **China Bayles series**

Bayless family series
Finlay, D G
see **Watchman chronicles series**

Baynes clan trilogy
McCord, John S
1 *Montana horseman* (1990)
2 *Texas comebacker* (1991)
3 *Wyoming giant* (1992)

Baynes series
Bell, Vicars
see **Doctor Douglas Baynes series**

Be a winner series
Coombs, Charles Ira
1 *Be a winner in baseball* (1973)
2 *Be a winner in ice hockey* (1974)
3 *Be a winner in football* (1974)
4 *Be a winner in tennis* (1975)
5 *Be a winner in basketball* (1975)
6 *Be a winner in track and field* (1976)
7 *Be a winner in horsemanship* (1976)
8 *Be a winner in soccer* (1977)
9 *Be a winner in skiing* (1977)
10 *Be a winner in windsurfing* (1983)

Bea and Lyon Wentworth series
Forrest, Richard
see **Lyon and Bea Wentworth series**

Beachcomber series
Banfield, Edmund James
1 *Confessions of a beachcomber* (1908)
2 *My tropic isle* (1911)
3 *Tropic days* (1918)
4 *Last leaves from Dunk Island* (1925)

Beagle series
Chanslor, Torrey
see **Lutie and Amanda Beagle series**
Gruber, Frank
see **Otis Beagle series**

Beaky Amyard series
Lister, Stephen
see **Kilakura series**

Beaky and his band series
Lloyd, Jeremy
see **Captain Beaky and his band series**

Beale series
Penny, Rupert
see **Chief Inspector Edward Beale series**

Beans series
Fowler, Richard
1 *Book-full of beans* (1978)
2 *Bus-full of beans* (1979)
3 *Bean ABC* (1980)
4 *Bean 123* (1981)

Beans series
Moffatt, Frank
see **Farmer Beans series**

Beany Malone series
Weber, Lenora Mattingly
1 *Meet the Malones* (1944)
2 *Beany Malone* (1948)
3 *Leave it to Beany* (1950)
4 *Beany and the beckoning road* (1952)
5 *Beany has a secret life* (1955)
6 *Make a wish for me* (1956)
7 *Happy birthday, dear Beany* (1957)
8 *More the merrier* (1958)
9 *Bright star falls* (1959)
10 *Welcome stranger* (1960)
11 *Pick a new dream* (1961)
12 *Tarry awhile* (1962)
13 *Something borrowed, something blue* (1963)
14 *Come back, wherever you are* (1969)
Companion volume: *Beany Malone cookbook*, 1971

Beany series
Bassett, Lisa
1 *Clock for Beany* (1985)
2 *Beany and Scamp* (1987)
3 *Beany wakes up for Christmas* (1988)

Bear and Duck series
Delton, Judy
1 *Pet for Bear and Duck* (1982)
2 *Bear and Duck on the run* (1985)

Bear child series
Rockwell, Anne Foote
1 *Bear child's book of hour* (1987)
2 *Bear child's book of special days* (1989)

Bear Creek series
Howard, Robert Ervin
see **Breckinridge Elkins series**

Bear Dinkum series
Curtis, Neil
1 *Bear Dinkum* (1988)
2 *Bear Dinkum drops his guts* (1990)

Bear for all seasons series
Roy, Anne
1 *Bear for all seasons* (1983)
2 *School bear days* (1983)

Bear hugs series
Alborough, Jez
1 *Where's my teddy?* (1992)
2 *It's the bear!* (1994)

Bear series
Asch, Frank
1 *Moon Bear* (1978)
2 *Starbaby* (1980)
3 *Happy birthday, Moon* (1982)
4 *Moon cake* (1983)
5 *Moongame* (1984)
6 *Skyfire* (1984)
7 *Bear shadow* (1985)
8 *Bear's bargain* (1985)
9 *Goodbye house* (1986)
10 *Moondance* (1993)

Bear series
Browne, Anthony
1 *Bear hunt* (1979)
2 *Bear goes to town* (1982)
3 *Little bear book* (1988)
4 *Bear-y tale* (1989)

Bear series
Campbell, Alan
see **Bromley Bear series**
Carlstrom, Nancy White
see **Jesse Bear series**
Cosgrove, Stephen Edward
see **Bumble B Bear series**
Dicks, Terrance
see **T.R.Bear series**
Kosikowski, Renate
see **Titus Bear series**
Kuratomi, Chizuko
see **Mister Bear series**
Latimer, Jim
see **James Bear series**
Lavelle, Sheila
see **Ursula Bear series**
McPhail, David Michael
see **Henry Bear series**
Oona, Katherine Deme
see **Bobbie Bear series**

Bear series
Prater, John
1 *Bear's bad mood* (1990)
2 *Bear's den* (1992)

Bear series
Pryor, Bonnie
see **Grandpa Bear series**
Runyon, Catherine
see **Mister and Mrs Bear series**
Tourtel, Mary
see **Rupert Bear series**
Van Stockum, Hilda
see **Jeremy Bear series**

Bear series
Yeoman, John
Illustrated by Quentin Blake
1 *Bear's winter house* (1969)
2 *Bear's water picnic* (1970)

Beard and Charleston series
Guthrie, Alfred Bertram
see **Sheriff Chick Charleston and Jason Beard series**

Bears series
Baker, Margaret Joyce
see **Three bears series**

Bears series
Dicks, Terrance
1 *Lost property* (1990)
2 *George and the dragon* (1991)
3 *Steaming Sam* (1992)

Bears series
Wild, Robin
1 *Bears' ABC book* (1977)
2 *Bears' counting book* (1978)

Beast master series
Norton, Andre
see **Arzor series**

Beast series
Smith, James V
1 *Beastmaker* (1988)
2 *Beaststalker* (1988)

Beast series
Stevens, Kathleen
1 *Beast in the bathtub* (1980)
2 *Beast and the babysitter* (1989)
3 *Bully for the Beast!* (1990)

Beast trilogy
Stallman, Robert
1 *Orphan* (1980)
2 *Captive* (1981)
3 *Beast* (1982)
Book of the beast
One volume edition entitled *The book of the beast*, 1982

Beasts in the field series
Fenton, Sylvia
Reminiscences of farm life
1 *All the beasts in the field* (1984)
2 *Creature comforts* (1985)

Beasts series
Belloc, Hilaire
Poems
1 *Bad child's book of beasts* (1896)
2 *More beasts, for worse children* (1897)

Beasts series
Creaton, David
1 *Beasts of my fields* (1977)
2 *Beasts and babies* (1978)
3 *Beasts go west* (1979)

Beasts series
Johnstone, William Wallace
1 *Devil's kiss* (1980)
2 *Devil's heart* (1983)
3 *Devil's touch* (1987)
4 *Devil's cat* (1987)
5 *Devil's laughter* (1992)

Beatrice Bradley series
Mitchell, Gladys
see **Dame Beatrice Bradley series**

Beatrice Chase series
This sequence has two authors
Oxenham, John
1 *My lady of the moor* (1916)
Chase, Beatrice
2 *Twelfth, an amethyst* (1929)

Beatrice series
Anderson, Catherine Corley
see **Sister Beatrice series**

Beatty trilogy
Bonner, Cindy
see **Haywood Beatty trilogy**

Beau Brummell series
Hamilton, Cosmo
1 *Brummell* (1907)
2 *Brummell again* (1909)

Beau Geste series
Wren, Percival Christopher
1 *Beau Geste* (1924)
2 *Beau Sabreur* (1926)
3 *Beau Ideal* (1928)
4 *Good Gestes* (1929)
5 *Spanish Maine* (1935)
Desert heritage

Beau Nash regime romance series
Castle, Agnes
1 *Bath comedy* (1900)
2 *Incomparable Bellairs* (1904)
3 *French Nan* (1905)
4 *Love gilds the scene and women guide the plot* (1912)
5 *Ways of Miss Barbara* (1914)

Beau Pepys series
Hammond, Gerald
1 *Loose screw* (1966)
2 *Fred in situ* (1965)
3 *Mud in his eye* (1967)

Beau Smith and Pogy Rogers series
Ross, Zola Helen
1 *Three down vulnerable* (1946)
2 *One corpse missing* (1948)

Beaufort family series
King, Betty
1 *Lady Margaret* (1965)
2 *Captive James* (1967)
3 *Lord Jasper* (1967)
4 *King's mother* (1969)
5 *Rose both red and white* (1970)
6 *Beaufort secretary* (1970)
7 *Beaufort bastard* (1973)

Beaufort series
Baker, James
see **Cardinal Henry Beaufort series**
Seymour, Arabella
see **Jane Beaufort series**

Beaumont series
Atkins, Meg Elizabeth
see **Inspector Henry Beaumont series**
Jance, Judith A
see **J P Beaumont series**

Beauregard series
Lang, Frances
see **Gillonne de Beauregard series**

Beautiful devil series
Dunn, *Detective*
1 *Beautiful devil* (1923)
2 *Queen of crooks* (1924)

Beautiful Gunner series
Lee, Norma
1 *Beautiful Gunner* (1953)
2 *Lover, say it with mink!* (1953)
3 *Another woman's man* (1954)
4 *Broadway jungle* (1954)

Beautiful Joe series
Saunders, Marshall
1 *Beautiful Joe* (1893)
The autobiography of a dog; revised edition 1907
2 *Beautiful Joe's paradise* (1902)

Beautiful room series
White, Edmund
Autobiographical fiction
1 *Boy's own story* (1982)
2 *Beautiful room is empty* (1988)

Beauty and the Beast trilogy
This sequence has two authors; based on a television series
Hambly, Barbara
1 *Beauty and the Beast* (1989)
Emerson, Ru
2 *Masques* (1990)
Hambly, Barbara
3 *Song of Orpheus* (1990)

Beauty of Canada series
Russell, Paul
1 *Beauty of Ontario* (1982)
2 *Beauty of Quebec* (1983)
3 *Beauty of the Maritimes* (1983)
4 *Beauty of British Columbia* (1984)

Beaver and Inspector Cam series
Cockin, Joan
see **Inspector Cam and Beaver series**

Beaver Towers trilogy
Hinton, Nigel
1 *Beaver Towers* (1980)
2 *Witch's revenge* (1981)
3 *Run to Beaver Towers* (1986)

Bebb tetralogy
Buechner, Frederick
see **Leo Bebb tetralogy**

Bech series
Updike, John
1 *Bech, a book* (1970)
2 *Bech is back* (1982)

Beck series
Bodkin, Matthias McDonnell
see **Paul Beck series**
Conway, Peter
see **Lucy Beck series**
Ryland, Clive
see **Inspector Beck series**
Sjowall, Maj
see **Inspector Martin Beck series**

Becket series
Eliot, Thomas Stearns
see **Thomas Becket series**

Beckett series
Crowe, John
see **Buena Costa County series**

Beckman family trilogy
Stirling, Jessica
1 *Deep well at noon* (1979)
Drums of time
2 *Blue evening gone* (1981)
3 *Gates of midnight* (1983)

Becky and Andrew series
Wells, Marian
see **Wedding dress series**

Becky Bryan series
Baxter, Betty
1 *Becky Bryan's secret* (1937)
2 *Unseen enemy* (1938)
3 *Daughter of the coast guard* (1938)

Becky Compton series
Jacberns, Raymond
1 *Becky Compton, ex-dux* (1909)
2 *Schoolgirls' battlefield* (1910)
3 *Uncomfortable term* (1911)

Becky series
Tudor, Tasha
1 *Becky's birthday* (1960)
2 *Becky's Christmas* (1961)

Becky Taylor series
Spencer, Sally
1 *Salt of the earth* (1993)
2 *Up our street* (1994)

Bed-knob and broomstick series
Norton, Mary
1 *Magic bed-knob* (1943)
2 *Bonfires and broomsticks* (1947)
One volume revised edition entitled *Bed-knob and broomstick*, 1957

Bed manners series
Hopton, Ralph
1 *Bed manners* (1936)
2 *Better bed manners* (1936)

Beddoes and Evans series
Jones, Roger William
see **Inspector Evans and Sergeant Beddoes series**

Bede and Bullock series
Byfield, Barbara
see **Simon Bede and Helen Bullock series**

Bedelia series
Parish, Peggy
see **Amelia Bedelia series**

Bedison series
Cobb, Thomas
see **Inspector Bedison series**

Bedtime story-books series
Burgess, Thornton Waldo
1 *Adventures of Reddy Fox* (1913)
2 *Adventures of Johnny Chuck* (1913)
3 *Adventures of Peter Cottontail* (1914)
4 *Adventures of Unc' Billy Possum* (1914)
5 *Adventures of Mister Mocker* (1914)
6 *Adventures of Jerry Muskrat* (1914)
7 *Adventures of Danny Meadow Mouse* (1915)
8 *Adventures of Grandfather Frog* (1915)
9 *Adventures of Chatterer the red squirrel* (1915)
10 *Adventures of Sammy Jay* (1915)
11 *Adventures of Buster Bear* (1916)
12 *Adventures of Old Mr Toad* (1916)
13 *Adventures of Prickly Porky* (1916)
14 *Adventures of Old Man Coyote* (1916)
15 *Adventures of Paddy the beaver* (1917)
16 *Adventures of poor Mrs Quack* (1917)
17 *Adventures of Bobby Coon* (1918)
18 *Adventures of Jimmy Skunk* (1918)
19 *Adventures of Bob White* (1919)
20 *Adventures of Ol' Mistah Buzzard* (1919)

Beebo series
This sequence has two authors; illustrated by Philippe Fix
Ast, Janine
1 *House that Beebo built* (1967)
Original edition entitled *Seraphin et le merveilleux chef d'oeuvre*
Gree, Alain
2 *Beebo and the Fizzimen* (1968)
Original edition entitled *Seraphin contre Seraphin*
3 *Beebo and the funny machine* (1968)
Original edition entitled *Defense de lire Seraphin*

Beechcroft series
Yonge, Charlotte Mary
1 *Scenes and characters* (1847)
2 *Dynevor Terrace* (1857)
3 *Stokesley secret* (1861)
4 *Pillars of the house* (1873)
Alternative title: Under wode, under rode
5 *Two sides of the shield* (1885)
6 *Beechcroft at Rockstone* (1888)
7 *Long vacation* (1895)
8 *Modern broods* (1900)
Alternative title: Developments unlooked for

Beef series
Bruce, Leo
see **Sergeant William Beef series**

Beef Wellington series
Davidson, Max
1 *Beef Wellington blues* (1985)
2 *Well done, Beef Wellington* (1992)

Beeke series
Brooks, Edwy Searles
see **Inspector William Beeke series**

Beekeepers series
Redgrove, Peter
1 *Beekeepers* (1980)
2 *Facilitators* (1982)
Alternative title: Mister Hole-in-the-Day

Beezus series
Cleary, Beverly
1 *Henry and Beezus* (1952)
2 *Beezus and Ramona* (1955)
Companion volume: *Beezus and Ramona diary*, 1986

Before noon trilogy
Sender, Ramon Jose
1 *Chronicle of dawn* (1942)
Original edition entitled *Cronica del Alba*
2 *Violent griffin* (1954)
Original edition entitled *Hipogripo violento*
3 *Villa Julieta* (1957)
Original edition entitled *La quinta Julieta*
One volume edition entitled *Before noon*, 1957

Beggar's Penny series
Coblentz, Catherine
1 *Beggar's Penny* (1943)
2 *Bells of Leyden sing* (1944)

Beginning to learn series
Allington, Richard L
1 *Shapes* (1979)
2 *Numbers* (1979)

Beginning to learn series

3 *Opposites* (1979)
4 *Colors* (1979)
5 *Looking* (1980)
6 *Hearing* (1980)
7 *Tasting* (1980)
8 *Smelling* (1980)
9 *Touching* (1980)
10 *Feelings* (1980)
11 *Thinking* (1981)
12 *Talking* (1981)
13 *Writing* (1981)
14 *Reading* (1981)
15 *Winter* (1981)
16 *Summer* (1981)
17 *Spring* (1981)
18 *Autumn* (1981)
19 *Letters* (1982)
20 *Words* (1982)
21 *Stories* (1982)
22 *Science* (1982)
23 *Time* (1982)
24 *Measuring* (1982)

Beginnings and ends series
Dickson, Gordon Rupert
1 *Beginnings* (1988)
2 *Ends* (1988)

Behaviorist trilogy
Skinner, Burrhus Frederic
Autobiography
1 *Particulars of my life* (1976)
2 *Shaping of a behaviorist* (1979)
3 *Matter of consequences* (1983)

Behind that mask series
Keeler, Harry Stephen
1 *Finger, finger!* (1938)
2 *Behind that mask* (1938)
Expanded from the original one-volume edition entitled *Behind that mask*, 1933

Behind the lines series
Adair, James B
see **World War III series**

Beiderbecke series
Plater, Alan
1 *Beiderbecke affair* (1985)
2 *Beiderbecke tapes* (1986)
3 *Beiderbecke connection* (1992)

Beklan Empire series
Adams, Richard
1 *Shardik* (1974)
2 *Maia* (1984)

Bel Air General series
Sutton, Jessica
1 *Bel Air General* (1987)
2 *Price of life* (1987)
3 *Masks and faces* (1987)
4 *Vital signs* (1988)
5 *Critical condition* (1988)
6 *Desperate remedy* (1988)
7 *Strong medicine* (1988)
9 *Kill or cure* (1989)
10 *High risk* (1989)
11 *Emergency* (1989)

Bel series
Carr, Charles
1 *Colonists of space* (1954)
2 *Salamander war* (1955)

Belcourt series
Rougvie, Cameron
see **Robert Belcourt series**

Belden series
Campbell, Julie
see **Trixie Belden series**

Beldrum and Blair series
Hay, Lindsay Fitzgerald
see **Archibald Beldrum and Nigel Blair series**

Belfer series
Pushker, Gloria
see **Toby Belfer series**

Belford series
Weber, Lenora Mattingly
see **Stacy and Katie Rose Belford series**

Belgariad series
Eddings, David
1 *Pawn of prophecy* (1982)
2 *Queen of sorcery* (1982)
3 *Magician's gambit* (1983)
Numbers 1-3 also published in one volume entitled *The Belgariad*, volume 1, 1985
4 *Castle of wizardry* (1984)
5 *Enchanters' end game* (1984)
Numbers 4 and 5 also published in one volume entitled *The Belgariad*, volume 2, 1985

Belgate trilogy
Robertson, Denise
1 *Land of lost content* (1985)
2 *Year of winter* (1986)
3 *Blue remembered hills* (1987)
One volume edition entitled *The land of lost content*, 1988

Belgrade Ballet School series
Curcija-Prodanovic, Nada
1 *Ballerina* (1961)
2 *Ballet on tour* (1972)

Belgravia trilogy
Bingham, Charlotte
1 *Belgravia* (1983)
2 *Country life* (1985)
3 *At home* (1986)

Belinda and Lalage series
Evans, Cherry
1 *Love from Belinda* (1962)
2 *Lalage in love* (1962)

Belinda, Ann and Mike series
Blyton, Enid
see **Mike, Belinda and Ann series**

Belinda Gordon series
Gervaise, Mary
1 *Pony for Belinda* (1959)
2 *Belinda rides to school* (1960)
3 *Belinda's other pony* (1961)
4 *Belinda wins her spurs* (1962)

Belinda, Jane and Cathy series
Bye, Beryl
see **Cathy, Belinda and Jane series**

Belinda series
Awdry, Wilbert
1 *Belinda the beetle* (1959)
2 *Belinda beats the band* (1961)

Belinda series
Blair, Tobin
1 *Belinda* (1902)
2 *Belinda engaged* (1903)

Belinda series
Blyton, Enid
1 *Humpty Dumpty and Belinda* (1949)
2 *Father Christmas and Belinda* (1951)

Belinda series
Brainerd, Eleanor Hoyt
1 *Concerning Belinda* (1905)
2 *Personal conduct of Belinda* (1910)

Belinda series
Brook, Judy
1 *Belinda* (1976)
2 *Belinda and Father Christmas* (1978)

Bell and Barnaby series
Oldfield, Pamela
see **Barnaby and Bell series**

Bell family series
Streatfeild, Noel
1 *Bell family* (1954)
Family shoes
2 *New Town* (1960)
New shoes

Bell series
Bullivant, Cecil Henry
see **Garnett Bell series**

Bell trilogy
Dyce, Gilbert
see **Jenny Bell trilogy**

Bella Pivar series
Black, William
1 *Bella* (1979)
2 *Bella's blessings* (1980)

Bellaire Troop series
Garis, Lilian C
see **Girl Scouts series**

Bellamy family series
Hawkesworth, John
see **Upstairs, downstairs series**

Bellamy series
Horler, Sydney
see **Sir Harker Bellamy series**
Jacobs, Thomas Curtis Hicks
see **Detective Superintendent John Bellamy series**

Bellary Bay series
Welcome, John
1 *Bellary Bay* (1979)
2 *Call to arms* (1985)

Bellbird series
Vernon, Barbara
Based on a television series
1 *Bellbird* (1970)
2 *Big day at Bellbird* (1971)

Belle Creole series
Hentz, Caroline Lee Whiting
1 *Linda* (1850)
The young pilot of the Belle Creole
2 *Robert Graham* (1855)

Belle Isle series
Gaunt, Michael
1 *Belle Isle* (1957)
2 *Invaders* (1959)

Belle of the ballet series
Beardmore, George
1 *Belle of the ballet's gala performance* (1956)
2 *Belle of the ballet's country holiday* (1957)

Belle series
Haedrich, Marcel
Translated from the French
1 *Belle, de Paris* (1968)
2 *Belle in diamonds* (1969)

Belle the bushie series
Richardson, Pat
1 *Belle the bushie* (1991)
2 *Belle on a broomstick* (1992)

Bellecroix and Roath series
Craig, David
see **Stephen Bellecroix and Sheila Roath series**

Bellefleur series
Oates, Joyce Carol
1 *Bellefleur* (1980)
2 *Bloodsmoor romance* (1982)
3 *Mysteries of Winterthurn* (1984)

Belleme series
Wren, Percival Christopher
see **Otho Belleme series**

Bellman series
De Andrea, William Louis
see **Clifford Driscoll series**

Bellman series
Barker, Kathleen Frances
1 *Bellman* (1933)
2 *Bellman carries on* (1934)

Belloni series
Meredith, George
see **Sandra Belloni series**

Bells series
Escott, John
1 *Alarm bells* (1981)
2 *Bells rescue* (1983)
3 *Burglar bells* (1983)
4 *Bell puzzle* (1984)

Bellwattle and Cruikshank series
Thurston, Ernest Temple
1 *Patchwork papers* (1910)
2 *Garden of resurrection* (1911)
Love story of an ugly man
3 *Tares* (1915)
4 *Sheepskins and grey russet* (1919)

Belot series
Aveline, Claude
see **Suite Policiere series**

Beloved cats series
Smyth, John George
1 *Beloved cats* (1963)
2 *Blue Magnolia* (1964)
3 *Ming* (1966)

Beloved son series
Turner, George Reginald
see **Ethical culture series**

Belvie family series
Ross, Jean
1 *Under a glass dome* (1956)
2 *Garden by the river* (1957)

Ben Allison series
Fisher, Clay
1 *Tall men* (1954)
2 *Crossing* (1958)
River of decision
3 *Return of the Tall Man* (1961)
4 *Outcasts of Canyon Creek* (1972)
5 *Apache ransom* (1974)

Ben and Arthur series
Billam, Rosemary
1 *Send for Ben* (1992)
2 *Ben and Arthur* (1992)

Ben and Carrie Porter series
Travis, Elizabeth
1 *Deadlines* (1987)
2 *Under the influence* (1989)
3 *Finders, keepers* (1990)

Ben and Frito series
McHargue, Georgess
1 *Funny bananas* (1975)
2 *Turquoise toad mystery* (1982)

Ben and Kate King series
Smith, Beatrice Schillinger
see **Kate and Ben King series**

Ben and Willard series
This sequence has two authors
Gilbert, Stephen
1 *Ratman's notebooks* (1968)
Willard
Ralston, Gilbert Alexander
2 *Ben* (1972)

Ben Anderson series
Compton, David Guy
1 *Medium for murder* (1963)
2 *Disguise for a dead gentleman* (1964)

Ben Bartholomew series
Richards, Kel
1 *Case of the vanishing corpse* (1990)
2 *Case of the secret assassin* (1992)
3 *Second death* (1993)
4 *Case of the Damascus dagger* (1994)

Ben Camden series
Graat, Heinrich
1 *Revenge of Increase Sewell* (1969)
2 *Devil and Ben Camden* (1970)
3 *Place of demons* (1972)

Ben Clancy series
Bachmann, Lawrence Paul
1 *Legend of Joseph Nokato* (1971)
2 *Ultimate act* (1972)

Ben Corbin series
Crane, Robert
1 *Sergeant Corbin's war* (1964)
2 *Sergeant and the Queen* (1964)
3 *Operation Vengeance* (1965)
4 *Paradise trap* (1967)
5 *Tongue of treason* (1967)
6 *Time running out* (1974)
Out of time

Ben Crandel series
Sinclair, Murray
1 *Tough luck L.A.* (1980)
2 *Only in L.A.* (1982)

Ben Dryden series
Hartmann, Michael
1 *Shadow of the leopard* (1978)
Hunted
2 *Days of thunder* (1980)

Ben Garden series
Pace, Tom
1 *Treasure hunt* (1970)
2 *Fisherman's hunt* (1971)

Ben Gates series
Kyle, Robert
1 *Blackmail, Inc.* (1958)
2 *Model for murder* (1959)
3 *Kill now, pay later* (1960)
4 *Some like it cool* (1962)
5 *Ben Gates is hot* (1964)

Ben Gold series
Turner, Clay
1 *Give a man a gun* (1971)
2 *Go west, Ben Gold* (1974)
3 *Goldd goes to the mountain* (1974)

Ben Gordon series
Ross, Ivan T
1 *Murder out of school* (1960)
2 *Requiem for a schoolgirl* (1961)
3 *Old students never die* (1962)
4 *Man who would do anything* (1963)
5 *Teachers's blood* (1964)

Ben Grant series
Collenette, Eric J
1 *Gruesome tide* (1988)
2 *Ninety feet to the sun* (1984)
3 *Gemini plot* (1985)
4 *Secret of the Kara Sea* (1987)
5 *Monday mutiny* (1987)
6 *Capful of glory* (1988)
7 *Sea-wolf hunter* (1989)

Ben Helm series
Fischer, Bruno
1 *Dead men grin* (1945)
2 *More deaths than one* (1947)
3 *Restless hands* (1949)
4 *Angels fell* (1950)
Flesh was cold
5 *Silent dust* (1950)
6 *Paper circle* (1951)
Stripped for murder

Ben Henry series
Weiss, Mike
1 *No go on Jackson Street* (1987)
2 *All points bulletin* (1989)
3 *Dry and thirsty ground* (1992)

Ben Jolson series
Goulart, Ron
1 *Sword swallower* (1968)
2 *Chameleon Corps, and other shape changers* (1972)
3 *Flux* (1974)
4 *Spacehawk, Inc.* (1974)
5 *Whiff of madness* (1976)

Ben Jonson series
Levi, Peter
1 *Grave witness* (1985)
2 *Knit one, drop one* (1986)

Ben Jurnet series
Haymon, Sylvia T
see **Inspector Ben Jurnet series**

Ben Kane series
Stone, Nick
1 *Kane's war* (1987)
2 *Assassin* (1987)
3 *Death waves* (1987)
4 *Poisoned treasure* (1987)
5 *Depth charge* (1987)
6 *Crackdown* (1987)

Ben Krahmer series
Krasney, Samuel A
see **Lieutenant Ben Krahmer series**

Ben Louis series
Russell, Enid Sherry
1 *She should have cried on Monday* (1968)
2 *Nice enough to murder* (1971)
3 *Dead easy* (1992)

Ben Lucias series
Howes, Royce
see **Captain Ben Lucias series**

Ben Martin series
Messmann, Jon
see **Revenger series**

Ben O'Malley series
Lysaght, Brian
1 *Special circumstances* (1983)
2 *Sweet deals* (1985)

Ben O'Neal and Teetoncey trilogy
Taylor, Theodore
see **Teetoncey and Ben O'Neal trilogy**

Ben Pedley series
Sterling, Stewart
see **Fire Marshal Ben Pedley series**

Ben Bedley series
Sterling, Stewart
1 *Five alarm funeral* (1942)
2 *Where there's smoke* (1946)
3 *Alarm in the night* (1949)
4 *Nightmare at noon* (1951)
5 *Hinges of hell* (1955)
6 *Candle for a corpse* (1957)
Too hot to kill
7 *Fire on Fear Street* (1958)
8 *Dying room only* (1960)
9 *Too hot to handle* (1961)

Ben Safford series
Dominic, R B
see **Congressman Ben Safford series**

Ben series
Bradman, Tony
1 *Let's go, Ben* (1990)
2 *Night, night, Ben* (1991)

Ben series
Foreman, Michael
1 *Ben's box* (1986)
2 *Ben's baby* (1987)

Ben Shock and Charity Tucker series
Buchanan, Patrick
1 *Murder of crows* (1970)
2 *Parliament of owls* (1971)
3 *Requiem of sharks* (1973)
4 *Sounder of swine* (1974)

Ben Slayton series
Sanders, Buck
This pseudonym is used by Thomas Larry Adcock and Jeffrey Frentzen as indicated against each title
1 *Clear and present danger* (1981) [Adcock]
2 *Star of Egypt* (1981) [Frentzen]
3 *Trail of the twisted cross* (1982) [Adcock]
4 *Starshine connection* (1982)
5 *Bayou Brigade* (1982) [Frentzen]

Ben, Sophie and Sarah series
Barrett, Peter
see **Sophie, Sarah and Ben series**

Ben Spence series
Allen, Michael
see **Superintendent Ben Spence series**

Ben Taylor series
Gifford, Griselda
1 *Youngest Taylor* (1963)
2 *Ben's expedition* (1965)

Ben the tramp series
Farjeon, Joseph Jefferson
1 *Number seventeen* (1926)
2 *Crook's shadow* (1927)
3 *House opposite* (1931)
4 *Murderer's trail* (1931)
Phantom fingers
5 *Ben sees it through* (1932)
6 *Little God Ben* (1935)
7 *Detective Ben* (1936)
8 *Number nineteen* (1952)
9 *Ben on the job* (1952)

Ben Tolliver series
Harvey, James Neal
1 *By reason of insanity* (1990)
2 *Painted ladies* (1992)
3 *Flesh and blood* (1994)

Ben, William and Mary series
Furminger, Jo
see **Mary, Ben and William series**

Benasque series
Caillou, Alan
see **Mike Benasque**

Benbow Smith and Frank Garratt series
Wentworth, Patricia
1 *Danger calling* (1931)
2 *Walk with care* (1933)

Bencolin series
Carr, John Dickson
see **Henri Bencolin series**

Bendelbinder and Silverthorn families series
Longstreet, Stephen
see **Dream seekers series**

Bendilow series
Wallace, Carlton
see **Superintendent Edmund Bendilow series**

Benedetti series
De Andrea, William Louis
see **Niccolo Benedetti series**

Benedict and Brazos series
Clay, E Jefferson
see **Duke Benedict and Hank Brazos series**

Benedict Arnold series
Knipe, Emilie Benson
1 *Continental dollar* (1923)
2 *Powder, patches and Patty* (1924)

Benedict Breeze series
Bayne, Isabella
1 *Death and Benedict* (1952)
2 *Cruel as the grave* (1956)

Benedict series
Lee, Elsie
see **Sam Benedict series**
Ronns, Edward
see **Jerry Benedict series**

Benham series
Home, Michael
see **John Benham series**

Benjamin Disraeli series
Edelman, Maurice
1 *Disraeli in love* (1972)
2 *Disraeli rising* (1975)

Benjamin Hooker series
Train, Arthur
1 *Man who rocked the earth* (1915)
2 *Moon maker* (1958)

Benjamin series
Baker, Alan
1 *Benjamin and the box* (1977)
2 *Benjamin bounces back* (1978)
3 *Benjamin's dreadful dream* (1980)
4 *Benjamin's portrait* (1986)
5 *Benjamin's balloon* (1990)
Companion volume: Benjamin's book, 1982

Benjamin series
Garfield, Brian Wynne
see **Paul Benjamin series**
McInerney, Judith Whitelock
see **Judge Benjamin series**

Benjamin Simon series
Dean, Gregory
see **Deputy Commissioner Benjamin Simon series**

Benjamin Tancred series
Cole, George Douglas Howard
see **Doctor Benjamin Tancred series**

Benjie and Simon series
Ballard, Martin
1 *Benjie's portion* (1969)
2 *Speaking drums of Ashanti* (1970)

Benjie series
Lexau, Joan M
1 *Benjie* (1964)
2 *Benjie on his own* (1970)

Benjie series
Walter, Francis V
Illustrated by Violet T Pearson
1 *Here's Benjie* (1976)
A child's animal story book
2 *Benjie and his friends* (1977)
3 *Benjie and the flood* (1978)

Benjy series
Graham, Margaret Bloy
1 *Benjy and the barking bird* (1972)
2 *Benjy's dog house* (1974)

Benn series
McKee, David
see **Mister Benn series**

Bennet family series
This sequence has three authors
Austen, Jane
1 *Pride and prejudice* (1813)

Bennet family series

Barrington, E
2 *Ladies* (1927)
A shining constellation of wit and beauty
Piper, Warrene
3 *Son of John Wintringham* (1930)
New lives
4 *Sun in his own house* (1931)
Full flower

Bennett Island series

Ogilvie, Elisabeth May
1 *High tide at noon* (1944)
2 *Storm tide* (1945)
3 *Ebbing tide* (1947)
4 *How wide the heart* (1959)
5 *Answer to the tide* (1978)
6 *Summer of the osprey* (1987)

Bennett series

Lewis, Elliott
see **Fred Bennett series**
Martin, Robert Lee
see **Jim Bennett series**
Stuart, Anne
see **Maggie Bennett series**
Wood, Ted
see **Reid Bennett series**

Benni Soldano series

Webster, Ernest
1 *Madonna of the black market* (1981)
2 *Cossack hide-out* (1981)
3 *Red alert* (1982)
4 *Venetian spy-glass* (1983)
5 *Verratoli inheritance* (1983)
6 *Million-dollar stand-in* (1983)

Bennion series

Adams, Herbert
see **Major Roger Bennion series**

Benny Cooperman series

Engel, Howard
1 *Suicide murders* (1980)
Suicide notice
2 *Ransom game* (1981)
3 *Murder on location* (1982)
4 *Murder sees the light* (1984)
5 *City called July* (1986)
6 *Victim must be found* (1988)
7 *Dead and buried* (1990)

Benny Kramer series

Weidman, Jerome
1 *Fourth Street East* (1970)
2 *Last respects* (1971)
3 *Tiffany Street* (1974)

Benny of Crab Island series

Hurt, Freda Mary
1 *Crab Island* (1965)
2 *Benny and the dolphin* (1968)
3 *Benny and the space boy* (1970)

Benny series

Garnett, Henry
1 *Rough water brown* (1955)
2 *Secret of the rocks* (1958)

Benny series

Wilmer, Diane
Illustrated by Nicola Smee
1 *Benny* (1985)
The story of a dog
2 *Benny and the football match* (1986)
3 *Benny and the fair* (1986)
4 *Benny and the builders* (1986)
5 *Benny and the jumble sale* (1986)

Benny series

Zach, Cheryl
1 *Benny and the crazy contest* (1991)
2 *Benny and the no-good teacher* (1992)

Benoir family series

Handl, Irene
1 *Sioux* (1965)
2 *Gold tipped pfitzer* (1973)

Benoni series

Hamsun, Knut
1 *Benoni* (1908)
Original edition entitled *Benoni*
2 *Rosa* (1908)
Original edition entitled *Rosa*

Benson Kellogg series

Spicer, Bart
1 *Act of anger* (1962)
2 *Kellogg Junction* (1969)

Benson series

Adler, David A
see **T F Benson series**
Ewing, Kathryn
see **Marcy Benson series**

Benson-Williams series

Jones, Richard
1 *Age of wonder* (1967)
2 *Tower is everywhere* (1971)

Bent series

Branson, Henry Clay
see **John Bent series**

Bentiron series

Poate, Ernest M
see **Doctor Bentiron series**

Bentley series

Dietrich, Robert
see **Steve Bentley series**
Macdonnell, James Edmond
see **Captain Peter Bentley series**

Benton series

Verral, Charles Spain
see **Brains Benton series**

Benvenuto Brown series

Gill, Elizabeth
1 *Strange holiday* (1931)
Crime coast
2 *What dread hand?* (1932)
3 *Crime de luxe* (1933)

Beppo Tate series

Palmer, Cyril Everard
1 *Wooing of Beppo Tate* (1972)
2 *Beppo Tate and Roy Penner* (1980)
Also contains *The runaway marriage brokers*

Berbora series

Sirota, Mike
1 *Berbora* (1978)
2 *Flight from Berbora* (1978)

Berenger series

Duff, Douglas Valder
see **Bill Berenger series**

Berenstain bears series

Berenstain, Stan
1 *Big honey hunt* (1962)
2 *Bike lesson* (1964)
3 *Bears' picnic* (1966)
4 *Bear Scouts* (1967)
5 *Bears' vacation* (1968)
Bears' holiday
6 *Inside, outside, upside down* (1968)
7 *Bears on wheels* (1969)
8 *Bears' Christmas* (1970)
9 *Old hat, new hat* (1970)
10 *Bears in the night* (1971)
11 *B book* (1971)
12 *C is for clown* (1972)
13 *Bears' almanac* (1973)
Berenstain bears' almanac
A year in bear country, holidays, seasons, weather, actual facts about snow, wind, rain, thunder, lightning, the sun, the moon and lots more
14 *Berenstain bears' nursery tales* (1973)
15 *He bear, she bear* (1974)
16 *Berenstain bears' new baby* (1974)
17 *Bears' nature guide* (1975)
Berenstain bears' nature guide
18 *Bear detectives* (1975)
Alternative title: The case of the missing pumpkin
19 *Berenstain bears' science fair* (1977)
20 *Berenstain bears and the spooky old tree* (1978)
21 *Papa's pizza* (1978)
A Berenstain bear sniffy book
22 *Berenstain bears go to school* (1978)
23 *Berenstain bears and the missing dinosaur bone* (1980)
24 *Berenstain bears' Christmas tree* (1980)
25 *Berenstain bears and the sitter* (1981)
26 *Berenstain bears go to the doctor* (1981)
27 *Berenstain bears' moving day* (1981)
28 *Berenstain bears visit the dentist* (1981)
29 *Berenstain bears get in a fight* (1982)
30 *Berenstain bears go to camp* (1982)
31 *Berenstain bears in the dark* (1982)
32 *Berenstain bears and the messy room* (1983)
33 *Berenstain bears and the truth* (1983)
34 *Berenstain bears and the wild, wild honey* (1983)
35 *Berenstain bears' soccer star* (1983)
36 *Berenstain bears go fly a kite* (1983)
37 *Berenstain bears to the rescue* (1983)
38 *Berenstain bears' trouble with money* (1983)
39 *Berenstain bears and the big election* (1984)
40 *Berenstain bears and too much TV* (1984)
Numbers 25, 28, 31, 32, 40 also published in one volume entitled *The Berenstain bears' take-along library*, 1985
41 *Berenstain bears shoot the rapids* (1984)
42 *Berenstain bears and the neighborly skunk* (1984)
43 *Berenstain bears and the dinosaurs* (1984)
44 *Berenstain bears meet Santa Bear* (1984)
45 *Berenstain bears and mama's new job* (1984)
46 *Berenstain bears and too much junk food* (1985)
47 *Berenstain bears on the moon* (1985)
48 *Berenstain bears learn about strangers* (1985)
49 *Berenstain bears' toy time* (1985)
50 *Berenstain bears forget their manners* (1985)
51 *Berenstain bears get stage fright* (1986)
52 *Berenstain bears, no girls allowed* (1986)
53 *Berenstain bears and the week at grandma's* (1986)
54 *Berenstain bears and too much birthday* (1986)
55 *Berenstain bears go out for the team* (1987)
56 *Berenstain bears, coughing catfish* (1987)
57 *Berenstain bears blaze a trail* (1987)
58 *Berenstain bears on the job* (1987)
59 *Berenstain bears and the trouble with friends* (1987)
60 *Berenstain bears and the missing honey* (1987)
61 *Berenstain bears and the big road race* (1987)
62 *Berenstain bears and the bad habit* (1987)
63 *Berenstain bears and the trouble at school* (1987)
64 *After the dinosaurs* (1988)
65 *Berenstain bears and the ghost of the forest* (1988)
66 *Berenstain bears get the gimmies* (1988)
67 *Berenstain bears and the double dare* (1988)
68 *Berenstain bears and the bad dream* (1988)
69 *Berenstain bears, ready, set, go!* (1988)
70 *Berenstain bears and too much vacation* (1989)
71 *Berenstain bears' trick or treat* (1989)
72 *Berenstain bears and the in-crowd* (1989)
73 *Berenstain bears and the slumber party* (1990)
74 *Berenstain bears and the prize pumpkin* (1990)
75 *Berenstain bears' trouble with pets* (1990)
76 *Berenstain bears are a family* (1991)
77 *Berenstain bears at the super-duper market* (1991)
78 *Berenstain bears say goodnight* (1991)
79 *Berentain bears' four seasons* (1991)
Companion volumes: *The Berenstain bears' counting book*, 1976, *The bears' activity book*, 1979, *The Berenstain bears' make and do book*, 1984, *The Berenstain bears' bath book*, 1985, *The Berenstain kids, I love colors*, 1987, also numerous Berenstain bears coloring books

Beresford series

Christie, Agatha
see **Tommy and Tuppence Beresford series**
Curling, Henry
see **Frank Beresford series**

Bergen series

Greene, Bette
see **Patty Bergen series**

Bergerac series

This sequence has two authors; based on a television series
Hardwick, Michael
1 *Bergerac* (1982)
Saville, Andrew
2 *Bergerac is back!* (1985)
3 *Crimes of the season* (1985)
4 *Bergerac and the Jersey rose* (1988)
5 *Bergerac and the moving fever* (1988)
6 *Bergerac and the fatal weakness* (1989)
7 *Bergerac and the traitor's child* (1989)

Bergman family series

Bergman, Ingmar
Translated from the Swedish; autobiographical novels
1 *Best intentions* (1993)
2 *Sunday's child* (1994)

Bergson series

Lindgren, Astrid
see **Bill Bergson series**

Beria papers series

Williams, Alan
1 *Beria papers* (1973)
2 *Gentleman traitor* (1974)

Berkeley Barnes and Larry Howe series

Franklin, Eugene
1 *Murder Trapp* (1971)
2 *Money murders* (1972)
3 *Bold house murders* (1973)

Berkeley series

Burland, Brian
see **James Berkeley series**

Berkley series
Meynell, Laurence Walter
see **Bluefeather series**

Berlin noir trilogy
Kerr, Philip
1 *March violets* (1989)
2 *Pale criminal* (1990)
3 *German requiem* (1991)
One volume edition entitled Berlin noir, 1993

Berlin series
Isherwood, Christopher
1 *Mister Norris changes trains* (1935)
2 *Sally Bowles* (1937)
3 *Goodbye to Berlin* (1939)
Last of Mister Norris
One volume editions entitled *The Berlin stories*, 1946, and *The Berlin of Sally Bowles*, 1975; dramatization entitled *I am a camera*, by John Van Druten, 1951

Bermuda Triangle series
Berlitz, Charles
1 *Bermuda Triangle* (1974)
2 *Without a trace* (1977)

Bernadette series
Saint-Laurent, Cecil
1 *Algerian adventure* (1960)
Original edition entitled *Les passagers pour Alger*
2 *Toujours Bernadette* (1961)
Original edition entitled *Agites d'Alger*

Bernal One series
Zebrowski, George
1 *Sunspacer* (1984)
2 *Stars will speak* (1985)

Bernal series
Serafin, David
see **Superintendent Luis Bernal series**

Bernard and Josee series
Sagan, Francoise
see **Josee and Bernard series**

Bernard Bray series
Sprigg, Christopher Saint John
see **Inspector Bernard Bray series**

Bernard Clare series
Farrell, James Thomas
1 *Bernard Clare* (1946)
Bernard Clayre
2 *Road between* (1949)
3 *Yet other waters* (1952)

Bernard Clayre series
Farrell, James Thomas
see **Bernard Clare series**

Bernard Feston series
Fitzgerald, Kevin
1 *Quiet under the sun* (1953)
2 *It's different in July* (1955)
3 *Dangerous to lean out* (1960)

Bernard McFoy series
Shrog, J M
1 *Hag Wood* (1936)
2 *White circle* (1936)

Bernard Samson series
Deighton, Len
1 *Berlin game* (1983)
2 *Mexico set* (1984)
3 *London match* (1985)
4 *Spy hook* (1988)
5 *Spy line* (1989)
6 *Spy sinker* (1990)
7 *Faith* (1994)

Bernard series
Gluck, Sinclair
see **Paul Bernard series**

Bernard series
Freschet, Berniece
1 *Bernard sees the world* (1976)
2 *Bernard of Scotland Yard* (1978)
3 *Bernard and the catnip caper* (1981)

Bernard Shaw series
Holroyd, Michael
1 *Search for love, 1856-1898* (1988)
2 *Pursuit of power, 1898-1918* (1989)
3 *Lure of fantasy, 1918-1950* (1991)

Bernard Simmons series
Lockridge, Frances
see **Assistant District Attorney Bernie Simmons series**

Bernard Smith series
Brooks, Jeremy
1 *Jampot Smith* (1960)
2 *Smith, as hero* (1965)

Bernard Young and Arnold Keene series
Wood, Eric
see **Arnold Keene and Bernard Young series**

Bernhard Gunther trilogy
Kerr, Philip
see **Berlin noir trilogy**

Bernhardt series
Wilcox, Collin
see **Alan Bernhardt series**

Bernie Rhodenbarr series
Block, Lawrence
1 *Burglars can't be choosers* (1977)
2 *Burglar in the closet* (1978)
3 *Burglar who liked to quote Kipling* (1979)
4 *Burglar who studied Spinoza* (1981)
5 *Burglar who painted like Mondrian* (1983)
6 *Burglar who traded Tad Williams* (1994)
Also a short story in *Sometimes they bite*, 1983

Bernie Ryng series
Taylor, Charles Doonan
1 *First salvo* (1985)
2 *Choke point* (1986)
3 *Counterstrike* (1988)
4 *Deep sting* (1991)

Bernie Simmons series
Lockridge, Frances
see **Assistant District Attorney Bernie Simmons series**

Bernstein series
Hurwitz, Johanna
see **Ali Baba Bernstein series**

Berresford series
Le Grand, Leon
see **Michael Berresford series**

Berry series
This sequence has two authors
Yates, Dornford
1 *Brother of Daphne* (1914)
2 *Courts of idleness* (1920)
3 *Berry and Company* (1921)
Short stories
4 *Jonah and Company* (1922)
Short stories
5 *Perishable goods* (1928)
6 *Adele and Company* (1931)
7 *And Berry came too* (1936)
Short stories
8 *House that Berry built* (1945)
9 *Berry scene* (1947)
Short stories
10 *As Berry and I were saying* (1952)
11 *B-Berry and I look back* (1958)
Omnibus volume: *The best of Berry*, 1989
Smithers, Jack
12 *Combined forces* (1983)
The latter-day adventures of Maj. Gen. Sir Richard Hannay, Captain Hugh, Bulldog, Drummond and Berry and Co.

Berserker series
Carlsen, Chris
1 *Shadow of the wolf* (1977)
2 *Bull chief* (1977)
3 *Horned warrior* (1979)

Berserker series
Saberhagen, Fred
1 *Berserker* (1967)
Berserker wars
The second title is an expanded edition
2 *Brother Assassin* (1969)
Brother Berserker
3 *Berserker's planet* (1975)
4 *Berserker man* (1979)
5 *Ultimate enemy* (1979)
6 *Berserker base* (1985)
Includes contributions from other authors
7 *Berserker throne* (1985)
8 *Blue death* (1985)
9 *Berserker attack* (1987)
10 *Berserker lies* (1991)

Bert McCall and Tony Costaine series
Macneil, Neil
see **Tony Costaine and Bert McCall series**

Bert Poole series
Brent of Bin Bin
1 *Up the country* (1928)
2 *Ten creeks run* (1930)
3 *Cockatoos* (1954)
4 *Gentlemen of Gyang Gyang* (1956)
5 *Back to Bool Bool* (1931)

Bert Swain series
Nathan, Paul
1 *Protocol for murder* (1994)
2 *No good deed* (1995)

Bertha Cool and Donald Lam series
Fair, A A
1 *Bigger they come* (1939)
Lam to the slaughter
2 *Turn on the heat* (1940)
3 *Gold comes in bricks* (1940)
4 *Spill the jackpot* (1941)
5 *Double or quits* (1941)
6 *Bats fly at dusk* (1942)
7 *Owls don't blink* (1942)
8 *Cats prowl at night* (1943)
9 *Give 'em an ax* (1944)
Axe to grind
10 *Crows can't count* (1946)
11 *Fools die on Friday* (1947)
12 *Bedrooms have windows* (1949)
13 *Top of the heap* (1952)
14 *Some women won't wait* (1953)
15 *Beware the curves* (1956)
16 *You can die laughing* (1957)
17 *Some slips don't show* (1957)
18 *Count of nine* (1958)
19 *Pass the gravy* (1959)
20 *Kept women can't quit* (1960)
21 *Bachelors get lonely* (1961)
22 *Shills can't cash chips* (1961)
Stop at the red light
23 *Try anything once* (1962)
24 *Fish or cut bait* (1963)
25 *Up for grabs* (1964)
26 *Cut thin to win* (1965)
27 *Widows wear weeds* (1966)
28 *Traps need fresh bait* (1967)
29 *All grass isn't green* (1970)

Bertha series
Charles, Eric
Illustrated by Steve Augarde; based on a television series
1 *Bertha and the great painting job* (1985)
2 *Bertha and the windmills* (1985)
3 *Bertha and the best machine competition* (1986)
4 *Bertha and a mouse in the works* (1986)
5 *Bertha and the flying bear* (1987)
6 *Bertha and the lost tom* (1987)

Bertie series
Bouma, Paddy
1 *Bertie visits granny* (1987)
2 *Bertie at the dentist's* (1987)

Bertie series
Felsen, Henry Gregor
1 *Bertie comes through* (1947)
2 *Bertie takes care* (1948)

Bertie series
Hattie, *Aunt*
see **Woodlawn series**

Bertie series
Lovesey, Peter
1 *Bertie and tinman* (1987)
From the detective memoirs of King Edward VII
2 *Bertie and the seven bodies* (1990)
3 *Bertie and the crime of passion* (1993)

Bertie Wooster and Jeeves series
Wodehouse, Pelham Grenville
see **Jeeves and Bertie Wooster series**

Bertin and Wahl series
Zweig, Arnold
see **Werner Bertin and Lenore Wahl series**

Bertram family series
Charles, Elizabeth
1 *Winifred Bertram and the world she lived in* (1866)
2 *Bertram family* (1876)

Bertram Lynch and Robert Deane series
Vandercook, John Womack
1 *Murder in Trinidad* (1933)
2 *Murder in Fiji* (1936)
3 *Murder in Haiti* (1956)
Out for a killing
4 *Murder in New Guinea* (1959)

Bertram Pleydell series
Yates, Dornford
see **Berry series**

Berurier series
San Antonio
The following titles are those which are translated into English of a large number of French titles in this sequence
1 *Stone dead* (1954)
Original edition entitled *C'est mort et ca ne sait pas*
2 *Tough justice* (1955)
Original edition entitled *Messieurs les hommes*
3 *Sub killers* (1958)
Original edition entitled *La rate au court bouillon*
4 *Thugs and bottles* (1960)
Original edition entitled *Du brut pour les brutes*
5 *Hatchet man* (1960)
Original edition entitled *Vas-y beru*
6 *From A to Z* (1961)
Original edition entitled *De A jusqu'a Z*
7 *Strangler* (1961)
Original edition entitled *La fin des haricots*
8 *Crooks' Hill* (1963)
Puck of Crooks' Hill
Original edition entitled *Le gala des emplumes*

Berurier series

9 *Knights of Arabia* (1964)
Original edition entitled *Berurier au serail*
10 *Alien archipelago* (1969)
Original edition entitled *L'archipel des malotrus*

Beryl and Alex series
Oliver, Marjorie Mary
see **Alex and Beryl series**

Beryl and Bill series
Burke, Thomas
see **Bill and Beryl series**

Beryl Humphries series
Powell, Margaret
1 *Beryl's lot* (1975)
2 *Beryl's lot, book two* (1976)

Besant series
Nethercot, Arthur Hobart
see **Annie Besant series**

Besserley series
Oppenheim, Edward Phillips
see **General Besserley series**

Bessey series
McKissack, Patricia Carwell
see **Messy Bessey series**

Bessie Bradford series
Mathews, Joanna Hooe
1 *Bessie at the seaside* (1867)
2 *Bessie in the city* (1868)
3 *Maggie and Bessie and their way to do good* (1868)
4 *Bessie and her friends* (1869)
5 *Bessie among the mountains* (1869)
6 *Bessie at school* (1869)
7 *Bessie on her travels* (1870)
8 *Bessie Bradford's secret* (1881)
9 *Bessie Bradford's prize* (1890)

Bessie Bunter series
Richards, Hilda
1 *Bessie Bunter of Cliff House* (1949)
2 *Bessie Bunter joins the circus* (1967)
3 *Bessie Bunter and the gold robbers* (1967)

Bessie Hipkiss series
Urquhart, Fred
1 *Ferret was Abraham's daughter* (1949)
2 *Jezebel's dust* (1951)

Bessie King series
Stewart, Jane L
see **Camp Fire Girls series**

Bessledorf series
Naylor, Phyllis Reynolds
1 *Mad gasser of Bessledorf Street* (1983)
2 *Bodies in the Bessledorf Hotel* (1986)
3 *Bernie and the Bessledorf ghost* (1990)
4 *Face in the Bessledorf Funeral Parlor* (1993)

Best and Barton series
Pearson, Parry
see **Jeremy Barton and Samuel Best series**

Best and Frend series
Chetwynd, Bridget
see **Petunia Best and Max Frend series**

Best enemies series
Leverich, Kathleen
1 *Best enemies* (1989)
2 *Best enemies again* (1991)

Best friends series
Bard, Mary
1 *Best friends* (1955)
2 *Best friends in summer* (1960)
3 *Best friends at school* (1961)

Best friends series
Cohen, Miriam
Illustrated by Lillian Hoban
1 *Best friends* (1971)
2 *New teacher* (1972)
3 *Tough Jim* (1974)
4 *When will I read?* (1977)
5 *Bee, my Valentine!* (1978)

Best friends series
Schwartz, Joel L
1 *Upchuck summer* (1982)
2 *Best friends don't come in threes* (1985)

Best friends series
Smith, Susan
1 *Sonya Begonia and the eleventh birthday blues* (1988)
2 *Angela and the king-size crusade* (1988)

Best friends series
Stahl, Hilda
1 *Chelsea and the outrageous phone bill* (1992)
2 *Big trouble for Roxie* (1992)
3 *Kathy and the babysitting hassle* (1992)
4 *Hannah and the special fourth of July* (1992)
5 *Roxie and Red Rose mystery* (1992)
6 *Kathy's new brother* (1992)
7 *Made-over Chelsea* (1992)
8 *no friends for Hannah* (1992)
9 *Tough choices for Roxie* (1993)
10 *Chelsea's special gift* (1993)
11 *Mystery at Bellwood Estate* (1993)
12 *Hannah's dangerous mystery* (1993)
13 *Hannah and the snowy highway* (1993)
14 *Chelsea and the alien invasion* (1993)
15 *Roxie's mail madness* (1993)

Best of friends series
Hindley, Judy
1 *Jim and Pete* (1985)
2 *Brave explorers* (1985)
3 *Polly's dance* (1985)
4 *Jane's amazing woolly jumper* (1985)

Best wishes series
Rylant, Cynthia
Autobiography
1 *But I'll be back again* (1989)
2 *Best wishes* (1992)

Bestiary trilogy
Forrester, John
1 *Bestiary Mountain* (1985)
2 *Secret of the round beast* (1986)
3 *Forbidden beast* (1988)

Bet you series
Cobb, Vicki
1 *Bet you can't!* (1980)
Science impossibilities to fool you
2 *Bet you can!* (1983)
Science possibilities to fool you

Beth Anne series
Ginther, Mary Pemberton
1 *Beth Anne herself* (1915)
2 *Beth Anne, really-for-truly* (1916)
3 *Beth Anne's new cousin* (1917)
4 *Beth Anne goes to school* (1919)

Beth Dean series
Hill, Margaret
1 *Goal in the sky* (1953)
2 *Hostess in the sky* (1955)
3 *Senior hostess* (1958)

Beth Lambert series
Greene, Bette
1 *Philip Hall likes me, I reckon maybe* (1974)
2 *Get on out of here, Philip Hall* (1981)

Beth series
Taggart, Marion Ames
1 *Beth's wonder-winter* (1914)
2 *Beth's old home* (1915)
3 *Beth of Old Chilton* (1916)

Bethlehem series
Steuben, Fritz
1 *Stable in Bethlehem* (1960)
2 *Way to Bethlehem* (1960)

Betsey Bobbet series
Holley, Marietta
1 *My opinions and Betsey Bobbet's* (1873)
A beacon light to guide women to life, liberty and pursuit of happiness which may be read by members of the sterner sect without injury to themselves or the book
2 *Betsey Bobbet* (1880)
A drama; scenes drawn from *My opinions and Betsey Bobbet's*, 1873

Betsy and Tim series
Rhodes, John
see **Tim and Betsy series**

Betsy Hale series
Ginther, Mary Pemberton
1 *Betsy Hale* (1923)
2 *Betsy Hale tries* (1923)
3 *Betsy Hale succeeds* (1923)

Betsy Ray series
Lovelace, Maud Hart
1 *Betsy-Tacy* (1940)
Revised edition 1979
2 *Betsy-Tacy and Tib* (1941)
Revised edition 1979
3 *Over the big hill* (1942)
Betsy and Tacy go over the big hill
Revised edition 1979
4 *Down town* (1943)
Betsy and Tacy go down town
Revised edition 1979
5 *Heaven to Betsy* (1945)
6 *Betsy in spite of herself* (1946)
7 *Betsy was a junior* (1947)
8 *Betsy and Joe* (1948)
9 *Betsy and the great world* (1952)
10 *Betsy's wedding* (1955)
Companion volumes: *Carney's house party*, 1949, *Emily of Deep Valley*, 1950, *Winona's pony cart*, 1953

Betsy series
Haywood, Carolyn
1 *B is for Betsy* (1939)
2 *Betsy and Billy* (1941)
3 *Back to school with Betsy* (1943)
4 *Betsy and the boys* (1945)
5 *Betsy's little star* (1950)
6 *Betsy and the circus* (1954)
7 *Betsy's busy summer* (1956)
8 *Betsy's winterhouse* (1958)
9 *Snowbound with Betsy* (1962)
10 *Betsy and Mr Kilpatrick* (1967)
11 *Merry Christmas from Betsy* (1970)
12 *Betsy's play school* (1977)

Betsy series
Wolde, Gunilla
see **Emma series**

Bettesworth series
Bourne, George
see **Frederick Bettesworth series**

Betty and Buster series
Dicks, Terrance
see **Adventures of Buster and Betty series**

Betty and John series
Williamson, Margaret
see **John and Betty series**

Betty Baird trilogy
Weikel, Anna Hamline
1 *Betty Baird* (1906)
2 *Betty Baird's ventures* (1907)
3 *Betty Baird's golden year* (1909)

Betty Gordon series
Emerson, Alice B
1 *Betty Gordon at Bramble Farm* (1920)
Alternative title: The mystery of a nobody
2 *Betty Gordon in Washington* (1920)
Alternative title: Strange adventures in a great city
3 *Betty Gordon in the land of oil* (1920)
Alternative title: The farm that was worth a fortune
4 *Betty Gordon at boarding school* (1921)
Alternative title: The treasure of Indian Chasm
5 *Betty Gordon at Mountain Camp* (1922)
Alternative title: The mystery of Ida Bellethorne
6 *Betty Gordon at Ocean Park* (1923)
Alternative title: School chums on the boardwalk
7 *Betty Gordon and her school chums* (1924)
Alternative title: Bringing the rebels to terms
8 *Betty Gordon at Rainbow Ranch* (1925)
Alternative title: Cowboy Joe's secret
9 *Betty Gordon in Mexican wilds* (1926)
Alternative title: The secret of the mountains
10 *Betty Gordon and the lost pearls* (1927)
Alternative title: A mystery of the seaside
11 *Betty Gordon on the campus* (1928)
Alternative title: The secret of the trunk room
12 *Betty Gordon and the Hale twins* (1929)
Alternative title: An exciting vacation
13 *Betty Gordon at Mystery Farm* (1930)
Alternative title: Strange doings at Rocky Ridge
14 *Betty Gordon on No-Trail Island* (1931)
Alternative title: Uncovering a queer secret
15 *Betty Gordon and the mystery girl* (1932)
Alternative title: The secret at Sundown Hall

Betty Lee series
Grove, Harriet Pyne
1 *Betty Lee, freshman* (1931)
2 *Betty Lee, sophomore* (1931)
3 *Betty Lee, junior* (1931)
4 *Betty Lee, senior* (1931)

Betty Leicester series
Jewett, Sarah Orne
1 *Betty Leicester* (1890)
2 *Betty Leicester's Christmas* (1899)

Betty Morton series
Govan, Margaret
1 *Trail of the red canoe* (1954)
2 *Trail of the broken snowshoe* (1956)

Betty series
Wevill, Lilian F
1 *Betty's first term* (1908)
2 *Betty's next term* (1912)

Betty Vivian series
Meade, Lillie Thomas
1 *Betty, a schoolgirl* (1894)
2 *Betty of the rectory* (1908)
3 *Betty Vivian* (1909)
A story of Haddo Court School

Betty Wales series
Warde, Margaret
1 *Betty Wales, freshman* (1904)
2 *Betty Wales, sophomore* (19105)
3 *Betty Wales, junior* (1906)
4 *Betty Wales, senior* (1907)
5 *Betty Wales, B.A.* (1908)
6 *Betty Wales and Company* (1909)
7 *Betty Wales on the campus* (1910)
8 *Betty Wales decides* (1911)
9 *Betty Wales girls and Mister Kidd* (1912)
10 *Betty Wales, business woman* (1917)

Between the lines series
Ames, Franklin T
1 *Between the lines in Belgium* (1915)
2 *Between the lines in France* (1915)
3 *Between the lines on the American Front* (1919)

Between two worlds trilogy
Mosco, Maisie
1 *Between two worlds* (1983)
2 *Sense of place* (1984)
3 *Price of fame* (1985)

Beulah Land trilogy
Coleman, Lonnie
1 *Beulah Land* (1973)
2 *Look away, Beulah Land* (1977)
3 *Legacy of Beulah Land* (1980)

Beulah series
Settle, Mary Lee
1 *Prisons* (1973)
Long road to paradise
2 *O Beulah Land* (1956)
3 *Know nothing* (1960)
4 *Scapegoat* (1980)
5 *Killing ground* (1982)
Companion volume: *Fight night at Sweet Saturday*, 1966

Bevan and Smith series
Forster, Peter
see **Alex Smith and Tony Bevan series**

Beverley series
Marsden, Antony
see **Jim Beverley series**

Beverly Gray series
Blank, Clair
1 *Beverly Gray, freshman* (1934)
2 *Beverly Gray, sophomore* (1934)
3 *Beverly Gray, junior* (1934)
4 *Beverly Gray, senior* (1934)
5 *Beverly Gray's career* (1935)
6 *Beverly Gray at the World's Fair* (1935)
7 *Beverly Gray on a world cruise* (1936)
8 *Beverly Gray in the Orient* (1937)
9 *Beverly Gray on a treasure hunt* (1938)
10 *Beverly Gray's return* (1939)
11 *Beverly Gray, reporter* (1940)
12 *Beverly Gray's romance* (1941)
13 *Beverly Gray's quest* (1942)
14 *Beverly Gray's problem* (1943)
15 *Beverly Gray's adventure* (1944)
16 *Beverly Gray's challenge* (1945)
17 *Beverly Gray's journey* (1946)
18 *Beverly Gray's assignment* (1947)
19 *Beverly Gray's mystery* (1948)
20 *Beverly Gray's vacation* (1949)
21 *Beverly Gray's fortune* (1950)
22 *Beverly Gray's secret* (1951)
23 *Beverly Gray's island mystery* (1952)
24 *Beverly Gray's discovery* (1953)
25 *Beverly Gray's scoop* (1954)
26 *Beverly Gray's surprise* (1955)

Beverly Hills 90210 series
Gilden, Mel
1 *Beverly Hills 90210* (1991)
2 *No secrets* (1992)
3 *Which way to the beach?* (1992)
4 *Tis the season* (1992)
5 *More than words* (1993)
6 *Summer love* (1993)
7 *Two hearts* (1993)
8 *Where the boys are* (1993)
Companion volume: *Stars of Beverly Hills 90210, their lives and loves*, by Randi Reisfeld, 1991

Beverly series
Brandon, Gordon
see **Michael and Terry Terence series**

Bevis series
Jefferies, Richard
1 *Wood magic* (1881)
Sir Bevis
A fable; the second title is an abridged edition
2 *Bevis* (1882)
The story of a boy

Bewitched series
This sequence has two authors
Hine, Alfred Blakelee
1 *Bewitched* (1965)
Johnston, William
2 *Opposite uncle* (1970)

Beyond trilogy
Leiber, Justin Fritz
1 *Beyond rejection* (1980)
2 *Beyond humanity* (1987)
3 *Beyond gravity* (1988)

Bianca series
Sharp, Margery
see **Miss Bianca series**

Bibi series
Michaelis, Karin
Translated from the Danish
1 *Bibi, a little Danish girl* (1927)
2 *Bibi goes travelling* (1930)
At least four other titles in this sequence not translated into English

Bible and literature series
Frye, Northrop
1 *Great code* (1982)
2 *Words with power* (1990)

Bible pictures and stories series
Evans, Adelaide Bee
1 *Easy steps in the Bible story, from creation to Joseph* (1911)
2 *Men of might* (1911)
3 *Stories of the kings, from David to Christ* (1911)
4 *Children's friend* (1911)

Bible series
Powell, Ivor
1 *Bible cameos* (1951)
2 *Bible pinnacles* (1952)
3 *Bible treasures* (1953)
4 *Bible windows* (1954)
5 *Bible highway* (1959)
6 *Bible gems* (1987)
7 *Bible names of Christ* (1988)
8 *Bible nuggets* (1991)
9 *Bible promises* (1993)

Bible stories series
Blyton, Enid
1 *In the beginning* (1985)
2 *Noah builds his ark* (1985)
3 *Baby in the bulrushes* (1985)
4 *David and Goliath* (1985)
5 *Samson, the strong giant* (1985)
6 *Burning bush* (1985)
7 *Path through the sea* (1985)
8 *Daniel in the lion's den* (1985)

Bible stories series
Oursler, Fulton
1 *Greatest book ever written* (1951)
Based on the *Old Testament*
2 *Greatest story ever told* (1949)
Based on the life and work of Jesus
3 *Greatest faith ever known* (1953)
Life of the early church based on the *Acts of the Apostles*

Bibleland series
Davidson, Alice Joyce
see **Alice In Bibleland series**

Biblical series
Asch, Sholem
1 *Nazarene* (1939)
2 *Apostle* (1943)
3 *Mary* (1949)
4 *Moses* (1951)
5 *Prophet* (1955)

Biblical series
Slaughter, Frank Gill
1 *Road to Bithynia* (1951)
A novel of Luke, the beloved physician
2 *Galileans* (1953)
A novel of Mary Magdalene
3 *Song of Ruth* (1954)
4 *Scarlet cord* (1956)
A novel of the woman of Jericho

Biblical series
Weinreb, Nathaniel Norsen
1 *Babylonians* (1953)
2 *Sorceress* (1953)
3 *Esther* (1955)

Bickley family series
Jahoda, Gloria
1 *Loving maid* (1960)
2 *Delilah's mountain* (1963)

Biddy and Tessie series
Warner, Priscilla Mary
1 *Biddy Christmas* (1948)
2 *Tessie growing up* (1952)
Tessie's caravan

Biff Brewster series
Adams, Andy
1 *Brazilian gold mine mystery* (1960)
2 *Mystery of the Chinese ring* (1960)
3 *Hawaiian sea hunt mystery* (1960)
4 *Mystery of the Mexican treasure* (1961)
5 *African ivory mystery* (1961)
6 *Alaska Ghost Glacier mystery* (1961)
7 *Mystery of the ambush in India* (1962)
8 *Mystery of the Caribbean pearls* (1962)
9 *Egyptian scarab mystery* (1963)
10 *Mystery of the Tibetan canvas* (1963)
11 *British spy ring mystery* (1964)
12 *Mystery of the Arabian stallion* (1964)
13 *Mystery of the Alpine pass* (1965)

Biff Corrigan series
Morton, William
1 *Masquerade* (1927)
2 *Mystery of the human bookcase* (1931)
3 *Murderer* (1932)
Also published as *The Piltditch puzzle*, under the author's real name William Blair Morton Ferguson

Biff Norris series
Runyan, John
1 *Biff Norris and the clue of the lonely landing strip* (1962)
2 *Biff Norris and the clue of the worn saddle* (1962)
3 *Biff Norris and the clue of the nervous stranger* (1962)
4 *Biff Norris and the clue of the golden ram* (1962)
5 *Biff Norris and the clue of the midnight stage* (1963)
6 *Biff Norris and the clue of the lavender mink* (1964)
7 *Biff Norris and the clue of the gold ring* (1965)
8 *Biff Norris and the clue of the angry fisherman* (1966)
9 *Biff Norris and the clue of the disappearing wolf* (1967)
10 *Biff Norris and the clue of the mysterious letter* (1968)
11 *Biff Norris and the clue of the half-burned book* (1969)

Biff series
Gould, Charles S
1 *Biff* (1945)
2 *Biff finds a clue* (1947)

Biffin series
Graham, Harry
see **Reginald Drake Biffin series**

Bifrost guardians series
Reichert, Mickey Zucker
1 *Godslayer* (1987)
2 *Shadow climber* (1988)
3 *Dragonrank master* (1989)
4 *Shadow's realm* (1990)
5 *By chaos cursed* (1991)

Big baby series
Oxenbury, Helen
Board books
1 *Tickle, tickle* (1987)
2 *Say goodnight* (1987)
3 *All fall down* (1987)
4 *Clap hands* (1987)

Big Bear series
Margolis, Richard Jules
1 *Wish again, Big Bear* (1973)
2 *Big Bear to the rescue* (1977)

Big Brain series
Brandner, Gary
1 *Aardvark affair* (1975)
2 *Beelzebub business* (1975)
3 *Energy zero* (1976)

Big Brother series
This sequence has two authors
Orwell, George
1 *Nineteen eighty four* (1949)
Dalos, Gyorgy
2 *Nineteen eighty five* (1983)
A historical report, Hongkong 2036, translated from the Hungarian
Companion volume: *Nineteen eighty five*, by Anthony Burgess, 1978

Big bug series
McKissack, Patricia Carwell
1 *Big bug book of counting* (1987)
2 *Big bug book of opposites* (1987)
3 *Big bug book of places to go* (1987)
4 *Big bug book of the alphabet* (1987)
5 *Big bug book of things to do* (1987)

Big drawing book series
Emberley, Ed
see **Ed Emberley's big drawing book series**

Big Ears series
Blyton, Enid
see **Noddy series**

Big Four trilogy
Barbour, Ralph Henry
1 *Four in camp* (1905)
2 *Four afoot* (1906)
3 *Four afloat* (1907)

Big Jim Rand series
Grover, Marshall
see **Nevada Jim series**

Big Jim Wade series
Short, Luke
1 *And the wind blows free* (1945)
2 *Savage range* (1980)

Big Mac series
Jungman, Ann
1 *Big Mac and the oil rig* (1987)
2 *Big Mac and the satellite* (1987)
3 *Big Mac goes to Mars* (1987)

Big machine series
Lynam, Terence
see **Sally and Tom series**

Big Max series
Platt, Kin
1 *Big Max* (1966)
2 *Big Max in the mystery of the missing moose* (1977)

Big Planet series
Vance, Jack
1 *Big Planet* (1957)
2 *Showboat world* (1975)
Magnificent showboats of the Lower Vissel River, Lune 23 South, Big Planet

Big red bus series
Wood, Leslie
1 *Count with us from the big red bus* (1978)
2 *Shapes we see from the big red bus* (1978)
3 *Patterns we see from the big red bus* (1978)
4 *Compare with us from the big red bus* (1978)
5 *Measure with us from the big red bus* (1978)
6 *Sets we see from the big red bus* (1978)

Big river, big man series
Duncan, Thomas
1 *End and a beginning* (1959)
2 *Inferno* (1959)
Not published separately; only published in the one volume edition entitled *Big river, big man*, 1959

Big sleep series
This sequence has two authors
Chandler, Raymond
1 *Big sleep* (1939)
Parker, Robert Brown
2 *Perchance to dream* (1991)

Big Sur series
Ross, Lillian
1 *Stranger* (1942)
2 *Blaze Allan* (1944)

Big Tom Holder trilogy
Wilson, Trevor Edward
1 *Newcomers* (1977)
2 *Yellow fever* (1979)
3 *Harvest of gold* (1983)

Big war series
Kay, Ross
1 *Search for the spy* (1914)
2 *Air scout* (1914)
3 *Dodging the North Sea mines* (1915)
4 *With Joffre on the battle line* (1915)
5 *Fighting in France* (1916)
6 *Battling on the Somme* (1917)
7 *With Pershing at the Front* (1918)
8 *Smashing the Hindenburg Line* (1919)
9 *Underground spy* (1920)

Biggles series
Johns, William Earl
1 *Camels are coming* (1932)
Contains 17 stories some of which were reissued in *Biggles of the Special Air Police*, 1953 and *Biggles, pioneer air fighter*, 1954
2 *Cruise of the Condor* (1933)
Biggles in the cruise of the Condor
Biggles and the cruise of the Condor
Serialized as *Wings of fortune*
3 *Biggles of the Camel Squadron* (1934)
Biggles goes to war
Contains 13 stories; reissued as *Biggles goes to war* as number 610 in the Boys' friend library, February 1938, not to be confused with the title of the same name published in May 1938
4 *Biggles flies again* (1934)
Contains 13 stories
5 *Biggles learns to fly* (1935)
Revised edition 1951
6 *Black peril* (1935)
Biggles and the plack peril
Biggles flies east
Serialized as *Winged menace*; reissued under the title *Biggles flies east* as number 621 in the Boys' friend library, May 1938, not the same as another book with the same title published in August 1935
7 *Biggles flies east* (1935)
Not to be confused with another book with the same title published in May 1938
8 *Biggles hits the trail* (1935)
Serialized as *The mountain of light*
9 *Biggles in France* (1935)
Some of the stories in this book were revised and reissued as *Spitfire parade*, 1941; others were reprinted in *Biggles of 266*, 1955
10 *Biggles and Company* (1936)
Serialized as *The gold flyers*; numbers 7, 8 and 10 also published in one volume entitled *The Biggles omnibus*, 1938
11 *Biggles in Africa* (1936)
12 *Biggles, air commodore* (1937)
13 *Biggles flies west* (1937)
14 *Biggles flies south* (1938)
15 *Biggles goes to war* (1938)
Not to be confused with another book with the same title published in February 1938
16 *Rescue flight* (1939)
Serialized as *Biggles' rescue flight*
17 *Biggles in Spain* (1939)
Serialized as *Wings over Spain*
18 *Biggles flies north* (1939)
Numbers 13, 14 and 18 also published in one volume entitled *The Biggles flying omnibus*, 1940
19 *Biggles, secret agent* (1940)
Serialized as *Castle Sinister*
20 *Biggles in the Baltic* (1940)
Serialized as *Storm troops of the Baltic skies*; numbers 15, 17 and 20 also published in one volume entitled *The third Biggles omnibus*, 1941
21 *Biggles in the South Seas* (1940)
Serialized as *Biggles' South Seas adventure*
22 *Biggles defies the swastika* (1941)
23 *Biggles sees it through* (1941)
24 *Biggles in the jungle* (1942)
25 *Biggles sweeps the desert* (1942)
26 *Biggles, charter pilot* (1943)
27 *Biggles in Borneo* (1943)
28 *Biggles fails to return* (1943)
29 *Biggles in the Orient* (1945)
30 *Biggles delivers the goods* (1946)
Numbers 28-30 also published in one volume entitled *The first Biggles omnibus*, 1953
31 *Sergeant Bigglesworth, C.I.D.* (1947)
32 *Biggles' second case* (1948)
33 *Biggles hunts big game* (1948)
34 *Biggles takes a holiday* (1949)
35 *Biggles breaks the silence* (1949)
Biggles in the Antarctic
36 *Biggles gets his men* (1950)
37 *Another job for Biggles* (1951)
38 *Biggles goes to school* (1951)
Serialized as *Biggles at school*
39 *Biggles works it out* (1951)
Numbers 31, 32, 37 and 39 also published in one volume entitled *The Biggles air detective omnibus*, 1956
40 *Biggles takes the case* (1952)
Contains 9 stories
41 *Biggles follows on* (1952)
42 *Biggles, air detective* (1952)
43 *Biggles and the black raider* (1953)
44 *Biggles in the blue* (1953)
45 *Biggles in the Gobi* (1953)
46 *Biggles cuts it fine* (1954)
47 *Biggles and the pirate treasure* (1954)
Contains 11 stories
48 *Biggles, foreign legionnaire* (1954)
49 *Biggles in Australia* (1955)
50 *Biggles' Chinese puzzle, and other Biggles adventures* (1955)
Contains 8 stories
51 *No rest for Biggles* (1956)
Numbers 34, 36, 37 and 51 also published in one volume entitled *The Biggles adventure omnibus*, 1965
52 *Biggles takes charge* (1956)
53 *Biggles makes ends meet* (1957)
54 *Biggles of the Interpol* (1957)
55 *Biggles on the home front* (1957)
56 *Biggles presses on* (1958)
Contains 11 stories
57 *Biggles on Mystery Island* (1958)
58 *Biggles buries a hatchet* (1958)
59 *Biggles in Mexico* (1959)
60 *Biggles' combined operation* (1959)
61 *Biggles at world's end* (1959)
62 *Biggles and the leopards of Zinn* (1960)
63 *Biggles goes home* (1960)
64 *Biggles and the poor rich boy* (1961)
65 *Biggles forms a syndicate* (1961)
66 *Biggles and the missing millionaire* (1961)
67 *Biggles goes alone* (1962)
68 *Orchids for Biggles* (1962)
69 *Biggles sets a trap* (1962)
70 *Biggles takes it rough* (1963)
71 *Biggles takes a hand* (1963)
72 *Biggles' special case* (1963)
73 *Biggles and the plane that disappeared* (1963)
74 *Biggles flies to work* (1963)
Contains 11 stories
75 *Biggles and the lost sovereigns* (1964)
Biggles and the lost treasure
76 *Biggles and the Black Mask* (1964)
77 *Biggles investigates, and other stories of the Air Police* (1964)
Contains 8 stories
78 *Biggles looks back* (1965)
79 *Biggles and the plot that failed* (1965)
80 *Biggles and the blue moon* (1965)
81 *Biggles scores a bull* (1965)
82 *Biggles in the Terai* (1966)
83 *Biggles and the gun-runners* (1966)
84 *Biggles sorts it out* (1967)
85 *Biggles and the dark intruder* (1967)
86 *Biggles and the penitent thief* (1967)
87 *Biggles and the deep blue sea* (1968)
88 *Boy Biggles* (1968)
89 *Biggles in the underworld* (1968)
90 *Biggles and the little green god* (1969)
91 *Biggles and the noble lord* (1969)
92 *Biggles sees too much* (1970)
Selections: *Biggles of the Royal Flying Corps*, 1978
Companion volumes: *The Biggles book of heroes*, 1959, *The Biggles book of treasure hunting*, 1962, also unfinished, unpublished volume entitled *Biggles does some homework*

Bignon series
Didelot, Francis
see **Commissaire Orestes Bignon series**

Bikie series
Hall, Stuart
1 *Bikie birds* (1973)
2 *Bikie hellcats* (1975)
3 *Bikie hell* (1976)

Bill Abbot and George Thorne series
Penn, John
see **Inspector George Thorne and Sergeant Bill Abbot series**

Bill and Beryl series
Burke, Thomas
1 *Bill and Beryl in Chinatown* (1935)
2 *Bill and Beryl in Old London* (1936)
3 *Bill and Beryl in Soho* (1936)

Bill and Coco Hastings series
Offord, Lenore Glen
1 *Murder on Russian Hill* (1938)
Murder before breakfast
2 *Clues to burn* (1942)

Bill and Joan series
Newcomb, Ellsworth
see **Joan and Bill series**

Bill and Mike Hendry series
Lee, Benjamin
see **Mike and Bill Hendry series**

Bill and Pete series
De Paola, Tomie
1 *Bill and Pete* (1978)
2 *Bill and Pete go down the Nile* (1987)

Bill and Susan series
Saville, Malcolm
see **Susan and Bill series**

Bill and Wade series
Weddle, Ferris
see **Clint Wade and Trapper Bill series**

Bill Anstruther series
Nicholas, Jerome
1 *Widow's peak* (1946)
2 *Asbestos mask* (1948)
3 *Whispering steel* (1949)
4 *Deirdre* (1952)

Bill Aveyard series
Fraser, James
see **Inspector Bill Aveyard series**

Bill Badger series
B B
1 *Wandering wind* (1957)
Bill Badger and the wandering wind
2 *Bill Badger's winter cruise* (1959)
3 *Bill Badger and the pirates* (1960)
4 *Bill Badger's finest hour* (1961)
5 *Bill Badger's whispering reeds adventure* (1962)
6 *Bill Badger's big mistake* (1963)
7 *Bill Badger and the big store robbery* (1967)
8 *Bill Badger's voyage to the world's end* (1969)

Bill Bailey series
Cookson, Catherine
1 *Bill Bailey* (1986)
2 *Bill Bailey's lot* (1987)
3 *Bill Bailey's daughter* (1988)
One volume edition entitled The Bailey chronicles, 1989

Bill Banning series
Easton, Nat
1 *Always the wolf* (1957)

2 *One good turn* (1957)
3 *Bill for damages* (1958)
4 *Mistake me not* (1958)
5 *Book for Banning* (1959)
6 *Right for trouble* (1960)
7 *Quick tempo* (1960)
8 *Moment on ice* (1960)
9 *Forgive me, lovely lady* (1961)

Bill Berenger series
Duff, Douglas Valder
1 *Bill Berenger's first case* (1948)
2 *Bill Berenger to the rescue* (1949)
3 *Bill Berenger wins command* (1950)
4 *Berenger's toughest case* (1951)

Bill Bergson series
Lindgren, Astrid
1 *Bill Bergson, master detective* (1946)
Original edition entitled *Maasterdetektiven Blomkvist*; revised edition 1981
2 *Bill Bergson lives dangerously* (1951)
Original edition entitled *Maasterdetektiven Blomkvist lever farligt*; revised edition 1981
3 *Bill Bergson and the white rose rescue* (1953)
Original edition entitled *Kalle Blomkvist och Rasmus*; revised edition 1981

Bill Beverly series
Brandon, Gordon
see **Michael and Terry Terence series**

Bill Bolton series
Sainsbury, Noel
1 *Bill Bolton, flying midshipman* (1933)
2 *Bill Bolton and the flying fish* (1933)
3 *Bill Bolton and hidden danger* (1933)
4 *Bill Bolton and the winged cartwheels* (1933)

Bill Bradley and Noel Mayberry series
Tree, Gregory
1 *Case against myself* (1950)
2 *Case against Butterfly* (1951)

Bill Britain series
Courage, John
1 *Spooks sometimes sing* (1946)
2 *Lakeland tragedy* (1947)
3 *Affair Ravel* (1948)
4 *Death of a gentleman* (1951)
5 *Dread cave* (1952)

Bill Bruce series
Arnold, Henry
1 *Bill Bruce and the pioneer aviators* (1928)
2 *Bill Bruce, the flying cadet* (1928)
3 *Bill Bruce becomes an ace* (1928)
4 *Bill Bruce on the Border Patrol* (1928)
5 *Bill Bruce and the Trans-continental Race* (1928)
6 *Bill Bruce on forest patrol* (1928)

Bill Cartwright series
Morgan, Patrick
see **Operation Hang Ten series**

Bill Cassidy series
Mulford, Clarence Edward
see **Hopalong Cassidy series**

Bill Crane series
Latimer, Jonathan
1 *Murder in the madhouse* (1935)
2 *Headed for a hearse* (1935)
Westland case
3 *Lady in the morgue* (1936)
4 *Dead don't care* (1938)
5 *Red gardenias* (1939)
Some dames are deadly

Bill Cromwell series
Gunn, Victor
see **Chief Inspector Bill Cromwell series**

Bill Davies series
Mason, Sara Elizabeth
see **Sheriff Bill Davies series**

Bill Decker series
Treat, Lawrence
1 *F as in flight* (1948)
2 *Over the edge* (1948)
3 *Big shot* (1951)

Bill Easter series
Blackburn, John
1 *Deep among the dead men* (1973)
2 *Mister Brown's bodies* (1975)
3 *Cyclops goblet* (1977)

Bill French series
Hale, Christopher
see **Lieutenant Bill French series**

Bill Gastner series
Havill, Steven F
1 *Heartshot* (1991)
2 *Bitter recoil* (1992)
3 *Twice buried* (1994)

Bill Grady series
Shriber, Ione Sandberg
see **Lieutenant Bill Grady series**

Bill Harland series
Allum, Tom
see **Hurricane Harland series**

Bill Harper and Shirley Leighton series
Ernst, Paul
see **Shirley Leighton and Bill Harper series**

Bill Hazard and Frank Drury series
Marlowe, Piers
see **Frank Drury and Inspector Bill Hazard series**

Bill Holmes series
Hughes, Gwilym Fielden
1 *Adventures of Bill Holmes* (1950)
2 *Bill Holmes and the red panthers* (1953)
3 *Bill Holmes and the fortune-teller* (1955)

Bill Houghton series
Culpan, Maurice
see **Inspector Bill Houghton series**

Bill, Jake and Ned series
Leyland, Eric
1 *Arizona round-up* (1951)
2 *Rustlers' trail* (1951)
3 *Outlaw Gulch* (1952)
4 *Indian Range* (1953)

Bill, Jed and Liza series
Parish, Peggy
see **Liza, Bill and Jed series**

Bill Kellaway series
Evans, Gwyn
1 *Hercules, Esq.* (1930)
Mister Hercules
2 *Homicide Club* (1931)
3 *Satan Ltd.* (1935)
4 *Return of Hercules* (1937)

Bill Kennedy series
Charteris, Leslie
1 *X Esquire* (1927)
2 *White rider* (1928)

Bill Kinderman series
Blatty, William Peter
see **Lieutenant Bill Kinderman series**

Bill Langley series
Meriton, Peter
1 *Three die at midnight* (1937)
American edition published under the author's real name John Hunter
2 *After Darvray died* (1938)

Bill Lennox series
Volumes of this sequence are variously published under the author's real name Willis Todhunter Ballard and his pseudonym John Shepherd
Ballard, Willis Todhunter
1 *Say yes to murder* (1942)
Also published as *The demise of a house*, under the pseudonym John Shepherd
2 *Murder can't stop* (1946)
3 *Dealing out death* (1948)
Shepherd, John
4 *Lights, camera, murder* (1960)
Ballard, Willis Todhunter
5 *Murder Las Vegas style* (1967)

Bill Lloyd series
Reed, Wallace
see **Sheriff Bill Lloyd series**

Bill Lockwood series
Latham, Brad
see **Hook series**

Bill Mitchell series
Wrenn, Harold Albert
see **William Mitchell series**

Bill Mitchum series
Wrexe, Charles
1 *Trail of no return* (1954)
2 *Blazing Colts* (1955)
3 *Marked bullets* (1955)
4 *Night rider* (1956)

Bill Murray series
Colin, Aubrey
see **Inspector Bill Murray series**

Bill of Grimley Grange series
Stones, Anthony
1 *Bill and the ghost of Grimley Grange* (1988)
2 *Bill and the maze at Grimley Grange* (1990)

Bill Owen series
Orczy, Emmuska
see **Old man in the corner series**

Bill Rice series
Stand, Marguerite
1 *Escape from murder* (1964)
2 *Death came with darkness* (1965)
3 *Death came with flowers* (1966)
4 *Death came in Lucerne* (1966)
5 *Death came with diamonds* (1966)
6 *Death came to Lighthouse Steps* (1968)
7 *Death came in the studio* (1969)
8 *Death came too soon* (1970)

Bill Rowlands series
Lucas, Norman
see **Superintendent Bill Rowlands series**

Bill Ryan series
Morgan, Michael
1 *Nine more lives* (1947)
Blonde body
2 *Decoy* (1953)

Bill Rye series
Spain, John
1 *Dig me a grave* (1942)
2 *Death is like that* (1943)

Bill Saville series
Daniel, Roland
1 *Society of the Spiders* (1928)
2 *Wu Fang* (1929)
3 *Remover* (1933)
4 *Blackmailer* (1934)
5 *Remover returns* (1935)
6 *Again the Remover* (1939)

Bill series
Adams, Georgie
see **Mister Bill series**
Green, Cliff
see **Riverboat Bill series**
James, Will
see **Uncle Bill series**
Stivens, Dal
see **Ironbark Bill series**
Wibberley, Leonard
see **Uncle Bill series**

Bill Slaker series
Redmond, Anton Edward
1 *Cancelled out* (1972)
2 *No exit* (1972)
3 *Dead is forever* (1973)

Bill Speed series
Donovan, Jean Beradine
1 *Laughing horse* (1961)
Mystery of the laughing horses
2 *Bill Speed on hot ice* (1962)
Disappearing diamonds
3 *Bill Speed, Special Squad* (1963)
White dynamite

Bill Tempest series
Shand, William
1 *Man called Tempest* (1957)
2 *Tempest weaves a shroud* (1957)
3 *Tempest in a tea-cup* (1958)

Bill Tern series
Wallace, Bryan Edgar
1 *Death packs a suitcase* (1961)
2 *Device* (1962)

Bill, the galactic hero series
Harrison, Harry
1 *Planet of robot slaves* (1989)
Bill, the galactic hero on the planet of tobot slaves
Bill, the galactic hero
2 *Bill, the galactic hero on the planet of bottled brains* (1990)
Co-author: Robert Sheckley
3 *Bill, the galactic hero on the planet of tasteless pleasure* (1991)
Co-author: David Bischoff
4 *Bill, the galactic hero on the planet of the zombie vampires* (1991)
Co-author: Jack Carroll Haldeman
5 *Bill, the galactic hero on the planet of ten thousand bars* (1991)
Co-author: David Bischoff
6 *Bill, the galactic hero on the planet of the hippies from hell* (1992)
Co-author: David Bischoff
7 *Final incoherent adventure* (1993)
Co-author: David Harris

Bill Thompson trilogy
Gallacher, Tom
1 *Apprentice* (1983)
2 *Journeyman* (1984)
3 *Survivor* (1985)

Bill Vallance series
Proudfoot, Walter
see **Inspector Bill Vallance series**

Bill Wiegand series
Lockridge, Frances
1 *Norths meet murder* (1940)
Mister and Mrs North meet murder
2 *Murder out of turn* (1941)
3 *Pinch of poison* (1941)
4 *Hanged for a sheep* (1942)
5 *Death on the aisle* (1942)
6 *Death takes a bow* (1943)
7 *Killing the goose* (1944)
8 *Payoff for the banker* (1945)

Bill Wiegand series

9 *Death of a tall man* (1946)
10 *Murder within murder* (1946)
11 *Untidy of murder* (1947)
12 *Murder is served* (1948)
13 *Dishonest murderer* (1949)
14 *Murder in a hurry* (1950)
15 *Murder comes first* (1951)
16 *Dead as a dinosaur* (1952)
17 *Curtain for a jester* (1952)
18 *Death has a small voice* (1953)
19 *Key to death* (1954)
20 *Death of an angel* (1955)
Mister and Mrs North and the poisoned playboy
21 *Voyage into violence* (1956)
22 *Tangled cord* (1957)
23 *Long skeleton* (1958)
24 *Murder is suggested* (1959)
25 *Judge is reversed* (1960)
26 *Murder has its points* (1961)
27 *Ticking clock* (1962)

Billabong series
Bruce, Mary Grant
1 *Little bush maid* (1910)
2 *Mates at Billabong* (1911)
3 *Norah at Billabong* (1913)
4 *From Billabong to London* (1915)
5 *Jim and Wally* (1916)
6 *Captain Jim* (1919)
7 *Back to Billabong* (1921)
8 *Billabong's daughter* (1924)
9 *Billabong adventurers* (1927)
10 *Bill of Billabong* (1931)
11 *Billabong's luck* (1933)
12 *Wings above Billabong* (1935)
13 *Billabong gold* (1937)
14 *Son of Billabong* (1939)
15 *Billabong riders* (1942)

Billie Bradley series
Wheeler, Janet D
1 *Billie Bradley and her inheritance* (1920)
Alternative title: The queer homestead at Cherry Corners
2 *Billie Bradley at Three Towers Hall* (1920)
Alternative title: Leading a needed rebellion
3 *Billie Bradley on Lighthouse Island* (1920)
Alternative title: The mystery of the wreck
4 *Billie Bradley and her classmates* (1921)
Alternative title: The secret of the locked tower
5 *Billie Bradley at Twin Lakes* (1922)
Alternative title: Jolly schoolgirls afloat and ashore
6 *Billie Bradley at Treasure Cove* (1928)
Alternative title: The old sailor's secret
7 *Billie Bradley at Sun Dial Lodge* (1929)
Alternative title: School chums solving a mystery
8 *Billie Bradley and the school mystery* (1930)
Alternative title: The girl from Oklahoma
9 *Billie Bradley winning the trophy* (1932)
Alternative title: Scoring against big odds

Billie Impett series
Ainsworth, Eustace
1 *Second Lieutenant Billie Impett and his orderly* (1917)
2 *Billie Impett and Doris* (1918)

Billiter series
Blaker, Richard
see **Hester Billiter series**

Billson series
Benson, Edward Frederic
see **Lucia Billson series**

Billy and Blaze series
Anderson, Clarence William
1 *Billy and Blaze* (1936)
2 *Blaze and the gypsies* (1937)
3 *Blaze and the forest fire* (1938)
4 *Blaze finds the trail* (1950)
5 *Blaze and Thunderbolt* (1955)
6 *Blaze and the mountain lion* (1959)
7 *Blaze and the Indian cave* (1964)
8 *Blaze and the lost quarry* (1966)
9 *Blaze and the gray spotted pony* (1968)
10 *Blaze shows the way* (1969)
11 *Blaze finds forgotten roads* (1970)

Billy and Owl series
Waddell, Martin
see **Owl and Billy series**

Billy Boyo and Albert Finn series
Niall, Ian
1 *Fishing for trouble* (1968)
2 *Owl hunters* (1969)

Billy Brown series
Kitt, Tamara
1 *Adventures of Silly Billy* (1961)
2 *Billy Brown makes something grand* (1961)
3 *Billy Brown, the baby sitter* (1962)
4 *Surprising pets of Billy Brown* (1962)

Billy Bunker series
Nokes, Ethel
1 *Nibs* (1934)
2 *Nibs in clover* (1939)

Billy Bunter series
Richards, Frank
1 *Billy Bunter of Greyfriars School* (1947)
2 *Billy Bunter's barring-out* (1948)
3 *Billy Bunter's banknote* (1948)
4 *Billy Bunter in Brazil* (1949)
5 *Billy Bunter's Christmas party* (1949)
Bunter's Christmas party
6 *Billy Bunter among the cannibals* (1950)
7 *Billy Bunter's benefit* (1950)
8 *Billy Bunter butts in* (1951)
9 *Billy Bunter's postal order* (1951)
10 *Billy Bunter and the blue Mauritius* (1952)
11 *Billy Bunter's beanfeast* (1952)
12 *Billy Bunter's brainwave* (1953)
13 *Billy Bunter's first case* (1953)
14 *Billy Bunter the bold* (1954)
15 *Bunter does his best* (1954)
Billy Bunter does his best
16 *Backing up Billy Bunter* (1955)
17 *Billy Bunter's double* (1955)
18 *Banishing of Billy Bunter* (1956)
19 *Lord Billy Bunter* (1956)
20 *Billy Bunter afloat* (1957)
21 *Billy Bunter's bolt* (1957)
22 *Billy Bunter the hiker* (1958)
23 *Billy Bunter's bargain* (1958)
24 *Bunter comes for Christmas* (1959)
Billy Bunter comes for Christmas
25 *Bunter out of bounds* (1959)
26 *Bunter keeps it dark* (1960)
27 *Bunter the bad lad* (1960)
28 *Billy Bunter at Butlin's* (1961)
29 *Billy Bunter's treasure-hunt* (1961)
30 *Bunter the ventriloquist* (1961)
31 *Billy Bunter's bodyguard* (1962)
32 *Bunter the caravanner* (1962)
33 *Just like Bunter* (1963)
34 *Big Chief Bunter* (1963)
35 *Bunter the stowaway* (1964)
36 *Thanks to Bunter* (1964)
37 *Bunter and the phantom of the towers* (1965)
38 *Bunter the racketeer* (1965)
39 *Bunter the sportsman* (1965)
40 *Bunter the tough guy of Greyfriars* (1965)
41 *Bunter's holiday cruise* (1965)
42 *Bunter's last fling* (1965)
43 *Billy Bunter and the man from South America* (1967)
44 *Billy Bunter and the school rebellion* (1967)
45 *Billy Bunter and the secret enemy* (1967)
46 *Billy Bunter's big top* (1967)
47 *Billy Bunter and the bank robber* (1968)
48 *Billy Bunter, sportsman* (1968)
49 *Billy Bunter and the crooked captain* (1968)
50 *Billy Bunter's convict* (1968)
Companion volumes *Billy Bunter's own*, 1953-59

Billy Clyde Puckett series
Jenkins, Dan
1 *Semi-tough* (1972)
2 *Life its ownself* (1984)

Billy Dancey series
Breeze, Paul
1 *While my guitar gently weeps* (1979)
2 *Back street runner* (1980)

Billy de Salis series
Pardoe, Margot
see **Bunkle series**

Billy Dupree series
Bexar, Phil
1 *Showdown in Gunsmoke* (1958)
2 *Outlaw marshal* (1959)
3 *Six-gun fury* (1959)
4 *Lone prairie* (1960)
5 *Cowtown fury* (1961)
6 *Trail to Slaughter Creek* (1961)
7 *Cowtown marshal* (1962)
8 *Texas terror* (1962)
9 *Maverick gunfighter* (1963)
10 *Rustler guns* (1964)

Billy Fisher series
Waterhouse, Keith
see **Billy Liar series**

Billy Forrester series
Rockwell, Thomas
1 *How to eat fried worms* (1973)
2 *How to fight a girl* (1987)
3 *How to get fabulously rich* (1990)

Billy Jack series
Christina, Frank
Screenplays
1 *Billy Jack* (1973)
2 *Trial of Billy Jack* (1974)
Novelization: *The trial of Billy Jack*, by Howard Liebling, 1974
3 *Billy Jack goes to Washington* (1977)

Billy Liar series
Waterhouse, Keith
1 *Billy Liar* (1959)
2 *Billy Liar on the moon* (1975)

Billy Nevers series
Glazner, Joseph Mark
1 *Smart money doesn't sing or dance* (1979)
2 *Fast money shoots from the hip* (1980)
3 *Dirty money can't wash both hands at once* (1980)
4 *Big Apple money is rotten to the core* (1981)
5 *Hot money can cook your goose* (1981)

Billy Prior series
Barker, Pat
1 *Regeneration* (1991)
2 *Eye in the door* (1993)

Billy Ray series
Roderus, Frank
1 *Billy Ray and the good news* (1987)
2 *Billy Ray's forty days* (1989)

Billy series
Holland, Marion
1 *Billy had a system* (1952)
2 *Billy's clubhouse* (1955)

Billy series
Porter, Eleanor Hodgman
see **Miss Billy series**

Billy Smith series
Sainsbury, Noel
1 *Billy Smith exploring Ace* (1928)
Alternative titles: Into the heart of savage New Guinea, and By airplane to New guinea
2 *Billy Smith, secret service ace* (1932)
Alternative title: Airplane adventures in Arabia
3 *Billy Smith, mystery ace* (1932)
Alternative title: Airplane discoveries in South America
4 *Billy Smith, trail eater ace* (1933)
Alternative title: Into the wilds of northern Alaska by airplane
5 *Billy Smith shangaied ace* (1934)
Alternative title: Malay pirates and Solomon Island cannibals

Billy Topsail series
Duncan, Norman
see **Doctor Luke series**

Bilsley Pack series
Travis, Falcon
see **Third bilsley Pack series**

Bim series
Lindsay, Frances
1 *Half-price bear* (1986)
2 *Bim, the very special bear* (1987)
3 *Runaway Bim* (1989)

Bimbo series
Blyton, Enid
1 *Bimbo and Topsy* (1943)
Revised edition 1981
2 *Bimbo, the little kitten* (1953)
3 *Bimbo and his cousin* (1954)
4 *Bimbo and Blackie* (1954)
5 *Bimbo and Blackie go camping* (1955)
6 *Christmas with Scamp and Bimbo* (1955)

Bindle series
Jenkins, Herbert
1 *Bindle* (1916)
2 *Night club* (1917)
3 *Adventures of Bindle* (1918)
4 *Mrs Bindle* (1921)
5 *Bindles on the rocks* (1924)

Bing Irvington series
Baldwin, Faith
see **Doctor Bing Irvington series**

Bing series
Blaylock, James Paul
see **Jonathan Bing series**

Bingham Harvard series
Vanardy, Varick
1 *Alias the night wind* (1913)
2 *Return of the night wind* (1914)
3 *Night wind's promise* (1914)
4 *Lady of the night wind* (1919)

Bingo Bones and the Boggart series
Roberts, K H
1 *Bingo Bones and the Boggart* (1982)
2 *Bingo, Boggart and the furry cubs* (1986)

Bingo Brown series
Byars, Betsy
1 *Burning questions of Bingo Brown* (1988)
2 *Bingo Brown and the language of love* (1989)
3 *Bingo Brown, gypsy lover* (1990)

Bingo Riggs and Handsome Kusak series
Rice, Craig
1 *Sunday pigeon murders* (1942)
2 *Thursday turkey murders* (1943)
3 *April Robin murders* (1958)
Completed by Ed McBain

Binklebys series
Williams, Ursula Moray
1 *Binklebys at home* (1951)
2 *Binklebys on the farm* (1953)

Binks family series
Winter, John Strange
1 *Binks family* (1899)
Story of a social evolution
2 *Married Miss Binks* (1900)

Binns series
Newton, William
see **Joey Binns series**

Binton series
Barth, Richard
see **Margaret Binton series**

Bio of a space tyrant series
Anthony, Piers
1 *Refugee* (1983)
2 *Mercenary* (1984)
3 *Politician* (1985)
4 *Executive* (1985)
5 *Statesman* (1986)
Companion volume: *Cut by emerald, Combat Command in the world of Piers Anthony's Bio of a space tyrant*, by Dana Kramer, 1987

Biography of Dom Manuel and his descendants series
Cabell, James Branch
see **Dom Manuel and his descendants series**

Biography series
Bentley, Edmund Clerihew
see **Clerihews series**

Bionic woman series
Lottman, Eileen
1 *Welcome home, Jaime* (1976)
Also published as *Double identity*, under the pseudonym Maud Willis
2 *Extracurricular activities* (1977)
Also published as *Question of life*, under the pseudonym Maud Willis

Biowarriors trilogy
Vardeman, Robert Edward
1 *Infinity plague* (1989)
2 *Crisis at Starlight* (1990)
3 *Space vectors* (1990)

Birch series
Lee, W W
see **Jefferson Birch series**

Bird Boys series
Langworthy, John Luther
1 *Bird Boys* (1912)
Alternative title: The young sky pilots' first air voyage
2 *Bird Boys on the wing* (1912)
Alternative title: Aeroplane chums in the tropics
3 *Bird Boys among the clouds* (1912)
Alternative title: Young aviators in a wreck
4 *Bird Boys' flight* (1914)
Alternative title: A hydroplane roundup
5 *Bird Boys' aeroplane wonder* (1914)
Alternative title: Young aviators on a cattle ranch

Bird of kinship series
Cowper, Richard
1 *Road to Corlay* (1978)
Revised edition 1979; based on a story entitled Piper and the gates of dawn, published in *The custodians, and other stories*, 1988
2 *Dream of kinship* (1981)
3 *Tapestry of time* (1982)

Bird series
Robertson, Don
see **Morris Bird III series**

Birdcage trilogy
Canning, Victor
1 *Birdcage* (1978)
2 *Satan sampler* (1979)
3 *Vanishing point* (1982)

Birdie Linnett and Nimue Hawthorne series
Linscott, Gillian
1 *Healthy body* (1984)
2 *Murder makes tracks* (1985)
3 *Knightfall* (1986)
4 *Whiff of sulphur* (1987)

Birdland series
Bancroft, Laura
1 *Bandit Jim Crow* (1906)
2 *Policeman Bluejay* (1911)
Babes in Birdland

Birds series
Ardley, Neil
1 *Birds of towns* (1975)
2 *Birds of the country* (1975)
3 *Birds of coasts, lakes and rivers* (1976)

Birdseye series
Spain, Nancy
see **Miriam Birdseye series**

Birdwell series
West, Jessamyn
see **Jess and Eliza Birdwell series**

Birdwood series
Rowe, Jennifer
see **Verity Birdwood series**

Birdy Birdwood series
Rowe, Jennifer
see **Verity Birdwood series**

Birdy Jones series
Hildick, Edmund Wallace
1 *Birdy Jones* (1963)
2 *Birdy and the group* (1968)
3 *Birdy swings north* (1969)
4 *Birdy in Amsterdam* (1970)
5 *Birdy Jones and the New York heads* (1974)

Birge Moreau series
Vanardy, Varick
see **Crewe series**

Birge series
Krasner, William
see **Sam Birge series**

Birkett series
Payne, Laurence
see **Chief Inspector Sam Birkett series**

Birman series
Jackson, Charles Reginald
see **Don Birman series**

Birmingham life series
Dayus, Kathleen
1 *Her people* (1982)
2 *Where there's life* (1985)
3 *All my days* (1988)

Birney series
Livingston, Jack
see **Joe Birney series**

Birth series
Miller, Jane
Photographic picture books
1 *Birth of a foal* (1977)
2 *Lambing time* (1978)
3 *Calf is born* (1981)
4 *Birth of piglets* (1984)

Birthday girls series
Thesman, Jean
1 *I'm not telling* (1992)
2 *Mirror, mirror* (1992)
3 *Who am I, anyway?* (1992)

Birthday series
Beccaria, Mijo
Translated from the French
1 *It's fun to be one* (1985)
2 *It's fun to be two* (1985)
3 *It's fun to be three* (1985)
4 *It's fun to be four* (1985)
5 *It's fun to be five* (1985)

Birthday series
Rush, Robert
1 *Birthday girl* (1983)
2 *Birthday treat* (1983)

Birthday tales series
Adams, Henry Cadwallader
1 *Falconshurst* (1869)
Alternative title: Birthday tales
2 *Falcon family* (1874)
Alternative title: Meta and Willy

Birthgrave trilogy
Lee, Tanith
1 *Birthgrave* (1975)
2 *Vazkor, son of Vazkor* (1978)
Shadowfire
3 *Quest for the white witch* (1978)

Birtley series
Alington, Cyril Augustine
see **Mister Birtley series**

Biscuits, buttons and pickles series
Taylor, E J
1 *Ivy Cottage* (1984)
2 *Goose eggs* (1984)
3 *Thorn witch* (1985)
4 *Rag doll press* (1985)

Bishop of Kenelminster series
Hope-Simpson, Jacynth
1 *Bishop of Kenelminster* (1961)
2 *Bishop's picture* (1962)

Bishop series
Ellery, Jan
see **Adrienne Bishop series**
Foreman, Leonard London
see **Rogue Bishop series**
Homes, Geoffrey
see **Robin Bishop series**
Jeier, Thomas
see **Matt Bishop series**
Montague, J J
see **Black Swan series**
Rattray, Simon
see **Hugo Bishop series**

Bits and Pieces series
Lindsay, Frances
see **Mister Bits and Pieces series**

Bitter sea series
Dillon, Eilis
1 *Across the bitter sea* (1973)
2 *Blood relations* (1977)

Bixby Wyler series
Leroe, Ellen Whitney
1 *Robot romance* (1984)
2 *Robot raiders* (1985)

Bjorndal family series
Gulbranssen, Trygve
Translated from the Norwegian
1 *Beyond sing the woods* (1933)
2 *Wind from the mountains* (1934)
Wind from the mountain

Black and Braddock series
Johnson, Susan
see **Blaze Braddock and Jon Hazard Black series**

Black and Wild series
Carter, Bruce
see **Danny Black and Johnny Wild series**

Black Avons series
Wallace, Edgar
1 *How they fared in the times of the Tudors* (1926)
2 *Roundhead and Cavalier* (1926)
3 *From Waterloo to the Mutiny* (1926)
4 *Europe in the melting pot* (1926)

Black Banner series
Trease, Geoffrey
see **Bannermere series**

Black Bat series
Jones, G Wayman
House pseudonym; the 34 titles in this sequence are those which have been reprinted in book form from the 62 titles which originally appeared in the *Black Book Detective magazine* between 1939 and 1953; the dates shown are those of the original magazine publication
1 *Brand of the black bat* (1939)
2 *Murder calls the Black Bat* (1939)
3 *Black Bat strikes again* (1939)
4 *Black Bat's challenge* (1940)
5 *Black Bat's spy trail* (1940)
6 *Black Bat's crusade* (1940)
7 *Black Bat's flame trail* (1940)
8 *Black Bat's triumph* (1940)
9 *Black Bat and the Trojan horse* (1940)
10 *Black Bat and the Dragon Trail* (1941)
11 *Black Bat's justice* (1941)
12 *Black Bat and the Red Menace* (1941)
13 *Black Bat's invisible enemy* (1941)
14 *Voice of doom* (1941)
15 *Blackout murders* (1942)
16 *Seventh column* (1943)
17 *Millions for a murderer* (1943)
18 *Captains of death* (1943)
19 *Without blood they die* (1943)
20 *Guardian in black* (1943)
21 *White witch* (1944)
22 *Murder on the loose* (1945)
23 *Murder among the dying* (1945)
24 *Blind man's bluff* (1946)
25 *Man behind the murder* (1946)
26 *Survivor murders* (1946)
27 *Masked man* (1947)
28 *Long-ago murders* (1947)
29 *Murder maker* (1948)
30 *Dennison documents* (1948)
31 *Murder's playground* (1949)
32 *Mission million* (1949)
33 *Black Bat fights for life* (1950)
34 *League of Faceless Men* (1951)

Black Beauty series
This sequence has five authors
Sewell, Anna
1 *Black Beauty, his grooms and companions* (1877)
The autobiography of a horse
Companion volume: *Strike at Shane's, a*

Black Beauty series

prize story of Indiana, by James S Shelton, 1893

Briggs, Phyllis

2 *Son of Black Beauty* (1954)

Pullein-Thompson, Christine

3 *Black Beauty's clan* (1975)
Co-authors: Diana Pullein-Thompson and Josephine Pullein-Thompson

3.1 *Black Ebony* (1975)

3.2 *Black Princess* (1975)

3.3 *Black Velvet* (1975)

4 *Black Beauty's family, book 1* (1978)

5 *Black Beauty's family, book 2* (1982)

Black Berets series

McCray, Mike

1 *Deadly reunion* (1984)
2 *Cold vengeance* (1984)
3 *Black palm* (1984)
4 *Contract White Lady* (1984)
5 *Louisiana firestorm* (1985)
6 *Death machine contract* (1985)
7 *Red man contract* (1985)
8 *D.C. death march* (1986)
9 *Night of the jaguar* (1986)
10 *Contract Terror Summit* (1986)
11 *Samurai contract* (1987)
12 *Akbar contract* (1987)
13 *Blue water contract* (1987)

Companion volumes: *Black Berets*, 1984, *L.A. payback*, 1985

Black Boar series

Wiat, Philippa

1 *Raven in the wind* (1978)
2 *Lord of the Black Boar* (1975)
3 *Sword of Woden* (1975)
4 *Tree of Vortigern* (1976)
5 *Atheling* (1977)
6 *Westerfalca* (1979)
7 *Lord of the Wolf* (1980)

Black boy series

Wright, Richard Nathaniel
see **Horror and the glory series**

Black brute trilogy

Tralins, Sandor Robert
see **Black stud trilogy**

Black Circle Gang series

Kennett, John

1 *Peril for the guy* (1955)
2 *Walk into peril* (1957)
3 *Peril all the way* (1959)

Black Company series

Cook, Glen
see **Chronicles of the Black Company series**

Black cop series

Gober, Don
see **James Rhodes series**

Black Cossacks series

Kessler, Leo

1 *Black Cossacks* (1975)
2 *Sabres of the Reich* (1976)
3 *Mountain of skulls* (1977)
4 *Breakthrough* (1979)

Black country series

Alldritt, Keith

1 *Good pit man* (1976)
2 *Lover next door* (1977)
3 *Elgar on the journey to Hanley* (1979)

Black Current trilogy

Watson, Ian

1 *Book of the River* (1984)
2 *Book of the Stars* (1984)
3 *Book of Being* (1985)

One volume edition entitled *The books of the Black Current*, 1986

Black Dragon series

Macavoy, Roberta Ann
see **Mayland Long and Martha Macnamara series**

Black Duke series

Dexter, Ross
see **Duke Lawson series**

Black Eagles series

Lansing, John

1 *Hanoi hellground* (1983)
2 *Mekong massacre* (1983)
3 *Nightmare in Laos* (1984)
4 *Pungi patrol* (1984)
5 *Saigon slaughter* (1984)
6 *AK-47 Firefight* (1985)
7 *Beyond the DMZ* (1985)
8 *Boocoo death* (1985)
9 *Bad scene at Bong Son* (1986)
10 *Cambodia kill-zone* (1986)
11 *Duel on the Song Cai* (1987)
Number 12 not identified
13 *Encore at Dien Bien Phu* (1987)
14 *Firestorm at Dong Nam* (1988)
15 *Ho's hellhounds* (1988)
16 *Monsoon hellhole* (1988)
17 *Mau Len death zone* (1988)
18 *Durong warrior* (1989)
19 *Hoa-Tien kill* (1989)
20 *Bo Binh command* (1990)
21 *Nguy Hiem war zone* (1990)

Black fire series

Roberts, Kenneth

1 *Blaze* (1969)
2 *Flame* (1970)

Black flame trilogy

Du Bois, William Edward Burghardt

1 *Ordeal of Mansart* (1957)
2 *Mansart builds a school* (1959)
3 *Worlds of color* (1961)

One volume edition entitled *The black flame*, 1976

Black harvest series

Cheetham, Ann

1 *Black harvest* (1983)
2 *Beggar's curse* (1984)
3 *Witch of Lagg* (1985)
4 *Pit* (1987)

Black Heart Crowle series

Hanson, Victor Joseph
see **Amos Crowle series**

Black Hole Travel Agency series

McKinney, Jack

1 *Event horizon* (1991)
2 *Artifact of the system* (1991)

Black John and Hazel series

Martin, Rhona

1 *Gallows wedding* (1978)
2 *Unicorn summer* (1984)

Black John series

Hendryx, James Beardsley

1 *Raw gold* (1933)
2 *Outlaws of Halfaday Creek* (1935)
Short stories
3 *Black John of Halfaday Creek* (1939)
Short stories
4 *Hard Rock Man* (1940)
5 *Czar of Halfaday Creek* (1940)
Short stories
6 *Law and order on Halfaday Creek* (1941)
Short stories
7 *Strange doings on Halfaday Creek* (1943)
Short stories
8 *Gold and guns on Halfaday Creek* (1943)
Short stories
9 *It happened on Halfaday Creek* (1944)
Short stories
10 *Way of the north* (1945)
11 *Skulduggery on Halfaday Creek* (1946)
Short stories
12 *Saga of Halfaday Creek* (1947)
Short stories
13 *Justice on Halfaday Creek* (1949)
Short stories
14 *Badmen on Halfaday Creek* (1950)
Short stories
15 *Murder on Halfaday Creek* (1951)
Short stories
16 *Sourdough gold* (1952)
17 *Intrigue on Halfaday Creek* (1953)
Short stories
18 *Terror on Halfaday Creek* (1963)
Short stories

Black majesty series

Nicole, Christopher

1 *Seeds of rebellion* (1984)
2 *Wild harvest* (1985)

Black man trilogy

Ryan, Isobel

1 *Black man's country* (1950)
2 *Black man's town* (1953)
3 *Black man's palaver* (1958)

Black Maria series

Slate, John

1 *Black Maria, M.A.* (1944)
2 *Maria marches on* (1945)
3 *One remained seated* (1946)
4 *Thy arm alone* (1947)
5 *Death in silhouette* (1950)

Black Marsden series

Harris, Wilson

1 *Black Marsden* (1972)
A tabula rasa comedy set in Scotland
2 *Companions of the day and night* (1975)
Set in Mexico

Black Nickum series

Robertson, Jean
see **Little Black Nickum series**

Black pearl series

Roberts, Willo Davis

1 *Dark dowry* (1978)
2 *Cade curse* (1978)
3 *Stuart stain* (1978)
4 *Devil's double* (1979)
5 *Radkin revenge* (1979)
6 *Hellfire heritage* (1979)
7 *Macomber menace* (1979)
8 *Gresham ghost* (1980)

Black Pilgrim series

Stanley, George

1 *Adventure of the Black Pilgrim* (1945)
2 *Further adventures of the Black Pilgrim* (1945)

Black Pony Inn series

Pullein-Thompson, Christine

1 *Strange riders at Black Pony Inn* (1976)
2 *Mystery at Black Pony Inn* (1976)
3 *Prince at Black Pony Inn* (1978)
4 *Secrets at Black Pony Inn* (1978)

Black roots trilogy

Tralins, Sandor Robert
see **Black stud trilogy**

Black Samurai series

Olden, Marc
see **Robert Sand series**

Black Sea trilogy

Tarsis, Valeriy

1 *Pleasure factory* (1967)
2 *Gay life* (1968)
3 *Thousand illusions* (1966)

Black series

Chance, John Newton
see **Superintendent Black series**

Garnett, Roger
see **Chief Inspector Jonathan Black series**

Jakes, John
see **Gavin Black series**

Manson, Will
see **Man called Black series**

Black series

Nazel, Joseph

1 *My name is Black* (1973)
2 *Black is black* (1974)

Black series

Pemberton, Max
see **Captain Black series**

Smith, Hendy
see **Johnny Black series**

Southall, Ivan
see **Simon Black series**

Black Sheep Squadron series

Jahn, Mike

1 *Devil in the slot* (1978)
2 *Hawk flies on Sunday* (1980)

Companion volume: *Baa baa Black Sheep*, by Gregory Boyington, 1958

Black stallion series

Farley, Walter

1 *Black stallion* (1941)
Abridged edition entitled *The black stallion picture book*, 1979
2 *Black stallion returns* (1945)
3 *Son of the black stallion* (1947)
4 *Island stallion* (1948)
5 *Black stallion and Satan* (1949)
Revised edition 1974
6 *Blood bay colt* (1950)
7 *Island stallion's fury* (1951)
8 *Black stallion's filly* (1952)
9 *Black stallion revolts* (1953)
10 *Black stallion's sulky colt* (1954)
11 *Island stallion races* (1955)
12 *Black stallion's courage* (1956)
13 *Black stallion's mystery* (1957)
14 *Horse-tamer* (1958)
15 *Black stallion and Flame* (1960)
Revised edition 1974
16 *Man o' War* (1962)
17 *Black stallion challenged* (1964)
Black stallion's challenge
18 *Black stallion's ghost* (1969)
19 *Black stallion and the girl* (1971)
20 *Black stallion legend* (1983)

Black Star series

McCulley, Johnston

1 *Black Star* (1921)
2 *Black Star's campaign* (1924)
3 *Black Star's return* (1926)
4 *Black Star's revenge* (1931)
Black Star again

Black stud trilogy

Tralins, Sandor Robert

1 *Black brute* (1969)
Black stud
2 *Runaway slave* (1969)
Rampage
3 *Slave's revenge* (1969)
Rampage

Black Swan series

Montague, J J

1 *Chinese kiss* (1974)
2 *Cong kiss* (1974)
3 *French kiss* (1974)

Black swan series

Taylor, Day

1 *Black swan* (1978)
2 *Moss rose* (1980)

Black Tiger series

O'Connor, Patrick

1 *Black Tiger* (1956)

2 *Mexican road race* (1957)
3 *Black Tiger at Le Mans* (1958)
4 *Black Tiger at Bonneville* (1960)
5 *Black Tiger at Indianapolis* (1962)

Black turret series
Wynnton, Patrick
1 *Black turret* (1925)
2 *Ten jewels* (1931)

Black Vulmea series
This sequence has two authors
Howard, Robert Ervin
1 *Black Vulmea's vengeance* (1977)
Smith, David Claude
2 *Witch of the Indies* (1977)

Black Widowers series
Asimov, Isaac
Short stories
1 *Tales of the Black Widowers* (1974)
2 *More tales of the Black Widowers* (1976)
3 *Casebook of the Black Widowers* (1980)
4 *Banquets of the Black Widowers* (1984)
5 *Puzzles of the Black Widowers* (1990)

Blackbeard series
Stahl, Ben
1 *Blackbeard's ghost* (1965)
2 *Secret of Red Skull* (1971)

Blackberry Farm series
Pilgrim, Jane
Illustrated by F Stocks May
1 *Emily the goat* (1949)
2 *Mrs Nibble* (1949)
3 *Henry goes visiting* (1950)
4 *Little Martha* (1950)
5 *Rusty the sheepdog* (1950)
6 *Christmas at Blackberry Farm* (1951)
7 *Mother Hen and Mary* (1951)
8 *Postman Joe* (1951)
9 *Adventures of Walter* (1952)
10 *Ernest Owl starts a school* (1952)
11 *Lucy Mouse keeps a secret* (1952)
12 *Birthday picnic* (1953)
13 *Mrs Squirrel and Hazel* (1953)
14 *Naughty George* (1953)
15 *Mrs Nibble moves house* (1957)
16 *Walter Duck and Winifred* (1958)
17 *Hide and seek at Blackberry Farm* (1959)
18 *Bunny in trouble* (1960)
19 *Sports day at Blackberry Farm* (1961)
20 *Poor Mister Nibble* (1962)
21 *Snow at Blackberry Farm* (1963)
22 *Mister Nibble calls the doctor* (1964)
Numbers 8, 10, 21, 22 also published in one volume entitled *Blackberry Farm storybook*, 1982
23 *Sam Sparrow* (1965)
24 *Saturday at Blackberry Farm* (1966)
25 *Mister Mole takes charge* (1967)
26 *Round the year at Blackberry Farm* (1985)
Companion volume: *First book of Blackberry Farm*, 1964

Blackbird series
Furminger, Jo
1 *Pony at Blackbird Cottage* (1975)
2 *Blackbirds ride a mystery trail* (1976)
3 *Blackbirds' pony trek* (1977)
4 *Blackbirds and the gift pony* (1978)
5 *Blackbirds' own gymkhana* (1979)
6 *Saddle up, Blackbirds* (1980)
7 *Blackbirds at the gallop* (1981)
8 *Blackbirds and the midnight horse* (1984)

Blackbird series
Warrington, Freda
see **Quest of the serpent series**

Blackboard Bear series
Alexander, Martha G
1 *Blackboard Bear* (1969)
2 *And my mean old mother will be sorry, Blackboard Bear* (1976)
3 *I sure am glad to see you, Blackboard Bear* (1976)
4 *We're in big trouble, Blackboard Bear* (1980)

Blackburn series
Afford, Max
see **Jeffery Blackburn series**

Blackcollar series
Zahn, Timothy
1 *Blackcollar* (1983)
2 *Backlash mission* (1986)

Blackfoot series
Schultz, James Willard
1 *My life as an Indian* (1906)
The story of a red woman and a white man in the lodges of the Blackfeet; serialized as *The lodges of the Blackfeet*
2 *Friends of my life as an Indian* (1923)

Blackford Oakes series
Buckley, William Frank
1 *Saving the Queen* (1976)
2 *Stained glass* (1978)
3 *Who's on first?* (1980)
4 *Marco Polo, if you can* (1982)
5 *Story of Henri Tod* (1984)
6 *See you later, alligator* (1985)
7 *High Jinx* (1986)
8 *Mongoose, R.I.P.* (1988)

Blackgrove series
Mackintosh, Ian
see **Tim Blackgrove series**

Blackheart series
Stuart, Anne
see **Catspaw series**

Blackie Ryan series
Greeley, Andrew Moran
see **Monsignor John Blackwood Ryan series**

Blackjack Endicott series
Roosevelt, Elliott
1 *President's man* (1991)
2 *New deal for death* (1993)

Blackoaks series
Carter, Ashley
1 *Master of Blackoaks* (1976)
2 *Secret of Blackoaks* (1978)
3 *Heritage of Blackoaks* (1982)
4 *Farewell to Blackoaks* (1984)

Blackshirt series
Graeme, Bruce
1 *Blackshirt* (1925)
Revised edition 1930
2 *Return of Blackshirt* (1927)
Revised edition 1927
3 *Blackshirt again* (1929)
Adventures of Blackshirt
4 *Alias Blackshirt* (1932)
5 *Blackshirt the audacious* (1935)
6 *Blackshirt the adventurer* (1936)
7 *Blackshirt takes a hand* (1937)
8 *Blackshirt counter-spy* (1938)
9 *Blackshirt interferes* (1939)
10 *Blackshirt strikes back* (1940)
Sequence continued by the author's son, Roderic Graeme
Graeme, Roderic
11 *Concerning Blackshirt* (1952)
12 *Blackshirt wins the trick* (1953)
13 *Blackshirt passes by* (1953)
14 *Salute to Blackshirt* (1954)
15 *Amazing Mister Blackshirt* (1955)
16 *Blackshirt meets the lady* (1956)
17 *Paging Blackshirt* (1957)
18 *Blackshirt helps himself* (1958)
19 *Double for Blackshirt* (1958)
20 *Blackshirt sets the pace* (1959)
21 *Blackshirt sees it through* (1960)
22 *Blackshirt finds trouble* (1961)
23 *Blackshirt takes the trail* (1962)
24 *Call for Blackshirt* (1963)
25 *Blackshirt on the spot* (1963)
26 *Blackshirt saves the day* (1964)
27 *Danger for Blackshirt* (1965)
28 *Blackshirt at large* (1966)
29 *Blackshirt in peril* (1967)
30 *Blackshirt stirs things up* (1969)

Blackshirt series
Graeme, David
see **Monsieur Blackshirt series**

Blackstone series
Falkirk, Richard
see **Edmund Blackstone series**

Blackstone's magical adventure series
Dennison, Milo
1 *America's secret king* (1986)
2 *Secrets of Stonehenge* (1986)

Blackthorne series
Marsh, Geoffrey
see **Lincoln Blackthorne series**

Blackwater series
McDowell, Michael M
1 *Flood* (1983)
2 *Levee* (1983)
3 *House* (1983)
4 *War* (1983)
5 *Fortune* (1983)
6 *Rain* (1983)
Omnibus volume entitled *Blackwater*, 1983

Blackwood family series
Reeman, Douglas
1 *Badge of glory* (1982)
2 *First to land* (1984)

Blackwood series
Starrett, Vincent
see **Riley Blackwood series**

Blacky Oakes series
Buckley, William Frank
see **Blackford Oakes series**

Blade series
Chisholm, Matt
see **Joe Blade series**
Jackson, Ken
see **Jud Blade series**
Lord, Jeffrey
see **Richard Blade series**

Blade series
Robbins, David
1 *First strike* (1989)
2 *Outlands strike* (1989)
3 *Vampire strike* (1989)
4 *Pipeline strike* (1989)
5 *Pirate strike* (1989)
6 *Crusher strike* (1990)
7 *Terror strike* (1990)
8 *Devil strike* (1990)
9 *L.A. strike* (1990)
10 *Dead zone strike* (1990)
11 *Quest strike* (1991)
12 *Death master strike* (1991)
13 *Vengeance strike* (1991)

Blaike family series
Muskett, Netta
1 *Crown of willow* (1957)
2 *High fence* (1959)

Blaine McCracken series
Land, Jon
1 *Omega command* (1986)
2 *Alpha deception* (1988)
3 *Gamma option* (1989)
4 *Omicron legion* (1991)

Blaine series
Davis, Lavinia Riker
see **Nora Hughes and Larry Blaine series**
Young, Carter Travis
see **Cullom Blaine series**

Blainey series
Newby, Percy Howard
see **Eric Blainey series**

Blair and Beldrum series
Hay, Lindsay Fitzgerald
see **Archibald Beldrum and Nigel Blair series**

Blair and Bloomfield series
Little, Jean
see **Emily Blair and Kate Bloomfield series**

Blair Emerson series
Amey, Linda
1 *Bury her sweetly* (1992)
2 *At dead of night* (1993)

Blair family series
Gowans, Elizabeth
1 *Stravaigers* (1984)
2 *Shepherd's warning* (1985)
3 *Sleeping warrior* (1986)

Blair series
Allen, Betsy
see **Connie Blair series**
Anderson, John Richard Lane
see **Major Peter Blair series**
Knight, Kathleen Moore
see **Margot Blair series**

Blaize series
Benson, Edward Frederic
see **David Blaize series**

Blake family series
Hodges, Arthur
1 *Man of substance* (1931)
2 *Glittering hour* (1933)

Blake series
Bly, Stephen Arthur
see **Crystal Blake series**
Chance, John Newton
see **Jonathan Blake series**
Conaway, Jim C
see **Jana Blake series**
Farrar, Stewart
see **Bridget and George Blake series**
Garis, Cleo Fausta
see **Arden Blake series**
Greene, Yvonne
see **Kelly Blake series**
Gunn, John
see **Andrew Blake series**
Lee, Edward
see **Red Blake series**
Masters, Zeke
see **Faro Blake series**
Mitchell, Silas Weir
see **Roland Blake series**
Powell, Richard
see **Arab and Andy Blake series**
Warner, Frank A
see **Bobby Blake series**

Blake Walker series
Norton, Andre
1 *Crossroads of time* (1956)
2 *Quest crosstime* (1965)
Crosstime agent

Blakeley series
Fitzhugh, Percy Keese
see **Roy Blakeley series**

Blakeney papers series
Clayton, Colin Guy
1 *Daughter of the Revolution* (1984)
2 *Such mighty rage* (1985)
3 *Bordeaux red* (1986)

Blakeney series
Orczy, Emmuska
see **Scarlet Pimpernel series**

Blake's Seven series
This sequence has three authors; based on a television series
Hoyle, Trevor
1 *Terry Nation's Blake's Seven* (1977)
2 *Project Avalon* (1979)
3 *Scorpio attack* (1981)
Attwood, Tony
4 *Afterlife* (1984)
Darrow, Paul
5 *Terry Nation's Avon, a terrible aspect* (1989)

Blancanales series
Stivers, Dick
see **Able Team series**

Blanche Hampton series
Barnes, Trevor
1 *Midsummer killing* (1989)
Midsummer night's killing
2 *Dead meat* (1991)
Pound of flesh
3 *Taped* (1992)

Bland series
Symons, Julian
see **Inspector Bland series**

Blandings Castle series
Wodehouse, Pelham Grenville
1 *Something fresh* (1915)
Something new
2 *Leave it to Psmith* (1923)
3 *Blandings Castle* (1935)
4 *Summer lightning* (1929)
Fish preferred
5 *Heavy weather* (1933)
6 *Lord Emsworth and others* (1937)
Crime wave at Blandings
7 *Uncle Fred in the springtime* (1939)
8 *Full moon* (1947)
9 *Pigs have wings* (1952)
10 *Service with a smile* (1961)
11 *Galahad at Blandings* (1965)
Brinkmanship of Galahad
12 *Plum pie* (1967)
Short stories
13 *Pelican at Blandings* (1969)
No nudes is good news
14 *Sunset at Blandings* (1977)
Unfinished at the author's death
One Blandings story in *Plum pie*, 1966

Blandings series
Hodgins, Eric
1 *Mister Blandings builds his dream house* (1946)
2 *Blandings way* (1950)

Blandish series
Chase, James Hadley
see **Carol Blandish series**

Blanket-making series
Early, Richard Elliott
see **Thomas Early series**

Blankhampton series
Winter, John Strange
1 *In quarters* (1885)
In quarters with the 25th
Chronicles of the 25th, Black Horse Dragoons
2 *Army society* (1886)
Alternative title: Life in a garrison town
3 *On march* (1886)
The story of a man of honour
4 *Garrison gossip gathered in Blankhampton* (1887)
5 *Beautiful Jim of Blankshire Regiment* (1888)
6 *Other man's wife* (1891)
7 *Soul of the bishop* (1893)
8 *Little Joan* (1903)
9 *Simple gentleman* (1906)
10 *Love of Philip Hampden* (1907)

Blatchington series
Cole, George Douglas Howard
see **Everard Blatchington series**

Blayde series
Wainwright, John
see **Superintendent Blayde series**

Blaydon family trilogy
Fielding, Gabriel
1 *In the time of Greenbloom* (1956)
2 *Brotherly love* (1954)
Numbers 1 and 2 overlap in time
3 *Through streets broad and narrow* (1960)

Blayne series
Blayne, Sebastian
see **Sebastian Blayne series**

Blayre series
Blayre, Christopher
see **University of Cosmopoli series**

Blaze and Billy series
Anderson, Clarence William
see **Billy and Blaze series**

Blaze Braddock and Jon Hazard Black series
Johnson, Susan
1 *Blaze* (1986)
2 *Silver flame* (1988)

Blaze series
Novak, Robert
see **Joe Blaze series**

Bleak Creek series
Grover, Marshall
1 *Bleak Creek* (1960)
2 *Peaceable man* (1960)
3 *Hit the leather* (1960)
4 *Tyler cache* (1960)
5 *No safe trail* (1960)
6 *Ride the wild river* (1961)
7 *Wanted in Texas* (1961)
8 *Gun against gun* (1961)
9 *Try me!* (1962)
10 *Colt hostages* (1962)
11 *Devil's trail* (1962)

Blenheim boy series
Passmore, Richard
War reminiscences
1 *Blenheim boy* (1981)
2 *Moving tent* (1982)

Blessed girl series
Lutyens, Emily
1 *Blessed girl* (1953)
2 *Birth of Rowland* (1956)
3 *Candles in the sun* (1957)

Blessing trilogy
Barnwell, William
1 *Blessing papers* (1980)
2 *Imram* (1981)
3 *Sigma curve* (1981)

Blessingay series
Barrett, Geoffrey John
see **Inspector Blessingay series**

Blessington series
Sherwood, John
see **Mister Charles Blessington series**

Bleys quartet
Dickson, Gordon Rupert
1 *Young Bleys* (1991)
2 *Final encyclopedia* (1984)
3 *Chantry guild* (1988)
4 *Bleys the man* (1993)

Bligh series
Bligh, Eric
see **Tooting Corner series**
Clark, Gail
see **Dulcie Bligh series**

Blind colt series
Rounds, Glen
1 *Blind colt* (1941)
2 *Stolen pony* (1942)
Revised edition 1969

Blind series
Bjarnhof, Karl
1 *Stars grow pale* (1956)
Original edition entitled *Stjernerne blegner*
2 *Good light* (1957)
Original edition entitled *Det gode lys*

Blind spot series
Hall, Austin
1 *Blind spot* (1951)
Co-author: Homer Eon Flint
2 *Spot of life* (1965)

Blinkins series
Teitelbaum, Michael
1 *Meet the Blinkins* (1986)
2 *Here come the Blinkins* (1986)
Coloring book

Blinkwell series
Fowler, Sydney
see **Professor Blinkwell series**

Blinky Bill adaptations series
Wall, Dorothy
1 *Let's call him Blinky Bill* (1970)
Meet Blinky Bill
Adapted by Carol Odell
2 *Blinky Bill and the rabbit's birthday party* (1971)
Adapted by Carol Odell
3 *Blinky Bill and Nutsy* (1972)
Adapted by Carol Odell
4 *Blinky Bill at Mister Smifkin's farm* (1974)
Adapted by Anne Marie Willis
5 *Blinky Bill and the guest house* (1975)
Adapted by Anne Marie Willis
6 *Blinky Bill and the pelicans* (1976)
Adapted by Anne Marie Willis
7 *Blinky Bill and the tree-warming* (1976)
Adapted by Anne Marie Willis; Numbers 5-7 also published in one volume editions entitled *Blinky Bill and his friends*, 1978, and *Blinky Bill and Nutsy have fun*, 1978
8 *Meet Blinky Bill, the mischievous koala* (1977)
Adapted by Betty Boaden
9 *Blinky Bill at Frog Hollow* (1977)
Adapted by Betty Boaden
10 *Blinky Bill and the bull ants* (1977)
Adapted by Betty Boaden
11 *Blinky Bill runs away* (1977)
Adapted by Betty Boaden
12 *Blinky Bill meets Nutsy* (1978)
Adapted by Betty Boaden
13 *Blinky Bill goes to school* (1982)
Illustrated by Louis Silvestro
14 *Blinky Bill goes to the doctor* (1982)
Illustrated by Louis Silvestro

Blinky Bill series
Wall, Dorothy
1 *Blinky Bill, the quaint little Australian* (1933)
2 *Blinky Bill grows up* (1934)
3 *Blinky Bill and Nutsy* (1937)
Numbers 1-3 also published in one volume entitled *The complete adventures of Blinky Bill*, 1939
4 *Blinky Bill joins the army* (1940)
Companion volumes: *Blinky Bill magic action, pop-up book*, 1935, *Blinky Bill dress-up book*, 1942, *A tiny story of Blinky Bill*, 1942, *Blinky Bill's ABC book*, 1947, *Fun with Blinky Bill*, 1953, *Blinky Bill cookbook*, by Mary Coleman, 1977

Bliss series
Booth, Christopher B
see **Jim Bliss series**
Peters, Elizabeth
see **Vicky Bliss series**
Remenham, John
see **Inspector Bliss series**

Blissberg series
Rosen, Richard
see **Harvey Blissberg series**

Blithe sheriff series
Buckley, Frederick Robert
1 *Blithe sheriff* (1926)
2 *Re-enter the blithe sheriff* (1927)

Blixen series
Larson, Charles
see **Nils-Frederick Blixen series**

Blizzard Wilson and Badger Coe series
Cameron, Caddo
see **Private Badger Coe and Sergeant Blizzard Wilson series**

Bloch series
Elkon, Jon
see **Tom Bloch series**

Block and Siscoe series
Haiblum, Isidore
see **Siscoe and Block series**

Blonde series
Carnelle, Inge
see **Jane Blonde series**

Blondie and Dagwood series
Young, Chic
Comic strips
1 *Blondie with Baby Dumpling and Daisy* (1939)
2 *Blondie and bouncing Baby Dumpling* (1940)
3 *Blondie, Baby Dumpling and all* (1941)
4 *Blondie and Dagwood's secret service* (1942)
5 *Blondie from A to Z* (1943)
6 *Blondie, Cookie and Daisy's pups* (1943)
7 *Blondie and Dagwood's snapshot clue* (1943)
8 *Blondie* (1944)
9 *Blondie and Dagwood's adventure in magic* (1944)
10 *Blondie and Dagwood's marvelous invention* (1947)
11 *Blondie and Dagwood's footlight folly* (1951)
12 *Blondie's family* (1954)
Cookie, Alexander and their dog
Companion volumes: *Blondie's soups, salads, sandwiches cook book*, 1947, also known as *Blondie's cook book*, *Blondie and Dagwood, a novel of the great American family*, by Helga Lund, 1947

Blood and fire series
Pegram, Lorna
1 *Blood and fire* (1978)
2 *Day among many* (1955)
3 *Long way from home* (1986)

Blood bond series
Johnstone, William Wallace
1 *Blood bond* (1989)
2 *Brotherhood of the gun* (1990)
3 *Gunshot Crossing* (1991)
4 *Gunsmoke and gold* (1992)
5 *Devil Creek crossfire* (1992)
6 *Shootout at Gold Creek* (1993)
7 *San Angelo showdown* (1994)

Blood heritage series
Tepper, Sheri S
1 *Blood heritage* (1986)
2 *Bones* (1987)

Blood hunt series
Killough, Lee
1 *Blood hunt* (1987)
2 *Bloodlinks* (1988)

Blood of Kerensky trilogy
Stackpole, Michael
1 *Lethal heritage* (1990)
2 *Blood legacy* (1990)
3 *Lost legacy* (1991)

Blood of the lamb series
Rogers, Mark Earl
1 *Expected one* (1991)
2 *Devouring void* (1991)

Blood oranges trilogy
Hawkes, John
1 *Blood oranges* (1971)
2 *Death, sleep and the traveller* (1974)
3 *Travesty* (1976)

Blood series
Morgan, Allan
see **Mark Blood series**
Peacock, Max
see **Colonel Blood series**
Sabatini, Rafael
see **Captain Blood series**

Blood sword series
Morris, Dave
1 *Blood sword* (1987)
2 *Kingdom of Wyrd* (1987)
3 *Demon's claw* (1987)
4 *Doomwalk* (1988)

Bloodbird series
Burton, Thomas
1 *Great grab* (1941)
And so divided
2 *Bloodbird* (1942)

Bloodheart series
Tresillian, Richard
1 *Bloodheart* (1985)
2 *Bloodheart royal* (1986)
3 *Bloodheart feud* (1988)

Bloodhound Gang series
Fleischman, Sid
1 *Bloodhound Gang in the case of the flying clock* (1981)
2 *Bloodhound Gang in the case of the cackling ghost* (1981)
3 *Bloodhound Gang in the case of the Princess Tomorrow* (1981)
4 *Bloodhound Gang in the case of the secret message* (1981)
5 *Bloodhound Gang's secret code book* (1982)
6 *Bloodhouse Gang in the case of the two hundred and sixty four pound burglar* (1982)

Bloodworth and Dahlquist series
Lochte, Dick
see **Leo Bloodworth and Serendipity Dahlquist series**

Bloody ratbags series
Cue, Kerry
Humour
1 *Crooks, chooks and bloody ratbags* (1983)
2 *Another bloody ratbag book* (1986)
3 *My ratbag relations* (1989)

Bloom series
Rosenthal, Lesley Sharon
see **Esmeralda Bloom series**
Warman, Erik
see **Inspector John Isidore Bloom series**

Bloomer girl series
Lee, Mabel
Autobiography
1 *Memories of a bloomer girl, 1894-1924* (1977)
2 *Memories beyond bloomers, 1924-1954* (1978)

Bloomfield and Blair series
Little, Jean
see **Emily Blair and Kate Bloomfield series**

Blossom and Ellerdine series
Wills, Cecil Melville
see **Superintendent Roger Ellerdine and Sergeant Cherry Blossom series**

Blossom Culp series
Peck, Richard
1 *Ghost belonged to me* (1975)
2 *Ghosts I have been* (1977)
3 *Dreadful future of Blossom Culp* (1983)
4 *Blossom Culp and the sleep of death* (1986)

Blossom series
Nelson, Michael
see **Captain Blossom series**

Blossom Shop series
Mullins, Iola May
1 *Blossom Shop* (1913)
A story of the South
2 *Anne of the Blossom Shop* (1914)
Alternative title: The growing up of Anne Carter
3 *Anne's wedding* (1916)
4 *Mount Blossom girls* (1918)
Alternative title: New paths from the Blossom Shop
5 *Tweedie* (1919)
6 *Uncle Mary* (1922)

Blossoms series
Byars, Betsy
1 *Blossoms meet the vulture lady* (1986)
2 *Blossoms and the green phantom* (1987)
3 *Blossom promise* (1987)
4 *Wanted, Mud Blossom* (1991)

Blounts of Avonleigh series
Diver, Maud
see **English scene series**

Blow and Manciple series
Hopkins, Kenneth
see **Doctor William Blow and Professor Gideon Manciple series**

Blue above the chimneys series
Fraser, Christine Marion
Autobiography
1 *Blue above the chimneys* (1980)
2 *Roses round the door* (1986)
3 *Green are my mountains* (1990)
4 *Noble beginnings* (1994)

Blue and the Gray afloat series
Optic, Oliver
1 *Taken by the enemy* (1888)
2 *Within the enemy lines* (1889)
3 *On the blockade* (1890)
4 *Stand by the union* (1891)
5 *Fighting for the right* (1892)
6 *Victorious Union* (1893)

Blue and the Gray on land series
Optic, Oliver
1 *Brother against brother* (1894)
Alternative title: War on the border
2 *In the saddle* (1895)
3 *Lieutenant at eighteen* (1895)
4 *On the staff* (1896)
5 *At the front* (1897)
6 *Undivided union* (1899)

Blue bird series
Maeterlinck, Maurice
1 *Blue bird* (1909)
A fairy play in six acts; original edition entitled *L'oiseau bleu*
2 *Betrothal* (1918)
Blue bird chooses
Tyltyl
Five act play; original edition entitled *Les fiancailles*; the second and third titles are children's editions

Blue Birds series
Roy, Lillian Elizabeth
1 *Blue Birds of happy times* (1914)
2 *Blue Birds' winter nest* (1916)
3 *Blue Birds' Uncle Ben* (1917)
4 *Blue Birds at Happy Hills* (1919)

Blue Bonnet series
This sequence has three authors
Jacobs, Caroline Emilia
1 *Texas Blue Bonnet* (1910)
2 *Blue Bonnet's ranch party* (1912)
Co-author: Edyth Ellerbeck Read
3 *Blue Bonnet in Boston* (1914)
Co-author: Lela Horn Richards
4 *Blue Bonnet keeps house* (1916)
Co-author: Lela Horn Richards
Richards, Lela Horn
5 *Blue Bonnet, debutante* (1917)
6 *Blue Bonnet of the Seven Stars* (1919)
7 *Blue Bonnet's family* (1929)

Blue bonnet series
Muir, Augustus
1 *Blue bonnet* (1926)
2 *Castles in the air* (1938)

Blue Door Theatre Company series
Brown, Pamela
1 *Swish of the curtain* (1941)
Revised edition 1971
2 *Maddy alone* (1945)
3 *Golden pavements* (1947)
4 *Blue Door venture* (1949)
5 *Maddy again* (1956)

Blue figurine trilogy
Bellairs, John
1 *Curse of the blue figurine* (1983)
2 *Mummy, the will and the crypt* (1983)
3 *Spell of the sorcerer's skull* (1984)

Blue Grass Seminary girls series
Burnett, Carolyn Judson
1 *Blue Grass Seminary girls' vacation adventures* (1916)
Alternative title: Shirley Willing to the rescue
2 *Blue Grass Seminary girls' Christmas holidays* (1916)
Alternative title: A four weeks tour with the glee club
3 *Blue Grass Seminary girls in the mountains* (1916)
Alternative title: Shirley Willing on a mission of peace
4 *Blue Grass Seminary girls on the water* (1916)
Alternative title: Exciting adventures on a summer cruise through the Panama Canal

Blue Harbour series
Wilson, Budge
1 *Best-worse Christmas present ever* (1984)
2 *House far from home* (1986)
3 *Mystery lights on Blue Harbour* (1987)

Blue Hawk series
Bittner, F Rosanne
see **Caleb Sax series**

Blue Hills series
Meredith, Gwen
1 *Lawsons* (1948)
2 *Blue Hills* (1950)
3 *Beyond Blue Hills* (1953)
4 *Into the sun* (1961)
Blue Hills in the sun

Blue horizon series
Stacpoole, Henry de Vere
1 *Blue horizon* (1908)
2 *In blue waters* (1917)

Blue Jean Billy Race series
Tyler, Charles Waller
1 *Blue Jean Billy* (1921)
2 *Quality Bill's girl* (1925)

Blue light series
Kaye, Marvin
1 *Cold blue light* (1983)
Co-author: Parke Godwin
2 *Ghosts of night and morning* (1987)

Blue Maguire and Spaceman Kowalski series
White, Teri
1 *Bleeding hearts* (1984)
2 *Tightrope* (1986)

Blue Mask series
Morton, Anthony
see **Baron series**

Blue Max series
Hunter, Jack Dayton
1 *Blue Max* (1964)
2 *Blood order* (1979)
3 *Tin cravat* (1981)

Blue Mitchell series
Luckey, William A
1 *Long ride to nowhere* (1987)
2 *Bad company* (1991)
3 *Cimarron blood* (1992)

Blue Mountains series
Brinsmead, Hesba Fay
see **Truelance family series**

Blue Pete series
Allan, Luke
1 *Blue Pete, half-breed* (1920)
A story of the cowboy West
2 *Return of Blue Pete* (1922)
3 *Blue Pete, detective* (1928)
4 *Blue Pete, horsethief* (1938)
5 *Vengeance of Blue Pete* (1939)
6 *Blue Pete, rebel* (1940)
7 *Blue Pete pays a debt* (1942)
8 *Blue Pete breaks the rules* (1943)
9 *Blue Pete, outlaw* (1944)
10 *Blue Pete's dilemma* (1945)
11 *Blue Pete's vendetta* (1947)
12 *Blue Pete to the rescue* (1947)
13 *Blue Pete and the Pinto* (1948)
14 *Blue Pete works alone* (1948)
15 *Blue Pete, unofficially* (1949)
16 *Blue Pete, Indian scout* (1950)
17 *Blue Pete at bay* (1952)
18 *Blue Pete rides the foothills* (1953)
19 *Blue Pete and the kid* (1953)
20 *Blue Pete in the badlands* (1954)

Blue Peter series
Baxter, Biddy
1 *Blue Peter book of limericks* (1976)
2 *Blue Peter book of odd odes* (1976)

Blue series
Brown, Rosel George
see **Sibyl Sue Blue series**

Blue Stacks series
Bernen, Robert
1 *Tales from the Blue Stacks* (1978)
2 *Hills* (1983)

Blue Steele series
Gunn, Tom
see **Sheriff Blue Steele series**

Blue water trilogy
Durell, Charles Pendexter
1 *Skipper of the Cynthia B* (1921)
2 *Heave short* (1923)
3 *Lights off shore* (1925)
Alternative title: The outlaws of the bay

Bluebeards series
Bradman, Tony
1 *Adventure on Skull Island* (1988)
2 *Mystery at Musket Bay* (1989)
3 *Peril at the pirate school* (1990)

Blueberry Mountain series
Meader, Stephen Warren
1 *Blueberry Mountain* (1941)
2 *Snow on Blueberry Mountain* (1961)

Blueberry series
Charlier, Jean Michel
see **Young Blueberry series**
Giraud, Jean
see **Lieutenant Mike S Blueberry series**

Bluefeather series
Meynell, Laurence Walter
1 *Bluefeather* (1928)
2 *Odds on Bluefeather* (1934)

Blues series
Campbell, Bebe Moore
1 *Your blues ain't like mine* (1992)
2 *Brothers and sisters* (1994)

Bluestar series
Moore, Arthur
1 *Trail of the Gatling* (1989)
2 *Steel box* (1989)
3 *Dead or alive* (1989)
4 *Murder road* (1990)
5 *Hunters* (1990)
6 *Outlaws* (1991)

Bluff and Bran series
Rutherford, Meg
1 *Bluff and Bran and the scarecrow* (1984)
2 *Bluff and Bran and the magpie* (1985)
3 *Bluff and Bran and the tree house* (1986)
4 *Bluff and Bran and the snowdrift* (1987)
5 *Bluff and Bran and the birthday* (1988)

Blundle and Gang series
Plain, Neil
see **Boris Blundle and Gang series**

Blunt series
Cranston, Maurice
see **Inspector Mortimer Blunt series**
Yates, Peter
see **Sandy Blunt series**

Blythe and Trevor series
Philips, Judson Pentecost
see **Carole Trevor and Max Blythe series**

Blythe family series
Turner, Mary
1 *Story of David Blythe* (1952)
2 *Another moon* (1953)

Blythe girls series
Hope, Laura Lee
House pseudonym
1 *Helen, Margy and Rose* (1925)
Alternative title: Facing the great world
2 *Margy's queer inheritance* (1925)
Alternative title: The worth of a name
3 *Rose's great problem* (1925)
Alternative title: Face to face with a crisis
4 *Helen's strange boarder* (1925)
Alternative title: The girl from Bronx Park
5 *Three on a vacation* (1925)
Alternative title: The mystery at Peach Farm
6 *Margy's secret mission* (1926)
Alternative title: Exciting days at Shadymore
7 *Rose's odd discovery* (1927)
Alternative title: The search for Irene Conroy
8 *Disappearance of Helen* (1928)
Alternative title: The art shop mystery
9 *Snowbound in camp* (1929)
Alternative title: The mystery at Elk Lodge
10 *Margy's mysterious visitor* (1930)
Alternative title: Guarding the Pepper fortune
11 *Rose's hidden talent* (1931)
12 *Helen's wonderful mistake* (1932)
Alternative title: The mysterious necklace

BMX bikers series
Spurgeon, Maureen
1 *BMX biker* (1985)
2 *BMX bikers and the Dirt Track Racers* (1985)

BMX Gang series
Lynam, Terence
Illustrated by David Mostyn
1 *BMX Gang on holiday* (1986)
BMX Bunch on vacation
2 *BMX Gang turns detective* (1986)
BMX Bunch turns detective
3 *Greg's first race* (1986)
4 *Andy joins the Gang* (1986)
Andy joins the BMX Bunch

BMX series
Graham, Caroline
1 *BMX star rider* (1985)
2 *BMX'ers battle it out!* (1985)

Bo Bradley series
Padgett, Abigail
1 *Child of silence* (1993)
2 *Strawgirl* (1994)
3 *Turtle baby* (1995)

Boadicea series
Sinclair, James
1 *Warrior queen* (1977)
2 *Canis the warrior* (1979)

Boas series
Baron, Alexander
see **Harryboy Boas series**

Boat builders series
Optic, Oliver
1 *All adrift* (1882)
Alternative title: The Goldwing Club
2 *Snug harbor* (1884)
Alternative title: The Champlain mechanics
3 *Square and compasses* (1884)
Alternative title: Building the house
4 *Stem to stern* (1885)
Alternative title: Building the boat
5 *All taut* (1887)
Alternative title: Rigging the boat
6 *Ready about* (1887)
Alternative title: Sailing the boat

Boat Club series
Optic, Oliver
1 *Boat Club* (1854)
Alternative title: Bunkers of Rippleton
2 *All aboard* (1855)
Alternative title: Life on the lake
3 *Poor and proud* (1856)
Alternative title: The fortunes of Katy Redburn
4 *Now or never* (1857)
Alternative title: The adventures of Bobby Bright
5 *Try again* (1858)
Alternative title: The trials and triumphs of Harry West
6 *Little by little* (1860)
Alternative title: The cruise of the Flyaway

Boat series
Pardoe, Margot
1 *Ghost boat* (1951)
2 *Boat seekers* (1953)
3 *Dutch boat* (1955)
4 *Nameless boat* (1957)
5 *Greek boat mystery* (1960)

Boat travel series
Millar, George
1 *Isabel and the sea* (1948)
A voyage in a ketch from England to Greece
2 *White boat from England* (1951)

Bob and Hilary Dean series
Henry, Margaret
1 *Unlucky dip* (1960)
2 *Householders* (1964)

Bob and Jilly series
Schmidt, Annie Maria Geertruida
1 *Bob and Jilly* (1956)
Original edition entitled *Jip and Janneke*
2 *Good luck, Mick and Mandy* (1961)
Original edition entitled *Daar gaan Jip en Janneke*
3 *Love from Mick and Mandy* (1961)
Original edition entitled *Een zoentje van Jip en Janneke*
4 *Take care Mick and Mandy* (1961)
Original edition entitled *Pas op, Jip en Janneke*
5 *Bob and Jilly are friends* (1964)
Originally published in *Jip en Janneke*, eerste boek, 1963 and *Jip en Janneke*, tweede boek, 1964
6 *Bob in Jilly in trouble* (1964)
Originally published in *Jip en Janneke*, eerste boek, 1963 and *Jip en Janneke*, tweede boek, 1964

Bob Bodden series
Coatsworth, Elizabeth
1 *Bob Bodden and the good ship Rover* (1968)
2 *Bob Bodden and the seagoing farm* (1970)

Bob Bodewicz series
Zenowich, Christopher
1 *Economics of the heart* (1990)
2 *Cost of living* (1989)

Bob Chase series
Warner, Frank A
1 *Bob Chase with the big moose hunters* (1929)
2 *Bob Chase after grizzly bears* (1929)
3 *Bob Chase in the tiger's lair* (1929)
4 *Bob Chase with the lion hunters* (1930)

Bob Christie series
Preston, James
see **Sergeant Bob Christie series**

Bob Christopher series
Irvine, Robert Ralstone
see **Robert Christopher series**

Bob Clifford series
Scott, Leroy
1 *Partners of the night* (1916)
2 *Mary Regan* (1918)
3 *Folly's gold* (1926)

Bob Dashaway series
Brady, Cyrus Townsend
1 *Bob Dashaway, treasure hunter* (1912)
A story of adventure in the strange South Seas
2 *Bob Dashaway in the frozen seas* (1913)

Bob Dexter series
Baker, Willard F
1 *Bob Dexter and the Storm Mountain mystery* (1923)
Alternative title: The secret of the log cabin
2 *Bob Dexter and the Beacon Beach mystery* (1925)
Alternative title: The wreck of the Sea Hawk
3 *Bob Dexter and the club house mystery* (1925)
Alternative title: The missing golden eagle
4 *Bob Dexter and the aeroplane mystery* (1930)
Alternative title: The secret of Jint San
5 *Bob Dexter and the seaplane mystery* (1931)
Alternative title: The secret of the white stones
6 *Bob Dexter and the red auto mystery* (1932)
Alternative title: The secret of the flying car
7 *Bob Dexter and the radio mystery* (1933)
Alternative title: The secret of the counterfeiters

Bob Dunbar and Gary Lunt series
Shirreffs, Gordon Donald
1 *Cold seas beyond* (1963)
2 *Hostile beaches* (1964)
3 *Enemy seas* (1965)
4 *Bolo battalion* (1966)
5 *Torpedoes away* (1967)
6 *Killer sea* (1968)

Bob Fulton series
Beatty, Jerome
1 *Bob Fulton's amazing soda-pop stretcher* (1963)
An international spy story
2 *Bob Fulton's terrific time machine* (1982)
An adventure in space and time

Bob Hamilton series
Burley, Andrew S
see **Uncle Sam's Army boys series**

Bob Hamilton series
Helmericks, Bud
1 *Oolak's brother* (1953)
2 *Arctic hunter* (1956)
3 *Arctic bush pilot* (1957)

Bob Howarth series
Farrimond, John
1 *Dust in my throat* (1963)
2 *Dust is forever* (1969)

Bob, Jerry and Ned series
Young, Clarence
see **Motor boys series**

Bob Koesler series
Kienzle, William Xavier
see **Father Robert Koesler series**

Bob Moran series
Verne, Henry
1 *Bob Moran and the Fawcett mystery* (1956)
2 *Bob Moran and the pirates of the air* (1956)
3 *Bob Moran and the sunken galley* (1957)
4 *Bob Moran and the buccaneer's board* (1957)
5 *Bob Moran in the valley of hell* (1960)
6 *Bob Moran and the fiery claw* (1960)

Bob Newman series
Forbes, Colin
see **Tweed, Grey and Newman series**

Bob Ponting series
Bolt, Ben
1 *Shot in the night* (1934)
2 *Five red stars* (1936)

Bob Pruitt and Jack McDuff series
Mitchell, Red
see **Doc McDuff and Popcorn Pruitt series**

Bob Steele series
Grayson, Donald
1 *Bob Steele's motorcycle* (1909)
Alternative title: True to his friends
2 *Bob Steele on high gear* (1909)
Alternative title: A prize worth winning
3 *Bob Steele from auto to airship* (1909)
Alternative title: A strange adventure in the air
4 *Bob Steele afloat in the clouds* (1909)
Alternative title: The boy who owned an airship
5 *Bob Steele's submarine cruise* (1909)
Alternative title: Captain Nemo's friend
6 *Bob Steele in strange waters* (1909)
Alternative title: Aboard a strange craft
7 *Bob Steele's motorboat* (1909)
Alternative title: The fellow they could not beat
8 *Bob Steele's winning race* (1909)
Alternative title: Fearless and true
9 *Bob Steele's new aeroplane* (1909)
Alternative title: The bird man
10 *Bob Steele's last flight* (1909)
Alternative title: The sale of the Comet

Bob Sullivan series
Mullally, Frederic
1 *Danse macabre* (1959)
Marianne
2 *Munich involvement* (1968)
3 *Malta conspiracy* (1972)

Bob Wakefield series
Miller, Blaine
1 *Bob Wakefield, naval aviator* (1936)
2 *Bob Wakefield, naval inspector* (1937)
3 *Bob Wakefield's flight log* (1940)

Bob Whitfield series
Moore, Richard A
1 *Death in the past* (1980)
2 *Death of a source* (1980)

Bob Wincourt and Jim Raine series
Hodge, Charles
see **Jim Raine and Bob Wincourt series**

Bob Zane series
Gardner, Erle Stanley
see **Whispering Sands series**

Bobbet series
Holley, Marietta
see **Betsey Bobbet series**

Bobbie Bear series
Oona, Katherine Deme
1 *Bobbie Bear goes to the beach* (1980)
2 *Bobbie Bear and the blizzard* (1980)

Bobbie series
Furminger, Justine
1 *Bobbie takes the reins* (1981)
2 *Bobbie's sponsored ride* (1982)

Bobbie Toppin series
Brookins, Dana
1 *Soul-eater* (1985)
2 *Manipulator* (1989)

Bobbsey twins new series
Hope, Laura Lee
see **New Bobbsey twins series**

Bobbsey twins series
Hope, Laura Lee
House pseudonym
1 *Bobbsey twins* (1904)
Meet the Bobbsey twins
Bobbsey twins of Lakeport
Alternative title: Merry days indoors and out; revised editions 1928, 1950, 1961; *Laura Lee Hope's The Bobbsey twins*, retold by Bennett Kline, 1940
2 *Bobbsey twins in the country* (1904)
Bobbsey twins' adventure in the country
Revised editions 1950, 1961
3 *Bobbsey twins at the seashore* (1907)
Bobbsey twins' secret at the seashore
Revised edition 1950, 1962
4 *Bobbsey twins at school* (1913)
Bobbsey twins' mystery at school
Revised edition 1962
5 *Bobbsey twins at Snow Lodge* (1913)
Bobbsey twins and the mystery at Snow Lodge
Revised edition 1960
6 *Bobbsey twins on a houseboat* (1915)
Revised edition 1955
7 *Bobbsey twins at Meadow Brook* (1915)
Bobbsey twins' mystery at Meadow Brook
Revised edition 1963
8 *Bobbsey twins at home* (1916)
Bobbsey twins big adventure at home
Revised edition 1960
9 *Bobbsey twins in a great city* (1917)
Bobbsey twins' search in the great city
Revised edition 1960
10 *Bobbsey twins on Blueberry Island* (1917)
Revised edition 1959
11 *Bobbsey twins on the deep blue sea* (1918)
Bobbsey twins' mystery on the deep blue sea
Revised edition 1965
12 *Bobbsey twins in Washington* (1919)
Bobbsey twins' adventure in Washington
Revised edition 1963
13 *Bobbsey twins in the great West* (1920)
Bobbsey twins' visit to the great West
Revised edition 1966
14 *Bobbsey twins at Cedar Camp* (1921)
Bobbsey twins and the Cedar Camp mystery
Revised edition 1967
15 *Bobbsey twins at the country fair* (1922)
Bobbsey twins and the country fair mystery
Revised edition 1960
16 *Bobbsey twins camping out* (1923)
Revised edition 1955
17 *Bobbsey twins and baby May* (1924)
Bobbsey twins' adventures with baby May
Revised edition 1968
18 *Bobbsey twins keeping house* (1925)
Bobbsey twins and the play house secret
Revised edition 1968
19 *Bobbsey twins at Cloverbank* (1926)
Bobbsey twins and the four-leaf clover mystery
Revised edition 1968
20 *Bobbsey twins at Cherry Corners* (1927)
Bobbsey twins in the mystery at Cherry Corners
Revised edition 1971
21 *Bobbsey twins and their schoolmates* (1928)
22 *Bobbsey twins treasure hunting* (1929)
23 *Bobbsey twins at Spruce Lake* (1930)
24 *Bobbsey twins' wonderful secret* (1931)
Bobbsey twins' wonderful winter secret
Revised edition 1962
25 *Bobbsey twins at the circus* (1932)
Bobbsey twins and the circus surprise
Revised edition 1960
26 *Bobbsey twins on an airplane trip* (1933)
27 *Bobbsey twins solve a mystery* (1934)
28 *Bobbsey twins on a ranch* (1935)
29 *Bobbsey twins in Eskimo Land* (1936)
30 *Bobbsey twins in a radio play* (1937)
31 *Bobbsey twins at Windmill Cottage* (1938)
32 *Bobbsey twins at Lighthouse Point* (1939)
33 *Bobbsey twins at Indian Hollow* (1940)
34 *Bobbsey twins at the ice carnival* (1941)
35 *Bobbsey twins in the land of cotton* (1942)
36 *Bobbsey twins in Echo Valley* (1943)
37 *Bobbsey twins on the pony trail* (1944)
38 *Bobbsey twins at Mystery Mansion* (1945)
39 *Bobbsey twins at Sugar Maple Hill* (1946)
40 *Bobbsey twins in Mexico* (1947)
41 *Bobbsey twins' toy shop* (1948)
42 *Bobbsey twins in Tulip Land* (1949)
43 *Bobbsey twins in Rainbow Valley* (1950)
44 *Bobbsey twins' own little railroad* (1951)
Bobbsey twins' own little railway
45 *Bobbsey twins at Whitesail Harbor* (1952)
Bobbsey twins at Whitesail Harbour
46 *Bobbsey twins and the horsehoe riddle* (1953)
47 *Bobbsey twins at Big Bear Pond* (1954)
48 *Bobbsey twins on a bicycle trip* (1955)
49 *Bobbsey twins' own little ferryboat* (1956)
50 *Bobbsey twins at Pilgrim Rock* (1957)
51 *Bobbsey twins' forest adventure* (1958)
52 *Bobbsey twins at London Tower* (1959)
Bobbsey twins at the Tower of London
53 *Bobbsey twins in the mystery cave* (1960)
54 *Bobbsey twins in Volcano Land* (1961)
55 *Bobbsey twins and the goldfish mystery* (1962)
56 *Bobbsey twins and the Big River mystery* (1963)
57 *Bobbsey twins and the Greek hat mystery* (1963)
58 *Bobbsey twins' search for the green rooster* (1965)
59 *Bobbsey twins and their camel adventure* (1966)
60 *Bobbsey twins and the mystery of the king's puppet* (1967)
61 *Bobbsey twins and the secret of Candy Castle* (1968)
62 *Bobbsey twins and the doodlebug mystery* (1969)
63 *Bobbsey twins and the talking fox mystery* (1970)
64 *Red, white and blue mystery* (1971)
65 *Doctor Funnybone's secret* (1972)
66 *Bobbsey twins and the tagalong giraffe* (1973)
67 *Bobbsey twins and the flying clown* (1974)
68 *Bobbsey twins on the sun-moon cruise* (1975)
69 *Bobbsey twins and the Freedom Bell mystery* (1976)
70 *Bobbsey twins and the Smoky Mountain mystery* (1977)
71 *Bobbsey twins in a TV mystery show* (1978)
72 *Coral turtle mystery* (1979)
73 *Blue poodle mystery* (1980)
74 *Secret in the pirate's cave* (1980)
75 *Dune buggy mystery* (1980)
76 *Missing pony mystery* (1981)
77 *Bobbsey twins and the rose parade mystery* (1981)
78 *Bobbsey twins and the camp fire mystery* (1981)
79 *Bobbsey twins and double trouble* (1982)
80 *Bobbsey twins and the mystery of the laughing dinosaur* (1983)
81 *Bobbsey twins and the music box mystery* (1983)
82 *Bobbsey twins and the ghost in the computer* (1984)
83 *Bobbsey twins and the scarecrow mystery* (1984)
84 *Bobbsey twins and the haunted house mystery* (1985)
85 *Bobbsey twins and the mystery of the Hindu temple* (1985)
86 *Bobbsey twins and the grinning gargoyle mystery* (1986)

Bobby Bax series
Collinson, Roger
1 *Boat and Bax* (1967)
2 *Butch and Bax* (1970)

Bobby Blake series
Warner, Frank A
1 *Bobby Blake at Rockledge School* (1915)
Alternative title: Winning the medal of honor
2 *Bobby Blake at Bass Cove* (1915)
Alternative title: The hunt for the motor boat Gem
3 *Bobby Blake on a cruise* (1915)
Alternative title: The castaways of Volcano Island
4 *Bobby Blake and his school chums* (1916)
Alternative title: The rivals of Rockledge
5 *Bobby Blake at Snowtop Camp* (1916)
Alternative title: Winter holidays in the big woods
6 *Bobby Blake on the school nine* (1917)
Alternative title: The champions of Monotook Lake League
7 *Bobby Blake on a ranch* (1918)
Alternative title: The secret of the mountain cave
8 *Bobby Blake on an auto tour* (1920)
Alternative title: The mystery of the deserted house
9 *Bobby Blake on the school eleven* (1921)
Alternative title: Winning the banner of blue and gold

Bobby Blake series

10 *Bobby Blake on a plantation* (1922)
Alternative title: Lost in the great swamp
11 *Bobby Blake in the frozen North* (1923)
Alternative title: The old eskimo's last message
12 *Bobby Blake on Mystery Mountain* (1926)

Bobby Brewster picture book series
Todd, Herbert Eatton
Illustrated by Val Biro
1 *Sick cow* (1974)
2 *George, the fire engine* (1976)
3 *Roundabout horse* (1978)
4 *King of beasts* (1979)

Bobby Brewster series
Todd, Herbert Eatton
1 *Bobby Brewster and the Winker's Club* (1949)
2 *Bobby Brewster* (1954)
3 *Bobby Brewster, bus conductor* (1955)
4 *Bobby Brewster's shadow* (1956)
5 *Bobby Brewster's bicycle* (1957)
6 *Bobby Brewster's camera* (1959)
7 *Bobby Brewster's wallpaper* (1961)
8 *Bobby Brewster's conker* (1963)
9 *Bobby Brewster, detective* (1964)
10 *Bobby Brewster's potato* (1964)
11 *Bobby Brewster and the ghost* (1966)
12 *Bobby Brewster's kite* (1967)
13 *Bobby Brewster's scarecrow* (1968)
14 *Bobby Brewster's torch* (1969)
15 *Bobby Brewster's balloon race* (1970)
16 *Bobby Brewster's first magic* (1970)
17 *Bobby Brewster's typewriter* (1971)
18 *Bobby Brewster's bee* (1972)
19 *Bobby Brewster's wishbone* (1974)
20 *Bobby Brewster's first fun* (1974)
21 *Bobby Brewster's bookmark* (1975)
22 *Bobby Brewster's tea-leaves* (1979)
23 *Bobby Brewster's lamp post* (1982)
24 *Bobby Brewster's old van* (1985)
25 *Bobby Brewster's hiccups* (1985)
26 *Bobby Brewster and the magic handyman* (1986)
27 *Bobby Brewster's jigsaw puzzle* (1986)

Bobby Cullen series
Fitzhugh, Percy Keese
1 *Uncle Sam's outdoor magic* (1916)
Bobby Cullen with the reclamation workers
2 *Bobby Cullen on the Mississippi* (1920)

Bobby of the Globe series
Hoare, Robert John
1 *Sinister hoard* (1958)
2 *Desperate venture* (1958)
3 *Secret in the Sahara* (1960)

Bobby Owen series
Punshon, Ernest Robertson
1 *Information received* (1933)
2 *Death among the sunbathers* (1934)
3 *Crossword mystery* (1934)
Crossword murder
4 *Mystery villa* (1934)
5 *Death of a beauty queen* (1935)
6 *Death comes to Cambers* (1935)
7 *Bath mysteries* (1936)
Bathtub murder case
8 *Mystery of Mr Jessop* (1937)
9 *Dusky hour* (1937)
10 *Dictator's way* (1938)
Death of a tyrant
11 *Comes a stranger* (1938)
12 *Suspects nine* (1939)
13 *Murder abroad* (1939)
14 *Four strange women* (1940)
15 *Ten star claws* (1941)
16 *Dark garden* (1941)
17 *Diabolic candelabra* (1942)
18 *Conqueror Inn* (1943)
19 *Night's cloak* (1944)
20 *Secrets can't be kept* (1944)
21 *There's a reason for everything* (1945)
22 *It might lead anywhere* (1946)
23 *Helen passes by* (1947)
24 *Music tells all* (1948)
25 *House of Goodwinsson* (1948)
26 *So many doors* (1949)
27 *Everybody always tells* (1950)
28 *Secret search* (1951)
29 *Golden dagger* (1951)
30 *Attending truth* (1952)
31 *Strange ending* (1953)
32 *Brought to light* (1954)
33 *Dark is the clue* (1955)
34 *Triple quest* (1955)
35 *Six were present* (1956)

Bobby series
Hammond, Ray
1 *Bobby catches a bug* (1983)
2 *Bobby meets a pirate* (1983)

Bobby Thiriet series
Berna, Paul
1 *Clue of the black cat* (1964)
2 *Mule on the motorway* (1967)
3 *Truckload of rice* (1968)

Bobo series
Rock, Nova
1 *Hat* (1960)
2 *Bobo and the crocodile* (1961)

Bob's Hill series
Burton, Charles Pierce
1 *Boys of Bob's Hill* (1905)
2 *Bob's Cave boys* (1909)
3 *Bob's Hill braves* (1910)
4 *Boy scouts of Bob's Hill* (1915)
5 *Camp Bob's Hill* (1915)
6 *Raven patrol of Bob's Hill* (1917)
7 *Trail makers* (1919)
8 *Bob's Hill trails* (1922)
9 *Treasure hunters of Bob's Hill* (1926)
10 *Bob's Hill meets the Andes* (1928)
12 *Bob's Hill on the air* (1934)
13 *Bob's Hill in Virginia* (1939)

Bockhorn series
Cohen, Barry
see **Asher Bockhorn series**

Bod series
Cole, Michael
1 *Bod's present* (1965)
2 *Bod's apple* (1965)
3 *Bod's dream* (1966)
4 *Bod and the cherry tree* (1966)
5 *Bod in the park* (1975)
6 *Bod and the birds* (1975)
7 *Bod and breakfast* (1977)
8 *Bod on the beach* (1977)
9 *Bod and the cake* (1977)
10 *Bod and the dog* (1977)
11 *Bod and the grasshopper* (1977)
12 *Bod and the kite* (1977)
Numbers 7-12 also published in one volume entitled *A lot of Bod*, 1977
13 *Bod and the tiger* (1977)

Bodden series
Coatsworth, Elizabeth
see **Bob Bodden series**

Bodewicz series
Zenowich, Christopher
see **Bob Bodewicz series**

Bodger series
Winton, John
see **Navy series**

Bodie the Stalker series
Hunter, Neil
1 *Trackdown* (1979)
2 *Bloody bounty* (1979)
3 *High hell* (1979)
4 *Killing trail* (1979)
5 *Hangtown* (1980)
6 *Day of the savage* (1980)

Bodkin series
Wodehouse, Pelham Grenville
see **Monty Bodkin series**

Bodley family series
Scudder, Horace Elisha
1 *Doings of the Bodley family in town and country* (1875)
2 *Bodleys telling stories* (1877)
3 *Bodleys on wheels* (1878)
4 *Bodleys afoot* (1879)
5 *Mister Bodley abroad* (1881)
6 *Bodley grandchildren and their journey in Holland* (1882)
7 *English Bodley family* (1884)
8 *Viking Bodleys* (1885)

Bodyguard series
Reinsmith, Richard
1 *Bodyguard* (1980)
2 *Blonde target* (1980)
3 *Extra body* (1980)
4 *Bury the past* (1980)
5 *Five and dime murders* (1980)
6 *Savage stars* (1981)
7 *Somebody to kill* (1982)
8 *Body in paradise* (1984)
9 *Model body* (1984)
10 *Nobody's perfect* (1984)
11 *Body for Christmas* (1984)

Boer War journal trilogy
Reitz, Deneys
1 *Commando* (1932)
2 *Afrikander* (1933)
Trekking on
3 *No outspan* (1943)

Boer War series
Young, Francis Brett
1 *They seek a country* (1937)
2 *City of gold* (1939)

Boffin series
Alexander, Louis George
see **Professor Boffin series**

Boffo series
Dickens, Frank
1 *Great motor-cycle race* (1976)
2 *Great air race* (1976)

Boffy series
Barry, Margaret Stuart
1 *Boffy and the teacher-eater* (1971)
2 *Boffy and the Mumford ghosts* (1974)

Bogen series
Weidman, Jerome
see **Harry Bogen series**

Boggart and Bingo Bones series
Roberts, K H
see **Bingo Bones and the Boggart series**

Boggs series
Ballew, Charles
see **Rim-Fire series**
Washburn, Mark
see **Sam Boggs series**

Bognor series
Heald, Tim
see **Simon Bognor series**

Bohemia series
Watson, Edmund Henry Lacon
1 *Attic in Bohemia* (1897)
A diary without dates
2 *Benedictine* (1898)
Sketches of married life

Bohler series
Konsalik, Heinz Gunther
see **Stalingrad series**

Bolan series
Pendleton, Don
see **Mack Bolan series**

Boland series
B B
1 *Forest of Boland Light Railway* (1955)
Forest of the Railway
2 *Wizard of Boland* (1959)

Boldness series
Pape, Richard
Autobiography
1 *Boldness be my friend* (1953)
Revised edition 1984
2 *Sequel to boldness* (1959)

Boldre series
Ditton, James
see **John Boldre series**

Bolescu series
Jungman, Ann
see **Count Boris Bolescu series**

Boleyn series
Reeve, Linda Dawn
see **Anne Boleyn series**

Bolitho series
Kent, Alexander
see **Captain Richard Bolitho series**

Bolivar Manchenil series
Douglass, Donald McNutt
1 *Rebecca's pride* (1956)
2 *Many brave hearts* (1958)
3 *Saba's treasure* (1961)

Bolo series
Laumer, Keith
1 *Bolo* (1976)
The annals of the Dinochrome Brigade
2 *Rogue Bolo* (1985)
Numbers 1 and 2 also published in one volume entitled *The compleat Bolo*, 1990
3 *Stars must wait* (1990)

Bolt series
Curtis, Richard
see **Dave Bolt series**
Hawkes, Robert
see **NARC series**
Martin, Cort
see **Jared Bolt series**

Bolton series
Sainsbury, Noel
see **Bill Bolton series**
Sutton, Margaret
see **Judy Bolton series**

Bom series
Blyton, Enid
1 *Bom, the little toy drummer* (1956)
2 *Bom and his magic drumstick* (1957)
3 *Bom goes adventuring* (1958)
4 *Bom goes to Ho Ho Village* (1958)
5 *Bom and the rainbow* (1959)
6 *Bom and the clown* (1959)
7 *Hullo Bom and Wuffy Dog* (1959)
8 *Bom goes to Magic Town* (1960)
9 *Here come Bom* (1960)
10 *Bom at the seaside* (1961)
11 *Bom goes to the circus* (1961)
Companion volumes: *Bom painting book*, 1957 and *Bom annual*, 1958 and 1959

Bomba series
Rockwood, Roy
House pseudonym
1 *Bomba the jungle boy* (1926)
Alternative title: The old naturalist's secret
2 *Bomba the jungle boy at the moving mountain* (1926)
Alternative title: The mystery of the caverns of fire

3 *Bomba the jungle boy at the giant cataract* (1926)
Alternative title: Chief Nascanora and his captives
4 *Bomba the jungle boy on Jaguar Island* (1927)
Alternative title: Adrift on the river of mystery
5 *Bomba the jungle boy in the abandoned city* (1927)
Alternative title: A treasure ten thousand years old
6 *Bomba the jungle boy on Terror Trail* (1928)
Alternative title: The mysterious men from the sky
7 *Bomba the jungle boy in the swamp of death* (1929)
Alternative title: The sacred alligators of Abarago
8 *Bomba the jungle boy among the slaves* (1929)
Alternative title: Daring adventures in the Valley of Skulls
9 *Bomba the jungle boy on the underground river* (1930)
Alternative title: The cave of bottomless pits
10 *Bomba the jungle boy and the lost explorers* (1930)
Alternative title: A wonderful revelation
11 *Bomba the jungle boy in a strange land* (1931)
Alternative title: Facing the unknown
12 *Bomba the jungle boy among the pygmies* (1931)
Alternative title: Battling with stealthy foes
13 *Bomba the jungle boy and the cannibals* (1932)
Alternative title: Winning against native dangers
14 *Bomba the jungle boy and the painted hunters* (1932)
Alternative title: A long search rewarded
15 *Bomba the jungle boy and the river demons* (1933)
Alternative title: Outwitting the savage medicine men
16 *Bomba the jungle boy and the hostile chieftain* (1934)
Alternative title: A hazardous trek to the sea
17 *Bomba the jungle boy trapped by the cyclone* (1935)
Alternative title: Shipwrecked on the swirling seas
18 *Bomba the jungle boy in the land of burning lava* (1936)
Alternative title: Outwitting superstitious natives
19 *Bomba the jungle boy in the perilous kingdom* (1937)
Alternative title: Braving strange hazards
20 *Bomba the jungle boy in the steaming grotto* (1938)
Alternative title: Victorious through flame and fury

Bomber Command series
Jackson, Robert
1 *Before the storm* (1972)
The story of the Royal Air Force Bomber Command, 1939-42
2 *Storm from the skies* (1974)
The strategic bombing offensive, 1943-1945

Bomber Command series
Taylor, Geoff
1 *Piece of cake* (1956)
2 *Return ticket* (1972)

Bonanza series
This series has five authors
Loomis, Noel
1 *Bonanza* (1960)
Thompson, Thomas
2 *One man with courage* (1966)
Cox, William Robert
3 *Black gold* (1966)
Owen, Dean
4 *Winter grass* (1968)
5 *Ponderosa kill* (1968)
Calder, Stephen
6 *Pioneer spirit* (1992)
7 *Ponderosa empire* (1992)
Companion volumes: *Killer lion*, by Steve Frazee, 1966, *The bubble gum kid*, by George S Elrich, 1967, *Treacher trail*, anonymous, 1968, *Bonanza annual*, 1960-1969

Bonanza series
Peterson, Richard Hermann
see **Western mining series**

Bonaparte series
Austin, Frederick Britten
see **Napoleon Bonaparte series**

Bonaparte series
Turnbull, Patrick
1 *Phantom called glory* (1961)
2 *Wingless eagle* (1962)

Bonaparte series
Upfield, Arthur William
see **Napoleon Bonaparte series**

Bond series
Fleming, Ian
see **James Bond series**
Martyn, Wyndham
see **Christopher Bond series**
Weinstein, Sol
see **Israel Bond series**

Bondmaster series
Tresillian, Richard
1 *Bondmaster* (1977)
2 *Blood of the Bondmaster* (1977)
3 *Bondmaster breed* (1979)
4 *Bondmaster fury* (1982)
5 *Bondmaster's revenge* (1983)
6 *Bondmaster buck* (1984)

Bondurant series
Edwards, James G
see **Inspector Victor Bondurant series**

Bone series
Staynes, Jill
see **Superintendent Bone series**

Bones and the Boggart series
Roberts, K H
see **Bingo Bones and the Boggart series**

Bones series
Carroll, Jonathan
1 *Bones of the moon* (1987)
2 *Sleeping in flame* (1988)
3 *Child across the sky* (1989)

Bones series
Wilson, Anthony Clifford
see **Norman and Henry Bones series**

Boneshaker series
Rogers, Paul
Short stories
1 *Boneshaker* (1989)
2 *Boneshaker rides again* (1990)

Boney series
Upfield, Arthur William
see **Napoleon Bonaparte series**

Bonhamy series
Gathorne-Hardy, Jonathan
see **Cyril Bonhamy series**

Bonhomme series
Brunhoff, Laurent de
1 *Bonhomme* (1965)
Original edition entitled *Bonhomme*, 1965
2 *Bonhomme and the huge beast* (1974)
Original edition entitled *Bonhomme et la grosse bete qui avait des escailles sur le dos*

Bonifacius series
Anckarsvard, Karin
1 *Bonifacius the Green* (1952)
Original edition entitled *Bonifacius den Grone*
2 *Bonifacius and Little Bonnie* (1958)
Original edition entitled *Bonifacius och Lill Bonnie*

Bonisseur de la Bath series
Bruce, Jean
see **Secret Agent O.S.S.117 series**

Bonner series
Harding, Richard
see **Outrider series**
Stout, Rex
see **Dol Bonner series**

Bonnie and Clyde series
This sequence has two authors; based on screenplays
Hirschfeld, Burt
1 *Bonnie and Clyde* (1967)
Brent, Lynton Wright
2 *Daughter of Bonnie and Clyde* (1971)

Bonnie Dundee series
Austin, Anne
see **James F Dundee series**

Bonnie Indermill series
Berry, Carole
1 *Letter of the law* (1987)
2 *Year of the monkey* (1988)
3 *Good night, sweet prince* (1990)
4 *Island girl* (1991)
5 *Nightmare point* (1993)
6 *Death of a difficult woman* (1994)

Bonnie McSmithers series
Alderson, Sue Ann
1 *Bonnie McSmithers, you're driving me dithers* (1974)
Revised edition 1987
2 *Bonnie McSmithers is at it again!* (1979)

Bonnie series
Caudill, Rebecca
1 *Happy little family* (1947)
2 *Schoolhouse in the woods* (1949)
3 *Up and down the river* (1951)
4 *Schoolroom in the parlor* (1959)

Bonny Lee series
Douglas, George
see **Inspector Bonny Lee series**

Bony series
Upfield, Arthur William
see **Napoleon Bonaparte series**

Boo series
Cartwright, Stephen
1 *Who did it?* (1987)
2 *Who likes honey?* (1988)
3 *Who says moo?* (1988)
4 *Who can hop?* (1988)
5 *Who is the tallest?* (1988)

Boo series
Runbeck, Margaret Lee
see **Miss Boo series**

Boogie Woogie Bears series
Kraus, Robert
1 *Boogie Woogie Bears go bacvk to nature* (1990)
2 *Boogie Woogie Bears' picnic* (1990)

Book of Avis series
Phillpotts, Eden
1 *Bred in the bone* (1932)
2 *Witches' cauldron* (1933)
3 *Shadow passes* (1933)
One volume edition entitled *The book of Avis*, 1936

Book of Isle series
Springer, Nancy
1 *Book of suns* (1977)
Silver sun
The second title is an expanded edition
2 *White hart* (1979)
3 *Sable moon* (1981)
4 *Black beast* (1982)
5 *Golden swan* (1983)
Numbers 4 and 5 also published in one volume entitled *The book of Vale*, 1984

Book of justice series
Arnett, Jack
1 *Genocide express* (1989)
2 *Zaitech sting* (1990)
3 *Death force* (1990)
4 *Panama dead* (1990)

Book of lost swords series
Saberhagen, Fred
1 *Woundhealer's story* (1986)
2 *Sightblinder's story* (1987)
3 *Stonecutter's story* (1988)
Numbers 1-3 also published in one volume entitled *The lost swords, the first triad*, 1988
4 *Farslayer's story* (1989)
5 *Coinspinner's story* (1989)
6 *Mindsword's story* (1990)
Numbers 4-6 also published in one volume entitled *The lost swords, the second triad*, 1991

Book of marvels series
Halliburton, Richard
1 *Occident* (1937)
Richard Halliburton's book of marvels
2 *Orient* (1938)
Richard Halliburton's second book of marvels
One volume edition entitled *Richard Halliburton's complete book of marvels*. 1941

Book of Sarah series
Christie, Robert Stuart
1 *Young experience* (1925)
2 *Gay application* (1925)

Book of small souls quartet
Couperus, Louis
1 *Small souls* (1902)
Original edition entitled *De kleine zielen*
2 *Later life* (1902)
Original edition entitled *Het late leven*
3 *Twilight of the soul* (1903)
Original edition entitled *Zielensschemering*
4 *Doctor Adriaan* (1903)
Original edition entitled *Het heilige weten*

Book of swords trilogy
Saberhagen, Fred
1 *First book of swords* (1983)
2 *Second book of swords* (1983)
3 *Third book of swords* (1984)
One volume edition entitled *The complete book of swords*, 1985; this sequence is followed by the **Book of lost swords series**

Book of the beast trilogy
Stallman, Robert
see **Beast trilogy**

Book of the new sun series
Wolfe, Gene
1 *Shadow of the torturer* (1980)
2 *Claw of the conciliator* (1981)
Numbers 1 and 2 also published in one volume editions entitled *The book of the new sun*, volumes 1 and 2, 1983, and *Shadow and claw*, 1994
3 *Sword of the Lictor* (1981)
4 *Citadel of the Autarch* (1983)
Numbers 3 and 4 also published in one volume entitled *Sword and citadel*, 1994
5 *Urth of the new sun* (1987)
Companion volumes: *The boy who hooked the sun, a tale from the Book of the wonders of Urth and sky*, 1985, and *Empires of foliage and flower, a tale from the Book of the wonders of Urth and sky*, 1987

Book of the Nomes trilogy
Pratchett, Terry
1 *Truckers* (1989)
2 *Diggers* (1990)
3 *Wings* (1990)

Book of the undead series
Meyers, Richard S
1 *Fear itself* (1991)
2 *Living hell* (1991)

Book of Wraeththu series
Constantine, Storm
1 *Enchantments of flesh and spirit* (1987)
2 *Bewitchments of love and hate* (1988)
3 *Fulfilments of fate and desire* (1989)

Book of years series
Morwood, Peter
1 *Horse lord* (1983)
2 *Demon lord* (1984)
3 *Dragon lord* (1986)
4 *Warlord's domain* (1989)

Bookman trilogy
Deal, Borden
1 *Loser* (1964)
2 *Advocate* (1968)
3 *Winner* (1973)

Books and games series
Gree, Alain
1 *Farm* (1971)
Original edition entitled *Le livre-jeu de la ferme*
2 *Home* (1971)
Original edition entitled *Le livre-jeu de la maison*
3 *Sailing* (1972)
Original edition entitled *Le livre-jeu des voiliers*
4 *All-color activity book of animals* (1973)
Original edition entitled *Le livre-jeu des animaux*
Eight more volumes in this sequence not translated into English

Books for me series
Wolff, Margaret
Illustrated by Val Hunt
1 *Me* (1978)
2 *All about me* (1978)
3 *My bathtime* (1978)
4 *My day* (1978)
5 *My garden* (1979)
6 *My birthday* (1979)
7 *Me at playschool* (1979)
8 *Me in the park* (1979)
9 *My new baby* (1979)
10 *Me in puddles* (1979)
11 *What can I do?* (1979)
12 *Me outside* (1979)
13 *My bedroom* (1980)
14 *Me shopping* (1980)
15 *My toys* (1980)
16 *My pussycat* (1980)
17 *My teddy* (1983)
18 *My truck* (1983)
19 *My dinner* (1983)
20 *What I wear* (1983)

Books from barely there series
Cosgrove, Stephen Edward
see **Barely there series**

Books of blood series
Barker, Clive
1 *Books of blood, volume I* (1984)
2 *Books of blood, volume II* (1984)
3 *Books of blood, volume III* (1984)
4 *Books of blood, volume IV* (1985)
Inhuman condition
The second title is an abridged edition
5 *Books of blood, volume V* (1985)
In the flesh
Books of blood V
6 *Books of blood, volume VI* (1985)
Books of blood VI

Books of Corum series
Moorcock, Michael
see **Corum series**

Books of Paradys series
Lee, Tanith
see **Secret books of Paradys series**

Books of the art series
Barker, Clive
1 *Great and secret show* (1989)
2 *Everville* (1994)

Books of the Kingdoms trilogy
Wells, Angus
see **Kingdoms trilogy**

Books of the Welsh Mabinogion series
Walton, Evangeline
see **Mabinogion series**

Bookshop series
Evans, Benjamin Ifor
1 *Shop on the King's Road* (1946)
2 *Church in the markets* (1949)

Boom series
Suhl, Yuri
see **Simon Boom series**

Boone and Kenton series
Ellis, Edward Sylvester
see **Daniel Boone and Simon Kenton series**

Boone Helm series
Slaughter, Jim
1 *Gunnison Butte* (1975)
2 *Shadow Range* (1975)
3 *Boone's law* (1976)
4 *Gunman's choice* (1976)
5 *Rendezvous on the South Desert* (1976)
6 *Blue Star Range* (1977)
7 *Guns of summer* (1977)
8 *Hangtree* (1977)
9 *Legend of Chilili* (1978)

Boone series
Messmann, Jon
see **Jefferson Boone series**

Boori series
Scott, Bill
1 *Boori* (1978)
2 *Darkness under the hills* (1980)

Booth series
Linklater, Joseph Lane
see **Silas Booth series**

Bootles series
Winter, John Strange
1 *Cavalry life* (1881)
Alternative title: Sketches and stories in barracks and out
2 *Regimental legends* (1883)
3 *Bootles' baby* (1885)
A story of the Scarlet Lancers
4 *Houp-la!* (1885)
5 *Pluck* (1886)
6 *Mignon's secret* (1886)
The story of a barrack bairn
7 *Mignon's husband* (1887)
8 *Bootles' children* (1888)
9 *Ferrers Court* (1890)
10 *Born soldier* (1894)
11 *Major's favourite* (1895)
12 *Blameless woman* (1895)
13 *Heart and sword* (1898)

Borak trilogy
Howard, Robert Ervin
see **El Borak trilogy**

Borba series
Machado de Assis, Joachim Maria
see **Quincas Borba series**

Bordelon series
Ogan, George
see **Johnny Bordelon series**

Borden series
Dougall, Bernard
see **Steve Borden series**

Border Boys series
Deering, Fremont B
1 *Border Boys on the trail* (1911)
2 *Border Boys across the frontier* (1911)
3 *Border Boys with the Mexican Rangers* (1911)
4 *Border Boys with the Texas Rangers* (1911)
5 *Border Boys in the Canadian Rockies* (1913)
6 *Border Boys along the St Lawrence* (1914)

Border Legion series
This sequence has two authors
Grey, Zane
1 *Border Legion* (1916)
Grey, Romer Zane
2 *Heritage of the Legion* (1972)

Border series
Derwent, Lavinia
1 *Breath of Border air* (1975)
2 *Another breath of Border air* (1977)
3 *Border bairn* (1978)
4 *God bless the Borders* (1981)
5 *Lady of the manse* (1984)
6 *Mouse in the manse* (1985)
7 *Beyond the Borders* (1988)
Omnibus volume: *Borders omnibus*, 1991

Border series
Grey, Zane
see **Zane family series**

Border trilogy
McCarthy, Cormac
1 *All the pretty horses* (1993)
2 *Crossing* (1994)
Third volume not yet published

Border trilogy
Pease, Howard
1 *Magnus Sinclair* (1904)
2 *Of Mistress Eve* (1906)
3 *Burning cresset* (1908)

Borderland series
Calderini, Priscilla
1 *Mount Subasio* (1985)
2 *Borderland* (1987)

Borderland series
Windling, Terri
1 *Borderland* (1986)
2 *Bordertown* (1986)
Companion volume: *Life on the border*, 1991

Borderland trilogy
Hunt, Greg
see **Hartman family trilogy**

Borg series
Hawkins, Ward
see **Harry Borg series**
Posey, Carl Alfred
see **Steven Borg series**

Borges series
Bonett, John
see **Inspector Borges series**

Borgia series
Bennetts, Pamela
see **Cesare Borgia series**

Borgia series
Gaunt, Richard
1 *Blood for a Borgia* (1968)
2 *Vendetta* (1968)
3 *Tyrant* (1969)
4 *Blood feud* (1970)
5 *Lucrezia Borgia's lover* (1971)

Borgia series
Plaidy, Jean
see **Lucrezia Borgia series**
Sabatini, Rafael
see **Cesare Borgia series**

Borgia trilogy
Huna, Ludwig
1 *Borgian bull* (1928)
Bulls of Rome
Original edition entitled *Die Stiere von Rom*
2 *Star of the Orsini* (1928)
Original edition entitled *Der Stern des Orsini*
3 *Maid of the Nettuno* (1928)
Original edition entitled *Das Madchen des Nettuno*

Borgneff and Mancuso series
Luckless, John
see **Eddie Mancuso and Vasily Borgneff series**

Borham series
Brodie, Gordon
see **John Borham series**

Boris Bear series
Bruna, Dick
1 *Boris Bear* (1989)
Original edition entitled *Boris Beer*
2 *Boris and Barbara* (1989)
Original edition entitled *Boris en Barbara*
3 *Boris on the mountain* (1989)
Original edition entitled *Boris op de berg*
Companion volume: *Through the year with Boris Bear*, 1986, original edition entitled *Lente, zommer, herfst en winter*

Boris Blundle and Gang series
Plain, Neil
Illustrated by Clive Stevens
1 *Mystery on Stuart Street* (1985)
2 *Fear in the deep* (1985)
3 *Danger in Danny's back yard* (1985)
4 *Noisy garbage-truck problem* (1985)
5 *Secret in the shed* (1985)
6 *Fishing for a job* (1986)
7 *Lonely vombatus* (1986)
8 *Invisible stranger* (1987)

Boris Bolescu series
Jungman, Ann
see **Count Boris Bolescu series**

Boris series
Jenkin-Pearce, Susie
see **Bad Boris series**

Born to believe trilogy
Longford, Frank Pakenham
Autobiography
1 *Born to believe* (1953)
2 *Five lives* (1964)
3 *Grain of wheat* (1974)

Borneo series
Keith, Agnes
Memoirs of life in Borneo before and during the Second World War
1 *Land below the wind* (1939)
2 *Three came home* (1948)
3 *White man returns* (1952)
4 *Bare feet in the palace* (1956)

Borodin family series
Arlen, Leslie
1 *Love and honor* (1980)
Love and honour
2 *War and passion* (1981)
3 *Fate and dreams* (1981)
4 *Hope and glory* (1982)
5 *Rage and desire* (1982)
6 *Fortune and fury* (1984)

Borribles series
De Larrabeiti, Michael
1 *Borribles* (1976)
2 *Borribles go for broke* (1981)
3 *Across the dark metropolis* (1986)

Borrowers series
Norton, Mary
1 *Borrowers* (1952)
2 *Borrowers afield* (1955)
3 *Borrowers afloat* (1959)
4 *Borrowers aloft* (1961)
Numbers 1-4 also published in one volume editions entitled *The Borrowers omnibus*, 1966 and *The complete adventures of the Borrowers*, 1967
5 *Poor Stainless* (1971)
6 *Borrowers avenged* (1982)

Borstal boy series
Behan, Brendan
1 *Borstal boy* (1958)
2 *Confessions of an Irish rebel* (1965)

Bosch series
Connelly, Michael
see **Harry Bosch series**

Boscobell series
Wills, Cecil Melville
see **Geoffrey Boscobell series**

Bosnian trilogy
Andric, Ivo
1 *Bridge on the Drina* (1945)
Original edition entitled *Na Drini cuprija*
2 *Bosnian story* (1945)
Bosnian chronicle
Original edition entitled *Travnicka kronika*
3 *Woman from Sarajevo* (1945)
Original edition entitled *Gospodjica*

Bostock and Harris series
Garfield, Leon
1 *Strange affair of Adelaide Harris* (1971)
2 *Bostock and Harris* (1979)
Alternative title: The night of the comet

Bostocks series
Darby, Catherine
see **Moon series**

Boswell series
Douglas, Felicity
see **Faye Boswell series**

Botternsikes and gumbles series
Wakefield, Sydney Alexander
see **Gumbles series**

Bottle, Hamish and David series
Kiddell, John
see **Hamish, David and Bottle series**

Bottom dogs series
Dahlberg, Edward
Autobiographical fiction
1 *Bottom dogs* (1929)
2 *From Flushing to Calvary* (1932)
3 *Those who perish* (1934)
One volume edition, including other unpublished work, 1976

Botts series
Upson, William Hazlett
see **Alexander Botts series**

Bouchard family series
De Jourlet, Marie
see **Windhaven series**

Bouchard family trilogy
Caldwell, Taylor
1 *Dynasty of death* (1938)
2 *Eagles gather* (1940)
3 *Final hour* (1944)

Bouncing series
Schuller, Gary
1 *Bouncing back* (1987)
How you can bounce back from failure to success or from limited success to unlimited success
2 *Bouncing higher* (1989)

Bound to succeed series
Stratemeyer, Edward L
1 *Richard Dare's venture* (1894)
Alternative title: Striking out for himself; revised edition 1899
2 *Oliver Bright's search* (1895)
Alternative title: The mystery of a mine; revised edition 1899
3 *To Alaska for gold* (1899)
Alternative title: The fortune hunters of the Yukon

Bound to win series
Stratemeyer, Edward L
Volumes in this sequence are published variously under the author's real name Edward L Stratemeyer and the two pseudonyms Ralph Bonehill and Arthur M Winfield
1 *Bound to be an electrician* (1897)
Alternative title: Franklin Bell's road to success
Winfield, Arthur M
2 *Schooldays of Fred Harley* (1897)
Alternative title: Rivals for all honors
Bonehill, Ralph
3 *Gun and sled* (1897)
Alternative title: The young hunters of Snow-Top Island
Stratemeyer, Edward L
4 *Shorthand Tom* (1897)
Alternative title: The exploits of a young reporter
Winfield, Arthur M
5 *Missing tin box* (1897)
Alternative title: The stolen railroad bonds
Bonehill, Ralph
6 *Young oarsmen of Lakeview* (1897)
Alternative title: The mystery of Hermit Island
Stratemeyer, Edward L
7 *Young auctioneers* (1897)
Alternative title: Polishing of a rolling stone
Winfield, Arthur M
8 *Poor but plucky* (1897)
Alternative title: The mystery of a flood
Bonehill, Ralph
9 *Rival bicyclists* (1897)
Rival cyclists
Alternative title: Fun and adventures on the wheel
Stratemeyer, Edward L
10 *Fighting for his own* (1897)
Alternative title: The fortunes of a young artist
Winfield, Arthur M
11 *By pluck, not luck* (1897)
Alternative title: Dan Granbury's struggle to rise
Bonehill, Ralph
12 *Leo the circus boy* (1897)
Alternative title: Life under the great white canvas

Bound to win trilogy
Ellis, Edward Sylvester
1 *Brave Billy* (1907)
2 *Plucky Dick* (1907)
Alternative title: Sowing and reaping
3 *Tam* (1907)
Alternative title: Holding the fort

Bounty Hunter series
Boyles, William
1 *Deadliest profession* (1981)
2 *Killing trade* (1981)
3 *Wild ride* (1981)
4 *Blood Mountain* (1982)

Bounty Hunter series
Fletcher, Aaron
1 *Bounty Hunter* (1977)
2 *Blood money* (1977)

Bounty Hunter series
Randall, Joshua
1 *Double the Bounty* (1987)
2 *Bounty on a lawman* (1987)
3 *Beauty and the Bounty* (1988)
4 *Bounty on a baron* (1988)
5 *Broadway Bounty* (1988)

Bounty Man series
Newton, Mike
1 *Vengeance ride* (1979)
2 *Massacre trail* (1979)

Bounty series
Downing, Todd
see **Peter Bounty series**

Bounty trilogy
Nordhoff, Charles
1 *Mutiny on the Bounty* (1932)
Mutiny!
2 *Men against the sea* (1933)
3 *Pitcairn's Island* (1934)
One volume edition entitled *The Bounty trilogy*, 1936

Bouquet series
Newman, Andrea
1 *Bouquet of barbed wire* (1969)
2 *Another bouquet* (1978)

Bourke and Ashton series
McNab, Claire
see **Inspector Carol Ashton and Sergeant Mark Bourke series**

Bourne and Curtis series
Somers, Paul
see **Hugh Curtis and Mollie Bourne series**

Bourne family trilogy
Hardwick, Michael
see **Cedar tree trilogy**

Bourne series
Finney, R C
see **Inspector Bourne series**
Galwey, Geoffrey Valentine
see **Inspector Daddy Bourne series**
Leach, Christopher
see **Dave Bourne series**

Bourne trilogy
Ludlum, Robert
1 *Bourne identity* (1980)
2 *Bourne supremacy* (1986)
3 *Bourne ultimatum* (1990)

Bow Street Runner series
Sturrock, Jeremy
American edition of this sequence published under the pseudonym J G Jeffreys
1 *Village of rogues* (1972)
Thief taker
2 *Wicked way to die* (1973)
3 *Wilful lady* (1975)
4 *Conspiracy of poisons* (1977)
5 *Suicide most foul* (1981)
6 *Captain Bolton's corpse* (1982)
7 *Pangersbourne murders* (1983)
8 *Thistlewood plot* (1987)

Bow Street series
Sebastian, Margaret
1 *Bow Street brangle* (1977)
2 *Bow Street gentleman* (1977)

Bowden series
Leeson, Robert
see **Alec Bowden series**

Bowdre series
Page, Jake
see **Mo Bowdre series**

Bowdrie series
L'Amour, Louis
see **Chick Bowdrie series**

Bowen series
Hines, Anna Grossnickle
see **Cassie Bowen series**

Bowen Tylor trilogy
Burroughs, Edgar Rice
1 *Land that time forgot* (1924)
Originally published in *Blue Book Magazine*, July 1918
2 *People that time forgot* (1963)
Originally published in *Blue Book Magazine*, October 1918
3 *Out of time's abyss* (1963)
Originally published in *Blue Book Magazine*, December 1918
One volume edition entitled *The land that time forgot*, 1924

Bowering series
Yeager, Dorian
see **Victoria Bowering series**

Bowie series
Martin, Charles Morris
see **Alamo Bowie series**

Bowker series
Parkman, Sydney
see **Captain Bowker series**

Bowman and Peart series
Burrows, Julie
see **Superintendent Bowman and Sergeant Peart series**

Bowman family trilogy
Eastlake, William
1 *Go in beauty* (1956)
2 *Bronc people* (1958)
3 *Portrait of an artist and twenty-six horses* (1963)

Bowman series
Howard, Hartley
see **Glenn Bowman series**

Bowmen series
Doyle, Arthur Conan
see **English bowmen series**

Boxcar children series
Warner, Gertrude Chandler
1 *Boxcar children* (1924)
Revised edition 1942
2 *Surprise island* (1949)
3 *Yellow house mystery* (1953)
4 *Mystery ranch* (1958)
5 *Mike's mystery* (1960)
6 *Blue Bay mystery* (1961)
7 *Woodshed mystery* (1962)
8 *Lighthouse mystery* (1963)
9 *Mountain top mystery* (1964)
10 *Schoolhouse mystery* (1965)
11 *Caboose mystery* (1966)
12 *Houseboat mystery* (1967)
13 *Snowbound mystery* (1968)
14 *Tree house mystery* (1969)
15 *Bicycle mystery* (1970)
16 *Mystery in the sand* (1971)
17 *Mystery behind the wall* (1973)
18 *Bus station mystery* (1974)
19 *Benny uncovers a mystery* (1976)
20 *Haunted cabin mystery* (1991)
21 *Deserted library mystery* (1991)
22 *Animal shelter mystery* (1991)
23 *Old motel mystery* (1991)
24 *Mystery of a hidden painting* (1992)
25 *Amusement park mystery* (1992)
26 *Mystery of the mixed-up zoo* (1992)
27 *Camp-out mystery* (1992)
28 *Mystery girl* (1992)
29 *Mystery cruise* (1992)
30 *Disappointed friend mystery* (1992)
31 *Mystery of the singing ghost* (1992)
32 *Mystery in the snow* (1992)
33 *Pizza mystery* (1993)
34 *Mystery horse* (1993)
35 *Mystery at the dog show* (1993)
36 *Castle mystery* (1993)
37 *Mystery of the lost village* (1993)
38 *Mystery of the purple pool* (1994)
39 *Ghost ship mystery* (1994)
40 *Canoe trip mystery* (1994)
41 *Mystery of the hidden beach* (1994)
42 *Mystery of the missing cat* (1994)
43 *Mystery on stage* (1994)
44 *Dinosaur mystery* (1995)

Boxcar children special series
Warner, Gertrude Chandler
1 *Mystery on the ice* (1993)
2 *Mystery in Washington, D.C.* (1994)
3 *Mystery at Snowflake Inn* (1994)

Boxer Unit SS series
Cort, Ned
1 *French entrapment* (1981)
2 *Alpine gambit* (1981)
3 *Operation Counter-Scorch* (1982)
4 *Target Norway* (1982)
5 *Partisan demolition* (1982)

Boxing series
Wilson, Peter
Essays
1 *Ringside seat* (1949)
2 *More ringside seats* (1959)

Boy adventurers series
Verrill, Alpheus Hyatt
1 *Boy adventurers in the forbidden land* (1922)
2 *Boy adventurers in the land of El Dorado* (1923)
3 *Boy adventurers in the land of the monkey men* (1923)
4 *Boy adventurers in the unknown land* (1924)

Boy Aeronauts series
Ashton, Lamar
see **Aeroplane boys series**

Boy allies of the army series
Hayes, Clair Wallace
1 *Boy allies at Liege* (1915)
Alternative title: Through lines of steel
2 *Boy allies on the firing line* (1915)
Alternative title: Twelve days battle along the Marne
3 *Boy allies with the Cossacks* (1915)
Alternative title: A wild dash over the Carpathians
4 *Boy allies in the trenches* (1915)
Alternative title: Midst shot and shell along the Aisne
5 *Boy allies in great peril* (1916)
Alternative title: With the Italian Army in the Alps
6 *Boy allies in the Balkan Campaign* (1916)
Alternative title: The struggle to save a nation
7 *Boy allies on the Somme* (1917)
Alternative title: Courage and bravery rewarded
8 *Boy allies at Verdun* (1917)
Alternative title: Saving France from the enemy
9 *Boy allies under the Stars and Stripes* (1918)
Alternative title: Leading the American troops to the firing line
10 *Boy allies with Haig in Flanders* (1918)
Alternative title: The fighting Canadians of Vimy Ridge
11 *Boy allies with Pershing in France* (1919)
Alternative title: Over the top at Chateau Thierry
12 *Boy allies with the great advance* (1919)
Alternative title: Driving the enemy through France and Belgium
13 *Boy allies with Marshall Foch* (1919)
Alternative title: The closing days of the Great World War

Boy allies of the navy series
Drake, Robert L
1 *Boy allies with the North Sea Patrol* (1915)
Alternative title: Striking the first blow at the German Fleet
2 *Boy allies under two flags* (1915)
Alternative title: Sweeping the enemy from the seas
3 *Boy allies with the Flying Squadron* (1915)
Alternative title: The naval raiders of the Great War
4 *Boy allies with the Terror of the Seas* (1915)
Alternative title: The last shot of the submarine D-16
5 *Boy allies under the sea* (1916)
Alternative title: The vanishing submarine
6 *Boy allies in the Baltic* (1916)
Alternative title: Through fields of ice to aid the Czar
7 *Boy allies at Jutland* (1917)
Alternative title: The greatest naval batle of history
8 *Boy allies with Uncle Sam's cruisers* (1918)
Alternative title: Convoying the American Army across the Atlantic
9 *Boy allies with the submarine D-32* (1918)
Alternative title: The fall of the Russian empire
10 *Boy allies with the victorious fleets* (1919)
Alternative title: The fall of the German Navy

Boy and man series
Hanson, Lawrence
Autobiography
1 *Shining morning face* (1948)
2 *Boy and man* (1952)

Boy aviators series
Lawton, Wilbur
1 *Boy aviators in Nicaragua* (1910)
Alternative title: In league with the insurgents
2 *Boy aviators on secret service* (1910)
Alternative title: Working with wireless
3 *Boy aviators in Africa* (1910)
Alternative title: An aerial ivory trail
4 *Boy aviators' treasure quest* (1910)
Alternative title: The golden galleon
5 *Boy aviators in record flight* (1910)
Alternative title: The rival aeroplane
6 *Boy aviators' Polar dash* (1910)
Alternative title: Facing death in the Antarctic
7 *Boy aviators' flight for a fortune* (1912)
8 *Boy aviators with the air raiders* (1915)

Boy explorers series
Miller, Warren Hastings
1 *Boy explorers in darkest New Guinea* (1921)
2 *Boy explorers in Borneo* (1922)
3 *Boy explorers and the ape-man of Sumatra* (1923)
4 *Boy explorers on tiger trails in Burma* (1925)
5 *Boy explorers in the Pirate Archipelago* (1926)

Boy fortune hunters series
Akers, Floyd
1 *Boy fortune hunters in Alaska* (1908)
Originally published as *Sam Steele's adventures on land and sea*, under the pseudonym Hugh Fitzgerald, 1906
2 *Boy fortune hunters in Egypt* (1908)
3 *Boy fortune hunters in Panama* (1908)
Originally published as *Sam Steele's adventures in Panama*, under the pseudonym Hugh Fitzgerald, 1906
4 *Boy fortune hunters in China* (1909)
5 *Boy fortune hunters in Yucatan* (1910)
6 *Boy fortune hunters in the South Seas* (1911)

Boy hunters series
Bonehill, Ralph
1 *Four boy hunters* (1906)
Alternative title: The outing of the gun club
2 *Guns and snowshoes* (1907)
Alternative title: The winter outing of the young hunters
3 *Young hunters of the lake* (1908)
Alternative title: Out with rod and gun
4 *Out with gun and camera* (1910)
Alternative title: The boy hunters in the mountains

Boy hunters series
Reid, Mayne
1 *Boy hunters* (1853)
Alternative title: Adventures in search of a white buffalo
2 *Young voyageurs* (1854)
Alternative title: The boy hunters in the north

Boy inventors series
Bonner, Richard
1 *Boy inventors' wireless triumph* (1912)
2 *Boy inventors and the vanishing gun* (1912)
3 *Boy inventors' diving torpedo boat* (1912)
4 *Boy inventors' flying ship* (1913)
5 *Boy inventors' electric hydroaeroplane* (1914)
6 *Boy inventors' radio-telephone* (1915)

Boy life among the Indians series
Goulding, Francis Robert
1 *Adventures among the Indians* (1871)
2 *Cousin Aleck* (1872)
Companion volume: *Boy life on the water*, 1872

Boy patrol series
Ellis, Edward Sylvester
1 *Boy patrol around the council fire* (1913)
2 *Boy patrol on guard* (1913)

Boy pioneer series
Ellis, Edward Sylvester
1 *Ned in the block-house* (1883)
2 *Ned in the woods* (1884)
3 *Ned on the river* (1884)

Boy ranchers series
Baker, Willard F
1 *Boy ranchers* (1921)
Alternative title: Solving the mystery at Diamond X
2 *Boy ranchers in camp* (1921)
Alternative title: The water fight at Diamond X
3 *Boy ranchers on the trail* (1921)
Alternative title: The Diamond X after cattle rustlers
4 *Boy ranchers among the Indians* (1922)
Alternative title: Trailing the Yaquis
5 *Boy ranchers at Spur Creek* (1923)
Alternative title: Fighting the sheep herders
6 *Boy ranchers in the desert* (1924)
Alternative title: Diamond X and the lost mine
7 *Boy ranchers on Roaring River* (1926)
Alternative title: Diamond X and the Chinese smugglers
8 *Boy ranchers in Death Valley* (1928)
Alternative title: Diamond X and the poison mystery
9 *Boy ranchers in Terror Canyon* (1930)
Alternative title: Diamond X winning out

Boy Scout Explorers series
Palmer, Don
1 *Boy Scout Explorers at Emerald Valley* (1955)
2 *Boy Scout Explorers at Treasure Mountain* (1955)
3 *Boy Scout Explorers at Headless Hollow* (1957)

Boy Scout series
Carter, Herbert
1 *Boy Scouts* (1909)
Boy Scouts at the Battle of Saratoga
2 *Boy Scouts' first campfire* (1913)
3 *Boy Scouts in the Blue Ridge* (1913)
4 *Boy Scouts on the trail* (1913)
5 *Boy Scouts in the Maine woods* (1913)
6 *Boy Scouts through the big timber* (1913)
7 *Boy Scouts in the Rockies* (1913)
8 *Boy Scouts on Sturgeon Island* (1914)
9 *Boy Scouts down in Dixie* (1914)
10 *Boy Scouts along the Susquehanna* (1915)
11 *Boy Scouts on war trials in Belgium* (1916)
12 *Boy Scouts afoot in France* (1917)

Boy Scouts of the Air series
Stuart, Gordon
1 *Boy Scouts of the Air at Eagle Camp* (1912)
2 *Boy Scouts of the Air at Greenwood School* (1912)

3 *Boy Scouts of the Air in Indian land* (1912)
4 *Boy Scouts of the Air in Northern wilds* (1912)
5 *Boy Scouts of the Air on Flathead Mountain* (1913)
6 *Boy Scouts of the Air on the Great Lakes* (1914)
7 *Boy Scouts of the Air in Belgium* (1915)
8 *Boy Scouts of the Air in the Lone Star Patrol* (1916)
9 *Boy Scouts of the Air on Lost Island* (1917)
10 *Boy Scouts of the Air on the French Front* (1918)
11 *Boy Scouts of the Air with Pershing* (1919)
12 *Boy Scouts of the Air in Dismal Swamp* (1920)
13 *Boy Scouts of the Air at Cape Peril* (1921)
14 *Boy Scouts of the Air on Baldcrest* (1922)

Boy Scouts series
Burgess, Thornton Waldo
1 *Boy Scouts of Woodcraft Camp* (1912)
2 *Boy Scouts on Swift River* (1913)
3 *Boy Scouts on lost trail* (1914)
4 *Boy Scouts in a trapper's camp* (1915)

Boy Scouts series
Corcoran, Brewer
1 *Boy Scouts of Kendallville* (1918)
2 *Boy Scouts of the Wolf Patrol* (1920)

Boy Scouts series
Fitzhugh, Percy Keese
1 *Along the Mohawk Trail* (1912)
Alternative title: Boy Scouts on Lake Champlain
2 *For Uncle Sam, boss* (1913)
Alternative title: Boy Scouts at Panama
3 *In the path of La Salle* (1914)
Alternative title: Boy Scouts on the Mississippi

Boy series
Aimwell, Walter
1 *Oscar* (1853)
Alternative title: The boy who had his own way
2 *Clinton* (1853)
Alternative title: Boy-life in the country
3 *Ella* (1855)
Alternative title: Turning over a new leaf
4 *Whistler* (1856)
Alternative title: The manly boy
5 *Marcus* (1857)
Alternative title: The boy-tamer
6 *Jessie* (1859)
Alternative title: Trying to be somebody
7 *Jerry* (1864)
Alternative title: The sailor boy ashore; unfinished at the author's death

Boy spies series
This sequence has two authors
Otis, James
1 *Boy spies with Lafayette* (1895)
2 *Boy spies of Philadelphia* (1897)
3 *Boy spies at the Battle of Bunker Hill* (1898)
4 *Boy spies of old New York* (1898)
5 *Boy spies with the Swamp Fox* (1899)
6 *Boy spies at Yorktown* (1899)
7 *Boy spies at the defense of Fort Henry* (1900)
Chipman, William Pendleton
8 *Boy spies of Fort Griswold* (1900)
Otis, James
9 *Boy spies with the Regulators* (1901)
10 *Boy spies in Detroit* (1904)
11 *Boy spies on Chesapeke Bay* (1907)
Chipman, William Pendleton
12 *Boy spies at the Battle of New Orleans* (1910)

Boy travellers series
Knox, Thomas Wallace
1 *Boy travellers in the Far East, part 1* (1879)
Adventures of two youths in a journey to Japan and China
2 *Boy travellers in the Far East, part 2* (1880)
Adventures of two youths in a journey to Siam and Java, with descriptions of Cochin China, Cambodia, Sumatra and the Malay archipelago
3 *Boy travellers in the Far East, part 3* (1881)
Adventures of two youths in a journey to Ceylon and India, with descriptions of Borneo, the Philippine Islands and Burmah
4 *Boy travellers in the Far East, part 4* (1882)
Adventures of two youths in a journey to Egypt and the Holy Land
5 *Boy travellers in the Far East, part 5* (1883)
Adventures of two youths in a journey through Africa
6 *Boy travellers in the Russian Empire* (1886)
Adventures of two youths in a journey in European and Asian Russia, with accounts of a tour across Siberia
7 *Boy travellers in South America* (1886)
Adventures of two youths in a journey in Ecuador, Peru, Bolivia, Brazil, Paraguay, Argentine Republic and Chili, with descriptions of Patagonia and Tierra del Fuego and voyages upon the Amazon and La Plata rivers
8 *Boy travellers in the Congo* (1887)
Adventures of two youths in a journey with Henry M Stanley through the Dark Continent
9 *Boy travellers in Australasia* (1889)
Adventures of two youths in a journey to the Sandwich, Marqueasa, Society, Samoan and Feejee islands
10 *Boy travellers in Mexico* (1889)
Adventures of two youths in a journey to northern and central Mexico, Campeachey and Yicatan, with a description of the republics of Central America and of the Nicaragua Canal
11 *Boy travellers in central Europe* (1889)
Adventures of two youths in a journey through France, Switzerland and Austria, with excursions among the Alps of Switzerland and the Tyrol
12 *Boy travellers in Great Britain and Ireland* (1890)
Adventures of two youths in a journey through Ireland, Scotland, Wales and England, with visits to the Hebrides and the Isle of Man
13 *Boy travellers in northern Europe* (1891)
Adventures of two youths in a journey through Holland, Germany, Denmark, Norway and Sweden, with visits to Heligoland and the Land of the Midnight Sun
14 *Boy travellers in southern Europe* (1893)
Adventures of two youths in a journey through Italy, southern France and Spain, with visits to Gibraltar and the islands of Sicily and Malta
15 *Boy travellers in the Levant* (1895)
Adventures of two youths in a journey through Morocco, Algeria, Tunis, Greece and Turkey, with visits to the islands of Rhodes and Cyprus and the site of ancient Troy
16 *In wild Africa* (1895)
Adventures of two youths in a journey through the Sahara Desert
17 *Land of the kangaroo* (1896)
Adventures of two youths in a journey through the great island continent
Companion volume: *The voyage of the Vivian to the North Pole and beyond, adventures of two youths in the open Polar sea,* 1884

Boy troopers series
Hayes, Clair Wallace
1 *Boy troopers on the trail* (1922)
2 *Boy troopers in the Northwest* (1922)
3 *Boy troopers on strike duty* (1922)
4 *Boy troopers among the wild mountaineers* (1922)

Boy volunteers series
Ward, Kenneth
1 *Boy volunteers on the Belgian Front* (1917)
2 *Boy volunteers with the French airmen* (1917)
3 *Boy volunteers with the British artillery* (1917)
4 *Boy volunteers with the submarine fleet* (1917)
5 *Boy volunteers with the American infantry* (1917)

Boyars trilogy
Dumitru, Petru
1 *Family jewels* (1956)
Original edition entitled *Cronica de familie*
2 *Prodigals* (1960)
Original edition entitled *Les plaisirs de jeunesse*
Third volume not published

Boyce series
Ward, Mary Augusta
see **Marcella Boyce series**

Boyd family series
Finlay, Eileen
1 *Hills of home* (1943)
2 *Storm Boyd's family* (1952)

Boyd series
Brown, Carter
see **Danny Boyd series**
Jackson, Giles
see **Nile Boyd series**
Westermann, John
see **Orin Boyd series**

Boyet Rhodes series
Aikman, Anthony
1 *Caves of Segada* (1985)
2 *Eye of Itza* (1986)
3 *Brokers of doom* (1987)

Boyne series
Macgowan, Alice
see **Jerry Boyne series**

Boyo and Finn series
Niall, Ian
see **Billy Boyo and Albert Finn series**

Boys and girls and I series
Molesworth, Mary Louisa
1 *Boys and I* (1883)
2 *Girls and I* (1892)

Boys' and girls' series
Blyton, Enid
1 *Boys' and girls' circus book* (1939)
2 *Boys' and girls' story book* (1940)

Boys at the Front series
Grant, Allan
1 *Cadet of Belgium* (1915)
2 *In defense of Paris* (1915)
3 *Fifty feet under the sea* (1915)
4 *Fighting the zeppelin* (1915)

Boys' book series
Crump, James Irving
1 *Boys' book of firemen* (1916)
2 *Boys' book of policemen* (1917)
3 *Boys' book of mounted police* (1917)
4 *Boys' book of railroads* (1917)
5 *Boys' book of forest rangers* (1924)
6 *Boys' book of Arctic exploration* (1925)
7 *Boys' book of the U.S. mails* (1926)
8 *Boys' book of airmen* (1927)
9 *Boys' book of coast guards* (1928)
10 *Boys' book of fisheries* (1933)
11 *Boys' book of newsreel hunters* (1933)
12 *Boys' book of cowboys* (1934)

Boys of business series
Chapman, Allen
1 *Young express agent* (1906)
Alternative title: Bart Stirling's road to success
2 *Two boy publishers* (1906)
Alternative title: From typecase to editor's chair
3 *Mail Order Frank* (1907)
Alternative title: A smart boy and his chances
4 *Business boy* (1908)
Business boy's pluck
Alternative title: Winning success
5 *Young land agent* (1911)
Nat Borden's find
Alternative title: The secret of the Borden Estate

Boys of Columbia High series
Forbes, Graham B
see **Columbia High School series**

Boys of pluck series
Chapman, Allen
see **Boys of business series**

Boy's possessions series
Sandberg, Inger
Illustrated by Lasse Sandberg
1 *Boy with one hundred cars* (1966)
Original edition entitled *Pojken med de hundra bilarna*
2 *Boy with many houses* (1968)
Original edition entitled *Pojken med de maanga husen*

Boys' Republic series
Buhet, Gil
1 *Honey siege* (1951)
2 *Grand catch* (1956)

Boy's series
Derleth, August
Poems
1 *Boy's way* (1947)
2 *It's a boy's world* (1948)

Boys' story of the railroad series
Stevenson, Burton Egbert
1 *Young section-hand* (1905)
2 *Young train despatcher* (1907)
3 *Young train master* (1909)
4 *Young apprentice* (1912)
Alternative title: Allan West's chum

Boysie Cumberbatch trilogy
Clarke, Austin Chesterfield
1 *Meeting point* (1967)
2 *Storm of fortune* (1973)
3 *Bigger light* (1975)

Boysie L Oakes series
Gardner, John Edmund
1 *Liquidator* (1964)

2 *Understrike* (1965)
3 *Amber nine* (1966)
4 *Madrigal* (1967)
5 *Founder member* (1969)
6 *Traitor's exit* (1970)
7 *Airline pirates* (1970)
Air apparent
8 *Assassination file* (1974)
Short stories
9 *Killer for a song* (1975)
Also two Oakes stories in *Hideaway*, 1968

Braby series
Dehan, Richard
see **Market place series**

Bracken and Woodward series
Blazer, J S
see **Donald Bracken and James Rowland Woodward series**

Brad Bradley series
Ronald, E B
see **Rupert Bradley series**

Brad Dolan series
Fuller, William
1 *Back country* (1954)
2 *Goat Island* (1954)
Local talent
3 *Pace that kills* (1956)
4 *Brad Dollan's blonde cargo* (1957)
5 *Girl in the frame* (1957)
6 *Brad Dolan's Miami manhunt* (1958)
7 *Tight squeeze* (1959)

Brad Ford series
Hobson, Hank
1 *Gallant affair* (1957)
2 *Death makes a claim* (1958)
3 *Big twist* (1959)
4 *Mission House murder* (1959)
5 *Beyond tolerance* (1960)

Brad Forrest series
Maitland, Hugh
1 *Brad Forrest's Hong Kong adventure* (1964)
2 *Brad Forrest's Los Angeles adventure* (1964)
3 *Brad Forrest's Madagascar adventure* (1964)
4 *Brad Forrest's Calgary adventure* (1964)
5 *Brad Forrest's New York adventure* (1965)
6 *Brad Forrest's Yucatan adventure* (1965)
7 *Brad Forrest's Halifax adventure* (1965)
8 *Brad Forrest's London adventure* (1965)

Brad Smith series
Bickham, Jack Miles
1 *Dropshot* (1990)
2 *Tiebreaker* (1990)
3 *Overhead* (1991)
4 *Breakfast at Wimbledon* (1991)
5 *Double fault* (1993)
6 *Davis Cup conspiracy* (1994)

Brad Spear series
Cunningham, Chet
see **Agent Brad Spear series**

Braddock and Black series
Johnson, Susan
see **Blaze Braddock and Jon Hazard Black series**

Braddock series
Bodine, J D
see **Pecos Kid series**

Brade series
Campbell, Harriette Russell
see **Simon Brade series**
Wolffe, Katherine
see **Captain Courtney Brade series**

Bradfield series
Witting, Clifford
see **Inspector Peter Bradfield series**

Bradford family series
Jenkins, Jerry Bruce
1 *In deep water* (1984)
2 *Mystery at Raider Stadium* (1984)
3 *Daniel's big decision* (1984)
4 *Before the judge* (1984)
5 *Daniel's big surprise* (1984)
6 *Two runaways* (1984)
7 *Clubhouse mystery* (1990)
8 *Daniel and the big blizzard* (1990)
9 *Yo Yo and midnight* (1990)
10 *Good sport, bad sport* (1990)
11 *Mystery at ballpark* (1990)
12 *Big trouble at the beach* (1990)

Bradford family series
Mathews, Joanna Hooe
1 *Fred Bradford's debt* (1882)
2 *Harry Bradford's crusade* (1883)
3 *Maggie Bradford's club* (1889)
4 *Maggie Bradford's school-mates* (1890)
5 *Bessie Bradford's prize* (1890)
6 *Maggie Bradford's fair* (1892)
7 *Frankie Bradford's bear* (1893)

Bradford series
Mathews, Joanna Hooe
see **Bessie Bradford series; Maggie Bradford series**
Warden, Mike
see **Hank Bradford series**

Bradfords series
Hatch, Richard Warren
1 *Into the wind* (1929)
2 *Leave the salt earth* (1933)

Bradley Adams series
Dekobra, Maurice
1 *She wore pink gloves* (1956)
Widow with pink gloves
Original edition entitled *La veuve aux ganta roses*
2 *Lady is a vamp* (1957)
Original edition entitled *Vamp ou vestale*

Bradley and Mayberry series
Tree, Gregory
see **Bill Bradley and Noel Mayberry series**

Bradley and Raymond series
Longmate, Norman
see **Inspector Bradley and Sergeant Raymond series**

Bradley series
Boone, Silas K
see **Phil Bradley series**
Mitchell, Gladys
see **Dame Beatrice Bradley series**
Padgett, Abigail
see **Bo Bradley series**

Bradley series
Palmer, Bernard
1 *Mysterious letter* (1975)
2 *Mystery of the new sky* (1975)
3 *Jon and the break-in mystery* (1976)
4 *Trena and the old diary* (1976)
5 *Homesteading in Standing Bear's territory* (1976)
6 *Princess Pat saves the day* (1977)
7 *Trena's rodeo vial* (1977)
8 *Mystery of the missing fossil* (1977)

Bradley series
Pentecost, Hugh
see **Luke Bradley series**
Robertson, Colin
see **Superintendent Bradley series**
Ronald, E B
see **Rupert Bradley series**
Wheeler, Janet D
see **Billie Bradley series**
White, Constance Mary
see **Saint Mark's Hospital series**

Bradshaw family series
Pugh, Nansi
1 *Miniature mystery* (1953)
2 *Bradshaws on the trail* (1963)

Bradshaw series
Dobyns, Stephen
see **Charlie Bradshaw series**
Johnston, Madeleine
see **Noah Bradshaw series**

Bradshaw trilogy
Kennedy, Adam
1 *No place to cry* (1986)
2 *Fires of summer* (1988)
3 *All dreams denied* (1989)

Brady Bunch series
Johnston, William
1 *Brady Bunch* (1969)
2 *Showdown at the PTA Corral* (1969)
3 *Count up to blast down* (1970)
4 *Quarterback who came to dinner* (1970)

Brady Coyne series
Tapply, William George
1 *Death at Charity's Point* (1984)
2 *Dutch blue error* (1985)
3 *Follow the sharks* (1985)
4 *Marine corpse* (1986)
Rodent of doubt
5 *Dead meat* (1987)
6 *Vulgar boatman* (1987)
7 *Void in hearts* (1988)
8 *Dead winter* (1989)
9 *Client privilege* (1989)
10 *Spotted cats* (1991)
11 *Tight lines* (1992)
12 *Snake eater* (1993)
13 *Seventh enemy* (1995)

Brady series
Faulcon, Robert
see **Nighthunter series**
Jance, Judith A
see **Joanna Brady series**
Macdonnell, James Edmond
see **Jim Brady series**
McRoyd, Allan
see **Inspector Franklin Brady series**

Bragg and Morton series
Harrison, Ray
see **Sergeant Joseph Bragg and Constable James Morton series**

Bragg series
Lynch, Jack
see **Peter Bragg series**
Wade, Henry
see **John Bragg series**

Brain and brawn series
Drysdale, William
1 *Young reporter* (1895)
A story of Printing House Square
2 *Fast mail* (1896)
The story of a train boy
3 *Beach patrol* (1897)
A story of the life-saving service
4 *Young supercargo* (1898)
A story of the merchant marine

Brain plant series
Meltzer, David
Poetry
1 *Lovely* (1969)
2 *Healer* (1969)
3 *Out* (1969)
4 *Glue factory* (1969)
One volume edition entitled *The brain plant tetralogy*, 1970

Brain series
Cecil, Henry
see **Colonel Brain series**

Brain Sharpeners series
Curtis, Philip
see **Mister Browser series**

Brains Benton series
This sequence has two authors
Verral, Charles Spain
1 *Case of the missing message* (1959)
Wyatt, George
2 *Case of the counterfeit coin* (1960)
3 *Case of the stolen dummy* (1961)
4 *Case of the roving Rolls* (1961)
5 *Case of the waltzing mouse* (1961)
6 *Case of the painted dragon* (1961)
7 *Case of the haunted hermit* (1962)

Brains Cunningham series
Thorne, Ernest Pollett
see **Major Brains Cunningham series**

Brains series
Dunstan, Keith
Autobiography
1 *No brains at all* (1990)
2 *No brains on Tuesday* (1991)
Collected wit and wisdom

Braithwaite series
Spence, Eleanor
see **Arabella Braithwaite series**

Brak series
Jakes, John
1 *Brak the barbarian* (1968)
Short stories
2 *Brak the barbarian versus the sorceress* (1969)
Sorceress
3 *Brak the barbarian versus the mark of the demons* (1969)
Mark of the demons
4 *When the idols walked* (1978)
5 *Fortunes of Brak* (1980)
Short stories

Bramble series
Maurois, Andre
see **Colonel Bramble series**

Brambleberrys series
Mayer, Marianna
Illustrated by Gerald McDermott
1 *Brambleberrys animal book of alphabet* (1991)
2 *Brambleberrys animal book of colors* (1991)
3 *Brambleberrys animal book of counting* (1991)
4 *Brambleberrys animal book of shapes* (1991)

Brambly Hedge series
Barklem, Jill
1 *Winter story* (1980)
2 *Autumn story* (1980)
3 *Spring story* (1980)
4 *Summer story* (1980)
Numbers 1-4 also published in one volume editions entitled *The big book of Brambly Hedge*, 1981 and *The four seasons of Brambly Hedge*, 1988
5 *Secret staircase* (1983)
6 *High hills* (1986)
7 *Sea story* (1990)
Companion volume: *Brambly Hedge pattern book*, by Sue Dolman, 1984

Bramley series
Broome, Adam
see **Inspector Bramley series**

Bran and Bluff series
Rutherford, Meg
see **Bluff and Bran series**

Bran Mak Morn trilogy
This sequence has four authors
Howard, Robert Ervin
1 *Bran Mak Morn* (1969)
Worms of the earth
The second title is an abridged edition
Wagner, Karl Edward
2 *Legion from the shadows* (1976)
Smith, David Claude
3 *For the witch of the mists* (1978)

Bran Tregare series
Busby, Francis Marion
1 *Star rebel* (1984)
2 *Alien debt* (1984)
Numbers 1 and 2 also published in one volume entitled *The rebel dynasty*, volume 1, 1987
3 *Rebel's quest* (1985)
4 *Rebel's seed* (1986)
Numbers 3 and 4 also published in one volume entitled *The rebel dynasty*, volume 2, 1988

Brand series
Brand, Hilary
see **Hilary Brand series**
Brent, R L
see **Liquidator series**
Connington, John Jervis
see **Mark Brand series**
Hinxman, Margaret
see **Detective Inspector Ralph Brand series**

Brand series
Hunter, Neil
1 *Gun for hire* (1978)
2 *Hardcase* (1978)
3 *Lobo* (1978)
4 *Kill* (1978)
5 *Day of the gun* (1978)
6 *Brotherhood of evil* (1978)
7 *Legacy of evil* (1978)
8 *Devil's gold* (1978)
9 *Gunloose* (1978)

Brand series
Knight, Brigid
see **Christina Brand series**

Brandd series
Harrison, Harry
see **Brion Brandd series**

Brandeis series
Ash, William
see **Kyle Brandeis series**

Branders Noble series
Martin, A Richard
1 *Cassiodore case* (1927)
2 *Death of the claimant* (1929)

Brandon and Lundstrom series
Peters, Bryan
1 *Hong Kong kill* (1958)
2 *Big H* (1961)

Brandon and Morgan series
Rogers, Rosemary
see **Ginny Brandon and Steve Morgan series**

Brandon Coyle series
Southworth, Emma Dorothy Eliza Nevitte
1 *Skeleton in the closet* (1893)
2 *Brandon Coyle's wife* (1893)

Brandon family series
Tinniswood, Peter
1 *Touch of Daniel* (1968)
2 *Mog* (1970)
3 *I didn't know you cared* (1973)
4 *Except you're a bird* (1974)
5 *Uncle Mort's North Country* (1986)
6 *Uncle Mort's South Country* (1990)

Brandon series
Austen, Jane
see **Eliza Brandon series**
Bensen, Donald R
see **Cole Brandon series**
Warren, Vernon
see **Mark Brandon series**

Brandreths series
Hope, Alexander James Beresford
1 *Strictly tied up* (1880)
Originally published anonymously
2 *Brandreths* (1882)

Brandstetter series
Hansen, Joseph
see **Dave Brandstetter series**

Brandy series
Graeme, Roderic
1 *Brandy ahoy!* (1951)
2 *Where's Brandy?* (1953)
3 *Brandy goes a cruising* (1954)

Brandyjack series
Funnell, Augustine
1 *Brandyjack* (1976)
2 *Rebels of Merka* (1976)

Branestawm series
Hunter, Norman
see **Professor Branestawm series**

Brangwen family series
Lawrence, David Herbert
1 *Rainbow* (1915)
2 *Women in love* (1921)

Brannigan family series
Hatcher, Robin Lee
see **Women West series**

Brannigan series
Mackenzie, Andrew
see **Superintendent Brannigan series**
McDermid, Val
see **Kate Brannigan series**
Newsom, Ed
see **Chagro Brannigan series**

Brannigan series
Ryan, Tom
1 *Brannigan* (1974)
2 *Man from Furnace Creek* (1975)
3 *Mark of the rattler* (1975)

Brannocks series
Braun, Matt
1 *Brannocks* (1986)
2 *Windward west* (1987)
3 *Rio Hondo* (1987)
4 *Distant land* (1988)

Brannon series
Bly, Stephen Arthur
see **Stuart Brannon series**

Branscombe series
Matheson, Hugh
see **Gregory Branscombe series**

Branson series
Meredith, Doris R
see **John Lloyd Branson series**

Brant series
Blaine, John
see **Rick Brant series**
Hopkins, Nevil Monroe
see **Mason Brant series**

Branwen series
Meaney, Dee Morrison
see **Lady Branwen series**

Branxome family series
Pilkington, Roger
1 *Jan's treasure* (1955)
2 *Chesterfield gold* (1957)
3 *Missing panel* (1958)
4 *Dahlia's cargo* (1959)
5 *Don John's ducats* (1960)
6 *Nepomuk of the river* (1962)
7 *Eisenbart mystery* (1963)

Braun series
Ewers, Hanns Heinz
see **Frank Braun series**

Brave and bold series
Alger, Horatio
1 *Brave and bold* (1874)
Alternative title: The fortunes of a factory boy
2 *Jack's ward* (1875)
Alternative title: The boy guardian
3 *Shifting for himself* (1876)
Alternative title: Gilbert Greyson's fortunes
4 *Wait and hope* (1877)
Alternative title: A plucky boy's luck

Brave and honest trilogy
Ellis, Edward Sylvester
1 *Brave Tom* (1894)
Alternative title: The battle that won
2 *Honest Ned* (1894)
3 *Righting the wrong* (1894)

Brave Fireman series
Bradbury, Bianca
1 *Brave Fireman* (1951)
2 *Brave Fireman and the firehouse cat* (1951)

Brave little toaster series
Disch, Thomas Michael
1 *Brave little toaster* (1986)
A bedtime story for small appliances
2 *Brave little toaster goes to Mars* (1988)

Brave new world series
Huxley, Aldous
see **New world series**

Bravo series
Hardwick, Mollie
see **Juliet Bravo series**

Brazil series
Chalker, Jack Laurence
see **Well world series**

Brazos and Benedict series
Clay, E Jefferson
see **Duke Benedict and Hank Brazos series**

Brazos trilogy
Graves, John
1 *Goodbye to a river* (1960)
2 *Hard scrabble* (1974)
Observations on a patch of land
3 *From a limestone ledge* (1980)
Some essays and other ruminations about country life in Texas

Bread-and-Butter series
Colver, Anne
see **Barbara Baum series**

Bread and oranges series
Warner, Susan Bagert
1 *Bread and oranges* (1875)
2 *Rapids of Niagara* (1875)

Breadwinners series
This sequence has two authors
Hay, John
1 *Breadwinners* (1883)
Templeton, Faith
2 *Drafted in* (1888)
A social study

Break series
Bratby, John
1 *Breakdown* (1960)
2 *Breakfast and elevenses* (1961)
3 *Brake-pedal down* (1962)
4 *Break 50 kill* (1963)

Breakenridge series
Cleary, Denis
1 *Hook* (1979)
Capricorn run
2 *Sahara strike* (1980)
3 *Wipe-out* (1980)

Breakfast table trilogy
Holmes, Oliver Wendell
1 *Autocrat of the breakfast table* (1858)
2 *Professor at the breakfast table* (1859)
3 *Poet at the breakfast table* (1872)

Breakout series
Lake, David John
1 *Walkers on the sky* (1976)
2 *Right hand of Dextra* (1977)
3 *Wildings of Westron* (1977)
4 *Gods of Xuma* (1978)
5 *Warlord of Xuma* (1983)
6 *Fourth hemisphere* (1980)

Breakthrough series
Smith, Betsy Covington
1 *Women in religion* (1978)
2 *Women in television* (1981)
3 *Women in law* (1984)
Co-author: Jeanne Gardener

Breck series
Orvis, Kenneth
see **Adam Breck series**
Palmer, Bernard
see **Kid Breckinridge series**

Breckenridge series
Vidal, Gore
see **Myra, Myron series**

Breckinridge Elkins series
Howard, Robert Ervin
1 *Gent from Bear Creek* (1937)
2 *Pride of Bear Creek* (1966)
3 *Mayhem on Bear Creek* (1979)
4 *Heroes of Bear Creek* (1983)

Breckinridge series
Palmer, Bernard
see **Kid Breckinridge series**

Breckland series
Home, Michael
1 *Return* (1933)
God and the rabbit
2 *In this valley* (1934)
3 *This string first* (1935)
4 *Questing man* (1936)
5 *Harvest is past* (1937)
6 *July at Fritham* (1939)
7 *No snow in Latching* (1949)
8 *Grain of the wood* (1950)
9 *Soundless years* (1951)
10 *Brackenford story* (1952)
11 *That was yesterday* (1955)

Bredder series
Holton, Leonard
see **Father Joseph Bredder series**

Bredon series
Knox, Ronald Arbuthnott
see **Miles Bredon series**

Breed series
Ballinger, Bill Sanborn
see **Barr Breed series**

Breed series
Muir, James A
1 *Lonely hunt* (1976)

2 *Silent kill* (1976)
3 *Cry for vengeance* (1977)
4 *Death stage* (1977)
5 *Gallows tree* (1978)
6 *Judas goat* (1978)
7 *Time of the Wolf* (1978)
8 *Blood debt* (1979)
9 *Blood-stock* (1979)
10 *Outlaw road* (1979)
11 *Dying and the damned* (1980)
12 *Killer's moon* (1980)
13 *Bounty hunter* (1980)
14 *Spanish gold* (1981)
15 *Slaughter time* (1981)
16 *Bad habits* (1981)
17 *Day of the gun* (1982)
18 *Colour of death* (1982)
19 *Blood Valley* (1983)
20 *Gundown* (1983)
21 *Blood hunt* (1984)
22 *Apache blood* (1985)

Breed series
Stone, Ned
see **Other Day Logan series**

Breen series
Karney, Jack
see **Jim Breen series**

Breeze series
Bayne, Isabella
see **Benedict Breeze series**

Bren Hardy series
Elliott, William James
1 *Bren Hardy, tough dame* (1942)
2 *Bren Hardy again* (1945)

Brenda Bear series
Coombes, Marion
1 *All about Brenda Bear* (1959)
2 *Brenda Bear's castle* (1960)
3 *More about Brenda Bear* (1961)

Brenda Phipps and Chief Inspector Walsh series
Hunt, Richard
see **Chief Inspector Walsh and Constable Brenda Phipps series**

Brenda series
Reed, Helen Leah
1 *Miss Theodora* (1898)
2 *Brenda, her school and her club* (1900)
3 *Brenda's summer at Rockley* (1901)
4 *Brenda's cousin at Radcliffe* (1902)
5 *Brenda's bargain* (1903)
6 *Amy in Acadia* (1905)
7 *Brenda's ward* (1906)

Brendel series
Masterman, John Cecil
see **Ernst Brendel series**

Brennan series
Raine, Norman Reilly
see **Tugboat Annie series**
Zackel, Fred
see **Michael Brennan series**

Brensham trilogy
Moore, John Cecil
1 *Portrait of Elmbury* (1945)
2 *Brensham Village* (1946)
3 *Blue field* (1948)

Brent series
Davison, Gilderoy
see **Mister Brent series**
Deming, Dorothy
see **Wendy Brent series**
Fennell, George
see **Mike Brent series**
Glidden, Minna Wesselhoft
see **Carey Brent series**
Kemp, Harold
see **Inspector James Brent series**
Marfield, Dwight
see **Dudley Brent series**
McFarlane, Leslie
see **Michael Brent series**
Oxenham, Elsie J
see **Robin Brent series**
Roy, Thomas Albert
see **Jimmy Brent series**

Brentford series
Hough, Stanley Bennett
see **Inspector Brentford series**

Brentford series
Rankin, Robert
1 *Antipope* (1981)
2 *Brentford triangle* (1982)
3 *East of Ealing* (1984)
Numbers 1-3 also published in one volume entitled *The Brentford trilogy*, 1988
4 *Sprouts of wrath* (1988)

Brentland series
Trevor, Meriol
1 *Fortunate marriage* (1976)
2 *Civil prisoners* (1977)
3 *Wanton fires* (1979)

Brer Anansi series
Makhanlall, David Paschal
see **Anansi series**

Brer Rabbit adventures series
Blyton, Enid
1 *Tales of Brer Rabbit* (1928)
2 *Heyo, Brer Rabbit!* (1938)
3 *Further adventures of Brer Rabbit* (1942)
4 *Brer Rabbit and his friends* (1948)
5 *Brer Rabbit again* (1963)
Revised edition 1982
6 *Brer Rabbit's a rascal* (1965)

Brer Rabbit series
Blyton, Enid
1 *Brer Rabbit book* (1948)
2 *Second Brer Rabbit book* (1950)
3 *Third Brer Rabbit book* (1952)
4 *Fourth Brer Rabbit book* (1953)
5 *Fifth Brer Rabbit book* (1954)
6 *Sixth Brer Rabbit book* (1955)
7 *Seventh Brer Rabbit book* (1957)
8 *Eighth Brer Rabbit book* (1958)

Brer Rabbit series
Derwent, Lavinia
1 *Brer Rabbit* (1938)
2 *More Brer Rabbit* (1940)
3 *Brer Rabbit again* (1942)

Bret and Delchard series
Marston, Edward
see **Gervase Bret and Ralph Delchard series**

Bret King series
Scott, Dan
1 *Mystery of Ghost Canyon* (1960)
2 *Secret of Hermit's Peak* (1960)
3 *Range rodeo mystery* (1960)
4 *Mystery of Rawhide Gap* (1960)
5 *Mystery at Blizzard Mesa* (1960)
6 *Secret of Fort Pioneer* (1961)
7 *Mystery of Comanche Caves* (1962)
8 *Phantom of Wolf Creek* (1963)
9 *Mystery of Bandit Gulch* (1964)

Bret Malone series
Dower, Penn
see **Marshal Bret Malone series**

Brethren of the White Cross series
De Mille, James
1 *B.O.W.C.* (1869)
2 *Boys of Grand Pre School* (1870)
3 *Lost in the fog* (1870)
4 *Fire in the woods* (1871)
5 *Picked up adrift* (1872)
6 *Treasure of the seas* (1872)

Brett Carstairs series
Horler, Sydney
1 *Man who walked with death* (1931)
2 *Spy* (1931)

Brett Macklin series
Ludlow, Ian
see **Vigilante series**

Brett Nightingale series
Kelly, Mary
see **Inspector Brett Nightingale series**

Brett series
Campbell, Keith
see **Mike Brett series**
Evans, Gwyn
see **Chester Brett series**
Garrett, Robert
see **Alan Brett series**
King, T Stanleyan
see **Dixon Brett series**
Monig, Christopher
see **Brian Brett series**
O'Hara, Kevin
see **Chico Brett series**
Tracy, Louis
see **Reginald Brett series**

Brevet Cable series
Callison, Brian
1 *Plague of sailors* (1971)
2 *Frenzy of merchantmen* (1977)
Act of war

Brevitt series
Patchett, Mary Elwyn
1 *Undersea treasure hunters* (1955)
Chance of treasure
2 *Caribbean adventurers* (1957)
3 *Outback adventure* (1957)
4 *Call of the bush* (1959)
5 *Quest of Ati Manu* (1960)

Brew Axbrewder series
Stephens, Reed
see **Mick Axbrewder series**

Brewer series
Hallahan, William Henry
see **Charley Brewer series**
McElroy, Hugh
see **Inspector William Brewer series**

Brews series
Loder, Vernon
see **Inspector Brews series**

Brewster picture book series
Todd, Herbert Eatton
see **Bobby Brewster picture book series**

Brewster series
Adams, Andy
see **Biff Brewster series**
Eisenberg, Lisa
see **Laura Brewster series**
Matthews, Ann
see **Punky Brewster series**
Merwin, Samuel
see **Amy Brewster series**
Roy, Lillian Elizabeth
see **Polly Brewster series**
Todd, Herbert Eatton
see **Bobby Brewster series**

Breynton series
Phelps, Elizabeth Stuart Ward
see **Gypsy Breynton series**

Brian and Peter Leonard series
Wain, John
see **Peter and Brian Leonard series**

Brian Brett series
Monig, Christopher
1 *Burned man* (1956)
Don't count the corpses
2 *Abra-cadaver* (1958)
3 *Once upon a crime* (1959)
4 *Lonely graves* (1960)

Brian Dinsmore Conway series
Stone, Simon
see **Sir Brian Dinsmore Conway series**

Brian Douglas series
Lee, John Darrell
1 *Caught in the act* (1968)
2 *Assignment in Algeria* (1971)
Killing wind

Brian Fordinghame series
Horler, Sydney
see **Sir Brian Fordinghame series**

Brian Grant series
Seth, Ronald
1 *Operation Retriever* (1953)
Operation Getaway
2 *Operation Lama* (1953)
3 *Operation Ormer* (1956)
4 *Spy and the atom-gun* (1957)
5 *Rockets on Moon Island* (1959)
6 *Smoke without fire* (1959)

Brian Guy series
Ridgway, Jason
1 *Adam's fall* (1960)
2 *People in glass houses* (1961)
3 *Hardly a man is now alive* (1962)
4 *Treasure of the Cosa Nostra* (1966)

Brian Lee series
Douglas, George
see **Inspector Bonny Lee series**

Brian Mulroney series
Murphy, Rae Allan
1 *Brian Mulroney, the boy from Baie Comeau* (1984)
Co-authors: Robert Chodos and Nick auf der Maur
2 *Selling out* (1988)
Co-authors: Robert Chodos and Eric Hamovitch; four years of the Mulroney government

Brian O'Malley series
Daniel, Roland
1 *Arrested for murder* (1950)
2 *Deadly mission* (1961)
3 *Devil woman* (1964)
4 *Female spy* (1964)

Brian Peterson series
Cody, James P
1 *Top secret kill* (1974)
2 *Search and destroy* (1974)
3 *French killing* (1975)
4 *Your daughter will die* (1975)

Brian series
O'Neill, Donal
1 *Crucible* (1986)
2 *Of gods and men* (1987)
March of a nation

Brice Kent series
Giles, Guy Elwyn
1 *Three died variously* (1941)
2 *Target for murder* (1943)

Brichter and Price series
Pulver, Mary Monica
see **Kori McLeod Price and Peter Brichter series**

Brick Street Boys series
Ahlberg, Allan
Illustrated by Janet Ahlberg
1 *Here are the Brick Street Boys* (1975)
2 *Place to play* (1975)
3 *Sam the referee* (1975)

4 *Fred's dream* (1976)
5 *Great marathon football match* (1976)

Brick-Top Corridon series
Marshall, Raymond
1 *Mallory* (1950)
2 *Why pick on me?* (1951)

Bricktop series
Horner, Lance
see **Golden stud series**

Bricky series
Nesdale, Ira
1 *Riverbend Bricky* (1960)
2 *Bricky and the hobo* (1964)

Briconi series
Baskerville, Beatrice
1 *By whose hand?* (1922)
2 *Saint Cloud affair* (1931)

Bricoule trilogy
Montherlant, Henry de
see **Alban de Bricoule trilogy**

Bride series
Nordtvedt, Matilda
1 *Something old, something new* (1981)
2 *Something borrowed, something blue* (1981)

Bride trilogy
Coulter, Catherine
1 *Sherbrooke bride* (1991)
2 *Hellion bride* (1992)
3 *Heiress bride* (1993)

Brides series
Bittner, F Rosanne
1 *Arizona bride* (1985)
2 *Texas bride* (1988)
3 *Tennessee bride* (1988)
4 *Oregon bride* (1990)

Bridge series
Connell, Evan Shelby
1 *Mrs Bridge* (1959)
2 *Mister Bridge* (1969)

Bridge series
Way, Peter
see **Crispin Bridge series**

Bridges over time series
Anand, Valerie
1 *Proud villeins* (1990)
2 *Ruthless yeoman* (1991)
3 *Women of Ashdon* (1992)
4 *Faithful lovers* (1993)
5 *Cherished wives* (1994)

Bridget and George Blake series
Farrar, Stewart
1 *Twelve maidens* (1974)
2 *Sword of Orley* (1977)

Bridget McSweeney series
Spencer, Thomas Edward
1 *Surprising adventures of Mrs Bridget McSweeney* (1906)
2 *Spring cleaning, and other stories* (1908)
3 *That droll lady* (1911)

Bridget O'Toole and Harry Garnish series
McConnell, Frank
see **Harry Garnish and Bridget O'Toole series**

Bridie McShane series
Hunter, Mollie
1 *Sound of chariots* (1972)
2 *Dragonfly years* (1983)
Hold on to love

Bridlington series
Vickers, Bette
1 *Fed up to the top attic* (1984)
2 *Life golden time* (1985)

Brief chronicles series
Stubbs, Jean
1 *Kit's Hill* (1978)
By our beginnings
2 *Ironmaster* (1981)
Imperfect joy
3 *Vivian inheritance* (1982)
4 *Northern correspondent* (1984)

Briercliffe series
Beeding, Francis
see **Ronald Briercliffe series**

Brigade Boys series
Palmer, Bernard
1 *Brigade Boys and the flight to danger* (1960)
2 *Brigade Boys and the phantom radio* (1960)
3 *Brigade Boys in the Arctic wilderness* (1961)
4 *Brigade Boys and the disappearing stranger* (1961)
5 *Brigade Boys and the basketball mystery* (1961)

Brigade of Guards series
Kersh, Gerald
1 *They die with their boots clean* (1941)
2 *Nine lives of Bill Nelson* (1942)
3 *Clean, bright and slightly oiled* (1946)
Short stories

Brigadier Dougal Munro and Captain Jack Carter series
Higgins, Jack
1 *Night of the fox* (1986)
2 *Cold harbour* (1990)

Brigadier Ffellowes series
Lanier, Sterling Edmund
1 *Peculiar exploits of Brigadier Ffellowes* (1972)
2 *Curious quests of Brigadier Ffellowes* (1986)

Brigadier Gerard series
Doyle, Arthur Conan
1 *Exploits of Brigadier Gerard* (1896)
Short stories
2 *Adventures of Gerard* (1903)

Brigadier Rayne series
Coke, Peter
Three-act plays
1 *Breath of spring* (1959)
2 *Midsummer mink* (1965)

Brigadier series
Tinniswood, Peter
1 *Tales from a long room* (1981)
2 *More tales from a long room* (1982)
Omnibus volume: *Collected tales from a long room*, 1982
3 *Brigadier down under* (1983)
4 *Brigadier in season* (1984)
5 *Brigadier's brief lives* (1984)
6 *Brigadier's tour* (1985)
Brigadier's last tour
Numbers 5 and 6 also published in one volume entitled *The brigadier's collection*, 1986
7 *Uncle Mort's North Country* (1986)

Brigadier Worrall series
Cousins, Edmund George
1 *To comfort the signora* (1951)
2 *Any kind of danger* (1951)

Brigante sereis
Torres, Edwin
see **Carlito series**

Briganti series
McCurtin, Peter
see **Assassins series**

Briggs series
Macdonald, Donald
see **Tommy Briggs series**
Marsh, Richard
see **Sam Briggs series**

Bright and bold series
Winfield, Arthur M
1 *Poor but plucky* (1905)
Alternative title: The mystery of a flood
2 *Schooldays of Fred Harley* (1905)
Alternative title: Rivals for all honors
3 *By pluck, not luck* (1905)
Alternative title: Dan Granbury's struggle to rise
4 *Missing tin box* (1905)
Alternative title: The stolen railroad bonds

Bright intervals series
Clements, Eileen Helen
1 *Let him die* (1939)
2 *Bright intervals* (1940)

Bright series
Richards, Laura Elizabeth
see **Honor Bright series**
Ruegg, Alfred Henry
see **Rosie Bright series**
Scannell, Dorothy
1 *Polly Bright* (1984)
2 *Jet Bright* (1985)

Bright trilogy
Caute, David
see **Confrontation trilogy**

Brighteyes series
Haggard, Henry Rider
see **Eric Brighteyes series**

Brighthope series
Trowbridge, John Townsend
1 *Father Brighthopes* (1853)
Alternative title: An old clergyman's vacation
2 *Hearts and faces* (1853)
Alternative title: Home life unveiled
3 *Burcliff, its sunshine and its clouds* (1854)
4 *Ironthorpe, the pioneer preacher* (1855)
Ironthorpe, the frontier preacher
5 *Old battle ground* (1860)

Brighton Boys series
Driscoll, James R
1 *Brighton Boys with the Flying Corps* (1918)
2 *Brighton Boys in the trenches* (1918)
3 *Brighton Boys with the Battle Fleet* (1918)
4 *Brighton Boys in the Radio Service* (1918)
5 *Brighton Boys with the Submarine Fleet* (1918)
6 *Brighton Boys with the Engineers at Cantigny* (1919)
7 *Brighton Boys at Chateay Thierry* (1919)
8 *Brighton Boys at Saint Mihiel* (1919)
9 *Brighton Boys in the Argonne Forest* (1920)
10 *Brighton Boys in Translantic flight* (1920)
11 *Brighton Boys in a submarine treasure ship* (1920)

Brightsea series
This sequence has two authors
Austen, Jane
1 *Sense and sensibility* (1811)
Gillespie, Jane
2 *Brightsea* (1987)

Brigid Donovan series
Saum, Karen
1 *Murder is relative* (1990)
2 *Murder is germane* (1991)

Brigitta and Devon series
Randall, Lindsey
see **Two hearts series**

Brill and Maxwell trilogy
Killough, Lee
1 *Doppelganger gambit* (1979)
2 *Spider play* (1986)
3 *Dragon's teeth* (1990)

Brillstone Apartments series
Heide, Florence Parry
1 *Brillstone break-in* (1977)
2 *Face at Brillstone window* (1978)
3 *Fear at Brillstone* (1978)
4 *Body in the Brillstone garage* (1979)
5 *Black magic at Brillstone* (1982)
6 *Time bomb at Brillstone* (1982)

Brim series
Gaunt, Michael
1 *Brim's boat* (1964)
2 *Brim sails out* (1966)
3 *Brim's valley* (1967)

Brimhall series
Delton, Judy
1 *Brimhall comes to stay* (1978)
2 *Brimhall turns to magic* (1979)
3 *Brimhall turns detective* (1983)
4 *Xmas gift for Brimhall* (1986)

Brimmer series
McHugh, Arona
see **Sally Brimmer series**

Brimming cup series
Canfield, Dorothy
1 *Brimming cup* (1921)
2 *Rough-hewn* (1923)

Brindle series
Fleischman, Sid
see **Max Brindle series**

Bringing up father series
McManus, George
see **Maggie and Jiggs series**

Bringle series
Owen, John
see **Edward Bringle series**

Brinkworth Bear series
West, Annie
1 *Brinkworth Bear's opposites book* (1987)
2 *Brinkworth Bear's colours book* (1987)
3 *Brinkworth Bear's alphabet book* (1987)
4 *Brinkworth Bear's counting book* (1987)

Brion Brandd series
Harrison, Harry
1 *Planet of the damned* (1962)
Sense of obligation
2 *Planet of no return* (1981)

Briscoe series
Hamill, Pete
see **Sam Briscoe series**

Britain series
Courage, John
see **Bill Britain series**

Britannia series
Frith, Henry
1 *Captain of cadets* (1889)
A story of the rule of Britannia
2 *Log of the Bombastes* (1890)

British Army trilogy
Lynn, Escott
1 *Knights of the air* (1918)
2 *Tommy of the Tanks* (1919)
3 *Lads of the Lothians* (1920)

British Empire trilogy
Farrell, James Gordon
1 *Troubles* (1970)
Set during the Irish rebellion of 1919
2 *Siege of Krishnapur* (1973)
Set during the Indian mutiny of 1857
3 *Singapore grip* (1979)
Set during the siege of Singapore in the Second World War
Companion volume: *The hill station*, an unfinished novel

British Empire trilogy
Morris, James Humphrey
1 *Heaven's command* (1973)
An Imperial progress
2 *Pax Britannica* (1968)
The climax of an Empire
3 *Farewell the trumpets* (1978)
An Imperial retreat

British India quartet
Scott, Paul
1 *Jewel in the crown* (1966)
2 *Day of the scorpion* (1968)
3 *Towers of silence* (1971)
4 *Division of the spoils* (1975)
One volume edition entitled *The Raj quartet*, 1976; companion volume: *Staying on*, 1977

British India trilogy
Masters, John
1 *Bugles and a tiger* (1956)
A personal adventure
2 *Road past Mandalay* (1961)
3 *Pilgrim son* (1971)
A personal odyssey

British International Airways series
Bunting, James
1 *Devil mountain* (1970)
2 *Flight of the lobster* (1971)
3 *Vapour trail* (1972)

British Isles series
McCormick, Donald
1 *Islands of England and Wales* (1974)
A guide to 138 English and Welsh islands
2 *Islands of Scotland* (1974)
A guide to 247 Scottish islands
3 *Islands of Ireland* (1974)
A guide to 110 Irish islands
Companion volume: *How to buy an island*, 1973

British law series
Bresler, Fenton Shea
1 *Within the law?* (1956)
Revised edition 1976
2 *Strictly legal* (1958)
3 *Strictly illegal* (1960)

British migrant series
Hart, Sydney
1 *Discharged dead* (1956)
A true story of Britain's submarines at war
2 *Pommie migrant* (1957)
Adventures of a British emigrant down under

British spy series
Churchill, Peter
1 *Of their own choice* (1952)
2 *Duel of wits* (1953)
3 *Spirit in the cage* (1954)
Experiences as a prisoner-of-war

British way series
Lindsay, Jack
1 *Betrayed spring* (1953)
2 *Rising tide* (1953)
3 *Moment of choice* (1955)
4 *Local habitation* (1957)
5 *Revolt of the sons* (1960)
6 *All on the never-never* (1961)
7 *Way the ball bounces* (1962)
8 *Masks and faces* (1963)
9 *Choice of times* (1964)

Britt Montero series
Buchanan, Edna
1 *Contents under pressure* (1992)
2 *Miami, it's murder* (1994)
3 *Suitable for framing* (1995)

Britt Saint Vincent series
Rossmann, John F
see **Mind Masters series**

Britton series
Smith, Guy Newman
see **Truckers series**

Broad acres series
Jacob, Naomi
1 *Sally Scarth* (1940)
2 *Loaded stick* (1934)
3 *Roots* (1931)
One volume edition entitled *Tales of the broad acres*, 1955

Broadcaster's Odyssey trilogy
Ebdon, John
Autobiography
1 *Ebdon's Odyssey* (1979)
2 *Ebdon's Iliad* (1983)
3 *Ebdon's England* (1985)

Broadcasting memoirs series
Hill, Charles
1 *Both sides of the hill* (1964)
2 *Behind the screen* (1974)

Broadstrop series
Kee, Robert
see **Simon Broadstrop series**

Brock Callahan series
Gault, William Campbell
1 *Ring around Rosa* (1955)
Murder in the raw
2 *Day of the Ram* (1956)
3 *Convertible hearse* (1957)
4 *Come die with me* (1959)
5 *Vein of violence* (1961)
6 *County kill* (1962)
7 *Dead hero* (1963)
8 *Bad Samaritan* (1980)
9 *Cana diversion* (1980)
10 *Death in Donegal Bay* (1984)
11 *Dead seed* (1985)
12 *Cat and mouse* (1988)

Brock Devlin series
Mitchell, Scott
1 *Some dames play rough* (1963)
2 *Sables spell trouble* (1963)
3 *Deadly persuasion* (1964)
4 *Lonely shroud* (1964)
5 *Come, sweet death* (1967)
6 *Double bluff* (1968)
7 *Knife-edged thing* (1969)
8 *Haven for the damned* (1971)
9 *You'll never get to heaven* (1972)
10 *Rage in Babylon* (1972)
11 *Girl in the wet-look bikini* (1973)
12 *Dead on arrival* (1974)
13 *Nice guys don't win* (1974)
14 *Over my dead body* (1974)
15 *Death's busy crossroads* (1975)
16 *Obsession* (1976)

Brock Potter series
Maling, Arthur
1 *Ripoff* (1976)
2 *Schroeder's game* (1977)
3 *Lucky devil* (1978)
4 *Koberg link* (1979)
5 *Taste of treason* (1983)

Brock series
Bingham, John
see **Superintendent Badger Brock series**
Skirrow, Desmond
see **John Brock series**
White, Reginald James
see **Inspector David Brock series**

Brock the badger series
Uttley, Alison
1 *Tales of the four pigs and Brock the badger* (1939)
2 *Six tales of the four pigs* (1941)
3 *Six tales of Brock the Badger* (1941)

Brockleby series
Keddell, Jim
1 *Tribesman's plunder* (1957)
2 *Red Sea patrol* (1959)

Brodie series
Edmonds, Harry
see **Hugh Brodie series**
Wylie, Ida Alexa Ross
see **Adam Brodie series**

Brody series
Brody, Marc
see **Marc Brody series**

Brogan McNally series
Tetlow, L D
1 *Ghost riders* (1986)
2 *Brogan, passing through* (1987)
3 *Brogan's Mexican stand-off* (1987)
4 *Brogan for sheriff* (1988)
5 *Fool's gold* (1989)
6 *Brogan and the bull* (1989)
7 *Shepherd's gold* (1990)
8 *Brogan takes toll* (1992)
9 *To earn a dollar* (1993)
10 *Brogan and the judge killer* (1993)

Brogan series
Breen, Jon Linn
see **Jerry Brogan series**
Poyer, Joe
see **Cole Brogan series**

Brogeen the leprechaun series
Lynch, Patricia
1 *Brogeen of the stepping stones* (1947)
2 *Brogeen follows the magic tune* (1952)
3 *Brogeen and the magic shoes* (1953)
4 *Brogeen and the bronze lizard* (1954)
5 *Brogeen and the Princess of Sheen* (1955)
6 *Brogeen and the lost castle* (1956)
7 *Cobbler's luck* (1957)
8 *Brogeen and the black enchanter* (1958)
9 *Stone house at Kilgobbin* (1959)
10 *Lost fisherman of Carrigmor* (1960)
11 *Longest way round* (1961)
12 *Brogeen and the little wind* (1962)
13 *Brogeen and the red fez* (1963)
14 *Guests at the beech tree* (1964)

Broken cup series
Browne, Edith Ophelia
1 *Broken cup* (1928)
2 *When the saints slept* (1930)

Broken house trilogy
South, Ambrose
1 *Broken house* (1932)
2 *Dwelling place* (1933)
3 *Renewal* (1933)

Broken images series
Graves, Robert
Selected letters, edited by Paul O'Prey
1 *In broken images, 1914-1946* (1982)
2 *Between moon and moon, 1946-1972* (1984)

Broken record series
Campbell, Roy
1 *Broken record* (1934)
2 *Light on a dark horse* (1951)

Bromden series
Kesey, Ken
see **Chief Bromden series**

Bromeliad trilogy
Pratchett, Terry
see **Book of the Nomes trilogy**

Bromley Barnes series
Barton, George
1 *Strange adventures of Bromley Barnes* (1918)
Short stories
2 *Mystery of the red flame* (1918)
3 *Ambassador's trunk* (1919)
4 *Pembroke Mason affair* (1920)

Bromley Bear series
Campbell, Alan
1 *Bromley climbs Uluru* (1993)
2 *Bromley to the rescue* (1993)
3 *Bromley and the hidden treasure* (1993)

Bromley Kay series
Walsh, James Morgan
1 *White mask* (1925)
2 *Man behind the curtain* (1927)
3 *League of missing men* (1927)
4 *Exit Simon Hex* (1930)

Broncho Bill series
O'Neil, Harry F
1 *Broncho Bill* (1935)
2 *Broncho Bill in Suicide Canyon* (1935)

Broncho Rider Boys series
Fowler, Frank
1 *Broncho Rider Boys at Keystone Ranch* (1914)
Alternative title: Three chums of the saddle and lariat
2 *Broncho Rider Boys down in Arizona* (1914)
Alternative title: A struggle for the great copper lode
3 *Broncho Rider Boys along the border* (1914)
Alternative title: The hidden treasure of the Zuni medicine man
4 *Broncho Rider Boys on the Wyoming Trail* (1914)
Alternative title: The mystery of the prairie stampede
5 *Broncho Rider Boys with the Texas Rangers* (1915)
Alternative title: The smugglers of the Rio Grande
6 *Broncho Rider Boys with Funston at Vera Cruz* (1916)
Alternative title: Upholding the honor of the Stars and Stripes

Bronson Beta series
Balmer, Edwin
1 *When worlds collide* (1933)
2 *After worlds collide* (1934)

Bronson series
Koehler, Robert Portner
see **Al Bronson series**
Rawls, Philip
see **Richard Bronson series**
Vernon, Rosemary
see **Frannie Bronson series**

Bronte series
Banks, Lynne Reid
1 *Dark quartet* (1976)
2 *Path to the silent country* (1977)

Brontosaurus series
McCrum, Robert
1 *Brontosaurus birthday cake* (1983)
2 *Brontosaurus superstar* (1985)
3 *Dream boat brontosaurus* (1987)

Bronwyn trilogy
Miller, Ron
1 *Palaces and prisons* (1991)
2 *Silk and steel* (1992)
3 *Hearts and armor* (1992)

Brook series
Wheatley, Dennis
see **Roger Brook series**

Brooke family series
Berrisford, Judith Mary
1 *Pony in the family* (1959)
2 *Colt in the family* (1962)
3 *Show jumper in the family* (1964)

Brooke series
Aiken, Joan
see **Felix Brooke series**
Crooker, Herbert
see **Clay Brooke series**
Sparhawk, Frances Campbell
see **Dorothy Brooke series**

Brook's Hospital series
Collins, Lynne
1 *To be a nurse* (1961)
2 *Dream for Nurse Tessa* (1962)

Brooks series
Gridban, Volsted
see **Clifford Brooks series**
Macpherson, Donald
see **Reggie Brooks series**
Rothwell, Henry Talbot
see **Michael Brooks series**

Brooks trilogy
Lipsyte, Roger
see **Contender trilogy**

Brookside series
Sharmat, Marjorie Weinman
see **Morris Brookside series**

Broom series
Hurt, Freda Mary
see **Inspector Herbert Broom series**
McInerny, Ralph
see **Andrew Broom series**

Brother and sister series
Lawrence, Josephine
1 *Brother and sister* (1921)
2 *Brother and sister's holidays* (1921)
3 *Brother and sister's schooldays* (1921)
4 *Brother and sister's vacation* (1922)
5 *Brother and sister at Bayport* (1922)
6 *Brother and sister keep house* (1927)

Brother Angelo series
Lieberman, Rosalie
1 *Man who sold Christmas* (1951)
2 *Man who captivated New York* (1960)

Brother Cadfael series
Peters, Ellis
1 *Morbid taste for bones* (1977)
2 *One corpse too many* (1979)
3 *Monk's-hood* (1980)
4 *Saint Peter's fair* (1981)
5 *Leper of Saint Giles* (1981)
6 *Virgin in the ice* (1982)
7 *Sanctuary sparrow* (1983)
8 *Devil's novice* (1983)
9 *Dead man's ransom* (1984)
10 *Pilgrim of hate* (1984)
11 *Excellent mystery* (1985)
12 *Raven in the Foregate* (1986)
13 *Rose rent* (1987)
14 *Hermit of Eyton Forest* (1987)
15 *Confession of Brother Halmin* (1988)
16 *Heretic's apprentice* (1989)
17 *Potter's field* (1989)
18 *Summer of the Danes* (1991)
19 *Holy thief* (1992)
20 *Brother Cadfael's penance* (1994)

Brother Nick series
Hayle, Felicity
see **Our brother Nick series**

Brotherhood of war series
Griffin, W E B
1 *Lieutenants* (1983)
2 *Captains* (1983)
3 *Majors* (1984)
4 *Colonels* (1985)
5 *Berets* (1985)
6 *Generals* (1986)
7 *New breed* (1987)
8 *Aviators* (1988)

Brotherly love trilogy
Fielding, Gabriel
see **Blaydon family trilogy**

Brothers in blood series
Saint James, Daniel
1 *Brothers in blood* (1991)
2 *Trackdown* (1992)
3 *Cold death* (1992)

Brothers of Gwynedd tetralogy
Pargeter, Edith
1 *Sunrise in the west* (1974)
2 *Dragon at noonday* (1975)
3 *Hounds of sunset* (1976)
4 *Afterglow and nightfall* (1977)

Brothers series
This sequence has two authors
Based on a television series
James, Janice
1 *Brothers* (1973)
2 *Brothers, book 2* (1974)
Mackenzie, Lee
3 *Brothers, book 3* (1974)
4 *Brothers, book 4* (1975)
5 *Brothers, book 5* (1976)

Brought up series
Jeffares, Alexander Norman
Poems
1 *Brought up in Dublin* (1987)
2 *Brought up to leave* (1987)

Brown and Ashton series
Stuart, Becky
see **Kellogg Brown and Carey Ashton series**

Brown and his sister Sue series
Hope, Laura Lee
see **Bunny Brown and his sister Sue series**

Brown Beggarman series
Daykin, Lilian
1 *Brown Beggarman series* (1958)
2 *More Brown Beggarman stories* (1960)

Brown cow series
Branfield, John
1 *Brown cow* (1983)
2 *Thin ice* (1983)

Brown Ears series
Lawhead, Stephen
1 *Brown Ears* (1989)
2 *Brown Ears at sea* (1991)

Brown family series
Boardman, M M
1 *Haps and mishaps of the Brown family* (1863)
2 *Sister's triumph* (1866)

Brown Mouse series
Uttley, Alison
see **Little Brown Mouse series**

Brown series
Alden, William Livingston
see **Jimmy Brown series**
Ames, Delano
see **Dagobert and Jane Brown series**
Boyd, Edward
see **Wanderlust Brown series**
Byars, Betsy
see **Bingo Brown series**
Cameron, Owen
see **Deputy Sheriff Jake Brown series**
Daly, Carroll John
see **Vee Brown series**
Gill, Elizabeth
see **Benvenuto Brown series**
Hughes, Thomas
see **Tom Brown series**
Kitt, Tamara
see **Billy Brown series**
Montrose, Graham
see **Angel Brown series**
Oldfield, Pamela
see **Melanie Brown series**
Paice, Margaret
see **Kathy Brown series**
Payes, Rachel
see **Forsythia Brown series**
Porter, Joyce
see **Edmund Brown series**
Roberts, Cecil
see **Mrs Brown series**
Russell, Steven
see **Bulldozer Brown series**
Sobol, Donald J
see **Encyclopedia Brown series**
Speed, Nell
see **Molly Brown series**
Stevenson, Dorothy Emily
see **Gerald Burleigh Brown series**
Wilcox, Barbara
see **Bunty Brown series**
Winstan, Matt
see **Reuben Brown series**

Brown trilogy
Barstow, Stan
see **Vic Brown trilogy**

Browne and Fanshaw series
Poole, Michael
see **Freddie Browne and Jim Fanshaw series**

Brownie Scout series
Wirt, Mildred Augustine
1 *Brownie Scouts at Snow Valley* (1949)
2 *Brownie Scouts in the circus* (1949)
3 *Brownie Scouts in the Cherry Festival* (1950)
4 *Brownie Scouts and their tree house* (1951)
5 *Brownie Scouts at Silver Beach* (1952)
6 *Brownie Scouts at Windmill Farm* (1953)

Brownie series
Blathwayt, Jean
1 *Lucy's Brownie road* (1970)
2 *Lucy's last Brownie challenge* (1972)
3 *Brownie discoverers* (1977)

Brownie series
Hann, Dorothy Owen
1 *All about a Brownie* (1928)
2 *What the Brownies did* (1930)
3 *Brownie from the caravans* (1933)
4 *Ten little Brownie girls* (1934)

Brownie stories series
Moss, Robert Alfred
1 *First challenge book of Brownie stories* (1980)
2 *Second challenge book of Brownie stories* (1981)

Brownies series
Anderson, Verily
1 *Amanda and the Brownies* (1960)
2 *Brownies and the golden hand* (1963)
3 *Brownies' day abroad* (1964)
4 *Brownies and the ponies* (1965)
5 *Brownies on wheels* (1966)
6 *Brownies and their animal friends* (1969)
7 *Brownie and the wedding day* (1974)
8 *Brownies and the christening* (1977)
Companion volumes: *Brownie cook-book*, 1972, *Camp fire cook-book*, 1976

Brownies series
Richardson, Dorothy
9 *Secret Brownies* (1979)
10 *Brownie venturers* (1982)
11 *Brownie explorers* (1983)
12 *Brownie rescuers* (1984)
13 *Brownie entertainers* (1985)
14 *Brownie elephant hunters* (1986)
15 *Brownie campaigners* (1987)
16 *Brownie foxwatchers* (1987)

Brownies series
Sykes, Pamela
see **Barnwell Brownie Guide Pack series**

Brownies series
Williams, Ursula Moray
1 *For Brownies* (1932)
2 *More for Brownies* (1934)

Browning series
Corris, Peter
see **Richard Browning series**

Brownstone trilogy
Eulo, Ken
see **Chandal Talon trilogy**

Browser series
Curtis, Philip
see **Mister Browser series**

Browser's dictionary series
Ciardi, John
1 *Browser's dictionary & native guide to the unknown American language* (1980)
2 *Second browser's dictionary & native guide to the unknown American language* (1987)
Omnibus volume: *The complete browser's dictionary, the best of John Ciardi's two Browser's dictionaries in a single compendium of curious expressions and intriguing facts*, 1988

Bruce and Ian series
Simons, Roger
1 *Island adventurer* (1962)
2 *Dolphin sailed north* (1964)

Bruce Baron series
Daniels, Norman A
1 *Baron of Hong Kong* (1967)
2 *Baron's mission to Peking* (1968)

Bruce McLintock series
Macvicar, Angus
1 *Golden Venus affair* (1972)
2 *Painted doll affair* (1973)

Bruce Murdoch series
Deane, Norman
Revised editions published under the author's real name John Creasey
1 *Secret errand* (1939)
2 *Dangerous journey* (1939)
3 *Unknown mission* (1940)
Revised edition 1972
4 *Withered Man* (1940)
5 *I am the Withered Man* (1941)
Revised edition 1972
6 *Where is the Withered Man?* (1942)
Revised edition 1972
7 *Incense of death* (1954)
Revised edition 1969

Bruce Perkins series
Lilly, Jean
1 *False face* (1929)
2 *Death in B-minor* (1934)
3 *Death thumbs a ride* (1940)

Bruce series
Arnold, Henry
see **Bill Bruce series**
Johnston, Ronald
see **James Bruce series**
Lindquist, Jennie Dorothea
see **Nancy Bruce series**
Ure, Jean
see **Nicola Bruce series**

Brumby series
Patchett, Mary Elwyn
see **Joey Meehan series**

Brummell series
Hamilton, Cosmo
see **Beau Brummell series**

Brunel series
Gavin, Catherine
see **French Resistance series**

Brunetti series
Leon, Donna
see **Commissario Guido Brunetti series**

Bruno and Sylvie series
Carroll, Lewis
see **Sylvie and Bruno series**

Bruno Farrell series
Mazzaro, Ed
see **Undercover series**

Bruno series
Raymond, Ernest
see **Daphne Bruno series**

Bruno Stachel series
Hunter, Jack Dayton
see **Blue Max series**

Brunt series
Hilton, John Buxton
see **Inspector Thomas Brunt series**

Brush series
Firmin, Peter
see **Basil Brush series**

Brussac family series
Banis, Victor Jerome
1 *This splendid earth* (1978)
2 *Earth and all it holds* (1980)

Brussac series
Gerard, Francis
see **Marquess de Brussac series**

Brussels series
Bronte, Charlotte
1 *Professor* (1857)
2 *Villette* (1853)
Number 1 acted as a first study for number 2

Brute family series
Hoban, Russell
1 *Little Brute family* (1966)
2 *Stone doll of Sister Brute* (1968)

Bryan Armitage series
Cobb, Belton
1 *Death with a difference* (1960)
2 *Search for Sergeant Baxter* (1961)
3 *Corpse in the cargo* (1961)
4 *Murder, men only* (1962)
5 *Death of a Peeping Tom* (1963)
6 *No shame for the devil* (1964)
7 *Dead girl's shoes* (1964)
8 *I never miss twice* (1965)
9 *Last drop* (1965)
10 *Some must watch* (1966)
11 *Stone for his head* (1966)
12 *Lost without trace* (1967)
13 *Security secrets sold here* (1967)
14 *Secret enquiry* (1968)
15 *Silence under threat* (1968)
16 *Scandal at Scotland Yard* (1969)
17 *Food for felony* (1969)
18 *Horrible man in Heron's Wood* (1970)
19 *Catch me, if you can* (1970)
20 *Suspicion in triplicate* (1971)
21 *I fell among thieves* (1971)

Bryan series
Baxter, Betty
see **Becky Bryan series**
Thurston, Ida Treadwell
see **Theodore Bryan series**

Bryant series
Grayson, Richard
see **John Bryant series**
Watmough, David
see **Davey Bryant series**

Bryce series
Scherf, Margaret
see **Emily and Henry Bryce series**

Bryden series
Phillpotts, Eden
see **Book of Avis series**

Brydon family series
Fidler, Kathleen
Originally written as radio stories
1 *Borrowed garden* (1944)
2 *Saint Jonathan's in the country* (1945)
Revised edition 1952
3 *Brydons at Smuggler's Creek* (1946)
4 *More adventures of the Brydons* (1947)
Revised edition 1971
5 *Brydons go camping* (1948)
6 *Brydons do battle* (1949)
7 *Brydons in summer* (1949)
8 *Surprises for the Brydons* (1950)
9 *Brydons in a pickle* (1950)
10 *Brydons look for trouble* (1950)
11 *Brydons get things going* (1951)
Revised edition 1971
12 *Brydons hunt for treasure* (1951)
13 *Brydons catch queer fish* (1952)
14 *Brydons stick at nothing* (1952)
15 *Brydons abroad* (1953)
16 *Brydons on the Broads* (1955)
Revised edition 1971
17 *Challenge to the Brydons* (1956)
18 *Brydons at Blackpool* (1960)
19 *Brydons go canoeing* (1963)

Brynchmachrye series
De Haan, Tom
1 *Mirror for princes* (1987)
2 *Child of good fortune* (1989)

Bryncoed series
Boore, Walter Hugh
1 *Valley and the shadow* (1963)
2 *Cry on the wind* (1967)

Bubb series
Craig, George
see **Sir Oliver Bubb series**

Bubbus series
Drake, Joan
see **Mister Bubbus series**

Buchan series
Boileau, Ethel
see **Hippy Buchan series**

Buchanan series
McCall, K T
see **Johnny Buchanan series**
Ward, Jonas
see **Tom Buchanan series**

Buchholz family series
Stinde, Julius
1 *Buchholzes in Italy* (1883)
Original edition entitled *Buchholzens in Italien*
2 *Buchholz family* (1886)
English edition in two volumes; original edition entitled *Die Familie Buchholz*, published in three volumes; includes *Frau Wilhelmine*; selections published as *Masterful Wilhelmine*, 1925
3 *[Frau Buchholz im Orient]* (1888)
No English edition
4 *[Wilhelmine Buchholz' Memoiren]* (1894)
[Frau Wilhelmine Buchholz' Memoiren]
No English edition
5 *[Hotel Buchholz]* (1897)
No English edition
One volume abridgement of the sequence published as *Hausfrau rampant*, 1916

Buck and Larry baseball series
Dawson, Elmer A
1 *Pick-up nine* (1930)
Alternative title: The Chester boys on the diamond
2 *Buck's winning hit* (1930)
Alternative title: The Chester boys making a record
3 *Larry's fadeaway* (1930)
Alternative title: The Chester boys saving the nine
4 *Buck's home run drive* (1931)
Alternative title: The Chester boys winning against the odds
5 *Larry's speedball* (1932)
Alternative title: The Chester boys and the diamond secret

Buck Duane series
This sequence has two authors
Grey, Zane
1 *Lone Star Ranger* (1915)
Grey, Romer Zane
2 *Lure of distant trails* (1969)
3 *Rider of distant trails* (1969)
4 *High Valley River* (1970)
5 *Long trail to nowhere* (1970)
6 *King of the range* (1970)
7 *Rustlers of the cattle range* (1970)
8 *Three deaths for Buck Duane* (1971)
9 *Track the man down* (1971)
Companion volume: *The last of the Duanes*, by Zane Grey, 1983

Buck Dunne series
Morgan, G J
1 *Trail of death* (1975)
2 *Border fury* (1975)
3 *Hell on wheels* (1975)

Buck Halliday series
Brady, Adam
1 *Ride for the devil!* (1979)
2 *Don't send a dude* (1981)

Buck Lawrence and Zeke Henderson series
Pritchett, Ron
1 *Peaceful guns* (1988)
2 *Cougar City* (1990)

Buck McKee and Tortilla Joe series
Floren, Lee
see **Buckshot McKee and Tortilla Joe series**

Buck Rogers series
This sequence has six authors
Nowlan, Philip Francis
1 *Armageddon 2419A.D.* (1962)
Originally published in *Amazing Science Fiction*, August 1928; this edition also includes *The airlords of Han*
2 *Buck Rogers on the moons of Saturn* (1934)
3 *Buck Rogers in the dangerous mission* (1934)
4 *Buck Rogers and the depth men of Jupiter* (1935)
5 *Strange adventures of the spider ship* (1935)
6 *Interplanetary war with Venus* (1938)
Omnibus volumes entitled *Buck Rogers in the 25th century*, 1-2, 7-8, 1964-68, *The collected works of Buck Rogers in the 25th century*, 1969, revised edition 1977
Niven, Larry
7 *Mordred* (1980)
Co-authors: John Eric Holmes and Jerry Pournelle
McEnroe, Richard S
8 *Warrior's blood* (1981)
Co-authors: Larry Niven and Jerry Pournelle
9 *Warrior's world* (1981)
Co-authors: Larry Niven and Jerry Pournelle
Niven, Larry
10 *Roger's Rangers* (1983)
Co-authors: John Silbersack and Jerry Pournelle
This sequence is followed by **Martian wars trilogy** and **Inner planets trilogy**

Buck Rogers teleplay series
Steele, Addison E
1 *Buck Rogers in the 25th century* (1978)
Based on a story and teleplay by Glen A Larson and Leslie Stevens
2 *That man on Beta* (1979)
Based on a teleplay by Bob Shane

Buck series
Marsden, Antony
see **Inspector Buck series**

Buckalew tetralogy
Kelton, Elmer
1 *Massacre at Goliad* (1965)
2 *After the bugles* (1967)
3 *Bowie's mine* (1971)
4 *Long way to Texas* (1976)
Originally published under the pseudonym Lee McElroy

Buckby series
Gloag, John
see **Lionel Buckby series**

Bucket series
Dahl, Roald
see **Charlie Bucket series**

Buckinghams series
Saville, Malcolm
1 *Master of Maryknoll* (1950)
2 *Buckinghams at Ravenswyke* (1952)
3 *Long passage* (1954)
4 *Palace for the Buckinghams* (1963)
5 *Secret of Villa Rosa* (1971)
6 *Diamond in the sky* (1974)

Buckle series
Brady, Nicholas
see **Ebenezer Buckle series**

Bucko trilogy
Westcott, C T
see **Eagleheart trilogy**

Bucks County trilogy
Schiddel, Edmund
1 *Devil in Bucks County* (1959)
2 *Scandal's child* (1963)
3 *Good and bad weather* (1965)
Devil's summer

Buckshot McKee and Tortilla Joe series
Floren, Lee
1 *Cottonwood pards* (1944)
Riders of death
2 *Milk River Range* (1949)
Shoot out at Milk River
3 *Troubled grass* (1952)
Story of the old Southwest
4 *Gunsmoke lawyer* (1957)
Powdersmoke lawyer
5 *Wyoming gun war* (1967)
6 *Saddle tramps* (1977)
7 *Gun chore* (1978)
8 *Rope the wild wind* (1980)
9 *High border riders* (1980)
10 *North to Powder River* (1980)

Buckskin Man tales series
Manfred, Frederick
1 *Lord Grizzly* (1954)
2 *Riders of judgment* (1957)
3 *Conquering horse* (1959)
4 *Scarlet plume* (1964)
5 *King of Spades* (1966)

Buckskin series
This sequence has two authors
LeBeau, Roy
1 *Rifle River* (1984)
2 *Gunstock* (1984)
3 *Pistoltown* (1984)
4 *Colt Creek* (1984)
5 *Gunsight Gap* (1985)
6 *Trigger Spring* (1985)
7 *Cartridge Coast* (1985)
8 *Hangfire Hill* (1985)
9 *Crossfire Country* (1985)
10 *Bolt-action* (1986)
11 *Trigger guard* (1986)
Numbers 10 and 11 also published in one volume 1989
12 *Recoil* (1986)
Dalton, Kit
13 *Gunpoint* (1986)
14 *Lever action* (1986)
15 *Scattergun* (1987)
16 *Winchester Valley* (1987)
17 *Gunsmoke Gorge* (1987)
18 *Remington Ridge* (1987)
19 *Shotgun Station* (1987)
20 *Pistol grip* (1987)
21 *Peacemaker Pass* (1988)
22 *Silver City carbine* (1988)
23 *California crossfire* (1988)
24 *Colt Crossing* (1989)
25 *Poder charge* (1989)
26 *Laramie chowdown* (1989)
27 *Double action* (1989)
28 *Apache rifles* (1990)
29 *Return fire* (1990)
30 *Rimfire revenge* (1991)
31 *Tombstone ten gauge* (1991)
32 *Death draw* (1992)
33 *Fifty-two caliber shoot-out* (1992)
34 *Trick shooter* (1992)
35 *Pistol whipped* (1993)
36 *Hogleg Hill* (1993)
37 *Colt forty-five vengeance* (1993)
38 *Derringer danger* (1994)
39 *Blazing six-gun* (1994)
40 *Six-gun kill* (1994)
Companion volumes: *The buckskin breed*, 1988, *Night rider's moon*, 1991

Buckskin series
McIntyre, John Thomas
1 *In Kentucky with Daniel Boone* (1913)
2 *In the Rockies with Kit Carson* (1913)
3 *In Texas with Davy Crockett* (1914)
4 *On the borders with Andrew Jackson* (1915)

Buckskin series
Stanley, Chuck
1 *Buckskin pards* (1949)
2 *Buckskin beau* (1950)

Bud Dugan series
Geller, Michael
1 *Mayhem on the Coney beat* (1979)
2 *Corpse for a candidate* (1980)
3 *Disco downbeat* (1980)
4 *Red hot and dangerous* (1982)

Budd series
Carlson, Dale
see **James Budd series**
Sinclair, Upton
see **World's end series**
Verner, Gerald
see **Superintendent Robert Budd series**

Buddy Mustard series
Daniel, Roland
1 *Crawshay jewel mystery* (1941)
2 *Black market* (1943)
3 *Evil shadows* (1944)
4 *Professor* (1944)
5 *Lady in scarlet* (1947)
6 *Dead man sings* (1949)
7 *Murder at a cottage* (1949)
8 *Arrow death* (1951)
9 *Three Sundays to live* (1952)
10 *Murder gang* (1954)
11 *Big racket* (1955)
12 *Man from Paris* (1958)
13 *Missing body* (1961)
14 *Big shot* (1962)
15 *Hangman waits* (1963)
16 *Gangster's daughter* (1965)
17 *Kidnapped wife* (1965)

Buddy series
Fitzhugh, Percy Keese
1 *Hervey Willetts* (1927)
2 *Skinny McCord* (1928)
3 *Spiffy Henshaw* (1929)
4 *Wigwag Weigand* (1929)
5 *Lefty Leighton* (1930)
6 *Story of Terrible Terry* (1930)

Budge and Toddie series
Habberton, John
1 *Helen's babies* (1876)
2 *Budge and Toddie* (1877)
Other people's children

Budge series
Adamson, Gareth
see **Mister Budge series**

Budgie series
Sarah, Duchess of York
1 *Budgie, the little helicopter* (1989)
2 *Budgie at Bendick's Point* (1989)

Buell series
Scherf, Margaret
see **Reverend Martin Buell series**

Buena Costa County series
Crowe, John
1 *Another way to die* (1972)
2 *Touch of darkness* (1972)
3 *Bloodwater* (1974)
4 *Crooked shadows* (1975)
5 *When they kill your wife* (1977)
6 *Close to death* (1979)

Buerklin series
Dunham, Mikel
see **Rhea Buerklin series**

Bufast series
Vesaas, Tarjei
see **Per Eilevson Bufast series**

Buffalo Bill series
Buntline, Ned
1 *Buffalo Bill, the king of the border men* (1881)
Buffalo Bill and his adventures in the West
2 *Buffalo Bill's first trail* (1888)
Alternative title: Will Cody, the Pony Express rider
3 *Buffalo Bill's best shot* (1890)
Alternative title: The heart of Spotted Tail
4 *Buffalo Bill's last victory* (1890)
Alternative title: Dove Eye, the lodge queen

Buffalo Bill series
Sherwood, Elmer
see **Young Buffalo Bill series**

Buffalo Hunter series
Hayes, Ralph Eugene
see **O'Brien, Buffalo Hunter series**

Buffalo Woman series
Johnson, Dorothy Marie
1 *Buffalo Woman* (1977)
2 *All the Buffalo returning* (1979)

Buffin series
Buckels, Alex
see **Bunny Buffin series**

Buffy and Company series
Dahlerup, Rina
Translated from the Danish
1 *Buffy cleans up* (1978)
2 *Friends again* (1978)

Buford Pusser series
Warren, Doug
see **Sheriff Buford Pusser series**

Bugaloos series
Stratton, Chris
1 *Bugaloos and the vile Vibes* (1971)
2 *Rock City rebels* (1971)
3 *Benita's platter pollution* (1971)

Bugg series
Cosgrove, Stephen Edward
1 *Bugglar boys* (1983)
2 *Dune Bugg* (1983)
3 *Eevil Weevil* (1983)
4 *Glance* (1983)
5 *Humbugg* (1983)
6 *Lord and Lady Bugg* (1983)
7 *Vee-Dubb* (1983)
8 *Love Bugg* (1983)
9 *Snugg* (1983)
10 *Tik Tok* (1983)
11 *June Bugg* (1984)
12 *Jitterbugg* (1984)
13 *Crick-ette* (1984)
14 *Cooty-Doo* (1984)
15 *Snugg and shoe fly flue* (1984)
16 *Shutterbugg* (1984)
17 *Katy-Didd* (1984)
18 *Doodle Bugg* (1984)
19 *BBOC* (1988)
20 *Buggly* (1988)
21 *Ugly Bugg* (1988)
22 *Bee Bopp* (1988)
23 *Scribble* (1988)
24 *Shrugg* (1988)
25 *Buzz* (1988)
26 *Chugga* (1988)
27 *Hugga Bugg* (1988)
28 *Barley* (1988)
29 *Betterfly* (1988)
30 *Bigg family* (1988)
31 *Brush Buggs* (1988)
32 *Bubble Bugg* (1988)
33 *Bubba Bugg* (1988)
34 *Bugg off* (1988)
35 *Buggaboo!* (1988)
36 *Buggita* (1988)
37 *Button* (1988)
38 *Chubba* (1988)
39 *Dragon fly* (1988)
40 *Fibber Bugg* (1988)
41 *Firefly* (1988)
42 *Flea flicker* (1988)
43 *Flitterfly* (1988)
44 *Fly baby fly* (1988)
45 *Fuss E Bugg* (1988)
46 *Hocus Locust* (1988)
47 *Little Buggaroo* (1988)
48 *Lullafly* (1988)
49 *Melody moth* (1988)
50 *Merry widow* (1988)
51 *Mizz Buggly* (1988)
52 *Popp fly* (1988)
53 *Skeeter* (1988)

Bugle Ann series
Kantor, Mackinlay
1 *Voice of Bugle Ann* (1935)
2 *Daughter of Bugle Ann* (1953)

Bugs Bunny series
Lewis, Jean
1 *Too many carrots* (1976)
2 *Bugs Bunny rides again* (1986)

Bugs Potter series
Korman, Gordon
1 *Who is Bugs Potter?* (1980)
2 *Bugs Potter, live at Nickaninny* (1983)

Bull and Macandrew series
Lariar, Lawrence
see **Ham Macandrew and Homer Bull series**

Bull Cochran series
Nighbert, David Franklin
1 *Strike zone* (1989)
2 *Squeezeplay* (1992)

Bull Hunter series
Manning, David
1 *Bull Hunter* (1924)
2 *Bull Hunter's romance* (1924)

Bull Rogers series
Brede, Arnold
1 *Climbed corpse* (1952)
2 *Outside job* (1952)

Bull series
Kennedy, Milward
see **Sir George Bull series**

Bulldog Drummond series
This sequence has four authors
Sapper
1 *Bulldog Drummond* (1920)
The adventures of a demobilized officer who found peace dull
2 *Black Gang* (1922)
3 *Third round* (1924)
Bulldog Drummond's third round
4 *Final count* (1926)
5 *Female of the species* (1928)
Bulldog Drummond and the female of the species
Bulldog Drummond meets a murderess
6 *Temple Tower* (1929)
7 *Return of Bulldog Drummond* (1932)
Bulldog Drummond returns
8 *Knock-out* (1933)
Bulldog Drummond strikes nack
9 *Bulldog Drummond at bay* (1935)
10 *Challenge* (1937)
Fairlie, Gerard
11 *Bulldog Drummond on Dartmoor* (1938)
12 *Bulldog Drummond attacks* (1939)
13 *Captain Bulldog Drummond* (1945)
14 *Bulldog Drummond stands fast* (1947)
15 *Hands off Bulldog Drummond* (1949)
16 *Calling Bulldog Drummond* (1951)
17 *Return of the Black Gang* (1954)
Reymond, Henry
18 *Deadlier than the male* (1966)
Based on a screenplay
Smithers, Jack
19 *Combined forces* (1983)
The latter-day adventures of Maj. Gen. Sir Richard Hannay, Captain Hugh, Bulldog, Drummond and Berry and Co.

Bulldog series
Cooper, Henry Saint John
1 *Bull-dogs and bull-dog breeding* (1905)
2 *Bulldogs and bulldog men* (1908)
3 *Bulldogs and all about them* (1914)

Bulldog tugboat series
Catherall, Arthur
1 *Ten fathoms deep* (1954)
2 *Jackals of the sea* (1955)
3 *Forgotten submarine* (1956)
4 *Java Sea duel* (1957)
5 *Sea wolves* (1959)
6 *Dangerous cargo* (1960)
7 *China Sea jigsaw* (1961)
8 *Prisoners under the sea* (1963)
9 *Strange invader* (1964)
Strange intruder
10 *Tanker trap* (1965)
11 *Death of an oil rig* (1967)
12 *Island of forgotten men* (1968)
13 *Red Sea rescue* (1969)
14 *Unwilling smuggler* (1971)

Bulldozer Brown series
Russell, Steven
1 *Bulldozer Brown* (1947)
2 *Bulldozer Brown in Africa* (1949)

Buller series
Hough, Richard Alexander
see **Archy Buller series**

Bullerby series
Lindgren, Astrid
1 *Six Bullerby children* (1947)
Original edition is the first part of *Alla vi barn i Bullerbyn*; revised edition 1975
2 *Children of Noisy Village* (1947)
Cherry time at Bullerby
Original edition is the second part of *Alla vi barn i Bullerbyn*; revised edition 1975; Numbers 1 and 2 published in one volume entitled *Bullerbyken*, 1961, Selections from 1 and 2 published as *All about the Bullerby children*, 1963
3 *Happy times in Noisy Village* (1949)
Happy days at Bullerby
Original edition entitled *Mera om oss barn i Bullerbyn*; revised edition 1975
4 *[Bara roligt i Bullerbyn]* (1952)
Revised edition 1975; no English edition
5 *[Bullerbybarnen]* (1957)
Revised edition 1969; no English edition
6 *[Tallbaka till Bullerbyn]* (1958)
Revised edition 1969; no English edition
7 *Christmas in Noisy Village* (1963)
Christmas at Bullerby
Original edition entitled *Jul i Bullerbyn*; revised edition 1980
8 *Springtime in Noisy Village* (1965)
Original edition entitled *Vaar i Bullerbyn*; revised edition 1975
9 *Day at Bullerby* (1966)
Original edition entitled *Barnensdag i Bullerbyn*; revised edition 1973

Bullfrog series
Dauer, Rosamond
1 *Bullfrog grows up* (1976)
2 *Bullfrog builds a horse* (1977)
3 *Bullfrog and Gertrude go camping* (1980)

Bullion series
Dix, Maurice Buxton
see **Superintendent Simon Bullion series**

Bullock and Bede series
Byfield, Barbara
see **Simon Bede and Helen Bullock series**

Bulls series
Bull, Peter
Memoirs of the author and his family
1 *To sea in a sieve* (1956)
2 *Bulls in the meadows* (1957)
3 *I know the face, but* (1959)
4 *I say, look here* (1965)
5 *It isn't all Greek to me* (1967)
6 *Life is a cucumber* (1973)

Bully brothers series
Thaler, Mike
1 *Trick the tooth fairy* (1993)
2 *Gobblin' Halloween* (1993)

Bulman series
This sequence has two authors; based on screenplays
Holdstock, Robert
1 *Bulman* (1984)
2 *One of our pigeons is missing* (1984)
Raymond, John
3 *Thin ice* (1987)

Bumble B Bear series
Cosgrove, Stephen Edward
Board books
1 *Christmas tree* (1984)
2 *Bumble B Bear takes a walk* (1984)
3 *Bumble B Bear rides in a car* (1984)
4 *Bumble B Bear in the garden* (1984)
5 *Bumble B Bear cleans up* (1984)
6 *Gift for the giving* (1984)

Bumble series
Eldon, Magdalen
1 *Bumble* (1950)
2 *Snow Bumble* (1951)
3 *Highland Bumble* (1952)

Bumble series
Treloar, Bruce
1 *Bumble's dream* (1981)
2 *Bumble's island* (1984)
3 *Bumble's journey* (1986)

Bumblemoose series
Andreus, Hans
see **Mister Bumblemoose series**

Bumbo series
Sinclair, Andrew
1 *Breaking of Bumbo* (1959)
2 *Beau Bumbo* (1985)

Bumper Morgan series
Wambaugh, Joseph
1 *New centurions* (1971)
2 *Blue knight* (1972)

Bumppo series
Cooper, James Fenimore
see **Leatherstocking series**

Bun, Josie and Click series
Blyton, Enid
see **Josie, Click and Bun series**

Bun series
Paterson, Bettina
1 *Bun and Mrs Tubby* (1986)
2 *Bun's birthday* (1987)

Bunburys series
English, David
Illustrated by Jan Brychta
1 *Bunbury tails* (1986)
2 *Bunnybados* (1986)
3 *Bunburys down under* (1987)
4 *Winter's tail* (1988)
5 *Bunburys play ball* (1989)
6 *Tail of two kittens* (1989)
7 *Rajbun's story* (1989)
8 *Le Buns twenty four hour race* (1989)
9 *Bunchester United* (1989)
10 *Bun Noel* (1989)

Bunby series
Jones, Harold
1 *There and back again* (1977)
2 *Silver bells and cockle-shells* (1979)

Bunce series
Curtiss, Elizabeth Mangam
see **Nathaniel Bunce series**
Davidson, Alan
see **Annabel Fidelity Bunce series**

Bunch and Alexander series
Wood, Andrew
1 *Mystery cruise* (1957)
2 *Noah's Ark river* (1959)

Bunch series
Thorndyke, Helen Louise
see **Honey Bunch series**

Bunchy series
Brisley, Joyce Lankester
1 *Bunchy* (1937)
2 *Another Bunchy book* (1951)

Buncle series
Stevenson, Dorothy Emily
see **Miss Buncle series**

Bundobust series
Stanford, John Keith
see **Lieutenant-Colonel James Gore-Bunbury series**

Bunduki series
Edson, John Thomas
1 *Bunduki* (1975)
2 *Bunduki and Dawn* (1976)
3 *Sacrifice for the Quagga god* (1976)
4 *Fearless master of the jungle* (1980)

Bundy series
Begbie, Harold
1 *Bundy in the Greenwood* (1902)
2 *Bundy on the sea* (1903)
The story of how Bundy with the Sandboy and the Mudlark set out across the sea to capture the golden apples of the sun

Bungle series
Strong, Jeremy
1 *Princess and Bungle* (1986)
2 *Bungle's ghost* (1987)

Bunjy Hearne series
Craig, Thurlow
see **Lieutenant Bunjy Hearne series**

Bunker series
Nokes, Ethel
see **Billy Bunker series**
Ross, Paul
see **Chopper Cop series**

Bunkers series
Hope, Laura Lee
see **Six little bunkers series**

Bunkle series
Pardoe, Margot
1 *Four plus Bunkle* (1939)
2 *Bunkle began it* (1942)
3 *Bunkle butts in* (1943)
4 *Bunkle bought it* (1945)
5 *Bunkle breaks away* (1947)
6 *Bunkle and Belinda* (1948)
7 *Bunkle baffles them* (1949)
8 *Bunkle went for six* (1950)
9 *Bunkle gets busy* (1961)
10 *Bunkle's brainwave* (1952)
11 *Bunkle scents a clue* (1953)
12 *Bunkle brings it off* (1961)

Bunn series
Atkey, Bertram
see **Smiler Bunn series**

Bunnicula series
Howe, James
1 *Bunnicula* (1979)
Co-author: Deborah Howe; a rabbit-tale of mystery
2 *Howliday Inn* (1982)
3 *Celery stalks at midnight* (1983)
4 *Nighty-nightmare* (1987)
5 *Harold and Chester in The fright before Christmas* (1989)
6 *Harold and Chester in Scared silly* (1989)
A Halloween treat
7 *Harold and Chester in Hot fudge* (1990)
8 *Harold and Chester in Creepy-crawly birthday* (1991)
9 *Return to Howliday Inn* (1992)
10 *Rabbit-cadabra!* (1993)
Companion volume: *The Bunnicula fun book*, 1993

Bunnies series
Carlson, Nancy
1 *Bunnies and their hobbies* (1984)
2 *Bunnies and their sports* (1987)

Bunnies series
Cartlidge, Michelle
see **Press and play series**

Bunnies series
Ehrlich, Amy
Adapted from Marie H Henry whose illustrations are used in these books
1 *Bunnies all day long* (1985)
Original edition entitled *Une journee comme une autre*
2 *Bunnies and their grandma* (1985)
Original edition entitled *Une journee chez grandmere*
3 *Bunnies on their own* (1986)
Original edition entitled *Le clairon de Praline*
4 *Bunnies at Christmas time* (1986)
Original edition entitled *Et si on invitait le Pere Noel*

Bunny Brown and his sister Sue series
Hope, Laura Lee
House pseudonym
1 *Bunny Brown and his sister Sue* (1916)
2 *Bunny Brown and his sister Sue on grandpa's farm* (1916)
3 *Bunny Brown and his sister Sue playing circus* (1916)
4 *Bunny Brown and his sister Sue at Camp Rest-a-While* (1916)
5 *Bunny Brown and his sister Sue at Aunt Lou's city home* (1916)
6 *Bunny Brown and his sister Sue in the big woods* (1917)
7 *Bunny Brown and his sister Sue on an auto tour* (1917)
8 *Bunny Brown and his sister Sue and their Shetland pony* (1918)
9 *Bunny Brown and his sister Sue giving a show* (1919)
10 *Bunny Brown and his sister Sue at Christmas Tree Cove* (1920)
11 *Bunny Brown and his sister Sue in the sunny South* (1921)
12 *Bunny Brown and his sister Sue keeping store* (1922)
13 *Bunny Brown and his sister Sue and their trick dog* (1923)
14 *Bunny Brown and his sister Sue at a sugar camp* (1924)
15 *Bunny Brown and his sister Sue on the rolling ocean* (1925)
16 *Bunny Brown and his sister Sue on Jack Frost Island* (1927)
17 *Bunny Brown and his sister Sue at Shore Acres* (1928)
18 *Bunny Brown and his sister Sue at Berry Hill* (1929)

19 *Bunny Brown and his sister Sue at Sky Top* (1930)
20 *Bunny Brown and his sister Sue at the summer carnival* (1931)

Bunny Buffin series
Buckels, Alex
1 *Stories of Bunny Buffin* (1945)
2 *Adventures of Bunny Buffin* (1953)

Bunny Chipstead series
Horler, Sydney
1 *In the dark* (1927)
Life for sale
2 *Chipstead of the Lone Hand* (1928)
3 *Secret agent* (1934)
4 *Enemy within the gates* (1940)

Bunny series
Cosgrove, Stephen Edward
see **Baby Bunny series**

Bunny series
Szekeres, Cyndy
1 *Things Bunny sees* (1990)
2 *What Bunny loves* (1990)

Bunny stories series
Jewett, John Howard
1 *Bunny stories for young people* (1892)
2 *More bunny stories for young people* (1900)

Bunny trouble series
Wilhelm, Hans
1 *Bunny trouble* (1985)
2 *More Bunny trouble* (1989)

Bunnykins series
Warrener
1 *Picnic for Bunnykins* (1984)
2 *Two Bunnykins out to tea* (1984)
3 *Bunnykins in the snow* (1985)
4 *Bunnykins in the kitchen* (1986)

Bunst series
Newton, David C
1 *Black ghost* (1947)
2 *Dangerous road* (1948)
Sequence continued under the author's real name John Newton Chance
Chance, John Newton
3 *Bunst the bold* (1950)
4 *Bunst and the brown voice* (1950)
5 *Bunst and the secret six* (1951)
6 *Bunst and the flying eye* (1953)

Bunter series
Richards, Frank
see **Billy Bunter series**
Richards, Hilda
see **Bessie Bunter series**

Bunting series
Greenwood, Robert
see **Mister Bunting series**

Bunty Brown series
Wilcox, Barbara
1 *Bunty Brown, probationer* (1940)
2 *Bunty Brown's bargain* (1941)
3 *Bunty Brown of the Flying Squad* (1943)

Bunyan series
McCormick, Dell J
see **Paul Bunyan series**

Bunyip series
Salmon, Michael
see **Alexander Bunyip series**

Bunyip series
Whitlock, Judith
1 *Green bunyip* (1962)
2 *Bunyip at the seaside* (1962)
3 *Bunyip and the brolga bird* (1963)
4 *Bunyip and the bushfire* (1964)
5 *Bunyip and the tiger cats* (1965)

Burchardt and Decker series
Bogen, M Arthur
1 *Double dealing* (1983)
2 *Barely undercover* (1983)
3 *Mind games* (1984)

Burdekin series
Campion, Sarah
see **Mister Moses Burdekin series**

Bure series
Lang, Maria
see **Christer Wick series**

Bureau thirteen series
Pollotta, Nick
1 *Bureau thirteen* (1991)
2 *Full moonstar* (1992)

Burford series
Macclure, Victor
see **Inspector Archie Burford series**

Burgess Cardigan series
Rico, Don
1 *Daisy dilemma* (1967)
2 *Man from P.A.N.S.Y.* (1967)

Burgess series
Franklin, Charles
see **Inspector Jim Burgess series**

Burghley series
Read, Conyers
see **William Cecil series**

Burgoyne series
Burgoyne, Peter
see **Peter Burgoyne series**

Burke series
Baker, Asa
see **Jerry Burke series**
Cullen, Robert
see **Colin Burke series**
Perdue, Virginia
see **Eleanora Burke series**
Trevor, Ralph
see **Superintendent Curtis Burke series**

Burke series
Vachss, Andrew
1 *Flood* (1985)
2 *Strega* (1987)
3 *Blue belle* (1988)
4 *Hard candy* (1989)
5 *Blossom* (1990)
6 *Sheila* (1993)
7 *Down in the zero* (1994)

Burke series
Webster, H M
see **Shamus Burke series**

Burlane series
Hoyt, Richard
see **James Burlane series**

Burlap Hall series
Ironside, Virginia
1 *Vampire master* (1987)
2 *Spaceboy at Burlap Hall* (1989)
3 *Phantom of Burlap Hall* (1991)
4 *Poltergeist of Burlap Hall* (1994)

Burlefoot series
Mykle, Agnar
see **Ash Burlefoot series**

Burleigh Brown series
Stevenson, Dorothy Emily
see **Gerald Burleigh Brown series**

Burma campaign series
Fergusson, Bernard
1 *Beyond the Chindwin* (1945)
An account of number 5 Column of the Wingate expedition to Burma
2 *Wild green earth* (1946)
An account of the 16th Brigade in General Wingate's second expedition into Burma, 1944

Burma surgeon trilogy
Seagrave, Gordon Stifler
Autobiography
1 *Burma surgeon* (1944)
2 *Burma surgeon returns* (1947)
3 *My hospital in the hills* (1957)

Burmann series
Cobb, Belton
see **Inspector Cheviot Burmann series**

Burnell series
Vivian, Francis
see **Inspector John Burnell series**

Burnett series
Lambourne, John
see **Jim Burnett series**
White, Stewart Edward
see **Andy Burnett series**
Whitman, Sidney Edgerton
see **Captain Cullah Burnett series**

Burning houses series
Harvey, Andrew
1 *Burning houses* (1986)
2 *Web* (1987)

Burnival series
Candy, Edward
see **Inspector Burnival series**

Burnley series
Ainsworth, Patricia
1 *Flickering candle* (1968)
2 *Candle rekindled* (1969)
3 *Steady burns the candle* (1970)
4 *Enchanted cup* (1980)

Burns Bannion series
Norman, Earl
1 *Kill me in Tokyo* (1958)
2 *Kill me in Shimbashi* (1959)
3 *Kill me in Yokohama* (1960)
4 *Kill me in Shinjuku* (1961)
5 *Kill me in Yoshiwara* (1961)
6 *Kill me in Atami* (1962)
7 *Kill me on the Ginza* (1962)
8 *Kill me in Roppongi* (1967)

Burns series
Abbey, Edward
see **Jack Burns series**
Barke, James
see **Immortal memory series**
Richmond, Grace Smith
see **Red Pepper Burns series**

Burnt boats series
Trease, Geoffrey
1 *Whiff of burnt boats* (1971)
2 *Laughter at the door* (1974)

Burr series
Kent, David
see **Jason Burr series**

Burrell series
Boothby, Guy
see **Jacob Burrell series**

Burrill series
Macleod, Adam Gordon
see **Sir William Burrill series**

Burris Weems series
Matthews, Greg
1 *Little red rooster* (1987)
2 *Gold flake hydrant* (1988)

Burroughs series
Murphy, Warren Burton
see **Digger Burroughs series**

Burton and Nichols series
Peters, Geoffrey
see **Inspector Trevor Nichols and Sergeant Tom Burton series**

Burton series
Beckett, Mark
see **Major Dick Burton series**
Dank, Milton
see **Edward Burton series**
Locke, Gladys Edson
see **Inspector Burton series**
Orczy, Emmuska
see **Old man in the corner series**

Burton trilogy
Penn, Margaret
see **Hilda Winstanley trilogy**

Burton Wulff series
Barry, Mike
1 *Night raider* (1973)
2 *Bay prowler* (1973)
3 *Boston avenger* (1973)
4 *Desert stalker* (1974)
5 *Havana hit* (1974)
6 *Chicago slaughter* (1974)
7 *Peruvian nightmare* (1974)
8 *Los Angeles holocaust* (1974)
9 *Miami marauder* (1974)
10 *Harlem showdown* (1975)
11 *Detroit massacre* (1975)
12 *Phoenix inferno* (1975)
13 *Killing run* (1975)
14 *Philadelphia blowup* (1975)

Bush boys series
Reid, Mayne
1 *Bush boys* (1856)
The adventures of a Cape farmer and his family in the wild Karoos of southern Africa
2 *Young yagers* (1857)
Alternative title: A narrative of hunting adventures in southern Africa
3 *Giraffe hunters* (1867)

Bush nurse series
Elliott, Mary
see **Clare Carson series**

Bush series
Dana, Mitchell
see **Dakota Bush series**

Bushies series
Magoffin, Richard
Anecdotes of rural life in western Queensland
1 *We bushies* (1968)
2 *Chops and gravy* (1972)

Bushwhacker series
Benton, Will
1 *Bushwhacker vengeance* (1964)
2 *Bushwhacker's moon* (1965)

Business and legal forms series
Crawford, Tad
1 *Business and legal forms for fine artists* (1990)
2 *Business and legal forms for authors and self-publishers* (1990)
3 *Business and legal forms for illustrators* (1990)
4 *Business and legal forms for graphic designers* (1990)
Co-author: Eva Doman Bruck
5 *Business and legal forms for photographers* (1991)

Buster and Betty series
Dicks, Terrance
see **Adventures of Buster and Betty series**

Buster series
Campbell, Rod
1 *Buster's morning* (1984)
2 *Buster's afternoon* (1984)

Buster series

3 *Buster's bedtime* (1984)
4 *Buster gets dressed* (1988)
5 *Buster keeps warm* (1988)

Busy baby's day series
Thompson, Carol
1 *Wake up time* (1987)
2 *Morning* (1987)
3 *Afternoon* (1987)
4 *Bedtime* (1987)

Busy Bear series
Margolin, Harriet
Illustrated by Carol Nicklaus
1 *Busy Bear's closet* (1985)
2 *Busy Bear's cupboard* (1985)
3 *Busy Bear's refrigerator* (1985)
4 *Busy Bear's room* (1985)

Busy Bears series
Killingback, Julia
1 *Monday is washing day* (1984)
2 *What's the time, Mrs Bear?* (1984)
3 *Catch the red bus* (1985)
4 *One, two, three, go!* (1985)
5 *Stars, squares and Busy Bears* (1986)
6 *Rain, rain, go away!* (1986)
7 *Wake up, Busy Bears!* (1987)
8 *Follow that bear* (1987)
9 *Busy Bears' picnic* (1988)
10 *Watch out, Busy Bears* (1988)
11 *Busy Bear to the rescue* (1988)
12 *Busy Bears at the fire station* (1988)
13 *Busy Bear firefighter counterpack* (1988)

Busy body series
Bentley, Nancy
Board books
1 *Let's go, feet!* (1987)
2 *Do this, hands!* (1987)
3 *Listen to this, ears!* (1987)
4 *What's on top, head?* (1987)

Busy O'Brien series
Poploff, Michelle
1 *Busy O'Brien and the great bubblegum blowout* (1990)
2 *Busy O'Brien and the caterpillar punch bunch* (1992)

But look trilogy
Kantor, Mackinlay
Reminiscences
1 *But look, the morn* (1947)
The story of a childhood
2 *Lobo* (1957)
3 *Missouri bittersweet* (1969)

Butch Cassidy and the Sundance Kid series
Essex, Saran
1 *Trail to Vengeance* (1988)
2 *Treacherous gun* (1990)

Butch Karp series
Tanenbaum, Robert K
see **Assistant District Attorney Butch Karp series**

Butch Lewis series
Klein, Dave
1 *Blind side* (1980)
2 *Hit and run* (1982)

Butcher series
Jason, Stuart
This pseudonym is used by several authors, including Michael Avallone and Lee Floren, whose authorship is indicated against those titles where it is known
1 *Kill quick or die* (1970)
2 *Come watch him die* (1971)
3 *Keepers of death* (1971)
4 *Blood debt* (1972)
5 *Deadly deal* (1973)
6 *Death race* (1973)
7 *Fire bomb* (1973)
8 *Kill time* (1973)
9 *Sealed with blood* (1973)
10 *Deadly doctor* (1974) [Floren]
11 *Valley of death* (1974) [Floren]
12 *Killer's cargo* (1974)
13 *Blood vengeance* (1975)
14 *African contract* (1975)
15 *Kill gently, but sure* (1975)
16 *Suicide in San Juan* (1975)
17 *Cubano caper* (1976)
18 *Grecian bloodbath* (1976)
19 *Mayday over Manhattan* (1976)
20 *Hollywood assassin* (1976)
21 *Instant dead* (1976)
22 *U.N. affair* (1976)
23 *Appointment in Iran* (1977)
24 *Venetian vendetta* (1977)
25 *Terror truckers* (1977)
26 *Corporate caper* (1977)
27 *Judas judge* (1979) [Avallone]
28 *Kill them silently* (1980) [Avallone]
29 *Slaughter in September* (1980) [Avallone]
30 *Coffin corner, U.S.A.* (1981) [Avallone]
31 *Death in yellow* (1981) [Avallone]
32 *Hoodoo horror* (1981) [Avallone]
33 *Go die in Afghanistan* (1982) [Avallone]
34 *Man from White Hat* (1982) [Avallone]
35 *Gotham Gore* (1982) [Avallone]

Butler and Audley series
Price, Anthony
see **Doctor David Audley and Jack Butler series**

Butler series
Anthony, David
see **Morgan Butler series**
Carr, John Dickson
see **Patrick Butler series**

Butler series
Kirk, Philip
1 *Hydra conspiracy* (1979)
2 *Smart bombs* (1979)
3 *Slayboys* (1979)
4 *Chinese roulette* (1979)
5 *Love me to death* (1980)
6 *Paris kill* (1980)
7 *Killer virus* (1980)
8 *Dead fall* (1980)
9 *Laser shuttle* (1980)
10 *Killer satellites* (1980)
11 *Q factor* (1984)
12 *Midas kill* (1984)

Butler series
Rey, Bret
see **Ned Butler series**

Butte family series
Rikhoff, Jean
1 *Buttes Landing* (1973)
2 *One of the Raymonds* (1974)
3 *Sweetwater* (1976)

Butten series
Barbette, Jay
see **Harry Butten series**

Buttercup Willie series
Oakden, David
1 *Buttercup Willie rides again* (1985)
2 *Buttercup Willie is a great help* (1987)

Butterfield Square series
York, Carol Beach
see **Miss Know It All series**

Butterflies series
Fountaine, Margaret
see **Victorian lady series**

Butterfly ball series
Aldridge, Alan
Verses
1 *Butterfly ball and the grasshopper's feast* (1973)
2 *Peacock party* (1979)

Butterfly days series
Fowkes, Aubrey
1 *Butterfly days* (1958)
2 *More butterfly days* (1958)

Buttermilk series
Cosgrove, Stephen Edward
1 *Buttermilk* (1986)
2 *Buttermilk Bear* (1987)

Butternut Bill series
McCall, Edith
1 *Butternut Bill* (1965)
2 *Butternut Bill and the bee tree* (1965)
3 *Butternut Bill and the big cash* (1965)
4 *Butternut Bill and the bear* (1965)
5 *Butternut Bill and Little River* (1966)
6 *Butternut Bill and the big pumpkin* (1966)
7 *Butternut Bill and his friends* (1968)
8 *Butternut Bill an the train* (1969)

Butterworth series
Green, Anna Katharine
see **Amelia Butterworth series**

Button family series
McCall, Edith
1 *Bucky Button* (1953)
2 *Buttons at the zoo* (1954)
3 *Buttons and the pet parade* (1954)
4 *Buttons at the farm* (1955)
5 *Buttons go camping* (1956)
6 *Buttons at the soap box derby* (1957)
7 *Buttons take a boat ride* (1957)
8 *Buttons and Mister Pete* (1957)
9 *Buttons and the Boy Scouts* (1958)
10 *Buttons and the Little League* (1958)
11 *Buttons and the whirlybird* (1959)
12 *Buttons see things that go* (1959)
Revised editions 1960-61

Buttonwoods series
Beiler, Edna
1 *Adventures with the Buttonwoods* (1960)
2 *Mitsy Buttonwood* (1963)

Buzz Cardigan series
Rico, Don
see **Burgess Cardigan series**

Buzzy Bear series
Marino, Dorothy
1 *Buzzy Bear goes south* (1964)
2 *Buzzy Bear goes camping* (1965)
3 *Buzzy Bear's busy day* (1967)
4 *Buzzy Bear and the rainbow* (1968)
5 *Buzzy Bear's first day at school* (1970)

By Jiminy series
Daniell, David Scott
see **Jiminy series**

Byrd series
Styles, Showell
see **Ensign Peter Byrd series**

Byrne series
Vivian, Evelyn Charles
see **Inspector Byrne series**

Byrnes series
Hawthorne, Julian
see **Inspector Byrnes series**

Byron O'Toole series
Thurston, Robert
see **Rugger series**

Byron series
Quennell, Peter
see **Lord Byron series**

Bystander series
Bairnsfather, Bruce
see **Old Bill series**

Bytes Brothers series
McCoy, Lois
1 *Bytes Brothers input an investigation* (1983)
2 *Bytes Brothers program a problem* (1983)
3 *Bytes Brothers enter the evidence* (1983)
4 *Bytes Brothers compute a clue* (1983)
5 *Bytes Brothers record a robbery* (1984)
6 *Bytes Brothers go to a getaway* (1984)

Byzantium series
Masefield, John
1 *Basilissa* (1940)
A tale of the Empress Theodora
2 *Conquer* (1941)
A tale of the Nika Rebellion in Byzantium

C

C.A.D.S. series
Sievert, John
This pseudonym is used by David Alexander, Jan Stacy and Ryder Syvertsen as indicated against each title
1 *C.A.D.S.* (1985) [Syvertsen; Stacy]
2 *Tech battleground* (1986) [Syvertsen]
3 *Tech commando* (1986) [Syvertsen]
4 *Tech strike force* (1987) [Syvertsen]
5 *Tech Satan* (1988) [Syvertsen]
6 *Tech inferno* (1988) [Syvertsen]
7 *Doom commander* (1989) [Syvertsen]
8 *Cybertech killing zone* (1989) [Syvertsen]
9 *Suicide attack* (1990) [Alexander]
10 *Recon by fire* (1990) [Alexander]
11 *Death zone attack* (1991) [Alexander]
12 *Tech assassins* (1991) [Alexander]

C.A.T. series
Andrews, Spike
1 *Tower of blood* (1982)
2 *Kidnap Hotel* (1983)
3 *Cult of the damned* (1983)

C Auguste Dupin series
Poe, Edgar Allan
see **Monsieur C Auguste Dupin series**

C.B.Greenfield series
Kallen, Lucille
1 *Introducing C.B.Greenfield* (1979)
2 *Tanglewood murder* (1980)

3 *No lady in the house* (1982)
4 *Piano bird* (1984)
5 *Little madness* (1986)

C D Sloan series
Aird, Catherine
see **Inspector C D Sloan series**

C.I.D. Room series
Alding, Peter
1 *C.I.D. Room* (1967)
All leads negative
2 *Circle of danger* (1968)
3 *Murder among thieves* (1969)
4 *Guilt without proof* (1970)
5 *Despite the evidence* (1971)
6 *Call back to crime* (1972)
7 *Field of fire* (1973)
8 *Murder line* (1974)
9 *Six days to death* (1975)
10 *Murder is suspected* (1977)
11 *Ransom town* (1979)
12 *Man condemned* (1981)
13 *Betrayed by death* (1982)
14 *One man's justice* (1983)

C J Watson series
Resciniti, Angelo G
1 *Mystery cases of C J Watson* (1980)
2 *C J Watson solves the dragon's blood mystery* (1980)
3 *C J Watson solves the spaceport mystery* (1980)

C.L.U.T.Z. series
Wilkes, Marilyn Z
1 *C.L.U.T.Z.* (1982)
2 *C.L.U.T.Z. and the fizzion formula* (1985)

C.O.B.R.A. series
Rosenberger, Joseph
1 *Heroin connection* (1986)
2 *Paris kill-ground* (1987)
3 *Red dragon* (1987)
4 *Nightmare in Panama* (1987)

C W Sughrue series
Crumley, James
1 *Last good kiss* (1978)
2 *Mexican tree duck* (1993)

Cab series
Pritchett, Victor Sawdon
Autobiography
1 *Cab at the door* (1968)
2 *Midnight oil* (1971)

Cabal series
Dunn, Saul
Also published under the author's real name Philip Dunn
1 *Cabal* (1978)
2 *Black moon* (1978)
3 *Evangelist* (1979)

Cabbagetown series
Garner, Hugh
1 *Cabbagetown* (1950)
Revised edition 1968
2 *Waste no tears* (1950)
Originally published under the pseudonym Jarvis Warwick
3 *Silence on the shore* (1962)
4 *Intruders* (1976)

Cabell series
Penton, Brian
see **Derek Cabell series**

Cable series
Callison, Brian
see **Brevet Cable series**

Cabot Cain series
Caillou, Alan
1 *Assault on Kolchak* (1969)
2 *Assault on Loveless* (1969)
3 *Assault on Ming* (1970)
4 *Assault on Fellawi* (1972)
5 *Assault on Agathon* (1972)
6 *Assault on Aimata* (1975)

Cabot series
Farley, Ralph Milne
see **Miles Cabot series**
Ketchum, Philip
see **Elijah Cabot Pickering series**
McDougald, Roman
see **Philip Cabot series**
Norman, John
see **Tarl Cabot series**
Scott, Gertrude Fisher
see **Jean Cabot series**

Cactus Clancy series
Cody, Stetson
1 *Cactus Clancy rides* (1949)
2 *Cactus justice* (1952)
3 *Trouble shooter* (1964)
4 *Lawdog's bite* (1965)
5 *Gunslick code* (1965)
6 *Sinister Valley* (1967)
7 *Guns along the Ruthless* (1973)

Cadbury series
Bates, Dianne
see **Grandma Cadbury series**

Cadbury series
Macbeth, George
1 *Samurai* (1975)
Cadbury and the Samurai
2 *Seven witches* (1978)
Cadbury and the seven witches
3 *Born losers* (1982)
Cadbury and the born losers

Caddie Woodlawn series
Brink, Carol Ryrie
1 *Caddie Woodlawn* (1935)
2 *Magical melons* (1944)

Cade series
Pike, Charles R
see **Jubal Cade series**

Cadee series
Dean, Spencer
see **Don Cadee series**

Cadet series
King, Charles
1 *Cadet days* (1894)
2 *To the front* (1908)

Cadfael series
Peters, Ellis
see **Brother Cadfael series**

Cadman series
Rushton, Charles
see **Inspector Cadman series**

Cadre trilogy
O'Riordan, Robert
1 *Cadre One* (1986)
2 *Cadre Lucifer* (1987)
3 *Cadre Messiah* (1988)

Cadwal chronicles series
Vance, Jack
1 *Araminta Station* (1987)
2 *Ecce and old earth* (1991)

Caesar and Cleopatra series
Mundy, Talbot
see **Tros of Samothrace series**

Caesar Cascabel series
Verne, Jules
1 *Travelling circus* (1890)
2 *Show on ice* (1890)
Originally published in one volume entitled *Cesar Cascabel*

Caesar series
Warner, Rex
1 *Young Caesar* (1958)
2 *Imperial Caesar* (1960)

Cage and Jennifer series
Saint Claire, Erin
see **Jennifer and Cage series**

Cage series
Israel, Peter
see **B F Cage series**
Riefe, Alan
see **Huntington Cage series**

Caged women series
This sequence has six authors; based on a television series
Sinclair, Murray
1 *Prisoner, Cell Block H* (1980)
Clement, Henry
2 *Franky Doyle story* (1980)
O'Shell, Maggie
3 *Karen Travers story* (1981)
Kerr, Michael
4 *Frustrations of Vera* (1981)
Michaels, Angela
5 *Reign of Queen Bea* (1981)
Carter, Mary
6 *Trials of Erica* (1981)

Cageworld series
Kapp, Colin
1 *Search for the sun!* (1981)
2 *Lost worlds of Cronus* (1982)
3 *Tyrant of Hades* (1982)
4 *Star-search* (1983)

Cain series
Caillou, Alan
see **Cabot Cain series**
Freeborn, Brian
see **Mister Cain series**

Cain series
Key, Sean A
1 *Mark of Cain* (1980)
2 *Cain's Chinese puzzle* (1981)

Cain series
Pickard, Nancy
see **Jenny Cain series**
Westerman, Percy Francis
see **Captain Cain series**

Caine series
Zochert, Donald
see **Nick Caine series**

Cainsforth series
Maske, John
see **Duncan Cainsforth series**

Cairn series
Loder, Vernon
see **Donald Cairn series**

Cairo Jim series
McSkimming, Geoffrey
1 *Cairo Jim and Doris in search of Martenarten* (1991)
Tale of archaeology, adventure and astonishment
2 *Cairo Jim on the trail to ChaCha Muchos* (1992)
Epic tale of rhythm

Cairo trilogy
Mahfouz, Naguib
Translated from the Arabic
1 *Palace walk* (1990)
2 *Palace of desire* (1991)
3 *Sugar Street* (1992)

Caithan Crusade series
Smith, Julie Dean
1 *Call of madness* (1990)
2 *Mission of magic* (1991)
3 *Sage of Sare* (1992)

Caithleen series
O'Brien, Edna
1 *Country girls* (1960)
2 *Lonely girl* (1962)
Girl with green eyes
3 *Girls in their married bliss* (1964)
One volume edition entitled *The country girls trilogy and epilogue*, 1986

Caitlin: forever trilogy
Pascal, Francine
see **Forever trilogy**

Caitlin: love trilogy
Pascal, Francine
see **Love trilogy**

Caitlin: promise trilogy
Pascal, Francine
see **Promise trilogy**

Caitlin Reece series
Douglas, Lauren Wright
1 *In the blood* (1989)
2 *Ninth life* (1990)
3 *Daughters of Artemis* (1991)
4 *Tiger's heart* (1992)
5 *Goblin market* (1993)
6 *Rage of maidens* (1994)

Caitlin series
Downer, Ann
1 *Spellkey* (1987)
2 *Glass salamander* (1989)

Caitlin trilogy
Campbell, Joanna
1 *Loving* (1985)
2 *Love lost* (1985)
3 *True love* (1986)

Cal, Veg and Aquilon trilogy
Anthony, Piers
see **Of man and mantra trilogy**

Caladon series
Mills, Craig
1 *Bane of Lord Caladon* (1982)
2 *Dreamer in discord* (1988)

Calamity Jane series
Edson, John Thomas
1 *Calamity, Mark and Belle* (1980)
Texas trio
2 *Cold deck, hot lead* (1969)
3 *Bull whip breed* (1965)
4 *Trouble trail* (1965)
5 *Cow thieves* (1965)
6 *Hide and Horn Saloon* (1983)
7 *Cut one, they all bleed* (1983)
8 *Calamity spells trouble* (1968)
9 *White stallion, red mare* (1970)
10 *Remittance kid* (1978)
11 *Whip and the war lance* (1979)
12 *Big hunt* (1967)
13 *Wanted, Belle Starr* (1986)

Calcutta series
This sequence has two authors; a broken love affair related by each of the lovers
Eliade, Mircea
1 *Bengal nights* (1993)
Devi, Maitreyi
2 *It does not die* (1994)

Calder series
Dailey, Janet
see **Webb Calder series**
Hammond, Gerald
see **Keith Calder series**

Caldwell and Phelan series
Ozaki, Milton K
see **Professor Caldwell and Lieutenant Phelan series**

Caldwell series
Hunter, E J
see **White Squaw series**

Cale series
Long, Patrick
see **Martyn Cale series**

Caleb Cluff series
North, Gil
see **Sergeant Caleb Cluff series**

Caleb Sax series
Bittner, F Rosanne
1 *Savage horizons* (1986)
2 *Frontier fires* (1987)
3 *Destiny's dawn* (1987)
4 *Tennessee bride* (1988)

Caleb Sweetwater series
Green, Anna Katharine
1 *Agatha Webb* (1899)
2 *Woman in the alcove* (1906)
3 *House of the whispering pines* (1910)
4 *Initials only* (1911)
5 *Mystery of the hasty arrow* (1917)

Caleb Thorn series
Coburn, L J
This pseudonym is used by John Barton Harvey and Laurence James as indicated against each title
1 *First shot* (1977)
[James]
2 *Raiders* (1977)
[Harvey]
3 *Brotherly death* (1978)
[James]
4 *Bloody Shiloh* (1978)
[Harvey]
5 *Death river* (1978)
[James]

Caledon series
Miller, Margaret Jessy
see **Kingdom of Caledon series**

Calhoun series
Hawkins, Clint
see **Saddletramp series**

Caliban series
Asimov, Isaac
1 *Caliban* (1993)
2 *Inferno* (1994)

Caliban series
Farmer, Philip Jose
see **Doc Caliban series**

Caliban series
Warren, Paulette
1 *Caliban's castle* (1976)
2 *Search in the shadows* (1976)
3 *Apprentice in terror* (1976)
4 *Lady Sinister* (1976)
5 *I take this stranger* (1977)
6 *Castle of dreams* (1977)

Caliban series
Williams, Tad
see **Tempest series**

Calico Jack series
Newte, Horace Wykeham Can
1 *Calico Jack* (1910)
A story of the music halls
2 *Gentle bigamist* (1920)

California Indian series
Curry, Jane Louise
1 *Down from the lonely mountain* (1965)
2 *Back in the beforetime* (1987)

California pioneer series
Schulte, Elaine
1 *Journey west* (1988)
2 *Golden dreams* (1989)
3 *Eternal passage* (1989)
4 *With wings as eagles* (1990)

California trilogy
Fritch, Elizabeth
1 *Passion's trail* (1983)
2 *Golden fires* (1984)
3 *Heart divided* (1984)

California trilogy
Moore, Arthur
1 *Sword and the cross* (1979)
2 *Flame and the dagger* (1979)
3 *Viper and the hawk* (1979)

California trilogy
White, Stewart Edward
1 *Gold* (1913)
A tale of the forty-niners
2 *Gray dawn* (1915)
Grey dawn
3 *Rose dawn* (1920)
One volume edition entitled *The story of California*, 1927

Californian Indian series
Austin, Mary
Sketches and stories
1 *Land of little rain* (1903)
2 *Flock* (1906)
3 *Lost borders* (1909)

Caliper Maxwell and Nogales Scott series
Macdonald, William Colt
see **Nogales Scott and Caliper Maxwell series**

Call home series
Burke, Fielding
1 *Call home the heart* (1932)
2 *Stone came rolling* (1935)

Call of fife and drum trilogy
Fast, Howard
1 *Conceived in liberty* (1939)
A novel of Valley Forge
2 *Unvanquished* (1947)
3 *Proud and the free* (1950)
One volume edition entitled *The call of fife and drum*, 1987

Call series
Cleaver, Vera
see **Luther family series**

Call to arms series
Nolan, Frederick
see **Davy Strong series**

Calladine family series
Bennett, Barbara
1 *There is a season* (1976)
2 *Beggar's virtue* (1979)
3 *Rough music* (1980)

Callaghan series
Chesney, Michael
see **Colonel Steel Callaghan series**
Cheyney, Peter
see **Slim Callaghan series**

Callahan and Gargano families trilogy
Seger, Maura
1 *Echo of thunder* (1985)
2 *Eye of the storm* (1985)
3 *Edge of dawn* (1985)

Callahan brothers series
Miller, Jim
see **Colt Revolver series**

Callahan Garrity series
Trocheck, Kathy Hogan
1 *Every crooked nanny* (1992)
2 *To live and die in Dixie* (1993)
3 *Homemade sin* (1994)

Callahan series
Ames, Francis Herbert
1 *That Callahan spunk!* (1965)
That Callahan blood!
2 *Callahans' gamble* (1970)
3 *Callahan goes south* (1976)

Callahan series
Gault, William Campbell
see **Brock Callahan series**

Callahan's Crosstime Saloon series
Robinson, Spider
1 *Callahan's Crosstime Saloon* (1977)
2 *Time travelers strictly cash* (1981)
3 *Callahan's secret* (1986)
Numbers 1-3 also published in one volume entitled *Callahan and company*, 1987 and *Callahan's crazy crosstime bar*, 1989
4 *Callahan's lady* (1989)
5 *Callahan touch* (1993)
6 *Of the wall at Callahan's* (1994)

Callan series
Mitchell, James
see **David Callan series**

Called to love, called to serve series
McGloin, Joseph Thaddeus
1 *Alive in the Lord!* (1979)
2 *Faith to share!* (1979)
3 *Christ with us!* (1979)
4 *Called to love, called to serve!* (1979)

Callendar family series
Verney, John
1 *Friday's tunnel* (1959)
2 *February's road* (1961)
3 *Ismo* (1964)
4 *Seven sunflower seeds* (1968)
5 *Samson's hoard* (1973)

Callie series
Curry, Jane Louise
1 *Beneath the hill* (1967)
2 *Daybreakers* (1970)
3 *Birdstones* (1977)

Callie series
Park, Ruth
1 *Callie's castle* (1985)
2 *Callie's family* (1988)

Callisto series
Carter, Lin
see **Jandar the Alien series**

Calloway Corners series
This sequence has four authors
Canfield, Sandra
1 *Maria* (1989)
Hughes, Tracy
2 *Jo* (1989)
Burton, Katherine
3 *Tess* (1989)
Richards, Penny
4 *Eden* (1989)

Calman Jacoby family series
Singer, Isaac Bashevis
1 *Manor* (1967)
2 *Estate* (1969)

Calouste Fisher series
Sellers, Michael
1 *Leonardo and others* (1980)
2 *From eternity to here* (1981)
3 *Cache on the rocks* (1982)

Calton and Kilsip series
Hume, Fergus
see **Detective Kilsip and Duncan Calton series**

Calverly series
Merwin, Samuel
see **Henry Calverly series**

Calvert series
Ferguson, William Blair Morton
see **Lightnin' Calvert series**

Calvert trilogy
Seger, Maura
1 *Sarah* (1987)
2 *Elizabeth* (1987)
3 *Catherine* (1988)

Calvin and Hobbes series
Watterson, Bill
Comic strips
1 *Calvin and Hobbes* (1987)
2 *Essential Calvin and Hughes* (1988)
3 *Something under the bed is drooling* (1988)
4 *Yukon ho!* (1989)
5 *Calvin and hobbes lazy Sunday book* (1989)
6 *Authoritative Calvin and Hobbes* (1990)
7 *Weirdos from another planet!* (1990)
8 *Revenge of the baby-sat* (1991)
9 *Scientific progress goes boink* (1991)
10 *Attack of the deranged mutant killer monster snow goons* (1992)
11 *Indispensible Calvin and Hobbes* (1992)
12 *Days are just packed* (1993)

Calvin Parks series
Richards, Laura Elizabeth
1 *Wooing of Calvin Parks* (1908)
2 *Up to Calvin's* (1910)
3 *On board the Mary Sands* (1911)

Calvin Willeford series
DeWeese, Gene
1 *Black suits from outer space* (1985)
Beepers from outer space
2 *Dandelion caper* (1986)
3 *Calvin nullifier* (1987)

Cam and Beaver series
Cockin, Joan
see **Inspector Cam and Beaver series**

Cam and Clayt series
Bickham, Jack Miles
see **John Campbell and Clayton Hartung series**

Cam Jansen series
Adler, David A
1 *Cam Jansen and the mystery of the stolen diamonds* (1980)
2 *Cam Jansen and the mystery of the UFO* (1980)
3 *Cam Jansen and the mystery of the dinodaur bones* (1981)
4 *Cam Jansen and the mystery of the television dog* (1981)
5 *Cam Jansen and the mystery of the gold coins* (1982)
6 *Cam Jansen and the mystery of the Babe Ruth baseball* (1982)
7 *Cam Jansen and the mystery of the circus clown* (1983)
8 *Cam Jansen and the mystery of the monster movie* (1984)
9 *Cam Jansen and the mystery of the carnival prize* (1984)
10 *Cam Jansen and the mystery at the monkey house* (1985)
11 *Cam Jansen and the mystery of the stolen corn popper* (1986)
12 *Cam Jansen and the mystery of Flight Fifty-four* (1989)
13 *Cam Jansen and the mystery at the haunted house* (1992)
Companion volume: *Cam Jansen activity book*, 1992

Cam Maccardle series
Halleran, Tucker
1 *Cool clear death* (1984)
2 *Sudden death finish* (1985)

Camber of Culdi trilogy
Kurtz, Katherine
see **Legends of Camber of Culdi trilogy**

Camber trilogy
Kurtz, Katherine
see **Heirs of Saint Camber trilogy**

Camberwell series
Fletcher, Joseph Smith
see **Ronald Camberwell series**

Camden series
Graat, Heinrich
see **Ben Camden series**

Camden Street kids series
Dicks, Terrance
1 *In the money* (1986)
2 *On T.V.* (1986)
3 *By the sea* (1987)
4 *School fair* (1987)

Camellion series
Rosenberger, Joseph
see **Death Merchant series**

Camelot series
Landis, Arthur Harold
1 *World called Camelot* (1976)
2 *Camelot in orbit* (1978)
3 *Magick of Camelot* (1981)
4 *Home, to Avalon* (1982)

Camelot series
White, Terence Hanbury
see **Once and future king series**

Cameron and Wu series
Sheridan, Juanita
see **Lily Wu and Janice Cameron series**

Cameron Downey series
Hendryx, James Beardsley
see **Corporal Cameron Downey series**

Cameron family trilogy
Joseph, Ronald S
1 *Kingdom* (1978)
2 *Power* (1978)
3 *Glory* (1980)

Cameron series
Connor, Ralph
see **North-West Mounted Police series**
Culp, John Hewett
see **Martin Cameron series**
Malcolm, Aleen
see **Daughters of Cameron series**
McCutchan, Philip
see **Donald Cameron series**
Wright, Wade
see **Paul Cameron series**

Camerons series
Duncan, Jane
1 *Camerons on the train* (1963)
2 *Camerons on the hills* (1963)
3 *Camerons at the castle* (1964)
4 *Camerons calling* (1966)
5 *Camerons ahoy!* (1968)

Camillo series
Guareschi, Giovanni
see **Don Camillo series**

Camillus and Hylas series
Ray, Mary
see **Early Christian series**

Cammie series
McIlvaine, Jane
1 *Cammie's choice* (1961)
2 *Cammie's challenge* (1962)
3 *Cammie's cousin* (1963)

Camp and tramp series
Allen, Willis Boyd
1 *Lost in Umbagog* (1894)
2 *Mammoth hunters* (1895)

Camp Crystal Lake series
Morse, Eric
see **Friday the thirteenth series**

Camp Fire Boys series
Clifton, Oliver Lee
1 *Camp Fire Boys at Log Cabin Bend* (1923)
2 *Camp Fire Boys in Muskrat Swamp* (1924)
3 *Camp Fire Boys' canoe cruise* (1925)
4 *Camp Fire Boys' tracking squad* (1926)

Camp Fire Girls series
Frey, Hildegarde Gertrude
see **Winnebagos series**

Camp Fire Girls series
Stewart, Jane L
1 *Camp Fire Girls at Long Lake* (1914)
Campfire Girl in summer camp
Alternative title: Bessie King in summer camp
2 *Camp Fire Girls at the seashore* (1914)
Campfire Girl's happiness
Alternative title: Bessie King's happiness
3 *Camp Fire Girls in the mountains* (1914)
Campfire Girl's adventure
Alternative title: Bessie King's strange adventure
4 *Camp Fire Girls in the woods* (1914)
Campfire Girl's first council fire
Alternative title: Bessie King's first council fire
5 *Camp Fire Girls on the farm* (1914)
Campfire Girl's chum
Alternative title: Bessie King's new chum
6 *Camp Fire Girls on the march* (1914)
Campfire Girl's test of friendship
Alternative title: Bessie king's test of friendship

Camp Fire girls series
Vandercook, Margaret
1 *Camp Fire girls at Sunrise Hill* (1913
2 *Camp Fire girls amid the snows* (1913)
3 *Camp Fire girls in the outside world* (1914)
4 *Camp Fire girls across the sea* (1914)
5 *Camp Fire girls' careers* (1915)
6 *Camp Fire girls in after years* (1915)
7 *Camp Fire girls at the edge of the desert* (1917)
8 *Camp Fire girls at the end of the trail* (1917)
9 *Camp Fire girls behind the lines* (1918)
10 *Camp Fire girls on the field of honor* (1918)
11 *Camp Fire girls in glorious France* (1919)
12 *Camp Fire girls in Merrie England* (1920)
13 *Camp Fire girls at Half Moon Lake* (1921)
14 *Camp Fire girls by the blue lagoon* (1921)

Camp Haunted Hills series
Coville, Bruce
1 *How I survived my summer vacation* (1988)
2 *Some of my best friends are monsters* (1988)
3 *Dinosaur that followed me home* (1990)

Camp Mehunkechoque series
Cooney, Caroline B
see **Vi and Marissa series**

Camp Sunnyside Friends series
Kaye, Marilyn
1 *No boys allowed* (1989)
2 *Cabin six plays Cupid* (1989)
3 *Color war!* (1989)
4 *New girl in Cabin six* (1989)
5 *Looking for trouble* (1990)
6 *Katie steals the show* (1990)
7 *Witch in Cabin six* (1990)
8 *Too many counselors* (1990)
9 *New and improved Sarah* (1990)
10 *Erin and the movie star* (1991)
11 *Problem with parents* (1991)
12 *Tennis trap* (1991)
13 *Big sister blues* (1991)
14 *Megan's ghost* (1991)
15 *Christmas break* (1991)
16 *Happily ever after* (1992)
17 *Camp Spaghetti* (1992)
18 *Balancing act* (1992)

Camp Sunnyside Friends specials series
Kaye, Marilyn
1 *My camp memory book* (1990)
2 *Christmas reunion* (1990)
3 *School daze* (1992)
4 *Spirit of Sunnyside* (1992)

Campaign trilogy
Alger, Horatio
1 *Frank's campaign* (1864)
2 *Paul Prescott's charge* (1865)
3 *Charlie Codman's cruise* (1866)

Campbell and Hartung series
Bickham, Jack Miles
see **John Campbell and Clayton Hartung series**

Campbell and Ross series
Henneker, Philip
see **Susan Campbell and Paul Ross series**

Campbell-Black series
Cooper, Jilly
see **Rupert Campbell-Black series**

Campbell series
Alcott, Louisa May
see **Rose Campbell series**
Colter, Eli
see **Pat Campbell series**
Douglas, Colin
see **David Campbell series**
Homes, Geoffrey
see **Humphrey Campbell series**

Campbells series
Lambert, Janet
1 *Precious days* (1957)
2 *For each other* (1959)
3 *Forever and ever* (1961)
4 *Five's a crowd* (1963)
5 *First of all* (1966)

Campfire Girls series
Benson, Irene Elliott
Numbers 1-6 also published under the pseudonym Stella M Francis
1 *Campfire Girls in the Alleghany Mountains* (1918)
Alternative title: A Christmas success against odds
2 *Campfire Girls in the country* (1918)
Alternative title: The secret Aunt Hannah forgot; originally published as *How Ethel Hollister became a Campfire Girl*, 1912
3 *Campfire Girls trip up the river* (1918)
Alternative title: Ethel Hollister's first lesson
4 *Campfire Girls outing* (1918)
Alternative title: Ethel Hollister's second summer in camp; originally published as *Ethel Hollister's summer as a Campfire Girl*, 1913
5 *Campfire Girls on a hike* (1918)
Alternative title: Lost in the Great North Woods
6 *Campfire Girls at Twin Lakes* (1918)
Aternative title: The quest of a summer vacation
7 *Campfire Girls in the forest* (1918)
Alternative title: The lost trail found
8 *Campfire Girls mountaineering* (1918)
Alternative title: Overcoming all obstacles
9 *Campfire Girls' lake camp* (1918)
Alternative title: Searching for new adventures
10 *Campfire Girls' rural retreat* (1918)
Alternative title: The quest of a secret

Campfire Girls series
De Vries, Julianne
1 *Campfire Girls as detectives* (1933)
2 *Campfire Girls at Holly House* (1933)
3 *Campfire Girls flying around me* (1933)
4 *Campfire Girls on Valiban Island* (1933)

Campfire Girls series
Hornibrook, Isabel
1 *Girls of the Morning-Glory Camp fire* (1916)
2 *Campfire Girls and Mount Greylock* (1917)
3 *Campfire Girls in war and peace* (1919)

Campfire girls series
Penrose, Margaret
1 *Campfire girls of Roselawn* (1930)
Alternative title: A strange message from the air; originally published as *The radio girls of Roselawn*, 1922
2 *Campfire girls on the program* (1930)
Alternative title: Singing and reciting at the sending station; originally published as *The radio girls on the program*, 1922
3 *Campfire girls on Station Island* (1930)
Alternative title: The wireless from the steam yacht; originally published as *The radio girls on Station Island*, 1922
4 *Campfire girls at Forest Lodge* (1930)
Alternative title: The strange hut in the swamp; originally published as *The radio girls at Forest Lodge*, 1924

Campfire Girls series
Sanderson, Margaret Love
1 *Campfire Girls at Hillside* (1913)
2 *Campfire Girls at Pine-Tree Camp* (1914)
3 *Campfire Girls at Top o' the World* (1916)
4 *Campfire Girls at Lookout Pass* (1917)
5 *Campfire Girls at Driftwood Heights* (1918)
6 *Campfire Girls in old Kentucky* (1919)
7 *Campfire girls on a yacht* (1920)
Co-author: Emma Keats
8 *Campfire Girls on Hurricane Island* (1921)

Campfire Girls series
Stewart, Jane L
see **Camp Fire Girls series**

Camping out series
Stephens, Charles Asbury
1 *Camping out, as recorded by Kit* (1867)
2 *Left on Labrador* (1872)
Alternative title: The cruise of the schooner-yacht Curlew
3 *Off to the geysers* (1872)
Alternative title: The young yachters in Iceland
4 *Lynx-hunting* (1872)
5 *Fox-hunting, as recorded by Raed* (1872)
6 *On the Amazons* (1872)
Alternative title: The cruise of the Rambler

Campion series
Allingham, Margery
see **Albert Campion series**
Batt, Elisabeth
see **Dinah Campion series**

Campus fever series
Wharton, Joanna
1 *Making the grade* (1985)
2 *All-nighter* (1985)
3 *Crash course* (1985)
4 *Illegal notion* (1985)
5 *Time out* (1986)
6 *Fast lane* (1986)
7 *Class act* (1986)
8 *Wild moves* (1986)

Campus series
Linn, James Weber
1 *This was life* (1936)
2 *Winds over the campus* (1936)

Camusfearna trilogy
Maxwell, Gavin
1 *Ring of bright water* (1960)
An adaptation for children is entitled *The otter's tale*
2 *Rocks remain* (1962)
3 *Raven seek thy brother* (1968)
Companion volumes: *The House of Elrig*, 1965, *The white island*, by John Lister-Kay, 1972; this sequence followed by the **Highland line series,** by Richard Frere

Can make and do series
Berry, Joy
1 *Great pretenders* (1977)
2 *More great pretenders* (1977)
3 *Puppets and pizazz* (1977)
4 *Puppet stages and props with pizazz* (1977)
5 *More puppets with pizazz* (1977)
6 *Rhythm and movement* (1977)
7 *Touch!* (1977)
8 *Listen!* (1977)
9 *Look!* (1978)
10 *Taste and smell* (1978)
11 *Game things* (1978)
12 *Seasonal and holiday happenings* (1978)

Canaan trilogy
Mackenzie, J Alexander
1 *Omega document* (1979)
2 *Jordan intercept* (1980)
3 *Rahab link* (1980)

Canada north series
Mowat, Farley
1 *Canada north* (1967)
2 *Great betrayal* (1976)
Canada north now

Canadian life series
McIntosh, Dave
Autobiography
1 *Seasons of my youth* (1984)
Life in rural Canada in the 1930s
2 *Terror in the starboard seat* (1980)
World War II memories of bombing missions over Germany
3 *Ottawa unbuttoned* (1987)
Alternative title: Who's running this country anyway?

Canadian North series
Mowat, Farley
Travels
1 *People of the deer* (1952)
2 *Desperate people* (1960)

Canadian prairie series
Grove, Frederick Philip
1 *Over prairie trails* (1922)
2 *Turn of the year* (1923)

Canadian trilogy
Wilson, Eric
1 *Murder on the Canadian* (1976)
2 *Vancouver nightmare* (1978)
3 *Terror in Winnipeg* (1979)

Canadian village life series
Redekopp, Elsa
1 *Wish and wonder* (1982)
A Manitoba village child
2 *Dream and wonder* (1986)
A child's view of Canadian village life

Canadian Western trilogy
Niven, Frederick
see **Flying years trilogy**

Canadians series
Wall, Robert Emmet
see **Newell family series**

Canals series
Bryce, Iris
1 *Canals are my home* (1979)
2 *Canals are my iris* (1982)

Canaris series
Winward, Walter
1 *Canaris fragments* (1982)
2 *Last and greatest art* (1983)

Canary series
Osgood, Mary A
see **Little Canary series**

Canavan series
Arthur, Burt
see **Johnny Canavan series**

Canby Hall series
Chase, Emily
1 *Roommates* (1983)
2 *Our roommate is missing* (1984)
3 *You're no friend of mine* (1984)
4 *Keeping secrets* (1984)
5 *Summer blues* (1984)
6 *Best friends forever* (1984)
7 *Four is a crowd* (1984)
8 *Big crush* (1985)
9 *Boy trouble* (1985)
10 *Make me a star* (1985)
11 *With friends like that* (1985)
12 *Who's the new girl* (1985)
13 *Here come the boys* (1985)
14 *What's a girl to do?* (1985)
15 *To tell the truth* (1985)
16 *Three of a kind* (1985)
17 *Graduation day* (1986)
18 *Making friends* (1986)
19 *One boy too many* (1986)
20 *Friends times three* (1987)
21 *Party time!* (1987)
22 *Troublemaker* (1987)
23 *But she's so cute* (1987)
24 *Princess who?* (1987)
25 *Ghosts of Canby Hall* (1987)
26 *Help wanted!* (1988)
27 *Roommate and the cowboy* (1988)
28 *Happy birthday, Jane* (1988)
29 *Roommate returns* (1988)
30 *Surprise!* (1988)
31 *Here comes the bridesmaid* (1988)
32 *Who's got* (1989)
Companion volumes: *Something old, something new*, 1986, *The almost summer carnival*, 1987

Canby Hall series
Hoh, Diane
1 *Girls of Canby Hall* (1987)
2 *Ghost of Canby Hall* (1987)

Candid recollections series
Nichols, Beverley
1 *Twenty five* (1926)
A young man's candid recollections of his elders and betters
2 *All I could never be* (1949)
Companion volume: *The unforgiving minute, some confessions from childhood to the outbreak of the Second World War*, 1978

Candle series
Ainsworth, Patricia
see **Burnley series**

Candy Kane series
Lambert, Janet
1 *Candy Kane* (1943)
2 *Whoa, Matilda!* (1944)
3 *One for the money* (1946)

Candy series
Daly, Ita
1 *Candy on the D.A.R.T.* (1989)
2 *Candy and Sharon Ole* (1990)

Candy series
Mamlok, Gwyneth
1 *Candy and Peppermint* (1965)
2 *Candy and the rocking horse* (1965)
3 *Candy and Ginger* (1966)
4 *Candy and the golden eagle* (1966)
5 *Candy in the tower* (1966)
6 *Candy and the pony* (1966)

Candy series
Reed, Maud Dorothy
1 *It was Candy's idea* (1955)
2 *Candy finds the clue* (1958)
3 *Candy does it again* (1960)
4 *Candy in the Alps* (1964)

Cane series
Courage, John
see **David Cane series**

Cannaways series
Shelby, Graham
1 *Cannaways* (1978)
2 *Cannaway concern* (1980)

Cannery Row series
Steinbeck, John
1 *Cannery Row* (1945)
2 *Sweet Thursday* (1954)

Cannon and Eddison series
Delving, Michael
see **Dave Cannon and Robert Eddison series**

Cannon series
Cannon, Curt
see **Curt Cannon series**

Cannon series
This sequence has three authors
Gallagher, Richard
1 *Murder by Gemini* (1971)
2 *Stewardess strangler* (1971)
Denver, Paul
3 *Golden bullet* (1973)
4 *Failing blonde* (1975)
Enefer, Douglas
5 *Farewell, little sister* (1978)
6 *Shoot-out* (1979)

Canoe and campfire series
Rathborne, Saint George
1 *Canoe mates in Canada* (1912)
Alternative title: Three boys afloat on the Saskatchewan
2 *Young fur takers* (1912)
Alternative title: Traps and trails in the wilderness
3 *Houseboat boys* (1912)
Alternative title: Drifting down to the sunny South
4 *Chums in Dixie* (1912)
Alternative title: The strange cruise of a motor boat
5 *Camp mates in Michigan* (1913)
Alternative title: With pack and paddle in the pine woods
6 *Rocky Mountain boys* (1913)
Alternative title: Camping in the big game country

Canon Tallis series
L'Engle, Madeleine
see **Poly and Charles O'Keefe series**

Canopus in Argus archives series
Lessing, Doris
1 *Re, colonised planet V, Shikasta* (1979)
Personal, psychological, historical documents relating to a visit by Johor, George Sherban, emissary, grade 9, 87th of the period of the last days
2 *Marriage between Zones Three, Four and Five* (1980)
As narrated by the chroniclers of Zone Three
3 *Sirian experiments* (1981)
The report by Ambien II of the Five
4 *Making of the representative for Planet Eight* (1982)
5 *Documents relating to the sentimental agents in the Volyen Empire* (1983)

Cantrell and Holden series
Chase, Elaine Raco
see **Roman Cantrell and Nikki Holden series**

Cantwell series
Boylan, Clare
see **Nan and Mary Cantwell series**

Canuck series
Moffatt, James
see **Johnny Canuck series**

Canute series
Williams, Patry
1 *I am Canute* (1938)
2 *God's warrior* (1942)

Canyon O'Grady series
Sharpe, Jon
1 *Dead men's trails* (1989)
2 *Silver slaughter* (1989)
3 *Machine gun madness* (1989)
4 *Shadow guns* (1989)
5 *Lincoln assignment* (1990)
6 *Comstock crazy* (1990)
7 *King of Colorado* (1990)
8 *Bleeding Kansas* (1990)
9 *Counterfeit madam* (1990)
10 *Great land swindle* (1990)
11 *Soldier's song* (1991)
12 *Railroad renegades* (1991)
13 *Assassin's trail* (1991)
14 *Colonel Death* (1991)
15 *Death ranch* (1991)
16 *Blood and gold* (1991)
17 *Killer's club* (1992)
18 *Blood bounty* (1992)
19 *Rio Grande ransom* (1992)
20 *California vengeance* (1992)
21 *Wyoming conspiracy* (1992)
22 *Colorado ambush* (1992)

23 *Louisiana gold race* (1993)
24 *Chicago six-guns* (1993)
25 *Rocky Mountain feud* (1993)

Canyon series
Caniff, Milton
see **Steve Canyon series**

Caoba series
Traven, B
see **Jungle series**

Cap Fog series
Edson, John Thomas
1 *You're a Texas Ranger, Alvin Fog* (1979)
2 *Rapido Clint* (1980)
3 *Justice of Company Z* (1980)
4 *Cap Fog, Texas Ranger, meet Mr J.G.Reeder* (1977)
5 *Return of Rapido Clint and Mr J.G.Reeder* (1984)
6 *Code of Dusty Fog* (1988)
7 *Rapido Clint strikes back* (1990)

Cap Kennedy series
Kern, Gregory
1 *Galaxy of the lost* (1973)
2 *Slave ship from Sergan* (1973)
3 *Monster of Metaleze* (1973)
4 *Enemy within the skull* (1974)
5 *Jewel of Jarhen* (1974)
6 *Seetee alert!* (1974)
7 *Gholan Gate* (1974)
8 *Eater of worlds* (1974)
9 *Earth enslaved* (1974)
10 *Planet of dread* (1974)
11 *Spawn of Laban* (1974)
12 *Genetic buccaneer* (1974)
13 *World aflame* (1974)
14 *Ghosts of Epidoris* (1975)
15 *Mimics of Dephene* (1975)
16 *Beyond the galactic lens* (1975)
17 *Galactiad* (1983)

Cap Millett series
Bowden, Jim
1 *Cap* (1978)
2 *Dollars of death* (1979)
3 *Shadow of Eagle Rock* (1982)
4 *Incident at Elm Creek* (1984)
5 *Hangmen's trail* (1986)

Cape Cod series
Bassett, Sara Ware
1 *Taming of Zenas Henry* (1915)
2 *Wayfarers at the Angels* (1917)
3 *Harbor Road* (1919)
4 *Flood tide* (1921)
5 *Granite and clay* (1922)
6 *Green dolphin* (1926)
7 *Bayberry Lane* (1931)
8 *Twin lights* (1932)
9 *Shiftinf sands* (1933)
10 *Turning tide* (1934)
11 *Hidden shoals* (1935)
12 *Eternal deeps* (1937)
13 *Shining headlands* (1937)
14 *Ocean heritage* (1940)
15 *White sail* (1949)

Capital crime series
Truman, Margaret
1 *Murder in the White House* (1980)
2 *Murder on Capitol Hill* (1981)
3 *Murder in the Supreme Court* (1982)
4 *Murder in the Smithsonian* (1983)
5 *Murder on Embassy Row* (1984)
6 *Murder at the FBI* (1985)
7 *Murder in Georgetown* (1986)
8 *Murder in the CIA* (1988)
9 *Murder at the Kennedy Center* (1989)
10 *Murder at the National Cathedral* (1990)
11 *Murder at the Pentagon* (1992)
12 *Murder on the Potomac* (1994)

Capitan Tiburon series
Silver, Richard
see **Captain Shark series**

Cap'n Bill and Trot series
Baum, Lyman Frank
see **Trot and Cap'n Bill series**

Cap'n Eri series
Lincoln, Joseph Crosby
see **Captain Eri series**

Cappy Ricks series
Kyne, Peter Bernard
1 *Cappy Ricks* (1916)
Alternative title: The subjugation of Matt Peasley
2 *Cappy Ricks retires* (1922)
3 *Cappy Ricks comes back* (1934)
4 *Cappy Ricks special* (1936)

Capri series
Mackenzie, Compton
1 *Vestal fire* (1927)
2 *Extraordinary women* (1928)

Capricorn series
Winslow, Pauline Glen
see **Superintendent Merlin Capricorn series**

Capsella series
Clarke, Judith
see **Al Capsella series**

Capshaw series
Stevenson, Drew
see **Sarah Capshaw series**

Captain Adam Horne series
Hill, Porter
1 *Bombay Marines* (1985)
2 *War chest* (1986)
3 *China flyer* (1987)

Captain Al Scabbard series
Crabb, Lawrence James
1 *Adventures of Captain Al Scabbard, no 1* (1981)
2 *Adventures of Captain Al Scabbard, no 2* (1981)

Captain Alexander Sheridan series
Stuart, Vivian
American editions published under the name V A Stuart
1 *Like victors and lords* (1964)
Victors and lords
2 *Brave captains* (1968)
3 *Sepoy mutiny* (1973)
Mutiny in Meerut
Mutiny at dawn
4 *Cannons of Lucknow* (1974)
Battle for Lucknow
5 *Heroic garrison* (1975)
6 *Escape from hell* (1976)
Sailors on horseback

Captain America series
This sequence has three authors
Binder, Otto
1 *Avengers battle the earth-wrecker* (1967)
White, Ted
2 *Great gold steal* (1968)
Silva, Joseph
3 *Holocaust for hire* (1979)

Captain Andrew Torrent series
Cores, Lucy
1 *Painted for the kill* (1943)
2 *Corpse de ballet* (1944)

Captain Andy and Sue McVeigh series
Macveigh, Sue
1 *Grand Central murder* (1939)
2 *Murder under construction* (1939)
3 *Streamlined murder* (1940)
4 *Corpse and the three ex-husbands* (1941)

Captain Apache series
Whitman, Sidney Edgerton
see **Captain Cullah Burnett series**

Captain Ashe series
Langoulant, Allan
1 *Ashe of the outback* (1992)
Co-authors: David Turton and Norman Jorgensen
2 *Ashe on parade* (1992)

Captain Barnaby series
White, Leslie Turner
1 *Harness bull* (1937)
Vice squad
2 *Homicide* (1937)

Captain Beaky and his band series
Lloyd, Jeremy
1 *Captain Beaky* (1976)
2 *Trial of Captain Beaky* (1980)
3 *Hissing Sid and the swimming lesson* (1980)
4 *Captain Beaky and the haunted wood* (1980)
5 *Search for Hissing Sid* (1980)
6 *Captain Beaky, volume 2* (1981)
7 *Woodland gospels according to Captain Beaky and his band* (1984)

Captain Ben Lucias series
Howes, Royce
1 *Night of the garter murder* (1937)
2 *Death dupes a lady* (1937)
3 *Murder at Maneuvers* (1938)
4 *Nasty name murders* (1939)
5 *Death rides a hobby* (1939)
6 *Case of the copy-hook killing* (1945)

Captain Black series
Pemberton, Max
1 *Iron pirate* (1891)
Shadow on the sea
A plain tale of strange happenings of the sea
2 *Captain Black* (1911)
A romance of the nameless ship

Captain Blood series
Sabatini, Rafael
1 *Captain Blood* (1922)
2 *Chronicles of Captain Blood* (1931)
Captain Blood returns
3 *Fortunes of Captain Blood* (1936)
One volume edition entitled *Saga of the sea*, 1953

Captain Blossom series
Nelson, Michael
1 *Captain Blossom* (1973)
Recollections of his struggle against the Third Reich and the British Army
2 *Captain Blossom soldiers on* (1974)
Alternative title: Run away, someone's coming

Captain Bowker series
Parkman, Sydney
1 *Plunder bar* (1934)
2 *Ship ashore* (1936)
3 *Facts about Floyd* (1938)
4 *Passing of Tony Blount* (1939)
5 *Captain Bowker* (1947)

Captain Cain series
Westerman, Percy Francis
1 *Pirate submarine* (1923)
2 *Captain Cain* (1924)

Captain Carew series
Broster, Dorothy Kathleen
1 *Sea without a haven* (1941)
2 *Captain's lady* (1947)

Captain Cobwebb series
Boshell, Gordon
1 *Captain Cobwebb* (1967)
2 *Captain Cobwebb's cowboys* (1968)
3 *Captain Cobwebb's cobra* (1971)
4 *Captain Cobwebb's adventurers* (1973)
5 *Captain Cobwebb and the red transistor* (1974)
6 *Captain Cobwebb and the Crustaks* (1975)
7 *Captain Cobwebb and the Chinese unicorn* (1976)
8 *Captain Cobwebb and the mischief man* (1977)
9 *Captain Cobwebb and the Quogs* (1978)
10 *Captain Cobwebb and the magic drops* (1979)
11 *Captain Cobwebb and the amazing cloud* (1980)

Captain Colin Huntington series
Condon, Richard
1 *Arigato* (1972)
2 *Bandicoot* (1978)

Captain Colin series
Wood, Clement
see **Inspector Colin series**

Captain Colson series
White, Alan
see **Commando series**

Captain Comstock series
Bishop, Gibs
1 *Lieutenant Comstock, U.S. Marines* (1922)
2 *Captain Comstock, USMC* (1923)

Captain Coppernob series
Bourne, Lawrence R
see **Coppernob series**

Captain Courtney Brade series
Wolffe, Katherine
1 *Attic room* (1942)
2 *Death's long shadow* (1946)

Captain Cullah Burnett series
Whitman, Sidney Edgerton
1 *Captain Apache* (1965)
2 *Change of command* (1966)

Captain Dack series
Meriton, Peter
1 *Captain Dack* (1939)
2 *Conspiracy* (1945)
3 *Plunder* (1948)

Captain Daley's crew series
Massey, Craig
1 *Captain Daley's crew and the missing houseboat* (1951)
2 *Captain Daley's crew at Thunderhead Lake* (1952)
3 *Captain Daley's crew in danger* (1953)
4 *Captain Daley's crew and peg-legged tramp* (1954)
5 *Captain Daley's crew and the jungle ship* (1957)

Captain Davy series
Bray, Donald
1 *Between two shores* (1984)
2 *Captain's wife* (1985)

Captain Demosthenes H de Goede trilogy
Leroux, Etienne
see **Welgevonden trilogy**

Captain Denzil Grigson series
Broome, Adam
see **Commissioner Denzil Grigson series**

Captain Deville McKeene series
Walker, Rowland
1 *Deville McKeene, the British ace* (1919)
2 *Exploits of Captain McKeene* (1926)

Captain Dormer series
Mottram, Ralph Hale
1 *Crime at Vanderlynden's* (1926)
2 *Our Mister Dormer* (1927)
3 *Boroughmonger* (1929)
4 *Castle Island* (1931)
5 *Banquet* (1934)
Companion volume: *The headless hound*, 1931

Captain Duncan Maclain series
Kendrick, Baynard
1 *Last express* (1937)
2 *Whistling hangman* (1937)
3 *Odor of violets* (1941)
Odour of violets
Eyes in the mist
4 *Blind man's bluff* (1943)
5 *Death knell* (1945)
6 *Out of control* (1945)
7 *You die today* (1952)
8 *Blind allies* (1954)
9 *Reservations for death* (1957)
10 *Clear and present danger* (1958)
11 *Aluminum turtle* (1960)
Spear gun murders
12 *Frankincense and murder* (1961)
Omnibus volumes: *Make mine Maclain*, 1947, *Murderer who wanted more*, 1951

Captain Edward Trapp series
Callison, Brian
1 *Trapp's war* (1974)
2 *Trapp's peace* (1979)
3 *Trapp and World War III* (1988)
4 *Crocodile Trapp* (1993)

Captain Eri series
Lincoln, Joseph Crosby
1 *Cap'n Eri* (1904)
A story of the coast
2 *Old Home House* (1907)

Captain Fantom series
Underhill, Charles
1 *Captain Fantom* (1978)
2 *Forging of Fantom* (1979)

Captain Felonius series
Cowley, Joy
1 *Captain Felonius* (1986)
2 *Happy birthday, Mrs Felonius* (1993)

Captain Firebrace series
Seafarer
1 *Captain Firebrace* (1958)
2 *Firebrace and the Java Queen* (1958)
3 *Captain Firebrace and Father Kelly* (1959)
4 *Smuggler's pay for Firebrace* (1959)

Captain Flint series
Craigie, Dorothy
1 *Captain Flint, detective* (1957)
2 *Captain Flint to the rescue* (1958)
3 *Captain Flint kidnapped* (1959)
4 *Captain Flint shipwrecked* (1960)

Captain Flynn series
Laurie-Long, Ernest
1 *Young Flynn* (1937)
2 *Fortunes of Flynn* (1938)
3 *Captain Flynn* (1939)
4 *Vengeance of Flynn* (1942)
5 *Flynn of the Martagon* (1934)
6 *Flynn, A.B.* (1936)
7 *Son of Flynn* (1940)
8 *Flynn's sampler* (1945)
9 *Lieutenant Flynn, RN* (1948)
10 *Captain Flynn, retd.* (1950)
11 *Ould Flynn* (1953)
12 *Blindness of Flynn* (1959)
13 *Captain Flynn, sheriff* (1962)

Captain Fox Elton series
White, Ared
1 *Spy net* (1931)
2 *Agent B-seven* (1934)

Captain Franklin Hatcher series
Merritt, Don
1 *Hatch's island* (1986)
2 *Hatch's conspiracy* (1987)
3 *Hatch's mission* (1987)

Captain Frass series
Chancellor, John
1 *Frass* (1929)
2 *Return of Frass* (1930)

Captain Future series
This sequence has three authors; its order is that of the original pulp publication from 1940 to 1946
Hamilton, Edmond
1 *Captain Future and the Space Emperor* (1969)
2 *Calling Captain Future* (1969)
3 *Captain Future's challenge* (1969)
4 *Galaxy mission* (1969)
5 *Magician of Mars* (1969)
6 *Quest beyond the stars* (1969)
7 *Outlaws of the moon* (1969)
8 *Comet kings* (1969)
9 *Planets in peril* (1969)
Sterling, Brett
10 *Tenth planet* (1969)
11 *Danger planet* (1968)
Wellman, Manly Wade
12 *Solar invasion* (1968)
Hamilton, Edmond
13 *Outlaw world* (1969)

Captain George Honegger series
Strange, John Stephen
1 *Murder gives a lovely light* (1941)
2 *All men are liars* (1948)
Come to judgment
3 *Eye witness* (1961)

Captain George Nash series
Butler, Ragan
1 *Captain Nash and the honour of England* (1975)
2 *Captain Nash and the Wroth inheritance* (1976)

Captain Gevert series
Kaufmann, Herbert
1 *Lost Sahara trail* (1955)
A story of men, camels, thirst and sand; original edition entitled *Der verlorene Karawanenweg*
2 *[Hammelpiste]* (1957)
No English edition
3 *City under the desert sands* (1957)
Original edition entitled *Die Stadt unter dem Wustensand*

Captain Grandison series
Bolt, Ben
1 *Mystery hand* (1932)
2 *Green arrow* (1933)

Captain Grant's children series
Verne, Jules
1 *Voyage round the world in search of castaways* (1868)
Among the cannibals
Castaways
Original edition entitled *Les enfants du Capitaine Grant*; also published in three volumes
1.1 *Mysterious document* (1868)
1.2 *On the track* (1868)
1.3 *Among the cannibals* (1868)
2 *Mysterious island* (1875)
Also published in three volumes
2.1 *Dropped from the clouds* (1875)
2.2 *Abandoned* (1875)
Marooned
2.3 *Secret of the island* (1875)

Captain Gregory Dangerfield series
Lloyd, Jeremy
1 *Further adventures of Captain Gregory Dangerfield* (1973)
2 *Continuing adventures of Captain Gregory Dangerfield* (1979)

Captain Gridley Nelson series
Fenisong, Ruth
1 *Murder needs a face* (1942)
2 *Murder needs a name* (1942)
3 *Butler died in Brooklyn* (1943)
4 *Murder runs a fever* (1943)
5 *Grim rehearsal* (1950)
6 *Dead yesterday* (1951)
7 *Deadlock* (1952)
8 *Wench is dead* (1953)
9 *Miscast for murder* (1954)
Too lovely to live
10 *Bite the hand* (1956)
Blackmailer
11 *Death of the party* (1958)
12 *But not forgotten* (1960)
Sinister assignment
13 *Dead weight* (1962)

Captain Gringo series
Thorne, Ramsay
1 *Renegade* (1979)
2 *Blood runner* (1979)
3 *Fear merchant* (1980)
4 *Death hunter* (1980)
5 *Macumba killer* (1980)
6 *Panama gunner* (1980)
7 *Death in high places* (1981)
8 *Over the Andes to hell* (1981)
9 *Hell raider* (1981)
10 *Great game* (1981)
11 *Citadel of death* (1982)
12 *Badlands brigade* (1982)
13 *Mahogany pirates* (1982)
14 *Harvest of death* (1982)
15 *Terror trail* (1982)
16 *Mexican marauder* (1982)
17 *Slaughter in Sinaloa* (1983)
18 *Cavern of doom* (1983)
19 *Hellfire in Honduras* (1983)
20 *Shots at sunrise* (1983)
21 *River of revenge* (1983)
22 *Payoff in Panama* (1983)
23 *Volcano of violence* (1984)
24 *Guatemala gunman* (1984)
25 *High sea showdown* (1984)
26 *Blood on the border* (1984)
27 *Savage safari* (1984)
28 *Slave raiders* (1984)
29 *Murder in Merida* (1985)
30 *Mayhem at Mission Bay* (1985)
31 *Shootout in Segovia* (1985)
32 *Death over Darien* (1985)
33 *Costa Rican carnage* (1985)
34 *Golden express* (1986)
35 *Standoff in the sky* (1986)
36 *Guns for Garcia* (1986)

Captain Hatteras series
Verne, Jules
see **Adventures of Captain Hatteras series**

Captain Havoc series
Healey, Ben
1 *Captain Havoc* (1977)
2 *Havoc in the Indies* (1979)

Captain Homer Clay series
Lauben, Philip
1 *Nice sound alibi* (1981)
2 *Surfeit of alibis* (1982)
3 *Sort of tragedy* (1985)

Captain Horn series
Stockton, Frank Richard
1 *Adventures of Captain Horn* (1895)
2 *Mrs Cliff's yacht* (1896)

Captain Jack Aubrey series
O'Brien, Patrick
1 *Master and commander* (1969)
2 *Post captain* (1972)
3 *Desolation Island* (1978)

Captain Jack Carter and Brigadier Dougal Munro series
Higgins, Jack
see **Brigadier Dougal Munro and Captain Jack Carter series**

Captain Jack Lorimer series
Standish, Winn
1 *Captain Jack Lorimer* (1906)
Alternative title: Young athletes of Millvale High
2 *Jack Lorimer's champions* (1907)
Alternative title: Sports on land and lake
3 *Jack Lorimer's holidays* (1908)
Alternative title: Millvale High in camp
4 *Jack Lorimer's substitute* (1909)
Alternative title: The acting captain of the team
5 *Jack Lorimer, freshman* (1912)
Alternative title: From Millvale High to Exmouth

Captain James Donald Macgregor series
Mason, Robert
1 *Cairo communique* (1942)
2 *More news from the Middle East* (1943)

Captain James Hind series
Foxall, Raymond
1 *Devil's smile* (1960)
2 *Devil's spawn* (1965)

Captain James Rollo series
Bushby, John
1 *Spanish general* (1981)
2 *Mondego Bay* (1983)

Captain January series
Richards, Laura Elizabeth
1 *Captain January* (1891)
2 *Star bright* (1927)

Captain John Cunningham series
Hammond, Gerald
1 *Dog in the dark* (1989)
2 *Doghouse* (1989)
3 *Whose dog are you?* (1990)
4 *Give a dog a name* (1992)
5 *Curse of the cockers* (1993)

Captain John Hunter series
Godwin, Felix
1 *Captain John Hunter series* (1964)
2 *Towers od pain* (1966)

Captain John Valcourt Justice series
Forrest, Anthony
1 *Captain Justice* (1981)
2 *Pandora secret* (1982)
3 *Secret agent against Napoleon* (1983)
4 *Balance of dangers* (1984)

Captain John Walton series
Frost, Kelman Dalgety
1 *Drinker of the wind* (1960)
2 *Sahara hostage* (1962)

Captain Jonas series
Wheeler, Anthony George
1 *Captain Jonas feeds the rary bird* (1986)
2 *Captain Jonas shelters the Gonk family* (1986)

Captain Jose da Silva series
Fish, Robert Lloyd
1 *Fugitive* (1962)
2 *Isle of the snakes* (1963)
3 *Shrunken head* (1963)
4 *Diamond bubble* (1965)
5 *Brazilian sleigh ride* (1965)
6 *Always kill a stranger* (1967)
7 *Bridge that went nowhere* (1968)

8 *Xavier affair* (1969)
9 *Green hell treasure* (1971)
10 *Trouble in Paradise* (1975)

Captain Justice series
Forrest, Anthony
see **Captain John Valcourt Justice series**

Captain Kennedy series
Kern, Gregory
see **Cap Kennedy series**

Captain Kenyon series
Macdonnell, James Edmond
1 *Convert* (1966)
2 *Down the throat* (1967)
3 *Combat assignment* (1967)

Captain Ketchup series
Stern, Simon
see **Astonishing adventures of Captain Ketchup series**

Captain Lingard series
Conrad, Joseph
1 *Rescue* (1920)
2 *Outcast of the islands* (1896)
3 *Almayer's folly* (1895)
A story of an Eastern river

Captain Lorrington King series
Johns, William Earl
see **Gimlet series**

Captain Lucy series
Havard, Aline
see **Lucy Gordon series**

Captain Madirankowitch series
Kruss, James
1 *Happy Islands behind the winds* (1966)
Original edition entitled *Die glucklichen Inseln hinter dem Winde*, Band I
2 *Return to the Happy Islands* (1967)
Original edition entitled *Die glucklichen Inseln hinter dem Winde*, Band II

Captain Mallory series
Maclean, Alistair
see **Navarone series**

Captain Martinus Harinxma trilogy
De Hartog, Jan
1 *Captain* (1966)
2 *Commodore* (1986)
3 *Centurion* (1989)

Captain McBain series
Stables, Gordon
1 *Cruise of the Snowbird* (1882)
2 *Wild adventures round the Pole* (1884)

Captain Merton Heimrich series
Lockridge, Frances
see **Inspector Merton Heimrich series**

Captain Mesquite series
Curry, Tom
1 *Captain Mesquite* (1941)
2 *Comstock Lode* (1941)
3 *Buffalo hunters* (1941)
4 *Mormon trail* (1942)
5 *Guns of the Sioux* (1945)
6 *Marshal of Wichita* (1946)
7 *Blood on the plains* (1947)
8 *Riding for Custer* (1947)

Captain Mettle series
Macnell, James
1 *Captain Mettle, VC* (1955)
2 *Mettle dives deep* (1956)
3 *Mettle at Woomera* (1957)

Captain Michael Triggington series
Allum, Tom
1 *Introducing Trigger* (1953)
2 *Trigger blazes the trail* (1954)

Captain Moffat series
Cousins, Edmund George
1 *Come like a storm* (1950)
2 *To comfort the signora* (1951)

Captain Najork series
Hoban, Russell
1 *How Tom beat Captain Najork and his hired sportsmen* (1974)
2 *Near thing for Captain Najork* (1975)

Captain Nemo series
Verne, Jules
1 *Twenty thousand leagues under the sea* (1870)
Original edition entitled *Vingt mille lieues sous les mers*; adaptation by Tom Barling, 1977
2 *Mysterious island* (1874)
Original edition entitled *L'ile mysterieuse*; also published in three parts
2.1 *Dropped from the clouds* (1874)
2.2 *Abandoned* (1874)
Marooned
2.3 *Secret of the island* (1874)

Captain O'Donnell series
Eyre, Donald Cuthbert
1 *Foxes have holes* (1948)
2 *Drumbeat* (1952)

Captain Owen Kettle series
Hyne, Charles John Cutcliffe
1 *Honour of thieves* (1895)
Little red captain
2 *Paradise coal-boat* (1897)
3 *Adventures of Captain Cattle* (1898)
4 *Further adventures of Captain Kettle* (1899)
Master of fortune
5 *Captain Kettle, KCB* (1903)
More adventures of Captin Kettle, KCB
6 *McTodd* (1903)
7 *Kate Meredith, financier* (1907)
Kate Meredith
8 *Escape agents* (1911)
9 *Marriage of Kettle* (1912)
Marriage of Captain Kettle
10 *Firemen hot* (1914)
11 *Captain Kettle on the war-path* (1916)
12 *Captain Kettle's bit* (1918)
13 *Red herrings* (1918)
Short stories
14 *Reverend Captain Kettle* (1925)
15 *President Kettle* (1929)
16 *Mister Kettle, third mate* (1931)
17 *Captain Kettle, ambassador* (1932)
18 *Ivory valley* (1932)
Also stories in *Derelict*, 1901, also published in a revised edition as *Mister Horrocks, purser*

Captain Peg-Leg series
Dawlish, Peter
1 *Captain Peg-Leg's war* (1939)
2 *Peg-Leg and the fur pirates* (1939)
3 *Peg-Leg and the invaders* (1940)
4 *Peg-Leg sweeps the sea* (1940)

Captain Percival Merewether series
Meacham, Ellis Kirby
1 *East Indiaman* (1968)
2 *On the company's service* (1971)
3 *For king and company* (1976)

Captain Peter Bentley series
Macdonnell, James Edmond
This sequence includes those works which have so far been identified as including the series character; however since there is much overlapping of characters in this author's numerous novels it is likely that this character will be found in other works
1 *Coffin Island* (1958)
2 *Command* (1958)
3 *Alarm, E-boats!* (1958)
4 *Battle ensign* (1958)
5 *Enemy in sight* (1958)
6 *Killer ship* (1958)
7 *Presumed sunk* (1958)
8 *Secret weapon* (1959)
9 *Surgeon* (1959)
10 *Coxswain* (1960)
11 *Escort ship* (1960)
12 *Blind eye* (1961)
13 *Battle fire* (1961)
14 *Lesson* (1961)
15 *Ordeal* (1961)
16 *Rocky* (1961)
17 *Battle line* (1962)
18 *Flotilla leader* (1962)
19 *Away boarders* (1962)
20 *Long haul* (1962)
21 *Conflict* (1963)
22 *Decision* (1963)
23 *Fire one!* (1963)
24 *Repel boarders* (1963)
25 *Abandon ship* (1963)
26 *Creeping attack* (1964)
27 *Big wind* (1964)
28 *Course to intercept* (1964)
29 *Killer group* (1964)
30 *Mistake* (1964)
31 *Pawn* (1964)
32 *Sabotage!* (1964)
33 *Flashpoint* (1965)
34 *Loom of ice* (1966)
35 *Snake boats* (1967)
36 *Unforgiving sea* (1967)
37 *Misfits* (1967)
38 *High command* (1968)
39 *Hunter-killer* (1968)
40 *Mission hopeless* (1968)
41 *Execute!* (1969)
42 *Battle hymn* (1970)
43 *Worst enemy* (1971)
44 *Verge of hell* (1972)
45 *Chain of violence* (1972)
46 *Trap* (1972)
47 *Iron claw* (1973)
48 *Council of captains* (1974)
49 *Operational immediate* (1975)

Captain Polly series
Jackson, Gabrielle Emilie
1 *Captain Polly of Annapolis* (1910)
2 *Captain Polly, an Annapolis co-ed* (1911)

Captain Prem Narayan series
Casberg, Melvin A
1 *Death stalks the Punjab* (1980)
2 *Five rivers to death* (1982)
3 *Dowry of death* (1984)

Captain Pugwash series
Ryan, John
1 *Captain Pugwash* (1957)
2 *Pugwash aloft* (1958)
3 *Pugwash and the ghost ship* (1962)
4 *Pugwash in the Pacific* (1973)
5 *Pugwash and the sea monster* (1976)
6 *Pugwash the smuggler* (1976)
7 *Captain Pugwash and the elephant* (1976)
8 *Captain Pugwash and the new ship* (1976)
9 *Captain Pugwash and the ruby* (1976)
10 *Captain Pugwash and the treasure chest* (1976)
11 *Pugwash and the buried treasure* (1980)
12 *Captain Pugwash and the mutiny* (1982)
13 *Pugwash and the fancy dress party* (1982)
14 *Quest of the golden handsake* (1983)
A cartoon book
15 *Pugwash and the wreckers* (1984)
16 *Pugwash and the midnight feast* (1984)
Numbers 12 and 16 also published in one volume 1985
17 *Battle of Bunkum Bay* (1984)
Companion volume: *Captain Pugwash cartoon book*, 1977

Captain Pyanfar series
Cherryh, Carolyn Janice
see **Chanur series**

Captain Redder series
Neuman, Fredric
1 *Seclusion room* (1978)
2 *Maneuvers* (1983)
Manoeuvres

Captain Richard Bolitho series
Kent, Alexander
1 *Richard Bolitho, midshipman* (1975)
2 *Midshipman Bolitho and the Avenger* (1978)
Numbers 1 and 2 also published in one volume entitled *Midshipman Bolitho*, 1991
3 *Stand into danger* (1980)
4 *In gallant company* (1977)
5 *Sloop of war* (1972)
Numbers 3-5 also published in one volume entitled *Bolitho omnibus*, 1991
6 *To glory we steer* (1968)
7 *Command a king's ship* (1973)
8 *Passage to mutiny* (1976)
9 *With all despatch* (1988)
10 *Form line of battle* (1969)
11 *Enemy in sight!* (1970)
12 *Flag captain* (1971)
13 *Signal, close action!* (1974)
14 *Inshore squadron* (1978)
15 *Tradition of victory* (1981)
16 *Success to the brave* (1983)
17 *Colours aloft!* (1986)
18 *Honour this day* (1987)
19 *Only victor* (1990)
Numbers 17-19 also published in one volume entitled *Bolitho*, 1993
20 *Beyond the reef* (1992)
21 *Darkening sea* (1993)

Captain Rizzi series
Sterling, Thomas
1 *Evil of the day* (1955)
Murder in Venice
2 *Silent siren* (1958)

Captain Samson series
Douglas, Gavin
1 *Rough passage* (1936)
Tall man
2 *Obstinate Captain Samson* (1936)
3 *Captain Samson, A.B.* (1937)

Captain Scarlet series
Theydon, John
1 *Captain Scarlet and the Mysterons* (1967)
Captain Scarlet
2 *Captain Scarlet and the silent saboteur* (1967)

Captain series
Leyland, Eric
1 *First adventure* (1949)
2 *Dead man's gold* (1947)
3 *Captain rides again* (1950)
4 *Captain intervenes* (1951)
5 *Captain strikes back* (1952)
6 *Captain on guard* (1952)

Captain Shark series
Silver, Richard
1 *By pirate's blood* (1975)
2 *Jaws of death* (1975)

Captain Shelby series
Robb, John
see **Shelby series**

Captain Smith series
Edingtons
1 *Studio murder mystery* (1929)
2 *House of the vanishing goblets* (1930)
Murder to music
3 *Monk's hood murders* (1931)

Captive series
Michaels, Fern
1 *Captive passions* (1977)
2 *Captive embraces* (1979)
3 *Captive splendors* (1980)
4 *Captive innocence* (1981)

Car wars adventure gamebook series
This sequence has four authors
Jackson, Steven Gary
1 *Battle road* (1986)
2 *Fuel's gold* (1986)
Co-authors: Creede Lambard and Sharleen Lambard
Haring, Scott D
3 *Dueltrack* (1987)
Lambard, Creede
4 *Badlands run* (1987)
Haring, Scott D
5 *Green circle blues* (1987)

Caran d'ache series
Plait, Dominique
see **Sebastian series**

Caravan family series
Blyton, Enid
1 *Caravan family* (1945)
2 *Run-Abouts' holiday* (1955)
3 *Four in a family* (1956)

Caravan series
Bellhouse, Lucy Wilered
1 *Caravan children* (1935)
2 *Caravan again* (1940)
3 *Caravan goes west* (1948)
4 *Caravan goes home* (1951)
5 *Christmas caravan* (1955)
6 *Winter caravan* (1960)

Caravan series
Finlay, Eileen
1 *Caravan passes* (1941)
2 *Full turn* (1942)
3 *Caravan turns* (1949)

Caravan series
Young, Emily Hilda
1 *Caravan island* (1940)
2 *River holiday* (1942)

Caraway series
Herbert, Alan Patrick
see **Admiral of the Fleet, Earl of Caraway series**

Carberry series
Rinehart, Mary Roberts
see **Tish series**
Symons, Beryl
see **Jane Carberry series**

Carbo series
Quartermain, James
see **Raven series**

Carbonari revolt series
Neumann, Alfred
1 *Rebels* (1927)
Original edition entitled *Rebellen*
2 *Guerra* (1928)
Original edition entitled *Guerra*

Carbonel series
Sleigh, Barbara
1 *Carbonel* (1955)
Carbonel, the king of the cats
2 *Kingdom of Carbonel* (1959)
3 *Carbonel and Calidor* (1978)

Carcoola series
Handford, Nourma
1 *Carcooola* (1950)
2 *Carcooola adventure* (1952)
3 *Carcoola holiday* (1953)
4 *Carcoola backstage* (1956)

Cardby series
Hume, David
see **Mick Cardby series**

Cardiff series
Gray, Dulcie
see **Inspector Cardiff series**

Cardigan series
Barrett, Monte
see **Peter Cardigan series**

Cardigan series
Chambers, Robert William
1 *Cardigan* (1901)
2 *Maid-at-arms* (1902)
3 *Hidden children* (1914)
4 *Painted minx* (1930)

Cardigan series
Rico, Don
see **Burgess Cardigan series**

Cardiman and Quong series
De Fraga, Geoff
see **Peter Cardiman and Quong series**

Cardinal Henry Beaufort series
Baker, James
1 *Gleaming dawn* (1896)
2 *Cardinal's page* (1898)

Cardinal series
Walton, Marion
see **Inspector James Cardinal series**

Cardinal sins and virtues series
Greeley, Andrew Moran
1 *Cardinal sins* (1981)
2 *Cardinal virtues* (1990)

Carding series
Collins, Gilbert
see **Hugh Carding series**

Cardles Farm series
Wall, Adrian
1 *Cardles Farm* (1945)
2 *Cardles Farm again* (1946)
3 *Cardles Farm once again* (1948)

Cardolini series
Gerrity, David
see **Frank Cardolini series**

Career adventure series
Martin, Robert
1 *October story* (1959)
2 *April story* (1960)
3 *September story* (1960)

Career series
Palmer, Bernard
1 *Student nurse* (1960)
Co-author: Marjorie Palmer
2 *Barbara Nichols, fifth grade teacher* (1960)
Co-author: Marjorie Palmer
3 *Big season* (1960)
4 *Mystery of the musty ledger* (1960)
5 *Peggy Archer, missionary candidate* (1961)
6 *Brad Foster, engineer* (1962)
7 *Karen Simms, private secretary* (1963)
Co-author: Marjorie Palmer
8 *Randy Warren, first term missionary* (1963)
9 *Cal Henderson, M.D.* (1963)
10 *Jim Shelton, radio engineer* (1964)
11 *Sandra Emerson, R.N.* (1966)
Co-author: Marjorie Palmer
12 *Lee Sloan, missionary pilot* (1966)
13 *Dennis Harper, missionary journalist* (1966)

Cares family series
Spykman, Elizabeth Choate
1 *Lemon and a star* (1955)
2 *Wild angel* (1957)
3 *Terrible, horrible Edie* (1960)
4 *Edie on the warpath* (1966)

Caretakers series
Dehn, Olive
see **Meredith children series**

Carew series
Broster, Dorothy Kathleen
see **Captain Carew series**

Carey Ashton and Kellogg Brown series
Stuart, Becky
see **Kellogg Brown and Carey Ashton series**

Carey Brent series
Glidden, Minna Wesselhoft
1 *Death strikes home* (1937)
Come dwell with death
2 *Long Island murders* (1937)

Carey family series
Welch, Ronald
1 *Knight crusader* (1954)
Set during the 12th century
2 *Hawk* (1967)
A story of seafaring life in Elizabethan times
3 *For the King* (1961)
A story of the Royalist cause in the English Civil War
4 *Captain of Dragoons* (1956)
A story of Marlborough's army
5 *Mohawk Valley* (1958)
A story of Wolfe's siege of Quebec
6 *Escape from France* (1960)
A story of the French Revolution
7 *Captain of Foot* (1959)
Set during the Peninsular War
8 *Ensign Carey* (1976)
9 *Nicholas Carey* (1963)
Set during the Crimean War
10 *Tank commander* (1972)
Set during the First World War

Carey series
Hoult, Norah
see **Augusta Hortense Carey series**
Lounsberry, Lionel
see **Kit Carey series**
Overton, Jenny
see **Creed series**

Carey trilogy
Greenfield, Irving A
see **Tom Carey trilogy**

Cargoe series
Peacey, Seton
see **William Cargoe series**

Caribbean series
Agard, John
1 *I din do nuttin, and other poems* (1983)
2 *Say it again, Granny!* (1986)
Twenty poems from Caribbean proverbs

Caribbean series
Lamming, George
1 *In the castle of my skin* (1953)
Set in a village in Barbados
2 *Emigrants* (1954)
3 *Water with berries* (1971)

Caribbean series
Nicole, Christopher
see **West Indies series**

Caribbean stories series
Sherlock, Philip
1 *Iguana's tail* (1969)
Crick crack stories
2 *Ears and tails and common sense* (1974)

Carl and Anna series
Frank, Leonhard
1 *Carl and Anna* (1927)
Original edition entitled *Karl und Anna*
2 *Brother and sister* (1929)
Original edition entitled *Bruder und Schwester*

Carl and Cathy series
Johnston, Dorothy Grunbock
see **Wagon train series**

Carl Burns series
Crider, Bill
1 *One dead dean* (1988)
2 *Dying voices* (1989)
3 *Dead on the island* (1991)
4 *Dangerous thing* (1994)

Carl Crader and Earl Jazine series
Hoch, Edward Dentinger
1 *Transvection machine* (1971)
2 *Fellowship of the hand* (1973)
3 *Frankenstein factory* (1975)

Carl Good series
Saber, Robert O
1 *Scented flesh* (1950)
2 *Deadly lover* (1951)
3 *Dove* (1951)
Chicago woman
4 *Murder doll* (1952)
5 *Too young to die* (1954)
6 *Sucker bait* (1955)

Carl Heller series
Roderus, Frank
1 *Oil rig* (1984)
2 *Rain rustlers* (1984)
3 *Video vandal* (1984)
4 *Turn-out man* (1985)
5 *Coyote Crossing* (1985)
6 *Dead heart* (1985)

Carl Kolchak series
Rice, Jeff
Based on television films
1 *Night stalker* (1973)
2 *Night strangler* (1974)

Carl Lyons series
Stivers, Dick
see **Able Team series**

Carl Masters series
Lynch, Lawrence L
1 *Against odds* (1894)
Also published under the author's real name Emma Murdoch Van Deventer
2 *Woman's tragedy* (1904)
Alternative title: The detective's task
3 *Man and master* (1908)

Carl Moore series
Ingersol, Jared
1 *Jade eye* (1970)
2 *Beautiful murder* (1970)
3 *Money murder* (1971)
4 *Man who stole heaven* (1971)

Carl series
Day, Alexandra
1 *Good dog, Carl* (1985)
2 *Carl goes shopping* (1989)

3 *Carl's Christmas* (1990)
4 *Carl's afternoon in the park* (1991)
5 *Carl's masquerade* (1992)
6 *Carl goes to daycare* (1993)

Carl Travis series
Jons, Hal
see **Marshal Carl Travis series**

Carl Wayward series
Treat, Lawrence
1 *B as in banshee* (1940)
Wail for the corpses
2 *D as in dead* (1941)
3 *H as in hangman* (1942)
4 *O as in omen* (1943)

Carl Wilcox series
Adams, Harold
1 *Murder* (1981)
2 *Paint the town red* (1983)
3 *Missing moon* (1983)
4 *Naked liar* (1985)
5 *Fourth widow* (1986)
6 *Barbed wire noose* (1987)
7 *Man who met the train* (1988)
8 *Man who missed the party* (1989)
9 *Man who was taller than God* (1992)
10 *Perfectly proper murder* (1993)
11 *Way with widows* (1994)

Carleton series
Ashmun, Margaret Eliza
see **Isabel Carleton series**

Carlingford series
Oliphant, Margaret Oliphant Wilson
1 *Salem Chapel* (1863)
2 *Rector* (1863)
Also includes The doctor's family
3 *Perpetual curate* (1864)
4 *Miss Marjoribanks* (1866)
5 *Phoebe, junior* (1876)

Carlisle and Laurence series
Dempster, Guy
see **Guy Laurence and Tony Carlisle series**

Carlisle chronicles series
Johnston, Norma
1 *Carlisle's hope* (1986)
2 *To Jess, with love and memories* (1986)
3 *Carlisles all* (1986)

Carlisle family series
Hallett, Phyllis
1 *White galloper* (1971)
2 *Jumping cats* (1977)

Carlito series
Torres, Edwin
1 *Carlito's way* (1975)
2 *After hours* (1979)

Carlo Reinhart series
Berger, Thomas
1 *Crazy in Berlin* (1958)
2 *Reinhart in love* (1962)
3 *Vital parts* (1970)
4 *Reinhart's women* (1981)

Carlona series
Petrocelli, Orlando Ralph
see **Giacomo Carlona series**

Carlos Brigante series
Torres, Edwin
see **Carlito series**

Carlotta Carlyle series
Barnes, Linda
1 *Lucky penny* (1986)
2 *Trouble of fools* (1987)
3 *Snake tattoo* (1989)
4 *Coyote* (1990)
5 *Steel guitar* (1991)
6 *Snapshot* (1993)

Carlotti series
Hawthorn, Mike
1 *Carlotti joins the team* (1959)
Set during the First World War
2 *Carlotti takes the wheel* (1959)

Carlsen series
Olsen, Violet
see **Marie Carlsen series**

Carlton series
Lavell, Edith
see **Linda Carlton series**

Carlton Todd series
Tresillian, Richard
see **Bondmaster series**

Carly and Danny series
Holmes, Marjorie
1 *Saturday night* (1959)
2 *Sunday morning* (1982)

Carlyle series
Du Barry, Michele
see **Angela Carlyle series**

Carmelo series
Dorman, Geoffrey
1 *Swooping vengeance* (1954)
2 *Shattering silence* (1955)

Carmichael series
Chase, Kip
see **Justine Carmichael series**
Cohen, Anthea
see **Nurse Agnes Carmichael series**
Durst, Paul
see **Michael Carmichael series**
Radford, Edwin
see **Superintendent Carmichael series**

Carmody series
McCurtin, Peter
1 *Hangtown* (1970)
2 *Slavers* (1970)
3 *Tough bullet* (1970)
4 *Screaming on the wire* (1972)
5 *Killers* (1972)
6 *Tall man riding* (1973)

Carnaby-King series
Walker, Peter Norman
see **Detective Sergeant Carnaby-King series**

Carnaby series
Emerson, David
see **Parson Carnaby series**

Carnaby trilogy
Fowler, Ellen Thornycroft
see **Isabel Carnaby trilogy**

Carnacki series
Hodgson, William Hope
1 *Carnacki, the ghost finder, and a poem* (1910)
2 *Carnacki, the ghost finder* (1913)
Expanded edition 1947; short stories

Carnecrane series
Williams, Mary
1 *Carnecrane* (1980)
2 *Return to Carnecrane* (1981)

Carnejoux series
Mauriac, Claude
see **Interior dialogue series**

Carnelian and Underwood series
Moorcock, Michael
see **Jherek Carnelian and Amelia Underwood series**

Carner series
Popkin, Zelda
see **Mary Carner Whittaker series**

Carney Wilde series
Spicer, Bart
1 *Dark light* (1950)
2 *Blues for the Prince* (1950)
3 *Golden door* (1951)
4 *Black sheep, run* (1951)
5 *Long green* (1952)
Shadow of fear
6 *Taming of Carney Wilde* (1954)
7 *Exit, running* (1959)

Caro series
Lapka, Fay S
1 *Dark is a color* (1990)
2 *Hoverlight* (1991)

Carol and Peter Garret series
Smythe, Pat
see **Peter and Carol Garret series**

Carol Ashton and Mark Bourke series
McNab, Claire
see **Inspector Carol Ashton and Sergeant Mark Bourke series**

Carol Blandish series
Chase, James Hadley
1 *No orchids for Miss Blandish* (1939)
Villain and the virgin
Revised edition 1961
2 *Twelve Chinks and a woman* (1940)
Twelve Chinamen and a woman
Doll's bad news
Second and third titles are a revised edition published 1950
3 *Flesh and the orchid* (1948)

Carol Gates series
Colburn, Laura
1 *Death in a small world* (1979)
2 *Death of a prima donna* (1979)
3 *Death through the mill* (1979)

Carol Page series
Boylston, Helen Dore
1 *Carol goes backstage* (1941)
Carol goes on the stage
2 *Carol plays summer stock* (1942)
Carol in repertory
3 *Carol on Broadway* (1944)
Carol comes to Broadway
4 *Carol on tour* (1946)

Carola Mountjoy series
Montague, Jeanne
see **Loves of Carola Mountjoy series**

Carole Trevor and Max Blythe series
Philips, Judson Pentecost
1 *Death syndicate* (1938)
2 *Death delivers a postcard* (1939)

Carolina Lightfoot trilogy
Sherwood, Valerie
1 *Lovesong* (1985)
2 *Windsong* (1986)
3 *Nightsong* (1986)

Carolina series
Arthur, Ruth Mabel
1 *Carolina's holiday, and other stories* (1957)
2 *Carolina's golden bird, and other stories* (1958)
3 *Carolina and Roberto* (1961)
4 *Carolina and the sea-horse, and other stories* (1964)

Carolina series
Fletcher, Inglis
1 *Roanoke Hundred* (1948)
2 *Bennett's welcome* (1950)
3 *Rogue's harbor* (1964)
4 *Raleigh's Eden* (1940)
5 *Men of Albemarle* (1942)
6 *Lusty wind for Carolina* (1944)
7 *Cormorant's brood* (1959)
8 *Wind in the forest* (1957)
9 *Scotswoman* (1954)
10 *Toil of the brave* (1946)
11 *Wicked lady* (1962)
12 *Queen's gift* (1952)
Companion volumes: *The wind in the forest*, 1957, *Cormorant's brood*, 1959, *Wicked lady*, 1962

Carolina series
Griswold, Francis
1 *Tides of Malvern* (1931)
2 *Sea island lady* (1939)

Carolina trilogy
Keyes, Frances Parkinson
see **Winslow family trilogy**

Caroline and Chrissy series
Quin-Harkin, Janet
see **Sugar and spice series**

Caroline and Mick Templeton series
Treadgold, Mary
see **Mick and Caroline Templeton series**

Caroline and Mike series
Delgado, Alan
see **Mike and Caroline series**

Caroline and Sara series
Shaw, Jane
1 *Breton holiday* (1939)
Breton adventure
2 *Bernese holiday* (1940)
Bernese adventure

Caroline Cherie series
Saint-Laurent, Cecil
see **Cherie series**

Caroline Hampton series
Ellis, Julie
1 *Hampton heritage* (1978)
2 *Hampton women* (1980)

Caroline of Ansbach series
Plaidy, Jean
1 *Queen in waiting* (1967)
2 *Caroline, the Queen* (1968)

Caroline series
Franzero, Carlo Maria
see **Mrs Caroline series**

Caroline series
Hale, Sylvia
1 *Caroline takes to dancing* (1960)
2 *Caroline joins the stars* (1961)

Caroline series
Mansbridge, Pamela
1 *Crime for Caroline* (1958)
2 *Flowers from Caroline* (1959)
3 *Caroline and the auction sale* (1961)
4 *No clues for Caroline* (1966)

Caroline series
Mason, Miriam Evangeline
1 *Caroline and her kettle named Maud* (1951)
2 *Caroline and the seven little words* (1967)

Caroline series
Vereker, Barbara
1 *Caroline at the film studios* (1955)
2 *Adventure for Caroline* (1956)
3 *Caroline in Scotland* (1957)
4 *Caroline in Wales* (1959)

Caroline Tate series
Lowry, Lois
1 *One hundredth thing about Caroline* (1985)
2 *Switch around* (1985)

Caroline trilogy
Richards, Lela Horn
1 *Then came Caroline* (1921)
2 *Caroline at college* (1922)
3 *Caroline's career* (1923)

Carolus Deene series
Bruce, Leo
1 *At death's door* (1955)
2 *Death of cold* (1956)
3 *Dead for a ducat* (1956)
4 *Dead man's shoes* (1958)
5 *Louse for the hangman* (1958)
6 *Our jubilee is death* (1959)
7 *Jack on the gallows tree* (1960)
8 *Furious old woman* (1960)
9 *Bone and a hank of hair* (1961)
10 *Die all, die merrily* (1961)
11 *Nothing like blood* (1962)
12 *Crack of doom* (1963)
Such is death
13 *Death in Albert Park* (1964)
14 *Death at Hallows End* (1965)
15 *Death on the Black Sands* (1966)
16 *Death at Saint Asprey's School* (1967)
17 *Death of a commuter* (1967)
18 *Death on Romney Marsh* (1968)
19 *Death with blue ribbon* (1969)
20 *Death on Allhallowe'en* (1970)
21 *Death by the lake* (1971)
22 *Death in the middle watch* (1974)
23 *Death of a bovver boy* (1974)

Carolus Herbert series
Leroux, Gaston
1 *Amazing adventures of Carolus Herbert* (1920)
Original edition entitled *Le capitaine Hyx*
2 *Veiled prisoner* (1923)

Carolus series
Ascher, Eugene
see **Lucian Carolus series**

Carolyn series
Byers, Irene
1 *Stage under the Cedars* (1970)
2 *Cameras on Carolyn* (1971)

Carolyn series
Endicott, Ruth Belmore
1 *Carolyn of the Corners* (1918)
2 *Carolyn of the sunny heart* (1919)

Carpenter and Parew series
Eldredge, Gilbert
see **Thibault Parew and Chips Carpenter series**

Carr and Kelly series
Petievich, Gerald
see **Charles Carr and Jack Kelly series**

Carr series
Bratby, John
see **Peter Carr series**
Leyland, Eric
see **Nicky and Simon Carr series**
Smith, Willard K
see **Inspector Dann Carr series**
Ure, Jean
see **Jamie Carr series**
Westerman, Percy Francis
see **Alan Carr series**
Willis, Ted
see **Rosie Carr series**

Carradine series
Robertson, Manning K
see **Steve Carradine series**

Carrados series
Bramah, Ernest
see **Max Carrados series**

Carrick series
Knox, Bill
see **Webb Carrick series**
Turner, Sheila
see **Mary Carrick series**

Carrie and Ben Porter series
Travis, Elizabeth
see **Ben and Carrie Porter series**

Carrie and Maxwell series
Clewes, Dorothy
1 *Missing from home* (1975)
2 *Testing year* (1977)

Carrie Wasserman series
Conford, Ellen
1 *Dear lovely Hart, I am desperate* (1975)
2 *We interrupt this semester for an important bulletin* (1979)

Carrie Willow series
Bawden, Nina
1 *Carrie's war* (1973)
2 *Rebel on a rock* (1978)

Carrier series
Douglass, Keith
1 *Carrier* (1991)
2 *Viper strike* (1991)

Carrigmore series
Reid, Meta Mayne
see **Tiffany series**

Carrington series
Clouston, Joseph Storer
see **F T Carrington series**
Netton, Budleigh
see **Derek Carrington series**

Carroll family series
Warwick, Audrey
1 *Pets in the barn* (1962)
2 *Hunt the piggies* (1962)

Carroll series
Cohen, Octavus Roy
see **David Carroll series**
Cronin, Archibald Joseph
see **Laurence Carroll series**
Donald, Winifred
see **Linda Carroll series**
Gordon, Grace
see **Patsy Carroll series**
Leigh, Robert
see **Sam Carroll series**
McCutcheon, Hugh
see **Jimmy Carroll series**

Carruthers series
Cox, Edmund Charles
see **John Carruthers series**
Marshall, James
1 *What's the matter with Carruthers?* (1972)
2 *Taking care of Carruthers* (1981)

Carruthers, Simpson and Briggs series
Fish, Robert Lloyd
see **Murder League series**

Carson and Hardisen series
Tate, Eleanora Elaine
see **Margie Carson and Ethel Hardisen series**

Carson series
Elliott, Mary
see **Clare Carson series**
Horner, Lance
see **Golden stud series**
Pruitt, Alan
see **Don Carson series**

Carstairs and Doan series
Davis, Norbert
see **Doan and Carstairs series**

Carstairs series
Carter, Lin
see **Eric Carstairs series**
Horler, Sydney
see **Brett Carstairs series**
Myles, Simon
see **Apples Carstairs series**

Carter and Bell series
Punshon, Ernest Robertson
1 *Unexpected legacy* (1929)
2 *Proof counter proof* (1931)
3 *Cottage murder* (1932)
4 *Genius in murder* (1932)
5 *Truth came out* (1932)

Carter and Munro series
Higgins, Jack
see **Brigadier Dougal Munro and Captain Jack Carter series**

Carter girls
Speed, Nell
This pseudonym is used by Emma Keats and Emma Sampson as indicated against each title
1 *Carter girls* (1917) [Sampson]
2 *Carter girls' week-end camp* (1918) [Sampson]
3 *Carter girls' mysterious neighbors* (1921) [Sampson]
4 *Carter girls of Carter House* (1924) [Keats]

Carter O'Brien series
Bridges, Ben
1 *Silver trail* (1986)
2 *Hard as nails* (1987)
3 *Mexico breakout* (1987)
4 *Hangman's noose* (1988)
5 *Deadly dollars* (1988)
6 *Squaw man* (1989)
7 *North of the border* (1990)
8 *Shoot to kill* (1990)
9 *Stagecoach to hell* (1991)
10 *Hell for leather* (1992)
11 *Marked for death* (1993)

Carter series
Burroughs, Edgar Rice
see **Martian series**
Carter, Nicholas
see **Nicholas Carter series**
Carter, Nick
see **Nick Carter series**
Darbyshire, Shirley
see **Nurse Carter series**
Dewhurst, Eileen
see **Inspector Neil Carter series**
Friend, Oscar
see **Simon Carter series**
Hume, David
see **Tony Carter series**
Lewis, Ted
see **Jack Carter series**
Long, Amelia Reynolds
see **Steve Carter series**
Smith, Francis Hopkinson
see **Colonel Carter series**
Wirt, Mildred Augustine
see **Dan Carter series**

Carter Street Detective Agency trilogy
Robertson, Keith
see **Neil and Swede trilogy**

Cartwright family series
Burnap, Jennifer
1 *Journey to Jamestown* (1973)
2 *Beyond the Blue Ridge* (1974)

Cartwright series
Morgan, Patrick
see **Operation Hang Ten series**
Palmer, Bernard
see **Felicia Cartwright series**

Caruso series
Paul, Barbara
see **Enrico Caruso series**

Carvajel series
Waltari, Mika
see **Michael Carvajel series**

Carver and Trask series
Wallingford, Lee
see **Frank Carver and Ginny Trask series**

Carver Bascombe series
Davis, Kenn
1 *Dark side* (1976)
2 *Forza trap* (1979)
3 *Dead to rights* (1981)
4 *Words can kill* (1984)
5 *Melting point* (1984)
6 *Nijinsky is dead* (1987)
7 *As October dies* (1987)
8 *Acts of homicide* (1989)
9 *Blood of poets* (1990)

Carver family series
Delderfield, Ronald Frederick
see **Avenue series**

Carver series
Canning, Victor
see **Rex Carver series**

Cary series
Bosher, Kate Lee Langley
see **Mary Cary series**

Caryll series
Fairlie, Gerard
see **Victor Caryll series**

Casamassima series
James, Henry
see **Princess Casamassima series**

Casca series
Sadler, Barry
1 *Eternal mercenary* (1979)
2 *God of death* (1979)
3 *War lord* (1980)
4 *Panzer soldier* (1980)
5 *Barbarian* (1981)
6 *Persian* (1982)
7 *Damned* (1982)
8 *Soldier of fortune* (1983)
9 *Sentinel* (1983)
10 *Conquistador* (1984)
11 *Legionnaire* (1984)
12 *African mercenary* (1984)
13 *Assassin* (1985)
14 *Phoenix* (1985)
15 *Pirate* (1985)
16 *Desert mercenary* (1986)
17 *Warrior* (1987)
18 *Cursed* (1987)
19 *Samurai* (1988)
20 *Soldier of Gideon* (1988)
21 *Trench soldier* (1989)
22 *Mongol* (1990)

Cascabel series
Verne, Jules
see **Caesar Cascabel series**

Case books series
Prescot, Julian
1 *Both sides of the case* (1958)
2 *Case continued* (1959)
3 *Case proceeding* (1960)
4 *Case for the accused* (1961)
5 *Case for trial* (1962)
6 *Case for hearing* (1963)
7 *Case for court* (1964)
8 *Case re-opened* (1965)
9 *Case counterfeit* (1967)

Case series
Spencer, John
see **Charley Case series**

White, Valerie
see **John Case series**

Casey Grant series
Rico, Don
1 *Ring-a-ding girl* (1969)
2 *Swinging virgin* (1969)
3 *So sweet, so deadly* (1970)

Casey Kellog and Al Krug series
Weston, Carolyn
1 *Poor, poor, Ophelia* (1972)
2 *Susannah screaming* (1975)
3 *Rouse the demon* (1976)

Casey Peters series
Moore, Harry F S
1 *Murder goes rolling along* (1942)
2 *Shed a bitter tear* (1944)

Casey Ruggles series
Tufts, Warren
Comic strips
1 *Whisperer* (1981)
2 *Black Barney* (1979)
3 *Pomo uprising* (1979)
4 *Juan Soto* (1979)
5 *Marchioness of Grofnek* (1981)
6 *Pearl galleon* (1981)

Casey Ryan series
Bower, Bertha Muzzy
1 *Casey Ryan* (1921)
2 *Trail of the white mule* (1922)

Casey series
Mead, Russell
see **Doctor Peter Casey series**

Casey Valentine series
Giff, Patricia Reilly
1 *Fourth-grade celebrity* (1979)
2 *Girl who knew it all* (1979)
3 *Left-handed shortstop* (1980)
4 *Winter worm business* (1981)
5 *Rat teeth* (1984)
6 *Love from the fifth grade celebrity* (1986)

Casey Wills series
Brown, Sam
1 *Big lonely* (1993)
2 *Long drift* (1995)

Cash Madigan series
Cassidy, Bruce
1 *While murder waits* (1957)
2 *Buried motive* (1957)

Cash series
Cleary, Denis
see **Theodore J Cash series**

Caspak trilogy
Burroughs, Edgar Rice
see **Bowen Tylor trilogy**

Caspar series
Hyman, Robin
Illustrated by Yutaka Sugita
1 *Caspar and the lion cub* (1974)
2 *Caspar and the rainbow bird* (1975)

Caspar series
Tourneur, Dina Kathelyn
1 *Caspar's ears* (1975)
Original edition entitled *L'oreille de Marmouset*
2 *Caspar's mouth* (1975)
Original edition entitled *La bouche de Marmouset*
3 *Caspar's hair* (1975)
Original edition entitled *Le cheveux de Marmouset*
4 *Caspar's feet* (1975)
Original edition entitled *Le pied de Marmouset*
5 *Caspar's hands* (1975)
Original edition entitled *Le main de Marmouset*
6 *Caspar's nose* (1975)
Original edition entitled *Le nez de Marmouset*
7 *Caspar plants a seed* (1976)
Original edition entitled *Marmouset plante une graine*
8 *Caspar finds a friend* (1977)
Original edition entitled *Marmouset soigne une tourterelle*
9 *Caspar loses his dog* (1979)
Original edition entitled *Marmouset a perdu son chien*

Caspian series
Burke, John Frederick
see **Doctor Alexander Caspian series**

Caspol trilogy
Adlard, Mark
see **Jan Caspol trilogy**

Cass Harty series
Dane, Joel Y
see **Sergeant Cass Harty series**

Cass Jameson series
Wheat, Carolyn
1 *Dead man's thoughts* (1983)
2 *Where nobody dies* (1986)

Cass series
Severn, Richard
see **Jeff Cass series**

Cassandra Reilly series
Wilson, Barbara Ellen
1 *Gaudi afternoon* (1990)
2 *Trouble in Transylvania* (1993)

Cassella series
Beinhart, Larry
see **Tony Cassella series**

Cassia series
Yep, Laurence Michael
1 *Serpent's children* (1984)
2 *Mountain light* (1985)

Cassidy and Sundance series
Essex, Saran
see **Butch Cassidy and the Sundance Kid series**

Cassidy series
Crosby, John Campbell
see **Horatio Cassidy series**
Mulford, Clarence Edward
see **Hopalong Cassidy series**

Cassie Bowen series
Hines, Anna Grossnickle
1 *Cassie Bowen takes witch lessons* (1985)
2 *Boys are yucko!* (1989)

Cassie Perkins series
Hunt, Angela Elwell
1 *No more broken promises* (1991)
2 *Forever friend* (1991)
3 *Basket of roses* (1991)
4 *Dream to cherish* (1992)
5 *Much-adored Sandy Shore* (1992)
6 *Love burning bright* (1992)
7 *Star light, star bright* (1993)
8 *Chance of a lifetime* (1993)
9 *Glory of love* (1993)

Cassie Swann series
Moody, Susan
1 *Takeover double* (1993)
2 *Grand slam* (1994)

Casson Duker series
Mole, William
1 *Hammersmith maggot* (1955)
Small venom
Shadow of a killer
2 *Goodbye is not worthwhile* (1956)
3 *Skin trap* (1957)
You pay for pity

Castang series
Freeling, Nicolas
see **Henri Castang series**

Castaways in time series
Adams, Robert
1 *Castaways in time* (1984)
2 *Seven magical jewels of Ireland* (1985)
3 *Of quests and kings* (1986)
4 *Of chiefs and champions* (1987)
5 *Of myths and monsters* (1988)
6 *Of beginnings and endings* (1989)

Castaways of the Jonathan series
Verne, Jules
see **Survivors of the Jonathan series**

Casteel-Tatterton family series
Andrews, Virginia Cleo
1 *Heaven* (1985)
2 *Dark angel* (1986)
3 *Fallen hearts* (1988)
4 *Gates of paradise* (1989)
5 *Web of dreams* (1990)

Castelferrante series
Buckley, Eunice
1 *Shadow of a god* (1956)
2 *Lay the ghosts* (1964)

Castle Brass series
Moorcock, Michael
see **Chronicles of Castle Brass series**

Castle of dark series
Lee, Tanith
1 *Castle of dark* (1978)
2 *Prince on a white horse* (1982)
One volume edition entitled *Dark castle, white horse*, 1986

Castle Perilous series
De Chancie, John
1 *Castle Perilous* (1987)
2 *Castle for rent* (1989)
3 *Castle kidnapped* (1989)
4 *Castle war!* (1990)
5 *Castle murders* (1991)
6 *Castle dreams* (1992)
7 *Castle Spellbound* (1992)

Castle Rising series
Cradock, Fanny
see **Lorme family series**

Castle School series
Little, Sylvia
1 *Castle School gets going* (1947)
2 *Twins at Castle School* (1947)
3 *Castle School on holiday* (1948)
4 *Blood royal at Castle School* (1949)
5 *Castle School on the screen* (1949)
6 *Castle School at the cross-roads* (1950)
7 *Castle School on the warpath* (1950)
8 *Castle School in the news* (1950)

Castle series
Davison, Gilderoy
see **Peter Castle series**
Michaels, Jan
see **Darby Castle series**
Winthrop, Elizabeth
see **William series**

Castledare series
Sinclair, Dee
1 *Night the ghost walked* (1969)
2 *Castledare vigilantes* (1969)

Castleman series
Kutak, Rosemary
see **Doctor Marc Castleman series**

Castles series
Gallagher, Patricia
1 *Castles in the air* (1976)
2 *No greater love* (1979)

Castleton and Craggs series
Alington, Cyril Augustine
see **Archdeacon series**

Cat and bat series
Danziger, Paula
1 *Cat ate my gymsuit* (1974)
2 *There's a bat in bunk five* (1980)

Cat and Dog series
Miller, Elizabeth
1 *Cat and Dog give a party* (1980)
2 *Cat and Dog have a contest* (1980)
3 *Cat and Dog raise the roof* (1980)
4 *Cat and Dog and the mixed-up week* (1980)
5 *Cat and Dog take a trip* (1980)
6 *Cat and Dog learn the ABCs* (1981)
Cat and Dog and the ABCs
7 *Cat and Dog have a parade* (1981)

Cat called Max series
Dicks, Terrance
1 *Magnificent Max* (1989)
2 *Max and the quiz kids* (1990)
3 *Majestic Max* (1990)
4 *Max's amazing summer* (1991)
5 *Max and the cat burglar* (1992)
6 *Max and the missing megastar* (1992)
7 *Max's old-fashioned Christmas* (1993)

Cat family series
Scarry, Richard
1 *Richard Scarry's the cat family takes a trip* (1992)
2 *Richard Scarry's the cat family's busy day* (1992)

Cat in the hat series
Seuss, Doctor
1 *Cat in the hat* (1957)
2 *Cat in the hat comes back!* (1958)
Companion volumes: *The Cat in the hat dictionary*, 1964, *The Cat in the hat songbook*, 1967

Cat Marsala series
D'Amato, Barbara
1 *Hardball* (1990)
2 *Hard tack* (1991)
3 *Hard luck* (1992)
4 *Hard women* (1993)
5 *Hard case* (1994)

Cat people trilogy
Moore, Wallace
see **Balzan of the cat people trilogy**

Cat Randall series
Gordons
see **Undercover Cat series**

CAT series
Andrews, Spike
see **C.A.T. series**

Cat series
Fowler, Richard
1 *Cat's car* (1988)
2 *Cat's cake* (1989)

Cat series
Nichols, Beverley
1 *Cat's ABC* (1960)
2 *Cat's XYZ* (1961)
Companion volume: *Cat book*, 1955

Cat series
Olsen, D B
see **Rachel and Jennifer Murdock series**

Cat series
Roe, JoAnn
1 *Castaway cat* (1984)
2 *Fisherman cat* (1988)
3 *Alaska cat* (1990)
4 *Samurai cat* (1993)

Catacombs series
Blashfield, Jean
1 *Faerie mound of dragonkind* (1987)
2 *Gnomes-one hundred, Dragons-zero* (1987)

Catacombs series
Oleck, Jack
1 *Tales from the crypt* (1972)
2 *Vault of horror* (1973)

Catalyst Club series
Dyer, George
1 *Catalyst Club* (1936)
2 *Long death* (1937)
3 *People ask death* (1940)

Catamount Camp series
Ellis, Edward Sylvester
1 *Catamount Camp* (1910)
2 *Captain of the Camp* (1910)
Alternative title: Ben, the young boss

Catastrophe practice series
Mosley, Nicholas
Plays
1 *Catastrophe practice* (1979)
Revised edition 1989; also includes *Cypher*, a novel
2 *Imago bird* (1980)
Revised edition 1989
3 *Serpent* (1981)
Revised edition 1990
4 *Judith* (1986)
Revised edition 1991
5 *Hopeful monsters* (1990)

Catch twenty two series
Heller, Joseph
1 *Catch twenty two* (1961)
2 *Closing time* (1994)

Catechisms and prayers series
Watts, Isaac
Based on *Catechisms, or, Instructions in the principles of the Christian religion*, 1730
1 *First set of catechisms and prayers* (1734)
Alternative title: The religion of little children
2 *Second set of catechisms* (1734)
A preservative from the sins and follies of childhood and youth
One volume edition entitled *Doctor Watts' chatechisms and prayers*, 1796

Catfish Bend series
Burman, Ben Lucien
1 *High water at Catfish Bend* (1952)
2 *Seven stars for Catfish Bend* (1956)
Numbers 1 and 2 published in one volume, 1975
3 *Owl hoots twice at Catfish Bend* (1961)
Numbers 1-3 also published in one volume entitled *Three from Catfish Bend*, 1967
4 *Blow a wild bugle for Catfish Bend* (1967)
Numbers 3 and 4 published in one volume, 1975
5 *High treason at Catfish Bend* (1977)
6 *Strange invasion at Catfish Bend* (1980)
7 *Thunderbolt at Catfish Bend* (1984)

Catfish series
Hurd, Edith Thatcher
1 *Catfish* (1970)
2 *Catfish and the kidnapped cat* (1974)

Catford Police series
Foxall, Peter Augustus
1 *Dishonest way to die* (1977)
2 *Act of terror* (1979)
3 *Sequel to yesterday's crime* (1979)
4 *To kill a call girl* (1980)
5 *Silent informer* (1981)

Cathedral cat series
Severn, June
1 *Cathedral cat* (1965)
2 *Close cats* (1968)

Cathedrals series
Goudge, Elizabeth
1 *City of bells* (1936)
Set in Wells
2 *Towers in the mist* (1938)
Set in Oxford
3 *Dean's watch* (1960)
Set in Ely
One volume edition entitled *Three cities of bells*, 1965

Catherine Alderly series
Robards, Karen
see **Lady Catherine Alderly series**

Catherine Cornelius series
Moorcock, Michael
1 *Cure for cancer* (1971)
Revised edition 1979
2 *Adventures of Una Persson and Catherine Cornelius in the twentieth century* (1976)

Catherine de Medici trilogy
Plaidy, Jean
1 *Madame Serpent* (1951)
2 *Italian woman* (1952)
3 *Queen Jezebel* (1953)
One volume edition entitled Catherine de Medici, 1969

Catherine de Valois trilogy
Williamson, Hugh Ross
1 *Florentine woman* (1970)
2 *Last of the Valois* (1971)
3 *Paris is worth a mass* (1971)

Catherine Legoix series
Benzoni, Juliette
1 *One love is enough* (1963)
Original edition entitled *Suffit d'un amour*, part 1
2 *Catherine* (1964)
Original edition entitled *Suffit d'un amour*, part 2
3 *Belle Catherine* (1966)
Original edition entitled *La belle Catherine*
4 *Catherine and Arnaud* (1967)
Original edition entitled *Catherine ma mie*
5 *Catherine and a time for love* (1968)
Original edition entitled *Catherine et le temps d'aimer*
6 *Snare for Catherine* (1973)
Original edition entitled *Piege pour Catherine*

Catherine of Calais series
De la Pasture, Elizabeth
1 *Catherine of Calais* (1901)
2 *Catherine's child* (1908)

Catherine series
Lloyd, Joanna
1 *Catherine goes to school* (1945)
2 *Catherine, head of the house* (1947)

Catherine the Great trilogy
Anthony, Evelyn
1 *Imperial Highness* (1953)
Rebel princess
2 *Curse not the king* (1954)
Royal intrigue
3 *Far fly the eagles* (1955)
The story of Alexander I and Napoleon

Catherine West and Geoffrey Macadam series
Campbell, Alice
see **Geoffrey Macadam and Catherine West series**

Cathie, Ian and Sovra series
Lyon, Elinor
see **Ian and Sovra series**

Catholic Stuarts series
Nolan, Winefride
1 *Rich inheritance* (1952)
A story of Catholic Elizabethan England
2 *Exiles from home* (1955)

Cathy and Carl series
Johnston, Dorothy Grunbock
see **Wagon train series**

Cathy and Chris Dollanganger series
Andrews, Virginia Cleo
see **Dollanganger family series**

Cathy and Company series
Schertle, Alice
1 *Cathy and Company and the green ghost* (1980)
2 *Cathy and company and Bumper the bully* (1980)
3 *Cathy and Company and mean Mister Meeker* (1980)
4 *Cathy and Company and the noisy neighbor* (1980)
5 *Cathy and Company and Hank the horse* (1980)

Cathy, Belinda and Jane series
Bye, Beryl
1 *Nobody's pony* (1967)
2 *Pony for sale* (1969)
3 *Belle's bridle* (1973)

Cathy Leonard series
Woolley, Catherine
1 *Room for Cathy* (1956)
2 *Miss Cathy Leonard* (1958)
3 *Cathy Leonard calling* (1960)
4 *Cathy's little sister* (1964)
5 *Chris in trouble* (1968)
6 *Cathy and the beautiful people* (1971)
7 *Cathy uncovers a secret* (1972)

Cathy series
Faber, Nancy Weingarten
1 *Cathy at the crossroads* (1965)
2 *Cathy's secret kingdom* (1966)

Cathy series
Guisewhite, Cathy
1 *Another Saturday night of wild and reckless abandon* (1982)
2 *Eat your way to a better relationship* (1983)
3 *How to get rich, fall in love, lose weight and solve all your problems* (1983)
By saying no
4 *Men should come with instruction booklets* (1984)
5 *Wake me up when I'm a size five* (1985)
6 *Stressed for success* (1986)
7 *Sorry I'm late, my hair won't start* (1986)
8 *Sales clerk made me buy it* (1986)
9 *My cologne backfired* (1986)
10 *Thin thighs in thirty years* (1986)
11 *Hand to hold, an opinion to reject* (1987)
12 *Two pies, one fork* (1987)
13 *It must be something in the ink* (1987)
14 *Why do all the right words come out of the wrong mouth?* (1988)

Cathy series
Mitchell, Yvonne
1 *Cathy away* (1964)
2 *Cathy at home* (1965)

Cathy Weston series
Conway, Peter
see **Inspector Cathy Weston series**

Caton series
Mason, Chuck
see **Lee Caton series**

Catrin series
Gower, Iris
1 *Copper cloud* (1976)
2 *Return to Tip Row* (1977)
One volume edition entitled *The loves of Catrin*, 1986

Catriona Chisholm series
Dwyer-Joyce, Alice
see **Doctor Catriona Chisholm series**

Cat's pawn series
Gadallah, Leslie
1 *Cat's pawn* (1987)
2 *Cat's gambit* (1990)

Cats series
Cass, Joan Evelyn
1 *Cat thief* (1961)
2 *Cat show* (1962)
3 *Cats go to market* (1969)
4 *Cats' adventures with car thieves* (1971)

Cats series
Lockridge, Frances
1 *Cats and people* (1950)
2 *Proud cat* (1951)
3 *Lucky cat* (1953)
4 *Nameless cat* (1954)
5 *Cat who rode cows* (1955)
Sequence continued by Richard Lockridge
Lockridge, Richard
6 *One lady, two cats* (1967)

Cats series
Tovey, Doreen
1 *Cats in the belfry* (1957)
2 *Cats in May* (1959)
3 *Donkey work* (1962)
4 *Life with grandma* (1964)
5 *Raining cats and donkeys* (1968)
6 *New boy* (1970)
7 *Double trouble* (1972)
8 *Making the horse laugh* (1974)
9 *Coming of Saska* (1977)
10 *Comfort of cats* (1979)
11 *Roses round the door* (1982)
12 *Waiting in the wings* (1986)

Catsfoot series
Robb, John
1 *Gun town marshal* (1959)
2 *Cry Apaches!* (1960)

Catspaw series
Stuart, Anne
1 *Catspaw* (1985)
2 *Catspaw II* (1988)

Catty Atkins series
Kelland, Clarence Budington
1 *Catty Atkins* (1920)
2 *Catty Atkins, riverman* (1921)
3 *Catty Atkins, sailorman* (1922)
4 *Catty Atkins, financier* (1922)
5 *Catty Atkins, bandmaster* (1924)

Catweazle series
Carpenter, Richard
1 *Catweazle* (1970)
2 *Catweazle and the magic zodiac* (1971)

Catwings series
Le Guin, Ursula Kroeber
1 *Catwings* (1988)
2 *Catwings return* (1989)

Caught in the spider's web series
Home-Gall, Edward Reginald
see **Human Bat series**

Caulder series
Knott, William Cecil
see **Vengeance Seeker series**

Cauldron series
Fowler, Sydney
see **Inspector Cauldron series**

Caution series
Cheyney, Peter
see **Lemmy Caution series**

Cautionary tales series
Belloc, Hilaire
Tales in verse and pictures
1 *Cautionary tales for children* (1907)
2 *New cautionary tales* (1930)

Cavalcade series
Coffman, Virginia
1 *Pacific cavalcade* (1981)
2 *Lombard cavalcade* (1982)
3 *Lombard heiress* (1982)

Cavalier series
Armstrong, Raymond
see **J Rockingham Stone series**

Cavalry trilogy
Cook, Will
see **United States Cavalry trilogy**

Cavalry trilogy
Hennessy, Max
1 *Soldier of the Queen* (1980)
2 *Blunted lance* (1981)
3 *Iron stallions* (1982)

Cavanaugh series
Carrington, G A
see **Marcus Cavanaugh series**

Cavender series
Tokson, Elliot
see **Alec Cavender series**

Cavendish series
Cooper, Charles
see **Russell Cavendish series**

Cavendish series
Douglas, Kathryn
1 *Cavendish chronicles* (1979)
Also published in three volumes
1.1 *Cavendish Square* (1979)
1.2 *Cavendish pride* (1979)
1.3 *Cavendish way* (1979)
2 *Vivian of Cavendish Square* (1982)

Caviar series
Buchwald, Art
Humorous autobiography
1 *I chose caviar* (1957)
2 *More caviar* (1958)

Caviar series
Thayer, Charles Wheeler
1 *Bears in the caviar* (1951)
Reminiscences as a diplomat in Moscow before the Second World War
2 *Hands across the caviar* (1952)
Reminiscences as a member of an American Military Mission to the Yugoslav partisans during the Second World War

Cawthorne series
Silverwood, Roger
see **Superintendent Cawthorne series**

Caxley series
Read, *Miss*
Pseudonym of Dora Jessie Saint
1 *Market Square* (1966)
2 *Howards of Caxley* (1967)
3 *Christmas mouse* (1973)

Caxton series
Brissenden, Robert Francis
see **Tom Caxton series**

Caxton trilogy
Lytton, Edward George Earle Lytton Bulwer-Lytton
see **Real and the ideal trilogy**

Cay series
Taylor, Theodore
1 *Timothy of the Cay* (1993)
2 *Cay* (1969)

Caywood Weston series
Thomas, Eugene
see **Mrs Caywood Weston series**

Ceb Barnes series
Nott, Loraine
1 *Ceb* (1989)
Exploits of an uncommon man
2 *Studmaster of Canning Downs* (1989)

Cecil series
Gore, Catherine Grace
1 *Cecil* (1841)
Alternative title: The adventures of a coxcomb
2 *Cecil, a peer* (1841)

Cecil series
Read, Conyers
see **William Cecil series**

Cecily Jolland series
Willard, Barbara
see **Mantlemass series**

Cedar Groves Junior High School series
Kenyon, Kate
1 *Junior High jitters* (1986)
2 *Class crush* (1986)
3 *Day the eighth grade ran the school* (1987)
4 *How dumb can you get?* (1987)
5 *Eighth grade to the rescue* (1987)
6 *Eighth grade hero?* (1987)
7 *Those crazy class pictures* (1987)
8 *Starting the eighth grade* (1988)
9 *Who's the Junior High hunk?* (1988)
10 *Big date* (1988)
11 *Great eighth grade switch* (1988)
12 *Revolt of the eighth grade* (1988)
13 *Who's haunting the eighth grade?* (1988)
14 *Junior High, private eyes* (1989)
15 *Night Eighth ran mall* (1989)

Cedar River daydreams series
Baer, Judy
1 *New girl in town* (1988)
2 *Trouble with a capital T* (1988)
3 *Jennifer's secret* (1989)
4 *Journey to nowhere* (1989)
5 *Broken promises* (1989)
6 *Intruder* (1989)
7 *Silent tears no more* (1990)
8 *Fill my empty heart* (1990)
9 *Yesterday's dream* (1991)
10 *Tomorrow's promise* (1991)
11 *Something old, something new* (1991)
12 *Vanishing star* (1991)
13 *No turning back* (1991)
14 *Second chance* (1991)
15 *Lost and found* (1992)
16 *Unheard voices* (1992)
17 *Lonely girl* (1992)
18 *More than friends* (1992)
19 *Never too late* (1993)
20 *Discovery* (1993)

Cedar series
Meader, Stephen Warren
1 *Red Horse Hill* (1930)
2 *Cedar's boy* (1949)

Cedar tree trilogy
Hardwick, Michael
1 *Cedar tree* (1976)
2 *Autumn of an age* (1977)
3 *Bough breaks* (1978)

Celebrity series
Maxwell, Elsa
Reminiscences of a famous party-giver
1 *R.S.V.P.* (1954)
I married the world
2 *Celebrity circus* (1963)

Celestine and Ernest series
Vincent, Gabrielle
see **Ernest and Celestine series**

Celestine series
Chica, Marcel
1 *Celestine decorates her house* (1978)
Original edition entitled *Celestine decore sa maison*
2 *Celestine goes to the market* (1978)
Original edition entitled *Celestine va au marche*
3 *Celestine to the rescue* (1979)
4 *Celestine high in the sky* (1979)
Original edition entitled *Celestine en plein ciel*

Celia Grant series
Sherwood, John
1 *Green trigger fingers* (1984)
2 *Botanist at bay* (1985)
3 *Mantrap garden* (1986)
4 *Flowers of evil* (1987)
5 *Death at the BBC* (1988)
6 *Menacing groves* (1988)
7 *Bouquet of thorns* (1989)
8 *Sunflower plot* (1991)
9 *Hanging garden* (1992)
10 *Creeping Jenny* (1993)
11 *Bones gather no moss* (1994)

Celia series
Brunner, Ethel
1 *Celia and her friends* (1917)
2 *Elopement* (1917)
Alternative title: Celia intervenes
3 *Celia once again* (1918)
4 *Celia's fantastic voyage* (1923)

Celibates' Club series
Zangwill, Israel
1 *Bachelors' Club* (1891)
2 *Old Maids' Club* (1892)
One volume edition entitled *The Celibates' Club*, 1905

Cellini series
Halliday, Michael
see **Doctor Emmanuel Cellini series**

Cellini Smith series
Reeves, Robert
1 *Dead and done for* (1939)
2 *No love lost* (1941)
Come out killing
The second title is an abridged edition
3 *Cellini Smith, detective* (1943)

Celtic fairy tales series
Jacobs, Joseph
1 *Celtic fairy tales* (1892)
2 *More Celtic fairy tales* (1895)
One volume edition entitled Celtic fairy tales, 1970

Cemetery Jones series
Cox, William Robert
1 *Cemetery Jones* (1985)
2 *Cemetery Jones and the Maverick Kid* (1986)
3 *Cemetery Jones and the dancing guns* (1987)
4 *Cemetery Jones and the gunslingers* (1988)
5 *Cemetary Jones and the Tombstone war* (1990)

Cemetery residents series
Culbertson, Judi
see **Guides to the cemeteries of the world's great cities series**

Cenotaph Road series
Vardeman, Robert Edward
1 *Cenotaph Road* (1983)
2 *Sorcerer's skull* (1983)
3 *World of mazes* (1983)
4 *Iron Tongue* (1984)
5 *Fire and fog* (1984)
6 *Pillar of night* (1984)

Centaur trilogy
Thiess, Frank
1 *Devil's shadow* (1925)
Original edition entitled *Der Leibhaftige*
2 *Gateway to life* (1926)
Original edition entitled *Das Tor zur Welt*
3 *Farewell to paradise* (1927)
Original edition entitled *Abschied vom Parodies*

Centennial history of the Civil War series
Catton, Bruce
1 *Coming fury* (1961)
2 *Terrible swift sword* (1963)
3 *Never call retreat* (1965)

Central America series
Larteguy, Jean
1 *No peace on earth* (1969)
2 *Freedom fighters* (1970)

Central Control series
Norton, Andre
1 *Star man's son, 2250AD* (1952)
Daybreak 2250AD
2 *Star rangers* (1953)
Last planet
3 *Star guard* (1955)

Central Crimes Bureau series
Geddes, Paul
see **Paul Venneker series**

Central High series
Morrison, Gertrude W
see **Girls of Central High series**

Central London Hospital series
Harrison, Elizabeth
1 *Physicians* (1966)
2 *Ravelston affair* (1967)
3 *Corridors of healing* (1968)
4 *Emergency call* (1970)
5 *Accident call* (1971)
6 *Ambulance call* (1972)
7 *Surgeon's call* (1973)
8 *On call* (1974)
9 *Hospital call* (1975)
10 *Dangerous call* (1976)
11 *To mend a heart* (1977)
12 *Young Doctor Goddard* (1978)
13 *Doctor called Caroline* (1979)
14 *Surgeon called Amanda* (1982)
15 *Surgeon's life* (1983)
16 *Marrying a doctor* (1984)
17 *Surgeon's affair* (1985)
18 *Surgeon at St Mark's* (1986)
19 *Surgeon she married* (1988)

Century of the detective series
Thorwald, Jurgen
Translated from the German
1 *Marks of Cain* (1965)
2 *Dead men tell tales* (1966)
3 *Proof of poison* (1966)

Century of the surgeon series
Thorwald, Jurgen
Translated from the German
1 *Century of the surgeon* (1959)
2 *Triumph of surgery* (1960)

Century series
Grier, Sydney Carlyon
1 *Power of the keys* (1907)
2 *Young man married* (1909)
3 *Path to honour* (1909)
4 *Keepers of the gate* (1911)
5 *Writ in water* (1913)
6 *England hath need of thee* (1916)

Cerebral palsy series
Brown, Christy
1 *My left foot* (1954)
Childhood story of Christy Brown
2 *Down all the days* (1970)
Autobiographical novel

Cerin Songweaver series
De Lint, Charles
1 *Oak king's daughter* (1979)
2 *Pattern of silver strings* (1981)
3 *Glass eyes of cotton strings* (1982)
4 *In mask and motley* (1983)
5 *Laughter in the leaves* (1984)
6 *Badger in the bag* (1985)
7 *Rafters were singing* (1986)
8 *Lark in the morning* (1987)

Cervantes series
Cook, Bruce
see **Antonio Cervantes series**

Cesar Cascabel series
Verne, Jules
see **Caesar Cascabel series**

Cesare Borgia series
Bennetts, Pamela
1 *Borgia prince* (1968)
2 *Borgia bull* (1968)

Cesare Borgia series
Sabatini, Rafael
1 *Shame of motley* (1908)
2 *Justice of the Duke* (1912)
3 *Banner of the Bull* (1915)
Three episodes in the career of Cesare Borgia; first episode published as *The Urbinian*, 1924

Chace series
Loder, Vernon
see **Inspector Chace series**

Chad Powell series
Sperry, Armstrong
1 *Rain forest* (1947)
2 *Thunder country* (1952)

Chaddie and Duncan Argylle McKail trilogy
Stringer, Arthur
see **Prairie trilogy**

Chadwick series
Cobden, Guy
see **John Chadwick series**
Jenkins, Jerry Bruce
see **Tara Chadwick series**

Chagro Brannigan series
Newsom, Ed
1 *Brannigan* (1981)
2 *Comanchero* (1981)
3 *Blood bullets* (1982)
4 *Peacekeeper* (1983)

Chairs series
Ilf, Ilya Arnoldovich
1 *Twelve chairs* (1928)
Diamonds to sit on
2 *Golden calf* (1931)
Little golden calf

Chalet School series
Brent-Dyer, Elinor Mary
1 *School at the Chalet* (1925)
2 *Jo of the Chalet School* (1926)
3 *Princess of the Chalet School* (1927)
4 *Head girl of the Chalet School* (1928)
5 *Rivals of the Chalet School* (1929)
6 *Eustacia goes to the Chalet School* (1930)
7 *Chalet School and Jo* (1931)
8 *Chalet girls in camp* (1932)
9 *Exploits of the Chalet girls* (1933)
10 *Chalet School and the Lintons* (1934)
Also published in two volumes entitled *The Chalet School and the Lintons* and *A rebel at the Chalet School*
11 *New house at the Chalet School* (1935)
12 *Jo returns to the Chalet School* (1936)
13 *New Chalet School* (1938)
United Chalet School
14 *Chalet School in exile* (1940)
15 *Chalet School goes to it* (1941)
Chalet School at war
16 *Highland twins and the Chalet School* (1942)
17 *Lavender laughs in the Chalet School* (1943)
18 *Gay from China at the Chalet School* (1944)
19 *Jo to the rescue* (1945)
20 *Three goes to Chalet School* (1949)
21 *Chalet School and the island* (1950)
22 *Peggy of the Chalet School* (1950)
23 *Carola storms the Chalet School* (1951)
24 *Wrong Chalet School* (1952)
25 *Shocks for the Chalet School* (1952)
26 *Chalet School in the Oberland* (1952)
27 *Bride leads the Chalet School* (1953)
28 *Changes for the Chalet School* (1953)
29 *Joey goes to the Oberland* (1954)
30 *Chalet School and Barbara* (1954)
31 *Chalet School does it again* (1955)
32 *Tom tackles the Chalet School* (1955)
33 *Chalet girl from Kenya* (1955)
34 *Mary-Lou of the Chalet School* (1956)
Mary-Lou at the Chalet School
35 *Genius at the Chalet School* (1956)
Revised edition 1969; also published in two volumes entitled *A genius at the Chalet School* and *Chalet School fete*
36 *Problem for the Chalet School* (1956)
37 *New mistress at the Chalet School* (1957)
38 *Excitement at the Chalet School* (1957)
39 *Coming-of-age of the Chalet School* (1958)
40 *Chalet School and Richenda* (1958)
41 *Trials for the Chalet School* (1959)
42 *Theodora and the Chalet School* (1959)
43 *Joey and Co. in Tirol* (1960)
44 *Ruey Richardson, Chaletian* (1960)
45 *Leader in the Chalet School* (1961)
46 *Chalet School wins the trick* (1961)
47 *Future Chalet School girl* (1962)
48 *Feud in the Chalet School* (1962)
49 *Chalet School triplets* (1963)
50 *Chalet School reunion* (1963)
51 *Jane and the Chalet School* (1964)
52 *Redheads at the Chalet School* (1964)
53 *Adrienne and the Chalet School* (1965)
54 *Summer term at the Chalet School* (1965)
55 *Challenge for the Chalet School* (1966)
56 *Two Sams at the Chalet School* (1967)
57 *Althea joins the Chalet School* (1969)
58 *Prefects of the Chalet School* (1970)

Chalice and Crying Eddie series
Mackenzie, Donald
see **Harry Chalice and Crying Eddie series**

Chalk series
Balaam
Autobiography of a teacher
1 *Chalk in my hair* (1953)
2 *Chalk gets in your eyes* (1955)

Challenge series
Collins, Warwick
1 *Challenge* (1990)
2 *New world* (1991)

Challenger series
Doyle, Arthur Conan
see **Professor Challenger series**

Challis series
Martin, Shane
see **Professor Ronald Challis series**
Nolan, William Francis
see **Bart Challis series**

Challoners series
Diver, Maud
1 *Lonely furrow* (1923)
2 *But yesterday* (1927)
3 *Wild bird* (1929)
4 *Ships of youth* (1931)

Chamberlayne series
Sewart, Alan
see **Detective Sergeant Chamberlayne series**

Chambers series
Kane, Henry
see **Peter Chambers series**

Chambrun series
Pentecost, Hugh
see **Pierre Chambrun series**

Chameleon Corps series
Goulart, Ron
see **Ben Jolson series**

Chameleon series
La Plante, Jerry
1 *Wrath of Garde* (1979)
2 *In Garde we trust* (1979)
3 *Garde save the world* (1979)

Champ and Djuna series
Queen, Ellery, Junior
see **Djuna and Champ series**

Champion series
Coles, P C J
1 *Champion's folly* (1984)
2 *Champion's chariot* (1985)
3 *Champion's calamity* (1987)

Champnell series
Marsh, Richard
see **Augustus Champnell series**

Chan series
Biggers, Earl Derr
see **Charlie Chan series**

Chance Malloy series
Dent, Lester
1 *Dead at the take-off* (1946)
High stakes
2 *Lady to kill* (1946)

Chance Purdue series
Spencer, Ross Harrison
1 *Dada caper* (1978)
2 *Reggis Arms caper* (1979)
3 *Stranger city caper* (1979)
4 *Abu Wahab caper* (1980)
5 *Radish River caper* (1981)

Chance series
Chance, John Newton
see **John Newton Chance series**
Cord, Barry
see **Dave Chance series**

Chance Sharpe series
Tanner, Clay
1 *Chance* (1986)
2 *Riverboat rampage* (1987)
3 *Dead man's hand* (1987)
4 *Gambler's revenge* (1987)
5 *Delta raiders* (1987)
6 *Mississippi rogue* (1987)
7 *Dakota showdown* (1987)
8 *Missouri massacre* (1987)
9 *Deadly deal* (1988)
10 *Bayou bluff* (1988)
11 *Gold fever* (1988)
12 *White water* (1988)

Chandal Talon trilogy
Eulo, Ken
1 *Brownstone* (1980)
2 *Bloodstone* (1981)
3 *Deathstone* (1982)

Chandler family series
Haas, Ben
1 *Chandler heritage* (1971)
2 *Daisy Canfield* (1973)

Chandler twins series
Deveraux, Jude
1 *Twin of ice* (1985)
2 *Twin of fire* (1985)

Chandos series
Yates, Dornford
see **Richard Chandos series**

Chane and Karlov series
Hayes, Ralph Eugene
see **Check Force series**

Chane series
Gant, Norman
1 *Chane* (1968)
2 *Black vengeance* (1968)
Vengeance of Chane

Chaney brothers series
Jacks, T J
1 *Glory dust* (1992)
2 *Chaney edge* (1992)

Chaney series
Garrison, Christian
see **Ace Chaney series**

Chang series
Apple, A E
see **Mister Chang series**

Changeling series
Zelazny, Roger
1 *Changeling* (1980)
2 *Madwand* (1981)
One volume edition entitled *Wizard world*, 1989

Changeling star series
Carver, Jeffrey Allan
1 *From a changeling star* (1989)
2 *Down the stream of stars* (1990)

Changeling trilogy
McKenney, Kenneth
1 *Moonchild* (1978)
2 *Changeling* (1985)
3 *Offspring* (1990)

Changes and chances series
Nevinson, Henry Woodd
Autobiography
1 *Changes and chances* (1923)

2 *More changes, more chances* (1925)
3 *Last changes, last chances* (1928)

Changes trilogy
Dickinson, Peter
1 *Devil's children* (1970)
2 *Heartsease* (1969)
3 *Weathermonger* (1968)
One volume editions entitled *The changes*, 1975 and *The changes trilogy*, 1985

Changewar series
Leiber, Fritz
1 *Big time* (1961)
2 *Change war* (1978)
Abridged edition entitled *Changewar*, 1983

Changewinds series
Chalker, Jack Laurence
1 *When the changewinds blow* (1987)
2 *Riders of the winds* (1988)
3 *War of the maelstrom* (1988)

Changing environment series
Muller, Jorg
1 *Changing countryside* (1973)
Original edition entitled *All jahre wieder saust der Presslufthammer nieder*
2 *Changing city* (1977)
Original edition entitled *Hier faullt ein Haus, dort steht ein Kran und ewig droht der Baggerzahn, oder die Veraenderung der Stadt*

Changing series
Armstrong, F W
1 *Changing* (1985)
2 *Devouring* (1987)

Channings series
Wood, Ellen
1 *Channings* (1862)
2 *Roland Yorke* (1869)

Chant series
Cross, David
1 *Chant* (1986)
2 *Silent killer* (1986)
3 *Code of blood* (1987)

Chantecoq series
Bernede, Arthur
1 *Mystery of the Louvre* (1929)
2 *Haunted house* (1930)

Chantry family series
L'Amour, Louis
1 *North to the rails* (1971)
2 *Ferguson rifle* (1973)
3 *Over on the dry side* (1975)
4 *Borden Chantry* (1978)
5 *Fair blows the wind* (1979)
6 *Ride the river* (1983)

Chanur series
Cherryh, Carolyn Janice
1 *Pride of Chanur* (1982)
2 *Chanur's venture* (1984)
3 *Kif strikes back* (1985)
4 *Chanur's homecoming* (1986)

Chaos gate trilogy
Cooper, Louise Antell
1 *Deceiver* (1991)
2 *Pretender* (1991)
3 *Avenger* (1992)

Chaos series
Kapp, Colin
1 *Patterns of chaos* (1972)
2 *Chaos weapon* (1977)

Chaos series
Smith, Shelley
see **Jacob Chaos series**

Chapman series
Sedley, Kate
see **Roger Chapman series**

Chapter series
Armitage, Aileen
1 *Chapter of innocence* (1988)
2 *Chapter of echoes* (1989)
3 *Chapter of shadows* (1990)

Character and environment series
Hardy, Thomas
see **Novels of character and environment series**

Chard series
Malim, Barbara
see **Simon Chard series**
Verner, Gerald
see **Peter Chard series**

Chariots of fire trilogy
Rusoff, Garry
1 *Chariots of fire* (1974)
Co-author: Michel Parry
2 *Throne of fire* (1975)
Co-author: Michel Parry
3 *Spear of fire* (1977)

Charisma Inc. series
Glick, Ruth
1 *Saber dance* (1988)
2 *Breahtless* (1988)
3 *Smoke screen* (1988)
4 *Desperado* (1988)
5 *Golden hawk* (1988)

Charity Rose series
Hunter, E J
see **Head hunter series**

Charity Ross series
Bickham, Jack Miles
1 *War on Charity Ross* (1967)
2 *Target, Charity Ross* (1968)

Charity Tucker and Ben Shock series
Buchanan, Patrick
see **Ben Shock and Charity Tucker series**

Charlecote series
Yonge, Charlotte Mary
see **Honor Charlecote series**

Charlemagne's champion series
Van Asten, Gail
1 *Charlemagne's champion* (1990)
2 *Dark sword's lover* (1990)

Charles A Baker series
Huston, Howard Chauncey
see **Detective Charles A Baker series**

Charles and James Latimer series
Gaite, Francis
see **James and Charles Latimer series**

Charles and Poly O'Keefe series
L'Engle, Madeleine
see **Poly and Charles O'Keefe series**

Charles Blessington series
Sherwood, John
see **Mister Charles Blessington series**

Charles Carr and Jack Kelly series
Petievich, Gerald
1 *Money men* (1981)
2 *One shot dead* (1983)
3 *To die in Beverly Hills* (1983)
4 *Quality of the informant* (1985)

Charles De Gaulle series
Crozier, Brian
see **De Gaulle series**

Charles Dexter series
Fredman, John
1 *Fourth agency* (1969)
2 *False Joanna* (1970)
3 *Epitaph to a bad cop* (1973)

Charles Douglas Kerrwood series
Duncan, Allan
see **Major Charles Douglas Kerrwood series**

Charles Duddleswell series
Boyd, Neil
see **Father Charles Duddleswell series**

Charles Harbord series
Liddell, Robert
1 *Unreal city* (1952)
2 *Rivers of Babylon* (1959)
3 *Object for a walk* (1966)

Charles Hillary series
McGrew, Fenn
see **Lieutenant Charles Hillary series**

Charles Honeybath series
Innes, Michael
1 *Mysterious commission* (1974)
2 *Honeybath's haven* (1977)
3 *Lord Mullion's secret* (1981)
4 *Appleby and Honeybath* (1983)

Charles Hood series
Mayo, James
1 *Hammerhead* (1964)
2 *Let sleeping girls lie* (1965)
3 *Shamelady* (1966)
4 *Once in a lifetime* (1968)
Sergeant Death
5 *Man above suspicion* (1969)
6 *Asking for it* (1971)

Charles Horne series
Tucker, Wilson
1 *Chinese doll* (1946)
2 *To keep or kill* (1947)
3 *Dove* (1948)
4 *Stalking man* (1949)
5 *Red herring* (1951)

Charles I series
Beardsworth, Millicent Monica
1 *King's servant* (1966)
2 *King's friend* (1968)
3 *King's endeavour* (1969)
4 *King's adversary* (1972)
5 *King's contest* (1975)
6 *King's victory* (1978)

Charles I trilogy
Lane, Jane
1 *Young and lonely king* (1969)
2 *Questing beast* (1970)
Based on the life of Pym, the Parliamentary leader, in the period before the Civil War
3 *Call of trumpets* (1971)
A novel of the Royalist cause in the Civil War

Charles I trilogy
Wingfield-Stratford, Esme
1 *Charles, King of England, 1600-1637* (1949)
2 *King Charles and King Pym, 1637-1643* (1949)
3 *King Charles the martyr, 1643-1649* (1950)
Companion volume: *King Charles and the conspirators*, 1937

Charles II series
Denis, Charlotte
1 *King's wench* (1975)
2 *King's bastard* (1977)

Charles II trilogy
Nepean, Evelyn Maud
1 *Lanterns of horn* (1923)
2 *Ivory and apes* (1921)
A Nell Gwyn novel
3 *My two kings, 1674-1686* (1917)
A novel of the Stuart Restoration

Charles II trilogy
Plaidy, Jean
1 *Wandering prince* (1956)
2 *Health unto His Majesty* (1956)
3 *Here lies our Sovereign Lord* (1957)
One volume edition entitled *Charles II*, 1972

Charles Kirk series
Blackburn, John
see **General Charles Kirk series**

Charles Knightley series
Horler, Sydney
see **Sir Charles Knightley series**

Charles Latimer series
Ambler, Eric
1 *Mask for Dimitrios* (1939)
Coffin for Dimitrios
2 *Intercom conspiracy* (1969)

Charles Lilburne and Rupert Inglis series
Walder, David
1 *Bags of swank* (1963)
2 *Short list* (1964)
3 *House party* (1966)

Charles Lyson series
Oppenheim, Edward Phillips
see **Major Charles Lyson series**

Charles Miller series
Keenan, William
see **Chief Superintendent Charles Miller series**

Charles Oakshott series
Challoner, Robert
see **Commander Lord Charles Oakshott series**

Charles Paris series
Brett, Simon
1 *Cast, in order of disappearance* (1975)
2 *So much blood* (1976)
3 *Star trap* (1977)
4 *Amateur corpse* (1978)
5 *Comedian dies* (1979)
6 *Dead side of the mike* (1980)
7 *Situation tragedy* (1981)
8 *Murder unprompted* (1982)
9 *Murder in the title* (1983)
10 *Not dead, only resting* (1984)
11 *Dead giveaway* (1985)
12 *What bloody man is that?* (1987)
13 *Series of murders* (1989)
14 *Corporate bodies* (1993)
15 *Reconstructed corpse* (1993)
A short story featuring Charles Paris is included in *A box of tricks*, 1985, also published as *Tickled to death*

Charles Proudfoot Bailey series
Borg, Jack
see **Hogleg Bailey series**

Charles Pry series
Large, Ernest Charles
1 *Asleep in the afternoon* (1938)
2 *Sugar in the air* (1937)

Charles Ripley series
Wainwright, John
see **Superintendent Charles Ripley series**

Charles Russell series
Haggard, William
see **Colonel Charles Russell series**

Charles series
Ainsworth, Ruth
1 *Charles stories, and others from Listen with mother* (1954)
2 *More about Charles, and other stories from Listen with mother* (1954)
3 *Five Listen with mother tales about Charles* (1957)

Charles series
Lang, Andrew
see **Pickle series**
Warner, Mignon
see **Mrs Edwina Charles series**

Charles Timothy Matthews series
Meredith, Doris R
see **Sheriff Charles Timothy Matthews series**

Charles Tremayne series
Mackenzie, Nigel
see **Inspector Charles Tremayne series**

Charles Venables series
Sprigg, Christopher Saint John
1 *Crime in Kensington* (1933)
2 *Fatality in Fleet Street* (1933)
3 *Perfect alibi* (1934)
4 *Death of a queen* (1935)

Charles Winter series
Egleton, Clive
1 *Winter touch* (1981)
Eisenhower deception
2 *Russian enigma* (1982)

Charles Wycliffe series
Burley, William John
see **Superintendent Charles Wycliffe series**

Charleston and Beard series
Guthrie, Alfred Bertram
see **Sheriff Chick Charleston and Jason Beard series**

Charleston series
Ripley, Alexandra
1 *Charleston* (1981)
2 *On leaving Charleston* (1984)

Charlesworth series
Brand, Christianna
see **Inspector Charlesworth series**
Fletcher, Joseph Smith
see **Sergeant Charlesworth series**
Sandys, James
see **James Charlesworth series**

Charley Brewer series
Hallahan, William Henry
1 *Foxcatcher* (1986)
2 *Tripletrap* (1989)

Charley Case series
Spencer, John
1 *Case for Charley* (1984)
2 *Charley gets the picture* (1985)

Charley Malarkey series
Kennedy, William
1 *Charley Malarkey and the belly-button machine* (1986)
2 *Charley Malarkey and the singing moose* (1994)

Charley Mitchell series
Wolff, William Almon
see **Lieutenant Charley Mitchell series**

Charley Moss series
Jackson, Jesse
1 *Call me Charley* (1945)
2 *Anchor man* (1947)
3 *Charley starts from scratch* (1958)

Charley Partanna series
Condon, Richard
see **Prizzi family series**

Charley series
Hodges, Margaret
1 *What's for lunch, Charley?* (1961)
2 *Sing out, Charley* (1968)

Charlie Adams series
Boyer, Richard Lewis
see **Doctor Charlie Adams series**

Charlie Agutter series
Llewellyn, Sam
1 *Dead reckoning* (1987)
2 *Blood orange* (1988)

Charlie Bradshaw series
Dobyns, Stephen
1 *Saratoga longshot* (1976)
2 *Saratoga swimmer* (1981)
3 *Saratoga headhunter* (1985)
4 *Saratoga snapper* (1986)
5 *Saratoga bestiary* (1988)
6 *Saratoga hexameter* (1990)
7 *Saratoga haunting* (1993)
8 *Saratoga backtalk* (1994)

Charlie Bucket series
Dahl, Roald
1 *Charlie and the chocolate factory* (1964)
2 *Charlie and the great glass elevator* (1972)
Omnibus volume entitled *The complete adventures of Charlie and Mr Willy Wonka*, 1978

Charlie Chan series
This sequence has three authors
Biggers, Earl Derr
1 *House without a key* (1925)
2 *Chinese parrot* (1926)
3 *Behind that curtain* (1928)
4 *Black camel* (1929)
5 *Charlie Chan carries on* (1930)
6 *Keeper of the keys* (1932)
Lynds, Dennis
7 *Charlie Chan returns* (1974)
Avallone, Michael
8 *Charlie Chan and the curse of the Dragon Queen* (1981)
Based on a screenplay by Stan Burns and George Axelrod

Charlie Clown series
Brook, Judy
1 *Charlie Clown at the seaside* (1986)
2 *Charlie Clown at the circus* (1986)

Charlie Ellis and Angela Mitchell series
Lavelle, Sheila
1 *My best fiend* (1980)
2 *Fiend next door* (1982)
3 *Trouble with the fiend* (1984)
4 *Holiday with the fiend* (1986)
5 *Disaster with the fiend* (1988)
6 *Calamity with the fiend* (1993)

Charlie Hope series
Eller, John
1 *Charlie and the iceman* (1981)
2 *Rage of heaven* (1983)

Charlie Miklejohn and Constance Leidl series
Wilhelm, Kate
1 *Hamlet trap* (1987)
2 *Dark door* (1988)
3 *Smart house* (1989)
4 *Sweet, sweet poison* (1990)

Charlie Moon series
Hughes, Shirley
1 *Here comes Charlie Moon* (1980)
2 *Charlie moon and the big bonanza bust up* (1982)

Charlie Mortdecai series
Bonfiglioli, Kyril
1 *Don't point that thing at me* (1972)
Mortdecai's endgame
2 *Something nasty in the woodshed* (1976)
3 *After you with the pistol* (1979)

Charlie Muffin series
Freemantle, Brian
1 *Charlie Muffin* (1977)
Charlie M
2 *Clap hands, here comes Charlie* (1978)
Here comes Charlie M
3 *Inscrutable Charlie Muffin* (1979)
4 *Charlie Muffin's Uncle Sam* (1980)
Charlie Muffin, U.S.A.
5 *Madrigal for Charlie Muffin* (1981)
6 *Charlie Muffin and Russian Rose* (1985)
7 *Blind run* (1986)
8 *Charlie Muffin San* (1987)
See Charlie run
9 *Runaround* (1988)
10 *Comrade Charlie* (1989)
11 *Charlie's apprentice* (1993)

Charlie Peace series
Barnard, Robert
1 *Bodies* (1986)
2 *Death in purple prose* (1987)
Cherry blossom corpse
3 *Death and the chaste apprentice* (1989)

Charlie Pearce and William Hart series
Gardner, Jerome
see **Dripspring series**

Charlie Resnick series
Harvey, John Barton
see **Inspector Charlie Resnick series**

Charlie Ryan series
Lenehan, John Christopher
1 *Masked blackmailer* (1933)
2 *Death dances thrice* (1933)
3 *Boston belle meets murder* (1935)
4 *Guilty but not insane* (1938)
5 *Driven to death* (1944)

Charlie Salter series
Wright, Eric
see **Inspector Charlie Salter series**

Charlie series
Allen, Joy
1 *Boots for Charlie* (1975)
2 *Teeth for Charlie* (1976)
3 *Move for Charlie* (1978)
4 *Stitches for Charlie* (1980)
5 *Cup final for Charlie* (1981)
6 *Goal for Charlie* (1984)
7 *Stick to it, Charlie* (1985)
8 *Adventure for Charlie* (1986)
9 *Computer for Charlie* (1987)
10 *County rovers for Charlie* (1988)
11 *Sports day for Charlie* (1990)
12 *Look out, Charlie* (1993)

Charlie series
Hurd, Edith Thatcher
see **Mister Charlie series**
Lane, Elizabeth
see **Uncle Charlie series**

Charlie Sparrow series
Ardies, Tom
1 *Their man in the White House* (1971)
2 *This suitcase is going to explode* (1972)
3 *Pandemic* (1973)

Charlie Spotted Moon series
Yarbro, Chelsea Quinn
1 *Ogilvie, Tallant and Moon* (1976)
Bad medicine
2 *Music when sweet voices die* (1979)
False notes
3 *Poison fruit* (1991)
4 *Cat's claw* (1992)

Charlie's Angels series
Franklin, Max
Based on a television series
1 *Charlie's Angels* (1977)
2 *Killing kind* (1977)
3 *Angels on a string* (1977)
4 *Angels in chains* (1977)
5 *Angels on ice* (1978)

Charlock series
Durrell, Lawrence
see **Revolt of Aphrodite series**

Charlotte and Emma Makepeace series
Farmer, Penelope
1 *Summer birds* (1962)
Revised edition 1985
2 *Emma in winter* (1966)
3 *Charlotte sometimes* (1969)

Charlotte Cheetham trilogy
Holmes, Barbara Ware
1 *Charlotte Cheetham, master of disaster* (1985)
2 *Charlotte the starlet* (1988)
3 *Charlotte Shakespeare and Annie the great* (1989)

Charlotte Eliot series
Filgate, Macartney
1 *Bravo Charlie* (1979)
Runway to death
2 *Delta November* (1979)

Charlotte Ellison Pitt and Inspector Thomas Pitt series
Perry, Anne
Set in London in the 1880s
1 *Cater Street hangman* (1979)
2 *Callander Square* (1980)
3 *Paragon Walk* (1981)
4 *Resurrection Row* (1981)
5 *Rutland Place* (1983)
6 *Bluegate Fields* (1984)
7 *Death in the Devil's Acre* (1985)
8 *Cardington Crescent* (1987)
9 *Silence in Hanover Close* (1988)
10 *Bethlehem Road* (1990)
11 *Face of a stranger* (1990)
12 *Highgate Rise* (1992)
13 *Belgrave Square* (1993)

Charlotte Graham series
Matteson, Stefanie
1 *Murder at the spa* (1990)
2 *Murder at teatime* (1991)
3 *Murder on the cliff* (1991)
4 *Murder on Silk Road* (1992)
5 *Murder at the falls* (1993)
6 *Murder on high* (1994)

Charlotte Morel series
Lodi, Maria
1 *Charlotte Morel* (1965)
2 *Dream* (1965)
3 *Siege* (1965)
Original edition in one volume entitled *Cherie, quand nous mourons*

Charlton Mead series
Wiat, Philippa
1 *Mistletoe bough* (1981)
2 *Bride in darkness* (1982)
3 *Wychwood* (1982)

Charlton School series
This sequence has two authors
Adams, William
1 *Cherry-stones* (1851)
Edited by Henry Cadwallader Adams; alternative title: Charlton School

Adams, Henry Cadwallader
2 *First of June* (1856)
Alternative title: Schoolboy rivalry

Charlton series
Witting, Clifford
see **Inspector Charlton series**

Charm bracelet series
Dickinson, Mary Anne
1 *Charm bracelet* (1994)
2 *Flower fairies* (1994)

Charmian Daniels series
Melville, Jennie
see **Sergeant Charmian Daniels series**

Charming people series
Arlen, Michael
1 *These charming people* (1923)
Man with the broken nose, and other stories
2 *May Fair* (1925)
Ace of Cads, and other stories
The last adventures of these charming people

Charrington series
Gathorne-Hardy, Jonathan
see **Jane Charrington series**

Chase Defoe series
Day, Deforest
1 *August ice* (1990)
2 *Cold killing* (1990)
3 *Fatal recall* (1991)

Chase Randel series
Wuamett, Victor
1 *Teardown* (1990)
2 *Deeds of trust* (1991)
3 *Artichoke hearts* (1991)

Chase series
Cort, Ned
see **Boxer Unit SS series**
Oxenham, John
see **Beatrice Chase series**
Tiltman, Marjorie Hessell
see **Quality Chase series**
Warner, Frank A
see **Bob Chase series**

Chatham series
Neebel, Richard
see **Erik Chatham series**

Chatham trilogy
Sherrard, Owen Aubrey
see **Lord Chatham trilogy**

Chatterbooks series
Berg, Leila
1 *Tickle* (1981)
2 *Hot, hot day* (1981)
3 *In a house I know* (1981)
4 *Our walk* (1981)

Chatterbooks series
Jessel, Camilla
1 *Away for the night* (1981)
2 *Moving house* (1981)
3 *Going to the doctor* (1981)
4 *Going to hospital* (1983)
5 *At playgroup* (1983)
6 *Lost and found* (1983)
7 *Baby-sitter* (1983)

Chatterbox series
Tarsky, Sue
1 *Who goes moo?* (1984)
2 *Open the door* (1984)
3 *I can* (1984)
4 *What goes beep?* (1984)
5 *Who goes splash?* (1985)

Chatterley series
Lawrence, David Herbert
see **Lady Chatterley series**

Chatterton series
Ayres, Ruby Mildred
see **Richard Chatterton series**

Chauncey O'Day series
Gaines, Audrey
1 *Old must die* (1939)
2 *While the wind howled* (1940)

Chautauqua series
Pansy
1 *Chautauqua girls at home* (1873)
2 *Four girls at Chautauqua* (1876)
3 *Eighty-seven* (1887)
4 *Four mothers at Chautauqua* (1913)

Chavasse series
Fallon, Martin
see **Paul Chavasse series**

Chavez series
Lindsey, Johanna
see **Hank Chavez series**

Check Force series
Hayes, Ralph Eugene
1 *One hundred megaton kill* (1975)
2 *Clouds of war* (1975)
3 *Judgment day* (1975)
4 *Peking plot* (1975)
5 *Nightmare Island* (1975)
6 *Seeds of doom* (1976)
7 *Fires of hell* (1976)

Check series
Staton, Knofel L
1 *Check your lifestyle* (1979)
Putting the Proverbs into practice
2 *Check your character* (1980)
Co-author: Julia Staton; putting the Beatitudes into practice
3 *Check your discipleship* (1982)
4 *Check your life with Christ* (1983)
5 *Check your morality* (1983)
Moral issues and the Bible
6 *Check your homelife* (1983)
7 *Check your commitment* (1985)
8 *Check your relationships* (1987)
Studies from Mark

Checkered flag series
Bamman, Henry A
1 *Wheels* (1967)
2 *Riddler* (1967)
3 *Bearcat* (1967)
4 *Smashup* (1967)
5 *Scramble* (1969)
6 *Flea* (1969)
7 *Grand Prix* (1969)
8 *Five Hundred* (1969)

Checkmate series
McFarlane, Leslie
1 *Agent of the Falcon* (1975)
2 *Dynamite Flynns* (1975)
3 *Mystery of Spider Lake* (1975)
4 *Squeeze play* (1975)
5 *Breakaway* (1976)
6 *Snow Hawk* (1976)

Chee series
Hillerman, Tony
see **Sergeant Jim Chee series**

Cheerful day series
Fairbrother, Nan
Memoirs
1 *Children in the house* (1954)
2 *Cheerful day* (1960)

Cheerful Yankee trilogy
Bacheller, Irving
1 *Coming up the road* (1928)
Memories of a north country boyhood
2 *Opinions of a cheerful Yankee* (1926)
3 *From stores of memory* (1938)

Cheerleaders series
This sequence has fifteen authors
Cooney, Caroline B
1 *Trying out* (1985)
Pike, Christopher
2 *Getting even* (1985)
Cooney, Caroline B
3 *Rumors* (1985)
Norby, Lisa
4 *Feuding* (1985)
Cooney, Caroline B
5 *All the way* (1985)
Sarasin, Jennifer
6 *Splitting* (1985)
Hoh, Diane
7 *Flirting* (1985)
Norby, Lisa
8 *Forgetting* (1985)
Theis, Jody Sorenson
9 *Playing games* (1985)
Hoh, Diane
10 *Betrayed* (1985)
Sarasin, Jennifer
11 *Cheating* (1985)
Hoh, Diane
12 *Staying together* (1986)
Norby, Lisa
13 *Hurting* (1986)
Sarasin, Jennifer
14 *Living it up* (1986)
Theis, Jody Sorenson
15 *Waiting* (1986)
Stanley, Carol
16 *In love* (1986)
Reynolds, Anne
17 *Taking risks* (1986)
Ellis, Carol
18 *Looking good* (1986)
Blake, Susan
19 *Making it* (1986)
Aks, Patricia
20 *Starting over* (1986)
Hoh, Diane
21 *Pulling together* (1986)
Steinke, Anne E
22 *Rivals* (1986)
Hoh, Diane
23 *Proving it* (1986)
Ellis, Carol
24 *Going strong* (1986)
Steinke, Anne E
25 *Stealing secrets* (1987)
Sarasin, Jennifer
26 *Taking over* (1987)
Hoh, Diane
27 *Spring fever* (1987)
Norby, Lisa
28 *Scheming* (1987)
Sarasin, Jennifer
29 *Falling in love* (1987)
Cooney, Caroline B
30 *Saying yes* (1987)
Ellis, Carol
31 *Showing off* (1987)
Sarasin, Jennifer
32 *Together again* (1987)
Steinke, Anne E
33 *Saying no* (1987)
Norby, Lisa
34 *Coming back* (1987)
Davis, Leslie
35 *Moving up* (1987)
Weber, Judith
36 *Changing loves* (1987)
Sarasin, Jennifer
37 *Acting up* (1988)
Norby, Lisa
38 *Talking back* (1988)
Davis, Leslie
39 *All or nothing* (1988)
Sarasin, Jennifer
40 *Getting serious* (1988)
Steinke, Anne E
41 *Having it all* (1988)
Ellis, Carol
42 *Fighting back* (1988)
Norby, Lisa
43 *Scheming* (1988)
44 *Telling lies* (1988)
Sarasin, Jennifer
45 *Here to stay* (1988)
Schurfranz, Vivian
46 *Overboard!* (1988)

Cheetham trilogy
Holmes, Barbara Ware
see **Charlotte Cheetham trilogy**

Chelmarsh series
Hardwick, Mollie
see **Doran Fairweather series**

Chemical warfare series
Spiers, Edward Michael
1 *Chemical warfare* (1986)
2 *Chemical weaponry* (1989)

Chequered flag series
Rutherford, Douglas
1 *Gunshot Grand Prix* (1972)
2 *Killer on the track* (1973)
3 *Rally to the death* (1974)
4 *Race against the sun* (1975)

Cheri series
Colette, Sidonie Gabrielle
1 *Cheri* (1920)
Original edition entitled *Cheri*
2 *Last of Cheri* (1926)
Original edition entitled *La fin de Cheri*
One volume edition 1951

Cheri-Bibi series
Leroux, Gaston
1 *Floating prison* (1921)
Wolves of the sea
Original edition entitled *Les cages flotantes*
2 *Cheri-Bibi and Cecily* (1921)
Missing men
Original edition entitled *Cheri-Bibi et Cecily*
3 *Cheri-Bibi, mystery man* (1921)
Dark road
Original edition entitled *Fatalitas*
4 *Dancing girl* (1924)
Nomads of the night
5 *New idol* (1925)
Original edition entitled *Le coup d'etat de Cheri-Bibi*

Cherie series
Saint-Laurent, Cecil
1 *Caroline Cherie* (1947)
Original edition entitled *Caroline Cherie*, part 1
2 *Loves of Caroline Cherie* (1947)
Original edition entitled *Caroline Cherie*, part 2
3 *Caroline in Italy* (1952)
Original edition entitled *Un caprice de Caroline Cherie*
4 *Caroline Cherie and Juan* (1958)
Original edition entitled *L'Espagne et Juan*
5 *Intrigues of Caroline Cherie* (1959)
Original edition entitled *Les caprices de Caroline*

Cherrington series
Daniel, Glyn
see **Sir Richard Cherrington series**

Cherrington trilogy
Hartley, Leslie Poles
see **Eustace and Hilda Cherrington trilogy**

Cherry Ames series
This sequence has two authors
Wells, Helen
1 *Cherry Ames, student nurse* (1943)
2 *Cherry Ames, senior nurse* (1944)
3 *Cherry Ames, army nurse* (1944)
4 *Cherry Ames, chief nurse* (1944)
5 *Cherry Ames, flight nurse* (1945)
6 *Cherry Ames, veterans' nurse* (1946)
Cherry Ames, soldiers' nurse

Cherry Ames series

7 *Cherry Ames, private duty nurse* (1946)
8 *Cherry Ames, visiting nurse* (1947)
9 *Cherry Ames, cruise nurse* (1948)
Tatham, Julie
10 *Cherry Ames at Spencer* (1949)
11 *Cherry Ames, night supervisor* (1950)
12 *Cherry Ames, mountaineer nurse* (1951)
13 *Cherry Ames, clinic nurse* (1952)
14 *Cherry Ames, dude ranch nurse* (1953)
15 *Cherry Ames, rest home nurse* (1954)
16 *Cherry Ames, country doctor's nurse* (1955)
Wells, Helen
17 *Cherry Ames, boarding-school nurse* (1955)
18 *Cherry Ames, department store nurse* (1956)
19 *Cherry Ames, camp nurse* (1957)
20 *Cherry Ames at Hilton Hospital* (1959)
21 *Cherry Ames, island nurse* (1960)
Mystery at Rogue's Cave
22 *Cherry Ames, rural nurse* (1961)
23 *Cherry Ames, staff nurse* (1962)
24 *Cherry Ames, companion nurse* (1964)
25 *Cherry Ames, jungle nurse* (1965)
26 *Mystery in the doctor's office* (1966)
27 *Ski nurse mystery* (1968)

Cherry and Duff series
Van Greenaway, Peter
see **Inspector Cherry and Sergeant Duff series**

Cherry Blossom and Roger Ellerdine series
Wills, Cecil Melville
see **Superintendent Roger Ellerdine and Sergeant Cherry Blossom series**

Cherry Delight series
Chase, Glen
House pseudonym
1 *Italian connection* (1972)
2 *Tong in cheek* (1972)
3 *Silverfinger* (1972)
4 *Up your ante* (1972)
5 *Crack shot* (1973)
6 *I'm Cherry, fly me!* (1973)
7 *Chuck you, Farley!* (1973)
8 *Hot rocks* (1974)
9 *Jersey bounce* (1974)
10 *Made in Japan* (1974)
11 *Broad jump* (1974)
12 *Fire in the hole* (1974)
13 *Over the hump* (1974)
14 *In a pinch* (1974)
15 *What a way to go* (1974)
16 *Busted* (1974)
17 *Treasure chest* (1974)
18 *Hang loose* (1974)
19 *In a bind* (1975)
20 *Always on Sunday* (1975)
21 *Mexican standoff* (1975)
22 *Roman candle* (1975)
23 *Lights, action, murder!* (1975)
24 *Big bankroll* (1975)
25 *Greek fire* (1977)
26 *Devil to pay* (1977)
27 *Moorland monster* (1977)
28 *Where the action is* (1977)
29 *Man who was God* (1978)

Cherrys series
Scott, Will
1 *Cherrys of River House* (1952)
2 *Cherrys and company* (1953)
3 *Cherrys by the sea* (1954)
4 *Cherrys and the Pringles* (1955)
5 *Cherrys and the galleon* (1956)
6 *Cherrys and the double arrow* (1957)
7 *Cherrys on Indoor Island* (1958)
8 *Cherrys on Zig-Zag Trail* (1959)
9 *Cherrys' mystery holiday* (1960)
10 *Cherrys and the silent rooom* (1961)
11 *Cherrys famous case* (1962)
12 *Cherrys to the rescue* (1963)
13 *Cherrys in the snow* (1964)
14 *Cherrys and the blue balloon* (1965)

Cherry-Tree Farm series
Kent, Margaret
see **Four seasons at Cherry-Tree Farm series**

Cherwell family series
Galsworthy, John
see **End of the chapter series**

Chesapeke steamboats series
Holly, David Chauncey
1 *Steamboat on the Chesapeke* (1987)
Emma Giles and the Tolchester Line
2 *Tidewater by steamboat* (1991)
A saga of the Chesapeke, the Weems Line on the Patuxent, Potomac and the Rappahannock

Chesnut trilogy
McDonald, Kay L
see **Ross Chesnut trilogy**

Chester boys series
Dawson, Elmer A
see **Buck and Larry baseball series**

Chester Brett series
Evans, Gwyn
1 *Mysterious Miss Death* (1937)
2 *Clue of the missing link* (1938)
3 *Triangle of terror* (1938)
4 *Case of the climbing corpse* (1939)

Chester C Tabor series
Cruz, Mark
see **Death Squad series**

Chester Cricket series
Selden, George
1 *Cricket in Times Square* (1960)
2 *Tucker's countryside* (1969)
3 *Harry Cat's pet puppy* (1974)
4 *Chester Cricket's pigeon ride* (1981)
5 *Chester Cricket's new home* (1983)
6 *Harry Kitten and Tucker Mouse* (1985)
7 *Old meadow* (1987)

Chester Drum series
Marlowe, Stephen
1 *Second longest night* (1955)
2 *Mecca for murder* (1956)
3 *Trouble is my name* (1957)
4 *Murder is my dish* (1957)
5 *Killers are my meat* (1957)
6 *Terror is my trade* (1958)
7 *Violence is my business* (1958)
8 *Homicide is my game* (1959)
9 *Double in trouble* (1959)
Co-author: Richard Scott Prather
10 *Danger is my line* (1960)
11 *Peril is my pay* (1960)
12 *Death is my comrade* (1960)
13 *Manhunt is my mission* (1961)
14 *Jeopardy is my job* (1962)
15 *Francesca* (1963)
16 *Drum beat, Berlin* (1964)
17 *Drum beat, Dominique* (1965)
18 *Drum beat, Madrid* (1966)
19 *Drum beat, Erica* (1967)
20 *Drum beat, Marianne* (1968)

Chester Fortune series
Stone, Thomas H
1 *Dead set* (1972)
2 *One horse race* (1972)

Chester Long series
Carpenter, Carleton
1 *Only her hairdresser knew* (1973)
2 *Deadhead* (1974)

Chester Nimmo trilogy
Cary, Joyce
1 *Except the Lord* (1953)
2 *Prisoner of grace* (1952)
3 *Not honour more* (1955)

Chester series
Pyke, Lillian Maxwell
see **Sheila Chester series**
Raymond, Evelyn Hunt
see **Dorothy Chester series**

Chester trilogy
De Born, Edith
see **Jimmy Chester trilogy**

Chet Gordon series
Millar, Kenneth
1 *Dark tunnel* (1944)
I die slowly
2 *Trouble follows me* (1946)
Night train

Chet Kinsman series
Bova, Ben
1 *Millenium* (1976)
2 *Kinsman* (1979)
One volume edition entitled *The Kinsman saga*, 1987

Chet Phelps series
Childerness, George
1 *Murder in false face* (1943)
2 *Too many murderers* (1944)

Cheviot Burmann series
Cobb, Belton
see **Inspector Cheviot Burmann series**

Cheyenne Jones series
Denver, Lee
1 *Gun code of Cheyenne Jones* (1971)
2 *Cheyenne swings a wide loop* (1971)
3 *Three slugs for Cheyenne* (1971)
4 *Cheyenne pays in lead* (1972)
5 *Lone trail for Cheyenne* (1973)
6 *Cheyenne bucks the law* (1975)
7 *Cheyenne Jones, the maverick marshal* (1977)
8 *Cheyenne's sixgun justice* (1980)
9 *Cheyenne's trail to Perdition* (1982)
10 *Cheyenne's two-gun shoot-out* (1983)
11 *Cheyenne at Dull Knife Pass* (1984)
12 *Close call for Cheyenne* (1988)

Cheyenne series
Cole, Judd
1 *Arrow keeper* (1992)
2 *Death chase* (1992)
3 *Renegade justice* (1993)
4 *Vision quest* (1993)
5 *Blood on the plains* (1993)
6 *Comanche raid* (1993)
7 *Comancheros* (1993)
8 *War party* (1993)
9 *Pathfinder* (1994)
10 *Buffalo hiders* (1994)
11 *Spirit path* (1994)
12 *Mankiller* (1994)
13 *Wendigo Mountain* (1995)

Cheyney series
Cosgrave, Patrick
see **Colonel Allen Cheyney series**

Cheysuli series
Roberson, Jennifer
see **Chronicles of the Cheysuli series**

Chi-Lo series
Macgregor, Reginald James
1 *Chi-Lo the admiral* (1947)
2 *Chi-Lo the general* (1947)

Chi Ming series
Marquand, Josephine
Illustrated by Pearl Binder
1 *Chi Ming and the tiger kitten* (1964)
2 *Chi Ming and the lion dance* (1969)
Sequence continued under the author's married name Josephine Gladstone
Gladstone, Josephine
3 *Chi Ming and the jade earring* (1974)

Chicago and the cat series
Koontz, Robin Michal
1 *Chicago and the cat* (1993)
2 *Camping trip* (1994)

Chicago Nordejoong series
McKernan, Victoria
1 *Osprey Reef* (1990)
2 *Point Deception* (1992)
3 *Crooked Island* (1994)

Chicago trilogy
Burnett, William Riley
1 *Little Caesar* (1929)
2 *Asphalt jungle* (1949)
3 *Little men, big world* (1951)
Companion volume: *Goodbye, Chicago*, 1981

Chichester Harbour series
Knight, Frank
1 *Mudlarks and mysteries* (1955)
2 *Family on the tide* (1956)
3 *Please keep off the mud* (1957)
4 *Shadows on the mud* (1960)

Chick Bowdrie series
L'Amour, Louis
Short stories
1 *Bowdrie* (1983)
2 *Bowdrie's law* (1984)

Chick Charleston and Jason Beard series
Guthrie, Alfred Bertram
see **Sheriff Chick Charleston and Jason Beard series**

Chick series
Quackenbush, Robert Mead
see **Sherlock Chick series**

Chick Swallow series
De Vries, Peter
1 *Comfort me with apples* (1939)
2 *Tents of wickedness* (1959)

Chick Varney series
Barry, Jerome
1 *Murder with your malted* (1941)
2 *Leopard cat's cradle* (1942)
Cat's cradle murder
3 *Lady of night* (1944)

Chicken and Rabbit series
Landa, Norbert
see **Rabbit and Chicken series**

Chicken Little Jane series
Ritchie, Lily Munsel
1 *Chicken Little Jane* (1918)
2 *Chicken Little Jane on the Big John* (1919)
3 *Adventures of Chicken Little Jane* (1920)
4 *Chicken Little Jane comes to town* (1921)
5 *Chicken Little Jane in the Rockies* (1926)

Chicken soup trilogy
Wesker, Arnold
Plays
1 *Chicken soup with barley* (1959)
2 *Roots* (1959)
3 *I'm talking about Jerusalem* (1960)

Chickenhawk series
Mason, Robert Caverly
Autobiography
1 *Chickenhawk* (1983)
2 *Back in the world* (1993)
Chickenhawk's life after Vietnam

Chico Brett series
O'Hara, Kevin
1 *Customer's always wrong* (1951)
2 *Exit and curtains* (1952)
3 *Sing, clubman, sing* (1952)
4 *Always tell the sleuth* (1953)
5 *It leaves them cold* (1954)
6 *Pace that kills* (1955)
7 *Keep your fingers cross* (1955)
8 *Women like to know* (1957)
9 *Danger, women at work!* (1958)
10 *Well, I'll be hanged* (1958)
11 *And here is the noose* (1959)
12 *Taking life easy* (1961)
13 *If anything should happen* (1962)
14 *Don't tell the police* (1963)
15 *Don't neglect the body* (1964)
16 *It's your funeral* (1966)

Chico Cervantes series
Cook, Bruce
see **Antonio Cervantes series**

Chief Bromden series
Kesey, Ken
1 *One flew over the cuckoo's nest* (1962)
2 *Sometimes a great notion* (1964)

Chief Fred Fellows series
Waugh, Hillary
1 *Sleep long, my love* (1959)
Jigsaw
2 *Road block* (1960)
3 *That night it rained* (1961)
4 *Late Mrs D* (1962)
5 *Born victim* (1962)
6 *Death and circumstance* (1963)
7 *Prisoner's plea* (1963)
8 *Missing man* (1964)
9 *End of a party* (1965)
10 *Pure poison* (1966)
11 *Con game* (1968)

Chief Inspector Alan Banks series
Robinson, Peter
1 *Gallows view* (1987)
2 *Dedicated man* (1988)
3 *Necessary end* (1989)
4 *Hanging valley* (1990)
5 *Past reason hated* (1991)
6 *Wednesday's child* (1992)

Chief Inspector Alan Markby and Meredith Mitchell series
Granger, Ann
see **Meredith Mitchell and Chief Inspector Alan Markby series**

Chief Inspector Andrew McMurdo series
Morland, Nigel
1 *She didn't like dying* (1948)
2 *No coupons for a shroud* (1949)
3 *Two dead charwomen* (1949)
4 *Corpse was no lady* (1950)
5 *Blood on the stars* (1951)
6 *He hanged his mother on Monday* (1951)
7 *Moon was made for murder* (1953)
8 *Death for sale* (1957)
9 *Death to the ladies* (1959)

Chief Inspector Barlow series
This sequence has five authors; based on a television series
Martin, Troy Kennedy
1 *Z cars* (1962)
Prior, Allan
2 *Z cars again* (1963)
Prendergast, William
3 *Z car detective* (1964)
4 *Calling all Z cars* (1966)
5 *Z car Squad* (1968)
Yarrow, Arnold
6 *Softly, softly casebook* (1973)
7 *Softly, softly murder casebook* (1973)
Short stories
Jones, Elwyn
8 *Barlow in charge* (1973)
9 *Barlow comes to judgement* (1974)
10 *Barlow casebook* (1975)
Short stories
11 *Barlow exposed* (1976)
12 *Barlow down under* (1977)
Companion volumes: *Softly, softly, five television scripts*, 1976, *The Ripper file*, by Elwyn Jones and John Lloyd, 1975

Chief Inspector Barnard series
Jacobs, Thomas Curtis Hicks
1 *Scorpion's trail* (1932)
2 *Kestrel House mystery* (1932)
3 *Sinister quest* (1934)
4 *Thirteenth chime* (1935)
5 *Silent terror* (1936)
6 *Laughing man* (1937)
7 *Identity unknown* (1938)
8 *Traitor spy* (1939)
9 *Brother Spy* (1940)
10 *Broken knife* (1941)
11 *Reward for treason* (1944)
12 *Black box* (1946)
13 *Red eyes of Kali* (1950)
14 *Death in the mews* (1955)

Chief Inspector Bill Cromwell series
Gunn, Victor
1 *Footsteps of death* (1939)
2 *Ironsides of the Yard* (1940)
3 *Ironsides smashes through* (1940)
4 *Ironsides' lone hand* (1941)
5 *Death's doorway* (1941)
6 *Mad Hatter's rock* (1942)
7 *Ironsides sees red* (1943)
Three novelettes
8 *Dead man laughs* (1944)
9 *Nice day for murder* (1945)
10 *Ironsides smells blood* (1946)
Three novelettes
11 *Death on the Shivering Sand* (1946)
12 *Three dates with death* (1947)
13 *Ironsides on the spot* (1948)
14 *Road to murder* (1949)
15 *Dead man's warning* (1949)
16 *lias the hangman* (1950)
17 *Murder on ice* (1951)
18 *Borgia Head mystery* (1951)
19 *Body vanishes* (1952)
20 *Death comes laughing* (1952)
21 *Whistling key* (1953)
22 *Crooked staircase* (1954)
23 *Crippled canary* (1954)
24 *Laughing grave* (1955)
25 *Painted dog* (1955)
26 *Dead men's bells* (1956)
27 *Golden monkey* (1957)
28 *Castle Dangerous* (1957)
29 *Sixty four thousand murder* (1958)
30 *Treble chance murder* (1958)
31 *Dead in a ditch* (1959)
32 *Next one to die* (1959)
33 *Death on Bodmir Moor* (1960)
34 *Death at Traitor's Gate* (1960)
35 *Devil in the name* (1961)
36 *Sweet smelling death* (1961)
37 *All change for murder* (1962)
38 *Body in the boot* (1963)
39 *Murder with a kiss* (1963)
40 *Murder at the motel* (1964)
41 *Black cap murder* (1965)
42 *Murder on Whispering Sands* (1965)
43 *Petticoat Lane murders* (1966)

Chief Inspector Bryan Armitage series
Cobb, Belton
see **Bryan Armitage series**

Chief Inspector Corby series
Cooper, Lettice
1 *Tea on Sunday* (1973)
2 *Unusual behaviour* (1986)

Chief Inspector Cummings series
McGuire, Paul
1 *Murder in Bostall* (1931)
Black rose murder
2 *Three dead men* (1931)
3 *Daylight murder* (1934)
Murder at high noon
4 *Murder in haste* (1934)
5 *Seven thirty Victoria* (1935)

Chief Inspector Dawson series
Copplestone, Bennet
1 *Lost naval papers* (1917)
Short stories
2 *Diversions of Dawson* (1923)

Chief Inspector Douglas Grant series
Millar, Florence N
1 *Grant's overture* (1946)
2 *Fishing is dangerous* (1946)

Chief Inspector Douglas Quantrill series
Radley, Sheila
1 *Death and the maiden* (1978)
Death in the morning
2 *Chief Inspector's daughter* (1980)
3 *Talent for destruction* (1982)
4 *Blood on the happy highway* (1983)
Quiet road to death
5 *Fate worse than death* (1985)
6 *Who saw him die?* (1987)
7 *This way out* (1989)

Chief Inspector Drewry series
Burnaby, Nigel
1 *Clue of the green-eyed girl* (1935)
2 *Two deaths for a penny* (1935)

Chief Inspector Duck Mallard series
Spiller, Andrew
1 *Queue up to listen* (1946)
2 *Crooked highway* (1947)
3 *What's in a name?* (1947)
4 *When crook meets crook* (1947)
5 *Murder has three dimensions* (1948)
6 *You can't get away with murder* (1948)
7 *And thereby hangs!* (1949)
8 *Brief candle* (1949)
9 *Phantom circus* (1950)
10 *Man who caught the 4.15* (1950)
11 *Birds of a feather* (1950)
12 *Who plays with sin* (1951)
13 *Alias Mr Orson* (1951)
14 *As they shall sow* (1951)
15 *Kiss the book* (1952)
16 *Evil that men do* (1953)
17 *They tell no tales* (1953)
18 *Murder is a shady business* (1954)
19 *Murder without malice* (1954)
20 *It's in the bag* (1955)
21 *Ring twice for murder* (1955)
22 *Black cap for murder* (1956)
23 *Brain Trust for murder* (1956)
24 *Curtain call for murder* (1957)
25 *Murder on a shoestring* (1958)
26 *Sing a song of murder* (1959)
27 *Man who dressed to kill* (1960)

Chief Inspector Edward Beale series
Penny, Rupert
1 *Talkative policeman* (1936)
2 *Policeman's holiday* (1937)
3 *Policeman in armour* (1937)
4 *Lucky policeman* (1938)
5 *Policeman's evidence* (1938)
6 *She had to have gas* (1939)
7 *Sweet poison* (1940)
8 *Sealed room murder* (1941)

Chief Inspector Frank Desouza series
Olbrich, Freny
Set in Bombay
1 *Desouza pays the price* (1978)
2 *Sweet and deadly* (1979)
3 *Desouza in stardust* (1979)

Chief Inspector George Bassett series
Ryland, Clive
1 *Murder in Queer Street* (1941)
2 *Monday never came* (1947)
3 *In walks murder* (1951)
4 *Case of the back seat girl* (1952)

Chief Inspector Gorham series
Cowdroy, Joan
1 *Framed evidence* (1936)
2 *Murder out of court* (1944)

Chief Inspector Gregory Saltfleet series
Wilson, Colin
1 *Schoolgirl murder case* (1974)
2 *Janus murder case* (1984)

Chief Inspector Harry Fathers series
Smith, Daniel Wybert
1 *Father's law* (1986)
2 *Serious crimes* (1987)

Chief Inspector Harry Martineau series
Procter, Maurice
1 *No proud chivalry* (1947)
2 *Each man's destiny* (1947)
3 *End of the street* (1949)
4 *Hurry the darkness* (1951)
5 *Rich is the treasure* (1952)
6 *Hell is a city* (1954)
Somewhere in this city
Murder, somewhere in this city
7 *Pub crawler* (1956)
8 *Midnight plumber* (1957)
9 *Three at the Angel* (1958)
10 *Man in ambush* (1958)
11 *Killer at large* (1959)
12 *Devil's due* (1960)
13 *Spearhead death* (1960)
14 *Devil was handsome* (1961)
15 *Body to spare* (1962)
16 *Devil in moonlight* (1962)
17 *Moonlight flitting* (1963)
Graveyard rolls
18 *Two men in twenty* (1964)
19 *Death has a shadow* (1965)
Homicide blonde
20 *His weight in gold* (1966)
21 *Rogue running* (1967)
22 *Exercise Hoodwink* (1967)
23 *Hideaway* (1968)
24 *Dog Man* (1969)

Chief Inspector Jonathan Black series
Garnett, Roger
1 *Death in Piccadilly* (1937)
2 *Croaker* (1938)
3 *Danger, death at work* (1939)
4 *Man died talking* (1943)

Chief Inspector Joshua Smarles series
Urquhart, Macgregor
1 *Frail on North Circular* (1962)
2 *Girl on the waterfront* (1962)
3 *Dig the missing* (1963)
4 *Bluebottle* (1964)
5 *Contact lens* (1964)
6 *Grey man* (1965)
7 *Bitter Lemon mob* (1966)
8 *Open mouth* (1967)

Chief Inspector Lars Kollin series
Hogstrand, Olle
1 *On the Prime Minister's account* (1971)
Original edition entitled *Maskerat Brott*
2 *Gambler* (1972)
Original edition entitled *Spelarna*
3 *Debt* (1973)
Original edition entitled *Skulden*

Chief Inspector Lennox series
Wainwright, John
1 *Evidence I shall give* (1974)
2 *Square dance* (1975)
3 *Landscape with violence* (1975)
4 *Pool of tears* (1977)
5 *Day of the peppercorn kill* (1977)
6 *Take murder* (1979)
7 *Dominoes* (1980)
8 *Spiral staircase* (1983)

Chief Inspector Lloyd and Sergeant Judy Hill series
McGown, Jill
1 *Perfect match* (1983)
2 *Redemption* (1988)
Murder at the old vicarage
3 *Death of a dancer* (1989)
Gone to her death

Chief Inspector Michael Tandy series
Shepherd, Neal
1 *Death flies low* (1938)
2 *Death walks softly* (1938)
3 *Death rides swiftly* (1939)
4 *Exit to music* (1940)
A problem in detection

Chief Inspector Peacock and Sergeant Steve Arrow series
Mantell, Laurie
see **Sergeant Steve Arrow and Chief Inspector Peacock series**

Chief Inspector Peter Jensen series
Wahloo, Per
1 *Murder on the thirty-first floor* (1964)
Thirty-first floor
Original edition entitled *Mord pa 31*
2 *Steel spring* (1968)
Original edition entitled *Stalspranget*

Chief Inspector Peter Parsons series
Scott, Jack S
1 *Time of fine weather* (1983)
2 *Little darling, dead* (1986)

Chief Inspector Reginald Wexford series
Rendell, Ruth
1 *From Doon with death* (1964)
2 *New lease of death* (1967)
Sins of the fathers
3 *Wolf to the slaughter* (1967)
4 *Best man to die* (1969)
5 *Guilty thing surprised* (1970)
6 *No more dying then* (1971)
7 *Murder being once done* (1972)
8 *Some lie and some die* (1973)
9 *Shake hands for ever* (1975)
10 *Sleeping life* (1978)
11 *Make death love me* (1979)
12 *Means of evil, and other stories* (1979)
Short stories
13 *Put on by Cunning* (1981)
Death notes
14 *Speaker of Mandarin* (1983)
15 *Unkindness of ravens* (1985)
16 *Veiled one* (1988)
17 *Simisola* (1994)

Chief Inspector Sam Birkett series
Payne, Laurence
1 *Nose on my face* (1961)
First body
2 *Too small for his shoes* (1962)
3 *Deep and crisp and even* (1964)
4 *Take the money and run* (1982)
5 *Dead for a ducat* (1986)

Chief Inspector Saunders series
Steele, V M
1 *Scarred wrists* (1935)
2 *Hunters of humans* (1936)
3 *Beloved of Ishmael* (1937)

Chief Inspector Thomas Littlejohn series
Bellairs, George
see **Detective Inspector Thomas Littlejohn series**

Chief Inspector Thompson series
Drax, Peter
1 *Murder by chance* (1936)
2 *Death by two hands* (1937)
Crime within crime
3 *Tune to a corpse* (1939)
Crime to music

Chief Inspector Walsh and Constable Brenda Phipps series
Hunt, Richard
1 *Murder in ruins* (1991)
2 *Death sounds grand* (1991)
3 *Death of a merry widow* (1992)

Chief Inspector Wilfred Dover series
Porter, Joyce
1 *Dover one* (1964)
2 *Dover two* (1965)
3 *Dover three* (1965)
4 *Dover and the unkindest cut of all* (1967)
5 *Dover goes to Pott* (1968)
6 *Dover strikes again* (1970)
7 *It's murder with Dover* (1973)
8 *Dover and the claret tappers* (1976)
9 *Dead easy for Dover* (1978)
10 *Dover beats the band* (1980)

Chief Inspector William Bastion series
Harrison, Richard
1 *Black widow* (1946)
2 *Bootlaces for Bastion* (1947)
3 *Brickbats for Bastion* (1948)
4 *Murder-on-sea* (1949)
5 *Rope over Jezebel* (1950)

Chief of Police Sutherland series
Eberhard, Frederick George
1 *Thirteenth murder* (1931)
2 *Microbe murders* (1935)

Chief Petty Officer William Walker series
Macdonnell, James Edmond
see **Hooky Walker series**

Chief Superintendent Charles Miller series
Keenan, William
1 *Lonely beat* (1967)
2 *Mosaic of death* (1969)
3 *Murder in melancholy* (1971)

Chief Superintendent Pat Stockton series
Joyce, Cyril
1 *Web to catch a spider* (1975)
2 *Elimination process* (1976)
3 *Twice a victim* (1977)
4 *Run a golden mile* (1978)
5 *Seize a passing stranger* (1978)
6 *Incidental murder* (1979)
7 *Sentence suspended* (1979)
8 *Hitch in time* (1980)
9 *Death of a left-handed woman* (1980)
10 *Errant witness* (1981)
11 *Calculated risk* (1981)
12 *Bullet for Betty* (1981)
13 *From the grave to the cradle* (1982)
14 *Errant target* (1982)
15 *Murder is a pendulum* (1983)
16 *Errant sleuth* (1983)
17 *Widows' beads* (1984)

Chief Superintendent Sebastian Griffin series
Charles, Wyndham
1 *Hogan's last case* (1982)
2 *No love for Miss Stent* (1983)

Child and the community series
Ford, Donald
1 *Deprived child and the community* (1955)
2 *Delinquent child and the community* (1957)

Childe cycle series
Dickson, Gordon Rupert
see **Dorsai series**

Childe series
Farmer, Philip Jose
see **Exorcism series**

Childermass trilogy
Lewis, Wyndham
see **Human age trilogy**

Childhood, boyhood and youth trilogy
Carossa, Hans
1 *Childhood* (1922)
Original edition entitled *Eine Kindheit*
2 *Boyhood and youth* (1928)
Original edition entitled *Verwandlungen einer Jugend*
3 *Year of sweet illusions* (1941)
Original edition entitled *Das Jahr der schonen Tauschungen*

Childhood of Alban de Bricoule trilogy
Montherlant, Henry de
see **Alban de Bricoule trilogy**

Childhood series
Howe, Bea
Reminiscences of childhood
1 *Galaxy of governesses* (1954)
2 *Child in Chile* (1957)

Childhood series
Peck, Winifred
1 *Little learning* (1952)
2 *Home for the holidays* (1955)

Childhood to university trilogy
Gorky, Maxim
Translated from the Russian
Autobiography
1 *My childhood* (1913)
Childhood
2 *My apprenticeship* (1915)
In the world
3 *My university days* (1923)
My universities

Children at Windylaw Farm series
Hardman, Diana
see **Windylaw Farm series**

Children need music series
Cass-Beggs, Barbara
1 *Your baby needs music* (1978)
Revised edition 1990
2 *Your child needs music* (1987)

Children of courage series
Sanford, Doris
1 *Don't be afraid of the darkness* (1992)
2 *Fire escape* (1992)
3 *My friend* (1992)
4 *Yes I can* (1992)

Children of crisis series
Coles, Robert
1 *Study in courage and fear* (1967)
2 *Migrants, sharecroppers, mountaineers* (1971)
3 *South goes north* (1971)
4 *Eskimos, Chicanos, Indians* (1978)
5 *Privileged ones* (1978)
The well-off and the rich in America

Children of other days series
Rutley, Cecily Marianne
1 *First children* (1924)
Old Stone Age
2 *Children of the downs* (1924)
New Stone Age
3 *Story of Strong* (1924)
Bronze Age
4 *Children of the lake villages* (1924)
Iron Age
5 *Centurion's son* (1924)
Roman period
6 *Cymric the Saxon* (1924)
Saxon period
7 *Children of the castle* (1928)
Norman period
8 *Gilbert the page* (1928)
Thirteenth century
9 *Children of Chaucer's day* (1930)
10 *Peter the prentice* (1930)
11 *Children of Tudor times* (1932)
12 *Children of Stuart days* (1932)
13 *Children of Georgian days* (1932)
15 *Hector of Hellas* (1934)
16 *Children of the Nile* (1934)
17 *Children of ancient Rome* (1935)
18 *Children of ancient Persia* (1936)

Children of Perestroika series
Adelman, Deborah
1 *Children of perestroika* (1991)
Moscow teenagers talk about their lives and the future
2 *Children of perestroika come of age* (1992)

Children of Ruth series
Sutton, Marvin
1 *Children of Ruth* (1933)
2 *Promised land* (1934)

Children of the fox trilogy
Walsh, Jill Paton
1 *Crossing to Salamis* (1977)
2 *Walls of Athens* (1977)
3 *Persian gold* (1978)
One volume edition entitled *Children of the fox*, 1978

Children of the Lion series
Danielson, Peter
1 *Children of the Lion* (1980)
2 *Shepherd Kings* (1981)
3 *Vengeance of the Lion* (1983)
4 *Lion in Egypt* (1984)
5 *Golden Paraoh* (1986)
6 *Lord of the Nile* (1986)
7 *Prophecy* (1987)
8 *Sword of glory* (1987)
10 *Exodus* (1989)
11 *Sea people* (1990)
12 *Promised land* (1990)
13 *Invaders* (1991)
14 *Trumpet and the swords* (1992)
15 *Prophets and warriors* (1993)
16 *Departed glory* (1993)
17 *Death of kings* (1994)

Children of the north series
Power, Maurice S
1 *Killing of yesterday's children* (1984)
2 *Lonely the man without heroes* (1986)
3 *Darkness in the eye* (1987)
One volume edition entitled *Children of the north*, 1991

Children of the stars series
Coulson, Juanita
1 *Tomorrow's heritage* (1981)
2 *Outward bound* (1982)
3 *Legacy of earth* (1989)
4 *Past of forever* (1989)

Children of the valley trilogy
French, Jackie
1 *Music from the sea* (1992)
2 *City in the sand* (1992)
3 *House of a hundred animals* (1993)

Children of Triad trilogy
Marks, Laurie J
1 *Delan the mislaid* (1989)
2 *Moonbane mage* (1990)
3 *Ara's field* (1991)

Children of violence series
Lessing, Doris
1 *Martha Quest* (1952)
2 *Proper marriage* (1954)
Numbers 1 and 2 also published in one volume entitled *Children of violence*, volume 1, 1965
3 *Ripple from the storm* (1958)
4 *Landlocked* (1965)
Numbers 3 and 4 also published in one volume entitled *Children of violence*, volume 2, 1966
5 *Four-gated city* (1969)

Children of Ynell series
Murphy, Shirley Rousseau
1 *Ring of fire* (1977)
2 *Wolf bell* (1979)
3 *Castle of Hape* (1980)
4 *Caves of fire and ice* (1980)
5 *Joining of the stone* (1981)

Children's life series
Solomon, Joan
1 *Kate's party* (1978)
2 *Spud comes to play* (1978)
3 *Day by the sea* (1978)
4 *Berron's tooth* (1978)
5 *Shabnam's day out* (1980)
6 *Bobbi's new year* (1980)
7 *Gifts and almonds* (1980)
8 *Present for mum* (1981)
9 *Sweet-tooth Sunil* (1984)

Child's play series
Costello, Matthew John
Based on moving pictures the first of which has not been novelized
1 *Child's play 2* (1990)
2 *Child's play 3* (1991)

Chill series
Sherman, Jory
see **Doctor Russell V Chillders series**

Chillders series
Sherman, Jory
see **Doctor Russell V Chillders series**

Chimmie Fadden series
Townsend, Edward Waterman
1 *Chimmie Fadden, Major Max, and other stories* (1891)
2 *Chimmie Fadden explain, Major Max expounds* (1895)
3 *Chimmie Fadden and Mister Paul* (1902)

Chimney corner stories series
Blyton, Enid
1 *Chimney corner stories* (1946)
2 *More chimney corner stories* (1955)

Chimney witch series
Whitehead, Victoria
1 *Chimney witches* (1986)
2 *Chimnmey witch chase* (1987)
3 *Chimney witch Christmas* (1988)
4 *Witches of Creaky-Cranky Castle* (1991)

Chimpy series
Judah, Aaron
see **Basil Chimpy series**

Chin Kwang Kham series
Foster, Richard
1 *Laughing Buddha murders* (1944)
2 *Invisible man murders* (1945)

China Bayles series
Albert, Susan Wittig
1 *Thyme of death* (1992)
2 *Witches' bane* (1993)
3 *Hangman's root* (1994)

China series
Hobart, Alice Tisdale
1 *Pidgin cargo* (1929)
River supreme
2 *Oil for the lamps of China* (1933)
3 *Yang and Yin* (1936)
4 *Their own country* (1940)

China Tate series
Johnson, Lissa Halls
1 *Sliced heather on toast* (1994)
2 *Secret in the kitchen* (1994)
3 *Project Black Bear* (1994)

China trilogy
Nicole, Christopher
1 *Crimson pagoda* (1983)
2 *Scarlet princess* (1984)
3 *Red dawn* (1985)

China trilogy
Roberts, Irene
1 *Moonpearl* (1983)
Revised edition 1986
2 *Time of the seventh moon* (1984)
3 *Hour of the tiger* (1985)

Chincoteague series
Henry, Marguerite
1 *Misty of Chincoteague* (1946)
Also published in six volumes entitled *The auction, The big race, The capture, Going home, The storm, The whirlpool*, 1987
2 *Sea Star, orphan of Chincoteague* (1949)
3 *Misty, the wonder pony* (1956)
4 *Stormy, Misty's foal* (1963)
Numbers 1-4 also published in one volume entitled *Misty treasury*, 1982
Companion volumes: *Sea Star, orphan of Chincoteague*, 1949, *A pictorial life story of Misty*, 1976
5 *Misty's twilight* (1992)

Chinese Civil War series
Standish, Robert
1 *Three bamboos* (1942)
2 *Small general* (1945)

Chinese color series
Owen, Frank
1 *Wind that tramps the world* (1929)
2 *Purple sea* (1930)

Chinese diaries series
Payne, Robert
1 *Forever China* (1945)
Chungking diary, December 1941-April 1944
2 *China awake* (1947)
1944-1946
One volume abridged edition entitled *Chinese diaries, 1941-1946*, 1969

Chinese in the New World series
Yee, Paul
Stories of the Chinese in the New World
1 *Tales from Gold Mountain* (1989)
2 *Roses sing on new snow* (1992)
A delicious tale

Chinese village series
Lin, Yutang
1 *Miss Tu* (1950)
2 *Widow Chuan* (1952)

Chip Hilton series
Bee, Clair
1 *Touchdown pass* (1948)
2 *Championship ball* (1948)
3 *Strike three!* (1949)
4 *Clutch hitter!* (1949)
5 *Hoop crazy* (1950)
6 *Pitchers' duel* (1950)
7 *Pass and a prayer* (1951)
8 *Dugout jinx* (1952)
9 *Freshman quarterback* (1952)
10 *Backboard fever* (1953)
11 *Fence busters* (1953)
12 *Ten seconds to play!* (1955)
13 *Fourth down showdown* (1956)
14 *Tournament crisis* (1957)
15 *Hardcourt upset* (1958)
16 *Pay-off pitch* (1958)
17 *No-hitter* (1959)
18 *Triple-threat trouble* (1960)
19 *Backcourt ace* (1961)
20 *Fuzzer basket* (1962)
21 *Comeback capers* (1963)
22 *Home run feud* (1964)

Chip Mitchell computer mystery series
D'Ignazio, Fred
1 *Case of the stolen computer brains* (1983)
2 *Case of the robot warriors* (1984)
3 *Case of the chocolate-covered bugs* (1985)

Chip series
McEvoy, Seth
see **Not quite human series**

Chipp series
Thiele, Colin
see **Tracy Chipp series**

Chips Carpenter and Thibault Parew series
Eldredge, Gilbert
see **Thibault Parew and Chips Carpenter series**

Chips Regan series
Brown, Roy Frederick
1 *Undercover boy* (1978)
2 *Chips and the crossword gang* (1979)
3 *Chips and the river rat* (1981)
4 *Chips and the Black Moth* (1982)

Chips series
Hilton, James
see **Mister Chips series**

Chips series
Hughes, Shirley
1 *Chips and Jessie* (1983)
2 *Another helping of Chips* (1986)

Chipstead series
Horler, Sydney
see **Bunny Chipstead series**

Chiri series
Kjelgaard, Jim
Story of a husky
1 *Snow dog* (1948)
2 *Wild trek* (1950)

Chisholm series
Cunningham, Chet
see **Wade Chisholm series**
Dwyer-Joyce, Alice
see **Doctor Catriona Chisholm series**
Eyles, Alfred W
see **Paul Chisholm series**

Chita series
Howard, Elizabeth Fitzgerald
1 *Chita's Christmas tree* (1989)
2 *Papa tells Chita a story* (1994)

Chitterwick series
Berkeley, Anthony
see **Ambrose Chitterwick series**

Chitty-Chitty-Bang-Bang series
Fleming, Ian
1 *Chitty-Chitty-Bang-Bang, the magical car, adventure number 1* (1964)
2 *Chitty-Chitty-Bang-Bang, the magical car, adventure number 2* (1964)
3 *Chitty-Chitty-Bang-Bang, the magical car, adventure number 3* (1965)
One volume edition, 1971
Companion volume: *Chitty-Chitty-Bang-Bang, the story of the film*, by John Frederick Burke, 1968

Chizzit series
Hall, Mary Bowen
see **Emma Chizzit series**

Chloris series
Platt, Kin
1 *Chloris and the creeps* (1973)
2 *Chloris and the freaks* (1975)
3 *Chloris and the weirdos* (1978)

Chocky series
This sequence has two authors
Wyndham, John
1 *Chocky* (1968)
Daniel, Mark
2 *Chocky's challenge* (1986)

Chocolate war series
Cormier, Robert
1 *Chocolate war* (1974)
2 *Beyond the chocolate war* (1985)

Choice series
Kravchenko, Viktor
1 *I chose freedom* (1946)
The personal and political life of a Soviet official
2 *I chose justice* (1951)

Choir school series
Mayne, William
1 *Swarm in May* (1955)
2 *Chorister's cake* (1956)
3 *Cathedral Wednesday* (1960)
4 *Words and music* (1963)

Choker series
Noonan, Michael
1 *Patchwork hero* (1958)
2 *December boys* (1963)

Chokra series
Michael, John
1 *Chokra* (1957)
2 *Chokra and Tags* (1958)

Chonkin series
Voinovich, Vladimir Nikolaevich
see **Private Ivan Chonkin series**

Choose your own adventure: Indiana Jones series
Brightfield, Richard
see **Indiana Jones choose your own adventure series**

Choose your own adventure series
This sequence has twenty seven authors
Packard, Edward
1 *Cave of time* (1979)
Mountain, Robert
2 *Journey under the sea* (1977)
Terman, Douglas
3 *By balloon to the Sahara* (1979)
Danger in the desert
Montgomery, Raymond A
4 *Space and beyond* (1980)
Packard, Edward
5 *Mystery of Chimney Rock* (1980)
Curse of the haunted mansion
6 *Your code name is Jonah* (1979)
7 *Third planet from Altair* (1979)
Exploration infinity
Message from space
8 *Deadwood City* (1978)
9 *Who killed Harlowe Thrombey?* (1981)
Montgomery, Raymond A
10 *Lost jewels of Nabooti* (1981)
11 *Mystery of the Maya* (1981)

Choose your own adventure series

Packard, Edward
12 *Inside UFO 54-40* (1982)
Montgomery, Raymond A
13 *Abominable snowman* (1982)
Packard, Edward
14 *Forbidden castle* (1982)
Montgomery, Raymond A
15 *House of danger* (1982)
Packard, Edward
16 *Survival at sea* (1982)
Montgomery, Raymond A
17 *Race forever* (1983)
Packard, Edward
18 *Underground kingdom* (1983)
Brightfield, Richard
19 *Secret of the pyramids* (1983)
Montgomery, Raymond A
20 *Escape* (1983)
Packard, Edward
21 *Hyperspace* (1983)
Goodman, Julius
22 *Space patrol* (1983)
Foley, Louise Munro
23 *Lost tribe* (1983)
Montgomery, Raymond A
24 *Lost on the Amazon* (1983)
25 *Prisoner of the ant people* (1983)
Brightfield, Richard
26 *Phantom submarine* (1983)
Goodman, Julius
27 *Horror of High Ridge* (1983)
Packard, Edward
28 *Mountain survival* (1984)
Montgomery, Raymond A
29 *Trouble on planet earth* (1984)
Brightfield, Richard
30 *Curse of Batterslea Hall* (1984)
Koltz, Tony
31 *Vampire express* (1984)
Goodman, Julius
32 *Treasure diver* (1984)
Brightfield, Richard
33 *Dragons' den* (1984)
Foley, Louise Munro
34 *Mystery of the Highland crest* (1984)
Graver, Fred
35 *Journey to Stonehenge* (1984)
Brightfield, Richard
36 *Secret treasure of Tibet* (1984)
Montgomery, Raymond A
37 *War with the Evil Power Master* (1984)
Leibold, Jay
38 *Sabotage* (1984)
Packard, Edward
39 *Supercomputer* (1984)
Goodman, Deborah Lerme
40 *Throne of Zeus* (1985)
Wallace, Jim
41 *Search for the mountain gorillas* (1985)
Foley, Louise Munro
42 *Mystery of Echo Lodge* (1985)
Leibold, Jay
43 *Grand Canyon odyssey* (1985)
Gilligan, Shannon
44 *Mystery of Ura Senke* (1985)
Packard, Edward
45 *You are a shark* (1985)
Brightfield, Richard
46 *Deadly shadow* (1985)
Kushner, Ellen
47 *Outlaws of Sherwood Forest* (1985)
Leibold, Jay
48 *Spy for George Washington* (1985)
Foley, Louise Munro
49 *Danger at Anchor Mine* (1985)
Packard, Edward
50 *Return to the Cave of Time* (1985)
Goodman, Deborah Lerme
51 *Magic of the unicorn* (1985)
Packard, Edward
52 *Ghost hunter* (1986)
Gilligan, Shannon
53 *Case of the silk king* (1986)
Foley, Louise Munro
54 *Forest of fear* (1986)
Goodman, Deborah Lerme
55 *Trumpet of terror* (1986)
Kushner, Ellen
56 *Enchanted kingdom* (1986)
Leibold, Jay
57 *Antimatter formula* (1986)
Kushner, Ellen
58 *Statue of Liberty adventure* (1986)
Koltz, Tony
59 *Terror Island* (1986)
Goodman, Deborah Lerme
60 *Vanished!* (1986)
Montgomery, Raymond A
61 *Beyond escape!* (1986)
Packard, Edward
62 *Sugarcane Island* (1986)
Original edition 1976
Kushner, Ellen
63 *Mystery of the secret room* (1986)
Siegman, Meryl
64 *Volcano!* (1987)
Foley, Louise Munro
65 *Mardi Gras mystery* (1987)
Leibold, Jay
66 *Secret of the ninja* (1987)
Hodgman, Ann
67 *Seaside mystery* (1987)
Packard, Andrea
68 *Secret of the sun god* (1987)
Wallace, Jim
69 *Rock and roll mystery* (1987)
Brightfield, Richard
70 *Invaders of the planet earth* (1987)
Packard, Edward
71 *Space vampire* (1987)
Montgomery, Raymond A
72 *Brilliant Doctor Wogan* (1987)
Leibold, Jay
73 *Beyond the Great Wall* (1987)
Newman, Marc
74 *Longhorn territory* (1987)
Brightfield, Richard
75 *Planet of the dragons* (1988)
Montgomery, Ramsey
76 *Mona Lisa is missing!* (1988)
Baglio, Ben M
77 *First Olympics* (1988)
Montgomery, Raymond A
78 *Return to Atlantis* (1988)
Foley, Louise Munro
79 *Mystery of the sacred stones* (1988)
Packard, Edward
80 *Perfect planet* (1988)
Gilligan, Shannon
81 *Terror in Australia* (1988)
Brightfield, Richard
82 *Hurricane!* (1988)
Montgomery, Raymond A
83 *Track of the bear* (1988)
Packard, Edward
84 *You are a monster* (1988)
Becket, Jim
85 *Inca gold* (1988)
Kushner, Ellen
86 *Knights of the Round Table* (1988)
Montgomery, Raymond A
87 *Exiled to earth* (1989)
Brightfield, Richard
88 *Master of kung fu* (1989)
Johnson, Seddon
89 *South Pole sabotage* (1989)
Packard, Edward
90 *Mutiny in space* (1989)
91 *You are a superstar* (1989)
Leibold, Jay
92 *Return of the ninja* (1989)
Hampton, Bill
93 *Captive!* (1989)
Montgomery, Raymond A
94 *Blood on the handle* (1989)
Packard, Edward
95 *You are a genius* (1989)
Montgomery, Raymond A
96 *Stock car champion* (1989)
Packard, Edward
97 *Through the black hole* (1990)
Leibold, Jay
98 *You are a millionaire* (1990)
99 *Revenge of the Russian ghost* (1990)
Packard, Edward
100 *Worst day of your life* (1990)
Johnson, Seddon
101 *Alien, go home!* (1990)
Brightfield, Richard
102 *Master of tae kwon do* (1990)
Montgomery, Ramsey
103 *Grave robbers* (1990)
Foley, Louise Munro
104 *Cobra connection* (1990)
Gilligan, Alison
105 *Treasure of the Onyx Dragon* (1990)
Brightfield, Richard
106 *Hijacked!* (1990)
Leibold, Jay
107 *Fight for freedom* (1990)
Brightfield, Richard
108 *Master of karate* (1990)
Montgomery, Raymond A
109 *Chinese dragons* (1991)
Packard, Edward
110 *Invaders from within* (1991)
Montgomery, Raymond A
111 *Smoke jumper* (1991)
Packard, Edward
112 *Skateboard champion* (1991)
Leibold, Jay
113 *Lost ninja* (1991)
Compton, Sara
114 *Daredevil Park* (1991)
Montgomery, Raymond A
115 *Island of time* (1991)
Packard, Edward
116 *Kidnapped!* (1991)
Leibold, Jay
117 *Search for Aladdin's lamp* (1991)
Packard, Edward
118 *Vampire invaders* (1991)
Gilligan, Shannon
119 *Terrorist trap* (1991)
Foley, Louise Munro
120 *Ghost train* (1992)
Number 121 not identified
Packard, Edward
122 *Magic master* (1992)
Montgomery, Raymond A
123 *Silver wings* (1992)
Packard, Edward
124 *Superbike* (1992)
Montgomery, Ramsey
125 *Outlaw gulch* (1992)
Brightfield, Richard
126 *Master of martial arts* (1992)
127 *Showdown* (1992)
Packard, Edward
128 *Viking raiders* (1992)
Gilligan, Alison
129 *Earthquake!* (1992)
Packard, Edward
130 *You are microscopic* (1992)
Leibold, Jay
131 *Surf monkeys* (1993)
Packard, Edward
132 *Luckiest day of your life* (1993)

Choose your own adventure super series

This sequence has two authors
Packard, Edward
1 *Journey to the year 3000* (1987)
Montgomery, Raymond A
2 *Danger zones* (1987)

Chopper Cop series

Ross, Paul
This pseudonym is used by Bill Amidon, Nathaniel Freedland and Dan Streib as indicated against each title
1 *Hitchhike killer* (1972)
[Streib]
2 *Valley of Death* (1972)
[Streib]
3 *Dynamite monster boogie concert* (1975)
[Amidon; Freedland]

Chopper cops series

Mackin, Rick
1 *Chopper cops* (1990)
2 *Gulf attack* (1990)
3 *Recon strike force* (1991)
4 *Sky war* (1991)

Chopper series

Hawkins, Jack
Adventure gamebooks
1 *Blood trails* (1987)
2 *Tunnel warriors* (1987)
3 *Jungle sweep* (1987)
4 *Red river* (1987)
5 *Renegade Mi As* (1987)
6 *Suicide mission* (1988)
7 *Kill zone* (1988)

Chopper series

Read, Mark Brandon
Reminiscences of a convicted criminal in Pentridge Gaol, based on letters to John Sylvester
1 *Chopper from the inside* (1991)
2 *Hits and memories* (1992)

Chrestomanci series

Jones, Diana Wynne
1 *Charmed life* (1977)
2 *Magicians of Caprona* (1980)
3 *Witch week* (1982)
4 *Lives of Christopher Chant* (1988)

Chris and Cathy Dollanganger series

Andrews, Virginia Cleo
see **Dollanganger family series**

Chris Devlin series

Kozlow, Mark J
1 *Gunfighter's trail* (1980)
2 *Hangtown mistake* (1981)
3 *Gunfighter and the Tong boss* (1981)
4 *Devlin in the canyon heat* (1981)

Chris Godfrey series

Walters, Hugh
1 *Blast off at Woomera* (1957)
Blast off at 0300
2 *Domes of Pico* (1958)
Menace from the moon
3 *Operation Columbus* (1960)
First on the moon
4 *Moon Base One* (1961)
Outpost on the moon
5 *Expedition Venus* (1962)
6 *Destination Mars* (1963)
7 *Terror by satellite* (1964)
8 *Mission to Mercury* (1965)
9 *Journey to Jupiter* (1965)
10 *Spaceship to Saturn* (1967)
11 *Mohole mystery* (1968)
Mohole menace
12 *Nearly Neptune* (1969)
Neptune One is missing
13 *First contact?* (1971)
14 *Passage to Pluto* (1973)
15 *Tony Hale, space detective* (1973)
16 *Murder on Mars* (1975)
17 *Caves of Drach* (1977)
18 *Boy astronaut* (1977)
19 *Last disaster* (1978)
20 *Blue aura* (1979)
21 *First family on the moon* (1979)
22 *Dark triangle* (1981)
23 *School on the moon* (1981)
24 *P-K* (1986)
The title stands for photokinesis

Chris Kilmoonie and Saul Grisman series

Morrell, David
1 *Brotherhood of the Rose* (1984)
2 *Fraternity of the Stone* (1985)
3 *League of Night and fog* (1987)
4 *Covenant of the Flame* (1991)

Chris Rockwell and Sarah Saber series

Linzee, David
see **Sarah Saber and Chris Rockwell series**

Chris series

Kooiker, Leonie
1 *Magic stone* (1978)

Original edition entitled *Heksensteen*
2 *Legacy of magic* (1981)
Original edition entitled *Her oerlanderboek*

Chrissy and Caroline series
Quin-Harkin, Janet
see **Sugar and spice series**

Christ and Antichrist trilogy
Merejkowski, Dmitri Sergeevich
Translated from the Russian
1 *Death of the gods* (1896)
Julian the Apostate
2 *Forerunner* (1901)
Romance of Leonardo da Vinci
Resurrection of the gods
Gods reborn
3 *Peter and Alexis* (1905)
Peter the Great

Christ series
Dixon, Roger
see **Jesus Christ series**
Oxenham, John
see **Jesus Christ series**

Christabel series
Hardy, Dorothy May
1 *Christabel at Cleave* (1951)
2 *Christable's Cornish adventure* (1954)

Christabel series
Latham, Katharine Wright
1 *Christabel* (1908)
Alternative title: The freaks and fancies of three little folk
2 *Christabel in France* (1910)
Alternative title: The further adventures of three little folk

Christer Wick series
Lang, Maria
1 *No more murders* (1951)
Original edition entitled *Inte flera mord*
2 *Death awaits thee* (1955)
Original edition entitled *Se, doden pa dig vantar*
3 *Wreath for the bride* (1957)
Original edition entitled *Kung Liljekonval*

Christian Daguerre series
Stevens, Carl
1 *Centaur conspiracy* (1983)
2 *Ride of the razorback* (1984)

Christian festivals trilogy
Weiser, Francis Xavier
1 *Christmas book* (1954)
2 *Easter book* (1955)
3 *Holy day book* (1957)

Christian mysteries series
Richards, Kel
see **Ben Bartholomew series**

Christian origins series
Allegro, John Marco
1 *Sacred mushroom and the cross* (1970)
Revised edition 1973; a study of the nature and origins of Christianity within the fertility cults of the ancient Near East
2 *End of a road* (1970)

Christian Queghan series
Hoyle, Trevor
1 *Seeking the mythical future* (1977)
2 *Through the eye of time* (1977)
3 *Gods look down* (1978)

Christian situations series
Krause, Jonathan
1 *Day God blew up my father's car* (1994)
2 *What would Jesus cook you for breakfast?* (1994)

Christian year series
Haughton, Rosemary
1 *Spring and Lent* (1962)
2 *Early summer, Easter and Whitsun* (1962)
3 *Autumn and Advent* (1962)
4 *Winter and Christmas* (1962)

Christiansson family trilogy
Bubb, Lillian
1 *April snow* (1951)
2 *Land of strangers* (1953)
3 *April harvest* (1959)

Christie Drayton series
Lambert, Janet
1 *Where the heart is* (1948)
2 *Treasure trouble* (1949)

Christie family series
Short, Agnes
1 *First fair wind* (1984)
2 *Running tide* (1986)
3 *Dragon seas* (1988)

Christie Opara series
Uhnak, Dorothy
1 *Bait* (1968)
2 *Witness* (1969)
3 *Ledger* (1970)

Christie series
Preston, James
see **Sergeant Bob Christie series**

Christie series
Paull, Minnie E
1 *Christie's next things* (1890)
2 *Christie's home-making* (1891)

Christie series
Walton, Catherine Augusta
1 *Christie's old organ* (1882)
Alternative title: Home sweet home
2 *Christie, the king's servant* (1898)

Christina Brand series
Knight, Brigid
1 *House of the swan* (1961)
2 *House of the bird of paradise* (1962)
3 *House of the seagull* (1963)

Christina Light series
James, Henry
see **Princess Casamassima series**

Christina Parsons series
Peyton, K M
see **Flambards series**

Christina series
Bell, John Joy
1 *Oh, Christina!* (1913)
2 *Courtin' Christina* (1914)

Christina Van Bell series
Saint James, Blakely
1 *Christina's quest* (1976)
2 *Christina's passion* (1976)
3 *Song for Christina* (1976)
4 *Christina's virtue* (1976)
5 *Chrstina's hunger* (1977)
6 *Christina's nights* (1977)
7 *Christina's desire* (1978)
8 *Christina's search* (1978)
9 *Christina's rapture* (1978)
10 *Christina's surrender* (1979)
11 *Christina's torment* (1979)
12 *Christina enchanted* (1980)
13 *Christina's pleasure* (1980)
14 *Christina's treasure* (1980)
15 *Christina's sins* (1980)
16 *Christina's promise* (1980)
17 *Christina's world* (1981)
18 *Christina's ecstasy* (1981)
19 *Kiss for Christina* (1981)
20 *Christina's obsession* (1981)
21 *Christina's bliss* (1981)
22 *Christina in love* (1981)
23 *Star for Christina* (1982)
24 *Christina's island* (1982)
25 *Christina's delight* (1982)
26 *Christina's touch* (1982)
27 *Christina's temptation* (1982)
28 *Christina's conquest* (1982)
29 *Festival for Christina* (1983)
30 *Christina's awakening* (1983)
31 *Diamond for Christina* (1983)
32 *Christina's fantasy* (1983)
33 *Christina's need* (1983)
34 *Christina's secret* (1983)
35 *Christina's thrills* (1983)
36 *Christina's paradise* (1983)
37 *Christina's favorite* (1983)
38 *Christina's voyage* (1984)
39 *Christina's challenge* (1984)
40 *Christina's wager* (1984)
41 *Christina's technique* (1984)
42 *Christina's essence* (1984)
43 *Christina's mystery* (1984)
44 *Christina's escapade* (1984)
45 *Christina's hunt* (1984)
46 *Christina's craving* (1984)
47 *Christina's sensation* (1984)

Christine and Susan Pratt series
Blair, Cynthia
see **Susan and Christine Pratt series**

Christine Andersen series
Mace, Merlda
1 *Headlong for murder* (1943)
2 *Blondes don't cry* (1945)

Christmas carol series
This sequence has two authors
Dickens, Charles
1 *Christmas carol* (1843)
A ghost story of Christmas; parody: *Christmas eve with the spirits, or, The canon's wanderings through ways unknown, with some further tidings of the lives of Scrooge and Tiny Tim*, published anonymously, 1869
Donaldson, Elaine
2 *Scrooge* (1970)
Based on a screenplay based on the character from Dicken's *A Christmas carol*

Christmas season series
Allen, James Lane
1 *Bride of the mistletoe* (1909)
2 *Doctor's Christmas eve* (1910)

Christmas stories series
Sawyer, Ruth
1 *This way to Christmas* (1916)
Revised edition 1970
2 *Long Christmas* (1941)
Short stories
3 *Christmas Anna angel* (1944)
4 *This is the Christmas* (1945)
A Serbian folk tale
5 *Maggie Rose, her birthday Christmas* (1952)
6 *Year of the Christmas dragon* (1960)
7 *Joy to the world* (1966)
Christmas legends

Christmas trilogy
Blake, Forrester
see **Johnny Christmas trilogy**
Van der Post, Laurens
see **Seed and the sower trilogy**

Christophe series
Bourne, Peter
see **Henri Christophe series**
Rolland, Romain
see **John Christopher series**

Christopher Adrian series
Silverman, Marguerite Ruth
see **Inspector Christopher Adrian series**

Christopher and Cressida series
Mauldsley, Daniel
1 *Solitaries of Sambuca* (1914)
Sequence continued under the author's real name Montgomery Carmichael
Carmichael, Montgomery
2 *Christopher and Cressida* (1924)

Christopher and Rufus series
Hastings, Ian
see **Rufus and Christopher series**

Christopher Blayre series
Blayre, Christopher
see **University of Cosmopoli series**

Christopher Bond series
Martyn, Wyndham
1 *Christopher Bond, adventurer* (1933)
2 *Spies of peace* (1934)
3 *Denmede mystery* (1936)
4 *Marrowby myth* (1938)
5 *Noonday devils* (1939)
6 *Capture* (1940)
7 *Shadow agent* (1941)
8 *Cairo crisis* (1945)
9 *Chromium cat* (1952)

Christopher Cool series
Lancer, Jack
1 *X marks the spy* (1967)
2 *Mission, Moonfire* (1967)
3 *Department of danger* (1967)
4 *Ace of shadows* (1968)
5 *Heads you lose* (1968)
6 *Trial by fury* (1969)

Christopher Cricket series
Gilmore, David Hunter
1 *Remarkable adventures of Cuthbert the Caterpillar and Wilfred the Wasp* (1941)
Also published with *The adventures of Drowsy the Drone*, and, *The lost ladybirds*, 1981
2 *Antony Ant and the earwig pirates* (1942)
3 *Tale of Gregory Grasshopper* (1942)
4 *Adventures of Catkin and Codlin* (1946)
5 *Tale of Christopher Cricket* (1946)
6 *Tale of Benjamin Bumble* (1947)
Numbers 4-6 also published in one volume entitled *Adventures of Catkin and Codlin, Christopher Cricket and Benjamin Bumble*, 1977
7 *Cruise of the Saucy Walnut* (1948)
Numbers 4-7 also published in one volume entitled *Christopher Cricket's favourite tales*, 1950 and *The delightful adventures of Catkin and Codlin and friends*, 1987; numbers 2, 3 and 7 also published in one volume entitled *Adventures of Antony Ant and the earwig pirates, Gregory Grasshopper, and, The cruise of the Saucy Walnut*, 1979
Companion volume: *The little world of D H Gilmore*, 1982

Christopher Dennis Sloan series
Aird, Catherine
see **Inspector C D Sloan series**

Christopher Fenn series
Stokes, Manning Lee
1 *Case of the Presidents' Heads* (1956)
2 *Case of the Judas spoon* (1957)

Christopher Fenton series
Mackenzie, Nigel
see **Professor Christopher Fenton series**

Christopher Gibson series
Montgomery, Ione
1 *Golden dress* (1940)
2 *Death won a prize* (1941)

Christopher Hand series
Page, Stanley Hart
1 *Sinister cargo* (1932)
2 *Resurrection murder case* (1932)
3 *Murder flies the Atlantic* (1933)
4 *Fool's gold* (1933)
5 *Tragic curtain* (1935)

Christopher Jensen series
Langley, Lee
see **Lieutenant Christopher Jensen series**

Christopher Kent series
Boswell, John
1 *Blue pheasant* (1958)
2 *Lost girl* (1959)

Christopher Marsden series
Backhouse, Elizabeth
see **Inspector Christopher Marsden series**

Christopher McKee series
Reilly, Helen
see **Inspector Christopher McKee series**

Christopher Perrin series
Waye, Cecil
1 *Figure of eight* (1931)
2 *Murder at Monk's Farm* (1931)
3 *End of the chase* (1932)
4 *Prime Minister's pencil* (1933)

Christopher Quarles series
Brebner, Percy
Short stories
1 *Christopher Quarles, college professor and master detective* (1914)
2 *Master detective* (1916)

Christopher Robin series
Milne, Alan Alexander
Verses
1 *When we were very young* (1924)
2 *Now we are six* (1927)
Revised edition 1961

Christopher Saxe series
Shane, Susannah
1 *Lady in danger* (1942)
2 *Lady in a million* (1943)
3 *Baby in the ash can* (1944)
4 *Diamonds in the dumplings* (1946)

Christopher series
Chaney, Jill
1 *Christopher's dig* (1972)
2 *Christopher's find* (1975)

Christopher series
De la Pasture, Elizabeth
see **Master Christopher series**
Irvine, Robert Ralstone
see **Robert Christopher series**

Christopher series
Isherwood, Christopher
1 *Kathleen and Frank* (1971)
Study of the author's parents and their influence on him, based on his mother's diaries
2 *Lions and shadows* (1938)
An education in the twenties
3 *Christopher and his kind, 1929-1939* (1976)
4 *October* (1983)
Record of one month in the author's life

Christopher series
McCarry, Charles
see **Paul Christopher series**

Christopher series
McKissack, Patricia Carwell
1 *Give it with love, Christopher* (1988)
Christopher learns about gifts and giving
2 *Speak up, Christopher* (1988)
Christopher learns the difference between right and wrong

Christopher series
Rolland, Romain
see **John Christopher series**
Steele, Curtis
see **James Christopher series**

Christopher Storm series
Barber, Willetta Ann
1 *Murder draws a line* (1940)
2 *Pencil points to murder* (1941)
3 *Drawn conclusion* (1942)
4 *Murder enters the picture* (1942)
5 *Noose is drawn* (1945)
6 *Drawback to murder* (1947)
7 *Deed is drawn* (1949)

Christopher Tietjens series
Ford, Ford Madox
see **Parade's end series**

Christos experience trilogy
Glaskin, Gerald Marcus
1 *Windows of the mind* (1974)
2 *Worlds within* (1976)
3 *Door to eternity* (1979)

Chronicle of Greystone Bay series
Grant, Charles Lewis
see **Chronicles of Greystone Bay series**

Chronicle of Prince Corum and the silver hand trilogy
Moorcock, Michael
1 *Bull and the spear* (1973)
2 *Oak and the ram* (1973)
3 *Sword and the stallion* (1974)
One volume edition entitled *The chronicles of Corum*, 1978

Chronicles of Aescendune trilogy
Crake, Augustus David
1 *Edwy the Fair* (1874)
Alternative title: The first chonicle of Aescendune; a tale of the days of St Dunstan
2 *Alfgar the Dane* (1875)
Alternative title: The second chonicle of Aescendune
3 *Rival heirs* (1882)

Chronicles of an age of darkness series
Cook, Hugh
1 *Wizards and the warriors* (1986)
Wizard war
2 *Wordsmiths and the warguild* (1987)
2.1 *Questing hero* (1987)
2.2 *Hero's return* (1987)
3 *Women and the warlords* (1987)
Oracle
4 *Walrus and the warwolf* (1988)
Lords of the sword
5 *Wicked and the witless* (1989)
6 *Wishstone and the wonderworkers* (1990)
7 *Wazir and the witch* (1990)
8 *Werewolf and the worlord* (1991)

Chronicles of ancient sunlight series
Williamson, Henry
Chronicles of a family from Victorian times to the Second World War
1 *Dark lantern* (1951)
2 *Donkey boy* (1952)
3 *Young Phillip Maddison* (1953)
Revised edition 1962
4 *How dear is life* (1954)
5 *Fox under my cloak* (1955)
6 *Golden virgin* (1957)
Revised edition 1963
7 *Love and the loveless* (1958)
A soldier's tale
8 *Test to destruction* (1960)
Revised edition 1964
9 *Innocent moon* (1961)
10 *It was the nightingale* (1962)
11 *Power of the dead* (1963)
Revised edition 1966
12 *Phoenix generation* (1965)
13 *Solitary war* (1966)
14 *Lucifer before sunrise* (1967)
15 *Gale of the world* (1969)

Chronicles of Arundel series
Roberts, Kenneth Lewis
1 *Arundel* (1930)
A chronicle of the Province of Maine and the secret expedition against Quebec
2 *Rabble in arms* (1933)
A chronicle of Arundel and the Burgoyne invasion
3 *Lively Lady* (1931)
A chronicle of Arundel, of privateering and of the circular prison on Dartmoor
4 *Captain Caution* (1934)

Chronicles of Barsetshire series
Trollope, Anthony
1 *Warden* (1855)
2 *Barchester Towers* (1857)
3 *Doctor Thorne* (1858)
4 *Framley Parsonage* (1861)
5 *Small house at Allington* (1864)
6 *Last chronicle of Barset* (1867)

Chronicles of Castle Brass series
Moorcock, Michael
This sequence follows the History of Runestaff series
1 *Count Brass* (1973)
2 *Champion of Garathorm* (1973)
3 *Quest for Tanelorn* (1975)
One volume edition entitled *The chronicles of Castle Brass*, 1985

Chronicles of counter-earth series
Norman, John
see **Tarl Cabot series**

Chronicles of Damar series
McKinley, Robin
1 *Hero and the crown* (1985)
2 *Blue sword* (1982)
3 *Knot in the grain, and other stories* (1994)

Chronicles of Galen Sword series
Reeves-Stevens, Garfield
1 *Shifter* (1990)
2 *Nightfeeder* (1991)

Chronicles of Greystone Bay series
Grant, Charles Lewis
1 *First chronicles of Greystone Bay* (1985)
2 *Doom city* (1987)
3 *SeaHarp Hotel* (1990)

Chronicles of Inverness series
Macintyre, Lorn
1 *Cruel in the shadow* (1979)
2 *Blind bend* (1981)

Chronicles of Kylix series
Carter, Lin
1 *Quest of Kadji* (1971)
2 *Wizard of Zao* (1978)

Chronicles of Morgaine series
Cherryh, Carolyn Janice
1 *Gate of Ivrel* (1976)
2 *Well of Shiuan* (1978)
3 *Fires of Azeroth* (1979)
Numbers 1-3 also published in one volume editions entitled *The book of Morgaine*, 1979 and The chronicles of Morgaine, 1985
4 *Exile's gate* (1988)
Companion volume: *The witchfires of Leth, a Crossroads adventure in the world of C.J.Cherryh's Morgaine*, by Dan Greenburg, 1987

Chronicles of Morgon trilogy
McKillip, Patricia Anne
see **Morgon trilogy**

Chronicles of Pennycress series
Toms, Patricia
1 *Mrs Sherwood's summer* (1965)
2 *Three fountains* (1966)
3 *Cottage on the Green* (1967)

Chronicles of the Black Company series
Cook, Glen
1 *Black Company* (1984)
2 *Shadows linger* (1984)
3 *White Rose* (1985)
Numbers 1-3 also published in one volume entitled *Annals of the Black Company*, 1986
4 *Shadow games* (1989)
First book of the South
5 *Dreams of steel* (1990)
6 *Silver spike* (1989)

Chronicles of the Cheysuli series
Roberson, Jennifer
1 *Shapechangers* (1984)
2 *Song of Homana* (1985)
3 *Legacy of the sword* (1986)
4 *Track of the white wolf* (1987)
5 *Pride of princes* (1988)
6 *Daughter of the lion* (1989)
7 *Flight of the raven* (1990)
8 *Tapestry of lions* (1992)

Chronicles of the custodians series
Middleton, Martin
1 *Circle of light* (1990)
2 *Triad of darkness* (1991)
3 *Sphere of influence* (1992)
4 *New age* (1994)
5 *New order* (1994)

Chronicles of the Deryni trilogy
Kurtz, Katherine
The third trilogy in the **World of the Eleven Kingdoms** series
1 *Deryni rising* (1970)
2 *Deryni checkmate* (1972)
3 *High Deryni* (1973)
One volume edition entitled *The chronicles of the Deryni*, 1985; companion volumes: *The Deryni archives*, 1986, *Deryni magic*, 1990, *Deryni challenge*, by Stephen Billias, 1988

Chronicles of the door series
Edwards, Gene
1 *Birth* (1990)
2 *Beginning* (1992)
3 *Escape* (1993)

Chronicles of the high inquest series
Sucharitkul, Somtow
1 *Light on the sound* (1982)
Revised edition 1986
2 *Throne of madness* (1983)
3 *Utopia hunters* (1984)
4 *Darkling wind* (1985)

Chronicles of the house of Kurt series
Hudson, Stephen
see **Kurt series**

Chronicles of the keeper trilogy
King, Bernard
1 *Destroying angel* (1987)
2 *Time-fighters* (1987)
3 *Skyfire* (1988)

Chronicles of the Kingdom of Prydain series
Alexander, Lloyd
see **Prydain series**

Chronicles of the king's tramp series
De Haven, Tom
1 *Walker of worlds* (1990)
2 *End-of-everything man* (1991)
3 *Last human* (1992)

Chronicles of the twelve kingdoms series
Friesner, Esther Mona
1 *Mustapha and his wise dog* (1985)
2 *Spells of mortal weaving* (1986)
3 *Witchwood cradle* (1987)
4 *Water kings' laughter* (1989)

Chronicles of the Vampires series
Rice, Anne
see **Vampire chronicles series**

Chronicles of Thomas Covenant: first series
Donaldson, Stephen Reeder
see **First chronicles of Thomas Covenant series**

Chronicles of Thomas Covenant: second series
Donaldson, Stephen Reeder
see **Second chronicles of Thomas Covenant series**

Chronicles of Tintagel series
Brandewyne, Rebecca
1 *Passion moon rising* (1988)
2 *Beyond the starlit frost* (1991)

Chronicles of Tornor trilogy
Lynn, Elizabeth Anne
1 *Watchtower* (1979)
2 *Dancers of Arun* (1979)
3 *Northern girl* (1980)

Chronicles of Tzu Hang series
Smeeton, Miles
Memoirs of travel
1 *Once is enough* (1959)
2 *Sunrise to windward* (1966)

Chronicles of wasted time series
Muggeridge, Malcolm
Autobiography
1 *Green stick* (1973)
2 *Infernal grove* (1974)

Chronicles trilogy
Echlin, Elizabeth Gladys
Reminiscences
1 *Keep off, death* (1939)
2 *Live unafraid* (1944)
3 *Vertigo* (1946)

Chronique d'Avebury series
Martine-Barnes, Adrienne
1 *Fire sword* (1984)
2 *Crystal sword* (1988)
3 *Rainbow sword* (1988)
4 *Sea sword* (1989)

Chronoplane wars trilogy
Kilian, Crawford
1 *Empire of time* (1978)
2 *Fall of the republic* (1987)
3 *Rogue emperor* (1988)

Chronos series
Bayley, Barrington John
1 *Collision course* (1973)
Collision with Chronos
2 *Fall of Chronopolis* (1974)
3 *Knights of the limits* (1978)
Short stories

Chrystal Falls series
This sequence has five authors
Hill, Meredith
1 *Wrong side of love* (1985)
Ransom, Candice Farris
2 *Breaking the rules* (1985)
Cooney, Caroline B
3 *Bad and the beautiful* (1985)
Lottman, Eileen
4 *Morning after* (1985)
Hill, Meredith
5 *Loss of innocence* (1986)
6 *Forbidden love* (1986)
Hoh, Diane
7 *Night to forget* (1986)

Chthon series
Anthony, Piers
see **Aton series**

Chu-Sheng series
Thomas, Eugene
1 *Shadow of Chu-Sheng* (1933)
2 *Yellow magic* (1934)

Chubb series
Brown, Roy Frederick
1 *Chubb on the trail* (1976)
2 *Chubb to the rescue* (1977)
3 *Chubb catches a cold* (1979)

Chuck Conley and Jerry Long series
Fox, James M
see **Jerry Long and Chuck Conley series**

Chuck Norris and the Karate Kommandos series
Weinberg, Larry
1 *Menace in space* (1986)
2 *Island of the walking dead* (1986)

Chuck series
White, Stewart Edward
see **Skookum Chuck series**

Chucky series
Brand, Christianna
see **Inspector Chucky series**

Chudleigh Hold series
Brent-Dyer, Elinor Mary
1 *Chudleigh Hold* (1954)
2 *Condor Crags adventure* (1954)
3 *Top secret* (1955)

Chuffertrain series
Kruss, James
see **Henrietta Chuffertrain series**

Chullunder Ghose series
Mundy, Talbot
1 *Nine unknown* (1924)
2 *Jimgrim* (1931)
Jimgrim Sahib
3 *C.I.D.* (1932)
4 *Gunga Sahib* (1933)
5 *Red flame of Erinpura* (1934)

Chulo trilogy
Calhoun, Wes
1 *Chulo* (1988)
2 *At Muerto Springs* (1989)
3 *Texas nighthawks* (1990)

Chumash series
Spinka, Penina Keen
Set in precolonial North America
1 *Mother's blessing* (1992)
2 *White Hare's horses* (1991)

Chums of Scranton High series
Ferguson, Donald
1 *Chums of Scranton High* (1919)
2 *Chums of Scranton High out for the pennant* (1919)
3 *Chums of Scranton High on the cinder path* (1919)
4 *Chums of Scranton High at ice hockey* (1919)

Chung Kuo series
Wingrove, David
1 *Middle kingdom* (1989)
2 *Broken wheel* (1990)
3 *White mountain* (1991)
4 *Stone within* (1992)
5 *Beneath the tree of heaven* (1993)
Three volumes yet to be published

Chunky series
Berg, Leila
1 *Adventures of Chunky* (1950)
2 *Trust Chunky* (1954)

Chup trilogy
Saberhagen, Fred
1 *Broken lands* (1968)
2 *Black mountains* (1971)
3 *Changeling earth* (1973)
Ardneh's world
One volume revised edition entitled *Empire of the East*, 1979

Church animals series
Austin, Margot
1 *Peter Churchmouse* (1943)
2 *Gabriel Churchkitten* (1958)
3 *Gabriel Churchkitten and the molts* (1959)
4 *Trumpet Churchdog* (1959)

Church Farm series
Hutchings, Monica Mary
1 *Chronicles of Church Farm* (1945)
2 *Romany Cottage, Silverlake* (1946)
The true story of an ordinary adventure
3 *Rural reflections* (1947)
4 *Hundredfold* (1948)

Church mice series
Oakley, Graham
1 *Church mouse* (1972)
2 *Church cat abroad* (1973)
3 *Church mice and the moon* (1974)
Numbers 1-3 also published in one volume entitled *The church mice chronicles*, 1986
4 *Church mice spread their wings* (1975)
5 *Church mice adrift* (1976)
6 *Church mice at bay* (1978)
7 *Church mice at Christmas* (1980)
8 *Church mice in action* (1982)
9 *Diary of a church mouse* (1987)

Church of England series
Howatch, Susan
1 *Glittering images* (1987)
2 *Glamorous powers* (1988)
3 *Ultimate prizes* (1989)
4 *Scandalous risks* (1991)
5 *Mystical paths* (1992)
6 *Absolute truths* (1994)

Church series
Howard, Vechel
see **Johnny Church series**

Church trilogy
Peters, Lance
see **Detective Sergeant Joe Church trilogy**

Churchill, Duke of Marlborough series
Kenyon, Frank Wilson
see **John Churchill, Duke of Marlborough series**

Churchill family series
Rowse, Alfred Leslie
1 *Early Churchills* (1956)
2 *Later Churchills* (1958)

Churchill series
Gilbert, Martin
see **Winston S Churchill series**

Chutney series
Hunt, Roderick
1 *Chutney and the fossil* (1977)
2 *Chutney on the river* (1977)
3 *Chutney at the circus* (1977)
4 *Chutney and the new boy* (1977)
5 *Chutney on the beach* (1977)
6 *Chutney in the snow* (1977)

Cicely Plantagenet trilogy
Wilson, Sandra
see **Lady Cicely Plantagenet trilogy**

Cicero Smith series
Ahlswede, Ann
see **Doctor Cicero Smith series**

Cija series
Gaskell, Jane
see **Atlan saga series**

Cilhendre Village series
Gallie, Menna
1 *Strike for a kingdom* (1959)
2 *Man's desiring* (1960)
3 *Small mine* (1962)

Cimarron series
Gentry, Georgina
1 *Cheyenne captive* (1987)
2 *Cheyenne princess* (1987)
3 *Cheyenne splendor* (1994)

Cimarron series
This sequence has two authors
Kelley, Leo Patrick
1 *Cimarron and the hanging judge* (1983)
2 *Cimarron rides the outlaw trail* (1983)
3 *Cimarron and the border bandits* (1983)
4 *Cimarron in the Cherokee Strip* (1983)
5 *Cimarron and the elk soldiers* (1983)
6 *Cimarron and the bounty hunters* (1983)
7 *Cimarron and the high rider* (1984)
8 *Cimarron in No Man's Land* (1984)
9 *Cimarron and the vigilantes* (1984)
10 *Cimarron and the medicine wolves* (1984)
11 *Cimarron on hell's highway* (1984)
12 *Cimarron and the war women* (1984)
13 *Cimarron and the bootleggers* (1984)
Baines, Lew
14 *Cimarron on the high plains* (1986)
Kelley, Leo Patrick
15 *Cimarron and the prophet's people* (1985)
16 *Cimarron and the scalp hunters* (1985)
Baines, Lew
17 *Cimarron and the Comancheros* (1985)
Kelley, Leo Patrick
18 *Cimarron and the gun hawks' gold* (1985)
Baines, Lew
19 *Cimarron on a Texas manhunt* (1986)
Kelley, Leo Patrick
20 *Cimarron and the red earth people* (1986)
21 *Cimarron and the manhunters* (1986)
22 *Cimarron and the hired guns* (1986)

Cinda Hollister series
Lambert, Janet
1 *Cinda* (1954)
2 *Fly away Cinda* (1956)
3 *Big deal* (1958)
4 *Triple trouble* (1965)
5 *Love to spare* (1967)

Cinderella series
Scannell, Florence
1 *Cinderella sisters* (1914)
2 *Peter's predicament* (1919)

Cindy and Nicole series
Cole, Jennifer
1 *Three's a crowd* (1986)

Cindy and Nicole series

2 *Too late for love* (1986)
3 *Kiss* (1986)
4 *Secrets at seventeen* (1986)
5 *Always a pair* (1986)
6 *On thin ice* (1986)
7 *Star quality* (1986)
8 *Making waves* (1987)
9 *Too many cooks* (1987)
10 *Out of the woods* (1987)
11 *Never a dull moment* (1987)
12 *Mollie in love* (1987)

Cindy series
Orgel, Doris
1 *Cindy's snowdrops* (1966)
2 *Cindy's sad and happy tree* (1967)

Cineverse trilogy
Gardner, Craig Shaw
1 *Slaves of the volcano god* (1989)
2 *Bride of the slime monster* (1990)
3 *Revenge of the fluffy bunnies* (1990)
One volume edition entitled *The Cineverse cycle*, 1991

Cingulum trilogy
Roberts, John Maddox
1 *Cingulum* (1985)
2 *Cloak of illusion* (1985)
3 *Sword, the jewel and the mirror* (1988)

Cipola series
Beebee, Chris
1 *Hub* (1987)
2 *Main event* (1989)

Circle C series
Rider, Brett
1 *Circle C moves in* (1944)
2 *Circle C carries on* (1948)

Circle of light series
Hancock, Niel
1 *Greyfax Grimwald* (1977)
2 *Faragon Fairingay* (1977)
3 *Calix Stay* (1977)
4 *Squaring the circle* (1977)
This sequence is followed by the **Wilderness of four series**

Circle of magic series
Doyle, Debra
1 *School of wizardry* (1990)
2 *Tornament and tower* (1990)
3 *City by the sea* (1990)
4 *Prince's players* (1990)
5 *Prisoners of Bell Castle* (1990)
6 *High King's daughter* (1990)

Circle series
Robertson, Jenny
1 *Circle of shadows* (1975)
2 *Circle of fire* (1979)

Circuit rider series
Harris, Corra
1 *Circuit rider's wife* (1910)
2 *Circuit rider's widow* (1916)
3 *My son* (1921)

Circuit trilogy
Snodgrass, Melinda Marilyn
1 *Circuit* (1986)
2 *Circuit breaker* (1987)
3 *Final circuit* (1988)

Circus series
Blyton, Enid
see **Mister Galliano's circus series**

Circus series
Spear, Diana
1 *Square pegs* (1959)
Across Australia by caravan
2 *Circus down under* (1960)

Circus train come aboard series
Barkan, Joanne
1 *Performers' car* (1993)
2 *Circus locomotive* (1993)
3 *Clown caboose* (1993)
4 *Animal car* (1993)

Circus trilogy
Longyear, Barry Brookes
1 *City of Baraboo* (1980)
2 *Circus world* (1980)
3 *Elephant song* (1982)

Cirret series
Hely, Elizabeth
see **Antoine Cirret series**

Cissie Marlow series
Dickson, Grierson
see **Superintendent Cissie Marlow series**

Cities in flight series
Blish, James
1 *They shall have stars* (1956)
Year 2018!
The second title is a revised edition
2 *Life for the stars* (1962)
3 *Earthman, come home* (1955)
4 *Triumph of time* (1958)
Clash of cymbals
One volume revised edition entitled *Cities in flight*, 1970

Cities of salt trilogy
Munif, Abdelrahman
Translated from the Arabic
1 *Cities of salt* (1984)
2 *Trench* (1985)
3 *Variations on night and day* (1989)

Cities of the interior series
Nin, Anais
1 *Ladders to fire* (1946)
2 *Children of the albatross* (1947)
3 *Four-chambered heart* (1950)
4 *Spy in the house of love* (1954)
5 *Seduction of the minotaur* (1961)
Solar barque
One volume edition entitled *Cities of the interior*, 1974

Cities of the red night trilogy
Burroughs, William Seward
1 *Cities of the red night* (1981)
A boy's book
2 *Place of dead roads* (1983)
3 *Western lands* (1987)
Companion volume: *The wild boys*, 1971, revised 1979

City detective series
M'Govan, James
see **James M'Govan series**

City in the dawn series
Allen, Hervey
see **Disinherited series**

City jitters series
Fowler, Christopher
Short stories
1 *City jitters* (1986)
2 *More city jitters* (1988)

City of London Police series
Bruton, Eric
1 *Hold out* (1961)
2 *Laughing policeman* (1963)
3 *Finsbury mob* (1964)
4 *Smithfield slayer* (1965)
5 *Wicked saint* (1965)
6 *Fire bug* (1967)

City of shadows series
Farrell, Simon
1 *Coreus the prince* (1987)
2 *Bardik the thief* (1987)

Civil War Raider series
Hogan, Ray
see **John Mosby series**

Civil War series
Altsheler, Joseph Alexander
1 *Guns of Bull Run* (1914)
2 *Guns of Shiloh* (1914)
3 *Sword of Antietam* (1914)
4 *Scouts of Stonewall* (1914)
5 *Star of Gettysburg* (1915)
6 *Rock of Chikamauga* (1915)
7 *Shades of the wilderness* (1916)
8 *Tree of Appomattox* (1916)

Civil War series
Edson, John Thomas
see **American Civil War series**
Ray, Delia
see **American Civil War series**
Softly, Barbara
see **English Civil War series**

Civil War society series
Smith, Francis Hopkinson
1 *Fortunes of Oliver Horn* (1902)
2 *Kennedy Square* (1911)

Civil War trilogy
Coffin, Charles Carleton
1 *My days and nights on the battlefield* (1864)
2 *Following the flag, from August 1861 to November 1862* (1865)
3 *Winning his way* (1866)

Civil War trilogy
Foote, Shelby
1 *Fort Sumter to Perryville* (1958)
2 *Fredericksburg to Meridian* (1963)
3 *Red River to Appomattox* (1974)

Civil War trilogy
Graham, Heather
1 *One wore blue* (1991)
2 *And one wore gray* (1992)
3 *And one rode west* (1992)

Civil War trilogy
Jakes, John
see **North and South trilogy**

Civil War trilogy
Kantor, Mackinlay
1 *Voice of Bugle Ann* (1935)
2 *Arouse and beware* (1936)
3 *Romance of Rosy Ridge* (1937)

Civilization and capitalism trilogy
Braudel, Fernand
Original edition entitled *Civilisation materielle et capitalisme, XVe-XVIIIe siecle*, 1967; this translation is from the revised edition entitled *Civilisation materielle, economie et capitalisme*
1 *Structures of everyday life* (1979)
The limits of the possible
2 *Wheels of commerce* (1979)
3 *Perspectives of the world* (1979)

Civilizations quartet
Harris, Wilson
1 *Black Marsden* (1972)
A tabula rasa comedy
2 *Companions of the day and night* (1975)
3 *Da Silva Da Silva's cultivated wilderness* (1977)
Also includes *Genesis of the clowns*
4 *Tree of the sun* (1978)

Clachan series
Armstrong, Sybil
Reminiscences of life in the Scottish Highlands
1 *Croft in Clachan* (1976)
2 *Clachan days* (1977)
3 *Hotel by Clachan* (1978)
4 *Electrics come to Clachan* (1979)
5 *Jamie in Clachan* (1980)

Clackworthy series
Booth, Christopher B
see **Amos Clackworthy series**

Claire Aldington series
Holland, Isabelle
1 *Flight of the archangel* (1985)
2 *Death at Saint Anselm's* (1985)
3 *Lover scorned* (1986)

Claire Malloy series
Hess, Joan
1 *Strangled prose* (1986)
2 *Murder at the Mimosa Inn* (1986)
3 *Dear Miss Demeanor* (1987)
4 *Really cute corpse* (1988)
5 *Diet to die for* (1989)
6 *Roll over and play dead* (1991)
7 *Death by the light of the moon* (1992)
8 *Poisoned pins* (1993)
9 *Tickled to death* (1994)

Clamart series
Rowland, Henry Cottrell
see **Frank Clamart series**

Clammer trilogy
Hopkins, William John
1 *Clammer* (1906)
2 *Meddlings of Eve* (1910)
3 *Clammer and the submarine* (1917)

Clan wars series
Morwood, Peter
1 *Greylady* (1993)
2 *Widowmaker* (1994)

Clancy and Cooper series
Beck, Kathrine Kristine
see **Iris Cooper and Jack Clancy series**

Clancy Martin series
Jackson, Wallace
see **Inspector Clancy Martin series**

Clancy series
Bachmann, Lawrence Paul
see **Ben Clancy series**
Cody, Stetson
see **Cactus Clancy series**
Pike, Robert L
see **Lieutenant Clancy series**
Thayer, Lee
see **Peter Clancy series**

Clane series
Gardner, Erle Stanley
see **Terry Clane series**

Clane series
Van Vogt, Alfred Elton
1 *Empire of the atom* (1956)
2 *Wizard of Linn* (1962)

Clanna series
Williams, Jeanne
1 *Island harp* (1993)
2 *Daughter of the storm* (1994)

Clansman series
Dixon, Thomas
1 *Clansman* (1904)
An historical romance of the Ku Klux Klan; filmed as *The birth of a nation*, 1915
2 *Fall of a nation* (1916)
The origin, meaning and destiny of American democracy

Clapp series
Miller, Wade
see **Lieutenant Austin Clapp series**

Clare Carson series
Elliott, Mary
A story of a bush nurse in the Australian outback
1 *Clare Carson at Wilga Junction* (1970)
2 *Clare Carson and the runaways* (1970)
3 *Clare Carson and the gold rush* (1970)
4 *Clare Carson and the sheep duffers* (1970)

Clare Savage series
Cliff, Michelle
1 *Abeng* (1984)
2 *Free enterprise* (1993)

Clare series
Farrell, James Thomas
see **Bernard Clare series**

Claremont series
Cranston, Claudia
see **Clarice Claremont series**

Clarence Dandridge series
Denuziere, Maurice
Translated from the French
1 *Plantation* (1977)
Bagatelle
Louisiana
2 *Virginia* (1979)

Clarence E Hemingway series
Maske, John
1 *Cherbourg mystery* (1934)
2 *Ghost of a cardinal* (1935)

Clarence Knight series
King, Frank
1 *Ghoul* (1928)
2 *Greenface* (1929)
3 *Owl* (1930)

Clarence series
Dalgleish, Joan
1 *Cats don't bark* (1978)
2 *Clarence settles down* (1986)

Clarence series
Lauber, Patricia
1 *Clarence, the TV dog* (1955)
2 *Clarence goes to town* (1957)
3 *Clarence turns sea dog* (1959)
Clarence takes a vacation
4 *Clarence and the burglar* (1973)
5 *Clarence and the cat* (1977)
Adapted from a chapter in *Clarence, the TV dog*, 1955

Clarice Claremont series
Cranston, Claudia
1 *Murder on Fifth Avenue* (1934)
2 *Murder maritime* (1935)

Clarissa Lovelace and Dan Valentine series
Aldyne, Nathan
see **Dan Valentine and Clarissa Lovelace series**

Clark and White series
Andrews, Stephen
see **Nobby Clark and Snowy White series**

Clark Clark Clark series
Baker, Samm Sinclair
1 *One touch of blood* (1955)
2 *Murder, very dry!* (1956)

Clark series
Thom, James Alexander
see **George Rogers Clark series**
Walden, Amelia
see **Lisa Clark series**
Young, Gordon Ray
see **Red Clark series**

Clarke series
Lewis, Irwin
see **Horace Clarke series**
Martin, Nancy
see **Anne Clarke series**

Clarkeville series
Lawton, Charles
1 *Clarkeville's battery* (1937)
Alternative title: Baseball versus gangsters
2 *Ros Hackney, halfback* (1937)
Alternative title: How Clarkeville's captain made good
3 *Winning forward pass* (1940)
Alternative title: Onward to the Orange Bowl game
4 *Home run Hennessey* (1941)
Alternative title: Winning the all-star game
5 *Touchdown to victory* (1942)
Alternative title: The Touchdown Express makes good

Clarkson-Parry series
Quin, Basil Godfrey
see **James Clarkson-Parry series**

Class of eighty eight series
Cooney, Linda A
1 *Freshman* (1987)
2 *Sophomore* (1987)
3 *Junior* (1987)
4 *Senior* (1987)

Class of eighty nine series
Cooney, Linda A
1 *Freshman* (1988)
2 *Sophomore* (1988)
3 *Junior* (1988)
4 *Senior* (1988)

Claude and Shirley series
Nixon, Joan Lowery
see **Shirley and Claude series**

Claude Greenway series
Thompson, Lloyd S
see **Shimoru Kyota series**

Claude Kirlin and F T Zevich series
Bourgeau, Art
1 *Lonely way to die* (1980)
2 *Most likely suspects* (1981)
3 *Elvis murders* (1985)
4 *Murder at the Cheatin' Heart Motel* (1985)

Claude Ravel series
Jones, Bradshaw
1 *Hamlet problem* (1962)
2 *Crooked phoenix* (1963)
3 *Tiger from the shadows* (1963)
4 *Death on a pale horse* (1964)
5 *Private vendetta* (1964)
6 *Embers of hate* (1966)
7 *Testament of evil* (1966)
8 *Den of savage men* (1967)
9 *Deadly trade* (1967)

Claude series
Gackenbach, Dick
1 *Claude the dog* (1974)
A Christmas story
2 *Claude and Pepper* (1976)
3 *Pepper and all the legs* (1978)
4 *What's Claude doing?* (1984)
5 *Claude has a picnic* (1993)

Claude series
Nixon, Joan Lowery
1 *If you say so, Claude* (1980)
2 *Beats me, Claude* (1986)
3 *Fat chance, Claude* (1987)
4 *You bet your britches, Claude* (1989)
5 *That's the spirit, Claude* (1990)

Claude Warrington-Reeve series
Bell, Josephine
1 *Easy prey* (1959)
2 *Well-known face* (1960)
3 *Flat tyre in Fulham* (1963)
Fiasco in Fulham
Room for a body

Claudia and Evan trilogy
Levin, Betty
1 *Sword of Culann* (1973)
2 *Griffon's nest* (1975)
3 *Forespoken* (1976)

Claudia series
Coates, Irene
1 *Claudia's war* (1983)
2 *Claudia's India* (1987)

Claudia series
Franken, Rose
1 *Claudia* (1939)
Story of a marriage
2 *Claudia and David* (1940)
3 *Another Claudia* (1943)
4 *Young Claudia* (1946)
5 *Marriage of Claudia* (1948)
6 *From Claudia to David* (1949)
7 *Fragile years* (1952)
Those fragile years
Return of Claudia
8 *Antic years* (1958)

Claudia series
Wallace, Barbara Brooks
1 *Claudia* (1969)
2 *Hello, Claudia!* (1982)
3 *Claudia and Duffy* (1982)

Claudia Valentine series
Day, Marele
1 *Life and crimes of Harry Lavender* (1988)
2 *Case of the Chinese boxes* (1990)
3 *Last tango of Dolores Delgado* (1992)
4 *Disappearance of Madalena Grimaldi* (1994)

Claudine Saint Cyr series
Wallace, Ian
1 *Doctor Orpheus* (1968)
A downtime myth
2 *Deathstar voyage* (1969)
3 *Purloined prince* (1971)
4 *Sign of the mute Medusa* (1977)
5 *Heller's leap* (1979)

Claudine series
Colette, Sidonie Gabrielle
1 *Claudine at school* (1900)
Original edition entitled *Claudine a l'ecole*
2 *Claudine in Paris* (1901)
Young lady of Paris
Original edition entitled *Claudine a Paris*
3 *Claudine married* (1902)
Indulgent husband
Original edition entitled *Claudine en menage*
4 *Claudine and Annie* (1903)
Innocent wife
Original edition entitled *Claudine s'en va*
5 *Retreat from love* (1907)
Original edition entitled *Retraite sentimentale*
6 *My mother's house* (1922)
Original edition entitled *La maison de Claudine*
7 *Morning glory* (1928)
Lesson in love
Break of day
Original edition entitled *Naissance du jour*
8 *Sido* (1930)
Original edition entitled *Sido*
9 *My apprenticeships* (1936)
Original edition entitled *Mes apprentissages*

Claudius series
Graves, Robert
1 *I, Claudius* (1934)
2 *Claudius the god and his wife Messalina* (1934)

Claudius the bee series
Leeming, John Fishwick
1 *Claudius the bee* (1936)
2 *Thanks to Claudius* (1937)

Clavengers series
Stuart, Dorothy Margaret
1 *Children's chronicle* (1944)
2 *Young Clavengers* (1947)

Clavering Grange series
Chetwynd-Hayes, Ronald
see **Tales of Clavering Grange series**

Claw series
Kirk, Matthew
1 *Day of fury* (1983)
2 *Vengeance road* (1983)
3 *Yellow stripe* (1983)
4 *Wild hunt* (1983)
5 *Blood for blood* (1983)
6 *Death in red* (1984)

Claw series
Paradis, Vincent A
see **Tut Claw series**

Clay Brooke series
Crooker, Herbert
1 *Hollywood murder mystery* (1930)
2 *Crime in Washington Mews* (1931)

Clay Harrison series
Robbins, Clifton
1 *Dusty death* (1931)
2 *Man without a face* (1932)
Mystery of Mister Cross
3 *Death on the highway* (1933)
4 *Smash and grab* (1934)
5 *Methylated murder* (1935)

Clay Loomis series
Sanders, Leonard
1 *Hamlet warning* (1976)
2 *Hamlet ultimatum* (1979)

Clay mining series
Summers, Rowena
Family history
1 *Killigrew clay* (1986)
2 *Clay country* (1987)
3 *Family ties* (1988)

Clay series
Gore-Browne, Robert
see **Lucien Clay series**
Lauben, Philip
see **Captain Homer Clay series**
Macgrath, Harold
see **Cutty Clay series**
Porcelain, Sidney E
see **Stephen Clay series**

Clay Torn series
Edwards, Hank
see **Judge Clay Torn series**

Clayburn series
Conroy, Al
Also published under the author's real name Marvin Hubert Albert
1 *Clayburn* (1961)
2 *Last train to Bannock* (1963)
3 *Three ride north* (1964)
4 *Man in black* (1965)

Clayhanger series
Bennett, Arnold
1 *Clayhanger* (1910)
2 *Hilda Lessways* (1911)
3 *These twain* (1916)
4 *Roll call* (1919)

Claymore family series
McNaught, Judith
see **Westmoreland series**

Claymore series
Claymore, Tod
see **Tod Claymore series**

Clayre series
Farrell, James Thomas
see **Bernard Clare series**

Clayt and Cam series
Bickham, Jack Miles
see **John Campbell and Clayton Hartung series**

Clayton Drew series
Fearn, John Russell
1 *Emperor of Mars* (1950)
2 *Warrior of Mars* (1950)
3 *Red men of Mars* (1950)
4 *Goddess of Mars* (1950)

Clayton Hartung and John Campbell series
Bickham, Jack Miles
see **John Campbell and Clayton Hartung series**

Clayton series
Gluck, Sinclair
see **Jack Clayton series**
Marsh, Jean Evelyn
see **Rick and Pete Clayton series**

Clayton trilogy
Shelynn, Jack
see **Sam Clayton trilogy**

Cleary series
Thomas, Audrey
see **Isobel Cleary series**

Cleek series
Hanshew, Thomas W
see **Hamilton Cleek series**

Clegg series
Warner, Anne
see **Susan Clegg series**

Clem series
Phillpotts, Beatrice
1 *Clem and the dancing bear* (1987)
2 *Clem and the runaway pig* (1987)
3 *Clem and the fancy dress party* (1987)
4 *Happy Christmas, Clem* (1987)

Clem Talbot series
Mulkeen, Thomas Patrick
1 *Honor thy godfather* (1973)
2 *My killer doesn't understand me* (1973)

Clemons series
Cook, Thomas H
see **Frank Clemons series**

Cleo series
Garis, Lilian C
1 *Cleo's conquest* (1927)
2 *Cleo's misty rainbow* (1927)

Cleopatra Jones series
Goulart, Ron
Based on screenplays
1 *Cleopatra Jones* (1973)
2 *Cleopatra Jones and the casino of gold* (1975)

Cleopatra series
Lindsay, Kathleen
1 *Enchantress of the Nile* (1965)
2 *Queen of the mirage* (1966)

Cleric quintet
Salvatore, Robert Anthony
1 *Canticle* (1991)
2 *In sylvan shadows* (1992)
3 *Night masks* (1992)
4 *Fallen fortress* (1993)
5 *Chaos obscure* (1994)

Clerihew series
Allen, Herbert Warner
see **Mister Clerihew series**

Clerihews series
Bentley, Edmund Clerihew
1 *Biography for beginners* (1905)
2 *More biography* (1929)
3 *Baseless biography* (1939)
One volume editions entitled *Clerihews complete*, 1951, and *The complete Clerihews*, 1981

Clerihews series
Horgan, Paul
1 *Gallery of Clerihews* (1984)
2 *Annotated Clerihew* (1984)
One volume edition entitled *The Clerihews of Paul Horgan*, 1985

Clerkenwell series
Bennett, Arnold
see **Elsie series**

Cleveland series
Fowler, Sydney
see **Inspector Cleveland series**

Clevely series
Lofts, Norah
1 *Bless this house* (1954)
2 *Afternoon of an autocrat* (1956)
Devil in Clevely

Clever Polly series
Storr, Catherine
see **Polly and the wolf series**

Clever Trevor series
Rogers, Alan
1 *Clever Trevor knows his animals* (1986)
2 *Clever Trevor knows his numbers* (1986)
3 *Clever Trevor knows his shapes* (1986)
4 *Clever Trevor knows his colours* (1986)

Click, Bun and Josie series
Blyton, Enid
see **Josie, Click and Bun series**

Clicky series
Blyton, Enid
1 *Clicky the clockwork clown* (1953)
2 *Clicky gets into trouble* (1958)
3 *Clicky and Tiptoe* (1960)
4 *Happy holiday, Clicky* (1961)

Cliff Hardy series
Corris, Peter
1 *Matrimonial causes* (1993)
2 *Dying trade* (1980)
3 *White meat* (1981)
4 *Marvellous boy* (1982)
Marvelous boy
5 *Empty beach* (1983)
6 *Heroin Annie, and other Cliff Hardy stories* (1984)
7 *Make me rich* (1985)
8 *Big drop, and other Cliff Hardy stories* (1985)
9 *Deal me out* (1986)
10 *Greenwich Apartments* (1986)
11 *January Zone* (1987)
12 *Man in the shadows* (1988)
Short stories
13 *O'Fear* (1990)
14 *Wet graves* (1991)
15 *Aftershock* (1991)
16 *Beware of the dog* (1992)
17 *Burn, and other stories* (1993)
18 *Casino* (1994)

Cliff House series
Moss, Nancy
1 *School on the precipice* (1954)
2 *Susan's stormy term* (1955)
3 *Strange quest at Cliff House* (1956)
4 *Cliff House monster* (1957)
5 *Riddle of Cliff House* (1957)

Cliff Monroe series
Hubel, James Lyon
see **Medico series**

Cliff series
Matterson, Neil
Strip cartoons
1 *Cliff* (1984)
2 *Cliffhanger* (1988)

Clifford Brooks series
Gridban, Volsted
1 *Thing of the past* (1953)
2 *Genial dinosaur* (1954)

Clifford Driscoll series
De Andrea, William Louis
1 *Cronus* (1984)
2 *Snark* (1985)
3 *Azrael* (1987)
4 *Atropos* (1990)

Clifford series
Bridwell, Norman
1 *Clifford, the big red dog* (1962)
2 *Clifford gets a job* (1965)
3 *Clifford takes a trip* (1966)
4 *Clifford's Halloween* (1966)
5 *Clifford's tricks* (1969)
6 *Clifford, the small red puppy* (1972)
7 *Clifford's riddles* (1974)
8 *Clifford's good deeds* (1975)
9 *Clifford at the circus* (1977)
10 *Clifford goes to Hollywood* (1980)
11 *Clifford's ABC* (1984)
12 *Clifford's story hour* (1984)
13 *Clifford's family* (1984)
14 *Clifford's kitten* (1984)
15 *Clifford's Christmas* (1984)
16 *Clifford's pals* (1985)
17 *Clifford's neighborhood* (1985)
18 *Clifford and the grouchy neigbors* (1985)
Numbers 1, 5, 16, 18 also published in one volume entitled *Clifford treasury*, number 1, 1991
19 *Count on Clifford* (1985)
20 *Clifford's manners* (1986)
21 *Clifford's birthday party* (1987)
22 *Clifford's sing along* (1987)
23 *Clifford wants a cookie* (1988)
24 *Clifford's puppy days* (1989)
Numbers 13, 14, 21, 24 also published in one volume entitled *Clifford treasury*, number 2, 1991
25 *Clifford, we love you* (1991)
26 *Clifford's animal sounds* (1991)
27 *Clifford's peekaboo* (1991)
28 *Clifford's bedtime* (1991)
29 *Clifford's bathtime* (1991)
30 *Clifford's noisy day* (1992)
31 *Clifford counts bubbles* (1992)
32 *Clifford's Thanksgiving visit* (1993)
33 *Clifford's springtime* (1994)
34 *Clifford, I love you* (1994)
Companion volumes: *Clifford's sticker book*, 1984, *Where is Clifford, a lift-a-flap book*, 1989, *Fun with Clifford activity book*, 1989, *Clifford's word book*, 1990, *Clifford's happy day, a pop-up book*, 1990, *Hello, Clifford, a puppet book*, 1991, *Clifford's big book of stories*, 1994

Clifford series
Scott, Leroy
see **Bob Clifford series**

Clifford Wells series
Bortner, Norman Stanley
see **Professor Clifford Wells series**

Clift series
Heath, Eric
see **Cornelius Clift series**

Clifton family series
Ross, Sutherland
1 *Vagabond treasure* (1956)
2 *Sword is the king* (1958)
3 *Drum and trumpet sound* (1960)

Clifton series
Robinson, George Bush
see **James Clifton series**

Climbing series
Bonington, Chris
Autobiography
1 *I chose to climb* (1966)
2 *Next horizon* (1973)

Climbing the rope series
Mannering, May
1 *Climbing the rope* (1868)
Alternative title: God helps those who try to help themselves
2 *Billy Grime's favourite* (1868)
Alternative title: Johnny Greenleaf's talent
3 *Cruise of the Dashaway* (1868)
Alternative title: Katie Putnam's voyage
4 *Little Spaniard* (1869)
Alternative title: Old Jose's grandson
5 *Salt-water Dick* (1869)
6 *Little maid of Oxbow* (1871)

Clint Lacey series
Tyler, Clarke
1 *Ride clear, stranger* (1955)
2 *Showdown at Singing Sands* (1956)
3 *Gunsmoke over Tumbling T* (1957)

Clint Wade and Trapper Bill series
Weddle, Ferris
1 *Blizzard rescue* (1959)
2 *Blazing mountain* (1961)
3 *Wilderness renegades* (1962)

Clint Webb series
Foster, Walter Bertram
1 *Swept out to sea* (1913)
Alternative title: Clint Webb among the whales
2 *Frozen ship* (1913)
Alternative title: Clint Webb among the sealers
3 *From sea to sea* (1914)
Alternative title: Clint Webb's cruise on the windjammer
4 *Sea express* (1914)
Alternative title: Clint Webb and the sea tramp

Clinton Driffield series
Connington, John Jervis
see **Sir Clinton Driffield series**

Clinton Judd series
Goldman, Lawrence Louis
Based on a television series
1 *Judd for the defense* (1968)
2 *Secret listeners* (1968)

Clinton series
Hagen, Miriam Ann
see **Hortense Clinton series**
Johns, William Earl
see **Rex Clinton series**

Clinton series
Marshall, Archibald
1 *Peter Binney, undergraduate* (1899)
2 *Richard Baldock* (1906)
An account of some episodes in his childhood, youth and early manhood and of the advice that was freely offered to him
3 *Exton Manor* (1907)

4 *Many Junes* (1908)
5 *Squire's daughter* (1909)
6 *Eldest son* (1911)
7 *Honour of the Clintons* (1913)
8 *Rank and riches* (1915)
Old order changeth
9 *Clinton, and others* (1920)
Clinton twins, and other stories

Clinton series
Stevens, William Oliver
see **Peewee Clinton series**

Clinton Shannon series
Roberts, Lee
see **Doctor Clinton Shannon series**

Clipper of the clouds series
Verne, Jules
see **Robur series**

Clipper series
Cross, Gillian
1 *Save our school* (1981)
2 *Mintyglo Kid* (1983)
3 *Swimathon!* (1986)

Clipper ship series
Knight, Frank
1 *Golden Monkey* (1953)
2 *Voyage to Bengal* (1954)
3 *Clipper to China* (1955)
4 *Bluenose pirate* (1956)
5 *He sailed with Blackbeard* (1958)

Clipper Street series
Ashley, Bernard
1 *Calling for Sam* (1987)
2 *Taller than before* (1987)
3 *Down-and-out* (1988)
4 *Royal visit* (1988)
5 *All I ever ask* (1989)
6 *Sally Cinderella* (1989)

Clippie Nancarrow series
Brinsmead, Hesba Fay
1 *Who calls from afar?* (1971)
2 *Echo in the wilderness* (1972)

Clive and Robin Lendrick series
Braine, John
1 *Stay with me till morning* (1970)
2 *Two of us* (1984)

Clive Granville series
McKenna, Marthe
1 *Lancer spy* (1937)
2 *Spy in khaki* (1941)

Clive series
Morrison, Emmeline
see **Lovice clive series**

Cloakmaster series
Cook, David
see **Spelljammer series**

Cloche series
Pilgrim, David
see **James De la Cloche series**

Clochemerle series
Chevallier, Gabriel
Translated from the French
1 *Clochemerle* (1936)
2 *Clochemerle-Babylon* (1954)
3 *Clochemerle-les Bains* (1963)

Clock trilogy
Bellairs, John
1 *House with a clock in its walls* (1973)
2 *Figure in the shadows* (1975)
3 *Letter, the witch and the ring* (1976)

Clocks of death trilogy
McQueen, James
1 *White light* (1990)
2 *Heavy knife* (1991)
Number 3 not yet published

Clodagh Laidlaw series
Hine, Muriel
1 *Flight* (1922)
2 *Spell of Siris* (1923)

Clogshop trilogy
Ackworth, John
1 *Clogshop chronicles* (1896)
2 *Beckside lights* (1897)
3 *Doxie Dent* (1899)

Closer look at series
Stonehouse, Bernard
1 *Closer look at whales and dolphins* (1978)
2 *Closer look at plant life* (1978)
3 *Closer look at reptiles* (1979)

Clothes of a king's son trilogy
Frankau, Pamela
1 *Sing for your supper* (1963)
2 *Slaves of the lamp* (1965)
3 *Over the mountains* (1967)

Clotilde series
Saint-Laurent, Cecil
Translated from the French
1 *Clotilde* (1957)
2 *Encore, Clotilde* (1958)

Cloud family series
Mathews, M E
1 *Redheads of Windyridge* (1950)
2 *Island in the lake* (1951)
3 *Sixpenny holiday* (1953)

Cloud Patrol series
This sequence has three authors
Crump, James Irving
1 *Cloud Patrol* (1929)
2 *Pilot of the Cloud Patrol* (1929)
Sherman, Harold Morrow
3 *Ding Palmer, air detective* (1930)
Fitzhugh, Percy Kees
4 *Mark Gilmore, scout of the air* (1930)
Crump, James Irving
5 *Craig of the Cloud Patrol* (1931)
Fitzhugh, Percy Kees
6 *Mark Gilmore, speed flyer* (1931)
7 *Mark Gilmore's lucky landing* (1931)

Cloud Valley series
Leeson, Robert
1 *Landing in Cloud Valley* (1991)
2 *Fire on the cloud* (1991)

Clouseau series
Albert, Marvin Hubert
see **Inspector Clouseau series**

Clover Club series
Langholm, A D
1 *Clover Club and the house of mystery* (1978)
2 *Clover Club and the adventure that fell out of the sky* (1980)

Clovis Crawfish series
Fontenot, Mary Alice
1 *Clovis Crawfish and his friends* (1962)
Revised edition 1985
2 *Clovis Crawfish and the big betail* (1963)
3 *Clovis Crawfish and the singing cigales* (1963)
4 *Clovis Crawfish and Petit Papillon* (1966)
5 *Clovis Crawfish and the spinning spider* (1968)
6 *Clovis Crawfish and the curious craupaud* (1970)
7 *Clovis Crawfish and Michelle Mantis* (1976)
8 *Clovis Crawfish and Etienne Escargot* (1979)
9 *Clovis Crawfish and the orphan Zo-Zo* (1983)
10 *Clovis Crawfish and Simeon Suce-Fleur* (1990)
11 *Clovis Crawfish and Bertile's bon voyage* (1991)
12 *Clovis Crawfish and Batiste bete puante* (1993)

Clovis Kelly series
Babbin, Jaqueline
1 *Prime time corpse* (1972)
2 *Bloody special* (1973)

Clovis Pel series
Hebden, Mark
see **Inspector Clovis Pel series**

Clovis series
Saki
Short stories
1 *Chronicles of Clovis* (1911)
2 *Beasts and super-beasts* (1914)
One volume edition entitled *The short stories of Saki*, 1930

Clown-Arounds series
Cole, Joanna
1 *Clown-Arounds* (1981)
2 *Clown-Arounds have a party* (1982)
3 *Get well, Clown-Arounds!* (1982)
4 *Clown-Arounds go on vacation* (1983)
5 *Sweet dreams, Clown-Arounds* (1985)

Clown series
Brook, Judy
see **Charlie Clown series**

Clown series
Judah, Aaron
1 *Clown of Bombay* (1963)
2 *Clown of fire* (1965)

Club of the Round Table series
Lawrence, Margery
1 *Nights of the Round Table* (1926)
A book of strange tales
2 *Terraces of night* (1932)

Clubfoot series
Williams, Valentine
1 *Man with the clubfoot* (1918)
English edition published under the pseudonym Douglas Valentine
2 *Okewood of the Secret Service* (1919)
Secret hand
Second title published under the pseudonym Douglas Valentine
3 *Return of Clubfoot* (1922)
Island gold
4 *Clubfoot the avenger* (1924)
5 *Three of Clubs* (1924)
6 *Crouching beast* (1928)
7 *Gold comfit box* (1932)
Mystery of the gold box
8 *Spider's touch* (1936)
9 *Courier to Marrakesh* (1944)

Clubman series
Burgin, George Brown
1 *Memoirs of a clubman* (1921)
2 *More memoirs, and some travels* (1922)
3 *Many memories* (1922)
4 *Some more memoirs* (1924)

Cluer series
Ferguson, William Blair Morton
see **Dan Cluer series**

Cluff series
North, Gil
see **Sergeant Caleb Cluff series**

Clume series
Goldman, Raymond Leslie
see **Asaph Clume series**

Clunk series
Bailey, Henry Christopher
see **Mister Joshua Clunk series**

Cluster series
Anthony, Piers
1 *Cluster* (1977)
Vicinity cluster
2 *Chaining the lady* (1978)
3 *Kirlian quest* (1978)
4 *Thousandstar* (1980)
5 *Viscous circle* (1982)

Clutha series
Munro, Hugh Macfarlane
1 *Who told Clutha* (1958)
2 *Clutha plays a bunch* (1959)
3 *Clue for Clutha* (1960)
4 *Clutha and the lady* (1973)
5 *Get Clutha* (1974)
6 *Evil innocence* (1976)
7 *Brain robbers* (1977)

Clyde and Bonnie series
Brent, Lynton Wright
see **Bonnie and Clyde series**

Clyde Valley series
Gavin, Catherine
1 *Clyde Valley* (1938)
2 *Hostile shore* (1940)

Clydeside series
Bowie, Janetta
1 *Penny buff* (1975)
A Clydeside school in the thirties
2 *Penny boss* (1976)
A Clydeside school in the fifties
3 *Penny change* (1977)
A Clydeside school in the seventies

Clymping and Pellew series
Gielgud, Val
see **Inspector Gregory Pellew and Viscount Clymping series**

Cname Sname series
This sequence has two authors
Manners, Carol
1 *Adventures of Cname Sname and the Wattle Fairy* (1986)
2 *Journey of Cname Sname in a UFO* (1986)
3 *Cname Sname goes riding with Emily Emu* (1986)
Smith, Peter Charles
4 *Cname Sname defends the America's Cup* (1986)

Coal series
Sinclair, Upton
1 *King Coal* (1917)
2 *Coal war* (1976)

Coarse plays series
Green, Michael
1 *Four plays for coarse actors* (1978)
Also known as *The coarse acting show;* contains *Streuth, Il fornicazione, A collier's Tuesday tea, All's well that ends as you like it*
2 *Coarse acting show 2* (1980)
Contains *Moby Dick, Last call for breakfast, The Cherry sisters, Henry the Tenth, part seven*
3 *Third coarse acting show* (1985)
Contains *A fish in her kettle, Present slaughter, The vagabond prince, Stalag 69, Julius and Cleopatra*

Coarse series
Green, Michael
Humour
1 *Art of coarse rugby* (1960)
2 *Art of coarse sailing* (1962)
Revised edition 1975
3 *Even coarser rugby* (1963)
Subtitle: What did you do to Ronald?
4 *Art of coarse acting* (1964)
How to wreck an amateur dramatic society; revised edition 1980
5 *Book of coarse sport* (1965)
Michael Green book of coarse sport

Coarse series

6 *Art of coarse golf* (1967)
7 *Roof over my head* (1969)
Art of coarse moving
8 *Art of coarse drinking* (1973)
9 *Art of coarse cruising* (1976)
10 *Even coarser sport* (1978)
11 *Art of coarse sex* (1981)
How to love better and die with a beautiful smile on your face
12 *Art of coarse office life* (1985)
Any number can play

Coarse series
Hughes, Spike
1 *Art of coarse cricket* (1954)
A study of its principles, traditions and practice; revised edition 1961
2 *Art of coarse travel* (1954)
Revised edition 1963
3 *Art of coarse gardening* (1968)
4 *Art of coarse bridge* (1970)
5 *Art of coarse cookery* (1971)
6 *Art of coarse entertaining* (1972)

Coastlanders series
Cronin, Bernard
1 *Coastlanders* (1918)
2 *Red Dawson* (1927)

Coates series
Rey, Bret
see **Ralph Coates series**

Cobb family series
Dunnett, Margaret
1 *Has anyone see Emily* (1968)
2 *Boy who saw Emmy* (1973)

Cobb series
De Andrea, William Louis
see **Matt Cobb series**
Hodges, Margaret
see **Joshua Cobb series**
Winsor, Roy
see **Ira Cobb series**

Cobra trilogy
Zahn, Timothy
1 *Cobra* (1985)
2 *Cobra strike* (1986)
3 *Cobra bargain* (1988)

Cobwebb series
Boshell, Gordon
see **Captain Cobwebb series**

Cochran series
Nighbert, David Franklin
see **Bull Cochran series**

Cochrane series
Evans, Alan
see **David Cochrane series**

Cockalorum series
Simkins, Wallis
see **Little cockalorum series**

Cockleshell Bay series
Trueman, Brian
see **Stories from Cockleshell Bay series**

Cockrill series
Brand, Christianna
see **Inspector Cockrill series**

Cocky chaff series
Nelson, Brian
1 *Major Mitchell's cocky chaff* (1981)
2 *Another load of cocky chaff* (1983)
3 *Cocky chaff flies again* (1990)
4 *What a heap of cocky chaff* (1990)

Coco and Bill Hastings series
Offord, Lenore Glen
see **Bill and Coco Hastings series**

Cocoon series
Saperstein, David
1 *Cocoon* (1985)
2 *Metamorphosis* (1988)

Code name Sebastian series
Johnson, James Leonard
1 *Code name Sebastian* (1967)
2 *Nine lives of Alphonse* (1968)
3 *Handful of dominoes* (1970)
4 *Piece of the moon is missing* (1974)

Codebreaker kids series
Stanley, George Edward
1 *Codebreaker kids* (1987)
2 *Codebreaker kids return* (1989)

Cody series
Brierley, David
1 *Cold war* (1979)
2 *Blood group O* (1980)
3 *Skorpion's death* (1985)
4 *Snowline* (1986)

Cody series
Buntline, Ned
see **Buffalo Bill series**

Cody's army series
Case, Jim
1 *Cody's army* (1986)
2 *Assault into Libya* (1986)
3 *Philippine hardpunch* (1987)
4 *Belfast blitz* (1987)
5 *D.C. firestrike* (1987)
6 *Hellfire in Haiti* (1988)

Cody's law series
Hart, Matthew S
1 *Gunmetal justice* (1991)
2 *Die lonesome* (1991)
3 *Border showdown* (1991)
4 *Bounty man* (1992)
5 *Mano a mano* (1992)
6 *Renegade trail* (1992)
7 *End of the line* (1992)
8 *Eagle Pass* (1993)
9 *Prisoners* (1993)
10 *Gallows waiting* (1994)

Coe and Mallin series
Ormerod, Roger
see **David Mallin and George Coe series**

Coe and Wilson series
Cameron, Caddo
see **Private Badger Coe and Sergeant Blizzard Wilson series**

Co-ed series
Lee, Alice Lester
1 *Freshman co-ed* (1910)
2 *Sophomore co-ed* (1911)
3 *Junior co-ed* (1912)
4 *Senior co-ed* (1913)

Coffee series
Blochman, Lawrence Goldtree
see **Doctor Daniel Webster Coffee series**

Coffee, tea or me girls series
Baker, Trudy
Humorous reminiscences of two flight attendants
1 *Coffee, tea or me?* (1967)
2 *Coffee, tea of me girls round-the-world diary* (1970)
3 *Coffee, tea or me girls lay it on the line* (1972)
4 *Coffee, tea or me girls get away from it all* (1974)

Coffin Ed Johnson and Grave Digger Jones series
Himes, Chester
see **Grave Digger Jones and Coffin Ed Johnson series**

Coffin series
Butler, Gwendoline
see **Inspector John Coffin series**

Coffyn series
Snedeker, Caroline Dale
see **Dencey Coffyb series**

Cogburn series
Portis, Charles
see **Rooster Cogburn series**

Cogg series
Sloan, Carolyn
see **Mister Cogg series**

Coggin trilogy
Oldmeadow, Ernest James
1 *Coggin* (1920)
2 *Hare* (1921)
3 *Wildfang* (1922)

Cohen and Comaday series
Cunningham, E V
see **John Comaday and Larry Cohen series**

Cohn series
Gary, Romain
see **Genghis Cohn series**

Coignard series
France, Anatole
see **Abbe Coignard series**

Colby series
Dodge, David
see **Al Colby series**

Cold cash war series
Asprin, Robert Lynn
1 *Cold cash war* (1977)
2 *Combat Command in the world of Robert Asprin's Cold cash warrior* (1989)
Co-author: Bill Fawcett

Cold Comfort Farm series
Gibbons, Stella
1 *Cold Comfort Farm* (1932)
2 *Christmas at Cold Comfort Farm, and other stories* (1940)
3 *Conference at Cold Comfort Farm* (1949)

Cold Sassy Tree series
Burns, Olive Ann
see **Tweedy family series**

Coldiron series
Parker, F M
see **Luke Coldiron series**

Colditz series
This sequence has eleven authors
Reid, Patrick Robert
1 *Colditz story* (1952)
2 *Latter days* (1953)
Latter days at Colditz
Numbers 1 and 2 also published in one volume entitled *Colditz*, 1962
3 *Colditz, the full story* (1984)
Neave, Airey
4 *They have their exits* (1953)
Romilly, Giles
5 *Privileged nightmare* (1954)
Hostages of Colditz
Eggers, Reinhold
6 *Colditz, the German story* (1961)
Translated and edited by Howard Gee
Green, Julius Morris
7 *From Colditz in code* (1971)
Platt, Jock Ellison
8 *Padre in Colditz* (1978)
Diary, edited by Margaret Duggan
Baybutt, Ron
9 *Camera in Colditz* (1982)
Champ, Jack
10 *Diggers of Colditz* (1985)
Rogers, Jim
11 *Tunnelling into Colditz* (1986)
A mining engineer in captivity
Pringle, Jack
12 *Colditz last stop* (1988)
Six escapes remembered
Companion volume: *Colditz recaptured, sixteen firsthand accounts*, compiled by Reinhold Eggers, edited by John Watton, 1973, also published as *Escape from Colditz*, 1991

Cole and Speare series
Davis, Frederick Clyde
see **Schyler Cole and Luke Speare series**

Cole Brandon series
Bensen, Donald R
1 *Mask of the Tracker* (1992)
2 *Fool's gold* (1992)
3 *Death in the hills* (1992)

Cole Brogan series
Poyer, Joe
1 *Shooting of the green* (1973)
Hell shot
3 *Contract* (1978)

Cole family series
Dawes, Frank Victor
1 *Family album* (1982)
2 *Inheritance* (1984)

Cole McCurtain series
Owens, Louis
1 *Sharpest sight* (1992)
2 *Bone game* (1994)

Cole series
Cawley, Winifred
see **Ralph Cole series**
Donahue, Jackson
see **Harlan Cole series**
Greenwald, Sheila
see **Rosy Cole series**

Coleman family and Jake Langston series
Brown, Sandra
1 *Sunset embrace* (1984)
2 *Another dawn* (1985)

Coleridge Tucker, Jennifer Norrington and Alessandro di Ganzarello series
Drummond, Ivor
see **Lady Jennifer, Sandro and Colly series**

Colette and Joc series
Barclay, Vera Charlesworth
see **Joc and Colette series**

Colfax series
Conley, Robert Jackson
see **Oliver Colfax series**

Colin and Patricia series
Rutley, Cecil Bernard
1 *Colin and Patricia in Canada* (1949)
2 *Colin and Patricia in South Africa and Southern Rhodesia* (1952)

Colin and Susan series
Garner, Alan
see **Alderley series**

Colin Andrew Macthrockle Glencannon series
Gilpatric, Guy
see **Mister Colin Andrew Macthrockle Glencannon series**

Colin Anstruther series
Plain, Josephine
1 *Secret of the sandbanks* (1934)
2 *Secret of the snows* (1935)
3 *Pazenger problem* (1936)

Colin Burke series
Cullen, Robert
1 *Soviet sources* (1990)
2 *Cover story* (1994)

Colin Garrett series
Brandner, Gary
see **Big Brain series**

Colin Gray series
Channing, Mark
1 *King Cobra* (1933)
2 *White python* (1934)
3 *Poisoned mountain* (1935)
4 *Nine lives* (1937)

Colin Harpur series
James, Bill
see **Superintendent Colin Harpur series**

Colin Huntington series
Condon, Richard
see **Captain Colin Huntington series**

Colin Keats and Gwynn Leith series
Shore, Viola Brothers
1 *Beauty-mask murder* (1930)
Beauty-mask mystery
2 *Murder on the glass floor* (1932)

Colin Knowles series
East, Roger
see **Superintendent Simmonds series**

Colin Ladbroke series
Campbell, Alice
1 *Death framed in silver* (1937)
2 *Door closed softly* (1939)
3 *They hunted a fox* (1940)

Colin O'Leary series
Scoggins, Charles Elbert
1 *House of dawn* (1935)
2 *Lost road* (1941)

Colin Panton series
Purser, Philip
1 *Peregrination twenty two* (1962)
2 *Twentymen* (1967)
3 *Holy Father's navy* (1971)

Colin Patten trilogy
Callow, Philip
1 *Going to the moon* (1968)
2 *Bliss body* (1969)
3 *Flesh of the morning* (1969)

Colin, Prill and Oliver series
Cheetham, Ann
see **Black harvest series**

Colin series
Benson, Edward Frederic
1 *Colin* (1923)
2 *Colin II* (1925)

Colin series
Wood, Clement
see **Inspector Colin series**

Colin Stryker series
Crawford, William
1 *Stryker* (1973)
2 *Cop-kill* (1974)
3 *Drug run* (1974)
4 *Deadly alliance* (1975)

Colin Thane and Phil Moss series
Knox, Bill
see **Inspector Colin Thane and Phil Moss series**

Coll series
Lewis, Roy Harley
see **Matthew coll series**

Collected travels series
Hone, Joseph
1 *Dancing waiters* (1975)
2 *Gone tomorrow* (1981)
3 *Duck soup in the Black Sea* (1988)

College sports series
Chadwick, Lester
1 *Rival pitchers* (1910)
2 *Quarterback's pluck* (1910)
3 *Batting to win* (1911)
4 *Winning touchdown* (1911)
5 *For the honor of Randall* (1912)
6 *Eight-oared victors* (1913)

Collier series
Dalton, Moray
see **Inspector Hugh Collier series**

Collin series
Heller, Frank
see **Mister Collin series**

Collins and Adams series
Masters, M
see **Hawkeye Collins and Amy Adams series**

Collins and McKechnie series
Hitchens, Bert
1 *F.O.B. murder* (1955)
2 *Man who followed women* (1959)

Collins and Tony series
Elwell, Felicia Rosemary
see **Mister Collins and Tony series**

Collins series
Hart, Carolyn Gimpel
see **Henrietta O'Dwyer Collins series**
Laurie-Long, Ernest
see **Lizzie Collins series**
Palmer, Bernard
see **Pat Collins series**
Ross, Marilyn
see **Barnabas Collins series**
Thompson, Victoria
see **Kid Collins series**
Wood, James
see **Jumbo Collins series**

Colly, Lady Jennifer and Sandro series
Drummond, Ivor
see **Lady Jennifer, Sandro and Colly series**

Colombine series
This sequence has two authors
Chenneviere, Sabine
1 *Colombine in the country* (1984)
Fert, Valerie
2 *Colombine on holiday* (1984)
Illustrated by Sabine Chenneviere
3 *Colombine and the birthday party* (1984)

Colonel Alastair Granby series
Beeding, Francis
1 *Six proud walkers* (1928)
2 *Five flamboys* (1929)
3 *Pretty sinister* (1929)
4 *Four armourers* (1930)
5 *League of discontent* (1930)
6 *Take it crooked* (1932)
7 *Two undertakers* (1933)
8 *One sane man* (1934)
9 *Eight crooked trenches* (1936)
Coffin for one
10 *Nine waxed faces* (1936)
11 *Hell let loose* (1937)
12 *Black arrows* (1938)
13 *Ten holy terrors* (1939)
14 *Not a bad show* (1940)
Secret weapon
15 *Eleven were brave* (1940)
16 *Twelve disguises* (1942)
17 *There are thirteen* (1946)

Colonel Allen Cheyney series
Cosgrave, Patrick
1 *Cheyney's law* (1977)
2 *Three colonels* (1979)
3 *Adventure of state* (1984)

Colonel Anthony Ruthven Gethryn series
Macdonald, Philip
1 *Rasp* (1924)
2 *White crow* (1928)
3 *Link* (1930)
4 *Noose* (1930)
5 *Choice* (1931)
Polferry riddle
Polferry mystery
6 *Persons unknown* (1931)
Maze
7 *Wraith* (1931)
8 *Crime conductor* (1931)
9 *Rope to spare* (1932)
10 *Nursemaid who disappeared* (1938)
Warrant for X
11 *List of Adrian Messenger* (1959)
Also one story featuring Gethryn in *Fingers of fear*, 1953, also published as *Something to hide*

Colonel Blood series
Peacock, Max
1 *Colonel Blood* (1946)
2 *Men of wrath* (1950)

Colonel Brain series
Cecil, Henry
1 *No bail for the judge* (1952)
2 *Natural causes* (1953)
3 *According to the evidence* (1954)
4 *Independent witness* (1963)

Colonel Bramble series
Maurois, Andre
1 *Silence of Colonel Bramble* (1918)
Original edition entitled *Les silences du colonel Bramble*; revised edition 1943
2 *General Bramble* (1920)
Original edition entitled *Le General Bramble*; rewritten as *Les discours du docteur O'Grady*, 1922

Colonel Carter series
Smith, Francis Hopkinson
1 *Colonel Carter of Cartersville* (1891)
2 *Colonel Carter's Christmas* (1903)

Colonel Charles Russell series
Haggard, William
1 *Slow burner* (1958)
2 *Venetian blind* (1959)
3 *Arena* (1961)
4 *Unquiet sleep* (1962)
5 *High wire* (1963)
6 *Antagonists* (1964)
7 *Powder barrel* (1965)
8 *Hard sell* (1965)
9 *Power house* (1966)
10 *Conspirators* (1967)
11 *Cool day for killing* (1968)
12 *Doubtful disciple* (1969)
13 *Hardliners* (1970)
14 *Bitter harvest* (1971)
Too many enemies
15 *Old masters* (1973)
Notch on the knife
16 *Scorpion's tail* (1975)
17 *Yesterday's enemy* (1976)
18 *Poison people* (1978)
19 *Visa to limbo* (1978)
20 *Median line* (1979)
21 *Money men* (1981)
22 *Mischief-makers* (1982)
23 *Need to know* (1984)
24 *Meritocrats* (1985)
25 *Expatriates* (1989)
26 *Vendettists* (1990)

Colonel Duncan Grant series
Seton, Graham
1 *W plan* (1929)
2 *Colonel Grant's tomorrow* (1931)
3 *Scar 77* (1936)
4 *K code plan* (1938)
5 *According to plan* (1938)
6 *V plan* (1941)
7 *Red colonel* (1947)

Colonel Gantian series
Dawe, Carlton
see **Leathermouth series**

Colonel Gore series
Brock, Lynn
1 *Deductions of Colonel Gore* (1924)
Barrington mystery
2 *Colonel Gore's second case* (1925)
3 *Colonel Gore's third case* (1927)
Kink
4 *Slip-carriage mystery* (1928)
5 *Mendip mystery* (1929)
Murder in the inn
6 *Q.E.D.* (1930)
Murder on the bridge
7 *Stoat* (1940)

Colonel Hugh North series
Mason, Francis Van Wyck
1 *Seeds of murder* (1930)
2 *Vesper service murders* (1931)
3 *Fort Terror murders* (1931)
4 *Yellow arrow murders* (1932)
5 *Branded spy murders* (1932)
6 *Shanghai Bund murders* (1933)
China Sea murders
The second title is a revised edition
7 *Sula Sea murders* (1933)
8 *Budapest Parade murders* (1935)
9 *Washington legation murders* (1935)
10 *Seven seas murders* (1936)
Four novelettes entitled *Shanghai sanctuary, The repeater, Port of intrigue, The munitions ship murders*
11 *Hong Kong air base murders* (1937)
12 *Cairo garter murders* (1938)
13 *Singapore exile murders* (1939)
14 *Bucharest ballerina murders* (1940)
15 *Rio Casino intrigue* (1941)
16 *Saigon singer* (1946)
17 *Dardanelles derelict* (1949)
18 *Himalayan assignment* (1952)
19 *Two tickets for Tangier* (1955)
20 *Gracious lily affair* (1957)
21 *Secret mission to Bangkok* (1960)
22 *Multi-million dollar murders* (1960)
Original edition entitled *The Castle Island case*, 1937 did not include Colonel North
23 *Trouble in Burma* (1962)
24 *Zanzibar intrigue* (1963)
25 *Maracaibo mission* (1965)
26 *Deadly orbit mission* (1968)

Colonel James Charlesworth series
Sandys, James
see **James Charlesworth series**

Colonel John Hardin series
Teed, Jack Hamilton
see **Gunships series**

Colonel John Primrose series
Ford, Leslie
1 *Strangled witness* (1934)
2 *Ill met by moonlight* (1937)
3 *Simple way of poison* (1937)
4 *Reno rendezvous* (1939)
Mister Cromwell is dead
5 *False to any man* (1939)
Snow-White murder
6 *Old lover's ghost* (1940)
7 *Murder of a fifth columnist* (1941)
Capital crime
8 *Murder in the O.P.M.* (1942)
Priority murder
9 *Siren in the night* (1943)
10 *All for the love of a lady* (1944)

Colonel John Primrose series

Crack of dawn
11 *Philadelphia murder story* (1945)
12 *Honolulu story* (1946)
Honolulu murder story
Honolulu murders
13 *Woman in black* (1947)
14 *Devil's stronghold* (1948)
15 *Washington whispers murder* (1953)
Lying jade

Colonel John Weatherford series
Grand, Gordon
1 *Silver horn, and other sporting tales* (1932)
2 *Colonel Weatherford and his friends* (1933)
3 *Old man, and other Colonel Weatherford stories* (1934)
4 *Southborough fox, and other Colonel Weatherford stories* (1939)

Colonel Matthew Tobin series
Caillou, Alan
1 *Dead Sea submarine* (1971)
2 *Terror in Rio* (1971)
3 *Congo war-cry* (1971)
4 *Afghan onslaught* (1971)
5 *Swamp war* (1973)
6 *Death charge* (1973)
7 *Garonsky missile* (1973)

Colonel Max Masterson series
Hawton, Hector
1 *Tower of darkness* (1950)
2 *Blue-eyed Buddha* (1951)
3 *Black emperor* (1952)
4 *Lost valley* (1953)

Colonel Miltiades Vaiden trilogy
Stribling, Thomas Sigismund
1 *Forge* (1931)
2 *Store* (1932)
3 *Unfinished cathedral* (1934)

Colonel Mostyn series
Hebden, Mark
1 *Mask of violence* (1970)
2 *Pride of dolphins* (1974)
3 *League of 89* (1977)

Colonel Munroe Tallant series
York, Andrew
1 *Tallant for trouble* (1977)
2 *Tallant for disaster* (1978)

Colonel Nur Bey series
Rathbone, Julian
1 *Diamonds bid* (1967)
2 *Hand out* (1968)
3 *Trip trap* (1972)
4 *Kill cure* (1975)

Colonel Ormiston series
Walsh, James Morgan
1 *Spies are abroad* (1933)
2 *Secret service girl* (1933)
3 *King's messenger* (1933)
4 *Spies in pursuit* (1934)
5 *Man from Whitehall* (1934)
6 *Spies never return* (1935)
7 *Tiger of the night* (1935)
8 *Silent man* (1935)
9 *Half acre* (1936)
10 *Spies' vendetta* (1936)
11 *Spies in Spain* (1937)

Colonel Paternoster series
Inchbald, Ralph
1 *Colonel Paternoster* (1951)
2 *Five inns* (1952)
3 *September story* (1955)

Colonel Peregrine White series
Spicer, Bart
1 *Day of the dead* (1955)
2 *Burned man* (1966)

Colonel Peter Blair series
Anderson, John Richard Lane
see **Major Peter Blair series**

Colonel Pyat series
Moorcock, Michael
1 *Byzantium endures* (1981)
Revised edition 1981
2 *Laughter of Carthage* (1984)

Colonel Race series
Christie, Agatha
1 *Man in the brown suit* (1924)
2 *Cards on the table* (1936)
3 *Death on the Nile* (1937)
4 *Sparkling cyanide* (1945)
Remembered death

Colonel Richard Barne series
Cousins, Edmund George
1 *Death by marriage* (1959)
2 *Death by treble chance* (1959)
3 *Fear of Mr Taltry* (1960)
4 *Murder in the top drawer* (1964)
5 *Body beyond the curtain* (1966)
6 *Death in a quiet place* (1967)

Colonel Rickman trilogy
White, Jon Manchip
1 *Nightclimber* (1968)
2 *Game of Troy* (1971)
3 *Garden game* (1973)
One volume edition entitled Fevers and chills, 1983

Colonel Robert Lee Ashley series
Steele, Chester K
1 *Diamond cross mystery* (1918)
2 *Golf course mystery* (1919)

Colonel Sellers series
Twain, Mark
1 *Gilded cage* (1873)
Adventures of Colonel Sellers
2 *American claimant* (1892)
Companion volume: *Colonel Sellers, a play*, 1874

Colonel Steel Callaghan series
Chesney, Michael
1 *Callaghan of Intelligence* (1938)
2 *Steel Callaghan* (1939)
3 *Callaghan meets his fate* (1939)

Colonel Verney series
Wheatley, Dennis
see **Molly Fountain series**

Colonel William T Bucko trilogy
Westcott, C T
see **Eagleheart trilogy**

Colonel Winston Creevy series
Lord, Jeremy
1 *Bannerman case* (1935)
2 *Sixty-nine diamonds* (1940)

Colonel Xavier Flynn series
Braine, John
1 *Pious agent* (1975)
2 *Finger of fire* (1977)

Colonel's children series
Supervielle, Jules
1 *Colonel's children* (1926)
Original edition entitled Le voleur d'enfants
2 *Survivor* (1928)
Original edition entitled Le survivant

Colonial Americans series
Fisher, Leonard Everett
1 *Glassmakers* (1964)
2 *Silvesrsmiths* (1964)
3 *Papermakers* (1965)
4 *Printers* (1965)
5 *Wigmakers* (1965)
6 *Hatters* (1965)
7 *Weavers* (1966)
8 *Cabinet makers* (1966)
9 *Tanners* (1966)
10 *Shoemakers* (1967)
11 *Schoolmasters* (1967)
12 *Peddlers* (1968)
13 *Doctors* (1968)
14 *Potters* (1969)
15 *Limners* (1969)
16 *Architects* (1970)
17 *Shipbuilders* (1971)
18 *Homemakers* (1973)
19 *Blacksmiths* (1976)

Colonial series
Stratemeyer, Edward L
1 *With Washington in the West* (1901)
Alternative title: A soldier boy's battles in the wilderness
2 *Marching on Niagara* (1902)
Alternative title: The soldier boys of the old frontier
3 *At the fall of Montreal* (1903)
Alternative title: A soldier boy's final victory
4 *On the trail of Pontiac* (1904)
Alternative title: The pioneer boys of the Ohio
5 *Fort in the wilderness* (1905)
Alternative title: The soldier boys of the Indian trails
6 *Trail and trading post* (1906)
Alternative title: The young hunters of the Ohio

Colonial series
Tomlinson, Everett Titsworth
1 *With flintlock and fife* (1903)
2 *Fort in the forest* (1904)
3 *Soldier of the wilderness* (1905)
4 *Young rangers* (1906)

Colonial trilogy
Ellis, Edward Sylvester
1 *Uncrowning a king* (1896)
American king
A story of King Phillip's war
2 *Cromwell of Virginia* (1904)
A story of Bacon's rebellion
3 *Last emperor of the old dominion* (1904)

Colonial trilogy
Irish, Lola
1 *And the wild birds sing* (1983)
2 *Place of the swan* (1986)
3 *House of O'Shea* (1990)

Colonised Planet Five series
Lessing, Doris
see **Canopus in Argus archives series**

Colonization of America series
Porter, Donald Clayton
see **White Indian series**

Colonizing series
Bergaust, Erik
1 *Colonizing the planets* (1975)
2 *Colonizing the sea* (1976)
3 *Colonizing space* (1978)

Colorado gold trilogy
Wells, Marian
see **Amy Randolph trilogy**

Colorado Jim series
Goodchild, George
1 *Colorado Jim* (1920)
Alternative title: The taming of Angela
2 *Jim goes north* (1926)

Colorado trilogy
Garlock, Dorothy
1 *Restless wind* (1986)
2 *Wayward wind* (1987)
3 *Wind of promise* (1987)

Colors, letters, numbers and words to talk about series
Lionni, Leon
1 *Colors to talk about* (1985)
2 *Letters to talk about* (1985)
3 *Numbers to talk about* (1985)
4 *Words to talk about* (1985)

Colossal Corcoran series
Morgan, W Ingram
1 *Colossal Corcoran in Central Africa* (1952)
2 *Colossal Corcoran in Mystery Valley* (1952)
3 *Colossal Corcoran on Smoke Island* (1952)
4 *Colossal Corcoran on Skull Atoll* (1952)
5 *Colossal Corcoran in the Caribbean Sea* (1952)
6 *Colossal Corcoran in the Hindu Kush mountains* (1952)

Colossus trilogy
Jones, Dennis Feltham
1 *Colossus* (1966)
2 *Fall of Colossus* (1974)
3 *Colossus and the crab* (1977)

Colour of Canada series
Brooks, Bill
Photographs with text
1 *Colour of Ontario* (1977)
2 *Colour of Alberta* (1978)
3 *Colour of British Columbia* (1980)

Colour out of space and time series
This sequence has two authors
Lovecraft, Howard Phillips
1 *Dunwich horror, and others* (1963)
Colour out of space, and others
Shea, Michael
2 *Colour out of time* (1984)
Color out of time

Colour story book series
Blyton, Enid
1 *Blue story book* (1945)
2 *Red story book* (1946)
3 *Green story book* (1947)
4 *Yellow story book* (1950)

ColSec trilogy
Hill, Douglas
1 *Exiles of ColSec* (1984)
2 *Caves of Klydor* (1984)
3 *ColSec rebellion* (1985)

Colson series
White, Alan
see **Commando series**

Colt Revolver series
Miller, Jim
1 *Gone to Texas* (1983)
2 *Comanche trail* (1984)
Co-author: James Collins
3 *War clouds* (1985)
4 *Riding shotgun* (1985)
5 *Orphans preferred* (1985)
6 *Campaigning* (1985)

Colt series
Abbot, Anthony
see **Thatcher Colt series**
Allen, Chester
see **Justice Colt series**
Hill, Morgan
see **Dan Colt series**

Colton series
Stagg, Clinton Holland
see **Thornley Colton series**

Coltrane series
Hagan, Patricia
1 *Love and war* (1978)
2 *Love and glory* (1982)

3 *Love's wine* (1985)
4 *Love and fury* (1986)
5 *Love and splendor* (1987)
6 *Love and dreams* (1988)
7 *Love and honor* (1989)
8 *Love and triumph* (1991)

Columbia High School series
Forbes, Graham B
House pseudonym
1 *Boys of Columbia High* (1912)
Alternative title: The all around rivals of the School; reissued as *Frank Allen's schooldays*, 1926
2 *Boys of Columbia High on the diamond* (1912)
Alternative title: Winning out by pluck; reissued as *Frank Allen, pitcher*, 1926
3 *Boys of Columbia High on the river* (1912)
Alternative title: The boat race plot that failed; reissued as *Frank Allen, head of the crew*, 1926
4 *Boys of Columbia High on the gridiron* (1912)
Alternative title: The struggle for the silver cup; reissued as *Frank Allen, captain of the team*, 1926
5 *Boys of Columbia High on the ice* (1912)
Alternative title: Out for the hockey championship; reissued as *Frank Allen playing to win*, 1926
6 *Boys of Columbia High in track athletics* (1913)
Alternative title: A long run that won; reissued as *Frank Allen and his rivals*, 1926
7 *Boys of Columbia High in winter sports* (1915)
Alternative titles: Stirring doings on skates and iceboats; reissued as *Frank Allen in winter sports*, 1926
8 *Boys of Columbia High in camp* (1920)
Alternative title: The rivalry of the Old School League; reissued as *Frank Allen in camp*, 1926
Reissued as part of the **Frank Allen series**, 1926-1927

Columbo series
This sequence has six authors; based on a television series
Lawrence, Alfred
1 *Columbo* (1972)
2 *Dean's death* (1975)
Clement, Henry
3 *Any old port* (1975)
4 *By dawn's early light* (1975)
Hays, Lee
5 *Murder by the book* (1976)
6 *Deadly state of mind* (1976)
Magee, Bill
7 *Columbo and the Samurai sword* (1980)
Harrington, William
8 *Grassy knoll* (1993)
9 *Helter skelter murders* (1994)

Colwin Grey series
Rees, Arthur John
1 *Threshold of fear* (1925)
2 *Simon of Hangletree* (1926)
Unquenchable flame
3 *Greymarsh* (1927)
4 *Investigations of Colwin Grey* (1932)
Short stories

Comaday and Cohen series
Cunningham, E V
see **John Comaday and Larry Cohen series**

Comanche John series
Cushman, Dan
1 *Montana, here I be!* (1950)
2 *Ripper from Rawhide* (1952)

Comanche trilogy
Anderson, Catherine
1 *Comanche moon* (1991)
2 *Comanche heart* (1992)
3 *Indigo blue* (1992)

Comanche trilogy
Jones, Douglas Clyde
1 *Season of yellow leaf* (1983)
2 *Barefoot brigade* (1982)
3 *Gone the dreams and dancing* (1984)

Combat Command series
This sequence has ten authors
Kramer, Dana
1 *Cut by emerald* (1987)
The world of Piers Anthony's **Bio of a space tyrant series**
Acres, Mark
2 *Shines the name* (1987)
The world of Robert A Heinlein's **Starship troopers series**
Denning, Troy
3 *Omega rebellion* (1987)
The world of Keith Laumer's **Star colony series**
Johnson, Todd
4 *Slammers down!* (1988)
The world of David Drake's **Hammer's Slammers series**
Keith, Andrew
5 *Legion of war* (1988)
The world of Jack Williamson's **The legion of space series**
Randall, Neil
6 *Black road war* (1988)
The world of Roger Zelazny's **Amber series**
Acres, Mark
7 *Lord of lances* (1988)
The world of Jerry E Pournelle's **Janissaries series**
Denning, Troy
8 *Dorsai's command* (1989)
Co-authors: Gordon Rupert Dickson and Cory Glaberson
Asprin, Robert Lynn
9 *Cold cash warrior* (1989)
The world of Robert Asprin's *Cold cash war*, 1977

Combat heroes series
Dever, Joe
1 *White warlord* (1986)
2 *Black baron* (1986)
3 *Emerald enchanter* (1986)
4 *Scarlet sorcerer* (1986)

Come aboard series
Barkan, Joanne
1 *Boxcar* (1992)
2 *Caboose* (1992)
3 *Locomotive* (1992)
4 *Passenger car* (1992)

Comfort Servosse series
Tourgee, Albion Winegar
Set in the American South following the Civil War
1 *Fool's errand* (1879)
2 *Invisible empire* (1883)

Coming Attractions trilogy
Strasser, Todd
1 *Rock 'n' roll nights* (1982)
2 *Turn it up!* (1984)
3 *Wildlife* (1987)

Cominsec series
Hayes, Ralph Eugene
see **Agent for Cominsec series**

Commander Adam Dalgleish series
James, Phyllis Dorothy
see **Commander Adam Dalgleish series**

Commander Adam Dalgleish series
James, Phyllis Dorothy
1 *Cover her face* (1962)
2 *Mind to murder* (1963)
3 *Unnatural causes* (1967)
4 *Shroud for a nightingale* (1971)
5 *Unsuitable job for a woman* (1972)
6 *Black tower* (1975)
7 *Death of an expert witness* (1977)
Numbers 4, 6, 7 also published in one volume entitled *Dalgliesh trilogy*, 1991
8 *Taste for death* (1986)
9 *Devices and desires* (1989)
10 *Children of men* (1992)

Commander Allan Dice series
Hill, Peter
1 *Fanatics* (1977)
2 *Washerman* (1979)

Commander Amanda Nightingale series
Revelli, George
see **Amanda Nightingale series**

Commander Craig series
Somers, Bart
1 *Beyond the black enigma* (1965)
2 *Abandon galaxy!* (1967)

Commander Esmonde Shaw series
McCutchan, Philip
1 *Gibraltar Road* (1960)
2 *Redcap* (1961)
3 *Bluebolt one* (1962)
4 *Man from Moscow* (1963)
5 *Warmaster* (1963)
6 *Moscow coach* (1964)
7 *Dead line* (1966)
8 *Skyprobe* (1966)
9 *Screaming dead balloons* (1968)
10 *Bright red business men* (1969)
11 *All-purpose bodies* (1969)
12 *Hartinger's mouse* (1970)
13 *This Drakotny* (1971)
14 *Sunstrike* (1979)
15 *Corpse* (1980)
16 *Werewolf* (1982)
17 *Rollerball* (1984)
18 *Greenfly* (1987)
19 *Boy who liked monsters* (1989)
20 *Spatchcock plan* (1990)

Commander Geoffrey Peace series
Jenkins, Geoffrey
1 *Twist of sand* (1959)
2 *Hunter-killer* (1966)

Commander George Gideon series
This sequence has two authors
Marric, J J
1 *Gideon's day* (1955)
Gideon of Scotland Yard
2 *Gideon's week* (1956)
Seven days to death
Play adaptation entitled *Gideon's fear*, 1967
3 *Gideon's night* (1957)
4 *Gideon's month* (1958)
5 *Gideon's staff* (1959)
6 *Gideon's risk* (1960)
7 *Gideon's fire* (1961)
8 *Gideon's march* (1962)
9 *Gideon's ride* (1963)
10 *Gideon's vote* (1964)
11 *Gideon's lot* (1964)
12 *Gideon's badge* (1966)
13 *Gideon's wrath* (1967)
14 *Gideon's river* (1968)
15 *Gideon's power* (1969)
16 *Gideon's sport* (1970)
17 *Gideon's art* (1971)
18 *Gideon's men* (1972)
19 *Gideon's press* (1973)
20 *Gideon's fog* (1975)
21 *Gideon's drive* (1976)
Butler, William Vivian
22 *Gideon's force* (1978)
23 *Gideon's law* (1981)
24 *Gideon's way* (1983)
25 *Gideon's raid* (1986)

Commander John Benedict Holland series
Macdonnell, James Edmond
see **Dutchy Holland series**

Commander Lawless series
Bennett, Rolf
1 *Adventures of Lieut. Lawless, R.N.* (1915)
2 *Commander Lawless, V.C.* (1916)

Commander Lord Charles Oakshott series
Challoner, Robert
1 *Run out the guns* (1984)
2 *Give fire!* (1986)
3 *Into battle!* (1987)

Commander Moreton Shade series
Boyle, Denis
1 *Strange corpse on Murder Mile* (1960)
2 *Death at Devil-Fish Point* (1961)

Commander Peter Bentley series
Macdonnell, James Edmond
see **Captain Peter Bentley series**

Commander Philip Hazard series
Stuart, Vivian
American editions published under the name V A Stuart
1 *Valiant sailors* (1964)
2 *Black Sea frigate* (1971)
Hazard's command
3 *Hazard of Huntress* (1972)
4 *Hazard in Circassia* (1973)
5 *Victory at Sebastopol* (1973)
6 *Massacre at Cawnpore* (1974)
7 *Hazard to the rescue* (1974)
8 *Guns to the Far East* (1975)
Shannon's brigade

Commander Pug Henry series
Wouk, Herman
1 *Winds of war* (1971)
2 *War and remembrance* (1978)

Commander Roger Waterlow series
Mackenzie, Compton
1 *Extremes meet* (1928)
2 *Three couriers* (1929)

Commander Sainsbury series
Macdonnell, James Edmond
This sequence includes those works which have so far been identified as including the series character; however since there is much overlapping of characters in this author's numerous novels it is likely that this character will be found in other works
1 *Stand-by to ram!* (1957)
2 *Lesson* (1961)
3 *Sainsbury, V.C.* (1962)
4 *U-boat* (1962)
5 *Course to intercept* (1964)
6 *Flashpoint* (1965)
7 *Execute!* (1969)
8 *Council of captains* (1974)
9 *Death of a destroyer* (1977)

Commander Toad series
Yolen, Jane
1 *Commander Toad and the planet of the grapes* (1982)
2 *Commander Toad and the big black hole* (1983)
3 *Commander Toad and the intergalactic spy* (1986)
4 *Commander Toad and the space pirates* (1987)

Commander Wally Phipps-Mangot series
Hackforth-Jones, Gilbert
1 *Fish out of water* (1954)
2 *Death of an admiral* (1956)

Commander William Mallett series
Macdonnell, James Edmond
This sequence includes those works which have so far been identified as including the series character; however since there is much overlapping of characters in this author's numerous novels it is likely that this character will be found in other works
1 *First lieutenant* (1962)
2 *Big Bill the bastard* (1976)
3 *Confirmed in command* (1976)

Commander Wraithlea series
Taylor, Philip Neville Walker
1 *Murder in the flagship* (1936)
2 *Murder in the game reserve* (1937)
3 *Murder in the Suez Canal* (1937)
4 *Murder in the Tajmahal* (1938)
5 *Admiral's a spy* (1941)
6 *Spylight* (1943)
7 *Spyrocket* (1944)

Commandments series
Sanders, Lawrence
see **Ten commandments series**

Commando series
White, Alan
1 *Long day's dying* (1965)
Death finds the day
2 *Long night's walk* (1968)
3 *Long drop* (1969)
4 *Long watch* (1971)
5 *Long midnight* (1972)
6 *Long fuse* (1973)
7 *Long summer* (1974)
8 *Long silence* (1976)
9 *Long hand of death* (1977)

Commissaire Orestes Bignon series
Didelot, Francis
1 *Many ways of death* (1955)
Original edition entitled *6 heures d'anguisse*
2 *Tenth leper* (1956)
Original edition entitled *Feu sur le mage*
3 *Warrant for arrest* (1961)
Original edition entitled *Mandat d'arret*
4 *Death on the Champs Elysees* (1963)
Original edition entitled *Bignon et la verite*

Commissaire Patras series
Grierson, Francis Durham
1 *Lady of despair* (1930)
2 *Heart in the box* (1936)
3 *Coward's Club* (1937)
4 *Man from Madagascar* (1937)

Commissaire Payran series
Nisot, Elizabeth
1 *Twelve to dine* (1935)
2 *Hazardous holiday* (1936)
3 *False witness* (1938)
4 *Unnatural deeds* (1939)

Commissario Achille Peroni series
Holme, Timothy
see **Inspector Achille Peroni series**

Commissario Guido Brunetti series
Leon, Donna
1 *Death at La Fenice* (1992)
2 *Death in a strange country* (1993)
3 *Dressed for death* (1994)
Anonymous Venetian

Commissario Trotti series
Williams, Timothy
1 *Converging parallels* (1982)
Red Citroen
2 *Puppeteer* (1985)
Metal green Mercedes
3 *Persona non grata* (1987)

Commissioner Denzil Grigson series
Broome, Adam
1 *Crowner's quest* (1930)
2 *Island of death* (1932)
3 *Queen's Hall murder* (1933)
4 *Crocodile club* (1935)
5 *Snakes and ladders* (1938)
6 *Flame of the forest* (1943)
7 *Dream murder* (1946)

Commissioner Robin McKay series
Morris, John
1 *Fever grass* (1969)
2 *Candywine development* (1970)
3 *Checkerboard caper* (1975)

Commissioner Sanders series
This sequence has two authors; short stories
Wallace, Edgar
1 *Sanders of the river* (1911)
2 *People of the river* (1912)
3 *Bosambo of the river* (1914)
4 *Bones* (1915)
5 *Bones of the river* (1923)
6 *Sanders* (1926)
Mister Commissioner Sanders
7 *Again Sanders* (1928)
Gerard, Francis
8 *Return of Sanders of the river* (1938)
9 *Law of the river* (1939)
10 *Justice of Sanders* (1951)
Wallace, Edgar
11 *Keepers of the king's peace* (1917)
12 *Lieutenant Bones* (1918)
13 *Sandi, the kingmaker* (1922)
Also stories featuring Sanders in *Bones in London*, 1921; companion volume: *River of stars*, 1913

Commonplace series
Stocks, Mary
Autobiography
1 *My commonplace book* (1970)
2 *Still more commonplace* (1973)

Commonwealth series
Foster, Alan Dean
see **Flinx of the Commonwealth series**

Commuter's wife series
Wright, Mabel Osgood
1 *Garden of a commuter's wife* (1901)
2 *People of the whirlpool* (1903)
From the experience book of a commuter's wife
3 *Woman errant* (1904)
Some chapters from the wonder book of Barbara, the commuter's wife
4 *Princess Flower Hat* (1910)
A comedy from the perplexity book of Barbara, the commuter's wife

Companions of Doctor Who series
This sequence has three authors
Attwood, Tony
1 *Turlough and the earthlink dilemma* (1985)
Marter, Ian
2 *Harry Sullivan's war* (1986)
Dudley, Terence
3 *K9 and company* (1987)

Compass adventures series
North, Joe
see **Adventures around the compass series**

Compleat enchanter series
De Camp, Lyon Sprague
see **Harold Shea series**

Compton series
Jacberns, Raymond
see **Becky Compton series**

Compulsive traveller series
Laurence, Murray
1 *High times in the middle of nowhere* (1986)
Revised edition 1991
2 *Accidentally in transit* (1991)

Computer detectives series
Harris, Lavinia
1 *Great rip-off* (1984)
2 *Soaps in the afternoon* (1985)
3 *Touch of madness* (1985)
4 *Cover up!* (1986)

Comrades from Canada series
Wynne, May
1 *Cousin from Canada* (1918)
2 *Comrades from Canada* (1919)

Comstock series
Bishop, Gibs
see **Captain Comstock series**

Comtat series
Ratel, Simonne
see **Isabelle Comtat series**

Con and Ginty series
Hallard, Peter
Set on the Great Barrier Reef
1 *Coral Reef castaway* (1958)
2 *Barrier Reef bandits* (1960)
3 *Guardian of the Reef* (1961)

Con Randollph series
Smith, Charles Merrill
see **Reverend Randollph series**

Conacher series
Knight, Adam
see **Steve Conacher series**

Conan Flagg series
Wren, M K
1 *Curiosity didn't kill the cat* (1973)
2 *Multitude of sins* (1975)
3 *Oh, bury me not* (1976)
4 *Nothing's certain but death* (1978)
5 *Season of death* (1981)
6 *Wake up, darlin' Corey* (1984)

Conan series
This sequence has thirteen authors
Howard, Robert Ervin
1 *Conan the conqueror* (1950)
Hyborean age
Hour of the dragon
2 *Sword of Conan* (1952)
3 *Coming of Conan* (1953)
4 *King Conan* (1954)
5 *Conan the barbarian* (1954)
6 *Tales of Conan* (1955)
Flame knife
Co-author: Lyon Sprague de Camp
De Camp, Lyon Sprague
7 *Return of Conan* (1957)
Co-author: Bjorn Nyberg
Howard, Robert Ervin
8 *Conan* (1967)
Co-authors: Lyon Sprague de Camp and Lin Carter
9 *Conan of Cimmeria* (1969)
Co-authors: Lyon Sprague de Camp and Lin Carter
10 *Conan the freebooter* (1968)
Co-author: Lyon Sprague de Camp; numbers 8-10 also published in one volume entitled *The Conan chronicles*, 1989
11 *Conan the wanderer* (1968)
Co-authors: Lyon Sprague de Camp and Lin Carter
12 *Conan the adventurer* (1966)
Co-author: Lyon Sprague de Camp
Carter, Lin
13 *Conan the buccaneer* (1971)
Co-author: Lyon Sprague de Camp; numbers 11-13 also published in one volume entitled *The Conan chronicles 2*, 1990
Howard, Robert Ervin
14 *Conan the warrior* (1967)
15 *Conan the usurper* (1967)
Co-author: Lyon Sprague de Camp
16 *Conan the avenger* (1968)
Co-authors: Lyon Sprague de Camp and Bjorn Nyberg
De Camp, Lyon Sprague
17 *Conan of Aquilonia* (1971)
Co-authors: Lin Carter and Robert Ervin Howard
Carter, Lin
18 *Conan of the isles* (1968)
Co-author: Lyon Sprague de Camp
Howard, Robert Ervin
19 *People of the black circle* (1974)
20 *Tower of the elephant* (1975)
21 *Red nails* (1975)
22 *Witch shall be born* (1975)
23 *Rogues in the house* (1976)
24 *Devil in iron* (1976)
25 *Hour of the dragon* (1977)
Carter, Lin
26 *Conan the swordsman* (1978)
Co-authors: Lyon Sprague de Camp and Bjorn Nyberg
Howard, Robert Ervin
27 *Queen of the black coast* (1978)
Wagner, Karl Edward
28 *Road of kings* (1979)
Carter, Lin
29 *Conan the liberator* (1979)
Co-author: Lyon Sprague de Camp
Offutt, Andrew Jefferson
30 *Sword of Skelos* (1979)
Anderson, Poul
31 *Conan the rebel* (1980)
De Camp, Lyon Sprague
32 *Conan and the spider god* (1980)
33 *Treasure of Tranicos* (1980)
Co-author: Robert Ervin Howard
Offutt, Andrew Jefferson
34 *Conan and the sorcerer* (1978)
Conan the mercenary
Jordan, Robert
35 *Conan the defender* (1982)
Carter, Lin
36 *Conan the barbarian* (1982)
Co-author: Lyon Sprague de Camp; based on a screenplay
Jordan, Robert
37 *Conan the invincible* (1982)
38 *Conan the unconquered* (1983)
39 *Conan the triumphant* (1983)
40 *Conan the magnificent* (1984)
41 *Conan the destroyer* (1984)
42 *Conan the victorious* (1984)
Ward, James Michael
43 *Conan the undaunted* (1984)
Moore, Roger Elwood
44 *Conan and the prophecy* (1984)
45 *Conan the outlaw* (1984)
Roberts, John Maddox
46 *Conan the valorous* (1985)
Perry, Steve
47 *Conan the fearless* (1986)
Carpenter, Leonard
48 *Conan the raider* (1986)
49 *Conan the renegade* (1986)
Howard, Robert Ervin
50 *Pool of the black one* (1986)
Roberts, John Maddox
51 *Conan the champion* (1987)
Perry, Steve
52 *Conan the defiant* (1987)
Roberts, John Maddox
53 *Conan the marauder* (1988)
Green, Roland James
54 *Conan the valiant* (1988)
Carpenter, Leonard
55 *Conan the warlord* (1988)
Roberts, John Maddox
56 *Conan the bold* (1989)
Carpenter, Leonard
57 *Conan the hero* (1989)
Perry, Steve
58 *Conan the indomitable* (1989)
Carpenter, Leonard
59 *Conan the great* (1990)

Perry, Steve
60 *Conan the formidable* (1990)
61 *Conan the free lance* (1990)
Green, Roland James
62 *Conan the guardian* (1991)
Carpenter, Leonard
63 *Conan the outcast* (1991)
Roberts, John Maddox
64 *Conan the rogue* (1991)
Green, Roland James
65 *Conan the relentless* (1992)
Carpenter, Leonard
66 *Conan of the Red Brotherhood* (1993)
Green, Roland James
67 *Conan and the gods of the mountain* (1993)
Roberts, John Maddox
68 *Conan and the treasure of Python* (1993)
Carpenter, Leonard
69 *Scourge of the bloody coast* (1994)
Companion volumes: *The Conan reader*, edited by Lyon Sprague de Camp, 1968, *The Conan swordbook*, edited by Leonard Sprague de Camp and George Scithers, 1969, *The Conan grimoire*, edited by Lyon Sprague de Camp and George Scithers, 1972, *The leopard of Poitain*, by Raul Garcia Capella, 1985; parody: *The black sorcerer of the Black Castle*, by Andrew Jefferson Offutt, 1976

Conception series
Smythe, R John
1 *Conception* (1969)
2 *Coming of Morikand* (1970)

Concordat series
Swycaffer, Jefferson Putnam
1 *Become the hunted* (1985)
2 *Not in our stars* (1984)
3 *Universal prey* (1985)
4 *Praesidium of Archive* (1986)

Concordat trilogy
Swycaffer, Jefferson Putnam
see **Tales of the Concordat trilogy**

Concordia series
Fleetwood, Frances
1 *Concordia* (1971)
2 *Concordia errant* (1973)

Condesa Guilia and Count de Quesnoy series
Wheatley, Dennis
see **Count de Quesnoy and Condesa Guilia series**

Condit family series
Baldwin, Faith
1 *American family* (1935)
Conflict
2 *Puritan strain* (1935)

Condo Kids series
Delton, Judy
Illustrated by Alan Tiegreen
1 *Hello Huckleberry Heights* (1990)
2 *Summer showdown* (1990)
3 *Artificial grandma* (1990)
4 *Huckleberry hash* (1990)
5 *Scary scary Huckleberry* (1990)
6 *Merry merry Huckleberry* (1990)

Condom poems series
Dacey, Philip
1 *Condom poems* (1979)
2 *Condom poems II* (1989)

Condon and Tom Kane series
Jordan, David
see **Tom Kane and Condon series**

Condor series
Grady, James
1 *Six days of the Condor* (1974)
Three days of the Condor
2 *Shadow of the Condor* (1975)

Condor series
Wright, Wade
see **Bart Condor series**

Confederate series
Randolph, Forrest A
1 *Confederate* (1984)
2 *Ride beyond glory* (1984)
3 *Sabre charge* (1985)
4 *Blood cavalry* (1985)

Confessions and impressions series
Mannin, Ethel
Autobiography
1 *Confessions and impressions* (1930)
2 *All experience* (1932)
Reminiscences of travel
3 *Privileged spectator* (1939)
4 *Brief voices* (1959)
A writer's story
5 *Stories from my life* (1973)

Confessions series
This sequence has two authors - Christopher Wood using the pseudonyms Rosie Dixon and Timothy Lea, and Laurence James using the pseudonym Jonathan May
Lea, Timothy
1 *Confessions of a window cleaner* (1971)
2 *Confessions of a driving instructor* (1972)
3 *Confessions of a hitch hiker* (1972)
4 *Confessions from a holiday camp* (1972)
5 *Confessions from a hotel* (1973)
6 *Confessions of a film extra* (1973)
7 *Confessions from the clink* (1973)
8 *Confessions of a private soldier* (1974)
May, Jonathan
9 *Confessions of a shop assistant* (1974)
Lea, Timothy
10 *Confessions of a travelling salesman* (1974)
Dixon, Rosie
11 *Confessions of a night nurse* (1974)
Lea, Timothy
12 *Confessions from the pop scene* (1974)
Confessions of a pop performer
Dixon, Rosie
13 *Confessions of a gym mistress* (1974)
Lea, Timothy
14 *Confessions from a health farm* (1974)
15 *Confessions from the shop floor* (1975)
16 *Confessions of a long distance lorry driver* (1975)
Dixon, Rosie
17 *Confessions of a lady courier* (1975)
Lea, Timothy
18 *Confessions of a plumber's mate* (1975)
Dixon, Rosie
19 *Confessions from an escort agency* (1975)
May, Jonathan
20 *Confessions of a travel courier* (1975)
21 *Confessions from the beat* (1975)
22 *Confessions of a games master* (1975)
Dixon, Rosie
23 *Confessions from a package tour* (1975)
Lea, Timothy
24 *Confessions of a private dick* (1975)
25 *Confessions from a luxury liner* (1976)
Dixon, Rosie
26 *Confessions of a babysitter* (1976)
Lea, Timothy
27 *Confessions from a nudist colony* (1976)
Dixon, Rosie
28 *Confessions of a personal secretary* (1976)
Lea, Timothy
29 *Confessions of a milkman* (1976)
May, Jonathan
30 *Confessions from a strip club* (1976)
31 *Confessions of a housewife* (1976)
32 *Confessions from a sex clinic* (1976)
Lea, Timothy
33 *Confessions of an ice cream man* (1977)
May, Jonathan
34 *Confessions of a stuntman* (1977)
35 *Confessions of a gasman* (1977)
36 *Confessions of an astronaut* (1978)
37 *Confessions from a stud farm* (1978)
Lea, Timothy
38 *Confessions from a haunted house* (1979)
May, Jonathan
39 *Confessions from the Olympics* (1980)

Confessions series
Macvicar, Angus
1 *Salt in my porridge* (1971)
Confessions of a minister's son
2 *Heather in my ears* (1974)
More confessions of a minister's son
3 *Rocks in my Scotch* (1977)
Still more confessions of a minister's son
4 *Silver in my sporran* (1979)
Confessions of a writing man
5 *Bees in my bonnet* (1982)
6 *Golf in my gallowses* (1983)
Confessions of a fairway fanatic
7 *Gremlin in the garden* (1985)
Confessions of a harassed horticulturalist
8 *Capers in my kirk* (1987)
Confessions of a would-be Christian

Conflict trilogy
Kemp, Peter Mant Macintyre
1 *Mine were of trouble* (1958)
Experiences during the Spanish Civil War
2 *No colours or crest* (1958)
The Special Operations Executive in the Second World War
3 *Alms for oblivion* (1961)
Experiences of war in Southeast Asia

Confrontation trilogy
Caute, David
1 *Demonstration* (1970)
A play
2 *Occupation* (1971)
A novel
3 *Illusion* (1971)
An essay on politics, theatre and the novel
One volume edition entitled *The confrontation*, 1971

Congo series
Hunter, Richard Wilkes
1 *Congo diamonds* (1965)
2 *Congo mercenary* (1965)
3 *Congo mercenary major* (1965)

Congo series
This sequence has two authors
Slade, Ruth
1 *King Leopold's Congo* (1962)
Aspects of the development of race relations in the Congo Independent State
Anstey, Roger
2 *King Leopold's legacy* (1966)
The Congo under Belgian rule, 1908-1960

Congressman Ben Safford series
Dominic, R B
1 *Murder sunny side up* (1968)
2 *Murder in high place* (1969)
3 *There is no justice* (1971)
Murder out of court
4 *Epitaph for a lobbyist* (1974)
5 *Murder out of commission* (1976)
6 *Attending physician* (1980)
7 *Unexpected developments* (1984)
Flaw in the system

Conisby series
Farnol, Jeffery
see **Martin Conisby series**

Conjurers series
Gurney, David
1 *Conjurers* (1972)
Demonists
2 *Devil in the atlas* (1976)
A study of modern satanism

Conjuror's years series
Stuart, Donald Robert
1 *Prince of my country* (1974)
2 *Walk, trot, canter and die* (1975)
3 *Drought foal* (1977)
4 *Wedgetail view* (1978)
5 *Crank back on roller* (1979)
6 *I think I'll live* (1981)

Conley and Long series
Fox, James M
see **Jerry Long and Chuck Conley series**

Conmara trilogy
Macmanus, Francis
see **Donnacha Mac Conmara trilogy**

Connection series
Moore, Robin
1 *Fifth estate* (1973)
2 *London switch* (1974)
London connection
Co-author: Al Dempsey
3 *Italian connection* (1975)
Co-author: Al Dempsey
4 *French connection II* (1975)
Co-author: Milt Machlin; based on a moving picture
5 *Set-up* (1975)
New York connection
Co-author: Milt Machlin
6 *Terminal connection* (1976)
7 *Black Sea caper* (1978)
Black Sea connection
Co-author: Hugh McDonald
8 *Gold connection* (1979)
Co-author: Julian Askin
Companion volumes: *The French connection, the world's most crucial narcotics investigation*, by Robin Moore, 1969, *Code name Richard*, by Richard Berdin, 1974

Connell series
Foxx, Jack
see **Dan Connell series**
Weatherhead, John
see **Professor David Connell series**

Connie Blair series
Allen, Betsy
1 *Riddle in red* (1948)
2 *Puzzle in purple* (1948)
3 *Secret of Black Cat Gulch* (1948)
4 *Clue in blue* (1948)
5 *Green Island mystery* (1949)
6 *Ghost wore white* (1950)
7 *Yellow warning* (1951)
8 *Gray menace* (1953)
9 *Brown satchel mystery* (1954)
10 *Peril in pink* (1955)
11 *Silver secret* (1956)
12 *Mystery of the ruby queens* (1958)

Connie Morgan series
Hendryx, James Beardsley
1 *Connie Morgan in Alaska* (1916)
2 *Connie Morgan with the Mounted* (1918)
Connie Morgan with the Northwest Mounted
3 *Connie Morgan in the lumber camps* (1919)
4 *Connie Morgan in the fur country* (1921)

5 *Connie Morgan in the cattle country* (1923)
6 *Connie Morgan with the forest rangers* (1925)
7 *Connie Morgan hits the trail* (1929)
Connie Morgan in the barren lands
8 *Connie Morgan, prospector* (1929)
9 *Connie Morgan in the Arctic* (1936)

Connington series
Irwin, Grace
see **Andrew Connington series**

Connor family series
Stolz, Mary
1 *Ready or not* (1953)
2 *Day and the way we met* (1956)

Connor series
Dolph, Jack
see **Doc Connor series**

Connors and Lingemann series
Kelly, Susan
see **Liz Connors and Jack Lingemann series**

Conquest of Mexico series
Madariaga, Salvador de
1 *Heart of jade* (1942)
Original edition entitled *El corazon de piedra verde*
2 *War in the blood* (1956)
Original edition entitled *Guerra en la sangre*

Conquest of series
Bankoff, George Alexis
1 *Conquest of disease* (1946)
The story of penicillin
2 *Conquest of pain* (1946)
Story of anaesthesia
3 *Conquest of tuberculosis* (1946)
4 *Conquest of brain mysteries* (1947)
The story and secrets of the human mind
5 *Story of cancer* (1947)
6 *Story of the unknown* (1947)
The story of the endocrine glands

Conquest of the United States series
Hancock, Harrie Irving
1 *Invasion of the United States* (1916)
Alternative title: Uncle Sam's boys at the capture of Boston
2 *In the battle for New York* (1916)
Alternative title: Uncle Sam's boys in the desperate struggle for the metropolis
3 *At the defense of Pittsburgh* (1916)
Alternative title: The struggle to save America's fighting steel supply
4 *Making the stand for Old Glory* (1916)
Alternative title: Uncle Sam's boys in the last frantic drive

Conquest series
Cabell, James Branch
1 *King was in his counting house* (1938)
2 *Hamlet had an uncle* (1940)
3 *First gentleman of America* (1942)
First American gentleman

Conquest series
Gray, Berkeley
see **Norman Conquest series**

Conrad chronicles series
Warren, Joanna
1 *Belle Meade* (1978)
2 *Dreamers* (1980)
3 *Destined* (1980)

Conrad Detective Agency series
King, Frank
see **Dormouse series**

Conrad Franks series
Wallace, John
1 *Sedan murder mystery* (1938)
2 *It's here* (1940)

Conrad Stargard series
Frankowski, Leo
see **Adventures of Conrad Stargard series**

Conrad's world series
Sherry, Norman
1 *Conrad's Eastern world* (1966)
2 *Conrad's Western world* (1971)
Companion volume: *Conrad and his world*, 1972

Conroy and Van Treece series
Tuttle, Wilbur Coleman
see **Henry Harrison Conroy and Judge Van Treece series**

Conroy series
Ames, Francis Herbert
see **Callahan series**
Asbury, Herbert
see **Inspector Thomas Conroy series**

Consett trilogy
Goolden, Barbara
1 *Goodbye to yesterday* (1976)
2 *In the melting pot* (1976)
3 *Unborn tomorrow* (1977)

Conshelf Ten series
Hughes, Monica
1 *Crisis on Conshelf Ten* (1975)
2 *Earthdark* (1977)

Considine family series
O'Brien, Kate
1 *Without my cloak* (1931)
2 *Ante-room* (1934)

Considine series
Wilmot, Robert Patrick
see **Steve Considine series**

Conspiracy series
Hayes, Ralph Eugene
see **Agent for Cominsec series**

Conspirators and police under Napoleon series
Thierry, Gilbert Augustin
1 *Plot of the Placards at Rennes, 1802* (1903)
Original edition entitled *Le complot des libelles*
2 *[Mysterieuse affaire Donnadieu, 1802]*(1909)
No English edition

Constable Brenda Phipps and Chief Inspector Walsh series
Hunt, Richard
see **Chief Inspector Walsh and Constable Brenda Phipps series**

Constable Craig series
Lees, Dan
1 *Our man in Morton Episcopi* (1979)
2 *Mayhem in Morton Episcopi* (1980)

Constable James Morton and Sergeant Joseph Bragg series
Harrison, Ray
see **Sergeant Joseph Bragg and Constable James Morton series**

Constable Kerr and Inspector Robert Fusil series
Alding, Peter
see **C.I.D. Room series**

Constable Meatyard series
Horler, Sydney
1 *Here is an S.O.S.* (1939)
2 *Man who loved spiders* (1948)

Constable series
Rhea, Nicholas
see **Aidensfield series**

Constable Thackeray and Sergeant Cribb series
Lovesey, Peter
see **Sergeant Cribb and Constable Thackeray series**

Constance Chatterley series
Lawrence, David Herbert
see **Lady Chatterley series**

Constance Daniels series
Stanley, George Edward
see **Doctor Constance Daniels series**

Constance Ethel Morrison-Burke series
Porter, Joyce
see **Honourable Constance Ethel Morrison-Burke series**

Constance Howard series
De Selincourt, Hugh
1 *Daughter of the morning* (1912)
2 *Realms of day* (1915)
3 *Evening light* (1931)
The life and letters of Susan Rivarol as related by Professor Owen Mansfield

Constance Leidl and Charlie Miklejohn series
Wilhelm, Kate
see **Charlie Miklejohn and Constance Leidl series**

Constantine series
Thynne, Molly
see **Doctor Constantine series**

Constanza and Flavia series
Bedford, Sybille
1 *Favourite of the gods* (1963)
Favorite of the gods
2 *Compass error* (1968)

Constructs series
Kostlanetz, Richard
Poems
1 *Constructs* (1975)
2 *Constructs two* (1978)
3 *Constructs three* (1991)
4 *Constructs four* (1991)
5 *Constructs five* (1991)
6 *Constructs six* (1991)

Consuelo series
Sand, George
1 *Consuelo* (1842)
Original edition entitled *Consuelo*
2 *Countess of Rudolstadt* (1843)
Original edition entitled *La comtesse de Rudolstadt*

Contact and commune series
Smith, Lester Neil
1 *Contact and commune* (1990)
2 *Converse and conflict* (1990)

Container series
Sanders, J R
1 *Container is ready* (1987)
2 *Intergalactic express* (1988)

Contemporary history series
France, Anatole
1 *Wicker-work woman* (1897)
Original edition entitled *Le mannequin d'osier*
2 *Elm-tree on the wall* (1897)
Original edition entitled *L'orme du mail*
3 *Amethyst ring* (1899)
Original edition entitled *L'anneau d'amethyste*
4 *Monsieur Bergeret in Paris* (1900)
Original edition entitled *Monsieur Bergeret a Paris*

Contemporary novels of Spain series
Perez Galdos, Benito
1 *[Fontana de ora]* (1870)
No English edition
2 *Shadow* (1870)
Original edition entitled *La sombra*; this title has three parts entitled *Celin, Tropiquillos, Theros*
3 *[Audaz]* (1871)
No English edition
4 *Dona Prefecta* (1876)
Lady Perfecta
Original edition entitled *Dona Perfecta*
5 *Gloria* (1877)
Original edition entitled *Gloria*
6 *Marianela* (1878)
Original edition entitled *Marianela*
7 *Leon Roch* (1879)
Original edition entitled *La familia de Leon Roch*
8 *Disinherited lady* (1881)
Original edition entitled *La desheredada*
9 *Our friend Manso* (1882)
Original edition entitled *El amigo Manso*
10 *[Doctor Centeno]* (1883)
No English edition
11 *Torment* (1884)
Original edition entitled *Tormento*
12 *Spendthrifts* (1884)
Original edition entitled *La de bringas*
13 *[Prohibido]* (1885)
No English edition
14 *Fortunata and Jacinta* (1887)
Original edition entitled *Fortunata y Jacinta*
15 *Miau* (1888)
Original edition entitled *Miau*
19 *[Incognita]* (1889)
No English edition
20 *[Torquemada en la hoguera]* (1889)
No English edition
21 *[Realidad]* (1890)
No English edition
22 *[Angel Guerra]* (1891)
No English edition
23 *Tristana* (1892)
Original edition entitled *Tristana*
24 *[Loca de la casa]* (1892)
No English edition
25 *[Torquemada en la Cruz]* (1892)
No English edition
26 *[Torquemada en el purgatorio]* (1894)
No English edition
27 *[Torquemado y San Pedro]* (1895)
No English edition
28 *[Nazarin]* (1895)
No English edition
29 *[Halma]* (1895)
No English edition
30 *Miseracordia* (1897)
Compassion
Original edition entitled *Miseracordia*
31 *[Abuelo]* (1897)
No English edition
32 *[Casandra]* (1905)
No English edition
33 *[Caballero encantado]* (1909)
No English edition
34 *[Razon de la sinrazon]* (1915)
No English edition

Contender trilogy
Lipsyte, Roger
1 *Contender* (1967)
2 *Brave* (1991)
3 *Chief* (1993)

Continent and Edinburgh series
Cammell, Charles Richard
Reminiscences
1 *Castles in the air* (1953)
2 *Heart of Scotland* (1956)

Continental Op series
Hammett, Dashiell
1 *Red harvest* (1929)
2 *Dain curse* (1929)
3 *One hundred and six thousand dollars blood money* (1943)
Blood money
Big knock-over
4 *Continental Op* (1945)
Short stories
5 *Return of the Continental Op* (1945)
Short stories
Short stories featuring the Continental Op in *Hammett homicides*, 1946, *Dead yellow women*, 1947, *Nightmare town*, 1948, *The creeping Siamese*, 1950, *Woman in the dark*, 1951, *A man named Thin*, 1962

Contrasts series
Laird, Elizabeth
1 *Wet and dry* (1987)
2 *Hot and cold* (1987)
3 *Light and dark* (1987)
4 *Heavy and light* (1987)

Conversations series
Berrigan, Daniel
1 *Geography of faith* (1971)
Conversations from the underground with Robert Coles
2 *Absurd convictions, modest hopes* (1972)
Conversations after prison with Lee Lockwood
Companion volume: *America is hard to find, letters from prison and writings from the underground*, 1972

Conversations series
Stravinsky, Igor
1 *Conversations with Igor Stravinsky* (1959)
2 *Memories and developments* (1960)
3 *Expositions and developments* (1962)
4 *Dialogues and a diary* (1963)
5 *Themes and episodes* (1970)

Convict trilogy
Hall, Rodney
see **Yandilli trilogy**

Convoy series
McCutchan, Philip
1 *Convoy commodore* (1986)
2 *Convoy north* (1987)
3 *Convoy south* (1988)
4 *Convoy east* (1989)
5 *Convoy of fear* (1990)
6 *Convoy homeward* (1992)

Conway series
Jennings, D K
see **Doctor Ralph Conway series**
Leather, Edwin
see **Rupert Conway series**
Morrison, Margaret
see **Elizabeth Conway series**
Stone, Simon
see **Sir Brian Dinsmore Conway series**

Conways series
Morgan, Geoffrey
1 *Cameras on the Conways* (1954)
2 *Conways ahoy* (1955)

Conyers and Dean series
Solmssen, Arthur Robert George
1 *Rittenhouse Square* (1968)
2 *Alexander's feast* (1971)
3 *Comfort letter* (1975)
4 *Takeover time* (1986)

Cook series
Tomlinson, Paul Greene
see **Tom Cook series**

Cool and Lam series
Fair, A A
see **Bertha Cool and Donald Lam series**

Cool series
Lancer, Jack
see **Christopher Cool series**

Coole series
Stephens, Michael
see **J Leland Coole series**

Cooley series
Thompson, Gene
see **Dade Cooley series**

Coombe series
Burnett, Frances Hodgson
see **House of Coombe series**

Coop series
Wangerin, Walter
1 *Book of the dun cow* (1978)
2 *Book of sorrows* (1985)

Cooper and Clancy series
Beck, Kathrine Kristine
see **Iris Cooper and Jack Clancy series**

Cooper family series
Giles, Janice Holt
see **Fowler family series**

Cooper series
Herman, Charlotte
see **Millie Cooper series**

Cooperman series
Engel, Howard
see **Benny Cooperman series**

Coopersmith series
Griffin, Robert J
1 *Coopersmith* (1968)
2 *Coopersmith's dolls* (1969)
3 *King Coopersmith* (1971)
4 *Genghis Coopersmith* (1972)

Coorain series
Conway, Jill Ker
Autobiography
1 *Road from Coorain* (1989)
Recollections of a harsh and beautiful journey into adulthood
2 *True north* (1994)

Cope series
Charlesworth, Maria Louisa
see **Mrs Dorothy Cope series**

Coping series
Skoglund, Elizabeth
1 *Coping* (1979)
2 *More than coping* (1987)

Coping series
Webb, Margot
1 *Coping with street gangs* (1990)
2 *Coping with overprotective parents* (1990)
3 *Coping with parents who are activists* (1992)

Copp series
Pendleton, Don
see **Joe Copp series**

Copper kingdom series
Gower, Iris
1 *Copper kingdom* (1983)
2 *Proud Mary* (1984)
3 *Spinner's wharf* (1985)
4 *Morgan's woman* (1986)
5 *Fiddler's Ferry* (1987)
6 *Black gold* (1988)

Coppering series
Meek, Victor
Reminiscences of a policeman
1 *Cops and robbers* (1962)
2 *Coppering lark* (1963)

Coppernob series
Bourne, Lawrence R
1 *Coppernob Buckland* (1925)
2 *Coppernob, Second Mate* (1927)
3 *Captain Coppernob* (1929)
Numbers 1-3 also published in one volume entitled *Coppernob omnibus*, 1933
4 *Coppernob, shipowner* (1931)

Coppinger tetralogy
Arnold, Bruce
1 *Singer at the wedding* (1978)
2 *Song of the nightingale* (1980)
3 *Muted swan* (1981)
4 *Running to paradise* (1983)

Coppins Bridge trilogy
Daish, Elizabeth
1 *Shop on Coppins Bridge* (1985)
2 *Family on Coppins Bridge* (1986)
3 *Ebb-tide at Coppins Bridge* (1988)
One volume edition entitled *Coppins Bridge saga*, 1992

Copplestone series
Avery, Gillian
see **Mister Copplestone series**

Copycats series
Bayley, Nicola
1 *Parrot cat* (1984)
2 *Elephant cat* (1984)
3 *Polar bear cat* (1984)
4 *Crab cat* (1984)
5 *Spider cat* (1984)
Companion volume: *Patchwork cat*, by Nicola Bayley and William Mayne, 1981

Coquenil series
Moffett, Cleveland
see **Paul Coquenil series**

Coquette series
McCormick, Renee
Translated from the French
1 *Little coquette* (1944)
The story of a French girlhood
2 *Rustle of petticoats* (1946)

Coral Island series
Ballantyne, Robert Michael
1 *Coral Island* (1858)
2 *Gorilla hunters* (1861)

Coramonde series
Daley, Brian
1 *Doomfarers of Coramonde* (1977)
2 *Starfollowers of Coramonde* (1979)

Corbett series
Edgar, Josephine
see **Viola Corbett series**
Hermes, Patricia
see **Kevin Corbett series**
Rockwell, Carey
see **Tom Corbett series**

Corbin series
Crane, Robert
see **Ben Corbin series**

Corby series
Cooper, Lettice
see **Chief Inspector Corby series**

Corcoran series
Morgan, W Ingram
see **Colossal Corcoran series**

Cord Diamondback series
Bishop, Pike
1 *Diamondback* (1983)
2 *Judgment at Poisoned Well* (1983)
3 *Snake Eyes* (1984)
4 *Dead man's hand* (1984)
5 *River race verdict* (1984)
6 *Shroud of vengeance* (1985)
7 *Old bone betrayed* (1985)
8 *Teton gamble* (1985)
9 *Poison Bay* (1985)

Cord series
Macleod, Robert
see **Talos Cord series**
Robbins, Harold
see **Jonas Cord series**
Rountree, Owen
see **Jim Cord series**

Cordelia Gray series
James, Phyllis Dorothy
1 *Unsuitable job for a woman* (1972)
2 *Skull beneath the skin* ()

Cordelia trilogy
Maclean, Catherine Macdonald
see **Tharrus trilogy**

Cordell series
Taylor, Janelle
1 *Follow the wind* (1990)
2 *Chase the wind* (1994)

Cordina series
Roberts, Nora
1 *Affaire royale* (1986)
2 *Command performance* (1987)
3 *Playboy prince* (1987)

Cordrey series
O'Hanlon, James
see **Jason Cordrey series**

Corduroy series
McCue, Lisa
1 *Corduroy's day* (1985)
2 *Corduroy's party* (1985)
3 *Corduroy's toys* (1985)
4 *Corduroy goes to the doctor* (1987)
5 *Corduroy on the go* (1987)
6 *Corduroy's busy street* (1987)

Corey Lane series
Zollinger, Norman
1 *Corey Lane* (1981)
2 *Rage in Chupadera* (1991)

Corey series
Borg, Jack
see **Thady Corey series**
Williamson, Tony
see **Lee Corey series**

Corfu series
Durrell, Gerald
Autobiography of a zoologist
1 *My family and other animals* (1956)
2 *Birds, beasts and relatives* (1969)
3 *Fillets of plaice* (1971)
4 *Garden of the gods* (1978)

Cork series
Hastings, Macdonald
see **Montague Cork series**
Swinson, Arthur
see **Sergeant Cork series**

Corlay series
Cowper, Richard
see **Bird of kinship series**

Corleone family series
Puzo, Mario
see **Godfather series**

Cormac Mac Art series
This sequence has three authors
Offutt, Andrew Jefferson
1 *Mists of doom* (1977)
2 *Tower of death* (1982)

Cormac Mac Art series

Co-author: Keith Taylor
3 *When death birds fly* (1980)
Co-author: Keith Taylor
Howard, Robert Ervin
4 *Tigers of the sea* (1974)
Offutt, Andrew Jefferson
5 *Sword of the Gael* (1975)
6 *Undying wizard* (1976)
7 *Sign of the moonbow* (1977)
Howard, Robert Ervin
8 *Hawks of Outremer* (1979)

Cormack and Woodward series
Baddock, James
1 *Radar job* (1986)

Cormorant series
Haley, George Elvey
1 *Cormorant ahoy!* (1952)
2 *Cormorant's commandos* (1954)
3 *Cormorant sails again* (1955)
4 *Cormorant on patrol* (1958)

Cormorant series
Knight, Arthur Lee
1 *Rajah of Monkey Island* (1892)
2 *Cruise of the Cormorant* (1893)
Alternative title: Treasure seekers of the Orient

Cormorant series
Verrill, Alpheus Hyatt
1 *Cruise of the Cormorant* (1915)
2 *In Morgan's wake* (1915)

Cornelius Clift series
Heath, Eric
1 *Death takes a dive* (1938)
2 *Murder in the museum* (1939)

Cornelius Plum series
King, Kay
1 *Life and times of Cornelius Plum* (1972)
2 *Six days in the life of Cornelius Plum* (1974)

Cornelius Rabbit series
Flynn, Mary
1 *Cornelius Rabbit of Tang* (1944)
2 *Cornelius on holidays* (1945)
3 *Cornelius in charge* (1946)

Cornelius series
Moorcock, Michael
see **Catherine Corbelius series; Jerry Cornelius series**

Cornell series
Michel, Milton Scott
see **Doctor Alexander Cornell series**
Moorcock, Michael
see **Jerry Cornell series**

Corner House Girls series
Hill, Grace Brooks
1 *Corner House Girls* (1915)
How they moved to Milton, what they found and what they did
2 *Corner House Girls at school* (1915)
How they entered, whom they met and whatthey did
3 *Corner House Girls under canvas* (1915)
How they reached Pleasant Cove and what happened afterward
4 *Corner House Girls in a play* (1916)
How they rehearsed, how they acted and what the play brought in
5 *Corner House Girls' odd find* (1916)
Where they made it and what the strange discovery led to
6 *Corner House Girls on a tour* (1917)
Where they went, what they saw and what they found
7 *Corner House Girls growing up* (1918)
What happened first, what came next and how it ended
8 *Corner House Girls snowbound* (1919)
How they went away, what they discovered and how it ended
9 *Corner House Girls on a houseboat* (1920)
How they sailed away, what happened on the voyage and what they discovered
10 *Corner House Girls among the gypsies* (1921)
How they met, what happened and how it ended
11 *Corner House Girls on Palm Island* (1922)
Looking for adventure, how they found it and what happened
12 *Corner House Girls solve a mystery* (1923)
What it was, where it was and who found it
13 *Corner House Girls facing the world* (1926)
Why they had to, how they did it and what came of it

Corner-stone series
Oldenbourg, Zoe
1 *World is not enough* (1946)
Original edition entitled *Argile et cendres*
2 *Corner-stone* (1953)
Original edition entitled *La pierre angulaire*

Cornford series
Kennedy, Milward
see **Inspector Cornford series**

Cornish and Drew series
Hanson, Virginia
see **Adam Drew and Katherine Cornish series**

Cornish island series
Atkins, Evelyn Edith
Memoirs
1 *We bought an island* (1976)
2 *Tales from our Cornish island* (1986)

Cornish series
Baker, Denys Val
1 *Sea's in the kitchen* (1962)
2 *Door is always open* (1963)
3 *We'll go round the world tomorrow* (1965)
4 *To sea with Sanu* (1967)
Numbers 1-4 also published in one volume entitled *Adventures before fifty*, 1969
5 *Life up the creek* (1971)
6 *Petrified mariner* (1972)
7 *Old mill by the stream* (1973)
8 *Spring at Land's End* (1974)
9 *Sunset over the Scillies* (1975)
10 *View from the valley* (1976)
11 *Long way to Land's End* (1977)
12 *Wind blows from the west* (1977)
13 *All this and Cornwall too* (1978)
14 *Family for all seasons* (1979)
15 *As the stream flows by* (1980)
16 *Upstream at the mill* (1981)
17 *Family at sea* (1981)
18 *Summer at the mill* (1982)
19 *Waterwheel turns* (1982)
20 *Down a Cornish lane* (1983)
21 *Family circles* (1983)
22 *Mill in the valley* (1984)
23 *When Cornish skies are smiling* (1984)
24 *My Cornish world* (1985)
25 *Cornish prelude* (1985)

Cornish series
McCulloch, Derek
1 *Cornish adventure* (1937)
2 *Cornish mystery* (1950)

Cornish series
Mackenzie, Andrew
see **Nicholas Cornish series**

Quiller-Couch, Arthur
see **Troy Town series**

Cornish trilogy
Davies, Robertson
see **Francis Cornish trilogy**

Cornishman series
Rowse, Alfred Leslie
Autobiography of a historian
1 *Cornish childhood* (1944)
2 *Cornishman at Oxford* (1965)
3 *Cornishman abroad* (1976)

Coronation Street series
Kershaw, H V
Based on a television series
1 *Early days* (1977)
2 *Trouble at the Rovers* (1977)
3 *Elsie Tanner fights back* (1977)
Companion volume: *The street where I live*, 1981

Coronet series
Bingham, Charlotte
Autobiography
1 *Coronet among the weeds* (1963)
2 *Coronet among the grass* (1972)

Corporal Allan Cameron series
Connor, Ralph
see **North-West Mounted Police series**

Corporal Cameron Downey series
Hendryx, James Beardsley
1 *Downey of the Mounted* (1926)
2 *Blood on the Yukon trail* (1930)
In the days of gold
Devil's gold
3 *Corporal Downey takes the trail* (1931)
4 *Yukon kid* (1934)
5 *Gambler's chance* (1941)
6 *It happened on Halfaday Creek* (1963)
Short stories
7 *Murder in the outlands* (1949)
8 *Badmen on Halfaday Creek* (1950)
Short stories

Corporal Downey series
Hendryx, James Beardsley
1 *Golden girl* (1920)
2 *Snowdrift* (1922)
A story of the land of the strong cold
3 *Challenge of the north* (1922)
4 *At the foot of the rainbow* (1924)
5 *Oak and iron* (1925)
Of these be the breed of the North
6 *Downey of the Mounted* (1926)
7 *Blood on the Yukon Trail* (1930)
8 *Blood of the North* (1930)
9 *Corporal Downey takes the trail* (1931)
10 *Yukon Kid* (1934)
11 *Edge of beyond* (1939)
12 *Gambler's chance* (1941)
13 *Sourdough gold* (1952)

Corps series
Griffin, W E B
1 *Semper fi* (1986)
2 *Call to arms* (1987)
3 *Counterattack* (1990)
4 *Battleground* (1991)
5 *Line of fire* (1992)
6 *Close combat* (1992)

Corpse series
Masefield, John
see **Autobiography of a corpse series**

Corpse series
Murray, Max
1 *Voice of the corpse* (1947)
2 *King and the corpse* (1948)
3 *Queen and the corpse* (1949)
No duty on a corpse
4 *Neat little corpse* (1950)
5 *Right honourable corpse* (1951)
6 *Good luck to the corpse* (1951)
7 *Doctor and the corpse* (1952)
8 *Sunshine corpse* (1954)
9 *Royal bed for a corpse* (1955)
10 *Breakfast with a corpse* (1956)
Corpse for breakfast
11 *Wait for a corpse* (1957)

Correspondence College series
Potter, Stephen
see **Lifemanship Correspondence College series**

Corridon series
Marshall, Raymond
see **Brick-Top Corridon series**

Corrigan and McLean series
Corrigan, Mark
see **Mark Corrigan and McLean series**

Corrigan series
Maddock, Reginald Bertram
1 *Corrigan and the white cobra* (1956)
2 *Corrigan and the yellow peril* (1957)
3 *Corrigan and the black riders* (1957)
4 *Corrigan and the tom of Opi* (1957)
5 *Corrigan and the golden pagoda* (1958)
6 *Corrigan and the dream makers* (1959)
7 *Corrigan and the blue crater* (1960)
8 *Corrigan and the green tiger* (1961)
9 *Corrigan and the red lions* (1962)
10 *Corrigan and the little people* (1963)

Corrigan series
Morton, William
see **Biff Corrigan series**
Queen, Ellery
see **Tim Corrigan series**

Corson series
Mulford, Clarence Edward
see **J C series**

Corti series
Inchbald, Peter
see **Inspector Franco Corti series**

Corum and the silver hand trilogy
Moorcock, Michael
see **Chronicle of Prince Corum and the silver hand trilogy**

Corum series
Moorcock, Michael
1 *Knight of the Swords* (1971)
2 *Queen of the Swords* (1971)
3 *King of the Swords* (1971)
One volume editions entitled *The swords trilogy*, 1986 and *The swords of Corum omnibus*, 1986
4 *Bull and the spear* (1973)
5 *Oak and the ram* (1973)
6 *Sword and the stallion* (1973)
Numbers 4-6 also published in one volume entitled *The Swords trilogy*, 1977

Corunna series
Morgan, Sally
see **My place series**

Corvette series
Monsarrat, Nicholas
1 *H M Corvette* (1942)
2 *East Coast corvette* (1943)
3 *Corvette command* (1944)
One volume edition entitled *Three corvettes*, 1945

Cory Barnett series
Miller, Ben E
1 *Death deal* (1969)
2 *Set-up* (1969)

Cory series
Siodmak, Curt
see **Doctor Patrick Cory series**

Coscuin chronicles series
Lafferty, Raphael Aloysius
1 *Flame is green* (1971)
2 *Devil is dead* (1971)
3 *Archipelago* (1979)
4 *Half a sky* (1984)

Cosmo series
McGirt, Dan
see **Jason Cosmo series**

Cosmopoli series
Blayre, Christopher
see **University of Cosmopoli series**

Cossacks series
Kessler, Leo
see **Black Cossacks series**

Costa Verde series
Yerby, Frank
1 *Old gods laugh* (1964)
2 *Hail the conquering hero* (1977)

Costaine and McCall series
Macneil, Neil
see **Tony Costaine and Bert McCall series**

Costello series
Hall, Richard
see **Patrick Costello series**

Cotswold Cider Company series
Stewart-Hargreaves, Eustace Hamilton Ian
Memoirs
1 *Hargreaves story* (1953)
2 *Man on the run* (1957)

Cotswold Ommony series
Mundy, Talbot
1 *Om* (1924)
Alternative title: The secret of Abhor Valley
2 *Jungle jest* (1931)

Cotswold vet series
Knowles, Anne
1 *Single in the field* (1984)
2 *Ark on the flood* (1985)

Cotswolds series
Lee, Laurie
Essays and reminiscences
1 *Cider with Rosie* (1959)
Edge of day
A boyhood in the west of England
2 *As I walked out one midsummer morning* (1969)
3 *I can't stay long* (1975)

Cotter and Keats series
Long, Martin
see **Inspector Keats and Tom Cotter series**

Cotterell series
Trench, John
see **Martin Cotterell series**

Cottingham series
Syrett, Netta
see **Rose Cottingham series**

Cotton series
Grayson, Rupert
see **Gun Cotton series**
Taylor, Sam S
see **Neal Cotton series**

Cotton trilogy
Scarborough, Dorothy
1 *In the land of cotton* (1923)
2 *Can't get a redbird* (1929)
3 *Stretch-berry smile* (1932)

Cougar and Shaddrock series
Fieldhouse, William
see **Shaddrock and Cougar series**

Could you ever series
Darling, David J
1 *Could you ever fly to the stars?* (1990)
2 *Could you ever meet an alien?* (1990)
3 *Could you ever speak chimpanzee?* (1990)
4 *Could you ever dig a hole to China?* (1990)
5 *Could you ever build a time machine?* (1990)
6 *Could you ever live forever?* (1991)

Coulson series
Mann, Jack
see **Rex Coulson series**

Coulter series
Fletcher, Aaron
see **Bounty Hunter series**

Count Alessandro di Ganzarello, Tucker and Norrington series
Drummond, Ivor
see **Lady Jennifer, Sandro and Colly series**

Count Boris Bolescu series
Jungman, Ann
1 *Count Boris Bolescu and the black pudding* (1989)
2 *Count Boris Bolescu and the Transylvanian tango* (1991)

Count de Quesnoy and Condesa Guilia series
Wheatley, Dennis
1 *Prisoner in the mask* (1957)
2 *Vendetta in Spain* (1961)

Count Dracula series
Jungman, Ann
1 *Count Dracula and the ghost* (1989)
2 *Count Dracula and the monster* (1989)
3 *Count Dracula and the victim* (1989)
4 *Count Dracula meets his match* (1989)
Companion volume: Dracula play, 1989

Count of Monte Cristo series
This sequence has two authors
Dumas, Alexandre
1 *Count of Monte Cristo* (1845)
Original edition entitled *Le comte de Monte-Cristo*
Flagg, Edmund
2 *Edmond Dantes* (1878)
Revised edition 1884; originally published anonymously

Count Ragoczy Saint-Germain series
Yarbro, Chelsea Quinn
1 *Hotel Transylvania* (1978)
A novel of forbidden love
2 *Palace* (1979)
3 *Blood games* (1980)
4 *Path of the eclipse* (1981)
5 *Tempting fate* (1982)
6 *Saint-Germain chronicles* (1983)
Short stories and an essay on the real Count
7 *Out of the house of life* (1990)
8 *Spider glass* (1991)

Count your way series
Haskins, Jim
1 *Count your way through China* (1987)
2 *Count your way through Japan* (1987)
3 *Count your way through Russia* (1987)
4 *Count your way through the Arab world* (1987)
5 *Count your way through Mexico* (1989)
6 *Count your way through Canada* (1989)
7 *Count your way through Africa* (1989)
8 *Count your way through Korea* (1989)
9 *Count your way through Israel* (1990)
10 *Count your way through India* (1990)
11 *Count your way through Italy* (1990)
12 *Count your way through Germany* (1990)

Countdown WWIII series
Davies, W X
1 *Operation North Africa* (1984)
2 *Operation Black Sea* (1984)
3 *Operation Choke Point* (1984)
4 *Operation Persian Gulf* (1984)

Counter Force series
Erskine, George
1 *Beware the Tektrons* (1988)
2 *Find the Tektrons* (1988)
Companion volume: *The official Counter Force reference book, the background on the Counter Force characters and the world they live in*, 1986

Counter Force series
Streib, Dan
see **Steve Crown series**

Counterearth series
Lupoff, Richard Allen
1 *Circumpolar!* (1984)
2 *Countersolar!* (1987)

Counter-earth series
Norman, John
see **Tarl Cabot series**

Counterforce series
Streib, Dan
see **Steve Crown series**

Counterpol series
Boland, John
1 *Counterpol* (1963)
2 *Counterpol in Paris* (1964)

Counter-terror series
Charles, Robert
1 *Hour of the Wolf* (1974)
2 *Flight of the Raven* (1975)
3 *Scream of a Dove* (1975)
4 *Clash of hawks* (1975)
5 *Prey of the falcon* (1976)
6 *Snarl of the lynx* (1977)
7 *Venom of the cobra* (1977)
8 *Arms of the mantis* (1977)

Countess series
White, Percy
1 *King's diary* (1895)
2 *Infatuation of the Countess* (1899)

Country and city series
Noonan, Diana
1 *Leaving the snow country* (1991)
2 *Sonnet for the city* (1992)

Country beat series
Quinain, Louis
A police constable's story
1 *Country beat* (1946)
2 *Policeman on the green* (1948)

Country child series
Uttley, Alison
1 *Country child* (1931)
2 *Farm on the hill* (1941)

Country doctor series
Bagster, Hubert
Reminiscences
1 *Country practice* (1957)
2 *Doctor's weekend* (1960)

Country doctor series
Duncan, Alex
1 *To be a country doctor* (1980)
2 *God and the doctor* (1981)
3 *Diary of a country doctor* (1982)
4 *Doctor affairs all told* (1983)

Country heart series
Bates, Herbert Ernest
1 *In the heart of the country* (1942)
2 *O, more than happy countryman* (1943)
Happy countryman
One volume revised edition entitled *The country heart*, 1949

Country house trilogy
Galsworthy, John
1 *Country house* (1907)
2 *Fraternity* (1909)
3 *Patrician* (1911)

Country life series
Bell, Adrian
Stories of country life in Suffolk
1 *Corduroy* (1930)
2 *Silver Ley* (1931)
3 *Cherry tree* (1932)
4 *Apple Acre* (1942)
5 *Sunrise to sunset* (1944)

Country life trilogy
Tiltman, Marjorie Hessell
Reminiscences of country life in Sussex
1 *Cottage pie* (1940)
2 *Little place in the country* (1944)
3 *Birds began to sing* (1952)

Country living series
McMullen, Jeanine
Autobiography
1 *My small country living* (1984)
2 *Wind in the ashtree* (1988)

Country music series
Emery, Ralph
Autobiography
1 *Memories* (1991)
2 *More memories* (1993)

Country practice series
Jackson, Arthur
Reminiscences
1 *Tales from a country practice* (1986)
2 *More tales from a country practice* (1987)
3 *Further tales from a country practice* (1989)

Country practice series
Poidevin, Leslie
1 *Goodbye doctor* (1986)
2 *Come in doctor* (1990)

Country rat series
Firmin, Peter
1 *Winter diary of a country rat* (1981)
2 *Midsummer notebook of a country rat* (1983)

Country vicarage series
Brode, Anthony
Memoirs
1 *Picture a country vicarage* (1956)
2 *To bed on Thursday* (1958)

Countrygoer series
Lofthouse, Jessica
1 *Lancashire countrygoer* (1962)
Revised edition 1974
2 *Countrygoer in the Dales* (1964)
3 *Countrygoers' North* (1965)
Revised edition 1972
4 *North Wales for the countrygoer* (1970)

Count's secret series
Gaboriau, Emile
1 *Count's millions* (1870)

Count's secret series

Original edition entitled *Pascal et Marguerite*
2 *Baron Trigault's vengeance* (1870)
Original edition entitled *Lia d'Argeles*
One volume edition entitled *The count's secret*, 1881, originally *Le vie infernale*

Couples series
This sequence has two authors
Cooney, Linda A
1 *Change of hearts* (1985)
2 *Fire and ice* (1985)
3 *Alone, together* (1985)
Cooper, M E
4 *Made for each other* (1985)
5 *Moving too fast* (1985)
6 *Crazy love* (1985)
7 *Sworn enemies* (1985)
8 *Making promises* (1986)
9 *Broken hearts* (1986)
10 *Secrets* (1986)
11 *More than friends* (1986)
12 *Bad love* (1986)
13 *Changing partners* (1986)
14 *Picture perfect* (1986)
15 *Coming on strong* (1987)
16 *Sweethearts* (1987)
17 *Dance with me* (1987)
18 *Kiss and run* (1987)
19 *Show some emotion* (1987)
20 *No contest* (1987)
21 *Teacher's pet* (1987)
22 *Slow dancing* (1987)
23 *Bye bye love* (1987)
24 *Something new* (1987)
25 *Love exchange* (1987)
26 *Head over heels* (1987)
27 *Sweet and sour* (1987)
28 *Love struck* (1987)
29 *Take me back* (1987)
30 *Falling for you* (1988)
31 *Prom date* (1988)
32 *Playing dirty* (1988)
33 *Mean to me* (1988)
34 *Don't get close* (1988)
35 *Break away* (1988)
Companion volumes: *Summer heat*, 1986, *Beach party*, 1987, *Sealed with a kiss*, 1988

Courage series
Shears, Sarah
1 *Child of gentle courage* (1974)
2 *Courage in darkness* (1974)
3 *Courage to serve* (1974)
4 *Courage in war* (1976)
5 *Courage in parting* (1977)

Court family series
Carroll, Joy
1 *Proud blood* (1978)
2 *Pride's Court* (1980)

Court of memory trilogy
McConkey, James
Autobiographical novels
1 *Crossroads* (1968)
2 *Tree house confessions* (1979)
3 *Stories from my life with the other animals* (1993)
Companion volume: *Court of memory*, 1983

Courtenay series
Berrow, Norman
see **Inspector Courtenay series**

Courtney Brade series
Wolffe, Katherine
see **Captain Courtney Brade series**

Courtney family series
Smith, Wilbur Addison
This sequence follows the **Sean Courtney series**
1 *Burning shore* (1985)
2 *Power of the sword* (1986)
3 *Rage* (1987)

Courtney series
Pearson, Ann
see **Maggie Courtney series**
Smith, Wilbur Addison
see **Sean Courtney series**

Cousin Annabelle series
O'Farrell, Kathleen
see **Lattimer children series**

Cousin Kate series
This sequence has two authors
Godwin, Catherine Grace
1 *Cousin Kate* (1836)
Alternative title: Punishment of pride
Bell, Catherine Douglas
2 *Autumn at Karnford* (1847)

Cousin Lucy series
Abbott, Jacob
1 *Cousin Lucy's stories* (1832)
2 *Cousin Lucy at study* (1841)
3 *Cousin Lucy at play* (1842)
4 *Cousin Lucy among the mountains* (1842)
5 *Cousin Lucy on the sea-shore* (1842)
6 *Cousin Lucy's conversation* (1842)

Cousins quartet
Mahy, Margaret
1 *Good Fortunes Gang* (1993)
2 *Fortunate name* (1993)
3 *Fortune branches out* (1994)
4 *Tangled Fortunes* (1994)

Cousins series
Alcott, Louisa May
see **Rose Campbell series**

Cousins series
McKenna, Colleen O'Shaughnessy
1 *Not quite sisters* (1993)
2 *Stuck in the middle* (1993)

Cove series
Coffman, Virginia
see **Lucifer Cove series**

Coven Tree series
Brittain, Bill
1 *Devil's donkey* (1981)
2 *Wish giver* (1983)
Three tales
3 *Doctor Dredd's wagon of wonders* (1987)
4 *Professor Popkin's prodigious polish* (1991)

Covenant Chronicles: first series
Donaldson, Stephen Reeder
see **First chronicles of Thomas Covenant series**

Covenant Chronicles: second series
Donaldson, Stephen Reeder
see **Second chronicles of Thomas Covenant series**

Cow camps series
James, Will
1 *Big enough* (1931)
2 *Sun up* (1931)
One volume abridged edition entitled *Young cowboy*, 1935

Cowboy and college life series
Stoddard, William Osborn
1 *Dab Kinzer* (1881)
A story of a growing boy
2 *Quartet* (1881)

Cowboy Sam series
Chandler, Edna Walker
1 *Cowboy Sam* (1951)
2 *Cowboy Sam and Freddy* (1951)
3 *Cowboy Sam and the rodeo* (1951)
4 *Cowboy Sam and the rustlers* (1952)
5 *Cowboy Sam and Porky* (1952)
6 *Cowboy Sam and Shorty* (1953)
7 *Cowboy Sam and the fair* (1953)
8 *Cowboy Sam and the Indians* (1954)
9 *Cowboy Sam and Miss lily* (1958)
10 *Cowboy Sam and Flop* (1958)
11 *Cowboy Sam and Dandy* (1958)
12 *Cowboy Sam and Sally* (1959)
13 *Cowboy Sam and the airplane* (1959)
14 *Cowboy Sam and Big Bill* (1960)
15 *Cowboy Sam and Freckles* (1960)

Cowboy series
Anglund, Joan Walsh
1 *Cowboy and his friend* (1961)
2 *Cowboy's secret life* (1964)

Cowleaze Farm series
Whitlock, Ralph
1 *Cowleaze Farm* (1948)
2 *Harvest at Cowleaze* (1951)
3 *Cowleaze Farm in winter* (1952)
4 *Year on Cowleaze Farm* (1964)

Cowperwood trilogy
Dreiser, Theodore
see **Frank Cowperwood trilogy**

Coxeman series
Conway, Troy
1 *Berlin Wall affair* (1967)
Don't bite off more than you can chew
2 *Hard act to follow* (1968)
3 *Billion dollar snatch* (1968)
4 *Wham, bang, thank you ma'am affair* (1968)
5 *It's getting harder all the time* (1968)
6 *Come one, come all* (1968)
7 *Last licks* (1968)
8 *Keep it up, Rod!* (1968)
9 *Man-eater* (1968)
10 *Best laid plans* (1969)
11 *It's what's up front that counts* (1969)
12 *Had any lately?* (1969)
13 *Whatever goes up* (1969)
14 *Good peace* (1969)
15 *It's rather fight than swish* (1969)
16 *Just a silly millimeter longer* (1969)
17 *Big broad jump* (1969)
18 *Sex machine* (1970)
19 *Blow your mind job* (1970)
20 *Cunning linguist* (1970)
21 *Will the real Rod please stand up* (1970)
22 *All screwed up* (1970)
23 *Master baiter* (1970)
24 *Turn the other sheik* (1970)
25 *It's not how long you make it* (1970)
26 *Son of a witch* (1971)
27 *Penetrator* (1971)
28 *Stiff proposition* (1971)
29 *Harder you try, the harder it gets* (1971)
30 *Up and coming* (1972)
31 *Cockeyed cuties* (1972)
32 *I can't believe I ate the whole thing* (1972)
33 *Eager beaver* (1973)
34 *Hard man is good to find* (1973)

Coyle and Dobie series
Cory, Desmond
see **John Dobie and Kate Coyle series**

Coyle and Donovan series
Philips, Judson Pentecost
1 *Odds on the hot seat* (1941)
2 *Fourteenth trump* (1942)

Coyle series
Southworth, Emma Dorothy Eliza Nevitte
see **Brandon Coyle series**

Coyne series
Tapply, William George
see **Brady Coyne series**

Coyote Jones series
Elgin, Suzette Haden
1 *Communipaths* (1970)
2 *Furthest* (1971)
3 *At the Seventh Level* (1972)
Numbers 1-3 also published in one volume entitled *Communipath worlds*, 1980
4 *Star anchored, star angered* (1979)
5 *Yonder comes the other end of time* (1986)

Crab Island series
Hurt, Freda Mary
see **Benny of Crab Island series**

Crabs series
Smith, Guy Newman
1 *Night of the crabs* (1976)
2 *Killer crabs* (1978)
3 *Origin of the crabs* (1979)
4 *Crabs on the rampage* (1981)
5 *Crabs' moon* (1984)
6 *Human sacrifice* (1988)

Crabtree family series
Norris, Kathleen
1 *Certain people of importance* (1922)
2 *Hildegarde* (1926)

Craddocks of Shallowford series
Delderfield, Ronald Frederick
1 *Horseman riding by* (1966)
1.1 *Long summer day* (1966)
1.2 *Post of honour* (1966)
2 *Green gauntlet* (1968)

Crader and Jazine series
Hoch, Edward Dentinger
see **Carl Crader and Earl Jazine series**

Cradle builder series
Schoenstedt, Walter
1 *In praise of life* (1939)
Germany, 1914-1933
2 *Cradle builder* (1940)

Craft series
Patterson, Innis
see **Sebald Craft series**

Crag series
Elvestad, Sven
see **Osborne Crag series**

Cragg and Fletcher series
Gruber, Frank
see **Johnny Fletcher and Sam Cragg series**

Cragg and Frayne series
Evans, Alan
1 *End of the running* (1966)
2 *Mantrap* (1967)

Craggs and Castleton series
Alington, Cyril Augustine
see **Archdeacon series**

Craggs series
Keating, Henry Reymond Fitzwalter
see **Mrs Craggs series**

Craghold series
Noone, Edwina
1 *Craghold legacy* (1971)
2 *Craghold curse* (1972)
3 *Craghold creatures* (1972)
4 *Craghold crypt* (1973)
5 *Craighold cross* (1975)

Craig adventures series
Sheldon, Ann
see **Linda Craig adventures series**

Craig Kennedy series
Reeve, Arthur Benjamin
1 *Silent bullet* (1912)
Black hand
Short stories
2 *Poisoned pen* (1911)

Short stories
3 *Dream doctor* (1914)
Short stories
4 *War terror* (1915)
Craig Kennedy, detective
Short stories
5 *Gold of the gods* (1915)
The mystery of the Incas
6 *Exploits of Elaine* (1915)
Based on a screenplay
7 *Social gangster* (1916)
Diamond queen
Short stories
8 *Romance of Elaine* (1916)
Based on a screenplay
9 *Triumph of Elaine* (1916)
Based on a screenplay
10 *Ear in the wall* (1916)
11 *Treasure train* (1917)
Short stories
12 *Adventuress* (1917)
13 *Panama plot* (1918)
Short stories
14 *Soul scar* (1919)
15 *Film mystery* (1921)
16 *Craig Kennedy listens in* (1923)
Short stories
17 *Atavar, the dream dancer* (1924)
18 *Fourteen points* (1925)
Short stories
19 *Craig Kennedy on the farm* (1925)
Short stories
20 *Boy Scout's Craig Kennedy* (1925)
Short stories
21 *Pandora* (1926)
22 *Radio detective* (1926)
Based on a screenplay
23 *Kidnap club* (1932)
24 *Clutching hand* (1934)
25 *Enter Craig Kennedy* (1935)
Co-author: Ashley Locke; four novelettes
26 *Stars scream murder* (1936)

Craig series
Benton, Kenneth
see **Peter Craig series**
Gray, Malcolm
see **Alan Craig series**
Jefferies, Ian
see **Sergeant Craig series**
Lees, Dan
see **Constable Craig series**
Littleton, Kay
see **Jean Craig series**
Munro, James
see **John Craig series**
Rowlands, Betty
see **Melissa Craig series**
Sheldon, Ann
see **Linda Craig series**
Somers, Bart
see **Commander Craig series**
Van Urk, Virginia
see **Tom Craig series**
Winter, Bevis
see **Steve Craig series**

Craigallan family series
Barclay, Tessa
1 *Sower went forth* (1980)
2 *Stony places* (1981)
3 *Harvest of thorns* (1983)
4 *Good ground* (1984)

Craine series
Healy, Eugene P
see **Paul Craine series**

Crammond series
Muir, Thomas
see **Roger Crammond series**

Cranberryport series
Devlin, Wende
1 *Cranberry Thanksgiving* (1971)
2 *Cranberry Christmas* (1976)
3 *Cranberry mystery* (1978)
4 *Cranberry Halloween* (1982)
5 *Cranberry Valentine* (1986)
6 *Cranberry birthday* (1988)
7 *Cranberry Easter* (1990)
8 *Cranberry summer* (1992)

Crandel series
Sinclair, Murray
see **Ben Crandel series**

Crane Hammond series
Carmichael, Fred
Three-act plays
1 *Exit the body* (1962)
2 *Exit who?* (1982)

Crane series
Christie, Kate
see **Harold Crane series**
Curtis, Wade
see **Paul Crane series**
Jackson, Alison
see **Leslie Crane series**
Latimer, Jonathan
see **Bill Crane series**
Stuart, Donald
see **Lionel Crane series**

Crane trilogy
Glemser, Bernard
see **Robert Crane trilogy**

Cranleigh series
Wright, Sydney Fowler
see **Marguerite Cranleigh series**

Cranley series
Storm, Michael
see **Nick Cranley series**

Cranmer series
Knickmeyer, Steve
see **Steve Cranmer series**

Cranshaw series
Mason, Dan
see **Lex Cranshaw series**

Cranston series
Grant, Maxwell
see **Shadow series**

Cranstone series
Bullock, Michael
see **Randolph Cranstone series**

Crathorne family series
Dodd, Catherine Isabel
see **Red Lattice series**

Craven series
Gaunt, Mary
see **Doctor Craven series**

Craw series
Bell, John Joy
see **Mister Craw series**

Crawfish-Man series
Edler, Timothy J
1 *Adventures of Crawfish-Man* (1979)
2 *Crawfish-Man rescues Ron Guidry* (1980)
3 *Crawfish-Man's fifty ways to keep your kids from using drugs* (1982)
4 *Crawfish-Man's night befo' Christmas* (1984)
5 *Crawfish-Man rescues the old beachcomber* (1985)

Crawfish series
Fontenot, Mary Alice
see **Clovis Crawfish series**

Crawford and Gordon series
Gilruth, Susan
see **Inspector Hugh Gordon and Liane Crawford series**

Crawford of Lymond series
Dunnett, Dorothy
see **Francis Crawford of Lymond series**

Crawford series
mann, Jessica
see **Thea Crawford series**

Crawford series
Cushman, Dan
1 *Naked ebony* (1951)
2 *Savage interlude* (1952)

Crawford trilogy
Reynolds, Mack
see **Home Crawford trilogy**

Crawley series
Corris, Peter
see **Pokerface series**

Craythorne series
Douglas, Arthur
see **Jonathan Craythorne series**

Crazy cut-outs series
Tong, Gary
1 *Crazy cut-outs* (1979)
2 *More crazy cut-outs* (1980)
3 *Crazy cut-outs from outer space* (1982)
4 *Crazy cut-out tricks and puzzles* (1983)
Companion volume: Crazy pop-ups, 1988

Crazy series
McNaughton, Colin
1 *Football crazy* (1980)
2 *Crazy bear* (1983)

Creasy series
Quinnell, A J
1 *Perfect kill* (1992)
2 *Blue ring* (1993)

Created legend trilogy
Sologub, Fedor
Translated from the Russian
1 *Drops of blood* (1907)
2 *Queen Ortruda* (1910)
3 *Smoke and ashes* (1913)

Creatures from the past series
Stidworthy, John
1 *Life begins* (1986)
2 *Day of the dinosaurs* (1986)
3 *Mighty mammals of the past* (1986)
4 *Human ape* (1986)
When humans began
One volume edition entitled Creatures from the past, 1987

Creed series
Harte, Bryce
see **Slate Creed series**
Newton, Mike
see **Lawman series**

Creed series
Overton, Jenny
1 *Creed country* (1969)
2 *Nightwatch winter* (1973)

Creed Wetherall series
Sutton, Stack
see **Marshal Creed Wetherall series**

Creepies series
Impey, Rose
1 *Flat man* (1988)
2 *Scare yourself to sleep* (1988)
3 *Jumble Joan* (1989)
4 *Ankle grabber* (1989)

Creeps series
Schoch, Tim
1 *Creeps* (1985)
2 *Summer camp creeps* (1987)

Creepy Crawley series
Corris, Peter
see **Pokerface series**

Creepy Creature Club series
Mooser, Stephen
1 *Monster of the outfield* (1989)
2 *My Halloween boyfriend* (1989)
3 *Monster holiday* (1989)
4 *Fright face context* (1990)
5 *Monster of the year* (1990)
6 *That's so funny, I forgot to laugh* (1990)
7 *Crazy mixed-up valences* (1990)
8 *Secrets of the scarry fun* (1991)
9 *Night of the vampire kitty* (1991)
10 *Man who ate a car* (1991)

Creighton series
Livingston, Armstrong
see **Peter Creighton series**

Cremer series
Cremer, Jan
see **Jan Cremer series**

Crescent children series
Melinsky, Renate
1 *Children of the Crescent* (1974)
2 *Crescent children on the green* (1974)

Cressida and Christopher series
Mauldsley, Daniel
see **Christopher and Cressida series**

Casside and Fabian series
Keyes, Frances Parkinson
see **Fabian and cresside series**

Cressy series
Chappell, Mollie
1 *Valley of lilacs* (1972)
2 *Cressy* (1973)

Crew Cats series
Smith, Sam
1 *Secret harbour* (1975)
A very nice book about boats
2 *Rover's regatta day* (1977)

Crewe series
Burnett, Frances Hodgson
see **Sara Crewe series**

Crewe series
Vanardy, Varick
1 *Two-faced man* (1918)
2 *Something doing* (1919)
Three novelettes

Crewe series
Watson, John Reay
1 *Hampstead mystery* (1916)
2 *Mystery of the Downs* (1918)

Cribb and Thackeray series
Lovesey, Peter
see **Sergeant Cribb and Constable Thackeray series**

Cribbage series
Traill, Peter
see **Mister Cribbage series**

Crichton series
Morice, Anne
see **Tessa Crichton Price series**

Cricket person series
Swanton, Ernest William
Reminiscences
1 *Sort of a cricket person* (1972)
Revised edition 1976
2 *Follow on* (1977)

Cricket series
Elias, Frank
1 *Cricket on the brain* (1905)
2 *Cricket at the breakfast table* (1909)

Cricket series
Gilmore, David Hunter
see **Christopher Cricket series**

Cricket series
McGilvray, Alan
1 *Game is not the same* (1985)
2 *Game goes on* (1987)
Companion volume: *McGilvray's back page of cricket*, 1989

Cricket series
Selden, George
see **Chester Cricket series**

Cricket series
Timlow, Elizabeth Weston
1 *Cricket* (1895)
2 *Cricket at the seashore* (1896)
3 *Eunice and Cricket* (1897)

Cricket trilogy
Jackson, Gabrielle Emilie
see **Little Miss Cricket trilogy**

Cricketer series
Walker, Max
Autobiography
1 *Cricketer at the crossroads* (1978)
2 *Back to Bay Thirteen* (1980)

Cricklepit School series
Kemp, Gene
1 *Turbulent term of Tyke Tiler* (1977)
2 *Gowi Corby plays chicken* (1979)
3 *Charlie Lewis plays for time* (1984)
4 *Juniper* (1986)

Criddle series
Strong, Ben
see **Professor Adrian Criddle series**

Crime and puzzlement series
Treat, Lawrence
Pictorial mysteries
1 *Crime and puzzlement I* (1986)
2 *Crime and puzzlement II* (1986)
3 *Crime and puzzlement III* (1988)

Crime Haters series
Ashe, Gordon
see **Patrick Dawlish series**

Crime minister series
Barclay, Ian
see **Richard Dartley series**

Crimebusters series
Arden, William
see **Three Investigators Crimebusters series**

Crimefighters series
Hulke, Malcolm
see **Roger Moore and the Crimefighters series**

Criminal Court series
Rossiter, John
1 *Manipulators* (1973)
2 *Villains* (1974)

Crimson chalice trilogy
Canning, Victor
1 *Crimson chalice* (1976)
2 *Circle of the gods* (1977)
3 *Immortal wound* (1978)
One volume edition entitled *The crimson chalice trilogy*, 1980

Crimson Clown series
McCulley, Johnston
1 *Crimson Clown* (1927)
Four novelettes
2 *Crimson Clown again* (1928)
Four novelettes

Crimson crystal adventure series
Lawson, Susan
see **Endless quest crimson crystal adventure series**

Crinkleroot series
Arnosky, Jim
1 *Crinkleroot's animal tracks and wildlife signs* (1979)
2 *Crinkleroot's guide to walking in wild places* (1990)
3 *Crinkleroot's guide to knowing the birds* (1992)

Crippled tree series
Han, Suyin
1 *Crippled tree* (1965)
China, biography, history, autobiography, 1917-1928
2 *Mortal flower* (1966)
China, autobiography, history, 1928-1938
3 *Birdless summer* (1968)
China, autobiography, history, 1938-1948
4 *My house has two doors* (1980)
China, autobiography, history, 1948-1979

Crisis Aversion Team series
Andrews, Spike
see **C.A.T. series**

Crisis of empire trilogy
Drake, David
1 *Honorable defense* (1988)
Co-author: Thomas Thurston Thomas
2 *Cluster command* (1989)
Co-author: William Corey Dietz
3 *War machine* (1989)
Co-author: Roger MacBride Allen

Crisp series
Matthew, Christopher
see **Simon Crisp series**

Crispin Bridge series
Way, Peter
1 *Super-Celeste* (1977)
Dirty tricks
2 *Icarus* (1980)
3 *Belshazzar's feast* (1982)

Crispin Paton series
Draper, Alfred
1 *Grey Seal* (1981)
2 *Restless waves* (1983)
3 *Raging of the deep* (1985)
4 *Storm over Singapore* (1986)
5 *Great avenging day* (1988)

Crispin Quane series
Kilvington, Edwin
1 *Mystery in glass* (1931)
2 *Window in the dark* (1932)

Crispin series
Foxall, Raymond
see **John Crispin series**

Crispin Tyler series
Evans, Kenneth
1 *Eich way to die* (1973)
2 *Blueprint to kill* (1975)

Crispy Critter series
Korman, Justine
1 *No place like home* (1987)
2 *Birthday band* (1987)
3 *Bedtime book* (1987)
Companion volume: *Four rhyming puzzle books*, 1987

Cristy Romano series
Hunt, Mabel Leigh
1 *Stars for Cristy* (1956)
2 *Cristy at Skippinhills* (1958)

Critterland desert series
Reese, Bob
see **Desert critterland series**

Critterland ocean series
Reese, Bob
see **Ocean critterland series**

Critterland readers series
Reese, Bob
1 *Scary Larry meets big Willie* (1983)
2 *Calico Jack and the desert critters* (1983)
3 *Rapid Robert and Hiss the snake* (1983)

Crockett series
Korman, Justine
see **Davy Crockett series**
Lang, Brad
see **Fred Crockett series**
McNeil, Everett
see **Davy Crockett series**

Crocodile series
Mahy, Margaret
School readers
1 *Crocodile's Christmas jandals* (1982)
Christmas crocodile's thongs
2 *Bubbling crocodile* (1983)
3 *Mrs Bubble's baby* (1983)
4 *Shopping with a crocodile* (1985)
5 *Crocodile in the garden, volume 1* (1983)
6 *Crocodile in the garden, volume 2* (1985)

Crocodile series
Watts, Marjorie Ann
1 *Crocodile medicine* (1977)
2 *Crocodile plaster* (1978)
3 *Crocodile teeth* (1986)
Alternative title: *Crocodile goes to the dentist*

Crocus series
Duvoisin, Roger
1 *Crocodile in the tree* (1972)
2 *Crocus* (1977)
3 *Importance of Crocus* (1980)

Croft trilogy
Giesy, John Ulrich
see **Jason Croft trilogy**

Crole series
Leitfred, Robert H
see **Simon Crole series**

Crombie series
Coxe, George Harmon
see **Sam Crombie series**

Cromwell series
Gunn, Victor
see **Chief Inspector Bill Cromwell series**

Cromwellian Ireland series
Moore, Frank Frankfort
1 *Castle Omeragh* (1903)
2 *Captain Latymer* (1907)

Crook series
Berry, Martha Eugenie
1 *Crooked and straight* (1867)
2 *Crook straightened* (1868)

Crook series
Gilbert, Anthony
see **Arthur Crook series**
West, Charles
see **Paul Crook series**

Crooked brownie series
Arthur, Ruth Mabel
1 *Crooked brownie* (1989)
2 *Crooked brownie in town* (1943)
3 *Crooked brownie at the seaside* (1943)

Crooked Snake series
Wrightson, Patricia
see **Society of the Crooked Snake series**

Crop circles series
Andrews, Colin
1 *Circular evidence* (1989)
2 *Crop circles* (1990)
The latest evidence

Crosley series
Tralins, Sandor Robert
see **Lee Crosley series**

Cross and the switchblade series
Wilkerson, David
1 *Cross and the switchblade* (1963)
2 *Twelve angels from hell* (1965)
3 *Beyond the cross and the switchblade* (1974)

Cross currents series
Porter, Eleanor Hodgman
1 *Cross currents* (1907)
The story of Margaret
2 *Turn of the tide* (1908)
The story of how Margaret solved her problem

Cross series
Kenan, Randall
see **Tims Creek series**

Crossroads adventures in the world of Pern series
Nye, Jody Lynn
see **World of Pern series**

Crossroads series
This sequence has two authors; based on a television series
Hulke, Malcolm
1 *New beginning* (1974)
2 *Warm breeze* (1975)
3 *Something old, something new* (1976)
4 *Time for living* (1976)
Miles, Keith
5 *Family affair* (1980)

Crosswicks journals series
L'Engle, Madeleine
Autobiography
1 *Circle of quiet* (1972)
2 *Summer of the great-grandmother* (1974)
3 *Irrational season* (1977)
4 *Two part invention* (1988)
The story of a marriage

Crossword series
Resnicow, Herbert
1 *Murder across and down* (1985)
2 *Seventh crossword* (1985)
3 *Crossword code* (1986)
4 *Crossword legacy* (1987)
5 *Crossword hunt* (1987)

Crouchback trilogy
Waugh, Evelyn
see **World War II trilogy**

Crow Feather series
Kelton, Elmer
1 *Slaughter* (1992)
2 *Far canyon* (1994)

Crow series
Brooke, Leonard Leslie
see **Johnny Crow series**
Lewis, Royston
see **Inspector John Crow series**
Lumley, Brian
see **Titus Crow series**
McCutcheon, George Barr
see **Anderson Crow series**

Crow series
Marvin, James W
1 *Red hills* (1979)
2 *Worse than death* (1979)
3 *Tears of blood* (1980)
4 *Black trail* (1980)
5 *Body guard* (1981)
6 *Sisters* (1981)
7 *One-eyed death* (1982)
8 *Good day* (1982)

Crow series
Norsworthy, George
see **Martin Crow series**

Crowder series
Pentecost, Hugh
see **George Crowder series**

Crowe series
Daniell, David Scott
see **Drummer Oliver Crowe series**

Crowle series
Hanson, Victor Joseph
see **Amos Crowle series**

Crown jewels series
Williams, Walter Jon
1 *Crown jewels* (1987)
2 *House of shards* (1988)

Crown of thorns series
Heenan, John Carmel
Autobiography
1 *Not the whole truth* (1971)
2 *Crown of thorns* (1974)

Crown series
Harknett, Terry
see **Superintendent John Crown series**

Crown series
Ling, Peter
1 *Crown house* (1988)
2 *Crown papers* (1989)

Crown series
Streib, Dan
see **Steve Crown series**

Crow's Nest series
Connor, Ralph
1 *Prospector* (1901)
A tale of Crow's Nest Pass
2 *Doctor at Crow's Nest* (1906)
Doctor
A tale of the Rockies

Crowther chronicles series
Armstrong, Thomas
1 *Crowthers of Bankdam* (1940)
2 *Pilling always pays* (1954)
3 *Sue Crowther's marriage* (1961)
4 *Our London office* (1966)
Companion volume: *A ring has no end*, 1971

Crowther series
Jacob, Naomi
1 *Susan Crowther* (1945)
2 *Honour's mistress* (1947)

Croyd series
Wallace, Ian
1 *Croyd* (1967)
A downtime fantasy
2 *Doctor Orpheus* (1968)
A downtime myth
3 *Deathstar voyage* (1969)
A downtime mystery cruise
4 *Voyage to Dari* (1974)
5 *Z-sting* (1978)
6 *Heller's leap* (1979)
7 *Lucifer comet* (1980)
8 *Megalomania* (1989)

Crucifixion trilogy
Cleeve, Brian
1 *House on the rock* (1980)
2 *Seven mansions* (1980)
3 *Fourth Mary* (1982)

Cruiskeen Lawn series
O'Brien, Flann
Humour
1 *Best of Myles* (1968)
2 *Further cuttings from Cruiskeen Lawn* (1976)
3 *Hair of the dogma* (1977)

Crumble Lane series
Allan, Mabel Esther
1 *Crumble Lane adventure* (1983)
2 *Trouble in Crumble Lane* (1984)
3 *Crumble Lane captives* (1986)
4 *Crumble Lane mystery* (1987)

Crunch and Des series
Wylie, Philip
1 *Big one gets away!* (1940)
2 *Salt water daffy* (1941)
3 *Fish and tin fish* (1944)
4 *Crunch and Des* (1948)
Selections: *The best of Crunch and Des*, 1954

Crusaders series
Scott, Walter
see **Tales of the Crusaders series**

Crusades series
Lamb, Harold
1 *Iron men and saints* (1930)
2 *Flame of Islam* (1931)
One volume edition entitled *The crusades*, 1962

Crusoe series
Defoe, Daniel
see **Robinson, Crusoe series**

Crusoe series
Severn, David
1 *Rick afire!* (1942)
2 *Cabin for Crusoe* (1943)
3 *Waggon for five* (1944)
4 *Hermit in the hills* (1945)
5 *Forest holiday* (1946)

Crying Eddie and Harry Chalice series
Mackenzie, Donald
see **Harry Chalice and Crying Eddie series**

Crystal Blake series
Bly, Stephen Arthur
1 *Crystal's solid gold discovery* (1986)
2 *Crystal's perilous ride* (1986)
3 *Crystal's rodeo debut* (1986)
4 *Crystal's mill town mystery* (1986)
5 *Crystal's blizzard trek* (1986)
6 *Crystal's grand entry* (1986)

Crystal Lake series
Hawke, Simon
see **Friday the thirteenth series**

Crystal series
Bayer, Sandy
1 *Crystal curtain* (1988)
2 *Crystal cage* (1991)

Crystal series
Forstchen, William R
1 *Crystal warriors* (1988)
2 *Crystal sorcerers* (1991)

Cthulhu Mythos series
This sequence has thirteen authors
Chappell, Fred
1 *Dagon* (1968)
Harvey, Jon M
2 *Cthulhu* (1976)
Tales
Berglund, Edward Paul
3 *Disciples of Cthulhu* (1976)
Mooney, Brian
4 *Cthulhu 2* (1977)
Guardians of the gate
Tales
Harvey, Jon M
5 *Cthulhu 3* (1978)
Tales
Foster, Alan Dean
6 *Horror on the beach* (1978)
Bloch, Robert
7 *Strange eons* (1978)
8 *Mysteries of the worm* (1979)
Stories
Diaper, John
9 *Arkham evil* (1983)
Wimble, Edward
10 *Death in Dunwich* (1983)
Diaper, John
11 *Pursuit of Kadath* (1983)
Clayton, Sheena
12 *Tide of desire* (1983)
Lumley, Brian
13 *Hero of dreams* (1986)
Shea, Michael
14 *Fat face* (1987)
Chappell, Fred
15 *Fred Chappell reader* (1987)
Includes Dagon, 1968
Lumley, Brian
16 *Elysia* (1989)
Kitsch, Hieronymous
17 *Heart of R'Lyeh* (1989)
Companion volumes: *Colour out of time*, by Michael Shea, 1984, *Cthulhu, the mythos and kindred horrors*, by Robert Ervin Howard, 1987

Cthulhu series
Derleth, August
1 *Mask of Cthulhu* (1958)
Short stories
2 *Trail of Cthulhu* (1962)

Cub series
Turner, Ethel
1 *Cub* (1915)
2 *Captain Cub* (1917)
3 *Brigid and the Cub* (1919)

Cuba series
Verrill, Alpheus Hyatt
1 *Cuba, past and present* (1914)
2 *Cuba of today* (1931)

Cubby Bear series
Burgess, Thornton Waldo
1 *Frightened baby* (1929)
2 *Farmer Brown's boy becomes curious* (1929)
3 *What Farmer Brown's boy did* (1929)
4 *Cubby Bear has a mind of his own* (1929)
5 *Imp of mischief* (1929)
6 *Cubby in Mother Brown's pantry* (1929)
7 *Woe-begone little bear* (1929)
8 *Cubby gets a bath* (1929)
9 *Milk and honey* (1929)
10 *Cubby finds an open door* (1929)

Cubby Bears series
Laird, Elizabeth
1 *Cubby Bears' birthday party* (1985)
2 *Cubby Bears go camping* (1985)
3 *Cubby Bears on the river* (1985)
4 *Cubby Bears go shopping* (1985)

Cubby, Mandy and Mops series
Blyton, Enid
see **Mandy, Mops and Cubby series**

Cubby series
Tucker, Jenni
1 *Cubbies galore* (1983)
2 *Snow Cubby* (1983)Δ118
3 *Tree-time Cubby* (1983)
4 *Cubby in a muddle* (1983)

Cuckoo series
Park, Ruth
1 *Fence around the cuckoo* (1993)
2 *Fishing in the Styx* (1993)

Cuckoo's saga series
Pohl, Frederik
1 *Farthest star* (1975)
2 *Wall around star* (1983)
One volume edition entitled *The saga of Cuckoo*, 1983

Cuculain trilogy
O'Grady, Standish James
1 *Coming of Cuculain* (1894)
2 *In the gates of the north* (1896)
3 *Triumph and passing of Cuculain* (1919)

Cucumbers trilogy
Moore, Lilian
1 *I'll meet you at the Cucumbers* (1988)
2 *Don't be afraid, Amanda* (1992)
3 *Adam Mouse's book of poems* (1992)

Cudjo's cave series
Trowbridge, John Townsend
1 *Cudjo's cave* (1863)
2 *Three scouts* (1863)

Cugel the Clever series
Vance, Jack
see **Adventures of Cugel the Clever series**

Culdi trilogy
Kurtz, Katherine
see **Legends of Camber of Culdi trilogy**

Cullah Burnett series
Whitman, Sidney Edgerton
see **Captain Cullah Burnett series**

Cullen Baker series
L'Amour, Louis
1 *First fast draw* (1959)
2 *Lando* (1962)

Cullen series
Fitzhugh, Percy Keese
see **Bobby Cullen series**
Thomson, David Robert Alexander
see **Daniel Cullen series**

Cullinan series
Martin, Oliver
see **Timothy Cullinan series**

Cullom Blaine series
Young, Carter Travis
1 *Blaine's law* (1974)
2 *Red grass* (1976)
3 *Winter drift* (1980)

Culp series
Peck, Richard
see **Blossom Culp series**

Cultural survey series
Biggle, Lloyd
1 *Still small voice of trumpets* (1968)
2 *World menders* (1971)

Culture series
Banks, Iain Menzies
1 *Consider Phlebas* (1987)
2 *Player of games* (1988)
3 *State of the art* (1989)
4 *Use of weapons* (1990)

Cumberbatch trilogy
Clarke, Austin Chesterfield
see **Boysie Cumberbatch trilogy**

Cumberland series
Arnow, Harriette
1 *Seedtime on the Cumberland* (1960)
2 *Flowering of the Cumberland* (1963)

Cumbrian series
Herbert, Kathleen
Set in England in the Dark Ages
1 *Queen of the lightning* (1983)
2 *Ghost in the sunlight* (1986)
3 *Bride of the spear* (1988)

Cummings series
McGuire, Paul
see **Chief Inspector Cummings series**
Martin, Charles Morris
see **Gospel Cummings series**

Cunningham series
Hammond, Gerald
see **Captain John Cunningham series**
Thorne, Ernest Pollett
see **Major Brains Cunningham series**

Cunningham trilogy
Edmondson, Garry Cotton
1 *Cunningham equations* (1986)
2 *Black magician* (1986)
3 *Maximum effort* (1987)

Cupid Delaney series
Leroe, Ellen Whitney
1 *Have a heart, Cupid Delaney* (1985)
2 *Meet your match, Cupid Delaney* (1990)

Cupid trilogy
Matthewman, Phyllis
1 *Winged Cupid* (1951)
2 *Cupid in Mayfair* (1958)
3 *Cupid under Capricorn* (1961)

Curdie series
Macdonald, George
see **Princess series**

Curdy and Minka series
White, Antonia
see **Minka and Curdy series**

Cure of souls trilogy
Shaw, Robert
1 *Flag* (1965)
2 *Man in the glass booth* (1967)
3 *Card from Morocco* (1969)

Curfew series
Brunner, John
see **Max Curfew series**

Curious George series
Krulick, Nancy E
1 *Curious George makes a splash* (1985)
2 *Curious George saves the day* (1986)
3 *I am curious about numbers* (1987)

Curious George series
This sequence has two authors
Rey, Hans Augusto
1 *Curious George* (1941)
2 *Curious George takes a job* (1947)
3 *Curious George rides a bike* (1952)
4 *Curious George gets a medal* (1957)
Rey, Margret
5 *Curious George flies a kite* (1958)
Rey, Hans Augusto
6 *Curious George learns the alphabet* (1963)
Rey, Margret
7 *Curious George goes to the hospital* (1966)
Illustrated by Hans Augusto Rey
8 *Curious George and the dump truck* (1984)
From number 8 the sequence is based on the Curious George films
9 *Curious George goes to the circus* (1984)
10 *Curious George goes to the aquarium* (1984)
11 *Curious George goes sledding* (1984)
12 *Curious George goes hiking* (1985)
13 *Curious George walks the pets* (1986)
14 *Curious George plays baseball* (1986)
15 *Curious George goes to a costume party* (1986)
16 *Curious George at the ballet* (1986)
17 *Curious George visits the police station* (1987)
18 *Curious George goes fishing* (1987)
19 *Curious George at the laundromat* (1987)
20 *Curious George visit4s the zoo* (1988)
21 *Curious George at the fire station* (1988)
22 *Curious George at the airport* (1988)
23 *Curious George and the pizza* (1988)
24 *Curious George at the beach* (1988)
25 *Curious George at the railroad station* (1988)
26 *Curious George goes to a restaurant* (1988)
27 *Curious George visits an amusement park* (1988)
28 *Curious George and the dinosaur* (1989)
29 *Curious George goes to an icecream shop* (1989)
30 *Curious George goes to school* (1989)
31 *Curious George goes to the dentist* (1989)
32 *Curious George bakes a cake* (1990)
33 *Curious George goes camping* (1990)
34 *Curious George goes to an air show* (1990)
35 *Curious George goes to a toy store* (1990)

Curious lobster series
Hatch, Richard Warren
1 *Curious lobster* (1937)
2 *Curious lobster's island* (1939)
One volume edition entitled *The lobster books*, 1951

Curlew Jon series
Edwin, Maribel
1 *Curlew Jon* (1953)
2 *Zigzag path* (1955)
3 *Double halfpenny* (1956)

Curlon series
Laumer, Keith
see **Mister Curlon series**

Curly Graham trilogy
Ames, James Bushnell
1 *Curly of the Circle-bar* (1919)
2 *Curly and the Aztec gold* (1920)
3 *Curly Graham, cowpuncher* (1924)

Curlytops series
Garis, Howard Roger
1 *Curlytops at Cherry Farm* (1918)
2 *Curlytops at Uncle Frank's ranch* (1918)
3 *Curlytops on Star Island* (1918)
4 *Curlytops snowed in* (1918)
5 *Curlytops at Silver Lake* (1920)
6 *Curlytops and their pets* (1921)
7 *Curlytops and their playmates* (1922)
8 *Curlytops in the woods* (1923)
9 *Curlytops at Sunset Beach* (1925)
10 *Curlytops touring around* (1927)
11 *Curlytops in summer camp* (1928)
12 *Curlytops growing up* (1928)
13 *Curlytops at Happy House* (1931)
14 *Curlytops at the circus* (1932)

Currain family series
Williams, Ben Ames
1 *House divided* (1947)
2 *Unconquered* (1953)

Curry and Hayes series
Fox, Brian
see **Alias Smith and Jones series**

Curt Cannon series
Cannon, Curt
1 *I'm Cannon, for hire* (1958)
2 *I like 'em tough* (1958)
Short stories

Curt Jaeger series
Mandell, Mark
see **Nazi hunter series**

Curt Stone series
Seward, Jack
1 *Cave of the Chinese skeletons* (1964)
2 *Frogman assassination* (1968)
3 *Eurasian virgins* (1969)
4 *Assignment, Find Cherry* (1969)
5 *Chinese pleasure girl* (1969)

Curtain falls trilogy
Druon, Maurice
1 *Magnates* (1949)
Original edition entitled *Les grandes familles*
2 *Feet of clay* (1951)
Original edition entitled *La chute des corps*
3 *Rendezvous in hell* (1956)
Original edition entitled *Rendez vous aux enfers*
One volume edition entitled *The curtain falls*, 1959

Curtis and Bourne series
Somers, Paul
see **Hugh Curtis and Mollie Bourne series**

Curtis and Yates series
Fetta, Emma Lou
see **Lyle Curtis and Susan Yates series**

Curtis Burke series
Trevor, Ralph
see **Superintendent Curtis Burke series**

Curtis Long series
Evans, Tabor
see **Longarm series**

Curwen and Stanton series
Vickers, Roy
see **Inspector Peter Curwen and Hugh Stanton series**

Curzon and Sallis series
Usher, Frank
see **Amanda Curzon and Oscar Sallis series**

Custard Kid series
Deary, Terry
1 *Custard Kid* (1978)
2 *Calamity Kate* (1980)

Custard series
Nash, Ogden
Poems
1 *Custard the dragon* (1959)
2 *Custard the dragon and the wicked knight* (1961)
One volume selection entitled *Custard and Company*, 1980

Custer series
Burroughs, Edgar Rice
see **Barney Custer series**
Johnston, Terry Conrad
see **General Armstrong Custer series**

Custer series
Standish, Buck
1 *Custer County* (1974)
2 *Custer Meadow* (1975)

Custer trilogy
Jones, Douglas Clyde
see **General George Custer trilogy**

Custodians series
Middleton, Martin
see **Chronicles of the custodians series**

Cut-Ups series
Marshall, James
1 *Cut-Ups* (1984)
2 *Cut-Ups cut loose* (1987)
3 *Cut-Ups at Camp Custer* (1989)
4 *Cut-Ups carry on* (1990)
5 *Cut-Ups crack up* (1992)

Cuthbert Higgins series
Gregg, Cecil Freeman
see **Inspector Cuthbert Higgins series**

Cuthbert series
Chesher, Kim
Illustrated by Yasuko Kimura
Originally published with Japanese text
1 *Cuthbert and the thingamabob* (1976)
2 *Cuthbert and the sea monster* (1977)
3 *Cuthbert and the long winter sleep* (1979)
4 *Cuthbert and the good ship Thingamabob* (1981)
5 *Cuthbert and the night walkers* (1982)

Cutler family series
Andrews, Virginia Cleo
1 *Dawn* (1990)
2 *Secrets of the morning* (1991)
3 *Twilight's child* (1992)
4 *Midnight whispers* (1992)
5 *Darkest hour* (1993)

Cutter series
Haugaard, Erik Christian
see **Oliver Cutter series**
McCoy, Duff
see **Jeb Cutter series**

Cutting series
Westbrook, Perry Dickie
see **Doctor Samuel Cutting series**

Cutty Clay series
Macgrath, Harold
1 *Drums of jeopardy* (1920)
2 *Wolves of chaos* (1929)

CV trilogy
Knight, Damon
1 *CV* (1985)
2 *Observers* (1988)
3 *Reasonable world* (1991)

Cyber and Starr series
Heath, Peter
see **Jason Starr and Adam Cyber series**

Cybernarc series
Cain, Robert
1 *Cybernarc* (1991)
2 *Gold dragon* (1991)

Cybernetic shogun series
Milan, Victor
1 *Cybernetic samurai* (1985)
2 *Cybernetic shogun* (1990)

Cyberspace trilogy
Gibson, William
see **Neuromancer trilogy**

Cyberstealth series
Lewitt, Shariann N
1 *Cyberstealth* (1989)
2 *Dancing vac.* (1990)

Cyborg commando trilogy
Mohan, Kim
1 *Planet in peril* (1987)

2 *Chase into space* (1988)
3 *Ultimate prize* (1988)

Cyborg series
Caidin, Martin
see **Six Million Dollar Man series**

Cycle of fire trilogy
Wurts, Janny
1 *Stormwarden* (1984)
2 *Keeper of the keys* (1988)
3 *Shadowfane* (1988)

Cycle of the West series
Neihardt, John Gneisenau
A verse epic
1 *Song of Hugh Glass* (1915)
2 *Song of three friends* (1919)
3 *Song of the Indian wars* (1925)
4 *Song of the messiah* (1935)
5 *Song of Jed Smith* (1941)
One volume edition entitled *A cycle of the West*, 1949; also published in two volumes entitled *The mountain men*, and *The twilight of the Sioux*, 1971

Cyclone series
Gregory, Lester
see **Kid Cyclone series**

Cygnet series
McKillip, Patricia Anne
1 *Sorceress and the cygnet* (1991)
2 *Vygnet and the Firebird* (1994)

Cynthia Doanides series
Kenneth, Claire
1 *Love riddle* (1958)
2 *May in Manhattan* (1959)

Cynthia Godwin and Vincent Stallard series
Beare, George
see **Vincent Stallard and Cynthia Godwin series**

Cyrano de Bergerac and D'Artagnon series
Feval, Paul
see **Years between series**

Cyril Bonhamy series
Gathorne-Hardy, Jonathan
1 *Terrible kidnapping of Cyril Bonhamy* (1978)
2 *Cyril Bonhamy versus Madam Big* (1981)
3 *Cyril Bonhamy and the great Father Christmas robbery* (1981)
4 *Cyril Bonhamy and the great drain robbery* (1983)
5 *Cyril Bonhamy and Operation Ping* (1985)
6 *Cyril of the apes* (1987)

Cyril Rapstoff series
Pullen, Alan
see **Sam and Lin series**

Cyril series
Palin, Michael
1 *Cyril and the House of Commons* (1986)
2 *Cyril and the dinner party* (1986)

Cyrus Hatch series
Davis, Frederick Clyde
see **Professor Cyrus Hatch series**

Cyrus Wilson series
Garnet, A H
1 *Santa Claus killer* (1981)
2 *Maze* (1982)

Cyteen series
Cherryh, Carolyn Janice
1 *Betrayal* (1988)
2 *Rebirth* (1988)
3 *Vindication* (1988)
One volume edition entitled *Cyteen*, 1988

D

D.A. series
Gardner, Erle Stanley
see **District Attorney series**

D.W. series
Brown, Marc
1 *D.W. flips!* (1987)
Roll over D.W.
2 *D.W. all wet* (1987)

Dabney family series
Street, James
1 *Oh promised land* (1940)
2 *Tap roots* (1942)
3 *By valour and arms* (1944)
4 *Tomorrow we reap* (1949)
5 *Mungo Dabney* (1950)

Dack series
Meriton, Peter
see **Captain Dack series**

Daddies and mommies at work series
Merriam, Frank
see **Mommies and daddies at work series**

Daddy and mummy series
Harper, Anita
1 *Mummy runs a cafe* (1973)
2 *Mummy is a health visitor* (1973)
3 *Daddy drives a bus* (1973)
4 *Daddy builds houses* (1973)

Daddy Bourne series
Galwey, Geoffrey Valentine
see **Inspector Daddy Bourne series**

Daddy Long Ears series
Kraus, Robert
1 *Daddy Long Easr Christmas surprise* (1989)
2 *Daddy Long Ears Halloween* (1990)

Dade Cooley series
Thompson, Gene
1 *Murder mystery* (1980)
2 *Nobody cared for Kate* (1983)
3 *Cup of death* (1988)

Daedalus quartet
Bickers, Richard Townshend
1 *Gifts of Jove* (1983)
2 *Time for haste* (1984)
3 *Too late the morrow* (1984)
4 *Sure recompense* (1985)

Daedalus series
Stableford, Brian Michael
1 *Florians* (1976)
2 *Critical threshold* (1977)
3 *Wildeblood's empire* (1977)
4 *City in the sun* (1978)
5 *Balance of power* (1979)
6 *Paradox of the sets* (1979)

Daffodil series
Butler, Maude Mary
1 *Waiting and serving* (1892)
Alternative title: The major's little sentinel
2 *Daffodil* (1893)
A brave little lady

Daft series
Parkinson, Michael
Humorous reminiscences of sport
1 *Football daft* (1968)
2 *Cricket mad* (1969)
3 *Bats in the pavilion* (1977)

Dag Bjorndal series
Gulbranssen, Trygve
see **Bjorndal family series**

Dag Fletcher series
Rankine, John
1 *Ring of Garamas* (1971)
2 *Interstellar Two-Five* (1966)
3 *Plantos affair* (1971)
4 *Bromius Phenomenon* (1973)
5 *One is one* (1968)
Companion volume: *The blockade of Sinitron*, 1966

Dagmar Schultz series
Hall, Lynn
1 *Secret life of Dagmar Schulz* (1988)
2 *Dagmar Schultz and the Angel Edna* (1989)
3 *Dagmar Schultz and the powers of darkness* (1989)
4 *Dagmar Schultz and the green-eyed monster* (1991)

Dagobert and Jane Brown series
Ames, Delano
1 *She shall have murder* (1948)
2 *Murder begins at home* (1949)
3 *Death of a fellow traveller* (1950)
Nobody wore black
4 *Corpse diplomatique* (1950)
5 *Body on page one* (1951)
6 *Murder, maestro, please* (1952)
7 *No mourning for the matador* (1953)
8 *Crime, gentlemen, please* (1954)
Coffin for Christopher
9 *Landscape with corpse* (1955)
10 *Crime out of mind* (1956)
11 *She wouldn't say who* (1957)
12 *Lucky Jane* (1959)
For old crime's sake

Daguerre series
Stevens, Carl
see **Christian Daguerre series**

Dagwood and Blondie series
Young, Chic
see **Blondie and Dagwood series**

Dahlgren series
Gotlieb, Phyllis
1 *O master Caliban!* (1976)
2 *Heart of red iron* (1989)

Dahlquist and Bloodworth series
Lochte, Dick
see **Leo Bloodworth and Serendipity Dahlquist series**

Dahomean series
Yerby, Frank
see **Hwesu series**

Dai Evans series
Stranger, Joyce
1 *Running foxes* (1965)
2 *Lakeland vet* (1972)

Dai-San series
Lustbader, Eric
see **Sunset Warrior series**

Daily bread series
Larsson, Gosta
1 *Our daily bread* (1934)
2 *Fatherland, farewell!* (1938)

Daily lives in Nghsi-Altai series
Nichols, Robert
1 *Red shift* (1977)
Co-author: Peter Schumann
2 *Arrival* (1977)
3 *Gahr City* (1978)
4 *Harditts in Sawna* (1979)
5 *Exile* (1979)

Dain series
Sheckley, Robert
see **Stephen Dain series**

Daine series
Pierce, Tamora
1 *Wild magic* (1992)
2 *Wolf-speaker* (1994)

Daintrey series
Knight, Peter
see **Anthony Daintrey series**

Dainty series
Brooks, Amy
see **Dorothy Dainty series**

Daisy and Dick Travers series
Samuels, Adelaide Florence
see **Dick and Daisy Travers series**

Daisy Jane Mott series
Jones, Jennifer
1 *Murder-on-Hudson* (1937)
2 *Murder al fresco* (1939)
3 *Dirge for a dog* (1939)

Daisy Peach series
Saint John, Mabel
1 *Daisy earns her living* (1917)
2 *Daisy Peach abroad* (1917)

Daisy Penny series
Joseph, Marie
1 *Better world than this* (1987)
2 *World apart* (1988)

Daisy Punkin series
Stahl, Hilda
1 *Daisy Punkin* (1991)
2 *Daisy Punkin and the bratty brother* (1992)

Daisy series
Bradman, Tony
1 *Daisy and the washing machine* (1986)
2 *Daisy goes swimming* (1986)
3 *Daisy and the babysitter* (1986)
4 *Daisy and the crying baby* (1986)
5 *Daisy feels ill* (1988)
6 *Daisy goes to playgroup* (1988)

Daisy series
Greig, Daisy
1 *Daisy* (1978)
2 *Daisy reminisces* (1979)

Daisy series
Kelley, Anne
1 *Daisy and the dog show* (1985)
2 *Daisy's discovery* (1985)

Daisy trilogy
Warner, Susan Bagert
1 *Melbourne House* (1864)
2 *Daisy* (1868)
3 *Daisy in the field* (1869)

Daisychain series
Ahlberg, Janet
1 *Ready, Teddy go!* (1983)
2 *Summer snowman* (1983)
3 *That's my baby!* (1983)
4 *Which witch?* (1983)
5 *Clowning about* (1984)
6 *Good old dolls* (1984)
7 *Monster munch* (1984)
8 *Rent-a-robot* (1984)
9 *One true Santa* (1985)

Daker trilogy
Moorcock, Michael
see **Eternal champion trilogy**

Dakkers series
Brett, Mike
see **Sam Dakkers series**

Dakota Bush series
Dana, Mitchell
1 *Beyond the law* (1972)
2 *Town without a prayer* (1972)
3 *Last buffalo* (1973)
4 *Gun shy* (1973)
5 *Incident in a Texas town* (1975)
6 *Beware the smiling stranger* (1977)

Dakota King series
Mackenzie, Jake
see **Secret files of Dakota King series**

Dakota series
Ralston, Gilbert Alexander
1 *Dakota warpath* (1973)
2 *Red revenge* (1974)
3 *Cat trap* (1974)
4 *Murder's money* (1975)
5 *Chain reaction* (1975)

Dakotas series
Davis, Kathryn
1 *At wind's edge* (1983)
2 *Endless sky* (1984)

Dalby series
Harper, Stephen
see **Healers series**

Dale Evans series
This sequence has two authors; based on a television series
Fannin, Cole
1 *Roy Rogers and Dale Evans* (1957)
Hale, Helen
2 *Dale Evans and danger in Crooked Canyon* (1958)

Dale family series
Antony, Jonquil
1 *Mrs Dale* (1958)
Ten years in the life of a doctor's family
2 *Dales of Parkwood Hill* (1959)
3 *Dear Doctor Dale* (1970)
Selections with household recipes entitled *Mrs Dale's bedside book*, 1951, and *Mrs Dale at home*, 1952; companion volume: *Mrs Dale's friendship book*, 1961

Dale of the Mounted series
Holliday, Joe
1 *Dale of the Mounted* (1951)
2 *Dale of the Mounted in the Arctic* (1953)
3 *Dale of the Mounted on the west coast* (1954)
4 *Dale of the Mounted in Newfoundland* (1955)
5 *Dew Line duty* (1957)
6 *Dale of the mounted in the Northwest* (1958)
7 *Submarine hunt* (1958)
8 *Atlantic assignment* (1959)
9 *Atomic plot* (1959)
10 *Pursuit on the Saint Lawrence* (1960)
11 *Manhunt at the UN* (1961)
12 *Dale of the mounted in Hong Kong* (1962)

Dale series
Cooper, John C
see **Inspector James Dale series**
Packard, Frank Lucius
see **Jimmie Dale series**
Penrose, Margaret
see **Dorohy Dale series**
Smith, Cicely Fox
see **Barty Dale series**

Dale Shand series
Enefer, Douglas
1 *Deadly quiet* (1961)
2 *Long chance* (1961)
3 *Dark kiss* (1964)
4 *Painted death* (1966)
5 *Long hot night* (1967)
6 *Girl chase* (1968)
7 *Girl in arms* (1968)
8 *Gilded kiss* (1969)
9 *Deadline dolly* (1970)
10 *Screaming orchid* (1971)
11 *Pacific Northwest* (1975)
12 *Seven nights at the resort* (1976)
13 *Ice in the sun* (1977)
14 *Goodbye blond* (1980)

Dale Thompson series
Holliday, Joe
see **Dale of the mounted series**

Dalemark series
Jones, Diana Wynne
1 *Cart and Cwidder* (1975)
2 *Drowned Ammet* (1977)
3 *Spellcoats* (1979)

D'Alembert family series
Smith, Edward Elmer
see **Family d'Alembert series**

Daleswoman series
Hauxwell, Hannah
Based on the television series entitled Too long a winter
1 *Seasons of my life* (1989)
The story of a solitary Daleswoman
2 *Daughter of the Dales* (1990)
The world of Hannah Hauxwell
3 *Innocent abroad* (1991)
The travels of Miss Hannah Hauxwell
5 *Hannah in North America* (1993)
Omnibus: *Hannah, the complete story*, 1991; companion volume: *Hannah's North Country*, 1993

Daley's crew series
Massey, Craig
see **Captain Daley's crew series**

Dalgleish series
James, Phyllis Dorothy
see **Commander Adam Dalgliesh series**

Dalgliesh series
James, Phyllis Dorothy
see **Commander Adam Dalgliesh series**

Dalla series
Stockley, Cynthia
1 *Dalla the lion cub* (1924)
A story of South Africa
2 *Leopard in the bush* (1927)

Dallas Henry series
Pairo, Preston
1 *Beach money* (1991)
2 *One dead judge* (1993)

Dallas O'Neil and the Baker Street Sports Club series
Jenkins, Jerry Bruce
1 *Secret baseball challenge* (1986)
2 *Scary basketball player* (1986)
3 *Mysterious football team* (1986)
4 *Angry gymnast* (1986)
5 *Bizarre hockey tournament* (1986)
6 *Weird soccer match* (1986)
7 *Strange swimming coach* (1986)
8 *Silent track star* (1986)

Dallas O'Neil mysteries series
Jenkins, Jerry Bruce
1 *Mystery of the kidnapped kid* (1988)
2 *Mystery of the mixed-up teacher* (1988)
3 *Mystery of the missing sister* (1988)
4 *Mystery of the scorpion threat* (1988)
5 *Mystery on the Midway* (1989)
6 *Mystery of the golden palomino* (1989)
7 *Mystery of the skinny sophomore* (1989)
8 *Mystery of the phony murder* (1989)

Dallas series
This sequence has three authors; based on a television series
O'Hara, John
1 *Ewings* (1972)
Companion volume: *The second Ewings, a fragment*, 1977
Raintree, Lee
2 *Dallas* (1978)
Hirschfeld, Burt
3 *Ewings of Dallas* (1980)
4 *Women of Dallas* (1981)
5 *Men of Dallas* (1981)

Dallas Webster series
Stanford, Don
1 *Slaughtered lovelies* (1950)
2 *Bargain in blood* (1951)

Dalloway series
Woolf, Virginia
see **Mrs Dalloway series**

Dalton Boys series
Lawson, W B
1 *Dalton Boys in California* (1893)
Alternative title: A bold hold-up at Ceres
2 *Dalton Boys and the MK and T robbery* (1899)

Dalton Prouse series
McCulley, Johnston
see **Crimson Clown series**

Dalziel and Pascoe series
Hill, Reginald
see **Superintendent Andrew Dalziel and Sergeant Pascoe series**

Damar series
McKinley, Robin
see **Chronicles of Damar series**

Damaris and Rachel series
Oxenham, Elsie J
see **Rachel and Damaris series**

Damaris series
Malet, Lucas
1 *Damaris* (1916)
2 *Damaris Hard* (1919)

Damask family series
Carr, Philippa
see **Daughters of England series**

Dame Beatrice Bradley series
Mitchell, Gladys
1 *Speedy death* (1929)
2 *Mystery of a butcher's shop* (1929)
3 *Longer bodies* (1930)
4 *Saltmarsh murders* (1932)
5 *Death at the opera* (1934)
Death in the wet
6 *Devil at Saxon wall* (1935)
7 *Dead man's Morris* (1936)
8 *Come away, death* (1937)
9 *Saint Peter's finger* (1938)
10 *Printer's error* (1939)
11 *Brazen tongue* (1940)
12 *Hangman's curfew* (1941)
13 *When last I died* (1941)
14 *Laurels are poison* (1942)
15 *Worsted viper* (1943)
16 *Sunset over Soho* (1943)
17 *My father sleeps* (1944)
18 *Rising of the moon* (1945)
19 *Here comes a chopper* (1946)
20 *Death and the maiden* (1947)
21 *Dancing Druids* (1948)
22 *Tom Brown's body* (1949)
23 *Groaning spinney* (1950)
24 *Devil's elbow* (1951)
25 *Echoing strangers* (1952)
26 *Merlin's furlong* (1953)
27 *Faintley speaking* (1954)
28 *Watson's choice* (1955)
29 *Twelve horses and the hangman's noose* (1956)
Hangman's noose
30 *Twenty-third man* (1957)
31 *Spotted hemlock* (1958)
32 *Man who grew tomatoes* (1959)
33 *Say it with flowers* (1960)
34 *Nodding canaries* (1961)
35 *My bones will keep* (1962)
36 *Adders on the heath* (1963)
37 *Death of a Delft blue* (1964)
38 *Pageant of murder* (1965)
39 *Croaking raven* (1966)
40 *Skeleton Island* (1967)
41 *Three quick and five dead* (1968)
42 *Dance to your Daddy* (1969)
43 *Gory dew* (1970)
44 *Lament for Leto* (1971)
45 *Hearse on May-Day* (1972)
46 *Murder of busy Lizzie* (1973)
47 *Javelin for Jonah* (1974)
48 *Winking at the brim* (1974)
49 *Convent on Styx* (1975)
50 *Late, late in the evening* (1976)
51 *Fault in the structure* (1977)
52 *Noonday and night* (1977)
53 *Wraiths and changelings* (1978)
54 *Mingled with venom* (1978)
55 *Nest of vipers* (1979)
56 *Mudflats of the dead* (1979)
57 *Uncoffin'd clay* (1980)
58 *Whispering knights* (1980)
59 *Death-cap dancers* (1981)
60 *Lovers, make moan* (1981)
61 *Here lies Gloria Mundy* (1982)
62 *Death of a borrowing mole* (1982)
63 *Greenstone griffins* (1983)
64 *Cold, lone and still* (1983)
65 *No winding-sheet* (1984)
66 *Crozier Pharaohs* (1984)

Damia series
McCaffrey, Anne
1 *Damia* (1991)
2 *Damia's children* (1993)
3 *Lyon's pride* (1994)

Damian McQuaid series
Rifkin, Shepard
1 *McQuaid* (1974)
2 *Snow rattlers* (1977)
3 *McQuaid in August* (1979)

Damiano Destrego trilogy
Macavoy, Roberta Ann
see **Lute trilogy**

Damiot series
McConnor, Vincent
see **Inspector Damiot series**

Damned series
Foster, Alan Dean
1 *Call to arms* (1991)
2 *False mirror* (1992)

Damon series
Conway, Troy
see **Coxeman series**

Damyo series
Morell, William
1 *Damyo* (1983)
2 *Damyo's revenge* (1984)

Dan and Grum series
Cockett, Mary
1 *Rolling on* (1960)
2 *Cottage by the lock* (1962)

Dan Banion series
Finnegan, Robert
1 *Lying ladies* (1946)
2 *Bandaged nude* (1946)
3 *Many a monster* (1948)

Dan Barry series
Brand, Max
1 *Untamed* (1919)
2 *Night horseman* (1920)
3 *Seventh man* (1921)
4 *Dan Barry's daughter* (1924)

Dan Brady series
Faulcon, Robert
see **Nighthunter series**

Dan Carter series
Wirt, Mildred Augustine
1 *Dan Carter, cub scout* (1949)
2 *Dan Carter and the river camp* (1949)
3 *Dan Carter and the money box* (1950)
4 *Dan Carter and the haunted castle* (1951)
5 *Dan Carter and the great carved face* (1952)
6 *Dan Carter and the cub honor* (1953)

Dan Cluer series
Ferguson, William Blair Morton
1 *Escape to destiny* (1944)
2 *Shayne case* (1947)

Dan Colt series
Hill, Morgan
1 *Twin colts* (1980)
2 *Quick and the deadly* (1980)
3 *Boot Hill brother* (1981)
4 *Ten must die* (1981)
5 *Bandits in blue* (1981)
6 *Midnight hangman* (1982)
7 *Last bullet* (1982)
8 *Dead man's noose* (1982)
9 *Last stage to Eternity* (1983)

Dan Connell series
Foxx, Jack
1 *Jade figurine* (1972)
2 *Dead run* (1975)

Dan Doner series
Shay, Frank
1 *Charming murder* (1930)
2 *Murder on Cape Cod* (1931)

Dan Durkin series
Chase, Arthur Minturn
see **Lieutenant Dan Durkin series**

Dan Fortune series
Collins, Michael
1 *Act of fear* (1967)
2 *Brass rainbow* (1969)
3 *Night of the toads* (1970)
4 *Walk a black wind* (1971)
5 *Shadow of a tiger* (1972)
6 *Silent scream* (1973)
7 *Blue death* (1975)
8 *Blood red dream* (1976)
9 *Nightrunners* (1978)
10 *Slasher* (1981)
11 *Freak* (1983)
12 *Minnesota Strip* (1987)
13 *Red Rosa* (1988)
14 *Castrato* (1989)
16 *Chasing eights* (1990)
17 *Irishman's horse* (1991)
18 *Cassandra in red* (1992)
19 *Crime, punishment, and resurrection* (1992)

Dan Fowler series
Eliot, George Fielding
see **G-men series**

Dan Gregory series
Jamieson, Leland
1 *Murder Island* (1935)
2 *G-men on Murder Island* (1947)

Dan Jordan series
Reed, Harlan
1 *Case of the crawling cockroach* (1937)
2 *Swing music murder* (1938)

Dan Kruger series
Cormany, Michael
1 *Lost daughter* (1988)
2 *Red winter* (1989)
3 *Rich or dead* (1990)
4 *Polaroid man* (1991)
5 *Skin deep is fatal* (1992)

Dan Lovett series
Arthur, Burt
1 *Nevada* (1949)
Trigger man
2 *Free lands* (1967)

Dan Mallett series
Parrish, Frank
1 *Fire in the barley* (1977)
2 *Sting of the honeybee* (1978)
3 *Snare in the dark* (1982)
4 *Bait on the hook* (1983)
5 *Face at the window* (1984)
Death in the rain
6 *Fly in the cobweb* (1986)
7 *Caught in the birdlime* (1987)
Bird in the net
8 *Voices from the dark* (1993)

Dan Matthews series
Wright, Harold Bell
1 *Shepherd of the hills* (1907)
2 *Calling of Dan Matthews* (1909)
3 *God and the groceryman* (1927)

Dan McCoy series
Bowden, Jim
1 *Return of the sheriff* (1960)
2 *Wayman's Ford* (1960)
3 *Two gun justice* (1961)
4 *Roaring Valley* (1962)
5 *Revenge in Red Springs* (1962)
6 *Black Water Canyon* (1963)
7 *Trail of revenge* (1964)
8 *Brazo feud* (1965)
9 *Guns along the Brazo* (1967)
10 *Gun loose* (1969)

Dan Morrison series
Shallit, Joseph
1 *Billion dollar body* (1947)
Case of the billion dollar body
2 *Lady, don't die on my doorstep* (1951)
3 *Yell bloody murder* (1951)
Yell ruddy murder
4 *Kiss the killer* (1952)
Juvenile moods

Dan Rhodes series
Crider, Bill
1 *Too late to die* (1986)
2 *Shotgun Saturday night* (1987)
3 *Cursed to death* (1988)
4 *Death on the move* (1989)
5 *Evil at the root* (1990)
6 *Blood marks* (1991)
7 *Booked for a hanging* (1992)
8 *Murder most fowl* (1994)

Dan series
Rosenbloom, Joseph
see **Deputy Dan series**

Dan Sleyter series
Murray, Earl
1 *Mountain sheriff* (1987)
2 *Lobo wolf* (1988)
3 *Canyon Mountain* (1988)
4 *Wild stallion* (1988)

Dan Storm quartet
Nelson, Lee
1 *Storm testament I* (1982)
2 *Storm testament II* (1983)
3 *Storm testament III* (1984)
4 *Storm testament IV* (1985)

Dan Track series
Ahern, Jerry
1 *Ninety-nine* (1984)
2 *Atrocity* (1984)
3 *Armageddon conspiracy* (1984)
4 *Hard way* (1984)
5 *Origin of a vendetta* (1985)
6 *Certain blood* (1985)
7 *Master of D.E.A.T.H.* (1985)
8 *Revenge of the master* (1985)
9 *D.E.A.T.H. hunters* (1985)
10 *Cocaine run* (1985)
11 *Ghost dancers* (1986)
12 *Drug runner* (1986)

Dan Valentine and Clarissa Lovelace series
Aldyne, Nathan
1 *Vermilion* (1980)
2 *Cobalt* (1982)
3 *Slate* (1984)
4 *Ivory* (1986)

Dana girls series
Keene, Carolyn
House pseudonym
1 *By the light of the study lamp* (1934) [McFarlane]
2 *In the shadow of the tower* (1934) [McFarlane]
3 *Secret at Lone Tree Cottage* (1934) [McFarlane]
4 *Three-cornered mystery* (1935) [McFarlane]
5 *Secret at the Hermitage* (1936)
6 *Circle of footprints* (1937)
7 *Mystery of the locked room* (1938)
8 *Clue in the cobweb* (1939)
9 *Secret at the gatehouse* (1940)
10 *Mysterious fireplace* (1941)
11 *Clue of the rusty key* (1942)
12 *Portrait in the sand* (1943)
13 *Secret in the old well* (1944)
14 *Clue in the ivy* (1952)
15 *Secret of the jade ring* (1953)
16 *Mystery at the crossroads* (1954)
17 *Ghost in the gallery* (1955)
Revised edition 1975
18 *Clue to the black flower* (1956)
19 *Winking ruby mystery* (1957)
Revised edition 1974
20 *Secret of the Swiss chalet* (1958)
Revised edition 1973
21 *Haunted lagoon* (1959)
Revised edition 1973
22 *Mystery of the bamboo bird* (1960)
Revised edition 1973
23 *Sierra gold mystery* (1961)
Revised edition 1973
24 *Secret of Lost Lake* (1963)
Revised edition 1974
25 *Mystery of the stone tiger* (1963)
Revised edition 1972
26 *Riddle of the frozen mountain* (1964)
Revised edition 1972
27 *Secret of the silver dolphin* (1965)
Revised edition 1972
28 *Mystery of the wax queen* (1966)
Revised edition 1972
29 *Secret of the minstrel's guitar* (1967)
Revised edition 1972
30 *Phantom surfer* (1968)
Revised edition 1972
31 *Curious coronation* (1976)
32 *Hundred-year mystery* (1977)
33 *Mountain-peak mystery* (1978)
34 *Witch's omen* (1979)

Danans trilogy
Taylor, Keith
1 *Sorcerers' sacred isle* (1989)
2 *Cauldron of plenty* (1989)
3 *Search for the starblade* (1990)

Danby series
Gard, Joyce
see **Mark Danby series**

Danby trilogy
Orwig, Sara
1 *San Antonio* (1989)
2 *Albuquerque* (1990)
3 *Denver* (1990)

Dance and Company series
Martin, Robert
1 *Mystery of the golden skulls* (1958)
2 *Mystery of the car bandits* (1958)
3 *Mystery of the friendly forger* (1958)
4 *Mystery of the long shadow* (1958)
5 *Mystery of the bullion robbery* (1960)
6 *Mystery of the TV crooks* (1960)
7 *Mystery of the motorway* (1961)
8 *Mystery of the poisoned puppet* (1962)
9 *Mystery of the pay-snatchers* (1963)
10 *Mystery of the missing passenger* (1964)

Dance of the gods series
Brenner, Mayer Alan
1 *Catastrophe's spell* (1989)
2 *Spell of intrigue* (1990)

Dance series
Kurten, Bjorn
Novels of the ice age
1 *Dance of the tiger* (1980)
Original edition entitled *Den svarta tigern*
2 *Singletusk* (1986)
Original edition entitled *Mammutens radare*

Dance to the music of time series
Powell, Anthony
1 *Question of upbringing* (1951)
2 *Buyer's market* (1952)
3 *Acceptance world* (1955)
Numbers 1-3 also published in one volume entitled *A dance to the music of time, first movement*, 1963
4 *At Lady Molly's* (1957)
5 *Casanova's Chinese restaurant* (1960)
6 *Kindly ones* (1962)
Numbers 4-6 also published in one volume entitled *A dance to the music of time, second movement*, 1964
7 *Valley of bones* (1964)
8 *Soldier's art* (1966)
9 *Military philosophers* (1968)
Numbers 7-9 also published in one volume entitled *A dance to the music of time, third movement*, 1971
10 *Books do furnish a room* (1971)
11 *Temporary kings* (1973)
12 *Hearing secret harmonies* (1975)
Numbers 10-12 also published in one volume entitled *A dance to the music of time, fourth movement*, 1976

Dancer series
Avallone, Michael
see **Girl from U.N.C.L.E. series**
Donleavy, James Patrick
see **Darcy Dancer series**

Dancer trilogy
Clayton, Jo
1 *Dancer's rise* (1993)
2 *Serpent waltz* (1994)
Number 3 not yet published

Dancer trilogy
Maxwell, Ann
1 *Fire dancer* (1982)
2 *Dancer's luck* (1983)
3 *Dancer's illusion* (1983)

Dancers at the end of time series
Moorcock, Michael
1 *Alien heat* (1972)

Dancers at the end of time series

2 *Hollow lands* (1974)
3 *End of all songs* (1976)
Numbers 1-3 also published in one volume entitled *The dancers at the end of time*, 1981
4 *Legends from the end of time* (1976)
5 *Transformation of Miss Mavis Ming* (1977)
Messiah at the end of time
Numbers 4 and 5 also published in one volume entitled *Tales from the end of time*, 1989

Companion volume: *The fireclown*, 1965, also published as *The winds of limbo*, 1969

Dancey series
Breeze, Paul
see **Billy Dancey series**

Dancing Gods series
Chalker, Jack Laurence
1 *River of Dancing Gods* (1984)
2 *Demons of the Dancing Gods* (1984)
3 *Vengeance of the Dancing Gods* (1985)
4 *Songs of the Dancing Gods* (1990)

Dancing meteorite series
Mason, Anne
1 *Dancing meteorite* (1984)
2 *Stolen law* (1986)

Dancy series
Hill, Lorna
see **Annette Dancy series**

Dandelion Cottage series
Rankin, Carroll Watson
1 *Dandelion Cottage* (1904)
2 *Girls of Gardenville* (1906)
3 *Adopting of Rosa Marie* (1908)
4 *Castaways of Pete's Patch* (1911)
5 *Girls of Highland Hall* (1921)

Dando series
Clive, William
see **Joseph Dando series**

Dandridge series
Denuziere, Maurice
see **Clarence Dandridge series**

Dandridge trilogy
Riefe, Barbara
1 *This ravaged heart* (1977)
2 *Far beyond desire* (1978)
3 *Fire and flesh* (1978)

Dane series
Ard, William
see **Timothy Dane series**
Dark, Rex
see **Bartholomew Dane series**

Dane Thorson series
Norton, Andre
1 *Sargasso of space* (1955)
Originally published under the pseudonym Andrew North
2 *Plague ship* (1956)
Originally published under the pseudonym Andrew North
3 *Voodoo planet* (1959)
Originally published under the pseudonym Andrew North
4 *Postmarked the stars* (1969)

Daneswood series
Matthewman, Phyllis
1 *Chloe takes control* (1940)
2 *Queerness of Rusty* (1941)
3 *Josie moves up* (1943)
4 *New role for Natasha* (1945)
5 *Justice for Jacqueline* (1946)
6 *Pat at the helm* (1948)
7 *Intrusion of Nicola* (1948)

Danforth series
Jackson, Marian J A
see **Miss Abigail Patience Danforth series**

Danger on the river trilogy
Janes, Joseph Robert
1 *Danger on the river* (1982)
2 *Spies for dinner* (1984)
3 *Murder in the market* (1985)

Danger zones series
Berry, Joy
1 *Abuse and neglect* (1984)
2 *Kidnapping* (1984)
3 *Sexual abuse* (1984)

Dangerfield series
Franklin, Charles
see **Maxine Dangerfield series**
Lloyd, Jeremy
see **Captain Gregory Dangerfield series**

Dangerman series
This sequence is by Wilfred McNeilly using his own name and three pseudonyms; based on a television series
Baker, William Howard
1 *Departure deferred* (1965)
2 *Storm over Rocktail* (1965)
Leslie, Peter
3 *Hell for tomorrow* (1965)
Ballinger, W A
4 *Exterminator* (1966)
McNeilly, Wilfred
5 *No way out* (1966)
Companion volume: *Target for tonight*, by Richard Telfair, 1962

Dangerous and deadly series
Vaughan, Marcia
1 *Dangerous and deadly Australian snakes* (1990)
2 *Dangerous and deadly Australian spiders* (1990)
3 *Dangerous and deadly Australian sea life* (1990)
4 *Dangerous and deadly Australian crocodiles* (1990)
5 *Dangerous and deadly Australian insects* (1990)
6 *Dangerous and deadly Australian plants* (1990)

Dangerous Davies series
Thomas, Leslie
1 *Dangerous Davies, the last detective* (1976)
2 *Dangerous in love* (1987)

Dangerous thoughts series
Finnegan, Robert
Essays on social and political subjects
1 *Dangerous thoughts* (1940)
2 *More dangerous thoughts* (1941)

Daniel Boone and Simon Kenton series
Ellis, Edward Sylvester
1 *Shod with silence* (1896)
2 *Phantom of the river* (1896)
3 *In the days of the pioneers* (1897)

Daniel Cullen series
Thomson, David Robert Alexander
1 *Daniel* (1962)
2 *Break in the sun* (1965)

Daniel Deronda series
Eliot, George
1 *Daniel Deronda* (1876)
Sequence continued by an anonymous author
Anonymous
2 *Gwendolen* (1878)

Daniel Kearney Associates series
Gores, Joe
see **DKA file series**

Daniel Keel series
Schock, T A
1 *Pratfall* (1981)
2 *Deadpan* (1981)
3 *Stopgap* (1981)

Daniel Kerr series
Orde, Lewis
1 *Lion's way* (1981)
2 *Lion's progress* (1987)

Daniel Kerry series
Rohmer, Sax
see **Red Kerry series**

Daniel Lacey series
Stall, Mike
1 *Killing mask* (1982)
2 *Wet job* (1982)

Daniel Port series
Rabe, Peter
1 *Dig my grave deep* (1956)
2 *It's my funeral* (1957)
3 *Out is death* (1957)
4 *Bring me another corpse* (1959)
5 *Time enough to die* (1959)

Daniel Rider series
Maguire, Gregory
1 *Lightning time* (1978)
2 *Lights on the lake* (1981)

Daniel series
Sandberg, Inger
Illustrated by Lasse Sandberg
1 *Daniel and the coconut cakes* (1968)
Original edition entitled *Mathias bakor kakor*
2 *Daniel's mysterious monster* (1968)
Original edition entitled *Mathias och trollet*
3 *Daniel's helping hand* (1969)
Original edition entitled *Mathias hjalper till*
4 *Daniel paints a picture* (1969)
Original edition entitled *Mathias maler en*

Daniel Skipton trilogy
Johnson, Pamela Hansford
1 *Unspeakable Skipton* (1959)
2 *Night and silence, who is here?* (1963)
An American comedy
3 *Cork Street, next to the hatters* (1965)
A novel in bad taste

Daniel Tremain series
Dengler, Sandy
1 *Socorro Island treasure* (1983)
2 *Chain five mystery* (1984)

Daniel Webster Coffee series
Blochman, Lawrence Goldtree
see **Doctor Daniel Webster Coffee series**

Daniel Webster series
Sale, Richard
1 *Lazarus number seven* (1942)
Death looks in
Lazarus murder seven
2 *Passing strange* (1942)
3 *Benefit performance* (1946)

Daniel Winter series
Telushkin, Joseph
see **Rabbi Daniel Winter series**

Daniels series
Baxter, Gregory
see **Superintendent Daniels series**
Melville, Jennie
see **Sergeant Charmian Daniels series**
Smith, Terence Lore
see **Webster Daniels series**
Stanley, George Edward
see **Doctor Constance Daniels series**
Tolles, Martha
see **Darci Daniels series**

Dann Carr series
Smith, Willard K
see **Inspector Dann Carr series**

Danning series
Von Elsner, Don
see **David Danning series**

Dannus series
Sirota, Mike
1 *Prisoner of Reglathium* (1978)
2 *Conquerors of Reglathium* (1978)
3 *Caves of Reglathium* (1978)
4 *Dark straits of Reglathium* (1978)
5 *Slaves of Reglathium* (1978)

Danny and Carly series
Holmes, Marjorie
see **Carly and Danny series**

Danny and David Delaney series
Patchett, Mary Elwyn
1 *Summer on Wild Horse Island* (1965)
2 *Summer on Boomerang Ranch* (1967)

Danny and Jack Kachiah series
Lesley, Craig
1 *Winterkill* (1984)
2 *River song* (1989)

Danny Black and Johnny Wild series
Carter, Bruce
1 *Perilous descent into a strange lost world* (1952)
Into a strange lost world
2 *Speed six!* (1953)

Danny Boyd series
Brown, Carter
1 *So deadly sinner* (1959)
Walk softly, witch
2 *Suddenly by violence* (1959)
3 *Terror comes creeping* (1959)
4 *Wayward wahine* (1960)
Wayward
5 *Dream is deadly* (1960)
6 *Savage Salome* (1961)
Rewritten from *Murder is my mistress*, 1954
7 *Seductress* (1961)
Sad-eyed seductress
8 *Ice-cold nude* (1962)
9 *Lover, don't come back!* (1962)
10 *Nymph to the slaughter* (1963)
11 *Passionate pagan* (1963)
12 *Silken nightmare* (1963)
13 *Catch me a phoenix!* (1965)
14 *Sometime wife* (1965)
15 *Black lace hangover* (1966)
16 *House of sorcery* (1967)
17 *Mini-murders* (1968)
18 *Murder is the message* (1969)
19 *Only the very rich?* (1969)
20 *Coffin bird* (1970)
21 *Sex clinic* (1971)
22 *Angry Amazons* (1972)
23 *Manhattan cowboy* (1973)
24 *So move the body* (1973)
25 *Early Boyd* (1975)
26 *Savage sisters* (1976)
27 *Pipes are calling* (1976)
28 *Rip-off* (1979)
29 *Strawberry blonde jungle* (1979)
30 *Death to a downbeat* (1980)
31 *Kiss Michelle goodbye* (1981)
32 *Real Boyd* (1984)

Danny Deck series
McMurtry, Larry
1 *All my friends are going to be strangers* (1972)
2 *Some can whistle* (1989)

Danny Dunn series
Williams, Jay
1 *Danny Dunn and the anti-gravity paint* (1956)
2 *Danny Dunn on a desert island* (1957)
3 *Danny Dunn and the homework machine* (1958)
Homework machine
4 *Danny Dunn and the weather machine* (1959)
5 *Danny Dunn on the ocean floor* (1960)
6 *Danny Dunn and the fossil cave* (1961)
7 *Danny Dunn and the heat ray* (1962)
8 *Danny Dunn, time traveller* (1963)
9 *Danny Dunn and the automatic house* (1967)
10 *Danny Dunn and the voice from space* (1967)
11 *Danny Dunn and the smallifying machine* (1969)
12 *Danny Dunn and the swamp monster* (1971)
13 *Danny Dunn, invisible boy* (1974)
14 *Danny Dunn, scientific detective* (1976)
15 *Danny Dunn and the universal glue* (1977)

Danny Fists trilogy
Camp, Walter Chauncey
1 *Danny Fists* (1913)
2 *Captain Danny* (1914)
3 *Danny the freshman* (1915)

Danny Fontaine series
Ard, William
1 *As bad as I am* (1959)
Wanted, Dany Fontaine
2 *When she was bad* (1960)

Danny Fox series
Thomson, David Robert Alexander
1 *Danny Fox* (1966)
2 *Danny Fox meets a stranger* (1968)
3 *Danny Fox at the palace* (1976)

Danny Leather series
Lawrence, David
1 *Dead orchid* (1958)
2 *Death has two hands* (1958)

Danny Levine series
Handler, David
1 *Kiddo* (1987)
2 *Boss* (1988)

Danny One series
Slote, Alfred
1 *My robot buddy* (1975)
2 *My trip to Alpha I* (1978)
3 *C.O.L.A.R.* (1981)
A tale of outer space
4 *Omega Station* (1983)
5 *Trouble on Janus* (1985)

Danny O'Neill series
Farrell, James Thomas
1 *Face of time* (1953)
2 *World I never made* (1936)
3 *No star is lost* (1938)
4 *Father and son* (1940)
5 *My days of anger* (1943)

Danny Orlis series
Palmer, Bernard
1 *Danny Orlis and the Point Barrow mystery* (1954)
2 *Danny Orlis and the Angle Inlet mystery* (1954)
3 *Danny Orlis and the strange forest fire* (1955)
4 *Danny Orlis and the hunters* (1955)
5 *Danny Orlis goes to school* (1955)
6 *Danny Orlis and the rocks that talk* (1955)
7 *Danny Orlis on Superstition Mountain* (1956)
8 *Danny Orlis makes the team* (1956)
9 *Danny Orlis changes schools* (1956)
10 *Danny Orlis and the wrecked plane* (1956)
11 *Danny Orlis and the big Indian* (1956)
12 *Danny Orlis and the sacred cave* (1957)
13 *Danny Orlis, star back* (1957)
14 *Danny Orlis and the boy who would not listen* (1957)
15 *Danny Orlis plays hockey* (1957)
16 *Danny Orlis and his big chance* (1958)
17 *Danny Orlis and the contrary Mrs Forester* (1958)
18 *Danny orlis and the man from the past* (1959)
19 *Danny Orlis, big brother* (1959)
20 *Danny Orlis on the Valiant* (1959)
21 *Danny Orlis and Marilyn's great trial* (1959)
22 *Danny Orlis and the mystery of the sunken ship* (1960)
23 *Danny Orlis and Ron Orlis in the Canadian wilderness* (1960)
24 *Danny Orlis in the mysterious Zanderland* (1960)
25 *Danny Orlis and the time of testing* (1961)
26 *Danny Orlis, bush pilot* (1961)
27 *Danny Orlis and Hal's great victory* (1962)
28 *Danny Orlis and the drug story mystery* (1962)
29 *Danny Orlis and Ron's call to service* (1963)
30 *Danny Orlis and the headstrong Linda Penner* (1963)
31 *Danny Orlis and the ordeal at camp* (1963)
32 *Danny Orlis and Linda's struggle* (1964)
33 *Danny Orlis and the ice fishing escapade* (1964)
34 *Danny Orlis and Linda's new mother* (1965)
35 *Danny Orlis and Ron in the Mexican jungle mystery* (1965)
36 *Danny Orlis and the defiant Kent Gilbert* (1965)
37 *Danny Orlis and Robin's big battle* (1965)
38 *Danny Orlis and the old mine mystery* (1966)
39 *Danny Orlis and Kent's encounter with law* (1966)
40 *Danny orlis and Robin's rebellion* (1966)
41 *Danny Orlis and Robin's big mistake* (1966)
42 *Danny Orlis and Jim's northern adventure* (1967)
43 *Danny Orlis and Kent Gilbert's tragedy* (1967)
44 *Danny Orlis and the teen-age marriage* (1967)
45 *Danny Orlis and the Guatemala adventure* (1967)
46 *Danny Orlis and Fritz McCloud, high school star* (1968)
47 *Danny Orlis and excitement at the Circle R* (1968)
48 *Danny Orlis and Jim Morgan's scholarship* (1968)
49 *Danny Orlis and trouble on the Circle R Ranch* (1968)
50 *Danny Orlis and the accident that shook Fairview* (1968)
51 *Danny Orlis, bid for victory* (1969)
52 *Danny Orlis and the dry gulch mystery* (1969)
53 *Danny Orlis and Johnny's new life* (1969)
54 *Danny Orlis and DeeDee's defiance* (1970)
55 *Danny Orlis and DeeDee's best friend* (1970)
56 *Danny Orlis and the football feud* (1971)
57 *Danny Orlis and the crisis at Cedarton* (1971)
58 *Danny Orlis and the bewildered runaway* (1971)
59 *Danny Orlis and the Mexican kidnapping* (1971)
60 *Danny Orlis and the Canadian caper* (1972)
61 *Danny Orlis and the Alaskan Highway adventure* (1972)
62 *Danny Orlis forced down* (1972)
63 *Danny Orlis and the live-in tragedy* (1972)
64 *Danny Orlis and the Colorado challenge* (1972)
65 *Danny Orlis and Doug's big disappointment* (1973)
66 *Danny Orlis and the ski slope emergency* (1973)
67 *Danny Orlis and the mystery at Northwest High* (1973)
68 *Danny Orlis and the girl who dared* (1974)
69 *Danny Orlis and the mysterious intruder* (1974)
70 *Danny Orlis and the Rock Point rebel* (1974)
71 *Danny Orlis and the model plane mystery* (1975)

Danny Saunders and Reuven Malter series
Potok, Chaim
1 *Chosen* (1966)
2 *Promise* (1969)

Danny Scipio series
Gates, Tudor
see **Vendetta series**

Danny series
Kunhardt, Edith
1 *Danny's birthday* (1986)
2 *Danny's mystery valentine!* (1987)
3 *Trick or treat, Danny?* (1988)
4 *Danny and the Easter egg* (1989)
5 *Danny's Christmas star* (1989)

Danny Smiricky series
Skvorecky, Josef
1 *Cowards* (1958)
Original edition entitled *Zbabelci*
2 *[Tankovy propor]* (1971)
No English edition
3 *Miracle game* (1972)
Original edition entitled *Mirakl*
4 *Bass saxophone* (1979)
A memoir entitled *Red music* and two novellas entitled *Bass saxophone*, and *Emoke*, originally published separately as *Legenda Emoke*, 1963
5 *Engineer of human souls* (1977)
Original edition entitled *Pribeh inzenyra lidskych dusi*; an entertainment on the old themes of life, women, fate, dreams, the working class, secret agents, love and death

Danny Spade series
Some volumes in this sequence are published under the author's real name Dail Ambler and some under the pseudonym Danny Spade
Spade, Danny
1 *Dame plays rough* (1950)
2 *You slay me* (1950)
3 *'Frisco Rock* (1951)
4 *Silk and cordite* (1951)
5 *Lady holds a gun* (1951)
6 *Waterfront rat* (1951)
7 *Move fast, brother* (1951)
8 *You'll play this my way* (1951)
9 *San Francisco by night* (1951)
10 *Don't die on me* (1951)
11 *So deep the river* (1951)
12 *Spades are trumps* (1951)
13 *Gun for sale* (1952)
Ambler, Dail
14 *Wildcat* (1952)
15 *Not killed, just dead* (1952)
Spade, Danny
16 *Dial death* (1952)
17 *Shadow of a gun* (1952)
18 *Dragnet* (1952)
19 *No more chances* (1952)
20 *Strong arm stuff* (1952)
21 *Hi-jack* (1952)
22 *Skid Row* (1952)
Ambler, Dail
23 *Duet for two guns* (1952)
Spade, Danny
24 *Calling Mr Spade* (1952)
Ambler, Dail
25 *Hold that tiger* (1952)
26 *Lady says when* (1952)
27 *What's with you* (1952)
Spade, Danny
28 *Twice as dead* (1952)
Ambler, Dail
29 *Johnny gets his* (1952)
Spade, Danny
30 *Kiss me as you go* (1953)
31 *Story of a killer* (1953)
32 *Lady likes to sin* (1953)
33 *Nothing to hide* (1953)
34 *That's all I need* (1953)
Ambler, Dail
35 *Danny Spade spells danger* (1953)
36 *Someone falling* (1954)
37 *Curtain of glass* (1954)
38 *Danny Spade sees red* (1954)
39 *Virgin collector* (1971)
40 *Three men for the job* (1975)

Danny the detective series
Barclay, Vera Charlesworth
1 *Danny the detective* (1918)
A story for Wolf Cubs
2 *Danny again* (1920)
3 *Danny's pack* (1928)
4 *Danny and the rattlesnakes* (1930)
Yarns for Scouts and Cubs

Danov family trilogy
Troyat, Henri
1 *My father's house* (1947)
Original edition entitled *Tant que la terre durera*
2 *Sackcloth and ashes* (1948)
Red and the white
Original edition entitled *Le sac et la cendre*
3 *Strangers in the land* (1950)
Strangers on earth
Original edition entitled *Etrangers sur la terre*

Dante series
Newman, Christopher
see **Joe Dante series**

Danvers family series
Cholmondeley, Mary
1 *Danvers jewels* (1887)
2 *Sir Charles Danvers* (1889)

Danvers series
Grinnell, George Bird
see **Jack Danvers series**
Wilde, Jennifer
see **Marietta Danvers series**

Danzig trilogy
Grass, Gunter
1 *Tin drum* (1959)
Original edition entitled *Die Blechtrommel*

Danzig trilogy

2 *Cat and mouse* (1961)
Original edition entitled *Katz und Maus*
3 *Dog years* (1963)
Original edition entitled *Hundejarre*
Companion volumes: *The flounder*, 1977, original edition entitled *Der Butt*, and, *The rat*, 1986, original edition entitled *Die Rattin*; one volume edition entitled *The Danzig trilogy*, 1987

Daphne Bruno series
Raymond, Ernest
1 *Daphne Bruno* (1925)
2 *Fulfilment of Daphne Bruno* (1926)

Daphne series
Topham, Anne
1 *Daphne in the Fatherland* (1912)
2 *Daphne in Paris* (1913)

Daphne Wrayne and her Four Adjusters series
Valentine
1 *Adjusters* (1930)
Three novelettes; sequence continued under the pseudonym Mark Cross
Cross, Mark
2 *Shadow of the Four* (1934)
3 *Grip of the Four* (1934)
4 *Hand of the Four* (1935)
5 *Way of the Four* (1936)
6 *Mark of the Four* (1936)
7 *Four strike home* (1937)
8 *Surprise for the Four* (1937)
9 *Four make holiday* (1938)
10 *Four get going* (1938)
11 *Challenge to the Four* (1939)
12 *Four at bay* (1939)
13 *It couldn't be murder* (1940)
14 *Find the professor* (1940)
15 *Murder in the pool* (1941)
16 *How was it done?* (1941)
17 *Mystery of Gruden's Gap* (1942)
18 *Green circle* (1942)
19 *Murder as arranged* (1943)
20 *Murder in the air* (1943)
21 *Murder in black* (1944)
22 *Mystery of Joan Marryat* (1945)
23 *Secret of the Grange* (1946)
24 *Strange affair at Graylands* (1948)
25 *Other than natural causes* (1949)
26 *Missing from his home* (1949)
27 *On the night of the 14th* (1950)
28 *Who killed Henry Wickenston?* (1951)
29 *Jaws of darkness* (1952)
30 *Black spider* (1953)
31 *Circle of freedom* (1953)
32 *Murder will speak* (1954)
33 *Strange case of Pamela Wilson* (1954)
34 *In the dead of night* (1955)
35 *Best laid schemes* (1955)
36 *When thieves fall out* (1956)
37 *Mystery of the corded box* (1956)
38 *Desperate steps* (1957)
39 *Over thin ice* (1958)
40 *Foul deeds will rise* (1958)
41 *When danger threatens* (1959)
42 *Not long to live* (1959)
43 *Third time unlucky* (1959)
44 *Wanted for questioning* (1960)
45 *Once too often* (1960)
46 *Once upon a time* (1961)
47 *Perilous hazard* (1961)

Da Polga series
Bond, Michael
see **Olga da Polga series**

Darblay series
Hardwick, Michael
see **Juliet Bravo series**

Darby Castle series
Michaels, Jan
1 *Sing a song of murder* (1978)
2 *Death on the Late Show* (1979)

Darby Prescott series
Wisler, Gary Clifton
1 *Illinois Prescott* (1987)
2 *Prescott's trail* (1989)
3 *Prescott's law* (1990)
4 *Prescott's challenge* (1990)

Darby series
Aresbys
see **Parrish Darby series**

Darci Daniels series
Tolles, Martha
1 *Darci and the dance contest* (1985)
2 *Darci in Cabin Thirteen* (1989)

Darcy Dancer series
Donleavy, James Patrick
1 *Destinies of Darcy Dancer, gentleman* (1977)
2 *Leila* (1983)

Darcy family trilogy
Park, Ruth
1 *Missus* (1985)
2 *Harp in the south* (1948)
3 *Poor man's orange* (1949)
Twelve and a half Plymouth Street

D'Arcy Oliveres series
Foster, David
1 *Dog Rock* (1985)
A postal pastoral
2 *Pale blue crochet coathanger* (1988)

Darcy series
Garrett, Randall
see **Lord Darcy series**
Goldin, Stephen
see **Rehumanization of Jade Darcy series**

Dare boys series
Cox, Stephen Angus
1 *Dare boys of 1776* (1910)
2 *Dare boys on the Hudson* (1910)
3 *Dare boys in Trenton* (1910)
4 *Dare boys on the Brandywine* (1910)
5 *Dare boys in the Red City* (1910)
6 *Dare boys after Benedict Arnold* (1910)
7 *Dare boys in Virginia* (1910)
8 *Dar boys with General Greene* (1910)
9 *Dare boys with Lafayette* (1910)
10 *Dare boys with the Swamp Fox* (1910)
11 *Dare boys at Vincennes* (1911)
12 *Dare boys in the North West* (1912)

Dare series
Brooks, Amy
see **Rosalie Dare series**
Eberhart, Mignon Good
see **Susan Dare series**
Lloyd, Hugh
see **Skippy Dare series**
Marshall, Archibald
see **Anthony Dare series**

Darenga trilogy
Mezo, Francine
see **Areia Darenga trilogy**

Darewell chums series
Chapman, Allen
1 *Darewell chums* (1908)
Alternative title: The heroes of the school
2 *Darewell chums in the city* (1908)
Alternative title: The disappearance of Nat Wilding
3 *Darewell chums in the woods* (1908)
Alternative title: Frank Roscoe's secret
4 *Darewell chums on a cruise* (1909)
Alternative title: Fenn Masterson's odd discovery
5 *Darewell chums in a winter camp* (1911)
Alternative title: Bart Keene's best shot

Darina Lisle series
Laurence, Janet
1 *Deepe coffyn* (1989)
2 *Tasty way to die* (1990)
3 *Hotel Morgue* (1991)
4 *Recipe for death* (1992)
5 *Death and the epicure* (1993)

Daring twins series
Baum, Lyman Frank
1 *Daring twins* (1911)
2 *Phoebe Daring* (1913)

Dark Ages series
Herbert, Kathleen
see **Cumbrian series**

Dark angel series
Graham, Jean
1 *Dark angel* (1977)
2 *Dark lord* (1980)

Dark border series
Zimmer, Paul Edwin
1 *Lost prince* (1982)
2 *King Chondos' ride* (1982)
3 *Gathering of heroes* (1987)

Dark castle series
Lee, Tanith
see **Castle of dark series**

Dark conspiracy series
Stackpole, Michael
1 *Gathering evil* (1991)
2 *Evil ascending* (1991)

Dark descent trilogy
Hartwell, David Geddes
1 *Colour of evil* (1990)
Color of evil
2 *Medusa in the shield* (1990)
3 *Fabulous, formless darkness* (1990)
One volume edition entitled *Dark descent* 1987

Dark elf trilogy
Salvatore, Robert Anthony
1 *Homeland* (1990)
2 *Exile* (1990)
3 *Sojourn* (1991)

Dark forces series
This sequence has nine authors
Logan, Les
1 *Game* (1983)
Bridges, Laurie
2 *Magic show* (1983)
Sparger, Rex
3 *Doll* (1983)
Bridges, Laurie
4 *Devil wind* (1983)
Sparger, Rex
5 *Bargain* (1983)
Bridges, Laurie
6 *Swamp witch* (1983)
Logan, Les
7 *Unnatural talent* (1983)
Siegel, Scott
8 *Companion* (1983)
Coville, Bruce
9 *Eyes of the tarot* (1983)
Siegel, Scott
10 *Beat the devil* (1983)
Coville, Bruce
11 *Waiting spirits* (1984)
Bridges, Laurie
12 *Ashton horror* (1984)
Weinberg, Larry
13 *Curse* (1984)
Scott, R C
14 *Blood sport* (1984)
Polcovar, Jane
15 *Charming* (1984)

Dark future series
This sequence has three authors
Yeovil, Jack
1 *Demon download* (1990)
2 *Krokodil tears* (1991)
3 *Comeback tour* (1991)
Alternative title: The sky belongs to the stars
Pringle, David
4 *Route 666* (1990)
Craig, Brian
5 *Ghost dancers* (1991)

Dark gate series
Jakes, John
see **Gavin Black series**

Dark Harbor series
Ross, Clarissa
1 *Ghost of Dark Harbor* (1974)
2 *Hearse for Dark Harbor* (1974)
3 *Dark Harbor hunting* (1975)
4 *Evil of Dark Harbor* (1975)
5 *Terror at Dark Harbor* (1975)

Dark hills trilogy
Stuart, Jesse
1 *Beyond dark hills* (1938)
2 *Thread that runs so true* (1949)
3 *Year of my rebirth* (1956)

Dark horse series
Herbert, Mary H
1 *Dark horse* (1990)
2 *Lightning's daughter* (1991)
3 *Valorian* (1993)

Dark is rising series
Cooper, Susan Mary
1 *Over sea, under stone* (1965)
2 *Dark is rising* (1973)
3 *Greenwitch* (1974)
4 *Grey king* (1975)
5 *Silver on the tree* (1977)
One volume edition entitled *The dark is rising sequence*, 1984

Dark Knight series
Smith, Ford
1 *Jarrum Creek Gang* (1952)
2 *Mystery at Calico Pass* (1952)
3 *Oklahoma gun-song* (1955)
4 *Guntrap Trail* (1955)

Dark pool series
Rienow, Leona Train
1 *Bewitched caverns* (1948)
2 *Dark pool* (1949)

Dark river series
Millin, Sarah Gertrude
1 *Dark river* (1919)
2 *Middle-class* (1921)
3 *Adam's rest* (1922)
4 *Jordans* (1923)

Dark series
Cheyney, Peter
see **Secret service series**

Dark shadows series
Ross, Marilyn
see **Barnabas Collins series**

Dark tower trilogy
King, Stephen
1 *Gunslinger* (1982)
2 *Drawing of the three* (1987)
3 *Waste lands* (1991)

Darkangel trilogy
Pierce, Meredith Ann
see **Aeriel trilogy**

Darkest America series
Barrett, Neal
1 *Through darkest America* (1986)
2 *Dawn's uncertain light* (1989)

Darkman series
Boyll, Randall
1 *Darkman* (1990)
2 *Chiller* (1992)

Darkness and dawn series
England, George Allen
1 *Darkness and dawn* (1964)
2 *Beyond the great oblivion* (1965)
3 *People of the abyss* (1966)
4 *Out of the abyss* (1967)
5 *Afterglow* (1967)
One volume edition entitled *Darkness and dawn*, 1914

Darkness series
Peretti, Frank E
1 *This present darkness* (1986)
2 *Piercing the darkness* (1989)

Darkover anthologies series
Bradley, Marion Zimmer
Written in collaboration with the Friends of Darkover
1 *Keeper's price, and other stories* (1980)
2 *Sword of chaos, and other stories* (1982)
3 *Other side of the mirror, and other Darkover stories* (1987)
4 *Red sun of Darkover* (1987)
5 *Four moons of Darkover* (1988)
6 *Domains of Darkover* (1990)
7 *Renunciates of Darkover* (1991)
8 *Leroni of Darkover* (1991)

Darkover series
Bradley, Marion Zimmer
1 *Stormqueen!* (1978)
2 *Two to conquer* (1980)
3 *Hawkmistress!* (1982)
4 *Darkover landfall* (1972)
5 *Spell sword* (1974)
6 *Forbidden tower* (1977)
7 *Shattered chain* (1976)
8 *Thendara House* (1983)
Numbers 7 and 8 also published in one volume entitled *Oath of the renunciates*, 1984
9 *City of sorcery* (1984)
10 *Star of danger* (1965)
11 *Winds of Darkover* (1970)
12 *Bloody sun* (1964)
Revised edition, including the short story *To keep the oath*, 1979
13 *Heritage of Hastur* (1975)
14 *Sharra's exile* (1981)
Numbers 13 and 14 also published in one volume entitled *Children of Hastur*, 1982
15 *Sword of Aldones* (1962)
16 *Planet savers* (1962)
Numbers 15 and 16 originally published in one volume
17 *World wreckers* (1971)
18 *Heirs of Hammerfell* (1989)

Darksword trilogy
Weis, Margaret
1 *Forging the Darksword* (1988)
2 *Doom of the Darksword* (1988)
3 *Triumph of the Darksword* (1988)
One volume edition entitled *The Darksword trilogy*, 1989

Darkwar trilogy
Cook, Glen
1 *Doomstalker* (1985)
2 *Warlock* (1985)
3 *Ceremony* (1986)

Darkworld detective series
This sequence has two authors
Reaves, Michael
1 *Darkworld detective* (1982)
Shirley, John
2 *Kamus of Kadizhar* (1988)
Alternative title: Black hole of Carcosa

Darkworld legends series
Bloomfield, Frena
1 *Dragon paths* (1973)
2 *Sky fleet of Atlantis* (1979)

Darling and Doolin series
Cookson, Catherine
see **Matty Doolin and Joe Darling series**

Darling and Fane series
Yardley, James
see **Kiss Darling and Angus Fane series**

Darling and Laurance series
Hart, Carolyn Gimpel
see **Annie Laurance and Max Darling series**

Darling series
Austin, Jane Goodwin
see **Dora Darling series**

D'Armond series
Stasheff, Christopher
see **Gramarye series**

Darn Cat Randall series
Gordons
see **Undercover Cat series**

Darnley Mills Railway series
Turner, Philip
1 *Steam on the line* (1968)
2 *Devil's Nob* (1970)
3 *Powder Quay* (1971)

Darnley Mills series
Turner, Philip
1 *Colonel Shepparton's clock* (1964)
Mystery of the colonel's clock
2 *Grange at High Force* (1965)
Adventure at High Force
3 *Sea Peril* (1966)
4 *War on the Darnel* (1969)
5 *Dunkirk summer* (1973)
6 *Skull Island* (1977)

Darren series
Lenton, Anthony
see **Graham Darren series**

Darrin series
Hancock, Harrie Irving
see **Dave Darrin series**

Darroch series
Mackinnon, Allan
see **Mike Darroch series**

Darrow series
White, Stewart Edward
see **Percy Darrow series**
Wirt, Mildred Augustine
see **Ruth Darrow series**

Darryl Krustov series
Keast, Francis
1 *Sunburst* (1984)
2 *Cloudburst* (1986)

D'Artagnon and Cyrano de Bergerac series
Feval, Paul
see **Years between series**

Dartanian series
Rainey, Rich
see **Alex Dartanian series**

Dartley series
Barclay, Ian
see **Richard Dartley series**

Dartmoor series
Phillpotts, Eden
1 *Children of the mist* (1898)
2 *Children of men* (1921)

Dartmoor trilogy
Trevena, John
1 *Furze the cruel* (1907)
2 *Heather* (1908)
3 *Granite* (1909)

Darwath trilogy
Hambly, Barbara
1 *Time of the dark* (1982)
2 *Walls of air* (1983)
3 *Armies of daylight* (1983)

Daryl series
Wilkinson, Laurence
see **Mike Daryl series**

Darzek series
Biggle, Lloyd
see **Jan Darzek series**

Dash and Dot series
West, Dorothy
see **Dot and Dash series**

Dashaway series
Brady, Cyrus Townsend
see **Bob Dashaway series**
Rockwood, Roy
see **Dave Dashaway series**

Dashwood family series
Rudd, Steele
1 *On an Australian farm* (1910)
2 *Dashwoods* (1911)

Dashwood series
Austen, Jane
see **Margaret Dashwood series**

Da Silva series
Beck, Kathrine Kristine
see **Jane Da Silva series**
Fish, Robert Lloyd
see **Captain Jose da Silva series**

Da Silva series
Harris, Wilson
1 *Da Silva Da Silva's cultivated wilderness* (1977)
2 *Tree of the sun* (1978)

Daughter of Tintagel series
Sampson, Fay
1 *Wise woman's telling* (1989)
2 *White nun's telling* (1989)
3 *Black Smith's telling* (1990)
4 *Taliesin's telling* (1991)
5 *Herself* (1991)
One volume edition entitled *Daughter of Tintagel omnibus*, 1992

Daughter series
Mahmoody, Betty
1 *Not without my daughter* (1987)
2 *For the love of a child* (1992)

Daughter series
Mayor, Flora Macdonald
1 *Rector's daughter* (1924)
2 *Squire's daughter* (1929)

Daughters of Cameron series
Malcolm, Aleen
1 *Taming* (1979)
2 *Ride out the storm* (1981)
3 *Daughters of Cameron* (1983)

Daughters of England series
Carr, Philippa
1 *Miracle of Saint Bruno's* (1972)
2 *Lion triumphant* (1974)
3 *Witch from the sea* (1975)
4 *Saraband for two sisters* (1976)
5 *Lament for a lost lover* (1977)
6 *Love-child* (1978)
7 *Song of the siren* (1980)
8 *Drop of the dice* (1981)
Will you love me in September?
9 *Adulteress* (1982)
10 *Zipporah's daughter* (1983)
Knave of hearts
11 *Voices in a haunted room* (1984)
12 *Return of the gypsy* (1985)
13 *Midsummer's eve* (1986)
14 *Pool of Saint Brunok* (1987)
15 *Changeling* (1989)

Daughters series
Vandergriff, Aola
1 *Daughters of the Southwind* (1977)
2 *Daughters of the wild country* (1978)
3 *Daughters of the far islands* (1979)
4 *Daughters of the opal skies* (1980)
5 *Daughters of the misty isles* (1981)
6 *Daughters of the shining city* (1982)
7 *Daughters of the storm* (1983)
8 *Daughters of the silver screen* (1984)

Dauntless series
Dawlish, Peter
1 *Dauntless finds her crew* (1947)
2 *Dauntless sails again* (1948)
Dauntless and the smugglers
3 *Dauntless and the Mary Baines* (1949)
Dauntless and the wreck of the Mary Baines
4 *Dauntless takes recruits* (1950)
Dauntless and the Poplar pirates
5 *Dauntless sails in* (1952)
6 *Dauntless in danger* (1954)
7 *Dauntless goes home* (1960)

Dave and Sam series
Singer, Marilyn
see **Sam and Dave series**

Dave Bolt series
Curtis, Richard
1 *Three million dollar turn-over* (1974)
2 *Death in the crease* (1975)
3 *Strike zone* (1975)
4 *Suicide squad* (1975)

Dave Bourne series
Leach, Christopher
1 *Tomorrow in Atlantis* (1972)
2 *Temporary open air life* (1973)
3 *Searching for skylights* (1977)

Dave Brandstetter series
Hansen, Joseph
1 *Fadeout* (1970)
2 *Death claims* (1973)
3 *Troublemaker* (1975)
4 *Man everybody was afraid of* (1978)
5 *Skinflick* (1979)
6 *Gravedigger* (1982)
7 *Nightwork* (1984)
8 *Little dog laughed* (1987)
9 *Early graves* (1987)
10 *Obedience* (1988)
11 *Boy who was buried this morning* (1990)
Numbers 8-11 also published in one volume entitled *Brandstetter*, volume 1, 1994
12 *Country of old men* (1991)
The last Dave Brandstetter mystery
Two stories featuring Brandstetter in *Brandstetter and others*, 1984

Dave Cannon and Robert Eddison series
Delving, Michael
1 *Smiling, the boy fell dead* (1966)
2 *Devil finds work* (1969)
3 *Die like a man* (1970)
4 *Shadow of himself* (1972)
5 *Wave of fatalities* (1975)
Bored to death
6 *No sign of life* (1978)

Dave Chance series
Cord, Barry
1 *Last chance at Devil's Canyon* (1959)
2 *Canyon showdown* (1967)

Dave Darrin series
Hancock, Harrie Irving
1 *Dave Darrin at Vera Cruz* (1914)
Alternative title: Fighting with the U.S. Navy in Mexico
2 *Dave Darrin on Mediterranean service* (1919)
Alternative title: With Dan Dalzell on European Day
3 *Dave Darrin's South American cruise* (1919)
Alternative title: The young naval tools of an infamous conspiracy
4 *Dave Darrin on the Asiatic station* (1919)
Alternative title: Winning lieutenant's commissions on the admiral's flagships
5 *Dave Darrin and the German submarines* (1919)
Alternative title: Making a clean-up of the Hun sea monsters
6 *Dave Darrin after the mine layers* (1919)
Alternative title: Hitting the enemy a hard naval blow

Dave Dashaway series
Rockwood, Roy
House pseudonym
1 *Dave Dashaway, the young aviator* (1913)
Alternative title: In the clouds for fame and fortune
2 *Dave Dashaway and his hydroplane* (1913)
Alternative title: Daring adventures over the Great Lakes
3 *Dave Dashaway and his giant airship* (1913)
Alternative title: A marvelous trip across the Atlantic
4 *Dave Dashaway around the world* (1913)
Alternative title: A young Yankee aviator among many nations
5 *Dave Dashaway, air champion* (1915)
Alternative title: Wizard work in the clouds

Dave Dawson series
Bowen, Robert Sidney
1 *Dave Dawson at Dunkirk* (1941)
2 *Dave Dawson with the RAF* (1941)
3 *Dave Dawson in Libya* (1941)
4 *Dave Dawson on convoy patrol* (1941)
5 *Dave Dawson, flight lieutenant* (1941)
6 *Dave Dawson at Singapore* (1942)
7 *Dave Dawson with the Pacific Fleet* (1942)
8 *Dave Dawson with the Air Corps* (1942)
9 *Dave Dawson with the commandos* (1942)
10 *Dave Dawson on the Russian front* (1943)
11 *Dave Dawson with the Flying Tigers* (1943)
12 *Dave Dawson on Guadalcanal* (1943)
13 *Dave Dawson at Casablanca* (1944)
14 *Dave Dawson with the Eighth Air Force* (1944)
15 *Dave Dawson at Tobruk* (1946)
16 *Dave Dawson over Berlin* (1946)

Dave Fearless series
Rockwood, Roy
House pseudonym
1 *Dave Fearless after a sunken treasure* (1905)
Alternative title: The search for a sunken treasure; originally serialized as *The rival ocean divers*, 1901
2 *Dave Fearless on a floating island* (1907)
Alternative title: The castaways of Floating Island; originally published as *The cruise of the treasure ship*, 1906
3 *Dave Fearless and the cave of mystery* (1908)
Alternative title: The secret of the island cave; also published as *Adrift on the Pacific*
4 *Dave Fearless among the icebergs* (1926)
Alternative title: The secret of the eskimo igloo
5 *Dave Fearless wrecked among savages* (1926)
Alternative title: The captives of the headhunters
6 *Dave Fearless and his big raft* (1926)
Alternative title: Alone on the broad Pacific
7 *Dave Fearless on Volcano Island* (1926)
Alternative title: The magic cave of blue fire
8 *Dave Fearless captured by apes* (1926)
Alternative title: In gorilla land
9 *Dave Fearless and the mutineers* (1926)
Alternative title: Prisoners on the ship of death
10 *Dave Fearless under the ocean* (1926)
Alternative title: Lost among the cannibals
11 *Dave Fearless in the black jungle* (1926)
Alternative title: Lost among the cannibals
12 *Dave Fearless near the South Pole* (1926)
Alternative title: The giant whales of Snow Island
13 *Dave Fearless caught by Malay pirates* (1926)
Alternative title: The secret of Bamboo Island
14 *Dave Fearless on the ship of mystery* (1927)
Alternative title: The strange hermit of Shark Cove
15 *Dave Fearless on the lost brig* (1927)
Alternative title: Abandoned in the big hurricane
16 *Dave Fearless at Whirlpool Point* (1927)
Alternative title: The mystery of the water cave
17 *Dave Fearless among the cannibals* (1927)
Alternative title: The defense of the hut in the swamp

Dave Fenner series
Chase, James Hadley
see **Carol Blandish series**

Dave Halloran series
Denver, Lee
see **Deputy Marshal Dave Halloran series**

Dave Hill series
Adkins, Bill
1 *Entry from San Sebastian* (1976)
2 *Prison at Obregon* (1976)
3 *Rivera Collection* (1976)

Dave Hunter series
Shirreffs, Gordon Donald
1 *Hell's forty acres* (1987)
2 *Maximilian's gold* (1988)
3 *Walking sands* (1990)

Dave Norton series
Malloch, Peter
see **Inspector Dave Norton series**

Dave Porter series
Stratemeyer, Edward L
1 *Dave Porter at Oak Hall* (1905)
Alternative title: The schooldays of an American boy
2 *Dave Porter in the South Seas* (1906)
Alternative title: The strange cruise of the Stormy Petrel
3 *Dave Porter's return to school* (1907)
Alternative title: Winning the medal of honor
4 *Dave Porter in the far North* (1908)
Alternative title: The pluck of an American schoolboy
5 *Dave Porter and his classmates* (1909)
Alternative title: For the honor of Oak Hall
6 *Dave Porter at Star Ranch* (1910)
Alternative title: The cowboy's secret
7 *Dave Porter and his rivals* (1911)
Alternative title: The chums and foes of Oak Hall
8 *Dave Porter on Oak Island* (1912)
Alternative title: A schoolboy's mysterious mission
9 *Dave Porter and the runaways* (1913)
Alternative title: Last days at Oak Hall
10 *Dave Porter in the gold fields* (1914)
Alternative title: The search for the Landslide Mine
11 *Dave Porter at Bear Camp* (1915)
Alternative title: The wild man of Mirror Lake
12 *Dave Porter and his double* (1916)
Alternative title: The disappearance of the Basswood fortune
13 *Dave Porter's great search* (1917)
Alternative title: The perils of a young civil engineer
14 *Dave Porter under fire* (1918)
Alternative title: A young army engineer in France
15 *Dave Porter's war honors* (1919)
Alternative title: At the Front with the Flying Engineers

Dave Robicheaux series
Burke, James Lee
1 *Neon rain* (1987)
2 *Heaven's prisoners* (1988)
3 *Black cherry blues* (1989)
4 *Mourning for flamingoes* (1990)
5 *Stained white radiance* (1992)
6 *In the electric mist with Confederate dead* (1993)

Dave Sanders series
Mulford, Clarence Edward
1 *Cottonwood Gulch* (1925)
2 *Hopalong Cassidy and the eagle's brood* (1931)

Dave Stevens series
Saddler, Allen
1 *Great brain robbery* (1965)
2 *Gilt edge* (1966)
3 *Talking Turkey* (1968)

Dave Wintino series
Lacy, Ed
see **Lieutenant Dave Wintino series**

D'Avebury series
Martine-Barnes, Adrienne
see **Chronique d'Avebury series**

Davenant family series
Charles, Elizabeth
see **Drayton family series**

Davenant series
Benson, Arthur Christopher
see **Molly Davenant series**
Hamilton, Frederic
see **P J Davenant series**

Davenport series
Sandford, John
see **Lucas Davenport series**

Davenports series
Dalgliesh, Alice
1 *Davenports are at dinner* (1948)
2 *Davenports and cherry pie* (1949)

Davey Bryant series
Watmough, David
The order of this sequence changes and will change with the inclusion of further volumes which fill gaps in the life of the central character beginning in 1926
1 *Ashes for Easter* (1972)
Short stories
2 *Love and the waiting game* (1975)
Short stories
3 *No more into the garden* (1978)
4 *Connecticut countess* (1984)
Short stories
5 *Fury* (1984)
Short stories
6 *Vibrations in time* (1986)
Short stories
7 *Year of fears* (1987)
8 *Families* (1990)

Davey Dillon series
Roddy, Lee
1 *D J Dillon and the pair-pulling bear dog* (1985)
2 *D J Dillon and the city bear's adventures* (1985)
3 *D J Dillon and Dooger, the grasshopper hound* (1985)
4 *D J Dillon and the ghost dog of Stony Ridge* (1985)
5 *D J Dillon and the mad dog of Lobo Mountain* (1986)
6 *D J Dillon and the legend of the white raccoon* (1986)
7 *D J Dillon and the mystery of the Black Hole Mine* (1987)
8 *D J Dillon and the ghost of the moaning mansion* (1987)
9 *D J Dillon and the hermit of Mad River* (1988)
10 *D J Dillon and the escape from the raging rapids* (1989)

David and Anne Layton series
Roberts, Marion
see **Anne and David Layton series**

David and Danny Delaney series
Patchett, Mary Elwyn
see **Danny and David Delaney series**

David and Frank Adams series
Saint James, Daniel
see **Brothers in blood series**

David and Goliath series
Dicks, Terrance
1 *Goliath and the buried treasure* (1984)
2 *Goliath and the burglar* (1984)
3 *Goliath and the dognappers* (1985)
4 *Goliath on holiday* (1985)
5 *Goliath at the dog show* (1986)
6 *Goliath in the snow* (1986)
7 *Goliath's Christmas* (1987)
8 *Goliath's Easter parade* (1987)
9 *Goliath goes to summer school* (1987)
10 *Goliath at the seaside* (1988)

11 *Goliath at sports day* (1988)
12 *Goliath and the Cub Scouts* (1989)
13 *Goliath's birthday* (1990)
14 *Teacher's pet* (1990)
15 *Big match* (1991)
16 *Goliath gets a job* (1991)
17 *David and Goliath on their own* (1992)
18 *Goliath and the school bully* (1993)

David and Pat series
Pullein-Thompson, Christine
1 *First rosette* (1956)
2 *Second mount* (1957)
3 *Three to ride* (1958)
4 *Lost pony* (1959)

David and Samuel series
Jenkins, Gwyn
see **Samuel and David series**

David and Uncle Bill series
Serraillier, Ian
1 *They raced for treasure* (1946)
2 *Flight to adventure* (1947)

David Audley and Jack Butler series
Price, Anthony
see **Doctor David Audley and Jack Butler series**

David Balfour series
This sequence has two authors
Stevenson, Robert Louis
1 *Kidnapped* (1886)
Memoirs of the adventures of David Balfour in the year 1751
2 *Catriona* (1893)
David Balfour
Smith, Arthur Douglas Howden
3 *Alan Breck again* (1934)
An account of the adventures of Ian MacDonnell of New York and his foster brother, Ho-No-We-Na-To, son to the Onondaga Royaneh in the course of a journey to Scotland in the year 1755 and of their experiences with the famous Alan Breck Stewart and the notorious spy, Pickle

David Blaize series
Benson, Edward Frederic
1 *David Blaize and the blue door* (1918)
2 *David Blaize* (1916)
3 *David of King's* (1924)
David Blaize of King's

David, Bottle and Hamish series
Kiddell, John
see **Hamish, David and Bottle series**

David Brock series
White, Reginald James
see **Inspector David Brock series**

David Callan series
Mitchell, James
1 *Magnum for Schneider* (1969)
Red file for Callan
Callan
2 *Russian roulette* (1973)
3 *Death and bright water* (1974)
4 *Smear job* (1975)

David Campbell series
Douglas, Colin
1 *Houseman's tale* (1976)
2 *Greatest breakthrough since lunchtime* (1977)
3 *Bleeders come first* (1979)
Numbers 1-3 also published in one volume entitled *The houseman's trilogy*, 1985
4 *Wellies from the Queen* (1981)
5 *Cure for living* (1983)
6 *For services to medicine* (1985)
7 *Ethics made easy* (1985)
8 *Hazards of the profession* (1988)

David Cane series
Courage, John
1 *Four doors to death* (1936)
2 *Death goes to the fair* (1937)
3 *Death on tour* (1937)
4 *Why murder Mrs Hope?* (1940)
5 *They all came back* (1945)

David Carroll series
Cohen, Octavus Roy
1 *Crimson alibi* (1919)
2 *Gray dusk* (1920)
Grey dusk
3 *Six seconds of darkness* (1921)
4 *Midnight* (1922)

David Chan series
Leader, Charles
1 *Wreath of poppies* (1975)
2 *Wreath from Bangkok* (1975)
3 *Wreath for Miss Wong* (1977)
4 *Wreath of cherry blossom* (1977)

David Cochrane series
Evans, Alan
1 *Thunder at dawn* (1978)
2 *Ship of force* (1979)
3 *Dauntless* (1980)
4 *Seek out and destroy* (1982)

David Colwyn series
Rees, Arthur John
1 *Shrieking pit* (1919)
2 *Hand in the dark* (1920)

David Connell series
Weatherhead, John
see **Professor David Connell series**

David Danning series
Von Elsner, Don
1 *Those who pray together slay together* (1961)
2 *Just not making mayhem like they used to* (1961)
3 *Don't just stand there, do someone* (1962)
4 *You can't do business with murder* (1962)
5 *Who says a corpse has to be dull* (1963)
6 *Pour a swindle through a loophole* (1964)
7 *Countdown for a spy* (1966)
8 *Bullet for your dreams* (1968)

David Dodd and Lucy Fountain series
Reade, Charles
1 *Love me little, love me long* (1859)
2 *Hard cash* (1863)

David Falkeyn and Nicholas Van Rijn series
Anderson, Poul
see **Polesotechnic League series**

David Garnett trilogy
Egleton, Clive
1 *Piece of resistance* (1970)
2 *Last post for a partisan* (1971)
3 *Judas mandate* (1972)

David Grant series
Mair, George Brown
1 *Death's foot forward* (1963)
2 *Miss Turquoise* (1964)
3 *Live, love and cry* (1965)
4 *Kisses from Satan* (1966)
5 *Girl from Peking* (1967)
6 *Black champagne* (1968)
7 *Goddesses never die* (1969)
8 *Wreath of camellias* (1970)
9 *Crimson jade* (1971)
10 *Paradise spells danger* (1973)

David Grierson series
Stuart, Ian
1 *Death from disclosure* (1976)
2 *End on the rocks* (1981)
3 *Garb of truth* (1982)
4 *Thrilling-sweet and rotten* (1983)
5 *Growing concern* (1985)

David Haham series
Haddad, Carolyn A
1 *Bloody September* (1976)
2 *Operation Apricot* (1978)

David Halliday series
Taylor, H Baldwin
1 *Duplicate* (1965)
2 *Triumvirate* (1966)

David Harcourt series
Sheridan, Matt
1 *Secret range* (1955)
2 *Wagons on the Ogden Road* (1957)

David Isaacs series
Gee, Joseph
1 *Isaacs* (1919)
2 *Isaacs reappears* (1926)

David John series
Fraser, Edith
1 *David John* (1958)
2 *David John hears about Jesus* (1961)
3 *David John again* (1962)
4 *David John finds out* (1965)

David Jones, R.N.V.R. series
Styles, Showell
1 *Indestructible Jones* (1967)
2 *Jones's private army* (1969)

David Lawrence series
Mackail, Denis
1 *Romance to the rescue* (1921)
2 *Summertime* (1923)

David Lofthouse and Rose Endel series
Marcus, Joanna
see **Romney Marsh series**

David Macfarlane quartet
McDonald, Gregory
see **Time squared quartet**

David Madden series
Disney, Doris Miles
1 *Unappointed rounds* (1956)
Post Office case
2 *Black mail* (1958)
3 *Mrs Meeker's money* (1961)

David Mallin and George Coe series
Ormerod, Roger
1 *Time to kill* (1974)
2 *Silence of the night* (1974)
3 *Full fury* (1975)
4 *Spoonful of Luger* (1975)
5 *Sealed with a loving kill* (1976)
6 *Colour of fear* (1976)
7 *Glimpse of death* (1976)
8 *Too late for the funeral* (1977)
9 *This murder came to mind* (1977)
10 *Dip into murder* (1978)
11 *Weight of evidence* (1978)
12 *Bright face of danger* (1979)
13 *Amnesia trap* (1979)
14 *Cart before the horse* (1979)
15 *More dead than alive* (1980)
16 *Double take* (1980)
17 *One deathless hour* (1981)
18 *Face value* (1983)
Hanging doll murder

David Markand series
Frank, Waldo
1 *Death and birth of Savid Markand* (1934)
2 *Bridegroom cometh* (1938)

David Martini series
Raine, Richard
1 *Wreath for America* (1967)
Corder index
2 *Night of the hawk* (1968)
3 *Bombshell* (1970)

David Meredith trilogy
Johnston, George Henry
1 *My brother Jack* (1964)
2 *Clean straw for nothing* (1969)
3 *Cartload of hay* (1971)

David Meynell series
Baker, Ivon
1 *Grave doubt* (1972)
2 *Peak performance* (1976)
3 *Death and variations* (1977)
4 *Blood on my sleeve* (1979)

David Middleton-Brown series
Charles, Kate
1 *Drink of deadly wine* (1992)
2 *Snares of death* (1993)
3 *Appointed to die* (1993)
4 *Dead man out of mind* (1994)

David Morgan series
Owen, Richard
1 *Eye of the gods* (1978)
2 *Nightmare* (1979)

David Morton series
Thomas, Gordon
1 *Deadly perfume* (1991)
2 *Godless icon* (1992)
3 *Organ hunters* (1994)

David Nairn series
Hartland, Michael
1 *Down among the dead men* (1983)
2 *Seven steps to treason* (1984)
3 *Third betrayal* (1986)

David, Peter and Sandy series
Hunter, Evan
1 *Last summer* (1968)
2 *Come winter* (1973)

David Polonsky series
Angoff, Charles
see **Polonsky family series**

David Powlett-Jones series
Delderfield, Ronald Frederick
see **To serve them all my days series**

David Ramsay and Andrea Reid series
Matschat, Cecile Hulse
see **Andrea Reid and David Ramsay series**

David Sheridan series
Davy, Colin
1 *Mariella, spy!* (1935)
2 *Agents of the League* (1936)

David Silver series
Hightower, Lynn S
1 *Alien blues* (1992)
2 *Alien eyes* (1993)
3 *Alien heat* (1994)

David Small series
Kemelman, Harry
see **Rabbi David Small series**

David Starr series
French, Paul
1 *David Starr, space ranger* (1952)
Also published as *Space ranger*, by Isaac Asimov
2 *Lucky Starr and the pirates of the asteroids* (1953)
Also published as *Pirates of the asteroids*, by Isaac Asimov
3 *Lucky Starr and the oceans of Venus* (1954)

David Starr series

Also published as *Oceans of Venus*, by Isaac Asimov
4 *Lucky Starr and the big sun of Mercury* (1956)
Also published as *Big sun of Mercury*, by Isaac Asimov
5 *Lucky Starr and the moons of Jupiter* (1957)
Also published as *Moons of Jupiter*, by Isaac Asimov
6 *Lucky Starr and the rings of Saturn* (1958)
Also published as *Rings of Saturn*, by Isaac Asimov

David Stuart series
Macdougall, James K
1 *Weasel hunt* (1977)
2 *Death and the maiden* (1978)

David Sullivan series
Deitz, Tom
1 *Windmaster's bane* (1986)
2 *Fireshaper's doom* (1987)
3 *Darkthunder's way* (1989)
4 *Sunshaker's war* (1990)
5 *Stoneskin's revenge* (1991)

David Webb and Ken Jackson series
Fraser, Anthea
see **Inspector David Webb and Sergeant Ken Jackson series**

David Wilshaw series
Pollard, Alfred Oliver
1 *David Wilshaw investigates* (1948)
2 *Poisoned pilot* (1950)
3 *Golden Buddha* (1951)
4 *Dead forger* (1952)
5 *Buckled wing* (1953)
6 *Missing diamond* (1955)

David Wintringham series
Bell, Josephine
see **Doctor David Wintringham series**

David Wright series
Straker, John Foster
1 *Coil of rope* (1962)
2 *Final witness* (1963)

Davidson series
Jackman, Stuart
see **Jesus Davidson series**

Davie series
Clinton-Baddeley, Victor Clinton
see **Doctor Davie series**

Davies series
Bennett, Margot
see **John Davies series**
Mason, Sara Elizabeth
see **Sheriff Bill Davies series**
Styles, Showell
see **Ann and John Davies series**

Davina Graham series
Anthony, Evelyn
1 *Defector* (1980)
2 *Avenue of the dead* (1981)
3 *Albatross* (1982)
4 *Company of Saints* (1983)

Davis and Quirk trilogy
Wakefield, Tom
see **Margaret Davis and Isobel Quirk trilogy**

Davis family series
Oke, Janette
1 *Love comes softly* (1979)
2 *Love's enduring promise* (1980)
3 *Love's long journey* (1982)
4 *Love's abiding joy* (1983)
5 *Love's unending legacy* (1984)

Davis series
Lord, Beman
see **Spaceship series**
North, Grace May
see **Virginia Davis series**
Ripley, Jack
see **John George Davis series**

Davis Troy series
Gardner, Alan Harold
1 *Escalator* (1963)
2 *Assignment Tahiti* (1965)
3 *Six-day week* (1966)
4 *Man who was too much* (1967)

Davison series
Fletcher, Robert James
see **Gilbert Davison series**

Davvie McLean series
Yates, Margaret Tayler
see **Anne Davenport McLean series**

Davy Crockett series
Korman, Justine
1 *Davy Crockett and the king of the river* (1991)
2 *Davy Crockett at the Alamo* (1991)
3 *Davy Crockett and the Creek Indians* (1991)
4 *Davy Crockett and the pirates at Cave-in-the-Rock* (1991)

Davy Crockett series
This sequence has two authors
McNeil, Everett
1 *Lost treasure cave* (1905)
Alternative title: Adventures with the cowboys of Colorado
2 *In Texas with Davy Crockett* (1908)
A story of the Texas war of independence
Singer, A L
3 *Davy Crockett and the pirates at Cave-In Rock* (1991)
4 *Davy Crockett and the king of the river* (1991)

Davy series
Bray, Donald
see **Captain Bray series**

Davy series
Lenski, Lois
1 *Davy's day* (1943)
2 *Surprise for Davy* (1947)
3 *Big little Davy* (1956)
4 *Davy and his dog* (1957)
5 *Davy goes places* (1961)

Davy series
Pangborn, Edgar
1 *Davy* (1964)
2 *Judgment of Eve* (1966)
3 *Company of glory* (1975)
4 *Still I persist in wondering* (1978)

Davy Strong series
Nolan, Frederick
1 *Promise of glory* (1983)
2 *Blind duty* (1983)

Davy Watson series
Mills, Robert E
1 *Showdown at Hell's Canyon* (1980)
2 *Across the High Sierras* (1980)
3 *Red Apache sun* (1981)
4 *Judge Colt* (1981)
5 *Warm flesh and hot lead* (1981)
6 *Long, hard ride* (1981)
7 *Trail of desire* (1981)
8 *Shootout at the Golden Slipper* (1982)
9 *Kansan's woman* (1982)
10 *Kansan's lady* (1982)

Dawes series
Greenwood, Robert
see **Rosie Dawes series**

Dawks series
Reid, Meta Mayne
see **Peyton children series**

Dawley trilogy
Sillitoe, Alan
see **Frank Dawley trilogy**

Dawlish series
Ashe, Gordon
see **Patrick Dawlish series**

Dawn Longchamp series
Andrews, Virginia Cleo
see **Cutler family series**

Dawn of magic series
Pauwels, Louis
1 *Dawn of magic* (1960)
Morning of the magicians
Original edition entitled *Le matin des magiciens*
2 *Eternal man* (1972)
Original edition entitled *L'homme eternel*

Daw's Hall series
Grahame, Iain
An account of the author's wildfowl farm
1 *Flying feathers* (1977)
2 *Ruffled feathers* (1978)

Dawson series
Bowen, Robert Sidney
see **Dave Dawson series**
Copplestone, Bennet
see **Chief Inspector Dawson series**
Milligan, Elsie
see **Penny Dawson series**

Dax series
Cumberland, Marten
see **Saturnin Dax series**

Day before yesterday series
Shafer, Sara Andrew
1 *Day before yesterday* (1904)
2 *Beyond chance of change* (1905)

Day of the seasons series
Miles, Betty
1 *Day of summer* (1960)
2 *Day of winter* (1961)
3 *Day of autumn* (1967)
4 *Day of spring* (1971)

Day of wrath trilogy
Stableford, Brian Michael
see **Dies irae trilogy**

Day series
Long, Helen Beecher
see **Do something series**
Wheatley, Dennis
see **Julian Day series**

Day when series
Peterson, Hans
1 *Day it snowed* (1959)
Original edition entitled *Nar vi snoeade inne*
2 *Day the chickens blew away* (1964)
Original edition entitled *Nar hoensen blaaste bort*
3 *When you are only small* (1970)
Original edition entitled *Nar man ar liten*

Daybreak series
Greenland, Colin
1 *Daybreak on a different mountain* (1984)
2 *Hour of the thin ox* (1987)
3 *Other voices* (1988)

Daydreamers series
Dolce, Janet Ellen
1 *If I had a hippo* (1988)
2 *If I knew how to fly a rocket* (1988)
3 *If I could be a circus clown* (1988)
4 *If I went sailing out to sea* (1988)

Daye Smith series
Usher, Frank
1 *Ghost of a chance* (1956)
2 *Lonely cage* (1956)
3 *Portrait of fear* (1957)
4 *Price of death* (1957)
5 *Death is waiting* (1958)
6 *First to kill* (1959)
7 *Death in error* (1959)
8 *Die, my darling* (1960)
9 *Shot in the dark* (1961)
10 *Faceless stranger* (1961)
11 *Fall into my grave* (1962)
12 *Who killed Rosie Gray?* (1962)
13 *Stairway to murder* (1964)

Days of Laura Ingalls Wilder series
This sequence follows the **Laura series**, by Laura Ingalls Wilder
Tedrow, Thomas L
1 *Missouri homestead* (1992)
2 *Children of promise* (1992)
3 *Good neighbors* (1992)
4 *Home to the prairie* (1992)
5 *World's Fair* (1992)
Number 6 not identified
7 *Great debate* (1992)
8 *Land of promise* (1992)

Days of my life series
Mais, Stuart Petre Brodie
1 *All the days of my life* (1937)
2 *Buffets and rewards* (1952)

Day's play series
Milne, Alan Alexander
Sketches first published in Punch
1 *Day's play* (1910)
2 *Holiday round* (1912)
3 *Once a week* (1914)
4 *Happy days* (1915)
Only published in the United States
5 *Sunny side* (1921)
Numbers 1, 2, 3, 5 also published in one volume entitled *Those were the days*, 1929

Days series
Green, Julian
Based on the author's journals
1 *Memories of happy days* (1942)
2 *Memories of evil days* (1976)

Days series
Margolin, Harriet
1 *Moving day* (1987)
2 *Shopping day* (1987)
3 *Swimming day* (1987)
4 *Tooth day* (1987)

Days series
Van Paassen, Pierre
1 *Days of our years* (1939)
2 *That day alone* (1942)

Dayworld series
Farmer, Philip Jose
1 *Dayworld* (1985)
2 *Dayworld rebel* (1987)
3 *Dayworld breakup* (1989)

Dazincourt trilogy
O'Riordan, Conal
see **Stanislaus Priest trilogy**

Dazzle series
O'Brien, Edna
1 *Dazzle* (1981)
2 *Christmas treat* (1982)
3 *Rescue* (1983)

D'Croy series
Williamson, Geoffrey
see **Silva d'Croy series**

Deacon series
Brean, Herbert
see **William Deacon series**

Dead and alive series
Baker, Howard
1 *All the gods are dead* (1983)
2 *Alive to the burning* (1985)

Dead Ends series
Vickers, Roy
see **Department of Dead Ends series**

Dead girls series
Ibarguengoitia, Jorge
1 *Dead girls* (1977)
Original edition entitled *La muertas*
2 *Two crimes* (1981)
Original edition entitled *Dos crimenes*

Dead man's trilogy
Broomall, Robert Walter
see **Jake Moran trilogy**

Dead Shot Dave series
Bowie, Jim
1 *Dead Shot Dave, the nerviest sport on record* (1892)
Alternative title: The card wizard of the Mississippi
2 *Dead Shot Dave in Butte* (1892)
Alternative title: Breaking the green cloth record
3 *Dead Shot Dave in Spokane* (1893)
Alternative title: A lone hand and a high stake
4 *Dead Shot Dave in Tacoma* (1893)
Alternative title: A fortune at one throw
5 *Dead Shot Dave in Denver* (1893)
Alternative title: Foiling the gamblers
6 *Dead Shot Dave in Chicago* (1893)
7 *Dead Shot Dave in Omaha* (1893)
Alternative title: The limit of the red and black
8 *Dead Shot Dave in Kentucky* (1893)
Alternative title: The Blue Grass Region horse thieves

Deadly Force series
Dixon, Mark
1 *Deadly force* (1987)
2 *Special delivery* (1987)

Deadly promise series
Nixon, Joan Lowery
1 *High trail to danger* (1991)
2 *Deadly promise* (1992)

Deal series
Aldrich, Bess Streeter
see **Abbie Deal series**
Standiford, Les
see **John Deal series**

Deal Woods series
Griswold, Latta
see **Deering series**

Dealer series
Wilson, Steve
1 *Dealer's move* (1978)
2 *Dealer's war* (1980)
3 *Dealer's wheels* (1982)

Dean Brothers series
Moray, Helga
1 *Clear to sail* (1974)
2 *Ruby fleet* (1976)
3 *Quest in the sun* (1978)

Dean college series
Lester, Pauline
see **Marjorie Dean college series**

Dean Grant series
Walker, Robert Wayne
1 *Dead man's float* (1989)
2 *Razor's edge* (1989)
3 *Burning obsession* (1990)
4 *Dying breath* (1990)

Dean high school series
Lester, Pauline
see **Marjorie Dean high school series**

Dean post-graduate series
Lester, Pauline
see **Marjorie Dean post-graduate series**

Dean series
Buck, Peter
see **Marc Dean series**
Francis, Basil
see **Sergeant Paul Dean series**
Henry, Margaret
see **Bob and Hilary Dean series**
Hill, Margaret
see **Beth Dean series**
Whelton, Paul
see **Garry Dean series**

Dean Street detectives series
Butler, Bill
1 *Voice from nowhere* (1984)
2 *Nightmare clowns* (1984)
3 *Corridor of ghosts* (1985)
4 *Spying machines* (1985)
5 *Fingers of flame* (1986)
6 *TV terror* (1986)

Deane and Lynch series
Vandercook, John Womack
see **Bertram Lynch and Robert Deane series**

Deane and McKenzie series
Borthwick, J S
see **Sarah Deane and Alex McKenzie series**

Deane series
Kirk, Ellen Olney
see **Dorothy Deane series**

Deans series
Fidler, Kathleen
1 *Deans move in* (1953)
2 *Deans follow a clue* (1954)
3 *Deans solve a mystery* (1954)
4 *Deans defy danger* (1955)
5 *Deans dive for treasure* (1956)
6 *Deans to the rescue* (1957)
7 *Deans' lighthouse adventure* (1959)
8 *Deans and Mr Popple* (1960)
9 *Deans' Dutch adventure* (1962)

Dear Dragon series
Hillert, Margaret
1 *Happy birthday, Dear Dragon* (1977)
2 *Happy Easter, Dear Dragon* (1981)
3 *I love you, Dear Dragon* (1981)
4 *It's Halloween time, Dear Dragon* (1981)
5 *Let's go, Dear Dragon* (1981)
6 *Merry Christmas, Dear Dragon* (1981)
7 *Help for Dear Dragon* (1985)
8 *It's circus time, Dear Dragon* (1985)
9 *Come to school, Dear Dragon* (1985)
10 *I need you, Dear Dragon* (1985)
11 *Go to sleep, Dear Dragon* (1985)
12 *Friend for Dear Dragon* (1985)

Dear Grandad series
Selway, Martina
1 *Don't forget to write* (1991)
2 *Dear Grandad, I hate Roland Roberts* (1993)
I hate Roland Roberts

Dear Judy series
Baer, Judy
1 *Dear Judy, what's it like at your house* (1992)
2 *Dear Judy, did you ever like a boy who didn't like you?* (1993)

Dear little girl series
Blanchard, Amy Ella
1 *Dear little girl* (1897)
2 *Dear little girl at school* (1910)
3 *Dear little girl's summer holidays* (1911)
4 *Dear little girl's Thanksgiving holidays* (1912)

Dear series
Aliki
1 *Keep your mouth closed, dear* (1972)
2 *Use your head, dear* (1983)

Dearborn V Pinch series
Green, Edith
1 *Rotten apples* (1977)
2 *Sneaks* (1979)
3 *Perfect fools* (1982)

Death and to-morrow series
De Polnay, Peter
1 *Crack of dawn* (1960)
A childhood fantasy
2 *Death and to-morrow* (1942)
Set in Hungary during the Second World War
3 *Fools of choice* (1955)
Remembrances of travel
4 *Door ajar* (1959)
Set on the Riviera

Death Dealer series
McCurtin, Peter
see **Jim Rainey series**

Death dealer series
Silke, James R
Illustrated by Frank Frazetta
1 *Prisoner of the horned helmet* (1988)
2 *Lords of destruction* (1989)
3 *Tooth and claw* (1989)
4 *Plague of knives* (1990)

Death Gate series
Weis, Margaret
1 *Dragon wing* (1990)
2 *Elven star* (1990)
3 *Fire sea* (1991)
4 *Serpent mage* (1992)
5 *Hand of chaos* (1993)
6 *Into the labyrinth* (1993)
7 *Seventh gate* (1994)

Death Merchant series
Rosenberger, Joseph
1 *Death Merchant* (1972)
2 *Operation Overkill* (1972)
3 *Psychotron plot* (1972)
4 *Satan strike* (1972)
5 *Chinese conspiracy* (1973)
6 *Albanian connection* (1973)
7 *Castro file* (1974)
8 *Billionaire mission* (1974)
9 *Laser war* (1974)
10 *Mainline plot* (1974)
11 *Manhattan wipeout* (1975)
12 *KGB frame* (1975)
13 *Mato Grosso horror* (1975)
14 *Vengeance of the Golden Hawk* (1976)
15 *Iron swastika plot* (1976)
16 *Invasion of the clones* (1976)
17 *Zemlya expedition* (1976)
18 *Nightmare in Algeria* (1976)
19 *Armageddon, USA!* (1976)
20 *Hell in Hindu land* (1977)
21 *Pole Star secret* (1977)
22 *Kondrashev chase* (1977)
23 *Budapest action* (1977)
24 *Kronos plot* (1977)
25 *Enigma project* (1977)
26 *Mexican hit* (1978)
27 *Surinam affair* (1978)
28 *Nipponese nightmare* (1978)
29 *Fatal formula* (1978)
30 *Shambhala strike* (1978)
31 *Operation Thunderbolt* (1979)
32 *Deadly manhunt* (1979)
33 *Alaska conspiracy* (1979)
34 *Operation Mind Murder* (1979)
35 *Massacre in Rome* (1979)
36 *Cosmic reality kill* (1979)
37 *Bermuda Triangle action* (1980)
38 *Burning blue death* (1980)
39 *Fourth Reich* (1980)
40 *Blueprint invisibility* (1980)
41 *Shamrock smash* (1980)
42 *High Command murder* (1980)
43 *Devil's trashcan* (1981)
44 *Island of the damned* (1981)
45 *Rim of fire conspiracy* (1981)
46 *Blood bath* (1981)
47 *Operation Skyhook* (1981)
48 *Psionics war* (1982)
49 *Night of the peacock* (1982)
50 *Hellbomb theft* (1982)
51 *Inca file* (1982)
52 *Flight of the phoenix* (1982)
53 *Judas scrolls* (1983)
54 *Apocalypse, USA* (1983)
55 *Slaughter in El Salvador* (1983)
56 *Afghanistan crashout* (1983)
57 *Rumanian operation* (1983)
58 *Silicon Valley connection* (1984)
59 *Burma probe* (1984)
60 *Methuselah factor* (1984)
61 *Bulgarian termination* (1984)
62 *Soul search project* (1985)
63 *Atlantean horror* (1985)
64 *Pakistan kill* (1985)
65 *Mission Deadly Snow* (1986)
66 *Cobra chase* (1986)
67 *Escape from Gulag Taria* (1986)
68 *Hindu trinity* (1987)
69 *Miracle mission* (1987)
70 *Greenland mystery* (1988)
Companion volume: *Apocalypse*, 1987

Death on Demand series
Hart, Carolyn Gimpel
see **Annie Laurance and Max Darling series**

Death on horseback series
Wellman, Paul Iselin
1 *Death on the prairie* (1934)
The terrible struggle for the Western plains
2 *Death in the desert* (1935)
One volume editions entitled *Death on horseback, seventy years of war for the American West*, 1947 and *The Indian Wars of the West*, 1954

Death row series
Chessman, Caryl
Autobiography of a prisoner condemned to death
1 *Cell 2455, death row* (1954)
2 *Trial by ordeal* (1955)
3 *Face of justice* (1957)

Death series
Kaye, Mary Margaret
1 *Death walked in Kashmir* (1953)
Death in Kashmir
2 *Death walked in Berlin* (1955)
Death in Berlin
3 *Death walked in Cyprus* (1956)
Death in Cyprus
4 *Later than you think* (1958)
It's later than you think
Death in Kenya
5 *House of Shade* (1959)
Death in Zanzibar
6 *Night on the island* (1960)
Death in the Andamans

Death series
Zorro
see **Doctor Death series**

Death Squad series
Colter, Frank
see **Gang war series**

Deathbell series
Smith, Guy Newman
1 *Deathbell* (1980)
2 *Demons* (1987)

Deathlands series
This sequence has two authors
Adrian, Jack
1 *Pilgrimage to hell* (1986)
Axler, James
2 *Red holocaust* (1986)
3 *Neutron solstice* (1987)
4 *Crater Lake* (1987)
5 *Homeward bound* (1988)
6 *Pony soldiers* (1988)
7 *Dectra chain* (1988)
8 *Ice and fire* (1988)
9 *Red equinox* (1989)
10 *Northstar rising* (1989)
11 *Time nomads* (1990)
12 *Latitude zero* (1991)
13 *Seedling* (1991)
14 *Dark carnival* (1992)
15 *Chill factor* (1992)
16 *Moon fate* (1992)
17 *Fury's pilgrims* (1993)
18 *Shockscape* (1993)
19 *Deep empire* (1993)
20 *Cold asylum* (1994)

Deathworld series
Harrison, Harry
see **Jason Din Alt series**

Deavors family series
McNeill, George
1 *Plantation* (1975)
2 *Rafaella* (1977)
3 *Hellions* (1979)

Deb Ralston series
Martin, Lee
1 *Too sane a murder* (1985)
2 *Conspiracy of strangers* (1986)
3 *Murder at the Blue Owl* (1987)
4 *Death warmed over* (1988)
5 *Deficit ending* (1990)
6 *Mensa murders* (1990)
7 *Hacker* (1992)
8 *Inherited murder* (1994)

Debbie learns series
Delahaye, Gilbert
Translated from the French
1 *Debbie learns to cook* (1983)
2 *Debbie learns to dance* (1984)

Debbie Miles series
Rosenberger, Joseph
see **C.O.B.R.A. series**

Debbie Preston, teenage reporter series
This sequence has two authors
Resnick, Sylvia
1 *Case of the gypsy's warning* (1972)
2 *Hollywood mystery* (1972)
3 *Donny Osmond mystery* (1973)
Stapleton, Doug
4 *Case of the superstar mystery* (1973)

Debbie series
Lenski, Lois
1 *Debbie and her grandma* (1967)
2 *Debbie and her family* (1969)
3 *Debbie herself* (1969)
4 *Debbie and her dolls* (1970)
5 *Debbie goes to nursery school* (1970)
6 *Debbie and her pets* (1971)

De Beauregard series
Lang, Frances
see **Gillonne de Beauregard series**

Deborah Krillet series
Askew, Alice
1 *Shulamite* (1904)
2 *Woman Deborah* (1910)

Deborah series
Davenat, Colette
1 *Deborah* (1970)
Springtime of love
Original edition entitled *Deborah*
2 *Many faces of love* (1971)
Original edition entitled *L'amour aux cents facettes*
3 *Deborah and the siege of Paris* (1973)
Original edition entitled *Paris des passions*

De Bricoule trilogy
Montherlant, Henry de
see **Alban de Bricoule trilogy**

De Brun series
Campbell, Marion
see **Richard De Brun series**

De Brussac series
Gerard, Francis
see **Marquess de Brussac series**

Decay of capitalism trilogy
Herbst, Josephine
1 *Pity is not enough* (1933)
2 *Executioner waits* (1934)
3 *Rope of gold* (1939)

Deception series
Mure, David
1 *Practise to deceive* (1977)
2 *Master of deception* (1980)
Tangled webs in London and the Middle East

Deceptions series
Michael, Judith
1 *Deceptions* (1985)
2 *Tangled web* (1994)

Decision series
Tolliver, Ruby Changes
1 *Summer of decision* (1979)
2 *Decision at sea* (1980)
3 *More than one decision* (1981)
4 *Decision at Brushy Creek* (1982)

Deck series
McMurtry, Larry
see **Danny Deck series**

Decker and Burchardt series
Bogen, M Arthur
see **Burchardt and Decker series**

Decker and Lazarus series
Kellerman, Faye
see **Sergeant Peter Decker and Rina Lazarus series**

Decker series
Albert, Andrew I
see **Paul Decker series**
Graber, Richard
see **Ray Decker series**
Riefe, Alan
see **Tyger Decker series**
Treat, Lawrence
see **Bill Decker series**

De Cock series
Baantjer, Albert Cornelis
see **Inspector De Kok series**

Decorative design series
Jackson, Frank George
1 *Lessons on decorative design* (1888)
2 *Theory and practice of design* (1894)

De Courdeval series
Rhodes, Daniel
see **Guilhelm de Courdeval series**

Decoy series
Robertson, Stephen
see **Ryne Lanark series**

Dedalus series
Joyce, James
see **Stephen Dedalus series**

Dee series
Cory, Desmond
see **Mister Dee series**
Gulik, Robert van
see **Judge Dee series**
Wesley, Elizabeth
see **Doctor Dorothy Dee series**

Dee Street series
Wakefield, Hannah
1 *Price you pay* (1987)
2 *February mourning* (1990)
Woman's own mystery

Deed of Paksenarrion series
Moon, Elizabeth
1 *Surrender none* (1990)
The legacy of Gird
2 *Sheepfarmer's daughter* (1988)
3 *Divided allegiance* (1988)
4 *Oath of gold* (1989)
5 *Liar's oath* (1993)

DeeDee Doner series
Shay, Frank
see **Dan Doner series**

Deedle Dumpy series
Schermele, Willy
Translated from the Dutch
1 *Deedle Dumpy and castles in the air* (1968)
2 *Deedle Dumpy meets Mimi the Mouse* (1968)
3 *Deedle Dumpy and Mimi the mouse meet Mister Owl* (1969)
4 *Deedle Dumpy and mimi's new friends* (1969)

Deene series
Bruce, Leo
see **Carolus Deene series**

Deenes series
Christian, Petra
see **Sally Deenes series**

Deep foot series
Vixen, Richard M
1 *Deep foot* (1977)
2 *Deeper foot* (1977)

Deep of the sky series
Ronan, Tom
1 *Deep of the sky* (1962)
An essay in ancestor worship
2 *Packhorse and pearling boat* (1964)
Memories of a mis-spent youth
3 *Once there was a bagman* (1966)

Deep sea hunters series
Verrill, Alpheus Hyatt
1 *Deep sea hunters* (1922)
Adventures on a whaler
2 *Deep sea hunters in the frozen seas* (1923)
3 *Deep sea hunters in the South Seas* (1924)

Deep sea series
Rockwood, Roy
House pseudonym
1 *Rival ocean divers* (1905)
Alternative title: The search for a sunken treasure; originally serialized as *The rival ocean divers,* 1901
2 *Cruise of the treasure ship* (1906)
Alternative title: The castaways of Floating Island
3 *Adrift on the Pacific* (1908)
Alternative title: The secret of the island cave; reissued as *Dave Fearless and the cave of mystery*, 1918
4 *Jack North's treasure hunt* (1908)
Alternative title: Daring adventures in South America

Deep South trilogy
Gluyas, Constance
1 *Savage Eden* (1976)
2 *Rogue's mistress* (1977)
3 *Flame of the South* (1979)

Deep throat series
Perkins, D M
see **Linda Lovelace series**

Deep Valley series
Lovelace, Maud Hart
see **Betsy Ray series**

Deepcore series
Adair, James B
1 *Deepcore* (1991)
2 *Boomer down* (1992)
3 *Crash dive* (1992)

Deep-sea adventure series
This sequence has two authors
Berres, Frances B
1 *Sea hunt* (1959)
Coleman, James Covington
2 *Treasure under the sea* (1959)
Berres, Frances B
3 *Submarine rescue* (1959)
Coleman, James Covington
4 *Pearl divers* (1959)
Berres, Frances B
5 *Frogmen in action* (1959)
6 *Danger below* (1962)
Coleman, James Covington
7 *Whale hunt* (1962)
8 *Rocket divers* (1962)
Berres, Frances B
9 *Storm island* (1962)
10 *Sea gold* (1962)
11 *Enemy agents* (1962)
12 *Castaways* (1962)

Deepwater series
Catran, Ken
1 *Deepwater black* (1992)
2 *Deepwater landing* (1993)

Deer trilogy
Holden, Philip
1 *Fawn* (1976)
First year in the life of a red deer
2 *Stag* (1980)
3 *White Patch* (1982)

Deerfoot the Showanoe series 1
Ellis, Edward Sylvester
see **Boy pioneer series**

Deerfoot the Showanoe series 2
Ellis, Edward Sylvester
see **Log cabin series**

Deerfoot the Showanoe series 3
Ellis, Edward Sylvester
see **New Deerfoot series**

Deerfoot the Showanoe series 4
Ellis, Edward Sylvester
1 *Hunters of the Ozark* (1887)
2 *Camp in the mountains* (1887)
3 *Last war trail* (1887)

Deering series
Griswold, Latta
1 *Deering of Deal* (1913)
Alternative title: The spirit of the school
2 *Winds of Deal* (1914)

A school story
3 *Deal Woods* (1915)
4 *Deering at Princeton* (1913)
A story of college life

Deerslayer series
Cooper, James Fenimore
see **Leatherstocking series**

Deets Shanahan series
Tierney, Ronald
1 *Stone veil* (1990)
2 *Steel web* (1991)
3 *Iron glove* (1992)

Defeat and victory series
Spears, Edward
1 *Liaison nineteen fourteen* (1930)
Nineteen fourteen
A narrative of the great defeat
2 *Prelude to victory* (1939)

Defender series
Ahern, Jerry
1 *Battle begins* (1988)
2 *Killing wedge* (1988)
3 *Out of control* (1988)
4 *Decision time* (1989)
5 *Entrapment* (1989)
6 *Escape* (1989)
7 *Vengeance* (1989)
8 *Justice denied* (1989)
9 *Death grip* (1990)
10 *Good fight* (1990)
11 *Challenge* (1990)
12 *No survivors* (1990)

Defoe series
Day, Deforest
see **Chase Defoe series**

De Gaulle series
Crozier, Brian
Biography
1 *Warrior* (1973)
2 *Statesman* (1974)

De Gier and Grijpstra series
Van de Wetering, Janwillem
1 *Outsider in Amsterdam* (1975)
2 *Tumbleweed* (1976)
3 *Corpse on the dike* (1976)
4 *Death of a hawker* (1977)
5 *Japanese corpse* (1977)
6 *Blond baboon* (1978)
7 *Maine massacre* (1979)
8 *Mind-murders* (1981)
9 *Streetbird* (1983)
10 *Rattle-rat* (1985)
11 *Hard rain* (1986)
12 *Sergeant's cat, and other stories* (1988)
13 *Just a corpse at twilight* (1994)

De Giret trilogy
Morgan, Denise
see **Ralph de Giret trilogy**

De Goede trilogy
Leroux, Etienne
see **Welgevonden trilogy**

DeGraaf series
D'Amato, Barbara
see **Doctor Garrett DeGraaf series**

De Grandin series
Quinn, Seabury
see **Jules de Grandin series**

Degrassi High School series
This sequence has six authors; based on a television series
Castellarin, Loretta
1 *Spike* (1990)
Nielsen, Susin
2 *Shane* (1990)
Roberts, Ken
3 *Stephanie Kaye* (1990)
Ellis, Kathryn
4 *Joey Jeremiah* (1990)
Nielsen, Susin
5 *Wheels* (1992)
6 *Melanie* (1992)
Sadiq, Nazneen
7 *Lucy* (1992)
Dunphy, Catherine
8 *Caitlin* (1992)

DeHavilland series
Chance, John Newton
see **Mister DeHavilland series**

Deirdre O'Hara trilogy
Gagnon, Maurice
1 *Inner ring* (1985)
2 *Dark night offshore* (1986)
3 *Doubtful motives* (1987)

De Kailern family series
De Born, Edith
1 *Schloss Fielding* (1957)
Fielding Castle
2 *House in Vienna* (1959)
3 *Flat in Paris* (1960)

Dekker series
Webb, Alex
see **Josh Dekker series**

De Kok series
Baantjer, Albert Cornelis
see **Inspector De Kok series**

Del and Tiger series
Roberson, Jennifer
see **Tiger and Del series**

Del Curb series
Hill, Douglas
1 *Fraxilly fracas* (1989)
2 *Colloghi conspiracy* (1990)

Del Whitby trilogy
Morressy, John
1 *Starbrat* (1972)
2 *Nail down the stairs* (1973)
Stardrift
3 *Under a calculating star* (1975)

De la Cloche series
Pilgrim, David
see **James De la Cloche series**

Delafield series
Forrest, Katherine V
see **Kate Delafield series**

De la Haye series
Turner, James Ernest
see **Nicholas de la Haye series**

Delamer series
Wisler, Gary Clifton
see **Willie Delamer series**

De Lancey series
Frost, Barbara
see **Marka de Lancey series**

Delancey series
Parkinson, Cyril Northcote
see **Richard Delancey series**

Delaney series
Archer, Frank
see **Inspector Joseph Delaney series**
Black, Thomas B
see **Al Delaney series**
Leroe, Ellen Whitney
see **Cupid Delaney series**
Maine, Charles Eric
see **Mike Delaney series**
Patchett, Mary Elwyn
see **Danny and David Delaney series**
Sanders, Lawrence
see **Edward X Delaney series**
Singer, Bant
see **Denis Delaney series**

Delaneys of Killaroo trilogy
This sequence has three authors
Hooper, Kay
1 *Adelaide, the enchantress* (1987)
Johansen, Iris
2 *Matilda, the adventuress* (1987)
Preston, Fayrene
3 *Sydney, the temptress* (1987)

Delaneys, the untamed years, second trilogy
This sequence has three authors
Johansen, Iris
1 *Satin ice* (1988)
Preston, Fayrene
2 *Silken thunder* (1988)
Hooper, Kay
3 *Velvet lightning* (1988)
Companion volume: *Christmas carol*, by Kay Hooper, 1992; this sequence is followed by **Delaneys of Killaroo trilogy**

Delaneys, the untamed years trilogy
This sequence has three authors
Johansen, Iris
1 *Wild silver* (1988)
Hooper, Kay
2 *Golden flames* (1988)
Preston, Fayrene
3 *Copper fire* (1988)
This sequence is followed by **Delaneys, the untamed years, second trilogy**

Delany series
Greenwald, Sheila
see **Mariah Delany series**

Delaroy series
Johns, William Earl
see **Steeley Delaroy series**

Delaware series
Kellerman, Jonathan
see **Alex Delaware series**

Delchard and Bret series
Marston, Edward
see **Gervase Bret and Ralph Delchard series**

Deleeuw series
Katz, Jon
see **Kit Deleeuw series**

Delgado series
Blackburn, Martin
1 *Sultan's turret* (1966)
2 *Ruler of Shahut* (1968)
3 *Market of the mountain men* (1968)
4 *Arabian nightmare* (1968)

Delia Scully series
Laverty, Maura
1 *Never no more* (1942)
2 *No more than human* (1944)

Delight series
Chase, Glen
see **Cherry Delight series**

Delight series
Milligan, Spike
1 *Transport of delight* (1975)
2 *Further transports of delight* (1986)

Delilah West series
O'Callaghan, Maxine
1 *Death is forever* (1980)
2 *Run from nightmare* (1981)
3 *Hit and run* (1989)

Dell Norton series
Palmer, Bernard
1 *Wild float trip* (1958)
2 *Vanishing mountain lion* (1958)
3 *Echo Mountain hermit* (1958)
4 *Dell Norton in the Ozarks* (1958)
5 *Dell Norton and the hidden cave* (1959)

Delmas trilogy
Deforges, Regine
see **Lea Delmas trilogy**

Delphond series
Halliday, Fred
see **Stanley Delphond series**

Deluge series
Wright, Sydney Fowler
see **Martin Webster series**

Demi series
Hitz, Demi
1 *Demi's find the animals A B C* (1985)
2 *Demi's count the animals one-two-three* (1986)
3 *Demi's opposites* (1987)
4 *Demi's reflective fables* (1988)
5 *Demi's Christmas surprise* (1990)
Companion volumes: *Find Demi's dinosaurs and animal game book*, 1989, *Find Demi's baby animals*, 1990

Democracy and truth trilogy
Capek, Karel
see **Truth and democracy trilogy**

Demon bike rider series
Leeson, Robert
1 *Demon bike rider* (1976)
2 *Challenge in the dark* (1978)
3 *Wheel of danger* (1986)

Demon crown trilogy
Vardeman, Robert Edward
1 *Glass warrior* (1989)
2 *Phantoms on the wind* (1989)
3 *Symphony of storms* (1990)
One volume edition entitled *The demon crown trilogy*, 1990

Demon headmaster series
Cross, Gillian
1 *Demon headmaster* (1982)
2 *Prime minister's brain* (1985)

Demon prince series
Vance, Jack
see **Kirth Gersen series**

Demon series
Lambert, William J
1 *Demon's stalk* (1970)
2 *Demon's coronation* (1971)

Demons trilogy
Friesner, Esther Mona
1 *Here be demons* (1988)
2 *Demon blues* (1989)
3 *Hooray for Hellywood* (1990)

Demonspawn series
Brennan, James Herbert
see **Sagas of the Demonspawn series**

De Mores series
Davis, Kathryn
see **Dakotas series**

Demosthenes H de Goede trilogy
Leroux, Etienne
see **Welgevonden trilogy**

Dempsey and Makepeace series
This sequence has three authors; based on a television series
Carr-Martindale, Jesse
1 *Make peace, not war* (1985)

Dempsey and Makepeace series

Raymond, John
2 *Blind eye* (1985)
3 *Lucky streak* (1985)
4 *Bogeyman* (1986)
5 *Jericho's scam* (1986)
Savage, Jack
6 *Love you to death* (1986)

Demu trilogy

Busby, Francis Marion
1 *Cage a man* (1973)
2 *Proud enemy* (1975)
3 *End of the line* (1980)
One volume edition entitled *The Demu trilogy*, 1980

Dencey Coffyn series

Snedeker, Caroline Dale
1 *Downright Dencey* (1927)
2 *Beckoning road* (1929)

Dene series

Sims, George Robert
see **Dorcas Dene series**
Verner, Gerald
see **Michael Dene series**
Williams, Valentine
see **Sergeant Trevor Dene series**

Denewood series

Knipe, Emilie Benson
1 *Lucky sixpence* (1912)
2 *Beatrice of Denewood* (1913)
3 *Peg o' the Ring, a maid of Denewood* (1915)
4 *Luck of Denewood* (1921)

Denis Delaney series

Singer, Bant
1 *You're wrong, Delaney* (1953)
Blind alley
Also published under the author's real name, Charles Shaw
2 *Have patience, Delaney* (1954)
3 *Don't slip, Delaney* (1954)
4 *Your move, Delaney* (1956)

Denis Grafton series

Dexter, William
1 *World in eclipse* (1954)
2 *Children of the void* (1955)

Denise and Ned Toodles series

Jackson, Gabrielle Emilie
1 *Denise and Ned Toodles* (1898)
2 *Another year with Denise and Ned Toodles* (1904)

Dennis Barrie series

Reynolds, Adrian
see **Professor Dennis Barrie series**

Dennis Devore series

Bennett, Dorothy
1 *Murder unleashed* (1935)
2 *Come and be killed* (1942)

Dennis Doyne series

Baines, Cuthbert
1 *Slip coach* (1927)
2 *Drug in the market* (1928)

Dennis Drury series

Sykes, William Stanley
see **Inspector Dennis Drury series**

Dennis Gatz series

Carroll, John Richard
1 *No way back* (1992)
2 *Out of the blue* (1993)

Dennis Tyler series

Diplomat
1 *Murder in the State Department* (1930)
2 *Murder in the Embassy* (1930)
3 *Scandal in the Chancery* (1931)
4 *Corpse on the White House lawn* (1932)
5 *Death in the Senate* (1933)
6 *Slow death at Geneva* (1934)
7 *Brain Trust murder* (1935)

Dennison's war series

Lassiter, Adam
1 *Dennison's war* (1984)
2 *Conte's run* (1985)
3 *Hell on wheels* (1985)
4 *King of the mountain* (1985)
5 *Triangle* (1985)
6 *Snowball in hell* (1986)

Denson series

Hoyt, Richard
see **John Denson series**

Dent series

Adams, Douglas Noel
see **Arthur Dent series**

Dentist series

Finch, Matthew
1 *Dentist in the chair* (1955)
2 *Teething troubles* (1956)
3 *Beauty bazaar* (1962)

Denton series

Hunt, Francis
see **Mary and Jerry Denton series**
Kane, Frank
see **Mickey Denton series**

Denver trilogy

Black, Hermina
see **Susan Denver trilogy**

Denzil Grigson series

Broome, Adam
see **Commissioner Denzil Grigson series**

Denzil series

Jordan, Sherryl
1 *Wednesday wizard* (1991)
2 *Denzil's dilemma* (1992)

Departing and return series

Thompson, Nancy
1 *At their departing* (1986)
2 *On their return* (1987)

Department K series

Howard, Hartley
see **Philip Scott series**

Department of Dead Ends series

Vickers, Roy
Short stories
1 *Department of Dead Ends* (1947)
2 *Murder will out* (1950)

Department Z series

Creasey, John
1 *Death miser* (1932)
2 *Redhead* (1933)
3 *First came a murder* (1934)
Revised edition 1969
4 *Death round the corner* (1935)
Revised edition 1971
5 *Mark of the crescent* (1935)
Revised edition 1970
6 *Thunder in Europe* (1936)
Revised edition 1970
7 *Terror trap* (1936)
Revised edition 1970
8 *Carriers of death* (1937)
Revised edition 1968
9 *Days of danger* (1937)
Revised edition 1970
10 *Death stands by* (1938)
Revised edition 1966
11 *Menace!* (1939)
Revised edition 1972
12 *Murder must wait* (1939)
Revised edition 1969
13 *Panic!* (1940)
14 *Death by night* (1940)
Revised edition 1971
15 *Island of peril* (1940)
Revised edition 1970
16 *Sabotage* (1941)
Revised edition 1972
17 *Go away death* (1941)
18 *Day of disaster* (1942)
19 *Prepare for action* (1942)
Revised edition 1966
20 *No darker crime* (1943)
21 *Dangerous quest* (1944)
Revised edition 1965
22 *Dark peril* (1944)
Revised edition 1965
23 *Peril ahead* (1946)
Revised edition 1969
24 *League of dark men* (1947)
Revised edition 1965
25 *Department of death* (1949)
26 *Enemy within* (1950)
27 *Dead or alive* (1951)
28 *Kind of prisoner* (1954)
29 *Black spider* (1957)

Deptford histories series

Jarvis, Robin
1 *Alchymists's cat* (1991)
2 *Oaken throne* (1993)

Deptford mice trilogy

Jarvis, Robin
1 *Dark portal* (1989)
2 *Crystal prison* (1989)
3 *Final reckoning* (1990)

Deptford trilogy

Davies, Robertson
1 *Fifth business* (1970)
2 *Manticore* (1972)
3 *World of wonders* (1976)
One volume edition entitled *The Deptford trilogy*, 1983

Depth force series

Greenfield, Irving A
1 *Depth force* (1984)
2 *Death dive* (1984)
3 *Bloody seas* (1985)
4 *Battle stations* (1985)
5 *Torpedo tomb* (1986)
6 *Sea of flames* (1986)
7 *Deep kill* (1986)
8 *Suicide run* (1987)
9 *Project discovery* (1988)
10 *Death cruise* (1988)
11 *Ice island* (1988)
12 *Harbor of doom* (1989)
13 *Warmonger* (1989)
14 *Deep rescue* (1990)
15 *Torpedo treasure* (1991)

Deputy Commissioner Benjamin Simon series

Dean, Gregory
1 *Case of Marie Corwin* (1933)
2 *Case of the fifth key* (1934)
3 *Murder on stilts* (1939)

Deputy Dan series

Rosenbloom, Joseph
1 *Deputy Dan and the bank robbers* (1985)
2 *Deputy Dan gets his man* (1985)

Deputy Marshal Dave Halloran series

Denver, Lee
1 *Gun fury* (1963)
2 *Trail to Maverick* (1965)
3 *Posse thunder* (1967)
4 *Payoff for Wells Fargo* (1967)
5 *Showdown at Sandy Gulch* (1968)
6 *Hungry gun* (1970)

Deputy Marshal Hooky Gibbs series

Tully, Paul
1 *Horsing blacksmith* (1985)
2 *Jehovahs' jailbreak* (1987)
3 *Bond jumper* (1987)
4 *Strychnine stand-off* (1988)
5 *Tale of three bullets* (1990)

Deputy Parr series

Anderson, Frederick Irving
1 *Notorious Sophie Lang* (1925)
Short stories
2 *Book of murder* (1930)
Short stories

Deputy Sheriff Jake Brown series

Cameron, Owen
1 *Catch a tiger* (1952)
2 *Fire trap* (1957)
Demon stirs

De Quesnoy and Guilia series

Wheatley, Dennis
see **Count de Quesnoy and Condesa Guilia series**

Derain family series

Thompson, Kate
1 *Great House* (1955)
2 *Mandevilla* (1958)
3 *Sugarbird* (1963)
4 *Richard's way* (1965)
5 *Painted caves* (1968)

Derben series

Foxall, Peter Augustus
see **Inspector Frank Derben series**

Derby Man series

McCarthy, Gary
1 *Derby Man* (1976)
2 *Showdown at Snakegrass Junction* (1978)
3 *Mustang fever* (1980)
4 *Pony express war* (1980)
5 *Silver shot* (1981)
6 *Explosion at Donner Pass* (1981)
7 *North chase* (1982)
8 *Rebel of Bodie* (1982)
9 *Rail warriors* (1982)
10 *Whiskey Creek* (1992)

Derek Cabell series

Penton, Brian
1 *Landtakers* (1934)
2 *Inheritors* (1936)
Giant's stride

Derek Carrington series

Netton, Budleigh
1 *Guns in the desert* (1937)
2 *Desert shadow* (1939)

Derek Flint series

This sequence has two authors
Pearl, Jack
1 *Our man Flint* (1965)
Street, Bradford
2 *In like Flint* (1967)

Derek Glover series

Mason, S C
1 *Murder at Bador* (1938)
2 *Man on the spot* (1938)

Derek Harding series

Worth, Maurice
1 *Golden pheasant mystery* (1927)
2 *Plaza mystery* (1928)
3 *Pagoda mystery* (1928)

Derek Thyrde series

Denham, Bertie
1 *Man who lost his shadow* (1979)
2 *Two Thyrdes* (1983)

Derek Torry series
Gardner, John Edmund
see **Detective Inspector Derek Torry series**

Deric series
Nusbaum, Deric
1 *Deric in Mesa Verde* (1926)
2 *Deric with the Indians* (1927)

De Richelieu series
Wheatley, Dennis
see **Duc de Richelieu series**

Dering series
Lisle, David
see **Isola Dering series**
Rives, Amelie
see **Barbara Dering series**

Dermott family series
McKenna, Stephen
1 *Dermotts rampant* (1931)
2 *Way of the phoenix* (1932)

De Rohan series
Graeme, David
see **Monsieur Blackshirt series**

Deryni trilogy
Kurtz, Katherine
see **Chronicles of the Deryni trilogy**

De Sales series
Boyle, Thomas
see **Detective Francis De Sales series**

Desdemona series
Keller, Beverly
1 *Desdemona, twelve going on desperate* (1986)
2 *Fowl play, Desdemona* (1989)
3 *Desdemona moves on* (1992)

Desert commandos series
Landsborough, Gordon
1 *Glasshouse gang* (1976)
2 *Desert marauders* (1976)
3 *Benghazi breakout* (1976)
4 *Dead commando* (1976)

Desert critterland series
Reese, Bob
1 *Lactus cactus* (1981)
2 *Tweedie-de-dee Tumbleweed* (1981)
3 *Rapid Robert Road-Runner* (1981)
4 *Critter race* (1981)
5 *Scary Larry the very, very hairy tarantula* (1981)
6 *Huzzard buzzard* (1981)

Desert Home series
Kopsen, Dorothy Blaxland
1 *Desert Home* (1954)
2 *Baileaus of Desert Home* (1956)

Desert queen series
Fitzgerald, Julia
1 *Taboo* (1985)
2 *Desert queen* (1986)

Desert series
Daniel, Jack
1 *Siege* (1974)
2 *Dispatch rider* (1980)
Originally announced as a trilogy

Desert trading post series
Hannum, Alberta
1 *Spin a silver dollar* (1945)
Spin a silver coin
Blue house
2 *Paint the wind* (1958)

Desert trilogy
Jernigan, Gisela
1 *Agave blooms just once* (1989)
2 *One green mesquite tree* (1989)
3 *Sonoran seasons* (1994)

Desert war series
Glubb, John Bagot
1 *Soldier with the Arabs* (1957)
2 *War in the desert* (1960)
An R.A.F. frontier campaign

De Silveira series
Cripps, Arthur Shearly
see **John Kent series**

Desire trilogy
Dreiser, Theodore
see **Frank Cowperwood trilogy**

Desire trilogy
Larkin, Rochelle T
1 *Mistress of desire* (1978)
2 *Harvest of desire* (1978)
3 *Torches of desire* (1980)

Desmond Drake series
Sea-Lion
1 *Meet Desmond Drake* (1952)
2 *Damn Desmond Drake* (1953)
3 *Desmond Drake goes west* (1956)

Desmond Merrion and Inspector Arnold series
Burton, Miles
see **Inspector Arnold and Desmond Merrion series**

Desmond Okewood series
Williams, Valentine
see **Clubfoot series**

Desmond series
Best, Herbert
1 *Desmond's first case* (1961)
2 *Desmond the dog detective* (1962)
Alternative title: The case of the lone stranger
3 *Desmond and the peppermint ghost* (1965)
4 *Desmond and Dog Friday* (1968)

Desmond series
Diver, Maud
1 *Captain Desmond, VC* (1907)
Revised edition 1914
2 *Great amulet* (1908)
3 *Candles in the wind* (1909)
Numbers 1-3 also published in one volume edition entitled *Men of the frontier force*, 1930
4 *Desmond's daughter* (1916)
5 *Wild bird* (1929)
6 *Ships of youth* (1931)
Study of marriage in modern India

Desmond Shannon series
Heberden, Mary Violet
1 *Death on the doormat* (1939)
2 *Subscription to murder* (1940)
3 *Fugitive from murder* (1940)
4 *Lobster pink murder* (1941)
5 *Aces, eights and murder* (1941)
6 *Murder follows Desmond Shannon* (1942)
7 *Murder makes a racket* (1942)
8 *Murder goes astray* (1943)
9 *Murder of a stuffed man* (1944)
10 *Vicious pattern* (1945)
11 *They can't all be guilty* (1947)
12 *Drinks on the victim* (1947)
13 *Case of the eight brothers* (1948)
14 *That's the spirit* (1950)
Ghosts can't kill
15 *Exit this way* (1950)
You'll fry tomorrow
16 *Tragic target* (1952)
17 *Murder unlimited* (1953)

Desmond the dinosaur series
Althea
1 *Desmond the dinosaur* (1968)
2 *Desmond the dusty dinosaur* (1969)
3 *Desmond goes to Scotland* (1969)
4 *Desmond meets a stranger* (1970)
5 *Desmond at the carnival* (1971)
6 *Desmond goes to New York* (1975)
7 *Desmond and the monsters* (1975)
8 *Desmond and the stranger* (1976)
9 *Desmond goes boating* (1977)
10 *Desmond and the fancy dress party* (1979)
11 *Desmond at the zoo* (1981)
12 *Desmond starts school* (1982)
13 *Desmond's birthday surprise* (1984)
Omnibus volumes: *The big Desmond story book*, 1979, *Desmond the dinosaur story book*, 1980, *Adventures of Desmond the dinosaur*, 1981

Desmond Thornton series
Lodwick, John
1 *Somewhere a voice is calling* (1953)
2 *Starless night* (1955)

Desouza series
Olbrich, Freny
see **Chief Inspector Frank Desouza series**

Despair trilogy
Burroughs, William Seward
1 *Junkie* (1953)
Junky
The second title is an expanded edition
2 *Queer* (1985)
Written over 30 years before publication
3 *Yage letters* (1963)
Co-author: Allen Ginsberg

Desperado series
Adams, Clifton
1 *Desperado* (1950)
2 *Noose for the Desperado* (1951)

D'Espinal series
Healey, Ben
see **Harcourt d'Espinal series**

Desteen series
Lanier, Sterling Edmund
see **Hiero Desteen series**

De Steur series
Morrison, Margaret
see **Annetze de Steur series**

Destiny makers series
Shupp, Mike
1 *With fate conspire* (1985)
2 *Morning of creation* (1986)
3 *Soldier of another fortune* (1988)
4 *Death's gray land* (1991)
Death's grey land
5 *Last reckoning* (1991)

Destiny of eagles series
Carnegie, Sacha
1 *Banners of love* (1968)
Scarlet banners of love
2 *Banners of war* (1970)
3 *Banners of power* (1972)
Kasia and the empress
4 *Banners of courage* (1976)
5 *Banners of revolt* (1977)

Destiny series
Grinnell, David
1 *Destiny's orbit* (1961)
2 *Destination, Saturn* (1967)
Co-author: Lin Carter

Destroyer series
This sequence has eight authors
Murphy, Warren Burton
1 *Created, the Destroyer* (1971)
2 *Death check* (1971)
3 *Chinese puzzle* (1972)
4 *Mafia fix* (1972)
5 *Doctor Quake* (1972)
6 *Death therapy* (1972)
7 *Union bust* (1973)
8 *Summit chase* (1973)
9 *Murder's shield* (1973)
10 *Terror squad* (1973)
11 *Kill or cure* (1973)
12 *Slave safari* (1973)
13 *Acid rock* (1973)
14 *Judgment day* (1974)
15 *Murder ward* (1974)
16 *Oil slick* (1974)
17 *Last war dance* (1974)
18 *Funny money* (1975)
19 *Holy terror* (1975)
20 *Assassins play-off* (1975)
21 *Deadly seeds* (1975)
22 *Brain drain* (1976)
23 *Child's play* (1976)
24 *King's curse* (1976)
25 *Sweet dreams* (1976)
Co-author: Richard S Meyers
26 *In enemy hands* (1977)
27 *Last temple* (1977)
Co-author: Richard S Meyers
28 *Ship of death* (1977)
29 *Final death* (1977)
Co-author: Richard S Meyers
30 *Mugger blood* (1977)
31 *Head men* (1977)
32 *Killer chromosomes* (1978)
33 *Voodoo die* (1978)
34 *Chained reaction* (1978)
35 *Last call* (1978)
36 *Power play* (1979)
37 *Bottom line* (1979)
38 *Bay City blast* (1979)
39 *Missing link* (1980)
40 *Dangerous games* (1980)
Co-author: Robert Joseph Randisi
41 *Firing line* (1980)
42 *Timber line* (1980)
Ghost writer: William Joy
43 *Midnight man* (1981)
Co-author: Robert Joseph Randisi
44 *Balance of power* (1981)
Ghost writer: Molly Cochran
45 *Spoils of war* (1981)
Ghost writer: Molly Cochran
46 *Next of kin* (1981)
Ghost writer: Molly Cochran
47 *Dying space* (1982)
Ghost writer: Molly Cochran
48 *Profit motive* (1982)
49 *Skin deep* (1982)
Ghost writer: Molly Cochran
50 *Killing time* (1982)
Ghost writer: Molly Cochran
51 *Shock value* (1983)
Ghost writer: Molly Cochran
52 *Fool's gold* (1983)
53 *Time trial* (1983)
Ghost writer: Molly Cochran
54 *Last drop* (1983)
Ghost writer: Molly Cochran
55 *Master's challenge* (1984)
Ghost writer: Molly Cochran
56 *Encounter group* (1984)
Ghost writer: Will Murray
57 *Date with death* (1984)
Ghost writers: Molly Cochran and Ed Hunsburger
58 *Total recall* (1984)
Co-author: Robert Joseph Randisi
59 *Arms of Kali* (1985)
60 *End of the game* (1985)
61 *Lords of the earth* (1985)
62 *Seventh stone* (1985)
Ghost writer: Ed Hunsburger
Sapir, Richard
63 *Sky is falling* (1986)
Ghost writer: Will Murray

64 *Last alchemist* (1986)
Ghost writer: Will Murray
65 *Lost yesterday* (1986)
Ghost writer: Will Murray
66 *Sue me* (1986)
67 *Look into my eyes* (1987)
68 *Old-fashioned war* (1987)
Murphy, Warren Burton
69 *Blood ties* (1987)
Ghost writer: Will Murray
70 *Eleventh hour* (1983)
Ghost writers: Molly Cochran and Will Murray
71 *Return engagement* (1988)
Ghost writer: Will Murray
72 *Sole survivor* (1988)
Ghost writer: Will Murray
73 *Line of succession* (1988)
Ghost writer: Will Murray
74 *Walking wounded* (1988)
Ghost writer: Will Murray
75 *Rain of terror* (1988)
Ghost writer: Will Murray
76 *Final crusade* (1989)
Ghost writer: Will Murray
77 *Coin of the realm* (1989)
Ghost writer: Will Murray
78 *Blue smoke and mirrors* (1989)
Ghost writer: Will Murray
79 *Shooting schedule* (1989)
Ghost writer: Will Murray
80 *Death sentence* (1990)
Ghost writers: Molly Cochran and Ed Hunsburger
81 *Hostile takeover* (1990)
Ghost writer: Will Murray
82 *Survival course* (1990)
Ghost writer: Will Murray
83 *Skull duggery* (1991)
Ghost writer: Will Murray
84 *Ground zero* (1991)
Ghost writer: Will Murray
85 *Blood lust* (1991)
Ghost writer: Will Murray
86 *Arabian nightmare* (1991)
Ghost writer: Will Murray
87 *Mob psychology* (1992)
88 *Ultimate death* (1992)
89 *Dark horse* (1992)
90 *Ghost in the machine* (1992)
91 *Cold warrior* (1993)
92 *Last dragon* (1993)
93 *Terminal transmission* (1993)
94 *Feeding frenzy* (1993)

Companion volumes: *Remo, the adventure begins*, by Richard Sapir, 1985, *The assassin's handbook*, by Will Murray, 1982, also published as *Inside Sinanju*, 1985

Destroyer series
Whiting, Charles
1 *Operation Afrika* (1974)
2 *Operation Stalag* (1974)
3 *Operation Caucasian Fox* (1974)
Operation Fox Hunt
4 *Operation Il Duce* (1974)
5 *Operation Kill Ike* (1975)
6 *Operation Werewolf* (1975)

Detective Charles A Baker series
Huston, Howard Chauncey
1 *With murder for some* (1953)
2 *Blind saw murder* (1954)

Detective Chief Superintendent Evans series
Sewart, Alan
1 *Turn-up* (1978)
2 *Very ordinary murder* (1979)
3 *Loop current* (1980)

Detective Ferguson series
Lincoln, Natalie Sumner
1 *Red seal* (1920)
2 *Unseen ear* (1921)

Detective Francis De Sales series
Boyle, Thomas
1 *Only the dead know Brooklyn* (1985)
2 *Post-mortem effects* (1988)

Detective Frank Pagan series
Armstrong, Campbell
1 *Jig* (1987)
2 *Mazurka* (1988)
3 *Mambo* (1990)

Detective Frank Sessions series
Waugh, Hillary
1 *Thirty Manhattan East* (1968)
2 *Young prey* (1969)
3 *Finish me off* (1970)

Detective Inspector Abraham Kozminski series
Downes, Quentin
1 *No smoke, no flame* (1952)
2 *Heads I win* (1953)
3 *They hadn't a clue* (1954)

Detective Inspector Alfred Stanley Rosher series
Scott, Jack S
1 *Poor old lady's dead* (1976)
2 *Better class of business* (1976)
Bastard's name was Bristow
3 *Shallow grave* (1977)
4 *Clutch of vipers* (1979)
5 *Gospel lamb* (1980)
6 *Distant view of death* (1981)
View from Deacon Hill
7 *Uprush of mayhem* (1982)
8 *Local lads* (1982)
9 *All the pretty people* (1983)
10 *Death in Irish Town* (1984)
11 *Knife between the ribs* (1987)

Detective Inspector Allport series
Everton, Francis
1 *Dalehouse murder* (1927)
2 *Hammer of doom* (1928)
3 *Young vanish* (1932)
4 *Murder may pass unpunished* (1936)

Detective Inspector Andrew Frampton series
Plummer, Thomas Arthur
1 *Shadowed by the C.I.D.* (1932)
2 *Shot at night* (1934)
3 *Frampton of the Yard* (1935)
4 *Dumb witness* (1936)
5 *Was the mayor murdered?* (1936)
Bonfire murder
6 *Man they feared* (1937)
7 *Death symbol* (1937)
8 *Man they put away* (1938)
9 *Five were murdered* (1938)
10 *Two men from the east* (1939)
11 *Muse Theatre murder* (1939)
12 *Melody of death* (1940)
13 *Black ribbon murders* (1940)
14 *Crime at Crooked Gables* (1941)
15 *Fool of the Yard* (1942)
16 *Devil's tea-party* (1942)
17 *Man who changed his face* (1943)
18 *Murder limps by* (1943)
19 *Murder by an idiot* (1944)
20 *Simon takes the rap* (1944)
21 *Murder in the village* (1945)
22 *Strangler* (1945)
23 *Man with the crooked arm* (1945)
24 *J for Jennie murders* (1945)
25 *Barush mystery* (1946)
26 *Pierced ear murders* (1947)
27 *Who fired the factory?* (1947)
28 *Silent four* (1947)
29 *Hunted!* (1948)
30 *Strychnine for one* (1949)
31 *Death haunts the repertory* (1950)
32 *Yellow disc murders* (1950)
33 *Murder of Doctor Gray* (1950)
34 *Murder at Marlington* (1951)
35 *Murder through Room 45* (1952)
36 *Frampton sees red* (1953)
37 *Westlade murders* (1953)
38 *Murder in Windy Coppice* (1954)
39 *Scream at midnight* (1954)
40 *Black rat* (1955)
41 *Murder in the surgery* (1955)
42 *Pagan Joe* (1956)
43 *Where was Trail murdered?* (1956)
44 *Condemned to live* (1957)
45 *Murder at Lantern Corner* (1957)
46 *Elusive killer* (1958)
47 *Hospital thief* (1959)
48 *Vestry murder* (1959)
49 *Spider man* (1961)
50 *Murder at Brownhill* (1962)

Detective Inspector Derek Torry series
Gardner, John Edmund
1 *Complete state of death* (1969)
Stone killer
2 *Corner men* (1974)

Detective Inspector Don Kerry series
Ashford, Jeffrey
1 *Counsel for the defence* (1960)
2 *Investigations are proceeding* (1961)
D.I.
3 *Will anyone who saw the accident* (1963)
Hit and run
4 *Enquiries are continuing* (1964)
Superintendent's room
5 *Forget what you saw* (1967)

Detective Inspector Du Cas series
Imbert-Terry, Henry
1 *Acid* (1928)
2 *Clay* (1931)
3 *Weeds* (1933)

Detective Inspector John Freeman series
Ironside, John
1 *Red symbol* (1910)
2 *Marten mystery* (1933)

Detective Inspector Leric series
Busby, Roger
1 *Robbery blue* (1969)
2 *Frighteners* (1970)
3 *Deadlock* (1971)
4 *Reasonable man* (1972)
5 *Pattern of violence* (1973)

Detective Inspector Manson series
Turner, Bill
1 *Bound to die* (1967)
2 *Sex trap* (1968)
3 *Circle of squares* (1969)
4 *Another little death* (1970)
5 *Solden's woman* (1972)

Detective Inspector Price series
Kelly, Vince
1 *Last minute clue* (1943)
2 *Sinister Street* (1944)

Detective Inspector Ralph Brand series
Hinxman, Margaret
1 *End of a good woman* (1976)
2 *One-way cemetery* (1977)
3 *Telephone never tells* (1982)
4 *Sound of murder* (1986)

Detective Inspector Rory Luccan series
Morland, Nigel
1 *Death when she wakes* (1951)
2 *Girl died singing* (1952)

Detective Inspector Thomas Littlejohn series
Bellairs, George
1 *Littlejohn on leave* (1941)
2 *Four unfaithful servants* (1942)
3 *Death of a busybody* (1942)
4 *Dead shall be raised* (1942)
Murder will speak
5 *Murder of a quack* (1943)
6 *Calamity at Harwood* (1943)
7 *He'd rather be dead* (1945)
8 *Death in the night watches* (1945)
9 *Crime at Halfpenny Bridge* (1946)
10 *Case of the scared rabbits* (1946)
11 *Case of the seven whistlers* (1948)
12 *Death on the last train* (1948)
13 *Outrage on Gallows Hill* (1948)
14 *Case of the famished parson* (1949)
15 *Case of the demented spiv* (1949)
16 *Case of the headless Jesuit* (1950)
Death brings in the new year
17 *Dead march for Penelope Blow* (1951)
Dead march for Penelope
18 *Death in dark glasses* (1952)
19 *Crime in Leper's Hollow* (1952)
20 *Knife for Harry Dodd* (1953)
21 *Half-mast for the Deemster* (1953)
22 *Corpses in Enderby* (1954)
23 *Cursing Stones murder* (1954)
24 *Death in Room Five* (1955)
25 *Death treads softly* (1956)
26 *Death drops the pilot* (1956)
27 *Death in High Provence* (1957)
28 *Death sends for the doctor* (1957)
29 *Corpse at the carnival* (1958)
30 *Murder makes mistakes* (1958)
31 *Bones in the wilderness* (1959)
32 *Toll the bell for murder* (1959)
33 *Death in the fearful night* (1960)
34 *Death in despair* (1960)
35 *Death of a tin god* (1961)
36 *Body in the dumb river* (1961)
Murder masquerade
37 *Death before breakfast* (1962)
38 *Tormentors* (1962)
39 *Death in the wasteland* (1963)
40 *Surfeit of suspects* (1964)
41 *Death of a shadow* (1964)
42 *Death spins the wheel* (1965)
43 *Intruder in the dark* (1966)
44 *Strangers among the dead* (1966)
45 *Death in desolation* (1967)
46 *Single ticket to death* (1967)
47 *Fatal alibi* (1968)
48 *Murder gone mad* (1969)
49 *Tycoon's death bed* (1970)
50 *Night they killed Joss Varran* (1970)
51 *Pomeroy, deceased* (1972)
52 *Murder adrift* (1972)
53 *Devious murder* (1973)
54 *Fear round about* (1975)
55 *Close all roads to Sospel* (1976)
All roads to Sospel
56 *Downhill ride of Leeman Popple* (1978)
57 *Old man dies* (1980)

Detective Kellerway series
Crauford, William Harold Lane
1 *Missing ace* (1931)
2 *Murder to music* (1936)

Detective Kilsip and Duncan Calton series
Hume, Fergus
1 *Mystery of a hansom cab* (1886)
Parody: *A blood-curdling romance, the mystery of a wheelbarrow, or, Gaboriau Garorooed, an idealistic story of a great rising colony*, by W Humer Ferguson, 1888
2 *Madam Midas* (1888)

Detective Knute Severson series
Wells, Tobias
1 *Matter of love and death* (1966)
2 *What should you know of dying?* (1967)
3 *Dead by the light of the moon* (1967)
4 *Murder most fouled up* (1968)
5 *Die quickly, dear mother* (1969)
6 *Young can die protesting* (1969)
7 *Dinky died* (1970)
8 *What to do until the undertaker comes* (1971)
9 *Foo dog* (1971)
Lotus affair
10 *How to kill a man* (1972)
11 *Die in the country* (1972)
12 *Brenda's murder* (1973)

13 *Have Mercy upon us* (1974)
14 *Hark, hark the watchdogs bark* (1975)
15 *Creature was stirring* (1977)

Detective Linley and Pel Pelham series
Martin, Archibald Edward
see **Pel Pelham and Detective Linley series**

Detective Mole series
Quackenbush, Robert Mead
1 *Detective Mole* (1976)
2 *Detective Mole and the secret clues* (1977)
3 *Detective Mole and the tip-top mystery* (1978)
4 *Detective Mole and the seashore mystery* (1979)
5 *Detective Mole and the circus mystery* (1980)
6 *Detective Mole and the Halloween mystery* (1981)
7 *Detective Mole and the haunted castle mystery* (1985)

Detective Norah Mulcahaney series
O'Donnell, Lillian
1 *Phone calls* (1972)
2 *Don't wear your wedding ring* (1973)
3 *Dial five seven seven R-A-P-E* (1974)
4 *Baby merchants* (1975)
5 *Leisure dying* (1976)
6 *No business being a cop* (1979)
7 *Children's zoo* (1981)
8 *Cop without a shield* (1983)
9 *Ladykiller* (1984)
10 *Casual affairs* (1985)
11 *Shadow in red* (1986)
12 *Other side of the door* (1987)
13 *Good night to kill* (1989)
14 *Pushover* (1992)
15 *Lockout* (1994)

Detective Peabody series
Thomson, Ruth
1 *Peabody's first case* (1978)
2 *Peabody's all at sea* (1978)
3 *Detective Peabody up in the air* (1980)

Detective Sergeant Carnaby-King series
Walker, Peter Norman
1 *Carnaby and the hijackers* (1967)
2 *Carnaby and the gaolbreakers* (1968)
3 *Carnaby and the assassins* (1968)
4 *Carnaby and the conspirators* (1969)
5 *Carnaby and the saboteurs* (1970)
6 *Carnaby and the eliminators* (1971)
7 *Carnaby and the demonstrators* (1972)
8 *Carnaby and the infiltrators* (1974)
9 *Carnaby and the kidnappers* (1976)
10 *Carnaby and the counterfeiters* (1980)
11 *Carnaby and the campaigners* (1984)

Detective Sergeant Chamberlayne series
Sewart, Alan
1 *In that rich earth* (1981)
2 *Romp in green heat* (1981)
3 *Smoker's cough* (1982)
4 *Drink, for once dead!* (1983)
5 *Dead man drifting* (1984)

Detective Sergeant Dennis Gatz series
Carroll, John Richard
see **Dennis Gatz series**

Detective Sergeant Elk series
Wallace, Edgar
see **Inspector Elk series**

Detective Sergeant Fuller series
Wallace, John
1 *Sedan murder mystery* (1938)
2 *Millionaire gangster again* (1942)

Detective Sergeant Joe Church trilogy
Peters, Lance
1 *Red collar gang* (1981)
Revised edition 1989
2 *Dirty half-mile* (1981)
3 *Civilian war zone* (1988)

Detective Sergeant Louis Solden series
Turner, Bill
see **Detective Inspector Manson series**

Detective Sergeant Pietro Tonelli series
Williams, Alexander
1 *Jinx Theatre murder* (1933)
2 *Death over Newark* (1933)
3 *Murder in the WPA* (1937)

Detective Sergeant Robert Mather series
Graeme, Bruce
1 *Quiet ones* (1970)
2 *Two and two make five* (1973)
3 *D notice* (1974)
4 *Snatch* (1976)
5 *Two-faced* (1977)
6 *Double trouble* (1978)
7 *Mather again* (1979)
8 *Invitation to Mather* (1980)
9 *Mather investigates* (1980)

Detective Sergeant Scamp series
Foxall, Peter Augustus
1 *Vultures in the smoke* (1972)
2 *Big time* (1973)
3 *Confessions of a convict* (1974)
4 *Scamp's law* (1975)
5 *No life for a loser* (1977)
6 *Taming the furies* (1978)
7 *Hostage of the damned* (1979)

Detective Sergeant Steytler series
Milne, Shirley
1 *Stiff silk* (1962)
2 *Hammer of justice* (1963)
3 *False witness* (1964)

Detective series
Thorp, Roderick
see **Joe Leland series**
Thorwald, Jurgen
see **Century of the detective series**

Detective Superintendent John Bellamy series
Jacobs, Thomas Curtis Hicks
1 *Grenson murder case* (1943)
2 *Curse of Khatra* (1947)
3 *With what motive?* (1948)
4 *Results of an accident* (1955)
5 *Broken alibi* (1957)
6 *Black trinity* (1959)
7 *Women are like that* (1960)

Detective Superintendent Roper series
Hart, Roy
1 *Seascape with dead figures* (1987)
2 *Pretty place for a murder* (1987)
3 *Fox in the night* (1988)
4 *Remains to be seen* (1989)
5 *Robbed blind* (1990)
6 *Breach of promise* (1990)

Determined detectives series
Christian, Mary Blount
1 *Mysterious case case* (1985)
2 *Merger on the Orient Expressway* (1986)
3 *Phantom of the operetta* (1986)
4 *Maltese feline* (1988)

Dethroned heiress series
Dupuy, Eliza Ann
Originally published anonymously
1 *Dethroned heiress* (1865)
2 *Hidden sin* (1866)

Detroit trilogy
Estleman, Loren D
1 *Whiskey River* (1990)
2 *Motown* (1991)
3 *King of the corner* (1992)

Detroit trilogy
Oates, Joyce Carol
see **Jules and Maureen Wendall trilogy**

Deutsch series
Christian, John
see **Richard Deutsch series**

Development series
Bryher, Winifred
1 *Development* (1920)
2 *Two selves* (1923)

Devenish series
Sudbery, Rodie
see **Polly Devenish series**

Deventer series
Anderson, John Richard Lane
see **Inspector Piet Deventer series**

Devereaux series
Granger, Bill
see **November Man series**
Roeburt, John
see **Johnny Devereaux series**

Deverry series
Kerr, Katharine
1 *Daggerspell* (1986)
2 *Darkspell* (1987)
3 *Bristling wood* (1989)
Dawnspell
4 *Dragon revenant* (1990)
Dragonspell
5 *Time of exile* (1991)
A novel of the Westlands

Devil Hardin series
Edson, John Thomas
see **Ole Devil Hardin series**

Devil series
Edwards, Olwen
1 *Devil's own* (1975)
2 *Devil's daughter* (1976)

Devil series
Johnstone, William Wallace
see **Beasts series**

Devil upon two sticks series
This sequence has two authors
Lesage, Alain Rene
1 *Asmodeus* (1707)
Devil upon crutches
Devil upon two sticks
Devil on two sticks
Original edition entitled *Le diable boiteux;* abridged edition entitled *The lame devil*, 1870; parody: *The devil upon crutches in England, or, Night scenes in London*, by a Gentleman of Oxford, 1755
Combe, William
2 *Devil upon two sticks in England* (1790)
Originally published anonymously

Devilday series
Hall, Angus
1 *Devilday* (1969)
Madhouse
2 *To play the devil* (1971)

Devildust and Maggie series
Alter, Judy
see **Maggie and Devildust series**

Devilgod series
Jallim, Collins
1 *Devilgod* (1985)
2 *Devilgod in the empire of the universal master* (1989)

Deville McKeene series
Walker, Rowland
see **Captain Deville McKeene series**

Deville series
Noy, John
see **Rufus Deville series**

De Villiers series
Muller, Mary
see **Anna and Johan de Villiers series**

Devil's dictionary series
This sequence has two authors
Bierce, Ambrose
1 *Devil's dictionary* (1911)
Based on *The cynic's word book*, 1906; revised edition entitled *The enlarged devil's dictionary*, edited by Ernest Jerome Hopkins, 1971
Williamson, Jerry Neal
2 *New devil's dictionary* (1985)

Devil's picture book series
Rayner, William
1 *Wheels of fortune* (1979)
2 *Knave of swords* (1980)
Originally announced as a trilogy

Devlin Kirk series
Burns, Rex
1 *Suicide season* (1987)
2 *Parts unknown* (1990)
3 *Body guard* (1991)
4 *Endangered species* (1993)

Devlin series
Buddee, Paul
see **Peter Devlin series**
Heatter, Basil
see **Timothy Devlin series**
Higgins, Jack
see **Liam Devlin series**
Kozlow, Mark J
see **Chris Devlin series**
Mitchell, Scott
see **Brock Devlin series**

Devlin Tracy series
Murphy, Warren Burton
1 *Trace* (1983)
2 *Trace and forty-seven miles of rope* (1984)
3 *When elephants forget* (1984)
4 *Once a mutt* (1984)
5 *Pigs get fat* (1985)
6 *Too old a cat* (1986)
7 *Getting up with fleas* (1987)

Devon and Brigitta series
Randall, Lindsey
see **Two hearts series**

Devon farm series
Addis, Faith
1 *Year of the cornflake* (1983)
2 *Green behind the ears* (1984)
3 *Buttered side down* (1985)
A slice of country life
4 *Down to earth* (1987)
5 *Taking the biscuit* (1989)

Devon School series
Knowles, John
1 *Separate peace* (1960)
2 *Peace breaks out* (1981)

Devon village series
Williamson, Henry
Short stories
1 *Tales of a Devon Village* (1945)
2 *Life in a Devon village* (1945)

Devonshire village series
Phillpotts, Eden
1 *There was an old woman* (1947)
2 *There was an old man* (1959)

Devore series
Bennett, Dorothy
see **Dennis Devore series**

Devotions series
Aaseng, Nathan
1 *I'm learning, Lord, but I still need help* (1981)
Story devotions for boys
2 *I'm searching, Lord, but I need your light* (1983)
3 *Which way are you leading me, Lord?* (1984)
Bible devotions for boys

Dewey annals series
Hagan, Chet
1 *Bon marche* (1988)
2 *From the ashes* (1989)

De Winter series
Du Maurier, Daphne
see **Rebecca De Winter series**

De Witt series
Rabe, Peter
see **Manny De Witt series**

Dexter Drake series
Barker, Elsa
1 *Cobra candlestick* (1928)
2 *C.I.D. of Dexter Drake* (1929)
3 *Redman Cave murder* (1930)

Dexter Dutton series
Fennell, Willie
1 *Life with Dexter* (1959)
2 *More life with Dexter* (1960)
3 *Third life with Dexter* (1960)
4 *Dexter loses his head* (1960)
5 *Dexter sings* (1960)
6 *Mad stuff* (1960)
7 *Dexter's fit* (1961)
8 *Dexter's court* (1961)
9 *Desert island wreckers* (1961)
10 *Dexter gets the point* (1961)
11 *Dexter and Ashleigh muddle on* (1962)
12 *Car-razy life with Dexter* (1962)
13 *Dexter detects* (1962)

Dexter series
Baker, Willard F
see **Bob Dexter series**
Fredman, John
see **Charles Dexter series**
Hackforth-Jones, Gilbert
see **Paul Dexter series**
Kennedy, Elliot
see **Griff Dexter series**
Marquand, John Phillips
see **Timothy Dexter series**
Sperry, Raymond
see **Larry Dexter series**

Dextra series
Lake, David John
1 *Right hand of Dextra* (1977)
2 *Wildings of Westron* (1977)

Diadem series
Clayton, Jo
1 *Diadem from the stars* (1977)
2 *Lamarchos* (1978)
3 *Irsud* (1978)
4 *Maeve* (1979)
5 *Star hunters* (1980)
6 *Nowhere hunt* (1981)
7 *Ghosthunt* (1983)
8 *Snares of ibex* (1984)
9 *Quester's endgame* (1986)
10 *Shadowplay* (1990)
11 *Shadowspeer* (1990)
12 *Shadowkill* (1991)

Diamond Outfit series
Grey, Zane
1 *Drift fence* (1932)
2 *Hash-Knife Outfit* (1933)

Diamond series
Horowitz, Anthony
see **Nick and Tim Diamond series**
Quartermain, James
see **Raven series**
Schorr, Mark
see **Red Diamond series**

Diamondback series
Bishop, Pike
see **Cord Diamondback series**

Diamonds series
Corbett, Scott
1 *Diamonds are trouble* (1967)
2 *Diamonds are more trouble* (1969)

Diana and Max series
Ziefert, Harriet
see **Max and Diana series**

Diana Forbes series
Mitton, Geraldine Edith
1 *Two-stringed fiddle* (1919)
2 *Green moth* (1922)
Co-author: James George Scott

Diana Logan and Matt Sutton series
White, James G
see **Gunslick series**

Diana Santee series
Green, Sharon
1 *Mind guest* (1984)
2 *Gateway to Xanadu* (1985)

Diana Tregarde series
Lackey, Mercedes
1 *Burning water* (1989)
2 *Children of the night* (1990)
3 *Jinx high* (1991)

Diana Winthrop series
Chambers, Kate
1 *Secret of the singing strings* (1983)
2 *Danger in the old fort* (1983)
3 *Case of the dog lover's legacy* (1983)
4 *Secrets of Beacon Hill* (1984)
5 *Legacy of Lucian Van Zandt* (1984)
6 *Threat of the pirate ship* (1984)

Dianas series
Herbert, Agnes
see **Two Dianas series**

Diane series
Cavanna, Betty
1 *Date for Diane* (1946)
2 *Diane's new love* (1955)
3 *Toujours Diane* (1957)

Diaries of Adam and Eve series
Twain, Mark
1 *Extracts from Adam's diary* (1904)
2 *Eve's diary* (1906)
One volume edition entitled *The diaries of Adam and Eve*, 1971

Diaries of Tom Goane series
Nolan, Christopher
see **Journals of Tom Goane series**

Diary series
Anonymous
1 *Diary of my honeymoon* (1910)
2 *Indiscretion of Lady Usher* (1913)

Dice Man series
Rhinehart, Luke
see **Wim series**

Dice series
Hill, Peter
see **Commander Allan Dice series**

Dick and Daisy Travers series
Samuels, Adelaide Florence
1 *Adrift in the world* (1872)
Alternative title: Dick and Daisy's early days
2 *Fighting the battle* (1872)
Alternative title: Dick and Daisy's city life
3 *Saved from the street* (1872)
Alternative title: Dick and Daisy's proteges
4 *Grandfather Milly's luck* (1872)
Alternative title: Dick and Daisy's reward
Companion volume: *Daisy Travers, or, The girls of Hive Hall*, 1876

Dick and Dolly series
Wells, Carolyn
1 *Dick and Dolly* (1909)
2 *Dick and Dolly's adventures* (1910)

Dick and Emmeline series
Stacpoole, Henry de Vere
1 *Blue lagoon* (1908)
2 *Garden of God* (1923)
3 *Gates of morning* (1925)

Dick and Janet series
Garis, Howard Roger
see **Two Wild Cherries series**

Dick and Tamily series
Robins, Patricia
1 *Long wait* (1962)
2 *Constant heart* (1964)
3 *Uncertain joy* (1966)

Dick Barton series
This sequence has four authors; based on a radio series
Jones, Elwyn
1 *Dick Barton, special agent* (1977)
Three novelettes
Radnor, Alan
2 *Case of the vanishing house* (1978)
Dorrell, Mike
3 *Mystery of the missing formula* (1978)
Pryce, Larry
4 *Gold bullion swindle* (1979)

Dick Burton series
Beckett, Mark
see **Major Dick Burton series**

Dick Donovan series
Donovan, Dick
1 *Man-hunter* (1888)
Stories from the note-book of a detective
2 *Caught at last!* (1889)
Leaves from the note-book of a detective
3 *Who poisoned Hetty Duncan, and other detective stories* (1890)
4 *Tracked and taken* (1890)
Stories from the note-book of a detective
Detective sketches
5 *Detective's triumphs* (1891)
Short stories
6 *Wanted!* (1892)
A detective's strange adventures
7 *In the grip of the law* (1892)
Short stories
8 *From information received* (1893)
Short stories
9 *Link by link* (1893)
Short stories
10 *From clue to capture* (1893)
Short stories
11 *Suspicion aroused* (1893)
Short stories
12 *Found and fettered* (1894)
Short stories
13 *Dark deeds* (1895)
Short stories
14 *Riddles read* (1896)
Short stories
15 *Tales of terror* (1899)
Short stories

Dick Grenville series
Fletcher, Lawrence
1 *Into the unknown* (1892)
A romance of South Africa
2 *Zero the slaver* (1892)
A romance of Equatorial Africa

Dick, Jane and Sally series
Montgomery, Elizabeth
1 *We look and see* (1940)
2 *We work and play* (1940)
3 *We come and go* (1940)
4 *Good times with our friends* (1941)
5 *Three friends* (1944)
6 *Five in the family* (1946)
7 *Girl next door* (1946)
8 *You* (1948)
9 *Happy days and our friends* (1948)
10 *Just like me* (1957)
11 *Being six* (1957)
12 *Seven or so* (1957)
13 *Eight to nine* (1957)
14 *Going on ten* (1958)
15 *About yourself* (1958)

Dick Kent series
Richards, Milton
1 *Dick Kent with the mounted police* (1927)
2 *Dick Kent in the far north* (1927)
3 *Dick Kent with the Eskimos* (1927)
4 *Dick Kent, fur trader* (1927)
5 *Dick Kent with the Malamute Mail* (1927)
6 *Dick Kent on special duty* (1928)
7 *Dick Kent at Half Way House* (1929)
8 *Dick Kent, Mounted Police deputy* (1933)
9 *Dick Kent's mysterious mission* (1933)
10 *Dick Kent and the mine mystery* (1934)

Dick Lingham series
Finch, Matthew
1 *Five are the symbols* (1964)
2 *Jones is a rainbow* (1965)
3 *Succubus* (1966)

Dick Marlow series
Bentley, John
1 *Dangerous waters* (1939)
Mister Marlow takes to Rye
2 *Prelude to trouble* (1939)
Mister Marlow chooses wine
3 *Front page murder* (1940)
Mister Marlow stops for brandy
4 *Rendezvous with death* (1941)
5 *Macedonian mixup* (1943)
6 *Dead do talk* (1944)

Dick Mason series
Armstrong, Raymond
see **Inspector Dick Mason series**

Dick McCunn series
Buchan, John
see **Dickson McCunn series**

Dick Morris and Jerry Scott series
Gulick, Bill
see **Junior Trail Blazers series**

Dick Pemberty series
Conde, Phillip
1 *Death from the air* (1936)
2 *Devil has wings* (1937)
3 *Pilot's graveyard* (1938)
4 *Spawn of the hawk* (1938)

5 *Death loop* (1938)
6 *Case of the crazy pilot* (1939)
7 *Mystery of the vanishing aerodrome* (1939)
8 *Secret of the scarlet letter* (1939)
9 *Death laughs aloft* (1940)

Dick Philip series
Pickering, Robert Easton
1 *Uncommitted man* (1967)
2 *Himself again* (1967)

Dick Ryder series
Watson, Henry Brereton Marriott
1 *Galloping Dick* (1896)
2 *High Toby* (1906)
3 *King's highway* (1910)
4 *As it chanced* (1916)

Dick Seldon series
Masterman, Walter Sidney
1 *Bloodhounds Bay* (1936)
2 *Border line* (1936)

Dick series
Alger, Horatio
see **Ragged Dick series**

Dick series
Bradby, Godfrey Fox
1 *Dick* (1906)
A story without a plot
2 *For this I had borne him* (1915)

Dick series
Rowe, John Gabriel
see **Sergeant Dick series**

Dick Talbot series
Aiken, Albert W
1 *Dick Talbot's clean out* (1892)
2 *Dick Talbot, the ranch king* (1892)

Dick Torreyton series
Charles, Ernest F
1 *Death crosses the line* (1937)
2 *Death comes ashore* (1938)
3 *Before the wind* (1938)

Dick Tracy cartoon series
This sequence has two authors; comic strips
Gould, Chester
1 *Exploits of Dick Tracy, detective* (1946)
2 *Celebrated cases of Dick Tracy, 1931-1951* (1970)
3 *Pruneface* (1975)
4 *Snowflake and Shaky* (1975)
5 *Dick Tracy, the thirties, tommy guns and hard times* (1978)
6 *Dick Tracy, America's most famous detective* (1987)
Moore, John
7 *Big city blues* (1990)
8 *Dick Tracy versus the underworld* (1990)
9 *Dick Tracy* (1990)
Companion volume : *Dick Tracy, a novelization of the comic strip,* by William Johnston, 1970

Dick Tracy film series
This sequence has two authors
Collins, Max Allan
1 *Dick Tracy* (1990)
Based on a screenplay; companion volume: *Dick Tracy,* by Peter Lerangis, 1990
Bonifer, Michael
2 *Dick Tracy, the official book of the movie* (1990)
Companion volumes: *Dick Tracy, the secret files,* by Martin Harry Greenberg, 1990, *Dick Tracy activity book,* by Peter Lerangis, 1990, *Dick Tracy, a catch-a-crook adventure,* by Peter Lerangis, 1990, *Dick Tracy fun book of puzzles and games,* by Nancy E Krulik, 1990

Dick Tracy series
This sequence has four authors
Gould, Chester
1 *Dick Tracy and the Woo Woo sisters* (1947)
Collins, Max Allan
2 *Dick Tracy meets Angel Top* (1980)
3 *Dick Tracy meets the punks* (1980)
Razzi, Jim
4 *Dick Tracy in hot water* (1990)
Gurelle, Andrew
5 *Dick Tracy on the trail of Blank* (1990)
Collins, Max Allan
6 *Dick Tracy and the nightmare machine* (1991)
7 *Dick Tracy goes to war* (1991)
8 *Dick Tracy meets his match* (1992)
Companion volumes: *Tracy's wartime memories,* 1986, *Dick Tracy casebook, favorite adventures, 1931-1990,* edited by Max Allan Collins and Dick Locher, 1990, *Dick Tracy, the official biography,* by Jay Meader, 1990, *Dick Tracy's fiendish foes, a sixtieth anniversary celebration,* edited by Max Allan Collins, 1991

Dick Travers series
Samuels, Adelaide Florence
1 *Palm land* (1872)
Alternative title: Dick Travers in the Chagos Islands
2 *Lost tar* (1872)
Alternative title: Dick Travers in Africa
3 *On the wave* (1872)
Alternative title: Dick Travers aboard the Happy Jack
4 *Little Cricket* (1872)
Alternative title: Dick Travers in London

Dick Weston series
Lund, Trygve
1 *Weston of the Royal North-West Mounted Police* (1928)
Weston of the North-West Mounted Police
2 *Up north* (1929)
Numbers 1 and 2 also published in one volume entitled *The Lone Trail omnibus,* 1936
3 *Murder of Dave Brandon* (1931)
A story of the Northwest Mounted Police
4 *Robbery at Portage Bend* (1933)
5 *Vanished prosepctor* (1937)

Dick Whelan series
Smith, Laurence Dwight
1 *Corpse with the listening ear* (1940)
2 *Follow this fair corpse* (1941)
Case of the rented coffin

Dick Wilson series
Sproul, Kathleen
1 *Birthday murder* (1932)
2 *Death and the professors* (1934)
Death among the professors
3 *Murder off key* (1934)
4 *Mystery of the closed car* (1935)

Dicken Quinney trilogy
Hennessy, Max
1 *Bright blue sky* (1982)
2 *Challenging heights* (1983)
3 *Once more the hawks* (1984)
4 *Crimson wind* (1985)

Dickerson series
Goldthwaite, Eaton Kenneth
see **Lieutenant Joseph Dickerson series**

Dickie and Dorrie series
Everett-Green, Evelyn
see **Hallowdene Hall series**

Dickie and Flora series
Stewart, Flora
see **Flora and Dickie series**

Dickson McCunn series
Buchan, John
1 *Huntingtower* (1922)
2 *Castle Gay* (1930)
3 *House of the four winds* (1935)

Did I ever tell series
Grender, Iris
1 *Did I ever tell you?* (1977)
2 *Second did I ever tell you book* (1978)
But that's another story
3 *Third did I ever tell you book* (1980)
4 *Did I ever tell you about my Irish great grandmother?* (1981)
5 *Did I ever tell you about my birthday party?* (1983)
6 *Did I ever tell you what the children told me?* (1985)

Didier series
Myers, Amy
see **Auguste Didier series**

Dido Twite series
Aiken, Joan
1 *Wolves of Willoughby Chase* (1962)
2 *Black hearts in Battersea* (1964)
3 *Night birds on Nantucket* (1966)
4 *Stolen lake* (1981)
5 *Cuckoo tree* (1971)
6 *Dido and pa* (1986)
7 *Whispering mountain* (1968)

Diego series
Kelsey, Vera
see **Lieutenant Diego series**

Dies Drear series
Hamilton, Virginia
1 *House of Dies Drear* (1968)
2 *Mystery of Drear House* (1987)

Dies irae trilogy
Stableford, Brian Michael
1 *Days of glory* (1971)
2 *In the kingdom of the beasts* (1971)
3 *Day of wrath* (1971)

Dig Allen series
Greene, Joseph
1 *Forgotten star* (1959)
2 *Captives in space* (1960)
3 *Journey to Jupiter* (1961)
4 *Trappers of Venus* (1961)
5 *Robots of Saturn* (1962)
6 *Lost city of Uranus* (1962)

Di Ganzarello, Tucker and Norrington series
Drummond, Ivor
see **Lady Jennifer, Sandro and Colly series**

Digburn series
Sanders, Bruce
see **Howard Digburn series**

Digby series
Byers, Irene
see **Tim Digby series**
Harvey, William Fryer
see **Athelstan Digby series**
Wray, I
see **Inspector Digby series**

Digger Burroughs series
Murphy, Warren Burton
1 *Smoked out* (1982)
2 *Fool's flight* (1982)
3 *Dead letter* (1982)
4 *Lucifer's weekend* (1982)
Co-author: Robert Joseph Randisi

Digger Driscoll series
Johns, William Earl
1 *Adventure bound* (1955)
2 *Adventure unlimited* (1957)

Digger Haig series
Courtier, Sidney Hobson
see **Inspector Digger Haig series**

Diggory and Gillian series
De la Roche, Mazo
see **Gillian and Diggory series**

Digit Dick series
Rees, Leslie
1 *Digit Dick on the Barrier Reef* (1942)
Digit Dick on the Great Barrier Reef
2 *Digit Dick and the Tasmanian devil* (1946)
3 *Digit Dick in Black Swan Island* (1952)
Revised edition 1972
4 *Digit Dick and the lost opals* (1957)
Revised edition 1971; numbers 1-4 published in one volume entitled *The big book of Digit Dick,* 1973
5 *Digit Dick and the zoo plot* (1981)

Di Griz series
Harrison, Harry
see **Jim Di Griz series**

Dilbert series
Robertson, Kate
1 *Dilbert wins his wings* (1977)
2 *Dilbert down under* (1977)
3 *Dilbert on safari* (1977)
4 *Dilbert and the dodo* (1977)

Dilbia series
Dickson, Gordon Rupert
1 *Spacial delivery* (1961)
2 *Spacepaw* (1969)

Dilke series
Gutteridge, Lindsay
see **Mathew Dilke series**

Dillon series
Higgins, Jack
1 *Eagle has flown* (1991)
2 *Eye of the storm* (1992)

Dillon series
Roddy, Lee
see **Davey Dillon series**

Dillworth trilogy
Spring, Howard
1 *Hard facts* (1944)
2 *Dunkerley's* (1946)
3 *Time and the hour* (1957)

Dilly series
Bradman, Tony
1 *Dilly the dinosaur* (1986)
2 *Dilly visits the dentist* (1986)
Dilly's muddy day
3 *Dilly tells the truth* (1987)
4 *Dilly and the horror film* (1987)
5 *Worst day ever* (1988)
Dilly goes swamp wallowing
6 *Dilly and the tiger* (1988)
7 *Dilly and the ghost* (1989)
8 *Dilly Dinosaur, superstar* (1989)
9 *Dilly the angel* (1990)
10 *Dilly speaks up* (1990)
11 *Dilly goes on holiday* (1990)
12 *Dilly goes to school* (1991)
13 *Dilly and his swamp lizard* (1991)
14 *Dilly and the big kids* (1991)
15 *Dilly's birthday party* (1991)
16 *Dilly and the pirates* (1992)
17 *Dilly, Dinosaur, detective* (1994)

Dilvish the Damned trilogy
Zelazny, Roger
1 *Bells of Shoredon* (1979)
2 *Changing land* (1981)
3 *Dilvish the Damned* (1982)

Dimarco series
Disney, Doris Miles
see **Jeff Dimarco series**

Dime series
Fantoni, Barry
see **Mike Dime series**

Dimsie series
Bruce, Dorita Fairlie
1 *Senior prefect* (1920)
Dimsie goes to school
2 *Dimsie moves up* (1921)
3 *Dimsie moves up again* (1922)
4 *Dimsie among the prefects* (1923)
5 *Dimsie grows up* (1924)
6 *Dimsie, head girl* (1926)
7 *Dimsie goes back* (1927)
8 *Dimsie intervenes* (1937)
9 *Dimsie carries on* (1942)
10 *Dimsie takes charge* (1985)
Short stories

Din Alt series
Harrison, Harry
see **Jason Din Alt series**

Dinah Campion series
Batt, Elisabeth
1 *House with the blind window* (1955)
2 *In search of Simon* (1956)

Dingle and Jones series
Osborne, Geoffrey
see **James Dingle and Glyn Jones series**

Dingleflop series
Heap, Jean Walmsley
1 *Dingleflop chimes* (1949)
2 *Dingleflop moon* (1953)

Dingo series
Wongar, B
1 *Marngit* (1992)
2 *Last pack of dingoes* (1993)

Dinkum Cavendish series
Cooper, Charles
see **Russell Cavendish series**

Dinkum oil series
Mills, Frederick John
1 *Dinkum oil* (1917)
Original Australian wit and humour
2 *Square dinkum* (1917)
More original Australian wit and humour
3 *New dunkum oil* (1944)
More Australian wit and humour and other ingredients

Dinny Gordon series
Emery, Anne
1 *Dinny Gordon, freshman* (1959)
2 *Dinny Gordon, sophomore* (1961)
3 *Dinny Gordon, junior* (1964)
4 *Dinny Gordon, senior* (1965)

Dinochrome Brigade series
Laumer, Keith
see **Bolo series**

Dinosaur days series
Lloyd, David
Illustrated by Peter Cross
1 *Early morning* (1985)
2 *Breakfast* (1985)
3 *Terrible thing* (1985)
4 *Silly games* (1985)

Dinosaur machines series
Bunting, Eve
1 *Day of the dinosaurs* (1975)
2 *Death of a dinosaur* (1975)
3 *Dinosaur trap* (1975)
4 *Escape from tyrannosaurus* (1975)

Dinosaur series
Salmon, Michael
1 *There's a dinosaur in the garden* (1985)
2 *Dinosaur who wanted to fly* (1988)
3 *Dinosaur who invented things* (1988)
4 *Dinosaur who wouldn't go to school* (1988)
5 *Dinosaur who forgot her birthday* (1988)
6 *Smallest dinosaur in the world* (1988)
7 *Dinosaur who couldn't sleep* (1988)

Dinosaur swamp series
Salmon, Michael
1 *Go away dinosaurs* (1989)
2 *Glub, the baby dinosaur* (1989)
3 *Cousin Roc comes to stay* (1989)
4 *Deep sea sauruses* (1989)
5 *Ice cave* (1989)
6 *Under the volcano* (1989)

Dinosaurs guide book series
Brown, Marc
1 *Dinosaurs, beware!* (1982)
Co-author: Stephen Krensky; a safety guide
2 *Dinosaurs divorce* (1986)
Co-author: Laurene Krasny Brown; a guide for changing families
3 *Dinosaurs travel!* (1988)
Co-author: Stephen Krensky; a guide for families on the go
4 *Dinosaurs alive and well* (1990)
A guide to good health

Dinosaurs series
Berenstain, Michael
1 *Biggest dinosaurs* (1989)
2 *Horned dinosaur* (1989)
Triceratops
3 *King of the dinosaurs* (1989)
Tyrabbosaurus rex
4 *Spike tailed dinosaurs* (1989)
Stegosaur
5 *Flying dinosaurs* (1991)
Pterodactyls

Dinosaurs series
Brown, Laurence Krasny
1 *Dinosaurs divorce* (1986)
A guide to changing families
2 *Dinosaurs travel* (1988)
A guide for families on the go
3 *Dinosaurs alive and well!* (1990)
Co-author: Marc Brown

Dinosaurs series
Ritthaler, Shelly
1 *Dinosaurs for lunch* (1993)
2 *Dinosaurs wild!* (1994)
3 *Dinosaurs alive!* (1994)

Dinsmore series
Finley, Martha Farquharson
see **Elsie Dinsmore series**

Dinwiddie series
Hassett, Margaret
see **Miss Dinwiddie series**

Dio series
Merejkowski, Dmitri Sergeevich
Translated from the Russian; set in ancient Crete and Egypt
1 *Birth of the gods* (1924)
2 *Akhnaton, King of Egypt* (1924)

Dion Quince series
Welch, Timothy L
1 *Tennis murders* (1976)
Sequence continued under the pseudonym Patrick Cake
Cake, Patrick
2 *Pro-Am murders* (1979)

Dionysus series
Priestley, Margaret
see **World Dionysus series**

Dionysus trilogy
Trevor, Meriol
see **World Dionysus trilogy**

Diplomat series
Vare, Daniele
Reminiscences
1 *Laughing diplomat* (1938)
2 *Two imposters* (1949)

Diplomatic series
Peyrefitte, Roger
1 *Diplomatic diversions* (1951)
Original edition entitled *Les ambassades*
2 *Diplomatic conclusions* (1953)
Original edition entitled *La fin des ambassades*

Dippers series
Willard, Barbara
1 *Dippers and Jo* (1960)
2 *Dippers and the high-flying kite* (1963)

Dipple trilogy
Norton, Andre
1 *Catseye* (1961)
2 *Judgment on Janus* (1963)
3 *Night of masks* (1969)

Dirk Gently series
Adams, Douglas Noel
1 *Dirk Gently's holistic detective gency* (1987)
2 *Long dark tea-time of the soul* (1989)

Dirk Pitt series
Cussler, Clive
1 *Pacific vortex!* (1983)
2 *Mediterranean caper* (1973)
Mayday!
3 *Iceberg* (1975)
4 *Raise the Titanic!* (1976)
5 *Vixen Zero Three* (1978)
6 *Night probe!* (1981)
7 *Deep six* (1984)
8 *Cyclops* (1986)
9 *Treasure* (1988)
10 *Dragon* (1990)
11 *Sahara* (1992)
12 *Inca gold* (1994)

Dirk Prine series
Garrisen, Paul
1 *Dirk's run* (1990)
2 *Dirk's revenge* (1990)
3 *Dirk's return* (1990)

Dirk Rogers series
Crisp, Frank
1 *Sea robbers* (1949)
2 *Haunted reef* (1950)
3 *Java wreckmen* (1955)
4 *Manila menfish* (1956)
5 *Manila stranger* (1957)
6 *Sea ape* (1958)
7 *Demon wreck* (1958)
8 *Giant of Jembu Gulf* (1959)
9 *Ice divers* (1960)
10 *Coral wreck* (1964)
11 *Sanguman* (1965)

Dirk series
Rybakov, Anatoli
Translated from the Russian
1 *Dirk* (1948)
2 *Bronze bird* (1956)

Dirk Spencer series
Winski, Norman
1 *Chicago deathwinds* (1984)
2 *L.A. massacre* (1984)
3 *Nevada nightmare* (1984)

Dirshan series
Lancour, Gene
1 *Lerios Mecca* (1973)
2 *War machines of Kalinth* (1977)
3 *Sword for the empire* (1978)
4 *Man-eaters of Cascalon* (1979)

Dirt bike racer series
Christopher, Matt
1 *Dirt bike racer* (1979)
2 *Dirt bike runaway* (1983)

Dirty Harry Callahan series
Hartman, Dane
This pseudonym is used by several authors including Leslie Horvitz and Richard S Meyers whose authorship is indicated against those titles where it is known; based on the character from the moving pictures
1 *Duel for cannons* (1981)
[Meyers]
2 *Death on the docks* (1981)
[Horvitz]
3 *Long death* (1981)
[Meyers]
4 *Mexico kill* (1982)
5 *Family skeletons* (1982)
[Meyers]
6 *City of blood* (1982)
7 *Massacre at Russian River* (1982)
8 *Hatchet men* (1982)
[Meyers]
9 *Killing connection* (1983)
10 *Blood of the strangers* (1983)
11 *Death in the air* (1983)
[Meyers]
12 *Dealer of death* (1983)
Companion volumes: *Dirty Harry*, by Philip Rock, 1971, *The enforcer*, by Mel Valley, 1973, *Sudden impact*, by Joe Stinson, 1984

Disability series
Hulme, Joy Nelson
1 *Other side of the door* (1990)
2 *Climbing the rainbow* (1992)

Disappointed man series
Barbellion, W N P
Autobiography
1 *Journal of a disappointed man* (1919)
2 *Last journal* (1920)

Disasters series
Reid, Colin
Humour
1 *Life with my wife, and other disasters* (1968)
2 *Do you take this woman, and more disasters* (1973)
3 *I kiss your little hand, madame, and more disasters abroad* (1977)

Disbro series
Martin, James E
see **Gil Disbro series**

Discoverers and creators series
Boorstin, Daniel Joseph
1 *Discoverers* (1983)
A history of man's search to know his world and himself
2 *Creators* (1993)
A history of heroes of the imagination

Discovering series
Simon, Seymour
1 *Discovering what earthworms do* (1969)
2 *Discovering what frogs do* (1969)
3 *Discovering what goldfish do* (1970)
4 *Discovering what gerbils do* (1971)
5 *Discovering what crickets do* (1973)
6 *Discovering what garter snakes do* (1975)
7 *Discovering what puppies do* (1977)

Discovery series
Clune, Frank
Memoirs of travel
1 *Rolling down the Lachlan* (1935)

2 *Roaming round the Darling* (1936)
3 *Free and easy land* (1938)
4 *Sky high to Shanghai* (1939)
5 *To the Isles of Spice* (1940)
6 *All aboard for Singapore* (1941)
7 *Prowling through Papua* (1942)
8 *Tobruk to Turkey with the army of the Nile* (1943)
9 *Song of India* (1946)
10 *Roaming round Australia* (1947)
11 *High-ho to London* (1948)
12 *Land of hope and glory* (1949)
13 *Ashes of Hiroshima* (1950)
14 *All roads lead to Rome* (1950)
15 *Hands across the Pacific* (1951)
16 *Somewhere in New Guinea* (1951)
17 *Castles in Spain* (1952)
18 *Flying Dutchmen* (1953)
19 *Land of Australia* (1953)

Discovery series
Macdonald, Suse
1 *Alphabatics* (1986)
2 *Numblers* (1988)
Co-author: Bill Oakes
3 *Once upon another* (1990)
4 *Space spinners* (1991)

Discursions series
Sitwell, Osbert
1 *Discursions on travel, art and life* (1925)
2 *Winters of content* (1932)
More discursions on travel, art and life
3 *Four continents* (1954)
More discursions on travel, art and life

Discworld series
Pratchett, Terry
1 *Colour of magic* (1983)
2 *Light fantastic* (1986)
3 *Equal rites* (1987)
4 *Mort* (1987)
5 *Sourcery* (1988)
6 *Wyrd sisters* (1988)
Starring three witches, also kings, daggers, crowns
7 *Pyramids* (1989)
The book of going forth
8 *Guards, guards!* (1989)
9 *Eric* (1989)
10 *Moving pictures* (1990)
11 *Reaper man* (1991)
12 *Witches abroad* (1991)
13 *Small gods* (1992)
14 *Lords and ladies* (1993)
15 *Men at arms* (1993)
16 *Soul music* (1994)

Disher series
Scott, Will
1 *Disher, detective* (1925)
Black stamp
2 *Shadows* (1928)
3 *Man* (1929)
Mask

Disinherited series
Allen, Hervey
1 *Forest and the fort* (1943)
2 *Bedford Village* (1944)
3 *Toward the morning* (1948)
Omnibus volume: *The city of the dawn*, 1950 contains abridgements of the three volumes with sections of a never-completed fourth

Disinherited series
Forster, Peter
see **Alex Smith and Tony Bevan series**

Disney's Annette series
Schroeder, Doris
see **Walt Disney's Annette series**

Disney's Oliver and company series
Korman, Justine
see **Oliver and company series**

Disraeli series
Edelman, Maurice
see **Benjamin Disraeli series**

Distant drums series
Carey, D L
see **Dorian Trozen series**

Distant lands series
Green, Julian
1 *Distant lands* (1991)
Original edition entitled *Les pays lointains*
2 *Stars of the South* (1995)
Original edition entitled *Les etoiles du Sud*

Distant prospect series
Berners, Gerald Hugh Tyrwhitt-Wilson
Autobiography
1 *First childhood* (1934)
2 *Distant prospect* (1945)

DiStefano trilogy
Janifer, Laurence Mark
see **Angelo DiStefano trilogy**

District Attorney series
Gardner, Erle Stanley
1 *D.A. calls it murder* (1937)
2 *D.A. holds a candle* (1938)
3 *D.A. draws a circle* (1939)
4 *D.A. goes to trial* (1940)
5 *D.A. cooks a goose* (1942)
6 *D.A. calls a turn* (1944)
7 *D.A. breaks a seal* (1946)
8 *D.A. takes a chance* (1948)
9 *D.A. breaks an egg* (1949)

District nurse series
Miller, Hugh
1 *District nurse* (1984)
2 *Snow on the wind* (1987)

District of Columbia series
Dos Passos, John
see **Spotswood family series**

District officer series
Bradley, Kenneth
Autobiography
1 *Diary of a district officer* (1943)
2 *Once a district officer* (1966)

Ditte trilogy
Nexo, Martin Andersen
1 *Ditte, girl alive!* (1917)
2 *Ditte, daughter of man* (1918)
3 *Ditte, beyond the stars* (1919)
Original one volume edition entitled *Ditte Menneskebarn*

Diver series
Sharp, Margery
see **Martha Diver series**

Diversions series
Wells, Carolyn
1 *Rainy day diversions* (1907)
2 *Pleasant day diversions* (1909)

Divine corners series
Baldwin, Faith
1 *Judy* (1930)
2 *Babs* (1931)
3 *Mary Lou* (1931)
4 *Myra* (1932)

Divine series
John, Stephen
see **Albert Divine series**

Divinity series
Agee, Jonis
1 *Pretend we've never met* (1989)
Short stories
2 *Sweet eyes* (1991)

Dixie T Struthers series
Sims, L V
1 *Death is a family affair* (1987)
2 *Murder is only skin deep* (1987)
3 *To sleep, perchance to dream* (1988)

Dixon Brett series
King, T Stanleyan
1 *Missing mayor* (1926)
2 *Yellow wolf* (1926)

Dixon of Dock Green series
This sequence has two authors
Willis, Ted
1 *Devil's churchyard* (1957)
2 *Seven gates to nowhere* (1958)
Hatton, Charles
3 *White Hart Lane mystery* (1960)

Dixon series
Bellairs, John
see **Johnny Dixon series**
Wayne, Dorothy
see **Dorothy Dixon series**
Willis, Ted
see **George Dixon series**
Wormser, Richard
see **Sergeant Joe Dixon series**

Dixon twins series
Markham, Marion M
1 *Halloween candy mystery* (1982)
2 *Christmas present* (1984)
3 *Thanksgiving Day parade* (1986)
4 *Birthday party* (1989)
5 *April Fool's Day mystery* (1991)
6 *Valentine's Day mystery* (1992)

Dizzy and Ali series
Shaw, Jane
see **Ali and Dizzy series**

Djuna and Champ series
Queen, Ellery, Junior
1 *Black dog mystery* (1941)
2 *Golden eagle mystery* (1942)
3 *Green turtle mystery* (1942)
4 *Red chipmunk mystery* (1946)
5 *Brown fox mystery* (1948)
6 *White elephant mystery* (1950)
7 *Yellow cat mystery* (1952)
8 *Blue herring mystery* (1954)

DKA file series
Gores, Joe
1 *Dead skip* (1972)
2 *Final notice* (1973)
3 *Gone, no forwarding* (1978)

Dmitry Korotoyev series
Ehrenburg, Ilya
Translated from the Russian
1 *Thaw* (1954)
2 *Spring* (1956)

Do and Dare Club series
Cooper, Wendy
1 *Cat strikes at night* (1959)
2 *Disappearing diamond* (1960)

Do series
Pratt, Henry
1 *Bit of a do* (1986)
2 *Fair do's* (1990)

Do something series
Long, Helen Beecher
1 *Janice Day at Poketown* (1914)
2 *Testing of Janice Day* (1915)
3 *How Janice Day won* (1916)
4 *Missing of Janice Day* (1917)
5 *Janice Day, the young homemaker* (1919)

Doan and Carstairs series
Davis, Norbert
1 *Sally's in the alley* (1943)
2 *Oh, murderer mine* (1946)

Doanides series
Kenneth, Claire
see **Cynthia Doanides series**

Dobbs series
Blake, Christina
see **Inspector Donald Dobbs series**
Saxe, R B
see **John Dobbs series**

Dobie and Coyle series
Cory, Desmond
see **John Dobie and Kate Coyle series**

Doc and Raider series
Hardin, J D
see **Raider and Doc series**

Doc Caliban series
Farmer, Philip Jose
1 *Feast unknown* (1969)
2 *Mad goblin* (1970)
Keeper of the secrets

Doc Connor series
Dolph, Jack
1 *Odds-on murder* (1948)
2 *Murder is mutuel* (1948)
3 *Murder makes the mare go* (1950)
4 *Hot tip* (1951)
5 *Dead angel* (1953)

Doc Hennessy and Angeltown Keeps series
Bancroft, Tex
see **Angeltown Keeps and Doc Hennessy series**

Doc McDuff and Popcorn Pruitt series
Mitchell, Red
1 *Rodeo* (1982)
2 *Slayride* (1982)

Doc Miller series
Petersen, Herman
1 *Murder in the making* (1940)
2 *Murder R.F.D.* (1942)

Doc Savage series
Robeson, Kenneth
This pseudonym is used by William G Bogart, Harold A Davis, Lester Dent, Laurence Donovan, Alan Hathway, Ryerson Johnson, Will Murray as indicated against each title
1 *Man of bronze* (1933)
[Dent]
2 *Thousand-headed man* (1964)
[Dent]
3 *Meteor menace* (1964)
[Dent]
4 *Polar treasure* (1965)
[Dent]
5 *Brand of the werewolf* (1965)
[Dent]
6 *Lost oasis* (1965)
[Dent]
7 *Monsters* (1965)
[Dent]
8 *Land of terror* (1933)
[Dent]
9 *Mystic Mullah* (1965)
[Dent]
10 *Phantom City* (1966)
[Dent]
11 *Fear Cay* (1966)
[Dent]
12 *Quest of Qui* (1966)
[Dent]
13 *Land of Always-Night* (1966)
[Dent; Johnson]
14 *Fantastic island* (1966)
[Dent; Johnson]
15 *Murder melody* (1967)
[Donovan]
16 *Spook Legion* (1967)
[Dent]
17 *Red skull* (1967)
[Dent]

Doc Savage series

18 *Sargasso Ogre* (1967)
[Dent]
19 *Pirate of the Pacific* (1967)
[Dent]
20 *Secret in the sky* (1967)
[Dent]
21 *Cold death* (1968)
[Donovan]; numbers 21 and 21 also published as one volume
22 *Czar of fear* (1968)
[Dent]
23 *Fortress of solitude* (1968)
[Dent]; numbers 22 and 23 also published as one volume
24 *Green eagle* (1968)
[Dent]
25 *Devil's playground* (1968)
[Hathway]; numbers 24 and 25 also published as one volume
26 *Death in silver* (1968)
[Dent]
27 *Mystery under the sea* (1968)
[Dent]; numbers 26 and 27 also published as one volume
28 *Deadly dwarf* (1968)
[Dent]
29 *Other world* (1968)
[Dent]
30 *Flaming falcons* (1968)
[Dent]
31 *Annihilist* (1968)
[Dent]
32 *Dust of death* (1969)
[Davis; Dent]
33 *Terror in the Navy* (1969)
[Dent]
34 *Mad eyes* (1969)
[Donovan]
35 *Squeaking Goblin* (1969)
[Dent]
36 *Resurrection day* (1969)
[Dent]
37 *Hex* (1969)
[Bogart; Dent]
38 *Red snow* (1969)
[Dent]
39 *World's Fair goblin* (1969)
[Bogart; Dent]
40 *Dagger in the sky* (1969)
[Dent]
41 *Merchants of disaster* (1969)
[Davis; Dent]
42 *Gold ogre* (1969)
[Dent]
43 *Man who shook the earth* (1969)
[Dent]
44 *Sea magician* (1970)
[Dent]
45 *Men who smiled no more* (1970)
[Donovan]
46 *Midas man* (1970)
[Dent]
47 *Land of long juju* (1970)
[Donovan]
48 *Feathered Octopus* (1970)
[Dent]
49 *Sea Angel* (1970)
[Dent]
50 *Devil on the Moon* (1970)
[Dent]
51 *Haunted ocean* (1970)
[Donovan]
52 *Vanisher* (1970)
[Dent]
53 *Mental wizard* (1970)
[Dent]
54 *He could stop the world* (1970)
[Donovan]
55 *Golden peril* (1970)
[Davis; Dent]
56 *Giggling ghosts* (1971)
[Dent]
57 *Poison Island* (1971)
[Dent]
58 *Munitions master* (1971)
[Davis]
59 *Yellow cloud* (1971)
[Dent]
60 *Majii* (1971)
[Dent]
61 *Living-fire menace* (1971)
[Davis]
62 *Pirate's ghost* (1971)
[Dent]
63 *Submarine mystery* (1971)
[Dent]
64 *Motion menace* (1971)
[Dent; Johnson]
65 *Green death* (1971)
[Davis]
66 *Mad Mesa* (1972)
[Dent]
67 *Freckled shark* (1972)
[Dent]
68 *Quest of the Spider* (1933)
[Dent]
69 *Mystery on the snow* (1972)
[Dent]
70 *Spook Hole* (1972)
[Dent]
71 *Murder mirage* (1973)
[Donovan]
72 *Metal Master* (1973)
[Dent]
73 *Seven agate devils* (1973)
[Dent]
74 *Derrick devil* (1973)
[Dent]
75 *Land of fear* (1973)
[Davis; Dent]
76 *Black spot* (1974)
[Donovan]
77 *South Pole terror* (1974)
[Dent]
78 *Crimson serpent* (1974)
[Davis; Dent]
79 *Devil Genghis* (1974)
[Dent]
80 *King maker* (1975)
[Davis; Dent]
81 *Stone man* (1976)
[Dent]
82 *Evil gnome* (1976)
[Dent]
83 *Red terrors* (1976)
[Dent]
84 *Mountain monster* (1976)
[Davis]
85 *Boss of terror* (1976)
[Dent]
86 *Angry ghost* (1977)
[Bogart; Dent]
87 *Spotted men* (1977)
[Bogart; Dent]
88 *Roar Devil* (1977)
[Dent]
89 *Magic island* (1977)
[Dent]
90 *Flying goblin* (1977)
[Bogart]
91 *Purple Dragon* (1978)
[Davis; Dent]
92 *Awful egg* (1978)
[Dent]
93 *Tunnel terror* (1979)
[Bogart]
94 *Hate genius* (1979)
[Dent]
95 *Red spider* (1979)
[Dent]
96 *Mystery on Happy Bones* (1979)
[Dent]
97 *Satan black* (1980)
[Dent]
98 *Cargo unknown* (1980)
[Dent]; numbers 97 and 98 published as one volume
99 *Hell below* (1980)
[Dent]
100 *Lost giant* (1980)
[Dent]; numbers 99 and 100 published as one volume
101 *Pharaoh's ghost* (1981)
[Dent]
102 *Time terror* (1981)
[Dent]; numbers 101 and 102 published as one volume
103 *Whisker of Hercules* (1981)
[Dent]
104 *Man who was scared* (1981)
[Dent]; numbers 103 and 104 published as one volume
105 *They died twice* (1981)
[Dent]
106 *Screaming man* (1981)
[Dent]; numbers 105 and 106 published as one volume
107 *Jiu San* (1981)
[Dent]
108 *Black, black witch* (1981)
[Dent]; numbers 107 and 108 published as one volume
109 *Shape of terror* (1982)
[Dent]
110 *Death had yellow eyes* (1982)
[Dent]; numbers 109 and 110 published as one volume
111 *One-eyed mystic* (1982)
[Dent]
112 *Man who fell up* (1982)
[Dent]; numbers 111 and 112 published as one volume
113 *Talking devil* (1982)
[Dent]
114 *Ten ton snakes* (1982)
[Dent]; numbers 113 and 114 published as one volume
115 *Pirate isle* (1983)
[Dent]
116 *Speaking stone* (1983)
[Dent]; numbers 115 and 116 published as one volume
117 *Golden man* (1984)
[Dent]
118 *Peril in the north* (1984)
[Dent]; numbers 117 and 118 published as one volume
119 *Laugh of death* (1984)
[Dent]
120 *King of terror* (1984)
[Dent]; numbers 119 and 120 published as one volume
121 *Three wild men* (1984)
[Dent]
122 *Fiery menace* (1984)
[Dent]; numbers 121 and 122 published as one volume
123 *Devils of the deep* (1984)
[Davis; Dent]
124 *Headless men* (1984)
[Hathway]; numbers 123 and 124 published as one volume
125 *Goblins* (1985)
[Dent]
126 *Secret of the Su* (1985)
[Dent]; numbers 125 and 126 published as one volume
127 *All-white elf* (1986)
[Dent]
128 *Running skeletons* (1986)
[Dent]
129 *Angry canary* (1986)
[Dent]
130 *Swooning lady* (1986)
[Dent]; numbers 127-130 published as *Doc Savage omnibus*, volume 1
131 *Mindless monsters* (1987)
[Hathway]
132 *Rustling death* (1987)
[Hathway]
133 *King Joe Cay* (1987)
[Dent]
134 *Thing that pursued* (1987)
[Dent]; numbers 131-134 published as *Doc Savage omnibus*, volume 2
135 *Spook of Grandpa Eben* (1987)
[Dent]
136 *Measures for a coffin* (1987)
[Dent]
137 *Three devils* (1987)
[Dent]
138 *Strange fish* (1987)
[Dent]; numbers 135-138 published as *Doc Savage omnibus*, volume 3
139 *Mystery island* (1987)
[Dent]
140 *Men of fear* (1987)
[Dent]
141 *Rock sinister* (1987)
[Dent]
142 *Pure evil* (1987)
[Dent]; numbers 139-142 published as *Doc Savage omnibus*, volume 4
143 *No light to die by* (1988)
[Dent]
144 *Monkey suit* (1988)
[Dent]
145 *Let's kill Ames* (1988)
[Dent]
146 *Once over lightly* (1988)
[Dent]
147 *I died yesterday* (1988)
[Dent]; numbers 143-147 published as *Doc Savage omnibus*, volume 5
148 *Awful dynasty* (1988)
[Bogart]
149 *Magic forest* (1988)
[Bogart; Dent]
150 *Fire and ice* (1988)
[Bogart; Dent]
151 *Disappearing lady* (1988)
[Bogart]; numbers 148-151 published as *Doc Savage omnibus*, volume 6
152 *Men vanished* (1988)
[Dent]
153 *Five fathoms dead* (1988)
[Dent]
154 *Terrible stork* (1988)
[Dent]
155 *Danger lies east* (1988)
[Dent]; numbers 152-155 published as *Doc Savage omnibus*, volume 7
156 *Mental monster* (1989)
[Dent]
157 *Pink lady* (1989)
[Dent]
158 *Weird valley* (1989)
[Dent]
159 *Trouble on parade* (1989)
[Dent]; numbers 156-159 published as *Doc Savage omnibus*, volume 8
160 *Invisible-box murders* (1989)
[Dent]
161 *Birds of death* (1989)
[Dent]
162 *Wee ones* (1989)
[Dent]
163 *Terror takes seven* (1989)
[Dent]; numbers 160-163 published as *Doc Savage omnibus*, volume 9
164 *Devil's black rock* (1989)
[Dent]
165 *Waves of death* (1989)
[Dent]
166 *Too-wise owl* (1989)
[Dent]
167 *Terror and the lonely widow* (1989)
[Dent]; numbers 164-167 published as *Doc Savage omnibus*, volume 10
168 *Se-Pah-Poo* (1990)
[Dent]
169 *Colors for murder* (1990)
[Dent]
170 *Three times a corpse* (1990)
[Dent]
171 *Death is a round black spot* (1990)
[Dent]
172 *Devil is Jones* (1990)
[Dent]; numbers 168-172 published as *Doc Savage omnibus*, volume 11
173 *Bequest of evil* (1990)
[Bogart]
174 *Death in little houses* (1990)
[Bogart; Dent]
175 *Target for death* (1990)
[Bogart]
176 *Death lady* (1990)
[Bogart]
177 *Exploding lake* (1990)
[Dent]; numbers 173-177 published as *Doc Savage omnibus*, volume 12
178 *Derelict of Skull Shoal* (1990)
[Dent]
179 *Terror wears no shoes* (1990)
[Dent]
180 *Green master* (1990)
[Dent]
181 *Return for Cormoral* (1990)
[Dent]

182 *Up from Earth's center* (1990) [Dent]; numbers 178-182 published as *Doc Savage omnibus*, volume 13
183 *Python Isle* (1991) [Dent; Murray]
Companion volumes: *Doc Savage, his apocalyptic life*, by Philip Jose Farmer, 1973, *Doc Savage, the supreme adventurer*, by John Leonard Nanovic, 1980, *The incredible radio exploits of Doc Savage*, by Lester Dent, 1982, *The invincible Doc Savage*, edited by Edward Grushkin, 1983, *The crazy Indian*, by William G Bogart, 1987, *Escape from Loki*, by Philip Jose Farmer, 1991; parody: *The living toilets*, by Kin I Disrobeson, 1973

Doc Summers series
Marlowe, Francis
1 *Hatton Garden mystery* (1934)
2 *Crime of Philip Garrison* (1935)
3 *In pursuit of a million* (1936)

Doc Travis trilogy
Cameron, Lou
1 *Doc Travis* (1975)
2 *North to Cheyenne* (1975)
3 *Guns of Durango* (1976)

Docker series
Pink, Hal
see **Inspector Docker series**

Doctor Adder trilogy
Jeter, Kevin W
1 *Doctor Adder* (1984)
2 *Glass hammer* (1985)
3 *Death arms* (1987)

Doctor Adolph Grundt series
Williams, Valentine
see **Clubfoot series**

Doctor Alexander Caspian series
Burke, John Frederick
1 *Devil's footsteps* (1976)
2 *Black charade* (1977)
3 *Ladygrove* (1978)

Doctor Alexander Cornell series
Michel, Milton Scott
1 *Black key* (1946)
Sequence continued under the pseudonym Milton Scott
Scott, Milton
2 *Dear, dead Harry* (1949)

Doctor Amy Prescott series
Hendricksen, Louise
1 *With deadly intent* (1993)
2 *Grave secrets* (1994)

Doctor Anthony Post series
Irving, Alexander
1 *Bitter ending* (1946)
2 *Symphony in two time* (1948)

Doctor Benjamin Tancred series
Cole, George Douglas Howard
1 *Doctor Tancred begins* (1935)
2 *Last will and testament* (1936)

Doctor Bentiron series
Poate, Ernest M
1 *Behind locked doors* (1923)
2 *Doctor Bentiron, detective* (1930)
Three novelettes

Doctor Bing Irvington series
Baldwin, Faith
1 *Station wagon set* (1938)
2 *Any village* (1971)

Doctor Bohler series
Konsalik, Heinz Gunther
see **Stalingrad series**

Doctor Bones series
This sequence has five authors
Leigh, Stephen
1 *Gilded sarcaphogus* (1967)
Wu, William Franking
2 *Cosmic bomber* (1989)
Wylde, Thomas
3 *Garukan blood* (1989)
Betancourt, John Gregory
4 *Dragons of Komako* (1989)
Stern, David
5 *Nightmare world* (1989)
Wylde, Thomas
6 *Journey to Rilla* (1990)

Doctor Burton series
Gunter, Archibald Clavering
1 *Doctor Burton* (1907)
2 *Doctor Burton's success* (1908)

Doctor Catriona Chisholm series
Dwyer-Joyce, Alice
1 *For I have lived today* (1971)
2 *Prescription for Melissa* (1974)

Doctor Charlie Adams series
Boyer, Richard Lewis
1 *Billingsgate shoal* (1982)
2 *Penny ferry* (1984)
3 *Daisy ducks* (1986)
4 *Moscow metal* (1987)
5 *Whale's footprint* (1988)
6 *Gone to earth* (1990)
7 *Yellow bird* (1991)

Doctor Christopher Blayre series
Blayre, Christopher
see **University of Cosmopoli series**

Doctor Cicero Smith series
Ahlswede, Ann
1 *Day of the hunter* (1960)
2 *Hunting wolf* (1960)
3 *Savage land* (1962)

Doctor Clinton Shannon series
Roberts, Lee
1 *Once a widow* (1957)
2 *If the shoe fits* (1959)
3 *Death of a ladies' man* (1960)
Also published under the author's real name Robert Lee Martin
4 *Suspicion* (1964)

Doctor Constance Daniels series
Stanley, George Edward
1 *Mini-mysteries* (1977)
2 *Crime lab* (1985)
3 *Ukrainian egg mystery* (1986)
4 *Italian spaghetti mystery* (1987)
5 *Mexican tamale mystery* (1988)

Doctor Constantine series
Thynne, Molly
1 *Crime at the Noah's Ark* (1931)
2 *Murder in the dentist chair* (1932)
3 *He dies and makes no sign* (1933)

Doctor Craven series
Gaunt, Mary
1 *Arm of the leopard* (1904)
2 *Fools rush in* (1906)
3 *Silent ones* (1909)

Doctor Daniel Webster Coffee series
Blochman, Lawrence Goldtree
1 *Diagnosis, homicide* (1950)
Short stories
2 *Recipe for homicide* (1952)
3 *Clues for Dr Coffee* (1964)
Short stories

Doctor David Audley and Jack Butler series
Price, Anthony
1 *Forty four vintage* (1978)
2 *Labyrinth makers* (1970)
3 *Alamut ambush* (1971)
4 *Colonel Butler's wolf* (1972)
5 *October men* (1973)
6 *Other paths to glory* (1974)
7 *Our man in Camelot* (1975)
8 *War game* (1976)
9 *Tomorrow's ghost* (1979)
10 *Hour of the donkey* (1980)
11 *Soldier no more* (1981)
12 *Old Vengeful* (1982)
13 *Gunner Kelly* (1983)
14 *Sion Crossing* (1984)
15 *Here be monsters* (1985)
16 *For the good of the state* (1986)
17 *New kind of war* (1987)
18 *Prospect of vengeance* (1988)
19 *Memory trap* (1989)

Doctor David Wintringham series
Bell, Josephine
1 *Murder in hospital* (1937)
2 *Death on the borough council* (1937)
3 *Fall over cliff* (1938)
4 *Death at half-term* (1939)
Curtain call for a corpse
5 *From natural causes* (1939)
6 *All is vanity* (1940)
7 *Trouble at Wrekin Farm* (1942)
8 *Death at the medical board* (1944)
9 *Death in clairvoyance* (1949)
10 *Summer school mystery* (1950)
11 *Bones in the barrow* (1953)
12 *Fires at Fairlawn* (1954)
13 *Death in retirement* (1956)
14 *China roundabout* (1956)
Murder on the merry-go-round
15 *Seeing eye* (1958)

Doctor Davie series
Clinton-Baddeley, Victor Clinton
1 *Death's bright dart* (1967)
2 *My foe outstrech'd beneath the tree* (1968)
3 *Only a matter of time* (1969)
4 *No case for the police* (1970)
5 *To study a long silence* (1972)
Completed by Mark Goullet after the author's death

Doctor Death series
Zorro
1 *Twelve must die* (1966)
2 *Gray creatures* (1966)
3 *Shriveling murders* (1966)
4 *Stories from Doctor Death* (1966)

Doctor Dolittle series
Lofting, Hugh
1 *Story of Doctor Dolittle* (1920)
Doctor Dolittle
2 *Voyages of Doctor Dolittle* (1922)
Doctor Dolittle and the pirates
3 *Doctor Dolittle's post office* (1923)
4 *Doctor Dolittle's circus* (1924)
5 *Doctor Dolittle's zoo* (1925)
6 *Doctor Dolittle's caravan* (1926)
7 *Doctor Dolittle's garden* (1927)
8 *Doctor Dolittle in the moon* (1928)
9 *Doctor Dolittle's return* (1933)
10 *Doctor Dolittle and the secret lake* (1948)
11 *Doctor Dolittle and the green canary* (1950)
12 *Doctor Dolittle's Puddlebury adventures* (1952)
Selection: *Doctor Dolittle, a treasury*, 1967
Companion volume: *Gub-Gub's book, an encyclopaedia of food*, 1932

Doctor Dorothy Dee series
Wesley, Elizabeth
1 *Doctor Dee* (1960)
2 *Doctor Dee's choice* (1962)
Doctor Dorothy's choice

Doctor Douglas Baynes series
Bell, Vicars
1 *Death under the stars* (1949)
2 *Two by day and one by night* (1950)
3 *Death has two doors* (1950)
4 *Death darkens council* (1952)
5 *Death and the night watches* (1955)
6 *Death walks by the river* (1959)

Doctor Edward Lester series
Levison, Eric
1 *Hidden eyes* (1920)
2 *Eye witness* (1921)
3 *Ashes of evidence* (1921)

Doctor Elwin Ransom trilogy
Lewis, Clive Staples
see **Space trilogy**

Doctor Emmanuel Cellini series
Halliday, Michael
American edition of this sequence published under the pseudonym Kyle Hunt
1 *Cunning as a fox* (1965)
2 *Wicked as the Devil* (1966)
3 *Sly as a serpent* (1967)
4 *Cruel as a cat* (1968)
5 *Too good to be true* (1969)
6 *Period of evil* (1970)
7 *As lonely as the damned* (1971)
8 *As empty as hate* (1972)
9 *As merry as hell* (1973)
10 *This man did I kill* (1974)
11 *Man who was not himself* (1976)

Doctor Esmond Ross series
Dwyer-Joyce, Alice
1 *Doctor Ross of Harton* (1966)
2 *Story of Doctor Esmond Ross* (1967)
3 *Verdict on Doctor Esmond Ross* (1968)
4 *Dial emergency for Doctor Ross* (1969)
5 *Message for Doctor Ross* (1971)

Doctor Eustace Hailey series
Wynne, Anthony
1 *Mystery of the evil eye* (1925)
Sign of evil
2 *Double-thirteen mystery* (1926)
Double thirteen
3 *Mystery of the ashes* (1927)
4 *Horseman of death* (1927)
5 *Sinners go secretly* (1927)
6 *Red Scar* (1928)
7 *Dagger* (1928)
8 *Fourth finger* (1929)
9 *Room with the iron shutters* (1929)
10 *Yellow crystal* (1930)
11 *Blue Vesuvius* (1930)
12 *Murder of a lady* (1931)
Silver scale mystery
13 *Silver arrow* (1931)
White arrow
14 *Case of the green knife* (1932)
Green knife
15 *Case of the red-haired girl* (1932)
Cotswold case
16 *Loving cup* (1933)
Death out of the night
17 *Case of the gold coins* (1933)
18 *Death of a banker* (1934)
19 *Toll-house murder* (1935)
20 *Holbein mystery* (1935)
Red lady
21 *Murder in thin air* (1936)
22 *Death of a golfer* (1937)
Murder in the morning
23 *Death of a king* (1938)
Murder calls Doctor Hailey
24 *Door nails never die* (1939)
25 *Horse on the hard* (1940)
26 *Emergency exit* (1941)
27 *Murder in a church* (1942)
28 *Death of a shadow* (1950)

Doctor Ferenc series
Savage, Richard
1 *Murder for fun* (1947)
2 *Horrible hat* (1948)
3 *Poison and the root* (1950)

Doctor Finlay series
Cronin, Archibald Joseph
1 *Adventures of a black bag* (1969)
2 *Doctor Finlay of Tannochnrae* (1978)
Companion volume: *On call with Doctor Finlay*, by Peter Haining, 1995

Doctor Frank King series
King, Frank
1 *Death of a halo* (1950)
2 *Death of a cloven hoof* (1951)
3 *Death changes his mind* (1953)
4 *Death has a double* (1955)

Doctor Frank Tarleton series
Upward, Allen
1 *Domino Club* (1926)
Club of Masks
2 *House of sin* (1926)
3 *Venetian key* (1927)

Doctor Fu-Manchu series
Rohmer, Sax
see **Fu-Manchu series**

Doctor Furnell series
Furnell, John
1 *Dark portal* (1950)
2 *God on the mountain* (1951)

Doctor Garrett DeGraaf series
D'Amato, Barbara
1 *Hands of healing murder* (1980)
2 *Eyes on Utopia murders* (1981)

Doctor Gideon Fell series
Carr, John Dickson
1 *Hag's Nook* (1933)
2 *Mad Hatter mystery* (1933)
3 *Blind barber* (1934)
Case of the blind barber
4 *Eight of swords* (1934)
5 *Death-watch* (1935)
6 *Three coffins* (1935)
Hollow man
7 *Arabian Nights murder* (1936)
8 *To wake the dead* (1937)
9 *Crooked hinge* (1938)
10 *Problem of the green capsule* (1939)
Black spectacles
11 *Problem of the wire cage* (1939)
12 *Man who could not shudder* (1940)
13 *Case of the constant suicides* (1941)
14 *Death turns the tables* (1941)
Seat of the scornful
15 *Till death do us part* (1944)
16 *He who whispers* (1946)
17 *Sleeping sphinx* (1947)
18 *Dead man's knock* (1948)
19 *Below suspicion* (1949)
20 *In spite of thunder* (1960)
21 *House at Satan's Elbow* (1965)
22 *Panic in Box C* (1966)
23 *Dark of the moon* (1967)
Doctor Fell also appears in three stories in *The third bullet, and other stories*, 1954, two stories in *The men who explained miracles*, 1963 and a radio play in *The door to doom, and other detections*, 1980; selection of stories and radio plays: *Doctor Fell, detective, and other stories*, 1947

Doctor Goodwin series
Merritt, Abraham
1 *Moon pool* (1919)
2 *Metal monster* (1946)

Doctor Gregor Maclean series
McLeave, Hugh
1 *Question of negligence* (1970)
2 *Borderline case* (1978)
3 *Double exposure* (1979)
4 *No face in the mirror* (1980)
Also published under the pseudonym Richard Copeland
5 *Death masque* (1986)

Doctor Henry Frost series
Bell, Josephine
1 *Upfold witch* (1964)
2 *Death on the reserve* (1966)

Doctor Henry Poggioli series
Stribling, Thomas Sigismund
see **Professor Henry Poggioli series**

Doctor Henry Pym series
Burley, William John
1 *Taste of power* (1966)
2 *Death in willow pattern* (1969)

Doctor Hillis Owen series
Wells, Anna Mary
1 *Talent for murder* (1942)
2 *Murderer's choice* (1943)
3 *Sin of angels* (1948)

Doctor Hudson series
Douglas, Lloyd Cassel
1 *Doctor Hudson's secret journal* (1939)
2 *Magnificent obsession* (1929)

Doctor Hugh Westlake series
Stagge, Jonathan
1 *Murder gone to earth* (1936)
Dogs do bark
2 *Murder or mercy* (1937)
Murder by prescription
3 *Stars spell death* (1939)
Murder in the stars
4 *Turn of the table* (1940)
Funeral for five
5 *Yellow taxi* (1942)
Call a hearse
6 *Scarlet circle* (1943)
Light from a lantern
7 *Death my darling daughters* (1945)
Death and the dear girls
8 *Death's old sweet song* (1946)
9 *Three fears* (1949)

Doctor Jack Mason series
Duncan, Alex
see **Country doctor series**

Doctor Jack series
Rathborne, Saint George
1 *Doctor Jack* (1890)
2 *Doctor Jack's wife* (1893)
3 *Doctor Jack's Paradise Mine* (1904)
4 *Doctor Jack and Company* (1906)
5 *Doctor Jack's talisman* (1906)
6 *Doctor Jack's widow* (1910)

Doctor James Wiscock series
Rice, William
1 *Doctor, darling!* (1975)
2 *Doctor, don't!* (1976)

Doctor James Yeo series
Treherne, John
1 *Trap* (1985)
2 *Mangrove chronicles* (1986)

Doctor Jane series
McElfresh, Adeline
1 *Doctor Jane* (1954)
2 *Calling Doctor Jane* (1957)
3 *Doctor Jane's mission* (1958)
4 *Doctor Jane comes home* (1959)
5 *Doctor Jane's choice* (1961)
6 *Challenge for Doctor Jane* (1963)
7 *Doctor Jane, interne* (1966)

Doctor Jason Love series
Leasor, James
1 *Passport to oblivion* (1964)
Where the spies are
2 *Passport to peril* (1966)
Spylight
3 *Passport in suspense* (1967)
Yang meridian
4 *Passport for a pilgrim* (1968)
5 *Week of love* (1969)
Short stories
6 *Love-all* (1971)
7 *Host of extras* (1973)
8 *Love and the land beyond* (1979)
9 *Frozen assets* (1989)
10 *Love down under* (1992)

Doctor Jekyll sequels series
This sequence, by three authors whose works have been inspired by Robert Louis Stevenson's novel, are listed in chronological order of publication
Estleman, Loren D
1 *Doctor Jekyll and Mister Holmes* (1979)
Hall, Willis
2 *Doctor Jekyll and Mister Hollins* (1988)
Tennant, Emma
3 *Two women of London* (1989)
The strange case of Ms Jekyll and Mrs Hyde

Doctor Jekyll series
This sequence has two authors
Stevenson, Robert Louis
1 *Strange case of Doctor Jekyll and Mister Hyde* (1886)
Doctor Jekyll and Mister Hyde
Adaptations: *The strange case of Doctor Jekyll and Mister Hyde*, by Raymond Harris, 1982, *Doctor Jekyll and Mister Hyde*, by Kate McMullan, 1984, *Doctor Jekyll and Mister Hyde*, by Tomas Ernesto Bethancourt, 1985, *The strange case of Doctor Jekyll and Mister Hyde*, by Joan Cameron, 1986, *Robert Louis Stevenson's Doctor Jekyll and Mister Hyde*, by Samantha Lee, 1987, *Doctor Jekyll and Mister Hyde*, by Rosemary Border, 1991; parody: *The adult version of Doctor Jekyll and Mister Hyde*, by Terry Stacy, 1970
Bloch, Robert
2 *Jekyll legacy* (1990)
Companion volumes: *The definitive Doctor Jekyll and Mister Hyde companion*, by Harry Maurice Geduld, 1983, *Doctor Jekyll and Mister Hyde after one hundred years*, by Gordon Hirsch and William Veeder, 1988

Doctor Joan Marvin series
Eyles, Leonora
1 *They wanted him dead* (1936)
2 *Death of a dog* (1936)

Doctor Johann Faustus series
Faustus, Johann
1 *Faustus* (1587)
Original edition entitled *Historia von Doctor Johann Fausten*, part 1; the history of the damnable life and deserved death of Doctor John Faustus
2 *Second report of Doctor Faustus* (1593)
Original edition entitled *Historia von Doctor Johann Fausten*, part 2; his appearance and the deeds of Wagner

Doctor John Evelyn Thorndyke series
This sequence has three authors
Freeman, Richard Austin
1 *Red thumb mark* (1907)
2 *John Thorndyke's cases* (1909)
Doctor Thorndyke's cases
Short stories
3 *Eye of Osiris* (1911)
Vanishing man
4 *Singing bone* (1912)
Adventures of Doctor Thorndyke
Short stories; including *The case of Oscar Brodski* (1912)
5 *Mystery of Thirty One New Inn* (1912)
6 *Silent witness* (1914)
7 *Great portrait mystery* (1918)
Short stories
8 *Helen Vardon's confession* (1922)
9 *Doctor Thorndyke's case book* (1923)
Blue scarab
Short stories
10 *Cat's eye* (1923)
11 *Mystery of Angelina Frood* (1924)
12 *Shadow of the Wolf* (1925)
13 *Puzzle lock* (1925)
Short stories
14 *D'Arblay mystery* (1926)
15 *Magic casket* (1927)
Short stories
16 *Certain Doctor Thorndyke* (1927)
17 *As a thief in the night* (1928)
18 *Mister Pottermack's oversight* (1930)
19 *Pontifex, Son and Thorndyke* (1931)
20 *When rogues fall out* (1932)
Doctor Thorndyke's discovery
21 *Doctor Thorndyke intervenes* (1933)
22 *For the defence, Doctor Thorndyke* (1934)
23 *Penrose mystery* (1936)
24 *Felo de se?* (1937)
Death at the inn
25 *Stoneware monkey* (1939)
26 *Mister Polton explains* (1940)
27 *Jacob Street mystery* (1942)
Unconscious witness
Omnibus volumes: *The famous cases of Doctor Thorndyke*, 1929, *The Doctor Thorndyke omnibus*, 1930, *Doctor Thorndyke's crime file*, 1941; *Doctor Thorndyke investigates*, 1930, includes five stories from earlier collections
Donaldson, Norman
28 *Goodbye, Donald Thorndyke* (1972)
Dirckx, John H
29 *Doctor Thorndyke's dilemma* (1974)

Doctor John Smith series
Pentecost, Hugh
1 *Memory of murder* (1947)
Novelettes
2 *Where the snow was red* (1949)
3 *Shadow of madness* (1950)

Doctor Joseph Kerkhoven trilogy
Wassermann, Jakob
1 *Maurizius case* (1928)
Original edition entitled *Der Fall Maurizius*
2 *Doctor Kerkhoven* (1932)
Original edition entitled *Etzel Andergast*
3 *Joseph Kerkhoven's third existence* (1934)
Original edition entitled *Joseph Kerkhovens dritte Existenz*

Doctor Joszef Venesz series
Thwaites, Frederick Joseph
1 *No rainbow in the sky* (1959)
2 *Beyond the rainbow* (1961)

Doctor Kay Scarpetta series
Cornwell, Patricia Daniels
1 *Postmortem* (1990)
2 *Body of evidence* (1991)
3 *All that remains* (1992)
4 *Cruel and unusual* (1993)
5 *Time since death* (1994)

Doctor Kildare junior series
This sequence has two authors
Ackworth, Robert Charles
1 *Doctor Kildare assigned to trouble* (1963)
Johnston, William
2 *Magic key* (1964)

Doctor Kildare series
This sequence has four authors
Brand, Max
1 *Secret of Doctor Kildare* (1940)
2 *Calling Doctor Kildare* (1940)
3 *Young Doctor Kildare* (1941)
4 *Doctor Kildare takes charge* (1941)
5 *Doctor Kildare's crisis* (1942)
6 *Doctor Kildare's trial* (1942)
7 *Doctor Kildare's search* (1943)
Also includes *Doctor Kildare's hardest case*

Ackworth, Robert Charles
8 *Doctor Kildare* (1962)
Daniels, Norman A
9 *Doctor Kildare's secret romance* (1962)
10 *Doctor Kildare's finest hour* (1963)
Johnston, William
11 *Heart has an answer* (1963)
12 *Faces of love* (1963)

Doctor Kirke Montgomery series
Mallory, Arthur
1 *Apperson's folly* (1930)
2 *Black Valley murders* (1930)
3 *Mysteries of Black Valley* (1930)

Doctor L Rees Pons series
King, Charles Daly
1 *Obelists at sea* (1932)
2 *Obelists en route* (1934)
3 *Obelists fly high* (1935)
4 *Careless corpse* (1937)
5 *Arrogant alibi* (1938)

Doctor Lancelot Priestley series
Rhode, John
1 *Paddington mystery* (1925)
2 *Doctor Priestley's quest* (1926)
3 *Ellerby case* (1926)
4 *Murders in Praed Street* (1928)
5 *Tragedy at the Unicorn* (1928)
6 *House on Tollard Ridge* (1929)
7 *Davidson case* (1929)
Murder at Bratton Grange
8 *Peril at Cranbury Hall* (1930)
9 *Pinehurst* (1930)
Doctor Priestley investigates
10 *Tragedy on the line* (1931)
11 *Hanging woman* (1931)
12 *Mystery at Greycombe Farm* (1932)
Fire at Greycombe Farm
13 *Dead men at the Folly* (1932)
14 *Motor rally mystery* (1933)
Doctor Priestley lays a trap
15 *Claverton mystery* (1933)
Claverton affair
16 *Venner crime* (1933)
17 *Robthorne mystery* (1934)
18 *Poison for one* (1934)
19 *Shot at dawn* (1934)
20 *Hendon's first case* (1935)
21 *Mystery at Olympia* (1935)
Murder at the motor show
22 *Corpse in the car* (1935)
23 *Death at breakfast* (1936)
24 *In face of the verdict* (1936)
In the face of the verdict
25 *Death in the hop fields* (1937)
Harvest murder
26 *Death on the board* (1937)
Death sits on the board
27 *Proceed with caution* (1937)
Body unidentified
28 *Invisible weapons* (1938)
29 *Bloody Tower* (1938)
Tower of evil
30 *Death pays a dividend* (1939)
31 *Death on Sunday* (1939)
Elm tree murder
32 *Death on the boat train* (1940)
33 *Murder at Lilac Cottage* (1940)
34 *Death at the helm* (1941)
35 *They watched by night* (1941)
Signal for death
36 *Fourth bomb* (1942)
37 *Dead on the track* (1943)
38 *Men die at Cyprus Lodge* (1943)
39 *Death invades the meeting* (1944)
40 *Vegetable duck* (1944)
Too many suspects
41 *Bricklayer's arms* (1945)
Shadow of a crime
42 *Lake House* (1946)
Secrets of the Lake House
43 *Death in Harley Street* (1946)
44 *Nothing but the truth* (1947)
Experiment in crime
45 *Death of an author* (1947)
46 *Paper bag* (1948)
Links in the chain
47 *Telephone call* (1948)
Shadow of an alibi
48 *Blackthorn House* (1949)
49 *Up the garden path* (1949)
Fatal garden
50 *Two graphs* (1950)
Double identities
51 *Family affairs* (1950)
Last suspect
52 *Doctor Goodwood's locum* (1951)
Affair of the substitute doctor
53 *Secret meeting* (1951)
54 *Death in Wellington Road* (1952)
55 *By registered post* (1952)
Mysterious suspect
56 *Death at the dance* (1952)
57 *Death at the inn* (1953)
Case of the forty thieves
58 *Dovebury murders* (1954)
59 *Death on the lawn* (1954)
60 *Domestic agency* (1955)
Grave matters
61 *Death of a grandmother* (1955)
Delayed payment
62 *Artist dies* (1956)
Death of an artist
63 *Open verdict* (1956)
64 *Robbery with violence* (1957)
65 *Death of a bridegroom* (1957)
66 *Murder at Derivale* (1958)
67 *Death takes a partner* (1958)
68 *Licensed for murder* (1958)
69 *Three cousins die* (1959)
70 *Twice dead* (1960)
71 *Fatal pool* (1960)
72 *Vanishing diary* (1961)

Doctor Lindsay series
Cameron, Isabel
1 *Doctor* (1923)
2 *More about the Doctor* (1925)
3 *Doctor calls again* (1935)
Numbers 1-3 published in one volume entitled *The Doctor omnibus*, 1937
4 *Doctor and his friends* (1938)
5 *More friends of the Doctor* (1939)

Doctor Lowell series
Merritt, Abraham
1 *Burn, witch, burn!* (1933)
2 *Creep, shadow!* (1934)
Creep, shadow, creep!

Doctor Luke series
Duncan, Norman
1 *Doctor Luke of the Labrador* (1904)
2 *Adventures of Billy Topsail* (1906)
3 *Billy Topsail and company* (1910)
4 *Billy Topsail, M.D.* (1916)

Doctor Manson series
Radford, Edwin
1 *Inspector Manson's success* (1944)
2 *Murder jigsaw* (1944)
3 *Crime pays no dividends* (1945)
4 *Murder isn't cricket* (1946)
5 *It's murder to live* (1947)
6 *Who killed Dick Whittington?* (1947)
7 *John Kyeling died* (1949)
8 *Heel of Achilles* (1950)
9 *Look in at murder* (1956)
10 *Death on the Broads* (1957)
11 *Death of a frightened editor* (1959)
12 *Death at the Chateau Noir* (1960)
13 *Murder on my conscience* (1960)
14 *Death's inheritance* (1961)
15 *Death takes the wheel* (1962)
16 *From information received* (1962)
17 *Cosy little murder* (1963)
18 *Murder of three ghosts* (1963)
19 *Hungry killer* (1964)
20 *Mask of murder* (1965)
21 *Murder magnified* (1965)
22 *Death of a gentleman* (1966)
23 *No reason for murder* (1967)
24 *Jones's little murder* (1967)
25 *Middlefold murders* (1967)
26 *Safety first murders* (1968)
27 *Trunk call for murder* (1968)
28 *Death of an ancient Saxon* (1969)
29 *Death of a peculiar rabbit* (1969)
30 *Two ways to murder* (1969)
31 *Murder is ruby red* (1970)
32 *Murder speaks* (1970)
33 *Greedy killers* (1971)
34 *Dead water* (1971)
35 *Death has two faces* (1972)

Doctor Marc Castleman series
Kutak, Rosemary
1 *Darkness of slumber* (1944)
2 *I am the Cat* (1948)

Doctor Martin Lestrange series
Hilton, Alec
1 *Consultant* (1968)
2 *Waiting for the night* (1969)

Doctor Mary Finney series
Head, Matthew
1 *Devil in the bush* (1945)
2 *Cabinda affair* (1949)
3 *Congo Venus* (1950)
4 *Murder at the Flea Club* (1955)

Doctor Mary Livingstone series
Allen, Julia
see **Mary Livingstone series**

Doctor McGurk series
White, Osmar
1 *Super-roo of Mungalongaloo* (1973)
2 *Further adventures of Doctor A.A.A. McGurk, M.D.* (1981)
3 *McGurk and the lost atoll* (1983)

Doctor McKinnon series
Macvicar, Angus
see **Jeremy Grant series**

Doctor Merlin series
Corbett, Scott
1 *Doctor Merlin's magic shop* (1973)
2 *Great custard pie panic* (1974)

Doctor Michael Gray series
Kuttner, Henry
1 *Murder of Ann Avery* (1956)
2 *Murder of Eleanor Pope* (1956)
3 *Murder of a mistress* (1957)
4 *Murder of a wife* (1958)

Doctor Moreau series
This sequence has two authors
Wells, Herbert George
1 *Island of Doctor Moreau* (1896)
Aldiss, Brian Wilson
2 *Moreau's other island* (1980)
Island called Moreau

Doctor Morelle series
Dudley, Ernest
1 *Meet Doctor Morelle* (1943)
2 *Meet Doctor Morelle again* (1944)
3 *Menace for Doctor Morelle* (1947)
4 *Doctor Morelle meets murder, and other new adventures* (1948)
Short stories
5 *Doctor Morelle and the drummer girl* (1950)
6 *Doctor Morelle takes a bow* (1957)
7 *Callers for Doctor Morelle* (1957)
8 *Mind of Doctor Morelle* (1958)
9 *Doctor Morelle and destiny* (1958)
10 *Confess to Doctor Morelle* (1959)
11 *Doctor Morelle at midnight* (1959)
12 *Alibi and Doctor Morelle* (1959)
13 *Nightmare for Doctor Morelle* (1960)
14 *Doctor Morelle and the doll* (1960)

Doctor Nassim Pride series
Petrie, Rhona
1 *Foreign bodies* (1967)
2 *Despatch of a dove* (1969)

Doctor Nikola series
Boothby, Guy
1 *Bid for fortune* (1895)
Doctor Nikola's vendetta
Enter Doctor Nikola!
2 *Doctor Nikola* (1896)
Doctor Nikola returns
3 *Lust of hate* (1898)
4 *Doctor Nikola's experiment* (1899)
5 *Farewell, Nikola!* (1901)

Doctor Norah North series
Duke, Madelaine
1 *Death of a holy murderer* (1975)
2 *Death at the wedding* (1976)
3 *Death of a Dandie Dinmont* (1978)

Doctor North series
Mitchell, Silas Weir
1 *Characteristics* (1892)
2 *Doctor North and his friends* (1900)

Doctor of Tanganyika series
White, Paul
1 *Doctor of Tanganyika* (1942)
2 *Jungle Doctor's progress* (1962)

Doctor O'Grady series
Maurois, Andre
1 *Discourses of Doctor O'Grady* (1922)
Original edition entitled *Les discours du docteur O'Grady*; based on *Le General Bramble*, 1920
2 *Return of Doctor O'Grady* (1950)
Original edition entitled *Les nouveaux discours du docteur O'Grady*

Doctor Owen Orient series
Lauria, Frank
1 *Doctor Orient* (1970)
2 *Raga Six* (1972)
3 *Lady Sativa* (1973)
4 *Baron Orgaz* (1974)
5 *Priestess* (1978)
6 *Seth papers* (1979)
7 *Blue limbo* (1991)

Doctor Palfrey series
Creasey, John
1 *Traitors' doom* (1942)
2 *Valley of fear* (1943)
Perilous country
Revised edition 1966
3 *Legion of the Lost* (1943)
Revised edition 1974
4 *Hounds of vengeance* (1945)
Revised edition 1969
5 *Death in the rising sun* (1945)
Revised edition 1970
6 *Shadow of doom* (1946)
Revised edition 1970
7 *House of the bears* (1946)
Revised edition 1962
8 *Sons of Satan* (1947)
9 *Dark harvest* (1947)
Revised edition 1962
10 *Wings of peace* (1948)
11 *Dawn of darkness* (1949)
12 *League of light* (1949)
13 *Man who shook the world* (1950)
14 *Prophet of fire* (1951)
15 *Children of hate* (1951)
Killers of innocence
Children of despair
Revised edition 1970
16 *Touch of death* (1954)
17 *Mists of fear* (1955)
18 *Flood* (1956)
19 *Plague of silence* (1958)
20 *Drought* (1959)
Dry spell
21 *Terror* (1962)
22 *Depths* (1963)
23 *Sleep!* (1964)
24 *Inferno* (1965)
25 *Famine* (1967)
26 *Blight* (1968)
27 *Oasis* (1969)

Doctor Palfrey series

28 *Smog* (1970)
29 *Unbegotten* (1971)
30 *Insulators* (1972)
31 *Voiceless ones* (1973)
32 *Thunder-maker* (1976)
33 *Whirlwind* (1979)

Doctor Patrick Cory series
Siodmak, Curt
1 *Donovan's brain* (1943)
2 *Hauser's memory* (1968)

Doctor Patrick Grant series
Yorke, Margaret
1 *Dead in the morning* (1970)
2 *Silent witness* (1972)
3 *Grave matters* (1973)
4 *Mortal remains* (1974)
5 *Cast for death* (1976)

Doctor Paul Holton series
Hunt, Charlotte
1 *Gilded sarcophagus* (1967)
2 *Cup of Thanatos* (1968)
Numbers 1 and 2 also published in one volume entitled *The casebook of Doctor Holton*, volume 1, 1978
3 *Lotus vellum* (1970)
4 *Thirteenth treasure* (1972)
Numbers 3 and 4 also published in one volume entitled *The casebook of Doctor Holton*, volume 2, 1978
5 *Touch of myrrh* (1974)
6 *Chambered tomb* (1975)

Doctor Paul Prye series
Millar, Margaret
1 *Invisible worm* (1941)
2 *Weak-eyed bat* (1942)
3 *Devil loves me* (1942)

Doctor Peter Casey series
Mead, Russell
1 *Moses bottle* (1980)
2 *Nightingale trivet* (1981)
3 *Third one* (1981)

Doctor Phibes series
Goldstein, William
Based on screenplays
1 *Doctor Phibes* (1971)
2 *Doctor Phibes rises again* (1972)

Doctor Quarshie series
Wyllie, John
1 *Skull still bone* (1975)
2 *Butterfly flood* (1975)
3 *To catch a viper* (1977)
4 *Death is a drum, beating forever* (1977)
5 *Pocket full of dead* (1978)
6 *Killer breath* (1979)
7 *Tiger in red weather* (1980)
8 *Long dark night of Baron Samedi* (1981)

Doctor Quartz series
Carter, Nicholas
1 *Doctor Quartz, magician* (1906)
2 *Doctor Quartz's quick move* (1906)

Doctor Quentin Pace series
Denbie, Roger
1 *Death on the Limited* (1933)
Timetable murder
2 *Death cruises south* (1934)

Doctor Quentin Toby series
Schley, Sturges Mason
1 *Who'd shoot a genius?* (1940)
Vengeance pulls the trigger
2 *Doctor Toby finds murder* (1941)
3 *Dream sinister* (1950)
Starry-eyed chipmonk

Doctor Rabbit series
Wahl, Jan
1 *Doctor Rabbit's foundling* (1977)
2 *Doctor Rabbit's last scout* (1979)

Doctor Ralph Conway series
Jennings, D K
1 *Surgeon at arms* (1961)
2 *Calling Doctor Conway* (1961)
3 *Wayward heart* (1961)
4 *Emergency call* (1961)
5 *Nurse Anne* (1962)
6 *Healing breed* (1962)
7 *Dedicated* (1962)
8 *They also serve* (1962)
9 *Long summer* (1962)
10 *Safari episode* (1962)
11 *And the glory* (1962)
12 *Danger in paradise* (1962)
13 *Doctor Sahib* (1962)
14 *White country* (1963)
15 *Spanish interlude* (1963)
16 *Time without end* (1963)
17 *Behind the sunset* (1963)
18 *Doctor in Mexico* (1963)
19 *To far horizons* (1963)
20 *Tall city* (1963)
21 *Young interns* (1963)
22 *To-day a stranger* (1963)
23 *Nurse on call* (1964)
24 *Hours of destiny* (1964)
25 *Wondering heart* (1964)
26 *Ward sister* (1964)
27 *Long days* (1964)
28 *Dark summer* (1964)
29 *When summer dies* (1965)

Doctor Rance Mandarin series
Zorro
see **Doctor Death series**

Doctor Richard Lasson series
Laqueur, Walter
1 *Missing years* (1980)
2 *Farewell to Europe* (1981)

Doctor Robert Frederickson series
Chesbro, George Clark
see **Mongo series**

Doctor Russell V Chillders series
Sherman, Jory
1 *Satan's seed* (1978)
2 *Chill* (1978)
3 *Bamboo demons* (1979)
4 *Vegas vampire* (1980)
Vampire
5 *Phoenix man* (1980)
6 *House of scorpions* (1980)
7 *Shadows* (1980)

Doctor Saint George Peachy and Barney Forge series
Starnes, Richard
see **Barney Forge and Doctor Saint George Peachy series**

Doctor Sam, Johnson series
De la Torre, Lillian
Short stories
1 *Doctor Sam, Johnson, detector* (1948)
2 *Detections of Doctor Sam, Johnson* (1960)
3 *Return of Doctor Sam, Johnson* (1985)
4 *Exploits of Doctor Sam, Johnson* (1985)

Doctor Samuel Cutting series
Westbrook, Perry Dickie
1 *Happy deathday* (1947)
2 *Red herring murder* (1949)
3 *Infra blood* (1950)

Doctor Samuel Johnson series
Moore, Frank Frankfort
Set in England at the time of Doctor Samuel Johnson
1 *Jessamy bride* (1897)
Based on the life of Mary Horneck
2 *Fanny's first novel* (1913)
Discovering Evelina
Based on the life of Fanny Burney

Doctor Scarlett series
Laing, Alexander
1 *Cadaver of Gideon Wyck* (1934)
2 *Doctor Scarlett* (1936)
3 *Methods of Doctor Scarlett* (1937)

Doctor Septimus Dodds series
Scott, Sutherland
1 *Murder without mourners* (1936)
2 *Murder is infectious* (1936)
3 *Crazy murder show* (1937)
Murder on stage
4 *Influenza mystery* (1938)
5 *A.R.P. murder* (1939)
6 *Murder in the mobile unit* (1940)
7 *Escape to murder* (1946)
8 *Operation urgent* (1947)
9 *Tincture of murder* (1951)
10 *Diagnosis, murder* (1954)
11 *Doctor Dodds' experiment* (1956)

Doctor series
Cameron, Isabel
see **Doctor Lindsay series**

Doctor series
Clifford, Robert
1 *Just here Doctor* (1977)
2 *Not there, Doctor* (1978)
3 *What next, Doctor?* (1979)
4 *Oh dear, Doctor* (1981)
5 *Look out, Doctor* (1983)
6 *Surely not, Doctor* (1985)
7 *There you are, Doctor* (1986)
8 *On holiday again, Doctor?* (1987)

Doctor series
Downe, Patrick
1 *Dear doctor* (1955)
2 *Doctor calls again* (1957)
3 *Come in, doctor* (1960)

Doctor series
Gordon, Richard
1 *Doctor in the house* (1946)
2 *Doctor at sea* (1953)
3 *Doctor at large* (1955)
4 *Doctor in love* (1957)
5 *Doctor and son* (1959)
6 *Doctor in clover* (1960)
7 *Doctor on toast* (1961)
8 *Doctor in the swim* (1962)
9 *Summer of Sir Launcelot* (1965)
10 *Love and Sir Launcelot* (1965)
11 *Doctor on the boil* (1970)
12 *Doctor on the brain* (1972)
13 *Doctor in the nude* (1973)
14 *Doctor on the job* (1976)
15 *Doctor in the nest* (1979)
16 *Doctor's daughters* (1981)
17 *Doctor on the ball* (1985)
18 *Doctor in the soup* (1986)

Doctor Skull series
Craig, Randolph
see **Octopus series**

Doctor Starr series
Johnston, William
1 *Doctor Starr* (1962)
2 *Doctor Starr in crisis* (1963)
3 *Love finds Doctor Starr* (1964)

Doctor Stephen Armitage series
McLeave, Hugh
1 *No face in the mirror* (1980)
Also published under the pseudonym Richard Copeland
2 *Second time round* (1981)

Doctor Steven Rushton series
Russell, Robert
1 *Go on, I'm listening* (1983)
2 *While you're here, doctor* (1985)

Doctor Strange series
This sequence has two authors
Rotsler, William
1 *Nightmare* (1979)
Varney, Allen
2 *Through six dimensions* (1987)

Doctor Stud series
Rice, William
see **Doctor James Wiscock series**

Doctor Syn series
This sequence has two authors
Thorndike, Russell
1 *Doctor Syn* (1915)
2 *Doctor Syn returns* (1935)
Scarecrow rides
3 *Further adventures of Doctor Syn* (1936)
4 *Doctor Syn on the high seas* (1936)
5 *Amazing quest of Doctor Syn* (1938)
6 *Courageous exploits of Doctor Syn* (1939)
7 *Shadow of Doctor Syn* (1944)
Crume, Vic
8 *Doctor Syn alias The Scarecrow* (1975)

Doctor Tina May series
Kemp, Sarah
1 *No escape* (1985)
2 *Lure of sweet death* (1986)
3 *What dread hand?* (1987)

Doctor Tom More series
Percy, Walker
1 *Love in the ruins* (1971)
The adventures of a bad Catholic at a time near the end of the world
2 *Thanatos syndrome* (1987)

Doctor Who Companions series
Attwood, Tony
see **Companions of Doctor Who series**

Doctor Who find your fate series
This sequence has four authors
Martin, David
1 *Search for the Doctor* (1986)
2 *Crisis in space* (1986)
Cover has author as Michael Holt
3 *Garden of evil* (1986)
Emms, William
4 *Mission to Venus* (1986)
Martin, Philip
5 *Invasion of the Ormazoids* (1986)
Baker, Jane
6 *Race against time* (1986)

Doctor Who new adventures series
Peel, John
see **Timewyrm series**

Doctor Who quiz book series
Holt, Michael
1 *Doctor Who quiz book of dinosaurs* (1982)
2 *Doctor Who quiz book of magic* (1983)
3 *Doctor Who quiz book of science* (1983)
4 *Doctor Who quiz book of space* (1983)
Companion volumes: *The Doctor Who quiz book*, by Nigel Robinson, 1982, *The second Doctor Who quiz book*, by Nigel Robinson, 1983, *The third Doctor Who quiz book*, by Nigel Robinson, 1985

Doctor Who scripts series
This sequence has six authors
Coburn, Anthony
1 *Tribe of Gum* (1987)
Davis, Gerry
2 *Tomb of the Cybermen* (1989)
Holmes, Robert
3 *Talons of Weng-Chiang* (1989)
Nation, Terry
4 *Daleks* (1989)
Coburn, Anthony
5 *Masters of Luxor* (1992)
Sloman, Robert
6 *Daemons* (1992)
Nation, Terry
7 *Power of Daleks* (1993)
Platt, Marc
8 *Ghost light* (1993)

Doctor Who series
This sequence has forty-six authors
Whitaker, David
1 *Doctor Who in an exciting adventure with the Daleks* (1963)
Doctor Who
Doctor Who and the Daleks
Strutton, Bill
2 *Doctor Who and the Zarbi* (1965)
Web planet
Whitaker, David
3 *Doctor Who and the Crusaders* (1965)
Hulke, Malcolm
4 *Doctor Who and the cave monsters* (1974)
Silurians
Dicks, Terrance
5 *Doctor Who and the Auton invasion* (1974)
Auton invasion
6 *Doctor Who and the day of the Daleks* (1974)
Day of the Daleks
Hulke, Malcolm
7 *Doctor Who and the doomsday weapon* (1974)
Dicks, Terrance
8 *Doctor Who and the abominable snowman* (1974)
Hulke, Malcolm
9 *Doctor Who and the sea-devils* (1974)
Letts, Barry
10 *Doctor Who and the daemons* (1974)
Davis, Gerry
11 *Doctor Who and the Cybermen* (1974)
Dicks, Terrance
12 *Doctor Who and the giant robot* (1974)
Giant robot
Robot
Hulke, Malcolm
13 *Doctor Who and the green death* (1975)
Dicks, Terrance
14 *Doctor Who and the terror of the Autons* (1975)
15 *Doctor Who and the planet of the spiders* (1975)
Planet of the spiders
Davis, Gerry
16 *Doctor Who and the tenth planet* (1976)
Hulke, Malcolm
17 *Doctor Who and the dinosaur invasion* (1976)
Dicks, Terrance
18 *Doctor Who and the Loch Ness Monster* (1976)
Terror of the Zygons
19 *Doctor Who and the three doctors* (1976)
Three doctors
Hayles, Brian
20 *Doctor Who and the ice warriors* (1976)
Dicks, Terrance
21 *Doctor Who and the revenge of the Cybermen* (1976)
Revenge of the Cybermen
22 *Doctor Who and the genesis of the Daleks* (1976)
Genesis of the Daleks
Numbers 18, 21, 22 also published in one volume entitled The adventures of Doctor *Who*, 1979
23 *Doctor Who and the web of fear* (1976)
Hulke, Malcolm
24 *Doctor Who and the space war* (1976)
Dicks, Terrance
25 *Doctor Who and the planet of the Daleks* (1976)
26 *Doctor Who and the pyramids of Mars* (1976)
27 *Doctor Who and the carnival of monsters* (1977)
Hinchcliffe, Philip
28 *Doctor Who and the seeds of doom* (1977)
Dicks, Terrance
29 *Doctor Who and the Dalek invasion of earth* (1977)
Dalek invasion of earth
Numbers 6, 25, 29 also published in one volume entitled *The Doctor Who omnibus*, 1983
30 *Doctor Who and the claws of Axos* (1977)
Marter, Ian
31 *Doctor Who and the ark in space* (1977)
Ark in space
Dicks, Terrance
32 *Doctor Who and the brain of Morbius* (1977)
Brain of Morbius
33 *Doctor Who and the planet of evil* (1977)
34 *Doctor Who and the mutants* (1977)
35 *Doctor Who and the deadly assassin* (1977)
36 *Doctor Who and the talons of Weng-Chiang* (1977)
37 *Doctor Who and the face of evil* (1978)
Hinchcliffe, Philip
38 *Doctor Who and the masque of Mandragora* (1978)
Dicks, Terrance
39 *Doctor Who and the time warrior* (1978)
40 *Doctor Who and death to the Daleks* (1978)
Death to the Daleks
41 *Doctor Who and the android invasion* (1978)
42 *Doctor Who and the horror of Fang Rock* (1978)
Davis, Gerry
43 *Doctor Who and the tomb of the Cybermen* (1978)
Marter, Ian
44 *Doctor Who and the Sontaron experiment* (1978)
Dicks, Terrance
45 *Doctor Who and the hand of fear* (1979)
46 *Doctor Who and the invisible enemy* (1979)
47 *Doctor Who and the robots of death* (1979)
Numbers 35, 37, 47 also published in one volume entitled *The further adventures of Doctor Who*, 1986
48 *Doctor Who and the image of the Fendahl* (1979)
Hulke, Malcolm
49 *Doctor Who and the war games* (1979)
Dicks, Terrance
50 *Doctor Who and the destiny of the Daleks* (1979)
51 *Doctor Who and the invasion of time* (1980)
52 *Doctor Who and the underworld* (1980)
53 *Doctor Who and the stones of blood* (1980)
54 *Doctor Who and the Armageddon factor* (1980)
Marter, Ian
55 *Doctor Who and the Ribos operation* (1980)
Dicks, Terrance
56 *Doctor Who and the androids of Tara* (1980)
Hinchcliffe, Philip
57 *Doctor Who and the keys of Marinus* (1980)
Hayles, Brian
58 *Doctor Who and the curse of Peladon* (1980)
Dicks, Terrance
59 *Doctor Who and the monster of Peladon* (1980)
60 *Doctor Who and the power of Kroll* (1980)
61 *Doctor Who and the horns of Nimon* (1980)
Fisher, David
62 *Doctor Who and the creature from the pit* (1981)
Dicks, Terrance
63 *Doctor Who and the nightmare of Eden* (1980)
Marter, Ian
64 *Doctor Who and the enemy of the world* (1981)
Dicks, Terrance
65 *Doctor Who and an unearthly child* (1981)
Unearthly child
66 *Doctor Who and the state of decay* (1982)
Lydecker, John
67 *Doctor Who and the warriors' gate* (1982)
Dicks, Terrance
68 *Doctor Who and the keeper of Traken* (1982)
Fisher, David
69 *Doctor Who and the leisure hive* (1982)
Saward, Eric
70 *Doctor Who and the visitation* (1982)
Smith, Andrew
71 *Full circle* (1982)
Dicks, Terrance
72 *Doctor Who and the sunmakers* (1982)
Bidmead, Christopher H
73 *Logopolis* (1982)
Grimwade, Peter
74 *Time flight* (1983)
Dicks, Terrance
75 *Meglos* (1983)
Bidmead, Christopher H
76 *Castrovalva* (1983)
Dicks, Terrance
77 *Four to doomsday* (1983)
Marter, Ian
78 *Earthshock* (1983)
Lydecker, John
79 *Terminus* (1983)
Dicks, Terrance
80 *Arc of infinity* (1983)
81 *Five doctors* (1983)
Grimwade, Peter
82 *Mawdryn undead* (1983)
Dicks, Terrance
83 *Snakedance* (1983)
84 *Kinda* (1983)
Clegg, Barbara
85 *Enlightenment* (1984)
Marter, Ian
86 *Dominators* (1984)
Dicks, Terrance
87 *Warriors of the deep* (1984)
Lucarotti, John
88 *Aztecs* (1984)
Dicks, Terrance
89 *Inferno* (1984)
Davis, Gerry
90 *Highlanders* (1984)
Bidmead, Christopher H
91 *Frontios* (1984)
Dicks, Terrance
92 *Caves of Androzani* (1984)
Grimwade, Peter
93 *Planet of fire* (1984)
Lucarotti, John
94 *Marco Polo* (1984)
Pringle, Eric
95 *Awakening* (1985)
Dicks, Terrance
96 *Mind of evil* (1985)
Cotton, Donald
97 *Myth makers* (1985)
Marter, Ian
98 *Invasion* (1985)
Dicks, Terrance
99 *Krotons* (1985)
Holmes, Robert
100 *Two doctors* (1985)
Cotton, Donald
101 *Gunfighters* (1985)
Dicks, Terrance
102 *Time monster* (1985)
Saward, Eric
103 *Twin dilemma* (1985)
Emms, William
104 *Galaxy four* (1985)
McCoy, Glen
105 *Timelash* (1985)
Martin, Philip
106 *Vengeance on Varus* (1988)
Baker, Pip
107 *Mark of the Rani* (1986)
Dudley, Terence
108 *King's demons* (1986)
Black, Ian Stuart
109 *Savages* (1986)
Pemberton, Victor
110 *Fury from the deep* (1986)
Davis, Gerry
111 *Celestial toymaker* (1986)
Dicks, Terrance
112 *Seeds of death* (1986)
Dudley, Terence
113 *Black orchid* (1986)
Short stories
Erickson, Paul
114 *Ark* (1986)
Ling, Peter
115 *Mind robber* (1986)
Dicks, Terrance
116 *Faceless ones* (1986)
Jones, Glyn
117 *Space museum* (1987)
Robinson, Nigel
118 *Sensorites* (1987)
Marter, Ian
119 *Reign of terror* (1987)
Cotton, Donald
120 *Romans* (1987)
Dicks, Terrance
121 *Ambassadors of death* (1987)
Lucarotti, John
122 *Massacre* (1987)
Black, Ian Stuart
123 *Macra terror* (1987)
Marter, Ian
124 *Rescue* (1987)
Baker, Pip
125 *Terror of the Vervoids* (1987)
Robinson, Nigel
126 *Time meddler* (1987)
Baker, Pip
127 *Time and the Rani* (1987)
Dicks, Terrance
128 *Mysterious planet* (1987)
Robinson, Nigel
129 *Underwater menace* (1988)
Dicks, Terrance
130 *Wheel in space* (1988)
Baker, Pip
131 *Ultimate foe* (1988)
Robinson, Nigel
132 *Edge of destruction* (1988)
Dicks, Terrance
133 *Smugglers* (1988)
Wyatt, Stephen
134 *Paradise Towers* (1988)
Kohill, Malcolm
135 *Delta and the Bannerman* (1989)
Black, Ian Stuart
136 *War machines* (1989)
Briggs, Ian
137 *Dragonfire* (1989)
Saward, Eric
138 *Attack of the Cybermen* (1989)
Martin, Philip
139 *Mindwarp* (1989)
Peel, John
140 *Chase* (1989)
141 *Mission to the unknown* (1989)
Also known as *The Daleks' master plan*, part 1
142 *Mutation of time* (1989)
Also known as *The Daleks' master plan*, part 2
Clarke, Kevin
143 *Silver nemesis* (1989)

Doctor Who series

Wyatt, Stephen
144 *Greatest show in the galaxy* (1989)
Dicks, Terrance
145 *Doctor Who and the planet of the giants* (1990)
Planet of the giants
Curry, Graeme
146 *Happiness patrol* (1990)
Dicks, Terrance
147 *Space pirates* (1990)
Aaronovitz, Ben
148 *Remembrance of the Daleks* (1990)
Platt, Marc
149 *Ghost light* (1990)
Munro, Rona
150 *Survival* (1990)
Briggs, Ian
151 *Curse of the Fenric* (1990)
Platt, Marc
152 *Battlefield* (1991)
Pemberton, Victor
153 *Pescatons* (1991)
Darvill-Evans, Peter
154 *Time lord* (1991)
Dicks, Terrance
155 *Mark of Mandragora* (1993)
Masque of Mandragora
Peel, John
156 *Power of the Daleks* (1993)
Bulis, Christopher
157 *Shadowland* (1993)
Peel, John
158 *Evil of the Daleks* (1993)
Banks, David
159 *Iceberg* (1993)
Blythe, Daniel
160 *Dimension riders* (1993)
Orman, Kate
161 *Left-handed humming bird* (1993)
Letts, Barry
162 *Paradise of death* (1994)
Companion volumes: *The Doctor Who monster book*, by Terrance Dicks, 1975, *Doctor Who crossword book*, by Nigel Robinson,1982, *Doctor Who, the making of a television series*, by Alan Road, 1982, *The Doctor Who technical manual*, by Mark Harris, 1983, *Doctor Who, the unfolding text*, by John Tulloch and Manuel Alvaredo, 1983, *Doctor Who, a celebration, two decades through time and space*, by Peter Haining, 1983, *The Doctor Who illustrated A-Z*, by Lesley Sandring, 1985, *Doctor Who timeview*, by Frank Bellamy, 1985, *The Doctor Who cookbook*, by Gary Downie, 1985, *The Doctor Who puzzle book*, by Michael Holt, 1985, *The Tardis inside out*, by John Nathan-Turner, 1985, *The companions*, by John Nathan-Turner, 1986, *The Doctor Who file*, edited by Peter Haining, 1986, *Doctor Who, the early years*, by Jeremy Bentham, 1986, *Travel with the Tardis*, by Jean Airey and Lurie Haldeman, 1986, *Doctor Who special effects*, by Mat Irvine, 1986, *Slipback*, by Eric Saward, 1986, *Encyclopaedia of the worlds of Doctor Who*, by David Saunders, 1987-1990, *The time-traveller's guide*, by Peter Haining, 1987, Doctor Who *fun book*, by Tim Quinn and Dicky Howett, 1987, *Doctor Who, twenty five glorious years*, by Peter Haining, 1988, The official Doctor Who and the Daleks book, by Terry Nation and John Peel, 1988, *Ultimate evil*, by Wally K Daly, 1989, *The nightmare fair*, by Graham Williams, 1989, *Mission to Magnus*, by Philip Martin, 1990, *Cybermen*, by David Banks, 1990, *The Gallifrey chronicles*, by John Peel, 1991

Doctor William Ames series

Freeman, Lucy
1 *Dream* (1971)
2 *Psychiatrist says murder* (1973)
3 *Case on cloud nine* (1975)

Doctor William Blow and Professor Gideon Manciple series

Hopkins, Kenneth
1 *She died because* (1957)
2 *Dead against my principles* (1960)
3 *Body blow* (1962)

Doctor Xargle series

Willis, Jeanne
1 *Doctor Xargle's book of earthhounds* (1989)
2 *Doctor Xargle's book of earthriggers* (1990)

Doctor Zed series

Penrose, Gordon
1 *It's Doctor Zed's zany brilliant book of science experiments* (1977)
Doctor Zed's zany brilliant book of science experiments
2 *Doctor Zed's dazzling book of science activities* (1982)
Selections from numbers 1-2 published as *Fooling around with science*, 1986
3 *Doctor Zed's science surprises* (1989)
4 *Sensational science activities with Doctor Zed* (1990)
5 *More science surprised from Doctor Zed* (1992)

Doctor Zhivago series

This sequence has two authors
Pasternak, Boris
1 *Doctor Zhivago* (1958)
Translated from the Russian
Mollin, Alexander
2 *Lara's child* (1994)

Doctor's little girl series

Taggart, Marion Ames
1 *Doctor's little girl* (1907)
2 *Sweet Nancy* (1909)
3 *Nancy, the doctor's little partner* (1911)
4 *Nancy Porter's opportunity* (1912)
5 *Nancy and the Coggs twins* (1914)

Dodd and Fountain series

Reade, Charles
see **David Dodd and Lucy Fountain series**

Doddles series

Adams, Agnes
1 *Doddles* (1920)
A school story
2 *Doddles makes things hum* (1927)

Dodds series

Scott, Sutherland
see **Doctor Septimus Dodds series**

Dodge Club series

De Mille, James
see **Young Dodge Club series**

Dodie, Lisa and Emmy series

Chastain, Madye Lee
see **Lisa, Emmy and Dodie series**

Dodo series

Bell, Vicars
Autobiography
1 *Dodo* (1950)
The story of a village schoolmaster
2 *This way home* (1951)
The story of a voyage in search of the earth

Dodo series

Benson, Edward Frederic
1 *Dodo* (1893)
A detail of to-day
2 *Dodo's daughter* (1913)
Dodo the second

Dodo series

Edwards, Lynne
1 *Dead as a dodo* (1973)
2 *Dodo is a solitary bird* (1977)
3 *Mad Dan Dodo in outer space* (1979)

Dog and Cat series

Miller, Elizabeth
see **Cat and Dog series**

Dog and Frog series

Astrop, John
see **Frog and Dog series**

Dog lover's mystery series

Conant, Susan
1 *Gone to the dogs* (1992)
2 *Bloodlines* (1993)
3 *Ruffly speaking* (1994)

Dog series

Cobbett, Pelham
Poems
1 *Dog* (1988)
Number 2 not yet published
3 *Zulu tak* (1990)
Number 4 not yet published
5 *Right on Rubens* (1992)

Dog series

Stranger, Joyce
1 *Two's company* (1977)
2 *Two for joy* (1982)
3 *Dog in a million* (1984)
4 *Dog days* (1986)

Dog stories series

Pollock, Mary
1 *Three boys and a circus* (1940)
2 *Adventures of Scamp* (1943)
One volume edition entitled *Dog stories*, by Enid Blyton, 1959

Dog trainer mystery series

Conant, Susan
1 *New leash on death* (1990)
2 *Dead and doggone* (1990)
3 *Bite of death* (1991)
4 *Paws before dying* (1991)

Dogmatix series

Goscinny, Rene
Illustrated by Albert Uderzo; translated from the French
1 *Dogmatix and the storm* (1972)
2 *Well-deserved tea party* (1972)
3 *Dogmatix makes a friend* (1972)
4 *Dogmatix and the boar hunt* (1972)
5 *Dogmatix and the ugly little eagle* (1983)
Original edition entitled *Idefix et le vilain petit aiglon*
6 *Dogmatix and the magic potion* (1983)
Original edition entitled *Idefix et la grande fringale*

Dogsbody series

Sinderby, Donald
1 *Dogsbody* (1928)
The story of a romantic subaltern
2 *Vagrant lover* (1929)

Dogtown Ghetto series

Bonham, Frank
1 *Durango Street* (1965)
2 *Mystery of the fat cat* (1968)
3 *Golden bees of Tulami* (1974)

Doight series

Symons, Beryl
see **Inspector Henry Doight series**

Doino Faber trilogy

Sperber, Manes
1 *Wind and the flame* (1950)
Burned bramble
2 *To dusty death* (1952)
3 *Lost bay* (1953)

Dol Bonner series

Stout, Rex
1 *Hand in the glove* (1937)
Crime on her hands
2 *Three for the chair* (1956)
Three novelettes entitled *Immune to murder, A window for death, Too many detectives*
3 *Plot it yourself* (1959)
Murder in style

Dolan and Sinclair series

Babson, Marian
see **Trixie Dolan and Evangeline Sinclair series**

Dolan series

Fuller, William
see **Brad Dolan series**

Dolf Morgette series

Boyer, Glenn G
1 *Guns of Morgette* (1982)
2 *Morgette in the Yukon* (1983)
3 *Morgette on the Barbary Coast* (1984)
4 *Return of Morgette* (1985)
5 *Morgette and the Alaskan bandits* (1988)

Dolittle series

Lofting, Hugh
see **Doctor Dolittle series**

Doll trilogy

Lawler, Ray
Plays
1 *Kid stakes* (1978)
2 *Other times* (1978)
3 *Summer of the seventeenth doll* (1957)
One volume edition entitled *The doll trilogy*, 1978

Dollanganger family series

Andrews, Virginia Cleo
1 *Garden of shadows* (1987)
2 *Flowers in the attic* (1979)
3 *Petals on the wind* (1980)
4 *If there be thorns* (1981)
5 *Seeds of yesterday* (1983)

Dollar series

This sequence has three authors
Millard, Joseph John
1 *Good, the bad and the ugly* (1967)
2 *For a few dollars more* (1967)
Fox, Brian
3 *Dollar to die for* (1968)
Millard, Joseph John
4 *Coffin full of dollars* (1971)
Chandler, Frank
5 *Fistfull of dollars* (1972)
Millard, Joseph John
6 *Devil's dollar sign* (1972)
7 *Million-dollar bloodhunt* (1973)
8 *Blood for a dirty dollar* (1973)

Dolling series

Clouston, Joseph Storer
see **Ursula Dolling series**

Dolls series

Stover, Marjorie Filley
1 *When the dolls awoke* (1985)
2 *Midnight in the doll house* (1990)

Dolly and Molly series

Gordon, Elizabeth
1 *Dolly and Molly and the farmer men* (1914)
2 *Dolly and Molly at the circus* (1914)
3 *Dolly and Molly at the seashore* (1914)
4 *Dolly and Molly on Christmas day* (1914)

Dolly and Ted series
Fowler, Richard
see **Ted and Dolly series**

Dolly series
Dunnett, Dorothy
see **Johnson and the yacht Dolly series**

Dolly trilogy
Scannell, Dorothy
Autobiography
1 *Mother knew best* (1974)
An East End childhood
2 *Dolly's war* (1975)
3 *Dolly's mixture* (1977)

Dolphins trilogy
Meyers, Roy
1 *Dolphin boy* (1967)
Dolphin rider
2 *Daughters of the dolphin* (1968)
3 *Destiny and the dolphins* (1969)

Dom and Katy series
Oldfield, Pamela
see **Katy and Dom series**

Dom Manuel and his descendants series
Cabell, James Branch
1 *Beyond life* (1919)
Dizain des demiurges
2 *Figures of earth* (1921)
A comedy of appearances
3 *Silver stallion* (1926)
A comedy of redemption
4 *Music from behind the moon* (1926)
An epitome
5 *Way of Ecben* (1929)
A comedietta involving a gentleman
6 *White robe* (1928)
A saint's summary; numbers 4-6 also published in one volume entitled *The witch-woman*, 1948
7 *Soul of Melicent* (1913)
Domnei
A comedy of woman-worship; the second title is a revised edition
8 *Chivalry* (1909)
Revised edition 1921
9 *Jurgen* (1919)
A comedy of justice; revised edition 1921
10 *Line of love* (1905)
Dizain des mariages; revised edition 1921
11 *High place* (1923)
A comedy of disenchantment
12 *Gallantry* (1907)
Short stories; revised edition 1922
13 *Something about Eve* (1927)
A comedy of fig-leaves
14 *Certain hour* (1916)
Dizain des poetes
15 *Cords of vanity* (1909)
A comedy of shirking; revised edition 1920
16 *From the hidden way* (1916)
Poetry; revised edition 1920
17 *Jewel merchants* (1921)
A play
18 *Rivet in grandfather's neck* (1915)
A comedy of limitations; revised edition 1922
19 *Eagle's shadow* (1904)
Revised edition 1923
20 *Cream of the jest* (1917)
A comedy of evasions; revised edition 1921
21 *Lineage of Lichfield* (1922)
An essay in eugenics; numbers 21 and 21 also published in one volume 1930
22 *Straws and prayer-books* (1924)
23 *Townsend of Lichfield* (1930)
Dizain des adieux
24 *Preface to the past* (1936)
25 *Sonnets from Antan* (1930)
Companion volumes: *The judging of Jurgen*, 1920, *Jurgen and the censor*, 1920

Dombey series
This sequence has two authors
Dickens, Charles
1 *Dombey and Son* (1848)
Johnston, Harry Hamilton
2 *Gay-Dombeys* (1919)

Domesday Book series
Masters, Edgar Lee
Novels in blank verse
1 *Domesday Book* (1920)
2 *Fate of the jury* (1929)

Domestic service series
Powell, Margaret
Autobiography
1 *Below stairs* (1968)
2 *Climbing the stairs* (1969)
3 *Treasure upstairs* (1970)
4 *London season* (1971)
5 *My mother and I* (1972)
6 *Margaret Powell in America* (1973)
7 *Albert, my consort* (1975)
8 *Margaret Powell down under* (1976)
9 *My children and I* (1977)

Domingo Santos series
Bannerman, W B
1 *Whispering riders* (1937)
2 *Bad End Valley* (1937)

Dominic and Helen series
Odgers, Sally Farrell
see **Helen and Dominic series**

Dominic Flandry series
Anderson, Poul
see **Sir Dominic Flandry series**

Dominie series
Neill, Alexander Sutherland
Reminiscences of a Scottish schoolteacher, later founder of Summerhill School
1 *Dominie's log* (1915)
2 *Dominie dismissed* (1916)
3 *Dominie in doubt* (1920)
4 *Booming of Bunkie* (1921)
5 *Dominie abroad* (1922)
6 *Dominie's five* (1924)

Dominique and Ambrose Frayne series
McIntosh, J T
see **Ambrose and Dominique Frayne series**

Dominique Aubry series
Travers, Hugh
see **Madame Dominique Aubry series**

Domino series
Kennedy, Adam
see **Roy Tucker series**

Don affair series
Konsalik, Heinz Gunther
see **Love on the Don series**

Don Bartholomew series
Carroll, John Richard
1 *Catspaw* (1988)
2 *Tropic of fear* (1990)

Don Birman series
Jackson, Charles Reginald
1 *Sunnier side* (1953)
Twelve Arcadian tales
2 *Lost weekend* (1945)

Don Cadee series
Dean, Spencer
1 *Frightened fingers* (1954)
2 *Scent of fear* (1954)
Smell of fear
3 *Marked down for murder* (1956)
4 *Murder on delivery* (1957)
5 *Dishonor among thieves* (1958)
6 *Merchant of murder* (1959)
7 *Price tag for murder* (1959)
8 *Murder after a fashion* (1960)
9 *Credit for a murder* (1961)

Don Camillo series
Guareschi, Giovanni
Translated from the Italian
1 *Little world of Don Camillo* (1950)
2 *Don Camillo and the prodigal son* (1952)
Don Camillo and his flock
3 *Don Camillo's dilemma* (1954)
Numbers 1 and 3 also published in one volume entitled *Don Camillo, his little world and his dilemma*, 1954
4 *Don Camillo and the devil* (1957)
Don Camillo takes the devil by the tail
5 *Comrade Don Camillo* (1963)
6 *Don Camillo meets Hell's Angels* (1969)
Don Camillo meets the flower children

Don Carson series
Pruitt, Alan
1 *Restless corpse* (1947)
2 *Typed for a corpse* (1951)

Don Juan series
Castaneda, Carlos
1 *Teachings of Don Juan* (1968)
A Yaqui tale of knowledge
2 *Separate reality* (1971)
3 *Journey to Ixtlan* (1972)
Numbers 1-3 also published in one volume entitled *Trilogy*, 1974
4 *Tales of power* (1974)
5 *Second ring of power* (1977)
6 *Eagle's gift* (1981)
7 *Fire from within* (1984)
8 *Power of silence* (1987)

Don Juan series
Duncan, Ronald
1 *Don Juan* (1954)
2 *Death of Satan* (1955)

Don Kerry series
Ashford, Jeffrey
see **Detective Inspector Don Kerry series**

Don Kirk series
Patten, Gilbert
1 *Boy cattle king* (1895)
Alternative title: Don Kirk
2 *Boy from the West* (1895)
3 *Don Kirk's mine* (1895)
Alternative title: The fight for a lost fortune

Don Micklem series
Marshall, Raymond
Also published under the pseudonym James Hadley Chase
1 *Mission to Venice* (1954)
2 *Mission to Siena* (1955)

Don Morgan series
Haig-Brown, Roderic Langmere
1 *Starbuck Valley winter* (1943)
2 *Saltwater summer* (1948)

Don Pancho series
Buckingham, Bruce
1 *Three bad nights* (1956)
2 *Broiled alive* (1957)

Don Q series
Prichard, Katherine
1 *Chronicles of Don Q* (1904)
Short stories
2 *New chronicles of Don Q* (1906)
Don Q in the Sierra
Short stories
3 *Don Q's love story* (1909)

Don Quixote series
This sequence has two authors
Cervantes Saavedra, Miguel de
1 *Don Quixote de la Mancha* (1615)
Adventures of Don Quixote de la Mancha
Original edition entitled *Don Quijote*, 1605-1615
Chesterton, Gilbert Keith
2 *Return of Don Quixote* (1927)

Don Sebastien series
Daniels, Les
1 *Black castle* (1978)
A novel of the macabre
2 *Silver skull* (1979)
A novel of sorcery
3 *Citizen vampire* (1981)
4 *Yellow fog* (1986)
Expanded edition 1988
5 *No blood spilled* (1991)

Don series
Sholokhov, Mikhail
Translated from the Russian
1 *Tales of the Don* (1926)
2 *And quiet flows the Don* (1928)
3 *Don flows home to the sea* (1932)
4 *Seeds of tomorrow* (1933)
5 *Harvest of the Don* (1940)
Numbers 4 and 5 also published in one volume editions entitled *Virgin soil upturned*, and, *Soil upturned*

Don Slade series
Drake, David
see **Hammer's Slammers series**

Don Sturdy series
Appleton, Victor
1 *Don Sturdy in the desert of mystery* (1925)
Desert of mystery
Alternative title: Autoing in the land of caravans
2 *Don Sturdy with the big snake hunters* (1925)
Big snake hunters
Alternative title: Lost in the jungles of the Amazon
3 *Don Sturdy in the tombs of gold* (1925)
Alternative title: The old Egyptian's great secret
4 *Don Sturdy across the North Pole* (1925)
Alternative title: Cast away in the land of ice
5 *Don Sturdy in the land of volcanoes* (1925)
Alternative title: The trail of the ten thousand smokes
6 *Don Sturdy in the port of lost ships* (1926)
Alternative title: Adrift in the Sargasso Sea
7 *Don Sturdy among the gorillas* (1927)
Alternative title: Adrift in the great jungle
8 *Don Sturdy captured by headhunters* (1928)
Alternative title: Adrift in the wilds of Borneo
9 *Don Sturdy in lion land* (1929)
Alternative title: The strange clearing in the jungle
10 *Don Sturdy in the land of giants* (1930)
Alternative title: Captives of the savage Patagonians
11 *Don Sturdy on the ocean bottom* (1931)
Alternative title: The strange cruise of the Phantom
12 *Don Sturdy in the temples of fear* (1932)
Alternative title: Destined for a strange sacrifice

Don Sturdy series

13 *Don Sturdy in Glacier Bay* (1933)
Alternative title: The mystery of the moving totem poles
14 *Don Sturdy trapped in the flaming wilderness* (1934)
Alternative title: Unearthing secrets in Central Asia
15 *Don Sturdy with the harpoon hunters* (1935)
Alternative title: The strange cruise of the whaling ship

Don Winslow series
Martinek, Frank V
1 *Don Winslow in the Navy* (1940)
2 *Don Winslow face to face with the Scorpion* (1940)
3 *Don Winslow breaks the spy net* (1941)
4 *Don Winslow saves the secret formula* (1941)

Donahue series
Hill, Katharine
see **Lorna Donahue series**

Donald and Jean series
Dickinson, William Croft
1 *Borrobil* (1944)
2 *Eildon tree* (1947)
3 *Flag from the isles* (1951)

Donald Bracken and James Rowland Woodward series
Blazer, J S
1 *Deal me out* (1973)
2 *Lend a hand* (1975)

Donald Briggs O'Meara series
Bannerman, David
see **Magic Man series**

Donald Cairn series
Loder, Vernon
1 *Men with double faces* (1937)
2 *Wolf in the fold* (1938)

Donald Cameron series
McCutchan, Philip
1 *Cameron, ordinary seaman* (1980)
2 *Cameron comes through* (1980)
3 *Cameron of the Castle Bay* (1981)
4 *Lieutenant Cameron, RNVR* (1981)
5 *Cameron's convoy* (1982)
6 *Cameron in the gap* (1982)
7 *Orders for Cameron* (1983)
8 *Cameron in command* (1983)
9 *Cameron and the Kaiserhof* (1984)
10 *Cameron's raid* (1985)
11 *Cameron's chase* (1986)
12 *Cameron's troop lift* (1987)
13 *Cameron's commitment* (1989)
14 *Cameron's crossing* (1993)

Donald Dobbs series
Blake, Christina
see **Inspector Donald Dobbs series**

Donald Duck series
Korman, Justine
1 *Some ducks have all the luck* (1987)
2 *Daffy Duck in Duck Troop to the rescue* (1990)
3 *Ducktales, down the drain* (1990)
4 *Huey, Dewey, Louie and the witch* (1990)
5 *Donald's dream* (1990)
6 *Donald's buried treasure* (1991)

Donald Dyke series
Rockwood, Harry
1 *Donald Dyke, the down-east detective* (1882)
2 *Dyke and Burr, the rival detectives* (1883)
Rival detectives
3 *Clarice Dyke, the femal detective* (1883)
4 *Mrs Donald Dyke, detective* (1900)

Donald Everhard series
Steward, Paull
1 *Dangerous men* (1926)
2 *Gaboreau* (1927)
3 *Gaboreau the terrible* (1927)

Donald Kendrick series
Mackinnon, Allan
1 *Dead on departure* (1964)
Report from Argyll
2 *No wreath for Manuela* (1965)
Man overboard

Donald Lam and Bertha Cool series
Fair, A A
see **Bertha Cool and Donald Lam series**

Donald Macdonald series
Tranter, Nigel Godwin
1 *Something very fishy* (1962)
2 *Give a dog a bad name* (1963)
3 *Pursuit* (1965)
4 *Fire and high water* (1967)

Donald Martin series
Bardsley, Michael
see **Superintendent Donald Martin series**

Donald McCarry series
Boland, John C
1 *Easy money* (1991)
2 *Brokered death* (1992)
3 *Rich man's blood* (1993)
4 *Death in Jerusalem* (1994)

Donald O'Dare series
Buncher, Walter
1 *Mother's secret* (1924)
2 *Donald O'Dare* (1925)

Donald O'Keefe Adams series
Sage, Dana
1 *Moon was red* (1944)
2 *Twenty two brothers* (1950)

Donald Reamer series
Duncan, William Murdoch
see **Superintendent Donald Reamer series**

Donald Robak series
Hensley, Joe Louis
1 *Deliver us to evil* (1971)
2 *Legislative body* (1972)
3 *Song of corpus juris* (1974)
4 *Killing in gold* (1978)
5 *Minor murders* (1979)
6 *Outcasts* (1981)
7 *Robak's cross* (1985)
8 *Robak's fire* (1986)
9 *Robak's fun* (1987)
Short stories
10 *Robak's run* (1990)

Donald series
Gorey, Edward
1 *Donald and the* (1969)
2 *Donald has a difficulty* (1970)

Donald Strachey series
Stevenson, Richard
1 *Death trick* (1981)
2 *On the other hand* (1984)

Donan series
Hood, Margaret Page
see **Gil Donan series**

Donavan series
Brown, Carter
see **Paul Donavan series**

Doner series
Shay, Frank
see **Dan Doner series**

Donkey series
Richards, James
Inspired by *Travels with a donkey in the Cevennes*, by Robert Louis Stevenson, 1879
1 *Donkey walk* (1967)
2 *Donkey in danger* (1970)

Donkey series
Towers, Joyce
1 *Seaside donkey* (1964)
2 *Flower garden donkeys* (1965)
3 *Winter donkey* (1966)
4 *Holiday camp donkeys* (1967)

Donkey trap series
Baker, Daisy
Reminiscences of travels in southern England
1 *Travels in a donkey trap* (1974)
2 *More travels in a donkey trap* (1976)

Donna Miro and Lorna Doria series
Graham, Heather
1 *Sensuous angel* (1985)
2 *Angel's share* (1985)

Donna Parker series
Martin, Marcia
1 *Donna Parker in Hollywood* (1956)
2 *Donna Parker at Cherrydale* (1957)
3 *Donna Parker, special agent* (1957)
4 *Donna Parker on her own* (1957)
5 *Spring to remember* (1960)
6 *Mystery at Arawak* (1962)
7 *Donna Parker takes a giant step* (1964)

Donna Rockford series
Woolfolk, Dorothy
1 *Who killed daddy?* (1980)
Mother, where are you?
2 *Death of a dancer* (1982)
3 *Murder in Washington* (1982)
Body on the beach
4 *Abby is missing* (1983)
5 *Mystery in Studio Thirteen* (1984)

Donna series
Larkin, Rochelle T
1 *Godmother* (1971)
2 *Honor thy Godmother* (1972)
3 *For Godmother and country* (1972)

Donnacha Mac Conmara trilogy
Macmanus, Francis
1 *Stand and give challenge* (1934)
2 *Candle for the proud* (1936)
3 *Men withering* (1939)

Donnegan series
Quick, Dorothy
see **Lieutenant Peter Donnegan series**

Donnellys series
Miller, Orlo
1 *Donnellys must die* (1962)
2 *Death to the Donnellys* (1975)

Donoghue series
Turnbull, Peter
see **P Division series**

Donovan and Coyle series
Philips, Judson Pentecost
see **Coyle and Donovan series**

Donovan series
Donovan, Dick
see **Dick Donovan series**

Donovan series
Lyall, Edna
1 *Donovan, a modern Englishman* (1882)
2 *We too* (1884)

Donovan series
Palmer, Vance
see **Macy Donovan series**
Saum, Karen
see **Brigid Donovan series**
Wright, Steve
see **Barry Donovan series**

Donovan's Devils series
Parker, Lee
1 *Assassination is set for July four* (1974)
2 *Blue print for execution* (1974)
3 *Guns of Mazatlan* (1975)

Don't bite the sun series
Lee, Tanith
1 *Don't bite the sun* (1976)
2 *Drinking sapphire wine* (1977)
One volume edition 1979

Don't series
Hastings, Beverly
1 *Don't talk to strangers* (1980)
2 *Don't walk home alone* (1985)
3 *Don't cry, little girl* (1987)
4 *Don't look back* (1991)

Don't series
Henderson, Kathy
1 *Don't interrupt!* (1988)
2 *Don't do that!* (1989)

Doodle series
Ryan, John
1 *Dodo's delight* (1977)
Alternative title: Doodle and the state secrets
2 *Doodle's homework* (1978)
Alternative title: The fuddi-duddi-dodo's great mathematical experiment

Dooki series
Hughes, Jean
1 *Doings of Dooki* (1938)
2 *Dooki and the little white dog* (1939)

Dooley series
Dunne, Finley Peter
see **Mister Dooley series**

Doolin and Darling series
Cookson, Catherine
see **Matty Doolin and Joe Darling series**

Doom-quest of Ara-Karn series
Corby, Adam
1 *Former king* (1981)
2 *Divine queen* (1982)

Doom trail series
Smith, Arthur Douglas Howden
1 *Doom trail* (1923)
2 *Beyond the sunset* (1923)

Doomsday Marshal series
Hogan, Ray
1 *Doomsday Marshal* (1975)
2 *Doomsday posse* (1977)
3 *Doomsday trail* (1979)
4 *Doomsday bullet* (1981)
5 *Doomsday canyon* (1984)
6 *Doomsday Marshal and the hanging judge* (1986)
7 *Doomsday Marshal and the Comancheros* (1988)
8 *Doomsday Marshal and the mountain man* (1993)

Doomsday series
Forman, James Douglas
1 *Call back yesterday* (1981)
2 *Doomsday plus twelve* (1984)

Doomsday warrior series
Stacy, Ryder
This pseudonym is used by Ryder Syvertsen alone for numbers 5-19 and with Jan Stacey for numbers 1-4
1 *Doomsday warrior* (1984)
2 *Red America* (1984)
3 *Last American* (1984)
4 *Bloody America* (1985)
5 *America's last declaration* (1985)
6 *American rebellion* (1985)
7 *American defiance* (1986)

8 *American glory* (1986)
9 *America's zero hour* (1986)
10 *American nightmare* (1987)
11 *American Eden* (1987)
12 *Death, American style* (1987)
13 *American paradise* (1988)
14 *American death orbit* (1988)
15 *American ultimatum* (1989)
16 *American overthrow* (1989)
17 *America's sword* (1990)
18 *American dream machine* (1990)
19 *America's final defense* (1991)

Doomstar series
Meyers, Richard S
1 *Doom star* (1978)
Doomstar
2 *Doom star, number two* (1979)
Return to Doomstar

Doone series
Blackmore, Richard Doddridge
see **Lorna Doone series**
Manning, David
see **Ronicky Doone series**
Reno, Clint
see **Vigilante series**

Door chronicles series
Edwards, Gene
see **Chronicles of the door series**

Door County trilogy
Blei, Norbert
1 *Door way* (1981)
2 *Door to Door* (1985)
3 *Neighborhood* (1987)

Doors into time series
McKean, Thomas
1 *Secret of the seven willows* (1991)
2 *Haunted circus* (1993)

Dop Doctor series
Dehan, Richard
1 *Dop Doctor* (1910)
One braver thing
2 *That which hath wings* (1918)

Dora Darling series
Austin, Jane Goodwin
1 *Dora Darling* (1865)
2 *Outpost* (1867)

Dora Myrl series
Bodkin, Matthias McDonnell
1 *Dora Myrl, the lady detective* (1900)
Short stories
2 *Capture of Paul Beck* (1909)
3 *Young Beck* (1911)
Short stories

Dorabella and Penny series
Bracken, Anne
see **Penny and Dorabella series**

Doran Chelmarsh series
Hardwick, Mollie
see **Doran Fairweather series**

Doran Fairweather series
Hardwick, Mollie
1 *Malice domestic* (1986)
2 *Parson's pleasure* (1987)
3 *Uneaseful death* (1988)
4 *Bandersnatch* (1989)
5 *Dreaming damozel* (1990)

Dorcas Dene series
Sims, George Robert
Short stories
1 *Dorcas Dene, detective* (1897)
2 *Dorcas Dene, detective, second series* (1898)

Doria and Miro series
Graham, Heather
see **Donna Miro and Lorna Doria series**

Dorian Silk series
Harvester, Simon
1 *Dragon road* (1956)
2 *Unsung road* (1960)
3 *Silk road* (1962)
4 *Red road* (1963)
5 *Assassins road* (1965)
6 *Treacherous road* (1966)
7 *Battle road* (1967)
8 *Zion road* (1968)
9 *Nameless road* (1969)
10 *Moscow road* (1970)
11 *Sahara road* (1972)
12 *Forgotten road* (1974)
13 *Siberian road* (1976)

Dorian Trozen series
Carey, D L
1 *Distant drums* (1991)
2 *Rise defiant* (1992)

Doring series
North, Grace May
see **Adele Doring series**

Doris Fein series
Bethancourt, Tomas Ernesto
1 *Doctor Doon, superstar* (1978)
2 *Doris Fein, superspy* (1979)
3 *Quartz boyar* (1980)
4 *Phantom of the casino* (1981)
5 *Mad Samurai* (1981)
6 *Deadly Aphrodite* (1982)
7 *Murder is no joke* (1982)
8 *Dead heat at Long Beach* (1983)
9 *Legacy of terror* (1984)

Doris Force series
Duncan, Julia K
1 *Doris Force at Locked Gates* (1931)
Alternative title: Saving a mysterious fortune
2 *Doris Force at Cloudy Cove* (1931)
Alternative title: The old miner's signature
3 *Doris Force at Raven Rock* (1932)
Alternative title: Uncovering the secret oil well
4 *Doris Force at Barry Manor* (1932)
Alternative title: Mysterious adventures between classes

Doris series
Hansen, Joyce
1 *Gift-giver* (1980)
2 *Yellow bird and me* (1986)

Dorm A series
Sinclair, Dee
see **Castledare series**

Dormer series
Mottram, Ralph Hale
see **Captain Dormer series**

Dormouse series
Clarke, Elf Lewis
see **Drowsy Dormouse series**

Dormouse series
King, Frank
1 *Enter the Dormouse* (1936)
2 *Dormouse, undertaker* (1937)
3 *Dormouse has nine lives* (1938)
4 *Dormouse, peacemaker* (1938)
5 *Dough for the Dormouse* (1938)
6 *This doll is dangerous* (1940)
7 *They vanish at night* (1941)
8 *What price dubloons?* (1942)
9 *Crooks' cross* (1943)
10 *Gestapo Dormouse* (1944)
11 *Sinister light* (1946)
12 *Catastrophe Club* (1947)
13 *Operation Halter* (1948)
14 *Operation Honeymoon* (1950)
15 *Case of the strange beauties* (1952)
16 *Big blackmail* (1954)
17 *Crooks' caravan* (1955)
18 *Empty flat* (1957)
19 *Two who talked* (1958)
20 *That charming crook* (1958)
21 *Case of the frightened brother* (1959)

Dormouse series
Taylor, Judy
see **Dudley Dormouse series**

Dorothy and Lorelei Lee series
Loos, Anita
see **Lorelie Lee and Dorothy series**

Dorothy Brooke series
Sparhawk, Frances Campbell
1 *Dorothy Brooke's schooldays* (1909)
2 *Dorothy Brooke's vacation* (1910)
3 *Dorothy Brooke's experiments* (1911)
4 *Dorothy Brooke at Ridgemore* (1912)
5 *Dorothy Brooke across the sea* (1913)

Dorothy Chester series
Raymond, Evelyn Hunt
1 *Dorothy Chester at Skyrie* (1907)
2 *Dorothy's house party* (1908)
3 *Dorothy's schooling* (1908)
4 *Dorothy's travels* (1908)
5 *Dorothy* (1909)
6 *Dorothy in California* (1909)
7 *Dorothy on a house boat* (1909)
8 *Dorothy on a ranch* (1909)
9 *Dorothy at Oak Knowe* (1910)
10 *Dorothy's tour* (1912)
11 *Dorothy's triumph* (1913)

Dorothy Cope series
Charlesworth, Maria Louisa
see **Mrs Dorothy Cope series**

Dorothy Dainty series
Brooks, Amy
1 *Dorothy Dainty* (1902)
2 *Dorothy's playmates* (1903)
3 *Dorothy Dainty at school* (1904)
4 *Dorothy Dainty at the shore* (1905)
5 *Dorothy Dainty in the city* (1906)
6 *Dorothy Dainty at home* (1907)
7 *Dorothy Dainty's gay times* (1908)
8 *Dorothy Dainty in the country* (1909)
9 *Dorothy Dainty's winter* (1910)
10 *Dorothy Dainty at the mountains* (1911)
11 *Dorothy Dainty's holidays* (1912)
12 *Dorothy Dainty's vacation* (1913)
13 *Dorothy Dainty's visit* (1914)
14 *Dorothy Dainty at Crestville* (1915)
15 *Dorothy Dainty's new friends* (1916)
16 *Dorothy Dainty at Glenmore* (1917)
17 *Dorothy Dainty at Foam Ridge* (1918)
18 *Dorothy Dainty at the stone house* (1919)
19 *Dorothy Dainty at Gem Island* (1920)
20 *Dorothy Dainty's red letter day* (1921)
21 *Dorothy Dainty's treasure chest* (1922)
22 *Dorothy Dainty's castle* (1923)

Dorothy Dale series
Penrose, Margaret
1 *Dorothy Dale, a girl of today* (1908)
2 *Dorothy Dale at Glenwood School* (1908)
3 *Dorothy Dale's great secret* (1909)
4 *Dorothy Dale and her chums* (1909)
5 *Dorothy Dale's queer holidays* (1910)
6 *Dorothy Dale's camping days* (1911)
7 *Dorothy Dale's school rivals* (1912)
8 *Dorothy Dale in the city* (1913)
9 *Dorothy Dale's promise* (1914)
10 *Dorothy Dale in the West* (1915)
11 *Dorothy Dale's strange discovery* (1916)
12 *Dorothy Dale's engagement* (1917)
13 *Dorothy Dale to the rescue* (1924)

Dorothy Deane series
Kirk, Ellen Olney
1 *Dorothy Deane* (1898)
2 *Dorothy and her friends* (1899)

Dorothy Dee series
Wesley, Elizabeth
see **Doctor Dorothy Dee series**

Dorothy Dixon series
Wayne, Dorothy
1 *Dorothy Dixon and the double cousin* (1933)
2 *Dorothy Dixon and the mystery plane* (1933)
3 *Dorothy Dixon solves the Conway case* (1933)
4 *Dorothy Dixon wins her wings* (1933)

Dorothy Dot series
Timlow, Elizabeth Weston
1 *Dorothy Dot* (1898)
2 *April-fool twins* (1908)

Dorothy Draycott series
Townsend, Virginia Frances
1 *Sirs, only seventeen!* (1894)
Dorothy Draycott's todays
2 *Dorothy Draycott's tomorrow* (1897)

Dorrance series
Wells, Carolyn
1 *Dorrace domain* (1905)
2 *Dorrance doings* (1906)

Dorrie and Dickie series
Everett-Green, Evelyn
see **Hallowdene Hall series**

Dorrie series
Coombs, Patricia
1 *Dorrie's magic* (1962)
2 *Dorrie and the blue witch* (1964)
3 *Dorrie's play* (1965)
4 *Dorrie and the seather box* (1966)
5 *Dorrie and the witch doctor* (1967)
6 *Dorrie and the wizard's spell* (1968)
7 *Dorrie and the haunted house* (1970)
8 *Dorrie and the birthday eggs* (1971)
9 *Dorrie and the goblin* (1972)
10 *Dorrie and the fortune teller* (1973)
11 *Dorrie and the amazing magic elixir* (1974)
12 *Dorrie and the witch's imp* (1975)
13 *Dorrie and the Hallowe'en plot* (1976)
14 *Dorrie and the dreamyard monsters* (1977)
15 *Dorrie and the Screebit ghost* (1979)
16 *Dorrie and the Witchville Fair* (1980)
17 *Dorrie and the witch's camp* (1983)
18 *Dorrie and the museum case* (1986)

Dorsai series
Dickson, Gordon Rupert
1 *Necromancer* (1962)
No room for man
2 *Tactics of mistake* (1971)
3 *Soldier, ask not* (1967)
4 *Genetic general* (1961)
Dorsai
The second title is a revised edition; numbers 1, 2, 4 also published in one volume entitled *Three to Dorsai*, 1975
5 *Spirit of Dorsai* (1979)
6 *Lost Dorsai* (1980)
7 *Young Bleys* (1991)
8 *Final encyclopedia* (1984)
9 *Chantry Guild* (1988)
10 *Bleys the man* (1993)
11 *Other* (1994)
Companion volumes: *Dorsai companion*, 1986, *Dorsai's command*, by Troy Denning, Gordon Rupert Dickson and Cory Glaberson, 1989

Dortmunder Gang series
Westlake, Donald Edwin
1 *Hot rock* (1970)
2 *Bank shot* (1972)
3 *Jimmy the Kid* (1974)
4 *Nobody's perfect* (1977)
5 *Why me?* (1983)
6 *Good behavior* (1985)
7 *Drowned hope* (1990)

Dose series
Dennys, Joyce
1 *Mrs Dose, the doctor's wife* (1930)
2 *Repeated doses* (1931)

Dossier series
This sequence has three authors
Gaboriau, Emile
1 *File number one hundred and thirteen* (1867)
Blackmailers
Dossier number one hundred and thirteen
File one hundred and thirteen
Young, Ernest A
2 *File number one hundred and fourteen* (1886)
Harper, Harry
3 *File number one hundred and fifteen* (1886)
Alternative title: A man of steel

Dot and Dash series
West, Dorothy
1 *Dot and Dash at the Maple Sugar Camp* (1938)
2 *Dot and Dash at Happy Hollow* (1938)
3 *Dot and Dash in the north woods* (1938)
4 *Dot and Dash in the Pumpkin Patch* (1939)
5 *Dot and Dash at the seashore* (1940)

Double act series
Denison, Muriel
Autobiography
1 *Overture and beginners* (1973)
2 *Double act* (1985)

Double feature series
Stamp, Terence
Autobiography
1 *Stamp album* (1987)
2 *Coming attractions* (1988)
3 *Double feature* (1989)

Double lives series
Plomer, William
Memoirs
1 *Double lives* (1943)
2 *At home* (1958)

Double O Seven series
Fleming, Ian
see **James Bond series**

Double O'Day series
Evans, Gwyn
1 *Bluebeard's keys* (1937)
2 *Iron mask* (1938)
3 *Coffins for two* (1939)
4 *Sleepless man* (1940)

Double-spiral war series
Norwood, Warren
1 *Midway between* (1984)
2 *Polar fleet* (1985)
3 *Final command* (1986)

Double Thirteen Club series
Marlowe, Piers
1 *Double Thirteen* (1947)
2 *Loaded dice* (1949)

Dougal Munro and Jack Carter series
Higgins, Jack
see **Brigadier Dougal Munro and Captain Jack Carter series**

Dougal series
Taylor, Andrew
see **William Dougal series**

Dougal series
Thompson, Eric
1 *Adventures of Dougal* (1971)
2 *Dougal's Scottish holiday* (1971)
3 *Dougal round the world* (1972)
4 *Misadventures of Dougal* (1972)
5 *Dougal strikes again* (1973)
Omnibus volume entitled *Best of Dougal*, 1973

Dougal Trocher series
Walker, David Harry
1 *Winter of madness* (1964)
2 *Black Dougal* (1973)

Douglas and Reeves series
Infante, Anne
see **Micky Douglas and inspector Reeves series**

Douglas Baynes series
Bell, Vicars
see **Doctor Douglas Baynes series**

Douglas convolution trilogy
Llewellyn, Edward
1 *Douglas convolution* (1979)
2 *Bright companion* (1980)
3 *Prelude to chaos* (1983)

Douglas Grant series
Millar, Florence N
see **Chief Inspector Douglas Grant series**

Douglas Perkins and Gerry Tate series
Babson, Marian
1 *Cover-up story* (1971)
2 *Murder on show* (1972)
Murder at the cat show
3 *Tourists are for trapping* (1989)
4 *In the teeth of adversity* (1990)

Douglas Quantrill series
Radley, Sheila
see **Chief Inspector Douglas Quantrill series**

Douglas Renfrew series
Erskine, Laurie York
1 *Renfrew of the Royal Mounted* (1922)
2 *Renfrew rides again* (1927)
3 *Renfrew rides the sky* (1928)
4 *Renfrew rides north* (1931)
5 *Renfrew's long trail* (1933)
6 *Renfrew rides the range* (1935)
7 *Renfrew in the valley of vanished men* (1936)
8 *One man came back* (1939)
9 *Renfrew flies again* (1941)

Douglas Selby series
Gardner, Erle Stanley
see **District Attorney series**

Douglas series
Crockett, Samuel Rutherford
1 *Black Douglas* (1899)
2 *Maid Margaret of Galloway* (1905)

Dougy and Gracey series
Moloney, James
1 *Dougie* (1993)
2 *Gracey* (1994)

Douglas series
Lee, John Darrell
see **Brian Douglas series**

Dover series
Porter, Joyce
see **Chief Inspector Wilfred Dover series**

Dove's End Football Club series
McCann, Sean
1 *Goals for glory* (1975)
2 *We are the champions* (1975)
3 *Golden goal* (1977)
4 *Shooting stars* (1978)
5 *Hot shot* (1979)
6 *Shoot on sight* (1981)
7 *Team that nobody wanted* (1982)

Dowbiggins series
Vipont, Elfrida
1 *Family at Dowbiggins* (1955)
2 *More about Dowbiggins* (1958)
Win for Henry Conyers
3 *Changes at Dowbiggins* (1960)
Boggarts and dreams

Dowling series
McInerny, Ralph
see **Father Roger Dowling series**

Down home series
Sandstrom, Eve K
1 *Death down home* (1990)
2 *Devil down home* (1991)
3 *Down home heifer heist* (1993)

Down North series
Duncan, Norman
1 *Harbor tales down North* (1918)
2 *Battles royal down North* (1918)

Down the long wind trilogy
Bradshaw, Gillian
see **Arthur and Gawain trilogy**

Downbelow Station trilogy
Cherryh, Carolyn Janice
1 *Downbelow Station* (1981)
2 *Merchanter's luck* (1982)
3 *Forty thousand in Gehenna* (1983)

Downes and Hopkins series
Sampson, Victor
see **Inspector Downes and Sergeant Hopkins series**

Downey series
Hendryx, James Beardsley
see **Corporal Cameron Downey series; Corporal Downey series**

Dowsabel series
Wood, Lorna
see **Hag Dowsabel series**

Doyle brothers series
Carroll, James
1 *Mortal friends* (1992)
2 *City below* (1994)

Doyle series
Newell, Audrey
see **Patrick Michael Doyle series**

Doyne series
Baines, Cuthbert
see **Dennis Doyne series**

Drac series
Jungman, Ann
see **Vlad the Drac series**

Draco series
Foster, Richard
see **Pete Draco series**

Dracon series
Longyear, Barry Brookes
1 *Enemy mine* (1985)
Co-author: David Gerrold
2 *Tomorrow testament* (1983)

Dracula horror series
Lory, Robert
Based on moving pictures concerning a modern descendant of Dracula
1 *Dracula returns* (1973)
2 *Hand of Dracula* (1973)
3 *Dracula's brother* (1973)
4 *Dracula's gold* (1973)
5 *Drums of Dracula* (1974)
6 *Witching of Dracula* (1974)
7 *Dracula's lost world* (1974)
8 *Dracula's disciple* (1975)
9 *Challenge to Dracula* (1975)

Dracula series
Jungman, Ann
see **Count Dracula series**

Dracula series
This sequence has nineteen authors
Stoker, Bram
1 *Dracula* (1897)
Also published as *The illustrated Dracula*, 1975, *The annotated Dracula*, edited by Leonard Woolf, 1975, *The essential Dracula*, completely illustrated and annotated edition, edited by Raymond T McNally and Radu Florescu, 1979; adaptations: *Dracula*, by Tom Barling, 1976, *Dracula*, by Stephanie Skinner, 1982, *Dracula*, by Joan Cameron, 1984; film adaptations: *Dracula*, by Ian Thorne, 1977, *Dracula, prince of darkness*, by John Frederick Burke, 1967, *Zoltan, hound of Dracula*, by Kenneth Rayner Johnson, 1977, also published as *Hounds of Dracula*, and as *Dracula's dog*
2 *Dracula's guest, and other weird stories* (1914)
Owen, Dean
3 *Brides of Dracula* (1960)
Based on a screenplay
Hall, Angus
4 *Scars of Dracula* (1971)
Based on a screenplay
Parry, Michel
5 *Countess Dracula* (1971)
Based on a screenplay
Samuels, Victor
6 *Vampire women* (1973)
Aubin, Etienne
7 *Dracula and the virgins of the undead* (1974)
Saberhagen, Fred
8 *Dracula tapes* (1975)
Kimberly, Gail
9 *Dracula began* (1976)
Tremayne, Peter
10 *Dracula unborn* (1977)
Bloodright
Dreadstone, Carl
11 *Dracula's daughter* (1977)
Also published under the pseudonym E K Leyton; based on a screenplay
Teed, Jack Hamilton
12 *Blood of Dracula* (1977)
Savory, Gerald
13 *Count Dracula* (1977)
Based on a screenplay
Saberhagen, Fred
14 *Holmes-Dracula file* (1978)
Set in 1897
Estleman, Loren D
15 *Sherlock Holmes versus Dracula* (1978)
Alternative title: The adventures of the sanguinary count; set in the 1890s
Tremayne, Peter
16 *Revenge of Dracula* (1978)
Saberhagen, Fred
17 *Old friend of the family* (1979)

Youngson, Jeanne
18 *Further perils of Dracula* (1979)
Tremayne, Peter
19 *Dracula, my love* (1980)
Saberhagen, Fred
20 *Thorn* (1980)
Drake, Asa
21 *Crimson kisses* (1981)
Saberhagen, Fred
22 *Dominion* (1982)
Garden, Nancy
23 *Prisoner of vampires* (1984)
Saberhagen, Fred
24 *Matter of taste* (1990)
Ruddy, Jon
25 *Bargain* (1990)
Aldiss, Brian Wilson
26 *Dracula unbound* (1991)
Companion volumes: *Shades of Dracula*, Bram Stoker's uncollected stories, edited by Peter Haining, 1982, *The adult version of Dracula*, by Hal Kantor, 1970, *The Dracula archives*, by Raymond Rudorff, 1971, *The Count Dracula book of classic vampire stories*, by Jeanne Youngson, 1981, *The Count Dracula cookbook*, by Jeanne Youngson, 1979, *Count Dracula Fan Club book of vampire stories*, by Jeanne Youngson, 1980, *Count Dracula's favorite Christmas cookie recipes*, by Jeanne Youngson, 1988, *The Dracula book*, by Donald Frank Glut, 1975, *The Dracula book of great vampire stories*, by Leslie Shepard, 1977, *The Dracula book of great horror stories*, by Leslie Shepard, 1981, *Dracula's diary*, by Michael Corby and Michael Geare, 1982, *Dracula's castle*, by James Herbert Brennan, 1986, *Dracula's brood, neglected vampire classics*, edited by Richard Dalby, 1987, *The Dracula centenary book*, by Peter Haining, 1987, *Dracula, prince of many faces, his life and his times*, by Radu Florescu and Raymond T McNally, 1975, *Dracula scrapbook*, by Peter Haining, 1976, *Dracula, the novel and the legend*, by Clive Leatherdale, 1985, *Dracula, the vampire and the critics*, by Margaret Louise Carter, 1988; parodies: *Dracutwig*, by Mallory T Knight, 1969, *Dhampire*, by Scott Baker, 1982, *Dracula go home*, by Kin Platt, 1979, *Dracula in love*, by John Shirley, 1983, *Dracula is a pain in the neck*, by Elizabeth Levy, 1983, *Seance for a vampire*, by Fred Saberhagen, 1994

Dracula series
Waddell, Martin
see **Little Dracula series**

Dracula trilogy
Ambrus, Victor Gyozo
1 *Dracula* (1980)
Everything you always wanted to know but were too afraid to ask
2 *Dracula's bedtime storybook* (1981)
Tales to keep you awake at night
3 *Son of Dracula* (1986)

Dracula's children series
Chetwynd-Hayes, Ronald
1 *Dracula's children* (1987)
2 *House of Dracula* (1987)

Dragnet series
This sequence has four authors
Knight, David
1 *Case number 561* (1956)
Deming, Richard
2 *Case of the courteous killer* (1958)
3 *Case of the crime king* (1959)
Tralins, Sandor Robert
4 *Dragnet '67* (1967)
Vowell, David
5 *Dragnet 1968* (1967)

Dragon and Susan series
Manning, Rosemary
see **Susan and R.Dragon series**

Dragon apparent series
Lewis, Norman
Reminiscences of travels
1 *Dragon apparent* (1951)
Travels in Indo-China
2 *Holden earth* (1952)
Travels in Burma

Dragon Green series
Thomas, Joyce Bissell
1 *Dragon Green* (1975)
2 *Prince of the Dragon Green* (1975)
One volume edition entitled *Dragon Green*, 1936

Dragon King trilogy
Lawhead, Stephen
1 *In the hall of the Dragon King* (1982)
2 *Warlords of Nin* (1983)
3 *Sword and the flame* (1984)

Dragon Lance chronicles series
Weis, Margaret
see **Dragonlance chronicles series**

Dragon lord series
This sequence has two authors
Drake, David
1 *Dragon lord* (1979)
Randall, Neil
2 *Storm of dust* (1987)
A Crossroads adventure in the world of David Drake's *Dragon lord*

Dragon prince series
Rawn, Melanie
1 *Dragon prince* (1988)
2 *Star scroll* (1989)
3 *Sunrunner's fire* (1990)

Dragon series
Anthony, Piers
1 *Dragon's gold* (1987)
2 *Serpent's silver* (1988)
3 *Chimaera's copper* (1990)
4 *Orc's opal* (1990)

Dragon series
Counsel, June
1 *Dragon in class four* (1984)
2 *Dragon in Spring term* (1988)
3 *Dragon in Summer* (1988)
4 *Dragon in top class!* (1994)

Dragon series
Dickson, Gordon Rupert
1 *Dragon and the George* (1976)
2 *Dragon knight* (1990)

Dragon series
Gannett, Ruth Stiles
1 *My father's dragon* (1948)
2 *Elmer and the dragon* (1950)
3 *Dragons of Blueland* (1951)

Dragon series
Hall, Lynn
1 *Horse called Dragon* (1971)
Wild mustang
2 *New day for Dragon* (1975)
3 *Dragon defiant* (1977)
4 *Dragon's delight* (1980)

Dragon series
Jungman, Ann
Illustrated by Derek Collard
1 *Dragon of Yang-Wong* (1978)
2 *Dragon becomes a pet* (1978)
3 *Dragon joins the army* (1978)
4 *Dragon in love* (1978)

Dragon series
Leedy, Loreen
1 *Number of dragons* (1985)
2 *Dragon ABC hunt* (1986)
3 *Dragon Halloween party* (1986)
Things to make and do
4 *Dragon Christmas* (1988)
Things to make and do
5 *Dragon Thanksgiving feast* (1990)
Things to make and do

Dragon series
Pilkey, Dav
1 *Friend for Dragon* (1991)
2 *Dragon gets by* (1991)
3 *Dragon's merry Christmas* (1991)
4 *Dragon's fat cat* (1992)
5 *Dragon's Halloween* (1992)

Dragon star series
Rawn, Melanie
1 *Stronghold* (1990)
2 *Dragon token* (1992)
3 *Skybowl* (1993)

Dragon warriors series
This sequence has two authors
Morris, Dave
1 *Dragon warriors* (1985)
2 *Way of wizardry* (1986)
Johnson, Oliver
3 *Eleven crystals* (1985)
Morris, Dave
4 *Out of the shadows* (1986)
Johnson, Oliver
5 *Power of darkness* (1986)
Morris, Dave
6 *Lands of legend* (1986)

Dragonard series
Gilchrist, Rupert
1 *Dragonard* (1975)
2 *Master of Dragonard Hill* (1976)
3 *Dragonard blood* (1977)
4 *Dragonard rising* (1978)
5 *Siege of Dragonard Hill* (1979)
6 *Guns of Dragonard* (1980)

Dragonard series
Jakes, John
1 *When the Star Kings die* (1967)
2 *Planet wizard* (1969)
3 *Tonight we steal the stars* (1969)

Dragonbards trilogy
Murphy, Shirley Rousseau
1 *Nightpool* (1985)
2 *Ivory lyre* (1987)
3 *Dragonbards* (1988)

Dragonbound trilogy
Miller, Carl
1 *Dragonbound* (1988)
2 *Warrior and the witch* (1990)
3 *Goblin plain war* (1991)

Dragonfall 5 series
Earnshaw, Brian
1 *Dragonfall 5 and the royal beast* (1972)
2 *Dragonfall 5 and the space cowboys* (1972)
3 *Dragonfall 5 and the empty planet* (1973)
4 *Dragonfall 5 and the hijackers* (1974)
5 *Dragonfall 5 and the master mind* (1975)
6 *Dragonfall 5 and the super horse* (1977)
7 *Dragonfall 5 and the haunted world* (1979)

Dragonfire series
Scott, Peter Graham
1 *Dragonfire* (1981)
2 *Feast of vultures* (1983)
Originally announced as a trilogy

DragonLance chronicles series
Weis, Margaret
1 *Dragons of the autumn twilight* (1984)
2 *Dragons of the winter night* (1985)
3 *Dragons of spring dawning* (1985)
One volume edition entitled *DragonLance chronicles*, 1988; companion volume: *The atlas of the DragonLance world*, by Karen Wynn Fonstad, 1987

DragonLance heroes series
This sequence has four authors
Knaak, Richard Allen
1 *Legend of Huma* (1988)
Berberick, Nancy Varian
2 *Stormblade* (1988)
Williams, Michael Leon
3 *Weasel's luck* (1988)
Knaak, Richard Allen
4 *Kaz, the minotaur* (1990)
Parkinson, Dan
5 *Gates of Thorbardin* (1990)
Williams, Michael Leon
6 *Galen beknighted* (1990)

DragonLance legends trilogy
Weis, Margaret
1 *Time of the twins* (1986)
2 *War of the twins* (1986)
3 *Test of the twins* (1986)
One volume edition entitled *The DragonLance legends*, 1988

DragonLance preludes II series
This sequence has six authors
Carter, Tonya R
1 *Riverwind the plainsman* (1990)
Kirchoff, Mary Lynn
2 *Flint the king* (1990)
Siegel, Barbara
3 *Tanis, the shadow years* (1990)

DragonLance preludes series
This sequence has three authors
Carter, Tonya R
1 *Darkness and light* (1989)
Kirchoff, Mary Lynn
2 *Kendermore* (1989)

DragonLance series
This sequence has five authors
Phillips, Terry
1 *Soulforge* (1985)
Niles, Douglas
2 *Lords of doom* (1986)
Weis, Margaret
3 *DragonLance adventures* (1987)
Stein, Kevin
4 *Brothers Majere* (1989)

DragonLance tales trilogy
Weis, Margaret
1 *Magic of Krynn* (1987)
2 *Kender, gully dwarves and gnomes* (1987)
3 *Love and war* (1987)
One volume edition entitled *DragonLance tales*, 1991

Dragonling series
Koller, Jackie French
1 *Dragonling* (1990)
2 *Dragon in the family* (1993)

Dragonmaster series
Brightfield, Richard
1 *Dragonmaster* (1984)
2 *Revenge of the Dragonmaster* (1985)

Dragonrealm series
Knaak, Richard Allen
1 *Firedrake* (1989)
2 *Icedragon* (1989)
3 *Wolfhelm* (1990)
4 *Shadow steed* (1990)

Dragonriders of Pern series
McCaffrey, Anne
see **Pern and the Red Planet series**

Dragon's blood trilogy
Yolen, Jane
see **Pit dragons trilogy**

Dragon's egg series
Forward, Robert Lull
1 *Dragon's egg* (1980)
2 *Starquake* (1985)

Dragon's pawn trilogy
Dennis, Carol Larkey
1 *Dragon's pawn* (1987)
2 *Dragon's knight* (1989)
3 *Dragon's queen* (1991)

Dragons series
Brightfield, Richard
1 *Battle of the dragons* (1986)
2 *Planet of the dragons* (1988)

Dragons series
Gentile, Gary
1 *Time for dragons* (1989)
2 *Dragons past* (1990)
3 *No future for dragons* (1990)

Dragons series
Gunnarsson, Thorarinn
1 *Make way for dragons!* (1990)
2 *Human, beware!* (1990)

Dragons trilogy
Salsitz, R A V
1 *Where dragons lie* (1985)
2 *Where dragons rule* (1986)
3 *Night of dragons* (1990)

Dragonsbane series
Hambly, Barbara
1 *Ladies of Mandrigyn* (1984)
2 *Dragonsbane* (1986)
3 *Silicon mage* (1988)

Dragonstar trilogy
Bischoff, David
1 *Day of the Dragonstar* (1983)
2 *Night of the Dragonstar* (1985)
3 *Dragonstar destiny* (1991)

Dragonsword series
Baudino, Gael
1 *Dragon sword* (1988)
Dragonsword
2 *Duel of dragons* (1991)

Dragoon and Gaines series
Diamond, Frank
see **Ransome Dragoon and Vicky Gaines series**

Draka trilogy
Stirling, Stephen Michael
1 *Marching through Georgia* (1988)
2 *Under the yoke* (1989)
3 *Stone dogs* (1990)

Drake series
Baker, William Howard
see **Dangerman series**
Barker, Elsa
see **Dexter Drake series**
Ellington, Richard
see **Steve Drake series**
Faulkner, William
see **Temple Drake series**
Krich, Rochelle Majer
see **Jessie Drake series**
Maguire, Michael
see **Simon Drake series**
Marlowe, Dan James
see **Earl Drake series**
Nielsen, Helen
see **Simon Drake series**
Sea-Lion
see **Desmond Drake series**
Turner, Judy
see **Sir Francis Drake series**
Wilcox, Collin
see **Stephen Drake series**

Drakov series
Winters, Jon
see **Anton Drakov series**

Drakulya series
Doherty, Paul C
1 *Prince of Drakulya* (1986)
2 *Lord Count Drakulya* (1986)

Drale series
Aronin, Ben
see **Raphael Drale series**

Drawing book series
Emberley, Ed
see **Ed Emberley's drawing book series**

Drawn from series
Shepard, Ernest Howard
Autobiography
1 *Drawn from memory* (1957)
2 *Drawn from life* (1961)

Dray Prescot series
Akers, Alan Burt
1 *Transit to Scorpio* (1972)
2 *Suns of Scorpio* (1973)
3 *Warrior of Scorpio* (1973)
4 *Swordships of Scorpio* (1973)
5 *Prince of Scorpio* (1974)
6 *Manhounds of Antares* (1974)
7 *Arena of Antares* (1974)
Numbers 6 and 7 also published in one volume, 1981
8 *Fliers of Antares* (1975)
9 *Bladesman of Antares* (1975)
10 *Avenger of Antares* (1975)
11 *Armada of Antares* (1976)
12 *Tides of Kregen* (1976)
13 *Renegades of Kregen* (1976)
14 *Krozair of Kregen* (1977)
15 *Secret Scorpio* (1977)
16 *Savage Scorpio* (1978)
17 *Captive Scorpio* (1978)
18 *Golden Scorpio* (1978)
Sequence continued under the pseudonym Dray Prescot
Prescot, Dray
19 *Life for Kregen* (1979)
20 *Sword for Kregen* (1979)
21 *Fortune for Kregen* (1979)
22 *Victory for Kregen* (1980)
23 *Beasts of Antares* (1980)
24 *Rebel of Antares* (1980)
25 *Legions of Antares* (1981)
26 *Allies of Antares* (1981)
27 *Mazes of Antares* (1982)
28 *Delia of Valla* (1982)
29 *Fires of Scorpio* (1983)
30 *Talons of Scorpio* (1983)
31 *Masks of Scorpio* (1984)
32 *Seg the bowman* (1984)
33 *Werewolves of Kregen* (1985)
34 *Witches of Kregen* (1985)
35 *Storm over Valla* (1985)
36 *Omens of Kregen* (1985)
37 *Warlord of Antares* (1988)

Draycott series
Townsend, Virginia Frances
see **Dorothy Draycott series**

Drayton family series
Charles, Elizabeth
1 *Draytons and the Davenants* (1867)
2 *On both sides of the sea* (1868)

Drayton series
Lambert, Janet
see **Christie Drayton series**

Drayton series
Randall, Rona
1 *Drayton legacy* (1985)
2 *Potter's niece* (1987)

Dread Empire series
Cook, Glen
1 *Shadow of all night falling* (1979)
2 *October's baby* (1980)
3 *All darkness met* (1980)
4 *Fire in his hands* (1984)
5 *With mercy toward none* (1985)
6 *Reap the east wind* (1987)
7 *Ill fate marshalling* (1988)

Dreadnaught boys series
Lawton, Wilbur
1 *Dreadnaught boys on battle practice* (1911)
2 *Dreadnaught boys aboard a destroyer* (1911)
3 *Dreadnaught boys on a submarine* (1911)
4 *Dreadnaught boys on aero service* (1912)
5 *Dreadnaught boys' world cruise* (1913)
6 *Dreadnaught boys in home waters* (1914)

Dreadnought series
Carey, Diane
1 *Dreadnought!* (1986)
2 *Battlestations!* (1986)

Dream dancer series
Morris, Janet Ellen
see **Kerrion Empire series**

Dream girls series
Joyce, Rosemary
1 *Anything to win* (1986)
2 *Love or glory* (1986)
3 *Tarnished victory* (1986)
4 *Bond of love* (1986)
5 *Up to no good* (1987)

Dream Lords trilogy
Cole, Adrian
1 *Plague of nightmares* (1975)
2 *Lord of nightmares* (1975)
3 *Bane of nightmares* (1976)

Dream of red mansions series
Ts'ao, Hsueh-ch'in
see **Dream of the red chamber series**

Dream of the red chamber series
Ts'ao, Hsueh-ch'in
Translated from the Chinese
1 *Golden days* (1792)
2 *Crab-Flower Club* (1792)
3 *Warning voice* (1792)
4 *Debt of tears* (1982)
5 *Dreamer wakes* (1982)
One volume editions entitled *A dream of the red chamber*, 1929, and *A dream of red mansions*, 1978-80

Dream Park series
Niven, Larry
1 *Dream Park* (1981)
2 *Barsoom project* (1989)
3 *Voodoo game* (1991)

Dream quest trilogy
Saint Alcorn, Lloyd
1 *Halberd, dream warrior* (1987)
2 *On the shoulders of giants* (1988)
3 *Serpent mound* (1989)

Dream seekers series
Longstreet, Stephen
1 *Dream seekers* (1979)
2 *Wheel of fortune* (1981)

Dreamer series
Duncan, William Murdoch
see **Superintendent Donald Reamer series**

Dreamers of the day series
Ross, David D
1 *Argus gambit* (1989)
2 *Eighth rank* (1991)

Dreamers series
Lehrer, Jim
Memoirs
1 *We were dreamers* (1975)
2 *Bus of my own* (1992)

Dreamhouse series
Wayman, Tony Russell
1 *World of the sleeper* (1967)
2 *Ads infinitum* (1971)

Dreamlands series
Lumley, Brian
1 *Hero of dreams* (1986)
2 *Ship of dreams* (1986)
3 *Mad moon of dreams* (1987)
4 *Iced on Aran, and other dreamquests* (1990)

DreamMaker series
Cosgrove, Stephen Edward
1 *Goldilocks* (1988)
2 *Billy Goats Gruff* (1988)
3 *Three blind mice* (1988)
4 *Humpty Dumpty* (1988)

Dreams of youth series
Winn, Godfrey
1 *Dreams fade* (1928)
2 *Fly away, youth* (1934)

Dreams trilogy
Quick, W T
1 *Dreams of flesh and sand* (1988)
2 *Dreams of gods and men* (1989)
3 *Singularities* (1990)

Dreamtime series
This sequence has two authors
Aboriginal myths in paintings
Mountford, Charles Pearcy
Illustrated by Ainslie Roberts
1 *Dreamtime* (1965)
This sequence has two authors
2 *Dawn of time* (1868)
3 *First sunrise* (1971)
Roberts, Melva Jean
4 *Dreamtime heritage* (1975)
Dreamtime, Aboriginal heritage

Dreamweaver series
Hilgartner, Beth
1 *Colors in the dreamweaver's loom* (1989)
2 *Feast of the trickster* (1991)

Dreamweaver's loom series
Hilgartner, Beth
1 *Colors in the dreamweaver's loom* (1989)
2 *Feast of the trickster* (1991)

Drenai series
Gemmell, David A
1 *Legend* (1985)
Against the horde
2 *King beyond the gate* (1985)
3 *Waylander* (1986)
4 *Quest for lost heroes* (1990)
One volume edition including *Druss the legend*, entitled *Drenai tales*, 1991

Drenee series
Roberts, Beth
1 *Magpie boy* (1989)
2 *Manganinnie* (1979)

Dresden doll trilogy
Andrews, Virginia Cleo
see **Dollanganger family series**

Drew and Cornish series
Hanson, Virginia
see **Adam Drew and Katherine Cornish series**

Drew files series
Keene, Carolyn
see **Nancy Drew files series**

Drew series
Fearn, John Russell
see **Clayton Drew series**
Garrett, William
see **James Drew series**
Keene, Carolyn
see **Nancy Drew series**
Ward, Christopher
see **Jonathan Drew series**

Drewer series
Landon, Hilary
see **Timothy Drewer series**

Drewry series
Burnaby, Nigel
see **Chief Inspector Drewry series**

Drex series
Evans, Gwyn
see **Quentin Drex series**

Drexel series
Usher, Gray
see **Superintendent Michael Drexel series**

Drexel Ware series
Andrews, Charlton
1 *Affair of the Malacca stick* (1936)
2 *Affair of the Syrian dagger* (1937)

Dria Meredith trilogy
Lambert, Janet
1 *Star dream* (1951)
2 *Summer for seven* (1952)
3 *High hurdles* (1955)

Driffield series
Connington, John Jervis
see **Sir Clinton Driffield series**

Drift of things series
Robinson, Roland Edward
Autobiography
1 *Drift of things* (1973)
Covers 1914-1952
2 *Shidt of sands* (1976)
Covers 1952-1962
3 *Letter to Joan* (1978)
Covers 1962-1973

Drifter Morgan series
Weston, Matt
1 *Morgan* (1970)
2 *Morgan's revenge* (1971)

Drina series
Estoril, Jean
1 *Ballet for Drina* (1957)
2 *Drina's dancing year* (1958)
3 *Drina dances in exile* (1959)
4 *Drina dances in Italy* (1959)
5 *Drina dances again* (1960)
6 *Drina dances in New York* (1961)
7 *Drina dances in Paris* (1962)
8 *Drina dances in Madeira* (1963)
9 *Drina dances in Switzerland* (1964)
10 *Drina goes on tour* (1965)
11 *Drina, ballerina* (1991)

Drinker of souls trilogy
Clayton, Jo
1 *Drinker of souls* (1986)
2 *Blue magic* (1988)
3 *Gathering of stones* (1989)
One volume edition entitled *The soul drinker*, 1989

Drinkwater series
Woodman, Richard
see **Nathaniel Drinkwater series**

Dripping series
Cresswell, Helen
see **Lizzie Dripping series**

Dripspring series
Gardner, Jerome
1 *Gunman's holiday* (1975)
2 *Dilemma at Dripspring* (1976)
3 *Underhand mail* (1976)
4 *Oldtimers* (1979)
5 *Confession at Dripspring* (1982)
6 *Jayhawk legacy* (1983)
7 *Pitchman healer* (1985)
8 *Rawhide redeemer* (1986)
9 *Owlhoot convention* (1988)
10 *Wide open town* (1990)

Driscoll series
De Andrea, William Louis
see **Clifford Driscoll series**
Johns, William Earl
see **Digger Driscoll series**
King, Rufus
see **Stuff Driscoll series**

Drive-in series
Lansdale, Joe Richard
1 *Drive-in* (1988)
A B-movie with blood and popcorn
2 *Drive-in 2* (1990)
Not just one of them sequels

Driving me crazy series
Vedral, Joyce Lauretta
1 *My parents are driving me crazy* (1986)
2 *Opposite sex is driving me crazy* (1988)
3 *My teenager is driving me crazy* (1989)

Drones Club series
Wodehouse, Pelham Grenville
1 *Young men in spats* (1936)
2 *Eggs, Beans and Crumpets* (1940)
3 *Few quick ones* (1959)

Drover series
Granger, Bill
see **Jimmy Drover series**

Drowsy Dormouse series
Clarke, Elf Lewis
1 *Drowsy Dormouse* (1944)
2 *Drowsy and Timmy go south* (1946)
3 *Farmer Drowsy* (1950)
4 *Drowsy's Christmas Eve* (1950)
5 *Drowsy and the beanstalk* (1952)
6 *Drowsy goes to school* (1952)

Druggist series
Kaye, Marvin
see **Marty Gold series**

Drum series
Gray, Rod
see **Lady from L.U.S.T. series**
Marlowe, Stephen
see **Chester Drum series**

Drumberley trilogy
Stevenson, Dorothy Emily
1 *Vittoria Cottage* (1949)
2 *Music in the hills* (1950)
3 *Winter and rough weather* (1951)
Shoulder the sky

Drummer Oliver Crowe series
Daniell, David Scott
1 *Mission for Oliver* (1953)
2 *Polly and Oliver* (1954)
3 *Polly and Oliver at sea* (1960)
4 *Polly and Oliver besieged* (1963)
5 *Polly and Oliver pursued* (1964)

Drummond series
Sapper
see **Bulldog Drummond series**

Drumtochty series
Maclaren, Ian
Sketches and stories of a Scottish village
1 *Beside the bonnie briar bush* (1894)
2 *Days of Auld Lang Syne* (1895)
3 *Kate Carnegie and those ministers* (1896)

Drury and Hazard series
Marlowe, Piers
see **Frank Drury and Inspector Bill Hazard series**

Drury Lane series
Ross, Barnaby
1 *Tragedy of X* (1932)
2 *Tragedy of Y* (1932)
3 *Tragedy of Z* (1933)
4 *Drury Lane's last case* (1933)
One volume edition entitled *The XYZ murders*, 1961

Drury series
Greene, L Patrick
see **Dynamite Drury series**
Sykes, William Stanley
see **Inspector Dennis Drury series**

Dryden series
Hartmann, Michael
see **Ben Dryden series**

Drylands series
Benton, Peggie
1 *One man against the drylands* (1972)
2 *Fight for the drylands* (1977)

Duane Braddock series
Bodine, J D
see **Pecos Kid series**

Duane series
Benton, John L
see **Stephen Duane series**
Grey, Romer Zane
see **Buck Duane series**

Dublin series
Joyce, Stanislaus
1 *My brother's keeper* (1958)
Memoirs of James Joyce
2 *Dublin diary of Stanislaus Joyce* (1962)

Duc de Richelieu series
Wheatley, Dennis
1 *Three inquisitive people* (1939)
2 *Forbidden territory* (1933)
3 *Devil rides out* (1935)
4 *Golden Spaniard* (1938)
5 *Strange conflict* (1941)
6 *Codeword, Golden Fleece* (1946)
7 *Second seal* (1950)
8 *Prisoner in the mask* (1957)
9 *Vendetta in Spain* (1961)
10 *Dangerous inheritance* (1965)
11 *Gateway to hell* (1970)

Ducane series
Bingham, John
1 *Double agent* (1966)
2 *Vulture in the sun* (1971)
3 *God's defector* (1976)
Ministry of Death

Du Cas series
Imbert-Terry, Henry
see **Detective Inspector Du Cas series**

Duchess Laura series
Lowndes, Marie Belloc
1 *Duchess Laura, certain days of her life* (1929)
Duchess intervenes
2 *Duchess Laura, further days of her life* (1933)

Duchess of Duke Street series
Hardwick, Mollie
Based on a television series
1 *Way up* (1976)
2 *Golden years* (1976)
Numbers 1 and 2 also published in one volume entitled *The Duchess of Duke Street*, 1977
3 *World keeps turning* (1976)

Duchess series
Nicholson, Celia Anna
1 *Hell and the duchess* (1928)
2 *Bridge is lost* (1930)

Duchy of Cornwall series
Quiller-Couch, Arthur
see **Troy Town series**

Duchy of Grand Fenwick series
Wibberley, Leonard
see **Grand Fenwick series**

Duck and Bear series
Delton, Judy
see **Bear and Duck series**

Duck Mallard series
Spiller, Andrew
see **Chief Inspector Duck Mallard series**

Duck series
Korman, Justine
see **Donald Duck series**

Duck series
Tyler, Jenny
1 *Duck on holiday* (1987)
2 *Duck and his friends* (1987)
3 *Duck in trouble* (1987)

Duck Street Gang series
Marray, Denis
1 *Duck Street Gang* (1984)
2 *Duck Street Gang returns* (1986)

Duddleswell series
Boyd, Neil
see **Father Charles Duddleswell series**

Dude McQuint series
Grove, Frederick Philip
1 *Great horse race* (1977)
2 *Match race* (1982)
3 *Search for the breed* (1986)
4 *Deception Trail* (1988)

Dudley Brent series
Marfield, Dwight
1 *Mystery of the east wind* (1930)
2 *Man with a paper skull* (1932)
3 *Sword in the pool* (1932)
4 *Mystery of King Cobra* (1933)

Dudley Dormouse series
Taylor, Judy
Illustrated by Peter Cross
1 *Dudley goes flying* (1986)
2 *Dudley and the monster* (1986)
3 *Dudley in a jam* (1986)
4 *Dudley and the strawberry snake* (1986)
5 *Dudley bakes a cake* (1987)

Dudley Graham series
Haines, Alice Calhoun
1 *Luck of the Dudley Grahams* (1907)
As related in extracts from Elizabeth Graham's diary
2 *Cock-a-doodle hill* (1909)

Dudley series
Drysdale, Margaret
see **Robert Dudley series**
Kendall, Ralph Selwood
see **L Division series**

Dudley series
Swede, George
1 *Dudley and the birdmen* (1985)
2 *Dudley and the Christmas thief* (1986)

Dudley series
Wilson, Derek
see **Robert Dudley series**

Due East series
Sayers, Valerie
1 *Due East* (1987)
2 *How I got him back* (1989)
Alternative title: Under the cold moon's shine
3 *Who do you love* (1991)
4 *Distance between us* (1994)

Duel of sorcery trilogy
Clayton, Jo
1 *Moongather* (1982)
2 *Moonscatter* (1983)
3 *Changer's moon* (1985)

Duelmaster series
Smith, Mark
1 *Challenge of the Magi* (1986)
2 *Blood Valley* (1986)
3 *Duelmaster* (1986)
4 *Shattered realm* (1987)
5 *Arena of death* (1987)

Duels in the air series
Townsend, Peter
Wartime reminiscences
1 *Duel of eagles* (1970)
2 *Duel in the dark* (1986)

Duets series
This sequence has two authors; bilingual English and Urdu
Stone, Susheila
1 *Nadeem makes samosas* (1987)
Dhanjal, Beryl
2 *Ranjit and the fire engines* (1987)
Stone, Susheila
3 *Where is Batool?* (1987)
Dhanjal, Beryl
4 *Sarah's birthday surprise* (1987)

Duff and Cherry series
Van Greenaway, Peter
see **Inspector Cherry and Sergeant Duff series**

Duff series
Armstrong, Charlotte
see **MacDougal Duff series**

Duffers of the deep series
Brown, Winifred
1 *Duffers on the deep* (1939)
Memoirs of travel before the Second World War
2 *No distress signals* (1952)
Experiences at a Catalina flying-boat base on Anglesey, 1940-1945
3 *Under six planets* (1955)
Memoirs of travel after the Second World War

Duffus January series
Smith, George Henry
1 *Druids' world* (1967)
2 *Witch queen of Lochlann* (1969)

Duffy House series
Evers, Crabbe
1 *Murder in Wrigley Field* (1991)
2 *Murderer's row* (1991)
3 *Bleeding Dodger Blue* (1991)
4 *Fear in Fenway* (1993)
5 *Tigers burning* (1994)

Duffy series
Fitzgerald, Nigel
see **Superintendent Duffy series**
Kavanagh, Dan
see **Nick Duffy series**

Dukay family series
Zilahy, Lajos
1 *Dukays* (1947)
2 *Angry angel* (1953)
3 *Century of scarlet* (1965)

Duke Benedict and Hank Brazos series
Clay, E Jefferson
1 *Fools' frontier* (1972)
2 *Sixgun says goodbye* (1972)
3 *Adios, Bandido* (1976)
Desperados on the loose
4 *Aces wild* (1980)
Badge for Brazos

Duke James series
Rizzi, Timothy
see **Major General Duke James series**

Duke Lawson series
Dexter, Ross
1 *Black Duke* (1977)
2 *Killing at Buffalo Crossing* (1978)
3 *Rainbow Kid* (1978)

Duke McCale series
Brown, Gerald
1 *Murder on Beacon Hill* (1941)
2 *Murder in plain sight* (1945)

Duke of Burgundy series
Morris, Ira J
1 *Kingdom for a song* (1963)
2 *Witch's son* (1964)

Duke of Marlborough series
Kenyon, Frank Wilson
see **John Churchill, Duke of Marlborough series**

Duke Renny series
Richmond, Philip
1 *Scarred hand* (1941)
2 *Reign of terror* (1942)
3 *Death in Hollywood* (1942)
4 *Chain murders* (1942)
5 *Jungle murders* (1943)
6 *Crime harvest* (1943)
7 *Riddle of the bleeding Venus* (1945)
Alternative title: Not a murderer!

Duke series
Cary, Lucian
1 *Duke steps out* (1929)
2 *Duke comes back* (1933)

Duke series
Meyerstein, Edward Henry William
see **Terence Duke series**

Duker series
Mole, William
see **Casson Duker series**

Dulcie Bligh series
Clark, Gail
1 *Dulcie Bligh* (1978)
2 *Baroness of Bow Street* (1979)

Dulcie trilogy
Everett-Green, Evelyn
1 *Dulcie's little brother* (1887)
Alternative title: Doings at Little Monksholm
2 *Dulcie and Tottie* (1889)
The story of an old-fashioned pair
3 *Dulcie's love story* (1891)

Duluoz series
Kerouac, Jack
see **Jack Duluoz series**

Duluth series
Quentin, Patrick
see **Peter Duluth series**

Dumarest series
Tubb, Edwin Charles
1 *Winds of Gath* (1967)
Gath
2 *Derai* (1968)
3 *Toyman* (1969)
4 *Kalin* (1969)
5 *Jester at Scar* (1970)
6 *Lallia* (1971)
7 *Technos* (1972)
8 *Veruchia* (1973)
9 *Mayenne* (1973)
10 *Jondelle* (1973)
Numbers 9 and 10 also published in one volume 1981
11 *Zenya* (1974)
12 *Eye of the Zodiac* (1975)
13 *Eloise* (1975)
14 *Jack of swords* (1976)
15 *Spectrum of a forgotten sun* (1976)
16 *Haven of darkness* (1977)
17 *Prison of night* (1977)
18 *Incident on Ath* (1978)
19 *Quillian Sector* (1978)
20 *Web of sand* (1979)
21 *Iduna's universe* (1979)
22 *Terra data* (1980)
23 *World of promise* (1980)
24 *Nectar of heaven* (1981)
25 *Terridae* (1981)
26 *Coming event* (1982)
27 *Earth is heaven* (1982)
28 *Melome* (1983)
29 *Angado* (1984)
Numbers 28 and 29 also published in one volume 1988
30 *Symbol of Terra* (1984)
31 *Temple of truth* (1985)
Numbers 30 and 31 also published in one volume 1989

Dumper series
Bartlett, Evelyn
1 *Dumper the kangaroo* (1955)
2 *Dumper and the circus* (1958)

Dumyat series
Fraser, Christine Marion
see **Light on Dumyat series**

Dunbar and Lunt series
Shirreffs, Gordon Donald
see **Bob Dunbar and Gary Lunt series**

Duncan and Mallory series
Asprin, Robert Lynn
1 *Duncan and Mallory* (1986)
2 *Bar-None Ranch* (1987)

Duncan Argylle and Chaddie McKail trilogy
Stringer, Arthur
see **Prairie trilogy**

Duncan Cainsforth series
Maske, John
1 *Dinard mystery* (1933)
2 *Saint-Malo mystery* (1933)

Duncan Calton and Detective Kilsip series
Hume, Fergus
see **Detective Kilsip and Duncan Calton series**

Duncan Grant series
Seton, Graham
see **Colonel Duncan Grant series**

Duncan Kincaid and Gemma James series
Crombie, Deborah
see **Superintendent Duncan Kincaid and Sergeant Gemma James series**

Duncan Maccallum series
Mackinnon, Allan
see **Inspector Duncan Maccallum series**

Duncan McClure series
Rudd, Steele
1 *Poor parson* (1907)
2 *Duncan McClure* (1909)

Duncan Maclain series
Kendrick, Baynard
see **Captain Duncan Maclain series**

Duncan Pattullo series
Stewart, John Innes Mackintosh
1 *Gaudy* (1974)
2 *Young Pattullo* (1975)
3 *Memorial service* (1976)
4 *Madonna of the Astrolabe* (1977)
5 *Full term* (1978)

Duncan Pride series
Frazer, Andrew
1 *Find Eileen Hardin, alive!* (1959)
2 *Fall of Marty Moon* (1960)

Duncan Prine series
Garrisen, Paul
see **Dirk Prine series**

Duncan series
Carter, Dorothy
see **Marise Duncan series**
Mulford, Clarence Edward
see **Wyatt Duncan series**
Ross, Cameron
see **Alistair Duncan series**
Walker, Holly Beth
see **Meg Duncan series**

Duncton chronicles series
Horwood, William
1 *Duncton Wood* (1979)
2 *Duncton quest* (1988)
3 *Duncton found* (1989)
4 *Duncton tales* (1991)

Dundas series
Rath, Virginia
see **Michael Dundas series**

Dundee series
Austin, Anne
see **James F Dundee series**

Dune series
Herbert, Frank
1 *Dune* (1965)
Illustrated Dune
2 *Dune messiah* (1969)
3 *Children of Dune* (1976)
Numbers 1-3 published as *The great Dune trilogy*, 1979
4 *God-emperor of Dune* (1981)
5 *Heretics of Dune* (1984)
6 *Chapter-House Dune* (1985)
Numbers 4-6 published as *The second great Dune trilogy*, 1987

Companion volumes: *Dune*, by Rosemary Border, 1980, *The Dune storybook*, by Joan Dennison Vinge, 1984, *The notebooks of Frank Herbert's Dune*, edited by Brian Herbert, 1988; parody: *National Lampoon's Doon*, by Ellis Werner, 1984

Dungeon series
Costikyan, Greg
1 *Another day, another dungeon* (1990)
2 *One quest, hold the dragons* (1994)

Dungeon series
This sequence has four authors
Lupoff, Richard Allen
1 *Black tower* (1988)
Coville, Bruce
2 *Dark abyss* (1989)
De Lint, Charles
3 *Valley of thunder* (1989)
Bailey, Robin Wayne
4 *Lake of fire* (1989)

De Lint, Charles
5 *Hidden city* (1990)
Lupoff, Richard Allen
6 *Final battle* (1990)

Dunk Island series
Banfield, Edmund James
see **Beachcomber series**

Dunkel series
Dugdale, Pamela
1 *Dunkel* (1959)
2 *Dunkel again* (1961)

Dunlap series
Palmer, Bernard
see **Jim Dunlap series**

Dunlop series
Corris, Peter
see **Luke Dunlop series**
Reeder, Colin
see **Adventures of Dunlop series**

Dunn series
Nelson, Hugh Lawrence
see **Jim Dunn series**
Williams, Jay
see **Danny Dunn series**

Dunn trilogy
Seymour, Beatrice Kean
see **Sally Dunn trilogy**

Dunne series
Morgan, G J
see **Buck Dunne series**

Dunny series
Hillier, Fred
see **Outhouse series**

Dunstan series
Sheppard, Alfred Tresidder
see **Ledgar Dunstan series**

Dupin series
Poe, Edgar Allan
see **Monsieur C Auguste Dupin series**

Dupree series
Bexar, Phil
see **Billy Dupree series**

Dupree series
Dimmock, Frederick Haydon
1 *Dupree in Alaska* (1939)
2 *Dupree's tenderfoot* (1949)

Dupuy series
Gilbert, Anthony
1 *Man in button boots* (1934)
2 *Courtier to death* (1936)
Dover train mystery

Durant and Wu series
Thomas, Ross
see **Artie Wu and Quincy Durant series**

Durdane trilogy
Vance, Jack
1 *Anome* (1971)
Faceless man
2 *Brave Free Men* (1972)
3 *Asutra* (1974)
One volume edition entitled *Durdane*, 1989

Durell series
Aarons, Edward Sidney
see **Sam Durell series**

Durkin series
Chase, Arthur Minturn
see **Lieutenant Dan Durkin series**
Stringer, Arthur
see **James Durkin series**

Durtal series
Huysmans, Joris Karl
1 *Down there* (1891)
Original edition entitled *La bas*
2 *En route* (1895)
3 *Cathedral* (1898)
Original edition entitled *La cathedrale*
4 *Oblate* (1903)
Original edition entitled *L'oblate*
5 *Crowds of Lourdes* (1906)
Original edition entitled *Les foules de Lourdes*

Durward series
Walpole, Hugh
see **Mister Durward series**

Dury and Judge series
Whitehead, David
see **Judge and Dury series**

Dus series
Watt-Evans, Lawrence
see **Lords of Dus series**

Dushau trilogy
Lichtenberg, Jacqueline
1 *Dushau* (1985)
2 *Farfetch* (1985)
3 *Outreach* (1986)

Dusky MacMorgan series
Striker, Randy
1 *Key West connection* (1981)
2 *Deep six* (1981)
3 *Cuban death-lift* (1981)
4 *Deadlier sex* (1981)
5 *Assassin's shadow* (1981)
6 *Everglades assault* (1982)
7 *Grand Cayman slam* (1982)

Dust on my shoes series
Pinney, Peter
Reminiscences of travels
1 *Dust on my shoes* (1952)
2 *Who wanders alone* (1954)
3 *Anywhere but here* (1956)
4 *Lawless and the lotus* (1963)
Selections: *Road to anywhere*, 1993

Dust series
Farrimond, John
see **Bob Howarth series**
Graaf, Peter
see **Joe Dust series**

Dust to dust series
Budd, Mavis
History of the author's family
1 *Dust to dust* (1966)
2 *Prospect of love* (1968)
3 *Fit for a duchess* (1970)

Dustin family series
Comfort, Mildred Houghton
1 *Winter on the Johnny Smoker* (1943)
2 *Treasure of the Johnny Smoker* (1947)

Dusty and Smudge series
Schmidt, Annie Maria Geertruida
Illustrated by Fiep Westendorp
1 *Dusty and Smudge spill the paint* (1973)
Original edition entitled *Opgesloten*
2 *Dusty and Smudge and the soap suds* (1973)
Original edition entitled *Schuim*
3 *Dusty and Smudge keep cool* (1973)
Original edition entitled *Allemaal kaal*
4 *Dusty and Smudge and the bride* (1973)
Original edition entitled *Floddertje en de bruid*
5 *Dusty and Smudge splash soup* (1973)
Original edition entitled *Moeder is ziek*
6 *Dusty and Smudge and the cake* (1973)
Original edition entitled *Tante is jarig*

Dusty Ayres and his Battle Birds series
Bowen, Robert Sidney
1 *Black lightning* (1966)
2 *Crimson doom* (1966)
3 *Purple tornado* (1966)
4 *Telsa raiders* (1966)
5 *Black Invaders versus the Battle Birds* (1966)

Dusty Jones and Wrangler Lewis series
Evans, Max
1 *Rounders* (1960)
2 *Great wedding* (1963)
One volume edition entitled *Rounders three*, 1990

Dusty Muller and Tiny Meldrum series
Glanville, Alec
see **Inspector Dusty Muller and Tiny Meldrum**

Dusty series
Sandberg, Inger
Illustrated by Lasse Sandberg
1 *Dusty wants to help* (1983)
Original edition entitled *Hjaelpa till, sa Pulvret*
2 *Dust wants to borrow everything* (1984)
Original edition entitled *Lana den, sa Pulvret*

Dutch in Spain series
Bevan, Tom
1 *Beggars of the sea* (1903)
A story of the Dutch struggle with Spain
2 *Grey Fox of Holland* (1908)

Dutch Mill Stable series
Grossman, Nancy Livright
1 *Judge is seeing double* (1988)
2 *If wishes were horses* (1988)
3 *Leg up for Lucinda* (1989)
4 *Only boy in the ring* (1989)

Dutch Republic series
Henty, George Alfred
1 *By pike and dyke* (1889)
A tale of the rise of the Dutch Republic
2 *By England's aid* (1890)
A story of the freeing of the Netherlands, 1584-1604

Dutch twins series
Perkins, Lucy Fitch
1 *Dutch twins* (1911)
2 *Kit and Kat* (1929)
3 *Dutch twins and little brother* (1939)
Completed by Eleanor Ellis Perkins

Dutch War of Independence series
Orczy, Emmuska
1 *Leatherface* (1916)
A tale of old Flanders
2 *Flower o' the lily* (1918)
3 *Laughing Cavalier* (1914)
4 *First Sir Percy* (1920)
An adventure of the Laughing Cavalier

Dutchy Holland series
Macdonnell, James Edmond
This sequence includes those works which have so far been identified as including the series character; however since there is much overlapping of characters in this author's numerous novels it is likely that this character will be found in other works
1 *Abandon and destroy* (1963)
2 *Collision course* (1964)
3 *Duel* (1965)
4 *Under sealed orders* (1965)
5 *Whispering death* (1965)
6 *White death* (1965)
7 *Foul ground* (1966)
8 *Hell ship* (1966)
9 *Point of departure* (1966)
10 *Behemoth* (1967)
11 *Unforgiving sea* (1967)
12 *Approved to scrap* (1968)
13 *Attack and be damned* (1968)
14 *Full fathom five* (1968)
15 *Full fathom five* (1968)
16 *Judas rat* (1968)
17 *Mission hopeless* (1968)
18 *Rat Island* (1968)
19 *Heading into hell* (1968)
20 *To the death* (1969)
21 *Operation Jackal* (1969)
22 *Strike force* (1969)
23 *Circle of fire* (1970)
24 *Last stand* (1970)
25 *Fog blind* (1970)
26 *Damn the torpedoes!* (1971)
27 *Torrent of fire* (1971)
28 *Northwest by north* (1971)
29 *First command* (1971)
30 *Standing into danger* (1971)
31 *False colours* (1972)
32 *Most immediate* (1972)
33 *Point blank* (1972)
34 *This ship is mine* (1972)
35 *Fire storm* (1973)
36 *Attack!* (1973)
37 *Council of captains* (1974)
38 *Kill* (1974)
39 *Court martial* (1975)
40 *Dark of the night* (1975)
41 *Liberty man* (1976)
42 *Shadow* (1977)
43 *Shadow* (1977)
44 *Stand off* (1977)
45 *Breaking point* (1979)
46 *Killers* (1982)

Dutiful daughter series
Beauvoir, Simone de
1 *Memoirs of a dutiful daughter* (1958)
Original edition entitled *Memoires d'un jeune fille rangee*
2 *Prime of life* (1960)
Original edition entitled *La force de l'age*
3 *Force of circumstance* (1963)
Original edition entitled *La force de choses*
4 *All said and done* (1972)
Original edition entitled *Tout compte fait*

Dutton series
Fennell, Willie
see **Dexter Dutton series**

Duty free series
Harvey, John Barton
Based on a television series
1 *Duty free* (1985)
2 *More duty free* (1986)

Duvivien series
Spain, Nancy
see **Johnny Duvivien series**

Dwarks series
Berenstain, Michael
1 *Dwarks* (1983)
2 *Dwarks meet Skunk Momma* (1984)
3 *Dwarks at the mall* (1985)

Dwyer series
Gorman, Edward
see **Jack Dwyer series**

Dying earth series
Vance, Jack
1 *Dying earth* (1950)
2 *Eyes of the Overworld* (1966)
3 *Morreion* (1979)
4 *Cugel's saga* (1983)
5 *Rhialto the marvellous* (1984)
Companion volumes: *A quest for Simbilis*, by Michael Shea, 1974, *Nifft the Lean*, by Michael Shea, 1982, and the **Adventures of Cugel the Clever series**

Dyke family trilogy
Hastings, Phyllis
see **Sussex trilogy**

Dyke series
Ferrars, Elizabeth
see **Toby Dyke series**
Rockwood, Harry
see **Donald Dyke series**

Dykes series
Bechdel, Alison
Comic strips
1 *Dykes to watch out for* (1986)
2 *More dykes to watch out for* (1988)
3 *New, improved, dykes to watch out for!* (1990)
4 *Dykes to watch out for, the sequel* (1992)

Dymek series
Riley, Frank
see **Father Anton Dymek series**

Dymoke series
Deeley, Roger
see **Martin Dymoke series**

Dynamite Drury series
Greene, L Patrick
1 *Dynamite Drury* (1929)
2 *Dynamite Drury again* (1930)
3 *Dynamite Drury patrols* (1946)

Dynamite series
Guenter, C H
see **Robert Urban series**

Dynamite series
Stine, Robert Lawrence
1 *Dynamite do-it-yourself pen pal kit* (1980)
2 *Dynamite's funny book of the sad facts of life* (1980)

Dynamite twins series
Newsham, Wendy
1 *At the seaside* (1987)
2 *Birthday party* (1987)

Dynasty series
Harrod-Eagles, Cynthia
see **Morland family series**

Dynes series
Robertson, Helen
see **Inspector Lathom Dynes series**

Dysart series
Wren, Percival Christopher
see **Sinbad Dysart series**

Dysart trilogy
Deegan, Jon J
1 *Corridors of time* (1953)
2 *Beyond the fourth door* (1954)
3 *Exiles in time* (1954)

E

E.T. series
Kotzwinkle, William
Based on screenplays
1 *E.T., the extraterrestrial, in his adventure on earth* (1982)
Companion volume: *E.T., the extraterrestrial storybook*, 1982
2 *Book of the green planet* (1985)
Companion volumes: *The storybook of the green planet*, 1985, *E.T., the extraterrestrial*, by M Howard Gelfland, 1983

Eady series
Thorne, Ernest Pollett
see **Quentin Eady series**

Eagle Child trilogy
Faulknor, Cliff
1 *White calf* (1965)
The story of Eagle Child, the Pilgan boy, who found a white buffalo calf said to have been sent by the above ones
2 *White peril* (1966)
3 *Smoke horse* (1968)

Eagle Force series
Schmidt, Dan
1 *Eagle Force* (1989)
2 *Death Camp Company* (1989)
3 *Flight six six six* (1989)
4 *Red fire storm* (1990)
5 *Ring of fire* (1990)
6 *Berserker* (1990)
7 *Edge of the blade* (1990)
8 *Hell's march* (1991)
9 *Armageddon, USA* (1991)

Eagle Hill series
Warner, Susan Bagert
1 *Little camp on Eagle Hill* (1873)
2 *Willow Brook* (1874)

Eagle series
Dorer, Nancy
1 *By daybreak the Eagle* (1979)
2 *Return of the Eagle* (1979)
3 *Wings of the Eagle* (1979)

Eagle series
Edwards, Paul
see **John Eagle series**

Eagle series
Macdonnell, James Edmond
1 *Brood of the Eagle* (1960)
2 *Eagles over Taranto* (1961)

Eagle Special Investigator series
Hastings, Macdonald
1 *Eagle Special Investigator* (1953)
2 *Adventure calling* (1955)
3 *Search for the little yellow men* (1956)

Eagleheart trilogy
Westcott, C T
1 *Silver wings and leather jackets* (1989)
2 *Broadsides and brass* (1989)
3 *Blood and bone* (1989)

Ealdwood series
Cherryh, Carolyn Janice
This sequence is expanded from *Ealdwood*, 1981
1 *Dreamstone* (1983)
2 *Tree of swords and jewels* (1983)
One volume editions entitled *Arafel's saga*, 1983 and *Ealdwood*, 1991

Earl Drake series
Marlowe, Dan James
1 *Name of the game is death* (1962)
Operation Overkill
2 *One endless hour* (1969)
Operation Endless Hour
3 *Operation Fireball* (1969)
4 *Flashpoint* (1970)
Operation Flashpoint
5 *Operation Breakthrough* (1971)
6 *Operation Checkmate* (1972)
7 *Operation Drumfire* (1972)
8 *Operation Stranglehold* (1973)
9 *Operation Whiplash* (1973)
10 *Operation Hammerlock* (1974)
11 *Operation Deathmaker* (1975)
12 *Operation Counterpunch* (1976)

Earl Dumarest series
Tubb, Edwin Charles
see **Dumarest series**

Earl Jazine and Carl Crader series
Hoch, Edward Dentinger
see **Carl Crader and Earl Jazine series**

Earl Morton series
Bosworth, Frank
1 *Mustang mesa* (1971)
2 *Rainey Valley* (1971)
3 *Singing Wind Trail* (1971)
4 *Long-riders* (1971)
5 *Sunday's guns* (1972)
6 *South slope* (1972)
7 *Rustler's Range* (1972)
8 *Bear-Claw Range* (1973)

Earl of Caraway series
Herbert, Alan Patrick
see **Admiral of the Fleet, Earl of Caraway series**

Earl of Ickenham series
Wodehouse, Pelham Grenville
see **Uncle Fred, Earl of Ickenham series**

Earl of Leicester series
Drysdale, Margaret
see **Robert Dudley series**

Earl of Millington series
Hackforth-Jones, Gilbert
see **Submarine Service series**

Earl of Montrose series
Tranter, Nigel Godwin
see **James Graham, Earl of Montrose series**

Earl of Moriston series
Laine, Annabel
1 *Reluctant heiress* (1978)
2 *Melancholy virgin* (1981)

Early bird astronomy series
Bendick, Jeanne
1 *Moons and rings* (1991)
Helpers in space
2 *Comets and meteors* (1991)
Visitors from space
3 *Artificial satellites* (1991)
Helpers in space
4 *Stars* (1991)
Lights in the night sky
5 *Universe* (1991)
Think big
6 *Sun* (1991)
Our very own star
7 *Planets* (1991)
Neighbors in space

Early Britain series
Treece, Henry
1 *Golden strangers* (1956)
Invaders
Set during the Celtic overthrow of the neolithic culture of Britain
2 *Dark island* (1952)
Savage warriors
Set during the Roman invasion of Britain
3 *Red queen, white queen* (1958)
Pagan queen
Set during Boadicea's rebellion against the Roman invaders
4 *Great captains* (1956)
Based on the Arthurian legends

Early Christian series
Goldthorpe, John
1 *Same scourge* (1954)
2 *No crown of glory* (1956)
3 *Hidden splendour* (1962)

Early Christian series
Kingsley, Florence Morse
1 *Titus* (1895)
A comrade of the Cross
2 *Stephen* (1896)
A soldier of the Cross
3 *Paul* (1897)
A herald of the Cross

Early Christian series
Mann, Deborah
1 *Woman called Mary* (1960)
Based on the life of Mary Magdalene
2 *Now Barabbas was a robber* (1969)
3 *Pilate's wife* (1976)
4 *Song of Salome* (1969)

Early Christian series
Ray, Mary
1 *Tent for the sun* (1971)
2 *Ides of April* (1974)
3 *Sword sleep* (1975)
4 *Beyond the desert gate* (1977)
5 *Rain from the west* (1980)

Early Christianity series
Nunez Alonso, Alejandro
No English translation of numbers 2-5
1 *Purple sash* (1956)
Original edition entitled *El lazo de purpura*; based on the life of the Emperor Tiberius
2 *[Hombre de Damasco]* (1958)
3 *[Denario de plata]* (1959)
4 *[Piedra y el Cesar]* (1960)
5 *[Columnas de fuego]* (1962)

Early Church series
Farrar, Frederic William
1 *Darkness and dawn* (1891)
Alternative title: Scenes in the days of Nero
2 *Gathering clouds* (1895)
A tale of the days of Saint Chrysostom

Early day series
Boswell, Annabella
1 *Some recollections of my early days written at different periods* (1908)
2 *Further recollections of my early days in Australia* (1911)

Early experiences series
Hawker, James Collins
1 *Early experiences in South Australia* (1899)
Covers 1838-1841
2 *Early experiences in South Australia, second series* (1901)
Covers 1842-1843

Early nature picture book series
Aaseng, Nathan
Illustrated by Alcuin C Dornisch
1 *Animal specialists* (1987)
2 *Horned animals* (1987)
3 *Man-eating animals* (1987)
4 *Prey animals* (1987)

Early series
Burch, Robert Joseph
see **Ida Early series**
Early, Richard Elliott
see **Thomas Early series**

Early settler life series
Kalman, Bobbie
1 *Early Christmas* (1981)
2 *Early stores and markets* (1981)
3 *Early travel* (1981)

4 *Early village life* (1981)
5 *Early schools* (1982)
6 *Early fmily home* (1982)
7 *Early settler children* (1982)
8 *Early settler storybook* (1982)
9 *Food for the settler* (1983)
10 *Early city life* (1983)
11 *Early artisans* (1983)
12 *Early health and medicine* (1983)
13 *Early pleasures and pastimes* (1983)

Earth inspectors series
This sequence has six authors
Packard, Edward
1 *America, why is there an eye on the pyramid on the one-dollar bill?* (1988)
Compton, Sara
2 *Amazon, where do fish swim through the treetops?* (1988)
Packard, Edward
3 *Olympus, what is the secret of the oracle?* (1988)
Foley, Louise Munro
4 *Australia, find the flying foxes!* (1988)
Compton, Sara
5 *Venice, who are the three?* (1989)
Packard, Edward
6 *Africa, where do elephants live underground?* (1989)
Brightfield, Richard
7 *China, why was an army made of clay?* (1989)
8 *U.S.A., what is the great American invention?* (1989)
Compton, Sara
9 *Europe, why was a city built to capture a castle?* (1989)
Meyer, Carolyn
10 *Japan, how do hands make peace?* (1989)
Stuart, Charles
11 *England, what is the secret of the stones?* (1990)
Packard, Edward
12 *Russia, what is the Golden Horde?* (1989)

Earth is ours trilogy
Moberg, Vilhelm
1 *Memory of youth* (1935)
Original edition entitled *Saenkt sedebetyg*
2 *Sleepless nights* (1937)
Original edition entitled *Soemloes*
3 *Earth is ours* (1939)
Original edition entitled *Giv oss jorden*
One volume edition entitled *Earth is ours*, 1940

Earth song trilogy
Webb, Sharon
1 *Earthchild* (1982)
2 *Earth song* (1983)
3 *Ram song* (1984)

Earth trilogy
Giono, Jean
see **Trilogy of earth**

Earthblood series
Axler, James
1 *Earthblood* (1993)
2 *Deep trek* (1994)

Earthclan series
Brin, David
1 *Sundiver* (1980)
2 *Startide rising* (1983)
Revised edition 1985
3 *Uplift war* (1987)
Numbers 2 and 3 also published in one volume entitled *Earthclan*, 1987

Earthdawn series
Kubasik, Christopher
1 *Longing ring* (1993)
2 *Mother speaks* (1994)
3 *Poisoned memories* (1994)

Earthminds trilogy
Sargent, Pamela
1 *Watchstar* (1980)
2 *Eye of the comet* (1984)
3 *Homesmind* (1984)

Earth's children series
Auel, Jean Marie
1 *Clan of the cave bear* (1980)
2 *Valley of horses* (1982)
3 *Mammoth hunters* (1985)
Numbers 1-3 also published in one volume entitled *Earth's children*, 1987
4 *Plains of passage* (1990)

Earth's End trilogy
Saberhagen, Fred
see **Chup trilogy**

Earthsea series
Le Guin, Ursula Kroeber
1 *Wizard of Earthsea* (1968)
2 *Tombs of Atuan* (1972)
3 *Farthest shore* (1973)
Numbers 1-3 also published in one volume editions entitled *The Earthsea*, 1977, and *The Earthsea trilogy*, 1979
4 *Tehanu* (1990)
The last book of Earthsea

Earthsearch series
Follett, James
1 *Earthsearch* (1981)
2 *Death ship* (1982)
3 *Torus* (1990)

Earthwise trilogy
Lowery, Linda
1 *Earthwise at play* (1992)
2 *Earthwise at home* (1992)
3 *Earthwise at school* (1992)
Companion volume: *Earthwise teachers' guide*, by Linda Lowery and Betty Botts, 1993

Easingden series
Sinclair, John George
1 *Easingden* (1926)
2 *Love in Easingden* (1928)

East and O'Hannay series
Rushton, Charles
see **James O'Hannay and Floyd East series**

East Anglia seasons series
Home, Michael
Reminiscences
1 *Autumn fields* (1944)
2 *Spring sowing* (1946)
3 *Winter harvest* (1967)
A Norfolk boyhood

East Anglian childhood series
Haymon, Sylvia T
1 *Opposite the cross keys* (1988)
2 *Quivering tree* (1990)

East country crimes series
Thurlow, David
1 *Essex triangle* (1990)
2 *Norfolk nightmare* (1991)
3 *Evil in East Anglia* (1993)

East End series
Barnes, Ron
1 *Licence to live* (1974)
Scenes from a post-war working life in Hackney
2 *Coronation cups and jam jars* (1976)
A portrait of an East End family through three generations

East End series
Braithwaite, Edward Ricardo
see **Sir series**

East End series
Flint, Elizabeth
1 *Hot bread and chips* (1963)
2 *Kipper stew* (1964)

East Kimberley series
Shaw, Bruce
1 *My country of the pelican dreaming* (1981)
Co-author: Grant Ngabidj; life of an Australian Aboriginal of Gudjerong
2 *Banggaiyerri* (1983)
Co-author: Jack Sullivan
3 *Countrymen* (1986)
Life histories of four Aboriginal men
4 *Bush time, station time* (1991)
Co-author: Waddi Boyoi; reminiscences of eighty years
5 *When the dust come in between* (1992)
Aboriginal viewpoints in the East Kimberley prior to 1982

East series
Lawrence, Hilda
see **Mark East series**

Eastenders series
Miller, Hugh
Based on a television series
1 *Home fires burning* (1985)
2 *Swings and roundabouts* (1986)
3 *Good intentions* (1986)
4 *Flower of Albert Square* (1986)
5 *Blind spots* (1986)
6 *Hopes and horizons* (1986)
7 *Baffled heart* (1987)
8 *Growing wild* (1987)
9 *Place in life* (1987)
10 *Single man* (1987)
11 *Taking chances* (1988)
12 *Elbow room* (1988)

Easter series
Barkan, Joanne
1 *Easter egg fun* (1991)
2 *Easter surprise* (1991)

Easter series
Blackburn, John
see **Bill Easter series**

Easter series
Drummond, Violet Hilda
see **Mrs Easter series**

Eastern Indians series
Gregor, Elmer Russell
1 *Running Fox* (1918)
2 *White Wolf* (1921)
3 *Spotted Deer* (1922)
4 *War Eagle* (1926)
5 *Mystery trail* (1927)
7 *Spotted pony* (1930)

Eastern nobody series
Moore, Donald
Travels in the Far East
1 *Far Eastern agent* (1952)
2 *We live in Singapore* (1955)

Eastern prince series
Chula Chakrabongse
1 *Twain have met* (1956)
Alternative title: An Eastern prince came west
2 *First class ticket* (1958)
The travels of a prince

Easthampton trilogy
Laker, Rosalind
1 *Warwyck's woman* (1978)
Warwyck's wife
2 *Claudine's daughter* (1979)
3 *Warwycks of Easthampton* (1980)
Warwyck's choice

Eastmans series
Pullein-Thompson, Christine
1 *Eastmans in Brittany* (1964)
2 *Eastmans move house* (1965)
3 *Eastmans find a boy* (1966)

Easy Company series
Howard, John Wesley
1 *Easy Company and the Suicide Boys* (1981)
2 *Easy Company and the medicine gun* (1981)
3 *Easy Company and the green arrows* (1981)
4 *Easy Company and the white man's path* (1981)
5 *Easy Company and the longhorns* (1981)
6 *Easy Company and the big medicine* (1981)
7 *Easy Company and the Black Hills* (1981)
8 *Easy Company and the Bitter Trail* (1981)
9 *Easy Company in Colter's Hell* (1981)
10 *Easy Company and the headline hunter* (1981)
11 *Easy Company and the engineers* (1981)
12 *Easy Company and the bloody flag* (1982)
13 *Easy Company and the Oklahoma Trail* (1982)
14 *Easy Company and the Cherokee beauty* (1982)
15 *Easy Company and the big blizzard* (1982)
16 *Easy Company and the long marchers* (1982)
17 *Easy Company and the bootleggers* (1982)
18 *Easy Company and the card sharps* (1982)
19 *Easy Company and the Indian doctor* (1982)
20 *Easy Company and the twilight sniper* (1982)
21 *Easy Company and the sheep ranchers* (1982)
22 *Easy Company at Hat Creek Station* (1982)
23 *Easy Company and the mystery trooper* (1982)
24 *Easy Company and the Cow Country Queen* (1983)
25 *Easy Company and the Bible salesman* (1983)
26 *Easy Company and the blood feud* (1983)
27 *Easy Company and the dog soldiers* (1983)
28 *Easy Company and the big name hunter* (1983)
29 *Easy Company and the gypsy riders* (1983)
30 *Easy Company and the bullwhackers* (1983)
31 *Easy Company and the Whiskey Trail* (1983)

Easy Rawlins series
Mosley, Walter
see **Ezekiel Rawlins series**

Easy series
Berry, Liz
1 *Easy connections* (1983)
2 *Easy freedom* (1985)

Easy series
Goulart, Ron
see **John Easy series**

Ebbie Entwhistle series
Webster, Frederick Annesley Michael
1 *Old Ebbie, detective up-to-date* (1923)

Ebbie Entwhistle series
2 *Old Ebbie returns* (1925)
3 *Crime scientist* (1930)

Ebbie series
Gudmundson, Shirley M
1 *Turtle net* (1965)
2 *Hurricane* (1966)

Eben Holden series
Bacheller, Irving
1 *Eben Holden* (1901)
A tale of the North Country
2 *Eben Holden's last day a-fishing* (1907)

Ebenezer Buckle series
Brady, Nicholas
1 *House of strange guests* (1932)
2 *Fair murder* (1933)
Carnival murder
3 *Ebenezer investigates* (1934)

Ebenezer Gryce series
Green, Anna Katharine
1 *Leavenworth case* (1878)
2 *Strange disappearance* (1880)
3 *Hand and ring* (1883)
4 *Behind closed doors* (1888)
5 *Matter of millions* (1890)
6 *Doctor, his wife and the clock* (1895)
7 *That affair next door* (1897)
8 *Lost man's lane* (1898)
9 *Circular study* (1900)
10 *One of my sons* (1901)
11 *Initials only* (1911)
12 *Mystery of the hasty arrow* (1917)
Also a short story featuring Ebenezer Gryce in *A difficult problem, and other stories*, 1900

Ebenezum series
Gardner, Craig Shaw
1 *Malady of magicks* (1986)
2 *Multitude of monsters* (1986)
3 *Night in the Netherhells* (1987)
Numbers 1-3 also published in one volume edition entitled *The exploits of Ebenezum*, 1987
4 *Difficulty with dwarves* (1987)

Ebony masters series
Lascaux, Simon
1 *Chains of rage* (1985)
2 *Bonds of shame* (1986)

Eclipse trilogy
Shirley, John
see **Song called youth trilogy**

Eco-Kids series
Makris, Kathryn
1 *Five Cat Club* (1994)
2 *Clean-up crew* (1994)
3 *Green team* (1994)

Ecolitan trilogy
Modesitt, Leland Exton
1 *Ecologic envoy* (1986)
2 *Ecolitan operation* (1989)
3 *Ecologic secession* (1990)

Ecotopia series
Callenbach, Ernest
1 *Ecotopia emerging* (1981)
2 *Ecotopia* (1975)
The notebooks and reports of William Weston
Companion volume: *The Ecotopian sketchbook, a book for drawing, coloring, writing, collaging, designing, thinking about and creating a new world*, by Judith S Clancy, 1981

Ecstasy series
Taylor, Janelle
see **Sioux series**

Ed and Am Hunter series
Brown, Fredric
1 *Fabulous clipjoint* (1947)
2 *Dead ringer* (1948)
3 *Bloody moonlight* (1949)
Murder in the moonlight
4 *Compliments of a fiend* (1950)
5 *Death has many doors* (1951)
6 *Late lamented* (1959)
7 *Mrs Murphy's underpants* (1963)

Ed and Warren Baer series
Resnicow, Herbert
1 *Dead room* (1987)
2 *Hot place* (1990)

Ed Emberley's big drawing book series
Emberley, Ed
1 *Ed Emberley's big green drawing book* (1979)
2 *Ed Emberley's big orange drawing book* (1980)
3 *Ed Emberley's big purple drawing book* (1981)
4 *Ed Emberley's big red drawing book* (1987)

Ed Emberley's drawing book series
Emberley, Ed
1 *Ed Emberley's drawing book of animals* (1970)
2 *Make a world* (1972)
3 *Ed Emberley's drawing book of faces* (1975)

Ed Emberley's little drawing books series
Emberley, Ed
1 *Ed Emberley's little drawing book of birds* (1973)
2 *Ed Emberley's little drawing book of farms* (1973)
3 *Ed Emberley's little drawing book of trains* (1973)
4 *Ed Emberley's little drawing book of weirdos* (1973)
5 *Ed Emberley's little drawing book of horses* (1990)
6 *Ed Emberley's little drawing book of fish* (1990)
7 *Ed Emberley's little drawing book of trucks* (1990)
8 *Ed Emberley's little drawing book of more weirdos* (1990)

Ed Fitzgerald series
Flynn, Don
1 *Murder isn't enough* (1983)
2 *Murder on the Hudson* (1985)

Ed Gunning series
Elliott, William James
1 *Freak racket* (1941)
2 *Snatched dame* (1942)
3 *Triggers are trumps* (1942)
4 *Gunning in England* (1946)

Ed Nelson series
Norman, Frank
1 *Dead butler caper* (1978)
2 *Too many crooks spoil the caper* (1979)
3 *Baskerville caper* (1981)

Ed Noon series
Avallone, Michael
1 *Tall Dolores* (1953)
2 *Spitting image* (1953)
3 *Dead game* (1954)
4 *Violence in velvet* (1956)
5 *Case of the Bouncing Betty* (1956)
6 *Case of the violent virgin* (1957)
7 *Crazy mixed-up corpse* (1957)
8 *Voodoo murders* (1957)
9 *Meanwhile back at the morgue* (1960)
10 *Alarming clock* (1961)
11 *Living bomb* (1963)
12 *There is something about a dame* (1963)
13 *Bedroom bolero* (1963)
Bolero murders
14 *Lust is no lady* (1964)
Brutal kook
15 *Fat death* (1966)
16 *February doll murders* (1966)
17 *Assassins don't die in bed* (1968)
18 *Horrible man* (1968)
19 *Flower-covered corpse* (1969)
20 *Doomsday bag* (1969)
Killer's highway
21 *Death dives deep* (1971)
22 *Little Miss Murder* (1971)
Ultimate client
23 *Shooting it again, Sam* (1972)
Moving graveyard
24 *London, bloody London* (1972)
Ed Noon in London
25 *Girl in the cockpit* (1972)
26 *Kill her, you'll like it!* (1973)
27 *Hot body* (1973)
28 *Killer on the keys* (1973)
29 *X-rated corpse* (1973)
30 *Big stiffs* (1977)
31 *Dark on Monday* (1978)

Ed Rivers series
Powell, Talmage
1 *Killer is mine* (1959)
2 *Girl's number doesn't answer* (1960)
3 *With a madman behind me* (1962)
4 *Start screaming* (1962)
5 *Corpus delectable* (1965)

Ed series
Tully, Tom
see **Little Ed series**

Eddie and Chalice series
Mackenzie, Donald
see **Harry Chalice and Crying Eddie series**

Eddie and Marty series
Slobodkin, Louis
see **Space ship series**

Eddie Felson series
Tevis, Walter Stone
see **Hustler series**

Eddie Limonov series
Limonov, Edward
Translated from the Russian
1 *Memoir of a Russian punk* (1986)
2 *It's me, Eddie* (1983)
3 *His butler's story* (1987)

Eddie Mancuso and Vasily Borgneff series
This sequence has three authors
Luckless, John
1 *Death freak* (1978)
Burkholz, Herbert
2 *Sleeping spy* (1983)

Eddie series
Haywood, Carolyn
see **Eddie Wilson series**

Eddie Shoestring series
Ableman, Paul
Based on a television series
1 *Shoestring* (1979)
2 *Shoestring's finest hour* (1980)

Eddie Spaghetti series
Frascino, Edward
1 *Eddie Spaghetti* (1978)
2 *Eddie Spaghetti on the home front* (1983)

Eddie Wilson series
Haywood, Carolyn
1 *Little Eddie* (1947)
2 *Eddie and the fire engine* (1949)
3 *Eddie and Gardenia* (1951)
4 *Eddie's pay dirt* (1953)
5 *Eddie and his big deals* (1955)
6 *Eddie makes music* (1957)
7 *Eddie and Louella* (1959)
8 *Annie Pat and Eddie* (1960)
9 *Eddie's green thumb* (1964)
10 *Eddie the dog holder* (1966)
11 *Ever-Ready Eddie* (1968)
12 *Eddie's happenings* (1971)
13 *Eddie's valuable property* (1975)
14 *Eddie's menagerie* (1978)
15 *Merry Christmas from Eddie* (1986)

Eddie Wright and Tony Lantz series
Mullen, Clarence
see **Tony Lantz and Eddie Wright series**

Eddison and Cannon series
Delving, Michael
see **Dave Cannon and Robert Eddison series**

Eddy series
Duffin, Andrew
1 *Hi, I'm Eddy and this is how I pray* (1993)
2 *Hi, I'm Eddy and I believe in Jesus* (1993)
3 *Hi, I'm Eddy and here's why I read the Bible* (1993)

Eden family series
Harris, Marilyn
1 *This other Eden* (1977)
2 *Prince of Eden* (1978)
3 *Eden passion* (1979)
4 *Women of Eden* (1980)
5 *Eden rising* (1982)
6 *American Eden* (1987)
7 *Eden and Honor* (1989)

Eden Grove series
Bennett, Dwight
1 *West of railhead* (1977)
2 *Texans* (1979)

Eden series
Miles, Rosalind
1 *Return to Eden* (1984)
2 *Bitter legacy* (1986)

Eden series
Pohl, Frederik
see **Jim Eden series**

Eden trilogy
Harrison, Harry
1 *West of Eden* (1984)
2 *Winter in Eden* (1986)
3 *Return to Eden* (1988)

Eden trilogy
Masters, John
see **Loss of Eden trilogy**

Eden trilogy
Morgan, Jill Meredith
1 *Desert Eden* (1991)
2 *Beyond Eden* (1992)
3 *Future Eden* (1992)

Edevart and August series
Hamsun, Knut
1 *Vagabonds* (1927)
Original edition entitled *Landstrykere*
2 *August* (1930)
Original edition entitled *August*
3 *Road leads on* (1933)
Original edition entitled *Men livet lever*

Edgar Allan Poe series
Steward, Barbara
1 *Evermore* (1970)
2 *Lincoln diddle* (1979)

Edgar Ewart series
Walter, Alexia E
see **Sir Edgar Ewart series**

Edge Hannegan series
Lovell, B E
1 *And incidentally, murder!* (1952)
2 *Rage to kill* (1957)

Edge meets Steele series
Gilman, George G
1 *Two of a kind* (1980)
2 *Matching pair* (1982)
3 *Double action* (1984)

Edge series
Gilman, George G
1 *Loner* (1971)
2 *Ten thousand dollars, American* (1972)
Ten grand
3 *Apache death* (1972)
4 *Killer's breed* (1972)
5 *Blood on silver* (1972)
6 *Blue, the grey and the red* (1973)
Red River
7 *California killing* (1973)
California kill
8 *Seven out of hell* (1973)
Hell's seven
9 *Bloody summer* (1973)
10 *Vengeance is black* (1973)
Black vengeance
11 *Sioux uprising* (1974)
12 *Biggest bounty* (1974)
Death's bounty
13 *Town called Hate* (1974)
Hated
14 *Big gold* (1974)
Tiger's gold
15 *Blood run* (1975)
Paradise loses
16 *Final shot* (1975)
17 *Vengeance Valley* (1975)
18 *Ten tombstones to Texas* (1975)
Ten tombstones
19 *Ashes and dust* (1976)
20 *Sullivan's law* (1976)
21 *Rhapsody in red* (1976)
22 *Slaugher Road* (1977)
23 *Echoes of war* (1977)
24 *Day democracy died* (1977)
Slaughterday
25 *Violence Trail* (1978)
26 *Savage dawn* (1978)
27 *Death drive* (1978)
28 *Eve of evil* (1978)
29 *Living, the dying and the dead* (1978)
30 *Waiting for a train* (1979)
Towering nightmare
31 *Guilty ones* (1979)
32 *Frightened gun* (1979)
33 *Hated* (1979)
Red fury
34 *Ride in the sun* (1980)
35 *Death deal* (1980)
36 *Town on trial* (1981)
37 *Vengeance at Ventura* (1981)
38 *Massacre mission* (1981)
39 *Prisoners* (1981)
40 *Montana melodrama* (1982)
41 *Killing claim* (1982)
42 *Bloody sunrise* (1982)
43 *Arapaho revenge* (1983)
44 *Blind side* (1983)
45 *House on the range* (1983)
46 *Godforsaken* (1984)
47 *Moving cage* (1984)
48 *School for slaughter* (1985)
49 *Revenge ride* (1985)
50 *Shadow of the gallows* (1985)
51 *Time for killing* (1986)
52 *Brutal border* (1986)
53 *Hitting paydirt* (1986)
54 *Backshot* (1987)
55 *Uneasy riders* (1987)
56 *Doom town* (1987)
57 *Dying is forever* (1987)
58 *Desperadoes* (1988)
59 *Terror town* (1988)
60 *Breed woman* (1989)
61 *Rifle* (1989)

Edgecombe series
Brady, Terence
see **Victoria Edgecombe series**

Edgwell series
Sidgwick, Ethel
see **Tony Edgwell series**

Edie Cares series
Spykman, Elizabeth Choate
see **Cares family series**

Edinburgh detective series
M'Govan, James
Reminiscences
1 *Secret confessions* (1883)
Alternative title: The experiences of an Edinburgh detective
2 *Edinburgh detective* (1883)
Alternative title: His last confession

Edinburgh life series
Kemp, Robert
see **Stories of Edinburgh life series**

Edison-Armstrong School series
Hurwitz, Johanna
1 *Class clown* (1987)
2 *Class president* (1990)
3 *School spirit* (1994)

Edith Jackson series
Guy, Rosa
1 *Friends* (1973)
2 *Edith Jackson* (1978)
3 *Ruby* (1976)

Edith Ottley trilogy
Leverson, Ada
1 *Love's shadow* (1908)
2 *Tenterhooks* (1912)
3 *Love at second sight* (1916)

Edith Trevor series
Lewis, Harriet
1 *Edith Trevor's secret* (1872)
2 *Cecil Rosse* (1872)

Edmund Bendilow series
Wallace, Carlton
see **Superintendent Edmund Bendilow series**

Edmund Blackstone series
Falkirk, Richard
1 *Blackstone* (1972)
2 *Blackstone's fancy* (1973)
3 *Beau Blackstone* (1973)
4 *Blackstone and the scourge of Europe* (1974)
5 *Blackstone underground* (1976)
6 *Blackstone on Broadway* (1977)

Edmund Brown series
Porter, Joyce
1 *Sour cream with everything* (1966)
2 *Chinks in the curtain* (1967)
3 *Neither a candle nor a pitchfork* (1969)
4 *Only with a bargepole* (1971)

Edmund Roersch series
Kastle, Herbert David
see **Sergeant Edmund Roersch series**

Edmund Talbot trilogy
Golding, William
see **Sea trilogy**

Edmund Trothe series
Llewellyn, Richard
1 *End of the rug* (1968)
2 *But we didn't get the fox* (1970)
3 *White horse to Banbury Cross* (1970)
4 *Night is a child* (1972)

Educated Evans series
Wallace, Edgar
Short stories
1 *Educated Evans* (1924)
2 *More educated Evans* (1926)
3 *Good Evans!* (1927)
Educated man

Edward and Elizabeth series
Brandenberg, Franz
1 *Secret for grandmother's birthday* (1975)
2 *No school today!* (1976)
3 *Robber, a robber!* (1976)
4 *I don't feel well* (1977)
5 *Picnic, hurrah!* (1978)

Edward and friends series
Cole, Michael
1 *Lionel's party* (1987)
Also includes *Edward and the camera*
2 *Edward gets the hiccups* (1987)
Also includes *Wilfred's treasure*
3 *Edward joins the band* (1988)
Also includes *Clive's kite*
4 *Lionel's car* (1988)
Also includes *Edward to the rescue*

Edward Beale series
Penny, Rupert
see **Chief Inspector Edward Beale series**

Edward Bringle series
Owen, John
1 *Running footman* (1931)
Alternative title: The sentimental servant
2 *Edward Bringle* (1935)

Edward Burton series
Dank, Milton
1 *Khaki wings* (1980)
2 *Red flight two* (1981)

Edward, Eleanor and Georgie Hall series
Langton, Jane
1 *Diamond in the window* (1962)
2 *Swing in the summerhouse* (1967)
3 *Astonishing stereoscope* (1971)
4 *Fledgling* (1980)
5 *Fragile flag* (1984)

Edward Fitzgerald series
Bodkin, Matthias McDonnell
see **Lord Edward Fitzgerald series**

Edward, Frank and Gerry series
Pearce, Agatha Hunt
1 *Porpoise Bay* (1951)
2 *Hyak Inlet* (1960)
3 *Rattlesnake Range* (1961)

Edward I series
Bennetts, Pamela
1 *Dragon for Edward* (1975)
2 *She-wolf* (1975)

Edward II series
Holt, Emily Sarah
1 *In all times of our tribulation* (1887)
The story of Piers Gavestone
2 *In convent walls* (1888)
The story of the Dispensers

Edward III series
Honeyman, Brenda
1 *Edward the warrior* (1975)
2 *All the king's sons* (1976)

Edward III series
Wiat, Philippa
1 *Queen-gold* (1985)
2 *Grey goose wing* (1986)
3 *Whyte Swan* (1986)

Edward Leithen series
Buchan, John
see **Sir Edward Leithen series**

Edward Lester series
Levison, Eric
see **Doctor Edward Lester series**

Edward Mansell series
Masefield, John
see **Autobiography of a corpse series**

Edward North series
Robertson, Colin
1 *Dusky limelight* (1950)
2 *North for danger* (1952)
3 *Lady, take care* (1952)
4 *No trial, no error* (1953)

Edward Razoni and William Jackson series
Murphy, Warren Burton
1 *One night stand* (1973)
2 *Dead end street* (1973)
3 *City in heat* (1973)
4 *Down and dirty* (1974)
5 *Lynch town* (1974)
6 *On the dead run* (1975)

Edward series
Dumas, Philippe
1 *Story of Edward* (1976)
Original edition entitled *Histoire d'Edouard*
2 *Lucy, Edward's daughter* (1977)
Original edition entitled *Lucie, la fille d'Edouard*

Edward series
Gordon, Giles
1 *About a marriage* (1972)
2 *One hundred scenes from married life* (1976)

Edward series
Morgan, Michaela
Illustrated by Sue Porter
1 *Edward gets a pet* (1987)
2 *Visitors for Edward* (1987)
3 *Edward hurts his knee* (1988)
4 *Edward loses his teddy bear* (1988)

Edward Tope series
Davis, Howard Charles
1 *Trouble in the bank* (1960)
2 *Tortured boy* (1961)

Edward Trapp series
Callison, Brian
see **Captain Edward Trapp series**

Edward Trelawny series
Long, Amelia Reynolds
1 *Shakespeare murders* (1939)
2 *Murder times three* (1940)
3 *Invitation to death* (1940)
Carter kidnapping case
4 *Triple cross murders* (1943)
5 *Symphony in murder* (1944)
6 *Death looks down* (1945)

Edward VII series
Butler, David
1 *Edward VII* (1974)
Prince of Hearts
2 *Peacemaker* (1975)

Edward VII series
Lovesey, Peter
see **Bertie series**

Edward VII series
Whittle, Tyler
1 *Bertie* (1974)
2 *Edward* (1975)

Edward X Delaney series
Sanders, Lawrence
Based on a minor character in *The Anderson tapes*, 1970
1 *First deadly sin* (1973)
2 *Second deadly sin* (1977)
3 *Third deadly sin* (1981)
4 *Fourth deadly sin* (1985)

Edward Yorke series
Pope, Dudley
see **Ned Yorke series**

Edwardian lady series
Tweedsmuir, Susan Buchan
Autobiography
1 *Lilac and the rose* (1952)
2 *Winter bouquet* (1954)
3 *Edwardian lady* (1966)

Edwardian Lancashire series
Bradley, Helen
Reproductions of paintings
1 *And Miss Carter wore pink* (1971)
Scenes from an Edwardian childhood
2 *Miss Carter came with us* (1973)
3 *In the beginning, said Great-Aunt Jane* (1975)
4 *Queen who came to tea* (1978)

Edwardian London trilogy
Willis, Frederick
1 *One hundred and one Jubilee Road* (1948)
A book of London yesterdays
2 *Peace and dripping toast* (1950)
3 *London general* (1953)

Edwardian series
Goodall, John Strickland
1 *Edwardian summer* (1976)
2 *Edwardian Christmas* (1977)
3 *Edwardian holiday* (1978)
4 *Edwardian season* (1979)
5 *Edwardian entertainments* (1981)

Edwardian trilogy
Vernon, Frances
1 *Gentlemen and players* (1984)
2 *Privileged children* (1982)
3 *Desirable husband* (1987)

Edwards series
De Clements, Barthe
see **Elsie Edwards series**
Russell, Charlotte Murray
see **Jane Amanda Edwards series**

Edwin George series
Goodrum, Charles Alvin
1 *Dewey decimated* (1977)
2 *Carnage of the realm* (1979)
Dead for a penny

Edwin Mould series
Wheeler, David
1 *Mould* (1967)
2 *Unimpeachable source* (1970)

Edwin series
Skelton, Peter
1 *Charm of hours* (1854)
2 *Promise of days* (1965)
3 *Blossom of months* (1974)

Edwina Charles series
Warner, Mignon
see **Mrs Edwina Charles series**

Eerie series
McHargue, Georgess
1 *Meet the werewolf* (1976)
2 *Meet the vampire* (1979)
3 *Meet the witches* (1983)

Effie Gray series
Lutyens, Mary
Biography based on letters
1 *Effie in Venice* (1965)
Young Mrs Ruskin in Venice
Her picture of society life with John Ruskin, 1849-52
2 *Millais and the Ruskins* (1967)
3 *Ruskins and the Grays* (1972)

Effingham series
Cooke, John Esten
1 *Virginia comedians* (1854)
From the mss of C Effingham, Esq
2 *Henry Saint John, gentleman* (1858)

Egerton series
Gilbert, Anthony
see **Scott Egerton series**

Egg Pandervil series
Bullett, Gerald
see **History of Pandervil series**

Eggs of things series
Kumin, Maxine W
1 *Eggs of things* (1963)
2 *More eggs of things* (1964)

Egholm series
Buchholtz, Johannes
1 *Egholm and his God* (1920)
Original edition entitled *Egholms Gud*
2 *Miracles of Clara van Haag* (1921)
Original edition entitled *Clara van Haags mirakler*

Ego series
Agate, James
Autobiography
1 *Ego* (1935)
2 *Ego 2* (1936)
3 *Ego 3* (1938)
4 *Ego 4* (1940)
5 *Ego 5* (1942)
6 *Ego 6* (1944)
7 *Ego 7* (1945)
8 *Ego 8* (1947)
9 *Ego 9* (1948)

Egypt, Maine series
Chute, Carolyn
1 *Beans of Egypt* (1985)
2 *Letourneau's used auto parts* (1988)

Egypt series
Broun, Daniel
see **Harry Egypt series**

Egypt series
Lorimer, Norma
1 *There was a king in Egypt* (1918)
2 *Shadow of Egypt* (1923)

Egyptian trilogy
Harris, Rosemary
1 *Moon in the cloud* (1968)
2 *Shadow on the sun* (1970)
3 *Bright and morning star* (1972)

Eichord series
Miller, Rex
see **Jack Eichord series**

Eight children series
Vestly, Anna Catharina
1 *Eight children and a truck* (1957)
Original edition entitled *Aatte smaa to stare og en lastebil*
2 *Eight children in the house* (1958)
Original edition entitled *Mormor og de atte ungene i skogen*
3 *Eight children in winter* (1959)
Original edition entitled *Marte og mormor og mormor og Morten*
4 *Eight children and Rosie* (1960)
Original edition entitled *En liten takk fra Anton*
5 *Eight children and a bulldozer* (1961)
Original edition entitled *Mormors promenade*

Eighteen Pine Street series
Johnson, Stacie
1 *Sort of sisters* (1992)
2 *Party* (1992)
3 *Prince* (1992)
4 *Test* (1993)
5 *Sky man* (1993)
6 *Fashion by Tasha* (1993)
7 *Intensive care* (1993)
8 *Dangerous games* (1993)
9 *Cindy's baby* (1993)
10 *Kwame's girl* (1994)

Eighteenth century London series
Garfield, Leon
see **Apprentices series**

Eighth champion of Christendom trilogy
Pargeter, Edith
1 *Eighth champion of Christendom* (1945)
Lame crusade
2 *Reluctant odyssey* (1946)
3 *Warfare accomplished* (1947)

Eighty Seventh Precinct series
McBain, Ed
1 *Cop hater* (1956)
2 *Mugger* (1956)
3 *Pusher* (1956)
4 *Con man* (1957)
5 *Killer's choice* (1958)
6 *Killer's payoff* (1958)
7 *Lady killer* (1958)
8 *Killer's wedge* (1959)
9 *'Til death* (1959)
10 *King's ransom* (1959)
11 *Give the boys a great big hand* (1960)
12 *Heckler* (1960)
13 *See them die* (1960)
14 *Lady, lady I did it!* (1961)
15 *Empty hours* (1962)
3 novelettes
16 *Like love* (1962)
17 *Ten plus one* (1963)
18 *Ax* (1964)
Axe
19 *He who hesitates* (1965)
20 *Doll* (1965)
21 *Eighty million eyes* (1966)
22 *Fuzz* (1968)
23 *Shotgun* (1969)
24 *Jigsaw* (1970)
25 *Hail, hail, the gangs all here!* (1971)
26 *Sadie when she died* (1972)
27 *Let's hear it for the deaf man* (1973)
28 *Hail to the Chief* (1973)
29 *Bread* (1974)
30 *Blood relatives* (1975)
31 *So long as you both shall live* (1976)
32 *Long time no see* (1977)
33 *Calypso* (1979)
34 *Ghosts* (1980)
35 *Heat* (1981)
36 *Ice* (1983)
37 *Lightning* (1984)
38 *Eight black horses* (1985)
39 *Another part of the city* (1985)
40 *Poison* (1987)
41 *Tricks* (1987)
42 *McBain's ladies* (1988)
Short stories
43 *McBain's ladies, too* (1989)
44 *Vespers* (1990)
45 *Widows* (1991)
46 *Kiss* (1992)
47 *Mischief* (1993)
48 *And all through the house* (1994)

Eigin series
Leiber, Justin Fritz
see **House of Eigin series**

Eileen Goudge's Swept away series
Goudge, Eileen
see **Swept away series**

Einstein Anderson series
Simon, Seymour
1 *Einstein Anderson, science sleuth* (1980)
2 *Einstein Anderson shocks his friends* (1980)
3 *Einstein Anderson makes up for lost time* (1981)
4 *Einstein Anderson tells a comet's tale* (1981)
5 *Einstein Anderson goes to bat* (1982)
6 *Einstein Anderson lights up the sky* (1982)
7 *Einstein Anderson sees through the invisible man* (1983)

Eisenberg and Kendall series
Chase, Philip
see **Aaron Eisenberg and William Kendall series**

Eisengrim trilogy
Davies, Robertson
see **Deptford trilogy**

Eisenhower series
Ambrose, Stephen Edward
1 *Eisenhower, soldier, general of the army, president-elect, 1890-1952* (1983)
2 *Eisenhower, the President* (1984)
One volume abridged edition entitled *Eisenhower, soldier and President*, 1990

El Borak trilogy
Howard, Robert Ervin
1 *Lost valley of Iskander* (1974)
2 *Son of the White Wolf* (1977)
3 *Three-bladed doom* (1977)

El Lazo series
Martin, Larry Jay
see **John Clinton Ryan series**

Elaine trilogy
Reeve, Arthur Benjamin
Based on screenplays
1 *Exploits of Elaine* (1915)
2 *Romance of Elaine* (1916)
3 *Triumph of Elaine* (1916)

Elana series
Engdahl, Sylvia Louise
1 *Enchantress from the stars* (1970)
2 *Far side of evil* (1971)

Eldorado series
Cameron, Donald
Autobiography
1 *Field of sighing* (1966)
2 *Sons of Eldorado* (1968)

Eldred Pottinger series
Diver, Maud
Set in Afghanistan during the first Afghan war, 1837-1841
1 *Hero of Herat* (1912)
2 *Judgement of the sword* (1913)

Eleanor, Georgie and Edward Hall series
Langton, Jane
see **Edward, Eleanor and Georgie Hall series**

Eleanor Marx series
Kapp, Eleanor
Biography of the wife of Karl Marx
1 *Family life, 1855-1883* (1972)
2 *Crowded years, 1884-1898* (1976)

Eleanor of Aquitaine series
Jones, Ellen
1 *Fatal crown* (1991)
2 *Beloved enemy* (1994)

Eleanor Roosevelt series
Lash, Joseph P
Biography
1 *Eleanor and Franklin* (1971)
2 *Eleanor, the years alone* (1972)

Eleanor Roosevelt series
Roosevelt, Elliott
1 *Murder and the First Lady* (1984)
2 *Hyde Park murder* (1985)
3 *Murder at Hobcaw Barony* (1986)
4 *White House pantry murder* (1987)
5 *Murder at the Palace* (1988)
6 *Murder in the Oval Office* (1989)
7 *Murder in the Rose Garden* (1989)
8 *Murder in the Blue Room* (1990)
9 *First class murder* (1991)
10 *Murder in the Red Room* (1992)
11 *Murder in the West Wing* (1992)
12 *Murder in the East Room* (1993)
13 *Royal murder* (1994)

Eleanora Burke series
Perdue, Virginia
1 *Case of the grieving monkey* (1941)
2 *Case of the foster father* (1942)

Eleanora Mousie series
Morris, Ann
Illustrated by Ruth Young
1 *Eleanora Mousie catches cold* (1987)
2 *Eleanora Mousie's gray day* (1987)
3 *Eleanora Mousie makes a mess* (1987)
4 *Eleanora Mousie in the dark* (1987)

Elected silence series
Merton, Thomas
1 *Seven-storey mountain* (1948)
Elected silence
The second title is an abridged edition
2 *Sign of Jonas* (1953)
Journal of a Trappist monk

Electric elephant series
Montgomery, Frances Trego
1 *Wonderful electric elephant* (1903)
2 *On a lark to the planets* (1904)

Electric High series
Thornton, Jane Foster
1 *Breakaway* (1984)
2 *Close harmony* (1984)
3 *Heartbreaker* (1984)
4 *On the edge* (1985)
5 *Star struck* (1985)

Elegant Edwardian series
Bloom, Ursula
Memoirs of the author's life and family
1 *Victorian vinaigrette* (1956)
2 *Elegant Edwardian* (1957)
3 *Youth at the gate* (1959)
4 *Down to the sea in ships* (1958)
5 *War isn't wonderful* (1961)
6 *Life is no fairytale* (1976)

Elena Olivirez series
Muller, Marcia
1 *Tree of death* (1983)
2 *Legend of the slain soldiers* (1985)
3 *Beyond the grave* (1986)
Co-author: Bill Pronzini

Elenium trilogy
Eddings, David
1 *Diamond throne* (1989)
2 *Ruby knight* (1990)
3 *Sapphire rose* (1991)

Elephant and mouse series
Grambling, Lois Goodwin
Illustrated by Deborah Maze
1 *Elephant and Mouse get ready for Christmas* (1990)
2 *Elephant and Mouse get ready for Easter* (1991)
3 *Elephant and Mouse celebrate Halloween* (1991)

Elephant series
Thurman, Mark
1 *Elephant's cold* (1979)
Revised edition 1985
2 *Elephant's new bicycle* (1980)
Revised edition 1985

Eleusinia series
Lytton, Edward George Earle Lytton Bulwer-Lytton
1 *Ernest Maltravers* (1837)
2 *Alice* (1838)
Alternative title: The mysteries
One volume edition entitled *The Eleusinia*, 1838

Eleven Kingdoms, first trilogy
Kurtz, Katherine
see **Legends of Camber of Culdi trilogy**

Eleven Kingdoms, fourth trilogy
Kurtz, Katherine
see **Histories of King Kelson trilogy**

Eleven Kingdoms, second trilogy
Kurtz, Katherine
see **Heirs of Saint Camber trilogy**

Eleven Kingdoms, third trilogy
Kurtz, Katherine
see **Chronicles of the Deryni trilogy**

Elfego O'Reilly series
Hawk, Alex
1 *Mexican standoff* (1971)
2 *Half-breed* (1971)

Elfie series
Wilhelm, Hans
1 *I'll always love you* (1985)
2 *Let's be friends again!* (1986)

Elfquest series
This sequence has four authors
Pini, Wendy
1 *Elfquest* (1982)
Alternative title: Journey to sorrow's end
Pini, Richard
2 *Blood of ten chiefs* (1986)
Co-authors: Lynn Abbey and Robert Lynn Asprin
3 *Wolfsong* (1988)
Co-authors: Lynn Abbey and Robert Lynn Asprin
4 *Winds of change* (1989)
5 *Against the wind* (1990)

Eli Holten series
Gentry, Buck
1 *Rowan's Raiders* (1981)
2 *Dakota massacre* (1981)
3 *Outlaw canyon* (1981)
4 *Cheyenne vengeance* (1982)
5 *Sioux slaughter* (1982)
6 *Bandit fury* (1982)
7 *Prairie bush* (1982)
8 *Pawnee rampage* (1983)
9 *Apache ambush* (1983)
10 *Traitor's gold* (1983)
11 *Yaqui terror* (1983)
12 *Yellowstone kill* (1983)
13 *Oglala outbreak* (1983)
14 *Cathouse Canyon* (1984)
15 *Texas tease* (1984)
16 *Virgin outpost* (1985)
17 *Breakneck bawdy house* (1985)
18 *Redskin thrust* (1985)
19 *Big top squaw* (1985)
20 *Big Baja bounty* (1986)
21 *Wildcat widow* (1986)
22 *Railhead roundup* (1986)
23 *Bedroll bait* (1986)
24 *Sioux swordsman* (1987)
25 *Rocky Mountain ball* (1987)
26 *Hangtown hustle* (1988)
27 *Apache trick* (1988)
28 *Cock of the walk* (1988)
29 *Comanchero lust* (1989)
30 *Hellfire mound* (1990)
31 *Hard rider* (1990)
32 *Stiff justice* (1991)
33 *Savage spread* (1992)
34 *Deep shooter* (1992)

Eli Pike series
Javor, Frank A
1 *Rim-world legacy and beyond* (1991)
2 *Scor-sting* (1990)
3 *Ice beast* (1990)

Elias Hackshaw series
Wilcox, Stephen F
1 *Twenty-acre plot* (1991)
2 *Nimby factor* (1992)
3 *Painted lady* (1993)

Elijah Baley series
Asimov, Isaac
1 *Caves of steel* (1954)
2 *Naked sun* (1957)
Numbers 1 and 2 are also published in one volume entitled *The robot novels*, 1971
3 *Robots of dawn* (1983)
4 *Robots and empire* (1985)
Companion volume: *The caves of steel*, by Rosemary Border, 1978

Elijah Cabot Pickering series
Ketchum, Philip
1 *Man who tamed Dodge* (1967)
2 *Man who turned outlaw* (1967)
3 *Man who sold Leadville* (1968)
4 *Cabot* (1969)

Eliot family trilogy
Goudge, Elizabeth
1 *Bird in the tree* (1940)
2 *Herb of grace* (1948)
Pilgrim's Inn
3 *Heart of the family* (1951)

Eliot Ness series
Collins, Max Allan
1 *Dark city* (1987)
2 *Butcher's dozen* (1988)
3 *Bullet proof* (1989)

Eliot series
Filgate, Macartney
see **Charlotte Eliot series**
Gordon, Lyndall
see **T.S.Eliot series**
Snow, Charles Percy
see **Strangers and brothers series**

Elisa series
Hurwitz, Johanna
1 *Russell and Elisa* (1989)
2 *E is for Elisa* (1991)

Elisabeth series
Holman, Felice
1 *Elisabeth, the bird watcher* (1963)
2 *Elisabeth, the treasure hunter* (1964)
3 *Elisabeth and the marsh mystery* (1966)

Elisha Macomber series
Knight, Kathleen Moore
1 *Death blew out the candle* (1935)
2 *Clue of the poor man's shilling* (1936)
Poor man's shilling
3 *Wheel that turned* (1936)
Murder gets Jean Holton
4 *Seven were veiled* (1937)
Seven were suspect
Death wears a veil
5 *Tainted token* (1938)
Case of the tainted token
6 *Acts of black night* (1938)
7 *Death came dancing* (1940)
8 *Trouble at Turkey Hill* (1946)
9 *Footbridge to death* (1947)
10 *Bait for murder* (1948)
11 *Bass Derby murder* (1949)
12 *Death goes to a reunion* (1952)
13 *Valse macabre* (1952)
14 *Akin to murder* (1953)
15 *Three of diamonds* (1953)
16 *Beauty is a beast* (1959)

Elisha trilogy
Wiesel, Elie
see **Night trilogy**

Eliza and Jess Birdwell series
West, Jessamyn
see **Jess and Eliza Birdwell series**

Eliza Brandon series
This sequence has two authors
Austen, Jane
1 *Sense and sensibility* (1811)
Aiken, Joan
2 *Eliza's daughter* (1994)

Eliza series
Pain, Barry
1 *Eliza* (1900)
2 *Eliza's husband* (1903)
3 *Eliza getting on* (1911)
4 *Exit Eliza* (1912)
5 *Eliza's son* (1913)

Elizabeth and Edward series
Brandenberg, Franz
see **Edward and Elizabeth series**

Elizabeth and Wynn series
Oke, Janette
1 *When comes the heart* (1983)
2 *When comes the spring* (1985)
3 *When breaks the dawn* (1986)
4 *When hope springs new* (1986)

Elizabeth Ann series
Bradburne, Elizabeth Sutton
1 *Elizabeth Ann* (1960)
2 *More of Elizabeth Ann* (1964)
3 *Elizabeth Ann again* (1968)
4 *Elizabeth Ann and her friends* (1969)

Elizabeth Ann series
Lawrence, Josephine
1 *Adventures of Elizabeth Ann* (1923)
2 *Elizabeth Ann at Maple Spring* (1923)
3 *Elizabeth Ann's six cousins* (1924)
4 *Elizabeth Ann and Doris* (1925)
5 *Elizabeth Ann's borrowed grandma* (1926)
6 *Elizabeth Ann's spring vacation* (1927)
7 *Elizabeth Ann and Uncle Doctor* (1928)
8 *Elizabeth Ann's houseboat* (1929)

Elizabeth Conway series
Morrison, Margaret
1 *Written for Elizabeth* (1934)
2 *Lady of justice* (1935)
3 *Betsybob* (1954)
4 *Undaunted* (1956)

Elizabeth Fytton series
Howard, Liz
1 *Elizabeth Fytton of Gawsworth* (1985)
2 *Master of Littlecote Manor* (1985)
3 *Squire of Holdenby* (1986)

Elizabeth Gail series
Stahl, Hilda
1 *Elizabeth Gail at the Johnson Farm* (1979)
2 *Elizabeth Gail and the secret box* (1979)

3 *Elizabeth Gail and the Teddy Bear mystery* (1979)
4 *Elizabeth Gail and the dangerous double* (1980)
5 *Elizabeth Gail and the trouble at Sandhill Ranch* (1980)
6 *Elizabeth Gail and the strange birthday party* (1980)
7 *Elizabeth Gail and the terrifying news* (1980)
8 *Elizabeth Gail and the frightened runaways* (1981)
9 *Elizabeth Gail and the trouble from the past* (1981)
10 *Elizabeth Gail and the silent piano* (1981)
11 *Elizabeth Gail and double trouble* (1982)
12 *Elizabeth Gail and the holiday mystery* (1982)
13 *Elizabeth Gail and the missing love letters* (1982)
14 *Elizabeth Gail and the music camp romance* (1983)
15 *Elizabeth Gail and the handsome stranger* (1983)
16 *Elizabeth Gail and the secret love* (1983)
17 *Elizabeth Gail and the summer for weddings* (1984)
18 *Elizabeth Gail and the time for love* (1984)
19 *Elizabeth Gail and the great canoe conspiracy* (1991)
20 *Elizabeth Gail and the hidden key mystery* (1992)
21 *Elizabeth Gail and the secret of the gold charm* (1992)

Elizabeth Glen series
Swan, Annie Shepherd
1 *Elizabeth Glen, M.B.* (1895)
The experience of a lady doctor
2 *Mrs Keith Hamilton, M.B.* (1897)

Elizabeth, her books series
Kay, Barbara
1 *Elizabeth, her folks* (1920)
2 *Elizabeth, her friends* (1920)

Elizabeth I series
Irwin, Margaret
Based on the life of Queen Elizabeth I
1 *Young Bess* (1944)
2 *Elizabeth, captive princess* (1948)
3 *Elizabeth and the Prince of Spain* (1953)

Elizabeth I series
Plowden, Alison
1 *Young Elizabeth* (1971)
2 *Danger to Elizabeth* (1973)
The Catholics under Elizabeth I
3 *Marriage with my kingdom* (1977)
The courtships of Elizabeth
4 *Elizabeth Regina* (1980)
The age of triumph, 1588-1603

Elizabeth I trilogy
Dessau, Joanna
1 *Red-haired brat* (1978)
2 *Absolute Elizabeth* (1978)
3 *Fantastical marvellous Queen* (1979)

Elizabeth Lamb Worthington series
Morison, Betty Jane
1 *Champagne and a gardener* (1983)
2 *Port and a star boarder* (1984)
3 *Beer and skittles* (1985)
4 *Voyage of the Chianti* (1987)

Elizabeth Macpherson series
McCrumb, Sharon
1 *Sick of shadows* (1984)
2 *Lovely in her bones* (1985)
3 *Highland laddie gone* (1986)
4 *Paying the piper* (1988)

Elizabeth, Peter Robin and Alastair series
Fitzgerald, Hilary
see **Alastair, Elizabeth and Peter Robin series**

Elizabeth Quigly series
Van Slyke, Helen
1 *Heart listens* (1973)
2 *Mixed blessing* (1975)

Elizabeth series
Glyn, Elinor
1 *Visits of Elizabeth* (1900)
2 *Elizabeth visits America* (1909)
Also a story entitled *Elizabeth's daughter*, in *The contract, and other stories*, 1913

Elizabeth series
Kilpatrick, Florence Antoinette
1 *Our Elizabeth* (1920)
2 *Our Elizabeth again* (1923)
3 *Our Elizabeth returns* (1933)
4 *Our Elizabeth in America* (1936)
5 *Elizabeth in Africa* (1940)
6 *Elizabeth in wartime* (1942)
7 *Elizabeth to the rescue* (1943)
8 *Elizabeth the sleuth* (1946)
9 *Elizabeth finds the body* (1949)

Elizabeth series
Russell, Mary Annette
1 *Elizabeth and her German garden* (1898)
2 *Solitary summer* (1899)
3 *Benefactress* (1901)
4 *Ordeal of Elizabeth* (1901)
5 *Adventures of Elizabeth in Rugen* (1904)

Elizabeth series
Westrup, Margaret
1 *Elizabeth's children* (1903)
Originally published anonymously
2 *Elizabeth in retreat* (1912)

Elizabeth Warrender series
Cole, George Douglas Howard
see **Mrs Elizabeth Warrender series**

Elizabethan age series
Rowse, Alfred Leslie
1 *England of Elizabeth* (1951)
The structure of society
2 *Expansion of Elizabethan England* (1955)

Elizabethan Catholics series
Nolan, Winefride
see **Catholic Stuarts series**

Elizabethan England trilogy
Neale, John Ernest
1 *Elizabethan House of Commons* (1949)
2 *Elizabeth I and her parliaments, 1558-1581* (1953)
3 *Elizabeth I and her parliaments, 1584-1601* (1957)

Elizabethan whodunits series
Marston, Edward
1 *Queen's head* (1989)
2 *Merry devils* (1989)
3 *Trip to Jerusalem* (1990)
4 *Nine giants* (1991)
5 *Mad courtesan* (1992)
6 *Silent woman* (1994)

Elizabethans and Spaniards series
Whittle, Tyler
see **Spaniards and Elizabethans series**

Elizalde series
Marshall, William Leonard
see **Battling Mendez series**

Elk series
Wallace, Edgar
see **Inspector Elk series**

Elkins series
Howard, Robert Ervin
see **Breckinridge Elkins series**

Ellen Augusta and Emily Mary Hall series
Sherrard, Owen Aubrey
see **Emily Mary and Ellen Augusta Hall series**

Ellen Grae series
Cleaver, Vera
1 *Ellen Grae* (1967)
2 *Lady Ellen Grae* (1968)
Numbers 1 and 2 also published in one volume 1977
3 *Grover* (1970)

Ellen, Melinda and Timothy series
Storey, Margaret
see **Timothy, Ellen and Melinda series**

Ellen Montgomery series
Wetherell, Elizabeth
1 *Wide wide world* (1851)
2 *Ellen Montgomery's bookshelf* (1854)

Ellen series
Lee, Marie G
1 *Finding my voice* (1992)
2 *Saying goodbye* (1994)

Ellen Timms series
Avery, Gillian
1 *Ellen's birthday* (1971)
2 *Ellen and the Queen* (1971)

Ellerdine and Blossom series
Wills, Cecil Melville
see **Superintendent Roger Ellerdine and Sergeant Cherry Blossom series**

Ellery Queen series
Queen, Ellery
This is the pseudonym of Frederic Dannay and Manfred Bennington Lee except where other authorship is indicated
1 *Greek coffin mystery* (1932)
2 *Roman hat mystery* (1929)
3 *French powder mystery* (1931)
4 *Dutch shoe mystery* (1931)
5 *Egyptian cross mystery* (1932)
6 *American gun mystery* (1933)
Death at the rodeo
7 *Siamese twin mystery* (1933)
8 *Adventures of Ellery Queen* (1934)
Short stories
9 *Chinese orange mystery* (1934)
10 *Spanish cape mystery* (1935)
11 *Halfway house* (1936)
12 *Door between* (1937)
13 *Devil to pay* (1938)
14 *Four of hearts* (1938)
15 *Dragon's teeth* (1939)
Virgin heiress
16 *New adventures of Ellery Queen* (1940)
Short stories
16.1 *Lamp of God* (1940)
17 *Last man club* (1940)
Based on a radio play
18 *Ellery Queen, master detective* (1941)
Vanishing corpse
Based on a screenplay
19 *Penthouse mystery* (1941)
Based on a screenplay
20 *Murdered millionaire* (1942)
Based on a radio play
21 *Perfect crime* (1942)
Based on a screenplay
22 *Calamity town* (1942)
23 *There was an old woman* (1943)
Quick and the dead
24 *Murderer is a fox* (1945)
25 *Ten days' wonder* (1948)
26 *Cat of many tails* (1949)
27 *Double, double* (1950)
Case of the seven murders
28 *Origin of evil* (1951)
29 *King is dead* (1952)
30 *Calendar of crime* (1952)
Short stories
31 *Scarlet letters* (1953)
32 *Q.B.I.* (1954)
Queen's Bureau of Investigation
Short stories
33 *Inspector Queen's own case* (1956)
34 *Finishing stroke* (1958)
35 *Player on the other side* (1963)
This title is by Theodore Sturgeon using the pseudonym
36 *And on the eighth day* (1964)
This title is by Avram Davidson using the pseudonym
37 *Fourth side of the triangle* (1965)
This title is by Avram Davidson using the pseudonym
38 *Queens full* (1965)
Short stories
39 *Study in terror* (1966)
Sherlock Holmes versus Jack the Ripper
This title is by Dannay and Lee with Paul Fairman using the pseudonym; based on a screenplay set in 1888
40 *Face to face* (1967)
41 *House of brass* (1968)
This title is by Avram Davidson using the pseudonym
42 *Q.E.D.* (1968)
Alternative title: Queen's experiments in detection; short stories
43 *Last woman in his life* (1970)
44 *Fine and private place* (1971)
Omnibus volumes: *Ellery Queen's big book*, 1938, *Ellery Queen's mystery parade*, 1944, *The case book of Ellery Queen*, 1949, *The Wrightsville murders*, 1956, *The Hollywood murders*, 1957, *The New York murders*, 1958, *The bizarre murders*, 1962

Elli Sari series
Ruthin, Margaret
1 *Reindeer girl* (1961)
Elli of the Northland
2 *Lapland nurse* (1962)

Ellie Gordon series
Berne, Karin
1 *Bare acquaintances* (1985)
2 *Shock value* (1985)
3 *False impressions* (1986)

Ellie Simons Haskell series
Cannell, Dorothy
1 *Thin woman* (1984)
An epicurean mystery
2 *Down the garden path* (1985)
A pastoral
3 *Widows' Club* (1988)
4 *Mum's the word* (1990)
5 *Femmes fatal* (1992)
6 *How to murder your mother-in-law* (1994)

Ellie's people series
Borntrager, Mary Christner
1 *Ellie* (1988)
2 *Rebecca* (1989)
3 *Rachel* (1990)
4 *Daniel* (1991)
5 *Reuben* (1992)
6 *Andy* (1993)
7 *Polly* (1994)

Elliot series
Roberts, Ann Victoria
see **Louisa Elliot series**

Elliott series
Taylor, Elizabeth Atwood
see **Maggie Elliott series**

Ellis and Gregg series
Koehler, Robert Portner
see **Avery Gregg and Tony Ellis series**

Ellis and Mitchell series
Lavelle, Sheila
see **Charlie Ellis and Angela Mitchell series**

Ellis Island series
Nixon, Joan Lowery
1 *Land of hope* (1992)
2 *Land of promise* (1993)
3 *Land of dreams* (1994)

Ellis McKay series
Strong, Leonard Alfred George
see **Police diversion series**

Ellis series
Collin, Paul Ries
see **Henry and Jane Ellis series**
Newell, Hope
see **Mary Ellis series**

Ellis Stack series
Fields, Frank
1 *Revenge of Ellis Stack* (1989)
2 *Stack's law* (1989)

Ellison series
Perry, Anne
see **Charlotte Ellison Pitt and Inspector Thomas Pitt series**

Ellon family trilogy
Goolden, Barbara
see **Consett trilogy**

Ellynne Aleese series
Miner, Jane Claypool
1 *Dreams can come true* (1981)
2 *Senior dreams can come true* (1985)

Elm Island series
Kellogg, Elijah
1 *Lion Ben of Elm Island* (1868)
2 *Charlie Bell* (1868)
3 *Ark of Elm Island* (1869)
4 *Boy farmers of Elm Island* (1869)
5 *Young ship builders of Elm Island* (1870)
6 *Hardscrabble of Elm Island* (1870)

Elm Street series
Cooper, Jeffrey
see **Nightmare on Elm Street series**

Elm Street series
Ripperger, Henrietta
1 *One hundred and twelve Elm Street* (1943)
2 *Bretons of Elm Street* (1946)

Elmer series
McKee, David
1 *Elmer* (1968)
The story of a patchwork elephant; revised edition 1989
2 *Elmer again and again* (1975)

Elmer the rat series
Cook, Patrick
1 *Elmer the rat* (1980)
2 *Elmer makes a break* (1982)
3 *Elmer runs wild* (1986)
4 *Elmer rides the rails* (1991)

Eloise series
Thompson, Kay
Illustrated by Hilary Knight; humour
1 *Kay Thompson's Eloise* (1955)
Eloise
2 *Kay Thompson's Eloise in Paris* (1958)
Eloise in Paris
3 *Kay Thompson's Eloise at Christmastime* (1958)
Eloise at Christmastime
4 *Kay Thompson's Eloise in Moscow* (1960)
Eloise in Moscow

Elric series
Moorcock, Michael
1 *Dreaming city* (1972)
Elric of Melnibone
The second title is a revised edition; abridged edition entitled *The dreaming jewels*, 1972
2 *Sailor on the seas of fate* (1976)
3 *Weird of the White Wolf* (1977)
Numbers 1-3 also published in one volume entitled *The Elric saga*, part one
4 *Sleeping sorceress* (1976)
Vanishing tower
5 *Stealer of souls, and other stories* (1963)
Bane of the black sword
Weird of the white wolf
The second and third titles are expanded editions
6 *Stormbringer* (1965)
Numbers 4-6 also published in one volume entitled *The Elric saga*, part two
Companion volumes: *The singing citadel*, 1970, *The jade man's eyes*, 1973, *The return to Melnibone*, a comic strip, 1973, *The great rock 'n' roll swindle*, 1980, *Elric at the end of time*, 1984, *The fortress of the pearl*, 1989, *The revenge of the rose*, 1991

Elsa series
Adamson, Joy
1 *Born free* (1960)
A lioness of two worlds; includes extracts from George Adamson's letters
2 *Living free* (1961)
The story of Elsa and her cubs
3 *Forever free* (1962)
Elsa's pride
4 *Elsa and her cubs* (1965)
Companion volume: *The searching spirit*, 1978

Elsa series
Virin, Anna
1 *Elsa tidies her house* (1974)
2 *Elsa's bears* (1974)
3 *Elsa in the night* (1976)
4 *Elsa's bears need the doctor* (1976)
5 *Elsa's bears in the playground* (1977)
6 *Elsa's bears learn to paint* (1977)

Elsewhere and Odd series
Roose-Evans, James
see **Odd and Elsewhere series**

Elsewhere trilogy
Windling, Terri
Tales of fantasy
1 *Elsewhere* (1981)
2 *Elsewhere II* (1982)
3 *Elsewhere III* (1984)

Elsie and Heiner series
Hoberg, Marielis
see **Heiner and Elsie series**

Elsie Dinsmore series
Finley, Martha Farquharson
1 *Elsie Dinsmore* (1867)
2 *Elsie's holidays at Roselands* (1868)
Holidays at Roselands
3 *Elsie's girlhood* (1872)
4 *Elsie's womanhood* (1875)
5 *Elsie's motherhood* (1876)
6 *Elsie's children* (1877)
7 *Elsie's widowhood* (1880)
8 *Grandmother Elsie* (1882)
9 *Elsie's new relations* (1883)
10 *Elsie at Nantucket* (1884)
11 *Two Elsies* (1885)
12 *Elsie's kith and kin* (1886)
13 *Elsie's friends at Woodburn* (1887)
14 *Christmas with Grandma Elsie* (1888)
15 *Elsie and the Raymonds* (1889)
16 *Elsie yachting with the Raymonds* (1890)
17 *Elsie's vacation and after events* (1891)
18 *Elsie at Viamede* (1892)
19 *Elsie at Ion* (1893)
20 *Elsie at the World's Fair* (1894)
21 *Elsie's journey on inland waters* (1895)
22 *Elsie at home* (1897)
23 *Elsie on the Hudson and elsewhere* (1898)
24 *Elsie in the South* (1899)
25 *Elsie's young folks in peace and war* (1900)
26 *Elsie's winter trip* (1902)
27 *Elsie and her loved ones* (1903)
28 *Elsie and her namesakes* (1905)
Companion volumes: *Mildred and Elsie*, 1881, *Mildred's married life and a winter with Elsie Dinsmore*, 1882

Elsie Edwards series
De Clements, Barthe
1 *Nothing's fair in fifth grade* (1981)
2 *Sixth grade can really kill you* (1985)
3 *How do you lose those ninth grade blues* (1983)
4 *Seventeen and in-between* (1984)

Elsie Lindtner series
Michaelis, Karin
Letters and fragments from a woman's diary
1 *Dangerous age* (1910)
Original edition entitled *Den farlige Alder*
2 *Elsie Lindtner* (1912)
Original edition entitled *Elsie Lindtner*

Elsie series
Bennett, Arnold
1 *Riceyman Steps* (1923)
2 *Elsie and the child* (1924)

Elsie series
Dunboyne, Marion Clifford Butler
see **Little Elsie series**

Elsie Silver series
Golding, Louis
1 *Five Silver daughters* (1934)
2 *Mister Emmanuel* (1939)
3 *Glory of Elsie Silver* (1945)
4 *Dangerous places* (1951)
5 *To the quayside* (1954)

Elsie Vanetti series
Lovell, Marc
1 *Blind hypnotist* (1976)
2 *Second Vanetti affair* (1977)

Elspeth and Anna Patterson trilogy
Stirling, Jessica
Set in Scotland in the 19th century
1 *Treasures on earth* (1985)
2 *Creature comforts* (1986)
3 *Hearts of gold* (1987)

Elspeth Marriner and Mack Fraser series
Merwin, Samuel Kimball
1 *House of many worlds* (1951)
2 *Three faces of time* (1955)
One volume edition entitled *The house of many worlds*, 1983

Elspeth Rodney series
Mannin, Ethel
1 *Cactus* (1935)
2 *Pure flame* (1936)

Elton series
Eiloart, Elizabeth
see **Ernie Elton series**
White, Ared
see **Captain Fox Elton series**

Elundium trilogy
Jefferies, Mike
see **Loremasters of Elundium trilogy**

Elven nations trilogy
This sequence has three authors
Carter, Tonya R
1 *Firstborn* (1991)
Niles, Douglas
2 *Kinslayer wars* (1991)
Carter, Tonya R
3 *Qualinesti* (1991)

Elver series
Dilnot, George
see **Horace Augustus Elver series**

Elvie's magic shop series
Coville, Bruce
1 *Jeremy Thatcher, dragon hatcher* (1991)
2 *Jennifer Murdley's toad* (1992)

Elvis Karlsson series
Gripe, Maria
1 *Julia's house* (1971)
Original edition entitled *Julias hus och Nattpappan*
2 *Elvis and his secret* (1972)
Original edition entitled *Elvis Karlsson*
3 *Elvis and his friends* (1973)
Original edition entitled *Elvis, Elvis!*
4 *[Den riktiga Elvis]* (1976)
No English edition
5 *[Att vara Elvis]* (1977)
No English edition
6 *[Bara Elvis]* (1979)
No English edition

Elwin Ransom trilogy
Lewis, Clive Staples
see **Space trilogy**

Elwood family series
Meyler, Eileen
1 *Adventure in Purbeck* (1955)
2 *Adventure in Dale House* (1956)
3 *Adventure on ponies* (1958)
4 *Adventure next door* (1960)
5 *Adventure at Hawthorn* (1961)
6 *Adventure with Whim* (1962)
7 *Adventure at Tremayne* (1963)

Elwyn Hughes series
Hardie, David William Ferguson
see **Inspector Elwyn Hughes series**

Elwyn Morgan series
Farrar, Stewart
see **Inspector Elwyn Morgan series**

Em series
Southworth, Emma Dorothy Eliza Nevitte
1 *Em* (1892)
2 *Em's husband* (1892)

Emancipator series
Aldridge, Ray
1 *Pharaoh contract* (1991)
2 *Emperor of everything* (1992)
3 *Orpheus machine* (1992)

Emanuel family series
Orlovitz, Gil
1 *Milkbottle H* (1968)
2 *Ice never F* (1970)
Originally planned as a trilogy

Emanuel Santana series
Truman, Timothy
1 *Four monsters* (1988)
2 *Mount fire* (1989)

Emanuel series
Craig, Christine
Illustrated by Karl Craig
1 *Emanuel and his parrot* (1970)
2 *Emanuel goes to market* (1971)

Emerald Canyon series
Clinton, Jeff
1 *Emerald Canyon* (1974)
2 *Showdown at Emerald Canyon* (1975)

Emerald enchanter series
Dever, Joe
1 *Emerald enchanter* (1986)
2 *Scarlet sorcerer* (1986)

Emergency series
Brown, Rollo Walter
1 *Firemakers* (1931)
A novel of environment
2 *Toward romance* (1932)
3 *Hilliken* (1933)
4 *As of the gods* (1937)

Emergency Ward 10 series
Falla, Roger
1 *Life in Emergency Ward 10* (1959)
2 *Love in Emergency Ward 10* (1960)
3 *Sisters of Emergency Ward 10* (1961)
4 *Case for Emergency Ward 10* (1962)
5 *Boy in Emergency Ward 10* (1965)

Emerson series
Amey, Linda
see **Blair Emerson series**
Peters, Elizabeth
see **Amelia Peabody Emerson series**

Emery series
Dilnot, George
see **Val Emery series**

Emigrants series
Moberg, Vilhelm
Translated from the Swedish
1 *Emigrants* (1949)
Original edition entitled *Utvandrarna*
2 *Unto a good land* (1953)
Original edition entitled *Invandrarna*
3 *Last letter home* (1959)
Original edition in two volumes entitled *Nybyggarne,* 1956 and *Sista brevet till Sverige,* 1959
3.1 *Settlers* (1956)
3.2 *Last letter home* (1959)

Emil Martin series
Taylor, Mary Ann
1 *Red is for shrouds* (1980)
2 *Return to murder* (1980)

Emil series
Kastner, Erich
1 *Emil and the detectives* (1928)
Original edition entitled *Emil und die Detektive*
2 *Emil and the three twins* (1935)
Original edition entitled *Emil und die drei Zwillinge*
3 *Thirty-fifth of May* (1933)
Alternative title: Conrad's ride to the South Seas; original edition entitled *Der 35 Mai, oder, Konrad reitet in die Suidsee*

Emil series
Lindgren, Astrid
1 *Emil in the soup tureen* (1963)
Original edition entitled *Emil i Loonnerberga;* revised edition 1980
2 *Emil's pranks* (1966)
Original edition entitled *Nya hyss av Emil i Loonneberga*; revised edition 1972
3 *Emil and piggy beast* (1970)
Emil and his clever pig
Original edition entitled *Aan lever Emil i Loonneberga;* revised edition 1979
4 *That Emil* (1972)
Original edition entitled *Den daar Emil*; picture book
5 *Emil and Lina's bad tooth* (1976)
Original edition entitled *Naar Emil skulle dra ut Lina's tand*; picture book

Emil Whippletree series
Hinkemeyer, Michael Thomas
see **Sheriff Emil Whippletree series**

Emily and Alice series
Starling, Jill
see **Alice and emily series**

Emily and Amy series
Vail, Amanda
1 *Love me a little* (1957)
2 *Bright young things* (1958)

Emily and Henry Bryce series
Scherf, Margaret
1 *Always murder a friend* (1948)
2 *Gun in Daniel Webster's bust* (1949)
3 *Green plaid pants* (1951)
Corpse with one shoe
4 *Glass on the stairs* (1954)
5 *Diplomat and the gold piano* (1963)
Death and the diplomat

Emily and Leo series
Brandenberg, Franz
see **Leo and Emily series**

Emily Blair and Kate Bloomfield series
Little, Jean
1 *Look through my window* (1970)
2 *Kate* (1971)

Emily Eyefinger series
Ball, Duncan
1 *Emily Eyefinger* (1992)
2 *Emily Eyefinger, secret agent* (1993)

Emily Mary and Ellen Augusta Hall series
Sherrard, Owen Aubrey
see **Victorian girls series**

Emily Pollifax series
Gilman, Dorothy
see **Mrs Emily Pollifax series**

Emily Seeton series
Carvic, Heron
see **Miss Emily Seeton series**

Emily series
Bedard, Michael
1 *Darker magic* (1989)
2 *Painted devil* (1994)

Emily series
Smith, Emma
1 *Emily* (1959)
Emily, the travelling guinea pig
The story of a traveller
2 *Emily's voyage* (1966)

Emily series
Stewart, Maureen
1 *Dear Emily* (1987)
2 *All about Emily* (1989)

Emily Starr trilogy
Montgomery, Lucy Maud
1 *Emily of New Moon* (1923)
2 *Emily climbs* (1925)
3 *Emily's quest* (1927)

Emily trilogy
Murdoch, Nina
see **Miss Emily trilogy**

Emma and Arthur series
Hoban, Russell
see **Arthur and Emma series**

Emma and Charlotte Makepeace series
Farmer, Penelope
see **Charlotte and Emma Makepeace series**

Emma Chizzit series
Hall, Mary Bowen
1 *Emma Chizzit and the Queen Anne killer* (1989)
2 *Emma Chizzit and the Sacramento stalker* (1991)
3 *Emma Chizzit and the NAPA nemesis* (1992)
4 *Emma Chizzit and the mother lode marauder* (1993)

Emma Greaves series
Black, Lionel
1 *Chance to die* (1965)
2 *Bait* (1966)
3 *Two ladies of Verona* (1967)
Lady is a spy

Emma Hamilton series
Foxell, Nigel
1 *Loving Emma* (1986)
2 *Emma expects* (1987)

Emma Harte series
Bradford, Barbara Taylor
1 *Woman of substance* (1979)
2 *Hold the dream* (1985)
3 *To be the best* (1988)

Emma McChesney series
Ferber, Edna
1 *Roast beef, medium* (1913)
Business adventures
2 *Personality plus* (1914)
3 *Emma McChesney and Co* (1915)
4 *Fanny herself* (1917)

Emma Marsh and Hank Fairbanks series
Dean, Elizabeth
1 *Murder is a collector's item* (1939)
2 *Murder is a serious business* (1940)
3 *Murder a mile high* (1944)

Emma series
Arundel, Honor
1 *High house* (1966)
2 *Emma's island* (1968)
3 *Emma in love* (1970)

Emma series
Hocken, Sheila
1 *Emma and I* (1977)
2 *Emma, V.I.P.* (1980)
3 *Emma's glory* (1981)
4 *Emma and Co.* (1983)
5 *After Emma* (1988)

Emma series
McPhail, David Michael
1 *Fix it!* (1984)
2 *Emma's pet* (1985)
3 *Emma's holiday* (1987)
Emma's vacation

Emma series
Stevenson, James
1 *Yuck!* (1984)
2 *Emma* (1985)
3 *Un-happy New Year, Emma!* (1989)
4 *Emma at the beach* (1990)

Emma series
Wolde, Gunilla
English text by Alison Winn
1 *Emma's baby brother* (1974)
Betsy's baby brother
2 *Emma quite contrary* (1974)
This is Betsy
3 *Emma and the measles* (1975)
Betsy and the chicken pox
4 *Emma goes to the dentist* (1975)
Betsy goes to the dentist
5 *Different Peter and Emma* (1975)
Betsy and Peter are different
6 *Emma and the vacuum cleaner* (1975)
Betsy and the vacuum cleaner
7 *Emma's first day at nursery school* (1976)
Betsy's first day at nursery school
8 *Emma enjoys nursery school* (1976)
9 *Emma's workshop* (1976)
Betsy's fixing day
10 *Emma and the doctor* (1976)
Betsy and the doctor

Emma Victor series
Wings, Mary
1 *She came too late* (1986)
2 *She came in a flash* (1988)

Emmanuel Cellini series
Halliday, Michael
see **Doctor Emmanuel Cellini series**

Emmanuel trilogy
Pontoppidan, Henrik
1 *Emmanuel* (1891)
Alternative title: Children of the soil; original edition entitled *Muld*
2 *Promised land* (1892)
Original edition entitled *Det forjaettede land*
3 *[Dommens dag]* (1895)
No English edition

Emmanuelle series
Arsan, Emmanuelle
Translated from the French
1 *Emmanuelle* (1967)
2 *Nea* (1975)
3 *Emmanuelle II* (1976)
Further experiences of Emmanuelle
4 *Laure* (1976)

Emmeline and Dick series
Stacpoole, Henry de Vere
see **Dick and Emmeline series**

Emmerdale Farm, retrospective series
Mackenzie, Lee
see **Annie Sugden series**

Emmerdale Farm series
This sequence has two authors; based on a television series
Mackenzie, Lee
1 *Legacy* (1977)
2 *Prodigal's progress* (1977)
3 *All that a man has* (1977)
4 *Lovers' meeting* (1977)
5 *Sad and happy summer* (1978)
6 *Sense of responsibility* (1979)
7 *Nothing stays the same* (1979)
8 *Couple at Demdyke Row* (1979)
9 *Whispers of scandal* (1979)
10 *Shadows from the past* (1980)
11 *Lucky for some* (1980)
12 *Face value* (1980)
13 *Good neighbours* (1981)
14 *Innocent victim* (1981)
15 *False witness* (1981)
16 *Homecoming* (1982)
17 *Old flames* (1982)
18 *Wedding bells* (1983)
19 *Family feuds* (1984)
20 *Young passions* (1985)
21 *Another door opens* (1986)

Ferguson, James
22 *Friend in need* (1987)
23 *Divided loyalties* (1988)
Companion volumes: *Emmerdale Farm, the official companion*, 1988, *Emmerdale Farm book of country love*, 1988

Emmett series
Stolz, Mary
1 *Emmett's pig* (1959)
2 *King Emmett the Second* (1991)

Emmie, Leo and Zack series
Ehrlich, Amy
see **Leo, Zack and Emmie series**

Emmis series
Burgess, Anthony
see **Richard Emmis series**

Emmy and Henry Tibbett series
Moyes, Patricia
see **Henry and Emmy Tibbett series**

Emmy, Dodie and Lisa series
Chastain, Madye Lee
see **Lisa, Emmy and Dodie series**

Emmy Lou series
Martin, George Madden
1 *Emmy Lou, her book and heart* (1902)
2 *Emmy Lou's road to grace* (1916)

Emmy series
Dunnett, Margaret
see **Cobb family series**

Emory series
Kootz, Samuel Melvin
see **Jason Emory series**

Emotions series
Hellner, Katarina
Illustrated by Tineke Daalder; translated from the Swedish
1 *Joan is sad* (1978)
2 *Joan is scared* (1978)
3 *Joan is angry* (1978)
4 *Joan is happy* (1978)

Emp series
Horler, Sydney
1 *Horror's head* (1932)
2 *Master of venom* (1949)
3 *Murderer at large* (1951)

Emperor Napoleon III series
Kenyon, Frank Wilson
1 *I, Eugenie* (1962)
2 *Imperial courtesan* (1967)

Emperor Shah Jahan series
Payne, Robert
1 *Great mogul* (1950)
Young Emperor
2 *Emperor* (1953)

Emphyrion series
Lawhead, Stephen
1 *Search for Fierra* (1985)
2 *Siege of Dome* (1986)
One volume edition entitled *Emphyrion*, 1990

Empire City quartet
Goodman, Paul
1 *State of nature* (1946)
2 *Dead of spring* (1950)
3 *Holy terror* (1959)
Numbers 1-3 also published in one volume entitled *Empire city*, 1959
4 *Grand piano* (1942)
Alternative title: The almanac of alienation
One volume edition entitled *Empire City*, 1977

Empire of the East trilogy
Saberhagen, Fred
see **Chup trilogy**

Empire Princess series
Diamond, Graham
see **Stacy series**

Empire series
Feist, Raymond Elias
1 *Daughter of the Empire* (1987)
2 *Servant of the Empire* (1990)
3 *Mistress of the empire* (1992)

Empires trilogy
This sequence has three authors
Cook, David
1 *Horselords* (1990)
Awlinson, Richard
2 *Dragonwall* (1990)
Lowder, James
3 *Crusade* (1991)

Empress of outer space series
Chandler, Arthur Bertram
1 *Empress of outer space* (1965)
2 *Space mercenaries* (1965)
3 *Nebula alert* (1967)

Empty house trilogy
Gutman, Claude
1 *Empty house* (1991)
Original edition entitled *Maison vide*
2 *Fighting back* (1992)

Enchanted forest series
Wrede, Patricia Collins
1 *Dealing with dragons* (1990)
2 *Searching for dragons* (1991)
3 *Calling on dragons* (1992)
4 *Talking to dragons* (1993)

Enchanted places series
Milne, Christopher
Autobiography
1 *Enchanted places* (1974)
2 *Path through the trees* (1979)
3 *Hollow on the hill* (1982)
The search for a personal philosophy

Enchanter's nightshade series
Morton, John Bingham
1 *Enchanter's nightshade* (1921)
2 *Penny royal* (1921)

Enchantress trilogy
Yorke, Katherine
1 *Enchantress* (1979)
2 *Falcon gold* (1980)
3 *Lady of the lakes* (1981)
One volume revised edition entitled *Enchantress saga*, by Nicola Thorne, 1985

Encyclopaedia Brown series
Sobol, Donald J
see **Encyclopedia Brown series**

Encyclopedia Brown series
Sobol, Donald J
1 *Encyclopedia Brown, boy detective* (1963)
2 *Encyclopedia Brown and the case of the secret pitch* (1965)
3 *Encyclopedia Brown finds the clues* (1966)
4 *Encyclopedia Brown gets his man* (1967)
5 *Encyclopedia Brown solves them all* (1968)
6 *Encyclopedia Brown keeps peace* (1969)
7 *Encyclopedia Brown saves the day* (1970)
8 *Encyclopedia Brown tracks them down* (1971)
9 *Encyclopedia Brown shows the way* (1972)
10 *Encyclopedia Brown takes the case* (1973)
11 *Encyclopedia Brown lends a hand* (1974)
12 *Encyclopedia Brown and the case of the dead eagles* (1975)
13 *Encyclopedia Brown and the case of the midnight visitor* (1977)
14 *Encyclopedia Brown carries on* (1980)
15 *Encyclopedia Brown sets the pace* (1981)
16 *Encyclopedia Brown and the case of the mysterious handprints* (1985)
17 *Encyclopedia Brown and the case of the treasure hunt* (1988)
18 *Encyclopedia Brown and the case of the disgusting sneakers* (1990)
19 *Encyclopedia Brown and the case of the two spies* (1994)
Companion volumes: *Encyclopedia Brown's record book of weird and wonderful facts*, 1979, *Encyclopedia Brown's second record book of weird and wonderful facts*, 1981, *Encyclopedia Brown's third record book of weird and wonderful facts*, 1981, *Encyclopedia Brown and the case of the exploding plumbing*, 1977, *Encyclopedia Brown takes the cake, a cook and case book*, 1984, *Encyclopedia Brown's book of strange but true crimes*, 1992

Encyclopedia Brown's wacky series
Sobol, Donald J
1 *Encyclopedia Brown's book of wacky crimes* (1982)
2 *Encyclopedia Brown's book of wacky spies* (1984)
3 *Encyclopedia Brown's book of wacky sports* (1984)
4 *Encyclopedia Brown's book of wacky animals* (1985)
5 *Encyclopedia Brown's book of wacky outdoors* (1987)
6 *Encyclopedia Brown's book of wacky cars* (1987)

End of the chapter series
Galsworthy, John
1 *Maid in waiting* (1931)
2 *Flowering wilderness* (1932)
3 *Over the river* (1933)
One volume edition entitled *End of the chapter*, 1934; companion volumes: *Caravan*, 1925, *On Forsyte 'change*, 1930

Endangered animals series
McClung, Robert Marshall
1 *Shag* (1960)
Last of the Plains buffalo
2 *Screamer* (1964)
Last of the Eastern panthers
3 *Black Jack* (1967)
Last of the big alligators
4 *Thor* (1971)
Last of the sperm whales
5 *Scoop* (1972)
Last of the brown pelicans
6 *Samson* (1973)
Last of the California grizzlies
7 *Rajpur* (1982)
Last of the Bengal tigers
Companion volumes: *Lost wild America, the story of our extinct and vanishing wildlife*, 1969, *Lost wild worlds, the story of our extinct and vanishing wildlife of the Eastern Hemisphere*, 1976, *Vanishing wildlife of Latin America*, 1981

Endagered animals series
Taylor, Dave
1 *Endangered grassland animals* (1992)
2 *Endangered forest animals* (1992)
3 *Endangered wetland animals* (1992)
4 *Endangered mountain animals* (1992)
5 *Endangered island animals* (1993)
6 *Endangered ocean animals* (1993)
7 *Endangered desert animals* (1993)
8 *Endangered savannah animals* (1993)

Endel and Lofthouse series
Marcus, Joanna
see **Romney Marsh series**

Ender Wiggins series
Card, Orson Scott
1 *Ender's game* (1985)
Revised edition 1991
2 *Speaker for the dead* (1986)
Revised edition 1991; numbers 1 and 2 also published in one volume entitled *Ender's war*, 1986
3 *Xenocide* (1991)

Enderby series
Burgess, Anthony
see **Mister Enderby series**

Endicott family trilogy
Daringer, Helen Fern
1 *Pilgrim Kate* (1949)
2 *Debbie of the Green Gate* (1950)
3 *Country cousin* (1951)

Endicott series
Roosevelt, Elliott
see **Blackjack Endicott series**

Endless and Company series
Ridge, Antonia
1 *Rom-Bom-Bom, and other stories* (1946)
2 *Hurrah for Muggins, and other stories* (1947)
3 *Endless and Company* (1948)
4 *Galloping Fred* (1950)

Endless frontier series
Pournelle, Jerry
1 *Endless frontier* (1979)
2 *Endless frontier, volume 2* (1982)
3 *Cities in space* (1991)

Endless quest crimson crystal adventure series
This sequence has three authors
Lawson, Susan
1 *Riddle of the griffon* (1985)
Moore, Roger Elwood
2 *Search for the Pegasus* (1985)
3 *Renegades of Luntar* (1985)
Clark, Mary
4 *Stop that witch!* (1985)

Endless quest series
This sequence has nineteen authors
Estes, Rose
1 *Dungeon of dread* (1982)
2 *Mountain of mirrors* (1982)
3 *Pillars of Pentegarn* (1982)
4 *Return to Brookmere* (1982)
5 *Revolt of the dwarves* (1983)
6 *Revenge of the rainbow dragons* (1983)
7 *Hero of Washington Square* (1983)
Blashfield, Jean
8 *Villains of Volturnus* (1983)
Carr, Mike
9 *Robbers and robots* (1983)
Estes, Rose
10 *Circus of fear* (1983)
Lowery, Linda
11 *Spell of the winter wizard* (1983)
Kirchoff, Mary Lynn
12 *Light on Quests Mountain* (1983)
Estes, Rose
13 *Dragon of doom* (1983)
McGuire, Catherine
14 *Raid on Nightmare Castle* (1983)
Kendall, John
15 *Under dragon's wing* (1984)
French, Laura
16 *Dragon's ransom* (1984)
Simon, Morris
17 *Captive planet* (1984)
McGowen, Tom
18 *King's quest* (1984)
Ward, James Michael
19 *Conan the undaunted* (1984)

Endless quest series

Moore, Roger Elwood
20 *Conan and the prophecy* (1984)
Martindale, T Chris
21 *Duel of the masters* (1984)
Weis, Margaret
22 *Endless catacombs* (1984)
Simon, Morris
23 *Blade of the young samurai* (1984)
McGuire, Catherine
24 *Trouble on Artule* (1984)
Moore, Roger Elwood
25 *Conan the outlaw* (1984)
Niles, Douglas
26 *Tarzan and the well of slaves* (1985)
Algozin, Bruce
27 *Lair of the Lich* (1985)
Simon, Morris
28 *Mystery of the ancients* (1985)
Fultz, Regina Oehler
29 *Tower of darkness* (1985)
Simon, Morris
30 *Fireseed* (1985)
Reinsmith, Richard
31 *Tarzan and the tower of diamonds* (1985)
Algozin, Bruce
32 *Prisoner of Elderwood* (1986)
Kirchoff, Mary Lynn
33 *Knights of illusion* (1986)
Algozin, Bruce
34 *Claw of the dragon* (1986)
Kirchoff, Mary Lynn
35 *Vision of doom* (1986)
Sherman, Josepha
36 *Song of the dark druid* (1987)

Endless summer series

Davidson, Linda
1 *Treading water* (1988)
2 *Too hot to handle* (1988)
3 *On the edge* (1988)
4 *Cool breezes* (1988)

Ends and means trilogy

Koestler, Arthur
1 *Gladiators* (1939)
Original edition entitled *Die Gladiatoren*
2 *Darkness at noon* (1940)
Original edition entitled *Sonnenfinsternis*
3 *Arrival and departure* (1943)
Original edition in English; revised edition 1966

Endworld series

Robbins, David
1 *Fox run* (1986)
2 *Thief River Falls run* (1986)
3 *Twin cities run* (1986)
4 *Kalispell run* (1987)
5 *Dakota run* (1987)
6 *Minnesota run* (1987)
7 *Armageddon run* (1987)
8 *Denver run* (1987)
9 *Capital run* (1988)
10 *New York run* (1988)
Numbers 9-10 also published in one volume 1991
11 *Liberty run* (1988)
12 *Houston run* (1988)
Numbers 11 and 12 also published in one volume 1991
13 *Anaheim run* (1988)
14 *Seattle run* (1989)
Numbers 13 and 14 also published in one volume 1991
15 *Nevada run* (1989)
16 *Miami run* (1989)
Numbers 15 and 16 also published in one volume 1991
17 *Atlanta run* (1989)
18 *Memphis run* (1989)
19 *Cincinnati run* (1990)
20 *Dallas run* (1990)
21 *Boston run* (1990)
22 *Green Bay run* (1990)
23 *Yellowstone run* (1990)
24 *New Orleans run* (1991)
25 *Spartan run* (1991)
26 *Madman run* (1991)
27 *Chicago run* (1991)
Companion volume: *Citadel run*, 1987

Enforcer series

Sugar, Andrew
1 *Enforcer* (1973)
Caribbean kill
2 *Calling Doctor Kill* (1973)
3 *Kill city* (1973)
4 *Kill deadline* (1973)
5 *Steel trap* (1975)
6 *Bio blitz* (1975)

England and the English series

Ford, Ford Madox
1 *Soul of London* (1905)
A survey of a modern city
2 *Heart of the country* (1906)
A survey of a modern land
3 *Spirit of the people* (1907)
An analysis of the English mind
One volume edition entitled *England and the English, an interpretation*, 1907

England reclaimed series

Sitwell, Osbert
1 *England reclaimed* (1927)
A book of eclogues
2 *Wrack at Tidesend* (1952)
A book of balnearics
3 *On the Continent* (1958)
A book of inquilinics

England series

Elliott, William James
see **Anthony England series**

English bowmen series

Doyle, Arthur Conan
1 *Sir Nigel* (1906)
2 *White Company* (1891)

English Civil War series

Bell, Josephine
1 *To serve a queen* (1972)
2 *In the King's absence* (1973)

English Civil War series

Gaunt, Richard
1 *Brother enemy* (1969)
2 *Iron Girdle* (1969)

English Civil War series

Ross, Sutherland
see **Clifton family series**

English Civil War series

Softly, Barbara
1 *Plain Jane* (1961)
2 *Place Mill* (1962)
3 *Stone in a pool* (1964)

English fairy tales series

Jacobs, Joseph
1 *English fairy tales* (1890)
2 *More English fairy tales* (1894)

English gentleman series

Sutherland, Douglas
Satirical reminiscences
1 *English gentleman* (1978)
2 *English gentleman's wife* (1979)
3 *English gentleman's child* (1979)
4 *English gentleman's mistress* (1980)
5 *Sutherland's war* (1984)
An English gentleman goes into battle
6 *English gentleman's good shooting guide* (1989)

English girl series

Maud, Constance Elisabeth
1 *English girl in Paris* (1902)
2 *Daughter of France* (1908)

English journey series

Priestley, John Boynton
Reminiscences
1 *English journey* (1934)
A rambling but truthful account of what one man saw and heard and felt and thought during a journey through England during autumn of the year 1933
2 *Midnight on the desert* (1937)
Winter in America, 1935-36
3 *Rain upon Godshill* (1939)
4 *Journey down a rainbow* (1955)
Co-author: Jacquetta Hawkes; travels in New Mexico and Texas
5 *Margin released* (1962)
6 *Instead of the trees* (1977)

English library series

Irwin, Raymond
History of English libraries up to 1850
1 *Origins of the English library* (1958)
2 *Heritage of the English library* (1964)
Companion volume: *The English library, sources and history*, 1966

English Revolution series

Crockett, Samuel Rutherford
1 *Men of the moss-hag* (1895)
2 *Lochinvar* (1897)

English scene series

Diver, Maud
1 *Unconquered* (1917)
2 *Strange roads* (1918)
3 *Strong hours* (1919)
4 *Coombe Saint Mary's* (1925)

English series

Broome, H B
see **Tom English series**
Stevenson, Drew
see **J Huntley English series**

English village series

Goodall, John Strickland
1 *Story of an English village* (1978)
2 *Story of a castle* (1986)
3 *Story of a high street* (1987)
4 *Story of a farm* (1989)
5 *Story of a seashore* (1990)

English walks series

Davies, Hunter
1 *Walk along the Wall* (1974)
Third edition 1993
2 *Walk around the Lakes* (1979)
Second edition 1993
3 *Walk along the tracks* (1982)
Second edition 1993
4 *Walk around London's parks* (1983)

English ways series

Hilton, Jack
1 *English ways* (1940)
A walk from the Pennines to Epsom Downs in 1939
2 *English ribbon* (1950)

Enid Blyton's story book series

Blyton, Enid
see **Story book series**

Ennal's Point series

Richards, Alun
Novels concerning the Lifeboat Service of the Bristol Channel
1 *Ennal's Point* (1977)
2 *Barque Whisper* (1979)

Enniscorthy series

Toibin, Colm
1 *South* (1990)
2 *Heather blazing* (1993)

Enough series

Sargeson, Frank
Memoirs
1 *Once is enough* (1973)
2 *More than enough* (1975)
3 *Never enough* (1977)
Place and people mainly

Enrico Caruso series

Paul, Barbara
1 *Cadenza for Caruso* (1984)
2 *Prima donna at large* (1985)
3 *Chorus of detectives* (1987)

Enrique Alvarez series

Jeffries, Roderic Graeme
see **Inspector Enrique Alvarez series**

Ensign Peter Byrd series

Styles, Showell
1 *Flying ensign* (1960)
Greencoats against Napoleon
2 *Byrd of the 95th* (1962)
Thunder over Spain

Enthala trilogy

Mayhar, Ardath
see **House of Enthala trilogy**

Entwhistle series

Webster, Frederick Annesley Michael
see **Ebbie Entwhistle series**

Environment series

Bentley, Phyllis
1 *Environment* (1922)
2 *Cat-in-the-manger* (1923)

Environmental awareness series

Snodgrass, Mary Ellen
1 *Acid rain* (1991)
2 *Air pollution* (1991)
3 *Land pollution* (1991)
4 *Solid waste* (1991)
5 *Toxic waste* (1991)
6 *Water pollution* (1991)

Eon series

Bear, Greg
1 *Eon* (1985)
2 *Eternity* (1988)

Eorthe series

Beamer, Charles
see **Legends of Eorthe series**

Ephraim Peck series

Derleth, August
see **Judge Ephraim Peck series**

Ephraim Tutt series

Train, Arthur
1 *Tutt and Mister Tutt* (1920)
Short stories
2 *By advice of counsel* (1921)
Short stories
3 *Hermit of Turkey Hollow* (1921)
The story of an alibi
4 *Tut, tut, Mister Tutt!* (1923)
Short stories
5 *Page Mister Tutt* (1926)
Short stories
6 *When Tutt meets Tutt* (1927)
Short stories
7 *Adventures of Ephraim Tutt* (1930)
8 *Tutt for Tutt* (1934)
Short stories
9 *Mister Tutt takes the stand* (1936)
Short stories
10 *Old man Tutt* (1938)
Short stories
11 *Mister Tutt comes home* (1941)
Short stories
12 *Yankee lawyer* (1943)
Autobiography of Ephraim Tutt
13 *Mister Tutt finds a way* (1945)
Short stories
Omnibus volumes: *Mister Tutt's case book*, 1936, *Mister Tutt at his best*, 1961

Epic of wheat series
Norris, Frank
1 *Octopus* (1902)
A story of California
2 *Pit* (1902)
A story of Chicago
Originally intended to be a trilogy

Epic tales of the five series
Duane, Diane
1 *Door into fire* (1979)
2 *Door into shadow* (1984)
3 *Door into sunset* (1993)

Epicure trilogy
Wechsberg, Joseph
Memoirs
1 *Looking for a bluebird* (1945)
2 *Sweet and sour* (1948)
3 *Blue trout and black truffles* (1953)

Episodes of the great Russian tragedy series
Piccard, Eulalie
1 *Death to the bourgeois* (1929)
Original edition entitled *Mort aux bourgeois, 1917- 21*
2 *Red university* (1933)
Original edition entitled *Universite rouge, 1921- 25*
3 *Kulaks* (1935)
Original edition entitled *Les Koulaks, 1925-30*
4 *Harmers* (1938)
Original edition entitled *Les nuisers, 1930-33*
5 *End of the revolution* (1943)
Original edition entitled *La fin d'une revolution, 1933-42*

Epton series
Underwood, Michael
see **Rosa Epton series**

Ereache O'Shea series
Yates, Renate
see **Inspector Ereache O'Shea series**

Erekose series
Moorcock, Michael
1 *Eternal champion* (1970)
Revised edition 1978
2 *Phoenix in obsidian* (1970)
Silver warriors
3 *Champion of Garathorn* (1973)
4 *Quest for Tanelorn* (1975)

Erewhon series
Butler, Samuel
1 *Erewhon* (1872)
Over the range
Revised edition 1872
2 *Erewhon revisited* (1901)
One volume edition 1927

Eri series
Lincoln, Joseph Crosby
see **Captain Eri series**

Eric Blainey series
Newby, Percy Howard
1 *Picnic at Sakkara* (1955)
2 *Revolution and roses* (1957)
3 *Guest and his going* (1959)

Eric Brighteyes series
This sequence has two authors
Haggard, Henry Rider
1 *Eric Brighteyes* (1891)
Skaldaspillir, Sigfriour
2 *Witch's welcome* (1979)

Eric Carstairs series
This sequence has four authors
Carter, Lin
1 *Journey to the underground world* (1979)
2 *Zanthodon* (1980)
3 *Hurok of the stone age* (1981)
4 *Darya of the bronze age* (1981)
5 *Eric of Zanthodon* (1982)

Eric Hazard series
Crosby, Lee
1 *Terror by night* (1938)
2 *Too many doors* (1941)
Doors to death
Revised edition 1965

Eric Ivorsen series
Spencer, Rick
1 *Icebound* (1983)
2 *All that glitters* (1983)
3 *Moneymaster* (1984)
4 *Terror merchant* (1984)
5 *Devil's mirror* (1984)

Eric John Stark series
Brackett, Leigh
1 *People of the Talisman* (1964)
2 *Secret of Sinharat* (1964)
3 *Ginger star* (1974)
4 *Hounds of Skaith* (1974)
5 *Reavers of Skaith* (1976)
Numbers 4 and 5 also published in one volume entitled *The book of Skaith*, 1976
6 *Eric John Stark, outlaw of Mars* (1982)
Also Skaith stories in *The halfling, and other stories*, 1973

Eric Kendall series
Muirden, James
1 *Space intruder* (1965)
2 *Moon-winners* (1965)

Eric Lund series
Wallis, Ruth Sawtell
1 *No bones about it* (1944)
2 *Cold bed in the clay* (1947)
3 *Forget my fate* (1950)

Eric Marsden series
Graham, Anthony
1 *Act of silence* (1964)
2 *Behind the arras* (1964)
3 *Veetols* (1965)

Eric Ravensmith series
Frost, Jason
see **Warlord series**

Eric Saveman series
Petersen, Paul
see **Smugglers series**

Eric series
Henri, Adrian
Illustrated by Roger Wade Walker
1 *Eric the punk cat* (1982)
2 *Eric and Frankie in Las Vegas* (1987)

Eric series
Sheridan, John
Illustrated by Malcolm Livingstone
1 *Eric, the wild car* (1978)
2 *Eric and the mad inventor* (1978)
3 *Eric and the lost planes* (1978)

Eric Ward series
Lewis, Royston
1 *Certain blindness* (1980)
2 *Dwell in danger* (1982)
3 *Limited vision* (1983)
4 *Once dying, twice dead* (1984)
5 *Blurred reality* (1985)
6 *Premium on death* (1986)
7 *Necessary dealing* (1989)

Eridanus series
Barbet, Pierre
1 *Napoleons of Eridanus* (1976)
Original edition entitled *Les grognards d'Eridan*
2 *Emperor of Eridanus* (1976)
Original edition entitled *L'empereur d'Eridan*

Erie Canal series
Edmonds, Walter Dumaux
1 *Erie water* (1933)
2 *Rome haul* (1929)
3 *Big barn* (1930)
4 *Mostly canallers* (1934)
Short stories

Erik Chatham series
Neebel, Richard
1 *Halo solution* (1979)
2 *Yunnan terminus* (1980)

Erik March series
Fickling, G G
1 *Naughty but dead* (1962)
2 *Case of the radioactive redhead* (1963)
3 *Crazy mixed-up nude* (1964)
4 *Stiff as a broad* (1971)

Erinn series
Castle, Frances
1 *Sister's tale* (1968)
2 *Tara's daughter* (1970)
3 *Thread of gold* (1971)

Ermineskin series
Kinsella, William Patrick
see **Silas Ermineskin series**

Ernest and Celestine series
Vincent, Gabrielle
1 *Ernest and Celestine* (1982)
2 *Bravo, Ernest and Celestine!* (1982)
3 *Ernest and Celestine's picnic* (1982)
4 *Smile, Ernest and Celestine* (1982)
5 *Merry Christmas, Ernest and Celestine* (1984)
6 *Ernest and Celestine's patchwork quilt* (1985)
7 *Breakfast time, Ernest Celestine* (1985)
8 *Where are you, Ernest and Celestine?* (1986)
9 *Feel better, Ernest!* (1988)
10 *Ernest and Celestine at the circus* (1989)

Ernest and Frank series
Day, Alexandra
see **Frank and Ernest series**

Ernest and Phoebe series
Gillmore, Inez Haynes
see **Phoebe and Ernest series**

Ernest Hemingway series
Griffin, Peter
1 *Along with youth* (1985)
The early years
2 *Less than a treason* (1990)
Hemingway in Paris

Ernest Lamb series
Wentworth, Patricia
see **Inspector Ernest Lamb series**

Ernest Ralph Gorse series
Hamilton, Patrick
1 *Hangover Square* (1941)
Alternative title: The man with two minds; a story of darkest Earl's Court in the year 1939
2 *West Pier* (1951)
3 *Mister Stimpson and Mister Gorse* (1953)
4 *Unknown assailant* (1955)

Ernest series
Libenzi, Ermanno
Translated from the Italian
1 *Adventures of Ernest in Africa* (1973)
2 *Ernest in the wild west* (1973)
Original edition entitled *Bacciccia nel far west*

Ernestine series
Pinkney, Gloria Jean
1 *Sunday outing* (1994)
2 *Back home* (1992)

Ernie Astorbilt series
Lazare, Lewis
1 *Ernie discovers excellence* (1984)
2 *Ernie discovers Washington* (1984)
3 *Ernie discovers Wall Street* (1984)
4 *Ernie goes abroad* (1984)

Ernie Elton series
Eiloart, Elizabeth
1 *Ernie Elton, the lazy boy* (1865)
2 *Ernie at school and what came of his going there* (1867)
Ernie Elton at school
One volume edition entitled *Ernie Elton at home and school*, 1867

Ernie Pratt series
Leslie, David Stuart
1 *Sbap crackle pop* (1970)
2 *Bad medicine* (1971)

Ernie series
Mallett, Jerry J
1 *Good old Ernie* (1983)
2 *Poor old Ernie* (1988)
3 *Just old Ernie* (1988)
4 *Clearly old Ernie* (1989)

Ernie series
Waddell, Martin
1 *Ernie's chemistry set* (1978)
2 *Ernie's flying trousers* (1978)

Ernst Brendel series
Masterman, John Cecil
1 *Oxford tragedy* (1933)
2 *Case of the four friends* (1957)
A diversion in pre-detection
Two stories featuring Brendel in *Bits and pieces*, 1961

Eros series
Resnick, Mike
see **Tales of the velvet comet series**

Erotic autobiography series
Lundin, John Philip
1 *Women* (1963)
2 *Ghosts of venery* (1965)
Mistresses

Erotic memoirs series
Villefranche, Anne Marie
Translated from the French
1 *Plaisir d'amour* (1982)
2 *Joie d'amour* (1983)
3 *Folies d'amour* (1984)
Numbers 1-3 also published in one volume entitled *Menage a trois*, 1986
4 *Mystere d'amour* (1988)
5 *Secrets d'amour* (1989)

Erridge series
Stein, Aaron Marc
see **Matt Erridge series**

Erskine series
Hamilton, Mary
see **Robert Erskine series**
Pansy
see **Ruth Erskine series**

Erskine trilogy
Barbour, Ralph Henry
1 *Behind the lines* (1902)
2 *Weatherby's innings* (1903)
3 *On your mark* (1904)

Erthring cycle series
Drew, Wayland
1 *Memoirs of Alcheringia* (1984)
2 *Gaian expedient* (1985)

3 *Master of Norriya* (1986)
One volume edition entitled *The Erthring cycle*, 1986

Escape from Tenopia series
This sequence has two authors
Packard, Edward
1 *Tenopia Island* (1986)
Brightfield, Richard
2 *Trapped in the sea kingdom* (1986)
3 *Terror on Kabran* (1986)
4 *Star system Tenopia* (1986)

Escape from the Kingdom of Frome series
This sequence has two authors
Packard, Edward
1 *Castle of Frome* (1986)
Brightfield, Richard
2 *Forest of the king* (1987)
3 *Caverns of Mornas* (1987)
4 *Battle of Astar* (1987)

Escape series
Bromfield, Louis
1 *Green bay tree* (1924)
2 *Possession* (1925)
Lilli Barr
3 *Early autumn* (1926)
4 *Good woman* (1927)

Escape series
Lane, Jane
see **Stuart series**

Escape series
Neave, Airey
1 *They have their exits* (1953)
2 *Saturday at M.I.9* (1969)
A history of underground escape lines in north-west Europe in 1940-5 by a leading organiser at M.I.9

Escape to the wild wood series
Mann, Phillip
1 *Land fit for heroes* (1993)
2 *Stand alone Stan* (1994)

Escobar trilogy
O'Dell, Scott
see **Julian Escobar trilogy**

Eskimos series
Nelson, Richard King
1 *Hunters of the northern ice* (1969)
2 *Hunters of the northern forest* (1973)
Second edition 1986

Esmeralda Bloom series
Rosenthal, Lesley Sharon
1 *Misadventures of Esmeralda Bloom* (1991)
2 *Milkshakes, men and melodies* (1994)
An American affair

Esmond Ross series
Dwyer-Joyce, Alice
see **Doctor Esmond Ross series**

Esmonde Shaw series
McCutchan, Philip
see **Commander Esmonde Shaw series**

ESP McGee series
This sequence has six authors
Packard, Edward
1 *ESP McGee* (1983)
Lawrence, Jim
2 *ESP McGee and the haunted mansion* (1983)
Ernst, Kathryn Fitzgerald
3 *ESP McGee and the mysterious magician* (1983)
McMahan, Ian
4 *ESP McGee and the ghost ship* (1984)
Shea, George
5 *ESP McGee to the rescue* (1984)
Rodgers, Jesse
6 *ESP McGee and the dolphin's message* (1984)

Espie Sanchez series
Dunnahoo, Terry
1 *Who cares about Espie Sanchez?* (1976)
2 *This is Espie Sanchez* (1976)
3 *Who needs Espie Sanchez?* (1977)

Essex series
Waldron, Simon
see **Steve Essex series**

Essington Holt series
Wallace, Robert
This pseudonym is used by Robin Wallace-Crabbe for this sequence
1 *To catch a forger* (1988)
2 *Axe to grind* (1989)
3 *Paint out* (1990)
4 *Finger play* (1991)

Essington series
Clouston, Joseph Storer
see **Mister Francis Mandell-Essington series**

Estcarp series
Norton, Andre
1 *Witch World* (1963)
2 *Web of the Witch World* (1964)
3 *Three against the Witch World* (1965)
4 *Warlock of the Witch World* (1967)
5 *Sorceress of the Witch World* (1968)

Ester Ried series
Pansy
1 *Ester Ried* (1870)
Esther Reid
2 *Ester Ried, asleep and awake* (1870)
3 *Julia Ried, listening and led* (1872)
4 *Ester Ried yet speaking* (1883)
5 *Julia Ried* (1887)
6 *Ester Ried's namesake* (1906)

Esther Reid series
Pansy
see **Ester Ried series**

Etching series
Ruark, Robert
see **Grenadine Etching series**

Eternal champion trilogy
Moorcock, Michael
1 *Eternal champion* (1970)
Revised edition 1978
2 *Phoenix in obsidian* (1970)
Silver warriors
3 *Dragon in the sword* (1973)

Eternal mercenary series
Sadler, Barry
see **Casca series**

Ethan Frame Fortune series
Foster, Alan Dean
see **Icerigger series**

Ethel Hardisen and Margie Carson series
Tate, Eleanora Elaine
see **Margie Carson and Ethel Hardisen series**

Ethel Hollister series
Benson, Irene Elliott
see **Campfire Girls series**

Ethel Morton series
Smith, Mabell Shipple Clarke
1 *Ethel Morton and the Christmas ship* (1915)
2 *Ethel Morton at Chautauqua* (1915)
3 *Ethel Morton at Rose House* (1915)
4 *Ethel Morton at Sweetbriar Lodge* (1915)
5 *Ethel Morton's surprise* (1915)
6 *Ethel Morton's holidays* (1915)

Ethel Thomas series
Fitzsimmons, Cortland
1 *Whispering window* (1936)
2 *Moving finger* (1937)
3 *Mystery at Hidden Harbor* (1938)
4 *Evil men do* (1941)

Ethelbert series
Hoyland, Rosemary
1 *Ethelbert* (1954)
The tale of a tiger
2 *Ethelbert goes to the moon* (1955)
3 *Ethelbert under the sea* (1956)
4 *Ethelbert and the witch doctor* (1959)

Ethical culture series
Turner, George Reginald
1 *Beloved son* (1978)
2 *Vaneglory* (1981)
3 *Yesterday's men* (1983)

Ethnic groups in America series
Wertsman, Vladimir
1 *Romanians in America, 1748-1974* (1975)
2 *Ukrainians in America, 1608-1975* (1976)
3 *Russians in America, 1727-1970* (1977)
4 *Armenians in America, 1618-1976* (1978)
Companion volumes: *Romanians in America and Canada, a guide to information sources*, 1980, *The Ukrainians in America and Canada, a guide to information sources*, 1981

Ethshar series
Watt-Evans, Lawrence
see **Legend of Ethshar series**

Etiquette series
Stevens, William Oliver
1 *Correct thing* (1934)
A guide book of etiquette for young men
2 *Right thing* (1935)
How to be decent though modern

Eucalyptus series
Hanrahan, Barbara
1 *Scent of eucalyptus* (1973)
2 *Kewpie doll* (1984)

Eugene Gant series
Wolfe, Thomas Clayton
1 *Look homeward, angel* (1929)
2 *Of time and the river* (1935)

Eugene Mulcahy series
Street, James
1 *Death in an armchair* (1936)
2 *Carbon monixide* (1937)
3 *Wastrel goes west* (1937)

Eugenia Potter series
Rich, Virginia
see **Mrs Eugenia Potter series**

Eunice Gottlieb series
Springstubb, Tricia
1 *Which way to the nearest wilderness?* (1984)
2 *Eunice Gottlieb and the unwhitewashed truth about life* (1987)
Why can't life be a piece of cake?
3 *Eunice, the egg salad, Gottlieb* (1988)

Euphoria University series
Lodge, David
see **Rummidge University series**

Eurasian series
Bruce, Henry
1 *Eurasian* (1913)
2 *Residency* (1914)
3 *Song of surrender* (1915)
4 *Wonder Mist* (1917)
A sea story
5 *Temple girl* (1919)
6 *Bride of Shiva* (1920)

Europa series
Briffault, Robert
1 *Europa* (1936)
2 *Europa in limbo* (1937)

Eustace and Hilda Cherrington trilogy
Hartley, Leslie Poles
1 *Shrimp and the anemone* (1944)
West window
2 *Sixth heaven* (1946)
3 *Eustace and Hilda* (1947)
One volume edition entitled *Eustace and Hilda, a trilogy*, 1958

Eustace Hailey series
Wynne, Anthony
see **Doctor Eustace Hailey series**

Ev Franklin series
Orenstein, Frank
1 *Murder on Madison Avenue* (1983)
2 *Man in the gray flannel shroud* (1984)

Evacuee trilogy
Pearson, Kit
1 *Sky is falling* (1989)
2 *Looking at the moon* (1991)
3 *Lights go on again* (1993)

Evan and Claudia trilogy
Levin, Betty
see **Claudia and Evan trilogy**

Evan Pinkerton series
Frome, David
1 *Hammersmith murders* (1930)
2 *Two against Scotland Yard* (1931)
By-pass murder
3 *Man from Scotland Yard* (1932)
Mister Simpson finds a body
4 *Eel pie murders* (1933)
Eel pie mystery
5 *Mister Pinkerton goes to Scotland Yard* (1934)
Arsenic in Richmond
6 *Mister Pinkerton finds a body* (1934)
Body in the turl
7 *Mister Pinkerton grows a beard* (1935)
Body in Bedford Square
8 *Mister Pinkerton has the clue* (1936)
9 *Black envelope* (1937)
Guilt is plain
10 *Mister Pinkerton at the Old Angel* (1939)
Mister Pinkerton and the Old Angel
11 *Passage for one* (1945)
12 *Homicide House* (1950)
Murder on the square

Evan Tanner series
Block, Lawrence
1 *Thief who couldn't sleep* (1966)
2 *Canceled Czech* (1966)
3 *Tanner's twelve swingers* (1967)
4 *Two for Tanner* (1967)
5 *Tanner's tiger* (1968)
6 *Here comes a hero* (1968)
7 *Me Tanner, you Jane* (1970)

Evangeline Sinclair and Trixie Dolan series
Babson, Marian
see **Trixie Dolan and Evangeline Sinclair series**

Evans and Beddoes series
Jones, Roger William
see **Inspector Evans and Sergeant Beddoes series**

Evans series
Fannin, Cole
see **Dale Evans series**
Graham, Peter
see **Michael Evans series**
Makin, William James
see **Inspector Evans series**
Paul, Elliot
see **Homer Evans series**
Sewart, Alan
see **Detective Chief Superintendent Evans series**
Stranger, Joyce
see **Dai Evans series**
Wallace, Edgar
see **Educated Evans series**

Eve and Adam series
Twain, Mark
see **Diaries of Adam and Eve series**

Eve Drum series
Gray, Rod
see **Lady from L.U.S.T. series**

Eve Gill series
Jepson, Selwyn
1 *Man running* (1948)
Outrun the constable
Killer by proxy
2 *Golden dart* (1949)
3 *Hungry spider* (1950)
4 *Black Italian* (1954)
5 *Laughing fish* (1960)
Verdict in question
6 *Fear in the wind* (1964)
7 *Third possibility* (1965)

Eve Macwilliams series
Blizard, Marie
1 *Late, lamented lady* (1946)
2 *Men in her death* (1947)

Eve series
Fowl
Illustrated by Anne Harriet Fish
1 *First book of Eve* (1916)
2 *New Eve* (1917)
3 *Third Eve book* (1919)

Eveli series
Spyri, Johanna
Translated from the German
1 *Eveli, the little singer* (1926)
2 *Eveli and Beni* (1926)

Evelyn Innes series
Moore, George
1 *Evelyn Innes* (1898)
2 *Sister Teresa* (1901)

Evelyn Temple series
Gorell, Ronald Gorell Barnes
1 *In the night* (1917)
2 *D.E.Q.* (1922)
3 *Red lilac* (1935)

Evelyn Waugh series
Stannard, Martin
1 *Evelyn Waugh, the early years, 1903-1939* (1987)
2 *No abiding city* (1992)
Evelyn Waugh, the later years, 1939-1966

Even gods err trilogy
Gourley, Frank Alan
1 *Fresh look at creation* (1979)
2 *Social order today* (1979)
3 *Of truth as related to self and society* (1976)

Evening tales series
Blyton, Enid
1 *Five o'clock tales* (1941)
2 *Six o'clock tales* (1942)
3 *Seven o'clock tales* (1943)
4 *Eight o'clock tales* (1944)

Evenings in Albany series
Bax, Clifford
Autobiography
1 *Evenings in Albany* (1942)
2 *Rosemary for remembrance* (1948)

Eventing trilogy
Akrill, Caroline
1 *Eventer's dream* (1981)
2 *Hoof in the door* (1982)
3 *Ticket to ride* (1982)
One volume edition entitled *Eventing trilogy*, 1984

Everard Blatchington series
Cole, George Douglas Howard
1 *Blatchington tangle* (1926)
2 *Burglars in Bucks* (1930)
Berkshire mystery
3 *Death in the quarry* (1934)
4 *Scandal at school* (1935)
Sleeping death

Everard Peter Quayle series
Cheyney, Peter
1 *Stars are dark* (1943)
London spy murders
2 *Dark street* (1944)
Dark street murders
3 *Dark interlude* (1947)
Terrible night
4 *Dark wanton* (1948)
Case of the dark wanton

Everard series
Fullerton, Alexander
see **Nick Everard series**

Everest series
Fitzgerald, Ross
see **Grafton Everest series**

Everest series
Hunt, John
1 *Ascent of Everest* (1953)
2 *Our Everest adventure* (1954)
The pictorial history from Kathmandu to the summit

Everett Anderson series
Clifton, Lucille
1 *Some of the days of Everett Anderson* (1970)
2 *Everett Anderson's Christmas coming* (1971)
3 *Good, says Jerome* (1973)
4 *Everett Anderson's year* (1974)
5 *Everett Anderson's friend* (1976)
6 *Everett Anderson's one-two-three* (1977)
7 *Everett Anderson's nine month long* (1978)
8 *Everett Anderson's goodbye* (1983)

Everett Anderson series
Daiger, Katherine S
see **Inspector Everett Anderson series**

Everhard series
Steward, Paull
see **Donald Everhard series**

Eversley Family series
Ley, Alice Chetwynd
1 *Clandestine betrothal* (1967)
2 *Toast of the town* (1968)

Everyday parenting series
Goldstein, Robin
1 *Everyday parenting* (1987)
The first five years
2 *More everyday parenting* (1991)
Six to nine years old

Everyday series
Rylant, Cynthia
1 *Everyday children* (1993)
2 *Everyday garden* (1993)
3 *Everyday house* (1993)
4 *Everyday school* (1993)
5 *Everyday town* (1993)

Everyperson series
Llewellyn-Jones, Derek
1 *Everywoman* (1971)
A gynaecological guide for life; sixth edition 1993
2 *Everybody* (1978)
Revised edition 1993
3 *Every man* (1981)
Third edition 1991
4 *Everygirl* (1986)
Co-author: Suzanne Abraham; second edition 1992
5 *Everywoman's middle years* (1992)
Co-author: Suzanne Abraham

Everything you need to survive series
Stine, Jane
1 *Brothers and sisters* (1983)
2 *First dates* (1983)
3 *Homework* (1983)
4 *Money problems* (1983)

Evesham Vale series
Archer, Fred
Reminiscences of country life in the Vale of Evesham in Worcestershire
1 *Under the parish lantern* (1969)
2 *Hawthorn hedge country* (1970)
3 *Secrets of Bredon Hill* (1971)
A country chronicle of the year 1900
4 *Lad of Evesham Vale* (1972)
5 *Muddy boots and Sunday suits* (1973)
Memories of a country childhood
6 *Golden sheaves, black horses* (1974)
7 *When village bells were silent* (1975)
8 *Poacher's pie* (1976)
9 *By hook and by crook* (1978)
10 *When Adam was a boy* (1979)
11 *Fred Archer, farmer's son* (1984)
12 *Distant scene* (1967)

Evonn and Stefan series
Cooper, Margaret Chilvers
see **Stefan and Evonn series**

Ewart series
Walter, Alexia E
see **Sir Edgar Ewart series**

Ewerton series
Morlan, A R
1 *Cat with the tulip face* (1991)
2 *Amulet* (1991)
3 *Dark journey* (1991)

Ewing family series
Raintree, Lee
see **Dallas series**

Ewok series
This sequence has three authors; it is based on a television series and is a companion to the **Luke Skywalker series** and the **Star wars series**
Howe, James
1 *How the Ewoks saved the trees* (1984)
An old Ewok legend
Weinberg, Larry
2 *Wicket and the dandelion warriors* (1985)
Dubowski, Cathy East
3 *Ring, the witch and the crystal* (1986)

Exchameleon series
Goulart, Ron
1 *Daredevils, Ltd* (1987)
2 *Starpirate's brain* (1987)
3 *Everybody's come to Cosmo's* (1988)

Exchange royal series
Bowen, Marjorie
1 *Exchange royal* (1940)
2 *Today is mine* (1941)

Executioner series
Pendleton, Don
see **Mack Bolan series**

Exile series
May, Julian
see **Pliocene exile series**

Exile series
Weiss, Peter
1 *Leavetaking* (1961)
Original edition entitled *Abschied von den Eltern*
2 *Vanishing point* (1962)
Original edition entitled *Fluchtpunkt*
One volume edition entitled *Exile*, 1966

Exiles trilogy
Bova, Ben
1 *Exiled from earth* (1971)
2 *Flight of exiles* (1972)
3 *End of exile* (1975)
One volume editions entitled *Exiles*, 1978, and *The exiles trilogy*, 1980

Exitorn series
Downing, Peggy
1 *Brill and the Dragators* (1987)
2 *Segra and Stargull* (1987)
3 *Segra in Diamond Castle* (1988)
4 *Brill and the Zinders* (1988)
5 *Segra and the magician* (1989)
6 *Brill and the puffire volcano* (1989)

Exley trilogy
Exley, Frederick
see **Frederick Exley trilogy**

Exorcism series
Farmer, Philip Jose
1 *Image of the beast* (1968)
2 *Blown* (1969)
Alternative title: Sketches among the ruins of my mind; numbers 1 and 2 also published in one volume entitled *Image of the beast*, 1979
3 *Traitor to the living* (1973)

Exorcist series
Blatty, William Peter
see **Lieutenant Bill Kinderman series**

Exoterra series
McBain, Gordon
1 *Path of Exoterra* (1981)
2 *Quest of the Dawnstar* (1984)

Expatriates trilogy
Wells, Mary
1 *Expatriates* (1987)
2 *Silk king* (1987)
3 *Tycoon* (1988)

Expeditor series
Edwards, Paul
see **John Eagle series**

Expendables series
Avery, Richard
Also published under the author's real name Edmund Cooper
1 *Deathworms of Kratos* (1975)
2 *Rings of Tantalus* (1975)
3 *War games of Zelos* (1975)
4 *Venom of Argus* (1976)

Explorations series
Knights, Lionel Charles
Essays in criticism
1 *Explorations* (1946)

2 *Further explorations* (1965)
3 *Explorations III* (1976)

Explorer series
This sequence has two authors
Gaskin, Carol
1 *Journey to the center of the atom!* (1987)
McEvoy, Seth
2 *Destination brain* (1987)
3 *In search of a shark* (1987)
4 *Escape from Jupiter* (1987)

Explorers trilogy
Hogg, Garry
1 *Explorers awheel* (1938)
2 *Explorers on the wall* (1939)
3 *Explorers afloat* (1940)

Exploring our universe series
Branley, Franklyn Mansfield
1 *Nine planets* (1958)
Revised edition 1978
2 *Moon, earth's natural satellite* (1960)
Revised edition 1971
3 *Sun, star number one* (1964)
4 *Earth, planet number three* (1966)
5 *Milky Way, galaxy number one* (1969)
6 *Comets, meteoroids and asteroids, mavericks of the solar system* (1974)
7 *Black holes, white dwarfs and superstars* (1975)
8 *Electromagnetic spectrum, key to the universe* (1979)

Exploring series
Gallant, Roy Arthur
1 *Exploring the moon* (1955)
Revised edition 1966
2 *Exploring the universe* (1956)
Nature of the universe
Revised edition 1968
3 *Exploring Mars* (1956)
Revised edition 1968
4 *Exploring the weather* (1957)
Nature of the weather
Revised edition 1969
5 *Exploring the planets* (1958)
Revised edition 1967
6 *Exploring chemistry* (1958)
7 *Exploring the sun* (1958)
8 *Exploring under the earth* (1960)

Exploring the seasons series
Markle, Sandra
1 *Exploring winter* (1984)
2 *Exploring summer* (1987)

Ex-Rangers series
Miller, Jim
1 *Rangers' revenge* (1990)
2 *Long rope* (1990)
3 *Hell with the hide off* (1991)
4 *Too many drifters* (1991)
5 *Rangers re-united* (1991)
6 *Six-hundred mile stretch* (1992)
7 *Stagecoach to Fort Dodge* (1992)
8 *Shootout in Sendero* (1992)
9 *Carston's law* (1993)
10 *Stranger from nowhere* (1993)
11 *South of the border* (1993)

Ex-Superintendent Tubby Green series
Goyne, Richard
1 *Introducing the Super* (1955)
2 *Missing minx* (1957)

Extinct birds series
Eckert, Allan Wesley
Documentary novels
1 *Great auk* (1963)
Last great auk
2 *Silent sky* (1965)
The incredible extinction of the passenger pigeon

Eye of time trilogy
Darby, Lyndan
1 *Crystal and steel* (1988)
2 *Bloodseed* (1988)
3 *Phoenix fire* (1989)

Eye series
Finch, Matthew
see **Stevie O'Dowda series**

Eye series
Nunn, Judy
1 *Eye in the storm* (1988)
2 *Eye in the city* (1991)

Eyefinger series
Ball, Duncan
see **Emily Eyefinger series**

Eyes of a child series
Pugh, Edwin
1 *Eyes of a child* (1917)
2 *Secret years* (1923)

Eyes trilogy
Gordon, Stuart
1 *One-Eye* (1973)
2 *Two eyes* (1974)
3 *Three eyes* (1975)
One volume edition entitled *The eyes trilogy*, 1978

Ezekiel Rawlins series
Mosley, Walter
1 *Devil in a blue dress* (1990)
2 *Red death* (1991)
3 *White butterfly* (1992)
4 *Black Betty* (1994)

Ezekiel series
Pratt, Lucy
1 *Ezekiel* (1909)
2 *Ezekiel expands* (1914)

Ezell Barnes series
Hilary, Richard
1 *Snakes in the grass* (1987)
2 *Pieces of cream* (1987)
3 *Pillow of the community* (1988)

F

F.A.T.E. series
Kern, Gregory
see **Cap Kennedy series**

F.B.I. series
G-Man
1 *Call in the Feds* (1951)
2 *Federal agent* (1952)
3 *F.B.I. special agent* (1952)
4 *F.B.I. showdown* (1952)

F Millard Smyth series
Boyd, Eunice Mays
1 *Murder breaks trail* (1943)
2 *Doom in the midnight sun* (1944)
3 *Murder wears mukluks* (1945)

F T Carrington series
Clouston, Joseph Storer
1 *Simon* (1919)
2 *Carrington's cases* (1920)
Short stories
3 *Beastmark the spy* (1941)

F T Zevich and Claude Kirlin series
Bourgeau, Art
see **Claude Kirlin and F T Zevich series**

Faber trilogy
Sperber, Manes
see **Doino Faber trilogy**

Fabian and Cresside series
Keyes, Frances Parkinson
1 *River road* (1946)
2 *Vail d'Alvery* (1947)
One volume edition entitled *The river road*, 1945

Fabian Donoghue series
Turnbull, Peter
see **P Division series**

Fabian series
Kersh, Gerald
see **Harry Fabian series**

Fables for young and old series
Richards, Laura Elizabeth
1 *Golden windows* (1903)
2 *Silver crown* (1906)
3 *Pig brother, and other fables and stories* (1908)
4 *Naughty comet, and other fables and stories* (1910)
Revised edition 1925

Fables in slang series
Ade, George
1 *Fables in slang* (1899)
2 *More fables* (1900)

Fabri series
Prescott, Hilda Frances Margaret
see **Friar Felix Fabri series**

Fabulous Five series
Haynes, Betsy
1 *Seventh grade rumors* (1988)
2 *Trouble with flirting* (1988)
3 *Popularity trap* (1988)
4 *Her Honor, Katie Shannon* (1988)

Fabulous Five super series
Haynes, Betsy
1 *In trouble* (1990)
2 *Caribbean adventure* (1990)
3 *Missing you* (1991)
4 *Yearbook memories* (1992)

Face to face series
Mehta, Ved
Autobiography of an Indian, blind from birth
1 *Face to face* (1958)
2 *Walking the Indian streets* (1961)

Faces of terror series
Litvinoff, Samuel
1 *Death out of season* (1973)
2 *Blood on the snow* (1975)
3 *Force of terror* (1978)

Faces series
Laird, Elizabeth
1 *Faces of Britain* (1986)
2 *Faces of U.S.A.* (1987)

Facing up series
Padoan, Gianni
Illustrated by Emanuela Collini
1 *Break-up* (1987)
Facing up to divorce
2 *Remembering grandad* (1987)
Facing up to death
3 *Danger kids* (1987)
Facing up to dangers in the home
4 *Follow my leader* (1988)

Factory series
Raymond, Derek
1 *Devil's home on leave* (1985)
2 *How the dead live* (1986)
3 *Devil's home on leave* (1985)
4 *How the dead live* (1986)

Fact'ry 'ands series
Dyson, Edward
1 *Fact'ry 'ands* (1906)
2 *Benno and some of the Push* (1911)
3 *Spats' fact'ry* (1914)
Includes some stories from *Fact'ry 'ands*, 1906

Fadden series
Townsend, Edward Waterman
see **Chimmie Fadden series**

Faded sun trilogy
Cherryh, Carolyn Janice
1 *Kesrith* (1978)
2 *Shon'jir* (1978)
3 *Kutath* (1979)
One volume edition entitled *The faded sun trilogy*, 1987

Fadiman Wace series
Simons, Roger
see **Inspector Fadiman Wace series**

Fading worlds series
Gravel, Geary
1 *Key for the nonesuch* (1990)
2 *Return of the Breakneck Boys* (1991)

Faery trilogy
Macdonald, George
1 *At the back of the north wind* (1870)
2 *Princess and the goblin* (1871)
3 *Princess and Curdie* (1882)

Fafhrd and Gray Mouser series
Leiber, Fritz
1 *Swords and deviltry* (1970)
2 *Swords against death* (1970)
3 *Swords in the mist* (1968)
Numbers 1-3 also published in one volume entitled *The three of swords*, 1989
4 *Swords against wizardry* (1968)
Numbers 1, 3, 4 also published in one volume entitled *Swords' masters*, 1990
5 *Swords of Lankhmar* (1968)
6 *Swords and ice magic* (1977)
Rime isle
7 *Bazaar of the bizarre* (1978)
8 *Knight and knave of swords* (1988)
Companion volumes: *Two sought adventure*, 1957, *Lankhmar, city of adventure*, by Bruce Nesmith, Douglas Niles and Ken Rolston, 1985, *Dragonsword of Lankhmar*, by James Michael Ward, 1986, *Fafhrd and me*, by Fritz Leiber, edited by John Gregory Betancourt, 1990

Faide series
Wade, Henry
see **Major Faide series**

Failure series
Kolyer, John
Autobiography
1 *Brief biography of a failure* (1980)
2 *Twenty years before the muse* (1990)

Fair rules series
Smith, David Claude
1 *Fair rules of evil* (1989)
2 *Eyes of night* (1991)

Fairacre series
Read, *Miss*
1 *Village school* (1955)
2 *Village diary* (1957)
3 *Storm in the village* (1958)
4 *Miss Clare remembers* (1962)
5 *Over the gate* (1964)
6 *Village Christmas* (1966)
7 *Fairacre festival* (1968)
8 *Emily Davis* (1971)
9 *Tyler's Row* (1972)
10 *Farther afield* (1974)
11 *No holly for Miss Quinn* (1976)
12 *Village affairs* (1977)

13 *White robin* (1979)
14 *Village centenary* (1980)
15 *Summer at Fairacre* (1985)

Fairbanks and Marsh series
Dean, Elizabeth
see **Emma Marsh and Hank Fairbanks series**

Fairbanks of the railroad series
Chapman, Allen
see **Ralph Fairbanks of the railroad series**

Fairfax series
Austen, Jane
see **Miss Jane Fairfax series**
Norris, Kathleen
see **Rachel Fairfax series**

Fairfield series
Chapman, Allen
see **Tom Fairfield series**

Fairground family series
Daykin, Lilian
1 *Fairground family* (1962)
2 *More about the fairground family* (1964)

Fairies series
Molesworth, Mary Louisa
1 *Fairies, of sorts* (1908)
2 *Fairies afield* (1911)

Fairley family trilogy
Hocking, Mary
1 *Good daughters* (1984)
2 *Indifferent heroes* (1985)
3 *Welcome strangers* (1986)

Fairmount girls series
Baker, Etta Anthony
1 *Girls of Fairmount* (1909)
2 *Frolics at Fairmount* (1910)
3 *Fairmount girls in school and camp* (1911)
4 *Fairmount quartette* (1914)

Fairr series
Venning, Michael
see **Michael Fairr series**

Fairview boys series
Gordon, Frederick
1 *Fairview boys afloat and ashore* (1914)
Originally published as *The young Crusoes of Pine Island*, 1912
2 *Fairview boys on Eagle Mountain* (1914)
Originally published as *Sammy Brown's treasure hunt*, 1912
3 *Fairview boys and their rivals* (1914)
Originally published as *Bob Bouncer's schooldays*, 1912
4 *Fairview boys at Camp Mystery* (1914)
Alternative title: The old hermit and his secret
5 *Fairview boys at Lighthouse Cove* (1914)
Alternative title: Carried out to sea
6 *Fairview boys on a ranch* (1917)
Alternative title: Riding with the cowboys

Fairweather and Free series
Lynde, Stan
see **Pardners series**

Fairweather series
Hardwick, Mollie
see **Doran Fairweather series**

Fairwood High School series
Norton, Nancy
see **Homeroom series**

Fairyland tales series
Chisholm, Louey
1 *In Fairyland* (1904)
2 *Enchanted land* (1906)

Faith and Spirit series
Urquhart, Colin
see **Spirit and faith series**

Faith healing series
Kerin, Dorothy
1 *Living touch* (1914)
2 *Fulfilling* (1952)

Faith healing series
Macmillan, William John
1 *Prelude to healing* (1957)
2 *Reluctant healer* (1952)
Companion volume: *This is my heaven*, 1948

Faith healing trilogy
Reminiscences
Woodard, Christopher Roy
1 *Doctor heals by faith* (1953)
2 *Doctor's faith holds fast* (1955)
3 *Doctor's faith is challenged* (1957)
Companion volume: *Healing through faith*, 1973

Faith, hope and charity trilogy
Mackenzie, Compton
1 *Altar steps* (1922)
2 *Parson's progress* (1923)
3 *Heavenly ladder* (1924)

Faith Palmer series
Woolley, Lazelle Thayer
1 *Faith Palmer at the Oaks* (1912)
2 *Faith Palmer at Fordyce Hall* (1913)
3 *Faith Palmer in New York* (1914)
4 *Faith Palmer in Washington* (1915)

Falcon family series
Darby, Catherine
1 *Falcon for a witch* (1975)
2 *King's Falcon* (1975)
Game of Falcons
3 *Fortune for a Falcon* (1975)
4 *Season of the Falcon* (1976)
5 *Falcon royal* (1976)
Pride of Falcons
6 *Falcon tree* (1976)
7 *Falcon and the moon* (1976)
8 *Falcon rising* (1976)
9 *Falcon sunset* (1976)
10 *Seed of the Falcon* (1978)
11 *Falcon's claw* (1978)
12 *Falcon to the lure* (1978)

Falcon series
Benzoni, Juliette
1 *Lure of the Falcon* (1976)
Original edition entitled *Le Gerfaut des brumes*
2 *Devil's diamonds* (1978)
Original edition entitled *Un collier pour le diable*

Falcon series
Crozier, John
1 *Murder in public* (1934)
2 *Kidnapped again* (1935)

Falcon series
Drake, Drexel
1 *Falcon's prey* (1936)
2 *Falcon cuts in* (1937)
3 *Falcon meets a lady* (1938)

Falcon series
Hohl, Joan
see **Flint Falcon series**

Falcon series
Lindsey, Robert
1 *Falcon and the snowman* (1979)
True story of friendship and espionage
2 *Flight of the Falcon* (1983)

Falcon series
Smith, Mark
1 *Renegade lord* (1985)
2 *Mechanon* (1985)
3 *Rack of Baal* (1985)
4 *Lost in time* (1985)
5 *Dying sun* (1986)
6 *At the end of time* (1986)

Falcon series
Yates, Dornford
see **Superintendent Richard Falcon series**

Falcon trilogy
Ramsay, Mark
1 *Falcon strikes* (1982)
2 *Black pope* (1982)
3 *Bloody cross* (1982)

Falconbridge series
Somers, Derek
see **Major John Falconbridge series**

Falconer and Thaine trilogy
De Blasis, Celeste
see **Wild Swan trilogy**

Falconer series
Harris, John
see **Martin Falconer series**

Falconhurst series
This sequence has three authors
Onstott, Kyle
1 *Mandingo* (1957)
2 *Drum* (1962)
3 *Master of Falconhurst* (1964)
Horner, Lance
4 *Falconhurst fancy* (1966)
5 *Mustee* (1967)
6 *Heir to Falconhurst* (1968)
7 *Flight to Falconhurst* (1971)
8 *Mistress of Falconhurst* (1973)
9 *Golden stud* (1975)
Six-fingered stud
Carter, Ashley
10 *Sword of the golden stud* (1977)
11 *Taproots of Falconhurst* (1978)
12 *Scandal of Falconhurst* (1980)
13 *Road to Falconhurst* (1983)
Rogue of Falconhurst
14 *Miz Lucretia of Falconhurst* (1985)
15 *Falconhurst fugitive* (1988)
16 *Mandingo Mansa* (1986)

Falcons-Height trilogy
Le Baron, Grace
1 *Little Miss Faith* (1894)
2 *Little daughter* (1895)
3 *Rosebud Club* (1896)

Falder series
Ward, Richard Heron
see **Neil Falder series**

Fales series
Knipe, Emilie Benson
see **Little Miss Fales series**

Falkenberg's Legion series
Pournelle, Jerry
1 *Mercenary* (1977)
Short stories
2 *West of honor* (1976)
Numbers 1 and 2 also published in one volume entitled *Falkenberg's Legion*, 1990
3 *Prince of mercenaries* (1989)
Short stories
4 *Go tell the Spartans* (1991)
Co-author: Stephen Michael Stirling

Falkenstein series
Egan, Lesley
see **Jesse Falkenstein series**

Falkeyn and Van Rijn series
Anderson, Poul
see **Polesotechnic League series**

Fall of night series
This sequence has two authors
Clarke, Arthur Charles
1 *Against the fall of night* (1953)
City and the stars
The second title is a revised edition
Benford, Gregory
2 *Beyond the fall of night* (1990)
Also includes *Against the fall of night*, by Arthur Charles Clarke, 1953

Fall of the first world trilogy
Smith, David Claude
1 *Master of evil* (1983)
2 *Sorrowing vengeance* (1983)
3 *Passing of the gods* (1983)

Fall of the towers trilogy
Delany, Samuel Ray
1 *Captives of the flame* (1963)
Out of the dead city
The second title is a revised edition
2 *Towers of Toron* (1964)
Revised edition 1968
3 *City of a thousand suns* (1965)
Revised edition 1968
One volume edition entitled *Fall of the towers*, 1970

Fallon trilogy
O'Neal, Reagan
1 *Fallon blood* (1980)
2 *Fallon pride* (1981)
3 *Fallon legacy* (1982)

Family at war series
Baker, Kathleen
see **Ashton family series**

Family d'Alembert series
Smith, Edward Elmer
1 *Imperial stars* (1976)
2 *Stranglers' moon* (1976)
3 *Clockwork traitor* (1976)
4 *Getaway world* (1977)
5 *Appointment at Bloodstar* (1978)
Bloodstar conspiracy
6 *Purity plot* (1978)
7 *Planet of treachery* (1982)
8 *Eclipsing binaries* (1983)
9 *Omicron invasion* (1984)
10 *Revolt of the galaxy* (1985)

Family flight series
Hale, Edward Everett
1 *Family flight through France* (1881)
2 *Family flight over Egypt and Syria* (1882)
3 *Family life through Spain* (1883)
This volume by Susan Hale
4 *Family flight around home* (1885)
5 *Family flight through Mexico* (1886)

Family from One End Street series
Garnett, Eve
see **Ruggles family series**

Family holiday series
Babson, Marian
1 *Death swap* (1985)
2 *Trail of ashes* (1985)

Family life series
Garland, Sarah
1 *Going shopping* (1982)
2 *Doing the washing* (1983)
3 *Having a picnic* (1984)
4 *Coming to tea* (1985)

Family secrets series
Leitch, David
1 *God stand up for bastards* (1973)
2 *Family secrets* (1984)
A writer's search for his parents and his past

Family series
Blyton, Enid
see **Mike, Belinda and Ann series**

Family series
Everett-Green, Evelyn
1 *Family* (1894)
2 *Sir Reginald's ward* (1899)

Family trilogy
Carrier, Jean Guy
1 *My father's house* (1974)
Short stories
2 *Family* (1977)
3 *Cage of bone* (1978)

Family voyage series
Caldwell, John
1 *Desperate voyage* (1949)
2 *Family at sea* (1958)
Across the Pacific from Los Angeles to Sydney in a 36 foot boat

Family without a name series
Verne, Jules
1 *Leader of the resistance* (1889)
2 *Into the abyss* (1889)
Originally published in one volume entitled *Famille sans nom*

Famous adventures series
Halliburton, Richard
1 *Flying carpet* (1932)
2 *Seven league boots* (1935)
3 *Richard Halliburton* (1940)
His story of his life's adventures as told in letters to his mother and father
One volume edition entitled *The famous adventures of Richard Halliburton*, 1947

Famous Boat Club series
Optic, Oliver
see **Boat Club series**

Famous Five adventure games series
Blyton, Enid
1 *Haunted railway game* (1984)
Based on *Five go off to camp*, 1948
2 *Wrecker's Tower game* (1984)
Based on *Five go down to the sea*, 1953
3 *Whispering Island game* (1985)
Based on *Five have a mystery to solve*, 1962
4 *Sinister Lake game* (1985)
Based on *Five on a hike together*, 1951
5 *Wailing lighthouse game* (1986)
Based on *Five go to Demon Rocks*, 1961
6 *Secret airfield game* (1986)
Based on *Five go to Billycock Hill*, 1957
7 *Shuddering Mountain game* (1988)
Based on *Five get into a fix*, 1958
8 *Missing scientist game* (1988)
Based on *Five have a wonderful time*, 1952

Famous Five and you series
Danby, Mary
1 *Search for treasure!* (1987)
Based on *Five on a treasure island*, by Enid Blyton, 1942
2 *Find adventure!* (1987)
Based on *Five go adventuring again*, by Enid Blyton, 1943
3 *Run away!* (1988)
Based on *Five run away together*, by Enid Blyton, 1944
4 *Search for smugglers!* (1988)
Based on *Five go to Smuggler's Top*, by Enid Blyton, 1945
5 *Take off!* (1989)
Based on *Five go off in a caravan*, by Enid Blyton, 1946
6 *Underground!* (1989)
Based on *Five on Kirrin Island again*, by Enid Blyton, 1947

Famous Five series
Blyton, Enid
1 *Five on a treasure island* (1942)
2 *Five go adventuring again* (1943)
Five find a secret way
Numbers 1-2 also published in one volume entitled *Famous Five bumper double*, 1986
3 *Five run away together* (1944)
Five run away to danger
4 *Five go to Smugglers' Top* (1945)
5 *Five go off in a caravan* (1946)
6 *Five on Kirrin Island again* (1947)
7 *Five go off to camp* (1948)
Five on the track of a spook train
8 *Five get into trouble* (1949)
Five caught in a treacherous plot
9 *Five fall into adventure* (1950)
10 *Five on a hike together* (1951)
Numbers 8-10 also published in one volume entitled *Fabulous Famous Five*, 1974
11 *Five have a wonderful time* (1952)
12 *Five go down to the sea* (1953)
13 *Five go to Mystery Moor* (1954)
14 *Five have plenty of fun* (1955)
15 *Five on a secret trail* (1956)
16 *Five go to Billycock Hill* (1957)
17 *Five get into a fix* (1958)
18 *Five on Finniston Farm* (1960)
19 *Five go to Demon Rocks* (1961)
20 *Five have a mystery to solve* (1962)
21 *Five are together again* (1963)
Continued by **Famous Five television series**

Famous Five television series
Voilier, Charles
1 *Famous Five and the Stately Homes Gang* (1981)
Original edition entitled *Les marquis appelle Les Cinq*
2 *Famous Five and the mystery of the emeralds* (1981)
Original edition entitled *Les Cinq sont les plus forts*
3 *Famous Five go on television* (1981)
Original edition entitled *Les Cinq a la television*
4 *Famous Five and the missing cheetah* (1981)
Original edition entitled *Les Cinq au Cap des Tempetes*
5 *Famous Five and the golden galleon* (1982)
Original edition entitled *Les Cinq et la galion d'or*
6 *Famous Five versus the Black Mask* (1982)
Original edition entitled *Les Cinq contre le Masque Noir*
7 *Famous Five in fancy dress* (1983)
Original edition entitled *Les Cinq au bal des espions*
8 *Famous Five and the blue bear mystery* (1983)
Original edition entitled *Les Cinq vendent la peau de l'ours*
9 *Famous Five and the cavalier's treasure* (1984)
Original edition entitled *La fortune sourit aux Cinq*
10 *Famous Five and the Inca god* (1984)
Original edition entitled *Les Cinq font de la brocante*
11 *Famous Five and the secret of the caves* (1984)
Original edition entitled *Les Cinq dans la cite secrete*
12 *Famous Five and the strange legacy* (1984)
Original edition entitled *Du neuf pour Les Cinq*
13 *Famous Five and the strange scientist* (1985)
Original edition entitled *Les Cinq jouent serre*
14 *Famous Five and the hijackers* (1985)
Original edition entitled *Les Cinq et les pirates du ciel*
15 *Famous Five and the knights' treasure* (1986)
Original edition entitled *Les Cinq et le tresor de Roquepine*
16 *Famous Five in deadly danger* (1986)
Original edition entitled *Les Cinq aux rendezvous du Diable*
17 *Famous Five and the pink pearls* (1987)
Original edition entitled *Les Cinq se mettent en quatre*
18 *Famous Five and the Z-rays* (1987)
Original edition entitled *Les Cinq et le rayon Z*

Famous last words series
Green, Jonathon
1 *Famous last words* (1979)
2 *Don't quote me* (1981)
Co-author: Don Atyeo

Fancy Free and Footloose Fairweather series
Lynde, Stan
see **Pardners series**

Fancy Hatch series
Hawkes, Zachary
1 *Fancy Hatch* (1984)
2 *Case deuce* (1984)
3 *Solomon King's mine* (1984)
4 *Odds against Sundown* (1985)

Fane and Darling series
Yardley, James
see **Kiss Darling and Angus Fane series**

Fane brothers series
Halliday, Michael
see **Martin and Richard Fane series**

Fang Mulheisen series
Jackson, Jon Anthony
see **Sergeant Fang Mulheisen series**

Fang series
Daniel, Roland
see **Wu Fang series**
Perry, Ritchie
see **Fenella Fang series**

Fanglith series
Dalmas, John
1 *Fanglith* (1985)
2 *Return to Fanglith* (1987)

Fanina series
Sabbagh, Pierre
1 *Fanina* (1965)
Original edition entitled *Fanina*
2 *Fanina, child of Rome* (1966)
Original edition entitled *Fanina, face au destin*

Fanks series
Hume, Fergus
see **Octavius Fanks series**

Fannin series
Markson, David
see **Harry Fannin series**

Fanny series
Lively, Penelope
1 *Fanny's sister* (1976)
2 *Fanny and the monsters* (1978)
3 *Fanny and the battle of Potter's Place* (1980)

Fanny Witch series
Strong, Jeremy
1 *Fanny Witch and the Bosnatch* (1985)
2 *Fanny Witch and the thunder lizard* (1987)

Fanshaw and Browne series
Poole, Michael
see **Freddie Browne and Jim Fanshaw series**

Fansler series
Cross, Amanda
see **Professor Kate Fansler series**

Fantastic voyage series
Asimov, Isaac
1 *Fantastic voyage* (1966)
2 *Destination brain* (1987)

Fantasy forest series
This sequence has nine authors
Ward, James Michael
1 *Ring, the sword and the unicorn* (1983)
Carr, Mike
2 *Ruins of Rangar* (1983)
Gray, Michael
3 *Shadowcastle* (1983)
Carr, Mike
4 *Keep of the ancient king* (1983)
Kendall, John
5 *Dungeon of darkness* (1984)
Blashfield, Jean
6 *Star rangers and the spy* (1984)
Simon, Morris
7 *Castle in the clouds* (1984)
Charette, Beverly
8 *Star rangers meet the solar robot* (1984)
Moore, Roger Elwood
9 *Jason's first quest* (1984)
Gray, Michael
10 *Lost wizard* (1984)

Fantasy illustrations series
Achilleos, Chris
1 *Beauty and the beast* (1978)
2 *Sirens* (1986)
3 *Medusa* (1988)

Fantasy quest book series
Fickling, David
Adventure game books
1 *Path of peril* (1984)
2 *Starflight zero* (1985)
3 *Helmquist* (1986)
4 *Ten doors of doom* (1987)

Fantazius Mallare series
Hecht, Ben
1 *Fantazius Mallare* (1922)
A mysterious oath
2 *Kingdom of evil* (1924)

Fantom series
Underhill, Charles
see **Captain Fantom series**

Fantomas series
This sequence has two authors; translated from the French
Souvestre, Pierre
1 *Fantomas* (1915)
2 *Exploits of Juve* (1916)
3 *Messengers of evil* (1917)
4 *Nest of spies* (1917)
5 *Royal prisoner* (1918)
6 *Slippery as sin* (1920)
Allain, Marcel
7 *Yellow document* (1919)
Souvestre, Pierre
8 *Limb of Satan* (1924)
Long arm of Fantomas
Allain, Marcel
9 *Lord or Terror* (1925)
10 *Juve in the dock* (1925)

11 *Fantomas recaptured* (1926)
12 *Revenge of Fontomas* (1927)
13 *Bulldog and Rats* (1928)

Far East series
Leasor, James
1 *Follow the drum* (1972)
2 *Mandarin-gold* (1973)
3 *Chinese widow* (1975)
4 *Jade gate* (1976)

Far East trilogy
Becker, Stephen
1 *Chinese bandit* (1975)
2 *Last mandarin* (1979)
3 *Blue-eyed Shan* (1982)

Far memory series
Grant, Joan
Based on the author's recollections of previous lives
1 *Life as Carola* (1939)
2 *Scarlet feather* (1945)
3 *Return to Elysium* (1947)
4 *So Moses was born* (1952)
Companion volume: *Time out of mind*, 1956

Far pavilions series
Cooper, Leo
Anecdotes about cricket
1 *Tales from far pavilions* (1984)
2 *Beyond the far pavilions* (1986)

Far Side series
Larson, Gary
Comic strips
1 *Far Side* (1982)
2 *Beyond the Far Side* (1983)
3 *In search of the Far Side* (1984)
4 *Bride of the Far Side* (1985)
5 *Valley of the Far Side* (1985)
6 *It came from the Far Side* (1986)
7 *Far Side observer* (1987)
8 *Hound of the Far Side* (1987)
9 *Night of the crash-test dummies* (1988)
10 *Wildlife preserves* (1989)
11 *Wiener dog art* (1990)
12 *Unnatural selections* (1991)
13 *Cows of our planet* (1992)
14 *Chickens are restless* (1993)
Companion volumes: *Far Side gallery*, no 1, 1984, no 2, 1986, no 3, 1988, no 4, 1993, *The prehistory of the Far Side*, 1989

Far stars and future times series
McEnroe, Richard S
1 *Shattered stars* (1984)
2 *Flight of honour* (1984)
3 *Skinner* (1985)

Faradawn trilogy
Ford, Richard
1 *Quest for the Faradawn* (1982)
2 *Melvaig's vision* (1984)
3 *Children of Ashgaroth* (1986)

Faraday series
Copper, Basil
see **Mike Faraday series**
Grant, William
see **Matthew Faraday series**
Pertwee, Roland
see **Patrick Faraday series**

Faraway tree series
Blyton, Enid
1 *Enchanted wood* (1939)
2 *Magic faraway tree* (1943)
3 *Folk of the faraway tree* (1946)
4 *Up the faraway tree* (1951)

Fardingdales series
Brent-Dyer, Elinor Mary
1 *Fardingales* (1950)
2 *Susannah adventure* (1953)

Farewell innocence series
Glynne-Jones, William
1 *Farewell innocence* (1950)
2 *Ride the white stallion* (1951)

Far-fetched pets series
Hamsa, Bobbie
1 *Your pet bear* (1980)
2 *Your pet beaver* (1980)
3 *Your pet elephant* (1980)
4 *Your pet camel* (1980)
5 *Your pet kangaroo* (1980)
6 *Your pet camel* (1980)
7 *Your pet gorilla* (1981)
8 *Your pet lion* (1981)
9 *Your pet giraffe* (1982)
10 *Your pet sea lion* (1982)

Fargo series
Benteen, John
see **Neal Fargo series**
Sharpe, Jon
see **Trailsman series**

Farm boy series
Mauzey, Merritt
1 *Cotton-farm boy* (1954)
2 *Texas ranch boy* (1955)
3 *Oilfield boy* (1957)
4 *Rice boy* (1958)
5 *Rubber boy* (1962)
6 *Salt boy* (1964)

Farm life series
Evans, George Ewart
1 *Ask the fellows who cut the hay* (1956)
2 *Horse in the furrow* (1960)
3 *Pattern under the plough* (1966)
4 *Farm and the village* (1969)
Aspects of folk life in East Anglia
Companion volume: *Where beards wag all*, 1970

Farm life series
Holgate, John
1 *Make a cow laugh* (1979)
A first year in farming
2 *On a pig's back* (1979)
Life on a small farm
3 *Sheep's eye view* (1979)

Farm poems series
Kherdian, David
Poetry
1 *Farm* (1979)
2 *Farm, book two* (1982)
3 *Threads of light* (1985)

Farm series
Haigh, Richard
1 *Farm* (1984)
2 *City* (1986)

Farm servant trilogy
Anstruther, Eileen Harriet
1 *Farm servant* (1916)
2 *Husband* (1919)
3 *Five in family* (1924)

Farmer Barnes series
Cunliffe, John Arthur
1 *Farmer Barnes buys a pig* (1964)
2 *Farmer Barnes and bluebell* (1966)
3 *Farmer Barnes at the country show* (1969)
Farmer Barnes at the country fair
4 *Farmer Barnes and the goats* (1971)
5 *Farmer Barnes goes fishing* (1972)
6 *Farmer Barnes and the snow picnic* (1974)
7 *Farmer Barnes fells a tree* (1977)
8 *Farmer Barnes and the harvest doll* (1977)
9 *Farmer Barnes' Guy Fawkes Day* (1978)

Farmer Beans series
Moffatt, Frank
1 *Farmer Beans and the pantry frog* (1988)
2 *Farmer Beans and the baby wallaby* (1991)

Farmer's creed trilogy
Porteous, Crichton
Autobiography
1 *Farmer's creed* (1938)
2 *Teamsman* (1939)
3 *Land truant* (1940)

Farming series
Donaldson, Frances Annesley
1 *Approach to farming* (1941)
2 *Four year's harvest* (1945)

Farmyard Cat series
Anello, Christine
Illustrated by Sharon Thompson
1 *Farmyard Cat* (1987)
2 *Farmyard Cat in trouble* (1993)

Farne series
Butler, Richard
see **Max Farne series**

Faro Blake series
Masters, Zeke
This pseudonym is used by several authors including Donald R Bensen and Ron Goulart whose authorship is indicated where it is known
1 *Big gamble* (1980)
[Bensen]
2 *Luck of the draw* (1980)
[Bensen]
3 *Threes are wild* (1980)
[Bensen]
4 *Diamond flush* (1981)
5 *Riverboat showdown* (1981)
[Bensen]
6 *Four of a kind* (1981)
[Bensen]
7 *Bottom deal* (1981)
8 *Ace in the hole* (1981)
[Bensen]
9 *Boomtown bustout* (1981)
10 *Mexican standoff* (1981)
[Bensen]
11 *Six-gun poker* (1981)
12 *Devil's jackpot* (1982)
13 *Fast shuffle* (1982)
[Bensen]
14 *Full house* (1982)
15 *Place your bets* (1982)
16 *Stacked deck* (1982)
[Bensen]
17 *Sucker bet* (1982)
18 *High card* (1982)
[Goulart]
19 *Call the turn* (1982)
20 *Inside straight* (1982)
21 *Deuces to open* (1982)
[Bensen]
22 *Loaded dice* (1982)
23 *Long odds* (1982)
[Bensen]
24 *Stagg night* (1982)
25 *Close to the vest* (1983)
[Bensen]
26 *Texas two-step* (1983)
27 *Down and dirty* (1983)
28 *Cashing in* (1983)
29 *Double or nothing* (1983)
30 *Devil's gambit* (1983)
31 *Up for grabs* (1983)

Faro series
Knight, Alanna
see **Inspector Faro series**

Farraday series
Caraker, Mary
see **Seven worlds series**

Farrant series
Gorell, Ronald Gorell Barnes
see **Harry Farrant series**
Larbalestier, Philip George
see **Inspector Michael Farrant series**

Farrar family series
Barne, Kitty
1 *Family footlights* (1939)
2 *Visitors from London* (1940)
3 *Dusty's windmill* (1949)
Windmill mystery

Farrel series
Brown, Carter
see **Mike Farrel series**
Hitchens, Dolores
see **John Farrel series**

Farrell series
Comstock, Jarrod
see **These lawless worlds series**
Mazzaro, Ed
see **Undercover series**

Farrow series
Ross, Angus
see **Mark Farrow series**

Farside of forever series
Green, Sharon
1 *Far side of forever* (1987)
2 *Hellbound magic* (1989)

Farstar and son series
Starr, Bill
1 *Way to Dawnworld* (1975)
2 *Treasure of Wonderwhat* (1976)

Farthing family series
Dodd, Catherine Isabel
1 *Farthing spinster* (1925)
2 *Queen Anne Farthings* (1928)

Farthing family series
Graveson, Caroline Cassandra
1 *Farthing family* (1950)
A story of London life in the seventeenth century
2 *London to Philadelphia* (1954)
A story of a Quaker family, 1670-1689

Farthing family trilogy
Gardner, John Edmund
see **Secret generations trilogy**

Farthing Wood series
Dann, Colin
1 *Animals of Farthing Wood* (1979)
2 *In the grip of winter* (1981)
3 *Fox's feud* (1982)
4 *Fox cub bold* (1982)
5 *Ram of Sweetriver* (1986)
6 *In the path of the storm* (1989)

Farthingale series
Gervaise, Mary
1 *Fireworks at Farthingale* (1954)
2 *Farthingale fete* (1955)
3 *Farthingale feud* (1957)
4 *Farthingale find* (1961)

Fashion features series
James, Judi
1 *First assignment* (1987)
2 *Double page spread* (1987)
3 *Features editor* (1987)

Fast Eddie Felson series
Tevis, Walter Stone
see **Hustler series**

Fast Lady and Gentleman series
Howard, Keble
1 *Fast Lady* (1925)
A tale of a motoring honeymoon
2 *Fast Gentleman* (1928)
A tale of the Norfolk Broads

Fat Albert series
Levy, Elizabeth
Based on a television series
1 *Shuttered window* (1981)
2 *Mister Big Time* (1981)
3 *Take two, they're small* (1981)
4 *Spare the rod* (1981)
5 *Mom or pop* (1981)
6 *Runt* (1981)

Fat Glenda series
Perle, Lila
1 *Me and Fat* (1972)
2 *Hey, remember Fat Glenda?* (1972)
3 *Fat Glenda's summer romance* (1981)

Fat of the land series
Seymour, John
Life as a farmer in Suffolk and Africa
1 *Fat of the land* (1961)
2 *On my own terms* (1963)
Revised edition 1980

Fatal gesture series
Foote, John Taintor
1 *Fatal gesture* (1933)
2 *Daughter of Delilah* (1936)

FATE series
Kern, Gregory
see **Cap Kennedy series**

Fate trilogy
Hugo, Victor Marie
1 *Les miserables* (1862)
Original edition entitled *Les miserables*
1.1 *Fantine* (1862)
1.2 *Cosette and Marius* (1862)
1.3 *Rue Plumet* (1862)
1.4 *Jean Valjean* (1862)
2 *Toilers of the sea* (1866)
Original edition entitled *Travailleurs de la mer*
3 *Notre Dame de Paris* (1830)
Original edition entitled *Notre Dame de Paris*

Fateful years trilogy
Dalton, Hugh
Autobiography
1 *Call back yesterday* (1953)
2 *Fateful years* (1957)
3 *High tide and after* (1962)

Father and Mother Goose series
Baum, Lyman Frank
see **Mother and Father Goose series**

Father and mother series
Bloom, Ursula
Biographies of the author's father and mother
1 *Parson extraordinary* (1963)
2 *Price above rubies* (1965)

Father Anton Dymek series
Riley, Frank
1 *Kocska formula* (1971)
2 *Jesus II* (1972)

Father Blackie Ryan series
Greeley, Andrew Moran
see **Monsignor John Blackwood Ryan series**

Father Brown series
Chesterton, Gilbert Keith
Short stories
1 *Innocence of Father Brown* (1911)
Annotated Innocence of Father Brown
2 *Wisdom of Father Brown* (1914)
3 *Incredulity of Father Brown* (1926)
4 *Secret of Father Brown* (1927)
5 *Scandal of Father Brown* (1935)
Omnibus volumes: *Father Brown, selected stories*, 1955, *The Father Brown omnibus*, 1983, *The best of Father Brown*, 1987

Father Charles Duddleswell series
Boyd, Neil
1 *Bless me, father* (1977)
2 *Father before Christmas* (1978)
3 *Father in a fix* (1979)
4 *Father under fire* (1980)
5 *Bless me again, father* (1981)

Father Christmas series
Briggs, Raymond
1 *Father Christmas* (1973)
2 *Father Christmas goes on holiday* (1975)
One volume edition entitled *The complete Father Christmas*, 1978

Father figures series
Martin, Kingsley
1 *Father figures* (1966)
Evolution of an editor, 1897-1931
2 *Editor* (1968)
Reminiscences of the editor of *New Statesman*, 1931-1945

Father Fox series
Watson, Clyde
Rhymes
1 *Father Fox's pennyrhymes* (1971)
2 *Catch me and kiss me and say it again* (1978)
Selections published as *Father Fox's feast of songs, musical adaptations*, 1983

Father Goose series
Mortimer, Chapman
1 *Father Goose* (1951)
2 *Mediterraneo* (1955)

Father Hayes trilogy
Leslie, Peter
1 *Father Hayes* (1976)
2 *Steeds of Satan* (1976)
3 *Holy spirit* (1977)

Father John Murphy series
This sequence has two authors; it is based on a character from the **Little house on the prairie television series**
Weinberg, Larry
1 *Father Murphy's promise* (1982)
Levy, Elizabeth
2 *Father Murphy's first miracle* (1983)

Father Joseph Bredder series
Holton, Leonard
1 *Saint maker* (1959)
2 *Pact with Satan* (1960)
3 *Secret of the doubting saint* (1961)
4 *Deliver us from wolves* (1963)
5 *Flowers by request* (1964)
6 *Out of the depths* (1966)
7 *Touch of Jonah* (1968)
8 *Problem in angels* (1970)
9 *Mirror of hell* (1972)
10 *Devil to play* (1974)
11 *Corner of paradise* (1977)

Father Joseph Shanley and Sammy Golden series
Webb, Jack
1 *Big sin* (1952)
2 *Naked angel* (1953)
Such women are dangerous
3 *Damned lovely* (1954)
4 *Broken doll* (1955)
5 *Bad blonde* (1956)
6 *Brass halo* (1957)
7 *Deadly sex* (1959)
8 *Delicate darling* (1959)
9 *Gilded witch* (1963)

Father Keogh series
Lindop, Audrey Erskine
1 *Singer not the song* (1953)
Bandit and the priest
2 *Judas figures* (1956)

Father Koala series
Richards, Kel
1 *Father Koala's nursery rhymes* (1992)
2 *Father Koala's fables* (1993)

Father Lascaut series
Jones, Lawrence Evelyn
1 *Trepidation in Downing Street* (1962)
2 *Father Lascaut hits back* (1964)

Father Robert Koesler series
Kienzle, William Xavier
1 *Rosary murders* (1979)
2 *Death wears a red hat* (1980)
3 *Mind over murder* (1981)
4 *Assault with intent* (1982)
5 *Shadow of death* (1983)
6 *Kill and tell* (1984)
7 *Sudden death* (1985)
8 *Deathbed* (1986)
9 *Deadline for a critic* (1987)
10 *Marked for murder* (1988)
11 *Eminence* (1989)
12 *Masquerade* (1990)
13 *Chameleon* (1991)
14 *Body count* (1992)
15 *Dead wrong* (1993)
16 *Bishop as pawn* (1994)

Father Roger Dowling series
McInerny, Ralph
1 *Her death of cold* (1977)
2 *Seventh station* (1977)
3 *Bishop as pawn* (1978)
4 *Lying three* (1979)
5 *Second vespers* (1980)
6 *Thicker than water* (1981)
7 *Loss of patients* (1982)
8 *Grass widow* (1983)
9 *Getting a way with murder* (1984)
10 *Rest in pieces* (1985)
11 *Basket case* (1987)
12 *Abracadaver* (1989)
Sleight of body
13 *Four on the floor* (1989)
Short stories
14 *Judas Priest* (1991)
15 *Desert sinner* (1992)
16 *Seed of doubt* (1993)

Father's and Mother's Day series
Sharmat, Marjorie Weinman
see **Mother's and Father's Day series**

Fathers series
Smith, Daniel Wybert
see **Chief Inspector Harry Fathers series**

Fatty series
Blyton, Enid
1 *Mystery of the burnt cottage* (1943)
2 *Mystery of the disappearing cat* (1944)
3 *Mystery of the secret room* (1945)
4 *Mystery of the spiteful letters* (1946)
5 *Mystery of the missing necklace* (1947)
6 *Mystery of the hidden house* (1948)
7 *Mystery of the pantomime cat* (1949)
8 *Mystery of the invisible thief* (1950)
9 *Mystery of the vanished prince* (1951)
10 *Mystery of the strange bundle* (1952)
11 *Mystery of Holly Lane* (1953)
12 *Mystery of Tally-Ho Cottage* (1954)
13 *Mystery of the missing man* (1956)
14 *Mystery of the strange messages* (1957)
15 *Mystery of Banshee Towers* (1961)
16 *Mystery that never was* (1961)

Faulkner series
Snell, Edmund
see **Reggie Faulkner series**

Faust series
Butler, Eliza Marian
A study of the Faust legend
1 *Myth of the magus* (1948)
2 *Ritual magic* (1949)
3 *Fortunes of Faust* (1952)

Faustus hexagram series
Broderick, Damien
1 *Judas mandala* (1982)
2 *Black grail* (1985)
Based on *Sorcerer's world*, 1970
3 *Dreaming dragons* (1980)
4 *Transmitters* (1984)
5 *Striped holes* (1988)

Faustus series
Faustus, Johann
see **Doctor Johann Faustus series**

Favian Markham series
Williams, Jon
see **Privateers and gentlemen series**

Fax Pack series
Pearce, Colin
1 *Date can be deadly* (1993)
2 *Never trust a friend* (1993)
3 *People can be animals* (1993)

Fay trilogy
Dell, Floyd
see **Felix Fay trilogy**

Faye Boswell series
Douglas, Felicity
1 *Within these walls* (1975)
2 *Governor* (1975)

Faye's folly series
Corbett, Elizabeth
1 *Faye's folly* (1941)
2 *Early summer* (1942)

Fear God and dread nought trilogy
Fisher, John Arbuthnot
Correspondence
1 *Making of an admiral, 1854-1904* (1952)
2 *Years of power, 1904-1914* (1956)
3 *Restoration, abdication and last years, 1914-1920* (1959)

Fear Street cheerleaders series
Stine, Robert Lawrence
1 *First evil* (1992)
2 *Second evil* (1992)
3 *Third evil* (1992)
4 *New evil* (1994)

Fear Street number ninety-nine series
Stine, Robert Lawrence
see **Ninety-nine Fear Street series**

Fear Street saga series
Stine, Robert Lawrence
1 *Betrayal* (1993)
2 *Secret* (1993)
3 *Burning* (1993)

Fear Street series
Stine, Robert Lawrence
1 *New girl* (1989)
2 *Wrong number* (1990)
3 *Missing* (1990)
4 *Halloween party* (1990)
5 *Surprise party* (1990)
6 *Stepsister* (1990)
7 *Ski weekend* (1991)
8 *Fire game* (1991)
9 *Lights out* (1991)
10 *Overnight* (1991)
11 *Haunted* (1991)

12 *Sleepwalker* (1991)
13 *Secret bedroom* (1991)
14 *Knife* (1992)
15 *Prom queen* (1992)
16 *First date* (1992)
17 *Best friend* (1992)
18 *Cheater* (1993)
19 *Sunburn* (1993)
20 *New boy* (1994)
21 *Dare* (1994)
22 *Bad dreams* (1994)
23 *Double date* (1994)
24 *Thrill club* (1994)
25 *One evil summer* (1994)
26 *Mind reader* (1994)

Fear Street super chiller series
Stine, Robert Lawrence
1 *Party summer* (1991)
2 *Silent night* (1991)
3 *Goodnight kiss* (1992)
4 *Broken hearts* (1993)
5 *Silent night 2* (1992)
6 *Dead lifeguard* (1994)

Fearless Freddy series
Gascoigne, Bamber
1 *Fearless Freddy's sunken treasure* (1982)
2 *Fearless Freddy's magic wish* (1982)

Fearless series
Rockwood, Roy
see **Dave Fearless series**

Fears series
Mayer, Mercer
1 *There's a nightmare in my closet* (1968)
There's a nightmare in my cupboard
2 *There's an alligator under my bed* (1987)

Fearsome series
Miller, Margaret Jessy
1 *Fearsome road* (1974)
2 *Fearsome island* (1975)
3 *Fearsome tide* (1976)

Feast of the animals series
Nickerson, Sheila Bunker
Illustrated by Dale De Armond
Alaskan bestiary in verse
1 *Feast of the animals* (1987)
2 *Feast of the animals II* (1991)

Feather Town series
Martin, Ann Matthews
1 *Fancy dance in Feather Town* (1988)
2 *Moving day in Feather Town* (1989)

Feathergrant series
Kenyon, Theda
see **Staceys of Feathergrant series**

Fedora
Cory, Desmond
see **Johnny Fedora series**

Feeley series
Lasswell, Mary
see **Mrs Feeley series**

Feelings series
Leonard, Marcia
Illustrated by Wendy Watson
1 *Angry* (1988)
2 *Happy* (1988)
3 *Scared* (1988)
4 *Silly* (1988)

Feeney family series
Kelly, Sheelagh
1 *Long way from heaven* (1985)
2 *For my brother's sins* (1986)
3 *Erin's child* (1987)

Feet first series
Matthews, Stanley
Memoirs
1 *Feet first* (1948)
2 *Feet first again* (1955)

Feet series
Weir, Molly
Autobiography of a radio broadcaster from Glasgow
1 *Shoes were for Sunday* (1970)
2 *Best foot forward* (1972)
3 *Toe on the ladder* (1973)
Numbers 1-3 also published in one volume entitled *Molly Weir's trilogy of Scottish childhood*, 1988
4 *Stepping into the spotlight* (1975)
5 *Walking into the Lyons' den* (1977)
6 *One small footprint* (1980)
7 *Spinning like a peerie* (1983)

Feiffer series
Marshall, William Leonard
see **Yellowthread Street series**

Feighan series
O'Donnell, Kevin
see **Journeys of McGill Feighan series**

Feilmar family series
Prior, Loveday
1 *Law unto themselves* (1934)
2 *Valley of exile* (1939)
3 *These times of travail* (1941)

Fein series
Bethancourt, Tomas Ernesto
see **Doris Fein series**

Felan series
Prior, Ann
1 *Sky cage* (1967)
2 *Mirror image* (1969)

Felicia Cartwright series
Palmer, Bernard
1 *Felicia Cartwright and the frantic search* (1958)
2 *Felicia Cartwright and the missing sideboard* (1958)
3 *Felicia Cartwright and the green medallion* (1958)
4 *Felicia Cartwright and the uncut diamond* (1958)
5 *Felicia Cartwright and the case of the twisted key* (1959)
6 *Felicia Cartwright and the case of the frightened student* (1959)
7 *Felicia Cartwright and the case of the lonely teacher* (1960)
8 *Felicia Cartwright and the case of the dancing fire* (1960)
9 *Felicia Cartwright and the case of the troubled rancher* (1961)
10 *Felicia Cartwright and the case of the storm scarred mountain* (1961)
11 *Felicia Cartwright and the case of the hungry fiddler* (1962)
12 *Felicia Cartwright and the case of the antique bookmark* (1963)
13 *Felicia Cartwright and the case of the lost puppy* (1965)
14 *Felicia Cartwright and the case of the knotted wire* (1966)
15 *Felicia Cartwright and the case of the honorable traitor* (1967)
16 *Felicia Cartwright and the case of the black phantom* (1968)
17 *Felicia Cartwright and the case of the lonely ski boot* (1969)
18 *Felicia Cartwright and the case of the bad-eyed girl* (1970)
19 *Felicia Cartwright and the case of the pink poodle* (1970)

Felicia series
Gould, Elizabeth Lincoln
1 *Felicia* (1908)
2 *Felicia's friends* (1909)
3 *Felicia's visits* (1910)
4 *Felicia's folks* (1911)

Feliciana series
Young, Stark
1 *So red the rose* (1934)
2 *Feliciana* (1935)

Felicity and Jonathan series
Cockett, Mary
see **Jonathan and Felicity series**

Felicity series
Tripp, Valerie
1 *Meet Felicity, an American girl* (1991)
2 *Felicity learns a lesson* (1991)
A school story
3 *Felicity's surprise* (1991)
A Christmas story
4 *Happy birthday, Felicity!* (1992)
A springtime story
5 *Changes for Felicity* (1992)
A winter story
6 *Felicity saves the day* (1992)
A summer story

Felicity Travers series
Deighton, Barbara
1 *Little learning* (1988)
2 *Good intentions* (1988)

Felidae series
Pirincci, Akif
Translated from the German
1 *Felidae* (1993)
2 *Felidae on the road* (1994)

Felimid Mac Fal series
Taylor, Keith
see **Bard series**

Felita series
Mohr, Nicholasa
1 *Felita* (1979)
2 *Going home* (1986)

Felix and Virginia Freer series
Ferrars, Elizabeth
see **Virginia and Felix Freer series**

Felix Boyd series
Campbell, Scott
1 *Below the dead-line* (1906)
2 *On the trail of Big Finger Street* (1906)
3 *Exploits of a private detective* (1909)
Short stories
4 *Adventures of felix Boyd* (1909)
Short stories
5 *Felix Boyd's revelations* (1909)
Short stories
6 *Felix Boyd's final problems* (1909)
Short stories

Felix Brooke series
Aiken, Joan
1 *Go saddle the sea* (1977)
2 *Bridle the wind* (1983)
3 *Teeth of the gale* (1988)

Felix Charlock series
Durrell, Lawrence
see **Revolt of Aphrodite series**

Felix Elizalde series
Marshall, William Leonard
see **Battling Mendez series**

Felix Fabri series
Prescott, Hilda Frances Margaret
see **Friar Felix Fabri series**

Felix Fay trilogy
Dell, Floyd
1 *Moon-Calf* (1920)
2 *Briary-bush* (1922)
3 *Souvenir* (1930)

Felix Heron series
Verner, Gerald
1 *Tudor garden mystery* (1966)
2 *Dead secret* (1967)

Felix Holliday series
Jones, Arthur E
1 *You know the way it is* (1956)
2 *Too dead to talk* (1957)
3 *It makes you think* (1958)

Felix series
Ford, Hilary
1 *Felix walking* (1958)
2 *Felix running* (1959)

Felix series
Kernahan, Jeannie Gwynne
1 *Devastation* (1904)
2 *Fate of Felix* (1905)

Fell Farm series
Lloyd, Marjorie
1 *Fell Farm holiday* (1951)
2 *Fell Farm for Christmas* (1954)
3 *Fell Farm campers* (1960)

Fell series
Carr, John Dickson
see **Doctor Gideon Fell series**
Godden, Rumer
see **Nona Fell series**
Kerr, M E
see **John Fell series**

Fellows series
Waugh, Hillary
see **Chief Fred Fellows series**
Woolley, Catherine
see **Ginnie Fellows series**

Fellowship of light trilogy
Mills, Robert E
1 *Star quest* (1978)
2 *Star fighters* (1978)
3 *Star force* (1978)

Fellside Farm series
Waterhouse, Arthur
1 *Raiders of the Fells* (1954)
2 *Fly of the Fells* (1957)

Felonius series
Cowley, Joy
see **Captain Felonius series**

Felse series
Peters, Ellis
see **Inspector George Felse series**

Felson series
Tevis, Walter Stone
see **Hustler series**

Feltham series
Mather, Berkely
see **Peter Feltham series**

Felthams series
Tute, Warren
1 *Felthams* (1950)
2 *Younger Felthams* (1953)

Felton series
Marsh, John
see **Ray Felton series**

Fen family series
Marshall, Sybil
Autobiography
1 *Silver new nothing* (1987)
Edwardian childhood in the Fen
2 *Pride of tigers* (1992)
A fen family and its fortune
Companion volume: *Fenland chronicle*, recollections of William Henry and Kate Mary Edwards, collected and edited by Sybil Marshall, 1980

Fen series
Crispin, Edmund
see **Gervase Fen series**

Fenby series
Hull, Richard
see **Inspector Fenby series**

Fender series
Geddes, Paul
see **Ludovic Fender series**

Fenella and Jeremy series
Byers, Irene
see **Jeremy and Fenella series**

Fenella Fang series
Perry, Ritchie
1 *Fenella Fang* (1986)
2 *Fenella Fang and the wicked witch* (1989)
3 *Fenella Fang and the time machine* (1991)

Fenella series
Gentleman, David
1 *Fenella in the south of France* (1967)
2 *Fenella in Greece* (1967)
3 *Fenella in Ireland* (1967)
4 *Fenella in Spain* (1967)

Fenfallow series
Hill, Pamela
1 *Fenfallow* (1987)
2 *Sutburys* (1988)

Fenland series
Wilson, Timothy R
1 *Master of Morholm* (1986)
2 *Ravished earth* (1988)

Fenn series
Stokes, Manning Lee
see **Christopher Fenn series**

Fennell series
Thorne, Ernest Pollett
see **Geoff Fennell series**

Fenner series
Booth, Louis F
see **Maxwell Fenner series**
Chase, James Hadley
see **Carol Blandish series**
Coxe, George Harmon
see **Jack Fenner series**

Fenrile trilogy
Rowley, Christopher
1 *War for eternity* (1983)
2 *Black ship* (1985)
3 *Founder* (1989)

Fenton Investigative Agency series
Overholser, Stephen
see **Molly Owens series**

Fenton series
Annesley, Michael
see **Lawrence Fenton series**
Chapman, Allen
see **Fred Fenton series**
Mackenzie, Nigel
see **Professor Christopher Fenton series**
Story, Jack Trevor
see **Horace Spurgeon Fenton series**

Fenwick and Susan series
Barth, John
1 *Sabbatical* (1982)
2 *Tidewater tales* (1987)

Fenwick series
Batchelor, Reg
see **Sergeant Fenwick series**
McMullan, Kate
see **Lila Fenwick series**
Whitby, Beatrice
see **Mary Fenwick series**

Feramontov quintet
Cory, Desmond
1 *Undertow* (1962)
Johnny goes under
2 *Hammerhead* (1963)
Shockwave
3 *Feramontov* (1966)
4 *Timelock* (1967)
5 *Sunburst* (1971)

Ferdinand and Isabella trilogy
Plaidy, Jean
1 *Castile for Isabella* (1960)
2 *Spain for the sovereigns* (1960)
3 *Daughters of Spain* (1961)
One volume edition entitled *Isabella and Ferdinand*, 1970

Ferenc series
Savage, Richard
see **Doctor Ferenc series**

Fergus McQueen series
Litchfield, Michael
see **Superintendent Fergus McQueen series**

Fergus O'Breen series
Boucher, Anthony
1 *Case of the crumpled knave* (1939)
2 *Case of the Baker Street Irregulars* (1940)
Blood on Baker Street
3 *Case of the solid key* (1941)
4 *Case of the seven sneezes* (1942)
Also two stories featuring O'Breen in *Far and away*, 1955 and one story featuring O'Breen in *The compleat werewolf, and other tales of fantasy and science fiction*, 1969

Ferguson series
Lincoln, Natalie Sumner
see **Detective Ferguson series**

Ferme l'Espagnole series
Mottram, Ralph Hale
see **Spanish Farm series**

Fernald series
Hicks, Clifford Byron
see **Alvin Fernald series**

Ferne Fleming series
Warfield, Catherine Ann
1 *Ferne Fleming* (1877)
2 *Cardinal's daughter* (1877)

Ferrall trilogy
Hill, Douglas
see **Huntsman trilogy**

Ferrara series
Bassani, Giorgio
1 *Prospect of Ferrara* (1956)
Five stories of Ferrara
Original edition entitled *Cinque storie ferraresi*
2 *Gold-rimmed spectacles* (1958)
Original edition entitled *Gli occhiali d'oro*
3 *Garden of the Finzi-Continis* (1962)
Original edition entitled *Il giardino dei Finzi-Contini*
4 *Behind the door* (1964)
Original edition entitled *Dietro la porta*
5 *Heron* (1968)
Original edition entitled *L'airone*
6 *Smell of hay* (1972)
Original edition entitled *L'odore del fieno*

Ferrara series
Rohmer, Sax
see **Anthony Ferrara series**

Ferris McClue series
Wickham, Harvey
1 *Clue of the primrose petal* (1921)
2 *Scarlet X* (1922)
3 *Boncoeur affair* (1923)
4 *Trail of the squid* (1924)

Ferroll series
Clive, Caroline
see **Paul Ferroll series**

Ferron series
Keene, Day
see **Les Ferron series**

Fertile earth series
Seymour, Aubrey
Autobiography
1 *Land where I belong* (1968)
2 *Fragrant the fertile earth* (1970)

Feston series
Fitzgerald, Kevin
see **Bernard Feston series**

Fevers and chills trilogy
White, Jon Manchip
see **Colonel Rickman trilogy**

Ffellowes series
Lanier, Sterling Edmund
see **Brigadier Ffellowes series**

Fiammetta series
Harker, Lizzie Allen
1 *Romance of the nursery* (1902)
2 *Concerning Paul and Fiammetta* (1906)

Fiddle series
Styles, Showell
see **Mister Fiddle series**

Fiddler on the roof series
Aleichem, Sholom
see **Tevye the milkman series**

Fidelity series
Du Bay, Sandra
1 *Mistress of the Sun King* (1980)
2 *Flame of Fidelity* (1981)
3 *Fidelity's flight* (1982)

Fidelity series
Fausset, Hugh l'Anson
1 *Modern prelude* (1933)
2 *Towards fidelity* (1952)
A meditation in middle life

Field Marshal Montgomery trilogy
Hamilton, Nigel
see **Montgomery of Alamein trilogy**

Fieldend series
Duke, Winifred
see **Harold Fieldend series**

Fielding family series
Dickens, Monica
1 *House at World's End* (1970)
2 *Summer at World's End* (1971)
3 *World's End in winter* (1972)
4 *Spring comes to World's End* (1973)

Fielding series
Emerson, Alice B
see **Ruth Fielding series**
Francis, Dick
see **Kit Fielding series**
Ingate, Mary
see **Ann Fielding series**
Sharp, David
see **Professor Henry Arthur Fielding series**

Fieldmouse children series
Brandenberg, Franz
1 *What can you make of it?* (1977)
2 *Nice new neighbors* (1977)
3 *Six new students* (1978)

Fieldmouse series
Wahl, Jan
see **Pleasant Fieldmouse series**

Fields of glory series
Rouaud, Jean
1 *Fields of glory* (1992)
2 *Of illustrious men* (1994)

Fields of honor series
Zlotnik, Donald E
1 *Medal of Honor* (1990)
2 *Distinguished Service Cross* (1991)
3 *Silver Star* (1991)
4 *Soldier's medal* (1991)
5 *Bronze Star* (1992)

Fiend series
Lavelle, Sheila
see **Charlie Ellis and Angela Mitchell series**

Fievel series
Teitelbaum, Michael
1 *Little lost Fievel* (1986)
2 *Escape from the Cossacks* (1986)
3 *Fievel's New York adventure* (1986)
4 *Mott Street maulers* (1986)
5 *Tony and Fievel* (1986)
6 *Fievel's boat trip* (1986)
7 *Fievel and Tiger* (1986)
8 *Fievel's friends* (1986)

Fifi series
Baldwin, Mary
1 *Follies of Fifi* (1907)
2 *Golden Square High School* (1908)

Fifteen series
This sequence has five authors
Steiner, Barbara
1 *Is there a cure for sophomore year?* (1986)
Haynes, Betsy
2 *Faking it* (1986)
Balluck, Georgia Ann
3 *So who wants to be popular anyway?* (1986)
Blake, Susan
4 *What they don't teach you in junior high* (1986)
Leonard, Marcia
5 *My little big sister* (1986)
Blake, Susan
6 *All out of grape jelly* (1986)

Fifteenth century London series
Harnett, Cynthia
1 *Ring out, Bow Bells!* (1953)
Drawbridge Gate
Based on the life of Dick Whittington
2 *Writing on the hearth* (1971)
Based on the life William Caxton
3 *Load of unicorn* (1959)
Caxton's challenge
Cargo of Madalena
A story of the rivalry between printers and scriveners in the early days of printing

Fifth Form series
Walker, Rowland
1 *Pickles of the Lower Fifth* (1921)
2 *Fifth Form detective* (1923)

Fifth grade magic series
Gormley, Beatrice
1 *Fifth grade magic* (1982)
Understudy magic
2 *More fifth grade magic* (1989)

Fifth grade monsters series
This sequence has two authors
Gilden, Mel
1 *M is for monster* (1987)
2 *Born to howl* (1987)
Hodgman, Ann
3 *There's a batwing in my lunchbox* (1988)
Gilden, Mel
4 *Pet of Frankenstein* (1988)
5 *Z is for zombie* (1988)
6 *Monster mashers* (1989)
7 *Things that go bark in the park* (1989)
8 *Yuckers!* (1989)
9 *Monster in Creeps Head Bay* (1990)
10 *How to be a vampire in one easy lesson* (1990)
11 *Island of the weird* (1990)
12 *Werewolf, come home* (1990)
13 *Monster boy* (1991)
14 *Troll patrol* (1991)
15 *Secret of Dinosaur Bog* (1991)

Fifth millenium series
This sequence has three authors
Stirling, Stephen Michael
1 *Snowbrother* (1985)
2 *Sharpest edge* (1986)
Co-author: Shirley Meier
3 *Cage* (1989)
Co-author: Shirley Meier
4 *Shadow's son* (1991)
Co-authors: Shirley Meier and Karen Wehrstein
5 *Shadow's daughter* (1991)
Wehrstein, Karen
6 *Lion's heart* (1991)
7 *Lion's soul* (1991)
Stirling, Stephen Michael
8 *Saber and Shadow* (1992)
Co-author: Shirley Meier

Fifth queen trilogy
Ford, Ford Madox
Based on the life of Katherine Howard
1 *Fifth queen and how she came to court* (1906)
2 *Privy Seal, his last venture* (1907)
3 *Fifth queen crowned* (1908)
One volume edition entitled *The fifth queen*, 1963

Fifty Second Precinct series
Pike, Robert L
see **Lieutenant Clancy series**

Figaro series
Beaumarchais, Pierre Augustin Caron de
1 *Barber of Seville* (1774)
Original edition entitled *Le barbier de Seville*; play on which the opera by Gioacchino Rossini is based
2 *Marriage of Figaro* (1784)
Original edition entitled *Le mariage de Figaro*; play on which the operas by Ernst von Dohnanyi and Wolfgang Amadeus Mozart are based

Fighter aces series
Toliver, Raymond F
1 *Fighter aces* (1965)
2 *Fighter aces of the Luftwaffe* (1977)
3 *Fighter aces of the U.S.A.* (1979)

Fighter series
Williams, David
1 *Bluebirds over* (1981)
2 *Vendetta* (1981)

Fighter Station series
Blake
Also published under the author's real name, Ronald Adam; experiences in the Royal Air Force in the Second World War
1 *Readiness at dawn* (1941)
2 *We rendezvous at ten* (1942)

Fighting fantasy gamebook series
This sequence has eighteen authors
Jackson, Steve
1 *Warlock of Firetop Mountain* (1982)
2 *Citadel of chaos* (1983)
Livingstone, Ian
3 *Forest of doom* (1983)
Jackson, Steve
4 *Starship traveler* (1983)
Livingstone, Ian
5 *City of thieves* (1983)
6 *Deathtrap dungeon* (1984)
7 *Island of the Lizard King* (1984)
Jackson, Steven Gary
8 *Scorpion swamp* (1984)
Livingstone, Ian
9 *Caverns of the snow witch* (1984)
Jackson, Steve
10 *House of hades* (1985)
House of hell
Smith, Mark
11 *Talisman of death* (1985)
Chapman, Andrew
12 *Space assassin* (1985)
Livingstone, Ian
13 *Freeway fighter* (1985)
14 *Temple of terror* (1986)
Chapman, Andrew
15 *Rings of Kether* (1986)
16 *Seas of blood* (1985)
Jackson, Steve
17 *Appointment with F.E.A.R.* (1985)
Waterfield, Robin
18 *Rebel planet* (1985)
Jackson, Steven Gary
19 *Demons of the deep* (1986)
Smith, Mark
20 *Sword of the samurai* (1986)
Livingstone, Ian
21 *Trial of champions* (1986)
Jackson, Steven Gary
22 *Robot commando* (1986)
Waterfield, Robin
23 *Masks of mayhem* (1986)
Jackson, Steve
24 *Creature of havoc* (1986)
Darvill-Evans, Peter
25 *Beneath Nightmare Castle* (1987)
Mason, Paul
26 *Riddling reaver* (1986)
Livingstone, Ian
27 *Crypt of the sorcerer* (1987)
Waterfield, Robin
28 *Phantoms of fear* (1987)
Davis, Graeme
29 *Midnight rogue* (1987)
Sharp, Luke
30 *Chasms of malice* (1987)
Waterfield, Robin
31 *Money spider* (1988)
Gascoigne, Marc
32 *Battleblade warrior* (1988)
Mason, Paul
33 *Slaves of the abyss* (1988)
Waterfield, Robin
34 *Water spider* (1988)
Allen, Martin
35 *Sky lord* (1988)
Martin, Keith
36 *Stealer of souls* (1988)
Darvill-Evans, Peter
37 *Portal of ancient evil* (1989)
Gascoigne, Marc
38 *Dyngeoneer* (1989)
Sharp, Luke
39 *Fangs of fury* (1989)
Gascoigne, Marc
40 *Blacksand!* (1990)
Hand, Stephen
41 *Legend of the shadow warriors* (1991)
Mason, Paul
42 *Black vein prophecy* (1990)
Jackson, Steve
43 *Keep of the Lich-Lord* (1990)
Darvill-Evans, Peter
44 *Spectral stalkers* (1991)
Gascoigne, Marc
45 *Demonstealer* (1991)
Martin, Keith
46 *Tower of destruction* (1991)
Companion volumes: *Fighting fantasy, an introductory role-playing game*, by Steve Jackson, 1984, *Titan, the fighting fantasy world*, by Steve Jackson and Ian Livingstone, 1986, *Fighting fantasy poster book*, by Steve Jackson and Ian Livingstone, 1990

Fighting Four series
Channel, A R
1 *Fighting Four* (1958)
2 *Tunnel busters* (1960)
3 *Operation V2* (1961)
4 *Mission accomplished* (1964)

Fighting saga of the S.A.S. series
Albany, James
see **S.A.S. series**

Fighting the sea series
Rand, Edward Augustus
1 *Fighting the sea* (1887)
Alternative title: Winter at the life-saving station
2 *Candle in the sea* (1892)
Alternative title: Winter at Seal's Head
3 *Mill at Sandy Creek* (1893)
4 *Salt-water hero* (1894)

Fikkan series
Shetterly, Will
see **Kevin Fikkan series**

Fillinger series
McGuire, Paul
see **Superintendent Fillinger series**

Fillmore series
Kaye, Marvin
1 *Incredible umbrella* (1979)
2 *Amorous umbrella* (1981)

Final friends series
Pike, Christopher
1 *Party* (1989)
2 *Dance* (1989)
3 *Graduation* (1989)

Finance series
Hill-Reid, William Scott
1 *Letters of an economic father* (1948)
2 *Letters from a bank parlour* (1953)

Finance trilogy
Warner, Charles Dudley
1 *Little journey in the world* (1889)
2 *Golden house* (1894)
3 *That fortune* (1899)

Financial series
Erdman, Paul
1 *Crash of '79* (1976)
2 *Panic of '89* (1986)

Finch series
Cleife, Philip
see **Martyn Finch series**
Erskine, Margaret
see **Inspector Septimus Finch series**
Thomson, June
see **Inspector Finch series**

Finchley series
Canning, Victor
see **Mister Finchley series**

Find my series
Threadgall, Colin
1 *Find my mother* (1993)
2 *Find my wheels* (1993)

Find-Outers and Dog series
Blyton, Enid
see **Fatty series**

Find series
Gree, Alain
1 *Find the yellow chicken* (1968)
Original edition entitled *Il y un petit poussin*
2 *Find the goldfish* (1968)
Original edition entitled *Il y un poisson rouge*
3 *Find the bee* (1968)
Original edition entitled *Il y une petite abeille*

Find your fate: Doctor Who series
Martin, David
see **Doctor Who find your fate series**

Find your fate: G.I. Joe series
This sequence has twelve authors
Affabee, Eric
1 *Operation star raider* (1985)
Sno, William
2 *Operation dragon fire* (1985)
Stine, Harlan William
3 *Operation terror trap* (1985)
Macrae, G V
4 *Operation robot assassin* (1985)
Affabee, Eric
5 *Everglades swamp terror* (1986)
G.I. Joe and the Everglades swamp terror
Siegel, Barbara
6 *Operation death stone* (1986)
Stine, Robert Lawrence
7 *Operation deadly decoy* (1986)
Stine, Harlan William
8 *Operation death-ray* (1986)
Stine, Robert Lawrence
9 *Operation mindbender* (1986)
Sno, William
10 *Operation night flight* (1986)
Ward, James Michael
11 *Operation weapons disaster* (1986)
Beach, Lynn
12 *Operation jungle doom* (1986)
Siegel, Barbara
13 *Operation snow job* (1987)
Edwards, K C
14 *Operation thunderbolt* (1987)
Beach, Lynn
15 *Operation time machine* (1987)
Stine, Harlan William
16 *Operation poison dart* (1987)
Siegel, Barbara
17 *Operation sink or swim* (1987)
Ballard, S M
18 *Operation killer comet* (1987)
Sno, William
19 *Operation tiger strike* (1987)
Stine, Robert Lawrence
20 *Serpentor and the mummy warrior* (1987)

Find your fate: Golden Girl series
Stine, Robert Lawrence
see **Golden Girl and the Guardians of the Gemstones trilogy**

Find your fate: Indiana Jones series
Stine, Robert Lawrence
see **Indiana Jones find your fate series**

Find your fate: James Bond series
Stine, Robert Lawrence
see **James Bond find your fate series**

Find your fate: Jem series
This sequence has five authors
Hallock, Rusty
1 *Jewels in the dark* (1986)
Waricha, Jean
2 *Video caper* (1986)
Stamper, Judith Bauer
3 *Secret of Rainbow Island* (1986)
Stine, Megan
4 *Double trouble* (1986)

Find your fate: Junior transformers series
Todd, Casey
see **Junior transformers find your fate series**

Find your fate: Morgan Swift series
Hughes, Sara
see **Morgan Swift find your fate series**

Finder's stone trilogy
Novak, Kate
1 *Azure bonds* (1988)
2 *Wyvern's spur* (1990)
3 *Song of the saurials* (1991)

Fingerling series
Laan, Dick
1 *Fingerling and his friends* (1952)
Original edition entitled *De avonturen van Pinkeltje en zijn vriendjes*
2 *Fingerling at the zoo* (1953)
Original edition in two volumes entitled *Pinkeltje in Artis*, 1952, and *Pinkeltje en het Grote Huis*, 1953
3 *Fingerling and the sandman* (1954)
Original edition entitled *Pinkeltje op zoek naar Klaas Vaak*
4 *Adventures of Fingerling* (1955)
Original edition entitled *De avonturen van Pinkeltje*
5 *Travels of Fingerling* (1955)
Original edition entitled *Pinkeltje op reis*
6 *Fingerling goes home* (1956)
Original edition entitled *Pinkeltje gaat naar Pinkeltjesland*

Fingermouse series
Cole, Michael
1 *Look out with Fingermouse* (1987)
2 *Look again with Fingermouse* (1987)

Fingers Finnegan series
Doherty, Berlie
1 *How green you are* (1982)
2 *Making of Fingers Finnegan* (1983)

Finlay series
Cronin, Archibald Joseph
see **Doctor Finlay series**

Finley series
Lupica, Mike
see **Peter Finley series**

Finn and Boyo series
Niall, Ian
see **Billy Boyo and Albert Finn series**

Finn Ferrall trilogy
Hill, Douglas
see **Huntsman trilogy**

Finn McCumhal series
Flint, Kenneth Covey
1 *Challenge of the clans* (1986)
2 *Storm shield* (1986)
3 *Dark druid* (1987)

Finn series
Dawson, Alec John
1 *Finn the wolfhand* (1908)
2 *Jan, son of Finn* (1917)

Finn series
Tannen, Mary
1 *Wizard children of Finn* (1981)
2 *Lost legend of Finn* (1982)

Finn series
Twain, Mark
see **Huckleberry Finn series**

Finnbranch trilogy
Hazel, Paul
1 *Yearwood* (1980)
2 *Undersea* (1982)
3 *Winterking* (1985)
One volume edition entitled *The Finnbranch*, 1986

Finnegan series
Doherty, Berlie
see **Fingers Finnegan series**
Forrest, Norman
see **John Finnegan series**

Finney series
Head, Matthew
see **Doctor Mary Finney series**

Fiona and Ken series
Tranter, Nigel Godwin
see **Ken and Fiona series**

Fiona Fitzgerald series
Adler, Warren
1 *American quartet* (1982)
2 *American sextet* (1982)
3 *Immaculate deception* (1991)
4 *Senator love* (1991)
5 *Witch of Watergate* (1992)
6 *Ties that bind* (1994)

Fiona series
Keller, Beverly
1 *Fiona's bee* (1975)
2 *Fiona's flea* (1981)
3 *Only Fiona* (1988)

Fionavar tapestry trilogy
Kay, Guy Gavriel
1 *Summer tree* (1984)
2 *Wandering fire* (1986)
3 *Darkest road* (1986)

Fiore family series
Longstreet, Stephen
1 *All or nothing* (1983)
2 *Our father's house* (1985)
3 *Sons and daughters* (1987)

Fiorina series
Buckley, Eunice
1 *For benefits received* (1960)
2 *Fiorina* (1961)

Fire, drought and flood trilogy
This sequence has two authors; poetry
Smith, Ivan
Illustrated by Clifton Pugh
1 *Death of a wombat* (1972)
2 *Dingo king* (1977)
Numbers 1 and 2 also published in one volume entitled *The wombat and the dingo*, 1984
Blashki, Pam
3 *Sometimes river* (1986)

Fire in the heart series
Murrow, Liza Ketchum
1 *West against the wind* (1987)
2 *Fire in the heart* (1989)
3 *Twelve days in August* (1993)

Fire Island series
Hirschfeld, Burt
1 *Fire Island* (1970)
2 *Cindy on Fire* (1971)
3 *Fire in the embers* (1972)
4 *Return to Fire Island* (1984)

Fire Marshal Ben Pedley series
Sterling, Stewart
1 *Five alarm funeral* (1942)
2 *Where there's smoke* (1946)
3 *Alarm in the night* (1949)
4 *Nightmare at noon* (1951)
5 *Hinges of hell* (1955)
6 *Candle for a corpse* (1957)
Too hot to kill
7 *Fire on Fear Street* (1958)
8 *Dying room only* (1960)
9 *Too hot to handle* (1961)

Fire of youth series
Muspratt, Eric
Autobiography
1 *My South Sea island* (1931)
2 *Wild oats* (1932)
3 *Journey home* (1933)
4 *Fire of youth* (1948)
The story of forty-five years wandering
Companion volume: *Ambition*, 1934

Fireball trilogy
Christopher, John
1 *Fireball* (1981)
2 *New found land* (1983)
3 *Dragon dance* (1986)
Dragondance

Firebird series
Tyers, Kathy
1 *Firebird* (1987)
2 *Fusion fire* (1988)

Firebrace series
Seafarer
see **Captain Firebrace series**

Firebrats series
Siegel, Barbara
1 *Burning land* (1987)
2 *Survivors* (1987)
3 *Thunder Mountain* (1987)
4 *Shockwave* (1988)

Firebringer trilogy
Pierce, Meredith Ann
1 *Birth of the Firebringer* (1985)
2 *Dark moon* (1992)
Third volume not yet published

Firecloud series
Spencer, Jake
see **John Firecloud series**

Firefly series
Ellis, Edward Sylvester
1 *Hunt on snow shoes* (1906)
2 *Cruise of the Firefly* (1906)
Co-author: William Pendleton Chipman

Firefox series
Thomas, Craig
1 *Firefox* (1977)
2 *Firefox down!* (1983)
3 *Winter hawk* (1987)

Fire-proof hero series
Jacobs, Barbara
1 *Fire-proof hero* (1986)
2 *Desperadoes* (1987)

Firlanders series
Power, Norman
1 *Forgotten kingdom* (1973)
2 *Fear in Firland* (1974)

First act series
Christie, Anne
1 *First act* (1983)
2 *My secret gorilla* (1981)
3 *Time to weep* (1987)

First Americans series
Sarabande, William
1 *Beyond the sea of ice* (1987)
2 *Corridor of storms* (1988)
3 *Forbidden land* (1989)
4 *Walkers of the wind* (1990)
5 *Sacred stones* (1991)

First blood series
Morrell, David
see **John Rambo series**

First Chronicles of Thomas Covenant series
Donaldson, Stephen Reeder
1 *Lord Foul's bane* (1977)
2 *Illearth war* (1977)
3 *Power that preserves* (1977)
One volume edition entitled *The first chronicles of Thomas Covenant, the Unbeliever*, 1983

First clash trilogy
Stil, Andre
Set during the Paris Commune of 1871
1 *Water tower* (1951)
Original edition entitled *Au chateau d'eau*
2 *Gun is unloaded* (1952)
Original edition entitled *Le coup du canon*
3 *Paris is with us* (1953)
Original edition entitled *Paris avec nous*

First directive series
McNamara, Joseph D
1 *First directive* (1984)
2 *Fatal command* (1987)

First hundred thousand series
Hay, Ian
1 *First hundred thousand* (1915)
An unofficial chronicle of a unit of K1
2 *Carrying on* (1917)

First Mountain Man trilogy
Johnstone, William Wallace
1 *First Mountain Man* (1991)
2 *Blood on the divide* (1992)
3 *Forty guns West* (1993)

First picture books series
Oxenbury, Helen
1 *Birthday party* (1983)
2 *Dancing class* (1983)
3 *Eating out* (1983)
4 *Check-up* (1983)
5 *Drive* (1983)
6 *First day at preschool* (1983)
7 *Gran and grandpa* (1984)
8 *Our dog* (1984)
9 *Visitor* (1984)

First read-alone mystery series
Nixon, Joan Lowery
Illustrated by Jim Cummins
1 *New Year's mystery* (1979)
2 *Halloween mystery* (1979)
3 *Valentine mystery* (1979)
4 *Happy birthday mystery* (1979)
5 *Thanksgiving mystery* (1980)
6 *April Fool mystery* (1980)
7 *Easter mystery* (1981)
8 *Christmas Eve mystery* (1981)

First round series
Lucas, Saint John
1 *First round* (1909)
2 *April folly* (1916)

First timers series
Petty, Kate
1 *New baby* (1987)
2 *Moving house* (1987)
3 *Starting school* (1987)
4 *Going to the doctor* (1987)
5 *Going to the dentist* (1988)
6 *Staying overnight* (1988)
7 *Splitting up* (1988)
8 *Taking care with strangers* (1988)

First words series
Burningham, John
1 *Sniff shout* (1984)
2 *Skip trip* (1984)
3 *Wobble pop* (1984)
4 *Slam bang!* (1985)
5 *Shuck baa* (1985)
6 *Jangle twang* (1985)

First words series
Emberley, Ed
1 *Home* (1987)
2 *Sounds* (1987)
3 *Animal* (1987)
4 *Cars, boats and planes* (1987)

First words series
Tyler, Jenny
1 *Toy words* (1987)
2 *Mealtime words* (1987)
3 *Bedtime words* (1987)
4 *Animal words* (1988)
5 *Outdoor words* (1988)
6 *Shopping words* (1988)
One volume edition entitled *Usborne book of first words*, 1989

First world trilogy
Smith, David Claude
see **Fall of the first world trilogy**

FirstFlight series
Claremont, Chris
1 *FirstFlight* (1987)
2 *Grounded!* (1991)

Firstworld chronicles series
Williamson, Philip G
1 *Dinbig of Khimmur* (1991)
2 *Legend of Shadd's torment* (1993)
3 *Flight from Enchantry* (1993)

Firth series
Peters, Ludovic
see **Ian Firth series**

Fischman series
Piesman, Marissa
see **Nina Fischman series**

Fish series
Geason, Susan
see **Syd Fish series**

Fisher and Hawk series
Green, Simon
see **Hawk and Fisher series**

Fisher series
Greenwood, Kerry
see **Phryne Fisher series**
Sellers, Michael
see **Calouste Fisher series**
Waterhouse, Keith
see **Billy Liar series**

Fisheries series
Street, Philip
1 *Between the tides* (1952)
2 *Beyond the tides* (1955)

Fisherman series
Grey, Zane
see **Tales of a fisherman series**

Fishery Protection Service series
Knox, Bill
see **Webb Carrick series**

Fishing series
Walsh, Bill
1 *Live bait* (1981)
2 *Cheat* (1982)
3 *Tight lines* (1984)

Fishmans series
Katz, H W
1 *Fishmans* (1938)
Original edition entitled *Die Fischmanns*
2 *Number twenty one Castle Street* (1940)
Original edition entitled *Schlossgasse, 21*

Fishpingle series
Vachell, Horace Annesley
1 *Fishpingle* (1917)
A romance of the countryside
2 *Soul of Susan Yellam* (1918)
A record

Fishy business series
Lee, Robert
1 *Fishy business* (1981)
2 *Microfish* (1983)
3 *Nervous wreck* (1985)
4 *King Conger* (1987)
5 *Red herring* (1989)

Fists trilogy
Camp, Walter Chauncey
see **Danny Fists trilogy**

Fitton series
Styles, Showell
see **Lieutenant Michael Fitton series**

Fitzgerald series
Bodkin, Matthias McDonnell
see **Lord Edward Fitzgerald series**
Flynn, Don
see **Ed Fitzgerald series**
Russell, Charlotte Murray
see **Homer Fitzgerald series**
Topor, Tom
see **Kevin Fitzgerald series**

Fitzgerald trilogy
Fitzgerald, John Dennis
see **Will Fitzgerald trilogy**

FitzHugh trilogy
Daley, Brian
see **Alacrity FitzHugh trilogy**

Five children series
Nesbit, Edith
1 *Five children and it* (1902)
2 *Phoenix and the carpet* (1904)
3 *Story of the amulet* (1906)
One volume edition entitled *The five children*, 1930

Five Civilized Tribes series
Culp, John Hewett
1 *Timothy Baines* (1969)
2 *Bright feathers* (1965)

Five dolls series
Clare, Helen
1 *Five dolls in a house* (1953)
2 *Five dolls and the monkey* (1956)
3 *Five dolls in the snow* (1957)
4 *Five dolls and their friends* (1959)
5 *Five dolls and the Duke* (1963)

Five Find-Outers series
Blyton, Enid
see **Fatty series**

Five Little Peppers series
Sidney, Margaret
1 *Five Little Peppers* (1880)
Five Little Peppers and how they grew
2 *Five Little Peppers midway* (1890)
3 *Five Little Peppers grown up* (1892)
4 *Phronsie Pepper* (1897)
5 *Stories Polly Pepper told* (1899)
6 *Adventures of Joel Pepper* (1900)
7 *Five Little Peppers abroad* (1902)
8 *Five Little Peppers at school* (1903)
9 *Five Little Peppers and their friends* (1904)
10 *Ben Pepper* (1905)
11 *Five Little Peppers in the little brown house* (1907)
12 *Our Davie Pepper* (1918)

Five Mavericks series
Cody, Stone
1 *Gun with the waiting notch* (1933)
Carol of Circle T
2 *Mustang Trail* (1933)
3 *Gun-smoke cure* (1933)
4 *Dangerous gold* (1934)
5 *Desert silver* (1935)
6 *Outlaw posse* (1936)
Based on a short story entitled *Charlie Parr's outlaw posse*
7 *Five against the law* (1936)

Five minute mysteries series
Weber, Ken
1 *Five minute mysteries* (1988)
2 *More five minute mysteries* (1991)

Five minute stories series
Richards, Laura Elizabeth
1 *Five minute stories* (1895)
2 *More five minute stories* (1903)
Companion volume: *Three five minute stories*, 1914

Five series
Blyton, Enid
see **Famous Five series**

Five towns series
Bennett, Arnold
1 *Man from the north* (1898)
2 *Anna of the Five Towns* (1902)
3 *Leonora* (1903)
4 *Great man* (1904)
5 *Sacred and profane love* (1905)
6 *Whom God hath joined* (1906)
7 *Old wives' tale* (1908)
8 *Helen with the high hand* (1910)
9 *Clayhanger* (1910)
10 *Card* (1911)
11 *Hilda Lessways* (1911)
12 *Regent* (1913)
13 *Price of love* (1914)
14 *These twain* (1916)
15 *Roll call* (1919)

Five Towns tales series
Bennett, Arnold
see **Tales of the Five Towns series**

Flack series
Maske, John
see **Jeremy Flack series**

Flag and frontier series
Bonehill, Ralph
1 *With Boone on the frontier* (1912)
Alternative title: The pioneer boys of old Kentucky
2 *Pioneer boys of the great Northwest* (1912)
Alternative title: With Lewis and Clark across the Rockies
3 *Pioneer boys of the gold fields* (1912)
Alternative title: The nugget hunters of '49
4 *With Custer in the Black Hills* (1912)
Alternative title: A young scout among the Indians
5 *Boys of the Fort* (1912)
Alternative title: A young captain's pluck
6 *Young bandmaster* (1912)
Alternative title: Concert, stage and battlefield
7 *Off for Hawaii* (1912)
Alternative title: The mystery of a great volcano
8 *Sailor boy with Dewey* (1912)
Alternative: Afloat in the Philippines
9 *When Santiago fell* (1912)
Alternative title: The war adventures of two chums

Flag lieutenant series
Drury, William Price
1 *Flag lieutenant* (1934)
Based on a play
2 *Flag lieutenant in China* (1934)

Flag of freedom series
Bonehill, Ralph
This sequence was reissued under the author's real name Edward L Stratemeyer and with different titles
1 *When Santiago fell* (1899)
Alternative title: The war adventures of two chums
2 *Sailor boy with Dewey* (1899)
Alternative title: Afloat in the Philippines
3 *Off for Hawaii* (1899)
Alternative title: The mystery of a great volcano
4 *Young bandmaster* (1900)
Alternative title: Concert, stage and battlefield
5 *Boys of the fort* (1901)
Alternative title: Young Captain's pluck
6 *With Custer in the Black Hills* (1902)
Alternative title: A young scout among the Indians

Flagg series
Cassells, John
see **Superintendent Flagg series**
Day, Will B
see **Steven Flagg series**
Johns, Veronica Parker
see **Webster Flagg series**
Randall, Clay
see **Amos Flagg series**
Wren, M K
see **Conan Flagg series**

Flambards series
Peyton, K M
1 *Flambards* (1967)
2 *Edge of the cloud* (1969)
3 *Flambards in summer* (1969)
Numbers 1-3 also published in one volume edition entitled *Flambards*, 1978
4 *Flambards divided* (1981)

Flame series
Leyland, Eric
1 *Flame of the Sierras* (1949)
2 *Flame takes over* (1950)
3 *Flame over Africa* (1951)
4 *Flame of the Amazon* (1952)
5 *Flame wins through* (1953)
6 *Flame takes a chance* (1953)
7 *Flame hits the trail* (1954)
8 *Flame hits back* (1954)
9 *Flame of the Sahara* (1955)
10 *Flame and the king's ransom* (1955)
11 *Flame sets the pace* (1956)
12 *Flame and the treasure trail* (1956)
13 *Flame takes command* (1957)
14 *Flame makes the grade* (1957)
15 *Flame, secret agent* (1958)
16 *Flame and the League of Five* (1959)

Flaming youth series
Fabian, Warner
1 *Flaming youth* (1923)
2 *Sailors' wives* (1924)

Flamm series
Wilson, Ivor
see **Gregory Flamm series**

Flandry series
Anderson, Poul
see **Sir Dominic Flandry series**

Flannelled fool series
Worsley, Thomas Cuthbert
Reminiscences of life in the 1930s
1 *Flannelled fool* (1966)
2 *Fellow travellers* (1971)

Flannery series
Campbell, Robert Wright
see **Jimmy Flannery series**

Flash Casey series
Coxe, George Harmon
1 *Silent are the dead* (1942)
2 *Murder for two* (1943)
3 *Flash Casey, detective* (1946)
Four novelettes
4 *Error of judgment* (1961)
One murder too many
5 *Man who died too soon* (1962)
6 *Deadly image* (1964)
Companion volume: *Dead heat,* by Paul Ayres, 1950

Flash Gordon series
Raymond, Alex
1 *Flash Gordon in the caverns of Mongo* (1937)
Sequence continued by Con Steffanson which is a pseudonym used by Ron Goulart and Bruce Cassidy as indicated against each title
Steffanson, Con
2 *Lion Men of Mongo* (1974)
[Goulart]
3 *Plague of sound* (1974)
[Goulart]
4 *Space circus* (1974)
[Goulart]
5 *Time trap of Ming XIII* (1974)
[Cassidy]; sequence continued by Carson Bingham
Bingham, Carson
6 *Witch Queen of Mongo* (1974)
7 *War of the Cybernauts* (1975)
Sequence continued by Arthur Byron Cover
Cover, Arthur Byron
8 *Flash Gordon* (1980)
Sequence continued by David Hagberg in titles which were published anonymously
Hagberg, David
9 *Massacre in the 22nd century* (1980)
10 *War of the citadels* (1980)
11 *Crisis on Citadel II* (1980)
12 *Forces from the Federation* (1981)
13 *Citadels under attack* (1981)
14 *Citadels on earth* (1981)
Companion volume: *The Flash Gordon book,* by Arthur Byron Cover and Lynn Haney, 1980

Flashman series
Fraser, George Macdonald
Based on the character of the school bully in *Tom Brown's schooldays,* by Thomas Hughes
1 *Flashman* (1969)
1839-1842
2 *Royal Flash* (1970)
1842-1843 and 1847-1848
3 *Flash for freedom!* (1971)
Set in America in the time of Abraham Lincoln
4 *Flashman at the Charge* (1973)
Set during the Crimean War
5 *Flashman in the great game* (1975)
Set during the Indian Mutiny
6 *Flashman's lady* (1977)
7 *Flashman and the Redskins* (1982)
Set during the Battle of Little Big Horn
8 *Flashman and the dragon* (1986)
Set during the Taiping Rebellion
9 *Flashman and the mountain of light* (1990)

Flat on my back series
Baxter, Alida
Humorous reminiscences
1 *Flat on my back* (1974)
2 *Up to my neck* (1975)
3 *Out on my ear* (1976)
4 *Upside-down under* (1978)

Flatchley series
McCulley, Johnston
see **Thunderbolt series**

Flatland series
This sequence has three authors
Abbott, Edwin Abbott
1 *Flatland* (1884)
A romance of many dimensions; originally published under the pseudonym A Square
Hinton, Charles Howard
2 *Episode of Flatland* (1907)
Alternative title: How a plane folk discovered the third dimension, to which is added an outline of the history of Unaea
Burger, Dionys
3 *Sphereland* (1965)
A fantasy about curved space and an expanding universe

Flavia and Constanza series
Bedford, Sybille
see **Constanza and Flavia series**

Flax of dream series
Williamson, Henry
1 *Beautiful years* (1921)
Revised edition 1929
2 *Dandelion days* (1922)
Revised edition 1930
3 *Dream of fair women* (1924)
Revised edition 1931; a tale of youth after the Great War
4 *Pathway* (1928)
Numbers 1-4 also published in one volume entitled *The flax of dreams,* 1936
5 *Star-Born* (1933)
Revised edition 1948
Companion volume: *Some notes on The flax of dreams, and other essays,* 1988

Flaxborough series
Watson, Colin
see **Inspector Purbright series**

Fleck series
Clapperton, Richard
see **Peter Fleck series**

Flecker series
Pullein-Thompson, Josephine
see **Inspector James Flecker series**

Fleet Air Arm training series
Hocking, Mary
1 *Time of war* (1968)
2 *Hopeful traveller* (1970)

Fleet series
Drake, David
1 *Fleet* (1988)
2 *Counterattack* (1988)
3 *Breakthrough* (1989)
4 *Sworn allies* (1990)
5 *Total war* (1990)
6 *Crisis* (1991)

Fleet Street eclogues series
Davidson, John
1 *Fleet Street eclogues* (1893)
2 *Second series of Fleet Street eclogues* (1896)

Fleming family series
Sutton, Graham
1 *Rowan tree* (1955)
2 *Shepherd's warning* (1946)
3 *Smoke across the fell* (1947)
4 *Fell days* (1948)
5 *North Star* (1949)
6 *Fleming of Honister* (1953)

Fleming series
Harvester, Simon
see **Roger Fleming series**
Warfield, Catherine Ann
see **Ferne Fleming series**

Fleming Stone series
Wells, Carolyn
1 *Clue* (1909)
2 *Gold bag* (1911)
3 *Chain of evidence* (1912)
4 *Maxwell mystery* (1913)
5 *Anybody but Anne* (1914)
6 *White alley* (1915)
7 *Curved blades* (1916)
8 *Mark of Cain* (1917)
9 *Vicky Van* (1918)
Elusive Vicky Van
10 *Diamond pin* (1919)
11 *Raspberry jam* (1920)
12 *Mystery of the sycamore* (1921)
13 *Mystery girl* (1922)
14 *Feathers left around* (1923)
15 *Spooky Hollow* (1923)
16 *Furthest fury* (1924)
17 *Prillilgirl* (1924)
18 *Anything but the truth* (1925)
19 *Daughter of the house* (1925)
20 *Bronze hand* (1926)
21 *Red-haired girl* (1926)
22 *All at sea* (1927)
23 *Where's Emily?* (1927)
24 *Crime in the crypt* (1928)
25 *Tannahill tangle* (1928)
26 *Tapestry room murder* (1929)
27 *Triple murder* (1929)
28 *Doomed five* (1930)
29 *Ghosts' high noon* (1930)
30 *Horror House* (1931)
31 *Umbrella murder* (1931)
32 *Fuller's earth* (1932)
33 *Roll-top desk mystery* (1932)
34 *Broken O* (1933)
35 *Clue of the eyelash* (1933)
36 *Master murderer* (1933)
37 *Eyes in the wall* (1934)
38 *In the tiger's cage* (1934)
39 *Visiting villain* (1934)
40 *Beautiful derelict* (1935)
41 *For goodness' sake* (1935)
42 *Wooden Indian* (1935)
43 *Huddle* (1936)
44 *Money musk* (1936)
45 *Murder in the bookshop* (1936)
46 *Mystery of the tarn* (1937)
47 *Radio studio murder* (1937)
48 *Gilt-edged guilt* (1938)
49 *Killer* (1938)
50 *Missing link* (1938)
51 *Calling all suspects* (1939)
52 *Crime tears on* (1939)
53 *Importance of being murdered* (1939)
54 *Crime incarnate* (1940)
55 *Devil's work* (1940)
56 *Murder on parade* (1940)
57 *Murder plus* (1940)
58 *Black night murders* (1941)
59 *Murder at the casino* (1941)
60 *Who killed Caldwell?* (1942)

Flesh traders series
Devine, Raynard
Also published under the author's real name Richard Tresillian
1 *Master of Black River* (1984)
2 *Black River affair* (1985)
3 *Black River breed* (1985)
4 *Revenge at Black River* (1985)

Flesh wounds trilogy
Holbrook, David
1 *Flesh wounds* (1966)
2 *Play of passion* (1978)
3 *Nothing larger than life* (1987)

Fletch series
McDonald, Gregory
1 *Fletch won* (1985)
2 *Fletch, too* (1986)
3 *Fletch* (1974)
4 *Carioca Fletch* (1984)
5 *Confess, Fletch* (1976)
Numbers 3-5 also published in one volume entitled *The Fletch chronicles,* 2, 1988
6 *Fletch's fortune* (1978)
7 *Fletch and the widow Bradley* (1981)
Numbers 1, 2, 7 also published in one volume entitled *The Fletch chronicles,* 1, 1988
8 *Fletch's moxie* (1982)
9 *Fletch and the man who* (1983)
Numbers 6, 8, 9 also published in one volume entitled *The Fletch chronicles,* 3, 1988
10 *Son of Fletch* (1993)
11 *Fletch reflected* (1994)

Fletcher and Cragg series
Gruber, Frank
see **Johnny Fletcher and Sam Cragg series**

Fletcher and Fury series
Jerina, Carol
see **Jack and Jill series**

Fletcher and Zenobia series
Gorey, Edward
1 *Fletcher and Zenobia* (1967)
2 *Fletcher and Zenobia save the circus* (1971)

Fletcher family series
Paice, Margaret
1 *Colour in the creek* (1976)
2 *Shadow of wings* (1978)
3 *Applewood* (1986)

Fletcher series
Anderson, James
see **Jessica Fletcher series**
Butterworth, William Edmund
see **Tony Fletcher series**
Davison, Geoffrey
see **Stephen Fletcher series**
Lee, Patrick
see **Six-Gun Samurai series**
McDonald, Gregory
see **Fletch series**
Rankine, John
see **Dag Fletcher series**

Fleur de Lys series
Carstairs, John Paddy
1 *Vinegar and brown paper* (1939)
2 *Sunshine and champagne* (1955)

Fleury Feverel Village series
Lamb, Lynton
see **Superintendent Quill and Inspector Glover series**

Flick series
Ehrlich, Jack
see **Robert Flick series**

Flicka series
O'Hara, Mary
1 *My friend Flicka* (1941)
Flicka
2 *Thunderhead* (1943)
3 *Green grass of Wyoming* (1946)
Companion volume: *Flicka's friend,* 1982

Flicker series
Millward, Edward J
see **Inspector Gil Flicker series**

Flickinger series
Hoover, Bessie Ray
1 *Pa Flickinger's folks* (1909)
2 *Opal* (1910)

Flight in Yiktor series
Norton, Andre
see **Krip Vorland series**

Flight over fire series
Jones, Jenny
1 *Fly by night* (1990)
2 *Edge of vengeance* (1991)

Flight series
Dale, Judith
see **Shirley Flight series**
Daniell, David Scott
see **Alison and John series**

Flim-flam man series
Owen, Guy
1 *Ballad of the flim-flam man* (1965)
2 *Flim-flam man and the apprentice grifter* (1972)
Companion volume: *The flim-flam man, and other stories*, 1980

Flint Falcon series
Hohl, Joan
1 *Nevada silver* (1987)
2 *Falcon's flight* (1987)

Flint series
Craigie, Dorothy
see **Captain Flint series**
Pearl, Jack
see **Derek Flint series**

Flintstones series
This sequence has two authors
Lewis, Jean
1 *Pebbles Flintstone* (1963)
2 *Bamm-Bamm and Pebbles Flintstone* (1963)
3 *Flintstones at the circus* (1963)
4 *Flintstone's picnic panic* (1965)
5 *Flintstones meet the Gruesomes* (1965)
Elias, Horace J
6 *Computer that went bananas* (1974)
7 *Gentlemen farmers* (1974)
8 *Fred and Barney lay an egg* (1974)
9 *Mayor for a day* (1974)
10 *Volunteer fireman* (1974)
11 *Bedrock connection* (1974)

Flinx of the Commonwealth series
Foster, Alan Dean
1 *For love of Mother-not* (1983)
2 *Tar-Aiym Krang* (1972)
3 *Orphan star* (1977)
4 *End of the matter* (1977)
5 *Bloodhype* (1973)
6 *Flinx in flux* (1988)
Companion volume: *A guide to the Commonwealth, the official guide to Alan Dean Foster's Humanx Commonwealth universe*, by Michael Goodwin and Robert Teague, 1985

Flip series
Dennis, Wesley
1 *Flip* (1941)
2 *Flip and the cows* (1942)
3 *Flip and the morning* (1951)

Flique series
Booth, Charles Gordon
see **Anatole Flique series**

Flo and Aston series
Benjamin, Floella
1 *Where's the giraffe?* (1987)
2 *How will we go?* (1987)
3 *How do you eat it?* (1988)

Floating city series
Verne, Jules
1 *Floating city* (1871)
Propellor Island
Alternative title: The pearl of the Pacific; original edition entitled *Une ville flottante*
2 *Blockade runners* (1871)
Original edition entitled *Les forceurs de blocus*
One volume edition 1874

Floating Outfit series
Edson, John Thomas
1 *Ysabel Kid* (1962)
2 *Forty four calibre man* (1969)
3 *Horse called Mogollon* (1971)
4 *Goodnight's dream* (1969)
5 *From hide and horn* (1969)
6 *Set Texas back on her feet* (1973)
Viridian's trail
7 *Hide and tallow men* (1974)
8 *Hooded riders* (1968)
9 *Quiet town* (1962)
Originally published under the pseudonym Chuck Nelson
10 *Trail boss* (1961)
11 *Wagons to Backsight* (1964)
12 *Troubled range* (1965)
13 *Sidewinder* (1967)
14 *Rangeland Hercules* (1968)
15 *McGraw's inheritance* (1968)
16 *Half breed* (1963)
17 *White Indians* (1981)
18 *Wildcats* (1965)
19 *Bad bunch* (1968)
20 *Fast gun* (1967)
21 *Cuchilo* (1969)
22 *Town called Yellowdog* (1966)
23 *Trigger fast* (1964)
24 *Making of a lawman* (1968)
25 *Trouble busters* (1965)
26 *Gentle giant* (1979)
27 *Decision for Dusty Fog* (1987)
28 *Diamonds, emeralds, cards and colts* (1988)
29 *Code of Dusty Fog* (1989)
30 *Set a-foot* (1978)
31 *Law of the gun* (1966)
32 *Peacemakers* (1965)
33 *To arms, to arms, in Dixie!* (1972)
34 *Hell in the Palo Duro* (1971)
35 *Go back to hell* (1972)
36 *South will rise again* (1972)
37 *Quest for Bowie's blade* (1974)
38 *Beguinage* (1978)
Texas assassin
39 *Beguinage is dead!* (1978)
40 *Master of triggernometry* (1981)
Trigger master
41 *Rushers* (1964)
42 *Buffalo are coming* (1985)
43 *Fortune hunters* (1965)
44 *Rio guns* (1962)
45 *Gun wizard* (1963)
46 *Texan* (1962)
47 *Old moccasins on the trail* (1981)
48 *Rio Hondo kid* (1963)
49 *Ole Devil's hands and feet* (1984)
50 *Waco's debt* (1962)
51 *Hard riders* (1962)
52 *Floating Outfit* (1967)
53 *Apache rampage* (1963)
54 *Rio Hondo war* (1964)
55 *Man from Texas* (1965)
56 *Gunsmoke thunder* (1963)
57 *Small Texan* (1969)
58 *Town tamers* (1969)
59 *Return to Backsight* (1966)
60 *Terror Valley* (1967)
61 *Guns in the night* (1966)
62 *Renegade* (1978)
63 *Lone Star killers* (1978)
64 *Mark Counter's kin* (1990)

Flood trilogy
Steen, Marguerite
1 *Sun is my undoing* (1941)
2 *Twilight on the Floods* (1949)
3 *Phoenix rising* (1952)
Jehovah blues

Floosie series
Standish, Walter
1 *Floosie goes astray* (1952)
2 *Floosie on the spot* (1952)
3 *Floosie passes by* (1952)
4 *Floosie takes a fall* (1952)

Flora and Dickie series
Stewart, Flora
Reminiscences of flower farming and beekeeping in Natal
1 *Flowering in the sun* (1956)
2 *I wore my rabbit* (1959)
3 *Bees in our bonnet* (1961)

Flora Hogg series
Lee, Austin
see **Miss Flora Hogg series**

Flora Lee series
Optic, Oliver
1 *Picnic party* (1863)
2 *Gold thimble* (1863)
3 *Do-Somethings* (1863)
4 *Christmas gift* (1863)
5 *Uncle Ben* (1863)
6 *Birthday party* (1863)

Flora McFlimsey series
Mariana
see **Miss Flora McFlimsey series**

Florence Monroe series
Bell, Margaret Elizabeth
1 *Watch the tall white sail* (1948)
2 *Totem casts a shadow* (1949)
3 *Love is forever* (1954)
4 *Daughter of Wolf House* (1957)

Florence series
Abbott, Jacob
1 *Florence and John* (1860)
2 *Grimkie* (1860)
3 *Orkney Islands* (1861)
4 *English Channel* (1863)
5 *Isle of Wight* (1864)
6 *Florence's return* (1868)

Florence series
Hope, Jane
1 *Call me Florence* (1953)
2 *Leave it to Florence* (1954)

Florentine series
Kruss, James
Translated from the German
1 *Florentine* (1967)
2 *Florentine on holiday* (1967)

Florian Slappey series
Cohen, Octavus Roy
1 *Florian Slappey goes abroad* (1928)
2 *Florian Slappey* (1938)
Short stories

Florida trilogy
Pratt, Theodore
1 *Barefoot mailman* (1943)
2 *Flame tree* (1950)
3 *Big bubble* (1951)

Flossie Teacake series
Davies, Hunter
1 *Flossie Teacake's fur coat* (1982)
2 *Flossie Teacake, again!* (1983)
3 *Flossie Teacake strikes back!* (1984)

Flower fairies series
Barker, Cicely Mary
1 *Flower fairies of the spring* (1923)
2 *Flower fairies of the summer* (1925)
3 *Flower fairies of the autumn* (1926)
4 *Book of flower fairies* (1927)
5 *Fairies of the trees* (1940)
Flower fairies of the trees
6 *Flower fairies of the garden* (1944)
7 *Flower fairies of the wayside* (1948)
8 *Flower fairies of the winter* (1985)
Selections: *Flower fairy picture book*, 1955; companion volumes: *A flower fairy alphabet*, 1934, *An ABC of flower fairies*, 1978

Flower fairy series
Marden, Fay
Based on the **Flower fairies series**, by Cicely Mary Barker
1 *Almond blossom fairy* (1986)
2 *Midsummer ball* (1986)
3 *Missing hazelnuts* (1986)
4 *Midwinter tale* (1986)

Flower-patch series
Klickmann, Flora
1 *Flower-patch among the hills* (1916)
2 *Between the larch-woods and the weir* (1917)
3 *Trail of the ragged robin* (1921)
4 *Flower-patch neighbours* (1928)
5 *Visitors at the flower-patch* (1931)
6 *Weeding the flower-patch* (1948)
Companion volume: *Flower-patch garden book*, 1933

Flower series
Field, Moira
see **Inspector Flower series**

Flower story book series
Blyton, Enid
1 *Daffodil story book* (1949)
2 *Bluebell story book* (1949)
3 *Poppy story book* (1950)
4 *Buttercup story book* (1951)
5 *Snowdrop story book* (1952)
6 *Marigold story book* (1954)
7 *Foxglove story book* (1955)

Flowerets series
Mathews, Joanna Hooe
1 *Violet's idol* (1870)
2 *Daisy's work* (1870)
3 *Rose's temptation* (1870)
4 *Lily's lesson* (1870)
5 *Hyacinth and her brother* (1870)
6 *Pinkie and the rabbits* (1870)

Flowerpot Men series
Bird, Maria
1 *Bill and Ben and the Potato Man* (1953)
2 *Nursery rhymes for Bill and Ben, the Flowerpot Men* (1954)
3 *Flowerpot Men and the bush baby* (1954)
4 *Flowerpot Men and the weathercock* (1954)

Flowers series
Harrison, Sarah
1 *Flowers of the field* (1980)
2 *Flower that's free* (1984)

Flowers series
Roberts, Nora
1 *Irish thoroughbred* (1992)
2 *Law is a lady* (1992)
3 *Irish rose* (1992)
4 *Storm warning* (1992)
5 *First impressions* (1992)
6 *Reflections* (1992)
7 *Night moves* (1992)
8 *Dance of dreams* (1992)
9 *Opposites attract* (1992)
10 *Island of flowers* (1992)
11 *Search for love* (1992)
12 *[laying the odds* (1992)
13 *Tempting fate* (1992)
14 *From this day* (1992)
15 *All the possibilities* (1992)
16 *Heart's victory* (1992)
17 *One man's art* (1992)
18 *Rules of the game* (1992)
19 *For now, forever* (1992)
20 *Her mother's keeper* (1992)
21 *Partners* (1992)
22 *Sullivan's woman* (1992)
23 *Summer deserts* (1993)
24 *This magic moment* (1993)
25 *Lessons learned* (1993)
26 *Right path* (1993)
27 *Art of deception* (1993)
28 *Untamed* (1993)
29 *Duel image* (1993)
30 *Second nature* (1993)
31 *One summer* (1993)
32 *Gabriel's angel* (1993)
33 *Name of the game* (1993)
34 *Will and a way* (1993)
35 *Affairs royale* (1993)
36 *Less of a stranger* (1993)

37 *Command performance* (1993)
38 *Blithe images* (1993)
39 *Playboy prince* (1994)
40 *Treasures lost, treasures found* (1994)
41 *Risky business* (1994)
42 *Loving Jack* (1994)
43 *Temptation* (1994)
44 *Best laid plans* (1994)
45 *Mind over matter* (1994)
46 *Welcoming* (1994)
47 *Boundary lines* (1994)
48 *Local hero* (1994)

Floyd East and James O'Hannay series
Rushton, Charles
see **James O'Hannay and Floyd East series**

Floyd Warner series
Morris, Wright
1 *Fire sermon* (1971)
2 *Life* (1973)

Fluster series
Ogden, Angela
see **Mrs Fluster series**

Flute series
Launay, Droo
see **Adam Flute series**

Flux and Anchor series
Chalker, Jack Laurence
see **Soul rider series**

Fly boys series
Morgan, Stanley
1 *Fly boys* (1974)
2 *Fly boys in London* (1975)
3 *Fly boys sky-jacked* (1976)

Flyaways series
Hardy, Alice Dale
1 *Flyaways and Cinderella* (1925)
2 *Flyaways and Little Red Riding Hood* (1925)
3 *Flyaways and Goldilocks* (1925)

Flyball series
Todd, Ruthven
see **Space Cat series**

Flying boys series
Ellis, Edward Sylvester
1 *Flying boys in the sky* (1911)
2 *Flying boys to the rescue* (1911)

Flying Doctor series
Noonan, Michael
1 *Flying Doctor* (1961)
2 *Flying Doctor on the Great Barrier Reef* (1962)
3 *Flying Doctor and the secret of the pearls* (1962)
4 *Flying Doctor shadows the mob* (1964)
5 *Flying Doctor hits the headlines* (1965)
6 *Flying Doctor under the desert* (1969)

Flying Fish trilogy
Collingwood, Harry
1 *Log of the Flying Fish* (1886)
A story of aerial and submarine peril and adventure
2 *With airship and submarine* (1907)
3 *Cruise of the Flying Fish, the air-ship-submarine* (1924)

Flying free series
Cate, Dick
1 *Flying free* (1975)
2 *Funny sort of Christmas* (1976)
3 *Old dog, new tricks* (1978)
4 *Nice day out?* (1979)

Flying girl series
Van Dyne, Edith
1 *Flying girl* (1911)
2 *Flying girl and her chum* (1912)

Flying nun series
This sequence has two authors
Rios, Tere
1 *Fifteenth pelican* (1965)
Flying nun
Johnston, William
Numbers 2-6 based on a television series
2 *Miracle at San Tanco* (1968)
3 *Littlest rebels* (1968)
4 *Mother of invention* (1969)
5 *Little green men* (1969)
6 *Underground picnic* (1970)

Flying Officer George Yeoman series
Jackson, Robert
1 *Hurricane Squadron* (1978)
Yeoman goes to war
2 *Squadron scramble* (1978)
Yeoman in the Battle of Britain
3 *Target Tobruk* (1979)
Yeoman in the Western Desert
4 *Malta victory* (1980)
Yeoman on the George Cross Island
5 *Mosquito Squadron* (1981)
Yeoman in the battle over Germany
6 *Operation Diver* (1981)
Yeoman on special missions
7 *Tempest Squadron* (1981)
Yeoman in the battle of the Ardennes
8 *Last battle* (1982)
Yeoman and the defeat of the Third Reich
9 *Operation Firedog* (1982)
Yeoman in guerrilla warfare
10 *Korean combat* (1983)
Yeoman in jet age warfare
11 *Venom Squadron* (1983)
Yeoman in the Suez crisis
12 *Hunter Squadron* (1984)
Yeoman in the Congo conflict

Flying sorcerer series
Ryan, John
1 *Frisco and Fred* (1985)
2 *Frisco and Fred and the space monster* (1986)

Flying U Ranch series
Bower, Bertha Muzzy
1 *Chip of the Flying U* (1906)
2 *Lonesome trail* (1909)
3 *Happy family* (1910)
4 *Flying U Ranch* (1914)
5 *Flying U's last stand* (1915)
6 *Heritage of the Sioux* (1916)
7 *Phantom herd* (1916)
8 *Dark horse* (1931)
9 *Whoop-up Trail* (1933)
10 *Flying U strikes* (1934)
11 *Trouble rides the wind* (1935)
12 *Spirit of the range* (1940)

Flying years trilogy
Niven, Frederick
1 *Flying years* (1935)
2 *Mine inheritance* (1940)
3 *Transplanted* (1944)

Flynn family quartet
Glover, Judith
see **Sussex quartet**

Flynn series
Braine, John
see **Colonel Xavier Flynn series**
Granger, Bill
see **Terry Flynn series**
James, Peter
see **Max Flynn series**
Laurie-Long, Ernest
see **Captain Flynn series**
McDonald, Gregory
see **Francis Xavier Flynn series**
O'Shea, Sean
see **Valentine Flynn series**

Focus pocus series
Gormley, Beatrice
1 *Mail-order wings* (1981)
2 *Focus pocus* (1985)

Fog Island series
Ross, Marilyn
1 *Phantom of Fog Island* (1971)
2 *Dark towers of Fog Island* (1975)
3 *Fog Island secret* (1975)
4 *Ghost ship of Fog Island* (1975)
5 *Horror of Fog Island* (1978)

Fog series
Cooney, Caroline B
1 *Fog* (1989)
2 *Snow* (1990)
3 *Fire* (1990)

Fog series
Edson, John Thomas
see **Cap Fog series**

Fogg series
Verne, Jules
see **Phileas Fogg series**

Foggy series
Rutherford, Meg
1 *Foggy's crown* (1989)
2 *Foggy and the mermaid* (1990)

Fogou series
Ireland, Kenneth
1 *Fogou* (1977)
2 *Cove* (1979)
3 *Quail message* (1980)

Foldaways series
Ahlberg, Allan
Illustrated by Colin McNaughton
1 *Circus* (1984)
2 *Families* (1984)
3 *Monsters* (1984)
4 *Zoo* (1984)

Folk tales series
Manning-Sanders, Ruth
1 *Book of giants* (1962)
2 *Book of dwarfs* (1963)
3 *Book of dragons* (1964)
4 *Book of witches* (1965)
5 *Book of wizards* (1966)
6 *Book of mermaids* (1967)
7 *Book of ghosts and goblins* (1968)
8 *Book of princes and princesses* (1969)
9 *Book of devils and demons* (1970)
10 *Book of charms and changelings* (1971)
11 *Book of ogres and trolls* (1972)
12 *Book of sorcerers and spells* (1973)
13 *Book of magic animals* (1974)
14 *Book of monsters* (1975)
15 *Book of enchantments and curses* (1976)
16 *Book of kings and queens* (1977)
17 *Book of marvels and magic* (1978)
18 *Book of spooks and spectres* (1979)
19 *Book of cats and creatures* (1981)
20 *Book of heroes and heroines* (1982)
21 *Book of magic adventures* (1983)
22 *Book of magic horses* (1984)

Folkungs series
Heidenstam, Verner von
see **Tree of the folkungs series**

Folliets and Peverills series
Leslie, Doris
1 *Folly's End* (1944)
2 *Peverills* (1946)
3 *Young wives' tale* (1971)

Followers of the sun trilogy
Fergusson, Harvey
1 *Wolf song* (1927)
2 *In those days* (1928)
3 *Blood of the conquerors* (1922)
One volume editions entitled *Followers of the sun*, 1936 and *The Santa Fe omnibus*, 1938

Folly series
Wells, Carolyn
1 *Folly in Fairyland* (1901)
2 *Folly in the forest* (1902)

Folly series
York, Jeremy
see **Superintendent Folly series**

Follyfoot Farm series
Dickens, Monica
1 *Follyfoot* (1971)
2 *Dora at Follyfoot* (1972)
Numbers 1 and 2 also published in one volume entitled *Follyfoot Farm*, 1973
3 *Horses of Follyfoot* (1975)
4 *Stranger at Follyfoot* (1976)

Fontaine series
Ard, William
see **Danny Fontaine series**

Fontana d'amore series
Leeming, John Fishwick
1 *It always rains in Rome* (1960)
2 *Girl like Wigan* (1961)
3 *Arnaldo my brother* (1962)

Fonzie series
Johnston, William
see **Happy days series**

Food and cooking series
Black, Margaret Katherine
1 *Food and cooking in mediaeval Britain* (1985)
2 *Food and cooking in nineteenth-century Britain* (1985)

Fool trilogy
Toy, Barbara
Reminiscences of travel
1 *Fool on wheels* (1955)
2 *Fool in the desert* (1956)
3 *Fool strikes oil* (1957)

Fools series
Knott, Tina Spencer
Reminiscences of life as proprietor of a laundrette
1 *Fools rush in* (1949)
2 *Keep it clean* (1958)

Football captain series
Wright, Billy
Autobiography
1 *Captain of England* (1950)
2 *World's my football pitch* (1953)
3 *Football is my passport* (1957)
4 *One hundred caps and all that* (1962)

Football series
Perry, Lawrence
1 *Fullback* (1916)
2 *Big game* (1918)

Footloose Fairweather and Fancy Free series
Lynde, Stan
see **Pardners series**

Footsteps series
Adler, Carole Schwerdtfeger
1 *Footsteps on the stairs* (1982)
2 *Binding ties* (1985)

For children series
Kelemen, Julie
1 *Lent is for children* (1987)
2 *Advent is for children* (1988)
3 *Prayer is for children* (1992)

Forbes series
Mitton, Geraldine Edith
see **Diana Forbes series**

Forbidden borders series
Gear, William Michael
1 *Requiem for the conqueror* (1991)
2 *Relic of empire* (1992)
3 *Countermeasures* (1993)

Forbidden game trilogy
Smith, Lisa J
1 *Hunter* (1994)
2 *Chase* (1994)
3 *Kill* (1994)

Forbidden planet series
Kaveney, Roz
1 *Tales from the forbidden planet* (1987)
2 *More tales from the forbidden planet* (1990)

Force series
Decker, Jake
see **Steve Sinclair series**

Ford series
Hobson, Hank
see **Brad Ford series**
Moore, Fenworth
see **Jerry Ford series**
Pendleton, Don
see **Ashton Ford series**
Wells, Carolyn
see **Alan Ford series**

Fordinghame series
Horler, Sydney
see **Sir Brian Fordinghame series**

Foreign adventure trilogy
Ellis, Edward Sylvester
1 *Lost in the forbidden land* (1906)
2 *River and jungle* (1906)
3 *Hunt of the white elephant* (1906)

Foreign Legion series
Surdez, Georges
1 *Demon caravan* (1931)
2 *They march from yesterday* (1932)

Foreign Office trilogy
Hurd, Douglas
1 *Send him victorious* (1968)
2 *Smile on the face of the tiger* (1969)
3 *Scotch on the rocks* (1971)

Foreman series
Rey, Bret
see **Will Foreman series**

Forensic fables series
O
1 *Forensic fables* (1926)
2 *Further forensic fables* (1928)
3 *Final forensic fables* (1929)
4 *Final forensic fables, second series* (1932)
Selections: *Fifty forensic fables*, 1949

Forerunner series
Norton, Andre
see **Planet Warlock series**

Forest and prairie trilogy
Ellis, Edward Sylvester
1 *Great cattle trail* (1894)
2 *Path in the ravine* (1895)
3 *Young ranchers* (1895)
Alternative title: Fighting the Sioux

Forest Glen series
Kellogg, Elijah
1 *Sowed by the wind* (1874)
2 *Wolf run* (1875)
3 *Brought to the front* (1875)
4 *Mission of Black Rifle* (1876)
5 *Forest Glen* (1877)
Alternative title: The Mohawk's friendship
6 *Burying the hatchet* (1878)

Forest King trilogy
Edwards, Claudia Jane
1 *Taming the Forest King* (1986)
2 *Horsewoman in Godsland* (1987)
3 *Bright and shining tiger* (1988)

Forest Lodge series
Rich, Louise Dickinson
see **Woods series**

Forest of Boland series
B B
see **Boland series**

Forest series
Dale, Norman
see **Tim Forest series**

Forest series
Foley, Winifred
1 *Child in the forest* (1974)
2 *Back to the forest* (1981)

Forest series
Steussy, Marti
1 *Forest of the night* (1987)
2 *Dreams of dawn* (1988)

Forest Service series
Atwater, Montgomery Meigs
see **Hank Winton series**

Forest trilogy
Hoover, Helen
Autobiography
1 *Gift of the deer* (1967)
2 *Place in the woods* (1969)
3 *Years of the forest* (1973)

Foresters series
Byers, Irene
1 *Foresters of Fourways* (1963)
2 *Foresters afield* (1966)

Forever hero trilogy
Modesitt, Leland Exton
1 *Dawn for a distant earth* (1987)
2 *Silent warrior* (1987)
3 *In endless twilight* (1988)

Forever trilogy
Pascal, Francine
1 *Dreams of forever* (1988)
2 *Forever and always* (1988)
3 *Together forever* (1988)

Forfarshire series
Barrie, James Matthew
see **Thrums series**

Forge and Peachy series
Starnes, Richard
see **Barney Forge and Doctor Saint George Peachy series**

Forgetting series
Stott, Mary
1 *Forgetting's no excuse* (1973)
2 *Before I go* (1985)
Reflections on my life and times

Forging of a rebel trilogy
Barea, Arturo
Autobiography
1 *Forge* (1941)
Original edition entitled *La forga*
2 *Track* (1943)
Original edition entitled *La ruta*
3 *Clash* (1946)
Original edition entitled *La llama*

Forgotten forest series
Gaskin, Carol
1 *War of the wizards* (1985)
2 *Magician's ring* (1985)
3 *Master of mazes* (1985)
4 *Forbidden towers* (1985)

Forgotten realms fantasy series
Awlinson, Richard
see **Avatar trilogy**

Forgotten realms trilogy
Niles, Douglas
see **Moonshae trilogy**

Forgotten season series
Conlon, Kathleen
1 *Forgotten season* (1980)
2 *Consequences* (1981)

Forlorn River Ranch series
Grey, Zane
1 *Forlorn River* (1927)
2 *Nevada* (1928)

Former days trilogy
Maclean, Norman
Autobiography
1 *Former days* (1945)
2 *Set free* (1949)
3 *Years of fulfilment* (1953)

Forrest series
Maitland, Hugh
see **Brad Forrest series**

Forrester family series
Warde, Joan
1 *No more romance* (1975)
2 *Perhaps it's love* (1976)
3 *Strange capers* (1976)

Forrester series
Grove, Harriet Pyne
see **Merilyn Forrester series**
L'Engle, Madeleine
see **Katherine Forrester series**
Rockwell, Thomas
see **Billy Forrester series**
Wees, Frances Shelley
see **Michael Forrester series**

Forsyte saga, second series
Galsworthy, John
see **Modern comedy series**

Forsyte saga, third series
Galsworthy, John
see **End of the chapter series**

Forsyte saga trilogy
Galsworthy, John
1 *Man of property* (1906)
2 *In Chancery* (1920)
3 *To let* (1921)
One volume edition entitled *The Forsyte saga*, 1922 which also contains two interludes entitled *Indian summer of a Forsyte* and *Awakening*

Forsythe and Sanderson series
Giroux, E X
see **Robert Forsythe and Abigail Sanderson series**

Forsythia Brown series
Payes, Rachel
1 *Forsythia finds murder* (1960)
2 *Memoirs of murder* (1964)

Forte family trilogy
Da Cruz, Daniel
1 *Ayes of Texas* (1982)
2 *Texas on the rocks* (1986)
3 *Texas triumphant* (1987)

Fortescue series
Brandon, Charles
see **John Fortescue series**

Fortuna West series
Hogan, Ray
1 *Fortuna West, lawman* (1983)
2 *Vengeance of Fortuna West* (1983)

Fortunato series
Green, Kate
see **Theresa Fortunato series**

Fortune and power series
Roche, Eliane
Original edition entitled *Chateauvallon*
1 *Berg family fortune* (1986)
2 *New money* (1986)

Fortune and Webley series
Maddock, Larry
see **Hannibal Fortune and Webley series**

Fortune family quartet
Mahy, Margaret
see **Cousins quartet**

Fortune grass series
Lethbridge, Mabel
Autobiography of a physically and socially handicapped woman
1 *Fortune grass* (1934)
2 *Against the tide* (1936)
3 *Homeward bound* (1967)

Fortune hunters series
Patchin, Frank Gee
see **Ted Jones series**

Fortune series
Bailey, Henry Christopher
see **Mister Reggie Fortune series**
Collins, Michael
see **Dan Fortune series**
Foster, Alan Dean
see **Icerigger series**
Fyfield, Frances
see **Sarah Fortune series**
Hill, Denise
see **Jane and Jeremy Fortune series**
Jacobs, Thomas Curtis Hicks
see **Temple Fortune series**
Stone, Thomas H
see **Chester Fortune series**

Fortune's Friends series
Reynolds, Kay
1 *Hell week* (1987)
2 *Lucky Lacey* (1987)

Fortunes of Richard Mahony trilogy
Richardson, Henry Handel
1 *Australia Felix* (1917)
2 *Way home* (1925)
3 *Ultima Thule* (1929)
One volume revised edition entitled *The fortunes of Richard Mahony*, 1930; companion volume: *The end of a childhood, and other stories*, 1934

Fortunes series
Barlow, Jane
1 *Kerrigan's quality* (1893)
2 *Founding of fortunes* (1902)

Fortunes series
Grant, Pamela
1 *Fortunes of Doria* (1924)
2 *Fortunes of Billy* (1925)
3 *Pranks of Doria* (1929)

Fortunes west series
Riefe, A R
1 *Tucson* (1988)
2 *Cheyenne* (1989)
3 *San Francisco* (1989)
4 *Salt Lake City* (1989)

Forty years series
Gorky, Maxim
see **Life of Klim Samgin series**

Forty-Five Acres series
Wildsmith, Alan
1 *Summer at Forty-Five Acres* (1975)
2 *Snowbound at Forty-Five Acres* (1976)

Forty-Five trilogy
Broster, Dorothy Kathleen
see **Jacobite trilogy**

Fosse series
Cannon, Elliott
see **Guy Fosse series**

Fossett trilogy
Hollis, Christopher
see **Robert Fossett trilogy**

Fossil family tales series
Green, Kate
1 *Everything a dinosaur could want* (1992)
2 *Between friends* (1992)
3 *Buddy Rock's race* (1992)
4 *T-bone's tent* (1992)
5 *Grumble day* (1992)
6 *Just about perfect* (1992)

Foster series
Buzo, Alexander
see **Prue Foster series**
Colver, Alice Ross
see **Joan Foster series**

Foundation series
Asimov, Isaac
1 *Prelude to Foundation* (1988)
2 *Foundation* (1951)
Thousand-year plan
The second title is an abridged edition
3 *Foundation and Empire* (1952)
Man who upset the universe
The second title is an abridged edition
4 *Second Foundation* (1953)
Numbers 2-4 published in one volume entitled *Foundation trilogy*, 1963, and as *An Isaac Asimov omnibus*, 1966
5 *Foundation's edge* (1982)
6 *Foundation and earth* (1986)
7 *Forward the Foundation* (1993)

Fountain and Dodd series
Reade, Charles
see **David Dodd and Lucy Fountain series**

Fountain series
Wheatley, Dennis
see **Molly Fountain series**

Four Adjusters series
Cross, Mark
see **Daphne Wrayne and her Four Adjusters series**

Four classmates series
Tomlinson, Paul Greene
1 *To the land of the caribou* (1914)
The adventures of four classmates on a cruise to Labrador
2 *In camp on Bass Island* (1915)
What happened to four classmates on the Saint Lawrence

Four Corners series
Blanchard, Amy Ella
1 *Four Corners* (1906)
2 *Four Corners in California* (1907)
3 *Four Corners at school* (1908)
4 *Four Corners abroad* (1909)
5 *Four corners in camp* (1910)
6 *Four Corners at college* (1911)
7 *Four Corners in Japan* (1912)
8 *Four Corners in Egypt* (1913)

Four Corners series
Burgin, George Brown
1 *Dance at Four Corners* (1894)
2 *Judge of the Four Corners* (1896)
3 *Old Man's marriage* (1897)
4 *Land of silence* (1904)
5 *Marble city* (1905)
6 *Devil's due* (1905)
7 *King of Four Corners* (1910)
8 *Dickie Dilver* (1912)
9 *Duke's twins* (1914)
10 *Herb of healing* (1915)
11 *Game of hearts* (1915)
12 *Hut by the river* (1916)
13 *Puller of strings* (1917)
14 *Manetta's marriage* (1922)
15 *Sally's sweetheart* (1923)
16 *Fleurette of Four Corners* (1925)
17 *Mariette's lovers* (1925)
18 *All things come round* (1929)
19 *Duke's strategem* (1931)
20 *Honour of Four Corners* (1934)

Four dolls series
Godden, Rumer
1 *Impunity Jane* (1954)
The story of a pocket doll
2 *Fairy doll* (1956)
3 *Story of Holly and Ivy* (1958)
4 *Candy Floss* (1960)
One volume edition entitled *Four dolls*, 1983

Four elements series
Coote, Roger
1 *Air* (1989)
2 *Earth* (1989)
3 *Fire* (1989)
4 *Water* (1989)

Four Gospels series
Zola, Emile
1 *Fruitfulness* (1899)
Original edition entitled *Fecondite*
2 *Work* (1901)
Travail
Original edition entitled *Travail*
3 *Truth* (1902)
Original edition entitled *Verite*
Projected fourth volume entitled *Justice* never published

Four hundred billion stars series
McAuley, Paul J
1 *Four hundred billion stars* (1988)
2 *Of the fall* (1989)
Secret harmonies
3 *Eternal light* (1991)

Four languages series
Hautzig, Esther Rudomin
Text in English Spanish, French, Russian
1 *In the park* (1968)
2 *At home* (1968)
3 *In school* (1969)

Four Little Blossoms series
Hawley, Mabel C
1 *Four Little Blossoms at Brookside Farm* (1920)
2 *Four Little Blossoms at Oak Hill School* (1920)
3 *Four Little Blossoms and their winter fun* (1920)
4 *Four Little Blossoms on Appletree Island* (1921)
5 *Four Little Blossoms through the holidays* (1922)
6 *Four Little Blossoms at Sunrise Beach* (1929)
7 *Four Little Blossoms indoors and out* (1930)

Four little pets series
Frees, Harry Whittier
Photographic picture books
1 *Four little kittens* (1934)
2 *Four little bunnies* (1935)
3 *Four little puppies* (1935)
4 *More about the four little kittens* (1938)
5 *Four little kittens' Christmas* (1939)

Four little troubles series
Marshall, James
1 *Eugene* (1975)
2 *Someone is talking about Hortense* (1975)
3 *Sing out Irene* (1975)

Four Lords of the Diamond series
Chalker, Jack Laurence
1 *Lilith, a snake in the grass* (1981)
2 *Cerberus, a wolf in the fold* (1982)
3 *Charon, a dragon at the gate* (1982)
4 *Medusa, a tiger by the tail* (1983)
One volume edition entitled *Four Lords of the diamond*, 1983

Four million series
Henry, O
1 *Four million* (1906)
2 *Trimmed lamp* (1907)
3 *Voice of the city* (1908)
4 *Strictly business* (1910)

Four pigs series
Uttley, Alison
see **Brock the badger series**

Four quartets series
Eliot, Thomas Stearns
Poetry
1 *Burnt Norton* (1936)
2 *East Coker* (1940)
3 *Dry Salvages* (1941)
4 *Little Gidding* (1942)
One volume edition entitled *Four quartets*, 1944

Four seasons at Cherry-Tree Farm series
Kent, Margaret
1 *Spring at Cherry-Tree Farm* (1942)
2 *Summer at Cherry-Tree Farm* (1942)
3 *Autumn at Cherry-Tree Farm* (1942)
4 *Winter at Cherry-Tree Farm* (1943)

Four square meals series
Muir, Frank
1 *What-a-Mess has breakfast* (1986)
2 *What-a-Mess has lunch* (1986)
3 *What-a-Mess has tea* (1986)
4 *What-a-Mess has supper* (1986)

Four winds of love series
Mackenzie, Compton
1 *East wind of love* (1937)
Also published in two volumes
2 *South wind of love* (1937)
Also published in two volumes
3 *West wind of love* (1940)
3.1 *West wind of love, book 1* (1940)
3.2 *West wind of love, book 2* (1940)
West to north
4 *North wind of love* (1940)
Also published in two volumes

Fours Crossing trilogy
Garden, Nancy
1 *Fours Crossing* (1981)
2 *Watersmeet* (1983)
3 *Door between* (1987)

Fourth Floor twins series
Adler, David A
1 *Fourth Floor twins and the fish snitch mystery* (1985)
2 *Fourth Floor twins and the fortune cookie chase* (1985)
3 *Fourth Floor twins and the talking bird trick* (1986)
4 *Fourth Floor twins and the Silver Ghost Express* (1986)
5 *Fourth Floor twins and the sky-scraper parade* (1987)
6 *Fourth Floor twins and the sand castle contest* (1988)

Fourth Form series
Chaundler, Christine
1 *Reputation of the Upper Fourth* (1919)
2 *Fourth Form detectives* (1921)
3 *Fourth Form rebel* (1922)
4 *Jan of the Fourth* (1923)
5 *Reforming the Fourth* (1927)
6 *Friends in the Fourth* (1929)
7 *Disgrace to the Fourth* (1930)

Fourth grade ghost series
Stine, Harlan William
see **Jeffrey and the fourth grade ghost series**

Fowler family series
Giles, Janice Holt
1 *Kentuckians* (1953)
2 *Hannah Fowler* (1956)
3 *Believers* (1957)
4 *Johnny Osage* (1960)
5 *Voyage to Santa Fe* (1962)
6 *Savanna* (1961)
7 *Great adventure* (1966)
8 *Land beyond the mountains* (1958)
9 *Run me a river* (1964)
10 *Six-horse hitch* (1969)

Fowler series
Eliot, George Fielding
see **G-men series**
Harris, Colver
see **Timothy Fowler series**
Richards, Paul
see **Grant Fowler series**

Fox Elton series
White, Ared
see **Captain Fox Elton series**

Fox series
Hardcastle, Michael
see **Mark Fox series**
Hardy, Adam
see **George Abercrombie Fox series**

Fox series
Marshall, Edward
1 *Three by the sea* (1981)
2 *Fox and his friends* (1982)
3 *Fox in love* (1982)
4 *Fox on wheels* (1983)
5 *Fox at school* (1983)
6 *Fox all week* (1984)
7 *Four on the shore* (1985)
Sequence continued under the name James Marshall
Marshall, James
8 *Fox on the job* (1988)
9 *Fox be nimble* (1990)
10 *Fox outfoxed* (1992)
11 *Fox on stage* (1993)

Fox series
Mounce, David R
see **Paul Fox series**
Nelson, Peter N
see **Mollie Fox series**
Radau, Hans
see **Little Fox series**

Fox series
Shakespeare, Brian
1 *Fox, part 1* (1980)
2 *Fox, part 2* (1980)

Fox series
Stout, Rex
  see **Tecumseh Fox series**
Thomson, David Robert Alexander
  see **Danny Fox series**

Fox trilogy
Parkinson, Dan
1 *Fox and the faith* (1989)
2 *Fox and the fury* (1989)
3 *Fox and the flag* (1990)

Fox trilogy
Walsh, Jill Paton
  see **Children of the fox trilogy**

Foxendale series
Kitchen, Fred
1 *Foxendale Farm* (1959)
2 *More adventures at Foxendale Farm* (1961)
3 *Winter at Foxendale* (1964)

Foxes of Ireland series
McCaughren, Tom
  Illustrated by Jeannette Dunne
1 *Run with the wind* (1983)
2 *Run to earth* (1984)
3 *Run swift, run free* (1986)
4 *Run to the ark* (1991)
5 *Run wild* (1993)

Foxwood series
Paterson, Cynthia
1 *Robbery at Foxwood* (1985)
2 *Foxwood treasure* (1985)
3 *Foxwood kidnap* (1986)
4 *Foxwood regatta* (1986)
5 *Foxwood smugglers* (1988)

Foxworth Hall series
Andrews, Virginia Cleo
  see **Dollanganger family series**

Foxx series
Tyler, Zack
1 *Foxx!* (1981)
2 *Foxx's gold* (1981)
3 *Foxx hunting* (1981)
4 *Foxx's herd* (1982)
5 *Foxx's vixen* (1982)
6 *Foxx's foe* (1983)

Foxy series
Montgomery, John
1 *Foxy* (1959)
2 *My friend Foxy* (1961)
3 *Foxy and the badgers* (1968)

Foxy Squirrel series
Judson, Clara Ingram
1 *Foxy Squirrel* (1921)
2 *Foxy Squirrel in the garden* (1929)

Foy series
Black, Lionel
  see **Superintendent Francis Foy series**

Fozbek series
Senn, Steve
1 *Double disappearance of Walter Fozbek* (1980)
2 *Ralph Fozbek and the amazing black hole patrol* (1986)

Fraggle Rock series
  This sequence has seven authors
Muntean, Michaela
1 *They call me Boober Fraggle* (1983)
Bruce, Sheilah B
2 *Radish day jubilee* (1983)
Stevenson, Jocelyn
3 *Red and the pumpkins* (1983)
4 *Fraggle Rock* (1984)
5 *Welcome to Fraggle Rock* (1984)
Abelson, Danny
6 *If I were king of the universe* (1984)
Gikow, Louise
7 *Sprocket's Christmas tale* (1984)
8 *What's a Fraggle?* (1984)
Muntean, Michaela
9 *Doozer disaster* (1984)
10 *What do Doozers do?* (1984)
11 *Tale of traveling Matt* (1984)
Perlberg, Deborah
12 *Wembley Fraggle gets the story* (1984)
Young, David
13 *Marooned in Fraggle Rock* (1984)

Fragments of autobiography series
John, Augustus
1 *Chiaroscuro* (1952)
2 *Finishing touches* (1964)
  One volume edition entitled *Autobiography*, 1975

Frame series
Brean, Herbert
  see **Reynold Frame series**

Frames series
Ball, Brian Neville
  see **Probability series**

Frampton series
Plummer, Thomas Arthur
  see **Detective Inspector Andrew Frampton series**

France series
Stevenson, Dorothy Emily
  see **Barbie France series**

Frances Baird series
Kauffman, Reginald Wright
1 *Miss Frances Baird, detective* (1906)
2 *My heart and Stephanie* (1910)

Frances in the fourth grade series
Cooper, Ilene
1 *Frances takes a chance* (1991)
2 *Frances dances* (1991)
3 *Frances Four-Eyes* (1991)
4 *Frances and friends* (1991)

Frances series
Hoban, Russell
1 *Bedtime for Frances* (1960)
2 *Baby sister for Frances* (1964)
3 *Bread and jam for Frances* (1964)
4 *Birthday for Frances* (1968)
5 *Best friends for Frances* (1969)
6 *Bargain for Frances* (1970)
Companion volume: *Egg thoughts, and other Frances songs*, 1972

Frances series
Saxon, Nancy
  see **Panky series**

Frances series
Warner, Priscilla Mary
1 *Friend for Frances* (1956)
2 *If it hadn't been for Frances* (1957)

Francesca da Rimini series
Fleetwood, Frances
  see **Concordia series**

Francesca Miles and Inspector Joe Barnaby series
Chan, Melissa
  see **Inspector Joe Barnaby and Francesca Miles series**

Francesca series
Shulman, Sandra
1 *Francesca, the Florentine* (1971)
  Florentine
2 *Francesca, madonna of the shadows* (1973)

Francie series
Hahn, Emily
1 *Francie* (1951)
2 *Francie again* (1953)
3 *Francie comes home* (1956)

Francis and Anne Woodward series
Lowndes, Joan Selby
1 *Royal chase* (1947)
2 *Tudor star* (1949)

Francis Cornish trilogy
Davies, Robertson
1 *Rebel angels* (1981)
2 *What's bred in the bone* (1985)
3 *Lyre of Orpheus* (1988)
One volume edition entitled *The Cornish trilogy*, 1991

Francis Crawford of Lymond series
Dunnett, Dorothy
  Ten years in the life of the younger son of an aristocratic Scottish family in the sixteenth century
1 *Game of kings* (1961)
2 *Queen's play* (1964)
3 *Disorderly knights* (1966)
4 *Pawn in frankincense* (1969)
5 *Ringed castle* (1971)
6 *Checkmate* (1975)

Francis De Sales series
Boyle, Thomas
  see **Detective Francis De Sales series**

Francis Drake series
Turner, Judy
  see **Sir Francis Drake series**

Francis Foy series
Black, Lionel
  see **Superintendent Francis Foy series**

Francis Macnab series
Ferguson, John
1 *Man in the dark* (1928)
2 *Murder on the marsh* (1930)
3 *Death comes to the Perigord* (1931)
4 *Grouse Moor mystery* (1934)
  Grouse Moor murder
5 *Death of Mister Dodsley* (1937)
Companion volume: *The dark Geraldine*, 1921

Francis Mandell-Essington series
Clouston, Joseph Storer
  see **Mister Francis Mandell-Essington series**

Francis Newnes series
Martindale, Cyril Charlie
  see **Mister Francis Newnes series**

Francis Pettigrew series
Hare, Cyril
1 *Tragedy at law* (1942)
2 *With a bare bodkin* (1946)
3 *When the wind blows* (1949)
  Wind blows death
4 *That yew trees shade* (1954)
  Death walks the woods
5 *He should have died hereafter* (1958)
  Untimely death

Francis Quarles series
Symons, Julian
1 *Murder, murder!* (1961)
  Short stories
2 *Francis Quarles investigates* (1965)
  Short stories

Francis Redmayne series
Darke, Marjorie
1 *Ride the iron horse* (1973)
2 *Star trap* (1974)

Francis series
Pirincci, Akif
  see **Felidae series**

Francis trilogy
Stern, David
1 *Francis, the army mule* (1945)
  Originally published under the pseudonym Peter Sterling
2 *Francis* (1946)
3 *Francis goes to Washington* (1948)

Francis Villiers series
Rodney, Bryan
1 *Owl hoots* (1945)
2 *Owl meets the Devil* (1949)
3 *Owl flies home* (1952)

Francis X Gordon trilogy
Howard, Robert Ervin
  see **El Borak trilogy**

Francis Xavier Flynn series
McDonald, Gregory
1 *Confess, Fletch* (1976)
2 *Flynn* (1977)
3 *Buck passes Flynn* (1981)
4 *Flynn's in* (1984)

Francis Xavier Killy series
Quinn, Simon
  see **Inquisitor series**

Franciscan prient series
Fisher, Clay
1 *Apache ransom* (1974)
2 *Black Apache* (1976)

Franco Corti series
Inchbald, Peter
  see **Inspector Franco Corti series**

Franco-Prussian War series
Everett-Green, Evelyn
1 *Castle of the White Flag* (1904)
2 *Ringed by fire* (1904)

Franco-Prussian War series
Margueritte, Paul
1 *Disaster* (1897)
  Original edition entitled *Desastre*
2 *[Troncons de Glaive]* (1900)
  No English edition
3 *Strasbourg* (1901)
  Original edition entitled *Les braves gens*
4 *Commune* (1904)
  Original edition entitled *La commune*

Franco-Prussian war trilogy
Chambers, Robert William
1 *Lorraine* (1898)
2 *Ashes of empire* (1899)
3 *Maids of paradise* (1903)

Francoeur family series
Plante, David
1 *Family* (1978)
2 *Woods* (1982)
3 *Foreigner* (1984)
4 *Country* (1981)
  Numbers 1, 2, 4 written as a trilogy and also published in one volume entitled *The Francoeur novels*, 1983
5 *Catholic* (1986)
6 *Native* (1988)

Francois Joubert series
Van der Post, Laurens
1 *Story like the wind* (1972)
2 *Far-off place* (1974)

Francois Villon trilogy
McCarthy, Justin Huntly
1 *If I were king* (1901)
2 *Needles and pins* (1907)
3 *Pretty maids all in arow* (1915)

Franconia series
Abbott, Jacob
1 *Malleville* (1850)
2 *Wallace* (1850)

3 *Mary Erskine* (1850)
4 *Mary Bell* (1850)
5 *Beechnut* (1850)
6 *Rodolphus* (1852)
7 *Ellen Linn* (1853)
8 *Stuyvesat* (1853)
9 *Caroline* (1853)
10 *Agnes* (1853)

Frank Allen series
Forbes, Graham B
Originally issued in part as **Boys of Columbia High series**, 1912-1920
House pseudonym
1 *Frank Allen's schooldays* (1926)
Alternative title: The all around rivals of Columbia High; originally issued as *The boys of Columbia High*, 1912
2 *Frank Allen playing to win* (1926)
Originally issued as *The boys of Columbia High on the ice*, 1912
3 *Frank Allen in winter sports* (1926)
Alternative title: Columbia High on skates and iceboats; originally issued as *The boys of Columbia High in winter sports*, 1915
4 *Frank Allen and his rivals* (1926)
Originally issued as *The boys of Columbia High in track athletics*, 1913
5 *Frank Allen, pitcher* (1926)
Originally issued as *The boys of Columbia High on the diamond*, 1912
6 *Frank Allen, head of the crew* (1926)
Originally issued as *The boys of Columbia High on the river*, 1912
7 *Frank Allen in camp* (1926)
Alternative title: Columbia High and the School League rivals; originally published as *The boys of Columbia High in camp*, 1920
8 *Frank Allen at Rockspur Ranch* (1926)
Alternative title: The old cowboy's secret
9 *Frank Allen at Gold Fork* (1926)
Alternative title: Locating the lost claim
10 *Frank Allen and his motor boat* (1926)
Alternative title: Racing to save a life
11 *Frank Allen, captain of the team* (1926)
Originally issued as *The boys of Columbia High on the gridiron*, 1912
12 *Frank Allen at Old Moose Lake* (1926)
Alternative title: The trail in the snow
13 *Frank Allen at Zero Camp* (1926)
Alternative title: The queer old man of the hills
14 *Frank Allen, snowbound* (1927)
Alternative title: Fighting for life in the big blizzard
15 *Frank Allen after big game* (1927)
Alternative title: With guns and snowshoes in the Rockies
16 *Frank Allen with the circus* (1927)
Alternative title: The old ringmaster's secret
17 *Frank Allen pitching his best* (1927)
Alternative title: The baseball rivals of Columbia High

Frank and David Adams series
Saint James, Daniel
see **Brothers in blood series**

Frank and Ernest series
Day, Alexandra
1 *Frank and Ernest* (1988)
2 *Frank and Ernest play ball* (1990)
3 *Frank and Ernest on the road* (1994)

Frank and fearless trilogy
Alger, Horatio
1 *Frank Hunter's peril* (1896)
2 *Frank and fearless* (1897)
3 *Young salesman* (1896)

Frank and Gail Mitchell series
Gordons
1 *Night before the wedding* (1968)
2 *Night after the wedding* (1979)

Frank Angel series
Christian, Frederick H
This pseudonym is used by Frederick Nolan for numbers 1-9 and by Michael R Linaker for numbers 10-14
1 *Kill Angel* (1972)
Bad day at Agua Caliente
2 *Send Angel* (1972)
Ride clear of Daranga
3 *Find Angel* (1973)
Ride out to Vengeance
4 *Trap Angel* (1973)
Ambush in Purgatory
5 *Frame Angel* (1974)
Shoot-out at Silver King
6 *Hang Angel* (1975)
Showdown at Trinidad
7 *Hunt Angel* (1975)
Massacre in Madison
8 *Take Angel* (1975)
Warn Angel
9 *Stop Angel!* (1976)
10 *Hell's Angel* (1978)
11 *Wild Angel* (1978)
12 *Angel's law* (1978)
13 *Angel's way* (1978)
14 *Long ride to hell* (1978)

Frank Arrow series
Deptula, Walter
1 *Naked mistress* (1974)
2 *Wine, women and death* (1974)
3 *Death list of Rico Scalisi* (1974)

Frank Beresford series
Curling, Henry
1 *Frank Beresford* (1858)
Alternative title: Life in the army
2 *Miser lord* (1859)

Frank Braun series
Ewers, Hanns Heinz
Translated from the German
1 *Sorcerer's apprentice* (1927)
2 *Alraune* (1929)

Frank Cardolini series
Gerrity, David
1 *Never contract* (1975)
2 *Plastic man* (1976)
3 *Numbers man* (1977)

Frank Carver and Ginny Trask series
Wallingford, Lee
1 *Cold tracks* (1991)
2 *Clear-cut murder* (1993)

Frank Clamart series
Rowland, Henry Cottrell
1 *Closing net* (1912)
2 *Return of Frank Clamart* (1923)

Frank Clemons series
Cook, Thomas H
1 *Sacrificial ground* (1988)
2 *Flesh and blood* (1989)
3 *Night secrets* (1990)

Frank Cowperwood trilogy
Dreiser, Theodore
1 *Financier* (1912)
2 *Titan* (1914)
3 *Stoic* (1948)

Frank Dawley trilogy
Sillitoe, Alan
1 *Death of William Posters* (1965)
2 *Tree on fire* (1967)
3 *Flame of life* (1974)

Frank Derben series
Foxall, Peter Augustus
see **Inspector Frank Derben series**

Frank Desouza series
Olbrich, Freny
see **Chief Inspector Frank Desouza series**

Frank Drury and Inspector Bill Hazard series
Marlowe, Piers
1 *Dead don't scare* (1963)
2 *Men in her death* (1964)
3 *Promise to kill* (1965)
4 *Knife for your heart* (1966)
5 *Hire me a hearse* (1968)
6 *Cash my chips, croupier* (1969)
7 *Killer in the shade* (1973)

Frank Frazetta's Death dealer series
Silke, James R
see **Death dealer series**

Frank Frobisher series
Cannan, Joanna
1 *And all I learned* (1951)
2 *All is discovered* (1962)

Frank Garratt and Benbow Smith series
Wentworth, Patricia
see **Benbow Smith and Frank Garratt series**

Frank, Gerry and Edward series
Pearce, Agatha Hunt
see **Edward, Frank and Gerry series**

Frank Hastings series
Wilcox, Collin
see **Lieutenant Frank Hastings series**

Frank Kerrigan series
Harrington, Joseph
see **Lieutenant Frank Kerrigan series**

Frank King series
King, Frank
see **Doctor Frank King series**

Frank Le Roux series
Brown, Hosanna
1 *I spy, you die* (1984)
2 *Death upon a spear* (1986)

Frank Luther series
Lanham, Edwin
1 *Murder on my street* (1958)
2 *No hiding place* (1962)

Frank Marker series
The sequence has two authors; based on the *Private Eye* television series
Marriott, Anthony
1 *Marker calls the tune* (1968)
Southcott, Audley
2 *Cross that palm when I come to it* (1974)

Frank Merriwell series
Frederic, Mike
1 *Frank Merriwell, freshman quarterback* (1965)
2 *Frank Merriwell, freshman pitcher* (1965)
3 *Frank Merriwell, sports car racer* (1965)

Frank Muir goes into series
Muir, Frank
1 *Frank Muir goes into* (1978)
2 *Second Frank Muir goes into* (1979)
3 *Third Frank Muir goes into* (1980)
4 *Fourth Frank Muir goes into* (1981)

Frank Pagan series
Armstrong, Campbell
see **Detective Frank Pagan series**

Frank Richmond series
Graham, Anthony
1 *Deadly lovers* (1966)
2 *Death business* (1967)

Frank Ryan series
Leonard, Elmore
1 *Swag* (1976)
Ryan's rules
2 *Unknown man number eighty nine* (1977)

Frank Sessions series
Waugh, Hillary
see **Detective Frank Sessions series**

Frank Shearer and Arthur Salisbury series
Crawford, Robert
see **Arthur Salisbury and Frank Shearer series**

Frank Slade series
Pennington, Link
1 *Days of '76* (1988)
2 *Escape from Montana* (1988)

Frank Tarleton series
Upward, Allen
see **Doctor Frank Tarleton series**

Frank Terrell series
Chase, James Hadley
1 *Soft centre* (1964)
2 *Way the cookie crumbles* (1965)
3 *Well now, my pretty* (1967)
4 *Ear to the ground* (1968)
5 *Believed violent* (1968)
6 *There's a hippie on the highway* (1970)

Frank Wady series
Mack Bride, Johnny
1 *Tenderfoot veteran* (1990)
2 *Dutch Pensey can ride* (1991)

Frankenstein sequels series
This sequence, by several authors whose works have been inspired by Mary Shelley's novel, are listed in chronological order of publication; some of the titles are based on screenplays
Egremont, Michael
1 *Bride of Frankenstein* (1935)
Janes, Henry Hurford
2 *Revenge of Frankenstein* (1958)
Fairman, Paul Warren
3 *Frankenstein wheel* (1972)
Myers, Robert John
4 *Cross of Frankenstein* (1975)
5 *Slave of Frankenstein* (1976)
Glut, Donald Frank
6 *Frankenstein lives again* (1977)
Revised edition 1981
7 *Terror of Frankenstein* (1977)
8 *Bones of Frankenstein* (1977)
9 *Frankenstein meets Dracula* (1977)
Dreadstone, Carl
10 *Bride of Frankenstein* (1977)
Tremayne, Peter
11 *Hound of Frankenstein* (1977)
Baxter, Alida
12 *Frankenstein is alive and well and living with Mrs Frankenstein* (1980)
Venables, Hubert
13 *Frankenstein diaries* (1980)
Martin, Les
14 *Bride* (1985)
McIntyre, Vondra Neil
15 *Bride* (1985)
Brennan, James Herbert
16 *Curse of Frankenstein* (1986)
Saberhagen, Fred
17 *Frankenstein papers* (1986)

Frankenstein series
This sequence has two authors
Shelley, Mary
1 *Frankenstein* (1818)
Alternative title: The modern Prometheus; adaptations by Dale Carlson, 1968, by Tom Barling, 1976, by Diana Stewart, 1981, by Tomas Ernesto Bethancourt, 1986, by David Campton, 1987; parodies: *Frankenstein '69*, by Ed Martin, 1969, *The adult version of Frankenstein*, by Hal Kantor, 1970, *Frankenstein and the whiz kid*, by Vic Crume, 1976; Companion volumes: *The Frankenstein legend, a tribute to Mary Shelley and Boris Karloff*, by Donald Frank Glut, 1973, *The Frankenstein catalog, being a complete listing of novels, translations, adaptations, stories, critical works, popular articles, series, fumetti, verse, stage plays, films, cartoons, puppetry, radio and television programs, comics, satire and humor, spoken and musical recordings, tapes and sheet music featuring Frankenstein's monster and or descended from Mary Shelley's novel*, by Donald Frank Glut, 1984
Aldiss, Brian Wilson
2 *Frankenstein unbound* (1973)

Frankenstein's aunt series
Pettersson, Allan Rune
1 *Frankenstein's aunt* (1980)
Original edition entitled *Frankensteins faster*
2 *Frankenstein's aunt returns* (1990)
Original edition entitled *Frankensteins faster, igen!*

Frankie series
Leslie, Madeline
see **Little Frankie series**

Franklin and Spence series
Jenkins, Jerry Bruce
see **Margo Franklin and Philip Spence series**

Franklin Brady series
McRoyd, Allan
see **Inspector Franklin Brady series**

Franklin family series
Shears, Sarah
1 *Village* (1984)
2 *Family fortunes* (1985)
3 *Young generation* (1986)

Franklin Hatcher series
Merritt, Don
see **Captain Franklin Hatcher series**

Franklin Parry and Leonard Harris series
Keverne, Richard
1 *William Cook, antique dealer* (1928)
Strange case of William Cook
2 *Menace* (1933)

Franklin Russell series
Baker, Richard Merriam
1 *Death stops the manuscript* (1936)
2 *Death stops the rehearsal* (1937)
3 *Death stops the bells* (1938)

Franklin series
Bourgeois, Paulette
Illustrated by Brenda Clark
1 *Franklin in the dark* (1989)
2 *Hurry up, Franklin* (1989)
3 *Franklin fibs* (1990)
4 *Franklin is lost* (1992)
5 *Franklin is bossy* (1993)

Franklin series
Orenstein, Frank
see **Ev Franklin series**

Franklyn Keen series
Long, Harman
1 *Seven to die* (1946)
2 *Golden cat* (1947)
3 *Corpse can't walk* (1950)

Franks series
Wallace, John
see **Conrad Franks series**

Frannie Bronson series
Vernon, Rosemary
1 *Popularity plan* (1981)
2 *Popularity summer* (1982)

Franny Scully series
Bleasdale, Alan
1 *Scully* (1975)
2 *Who's been sleeping in my bed?* (1977)

Frant series
Fearon, Diana
see **Arabella Frant series**

Franzon series
Bjorn, Thyra Ferre
see **Pastor Pontus Franzon series**

Fraser and Marriner series
Merwin, Samuel Kimball
see **Elspeth Marriner and Mack Fraser series**

Fraser family trilogy
Main, Carol
1 *White planet* (1982)
2 *Planet of evil* (1983)
3 *Planet of adventure* (1986)

Fraser series
Bailey, Elliot
see **Inspector Geoffrey Fraser series**
Boyd, James
see **James Fraser series**
Desmond, Hugh
see **Alan Fraser series**
Wood, James
see **James Fraser series**

Fraser Todd series
Jones, Henry Llewellyn
1 *Under the shadow* (1928)
2 *Case is altered* (1929)

Frass series
Chancellor, John
see **Captain Frass series**

Frayne and Cragg series
Evans, Alan
see **Cragg and Frayne series**

Frayne series
McIntosh, J T
see **Ambrose and Dominique Frayne series**

Frazer series
Durbridge, Francis
see **Tim Frazer series**

Frazetta's Death dealer series
Silke, James R
see **Death dealer series**

Freaks series
Harris, Rosemary
see **Orion series**

Freckles series
Porter, Gene Stratton
see **Limberlost series**

Fred and Frisco series
Ryan, John
see **Flying sorcerer series**

Fred and I series
Pudney, John
1 *Saturday adventure* (1950)
2 *Sunday adventure* (1951)
3 *Monday adventure* (1952)
4 *Tuesday adventure* (1953)
5 *Wednesday adventure* (1954)
6 *Thursday adventure* (1955)
7 *Friday adventure* (1956)
8 *Spring adventure* (1961)
9 *Summer adventure* (1962)
10 *Autumn adventure* (1964)
11 *Winter adventure* (1965)

Fred Bennett series
Lewis, Elliott
1 *Two heads are better* (1980)
2 *Dirty linen* (1980)
3 *People in glass houses* (1981)
4 *Double trouble* (1981)
5 *Here today, dead tomorrow* (1982)
6 *Bennett's world* (1982)
7 *Death and the single girl* (1983)

Fred Carver series
Lutz, John
1 *Tropical heat* (1986)
2 *Scorcher* (1987)
3 *Kiss* (1988)
4 *Flame* (1989)
5 *Blood fire* (1991)
6 *Hot* (1992)
7 *Spark* (1993)
8 *Torch* (1994)

Fred Crockett series
Lang, Brad
1 *Crockett on the loose* (1975)
2 *Perdition Express* (1976)
3 *Brand of fear* (1976)

Fred Fellows series
Waugh, Hillary
see **Chief Fred Fellows series**

Fred Fenton series
Chapman, Allen
1 *Fred Fenton the pitcher* (1913)
Alternative title: The rivals of Riverport School
2 *Fred Fenton in the line* (1913)
Alternative title: The football boys of Riverport School
3 *Fred Fenton on the crew* (1913)
Alternative title: The young oarsmen of Riverport School
4 *Fred Fenton on the track* (1913)
Alternative title: The athletes of Riverport School
5 *Fred Fenton, marathon runner* (1915)
Alternative title: The great race at Riverport School

Fred series
Edwards, Pat
1 *Fred's birthday* (1987)
2 *Fred makes a shelf* (1987)
3 *Get some bread, Fred* (1987)
4 *Fred and the wasp* (1990)
5 *Fred and the skateboard* (1990)
6 *Fred's letters* (1990)
7 *Fred at the beach* (1990)
8 *Fred in space* (1990)
9 *When Fred went to school* (1990)
10 *Fred's Father Christmas story* (1990)
11 *Fred's photo album* (1990)
12 *Where's Fred's trumpet* (1992)
13 *Fred makes a table* (1992)
14 *Time to go on a diet, Fred* (1992)

Freddie Browne and Jim Fanshaw series
Poole, Michael
1 *Browne's first case* (1935)
2 *Browne follows the clue* (1936)
3 *Brown's fifty thousand pound mystery* (1937)
4 *Missing bank manager* (1938)
5 *Mystery at Merrilees* (1939)
6 *Gwythyn clay mystery* (1940)
7 *Browne of the Secret Service* (1940)
8 *Browne fights the fifth column* (1942)

Freddie Freightliner series
George, David Lester
Illustrated by Bob Reese
1 *Freddie Freightliner goes to Kennedy Space Center* (1983)
2 *Freddie Freightliner learns to talk!* (1983)
3 *Freddie Freightliner to the rescue* (1983)

Freddie series
Scott, Mary
1 *Families are fun* (1957)
2 *No sad songs* (1960)
3 *Freddie* (1965)

Freddie series
Wainwright, Sheila
Illustrated by Francis Wainwright
1 *Freddie and the Star of Africa* (1984)
2 *Freddie and the Bank of England mystery* (1985)

Freddy Krueger series
Cooper, Jeffrey
see **Nightmare on Elm Street series**

Freddy Philpotts series
Caldwell, Alfred Betts
1 *Coffee for none* (1934)
2 *Turquoise hazard* (1936)
3 *No tears shed* (1937)
4 *Death rattle* (1940)

Freddy series
Gascoigne, Bamber
see **Fearless Freddy series**

Freddy the pig series
Brooks, Walter Rollin
1 *To and again* (1927)
Freddy goes to Florida
Freddy's first adventure
2 *More to and again* (1930)
Freddy the explorer
Freddy goes to the North Pole
3 *Freddy the detective* (1932)
4 *Story of Freginald* (1936)
Freddy and Freginald
5 *Clockwork twin* (1937)
6 *Wiggins for president* (1939)
Freddy the politician
7 *Freddy's cousin Weedly* (1940)
8 *Freddy and the ignoramus* (1941)
9 *Freddy and the perilous adventure* (1942)
10 *Freddy and the Bean Home news* (1943)
11 *Freddy and Mister Camphor* (1944)
12 *Freddy and the popinjay* (1945)
13 *Freddy the Pied Piper* (1946)
14 *Freddy the magician* (1947)
15 *Freddy goes camping* (1948)
16 *Freddy plays football* (1949)
17 *Freddy the cowboy* (1950)
18 *Freddy rides again* (1951)
19 *Freddy the pilot* (1952)
20 *Freddy and the space ship* (1953)
21 *Freddy and the men from Mars* (1954)
22 *Freddy and the baseball team from Mars* (1955)
23 *Freddy and Simon the dictator* (1956)
24 *Freddy and the flying saucer plans* (1957)

Freddy the pig series

25 *Freddy and the dragon* (1958)
Companion volume: *The collected poems of Freddy the pig*, 1953

Frederic Belot series
Aveline, Claude
see **Suite Policiere series**

Frederick Bettesworth series
Bourne, George
Documentary novels based on journals kept by the employer of a labourer and his family
1 *Bettesworth book* (1901)
Talks with a Surrey peasant
2 *Memoirs of a Surrey labourer* (1907)
A record of the last years of the labourer
3 *Lucy Bettesworth* (1913)

Frederick Dealtry Lugard series
Perham, Margery
1 *Years of adventure, 1858-1898* (1956)
2 *Years of authority, 1898-1945* (1960)

Frederick Exley trilogy
Exley, Frederick
Autobiographical fiction
1 *Fan's notes* (1968)
2 *Pages from a cold island* (1975)
3 *Last notes from home* (1988)

Frederick Hunt series
Day, Lillian
1 *Murder in time* (1935)
2 *Death comes on Friday* (1937)

Frederick Nutsell series
Hughes, Dean
see **Nutty Nutsell series**

Frederick series
Lionni, Leon
1 *Frederick* (1967)
2 *Frederick and his friends* (1989)
Companion volume: *Frederick's fables*, 1985, also published as *Frederick's tales*

Fredrickson series
Chesbro, George Clark
see **Mongo series**

Free agent series
Chapman, Eddie
1 *Eddie Chapman story* (1953)
Co-author: Frank Owen
2 *Free agent* (1955)

Free and Fairweather series
Lynde, Stan
see **Pardners series**

Free forest series
White, Stewart Edward
1 *Conjuror's house* (1903)
Call of the North
2 *Silent places* (1904)

Free traders series
Norton, Andre
see **Krip Vorland series**

Freedom fighters series
Scofield, Jonathan
1 *Tomahawk and long rifles* (1981)
2 *Muskets of '76* (1981)
3 *King's cannon* (1981)
4 *Guns at twilight* (1981)
5 *Bullets on the border* (1981)
6 *Storm in the south* (1981)
7 *Turning of the tide* (1981)
8 *Frontier war* (1981)
9 *Shellfire on the bay* (1981)
10 *Volunteers for glory* (1981)
11 *Bayonets in No-Man's Land* (1982)
12 *Armageddon in the West* (1982)
13 *Pacific hellfire* (1982)
14 *Far shores of danger* (1982)
15 *Junglefire* (1982)

Freedom series
Martin, Bill
1 *Adam's balm* (1970)
2 *America, I know you* (1970)
3 *Freedom's apple tree* (1970)
4 *Gentle, gentle Thursday* (1970)
Co-author: Gene D Shepherd
5 *I am freedom's child* (1970)
6 *I reach out to the morning* (1970)
7 *It's America for me* (1970)
8 *Once there were bluebirds* (1970)
9 *Poor old Uncle Sam* (1970)
10 *Spoiled tomatoes* (1970)

Freedom series
Murray, Mary
1 *Escape* (1965)
A thousand miles to freedom
2 *Hunted* (1967)
A coastwatcher's story

Freedom's Rangers series
Andrews, Keith William
1 *Freedom's Rangers* (1989)
2 *Raiders of the revolution* (1989)
3 *Search and destroy* (1990)
4 *Treason in time* (1990)
5 *Sink the armada* (1990)
6 *Snow kill* (1991)

Freeman series
Ironside, John
see **Detective Inspector John Freeman series**
Treat, Lawrence
see **Jub Freeman series**

Freeman trilogy
Collier, James Lincoln
see **Willy Freeman trilogy**

Freemantle series
Ingraham, Joseph Holt
1 *Freemantle* (1845)
Alternative title: The privateersman
2 *Norman* (1845)
Alternative title: The privateersman's bride

Freer series
Ferrars, Elizabeth
see **Virginia and Felix Freer series**

Freeway warrior series
Dever, Joe
1 *Highway holocaust* (1988)
2 *Slaughter Mountain run* (1988)
Mountain run
3 *Omega zone* (1989)
4 *California countdown* (1989)

Freightliner series
George, David Lester
see **Freddie Freightliner series**

Fremont trilogy
Zola, Emile
see **Abbe Pierre Fremont trilogy**

French and Indian war series
Altsheler, Joseph Alexander
1 *Hunters of the hills* (1916)
2 *Shadow of the North* (1917)
3 *Rulers of the Lakes* (1917)
4 *Masters of the Peaks* (1918)
5 *Lords of the wild* (1919)
6 *Sun of Quebec* (1919)

French and Indian war series
Robbins, Orison
1 *Boy of old Quebec* (1926)
2 *Boy of old French West* (1927)
3 *Escaping the Monawks* (1929)

French campaign series
Erckmann, Emile
1 *Conscript* (1864)
History of a conscript of 1813
Original edition entitled *Histoire d'un conscrit de 1813*
2 *Waterloo* (1865)
Original edition entitled *Waterloo, suite du conscrit de 1813*; the story of the 100 days

French Front series
Hocking, Joseph
see **Great War, French Front series**

French history trilogy
Thompson, James Matthew
1 *French Revolution* (1943)
2 *Napoleon Bonaparte, his rise and fall* (1952)
3 *Louis Napoleon and the Second Empire* (1954)

French Resistance series
Gavin, Catherine
1 *Traitors' gate* (1976)
Set in London and Brazil
2 *None dare call it treason* (1978)
Set in Vichy France
3 *How sleep the brave* (1980)

French Revolution series
Bowen, Marjorie
1 *Giant in chains* (1938)
Prelude to Revolution, 1775-1791; sequence continued under the pseudonym George Preedy
Preedy, George Runnell
2 *Laurell'd captains* (1935)
3 *Primula* (1940)

French Revolution series
Dymoke, Juliet
1 *White cockade* (1979)
2 *March to Corunna* (1985)
3 *Queen's diamond* (1985)
4 *Two flags for France* (1986)

French Revolution trilogy
Gras, Felix
1 *Reds of the Midi* (1896)
2 *Terror* (1898)
3 *White Terror* (1899)

French Revolution trilogy
Plaidy, Jean
see **Louis XV trilogy**

French series
Crofts, Freeman Wills
see **Inspector Joseph French series**
Gollin, James
see **Philomel Foundation series**
Hale, Christopher
see **Lieutenant Bill French series**

Frend and Best series
Chetwynd, Bridget
see **Petunia Best and Max Frend series**

Frere series
Elliott, William James
see **Royston Frere series**

Fresh series
Aiken, Albert W
1 *Fresh of Frisco* (1879)
Alternative title: The heiress of Buenaventure
2 *Fresh at Santa Fe* (1891)
3 *Fresh in Montana* (1891)
Alternative title: Jackson Blake's full hand at hardtack
4 *Fresh, the race-track sport* (1894)
Alternative title: Kentucky Sharpers brought to bay

Freshman dorm series
Cooney, Linda A
1 *Freshman dorm* (1990)
2 *Freshman lies* (1990)
3 *Freshman guys* (1990)
4 *Freshman nights* (1990)
5 *Freshman dreams* (1991)
6 *Freshman games* (1991)
7 *Freshman loves* (1991)
8 *Freshman secrets* (1991)
9 *Freshman schemes* (1991)
10 *Freshman changes* (1991)
11 *Freshman fling* (1991)
12 *Freshman rivals* (1991)
13 *Freshman flames* (1991)
14 *Freshman choices* (1991)
15 *Freshman heartbreak* (1992)
16 *Freshman feud* (1992)
17 *Freshman follies* (1992)
18 *Freshman wedding* (1992)
19 *Freshman promises* (1992)
20 *Freshman affair* (1992)
21 *Freshman truths* (1992)
22 *Freshman scandal* (1992)
23 *Freshman roommate* (1993)
24 *Freshman obsession* (1993)
25 *Freshman heat* (1993)
26 *Freshman taboo* (1993)
27 *Freshman passion* (1993)
28 *Freshman celebrity* (1993)
29 *Freshman breakup* (1993)
30 *Freshman temptation* (1993)

Frewin family series
Maynard, Nan
1 *Weep not, my wanton* (1964)
2 *Red roses dying* (1974)

Freya Matthews and Guy Plante series
Palmer, John
see **Guy Plante and Freya Matthews series**

Friar Felix Fabri series
Prescott, Hilda Frances Margaret
1 *Friar Felix at large* (1950)
Jerusalem journey
A fifteenth-century pilgrimage to the Holy Land
2 *Once to Sinai* (1957)

Fricka Hammond series
Atkinson, Mary Evelyn
1 *Castaway camp* (1951)
2 *Hunter's moon* (1952)
3 *Barnstormers* (1953)
4 *Unexpected adventure* (1955)
5 *Riders and raids* (1955)

Friday the thirteenth series
Hawke, Simon
Based on moving pictures
1 *Friday the thirteenth, part I* (1987)
2 *Friday the thirteenth, part II* (1988)
3 *Friday the thirteenth, part III* (1988)
Companion volume: *Friday the thirteenth, part III, 3-D*, by Michael Avallone, 1982; parts IV and V not novelized
6 *Jason lives* (1986)

Friday the thirteenth series
Morse, Eric
1 *Mother's Day* (1994)
2 *Jason's curse* (1994)
3 *Carnival* (1994)
4 *Road trip* (1994)

Friedman series
Friedman, Kinky
see **Kinky Friedman series**
Plain, Belva
see **Anna Friedman series**

Friedrich trilogy
Richter, Hans Peter
1 *Friedrich* (1961)

Original edition entitled *Damals war es Friedrich*
2 *I was there* (1962)
Original edition entitled *Wir waren dabei*
3 *Time of the young soldiers* (1967)
Original edition entitled *Zeit der jungen Soldaten*

Friend series
Cawley, Winifred
see **Jinnie Friend series**

Friendly Farm series
How, Ruth W
1 *Friendly Farm* (1946)
2 *Adventures at Friendly Farm* (1948)

Friendly series
Gee, Herbert Leslie
1 *Winter journey* (1938)
Some account of a friendly man's adventures
2 *Friendly house* (1939)
3 *Friendly year* (1940)
4 *Friendly folk* (1942)
5 *Busy streets* (1950)
6 *They come to my door* (1950)
7 *As it happened* (1955)
8 *Chance acquaintances* (1955)
9 *One fine day* (1956)
10 *On my way* (1956)
11 *Good Samaritans* (1957)
12 *Gallant folk* (1957)

Friendly Terrace series
Smith, Harriet Lummis
1 *Girls of Friendly Terrace* (1928)
Alternative title: Peggy Raymond's success
2 *Peggy Raymond's vacation* (1928)
Alternative title: Friendly Terrace transplanted
3 *Peggy Raymond's school days* (1928)
Alternative title: Old girls and new
4 *Friendly Terrace quartet* (1928)
Alternative title: How Peggy and Priscilla and Amy and Ruth did their share on the farm and in the shop
5 *Peggy Raymond's way* (1928)
Alternative title: Blossom time at Friendly Terrace

Friends like these series
Foster, Alan Dean
Short stories
1 *With friends like these* (1983)
2 *Who needs enemies* (1984)

Friendship village series
Gale, Zora
1 *Friendship village* (1908)
2 *Friendship village love stories* (1909)
3 *Mothers to men* (1911)
4 *Neighborhood stories* (1914)
5 *Peace in Friendship village* (1919)

Fripsey series
Chastain, Madye Lee
1 *Bright days* (1952)
2 *Fripsey summer* (1953)
3 *Fripsey fun* (1955)
4 *Leave it to the Fripseys* (1957)

Frisco and Fred series
Ryan, John
see **Flying sorcerer series**

Frito and Ben series
McHargue, Georgess
see **Ben and Frito series**

Frobisher series
Cannan, Joanna
see **Frank Frobisher series**

Frodesley series
Lance, Leslie
see **Nurse Verena Frodesley series**

Frog and Dog series
Astrop, John
1 *Frog and Dog at the sea* (1986)
2 *Frog and Dog have a party* (1986)
3 *Frog and Dog find a treasure* (1986)
4 *Frog and Dog go to the moon* (1986)

Frog and Toad series
Lobel, Arnold
1 *Frog and Toad are friends* (1970)
2 *Frog and Toad together* (1972)
3 *Frog and Toad all year* (1976)
4 *Days with Frog and Toad* (1979)
Omnibus volume: *Frog and Toad tales*, 1981; companion volumes: *The Frog and Toad coloring book*, 1981, *The Frog and Toad pop-up book*, 1986

Frog band series
Smith, Jim
1 *Frog band and the onion seller* (1976)
2 *Frog band and the Durrington dormouse* (1978)
3 *Frog band and the mystery of Lion Castle* (1978)
4 *Frog band and the owlnapper* (1980)

Frog series
Mayer, Mercer
1 *Boy, a dog and a frog* (1967)
2 *Frog, where are you?* (1969)
3 *Frog on his own* (1973)
4 *Frog goes to dinner* (1974)

Froggy series
Brenda
1 *Froggy's little brother* (1875)
2 *More about Froggy* (1914)

Froggy series
London, Jonathan
Illustrated by Frank Remkiewicz
1 *Froggy gets dressed* (1992)
2 *Let's go, Froggy!* (1994)

Frogs series
Leeson, Robert
1 *Never kiss frogs!* (1988)
2 *One frog too many* (1991)

From thief to king series
Williams, Michael Leon
1 *Sorcerer's apprentice* (1990)
2 *Forest lord* (1991)

Frome series
Packard, Edward
see **Escape from the Kingdom of Frome series**

Frontier America series
Chambers, Catherine E
see **Adventures in frontier America series**

Frontier Boys series
Roosevelt, Wyn
1 *Frontier Boys on Overland Trail* (1908)
Alternative title: Across the plains of Kansas
2 *Frontier Boys in Colorado* (1908)
Alternative title: Captured by Indians
3 *Frontier Boys in the Grand Canyon* (1908)
Alternative title: A search for treasure
4 *Frontier Boys in Mexico* (1908)
Alternative title: Mystery Mountain
5 *Frontier Boys in the Rockies* (1909)
Alternative title: Lost in the mountains
6 *Frontier Boys on the coast* (1909)
Alternative title: In the pirate's power
7 *Frontier Boys in Hawaii* (1909)
Alternative title: The mystery of the hollow mountain
8 *Frontier Boys in the Sierras* (1909)
Alternative title: The lost mine
9 *Frontier Boys in the saddle* (1910)
10 *Frontier Boys in Frisco* (1911)
11 *Frontier Boys in the South Seas* (1912)

Frontier girl series
Curtis, Alice Turner
1 *Frontier girl of Virginia* (1929)
2 *Frontier girl of Massachusetts* (1930)
3 *Frontier girl of New York* (1931)
4 *Frontier girl of Chesapeke Bay* (1934)
5 *Frontier girl of Pennsylvania* (1937)

Frontier rakers series
Norman, David
1 *Frontier rakers* (1981)
2 *Forty-niners* (1981)
3 *Gold fever* (1981)
4 *Silver City* (1982)
5 *Montana Pass* (1982)
6 *Santa Fe dream* (1983)

Frontier series
Bonehill, Ralph
This sequence was reissued under the author's real name Edward L Stratemeyer and with different titles
1 *With Boone on the frontier* (1903)
Alternative title: The pioneer boys of old Kentucky
2 *Pioneer boys of the great Northwest* (1904)
Alternative title: With Lewis and Clark across the Rockies
3 *Pioneer boys of the gold fields* (1906)
Alternative title: The nugget hunters of '49

Frontier series
Stanley, Chuck
1 *Frontier renegade* (1956)
2 *Frontier medico* (1956)

Frontier series
Stratemeyer, Edward L
1 *Boys of the wilderness* (1932)
Alternative title: Down in old Kentucky
2 *Boys of the great Northwest* (1932)
Alternative title: Across the Rockies
3 *Boys of the gold fields* (1932)
Alternative title: The nugget hunters

Frontier women series
This sequence has two authors
Brown, Kitt
1 *Kentucky spitfire, Caitlyn McGregor* (1981)
Foster, Jeanne
2 *Missouri flame, Deborah Leigh* (1981)
Brown, Kitt
3 *Texas wildflower, Laurian Kane* (1982)
Foster, Jeanne
4 *Wyoming glory, Eden Richards* (1982)

Frontiers of America series
McCall, Edith
1 *Log fort adventures* (1958)
2 *Steamboats to the West* (1959)
3 *Hunters blaze the trail* (1959)
4 *Explorers in a new world* (1960)
5 *Men on iron horses* (1960)
6 *Settlers on a strange shore* (1960)
7 *Heroes of the Western outposts* (1960)
8 *Pioneers of the early waterways* (1961)
9 *Wagons over the mountains* (1961)
10 *Cumberland Gap and trails West* (1961)
11 *Mail riders* (1961)
12 *Gold rush adventures* (1962)
13 *Pioneering on the Plains* (1962)
14 *Pirates and privateers* (1963)
15 *Pioneer show folk* (1963)
16 *Pioneer traders* (1964)
17 *Cowboys and cattle drives* (1964)
18 *Fort in the wilderness* (1968)
19 *Stalwart men of early Texas* (1970)
A teacher's guide to this sequence was published in 1980

Frontiersman series
Pocock, Roger
Autobiography
1 *Frontiersman* (1903)
Following the frontier
2 *Chorus to adventurers* (1931)
The later life of Roger Pocock, a frontiersman

Frost in May series
White, Antonia
1 *Frost in May* (1933)
2 *Lost traveller* (1950)
3 *Sugar house* (1952)
4 *Beyond the glass* (1954)

Frost series
Bell, Josephine
see **Doctor Henry Frost series**
Horler, Sydney
see **Nighthawk series**
Kilgore, Axel
see **They call me the Mercenary series**
Lee, Laurel
see **Barnaby Frost series**
Smith, Herbert Maynard
see **Inspector Frost series**

Frost trilogy
Bailey, Robin Wayne
1 *Frost* (1983)
2 *Skull Gate* (1985)
3 *Bloodsongs* (1986)

Frostflower series
Karr, Phyllis Ann
1 *Frostflower and Thorn* (1980)
2 *Frostflower and Windbourne* (1982)

Frozen north series
Rutzebeck, Hjalmar
1 *Alaska man's luck* (1921)
A fight for life and love in the frozen north
2 *My Alaskan idyll* (1922)

Fruits of the earth series
Gide, Andre
1 *Fruits of the earth* (1897)
Original edition entitled *Les nourritures terrestres*
2 *Later fruits of the earth* (1935)
Original edition entitled *Les nouvelles nourritures*
One volume edition entitled *Fruits of the earth*, 1949

Fry series
Fry, Pete
see **Pete Fry series**

Fu-Manchu series
Rohmer, Sax
1 *Mystery of Doctor Fu-Manchu* (1913)
Insidious Doctor Fu-Manchu
2 *Devil doctor* (1916)
Return of Doctor Fu-Manchu
3 *Si-Fan mysteries* (1917)
Hand of Fu-Manchu
4 *Golden scorpion* (1919)
5 *Daughter of Fu-Manchu* (1931)
6 *Mask of Fu-Manchu* (1932)

7 *Bride of Fu-Manchu* (1933)
Fu-Manchu's bride
8 *Trail of Fu-Manchu* (1934)
9 *President Fu-Manchu* (1936)
Serialized as The invisible president
10 *Drums of Fu-Manchu* (1939)
11 *Island of Fu-Manchu* (1941)
12 *Shadow of Fu-Manchu* (1948)
13 *Re-enter Fu-Manchu* (1957)
Re-enter Doctor Fu-Manchu
14 *Emperor Fu-Manchu* (1959)
15 *Wrath of Fu-Manchu, and other stories* (1973)
Also one story featuring Fu-Manchu in *The secret of Holm Peel, and other strange stories*, 1970
Van Ash, Cay
16 *Fires of Fu Manchu* (1987)
Companion volumes: *Ten years beyond Baker Street, Sherlock Holmes matches wits with the diabolical Doctor Fu Manchu*, 1984, *The passing of Fu Manchu*, by Jon Michael Suter, 1976

Fugitives series
Mackenzie, Donald
Autobiography
1 *Fugitives* (1955)
Occupation, thief
2 *Gentleman in crime* (1956)

Full tilt series
Murphy, Dervla
1 *Full tilt* (1965)
Ireland to India with a bicycle
2 *Tibetan foothold* (1966)

Fuller series
Vaughan, Carter A
see **Lieutenant Gordon Fuller series**
Wallace, John
see **Detective Sergeant Fuller series**

Fullie series
Glyn, Caroline
1 *Unicorn girl* (1966)
2 *Heights and depths* (1968)
3 *Tree* (1969)

Fulton series
Beatty, Jerome
see **Bob Fulton series**

Fun with arithmetic series
Daniel, Rebecca
1 *Fun with addition* (1979)
2 *Fun with subtraction* (1979)
3 *Fun with multiplication* (1979)
4 *Fun with division* (1979)

Fun with Sally series
Carruth, Jean
1 *Sally and her puppy* (1963)
Contains *Grandpa's surprise*, and *Sally in the jungle*
2 *Sally on holiday* (1963)
Contains *Fun at the seaside*, and *Adventure in the snow*
3 *Sally on the farm* (1963)
Contains *Cowboys and Indians*, and *The new camera*

Fungus the bogeyman series
Briggs, Raymond
1 *Fungus the bogeyman* (1977)
2 *Fungus the bogeyman plop-up book* (1982)

Funny animals series
Browne, Eileen
1 *Numbers* (1986)
2 *Colours* (1986)

Funny bunnies series
Quackenbush, Robert Mead
1 *Funny bunnies* (1984)
2 *Funny bunnies on the run* (1989)

Funny Farm series
Kanno, Wendy
1 *Holey Moley Cow* (1984)
2 *Waldo Duck* (1984)
3 *Bags the lamb* (1984)
4 *Elmo the pig* (1984)
5 *Sampson the horse* (1984)
6 *Funny Farm house* (1984)

Funny game series
Johnston, Brian
Humorous reminiscences of cricket and broadcasting
1 *It's been a lot of fun* (1974)
2 *It's a funny game* (1978)

Funny names series
Cross, Diana Harding
Illustrated by Jan Brett
1 *Some birds have funny names* (1981)
2 *Some plants have funny names* (1983)

Funny ones series
Hough, Charlotte
1 *Three little funny ones* (1962)
2 *More funny ones* (1965)

Funnybones series
Ahlberg, Allan
Illustrated by Andre Amstutz
1 *Black cat* (1990)
2 *Pet shop* (1990)
3 *Dinosaur dreams* (1991)
4 *Mystery tour* (1991)
5 *Skeleton crew* (1991)
6 *Bumps in the night* (1991)
7 *Give the dog a bone* (1991)
8 *Ghost train* (1992)
Companion volume: *Funnybones*, 1980

Funnyman series
Mooser, Stephen
Illustrated by Tomie de Paola
1 *Funnyman's first case* (1981)
2 *Funneyman and the penny dodo* (1984)
3 *Funnyman meets the monster from outer space* (1987)

Fur country series
Verne, Jules
Original edition entitled Le pays des fourrures
1 *Sun in eclipse* (1873)
2 *Through the Behring Strait* (1873)

Furling series
Grierson, Francis Durham
see **Richard Furling series**

Furlong series
Thurston, Ernest Temple
see **Richard Furlong series**

Furneaux series
Holmes, Gordon
see **Inspector Furneaux series**

Furnell series
Furnell, John
see **Doctor Furnell series**

Furness series
Cottenham, Mark Pepys
see **Tom Furness series**

Furnival series
Haynes, Annie
see **Inspector Furnival series**
Phillips, Stella
see **Inspector Matthew Furnival series**

Furry Forest series
Graham, Rosemary
1 *Furry Forest bears* (1956)
2 *Mustard and company* (1960)

Furry tales series
Lee, Leslie
1 *Furry tales* (1950)
2 *More furry tales* (1953)

Fursey series
Wall, Mervyn
1 *Unfortunate Fursey* (1946)
2 *Return of Fursey* (1948)
One volume edition entitled *The complete Fursey*, 1985

Fury and Fletcher series
Jerina, Carol
see **Jack and Jill series**

Fury series
Austin, Jim
see **John Fury series**

Fury series
Miller, Albert Griffith
1 *Fury, stallion of Broken Wheel Ranch* (1959)
2 *Fury and the mustangs* (1960)
3 *Fury and the white mare* (1962)

Furys chronicle series
Hanley, James
1 *Furys* (1935)
2 *Secret journey* (1936)
3 *Our time is gone* (1940)
4 *Winter song* (1950)
5 *End and a beginning* (1958)

Furze series
Kyle, Elisabeth
1 *Visitors from England* (1941)
2 *Vanishing island* (1942)
Disappearing island
3 *Seven sapphires* (1944)
4 *Holly Hotel* (1945)
5 *West wind* (1948)
6 *House on the hill* (1949)

Fusil and Kerr series
Alding, Peter
see **C.I.D. Room series**

Future at war series
Bretnor, Reginald
1 *Thor's hammer, on or near earth* (1979)
2 *Spear of Mars* (1980)
3 *Orion's sword* (1980)
War in interstellar and intergalactic space

Future history series
Anderson, Poul
1 *Let the spacemen beware!* (1963)
Night face
2 *Day of their return* (1973)
3 *People of the wind* (1973)
Numbers 2 and 3 also published in one volume, 1982
Companion volume: *The trouble twisters*, 1966

Future history series
Heinlein, Robert Anson
1 *Green hills of earth* (1951)
Short stories
2 *Man who sold the moon* (1950)
Short stories
3 *Universe* (1951)
Orphans of the sky
4 *Revolt in 2100* (1953)
5 *Methuselah's children* (1958)
Selections published as *The past through tomorrow*, 1967
7 *Time enough for love* (1973)
Selections published as *The notebooks of Lazarus Long*, 1978
8 *Cat who walks through walls* (1985)
9 *To sail beyond the sunset* (1987)
The life and loves of Maureen Johnson, being the memoirs of a somewhat irregular lady

Future history series
Pournelle, Jerry
1 *Mote in God's eye* (1974)
Co-author: Larry Niven
2 *Mercenary* (1977)
Short stories
3 *West of honor* (1976)
Numbers 2 and 3 also published in one volume entitled *Future history*, 1980
4 *Prince of mercenaries* (1989)
Short stories
5 *Go tell the Spartans* (1991)
Co-author: Stephen Michael Stirling
Companion volume: *A spaceship for the king*, 1973, revised edition entitled *King David's spaceship*, 1980

Future past series
Karl, Jean Edna
1 *Turning place* (1976)
Worlds end and after
2 *Strange tomorrow* (1985)

Future series
Sterling, Brett
see **Captain Future series**

Fuzzy Rabbit series
Billam, Rosemary
see **Alpaca series**

Fuzzy series
This sequence has three authors
Piper, Horace Beam
1 *Little Fuzzy* (1962)
Adventures of little Fuzzy
The second title is an abridgement by Benson Parker, 1983
2 *Other human race* (1964)
Fuzzy sapiens
3 *Fuzzies and other people* (1984)
Tuning, William
4 *Fuzzy bones* (1984)
Mayhar, Ardath
5 *Golden dream* (1982)

Fuzzy tales series
Ross, Katharine
Illustrated by Lisa McCue
1 *Fuzzy fussy tale* (1987)
2 *Fuzzy sleepy tale* (1987)
3 *Fuzzy wake up tale* (1987)
4 *Fuzzy friendly tale* (1987)
Companion volume: *The Fuzzytail friends' great egg hunt*, 1988

Fuzzypeg series
Uttley, Alison
1 *Story of Fuzzypeg, the hedgehog* (1932)
2 *Fuzzypeg goes to school* (1938)
3 *Fuzzypeg's brother* (1971)

Fyles series
Cullum, Ridgwell
see **Inspector Stanley Fyles series**

Fynn series
Rayner, William
see **Missouri series**

Fytton series
Howard, Liz
see **Elizabeth Fytton series**

G

G D H Pringle series
Livingston, Nancy
1 *Trouble at Aquitaine* (1985)
2 *Fatality at Bath and Wells* (1986)
3 *Incident at Parga* (1987)
4 *Death in a distant land* (1988)
5 *Death in close-up* (1989)
6 *Mayhem in Parva* (1990)
7 *Unwillingly to Vegas* (1991)
8 *Quiet murder* (1992)

G-Eight series
Hogan, Robert Jasper
1 *Bat Staffel* (1969)
2 *Aces of the White Death* (1970)
3 *Purple aces* (1970)
4 *Bombs from the murder wolves* (1971)
5 *Fangs of the Sky Leopard* (1971)
6 *Flight from the grave* (1971)
7 *Mark of the vulture* (1971)
8 *Vultures of the White Death* (1971)
9 *Scourge of the steel mask* (1985)
10 *G-Eight and his battle aces* (1985)

G for Georgia series
Gervaise, Mary
1 *Pony of your own* (1950)
2 *Ponies and holidays* (1950)
3 *Ponies in clover* (1952)
4 *Ponies and mysteries* (1953)
5 *Pony from the farm* (1954)
6 *Pony clue* (1955)
7 *Pony Island* (1957)
8 *Vanishing pony* (1958)
9 *Puzzle for ponies* (1964)
10 *Secret of Pony Pass* (1965)

G.I.Joe series
Affabee, Eric
see **Find your fate: G.I. Joe series**

G.I.Joe series
This sequence has five authors
Stine, Robert Lawrence
1 *Siege of Serpentor* (1988)
Becker, Margot
2 *Divide and conquer* (1988)
Ballard, S M
3 *Fool's gold* (1988)
Beach, Lynn
4 *Invisibility Island* (1988)
Stine, Robert Lawrence
5 *Jungle raid* (1988)
Lerangis, Peter
6 *Sultan's secret* (1988)

G-man's son series
Robinson, Warren F
1 *G-man's son* (1936)
2 *G-man's son ar Porpoise Island* (1937)
3 *Phantom whale* (1937)

G-men series
This sequence has two authors
Eagle, William
1 *G-Men in the professor's ring* (1936)
Smith, Lawrence Dwight
2 *G-men in jeopardy* (1938)
3 *G-men tarp the spy ring* (1939)
Eliot, George Fielding
1 *Federal bullets* (1936)
2 *Purple legion* (1936)
3 *Navy spy murders* (1937)

G.O.D. Inc. series
Chalker, Jack Laurence
1 *Labyrinth of dreams* (1987)
2 *Shadow dancers* (1987)
3 *Maze in the mirror* (1989)

Gaboreau series
Steward, Paull
see **Donald Everhard series**

Gabriel series
Gosling, Paula
see **Sheriff Matt Gabriel series**

Gabriel Wager series
Burns, Rex
1 *Alvarez journal* (1975)
2 *Farnsworth score* (1977)
3 *Speak for the dead* (1978)
4 *Angle of attack* (1979)
5 *Avenging angel* (1983)
6 *Strip search* (1984)
7 *Ground money* (1986)
8 *Killing zone* (1988)

Gabrielle Allan series
West, Joyce
1 *Drovers road* (1953)
2 *Cape Lost* (1963)
3 *Golden country* (1965)

Gaby series
Berna, Paul
1 *Hundred million francs* (1955)
Horse without a head
Original edition entitled *Le cheval sans tete*
2 *Street musician* (1956)
Original edition entitled *Le piano a bretelle*
3 *Gaby and the new money fraud* (1961)
Original edition entitled *Le bout du monde*
4 *Mystery of Saint-Salgue* (1962)
Original edition entitled *La pirate du souvenir*

Gaddy series
Gage, Wilson
see **Mrs Gaddy series**

Gaden series
Powell, Percival Henry
see **Superintendent Gaden series**

Gadfly series
Voynich, Ethel Lillian
1 *Put off thy shoes* (1945)
2 *Gadfly* (1897)
3 *Interrupted friendship* (1910)

Gadgets Schwartz series
Stivers, Dick
see **Able Team series**

Gad's Hall series
Lofts, Norah
1 *Gad's Hall* (1977)
2 *Haunted house* (1978)
Haunting of Gad's Hall
One volume edition 1979

Gaea trilogy
Varley, John
1 *Titan* (1979)
2 *Wizard* (1980)
3 *Demon* (1984)

Gaean series
Vance, Jack
1 *Trullion* (1973)
Alastor 2262
2 *Gray Prince* (1975)
3 *Marune* (1975)
Alastor 933
4 *Maske* (1976)
Thaery
5 *Wyst* (1978)
Alastor 1716
6 *Galactic Effectuator* (1980)

Gaff Lee series
Stewart, William Thomas
1 *Gaff Lee, detective* (1940)
A tale of Japanese espionage in Hong Kong
2 *Yellow spies* (1942)
3 *Japanese Ronin* (1943)
4 *Red agents* (1944)

Gaffney series
Ison, Graham
see **Superintendent John Gaffney series**

Gail and Frank Mitchell series
Gordons
see **Frank and Gail Mitchell series**

Gail and Mitch
Gordons
see **Frank and Gail Mitchell series**

Gail Gardner series
Sutton, Margaret
1 *Gail Gardner, junior cadet nurse* (1943)
2 *Gail Gardner wins her cap* (1944)

Gail McGurk series
Marfield, Dwight
1 *Mystery of the east wind* (1930)
2 *Man with a paper skull* (1932)
3 *Sword in the pool* (1932)
4 *Mystery of the king cobra* (1933)

Gail series
Frances, Stephen Daniel
see **John Gail series**
Stahl, Hilda
see **Elizabeth Gail series**

Gaines and Dragoon series
Diamond, Frank
see **Ransome Dragoon and Vicky Gaines series**

Gair Mainwaring series
Carnegie, Sacha
see **Major Gair Mainwaring series**

Galactic adventure series
Somers, Bart
see **Commander Craig series**

Galactic Center series
Benford, Gregory
1 *Deeper than the darkness* (1970)
Stars in shroud
The second title is a revised edition, 1978
2 *In the ocean of night* (1977)
3 *Great Sky River* (1987)
4 *Tides of light* (1989)
5 *Furious gulf* (1994)

Galactic connectivity series
Belden, David
1 *Children of Arabic* (1987)
2 *To warm the earth* (1988)

Galactic hero series
Harrison, Harry
see **Bill, the galactic hero series**

Galactic Midway series
Resnick, Mike
see **Tales of the Galactic Midway series**

Galactica series
Larson, Glen A
see **Battlestar Galactica series**

Galapagos series
Reminiscences of travel
Conway, Ainslie
1 *Enchanted islands* (1948)

Galaxy Five series
Kelley, Leo Patrick
1 *Good-bye to earth* (1979)
2 *On the red world* (1979)
3 *Vacation in space* (1979)
4 *Dead moon* (1979)
5 *Where no sun shines* (1979)
6 *King of the stars* (1979)

Galaxy Gang series
Dank, Milton
1 *Computer caper* (1983)
2 *UFO has landed* (1983)
3 *Three-D traitor* (1984)
4 *Treasure code* (1985)
5 *Computer game murder* (1985)

Gale Gallagher series
Gallagher, Gale
1 *I found him dead* (1947)
2 *Chord in crimson* (1949)

Gale series
Craig, David
see **Peter Gale series**
Leyland, Eric
see **Steven Gale series**
Verner, Gerald
see **Simon Gale series**

Galen LeBeau series
Crafton, Dennis
see **Lobo series**

Galen Sword series
Reeves-Stevens, Garfield
see **Chronicles of Galen Sword series**

Gales series
Traven, B
see **Gerard Gales series**

Gall series
Phillips, James Atlee
see **Joe Gall series**

Gallagher series
Gallagher, Gale
see **Gale Gallagher series**
Savarin, Julian Jay
see **Gordon Gallagher series**

Gallant series
Suthren, Victor
see **Paul Gallant series**

Gallants series
Cohen, Albert
Translated from the French
1 *Solal of the Solals* (1933)
2 *Nail cruncher* (1940)

Galldora series
Sedgwick, Modwena
1 *Adventures of Galldora* (1960)
2 *New adventures of Galldora* (1961)
3 *Rag doll called Galldora* (1971)
One volume edition entitled *The Galldora omnibus*, 1973

Galletin series
Parker, F M
see **Tom Galletin series**

Galliano's circus series
Blyton, Enid
see **Mister Galliano's circus series**

Galloway series
Crockett, Samuel Rutherford
1 *Cleg Kelly, the Arab of the streets* (1896)
2 *Kit Kennedy* (1899)
Companion volume: *Bog-myrtle and peat*, 1895

Galloway series
Niall, Ian
1 *Galloway childhood* (1967)
2 *Galloway shepherd* (1970)

Galloway series
Poyer, David
see **Tiller Galloway series**

Gallowglass series
Stasheff, Christopher
see **Gramarye series**

Gallows Detective Agency series
Flynn, Jay
see **Jim Bannerman series**

Gal's gossip series
Binstead, Arthur Morris
1 *Gal's gossip* (1899)
2 *More gal's gossip* (1901)

Galt and Tower series
France, Victor
see **Oliver Galt and Hugo Tower series**

Galt series
Gollomb, Joseph
1 *Portrait invisible* (1928)
2 *Subtle trail* (1929)
3 *Curtain of storm* (1933)

Galt series
Lovell, Marc
see **Elsie Vanetti series**

Gamadge series
Daly, Elizabeth
see **Henry Gamadge series**

Gamboney series
Torr, Iain
1 *Time of change* (1965)
2 *Sundown* (1968)

Game series
Chase, Robert Reynolds
1 *Game of fox and lion* (1986)
2 *Crucible* (1991)

Game series
Dank, Milton
1 *Dangerous game* (1977)
2 *Game's end* (1979)

Game, set and match trilogy
Deighton, Len
1 *Berlin game* (1983)
2 *Mexico set* (1984)
3 *London match* (1985)
One volume edition entitled *Game, set and match*, 1985

Gamearth trilogy
Anderson, Kevin James
1 *Gamearth* (1989)
2 *Gameplay* (1989)
3 *Game's end* (1990)

Gamekeeper trilogy
Speakman, Frederick James
Reminiscences
1 *Keeper's tale* (1962)
2 *Forest by night* (1965)
3 *Out of the wild* (1967)

Gamester wars series
Forstchen, William R
1 *Alexandrian ring* (1987)
2 *Assassin gambit* (1988)
3 *Napoleon wager* (1993)

Gaming magi series
Bischoff, David
1 *Destiny dice* (1985)
2 *Wraith board* (1985)
3 *Unicorn gambit* (1986)

Gandalara cycle series
Garrett, Randall
1 *Steel of Raithskar* (1981)
2 *Glass of Dyskornis* (1982)
3 *Bronze of Eddarta* (1983)
Numbers 1-3 also published in one volume entitled *The Gandalara cycle*, volume 1, 1986
4 *Well of darkness* (1983)
5 *Search for Ka* (1984)
6 *Return to Eddarta* (1985)
Numbers 4-6 also published in one volume entitled *The Gandalara cycle*, volume 2, 1986
7 *River wall* (1986)

Gandelyn the Jester trilogy
Onions, Oliver
1 *Poor man's tapestry* (1946)
2 *Arras of youth* (1949)
3 *Penny for the harp* (1952)

Gandhi series
Brown, Judith Margaret
1 *Gandhi's rise to power* (1972)
Indian politics, 1918-1922
2 *Gandhi and civil disobedience* (1977)
The Mahatma in Indian politics, 1928-1977
Companion volume: *Gandhi, prisoner of hope*, 1989

Gane series
Woodman, Michael
see **Paul Gane series**

Ganesh Ghote series
Keating, Henry Reymond Fitzwalter
see **Inspector Ganesh Ghote series**

Gang series
Catling, Gordon
1 *Gang on the Broads* (1958)
2 *Gang in the Western Isles* (1959)

Gang Smasher series
Clevely, Hugh
see **John Martinson series**

Gang war series
Colter, Frank
1 *Gang war* (1975)
2 *Killers for hire* (1975)

Gangster series
Daniel, Roland
1 *Gangster* (1932)
2 *Gangster's last shot* (1939)
3 *Gangster's daughter* (1965)

Gangsters series
Martin, Philip
see **John Kline series**

Gannon series
Ballenger, Dean
see **Mike Gannon series**

Gant series
Wolfe, Thomas Clayton
see **Eugene Gant series**

Gantian series
Dawe, Carlton
see **Leathermouth series**

Gants series
Abshire, Richard
1 *Gants* (1985)
2 *Shaman tree* (1989)

Gantt series
Strange, John Stephen
see **Barney Gantt series**

Ganymede series
Del Rey, Lester
1 *Outpost of Jupiter* (1963)
2 *Runaway robot* (1965)

Ganymede series
Resnick, Mike
1 *Goddess of Ganymede* (1967)
2 *Pursuit on Ganymede* (1968)

Ganz series
Sachs, Marilyn
see **Veronica Ganz series**

Ganzarello, Tucker and Norrington series
Drummond, Ivor
see **Lady Jennifer, Sandro and Colly series**

Gap series
Donaldson, Stephen Reeder
1 *Gap into conflict* (1990)
The real story
2 *Gap into vision* (1991)
Forbidden knowledge
3 *Gap into power* (1992)
A dark and hungry god arises
4 *Chaos and order* (1994)

Gappy, Jim and Jane series
Beresford, Elisabeth
1 *Television mystery* (1957)
2 *Flying Doctor mystery* (1958)
3 *Trouble at Tullington Castle* (1958)
4 *Gappy goes west* (1959)
5 *Tullington film-makers* (1960)
6 *Strange hiding place* (1962)
7 *Missing formula mystery* (1963)
8 *Flying Doctor to the rescue* (1964)
9 *Game, set and match* (1965)
10 *Black Mountain mystery* (1967)

Garaway Trenton series
Carstairs, John Paddy
1 *Gardenias bruise easily* (1958)
2 *No wooden overcoat* (1959)
3 *Touch of a French pom-pom* (1960)
4 *Pardon my gun* (1962)
5 *Concrete kimono* (1965)
6 *Smell of peardrops* (1966)
7 *No thanks for the shroud* (1967)

Garde series
La Plante, Jerry
see **Chameleon series**

Garden open series
Nichols, Beverley
see **Open garden series**

Garden series
Andrews, Lucilla
see **Wally's Ward series**
Pace, Tom
see **Ben Garden series**

Garden series
Strong, Leonard Alfred George
1 *Garden* (1931)
2 *Sea wall* (1933)

Gardener series
Mann, Phillip
see **Story of the gardener series**

Gardening tools series
Barkan, Joanne
see **My first gardening tools series**

Gardner and Redmond series
Quin-Harkin, Janet
see **Toni Redmond and Jill Gardner series**

Gardner Lawson series
Warfield, Gallatin
1 *State vs. justice* (1992)
2 *Silent son* (1994)

Gardner series
Sutton, Margaret
see **Gail Gardner series**

Garfield series
Franklin, Charles
see **Grant Garfield series**

Garfin series
Brett, Martin
see **Mike Garfin series**

Gargano and Callahan families trilogy
Seger, Maura
see **Callahan and Gargano families trilogy**

Garibaldi and the new Italy series
Huch, Ricarda Octavia
1 *Defeat* (1906)
Original edition entitled *Die oesteidigung Roms*
2 *Victory* (1907)
Original edition entitled *Der Kampf um Rom*

Garibaldi series
Hofmeyer, Hans
1 *Garibaldi's ski-boat* (1960)
2 *Fly away Paul* (1963)

Garibaldi trilogy
Trevelyan, George Macaulay
see **Giuseppe Garibaldi trilogy**

Garillon trilogy
Harris, Deborah Turner
see **Mages of Garillon trilogy**

Garland family series
Allan, Mabel Esther
1 *Ballet family* (1963)
2 *Ballet family again* (1964)
Dancing Garlands

Garman and Worse series
Kielland, Alexander Lange
1 *Garman and Worse* (1880)
Original edition entitled *Garman og Worse*
2 *Skipper Worse* (1882)
Original edition entitled *Skipper Worse*

Garnet series
Leigh, Petra
1 *Garnet* (1978)
2 *Rosewood* (1979)

Garnett Bell series
Bullivant, Cecil Henry
1 *Garnett Bell, detective* (1920)
Short stories
2 *Blood money* (1924)

Garnett series
Philmore, R
see **Inspector Garnett series**

Garnett trilogy
Egleton, Clive
see **David Garnett trilogy**

Garnish and O'Toole series
McConnell, Frank
see **Harry Garnish and Bridget O'Toole series**

Garratt and Smith series
Wentworth, Patricia
see **Benbow Smith and Frank Garratt series**

Garret series
Smythe, Pat
see **Peter and Carol Garret series**

Garrett and Torres series
Moore, Arthur
see **Bluestar series**

Garrett DeGraaf series
D'Amato, Barbara
see **Doctor Garrett DeGraaf series**

Garrett dossier series
Nolan, Frederick
1 *Sweet sister death* (1989)
Also published under the pseudonym Donald Severn as *A time to die*
2 *Alert state black* (1989)
Originally published under the pseudonym Donald Severn
3 *Designated assassin* (1990)
4 *Rat run* (1991)
5 *Maximal demotion* (1991)
6 *Soft target* (1992)

Garrett Maynard series
Swiggett, Howard
1 *Corpse in the derby hat* (1937)
Stairs lead nowhere
2 *Most secret, most immediate* (1944)

Garrett series
Brandner, Gary
see **Big Brain series**

Garrett series
Cook, Glen
1 *Sweet silver blues* (1987)
2 *Bitter gold hearts* (1988)
3 *Cold copper tears* (1988)
Numbers 1-3 also published in one volume entitled *The Garrett files*, 1989
4 *Old tin sorrows* (1989)
5 *Dread brass shadows* (1990)
6 *Red iron nights* (1991)

Garrett series
Larsen, Gaylord D
see **Henry Garrett series**

Garrison series
Kirby, Dallas
see **Victor Garrison series**
Rovin, Jeff
see **Roger Garrison series**

Garrison's Gorillas series
Pearl, Jack
1 *Garrison's Gorillas* (1967)
2 *Garrison's Gorillas and the fear formula* (1968)

Garrity series
Nixon, Allan
see **Tony Garrity series**
Trocheck, Kathy Hogan
see **Callahan Garrity series**

Garry Dean series
Whelton, Paul
1 *Death and the devil* (1944)
Flash, hold for murder
2 *Call the lady indiscreet* (1946)
3 *Angels are painted fair* (1947)
Lures of death
4 *Women are skin deep* (1948)
Uninvited corpse
5 *Pardon my blood* (1950)
6 *In comes death* (1951)

Garry Grayson football series
Dawson, Elmer A
1 *Garry Grayson's High Street Eleven* (1926)
Alternative title: The football boys of Lenox
2 *Garry Grayson at Lenox High* (1926)
Alternative title: The champions of the Football League
3 *Garry Grayson's football rivals* (1926)
Alternative title: The secret of the stolen signals
4 *Garry Grayson showing his speed* (1927)
Alternative title: A daring run on the gridiron
5 *Garry Grayson at Stanley Prep* (1927)
Alternative title: The football rivals of Riverview
6 *Garry Grayson's winning kick* (1928)
Alternative title: Battling for honor
7 *Garry Grayson hitting the line* (1929)
Alternative title: Stanley Prep on a new gridiron
8 *Garry Grayson's winning touchdown* (1930)
Alternative title: Putting Passmore Tech on the map
9 *Garry Grayson's double signals* (1931)
Alternative title: Vanquishing the football plotters
10 *Garry Grayson's forward pass* (1932)
Alternative title: Winning in the final quarter

Garry Halliday series
Blake, Justin
1 *Garry Halliday and the disappearing diamonds* (1960)
2 *Garry Halliday and the ray of death* (1961)
3 *Garry Halliday and the kidnapped five* (1962)
4 *Garry Halliday and the sands of time* (1963)
5 *Garry Halliday and the Flying Foxes* (1965)

Garry Raymond series
Thwaites, Frederick Joseph
see **Mad doctor series**

Garstang series
Walling, Robert Alfred John
1 *Stroke of one* (1931)
2 *Behind the yellow blind* (1932)
Murder at midnight

Garth Pig series
Rayner, Mary
see **Mister and Mrs Pig series**

Garth Ryland series
Riggs, John Raymond
1 *Last laugh* (1984)
2 *Let sleeping dogs lie* (1985)
3 *Glory hound* (1986)
Hunting ground
4 *Haunt of the nightingale* (1988)
5 *Wolf in sheep's clothing* (1989)
6 *One man's poison* (1991)
7 *Dead letter* (1992)
8 *Dragon lives forever* (1992)
9 *Cold hearts and gentle people* (1994)

Garth series
Blayn, Hugo
see **Inspector Garth series**

Garth series
Camp, Wadsworth
1 *Gray mask* (1920)
2 *Communicating door* (1923)
Short stories including some featuring other characters

Garton series
Hackforth-Jones, Gilbert
see **Joe Garton series**

Gary Lunt and Bob Dunbar series
Shirreffs, Gordon Donald
see **Bob Dunbar and Gary Lunt series**

Gary Spector trilogy
Strasser, Todd
see **Coming attractions trilogy**

Gastner series
Havill, Steven F
see **Bill Gastner series**

Gaston Max series
Rohmer, Sax
1 *Yellow claw* (1915)
2 *Golden scorpion* (1919)
3 *Day the world ended* (1930)
4 *Seven sins* (1943)

Gasworks Alley Gang series
Hatcher, Jo
1 *Gasworks Alley Gang* (1960)
2 *Gasworks Alley Gang goes west* (1961)

Gate of Eden trilogy
Corlett, William
1 *Gate of Eden* (1974)
2 *Land beyond* (1975)
3 *Return to the gate* (1975)

Gate of ivory series
Egan, Doris
1 *Gate of ivory* (1989)
2 *Two-bit heroes* (1992)
3 *Guilt-edged ivory* (1992)

Gates of Lucifer series
Eshbach, Lloyd Arthur
1 *Land beyond the gate* (1984)
2 *Armlet of the gods* (1986)
3 *Sorceress of Scath* (1988)
4 *Scroll of Lucifer* (1990)

Gates series
Colburn, Laura
see **Carol Gates series**
Kyle, Robert
see **Ben Gates series**

Gateway series
Pohl, Frederik
see **Heechee series**

Gatling series
Slade, Jack
1 *Zuni gold* (1989)
2 *Outlaw empire* (1989)
3 *Border war* (1989)
4 *South of the border* (1989)
5 *War wagon* (1990)
6 *Butte bloodbath* (1990)

Gator series
Kraus, Robert
see **Miss Gator series**

Gatz series
Carroll, John Richard
see **Dennis Gatz series**

Gaunt series
Braddon, George
see **Michael Gaunt series**

Gaunt series
Downie, James Millar
1 *Gaunt of Pacific Command* (1948)
2 *Secret of the loch* (1949)
3 *Gaunt of the Pearl Seas patrol* (1950)

Gaunt series
Macleod, Robert
see **Jonathan Gaunt series**

Gaunt woman series
Gilligan, Edmund
1 *Gaunt woman* (1943)
2 *Ringed horizon* (1943)

Gauntlet series
Leyland, Eric
see **Six Gun Gauntlet series**

Gautier series
Grayson, Richard
see **Inspector Gautier series**

Gauvinier series
De Selincourt, Hugh
1 *Cricket match* (1924)
2 *Game of the season* (1931)
3 *Gauvinier takes to bowls* (1949)

Gavin and Norah trilogy
Pearson, Kit
see **Evacuee trilogy**

Gavin Black series
Jakes, John
1 *Master of the dark gate* (1970)
2 *Witch of the dark gate* (1972)

Gavin series
Quinn, John
see **Rod Gavin series**

Gavin Stevens trilogy
Faulkner, William
1 *Sanctuary* (1931)
2 *Intruder in the dust* (1948)
3 *Knight's gambit* (1949)
Short stories

Gawain and Arthur trilogy
Bradshaw, Gillian
see **Arthur and Gawain trilogy**

Gay Allan series
West, Joyce
see **Gabrielle Allan series**

Gay spirit and soul series
Thompson, Mark
Essays and interviews
1 *Gay spirit* (1987)
Myth and meaning
2 *Gay soul* (1994)
The inner lives of gay men

Gaye series
Freed, Artelle
see **Melanie Gaye series**

Gaylord series
Duncan, William Murdoch
see **Superintendent Gaylord series**

Gaylord series
Malpass, Eric Lawson
1 *Morning's at seven* (1965)
2 *At the height of the moon* (1967)
3 *Fortinbras has escaped* (1970)
4 *Long long dances* (1978)
5 *Summer awakening* (1978)

Gaynor and Katheryn Scarlett series
Maynard, Nan
see **Katheryn and Gaynor Scarlett series**

Gaynor women series
Coffman, Virginia
1 *Gaynor women* (1978)
2 *Dinah Faire* (1979)

Gays series
Brown, Ethel C
see **Three Gays series**

Gaywood family series
Seymour, Beatrice Kean
see **Malling-Gaywood family series**

Gees series
Mann, Jack
see **Gregory George Gordon Green series**

Gemma and Jo series
Dixon, Rachel
see **Jo and Gemma series**

Gemma James and Duncan Kincaid series
Crombie, Deborah
see **Superintendent Duncan Kincaid and Sergeant Gemma James series**

Gemma series
Gilbert, Pamela
1 *Gemma and the witch* (1983)
2 *Gemma and the witch's house* (1986)

Gemma series
Streatfeild, Noel
1 *Gemma* (1968)
2 *Gemma and sisters* (1968)
3 *Gemma alone* (1969)
4 *Goodbye Gemma* (1969)

Gems and jewels series
Oyved, Moysheh
see **Jewels and gems series**

Gene Autry series
This sequence has three authors
Hamilton, Bob
1 *Gene Autry and the Thief River outlaws* (1944)
2 *Gene Autry and the redwood pirates* (1946)
Hutchinson, William Henry
3 *Gene Autry and the Golden Ladder Gang* (1950)
Miller, Snowden
4 *Gene Autry and the badmen of Broken Arrow* (1951)
Hutchinson, William Henry
5 *Gene Autry and the Big Valley grab* (1952)
Cole, Fannin
6 *Gene Autry and the ghost riders* (1955)
7 *Gene Autry and the golden stallion* (1954)
Companion volume: *Gene Autry and the red shirt*, by Elizabeth Beecher, 1951

Gene Autry tell-a-tale series
This sequence has two authors
Autry, Gene
1 *Gene Autry goes to the circus* (1950)
Beecher, Elizabeth
2 *Gene Autry makes a new friend* (1952)
3 *Gene Autry and the lost dogie* (1953)
Companion volume: *Gene Autry and Champion*, by Monica Hill, 1956

General Armstrong Custer series
Johnston, Terry Conrad
1 *Long winter gone* (1990)
2 *Seize the sky* (1991)
3 *Whisper of the wolf* (1991)

General Besserley series
Oppenheim, Edward Phillips
Short stories
1 *General Besserley's puzzle box* (1935)
2 *General Besserley's second puzzle box* (1939)

General Charles Kirk series
Blackburn, John
1 *Scent of new-mown hay* (1958)
Reluctant spy
2 *Sour apple tree* (1958)
3 *Broken boy* (1959)
4 *Gaunt woman* (1962)
5 *Colonel Bogus* (1964)
Packed for murder
6 *Ring of roses* (1965)
Wreath of roses
7 *Nothing but the night* (1968)
8 *Young man from Lima* (1968)
9 *For fear of little men* (1972)

General George Custer trilogy
Jones, Douglas Clyde
1 *Court-martial of George Armstrong Custer* (1976)
2 *Arrest Sitting Bull* (1977)
3 *Creek called Wounded Knee* (1978)

General Hospital series
Hirschfeld, Burt
Based on a television series
1 *General Hospital* (1963)
2 *Emergency entrance* (1965)

General hospital series
Marquis, Max
1 *Care takers* (1975)
2 *Matter of life* (1977)

General Janusz Prus trilogy
Kuniczak, Wieslaw Stanislaw
see **Polish war trilogy**

General Le Grande and GENOPS series
Blacker, Irwin Robert
1 *Kilroy gambit* (1960)
2 *Chain of command* (1965)
3 *Search and destroy* (1966)
Valley of Hanoi
4 *To hell in a basket* (1967)

General Ogle-Oxley series
French, Fergus
1 *Smouldering fuse* (1970)
2 *Invitation to die* (1970)

General Povin series
Trenhaile, John
1 *Kyril* (1981)
Man called Kyril
2 *View from the square* (1983)
3 *Nocturne for the General* (1985)

General practice series
Tibber, Robert
1 *General practice* (1967)
2 *Practice makes perfect* (1969)

General practitioner series
Smith, Francis Maylett
Autobiography
1 *Surgery at Aberffrwd* (1981)
2 *General practitioner's progress to the Black Country* (1984)

General practitioner series
Tibber, Robert
1 *No white coat* (1957)
2 *Love on my list* (1958)
3 *Patients of a saint* (1961)

Generals series
Drake, David
1 *Forge* (1991)
2 *Hammer* (1992)
3 *Anvil* (1993)
4 *Steel* (1993)

Generation series
Spencer, Colin
see **Simpson family series**

Generations series
Rutherford, Edward
1 *Sarum* (1987)
The novel of England
2 *Russka* (1991)
The novel of Russia

Genesis quest series
Moffitt, Donald
1 *Genesis quest* (1986)
2 *Second genesis* (1986)

Genghis Cohn series
Gary, Romain
1 *Dance of Genghis Cohn* (1967)
Original edition entitled *Le danse de Gengis Cohn*
2 *Guilty head* (1968)
Original edition entitled *La tete coupable*

Genie series
Leeson, Robert
see **Alec Bowden series**

Genie trilogy
Fine, Anne
1 *Sudden puff of glittering smoke* (1989)
2 *Sudden swirl of icy wind* (1990)
3 *Sudden glow of gold* (1991)
One volume edition entitled *The genie trilogy*, 1992

Genji series
Murasaki Shibuku
Originally published in Japanese between 1001 and 1015
1 *Tale of Genji* (1925)
2 *Sacred tree* (1926)
3 *Wreath of cloud* (1927)
4 *Blue trousers* (1928)
5 *Lady of the boat* (1932)
6 *Bridge of dreams* (1933)
One volume edition entitled *The tale of Genji*, 1935

Genki boys series
Kelly, Terence
1 *Fepow* (1985)
The story of a voyage beyond belief
2 *Genki boys* (1966)

GENOPS and General Le Grande series
Blacker, Irwin Robert
see **General Le Grande and GENOPS series**

Gentian trilogy
Watson, Julia
1 *Mistress for the Valois* (1969)
2 *King's mistress* (1970)
3 *Wolf and the unicorn* (1971)

Gentle house series
Rose, Anna Perrott
1 *Room for one more* (1951)
2 *Gentle house* (1955)

Gentle series
Kirkbride, Ronald
1 *Winds blow gently* (1947)
2 *Spring is not gentle* (1949)

Gentleman Jack series
Daly, Jim
1 *Gentleman Jack* (1892)
Alternative title: From student to pugilist
2 *Gentleman Jack's debut* (1893)
Alternative title: The ring champion on the stage
3 *Gentleman Jack's tour* (1893)
Alternative title: The ring champion and his enemies
4 *Gentleman Jack's mix-up* (1893)
Alternative title: Settled outside of the prize ring
5 *Gentleman Jack's soft mark* (1893)
Alternative title: Knocked out in three rounds
6 *Gentleman Jack's big hit* (1893)
Alternative title: Downing the prize ring fakirs

Gentleman Jim series
Briggs, Raymond
Comic strips
1 *Gentleman Jim* (1980)
2 *When the wind blows* (1982)
Written for adults; dramatized as *When the wind blows*, 1983

Gentleman series
Castronovo, David
1 *English gentleman* (1987)
Images and ideals in literature and society
2 *American gentleman* (1991)
Social prestige and the modern literary mind

Gentlemen of the west series
Owens, Agnes
1 *Gentlemen of the west* (1984)
2 *Like birds in the wilderness* (1987)

Gentlemen series
Boland, John
see **John George Norman Hyde series**

Gently series
Adams, Douglas Noel
see **Dirk Gently series**
Hunter, Alan
see **Inspector George Gently series**

Geodyssey series
Anthony, Piers
1 *Isle of woman* (1993)
2 *Shame of man* (1994)

Geoff and Jim Harrington series
Thorn, Ismay
1 *Quite unexpected* (1889)
2 *Flock of four* (1889)
3 *Geoff and Jim* (1891)
4 *Captain Geoff* (1892)
5 *Jim* (1893)
6 *Harringtons at home* (1894)

Geoff Fennell series
Thorne, Ernest Pollett
1 *They never came back* (1961)
2 *Assignment Haiti* (1963)
3 *Moscow file* (1967)

Geoffrey and Lenore series
Sherwood, Valerie
1 *This towering passion* (1978)
2 *Her shining splendor* (1980)

Geoffrey Austin series
Sheehan, Patrick Augustine
1 *Geoffrey Austin, student* (1895)
2 *Triumph of failure* (1899)

Geoffrey Aylett series
Meik, Vivian
1 *Devils' drums* (1933)
2 *Veils of fear* (1934)

Geoffrey Boscobell series
Wills, Cecil Melville
1 *Author in distress* (1934)
Number eighteen
2 *Death at the Pelican* (1934)
3 *Death treads* (1935)
4 *Then came the police* (1935)
5 *Chamois murder* (1935)
6 *Fatal accident* (1936)
7 *Defeat of a detective* (1936)
8 *On the night in question* (1937)
9 *Body in the dawn* (1938)
10 *Case of the Calabar bean* (1939)
11 *Case of the R.E. pipe* (1940)
12 *Clue of the lost hour* (1949)
13 *Clue of the golden earring* (1950)

Geoffrey Fraser series
Bailey, Elliot
see **Inspector Geoffrey Fraser series**

Geoffrey Gillard series
Turpin, Allan
1 *My flat and her apartment* (1964)
2 *Box* (1965)
3 *Beatrice and Bertha* (1966)
4 *Innocent employments* (1967)
5 *Laughing cavalier* (1969)

Geoffrey Glass series
Redgrove, Peter
1 *Glass cottage* (1976)
2 *God of Glass* (1979)

Geoffrey Landon series
Sinstadt, Gerald
1 *Fidelio score* (1965)
2 *Whisper in a lonely place* (1966)
Ship of spies

Geoffrey Macadam and Catherine West series
Campbell, Alice
1 *Spiderweb* (1936)
2 *No light came on* (1943)

Geoffrey Melville series
Edelman, Maurice
1 *Minister* (1961)
2 *Prime minister's daughter* (1964)

Geoffrey Mildmay series
Wilkinson, Burke
1 *Proceed at will* (1948)
2 *Run, mongoose* (1950)
Black Judas
3 *Last clear chance* (1954)
4 *Night of the short knives* (1964)

Geoffrey Peace series
Jenkins, Geoffrey
see **Commander Geoffrey Peace series**

Geoffrey Skene series
Mottram, Ralph Hale
1 *Spanish Farm* (1924)
2 *Sixty-four, ninety-four!* (1925)
3 *Europa's beast* (1930)
Rich man's daughter
4 *Come to the bower* (1949)
5 *One hundred and twenty-eight witnesses* (1951)
6 *Over the wall* (1955)

Geoffrey Slade series
Lester, Frank
1 *Corpse wore rubies* (1958)
2 *Death and the south wind* (1958)
3 *Golden murder* (1959)

Geoffrey Weston series
Haughey, Thomas Brace
1 *Case of the invisible thief* (1978)
2 *Case of the frozen scream* (1979)
3 *Case of the Maltese treasure* (1979)
4 *Case of the kidnapped shadow* (1980)
5 *Case of the hijacked moon* (1981)

Geordie Mactaggart series
Walker, David Harry
1 *Geordie* (1950)
2 *Come back, Geordie* (1966)

George Abercrombie Fox series
Hardy, Adam
1 *Press gang* (1973)
2 *Prize money* (1973)
3 *Siege* (1973)
Savage siege
4 *Treasure* (1973)
Treasure map
5 *Powder monkey* (1973)
Sailor's blood
6 *Blood for breakfast* (1974)
Sea of gold
7 *Court martial* (1974)
8 *Battle smoke* (1974)
9 *Cut and thrust* (1974)
10 *Boarders away!* (1975)
11 *Fireship* (1975)
12 *Blood beach* (1975)
13 *Sea flame* (1976)
14 *Close quarters* (1977)

George and Bridget Blake series
Farrar, Stewart
see **Bridget and George Blake series**

George and Martha series
Marshall, James
1 *George and Martha* (1972)
2 *George and Martha encore* (1973)
3 *George and Martha rise and shine* (1975)
4 *George and Martha one fine day* (1978)
5 *George and Martha, tons of fun* (1980)
6 *George and Martha back in town* (1984)
7 *George and Martha 'round and 'round* (1988)

George and Martha Washington Parke series
Curtis, Alice Turner
see **Little Washingtons series**

George and Matilda Mouse series
Buchanan, Heather S
see **Tales of George and Matilda Mouse series**

George and Paola series
Sampson, George
see **Paola and George series**

George and Zoe series
Arendt, Veronique
see **Zoe and George series**

George Annesley series
Everton, Francis
see **Inspector George Annesley series**

George Barclay series
Paul, Ernest
1 *Jewels in jeopardy* (1967)
2 *Komespi affair* (1968)
3 *Curtains for Komespi* (1968)
4 *Golden fleece* (1969)
5 *Silent murders* (1969)
6 *Reluctant cloak and dagger man* (1971)

George Bassett series
Ryland, Clive
see **Chief Inspector George Bassett series**

George Bull series
Kennedy, Milward
see **Sir George Bull series**

George Coe and David Mallin series
Ormerod, Roger
see **David Mallin and George Coe series**

George Crowder series
Pentecost, Hugh
1 *Choice of violence* (1961)
2 *Around dark corners* (1970)
Short stories
3 *Copycat killers* (1983)
4 *Price of silence* (1984)
5 *Murder sweet and sour* (1985)
6 *Death by fire* (1986)

George Custer trilogy
Jones, Douglas Clyde
see **General George Custer trilogy**

George Dixon of Dock Green series
Willis, Ted
see **Dixon of Dock Green series**

George Dixon series
Willis, Ted
1 *Blue lamp* (1950)
2 *Dixon of Dock Green* (1961)
Co-author: Paul Graham
Companion volumes: *Dixon of Dock Green, my life*, by Ted Willis with Charles Hatton, 1960, *Dixon of Dock Green, short stories*, by Rex Edwards, 1974

George Emlyn series
Williams, Emlyn
Autobiography
1 *George* (1961)
Covers 1905-1927
2 *Emlyn* (1973)
Covers 1927-1935

George Felse series
Peters, Ellis
see **Inspector George Felse series**

George Gently series
Hunter, Alan
see **Inspector George Gently series**

George Gideon series
Marric, J J
see **Commander George Gideon series**

George H Ghastly series
Perry, Ritchie
1 *George H Ghastly* (1981)
2 *George H Ghastly to the rescue* (1981)
3 *George H Ghastly and the little horror* (1985)

George Hanlon series
Evans, Edward Everett
1 *Man of many minds* (1953)
2 *Alien minds* (1955)

George Hanson series
Emerson, David
1 *Surgeon of Sedbridge* (1955)
2 *Warden of Grey's* (1957)

George Harlequin series
West, Morris Langlo
1 *Big story* (1957)
Crooked road
2 *Harlequin* (1974)

George Hawkins, Tommy Malins and Anthony Mornington series
Dix, Maurice Buxton
see **Tommy Malins, Anthony Mornington and George Hawkins series**

George Herbert Henry series
Sharkey, Jack
1 *Murder, maestro, please* (1970)
2 *Death for Auld Lang Syne* (1962)

George Higgs series
Butler, Samuel
see **Erewhon series**

George Honegger series
Strange, John Stephen
see **Captain George Honegger series**

George Judd series
Bruton, Eric
see **City of London Police series**

George Kennedy series
Kennedy, George
1 *Murder on location* (1983)
2 *Murder on high Avon* (1984)

George Le Fanu Gurney trilogy
Llewellyn, Sam
1 *Gurney's revenge* (1977)
Sea Devil
2 *Gurney's reward* (1978)
Sea Devil 2
3 *Gurney's release* (1979)

George Lydney series
Fox, Sebastian
1 *One man's poison* (1956)
2 *Odd woman out* (1958)

George Mado series
Tute, Warren
1 *Matter of diplomacy* (1969)
2 *Powder train* (1970)
3 *Tarnham connection* (1971)
4 *Resident* (1973)
5 *Next Saturday in Milan* (1975)
6 *Cairo sleeper* (1977)

George Maitland series
Severy, Martin
1 *Darrow enigma* (1904)
2 *Mystery of June thirteen* (1905)
3 *Maitland's master mystery* (1912)

George Maledon and Judge Issac C Parker series
Gardner, Jerome
see **Hanging Judge series**

George Man series
Heller, Keith
1 *Man's storm* (1985)
Set in London in 1703
2 *Man's illegal life* (1984)
Set in London in 1722
3 *Man's loving family* (1986)
A story of London's Paris Watch, 1727

George Marshall series
Barrington, Pamela
see **Inspector George Marshall series**

George Martin series
Beeding, Francis
see **Inspector George Martin series**

George Masters series
Clark, Douglas
see **Inspector George Masters series**

George Muir series
Grierson, Francis Durham
see **Inspector George Muir series**

George Nash series
Butler, Ragan
see **Captain George Nash series**

George O'Brien series
This sequence has three authors; based on a series of moving pictures
O'Brien, George
1 *Cowboy millionaire* (1935)
Packer, Eleanor
2 *George O'Brien in Gun law* (1938)
3 *George O'Brien and the Arizona bad man* (1939)
Du Bois, Gaylord
4 *George O'Brien and the hooded riders* (1940)

George Orwell series
Stansky, Peter
1 *Unknown Orwell* (1970)
2 *Orwell, the transformation* (1980)

George Palmer-Jones series
Cleeves, Ann
1 *Bird in the hand* (1986)
2 *Come death and high water* (1987)
3 *Murder in paradise* (1988)
4 *Prey to murder* (1989)
5 *Another man's poison* (1992)
6 *Mill on the shore* (1994)

George Proteron series
Stanford, John Keith
see **Life and death of George Proteron series**

George Rason series
Vickers, Roy
see **Inspector George Rason series**

George Riam series
Woodbury, David Oakes
1 *Five days to oblivion* (1963)
2 *Mister Faraday's formula* (1965)

George Roberts series
Symons, Maurice
1 *Girl in Ocean View* (1961)
2 *Pattern of murder* (1962)
3 *Lot forty one, dead auctioneer* (1964)

George Rogers Clark series
Thom, James Alexander
1 *Long knife* (1979)
2 *From sea to shining sea* (1984)

George Rogers series
Ross, Jonathan
see **Superintendent George Rogers series**

George series
Carlson, Nancy
see **Loudmouth George series**
Colt, Clem
see **Pony George series**
Goodrum, Charles Alvin
see **Edwin George series**

George series
Havilton, Jeffrey
1 *George pulls it off* (1932)
2 *George goes one better* (1935)

George series
Krulick, Nancy E
see **Curious George series**

George series
McCann, Helen
1 *What do we do now, George?* (1991)
2 *What's French for help, George?* (1993)

George Sherston trilogy
Sassoon, Siegfried
see **Sherston trilogy**

George Smiley series
Le Carre, John
1 *Call for the dead* (1961)
Deadly affair
2 *Murder of quality* (1962)
Numbers 1 and 2 also published in one volume entitled *The incongruous spy*, 1964
3 *Spy who came in from the cold* (1963)
4 *Looking-glass war* (1965)
5 *Tinker, tailor, soldier, spy* (1974)
6 *Honourable schoolboy* (1977)
Honorable schoolboy
7 *Smiley's people* (1980)
Numbers 5 and 7 also published in one volume entitled *The quest for Karla*, 1982

George Stable series
Collier, James Lincoln
1 *Teddy bear habit* (1967)
2 *Rich and famous* (1975)

George Stanhope Berkley series
Meynell, Laurence Walter
see **Bluefeather series**

George Thomassy series
Stein, Sol
1 *Magician* (1971)
2 *Other people* (1979)
3 *Touch of treason* (1985)

George Thorne and Bill Abbot series
Penn, John
see **Inspector George Thorne and Sergeant Bill Abbot series**

George Travers series
Barrington, Pamela
see **Inspector George Travers series**

George trilogy
Ward, Anthony
1 *Tent of God* (1963)
2 *River Slea* (1965)
3 *Our human condition* (1970)

George W Hayduke series
Abbey, Edward
1 *Monkey Wrench Gang* (1975)
2 *Hayduke lives!* (1990)

George Washington series
Flexner, James Thomas
1 *Forge of experience, 1732-1775* (1965)
2 *George Washington in the American Revolution, 1775-1783* (1968)
3 *George Washington and the new nation, 1783-1793* (1970)
4 *Anguish and farewell, 1793-1799* (1972)
Companion volume: *Washington, the indispensable man*, 1974

George Webber series
Wolfe, Thomas Clayton
1 *Web and the rock* (1939)
2 *You can't go home again* (1940)

George White series
Mannon, M M
see **Sheriff George White series**

George Williams series
Di Mona, Joseph
1 *Last man at Arlington* (1973)
2 *Benedict Arnold connection* (1977)
3 *To the Eagle's nest* (1980)
Eagle's nest

George Willis series
Hughes, William
1 *Split on red* (1979)
2 *Odds on gold* (1980)
3 *Cover zero* (1981)
4 *French deal* (1982)

Georgetown trilogy
Heath, Roy Aubrey Kelvin
1 *From the heat of the day* (1979)
2 *One generation* (1980)
3 *Genetha* (1981)

Georgia Lee Maxwell series
Friedman, Mickey
1 *Magic mirror* (1988)
Deadly reflections
2 *Temporary ghost* (1989)

Georgia series
Gervaise, Mary
see **G for Georgia series**

Georgia trilogy
York, Georgia
1 *Savage key* (1979)
2 *Savannah Grey* (1981)
3 *Savage conquest* (1983)

Georgian series
McCulloch, Sarah
1 *Not quite a lady* (1980)
2 *Lady for Ludovic* (1981)
3 *Most insistent lady* (1981)
4 *Merely a gentleman* (1982)
5 *Perfect gentleman* (1982)

Georgian series
Plaidy, Jean
1 *Princess of Celle* (1967)
2 *Queen in waiting* (1967)
3 *Caroline, the Queen* (1968)
4 *Prince and the Quakeress* (1968)
5 *Third George* (1969)
6 *Perdita's prince* (1969)
7 *Sweet lass of Richmond Hill* (1970)
8 *Indiscretions of the Queen* (1970)
9 *Regent's daughter* (1971)
10 *Goddess of the Green Room* (1971)
11 *Victoria in the wings* (1972)

Georgiana and Imogene series
Sherwood, Valerie
see **Imogene and Georgiana series**

Georgians series
Harben, William Nathaniel
1 *Abner Daniel* (1902)
2 *Georgians* (1904)
3 *Gilbert Neal* (1908)

Georgie, Edward and Eleanor Hall series
Langton, Jane
see **Edward, Eleanor and Georgie Hall series**

Georgie Pony Club series
Whitbread, Elizabeth
1 *Good year for riding* (1982)
2 *Good Christmas for riding* (1985)
3 *Good horse for riding* (1988)

Georgie series
Bright, Robert
1 *Georgie* (1944)
2 *Georgie to the rescue* (1956)
3 *Georgie's Halloween* (1958)
4 *Georgie and the robbers* (1963)
5 *Georgie and the magician* (1966)
6 *Georgie and the noisy ghost* (1971)
7 *Georgie goes west* (1973)
8 *Georgie's Christmas carol* (1975)
9 *Georgie and the buried treasure* (1979)
10 *Georgie and the ball of yarn* (1983)
11 *Georgie and the baby birds* (1983)
12 *Georgie and the little dog* (1983)
13 *Georgie and the runaway balloon* (1983)

Georgina series
Jellinek, Joanna
Illustrated by Agnes Molnar
1 *Georgina and the dragon* (1977)
2 *Raviola sneezes* (1980)

Gerald Burleigh Brown series
Stevenson, Dorothy Emily
1 *Gerald and Elizabeth* (1969)
2 *House of the deer* (1970)

Gerald Frost series
Horler, Sydney
see **Nighthawk series**

Gerald Knave trilogy
Janifer, Laurence Mark
1 *Survivor* (1977)
2 *Knave in hand* (1979)
3 *Knave and the game* (1987)
Short stories

Gerald Lissendale series
Horler, Sydney
1 *Secret service man* (1929)
2 *Closed door* (1948)
3 *Blade is bright* (1952)

Gerald Otley quartet
Waddell, Martin
1 *Otley* (1966)
2 *Otley pursued* (1967)
3 *Otley forever* (1968)
4 *Otley victorious* (1969)

Geraldine series
Agnew, Emily C
1 *Geraldine* (1838)
2 *Rome and the Abbey* (1849)
A tale of conscience

Gerard and O'Roarke series
Dentinger, Jane
see **Jocelyn O'Roarke and Phillip Gerard series**

Gerard Gales series
Traven, B
1 *Death ship* (1926)
Original edition entitled *Das Totenschiff*
2 *Cotton-pickers* (1926)
Original edition entitled *Die Baumwoll pflucker*; revised edition entitled *Der Wobbly*
3 *Bridge in the jungle* (1929)
Original edition entitled *Die Brucke im Dschungel*

Gerard series
Doyle, Arthur Conan
see **Brigadier Gerard series**

Gerard Sorme trilogy
Wilson, Colin
1 *Ritual in the dark* (1960)
2 *Man without a shadow* (1963)
Sex diary of Gerard Sorme
The diary of an existentialist
3 *God of the labyrinth* (1970)
Hedonists

Gerber series
Helm, Eric
see **Scorpion Squad series**

Gerin series
Iverson, Eric
1 *Wereblood* (1979)
2 *Werenight* (1979)

German occupation series
Habe, Hans
see **Occupied German series**

German raider series
This sequence has two authors as told to Arthur Victor Sellwood
Mohr, Ulrich
1 *Atlantis* (1955)
The story of a German surface raider
Fehler, Johann Heinrich
2 *Dynamite for hire* (1956)

German revolution series
Doblin, Alfred
1 *People betrayed* (1949)
Selections translated from *Verratenes Volk*, 1948, and, *Heimkehr der Fronttruppen*, 1949; contains *People betrayed*, and *The troops return*
2 *Karl and Rosa* (1950)
Original edition entitled *Karl und Rosa*

German Shepherd series
Stranger, Joyce
2 *Three's a pack* (1980)

German terror series
Toynbee, Arnold Joseph
1 *German terror in Belgium* (1917)
2 *German terror in France* (1917)

Germans in South Africa series
Bancroft, Francis
1 *Armed protest* (1918)
2 *Great possessions* (1919)

Germany between the wars series
Fallada, Hans
1 *Little man, what now?* (1932)
Original edition entitled *Kleiner Mann, was nun?*
2 *Who once eats out of the tin bowl* (1934)
Original edition entitled *Wer einmal aus dem Blechnapf frisst*
3 *Iron Gustav* (1938)
Original edition entitled *Der eiserne Gustav*

Gerry Barnes series
Bowen, Robert Sidney
1 *Make mine murder* (1946)
2 *Murder gets around* (1947)

Gerry, Edward and Frank series
Pearce, Agatha Hunt
see **Edward, Frank and Gerry series**

Gerry Lee series
Hopkins, Kenneth
1 *Girl who died* (1955)
2 *Forty-first passenger* (1958)
3 *Pierce with a skin* (1960)
4 *Campus corpse* (1963)

Gerry North series
North, Gerry
1 *Meet Gerry North* (1959)
2 *Gerry North collects* (1959)

Gerry Tate and Douglas Perkins series
Babson, Marian
see **Douglas Perkins and Gerry Tate series**

Gerry Vinson series
Norman, Mick
1 *Angels from hell* (1973)
2 *Angel challenge* (1973)
3 *Guardian Angels* (1974)
4 *Angels on my mind* (1974)

Gersen series
Vance, Jack
see **Kirth Gersen series**

Gertrude Haddon trilogy
Southworth, Emma Dorothy Eliza Nevitte
1 *Only a girl's heart* (1893)
2 *Rejected bride* (1894)
3 *Gertrude Haddon* (1894)

Gertrude series
Hughes, Richard Arthur Warren
1 *Gertrude's child* (1966)
2 *Gertrude and the mermaid* (1979)

Gervase Bret and Ralph Delchard series
Marston, Edward
1 *Wolves of Savernake* (1993)
2 *Ravens of Blackwater* (1994)

Gervase Fen series
Crispin, Edmund
1 *Case of the gilded fly* (1944)
Obsequies at Oxford
2 *Holy disorders* (1945)
3 *Moving toyshop* (1946)
4 *Swan song* (1947)
Dead and dumb
5 *Love lies bleeding* (1948)
6 *Buried for pleasure* (1948)
7 *Frequent hearses* (1950)
Sudden vengeance
8 *Long divorce* (1951)
Noose for her
9 *Beware of the trains* (1953)
Sixteen stories
10 *Glimpses of the moon* (1977)
11 *Fen country* (1979)
Twenty six short stories

Get up and go series
Isherwood, Shirley
1 *Is that you Mrs Pinkerton-Trunks, and other stories* (1984)
2 *Surprise for Mrs Pinkerton-Trunks* (1985)

Gethryn series
Macdonald, Philip
see **Colonel Anthony Ruthven Gethryn series**

Gevert series
Kaufmann, Herbert
see **Captain Gevert series**

Ghastly series
Perry, Ritchie
see **George H Ghastly series**

Ghent series
Francis, Basil
see **Inspector Ghent series**

Ghetto series
Zangwill, Israel
1 *Children of the ghetto* (1892)
2 *Ghetto tragedies* (1893)
3 *Dreamers of the ghetto* (1898)
4 *They that walk in darkness* (1899)
5 *Ghetto comedies* (1907)

Ghose series
Mundy, Talbot
see **Chullunder Ghose series**

Ghost and weirdo series
Windsor, Patricia
see **Weirdo and ghost series**

Ghost dog series
Cate, Dick
1 *Ghost dog* (1987)
2 *Twisters* (1987)

Ghost horse quartet
Highwater, Jamake
1 *Legend days* (1984)
2 *Ceremony of innocence* (1984)
3 *I wear the morning star* (1986)
4 *Kill hole* (1988)

Ghost house series
McNally, Clare
1 *Ghost house* (1979)
2 *Ghost house revenge* (1981)
One volume edition 1981

Ghost series
Ball, Duncan
1 *Ghost and the goggle box* (1984)
2 *Ghost and the gory story* (1987)
3 *Ghost and the shutterbug* (1989)

Ghost series
Edwards, Pat
1 *Ghost and Katie Donigan* (1981)
2 *Ghost of Fisher's Creek* (1981)
3 *Ghost, ghost are you scared?* (1987)

Ghost series
Fleischman, Sid
1 *Ghost in the noonday sun* (1965)
2 *Ghost on Saturday night* (1974)

Ghost series
Saxe, R B
see **John Dobbs series**
Starrett, Vincent
see **Walter Ghost series**

Ghost Squad series
Hildick, Edmund Wallace
1 *Ghost Squad breaks through* (1984)
2 *Ghost Squad and the Halloween conspiracy* (1985)
3 *Ghost Squad flies Concorde* (1985)
4 *Ghost Squad and the ghoul of Grunberg* (1986)
5 *Ghost Squad and the prowling hermits* (1987)
6 *Ghost Squad and the menace of the Malevs* (1988)

Ghost stories series
James, Montague Rhodes
1 *Ghost stories of an antiquary* (1904)
2 *More ghost stories of an antiquary* (1911)
More ghost stories
3 *Thin ghost and others* (1919)
4 *Warning to the curious, and other ghost stories* (1925)

Ghost trilogy
Coville, Bruce
1 *Ghost in the third row* (1987)
2 *Ghost wore grey* (1988)
3 *Ghost in the big brass bed* (1991)

Ghost Who Walks series
Falk, Lee
see **Phantom series**

Ghostbusters series
This sequence has two authors; based on screenplays
Digby, Anne
1 *Ghostbusters* (1984)
Naha, Ed
2 *Ghostbusters 2* (1989)
Junior versions by Barbara B Hiller, 1989 and Robert Lawrence Stine, 1989
Companion volumes: *Ghostbusters, the supernatural spectacular*, by Richard Muller, 1985, *Witch way out*, by Mark Daniel, 1988, *Movie magic*, by Mark Daniel, 1988

Ghoster trilogy
McKeone, Lee
1 *Ghoster* (1988)
2 *Backblast* (1989)
3 *Starfire down* (1991)

Ghostly tales series
Ainsworth, Ruth
1 *Phantom cyclist, and other stories* (1971)
Phantom cyclist, and other ghost stories
2 *Phantom fisherboy* (1974)
Tales of mystery and magic
3 *Phantom roundabout, and other ghostly tales* (1977)
Phantom carousel, and other ghostly tales

Ghostworld series
Siegel, Barbara
1 *Beyond terror* (1991)
2 *Midnight chill* (1991)

Ghote series
Keating, Henry Reymond Fitzwalter
see **Inspector Ganesh Ghote series**

Giacomo Carlona series
Petrocelli, Orlando Ralph
1 *Pact* (1973)
2 *Olympia's inheritance* (1974)
3 *Carlona legacy* (1981)

Giant Alexander series
Herrman, Frank
Illustrated by George Him
1 *Giant Alexander* (1964)
2 *Giant Alexander and the circus* (1966)
3 *Giant Alexander in America* (1968)
4 *Giant Alexander and Hannibel the elephant* (1971)
One volume edition entitled *All about the Giant Alexander*, 1975

Giant raft series
Verne, Jules
Originally published in one volume entitled La Jangada
1 *Giant raft, part 1* (1881)
Jangada, part 1
Down the Amazon
Eight hundred leagues on the Amazon
2 *Giant raft, part 2* (1882)
Jangada, part 2
Cryptogram
2.1 *Conspirators of Trieste* (1882)
2.2 *Captives of Antekirtta* (1882)

Giant series
Cunliffe, John Arthur
1 *Giant who stole the world* (1971)
2 *Giant who swallowed the wind* (1972)
3 *Giant Kippernose, and other stories* (1972)
4 *Giant Brog and the motorway* (1976)
5 *Sara's giant and the upside-down house* (1980)

Giant series
Grater, Michael
1 *On Sunday the giant* (1988)
2 *On Monday the giant* (1988)
3 *On Tuesday the giant* (1988)

Giant series
Hogan, James Patrick
see **Minervan experiment series**

Giant under the snow series
Gordon, John
1 *Giant under the snow* (1968)
2 *Ride the wind* (1989)

Giants in the earth trilogy
Webb, Michael
1 *Master's quilt* (1991)
2 *Balaam's error* (1992)

Gibbie series
Macdonald, George
see **Sir Gibbie series**

Gibbon series
Cooper, Barbara
see **Inspector Gibbon series**

Gibbs series
Tully, Paul
see **Deputy Marshal Hooky Gibbs series**

Gibby Gibson series
Stone, Hampton
see **Jeremiah X Gibson series**

Gibson series
Bentley, John
see **Glen Gibson series**
Montgomery, Ione
see **Christopher Gibson series**
Stone, Hampton
see **Jeremiah X Gibson series**

Gideon Fell series
Carr, John Dickson
see **Doctor Gideon Fell series**

Gideon Manciple and William Blow series
Hopkins, Kenneth
see **Doctor William Blow and Professor Gideon Manciple series**

Gideon Oliver series
Elkins, Aaron J
see **Professor Gideon Oliver series**

Gideon Page series
Stockley, Grif
1 *Expert testimony* (1991)
2 *Probable cause* (1992)
3 *Religious conviction* (1994)

Gideon series
Marric, J J
see **Commander George Gideon series**

Gideon series
This sequence has two authors
Rabier, Benjamin
1 *Gideon in Africa* (1928)
Original edition entitled *Gedeon en Afrique*
2 *Gideon in the forest* (1930)
Original edition entitled *Gedeon dans le foret*
Ratye, Helene
3 *Gideon* (1976)
Original edition entitled *Gedeon*
4 *Gideon's house* (1976)
Original edition entitled *La maison de Gedeon*
5 *Gideon on the riverbank* (1976)

Original edition entitled *Gedeon au bord de l'eau*
6 *Gideon and his friends* (1977)
Original edition entitled *Gedeon et ses amis*

Gidleigh series
Truss, Seldon
see **Inspector Gidleigh series**

Giff Speer series
Tracy, Don
1 *Deadly to bed* (1960)
2 *Naked she died* (1962)
3 *Fun and deadly games* (1968)
4 *Look down on her dying* (1968)
5 *Pot of trouble* (1971)
6 *Flats fixed, among other things* (1974)
7 *High, wide and ransom* (1976)
8 *Death calling, collect* (1976)
9 *Big X* (1976)

Gifford series
Lejeune, Anthony
see **Adam Gifford series**

Gift horse series
Knef, Hildegard
Autobiography
1 *Gift horse* (1970)
Original edition entitled *Der geschenkte Gaul*
2 *Verdict* (1975)
Original edition entitled *Das Urteil*

Gifted kids survival guide series
This sequence has two authors
Galbraith, Judy
1 *Gifted kids survival guide, for ages ten and under* (1983)
2 *Gifted kids survival guide, for ages eleven to eighteen* (1983)
Delisle, James
3 *Gifted kids survival guide II* (1987)
For ages 11-18

Giftwish series
Martin, Graham
1 *Giftwish* (1980)
2 *Catchfire* (1981)

Gigglemajig series
Mooser, Stephen
1 *Numbers up!* (1989)
2 *Square deal* (1989)
3 *Flying colors* (1989)
4 *Tons of fun from A-Z* (1989)

Gil Disbro series
Martin, James E
1 *Mercy trap* (1989)
2 *Flip side of life* (1990)
3 *And then you die* (1992)
4 *Fine and private place* (1994)

Gil Donan series
Hood, Margaret Page
1 *Silent women* (1954)
2 *Scarlet thread* (1956)
3 *In the dark night* (1957)
Murders on Fox Island
4 *Bell on Lonely* (1959)
5 *Drown the wind* (1961)

Gil Flicker series
Millward, Edward J
see **Inspector Gil Flicker series**

Gil Hamilton series
Niven, Larry
1 *Long ARM of Gil Hamilton* (1976)
2 *Patchwork girl* (1980)

Gil Henry series
Grafton, Cornelius Warren
1 *Rat began to gnaw the rope* (1943)
2 *Rope began to hang the butcher* (1944)

Gil Kennedy series
Venters, Archie
1 *Kennedy's killing* (1980)
2 *Blood on the rocks* (1983)

Gil Vine series
Sterling, Stewart
1 *Dead wrong* (1947)
2 *Dead sure* (1949)
3 *Dead of night* (1950)
4 *Alibi baby* (1955)
5 *Dead right* (1956)
Hotel murders
6 *Dead to the world* (1958)
Blonde in Suite Fourteen
7 *Body in the bed* (1959)
8 *Dead certain* (1960)
Two novelettes

Gilbert and Ellice Islands series
Grimble, Arthur
1 *Pattern of islands* (1952)
We chose the islands
2 *Return to the islands* (1957)

Gilbert Davison series
Fletcher, Robert James
1 *Half devil, half tiger* (1929)
Co-author: Alex McLachlan
2 *By misadventure* (1930)
3 *Missing doctor* (1930)

Gilbert Gurney series
Hook, Theodore Edward
1 *Gilbert Gurney* (1836)
2 *Gurney married* (1839)

Gilbert Larose series
Gask, Arthur
1 *Cloud the smiter* (1926)
2 *Dark highway* (1928)
3 *Lonely house* (1929)
4 *Shadow of Larose* (1931)
5 *House on the island* (1932)
6 *Gentlemen of crime* (1932)
7 *Judgment of Larose* (1934)
8 *Hidden door* (1934)
9 *Poisoned goblet* (1935)
10 *Hangman's knot* (1936)
11 *Master spy* (1937)
12 *Night of the storm* (1937)
13 *Grave digger of Monk's Arden* (1938)
14 *Vengeance of Larose* (1939)
15 *Destroyer* (1939)
16 *House on the fens* (1940)
17 *Tragedy of the silver moon* (1940)
18 *Beachy Head murder* (1942)
19 *His prey was man* (1942)
20 *Mystery of Fell Castle* (1944)
21 *Man of death* (1946)
22 *Dark mill stream* (1947)
23 *Unfolding years* (1947)
24 *House with the high wall* (1948)
25 *Storm breaks* (1949)
26 *Vaults of Blackarden Castle* (1950)
27 *Silent dead* (1950)
28 *Marauders by night* (1951)
29 *Crime upon crime* (1952)

Gilbert Nash series
Tucker, Wilson
1 *Time masters* (1953)
2 *Time bomb* (1957)
Tomorrow plus X

Gilbreth family series
Gilbreth, Frank Bunker
Humorous reminiscences of the authors' family life
1 *Cheaper by the dozen* (1948)
2 *Belles on their toes* (1950)
3 *Innside Nantucket* (1954)

Giles series
Pullein-Thompson, Christine
1 *Giles and the elephant* (1960)
2 *Giles and the greyhound* (1961)
3 *Giles and the canal* (1962)

Giles Tumulty series
Williams, Charles Walter Stansby
see **Sir Giles Tumulty series**

Giles Yeoman series
Woodhouse, Martin
1 *Tree Frog* (1966)
2 *Rock baby* (1968)
Bush baby
3 *Mama doll* (1972)
4 *Blue bone* (1973)
5 *Moon Hill* (1976)

Gilette and Lewis series
Gresham, Elizabeth
see **Jenny Gilette and Hunter Lewis series**

Gilgamesh series
Silverberg, Robert
1 *Gilgamesh the king* (1984)
2 *To the land of the living* (1989)

Gill series
Jepson, Selwyn
see **Eve Gill series**

Gillard series
Duffy, Margaret
see **Patrick Gillard series**
Turpin, Allan
see **Geoffrey Gillard series**

Gilles Goelo series
Benzoni, Juliette
see **Falcon series**

Gilles series
Decrest, Jacques
see **Superintendent Gilles series**

Gillian and Diggory series
De la Roche, Mazo
1 *Beside a Norman tower* (1934)
2 *Very house* (1937)

Gillian and Penny series
Byers, Irene
see **Penny and Gillian series**

Gillian Lindsay series
Finlay, Winifred
1 *Witch of Redesdale* (1951)
2 *Peril in Lakeland* (1953)
3 *Peril in the Pennines* (1953)

Gilliant series
Wainwright, John
see **Superintendent Gilliant series**

Gillonne de Beauregard series
Lang, Frances
1 *Well-wisher* (1967)
2 *Duke's daughter* (1967)
3 *Malcontent* (1968)

Gilly and Gus series
Anson, Brian
see **Gus and Gilly series**

Gilly series
Duncan, William Murdoch
see **Mister Gilly series**

Gilmartin series
Barry, Charles
see **Superintendent Lawrence Gilmartin series**

Gilmore series
Fitzhugh, Percy Keese
see **Mark Gilmore series**

Giltspur trilogy
Macraois, Cormac
1 *Battle below Giltspur* (1988)
2 *Dance of the midnight fire* (1989)
3 *Lightning over Giltspur* (1991)

Gimblet series
Bryce, Charles, *Mrs*
see **Mister Gimblet series**

Gimiendo Hernandez Quinto series
Norman, James
1 *Murder chop chop* (1942)
2 *Inch of time* (1944)
3 *Night walkers* (1946)

Gimlet series
Johns, William Earl
1 *King of the Commandos* (1943)
2 *Gimlet goes again* (1944)
3 *Gimlet comes home* (1946)
4 *Gimlet mops up* (1947)
5 *Gimlet's Oriental quest* (1948)
6 *Gimlet lends a hand* (1949)
7 *Gimlet bores in* (1950)
8 *Gimlet off the map* (1951)
9 *Gimlet gets the answer* (1952)
10 *Gimlet takes a job* (1954)

Gina series
Stratton, Alan
1 *Lady* (1986)
2 *Gina* (1988)

Ginger and Patty series
Lambert, Janet
see **Patty and Ginger series**

Ginger and Peter series
Dale, Norman
see **Peter and Ginger series**

Ginger Ella trilogy
Hueston, Ethel
1 *Ginger Ella* (1928)
2 *Ginger and Speed* (1929)
3 *For Ginger's sake* (1930)

Ginger Jenkins series
Andrew, Prudence
1 *Ginger over the wall* (1962)
2 *Ginger and Batty Billy* (1963)
3 *Ginger and No 10* (1964)
4 *Ginger among the pigeons* (1966)

Ginger Meggs series
This sequence has three authors
Bancks, James Charles
1 *Adventures of Ginger Meggs* (1924)
2 *Further adventures of Ginger Meggs, series 2* (1925)
3 *More adventures of Ginger Meggs, series 3* (1926)
4 *Further adventures of Ginger Meggs, series 4* (1927)
5 *More adventures of Ginger Meggs, series 5* (1928)
6 *More adventures of Ginger Meggs, series 6* (1929)
7 *Ginger Meggs in a 7th series of adventures* (1930)
8 *More adventures of Ginger Meggs, series 8* (1931)
9 *Ginger Meggs in a 9th series of adventures* (1932)
10 *More adventures of Ginger Meggs, series 10* (1933)
11 *Further adventures of Ginger Meggs, series 11* (1934)
12 *More adventures of Ginger Meggs, series 12* (1935)
13 *More adventures of Ginger Meggs, series 13* (1936)
14 *More adventures of Ginger Meggs, series 14* (1937)
15 *More adventures of Ginger Meggs, series 15* (1938)
16 *More adventures of Ginger Meggs, series 16* (1939)
17 *More adventures of Ginger Meggs, series 17* (1940)
18 *More adventures of Ginger Meggs, series 18* (1941)
19 *More adventures of Ginger Meggs, series 19* (1942)

20 *More adventures of Ginger Meggs, series 20* (1943)
21 *More adventures of Ginger Meggs, series 21* (1944)
22 *More adventures of Ginger Meggs, series 22* (1945)
23 *More adventures of Ginger Meggs, series 23* (1946)
24 *More adventures of Ginger Meggs, series 24* (1947)
25 *More adventures of Ginger Meggs, series 25* (1948)
26 *More adventures of Ginger Meggs, series 26* (1949)
27 *More adventures of Ginger Meggs, series 27* (1950)
28 *Ginger Meggs and Herbert the billy goat* (1956)
29 *Ginger Meggs' lucky break* (1957)
30 *Ginger Meggs and the country cousin* (1958)
Selections from numbers 1-30 published as *The golden years of Ginger Meggs*, 1921-1952, 1978

Peach, Bill
31 *Summer lightning* (1975)
32 *Ginger Meggs meets the test* (1976)

Kemsley, James
33 *Ginger Meggs at large* (1985)
34 *Comic adventures of Ginger Meggs* (1986)
35 *Look inside Ginger Meggs* (1987)
36 *It's Sunday, Ginger Meggs* (1988)
Numbers 33 and 36 also published in one volume entitled *The infamous adventures of Ginger Meggs,* 1987
37 *Wake up, Ginger Meggs* (1989)

Companion volumes: *Ginger Meggs annual*, by Ron Vivian, 1952-1959

Ginger Pennylove series
Martin, Robert
1 *Gangster pie* (1958)
2 *Laughing carpenter* (1958)
3 *Born mechanic* (1959)
4 *Chinese box* (1962)

Ginger series
Johnston, Dorothy Grunbock
1 *Ginger at Dogfish Bay* (1949)
2 *Ginger in Alaska* (1951)
3 *Ginger and the turkey raids* (1952)
4 *Ginger and the glacier express* (1953)
5 *Ginger in the jungles* (1954)
6 *Ginger and the witch doctor* (1955)

Ginger Tintagel series
Draco, F
see **Lord and Lady Tintagel series**

Gingerbread Man series
Walker, Elizabeth
1 *Adventures of the Gingerbread Man* (1986)
2 *Gingerbread Man in winter* (1987)

Gingerbread series
Althea
1 *Gingerbread band* (1974)
2 *Gingerbread men* (1975)

Ginnie Fellows series
Woolley, Catherine
1 *Ginnie and Geneva* (1948)
2 *Ginnie joins in* (1951)
3 *Ginnie and the new girl* (1954)
4 *Ginnie and the mystery house* (1957)
5 *Ginnie and the mystery doll* (1960)
6 *Ginnie and her juniors* (1963)
7 *Ginnie and the cooking contest* (1966)
8 *Ginnie and the wedding bells* (1967)
9 *Ginnie and the mystery cat* (1969)
10 *Ginnie and the mystery light* (1973)
11 *Ginnie and Geneva cookbook* (1975)

Ginnie Nixon series
Murray, Lillian
see **Virginia Nixon series**

Ginny Brandon and Steve Morgan series
Rogers, Rosemary
1 *Sweet savage love* (1974)
2 *Dark fires* (1975)
3 *Lost love, last love* (1980)
4 *Bound by desire* (1988)

Ginny Gordon series
Campbell, Julie
1 *Ginny Gordon and the mystery of the disappearing candlesticks* (1948)
2 *Ginny Gordon and the missing heirloom* (1950)
3 *Ginny Gordon and the mystery of the old barn* (1951)
4 *Ginny Gordon and the lending library* (1954)
5 *Ginny Gordon and the broadcast mystery* (1956)

Ginny Trask and Frank Carver series
Wallingford, Lee
see **Frank Carver and Ginny Trask series**

Ginty and Con series
Hallard, Peter
see **Con and Ginty series**

Giovanna and Mario series
De Polnay, Peter
see **Mario and Giovanna series**

Gipsy trilogy
Saint John, Mabel
1 *Gipsy, schoolgirl* (1922)
2 *Gipsy born!* (1922)
3 *Gipsy, actress* (1923)

Giradoux manuscript trilogy
Rusoff, Garry
see **Chariots of fire trilogy**

Giret trilogy
Morgan, Denise
see **Ralph de Giret trilogy**

Girl aviators series
Burnham, Margaret
1 *Girl aviators and the phantom airship* (1911)
2 *Girl aviators on golden wings* (1911)
3 *Girls aviators sky cruise* (1911)
4 *Girl aviators' motor butterfly* (1912)

Girl factory series
Murphy, Robert Franklin
1 *Girl factory* (1975)
Man made woman
2 *King's mate* (1975)

Girl from B.U.S.T. series
Carnelle, Inge
see **Jane Blonde series**

Girl from H.A.R.D. series
Moffatt, James
1 *Girl from H.A.R.D.* (1973)
2 *Virginia Box and the Unsatisfied* (1974)
3 *Perfect assignment* (1975)

Girl from P.U.S.S.Y.C.A.T. series
Mark, Ted
1 *Girl from P.U.S.S.Y.C.A.T.* (1965)
2 *Doctor Nyet* (1966)
3 *Pussycat, Pussycat* (1966)
4 *Nude who never* (1966)
5 *Nude who did* (1967)
6 *Nude who wore black* (1967)
7 *Pussycat transplant* (1968)

Girl from U.N.C.L.E.series
This sequence has three authors
Avallone, Michael
1 *Birds of a feather affair* (1966)
2 *Blazing affair* (1966)

Latter, Simon
3 *Global globules affair* (1967)
4 *Golden boats of Taradata affair* (1967)

Leslie, Peter
5 *Cornish pixie affair* (1967)

Girl reporter series
Edwards, Sylvia
see **Sally Baxter series**

Girl Scout series
Wirt, Mildred Augustine
1 *Girl Scouts at Penguin Pass* (1953)
Alternative title: Trail of the snowman
2 *Girl Scouts at Singing Sands* (1955)
3 *Girl Scouts at Mystery Mansion* (1957)

Girl Scouts series
Fairfax, Virginia
1 *Mysterious camper* (1933)
2 *Secret of Camp Pioneer* (1933)
3 *Secret of Halliday House* (1933)
4 *Trail of the Gypsy Eight* (1933)
5 *Curious quest* (1934)
6 *Camp's strange visitors* (1936)

Girl Scouts series
Galt, Katherine Keene
see **Rosanna series**

Girl Scouts series
Garis, Lilian C
1 *Girl Scout pioneers* (1920)
Alternative title: Winning the first B.C.
2 *Girl Scouts at Bellaire* (1920)
Alternative title: Maid Mary's awakening
3 *Girl Scouts at Sea Crest* (1920)
Alternative title: The wig wag rescue
4 *Girl Scouts at Camp Comealong* (1921)
5 *Girl Scouts at Rocky Ledge* (1922)
Alternative title: Nora's real vacation

Girl Scouts series
Lavell, Edith
1 *Girl Scouts at camp* (1922)
2 *Girl Scouts at Miss Allen's school* (1922)
3 *Girl Scouts' canoe trip* (1922)
4 *Girl Scouts' good turn* (1922)
5 *Girl Scouts' rivals* (1922)
6 *Girl Scouts on the ranch* (1923)
7 *Girl Scouts' motor trip* (1924)
8 *Girl Scouts' vacation* (1924)
9 *Girl Scouts' captain* (1925)
10 *Girl Scouts' director* (1925)

Girl Scouts series
Roy, Lillian Elizabeth
1 *Girl Scouts at Dandelion Camp* (1921)
2 *Girl Scouts in the Adirondacks* (1921)
3 *Girl Scouts in the Rockies* (1921)
4 *Girl Scouts in Arizona and New Mexico* (1923)
5 *Girl Scouts in the Redwoods* (1926)
6 *Girl Scouts in the magic city* (1927)
7 *Girl Scouts in Glacier Park* (1928)

Girl Scouts series
Vandercook, Margaret
1 *Girl Scouts of the Eagles Wing* (1921)
2 *Girl Scouts of the Round Table* (1921)
3 *Girl Scouts in Beechwood Forest* (1921)
4 *Girl Scouts and the open road* (1923)
5 *Girl Scouts in Mystery Valley* (1923)

Girl Scouts trilogy
Roy, Lillian Elizabeth
1 *Natalie, a garden scout* (1921)
2 *Norma, a flower scout* (1925)
3 *Janet, a stock-farm scout* (1925)

Girl series
Harriman, Karl Edwin
1 *Girl and the deal* (1905)
2 *Girl out there* (1906)

Girland series
Chase, James Hadley
see **Mark Girland series**

Girls in trouble series
Hart, Alison
1 *House of shame* (1975)
2 *Prisoner of love* (1976)
3 *Act of outrage* (1976)
4 *Lies of passion* (1976)
5 *Sins of surrender* (1976)

Girl's journey series
Bagnold, Enid
1 *Happy foreigner* (1920)
2 *Door of life* (1938)
Squire

One volume edition entitled *The girl's journey*, 1954

Girls of Canby Hall series
Chase, Emily
see **Canby Hall series**

Girls of Central High series
Morrison, Gertrude W
1 *Girls of Central High* (1914)
Alternative title: Rivals for all honors
2 *Girls of Central High on Lake Luna* (1914)
Alternative title: The crew that won
3 *Girls of Central High at basketball* (1914)
Alternative title: The great gymnasium mystery
4 *Girls of Central High on the stage* (1914)
Alternative title: The play that took the prize
5 *Girls of Central High on track and field* (1914)
Alternative title: The girl champions of the School League
6 *Girls of Central High in camp* (1915)
Alternative title: The old professor's secret
7 *Girls of Central High aiding the Red Cross* (1919)
Alternative title: Amateur theatricals for a worthy cause

Girls series
Montherlant, Henry de
1 *Young girls* (1936)
Original edition entitled *Les jeunes filles*
2 *Pity for women* (1936)
Original edition entitled *Pitie pour les femmes*; numbers 1 and 2 also published in one volume entitled *Pity for women*, 1937
3 *Demon of good* (1937)
Original edition entitled *Le demon du biens*
4 *Lepers* (1939)
Original edition entitled *Les lepreuses*; numbers 3 and 4 also published in one volume entitled *The lepers*, 1940 and as *Coastals and hippogriff*, 1940

One volume edition entitled *The girls*, 1968

Girls series
Tomkinson, Constance
see **Les Girls series**

Girls series
Whitney, Adeline Dutton Train
1 *We girls* (1870)
2 *Real folks* (1871)
3 *Other girls* (1873)

Girty series
Truman, Timothy
see **Simon Girty series**

Gitanjali series
Tagore, Rabindranath
Translated from the Bengali
1 *Gitanjali* (1909)
Song offerings
2 *Fruit-gathering* (1916)

Giuliano Sansevero series
Giovene, Andrea
Originally published as *Autobiografia de Giuliano Sansevero*, volumes 1-3
1 *Book of Giuliano Sansevero* (1966)
2 *Dilemma of love* (1967)
3 *Dice of war* (1967)

Giuseppe Garibaldi trilogy
Trevelyan, George Macaulay
1 *Defence of the Roman Republic, 1848-9* (1907)
2 *Garibaldi and the Thousand, Naples and Sicily, 1858-60* (1909)
3 *Garibaldi and the making of Italy* (1911)

Glade of dreams series
Farrell, Simon
1 *Darian, master magician* (1987)
2 *Issel, warrior king* (1987)

Glamour Airlines series
Morgan, Stanley
see **Fly boys series**

Glasgow series
O'Connor, Patrick
1 *Down the Bath rocks* (1971)
A boy's own penny wonder
2 *In a marmalade saloon* (1974)

Glasgow series
Rae, Hugh Crauford
1 *Skinner* (1965)
2 *Night pillow* (1967)
3 *Few small bones* (1968)
House at Balnesmoor

Glasgow trilogy
Davis, Margaret Thomson
1 *Breadmakers* (1972)
2 *Baby might be crying* (1973)
3 *Sort of peace* (1973)

Glass family series
Salinger, Jerome David
1 *Nine stories* (1953)
For Esme, with love and squalor
2 *Franny and Zooey* (1961)
3 *Raise the roof beam, carpenter and Seymour* (1963)

Glass series
Redgrove, Peter
see **Geoffrey Glass series**

Glass series
Steen, Marguerite
1 *Looking glass* (1966)
2 *Pier glass* (1968)

Glasshouse gang series
Landsborough, Gordon
see **Desert commandos series**

Glassmakers series
Baker, Donna
1 *Crystal* (1988)
2 *Black cameo* (1988)
3 *Chalice* (1989)

Glen Carrig trilogy
Hodgson, William Hope
1 *Boats of the Glen Carrig* (1907)
2 *House on the borderlands* (1908)
3 *Ghost pirates* (1909)

Glen folk series
Cameron, Isabel
1 *Folk of the Glen* (1937)
2 *White bell heather* (1938)
3 *But and ben* (1948)
4 *Tattered tartan* (1950)
5 *Heather mixture* (1952)
6 *Kirk of the Corrie* (1956)

Glen Gibson series
Bentley, John
1 *Bullets make holes* (1945)
2 *Pattern for perfidy* (1946)
3 *Call off the corpse* (1947)
Kill me again
4 *It was murder, they said* (1947)
5 *Obsession for two* (1949)

Glen Morrock series
Mackinnon, Allan
1 *Boys of Glen Morrock* (1961)
2 *Cracksman's holiday* (1962)

Glen series
Swan, Annie Shepherd
see **Elizabeth Glen series**

Glencannon family trilogy
Smith, George
1 *Devil's breed* (1980)
2 *Rogues* (1980)
3 *Fire brands* (1980)

Glencannon series
Gilpatric, Guy
see **Mister Colin Andrew Macthrockle Glencannon series**

Glenda series
Gordon, Glenda
1 *Better to arrive* (1968)
2 *Old warriors* (1970)

Glenda series
Perle, Lila
see **Fat Glenda series**

Glendale Police Department series
Egan, Lesley
see **Jesse Falkenstein series; Vic Varallo series**

Glendower and Spring series
Arnold, Margot
see **Penelope Spring and Sir Tobias Glendower series**

Glengarry series
Connor, Ralph
1 *Man from Glengarry* (1901)
2 *Glengarry school days* (1902)
Glengarry days
3 *Girl from Glengarry* (1933)
Glengarry girl
4 *Torches through the bush* (1934)

Glenloch girls series
Remick, Grace May
1 *Glenloch girls* (1909)
2 *Glenloch girls abroad* (1910)
3 *Glenloch girls' club* (1911)
4 *Glenloch girls at Camp West* (1912)

Glenn Bowman series
Howard, Hartley
1 *Last appointment* (1951)
2 *Last deception* (1951)
3 *Last vanity* (1952)
4 *Death of Cecilia* (1952)
5 *Other side of the door* (1953)
6 *Bowman strikes again* (1953)
7 *Bowman on Broadway* (1954)
8 *Bowman at a venture* (1954)
9 *No target for Bowman* (1955)
10 *Sleep for the wicked* (1955)
11 *Hearse for Cinderella* (1956)
12 *Bowman touch* (1956)
13 *Key to the morgue* (1957)
14 *Long night* (1957)
15 *Sleep, my pretty one* (1958)
16 *Big snatch* (1958)
17 *Armitage secret* (1959)
18 *Deadline* (1959)
19 *Extortion* (1960)
20 *Fall guy* (1960)
21 *Time bomb* (1961)
22 *I'm no hero* (1961)
23 *Count-down* (1962)
24 *Portrait of a beautiful harlot* (1966)
25 *Routine investigation* (1967)
26 *Secret of Simon Cornell* (1969)
27 *Cry on my shoulder* (1970)
28 *Room thirty seven* (1970)
29 *Million dollar snapshot* (1971)
30 *Murder one* (1971)
31 *Epitaph for Joanna* (1972)
32 *Nice day for a funeral* (1972)
33 *Highway to murder* (1973)
34 *Dead drunk* (1974)
35 *Treble cross* (1975)
36 *Payoff* (1976)
37 *One-way ticket* (1978)
38 *Sealed envelope* (1979)

Glenn series
Lee, Robert Corwin
see **Michael Glenn series**

Glenne series
Braun, Maurice-Gilles
see **Al Glenne series**

Glits series
Adler, Carole Schwerdtfeger
1 *Magic of the Glits* (1979)
2 *Some other summer* (1982)

Glittering series
Howatch, Susan
see **Church of England series**

Global 2000 series
Basile, Gloria Vitanza
1 *Eye of the eagle* (1983)
2 *Jackal Helix* (1984)
3 *Sting of the scorpion* (1984)

Global war series
Randle, Kevin
1 *Dawn of conflict* (1991)
2 *Border winds* (1992)

Glogauer series
Moorcock, Michael
see **Karl Glogauer series**

Gloom series
King, Frank
see **Superintendent Gloom series**

Gloop series
Thiele, Colin
1 *Gloop the gloomy bunyip* (1962)
2 *Gloop the bunyip* (1970)
One volume edition including revised edition of *Gloop the gloomy bunyip*, 1970

Gloria series
Garis, Lilian C
1 *Girl and her dad* (1923)
2 *Gloria at boardinf school* (1924)

Gloria series
Southworth, Emma Dorothy Eliza Nevitte
1 *Gloria* (1891)
2 *David Lindsay* (1891)

Glory Road series
This sequence has two authors
Heinlein, Robert Anson
1 *Glory Road* (1963)
Costello, Matthew John
2 *Fate's trick* (1988)

Glover and Quill series
Lamb, Lynton
see **Superintendent Quill and Inspector Glover series**

Glover series
Evermay, March
see **Inspector Glover series**
Mason, S C
see **Derek Glover series**

Glowrey series
Lejeune, Anthony
1 *Professor in peril* (1987)
2 *Key without a door* (1988)

Glyn Jones and James Dingle series
Osborne, Geoffrey
see **James Dingle and Glyn Jones series**

Glyn Morgan series
Lambert, Rosa
1 *Monsieur Faux-Pas* (1928)
Death goes to Brussels
2 *Mediterranean murder* (1930)
3 *Mystery of the golden wings* (1935)
4 *Crime in quarantine* (1938)

Glyndon series
Lytton, Edward George Earle Lytton Bulwer-Lytton
1 *Falkland and Zicci* (1841)
2 *Zanoni* (1842)

Glynmawr series
Williams, Raymond
1 *Border country* (1960)
2 *Second generation* (1964)

Gnarlsmyre series
Jefferies, Mike
see **Heirs to Gnarlsmyre series**

Gnome series
Friesner, Esther Mona
1 *Gnome man's land* (1991)
2 *Harpy high* (1991)
3 *Unicorn U* (1992)

Gnomes series
Huygen, Willibrord
1 *Gnomes* (1977)
Original edition entitled *Leven en werken van de kabouter*
2 *Secrets of the gnomes* (1982)
Original edition entitled *De oproep der kabouters*

Gnomobile series
This sequence has two authors
Sinclair, Upton
1 *Gnomobile* (1936)
Carey, Mary Virginia
2 *Gnomemobile* (1967)
Based on a moving picture

Go for it series
Gutman, Bill
1 *Tennis* (1989)
2 *Softball* (1989)
3 *Basketball* (1989)
4 *Field hockey* (1989)
5 *Wrestling* (1989)
6 *Track and field* (1989)
7 *Ice hockey* (1989)
8 *Football* (1989)
9 *Baseball* (1989)
10 *Soccer* (1989)
11 *Swimming* (1989)
12 *Volleyball* (1989)

Goalposts series
Sanders, Bill
1 *Goalposts, devotions for guys* (1990)
2 *Goalposts, devotions for girls* (1990)

Goane series
Nolan, Christopher
see **Journals of Tom Goane series**

Gobbolino series
Williams, Ursula Moray
1 *Adventures of the little wooden horse* (1938)
2 *Gobbolino the witch's cat* (1942)
Abridged edition 1970
3 *Further adventures of Gobbolino and the little wooden horse* (1984)

Goblin series
Edgerton, Teresa
1 *Goblin moon* (1991)
2 *Gnome's engine* (1991)

Goblin series
Grimm, Geraldine
see **King Goblin series**

Godbold series
Bolt, Ben
see **Inspector Godbold series**

Godden series
Kaye-Smith, Sheila
see **Joanna Godden series**

Godfather series
Puzo, Mario
1 *Godfather* (1969)
2 *Sicilian* (1984)
Companion volume: *The Godfather papers, and other confessions*, 1972

Godfrey Marten series
Turley, Charles
1 *Godfrey Marten, schoolboy* (1902)
2 *Godfrey Marten, undergraduate* (1904)

Godfrey series
Caldwell, Taylor
see **Listener series**
Stevenson, Burton Egbert
see **Jim Godfrey series**
Walters, Hugh
see **Chris Godfrey series**

Godfrey Tallboys series
Lofts, Norah
see **Sir Godfrey Tallboys series**

Godin series
John, Owen
see **Haggai Godin series**

Godmother series
Larkin, Rochelle T
see **Donna series**

God's gift to children series
Christian, Mary Blount
1 *Grandmothers* (1982)
2 *Grandfathers* (1982)

Gods in a vortex series
Houston, David
1 *Gods in a vortex* (1979)
2 *Wingmaster* (1981)

Gods of Ireland series
Flynn, Casey
1 *Most ancient song* (1991)
2 *Enchanted isles* (1992)

Gods of Pegana series
Dunsany, Edward John Moreton Drax Plunkett
1 *Gods of Pegana* (1905)
2 *Time and the gods* (1906)

God's wonderful railway series
Rowlands, Avril
1 *Permanent way* (1980)
2 *Clear ahead* (1980)
3 *Fire on the line* (1981)

God's wonderful word series
DeJonge, Joanne E
1 *God's wonderful word* (1978)
2 *More about God's wonderful word* (1981)

Godspeed series
Lee, Laurel
Memoirs based on journals
1 *Godspeed* (1988)
Hitchhiking home
2 *Walking through the fire* (1977)
A hospital journal
3 *Signs of spring* (1979)
4 *Mourning into dancing* (1984)

Godwin and Stallard series
Beare, George
see **Vincent Stallard and Cynthia Godwin series**

Godwin series
Leslie, Colin
see **House of Godwin series**

Goede trilogy
Leroux, Etienne
see **Welgevonden trilogy**

Goelo series
Benzoni, Juliette
see **Falcon series**

Goff family trilogy
Hennessy, Max
see **Cavalry trilogy**

Gog and Magog trilogy
Sinclair, Andrew
see **Albion trilogy**

Goggle series
Plagemann, Bentz
see **Wallace family series**

Gogo series
Rockwell, Anne Foote
1 *Gogo's pay day* (1978)
2 *Gogo's car breaks down* (1978)

Going ape series
Reese, Bob
1 *Apricot ape* (1984)
2 *Ape escape* (1984)
3 *Honest ape* (1984)
4 *Ape team* (1984)
5 *Going bananas* (1984)
6 *Jungle train* (1984)

Going bananas series
Keller, Charles
1 *Going bananas* (1975)
2 *Still going bananas* (1980)

Going for it series
This sequence has six authors
Chandler, A C
1 *Making waves* (1985)
Larsen, Rebecca
2 *Balancing act* (1985)
Gutman, Bill
3 *Summer dreams* (1985)
Bittman, Sam
4 *Out of control* (1985)
Steiner, Merrilee
5 *Bareback* (1986)
Rees, E M
6 *Thin ice* (1986)

Going places series
Scarry, Richard
Board books
1 *Going places on the water* (1987)
2 *Going places in the air* (1987)
3 *Going places in the car* (1987)
4 *Going places with Goldbug* (1987)

Going to my class series
Kuklin, Susan
1 *Going to my ballet class* (1989)
2 *Going to my nursery school* (1990)
3 *Going to my gymnastics class* (1991)

Going to school series
This sequence has two authors
Pragoff, Fiona
1 *I go to nursery school* (1985)
Heaslip, Peter
2 *Starting school* (1986)
Illustrated by Fiona Pragoff

Going to the wars series
Verney, John
Autobiography
1 *Verney abroad* (1954)
Humorous reminiscences
2 *Going to the wars* (1955)
A journey in various directions
3 *Dinner of herbs* (1966)

Gold class trilogy
This sequence has three authors
Johansen, Iris
1 *Lady and unicorn* (1984)
Preston, Fayrene
2 *For the love of Sami* (1984)
Hooper, Kay
3 *C J's fate* (1984)

Gold Hawk series
Clifford, Martin
see **Tom Merry series**

Gold Man series
Cunningham, Chet
see **Jim Steel series**

Gold series
Allen, Gina
see **History of gold series**
Cohen, Octavus Roy
see **Max Gold series**
Kahn, Michael A
see **Rachel Gold series**
Kaye, Marvin
see **Marty Gold series**
Paulsen, Gary
see **Lieutenant Ronnie Gold series**
Resnicow, Herbert
see **Alexander Magnus and Norma Gold series**
Turner, Clay
see **Ben Gold series**

Golden Amazon series
Fearn, John Russell
1 *Golden Amazon* (1944)
2 *Golden Amazon returns* (1948)
Deathless Amazon
3 *Golden Amazon's triumph* (1950)
4 *Amazon's diamond quest* (1953)
5 *Amazon strikes again* (1954)
6 *Twin of the Amazon* (1954)
7 *Conquest of the Amazon* (1976)

Golden and Shanley series
Webb, Jack
see **Father Joseph Shanley and Sammy Golden series**

Golden boomerang series
This sequence has three authors; based on a radio serial
Bingham, Lorna
1 *Search for the golden boomerang* (1941)
Edwards, George
2 *Boomerang stories for the children* (1942)
Martin, Marianne
3 *Further adventures of Tuckonie* (1942)
Edwards, George
4 *Lost tribe* (1943)
Bingham, Lorna
5 *Tuckonie's warrior friend* (1944)
Martin, Marianne
6 *Bushland tales* (1945)
7 *Tuckonie on tour* (1946)

Golden Boy series
Palmer, Bernard
1 *Golden Boy* (1954)
2 *Golden Boy, outlaw* (1954)
3 *Golden Boy and the counterfeiters* (1958)

Golden carpet series
De Chair, Somerset
Autobiography
1 *Golden carpet* (1943)
2 *Buried pleasure* (1986)

Golden chronicles series
Veryan, Patricia
1 *Practice to deceive* (1985)
2 *Journey to enchantment* (1986)
3 *Tyrant* (1987)
4 *Love alters not* (1987)
5 *Cherished enemy* (1987)
6 *Dedicated villain* (1989)
Companion volumes: *Mistress of Willowvale*, 1980, *Some brief folly*, 1981, *The wagered widow*, 1984

Golden dragon fantasy gamebooks series
This sequence has three authors
Morris, Dave
1 *Crypt of the vampire* (1984)
2 *Temple of flame* (1984)
Johnson, Oliver
3 *Lord of Shadow Keep* (1985)
Morris, Dave
4 *Eye of the dragon* (1985)
Johnson, Oliver
5 *Curse of the pharaoh* (1985)
Morris, Dave
6 (1985)

Golden echo trilogy
Garnett, David
Autobiography
1 *Golden echo* (1953)
2 *Flowers of the forest* (1955)
3 *Familiar faces* (1962)

Golden Girl and the Guardians of the Gemstones trilogy
This sequence has three authors
Stine, Robert Lawrence
1 *Golden Girl and the vanishing unicorn* (1986)
Storey, Alice
2 *Golden Girl in the land of dreams* (1986)
Sherman, Josepha
3 *Golden Girl and the crystal of doom* (1986)

Golden Hawk series
Knott, William Cecil
1 *Golden Hawk* (1986)
2 *Blood hunt* (1986)
3 *Grizzly pass* (1987)
4 *Hell's children* (1987)
5 *Kill Hawk* (1987)
6 *Scalper's trail* (1987)
7 *Eyes of the cat* (1988)
8 *Captive's trail* (1988)
9 *Searchers* (1988)

Golden key series
Sheldon, Georgie
1 *Golden key* (1905)
Alternative title: Heart's silent worship
2 *Heritage of love* (1905)

Golden lamp trilogy
Macgregor, Alasdair Alpin
1 *Golden lamp* (1964)
Portrait of a landlady

Golden lamp trilogy

2 *Land of the mountains and the flood* (1965)
3 *Enchanted isles* (1967)
Hebridean portraits and memories

Golden Orchard series
Castelhun, Dorothea
see **Penelope series**

Golden Path series
Gervaise, Mary
see **Marstons series**

Golden stallion series
Montgomery, Rutherford George
1 *Capture of the golden stallion* (1951)
2 *Golden stallion's revenge* (1953)
3 *Golden stallion to the rescue* (1954)
4 *Golden stallion's victory* (1954)
5 *Golden stallion and the wolf dog* (1958)
6 *Golden stallion's adventure at Redstone* (1959)
7 *Golden stallion and the mysterious feud* (1967)
Companion volume: The golden stallion picture book, 1962

Golden stud series
This sequence has two authors
Horner, Lance
1 *Golden stud* (1975)
Six-fingered stud
Carter, Ashley
2 *Sword of the golden stud* (1977)

Golden valley series
Browne, Belmore
1 *Quest of the golden valley* (1916)
2 *White blanket* (1918)

Golden volcano series
Verne, Jules
Originally published in one volume entitled *Le volcan d'or*
1 *Claim on Forty Mile Creek* (1906)
2 *Flood and flame* (1906)

Goldengrove series
Walsh, Jill Paton
1 *Goldengrove* (1972)
2 *Unleaving* (1976)

Goldenrod series
Slater, Jim
1 *Goldenrod* (1978)
2 *Goldenrod and the kidnappers* (1979)

Goldfeder series
Goldreich, Gloria
see **Leah Goldfeder series**

Golf series
Hepworth, George Hughes
see **Hiram Golf series**

Goliath and David series
Dicks, Terrance
see **David and Goliath series**

Golightly series
Pike, Geoffrey
see **Henry Golightly series**

Gollantz series
Jacob, Naomi
1 *Founder of the house* (1935)
2 *That wild lie* (1930)
3 *Young Emmanuel* (1932)
4 *Four generations* (1934)
5 *Private Gollantz* (1943)
6 *Gollantz, London, Paris, Milan* (1948)
7 *Gollantz and Partners* (1958)

Golliwogg series
Upton, Bertha
1 *Adventures of two Dutch dolls and a golliwogg* (1895)
Originally published anonymously
2 *Golliwogg's bicycle club* (1896)
3 *Golliwogg at the seaside* (1898)
4 *Golliwogg in war* (1899)
5 *Golliwogg's polar adventure* (1900)
6 *Golliwogg's auto go-cart* (1901)
7 *Golliwogg's air-ship* (1902)
8 *Golliwogg's circus* (1903)
9 *Golliwogg in Holland* (1904)
10 *Golliwogg's fox-hunt* (1905)
11 *Golliwogg's desert island* (1906)
12 *Golliwogg's Christmas* (1907)
13 *Golliwogg in the African jungle* (1909)

Gom in the Legends of Ulm series
Chetwin, Grace
see **Tales of Gom in the Legends of Ulm series**

Gombarov trilogy
Cournos, John
see **John Gombarov trilogy**

Goncalo de Silveira series
Cripps, Arthur Shearly
see **John Kent series**

Gondwane epic series
Carter, Lin
1 *Warrior of World's End* (1974)
2 *Enchantress of World's End* (1975)
3 *Immortal of World's End* (1976)
4 *Barbarian of World's End* (1977)
5 *Pirate of World's End* (1978)
6 *Giant of World's End* (1969)

Gone-Away series
Enright, Elizabeth
see **Portia and Julian series**

Gonji series
Rypel, Thadeus Chester
1 *Deathwind of Vedun* (1982)
2 *Samurai steel* (1982)
3 *Samurai combat* (1983)
4 *Fortress of lost worlds* (1985)
5 *Gonji* (1985)

Good answers to tough questions series
Berry, Joy
1 *Step families* (1990)
2 *About change and moving* (1990)
3 *About death* (1990)
4 *About divorce* (1990)
5 *About physical disabilities* (1990)
6 *About substance abuse* (1990)

Good fortune trilogy
Alger, Horatio
1 *Walter Sherwood's probation* (1897)
2 *Young bank messenger* (1898)
3 *Boy's fortune* (1898)
Alternative title: The strange adventures of Ben Baker

Good keen series
Crump, Barry
1 *Good keen man* (1960)
2 *Good keen girl* (1970)

Good life series
Esmonde, John
Based on a television series
1 *Good life* (1976)
2 *More of the good life* (1977)

Good master series
Seredy, Kate
1 *Good master* (1935)
2 *Singing tree* (1939)

Good news of Jesus series
Haughton, Rosemary
1 *Matthew's good news of Jesus* (1968)
2 *Mark's good news of Jesus* (1968)
3 *Luke's good news of Jesus* (1968)
4 *John's good news of Jesus* (1968)

Good old times series
Kellogg, Elijah
1 *Good old times* (1877)
2 *Strong arm and a mother's blessing* (1880)
3 *Unseen hand* (1881)
4 *Live Oak boys* (1883)
Alternative title: The adventures of Richard Constable afloat and ashore

Good series
Davis, George
see **Roag's Syndicate series**
Saber, Robert O
see **Carl Good series**

Good times series
Baker, Russell
Autobiography of a humorist
1 *Growing up* (1982)
2 *Good times* (1989)
Companion volumes: *So this is depravity*, 1980, *The rescue of Miss Yaskell, and other pipe dreams*, 1983

Good while it lasted series
Longhurst, Henry
Memoirs of a journalist
1 *It was good while it lasted* (1941)
2 *I wouldn't have missed it* (1945)
3 *You never know till you get there* (1949)
4 *My life and soft times* (1971)

Good wolf series
Burnett, Frances Hodgson
1 *Good wolf* (1908)
2 *Barty Crusoe and his man Saturday* (1909)

Goodbody series
Burstein, John
see **Slim Goodbody series**

Goodbye to all that series
Graves, Robert
Autobiography
1 *Goodbye to all that* (1929)
Revised edition 1957
2 *But it still goes on* (1930)
A miscellany

Goodey series
Alverson, Charles
see **Joe Goodey series**

Goodlooks series
Tully, John
see **Johnny Goodlooks series**

Goodwin and Wolfe series
Stout, Rex
see **Nero Wolfe and Archie Goodwin series**

Goodwin series
Merritt, Abraham
see **Doctor Goodwin series**

Goon cartoons series
Milligan, Spike
1 *Goon cartoons* (1982)
2 *More Goon cartoons* (1983)

Goonies series
This sequence has two authors
Kahn, James
1 *Goonies* (1985)
Rotsler, William
2 *Cavern of horror* (1985)

Goose series
Colson, John Henry Charles
Humorous reminiscences of yachting
1 *Goose and I* (1963)
2 *Goose up the creek* (1964)
3 *Goose at sea* (1966)

Goosebumps series
Stine, Robert Lawrence
1 *Welcome to Dead House* (1992)
2 *Stay out of the basement* (1992)
3 *Monster blood* (1992)
4 *Say cheese and die* (1992)
5 *Curse of the mummy's tomb* (1993)
6 *Let's get invisible* (1993)
7 *Night of the living dummy* (1993)
8 *Girl who cried monster* (1993)
9 *Welcome to Camp Nightmare* (1993)
10 *Ghost next door* (1993)
11 *Haunted mask* (1993)
Number 12 not identified
13 *Piano lessons can be murder* (1993)
14 *Werewolf of Fever Swamp* (1993)
15 *You can't scare me!* (1994)
16 *Call waiting* (1994)
17 *Why I'm afraid of Bess* (1994)
18 *Monster blood 2* (1994)
19 *Deep trouble* (1994)
20 *Scarecrow walks at midnight* (1994)
21 *Go eat worms!* (1994)
22 *Ghost Beach* (1994)

Goosehill Gang series
Christian, Mary Blount
1 *Vanishing sandwich* (1976)
2 *Test paper thief* (1976)
3 *Disappearing dues* (1976)
4 *Chocolate cake caper* (1976)
5 *C.B. convoy caper* (1977)
6 *Pocket park problem* (1977)
7 *Runaway house mystery* (1977)
8 *May basket mystery* (1977)
9 *Stitch in time solution* (1978)
10 *Ghost in the garage* (1978)
11 *Shadow in the shade* (1978)
12 *Christmas shoe thief* (1978)
Companion volumes: *The Goosehill Gang cookbook*, 1978, *The Goosehill Gang craft book*, 1978

Gopher series
Quackenbush, Robert Mead
see **Sheriff Sally Gopher series**

Gor series
Norman, John
see **Tarl Cabot series**

Gorbals trilogy
Glasser, Ralph
Autobiography
1 *Growing up in the Gorbals* (1986)
2 *Gorbals boy at Oxford* (1988)
3 *Gorbals voices, siren songs* (1990)

Gord the Rogue series
Gygax, Gary
1 *Sea of death* (1987)
2 *Night arrant* (1987)
Short stories
3 *City of hawks* (1987)
4 *Come endless darkness* (1988)
5 *Dance of demons* (1988)

Gordianus the Finder series
Saylor, Steven
see **Roma sub rosa series**

Gordon and Crawford series
Gilruth, Susan
see **Inspector Hugh Gordon and Liane Crawford series**

Gordon Fuller series
Vaughan, Carter A
see **Lieutenant Gordon Fuller series**

Gordon Gallagher series
Savarin, Julian Jay
1 *Waterhole* (1982)
2 *Wolfrun* (1984)
3 *Windshear* (1985)
4 *Naja* (1986)
5 *Quiraing list* (1988)

Gordon Knollis series
Vivian, Francis
see **Inspector Gordon Knollis series**

Gordon Liddy is my muse series
Batchelor, John Calvin
1 *Gordon Liddy is my muse by Tommy Tip Paine* (1990)
2 *Walking the cat by Tommy Tip Paine* (1991)

Gordon Muldrew series
Allan, Luke
see **Blue Pete series; Tiger Lillie series**

Gordon Ross series
Gorell, Ronald Gorell Barnes
see **Inspector Gordon Ross series**

Gordon series
Bear, Greg
see **Law series**
Berne, Karin
see **Ellie Gordon series**
Burr, Sybil
see **Holly Gordon series**
Campbell, Julie
see **Ginny Gordon series**
Ebersohn, Wessel
see **Yudel Gordon series**
Emerson, Alice B
see **Betty Gordon series**
Gervaise, Mary
see **Belinda Gordon series**
Grey, Estelle
see **Julie Gordon series**
Hamilton, Edmond
see **John Gordon series**
Havard, Aline
see **Lucy Gordon series**
McDermid, Val
see **Lindsay Gordon series**
Raymond, Alex
see **Flash Gordon series**
Ross, Ivan T
see **Ben Gordon series**
Shiplett, June Lund
see **Stacey Gordon series**
Wager, Walter
see **Alison Gordon series**

Gordon Stewart series
Treece, Henry
1 *Ask for King Billy* (1955)
2 *Don't expect any mercy!* (1958)
3 *Killer in dark glasses* (1965)
4 *Bang, you're dead!* (1966)

Gordon trilogy
Howard, Robert Ervin
see **El Borak trilogy**

Gore-Bunbury series
Stanford, John Keith
see **Lieutenant- Colonel James Gore-Bunbury series**

Gore series
Brock, Lynn
see **Colonel Gore series**

Gorgeous guys and girls series
Sharmat, Marjorie Weinman
1 *How to meet a gorgeous guy* (1983)
2 *How to meet a gorgeous girl* (1984)

Gorham series
Cowdroy, Joan
see **Chief Inspector Gorham series**

Gorilla series
Grater, Michael
see **Alf Gorilla series**

Gorman MP series
Birmingham, George A
1 *Gossamer* (1915)
2 *Island mystery* (1918)
3 *Lady Bountiful* (1921)

Gormenghast trilogy
Peake, Mervyn
see **Titus Groan trilogy**

Gorodish series
Delacorta
see **Serge Gorodish series**

Gorse series
Hamilton, Patrick
see **Ernest Ralph Gorse series**

Gorsefield Green series
Kaye, Barbara
1 *Black market Green* (1950)
2 *Rebellion on the Green* (1953)

Goshawk series
O'Duffy, Eimar
see **King Goshawk series**

Gosling series
Cunliffe, John Arthur
see **Mister Gosling series**

Gospel Cummings series
Martin, Charles Morris
1 *Lobo breed* (1951)
2 *Repentance at Boot Hill* (1951)
Boot Hill gospel

Gospel magic series
Westphail, Arnold Carl
1 *Gospel magic with home made stuff and things* (1972)
2 *Gospel magic made easy* (1982)
3 *Gospel magic you can do* (1985)
4 *Bible magic tricks for children's church* (1987)
5 *Magic messages for pulpit, pew and pint sized people* (1987)
Companion volumes: *Visual evangels*, numbers 1-6, 1979

Goss series
Willock, Colin Dennistoun
see **Nathaniel Ironsides Goss series**

Gotch series
Wetjen, Albert Richard
see **Shark Gotch series**

Gotobed trilogy
Quantrill, Malcolm
1 *Gotobed dawn* (1962)
2 *Gotobedlam* (1962)
3 *John Gotobed alone* (1964)

Gottlieb series
Springstubb, Tricia
see **Eunice Gottlieb series**

Gotty series
Copping, John Edward
1 *Gotty and the guv'nor* (1907)
2 *Gotty in furrin parts* (1908)

Goulburn series
Fletcher, Joseph Smith
see **Richard Goulburn series**

Gould series
Kalish, Robert
see **Skipper Gould series**
Milton, Joseph
see **Bart Gould series**
Obstfeld, Raymond
see **Harry Gould series**

Gourlay series
Ronald, James
see **Quentin Gourlay series**

Gow family series
Hepple, Anne
1 *House of Gow* (1948)
2 *Jane of Gowlands* (1949)

Grace family quartet
Swinnerton, Frank
see **Prothero quartet**

Grace Hamilton series
Worboise, Emma Jane
1 *Grace Hamilton's schooldays* (1856)
2 *Kigsdown Lodge* (1858)

Grace Harlowe at college series
Flower, Jessie Graham
1 *Grace Harlowe's first year at Overton College* (1914)
2 *Grace Harlowe's second year at Overton College* (1914)
3 *Grace Harlowe's third year at Overton College* (1914)
4 *Grace Harlowe's fourth year at Overton College* (1914)
5 *Grace Harlowe's return to Overton Campus* (1915)
6 *Grace Harlowe's problem* (1916)
7 *Grace Harlowe's golden summer* (1917)

Grace Harlowe at high school series
Flower, Jessie Graham
1 *Grace Harlowe's plebe year at high school* (1910)
Alternative title: The merry doings of the Oakdale freshmen girls
2 *Grace Harlowe's sophomore year at high school* (1911)
Alternative title: The record of the girl chums in work and athletics
3 *Grace Harlowe's junior year at high school* (1911)
Alternative title: Fast friends in the sororities
4 *Grace Harlowe's senior year at high school* (1911)
Alternative title: The parting of the ways

Grace Harlowe overseas series
Flower, Jessie Graham
1 *Grace Harlowe overseas* (1920)
2 *Grace Harlowe with the American Army on the Rhine* (1920)
3 *Grace Harlowe with the Marines at Chateau Thierry* (1920)
4 *Grace Harlowe with the Red Cross in France* (1920)
5 *Grace Harlowe with the US troops in the Argonne* (1920)
6 *Grace Harlowe with the Yankee Shock Boys at Saint Quentin* (1920)

Grace Harlowe's Overland Riders series
Flower, Jessie Graham
1 *Grace Harlowe's Overland Riders among the Kentucky Mountains* (1921)
2 *Grace Harlowe's Overland Riders in the Great North Woods* (1921)
3 *Grace Harlowe's Overland Riders on the Great American Desert* (1921)
4 *Grace Harlowe's Overland Riders on the Old Apache Trail* (1921)
5 *Grace Harlowe's Overland Riders at Circle O Ranch* (1923)
6 *Grace Harlowe's Overland Riders in the Black Hills* (1923)
7 *Grace Harlowe's Overland Riders in the High Sierras* (1923)
8 *Grace Harlowe's Overland Riders in the Yellowstone National Park* (1923)
9 *Grace Harlowe's Overland Riders among the border guerillas* (1924)
10 *Grace Harlowe's Overland Riders on the lost river* (1924)

Grace Jones series
Langton, Jane
1 *Boyhood of Grace Jones* (1972)
2 *Her Majesty, Grace Jones* (1974)
Majesty of Grace

Grace Latham series
Ford, Leslie
This sequence and the **Colonel John Primrose series** coincide in many titles
1 *Ill met by moonlight* (1937)
2 *Simple way of poison* (1938)
3 *Three bright pebbles* (1938)
4 *Reno rendezvous* (1939)
Mister Cromwell is dead
5 *False to any man* (1939)
Snow-White murder
6 *Old lover's ghost* (1940)
7 *Murder of a fifth columnist* (1941)
Capital crime
8 *Murder in the O.P.M.* (1942)
Priority murder
9 *Siren in the night* (1943)
10 *All for the love of a lady* (1944)
Crack of dawn
11 *Philadelphia murder story* (1945)
12 *Honolulu story* (1946)
Honolulu murder story
Honolulu murders
13 *Woman in black* (1947)
14 *Devil's stronghold* (1948)
15 *Washington whispers murder* (1953)
Lying jade

Grace Severance series
Scherf, Margaret
1 *Banker's bones* (1968)
2 *Beautiful birthday cake* (1971)
3 *To cache a millionaire* (1972)
4 *Beaded banana* (1978)

Gracey and Dougy series
Moloney, James
see **Dougy and Gracey series**

Grady Mulvane series
Heuman, William
1 *Stagecoach west* (1957)
2 *Violence Valley* (1958)
3 *Then came Mulvane* (1959)
4 *Bullets for Mulvane* (1960)
5 *Mulvane's war* (1960)
6 *Mulvane on the prod* (1962)

Grady series
Shriber, Ione Sandberg
see **Lieutenant Bill Grady series**

Grae series
Cleaver, Vera
see **Ellen Grae series**

Grafton Everest series
Fitzgerald, Ross
1 *Pushed from the wings* (1986)
2 *All about anthrax* (1987)
3 *Busy in the fog* (1990)

Grafton School trilogy
Barbour, Ralph Henry
1 *Rivals for the team* (1916)
2 *Winning his game* (1917)
3 *Hitting the line* (1917)

Grafton series
Coonts, Stephen
see **Jake Grafton series**
Dexter, William
see **Denis Grafton series**

Graham Darren series
Lenton, Anthony
1 *Murder beat* (1971)
2 *Murder city* (1972)

Graham, Earl of Montrose series
Tranter, Nigel Godwin
see **James Graham, Earl of Montrose series**

Graham Lorimer series
Stuart, Ian
1 *Sandscreen* (1987)
2 *Margin* (1988)
3 *Master plan* (1990)

Graham series
Anthony, Evelyn
see **Davina Graham series**
Arliss, Joen
see **Kate Graham series**
Chase, Lesley
see **Jill Graham series**
Keable, Robert
see **Peter Graham series**
Lorimer, George Horace
see **John Graham series**
Matteson, Stefanie
see **Charlotte Graham series**
Richardson, Jean
see **Moth Graham series**
Russell, Richard
see **Angel Graham series**
Thomson, Basil
see **Peter Graham series**
Welcome, John
see **Richard Graham series**

Graham trilogy
Ames, James Bushnell
see **Curly Graham trilogy**
Banks, Lynne Reid
see **Jane Graham trilogy**

Graham's Gang series
This sequence has two authors; based on a television series
Challen, John
1 *Graham's Gang* (1978)
Farrimond, John
2 *Hills of heaven* (1978)

Grail series
Cousins, Edmund George
see **Larry Grail series**

GrailQuest series
Brennan, James Herbert
1 *Castle of darkness* (1984)
2 *Den of dragons* (1984)
3 *Gateway of doom* (1984)
4 *Voyage of terror* (1985)
5 *Kingdom of horror* (1985)
6 *Realm of chaos* (1986)

Grain of truth series
Webster, Jack
Autobiography
1 *Grain of truth* (1981)
2 *Another grain of truth* (1988)

Grainger series
Sinclair, Fiona
see **Inspector Paul Grainger series**
Stableford, Brian Michael
see **Star Pilot Grainger series**

Gramarye series
Stasheff, Christopher
1 *Escape velocity* (1983)
2 *Warlock in spite of himself* (1969)
Numbers 1 and 2 also published in one volume entitled *To the magic born*, 1986
3 *King Kobold* (1971)
King Kobold revived
The second title is a revised edition; numbers 1-3 also published in one volume entitled *Warlock of the magic horn*, 1990
4 *Warlock unlocked* (1982)
5 *Warlock enlarged* (1985)
Numbers 4 and 5 also published in one volume entitled *Warlock enlarged*, 1986; numbers 3-5 also published in one volume entitled *Warlock enlarged*, 1991
6 *Warlock wandering* (1986)
7 *Warlock is missing* (1986)
Numbers 6 and 7 also published in one volume entitled *Warlock's night out*, 1988
8 *Warlock heretical* (1987)
Numbers 6-8 also published in one volume entitled *Warlock's night out*, 1991
9 *Warlock's companion* (1988)
10 *Warlock insane* (1989)
Numbers 8- 10 also published in one volume entitled *Odd warlock out*, 1989
11 *Warlock rock* (1990)
12 *Warlock and son* (1991)
Companion volume: *A warlock's blade, a Crossroads adventure in the world of Christopher Stasheff's Warlock of Gramarye*, by Megahn Perry and Mark Christopher Perry, 1987

Gramport series
Barnett, Glyn
see **Inspector Gramport series**

Gramps Wiggins series
Gardner, Erle Stanley
1 *Case of the turning tide* (1941)
2 *Case of the smoking chimney* (1943)

Gran Gorilla series
Waddell, Martin
see **Great Gran Gorilla series**

Gran series
Cole, Michael
1 *Gran gliding* (1983)
2 *Gran's old bones* (1983)
3 *Gran's pets* (1983)
4 *Gran's good news* (1983)
5 *Gran knits* (1985)
6 *Gran's game* (1985)
7 *Gran camping* (1985)
8 *Gran's goats* (1985)

Granby series
Beeding, Francis
see **Colonel Alastair Granby series**

Grand Canyon series
Reese, Bob
1 *Abert and Kaibab* (1987)
2 *Wild turkey run* (1987)
3 *Coco's berry party* (1987)
4 *Slitherfoot* (1987)
5 *Ravens roost* (1987)
6 *Surefoot* (1987)

Grand Fenwick series
Wibberley, Leonard
1 *Beware of the mouse* (1957)
2 *Mouse that roared* (1955)
Wrath of grapes
3 *Mouse on the moon* (1962)
4 *Mouse on Wall Street* (1969)
5 *Mouse that saved the West* (1981)
The true and secret history of how the world oil crisis was solved by the Duchy of Grand Fenwick

Grand Prix series
Ashford, Jeffrey
1 *Grand Prix Monaco* (1968)
2 *Grand Prix United States* (1971)
3 *Grand Prix Britain* (1973)

Grand Trunk Road series
Wiles, John
Reminiscences of travel
1 *Grand Trunk Road* (1972)
2 *Delhi is far away* (1974)

Granddad with snails series
Baldwin, Michael
Autobiography
1 *Granddad with snails* (1960)
2 *In step with a goat* (1963)

Grandfather and Thomas series
Stolz, Mary
see **Thomas and Grandfather series**

Grandfather's problems series
Stevenson, James
1 *Great big especially beautiful Easter egg* (1983)
2 *What's under my bed?* (1984)
3 *Worse than Willie* (1984)
4 *There's nothing to do* (1986)
5 *No friends* (1986)
6 *Will you please feed our cat?* (1987)

Grandin series
Quinn, Seabury
see **Jules de Grandin series**

Grandison series
Bolt, Ben
see **Captain Grandison series**

Grandith series
Farmer, Philip Jose
see **Lord Grandith series**

Grandma Bagley series
Pochocki, Ethel
1 *Grandma Bagley leads the way* (1989)
2 *Grandma Bagley to the rescue* (1989)

Grandma Cadbury series
Bates, Dianne
1 *Grandma Cadbury's trucking tales* (1987)
2 *Grandma Cadbury's safari tours* (1989)
3 *Grandma Cadbury's bikie gang* (1993)

Grandma series
Arnold, Emily
1 *Grandma mixup* (1988)
2 *Grandmas at the lake* (1990)
3 *Grandma at bat* (1993)

Grandma series
Haines, Alice Calhoun
see **According to grandma series**

Grandma's attic series
Richardson, Arleta
1 *In grandma's attic* (1974)
2 *More stories from grandma's attic* (1979)
3 *Still more stories from grandma's attic* (1980)
4 *Treasures from grandma's attic* (1984)
Companion volume: *Christmas stories from grandma*, 1991

Grandmaster series
Murphy, Warren Burton
1 *Grandmaster* (1984)
2 *High Priest* (1987)

Grandmother Lucy series
Wood, Joyce
Illustrated by Frank Francis
1 *Grandmother Lucy and her hats* (1968)
2 *Grandmother Lucy goes for a picnic* (1970)
3 *Grandmother Lucy in her garden* (1972)
4 *Grandmother Lucy's birthday* (1974)

Grandmother Oma series
Kleberger, Ilse
1 *Grandmother Oma* (1966)
Original edition entitled *Unsre Oma*
2 *Grandmother Oma and the green caravan* (1967)
Traveling with Oma
Original edition entitled *Ferien mit Oma*
3 *[Villa Oma]* (1972)
No English edition
4 *[Zwei punkt Zero fuer Oma]* (1979)
No English edition

Grandmother series
Molesworth, Mary Louisa
1 *Grandmother dear* (1878)
2 *Christmas posy* (1888)

Grandon trilogy
Kline, Otis Adelbert
1 *Planet of peril* (1929)
2 *Prince of peril* (1930)
The weird adventures of Zinlo, man of three worlds, upon the mysterious planet of Venus
3 *Port of peril* (1949)

Grandpa Bear series
Pryor, Bonnie
1 *Grandpa Bear* (1985)
2 *Grandpa Bear's Christmas* (1986)

Grandpa series
Stevenson, James
1 *Could be worse!* (1977)
2 *That terrible Halloween night* (1980)
3 *What's under my bed?* (1983)
4 *Grandpa's great city tour* (1983)
An alphabet book
5 *That dreadful day* (1985)
6 *No friends* (1986)
7 *Grandpa's too-good garden* (1989)

Grandparents series
Baker, Jeannie
1 *Grandfather* (1977)
2 *Grandmother* (1978)

Grandparents series
Buckley, Helen Elizabeth
Illustrated by Paul Galdone
1 *Grandfather and I* (1959)
2 *Grandmother and I* (1961)

Grandparents series
Storr, Catherine
1 *Fast move* (1987)
2 *Find the specs* (1987)
3 *Gran builds a house* (1987)
4 *Grandpa's birthday* (1987)

Grandpa's little girls series
Curtis, Alice Turner
1 *Grandpa's little girls* (1907)
2 *Grandpa's little girls at school* (1908)
3 *Grandpa's little girls and their freidns* (1909)
4 *Grandpa's little girls' house-boat party* (1910)
5 *Grandpa's little girls and Miss Abitha* (1911)
6 *Grandpa's little girls grown up* (1912)

Grandverger series
Sernine, Daniel
1 *Scorpion's treasure* (1990)
Original edition entitled *Le tresor du Scorpion*
2 *Sword of Arhapal* (1990)
Original edition entitled *L'epee Arhapal*

Grange Hill series
This sequence has five authors; based on a television series
Redmond, Phil
1 *Grange Hill stories* (1979)
Leeson, Robert
2 *Grange Hill goes wild* (1980)
3 *Grange Hill rules, OK?* (1980)
4 *Grange Hill for sale* (1981)
5 *Grange Hill home and away* (1982)
Redmond, Phil
6 *Tucker and Co.* (1982)
Needle, Jan
7 *Great days at Grange Hill* (1984)
Redmond, Phil
8 *Grange Hill on the run* (1986)
9 *Grange Hill after hours* (1986)
10 *Grange Hill graffiti* (1986)
11 *Grange Hill rebels* (1987)
Co-author: David Angus
12 *Grange Hill heroes* (1987)
Co-author: David Angus

13 *Grange Hill partners* (1988)
Co-author: David Angus
14 *Ziggy's working holiday* (1988)
Co-author: Margaret Simpson
Companion volumes: *Grange Hill, playscript*, volumes 1-2, 1985

Granny series
Parish, Peggy
1 *Granny and the Indians* (1969)
2 *Granny and the desperadoes* (1970)
3 *Granny, the baby and the big gray thing* (1972)

Grant and Noble series
Mackintosh, May
see **Laurie Grant and Stewart Noble series**

Grant Fowler series
Richards, Paul
This pseudonym is used by Chet Cunningham, Jon Messmann, George Snyder and Dan Streib as indicated against each title
1 *Our spacecraft is missing* (1970)
[Messmann; Snyder]
2 *President has been kidnapped!* (1971)
[Snyder; Streib]
3 *Moscow at high noon is the target* (1973)
[Cunningham; Streib]

Grant Garfield series
Franklin, Charles
1 *Exit without permit* (1946)
2 *Cocktails with a stranger* (1947)
3 *Rope of sand* (1948)
4 *Storm in an inkpot* (1949)
5 *Mask of Kane* (1949)
6 *She'll love you dead* (1950)
7 *One night to kill* (1950)
8 *Maid for murder* (1951)
9 *Escape to death* (1951)
10 *No other victim* (1952)
11 *Gallows for a fool* (1952)
12 *Stranger came back* (1953)
13 *Stop that man* (1954)
14 *Girl in shadow* (1955)
15 *Out of time* (1956)
16 *Death on my shoulder* (1958)
17 *Guilty you must be* (1959)
18 *Breathe no more* (1959)
19 *Handful of sinners* (1960)
20 *Fear runs softly* (1961)

Grant Kirby series
Richards, Clay
1 *Marble jungle* (1961)
2 *Death of an angel* (1963)

Grant Rushton series
Teed, George Hamilton
1 *Murder ship* (1935)
2 *Five in fear* (1936)
3 *Crooks' vendetta* (1939)
4 *Bottom of Suez* (1939)
5 *Voodoo Island* (1939)

Grant series
Collenette, Eric J
see **Ben Grant series**
Daniel, Roland
see **Michael Grant series**
Douglas, Amanda Minnie
see **Helen Grant series**
Ethan, John B
see **Victor Grant series**
Freeborn, Brian
see **Mister Cain series**
Garland, John
see **Ross Grant series**
Macvicar, Angus
see **Jeremy Grant series**
Mair, George Brown
see **David Grant series**
Millar, Florence N
see **Chief Inspector Douglas Grant series**
Redwood, Alec
see **Michael Grant series**
Rico, Don
see **Casey Grant series**
Seth, Ronald
see **Brian Grant series**
Seton, Graham
see **Colonel Duncan Grant series**
Sherwood, John
see **Celia Grant series**
Tey, Josephine
see **Inspector Alan Grant series**
Thomas, Craig
see **Firefox series**
Walker, Robert Wayne
see **Dean Grant series**
Yorke, Margaret
see **Doctor Patrick Grant series**

Grant Simon series
Pentecost, Hugh
1 *Obituary Club* (1958)
2 *Lonely target* (1959)

Grant Vickery series
Hobart, Robertson
1 *Case of the shaven blonde* (1959)
2 *Dangerous cargoes* (1960)

Grant's children series
Verne, Jules
see **Captain Grant's children**

Grants of Rothiedrum series
Fraser, Christine Marion
see **King's series**

Granville series
McKenna, Marthe
see **Clive Granville series**

Grape family series
Grape, Oliver
1 *Crumpet voluntary* (1974)
2 *It's a knock-up* (1975)

Graper girls series
Corbett, Elizabeth
1 *Graper girls* (1931)
2 *Graper girls go to college* (1932)
3 *Growing up with the Grapers* (1934)
4 *Beth and Ernestine Graper* (1936)

Grass castles series
Durack, Mary
Family history
1 *Kings in grass castles* (1959)
2 *Sons in the saddle* (1983)

Grass quartet
Simon, Claude
1 *Grass* (1958)
Original edition entitled *L'herbe*
2 *Flanders Road* (1960)
Original edition entitled *La Route des Flandres*
3 *Palace* (1962)
Original edition entitled *La palace*
4 *Histoire* (1967)
Original edition entitled *Histoire*

Grass series
Nash, Padder
1 *Grass* (1982)
2 *Grass's fancy* (1982)
3 *Coup de Grass* (1983)
4 *Grass in idleness* (1983)
5 *Wayward seeds of Grass* (1983)
6 *Grass and Supergrass* (1984)
7 *Grass makes hay* (1985)
8 *Sheep Grass* (1986)

Grasshopper series
Slater, Jim
1 *Grasshopper and the unwise owl* (1979)
2 *Grasshopper and the pickle factory* (1980)
3 *Grasshopper and the poisoned river* (1982)

Graustark series
McCutcheon, George Barr
1 *Graustark* (1901)
Story of a love behind a throne
2 *Beverly of Graustark* (1904)
3 *Truxton King* (1909)
4 *Prince of Graustark* (1914)
5 *East of the setting sun* (1924)
6 *Inn of the hawk and the raven* (1926)

Grave Digger Jones and Coffin Ed Johnson series
Himes, Chester
All titles except number 8, originally published in French
1 *For love of Imabelle* (1957)
Rage in Harlem
2 *Real cool killers* (1959)
3 *Crazy kill* (1959)
4 *Big gold dream* (1960)
5 *All shot up* (1960)
6 *Cotton comes to Harlem* (1965)
7 *Heat's on* (1966)
Come back, Charleston Blue
8 *Blind man with a pistol* (1969)
Hot day, hot night
9 *Plan B* (1983)

Graves series
Makin, William James
see **Inspector Graves series**

Gray and Lindon series
Whitman, Charles
see **Inspector Lindon and Sergeant Gray series**

Gray Bunny series
Crabb, Minnie Rowe
1 *Mrs Gray Bunny's children* (1936)
2 *Gray Bunny children still learning* (1937)

Gray lands series
Meade, Richard
1 *Sword of Morning Star* (1969)
2 *Exile's quest* (1970)

Gray Mouser and Fafhrd series
Leiber, Fritz
see **Fafhrd and Gray Mouser series**

Gray Phantom series
Landon, Herman
1 *Gray Phantom* (1921)
Grey Phantom
2 *Gray Phantom's return* (1922)
Grey Phantom's return
3 *Gray terror* (1923)
Grey terror
4 *Hands unseen* (1924)
5 *Gray magic* (1925)
Grey Phantom's triumph

Gray series
Blank, Clair
see **Beverly Gray series**
Brown, Helen Dawes
see **Anna Lavinia series**
Channing, Mark
see **Colin Gray series**
James, Phyllis Dorothy
see **Cordelia Gray series**
Kuttner, Henry
see **Doctor Michael Gray series**
Lanham, Edwin
see **Lieutenant Gray series**
Lutyens, Mary
see **Effie Gray series**
Mace, Helen
see **Noel Vickery series**
Moore, Patrick
see **Maurice Gray series**
Piper, Peter
see **Inspector Gray series**
Tranter, Nigel Godwin
see **Patrick Gray series**

Graydon McKelvie series
Harvey, Marion
1 *Mystery of the hidden room* (1922)
2 *Vengeance of the ivory skull* (1923)
3 *House of seclusion* (1925)
4 *Dragon of Lung Wang* (1928)

Graydon series
Wheeler, H E
see **Kendal Graydon series**

Grayle series
Sayer, Walter William
see **Barnaby Grayle series**

Grayleigh series
Robertson, Colin
see **Peter Grayleigh series**

Grayson football series
Dawson, Elmer A
see **Garry Grayson football series**

Grease series
De Christoforo, Ron
1 *Grease* (1978)
Based on the screenplay by Bronte Woodard; sequence continued by William Rotsler
Rotsler, William
2 *Grease 2* (1982)
Based on the screenplay by Ken Finkleman

Great Alta series
Yolen, Jane
1 *Sister Light, Sister Dark* (1988)
2 *White Jenna* (1989)
One volume edition entitled *The books of Great Alta*, 1990

Great Australian legends series
Hardy, Frank
1 *Great Australian legends* (1988)
2 *Retreat Australia fair, and other great Australian legends* (1990)

Great Brain series
Fitzgerald, John Dennis
see **Tom's Great Brain series**

Great Captain trilogy
Morrow, Honore Willsie
1 *Forever free* (1927)
2 *With malice toward none* (1928)
3 *Last full measure* (1930)
One volume edition entitled *Great captain*, 1930

Great Central Library series
Tiptree, James
1 *Brightness falls from the air* (1985)
2 *Starry rift* (1986)

Great circle trilogy
Anthony, Piers
see **Battle circle trilogy**

Great Dune trilogy
Herbert, Frank
see **Paul Atreides trilogy**

Great escapes series
Lloyd, David
Illustrated by Barbara Firth
1 *Jack the dog* (1984)
2 *Lady Loudly the goose* (1984)
3 *Mot the mouse* (1984)
4 *Tumult the rabbit* (1985)
5 *Waldo the tortoise* (1985)
6 *Romeo and Juliet the lovebirds* (1985)

Great ghosts series
Chambers, Aidan
1 *Great British ghosts* (1974)
2 *Great ghosts of the world* (1974)

Great Gran Gorilla series
Waddell, Martin
1 *Great Gran Gorilla and the robbers* (1988)
2 *Great Gran Gorilla to the rescue* (1988)

Great housewives series
Swain, Sally
1 *Great housewives of art* (1988)
2 *Great housewives of art revisited* (1991)

Great Imperium trilogy
Carter, Lin
see **History of the Great Imperium trilogy**

Great marvel series
Rockwood, Roy
House pseudonym
1 *Through the air to the North Pole* (1906)
Alternative title: The wonderful cruise of the Electric Monarch
2 *Under the ocean to the South Pole* (1907)
Alternative title: The strange cruise of the submarine wonder
3 *Five thousand miles underground* (1908)
Alternative title: The mystery of the center of the earth
4 *Through space to Mars* (1910)
Alternative title: The longest journey on record
5 *Lost on the moon* (1911)
Alternative title: In quest of the field of diamonds
6 *On the torn-away world* (1913)
Alternative title: The captives of the great earthquake
7 *City beyond the clouds* (1925)
Alternative title: Captured by the red dwarfs
8 *By air express to Venus* (1929)
Alternative title: Captives of a strange people
9 *By space ship to Saturn* (1935)
Alternative title: Exploring the ringed planet

Great McGonnigle series
Corbett, Scott
1 *Great McGonnigle's gray ghost* (1975)
2 *Great McGonnigle's key play* (1976)
3 *Great McGonnigle rides shotgun* (1977)
4 *Great McGonnigle switches pitches* (1980)

Great Merlini series
Rawson, Clayton
1 *Death from a top hat* (1938)
2 *Footprints on the ceiling* (1939)
3 *Headless lady* (1940)
4 *No coffin for the corpse* (1942)
5 *Great Merlini* (1979)
Short stories

Great mysteries series
Roop, Peter
1 *Dinosaurs* (1988)
2 *Poltergeists* (1988)
3 *Solar system* (1988)
4 *Stonehenge* (1989)

Great newspaper series
Garis, Howard Roger
1 *From office boy to reporter* (1907)
Young reporter at the big flood
Alternative titles: The first step in journalism, and The perils of news gathering; reissued as *Larry Dexter at the big flood*, by Raymond Sperry, 1926
2 *Larry Dexter, the young reporter* (1907)
Young reporter and the land swindlers
Alternative titles: Strange adventures in a big city, and Queer adventures in a great city; reissued as *Larry Dexter and the land swindlers*, by Raymond Sperry, 1926
3 *Larry Dexter's great search* (1907)
Young reporter and the missing millionaire
Alternative titles: The hunt for a missing millionaire, and A strange disappearance; reissued as *Larry Dexter and the missing millionaire*, by Raymond Sperry, 1926
4 *Larry Dexter and the bank mystery* (1912)
Young reporter and the bank mystery
Alternative titles: A young reporter in Wall Street, and Stirring doings in Wall Street; reissued as *Larry Dexter and the bank mystery*, by Raymond Sperry, 1926
5 *Larry Dexter and the stolen boy* (1915)
Young reporter and the stolen boy
Alternative titles: Young reporter on the Lakes, and A chase on the Great Lakes; reissued as *Larry Dexter and the stolen boy*, by Raymond Sperry, 1926
6 *Larry Dexter in Belgium* (1915)
Young reporter at the battle front
Alternative title: A war correspondent's double mission; reissued as *Larry Dexter at the battle front*, by Raymond Sperry, 1926

Great return series
Ramsay, Jay
Poetry
1 *Opening* (1988)
2 *Knife in the light* (1988)
A stage-poem
3 *Hole* (1988)
Numbers 1-3 published in one volume
4 *In the valley of shadow* (1988)
A cine-poem-cum-fantasy
5 *Divinations* (1988)
Numbers 4-5 published in one volume

Great river series
Ellis, Edward Sylvester
1 *Down the Mississippi* (1886)
2 *Up the Tapajos* (1886)
3 *Lost in the wilds* (1886)

Great Russian tragedy series
Piccard, Eulalie
see **Episodes of the great Russian tragedy series**

Great Skinner series
Tolan, Stephanie Stein
1 *Great Skinner strike* (1983)
2 *Great Skinner enterprise* (1986)
3 *Great Skinner getaway* (1987)
4 *Great Skinner homestead* (1988)

Great Uncle Prickles series
Adams, Georgie
1 *Great Uncle Prickles and the moon balloon* (1985)
2 *Great Uncle Prickles and the river boat* (1985)

Great War, French Front series
Hocking, Joseph
1 *All for a scrap of paper* (1914)
2 *Dearer than life* (1915)
3 *Curtain of fire* (1917)

Great War, Greek front series
Hocking, Joseph
1 *Tommy* (1916)
2 *Tommy and the Maid of Athens* (1917)
3 *Price of a throne* (1918)

Great war of the white man series
Zweig, Arnold
see **Werner Bertin and Lenore Wahl series**

Great War series
Lynn, Escott
1 *In khaki for the King* (1915)
2 *Oliver Hastings, V.C.* (1916)

Great War series
Strang, Herbert
see **Stories of the Great War series**

Great Warr trilogy
Pepys, Samuel, junior
1 *Diary of the Great Warr* (1916)
2 *Second diary of the Great Warr* (1917)
3 *Last diary of the Great Warr* (1919)

Great West series
Altsheler, Joseph Alexander
1 *Great Sioux trail* (1918)
2 *Lost hunters* (1918)

Great West series
Sabin, Edward Legrand
1 *Boy settler* (1916)
Alternative title: Terry in the new West
2 *Great Pike's Peak Rush* (1917)
Alternative title: Terry in the new gold fields
3 *On the overland stage* (1918)
Alternative title: Terry as a king whip cub
4 *Opening the iron trail* (1919)
Alternative title: Terry as a U Pay man

Great Western Railway series
Morgan, Bill
see **Morgan family series**

Great Western series
Optic, Oliver
1 *Going West* (1876)
Alternative title: The perils of a poor boy
2 *Out West* (1877)
Alternative title: Roughing it on the Great Lakes
3 *Lake breezes* (1879)
Alternative title: The cruise of the Sylvania
4 *Going South* (1879)
Alternative title: Yachting on the Atlantic coast
5 *Down South* (1880)
Alternative title: Yacht adventures in Florida
6 *Up the river* (1882)
Alternative title: Yachting on the Mississippi

Greataway series
Coney, Michael Greatrex
1 *Celestial steam locomotive* (1983)
2 *Gods of the Greataway* (1984)
3 *Fang, the gnome* (1988)
4 *King of the scepter'd isle* (1989)

Greatest heiress series
Oliphant, Margaret Oliphant Wilson
1 *Greatest heiress in England* (1880)
2 *Sir Tom* (1883)

Greatest series
Oursler, Fulton
see **Bible stories series**

Great-grandmother's girls series
Champney, Elizabeth Williams
1 *Great-grandmother's girls in New France* (1887)
The history of little Eunice Williams
2 *Great-grandmother's girls in New Mexico* (1888)

Greaves series
Black, Lionel
see **Emma Greaves series**

Greek Civil War trilogy
Forman, James Douglas
1 *Skies of Crete* (1963)
2 *Ring the Judas bell* (1965)
3 *Shield of Achilles* (1966)

Greek island series
Clift, Charmian
1 *Mermaid singing* (1958)
2 *Peel me a lotus* (1959)

Greek legends series
Vautier, Ghislaine
1 *Shining stars* (1980)
Original edition entitled *Quand brillant les etoiles*; Greek legends of the Zodiac
2 *Way of the stars* (1982)
Original edition entitled *Les lois du ciel*; Greek legends of the constellations

Greek mythology series
Garfield, Leon
1 *God beneath the sea* (1970)
2 *Golden shadow* (1973)

Greek travels series
Fermor, Patrick Leigh
1 *Mani* (1958)
Travels in the southern Peloponnese
2 *Roumeli* (1966)
Travels in northern Greece

Greek trilogy
Treece, Henry
1 *Oedipus* (1964)
Eagle king
2 *Jason* (1961)
3 *Electra* (1963)
Amber princess

Greek War of Independence series
Benson, Edward Frederic
1 *Vintage* (1898)
2 *Capsina* (1899)

Green fingers series
Arkell, Reginald
Humour about gardening
1 *Green fingers* (1934)
A present for a good gardener
2 *More green fingers* (1938)
Another present for a good gardener
3 *Green fingers again* (1942)
Verse

Green forest series
Burgess, Thornton Waldo
1 *Lightfoot the deer* (1921)
2 *Blacky the crow* (1922)
3 *Whitefoot the wood mouse* (1922)
4 *Buster Bear's twins* (1923)

Green Gables series
Montgomery, Lucy Maud
see **Avonlea series**

Green girl series
Wilmott, Phyllis
Autobiography
1 *Growing up in a London village* (1979)
2 *Green girl* (1983)

Green glade trilogy
Trevor, Elleston
1 *Into the happy glad* (1943)
Originally published under the author's real name Trevor Dudley-Smith
2 *By a silver stream* (1944)
Originally published under the author's real name Trevor Dudley-Smith
3 *Green glade* (1959)

Green harvest trilogy
Oldfield, Pamela
see **Kent trilogy**

Green Hornet series
This sequence has three authors
Striker, Fran
1 *Green Hornet returns* (1941)
2 *Green Hornet cracks down* (1942)
Friend, Ed
3 *Green Hornet in the infernal light* (1966)
Based on a television series
Keith, Brandon
4 *Case of the disappearing doctor* (1966)
Based on a television series

Green Knowe series
Boston, Lucy Maria
1 *Children of Green Knowe* (1954)
2 *Chimneys of Green Knowe* (1958)
Treasure of Green Knowe
3 *River at Green Knowe* (1959)
4 *Stranger at Green Knowe* (1961)
5 *Enemy at Green Knowe* (1964)
6 *Guardians of the house* (1974)
7 *Stones of Green Knowe* (1976)
Companion volumes: *The house that grew*, 1969, *Memory in a house*, 1973

Green lion trilogy
Edgerton, Teresa
1 *Child of Saturn* (1989)
2 *Moon in hiding* (1989)
3 *Work of the sun* (1990)

Green Meadow series
Burgess, Thornton Waldo
1 *Happy Jack* (1918)
2 *Mrs Peter Rabbit* (1919)
3 *Bowser the hound* (1920)
4 *Old Granny Fox* (1920)
One volume edition entitled *The Burgess big book of Green Meadow stories*, 1932

Green musketeers series
Saint Antoine, Sara
1 *Green musketeers and the fabulous frogs* (1994)
2 *Green musketeers and the incredible energy escapade* (1994)

Green Planet series
Petaja, Emil
1 *Lord of the Green Planet* (1967)
2 *Doom of the Green Planet* (1968)

Green sailors series
Hackforth-Jones, Gilbert
1 *Green sailors* (1951)
2 *Green sailors on holiday* (1952)
3 *Green sailors ahoy* (1953)
4 *Green sailors, beware* (1954)
5 *Green sailors and blue water* (1955)
6 *Green sailors and fair winds* (1956)
7 *Green sailors to Gibraltar* (1957)
8 *Green sailors in the Caribbean* (1958)
9 *Green sailors in the Galapagos* (1960)
10 *Green sailors in the South Seas* (1961)

Green series
Bede, Cuthbert
see **Mister Verdant Green series**

Green series
Brophy, John
1 *Green glory* (1940)
2 *Green ladies* (1940)

Green series
Clark, Douglas
see **Inspector George Masters series**
Goyne, Richard
see **Ex-Superintendent Tubby Green series**
Hentoff, Nat
see **Noah Green series**
Keith, Carlton
see **Jeff Green series**
Mann, Jack
see **Gregory George Gordon Green series**
Nichols, Beverley
see **Mister Horatio Green series**
Saint John, Mabel
see **Pollie Green series**
Starr, Leonard
see **Kelly Green series**

Green-sky trilogy
Snyder, Zilpha Keatley
1 *Below the root* (1975)
2 *And all between* (1976)
3 *Until the celebration* (1977)

Green Star series
Carter, Lin
1 *Under the Green Star* (1972)
2 *When the Green Star calls* (1973)
3 *By the light of the Green Star* (1974)
4 *As the Green Star rises* (1975)
5 *In the Green Star's glow* (1976)

Green stone trilogy
Cabell, James Branch
see **It happened in Florida trilogy**

Green Street series
Weir, Rosemary
1 *Number ten Green Street* (1958)
2 *Great days in Green Street* (1960)

Green Willow Farm series
Gould, Elizabeth
1 *Friends at the Farm* (1935)
2 *Tales of farm and home* (1935)
3 *Farm stories* (1936)
4 *Jolly pets* (1936)
5 *Green Willow Farm* (1944)
6 *Country days* (1944)
7 *Farm holidays* (1944)
8 *Happy days on the Farm* (1944)
9 *My book of the Farm* (1944)

Greenacres series
Forrester, Izola Louise
1 *Greenacre girls* (1915)
2 *Jean of Greenacres* (1917)
3 *Kit of Greenacre Farm* (1919)

Greenbriar Queen trilogy
Gilluly, Sheila
1 *Greenbriar Queen* (1988)
2 *Crystal keep* (1988)
3 *Ritnym's daughter* (1989)

Greenbush series
Dallas, Ruth
see **Jean, Robbie, Sophie and Helen series**

Greenery Street trilogy
Mackail, Denis
1 *Greenery Street* (1925)
2 *Tales from Greenery Street* (1928)
3 *Ian and Felicity* (1932)
Peninsula Place

Greenfield series
Brown, Ruth Alberta
see **Peace Greenfield series**
Kallen, Lucille
see **C.B.Greenfield series**

Greenhorn trilogy
Tibble, Anne
Autobiography
1 *Greenhorn* (1973)
2 *One woman's story* (1976)
3 *Alone* (1979)

Greenhouse series
James, Dakota
1 *Greenhouse* (1984)
It will happen in 1997
2 *Milwaukee the beautiful* (1986)

Greenleaf series
Yardley, Herbert Osborn
see **Mister Greenleaf series**

Greensleeves series
Duncan, William Murdoch
1 *Mystery on the Clyde* (1945)
2 *Straight ahead for danger* (1946)
3 *Cult of the queer people* (1949)

Greenstone land trilogy
Kalman, Yvonne
see **Yardley family trilogy**

Greenway series
Holmes, Robert
see **Walter Greenway series**
McMurtry, Larry
see **Aurora Greenway series**
Thompson, Lloyd S
see **Shimoru Kyota series**

Greenwich Village trilogy
This sequence has three authors
Anderson, Chester
1 *Butterfly kid* (1967)
Kurland, Michael
2 *Unicorn girl* (1969)
Waters, Thomas Allen
3 *Probability pad* (1970)

Greenwood series
Baker, George Philip
1 *Magic tale of Harvanger and Yolande* (1914)
2 *Romance of Palombris and Pallogris* (1915)

Greenwood series
Barr, Pat
see **Alice Greenwood series**
Wicking, George Walter
see **Inspector Greenwood series**

Greer series
Gayle, Newton
see **James Greer series**

Greg Allard trilogy
Joyce, Cyril
1 *Errant witness* (1981)
2 *Errant target* (1982)
3 *Errant sleuth* (1983)

Greg Ballard series
Sinclair, Dennis
1 *Third Force* (1976)
2 *Blood brothers* (1977)
3 *Friends of Lucifer* (1977)

Greg Marlowe series
Marlowe, Greg
This pseudonym is used by at least two authors including Leslie T Barnard and James McCormick whose authorship is indicated against those titles where it is known
1 *Behind the enemy* (1952) [Barnard]
2 *Death mask of war* (1952) [Barnard]
3 *Burma battle* (1953)
4 *Espionage!* (1953) [McCormick]

Gregg and Ellis series
Koehler, Robert Portner
see **Avery Gregg and Tony Ellis series**

Gregg Haljan series
Cummings, Ray
1 *Brigands of the moon* (1931)
2 *Wandl the invader* (1961)

Gregor Maclean series
McLeave, Hugh
see **Doctor Gregor Maclean series**

Gregory and Bassett series
Stratton, Roy
see **Scott Gregory and Justin Bassett series**

Gregory Branscombe series
Matheson, Hugh
1 *Third force* (1959)
2 *Balance of fear* (1961)

Gregory Dangerfield series
Lloyd, Jeremy
see **Captain Gregory Dangerfield series**

Gregory Flamm series
Wilson, Ivor
1 *But not for love* (1962)
2 *That feeds on men* (1963)
3 *Lilies that fester* (1964)
4 *Empty tigers* (1965)

Gregory George Gordon Green series
Mann, Jack
1 *Gees' first case* (1936)
2 *Grey shapes* (1937)
3 *Nightmare Farm* (1937)
4 *Kleinert case* (1938)
5 *Maker of shadows* (1938)
6 *Ninth life* (1939)
7 *Glass too many* (1940)
8 *Her ways are death* (1941)

Gregory Hiller series
Laflin, Jack
1 *Spy who loved America* (1964)
2 *Silent kind of war* (1965)
3 *Spy in white gloves* (1965)
4 *Reluctant spy* (1966)
5 *Spy who didn't* (1966)

Gregory Keen series
Hardy, Lindsay
1 *Requiem for a redhead* (1953)
2 *Nightshade ring* (1954)
3 *Faceless ones* (1956)
Twenty-six hours

Gregory Lewis series
Frome, David
see **Major Gregory Lewis series**

Gregory Pavlov and O'Shaughnessey series
Ryan, Jessica
1 *Man who asked why* (1945)
Clue of the frightening coin
2 *Exit Harlequin* (1947)

Gregory Pellew and Viscount Clymping series
Gielgud, Val
see **Inspector Gregory Pellew and Viscount Clymping series**

Gregory Quest series
Moore, Patrick
1 *Quest of the Spaceways* (1955)
2 *World of mists* (1956)

Gregory Quist series
Macdonald, William Colt
1 *Thunderbird Trail* (1946)
2 *Gunsight Range* (1949)
3 *Three-Notch Cameron* (1952)
4 *Law and order, unlimited* (1953)
5 *Mascarada Pass* (1954)
6 *Destination danger* (1955)
Whiplash
7 *Comanche scalp* (1955)
8 *Devil's drum* (1956)
Hellgate
9 *Action at Arcanum* (1958)
10 *Tombstone for a troubleshooter* (1960)
Trouble shooter
11 *Osage bow* (1964)
12 *Incident at Horcado City* (1969)

Gregory Sallust series
Wheatley, Dennis
1 *Contraband* (1936)
2 *Black August* (1934)
3 *Scarlet imposter* (1940)
4 *Faked passports* (1940)
5 *Black baroness* (1940)
6 *V for vengeance* (1942)
7 *Come into my parlour* (1946)
8 *Island where time stands still* (1954)
9 *Traitor's Gate* (1958)
10 *They used dark forces* (1964)
11 *White witch of the South Seas* (1968)

Gregory Saltfleet series
Wilson, Colin
see **Chief Inspector Gregory Saltfleet series**

Gregory series
Gibbon, Percival
see **Miss gregory series**
Jamieson, Leland
see **Dan Gregory series**

Gregory series
Stobbs, William
1 *Gregory's garden* (1984)
2 *Gregory's dog* (1984)

Gregory Trent series
Seifert, Adele
1 *Three blind mice* (1942)
2 *Shadows tonight* (1939)
3 *Deeds ill done* (1939)
Kill your own snakes

Gremlins series
This sequence has two authors
Gipe, George
1 *Gremlins* (1984)
Bischoff, David
2 *New batch* (1990)
Companion volume: *The Gremlins story book*, by Mary Virginia Carey, 1984

Grenadine Etching series
Ruark, Robert
1 *Grenadine Etching, her life and loves* (1947)
2 *Grenadine's spawn* (1952)

Grenfell and Wright series
Moore, Patrick
1 *Master of the moon* (1952)
2 *Island of fear* (1954)

Grenville series
Fletcher, Lawrence
see **Dick Grenville series**
Padfield, Peter
see **Guy Grenville series**

Gresham trilogy
Avery, Gillian
see **Julia and Henry Gresham trilogy**

Greta series
Haynes, Ambrose
1 *Greta's dream* (1961)
2 *Greta's decision* (1963)
3 *Greta's victory* (1965)

Gretchen and Kobie series
Ransom, Candice Farris
see **Growing up series**

Greville family trilogy
Rock, Phillip
1 *Passing bells* (1979)
2 *Circles of time* (1981)
3 *Future arrived* (1985)

Grey Eagle series
Taylor, Janelle
see **Sioux series**

Grey family series
Wiat, Philippa
1 *Five gold rings* (1982)
2 *Children of the spring* (1983)

Grey ghost series
Middleton, Jessie Adelaide
1 *Grey ghost book* (1912)
2 *Another grey ghost book* (1914)
With a chapter on prophetic dreams and a note on vampires
3 *White ghost book* (1916)

Grey mouse series
Dubois, Ivy Millicent
1 *Little grey mouse* (1960)
2 *More adventures of the grey mouse family* (1963)

Grey, Newman and Tweed series
Forbes, Colin
see **Tweed, Grey and Newman series**

Grey Phantom series
Landon, Herman
see **Gray Phantom series**

Grey Rabbit series
Uttley, Alison
see **Little Grey Rabbit series**

Grey Seal series
Draper, Alfred
see **Crispin Paton series**

Grey series
Bellamy, Robert Lowe
see **Scout Grey series**
Cory, Desmond
see **Lindy Grey series**
Jenkins, Jerry Bruce
see **Jennifer Grey series**
Preston, Florence
see **Kathrine Grey series**
Rees, Arthur John
see **Colwin Grey series**
Smith, Martin Cruz
see **Roman Grey series**
Thurston, Ernest Temple
see **John Grey series**

Grey Shadow series
Rochester, George Ernest
1 *Grey Shadow* (1936)
2 *Return of Grey Shadow* (1949)

Grey Six series
Styles, Showell
1 *Cubs of the castle* (1969)
2 *Cubs on the job* (1972)

Greycliff girls series
Grove, Harriet Pyne
1 *Cathaline at Greycliff* (1923)
2 *Girls of Greycliff* (1923)
3 *Greycliff wings* (1923)
4 *Greycliff girls in camp* (1923)
5 *Greycliff heroines* (1923)
6 *Greycliff girls ranching* (1925)
7 *Greycliff girld' great adventure* (1925)
8 *Greycliff girls in Georgia* (1925)

Greycourt series
Eastways, W W
1 *Greycourt* (1939)
2 *Girls of Greycourt* (1944)

Greyfriars series
Richards, Frank
see **Billy Bunter series**

Greyhaven Manor series
Michaels, Barbara
1 *Black rainbow* (1982)
2 *Someone in the house* (1981)

Greyhawk series
This sequence has two authors
Gygax, Gary
1 *Saga of old city* (1985)
A novel of swordplay, thievery and magic
2 *Artifact of evil* (1986)
A novel of fantastic action in a world where magic is law
Estes, Rose
3 *Master Wolf* (1987)
A novel of quest and romance, sorcery and death
4 *Price of power* (1987)
A journey into an incredible world of magic and peril
5 *Demon hand* (1988)
A journey to a land of wizards, demons and magical gems
6 *Name of the game* (1988)
A journey to a lland of wizards, kings and magical gems
7 *Eyes have it* (1989)
An adventure in a land of wizards, demons and fire-breathing dragons
Companion volume: *Greyhawk adventures, a compendium of Greyhawk campaign ideas for the AD&D playing system*, by James Michael Ward, 1988

Greyhawk trilogy
Estes, Rose
see **Mika trilogy**

Greyhouse series
Bell, Robert Stanly Warren
1 *Tales of Greyhouse* (1901)
2 *Green at Greyhouse* (1908)
3 *Secret seven* (1915)
4 *Greyhouse days* (1918)
5 *Polson of Greyhouse* (1932)
6 *J.O.Jones and how he earned his living* (1903)
7 *Smith's week* (1915)

Greylock of Godshome series
McGeary, Duncan
1 *Snowcastles* (1982)
2 *Icetowers* (1982)

Greystone Bay series
Grant, Charles Lewis
see **Chronicles of Greystone Bay series**

Greystone Tavern series
Bronte, Louisa
1 *Greystone Tavern* (1975)
2 *Gathering at Greystone* (1976)
3 *Freedom trail to Greystone* (1976)
4 *Casino Greystone* (1976)
5 *Moonlight at Greystone* (1976)
6 *Greystone heritage* (1976)

Gribble the dragon series
Ruffell, Ann
1 *Dragon fire* (1979)
2 *Dragon water* (1980)
3 *Dragon earth* (1981)
4 *Dragon air* (1981)
Companion volume: Dragon wanted, 1986

Grichka series
Guillot, Rene
1 *Grishka and the bear* (1958)
Original edition entitled *Grichka et son ours*
2 *Grichka and the wolves* (1960)
Grichka and Brother Bear
Pascal and the lioness
Original edition entitled *Grichka et les loups*; the third title is an abridged edition
3 *[Marque de Grichka]* (1962)
No English edition
4 *[Grichka et les turbans jaunes]* (1964)
No English edition

Griddle series
Polsky, Thomas
see **L F Griddle series**

Gridiron series
Gault, William Campbell
1 *Mister Fullback* (1953)
2 *Mister Quarterback* (1955)
3 *Bruce Benedict, quarterback* (1957)
4 *Backfield challenge* (1967)
5 *Quarterback gamble* (1970)
7 *Cut-rate quarterback* (1977)

Gridiron series
James, Laurence
1 *First and ten* (1987)
2 *Second and five* (1987)
3 *Third and goal* (1987)
4 *Touchdown!* (1987)

Gridley Nelson series
Fenisong, Ruth
see **Captain Gridley Nelson series**

Grief series
Cramer, Helen Catherine
Poems
1 *Tomorrow's dawn* (1983)
Alternative title: Love is immortal, death but an horizon; a mother's walk through the first year of grief
2 *Day by day* (1986)
A mother's walk through grief

Grier series
Mitchell, Lane
see **Jimmy Grier series**

Grierson series
Stuart, Ian
see **David Grierson series**
Wurr, H J
see **Inspector Grierson series**

Griff and Tommy series
Griffiths, John
1 *Griff and Tommy* (1956)
2 *Griff and Tommy and the golden image* (1964)

Griff Dexter series
Kennedy, Elliot
1 *Big loser* (1972)
2 *Bullets are final* (1973)
3 *That fatal feeling* (1974)
4 *Never say dead* (1974)
5 *Dead sleep late* (1975)
6 *No love in a bullet* (1976)

Griff Lomax series
Sutcliffe, Halliwell
Set on the moors of Yorkshire
1 *Man of the moors* (1897)
2 *Through sorrow's gates* (1904)

Griff Stark series
Randolph, Forrest A
see **Confederate series**

Griffin Moss and Sabine Stroheim trilogy
Bantock, Nick
1 *Griffin and Sabine* (1991)
An extraordinary correspondence
2 *Sabine's notebook* (1992)
In which the extraordinary correspondence of Griffin and Sabine continues
3 *Golden mean* (1993)

Griffin series
Charles, Wyndham
see **Chief Superintendent Sebastian Griffin series**
Sallis, James
see **Lew Griffin series**

Griggs series
Crawford, Francis Marion
see **Paul Griggs series**

Grigson series
Broome, Adam
see **Commissioner Denzil Grigson series**

Grijpstra and De Gier series
Van de Wetering, Janwillem
see **De Gier and Grijpstra series**

Grill room series
Oppenheim, Edward Phillips
see **Major Charles Lyson series**

Grimes series
Chandler, Arthur Bertram
see **John Grimes series**

Grimley Grange series
Stones, Anthony
see **Bill of Grimley Grange series**

Grimm series
Holmes, Bryan John
see **Reaper series**

Grimpwinkle series
Drake, Joan
see **Mister Grimpwinkle series**

Grimsen trilogy
Winther, Sophus Keith
1 *Take all to Nebraska* (1935)
2 *Mortgage your heart* (1937)
3 *This passion never dies* (1938)

Gringo series
Thorne, Ramsay
see **Captain Gringo series**

Gringos series
Sandon, J D
This pseudonym is used by John Barton Harvey and Angus Wells as indicated against each title
1 *Guns across the river* (1979) [Wells]
2 *Cannons in the rain* (1979) [Harvey]
3 *Fire in the wind* (1979) [Wells]
4 *Border affair* (1979) [Harvey]
5 *Easy money* (1980) [Wells]
6 *Mazatlan* (1980) [Harvey]
7 *One too many mornings* (1981) [Wells]
8 *Wheels of thunder* (1981) [Harvey]
9 *Durango* (1982) [Harvey]
10 *Survivors* (1982) [Wells]

Grischa Pavlov and O'Shaughnessey series
Ryan, Jessica
see **Gregory Pavlov and O'Shaughnessey series**

Grischa series
Zweig, Arnold
see **Werner Bertin and Lenore Wahl series**

Grisenbaum family series
Scott, Barbara Montagu
1 *Which, then, be fool?* (1944)
2 *And which, the knave?* (1946)

Grishka series
Guillot, Rene
see **Grichka series**

Grisman and Kilmoonie series
Morrell, David
see **Chris Kilmoonie and Saul Grisman series**

Grofield series
Stark, Richard
see **Alan Grofield series**

Grogan and Manning series
Neville, Margot
see **Inspector Grogan and Sergeant Manning series**

Groggs series
Bentley, Anne
1 *Groggs have a wonderful summer* (1980)
2 *Groggs' day out* (1981)

Groode series
Griswold, George
see **Mister Groode series**

Groosham Grange series
Horowitz, Anthony
1 *Groosham Grange* (1988)
2 *Unholy grail* (1991)

Grope series
Mann, Francis Oscar
see **Albert Grope series**

Gross series
Wohl, James Paul
see **Sam Gross series**

Ground Zero series
Helm, Eric
1 *Ground Zero* (1986)
2 *P.O.W.* (1986)
3 *Unconfirmed kill* (1986)
4 *Fall of Camp A-555* (1987)
5 *Soldier's medal* (1987)
6 *Kit Carson scout* (1987)
7 *Hobo woods* (1987)
8 *Guidelines* (1987)
9 *Ville* (1987)
10 *Incident at Plei Soi* (1988)
11 *Tet* (1988)
12 *Iron Triangle* (1988)
13 *Red dust* (1988)
14 *Hamlet* (1988)
15 *Moon cusser* (1988)
16 *Dragon's jaw* (1989)
17 *Cambodian sanctuary* (1989)
18 *Payback* (1989)
19 *Macv* (1989)
20 *Tan Son Nhut* (1989)
21 *Puppet soldiers* (1989)
Number 22 not identified
23 *Warrior* (1990)
24 *Target* (1990)
25 *Warlord* (1990)
26 *Spike* (1990)
27 *Recon* (1990)

Group Captain Alan Metcalfe series
Finkel, George
1 *Mystery of Secret Beach* (1962)
2 *Ship in hiding* (1963)
3 *Cloudmaker* (1965)
4 *Singing sands* (1966)

Groupie Metcalfe series
Finkel, George
see **Group Captain Alan Metcalfe series**

Grouser series
Brooks, Edwy Searles
see **Inspector William Beeke series**

Growing up series
Beers, Victor Gilbert
1 *Growing up with Jesus* (1987)
2 *Growing up with my family* (1987)
3 *Growing up to praise God* (1987)
4 *Growing up with God's friends* (1987)

Growing up series
Ransom, Candice Farris
1 *Almost ten and a half* (1990)
2 *Going on twelve* (1988)
3 *Thirteen* (1986)
4 *Fourteen and holding* (1987)
5 *Fifteen at last* (1987)

Growing up series
Richardson, Arleta
1 *Sixteen and away from home* (1985)
2 *Eighteen and on her own* (1986)
3 *Nineteen and wedding bells ahead* (1987)

Growing up series
Stevenson, James
1 *When I was nine* (1986)
2 *Higher on the door* (1987)

Growth trilogy
Tarkington, Booth
1 *Magnificent Ambersons* (1918)
2 *Turmoil* (1915)
3 *Midlander* (1923)
National Avenue

Grub-and-Stakers series
Craig, Alisa
see **Osbert Monk series**

Grug series
Prior, Ted
1 *Grug* (1979)
2 *Grug and the big red apple* (1979)
3 *Grug and the green paint* (1979)
4 *Grug and his garden* (1979)
5 *Grug learns to swim* (1982)
6 *Grug and the rainbow* (1982)
7 *Grug meets Snoot* (1982)
8 *Grug in the playground* (1982)
9 *Grug has a birthday* (1983)
10 *Grug goes fishing* (1983)
11 *Grug goes to school* (1983)
12 *Grug at the beach* (1983)
13 *Grug and his bicycle* (1985)
14 *Grug plays soccer* (1985)
15 *Grug at the snow* (1985)
16 *Grug at the zoo* (1985)
17 *Grug builds a car* (1989)
18 *Grug plays cricket* (1989)
19 *Grug learns to cook* (1989)
20 *Grug and his music* (1989)
21 *Grug learns to dance* (1992)
22 *Grug builds a boat* (1992)
23 *Grug and his kite* (1992)
24 *Grug goes shopping* (1992)

Grum and Dan series
Cockett, Mary
see **Dan and Grum series**

Grump series
Sampson, Derek
1 *Grump and the hairy mammoth* (1971)
2 *Grump strikes back* (1973)

Grundt series
Williams, Valentine
see **Clubfoot series**

Grundy series
James, Charles Thomas Clement
see **Mrs Grundy series**

Grunter series
Shelley, Noreen
see **Piggy Grunter series**

Grunts series
Selway, Martina
1 *Grunts, what a day!* (1982)
2 *Grunts go on a picnic* (1982)

Gryce series
Green, Anna Katharine
see **Ebenezer Gryce series**

Guadalcanal series
Hammel, Eric Maxwell
1 *Starvation island* (1987)
2 *Carrier battles* (1987)
3 *Decision at sea* (1988)

Guara series
Farrell, Anne
see **Mitchell family series**

Guard within series
Ferguson, Sarah
Reminiscences as a psychiatric patient
1 *To the place of shells* (1975)
2 *Guard within* (1976)

Guardians of the flame series
Rosenberg, Joel
1 *Sleeping dragon* (1983)
2 *Sword and the chain* (1984)
3 *Silver crown* (1985)
Numbers 1-3 also published in one volume entitled *The warriors,* 1985
4 *Heir apparent* (1987)
5 *Warrior lives* (1989)
Numbers 4 and 5 also published in one volume entitled *The heroes*, 1989
6 *Road to Ehnevor* (1991)
7 *Road home* (1995)
Announced as *The road to forever*

Guardians of the Gemstones trilogy
Stine, Robert Lawrence
see **Golden Girl and the Guardians of the Gemstones trilogy**

Guardians of the tall stones series
Caldecott, Moyra
see **Sacred stones series**

Guardians of the Three series
This sequence has six authors
Fawcett, Bill
1 *Lord of Cragsclaw* (1989)
Morwood, Peter
2 *Keeper of the city* (1989)
Costello, Matthew John
3 *Wizard of Tizare* (1990)
Lovejoy, Jack
4 *Defenders of Ar* (1990)

Guardians series
Austin, Richard
1 *Guardians* (1985)
2 *Trial by fire* (1985)
3 *Thunder of hell* (1985)
4 *Night of the phoenix* (1985)
5 *Armageddon run* (1985)
6 *War zone* (1986)
7 *Brute force* (1987)
8 *Desolation Road* (1987)
9 *Vengeance day* (1987)
10 *Freedom fight* (1988)
11 *Valley of the gods* (1988)
12 *Plague years* (1988)
13 *Devil's deal* (1989)
14 *Death from above* (1990)
15 *Snake eyes* (1990)
16 *Death charge* (1991)

Guardians series
Baker, William Howard
1 *Guardians* (1967)
Saxon, Peter
This pseudonym is used for numbers 2-7 of this sequence and is used by William Howard Baker, Rex Dolphin, Wilfred Glassford McNeilly, Ross Richards and Martin Thomas as indicated against each title
2 *Through the dark curtain* (1968)
Dark ways to death [Richards]

3 *Curse of Rathlaw* (1968)
[Thomas; Baker]
4 *Killing bone* (1969)
[Baker]
5 *Dark ways to death* (1968)
[Baker; McNeilly]
6 *Haunting of Alan Mais* (1969)
[Baker; McNeilly]
7 *Vampires of Finistere* (1970)
[Dolphin]

Guardians series
Weis, Margaret
see **Star of the guardians series**

Guarnaccia series
Nabb, Magdalen
see **Marshal Guarnaccia series**

Guatemala trilogy
Asturias, Miguel Angel
1 *Cyclone* (1950)
Strong wind
Original edition entitled *Viento fuerte*
2 *Green Pope* (1954)
Original edition entitled *El Papa Verde*
3 *Eyes of the interred* (1960)
Original edition entitled *Los ojos de los enterrados*

Guelpa series
Thompson, Vance
see **Mister Guelpa series**

Guessing game series
Ziefert, Harriet
Illustrated by Arnold Lobel
1 *Bear gets dressed* (1986)
2 *Bear all year* (1986)
3 *Bear goes shopping* (1986)
4 *Bear's busy morning* (1986)

Guiana series
Harris, Wilson
1 *Palace of the peacock* (1960)
2 *Far journey of Oudin* (1961)
3 *Whole armour* (1962)
4 *Secret ladder* (1963)

Guide, philosopher and friend trilogy
Dark, Sidney
Reminiscences and essays
1 *Not such a bad life* (1941)
2 *I sit and I think and I wonder* (1943)
3 *On the outskirts* (1951)

Guides to the cemeteries of the world's great cities series
Culbertson, Judi
1 *Permanent Parisians* (1986)
A guide to the cemeteries of Paris
2 *Permanent New Yorkers* (1987)
A biographical guide to cemeteries of New York
3 *Permanent Californians* (1989)
A biographical guide to the cemeteries of California
4 *Permanent Londoners* (1990)
Illustrated guide to the cemeteries of London

Guido Brunetti series
Leon, Donna
see **Commissario Guido Brunetti series**

Guild series
Gorman, Edward
see **Leo Guild series**

Guilhelm de Courdeval series
Rhodes, Daniel
1 *Next, after Lucifer* (1987)
2 *Adversary* (1988)

Guilia and De Quesnoy series
Wheatley, Dennis
see **Count de Quesnoy and Condesa Guilia series**

Guillaume and Penelope series
Baron, Nicole de
see **Penelope and Guillaume series**

Guinea pig board books series
Duke, Kate
1 *What bounces?* (1986)
2 *Clean-up day* (1986)
3 *Bedtime* (1986)
4 *Playground* (1986)

Guinea pig series
Duke, Kate
1 *Guinea pig ABC* (1983)
2 *Guinea pigs far and near* (1984)
3 *What would a guinea pig do?* (1988)

Guinevere Jones series
Castle, Jayne
1 *Desperate game* (1986)
2 *Chilling deception* (1986)
3 *Sinister touch* (1986)
4 *Fatal fortune* (1986)

Guinevere trilogy
Newman, Sharan
1 *Guinevere* (1981)
2 *Chessboard queen* (1983)
Guinevere, queen of the summer stars
3 *Guinevere evermore* (1985)

Guinevere trilogy
Woolley, Persia
1 *Child of the northern spring* (1987)
2 *Queen of the summer stars* (1990)
Guinevere, queen of the summer stars
3 *Legend in autumn* (1991)

Guinness series
Guild, Nicholas
see **Ray Guinness series**

Gulf Coast series
Thomas, D
1 *Gulf Coast run* (1980)
2 *Gulf Coast goods* (1981)

Gull series
Stuart, Anthony
see **Vladimir Gull series**

Gulliver Queen series
Queen, Ellery, Junior
1 *Mystery of the merry magician* (1961)
2 *Mystery of the vanished victim* (1962)
3 *Purple bird mystery* (1965)

Gulliver series
Burnett, George
see **Inspector Gulliver series**

Gulls' Point series
Nicholson, Joyce
1 *Adventure at Gulls' Point* (1955)
2 *Gulls' Point and Pineapple* (1957)

Gulls series
Wood, Kenneth
1 *Gulls* (1974)
2 *Period of violence* (1977)

Gumbles series
Wakefield, Sydney Alexander
1 *Bottersnikes and gumbles* (1967)
2 *Gumbles on guard* (1975)
3 *Gumbles in summer* (1979)
4 *Gumbles in trouble* (1990)

Gumble's Yard series
Townsend, John Rowe
see **Uncle Walter series**

Gumbo Grove series
Tate, Eleanora Elaine
1 *Secret of Gumbo Grove* (1987)
2 *Thank you, Doctor Martin Luther King, junior!* (1990)

Gumby Gang series
Oldfield, Pamela
1 *Adventures of the Gumby Gang* (1978)
2 *Gumby Gang again* (1978)
3 *More about the Gumby Gang* (1979)
4 *Gumby Gang strikes again* (1980)
5 *Gumby Gang on holiday* (1983)
6 *Return of the Gumby Gang* (1986)

Gumdrop series
Biro, Val
1 *Gumdrop* (1967)
The adventures of a vintage car
2 *Gumdrop and the farmer's friend* (1968)
3 *Gumdrop on the rally* (1969)
4 *Gumdrop on the move* (1970)
5 *Gumdrop goes to London* (1971)
6 *Gumdrop finds a friend* (1973)
Revised edition 1978
7 *Gumdrop in double trouble* (1975)
8 *Gumdrop and the steamroller* (1976)
9 *Gumdrop on the Brighton run* (1976)
10 *Gumdrop posts a letter* (1976)
Gumdrop and the birthday surprise
11 *Gumdrop has a birthday* (1977)
12 *Gumdrop gets his wings* (1979)
13 *Gumdrop finds a ghost* (1980)
14 *Gumdrop and the secret switches* (1981)
15 *Gumdrop and Horace* (1982)
16 *Gumdrop makes a start* (1982)
17 *Gumdrop races a train* (1982)
18 *Gumdrop at sea* (1983)
19 *Gumdrop goes to school* (1983)
20 *Gumdrop at the zoo* (1983)
21 *Gumdrop gets a lift* (1983)
22 *Gumdrop in a hurry* (1983)
Gumdrop beats the clock
23 *Gumdrop's magic journey* (1984)
24 *Gumdrop goes fishing* (1984)
25 *Gumdrop has a tummy-ache* (1984)
26 *Gumdrop is the best car* (1984)
Gumdrop is the best
27 *Gumdrop on the farm* (1984)
28 *Gumdrop and the monster* (1985)
29 *Gumdrop and the farmyard caper* (1985)
30 *Gumdrop and the great sausage caper* (1985)
31 *Gumdrop catches a cold* (1985)
32 *Gumdrop floats away* (1985)
33 *Gumdrop to the rescue* (1986)
34 *Gumdrop for ever!* (1987)
35 *Gumdrop and the dinosaur* (1988)
36 *Gumdrop and the pirates* (1989)
37 *Gumdrop and the elephant* (1990)
38 *Gumdrop and the bulldozer* (1991)
39 *Gumdrop's merry Christmas* (1992)
Omnibus volume: *The bumper Gumdrop omnibus*, 1989

Gummidge series
Todd, Barbara Euphan
see **Worzel Gummidge series**

Gumnut Land series
Gibbs, May
1 *Gum blossom babies* (1916)
2 *Gumnut babies* (1916)
3 *Boronia babies* (1917)
4 *Flannel flowers and other bush babies* (1917)
5 *Wattle babies* (1918)
6 *Snugglepot and Cuddlepie* (1918)
Adaptations from sections of this title: *Snugglepot and Cuddlepie meet Mister Lizard*, 1970, *Snugglepot and Cuddlepie find Ragged Blossom*, 1974, Snugglepot and *Cuddlepie on board the Snag*, 1975
7 *Little Ragged Blossom* (1920)
8 *Little Obelia, and further adventures of Ragged Blossom, Snugglepot and* (1921)
Cuddlepie
Numbers 6-8 also published in one volume entitled *The complete adventures of Snugglepot and Cuddlepie*, 1940
9 *Nuttybub and Nittersing* (1923)
10 *Chucklebud and Wunkydoo* (1924)
Two little Gumnuts
11 *Bib and Bub* (1925)
12 *Further adventures of Bib and Bub* (1927)
13 *More funny stories about old friends, Bib and Bub* (1928)
14 *Bib and Bub in Gumnut Town* (1929)
15 *Scotty in Gumnut Land* (1941)
16 *Mister and Mrs Bear and friends* (1943)
Companion volumes: *Bib and Bub painting book, new stories in cartoon form*, 1932, and *Gumnuts, verse*, 1943

Gumption series
Barry, Margaret Stuart
see **Maggie Gumption series**

Gumpy series
Burningham, John
see **Mister Gumpy series**

Gun Club series
Verne, Jules
1 *From the earth to the moon* (1865)
American Gun Club
Baltimore Gun Club
Passage direct in 97 hours and 20 minutes; original edition entitled *De la terre a la lune*
2 *Round the moon* (1870)
Around the moon
Original edition entitled *Autour de la lune*
3 *Purchase of the North Pole* (1889)
Original edition entitled *Sans dessus dessous*

Gun Cotton series
Grayson, Rupert
1 *Gun Cotton* (1929)
Gunston Cotton, Secret Service agent
2 *Death rides the forest* (1930)
3 *Gun Cotton, adventurer* (1933)
4 *Gun Cotton, secret agent* (1934)
Secret agent in Africa
5 *Escape with Gun Cotton* (1934)
6 *Gun Cotton goes to Russia* (1936)
7 *Gun Cotton in Hollywood* (1936)
8 *Gun Cotton outside the law* (1937)
9 *Gun Cotton, adventure nine* (1937)
10 *Gun Cotton, ace high* (1937)
11 *Gun Cotton in Mexico* (1937)
12 *Gun Cotton at Blind Man's Hood* (1938)
13 *Gun Cotton, secret airman* (1939)
14 *Murder at the bank* (1939)
15 *Secret agent in Africa* (1939)

Gun in cheek series
Pronzini, Bill
1 *Gun in cheek* (1982)
A study of alternative crime fiction
2 *Son of Gun in cheek* (1987)

Gun lust series
Fieldhouse, William
see **Shaddrock and Cougar series**

Guna series
Alderman, Gill
1 *Archivist* (1989)
A black romance
2 *Land beyond* (1990)

Gundam mobile suit trilogy
Tomino, Yoshiyuki
Translated from the Japanese
1 *Awakening* (1990)
2 *Escalation* (1990)
3 *Confrontation* (1991)

Gunjer series
Haiblum, Isidore
1 *Interworld* (1977)
2 *Outerworld* (1979)
3 *Specterworld* (1991)

Gunn series
Muir, James A
see **Breed series**

Gunn series
Sherman, Jory
1 *Dawn of revenge* (1980)
2 *Mexican showdown* (1980)
3 *Death's Head Trail* (1980)
4 *Bloody justice* (1980)
5 *Winter hell* (1981)
6 *Duel in purgatory* (1981)
7 *Law of the rope* (1981)
8 *Apache arrows* (1981)
9 *Boothill bounty* (1981)
10 *Hard bullets* (1981)
11 *Trial by sixgun* (1982)
12 *Widowmaker* (1982)
13 *Arizona hardcase* (1982)
14 *Buff runners* (1982)
15 *Drygulched* (1983)
16 *Wyoming wanton* (1983)
17 *Tucson twosome* (1983)
18 *Golden lady* (1983)
19 *High mountain hussy* (1984)
20 *Ten-gallon tease* (1984)
21 *Sweet Texas tart* (1984)
22 *Kansas kitten* (1985)
23 *Bedroll beauty* (1985)
24 *Frontier Fanny* (1986)
25 *Trail tramp* (1986)
26 *Gold shaft, gold shaft* (1986)
27 *Two for the money* (1987)
28 *Two easy pieces* (1987)
29 *Mine shaft* (1987)

Gunnar Matson series
James, Breni
see **Sergeant Gunnar Matson series**

Gunner Asch series
Kirst, Hans Hellmut
1 *Zero eight fifteen* (1954)
Revolt of Gunner Asch
Original edition entitled *Null Acht Funftzehen*
2 *Zero eight fifteen, 2* (1954)
Gunner Asch goes to war
Forward Gunner Asch!
Original edition entitled *Null Acht Funftzehen, die seitsamen Kriegserlehnisse de Soldaten Asch*
3 *Return of Gunner Asch* (1955)
Original edition entitled *Null Acht Funftzehen bis zum Ende*
4 *What became of Gunner Asch?* (1963)
Original edition entitled *Null Acht Funftzehen Heute*

Gunning series
Elliott, William James
see **Ed Gunning series**

Gunship series
Zeybel, Henry
1 *First ace* (1986)
2 *Spectre of death* (1987)
3 *Wings of fire* (1988)

Gunships series
Teed, Jack Hamilton
1 *Killing zone* (1983)
2 *Fire force* (1983)
3 *Cobra kill* (1984)
4 *Sky fire* (1986)

Gunslick series
White, James G
1 *Man pursued* (1990)
2 *Rawhiders* (1990)
3 *Long ride to vengeance* (1990)

Gunslinger series
Garrett, Charles C
This pseudonym is used by Laurence James and Angus Wells as indicated against each title
1 *Massacre trail* (1977) [James]
2 *Golden gun* (1978) [Wells]
3 *White Apache* (1978) [James]
4 *Fifty calibre kill* (1978) [Wells]
5 *Arizona bloodline* (1979) [James]
6 *Rebel vengeance* (1979) [Wells]
7 *Death canyon* (1979) [James]
8 *Peacemaker* (1980) [Wells]
9 *Russian lode* (1980) [Wells]
10 *Blood target* (1981) [James]

Gunsmith series
Roberts, J R
1 *Macklin's woman* (1982)
2 *Chinese gunmen* (1982)
3 *Woman hunt* (1982)
4 *Guns of Abilene* (1982)
5 *Three guns of glory* (1982)
6 *Leadtown* (1982)
7 *Longhorn war* (1982)
8 *Quanah's revenge* (1982)
9 *Heavyweight gun* (1982)
10 *New Orleans five* (1982)
11 *One-handed gun* (1982)
12 *Canadian payroll* (1983)
13 *Draw to an inside death* (1983)
14 *Dead man's hand* (1983)
15 *Bandit gold* (1983)
16 *Buckskins and sixguns* (1983)
17 *Silver war* (1983)
18 *High noon at Lancaster* (1983)
19 *Bandido blood* (1983)
20 *Dodge City gang* (1983)
21 *Sasquatch hunt* (1983)
22 *Bullets and ballots* (1983)
23 *Riverboat gang* (1983)
24 *Killer grizzly* (1984)
25 *North of the border* (1984)
26 *Eagle's Gap* (1984)
27 *Chinatown hell* (1984)
28 *Panhandle search* (1984)
29 *Wildcat roundup* (1984)
30 *Ponderosa war* (1984)
31 *Trouble rides a fast horse* (1984)
32 *Dynamite justice* (1984)
33 *Posse* (1984)
34 *Night of the gila* (1984)
35 *Bounty women* (1985)
36 *Black Pearl Saloon* (1985)
37 *Gundown in Paradise* (1985)
38 *King of the border* (1985)
39 *El Paso salt war* (1985)
40 *Ten Pines killer* (1985)
41 *Hell with a pistol* (1985)
42 *Wyoming cattle kill* (1985)
43 *Golden horseman* (1985)
44 *Scarlet gun* (1985)
45 *Navaho devil* (1985)
46 *Wild Bill's ghost* (1985)
47 *Miner's showdown* (1986)
48 *Archer's revenge* (1986)
49 *Showdown in Raton* (1986)
50 *When legends meet* (1986)
51 *Desert hell* (1986)
52 *Diamond gun* (1986)
53 *Denver duo* (1986)
54 *Hell on wheels* (1986)
55 *Legend-maker* (1986)
56 *Walking dead man* (1986)
57 *Crossfire Mountain* (1986)
58 *Deadly healer* (1986)
59 *Trail drive war* (1987)
60 *Geronimo's trail* (1987)
61 *Comstock gold fraud* (1987)
62 *Boom town killer* (1987)
63 *Texas crackdown* (1987)
64 *Fast draw league* (1987)
65 *Showdown in Rio Malo* (1987)
66 *Outlaw trail* (1987)
67 *Homesteader guns* (1987)
68 *Five card death* (1987)
69 *Trail drive to Montana* (1987)
70 *Trial by fire* (1987)
71 *Old Whistler Gang* (1988)
72 *Daughter of gold* (1988)
73 *Apache gold* (1988)
74 *Plains murder* (1988)
75 *Deadly memories* (1988)
76 *nevada timber war* (1988)
77 *New Mexico showdown* (1988)
78 *Barbed wire and bullets* (1988)
79 *Death express* (1988)
80 *When legends die* (1988)
81 *Six-gun justice* (1988)
82 *Mustang hunters* (1988)
83 *Texas ransom* (1989)
84 *Vengeance town* (1989)
85 *Winner take all* (1989)
86 *Message from a dead man* (1989)
87 *Ride for vengeance* (1989)
88 *Takersville shoot* (1989)
89 *Blood on the land* (1989)
90 *Six-gun sideshow* (1989)
91 *Mississippi massacre* (1989)
92 *Arizona triangle* (1989)
93 *Brothers of the gun* (1989)
94 *Stagecoach thieves* (1989)
95 *Judgement at Firecreek* (1990)
96 *Dead man's jury* (1990)
97 *Hands of the strangler* (1990)
98 *Nevada death trap* (1990)
99 *Wagon train to hell* (1990)
100 *Ride for revenge* (1990)
101 *Dead ringer* (1990)
102 *Trail of the assassin* (1990)
103 *Shoot out at Cross Fork* (1990)
104 *Buckskin's trail* (1990)
105 *Helldorado* (1990)
106 *Hanging judge* (1990)
107 *Bounty hunters* (1990)
108 *Tombstone at Little Horn* (1990)
109 *Killer's race* (1991)
110 *Wyoming range war* (1991)
111 *Grand Canyon* (1991)
112 *Guns don't argue* (1991)
113 *Saint Louis showdown* (1991)
114 *Frontier justice* (1991)
115 *Game of death* (1991)
116 *Oregon strangler* (1991)
117 *Blood brothers* (1991)
118 *Scarlet fury* (1991)
119 *Arizona ambush* (1991)
120 *Vengeance trail* (1991)
121 *Deadly derringer* (1992)
122 *Stagecoach killers* (1992)
123 *Five against death* (1992)
124 *Mustang man* (1992)
125 *Godfather* (1992)
126 *Killer's gold* (1992)
127 *Ghost town* (1992)
128 *Caliente gold robbery* (1992)
129 *Golden Gate killers* (1992)
130 *Road to Testimony* (1992)
131 *Witness* (1992)
132 *Great riverboat race* (1992)
133 *Two guns for justice* (1993)
134 *Outlaw women* (1993)
135 *Last bounty* (1993)
136 *Valley massacre* (1993)
137 *Nevada guns* (1993)
138 *Deadly gold* (1993)
139 *Vigilante hunt* (1993)
140 *Samurai hunt* (1993)
141 *Gambler's blood* (1993)
142 *Wyoming justice* (1993)

Gunsmoke series
Flynn, Jackson
Based on a television series
1 *Renegades* (1974)
2 *Shootout* (1974)
3 *Duel at Dodge City* (1974)
4 *Cheyenne vengeance* (1975)
Companion volumes: *Showdown on Front Street*, by Paul S Newman, 1969, *Gunsmoke*, by Chris Stratton, 1970

Gunston Cotton series
Grayson, Rupert
see **Gun Cotton series**

Gunther series
Mayor, Archer Huntington
see **Lieutenant Joe Gunther series**

Gunther trilogy
Kerr, Philip
see **Berlin noir trilogy**

Gunzberg family series
High, Monique Raphel
1 *Four winds of heaven* (1980)
2 *Encore* (1981)

Gurney series
Hook, Theodore Edward
see **Gilbert Gurney series**

Gurney trilogy
Llewellyn, Sam
see **George Le Fanu Gurney trilogy**

Gus and Gilly series
Anson, Brian
1 *Gus and Gilly* (1969)
2 *Winter journey* (1969)

Gus and me series
Anthony, Frank Sheldon
see **Gus Tomlins series**

Gus series
Thayer, Jane
Illustrated by Sid Fleischman
1 *Gus was a friendly ghost* (1962)
2 *What's a ghost going to do* (1966)
3 *Gus was a Christmas ghost* (1969)
4 *Gus and the baby ghost* (1972)
5 *Gus was a Mexican ghost* (1974)
6 *Gus was a gorgeous ghost* (1978)
7 *Gus was a real dumb ghost* (1982)
8 *Gus loved his happy home* (1989)

Gus Tomlins series
Anthony, Frank Sheldon
Short stories reprinted from New Zealand newspapers
1 *Me and Gus* (1938)
Revised edition 1951
2 *More me and Gus* (1952)
3 *Me and Gus again* (1955)
Numbers 1-3 also published as *The complete me and Gus*, 1963
4 *Gus Tomlins* (1977)
Includes some stories already published in book form and a previously unpublished novel

Gussie and Sophie series
Sharmat, Marjorie Weinman
see **Sophie and Gussie series**

Guthrie McCabe trilogy
Cook, Will
1 *Tough Texan* (1960)
2 *Peacemaker* (1965)
3 *Outcasts* (1965)

Gutsy Morgan series
Johnson, Duff
1 *Rocky mountain* (1951)
2 *Chiseller* (1951)

Guttman series
Goldstein, Arthur David
see **Max Guttman series**

Guy and Harriet Pringle series
Manning, Olivia
1 *Great fortune* (1960)
2 *Spoilt city* (1962)
3 *Friends and heroes* (1965)
Numbers 1-3 also published in one volume entitled *The Balkan trilogy*, 1990
4 *Danger tree* (1977)
5 *Battle lost and won* (1978)
6 *Sum of things* (1980)
Numbers 4-6 also published in one volume entitled *The Levant trilogy*, 1988

Guy Bannister series
Crossley, Maude
1 *Forbidden hour* (1925)
Co-author: Charles King
2 *Crookery Inn* (1931)

Guy Crouchback trilogy
Waugh, Evelyn
see **World War II trilogy**

Guy Fosse series
Cannon, Elliott
1 *Dumbo Dossier* (1975)
2 *Big chip* (1976)

Guy Grenville series
Padfield, Peter
1 *Lion's paw* (1978)
2 *Unquiet gods* (1980)
3 *Gold chains of empire* (1982)

Guy Laurence and Tony Carlisle series
Dempster, Guy
1 *Fleet wings* (1941)
2 *East with the admiral* (1945)
3 *Southward bound* (1947)

Guy Northeast series
Cannan, Joanna
see **Inspector Guy Northeast series**

Guy Plante and Freya Matthews series
Palmer, John
1 *Above and below* (1967)
2 *So much for Gennaro* (1968)

Guy Random series
Anderson, Oliver
1 *Painless extractions* (1952)
2 *Random rendezvous* (1955)
3 *Random mating* (1956)
4 *Random rapture* (1958)
5 *Random at random* (1959)
6 *Random all round* (1960)

Guy series
Ridgway, Jason
see **Brian Guy series**

Guy Silvestri series
Rennert, Maggie
1 *Circle of death* (1974)
2 *Operation Alcestis* (1975)
3 *Operation Calpurnia* (1976)

Guyon series
Madden, M S
see **Sir Guyon series**

Gwalchmai trilogy
Bradshaw, Gillian
see **Arthur and Gawain trilogy**

Gwalchmai trilogy
Munn, Harold Warner
1 *King of the world's edge* (1966)
2 *Ship from Atlantis* (1967)
Numbers 1 and 2 also published in one volume entitled *Merlin's godson*, 1976
3 *Merlin's ring* (1974)

Gwenda series
Batchelor, Margaret
1 *Little Rhodesian* (1922)
2 *Gwenda's friend from home* (1924)

Gwynedd tetralogy
Pargeter, Edith
see **Brothers of Gwynedd tetralogy**

Gwyneth series
Ford, Donald
1 *Following seasons* (1959)
2 *Catch of time* (1960)

Gwynett trilogy
Hayes, Frederick William
1 *Kent squire* (1900)
2 *Gwynett of Thornhaugh* (1900)
3 *Shadow of a throne* (1904)

Gwynn Leith and Colin Keats series
Shore, Viola Brothers
see **Colin Keats and Gwynn Leith series**

Gwynne trilogy
Sumner, Richard
see **Nell Gwynne trilogy**

Gymnast Gilly series
Aykroyd, Peter
1 *Gymnast Gilly the novice* (1986)
2 *Gymnast Gilly the dancer* (1986)
3 *Gymnast Gilly the champ* (1988)
4 *Gymnast Gilly the expert* (1988)

Gymnasts series
Levy, Elizabeth
1 *Beginners* (1988)
2 *First meet* (1988)
3 *Nobody's perfect* (1988)
4 *Winner* (1989)
5 *Trouble in the gym* (1989)
6 *Bad break* (1989)
7 *Tumbling ghosts* (1989)
8 *Captain of the team* (1989)
9 *Crush on the coach* (1990)
10 *Boys in the gym* (1990)
11 *Mystery at the meet* (1990)
12 *Out of control* (1990)
13 *First date* (1990)
14 *World class gymnast* (1990)
15 *Nasty competition* (1991)
16 *Fear of falling* (1991)
17 *Gymnast commandoes* (1991)
18 *New coach* (1991)
19 *Tough at the top* (1991)
20 *Gymnasts's gift* (1991)
21 *Team trouble* (1992)

Gyp Kidnadze series
Vincent, Kitty
1 *Number three* (1924)
2 *Ruby cup* (1928)
3 *Untold tale* (1934)

Gypsy Breynton series
Phelps, Elizabeth Stuart Ward
1 *Gypsy Breynton* (1866)
2 *Gypsy's sowing and reaping* (1866)
3 *Gypsy's cousin Joy* (1866)
4 *Gypsy's year at golden Crescent* (1867)

Gypsy life series
Reeve, Dominic
1 *Smoke in the lanes* (1958)
2 *No place like home* (1960)

Gypsy Rose Lee series
Lee, Gypsy Rose
These novels were ghostwritten by Craig Rice from ideas by Gypsy Rose Lee
1 *G-string murders* (1941)
Striptease murders
Lady of burlesque
2 *Mother finds a body* (1942)

Gypsy series
Borrow, George
1 *Lavengro* (1851)
2 *Romany Rye* (1857)

Gypsy series
Goulart, Ron
1 *Quest of the gypsy* (1976)
2 *Eye of the vulture* (1977)

Gypsy series
Wagner, Sharon
1 *Gypsy from nowhere* (1972)
2 *Gypsy and Nimblefoot* (1975

H

H.A.R.D. series
Moffatt, James
see **Girl from H.A.R.D. series**

H Emp series
Horler, Sydney
see **Emp series**

H.O.W.L. High series
Leroe, Ellen Whitney
1 *H.O.W.L. High* (1989)
2 *Heebie jeebies at H.O.W.L. High* (1991)
3 *H.O.W.L. High goes bats!* (1992)

Haakon series
Neilson, Eric
1 *Golden ax* (1984)
2 *Viking's revenge* (1984)
3 *Haakon's iron hand* (1984)
4 *War god* (1984)

Habbakuk Parton series
Evans, John
1 *Portobello virgin* (1986)
2 *Mexico novice* (1988)
3 *Alamo design* (1989)

Habitats series
Coote, Roger
1 *Life in the air* (1989)
2 *Life on the land* (1989)
3 *Life in the sea* (1989)
4 *Life underground* (1989)

Habsburg series
Hamilton, Julia
1 *Changeling queen* (1977)
2 *Emperor's daughter* (1978)
The story of Marguerite of Austria, Regent of the Netherlands, daughter of Maximilian I, Holy Roman Emperor and aunt of Charles V, the Great
3 *Pearl of the Habsburgs* (1978)
The continuing story of Marguerite
4 *Snow queen* (1978)
Based on the life of Isabella, Quuen of Denmark
5 *Habsburg inheritance* (1980)

Hacker series
Bartlett, James Y
see **Pete Hacker series**

Hackshaw series
Wilcox, Stephen F
see **Elias Hackshaw series**

Haddon series
Jones, Howard
see **John Haddon series**

Haddon trilogy
Southworth, Emma Dorothy Eliza Nevitte
see **Gertrude Haddon trilogy**

Hades series
Kummer, Frederic Arnold
1 *Ladies in Hades* (1928)
A story of hell's smart set
2 *Gentlemen in Hades* (1930)
The story of a damned debutante
One volume edition entitled *Shades of Hades*, 1978

Hadley family series
Clewes, Dorothy
1 *Adventures of the scarlet daffodil* (1952)
Mystery of the scarlet daffodil
2 *Adventure of the Blue Admiral* (1954)
Mystery of the Blue Admiral
3 *Adventure on Rainbow Island* (1957)
Mystery on Rainbow Island
4 *Jade green Cadillac* (1958)
Mystery of the jade-green Cadillac
5 *Lost tower treasure* (1960)
Mystery of the lost tower treasure
6 *Singing strings* (1961)
Mystery of the singing strings
7 *Purple mountain* (1962)
Golden eagle
8 *Operation Smuggle* (1964)
Mystery of the midnight smugglers

Hadley series
Porter, Mark
see **Win Hadley series**

Hadlows series
Walker, Victoria
1 *Winter of enchantment* (1969)
2 *House called Hadlows* (1972)

Hadon of ancient Opar series
Farmer, Philip Jose
see **Opar series**

Hadrian series
Lycett-Green, Candida
Stories in verse
1 *Adventures of Hadrian the hedgehog* (1968)
2 *Hadrian in the Orient* (1969)

Haffertee Hamster series
Perkins, Janet
1 *Haffertee Hamster Diamond* (1977)
Haffertee Hamster
2 *Haffertee finds a place of his own* (1977)
Haffertee Hamster's new house
Haffertee's new house
3 *Haffertee goes exploring* (1977)
4 *Haffertee's first Christmas* (1977)
5 *Haffertee starts school* (1983)
Haffertee goes to school
6 *Haffertee's first Easter* (1984)
7 *Haffertee goes on holiday* (1993)
8 *Haffertee goes to hospital* (1993)

Hafod Garden series
West, Elizabeth
1 *Hovel in the hills* (1979)
2 *Garden in the hills* (1980)
Companion volume: *Kitchen in the hills*, 1981

Hag Dowsabel series
Wood, Lorna
1 *People in the garden* (1954)
2 *Rescue by broomstick* (1956)
3 *Hag calls for help* (1957)
4 *Seven-league ballet shoes* (1959)
5 *Hags on holiday* (1960)
6 *Hag in the castle* (1962)
7 *Hags by starlight* (1970)

Hagan series
Knudson, Rozanne Ruth
see **Zan Hagan series**

Hagar the horrible series
Browne, Dik
Comic strips
1 *Hagar the horrible* (1977)
2 *Hagar the horrible, number two* (1978)
3 *Have you been uptight lately?* (1980)
4 *Big bands are back* (1981)
5 *Hagar the horrible and the basilisk* (1981)
6 *Bring 'em back alive* (1981)
7 *Midnight munchies* (1982)
8 *On the loose* (1983)
9 *On the rack* (1983)
10 *Vikings are fun* (1983)
11 *Brutish are coming* (1983)
12 *Sacking Paris on a budget* (1983)
13 *Hagar and the golden maiden* (1983)
14 *Hagar at work* (1983)
15 *Born leader* (1983)
16 *My feet are really drunk* (1983)
17 *Animal haus* (1983)
18 *Helga's revenge* (1983)
19 *Hear no evil* (1984)
20 *Simple life* (1984)
21 *Happy hour* (1984)
22 *Room for one more* (1984)
23 *Excuse me!* (1984)
24 *Hagar hits the mark* (1984)
25 *Hagar's knight out* (1984)
26 *All the world loves a lover* (1985)
27 *Sack time* (1985)
28 *Face stuffer's anonymous* (1985)
29 *Cang Wan* (1985)
30 *Horns of plenty* (1985)
31 *Gangway* (1985)
32 *Pillage idiot* (1986)
33 *Norse code* (1986)
34 *Roman holiday* (1986)
35 *Out on a limb* (1986)
36 *Spring cleaning* (1987)
37 *Hi dear, your hair looks great* (1988)
38 *Strapped for cash* (1988)
39 *Smotherly love* (1989)
40 *Look sharp* (1989)
41 *Silly sailing* (1990)
42 *Start the invasion without me* (1990)
43 *Piece of the pie* (1990)
44 *We're doing lunch* (1991)
45 *Hagar again and again* (1991)
46 *I dream of genie* (1991)
47 *Fish fly!* (1991)
48 *I see London, I see France* (1991)
49 *Special delivery* (1992)
50 *Another fish story* (1992)
51 *Motley crew* (1992)
52 *Things that go bump* (1992)
Companion volumes: *The wit and wisdom of Hagar the horrible*, 1974, *The best of Hagar the horrible*, 1981, *Hagar the horrible's activity book*, 1982, *Hagar the horrible's puzzlers*, 1982, *The very best of Hagar*, 1982, *Hagar the horrible tall tales*, 1983, *Hagar the horrible's very nearly complete Viking handbook*, 1985, *Hagar the horrible handyman special*, 1989

Hagart series
Smith, Alexander
see **Alfred Hagart series**

Hagen series
Hooper, Kay
1 *In Serena's web* (1987)
2 *Raven on the wing* (1987)
3 *Rafferty's wife* (1987)
4 *Zach's law* (1987)
5 *Fall of Lucas Kendrick* (1988)
6 *Unmasking Kelsey* (1988)
7 *Outlaw Derek* (1988)
8 *Shades of gray* (1988)
9 *Captain's paradise* (1988)
10 *It takes a thief* (1989)
11 *Aces high* (1989)

Haggai Godin series
John, Owen
1 *Thirty days hath September* (1966)
2 *Disinformer* (1967)
3 *Beam of black light* (1968)
4 *Dead on time* (1969)
5 *Shadow in the sea* (1972)
6 *Sabotage* (1973)
7 *Getaway* (1976)

Haggard trilogy
Nicole, Christopher
1 *Haggard* (1980)
2 *Haggard's inheritance* (1981)
Inheritors
3 *Young Haggards* (1982)

Haggerty series
Lindsay, Elizabeth
see **Heggerty Haggerty series**
Schutz, Benjamin Merrill
see **Leo Haggerty series**

Haggity series
Overgard, William
see **Hero Haggity series**

Haham series
Haddad, Carolyn A
see **David Haham series**

Haig series
Courtier, Sidney Hobson
see **Inspector Digger Haig series**
Haig, Alec
see **Alec Haig series**
Harrison, Chip
see **Leo Haig series**

Hail and farewell trilogy
Moore, George
1 *Ave* (1911)
2 *Salve* (1912)
3 *Vale* (1914)

Haila and Jeff Troy series
Roos, Kelley
see **Jeff and Haila Troy series**

Hailey series
Wynne, Anthony
see **Doctor Eustace Hailey series**

Hain series
Le Guin, Ursula Kroeber
1 *Lathe of heaven* (1971)
2 *Dispossessed* (1974)
Number 2 is followed by a short story, *Vaster than empires, and more slow*, which is not published separately
3 *Word for world is forest* (1976)
4 *Rocannon's world* (1966)
5 *Planet of exile* (1966)
6 *City of illusions* (1967)
7 *Left hand of darkness* (1969)

Haines series
Serling, Robert
see **Jeremy Haines series**

Hairy book series
Cole, Babette
1 *Hairy book* (1984)
2 *Slimy book* (1985)
3 *Smelly book* (1987)
4 *Silly book* (1989)
5 *Neastly birthday book* (1990)

Hairy Maclary series
Dodd, Lynley
1 *Hairy Maclary from Donaldson's Dairy* (1983)
2 *Hairy Maclary's bone* (1984)
3 *Hairy Maclary's scattercat* (1985)
4 *Hairy Maclary's catterwaul caper* (1987)
5 *Hairy Maclary's rumpus at the vet* (1989)
6 *Hairy Maclary's showbusiness* (1991)

Hajji Baba series
Morier, James
1 *Adventures of Hajji Baba of Ispahan* (1824)
2 *Hajji Baba in England* (1828)

Hakon and Helga series
Haugaard, Erik Christian
1 *Hakon of Rogen's Saga* (1963)
2 *Slave's tale* (1965)

Hal and Roger Hunt series
Price, Willard
1 *Amazon adventure* (1951)
2 *South Sea adventure* (1952)
3 *Underwater adventure* (1954)
4 *Volcano adventure* (1956)
5 *Whale adventure* (1960)
6 *African adventure* (1963)
7 *Elephant adventure* (1964)
8 *Safari adventure* (1966)
9 *Lion adventure* (1967)
10 *Gorilla adventure* (1969)
11 *Diving adventure* (1969)
12 *Cannibal adventure* (1972)
13 *Tiger adventure* (1979)
14 *Arctic adventure* (1980)

Hal Keen series
Lloyd, Hugh
1 *Hermit of Gordon's Creek* (1931)
2 *Kidnapped in the jungle* (1931)
3 *Copperhead Trail mystery* (1931)
4 *Smugglers' secret* (1931)
5 *Mysterious Arab* (1931)
6 *Clue at Skeleton Rocks* (1931)
7 *Lonesome Swamp mystery* (1932)
8 *Doom of Stark House* (1933)
9 *Lost mine of the Amazon* (1933)
10 *Mystery at Dark Star Ranch* (1934)

Hal series
Ure, Jean
1 *Plague nineteen ninety* (1989)
2 *Come, lucky April* (1992)
4 *Watchers at the shrine* (1994)

Hale series
Coxe, George Harmon
see **Max Hale series**
Garis, Lilian C
see **Barbara Hale series**
Knotts, Raymond
see **Jim Hale series**
Sandford, Ken
see **Max Hale series**

Hales series
Ingate, Mary
see **Ann Fielding series**

Half a life series
Barnes, James Strachey
Autobiography
1 *Half a life* (1933)
2 *Half a life left* (1937)

Half way series
Roberts, Cecil
Autobiography
1 *Half way* (1931)
2 *One year of life* (1952)

Halfaday Creek series
Hendryx, James Beardsley
see **Black John series**

Half-angel series
Lea, Fanny Heaslip
1 *Good-bye summer* (1932)
2 *Half-angel* (1933)

Halfhyde series
McCutchan, Philip
see **Lieutenant Saint Vincent Halfhyde series**

Haljan series
Cummings, Ray
see **Gregg Haljan series**

Hall series
Daly, Carroll John
see **Satan Hall series**
Grant, Robert
see **Jack Hall series**
Hambledon, Phyllis
see **Inspector Tubby Hall series**
Langton, Jane
see **Edward, Eleanor and Georgie Hall series**
Sherrard, Owen Aubrey
see **Emily Mary and Ellen Augusta Hall series**

Hall sisters series
Hall, Emily
Pages from the diaries, edited by Anthony Reginald Mills
1 *Two Victorian girls* (1966)
Accompanying text by Owen Aubrey Sherrard
2 *Halls of Ravenswood* (1967)
3 *Two Victorian ladies* (1969)

Hallam and Spratt series
Douglas, George
see **Inspector Hallam and Sergeant Spratt series**

Hallam series
Washburn, Livia Jane
see **Lucas Hallam series**

Haller series
Byrd, Max
see **Mike Haller series**

Haller series
Hughes, Dean
1 *Hooper Haller* (1981)
2 *Jenny Haller* (1983)

Hallersage series
Townsend, John Rowe
1 *Hell's Edge* (1963)
2 *Hallersage sound* (1966)

Halley series
Francis, Dick
see **Sid Halley series**

Halli Thordason series
Boucher, Alan Estcourt
1 *Path of the Raven* (1960)
2 *Greenland farers* (1961)
3 *Wineland adventure* (1963)
4 *Raven's flight* (1964)
5 *Land seekers* (1964)
One volume abridged edition entitled *The sword of the raven*, 1969

Halliday series
Blake, Justin
see **Garry Halliday series**
Brady, Adam
see **Buck Halliday series**
Fredman, Mike
see **Willie Halliday series**
Taylor, H Baldwin
see **David Halliday series**

Halliwell boys series
Palmer, Bernard
1 *Halliwell boys on crusade* (1957)
2 *Halliwell boys and the disappearing staircase* (1958)
3 *Halliwell boys on the secret expedition* (1958)
4 *Halliwell boys on a dangerous voyage* (1958)
5 *Halliwell boys and the mysterious treasure map* (1960)
6 *Halliwell boys and the missing film mystery* (1960)
7 *Halliwell boys on Forbidden Mountain* (1962)
8 *Halliwell boys on a secret African safari* (1962)

Halloran series
Denver, Lee
see **Deputy Marshal Dave Halloran series**

Halloran series
Gethin, David
1 *Jack Lane's Browning* (1984)
Point of honor
2 *Dane's testament* (1986)

Halloran series
Lapierre, Janet
see **Meg Halloran series**

Hallowdene Farm series
Pocock, Doris Alice
1 *Secret of Hallowdene Farm* (1923)
2 *Summer at Hallowdene Farm* (1926)

Hallowdene Hall series
Everett-Green, Evelyn
1 *Dickie and Dorrie* (1906)
2 *Dickie and Dorrie at school* (1911)

Halloween howls series
Maestro, Giulio
1 *Halloween howls* (1983)
Riddles that are a scream
2 *More Halloween howls* (1992)

Halloween series
This sequence has three authors
Richards, Curtis
1 *Halloween* (1979)
Martin, Jack
2 *Halloween II* (1981)
3 *Halloween III* (1982)
Season of the witch
Grabowsky, Nicholas
4 *Halloween IV* (1988)

Halstead series
Hayes, William Edward
see **Arthur Halstead series**

Halvorsson series
Anckarsvard, Karin
see **Jon Halvorsson series**

Ham Macandrew and Homer Bull series
Lariar, Lawrence
1 *Death paints the picture* (1943)
Death is the host
2 *He died laughing* (1943)
3 *Man with the lumpy nose* (1944)
4 *Girl with the frightened eyes* (1945)

Hambledon series
Coles, Manning
see **Tommy Hambledon series**
Dellbridge, John
see **Rupert Hambledon series**

Hamel series
Van Gieson, Judith
see **Neil Hamel series**

Hamey series
Keevil, John Joyce
see **Baldwin Hamey series**

Hamilton Cleek series
Hanshew, Thomas W
The authors shown are those taken from the title pages of the individual titles; in some cases other authors actually wrote the volumes as indicated against each title
1 *Man of the forty faces* (1910)
Cleek, the master detective
Cleek, the man of forty faces
The third title is a revised edition
2 *Cleek of Scotland Yard* (1914)
3 *Riddle of the night* (1915)
Actually written by Mary E Hanshew and Hazel Phillips Hanshew
4 *Cleek's greatest riddles* (1916)
Cleek's government cases
5 *Riddle of the purple emperor* (1916)
Actually written by Mary E Hanshew and Hazel Phillips Hanshew
Hanshew, Mary E
6 *Frozen flame* (1920)
Riddle of the frozen flame
Actually written by Hazel Phillips Hanshew
7 *Riddle of the mysterious light* (1921)
Actually written by Hazel Phillips Hanshew
8 *House of discord* (1922)
Riddle of the spinning wheel
Actually written by Hazel Phillips Hanshew
9 *Amber junk* (1924)
Riddle of the amber ship
Actually written by Hazel Phillips Hanshew
10 *House of the seven keys* (1925)
Actually written by Hazel Phillips Hanshew
Hanshew, Hazel Phillips
11 *Riddle of the winged death* (1931)
12 *Murder in the hotel* (1932)

Hamilton College series
Lester, Pauline
see **Marjorie Dean college series**

Hamilton family series
Plowman, Stephanie
1 *Three lives for the Czar* (1969)
2 *My kingdom for a grave* (1970)

Hamilton series
Burley, Andrew S
see **Uncle Sam's Army boys series**
Cookson, Catherine
see **Maisie Leviston series**
Foxell, Nigel
see **Emma Hamilton series**
Frost, Frederick
see **Secret service series**
Helmericks, Bud
see **Bob Hamilton series**
Hogarth, Grace Allen
see **Helen Hamilton series**
Niven, Larry
see **Gil Hamilton series**
Plowman, Stephanie
see **Alexei Hamilton series**
Schumacher, Heinrich
see **Lady Hamilton series**
Wiggin, Kate Douglas
see **Penelope Hamilton series**
Worboise, Emma Jane
see **Grace Hamilton series**

Hamish, David and Bottle series
Kiddell, John
1 *Eulowirree walkabout* (1968)
2 *Community of men* (1969)

Hamish Macbeth series
Beaton, M C
1 *Death of a gossip* (1985)
2 *Death of a cad* (1986)
3 *Death of an outsider* (1988)
4 *Death of a perfect wife* (1989)
5 *Death of a hussy* (1990)
6 *Death of a snob* (1991)
7 *Death of a prankster* (1992)
8 *Death of a glutton* (1993)
9 *Death of a travelling man* (1993)
10 *Death of a charming man* (1994)

Hamish Oath series
Durrant, Digby
1 *With my little eye* (1975)
2 *Trunch* (1978)

Hamlet Club series
Oxenham, Elsie J
see **Abbey girls first generation series**

Hammer series
Spillane, Mickey
see **Mike Hammer series**

Hammer's Slammers series
Drake, David
1 *Hammer's Slammers* (1979)
Expanded edition 1987
2 *Cross the stars* (1984)
3 *At any price* (1985)
4 *Counting the cost* (1987)
5 *Rolling hot* (1989)
6 *Warrior* (1991)
Companion volume: *Slammer's down, Combat Command in the world of David Drake's Hammer's Slammers*, by Todd Johnson, 1988

Hammersmith series
Hall, Lynn
see **Zelda Hammersmith series**

Hammond High School series
Steiner, Barbara
see **Fifteen series**

Hammond series
Atkinson, Mary Evelyn
see **Fricka Hammond series**
Carmichael, Fred
see **Crane Hammond series**

Hammond trilogy
Campbell, Daisy Rhodes
see **Virginia Hammond trilogy**

Hampton Hume series
Bird, Brandon
1 *Death in four colors* (1950)
2 *Never wake a dead man* (1950)
3 *Downbeat for a dirge* (1952)
Dead and gone

Hampton series
Ellis, Julie
see **Caroline Hampton series**

Hampton series
Ellis, Odette
1 *Hampton heritage* (1978)
2 *Hampton women* (1980)

Hamster series
Perkins, Janet
see **Haffertee Hamster series**

Hana Shaner series
Greth, Roma
1 *Now you don't* (1988)
2 *Plain murder* (1989)

Hanaud series
Mason, Alfred Edward Woodley
see **Inspector Hanaud series**

Hand over hand series
De Banke, Cecile
Autobiography
1 *Hand over hand* (1957)
2 *Bright weft* (1958)
Life in South Africa, 1916-1929
3 *American plaid* (1961)

Hand series
Page, Stanley Hart
see **Christopher Hand series**
Priestley, Brian
see **Willy Hand series**

Handful of men series
Duncan, Dave
1 *Cutting edge* (1993)
2 *Upland outlaws* (1993)
3 *Stricken field* (1993)
4 *Living god* (1994)

Handsome Kusak and Bingo Riggs series
Rice, Craig
see **Bingo Riggs and Handsome Kusak series**

Handtalk series
Charlip, Remy
1 *Handtalk* (1974)
An ABC of finger spelling and sign language
2 *Handtalk birthday* (1987)
A number and story book in sign language

Handyman series
Messmann, Jon
see **Jefferson Boone series**

Hang Ten series
Morgan, Patrick
see **Operation Hang Ten series**

Hanging Judge series
Gardner, Jerome
1 *Hangman and the Ladies' League* (1984)
2 *Blood-tie* (1984)
3 *Hangman's apprentice* (1985)
4 *Tumbleweed twosome* (1986)
5 *Get Maledon!* (1986)
6 *Parker ransom* (1987)
7 *Hanging week* (1987)
8 *Double on Death Row* (1988)
9 *Date with a noose* (1990)
10 *Maledon calls the shots* (1990)

Hanging Rock series
Lindsay, Joan
1 *Picnic at Hanging Rock* (1967)
2 *Secret of Hanging Rock* (1987)
The previously suppressed final chapter

Hangman series
Foley, Craig
1 *Quick drop* (1989)
2 *Blood knot* (1989)
3 *Air dance* (1989)
4 *Yuma run* (1990)
5 *Gallows gal* (1990)
6 *Outlaw rope* (1990)

Hank Bradford series
Warden, Mike
1 *Dead ringer* (1980)
2 *Bitter homicide* (1980)
3 *Model for murder* (1981)

Hank Brazos and Duke Benedict series
Clay, E Jefferson
see **Duke Benedict and Hank Brazos series**

Hank Chavez series
Lindsey, Johanna
1 *Glorious angel* (1982)
2 *Heart of thunder* (1983)

Hank Fairbanks and Emma Marsh series
Dean, Elizabeth
see **Emma Marsh and Hank Fairbanks series**

Hank Frost series
Kilgore, Axel
see **They call me the Mercenary series**

Hank Hyer series
Steel, Kurt
1 *Murder of a dead man* (1935)
Abridged edition entitled *The traveling corpses*, 1942
2 *Murder for what?* (1936)
3 *Murder goes to college* (1936)
4 *Murder in G-sharp* (1937)

Abridged edition entitled *Strangler's holiday*, 1942
5 *Crooked shadow* (1939)
6 *Judas, Incorporated* (1939)
7 *Dead of night* (1940)
8 *Madman's buff* (1941)
9 *Ambush House* (1943)

Hank Janson series

Janson, Hank

This pseudonym is used by several authors including Stephen Daniel Frances, Harry Hobson, Harold Ernest Kelly, James Moffatt, Victor George Charles Norwood and Colin Simpson whose authorship is indicated against those titles where it is known; it has not been established whether the series character Hank Janson appears in all titles in this sequence which, for convenience, are listed in order of their first publication

1 *When dames get tough* (1946) [Frances]
2 *One man in his time* (1946) [Frances]; also published under the author's real name
3 *Gun moll for hire* (1948) [Frances]
4 *Lady, mind that corpse* (1948) [Frances]
5 *This woman is death* (1948)
6 *Angel, shoot to kill* (1949) *Outcast* [Frances]
7 *Sister, don't hate me* (1949) *Prey for a newshawk* [Frances]
8 *No regrets for Clara* (1949) *Rave for a roughneck*
9 *Lilies for my lovely* (1949) [Frances]
10 *Blonde on the spot* (1949) [Frances]
11 *Gunsmoke in her eyes* (1949) [Frances]
12 *Honey, take ny gun* (1949) [Frances]
13 *Slay-ride for Cutie* (1949) [Frances]
14 *Smart girls don't talk* (1949) [Frances]
15 *Sweetheart, here's your grave!* (1949) *Situation, grave!* [Frances]
16 *Lola brought her wreath* (1950) *Dowtown doll* [Frances]
17 *Lady has a scar* (1950) *Sentence for sin* [Frances]
18 *Some look better dead* (1950) *Play it quiet* [Frances]
19 *Sweetie hold me tight* (1950) *Come quickly, honey* [Frances]
20 *Torment for Trixy* (1950) *Suddenly it's sin* [Frances]
21 *Don't dare me, Sugar* (1950) [Frances]
22 *Jane with green eyes* (1950) [Frances]
23 *Bride wore weeds* (1950) [Frances]
24 *Lady toll that bell* (1950) *Beloved traitor* [Frances]
25 *Broads don't scare easy* (1951) *Don't scare easy* [Frances]
26 *Baby, don't dare squeal* (1951) *Cool Sugar* [Frances]
27 *Death wore a petticoat* (1951) [Frances]
28 *Don't mourn me, toots* (1951) [Frances]
29 *Milady took the rap* (1951) [Frances]
30 *This dame dies soon* (1951) *Too soon to die* [Frances]
31 *It's always Eve that weeps* (1951) [Frances]
32 *Trails can be so tough* (1951) *Bad girl* [Frances]
33 *Hotsy, you'll be chilled* (1951) [Frances]
34 *Women hate till death* (1951) *Hate* [Frances]
35 *Skirts bring me sorrow* (1952) *Bring me sorrow* [Frances]
36 *Accused* (1952)
37 *Auctioned* (1952) [Frances]
38 *Conflict* (1952) [Frances]
39 *Corruption* (1952) *Secret session* [Frances]
40 *Filly wore a rod* (1952) *Lose this gun* [Frances]
41 *Kille her if you can* (1952) [Frances]
42 *Killer* (1952) [Frances]
43 *Murder* (1952) [Frances]
44 *Sadie, don't cry now* (1952) *Don't cry now* *Delicious danger* [Frances]
45 *Suspense* (1952) [Frances]
46 *Tension* (1952) [Frances]
47 *Whiplash* (1952) [Frances]
48 *Amok* (1953) *Fireball* [Frances]
49 *Britain's great flood disaster* (1953) [Frances]
50 *Desert fury* (1953) [Frances]
51 *Nyloned avenger* (1953) *Sultry avenger*
52 *Perfumed nemesis* (1953)
53 *Persian pride* (1953)
54 *Pursuit* (1953) *Flight from fear* [Frances]
55 *Silken menace* (1953) *Silken snare*
56 *Torment* (1953)
57 *Unseen assassin* (1953)
58 *Vengeance* (1953) *This hood for hire*
59 *Woman trap* (1953)
60 *Contaband* (1955) [Frances]
61 *Forty eight hours* (1955) [Frances]
62 *Framed* (1955) [Frances]
63 *Menace* (1955) [Frances]
64 *Tomorrow and today* (1955) [Frances]
65 *Untamed* (1955)
66 *Deadly mission* (1956) [Frances]
67 *Big lie* (1956)
68 *Cactus* (1956) [Frances]
69 *Devil's highway* (1956) [Frances]
70 *Escape* (1956) [Frances]
71 *Hell's angel* (1956) [Frances]
72 *One against time* (1956)
73 *Strange destiny* (1956)
74 *They die alone* (1956)
75 *Sinister rapture* (1957)
76 *Enemy of man* (1958)
77 *Hellcat* (1958)
78 *Revolt* (1958)
79 *Sweet fury* (1958)
80 *Mistress of fear* (1958) [Frances]
81 *Amorous captive* (1958) [Frances]; originally published in three volumes
82 *Avenging nymph* (1958) [Frances]
83 *Kill this man* (1958)
84 *Sugar and vice* (1958)
85 *Bewitched* (1958)
86 *Jack Spot* (1958) [Frances]
87 *Drop dead, sucker!* (1959) [Norwood]
88 *Invasion* (1959) [Frances]
89 *Murder magnifique* (1959) [Norwood]
90 *Obsession* (1959)
91 *Torrid temptress* (1959)
92 *Wild girl* (1959)
93 *All tramps are trouble* (1960)
94 *Cupid turns killer* (1960)
95 *Cutie on call* (1960) [Frances]
96 *Ecstasy* (1960) [Frances]
97 *Hell of a dame* (1960)
98 *Passionate* (1960)
99 *Quiet waits the grave* (1960)
100 *Ripe for rapture* (1960)
101 *Slaves for seduction* (1960)
102 *This wicked sex* (1960)
103 *Break for a lovely* (1961)
104 *Crowns can kill* (1961) [Hobson]
105 *Destination dames* (1961) [Frances]
106 *Hell's belles* (1961)
107 *Janson, go home* (1961) [Hobson]
108 *Lady, lie low* (1961)
109 *Late night revel* (1961)
110 *Master mind* (1961) [Hobson]
111 *Reluctant hostess* (1961)
112 *Scent from heaven* (1961)
113 *She sleeps to conquer* (1961)
114 *Short-term wife* (1961)
115 *Venus makes three* (1961)
116 *Angel astray* (1962) [Frances]
117 *Beauty and the beat* (1962) [Hobson]
118 *Blood bath* (1962) [Norwood]
119 *Chicago chick* (1962) [Hobson]
120 *Crime on my hands* (1962)
121 *Dig thos heels* (1962) [Frances]
122 *Exclusive* (1962) [Frances]
123 *Grape vine* (1962) [Hobson]
124 *Honey for me* (1962)
125 *Kille me for kicks* (1962) [Norwood]
126 *Like crazy* (1962) [Hobson]
127 *Like lethal* (1962) [Hobson]
128 *Like poison* (1962) [Hobson]
129 *Nymph in the night* (1962)
130 *Run for lover* (1962)
131 *Savage sequel* (1962)
132 *She waif* (1962)
133 *Take this, Sweetie* (1962) [Hobson]
134 *Twist for two* (1962)
135 *Uncommon market* (1962) [Hobson]
136 *Uncover agent* (1962) [Hobson]
137 *Vagabond vamp* (1962)
138 *Way out wanton* (1962)
139 *Brand image* (1963) [Frances]
140 *Brazen seductress* (1963)
141 *Dateline Darlene* (1963) [Hobson]
142 *Dateline Debbie* (1963) [Hobson]
143 *Dateline Diane* (1963) [Hobson]
144 *Daughter of shame* (1963) [Frances]
145 *Fast buck* (1963) [Hobson]
146 *Go with a jerk* (1963) [Norwood]
147 *Heartache* (1963) [Frances]
148 *Hilary's terms* (1963) [Frances]
149 *Hot line* (1963) [Kelly]
150 *I for intrigue* (1963) [Frances]
151 *Kill her with passion* (1963)
152 *Love and lamentation* (1963) [Hobson]
153 *Love makers* (1963) [Hobson]
154 *Lover* (1963)
155 *Nerve centre* (1963)
156 *Nice way to die* (1963)
157 *Passion pact* (1963)
158 *Playgirl* (1963) [Norwood]
159 *Raw deal* (1963) [Norwood]
160 *Second string* (1963) [Frances]
161 *Sensuality* (1963) [Norwood]
162 *Strange ritual* (1963) [Norwood]
163 *V for vitality* (1963)
164 *Visit from a broad* (1963) [Hobson]
165 *Cold dead coed* (1964)
166 *Crimebeat crisis* (1964) [Hobson]
167 *Depravity* (1964) [Moffatt]
168 *Design for dupes* (1964) [Frances]
169 *Dish ran away* (1964) [Moffatt]
170 *Doctor Fix* (1964) [Hobson]
171 *Double take* (1964) [Frances]
172 *Exotic seductress* (1964)
173 *Expectant nymph* (1964)
174 *Fan fare* (1964) [Hobson]
175 *Fanny* (1964)
176 *Flower of desire* (1964) [Frances]
177 *Girl in hand* (1964) [Frances]
178 *Her weapon is passion* (1964)
179 *Hot house* (1964)
180 *It's bedtime, baby!* (1964)
181 *Lake loot* (1964) [Hobson]
182 *Last lady* (1964) [Moffatt]
183 *Limbo lover* (1964) [Hobson]
184 *Love secretaries* (1964) [Moffatt]
185 *Passionate playmate* (1964)
186 *Patterned rape* (1964) [Moffatt]
187 *Sex angle* (1964) [Frances]
188 *Sexy vixen* (1964)
189 *Soft cargo* (1964) [Frances]

Hank Janson series

190 *Square one* (1964) [Hobson]
191 *That brain again* (1964) [Hobson]
192 *Tigress* (1964)
193 *Top ten* (1964) [Norwood]
194 *Voodoo violence* (1964)
195 *Will-power* (1964) [Norwood]
196 *Abomination* (1965) [Moffatt]
197 *Affairs of Paula* (1965)
198 *Backlash of infamy* (1965) [Moffatt]
199 *Becky* (1965)
200 *Berlin briefing* (1965) [Hobson]
201 *Catch me a renegade* (1965) [Moffatt]
202 *Counter-feat* (1965) [Frances]
203 *Devil and the deep* (1965) [Moffatt]
204 *Flashpoint* (1965) [Frances]
205 *Furtive plame* (1965)
206 *Jazz jungle* (1965) [Frances]
207 *Junk market* (1965) [Frances]
208 *Lust for vengeance* (1965)
209 *Missile mob* (1965) [Hobson]
210 *Model in mayhem* (1965) [Moffatt]
211 *Mympho named Sylvia* (1965)
212 *Roxy by proxy* (1965) [Hobson]
213 *Say it with a candy* (1965) [Frances]
214 *Sweet talk* (1965) [Moffatt]
215 *Tailsting* (1965) [Hobson]
216 *Why should Sylvia?* (1965) [Moffatt]
217 *Darling delinquent* (1966) [Hobson]
218 *Escalation* (1966) [Hobson]
219 *Helldorado* (1966) [Hobson]
220 *Physical attraction* (1966) [Hobson]
221 *Liquor is quicker* (1966) [Hobson]
222 *Nefarious quest* (1966) [Frances]
223 *Mayfair slayride* (1966) [Hobson]
224 *Khrush* (1966) [Frances]
225 *Dead certainty* (1966) [Frances]
226 *Riviera showdown* (1966) [Hobson]
227 *Bid for beauty* (1966) [Simpson]
228 *Big H* (1966) [Hobson]
229 *Make mine mink* (1966) [Hobson]
230 *Casino strip* (1967) [Hobson]
231 *Casinopoly* (1967) [Norwood]
232 *Deadly horse-race* (1967) [Hobson]
233 *F.E.U.D.* (1967) [Hobson]
234 *Hell brood* (1967) [Simpson]
235 *Ladybirds are in* (1967) [Hobson]
236 *One way split* (1967) [Hobson]
237 *Operation Obliterate* (1967) [Hobson]
238 *Same difference* (1967) [Norwood]
239 *Take two blondes* (1967) [Simpson]
240 *Young wolves* (1967) [Norwood]
241 *Zero takes all* (1967) [Hobson]
242 *Crunch* (1968) [Simpson]
243 *Micro kill* (1968) [Simpson]
244 *Shalom, my love* (1968) [Hobson]
245 *Sprung!* (1968) [Hobson]
246 *Cat's paw* (1969) [Simpson]
247 *Covering fire* (1969) [Simpson]
248 *Globe probe* (1969) [Hobson]
249 *Spy in my bed* (1969) [Hobson]
250 *Big round bed* (1970) [Hobson]
251 *Frame and fortune* (1970) [Simpson]
252 *Infiltrators* (1970) [Hobson]
253 *Lament for a lover* (1970) [Hobson]
254 *Long arm* (1970) [Hobson]
255 *Twilight tigress* (1970) [Simpson]
256 *Ultimate deterrent* (1970) [Hobson]
257 *Villon of the piece* (1970) [Hobson]
258 *Caribbean caper* (1971) [Hobson]
259 *Grass widow* (1971) [Simpson]
260 *Kay assignation* (1971) [Hobson]
261 *Liz assignation* (1971)

Hank Moody series
Chambers, Robert
1 *Moth in a rag shop* (1968)
Village East
2 *Divide by seven* (1969)
Lesser evil
3 *Neon preacher* (1977)

Hank Prank series
Older, Jules
1 *Hank Prank and hot Henrietta* (1984)
2 *Hank Prank in love* (1985)
3 *Hot Henrietta and Nailbiters United* (1987)

Hank the cowdog series
Erickson, John R
1 *Hank the cowdog* (1983)
2 *Further adventures of Hank the cowdog* (1983)
3 *It's a dog's life* (1984)
4 *Murder in the middle pasture* (1984)
5 *Faded love* (1985)
6 *Let sleepign dogs lie* (1986)
7 *Curse of the incredible priceless corncob* (1989)
8 *Case of the one-eyed killer stud horse* (1989)
9 *Case of the Halloween ghost* (1989)
10 *Every dog has his day* (1989)
11 *Lost in the dark enchanted forest* (1989)
12 *Fiddle-playing fox* (1989)
13 *Wounded buzzard on Christmas eve* (1989)
14 *Monkey business* (1990)
15 *Case of the missing cat* (1990)
16 *Lost in the blinded blizzard* (1991)
17 *Case of the car-barkaholic dog* (1991)
18 *Case of the hooking bull* (1992)
19 *Case of the midnight rustler* (1992)

Hank Winton series
Atwater, Montgomery Meigs
1 *Hank Winton, smoke chaser* (1947)
2 *Smoke patrol* (1949)
3 *Avalanche patrol* (1951)
4 *Rustlers on the High Range* (1952)
5 *Trouble hunters* (1956)

Hanks series
Hess, Joan
see **Arly Hanks series**

Hanlon series
Evans, Edward Everett
see **George Hanlon series**
Merrick, Mollie
see **Red Hanlon series**

Hannah Land series
Mackay, Amanda
1 *Death is academic* (1976)
2 *Death on the Eno* (1981)
Death on the river

Hannah Maine series
Power, Phyllis Mary
1 *Lost in the outback* (1954)
2 *Nursing in the outback* (1959)

Hannah Van Doren series
Babcock, Dwight Vincent
1 *Homicide for Hannah* (1941)
Murder for Hannah
2 *Gorgeous ghoul* (1943)
Gorgeous ghoul murder case
3 *Hannah says foul play* (1946)

Hannasyde series
Heyer, Georgette
see **Superintendent Hannasyde series**

Hannay series
Buchan, John
see **Richard Hannay series**

Hannegan series
Lovell, B E
see **Edge Hannegan series**

Hannibal Fortune and Webley series
Maddock, Larry
1 *Flying saucer gambit* (1966)
2 *Golden goddess gammbit* (1967)
3 *Emerald elephant gambit* (1967)
4 *Time trap gambit* (1969)

Hannibal Hayes and Kid Curry series
Fox, Brian
see **Alias Smith and Jones series**

Hannon series
Law, Winifred
see **Ralph Hannon series**

Hanover succession series
Meadows, Rose
1 *Show must go on* (1968)
2 *Bouquet of brides* (1970)
3 *Pretty maids all in a row* (1976)
4 *Slander most savage* (1977)

Hans Barlach series
Durrenmatt, Friedrich
see **Kommissar Hans Barlach series**

Hansa trilogy
Rolvaag, Ole Edvart
see **Per Hansa trilogy**

Hanscombe and Sommers series
Whalley, Peter
see **Harry Sommers and Jill Hanscombe series**

Hansen series
Pournelle, Jerry
see **Laurie Jo Hansen series**

Hanson series
Emerson, David
see **George Hanson series**

Hanvey series
Cohen, Octavus Roy
see **Jim Hanvey series**

Hapi series
Bermingham, Iris
1 *Hapi and the Morepork* (1973)
2 *Hapi and the forbidden island* (1977)

Happy countryman series
Warren, Clarence Henry
Reminiscences of country life in Essex
1 *Happy countryman* (1939)
2 *England is a village* (1940)
3 *Land is yours* (1943)
4 *Miles from anywhere* (1945)
5 *Adam was a ploughman* (1947)
6 *Scythe in the apple tree* (1953)
7 *Content with what I have* (1967)

Happy days series
Johnston, William
Based on a television series
1 *Ready to go steady* (1974)
2 *Fonzie drops in* (1974)
3 *Invaders* (1975)
4 *Fonzie, Fonzie superstar* (1976)
5 *Fonz and Lazonga* (1976)
6 *Bike tycoon* (1976)
7 *Dear Fonzie* (1977)
8 *Fonzie goes to college* (1977)
9 *Fonzie drops in* (1978)

Happy Family series
Bower, Bertha Muzzy
see **Flying U Ranch series**

Happy family series
Ahlberg, Allan
1 *Mister Biff the boxer* (1980)
2 *Mister Cosmo the conjuror* (1980)
3 *Miss Jump the jockey* (1980)
4 *Master Salt the sailor's son* (1980)
5 *Mrs Plug the plumber* (1980)
6 *Mrs Wobble the waitress* (1980)
7 *Miss Brick the builder's baby* (1981)
8 *Mister Buzz the beeman* (1981)
9 *Mister and Mrs Hay the horse* (1981)
10 *Mrs Lather's laundry* (1981)
11 *Master Money the millionaire* (1981)
12 *Mister Tick the teacher* (1981)
13 *Master Bun the baker's boy* (1988)
14 *Mister Creep the crook* (1988)
15 *Miss Dose the doctor's daughter* (1988)
16 *Mrs Jolly's joke shop* (1988)

Happy fields trilogy
Raine, Kathleen
Autobiography
1 *Farewell, happy fields* (1973)
2 *Land unknown* (1975)
3 *Lion's mouth* (1977)

Happy glade series
Dudley-Smith, Trevor
1 *Into a happy glade* (1943)
2 *By a silver stream* (1944)

Happy Hollisters series
West, Jerry
House pseudonym
1 *Happy Hollisters* (1953)
2 *Happy Hollisters and the Indian treasure* (1953)
3 *Happy Hollisters at Sea Gull Beach* (1953)
4 *Happy Hollisters on a river trip* (1953)
5 *Happy Hollisters and the trading post mystery* (1954)

6 *Happy Hollisters at Mystery Mountain* (1954)
7 *Happy Hollisters at Snowflake Camp* (1954)
8 *Happy Hollisters and the merry-go-round mystery* (1955)
9 *Happy Hollisters and the secret fort* (1955)
10 *Happy Hollisters at Circus Island* (1955)
11 *Happy Hollisters and the old clipper ship* (1956)
12 *Happy Hollisters at Pony Hill Farm* (1956)
13 *Happy Hollisters at Lizard Cove* (1957)
14 *Happy Hollisters and the scarecrow mystery* (1957)
15 *Happy Hollisters and the mystery of the totem faces* (1958)
16 *Happy Hollisters and the ice carnival mystery* (1958)
17 *Happy Hollisters and the mystery in Skyscraper City* (1959)
18 *Happy Hollisters and the mystery of the little mermaid* (1960)
19 *Happy Hollisters and the mystery at Missile Town* (1961)
20 *Happy Hollisters and the cowboy mystery* (1961)
21 *Happy Hollisters and the haunted house mystery* (1962)
22 *Happy Hollisters and the secret of the lucky coins* (1962)
23 *Happy Hollisters and the Castle Rock mystery* (1963)
24 *Happy Hollisters and the cuckoo clock mystery* (1963)
25 *Happy Hollisteres and the Swiss echo mystery* (1963)
26 *Happy Hollisters and the sea turtle mystery* (1964)
27 *Happy Hollisters and the whistle-pig mystery* (1964)
28 *Happy Hollisters and the Punch and Judy mystery* (1964)
29 *Happy Hollisters and the ghost horse mystery* (1965)
30 *Happy Hollisters and the mystery of the golden witch* (1966)
31 *Happy Hollisters and the mystery of the Mexican idol* (1967)
32 *Happy hollisters and the monster mystery* (1969)
33 *Happy Hollisters and the mystery of the midnight trolls* (1970)

Happy House series
Blyton, Enid
1 *Children at Happy House* (1946)
2 *Happy House children again* (1947)
3 *Happy House children* (1966)

Happy lion series
Fatio, Louise
1 *Happy lion* (1954)
2 *Happy lion in Africa* (1955)
3 *Happy lion roars* (1957)
4 *Three happy lions* (1959)
5 *Happy lion's quest* (1961)
6 *Happy lion and the bear* (1964)
7 *Happy lion's vacation* (1967)
Happy lion's holiday
8 *Happy lion's treasure* (1971)
9 *Happy lion's rabbits* (1974)
10 *Happy lioness* (1980)

Happy mountain series
Chapman, Maristan
1 *Happy mountain* (1928)
2 *Homeplace* (1929)
3 *Weather tree* (1932)
4 *Glen Hazard* (1933)

Happy Rascals series
Howard, Francis Morton
1 *Happy Rascals* (1920)
2 *Little shop in Fore Street* (1921)
3 *'Orace and Co.* (1923)
4 *Cakes and ale* (1927)

Happy Rebus series
Adler, David A
1 *Happy Hannukah, Rebus* (1989)
2 *Happy Thanksgiving, Rebus* (1991)

Happy thoughts series
Burnand, Francis Cowley
1 *Happy thoughts* (1866)
2 *Happy-Thought Hall* (1872)
3 *More happy thoughts* (1879)

Haps and mishaps series
Mathews, Joanna Hooe
1 *Little friends at Glenwood* (1876)
2 *Broken mallet and the pigeon's eggs* (1877)
3 *Blackberry jam* (1878)
4 *Milly's whims* (1878)

Harald Hardrada series
Treece, Henry
1 *Last of the Vikings* (1964)
Last Viking
2 *Swords from the North* (1967)

Harald series
Carrick, Donald
1 *Harald and the giant knight* (1982)
2 *Harald and the great stag* (1988)

Harald series
Maron, Margaret
see **Lieutenant Sigrid Harald series**

Harbord series
Liddell, Robert
see **Charles Harbord series**

Harcourt d'Espinal series
Healey, Ben
1 *Vespucci papers* (1972)
2 *Stone baby* (1973)
3 *Horstmann inheritance* (1975)
4 *Last ferry from the Lido* (1981)
Midnight ferry to Venice

Harcourt series
Sheridan, Matt
see **David Harcourt series**

Hard corps series
Bainbridge, Chuck
1 *Hard corps* (1986)
2 *Beirut contract* (1987)
3 *White heat* (1987)
4 *Slave trade* (1987)
5 *Mercenary justice* (1988)
6 *American nightmare* (1988)
7 *Scorched earth* (1989)
8 *Devil's plunder* (1989)

Hard money trilogy
Kelland, Clarence Budington
1 *Hard money* (1930)
2 *Gold* (1931)
3 *Jealous house* (1934)

Hardacre series
Skelton, Clement Lister
1 *Hardacre* (1977)
2 *Hardacre's luck* (1984)

Hardie family series
Melville, Anne
1 *House of Hardie* (1987)
2 *Grace Hardie* (1988)

Hardin series
Alexander, David
see **Bart Hardin series**
Derrick, Lionel
see **Mark Hardin series**
Edson, John Thomas
see **Ole Devil Hardin series**
Reynolds, Mack
see **Bat Hardin series**
Teed, Jack Hamilton
see **Gunships series**

Harding and Maitland series
Woods, Sara
see **Sir Nicholas Harding and Antony Maitland series**

Harding family series
Knight, Brigid
see **Ashenden series**

Harding series
Duff, Douglas Valder
see **Jack Harding series**
Stanners, Harold H
see **Professor Harding series**
Worth, Maurice
see **Derek Harding series**

Hardisen and Carson series
Tate, Eleanora Elaine
see **Margie Carson and Ethel Hardisen series**

Hardman series
Dennis, Ralph
see **Jim Hardman series**

Hardrada series
Treece, Henry
see **Harald Hardrada series**

Hardwick family series
Heath-Miller, Mavis
1 *Wrong side of the Park* (1975)
2 *Storm above the Park* (1976)
3 *Time for silence* (1977)
4 *Day before yesterday* (1978)

Hardwired trilogy
Williams, Walter Jon
1 *Hardwired* (1986)
2 *Voice of the whirlwind* (1987)
3 *Solip system* (1989)

Hardy boys case files series
Dixon, Franklin W
House name
1 *Dead on target* (1986)
2 *Evil, Inc.* (1986)
3 *Cult of crime* (1986)
4 *Lazarus plot* (1987)
5 *Edge of destruction* (1987)
6 *Crowning terror* (1987)
7 *Deathgame* (1987)
8 *See no evil* (1987)
9 *Genius thieves* (1987)
10 *Hostages of hate* (1987)
11 *Brother against brother* (1988)
12 *Perfect getaway* (1988)
13 *Borgia dagger* (1988)
14 *Too many traitors* (1988)
15 *Blood relations* (1988)
16 *Line of fire* (1988)
17 *Number file* (1988)
18 *Killing in the market* (1988)
19 *Nightmare in Angel City* (1988)
20 *Witness to murder* (1988)
21 *Street spies* (1988)
22 *Double exposure* (1988)
23 *Disaster for hire* (1989)
24 *Scene of the crime* (1989)
25 *Borderline case* (1989)
26 *Trouble in the pipeline* (1989)
27 *Nowhere to run* (1989)
28 *Countdown to terror* (1989)
29 *Thick as thieves* (1989)
30 *Deadliest dare* (1989)
31 *Without a trace* (1989)
32 *Blood money* (1989)
33 *Collision course* (1989)
34 *Final cut* (1989)
35 *Dead season* (1990)
36 *Running on empty* (1990)
37 *Danger zone* (1990)
38 *Diplomatic deceit* (1990)
39 *Flesh and blood* (1990)
40 *Fright wave* (1990)
41 *Highway robbery* (1990)
42 *Last laugh* (1990)
43 *Strategic moves* (1990)
44 *Castle Fear* (1990)
45 *In self-defense* (1990)
46 *Foul play* (1990)
47 *Flight into danger* (1991)
48 *Rock 'n' revenge* (1991)
49 *Dirty deeds* (1991)
50 *Power play* (1991)
51 *Choke hold* (1991)
52 *Uncivil war* (1991)
53 *Web of horror* (1991)
54 *Deep trouble* (1991)
55 *Beyond the law* (1991)
56 *Height of danger* (1991)
57 *Terror on track* (1991)
58 *Spiked!* (1991)
59 *Open season* (1992)
60 *Deadfall* (1992)
61 *Grave danger* (1992)
62 *Final gambit* (1992)
63 *Cold sweat* (1992)
64 *Endangered species* (1992)
65 *No mercy* (1992)
66 *Phoenix equation* (1992)
67 *Lethal cargo* (1992)
68 *Rough riding* (1992)
69 *Mayhem in motion* (1992)
70 *Rigged for revenge* (1992)
71 *Real horror* (1993)
72 *Screamers* (1993)
73 *Bad rap* (1993)
74 *Road pirates* (1993)
75 *No way out* (1993)
76 *Tagged for terror* (1993)
77 *Survival run* (1993)
78 *Ring of evil* (1993)
79 *Danger unlimited* (1993)
80 *Dead of the night* (1993)
81 *Sheer terror* (1993)
82 *Poisoned paradise* (1993)
83 *Toxic revenge* (1994)
84 *False alarm* (1994)
85 *Winner takes all* (1994)
86 *Virtual villainy* (1994)
87 *Dead man in Deadwood* (1994)
88 *Inferno of fear* (1994)
89 *Darkness falls* (1994)
90 *Deadly engagement* (1994)
91 *Hot wheels* (1994)
92 *Sabotage at sea* (1994)
93 *Mission Mayhem* (1994)
94 *Taste for terror* (1994)

Hardy boys series
Dixon, Franklin W
House name
1 *House on the cliff* (1927)
Revised edition 1959
2 *Tower treasure* (1927)
Revised edition 1959
3 *Secret of the old mill* (1927)
Revised edition 1962; numbers 1-3 also published in one volume, 1959
4 *Shore Road mystery* (1928)
Revised edition 1962
5 *Hunting for hidden gold* (1928)
Revised edition 1963
6 *Missing chums* (1928)
Revised edition 1964
7 *Mystery of Cabin Island* (1929)
Revised edition 1965
8 *Secret of the caves* (1929)
Revised edition 1966
9 *Great airport mystery* (1930)
Revised edition 1965
10 *What happened at midnight?* (1931)
Revised edition 1967
11 *While the clock ticked* (1932)
Revised edition 1962
12 *Footprints under the window* (1933)
Revised edition 1965
13 *Mark on the door* (1934)
Revised edition 1967
14 *Hidden harbor mystery* (1935)
Revised edition 1961
15 *Sinister signpost* (1936)
Revised edition 1968
16 *Figure in hiding* (1937)
Revised edition 1965

17 *Secret warning* (1938)
Revised edition 1966
18 *Twisted claw* (1939)
Revised edition 1969
19 *Disappearing floor* (1940)
Revised edition 1964
20 *Mystery of the flying express* (1941)
Revised edition 1970
21 *Clue of the broken blade* (1942)
Revised edition 1970
22 *Flickering torch mystery* (1943)
Revised edition 1971
23 *Melted coins* (1944)
Revised edition 1970
24 *Short-wave mystery* (1945)
Revised edition 1966
25 *Secret panel* (1946)
Revised edition 1969
26 *Phantom freighter* (1947)
Revised edition 1970
27 *Secret of Skull Mountain* (1948)
Revised edition 1966
28 *Sign of the crooked arrow* (1949)
Revised edition 1970
29 *Secret of the lost tunnel* (1950)
Revised edition 1968
30 *Wailing siren mystery* (1951)
Revised edition 1968
31 *Secret of Wildcat Swamp* (1952)
Revised edition 1969
32 *Yellow feather mystery* (1953)
Revised edition 1969
33 *Crisscross shadow* (1953)
Revised edition 1971
34 *Hooded hawk mystery* (1954)
Revised edition 1971
35 *Clue in the embers* (1955)
Revised edition 1972
36 *Secret of Pirates' Hill* (1957)
Revised edition 1972
37 *Ghost at Skeleton Rock* (1957)
Revised edition 1966
38 *Mystery at Devil's Paw* (1959)
Revised edition 1973
39 *Mystery of the Chinese junk* (1960)
40 *Mystery of the desert giant* (1961)
41 *Clue of the screeching owl* (1962)
42 *Viking symbol mystery* (1963)
43 *Mystery of the Aztec warrior* (1964)
44 *Haunted fort* (1965)
45 *Mystery of the spiral bridge* (1966)
46 *Secret agent on Flight 101* (1967)
47 *Mystery of the whale tattoo* (1968)
48 *Arctic patrol mystery* (1969)
49 *Bombay boomerang* (1970)
50 *Danger on Vampire Trail* (1971)
51 *Masked monkey* (1972)
52 *Shattered helmet* (1973)
53 *Clue of the hissing serpent* (1974)
54 *Mysterious caravan* (1975)
55 *Witchmaster's key* (1976)
56 *Jungle pyramid* (1977)
57 *Firebird rocket* (1978)
58 *Sting of the scorpion* (1979)
59 *Night of the werewolf* (1979)
60 *Mystery of the Samurai sword* (1979)
61 *Pentagon spy* (1980)
62 *Apeman's secret* (1980)
63 *Mummy case* (1980)
64 *Mystery of Smuggler's Cove* (1980)
65 *Stone idol* (1981)
66 *Vanishing thieves* (1981)
67 *Outlaw's silver* (1981)
68 *Deadly chase* (1981)
69 *Four-headed dragon* (1981)
70 *Infinity clue* (1981)
71 *Track of the zombie* (1982)
72 *Voodoo plot* (1982)
73 *Billion dollar ransom* (1982)
74 *Tic-tac-terror* (1982)
75 *Trapped at sea* (1982)
76 *Game plan for disaster* (1982)
77 *Crimson flame* (1983)
78 *Cave-in!* (1983)
79 *Sky sabotage* (1983)
80 *Roaring river mystery* (1984)
81 *Demon's den* (1984)
82 *Blackwing puzzle* (1984)
83 *Swamp monster* (1985)
84 *Revenge of the desert phantom* (1985)
85 *Skyfire puzzle* (1985)
86 *Mystery of the silver star* (1987)
87 *Program for destruction* (1987)
88 *Tricky business* (1988)
89 *Sky blue frame* (1988)
90 *Danger on the diamond* (1988)
91 *Shield of fear* (1988)
92 *Shadow killers* (1988)
93 *Serpent's tooth mystery* (1988)
94 *Breakdown in Axeblade* (1989)
95 *Danger on the air* (1989)
96 *Wipeout* (1989)
97 *Cast of criminals* (1989)
98 *Spark of suspicion* (1989)
99 *Dungeon of doom* (1989)
100 *Secret of the island treasure* (1990)
101 *Money hunt* (1990)
102 *Terminal shock* (1990)
103 *Million dollar nightmare* (1990)
104 *Tricks of the trade* (1990)
105 *Smoke screen mystery* (1990)
106 *Attack of the video villains* (1991)
107 *Panic on Gull Island* (1991)
108 *Fear on wheels* (1991)
109 *Prime-time crime* (1991)
110 *Secret of Sigma Seven* (1991)
111 *Three-ring terror* (1991)
112 *Demolition mission* (1992)
113 *Radical moves* (1992)
114 *Case of the counterfeit criminals* (1992)
115 *Sabotage at Sports City* (1992)
116 *Rock 'n' roll renegades* (1992)
117 *Baseball card conspiracy* (1992)
118 *Danger in the fourth dimension* (1993)
119 *Trouble at Coyote Canyon* (1993)
120 *Case of the cosmic kidnapping* (1993)
121 *Mystery in the old mine* (1993)
122 *Carnival of crime* (1993)
123 *Robot's revenge* (1993)
124 *Mystery with a dangerous boat* (1994)
125 *Mystery on Makatunk Island* (1994)
126 *Racing with disaster* (1994)
127 *Reel thrills* (1994)
128 *Day of the dinosaur* (1994)
129 *Treasure at Dolphin Bay* (1994)
Companion volumes: *The Hardy boys' detective handbook*, 1959, revised 1972, *The Hardy boys' handbook*, 1980, *The Hardy boys' who-dunnit mystery book*, 1980, *The Hardy boys and Nancy Drew meet Dracula*, by Glen A Larsen and Michael Sloan, 1978

Hardy series
Corris, Peter
see **Cliff Hardy series**
Currey, Edward Hamilton
see **Ian Hardy series**
Elliott, William James
see **Bren Hardy series**
Gittings, Robert
see **Thomas Hardy series**
Meyers, Martin
see **Patrick Hardy series**

Hare series
Clewes, Dorothy
see **Henry Hare series**
Holland, Muriel
see **Mister Hare series**

Hare's choice trilogy
Hamley, Dennis
1 *Hare's choice* (1987)
2 *Badger's fate* (1992)
3 *Hawk's vision* (1993)

Hargrave journal series
Lavender, William
1 *Children of the river* (1980)
2 *Journey to quiet waters* (1980)
3 *Fields above the sea* (1980)

Harilek series
Ganpat
see **Harry Lake series**

Harinxma trilogy
De Hartog, Jan
see **Captain Martinus Harinxma trilogy**

Hark series
Stine, Robert Lawrence
1 *Badlands of Hark* (1985)
2 *Invaders of Hark* (1985)

Harker Bellamy series
Horler, Sydney
see **Sir Harker Bellamy series**

Harker series
Masefield, John
see **Kay Harker series; Sard Harker series**
Olden, Marc
see **Hawthorne Albert Harker series**

Harkness series
Warwick, Milligan
see **William Harkness series**

Harlan Cole series
Donahue, Jackson
1 *Pray to the hustlers' god* (1977)
2 *Lady loved too well* (1978)

Harland series
Allum, Tom
see **Hurricane Harland series**
Foley, Rae
see **John Harland series**

Harlequin series
West, Morris Langlo
see **George Harlequin series**

Harley Manners series
Dutton, Charles Judson
1 *Streaked with crimson* (1929)
2 *Shadow of evil* (1930)
3 *Murder in a library* (1931)
4 *Poison unknown* (1932)
Vanishing murderer
5 *Circle of death* (1933)
6 *Black fog* (1934)

Harley series
Cleaver, Hylton
1 *Brother o' mine* (1919)
2 *Harley First XI* (1919)
3 *Captains of Harley* (1920)
4 *Roscoe makes good* (1920)

Harley series
Rohmer, Sax
see **Paul Harley series**
Tack, Alfred
see **John Harley series**

Harley Street series
Byam, William
Memoirs of a doctor
1 *Road to Harley Street* (1983)
2 *Doctor Byam in Harley Street* (1982)

Harley Street series
Mitchell, Alan Williams
1 *Harley Street hypnotist* (1959)
2 *Harley Street psychiatrist* (1960)

Harlowe series
Flower, Jessie Graham
see **Grace Harlowe series**

Harlowe's Overland Riders series
Flower, Jessie Graham
see **Grace Harlowe's Overland Riders series**

Harman series
Walsh, James Morgan
see **Mike Harman series**

Harmas series
Chase, James Hadley
see **Steve Harmas series**

Harmon series
Elman, Richard Martin
see **Professor Robert Harmon series**

Harold and Lizzie series
Winthrop, Elizabeth
see **Lizzie and Harold series**

Harold Atha series
Heppenstall, Rayner
1 *Connecting door* (1962)
2 *Woodshed* (1962)

Harold Crane series
Christie, Kate
1 *Smith* (1954)
2 *Harold in London* (1956)

Harold Fieldend series
Duke, Winifred
1 *Bastard verdict* (1931)
2 *Dark hill* (1932)
3 *Sown wind* (1932)
4 *Finale* (1933)
5 *These are they* (1933)
6 *Magpies' hoard* (1934)

Harold Shea series
De Camp, Lyon Sprague
1 *Incomplete enchanter* (1941)
Incompleat enchanter
2 *Castle of iron* (1950)
Numbers 1 and 2 also published in one volume entitled *The compleat enchanter*, 1975
3 *Wall of serpents* (1960)
Enchanter compleated
Numbers 1-3 also published in one volume editions entitled *Intrepid enchanter*, 1988 and *The complete compleat enchanter*, 1989
4 *Sir Harold and the gnome king* (1991)
Companion volume: *Prospero's island, a Crossroads adventure in the world of L.Sprague de Camp and Fletcher Pratt's The incomplete enchanter*, by Tom Wham, 1987

Harpe series
Lawrence, James D
see **Angela Harpe series**

Harper series
Aylward, Marcus
1 *Harper's folly* (1984)
2 *Harper's luck* (1985)

Harper series
Brown, Walter C
see **Inspector Stephen Harper series**
Ernst, Paul
see **Shirley Leighton and Bill Harper series**

Harpers series
This sequence has three authors
Awlinson, Richard
1 *Parched sea* (1991)
Cunningham, Elaine
2 *Elfshadow* (1991)
Rabe, Jean
3 *Red magic* (1991)

Harpur series
James, Bill
see **Superintendent Colin Harpur series**

Harrad College series
Rimmer, Robert Henry
1 *Harrad experiment* (1966)
2 *Premar experiments* (1975)
Companion volume: *The Harrad letters to Robert H Rimmer,* including his *Apology from a man in search of a fulcrum,* and the original introduction to *The Harrad experiment*, 1969

Harragan series
Harragan, Steve
see **Steve Harragan series**

Harriet and Guy Pringle series
Manning, Olivia
see **Guy and Harriet Pringle series**

Harriet Jeffries and Inspector John Sanders series
Sale, Medora
see **Inspector John Sanders and Harriet Jeffries series**

Harriet M Welsh series
Fitzhugh, Louise
1 *Harriet, the spy* (1964)
2 *Long secret* (1965)

Harriet series
Carlson, Nancy
1 *Harriet's recital* (1982)
2 *Harriet's Halloween candy* (1982)
3 *Harriet and the roller coaster* (1982)
4 *Harriet and the garden* (1982)
5 *Harriet and Walt* (1982)

Harriet series
Maestro, Betsy Crippen
Illustrated by Giulio Maestro
1 *Harriet goes to the circus* (1977)
A number concept book
2 *Harriet reads signs and more signs* (1981)
A word concept book
3 *Around the clock with Harriet* (1984)
A book about telling time
4 *Harriet the elephant* (1984)
5 *Harriet at play* (1984)
6 *Harriet at school* (1984)
7 *Harriet at home* (1984)
8 *Harriet at work* (1984)
9 *Through the year with Harriet* (1985)
10 *Dollars and cents for Harriet* (1988)

Harriet the Troublemaker series
Waddell, Martin
1 *Harriet and the crocodiles* (1982)
2 *Harriet and the haunted school* (1984)
3 *Harriet and the robot* (1985)
4 *Harriet and the flying teachers* (1987)

Harriet Unwin series
Hervey, Evelyn
1 *Governess* (1984)
2 *Man of gold* (1985)
3 *Into the valley of death* (1986)

Harriet Vane series
Sayers, Dorothy Leigh
1 *Strong poison* (1930)
2 *Have his carcass* (1932)
3 *Gaudy night* (1935)
4 *Busman's honeymoon* (1937)

Harrigan and Hoeffler series
O'Malley, Patrick
1 *Affair of the red mosaic* (1961)
2 *Affair of Swan Lake* (1962)
3 *Affair of Jolie Madame* (1963)
4 *Affair of Chief Strongheart* (1964)
5 *Affair of John Donne* (1964)
6 *Affair of the bumbling Briton* (1965)
7 *Affair of the blue pig* (1965)

Harrington series
Thorn, Ismay
see **Geoff and Jim Harrington series**

Harris and Bostock series
Garfield, Leon
see **Bostock and Harris series**

Harris and Perry series
Keverne, Richard
see **Franklin Parry and Leonard Harris series**

Harris series
Black, Gavin
see **Paul Harris series**
Cronin, Michael
see **Sam Harris series**
Dean, Amber
see **Albie Harris series**
Fitzhugh, Percy Keese
see **Pee-Wee Harris series**
Gallico, Paul
see **Mrs Harris series**
Macrae, Travis
see **Jim and Kate Harris series**

Harris series
Remkiewicz, Frank
1 *Last time I saw Harris* (1991)
2 *There's only one Harris* (1993)

Harris series
Woodley, Richard
see **Man from Atlantis series**

Harris trilogy
Oldfield, Pamela
see **Kent trilogy**

Harrison High series
Farris, John
1 *Harrison High* (1959)
2 *Girl from Harrison High* (1968)
3 *Trouble at Harrison High* (1970)
4 *Shadow on Harrison High* (1972)
5 *Return to Harrison High* (1973)

Harrison Hull series
Burns, Ron
1 *Mysterious death of Meriwether Lewis* (1993)
2 *Enslaved* (1994)

Harrison Keith series
Carter, Nicholas
This pseudonym is used by several authors including S A D Cox, Frederick William Davis, Frederick Van Rensselaar Dey, Walter Bertram Foster, George Charles Jenks, Larned, Lincoln, Eugene T Sawyer whose authorship is indicated where it is known
1 *Harrison Keith, sleuth* (1907) [Dey]
2 *Harrison Keith's warning* (1907) [Sawyer]
3 *Harrison Keith's chance clue* (1907) [Lincoln]
4 *Harrison Keith's greatest task* (1907) [Foster]
5 *Harrison Keith's struggle* (1907)
6 *Harrison Keith's triumph* (1907) [Sawyer]
7 *Harrison Keith's big stakes* (1907) [Lincoln]
8 *Harrison Keith's dilemma* (1907) [Sawyer]
9 *Harrison Keith's danger* (1907) [Sawyer]
10 *Harrison Keith's oath* (1907) [Lincoln]
11 *Harrison Keith's wireless message* (1908) [Sawyer]
12 *Harrison Keith's crooked trail* (1908) [Foster]
13 *Harrison Keith's double mystery* (1908) [Jenks]
14 *Harrison Keith's fight for life* (1908) [Foster]
15 *Harrison Keith's mystic letter* (1908) [Foster]
16 *Harrison Keith's drag net* (1908) [Foster]
17 *Harrison Keith's chance shot* (1908) [Jenks]
18 *Harrison Keith's weird partner* (1908) [Foster]
19 *Harrison Keith's diamond case* (1908) [Sawyer]
20 *Harrison Keith's tact* (1908) [Foster]
21 *Harrison Keith's time lock case* (1908) [Foster]
22 *Harrison Keith's strange summons* (1908) [Foster]
23 *Harrison Keith's queer clue* (1908) [Jenks]
24 *Harrison Keith and the phantom heiress* (1909) [Larned]
25 *Harrison Keith's close quarters* (1909) [Davis]
26 *Harrison Keith at bay* (1909) [Larned]
27 *Harrison Keith's padlock mystery* (1909) [Davis]
28 *Harrison Keith's cameo case* (1909) [Larned]
29 *Harrison Keith's triple tragedy* (1909) [Davis]
30 *Harrison Keith's double cross* (1909) [Davis]
31 *Harrison Keith's abduction tangle* (1909) [Larned]
32 *Harrison Keith's battle of nerve* (1909) [Larned]
33 *Harrison Keith's dual role* (1909) [Davis]
34 *Harrison Keith's haunted client* (1909) [Larned]
35 *Harrison Keith's mummy mystery* (1909) [Larned]
36 *Harrison Keith's lucky strike* (1909) [Jenks]
37 *Harrison Keith's green diamond* (1909) [Larned]
38 *Harrison Keith, magician* (1909) [Davis]
39 *Harrison Keith's death compact* (1909) [Davis]
40 *Harrison Keith's sparkling trail* (1909) [Larned]
41 *Harrison Keith's river front ruse* (1909) [Larned]
42 *Harrison Keith's wager* (1910) [Larned]
43 *Harrison Keith's studio crime* (1910) [Larned]
44 *Harrison Keith's labyrinth* (1910) [Larned]
45 *Harrison Keith's river mystery* (1910) [Larned]
46 *Harrison Keith's death watch* (1910) [Larned]
47 *Harrison Keith's poison problem* (1910)
48 *Harrison Keith, star reporter* (1910) [Larned]
49 *Harrison Keith's cyclone clue* (1910) [Larned]
50 *Harrison Keith's perilous contract* (1910) [Cox]
Companion volume: *The adventures of Harrison Keith, detective*, 1899

Harrison series
Berry, Stephen Ames
see **John Harrison series**
Robbins, Clifton
see **Clay Harrison series**

Harrison Wilke series
Roderus, Frank
1 *Leaving Kansas* (1983)
2 *Reaching Colorado* (1984)
3 *Finding Nevada* (1985)

Harrow School series
Vachell, Horace Annesley
1 *Hill* (1905)
A romance of friendship, based on an idea suggested by *Brothers*, 1904
2 *John Verney* (1911)
3 *Lord Samarkand* (1938)

Harrow series
Adams, Shipley
see **Inspector Harrow series**

Harry Adkins series
Foxall, Raymond
1 *Little Ferret* (1968)
2 *Brandy for the parson* (1970)
3 *Dark forest* (1972)
4 *Silver goblet* (1974)
5 *Last Jacobite* (1980)

Harry and Laura series
Eagar, Frances
see **Laura and Harry series**

Harry Angstrom series
Updike, John
see **Rabbit Angstrom series**

Harry Barnaby series
Neill, Robert
see **Sir Harry Barnaby series**

Harry Bogen series
Weidman, Jerome
1 *I can get it for you wholesale* (1937)
2 *What's in it for me* (1938)

Harry Borg series
Hawkins, Ward
1 *Red flame burning* (1985)
2 *Sword of fire* (1985)
3 *Blaze of wrath* (1986)
4 *Torch of fear* (1987)

Harry Bosch series
Connelly, Michael
1 *Black echo* (1992)
2 *Black ice* (1993)
3 *Concrete blonde* (1994)

Harry Butten series
Barbette, Jay
1 *Final copy* (1952)
2 *Dear, dead days* (1953)
Death's long shadow
3 *Deadly doll* (1958)
4 *Look behind you* (1960)

Harry Chalice and Crying Eddie series
Mackenzie, Donald
1 *Salute from a dead man* (1966)
2 *Death is a friend* (1967)
3 *Sleep is for the rich* (1971)
Chalice caper

Harry Egypt series
Broun, Daniel
1 *Subject of Harry Egypt* (1963)
2 *Egypt's choice* (1963)

Harry Fabian series
Kersh, Gerald
1 *Night and the city* (1938)
2 *Song of the flea* (1948)

Harry Fannin series
Markson, David
1 *Miss Doll, go home* (1965)
2 *Epitaph for a tramp* (1959)
Fannin
3 *Epitaph for a dead heat* (1961)

Harry Farrant series
Gorell, Ronald Gorell Barnes
1 *Devouring fire* (1928)
2 *Red lilac* (1935)

Harry Fathers series
Smith, Daniel Wybert
see **Chief Inspector Harry Fathers series**

Harry Feiffer series
Marshall, William Leonard
see **Yellowthread Street series**

Harry Garnish and Bridget O'Toole series
McConnell, Frank
1 *Murder among friends* (1985)
2 *Blood lake* (1987)

Harry Gould series
Obstfeld, Raymond
1 *Goulden fleece* (1979)
2 *Dead-end option* (1980)
3 *Dead heat* (1981)
4 *Dead bolt* (1982)

Harry Grant series
Freeborn, Brian
see **Mister Cain series**

Harry Henderson series
Stowe, Harriet Beecher
1 *My wife and I* (1871)
Alternative title: Harry Henderson's history
2 *We are our neighbors* (1875)
Alternative title: The records of an unfashionable street

Harry Horne series
Gonzales, John
1 *End of a JD* (1960)
2 *Someone's sleeping in my bed* (1962)
3 *Follow that hearse!* (1963)

Harry James and Sergeant Honeybody series
Giles, Kenneth
see **Inspector Harry James and Sergeant Honeybody series**

Harry Keel series
Trimnell, Robert L
see **Loner series**

Harry Kitten and Tucker Mouse series
Selden, George
see **Chester Cricket series**

Harry Lake series
Ganpat
1 *Harilek* (1923)
A romance of modern central Asia
2 *Wrexham's romance* (1935)
One volume edition entitled *Adventures in Sakaeland*, 1978

Harry Long series
Fulman, Al
1 *Last of the Wild Bunch* (1966)
2 *Portrait of a killer* (1968)

Harry Macneil series
Jeffers, Harry Paul
1 *Rubout at the Onyx* (1981)
2 *Murder on mike* (1984)

Harry Martineau series
Procter, Maurice
see **Chief Inspector Harry Martineau series**

Harry Maxim series
Lyall, Gavin
see **Major Harry Maxim series**

Harry Monroe series
Hannah, Barry
1 *Geronimo Rex* (1972)
2 *Nightwatchmen* (1973)

Harry Orwell series
Based on a television series
Hays, Lee
1 *Harry-O* (1975)
2 *Harry-O 2* (1976)
High cost of living

Harry Palmer series
Deighton, Len
see **Secret file series**

Harry Porter series
Naha, Ed
1 *Paradise plot* (1980)
2 *Suicide plague* (1982)

Harry Preleshnik series
Ka-tzetnik 135633
Translated from the Hebrew
1 *House of dolls* (1953)
2 *House of love* (1966)

Harry Reilly series
Corbin, Gary
1 *Last time I saw Mary* (1963)
2 *Cosa Nostra circus* (1964)

Harry Ryder series
Footman, Robert
1 *Once a spy* (1985)
2 *Always a spy* (1986)

Harry Sellers series
Denton, Derek
1 *Don't go near the magic shop* (1983)
2 *Hiders and seekers* (1983)
3 *House in the dunes* (1986)

Harry series
Chalmers, Mary
1 *Throw a kiss, Harry* (1958)
2 *Take a nap, Harry* (1964)
3 *Be good, Harry* (1967)
4 *Merry Christmas, Harry* (1977)
5 *Come to the doctor, Harry* (1981)

Harry series
Keith, Shona
1 *Harry's new hobby* (1979)
2 *Harry goes to a fancy-dress party* (1979)
3 *Harry's baggy jumper* (1979)

Harry series
Kline, Suzy
see **Horrible Harry series**

Harry series
Lavelle, Sheila
1 *Harry's aunt* (1985)
2 *Harry's horse* (1987)
3 *Harry's dog* (1988)
4 *Harry's hamster* (1990)
5 *Harry's cat* (1992)

Harry series
Porte, Barbara Ann
1 *Harry's dog* (1984)
2 *Harry's mom* (1985)
3 *Harry in trouble* (1989)

Harry series
Ridgway, Bill
see **Lucky Harry series**

Harry series
Waterman, Jill
1 *Harry's colours* (1978)
2 *Harry's spots* (1979)
3 *Harry's stripes* (1980)
4 *Harry's shapes* (1982)
5 *Harry's numbers* (1983)
6 *Harry's sizes* (1985)
7 *Harry's alphabet* (1985)

Harry Sommers and Jill Hanscombe series
Whalley, Peter
1 *Robbers* (1986)
2 *Bandits* (1986)
3 *Villains* (1987)
4 *Rogues* (1988)
5 *Crooks* (1988)

Harry Stoner series
Valin, Jonathan
1 *Lime pit* (1980)
2 *Final notice* (1980)
3 *Dead letter* (1981)
4 *Day of wrath* (1982)
5 *Natural causes* (1983)
6 *Life's work* (1986)
7 *Fire Lake* (1987)
8 *Extenuating circumstances* (1989)
9 *Second chance* (1991)
10 *Music lovers* (1993)
11 *Missing* (1994)

Harry the dirty dog series
Zion, Gene
1 *Harry the dirty dog* (1956)
2 *No roses for Harry* (1958)
3 *Harry and the lady next door* (1960)
4 *Harry by the sea* (1965)

Harry Thomas trilogy
Hall, Patrick
1 *India man* (1968)
2 *Sun and grey shadow* (1974)
Third volume not yet published

Harry Timberlake series
Marquis, Max
1 *Vengeance* (1990)
2 *Deadly doctors* (1992)
Twelfth man
3 *Elimination* (1992)
4 *Undignified death* (1994)

Harry Tong series
Burgess, Eric
1 *Killing frost* (1961)
2 *Closely confined* (1962)
3 *Deadly deceit* (1963)
4 *Exit Pretty Poll* (1968)

Harry Wilson series
Alden, William Livingston
see **Moral Pirates series**

Harryboy Boas series
Baron, Alexander
1 *Lowlife* (1963)
2 *Strip Jack naked* (1966)

Hart and Pearce series
Gardner, Jerome
see **Dripspring series**

Hart Muldoon series
Flagg, John
1 *Woman of Cairo* (1953)
2 *Dear, deadly beloved* (1954)
3 *Murder in Monaco* (1957)
4 *Death's lovely mask* (1958)
5 *Paradise gun* (1961)

Hart series
Glemser, Bernard
see **Nicholas Hart series**
Harvey, John Barton
see **Wes Hart series**

Harte series
Bradford, Barbara Taylor
see **Emma Harte series**

Hartlake Hospital series
Collins, Lynne
1 *Heartache Hospital* (1981)
2 *Rogue registrar* (1982)
3 *Second-year love* (1982)
4 *Doctor in pursuit* (1982)
5 *First-year's fancy* (1983)
6 *Surgeon on Skora* (1984)
7 *Sigh for a surgeon* (1984)
8 *Surgeon in disgrace* (1985)

Hartley and Stevens series
Tuttle, Wilbur Coleman
see **Hashknife Hartley and Sleepy Stevens series**

Hartley series
Ellinger, Geoffrey
see **Roger Hartley series**

Hartman family trilogy
Hunt, Greg
1 *Borderland* (1987)
2 *Exiles* (1988)
3 *Renegades* (1988)

Hartung and Campbell series
Bickham, Jack Miles
see **John Campbell and Clayton Hartung series**

Hartwarp series
Pudney, John
1 *Hartwarp light railway* (1962)
2 *Hartwarp dump* (1962)
3 *Hartwarp circus* (1963)
4 *Hartwarp balloon* (1963)
5 *Hartwarp bakehouse* (1964)
6 *Hartwarp explosion* (1965)
7 *Hartwarp jets* (1967)

Harty series
Dane, Joel Y
see **Sergeant Cass Harty series**

Harum Scarum series
Stuart, Esme
1 *Harum Scarum* (1896)
2 *Harum Scarum's fortune* (1909)
3 *Harum Scarum married* (1917)

Harvard series
Gibbs-Smith, Charles Harvard
see **Paul Harvard series**
Vanardy, Varick
see **Bingham Harvard series**

Harvest in the north series
Hodson, James Lansdale
1 *Harvest in the north* (1934)
2 *God's in his heaven* (1935)

Harvey Blissberg series
Rosen, Richard
1 *Strike three you're dead* (1984)
2 *Fadeaway* (1986)
3 *Saturday night dead* (1988)

Harvey Krim series
Cunningham, E V
1 *Lydia* (1964)
2 *Cynthia* (1968)

Harvey Landon series
Pattinson, James
1 *Contact Mister Delgado* (1959)
2 *Liberators* (1961)
3 *Last stronghold* (1968)
4 *Sinister stars* (1971)

Harvey Tuke series
Browne, Douglas Gordon
see **Mister Harvey Tuke series**

Harvie family series
Allan, Mabel Esther
1 *Over the sea to school* (1950)
2 *School in danger* (1952)
3 *At school in Skye* (1957)

Hasford family series
Jones, Douglas Clyde
1 *Elkhorn Tavern* (1980)
2 *Winding stair* (1979)
Winding stair massacre
3 *Weedy Rough* (1981)
4 *Barefoot brigade* (1982)
5 *Roman* (1986)
6 *Come winter* (1989)

Hashknife Hartley and Sleepy Stevens series
Tuttle, Wilbur Coleman
1 *Medicine man* (1925)

2 *Thicker than water* (1927)
3 *Hashknife of the Double Bar S* (1927)
Arizona ways
4 *Dead-line* (1927)
5 *Hashknife lends a hand* (1927)
6 *Shotgun gold* (1927)
7 *Morgan Trail* (1928)
8 *Hashknife of the Canyon Trail* (1928)
9 *Hidden blood* (1929)
10 *Tumbling River Range* (1929)
11 *Mystery of the red triangle* (1929)
12 *Hashknife of Stormy River* (1931)
13 *Valley of twisted trails* (1931)
14 *Santa Dolores stage* (1934)
Twisted trails
15 *Rifled gold* (1934)
16 *Ghost trails* (1940)
17 *Valley of vanishing herds* (1942)
18 *Wolf pack of Lobo Butte* (1945)
Wolf Creek Valley
19 *Trouble trailer* (1946)
20 *Salt for the tiger* (1952)
21 *Mission River justice* (1955)
22 *Shadow shooter* (1955)
23 *Diamond hitch* (1962)
24 *Passengers for Painted Rock* (1962)
25 *Valley of suspicion* (1964)
26 *Double-crossers of Ghost Tree* (1965)
27 *Road to the moon* (1965)
28 *Payroll of fate* (1966)
29 *Lone Wolf* (1967)
30 *Medicine maker* (1967)
31 *Vanishing brands* (1977)
32 *Red trail of a point forty-one* (1978)
33 *Trouble at War Eagle* (1991)
Published with *The redhead of Aztec Wells* which is not part of this sequence

Haskell series
Cannell, Dorothy
see **Ellie Simons Haskell series**
Sutherland, William
see **Inspector Haskell series**

Hastings series
Givens, Charles Garland
see **Jimmy Hastings series**
Hall, Parnell
see **Stanley Hastings series**
Hay, James
see **Jefferson Hastings series**
Offord, Lenore Glen
see **Bill and Coco Hastings series**
Wilcox, Collin
see **Lieutenant Frank Hastings series**

Haswell series
Adams, Herbert
see **Jimmy Haswell series**

Hatch series
Campbell, Robert Wright
see **Jake Hatch series**
Davis, Frederick Clyde
see **Professor Cyrus Hatch series**
Hawkes, Zachary
see **Fancy Hatch series**
Merritt, Don
see **Captain Franklin Hatcher series**

Hatcher series
Banks, Oliver
see **Amos Hatcher series**
Blume, Judy
see **Peter Hatcher series**
Merritt, Don
see **Captain Franklin Hatcher series**

Hate series
Braddon, Russell
Autobiography of a journalist
1 *Naked island* (1952)
Experiences in Changi Prison
2 *End of a hate* (1958)
Includes a short story, Song of war

Hatfield series
Cole, Jackson
see **Jim Hatfield series**
Rogers, Samuel
see **Professor Paul Hatfield series**

Hatherleigh series
Cooper, Charles
see **John Hatherleigh series**

Hatteras series
Verne, Jules
see **Adventures of Captain Hatteras series**

Hattie Rabbit series
Gackenbach, Dick
1 *Hattie Rabbit* (1976)
2 *Hattie be quiet, Hattie be good* (1977)
3 *Mother Rabbit's son Tom* (1977)
4 *Hattie, Tom and the Chicken Witch* (1980)
A play and a story
5 *Hurray for Hattie Rabbit!* (1986)

Hattie series
Frost, Marie Hibma
1 *Meet Hattie* (1994)
2 *Hattie's faraway family* (1994)
3 *Hattie's holiday fun* (1994)
4 *Hattie's adventures* (1994)

Haunted Britain series
Alexander, Marc
1 *Haunted inns* (1973)
2 *Haunted castles* (1974)
3 *Haunted churches and abbeys of Britain* (1978)
4 *Haunted pubs in Britain and Ireland* (1984)

Haunted houses series
Chambers, Aidan
1 *Haunted houses* (1971)
2 *More haunted houses* (1973)

Haunted seventh series
Ross, Charles
1 *Haunted seventh* (1922)
2 *When the devil was sick* (1924)

Haunting with Louisa series
Cates, Emily
1 *Ghost in the attic* (1990)
2 *Mystery of Misty Island Inn* (1990)
3 *Ghost ferry* (1991)

Hautley Quicksilver series
Carter, Lin
1 *Thief of Thoth* (1968)
2 *Purloined planet* (1969)

Haven series
Diamond, Graham
1 *Haven* (1977)
2 *Lady of the Haven* (1978)
3 *Dungeons of Kuba* (1979)
4 *Falcon of Eden* (1980)
5 *Beasts of Hades* (1981)

Haven series
Lucas, Edward Verrall
see **Richard Haven series**

Havengore series
Geston, Mark Symington
1 *Lords of the starship* (1967)
2 *Out of the mouth of the dragon* (1969)

Haverard family series
Vipont, Elfrida
1 *Lark in the morn* (1948)
2 *Lark on the wing* (1950)
3 *Spring of the year* (1957)
4 *Flowering spring* (1960)
5 *Pavilion* (1969)

Havers and Lynley series
George, Elizabeth
see **Inspector Thomas Lynley and Sergeant Barbara Havers series**

Havilland series
Gielgud, Val
see **Antony Havilland series**

Havisham series
Dickens, Charles
see **Miss Havisham series**

Havoc series
Healey, Ben
see **Captain Havoc series**
Jakes, John
see **Johnny Havoc series**

Hawaii Five-O series
This sequence has two authors; based on a television series
Avallone, Michael
1 *Hawaii Five-O* (1968)
2 *Terror in the sun* (1969)
Harris, Herbert
3 *Angry battalion* (1976)

Hawaii kai series
Stump, Jane Barr
1 *Our Hawaii kai* (1979)
2 *Hawaii kai chronicles* (1980)

Hawaii series
McKee, Ruth Eleanor
1 *Lord's anointed* (1934)
2 *After a hundred years* (1935)

Hawbucks series
Masefield, John
1 *Reynard the fox* (1919)
Alternative title: The Ghost Heath run; a story in verse
2 *Hawbucks* (1929)

Hawick series
Tranter, Nigel Godwin
1 *Cheviot Chase* (1952)
2 *Night riders* (1954)

Hawk and Fisher series
Green, Simon
1 *Hawk and Fisher* (1990)
No haven for the guilty
2 *Winner takes all* (1991)
Devil take the hindmost
3 *God killer* (1991)
4 *Wolf in the fold* (1991)
5 *Guard against dishonor* (1991)
6 *Bones of haven* (1992)

Hawk Macrae series
Barker, Albert
1 *Big fix* (1973)
2 *If anything should happen to me* (1973)
3 *Dragon in spring* (1973)
4 *Blood of angels* (1973)
5 *Diamond fix* (1974)

Hawk series
Brady, William S
see **Jared Hawk series**
James, Leigh Franklin
see **John Cooper Baines series**
Leyland, Eric
see **Hunter Hawk series**
Sanders, Brett
see **Web Steele series**
Streib, Dan
see **Michael Hawk series**

Hawke series
Cunningham, Chet
see **Matt Hawke series**
Patrick, Michael
see **Tommy Hawke series**

Hawkehurst series
Braddon, Mary Elizabeth
see **Valentine Hawkehust series**

Hawker series
Ramm, Carl
see **James Hawker series**

Hawkes series
Ephesian
see **A B C Hawkes series**

Hawkeye Collins and Amy Adams series
Masters, M
1 *Secret of the long-lost cousin, and other mysteries* (1983)
2 *Case of the chocolate snatcher, and other mysteries* (1983)
3 *Case of the video game smugglers, and other mysteries* (1983)
4 *Case of the mysterious dognapper, and other mysteries* (1983)
5 *Case of the clever computer crooks, and other mysteries* (1983)
6 *Case of the chocolate chip cookies, and other mysteries* (1983)
7 *Case of the star ship Mars, and other mysteries* (1983)
8 *Secret of the software spy, and other mysteries* (1983)
9 *Case of the toilet paper decorator, and other mysteries* (1984)
10 *Secret of the Loon Lake monster, and other mysteries* (1984)
11 *Case of the haunted house, and other mysteries* (1984)
12 *Secret of the video game scorer, and other mysteries* (1984)
13 *Case of the phony Frankenstein, and other mysteries* (1984)
14 *Case of the clever marathon cheat, and other mysteries* (1984)

Hawkeye series
Irwin, Ann
1 *Hawkeye adventure* (1966)
2 *Hawkeye lore* (1968)

Hawkin series
Harrison, Harry
see **Tony Hawkin series**

Hawkins, Malins and Mornington series
Dix, Maurice Buxton
see **Tommy Malins, Anthony Mornington and George Hawkins series**

Hawkins series
Allen, Richard
see **Joe Hawkins series**
Dickens, Frank
see **Albert Henry Hawkins series**
Hunter, Kristin
see **Lourette Hawkins series**

Hawkins series
Wallace, Barbara Brooks
1 *Hawkins* (1977)
2 *Hawkins and the soccer solution* (1981)

Hawklan series
Taylor, Roger
1 *Call of the sword* (1988)
2 *Fall of Fyorland* (1989)
3 *Waking of Orthlund* (1989)
4 *Into Narsindal* (1990)

Hawklords series
Butterworth, Michael
1 *Time of the hawklords* (1976)
Co-author: Michael Moorcock
2 *Queens of Deliria* (1977)

Hawkmoon series
Moorcock, Michael
see **History of Runestaff series**

Hawks series
Ballinger, Bill Sanborn
see **Joaquin Hawks series**

Hawksmoor series
Armitage, Aileen
1 *Hawksmoor* (1981)
2 *Hunter's moon* (1984)
3 *Touchstone* (1986)
4 *Hawkrise* (1988)

Hawkwood series
Cole, Hubert
see **Sir John Hawkwood series**

Hawthorne Albert Harker series
Olden, Marc
1 *Harker file* (1976)
2 *Dead and paid for* (1976)
3 *They've killed Anna* (1977)
4 *Kill the reporter* (1978)

Hawthorne and Linnett series
Linscott, Gillian
see **Birdie Linnett and Nimue Hawthorne series**

Hawthorne College series
Blake, Susan
1 *All-nighter* (1987)
2 *Crash course* (1987)
3 *Major changes* (1987)
4 *Extra credit* (1987)
5 *Teacher's pet* (1987)
6 *School's out* (1987)
7 *Final exam* (1987)
8 *Class act* (1988)
9 *Higher education* (1988)
10 *Multiple choice* (1988)
11 *Making the grade* (1988)
12 *No contest* (1988)
13 *Model student* (1988)
14 *Fever* (1988)
15 *Study break* (1988)

Hawthorne series
Ogilvie, Elisabeth May
see **Jennie Hawthorne series**

Haydon series
Lindsey, David L
see **Stuart Haydon series**

Hayduke series
Abbey, Edward
see **George W Hayduke series**

Hayes and Curry series
Fox, Brian
see **Alias Smith and Jones series**

Hayes series
Davis, Dorothy Salisbury
see **Julie Hayes series**
Lacy, Ed
see **Lee Hayes series**

Hayes trilogy
Leslie, Peter
see **Father Hayes trilogy**
Lewis, Colin
see **Howard Hayes trilogy**

Hayfield series
Repp, Ed Earl
see **Jim Hayfield series**

Haynes series
Symons, Julian
see **Sheridan Haynes series**

Haywood Beatty trilogy
Bonner, Cindy
1 *Lily* (1992)
2 *Looking after Lily* (1994)
Number three not yet published

Hazard and Drury series
Marlowe, Piers
see **Frank Drury and Inspector Bill Hazard series**

Hazard family trilogy
Jakes, John
see **North and South trilogy**

Hazard series
Crosby, Lee
see **Eric Hazard series**
Stuart, Vivian
see **Commander Philip Hazard series**

Hazel and Black John series
Martin, Rhona
see **Black John and Hazel series**

Hazel series
Warner, Susan Bagert
see **Wych Hazel series**

Hazell series
Yuill, P B
see **James Hazell series**

Hazelrigg series
Gilbert, Michael Francis
see **Inspector Hazelrigg series**
Wren, Percival Christopher
see **Major Hazelrigg series**

Hazlitt Woar series
Yates, George Worthing
1 *Body that came by post* (1937)
2 *Body that wasn't uncle* (1939)
3 *If a body* (1941)

Hazzard series
Bowles, Colin
see **Mike Hazzard series**

He, she and it trilogy
Abarbanell, Jacob Ralph
1 *He* (1887)
2 *She* (1887)
3 *It* (1887)
A wild, weird history of marvellous, miraculous, phrantasmagorial adventures

Head series
Vivian, Evelyn Charles
see **Inspector Head series**

Headcorn series
Campbell, Alice
see **Inspector Headcorn series**

Headhunter series
Hunter, E J
1 *Arizona hellcat* (1987)
2 *Texas tumble* (1987)
3 *Hard-riding* (1988)
4 *Sin city* (1988)
5 *Mile-high madness* (1988)
6 *Arizona bustout* (1989)
7 *Tombstone temptress* (1989)
8 *Nevada claim stripper* (1990)
9 *Tools of the trade* (1990)
10 *Red hot roundup* (1991)
11 *Hardcase squeeze* (1992)
12 *Rough shaft* (1992)
13 *Desert spread* (1993)

Headhunters series
Weisman, John
1 *Heroin triple-cross* (1974)
2 *Three faces of death* (1974)
3 *Starlight Motel incident* (1974)
4 *Quadrophonic homicide* (1975)

Headley series
Morris, Thomas Baden
see **Inspector Headley series**

Headlines series
Hall, Malcolm
1 *Headlines* (1974)
2 *Forecast* (1979)

Heads, bodies, legs series
Oxenbury, Helen
see **Seven hundred and twenty nine series**

Heald series
Hossent, Harry
see **Max Heald series**

Healers series
Harper, Stephen
1 *Future deferred* (1974)
2 *Wednesday's child* (1975)
3 *Wilderness boy* (1975)
4 *Nerve end* (1975)
5 *Blind spot* (1976)

Health facts series
Bailey, Donna
1 *All about your senses* (1990)
2 *All about birth and growth* (1990)
3 *All about your brain* (1990)
4 *All about heart and blood* (1990)
5 *All about your skeleton* (1990)
6 *All about digestion* (1990)
7 *All about your lungs* (1990)
8 *All about skin, hair and teeth* (1990)

Hearne series
Craig, Thurlow
see **Lieutenant Bunjy Hearne series**

Heart of a woman series
Angelou, Maya
Autobiography
1 *I know why the caged bird sings* (1970)
Childhood to 16 years
2 *Gather together in my name* (1974)
17- 25 years
3 *Singin' and swingin' and gettin' merry like Christmas* (1976)
4 *Heart of a woman* (1981)
5 *All God's children need traveling shoes* (1986)
Set in Ghana between 1963 and 1966

Heart of the dreaming series
Morrissey, Di
1 *Heart of the dreaming* (1991)
2 *Follow the morning star* (1993)

Heart throbs series
Chapple, Joseph Mitchell
1 *Heart throbs in prose and verse dear to the American people, part 1* (1905)
2 *Heart throbs in prose and verse dear to the American people, part 2* (1911)
Abridged edition of numbers 1 and 2 published as *Favorite heart throbs of famous people*, 1929
3 *More heart throbs contributed by the people* (1932)

Heart to heart series
This sequence has six authors
Tyler, Vicki
1 *Someday soon* (1985)
Ellis, Carol
2 *Summer to summer* (1985)
Norby, Lisa
3 *Waiting in the wings* (1985)
York, Carol Beach
4 *Making a wish* (1985)
Miller, Sandy
5 *This song is for you* (1985)
York, Carol Beach
6 *Likely story* (1985)
Connell, Abby
7 *Spring fever* (1985)
Tyler, Vicki
8 *Senior year* (1986)
Norby, Lisa
9 *Friendly rivals* (1986)

Heartbeat series
Rhea, Nicholas
see **Aidensfield series**

Heartlight series
Barron, Tom A
1 *Heartlight* (1990)
2 *Ancient one* (1992)

Heartquest series
This sequence has four authors
Black, Jeannie
1 *Ring of the ruby dragon* (1983)
Simon, Madeleine
2 *Talisman of Valdegarde* (1983)
Lowery, Linda
3 *Secret sorcerers* (1983)
Simon, Madeleine
4 *Isle of illusion* (1983)
Lowery, Linda
5 *Moon dragon summer* (1984)
Novak, Kate
6 *Lady of the winds* (1984)

Hearts and masks series
McGrath, Harold
1 *Hearts and masks* (1905)
2 *Deuces wild* (1913)

Heath series
Tyler, Alison
see **Jennifer Heath series**

Heathcliff series
This sequence has two authors
Bronte, Emily
1 *Wuthering Heights* (1847)
Caine, Jeffrey
2 *Heathcliff* (1977)

Heather, oak and olive trilogy
Sutcliff, Rosemary
1 *Chief's daughter* (1967)
2 *Circlet of oak leaves* (1968)
3 *Crown of white olive* (1972)
This title only published in the omnibus volume *Heather, oak and olive*, 1972

Heather series
Wynne, May
1 *Story of Heather* (1912)
2 *Heather the Second* (1938)

Heaven and Hell trilogy
Blamires, Harry
1 *Devil's hunting-grounds* (1954)
2 *Cold war in Hell* (1955)
3 *Blessing unbounded* (1955)
Highway to heaven

Heaven chronicles series
Vinge, Joan Dennison
1 *Outcasts of Heaven Belt* (1978)
2 *Legacy* (1991)
One volume edition entitled *Heaven chronicles*, 1991

Heaven lies about us series
Spring, Howard
1 *Heaven lies about us* (1939)
2 *In the meantime* (1942)
3 *And another thing* (1946)

Heaven series
Edwards, Charlotte
1 *Heaven on the doorstep* (1958)
2 *Heaven in the house* (1959)

Heavenly bodies series
Boylan, James Finney
1 *Planets* (1991)
2 *Constellations* (1994)

Heavenly twins series
Grand, Sarah
1 *Ideala* (1888)
Originally published anonymously
2 *Heavenly twins* (1893)

Heavers series
Clydesdale, Abby
see **Alys Heavers series**

Heavy woollen district series
Boothroyd, Derrick
1 *Value for money* (1953)
2 *Shoddy kingdom* (1955)

Hebridean boyhood series
Macdonald, Finlay J
Autobiography
1 *Crowdie and cream* (1982)
2 *Crotal and white* (1983)

Hebrides series
Beckwith, Lillian
1 *About my father's business* (1971)
An account of childhood in Cheshire before moving to the Hebrides
2 *Hills is lonely* (1959)
3 *Sea for breakfast* (1961)
4 *Loud halo* (1964)
5 *Rope, in case* (1968)
6 *Lightly poached* (1973)
7 *Beautiful just* (1975)
8 *Bruach bland* (1978)

Hebrides series
Black, William
1 *Princess of Thule* (1874)
2 *Maid of Killeena, and other stories* (1874)

Hec Ramsey series
This sequence has two authors; based on a television series
Owen, Dean
1 *Hec Ramsey* (1973)
Millard, Joe
2 *Hunted* (1974)

Hector and Art series
Gunn, Neil Miller
see **Young Art and old Hector series**

Hector and Prudence series
Koscielniak, Bruce
1 *Hector and Prudence* (1990)
2 *All aboard!* (1990)

Hector Penguin series
Fatio, Louise
1 *Hector Penguin* (1973)
2 *Hector and Christina* (1977)

Hector Servadac series
Verne, Jules
1 *To the sun?* (1877)
Astounding adventures among the comets
2 *Off on a comet!* (1877)
Homeward bound
Anomalous phenomena
Original edition in one volume entitled *Hector Servadac;* one volume English editions entitled *Hector Servadac, or, The career of a comet*, 1878, *Astounding adventures among the comets*, 1910, *Space novels by Jules Verne*, 1960; one volume abridged edition entitled *Off on a comet*, 1957

Hed trilogy
McKillip, Patricia Anne
see **Morgon trilogy**

Hedgerow tales series
Wynne-Jones, Pat
Illustrated by Sandra Fernandez
Rewritten from *Parables of nature*, by Margaret Gatty, 1874
1 *Story of Charlotte the Caterpillar* (1984)
2 *Story of Benjamin Bee* (1984)
3 *Story of Jeremy Cricket* (1984)
4 *Story of Robin Redbreast* (1984)

Hedley series
Healey, Ben
see **Paul Hedley series**

Heechee series
Pohl, Frederik
1 *Gateway* (1977)
2 *Beyond the blue event horizon* (1980)
3 *Heechee rendezvous* (1984)
4 *Annals of the Heechee* (1987)
5 *Gateway trip* (1990)
Tales and vignettes of the Heechee

Heerden series
Sharpe, Tom
see **Kommandant Van Heerden series**

Heffalump series
Nilsson, Eleanor Ann
1 *Heffalump?* (1989)
2 *Heffalump and the toy hospital* (1989)

Hefferman series
Meynell, Laurence Walter
see **Hooky Hefferman series**

Heggerty Haggerty series
Lindsay, Elizabeth
1 *Heggerty Haggerty and the dreadful drought* (1980)
2 *Heggerty Haggerty and the Hallowe'en ghosts* (1984)
3 *Heggerty Haggerty and the magic medicine* (1984)
4 *Heggerty Haggerty and the day at the fair* (1984)
5 *Heggerty Haggerty and the treasure hunt* (1984)
6 *Heggerty Haggerty and the great running race* (1985)
7 *Heggerty Haggerty and the amazing loaf of bread* (1985)
Numbers 6 and 7 also published in one volume entitled *Heggerty Haggerty red storybook*, 1985
8 *Heggerty Haggerty and the day at the farm* (1985)
9 *Heggerty Haggerty and the flying saucer* (1985)
Numbers 8 and 9 also published in one volume entitled *Heggerty Haggerty yellow storybook*, 1985

Heidi series
This sequence has two authors
Spyri, Johanna
1 *Heidi* (1880)
Original edition entitled *Heidis Lehr und Wanderjahre*
Tritten, Charles
2 *Heidi grows up* (1938)
3 *Heidi's children* (1950)

Heimrich series
Lockridge, Frances
see **Inspector Merton Heimrich series**

Heiner and Elsie series
Hoberg, Marielis
1 *One summer on Majorca* (1955)
Original edition entitled *Heiner und Elsie auf Mallorca*
2 *Voyage to Africa* (1956)
Original edition entitled *Heiner und Elsie fahren nach Afrika*

Heinrich series
Fremd, Angelika
see **Inge Heinrich series**

Heiress series
Gellis, Roberta
1 *English heiress* (1980)
2 *Cornish heiress* (1981)
3 *Kent heiress* (1982)
4 *Fortune's bride* (1983)
5 *Woman's estate* (1984)

Heirs and assigns series
Cabell, James Branch
see **Conquest series**

Heirs of Saint Camber trilogy
Kurtz, Katherine
The second trilogy in the **World of the Second Kingdoms series**
1 *Harrowing of Gwynedd* (1989)
2 *King Javan's year* (1992)
3 *Bastard prince* (1994)

Heirs to Byzantium trilogy
Shwartz, Susan
1 *Byzantium's crown* (1987)
2 *Woman of flowers* (1987)
3 *Queensblade* (1988)

Heirs to Gnarlsmyre series
Jefferies, Mike
1 *Glitterspike Hall* (1989)
2 *Hall of whispers* (1990)

Hel trilogy
Drake, Asa
1 *Warrior witch of Hel* (1985)
2 *Death riders of Hel* (1986)
3 *Werebeasts of Hel* (1986)

Heldar series
Hamilton, Henrietta
see **Johnny and Sally Heldar series**

Helen and Dominic series
Odgers, Sally Farrell
1 *Another good friend* (1991)
2 *All the sea between* (1991)

Helen and Marmaduke series
Monkhouse, Allan
1 *My daughter Helen* (1922)
2 *Marmaduke* (1924)

Helen and Roger Mifflin series
Morley, Christopher
see **Roger and Helen Mifflin series**

Helen Bullock and Simon Bede series
Byfield, Barbara
see **Simon Bede and Helen Bullock series**

Helen Grant series
Douglas, Amanda Minnie
1 *Helen Grant's schooldays* (1903)
2 *Helen Grant's friends* (1904)
3 *Helen Grant at Aldred House* (1905)
4 *Helen Grant in college* (1906)
5 *Helen Grant, senior* (1907)
6 *Helen Grant, graduate* (1908)
7 *Helen Grant, teacher* (1909)
8 *Helen Grant's decision* (1910)
9 *Helen Grant's harvest year* (1911)

Helen Hamilton series
Hogarth, Grace Allen
1 *Funny guy* (1955)
2 *Sister for Helen* (1976)

Helen, Jean, Robbie and Sophie series
Dallas, Ruth
see **Jean, Robbie, Sophie and Helen series**

Helen Johnson series
Dewhurst, Eileen
1 *Whoever I am* (1972)
2 *Playing safe* (1985)

Helen Keremos series
Zaremba, Eve
1 *Reason to kill* (1978)
2 *Work for a million* (1986)

Helen Markam series
Dewhurst, Eileen
see **Helen Johnson series**

Helen Ritchie series
Deland, Margaret
1 *Awakening of Helen Ritchie* (1906)
2 *Iron woman* (1911)

Helen Roderick series
Campbell, Alice
1 *Click of the gate* (1932)
2 *Desire to kill* (1934)

Helen series
Carter, Dorothy
see **Wren Helen series**

Helen series
Gilchrist, Beth Bradford
1 *Helen Over-the-Wall* (1912)
The adventure with the fairy godmother
2 *Helen and the uninvited guests* (1913)
The adventure with the yellow goggles lady
3 *Helen and the Find-Out Club* (1914)
The adventure with the girl across the street
4 *Helen and the fifth cousins* (1915)
The adventure with Judith the hermit and some other people

Helen series
Graeme, Linda
1 *Helen, ballet student* (1955)
2 *Helen in musical comedy* (1957)
3 *Helen, television dancer* (1958)

Helena trilogy
Johnson, Pamela Hansford
1 *Too dear for my possessing* (1940)
2 *Avenue of stone* (1947)
3 *Summer to decide* (1948)

Helene series
Mallet-Joris, Francoise
1 *Illusionist* (1951)
Into the labyrinth
Original edition entitled *Le rempart des beguines*
2 *Red room* (1955)
Original edition entitled *La chambre rouge*

Helga and Hakon series
Haugaard, Erik Christian
see **Hakon and Helga series**

Helga Rolfe series
Chase, James Hadley
This sequence overlaps with the **Herman Radnitz series**
1 *Ace up my sleeve* (1971)
2 *Joker in the pack* (1975)
3 *I hold the four aces* (1977)
One volume edition entitled *Meet Helga Rolfe*, 1984

Helicopter series
Bellhouse, Lucy Wilered
1 *Helicopter children* (1956)
2 *Helicopter flies again* (1957)

Heliobas series
Corelli, Marie
1 *Romance of two worlds* (1886)
2 *Ardath* (1889)
The story of a dead self

Heller series
Hubbard, Lafayette Ronald
see **Mission earth series**

Kellerman, Dan
see **Jesse Heller series**
Roderus, Frank
see **Carl Heller series**

Heller series
Whitehead, David
1 *Heller* (1990)
2 *Heller in the Rockies* (1992)

Helliconia trilogy
Aldiss, Brian Wilson
1 *Helliconia spring* (1982)
2 *Helliconia summer* (1983)
3 *Helliconia winter* (1985)
One volume edition entitled *The Helliconia trilogy*, 1985

Hellier series
Cronin, Michael
see **James Hellier series**

Hello Kitty series
Harris, Robin
1 *Hello Kitty sleeps over* (1982)
2 *Hello Kitty's bedtime search* (1982)
Sequence continued under the pseudonym Sarah Bright
Bright, Sarah
3 *Hello Kitty's paper kiss* (1982)
4 *Hello Kitty's happy Christmas* (1984)
5 *Hello Kitty's early day* (1984)
6 *Hello Kitty's special present* (1984)
Companion volumes: *Hello Kitty on the go*, by Scott Sullivan, 1982, *Hello Kitty's button book*, by J M Gray, 1984, *Hello Kitty can count*, by Scott Sullivan, 1984

Hello series
Allen, Jane
1 *Hello to ponies* (1979)
2 *Hello to riding* (1980)

Hello series
Gordon, Mike
1 *Hello I'm Mouse* (1987)
2 *Hello I'm Bear* (1987)
3 *Hello I'm Frog* (1987)
4 *Hello I'm Rabbit* (1987)

Hell's Angels series
Cave, Peter
1 *Chopper* (1971)
2 *Mama* (1972)
3 *Run* (1972)
4 *Judas freaks* (1972)
5 *Rogue Angels* (1973)
6 *Speed freaks* (1973)
7 *White line fever* (1975)
8 *West Coast wildcatting* (1975)

Hell's Angels series
Norman, Mick
see **Gerry Vinson series**

Helm series
Fischer, Bruno
see **Ben Helm series**
Hamilton, Donald
see **Matt Helm series**
Slaughter, Jim
see **Boone Helm series**

Helmer series
Ibsen, Henrik
see **Nora Helmer series**

Helmsman series
Baldwin, Bill
1 *Helmsman* (1985)
2 *Galactic convoy* (1987)
3 *Trophy* (1990)
4 *Mercenaries* (1991)
5 *Defenders* (1992)
6 *Siege* (1994)

Helmuth series
Ellis, Edward Sylvester
see **Arthur Helmuth series**

Help me be good series
Berry, Joy
see **Let's talk about series**

Help series
Downing, Peggy
1 *Help, I'm shrinking!* (1986)
2 *Help, I'm drowning, and other emergencies* (1987)

Help your child to read series
Ahlberg, Allan
1 *Fast Frog* (1982)
2 *Silly sheep* (1982)
3 *Double ducks* (1982)
4 *Bad Bear* (1982)
5 *Poorly Pig* (1982)
6 *Rubber Rabbit* (1982)
Numbers 1-6 also published in one volume entitled *Fast Frog and friends*, 1984
7 *Hip-Hippo-Ray* (1983)
8 *King Kangaroo* (1983)
9 *Mister Wolf* (1983)
10 *Spider Spy* (1983)
11 *Tell-Tale Tiger* (1983)
12 *Travelling moose* (1983)

Helpless Annie series
Tuite, Hugh
1 *Helpless Annie* (1927)
2 *Helpless Annie's idears* (1928)

Helsing series
Mathewson, Joseph
see **Alicia von Helsing series**

Hemingway series
Heyer, Georgette
see **Inspector Hemingway series**
Maske, John
see **Clarence E Hemingway series**

Hemispheres series
Lake, David John
see **Breakout series**

Hemlock series
Trevanian
see **Jonathan Hemlock series**

Hemsworthy series
Courtney, Edith
see **Kit Hemsworthy series**

Hemyock series
Browne, Douglas Gordon
see **Major Maurice Hemyock series**

Henderson and Lawrence series
Pritchett, Ron
see **Buck Lawrence and Zeke Henderson series**

Henderson series
Barrington, Pamela
see **Inspector Henderson series**
Peel, Hazel Mary
see **Ann and Jim Henderson series**
Richardson, Dorothy Miller
see **Pilgrimage series**
Stowe, Harriet Beecher
see **Harry Henderson series**

Hendrik Van Kill series
Bayne, Spencer
1 *Murder recalls Van Kill* (1939)
2 *Turning sword* (1941)
3 *Agent extraordinary* (1942)

Hendry series
Berkley, Tom
see **Algernon Alexander Gunning Hendry series**
Lee, Benjamin
see **Mike and Bill Hendry series**

Henk Strydom series
Nortje, Peter Henry
1 *Wild goose summer* (1959)
Original edition entitled *Pennie ze vuur*
2 *Green ally* (1960)
Original edition entitled *Die groen ghoen*

Henlake series
Hinde, Thomas
1 *Village* (1966)
2 *High* (1968)

Hennessy and Keeps series
Bancroft, Tex
see **Angeltown Keeps and Doc Hennessy series**

Henniker-Haddon series
Avery, Gillian
see **Maria Henniken-Haddon series**

Hennings series
Breen, Jon Linn
see **Rachel Hennings series**

Henny series
Erlbach, Arlene
1 *Guys, dating and other disasters* (1987)
2 *Drop out blues* (1988)

Henri Bencolin series
Carr, John Dickson
1 *It walks by night* (1930)
2 *Castle Skull* (1931)
3 *Lost gallows* (1931)
4 *Corpse in the waxworks* (1932)
Waxworks murder
5 *Poison in jest* (1932)
6 *Four false weapons* (1937)
Henri Bencolin also appears in four stories in *The door to doom, and other detections*, 1980

Henri Castang series
Freeling, Nicolas
1 *Dressing of diamond* (1974)
2 *What are the bugles blowing for?* (1975)
Bugles blowing
3 *Lake isle* (1976)
Sabine
4 *Night lords* (1978)
5 *Castang's city* (1980)
6 *Wolfnight* (1982)
7 *Back of the North Wind* (1983)
8 *No part in your death* (1984)
9 *City solitary* (1985)
10 *Cold iron* (1986)
11 *Lady Macbeth* (1988)
12 *Not as far as Velma* (1989)

Henri Christophe series
Bourne, Peter
1 *Black saga* (1947)
Drums of destiny
2 *Black gold* (1964)

Henrietta and Nosey series
Pizer, Abigail
1 *Henrietta Goose* (1985)
2 *Nosey Gilbert* (1987)

Henrietta Chuffertrain series
Kruss, James
1 *Henrietta Chuffertrain* (1958)
Original edition entitled Henriette Bimmelbahn
2 *Holiday with Henrietta* (1967)

Henrietta Hen series
Judah, Aaron
1 *Adventures of Henrietta Hen* (1958)
2 *Henrietta in the snow* (1960)
3 *Henrietta in love* (1961)

Henrietta O'Dwyer Collins series
Hart, Carolyn Gimpel
1 *Dead Man's Island* (1993)
2 *Scandal in Fair Haven* (1994)

Henrietta series
Dennys, Joyce
1 *Henrietta's war* (1985)
News from the home front, 1939-1942
2 *Henrietta sees it through* (1986)
More news from the home front, 1942-1945

Henrietta series
Hale, Kathleen
1 *Henrietta the faithful hen* (1943)
2 *Henrietta's magic egg* (1973)

Henrietta series
Hoff, Syd
1 *Henrietta lays some eggs* (1977)
2 *Henrietta, circus star* (1977)
3 *Henrietta, the early bird* (1978)
4 *Henrietta goes to the fair* (1979)
5 *Henrietta's Halloween* (1980)
6 *Henrietta's Fourth of July* (1981)
7 *Happy birthday, Henrietta!* (1983)

Henrietta series
Rosen, Winifred
1 *Henrietta, the wild woman of Borneo* (1975)
2 *Henrietta and the day of the iguana* (1978)
3 *Henrietta and the gong from Hong Kong* (1981)

Henry Adams trilogy
Samuels, Ernest
1 *Young Henry Adams* (1948)
2 *Henry Adams, the middle years* (1958)
3 *Henry Adams, the major phase* (1964)
One volume revised and abridged edition entitled *Henry Adams*, 1989

Henry and Emily Bryce series
Scherf, Margaret
see **Emily and Henry Bryce series**

Henry and Emmy Tibbett series
Moyes, Patricia
1 *Dead men don't ski* (1958)
2 *Sunken sailor* (1961)
Down among the dead men
3 *Death on the agenda* (1962)
4 *Murder a la mode* (1963)
5 *Falling star* (1964)
6 *Johnny under ground* (1965)
7 *Murder fantastical* (1967)
8 *Death and the Dutch uncle* (1968)
9 *Who saw her die?* (1970)
Many deadly returns
10 *Season of snows and mists* (1971)
11 *Curious affair of the third dog* (1973)
12 *Black widower* (1975)
13 *To kill a coconut* (1977)
Coconut killings
14 *Who is Simon Warwick?* (1978)
15 *Angel death* (1980)
16 *Six-letter word for death* (1983)
17 *Night ferry to death* (1985)
18 *Black girl, white girl* (1990)
19 *Twice in a blue moon* (1993)

Henry and Jane Ellis series
Collin, Paul Ries
1 *Parcel for Henry* (1970)
2 *Up Pepper Alley, down Goose Lane* (1971)
3 *Calling bridge* (1976)

Henry and Julia Gresham trilogy
Avery, Gillian
see **Julia and Henry Gresham trilogy**

Henry and Mudge series
Rylant, Cynthia
1 *Henry and Mudge* (1987)
2 *Henry and Mudge in puddle trouble* (1987)
3 *Henry and Mudge in the green time* (1987)
4 *Henry and Mudge under the yellow moon* (1987)
5 *Henry and Mudge in the sparkle days* (1988)
6 *Henry and mudge and the forever sea* (1989)
7 *Henry and Mudge get the cold shivers* (1989)
8 *Henry and Mudge and the happy cat* (1990)
9 *Henry and Mudge and the bedtime thumps* (1991)
10 *Henry and Mudge take the big test* (1991)
11 *Henry and Mudge and the long weekend* (1992)
12 *Henry and Mudge and the wild wind* (1992)
13 *Henry and Mudge and the careful cousin* (1994)

Henry and Norman Bones series
Wilson, Anthony Clifford
see **Norman and Henry Bones series**

Henry and Susannah Kable series
Whittaker, June Lovina
1 *Raking of the embers* (1981)
2 *Flame in the morning* (1983)

Henry and Voula series
Stewart, Maureen
1 *Henry and Voula* (1989)
Off-beat love story
2 *Henry goes green* (1990)
3 *Please write back* (1990)
More letters from Henry and Voula

Henry Arthur Fielding series
Sharp, David
see **Professor Henry Arthur Fielding series**

Henry Bear series
McPhail, David Michael
1 *Henry Bear's park* (1976)
2 *Stanley, Henry Bear's friend* (1979)

Henry Beaufort series
Baker, James
see **Cardinal Henry Beaufort series**

Henry Beaumont series
Atkins, Meg Elizabeth
see **Inspector Henry Beaumont series**

Henry Calverly series
Merwin, Samuel
1 *Temperamental Henry* (1917)
2 *Henry is twenty* (1918)
3 *Passionate pilgrim* (1919)

Henry Chinaski series
Bukowski, Charles
1 *Ham on rye* (1982)
2 *Post office* (1971)
3 *Hollywood* (1989)
Also some stories featuring Henry Chinaski in *Hot water music*, 1983

Henry Doight series
Symons, Beryl
see **Inspector Henry Doight series**

Henry Frost series
Bell, Josephine
see **Doctor Henry Frost series**

Henry Gamadge series
This sequence has two authors
Daly, Elizabeth
1 *Unexpected night* (1940)
2 *Deadly nightshade* (1940)
3 *Murders in volume two* (1941)
4 *House without the door* (1942)
5 *Evidence of things seen* (1943)
6 *Nothing can rescue me* (1943)
7 *Arrow pointing nowhere* (1944)
Murder listens in
8 *Book of the dead* (1944)
9 *Any shape or form* (1945)
10 *Somewhere in the house* (1946)
11 *Wrong way down* (1946)
Shroud for a lady
12 *Night walk* (1947)
13 *Book of the lion* (1948)
14 *And dangerous to know* (1949)
15 *Death and letters* (1950)
16 *Book of the crime* (1951)
Boylan, Eleanor
17 *Working murder* (1989)
18 *Murder observed* (1990)

Henry Garrett series
Larsen, Gaylord D
1 *Kilbourne connection* (1980)
2 *Trouble crossing the Pyrenees* (1983)

Henry Golightly series
Pike, Geoffrey
1 *Henry Golightly* (1974)
2 *Golightly adrift* (1977)

Henry Hare series
Clewes, Dorothy
1 *Henry Hare's boxing match* (1950)
2 *Henry Hare's earthquake* (1950)
3 *Henry Hare, painter and decorator* (1951)
4 *Henry Hare and the kidnapping of Selina Squirrel* (1951)

Henry Harrison Conroy and Judge Van Treece series
Tuttle, Wilbur Coleman
1 *Henry the sheriff* (1936)
Sheriff of Tonto Town
2 *Wild Horse Valley* (1938)
3 *Ghost guns* (1957)
4 *Shame of Arizona* (1957)
5 *Danger trail* (1958)
6 *Silver buckshot* (1959)
7 *Galloping gold* (1961)

Henry Holland series
Andover, Henry
1 *Death on the pack road* (1931)
2 *Dennisdale tragedy* (1936)

Henry Hollins series
Hall, Willis
1 *Summer of the dinosaur* (1977)
Henry Hollins and the dinosaur
2 *Last vampire* (1982)
3 *Inflatable shop* (1984)
4 *Dragon days* (1984)
5 *Doctor Jekyll and Mister Hollins* (1988)

Henry Huggins series
Cleary, Beverly
1 *Henry Huggins* (1950)
2 *Henry and Beezus* (1952)
3 *Henry and Ribsy* (1954)
4 *Beezus and Ramona* (1955)
5 *Henry and the paper route* (1957)
6 *Henry and the clubhouse* (1962)

Henry Hyland West series
Nazel, Joseph
see **Iceman series**

Henry I trilogy
Dymoke, Juliet
1 *Of the Ring of Earls* (1970)
2 *Henry of the high rock* (1971)
3 *Lion's legacy* (1974)

Henry II series
Butler, Margaret
1 *Lion of England* (1973)
2 *Lion of justice* (1975)
3 *This turbulent priest* (1977)

Henry II trilogy
Norman, Diana
1 *Morning gift* (1985)
2 *Fitzempress' law* (1980)
3 *King of the last days* (1981)

Henry James series
Edel, Leon
1 *Untried years, 1843-1870* (1953)
2 *Conquest of London, 1870-1883* (1962)
3 *Middle years, 1884-1894* (1963)
4 *Treacherous years, 1895-1901* (1969)
5 *Master, 1901-1916* (1972)

Henry, King of France series
Mann, Heinrich
1 *King Wren* (1935)
Young Henry of Navarre
Original edition entitled Die Jugend des Konigs Henri Quatre
2 *Last days of Henri Quatre* (1938)
Original edition entitled *Die Vollendung des Konigs Henri Quatre*
One volume edition entitled *Henri Quatre, King of France*, 1938

Henry Marquis series
Post, Melville Davisson
see **Sir Henry Marquis series**

Henry Maxwell series
Graeme, Bruce
1 *Blind date for a private eye* (1969)
2 *D notice* (1974)

Henry Maxwell series
Sheldon, Charles Monroe
1 *In His steps* (1896)
Dramatization published in 1912
2 *Jesus is here* (1914)
Reprinted from the *Christian Herald*
3 *In His steps to-day* (1921)
A dialogue

Henry Merrivale series
Dickson, Carter
see **Sir Henry Merrivale series**

Henry Morane series
Farrington, Robert
1 *Killing of Richard the Third* (1971)
2 *Tudor agent* (1974)

Henry Peckover series
Kenyon, Michael
see **Inspector Henry Peckover series**

Henry Poggioli series
Stribling, Thomas Sigismund
see **Professor Henry Poggioli series**

Henry Pratt series
Nobbs, David
1 *Second from last in the sack race* (1983)
2 *Pratt of the Argus* (1988)

Henry Prince series
Gregg, Cecil Freeman
1 *Ten black pearls* (1935)
Murder of Estelle Cantor
2 *Henry Prince in action* (1936)
3 *Return of Henry Prince* (1943)

Henry Pym series
Burley, William John
see **Doctor Henry Pym series**

Henry Reed series
Robertson, Keith
1 *Henry Reed, Inc.* (1958)
2 *Henry Reed's journey* (1963)
3 *Henry Reed's baby-sitting service* (1966)
4 *Henry Reed's big show* (1970)
5 *Henry Reed's think tank* (1986)

Henry Scruggs series
Conroy, Richard Timothy
1 *Smithsonian snafu* (1992)
2 *Mister Smithson's bones* (1993)
3 *Old ways in the new world* (1994)

Henry series
Barry, Joe
see **Rush Henry series**

Henry series
Joynson, Cecile
1 *In spite of Henry* (1958)
2 *In search of Henry* (1960)
3 *Yes, Henry* (1965)

Henry series
Keller, Holly
1 *Too big* (1983)
2 *Henry's picnic* (1985)

Henry series
Peppe, Rodney
1 *Henry's exercises* (1975)
Revised edition 1978
2 *Henry's garden* (1975)
3 *Henry's sunbathe* (1975)
Revised edition 1978
4 *Henry's aeroplane* (1978)
5 *Henry eats out* (1978)
6 *Henry's toy cupboard* (1978)
7 *Hello Henry* (1984)
8 *Hurrah for Henry!* (1984)

Henry series
Quackenbush, Robert Mead
1 *Henry's awful mistake* (1980)
2 *Henry's important date* (1981)
3 *Henry goes west* (1982)
4 *Henry babysits* (1983)
5 *Henry's world tour* (1992)

Henry series
Sharkey, Jack
see **George Herbert Henry series**

Henry series
Taylor, Mark
1 *Henry the explorer* (1966)
2 *Henry explores the jungle* (1988)
3 *Henry the castaway* (1970)
4 *Henry explores the mountains* (1975)

Henry series
Thatcher, Dora
1 *Henry the helicopter* (1956)
2 *Henry to the rescue* (1959)
3 *Henry the hero* (1960)
4 *Hovering with Henry* (1961)
5 *Henry in the news* (1963)
6 *Henry's busy winter* (1964)
7 *Henry joins the police* (1966)
8 *Henry and the astronaut* (1968)
9 *Henry and the traction engine* (1970)
10 *Henry in the mountains* (1970)
11 *Henry in Iceland* (1973)
12 *Henry on safari* (1975)
Companion picture books: *Henry's exciting flight*, 1961, *Henry's mountain adventure*, 1963, and, *Henry goes to town*, 1964

Henry series
Tippett, James Sterling
1 *Henry and the garden* (1936)
2 *Stories about Henry* (1936)
3 *Henry and his friends* (1939)
Co-author: Melvern J Barker
4 *Here and there with Henry* (1943)
Revised entitled including a special section entitled *A trip to Texas*, 1947

Henry series
Weiss, Mike
see **Ben Henry series**
Wouk, Herman
see **Commander Pug Henry series**

Henry Sontag series
Tuttle, Wilbur Coleman
see **Sad Sontag series**

Henry Spearman series
Jevons, Marshall
1 *Murder at the margin* (1978)
2 *Fatal equilibrium* (1985)

Henry Tyson series
Kummer, Frederic Arnold
see **Judge Henry Tyson series**

Henry V series
Rofheart, Martha
1 *Cry God for Harry* (1972)
Fortune made his sword
2 *Cry God for Glendower* (1973)
Glendower country

Henry VII series
Nichols, Wallace Bertram
1 *Wonder for wise men* (1930)
2 *Torryzany* (1931)

Henry W Wiggen series
Harris, Mark
1 *Southpaw* (1953)
2 *Bang the drug slowly* (1956)
3 *Ticket for a seamstick* (1957)
4 *It looked like for ever* (1979)

Henry Wilson series
Cole, George Douglas Howard
see **Superintendent Henry Wilson series**

Henry Wilt series
Sharpe, Tom
1 *Wilt* (1984)
2 *Wilt alternative* (1980)
3 *Wilt on high* (1985)

Heorot series
Niven, Larry
1 *Legacy of Heorot* (1987)
Co-authors: Jerry Pournelle and Steven Barnes
2 *Dragons of Heorot* (1994)
Co-authors: Jerry Pournelle and Steven Barnes

Hepburn series
Gorell, Ronald Gorell Barnes
see **Inspector Maurice Hepburn series**

Her father's sins series
Cox, Josephine
1 *Her father's sins* (1987)
2 *Let loose the tigers* (1988)

Heracles trilogy
Leslie, Richard
1 *Trouble in the wind* (1984)
2 *Fateful dawn* (1984)
3 *Under a shrieking sky* (1984)

Herald Childe series
Farmer, Philip Jose
see **Exorcism series**

Herald-Mage trilogy
Lackey, Mercedes
see **Last Herald-Mage trilogy**

Heralds of Valdemar trilogy
Lackey, Mercedes
1 *Arrows of the queen* (1987)
2 *Arrow's flight* (1987)
3 *Arrow's fall* (1988)

Her-Bak series
Schwaller de Lubicz, Isha
see **Homo sapiens series**

Herbert Broom series
Hurt, Freda Mary
see **Inspector Herbert Broom series**

Herbert series
Cutler, Ivor
1 *Herbert the chicken* (1984)
2 *Herbert the elephant* (1984)

Herbert series
Wilson, Hazel
1 *Herbert* (1950)
2 *Herbert's space trip* (1965)

Herbert Somerville series
Yonge, Charlotte Mary
see **Lady Herbert Somerville series**

Herbie Jones series
Kline, Suzy
1 *Herbie Jones* (1985)
2 *What's the matter with Herbie Jones?* (1986)
3 *Herbie Jones and the class gift* (1987)
4 *Herbie Jones and the monster ball* (1988)
5 *Herbie Jones and Hamburger Head* (1989)
7 *Herbie Jones reader's theater* (1992)
8 *Herbie Jones and the dark attic* (1992)
9 *Herbie Jones and the birthday showdown* (1993)

Herbie Kruger series
Gardner, John Edmund
1 *Nostradamus traitor* (1978)
2 *Garden of weapons* (1980)
3 *Quiet dogs* (1982)
4 *Secret houses* (1987)
5 *Secret families* (1989)

Herbie series
This sequence has three authors
Cebulash, Mel
1 *Love Bug* (1969)
2 *Herbie rides again* (1974)
Crume, Vic
3 *Herbie goes to Monte Carlo* (1977)
Claro, Joe
4 *Herbie goes bananas* (1980)
5 *Herbie the matchmaker* (1982)

Hercule Poirot series
Christie, Agatha
1 *Mysterious affair at Styles* (1920)
2 *Murder on the links* (1923)
3 *Poirot investigates* (1924)
Short stories
4 *Murder of Roger Ackroyd* (1926)
5 *Big four* (1927)
6 *Mystery of the Blue Train* (1928)
7 *Peril at End House* (1932)
8 *Lord Edgware dies* (1933)
Thirteen at dinner
9 *Murder on the Orient Express* (1934)
Murder in the Calais coach
10 *Murder in three acts* (1934)
Three act tragedy
11 *Death in the clouds* (1935)
Death in the air
12 *ABC murders* (1936)
Alphabet murders
13 *Murder in Mesopotamia* (1936)
14 *Cards on the table* (1936)
15 *Dumb witness* (1937)
Poirot loses a client
Murder at Littlegreen House
Mystery at Littlegreen House
16 *Death on the Nile* (1937)
17 *Murder in the mews, and three other Poirot cases* (1937)
Dead man's mirror, and other stories
Three novelettes entitled *Dead man's mirror, Murder in the mews, Triangle at Rhodes*
18 *Appointment with death* (1938)
19 *Hercule Poirot's Christmas* (1938)
Murder for Christmas
Holiday for murder
20 *Sad cypress* (1940)
21 *One, two, buckle my shoe* (1940)
Patriotic murders
Overdose of death
22 *Evil under the sun* (1941)
23 *Five little pigs* (1942)
Murder in retrospect
24 *Hollow* (1946)
Murder after hours
25 *Labours of Hercules* (1947)
Short stories
26 *Taken at the flood* (1948)
There is a tide
27 *Mrs McGinty's dead* (1952)
Blood will tell
28 *After the funeral* (1953)
Funerals are fatal
Murder at the gallop
29 *Hickory, dickory, dock* (1955)
Hickory, dickory, death
30 *Dead man's folly* (1956)
31 *Cat among the pigeons* (1959)
32 *Adventure of the Christmas pudding, and a selection of entrees* (1960)
Includes one Miss Marple story
33 *Clocks* (1963)
34 *Third girl* (1966)
35 *Hallowe'en party* (1969)
36 *Elephants can remember* (1972)
37 *Poirot's early cases* (1974)
Hercule poirot's early cases
38 *Curtain* (1975)

Omnibus volumes: *Hercule Poirot's casebook*, 1984, *The underdog, and other stories*, 1951; ; short stories published in pamphlet form: *Poirot and the regatta mystery*, 1943, *Poirot on holiday*, 1943, *Poirot knows the murderer*, 1946, *Poirot lends a hand*, 1946; also stories featuring Poirot in *The regatta mystery*, 1939, one story in *Witness for the prosecution*, 1948, three stories in *The mousetrap, and other stories*, 1950, four stories in *Double sin, and other stories*, 1961; companion volume: *The pale horse*, 1961; see also the **Mrs Ariadne Oliver series** which overlaps with many of the volumes in this sequence; companion volume: *The life and times of Hercule Poirot*, by Anne Hart, 1990

Hercule Renard series
Audemars, Pierre
1 *Hercule and the gods* (1944)
2 *Temptations of Hercule* (1945)
3 *Obligations of Hercule* (1947)
4 *Confession of Hercule* (1947)

Herdman family series
Robinson, Barbara
1 *Best Christmas pageant ever* (1972)
2 *Worst best school year ever* (1994)

Here come series
Goudey, Alice Edwards
1 *Here come the bears!* (1954)
2 *Here come the deer!* (1955)
3 *Here come the elephants!* (1955)
4 *Here come the lions!* (1956)
5 *Here come the whales!* (1956)
6 *Here come the seals!* (1957)
7 *Here come the beavers!* (1957)
8 *Here come the wild dogs!* (1958)
9 *Here come the raccoons!* (1959)
10 *Here come the bees!* (1960)
11 *Here come the dolphins!* (1961)
12 *Here come the squirrels!* (1962)
13 *Here come the cottontails!* (1965)

Heredity series
Holmes, Oliver Wendell
1 *Elsie Venner* (1861)
A romance of destiny
2 *Guardian angel* (1867)

Here's the church series
Watkins, Peter
1 *Here's the church* (1980)
2 *Here's the year* (1981)
3 *Here are the people* (1984)

Heritage of Shannara series
Brooks, Terry
1 *Scions of Shannara* (1990)
2 *Druid of Shannara* (1991)
3 *Elf Queen of Shannara* (1992)
4 *Talismans of Shannara* (1993)

Heritage series
Bronte, Louisa
see **American dynasty series**

Heritage series
Fidler, Kathleen
1 *Tales of the North Country* (1952)
2 *Tales of London* (1953)
3 *Tales of the Midlands* (1954)
4 *Tales of Scotland* (1956)
5 *Look to the West* (1957)
Tales of Liverpool
6 *Tales of the Islands* (1959)
7 *Tales of pirates and castaways* (1960)
8 *Tales of the West Country* (1961)
9 *True tales of treasure* (1962)
10 *Tales of the South Country* (1962)
11 *True tales of escapes* (1965)
12 *True tales of mystery* (1967)
13 *True tales of castles* (1969)

Heritage series
Hummel, George Frederick
1 *Heritage* (1935)
2 *Tradition* (1936)

Heritage universe series
Sheffield, Charles
1 *Summertide* (1990)
2 *Divergence* (1991)

Herman Brierly series
Levinrew, Will
see **Professor Herman Brierly series**

Herman Jozef series
Rooke, Daphne
1 *Double Ex* (1971)
2 *Horse of his own* (1976)

Herman Radnitz series
Chase, James Hadley
This sequence overlaps with the **Helga Rolfe series**
1 *This is for real* (1965)
2 *Believed violent* (1968)
3 *Whiff of money* (1969)
4 *You're dead without money* (1972)

Herman series
Unger, Jim
Comic strips
1 *Apart from a little dampness, Herman, how's everything?* (1975)
2 *And you wonder, Herman, why I never want to go to Italian restaurants* (1977)
3 *Latest Herman* (1981)
4 *Herman Sundays* (1982)
5 *Herman, you were a much stronger man on our first honeymoon* (1983)
6 *Herman and the extraterrestrials* (1983)
7 *Herman out to lunch* (1983)
8 *Herman, M.D.* (1983)
9 *Where's the kids, Herman?* (1984)
10 *People are starting to complain about too much violence on cave walls* (1984)
11 *Herman, dinner's served, as soon as the smoke clears!* (1985)
12 *Any other complaints, Herman?* (1985)
13 *What are we up to, Herman?* (1985)
14 *Now what are you up to, Herman?* (1985)

15 *It's called Midnight Surrender, Herman* (1986)
16 *Feeling run doqwn again, Herman!* (1986)
17 *Cat's got your teeth again* (1986)
18 *Herman, you can get in the bathroom now* (1987)
19 *They're gonna settle out of court, Herman* (1989)
20 *Herman over the wall* (1990)
21 *She just wants the hot wax!* (1991)

Herman the helper series
Kraus, Robert
1 *Herman the helper lends a hand* (1981)
2 *Herman the helper cleans up* (1981)

Herman treasury series
Unger, Jim
Comic strips
1 *First treasury of Herman* (1979)
2 *Second Herman treasury* (1980)
3 *Herman, the third treasury* (1982)
4 *Herman, the fourth treasury* (1984)
5 *Herman treasury five* (1986)
6 *Herman, the sixth treasury* (1988)
7 *Herman over the wall* (1990)
8 *Herman eight* (1992)

Hermann Kohler and Jean-Louis Saint-Cyr series
Janes, Joseph Robert
see **Jean-Louis Saint-Cyr and Hermann Kohler series**

Hermione Lester series
Hichens, Robert
1 *Call of the blood* (1906)
2 *Spirit in prison* (1908)

Hermoine series
Cooke, Kaz
see **Modern girl series**

Herne the Hunter series
McLaglen, John J
This pseudonym is used by John Barton Harvey and Laurence James as indicated against each title
1 *White death* (1976) [James]
2 *River of blood* (1976) [Harvey]
3 *Black widow* (1977) [James]
4 *Shadow of the vulture* (1977) [Harvey]
5 *Apache squaw* (1977) [James]
6 *Death in gold* (1977) [Harvey]
7 *Death rites* (1978) [James]
8 *Cross-draw* (1978) [Harvey]
9 *Massacre!* (1978) [James]
10 *Vigilante!* (1979) [Harvey]
11 *Silver threads* (1979) [James]
12 *Sun dance* (1980) [Harvey]
13 *Billy the Kid* (1980) [Harvey]
14 *Death school* (1980) [James]
15 *Till death* (1980) [Harvey]
16 *Geronimo* (1981) [James]
17 *Hanging* (1981) [James]
18 *Dying ways* (1982) [Harvey]
19 *Bloodline* (1982) [James]
20 *Hearts of gold* (1982) [Harvey]
21 *Pony express* (1983) [James]
22 *Wild blood* (1983) [Harvey]
23 *Texas massacre* (1984) [James]
24 *Last hurrah!* (1984) [James]

Hero Haggity series
Overgard, William
1 *Pieces of a Hero* (1973)
2 *Once more the Hero* (1974)

Hero series
Gallico, Paul
see **Alexander Hero series**
Kelly, Bill
see **Pepperoni Hero series**
Leigh, Roberta
see **Mister Hero series**

Hero series
Peyton, K M
1 *Prove yourself a hero* (1977)
2 *Free rein* (1983)
Last ditch

Hero series
Welsh, Ken
1 *Hail for the hero!* (1979)
2 *Fear for the hero!* (1981)

Herod family series
Perowne, Stewart
1 *Life and times of Herod the Great* (1956)
2 *Later Herods* (1958)
The political background of the *New Testament*

Heroes in hell series
This sequence has four authors
Morris, Janet Ellen
1 *Heroes in hell* (1986)
2 *Rebels in hell* (1986)
3 *Gates of hell* (1986)
Co-author: Carolyn Janice Cherryh
4 *Masters in hell* (1988)
5 *Kings in hell* (1987)
Co-author: Carolyn Janice Cherryh
6 *Angels in hell* (1987)
7 *Crusaders in hell* (1987)
Cherryh, Carolyn Janice
8 *Legions of hell* (1987)
Morris, Janet Ellen
9 *War in hell* (1988)
10 *Little Helliad* (1988)
Co-author: Chris Morris
11 *Explorers in hell* (1989)
Co-author: David Drake
12 *Prophets in hell* (1989)
Companion volume: Basileus, by Janet Morris and Caroline Janice Cherryh, published in *Rhialto the Marvellous*, by Jack Vance, 1985

Heroes, Inc. series
Crocco, Kyle
1 *Heroes, Inc.* (1991)
2 *Heroes wanted* (1991)

Heroes of the misty isle series
Dengler, Sandy
1 *Dublin crossing* (1993)
Romance and adventyure in the Viking era
2 *Shamrock shore* (1994)
In the footsteps of Patrick through the hills of Erin
3 *Emerald sea* (1994)
The quest of Brendan the Navigator

Heroes series
Eckhardt, Kurt
1 *Heroes without honour* (1980)
2 *Stalingrad heroes* (1980)
3 *Heroes of Cassino* (1980)
4 *Achtung, Normandy!* (1981)

Heron family series
Belle, Pamela
1 *Moon in the water* (1983)
2 *Chains of fate* (1984)
3 *Alathea* (1985)
4 *Lodestar* (1987)

Heron Murmur series
Harvester, Simon
1 *Chinese hammer* (1960)
2 *Troika* (1962)
Flying horse

Heron saga series
Oldfield, Pamela
1 *Rich earth* (1980)
2 *This ravished land* (1980)
3 *After the storm* (1981)
4 *White water* (1982)

Heron series
Brogan, Colm
see **Patrick Heron series**
Roberts, Constance Evelyn
see **Pikey's Steep series**

Heron series
Treadgold, Mary
1 *Heron ride* (1962)
2 *Return to the Heron* (1963)

Heron series
Verner, Gerald
see **Felix Heron series**

Heron's Neck series
Ladd, Elizabeth
see **Meg of Heron's Neck series**

Herries ancestors series
Walpole, Hugh
1 *Bright pavilions* (1940)
2 *Katherine Christian* (1943)
Unfinished novel

Herries saga series
Walpole, Hugh
1 *Rogue Herries* (1930)
2 *Judith Paris* (1931)
3 *Fortress* (1932)
4 *Vanessa* (1933)

Herring series
Torrie, Malcolm
see **Timothy Herring series**

Herrivell series
Bentley, John
see **Sir Richard Herrivell series**

Hervey Russell series
Jameson, Storm
1 *Farewell night, welcome day* (1939)
Captain's wife
2 *That was yesterday* (1932)
3 *Company parade* (1934)
4 *Love in winter* (1935)
5 *None turn back* (1936)
6 *Journey of Mary Hervey Russell* (1945)

Hervey series
Jameson, Storm
see **Triumph of time series**

Hesketh and Jane Oliphant series
Newby, Percy Howard
1 *Step to silence* (1952)
2 *Retreat* (1953)

Hester Billiter series
Blaker, Richard
1 *Here lies a most beautiful lady* (1935)
2 *But beauty vanishes* (1936)

Hester Prynne series
This sequence has two authors
Bigsby, Christopher
1 *Hester* (1994)
Hawthorne, Nathaniel
2 *Scarlet letter* (1850)

Hester trilogy
Baird, Jean Katherine
1 *Coming of Hester* (1909)
2 *Hester's counterpart* (1910)
A story of boarding school life
3 *Hester's wage-earning* (1912)

Heston series
Macnaghten, Patrick
see **Jack Heston series**

Hestviken series
Undset, Sigrid
see **Master of Hestviken series**

Hetherege series
Bernard, Robert
see **Millicent Hetherege series**

Hetta Atherley series
Bridge, Ann
1 *Portuguese escape* (1958)
2 *Episode at Toledo* (1966)

Hetty trilogy
Kilpatrick, Florence Antoinette
1 *Wild Cat Hetty* (1927)
2 *Hetty married* (1928)
3 *Hetty's son* (1929)

Hewes-Bradford series
Hamilton, Adam
see **Peacemaker series**

Hewison series
Douglas, G A H
see **Rab Hewison series**

Hewitt series
Morrison, Arthur
see **Martin Hewitt series**
Reese, John
see **Jefferson Hewitt series**

Heydon series
Du Jardin, Rosamond
see **Tobey and Midge Heydon series**

Heynitz series
Le Queux, William
see **Otto von Heynitz series**

Heysen series
Hamilton, Ian Sydney
see **Pete Heysen series**

Heysten series
Ammers-Kuller, Jo van
see **Jenny Heysten series**

Hi and Lois series
Walker, Mort
Illustrated by Dik Browne
Cartoon strips
1 *Home, sweat home* (1983)
2 *Spring dreams* (1983)
3 *Hi honey, I'm home* (1984)
4 *Is dinner ready?* (1984)
5 *Mom, where's my homework?* (1984)
6 *Saturday night fever* (1984)
7 *How do you spell dad?* (1985)
8 *Trixie a la mode* (1986)
9 *Good housekeeping* (1986)
10 *Dawg day afternoon* (1986)
11 *Sleepbusters* (1987)
12 *Say cheese* (1987)
13 *House calls* (1988)
14 *Modern chaos* (1989)
15 *Croquet for a day* (1989)
16 *Couch potatos!* (1990)
17 *Wheels of fortune* (1990)
18 *Happy campers* (1990)
19 *Say cheese* (1991)
20 *Mister Popularity!* (1991)
21 *Play ball!* (1991)
22 *Up two late* (1991)
23 *Baby talk* (1991)

Hickey trilogy
Kuhlken, Ken
see **Tom Hickey trilogy**

Hicks series
Hicks, D L
see **Milton Hicks series**

Hidden journey series
Chard, Brigid
1 *Hidden journey* (1976)
2 *Shepherd's crook* (1977)

Hidden life series
This sequence has two authors
Schwartz, David Martin
Photographs by Dwight Kuhn
1 *Hidden life of the pond* (1988)
2 *Hidden life of the forest* (1988)
3 *Hidden life of the meadow* (1988)
Wiewandt, Thomas
4 *Hidden life of the desert* (1990)

Hidden meanings series
Allen, Charlotte Vale
1 *Hidden meanings* (1976)
2 *Another kind of magic* (1977)

Hidden people series
Miller, Leo Edward
1 *Hidden people* (1920)
Story of a search for Incan treasure
2 *In the tiger's lair* (1921)

Hiero Desteen series
Lanier, Sterling Edmund
1 *Hiero's journey* (1973)
2 *Unforsaken Hiero* (1983)
One volume edition entitled *Hiero Desteen*, 1984

Hieronymous Bosch series
Connelly, Michael
see **Harry Bosch series**

Higby series
Heuman, William
see **Horace higby series**

Higgins series
Darlington, William Aubrey
see **Alf Higgins series**
Davis, Means
see **Matthew Higgins series**
Gregg, Cecil Freeman
see **Inspector Cuthbert Higgins series**

Higgs series
Butler, Samuel
see **Erewhon series**

High Chaparral series
This sequence has three authors; based on a television series
Sotona, Wayne
1 *Hell and high water* (1968)
Friend, Ed
2 *Coyote gold* (1968)
Frazee, Steve
3 *Apache way* (1969)

High Fell series
Brown, Alfred John
Reminiscences of life as a hotelkeeper
1 *I bought a hotel* (1949)
2 *Farewell High Fell* (1952)

High Hallack series
Norton, Andre
1 *Crystal gryphon* (1972)
2 *Spell of the Witch World* (1972)
3 *Year of the unicorn* (1965)
4 *Jargoon pard* (1974)
5 *Gryphon in glory* (1981)
6 *Gryphon's eyrie* (1984)
Co-author: Ann Carol Crispin

High inquest series
Sucharitkul, Somtow
see **Chronicles of the high inquest series**

High point series
Bunting, Eve
1 *Pitcher to center field* (1974)
2 *Surfing country* (1975)
3 *Springboard to summer* (1975)

High seas fleet series
Humble, Richard
1 *Hitler's high seas fleet* (1971)
2 *Japanese high seas fleet* (1973)

High treason series
Upward, Allen
1 *High treason* (1903)
2 *Romance of politics* (1904)
The fourth conquest of England

Highcliff series
Little, Sylvia
1 *New school at Highcliff* (1951)
2 *Highcliff, top of the form* (1952)
3 *Puzzles at Highcliff* (1960)
4 *Highcliff on tour* (1960)

Highclyffe Hall series
Brandewyne, Rebecca
1 *Upon a moon-dark moor* (1988)
2 *Across a starlit sea* (1989)

Highland line series
Frere, Richard
1 *Maxwell's ghost* (1976)
An epilogue to Gavin Maxwell's **Camusfearna trilogy**
2 *Beyond the Highland line* (1984)

Highland maid series
Swan, Annie Shepherd
1 *Maid of the isles* (1924)
2 *Macleod's wife* (1924)

Highland quest series
Milroy, Clarita
1 *Highland quest* (1956)
2 *Secret of the caves* (1857)

Highland series
Leigh, Margaret Mary
Autobiography
1 *Highland homespun* (1936)
2 *Harvest of the moor* (1937)
3 *My kingdom for a horse* (1939)
4 *Spade among the rushes* (1949)
5 *Fruit in the seed* (1952)

Highland series
Mackenzie, Compton
1 *Monarch of the Glen* (1941)
2 *Keep the Home Guard turning* (1943)
3 *Whisky galore* (1947)
Tight little island
4 *Hunting the fairies* (1949)
5 *Rival monster* (1952)
6 *Ben Nevis goes east* (1954)
7 *Rockets galore* (1957)
8 *Stolen soprano* (1965)

Highland vet series
Stevenson, Robert
Memoirs
1 *Highland vet* (1963)
2 *Vets rush in* (1977)
3 *Vets rush out* (1979)
4 *Vet in Tibet* (1981)

Highlands series
Tarrant, Elizabeth
1 *Summer term at Highlands* (1949)
2 *New girl at Highlands* (1950)
3 *Lodgers at Highlands* (1950)
4 *Amazing affair at Highlands* (1951)

Highlands youth series
Thomson, David
1 *Nairn in darkness and light* (1987)
Childhood in the 1920s
2 *Woodbrook* (1974)

High-low mysteries series
Christian, Mary Blount
1 *Deadline for danger* (1982)
2 *Dead man in Catfish Bay* (1985)
3 *Mystery at Camp Triumph* (1986)

Highroad trilogy
Rasmussen, Alis A
1 *Passage of stars* (1990)
2 *Revolution's shore* (1990)
3 *Price of ransom* (1990)

High-tech world series
Skurzynski, Gloria
see **Your high-tech world series**

Highway series
Weston, Garnett
1 *Murder in haste* (1935)
Death never forgets
2 *Dead man are dangerous* (1937)
3 *Undertaker dies* (1940)

Hilary and Bob Dean series
Henry, Margaret
see **Bob and Hilary Dean series**

Hilary Brand series
Brand, Hilary
1 *News girl* (1963)
2 *Brand T* (1964)
3 *Peak of frenzy* (1964)
4 *All, or something* (1965)
5 *Flair for affairs* (1966)
6 *Strictly wild* (1966)
7 *Running scared* (1966)

Hilary Dunsany Bailey and Hilea Bailey series
Bailey, Hilea
see **Hilea Bailey and Hilary Dunsany Bailey series**

Hilary Quayle series
Kaye, Marvin
1 *Lively game of death* (1972)
2 *Grand Ole Opry murders* (1974)
3 *Bullets for Macbeth* (1976)
4 *Laurel and Hardy murders* (1977)
5 *Soap opera slaughters* (1982)

Hilary series
Ellis, Vivian
1 *Hilary's tune* (1960)
2 *Hilary's holidays* (1961)

Hilary Tamar series
Caudwell, Sarah
see **Professor Hilary Tamar series**

Hilda Adams series
Rinehart, Mary Roberts
see **Nurse Hilda Adams series**

Hilda and Eustace Cherrington trilogy
Hartley, Leslie Poles
see **Eustace and Hilda Cherrington trilogy**

Hilda Burton trilogy
Penn, Margaret
see **Hilda Winstanley trilogy**

Hilda Hughes tetralogy
Hufford, Susan
1 *Midnight sailing* (1975)
2 *Devil's sonata* (1976)
3 *Delicate deceit* (1976)
4 *Satan's sunset* (1977)

Hilda series
Garrard, Phillis
1 *Hilda at school* (1929)
2 *Doings of Hilda* (1932)
3 *Hilda's adventures* (1938)
4 *Hilda, fifteen* (1944)

Hilda series
Ginther, Mary Pemberton
1 *Hilda of Grey Cottage* (1922)
2 *Hilda of Landis and Co.* (1924)
3 *Hilda of the green smock* (1925)
4 *Hilda of the Three Star Ranch* (1926)

Hilda Trenton series
Lyon, Dana
1 *Tentacles* (1950)
2 *Spin the web tight* (1963)

Hilda Winstanley trilogy
Penn, Margaret
1 *Manchester fourteen miles* (1947)
2 *Foolish virgin* (1951)
3 *Young Mrs Burton* (1954)

Hildegarde series
Richards, Laura Elizabeth
1 *Queen Hildegarde* (1889)
2 *Hildegarde's holiday* (1891)
3 *Hildegarde's home* (1892)
4 *Hildegarde's neighbors* (1895)
5 *Hildegarde's harvest* (1897)

Hildegarde Withers series
Palmer, Stuart
1 *Penguin pool murder* (1931)
2 *Murder on wheels* (1932)
3 *Murder on the blackboard* (1932)
4 *Puzzle of the pepper tree* (1933)
5 *Puzzle of the silver Persian* (1934)
6 *Puzzle of the red stallion* (1936)
Puzzle of the briar pipe
7 *Puzzle of the blue banderilla* (1937)
8 *Puzzle of the happy hooligan* (1941)
9 *Miss Withers regrets* (1947)
10 *Riddles of Hildegarde Withers* (1947)
11 *Four lost ladies* (1949)
12 *Monkey murder, and other Hildegarde Withers stories* (1950)
13 *Green ace* (1950)
At one fell swoop
14 *Nipped in the bud* (1952)
Trap for a redhead
15 *Cold poison* (1954)
Exit laughing
16 *People versus Withers and Malone* (1963)
Co-author: Craig Rice
17 *Hildegarde Withers makes the scene* (1969)
Co-author: Fletcher Flora

Hilea Bailey and Hilary Dunsany Bailey series
Bailey, Hilea
1 *What night will bring* (1939)
2 *Give thanks to death* (1940)
3 *Smiling corpse* (1941)
4 *Breathe no more, my lady* (1946)

Hill and Lloyd series
McGown, Jill
see **Chief Inspector Lloyd and Sergeant Judy Hill series**

Hill Farm trilogy
Ruck, Ruth Janette
Reminiscences of farm life
1 *Place of stones* (1961)
2 *Hill Farm story* (1966)
3 *Along came a llama* (1978)

Hill of summer series
Drury, Allen
see **Soviet conquest series**

Hill series
Adkins, Bill
see **Dave Hill series**
Birch, Claire
see **Lucy Hill series**
Hawton, Hector
see **Asmun Hill series**

Hill series
Rigby, Ray
1 *Hill* (1965)
2 *Hill of sand* (1981)

Hill series
Smith, Eunice Young
see **Jennifer Hill series**
Walters, Hugh
see **Peter Hill series**

Hillary series
McGrew, Fenn
see **Lieutenant Charles Hillary series**

Hiller series
Laflin, Jack
see **Gregory Hiller series**

Hillingtons trilogy
Beresford, John Davys
1 *Old people* (1931)
2 *Middle generation* (1932)
3 *Young people* (1933)

Hillis Owen series
Wells, Anna Mary
see **Doctor Hillis Owen series**

Hills and jungles series
Smeeton, Miles
Autobiography
1 *Taste of the hills* (1961)
2 *Change of jungles* (1962)

Hills of home trilogy
Fraser, Amy Stewart
Autobiography
1 *Hills of home* (1973)
2 *In memory long* (1977)
3 *Roses in December* (1981)

Hillsbridge series
Tanner, Janet
1 *Black mountains* (1981)
2 *Emerald valley* (1985)
3 *Hills and the valley* (1988)

Hilton and Warne families series
Nicole, Christopher
see **West Indies series**

Hilton School trilogy
Barbour, Ralph Henry
1 *Half-back* (1890)
2 *For the honour of the school* (1900)
3 *Captain of the crew* (1901)

Hilton series
Bee, Clair
see **Chip Hilton series**
Coryell, Jubert V
see **Sam Hilton series**
Lonsdale, Bertha
see **Molly Hilton series**

Himalayan series
Hillary, Louise
1 *Yak for Christmas* (1968)
The story of a Himalayan holiday
2 *High time* (1973)
Companion volume: *Keep calm if you can, round the world with the Hillary family*, 1964

Himalayas series
Reid, Mayne
1 *Plant hunters* (1858)
Alternative title: Adventures among the Himalaya mountains
2 *Cliff climbers* (1864)
Alternative title: The lone home in the Himalayas

Himself series
Bird, Kenneth
1 *Dog called Himself* (1968)
2 *Himself and Macafferty's queen* (1969)
3 *Stardom for Himself* (1970)
4 *Himself in a yellow balloon* (1971)
5 *Himself and a missing uncle* (1972)
6 *Not a word for Himself* (1973)
7 *Himself and Whistler's niece* (1974)
8 *Himself and the Rooney rebellion* (1975)
9 *Himself and the Kerry crucher* (1976)
10 *Himself beats the Bill* (1977)
11 *Himself and the fake Santas* (1978)
12 *Himself and tomorrow's ogre* (1979)
13 *Himself and the golden ghost* (1980)

Hind series
Foxall, Raymond
see **Captain James Hind series**

Hines series
Nickson, Arthur
see **Rusty Himes series**

Hipkiss series
Urquhart, Fred
see **Bessie Hipkiss series**

Hippo, Potto and Mouse series
Hargreaves, Roger
1 *Potto finds a job* (1976)
2 *Mouse gets caught* (1976)
3 *Hippo, Potto and Mouse* (1976)
4 *Hippo leaves home* (1976)

Hippo series
Thaler, Mike
1 *It's me, Hippo!* (1983)
2 *Hippo lemonade* (1986)
3 *Come and play, Hippo* (1989)

Hippopotamus series
Edwards, Hazel
Illustrated by Deborah Niland
1 *There's a hippopotamus on our roof eating cake* (1980)
2 *My hippopotamus is on our caravan roof getting sunburnt* (1989)
3 *Hey Hippopotamus, do babies eat cake too?* (1992)

Hippy Buchan series
Boileau, Ethel
1 *Hippy Buchan* (1924)
2 *Arches of the years* (1930)

Hipster series
Huddy, Delia
1 *Hush-a-bye baby* (1978)
2 *Gate crashers* (1978)
3 *Blow up!* (1978)
4 *No ladder for Tom Bates* (1978)

Hiram Golf series
Hepworth, George Hughes
1 *Hiram Golf's religion* (1893)
Alternative title: The shoemaker by the grace of God
2 *They met in heaven* (1894)

Hiram Holliday series
Gallico, Paul
1 *Adventures of Hiram Holliday* (1939)
2 *Secret front* (1940)

Hiram Odom series
Boniface, Marjorie
see **Sheriff Hiram Odom series**

Hiram Potter series
Foley, Rae
1 *Death and Mister Potter* (1955)
Peacock is a bird of prey
2 *Last gamble* (1956)
3 *Run for your life* (1957)
4 *Where is Nancy Bostwick?* (1958)
Where is Mary Bostwick?
5 *Dangerous to me* (1959)
6 *It's murder, Mister Potter* (1961)
Curtain call
7 *Repent at leisure* (1962)
Deadly noose
8 *Back door to death* (1963)
Nightmare honeymoon
9 *Fatal lady* (1964)
10 *Call it accident* (1965)
11 *Calculated risk* (1970)

Hiram series
Todd, Burbank L
see **Back to the soil series**

Hiroshima series
Morris, Edita
1 *Flowers of Hiroshima* (1959)
2 *Seeds of Hiroshima* (1965)

Hiscock series
Potter, Jeremy
see **Inspector Hiscock series**

Hissing Sid series
Lloyd, Jeremy
see **Captain Beaky and his band series**

Historian series
Bryant, Arthur
Autobiography
1 *Historian's holiday* (1951)
2 *Lion and the unicorn* (1969)
A historian's testament

Historian series
Clark, Manning
1 *Puzzles of childhood* (1989)
2 *Quest for grace* (1990)

Historic communities series
Kalman, Bobbie
1 *Gristmill* (1990)
2 *Kitchen* (1990)
3 *Home crafts* (1990)
4 *Visiting a village* (1990)
5 *Tools and gadgets* (1992)
6 *Colonial town, Williamsburg* (1992)
7 *Colonial crafts* (1992)
8 *Colonial life* (1992)
9 *Eighteenth century clothing* (1993)
10 *Nineteenth century clothing* (1993)

Historical illuminatus trilogy
Wilson, Robert Anton
1 *Earth will shake* (1982)
2 *Widow's son* (1985)
3 *Nature's god* (1991)

Historical Western series
Gruber, Frank
1 *Peace marshal* (1939)
2 *Outlaw* (1941)
3 *Gunsight* (1942)
4 *Fighting man* (1948)
5 *Broken lance* (1949)
6 *Smoky road* (1952)
Lone gunhawk
7 *Fort Starvation* (1953)
8 *Quantrell's raiders* (1954)
9 *Bitter sage* (1954)
10 *Johnny Vengeance* (1954)
11 *Bugles west* (1954)
12 *Highwayman* (1955)
Ride to hell
13 *Buffalo grass* (1956)
14 *Lonesome river* (1957)
15 *Tales of Wells Fargo* (1958)
16 *This gun is still* (1967)
17 *Dawn riders* (1968)

Histories mysteries series
Larsen, Anita
1 *Rosenbergs* (1992)
2 *Amelia Earhart, missing, declared dead* (1992)
3 *Montezuma's missing treasure* (1992)
4 *Raoul Wallenberg, missing diplomat* (1992)
5 *Roanoke missing persons case* (1992)

Histories of King Kelson trilogy
Kurtz, Katherine
The fourth trilogy in the **World of the Eleven Kingdoms series**
1 *Bishop's heir* (1984)
2 *King's justice* (1985)
3 *Quest for Saint Camber* (1986)

History atlas series
Gilbert, Martin
1 *Recent history atlas, 1870 to the present day* (1966)
Recent history atlas, 1860-1960
The second title is the third edition, 1977
2 *British history atlas* (1969)
3 *American history atlas* (1969)
Revised edition 1985
4 *Jewish history atlas* (1969)
Revised edition 1985
5 *First World War history atlas* (1970)
First World War atlas
Atlas of World War I
6 *Russian history atlas* (1972)
Imperial Russian history atlas
7 *Jerusalem illustrated history atlas* (1977)
Jerusalem history atlas
8 *Soviet history atlas* (1979)

History of a selfish man series
Hayes, Douglas
1 *My father in his dizziebell* (1968)
2 *Shy young man* (1969)
3 *War of thirty nine* (1970)
4 *Tomorrow the apricots* (1971)
5 *Player's hide* (1972)
6 *Quite a good address* (1973)

History of a society series
Behaine, Rene
French title of the series: *Histoire d'une societe*; only volumes 2, 4 and 12 translated into English
1 *[Alfred Varambaud, Celine Arnelle, Michel Varambaud]* (1904)
[Nouveaux venus]
2 *Survivors* (1914)
Original edition entitled *Les survivants*
3 *[Si jeunesse savait]* (1919)
4 *Conquest of life* (1924)
Original edition entitled *La conquete de la vie*
5 *[Enchantement du feu]* (1926)
6 *[Avec les yeux de l'esprit]* (1928)
7 *[Au prix meme du bonheur]* (1930)
8 *[Dans la foule horrible des hommes]* (1932)
9 *[Solitude et le silence]* (1933)
10 *[Signes dans le ciel]* (1935)
11 *[O peuple infortune]* (1936)
12 *Day of glory* (1939)
Original edition entitled *Le jour de gloire*
13 *[Sous le char de Kali]* (1947)
14 *[Moisson des morts]* (1957)
15 *[Aveugle devant son miroir]* (1958)
16 *[Seul amour]* (1959)

History of American painting series
Flexner, James Thomas
1 *First flowers of our wilderness* (1947)
The colonial period
2 *Light of distant skies* (1954)
1760-1835
3 *That wilder image* (1962)
The native school from Thomas Cole to Winslow Homer
Companion volume: *A short history of American painting*, 1950, also published as *Pocket history of American painting*

History of Britain and the British people series
Bryant, Arthur
1 *Set in a silver sea* (1984)
The island peoples from earliest times to the fifteenth century
2 *Freedom's own island* (1986)
The British oceanic expansion
3 *Search for justice* (1990)

History of civilization series
Smith, Edward Elmer
see **Lensman series**

History of gold series
Allen, Gina
1 *Gold!* (1964)
2 *Gold is* (1969)

History of Middle Earth series
Tolkien, John Ronald Reuel
Edited by Christopher Tolkien after his father's death
1 *Book of lost tales, part 1* (1983)
2 *Book of lost tales, part 2* (1984)
3 *Lays of Beleriand* (1985)
4 *Shaping of Middle Earth* (1986)
The Quenta, the Ambarkanta and the annals
5 *Lost road, and other writings* (1987)
Language and legend before the Lord of the Rings
6 *Return of the shadow* (1988)
7 *Treason of Isengard* (1989)
8 *War of the Ring* (1990)
9 *Sauron defeated* (1992)
10 *Morgoth's ring* (1993)

History of Pandervil series
Bullett, Gerald
1 *Egg Pandervil* (1928)
2 *Nicky, son of Egg* (1929)
One volume edition entitled *The Pandervils, Egg and Nicky*, 1930

History of Rhodesia series
Gann, Lewis Henry
1 *History of Northern Rhodesia* (1964)
Early days to 1953
2 *History of Southern Rhodesia* (1965)

History of Runestaff series
Moorcock, Michael
1 *Jewel in the skull* (1967)
Revised edition 1977
2 *Sorcerer's amulet* (1968)
Mad god's amulet
3 *Sword of the dawn* (1968)
Revised edition 1977
4 *Secret of the Runestaff* (1969)
Runestaff
One volume edition entitled *The history of the Runestaff*, 1979; followed by **Chronicles of Castle Brass series**

History of seafaring series
Armstrong, Richard
1 *Early mariners* (1967)
2 *Discoverers* (1968)
3 *Merchant men* (1969)

History of sexuality series
Foucault, Michel
1 *History of sexuality* (1976)
Original edition entitled *La volonte de savoir*
2 *Use of pleasure* (1984)
Original edition entitled *L'usage des plaisirs*
3 *Care of the self* (1984)
Original edition entitled *Souci de soi*

History of the future series
Heinlein, Robert Anson
see **Future history series**

History of the Great Imperium trilogy
Carter, Lin
1 *Man without a planet* (1966)
2 *Star rogue* (1970)
3 *Outworlder* (1971)

History of the Lord of the Rings series
Tolkien, John Ronald Reuel
Edited by Christopher Tolkien
1 *Return of the shadow* (1988)
2 *Treason of Isengard* (1989)
3 *War of the Ring* (1990)
4 *Sauron defeated* (1992)

History of the Plantagenets tetralogy
Costain, Thomas Bertram
1 *Conquerors* (1949)
Conquering family
2 *Magnificent century* (1951)
3 *Three Edwards* (1958)
4 *Last Plantagenets* (1962)

History's most fascinating women series
Peters, Maureen
1 *Princess of desire* (1970)
2 *Virgin Queen* (1972)
3 *Queen who never was* (1972)
4 *Destiny's lady* (1973)

Hit and Run Gang series
Kroll, Steven
1 *New kid in town* (1992)
2 *Playing favorites* (1992)
3 *Slump* (1992)
4 *Streak* (1992)
5 *Pitching trouble* (1994)
6 *You're out!* (1994)

Hitch-hiker series
Adams, Douglas Noel
see **Arthur Dent series**

Hite report series
Hite, Shere
1 *Hite report* (1976)
A nationwide study of female sexuality
2 *Hite report on male sexuality* (1981)
3 *Hite report of the family* (1994)
Eroticism and power between parents and children

Hite series
Burke, Richard
see **Quinny Hite series**

Hitman series
Carr, Kirby
1 *Who killed you, Candy Castle?* (1974)
2 *Let me kill you sweetheart!* (1974)
3 *Girls who came to murder* (1974)
4 *They're coming to kill you, Jane!* (1975)
5 *You die next, Jill Baby!* (1975)
6 *Don't bet on living, Alice!* (1975)
7 *You're hired, you're dead* (1975)

Hitman series
Davies, Frederick
1 *Death of a hitman* (1982)
2 *Snow in Venice* (1983)

Hitman series
Winski, Norman
see **Dirk Spencer series**

Hive series
Bass, T J
1 *Half-past human* (1971)
2 *God-whale* (1974)

Ho series
Farren, Mick
see **Jeb Stuart Ho series**

Hoani Mata series
Grayland, Valerie Merle
1 *Dead men of Eden* (1962)
2 *Night of the reaper* (1963)
3 *Grave-digger's apprentice* (1964)
4 *Jest of darkness* (1965)

Hoaryhead series
Abbott, Jacob
1 *Hoaryhead* (1838)
Alternative title: Truth through fiction
2 *Hoaryhead and M'Donner* (1838)

Hob Lane series
Leeson, Robert
1 *April fool at Hob Lane School* (1992)
2 *No sleep for Hob Lane* (1992)
3 *Ghosts at Hob Lane* (1993)

Hob stories series
Mayne, William
1 *Yellow book of Hob stories* (1984)
2 *Blue book of Hob stories* (1984)
3 *Green book of Hob stories* (1984)
4 *Red book of Hob stories* (1984)

Hobbes and Calvin series
Watterson, Bill
see **Calvin and Hobbes series**

Hobbs series
Lewis, Michael
see **Sergeant Hobbs series**

Hobby Horse Cottage series
Read, *Miss*
1 *Hobby Horse Cottage* (1958)
2 *Hob and the horse-bat* (1965)

Hobo Dog series
Hurd, Thacher
1 *Hobo Dog* (1980)
2 *Hobo Dog's Christmas tree* (1983)
3 *Hobo Dog in the ghost town* (1985)

Hobstones series
Bagshaw, Joyce Margaret
1 *Hobstones* (1966)
2 *Beyond the grass bank* (1969)

Hockaday series
Adcock, Thomas
see **Neil Hockaday series**

Hockney series
De Borchgrave, Arnaud
see **Robert Hockney series**

Hodson series
Bidwell, Margaret
see **Mister Hodson series**

Hoeffler and Harrigan series
O'Malley, Patrick
see **Harrigan and Hoeffler series**

Hoenig trilogy
Dickson, Gordon Rupert
see **Robby Hoenig trilogy**

Hofer series
Westall, William
see **Andreas Hofer series**

Hogg series
Lee, Austin
see **Miss Flora Hogg series**

Hogget series
Mitchell, James
see **Ron Hogget series**

Hoggie series
Watson, Julian
1 *Hoggie* (1949)
2 *Hoggie and bear* (1950)

Hogglespike series
Drew, Patricia
1 *Hogglespike* (1971)
2 *Hogglespike and Thistle* (1972)
3 *Hogglespike in danger* (1973)

Hogleg Bailey series
Borg, Jack
1 *Hellbent trail* (1954)
2 *Sheriff of Clinton* (1954)
3 *Cannon Kid* (1955)
4 *Big Cherokee* (1955)
5 *Sheriff's deputy* (1956)
6 *Bushwack Canyon* (1956)
7 *Bronco justice* (1957)
8 *Gunsmoke feud* (1957)
9 *Rawhide tenderfoot* (1958)
10 *Kansas trail* (1958)
11 *Badlands fury* (1959)
12 *Rustlers' Range* (1959)
13 *Range wolves* (1960)
14 *Saddle tramp* (1960)
15 *Horsethieves hang high* (1961)
16 *Kid with a Colt* (1961)
17 *Guns of the lawless* (1962)
18 *Cast a wide loop* (1963)
19 *Texas wolves* (1963)
20 *Gun feud at Sun Creek* (1964)
21 *Rope for a rustler* (1965)
22 *Stagecoach to Concho* (1966)
23 *Owlhooter* (1968)
24 *Dry Valley war* (1968)

Hoka series
Anderson, Poul
1 *Earthman's burden* (1957)
2 *Star Prince Charlie* (1975)
3 *Hoka!* (1983)

Hoke Moseley series
Willeford, Charles
1 *Miami blues* (1984)
2 *New hope for the dead* (1985)
3 *Sideswipe* (1987)

Holbrooke series
Pullein-Thompson, Josephine
see **Major Holbrooke series**

Hold my hand series
Davis, John Gordon
1 *Hold my hand, I'm dying* (1967)
2 *Seize the reckless wind* (1984)

Holden and Cantrell series
Chase, Elaine Raco
see **Roman Cantrell and Nikki Holden series**

Holden series
Bacheller, Irving
see **Eben Holden series**

Holder trilogy
Wilson, Trevor Edward
see **Big Tom Holder trilogy**

Holderly Hall series
Cameron, Kate
1 *Legend of Holderly Hall* (1974)
2 *Shadows of the past* (1974)
3 *Voices in the fog* (1975)
4 *Deadly nightshade* (1975)
5 *Music from the past* (1975)
6 *Portraits of the past* (1975)

Holes series
Lehmann, Rudolf Chambers
see **Picklock Holes series**

Holiday series
Haywood, Carolyn
1 *Christmas fantasy* (1972)
2 *Valentine fantasy* (1976)
3 *Halloween treats* (1981)

Holiday series
Mortimer, Derek
see **Tom Holiday series**
Prelutsky, Jack
see **It's a holiday series**

Holiday stories series
Blyton, Enid
1 *Holiday annual stories* (1967)
2 *Holiday magic stories* (1967)

3 *Holiday pixie stories* (1967)
4 *Holiday toy stories* (1967)

Holidays and festivals series
Kalman, Bobbie
1 *We celebrate Christmas* (1985)
2 *We celebrate Easter* (1985)
3 *We celebrate Hallowe'en* (1985)
4 *We celebrate New Year* (1985)
5 *We celebrate spring* (1985)
6 *We celebrate family days* (1986)
7 *We celebrate Hanukkah* (1986)
8 *We celebrate Valentine's Day* (1986)
9 *We ecelbrate the harvest* (1986)
10 *We celebrate winter* (1986)

Holland and Kitten series
Gover, Robert
see **Kitten series**

Holland series
Andover, Henry
see **Henry Holland series**
Hunt, Angela Elwell
see **Nicki Holland series**
Macdonnell, James Edmond
see **Dutchy Holland series**
Myers, Paul
see **Mark Holland series**

Holliday series
Gallico, Paul
see **Hiram Holliday series**
Jones, Arthur E
see **Felix Holliday series**

Hollingbury family series
Boscawen, Linda
1 *We never knew Uncle* (1952)
Original edition entitled *Himmelvolk*
2 *We live in Lemon Yard* (1955)

Hollis series
Peyton, K M
see **Ruth Hollis series**

Hollister series
Benson, Irene Elliott
see **Campfire Girls series**
Lambert, Janet
see **Cinda Hollister series**

Hollisters series
West, Jerry
see **Happy Hollisters series**

Holloway children series
Henson, Jean
1 *River detectives* (1947)
2 *Detectives in the hills* (1949)
3 *Detectives by the sea* (1950)
4 *Detectives abroad* (1952)
5 *Detectives in Wales* (1953)

Holly Beckman trilogy
Stirling, Jessica
see **Beckman family trilogy**

Holly Gordon series
Burr, Sybil
1 *Lantern of the north* (1954)
2 *My candle the moon* (1955)
3 *Saint Bride blue* (1956)
4 *Full fathom forty* (1957)
5 *Operation Blindbell* (1960)

Holly Hills series
Fleischer, Leonore
1 *Hearts and diamonds* (1986)
2 *Four Jessicas* (1986)
3 *Wrong name for Angela* (1986)

Holly series
Alexander, Lloyd
see **Vesper Holly series**
Postgate, Raymond
see **Inspector Holly series**

Hollys series
Prime, Heather
1 *Hollys of Tooting Steps* (1953)
2 *Hollys on wheels* (1954)

Hollywood daughters trilogy
Nixon, Joan Lowery
1 *Star baby* (1989)
2 *Overnight sensation* (1990)
3 *Encore* (1990)

Hollywood detective series
Rovin, Jeff
see **Roger Garrison series**

Hollywood series
Collins, Jackie
1 *Hollywood wives* (1983)
2 *Hollywood husbands* (1986)
3 *Hollywood kids* (1994)

Hollywood series
Lefcourt, Peter
1 *Deal* (1991)
2 *Di and I* (1994)

Hollywood trilogy
Robbins, Harold
1 *Dream merchants* (1949)
2 *Carpetbaggers* (1961)
3 *Inheritors* (1969)

Hollywood wars series
Cooper, Ilene
1 *My co-star, my enemy* (1993)
2 *Lights, camera, attitude* (1993)
3 *Seeing red* (1993)
4 *Trouble in paradise* (1993)

Holm series
Bojer, Johan
see **Peer Holm series**

Holman series
Brown, Carter
see **Rick Holman series**

Holmes series
Bark, Conrad Voss
see **Mister William Holmes series**
Doyle, Arthur Conan
see **Sherlock Holmes series**
Hughes, Gwilym Fielden
see **Bill Holmes series**

Holmes' youth series
Frow, Gerald
see **Young Sherlock Holmes series**

Holt family series
Ross, Dana Fuller
1 *Oregon legacy* (1989)
2 *Oklahoma pride* (1990)
3 *Caroline courage* (1991)
4 *California glory* (1991)
5 *Hawaii heritage* (1991)
6 *Sierra triumph* (1992)
7 *Yukon justice* (1992)

Holt series
Campbell, Bruce
see **Ken Holt series**
Durbridge, Francis
see **Philip Holt series**
Tully, John
see **Inspector Holt series**
Wallace, Robert
see **Essington Holt series**

Holten series
Gentry, Buck
see **Eli Holten series**

Holton series
Hunt, Charlotte
see **Doctor Paul Holton series**
Leigh, Stephen
see **Doctor Holton series**

Holy flower trilogy
Haggard, Henry Rider
1 *Holy flower* (1915)
Allan and the holy flower
2 *Ivory child* (1916)
3 *Ancient Allan* (1920)

Holy Ireland series
Hoult, Norah
1 *Holy Ireland* (1935)
2 *Coming from the fair* (1937)

Homburg trilogy
Gainham, Sarah
see **Viennese trilogy**

Home and after life series
Sewell, Elizabeth Missings
1 *Journal of a home life* (1867)
2 *After life* (1868)

Home and away series
This sequence has four authors; based on a television series
Darroll, Sally
1 *Dangerous ride* (1989)
Howarth, Trish
2 *Carly's crisis* (1989)
Pearce, Margaret
3 *Bobby and Frank* (1989)
Butler, Mark
4 *Family matters* (1989)

Home for animals series
Burkett, Molly
1 *Foxes, owls and all* (1977)
Lively, humorous tales of an animal-crazy household
2 *Home for animals* (1979)

Home influence series
Aguilar, Grace
1 *Home influence* (1847)
A tale for mothers and daughters
2 *Mother's recompense* (1851)

Home Run Kid series
Christopher, Matt
1 *Kid who only hit homers* (1972)
2 *Return of the Home Run Kid* (1992)

Home series
Bial, Raymond
1 *Amish home* (1993)
2 *Frontier home* (1993)
3 *Shaker home* (1994)

Home series
Cooper, James Fenimore
1 *Homeward bound* (1838)
Alternative title: The chase
2 *Home as found* (1838)
Alternative title: Home

Home stories series
Arthur, Timothy Shay
1 *Hidden wings, and other stories* (1864)
2 *Sowing the wind, and other stories* (1864)
3 *Sunshine at home, and other stories* (1864)
4 *Peacemaker, and other stories* (1868)
5 *Not anything for peace, and other stories* (1869)
6 *After a shadow* (1869)

Homer Bull and Ham Macandrew series
Lariar, Lawrence
see **Ham Macandrew and Homer Bull series**

Homer Clay series
Lauben, Philip
see **Captain Homer Clay series**

Homer Crawford trilogy
Reynolds, Mack
1 *Blackman's burden* (1972)
2 *Border, breed, nor birth* (1972)
3 *Best ye breed* (1978)

Homer Evans series
Paul, Elliot
1 *Mysterious Mickey Finn* (1939)
Alternative title: Murder at the Cafe du Dome
2 *Hugger-mugger in the Louvre* (1940)
3 *Fracas in the foothills* (1940)
4 *Mayhem in B flat* (1940)
5 *I'll hate myself in the morning* (1945)
Also includes *Summer in December*
6 *Murder on the Left Bank* (1951)
7 *Black gardenia* (1952)
8 *Waylaid in Boston* (1953)
9 *Black and the red* (1956)

Homer Fitzgerald series
Russell, Charlotte Murray
1 *Lament for William* (1947)
2 *Careless Mrs Christian* (1949)
3 *Between us and evil* (1950)
4 *June, moon and murder* (1952)

Homer Kelly series
Langton, Jane
1 *Transcendental murder* (1964)
Minute man murder
2 *Dark Nantucket noon* (1975)
3 *Memorial hall murder* (1978)
4 *Natural enemy* (1982)
5 *Emily Dickinson is dead* (1984)
6 *Good and dead* (1986)
7 *Murder at the Gardner* (1988)
8 *Dante game* (1991)
9 *God in Concord* (1992)

Homer series
Baker, Margaret Joyce
1 *Nonsense, said the tortoise* (1949)
Homer the tortoise
2 *Homer sees the Queen* (1953)
3 *Homer goes to Stratford* (1958)
4 *Homer in orbit* (1961)
5 *Homer goes west* (1965)

Homeroom series
Norton, Nancy
1 *Strange times at Fairwood High* (1988)
2 *Princess of Fairwood High* (1988)
3 *Triple trouble at Fairwood High* (1988)

Homes series
Fish, Robert Lloyd
see **Schlock Homes series**

Homewood trilogy
Wideman, John Edgar
1 *Damballah* (1981)
Short stories
2 *Hiding place* (1981)
Short stories
3 *Sent for you yesterday* (1983)
One volume edition entitled *The Homewood trilogy*, 1985
Companion volume: *Reuben*, 1987

Homo sapiens series
Schwaller de Lubicz, Isha
1 *Her-Bak, Chick-Pea* (1953)
Original edition entitled *Her-Bak, Pois Chiche*
2 *Her-Bak, Egyptian initiate* (1956)
Original edition entitled *Her-Bak, disciple de la sagesse egyptienne*
Companion volumes: *Sacred science, the king of pharaonic theocracy*, 1961, and *The Egyptian miracle, an introduction to the wisdom of the temple*, 1963

Homochito County series
Douglas, Ellen
1 *Family's affairs* (1962)
2 *Black cloud, white cloud* (1963)
Two novellas and two stories
3 *Where the dreams cross* (1968)

Homochito County series

4 *Apostles of light* (1973)
5 *Rock cried out* (1979)

Homosexuality series
West, Donald James
1 *Homosexuality* (1960)
2 *Homosexuality re-examined* (1977)

Honegger series
Strange, John Stephen
see **Captain George Honegger series**

Honest Jim series
Finley, Martha Farquharson
1 *Honest Jim* (1872)
2 *Contented Jim* (1872)
3 *How Jim did it* (1872)
4 *Twin babies* (1872)
5 *Neil, the beggar boy* (1872)
6 *Neil in the country* (1872)

Honest women series
Nelson, Betty Palmer
1 *Private knowledge* (1990)
2 *Weight of light* (1992)
3 *Pursuit of bliss* (1992)
4 *Uncertain April* (1994)

Honey B series
Goldin, Stephen
1 *Scavenger hunt* (1976)
2 *Finish line* (1976)

Honey Bunch series
Thorndyke, Helen Louise
House pseudonym
1 *Just a little girl* (1923)
2 *Her first visit to the city* (1923)
3 *Her first days on the farm* (1923)
4 *Her first visit to the seashore* (1924)
5 *Her first little garden* (1924)
6 *Her first days in camp* (1925)
7 *Her first auto tour* (1926)
8 *Her first trip on the ocean* (1927)
9 *Her first trip west* (1928)
10 *Her first summer on an island* (1929)
11 *Her first trip on the Great Lakes* (1930)
12 *Her first trip in an airplane* (1931)
13 *Her first visit to the zoo* (1932)
14 *Her first big adventure* (1933)
15 *Her first big parade* (1934)
16 *Her first little mystery* (1935)
17 *Her first little circus* (1936)
18 *Her first little treasure hunt* (1937)
19 *Her first little club* (1938)
20 *Her first trip in a trailer* (1939)
21 *Her first trip to a big fair* (1940)
22 *Her first twin playmates* (1941)
23 *Her first costume party* (1943)
24 *Her first trip on a houseboat* (1945)
25 *Her first winter at Snowtop* (1946)
26 *Her first trip to the big woods* (1947)
27 *Her first little pet show* (1948)
28 *Her first trip to a lighthouse* (1949)
Honey Bunch and Norman on Lighthouse Island
29 *Her first visit to a pony ranch* (1950)
30 *Her first tour of Toy Town* (1951)
Honey Bunch and Norman tour Toy Town
31 *Her first visit to Puppyland* (1952)
32 *Her first trip to Reindeer Farm* (1953)
Honey Bunch and Norman visit Reindeer Farm
33 *Honey Bunch and Norman ride with the sky mailman* (1954)
34 *Honey Bunch and Norman visit Beaver Lodge* (1955)
35 *Honey Bunch and Norman* (1957)
36 *Honey Bunch and Norman play detective at Niagara Falls* (1957)
37 *Honey Bunch and Norman in the Castle of Magic* (1959)
38 *Honey Bunch and Norman solve the pine cone mystery* (1960)
39 *Honey Bunch and Norman and the paper lantern mystery* (1961)
40 *Honey Bunch and Norman and the painted pony* (1962)
41 *Honey Bunch and Norman and the walnut tree mystery* (1963)

Honey family trilogy
Black, Margaret Katherine
1 *In the shop* (1961)
2 *Velvet and Rough* (1961)
3 *At home and away* (1961)

Honey machine series
Hunt, Peter
1 *Sue and the honey machine* (1989)
2 *Fay Cow and the missing milk* (1989)
Fay Cow and the honey machine

Honey-pot series
Barcynska, Helena Margareta
1 *Honey-pot* (1916)
A story of the stage
2 *Love Maggy* (1918)
3 *Pretty dear* (1920)
Rose o' the sea
4 *Back to the honey-pot* (1925)

Honey the dolphin series
Gilbert, Harry
1 *Dolphin that spoke* (1985)
2 *Dolphin that walked* (1985)

Honey West series
Fickling, G G
1 *This girl for hire* (1957)
2 *Girl on the loose* (1958)
3 *Gun for Honey* (1958)
4 *Girl on the prowl* (1959)
5 *Honey in the flesh* (1959)
6 *Dig a dead doll* (1960)
7 *Kiss for a killer* (1960)
8 *Blood and Honey* (1961)
9 *Bombshell* (1964)
10 *Honey on her tail* (1971)
11 *Stiff as a broad* (1971)

Honeybath series
Innes, Michael
see **Charles Honeybath series**

Honeybody and James series
Giles, Kenneth
see **Inspector Harry James and Sergeant Honeybody series**

Honeycutt Street series
Nixon, Joan Lowery
1 *Honeycutt Street celebrities* (1991)
2 *Haunted house on Honeycutt Street* (1991)

Honeywood series
Creswell, Harry Bulkeley
1 *Honeywood file* (1929)
2 *Honeywood settlement* (1930)
3 *Grig* (1942)
4 *Grig in retirement* (1943)

Hong Kong series
Ford, James Allan
1 *Brave white flag* (1961)
2 *Season of escape* (1963)

Honor Bright series
Richards, Laura Elizabeth
1 *Honor Bright* (1920)
2 *Honor Bright's new adventure* (1925)

Honor Bright series
Whitaker, Evelyn
1 *Honor Bright* (1882)
2 *Peas-Blossom* (1883)

Honor Charlecote series
Yonge, Charlotte Mary
1 *Hopes and fears* (1860)
2 *Pillars of the house* (1873)
Alternative title: Under wode, under rode

Honourable Bill Beverly series
Brandon, Gordon
see **Michael and Terry Terence series**

Honourable Constance Ethel Morrison-Burke series
Porter, Joyce
1 *Rather a common sort of crime* (1970)
2 *Meddler and her murder* (1972)
3 *Package included murder* (1975)
4 *Who the heck is Sylvia?* (1977)
5 *Cart before the crime* (1979)

Honourable Richard Rollison series
Creasey, John
see **Toff series**

Hood series
Dark, James
see **Mark Kingsley Hood series**
Mayo, James
see **Charles Hood series**
Rich, Nicholas
see **Adam Hood series**

Hooded Swan series
Stableford, Brian Michael
see **Star Pilot Grainger series**

Hood's Army trilogy
Elliott, Nathan
1 *Earth invaded* (1986)
2 *Staveworld* (1986)
3 *Liberators* (1986)

Hoods series
Torrio, Vincente
1 *Executioner* (1975)
2 *Bootlegger* (1975)
3 *Politician* (1976)
4 *Dealer* (1976)

Hook, line and sinker trilogy
Deighton, Len
1 *Spy hook* (1988)
2 *Spy line* (1989)
3 *Spy sinker* (1990)
One volume edition entitled *Hook, line and sinker*, 1991

Hook series
Lane, Gret
see **Inspector Hook series**

Hook series
Latham, Brad
1 *Gilded canary* (1981)
2 *Sight unseen* (1981)
3 *Hate is thicker than blood* (1981)
4 *Death of Lorenzo Jones* (1982)
5 *Corpses in the cellar* (1982)

Hook series
Tolman, Hildegarde
see **Sam Hook series**
Zetford, Tully
see **Ryder Hook series**

Hooky Gibbs series
Tully, Paul
see **Deputy Marshal Hooky Gibbs series**

Hooky Hefferman series
Meynell, Laurence Walter
1 *Frightened man* (1952)
2 *Danger round the corner* (1952)
3 *Too clever by half* (1953)
4 *Death by arrangement* (1972)
5 *Little matter of arson* (1972)
6 *Thirteen trumpeters* (1973)
7 *Fatal flaw* (1973)
8 *Fairly innocent little man* (1974)
9 *Don't stop for Hooky Hefferman* (1975)
10 *Hooky and the crock of gold* (1975)
11 *Lost half hour* (1976)
12 *Hooky gets the wooden spoon* (1977)
13 *Papersnake* (1978)
14 *Hooky and the villainous chauffeur* (1979)
15 *Hooky and the prancing horse* (1980)
16 *Hooky goes to blazes* (1981)
17 *Silver guilt* (1983)
18 *Open door* (1984)
19 *Affair at Barworld* (1985)
20 *Hooky catches a Tartar* (1986)
21 *Hooky on loan* (1987)
22 *Hooky hooked* (1988)

Hooky Walker series
Macdonnell, James Edmond
This sequence includes those works which have so far been identified as including the series character; however since there is much overlapping of characters in this author's numerous novels it is likely that this character will be found in other works
1 *Frogman* (1958)
2 *Mutiny* (1958)
3 *Night encounter* (1961)
4 *Buffer* (1963)
5 *Captain Mettle, VC* (1979)

Hooley series
Craigie, Dorothy
see **Tim Hooley series**

Hooper series
Sorenson, Jane
see **Katie Hooper series**

Hooray for arithmetic facts series
Daniel, Rebecca
1 *Hooray for addition facts!* (1989)
2 *Hooray for subtraction facts!* (1989)
3 *Hooray for multiplication facts!* (1989)
4 *Hooray for division facts!* (1989)

Hoorka trilogy
Leigh, Stephen
see **Neweden trilogy**

Hopalong Cassidy series
This sequence has two authors
Mulford, Clarence Edward
1 *Bar- 20* (1907)
Hopalong Cassidy's round-up
Short stories
2 *Hopalong Cassidy* (1908)
3 *Bar- 20 days* (1910)
Hopalong Cassidy's private war
Short stories
4 *Buck Peters, ranchman* (1912)
Co-author: John Wood Clay
5 *Coming of Cassidy and the others* (1913)
Coming of Hopalong Cassidy
Short stories
6 *Man from Bar- 20* (1918)
A story of the cow-country
7 *Johnny Nelson* (1920)
8 *Bar- 20 three* (1921)
Hopalong Cassidy sees red
9 *Tex* (1922)
Tex of Bar- 20
10 *Hopalong Cassidy returns* (1924)
11 *Hopalong Cassidy's protege* (1926)
Hopalong Cassidy's saddle mate
12 *Bar- 20 rides again* (1926)
Hopalong Cassidy's Bar- 20 rides again
13 *Hopalong Cassidy and the eagle's brood* (1931)
14 *Trail dust* (1934)
Hopalong Cassidy and the trail herd
The second title is an abridged edition
15 *Hoplaong Cassidy takes cards* (1937)
16 *Hopalong Cassidy serves a writ* (1941)

Burns, Tex
17 *Hopalong Cassidy and the rustlers of West Fork* (1951)
18 *Hopalong Cassidy and the trail to Seven Pines* (1951)
19 *Hopalong Cassidy and the riders of High Rock* (1951)
20 *Hopalong Cassidy, trouble shooter* (1952)
Companion volume: *Hopalong Cassidy and the five men of evil, comic strips,* by Royal King Cole and Dan Spiegle, 1991

Hope and Trevellyan series
Kelly, Susan
see **Alison Hope and Inspector Nick Trevellyan series**

Hope series
Eller, John
see **Charlie Hope series**
McBain, Ed
see **Matthew Hope series**

Hope series
Mandelstam, Nadezhda
1 *Hope against hope* (1970)
2 *Hope abandoned* (1972)

Hope series
Wouk, Herman
1 *Hope* (1993)
2 *Glory* (1994)

Hopewell series
Campbell, Drusilla
1 *Broken promises* (1982)
2 *Silent dreams* (1982)
3 *Stolen passions* (1982)
4 *Tomorrow's journey* (1982)

Hopkins and Downes series
Sampson, Victor
see **Inspector Downes and Sergeant Hopkins series**

Hopkins series
Daniel, Roland
see **John Hopkins series**

Hopkins trilogy
Ellroy, James
see **Sergeant Lloyd Hopkins trilogy**

Hopper series
Pfister, Marcus
Translated from the German
1 *Hopper hunts for spring* (1992)
2 *Hopper's Easter surprise* (1992)

Hopper Street trilogy
Gondosch, Linda
1 *Who needs a bratty brother?* (1985)
2 *Witches of Hopper Street* (1986)
3 *Who's afraid of Haggerty House?* (1987)

Hoppity and Sara series
Leigh, Roberta
see **Sara and Hoppity series**

Hopton series
Woodiwiss, John Cecil
see **Inspector Hopton series**

Horace Augustus Elver series
Dilnot, George
1 *Crook's castle* (1934)
2 *Murder masquerade* (1935)
3 *Great rail racket* (1936)
4 *Murder at Scotland Yard* (1937)

Horace Clarke series
Lewis, Irwin
1 *Day they invaded New York* (1964)
2 *Day New York trembled* (1967)

Horace Higby series
Heuman, William
1 *Horace Higby and the field goal* (1965)
2 *Horace Higby and the scientific pitch* (1968)
3 *Horace Higby and the gentle fullback* (1970)
4 *Horace Higby, coxswain of the crew* (1971)

Horace Rumpole series
Mortimer, John
1 *Rumpole of the Bailey* (1978)
2 *Trials of Rumpole* (1979)
Numbers 1-2 also published in one volume entitled *Rumpole*, 1980
3 *Rumpole's return* (1980)
Numbers 1-3 also published in one volume entitled *The first Rumpole omnibus,* 1983
4 *Rumpole for the defence* (1982)
Numbers 3-4 also published in one volume entitled *Regina versus Rumpole*, 1981
5 *Rumpole and the golden thread* (1983)
6 *Rumpole's last case* (1987)
Numbers 4-6 also published in one volume entitled *The second Rumpole omnibus*, 1987
7 *Rumpole and the age of miracles* (1988)
8 *Rumpole a la carte* (1990)
9 *Rumpole on trial* (1992)

Horace Spurgeon Fenton series
Story, Jack Trevor
1 *Hitler needs you* (1970)
2 *One mad last embrace* (1970)

Horace Stubbs series
Aldiss, Brian Wilson
1 *Hand-reared boy* (1970)
2 *Soldier erect* (1971)
3 *Rude awakening* (1978)
One volume edition entitled *The Horatio Stubbs saga*, 1985

Horace Thomas Cross series
Kenan, Randall
see **Tims Creek series**

Horatio Cassidy series
Crosby, John Campbell
1 *Party of the year* (1979)
2 *Men in arms* (1983)
3 *Take no prisoners* (1985)

Horatio Green series
Nichols, Beverley
see **Mister Horatio Green series**

Horatio Hornblower cadet series
Forester, Cecil Scott
1 *Hornblower goes to sea* (1954)
2 *Hornblower takes command* (1954)
3 *Hornblower in captivity* (1955)
4 *Hornblower's triumph* (1955)

Horatio Hornblower series
Forester, Cecil Scott
1 *Mister Midshipman Hornblower* (1950)
2 *Lieutenant Hornblower* (1952)
3 *Hornblower and the Hotspur* (1962)
4 *Hornblower and the crisis* (1967)
Hornblower during the crisis
Incomplete at the author's death
5 *Hornblower and the Atropos* (1953)
Numbers 1, 2, 5 also published in one volume entitled *Young Hornblower*, 1960
6 *Happy return* (1937)
Beat to quarters
7 *Ship of the line* (1938)
8 *Flying colours* (1938)
Numbers 6-8 also published in one volume entitled *Captain Horatio Hornblower*, 1939
9 *Commodore* (1945)
Commodore Hornblower
10 *Lord Hornblower* (1946)
11 *Hornblower in the West Indies* (1958)
Admiral Hornblower in the West Indies
Numbers 9-11 also published in one volume entitled *The indomitable Hornblower*, 1963
Companion volumes: *The Hornblower companion*, 1964, *The life and times of Horatio Hornblower*, by Cyril Northcote Parkinson, 1970

Horatio Nelson series
Frye, Pearl
see **Lord Horatio Nelson series**

Horatio Stubbs series
Aldiss, Brian Wilson
see **Horace Stubbs series**

Horn series
Sloane, Ben
1 *Hot zone* (1990)
2 *Blown dead* (1990)
3 *Outland strip* (1991)
4 *Ultimate weapon* (1991)

Horn series
Stockton, Frank Richard
see **Captain Horn series**

Hornblower cadet series
Forester, Cecil Scott
see **Horatio Hornblower cadet series**

Hornblower saga series
Roberts, Nora
1 *Time was* (1989)
2 *Times change* (1990)

Hornblower series
Forester, Cecil Scott
see **Horatio Hornblower series**

Horne series
Gonzales, John
see **Harry Horne series**
Hill, Porter
see **Captain Adam Horne series**
Mackenzie, Pierce
see **T G Horne series**
Tucker, Wilson
see **Charles Horne series**

Hornett family series
This sequence has three authors; novels based on plays by Philip King and Falkland Cary
Duff, Reginald Eustace Bluett
1 *Sailor, beware!* (1957)
Steen, Shiela
2 *Watch it, sailor!* (1961)

Hornsley series
Salter, Elizabeth
see **Inspector Michael Hornsley series**

Horowitz series
Delman, David
see **Lieutenant Jason Horowitz series**

Horribilly series
Osborne, Maureen
1 *Here comes the Horribilly* (1979)
2 *Horribilly goes to school* (1979)

Horrible Harry series
Kline, Suzy
1 *Horrible Harry in Room 2B* (1988)
2 *Horrible Harry and the green slime* (1989)
3 *Horrible Harry and the ant invasion* (1989)
4 *Horrible Harry's secret* (1990)
5 *Horrible Harry and the Christmas surprise* (1991)
6 *Horrible Harry and the kickball wedding* (1992)

Horror and the glory series
Wright, Richard Nathaniel
Autobiography
1 *Black boy* (1945)
A record of childhood and youth
2 *American hunger* (1977)

Horror High series
Adams, Nicholas
This pseudonym is used by Clay Coleman, Debra Doyle, Bruce Fretts, James Douglas Macdonald and Sherwood Smith as indicated against each title
1 *Mister Popularity* (1990)
Voice of evil
[Coleman]
2 *Resolved, you're dead* (1990)
You're dead
[Coleman]
3 *Heartbreaker* (1991)
[Coleman]
4 *New kid on the block* (1991)
Deadly secret
[Coleman]
5 *Hard rock* (1991)
[Coleman]
6 *Sudden death* (1991)
[Fretts]
7 *Pep rally* (1991)
Blood game
[Doyle; Macdonald]
8 *Final curtain* (1991)
[Smith]

Horror series
Dicks, Terrance
1 *Cry vampire!* (1981)
2 *Marvin's monster* (1982)
3 *Wereboy!* (1982)
4 *Demon of the dark* (1983)
5 *War of the witches* (1983)

Horrorscope series
Lory, Robert
1 *Green flames of Aries* (1974)
2 *Revenge of Taurus* (1974)
3 *Curse of Leo* (1974)
4 *Gemini smile, Gemini kill* (1975)

Horse book series
Bolton, Evelyn
1 *Stable of fear* (1974)
2 *Lady's girl* (1974)
3 *Goodbye Charlie* (1974)
4 *Ride when you're ready* (1974)
5 *Wild horses* (1974)
6 *Dream Dancer* (1974)

Horse crazy series
Vail, Virginia
1 *Horseback summer* (1990)
2 *Happy trails* (1990)
3 *Good sports* (1990)
4 *Horse play* (1990)
5 *Riding home* (1990)

Horse series
Hardcastle, Michael
1 *Saturday horse* (1977)
2 *Switch horse* (1980)

Horse series
Johnson, Dorothy Marie
see **Man called Horse series**

Horse series
Stanton, Mary
1 *Heavenly horse from the outermost west* (1988)
2 *Piper at the gate* (1989)
Piper at the gates of dawn

Horseclans series
Adams, Robert
1 *Coming of the Horseclans* (1975)
Revised edition 1982
2 *Swords of the Horseclans* (1977)
3 *Revenge of the Horseclans* (1977)
Numbers 1-3 also published in one volume entitled *Tales of the Horseclans*, 1985
4 *Cat of silvery hue* (1979)
5 *Savage mountains* (1980)
6 *Patrimony* (1980)
7 *Horseclans odyssey* (1981)
8 *Death of a legend* (1981)
9 *Witch goddess* (1982)
10 *Bili the Axe* (1983)
11 *Champion of the last battle* (1983)
12 *Woman of the Horseclans* (1983)
13 *Horses of the north* (1985)
14 *Man called Milo Morai* (1986)
15 *Memories of Milo Morai* (1986)
16 *Trumpets of war* (1987)
17 *Madman's army* (1987)
18 *Clan of the cats* (1988)
Companion volumes: *Friends of the Horseclans*, by Robert Adams and Pamela Crippen Adams, 2 volumes, 1987-1989

Horsegirl series
Ash, Constance
1 *Horsegirl* (1988)
2 *Stalking horse* (1990)
An evening-length opera ballet in five acts

Horses series
Hearne, Vicki
Poetry
1 *Nervous horses* (1980)
2 *In the absence of horses* (1983)

Horsin' around series
Coldsmith, Don
1 *Horsin' around* (1975)
2 *Horsin' around again* (1982)

Hortense Clinton series
Hagen, Miriam Ann
1 *Plant me now* (1947)
2 *Dig me later* (1949)
3 *Murder, but natch* (1951)

Hortense series
Foster, Edna Abigail
1 *Hortense* (1902)
A difficult child
2 *Cordelia's pathway out* (1905)

Horton and Jordan series
Butler, Leslie
1 *Night and the judgment* (1964)
2 *Recover or kill* (1965)
3 *Man who crawled away* (1966)

Horton series
Kilbourne, Fannie
see **William Horton series**

Hospital life series
Jones, Irene Heywood
1 *Sister* (1982)
2 *Senior sister* (1983)

Hospital trilogy
Timperley, Rosemary
1 *Washers-up* (1968)
2 *Tragedy business* (1969)
3 *Doctor Z* (1970)

Hospitalities series
Tennant, Emma
1 *House of hospitalities* (1987)
2 *Wedding of cousins* (1988)

Hostage crisis series
This sequence has two authors
Mann, Sunnie
1 *Holding on* (1990)
Mann, Jackie
2 *Yours till the end* (1992)
Two survivors of the hostage crisis, their amazing story

Hosteen series
Norton, Andre
see **Arzor series**

Hosteen Storm series
Norton, Andre
see **Arzor series**

Hot corner series
Bowen, Robert Sidney
1 *Hot corner* (1951)
2 *Hot corner blues* (1964)

Hot pursuit series
This sequence has two authors
Francis, Jaye
1 *Melissa* (1991)
Moss, Merrilee
2 *Franca* (1991)
3 *Louise* (1991)
Francis, Jaye
4 *Rebecca* (1991)
5 *Troy* (1993)
Moss, Merrilee
6 *Kristi* (1993)
7 *Semra* (1993)
Francis, Jaye
8 *Belle* (1993)

Hot rod series
Bowen, Robert Sidney
1 *Hot rod angels* (1960)
2 *Hot rod rodeo* (1964)
3 *Hot rod pareol* (1964)
4 *Hot rod showdown* (1967)
5 *Hot rod outlaws* (1968)
6 *Hot rod doom* (1973)

Hotel Destiny series
Hughes, Zach
1 *Adlon link* (1981)
2 *Fortress London* (1981)
3 *Fires of Paris* (1981)
4 *Tower of treason* (1982)

Hotel Quadriga series
Glanfield, Jenny
1 *Hotel Quadriga* (1988)
2 *Viktoria* (1989)
3 *Children of their time* (1994)

Hotel series
Bemelmans, Ludwig
1 *At your service* (1941)
The way of life in a hotel
2 *Hotel Splendide* (1941)
3 *Hotel Bemelmans* (1946)

Hotel series
Johnstone, Nancy
1 *Hotel in Spain* (1937)
2 *Hotel in flight* (1939)

Hotel series
Nicol, Jean
1 *Hotel Regina* (1967)
2 *Home is the hotel* (1976)
3 *Bertioni's Hotel* (1983)

Hotline series
Meyer, Carolyn
1 *Because of Lissa* (1990)
2 *Problem with Sidney* (1990)
3 *Gillian's choice* (1991)
4 *Two faces of Adam* (1991)

Hotshots series
Blacker, Terence
1 *Pride and penalties* (1994)
2 *Shooting star* (1994)

Hotzenplotz series
Preussler, Otfried
see **Robber Hotzenplotz series**

Houghton series
Culpan, Maurice
see **Inspector Bill Houghton series**

Hound and Bear series
Gackenbach, Dick
1 *Hound and Bear* (1976)
2 *More from Hound and Bear* (1979)

Hound and the Falcon trilogy
Tarr, Judith
1 *Isle of glass* (1985)
2 *Golden Horn* (1985)
3 *Hounds of God* (1986)
One volume edition entitled *The Hound and the Falcon*, 1986

Hound Dog Zip series
Steele, William Owen
1 *Hound Dog Zip to the rescue* (1970)
2 *Triple trouble for Hound Dog Zip* (1972)

Hound series
Sivers, Brenda
see **Shelock Hound series**

Hours of gladness series
Maeterlinck, Maurice
1 *Double garden* (1904)
Original edition entitled *Le double jardin*
2 *Intelligence of flowers* (1907)
Measure of the hours
Original edition entitled *L'intelligence des fleurs*
One volume edition entitled *Hours of gladness*, 1912; selections published as *News of spring, and other nature studies*, 1913

House for the season series
Chesney, Marion
1 *Miser of Mayfair* (1986)
2 *Plain Jane* (1986)
3 *Wicked godmother* (1987)
4 *Rake's progress* (1987)
5 *Adventuress* (1987)
6 *Milady in love* (1987)
7 *Rainbird's revenge* (1988)

House in the park series
Ommanney, Francis Downes
Autobiography
1 *House in the park* (1944)
2 *River bank* (1966)

House of Barnery series
Chardonne, Jacques
1 *Wife of Jean Barnery* (1934)
Original edition entitled *La femme de Jean Barnery*
2 *Pauline* (1934)
Original edition entitled *Pauline*

House of Coombe series
Burnett, Frances Hodgson
1 *Head of the House of Coombe* (1922)
2 *Robin* (1922)

House of earth series
Buck, Pearl Sydenstricker
see **Wang family series**

House of Eigin series
Leiber, Justin Fritz
1 *Sword and the eye* (1985)
2 *Sword and the tower* (1986)

House of Enthala trilogy
Mayhar, Ardath
1 *Lords of the triple moons* (1983)
2 *Runes of the lyre* (1982)
3 *Soul-singer of Tyrnos* (1981)

House of evil series
Stine, Robert Lawrence
see **Ninety-nine Fear Street series**

House of Godwin series
Leslie, Colin
1 *Farrago of foxes* (1976)
2 *Feud royal* (1977)

House of Kurt series
Hudson, Stephen
see **Kurt series**

House of Niccolo series
Dunnett, Dorothy
1 *Niccolo rising* (1986)
2 *Spring of the ram* (1987)
3 *Race of scorpions* (1989)
4 *Scales of gold* (1991)
5 *Unicorn hunt* (1993)

House of Nire series
Kita, Morio
see **Kiichiro Nire series**

House of Stuart series
Tranter, Nigel Godwin
see **Stuart series**

House of Zeor series
Lichtenberg, Jacqueline
see **Sime-Gen series**

House series
Evers, Crabbe
see **Duffy House series**

House series
Holland, Elizabeth
1 *House in the north* (1963)
2 *House by the sea* (1965)

House that sailed away trilogy
Hutchins, Pat
1 *House that sailed away* (1976)
2 *Follow that bus* (1977)
3 *Mona Lisa mystery* (1981)

House-boat series
Bangs, John Kendrick
see **Associated shades series**

Household library series
Arthur, Timothy Shay
1 *Married life, its shadows and sunshine* (1851)
2 *Seed-time and harvest* (1851)
Alternative title: Whatever a man soweth, that shall he also reap
3 *Stories for young housekeepers* (1851)
4 *Two wives* (1851)
Alternative title: Lost and won
5 *Woman's trials* (1851)
Alternative title: Tales and sketches from the life around us
6 *Words for the wise* (1851)

Houston series
De Puy, Edward Spence
see **Sam Houston series**

Hovden series
Hamre, Leif
see **Peter Hovden series**

How animals series
Freedman, Russell
1 *How animals learn* (1969)
Co-author: James E Morriss
2 *Growing up wild* (1975)
How young animals survive
3 *Hanging on* (1977)
How animals carry their young
4 *How birds fly* (1977)
5 *How animals defend their young* (1978)

How does your garden grow series
Tarsky, Sue
1 *Prickly plant book* (1980)
2 *Window box book* (1986)
3 *Potted plant book* (1981)

How in the world series
Groves, Seli
1 *How in the world do we recycle glass?* (1992)
2 *How in the world do we recycle paper?* (1992)

How it feels series
Kremenetz, Jill
Photographic picture books
1 *How it feels when a parent dies* (1981)
2 *How it feels to be adopted* (1982)
3 *How it feels when parents divorce* (1984)
4 *How it feels to fight for your life* (1989)
5 *How it feels to live with a physical disability* (1992)

How series
McCall, Edith
1 *How we get our mail* (1961)
2 *How airplanes help us* (1961)
3 *How we get our clothing* (1961)
4 *How we get cloth* (1961)

How to be the perfect wife series
Bradford, Barbara Taylor
1 *Etiquette to please him* (1969)
2 *Entertaining to please him* (1969)
3 *Fashions that please him* (1970)

How to hide an animal series
Heller, Ruth M
1 *How to hide a polar bear and other mammals* (1985)
2 *How to hide a butterfly and other insects* (1985)
3 *How to hide an octopus and other sea creatures* (1985)
4 *How to hide a crocodile and other reptiles* (1986)
5 *How to hide a whip-poor-will and other birds* (1986)
6 *How to hide a grey tree frog and other amphibians* (1986)

How to rise trilogy
Alger, Horatio
1 *Jed, the poorhouse boy* (1899)
2 *Rupert's ambition* (1899)
3 *Lester's luck* (1901)

How to series
Baker, Stephen
1 *How to live with a neurotic dog* (1960)
2 *How to play golf in the low 120s* (1962)
3 *How to look like somebody in business without being anybody* (1963)
4 *How to live with a neurotic wife* (1970)
5 *How to live with a neurotic husband* (1970)
6 *How to be analyzed by a neurotic psychoanalyst* (1970)
7 *How to live with a neurotic cat* (1985)

How to series
Deem, James Morgan
1 *How to find a ghost* (1988)
2 *How to catch a flying saucer* (1991)
3 *How to hunt buried treasure* (1992)
4 *How to travel through time* (1993)
5 *How to read your mother's mind* (1994)

How to talk to your animals series
George, Jean Craighead
1 *How to talk to your dog* (1986)
2 *How to talk to your cat* (1986)
Originally published in one volume entitled *How to talk to your animals*, 1985

Howard Digburn series
Sanders, Bruce
1 *Secret dragnet* (1956)
2 *To catch a spy* (1958)
3 *Code of dishonour* (1964)
4 *Feminine for spy* (1967)

Howard Hayes trilogy
Lewis, Colin
1 *Golden grin* (1980)
2 *Acid test* (1982)
3 *Hot rain* (1983)

Howard series
Bracken, Anne
see **Jon and Julie Howard series**
Ellis, Novalyne Price
see **Robert Ervin Howard series**
Howard, Tom
see **Sergeant Tom Howard series**
Kenney, Susan
see **Roz Howard series**

Howard series
Lawhead, Stephen
1 *Howard had a spaceship* (1986)
2 *Howard had a submarine* (1987)
3 *Howard had a hot air balloon* (1988)
4 *Howard had a shrinking machine* (1988)

Howard series
McCutcheon, Hugh
see **Anthony Howard series**
Sims, George
see **Nicholas Howard series**

Howard series
Wiat, Philippa
1 *Like as the roaring waves* (1972)
2 *Queen's fourth husband* (1976)
3 *Lion without claws* (1976)
4 *Maid of gold* (1978)
5 *Yet a lion* (1978)
6 *Wear a green kirtle* (1987)

Howard series
Williams, Eric Ernest
see **Peter Howard series**

Howard trilogy
Argo, Ellen
see **Julia Howard trilogy**
Ford, Ford Madox
see **Fifth queen trilogy**

Howard's way series
Brason, John
Based on a television series
1 *Howard's way* (1985)
2 *Howard's way II* (1986)
3 *Howard's way III* (1987)

Howarth family series
Stubbs, Jean
see **Brief chronicles series**

Howarth series
Farrimond, John
see **Bob Howarth series**

Howden series
Mills, Woosnam
see **Sir John Howden series**

Howe and Barnes series
Franklin, Eugene
see **Berkeley Barnes and Larry Howe series**

Howell family series
Thompson, Valerie
1 *Rough road south* (1975)
2 *Gold on the wind* (1977)

Howie Rook series
Palmer, Stuart
1 *Unhappy hooligan* (1956)
Death in grease paint
2 *Rook takes knight* (1968)

Howl series
Jones, Diana Wynne
1 *Howl's moving castle* (1986)
2 *Castle in the air* (1991)

Howling series
Brandner, Gary
1 *Howling* (1977)
2 *Howling II* (1979)
Return of the Howling
3 *Howling III* (1985)
Echoes

Howton trilogy
Haworth, Elizabeth
Life in Victorian Lancashire
1 *Mistress of Howton* (1979)
2 *Farrers of Howton* (1979)
3 *Howton inheritance* (1980)

Hoyland series
Mann, Jessica
see **Tamara Hoyland series**
Williams, Philip Claxton
see **Mister Hoyland series**

Hub series
Schmitz, James Henry
1 *Tale of two clocks* (1962)
Legacy
2 *Nice day for screaming, and other tales of The Hub* (1965)
3 *Demon breed* (1968)
4 *Pride of monsters* (1970)

Hubbard series
Seuffert, Muir
see **Mike Hubbard series**

Hubble series
Murphy, Jill
see **Worst Witch series**

Hubbles series
Horseman, Elaine
1 *Hubble's bubble* (1964)
2 *Hubbles' treasure hunt* (1965)
3 *Hubbles and the robot* (1968)

Hubbo O'Driscoll series
Doyle, Brian
1 *Easy Avenue* (1988)
2 *Covered bridge* (1990)

Hubert Bonisseur de la Bath series
Bruce, Jean
see **Secret Agent O.S.S.117 series**

Huckleberry Finn series
This sequence has three authors
Twain, Mark
1 *Adventures of Huckleberry Finn* (1884)
Huckleberry Finn
Comic strip version entitled *The adventures of Huckleberry Finn*, by Clare Dwiggins, 1990
2 *Huck Finn and Tom Sawyer among the Indians, and other unfinished stories* (1983)
Matthews, Greg
3 *Further adventures of Huckleberry Finn* (1983)
Wood, Clement
4 *More adventures of Huckleberry Finn* (1941)
Companion volume: *The true adventures of Huckleberry Finn*, by John Seelye, 1970

Hudson River trilogy
Barbour, Ralph Henry
1 *Crimson sweater* (1906)
2 *Tom, Dick and Harriet* (1907)
3 *Harry's island* (1908)

Hudson series
Douglas, Lloyd Cassel
see **Doctor Hudson series**
Gilchrist, Ellen
see **Anna Hudson series**

Huff series
Edwards, Charman
see **Percy Aloysius Huff series**

Huffam series
Mackenzie, Compton
see **Oliver Huffam series**

Huffy Puffy series
Derwent, Lavinia
1 *Huffy Puffy* (1955)
2 *Huffy Puffy the little red engine* (1958)

Huggetts series
Constanduros, Mabel
1 *Here come the Huggetts* (1949)
2 *Vote for Huggett* (1949)
3 *Huggetts abroad* (1949)

Huggins series
Cleary, Beverly
see **Henry Huggins series**

Hugh and John series
Iseborg, Harry
see **John and Hugh series**

Hugh Brodie series
Edmonds, Harry
1 *Clockmaker of Heidelberg* (1949)
2 *Rockets* (1951)
Operation Manhattan
3 *Orphans of Brandenberg* (1953)

Hugh Carding series
Collins, Gilbert
1 *Post-mortem* (1930)
2 *Phantom tourer* (1931)
Murder at Brambles
3 *Channel million* (1932)
4 *Dead walk* (1933)
5 *Death meets the king's messenger* (1934)
6 *Poison pool* (1935)
7 *Haven of unrest* (1936)

Hugh Collier series
Dalton, Moray
see **Inspector Hugh Collier series**

Hugh Corbett series
Doherty, Paul C
1 *Satan in Saint Mary's* (1985)
2 *Crown in darkness* (1988)
3 *Spy in Chancery* (1988)
4 *Angel of death* (1989)
5 *Prince of darkness* (1991)
6 *Murder wears a cowl* (1992)
7 *Assassin in the greenwood* (1993)

Hugh Curtis and Mollie Bourne series
Somers, Paul
1 *Beginner's luck* (1958)
2 *Operation piracy* (1958)
3 *Shivering mountain* (1959)

Hugh Gordon and Liane Crawford series
Gilruth, Susan
see **Inspector Hugh Gordon and Liane Crawford series**

Hugh Melling series
Phillips, Leon
1 *Fire in his hand* (1979)
2 *Phoenix reaction* (1980)
3 *Ritual fire dance* (1981)

Hugh Monroe series
Schultz, James Willard
1 *Rising Wolf, the white Blackfoot* (1919)

Hugh Monroe series

Hugh Monroe's story of his first year on the plains
2 *Red Crow's brother* (1927)
Hugh Monroe's story of his second year on the plains

Hugh North series
Mason, Francis Van Wyck
see **Colonel Hugh North series**

Hugh Pine trilogy
Van de Wetering, Janwillem
1 *Hugh Pine* (1980)
2 *Hugh Pine and the good place* (1986)
3 *Hugh Pine and something else* (1989)

Hugh Rendal series
Portman, Lionel
1 *Hugh Rendal* (1905)
A public school story
2 *Progress of Hugh Rendal* (1907)
A 'varsity story

Hugh Rennert series
Downing, Todd
1 *Murder on tour* (1933)
2 *Cat screams* (1934)
3 *Vultures in the sky* (1935)
4 *Case of the unconquered sisters* (1936)
5 *Last trumpet* (1937)
6 *Night over Mexico* (1937)

Hugh Rudd series
Davis, Howard Charles
1 *Waxworks spies* (1962)
2 *Murder starts from Fishguard* (1966)

Hugh Stanton and Inspector Peter Curwen series
Vickers, Roy
see **Inspector Peter Curwen and Hugh Stanton series**

Hugh Westlake series
Stagge, Jonathan
see **Doctor Hugh Westlake series**

Hughes and Blaine series
Davis, Lavinia Riker
see **Nora Hughes and Larry Blaine series**

Hughes series
Hardie, David William Ferguson
see **Inspector Elwyn Hughes series**
Martin, Aylwin Lee
see **Matt Hughes series**

Hughes tetralogy
Hufford, Susan
see **Hilda Hughes tetralogy**

Hugo and Josephine trilogy
Gripe, Maria
1 *Josephine* (1961)
Original edition entitled *Josefin*
2 *Hugo and Josephine* (1962)
Original edition entitled *Hugo och Josefin*
3 *Hugo* (1966)
Original edition entitled *Hugo*

Hugo Baron series
Brett, John Michael
1 *Diecast* (1963)
Originally published under the pseudonym Michael Brett
2 *Plague of dragons* (1965)
3 *Cargo of spent evil* (1966)

Hugo Bishop series
Rattray, Simon
American editions published under the pseudonym Adam Hall
1 *Knight sinister* (1951)
2 *Queen in danger* (1952)
3 *Bishop in check* (1953)
4 *Dead silence* (1954)
Pawn in jeopardy
5 *Dead circuit* (1955)
Rook's gambit
6 *Dead sequence* (1957)

Hugo series
Ross, Tony
1 *Hugo and the wicked winter* (1977)
2 *Hugo and the man who stole colours* (1977)
3 *Hugo and Oddsock* (1978)
4 *Hugo and the ministry of Holidays* (1980)

Hugo Tower and Oliver Galt series
France, Victor
see **Oliver Galt and Hugo Tower series**

Hugo Wolfram series
Graves, Richard Latshaw
1 *Black gold of Malverde* (1973)
2 *Platinum bullet* (1974)
3 *Cobalt sixty* (1975)
4 *Quicksilver* (1976)

Hugs and kisses series
McLerran, Alice
Illustrated by Mary Morgan
1 *Hugs* (1993)
2 *Kisses* (1993)

Huguenot series
Johnson, William Henry
1 *King's henchman* (1898)
2 *King or knave, which wins?* (1899)
An old tale of Huguenot days

Huish series
Horler, Sydney
see **Martin Huish series**

Hulk series
Silva, Joseph
see **Incredible Hulk series**

Hull series
Burns, Ron
see **Harrison Hull series**

Hulzein family series
Busby, Francis Marion
see **Bran Tregare series**

Human age trilogy
Lewis, Wyndham
1 *Childermass* (1928)
2 *Monstre gai* (1955)
3 *Malign fiesta* (1953)
Numbers 2 and 3 also published in one volume entitled *The human age*, volume 2, 1955

Human Bat series
Home-Gall, Edward Reginald
1 *Human Bat* (1950)
Caught in the spider's web
2 *Human Bat versus the robot gangster* (1950)

Human behaviour trilogy
Brierley, John Keith
1 *Biology and the social crisis* (1967)
2 *Natural history of man* (1970)
3 *Thinking machine* (1973)

Human boy series
Phillpotts, Eden
1 *Human boy* (1899)
2 *Human boy again* (1908)
3 *From the angle of seventeen* (1912)
4 *Human boy and the War* (1916)
5 *Human boy's diary* (1924)
One volume edition entitled *The complete human boy*, 1930

Human happiness series
Dudley, Owen Francis
see **Problems of human happiness series**

Human predicament series
Hughes, Richard Arthur Warren
1 *Fox in the attic* (1961)
2 *Wooden shepherdess* (1973)

Human race club series
Berry, Joy
1 *Lean mean machine* (1987)
2 *Letter on light blue stationery* (1987)
3 *Battle at the McGoverns'* (1987)
4 *Fair weather friend* (1987)
5 *What happened to A.J.?* (1987)
6 *High price to pay* (1987)
7 *Casey's revenge* (1987)
8 *Saturday night stalker* (1987)

Human relations series
Matthews, Andrew
1 *Being happy!* (1988)
2 *Making friends* (1990)
A guide to getting along with people

Humanoids series
Williamson, Jack
1 *Humanoids* (1949)
Revised edition 1980
2 *Humanoid touch* (1980)

Humble powers trilogy
Horgan, Paul
1 *Devil in the desert* (1952)
A legend of life and death in the Rio Grande
2 *One red rose for Christmas* (1952)
3 *To the castle* (1952)
One volume edition entitled *Humble powers*, 1954

Humble series
Seton, Hilary
see **Minty Humble series**

Humbold series
Haswell, Peter
1 *Humbold gets his wheels* (1987)
2 *Humbold's pitch black day* (1987)

Humboldt series
Huddy, Delia
see **Tom Humboldt series**

Humbug series
Balian, Lorna
1 *Humbug witch* (1965)
2 *Humbug rabbit* (1974)
3 *Bah, Humbug!* (1977)
4 *Humbug potion* (1984)

Hume series
Bird, Brandon
see **Hampton Hume series**
Duncan, William Murdoch
see **Laurie Hume series**

Humphrey Campbell series
Homes, Geoffrey
1 *Then there were three* (1938)
2 *No hands on the clock* (1939)
3 *Finders keepers* (1940)
4 *Forty whacks* (1941)
Stiffs don't vote
5 *Six silver handles* (1944)
Case of the unhappy angels

Humphrey the Hippo series
Riddell, Chris
1 *Humphrey the Hippo* (1986)
2 *Humphrey of the Rovers* (1986)
3 *Humphrey goes to the ball* (1986)
4 *Humphrey's new trousers* (1986)

Humphries series
Powell, Margaret
see **Beryl Humphries series**

Hundred Years' War series
Burne, Alfred Higgins
1 *Crecy War* (1955)
A military history of the Hundred Years' War from 1337 to the Peace of Bretigny, 1360
2 *Agincourt War* (1956)
A military history of the Hundred Years' War from 1369 to 1453

Hunky series
Williamson, Thames
1 *Hunky* (1929)
2 *In Krusach's house* (1931)

Hunniwell boys series
Wyman, Levi Parker
1 *Hunniwell boys in the air* (1928)
2 *Hunniwell boys' victory* (1928)
3 *Hunniwell boys in the secret service* (1928)
4 *Hunniwell boys and the platinum mystery* (1928)
5 *Hunniwell boys' longest flight* (1928)
6 *Hunniwell boys in the Gobi Desert* (1930)
7 *Hunniwell boys in the Caribbean* (1930)
8 *Hunniwell boys' non-stop flight around the world* (1931)

Hunt series
Day, Lillian
see **Frederick Hunt series**
Price, Willard
see **Hal and Roger Hunt series**
Wellard, James
see **Lucius Hunt series**

Hunter Hawk series
Leyland, Eric
1 *Outlaws of the air* (1957)
2 *Atom 'plane mystery* (1958)
3 *Smugglers of the skies* (1958)
4 *Commandos of the clouds* (1959)
5 *Comet round the world* (1959)
6 *Secret weapon* (1960)
7 *Bandit gold* (1962)

Hunter Lewis and Jenny Gilette series
Gresham, Elizabeth
see **Jenny Gilette and Hunter Lewis series**

Hunter series
Ballard, Willis Todhunter
see **Lieutenant Max Hunter series**
Brown, Fredric
see **Ed and Am Hunter series**
Conway, Norman
see **Adam hunter series**
Dean, Robert George
see **Tony Hunter series**

Hunter series
Estes, Rose
1 *Hunter* (1990)
2 *Hunter on Arena* (1991)

Hunter series
Fisher, Vardis
see **In tragic life series**
Godwin, Felix
see **Captain John Hunter series**
Grey, Peter
see **Kit Hunter series**
Hayes, Ralph Eugene
see **John Yard series**
Manning, David
see **Bull Hunter series**
Marcus, Arthur A
see **Pete Hunter series**
Morse, Larry Alan
see **Sam Hunter series**
Newton, Mike
see **Jon Steel series**

Procter, Maurice
see **Superintendent Philip Hunter series**
Sauter, Eric
see **Robert Lee Hunter series**
Shirreffs, Gordon Donald
see **Dave Hunter series**

Hunters series
Tabori, Paul
1 *Doomsday brain* (1967)
2 *Invisible eye* (1967)
3 *Torture machine* (1969)

Hunters series
Wetanson, Burt
1 *Hunters* (1978)
2 *Treasure hunters* (1983)

Hunting adventures on land and sea series
Knox, Thomas Wallace
1 *Young Nimrods in North America* (1881)
2 *Young Nimrods around the world* (1882)

Hunting series
Cole, Tom
1 *Hell west and crooked* (1990)
2 *Last paradise* (1990)

Huntington Cage series
Riefe, Alan
1 *Lady killers* (1975)
2 *Conspirators* (1975)
3 *Black widower* (1975)
4 *Silver puma* (1975)
5 *Bullet-proof man* (1975)
6 *Killer with the golden touch* (1975)

Huntington series
Condon, Richard
see **Captain Colin Huntington series**

Huntoon Rogers series
Knight, Clifford
1 *Affair of the scarlet crab* (1937)
2 *Affair of the heavenly voice* (1937)
3 *Affair at Palm Springs* (1938)
4 *Affair of the ginger lei* (1938)
5 *Affair of the black sombrero* (1939)
6 *Affair on the painted desert* (1939)
7 *Affair in Death Valley* (1940)
8 *Affair of the circus queen* (1940)
9 *Affair of the skiing clown* (1941)
10 *Affair of the crimson gull* (1941)
11 *Affair of the limping sailor* (1942)
12 *Affair of the splintered heart* (1942)
13 *Affair of the fainting butler* (1943)
14 *Affair of the jade monkey* (1943)
15 *Affair of the dead stranger* (1944)
16 *Affair of the corpse escort* (1946)
17 *Affair of the golden buzzard* (1946)
18 *Affair of the sixth button* (1947)

Huntsman trilogy
Hill, Douglas
1 *Huntsman* (1982)
2 *Warriors of the wasteland* (1983)
3 *Alien citadel* (1984)

Huricane Castle series
Nixon, Joan Lowery
1 *Mystery of Hurricane Castle* (1964)
2 *Mystery of the haunted woods* (1967)

Hurricane Harland series
Allum, Tom
1 *Hurricane Harland blows in* (1953)
2 *Hurricane Harland hits out* (1954)
3 *Hurricane Harland takes the plunge* (1955)
4 *Hurricane Harland crashes the gate* (1958)

Hurricane Williams trilogy
Young, Gordon Ray
1 *Wild blood* (1923)
2 *Hurricane Williams* (1924)
3 *Hurricane Williams' vengeance* (1925)

Hurts of childhood series
Sanford, Doris
1 *Don't look at me* (1986)
A child's book about feeling different
2 *I can't talk about it* (1986)
A child's book about sexual abuse
3 *It must have hurt a lot* (1986)
A child's book about death
4 *Please come home* (1986)
A child's book about divorce
5 *I can say no* (1987)
A child's book about drug abuse
6 *I know the world's worst secret* (1987)
A child's book about living with an alcoholic parent
7 *Don't make me go back, mommy* (1990)

Husband series
Kamins, Jeanette
1 *Everything but a husband* (1962)
2 *Husband isn't everything* (1966)

Husbands and wives series
Atherton, Gertrude Franklin
see **Wives and husbands series**

Husky series
Thwaites, Frederick Joseph
Reminiscences of travel
1 *Husky be my guide* (1956)
2 *Press on regardless* (1960)

Hussey series
Dunne, Colin
see **Joe Hussey series**

Hustler series
Tevis, Walter Stone
1 *Hustler* (1959)
2 *Colour of money* (1984)

Hustlers Club series
Campbell, Julie
see **Ginny Gordon series**

Hutch and Starsky series
Franklin, Max
see **Starsky and Hutch series**

Hutton Seary series
Ross, John
see **Major Hutton Seary series**

Huuygens series
Fish, Robert Lloyd
see **Kek Huuygens series**

Huw Morgan series
Llewellyn, Richard
1 *How green was my valley* (1939)
2 *Up, into the singing mountain* (1960)
3 *Down where the moon is small* (1966)
4 *Green, green my valley now* (1975)

Huxley Pig series
Peppe, Rodney
1 *Here comes Huxley Pig* (1989)
2 *Huxley Pig at the circus* (1989)
3 *Huxley Pig in the haunted house* (1989)
4 *Huxley Pig the clown* (1989)
5 *Huxley Pig's aeroplane* (1990)
6 *Huxley Pig at the beach* (1990)
7 *Huxley Pig at the restaurant* (1990)
8 *Huxley Pig's dressing up book* (1991)
9 *Huxley Pig's model car* (1991)

Hwesu series
Yerby, Frank
1 *Dahomean* (1971)
Man from Dahomey
2 *Darkness at Ingraham's Crest* (1979)

Hybrid universe series
Hansen, Karl
1 *War games* (1981)
2 *Dream games* (1985)

Hyde series
Boland, John
see **John George Norman Hyde series**
Brent, Nigel
see **Barney Hyde series**
Wolff, Benjamin
see **John Byron Hyde series**

Hydronauts series
Biemiller, Carl Ludwig
1 *Hydronauts* (1970)
2 *Follow the whales* (1973)
Hydronauts meet the otter-people
3 *Escape from the crater* (1974)
Reunion
One volume edition entitled *The hydronaut adventures*, 1981

Hylas and Camillus series
Ray, Mary
see **Early Christian series**

Hylas trilogy
Baker, George
see **Trojan War trilogy**

Hylor trilogy
Wilder, Cherry
see **Rulers of Hylor trilogy**

Hyman Kaplan series
Ross, Leonard Q
1 *Education of Hyman Kaplan* (1937)
Sequence continued under the author's real name Leo Rosten
Rosten, Leo
2 *Return of Hyman Kaplan* (1959)
One volume abridged edition entitled *O Kaplan, my Kaplan*, 1976

Hyperion series
Simmons, Dan
1 *Hyperion* (1989)
2 *Fall of Hyperion* (1990)
One volume edition entitled *Hyperion cantos*, 1990

I

I am growing up series
Aston, Elizabeth
1 *Where is my buggy* (1986)
2 *Katie gets a bed* (1986)
3 *Time to sleep* (1986)
4 *Tom's new shoes* (1986)

I am series
Fitzhugh, Louise
1 *I am three* (1982)
2 *I am four* (1982)
3 *I am five* (1978)

I am series
Mayer, Mercer
1 *I am helping* (1992)
2 *I am hiding* (1992)
3 *I am playing* (1992)
4 *I am sharing* (1992)

I can do it series
Erickson, Karen
Illustrated by Maureen Roffey
1 *Playing story* (1985)
2 *Shhh story* (1985)
3 *Tidy-up story* (1985)
4 *Sharing story* (1985)
5 *Getting-dressed story* (1987)
6 *Night-time story* (1987)
7 *Make-a-mistake story* (1987)
8 *Angry story* (1987)
11 *I'm brave!* (1989)
12 *Waiting my turn* (1989)
13 *Do I have to go home?* (1989)
14 *I like helping* (1989)

I can do it series
Watanabe, Shigeo
Illustrated by Yasuo Ohtomo
1 *How do I put it on?* (1977)
2 *How do I eat it?* (1979)
3 *Hallo, how are you?* (1979)
4 *Ready, steady, go!* (1980)
5 *I can do it!* (1981)
6 *I'm the king of the castle* (1982)
7 *I can build a house* (1983)
8 *I'm going for a walk* (1983)
9 *I'm playing with papa!* (1985)
10 *I'm having a bath with papa!* (1986)

I can jump puddles series
Marshall, Alan
Reminiscences
1 *I can jump puddles* (1955)
2 *This is the grass* (1962)
3 *In mine own heart* (1963)

I can series
Asch, Frank
1 *I can blink* (1985)
2 *I can roar* (1985)

I can series
Bruna, Dick
1 *I can read* (1965)
Original edition entitled *Ik kan lezen*
2 *I can read more* (1965)
Original edition entitled *Ik kan nog meer lezen*
3 *I can count* (1968)
Original edition entitled *Telboek*
4 *I can count more, 13- 24* (1972)
Original edition entitled *Telboek twee*
5 *I can read difficult words* (1976)
Original edition entitled *Ik kan moeilijke woorden lezen*
6 *I can dress myself* (1976)
Original edition entitled *Ik kan nog weel meer lezen*

I don't want to series
Jungman, Ann
1 *I don't want to live in a house* (1988)
2 *I don't want to go to school* (1988)
3 *I don't want to go in a car* (1989)
4 *I don't want to play with my friends* (1989)

I hate series
Dragonwagon, Crescent
1 *I hate my brother Harry* (1983)
2 *I hate my sister Maggie* (1989)

I knock at the door series
O'Casey, Sean
Autobiography
1 *I knock at the door* (1939)
2 *Pictures in the hallway* (1942)
3 *Drums under the window* (1945)
4 *Inishfallen fare thee well* (1949)
5 *Rose and crown* (1952)
6 *Sunset and evening star* (1954)
7 *Green crow* (1957)

I know series
Bruna, Dick
1 *I know about numbers* (1980)
Original edition entitled *Ik kan sommen maken*
2 *I know more about numbers* (1980)
Original edition entitled *Ik kan nog meer sommen maken*
3 *I know about shapes* (1982)
Original edition entitled *Rond, vierkant, driehoekig*

I know series
Gree, Alain
1 *I know about flowers* (1970)
Original edition entitled *J'apprends a reconnaitre les fleurs*
2 *I know about cars* (1970)
Original edition entitled *J'apprends les autos*
3 *I know about colours* (1970)
Original edition entitled *J'apprends a reconnaitre les souleurs*
4 *I know about counting* (1970)
Original edition entitled *J'apprends a compter*
5 *I know about our world* (1970)
Original edition entitled *J'apprends la geographie*
6 *[J'apprends a voyager]* (1970)
No English edition
7 *I know about animals* (1970)
Original edition entitled *J'apprends a reconnaitre les animaux*

I like series
Curry, Peter
1 *I like wearing* (1986)
2 *I like playing* (1986)
3 *I like driving* (1986)
4 *I like eating* (1986)

I lived series
Baume, Eric
Autobiography
1 *I lived these years* (1941)
2 *I've lived another year* (1942)

I read series
Hoban, Tana
1 *I read signs* (1983)
2 *I read symbols* (1983)

I series
Keeler, Harry Stephen
see **Mysterious Mister I series**

I should have stayed in bed series
Lexau, Joan M
1 *I should have stayed in bed!* (1965)
2 *Rooftop mystery* (1968)

I spy series
Marzollo, Jean
Picture riddles
1 *I spy* (1992)
2 *I spy Christmas* (1992)
3 *I spy funhouse* (1993)
4 *I spy mystery* (1993)

I spy series
Tiger, John
1 *I spy* (1965)
2 *Masterstroke* (1966)
3 *Superkill* (1967)
4 *Countertrap* (1967)
5 *Doomdate* (1967)
6 *Wipeout* (1967)
7 *Death-twist* (1968)
Companion volume: *Message from Moscow*, by Brandon Keith, 1966

I swore series
French, Harold
Theatrical memoirs
1 *I swore I never would* (1970)
2 *I thought I never could* (1973)

I walk alone series
Wallace, Kathleen
1 *I walk alone* (1930)
2 *Without a stair* (1932)

I want series
Lindgren, Astrid
1 *I don't want to go to bed* (1947)
Original edition entitled *Jag vill inte gaa och laagga mei*; revised edition 1969
2 *I want to go to school* (1951)
Original edition entitled *Jag vill ock-saa gaa i skolan*; revised edition 1959
3 *I want a brother or sister* (1954)
Original edition entitled *Jag vill ock-saa ha et syskon*

I want to be series
Greene, Carla
1 *I want to be an animal doctor* (1956)
2 *I want to be a baker* (1956)
3 *I want to be a train engineer* (1956)
4 *I want to be an orange grower* (1956)
5 *I want to be a bus driver* (1957)
6 *I want to be a coal miner* (1957)
7 *I want to be a dairy farmer* (1957)
8 *I want to be a fisherman* (1957)
9 *I want to be a nurse* (1957)
10 *I want to be a pilot* (1957)
11 *I want to be a teacher* (1957)
12 *I want to be a zoo keeper* (1957)
13 *I want to be a doctor* (1958)
14 *I want to be a news reporter* (1958)
15 *I want to be a policeman* (1958)
16 *I want to be a postman* (1958)
17 *I want to be a road builder* (1958)
18 *I want to be a storekeeper* (1958)
19 *I want to be a telephone operator* (1958)
20 *I want to be a truck driver* (1958)
21 *I want to be a ballet dancer* (1959)
22 *I want to be a carpenter* (1959)
23 *I want to be a farmer* (1959)
24 *I want to be a fireman* (1959)
25 *I want to be a mechanic* (1959)
26 *I want to be a restaurant owner* (1959)
27 *I want to be a cowboy* (1960)
29 *I want to be a dentist* (1960)
29 *I want to be a librarian* (1960)
30 *I want to be an airplane hostess* (1960)
31 *I want to be a baseball player* (1961)
32 *I want to be a homemaker* (1961)
33 *I want to be a scientist* (1961)
34 *I want to be a space pilot* (1961)
35 *I want to be a musician* (1962)
36 *I want to be a ship captain* (1962)

I wonder about series
Watson, Jean
1 *I wonder about me* (1983)
2 *I wonder about plants* (1983)
3 *I wonder about farm animals* (1983)
4 *I wonder about zoo animals* (1983)

Ian and Angela Kendall series
Baxter, Gillian
see **Angela and Ian Kendall series**

Ian and Bruce series
Simons, Roger
see **Bruce and Ian series**

Ian and Sovra series
Lyon, Elinor
1 *House in hiding* (1950)
2 *We daren't go hunting* (1951)
3 *Hunt away home* (1953)
4 *Daughters of Aradale* (1957)
5 *Cathie runs wild* (1960)
6 *Carver's journey* (1962)
Secret of Hermit's Bay
7 *Dream hunters* (1966)
8 *Strangers at the door* (1967)
9 *King of Grey Corrie* (1975)
10 *Floodmakers* (1976)

Ian Firth series
Peters, Ludovic
1 *Snatch of music* (1962)
2 *Tarakian* (1963)
3 *Two sets to murder* (1963)
4 *Out by the river* (1964)
5 *Two after Malic* (1965)
6 *Riot '71* (1967)

Ian Hardy series
Currey, Edward Hamilton
1 *Ian Hardy, naval cadet* (1914)
2 *Ian Hardy, midshipman* (1915)
3 *Ian Hardy, senior midshipman* (1916)
4 *Ian Hardy, fighting the Moors* (1917)

Ian Macarthur series
Jepson, Selwyn
1 *Qualified adventurer* (1922)
Manchu Jade
2 *That fellow Macarthur* (1923)

Ian Quayle series
Caillou, Alan
1 *League of hawks* (1986)
2 *Sword of God* (1987)

Ian Ross series
Wood, James
1 *Northern mission* (1954)
2 *Great river* (1955)

Ice prophet trilogy
Forstchen, William R
1 *Ice prophet* (1983)
2 *Flame upon the ice* (1984)
3 *Darkness upon the ice* (1985)

Iceman series
Nazel, Joseph
1 *Billion dollar death* (1974)
2 *Golden shaft* (1974)
3 *Slick revenge* (1974)
4 *Sunday fix* (1974)
5 *Spinning target* (1974)
6 *Canadian kill* (1974)
7 *Shakedown* (1975)

Icequake series
Kilian, Crawford
1 *Icequake* (1979)
2 *Tsunami* (1983)

Icerigger series
Foster, Alan Dean
1 *Icerigger* (1974)
2 *Mission to Moulokin* (1979)
3 *Deluge drivers* (1987)

Icewind Dale trilogy
Salvatore, Robert Anthony
1 *Crystal shard* (1988)
2 *Streams of silver* (1989)
3 *Halfling's gem* (1990)

Ida Early series
Burch, Robert Joseph
1 *Ida Early comes over the mountain* (1980)
2 *Christmas with Ida Early* (1983)

Ida series
Chorao, Kay
1 *Magic eye for Ida* (1973)
2 *Ida makes a movie* (1974)
3 *Ida and Betty and the secret eggs* (1991)

Identity of France series
Braudel, Fernand
1 *History and environment* (1986)
2 *People and production* (1986)
Originally published in three volumes entitled *L'identite de la France*

Idwal Rees series
Mather, Berkely
1 *Pass beyond Kashmir* (1960)
2 *Terminators* (1971)
3 *Snowline* (1973)

If this be I series
Deland, Margaret
Autobiography
1 *If this be I, as I suppose it be* (1935)
2 *Golden yesterdays* (1941)

Igor Kerinsky series
Ryan, Jim
1 *Bludgeon* (1973)
2 *Vengeance business* (1973)

Ijon Tichy series
Lem, Stanislaw
1 *Futurological congress* (1971)
Original edition entitled *Bezsennosc*
2 *Star diaries* (1957)
Original edition entitled *Dzienniki gwiazdowe*, part 1
3 *Memoirs of a space traveler* (1957)
Original edition entitled *Dzienniki gwiazdowe*, part 2; selections from *Dzienniki gwiazdowe* translated as *Mortal engines*, 1957
4 *Peace on earth* (1994)

Ike and Mama series
Snyder, Carol
1 *Ike and Mama and the once-a-year suit* (1978)
2 *Ike and Mama and the block wedding* (1979)
3 *Ike and Mama and the once-a-life-time movie* (1981)
4 *Ike and Mama and the trouble at school* (1983)

Iktomi series
Goble, Paul
Plains Indian stories
1 *Iktomi and the boulder* (1988)
2 *Iktomi and the berries* (1989)
3 *Iktomi and the buffalo skull* (1990)
4 *Iktomi and the ducks* (1990)

Ilbarana series
Stuart, Donald
1 *Ilbarana* (1971)
2 *Malloonkai* (1976)
This character is the son of Ilbarana who is separated from his father for most of his life

Iliad adaptations series
Logue, Christopher
1 *Kings* (1991)
Adapted from Books 1 and 2
2 *Patrocleia* (1962)
Adapted from Book 16
3 *War music* (1981)
Adapted from Books 16- 19
4 *Pax* (1967)

I'll cry tomorrow series
Roth, Lillian
Autobiography
1 *I'll cry tomorrow* (1954)
2 *Beyond my worth* (1959)

I'll tell you a story series
Blyton, Enid
1 *I'll tell you a story* (1942)
2 *I'll tell you another story* (1942)

Illuminatus series
This sequence has two authors
Shea, Robert
1 *Eye in the pyramid* (1975)
2 *Golden apple* (1975)
3 *Leviathan* (1975)
Numbers 1-3 also published in one volume entitled *Illuminatus trilogy*, 1984
Wilson, Robert Anton
4 *Right where you are sitting now* (1982)

Illusionist series
Radford, John P
1 *Most happy con man* (1974)
2 *All our aircraft are missing* (1974)
3 *Parisian pigeon drop* (1974)
4 *Game show girls* (1975)

Illustrated Dune trilogy
Herbert, Frank
see **Paul Atreides trilogy**

I'm a little series
Tubby, I M
1 *I'm a little airplane* (1982)
2 *I'm a little fish* (1982)
3 *I'm a little house* (1982)
4 *I'm a little tugboat* (1982)

Image men series
Priestley, John Boynton
1 *Out of town* (1968)
2 *London end* (1968)
One volume edition entitled *The image men*, 1969

Imagine living here series
Cobb, Vicki
Illustrated by Barbara Lavallee
1 *This place is cold* (1989)
2 *This place is dry* (1989)
3 *This place is wet* (1990)
4 *This place is high* (1990)
5 *This place is lonely* (1991)
6 *This place is crowded* (1992)

Imamu Jones series
Guy, Rosa
1 *Disappearance* (1979)
2 *New guys around the block* (1983)
3 *And I heard a bird sing* (1987)

Imaro trilogy
Saunders, Charles Robert
1 *Imaro* (1981)
2 *Quest for Cush* (1984)
3 *Trail of Bohu* (1985)

Immigrant trilogy
Rolvaag, Ole Edvart
see **Per Hansa trilogy**

Immortal memory series
Barke, James
Based on the life of the poet Robert Burns
1 *Wind that shakes the barley* (1946)
2 *Song in the green thorn tree* (1947)
3 *Wonder of all the gay world* (1949)
4 *Crest of the broken wave* (1953)
5 *Well of the silent harp* (1954)
6 *Bonnie Jean* (1959)
Based on the life of Burns's widow

Imogene and Georgiana series
Sherwood, Valerie
1 *Bold breathless love* (1981)
2 *Rash reckless love* (1981)
3 *Wild willful love* (1982)
4 *Rich radiant love* (1983)

Imp trilogy
Krymov, Vladimir
Translated from the Russian
1 *Out for a million* (1926)
2 *He's got a million* (1926)
3 *End of the imp* (1926)

Imperial stars series
Pournelle, Jerry
1 *Stars at war* (1986)
2 *Republic and empire* (1987)
3 *Crash of empire* (1989)

Imperium series
Laumer, Keith
see **Mister Curlon series**

Impertinence series
Arnott, Peter
Memoirs of an engineer's life in India
1 *This impertinence* (1941)
2 *More impertinence* (1948)

Impett series
Ainsworth, Eustace
see **Billie Impett series**

Impressions series
Smyth, Ethel Mary
Autobiography
1 *Impressions that remained* (1919)
2 *Streaks of life* (1921)
3 *Final burning of boats* (1928)
4 *As time went by* (1936)
5 *What happened next* (1940)

Imprisoned missionary series
Bull, Geoffrey Taylor
1 *When iron gates yield* (1955)
The account of a British missionary to Tibet imprisoned in China for three years
2 *God holds the key* (1959)
A record of meditations and reflections during imprisonment in China, October 1950 to December 1953

Improbable life trilogy
Roland, Betty
Reminiscences
1 *Improbable life* (1989)
2 *This is the South Coast news and I'm Paul Murphy* (1990)
3 *Five South Coast seasons* (1992)

In a quiet land series
O'Donoghue, John
1 *In a quiet land* (1957)
2 *In a strange land* (1958)
3 *In Kerry long ago* (1960)

In crowd series
Harrell, Janice
1 *Gangs all here* (1988)
2 *Dear Doctor Heartbreak* (1988)
3 *Your daily horoscope* (1988)
4 *So long, senior year* (1988)

In his little black waistcoat series
Kiddell-Monroe, Joan
1 *In his little black waistcoat* (1939)
2 *In his little black waistcoat to China* (1947)
3 *In his little black waistcoat to India* (1948)
4 *In his little black waistcoat to Tibet* (1949)

In love series
Delisle, Francoise
Autobiography
1 *Francoise, in love with love* (1962)
2 *Friendship's odyssey* (1946)
In love with life; revised edition 1964; an account of life with Havelock Ellis
Companion volume: *My life*, by Havelock Ellis, 1940

In my own time series
Lehmann, John
Autobiography of a publisher
1 *Whispering gallery* (1955)
2 *I am my brother* (1955)
3 *Ample proposition* (1966)

In my world series
Kalman, Bobbie
1 *All about me* (1985)
Activity guide
2 *Come to my place* (1985)
3 *Fun with my friends* (1985)
4 *Happy to be me* (1985)
5 *My busy body* (1985)
6 *I lile school* (1985)
7 *People in my family* (1985)
8 *Animal worlds* (1986)
9 *Food we eat* (1986)
10 *I live in a city* (1986)
11 *People at work* (1986)
12 *Time and the seasons* (1986)
13 *How we communicate* (1986)
14 *How we travel* (1986)
15 *Life through the ages* (1986)
16 *People at play* (1986)
17 *Natural resources* (1987)
18 *Our earth* (1987)
19 *People and places* (1987)

In our neighborhood series
Sanford, Doris
1 *Brian was adopted* (1989)
2 *David has AIDS* (1989)
3 *Lisa's parents fight* (1989)
4 *Maria's grandmother gets mixed up* (1989)

In the ditch series
Emecheta, Buchi
1 *In the ditch* (1972)
2 *Second class citizen* (1974)

In the Lord series
Hinnebusch, Paul
1 *Friendship in the Lord* (1974)
2 *Community in the Lord* (1975)

In the mill series
Masefield, John
Autobiography
1 *In the mill* (1941)
2 *New chum* (1944)
3 *Grace before ploughing* (1966)

In time of trouble series
Cockburn, Claud
Autobiography of a journalist
1 *In time of trouble* (1956)
2 *Crossing the line* (1958)
3 *View from the west* (1961)

In times of series
Watson, Jean
Meditations on Christian life
1 *In times of success* (1979)
2 *In times of sorrow* (1979)
3 *In times of need* (1979)
4 *In times of joy* (1979)
5 *In times of growth* (1979)
6 *In times of doubt* (1979)
7 *In times of courage* (1979)
8 *In times of change* (1979)

Incarnations of immortality series
Anthony, Piers
1 *On a pale horse* (1983)
2 *Bearing an hour glass* (1984)
3 *With a tangled skein* (1985)
4 *Wielding a red sword* (1986)
5 *Being a green mother* (1987)
6 *For love of evil* (1988)
7 *And eternity* (1990)

Inch series
Straker, John Foster
see **Johnny Inch series**

Incomer series
Elphinstone, Margaret
1 *Incomer* (1987)
2 *Sparrow's flight* (1989)

Incorporated knight series
De Camp, Lyon Sprague
1 *Incorporated knight* (1987)
2 *Pixilated peeress* (1991)

Incredibilia series
Hunter, Norman
see **Kingdom of Incredibilia series**

Incredible adventures series
This sequence has three authors
Waedt, Carl F
1 *Incredible adventures, number 1* (1977)
2 *Incredible adventures, number 2* (1977)
Cummings, Ray
3 *Into the fourth dimension* (1981)

Incredible Brazilian trilogy
Ghose, Zulfikar
1 *Native* (1972)
2 *Beautiful empire* (1975)
3 *Different world* (1978)

Incredible drawing dog series
Myers, David
see **Sebastian, the incredible drawing dog series**

Incredible Hulk series
This sequence has three authors
Silva, Joseph
1 *Stalker from the stars* (1978)
Meyers, Richard S
2 *Cry of the beast* (1979)
Kupperberg, Paul
3 *Murdermoon* (1979)

Incredible true adventures series
Wulffson, Don L
1 *Incredible true adventures* (1986)
2 *More incredible true adventures* (1989)

Incubus trilogy
Tigges, John
1 *Garden of the incubus* (1982)
2 *Unto the altar* (1985)
3 *Kiss not the child* (1985)

Indermill series
Berry, Carole
see **Bonnie Indermill series**

India quartet
Scott, Paul
see **British India quartet**

India series
Eyton, John
1 *Kulla of the carts* (1926)
2 *Bulbulla* (1928)

Indian chiefs series
Tomlinson, Everett Titsworth
see **American Indian chiefs series**

Indian family series
Wernher, Hilda
1 *My Indian family* (1945)
2 *My Indian son-in-law* (1949)

Indian heritage series
Lederer, Paul Joseph
1 *Manitou's daughter* (1982)
2 *Shawnee dawn* (1982)
3 *Seminole skies* (1983)
4 *Cheyenne dreams* (1985)
5 *Way of the wind* (1985)
6 *North Star* (1987)
7 *Far dreamer* (1987)

Indian history trilogy
Grier, Sydney Carlyon
1 *In furthest Ind* (1894)
A novel based on the career of Edward Carlyon in the East India Company
2 *Like another Helen* (1899)
Set during the Black Hole of Calcutta period
3 *Great proconsul* (1904)
Based on the career of Warren Hastings as the first Governor General of India, as described by Mrs Hester Ward, a member of his family

Indian history trilogy
Taylor, Philip Meadows
1 *Tara* (1863)
A Mahratta tale
2 *Ralph Darnell* (1865)
3 *Seeta* (1872)

Indian life series
Deming, Therese
1 *Little Eagle* (1931)
2 *Indians in winter camp* (1931)

Indian life series

3 *Red people of the wooded country* (1932)
4 *Indians of the pueblos* (1936)
5 *Indians of the wigwams* (1938)

Indian mutiny trilogy
Pearce, Charles Edward
1 *Love besieged* (1907)
A romance of the residence in Lucknow
2 *Red revenge* (1911)
A romance of Cawnpore
3 *Star of the East* (1912)
A romance of Delhi

Indian mystic love stories series
Bain, Francis William
1 *Digit of the moon, and other love stories from the Hindoo* (1901)
2 *Descent of the sun* (1903)
A cycle of birth
3 *Heifer of the dawn* (1904)
4 *In the Great God's hair* (1904)
5 *Draught of the blue* (1905)
6 *Essence of the dusk* (1906)
7 *Incarnation of the snow* (1908)
8 *Mine of faults* (1909)
9 *Ashes of a god* (1911)
10 *Bubbles of the foam* (1912)
11 *Syrup of the bees* (1914)
12 *Livery of Eve* (1917)
13 *Substance of a dream* (1919)

Indian romance series
White, Edmund Valentine
1 *Path* (1914)
2 *Pilgrimage of Premnath* (1918)

Indian series
Banks, Lynne Reid
see **Omri series**
Lewin, Hugh
see **Little Indian series**

Indian tribes series
Edwards, Cassie
see **Savage series**

Indian trilogy
Masters, John
1 *Nightrunners of Bengal* (1951)
2 *Deceivers* (1952)
3 *Bhowani Junction* (1954)
One volume edition entitled *An Indian trilogy*, 1978

Indian trilogy
Mundy, Talbot
1 *Guns of the gods* (1921)
2 *Nine unknown* (1924)
3 *Ramsden* (1926)
Devil's guard

Indian trilogy
Thompson, Edward
1 *Indian day* (1927)
2 *Farewell to India* (1931)
3 *End of the hours* (1938)

Indian Two Feet series
Friskey, Margaret
1 *Indian Two Feet and his horse* (1959)
2 *Indian Two Feet and his eagle feather* (1967)
3 *Indian Two Feet and the wolf cubs* (1971)
4 *Indian Two Feet and the grizzly bear* (1974)
5 *Indian Two Feet and the ABC moose hunt* (1977)
6 *Indian Two Feet rides alone* (1980)

Indian War trilogy
Eggleston, George Cary
1 *Big brother* (1875)
2 *Captain Sam* (1876)
Alternative title: The boy scouts of 1814
3 *Signal boys* (1877)
Alternative title: Captain Sam's company

Indiana Jones choose your own adventure series
Brightfield, Richard
1 *Valley of the kings* (1992)
2 *South of the border* (1992)

Indiana Jones explores series
Malam, John
1 *Indiana Jones explores Egypt* (1992)
2 *Indiana Jones explores the Incas* (1993)

Indiana Jones find your fate series
This sequence has six authors
Stine, Robert Lawrence
1 *Indiana Jones and the curse of Horror Island* (1984)
Estes, Rose
2 *Indiana Jones and the lost treasure of Sheba* (1984)
Stine, Robert Lawrence
3 *Indiana Jones and the giants of the silver tower* (1984)
Helfer, Andrew
4 *Indiana Jones and the cup of the vampire* (1984)
Wenk, Richard
5 *Indiana Jones and the eye of the fates* (1984)
6 *Indiana Jones and the Legion of Death* (1984)
Stine, Robert Lawrence
7 *Indiana Jones and the cult of the mummy's crypt* (1985)
Stine, Harlan William
8 *Indiana Jones and the dragon of vengeance* (1985)
Weiss, Ellen
9 *Indiana Jones and the gold of Genghis Khan* (1985)
Stine, Robert Lawrence
10 *Indiana Jones and the ape slaves of Howling Island* (1987)
Stine, Harlan William
11 *Indiana Jones and the mask of the elephant* (1987)

Indiana Jones series
This sequence has three authors
Black, Campbell
1 *Raiders of the lost ark* (1981)
Companion volumes: *Raiders of the lost ark, a storybook based on the movie*, by Les Martin, 1981, *Indiana Jones and the raiders of the lost ark, a storybook based on the movie*, by Michael French, 1984
Kahn, James
2 *Indiana Jones and the temple of doom* (1984)
Companion volumes: *Indiana Jones and the temple of doom, the illustrated screenplay*, by Willard Huyck and Gloria Katz, 1984, *Indiana Jones and the temple of doom, a storybook based on the movie*, by Michael French, 1984, *Indiana Jones and the temple of doom*, by Les Martin, 1984
Macgregor, Rob
3 *Indiana Jones and the last crusade* (1989)
Companion volumes: *Indiana Jones and the last crusade*, by Les Martin, 1989, *Indiana Jones and the last crusade, a storybook based on the movie*, by Anne Digby, 1989
4 *Indiana Jones and the peril at Delphi* (1991)
5 *Indiana Jones and the dance of the giants* (1991)
6 *Indiana Jones and the seven veils* (1991)
7 *Indiana Jones and the unicorns legacy* (1991)
8 *Indiana Jones and genesis* (1992)
9 *Indiana Jones and the interior world* (1992)
Companion volumes: *Tales for the telling, Summer session, Gross purposes*, by Karen Ripley, 1983, *Indiana Jones, his life and adventure*, anonymous, 1989

Indiana Jones the Younger series
Martin, Les
see **Young Indiana Jones series**

Indigo series
Cooper, Louise Antell
1 *Nemesis* (1988)
2 *Inferno* (1988)
3 *Infanta* (1989)
4 *Nocturne* (1989)
5 *Troika* (1989)
6 *Avatar* (1989)

Indo-China series
Brodrick, Alan Hough
Reminiscences of travel
1 *Little China* (1942)
The Annamese lands
2 *Little vehicle* (1949)
Cambodia and Laos

Industries of England series
Phillpotts, Eden
1 *Brunel's tower* (1915)
2 *Old Delabole* (1915)
3 *Green alleys* (1916)
4 *Nursery* (1917)
Banks of Colne
5 *Spinners* (1918)
6 *Storm in a teacup* (1919)

Infirm glory series
Winn, Godfrey
1 *Infirm glory* (1967)
Also published in two volumes
1.1 *Green years* (1967)
1.2 *Growing years* (1967)
2 *One positive hour* (1970)

Inge Heinrich series
Fremd, Angelika
1 *Heartland* (1989)
2 *Glass inferno* (1992)

Ingelram series
Household, Geoffrey
see **Raymond Ingelram series**

Ingemar Johansson series
Joensson, Reidar
1 *My life as a dog* (1983)
Original edition entitled *Mitt liv som hund*
2 *My father, his son* (1991)
Original edition entitled *En hund begraven*

Ingenuity series
Hardy, Thomas
see **Novels of ingenuity series**

Inglis and Lilburne series
Walder, David
see **Charles Lilburne and Rupert Inglis series**

Ingram series
Williams, Charles
see **John Ingram series**

Ingrid and Vic Brown trilogy
Barstow, Stan
see **Vic Brown trilogy**

Inheritance trilogy
Chesher, Kim
1 *Fifth quarter* (1976)
2 *Carnford inheritance* (1977)
3 *Finn bequest* (1978)

Inheritor series
Bradley, Marion Zimmer
see **Leslie Barnes series**

Injun and Whitey series
Hart, William Surrey
1 *Injun and Whitey* (1920)
2 *Injun and Whitey strike out for themselves* (1921)
3 *Injun and Whitey to the rescue* (1922)

Ink-Bottle Club series
Smith, Sarah Stafford
1 *Ink-Bottle Club* (1967)
2 *Ink-Bottle Club abroad* (1969)

Inland trilogy
Halam, Ann
1 *Daymaker* (1987)
2 *Transformations* (1988)
3 *Skybreaker* (1990)

Inland voyage series
Stevenson, Robert Louis
Memoirs of travel
1 *Inland voyage* (1878)
2 *Travels with a donkey* (1879)

Inner planets trilogy
This sequence has three authors
Miller, John Joseph
1 *First power play* (1990)
Murdock, Melinda Seabrooke
2 *Prime squared* (1990)
Bloom, Britton
3 *Matrix cubed* (1991)

Innes series
Moore, George
see **Evelyn Innes series**

Innings series
Cardus, Neville
Memoirs and reminiscences of cricket
1 *Autobiography* (1947)
2 *Second innings* (1950)
3 *Full score* (1970)
4 *Cardus on cricket* (1977)
5 *Cardus in the covers* (1978)
6 *Cardus for all seasons* (1985)
Companion volume: *The summer game*, 1948

Innkeeper series
Fothergill, John
Reminiscences
1 *Innkeeper's diary* (1931)
2 *Confessions of an innkeeper* (1938)
3 *My three inns* (1949)

Innocent series
Guth, Paul
No English translation of numbers 1-3, 5, 6
1 *[Memoirs d'un naif]* (1953)
2 *[Naif sous les drapeaux]* (1954)
3 *[Naif aux quarantes enfants]* (1955)
4 *Innocent tenant* (1956)
Original edition entitled *Le naif locataire*
5 *[Mariage du naif]* (1957)
6 *[Naif amoureux]* (1958)

Innocent series
Smith, Frederick Escreet
1 *Rage of the innocent* (1986)
2 *In presence of my foes* (1988)

Innocents series
Twain, Mark
1 *Innocents abroad* (1869)
2 *Innocents at home* (1872)
Companion volumes: *Roughing it*, 1872, *Traveling with the Innocents abroad, Mark Twain's original reports from Europe and the Holy Land*, 1958

Inquiries Inc. series
Linzee, David
see **Sarah Saber and Chris Rockwell series**

Inquisition war series
This sequence has three authors
Jones, Neal
1 *Deathwing* (1990)
Watson, Ian
2 *Inquisitor* (1990)
3 *Space marine* (1993)
Companion volume: *Warhammer forty thousand*, by Neal Jones and David Pringle, 1990

Inquisitor series
Quinn, Simon
1 *His Eminence, Death* (1974)
2 *Nuplex Red* (1974)
3 *Devil in Kansas* (1974)
4 *Last time I saw hell* (1974)
5 *Midas coffin* (1975)
6 *Last rites for the vulture* (1975)

Insanity fair trilogy
Reed, Douglas
1 *Insanity fair* (1938)
2 *Disgrace abounding* (1939)
3 *Prophet at home* (1941)

Insect life series
Maeterlinck, Maurice
1 *Life of the bee* (1901)
Original edition entitled *La vie des abeilles*; selections published as *The swarm*, 1906; children's edition published as *The children's life of the bee*, 1920
2 *Life of the white ant* (1926)
Original edition entitled *La vie des termites*
3 *Life of the ant* (1930)
Original edition entitled *La vie des fourmis*

Inside business series
Aaseng, Nathan
1 *Better mousetraps* (1989)
Product improvements that led to success
2 *Fortunate fortunes* (1989)
Business successes that began with a lucky break
3 *Problem solvers* (1989)
People who turned problems into products
4 *Rejects* (1989)
People and products that outsmarted the experts
5 *Unsung heroes* (1989)
Unheralded people who invented famous products
6 *Close calls* (1990)
From the brink of ruin to business success
7 *From rags to riches* (1990)
People who started businesses from scratch
8 *Midstream changes* (1990)
People who started over and made it work

Inside-outside series
Munro, Roxie
1 *Inside-outside book of New York City* (1985)
2 *Inside-outside book of Washington D.C.* (1987)
3 *Inside-outside book of London* (1989)
4 *Inside-outside book of Paris* (1992)

Inspector Achille Peroni series
Holme, Timothy
1 *Neapolitan streak* (1980)
2 *Funeral of gondolas* (1981)
3 *Devil and the Dolce Vita* (1982)
4 *Assisi murders* (1985)
5 *At the lake of sudden death* (1987)

Inspector Adam Quill series
Brahms, Caryl
1 *Bullet in the ballet* (1937)
2 *Casino for sale* (1938)
Murder a la Stroganoff
3 *Envoy on excursion* (1940)

Inspector Adams series
Hollingsworth, Leonard
see **Superintendent Adams series**

Inspector Alan Grant series
Tey, Josephine
1 *Man in the queue* (1929)
Killer in the crowd
Originally published under the pseudonym Gordon Daviot
2 *Shilling for candles* (1936)
3 *Franchise affair* (1948)
4 *To love and be wise* (1950)
5 *Daughter of time* (1951)
6 *Singing sands* (1952)

Inspector Anders series
Jobson, Hamilton
1 *Therefore I killed him* (1968)
2 *Smile and be a villain* (1969)
3 *Naked to my enemy* (1970)
4 *Silent cry* (1970)
5 *House with blnd eyes* (1971)
6 *Shadow that caught fire* (1972)
7 *Sand pit* (1972)
8 *Contact with a killer* (1974)
9 *Evidence you will hear* (1975)
10 *Waiting for Thursday* (1977)
11 *Judge me tomorrow* (1978)
12 *To die a little* (1979)
13 *Exit to violence* (1979)
14 *Don't tell the press* (1981)
15 *Sleeping tiger* (1982)

Inspector Archie Burford series
Macclure, Victor
1 *Case of the dead producer* (1930)
2 *Counterfeit murders* (1932)
3 *Death behind the door* (1933)
4 *Clue of the dead goldfish* (1933)
5 *Death on the set* (1934)
6 *Hi-spy-kick-the-can* (1936)
7 *Diva's emeralds* (1937)

Inspector Armstrong series
White, Alan
1 *Armstrong* (1973)
American edition published under the pseudonym Alec Whitney
2 *Death in duplicate* (1974)
3 *Death in darkness* (1975)
American edition published under the pseudonym Alec Whitney

Inspector Arnold and Desmond Merrion series
Burton, Miles
1 *Secret of High Eldersham* (1930)
Mystery of High Eldersham
2 *Three crimes* (1931)
3 *Menace on the Downs* (1931)
4 *Death of Mr Gantley* (1932)
5 *Fate at the fair* (1933)
6 *Tragedy at the thirteenth hole* (1933)
7 *Death at the crossroads* (1933)
8 *Charabanc mystery* (1934)
9 *To catch a thief* (1934)
10 *Devereux Court mystery* (1935)
11 *Milk-churn murders* (1935)
Clue of the silver brush
12 *Death in the tunnel* (1936)
Dark is the tunnel
13 *Murder of a chemist* (1936)
14 *Where is Barbara Prentice?* (1936)
Clue of the silver cellar
15 *Death at the club* (1937)
Clue of the fourteen keys
16 *Murder in Crown Passage* (1937)
Man with tattooed face
17 *Death at low tide* (1938)
18 *Platinum cat* (1938)
19 *Death leaves no card* (1939)
20 *Mister Babbacombe dies* (1939)
21 *Murder in the coalhole* (1940)
Written in dust
22 *Mister Westerby missing* (1940)
23 *Death takes a flat* (1940)
Vacancy with corpse
24 *Death of two brothers* (1941)
25 *Up the garden path* (1941)
Death visits Downspring
26 *This undesirable residence* (1942)
Death at Ash House
27 *Dead stop* (1943)
28 *Murder, M.D.* (1943)
Who killed the doctor?
29 *Four-ply yarn* (1944)
Shadow on the cliff
30 *Three corpse trick* (1944)
31 *Not a leg to stand on* (1945)
32 *Early morning murder* (1945)
Accidents do happen
33 *Cat jumps* (1946)
34 *Situation vacant* (1946)
35 *Heir to Lucifer* (1947)
36 *Will in the way* (1947)
37 *Death in shallow water* (1948)
38 *Devil's reckoning* (1949)
39 *Death takes the living* (1949)
Disappearing parson
40 *Look alive* (1949)
41 *Ground for suspicion* (1950)
42 *Village afraid* (1950)
43 *Beware your neighbour* (1951)
44 *Murder out of school* (1951)
45 *Murder on duty* (1952)
46 *Something to hide* (1953)
47 *Heir to murder* (1953)
48 *Murder in absence* (1954)
49 *Unwanted corpse* (1954)
50 *Murder unrecognized* (1955)
51 *Crime in time* (1955)
52 *Found drowned* (1956)
53 *Death in a duffle coat* (1956)
54 *Chinese puzzle* (1957)
55 *Moth-watch murder* (1957)
56 *Bones in the brickfield* (1958)
57 *Death takes a detour* (1958)
58 *Return from the dead* (1959)
59 *Smell of smoke* (1959)
60 *Legacy of death* (1960)
61 *Death paints a picture* (1960)

Inspector Auguste Jantry series
Graeme, Bruce
1 *Case of books* (1946)
2 *Cherchez la femme* (1951)
3 *Lady in black* (1952)

Inspector Barlow series
Martin, Troy Kennedy
see **Chief Inspector Barlow series**

Inspector Barlowe series
Smith, C I D
1 *Thy guilt is great* (1939)
2 *No epitaph for Mister Zarke* (1941)

Inspector Barnaby series
Shaw, Howard
1 *Killing no murder* (1972)
Originally published under the pseudonym Colin Howard
2 *Death of a don* (1981)

Inspector Barry series
Rowe, Anne
1 *Too much poison* (1944)
Cobra venom
2 *Up to the hilt* (1945)
3 *Deadly intent* (1946)

Inspector Basil series
Hobson, Polly
1 *Murder won't out* (1964)
2 *Titty's dead* (1968)
Terrible thing has happened to Miss Dupont
3 *Three Graces* (1970)

Inspector Bass series
Truss, Seldon
1 *Rooksmiths* (1936)
Later edition entitled *Deadline for a diplomat* does not include Inspector Bass
2 *Foreign bodies* (1938)
Sequence continued under the pseudonym George Selmark
Selmark, George
3 *Murder in silence* (1939)

Inspector Beck series
Ryland, Clive
1 *Blind beggar murder* (1935)
2 *Case against Alder* (1941)
3 *Murder on Bag Hill* (1945)

Inspector Bedison series
Cobb, Thomas
1 *Crime without a clue* (1929)
2 *Inspector Bedison and the Sunderland case* (1931)
3 *Inspector bedison risks it* (1931)
4 *Who closed the casement?* (1932)

Inspector Ben Jurnet series
Haymon, Sylvia T
1 *Death and the pregnant virgin* (1980)
2 *Ritual murder* (1982)
3 *Stately homicide* (1984)
4 *Death of a god* (1987)
5 *Very particular murder* (1989)
6 *Death of a warrior queen* (1991)
7 *Beautiful death* (1993)

Inspector Bernard Bray series
Sprigg, Christopher Saint John
1 *Crime in Kensington* (1933)
Pass the body
2 *Perfect alibi* (1934)
3 *Death of an airman* (1934)

Inspector Bill Aveyard series
Fraser, James
1 *Evergreen death* (1968)
2 *Cock-pit of roses* (1969)
3 *Deadly nightshade* (1970)
4 *Death in a pheasant's eye* (1971)
5 *Blood on a widow's cross* (1972)
6 *Five-leafed clover* (1973)
7 *Wreath of lords and ladies* (1974)
8 *Who steals my name?* (1976)
9 *Hearts ease in death* (1977)

Inspector Bill Hazard and Frank Drury series
Marlowe, Piers
see **Frank Drury and Inspector Bill Hazard series**

Inspector Bill Houghton series
Culpan, Maurice
1 *Nice place to die* (1965)
2 *Minister of Injustice* (1966)
3 *In a deadly vein* (1967)
4 *Vasiliko affair* (1968)
5 *Bloody success* (1969)

Inspector Bill Murray series
Colin, Aubrey
1 *Hands of death* (1963)
2 *Death comes to dinner* (1965)

Inspector Bill Vallance series
Proudfoot, Walter
1 *Crime in the arcade* (1931)
2 *Arrest* (1933)
3 *Conspiracy* (1933)

Inspector Bland series
Symons, Julian
1 *Immaterial murder* (1945)
2 *Man called Jones* (1947)
3 *Bland beginning* (1949)

Inspector Blessingay series
Barrett, Geoffrey John
1 *He died twice* (1968)
2 *Guilty, be damned!* (1968)
3 *Cup that kills* (1969)
4 *His own funeral* (1972)

Inspector Bliss series
Remenham, John
1 *Canal mystery* (1928)
2 *Arsenic* (1930)
3 *Dump* (1931)

Inspector Bonny Lee series
Douglas, George
1 *Death in darkness* (1973)
2 *Death on the doorstep* (1973)
3 *Dead on the dot* (1974)
4 *Crime without reason* (1975)
5 *Death in retreat* (1976)
6 *End of the line* (1977)
7 *Unholy terror* (1978)

Inspector Borges series
Bonett, John
1 *Better dead* (1964)
Better off dead
2 *Private face of murder* (1966)
3 *This side murder?* (1967)
Murder on the Costa Brava
4 *Sound of murder* (1970)
5 *No time to kill* (1972)
6 *Perish the thought* (1984)

Inspector Bourne series
Finney, R C
1 *Meet Inspector Bourne* (1945)
2 *Honeymoon murder* (1947)
3 *Death in the mist* (1947)
4 *Three point murder* (1949)
5 *Crimson hand* (1949)
6 *Find the lady* (1949)
7 *Lover's feud* (1949)
8 *Talking clues* (1949)
9 *Coleville skeleton* (1950)
10 *Death takes a ride* (1951)
11 *Love's prisoner* (1952)

Inspector Bradley and Sergeant Raymond series
Longmate, Norman
1 *Death won't wash* (1957)
2 *Head for death* (1958)
3 *Strip death naked* (1959)
4 *Vote for death* (1960)
5 *Death in office* (1961)

Inspector Bramley series
Broome, Adam
1 *Oxford murders* (1929)
2 *Cambridge murders* (1936)

Inspector Brentford series
Hough, Stanley Bennett
1 *Bronze Perseus* (1959)
Tender killer
2 *Dear daughter dead* (1965)
3 *Sweet sister seduced* (1968)
4 *Fear fortune, father* (1974)

Inspector Brett Nightingale series
Kelly, Mary
1 *Cold coming* (1956)
2 *Dead man's riddle* (1957)
3 *Christmas egg* (1958)

Inspector Brews series
Loder, Vernon
1 *Essex murders* (1930)
Death pool
2 *Death of an editor* (1931)

Inspector Buck series
Marsden, Antony
1 *Death on the Downs* (1929)
2 *Death strikes from the rear* (1934)

Inspector Burnival series
Candy, Edward
1 *Which doctor?* (1953)
2 *Bones of contention* (1954)
3 *Words for a murder perhaps* (1971)

Inspector Burton series
Locke, Gladys Edson
1 *Red cavalier* (1922)
2 *Scarlet macaw* (1923)
3 *Purple mist* (1924)
4 *House on the Downs* (1925)

Inspector Byrne series
Vivian, Evelyn Charles
1 *Girl in the dark* (1933)
2 *Man with a scar* (1940)
3 *Vain escape* (1952)

Inspector Byrnes series
Hawthorne, Julian
1 *American penman* (1887)
2 *Great bank robbery* (1887)
3 *Tragic mystery* (1887)
4 *Another's crime* (1888)
5 *Section five hundred and fifty eight* (1888)
Alternative title: The fatal letter

Inspector C D Sloan series
Aird, Catherine
1 *Religious body* (1966)
2 *Henrietta who?* (1968)
3 *Complete steel* (1969)
Stately home murder
4 *Late phoenix* (1970)
5 *His burial too* (1973)
6 *Slight mourning* (1975)
7 *Parting breath* (1977)
8 *Some die eloquent* (1979)
9 *Passing strange* (1980)
10 *Last respects* (1982)
11 *Harm's Way* (1984)
12 *Dead liberty* (1986)
13 *Body politic* (1990)
14 *Going concern* (1993)

Inspector Cadman series
Rushton, Charles
1 *Murder out of tune* (1939)
2 *Murder on trust* (1943)
3 *No beast so fierce* (1950)
4 *Furnace for a foe* (1951)
5 *Devil's power* (1952)

Inspector Cam and Beaver series
Cockin, Joan
1 *Curiosity killed the cat* (1947)
2 *Villainy at vespers* (1949)
3 *Deadly earnest* (1952)

Inspector Cardiff series
Gray, Dulcie
1 *Epitaph for a dead actor* (1960)
2 *Died in the red* (1968)

Inspector Carol Ashton and Sergeant Mark Bourke series
McNab, Claire
1 *Lessons in murder* (1988)
2 *Fatal reunion* (1989)
3 *Death down under* (1989)
4 *Cop out* (1991)
5 *Dead certain* (1992)
Off key
6 *Body guard* (1994)

Inspector Cathy Weston series
Conway, Peter
1 *Cradle snatch* (1978)
2 *Dancing bear* (1978)

Inspector Cauldron series
Fowler, Sydney
1 *Bout with the Mildew Gang* (1941)
2 *Second bout with the Mildew Gang* (1942)
3 *End of the Mildew Gang* (1944)

Inspector Chace series
Loder, Vernon
1 *Murder from three angles* (1934)
2 *Death at the horse show* (1935)

Inspector Charles Tremayne series
Mackenzie, Nigel
1 *Killer at large* (1961)
2 *Race toward death* (1963)
3 *Night of fear* (1964)

Inspector Charlesworth series
Brand, Christianna
1 *Death in high heels* (1941)
2 *London particular* (1952)
Fog of doubt
3 *Rose in darkness* (1979)
4 *Death of Jezebel* (1948)

Inspector Charlie Chan series
Biggers, Earl Derr
see **Charlie Chan series**

Inspector Charlie Resnick series
Harvey, John Barton
1 *Lonely hearts* (1989)
2 *Rough treatment* (1990)
3 *Cutting edge* (1991)
4 *Off minor* (1992)
5 *Wasted years* (1993)
6 *Cold light* (1994)

Inspector Charlie Salter series
Wright, Eric
1 *Night the gods smiled* (1983)
2 *Smoke detector* (1984)
3 *Death in the old country* (1985)
4 *Single death* (1986)
Man who changed his name
5 *Body surrounded by water* (1987)
6 *Question of murder* (1988)
7 *Sensitive case* (1990)
8 *Final cut* (1991)
9 *Fine Italian mind* (1992)
10 *Death by degrees* (1993)

Inspector Charlton series
Witting, Clifford
1 *Murder in blue* (1937)
2 *Midsummer murder* (1937)
3 *Case of the Michaelmas goose* (1938)
4 *Catt out of the bag* (1939)
5 *Measure for murder* (1941)
6 *Subject, murder* (1945)
7 *Let X be the murderer* (1947)
8 *Dead on time* (1948)
9 *Bullet for Rhino* (1950)
10 *Case of the Busy Bees* (1952)
11 *Silence after dinner* (1953)

Inspector Cherry and Sergeant Duff series
Van Greenaway, Peter
1 *Medusa touch* (1973)
2 *Doppelganger* (1975)
3 *Destiny man* (1977)
4 *Cassandra Bell* (1981)
5 *Lazarus lie* (1982)
6 *Killing cup* (1987)

Inspector Cheviot Burmann series
Cobb, Belton
1 *No alibi* (1936)
2 *Poisoner's mistake* (1936)
3 *Fatal dose* (1937)
4 *Quickly dead* (1937)
5 *Like a guilty thing* (1938)
Revised edition 1959
6 *Fatal holiday* (1938)
7 *Inspector Burmann's busiest day* (1939)
8 *Death defies the doctor* (1939)
9 *Inspector Burmann's blackout* (1941)
10 *Double detection* (1945)
11 *Death in the 13th dose* (1946)
12 *No mercy for Margaret* (1952)
13 *Next door to death* (1952)
14 *Detective in distress* (1953)
15 *Corpse incognito* (1953)
16 *Need a body tell?* (1954)
17 *Willing witness* (1955)
18 *Drink alone and die* (1956)
19 *Corpse at Casablanca* (1956)
20 *Doubly dead* (1957)
21 *Poisoner's base* (1957)
22 *Missing scapegoat* (1958)
23 *With intent to kill* (1958)
24 *Don't lie to the police* (1960)
25 *Death with a difference* (1960)
26 *Search for Sergeant Baxter* (1961)
27 *Corpse in the cargo* (1961)
28 *Murder, men only* (1962)
29 *Death of a peeping tom* (1963)
30 *No shame for the devil* (1964)
31 *Dead girl's shoes* (1964)
32 *I never miss twice* (1965)
33 *Last drop* (1965)
34 *Some must watch* (1966)
35 *Stone for his head* (1966)
36 *Lost without trace* (1967)
37 *Security secrets sold here* (1967)
38 *Secret inquiry* (1968)
39 *Silence under threat* (1968)
40 *Horrible man in Heron's Wood* (1970)
41 *Catch me, if you can* (1970)
42 *Suspicion in triplicate* (1971)

Inspector Christopher Adrian series
Silverman, Marguerite Ruth
1 *Vet it was that died* (1945)
2 *Who should have died* (1948)
3 *Nine had no vet* (1951)

Inspector Christopher Dennis Sloan series
Aird, Catherine
see **Inspector C D Sloan series**

Inspector Christopher Marsden series
Backhouse, Elizabeth
1 *Death came uninvited* (1957)
2 *Night has eyes* (1961)

Inspector Christopher McKee series
Reilly, Helen
1 *Diamond feather* (1930)
2 *Murder in the mews* (1931)
3 *Line-up* (1934)
4 *McKee of Centre Street* (1934)
5 *Mister Smith's hat* (1936)
6 *Dead man control* (1936)
7 *All concerned notified* (1939)
8 *Dead for a ducat* (1939)
9 *Dead can tell* (1940)
10 *Death demands an audience* (1940)
11 *Murder in Shinbone Alley* (1940)
12 *Mourned on Sunday* (1941)
13 *Three women in black* (1941)
14 *Name your poison* (1942)
15 *Opening door* (1944)
16 *Murder on Angler's Island* (1945)
17 *Silver leopard* (1946)
18 *Farm-house* (1947)
19 *Staircase four* (1949)
20 *Murder at Arroways* (1950)
21 *Lament for the bride* (1951)
22 *Double man* (1952)
23 *Velvet hand* (1953)
24 *Tell her it's murder* (1954)
25 *Compartment K* (1955)
Murder rides the express
26 *Canvas dagger* (1956)
27 *Ding, dong bell* (1958)
28 *Not me, Inspector* (1959)
29 *Follow me* (1960)
30 *Certain sleep* (1961)
31 *Day she died* (1962)

Inspector Chucky series
Brand, Christianna
1 *Death of Jezebel* (1948)
2 *Cat and mouse* (1950)

3 *Ring of roses* (1977)
Also published under the pseudonym Mary Ann Ashe

Inspector Clancy Martin series
Jackson, Wallace
1 *Two knocks for death* (1934)
2 *Diamonds of death* (1936)
3 *Sinister madonna* (1937)

Inspector Cleveland series
Fowler, Sydney
1 *By Saturday* (1931)
2 *Hanging of Constance Hillier* (1931)
3 *Crime and Co.* (1931)
Hand-print mystery
4 *Arresting Delia* (1933)

Inspector Clouseau series
This sequence has two authors; based on screenplays
Albert, Marvin Hubert
1 *Pink Panther* (1964)
Waldman, Frank
2 *Pink Panther strikes again* (1976)
3 *Return of the Pink Panther* (1977)

Inspector Clovis Pel series
This sequence has two authors
Hebden, Mark
1 *Death set to music* (1979)
2 *Pel and the faceless corpse* (1979)
3 *Pel under pressure* (1980)
4 *Pel is puzzled* (1981)
5 *Pel and the staghound* (1982)
6 *Pel and the bombers* (1982)
7 *Pel and the predators* (1984)
8 *Pel and the pirates* (1984)
9 *Pel and the prowler* (1985)
10 *Pel and the Paris mob* (1986)
11 *Pel among the Pueblos* (1987)
12 *Pel and the touch of pitch* (1987)
13 *Pel and the picture of innocence* (1988)
14 *Pel and the party spirit* (1989)
15 *Pel and the missing person* (1990)
16 *Pel and the promised land* (1991)
17 *Pel and the sepulchre job* (1992)
Hebden, Juliet
18 *Pel picks up the pieces* (1993)
19 *Pel and the perfect partner* (1994)

Inspector Cockrill series
Brand, Christianna
1 *Heads you lose* (1941)
2 *Green for danger* (1943)
3 *Crooked wreath* (1946)
Suddenly at his residence
4 *Death of Jezebel* (1948)
5 *London particular* (1952)
Fog of doubt
6 *Tour de force* (1955)
7 *Three-cornered halo* (1957)
8 *What dread hand* (1968)
Short stories

Inspector Colin series
Wood, Clement
1 *Shadow from the Bogue* (1928)
2 *Tabloid murders* (1930)

Inspector Colin Thane and Phil Moss series
Knox, Bill
1 *Deadline for a dream* (1957)
In at the kill
2 *Death department* (1959)
3 *Leave it to the hangman* (1960)
4 *Little drops of blood* (1962)
5 *Sanctuary isle* (1962)
Grey sentinels
6 *Man in the bottle* (1963)
Killing game
7 *Taste of proof* (1965)
8 *Deep fall* (1966)
Ghost car
9 *Justice on the rocks* (1967)
10 *Tallyman* (1969)
11 *Children of the mist* (1970)
Who shot the bull?
12 *To kill a witch* (1971)
13 *Draw batons!* (1973)
14 *Rally to kill* (1975)
15 *Pilot error* (1977)
16 *Live bait* (1978)
17 *Killing in antiques* (1981)
18 *Hanging tree* (1983)
19 *Crossfire killings* (1986)
20 *Interface man* (1989)

Inspector Cornford series
Kennedy, Milward
1 *Corpse on the mat* (1929)
Man who rang the bell
2 *Corpse guard parade* (1929)

Inspector Courtenay series
Berrow, Norman
1 *Secret dancer* (1936)
2 *One thrilling night* (1937)

Inspector Curtis Burke series
Trevor, Ralph
see **Superintendent Curtis Burke series**

Inspector Cuthbert Higgins series
Gregg, Cecil Freeman
1 *Murdered manservant* (1928)
Body in the safe
2 *Three daggers* (1929)
3 *Murder on the bus* (1930)
4 *Brazen confession* (1930)
I have killed a man
5 *Rutland mystery* (1931)
6 *Double solution* (1932)
7 *Inspector Higgins hurries* (1932)
8 *Body behind the bar* (1932)
9 *Duke's last trick* (1933)
10 *Inspector Higgins sees it through* (1934)
11 *Execution of Diamond Deutsch* (1934)
Execution of Deutsch
Murder in the park
12 *Ten black pearls* (1935)
Black pearls
13 *Danger at Cliff House* (1935)
14 *Tragedy at Wembley* (1936)
15 *Wrong house* (1937)
16 *Mystery at Moor Street* (1938)
17 *Who dialled 999?* (1939)
18 *Danger in the dark* (1939)
19 *Fatal error* (1940)
20 *Vandor mystery* (1942)
21 *Two died at three* (1943)
22 *Melander's millions* (1944)
23 *Old manor* (1945)
24 *Exit Harlequin* (1946)
25 *Murder at midnight* (1947)
26 *Man with a monocle* (1948)
27 *Ugly customer* (1949)
28 *From information received* (1950)
29 *Inspector Higgins goes fishing* (1951)
30 *Accidental murder* (1952)
31 *Sufficient rope* (1953)
32 *Night flight to Zurich* (1954)
33 *Chief constable* (1955)
34 *Dead on time* (1956)
35 *Obvious solution* (1958)
36 *Professional jealousy* (1960)

Inspector Daddy Bourne series
Galwey, Geoffrey Valentine
1 *Murder on leave* (1946)
2 *Lift and the drop* (1948)
3 *Full fathom five* (1951)

Inspector Damiot series
McConnor, Vincent
1 *Provence puzzle* (1980)
2 *Riviera puzzle* (1981)
3 *Paris puzzle* (1982)

Inspector Dann Carr series
Smith, Willard K
1 *Bowery murder* (1929)
2 *Sultan's skull* (1933)

Inspector Dave Norton series
Malloch, Peter
1 *Blood on pale fingers* (1969)
2 *Slugger* (1971)

Inspector David Brock series
White, Reginald James
1 *Smartest grave* (1961)
2 *Women of Peasenhall* (1969)

Inspector David Webb and Sergeant Ken Jackson series
Fraser, Anthea
1 *Shroud for Delilah* (1984)
2 *Necessary end* (1985)
3 *Pretty maids all in a row* (1986)
4 *Death speaks softly* (1987)
5 *Nine bright shiners* (1987)
6 *Six proud walkers* (1988)
7 *April rainers* (1989)
8 *Symbols at your door* (1990)
9 *Three, three the rivals* (1992)
10 *Gospel makers* (1994)

Inspector De Kok series
Baantjer, Albert Cornelis
1 *De Kok and the somber nude* (1964)
Original edition entitled *De Cock en het sombrere naakt*
2 *De Kok and the Sunday strangler* (1965)
Original edition entitled *De Cock en de wurger op zondag*; numbers 2 and 3 also published in one volume entitled *Murder in Amsterdam*, 1993
3 *De Kok and the corpse on Christmas eve* (1965)
Original edition entitled *De Cock en het lijk in de kerstnacht*
4 *De Kok and the dead harlequin* (1968)
Original edition entitled *De Cock en de dode harlekijn*
5 *De Kok and the sorrowing tomcat* (1969)
Original edition entitled *De Cock en de treurende kater*
6 *De Kok and the disillusioned corpse* (1970)
Original edition entitled *De Cock en de ontgoodshelde dode*
7 *De Kok and the careful killer* (1971)
Original edition entitled *De Cock en de zorgvuldige moordenaar*
8 *De Kok and the romantic murder* (1972)
Original edition entitled *De Cock en de romance in moord*
9 *De Kok and the dying stroller* (1972)
Original edition entitled *De Cock en de stervende wandelaar*
10 *De Kok and the corpse at the church wall* (1973)
Original edition entitled *De Cock en het lijk aan de kerkmuur*
11 *De Kok and the dancing death* (1974)
Original edition entitled *De Cock en de dansende dood*
12 *De kok and the naked lady* (1978)
Original edition entitled *De Cock en de naakte juffer*
13 *De Kok and the brothers of the easy death* (1979)
Original edition entitled *De Cock en de broeders van de zachte dood*
14 *De Kok and the deadly accord* (1980)
Original edition entitled *De Cock en het dodelijk akkoord*
15 *De Kok and the murder in seance* (1981)
Original edition entitled *De Cock en moord in seance*
16 *De Kok and murder in ecstacy* (1982)
Original edition entitled *De Cock en moord in extase*
17 *De Kok and the begging death* (1982)
Original edition entitled *De Cock en de smekende dood*
18 *De Kok and the geese of death* (1983)
Original edition entitled *De Cock en de gabzen van de dood*
19 *De Kok and murder by melody* (1983)
Original edition entitled *De Cock en moord op melodie*
20 *De Kok and the death of a clown* (1984)
Original edition entitled *De Cock en de dood van een clown*
21 *De Kok and variations on murder* (1984)
Original edition entitled *De Cock en een variant op moord*; numbers 22 to 30 not yet translated
31 *De Kok and murder on the menu* (1990)
Original edition entitled *De Cock en moord a la carte*
Numbers 32 to 40 not yet translated

Inspector Dennis Drury series
Sykes, William Stanley
1 *Missing money-lender* (1931)
Man who was dead
2 *Harness of death* (1932)
3 *Ray of doom* (1935)

Inspector Dick Mason series
Armstrong, Raymond
1 *Dangerous limelight* (1947)
2 *Sinister playhouse* (1949)
3 *Sinister Widow* (1951)
4 *Sinister Widow again* (1952)
5 *Sinister Widow returns* (1953)
6 *Sinister Widow comes back* (1956)
7 *Widow and the cavalier* (1957)
8 *Sinister Widow down under* (1958)
9 *Sinister Widow at sea* (1959)

Inspector Digby series
Wray, I
1 *Vye murder* (1930)
2 *Murder, and Ariadne* (1931)

Inspector Digger Haig series
Courtier, Sidney Hobson
1 *Now seek my bones* (1957)
2 *Death in dream time* (1959)
3 *Swing high, sweet murder* (1962)
4 *Ringnecker* (1965)
5 *See who's dying* (1967)
6 *No obelisk for Emily* (1970)

Inspector Docker series
Pink, Hal
1 *Green triangle mystery* (1938)
2 *Strelsen Castle mystery* (1939)
3 *Black sombrero mystery* (1940)
4 *Rodeo murder mystery* (1941)
5 *Test match mystery* (1941)

Inspector Donald Dobbs series
Blake, Christina
1 *Fragrant death* (1980)
2 *Deadly legacy* (1981)

Inspector Douglas Quantrill series
Radley, Sheila
see **Chief Inspector Douglas Quantrill series**

Inspector Downes and Sergeant Hopkins series
Sampson, Victor
1 *Murder of Paul Rougier* (1928)
2 *Komani mystery* (1930)

Inspector Duck Mallard series
Spiller, Andrew
see **Chief Inspector Duck Mallard series**

Inspector Duffy series
Fitzgerald, Nigel
see **Superintendent Duffy series**

Inspector Duncan Maccallum series
Mackinnon, Allan
1 *Nine days' murder* (1945)
Money on the black
2 *House of darkness* (1947)

Inspector Dusty Muller and Tiny Meldrum series
Glanville, Alec
1 *Death goes ashore* (1936)
2 *Body in the trawl* (1938)

Inspector Edward Beale series
Penny, Rupert
see **Chief Inspector Edward Beale series**

Inspector Elk series
Wallace, Edgar
1 *Nine bears* (1910)
Other man
Silinski, master criminal
Cheaters
The second, third and fourth titles are a revised edition
2 *Fellowship of the Frog* (1925)
3 *Joker* (1926)
Colossus
4 *Twister* (1928)
5 *India-rubber men* (1929)
6 *White Face* (1930)

Inspector Ellis McKay series
Strong, Leonard Alfred George
see **Police diversion series**

Inspector Elwyn Hughes series
Hardie, David William Ferguson
1 *Iron egg* (1947)
2 *Riddle of the Cambrian Venus* (1949)
3 *Case of the praying evangelist* (1950)
4 *Grave for Miss Carling* (1952)

Inspector Elwyn Morgan series
Farrar, Stewart
1 *Snake on 99* (1958)
2 *Zero in the gate* (1960)
3 *Death in the wrong bed* (1963)

Inspector Enrique Alvarez series
Jeffries, Roderic Graeme
1 *Mistakenly in Mallorca* (1974)
2 *Two-faced death* (1976)
3 *Troubled deaths* (1977)
4 *Murder begets murder* (1979)
5 *Just desserts* (1980)
6 *Unseemly end* (1981)
7 *Deadly petard* (1983)
8 *Three and one make five* (1984)
9 *Layers of deceit* (1985)
10 *Almost murder* (1986)
11 *Relatively dangerous* (1987)
12 *Death trick* (1988)
13 *Dead clever* (1989)
14 *Too clever by half* (1990)
15 *Murder's long memory* (1991)
16 *Murder confounded* (1993)

Inspector Ereache O'Shea series
Yates, Renate
1 *Social death* (1984)
2 *Rural pursuits* (1988)

Inspector Ernest Lamb series
Wentworth, Patricia
1 *Blind side* (1939)
2 *Who pays the piper?* (1940)
Account rendered
3 *Pursuit of a parcel* (1942)

Inspector Evans and Sergeant Beddoes series
Jones, Roger William
1 *Saving Grace* (1986)
2 *Cop out* (1987)
3 *Green reapers* (1988)

Inspector Evans series
Makin, William James
1 *Murder at Covent Garden* (1930)
Covent Garden murder
2 *Red mask* (1935)

Inspector Everett Anderson series
Daiger, Katherine S
1 *Fourth degree* (1931)
2 *Murder on Ghost Tree Island* (1934)

Inspector Fabian Donoghue series
Turnbull, Peter
see **P Division series**

Inspector Fadiman Wace series
Simons, Roger
1 *Houseboat killings* (1959)
2 *Frame for murder* (1960)
3 *Murder joins the chorus* (1960)
4 *Arrangement for murder* (1961)
5 *Gamble with death* (1961)
6 *Killing chase* (1962)
7 *Silver and death* (1963)
8 *Bullet for a beast* (1964)
9 *Dead reckoning* (1965)
10 *Veil of death* (1966)
11 *Taxed to death* (1967)
12 *Death on display* (1968)
13 *Murder first class* (1969)
14 *Reel of death* (1970)
15 *Picture of death* (1973)
16 *Murder by design* (1974)

Inspector Faro series
Knight, Alanna
1 *Enter second murderer* (1989)
2 *Blood line* (1989)
3 *Deadly beloved* (1990)
4 *Killing cousins* (1990)
5 *Quiet death* (1991)

Inspector Fenby series
Hull, Richard
1 *Murderers of Monty* (1937)
2 *Excellent intentions* (1938)
Beyond reasonable doubt

Inspector Fillinger series
McGuire, Paul
see **Superintendent Fillinger series**

Inspector Finch series
Thomson, June
American editions have the series character Inspector Rudd
1 *Not one of us* (1971)
2 *Death cap* (1973)
3 *Long revenge* (1974)
4 *Case closed* (1977)
5 *Question of identity* (1977)
6 *Deadly relations* (1979)
Habit of loving
7 *Alibi in time* (1980)
8 *Shadow of a doubt* (1981)
9 *To make a killing* (1982)
Portrait of Lilith
10 *Sound evidence* (1984)
11 *Dying fall* (1985)
12 *Dark stream* (1986)
13 *No flowers, by request* (1987)
14 *Rosemary for remembrance* (1988)
15 *Spoils of time* (1989)
16 *Past reckoning* (1990)

Inspector Flagg series
Cassells, John
see **Superintendent Flagg series**

Inspector Flower series
Field, Moira
1 *Forign body* (1950)
2 *Gunpowder, treason and plot* (1951)

Inspector Franco Corti series
Inchbald, Peter
1 *Tondo for short* (1981)
2 *Sweet short grass* (1982)
3 *Short break in Venice* (1983)
4 *Or the bambino dies* (1985)

Inspector Frank Derben series
Foxall, Peter Augustus
1 *Murder machine* (1976)
2 *Inspector Derben's war* (1976)
3 *Inspector Derben and the widow maker* (1977)
4 *Hell's Angel kidnapping* (1978)

Inspector Franklin Brady series
McRoyd, Allan
1 *Golden goose murders* (1938)
2 *Double shadow murders* (1939)
3 *Death in costume* (1940)

Inspector Frost series
Smith, Herbert Maynard
1 *Inspector Frost's jigsaw* (1929)
2 *Inspector Frost in the city* (1930)
3 *Inspector Frost and Lady Brassingham* (1930)
4 *Inspector Frost and the Waverdale fire* (1931)
5 *Inspector Frost in Crevenna Cove* (1933)
6 *Inspector Frost and the Whitbourne murder* (1939)
7 *Inspector Frost in the background* (1941)

Inspector Furneaux series
Holmes, Gordon
1 *By force of circumstance* (1909)
Also published under the author's real name Louis Tracy
2 *De Bercy affair* (1910)
Feldisham mystery
Sequence continued under the author's real name Louis Tracy

Tracy, Louis
3 *Case of Mortimer Fenley* (1915)
Strange case of Mortimer Fenley
4 *Number seventeen* (1915)
5 *Postmaster's daughter* (1916)
6 *House of peril* (1922)
7 *Token* (1924)
8 *Passing of Charles Lanson* (1924)
9 *Black cat* (1925)
10 *Gleave mystery* (1926)
11 *Law of the talon* (1926)
12 *Woman in the case* (1927)
13 *Third miracle* (1927)
Lastingham murder
14 *One girl in a million* (1928)
Manning-Burke murder
15 *What would you have done?* (1928)
Sandling case

Inspector Furnival series
Haynes, Annie
1 *Abbey Court murder* (1923)
2 *House in Charlton Crescent* (1926)
3 *Crow's Inn tragedy* (1927)

Inspector Ganesh Ghote series
Keating, Henry Reymond Fitzwalter
1 *Perfect murder* (1964)
2 *Inspector Ghote's good crusade* (1966)
3 *Inspector Ghote caught in meshes* (1967)
4 *Inspector Ghote hunts the peacock* (1968)
5 *Inspector ghote plays a joker* (1969)
6 *Inspector Ghote breaks an egg* (1970)
7 *Inspector Ghote goes by train* (1971)
8 *Inspector ghote trusts the heart* (1972)
9 *Bats fly up for Inspector Ghote* (1974)
10 *Filmi, filmi, Inspector Ghote* (1976)
11 *Inspector Ghote draws a line* (1979)
12 *Go west, Inspector Ghote* (1981)
13 *Sheriff of Bombay* (1984)
14 *Under a monsoon cloud* (1986)
15 *Body in the billiard room* (1987)
16 *Dead on time* (1988)
17 *Inspector Ghote, his life and times* (1989)
18 *Iciest sin* (1990)

Inspector Garnett series
Philmore, R
1 *Death in arms* (1939)
2 *Procession of two* (1940)

Inspector Garth series
Blayn, Hugo
1 *Except for one thing* (1947)
2 *Five matchboxes* (1948)
3 *Flashpoint* (1950)
4 *What happened to Hammond?* (1951)
5 *Silvered cage* (1955)
Companion volume: *Vision sinister*, by Nat Karta, 1954

Inspector Gautier series
Grayson, Richard
Set in Paris around 1900
1 *Murders at Impass Louvain* (1978)
2 *Monterant affair* (1980)
3 *Death of Abbe Didier* (1981)
4 *Montmartre murders* (1982)
5 *Crime without passion* (1983)
6 *Death on voyage* (1986)
7 *Death on the cards* (1988)

Inspector Geoffrey Fraser series
Bailey, Elliot
1 *Death in quiet places* (1933)
2 *No crime so great* (1936)
3 *Revenge at nightfall* (1937)

Inspector George Annesley series
Everton, Francis
1 *Murder at Plenders* (1930)
Murder through the window
2 *Murder may pass unpunished* (1936)

Inspector George Felse series
Peters, Ellis
1 *Fallen into the pit* (1951)
Originally published under the author's real name Edith Pargeter
2 *Death and the joyful woman* (1961)
3 *Flight of a witch* (1961)
4 *Nice derangement of epitaphs* (1965)
Who lies here?
5 *Piper on the mountain* (1966)
6 *Black is the colour of my true love's heart* (1967)
7 *Grass-widow's tale* (1968)
8 *House of green turf* (1969)
9 *Mourning raga* (1969)
10 *Knocker on death's door* (1970)
11 *Death to the landlords!* (1972)
12 *City of gold and shadows* (1973)
13 *Rainbow's End* (1978)

Inspector George Gently series
Hunter, Alan
1 *Gently does it* (1955)
2 *Gently by the shore* (1956)
3 *Gently down the stream* (1957)
4 *Landed Gently* (1957)
5 *Gently through the mill* (1958)
6 *Gently in the sun* (1959)
Numbers 1, 5, 6 also published in one volume entitled *Gently in an omnibus*, 1966
7 *Gently with the painters* (1960)
8 *Gently to the summit* (1961)
9 *Gently go man* (1961)
10 *Gently where the roads go* (1962)
11 *Gently floating* (1963)
Numbers 9-11 also published in one volume entitled *Gently in another omnibus*, 1969
12 *Gently Sahib* (1964)
13 *Gently with the ladies* (1965)

14 *Gently north-west* (1967)
Gently in the Highlands
15 *Gently continental* (1967)
16 *Gently coloured* (1969)
17 *Gently with the innocents* (1970)
18 *Gently at a gallop* (1971)
19 *Vivienne* (1972)
Alternative title: Gently where she lay
20 *Gently French* (1973)
21 *Gently in trees* (1974)
Gently through the woods
22 *Gently with love* (1975)
23 *Gently where the birds are* (1976)
24 *Gently instrumental* (1977)
25 *Gently to a sleep* (1978)
26 *Honfleur decision* (1980)
27 *Gabrielle's way* (1981)
Scottish decision
28 *Fields of heather* (1981)
Death on the heath
29 *Gently between tides* (1983)
30 *Amorous Leander* (1984)
Death on the broadlands
31 *Unhung man* (1984)
Unhanged man
32 *Once a prostitute* (1984)
33 *Chelsea ghost* (1985)
34 *Goodnight sweet prince* (1986)
35 *Strangling man* (1987)
36 *Traitor's end* (1988)
37 *Gently with the millions* (1989)
38 *Gently scandalous* (1990)
39 *Gently to a kill* (1992)
40 *Gently tragic* (1992)
41 *Gently in the glens* (1993)

Inspector George Judd series
Bruton, Eric
see **City of London Police series**

Inspector George Marshall series
The volumes in this sequence are published variously under the author's real name Pamela Barrington and the pseudonym Charles Barling
Barrington, Pamela
1 *Rest is silence* (1951)
2 *Account rendered* (1953)
3 *Night of violence* (1959)
4 *By some person unknown* (1960)
Barling, Charles
5 *Motive for murder* (1963)
Barrington, Pamela
6 *Final judgement* (1964)
Barling, Charles
7 *Appointment with death* (1964)
8 *Time to kill* (1965)
Barrington, Pamela
9 *Cage without bars* (1966)
10 *Slow poison* (1967)
11 *Game of murder* (1967)
Barling, Charles
12 *Confession of murder* (1967)
13 *Marked man* (1968)

Inspector George Martin series
Beeding, Francis
1 *Norwich victims* (1935)
2 *No fury* (1936)
Murdered one by one
3 *He could not have slipped* (1939)

Inspector George Masters series
Clark, Douglas
1 *Nobody's perfect* (1969)
2 *Death after evensong* (1969)
3 *Deadly pattern* (1970)
4 *Sweet poison* (1970)
5 *Sick to death* (1971)
6 *Premeditated murder* (1975)
7 *Dread and water* (1976)
8 *Table d'hote* (1977)
9 *Gimmel flask* (1977)
10 *Libertines* (1978)
11 *Heberden's seat* (1979)
12 *Poacher's bag* (1980)
13 *Golden rain* (1980)
14 *Roast eggs* (1981)
15 *Longest pleasure* (1981)
16 *Shelf life* (1982)
17 *Doone Walk* (1982)
18 *Monday theory* (1983)
19 *Vicious circle* (1983)
20 *Dead letter* (1984)
21 *Bouquet garni* (1984)
22 *Jewelled eye* (1985)
23 *Performance* (1985)
24 *Storm centre* (1986)
25 *Big grouse* (1986)
26 *Plain sailing* (1987)

Inspector George Muir series
Grierson, Francis Durham
1 *Covenant with death* (1938)
2 *Cabaret crime* (1938)
3 *Mystery of the two-faced man* (1939)
4 *Ink Street murder* (1940)
5 *Mad Hatter murder* (1941)
6 *Thrice Judas* (1942)
7 *Crimson cat* (1944)
8 *Entertaining murder* (1945)
9 *He had it coming to him* (1948)
10 *No wreaths for the duchess* (1948)
11 *Buddha of Fleet Street* (1949)
12 *Strange case of Edgar Heriot* (1950)
13 *Boomerang murder* (1951)
14 *Traitor's cross* (1952)
15 *Madame Shadow* (1952)

Inspector George Rason series
Vickers, Roy
1 *Hounded down* (1923)
Originally published under the pseudonym David Durham
2 *Exploits of Fidelity Dove* (1924)
Short stories; originally published under the pseudonym David Durham
3 *Murder will out* (1950)
Also five stories featuring Rason in *Eight murders in the suburbs*, 1954, two stories featuring Rason in *Seven chose murder*, 1959 and one story featuring Rason in *Best detective stories*, edited by Edmund Crispin, 1965

Inspector George Rogers series
Ross, Jonathan
see **Superintendent George Rogers series**

Inspector George Thorne and Sergeant Bill Abbot series
Penn, John
1 *Notice of death* (1982)
Ad for murder
2 *Deceitful death* (1983)
Stag dinner death
3 *Will to kill* (1983)
4 *Mortal term* (1984)
5 *Deadly sickness* (1985)
6 *Unto the grave* (1986)
7 *Barren revenge* (1986)
8 *Accident prone* (1987)
9 *Outrageous exposures* (1988)
10 *Feast of death* (1989)
11 *Killing to hide* (1990)
12 *Death's long shadow* (1991)
13 *Legacy of death* (1992)
14 *Haven of danger* (1993)
15 *Widow's end* (1993)

Inspector George Travers series
Barrington, Pamela
1 *Mortimer story* (1952)
2 *Among those present* (1953)
3 *Gentle killer* (1961)
Sequence continued under the pseudonym Charles Barling
Barling, Charles
4 *Afternoon of violence* (1963)

Inspector Ghent series
Francis, Basil
1 *Death on the roof* (1946)
2 *Death in act four* (1954)

Inspector Gibbon series
Cooper, Barbara
1 *Target for malice* (1964)
2 *Drown him deep* (1966)
3 *Who is my enemy?* (1967)

Inspector Gidleigh series
Truss, Seldon
1 *Draw the blinds* (1936)
Crooks' shepherd
2 *Man who played patience* (1937)
3 *Footsteps behind them* (1937)
4 *Disappearance of Julie Hintz* (1940)
5 *Sweeter for his going* (1950)
6 *Ladies always talk* (1950)
Why slug a postman?
7 *Never fight a lady* (1951)
8 *Death was no lady* (1950)
9 *High wall* (1954)
Other side of the wall
10 *Long night* (1956)
False face
11 *Barberton intrigue* (1956)
Store of wrath
12 *Truth about Claire Veryan* (1957)
13 *In secret places* (1958)
14 *Hidden men* (1959)
Man to match the hour
15 *One man's death* (1960)
One man's enemies
16 *Seven years dead* (1961)
17 *Time to hate* (1962)
18 *Technique for treachery* (1963)
19 *Walk a crooked mile* (1964)
20 *Town that went sick* (1965)

Inspector Gil Flicker series
Millward, Edward J
1 *Body lies* (1936)
2 *Aero Club mystery* (1939)

Inspector Gloom series
King, Frank
see **Superintendent Gloom series**

Inspector Glover and Superintendent Quill series
Lamb, Lynton
see **Superintendent Quill and Inspector Glover series**

Inspector Glover series
Evermay, March
1 *They talked of poison* (1938)
2 *This death was murder* (1940)

Inspector Godbold series
Bolt, Ben
1 *Shot in the night* (1934)
2 *Green lantern* (1935)

Inspector Gordon Knollis series
Vivian, Francis
1 *Three short men* (1939)
2 *Death of Mr Lomas* (1941)
3 *Sable messenger* (1947)
4 *Threefold cord* (1947)
5 *Ninth enemy* (1948)
6 *Laughing dog* (1949)
7 *Singing masons* (1950)
8 *Sleeping island* (1951)
9 *Elusive bowman* (1951)
10 *Ladies of Locksley* (1953)
11 *Darkling death* (1956)

Inspector Gordon Ross series
Gorell, Ronald Gorell Barnes
1 *Let not thy left hand* (1949)
2 *Murder at Manor House* (1954)

Inspector Gramport series
Barnett, Glyn
1 *Call-box murder* (1935)
2 *Murder on Monday* (1936)
3 *I know Mrs Long* (1937)
4 *Find the lady* (1946)
5 *Silent street* (1958)

Inspector Graves series
Makin, William James
1 *Gipsy in evening dress* (1935)
2 *Murder at full moon* (1937)

Inspector Gray series
Piper, Peter
1 *Murder after the blitz* (1943)
2 *Death in the Canongate* (1952)
Corpse that came back

Inspector Green series
Clark, Douglas
see **Inspector George Masters series**

Inspector Greenwood series
Wicking, George Walter
1 *Glory box mystery* (1936)
2 *Mysterious valley* (1938)

Inspector Gregory Pellew and Viscount Clymping series
Gielgud, Val
1 *Gallows' foot* (1958)
2 *Too bed at noon* (1960)
3 *And died so?* (1961)
4 *Goggle-box affair* (1963)
Through a glass darkly
5 *Prinvest-London* (1965)
6 *Conduct of a member* (1967)
7 *Necessary end* (1969)
8 *Candle-holders* (1970)
9 *Black Sambo affair* (1972)
10 *In such a night* (1974)
11 *Fearful thing* (1975)

Inspector Grierson series
Wurr, H J
1 *Giant hunchback* (1939)
2 *Who dies next?* (1939)

Inspector Grogan and Sergeant Manning series
Neville, Margot
1 *Murder in Rockwater* (1944)
Lena hates men
2 *Murder and gardenias* (1946)
3 *Murder in a blue room* (1948)
4 *Murder of a nymph* (1949)
5 *Murder before marriage* (1951)
6 *Seagull said murder* (1952)
7 *Murder of the well-beloved* (1953)
8 *Murder and poor Jenny* (1954)
9 *Murder of Olympia* (1956)
10 *Murder to welcome her* (1957)
Serialized as *Murder was her welcome*
11 *Flame of murder* (1958)
12 *Sweet night for murder* (1959)
13 *Confession of murder* (1960)
14 *Murder beyond the pale* (1961)
15 *Drop dead* (1962)
16 *Come see me die* (1963)
17 *My bad boy* (1964)
18 *Ladies in the dark* (1965)
19 *Head on the sill* (1966)

Inspector Gulliver series
Burnett, George
1 *Violent security* (1962)
2 *Sheep and the wolves* (1962)

Inspector Guy Northeast series
Cannan, Joanna
1 *They rang up the police* (1939)
2 *Death at The Dog* (1940)

Inspector Hallam and Sergeant Spratt series
Douglas, George
1 *Odd woman out* (1966)
2 *Unwanted witness* (1966)
3 *Death went hunting* (1967)
4 *Death unheralded* (1967)
5 *Death in duplicate* (1968)
6 *Devil to pay* (1969)
7 *Dead reckoning* (1969)
8 *Murder unmourned* (1970)

Inspector Hallam and Sergeant Spratt series

9 *Crime most foul* (1971)
10 *Time to die* (1971)
11 *One to jump* (1972)

Inspector Hanaud series
Mason, Alfred Edward Woodley
1 *At the Villa Rose* (1910)
2 *House of the Arrow* (1924)
3 *Prisoner in the opal* (1928)
4 *They wouldn't be chessmen* (1935)
5 *House in Lordship Lane* (1946)

Inspector Harrow series
Adams, Shipley
1 *Murder unsolved* (1947)
2 *Money by menaces* (1948)
3 *Murder in the first person* (1948)
4 *Murder well begun* (1948)

Inspector Harry Feiffer series
Marshall, William Leonard
see **Yellowthread Street series**

Inspector Harry James and Sergeant Honeybody series
Giles, Kenneth
1 *Some beasts no more* (1965)
2 *Big greed* (1966)
3 *Provenance of death* (1966)
Picture of death
4 *Death in diamonds* (1967)
5 *Death and Mister Prettyman* (1967)
6 *Death among the stars* (1968)
7 *Death cracks a bottle* (1969)
8 *Death in the church* (1970)
9 *Murder pluperfect* (1970)
10 *File on death* (1973)

Inspector Haskell series
Sutherland, William
1 *Behind the head-lines* (1933)
2 *Proverbial murder case* (1935)

Inspector Hazelrigg series
Gilbert, Michael Francis
1 *Close quarters* (1947)
2 *They never looked inside* (1948)
He didn't mind danger
3 *Doors open* (1949)
4 *Smallbone deceased* (1950)
5 *Death has deep roots* (1951)
6 *Fear to tread* (1953)
7 *Amateur in violence* (1973)
Short stories
Two stories featuring Hazelrigg in *Stay of execution, and other stories of legal practice*, 1971, and two in *Amateur violence*, 1973

Inspector Head series
Vivian, Evelyn Charles
1 *Shadow on the house* (1934)
2 *Accessory after* (1934)
3 *Seventeen cards* (1935)
4 *Cigar for Inspector Head* (1935)
5 *Who killed Gatton?* (1936)
6 *With intent to kill* (1936)
7 *Tramp's evidence* (1937)
Barking dog murder case
8 *Point thirty eight automatic* (1937)
9 *Evidence in blue* (1938)
Man in gray
10 *Rainbow puzzle* (1938)
11 *Problem by rail* (1939)
12 *Touch and go* (1939)

Inspector Headcorn series
Campbell, Alice
1 *Death framed in silver* (1937)
2 *They hunted a fox* (1940)
3 *No murder of mine* (1941)
Borrowed cottage
4 *Cockroach sings* (1946)
With bated breath
5 *Bloodstained toy* (1948)

Inspector Headley series
Morris, Thomas Baden
1 *Papyrus murder* (1958)
2 *Death among the orchids* (1959)
3 *Mandrakes in the cupboard* (1960)
4 *Orchids with murder* (1966)

Inspector Hemingway series
Heyer, Georgette
Inspector Hemingway has a supporting role in numbers 1-4 and is the central character in numbers 5-8
1 *Death in the stocks* (1935)
Merely murder
2 *Behold, here's poison!* (1936)
3 *They found him dead* (1937)
4 *Blunt instrument* (1938)
5 *No wind of blame* (1939)
6 *Envious Casca* (1941)
7 *Duplicate death* (1951)
8 *Detection unlimited* (1953)

Inspector Henderson series
Barrington, Pamela
1 *Accessory to murder* (1968)
Sequence continued under the pseudonym Charles Barling
Barling, Charles
2 *Death of a shrew* (1968)

Inspector Henry Beaumont series
Atkins, Meg Elizabeth
1 *By the north door* (1975)
2 *Samain* (1976)
3 *Palimpsest* (1981)
4 *Tangle* (1988)

Inspector Henry Doight series
Symons, Beryl
1 *Devine Court mystery* (1928)
2 *Leering house* (1929)
3 *Opal murder case* (1932)

Inspector Henry Peckover series
Kenyon, Michael
1 *Deep pocket* (1978)
Molehill file
2 *Zigzag* (1981)
Elgar variations
3 *God Squad bod* (1982)
Man at the wheel
4 *Free-range wife* (1983)
5 *Peckover holds the baby* (1988)
6 *Kill the butler!* (1991)
7 *French affair* (1992)
8 *Peckover joins the choir* (1994)

Inspector Henry Tibbett series
Moyes, Patricia
see **Henry and Emmy Tibbett series**

Inspector Herbert Broom series
Hurt, Freda Mary
1 *Body at Bowman's Hollow* (1959)
2 *Death by request* (1960)
3 *Sweet death* (1961)
4 *Acquainted with murder* (1962)
5 *Death and the bridegroom* (1963)
6 *Cold and unhonoured* (1964)
7 *Cause for malice* (1966)

Inspector Hiscock series
Potter, Jeremy
1 *Death in office* (1965)
2 *Foul play* (1967)
3 *Dance of death* (1968)

Inspector Holly series
Postgate, Raymond
1 *Somenody at the door* (1943)
2 *Ledger is kept* (1953)

Inspector Holt series
Tully, John
1 *Inspector Holt and the fur van* (1977)
2 *Inspector Holt gets his man* (1977)
3 *Where is Bill Ojo* (1978)
4 *Bridge* (1979)

Inspector Hook series
Lane, Gret
1 *Three died that night* (1937)
2 *Red mirror mystery* (1938)

Inspector Hopton series
Woodiwiss, John Cecil
1 *Death's visiting card* (1936)
2 *Ebony torso* (1939)

Inspector Hugh Collier series
Dalton, Moray
1 *One by one they disappeared* (1929)
2 *Night of fear* (1931)
3 *Harvest of tares* (1933)
4 *Belgrave Manor crime* (1935)
5 *Strange case of Harriet Hall* (1936)
6 *Mystery of the kneeling woman* (1936)
7 *Death in the dark* (1938)
8 *Death in the forest* (1939)
9 *Longbridge murders* (1945)
10 *Condamine case* (1947)
11 *Case of the dark stranger* (1948)
12 *Inquest on Miriam* (1949)
13 *Death of a spinster* (1951)

Inspector Hugh Gordon and Liane Crawford series
Gilruth, Susan
1 *Sweet revenge* (1951)
2 *Death in ambush* (1952)
3 *Postscript to Penelope* (1954)
4 *Corpse for Charybdis* (1956)
5 *To this favour* (1957)
6 *Drown her remembrance* (1961)
7 *Snake is living yet* (1963)

Inspector J Rason series
Volumes in this sequence are published variously under the author's real name Roy Vickers and his pseudonyms Sefton Kyle and David Durham
Vickers, Roy
1 *Mystery of the scented death* (1921)
Kyle, Sefton
2 *Man in the shadow* (1924)
Durham, David
3 *Pearl-headed pin* (1925)
Kyle, Sefton
4 *Hawk* (1930)
Vickers, Roy
5 *Bardelow's heir* (1933)
Kyle, Sefton
6 *Red hair* (1933)
Vickers, Roy
7 *Money buys everything* (1934)
Kyle, Sefton
8 *Life he stole* (1934)
Vickers, Roy
9 *Kidnap Island* (1935)
Kyle, Sefton
10 *Silence* (1935)
Vickers, Roy
11 *Man in the red mask* (1935)
Kyle, Sefton
12 *Body in the safe* (1937)
Vickers, Roy
13 *Terror of tongues!* (1937)
14 *Girl in the news* (1937)
Kyle, Sefton
15 *During His Majesty's pleasure* (1938)
Vickers, Roy
16 *Life between* (1938)
17 *She walked in fear* (1940)

Inspector Jack Laidlaw series
McIlvanney, William
1 *Laidlaw* (1977)
2 *Papers of Tony Veitch* (1983)
3 *Big man* (1985)

Inspector Jack Pearson series
Daniel, Roland
1 *Crackswoman* (1932)
2 *Crimson shadow* (1935)
3 *Gangster's last shot* (1939)
4 *Murder at Little Malling* (1946)

Inspector Jack Strickland series
Balfour, Hearnden
1 *Paper chase* (1927)
Gentleman from Texas
2 *Enterprising burglar* (1928)
3 *Anything might happen* (1931)
Murder and the red-haired girl

Inspector James Brent series
Kemp, Harold
1 *Murder humane* (1947)
2 *Dead snake's venom* (1948)
3 *As the devil burned* (1949)
4 *Heat not a furnace* (1952)
5 *Death of a dwarf* (1955)
6 *Red for murder* (1957)
7 *Mark for a witch* (1959)

Inspector James Cardinal series
Walton, Marion
1 *Cardinal error* (1973)
2 *Paduan conspiracy* (1973)

Inspector James Dale series
Cooper, John C
1 *Body was of no account* (1957)
2 *Death in aberration* (1958)

Inspector James Flecker series
Pullein-Thompson, Josephine
1 *Gin and murder* (1959)
2 *They died in the spring* (1960)
3 *Murder strikes pink* (1963)

Inspector James Miller series
Dix, Maurice Buxton
1 *Murder at Grassmere Abbey* (1933)
2 *Fleetwood Mansions mystery* (1934)

Inspector James series
Bax, Roger
1 *Blueprint for murder* (1948)
Trouble with murder
2 *Grave case of murder* (1951)

Inspector Jean Darblay series
Hardwick, Michael
see **Juliet Bravo series**

Inspector Jim Burgess series
Franklin, Charles
1 *Guilt for innocence* (1960)
2 *Kill me and live* (1961)
3 *Bath of acid* (1962)
4 *Murder before dinner* (1963)

Inspector Joe Barnaby and Francesca Miles series
Chan, Melissa
1 *Too rich* (1991)
2 *One too many* (1993)

Inspector Joel Saber series
Holt, Gavin
1 *Theme is murder* (1938)
2 *Green for danger* (1939)
3 *Swing it, death* (1940)
4 *Give a man rope* (1942)
5 *Begonia Walk* (1946)
Send no flowers
6 *Ladies in ermine* (1947)

Inspector John Burnell series
Vivian, Francis
1 *Arms of death* (1938)
2 *Dark moon* (1939)

Inspector John Coffin series
Butler, Gwendoline
1 *Dead in a row* (1957)
2 *Dull dead* (1957)
3 *Murdering kind* (1958)
4 *Interloper* (1959)
5 *Death lives next door* (1960)
Dine and be dead
6 *Make me a murderer* (1961)
7 *Coffin in Oxford* (1962)
8 *Coffin for baby* (1963)
9 *Coffin waiting* (1964)
10 *Coffin in Malta* (1964)
11 *Nameless Coffin* (1966)
12 *Coffin following* (1968)

13 *Coffin's dark number* (1969)
14 *Coffin from the past* (1970)
15 *Coffin for Pandora* (1973)
Olivia
16 *Coffin for the canary* (1974)
Sarsen Place
17 *Coffin on the water* (1986)
18 *Coffin in fashion* (1987)
19 *Coffin underground* (1988)
20 *Coffin in the black museum* (1989)
21 *Coffin and the paper man* (1990)
22 *Coffin on Murder Street* (1991)
23 *Cracking open a Coffin* (1992)
24 *Coffin for Charley* (1993)

Inspector John Crow series
Lewis, Royston
1 *Lover too many* (1969)
2 *Wolf by the ears* (1970)
3 *Error of judgment* (1971)
4 *Secret singing* (1972)
5 *Blood money* (1973)
6 *Question of degree* (1974)
7 *Part of virtue* (1975)
8 *Witness my death* (1976)
9 *Nothing but foxes* (1977)
10 *Uncertain sound* (1978)
11 *Inevitable fatality* (1978)
12 *Relative distance* (1981)

Inspector John Isidore Bloom series
Warman, Erik
1 *Relative to murder* (1940)
2 *Pattern for murder* (1943)

Inspector John Jay Jackson series
Lindsay, David T
1 *Inspector Jackson investigates* (1936)
2 *Another case for Inspector Jackson* (1937)
3 *Man nobody knew* (1938)
4 *Inspector Jackson goes north* (1939)

Inspector John Joseph Lintott series
Stubbs, Jean
1 *Dear Laura* (1973)
2 *Painted face* (1974)
3 *Golden crucible* (1976)

Inspector John Martin series
Robertson, Colin
1 *Night shadows* (1935)
2 *Fake* (1937)
3 *Stalking stranger* (1939)

Inspector John Sanders and Harriet Jeffries series
Sale, Medora
1 *Murder in focus* (1989)
2 *Murder in a good cause* (1990)
3 *Pursued by shadows* (1992)
4 *Short cut to Santa Fe* (1994)

Inspector John Walk series
Daniel, Roland
1 *Dead man's vengeance* (1931)
2 *Ann turns detective* (1932)
3 *Stool pigeon* (1936)
4 *Missing lady* (1937)
5 *Human vultures* (1939)

Inspector John Webber and Lizzie Thomas series
Oliver, Anthony
see **Lizzie Thomas and Inspector John Webber series**

Inspector Johnson series
Batchelor, Denzil
1 *Man who loved chocolates* (1961)
2 *On the brink* (1964)
3 *Sedulous ape* (1965)

Inspector Jolivet series
Shepherd, Joan
1 *Girl on the Left Bank* (1953)
2 *Tender is the knife* (1956)

Inspector Jonas Morck series
Orum, Poul
1 *Whipping-boy* (1972)
Scapegoat
Original edition entitled *Syndebuk*
2 *Nothing but the truth* (1974)
Original edition entitled *Kun sandheden*

Inspector Joseph Delaney series
Archer, Frank
1 *Malabang pearl* (1964)
2 *Widow watchers* (1965)
3 *Turquoise spike* (1967)

Inspector Joseph French series
Crofts, Freeman Wills
1 *Inspector French's greatest case* (1925)
2 *Inspector French and the Cheyne mystery* (1926)
Cheyne mystery
3 *Inspector French and the Starvel tragedy* (1927)
Starvel Hollow tragedy
4 *Sea mystery* (1928)
5 *Box office murders* (1929)
Purple sickle murders
6 *Sir John Magill's last journey* (1930)
7 *Mystery in the Channel* (1931)
Mystery in the English Channel
8 *Sudden death* (1932)
9 *Death on the way* (1932)
Double death
10 *Hog's Back mystery* (1933)
Strange case of Doctor Earle
11 *Twelve thirty from Croydon* (1934)
Wilful and premeditated
12 *Mystery on Southampton Water* (1934)
Crime on the Solent
13 *Crime at Guildford* (1935)
Crime at Nornes
14 *Loss of the Jane Vosper* (1936)
15 *Man overboard!* (1936)
Cold-blooded murder
The second title is an abridged edition
16 *Found floating* (1937)
17 *End of Andrew Harrison* (1938)
Futile alibi
18 *Antidote to venom* (1938)
19 *Fatal venture* (1939)
Tragedy in the hollow
20 *Golden ashes* (1940)
21 *James Tarrant, adventurer* (1941)
Circumstantial evidence
22 *Losing game* (1941)
23 *Fear comes to Chalfont* (1942)
24 *Affair at Little Wokeham* (1943)
Double tragedy
25 *Enemy unseen* (1945)
26 *Death of a train* (1946)
27 *Murderers make mistakes* (1947)
Short stories
28 *Silence for the murderer* (1948)
29 *French strikes oil* (1951)
Dark journey
30 *Many a slip* (1955)
Short stories
31 *Mystery of the sleeping car express* (1956)
Short stories
32 *Anything to declare?* (1957)

Inspector Jules Maigret series
Simenon, Georges
1 *Strange case of Peter the Lett* (1931)
Maigret and the enigmatic Lett
Original edition entitled *Pietr-le-Letton*; also published as *The case of Peter the Lett* in *Inspector Maigret investigates*, 1934
2 *Sailor's rendezvous* (1931)
Original edition entitled *Au rendez-vous des terre-nuevas*; published with *The Saint-Fiacre affair* in *Maigret keeps a rendezvous*, 1940
3 *Maigret meets a milord* (1931)
Original edition entitled *Le charretier de la Providence*; also published as *The crime at Lock 14* in *Triumph of Inspector Maigret*, 1934
4 *Maigret and the Concarneau murders* (1931)
Original edition entitled *Le chien jaune*; also published as *A face for a clue* in *The patience of Maigret*, 1939
5 *At the Gai-Moulin* (1931)
Original edition entitled *La danseuse du Gai-Moulin*; published with *A crime in Holland* in *Maigret abroad*, 1940
6 *Maigret stonewalled* (1931)
Original edition entitled *Monsieur Gallet decede*; also published as *The death of Monsieur Gallet* in *Introducing Inspector Maigret*, 1933
7 *Maigret at the crossroads* (1931)
Original edition entitled *La nuit du carrefour*; also published as *The crossroad murders* in *Inspector Maigret investigates*, 1933
8 *Maigret and the hundred gibbets* (1931)
Original edition entitled *Le pende de Saint-Pholien*; also published as *The crime of Inspector Maigret* in *Inspector Maigret investigates*, 1933
9 *Crime in Holland* (1931)
Original edition entitled *Un crime en Hollande*; published with *At the Gai-Moulin* in *Maigret abroad*, 1940
10 *Maigret's war of nerves* (1931)
Original edition entitled *Le tete d'un homme*; also published as *A battle of nerves* in *The patience of Maigret*, 1939
11 *Maigret goes home* (1932)
Original edition entitled *L'affair Saint-Fiacre*; also published as *The Saint-Fiacre affair* in *Maigret keeps a rendezvous*, 1940
12 *Flemish shop* (1932)
Original edition entitled *Chez les Flamands*; also published with *The guingeutte by the Seine* in *Maigret to the rescue*, 1940
13 *Madman of Bergerac* (1932)
Original edition entitled *Le four de Bergerac*; also published with *Liberty Bar* in *Maigret travels south*, 1940
14 *Guingette by the Seine* (1932)
Original edition entitled *La guingette a deux sous*; published with *The Flemish shop* in *Maigret to the rescue*, 1940
15 *Liberty Bar* (1932)
Original edition entitled *Liberty Bar*; published with *The madman of Bergerac* in *Maigret travels south*, 1940
16 *Maigret mystified* (1932)
Original edition entitled *L'ombre chinois*; also published as *The shadow in the courtyard* in *The triumph of Inspector Maigret*, 1934
17 *Death of a harbourmaster* (1932)
Original edition entitled *Le port des Brunes*; published with *The man from everywhere*, a non-Maigret story in *Maigret and Monsieur L'Abbe*, 1941
18 *Lock at Charenton* (1933)
Original edition entitled *L'ecluse no 1*; published with *Maigret returns* in *Maigret sits it out*, 1941
19 *Maigret returns* (1934)
Original edition entitled *Maigret*; published with *The lock at Charenton* in *Maigret sits it out*, 1941
20 *Maigret and the spinster* (1942)
Original edition entitled *Cecile est morte*
21 *Maigret in exile* (1942)
Original edition entitled *La maison du juge*
22 *Maigret and the Hotel Majestic* (1942)
Original edition entitled *Maigret et les Caves du Majestic*
23 *Maigret and the toy village* (1944)
Original edition entitled *Felicie est la*
24 *Maigret's rival* (1944)
Original edition entitled *L'inspecteur cadavre*
25 *To any lengths* (1944)
Maigret and the fortune teller
Original edition entitled *Signe Picpus*; published with *A summer holiday* in Maigret *on holiday*, 1950
26 *Maigret in New York's underworld* (1947)
Maigret in New York
Inspector Maigret in New York's underworld
Original edition entitled *Maigret a New York*
27 *Maigret in retirement* (1947)
Original edition entitled *Maigret se fache*; also published in *Maigret's Christmas*, 1976
28 *Maigret's pipe* (1947)
Short stories; original edition entitled *La pipe de Maigret*
29 *Maigret's dead man* (1948)
Maigret's special murder
Original edition entitled *Maigret et son mort*
30 *No vacation for Maigret* (1948)
Original edition entitled *Les vacances de Maigret*; also published with *A summer holiday* in *Maigret on holiday*, 1950
31 *Maigret and the coroner* (1949)
Maigret at the coroner's
Original edition entitled *Maigret chez le coroner*
32 *Maigret and the old lady* (1949)
Original edition entitled *Maigret et la vieille dame*; also published in *The second Maigret omnibus*, 1964 and in *Maigret cinq*, 1965
33 *My friend Maigret* (1949)
Methods of Maigret
Original edition entitled *Mon ami Maigret*
34 *Maigret's first case* (1949)
Original edition entitled *La premier enquete de Maigret*; also published in *The second Maigret omnibus*, 1964, and in *Maigret cinq*, 1965
35 *Madame Maigret's own case* (1950)
Madame Maigret's friend
Original edition entitled *L'amie de Madame Maigret*
36 *[Le petit cochon sans queue]* (1950)
[Maigret et les petits cochons sans queues]
No English edition
37 *Inspector Maigret and the strangled stripper* (1951)
Original edition entitled *Maigret au Picratt's*; also published as *Maigret in Montmartre* in *Maigret right and wrong*, 1954
38 *Maigret takes a room* (1951)
Maigret rents a room
Original edition entitled *Maigret en meuble*
39 *Maigret and the burglar's wife* (1951)
Inspector Maigret and the burglar's wife
Original edition entitled *Maigret et la grande perche*

Inspector Jules Maigret series

40 *Maigret's memoirs* (1951)
Original edition entitled *Les memoires de Maigret*
41 *Maigret and the gangsters* (1952)
Maigret and the killers
Original edition entitled *Maigret, Lognon et les gangsters*
42 *Maigret's revolver* (1952)
Original edition entitled *Le revolver de Maigret*
43 *Maigret and the man on the bench* (1953)
Maigret and the man on the boulevard
Original edition entitled *Maigret et l'homme du banc*
44 *Maigret afraid* (1953)
Original edition entitled *Maigret a peur*
45 *Maigret's mistake* (1953)
Original edition entitled *Maigret se trompe*; published with *Maigret in Montmartre* in *Maigret right and wrong*, 1954 and in *A Maigret omnibus*, 1962 and in *Five times Maigret*, 1964
46 *Maigret goes to school* (1954)
Original edition entitled *Maigret a l'ecole*; also published in *A Maigret omnibus*, 1962 and in *Five times Maigret*, 1964
47 *Maigret and the Calme Report* (1954)
Maigret and the minister
Original edition entitled *Maigret chez le ministre*
48 *Maigret and the dead girl* (1954)
Inspector Maigret and the dead girl
Original edition entitled *Maigret et la jeune morte*; also published in *The second Maigret omnibus*, 1964 and in *Maigret cinq*, 1965
49 *Maigret sets a trap* (1955)
Original edition entitled *Maigret tend un piege*
50 *Maigret and the headless corpse* (1955)
Original edition entitled *Maigret et le corps sans tete*
51 *Maigret's failure* (1956)
Original edition entitled Un echec de Maigret; also published in *A Maigret quartet*, 1972
52 *Maigret's little joke* (1957)
None of Maigret's business
Original edition entitled *Maigret s'amuse*
53 *Maigret and the millionaiures* (1958)
Original edition entitled *Maigret voyage*
54 *Maigret has scruples* (1959)
Original edition entitled *Les scrupules de Maigret*; also published with *Maigret and the reluctant witnesses* in *Versus Inspector Maigret*, 1960 and in *A Maigret omnibus*, 1962 and in *Five times Maigret*, 1964
55 *Maigret has doubts* (1959)
Original edition entitled *Une confidence de Maigret*
56 *Maigret and the reluctant witnesses* (1959)
Original edition entitled *Maigret et les temoins recalcitrants*; also published with *Maigret has scruples* in *Versus Inspector Maigret*, 1960 and in A Maigret omnibus, 1962 and in *Five times Maigret*, 1964
57 *Maigret in court* (1960)
Original edition entitled *Maigret aux assises*
58 *Maigret in society* (1960)
Original edition entitled *Maigret et les vieillards*; also published in *A Maigret quartet*, 1972
59 *Maigret and the lazy burglar* (1961)
Original edition entitled *Maigret et le voleur parasseux*; also published in *A Maigret quartet*, 1972
60 *Maigret and the black sheep* (1962)
Original edition entitled *Maigret et els braves gens*
61 *Maigret and the Saturday caller* (1962)
Original edition entitled *Maigret et le client du Samedi*
62 *Maigret and the surly inspector* (1962)
Original edition entitled *Maigret et l'inspecteur malgracieux*; also published in *Maigret's Christmas*, 1976
63 *Maigret loses his temper* (1963)
Original edition entitled *Le colere de Maigret*
64 *Maigret and the dosser* (1963)
Maigret and the bum
Original edition entitled *Maigret et le clochard*
65 *Maigret and the apparition* (1964)
Maigret and the ghost
Original edition entitled *Maigret et le fantome*
66 *Maigret on the defensive* (1964)
Original edition entitled *Maigret se defend*
67 *Patience of Maigret* (1965)
Maigret bides his time
Original edition entitled *La patience de Maigret*
68 *Maigret and the Nahour case* (1966)
Original edition entitled *Maigret et l'affair Nahour*; also published with *Maigret's pickpocket*
69 *Maigret's pickpocket* (1967)
Original edition entitled *Le voleur de Maigret*; also published with *Maigret and the Nahour case*
70 *Maigret's boyhood friend* (1968)
Original edition entitled *L'ami d'enfance de Maigret*
71 *Maigret in Vichy* (1968)
Maigret takes the waters
Original edition entitled *Maigret a Vichy*
72 *Maigret hesitates* (1968)
Original edition entitled *Maigret hesite*
73 *Maigret and the killer* (1969)
Original edition entitled *Maigret et le tueur*; also published in *The seventh Maigret omnibus*
74 *Maigret and the madwoman* (1970)
Original edition entitled *La folle de Maigret*
75 *Maigret and the wine merchant* (1970)
Original edition entitled *Maigret et le marchand de vin*
76 *Maigret and the loner* (1971)
Original edition entitled *Maigret et l'homme tout seul*
77 *Maigret and the flea* (1971)
Maigret and the informer
Original edition entitled *Maigret et l'indicateur*
78 *Maigret and Monsieur Charles* (1972)
Original edition entitled *Maigret et Monsieur Charles*

Companion volume: *The short cases of Inspector Maigret*, 1959

Inspector Julian Rivers series
Carnac, Carol
1 *Double for detection* (1945)
2 *Striped suitcase* (1946)
3 *Clue sinister* (1947)
4 *Over the garden wall* (1948)
5 *Upstairs downstairs* (1950)
Upstairs and downstairs
6 *Copy for crime* (1950)
7 *It's her own funeral* (1951)
8 *Crossed skies* (1952)
9 *Murder as a fine art* (1953)
10 *Policeman at the door* (1953)
11 *Impact of evidence* (1954)
12 *Murder among members* (1955)
13 *Rigging the evidence* (1955)
14 *Double turn* (1956)
Late Miss Trimming
15 *Long shadows* (1958)
Affair at Helen's Court

Inspector Kane series
Scarlett, Roger
1 *Beacon Hill murders* (1930)
2 *Back Bay murders* (1930)
3 *Cat's paw* (1931)
4 *Murder among the Angells* (1932)
5 *In the first degree* (1933)

Inspector Keats and Tom Cotter series
Long, Martin
1 *Music room* (1990)
2 *Dark gateway* (1987)
3 *Garden house* (1989)

Inspector Kelsey series
Page, Emma
1 *Every second Thursday* (1981)
2 *Last walk home* (1982)
3 *Cold light of day* (1983)
4 *Scent of death* (1985)
5 *Final moments* (1987)
6 *Violent end* (1988)
7 *Deadlock* (1990)
8 *Mortal remains* (1992)

Inspector Kendall series
Farjeon, Joseph Jefferson
1 *Thirteen guests* (1936)
2 *Seven dead* (1939)

Inspector Kilby series
Lenehan, John Christopher
1 *Tunnel mystery* (1929)
2 *Silecroft case* (1931)
3 *Mansfield mystery* (1932)

Inspector Knickman series
Eichler, Alfred
1 *Murder in the radio department* (1943)
2 *Death at the mike* (1946)
3 *Death of an ad man* (1954)
Hearse for the boss
4 *Death of an artist* (1955)
5 *Moment for murder* (1956)
6 *Bury in haste* (1957)

Inspector Lancelot Carolus Smith series
Berrow, Norman
1 *Three tiers of fantasy* (1947)
2 *Bishop's sword* (1948)
3 *Spaniard's thumb* (1949)
4 *Don't go out after dark* (1950)
5 *Footprints of Satan* (1950)

Inspector Lane Parry series
Sarsfield, Maureen
1 *Green December fills the graveyard* (1945)
2 *Dinner for none* (1948)
Party for Lawty

Inspector Lathom Dynes series
Robertson, Helen
1 *Venice of the Black Sea* (1956)
2 *Crystal-gazers* (1957)
3 *Chinese goose* (1960)
Swan song

Inspector Lecain series
Didelot, Francis
1 *Murder in the bath* (1933)
2 *Death of the deputy* (1934)
Original edition entitled *L'assassin du depute*

Inspector Leonidas Prike series
Blochman, Lawrence Goldtree
1 *Bombay mail* (1934)
2 *Bengal fire* (1937)
3 *Red snow at Darjeeling* (1938)

Inspector Lindon and Sergeant Gray series
Whitman, Charles
1 *Doctor Death* (1970)
2 *Death out of focus* (1970)
3 *Death suspended* (1971)

Inspector Lott series
Wade, Henry
1 *Dying alderman* (1930)
2 *Hanging captain* (1932)

Inspector Lovick series
Wilson, Gertrude Mary
1 *Bury that poker* (1957)
2 *I was murdered* (1957)
3 *Thirteen Stannergate* (1958)
4 *Shadows on the landing* (1959)
5 *It rained that Friday* (1960)
6 *Witchwater* (1961)
7 *Three fingered death* (1961)
8 *Roberta died* (1962)
9 *Nightmare cottage* (1963)
10 *Murder on Monday* (1963)
11 *Shot at dawn* (1964)
12 *Devil's Skull* (1965)
13 *Headless man* (1967)
14 *Cake for Caroline* (1967)
15 *Do not sleep* (1968)
16 *Death is buttercups* (1969)
17 *Dial of death caps* (1970)
18 *Bus ran late* (1971)
19 *She kept on dying* (1972)
20 *Gypsies don't have them* (1974)
21 *She sees things* (1975)
22 *Death on a broomstick* (1977)

Inspector Luckraft series
Rees, Arthur John
1 *Island of destiny* (1923)
2 *Sign of Hangletree* (1926)
Unquenchable flame
3 *Pavilion by the lake* (1930)
4 *Tragedy at Twelvetrees* (1931)
5 *River mystery* (1932)
6 *Aldringham's last chance* (1933)
7 *Corpse that traveled* (1938)
8 *Single clue* (1940)

Inspector Luis Bernal series
Serafin, David
see **Superintendent Luis Bernal series**

Inspector Luke Thanet series
Simpson, Dorothy
1 *Night she died* (1981)
2 *Six feet under* (1982)
3 *Puppet for a corpse* (1983)
4 *Close her eyes* (1984)
5 *Last seen alive* (1985)
6 *Dead on arrival* (1986)
7 *Element of doubt* (1987)
8 *Suspicious death* (1988)
9 *Dead by morning* (1989)
10 *Doomed to die* (1991)
11 *Wake the dead* (1992)
12 *No laughing matter* (1993)

Inspector Lyle series
Wainwright, John
1 *Brainwash* (1979)
2 *Duty elsewhere* (1979)
3 *Dominoes* (1980)
4 *Man who wasn't there* (1989)

Inspector Lyon series
Winn, Patrick
1 *Postscript to murder* (1964)
2 *Colour of murder* (1965)
3 *Fact X* (1966)
4 *Dead innocent* (1966)

Inspector Macdonald series
Lorac, E C R
1 *Murder on the burrows* (1931)
2 *Affair at Thor's Head* (1932)
3 *Greenwell mystery* (1932)
4 *Death on the Oxford Road* (1933)

5 *Case of Colonel Marchand* (1933)
6 *Murder in Saint John's Wood* (1934)
7 *Murder in Chelsea* (1934)
8 *Organ speaks* (1935)
9 *Crime counter crime* (1936)
10 *Pall for a painter* (1936)
11 *Post after post-mortem* (1936)
12 *These names make clues* (1937)
13 *Bats in the belfry* (1937)
14 *Devil and the C.I.D.* (1938)
15 *Slippery staircase* (1938)
16 *Black beadle* (1939)
17 *John Brown's body* (1939)
18 *Tryst for a tragedy* (1940)
19 *Death at Dyke's Corner* (1940)
20 *Case in the clinic* (1941)
21 *Rope's end, rogue's end* (1942)
22 *Sixteenth stair* (1942)
23 *Death came softly* (1943)
24 *Fell murder* (1944)
25 *Checkmate to murder* (1944)
26 *Murder by matchlight* (1945)
27 *Fire in the hatch* (1946)
28 *Theft of the iron dogs* (1946)
Murderer's mistake
29 *Relative to poison* (1947)
30 *Death before dinner* (1948)
Screen for murder
31 *Part for a poisoner* (1948)
Place for a poisoner
32 *Still waters* (1949)
33 *Policeman in the precinct* (1949)
And then put out the light
34 *Accident by design* (1950)
35 *Murder of a martinet* (1951)
I could murder her
36 *Dog it was that died* (1952)
37 *Murder in the mill-race* (1952)
Speak justly of the dead
38 *Crook o' lune* (1953)
Shepherd's crook
39 *Let well alone* (1954)
40 *Shroud of darkness* (1954)
41 *Ask a policeman* (1955)
42 *Murder in Vienna* (1956)
43 *Dangerous domicile* (1957)
44 *Picture of death* (1957)
45 *Murder on a monument* (1958)
46 *Death in triplicate* (1958)
People will talk
47 *Dishonour among thieves* (1959)
Last escape

Inspector Mace series
Keverne, Richard
1 *White gas* (1937)
2 *Open verdict* (1940)

Inspector Mackay series
Cushing, E Louise
1 *Murder without regret* (1954)
2 *Blood on my rug* (1956)
3 *Unexpected corpse* (1957)

Inspector Macsporran series
Hill, Lawrence
1 *Dagger drawn* (1939)
2 *Corpse without boots* (1940)

Inspector Madoc Rhys series
Craig, Alisa
1 *Pint of murder* (1980)
2 *Murder goes mumming* (1981)
3 *Dismal thing to do* (1986)
4 *Trouble in the brasses* (1989)
5 *Wrong rite* (1992)

Inspector Malcome Steele series
Scott, Mansfield
1 *Behind red curtains* (1919)
2 *Black circle* (1928)
3 *Spider's web* (1929)

Inspector Mallett series
Hare, Cyril
1 *Tenant for death* (1937)
2 *Death is no sportsman* (1938)
3 *Suicide excepted* (1939)
4 *Tragedy at law* (1942)
5 *With a bare bodkin* (1946)
6 *He should have died hereafter* (1958)
Untimely death

Inspector Manderton series
Williams, Valentine
1 *Yellow streak* (1922)
2 *Orange divan* (1923)
3 *Eye in attendance* (1927)
4 *Death answers the bell* (1931)

Inspector Manson series
Radford, Edwin
see **Doctor Manson series**

Inspector Marcus Maclurg series
Petrie, Rhona
1 *Death in Deakins Wood* (1963)
2 *Murder by precedent* (1964)
3 *Running deep* (1965)
4 *Dead loss* (1966)
5 *Maclurg goes west* (1968)

Inspector Margetson series
Keate, Edith Murray
see **Superintendent Margetson series**

Inspector Marshall series
Newman, Bernard
1 *Spy* (1935)
2 *Secret servant* (1935)
3 *German spy* (1936)
4 *Mussolini murder plot* (1939)

Inspector Martin Beck series
Sjowall, Maj
1 *Roseanna* (1965)
Original edition entitled *Roseanna*
2 *Man who went up in smoke* (1966)
Original edition entitled *Mannen som Gick Upp in Rok*
3 *Man on the balcony* (1967)
Original edition entitled *Mannen pa Balkongen*
4 *Laughing policeman* (1968)
Original edition entitled *Den Skrattande Polisen*
5 *Fire engine that disappeared* (1969)
Original edition entitled *Brandbilen som Forsvann*
6 *Murder at the Savoy* (1970)
Original edition entitled *Polis, Polis, Potatismos!*
7 *Abominable man* (1971)
Original edition entitled *Den Vedervardige Mannen fram Saffle*
8 *Locked room* (1972)
Original edition entitled *Det Slutna Rummet*
9 *Cop killer* (1975)
Original edition entitled *Polis-mordaren*
10 *Terrorists* (1975)
Original edition entitled *Terror-isterna*

Inspector Martin Laidman series
Seaton, Stuart
1 *Don't take it to heart* (1955)
2 *Dust in your eye* (1957)

Inspector Martin series
Amberley, Richard
1 *Incitement to murder* (1968)
2 *Dead on stone* (1969)
3 *Ordinary accident* (1971)

Inspector Matthew Furnival series
Phillips, Stella
1 *Down to death* (1967)
2 *Hidden wrath* (1968)
3 *Death in Arcady* (1969)
4 *Death makes the scene* (1970)
5 *Death in sheep's clothing* (1971)

Inspector Maurice Hepburn series
Gorell, Ronald Gorell Barnes
1 *D.E.Q.* (1922)
2 *Devil's drum* (1929)
3 *Murder at Mavering* (1943)

Inspector Maurice Ygrec series
Rippon, Marion
1 *Hand of Solange* (1969)
2 *Behold, the Druid weeps* (1970)
3 *Ninth tentacle* (1974)
4 *Lucien's tombs* (1979)

Inspector Maury series
Walsh, James Morgan
see **Tiger Bay series**

Inspector Max Kauffman series
Chastain, Thomas
1 *Pandora's box* (1974)
2 *Nine hundred and eleven* (1976)
Christmas bomber
3 *Vital statistics* (1977)
Kauffman has a subsidiary role in this title
4 *High voltage* (1979)
5 *Diamond exchange* (1981)

Inspector Maxwell Quayne series
Symonds, Francis Addington
see **Superintendent Maxwell Quayne series**

Inspector May series
Taylor, Selman
1 *Marshmead murders* (1967)
2 *Murder grows roots* (1970)

Inspector McCaig series
Rae, Hugh Crauford
see **Superintendent McCaig series**

Inspector McGregor series
Kane, Henry
1 *Midnight man* (1965)
Other sins only speak
2 *Conceal and disguise* (1966)
3 *Laughter in the alehouse* (1968)

Inspector McKeller series
McCutcheon, Hugh
1 *Angel of light* (1951)
Murder at the Angel
2 *None shall sleep tonight* (1953)
3 *Cover her face* (1954)

Inspector McLean series
Goodchild, George
1 *McLean of Scotland Yard* (1929)
Short stories
2 *McLean investigates* (1930)
Short stories
3 *McLean at the Golden Owl* (1930)
Short stories
4 *How now, McLean* (1931)
Short stories
5 *Chief Inspector McLean* (1932)
Short stories
6 *Triumph of McLean* (1933)
7 *Yes, Inspector McLean* (1934)
8 *McLean prevails* (1935)
Short stories
9 *McLean knows best* (1935)
Short stories
10 *Death on the Centre Court* (1935)
11 *Lead on, McLean* (1936)
Short stories
12 *McLean remembers* (1936)
13 *McLean finds a way* (1936)
Short stories
14 *McLean takes charge* (1937)
Short stories
15 *McLean plays a hand* (1937)
16 *Call McLean* (1937)
Short stories
17 *Having no hearts* (1937)
Short stories
18 *McLean incomporable* (1938)
Short stories
19 *Again McLean* (1939)
Short stories
20 *McLean sees it through* (1939)
Short stories
21 *McLean excels* (1939)
Short stories
22 *McLean intervenes* (1939)
Short stories
23 *Up, McLean* (1940)
24 *McLean deduces* (1940)
Short stories
25 *McLean the magnificent* (1940)
Short stories
26 *McLean non-stop* (1941)
Short stories
27 *McLean keeps going* (1941)
Short stories
28 *McLean takes a holiday* (1942)
Inspector McLean 's holiday
The second title is a revised edition
29 *Uncle Oscar's niece* (1944)
30 *Hail McLean* (1945)
Short stories
31 *Inspector McLean's casebook* (1948)
Short stories
32 *Companion to Sirius* (1949)
33 *Efford triangle* (1950)
34 *McLean carries on* (1950)
Short stories
35 *McLean predominant* (1951)
Short stories
36 *McLean to the dark tower came* (1951)
37 *McLean steps in* (1952)
Short stories
38 *Last redoubt* (1952)
39 *Well caught McLean* (1953)
40 *Double acrostic* (1954)
41 *Trust McLean* (1954)
42 *Find the lady* (1955)
Short stories
43 *Watch McLean* (1955)
44 *McLean solves it* (1956)
Short stories
45 *Next of kin* (1957)
Short stories
46 *Forever McLean* (1957)
Short stories
47 *McLean disposes* (1958)
Short stories
48 *Tiger, tiger* (1959)
Short stories
49 *McLean scores again* (1959)
Short stories
50 *Follow McLean* (1961)
51 *Savage encounter* (1962)
52 *McLean invincible* (1963)
Short stories
53 *Laurels for McLean* (1964)
Short stories
54 *McLean takes over* (1966)
Short stories
55 *McLean knows the answer* (1967)

Inspector Medford series
Roth, Holly
1 *Shadow of a lady* (1957)
2 *Operation doctors* (1962)
Too many doctors

Inspector Meredith series
Bude, John
1 *Cornish coast murder* (1935)
2 *Lake District murder* (1935)
3 *Sussex Downs murder* (1936)
4 *Cheltenham Square murder* (1937)
5 *Loss of a head* (1938)
6 *Hand on the alibi* (1939)
7 *Death on paper* (1940)
8 *Death of a cad* (1940)
9 *Slow vengeance* (1941)
10 *Death knows no calendar* (1942)
11 *Death deals a double* (1943)
12 *Death in white pyjamas* (1944)
13 *Death in ambush* (1945)
14 *Trouble a-brewing* (1946)
15 *Death makes a prophet* (1947)

16 *Dangerous sunlight* (1948)
17 *Glut of red herrings* (1949)
18 *Death steals the show* (1950)
19 *Constable and the lady* (1951)
20 *Death on the Riviera* (1952)
21 *When the case was opened* (1952)
22 *Twice dead* (1953)
23 *So much in the dark* (1954)
24 *Shift of guilt* (1956)
25 *Telegram from Le Tourquet* (1956)
26 *Another man's shadow* (1957)

Inspector Merton Heimrich series
Lockridge, Frances
1 *Death of a tall man* (1946)
2 *Think of death* (1947)
3 *I want to go home* (1948)
4 *Spin your web, lady!* (1949)
5 *Foggy, foggy death* (1950)
6 *Client is cancelled* (1951)
7 *Death by association* (1952)
Trial by terror
8 *Stand up and die* (1953)
9 *Death and the gentle bull* (1954)
Killer in the straw
10 *Burnt offering* (1955)
English edition published under the pseudonym Francis Richards
11 *Let dead enough alone* (1956)
English edition published under the pseudonym Francis Richards
12 *Practice to deceive* (1957)
English edition entitled *Practise to deceive*, published under the pseudonym Francis Richards
13 *Accent on murder* (1958)
English edition published under the pseudonym Francis Richards
14 *Show red for danger* (1960)
English edition published under the pseudonym Francis Richards
15 *With one stone* (1961)
English edition entitled *No dignity in death*, published under the pseudonym Francis Richards
16 *First come, first kill* (1962)
English edition published under the pseudonym Francis Richards
17 *Distant clue* (1963)
English edition published under the pseudonym Francis Richards; American editions from number 18 by Richard Lockridge
Lockridge, Richard
18 *Murder can't wait* (1964)
English edition published under the pseudonym Francis Richards
19 *Murder roundabout* (1966)
English edition published under the pseudonym Francis Richards
20 *With option to die* (1967)
English edition published under the pseudonym Francis Richards
21 *Risky way to kill* (1969)
22 *Inspector's holiday* (1971)
23 *Not I, said the sparrow* (1973)
24 *Dead run* (1976)
25 *Tenth life* (1977)

Inspector M'Guire series
Warren, John Russell
1 *Murder from three angles* (1939)
2 *Gas-mask murder* (1939)
Murder in the blackout
3 *Time for a murder* (1941)
Also published under the pseudonym Gilbert Coverack
4 *Magpie murder* (1942)
Also published under the pseudonym Gilbert Coverack

Inspector Michael Farrant series
Larbalestier, Philip George
1 *Darling, don't be dumb* (1950)
2 *Black shrouds the bride* (1951)
3 *Death casts no shadow* (1951)

Inspector Michael Hornsley series
Salter, Elizabeth
1 *Death in a mist* (1967)
2 *Will to survive* (1958)
3 *There was a witness* (1960)
4 *Voice of the peacock* (1962)
5 *Once upon a tombstone* (1965)

Inspector Michael Regan series
Hale, Edgar
1 *Devil's tears* (1946)
2 *Death dealt the cards* (1947)
3 *Never shoot a lady* (1947)
4 *Death came back* (1948)
5 *So the lady died* (1949)

Inspector Miguel Menendes series
Blanc, Suzanne
1 *Green stone* (1961)
2 *Yellow villa* (1964)
3 *Rose window* (1967)

Inspector Mike Kenny series
Dillon, Eilis
1 *Death at Crane's Court* (1953)
2 *Death in the quadrangle* (1956)

Inspector Millwall series
Sandys, James
1 *Vengeance due* (1938)
2 *This is death calling* (1943)
3 *Green eye of death* (1943)

Inspector Mitchell series
Lincoln, Natalie Sumner
1 *I spy* (1916)
2 *Nameless man* (1917)
3 *Three strings* (1918)
4 *Moving finger* (1918)
5 *Cat's paw* (1922)
6 *Meredith mystery* (1923)
7 *Missing initial* (1925)
8 *Blue car mystery* (1926)
9 *P.P.C. Appleton* (1927)
10 *Dancing silhouette* (1927)

Inspector Montero and Adam Ludlow series
Nash, Simon
1 *Dead of a counterplot* (1962)
2 *Killed by scandal* (1962)
3 *Death over deep water* (1963)
4 *Dead woman's ditch* (1964)
5 *Unhallowed murder* (1966)

Inspector Morse series
Dexter, Colin
1 *Last bus to Woodstock* (1975)
2 *Last seen wearing* (1976)
3 *Silent world of Nicholas Quinn* (1977)
4 *Service of all the dead* (1979)
5 *Dead of Jericho* (1981)
6 *Riddle of the third mile* (1983)
7 *Secret of Annexe 3* (1986)
8 *Wench is dead* (1989)
9 *Jewel that was ours* (1991)
10 *Way through the woods* (1992)
11 *Morse's greatest mystery, and other stories* (1993)

Inspector Mortimer Blunt series
Cranston, Maurice
1 *Tomorrow we'll be sober* (1946)
2 *Philosopher's hemlock* (1947)

Inspector Mosley series
Greenwood, John
1 *Murder, Mister Mosley* (1983)
2 *Mosley by moonlight* (1984)
3 *Mosley went to mow* (1985)
Missing Mister Mosley
4 *Mists over Mosley* (1986)
5 *Mind of Mister Mosley* (1987)
6 *What, me, Mister Mosley?* (1987)

Inspector Neil Carter series
Dewhurst, Eileen
1 *Curtain fall* (1977)
2 *Drink this* (1980)
3 *Trio in three flats* (1981)
4 *There was a little girl* (1984)
5 *Nice little business* (1987)

Inspector Neville Langham series
Daniel, Roland
1 *Rosario murder case* (1930)
2 *Brown murder case* (1930)

Inspector Newsom series
Stewart, Flora
1 *Deadly nightcap* (1966)
2 *Blood relations* (1967)

Inspector Newton series
Conway, Peter
1 *Victims of circumstance* (1977)
2 *Thirty days to live* (1979)
3 *Nut case* (1980)
4 *Needle track* (1981)
5 *Dead drunk* (1982)
6 *Cryptic clue* (1984)

Inspector Nick Trevellyan and Alison Hope series
Kelly, Susan
see **Alison Hope and Inspector Nick Trevellyan series**

Inspector Noel Macleod series
McLean, Allan Campbell
1 *Carpet-slipper murder* (1956)
2 *Death on All Hallows* (1958)
3 *Murder by invitation* (1959)

Inspector Noel Tracy series
Fraser, Alex
1 *Three wives* (1957)
2 *Constables don't count* (1957)
3 *Death is so final* (1958)
4 *Bury their dead* (1958)
5 *High tension* (1959)
6 *Dark places* (1960)

Inspector Ord series
Allen, Austen
1 *Menace to Mrs Kershaw* (1929)
2 *Dead mouse* (1930)
3 *Live wires* (1931)
4 *Loose rib* (1932)

Inspector Pardoe series
Bowers, Dorothy
1 *Postscript to poison* (1938)
2 *Shadows before* (1939)
3 *Deed without a name* (1940)
4 *Fear for Miss Betony* (1942)
Fear and Miss Betony

Inspector Parker series
Austwick, John
1 *Highland homicide* (1957)
2 *Murder in the borough library* (1959)

Inspector Patrick Aloysius McCarthy series
This sequence has two authors
Brandon, John Gordon
1 *Red altars* (1930)
Secret brotherhood
2 *Black joss* (1931)
3 *West End* (1933)
4 *Murder in Mayfair* (1934)
5 *One-minute murder* (1935)
6 *Riverside mystery* (1935)
7 *Pawnshop murder* (1936)
8 *Snatch game* (1936)
9 *Case of the withered hand* (1936)
10 *Death tolls the gong* (1936)
11 *Dragnet* (1936)
12 *McCarthy, C.I.D.* (1936)
13 *Murder at the Yard* (1936)
14 *Bond Street murder* (1937)
15 *Death in Downing Street* (1937)
16 *Hand of Seeta* (1937)
17 *Mail-van mystery* (1937)
18 *Murder in Soho* (1937)
19 *Night club murder* (1938)
20 *Regent Street raid* (1938)
21 *Bonus for murder* (1938)
22 *Cork Street crime* (1938)
23 *Fifty pound marriage case* (1938)
Two hundred and fifty pound marriage case
24 *Frame-up* (1938)
25 *Mark of the Tong* (1938)
26 *Finger-prints never lie* (1938)
27 *Crooked five* (1939)
28 *Death on delivery* (1939)
29 *Mister Pennington comes through* (1939)
30 *Scream in Soho* (1940)
31 *Yellow gods* (1940)
32 *Mister Pennington goes nap* (1940)
33 *Death in the quarry* (1941)
34 *Mister Pennington barges in* (1941)
35 *Transport murders* (1942)
36 *Blue-print murders* (1942)
37 *Death comes swiftly* (1942)
38 *Mister Pennington sees red* (1942)
39 *Death in Jermyn Street* (1942)
40 *Death in D Division* (1943)
41 *Death in duplicate* (1945)
42 *Candidate for a coffin* (1946)
43 *M for murder* (1949)
44 *Corpse rode on* (1951)
45 *Murderer's stand-in* (1953)
46 *Call-girl murders* (1954)
47 *Death of a Greek* (1955)
48 *Murder on the beam* (1956)
49 *Death of a socialite* (1957)
50 *Murder in Pimlico* (1958)
51 *Corpse from the City* (1958)
52 *Death stalks in Soho* (1959)
53 *Espionage killings* (1959)
Brandon, Gordon
54 *Murder comes smiling* (1959)
55 *Death of a mermaid* (1960)

Inspector Paul Grainger series
Sinclair, Fiona
1 *Scandalize my name* (1960)
2 *Dead of a physician* (1961)
But the patient died
3 *Meddle with the Mafia* (1963)
4 *Three slips to a noose* (1964)
5 *Most unnatural murder* (1965)

Inspector Penk series
Gore, William
1 *Death in the wheelbarrow* (1935)
Also published under the author's real name Jan Gordon
2 *Murder most artistic* (1937)
Mystery of the painted nude

Inspector Peter Bradfield series
Witting, Clifford
1 *Case of the Michaelmas goose* (1938)
2 *Subject, murder* (1945)
3 *Let X be the murderer* (1947)
4 *Dead on time* (1948)
5 *Case of the Busy Bees* (1952)
6 *Silence after dinner* (1953)
7 *There was a crooked man* (1960)
8 *Driven to kill* (1961)
9 *Crime in whispers* (1964)

Inspector Peter Curwen and Hugh Stanton series
Vickers, Roy
1 *Six came to dinner* (1949)
2 *Gold and wine* (1949)
3 *They can't hang Caroline* (1950)
4 *Murder in two flats* (1951)
5 *Find the innocent* (1949)
Girl who wouldn't talk
Includes only Curwen
One story featuring Curwen in *Eight murders in the suburbs*, 1954, one story featuring Curwen in *Double image, and other stories*, 1955, and two stories featuring Curwen in *Seven chose murder*, 1959

Inspector Peter McGarr series
Gill, Bartholomew
1 *McGarr and the politician's wife* (1977)
2 *McGirr and the Sienese conspiracy* (1977)
3 *McGirr on the cliffs of Moher* (1978)
4 *McGarr at the Dublin Horse Show* (1979)
5 *McGarr and the P.M. of Belgrave Square* (1983)
6 *McGarr and the method of Descartes* (1984)
7 *McGarr and the legacy of a woman scorned* (1986)
8 *Death of a Joyce scholar* (1989)
9 *Death of love* (1992)
10 *Death on a wild, cold river* (1993)

Inspector Pettengill series
Rowe, Anne
1 *Little dog barked* (1942)
2 *Painted monster* (1945)

Inspector Pierre Allain and Superintendent William Stevens series
Graeme, Bruce
see **Superintendent William Stevens and Inspector Pierre Allain series**

Inspector Piet Deventer series
Anderson, John Richard Lane
1 *Sprig of sea lavender* (1978)
2 *Festival* (1979)
3 *Late delivery* (1982)

Inspector Piet Van der Valk series
Freeling, Nicolas
1 *Love in Amsterdam* (1962)
Death in Amsterdam
2 *Because of the cats* (1963)
3 *Gun before butter* (1963)
Question of loyalty
4 *Double-barrel* (1964)
5 *Criminal conversation* (1965)
6 *King of the rainy country* (1966)
7 *Strike out where not applicable* (1967)
8 *Tsing-boum!* (1969)
Tsing-boom!
9 *Over the high side* (1970)
Lovely ladies
10 *Long silence* (1972)
Aupres de ma blonde
11 *Sand castles* (1989)
This sequence is continued in the **Arlette Van der Valk series** after the death of Inspector Van der Valk in A long silence

Inspector Pitt series
Straker, John Foster
1 *Postman's knock* (1954)
2 *Pick up the pieces* (1955)
3 *Ginger horse* (1956)
4 *Gun to play with* (1956)
5 *Good-bye, Aunt Charlotte!* (1958)
6 *Death of a good woman* (1961)
7 *Murder for Missemily* (1961)

Inspector Pointer series
Fielding, A
1 *Eames-Erskine case* (1924)
2 *Charteris mystery* (1925)
3 *Footsteps that stopped* (1926)
4 *Clifford affair* (1927)
Clifford mystery
5 *Net around Joan Ingleby* (1928)
6 *Cluny problem* (1929)
7 *Mysterious partner* (1929)
8 *Murder at the Nook* (1929)
9 *Craig poisoning mystery* (1930)
10 *Wedding chest mystery* (1930)
11 *Upfold Farm mystery* (1931)
12 *Death of John Tait* (1932)
13 *Westwood mystery* (1932)
14 *Tall House mystery* (1933)
15 *Cautley conundrum* (1934)
Cautley mystery
16 *Paper chase* (1934)
Paper chase mystery
17 *Tragedy at Beechcroft* (1935)
18 *Case of the missing diary* (1935)
19 *Case of the two pearl necklaces* (1936)
20 *Mystery at the rectory* (1936)
21 *Scarecrow* (1937)
22 *Black cats are lucky* (1937)
23 *Pointer to a crime* (1944)

Inspector Poole series
Wade, Henry
1 *Duke of York Steps* (1929)
2 *No friendly drop* (1931)
Revised edition 1932
3 *Policeman's lot* (1933)
Short stories
4 *Constable, guard thyself!* (1934)
5 *Bury him darkly* (1936)
6 *Lonely Magdalen* (1940)
Revised edition 1946
7 *Too soon to die* (1953)
8 *Gold was our grave* (1954)

Inspector Porfiry Petrovich Rostnikov series
Kaminsky, Stuart Melvin
1 *Rostnikov's corpse* (1981)
Death of a dissident
2 *Black night in Red Square* (1983)
3 *Red chameleon* (1985)
4 *Fine red rain* (1987)
5 *Cold red sunrise* (1988)
6 *Man who walked like a bear* (1990)
7 *Rostnikov's vacation* (1991)
8 *Death of a Russian priest* (1992)
9 *Hard currency* (1995)

Inspector Posse series
Alington, Adrian
1 *Vanishing celebrities* (1938)
2 *Amazing test match crime* (1939)

Inspector Prentis series
Backhouse, Elizabeth
1 *Web of shadows* (1960)
2 *Death climbs a hill* (1963)

Inspector Purbright series
Watson, Colin
1 *Coffin, scarcely used* (1958)
2 *Bump in the night* (1960)
3 *Hopjoy was here* (1962)
4 *Lonelyheart 4122* (1967)
5 *Charity ends at home* (1968)
6 *Flaxborough Crab* (1969)
Just what the doctored ordered
7 *Broomsticks over Flaxborough* (1972)
Kissing covens
8 *Naked nuns* (1975)
Six nuns and a shotgun
9 *One man's meat* (1977)
It shouldn't happen to a dog
10 *Blue murder* (1979)
11 *Plaster sinners* (1980)
12 *Whatever's been going on at Mumblesby* (1982)

Inspector Quaile series
Walsh, James Morgan
1 *Hand of doom* (1927)
2 *Tempania mystery* (1929)
3 *Lady Incognito* (1932)

Inspector Rae Norse series
Esteven, John
1 *Door of death* (1928)
2 *Voodoo* (1930)

Inspector Reeves and Micky Douglas series
Infante, Anne
see **Micky Douglas and inspector Reeves series**

Inspector Reginald Wexford series
Rendell, Ruth
see **Chief Inspector Reginald Wexford series**

Inspector Reynolds series
Hamilton, Elaine
1 *Some unknown hand* (1930)
Westminster mystery
2 *Murder in the fog* (1931)
3 *Chelsea mystery* (1932)
4 *Green death* (1932)
5 *Peril at midnight* (1934)
6 *Tragedy in the dark* (1935)
7 *Casino mystery* (1936)
8 *Murder before Tuesday* (1937)

Inspector Richard Jury series
Grimes, Martha
1 *Man with a load of mischief* (1981)
2 *Old fox deceiv'd* (1982)
3 *Anodyne necklace* (1983)
4 *Dirty duck* (1984)
5 *Jerusalem Inn* (1984)
6 *Help the poor struggler* (1985)
7 *Deer leap* (1985)
8 *I am the only running footman* (1986)
9 *Five Bills and Bladebone* (1988)
10 *Old silent* (1989)
11 *Send Bygraves* (1989)
12 *Old Contemptibles* (1991)
13 *End of the pier* (1992)
14 *Horse you came in with* (1993)

Inspector Richard Left series
Forsyte, Charles
1 *Diplomatic death* (1961)
2 *Diving death* (1962)
Dive into danger
3 *Double death* (1965)

Inspector Richard Ringwood series
Farrer, Katharine
1 *Missing link* (1952)
2 *Cretan counterfeit* (1954)
3 *Gownsman's gallows* (1957)

Inspector Richard Tuck series
Lewis, Lange
see **Lieutenant Richard Tuck series**

Inspector Richardson series
Thomson, Basil
see **Superintendent Richardson series**

Inspector Rip Irving and Sergeant Patrick Shirley series
Mills, Osmington
see **Sergeant Patrick Shirley and Inspector Rip Irving series**

Inspector Robert Fusil and Constable Kerr series
Alding, Peter
see **C.I.D. Room series**

Inspector Robert Staunton series
Hill, Peter
1 *Hunters* (1976)
2 *Liars* (1977)
3 *Enthusiast* (1978)
4 *Savages* (1980)

Inspector Robert Strong series
Robertson, Colin
1 *Painted faces* (1935)
2 *Marble tomb mystery* (1936)
3 *White menace* (1938)
4 *Soho spy* (1940)

Inspector Roderick Alleyn series
Marsh, Ngaio
1 *Man lay dead* (1934)
2 *Enter a murderer* (1935)
3 *Nursing-home murder* (1935)
Co-author: Henry Jellett
4 *Death in ecstasy* (1936)
5 *Vintage murder* (1937)
6 *Artists in crime* (1938)
7 *Death in a white tie* (1938)
8 *Overture to death* (1939)
9 *Death of a peer* (1940)
Surfeit of lampreys
10 *Death at the bar* (1940)
11 *Death and the dancing footman* (1941)
12 *Colour scheme* (1943)
13 *Died in the wool* (1945)
14 *Final curtain* (1947)
15 *Swing, brother, swing* (1949)
Wreath for Rivera
16 *Opening night* (1951)
Night at the Vulcan
17 *Spinsters in jeopardy* (1953)
Bride of death
18 *Scales of justice* (1955)
19 *Death of a fool* (1956)
Off with his head
20 *Singing in the shrouds* (1958)
21 *False scent* (1959)
22 *Hand in glove* (1962)
23 *Dead water* (1963)
24 *Killer Dolphin* (1966)
Death at the Dolphin
25 *Clutch of constables* (1968)
26 *When in Rome* (1970)
27 *Tied up in tinsel* (1972)
28 *Black as he's painted* (1974)
29 *Last ditch* (1976)
30 *Grave mistake* (1978)
31 *Photo-finish* (1980)
32 *Light thickens* (1982)

Inspector Rodway series
Ryland, John Knox
1 *Tragedy near Tring* (1934)
2 *Easter guests mystery* (1935)
3 *Death meets the coroner* (1936)

Inspector Roger Tearle series
Corbett, Scott
1 *Case of the gone goose* (1966)
2 *Case of the fugitive firebug* (1969)
3 *Case of the ticklish tooth* (1971)
4 *Case of the silver skull* (1974)
5 *Case of the burgled blessing box* (1975)

Inspector Roger West series
Creasey, John
1 *Inspector West takes charge* (1942)
Revised edition 1963
2 *Inspector West leaves town* (1943)
Getaway for Inspector West
Go away to murder
3 *Inspector West at home* (1944)
4 *Inspector West regrets* (1945)
Revised edition 1965
5 *Holiday for Inspector West* (1945)
6 *Triumph for Inspector West* (1948)
Case against Paul Raeburn
7 *Battle for Inspector West* (1948)
8 *Inspector West kicks off* (1949)
Sport for Inspector West
9 *Inspector West cries wolf* (1950)
Creepers
10 *Inspector West alone* (1950)
11 *Puzzle for inspector West* (1951)
Dissemblers
12 *Case for Inspector West* (1951)
Figure in the dust
13 *Inspector West at bay* (1952)
Blind spot
Case of the acid throwers
14 *Send Inspector West* (1953)
Send Superintendent West
The second title is a revised edition
15 *Gun for Inspector West* (1953)
Give a man a gun
16 *Beauty for Inspector West* (1954)
Beauty queen killer
So young, so cold, so fair
17 *Inspector West makes haste* (1955)
Gelignite gang
Night of the watchman
Murder makes haste

Inspector Roger West series

18 *Two for Inspector West* (1955)
Murder, one, two, three
Murder tips the scales
19 *Prince for Inspector West* (1956)
Death of an assassin
20 *Parcels for Inspector West* (1956)
Death of a postman
21 *Accident for Inspector West* (1957)
Hit and run
22 *Find Inspector West* (1957)
Trouble at Saxby's
Doorway to death
23 *Strike for death* (1958)
Killing strike
24 *Murder, London-New York* (1958)
25 *Death of a racehorse* (1959)
26 *Case of the innocent victims* (1960)
27 *Murder on the line* (1960)
89 *Scene of the crime* (1961)
29 *Death in cold print* (1961)
30 *Policeman's dread* (1962)
31 *Hang the little man* (1963)
32 *Look three ways at murder* (1964)
33 *Murder, London-Australia* (1965)
34 *Murder, London-South Africa* (1966)
35 *Executioners* (1967)
36 *So young to burn* (1968)
37 *Murder, London-Miami* (1969)
38 *Part for a policeman* (1970)
39 *Alibi?* (1971)
Alibi for Inspector West
40 *Splinter of glass* (1972)
41 *Theft of Magna Carta* (1973)
42 *Extortioners* (1974)
43 *Sharp rise in crime* (1978)

Inspector Ronald Price series
Cannan, Joanna
1 *Murder included* (1950)
Poisonous relations
Taste of murder
2 *Body in the beck* (1952)
3 *Long shadows* (1955)
4 *And be a villain* (1958)
5 *All is discovered* (1962)

Inspector Ross Paterson series
Field, Katherine
1 *Disappearance of a niece* (1941)
2 *Two-five to Mardon* (1942)
3 *Murder to follow* (1944)

Inspector Rudd series
Thomson, June
see **Inspector Finch series**

Inspector Ryvet series
Carnac, Carol
1 *Triple death* (1936)
2 *Missing rope* (1937)
3 *Murder at Mornington* (1937)
4 *When the devil was sick* (1939)
5 *Case of the first-class carriage* (1939)
6 *Death in the diving-pool* (1940)

Inspector Saint Clair series
Luigi, Belli
1 *Lightning crime* (1949)
2 *Toppling terror* (1950)
3 *Master-mind menace* (1950)
4 *Freezing peril strikes* (1951)

Inspector Sanderson series
Hume, David
1 *Call in the Yard* (1935)
2 *Crime combine* (1936)

Inspector Sands series
Millar, Margaret
1 *Devil loves me* (1942)
2 *Wall of eyes* (1943)
3 *Iron gates* (1945)
Taste of fears

Inspector Savage series
Wright, June
1 *Faculty of murder* (1961)
2 *Make-up for murder* (1966)

Inspector Schmidt series
Bagby, George
1 *Murder at the piano* (1935)
2 *Ring around a murder* (1936)
3 *Murder half-baked* (1937)
4 *Murder on the nose* (1938)
5 *Bird walking weather* (1939)
6 *Corpse with the purple thighs* (1939)
7 *Corpse wore a wig* (1940)
Bloody wig murders
8 *Here comes the corpse* (1941)
9 *Red is for killing* (1941)
10 *Murder calling 50* (1942)
11 *Dead on arrival* (1946)
12 *Original carcase* (1946)
Body for the bride
13 *Twin killing* (1947)
14 *Starting gun* (1948)
15 *In cold blood* (1948)
16 *Drop dead* (1949)
17 *Coffin corner* (1949)
18 *Blood will tell* (1950)
19 *Death ain't commercial* (1951)
20 *Scared to death* (1952)
21 *Corpse with sticky fingers* (1952)
22 *Give the little corpse a great big hand* (1953)
Big hand for the corpse
23 *Dead drunk* (1953)
24 *Body in the basket* (1954)
25 *Dirty way to die* (1955)
Shadow on the window
26 *Dead storage* (1956)
27 *Cop killer* (1956)
28 *Dead wrong* (1957)
29 *Three-time losers* (1958)
30 *Real gone goose* (1959)
31 *Evil genius* (1961)
32 *Murder's little helper* (1963)
33 *Mysteriouser and mysteriouser* (1965)
Murder in Wonderland
34 *Dirty pool* (1966)
Bait for a killer
35 *Corpse candle* (1967)
36 *Another day, another death* (1968)
37 *Honest reliable corpse* (1969)
38 *Killer boy was here* (1970)
39 *Two in the bush* (1976)
40 *My dead body* (1976)
41 *Innocent bystander* (1976)
42 *Tough get going* (1977)
43 *Better dead* (1978)
44 *Guaranteed to fade* (1978)
45 *I could have died* (1979)
46 *Mugger's day* (1979)
47 *Country and fatal* (1980)
48 *Question of quarry* (1981)
49 *Sitting duck* (1981)
50 *Golden creep* (1982)
51 *Most wanted* (1983)

Inspector Scott Stuart series
Coffin, Geoffrey
1 *Murder in the Senate* (1935)
Also published under the author's real name Francis Van Wyck Mason
2 *Forgotten fleet mystery* (1936)

Inspector Semlake series
Varnam, John
1 *Death rehearses* (1950)
2 *Travelling deadman* (1951)
3 *Beware of the dog* (1954)

Inspector Septimus Finch series
Erskine, Margaret
1 *And being dead* (1938)
Limping man
Painted mask
2 *Whispering house* (1947)
Voice of the house
3 *I knew McBean* (1948)
Caravan of night
4 *Give up the ghost* (1949)
5 *Disappearing bridegroom* (1950)
Silver ladies
6 *Death of our dear one* (1952)
Look behind you, lady
Don't look behind you
7 *Dead by now* (1953)
Revised edition 1972
8 *Fatal relations* (1955)
Old Mrs Ommanney is dead
Dead don't speak
9 *Voice of murder* (1956)
10 *Sleep no more* (1958)
11 *House of the enchantress* (1959)
Graveyard plot
12 *Woman at Belguardo* (1961)
13 *House in Belmont Square* (1963)
Number nine Belmont Square
14 *Take a dark journey* (1965)
Family at Tammerton
15 *Case with three husbands* (1967)
16 *Ewe lamb* (1968)
17 *Case of Mary Fielding* (1970)
18 *Brood of folly* (1971)
19 *Besides the wench is dead* (1973)
20 *Harriet farewell* (1975)
21 *House in Hook Street* (1978)

Inspector Severn series
Bromley, Gordon
1 *In the ansence of the body* (1972)
2 *Chance to poison* (1973)
3 *Midsummer night's crime* (1977)

Inspector Sevrel series
Worth, Cedric
1 *Trail of the serpent* (1940)
2 *Corpse that knew everybody* (1941)

Inspector Shelley series
Rowland, John
1 *Bloodshed in Bayswater* (1935)
2 *Professor dies* (1936)
3 *Death on Dartmoor* (1936)
4 *Suicide alibi* (1937)
5 *Dangerous company* (1937)
6 *Murder in the museum* (1938)
7 *Devil comes to Devon* (1938)
8 *Slow poison* (1939)
9 *Cornish Riviera mystery* (1939)
10 *Crooked house* (1940)
11 *Spy with a scar* (1940)
12 *Gunpowder Alley* (1941)
13 *Death of Neville Norway* (1942)
14 *Death beneath the river* (1943)
15 *Grim souvenir* (1944)
16 *Puzzle in pyrotechnics* (1947)
17 *Orange-tree mystery* (1949)
18 *Time for killing* (1950)
19 *Calamity in Kent* (1950)

Inspector Sherwood series
Bude, John
1 *Two ends to the town* (1955)
2 *Night the fog came down* (1958)
3 *Twist of the rope* (1958)

Inspector Sholto Lestrade series
Trow, Meirion James
Based on the character from the **Sherlock Holmes series**, by Sir Arthur Conan Doyle
1 *Lestrade and the sawdust ring* (1993)
Set in 1879
2 *Lestrade and the sign of nine* (1992)
Set in 1886
3 *Lestrade and the Ripper* (1888)
Set in 1888
4 *Adventures of Inspector Lestrade* (1985)
Supreme adventures of Inspector Lestrade
Set in 1891
5 *Brigade* (1986)
Set in 1892
6 *Lestrade and the dead man's hand* (1992)
Set in 1895
7 *Lestrade and the guardian angel* (1990)
Set in 1896
8 *Lestrade and the hallowed house* (1987)
Set in 1901
9 *Lestrade and the gift of the prince* (1991)
Set in 1903-4
10 *Lestrade and the deadly game* (1990)
Set in 1908
11 *Lestrade and the leviathan* (1987)
Set in 1911
12 *Lestrade and the brother of death* (1988)
Set in 1912
13 *Lestrade and the magpie* (1991)
Set in 1920

Inspector Sidney Kenyon series
Crisp, Norman James
1 *Gotland deal* (1976)
2 *Odd job man* (1977)
3 *London deal* (1978)

Inspector Silver series
Holt, Henry
1 *Mayfair mystery* (1929)
2 *Midnight mail* (1931)
3 *Necklace of death* (1931)
4 *Wolf's claw* (1932)
Wolf
5 *Murderer's luck* (1932)
6 *Gallows Grange* (1933)
Call out the Flying Squad
7 *Scarlet messenger* (1933)
8 *Calling all cars* (1934)
Sinister shadow
9 *Murder at the bookstall* (1934)
10 *Tiger of Mayfair* (1935)
11 *There has been a murder* (1936)
12 *Calling Scotland Yard* (1944)
13 *Motley and murder* (1945)
14 *Murder, my sweet* (1950)
15 *Wreath for the lady* (1959)
16 *Don't shoot, darling* (1961)

Inspector Simon Ashton series
Antill, Elizabeth
1 *Murder in mid-Atlantic* (1950)
2 *Death on the Barrier Reef* (1952)

Inspector Simon Manton series
Underwood, Michael
see **Superintendent Simon Manton series**

Inspector Simon Spears series
Gielgud, Val
1 *Death at Broadcasting House* (1934)
London calling
2 *Death as an extra* (1935)
3 *Death in Budapest* (1937)

Inspector Sims and Professor Wells series
Grierson, Francis Durham
1 *Limping man* (1924)
2 *Secret judges* (1925)
3 *Lost pearl* (1925)
4 *Zoo murder* (1926)
Murder in the garden
5 *Smiling death* (1927)
6 *White camellia* (1928)
7 *Blue bucket mystery* (1929)
8 *Yellow rat* (1929)
Murder at the wedding
9 *Mysterious mademoiselle* (1930)
10 *Murder at Lancaster Gate* (1934)
11 *Murder in black* (1935)
12 *Death on deposit* (1935)

Inspector Skane series
Marfield, Dwight
1 *Mystery of the east wind* (1930)
2 *Man with a paper skull* (1932)
3 *Sword in the pool* (1932)
4 *Mystery of King Cobra* (1933)
5 *Mandarin's sapphire* (1938)

Inspector Skarratt series
Fletcher, Joseph Smith
1 *Marchester Royal* (1909)
2 *Wolves and the lamb* (1914)
3 *Secret of secrets* (1929)

Inspector Slane series
Maddock, Stephen
1 *Exit only* (1947)
2 *East of Piccadilly* (1948)
3 *Keep your fingers crossed* (1949)
4 *Private line* (1950)

Inspector Smart series
Fowler, Richard
1 *Inspector Smart gets the message* (1982)
2 *Inspector Smart's international mystery tour* (1983)

Inspector Smith series
Troy, Simon
1 *Road to Rhuine* (1952)
2 *Half way to murder* (1955)
3 *Tonight and tomorrow* (1957)
4 *Drunkard's end* (1960)
5 *Second cousin removed* (1961)
6 *Waiting for Oliver* (1962)
7 *Don't play with the rough boys* (1963)
8 *Cease upon the midnight* (1964)
9 *No more a-roving* (1965)
10 *Sup with the devil* (1967)
11 *Swift to its close* (1969)
12 *Blind man's garden* (1970)

Inspector Spearpoint series
Arthur, Frank
1 *Who killed Netta Maul?* (1948)
Suva Harbour mystery
2 *Another mystery in Suva* (1950)
3 *Murder in the tropic night* (1961)
4 *Throbbing dark* (1963)

Inspector Speed series
Donovan, Jean Beradine
see **Bill Speed series**

Inspector Stanley Fyles series
Cullum, Ridgwell
1 *Law breakers* (1914)
2 *Law of the gun* (1918)

Inspector Stephen Harper series
Brown, Walter C
1 *Second chance* (1929)
2 *Laughing death* (1932)
3 *Murder at Mocking House* (1933)

Inspector Stephen Ramsay series
Cleeves, Ann
1 *Lesson in dying* (1990)
2 *Murder in my backyard* (1991)
3 *Day in the death of Dorothy Cassidy* (1992)

Inspector Steven Mitchell series
Bell, Josephine
1 *Murder in hospital* (1937)
2 *Fall over cliff* (1938)
3 *Port of London murders* (1938)
4 *Death at half-term* (1939)
Curtain call for a corpse
5 *Death in clairvoyance* (1940)
6 *Summer school mystery* (1950)
7 *Bones in the barrow* (1953)
8 *China roundabout* (1956)
Murder on the merry-go-round
9 *Seeing eye* (1958)
10 *Easy prey* (1959)
11 *Well-known face* (1960)
12 *Flat tyre in Fulham* (1963)
Fiasco in Fulham
Room for a body

Inspector Stoddart series
Haynes, Annie
1 *Crime at Tattenham Corner* (1929)
2 *Who killed Charmian Karslake?* (1929)
3 *Crysal beads murder* (1930)

Inspector Storm series
Walsh, James Morgan
1 *Silver greyhound* (1928)
2 *Whisperer* (1931)

Inspector Strang series
Carnac, Carol
1 *Double turn* (1956)
2 *Death of a ladykiller* (1959)

Inspector Strickland series
Dilnot, George
1 *Crooks' game* (1927)
2 *Black ace* (1929)

Inspector Swain series
Thomas, Donald
1 *Belladonna* (1984)
Mad Hatter summer
A Lewis Carroll nightmare
2 *Ripper's apprentice* (1986)
3 *Jekyll, alias Hyde* (1988)

Inspector Swinton series
Flower, Pat
1 *Wax flowers for Gloria* (1958)
2 *Goodbye, sweet William* (1959)
3 *Wreath of water-lilies* (1960)
4 *One rose less* (1961)
5 *Hell for Heather* (1962)
6 *Term of terror* (1963)
7 *Friends of the family* (1966)

Inspector Swinton series
Greig, Ian
1 *King's Club murder* (1930)
Silver king mystery
2 *Tragedy of the Chinese mine* (1930)
3 *Murder at Lintercombe* (1931)
4 *Baxter's second death* (1932)
5 *False scent* (1933)

Inspector Taff Roberts series
Parker, Roger
1 *Riot* (1986)
2 *Abuse of justice* (1988)

Inspector Tami Shimoni series
Hesky, Olga
1 *Serpent's smile* (1966)
2 *Time for treason* (1967)
3 *Sequin syndicate* (1969)
4 *Different night* (1970)

Inspector Terry Sneed series
Newman, Gordon F
1 *Sir, you bastard* (1970)
Rogue cop
2 *You nice bastard* (1972)
3 *Price* (1974)
You flash bastard

Inspector Thew series
Browne, Douglas Gordon
1 *Cotfold conundrums* (1933)
2 *Plan XVI* (1934)

Inspector Thomas Brunt series
Hilton, John Buxton
1 *Gamekeeper's gallows* (1976)
2 *Rescue from The Rose* (1976)
3 *Dead-nettle* (1977)
4 *Mister Fred* (1983)
5 *Quiet stranger* (1985)
6 *Slickensides* (1987)

Inspector Thomas Conroy series
Asbury, Herbert
1 *Devil of Pei-Ling* (1927)
Crimson rope
2 *Tick of the clock* (1928)

Inspector Thomas Lynley and Sergeant Barbara Havers series
George, Elizabeth
1 *Great deliverance* (1988)
2 *Payment in blood* (1989)
3 *Well-schooled in murder* (1990)
4 *Suitable vengeance* (1992)
5 *For the sake of Elena* (1992)
6 *Missing Joseph* (1993)
7 *Playing for the Ashes* (1994)

Inspector Thomas Pitt series
Perry, Anne
see **Charlotte Ellison Pitt and Inspector Thomas Pitt series**

Inspector Tobin series
Hughes, Dorothy Belle
1 *So blue marble* (1940)
2 *Cross-eyed bear* (1940)
Cross-eyed bear murders
3 *Fallen sparrow* (1942)

Inspector Todd series
Halstead, John
1 *Black Nat* (1932)
2 *Black Arab* (1933)
3 *Black Templar* (1934)
4 *Black fear* (1935)
5 *Black flame* (1936)
6 *Black hate* (1937)

Inspector Tom Anderson series
Southworth, Louis
1 *Felon in disguise* (1966)
2 *Corpse on London Bridge* (1969)

Inspector Tom Barnaby series
Graham, Caroline
1 *Killings at Badger's Drift* (1987)
2 *Death of a hollow man* (1989)

Inspector Tom Maybridge series
Gill, B M
1 *Victims* (1981)
Suspect
2 *Seminar for murder* (1985)

Inspector Tom Pollard series
Lemarchand, Elizabeth
see **Superintendent Tom Pollard series**

Inspector Tope series
Williams, Ben Ames
1 *Death on Scurvy Street* (1929)
Bellmer mystery
2 *Money musk* (1932)
Lady in peril

Inspector Treadgold series
Weymouth, Anthony
1 *Frozen death* (1934)
2 *Doctors are doubtful* (1935)
3 *No, Sir Jeremy* (1935)
4 *Hard liver* (1936)
5 *Cornish crime* (1937)
6 *Tempt me not* (1937)
7 *Inspector Treadgold investigates* (1941)

Inspector Trevor Nichols and Sergeant Tom Burton series
Peters, Geoffrey
1 *Claw of a cat* (1964)
2 *Eye of a serpent* (1964)
3 *Whirl of a bird* (1965)
4 *Twist of a stick* (1966)
5 *Flick of a fin* (1967)
6 *Mark of a buoy* (1967)
7 *Chill of a corpse* (1968)

Inspector Tubby Hall series
Hambledon, Phyllis
1 *Keys for the criminal* (1958)
2 *Murder and Miss Ming* (1959)
3 *Death of an uncle* (1962)

Inspector Victor Bondurant series
Edwards, James G
1 *Murder in the surgery* (1935)
2 *Private pavilion* (1935)
3 *F Corridor* (1936)
4 *Odor of bitter almonds* (1938)
5 *Death elects a mayor* (1939)
6 *Death among doctors* (1942)
7 *But the patient died* (1948)

Inspector Wade Paris series
Benson, Ben
1 *Beware the pale horse* (1951)
2 *Alibi at dusk* (1951)
3 *Lily in her coffin* (1952)
4 *Stamped for murder* (1952)
5 *Target in taffeta* (1953)
6 *Burning fuse* (1954)
7 *Ninth hour* (1956)
8 *Affair of the exotic dancer* (1958)
9 *Blonde in black* (1958)
10 *Huntress is dead* (1960)

Inspector Wake series
Kingston, Charles
1 *Brighton beach mystery* (1936)
2 *Murder in Piccadilly* (1936)
3 *Circle of guilt* (1937)
4 *Rigdale puzzle* (1937)
5 *Murder in disguise* (1938)
6 *Death came back* (1944)
7 *Fear followed on* (1945)

Inspector Walter McDumont series
Garner, Hugh
1 *Sin sniper* (1970)
Stone cold dead
2 *Death in Don Mills* (1975)
3 *Murder has your number* (1978)

Inspector Widgeon series
Thomas, Alan
1 *Death of Laurence Vining* (1928)
2 *Death of the Home Secretary* (1933)

Inspector Wield series
Glint Green
1 *Strands of red hair!* (1931)
2 *Devil spider* (1932)
3 *Beauty, a snare* (1933)
4 *Poison death* (1933)

Inspector Wilfred Dover series
Porter, Joyce
see **Chief Inspector Wilfred Dover series**

Inspector Wilkins series
Anderson, James
1 *Affair of the blood-stained egg cosy* (1975)
2 *Affair of the mutilated mink coat* (1981)

Inspector Wilkins series
Beeding, Francis
1 *Death walks in Eastrepps* (1931)
2 *Murder intended* (1932)

Inspector Wilkins series
Thomas, Murray
1 *Buzzards pick the bones* (1932)
2 *Inspector Wilkins sees red* (1934)
3 *Inspector Wilkins reads the proofs* (1935)

Inspector William Austen series
Hocking, Anne
1 *Little victims play* (1938)
2 *Ill deeds done* (1938)
3 *So many doors* (1939)
4 *Old Mrs Fitzgerald* (1939)
Deadly is the evil tongue
5 *Wicked flea* (1940)
6 *Night's candles* (1941)
7 *Miss Milverton* (1941)
Poison is a bitter brew
8 *One shall be taken* (1942)
9 *All my pretty chickens* (1943)
Death loves a shining mark
10 *Six green bottles* (1943)
11 *Nile green* (1943)
12 *Vultures gather* (1945)

Inspector William Austen series

13 *Death at the wedding* (1946)
14 *Prussian blue* (1947)
Finishing touch
15 *At The Cedars* (1949)
16 *Death disturbs Mr Jefferson* (1950)
17 *Best laid plans* (1950)
18 *Mediterranean murder* (1951)
Killing kin
19 *There's death in the cup* (1952)
20 *Evil men do* (1953)
21 *Death among the tulips* (1953)
22 *And no one wept* (1954)
23 *Poison in paradise* (1955)
24 *Reason for murder* (1955)
25 *Murder at mid-day* (1956)
26 *Simple way of poison* (1957)
27 *Relative murder* (1957)
28 *Epitaph for a nurse* (1958)
Victim must be found
29 *To cease upon the midnight* (1959)
30 *Poisoned chalice* (1959)
31 *Thin-spun life* (1960)
32 *Candidates for murder* (1961)
33 *He had to die* (1962)
34 *Murder cries out* (1968)
Completed by Evelyn Healey

Inspector William Baker series
Mills, Osmington
see **Superintendent William Baker series**

Inspector William Beeke series
Brooks, Edwy Searles
1 *Strange case of the antlered man* (1935)
2 *Grouser investigates* (1936)

Inspector William Brewer series
McElroy, Hugh
1 *Silver Venus* (1942)
2 *Curtains of the dark* (1944)
3 *Unkindly cup* (1946)
4 *House of Malory* (1948)

Inspector William McAlpin series
Smithies, Richard Hugo Ripman
1 *Academic question* (1965)
Death gets an A
2 *Disposing mind* (1966)
Death takes a gamble

Inspector William Monk series
Perry, Anne
1 *Sudden, fearful death* (1993)
2 *Dangerous mourning* (1994)
3 *Sins of the wolf* (1994)

Inspector William Winter series
Butler, Gwendoline
1 *Receipt for murder* (1956)
2 *Dead in a row* (1957)
3 *Dull dead* (1958)
4 *Murdering kind* (1958)

Inspector Williams series
Clevely, Hugh
1 *Hell to pay* (1930)
Call the Yard!
2 *Frazer butts in* (1931)
3 *Further outlook unsettled* (1932)
4 *Amateur crook* (1936)
5 *Death's counterfeit* (1937)

Inspector Wilton Jacks series
Wallis, James Harold
1 *Murder by formula* (1931)
2 *Servant of death* (1932)
3 *Capital city mystery* (1932)
4 *Mystery of Vaucluse* (1933)
5 *Cries in the night* (1933)
6 *Murder mansion* (1934)
House of murder

Inspector Wittler series
McGuire, Paul
1 *Murder in Bostall* (1931)
Black rose murder
2 *Prologue to the gallows* (1936)
3 *Threepence to Marble Arch* (1936)
4 *W One* (1937)

Inspector Woods series
Muir, Dorothy Erskine
1 *In muffled night* (1933)
2 *Five to five* (1934)

Inspector Wren series
Temple-Ellis, N A
1 *Three went in* (1934)
2 *Dead in no time* (1935)
Murder in the ruins
3 *Death of a decent fellow* (1941)

Inspector Wright series
Scott, Mary
1 *Fatal lady* (1960)
2 *Mangrove murder* (1963)
3 *No red herrings* (1964)

Inspector York series
Durham, Mary
1 *Hate is my livery* (1945)
2 *Why pick on Pickles?* (1946)
3 *Keeps death his court* (1946)
4 *Crime insoluble* (1947)
5 *Murder by multiplication* (1948)

Instrumentality series
Smith, Cordwainer
1 *You will never be the same* (1963)
Short stories
2 *Planet buyer* (1964)
3 *Space lords* (1965)
Short stories
4 *Quest of three worlds* (1966)
Short stories
5 *Underpeople* (1968)
Short stories; numbers 2 and 5 also published as *Norstrilia*, 1975
6 *Under old earth, and other explorations* (1970)
7 *Stardreamer* (1971)
Short stories
8 *Instumentality of mankind* (1979)

Intelligence Corps series
Frow, Marion
1 *Intelligence Corps and Anna* (1944)
2 *Intelligence Corps saved the island* (1946)
3 *Four stowaways and Anna* (1947)

Intergalactic kitchen series
Rodgers, Frank
1 *Intergalactic kitchen* (1990)
2 *Intergalactic kitchen goes prehistoric* (1991)

Interior dialogue series
Mauriac, Claude
1 *All women are fatal* (1957)
Femmes fatales
Original edition entitled *Femmes fatales*
2 *Dinner party* (1959)
Dinner in town
Original edition entitled *Le diner en ville*
3 *Marquise went out at five* (1961)
Original edition entitled *La marquise sortit a cinq heures*
4 *[Agrandissement]* (1961)
No English edition

Intersect File series
Cannon, John
1 *Web of terror* (1980)
2 *Death cruise* (1980)

Interstellar Patrol series
Hamilton, Edmond
1 *Outside the universe* (1964)
2 *Crashing suns* (1965)

Intimate secrets series
Flanagan
1 *Intimate secrets of an escort girl* (1975)
2 *Intimate secrets of a magazine writer* (1975)
3 *Intimate secrets of an actress* (1975)

Into their labours trilogy
Berger, John
1 *Pig earth* (1979)
Short stories
2 *Once in Europa* (1987)
Short stories
3 *Lilac and flag* (1990)
An old wives' tale of a city

Invaders series
This sequence has four authors; based on a television series
Laumer, Keith
1 *Invaders* (1967)
Also published as *The meteor men* under the pseudonym Anthony Le Baron
2 *Enemies from beyond* (1967)
Bernard, Rafe
3 *Halo highway* (1967)
Army of the undead
Newman, Paul S
4 *Alien missile threat* (1967)
Leslie, Peter
5 *Night of the trilobites* (1968)
6 *Autumn accelerator* (1969)
Companion volume: *Dam of death*, by Jack Pearl, 1967

Inverness series
Macintyre, Lorn
see **Chronicles of Inverness series**

Invincible questions series
Stanton, David
1 *Remember me* (1957)
2 *On a balcony* (1958)
3 *Segaki* (1958)

Invincible questions trilogy
Stacton, David
1 *Remember me* (1957)
2 *On a balcony* (1958)
3 *Segaki* (1958)

Invisibles series
Hurwood, Bernhardt Jackson
1 *Invisibles* (1971)
2 *Mind master* (1973)

Involvement in history series
Birt, David
1 *Middle Ages I, 1066-1154* (1978)
2 *Middle Ages II, 1154-1327* (1979)
3 *Middle Ages III, 1327-1485* (1979)

Ione Muffet series
Fine, Anne
1 *Summer-house loon* (1978)
2 *Other, darker Ned* (1979)

Ionia series
Stark, Freya
Travels
1 *Ionia* (1954)
A quest
2 *Lycian shore* (1956)

Iowa pioneer life series
Quick, Herbert
1 *Vandemark's folly* (1922)
2 *Hawkeye* (1923)
3 *Invisible woman* (1925)

Ira Cobb series
Winsor, Roy
1 *Corpse that walked* (1974)
2 *Always lock your bedroom door* (1976)
3 *Three motives for murder* (1976)

Ira Penaluna trilogy
Harris, John
1 *Mustering of the hawks* (1972)
2 *Mercenaries* (1969)
Jade wind
3 *Courtney entry* (1970)

Ira series
Waber, Bernard
1 *Ira sleeps over* (1972)
2 *Ira says goodbye* (1988)

Ira Yedder series
Bond, Evelyn
1 *Doomway* (1971)
2 *Girl from nowhere* (1972)
3 *Devil's footprints* (1972)
4 *Dark sonata* (1972)

Ire series
Crow, Duncan
see **Simon Ire series**

Ireland series
Mariz, Linda
see **Laura Ireland series**

Irene Adler series
Douglas, Carole Nelson
Based on a character from a story by Sir Arthur Conan Doyle
1 *Good night, Mister Holmes* (1990)
2 *Good morning, Irene* (1991)
3 *Irene at large* (1992)
4 *Irene's last waltz* (1994)

Irene series
Burke, Jan
1 *Goodnight, Irene* (1993)
2 *Sweet dreams, Irene* (1994)

Ireta adventure series
McCaffrey, Anne
1 *Dinosaur Planet* (1977)
2 *Dinosaur Planet survivors* (1984)
One volume edition entitled *The Ireta adventure*, 1985

Iris and Maggie series
Jukes, Mavis
see **Maggie and Iris series**

Iris Cooper and Jack Clancy series
Beck, Kathrine Kristine
1 *Death in a deckchair* (1984)
2 *Murder in a mummy case* (1986)
3 *Peril under the palms* (1989)

Iris series
Atkins, Meg Elizabeth
see **Inspector Henry Beaumont series**

Iris Thorne series
Pugh, Dianne G
1 *Cold call* (1993)
2 *Slow squeeze* (1994)

Irish childhood series
Hamilton, Elizabeth
Reminiscences
1 *River full of stars* (1954)
2 *Irish childhood* (1963)

Irish history series
McCaughren, Tom
1 *Legend of the golden key* (1983)
2 *Legend of the phantom highwayman* (1983)
3 *Legend of the Corrib king* (1984)
4 *Children of the forge* (1985)
5 *Silent sea* (1987)

Irish labourer trilogy
O'Donoghue, John
Reminiscense of farm life in Kerry
1 *In a quiet land* (1957)
2 *In a strange land* (1958)
Account of an interlude in England
3 *In Kerry long ago* (1960)

Irish Monte Cristo series
Robertson, Alexander
1 *Irish Monte Cristo's search* (1889)
Alternative title: The Bonanza King in New York
2 *Irish Monte Cristo abroad* (1889)
Alternative title: The secrets of the catacombs
3 *Irish Monte Cristo's trail* (1890)
Alternative title: Hunted from the Pyramids to Berlin

Irish R.M. series
Somerville, Edith Oenone
1 *Some experiences of an Irish R.M.* (1899)
2 *All on the Irish shore* (1903)
3 *Some Irish yesterdays* (1906)
4 *Further experiences of an Irish R.M.* (1908)
5 *In Mister Knox's country* (1915)

Irish series
Child, Nellise
see **Jeremiah Irish series**

Irissa and Kendric trilogy
Douglas, Carole Nelson
1 *Six of swords* (1982)
2 *Exiles of the Rynth* (1984)
3 *Keepers of Edanvani* (1987)

Iron angel series
Morressy, John
1 *Ironbrand* (1980)
2 *Graymantle* (1981)
3 *Kingsbane* (1982)
4 *Time of the annihilator* (1985)

Iron Duke series
Tunis, John Roberts
1 *Iron Duke* (1938)
2 *Duke decides* (1939)

Iron rails trilogy
Shane, Bart
1 *Iron rails* (1979)
2 *Rails west* (1980)
3 *Railhead* (1980)

Iron tower trilogy
McKiernan, Dennis L
1 *Dark tide* (1984)
2 *Shadows of doom* (1984)
3 *Darkest day* (1984)
This sequence is followed by the **Silver call series**

Ironbark Bill series
Stivens, Dal
1 *Gambling ghost, an other tales* (1953)
2 *Ironbark Bill* (1955)

Ironsides Cromwell series
Gunn, Victor
see **Chief Inspector Bill Cromwell series**

Ironsides Goss series
Willock, Colin Dennistoun
see **Nathaniel Ironsides Goss series**

Iroquois series
This sequence has four authors
Graymont, Barbara
1 *Iroquois in the American Revolution* (1972)
Hauptman, Laurence Marc
2 *Iroquois and the Civil War years* (1992)
From battlefield to reservation
3 *Iroquois and the New Deal* (1981)
4 *Iroquois struggle for survival* (1986)
World War II to Red Power
Vesey, Christopher
5 *Iroquois land claims* (1988)

Irtenyev trilogy
Tolstoi, Leo Nikolaevich
see **Nicholas Irtenyev trilogy**

Irving and Shirley series
Mills, Osmington
see **Sergeant Patrick Shirley and Inspector Rip Irving series**

Irving family trilogy
Irving, Laurence
The lives of the author's theatrical ancestors
1 *Henry Irving* (1951)
The actor and his world
2 *Successors* (1967)
3 *Precarious crust* (1971)

Irving Martin Reddy series
Zacharia, Irwin
1 *Brotherhood of evil* (1982)
2 *Princess of darkness* (1982)
3 *Reddy or not* (1982)
4 *Three to get Reddy* (1982)

Irving series
Grex, Leo
see **Paul Irving series**

Irving Todd series
Conde, Phillip
1 *Murder in the cockpit* (1936)
2 *Corpse in the clouds* (1937)
3 *Death takes the joystick* (1937)
4 *Skyway vampire* (1938)
5 *Murder at ten thousand feet* (1938)
6 *Dead reckoning* (1938)

Irvington series
Baldwin, Faith
see **Doctor Bing Irvington series**

Irwin M Fletcher series
McDonald, Gregory
see **Fletch series**

Is it series
Hoban, Tana
1 *Is it red, is it yellow, is it blue?* (1978)
2 *Is it rough, is it smooth, is it shiny?* (1984)
3 *Is it larger, is it smaller?* (1985)

Is-land trilogy
Frame, Janet
Autobiography
1 *To the is-land* (1983)
2 *Angel at my table* (1984)
3 *Envoy from mirror city* (1984)

I's series
Zukofsky, Louis
Poetry
1 *I's* (1963)
2 *After I's* (1964)

Is there anybody there series
Wilson, Jacqueline
1 *Spirit raising* (1990)
2 *Crystal gazing* (1990)

Is this a title, it is not series
Means, Eldred Kurtz
Short stories
1 *E K Means* (1918)
2 *More E K Means* (1919)
3 *Further E K Means* (1920)

Isaac Asimov's Robot city series
Kube-McDowell, Michael Paul
see **Robot city series**

Isaac Asimov's Robots and aliens series
Leigh, Stephen
see **Robots and aliens series**

Isaac C Parker and George Maledon series
Gardner, Jerome
see **Hanging Judge series**

Isaac Sidel series
Charyn, Jerome
1 *Blue Eyes* (1975)
2 *Marilyn the wild* (1976)
3 *Education of Patrick Silver* (1976)
4 *Secret Isaac* (1978)
Numbers 1-4 also published in one volume entitled *The Isaac quartet*, 1984
5 *Good policeman* (1990)

Isaacs series
Gee, Joseph
see **David Isaacs series**

Isaac's universe series
Greenberg, Martin Harry
1 *Diplomacy Guild* (1990)
2 *Phases in chaos* (1991)

Isabel Carleton series
Ashmun, Margaret Eliza
1 *Isabel Carleton's year* (1916)
2 *Heart of Isabel Carleton* (1917)
3 *Isabel Carleton's friends* (1918)
4 *Isabel Carleton in the West* (1919)
5 *Isabel Carleton at home* (1920)

Isabel Carnaby trilogy
Fowler, Ellen Thornycroft
1 *Concerning Isabel Carnaby* (1898)
2 *In subjection* (1906)
3 *Ten degrees backward* (1915)

Isabel series
Castaneda, Omar S
1 *Among the volcanoes* (1993)
2 *Imagining Isabel* (1994)

Isabella and Ferdinand trilogy
Plaidy, Jean
see **Ferdinand and Isabella trilogy**

Isabelle Comtat series
Ratel, Simonne
Translated from the French
1 *High house* (1934)
House in the hills
2 *Green grape* (1937)

Isabelle series
Greene, Constance Clarke
1 *Isabelle the itch* (1973)
2 *Isabelle shows her stuff* (1984)
3 *Isabelle and little orphan Frannie* (1988)

Isadora Wing series
Jong, Erica
1 *Fear of flying* (1973)
2 *How to save your own life* (1977)
3 *Parachutes and kisses* (1984)

Isen series
Ruggero, Ed
see **Mark Isen series**

Isher Empire series
Van Vogt, Alfred Elton
1 *Weapon shops of Isher* (1951)
2 *Weapon makers* (1947)
One against eternity
Revised edition 1952

Ishi series
Kroeber, Theodora
Stories of indigenous people of California
1 *Ishi in two worlds* (1961)
2 *Ishi, last of his tribe* (1964)

Isis trilogy
Hughes, Monica
1 *Keeper of the Isis Light* (1980)
2 *Guardian of Isis* (1981)
3 *Isis pedlar* (1982)

Iskirlak series
Fleming, Joan
see **Nuri Iskirlak series**

Island farm series
Lockley, Ronald Mathias
1 *Myself when young* (1979)
The making of a naturalist
2 *Dream island* (1930)
A record of a simple life
3 *Island days* (1934)
Revised one volume edition of Numbers 2 and 3 published as *Dream island days*, 1943
4 *Inland farm* (1943)
5 *Island farmers* (1948)
6 *Golden year* (1948)
7 *Island* (1969)
8 *Orielton* (1977)
The human and natural history of a Welsh manor

Island of Sodor series
Awdry, Wilbert
see **Sodor series**

Island of stone series
Hunter, Claire
1 *Island of stone* (1981)
2 *Fiercely the tempest* (1984)

Island series
Durrell, Lawrence
1 *Prospero's cell* (1945)
Revised edition 1975; Corfu
2 *Reflections on a marine Venus* (1953)
Revised edition 1960; Rhodes
3 *Bitter lemons* (1957)
Cyprus
4 *Sicilian carousel* (1977)
5 *Greek islands* (1978)

Island series
Grier, Sydney Carlyon
1 *Rearguard* (1915)
2 *Kingdom of waste lands* (1917)

Island series
Manners, Alexandra
see **Karran Kinrade series**

Island trilogy
Wilson, Jeanne
1 *Weep in the sun* (1976)
2 *Troubled heritage* (1977)
3 *Mulatto* (1978)

Islanders series
Knowles, Gaye
1 *Islanders* (1948)
2 *Islanders' secret cave* (1949)
3 *Islanders' strange holiday* (1950)
4 *Islanders follow a clue* (1952)
5 *Islanders in danger* (1953)

Islanders series
O'Donnell, Peadar
1 *Storm* (1926)
2 *Islanders* (1928)

Islandia series
This sequence has three authors
Wright, Austin Tappan
1 *Islandia* (1942)
Saxton, Mark
2 *Islar* (1969)
3 *Two kingdoms* (1979)
4 *Havoc in Islandia* (1982)
Farmer, Richard Neil
5 *Islandia revisited* (1983)
Companion volume: *The Islandian world of Austin Wright*, by Lawrence Clark Powell, 1957

Islands series
Mayne, William
1 *Glass ball* (1961)
2 *Day without wind* (1964)
3 *Old Zion* (1966)

Isle of the dead series
Zelazny, Roger
1 *Isle of the dead* (1969)
2 *To die in Italbar* (1973)

Isle series
Springer, Nancy
see **Book of Isle series**

Isobel Cleary series
Thomas, Audrey
1 *Songs my mother taught me* (1973)
2 *Mrs Blood* (1970)
3 *Blown figures* (1974)

Isobel Quirk and Margaret Davis trilogy
Wakefield, Tom
see **Margaret Davis and Isobel Quirk trilogy**

Isola Dering series
Lisle, David
1 *Painter of souls* (1911)
2 *What is love?* (1913)

Israel Bond series
Weinstein, Sol
1 *Loxfinger* (1965)
2 *Matzohball* (1966)
3 *On the secret service of His Majesty the Queen* (1966)
4 *You only live until you die* (1968)

Israeli armed services series
Stevenson, William Henri
1 *Zanek* (1971)
A chronicle of the Israeli Air Force
2 *Strike Zion!* (1967)
3 *Ninety minutes at Entebbe* (1976)

Israeli commandos series
Sugar, Andrew
1 *Aswan assignment* (1974)
2 *Fireball assignment* (1974)
3 *Kamikaze assignment* (1975)
4 *Alps assignment* (1975)

Israeli Security Branch series
Arvay, Harry
1 *Eleven bullets for Mohammed* (1975)
2 *Operation Kuwait* (1975)
3 *Meirovitz plan* (1975)
4 *Moscow intercept* (1975)
5 *Piraeus plot* (1975)
6 *Damascus countdown* (1976)
7 *Stranglehold* (1976)
8 *Togo commando* (1976)
9 *Swiss deal* (1976)
10 *Blow the four winds* (1977)
11 *Triad 21* (1977)
12 *Society of fear* (1979)

Issi Noho series
Chatfield, Keith
Based on a television series
1 *Issi Noho* (1974)
2 *Issi pandemonium* (1975)
3 *Issi's magic tonic* (1976)

It all started with series
Armour, Richard
1 *It all started with Columbus* (1953)
It all would have startled Columbus
The second title is a revised edition; an unexpurgated, unabridged and unlikely history of the United States from Christopher Columbus to the present for those who, having perused a volume of history in school, swore they would never read another
2 *It all started with Europa* (1955)
An undigested history of Europe from prehistoric man to the present proving that we remember best whatever is least appropriate
3 *It all started with Eve* (1956)
A brief account of certain famous women, each of them richly endowed with some quality that drives men mad, omitting no impertinent and unbelievable fact and based upon a stupendous amount of first-hand and second-hand research, some of it in books
4 *It all started with Marx* (1958)
5 *It all started with Hippocrates* (1966)
A mercifully brief history of medicine
6 *It all started with stones and clubs* (1967)
A short history of war and weaponry from earliest times to the present, noting the gratifying progress made by man since his first crude, small-scale efforts to do away with those who disagreed with him
7 *It all started with freshman English* (1973)
8 *It all started with nudes* (1977)
An artful history of art

It happened in Florida trilogy
Cabell, James Branch
1 *Saint John's* (1942)
A parade of diversities
2 *There were two pirates* (1946)
A comedy of division
3 *Devil's own dear son* (1949)
A comedy of the fatted calf

It takes a thief series
Brewer, Gil
see **Al Mundy series**

Italia perversa trilogy
Appignanesi, Richard
1 *Stalin's orphans* (1985)
2 *Mosque* (1985)
3 *Destroying America* (1985)

Italian Resistance series
Lett, Gordon
1 *Rossano* (1955)
2 *Many-headed monster* (1957)

Ithkar series
Adams, Robert
see **Magic in Ithkar series**

It's a holiday series
Prelutsky, Jack
1 *It's Halloween* (1977)
2 *It's Christmas* (1981)
3 *It's Thanksgiving* (1982)
4 *It's Valentine's Day* (1983)

It's alive series
This sequence has two authors
Woodley, Richard
1 *It's alive!* (1977)
Dixon, James
2 *It lives again* (1978)

It's easy to have series
Goldsmith, John
1 *It's easy to have a ladybird to stay* (1981)
2 *It's easy to have a wood-lice to stay* (1981)
3 *It's easy to have ants to stay* (1981)

It's fun series
Beccaria, Mijo
see **Birthday series**

Ivan Chonkin series
Voinovich, Vladimir Nikolaevich
see **Private Ivan Chonkin series**

Ivan Kovakin series
Olcott, Anthony
1 *Murder at the Red October* (1981)
2 *May Day in Magadan* (1983)

Ivanhoe Keeler series
Stong, Philip
1 *Buckskin breeches* (1937)
2 *Ivanhoe Keeler* (1941)

Iveagh series
Sidgwick, Ethel
see **Wickford series**

Iverson trilogy
Jordan, Elizabeth Garver
see **May Iverson trilogy**

Ivor Llewellyn series
Wodehouse, Pelham Grenville
1 *Lack of the Bodkins* (1935)
2 *Bachelors anonymous* (1973)

Ivor Maddox series
Linington, Elizabeth
see **Sergeant Ivor Maddox series**

Ivor the engine series
Postgate, Oliver
Illustrated by Peter Firmin
1 *Ivor the engine* (1977)
2 *Snowdrifts* (1977)
3 *Dragon* (1979)
4 *Elephant* (1979)
5 *Foxes* (1982)
6 *Ivor's birthday* (1984)

Ivorsen series
Spencer, Rick
see **Eric Ivorsen series**

Ivory trail series
Mundy, Talbot
1 *Ivory trail* (1919)
2 *Eye of Zeitoon* (1920)

Ivy and Peat Moss series
Berenstain, Michael
see **Peat Moss and Ivy series**

Ivy Compton-Burnett series
Spurling, Hilary
1 *Ivy when young* (1974)
1884-1919
2 *Secrets of a woman's heart* (1984)
1920-1969

Ivy Hall trilogy
Brown, Ruth Alberta
1 *Tabitha at Ivy Hall* (1911)
2 *Tabitha's glory* (1912)
3 *Tabitha's vacation* (1913)

J

J A Remington series
Ladline, Robert
1 *Shoe fits* (1936)
2 *Devil in Downing Street* (1937)
3 *Sky's the limit* (1937)
4 *When fools endanger us* (1938)
5 *Sinister craft* (1939)
6 *Stop that man!* (1940)

J Aubrey Whitford series
Roderus, Frank
1 *J A Whitford and the great California gold hunt* (1990)
2 *His Royal Highness, J Aubrey Whitford* (1992)

J C K Masters series
Rud, Anthony Melville
1 *Rose bath riddle* (1934)
2 *House of the damned* (1934)
3 *Stuffed men* (1935)

J C series
Mulford, Clarence Edward
1 *Corson of the J C* (1927)
2 *Me 'n' Shorty* (1929)
3 *Deputy sheriff* (1930)
4 *Hopalong Cassidy and the eagle's brood* (1931)
5 *Round-up* (1933)
6 *On the trail of the Tumbling T* (1935)

J C Stonewall series
Roberts, Mark Kelly
see **Soldier for hire series**

J D Polson series
Bond, Michael
1 *J D Polson and the Liberty Head dime* (1980)
2 *J D Polson and the Dillogate affair* (1981)
3 *J D Polson of the great unveiling* (1982)

J G Reeder series
Wallace, Edgar
see **Mr J G Reeder series**

J Huntley English series
Stevenson, Drew
1 *Case of the horrible swamp monster* (1984)
2 *Case of the visiting vampire* (1986)
3 *Case of the wandering werewolf* (1987)

J J Jamison series
Taylor, Laurie Aylma
1 *Footnote to murder* (1983)
One for the books
2 *Only half a hoax* (1983)
3 *Deadly objectives* (1984)
4 *Shed light on death* (1985)

J J Meldon series
Birmingham, George A
see **Reverend J J Meldon series**

J Leland Coole series
Stephens, Michael
1 *Season of Coole* (1984)
2 *Brooklyn book of the dead* (1994)

J P Beaumont series
Jance, Judith A
1 *Until proven guilty* (1985)
2 *Injustice for all* (1986)
3 *Trial by fury* (1986)
4 *Taking the Fifth* (1987)
5 *Improbable cause* (1988)
6 *More perfect union* (1988)
7 *Dismissed with prejudice* (1989)
8 *Minor in possession* (1990)
9 *Payment in kind* (1991)
10 *Without due process* (1992)
11 *Failure to appear* (1993)
12 *Lying in wait* (1994)

J R Kazallon series
Verne, Jules
1 *Survivors of the Chancellor* (1875)
Chancellor
Wreck of the Chancellor
2 *Martin Paz* (1875)
Pearl of Lima
Original edition in one volume entitled *Le Chancellor*

J R Leroy series
Perowne, Barry
see **Rick Leroy series**

J Rason series
Vickers, Roy
see **Inspector J Rason series**

J Rockingham Stone series
Armstrong, Raymond
1 *Midnight cavalier* (1954)
2 *Cavalier of the night* (1956)
3 *Widow and the cavalier* (1956)
4 *Sinister widow comes back* (1957)

J series
Swan, Phyllis
see **Anna J series**

J T Spanner series
Chastain, Thomas
1 *Pandora's box* (1974)
2 *Vital statistics* (1977)

J.T.'s ladies series
Edson, John Thomas
1 *J.T.'s ladies* (1980)
2 *More J.T.'s ladies* (1987)
3 *J.T.'s ladies ride again* (1989)

Jabal Jarrett series
Bream, Freda
see **Reverend Jabal Jarrett series**

Jabez Twombley series
Williams, Sidney
1 *Murder of Miss Betty Sloan* (1935)
2 *Aconite murders* (1956)

Jacare series
Norwood, Victor George Charles
1 *Untamed* (1951)
2 *Caves of death* (1951)
3 *Temple of the dead* (1951)
4 *Skull of Kanaima* (1951)
5 *Island of creeping death* (1952)
6 *Cry of the beast* (1953)
7 *Drums along the Amazon* (1953)

Jack Albany series
Godey, John
1 *Thrill a minute with Jack Albany* (1967)
Reluctant assassin
2 *Never put off till tomorrow what you can kill today* (1970)

Jack and Danny Kachiah series
Lesley, Craig
see **Danny and Jack Kachiah series**

Jack and Jill series
Jerina, Carol
1 *Tall dark alibi* (1988)
2 *Sweet jeopardy* (1988)

Jack and Sophie series
Taylor, Judy
see **Sophie and Jack series**

Jack Anderson series
Travers, J M
1 *Detective Jack Anderson* (1884)
2 *Detective Jack Anderson* (1886)
The 1884 title and the 1886 title are different stories

Jack Atherley series
Ashton, Charles
1 *Murder in make-up* (1934)
2 *Tragedy after tea* (1935)
3 *Death greets a guest* (1936)
4 *Calamity comes to Flenton* (1936)
5 *Stone dead* (1939)
6 *Death for two* (1940)
7 *Here's murder done* (1943)
8 *Murder at Melton Peveril* (1946)
9 *Dance for a dead uncle* (1948)

Jack Aubrey and Stephen Maturin series
O'Brian, Patrick
1 *Master and commander* (1969)
2 *Post captain* (1972)
3 *HMS Surprise* (1973)
4 *Mauritius command* (1977)
5 *Desolation Island* (1978)
6 *Fortune of war* (1979)
7 *Surgeon's mate* (1980)
8 *Ionian mission* (1981)
9 *Treason's harbour* (1983)
10 *Far side of the world* (1984)
11 *Reverse of the medal* (1986)
12 *Letter of Marque* (1988)
13 *Thirteen-gun salute* (1989)
14 *Nutmeg of Consolation* (1991)
15 *Wine-dark sea* (1993)

Jack Aubrey series
O'Brien, Patrick
see **Captain Jack Aubrey series**

Jack Beaumont and Susan Bright series
McDowell, Michael
1 *Jack and Susan in 1913* (1986)
2 *Jack and Susan in 1933* (1987)
3 *Jack and Susan in 1953* (1985)

Jack Burns series
Abbey, Edward
1 *Brave cowboy* (1956)
2 *Good news* (1980)

Jack Butler and Doctor David Audley series
Price, Anthony
see **Doctor David Audley and Jack Butler series**

Jack Carter and Dougal Munro series
Higgins, Jack
see **Brigadier Dougal Munro and Captain Jack Carter series**

Jack Carter series
Lewis, Ted
1 *Jack's return home* (1970)
Get Carter
2 *Jack Carter's law* (1974)
Jack Carter and the law
3 *Jack Carter and the Mafia pigeon* (1977)

Jack Clancy and Iris Cooper series
Beck, Kathrine Kristine
see **Iris Cooper and Jack Clancy series**

Jack Clayton series
Gluck, Sinclair
1 *House of the missing* (1923)
Golden panther
2 *Dragon in harness* (1927)

Jack Danvers series
Grinnell, George Bird
1 *Jack, the young ranchman* (1899)
Alternative title: A boy's adventures in the Rockies
2 *Jack among the Indians* (1900)
Alternative title: A boy's summer on the Buffalo Plains
3 *Jack in the Rockies* (1904)
Alternative title: A boy's adventures with a pack train
4 *Jack, the young canoeman* (1906)
An Eastern boy's voyage in a Chinook canoe
5 *Jack, the young trapper* (1907)
An Eastern boy's fur hunting in the Rocky Mountains
6 *Jack, the young explorer* (1908)
Experiences in the unknown Northwest
7 *Jack, the young cowboy* (1913)
An Eastern boy's experience with a Western round-up

Jack Duluoz series
Kerouac, Jack
1 *Visions of Gerard* (1963)
2 *Doctor Sax* (1959)
3 *Maggie Cassidy* (1959)
Springtime Mary
4 *Town and the city* (1950)
5 *Vanity of Duluoz* (1968)
6 *On the road* (1957)
7 *Visions of Cody* (1959)
Visions of Neal
8 *Subterraneans* (1958)
9 *Tristessa* (1960)
10 *Dharma bums* (1958)
11 *Desolation's angels* (1965)
12 *Big Sur* (1962)
13 *Satori in Paris* (1966)

Jack Dwyer series
Gorman, Edward
1 *Rough cut* (1985)
2 *New, improved murder* (1986)
3 *Murder straight up* (1986)
4 *Murder in the wings* (1986)
5 *Autumn dead* (1987)
6 *Cry of shadows* (1990)
7 *Night remembers* (1991)

Jack Eichord series
Miller, Rex
1 *Slob* (1987)
2 *Frenzy* (1988)
3 *Stone shadow* (1989)
4 *Slice* (1990)
5 *Iceman* (1990)

Jack Fenner series
Coxe, George Harmon
1 *Murder with pictures* (1935)
2 *Camera clue* (1938)
3 *Four frightened women* (1939)
Frightened women
4 *Charred witness* (1942)
5 *Fenner* (1971)
6 *Silent witness* (1973)
7 *No place for murder* (1975)

Jack Hall series
Grant, Robert
1 *Jack Hall* (1888)
Alternative title: The schooldays of an American boy
2 *Jack in the bush* (1888)
Alternative title: A summer on a salmon river

Jack Harding series
Duff, Douglas Valder
1 *Harding's mountain treasure* (1938)
2 *Harding and the Palestine police* (1938)
3 *Harding and the screaming mantle* (1939)
4 *Jack Harding's quest* (1939)

Jack Hazard series
Trowbridge, John Townsend
1 *Jack Hazard and his fortunes* (1871)
2 *Chance for himself* (1872)
Alternative title: Jack Hazard and his treasure
3 *Doing his best* (1873)
4 *Fast friends* (1874)
5 *Young surveyor* (1875)
Alternative title: Jack on the prairies
Companion volume: *Lawrence's adventures, among the ice-cutters, glass-makers, coal-miners, iron-men and ship-builders,* 1870

Jack Heston series
Macnaghten, Patrick
1 *Car that Jack built* (1965)
2 *Right line* (1966)

Jack-in-the-box series
Taggart, Marion Ames
1 *At Greenacres* (1921)
2 *Queer little man* (1921)
3 *Bottle imp* (1921)
4 *Poppy's pluck* (1921)

Jack Jordan series
Du Bois, William
1 *Case of the deadly diary* (1940)
2 *Case of the frightened fish* (1940)
3 *Case of the haunted brides* (1941)

Jack Journey series
Nash, Jay Robert
1 *Crime story* (1981)
2 *Mafia diaries* (1984)

Jack Kelly and Charles Carr series
Petievich, Gerald
see **Charles Carr and Jack Kelly series**

Jack Kyle series
Abshire, Richard
1 *Dallas drop* (1989)
2 *Turnaround Jack* (1990)
3 *Dallas deception* (1992)

Jack Laidlaw series
McIlvanney, William
see **Inspector Jack Laidlaw series**

Jack LeVine series
Bergman, Andrew
1 *Big kiss-off of 1944* (1974)
2 *Hollywood and LeVine* (1975)

Jack Le Vine series
Le Vine, Jack
1 *Big kiss-off of 1944* (1974)
2 *Hollywood and Vine* (1975)

Jack Lingemann and Liz Connors series
Kelly, Susan
see **Liz Connors and Jack Lingemann series**

Jack Locke series
Herman, Richard
1 *Warbirds* (1989)
2 *Force of eagles* (1990)
3 *Firebreak* (1991)
4 *Call to duty* (1993)

Jack Lorimer series
Standish, Winn
see **Captain Jack Lorimer series**

Jack Lovel series
Currington, Owen Josiah
1 *Bad night's work* (1974)
2 *Break-out* (1978)

Jack Lund series
Tralins, Sandor Robert
1 *Flight signals* (1990)
2 *Signal, Intruder* (1991)
3 *Signal, Blackbird* (1992)

Jack McBumby series
McArthur, John
1 *Day in the hay* (1960)
2 *How now brown cow* (1962)

Jack McDuff and Bob Pruitt series
Mitchell, Red
see **Doc McDuff and Popcorn Pruitt series**

Jack Mason series
Duncan, Alex
see **Country doctor series**

Jack Meredith and Uncle George series
Leyland, Eric
1 *Mystery trail* (1942)
2 *Treasure in Devon* (1954)

Jack Merrill series
Deering, Fremont B
see **Border Boys series**

Jack Novak series
Hunt, Everette Howard
1 *Cozumel* (1985)
2 *Guadalajara* (1986)
3 *Mazatlan* (1987)

Jack Odin series
Kelleam, Joseph Everidge
1 *Little men* (1960)
2 *Hunters of space* (1960)

Jack Pearson series
Daniel, Roland
see **Inspector Jack Pearson series**

Jack Pike series
Meek, Joseph
see **Mountain Jack Pike series**

Jack Prester series
Dengler, Sandy
1 *Death Valley* (1993)
2 *Model murder* (1993)
3 *Murder on the Mount* (1994)

Jack Ranger series
Young, Clarence
1 *Jack Ranger's schooldays* (1907)
Alternative title: The rivals of Washington Hall
2 *Jack Ranger's western trip* (1908)
Alternative title: From boarding school to ranch and range
3 *Jack Ranger's school victories* (1908)
Alternative title: Track, gridiron and diamond
4 *Jack Ranger's ocean cruise* (1909)
Alternative title: The wreck of the Polly Ann
5 *Jack Ranger's gun club* (1910)
Alternative title: From schoolroom to camp and trail
6 *Jack Ranger's treasure box* (1911)
Alternative title: The outing of the schoolboy yachtsmen

Jack Rann series
Huet, M M
Originally published anonymously
1 *Jack Rann's life and adventures* (1854)
Jack Rann
2 *Kit Clayton* (1855)
Alternative title: The hero of the road

Jack Regan series
Martin, Ian Kennedy
see **Sweeney series**

Jack Reid series
Howard, Tom
1 *Dead lucky* (1990)
2 *Death at his private zoo* (1991)

Jack Ryan series
Clancy, Tom
1 *Patriot games* (1987)
2 *Hunt for Red October* (1984)
3 *Cardinal of the Kremlin* (1988)
4 *Clear and present danger* (1989)
5 *Debt of honor* (1994)

Jack series
Barnum, Phineas Taylor
see **Lion Jack series**
Daly, Jim
see **Gentleman Jack series**

Jack series
Haley, Gail Einhart
1 *Jack and the bean tree* (1986)
2 *Jack and the fire dragon* (1988)

Jack series
Newte, Horace Wykeham Can
see **Calico Jack series**
Rathborne, Saint George
see **Doctor Jack series**
Wilson, Steve
see **Dealer series**

Jack Sharp series
Travers, J M
1 *Jack Sharp, keenest detective in Gotham* (1884)
2 *Jack Sharp in Florida* (1887)

Jack Stenton series
Dexter, Ted
1 *Testkill* (1976)
2 *Deadly putter* (1979)

Jack Stone series
Kincaid, J D
1 *Corrigan's revenge* (1989)
2 *Fourth of July* (1990)
3 *Showdown at Medicine Creek* (1990)
4 *Sheriff of Fletcher County* (1990)
5 *Coyote winter* (1990)

Jack Storm series
Stevens, Steve
1 *Man called Storm* (1971)
2 *Storm across the border* (1971)
3 *Storm in Arizona* (1972)
4 *Storm in the mountains* (1973)
5 *Storm on the trail* (1974)
6 *Storm in Wyoming* (1975)
7 *Storm in Montana* (1976)

Jack Straw series
Crump, James Irving
1 *Jack Straw in Mexico* (1914)
How the engineers defended the great hydro-electric plant
2 *Jack Straw, lighthouse builder* (1915)

Jack Strickland series
Balfour, Hearnden
see **Inspector Jack Strickland series**

Jack Stryker series
Gosling, Paula
see **Lieutenant Jack Stryker series**

Jack Sullivan series
Cutter, John
see **Specialist series**

Jack Sumner series
Goulart, Ron
see **Barnum series**

Jack Tallon series
Ball, John
1 *Police Chief* (1977)
2 *Trouble for Tallon* (1981)
3 *Chief Tallon and the S.O.R.* (1984)

Jack the bodiless series
May, Julian
1 *Jack the bodiless* (1992)
2 *Diamond mask* (1994)

Jack, the giant-killer series
De Lint, Charles
1 *Jack, the giant-killer* (1987)
2 *Drink down the moon* (1990)

Jack the Kaiser killer series
Lardner, Ring
1 *Treat 'em rough* (1918)
2 *Real dope* (1919)

Jack the outlaw series
Snowden, James Keighley
see **King Jack series**

Jack Thompson series
Cameron, Evelyn
see **Sheriff Jack Thompson series**

Jack Wigan series
Farmer, Bernard James
see **Sergeant Jack Wigan series**

Jackie and Babs series
Berrisford, Judith Mary
1 *Jackie won a pony* (1958)
2 *Ten ponies and Jackie* (1959)
3 *Jackie's pony patrol* (1961)
4 *Jackie and the pony trekkers* (1963)
5 *Jackie's pony camp summer* (1968)
6 *Jackie and the pony boys* (1970)
8 *Jackie and the misfit pony* (1975)
9 *Jackie on Pony Island* (1977)
10 *Jackie and the pony thieves* (1978)
11 *Jackie and the phantom ponies* (1979)

Jackman series
Pinkerton, Kathrene
see **Ann Jackman series**

Jacko Jackson series
Palmer, Frank
see **Jim Jackson series**

Jacks series
Wallis, James Harold
see **Inspector Wilton Jacks series**

Jackson and Razoni series
Murphy, Warren Burton
see **Edward Razoni and William Jackson series**

Jackson and Webb series
Fraser, Anthea
see **Inspector David Webb and Sergeant Ken Jackson series**

Jackson family series
Wensell, Ulises
1 *Jenny and Steve* (1977)
2 *Mum and dad* (1977)
3 *David* (1977)
4 *Smudge* (1977)
5 *Granny and Grandad Parker* (1978)
6 *Grandma and Grandpa Jackson* (1978)
7 *Our friends* (1978)
8 *Uncle George and aunt Mary* (1978)
9 *Everyday life* (1978)
10 *Our home* (1978)

Jackson Fury and Jillian Fletcher series
Jerina, Carol
see **Jack and Jill series**

Jackson series
Arden, William
see **Kane Jackson series**

Jackson series
Ball, Brian Neville
1 *Jackson's house* (1974)
2 *Jackson's friend* (1975)
3 *Jackson's holiday* (1977)
4 *Jackson and the magpies* (1978)

Jackson series
Buckman, Sam
see **Storm Jackson series**
Craig, Philip R
see **Martha's Vineyard series**
Frankau, Gilbert
see **Peter Jackson series**
Guy, Rosa
see **Edith Jackson series**
Kinsella, William Patrick
see **Shoeless Joe Jackson series**
Lindsay, David T
see **Inspector John Jay Jackson series**
Palmer, Frank
see **Jim Jackson series**
Rigby, Ray
see **Private Johnny Jackson series**
Scott, James Maurice
see **Jeremy Jackson series**
Thomas, Joyce Carol
see **Abyssinia Jackson series**
Turnbull, Margaret
see **Juliet Jackson series**

Jacky Ryderbeit series
Johns, Larry
1 *Power play* (1980)
2 *Thunder Island* (1980)
3 *Czechmate* (1980)
4 *Dangola script* (1981)
5 *Time to die* (1981)

Jacob and Joachim series
Clevin, Jorgen
1 *Jacob and Joachim* (1965)
Original edition entitled *Jakob og Joakim*
2 *Jacob and Joachim's rescue service* (1971)
Original edition entitled *Jakob og Joakims redningskorps*
3 *Jacob and Joachim on holiday* (1973)

Jacob Asch series
Lyons, Arthur
1 *Dead are discreet* (1974)
2 *All God's children* (1975)
3 *Killing floor* (1976)
4 *Dead ringer* (1977)
5 *Castles burning* (1980)
6 *Hard trade* (1982)
7 *At the hands of another* (1983)
8 *Three with a bullet* (1985)
9 *Fast fade* (1987)
10 *Other people's money* (1989)
11 *False pretenses* (1994)

Jacob Burrell series
Boothby, Guy
1 *Mystery of the clasped hands* (1901)
2 *Millionaire's love story* (1901)

Jacob Chaos series
Smith, Shelley
1 *Background for murder* (1942)
2 *He died of murder!* (1947)

Jacob Horowitz series
Delman, David
see **Lieutenant Jason Horowitz series**

Jacob Kaiser series
Collins, Alan
1 *Boys from Bondi* (1988)
2 *Going home* (1993)

Jacob Lomax series
Allegretto, Michael
1 *Death on the rocks* (1987)
2 *Blood stone* (1988)
3 *Dead of winter* (1989)

Jacob series
Klein, Zachary
see **Matthew Jacob series**
Soya, Carl Erik
see **Seventeen series**

Jacob Stahl series
Beresford, John Davys
1 *Early history of Jacob Stahl* (1911)
2 *Candidate for truth* (1912)
3 *Invisible event* (1915)

Jacob Two-Two series
Richler, Mordecai
1 *Jacob Two-Two meets the hooded fang* (1975)
2 *Jacob Two-Two and the dinosaur* (1987)

Jacobean trilogy
Bell, Josephine
1 *Jacobean adventure* (1969)
2 *Over the seas* (1970)
3 *Dark and the light* (1971)

Jacobite trilogy
Broster, Dorothy Kathleen
1 *Flight of the heron* (1925)
2 *Gleam in the north* (1927)

3 *Dark mile* (1929)
One volume edition entitled *A Jacobite trilogy*, 1984

Jacoby family series
Singer, Isaac Bashevis
see **Calman Jacoby family series**

Jacoby series
Randisi, Robert Joseph
see **Miles Jacoby series**
Smith, J C S
see **Quentin Jacoby series**

Jacoby's Corners trilogy
Falstaff, Jack
1 *Jacoby's Corners* (1940)
2 *Big snow* (1941)
3 *Come back to Wayne County* (1942)

Jacovich series
Roberts, Les
see **Milan Jacovich series**

Jacqueline Kirby series
Peters, Elizabeth
1 *Seventh sinner* (1972)
2 *Murders of Richard III* (1974)
3 *Love talker* (1980)
4 *Die for love* (1984)
5 *Naked once more* (1989)

Jacques Brunel series
Gavin, Catherine
see **French Resistance series**

Jacques Moran series
Beckett, Samuel
All volumes translated from the French by the author
1 *Molloy* (1951)
Original edition entitled *Molloy*
2 *Malone dies* (1951)
Original edition entitled *Malone meurt*
3 *Unnamable* (1953)
Original edition entitled *L'innommable*
One volume edition entitled *Three novels*, 1959

Jade Darcy series
Goldin, Stephen
see **Rehumanization of Jade Darcy series**

Jade demons quartet
Vardeman, Robert Edward
1 *Quaking lands* (1985)
2 *Frozen waves* (1985)
3 *Crystal clouds* (1985)
4 *White fire* (1986)
One volume edition entitled *The jade demons quartet*, 1987

Jaeger series
Mandell, Mark
see **Nazi hunter series**

Jaffe series
Schorr, Mark
see **Red Diamond series**

Jaffee gags series
Jaffee, Al
see **Al Jaffee gags series**

Jafta series
Lewin, Hugh
1 *Jafta* (1981)
2 *My father* (1981)
Jafta's father
3 *My mother* (1981)
Jafta's mother
Jafta and his mother
4 *Wedding* (1981)
Jafta and the wedding
5 *Journey* (1983)
6 *Town* (1983)
7 *Homecoming* (1992)

Jagger series
Garner, William
see **Mike Jagger series**

Jaggers family series
West, Paul
1 *Alley Jaggers* (1966)
2 *I'm expecting to live quite soon* (1970)
3 *Bela Lugosi's white Christmas* (1972)

Jago series
Peel, Hazel Mary
1 *Jago* (1966)
2 *Untamed!* (1969)

Jago series
Thompson, Ernest Victor
see **Nathan Jago series**

Jagua Nana series
Ekwensi, Cyprian
1 *Jagua Nana* (1961)
2 *Jagua Nana's daughter* (1987)

Jahan series
Payne, Robert
see **Emperor Shah Jahan series**

Jahdu series
Hamilton, Virginia
1 *Time-ago tales of Jahdu* (1969)
2 *Time-ago lost* (1973)
3 *Jahdu* (1980)
4 *All Jahdu storybook* (1991)

Jailbird Jackson series
Lindsay, David T
see **Inspector John Jay Jackson series**

Jake and Jody series
Levy, Elizabeth
see **Jody and Jake series**

Jake and Lenny series
Townson, Hazel
see **Lenny and Jake series**

Jake and Sally series
Cosgrove, Brian
see **Sally and Jake series**

Jake and the Kid series
Mitchell, William Ormond
Short stories
1 *Jake and the Kid* (1961)
2 *According to Jake and the Kid* (1989)

Jake Barrow series
Quarry, Nick
1 *Trail of a tramp* (1958)
2 *Hoods come calling* (1958)
3 *Girl with no place to hide* (1959)
4 *No chance in hell* (1960)
5 *Till it hurts* (1960)
6 *Some die hard* (1961)

Jake Brand series
Brent, R L
see **Liquidator series**

Jake Brown series
Cameron, Owen
see **Deputy Sheriff Jake Brown series**

Jake Coulter series
Fletcher, Aaron
see **Bounty Hunter series**

Jake Grafton series
Coonts, Stephen
1 *Flight of the intruder* (1986)
2 *Final flight* (1988)
3 *Minotaur* (1989)
4 *Under siege* (1990)
5 *Red horseman* (1993)
6 *Intruders* (1994)

Jake Hatch series
Campbell, Robert Wright
1 *Plugged nickle* (1988)
2 *Red cent* (1989)

Jake Langston and Coleman family series
Brown, Sandra
see **Coleman family and Jake Langston series**

Jake Lassiter series
Levine, Paul
1 *To speak for the dead* (1990)
2 *Night vision* (1991)
3 *False dawn* (1993)
4 *Slashback* (1995)

Jake Maroc series
Lustbader, Eric
1 *Jian* (1985)
2 *Shan* (1987)

Jake Moran trilogy
Broomall, Robert Walter
1 *Dead man's canyon* (1986)
2 *Dead man's crossing* (1987)
3 *Dead man's town* (1988)

Jake, Ned and Bill series
Leyland, Eric
see **Bill, Jake and Ned series**

Jake Neuman series
Oster, Jerry
1 *Sweet justice* (1985)
Rough justice
2 *Nowhere man* (1987)

Jake Samson and Rosie Vincente series
Singer, Shelley
1 *Samson's deal* (1983)
2 *Free draw* (1984)
3 *Full house* (1986)
4 *Spit in the ocean* (1987)
5 *Suicide king* (1988)

Jake Winkman series
Von Elsner, Don
1 *How to succeed at murder without really trying* (1963)
Jake of diamonds
2 *Ace of spies* (1966)
3 *Jack of Hearts* (1968)
4 *Everything's Jake with me* (1980)
Selections: The best of Jake Winkman, 1981

Jakob Abs series
Johnson, Uwe
1 *Speculations about Jakob* (1959)
Original edition entitled *Mutmassungen uber Jakob*
2 *Anniversaries* (1972)
From the life of Gesine Cesspahl, August 1967-February 1968; translated from volume 1 and part of volume 2 of *Jahrestage*, 1970-1972
3 *Anniversaries II* (1983)
From the life of Gesine Cesspahl; translated from volumes 3 and 4 and part of volume 2 of *Jahrestage*, 1972-1983

Jakob and Melchior series
Meynell, Esther
1 *Grave fairytale* (1931)
2 *Quintet* (1933)

Jalav series
Green, Sharon
1 *Crystals of Mida* (1982)
2 *Oath to Mida* (1983)
3 *Chosen of Mida* (1984)
4 *Will of the gods* (1985)
5 *To battle the gods* (1986)

Jali series
Myers, Leopold Hamilton
see **Prince Jali series**

Jalna series
De la Roche, Mazo
see **Whiteoak series**

Jam and Jim series
Littler, Angela
see **Jim and Jam series**

Jamaica series
Havill, Juanita
Illustrated by Anne Sibley O'Brien
1 *Jamaica's find* (1986)
2 *Jamaica Tag-Along* (1989)
3 *Jamaica and Brianna* (1993)

James, Alan and Roslin series
Lyon, Elinor
1 *King of Grey Corrie* (1975)
2 *Floodmakers* (1976)

James and Anna series
Boden, Hilda
see **Anna and James series**

James and Charles Latimer series
Gaite, Francis
American editions published under the pseudonym Manning Coles
1 *Brief candles* (1954)
2 *Family matter* (1955)
Happy returns
3 *Come and go* (1958)

James and gang series
Hiser, Constance
1 *No bean sprouts, please!* (1989)
2 *Ghosts in fourth grade* (1991)
3 *Dog on third base* (1991)
4 *Critter sitters* (1992)

James and Honeybody series
Giles, Kenneth
see **Inspector Harry James and Sergeant Honeybody series**

James and Kincaid series
Crombie, Deborah
see **Superintendent Duncan Kincaid and Sergeant Gemma James series**

James and Peg series
Batchelor, Mary
see **Peg and James series**

James and Susan series
Jones, Joan Clement
1 *James and Susan in the country* (1959)
2 *James and Susan at the seaside* (1961)

James Armitage trilogy
Kelsey, Franklyn
1 *Island in the mist* (1937)
2 *Children of the sun* (1939)
3 *Prowlers of the deep* (1942)

James Bear series
Latimer, Jim
1 *James Bear's pie* (1992)
2 *James Bear and the goose gathering* (1994)

James Berkeley series
Burland, Brian
1 *Fall from aloft* (1968)
2 *Few flowers for Saint George* (1969)

James Bond find your fate series
This sequence has four authors
Stine, Robert Lawrence
1 *James Bond in Win, place or die* (1985)

James Bond find your fate series

Siegel, Barbara
2 *James Bond in Strike it deadly* (1985)
Favors, Jean M
3 *James Bond in Programmed for danger* (1985)
Otfinoski, Steven
4 *James Bond in Barracuda run* (1985)

James Bond junior series

Vincent, John
1 *View to a thrill* (1991)
2 *Eiffel target* (1992)
3 *Live and let's dance* (1992)
4 *Sandblast!* (1992)
5 *Sword of death* (1992)
6 *High stakes* (1992)

James Bond series

This sequence has four authors
Fleming, Ian
1 *Casino Royale* (1953)
You asked for it
2 *Live and let die* (1954)
3 *Moonraker* (1955)
Too hot to handle
4 *Diamonds are forever* (1956)
Numbers 2-4 also published in one volume entitled *More gilt-edged Bonds*, 1965
5 *From Russia, with love* (1957)
6 *Doctor No* (1958)
Numbers 1, 5, 6 also published in one volume entitled *Gilt-edged Bonds*, 1961
7 *Goldfinger* (1959)
8 *For your eyes only* (1960)
Five secret occasions in the life of James Bond
9 *Thunderball* (1961)
10 *Spy who loved me* (1961)
Numbers 8-10 also published in one volume entitled *Bonded Fleming*, 1965
11 *On Her Majesty's secret service* (1963)
12 *You only live twice* (1964)
13 *Man with the golden gun* (1965)
14 *Octopussy* (1965)
Also includes *The living daylights*
Markham, Robert
15 *Colonel Sun* (1968)
Wood, Christopher
16 *James Bond, the spy who loved me* (1977)
Based on a screenplay
17 *James Bond and the Moonraker* (1979)
Gardner, John Edmund
18 *Licence renewed* (1981)
19 *For special services* (1982)
20 *Icebreaker* (1983)
21 *Role of honour* (1984)
22 *Nobody lives forever* (1986)
23 *No deals, Mister Bond* (1987)
24 *Scorpius* (1988)
25 *Win, lose or die* (1989)
26 *Brokenclaw* (1990)
27 *Man from Barbarossa* (1991)
28 *Death is forever* (1992)
29 *Never send flowers* (1993)
30 *Seafire* (1994)
Companion volume: *James Bond, the authorized biography of 007*, by John Pearson, 1973

James Brent series

Kemp, Harold
see **Inspector James Brent series**

James Bruce series

Johnston, Ronald
1 *Disaster at Dungeness* (1964)
Collision ahead
2 *Angry ocean* (1968)
3 *Sea story* (1980)

James Budd series

Carlson, Dale
1 *Mystery of the madman at Cornwall Cragg* (1984)
2 *Secret of Operation Brain* (1984)
3 *Mystery of the lost princess* (1984)
4 *Mystery of the galaxy game* (1984)

James Burlane series

Hoyt, Richard
1 *Trotsky's run* (1982)
2 *Head of state* (1985)

James Cardinal series

Walton, Marion
see **Inspector James Cardinal series**

James Cartwright Holland and Kitten series

Gover, Robert
see **Kitten series**

James Castleton and John Craggs series

Alington, Cyril Augustine
see **Archdeacon series**

James Charlesworth series

Sandys, James
1 *Stripe for a stripe* (1938)
2 *Hand without mercy* (1940)
3 *Green eye of death* (1943)
4 *Death is merciful* (1948)

James Christopher series

Steele, Curtis
1 *Masked invasion* (1974)
2 *Invisible empire* (1966)
3 *Yellow scourge* (1974)
4 *Revolt of the devil men* (1975)
5 *Cavern of the damned* (1980)
6 *Master of broken men* (1966)
7 *Legions of starvation* (1980)
8 *Army of the dead* (1966)
9 *March of the flame marauders* (1966)
10 *Blood reign of the dictator* (1966)
11 *Invasion of the yellow warlords* (1966)
12 *Legions of the Death Master* (1966)
13 *Hosts of the flaming death* (1966)
14 *Scourge of the invisible death* (1980)

James Clarkson-Parry series

Quin, Basil Godfrey
1 *Death box* (1929)
2 *Murder rehearsal* (1931)
3 *Mistigris* (1932)
4 *Phantom murderer* (1932)

James Clifton series

Robinson, George Bush
1 *Mate and the midshipman* (1966)
2 *Secret of the narrow seas* (1966)
3 *Eye of the pelican* (1966)

James Dale series

Cooper, John C
see **Inspector James Dale series**

James De la Cloche series

Pilgrim, David
1 *No common glory* (1941)
2 *Grand design* (1944)

James Dingle and Glyn Jones series

Osborne, Geoffrey
1 *Power bug* (1968)
2 *Balance of fear* (1968)
3 *Traitor's gait* (1969)
4 *Checkmate for China* (1969)
5 *Death's no antidote* (1971)

James Donald Macgregor series

Mason, Robert
see **Captain James Donald Macgregor series**

James Drew series

Garrett, William
1 *Secret of the hills* (1920)
Treasure royal
2 *Friday to Monday* (1923)
3 *Doctor Ricardo* (1925)

James Durkin series

Stringer, Arthur
1 *Wire tappers* (1906)
2 *Phantom wires* (1907)

James F Dundee series

Austin, Anne
1 *Black pigeon* (1929)
2 *Murder backstairs* (1930)
3 *Avenging parrot* (1930)
4 *Murder at bridge* (1931)
5 *One drop of blood* (1932)
6 *Murdered but not dead* (1939)

James Flecker series

Pullein-Thompson, Josephine
see **Inspector James Flecker series**

James Fraser series

Boyd, James
1 *Drums* (1925)
Set during the American Revolution
2 *Marching on* (1927)
Set during the American Civil War

James Fraser series

Wood, James
1 *Northern mission* (1954)
2 *Rain Island* (1957)
3 *Sealer* (1959)
4 *Lisa Bastian* (1960)
5 *Bay of Seals* (1964)
6 *Fire Rock* (1965)
7 *Friday run* (1967)
8 *Three blind mice* (1969)

James Gore-Bunbury series

Stanford, John Keith
see **Lieutenant-Colonel James Gore-Bunbury series**

James Graham, Earl of Montrose series

Tranter, Nigel Godwin
1 *Young Montrose* (1972)
2 *Montrose, the Captain-General* (1973)

James Greer series

Gayle, Newton
1 *Death follows a formula* (1935)
2 *Murder in the haunted sentry box* (1935)
Sentry box murder
3 *Murder at twenty eight ten* (1936)
4 *Death in the glass* (1937)
5 *Sinister crag* (1938)

James Hawker series

Ramm, Carl
1 *Florida firefight* (1984)
2 *L.A. wars* (1984)
3 *Chicago assault* (1984)
4 *Deadly in New York* (1984)
5 *Houston attack* (1985)
6 *Vegas vengeance* (1985)
7 *Detroit combat* (1985)
8 *Atlanta extreme* (1986)
9 *Terror in D.C.* (1986)
10 *Denver strike* (1986)
11 *Operation Norfolk* (1987)

James Hazell series

Yuill, P B
1 *Hazell plays Solomon* (1974)
2 *Hazell and the three card trick* (1975)
3 *Hazell and the menacing jester* (1976)

James Hellier series

Cronin, Michael
1 *Man alive* (1968)
2 *Dead loss* (1970)
3 *Emergency exit* (1970)
4 *Long memory* (1971)
5 *Escape at sunrise* (1972)
6 *Big C* (1973)

James Hind series

Foxall, Raymond
see **Captain James Hind series**

James III series

Aiken, Joan
see **Dido Twite series**

James Jameson series

Philip, Alexander John
1 *Complete change* (1926)
2 *Small change* (1947)

James Jenner series

Milne, John
1 *Dead birds* (1986)
2 *Shadow play* (1987)
Moody man
3 *Daddy's girl* (1988)

James M'Govan series

M'Govan, James
Short stories
1 *Brought to bay* (1878)
Alternative title: Experiences of a city detective
2 *Hunted down* (1878)
Alternative title: Recollections of a city detective
3 *Strange clues* (1881)
Alternative title: Chronicles of a city detective
4 *Traced and tracked* (1884)
Alternative title: Memoirs of a city detective
5 *Solved mysteries* (1888)
Alternative title: Revelations of a city detective
6 *Criminals caught* (1921)
Alternative title: Records of a city detective
7 *Invisible pickpocket* (1922)
Alternative title: Records of a city detective

James Malcolm series

Graham, Neill
see **Solo Malcolm series**

James Mallaby series

Norman, Bruce
1 *Thousand hands* (1926)
2 *Black pawn* (1927)

James Matthews and Philip Strong series

Oursler, William
see **Philip Strong and James Matthews series**

James Miller series

Dix, Maurice Buxton
see **Inspector James Miller series**

James Montgomerie series

Heaton, Rose Henniker
1 *Dinner with James* (1931)
2 *Chez James* (1932)
Co-author: Sir Damian Swann; the wisdom and foolishness of James, being a collection of papers concerning that estimable and loveable English gentleman, gathered by his disappearing family, and rearranged by his old friends
3 *Contract with James* (1933)
Co-author: Phyllis Bosworth; revised edition 1935
4 *Cruising with James* (1934)

James Morgan series

Coburn, Andrew
1 *No way home* (1992)
2 *Voices in the dark* (1994)

James Morton and Joseph Bragg series
Harrison, Ray
see **Sergeant Joseph Bragg and Constable James Morton series**

James Ogilvie series
Macneil, Duncan
1 *Drums along the Khyber* (1969)
2 *Lieutenant of the Line* (1970)
3 *Sadhu of the mountain peak* (1971)
4 *Gates of Kunarja* (1972)
5 *Red Daniel* (1973)
6 *Subaltern's choice* (1974)
7 *By command of the Viceroy* (1975)
8 *Mullah from Kashmir* (1976)
9 *Wolf in the fold* (1977)
10 *Charge of cowardice* (1978)
11 *Restless frontier* (1979)
12 *Cunningham's revenge* (1980)
13 *Train at Bundarbar* (1981)
14 *Matter for the regiment* (1982)

James O'Hannay and Floyd East series
Rushton, Charles
1 *Trail of blood* (1929)
2 *Master of fear* (1930)

James Packard series
Galway, Robert Conington
1 *Assignment New York* (1963)
2 *Assignment London* (1963)
3 *Assignment Andalusia* (1965)
4 *Assignment Malta* (1966)
5 *Assignment gaolbreak* (1968)
6 *Assignment Argentina* (1969)
7 *Assignment Fenland* (1969)
8 *Assignment sea bed* (1969)
9 *Assignment Sydney* (1970)
10 *Assignment death squad* (1970)
11 *Negative man* (1971)

James Pibble series
Dickinson, Peter
see **Superintendent James Pibble series**

James Rankin series
Grady, James
1 *Runner in the street* (1984)
2 *Hard bargains* (1985)

James Rhodes series
Gober, Don
1 *Black cop* (1974)
2 *Doomsday Squad* (1975)
3 *Killer cop* (1975)
4 *Killing ground!* (1976)

James River trilogy
Deveraux, Jude
1 *Counterfeit lady* (1984)
2 *Lost lady* (1985)
3 *River lady* (1985)

James Rollo series
Bushby, John
see **Captain James Rollo series**

James Rowland Woodward and Donald Bracken series
Blazer, J S
see **Donald Bracken and James Rowland Woodward series**

James Rufus Wallingford series
Chester, George Randolph
1 *Get-Rich-Quick Wallingford* (1908)
2 *Young Wallingford* (1910)
3 *Wallingford in his prime* (1913)
4 *Wallingford and Blackie Daw* (1913)
5 *Son of Wallingford* (1921)
Co-author: Lillian Eleanor Chester

James Segrove series
Vickers, Roy
1 *Vengeance of Henry Jerroman* (1923)
2 *Woman accused* (1923)
Originally published under the pseudonym David Durham
3 *Ishmael's wife* (1924)
4 *Four past four* (1925)

James series
Bax, Roger
see **Inspector James series**

James series
Clarke, Pauline
1 *James and the policeman* (1957)
2 *James and the robbers* (1959)
3 *James and the smugglers* (1961)
4 *James and the black van* (1963)

James series
Edel, Leon
see **Henry James series**

James series
Kathryn
1 *James* (1966)
2 *James and the hat* (1967)
3 *James and Lucy* (1968)

James series
Lawson, W B
see **Jesse James series**
O'Brien, Meg
see **Jessica James series**
Patchett, Mary Elwyn
see **Jeff James series**
Rizzi, Timothy
see **Major General Duke James series**
Rooke, Anne
see **Robert James series**
Scott, Denis
see **Mike James series**
Walsh, Maurice
see **Thomasheen James series**
Wilson, David Henry
see **Jeremy James series**

James Slade series
Deeping, Warwick
1 *Slade* (1943)
2 *Mister Gurney and Mister Slade* (1944)
Cleric's secret

James Steele series
Bancroft, John
1 *Guardian honour* (1961)
2 *Ring of truth* (1962)

James Strange series
Quinn, Eleanor Baker
1 *One man's muddle* (1936)
2 *Death is a restless sleeper* (1940)

James Tierney series
Moroso, John Antonio
1 *People against Nancy Preston* (1921)
2 *Listening man* (1924)

James V trilogy
Tranter, Nigel Godwin
1 *Riven realm* (1984)
2 *James, by the grace of God* (1985)
3 *Rough wooing* (1986)

James Wainwright series
Mather, Berkely
1 *Springers* (1968)
Spy for a spy
2 *Break in the line* (1970)
Break

James Warren series
Warren, James
1 *Lady was disturbed* (1956)
2 *Runaway corpse* (1957)
Disappearing corpse

James Weston series
Warren, James
1 *No sleep at all* (1941)
2 *She fell among actors* (1944)
3 *Cold steel* (1957)
4 *Brush of death* (1958)

James Wiscock series
Rice, William
see **Doctor James Wiscock series**

James Yeo series
Treherne, John
see **Doctor James Yeo series**

Jameson family series
Slote, Alfred
see **Danny One series**

Jameson series
Jones, Neil Ronald
see **Professor Jameson series**
Philip, Alexander John
see **James Jamesons series**
Wheat, Carolyn
see **Cass Jameson series**

Jamie and Jean Stewart series
Fitz Roy, Olivia
1 *Island of birds* (1954)
2 *Hunted head* (1956)

Jamie Carr series
Ure, Jean
1 *Proper little Nooryeff* (1982)
What if they saw me now?
2 *You win some, you lose some* (1984)

Jamie series
Denton, John
1 *Jamie* (1958)
The story of a puffer
2 *Jamie and Jock's present* (1959)

Jamie series
Roland, Betty
1 *Forbidden bridge* (1961)
2 *Jamie's discovery* (1963)
3 *Jamie's summer visitor* (1964)
4 *Jamie's other grandmother* (1970)

Jamie Stuart series
Kerr, Robert
1 *Stuart legacy* (1973)
2 *Black pearls* (1975)
3 *Dark lady* (1975)

Jamieson series
Bridge, Ann
see **Julia Probyn series**

Jamison series
Taylor, Laurie Aylma
see **J J Jamison series**

Jamnar series
Van Arnam, Dave
1 *Star barbarian* (1969)
2 *Lord of blood* (1970)

Jamskoni Airline series
Barry, Clive
1 *Spear grinner* (1963)
2 *Fly Jamskoni* (1969)

Jan Argand series
Rathbone, Julian
1 *Euro-killers* (1979)
2 *Base case* (1981)
3 *Watching the detectives* (1983)

Jan Caspol trilogy
Adlard, Mark
1 *Interface* (1971)
2 *Volteface* (1972)
3 *Multiface* (1975)

Jan Cremer series
Cremer, Jan
1 *I, Jan Cremer* (1964)
Original edition entitled Ik Jan Cremer
2 *Jan Cremer 2* (1965)
Original edition entitled Ik Jan Cremer, tweede boek

Jan Darzek series
Biggle, Lloyd
1 *All the colors of darkness* (1963)
All the colours of darkness
2 *Watchers of the dark* (1966)
3 *This darkening universe* (1976)
4 *Silence is deadly* (1977)
5 *Whirligig of time* (1979)

Jan Perry series
Sedgwick, Modwena
1 *Jan Perry stories* (1955)
2 *More Jan Perry stories* (1957)
3 *New Jan Perry stories* (1959)

Jan series
Carter, Dorothy
1 *Jan's flying start* (1947)
2 *Jan flies down under* (1948)

Jan series
Cockett, Mary
1 *Jan the market boy* (1957)
2 *Seven days with Jan* (1960)

Jan series
Kline, Otis Adelbert
1 *Call of the savage* (1937)
Jan of the jungle
2 *Jan in India* (1974)

Jan series
Leeson, Robert
1 *It's my life* (1980)
2 *Jan alone* (1989)

Jan series
Roggeveen, Leonard
1 *Here comes Jan* (1960)
Original edition entitled *Hier is Jan-Jaap*
2 *Jan's birthday* (1961)
Original edition entitled *Jan-Jaap is jarig*

Jana Blake series
Conaway, Jim C
1 *Deadlier than the male* (1977)
2 *They do it with mirrors* (1977)

Jancy series
Bracken, Anne
1 *Jancy wins through* (1945)
2 *Jancy scores again* (1947)
3 *Jancy in pursuit* (1950)
4 *Jancy stands alone* (1955)

Jandar the Alien series
Carter, Lin
1 *Jandar of Callisto* (1972)
2 *Black legion of Callisto* (1972)
3 *Sky pirates of Callisto* (1973)
4 *Mad empress of Callisto* (1975)
5 *Mind wizards of Callisto* (1975)
6 *Lankar of Callisto* (1975)
7 *Ylana of Callisto* (1977)
8 *Renegade of Callisto* (1978)

Jane Allen series
Bancroft, Edith
1 *Jane Allen of the sub-team* (1917)
2 *Jane Allen, right guard* (1918)
3 *Jane Allen, center* (1920)
4 *Jane Allen, junior* (1921)
5 *Jane Allen, senior* (1922)

Jane Amanda Edwards series
Russell, Charlotte Murray
1 *Murder at the old stone house* (1935)

Jane Amanda Edwards series

2 *Death of an eloquent man* (1936)
3 *Tiny diamond* (1937)
4 *Night on the pathway* (1938)
Night on the Devil's Pathway
5 *Clue of the naked eye* (1939)
6 *I heard the death bell* (1940)
7 *Message of the mute dog* (1942)
8 *No time for crime* (1945)
9 *Bad neighbor murder* (1946)
10 *Ill met in Mexico* (1948)
11 *Careless Mrs Christian* (1949)
12 *Hand me a crime* (1949)
13 *Cook up a crime* (1951)

Jane and Dagobert Brown series
Ames, Delano
see **Dagobert and Jane Brown series**

Jane and Henry Ellis series
Collin, Paul Ries
see **Henry and Jane Ellis series**

Jane and Hesketh Oliphant series
Newby, Percy Howard
see **Hesketh and Jane Oliphant series**

Jane and Jeremy Fortune series
Hill, Denise
1 *Pony for two* (1965)
2 *Coco, the gift horse* (1966)

Jane and Toby series
Thwaite, Ann
1 *Toby stays with Jane* (1962)
2 *Seaside holiday for Jane and Toby* (1962)
3 *Toby moves house* (1965)
4 *Jane and toby start school* (1965)

Jane Bailey series
Dobson, Margaret
1 *Touchstone* (1987)
2 *Primrose* (1987)
3 *Soothsayer* (1987)
4 *Nightcap* (1987)

Jane Beaufort series
Seymour, Arabella
1 *Maid of destiny* (1971)
2 *Bitter chalice* (1972)

Jane Blonde series
Carnelle, Inge
1 *Girl from B.U.S.T.* (1966)
2 *Joy ride* (1967)

Jane Canary series
Edson, John Thomas
see **Calamity Jane series**

Jane Carberry series
Symons, Beryl
1 *Jane Carberry, detective* (1940)
2 *Jane Carberry investigates* (1940)
3 *Magnet for murder* (1941)
4 *Jane Carberry and the laughing fountain* (1943)
5 *Jane Carberry's week-end* (1947)

Jane, Cathy and Belinda series
Bye, Beryl
see **Cathy, Belinda and Jane series**

Jane Charrington series
Gathorne-Hardy, Jonathan
1 *Jane's adventures in and out of the book* (1966)
2 *Jane's adventures on the Island of Peeg* (1968)
Operation Peeg
3 *Jane's adventures in a balloon* (1975)
Airship Ladyship adventure

Jane Da Silva series
Beck, Kathrine Kristine
1 *Hopeless case* (1992)
2 *Amateur night* (1993)
3 *Electric city* (1994)

Jane Fairfax series
Austen, Jane
see **Miss Jane Fairfax series**

Jane, Gappy and Jime series
Beresford, Elisabeth
see **Gappy, Jim and Jane series**

Jane Graham trilogy
Banks, Lynne Reid
1 *L-shaped room* (1960)
2 *Backward shadow* (1970)
3 *Two is lonely* (1974)

Jane Jeffry series
Churchill, Jill
1 *Grime and punishment* (1989)
2 *Farewell to yarns* (1991)
3 *Quiche before dying* (1993)
4 *Class menagerie* (1994)

Jane Lawless series
Hart, Ellen
1 *Hallowed murder* (1989)
2 *Vital lies* (1991)
3 *Stage fright* (1992)
4 *Killing cure* (1993)
5 *Small sacrifice* (1994)

Jane Marple series
Christie, Agatha
see **Miss Jane Marple series**

Jane Martin series
Bunting, Eve
1 *Jane Martin, dog detective* (1981)
2 *Jane Martin and the case of the ice-cream dog* (1981)

Jane Saint series
Saxton, Josephine
1 *Travails of Jane Saint* (1980)
Travails of Jane Saint, and other stories
The second title is an expanded edition
2 *Consciousness machine* (1989)
Alternative title: Jane Saint and the backlash

Jane Scott series
Gaye, Carol
1 *Jane Scott* (1964)
2 *Jane Scott again* (1965)
3 *Jane Scott meets the doctor* (1965)
4 *Jane Scott married* (1965)
5 *Jane Scott meets the Pops* (1966)
6 *Jane Scott, crime reporter* (1967)

Jane series
Barclay, Vera Charlesworth
1 *Jane, will you behave* (1936)
2 *Jane versus Jonathan* (1937)
3 *Jane and Tommy Tomkins* (1938)
4 *Jane and the pale faces* (1945)

Jane series
Farnol, Jeffery
1 *Book for Jane* (1937)
2 *New book for Jane* (1939)

Jane series
Hall, Eliza Calvert
see **Aunt Jane series**
Lavelle, Sheila
see **Jupiter Jane series**
McElfresh, Adeline
see **Doctor Jane series**

Jane series
Price, Evadne
1 *Just Jane* (1928)
2 *Meet Jane* (1930)
3 *Enter, Jane* (1932)
4 *Jane the fourth* (1937)
5 *Jane the unlucky* (1939)
6 *Jane the popular* (1939)
7 *Jane the sleuth* (1939)
8 *Jane the patient* (1940)
9 *Jane gets busy* (1940)
10 *Jane at war* (1947)

Jane series
Stone, Gene
1 *Jane and the owl* (1920)
2 *Adventures of Jane* (1921)

Jane Somers series
Somers, Jane
1 *Diary of a good neighbour* (1983)
2 *If the old could* (1984)
One volume edition entitled *The diaries of Jane Somers*, published under the author's real name, Doris Lessing, 1984

Jane, Stephen and Sandy series
Macgibbon, Jean
see **Sandy, Jane and Stephen series**

Jane Stuart series
Remick, Grace May
1 *Jane Stuart, twin* (1913)
2 *Jane Stuart's chum* (1914)
3 *Jane Stuart at Rivercroft* (1915)
4 *Jane Stuart, comrade* (1916)

Jane Taylor series
Ridley, Sheila
see **Nurse Jane Taylor series**

Jane Whitcomb series
Mitchell, James
1 *Woman to be loved* (1990)
2 *Impossible woman* (1992)
3 *Leading lady* (1993)

Jane Winfield and Andrew Quentin series
Peterson, Audrey
1 *Nocturne murder* (1987)
2 *Death in Wessex* (1989)
3 *Murder in Burgundy* (1989)
4 *Deadly rehearsal* (1990)
5 *Elegy in a country graveyard* (1990)
6 *Lament for Christobel* (1991)
7 *Dartmoor burial* (1992)
8 *Death too soon* (1994)

Janet and Dick series
Garis, Howard Roger
see **Two Wild Cherries series**

Janet and Peter Barron series
Darby, Ruth
see **Peter and Janet Barron series**

Janet and Phyllis series
Whitehill, Dorothy
1 *Janet, a twin* (1920)
2 *Phyllis, a twin* (1920)
3 *Twins in the South* (1920)
4 *Twins in the West* (1920)
5 *Twins summer vacation* (1920)
6 *Twins and Tommy junior* (1922)
7 *Twins at home* (1925)
8 *Twins' wedding* (1926)
9 *Twins adventuring* (1927)
10 *Twins at camp* (1928)
11 *Twins abroad* (1929)
12 *Twins a-visiting* (1930)
13 *Twins and Tim* (1932)

Janet and Sidney series
Ray, Anna Chapin
see **Sidney and Janet series**

Janet Lennon series
Meyers, Barlow
1 *Janet Lennon and the angels* (1962)
2 *Adventure at Two Rivers* (1962)
3 *Janet Lennon at Camp Calamity* (1962)

Janet Meredith series
Arundel, Honor
1 *Terrible temptation* (1971)
2 *Blanket word* (1973)
Love is a blanket word

Janet Reachfar series
Duncan, Jane
1 *Herself and Janet Reachfar* (1975)
2 *Janet Reachfar and the kelpie* (1976)
3 *Janet Reachfar and Chickabird* (1978)

Janet trilogy
Le Baron, Grace
1 *Queer Janet* (1897)
2 *Jessica's triumph* (1901)
3 *Children of Bedford Court* (1905)

Janeways series
Brent-Dyer, Elinor Mary
1 *Thrilling term at Janeways* (1927)
2 *Caroline the second* (1937)

Janey series
Pearl, Irene
1 *Janey* (1953)
2 *Janey and her friends* (1953)
3 *More Janey stories* (1957)

Jangada series
Verne, Jules
see **Giant raft series**

Janice Cameron and Lily Wu series
Sheridan, Juanita
see **Lily Wu and Janice Cameron series**

Janice Day series
Long, Helen Beecher
see **Do something series**

Janie B Jones series
Park, Barbara
1 *Janie B Jones and the stupid smelly bus* (1992)
2 *Janie B Jones and the little monkey business* (1993)
3 *Janie B Jones and her big fat mouth* (1993)
4 *Janie B Jones and some sneaky spying* (1994)

Janie Marshal series
Simpson, Dorothy
1 *Island in the Bay* (1956)
2 *Honest dollar* (1957)
3 *Lesson for Janie* (1958)
4 *Matter of pride* (1959)
5 *New horizons* (1961)
6 *Visitor from the sea* (1965)

Janine series
Thomas, Iolette
1 *Janine and the new baby* (1986)
2 *Janine and the carnival* (1987)

Janine West series
Welles, Elizabeth
1 *Fahnworth Manor* (1976)
2 *Captain's Walk* (1976)
3 *Waterview Manor* (1976)
4 *Spaniard's Gift* (1977)
5 *Seagull Crag* (1977)
6 *Mountainside Acres* (1977)

Janisseries trilogy
Pournelle, Jerry
1 *Janisseries* (1979)
2 *Clan and crown* (1982)
Co-author: Roland Green
3 *Storms of victory* (1987)
Co-author: Roland Green
Companion volume: *Lord of the Lances, Combat Command in the world of Jerry E Pournelle's Janisseries*, by Mark Acres, 1988

Jansen series
Adler, David A
see **Cam Jansen series**

Jansson series
Matera, Lia
see **Willa Jansson series**
Peterson, Hans
see **Pelle Jansson series**

Jantry series
Graeme, Bruce
see **Inspector Albert Jantry series**

January series
Richards, Laura Elizabeth
see **Captain January series**
Smith, George Henry
see **Duffus January series**

Janus series
Norton, Andre
1 *Judgment on Janus* (1963)
2 *Victory on Janus* (1966)

Janusz Prus trilogy
Kuniczak, Wieslaw Stanislaw
see **Polish war trilogy**

Japan series
Morris, James Humphrey
Japan before and after the Second World War
1 *Traveller from Tokyo* (1943)
2 *Phoenix cup* (1948)

Japan trilogy
Nicole, Christopher
1 *Sun rises* (1984)
2 *Sun and the dragon* (1985)
3 *Sun on fire* (1985)

Japanese-American evacuation series
Uchida, Yoshiko
1 *Journey to Topaz* (1971)
Revised edition 1985
2 *Journey home* (1978)

Japanese marriage series
Sladen, Douglas
1 *Japanese marriage* (1895)
2 *Playing the game* (1904)
When we were lovers in Japan

Japhet series
Horrabin, James Francis
see **Noah family series**

Jar of dreams trilogy
Uchida, Yoshiko
see **Rinko trilogy**

Jardino series
Singer, Norman
see **Robbie Jardino series**

Jared Bolt series
Martin, Cort
1 *First blood* (1981)
2 *Dead man's bounty* (1981)
3 *Showdown at Black Mesa* (1981)
4 *Guns of Taos* (1981)
5 *Shootout at Santa Fe* (1982)
6 *Tombstone honeypot* (1982)
7 *Rawhide woman* (1982)
8 *Hard in the saddle* (1982)
9 *Badman's bordello* (1983)
10 *Bawdy house* (1983)
11 *Last bordello* (1983)
12 *Hangtown harlots* (1983)
13 *Montana mistress* (1984)
14 *Virginia City virgin* (1984)
15 *Bordello backshooter* (1984)
16 *Hardcase hussy* (1985)
17 *Lone-Star stud* (1985)
18 *Queen of Hearts* (1985)
19 *Palomino stud* (1986)
20 *Sixguns and silk* (1986)
21 *Deadly withdrawal* (1986)
22 *Climax Mountain* (1987)
23 *Hook or crook* (1987)
24 *Rawhide Jezebel* (1987)
25 *Hot on the warpath* (1988)
26 *Maverick mistress* (1988)

Jared Hawk series
Brady, William S
This pseudonym is used by John Barton Harvey and Angus Wells as indicated against each title
1 *Sudden guns* (1978) [Wells]
2 *Blood money* (1979) [Harvey]
3 *Death's bounty* (1979) [Wells]
4 *Killing time* (1980) [Harvey]
5 *Fool's gold* (1980) [Wells]
6 *Blood kin* (1980) [Harvey]
7 *Gates of death* (1980) [Wells]
8 *Desperadoes* (1981) [Harvey]
9 *Widowmaker* (1981) [Wells]
10 *Dead man's hand* (1981) [Harvey]
11 *Sierra gold* (1981) [Harvey]
12 *Death and Jack Slade* (1982) [Harvey]
13 *Killers' breed* (1982) [Wells]
14 *Border war* (1983) [Wells]
15 *Killer!* (1983) [Harvey]

Jarnhan series
Dalmas, John
see **Nils Jarnhan series**

Jarrett series
Bream, Freda
see **Reverend Jabal Jarrett series**

Jarryn series
Davis, Elizabeth Jane
1 *Jarryn's miracle* (1990)
2 *Jarryn's test* (1991)
3 *Tank's choice* (1992)

Jarvis series
Davis, Dorothy Salisbury
see **Mrs Norris and Jasper Tully series**

Jason Beard and Chick Charleston series
Guthrie, Alfred Bertram
see **Sheriff Chick Charleston and Jason Beard series**

Jason Bourne trilogy
Ludlum, Robert
see **Bourne trilogy**

Jason Burr series
Kent, David
1 *Jason Burr's first case* (1941)
2 *Knife is silent* (1947)

Jason Cordrey series
O'Hanlon, James
1 *Murder at Malibu* (1937)
2 *Murder at three hundred to one* (1938)
3 *Murder at Coney Island* (1939)
4 *As good as murdered* (1940)
5 *Murder at Horsethief* (1941)

Jason Cosmo series
McGirt, Dan
1 *Jason Cosmo* (1989)
2 *Royal chaos* (1990)

Jason Croft trilogy
Giesy, John Ulrich
1 *Palos of the Dog Star Pack* (1965)
2 *Mouthpiece of Zitu* (1965)
3 *Jason, son of Jason* (1966)

Jason Din Alt series
Harrison, Harry
1 *Deathworld* (1960)
Deathworld 1
2 *Deathworld 2* (1964)
Ethical engineer
3 *Deathworld 3* (1968)
One volume edition entitled *Deathworld trilogy*, 1974

Jason Emory series
Kootz, Samuel Melvin
1 *Puzzle in paint* (1943)
2 *Puzzle in petticoats* (1944)

Jason Galt series
Lovell, Marc
see **Elsie Vanetti series**

Jason Jones and Necessary Smith series
Crossen, Kendell Foster
1 *Case of the curious heel* (1944)
2 *Case of the phantom fingerprints* (1945)

Jason King series
Miall, Robert
Based on a television series
1 *Jason King* (1972)
2 *Kill Jason King!* (1972)

Jason Love series
Leasor, James
see **Doctor Jason Love series**

Jason Lynx series
Orde, A J
1 *Little neighborhood murder* (1989)
2 *Death and the dogwalker* (1990)
3 *Death for old times' sake* (1992)

Jason Russell series
Yarbro, Chelsea Quinn
see **Sheriff Jason Russell series**

Jason series
Chance, John Newton
1 *Jason affair* (1953)
Up to her neck
2 *Jason and the sleep game* (1954)
3 *Jason murders* (1954)
4 *Jason goes west* (1955)

Jason series
Greer, Gery
1 *Jason and the aliens down the street* (1991)
2 *Jason and the lizard pirates* (1992)
3 *Jason and the escape from Bat Planet* (1993)

Jason series
Jason
1 *Murder uncensored* (1958)
2 *Death is a circus* (1958)
3 *High litre Lolita* (1958)
4 *Vanishing Venus* (1958)
5 *Honolulu slay ride* (1959)
6 *Damsel for discount* (1959)
7 *Maiden you slay me* (1959)
8 *Odds on its murder* (1959)
9 *Three's a shroud* (1959)
10 *Blackmail whoops it up* (1959)

Jason series
Michel, Milton Scott
see **Wood Jason series**
Sugar, Andrew
see **Enforcer series**

Jason Starr and Adam Cyber series
Heath, Peter
1 *Mind brothers* (1967)
2 *Assassins for tomorrow* (1967)
3 *Men who die twice* (1968)

Jason Striker series
Anthony, Piers
1 *Kiai!* (1974)
2 *Mistress of death* (1974)
3 *Bamboo bloodbath* (1974)
4 *Ninja's revenge* (1975)
5 *Amazon slaughter* (1976)

Jason Trask series
Heron, Jack
1 *Trask the avenger* (1982)
2 *Trask and the fighting Irishman* (1983)

Jason Winter series
Gaston, Bill
see **Lieutenant Jason Winter series**

Jason Wright series
Marks, James Macdonald
1 *Jason* (1973)
Hijacked
2 *Triangle* (1974)

Jaspard family series
Ponsonby, Doris Almon
1 *Family of Jaspard* (1950)
1.1 *General* (1950)
1.2 *Fortunate adventure* (1950)
2 *Bristol cousins* (1951)

Jasper Club series
Cockett, Mary
1 *Jasper Club* (1959)
2 *There for the picking* (1966)

Jasper series
McQuillan, Karin
see **Jazz Jasper series**

Jasper Shrig of Bow Street series
Farnol, Jeffery
see **Mister Jasper Shrig of Bow Street series**

Jasper Tully and Mrs Norris series
Davis, Dorothy Salisbury
see **Mrs Norris and Jasper Tully series**

Jasperodus series
Bayley, Barrington John
1 *Soul of the robot series* (1974)
2 *Rod of light* (1984)

Jaws series
This sequence has two authors; based on screenplays
Benchley, Peter
1 *Jaws* (1974)
Searls, Hank
2 *Jaws 2* (1978)
Companion volume: *The Jaws log*, by Carl Gottlieb, 1975

Jay and Tony series
Hardcastle, Michael
see **Tony and Jay series**

Jay Goldstein and Carlos Cruz series
Wallace, Marilyn
1 *Case of loyalties* (1986)
2 *Primary target* (1988)

Jay McGraw series
Champlin, Tim
1 *Colt lightning* (1989)
2 *King of the highbinders* (1989)

Jay series
VerDorn, Bethea
see **Baby Jay series**

Jays series
Smedley, Elisabeth
1 *Jays* (1940)
2 *Jays write a book* (1941)
3 *Job for the Jays* (1951)

Jays series
Smythe, Pat
see **Three Jays series**

Jazine and Crader series
Hoch, Edward Dentinger
see **Carl Crader and Earl Jazine series**

Jazz age series
Farrell, James Thomas
see **Universe of time series**

Jazz and Jasper series
Gerhardi, William Alexander
1 *Jazz and Jasper* (1928)
The story of Adams and Eva
2 *Eva's apples* (1928)

Jazz Jasper series
McQuillan, Karin
1 *Deadly safari* (1990)
2 *Elephants' graveyard* (1993)
3 *Cheetah chase* (1994)

Jean and Anna series
Lyon, Elinor
1 *Day that got lost* (1968)
2 *Wishing pool* (1970)

Jean and Donald series
Dickinson, William Croft
see **Donald and Jean series**

Jean and Jamie Stewart series
Fitz Roy, Olivia
see **Jamie and Jean Stewart series**

Jean and Pat Abbott series
Crane, Frances
see **Pat and Jean Abbott series**

Jean Cabot series
Scott, Gertrude Fisher
1 *Jean Cabot at Ashton* (1912)
2 *Jean Cabot in the British Isles* (1913)
3 *Jean Cabot in cap and gown* (1914)
4 *Jean Cabot in the house with the blue shutters* (1915)

Jean Christophe series
Rolland, Romain
see **John Christopher series**

Jean Craig series
Littleton, Kay
1 *Jean Craig grows up* (1948)
2 *Jean Craig in New York* (1948)
3 *Jean Craig finds romance* (1948)
4 *Jean Craig, nurse* (1949)
5 *Jean Craig, graduate nurse* (1950)

Jean Darblay series
Hardwick, Michael
see **Juliet Bravo series**

Jean Henri Saint Amand series
Teilhet, Darwin Le Ora
1 *Murder in the air* (1931)
2 *Death flies high* (1931)

Jean Hunter series
Swinburne, Doreen
1 *Jean tours a hospital* (1943)
2 *Jean at Jo's hospital* (1959)
3 *Jean, S.R.N.* (1960)
4 *Jean's new junior* (1964)

Jean Macaque series
Cloete, Stuart
1 *Thousand and one nights of Jean Macaque* (1965)
2 *More nights of Jean Macaque* (1975)

Jean Mary series
Lee, Ella
1 *Jean Mary's adventures* (1931)
2 *Jean Mary in Virginia* (1931)
3 *Jean Mary's romance* (1931)
4 *Jean Mary's summer mystery* (1931)
5 *Jean Mary solves the mystery* (1933)

Jean Nerac series
Soubiran, Andre
1 *Doctors* (1949)
Original edition entitled *Les hommes en blanc*
2 *Healing oath* (1951)
Original edition entitled *Le grand metier*
3 *Goodbye, Doctor Roch* (1958)
Original edition entitled *Au revoir*

Jean, Robbie, Sophie and Helen series
Dallas, Ruth
Stories of pioneer life in New Zealand
1 *Children in the bush* (1969)
2 *Wild boy in the bush* (1971)
3 *Big flood in the bush* (1972)

Jean Robertson series
Sandison, Janet
see **Apology for the life of Jean Robertson series**

Jean series
Cannan, Joanna
1 *Pony for Jean* (1936)
2 *Another pony for Jean* (1938)
3 *More ponies for Jean* (1943)

Jean series
Wynne, May
1 *Jean plays her part* (1926)
2 *Jean of the lumber camp* (1927)

Jean Thomas series
Martin, Nancy
1 *Jean behind the counter* (1960)
2 *Jean, teenage fashion buyer* (1964)

Jeanette series
Lunt, Alice
1 *Jeanette's first term* (1960)
2 *Jeanette in the summer term* (1962)

Jean-Louis Saint-Cyr and Hermann Kohler series
Janes, Joseph Robert
1 *Mayhem* (1992)
Mirage
2 *Carousel* (1992)
3 *Kaleidoscope* (1993)
4 *Salamander* (1994)

Jeanne series
Colver, Alice Ross
1 *Jeanne* (1922)
2 *Jeanne's house* (1923)
3 *Jeanne's happy year* (1925)
4 *Jeanne at Rainbow Lodge* (1926)

Jeanne-Marie series
Francoise
Translated from the French
1 *Jeanne-Marie counts her sheep* (1955)
2 *Jeanne-Marie in gay Paris* (1957)
3 *Spring-time for Jeanne-Marie* (1958)
4 *Jeanne-Marie at the fair* (1959)
5 *Big rain* (1962)
6 *Noel for Jeanne-Marie* (1966)

Jeannot and Lydie series
Danoen, Emile
1 *Dust in the wind* (1951)
Original edition entitled *Une maison soufflee aux vents*
2 *Wind rises* (1952)
Original edition entitled *Idyll dans un Quatier Mure*

Jean-Pierre series
Gallico, Paul
1 *Day the guinea-pig talked* (1963)
2 *Day Jean-Pierre was pignapped* (1964)
3 *Day Jean-Pierre went round the world* (1965)
4 *Day Jean-Pierre joined the circus* (1969)

Jeb Cutter series
McCoy, Duff
1 *Panhandle payback* (1990)
2 *Gut shot* (1990)
3 *Savage blood* (1991)
4 *Sixgun slaughter* (1991)

Jeb Stuart Ho series
Farren, Mick
1 *Quest of the DNA cowboys* (1976)
2 *Synaptic manhunt* (1976)
3 *Neural atrocity* (1977)
4 *Last stand of the DNA cowboys* (1989)

Jebediah Travis Herne series
McLaglen, John J
see **Herne the Hunter series**

Jed, Liza and Bill series
Parish, Peggy
see **Liza, Bill and Jed series**

Jed McLane series
Honig, Donald
1 *Adventures of Jed McLane* (1967)
2 *Jed McLane and Storm Cloud* (1968)
3 *Jed McLane and the stranger* (1969)

Jed series
Marzollo, Jean
1 *Jed's junior space patrol* (1982)
2 *Jed and the space bandits* (1987)

Jedediah Killinger series
Palmer, P K
1 *Turquoise-yellow case* (1974)
2 *Rainbow-seagreen case* (1974)

Jeeves and Bertie Wooster series
Wodehouse, Pelham Grenville
1 *My man Jeeves* (1920)
2 *Inimitable Jeeves* (1923)
Jeeves
3 *Carry on, Jeeves* (1925)
4 *Very good, Jeeves* (1930)
5 *Thank you, Jeeves* (1934)
6 *Right-ho, Jeeves* (1934)
Brinkley Manor
7 *Code of the Woosters* (1938)
8 *Joy in the morning* (1947)
Jeeves in the morning
9 *Mating season* (1949)
10 *Ring for Jeeves* (1953)
Return of Jeeves
11 *Jeeves and the feudal spirit* (1954)
Bertie Wooster sees it through
12 *Jeeves in the offing* (1960)
How right you are, Jeeves
13 *Stiff upper lip, Jeeves* (1963)
14 *Much obliged, Jeeves* (1971)
Jeeves and the tie that binds
15 *Aunts aren't gentlemen* (1974)
Cat-nappers
Also one Jeeves story in *The man with two left feet*, 1933 and one story featuring Jeeves in *Plum pie*, 1967; companion volume: *Jeeves, a gentleman's personal gentleman*, by Cyril Northcote Parkinson, 1981

Jeff and Haila Troy series
Roos, Kelley
1 *Made up to kill* (1940)
Made up for murder
2 *If the shroud fits* (1941)
Dangerous blondes
3 *Frightened stiff* (1942)
4 *Sailor, take warning!* (1944)
5 *There was a crooked man* (1945)
6 *Ghost of a chance* (1947)
7 *Murder in any language* (1948)
8 *Triple threat* (1949)
Beauty marks the spot
The second title is an abridged edition
9 *One false move* (1966)

Jeff Carson series
Horner, Lance
see **Golden stud series**

Jeff Cass series
Severn, Richard
1 *Stalk a long shadow* (1967)
2 *Game for hawks* (1968)
3 *Killing match* (1970)

Jeff Dimarco series
Disney, Doris Miles
1 *Dark road* (1946)
Dead stop
2 *Family skeleton* (1949)
3 *Straw man* (1951)
Case of the straw man
4 *Trick or treat* (1955)
Halloween murder
5 *Method in madness* (1957)
Quiet violence
Too innocent to kill
6 *Did she fall or was she pushed?* (1959)
7 *Find the woman* (1962)
8 *Chandler policy* (1971)

Jeff Green series
Keith, Carlton
1 *Diamond-studded typewriter* (1958)
Gem of a murder
2 *Missing presumed dead* (1961)
3 *Rich uncle* (1963)
4 *Crayfish dinner* (1966)
Elusive epicure
5 *Taste of sangria* (1968)
Missing bookkeeper

Jeff Jackson series
Craig, Philip R
see **Martha's Vineyard series**

Jeff James series
Patchett, Mary Elwyn
1 *Warrimoo* (1961)
2 *Dangerous assignment* (1962)
3 *Venus project* (1963)
4 *Tiger in the dark* (1964)

Jeff Layne series
Kelton, Elmer
see **Crow Feather series**

Jeff Marle series
Carr, John Dickson
see **Henri Bencolin series**

Jeff Plummer series
Lees, Dan
1 *Rainbow conspiracy* (1971)
2 *Zodiac* (1972)
3 *Rape of a quiet town* (1973)
4 *Elizabeth R.I.P.* (1974)

Jeff Pride series
O'Neill, Archie
1 *Da Vinci rose* (1973)
2 *Duplicate stiff* (1974)
3 *High bid for murder* (1974)

4 *Ginzberg circle* (1974)
Sequence continued under the author's real name Jim Henaghan
Henaghan, Jim
5 *Azor!* (1977)

Jeff Saunders series
Bar-Zohar, Michael
1 *Third truth* (1972)
Original edition entitled *La troisieme verite*
2 *Spy who died twice* (1973)
Translated from the Hebrew

Jeff Strange series
Gaines, Audrey
1 *Omit flowers* (1946)
2 *No crime like the present* (1952)

Jeff Tellford series
Fisher, Douglas George
1 *What's wrong at Pyford?* (1950)
2 *Poison pen at Pyford* (1951)
3 *Death at Pyford Hall* (1952)

Jeff Tyler series
Potter, J L
1 *Room at the bottom* (1962)
2 *Kill, sweet Charity, kill* (1962)
3 *Or murder for free* (1962)

Jeffers series
Brennan, James Herbert
see **Barmy Jeffers series**

Jefferson Birch series
Lee, W W
1 *Rogue's gold* (1989)
2 *Rustler's venom* (1990)
3 *Rancher's blood* (1991)
4 *Robber's trail* (1992)
5 *Outlaw's fortune* (1993)

Jefferson Boone series
Messmann, Jon
1 *Moneta papers* (1973)
2 *Game of terror* (1973)
3 *Murder today, money tomorrow* (1973)
4 *Swiss secret* (1974)
5 *Ransom* (1975)
6 *Inheritors* (1975)

Jefferson Hastings series
Hay, James
1 *Melwood mystery* (1920)
2 *No clue* (1920)
3 *Bellamy case* (1925)

Jefferson Hewitt series
Reese, John
1 *Weapon heavy* (1973)
2 *They don't shoot cowards* (1973)
3 *Sharpshooter* (1974)
4 *Texas gold* (1975)
5 *Wes Hardin's gun* (1975)
6 *Hangman's Springs* (1976)
7 *Cherokee diamondback* (1977)
8 *Sequoia shootout* (1977)
9 *Pair of deuces* (1978)
10 *Dead Eye* (1978)
11 *Two thieves and a puma* (1980)

Jefferson series
Johnson, Pat
see **Julie Jefferson series**

Jefferson Shields series
Carlon, Patricia
1 *Souvenir* (1970)
2 *Death by demonstration* (1970)

Jefferson's war series
Randle, Kevin
1 *Galactic silver star* (1990)
2 *Price of command* (1990)
3 *Lost colony* (1991)
4 *January platoon* (1991)
5 *Death of a regiment* (1991)
6 *Chain of command* (1992)

Jeffery Blackburn series
Afford, Max
1 *Blood on his hands* (1936)
Ear for murder
2 *Death's mannikins* (1937)
Dolls of death
A sober account of certain diabolical happenings, not untinged with the odour of brimstone, which befell a respectable family living at Exmoor in this present year
3 *Dead are blind* (1937)
4 *Owl of darkness* (1942)
Fly by night
5 *Sheep and the wolves* (1947)

Jeffrey and Anne McNeill series
Du Bois, Theodora
see **Anne and Jeffrey McNeill series**

Jeffrey and the fourth grade ghost series
Stine, Harlan William
1 *Max is back* (1989)
2 *Baseball card fever* (1989)
3 *Max's secret formula* (1989)
4 *Mad science* (1990)
5 *Camp Duck Down* (1990)
6 *Big brother blues* (1990)

Jeffrey and the third grade ghost series
Stine, Harlan William
1 *Mysterious Max* (1988)
2 *Haunted Halloween* (1988)
3 *Christmas visitors* (1988)
4 *Pet day surprise* (1989)
5 *Max onstage* (1989)
6 *Max saves the day* (1989)

Jeffrey series
Webster, Henry Kitchell
see **Arthur Jeffrey series**

Jeffrey's ghost series
Adler, David A
1 *Jeffrey's ghost and the leftover baseball team* (1984)
2 *Jeffrey's ghost and the fifth grade dragon* (1985)
3 *Jeffrey's ghost and the Ziffel Fair* (1987)

Jeffreys series
Chappell, Mollie
see **Tiddy Jeffreys series**

Jeffries and Sanders series
Sale, Medora
see **Inspector John Sanders and Harriet Jeffries series**

Jeffry series
Churchill, Jill
see **Jane Jeffry series**

Jellipot series
Fowler, Sydney
see **Mister Jellipot series**

Jem series
Hallock, Rusty
see **Find your fate: Jem series**

Jemima Shore series
Fraser, Antonia
1 *Quiet as a nun* (1977)
2 *Wild island* (1978)
3 *Splash of red* (1981)
4 *Cool repentance* (1982)
5 *Oxford blood* (1985)
6 *Your royal hostage* (1987)
7 *Cavalier case* (1990)
8 *Jemima Shore at the sunny grave, and other stories* (1991)
Also four stories featuring Jemima Shore in *Jemima Shore's first case, and other stories*, 1986

Jenkins series
Andrew, Prudence
see **Ginger Jenkins series**
Mulford, Clarence Edward
see **Mesquite Jenkins series**
Rosenhayn, Paul
see **Joe Jenkins series**

Jenkinson Talbot Merridrew series
Fearn, John Russell
1 *Valley of the doomed* (1949)
2 *Merridrew rides again* (1950)
3 *Merridrew marches on* (1951)
4 *Merridrew fights again* (1952)
5 *Merridrew follows the trail* (1953)

Jenner series
Milne, John
see **James Jenner series; Jimmy Jenner series**

Jennie Hawthorne series
Ogilvie, Elisabeth May
1 *Jennie about to be* (1984)
2 *World of Jennie G* (1985)

Jennie series
Gallico, Paul
1 *Jennie* (1950)
2 *Thomasina* (1957)

Jennifer and Cage series
Saint Claire, Erin
1 *Led astray* (1985)
2 *Devil's own* (1987)

Jennifer and John series
Denes, Gee
see **John and Jennifer series**

Jennifer and Rachel Murdock series
Olsen, D B
see **Rachel and Jennifer Murdock series**

Jennifer Grey series
Jenkins, Jerry Bruce
1 *Heartbeat* (1983)
2 *Three days in winter* (1983)
3 *Too late to tell* (1984)
4 *Gateway* (1984)
5 *Calling* (1984)
6 *Veiled threat* (1985)

Jennifer Heath series
Tyler, Alison
1 *Chase the wind* (1987)
2 *Chase the storm* (1987)
3 *Chase the sun* (1987)

Jennifer Hill series
Smith, Eunice Young
1 *Jennifer wish* (1949)
2 *Jennifer gift* (1950)
3 *Jennifer prize* (1951)
4 *Jennifer is eleven* (1953)
5 *Jennifer dances* (1954)
6 *High heels for Jennifer* (1964)

Jennifer Norrington, Alessandro di Ganzarello and Coleridge Tucker series
Drummond, Ivor
see **Lady Jennifer, Sandro and Colly series**

Jennifer series
Lister, Gladys
1 *Jennifer stands by* (1941)
2 *Whither Jennifer* (1948)

Jennifer series
This sequence has two authors
Smith, Thorne
1 *Passionate witch* (1941)
Completed by Norman Matson
Matson, Norman
2 *Bats in the belfry* (1943)

Jennifer series
Sorenson, Jane
1 *It's me, Jennifer* (1984)
2 *It's your move, Jennifer* (1984)
3 *Jennifer's new life* (1984)
4 *Jennifer says goodbye* (1984)
5 *Another Jennifer* (1986)

Jennings series
Buckeridge, Anthony
1 *Jennings goes to school* (1950)
2 *Jennifer follows a clue* (1951)
3 *Jennings' little hut* (1951)
4 *Jennings and Darbishire* (1952)
5 *Jennings' diary* (1953)
6 *According to Jennings* (1954)
7 *Our friend Jennings* (1955)
8 *Thanks to Jennings* (1957)
9 *Take Jennings for instance* (1958)
10 *Jennings, as usual* (1959)
11 *Trouble with Jennings* (1960)
12 *Just like Jennings* (1961)
13 *Leave it to Jennings* (1963)
14 *Jennings, of course!* (1964)
15 *Especially Jennings* (1965)
16 *Bookful of Jennings* (1966)
Best of Jennings
The second title is a revised edition
17 *Jennings abounding* (1967)
18 *Jennings in particular* (1968)
19 *Trust Jennings* (1969)
20 *Jennings report* (1970)
21 *Typically Jennings* (1971)
22 *Speaking of Jennings* (1973)
23 *Jennings at large* (1977)
Companion volume: *Jennings abounding*, a play, 1980

Jenny and Mirabelle series
Gifford, Griselda
1 *Jenny and the sheep thieves* (1975)
2 *Mirabelle's secret* (1976)

Jenny and Oliver series
Segal, Erich
see **Oliver and Jenny series**

Jenny and Simon series
Jones, Olive
see **Barfield series**

Jenny and Sue series
Macpherson, Bruce
1 *Lost koala* (1962)
2 *Sea urchin* (1963)
Happy holiday with the little sea urchin

Jenny Archer series
Conford, Ellen
1 *Job for Jenny Archer* (1988)
2 *Case for Jenny Archer* (1988)
3 *Jenny Archer, author* (1989)
4 *What's cooking, Jenny Archer?* (1989)
5 *Jenny Archer to the rescue* (1990)

Jenny Bell trilogy
Dyce, Gilbert
1 *Bella Donna* (1864)
Alternative title: The cross before the name; sequence continued under the author's real name Percy Fitzgerald
Fitzgerald, Percy
2 *Jenny Bell* (1866)
3 *Seventy five Brooke Street* (1867)

Jenny Cain series
Pickard, Nancy
1 *Generous death* (1984)
2 *Say no to murder* (1985)
3 *No body* (1986)
4 *Marriage is murder* (1987)
5 *Dead crazy* (1989)
6 *Bum steer* (1990)
7 *I.O.U.* (1991)
8 *But I wouldn't want to die there* (1993)
9 *Confession* (1994)

Jenny Dean series
Carlson, Dale
1 *Mystery of the shining children* (1983)
2 *Mystery of the hidden trap* (1983)
3 *Secret of the third eye* (1983)
4 *Secret of the invisible city* (1984)

Jenny Gilette and Hunter Lewis series
Gresham, Elizabeth
1 *Puzzle in porcelain* (1945)
Originally published under the pseudonym Robin Grey
2 *Puzzle in pewter* (1947)
Originally published under the pseudonym Robin Grey
3 *Puzzle in paisley* (1972)
4 *Puzzle in parquet* (1973)
5 *Puzzle in patchwork* (1973)
6 *Puzzle in parchment* (1973)

Jenny Heysten series
Ammers-Kuller, Jo van
1 *House of joy* (1922)
Original edition entitled *Het huisen der Vreugden*
2 *Jenny Heysten's career* (1930)
Original edition entitled *Jenny Heysten*

Jenny Linsky series
Averill, Esther
1 *Cat Club* (1944)
The life and times of Jenny Linsky
2 *Adventures of Jack Ninepins* (1944)
3 *School for cats* (1947)
4 *Jenny's first party* (1948)
5 *Jenny's moonlight adventure* (1949)
6 *When Jenny lost her scarf* (1951)
7 *Jenny's adopted brothers* (1952)
8 *How the brothers joined the Cat Club* (1953)
9 *Jenny's birthday book* (1954)
10 *Jenny goes to sea* (1957)
11 *Jenny's bedside book* (1959)
12 *Fire Cat* (1961)
13 *Hotel cat* (1969)
Numbers 1, 4, 6, 7, 8 also published in one volume entitled *Jenny and the Cat Club*, 1973

Jenny Pearl and Maurice Avery series
Mackenzie, Compton
1 *Carnival* (1912)
2 *Coral* (1925)

Jenny Rorke series
Hine, Muriel
1 *Wild rye* (1931)
2 *Jenny Rorke* (1932)

Jenny series
Fujikawa, Gyo
1 *Jenny learns a lesson* (1980)
2 *Jenny and Jupie* (1981)
3 *Jenny and Jupie to the rescue* (1982)

Jenny series
Martyn, Harriet
see **Blacombe Hall series**

Jenny series
Mazer, Norma Fox
1 *Figure of speech* (1973)
2 *When we first met* (1982)

Jenny series
Merriam, Lillie Fuller
1 *Jenny's bird house* (1910)
2 *Jenny and Tito* (1914)

Jenny series
Moss, Roberta
1 *Jenny of the Fourth* (1953)
2 *Jenny's exciting term* (1954)
3 *Shy girl at Southdown* (1957)

Jenny trilogy
Wells, Marian
see **Starlight trilogy**

Jenny Winfield series
Blake, Vanessa
1 *Gay gallant* (1971)
2 *Bride of chance* (1972)
Bride of misfortune

Jenny Wren series
Young, Emily Hilda
1 *Jenny Wren* (1932)
2 *Curate's wife* (1934)

Jensen series
Wahloo, Per
see **Chief Inspector Peter Jensen series**

Jeremiah and Mrs Ming series
Jennings, Sharon
1 *Jeremiah and Mrs Ming* (1990)
2 *When Jeremiah found Mrs Ming* (1992)

Jeremiah Irish series
Child, Nellise
1 *Murder comes home* (1933)
2 *Diamond ransom murders* (1934)

Jeremiah X Gibson series
Stone, Hampton
1 *Corpse in the corner saloon* (1948)
2 *Girl with the hole in her head* (1949)
3 *Needle that wouldn't hold still* (1950)
4 *Murder that wouldn't stay solved* (1951)
5 *Corpse that refused to stay dead* (1952)
6 *Corpse who had too many friends* (1953)
7 *Man who had too much to lose* (1955)
8 *Strangler wwho couldn't let go* (1956)
Strangler
9 *Girl who kept knocking them dead* (1957)
10 *Man who was three jumps ahead* (1959)
11 *Man who looked death in the eye* (1961)
12 *Babe with the twistable arm* (1962)
13 *Real serendipitous kill* (1964)
14 *Kid was last seen hanging ten* (1966)
15 *Funniest killer in town* (1967)
16 *Corpse was no bargain at all* (1968)
17 *Swinger who swung by the neck* (1970)
18 *Kid who came home with a corpse* (1972)

Jeremy, Algy and Peter series
Scott, Philip
see **Algy, Peter and Jeremy series**

Jeremy and Fenella series
Byers, Irene
1 *Strange story of Pippin Wood* (1956)
2 *Missing masterpiece* (1957)

Jeremy and Jane Fortune series
Hill, Denise
see **Jane and Jeremy Fortune series**

Jeremy and Lynette series
Adler, Carole Schwerdtfeger
see **Glits series**

Jeremy Barton and Samuel Best series
Pearson, Parry
1 *Midshipmen cruise south* (1950)
2 *South with the Kittiwake* (1952)

Jeremy Bear series
Van Stockum, Hilda
1 *Jeremy Bear* (1963)
2 *Little old bear* (1963)
3 *Bennie and the new baby* (1964)
4 *New baby is lost* (1964)

Jeremy Flack series
Maske, John
1 *Saint-Malo mystery* (1933)
2 *Cherbourg mystery* (1934)
3 *Ghost of a cardinal* (1935)

Jeremy Grant series
Macvicar, Angus
1 *Lost planet* (1953)
2 *Return of the lost planet* (1954)
3 *Secret of the lost planet* (1955)
4 *Red fire on the lost planet* (1959)
5 *Peril on the lost planet* (1960)
6 *Space agent from the lost planet* (1961)
7 *Space Agent and the Isles of Fire* (1962)
8 *Space Agent and the ancient peril* (1964)

Jeremy Haines series
Serling, Robert
1 *President's plane is missing* (1967)
2 *Air Force One is haunted* (1985)

Jeremy Jackson series
Scott, James Maurice
1 *Snowstone* (1936)
2 *Silver land* (1937)

Jeremy James series
Wilson, David Henry
1 *Elephants son't sit on cars* (1977)
2 *Getting rich with Jeremy James* (1979)
3 *Beside the sea with Jeremy James* (1980)
4 *How to stop a train with one finger* (1984)
5 *Do goldfish play the violin?* (1985)

Jeremy Locke series
Challis, Mary
1 *Burden of proof* (1980)
2 *Crimes past* (1980)
3 *Ghost of an idea* (1981)
4 *Very good hater* (1981)

Jeremy Moon series
Strickland, Brad
1 *Moon dreams* (1988)
2 *Nul's quest* (1989)
3 *Wizard's mole* (1991)

Jeremy Mouse series
Althea
1 *Jeremy Mouse* (1973)
2 *Jeremy Mouse and cat* (1980)
3 *Jeremy Mouse was hungry* (1981)

Jeremy series
Duff, Douglas Valder
1 *Ship slayers* (1953)
2 *Miracle man* (1953)
3 *Operation sunpower* (1955)

Jeremy series
Hermes, Patricia
1 *What if they knew?* (1980)
2 *Place for Jeremy* (1987)

Jeremy series
Lethbridge, Peter
1 *Holiday adventurers* (1948)
2 *Lakeland adventure* (1949)
3 *Boy from London* (1951)
4 *Danger in the hills* (1953)
5 *Beresfords in Tarndale* (1954)

Jeremy series
Montague, Jeffrey
see **John Jeremy series**

Jeremy series
Theulet-Luzie, Bernadette
1 *Jeremy in town* (1985)
2 *Jeremy at the circus* (1985)

Jeremy Shafto series
Feist, Aubrey
1 *High Barbary* (1950)
2 *Spread Eagle* (1951)

Jeremy Six series
Wynne, Brian
see **Marshal Jeremy Six series**

Jeremy Smith series
Smee, Donald
1 *Jeremy Smith to the rescue* (1958)
2 *Jeremy Smith investigates* (1959)
3 *Jeremy Smith in trouble* (1960)
4 *Jeremy Smith shows the way* (1961)

Jeremy Sturrock series
Sturrock, Jeremy
see **Bow Street Runner series**

Jeremy trilogy
Walpole, Hugh
1 *Jeremy* (1919)
2 *Jeremy and Hamlet* (1923)
3 *Jeremy at Crale* (1927)

Jericho series
Pentecost, Hugh
see **John Jericho series**

Jericho series
Wellman, Paul Iselin
1 *Walls of Jericho* (1947)
2 *Chain* (1949)
3 *Jericho's daughters* (1956)

Jern series
Norton, Andre
see **Murdoc Jern series**

Jerningham series
Myers, Isabel Briggs
see **Peter Jerningham series**

Jerome and Return Kingdom series
Braden, James Andrew
see **John Jerome and Return Kingdom series**

Jerome Aylwin series
Curry, Avon
1 *Derry down death* (1960)
2 *Dying high* (1961)

Jerome Coignard series
France, Anatole
see **Abbe Coignard series**

Jerry and Mary Denton series
Hunt, Francis
see **Mary and Jerry Denton series**

Jerry and Pam North series
Lockridge, Frances
see **Mister and Mrs North series**

Jerry and Vic series
Dines, Glen
1 *Mysterious machine* (1957)
2 *Fabulous flying bicycle* (1960)

Jerry Benedict series
Ronns, Edward
1 *No place to live* (1947)
Lady, the guy is dead
Also published under the author's real name Edward Sidney Aarons; the second title is an abridged edition
2 *Gift of death* (1948)

Jerry Boyne series
Macgowan, Alice
1 *Million dollar suitcase* (1922)
2 *Mystery woman* (1924)
3 *Shaken down* (1925)
4 *Seventh passenger* (1926)
5 *Who is this man?* (1927)

Jerry Brogan series
Breen, Jon Linn
1 *Listen for the click* (1983)
Vicar's roses
2 *Gathering place* (1984)
3 *Triple crown* (1985)
4 *Loose lips* (1990)
5 *Hot air* (1991)

Jerry Burke series
Baker, Asa
1 *Mum's the word for murder* (1938)
Also published under the pseudonym Brett Halliday
2 *Kissed corpse* (1939)

Jerry Cornelius series
Moorcock, Michael
1 *Final programme* (1968)
Last days of man on earth
Revised edition 1969
2 *Cure for cancer* (1971)
Revised edition 1979
3 *English assassin* (1972)
Revised edition 1979
4 *Condition of Muzak* (1977)
Numbers 1-4 also published in one volume entitled *The Cornelius chronicles*, volume 1, 1977
5 *Lives and times of Jerry Cornelius* (1976)
6 *Entropy tango* (1981)
Numbers 5-6 also published in one volume entitled *The Cornelius chronicles*, volume 2, 1986
7 *Adventures of Una Persson and Catherine Cornelius in the twentieth century* (1976)
Number 7 with *The alchemist's question* also published as *The Cornelius chronicles*, volume 3, 1986
Companion volumes: *The name of the catastrophe*, by Michael Moorcock and Langdon Jones, 1971, and, *The opium generals, and other stories*, 1984

Jerry Cornell series
Moorcock, Michael
1 *Chinese agent* (1970)
Rewritten from *Somewhere in the night*, by Bill Barclay, 1966
2 *Russian intelligence* (1980)
Rewritten from *Printer's devil*, by Bill Barclay, 1966

Jerry Ford series
Moore, Fenworth
1 *Wrecked on Cannibal Island* (1931)
Alternative title: Jerry Ford's adventure among savages
2 *Lost in the caves of gold* (1931)
Alternative title: Jerry Ford among the mountains of mystery
3 *Cast away in the land of snow* (1931)
Alternative title: Jerry Ford among the polar bears
4 *Prisoners on the pirate ship* (1932)
Alternative title: Jerry Ford among the polar bears; one volume edition entitled *Thrilling stories for boys*, 1937

Jerry Johnson trilogy
De Clements, Barthe
1 *Five-finger discount* (1989)
2 *Monkey see, monkey do* (1990)
3 *Breaking out* (1991)

Jerry Kennedy series
Higgins, George Vincent
1 *Judgment of Deke Hunter* (1976)
2 *Kennedy for the defense* (1980)
3 *Rat on fire* (1981)
4 *Penance for Jerry Kennedy* (1985)

Jerry Long and Chuck Conley series
Fox, James M
1 *Code three* (1953)
Dead shot
2 *Free ride* (1957)
Cell car fifty four
3 *Dead pigeon* (1967)
Dead canary

Jerry Mooney series
O'Neil, Kerry
1 *Mooney moves around* (1939)
2 *Ninth floor, Middle City Tower* (1943)
3 *Death strikes at Heron House* (1944)

Jerry, Ned and Bob series
Young, Clarence
see **Motor boys series**

Jerry Roe series
Roper, Lester V
1 *Red horse caper* (1975)
2 *Emerald chicks caper* (1976)

Jerry Scant series
Knight, Leonard Alfred
1 *Deadman's Bay* (1930)
2 *Creaking tree mystery* (1931)
3 *Creeping death* (1933)
4 *Murder by experiment* (1935)
5 *Solander box mystery* (1940)
6 *Dancing stones* (1946)

Jerry Scott and Dick Morris series
Gulick, Bill
see **Junior Trail Blazers series**

Jerry series
Darby, Joan
1 *Jerry finds ants* (1964)
2 *Jerry finds bees* (1967)
3 *Jerry finds spiders* (1969)

Jerry series
London, Jack
1 *Jerry of the islands* (1917)
2 *Michael, brother of Jerry* (1918)

Jerry series
Saddler, Allen
1 *Jerry and the monsters* (1986)
2 *Jerry and the inventions* (1988)

Jerry Todd series
Freeman, Martin Joseph
1 *Case of the blind mouse* (1935)
2 *Scarf on the scarecrow* (1938)

Jersey series
Wuorio, Eva Lis
1 *October treasure* (1966)
2 *Forbidden adventure* (1967)

Jerusalem quartet
Whittemore, Edward
1 *Sinai tapestry* (1977)
2 *Jerusalem poker* (1978)
3 *Nile shadows* (1983)
4 *Jericho mosaic* (1987)

Jerusalem series
Finn, Elizabeth Anne MacCaul
Tales illustrating customs and incidents in modern Jerusalem
1 *Home in the Holy Land* (1866)
2 *Third year in Jerusalem* (1869)

Jerusalem series
Harry, Myriam
1 *Conquest of Jerusalem* (1903)
Original edition entitled *La conquete de Jerusalem*
2 *Little daughter of Jerusalem* (1914)
Original edition entitled *La petite fille de Jerusalem*

Jerusalem series
Lagerlof, Selma
1 *Jerusalem* (1901)
Original edition entitled *I dalarna*
2 *Holy City* (1901)
Original edition entitled *I det helige landet*

Jess and Eliza Birdwell series
West, Jessamyn
1 *Friendly persuasion* (1945)
Short stories
2 *Except for me and thee* (1969)

Jess Roden series
Cunningham, Albert Benjamin
see **Sheriff Jess Roden series**

Jess the cat series
Cunliffe, John Arthur
1 *Jess and the fish* (1992)
2 *Jess goes hunting* (1992)
3 *Jess's new bed* (1992)
4 *Song for Jess* (1992)

Jesse Bear series
Carlstrom, Nancy White
1 *Jesse Bear, what will you wear?* (1986)
2 *Better not get wet, Jesse Bear* (1988)
3 *It's about time, Jesse Bear, and other rhymes* (1990)

Jesse Falkenstein series
Egan, Lesley
1 *Case for appeal* (1961)
2 *Against the evidence* (1962)
3 *My name is death* (1964)
4 *Some avenger, rise!* (1966)
5 *Serious investigation* (1968)
6 *In the death of a man* (1970)
7 *Paper chase* (1972)
8 *Blind search* (1977)
9 *Look back on death* (1978)
10 *Motive in shadow* (1980)
11 *Miser* (1981)
12 *Little boy lost* (1983)
13 *Chain of violence* (1985)

Jesse Heller series
Kellerman, Dan
1 *Blood run* (1985)
2 *Hellrider* (1985)

Jesse James series
Lawson, W B
1 *Jesse James at Coney Island* (1898)
Alternative title: The Wall Street banker's secret
2 *Jesse James at Long Beach* (1898)
3 *Jesse James' double* (1898)
Alternative title: The man from Missouri
4 *Jesse James in New York* (1898)
Alternative title: A plot against a millionaire
5 *Jesse James' oath* (1898)
Alternative title: Tracked to death
6 *Frank James in St Louis* (1898)
Alternative title: The mysteries of a great city
7 *Bob Ford, the slayer of Jesse James* (1898)
Alternative title: The dramatic life and death of a noted desperado

Jessica Fletcher series
Anderson, James
Based on a television series
1 *Affair of the mutilated mink* (1981)
2 *Murder of Sherlock Holmes* (1985)
3 *Hooray for homicide* (1985)
4 *Lovers and other killers* (1986)

Jessica James series
O'Brien, Meg
1 *Daphne decisions* (1988)
2 *Salmon in the soup* (1990)
3 *Eagles die too* (1992)

Jessica series
Stretton, Hesba
1 *Jessica's first prayer* (1867)
2 *Jessica's mother* (1893)

Jessica Trent series
Raymond, Evelyn Hunt
1 *Jessica Trent, her life on a ranch* (1902)
2 *Jessica, the heiress* (1904)
3 *Jessica Trent's inheritance* (1907)

Jessie Drake series
Krich, Rochelle Majer
1 *Till death do us part* (1992)
2 *Fair game* (1993)
3 *Nowhere to run* (1994)
4 *Angel of death* (1994)

Jessie series
Pullein-Thompson, Christine
1 *Home for Jessie* (1986)
2 *Please save Jessie* (1987)

Jessie series
Ziefert, Harriet
1 *Hurry up, Jessie* (1987)
2 *Good night, Jessie!* (1987)

Jessie Walters and Michael Skye series
Hart, Bruce
1 *Sooner or later* (1978)
2 *Waiting games* (1981)

Jesus Christ series
Dixon, Roger
1 *Messiah* (1975)
2 *Christ on trial* (1973)
Based on an original story by Basil Bovat
3 *Going to Jerusalem* (1977)

Jesus Christ series
Oxenham, John
1 *Hidden years* (1925)
2 *Anno Domini* (1932)
Master's golden years
3 *Splendour of the dawn* (1930)
Companion volume: *God's candle*, 1929

Jesus Davidson series
Jackman, Stuart
1 *Davidson affair* (1966)
2 *Slingshot* (1974)
3 *Burning men* (1976)

Jesus on horseback trilogy
Reese, John
1 *Angel Range* (1973)
2 *Blowholers* (1974)
Lonesome cowboys
3 *Land baron* (1974)
One volume edition entitled *Jesus on horseback*, 1971

Jesus series
Daniel, Rebecca
see **Life of Jesus series**

Jet Morgan series
Chilton, Charles
1 *Journey into space* (1954)
2 *Red planet* (1956)
3 *World in peril* (1960)

Jethro Stanton series
Clews, Roy
1 *Young Jethro* (1975)
2 *King's bounty* (1976)
3 *Drums of war* (1978)

Jets series
Thomson, Pat
1 *Jacko* (1989)
2 *Rhyming Russell* (1991)
3 *Messages* (1992)

Jettero Heller series
Hubbard, Lafayette Ronald
see **Mission earth series**

Jewel in the crown quartet
Scott, Paul
see **British India quartet**

Jewel series
Burnham, Clara Louise
1 *Jewel* (1903)
2 *Jewel's story book* (1905)

Jewel series
Thompson, Ames
1 *Adventure boys and the valley of diamonds* (1927)
2 *Adventure boys and the river of emeralds* (1927)
3 *Adventure boys and the lagoon of pearls* (1927)
4 *Adventure boys and the temple of rubies* (1928)
Numbers 1-4 also published in one volume entitled *Strange adventure stories for boys*, 1935
5 *Adventure boys and the island of sapphires* (1929)

Jewelled men series
Veryan, Patricia
see **Tales of the jewelled men series**

Jewels and gems series
Oyved, Moysheh
1 *Visions and jewels* (1926)
2 *Gems and life* (1927)

Jewish colonist series
Memmi, Albert
1 *Colonizer and the colonized* (1957)
Original edition entitled *Portrait du colonise precede du protait du colonisateur*
2 *Portrait of a Jew* (1962)
Original edition entitled *Portrait d'un Juif*
3 *Liberation of a Jew* (1962)
Original edition entitled *La liberation d'un Juif*

Jewish emigrants series
Gold, Herbert
1 *Fathers* (1967)
2 *Family* (1981)

Jewish family series
Halter, Marek
1 *Book of Abraham* (1983)
Original edition entitled *Le memoire d'Abraham*
2 *Children of Abraham* (1990)
Translated from the French

Jewish holidays series
Drucker, Malka
1 *Hanukkah* (1980)
Eight nights
2 *Passover* (1981)
A season of freedom
3 *Rosh Hashanah and Yom Kippur* (1981)
4 *Sukkot* (1982)
A time to rejoice
5 *Shabbat* (1983)
A peaceful island
6 *Celebrating life* (1984)
Jewish rites of passage

Jewish series
Zangwill, Israel
see **Ghetto series**

Jewish tales series
McDaniel, Becky Bring
1 *Only nine chairs* (1982)
A tall tale for Passover
2 *Poppy seeds too* (1982)
A twisted tale for Shabbat
3 *Modi'in Motel* (1986)
Co-author: Karen Ostrove; an idol tale for Hanukkah
4 *Fins and scales* (1992)
Co-author: Karen Ostrove; a Kosher tale

Jews in Arab lands series
Stillman, Norman Arthur
1 *Jews of Arab lands* (1979)
2 *Jews of Arab lands in modern times* (1991)

Jhereg series
Brust, Steven
1 *Jhereg* (1983)
2 *Yendi* (1984)
3 *Teckla* (1987)
Numbers 1-3 also published in one volume entitled *Taltos the assassin*, 1991
4 *Taltos* (1988)
Taltos and the paths of the dead
5 *Phoenix* (1990)
Companion volume: *Dzurlord, a Crossroads adventure in the world of Steven Brust's Jhereg*, by Architects Adventure, 1987

Jherek Carnelian and Amelia Underwood series
Moorcock, Michael
1 *Alien heart* (1973)
2 *Hollow lands* (1974)
3 *End of all songs* (1976)
4 *Legends from the end of time* (1976)
5 *Messiah at the end of time* (1978)

Jigger Moran series
Roeburt, John
1 *Jigger Moran* (1944)
Case of the tearless widow
Wine, women and murder
2 *There are dead men in Manhattan* (1946)
Manhattan underworld
Murder in Manhattan
Triple cross
3 *Corpse on the town* (1950)
Case of the hypnotised virgin
The second title is a revised edition

Jiggers Masters series
Rud, Anthony Melville
see **J C K Masters series**

Jiggs and Maggie series
McManus, George
see **Maggie and Jiggs series**

Jiggs series
Gilman, Phoebe
see **Jillian Jiggs series**

Jill and Joe series
Cole, Margaret Alice
1 *Jill and Joe on holiday* (1961)
2 *Jill and Joe's return* (1962)

Jill and Limpet series
Willard, Barbara
1 *Dog and a half* (1964)
2 *Surprise Island* (1966)

Jill and Prince series
Dickins, Joan
1 *Jill and Prince the pony* (1957)
2 *Jill and Prince triumph again* (1962)

Jill Gardner and Toni Redmond series
Quin-Harkin, Janet
see **Toni Redmond and Jill Gardner series**

Jill Graham series
Chase, Lesley
1 *Jill Graham and the secret of Druids Wood* (1974)
Jill Graham and the secret of the silent pool
2 *Jill Graham and the riddle of the dwarf's shadow* (1975)
3 *Jill Graham and the adventure of the man who vanished* (1975)
4 *Jill Graham and the mystery of the haunted priory* (1976)

Jill Hanscombe and Harry Sommers series
Whalley, Peter
see **Harry Sommers and Jill Hanscombe series**

Jill Nolan series
McElfresh, Adeline
1 *Jill Nolan, surgical nurse* (1962)
2 *Jill Nolan, R.N.* (1962)
3 *Jill Nolan's choice* (1963)
4 *Nurse Nolan's private duty* (1966)

Jill Robinson and me series
Digby, Anne
see **Me and Jill Robinson series**

Jill series
Conquest, Joan
1 *Desert love* (1920)
2 *Hawk of Egypt* (1922)

Jill series
Ferguson, Ruby
1 *Jill enjoys her pony* (1949)
2 *Jill's gymkhana* (1949)
3 *Stable for Jill* (1951)
4 *Jill has two ponies* (1952)
5 *Jill's riding club* (1956)
6 *Rosettes for Jill* (1957)
7 *Jill and the perfect pony* (1959)
8 *Pony jobs for Jilll* (1960)
9 *Jill's pony trek* (1962)

Jill series
Hastings, Valerie
1 *Jill at Hazelmore* (1964)
2 *Jill investigates* (1965)

Jill series
Page, Gertrude
1 *Jill's Rhodesian philosophy* (1910)
Alternative title: The dam farm
2 *Jill on a ranch* (1921)

Jill Smith series
Dunlap, Susan
1 *Karma* (1984)
2 *As a favor* (1984)
3 *Not exactly a Brahmin* (1985)
4 *Too close to the edge* (1987)
5 *Dinner to die for* (1987)
6 *Diamond in the buff* (1990)
7 *Time expired* (1992)

Jillian Fletcher and Jackson Fury series
Jerina, Carol
see **Jack and Jill series**

Jillian Jiggs series
Gilman, Phoebe
1 *Jillian Jiggs* (1988)
2 *Wonder pigs of Jillian Jiggs* (1988)

Jillies series
Saville, Malcolm
1 *Redshank's warning* (1948)
2 *Two fair plaits* (1948)
3 *Strangers of Snowfell* (1949)
4 *Sign of the alpine rose* (1950)
5 *Luck of Sallowby* (1952)
6 *Ambermere treasure* (1953)
Secret of the Ambermere treasure

Jilly and Bob series
Schmidt, Annie Maria Geertruida
see **Bob and Jilly series**

Jilly and Peanut Butter series
Haas, Dorothy
see **Peanut Butter and Jilly series**

Jilly series
Dickinson, Mary
1 *Jilly, you look terrible* (1985)
2 *Jilly's boat trip* (1986)
3 *Jilly takes over* (1987)

Jim and Ann Henderson series
Peel, Hazel Mary
see **Ann and Jim Henderson series**

Jim and Geoff Harrington series
Thorn, Ismay
see **Geoff and Jim Harrington series**

Jim and Jam series
Littler, Angela
1 *Jim and Jam and the band* (1985)
2 *Jim and Jam at the beach* (1985)
3 *Jim and Jam and the builders* (1985)
4 *Jim and Jam have a party* (1985)

Jim and Kate Harris series
Macrae, Travis
1 *Death in view* (1960)
2 *Twenty per cent* (1961)
Multiple murder

Jim and Ticktock series
Robertson, Keith
see **Ticktock and Jim series**

Jim Bannerman series
Flynn, Jay
1 *Bannerman* (1976)
2 *Border incident* (1976)

Jim Bannister series
Newton, Dwight Bennett
1 *On the dodge* (1962)
2 *Savage hills* (1964)
3 *Bullets in the wind* (1964)
4 *Manhunters* (1966)
5 *Hideout valley* (1967)
6 *Wolf pack* (1968)
7 *Judas horse* (1969)
8 *Syndicate gun* (1972)
9 *Range tramp* (1973)
10 *Bounty on Bannister* (1975)
11 *Broken spur* (1977)

Jim Bennett series
Martin, Robert Lee
1 *Dark dream* (1951)
2 *Sleep, my love* (1952)
3 *Tears for the bride* (1954)
4 *Widow and the web* (1954)
5 *Echoing shore* (1955)
Tough die hard
6 *Just a corpse at twilight* (1955)
7 *Catch a killer* (1956)
8 *Hand-picked for murder* (1957)
9 *Killer among us* (1958)
10 *Key to the morgue* (1958)
11 *To have and to kill* (1960)
12 *She, me and murder* (1962)
13 *Coffin for two* (1962)
14 *Bargain for death* (1964)

Jim Beverley series
Marsden, Antony
1 *Man in the sandhills* (1927)
2 *Moonstone mystery* (1928)

Jim Bliss series
Booth, Christopher B
1 *Seaside mystery* (1925)
2 *Killing jazz* (1928)

Jim Brady series
Macdonnell, James Edmond
1 *Jim Brady, leading seaman* (1954)
2 *Commander Brady* (1956)
3 *Subsmash!* (1960)
4 *Close and investigate* (1965)
5 *Petty Officer Brady* (1968)
6 *Mission hopeless* (1968)

Jim Breen series
Karney, Jack
1 *Knave of Diamonds* (1959)
2 *Layout for murder* (1960)

Jim Burgess series
Franklin, Charles
see **Inspector Jim Burgess series**

Jim Burnett series
Lambourne, John
1 *Kingdom that was* (1931)
2 *Second leopard* (1932)

Jim Chee series
Hillerman, Tony
see **Sergeant Jim Chee series**

Jim Clancy series
Cody, Stetson
see **Cactus Clancy series**

Jim Cord series
Rountree, Owen
1 *Cord* (1982)
2 *Nevada war* (1982)
3 *Black Hills duel* (1983)
4 *Gunman winter* (1983)
5 *Hunt the man down* (1984)
6 *King of Colorado* (1984)
7 *Gunsmoke River* (1985)
8 *Paradise Valley* (1986)
9 *Brimstone Basin* (1986)

Jim Di Griz series
Harrison, Harry
1 *Stainless steel rat* (1961)
2 *Stainless steel rat's revenge* (1970)
3 *Stainless steel rat saves the world* (1973)
Numbers 1-3 also published in one volume entitled *The adventures of the stainless steel rat*, 1977
4 *Stainless steel rat wants you* (1978)
5 *Stainless steel rat for president* (1982)
6 *Stainless steel rat is born* (1985)
7 *Stainless steel rat gets drafted* (1987)
8 *Stainless steel visions* (1993)
9 *Stainless steel rat sings the blues* (1994)
Companion volume: *You can be the stainless steel rat, an interacive game book*, 1985

Jim Dunlap series
Palmer, Bernard
This sequence has some volumes which are revised from volumes in the **Pat Collins series** and some new volumes
1 *Jim Dunlap and the strange Doctor Brockton* (1967)
Revised edition of *Pat Collins and the peculiar Doctor Brockton*, 1957
2 *Jim Dunlap and the secret rocket formula* (1967)
Revised edition of *Pat Collins and the secret engine*, 1957
3 *Jim Dunlap and the wingless plane* (1968)
Revised edition of *Pat Collins and the wingless plane*, 1957
4 *Jim Dunlap and the mysterious orbiting rocket* (1968)
Revised edition of *Pat Collins and the mysterious orbiting rocket*, 1958
5 *Jim Dunlap and the long lunar walk* (1974)
6 *Jim Dunlap and the mysterious spy* (1974)

Jim Dunn series
Nelson, Hugh Lawrence
1 *Ring the bell at zero* (1949)
2 *Murder comes high* (1950)
3 *Gold in every grave* (1951)
4 *Season for murder* (1952)
5 *Sleep is deep* (1952)
6 *Kill with care* (1953)
7 *Fence* (1953)
8 *Suspect* (1954)

Jim Eden series
Pohl, Frederik
1 *Undersea quest* (1954)
2 *Undersea fleet* (1956)
3 *Undersea city* (1958)

Jim Fanshaw and Freddie Browne series
Poole, Michael
see **Freddie Browne and Jim Fanshaw series**

Jim Godfrey series
Stevenson, Burton Egbert
1 *Holladay case* (1903)
2 *Marathon mystery* (1904)
3 *That affair at Elizabeth* (1907)
4 *Mystery of the Boule cabinet* (1912)
5 *Gloved hand* (1912)
6 *House next door* (1932)

Jim Hale series
Knotts, Raymond
1 *And the deep blue sea* (1944)
Also published under the pseudonym Gordon Volk
2 *Meeting by moonlight* (1946)

Jim Hanvey series
Cohen, Octavus Roy
1 *Jim Hanvey, detective* (1923)
Short stories
2 *May Day mystery* (1929)
3 *Backstage mystery* (1930)
Curtain at eight
4 *Star of earth* (1932)
5 *Scrambled yeggs* (1934)
Short stories
One story featuring Hanvey in *Detours*, 1927

Jim Hardman series
Dennis, Ralph
1 *Atlanta deathwatch* (1974)
2 *Charleston knife's back in town* (1974)
3 *Golden girl and all* (1974)
4 *Pimp for the dead* (1974)
5 *Down among the jocks* (1974)
6 *Murder's not an odd job* (1974)
7 *Working for the man* (1974)
8 *Deadly cotton heart* (1976)
9 *One-dollar rip-off* (1977)
10 *Hump's first case* (1977)
11 *Last of the Armageddon wars* (1977)
12 *Buy back blues* (1977)

Jim Hatfield series
Cole, Jackson
This pseudonym is used by several authors including Oscar Schisgall and Leslie Scott whose authorship is indicated against those titles where it is known
1 *Black gold* (1935)
[Schisgall]
2 *Lone Star silver* (1939)
[Scott]
3 *Outlawed* (1939)
[Scott]
4 *Lone Star law* (1939)
[Scott]; based on a story entitled *Lone Star brand*
5 *Lone Star legion* (1940)
[Schisgall]
6 *Lone Star terror* (1940)
[Schisgall]
7 *Riders of the Rimrock Trail* (1942)
Smoke against the sky
8 *Lone Star treasure* (1944)
9 *Guns of Mist River* (1950)
[Scott]
10 *Texas fury* (1951)
[Scott]
11 *Thunder Range* (1952)
[Scott]
12 *Border hell* (1952)
[Scott]
13 *Death raiders* (1952)
[Scott]
14 *Trigger law* (1952)
15 *Empire trail* (1952)
[Scott]
16 *Massacre Canyon* (1953)
[Scott]
17 *Killer country* (1953)
[Scott]
18 *Gun-runners* (1953)
[Scott]
19 *Land grab* (1953)
[Scott]
20 *Texas tornado* (1954)
[Scott]
21 *Guntown* (1954)
22 *Bullets high* (1954)
23 *Texas manhunt* (1955)
24 *Gunsmoke trail* (1955)
25 *Trouble shooter* (1955)
26 *Gun-blaze* (1955)
[Scott]
27 *Two-gun devil* (1955)
From number 28 the titles are reprints from *Texas Rangers magazine* from 1938 to the 1950s
28 *Tombstone Trail* (1967)
29 *Kiowa killer* (1955)
30 *Vanishing Vaqueros* (1955)
31 *Brand of the lawless* (1968)
32 *Frontier legion* (1968)
33 *Gun harvest* (1968)
34 *Guns of El Gato* (1968)
35 *Hell-benders* (1968)
36 *Range of No Return* (1968)
37 *Texas trigger* (1968)
38 *Outlaw empire* (1968)
39 *Badman's revenge* (1969)
40 *Drygulchers* (1969)
41 *Fast draw* (1969)
42 *Bullets on the border* (1969)
43 *Gunslinger's range* (1969)
44 *Guns of vengeance* (1969)
45 *Red River showdown* (1969)
46 *Six-gun fury* (1969)
47 *Trouble on Trinity Range* (1969)
48 *Trail Town guns* (1969)
49 *Outlaws of the Big Bend* (1969)
50 *Badmen of Bordertown* (1970)
51 *Black hat riders* (1970)
52 *Dead Man's Canyon* (1970)
53 *Free range* (1970)
54 *Outlaw Valley* (1970)
55 *Two guns for Texas* (1970)
56 *West of the Pecos* (1970)
57 *Six-gun syndicate* (1970)
58 *Six-gun hills* (1970)
59 *Texas showdown* (1970)
60 *Gunfire land* (1971)
61 *Gun-down on the Rio* (1971)
62 *Hell in paradise* (1971)
63 *Outlaw hell* (1971)
64 *Pecos poison* (1971)
65 *Shootout trail* (1971)
66 *Trouble Range* (1971)
67 *Power of the range* (1971)
68 *Six-gun country* (1972)
69 *Riders of the shadows* (1972)
70 *Red runs of the Rio* (1972)
71 *Red marauders* (1972)
72 *Panhandle bandits* (1972)
73 *Mesquite marauders* (1972)
74 *Lone Star peril* (1972)
75 *Death rides the Rio* (1972)
76 *Guns across the Pecos* (1972)
77 *Brass circle* (1973)
78 *Gunsmoke empire* (1973)
79 *Riders of the mesquite trail* (1973)
80 *Vaquero guns* (1973)
81 *Peril rides the Pecos* (1973)
82 *Riders* (1974)
83 *Lobo legion* (1974)
84 *Bayou guns* (1974)
85 *Death rides the Star Route* (1974)
86 *Dinero of doom* (1975)
87 *Guns of Fort Griffin* (1975)
88 *Lobo colonel* (1975)
89 *Lost River loot* (1975)
90 *Skeleton riders* (1975)
91 *Tin-star target* (1975)
92 *Land pirates* (1976)
93 *Bugles on the Bighorn* (1976)
94 *Crown for Azora* (1976)
95 *On to Cheyenne* (1976)
96 *Passport to Perdition* (1976)
97 *Raiders of the valley* (1976)
98 *Santa Fe Trail* (1976)
99 *Trail of the iron horse* (1976)
100 *Gun fight at Deep River* (1977)
101 *White gold of Texas* (1977)

Jim Hayfield series
Repp, Ed Earl
1 *Colt courier of the Rio* (1952)
2 *Desperado* (1954)

Jim Hedgehog series
Hoban, Russell
1 *Jim Hedgehog and the lonesome tower* (1990)
2 *Jim Hedgehog's supernatural Christmas* (1992)

Jim Jackson series
Palmer, Frank
1 *Testimony* (1992)
2 *Unfit to plead* (1992)
3 *Bent grasses* (1993)
4 *Blood brother* (1993)

Jim, Jane and Gappy series
Beresford, Elisabeth
see **Gappy, Jim and Jane series**

Jim Lacy series
Grey, Zane
see **Nevada Jim Lacy series**

Jim Larkin series
Russell, Martin
1 *Deadline* (1971)
2 *Concrete evidence* (1972)
3 *Crime wave* (1974)
4 *Phantom holiday* (1974)
5 *Murder by the mile* (1975)

Jim Little series
Parker, Maude
1 *Which Mrs Torr?* (1951)
2 *Intriguer* (1952)
Blood will tell
3 *Murder in Jackson Hole* (1955)
Final crossroads

Jim Maitland series
Daniel, Roland
1 *Z case* (1947)
2 *Man who sold secrets* (1948)

Jim Maitland series
Sapper
American editions of these titles published under the author's real name, Herman Cyril McNeile
1 *Jim Maitland* (1923)
Short stories
2 *Island of terror* (1931)
Guardians of the treasure

Jim Malone series
Jacobs, Thomas Curtis Hicks
1 *Let him stay dead* (1961)
2 *Red net* (1962)

Jim Mason series
Gregor, Elmer Russell
1 *Jim Mason, backwoodsman* (1923)
2 *Jim Mason, scout* (1923)
3 *Captain Jim Mason* (1924)
4 *Mason and his rangers* (1926)
5 *Three wilderness scouts* (1930)

Jim O'Neill series
Disney, Doris Miles
1 *Compound for death* (1943)
2 *Murder on a tangent* (1945)
3 *Appointment at nine* (1947)
4 *Fire at will* (1950)
5 *Last straw* (1954)
Driven to kill

Jim Piron series
McGirr, Edmund
1 *Funeral was in Spain* (1966)
2 *Here lies my wife* (1967)
3 *Hearse with horses* (1967)
4 *Lead-lined coffin* (1968)
5 *Entry of death* (1969)
6 *Death pays the wages* (1970)
7 *No better fiend* (1971)
8 *Bardel's murder* (1973)
9 *Murderous journey* (1974)

Jim Qwilleran series
Braun, Lilian Jackson
1 *Cat who could read backwards* (1966)
2 *Cat who ate Danish modern* (1967)
3 *Cat who turned on and off* (1968)
4 *Cat who saw red* (1986)
5 *Cat who played Brahms* (1987)
6 *Cat who played Post Office* (1987)
7 *Cat who knew Shakespeare* (1988)
8 *Cat who sniffed glue* (1988)
9 *Cat who had fourteen tales* (1988)
Short stories
10 *Cat who went underground* (1989)
11 *Cat who talked to ghosts* (1990)
12 *Cat who lived high* (1990)
13 *Cat who knew a cradinal* (1991)
14 *Cat who moved a mountain* (1992)
15 *Cat who wasn't there* (1992)
16 *Cat who went into the closet* (1993)
17 *Cat who came to breakfast* (1994)

Jim Raine and Bob Wincourt series
Hodge, Charles
1 *Raven's causeway* (1946)
2 *House of the winds* (1948)

Jim Rainey series
McCurtin, Peter
1 *Massacre at Umtali* (1976)
2 *Deadliest game* (1976)
3 *Spoils of war* (1976)
4 *Guns of Palembang* (1977)
5 *First blood* (1977)
6 *Ambush at Derati Wells* (1977)
7 *Operation Hong Kong* (1977)
8 *Body count* (1977)
9 *Battle pay* (1978)
10 *Yellow rain* (1984)
11 *Green hell* (1984)
12 *Moro* (1984)
13 *Kalahari* (1984)
14 *Golden triangle* (1984)
15 *Death squad* (1985)
16 *Bloodbath* (1985)
17 *Somali smashout* (1985)
18 *Blood island* (1985)

Jim Rand series
Grover, Marshall
see **Nevada Jim series**

Jim Reardon series
Pike, Robert L
see **Lieutenant Jim Reardon series**

Jim Reno series
Morris, Gilbert
1 *Drifter* (1986)
2 *Deputy* (1986)
3 *Runaway* (1987)
4 *Vigilante* (1987)

Jim Rush series
Grant-Adamson, Lesley
1 *Life of adventure* (1992)
2 *Dangerous games* (1993)

Jim Ryan series
Ernst, Paul
1 *Hangman's hat* (1951)
2 *Bronze mermaid* (1952)

Jim Saddler series
Curry, Gene
1 *Dirty way to die* (1979)
2 *Wildcat woman* (1979)
3 *Colorado crossing* (1979)
4 *Hot as a pistol* (1980)
5 *Wild, wild women* (1980)
6 *Ace in the hole* (1981)
7 *Yukon ride* (1981)

Jim Sader series
Hitchens, Dolores
1 *Sleep with strangers* (1955)
2 *Sleep with slander* (1960)

Jim Sands series
Casey, Robert J
1 *Secret of Thirty-Seven Hardy Street* (1929)
2 *Secret of the bungalow* (1930)
3 *News reel* (1932)
Secret of the dark room
4 *Hot ice* (1933)
5 *Third owl* (1934)

Jim series
Briggs, Raymond
see **Gentleman Jim series**
Conrad, Stephen
see **Mrs Jim series**
McSkimming, Geoffrey
see **Cairo Jim series**
Sillitoe, Alan
see **Marmalade Jim series**

Jim Sheridan series
Torrio, Vincente
see **Hoods series**

Jim Sinclair series
Mann, Edward Beverly
see **Whistler series**

Jim Starling series
Hildick, Edmund Wallace
1 *Jim Starling* (1958)
2 *Jim Starling and the agency* (1958)
3 *Jim Starling's holiday* (1960)
4 *Jim Starling and the Colonel* (1960)
5 *Jim Starling goes to town* (1963)
6 *Jim Starling takes over* (1964)
Revised edition 1971
7 *Jim Starling and the spotted dog* (1964)

Jim Steel series
Cunningham, Chet
Large print editions of these titles are published under the pseudonym Jess Cody
1 *Gold wagon* (1972)
2 *Die of Gold* (1973)
3 *Bloody Gold* (1975)
4 *Devil's Gold* (1980)
5 *Gold train* (1981)
6 *Aztec Gold* (1982)

Jim Steele series
Chambers, Dana
1 *Some day I'll kill you* (1939)
2 *Too like the lightning* (1939)
Too like the dead
3 *She'll be dead by morning* (1940)
4 *Blonde died first* (1941)
5 *Frightened man* (1942)
6 *Last secret* (1943)
7 *Darling this is death* (1945)
8 *Case of Caroline Animus* (1946)
Dear dead woman
9 *Death against Venus* (1946)
10 *Rope for an ape* (1947)

Jim Stevens series
Smith, David
1 *Leo conversion* (1980)
2 *Timbuktu* (1983)

Jim Strang series
Dilnot, George
1 *Secret service man* (1916)
2 *Counter-spy* (1942)

Jim Wade series
Short, Luke
see **Big Jim Wade series**

Jimbo series
Maddocks, Peter
1 *Jimbo and the whale* (1986)
2 *Jimbo and the UFO* (1986)

Jimbo's journeys series
Maddocks, Peter
1 *France* (1987)
2 *Spain* (1987)

Jimgrim series
Mundy, Talbot
1 *Nine unknown* (1924)
2 *Ramsden* (1926)
Devil's guard
3 *Hundred days* (1930)
4 *Woman Ayisha* (1930)
5 *Jimgrim* (1931)
Jimgrim Sahib
6 *Jungle jest* (1931)
7 *Lost trooper* (1931)
8 *Lion of Petra* (1932)
9 *King in check* (1933)
Affair in Araby
10 *Mystery of Khufri's tomb* (1933)
11 *Jimgrim and Allah's peace* (1934)
12 *Seventeen thieves of El-Kalil* (1935)
13 *Thunder Dragon Gate* (1937)
14 *Old ugly face* (1939)

Jiminy series
Daniell, David Scott
1 *By Jiminy* (1962)
2 *Saved by Jiminy* (1963)
3 *By Jiminy ahoy* (1963)
4 *By Jiminy in the jungle* (1964)
5 *By Jiminy in the Highlands* (1966)

Jimmie Dale series
Packard, Frank Lucius
1 *Adventures of Jimmie Dale* (1917)
2 *Further adventures of Jimmie Dale* (1917)
3 *Jimmie Dale and the phantom clue* (1922)
4 *Jimmie Dale and the blue envelope murder* (1930)
5 *Jimmie Dale and the missing hour* (1935)

Jimmie Haswell series
Adams, Herbert
see **Jimmy Haswell series**

Jimmie Jarvis series
Davis, Dorothy Salisbury
see **Mrs Norris and Jasper Tully series**

Jimmie Rezaire series
Armstrong, Anthony
1 *Trail of fear* (1927)
Jimmie Rezaire
2 *Secret trail* (1928)
3 *Trail of the Lotto* (1929)
4 *Trail of the black king* (1931)
5 *Poison trail* (1932)

Jimmy Brent series
Kemp, Harold
see **Inspector James Brent series**

Jimmy Brent series
Roy, Thomas Albert
1 *Curse of the turtle* (1977)
2 *Vengeance of the dolphin* (1980)

Jimmy Brown series
Alden, William Livingston
1 *Adventures of Jimmy Brown* (1885)
2 *Jimmy Brown trying to find Europe* (1889)
Jimmy Brown in Europe

Jimmy Bundobust series
Stanford, John Keith
see **Lieutenant-Colonel James Gore-Bunbury series**

Jimmy Carroll series
McCutcheon, Hugh
1 *Treasure of the sun* (1964)
2 *Black attendant* (1966)
3 *Scorpion's nest* (1967)
4 *Hot wind from hell* (1968)
5 *Something wicked* (1970)
6 *Night watch* (1978)

Jimmy Chester trilogy
De Born, Edith
1 *Disintegrator* (1969)
2 *Fight for Pelignac* (1970)
3 *End of the struggle* (1972)

Jimmy Drover series
Granger, Bill
1 *Drover* (1991)
2 *Drover and the zebras* (1992)
3 *Drover and the designated hitter* (1994)

Jimmy Flannery series
Campbell, Robert Wright
1 *Junkyard dog* (1986)
2 *Six hundred pound gorilla* (1987)
3 *Hip-deep in alligators* (1987)
4 *Thinning the turkey herd* (1988)
5 *Cat's meow* (1988)
6 *Nibbled to death by ducks* (1989)
7 *Gift horse's mouth* (1990)
8 *In a pig's eye* (1991)

Jimmy Grier series
Mitchell, Lane
1 *Boys of the big top* (1952)
2 *Codeword, Bontry* (1953)
3 *Trouble in the big top* (1956)

Jimmy Hastings series
Givens, Charles Garland
1 *Rose petal murders* (1935)
2 *Jig-time murders* (1936)

Jimmy Haswell series
Adams, Herbert
1 *Secret of Bogey House* (1924)
2 *Crooked lip* (1926)
3 *Queen's Gate mystery* (1927)
4 *Empty bed* (1928)
5 *Rogues fall out* (1928)
6 *Golden ape* (1930)
7 *Crime in the Dutch garden* (1930)
8 *Paulton plot* (1931)
9 *Woman in black* (1932)

Jimmy Jenner series
Milne, John
1 *Dead birds* (1986)
2 *Shadow play* (1987)
3 *Daddy's girl* (1988)

Jimmy Lane series
Ryerson, Florence
1 *Seven suspects* (1930)
2 *Fear of fear* (1931)
3 *Blind man's buff* (1933)
Sleep no more
4 *Shadows* (1934)

Jimmy Langry series
Leslie, Francis
1 *Study of death* (1943)
2 *Who keeps the keys?* (1948)

Jimmy Price series
Chichester, John Jay
1 *Bigamist* (1925)
2 *House of the moving room* (1926)

Jimmy Rehm series
Herber, William
1 *King-sized murder* (1954)
Some die slow
2 *Live bait for murder* (1955)

Jimmy Roxton series
Maddock, Reginald Bertram
1 *Rocky and the lions* (1957)
2 *Rocky and the elephant* (1962)

Jimmy series
Crompton, Richmal
1 *Jimmy* (1949)
2 *Jimmy again* (1951)
3 *Jimmy the Third* (1965)

Jimmy series
Morton, John
1 *Jimmy and the giant cleaner* (1971)
2 *Jimmy and the rubber boat* (1971)
3 *Jimmy and the ladder* (1972)
4 *Jimmy and the plant food* (1972)

Jimmy Treynor series
Livingston, Armstrong
1 *Doublecross* (1929)
2 *Monster in the pool* (1929)
3 *Murder trap* (1930)
4 *In cold blood* (1931)
5 *Night of crime* (1938)

Jimmy Waghorn series
Rhode, John
see **Doctor Lancelot Priestley series**

Jimmy Weston series
Warren, James
see **James Weston series**

Jimmy Zest series
McBratney, Sam
1 *Jimmy Zest* (1982)
2 *Zesty* (1984)
3 *Jimmy Zest All-Stars* (1985)

Jimmy's boa series
Noble, Trinka Hakes
1 *Day Jimmy's boa at the washing* (1979)
2 *Jimmy boa's bounces back* (1984)

Jim-Twin Allen series
Dunning, Hal
see **White Wolf series**

Jindi series
Smith, Joan Watson
1 *Jindi, the piccaninny fairy* (1968)
2 *Rosella and the raincloud* (1968)
3 *Mopoke and the necklace* (1968)
Prepublication title: *Jindi and the bunyip*
Companion volume: *Jindi's Australian ABC, a verse and animal picture book*, 1968

Jingalo series
Housman, Laurence
Satires on English life and institutions
1 *King John of Jingalo* (1912)
2 *Royal runaway and Jingalo in revolution* (1914)

Jinian trilogy
Tepper, Sheri S
1 *Jinian Footseer* (1985)
2 *Dervish daughter* (1986)
3 *Jinian Star Eye* (1986)
One volume edition entitled *The end of the game*, 1987

Jinks Gang series
Severy, Richard
1 *Mystery pig* (1983)
2 *Unicorn trap* (1984)
3 *Rat's castle* (1985)
4 *Hi Jinks!* (1986)

Jinnie Friend series
Cawley, Winifred
Set during the General Strike in England in 1926
1 *Silver everywhere* (1976)
2 *Gran at Coalgate* (1974)

Jinny series
Leitch, Patricia
1 *For the love of a horse* (1976)
2 *Devil to ride* (1976)
3 *Summer riders* (1977)
4 *Night of the red horse* (1978)
5 *Gallop to the hills* (1979)
6 *Horse in a million* (1980)
7 *Magic pony* (1982)
8 *Ride like the wind* (1983)
9 *Chestnut gold* (1984)
10 *Jump for the moon* (1985)
11 *Horse of fire* (1986)

Jinx and Wendy series
Hastings, Valerie
see **Wendy and Jinx series**

Jo and Gemma series
Dixon, Rachel
1 *Marshmallow* (1992)
2 *Max and the fire crystals* (1992)

Jo Lacey series
Dart, Dorothy
1 *Jo's search* (1984)
2 *Jo's choice* (1988)

Jo March series
Alcott, Louisa May
1 *Little women* (1868)
Alternative title: Meg, Jo, Beth and Amy
2 *Good wives* (1869)
Little women married
Numbers 1-2 also published in one volume entitled *Little women*, in many editions
3 *Little men* (1871)
Life at Plumfield with Jo's boys
4 *Jo's boys, and how they turned out* (1886)

Jo Salis series
Greener, William Oliver
1 *Exploits of Jo Salis, a British spy* (1905)
2 *Secret agent in Port Arthur* (1905)

Jo series
Hastings, Valerie
1 *Jo and the skiffle group* (1958)
2 *Jo and Coney's Cavern* (1959)
3 *Jo and the limping boy* (1961)

Jo, Zette and Jocko series
Herge
see **Adventures of Jo, Zette and Jocko series**

Joachim and Jacob series
Clevin, Jorgen
see **Jacob and Joachim series**

Joachim series
Baumann, Kurt
1 *Joachim the dustman* (1972)
Original edition entitled *Joachim der Strassenkehrer*
2 *Joachim the policeman* (1973)

Joan and Bill series
Newcomb, Ellsworth
1 *Anchor for her heart* (1947)
2 *Windows on the sea* (1948)
3 *Stars above* (1949)
4 *With this ring* (1951)

Joan Foster series
Colver, Alice Ross
1 *Joan Foster, freshman* (1942)
The story of a girl of today
2 *Joan Foster, sophomore* (1948)
3 *Joan Foster, junior* (1949)
4 *Joan Foster, senior* (1950)
5 *Joan Foster in Europe* (1951)
6 *Joan Foster, bride* (1952)

Joan Marvin series
Eyles, Leonora
see **Doctor Joan Marvin series**

Joan series
Black, Veronica
see **Sister Joan series**

Joan series
Elliot, Emilia
1 *Joan of Juniper Inn* (1907)
2 *Joan's jolly vacation* (1909)
3 *Patricia* (1910)
4 *S.W.F. Club* (1912)
Sequence continued by Caroline Emilia Jacobs, the author's real name, and Lucy Mansfield Mason
Jacobs, Caroline Emilia
5 *Joan's California summer* (1917)

Joan series
Garis, Lilian C
1 *Joan, just girl* (1924)
2 *Joan's garden of adventure* (1924)

Joan series
Hellner, Katarina
see **Emotions series**

Joan Winter series
Bensusan, Samuel Levy
1 *Joan Winter* (1933)
2 *Maurice Dravidoff* (1934)

Joanna Bradley series
White, Constance Mary
see **Saint Mark's Hospital series**

Joanna Brady series
Jance, Judith A
1 *Desert heat* (1993)
2 *Tombstone courage* (1994)

Joanna Godden series
Kaye-Smith, Sheila
1 *Joanna Godden* (1921)
2 *Joanna Godden married, and other stories* (1926)

Joanna series
Boden, Hilda
1 *Joanna's special pony* (1960)
2 *Joanna rides the hills* (1961)

Joanna Stark series
Muller, Marcia
1 *Cavalier in white* (1986)
2 *There hangs the knife* (1988)
3 *Dark star* (1989)

Joanne and Windhawk series
O'Banyon, Constance
1 *Savage desire* (1983)
2 *Savage splendor* (1983)
3 *Savage winter* (1985)
4 *Savage summer* (1986)
5 *Savage spring* (1988)
6 *Savage autumn* (1988)

Joaquin Hawks series
Ballinger, Bill Sanborn
1 *Chinese mask* (1965)
2 *Spy in Bangkok* (1965)
3 *Spy in the jungle* (1965)
4 *Spy at Angkor Wat* (1966)
5 *Spy in the Java Sea* (1966)

Joc and Colette series
Barclay, Vera Charlesworth
1 *Joc, Colette and the animals* (1934)
2 *Joc, Colette and the birds* (1934)
3 *Joc and Colette on the seashore* (1935)
4 *Joc and Colette at the Natural History Museum* (1935)

Jocelyn O'Roarke and Phillip Gerard series
Dentinger, Jane
1 *Murder on cue* (1983)
2 *First hit of the season* (1984)
3 *Death mask* (1988)
4 *Dead pan* (1992)
5 *Queen is dead* (1993)

Jocelyn series
Meyler, Eileen
1 *Gloriet Tower* (1956)
2 *Castle on the rock* (1957)

Jock Carlona series
Petrocelli, Orlando Ralph
see **Giacomo Carlona series**

Jock Patterson series
Walker, Peter Norman
see **Panda One series**

Jock Sergeant series
Da Cruz, Daniel
1 *Double kill* (1973)
2 *Deep kill* (1974)
3 *Sky kill* (1974)
4 *Fire kill* (1976)

Jock series
Taylor, Allan K
see **Uncle Jock series**

Jocko, Jo and Zette series
Herge
see **Adventures of Jo, Zette and Jocko series**

Jodi series
Work, Virginia
1 *Mystery of the missing message* (1980)
2 *Secret of the silver box* (1980)
3 *Curse of the broken feather* (1981)
4 *Mystery at Miser's Mountain* (1982)
5 *Secret of the Alaskan gift* (1983)

Jody and Jake series
Levy, Elizabeth
1 *Case of the frightened rock star* (1980)
2 *Case of the counterfeit race horse* (1980)
3 *Case of the fired-up gang* (1981)
Case of the fire raising gang
4 *Case of the wild river ride* (1981)
5 *Case of the mile high race* (1983)

Jody series
Sharmat, Marjorie Weinman
see **Notice me series**

Joe and Jill series
Cole, Margaret Alice
see **Jill and Joe series**

Joe and Judith Racina series
Keyes, Frances Parkinson
1 *Dinner at Antoine's* (1948)
2 *Royal box* (1954)

Joe and McKee series
Floren, Lee
see **Buckshot McKee and Tortilla Joe series**

Joe and Reynolds series
Martin, Charles Morris
see **Roaming Reynolds and Texas Joe series**

Joe and Timothy series
Edwards, Dorothy
1 *Tales of Joe and Timothy* (1969)
2 *Joe and Timothy together* (1971)

Joe Bain series
Vance, John Holbrook
see **Sheriff Joe Bain series**

Joe Barnaby and Francesca Miles series
Chan, Melissa
see **Inspector Joe Barnaby and Francesca Miles series**

Joe Birney series
Livingston, Jack
1 *Piece of the silence* (1982)
2 *Die again, Macready* (1984)
3 *Nightmare file* (1987)

Joe Blade series
Chisholm, Matt
1 *Indian incident* (1978)
2 *Tucson conspiracy* (1978)
3 *Laredo assignment* (1979)
4 *Pecos manhunt* (1979)
5 *Colorado virgins* (1979)
6 *Mexican proposition* (1979)
7 *Arizona climax* (1980)
8 *Nevada mustang* (1980)
9 *Montana deadlock* (1980)
10 *Cheyenne trap* (1980)
11 *Navaho trail* (1981)
12 *Last act* (1981)

Joe Blaze series
Novak, Robert
1 *Big payoff* (1974)
2 *Thrill killers* (1974)
3 *Concrete cage* (1974)

Joe Bob series
Briggs, Joe Bob
1 *Joe Bob goes to the drive-in* (1987)
2 *Joe Bob goes back to the drive-in* (1990)

Joe Church trilogy
Peters, Lance
see **Detective Sergeant Joe Church trilogy**

Joe Copp series
Pendleton, Don
1 *Copp for hire* (1987)
2 *Copp on fire* (1988)
3 *Copp in deep* (1989)
4 *Copp in the dark* (1990)
5 *Copp on ice* (1991)
6 *Copp in shock* (1992)

Joe Dante series
Newman, Christopher
1 *Midtown South* (1986)
2 *Sixth Precinct* (1987)
3 *Backfire* (1990)
4 *Midtown North* (1991)
5 *Nineteenth Precinct* (1992)
6 *Precinct command* (1993)
7 *Dead end game* (1994)

Joe Darling and Matty Doolin series
Cookson, Catherine
see **Matty Doolin and Joe Darling series**

Joe Delaney series
Archer, Frank
see **Inspector Joseph Delaney series**

Joe Dixon series
Wormser, Richard
see **Sergeant Joe Dixon series**

Joe Dust series
Graaf, Peter
1 *Dust and the curious boy* (1957)
Give the devil his due
2 *Daughter fair* (1958)
3 *Sapphire conference* (1959)

Joe Gall series
Phillips, James Atlee
1 *Pagoda* (1942)
Sequence continued under the pseudonym Philip Atlee
Atlee, Philip
2 *Green wound* (1963)
Green wound contract
3 *Silken baroness* (1966)
Silken baroness contract
4 *Death bird contract* (1966)
5 *Irish beauty contract* (1966)
6 *Paper pistol contract* (1966)
7 *Star ruby contract* (1967)
8 *Skeleton coast contract* (1968)
9 *Rockabye contract* (1968)
10 *Ill wind contract* (1969)
11 *Trembling earth contract* (1969)
12 *Fer-de-lance contract* (1970)
13 *Canadian bomber contract* (1971)
14 *White wolverine contract* (1971)
15 *Judah Lion contract* (1972)
16 *Kiwi contract* (1972)
17 *Shankill Road contract* (1973)
18 *Spice route contract* (1973)
19 *Kowloon contract* (1974)
20 *Underground cities contract* (1974)
21 *Black Venus contract* (1975)
22 *Makassar Strait contract* (1976)
23 *Last domino contract* (1976)

Joe Garton series
Hackforth-Jones, Gilbert
1 *Danger below* (1963)
2 *I am the captain* (1963)

Joe Goodey series
Alverson, Charles
1 *Fighting back* (1973)
2 *Goodey's last stand* (1975)
3 *Not sleeping, just dead* (1977)

Joe Gunther series
Mayor, Archer Huntington
see **Lieutenant Joe Gunther series**

Joe Hawkins series
Allen, Richard
1 *Skinhead* (1970)
2 *Suedehead* (1971)

Joe Hussey series
Dunne, Colin
1 *Retrieval* (1984)
2 *Ratcatcher* (1985)
3 *Hooligan* (1987)

Joe Jackson series
Kinsella, William Patrick
see **Shoeless Joe Jackson series**

Joe Jenkins series
Rosenhayn, Paul
Short stories
1 *Joe Jenkins, detective* (1929)
2 *Joe Jenkins' case book* (1930)

Joe Karns series
DeWeese, Gene
1 *Gates of the universe* (1975)
2 *Now you see it, him, them* (1975)
3 *Charles Fort never mentioned wombats* (1977)

Joe Keller series
Demille, Nelson
1 *Smack man* (1975)
2 *Cannibal* (1975)
3 *Night of the phoenix* (1975)
4 *Death squad* (1975)

Joe Kelly series
Avery, Robert
1 *Murder a day* (1940)
2 *Corpse in Company K* (1942)

Joe Kenmore trilogy
Leinster, Murray
1 *Space platform* (1953)
2 *Space tug* (1953)
3 *City on the moon* (1957)

Joe Lampton series
Braine, John
1 *Room at the top* (1957)
2 *Life at the top* (1962)

Joe Lathom series
Page, Gertrude
1 *Where the strange roads go down* (1913)
2 *Follow after* (1915)

Joe Leaphorn series
Hillerman, Tony
see **Lieutenant Joe Leaphorn series**

Joe Leland series
Thorp, Roderick
1 *Detective* (1966)
2 *Nothing last forever* (1979)

Joe Lunn series
Cooper, William
see **Scenes from life series**

Joe Maguire series
Radford, John P
see **Illusionist series**

Joe Mauser series
Reynolds, Mack
1 *Mercenary from tomorrow* (1968)
2 *Earth war* (1963)
Numbers 1 and 2 also published in one volume entitled *Joe Mauser, mercenary from tomorrow*, edited by Michael A Banks, 1986
3 *Time gladiator* (1966)
Sweet dreams, sweet princes
The second title is a revised edition, edited by Michael A Banks, 1986
4 *Fracas factor* (1978)

Joe Medford series
Starr, Jimmy
1 *Three short biers* (1945)
2 *Heads you lose* (1950)
3 *Corpse came C.O.D.* (1951)

Joe Meehan series
Patchett, Mary Elwyn
see **Joey Meehan series**

Joe Morrison series
Whittingham, Richard
1 *State Street* (1991)
2 *Their kind of town* (1994)

Joe Muller series
This sequence has two authors
Colbron, Grace Isabel
1 *Joe Muller, detective* (1910)
Short stories
Groner, Augusta
2 *Man with the black cord* (1911)
3 *Mene tekel* (1912)
A tale of strange happenings
4 *Lady in blue* (1922)
Co-author: Grace Isabel Colbron
Colbron, Grace Isabel
5 *Club car mystery* (1928)

Joe Petrosino series
Nolan, Frederick
see **Lieutenant Joe Petrosino series**

Joe Puma series
This sequence has two authors
Scott, Roney
1 *Shakedown* (1953)
Gault, William Campbell
2 *End of a call girl* (1958)
Don't call tonight
3 *Night lady* (1958)
4 *Wayward widow* (1959)
5 *Sweet wild wench* (1959)
6 *Million dollar tramp* (1960)
7 *Hundred-dollar girl* (1961)
8 *Cana diversion* (1980)

Joe Quinney series
Vachell, Horace Annesley
1 *Quinneys'* (1914)
2 *Quinney's adventures* (1924)
3 *Joe Quinney's Jodie* (1936)
4 *Quinney's for quality* (1938)

Joe Reddman series
Downing, Warwick
1 *Player* (1974)
2 *Mountains west of town* (1975)
3 *Gambler, the minstrel and the dance hall queen* (1976)

Joe Ryker series
This sequence has two authors
Demille, Nelson
1 *Sniper* (1974)
2 *Hammer of God* (1974)
3 *Terrorists* (1974)
4 *Agent of death* (1974)
Hamill, Edson T
5 *Motive for murder* (1975)
6 *Child killer* (1975)
7 *Sadist* (1975)
8 *Slasher* (1976)

Joe Sanford series
Proud, Franklin M
1 *Golden triangle* (1976)
2 *Walking wind* (1979)

Joe series
Chadwick, Lester
see **Baseball Joe series**
Morgan, Geoffrey
see **Orphan series**

Joe series
Prince, Alison
1 *Joe movs house* (1972)
2 *Joe and the nursery school* (1972)

Joe series
Roberts, Doreen
1 *Joe at the fair* (1972)
2 *Joe's day at the market* (1973)

Joe series
Saunders, Marshall
see **Beautiful Joe series**

Joe Silva series
Oleksiw, Susan
1 *Murder in Mellingham* (1993)
2 *Double take* (1994)

Joe Streeter series
Burke, Jackson Frederick
1 *Kama Sutra tango* (1977)
2 *Crazy woman blues* (1978)

Joe Strong series
Barnum, Vance
1 *Joe Strong, the boy wizard* (1916)
Alternative title: The mysteries of magic exposed
2 *Joe Strong on the trapeze* (1916)
Alternative title: The daring feats of a young circus performer
3 *Joe Strong, the boy fish* (1916)
Alternative title: Marvelous doings in a big tank
4 *Joe Strong on the high wire* (1916)
Alternative title: Motorcycle perils of the air
5 *Joe Strong and his wings of steel* (1916)
Alternative title: A young acrobat in the clouds
6 *Joe Strong and his box of mystery* (1916)
Alternative title: The ten thousand dollar prize trick
7 *Joe Strong, the boy fire-eater* (1916)
Alternative title: The most dangerous performance on record

Joel Saber series
Holt, Gavin
see **Inspector Joel Saber series**

Joey Binns series
Newton, William
1 *Someone has to take the fall* (1979)
2 *Smell of money* (1980)
3 *Set-up* (1981)
4 *Rio contract* (1982)

Joey Meehan series
Patchett, Mary Elwyn
1 *Brumby* (1958)
2 *Comne home, brumby* (1961)
Brumby, come home
3 *Circus brumby* (1962)
4 *Stranger in the herd* (1964)
5 *Brumby foal* (1965)
6 *Long ride* (1970)
7 *Rebel brumby* (1972)

Joey series
Joey
1 *Hit number twenty nine* (1974)
2 *Joey Kills* (1975)
3 *Joey collects* (1980)

Joey series
McGinley, Phyllis
1 *Horse who lived upstairs* (1944)
2 *Horse who had his picture in the paper* (1951)

Joey series
Martin, Robert
1 *Joey of Jasmine Street* (1954)
2 *Joey and the river pirates* (1954)
3 *Joey and the mail robbers* (1955)
4 *Joey and the Blackbird Gang* (1956)
5 *Joey and the helicopter* (1956)
6 *Joey and the magic eye* (1956)
7 *Joey and the square of gold* (1957)
8 *Joey and the city ghosts* (1957)
9 *Joey and the Royalist treasure* (1957)
10 *Joey and the squib* (1957)
11 *Joey, soap box driver* (1958)
12 *Joey and the smugglers' legend* (1958)
13 *Joey and the magic pony* (1958)
14 *Joey and the secret engine* (1960)
15 *Joey and the master plan* (1961)
16 *Joey and the detectives* (1963)
17 *Joey and the magician* (1963)
18 *Joey and the pickpocket* (1964)
19 *Joey and the train robbers* (1965)

Johan and Anna de Villiers series
Muller, Mary
see **Anna and Johan de Villiers series**

Johan series
Sandberg, Inger
Illustrated by Lasse Sandberg
1 *Johan's year* (1965)
Original edition entitled *Johan*
2 *Johan at school* (1969)
Original edition entitled *Johan i 2:an*
3 *[En fin dag foer Johan]* (1981)
No English edition

Johann Faustus series
Faustus, Johann
see **Doctor Johann Faustus series**

Johansson series
Joensson, Reidar
see **Ingemar Johansson series**

Johel series
Oman, Carola
1 *Ferry the Fearless* (1936)
2 *Johel* (1937)

John Abbot series
Whitaker, Beryl
1 *Of mice and murder* (1967)
2 *Matter of blood* (1967)
3 *Chained crocodile* (1967)
4 *Man who wasn't there* (1968)

John Abraham Lincoln series
Dodge, David
1 *Hooligan* (1969)
Hatchetman
2 *Troubleshooter* (1971)

John Adam series
Wood, Christopher
1 *John Adam, samurai* (1971)
2 *John Adam in Eden* (1973)

John Allison series
Meade, Richard
1 *Beyond the Danube* (1967)
Danube runs red
Gun runner
2 *Score of arms* (1969)
Last fraulein

John and Alison series
Daniell, David Scott
see **Alison and John series**

John and Ann Davies series
Styles, Showell
see **Ann and John Davies series**

John and Anne Webb series
Presnell, Frank G
1 *Send another coffin* (1939)
2 *No mourners present* (1940)

John and Betty series
Williamson, Margaret
1 *John and Betty's English history visit* (1910)
2 *John and Betty's Scotch history visit* (1912)
3 *John and Betty's Irish history visit* (1914)

John and friends series
Graham, Bob
1 *Here comes Theo* (1983)
2 *Here comes John* (1983)
3 *Bathtime for John* (1985)
4 *Where is Sarah?* (1985)

John and Hugh series
Iseborg, Harry
1 *John and the big dog* (1962)
Original edition entitled *Jan och den stora hunden*; adapted by Patricia Crampton
2 *John sails his boat* (1963)
Original edition entitled *Jan seglar Bidewind*; adapted by Hanne Barnes
3 *John's day at sea* (1966)
Original edition entitled *Jan och den grona baten*; adapted by Patricia Crampton
4 *John and the red parrot* (1966)
Original edition entitled *Jan och den roda papegojan*; adapted by Patricia Crampton

John and Jennifer series
This sequence has five authors
Denes, Gee
Illustrated by Gee Denes
1 *Jennifer goes to school* (1945)
Higgins, Valerie
2 *John and Jennifer at the zoo* (1946)
Harris, Elsie May
3 *Christmas at Timothy's* (1947)
Desmond, D J
4 *John and Jennifer at the farm* (1948)
Harris, Elsie May
5 *John and Jennifer at the circus* (1949)
6 *John and Jennifer and their pets* (1952)
7 *John and Jennifer go travelling* (1952)
8 *John and Jennifer's treasure hunt* (1953)
9 *John and Jennifer go camping* (1954)
Ritson, Kitty
10 *John and Jennifer's pony club* (1955)
Harris, Elsie May
11 *John and Jennifer go to London* (1956)
Denes, Gee
12 *John and Jennifer go sailing* (1957)
13 *John and Jennifer's concert party* (1958)
14 *John and Jennifer at London Airport* (1959)

John and Lorraine series
Zindel, Paul
see **Pigman series**

John and Mary series
Blyton, Enid
1 *Great big fish* (1966)
2 *How John got his ducklings* (1966)
3 *Dog who would go digging* (1966)
4 *Wheel that ran away* (1967)
5 *Three sailors* (1967)
6 *Kitten that disappeared* (1967)
7 *Little brown bear* (1968)
8 *Tim gets a chance* (1968)
9 *Granny's lovely necklace* (1968)

John and Mary series
James, Grace
1 *John and Mary* (1935)
2 *More about John and Mary* (1936)
3 *John and Mary abroad* (1937)
4 *John and Mary, detectives* (1938)
5 *John and Mary's secret society* (1939)
6 *John and Mary's visitors* (1940)
7 *New friends for John and Mary* (1941)
8 *John and Mary and Miss Rose Brown* (1942)
9 *John and Mary at school* (1944)
10 *John and Mary's youth club* (1945)
11 *John and Mary at Riverton* (1947)
12 *Adventures of John and Mary* (1948)
13 *John and Mary's aunt* (1950)
14 *John and Mary in Rome* (1954)
15 *John and Mary's fairy-tales* (1955)
16 *John and Mary by land and sea* (1956)
17 *John and Mary's Japanese fairy-tales* (1957)
18 *John and Mary and Lisetta* (1958)
19 *John and Mary's treasures* (1960)
20 *John and Mary revisit Rome* (1963)

John and Sally Heldar series
Hamilton, Henrietta
see **Johnny and Sally Heldar series**

John and Sally Strang series
Brinton, Henry
1 *Death to the windward* (1954)
2 *One down and two to slay* (1954)
Two to slay
3 *Now like to die* (1955)
4 *Drug on the market* (1956)
5 *Coppers and gold* (1957)
6 *Ill will* (1957)
7 *Ordinary day* (1959)
Apprentice to fear
8 *Purple-six* (1962)

John and Suzy Marshall series
Fox, James M
1 *Don't try anything funny* (1943)
2 *Journey into danger* (1943)
3 *Hell on the way* (1943)
4 *Cheese from a mousetrap* (1944)
5 *Lady regrets* (1947)
6 *Death commits bigamy* (1948)
7 *Inconvenient bride* (1948)
8 *Gentle hangman* (1950)
9 *Aleutian pink mink* (1951)
Fatal in furs
10 *Iron virgin* (1951)
11 *Shroud for Mr Bundy* (1952)
12 *Scarlet slippers* (1952)
13 *Bright serpent* (1953)
Rites for a killer

John and Wallace Mahoney series
Flannery, Sean
see **Wallace and John Mahoney series**

John Appleby series
Innes, Michael
see **Sir John Appleby series**

John Archer series
Gibbs, Anthony
1 *Here lies tomorrow* (1949)
2 *Daybreak* (1950)

John Barnes series
Ottolengui, Rodrigues
1 *Artist in crime* (1892)
2 *Conflict of evidence* (1893)
3 *Modern wizard* (1894)
4 *Crime of the century* (1896)
5 *Final proof* (1898)
Alternative title: The value of evidence

John Barrin series
Lane, Gret
1 *Curlew Coombe mystery* (1930)
2 *Hotel Cremona mystery* (1932)
3 *Unknown enemy* (1933)
4 *Death visits the summer-house* (1939)
5 *Death in Mermaid Lane* (1940)
6 *Death prowls the cove* (1942)
7 *Guest with the scythe* (1943)

John Bartley series
Dutton, Charles Judson
1 *Underwood mystery* (1921)
2 *Out of the darkness* (1922)
3 *Shadow on the glass* (1923)
4 *House by the road* (1924)
5 *Second bullet* (1925)
Westwood mystery
6 *Crooked cross* (1926)
7 *Flying clues* (1927)
8 *Clutching hand* (1928)

John Barton trilogy
Gibbs, Philip
1 *This nettle, danger* (1939)
2 *Broken pledges* (1939)
3 *Interpreter* (1943)

John Bellamy series
Jacobs, Thomas Curtis Hicks
see **Detective Superintendent John Bellamy series**

John Benedict Holland series
Macdonnell, James Edmond
see **Dutchy Holland series**

John Benham series
Home, Michael
1 *Strange prisoner* (1947)
2 *Amber file* (1953)

John Bent series
Branson, Henry Clay
1 *I'll eat you last* (1941)
I'll kill you last
2 *Pricking thumb* (1942)
3 *Case of the giant killer* (1944)
4 *Fearful passage* (1945)
5 *Last year's blood* (1947)
6 *Leaden bubble* (1949)
7 *Beggar's choice* (1953)

John Blackwood Ryan series
Greeley, Andrew Moran
see **Monsignor John Blackwood Ryan series**

John Boldre series
Ditton, James
1 *Bigger they are* (1973)
2 *You're fairly welcome* (1973)
3 *Escapemanship* (1975)

John Bolt series
Hawkes, Robert
see **NARC series**

John Borham series
Brodie, Gordon
1 *Lady had a tiger* (1968)
2 *Poison of poppies* (1968)
3 *Who called diamonds?* (1970)

John Bragg series
Wade, Henry
1 *Here comes the copper* (1938)
Short stories
2 *Released for death* (1938)

John Breck series
Palmer, Bernard
see **Kid Breckinridge series**

John Brock series
Skirrow, Desmond
1 *It won't get you anywhere* (1966)
2 *I was following this girl* (1967)
3 *I'm trying to give it up* (1968)

John Bryant series
Grayson, Richard
1 *Spiral path* (1955)
2 *Death in melting* (1957)
3 *Madman's whisper* (1958)
4 *Dead so soon* (1960)

John Bunyan series
Brown, Charles
1 *Wonderful journey* (1908)
Talks with young people on *The Pilgrim's progress from this world to that which is to come*, by James Bunyan, 1678
2 *Children on the King's Highway* (1909)
Talks with young people on *The Pilgrim's progress from this world to that which is to come*, part 2, by James Bunyan, 1684
3 *Oldest city in the world, its sieges and battles* (1919)
Addresses to children on *The holy war*, by John Bunyan, 1682

John Burnell series
Vivian, Francis
see **Inspector John Burnell series**

John Byron Hyde series
Wolff, Benjamin
1 *Hyde and seek* (1984)
2 *Hyde in deep cover* (1985)

John Campbell and Clayton Hartung series
Bickham, Jack Miles
1 *Gunman's gamble* (1958)
2 *Feud fury* (1959)
3 *Killer's paradise* (1959)
4 *Useless gun* (1960)
5 *Gunmen can't hide* (1961)
6 *Hangman's territory* (1961)

John Carruthers series
Cox, Edmund Charles
Short stories
1 *John Carruthers, Indian policeman* (1905)
2 *Achievements of John Carruthers* (1911)

John Carter series
Burroughs, Edgar Rice
see **Martian series**

John Case series
White, Valerie
1 *Case* (1954)
2 *Case for treachery* (1955)

John Chadwick series
Cobden, Guy
1 *Murder was my neighbour* (1955)
2 *My guess was murder* (1956)
3 *Murder was their medicine* (1957)
4 *Murder for his money* (1960)
5 *Murder for her birthday* (1960)
6 *Murder inherited* (1961)
7 *I saw murder* (1962)

John Christian Falkenberg series
Pournelle, Jerry
see **Falkenberg's Legion series**

John Christopher series
Rolland, Romain
1 *Dawn and morning* (1910)
Originally published in two volumes entitled *L'autre*, 1904, and *Le matin*, 1904; English titles *Dawn*, and *Morning*
2 *Storm and stress* (1910)
Originally published in two volumes entitled *L'adolescent*, 1905, and, *La revolte*, 1906-07; English titles *Youth*, and, *Revolt*
3 *John Christopher in Paris* (1911)
Originally published in three volumes entitled *La foire sur la place*, 1908, *Antoinette*, 1908, *Dans la maison*, 1909; English titles *The market place*, *Antoinette*, and, *The house*
4 *Journey's end* (1913)
Originally published in three volumes entitled *Les amies*, 1910, *Le buisson ardent*, 1911, *La nouvelle journee*, 1912; English titles *Love and friendship*, *The burning bush*, and, *The new dawn*

John Churchill, Duke of Marlborough series
Kenyon, Frank Wilson
1 *Seeds of time* (1961)
2 *Glory and the dream* (1963)

John Clinton Ryan series
Martin, Larry Jay
1 *El Lazo* (1991)
2 *Against the seventh flag* (1991)
3 *Devil's bounty* (1991)
4 *Benicia belle* (1992)
5 *Rush to destiny* (1992)
6 *Shadow of the grizzly* (1993)

John Cody series
Case, Jim
see **Cody's army series**

John Coffin series
Butler, Gwendoline
see **Inspector John Coffin series**

John Comaday and Larry Cohen series
Cunningham, E V
1 *Penelope* (1965)
2 *Margie* (1966)

John Cooper Baines series
James, Leigh Franklin
1 *Hawk and the Dove* (1980)
2 *Wings of the Hawk* (1981)
3 *Revenge of the Hawk* (1981)
4 *Flight of the Hawk* (1982)
5 *Night of the Hawk* (1983)
6 *Cry of the Hawk* (1984)
7 *Quest of the Hawk* (1985)
8 *Shadow of the Hawk* (1985)

John Craggs and James Castleton series
Alington, Cyril Augustine
see **Archdeacon series**

John Craig series
Munro, James
1 *Man who sold death* (1964)
2 *Die rich, die happy* (1965)
3 *Money that money can't die* (1967)
4 *Innocent bystanders* (1969)

John Crane and Tall Bird trilogy
Gulick, Bill
see **Northwest destiny trilogy**

John Crispin series
Foxall, Raymond
1 *Society of the dispossessed* (1976)
2 *Amorous rogue* (1977)
3 *Noble pirate* (1978)

John Crow series
Lewis, Royston
see **Inspector John Crow series**

John Crown series
Harknett, Terry
see **Superintendent John Crown series**

John Cunningham series
Hammond, Gerald
see **Captain John Cunningham series**

John Daker trilogy
Moorcock, Michael
see **Eternal champion trilogy**

John Davies series
Bennett, Margot
1 *Time to change hats* (1945)
2 *Away went the little fish* (1946)

John Deal series
Standiford, Les
1 *Done Deal* (1993)
2 *Raw Deal* (1994)

John Denson series
Hoyt, Richard
1 *Decoys* (1980)
2 *Thirty for a Harry* (1981)
3 *Siskiyou two-step* (1983)
Siskiyou
The second title is a revised edition
4 *Fish story* (1985)

John Dobbs series
Saxe, R B
1 *Ghost knows his greengages* (1940)
2 *Ghost does a Richard III* (1943)
3 *Ghost pulls the jackpot* (1945)

John Dobie and Kate Coyle series
Cory, Desmond
1 *Strange attractor* (1991)
Catalyst
2 *Mask of Zeus* (1992)
3 *Dobie paradox* (1993)

John Dortmunder series
Westlake, Donald Edwin
see **Dortmunder Gang series**

John Drake series
Baker, William Howard
see **Dangerman series**

John Eagle series
Edwards, Paul
This pseudonym is used by Paul Eiden, Robert Lory and Mannig Lee Stokes as indicated against each title
1 *Needles of death* (1973)
[Stokes]
2 *Brain scavengers* (1973)
[Stokes]
3 *Laughing death* (1973)
[Lory]
4 *Fist of Fatima* (1973)
[Lory]
5 *Valley of vultures* (1973)
[Stokes]
6 *Glyphs of gold* (1974)
[Lory]
7 *Ice goddess* (1974)
[Eiden]
8 *Death devils* (1974)
[Lory]
9 *Deadly cyborgs* (1975)
[Eiden]
10 *Holocaust auction* (1975)
[Lory]
11 *Poppies of death* (1975)
[Eiden]
12 *Green goddess* (1975)
[Stokes]
13 *Operation Weatherkill* (1975)
[Eiden]
14 *Silverskull* (1975)
[Stokes]

John Easy series
Goulart, Ron
1 *If dying was all* (1971)
2 *Too sweet to die* (1972)
3 *Same lie twice* (1973)
4 *One grave too many* (1974)

John Evelyn Thorndyke series
Freeman, Richard Austin
see **Doctor John Evelyn Thorndyke series**

John Everett Millais and Effie Gray series
Lutyens, Mary
see **Effie Gray series**

John Falconbridge series
Somers, Derek
see **Major John Falconbridge series**

John Farrel series
Hitchens, Dolores
1 *End of the line* (1957)
2 *Grudge* (1963)

John Fell series
Kerr, M E
1 *Fell* (1987)
2 *Fell back* (1987)
3 *Fell down* (1991)

John Finnegan series
Forrest, Norman
1 *Death took a publisher* (1936)
2 *Death took a Greek god* (1937)

John Firecloud series
Spencer, Jake
1 *Swamp Master* (1992)
2 *Hell on earth* (1992)

John Flatchley series
McCulley, Johnston
see **Thunderbolt series**

John Fortescue series
Brandon, Charles
1 *Mystery of King's Everard* (1924)
2 *Missing banker* (1927)
3 *Phantom musketeer* (1929)

John Francis Cuddy series
Healy, Jeremiah
1 *Blunt darts* (1984)
2 *Staked goat* (1986)
Tethered goat
3 *So like sleep* (1987)
4 *Swan dive* (1988)
5 *Yesterday's news* (1989)
6 *Right to die* (1991)
7 *Shallow graves* (1992)
8 *Foursome* (1993)
9 *Act of God* (1994)

John Franklin Cornelius Scotter series
Warriner, Thurman
see **Mister Scotter series**

John Freeman series
Ironside, John
see **Detective Inspector John Freeman series**

John Fury series
Austin, Jim
1 *Fury* (1992)
2 *Blood ransom* (1992)

John Gaffney series
Ison, Graham
see **Superintendent John Gaffney series**

John Gail series
Frances, Stephen Daniel
1 *This woman is death* (1965)
2 *To love and yet to die* (1966)
3 *Sad and tender flesh* (1966)
Ambassador's plot
4 *Caress of conquest* (1968)
5 *Hate is for the hunted* (1968)
6 *Sweet shame of fury* (1968)
7 *Cry for my lovely* (1971)

John George Davis series
Ripley, Jack
1 *Davis doesn't live here anymore* (1971)
2 *Pig got up and slowly walked away* (1971)
3 *My word you should have seen us* (1972)
4 *My god, how the money rolls in* (1972)
Sequence continued under the author's real name John Wainwright
Wainwright, John
5 *Devil you don't* (1973)

John George Norman Hyde series
Boland, John
1 *League of Gentlemen* (1958)
2 *Gentlemen reform* (1961)
3 *Gentlemen at large* (1962)

John Godfrey series
Caldwell, Taylor
see **Listener series**

John Gombarov trilogy
Cournos, John
1 *Mask* (1920)
2 *Wall* (1921)
3 *Babel* (1922)

John Gordon series
Hamilton, Edmond
1 *Star Kings* (1949)
Beyond the moon
2 *Return to the stars* (1970)
One volume edition entitled *Chronicles of the Star Kings*, 1986

John Graham series
Lorimer, George Horace
1 *Letters from a self-made merchant to his son* (1902)
2 *Old Gorgon Graham* (1904)

John Grey series
Thurston, Ernest Temple
1 *City of beautiful nonsense* (1909)
2 *World of wonderful reality* (1919)

John Grimes series
Chandler, Arthur Bertram
1 *Rendezvous on a lost world* (1961)
2 *Beyond the Galactic Rim* (1963)
3 *Into the alternate universe* (1964)
Published with *The coils of time* which is not part of the sequence
4 *Road to the Rim* (1967)
5 *Contraband from Otherspace* (1967)
Numbers 1 and 3 also published in one volume, 1979
6 *False fatherhood* (1968)
Spartan planet
7 *Rim gods* (1968)
Short stories
8 *To prime the pump* (1971)
9 *Dark dimensions* (1971)
Short stories; numbers 5 and 7 also published in one volume, 1978
10 *Alternate orbits* (1971)
Commodore at sea
Short stories; numbers 4 and 8 also published in one volume, 1979
11 *Inheritors* (1972)
Published with *The gateway to Never*
12 *Hard way up* (1972)
Short stories; numbers 2 and 10 also published in one volume, 1978
13 *Big black mark* (1975)
14 *Broken cycle* (1975)
15 *Way back* (1976)
16 *Star courier* (1977)
17 *Far traveller* (1977)
Far traveler
18 *To keep the ship* (1978)
19 *Matilda's stepchildren* (1979)
20 *Star loot* (1980)
21 *Anarch lords* (1981)
22 *Up to the sky in ships* (1982)
Short stories
23 *Last Amazon* (1984)
24 *Wild ones* (1985)
25 *Kelly country* (1985)

John Haddon series
Jones, Howard
1 *Beware the hunter* (1961)
2 *Web of Caesar* (1962)

John Hardin series
Teed, Jack Hamilton
see **Gunships series**

John Harland series
Foley, Rae
1 *Hundredth door* (1950)
2 *Ape in velvet* (1951)

John Harley series
Tack, Alfred
1 *Selling's murder* (1946)
2 *Interviewing's killing* (1947)
3 *Prospect's dead* (1948)
4 *Death takes a dive* (1950)

John Harrison series
Berry, Stephen Ames
1 *Biofab war* (1984)
2 *Battle for Terra Two* (1986)
3 *AI war* (1987)
4 *Final assault* (1988)

John Hatherleigh series
Cooper, Charles
1 *Turkish spy* (1932)
2 *Satan's mercy* (1934)

John Hawkwood series
Cole, Hubert
see **Sir John Hawkwood series**

John Hopkins series
Daniel, Roland
1 *Rosario murder case* (1930)
2 *Shooting of Sergius Leroy* (1932)

John Howden series
Mills, Woosnam
see **Sir John Howden series**

John Hunter series
Godwin, Felix
see **Captain John Hunter series**

John Ingram series
Williams, Charles
1 *Aground* (1960)
2 *Dead calm* (1963)
Companion volume: *Man on a leash*, 1973 in which the central character is the son of John Ingram

John Isidore Bloom series
Warman, Erik
see **Inspector John Isidore Bloom series**

John J Shannon series
Adams, Cleve Franklin
1 *Private eye* (1942)
2 *No wings on a cop* (1950)
Co-author: Robert Leslie Bellem

John Jay Jackson series
Lindsay, David T
see **Inspector John Jay Jackson series**

John Jeremy series
Montague, Jeffrey
1 *John Jeremy, cracksman* (1936)
2 *Mandarin's pearl* (1942)

John Jericho series
Pentecost, Hugh
1 *Sniper* (1965)
2 *Hide her from every eye* (1965)
3 *Creeping hours* (1966)
4 *Dead woman of the year* (1967)
5 *Girl with six fingers* (1969)
6 *Plague of violence* (1970)

John Jerome and Return Kingdom series
Braden, James Andrew
1 *Far past the frontier* (1902)
Also published in two volumes entitled *Far past the frontier*, and *Two boy pioneers*
2 *Connecticut boys in the western reserve* (1903)
Also published in two volumes entitled *Connecticut boys in the western reserve*, and *The lone Indian*
3 *Captives three* (1904)
Also published in two volumes entitled *Captives three*, and The cabin in the *clearing*
4 *Trail of the Seneca* (1907)
Also published in two volumes entitled *The trail of the Seneca*, and *In the camp of the Delawares*

John Jolly series
Blyton, Enid
1 *John Jolly at Christmas time* (1942)
2 *John Jolly by the sea* (1943)
3 *John Jolly on the farm* (1943)
4 *John Jolly at the circus* (1945)

John Jorrocks series
Surtees, Robert Smith
see **Mister John Jorrocks series**

John Joseph Lintott series
Stubbs, Jean
see **Inspector John Joseph Lintott series**

John Joseph Malone series
Rice, Craig
1 *Eight faces at three* (1939)
Death at three
2 *Corpse steps out* (1940)
3 *Wrong murder* (1940)
4 *Right murder* (1941)
5 *Trial by fury* (1941)
6 *Big midget murders* (1942)
7 *Having wonderful crime* (1943)
8 *Lucky stiff* (1945)
9 *Fourth postman* (1948)
10 *Knocked for a loop* (1957)
Double frame
11 *My kingdom for a hearse* (1957)
12 *Name is Malone* (1958)
Short stories
13 *People versus Withers and Malone* (1963)
Co-author: Stuart Palmer; short stories
14 *But the doctor died* (1967)
Companion volume: *The pickled poodles*, by Larry Mark Harris, 1960

John Keats series
Gittings, Robert
1 *John Keats, the living year* (1954)
21 September 1818 to 21 September 1819
2 *Mask of Keats* (1956)
A study of problems

John Keith series
Daniels, Norman A
see **Man from A.P.E. series**

John Kent series
Cripps, Arthur Shearly
1 *Martyr's servant* (1915)
1553-1563
2 *Martyr's heir* (1916)
1563-1594

John Kline series
Martin, Philip
Based on a television series
1 *Gangsters* (1977)
2 *Gangsters, number two* (1977)

John Lloyd Branson series
Meredith, Doris R
1 *Murder by impulse* (1988)
2 *Murder by deception* (1989)
3 *Murder by masquerade* (1990)
4 *Murder by reference* (1991)
5 *Murder by sacrilege* (1993)

John Locke series
Barnao, Jack
1 *Hammerlocke* (1987)
2 *Lockestep* (1988)
3 *Timelocke* (1991)

John Locke series
Silliphant, Stirling
1 *Steel tiger* (1983)
2 *Maracaibo* (1985)
3 *Bronze bell* (1985)
4 *Silver star* (1986)

John Macall series
Fairlie, Gerard
see **Johnny Macall series**

John Macinnes series
Finlay, Campbell Kirkman
1 *Fisherman's gold* (1960)
2 *Shepherd's purse* (1961)
3 *Farewell to the Western Isles* (1964)

John Mannering series
Morton, Anthony
see **Baron series**

John Manning series
Dines, Michael
see **Johnny Manning series**

John Marne series
Keenan, William
see **Chief Superintendent Charles Miller series**

John Marsh series
Chance, John Newton
1 *Case of the death computer* (1967)
2 *Case of the fear makers* (1967)
3 *Thug executive* (1967)

John Marshall series
Denning, Mark
1 *Shades of gray* (1976)
2 *Die fast, die happy* (1976)
3 *Beyond the prize* (1978)
4 *Golden lure* (1981)

John Marshall Tanner series
Greenleaf, Stephen
1 *Grave error* (1979)
2 *Death bed* (1980)
3 *State's evidence* (1982)
4 *Fatal obsession* (1983)
5 *Beyond blame* (1986)
6 *Toll call* (1987)
7 *Bookcase* (1991)
8 *Blood type* (1992)
9 *Southern Cross* (1993)
10 *False conception* (1994)

John Martinson series
Clevely, Hugh
1 *Gang Smasher* (1929)
2 *Gang Smasher again* (1938)

John Maxwell Senhouse and Sanchia series
Hewlett, Maurice
see **Sanchia and John Maxwell Senhouse series**

John Melrose series
Mills, Woosnam
1 *Grim Chancery* (1937)
2 *Knaves rampant* (1938)
3 *Dark encounter* (1938)
4 *Biting fortune* (1939)

John Meredith series
Gerard, Francis
see **Sir John Meredith series**

John Milano series
Ellin, Stanley
1 *Star light, star bright* (1979)
2 *Dark fantastic* (1983)

John Milton Schwab series
Wheatley, Dennis
see **Lieutenant John Milton Schwab series**

John Moore series
Logue, John
1 *Follow the leader* (1979)
2 *Replay, murder* (1983)

John Morpurgo trilogy
Garner, William
1 *Think big, think dirty* (1983)
2 *Rats' Alley* (1984)
3 *Zones of silence* (1985)

John Mosby series
Hogan, Ray
1 *Ghost raider* (1960)
2 *Raider's revenge* (1960)
3 *Rebel raid* (1961)
4 *Rebel in Yankee blue* (1962)
5 *Hell to Hallelujah* (1962)
6 *Rebel ghost* (1964)
7 *Night raider* (1964)
8 *Mosby's last raid* (1966)

John Moseby series
Sharp, Alan
1 *Green tree in Gedde* (1965)
2 *Wind shifts* (1967)
Originally announced as a trilogy

John Murphy series
Weinberg, Larry
see **Father John Murphy series**

John Newton Chance series
Chance, John Newton
1 *Screaming fog* (1944)
Death stalks the cobbled square
2 *Red knight* (1945)
3 *Eye in darkness* (1946)
4 *Man in my shoes* (1952)

John Nolan series
Nicolai, Charles
1 *Killer is loose* (1943)
2 *Death at Chestnut Hill* (1955)
3 *Murder in the Fine Arts* (1964)

John Norris series
Elliott, Richard
1 *Sword of Allah* (1984)
2 *Burnt lands* (1985)

John Oldcastle series
Lindsay, Philip
see **Sir John Oldcastle series**

John Patrick Blackheart series
Stuart, Anne
see **Catspaw series**

John Paul Jones series
Brady, Cyrus Townsend
1 *Grip of honor* (1900)
A story of the American Revolution
2 *My lady's slipper* (1905)

John Piper and Quinn series
Carmichael, Harry
Piper and Quinn appear in all titles except numbers 2, 4, 6, 11 which feature Piper only and number 27 which features Quinn only
1 *Death leaves a diary* (1952)
2 *Vanishing trick* (1952)
3 *Deadly nightcap* (1953)
4 *School for murder* (1953)
5 *Why kill Johnnie?* (1954)
6 *Death counts three* (1954)
Screaming rabbit
7 *Money for murder* (1955)
8 *Noose for a lady* (1955)
9 *Dead of the night* (1956)
10 *Justice enough* (1956)
11 *Emergency exit* (1957)
12 *Put out that star* (1957)
Into thin air
13 *James Knowland, deceased* (1958)
14 *Or be he dead* (1958)
15 *Stranglehold* (1959)
Marked man
16 *Seeds of hate* (1960)
17 *Requiem for Charles* (1960)
Late unlamented
18 *Alibi* (1961)
19 *Link* (1962)
20 *Of unsound mind* (1962)
21 *Vendetta* (1963)
22 *Flashback* (1964)
23 *Safe secret* (1964)
24 *Post mortem* (1965)
25 *Suicide clause* (1966)
26 *Murder by proxy* (1967)
27 *Slightly bitter taste* (1968)
28 *Remote control* (1970)
29 *Death trap* (1970)
30 *Quiet woman* (1971)
31 *Most deadly hate* (1971)
32 *Naked to the grave* (1972)
33 *Too late for tears* (1973)
34 *Candles for the dead* (1973)
35 *Motive* (1974)
36 *False evidence* (1976)
37 *Grave for two* (1977)
38 *Life cycle* (1978)

John Prentice series
Sea-Lion
1 *Phantom fleet* (1945)
2 *Sink me the ship* (1946)
3 *Sea of troubles* (1947)
4 *Cargo for crooks* (1948)
5 *When danger threatens* (1949)

John Primrose series
Ford, Leslie
see **Colonel John Primrose series**

John Putnam Thatcher series
Lathen, Emma
1 *Banking on death* (1961)
2 *Place for murder* (1963)
3 *Accounting for murder* (1964)
4 *Murder makes the wheels go round* (1966)
5 *Death shall overcome* (1966)
6 *Murder against the grain* (1967)
7 *Stitch in time* (1968)
8 *Come to dust* (1968)
9 *When in Greece* (1969)
10 *Murder to go* (1969)
11 *Pick up sticks* (1970)
12 *Ashes to ashes* (1971)
13 *Longer the thread* (1971)
14 *Murder without icing* (1972)
15 *Sweet and low* (1974)
16 *By hook or by crook* (1975)
17 *Double, double, oil and trouble* (1978)
18 *Going for the gold* (1981)
19 *Green grow the dollars* (1982)
20 *Something in the air* (1988)
21 *East is east* (1991)
22 *Right on the money* (1993)

John Quickshott series
Church, Richard
1 *Porch* (1937)
2 *Stronghold* (1939)
3 *Room within* (1940)

John Quicksilver series
Daniel, Roland
1 *Quicksilver* (1953)
2 *Great secret* (1958)

John Rambo series
Morrell, David
1 *First blood* (1972)
2 *Blood oath* (1982)
3 *First blood 2* (1985)
4 *Rambo 3* (1988)

John Raven series
Mackenzie, Donald
see **Johnny Raven series**

John Rawlings series
Minahan, John
see **Little John Rawlings series**

John Regan trilogy
Cordell, Alexander
1 *White cockade* (1970)
2 *Witches' Sabbath* (1970)
3 *Healing blade* (1971)

John Reisman series
Nathanson, E M
1 *Dirty dozen* (1965)
2 *Dirty distant war* (1970)

John Rickshaw series
England, Edward Oliver
1 *John the junior reporter* (1953)
2 *Junior reporter's rival* (1956)

John Ringrose series
Phillpotts, Eden
1 *Voice from the dark* (1925)
2 *Marylebone miser* (1926)
Jig-saw

John Ripley series
Gordons
1 *FBI story* (1950)
2 *Case file, FBI* (1953)
3 *Captive* (1957)
4 *Operation terror* (1961)
Experiment in terror
5 *Informant* (1973)

John Ruskin and Effie Gray series
Lutyens, Mary
see **Effie Gray series**

John Rye series
Hogan, Ray
see **Doomsday Marshal series**

John Samson series
Tripp, Miles
1 *Obsession* (1973)
2 *Once a year man* (1977)
3 *Wife-smuggler* (1978)
4 *Cruel victim* (1979)
5 *High heels* (1980)
6 *Going solo* (1981)
7 *One lover too many* (1983)
8 *Some predators are male* (1985)
9 *Death of a man-tamer* (1987)
10 *Frightened wife* (1987)
11 *Cords of vanity* (1989)
12 *Video vengeance* (1990)
13 *Dimension of deceit* (1993)

John Sanders and Harriet Jeffries series
Sale, Medora
see **Inspector John Sanders and Harriet Jeffries series**

John Saumerez series
Dane, Clemence
see **Sir John Saumerez series**

John Savage series
Trevor, James
1 *Savage game* (1967)
2 *Savage height* (1969)

John Scott series
Picard, Sam
1 *Notebooks* (1969)
2 *Man who never was* (1971)
3 *Dead man running* (1971)

John series
Bagdon, Paul
see **Scrapper John series**

John series
Chadwick, Doris
1 *John of the Sirius* (1955)
2 *John of Sydney Cove* (1957)
3 *John and Nanbaroo* (1962)

John series
Hendryx, James Beardsley
see **Black John series**
Warner, Anne
see **Uncle John series**

John Shaft series
Tidyman, Ernest
1 *Shaft* (1970)
2 *Shaft among the Jews* (1972)
3 *Shaft's big score* (1972)
4 *Shaft has a ball* (1973)
5 *Goodbye, Mister Shaft* (1973)
6 *Shaft's carnival of killers* (1974)
7 *Last Shaft* (1975)

John Silence series
Blackwood, Algernon
1 *John Silence, physician extraordinary* (1908)
2 *Day and night stories* (1917)
Tales of the mysterious and macabre

John Slade series
Essex, Richard
1 *Slade of the Yard* (1932)
2 *Slade scores again* (1933)
3 *Lessinger comes back* (1935)
4 *Murder in the bank* (1936)

John Slocum series
Logan, Jake
House pseudonym
1 *Ride, Slocum, ride* (1975)
2 *Hanging justice* (1975)
3 *Slocum and the widow Kate* (1975)
4 *Across the rio Grande* (1975)
5 *Comanche's woman* (1975)
6 *Slocum's gold* (1976)
7 *Bloody trail to Texas* (1976)
8 *North to Dakota* (1976)
9 *Slocum's woman* (1977)
10 *White hell* (1977)
11 *Ride for revenge* (1977)
12 *Outlaw blood* (1977)
13 *Montana showdown* (1977)
14 *See Texas and die* (1977)
15 *Iron mustang* (1978)
16 *Slocum's blood* (1978)
17 *Slocum's fire* (1978)
18 *Slocum's revenge* (1978)
19 *Slocum's hell* (1978)
20 *Slocum's grave* (1978)
21 *Shotgun from hell* (1978)
22 *Dead man's hand* (1979)
23 *Fighting vengeance* (1980)
24 *Slocum's slaughter* (1980)
25 *Rough rider* (1980)
26 *Slocum's rage* (1981)
27 *Hellfire* (1981)
28 *Slocum's code* (1981)
29 *Slocum's raid* (1981)
30 *Slocum's flag* (1981)
31 *Slocum's run* (1981)
32 *Slocum's gamble* (1982)
33 *Slocum's debt* (1982)
34 *Slocum and the mad major* (1982)
35 *Necktie party* (1982)
36 *Canyon bunch* (1982)
37 *Blazing guns* (1982)
38 *Swamp foxes* (1982)
39 *Law comes to Cold Rain* (1982)
Numbers 40 to 49 were allocated to reprints of earlier titles
50 *Slocum's drive* (1983)
51 *Jackson Hole trouble* (1983)
52 *Silver City shootout* (1983)
53 *Slocum and the law* (1983)
54 *Apache sunrise* (1983)
55 *Slocum's justice* (1983)
56 *Nebraska burnout* (1983)
57 *Slocum and the cattle queen* (1983)
58 *Slocum's women* (1983)
59 *Slocum's command* (1983)
60 *Slocum gets even* (1983)
61 *Slocum and the lost Dutchman mine* (1984)
62 *High country holdup* (1984)
63 *Guns of South Pass* (1984)
64 *Slocum and the hatchet men* (1984)
65 *Bandit gold* (1984)
66 *South of the border* (1984)
67 *Dallas madam* (1984)
68 *Texas showdown* (1984)
69 *Slocum in Deadwood* (1984)
70 *Slocum's winning hand* (1984)
71 *Slocum and the gun runners* (1984)
72 *Slocum's pride* (1984)
73 *Slocum's crime* (1984)
74 *Nevada swindle* (1985)
75 *Slocum's good deed* (1985)
76 *Slocum's stampede* (1985)
77 *Gunplay at Hobb's Hole* (1985)
78 *Journey of death* (1985)
79 *Slocum and the avenging gun* (1985)
80 *Slocum rides alone* (1985)
81 *Sunshine Basin war* (1985)
82 *Vigilante justice* (1985)
83 *Jailbreak moon* (1985)
84 *Six-gun bride* (1985)
85 *Mescalero dawn* (1985)
86 *Denver gold* (1986)
87 *Slocum and the Bozeman Trail* (1986)
88 *Slocum and the horse thieves* (1986)
89 *Slocum and the noose of hell* (1986)
90 *Cheyenne bloodbath* (1986)
91 *Blazing express* (1986)
92 *Slocum and the Silver Ranch fight* (1986)
93 *Slocum and the long wagon train* (1986)
94 *Slocum and the deadly feud* (1986)
95 *Slocum and the Indian ghost* (1986)
96 *Rawhide and justice* (1986)
97 *Seven graves to Laredo* (1986)
98 *Slocum and the Arizona cowboys* (1987)
99 *Sixgun cemetery* (1987)
100 *Slocum's deadly game* (1987)
101 *Hell's fury* (1987)
102 *High, wide and deadly* (1987)
103 *Slocum and the wild stallion chase* (1987)
104 *Slocum and the Laredo showdown* (1987)
105 *Slocum and the claim jumpers* (1987)
106 *Slocum and the Cherokee manhunt* (1987)
107 *Sixguns at Silverado* (1987)
108 *Slocum at the El Paso blood feud* (1987)
109 *Slocum and the blood rage* (1988)
110 *Slocum and the Cracker Creek killers* (1988)
111 *Slocum and the Red River renegade* (1988)
112 *Slocum and the gunfighter's greed* (1988)
113 *Sixgun law* (1988)
114 *Slocum and the Arizona kidnappers* (1988)
115 *Slocum and the hanging tree* (1988)
116 *Slocum and the Abilene swindle* (1988)
117 *Blood at the crossing* (1988)
118 *Slocum and the buffalo hunters* (1988)
119 *Slocum and the preacher's daughter* (1988)
120 *Slocum and the gunfighter's return* (1988)
121 *Rawhide breed* (1989)
122 *Gold fever* (1989)
123 *Death trap* (1989)
124 *Slocum and the crooked judge* (1989)
125 *Slocum and the Tong warriors* (1989)
126 *Slocum and the outlaw's trail* (1989)
127 *Slow death* (1989)
128 *Slocum and the Plains massacre* (1989)
129 *Slocum and the Idaho breakout* (1989)
130 *Stalker's moon* (1989)
131 *Mexican silver* (1989)
132 *Slocum's debt* (1989)
133 *Slocum and the cattle war* (1990)
134 *Colorado killers* (1990)
135 *Ride to vengeance* (1990)
136 *Revenge of the gunfighter* (1990)
137 *Texas trail drive* (1990)
138 *Wyoming cattle war* (1990)
139 *Vengeance road* (1990)
140 *Slocum and the town tamer* (1990)
141 *Noose for Slocum* (1990)
142 *Nevada gunner* (1990)
143 *Horse thief war* (1990)
144 *Slocum and the Plains rampage* (1991)
145 *Slocum and the death dealer* (1991)
146 *Desolation Point* (1991)
147 *Slocum and the Apache raiders* (1991)
148 *Slocum's fortune* (1991)
149 *Slocum and the deadwood treasure* (1991)
150 *Slocum and the trail of death* (1991)
151 *Slocum and the stagecoach bandits* (1991)
152 *Slocum and the hanging party* (1991)
153 *Grandville Bank heist* (1991)
154 *Slocum's standoff* (1991)
155 *Slocum and the death council* (1991)
156 *Slocum and the timber king* (1992)
157 *Slocum and the railroad baron* (1992)
158 *Slocum and the river chase* (1992)
159 *Tombstone gold* (1992)
160 *Slocum and the sharpshooter* (1992)
161 *Death's head* (1992)
162 *Silver Town showdown* (1992)
163 *Slocum and the bushwhackers* (1992)
164 *Slocum and the Wyoming frame-up* (1992)
165 *San Angelo shootout* (1992)
166 *Blood fever* (1992)
167 *Helltown trail* (1993)
168 *Sheriff Slocum* (1993)
169 *Virginia City showdown* (1993)
170 *Slocum and the forty thieves* (1993)
171 *Powder River massacre* (1993)
172 *Final draw* (1993)
173 *Slocum and the tin star swindle* (1993)
174 *Slocum and the nightriders* (1993)
175 *Revenge at Devil's Tower* (1993)
176 *Slocum at Outlaw's Haven* (1993)
177 *Ambush at Apache Rocks* (1993)
178 *Hell to midnight* (1993)
179 *Slocum and the buffalo soldiers* (1994)
180 *Slocum and the phantom gold* (1994)
181 *Ghost train* (1994)
182 *Slocum and the invaders* (1994)
183 *Slocum and the mountain of gold* (1994)
184 *Slocum and the cowtown kill* (1994)
185 *Pikes Peak shoot-out* (1994)
186 *Blood trail* (1994)
187 *Slocum and the gold slaves* (1994)

John Smith series
Pentecost, Hugh
see **Doctor John Smith series**

John Smith series
Plum, Mary
1 *Killing of Judge McFarlane* (1930)
2 *Dead man's secret* (1931)
3 *Murder at the hunting club* (1932)
4 *Murder at the World's Fair* (1933)
Broken vase mystery

John Smith series
Sangster, Jimmy
1 *Private I* (1967)
2 *Foreign exchange* (1968)

John Snow series
Sawkins, Raymond
see **Superintendent John Snow series**

John Solomon trilogy
Bedford-Jones, Henry
1 *Solomon's quest* (1924)
2 *Seal of John Solomon* (1924)
3 *Gentleman Solomon* (1925)
Shawl of Solomon

John Spencer series
Smith, Lou
1 *Fear and the dead man* (1968)
2 *Psycho in focus* (1969)
3 *Secret of MI6* (1975)
4 *Primrose, the fourth man* (1976)
Fourth man
5 *Master plot* (1976)

John Stark series
Hedges, Joseph
1 *Funeral rites* (1973)
2 *Arms for oblivion* (1973)
3 *Chinese coffin* (1973)
4 *Gold-plated hearse* (1974)
5 *Rainbow coloured shroud* (1974)
6 *Corpse on ice* (1975)
7 *Mile deep grave* (1975)
8 *Mexican mourning* (1975)
9 *Stainless steel wreath* (1975)
10 *Chauffeur driven pyre* (1976)
11 *Gates of death* (1976)
12 *Angel of destruction* (1977)

John Stone series
Edwards, Josh
1 *Searcher* (1990)
2 *Lynch law* (1990)
3 *Tin badge* (1991)
4 *Warpath* (1991)
5 *Hellfire* (1991)
6 *Devil's brand* (1991)
7 *Stampede* (1992)
8 *Reckless guns* (1992)
9 *Fort Hayes bustout* (1992)
10 *Boom town* (1992)
11 *Bloody Sunday* (1993)
12 *Barbary Coast* (1993)

John Strong series
Acres, Mark
see **Sniper series**

John Stryker series
Barnes, Dallas
see **Sergeant John Stryker series**

John Stubbs series
Campbell, R T
see **Professor John Stubbs series**

John Tarleton series
Van de Water, Frederic Franklin
1 *Still waters* (1929)
2 *Plunder* (1933)

John Taunt series
Murray, William Hutchinson
1 *Five frontiers* (1958)
Appointment in Tibet
2 *Spurs of Troodos* (1960)

John Thunstone trilogy
Wellman, Manly Wade
1 *Lonely vigils* (1981)
2 *What dreams may come* (1983)
3 *School of darkness* (1985)

John Tibbet series
Payne, Laurence
1 *Spy for sale* (1969)
2 *Even my foot's asleep* (1971)

John to James series
Kater, John
Illustrated by Nancy Willard
1 *Letter of John to James* (1981)
2 *Another letter of John to James* (1982)

John Touchwood series
Mackenzie, Compton
1 *Poor relations* (1919)
2 *April fools* (1930)
3 *Buttercups and daisies* (1931)
4 *Water on the brain* (1933)

John Tracy series
Wallace, Trevor
1 *Skyriders* (1937)
2 *Galahad of the air* (1937)
3 *Mystery of D's 24* (1937)
4 *Cargo for death* (1938)

John Trelawney series
Goodchild, George
1 *Q 33* (1933)
2 *Mister Q 33* (1935)
3 *Q 33, spycatcher* (1937)

John Valcourt Justice series
Forrest, Anthony
see **Captain John Valcourt Justice series**

John Walk series
Daniel, Roland
see **Inspector John Walk series**

John Walters series
Sapper
Short stories
1 *Lieutenant and others* (1915)
2 *No man's land* (1917)
3 *Human touch* (1918)
Selection: *John Walters*, 1928

John Walton series
Frost, Kelman Dalgety
see **Captain John Walton series**

John Waltz series
McCormick, Claire
1 *Resume for murder* (1982)
2 *Club Paradis murders* (1983)
3 *Murder in cowboy bronze* (1985)

John Warwick series
McCulley, Johnston
see **Spider series**

John Weatherford series
Grand, Gordon
see **Colonel John Weatherford series**

John Webber and Lizzie Thomas series
Oliver, Anthony
see **Lizzie Thomas and Inspector John Webber series**

John Wentley series
Westerman, John Francis Cyril
1 *John Wentley takes charge* (1938)
2 *John Wentley investigates* (1939)
3 *John Wentley wins through* (1940)

John Yard series
Hayes, Ralph Eugene
1 *Scavenger kill* (1975)
2 *Night of the jackals* (1975)
3 *Taste for blood* (1975)
4 *Track of the beast* (1975)
5 *Deadly prey* (1975)

John Yardley series
Garnett, Roger
1 *Starr Bedford dies* (1937)
2 *Death spoke sweetly* (1946)

Johnnie Ray Rousseau series
Duplechan, Larry
1 *Eight days a week* (1985)
2 *Blackbird* (1986)
3 *Captain Swing* (1993)
Companion volume: *Tangled up in blue*, 1989

Johnny Adrano series
Bradley, Michael
1 *Corsican cross* (1974)
2 *Kill the hack!* (1974)
3 *Swiss shot* (1974)
4 *Blood bargain* (1974)

Johnny Aloha series
Keene, Day
1 *Dead in bed* (1959)
2 *Payola* (1960)

Johnny Amsterdam series
Lawrence, Michael
1 *Naked and alone* (1953)
2 *I like it cool* (1960)

Johnny and Sally Heldar series
Hamilton, Henrietta
1 *Two hundred ghost* (1956)
2 *Death at one blow* (1957)
3 *At night to die* (1959)
4 *Answer in the negative* (1959)

Johnny Anthem series
Reno, James
see **Texas Anthem series**

Johnny April series
Roscoe, Mike
1 *Death is a round black ball* (1952)
2 *Riddle me this* (1952)
3 *Slice of hell* (1954)
4 *One tear for my grave* (1955)
5 *Midnight eye* (1958)

Johnny Black series
Smith, Hendy
1 *Johnny Black, footballer* (1981)
2 *Johnny Black, special agent* (1981)
3 *Johnny Black, show-jumper* (1981)
4 *Johnny Black, pilot* (1981)
5 *Johnny Black, racing driver* (1981)
6 *Johnny Black stops dreaming* (1981)

Johnny Bordelon series
Ogan, George
1 *To kill a judge* (1980)
2 *Murder in the wind* (1980)
3 *Murder by proxy* (1983)

Johnny Buchanan series
McCall, K T
1 *Sweet but deadly* (1956)
2 *Sweet but sinful* (1957)
3 *Shroud for her shame* (1957)
4 *Redhead for free* (1957)
5 *Fatally female* (1957)
6 *Deadly but delectable* (1957)
7 *Lady's a decoy* (1957)
8 *Dance with me deadly* (1957)
9 *Ma'mselle it's murder* (1957)
10 *Velvet vixen* (1957)
11 *Killer orchid* (1957)
12 *Killer in the chorus* (1957)
13 *Tornado in town* (1957)
14 *Playgirl for keeps* (1958)
15 *Mm-mmm-minx* (1958)
16 *Caviar to kill* (1958)
17 *Black lace blackmail* (1958)
18 *Babe up in arms* (1958)
19 *Angel hold fire* (1958)
20 *Dame on the make* (1958)
21 *Million dollar mayhem* (1958)
22 *Stripper strikes out* (1958)

Johnny Canavan series
Arthur, Burt
1 *Texan* (1946)
Also published under the author's real name, Herbert Shappiro
2 *Stirrups in the dust* (1950)
3 *Return of the Texan* (1956)
4 *Gunsmoke in Nevada* (1957)
5 *Walk tall, ride tall* (1963)
Co-author: Budd Arthur
6 *Action at Truxton* (1965)
Co-author: Budd Arthur
7 *Canavan's trail* (1980)
Co-author: Budd Arthur

Johnny Canuck series
Moffatt, James
1 *Blue Line murder* (1965)
2 *Terror-go-round* (1966)

Johnny Christmas trilogy
Blake, Forrester
1 *Johnny Christmas* (1948)
2 *Wilderness passage* (1953)
3 *Franciscan* (1963)

Johnny Church series
Howard, Vechel
1 *Murder with love* (1959)
2 *Murder on her mind* (1959)

Johnny Crow series
Brooke, Leonard Leslie
1 *Johnny Crow's garden* (1903)
2 *Johnny Crow's party* (1907)
3 *Johnny Crow's new garden* (1935)

Johnny Devereaux series
Roeburt, John
1 *Tough cop* (1949)
2 *Hollow man* (1954)

Johnny Dixon series
Bellairs, John
1 *Curse of the blue figurine* (1983)
2 *Mummy, the will and the crypt* (1983)
3 *Spell of the sorcerer's skull* (1984)
4 *Revenge of the wizard's ghost* (1985)
5 *Eyes of the killer robot* (1986)
6 *Trolly to yesterday* (1989)
7 *Chessmen of doom* (1989)
8 *Secret of the underground room* (1990)

Johnny Duvivien series
Spain, Nancy
1 *Poison in play* (1946)
2 *Death before wicket* (1946)
3 *Murder, bless it!* (1948)
4 *Death goes on skis* (1949)
5 *Poison for teacher* (1949)

Johnny Fedora series
Cory, Desmond
1 *Secret ministry* (1951)
Nazi assassins
2 *This traitor, death* (1952)
Gestapo file
3 *Dead man falling* (1953)
Hitler diamonds
4 *Intrigue* (1954)
Trieste
5 *Height of day* (1954)
Dead man alive
6 *High requiem* (1955)
7 *Johnny goes north* (1956)
Swastika hunt
8 *Johnny goes east* (1958)
Mountainhead
9 *Johnny goes west* (1958)
10 *Johnny goes south* (1959)
Overload
11 *Head* (1960)
12 *Undertow* (1962)
Johnny goes under
13 *Hammerhead* (1953)
Shockwave
14 *Feramontov* (1965)
15 *Timelock* (1967)
16 *Sunburst* (1971)

Johnny Fletcher and Sam Cragg series
Gruber, Frank
1 *French key* (1940)
French key mystery
Once over deadly
2 *Laughing fox* (1940)
3 *Hungry dog* (1941)
Hungry dog murders
Die like a dog
4 *Navy colt* (1941)
5 *Talking clock* (1941)
6 *Gift horse* (1942)
7 *Mighty blockhead* (1942)
Corpse moved upstairs
8 *Silver tombstone* (1945)
Silver tombstone mystery
9 *Honest dealer* (1947)
10 *Whispering master* (1947)
11 *Scarlet feather* (1948)
Gamecock murders
12 *Leather duke* (1949)
Job of murder
13 *Limping goose* (1954)
Murder one
14 *Swing low, swing dead* (1964)

Johnny Goodlooks series
Tully, John
1 *Johnny Goodlooks* (1977)
2 *Johnny and the Yank* (1978)

Johnny Havoc series
Jakes, John
1 *Johnny Havoc* (1960)
2 *Johnny Havoc meets Zelda* (1962)
Havoc for sale
3 *Johnny Havoc and the doll who had It* (1963)
Holiday for Havoc
4 *Making it big* (1968)
Johnny Havoc and the siren in red

Johnny Inch series
Straker, John Foster
1 *Sin and Johnny Inch* (1968)
2 *Tight circle* (1970)
3 *Letter for Obi* (1971)
4 *Goat* (1972)

Johnny Jackson series
Rigby, Ray
see **Private Johnny Jackson series**

Johnny Jones series
Stuart-Young, John Morag
1 *Johnny Jones, guttersnipe* (1926)
2 *What does it matter?* (1927)

Johnny Killain series
Marlowe, Dan James
1 *Doorway to death* (1959)
2 *Killer with a key* (1959)
3 *Doom service* (1960)
4 *Fatal frails* (1960)
5 *Shake a crooked town* (1961)

Johnny Lamb series
Donavan, John
see **Sergeant Johnny Lamb series**

Johnny Liddell series
Kane, Frank
1 *About face* (1947)
Death about face
Fatal foursome
2 *Green light for death* (1949)
3 *Slay ride* (1950)
4 *Dead weight* (1951)
5 *Bullet proof* (1951)
6 *Bare trap* (1952)
7 *Poisons unknown* (1953)
8 *Grave danger* (1954)
9 *Red hot ice* (1955)
10 *Real gone guy* (1956)
11 *Living end* (1957)
12 *Trigger mortis* (1958)
13 *Johnny Liddell's morgue* (1956)
Short stories
14 *Time to prey* (1960)
15 *Short bier* (1960)
16 *Mourning after* (1961)
17 *Stacked deck* (1961)
Short stories
18 *Due or die* (1961)
19 *Crime of their life* (1962)
20 *Dead rite* (1962)
21 *Ring-a-ding-ding* (1963)
22 *Johnny come lately* (1963)
23 *Hearse class male* (1963)
24 *Final curtain* (1964)
25 *Barely seen* (1964)
26 *Fatal undertaking* (1964)
27 *Guilt edged frame* (1964)
28 *Two to tangle* (1965)
29 *Esprit de corpse* (1965)
30 *Maid in Paris* (1966)
31 *Margin for terror* (1967)

Johnny Lion series
Hurd, Edith Thatcher
1 *Johnny Lion's book* (1965)
2 *Johnny Lion's bad day* (1970)
3 *Johnny Lion's rubber boots* (1972)

Johnny Logan series
Newton, Dwight Bennett
1 *Massacre Valley* (1973)
2 *Trail of the bear* (1975)
3 *Land grabbers* (1975)

Johnny Macall series
Fairlie, Gerard
1 *Winner take all* (1953)
2 *No sleep for Macall* (1955)
3 *Deadline for Macall* (1956)
4 *Double the bluff* (1957)
5 *Macall gets curious* (1959)
6 *Please kill my cousin* (1961)

Johnny McCoy series
Wolfe, John
1 *Wrong target* (1978)
2 *Drilling for death* (1980)

Johnny Maguire series
Himmel, Richard
1 *I'll find you* (1950)
It's murder, Maguire
2 *I have Gloria Kirby* (1951)
Name's Maguire
3 *Chinese keyhole* (1951)
4 *Two deaths must die* (1954)
5 *Rich and the damned* (1958)

Johnny Malone series
Findley, Ferguson
1 *My old man's badge* (1950)
Killer cop
2 *Waterfront* (1951)
Remember that face!

Johnny Manning series
Dines, Michael
1 *Operation, deadline* (1967)
2 *Operation, to kill a man* (1968)
3 *Operation, kill or be killed* (1969)

Johnny May series
Branscum, Robbie
1 *Johnny May* (1975)
2 *Adventures of Johnny May* (1984)
3 *Johnny May grows up* (1987)

Johnny Morini series
Conroy, Al
1 *Soldato!* (1972)
2 *Death grip!* (1972)
3 *Stranglehold!* (1973)
4 *Murder mission!* (1973)
5 *Blood run!* (1973)

Johnny Nelson series
Mulford, Clarence Edward
1 *Man from Bar-21* (1918)
A story of the cow-country
2 *Johnny Nelson* (1920)
3 *Bar-21 three* (1921)
Hopalong Cassidy sees red
4 *Mesquite Jenkins* (1928)
5 *Hopalong Cassidy and the eagle's brood* (1931)
6 *Mesquite Jenkins, Tumbleweed* (1932)

Johnny Ortiz series
Stern, Richard Martin
1 *Murder in the walls* (1971)
2 *You don't need an enemy* (1971)
3 *Death in the snow* (1973)
4 *Tsunami* (1988)
5 *Tangled murders* (1989)
6 *Missing man* (1990)
7 *Interloper* (1990)

Johnny Perfect series
Noel, Jeffrey
1 *Trouble with guns* (1976)
2 *Trouble with crime* (1976)

Johnny Phelan series
Duff, James P
1 *Some die young* (1956)
2 *Who dies there?* (1956)

Johnny Powers series
Rayter, Joe
1 *Victim was important* (1954)
2 *Asking for trouble* (1955)
3 *Stab in the dark* (1955)

Johnny Preston series
Chester, Peter
1 *Killing comes easy* (1958)
2 *Murder forestalled* (1960)

Johnny Raven series
Mackenzie, Donald
1 *Zaleski's percentage* (1974)
2 *Raven in flight* (1976)
3 *Raven and the ratcatcher* (1977)
4 *Raven and the Kamikaze* (1977)
5 *Rave settles a score* (1978)
6 *Raven feathers his nest* (1979)
Raven after dark
7 *Raven and the paperhangers* (1980)
8 *Raven's revenge* (1982)
9 *Raven's longest night* (1983)
10 *Raven's shadow* (1984)

Johnny Rock series
Rossi, Bruno
see **Sharpshooter series**

Johnny Ross series
Waldo, Dale
1 *Beat the drums slowly* (1961)
2 *No man rides alone* (1965)
3 *Once in the saddle* (1969)

Johnny Saturday series
Goldman, Lawrence Louis
1 *Fall guy for murder* (1943)
2 *Tiger by the tail* (1946)

Johnny Saxon series
Bogart, William
1 *Hell on Friday* (1941)
Murder man
2 *Murder is forgetful* (1944)
3 *Queen City murder case* (1946)

Johnny series
Bisset, Donald
1 *Johnny here and there* (1980)
2 *Johnny and the tin tortoise* (1982)

Johnny series
Martin, Robert
see **Career adventure series**

Johnny Smoker series
Comfort, Mildred Houghton
see **Dustin family series**

Johnny Texas series
Hoff, Carol
1 *Johnny Texas* (1950)
2 *Johnny Texas on the San Antonio road* (1953)

Johnny Vallon series
Cheyney, Peter
1 *You can call it a day* (1949)
Man nobody saw
2 *Lady, behave!* (1950)
Lady, beware!
3 *Dark Bahama* (1950)
I'll bring her back

Johnny Wild and Danny Black series
Carter, Bruce
see **Danny Black and Johnny Wild series**

Johnson and friends series
Patterson, John
1 *Beginnings* (1991)
2 *Battle of the bed* (1992)

Johnson and Jones series
Himes, Chester
see **Grave Digger Jones and Coffin Ed Johnson series**

Johnson and the yacht Dolly series
Dunnett, Dorothy
Numbers 1-5 originally published under the name Dorothy Halliday
1 *Dolly and the singing bird* (1968)
Photogenic soprano
Rum affair
2 *Dolly and the cookie bird* (1970)
Murder in the round
Ibiza surprise
3 *Dolly and the doctor bird* (1971)
Match for a murderer
4 *Dolly and the starry bird* (1973)
Murder in focus
5 *Dolly and the nanny bird* (1976)
Split code
6 *Dolly and the bird of paradise* (1983)
Tropical issue
7 *Moroccan traffic* (1991)

Johnson family trilogy
Chambers, Robert William
see **American Revolution trilogy**

Johnson series
Batchelor, Denzil
see **Inspector Johnson series**
Clifford, James Lowry
see **Samuel Johnson series**
Dewhurst, Eileen
see **Helen Johnson series**
Moore, Frank Frankfort
see **Doctor Samuel Johnson series**
Nelson, Hugh Lawrence
see **Steve Johnson series**
Savage, Buck
see **Speed Johnson series**

Johnson trilogy
De Clements, Barthe
see **Jerry Johnson trilogy**

Johnsons trilogy
Teague, Mark
1 *Trouble with the Johnsons* (1989)
2 *Moog-Moog, space barber* (1990)
3 *Frog medicine* (1991)

Johnstone trilogy series
Stevenson, Dorothy Emily
see **Drumberley trilogy**

Joke Shop series
Fuller, Roy
Poetry
1 *From the Joke Shop* (1975)
2 *Joke Shop annexe* (1975)

Joke shop trilogy
Enright, Dennis Joseph
1 *Joke shop* (1976)
2 *Wild ghost chase* (1978)
3 *Beyond Land's End* (1979)

Jolivet series
Shepherd, Joan
see **Inspector Jolivet series**

Jolland series
Willard, Barbara
see **Mantlemass series**

Jolly postman series
Ahlberg, Janet
1 *Jolly postman* (1986)
Alternative title: Other people's letters
2 *Jolly Christmas postman* (1991)

Jolly Roger series
Leyland, Eric
1 *Jolly Roger, buccaneer* (1954)
2 *Jolly Roger sails again* (1955)

Jolly series
Blyton, Enid
see **John Jolly series**

Jolly super series
Cooper, Jilly
Humorous pieces
1 *Jolly super* (1971)
2 *Jolly super too* (1973)
3 *Jolly superlative* (1975)
4 *Superjilly* (1977)
5 *Supercooper* (1980)
6 *Jolly marsupial* (1982)

Jolson series
Goulart, Ron
see **Ben Jolson series**

Jon and Julie Howard series
Bracken, Anne
1 *Twins take charge* (1946)
2 *Twins to the rescue* (1947)

Jon Halvorsson series
Anckarsvard, Karin
1 *Doctor's boy* (1963)
Original edition entitled *Doktorns pojk*
2 *Struggle at Soltuna* (1966)
Original edition entitled *Svenssons pojk*

Jon Hazard Black and Blaze Braddock series
Johnson, Susan
see **Blaze Braddock and Jon Hazard Black series**

Jon series
Edwin, Maribel
see **Curlew Jon series**

Jon Steel series
Newton, Mike
1 *Ripper* (1978)
2 *Satan ring* (1978)

Jonah Mansel series
Yates, Dornford
1 *Berry and Company* (1921)
Short stories
2 *Jonah and Company* (1922)
Short stories
3 *Blind corner* (1927)
4 *Perishable goods* (1928)
5 *Adele and Company* (1931)
6 *She fell among thieves* (1935)
7 *Gale warning* (1939)
8 *Shoal water* (1940)
9 *Eye for a tooth* (1943)
10 *House that Berry built* (1945)
11 *Red in the morning* (1946)
Were death denied
12 *Cost price* (1949)
Laughing bacchante
13 *Ne'er-do-well* (1954)

Jonas Cord series
Robbins, Harold
1 *Carpetbaggers* (1961)
2 *Raiders* (1995)

Jonas Morck series
Orum, Poul
see **Inspector Jonas Morck series**

Jonas Quarrel and Verity Ames series
Krentz, Jayne Ann
see **Verity Ames and Jonas Quarrel series**

Jonas series
Abbott, Jacob
1 *Jonas a judge* (1832)
2 *Caleb in town* (1833)
3 *Caleb in the country* (1839)
4 *Jonas's stories* (1839)
5 *Jonas on a farm in the summer* (1842)
6 *Jonas on a farm in the winter* (1842)

Jonas series
Wheeler, Anthony George
see **Captain Jonas series**

Jonas Wilde series
York, Andrew
1 *Eliminator* (1966)
2 *Co-ordinator* (1967)
3 *Predator* (1968)
4 *Deviator* (1969)
5 *Dominator* (1969)
6 *Infiltrator* (1971)
7 *Expurgator* (1972)
8 *Captivator* (1973)
9 *Fascinator* (1975)

Jonas Wishet series
Porteous, Crichton
1 *Cottage* (1941)
2 *Sons of the farm* (1948)
3 *Battle mound* (1955)

Jonathan Amory series
Du Soe, Robert C
1 *Boatswain's boy* (1950)
2 *Your orders, sir* (1953)

Jonathan and Felicity series
Cockett, Mary
1 *Jonathan on the farm* (1954)
2 *Jonathan and Felicity* (1955)
3 *Fourteen stories about Jonathan* (1956)
4 *More about Jonathan* (1957)
5 *When Felicity was small* (1959)
6 *Out with Felicity and Jonathan* (1962)

Jonathan Anders series
Nicole, Christopher
The English edition of this sequence is listed separately; it was published under the pseudonym, Andrew York and with different volume titles
1 *Operation destruct* (1969)
2 *Operation manhunt* (1970)
3 *Operation Neptune* (1972)

Jonathan Anders series
York, Andrew
The American edition of this sequence is listed separately; it was published under the author's real name, Christopher Nicole and with different volume titles
1 *Doom fisherman* (1969)
2 *Manhunt for a general* (1970)
3 *Appointment in Kiltone* (1972)

Jonathan Bing series
Blaylock, James Paul
1 *Elfin ship* (1982)
2 *Disappearing dwarf* (1983)
3 *Stone giant* (1989)

Jonathan Black series
Garnett, Roger
see **Chief Inspector Jonathan Black series**

Jonathan Blake series
Chance, John Newton
1 *Affair at Dead End* (1966)
2 *Double death* (1966)
3 *Mask of pursuit* (1967)
4 *Death women* (1967)
5 *Hurricane drift* (1967)
6 *Dead man's shoes* (1968)
7 *Mantrap* (1968)
8 *Death of the wild bird* (1968)
9 *Fate of the lying jade* (1968)
10 *Rogue aunt* (1968)
11 *Halloween murders* (1968)
12 *Involvement in Austria* (1969)
13 *Abel coincidence* (1969)
14 *Killer reaction* (1969)
15 *Killing experiment* (1969)
16 *Ice maidens* (1969)
17 *Mists of treason* (1970)
18 *Mirror train* (1970)
19 *Ring of liars* (1970)
20 *Three masks of death* (1970)
21 *Wreath of bones* (1971)
22 *Cat watchers* (1971)
23 *Faces of a bad girl* (1971)
24 *Man with two heads* (1972)
25 *Last train to Limbo* (1972)
26 *Dead tale-tellers* (1972)
27 *Bad dream of death* (1972)
28 *Farm villains* (1973)
29 *Grab operators* (1973)
30 *Starfish affair* (1974)
31 *Girl in the crime belt* (1974)
32 *Shadow of the killer* (1974)
33 *Canterbury kilgrims* (1974)
34 *Hill fog* (1975)
35 *Devil's Edge* (1975)
36 *Monstrous regiment* (1975)
37 *Murder maker* (1976)
38 *Return to Death Valley* (1976)
39 *Fall-out of thieves* (1976)
40 *Frightened fisherman* (1977)
41 *House of the dead ones* (1977)
42 *Motive for a kill* (1977)
43 *Ducrow folly* (1978)
44 *Drop of hot gold* (1979)
45 *Guilty witnesses* (1979)
46 *Mayhem madchen* (1980)
47 *Reluctant agent* (1988)

Jonathan Craythorne series
Douglas, Arthur
1 *Goods* (1985)
2 *Last rights* (1986)
3 *Very wrong number* (1987)
4 *Worm turns* (1988)

Jonathan Drew series
Ward, Christopher
1 *Strange adventures of Jonathan Drew, a rolling stone* (1932)
His travels through Massachusetts, Connecticut, Rhode Island, New York, Pennsylvania, Virginia, Ohio, Indian, Illinois, Missouri and Kentucky in the years 1821-24, together with some account of the people he met, the things they did and said, the songs they sang and the roads they travelled, as taken down
2 *Yankee rover* (1932)
Jonathan Drew, rover
The adventures of Jonathan Drew during his travels in the South and Far West by road, river and trail in the years 1824-29, together with some account of the people he met, white, black and red, good, bad and indifferent, his friends and enemies and what they did or tried to do, as taken down

Jonathan Gaunt series
Macleod, Robert
American editions published under the pseudonym Noah Webster
1 *Property in Cyprus* (1970)
Flickering death
2 *Killing in Malta* (1972)
3 *Burial in Portugal* (1973)
4 *Witchdance in Bavaria* (1975)
5 *Pay-off in Switzerland* (1977)
6 *Incident in Iceland* (1979)
7 *Problem in Prague* (1981)
8 *Legacy from Tenerife* (1984)
9 *Money mountain* (1987)
Flight from Paris

Jonathan Grimm series
Holmes, Bryan John
see **Reaper series**

Jonathan Hemlock series
Trevanian
1 *Eiger sanction* (1972)
2 *Loo sanction* (1973)

Jonathan Kane series
Barrie, Alexander
1 *Fly for three lives* (1975)
Abridged edition 1977
2 *Operation midnight* (1975)
Abridged edition 1977
3 *Let them all starve* (1976)
Abridged edition 1977
4 *Jonathan Kane's jungle run* (1977)
Jungle run
Second title is an abridged edition
5 *Jonathan Kane climbs high* (1978)
Climbing high
Second title is an abridged edition

Jonathan Knox series
McDowell, Emmett
1 *Stamped for death* (1958)
2 *Bloodline to murder* (1960)
3 *In at the kill* (1960)
Also one novelette featuring Knox in *Three for the gallows*, 1958

Jonathan Lamb series
Foster, Kingsley
1 *Dangerous waters* (1948)
2 *Danger for two* (1949)
3 *Jonathan Lamb, adventurer* (1950)
4 *Jonathan Lamb in peril* (1951)
5 *Jonathan Lamb, detective* (1952)

Jonathan Marks series
Barns, Glenn Miller
1 *Murder is a gamble* (1952)
2 *Murder walks the stairs* (1954)
3 *Murder is insane* (1956)

Jonathan Salt series
Salt, Jonathan
1 *Strange fortune* (1976)
2 *Avenger at large* (1977)

Jonathan series
Verne, Jules
see **Survivors of the Jonathan series**

Jonathan's ghost series
Dicks, Terrance
1 *Jonathan's ghost* (1988)
2 *Spitfire summer* (1989)
3 *Jonathan and the superstar* (1991)

Jones and Bates series
Floren, Lee
see **Judge Lemanuel Bates and Tobacco Jones series**

Jones and Dingle series
Osborne, Geoffrey
see **James Dingle and Glyn Jones series**

Jones and Johnson series
Himes, Chester
see **Grave Digger Jones and Coffin Ed Johnson series**

Jones and Lewis series
Evans, Max
see **Dusty Jones and Wrangler Lewis series**

Jones and Smith series
Crossen, Kendell Foster
see **Jason Jones and Necessary Smith series**

Jones, R.N.V.R. series
Styles, Showell
see **David Jones, R.N.V.R. series**

Jones series
Baynes, Jack
see **Morocco Jones series**
Black, Campbell
see **Indiana Jones series**
Brady, Cyrus Townsend
see **John Paul Jones series**
Castle, Jayne
see **Guinevere Jones series**
Cooper, James Fenimore
see **Paul Jones series**
Cox, William Robert
see **Cemetery Jones series**
Denver, Lee
see **Cheyenne Jones series**
Drake, Stan
see **Juliet Jones series**
Elgin, Suzette Haden
see **Coyote Jones series**
Fielding, Henry
see **Tom Jones series**
Fuller, Timothy
see **Jupiter Jones series**

Jones series
Gibb, Lee
1 *Joneses, how to keep up with them* (1959)
2 *Higher Jones* (1961)

Jones series
Guy, Rosa
see **Imamu Jones series**
Hildick, Edmund Wallace
see **Birdy Jones series**
Jones, Joanna
see **Nurse Jones series**
Kline, Suzy
see **Herbie Jones series**
Langton, Jane
see **Grace Jones series**
Mundy, Max
see **Russell Jones series**
Nickson, Arthur
see **Rusty Himes series**
Patchin, Frank Gee
see **Ted Jones series**
Steirman, Hy
see **Zachary Jones series**
Stokes, Manning Lee
see **Barnabas Jones series**
Stuart-Young, John Morag
see **Johnny Jones series**
Telfair, Richard
see **Wyoming Jones series**
Wayne, Les
see **Arvada Jones series**

Jones trilogy
Madison, Holt
see **Batwing Jones trilogy**

Joneses series
Gibb, Lee
see **Jones series**

Jongor trilogy
Williams, Robert Moore
1 *Jongor of Lost Land* (1970)
2 *Return of Jongor* (1970)
3 *Jongor fights back* (1970)

Jonnesty series
Mantle, Winifred
1 *Jonnesty* (1973)
2 *Jonnesty in winter* (1975)

Jonny Briggs series
Eadington, Joan
1 *Jonny Briggs* (1977)
Golden belt
2 *Jonny Briggs and the ghost* (1978)
3 *Jonny Briggs and the Whitby week-end* (1979)
Numbers 1-3 also published in one volume entitled *The adventures of Jonny Briggs*, 1979
4 *Jonny Briggs and the great razzle dazzle* (1981)
5 *Jonny Briggs and the giant cave* (1982)
6 *Jonny Briggs and the galloping wedding* (1983)
7 *Jonny Briggs and the jubilee concert* (1983)
8 *World of Jonny Briggs* (1985)
9 *Stand up Jonny Briggs* (1986)
10 *Jonny Briggs and the secret sunflowers* (1988)
11 *Jonny Briggs and the silver surprise* (1989)
12 *Well done, Jonny Briggs!* (1991)

Jonny series
Biemiller, Carl Ludwig
1 *Magic ball from Mars* (1953)
2 *Starboy* (1956)

Jonson series
Levi, Peter
see **Ben Jonson series**

Jonty series
Hogg, Garry
1 *Sealed orders* (1948)
2 *Secret of Hollow Hill* (1950)
3 *Norwegian journey* (1951)
4 *Norwegian holiday* (1952)

5 *Riddle of Dooley Castle* (1953)
6 *Granite Men* (1954)
7 *Portuguese journey* (1954)
8 *Bavarian journey* (1958)

Jordache family series
Shaw, Irwin
1 *Rich man, poor man* (1970)
2 *Beggarman, thief* (1977)

Jordan and Horton series
Butler, Leslie
see **Horton and Jordan series**

Jordan family series
Marton, Francesca
1 *Attic and area* (1948)
2 *Mrs Betsey* (1954)
Alternative title: Widowed and wed

Jordan series
Du Bois, William
see **Jack Jordan series**
Foote, Shelby
see **Lake Jordan series**
Garis, Lilian C
see **Judy Jordan series**
Laurenson, Robert Mark
see **Marc Jordan series**
Masur, Harold Q
see **Scott Jordan series**
Post, Mary Brinker
see **Annie Jordan series**
Reed, Harlan
see **Dan Jordan series**

Jordons series
Lambert, Janet
1 *Just Jennifer* (1945)
2 *Friday's child* (1947)
3 *Confusion by Cupid* (1950)
4 *Dream for Susan* (1954)
5 *Love taps gently* (1955)
6 *Song in their hearts* (1956)
7 *Myself and I* (1957)
8 *Stars hang high* (1960)
9 *Wedding bells* (1961)
10 *Bright tomorrow* (1965)
11 *Here's Marny* (1969)

Jorian series
De Camp, Lyon Sprague
1 *Goblin tower* (1968)
2 *Clocks of Iraz* (1970)
3 *Fallible fiend* (1973)
4 *Unbeheaded king* (1983)
Numbers 1, 2 and 4 also published in one volume entitled *The reluctant king*, 1985

Jorj X McKie series
Herbert, Frank
1 *Whipping star* (1970)
Revised edition 1977
2 *Dosadi experiment* (1977)

Jorkens series
Dunsany, Edward John Moreton Drax Plunkett
1 *Travel tales of Mister Joseph Jorkens* (1931)
2 *Mister Jorkens remembers Africa* (1934)
Jorkens remembers Africa
3 *Jorkens has a large whisky* (1940)
4 *Fourth book of Jorkens* (1948)
5 *Jorkens borrows another whisky* (1954)

Jorrocks series
Surtees, Robert Smith
see **Mister John Jorrocks series**

Jory series
Bass, Milton R
1 *Jory* (1969)
2 *Mister Jory* (1976)
3 *Sheriff Jory* (1987)
4 *Gunfighter Jory* (1987)

Jose da Silva series
Fish, Robert Lloyd
see **Captain Jose da Silva series**

Jose Manuel Madero series
Homes, Geoffrey
1 *Street of the crying woman* (1942)
Seven died
Case of the Mexican knife
2 *Hill of the terrified monk* (1943)
Dead as a dummy

Josee and Bernard series
Sagan, Francoise
1 *Those without shadows* (1957)
Original edition entitled *Dans un mois, dans un an*
2 *Wonderful clouds* (1961)
Original edition entitled *Les merveilleux nuages*

Josef Tanaka series
La Plante, Richard
1 *Mantis* (1993)
2 *Leopard* (1994)

Joseph and his brothers series
Mann, Thomas
1 *Tales of Jacob* (1933)
Original edition entitled *Die Geschichten Jaakobs*
2 *Young Joseph* (1934)
Original edition entitled *Der junge Joseph*
3 *Joseph in Egypt* (1936)
Original edition entitled *Joseph in Agypten*
4 *Joseph the provider* (1943)
Original edition entitled *Joseph der Ernahrer*

Joseph Balsamo series
Dumas, Alexandre
see **Memoirs of a physician series**

Joseph Bragg and James Morton series
Harrison, Ray
see **Sergeant Joseph Bragg and Constable James Morton series**

Joseph Bredder series
Holton, Leonard
see **Father Joseph Bredder series**

Joseph Dando series
Clive, William
1 *Dando on Delhi Ridge* (1971)
2 *Dando and the Summer Palace* (1972)
3 *Tunes that they play* (1973)
4 *Dando and the mad emperor* (1974)
5 *Blood of an Englishman* (1975)
A novel of the siege of Cawnpore

Joseph Delaney series
Archer, Frank
see **Inspector Joseph Delaney series**

Joseph Dickerson series
Goldthwaite, Eaton Kenneth
see **Lieutenant Joseph Dickerson series**

Joseph French series
Crofts, Freeman Wills
see **Inspector Joseph French series**

Joseph Jorkens series
Dunsany, Edward John Moreton Drax Plunkett
see **Jorkens series**

Joseph Kerkhoven trilogy
Wassermann, Jakob
see **Doctor Joseph Kerkhoven trilogy**

Joseph Khassan series
Dawson, Alec John
1 *Joseph Khassan, half-caste* (1901)
2 *Hidden manna* (1902)

Joseph Madden series
Santiago, V J
1 *Eye for an eye* (1975)
2 *Detour to a funeral* (1975)
3 *Kill or be killed* (1976)
4 *Knock, knock, you're dead* (1976)
5 *Dead end delivery* (1976)
6 *This gun for justice* (1978)

Joseph Rouletabille series
Leroux, Gaston
1 *Mystery of the yellow room* (1907)
Original edition entitled *Le mystere de la chambre jaune*
2 *Perfume of the lady in black* (1908)
Original edition entitled *Le parfum de la dame en noir*
3 *Secret of the night* (1914)
4 *Slave bangle* (1925)
Phantom clue
5 *Sleuth hound* (1926)
Octopus of Paris
At least four other titles in this sequence have not been translated into English

Joseph Shanley and Sammy Golden series
Webb, Jack
see **Father Joseph Shanley and Sammy Golden series**

Josephina series
Engel, Diana
1 *Josephina, the great collector* (1988)
2 *Josephina hates her name* (1989)

Josephine and Hugo trilogy
Gripe, Maria
see **Hugo and Josephine trilogy**

Josephine and Napoleon series
Chambers, Rosamund Mary
see **Napoleon and Josephine series**

Josephine and Simon Leyton series
Becker, Jillian
see **Simon and Josephine Leyton series**

Josephine series
Cradock, Henry Cowper, *Mrs*
1 *Josephine and her dolls* (1915)
2 *Josephine's happy family* (1916)
3 *Josephine is busy* (1918)
Numbers 1-3 also published in one volume entitled *The big book of Josephine*, 1919
4 *Josephine's birthday* (1919)
5 *Josephine, John and the puppy* (1920)
Numbers 2, 3, 5 also published in one volume entitled *Josephine's dolly book*, 1934
6 *Josephine keeps school* (1925)
Numbers 4-6 also published in one volume entitled *The bonny book of Josephine*, 1926
7 *Josephine goes shopping* (1926)
8 *Josephine's Christmas party* (1927)
9 *Josephine keeps house* (1931)
10 *Josephine's pantomime* (1939)
11 *Josephine goes travelling* (1940)

Josephine series
Mure, Geoffrey
1 *Josephine* (1937)
A fairy thriller
2 *Boots and Josephine* (1939)

Joseph's Landing series
Haldeman, Charles
1 *Sun's attendant* (1963)
2 *Snowman* (1965)

Josephus trilogy
Feuchtwanger, Lion
1 *Josephus* (1932)
Original edition entitled *Der judische Krieg*
2 *Jew of Rome* (1935)
Original edition entitled *Die Sohne*
3 *Josephus and the emperor* (1942)
Day will come
Original edition entitled *Der Tag wird Kommen*

Josey Wales series
Carter, Forrest
1 *Rebel outlaw, Josey Wales* (1973)
Gone to Texas
Outlaw Josey Wales
2 *Vengeance trail of Josey Wales* (1976)
One volume edition entitled *Josey Wales, two Westerns*, 1989

Josh Dekker series
Webb, Alex
1 *Blood run* (1985)
2 *Dekker's demons* (1985)

Josh Krales series
Gould, Heywood
1 *One dead debutante* (1975)
2 *Glitterburn* (1977)

Joshua Bain trilogy
Mackenzie, J Alexander
see **Canaan trilogy**

Joshua Clunk series
Bailey, Henry Christopher
see **Mister Joshua Clunk series**

Joshua Cobb series
Hodges, Margaret
1 *Hatching of Joshua Cobb* (1967)
2 *Making of Joshua Cobb* (1971)
3 *Freewheeling of Joshua Cobb* (1974)

Joshua Creed series
Newton, Mike
see **Lawman series**

Joshua series
Girzone, Joseph Francis
1 *Joshua* (1983)
A parable for today
2 *Joshua and the children* (1988)
3 *Joshua in the Holy Land* (1992)

Joshua Smarles series
Urquhart, Macgregor
see **Chief Inspector Joshua Smarles series**

Joshua T Bates series
Shreve, Susan Richards
1 *Flunking of Joshua T Bates* (1984)
2 *Joshua T Bates in charge* (1992)

Josiah and Samantha Allen series
Holley, Marietta
see **Samantha and Josiah Allen series**

Josiah C Hedges series
Gilman, George G
see **Edge series**

Josie, Click and Bun series
Blyton, Enid
1 *Little tree house* (1940)
Josie, Click and Bun and the little tree house
2 *Further adventures of Josie, Click and Bun* (1941)
3 *Josie, Click and Bun again* (1946)
4 *More about Josie, Click and Bun* (1947)
5 *Welcome Josie, Click and Bun* (1952)

Josie O'Gorman and Mary Louise series
Van Dyne, Edith
see **Mary Louise and Josie O'Gorman series**

Josie Smith series
Nabb, Magdalen
1 *Josie Smith* (1988)
2 *Josie Smith at the seaside* (1989)
3 *Josie Smith at school* (1990)
4 *Josie Smith and Eileen* (1991)
5 *Josie Smith's Christmas* (1992)
6 *Josie Smith in hospital* (1993)

Joslyn series
Westlake, Donald Edwin
see **Sara Joslyn series**

Jossy's Giants series
Waddell, Sid
1 *Jossy's Giants* (1986)
2 *Glipton Romeos* (1987)

Joszef Venesz series
Thwaites, Frederick Joseph
see **Doctor Joszef Venesz series**

Joubert series
Van der Post, Laurens
see **Francois Joubert series**

Journal of an antique dealer series
Bremond d'Ars, Yvonne de
1 *In the heart of Paris* (1959)
Original edition entitled *C'est arrive en plein*
2 *Antique dealer's tale* (1962)
Original edition entitled *Un etrange petit theatre*
3 *Chest with a secret* (1963)
Original edition entitled *Journal d'une antiquaire*
4 *Mysterious chateau* (1963)
Original edition entitled *Le chateau fantasque*

Journal of an artist series
Truitt, Anne
1 *Daybook* (1982)
2 *Turn* (1986)

Journal series
Gide, Andre
Translated from the French
1 *Journals, 1889-1913* (1947)
2 *Journals, 1914-1927* (1948)
3 *Journals, 1928-1939* (1951)
4 *Journals, 1939-1949* (1954)
Original edition entitled *Journal*, published in three volumes, 1939-1950
5 *Secret drama of my life* (1947)
Et nunc manet in te
Original edition entitled *Et nunc manet in te*; the second title is an enlarged edition
6 *Intimate journal* (1951)
Original edition entitled *Journal intime*
7 *So be it* (1952)
Original edition entitled *Ainsi soit-il*
Companion volume *If it die*, originally published as *Si le grain ne meurt*, 1920

Journals of Bartholomew Bandy series
Jack, Donald
1 *Three cheers for me* (1962)
Revised edition 1973
2 *That's me in the middle* (1973)
3 *It's me again* (1975)
4 *Me Bandy, you Cissie* (1979)
5 *Me too* (1983)
6 *This one's on me* (1988)
7 *Me so far* (1989)

Journals of Tom Goane series
Nolan, Christopher
1 *Journal of young rake* (1977)
2 *Journal of a navvy* (1977)
3 *Journal of a prize-fighter* (1977)
4 *Journal of a jailbird* (1978)
5 *Journal of a cavalry officer* (1978)
6 *Journal of a slaver* (1978)

Journey from obscurity trilogy
Owen, Harold
Biography of Wilfred Owen and his family
1 *Childhood* (1963)
2 *Youth* (1964)
3 *War* (1965)

Journey into war series
Donaldson, Margaret
1 *Journey into war* (1979)
2 *Moon's on fire* (1980)

Journey series
Anno, Mitsumasa
see **Anno's journey series**
Messner-Loebs, William
see **Wolverine MacAlister series**
Nash, Jay Robert
see **Jack Journey series**

Journey series
Sutherland, Halliday
1 *Lapland journey* (1938)
2 *Hebridean journey* (1939)
3 *Southward journey* (1942)
4 *Spanish journey* (1948)
5 *Irish journey* (1956)

Journey through history series
Coote, Roger
1 *Prehistoric times* (1989)
2 *Greek and Roman times* (1989)
3 *Moddle Ages* (1989)
4 *Renaissance* (1989)
5 *Georgians and Victorians* (1989)
6 *Modern times* (1989)

Journey to nature series
Mowbray, Jeanie Pearl
1 *Journey to nature* (1901)
2 *Tangled up in Beulah Land* (1902)

Journeyman series
Yates, Elizabeth
1 *Patterns on the wall* (1943)
Journeyman
2 *Hue and cry* (1953)

Journeys of McGill Feighan series
O'Donnell, Kevin
1 *Caverns* (1981)
2 *Reefs* (1981)
3 *Lava* (1982)
4 *Cliffs* (1986)

Journeys series
Coote, Roger
1 *Journey by car* (1989)
2 *Journeys by plane* (1989)
3 *Journey by boat* (1989)
4 *Journey by train* (1989)

Jousse series
Berna, Paul
see **Michael Jousse series**

Joy Payton series
Whitehill, Dorothy
1 *Joy and Gypsy Joe* (1927)
2 *Joy and Pam* (1927)
3 *Joy and her chums* (1928)
4 *Joy and Pam at Brookside* (1929)
5 *Joy and Pam a-sailing* (1930)
6 *Joy and Pam as seniors* (1932)

Joy series
Powys, Littleton Charles
Autobiography
1 *Joy of it* (1937)
2 *Still the joy of it* (1956)

Joy Sparton series
Johnson, Ruth Ingrid
1 *Joy Sparton of Parsonage Hill* (1958)
2 *Joy Sparton and the vacation mixup* (1959)
3 *Joy Sparton and the money mixup* (1960)
4 *Joy Sparton and her problem twin* (1963)

Joyce Payton series
Whitehill, Dorothy
see **Joy Payton series**

Joyce series
Cornell, Louis
see **Michael Joyce series**

Joyce series
Kerry, Lois
1 *Love song for Joyce* (1958)
2 *Promise for Joyce* (1959)

Jozef series
Rooke, Daphne
see **Herman Jozef series**

Juan Llorca series
Ames, Delano
1 *Man in the tricorn hat* (1960)
2 *Man with three Jaguars* (1961)
3 *Man with three chins* (1965)
4 *Man with three passports* (1967)

Juan series
Linklater, Eric
1 *Juan in America* (1931)
2 *Juan in China* (1937)

Jub Freeman series
Treat, Lawrence
1 *V as in victim* (1945)
2 *H as in hunted* (1946)
3 *Q as in quicksand* (1947)
Step into quicksand
4 *T as in trapped* (1947)
5 *F as in flight* (1948)
6 *Over the edge* (1948)
7 *Big shot* (1951)
8 *Weep for a wanton* (1956)
9 *Lady, drop dead* (1960)
10 *P as in police* (1970)
Short stories

Jubal Cade series
Pike, Charles R
This pseudonym is used by Terry Harknett and Angus Wells as indicated against each title
1 *Killing trail* (1974) [Harknett]
2 *Double cross* (1974) [Harknett]
3 *Hungry gun* (1975) [Harknett]
4 *Killer silver* (1975) [Wells]
5 *Vengeance hunt* (1976) [Wells]
6 *Burning man* (1976) [Wells]
7 *Golden dead* (1976) [Wells]
8 *Death wears grey* (1976) [Wells]
9 *Days of blood* (1977) [Wells]
10 *Killing ground* (1977) [Wells]
11 *Brand of vengeance* (1978) [Wells]
12 *Bounty road* (1978) [Wells]
13 *Ashes and blood* (1979) [Wells]
14 *Death pit* (1980) [Wells]
15 *Angel of death* (1980) [Wells]
16 *Mourning is red* (1981) [Wells]
17 *Bloody Christmas* (1981) [Wells]
18 *Time of the damned* (1982) [Wells]
19 *Waiting game* (1982) [Wells]
20 *Spoils of war* (1982) [Wells]
21 *Violent land* (1983) [Wells]
22 *Gallows bait* (1983) [Wells]

Jubal trilogy
Daniels, Norman A
1 *Jubal* (1970)
2 *Slave rebellion* (1970)
3 *Voodoo slave* (1970)

Jubilee is my street
Maynard, Nan
1 *This is my street* (1962)
2 *Crumb for every shadow* (1974)

Jud Blade series
Jackson, Ken
1 *Cutting edge* (1970)
2 *Sticking point* (1971)

Jud Walton series
Elton, Wallace
1 *Killer's heritage* (1955)
2 *Gunman's holiday* (1956)
3 *Dark gunman* (1957)
4 *Gunfighters' Hollow* (1957)
5 *Avenger's trail* (1958)

Judd series
Bruton, Eric
see **City of London Police series**
Goldman, Lawrence Louis
see **Clinton Judd series**

Judge and Dury series
Whitehead, David
1 *Hang 'em all* (1989)
2 *Riding for justice* (1990)
3 *Law of the gun* (1991)

Judge Benjamin series
McInerney, Judith Whitelock
1 *Judge Benjamin, superdog* (1982)
Superdog
2 *Superdog secret* (1983)
3 *Superdog rescue* (1984)
4 *Superdog surprise* (1985)
5 *Superdog gift* (1986)

Judge Clay Torn series
Edwards, Hank
1 *Judge* (1990)
2 *War clouds* (1991)
3 *Gun glory* (1991)
4 *Texas feud* (1991)
5 *Steel justice* (1991)
6 *Lawless land* (1992)
7 *Bad blood* (1992)
8 *River raid* (1992)
9 *Border way* (1993)
10 *Death warrant* (1993)

Judge Deborah Knott series
Maron, Margaret
1 *Bootlegger's daughter* (1992)
2 *Southern discomfort* (1993)
3 *Shooting at loons* (1994)

Judge Dee series
Gulik, Robert van
Based on the 18th century Chinese novel *Dee goong an*, three murder cases solved by Judge Dee, translated by Robert van Gulik, 1949

1 *Chinese maze murders* (1956)
Dutch edition entitled *Labyrint in Lan-Fang*
2 *New Year's Eve in Lan-Fang* (1958)
3 *Chinese bell murders* (1958)
Original edition entitled *Klokken van Kao-Yang*
4 *Chinese gold murders* (1958)
Original edition entitled *Fantoom in Foe-Lai*
5 *Chinese lake murders* (1959)
Original edition entitled *Meer van Mier-Yuan*
6 *Chinese nail murders* (1960)
Original edition entitled *Nagels in Ning-Tsao*
7 *Red pavilion* (1961)
Original edition entitled *Het rode paviljoen*
8 *Judge Dee at work* (1961)
Original edition entitled *Zes zaken voor rechter Tie*
9 *Haunted monastery* (1962)
Original edition entitled *Het spookklooster*; numbers 1 and 9 also published in one volume, 1976
10 *Lacquer screen* (1962)
Original edition entitled *Het Chinese lakscherm*
11 *Emperor's pearl* (1963)
Original edition entitled *De parel van de keizer*
12 *Murder in Canton* (1964)
Original edition entitled *Moord in Canton*
13 *Willow Pattern* (1965)
Dutch edition entitled *Het Wilgenpatroon*
14 *Monkey and the tiger* (1965)
15 *Phantom of the temple* (1966)
Dutch edition entitled *Het spook in de tempel*
16 *Necklace and calabash* (1967)
Original edition entitled *Halssnoer en kalabas*
17 *Poets and murder* (1968)
Fox-magic murders
Original edition entitled *Moord op het Maanfeest*

Judge Ephraim Peck series
Derleth, August
1 *Murder stalks the Wakely family* (1934)
Death stalks the Wakely family
2 *Man on all fours* (1934)
3 *Three who died* (1935)
4 *Sign of fear* (1935)
5 *Sentence deferred* (1939)
6 *Narracong riddle* (1940)
7 *Seven who waited* (1943)
8 *Mischief in the lane* (1944)
9 *No future for Luana* (1945)
10 *Fell purpose* (1953)

Judge Henry Tyson series
Kummer, Frederic Arnold
1 *Scarecrow murders* (1938)
2 *Twisted face* (1938)
Clue of the twisted face

Judge Isaac C Parker and George Maledon series
Gardner, Jerome
see **Hanging Judge series**

Judge Lemanuel Bates and Tobacco Jones series
Floren, Lee
1 *Bonanza at Wishbone* (1946)
2 *Puma pistoleers* (1948)
Also published under the pseudonym Dave Wilson
3 *Double Cross Ranch* (1950)
Also published under the pseudonym Will Watson
4 *Broomtail Basin* (1952)
Originally published under the pseudonym Brett Austin
5 *Guns of Montana* (1952)
Originally published under the pseudonym Brett Austin; sequence continued under the pseudonym Lew Smith
Smith, Lew
6 *Boothill Court* (1954)
7 *Dusty wheels* (1955)
Sequence continued by Lee Floren
Floren, Lee
8 *Guns along the Arrowhead* (1957)
9 *Cow-thief Trail* (1958)
10 *Wyoming showdown* (1970)

Judge Manfred series
Hilliard, Alec Rowley
1 *Justice be damned* (1944)
2 *Outlaw Island* (1947)

Judge Priest series
Cobb, Irwin Shrewsbury
1 *Back home* (1912)
Short stories
2 *Escape of Mister Trimm* (1913)
Short stories
3 *Old Judge Priest* (1916)
Short stories
4 *Snake doctor, and other stories* (1923)
Short stories
5 *Down yonder with Judge Priest* (1932)
Short stories
6 *Faith, hope and charity* (1934)
Short stories
7 *Judge Priest turns detective* (1937)

Judge trilogy
Parry, Edward Abbott
Reminiscences and autobiography
1 *What the judge saw* (1912)
Twenty-five years in Manchester by one who has done it
2 *What the judge thought* (1922)
3 *My own way* (1932)

Judge Van Treece and Henry Harrison Conroy series
Tuttle, Wilbur Coleman
see **Henry Harrison Conroy and Judge Van Treece series**

Judith and Joe Racina series
Keyes, Frances Parkinson
see **Joe and Judith Racina series**

Judith Lee series
Marsh, Richard
Short stories
1 *Judith Lee, some pages from her life* (1912)
2 *Adventures of Judith Lee* (1916)

Judith Norton series
Finlay, Winifred
1 *Cotswold holiday* (1954)
2 *Judith in Hanover* (1955)
3 *Storm over Cheviot* (1955)
4 *Lost silver of Langdon* (1961)
5 *Lost emeralds of Black Howe* (1961)
6 *Castle for four* (1966)

Judith Taverner Worth series
Heyer, Georgette
1 *Regency buck* (1935)
2 *Infamous army* (1937)

Judith the Tinker series
Reid, Meta Mayne
see **Kate and lynn series**

Judy Abbott series
Webster, Jean
1 *Daddy-Long-Legs* (1912)
2 *Dear Enemy* (1915)

Judy and Leland Pefley series
Perdue, Tito
see **Leland and Judy Pefley series**

Judy Bolton series
Sutton, Margaret
1 *Vanishing shadow* (1932)
2 *Haunted attic* (1932)
3 *Invisible chimes* (1932)
4 *Seven strange clues* (1932)
5 *Ghost parade* (1933)
6 *Yellow phantom* (1933)
7 *Mystic ball* (1934)
8 *Voice in the suitcase* (1935)
9 *Mysterious half cat* (1936)
10 *Riddle of the double ring* (1937)
11 *Unfinished house* (1938)
12 *Midnight visitor* (1939)
13 *Name on the bracelet* (1940)
14 *Clue in the patchwork quilt* (1941)
15 *Mark on the mirror* (1942)
16 *Secret of the barred window* (1943)
17 *Rainbow riddle* (1946)
18 *Living portrait* (1947)
19 *Secret of the musical tree* (1948)
20 *Warning on the window* (1949)
21 *Clue of the stone lantern* (1950)
22 *Spirit of Fog Island* (1951)
23 *Black cat's clue* (1952)
24 *Forbidden chest* (1953)
25 *Haunted road* (1954)
26 *Clue in the ruined castle* (1955)
27 *Trail of the green doll* (1956)
28 *Haunted fountain* (1957)
29 *Clue of the broken wing* (1958)
30 *Phantom friend* (1959)
31 *Discovery at the Dragon's Mouth* (1960)
32 *Whispered watchword* (1961)
33 *Secret quest* (1962)
34 *Puzzle in the pond* (1963)
35 *Hidden clue* (1964)
36 *Pledge of the twin knights* (1965)
37 *Search for the glowing hat* (1964)
38 *Secret of the sand castle* (1964)

Judy Hill and Chief Inspector Lloyd series
McGown, Jill
see **Chief Inspector Lloyd and Sergeant Judy Hill series**

Judy Jo series
Hill, Mabel Betsy
1 *Down-along Apple Market Street* (1934)
2 *Summer comes to Apple Market Street* (1937)
3 *Surprise for Judy Jo* (1940)
4 *Jack o' Lantern for Judy Jo* (1940)
5 *Along comes Judy Jo* (1943)
6 *Snowed-in family* (1951)
7 *Judy Jo's magic island* (1953)

Judy Jordan series
Garis, Lilian C
1 *Judy Jordan* (1931)
2 *Judy Jordan's discovery* (1931)

Judy Lawler series
Cole, Margaret Alice
1 *Holiday camp mystery* (1959)
2 *Thrilling holiday* (1962)
3 *Another thrilling holiday* (1964)
4 *Another holiday camp mystery* (1967)

Judy series
Baer, Judy
see **Dear Judy series**

Judy series
Haar, Jaap ter
1 *Judy at the zoo* (1966)
Original edition entitled *Lotje in de dierentuin*
2 *Judy and the baby elephant* (1967)
Original edition entitled *De kleine olifant*

Judy series
Nichols, Beverley
1 *Tree that sat down* (1945)
2 *Stream that stood still* (1948)
One volume abridged edition of numbers 1 and 2, 1960
3 *Mountain of magic* (1950)
4 *Wickedest witch in the world* (1971)

Judy series
Shoesmith, Kathleen Anne
1 *Judy in the garden* (1967)
2 *Judy in the wind* (1967)
3 *Judy in the snow* (1967)
4 *Judy on the sand* (1967)

Jug Valley Juniors series
Digby, Anne
1 *Boy v girls at Jug Valley Juniors* (1992)
2 *Headmaster's ghost at Jug Valley Juniors* (1992)
3 *Hands up at Jug Valley Juniors* (1992)
4 *Photofit mystery at Jug Valley Juniors* (1992)
5 *Poison pen at Jug Valley Juniors* (1993)
6 *Magic man at Jug Valley Juniors* (1993)

Jug Watson series
Zachary, Hugh
see **Sheriff Jug Watson series**

Jugedinski series
Swan, Phyllis
see **Anna J series**

Jules and Maureen Wendall trilogy
Oates, Joyce Carol
1 *Garden of earthly delights* (1967)
2 *Them* (1969)
3 *Wonderland* (1971)

Jules de Grandin series
Quinn, Seabury
Short stories
1 *Phantom-fighter* (1966)
2 *Adventures of Jules de Grandin* (1976)
3 *Casebook of Jules de Grandin* (1976)
4 *Hellfire files of Jules de Grandin* (1976)
5 *Skeleton closet of Jules de Grandin* (1976)
6 *Devil's bride* (1976)
A novel
7 *Horror chambers of Jules de Grandin* (1977)

Jules Maigret series
Simenon, Georges
see **Inspector Jules Maigret series**

Julia and Henry Gresham trilogy
Avery, Gillian
1 *To tame a sister* (1960)
2 *Greatest Gresham* (1962)
3 *Peacock House* (1963)

Julia Arbuthnot series
Croy, Catherine
1 *In silks she goes* (1933)
2 *Hungry locust* (1934)

Julia Homburg trilogy
Gainham, Sarah
see **Viennese trilogy**

Julia Howard trilogy
Argo, Ellen
1 *Jewel of the seas* (1977)
2 *Crystal star* (1979)
3 *Yankee girl* (1980)

Julia Jamieson series
Bridge, Ann
see **Julia Probyn series**

Julia Probyn series
Bridge, Ann
1 *Lighthearted quest* (1956)
2 *Portuguese escape* (1958)
3 *Numbered account* (1960)
Numbers 1-3 also published in one volume entitled *Julia involved*, 1962
4 *Tightening string* (1962)
5 *Dangerous islands* (1963)
6 *Emergency in the Pyrenees* (1965)
7 *Episode at Toledo* (1966)
8 *Malady in Madeira* (1969)
9 *Julia in Ireland* (1973)

Julia Redfern series
Cameron, Eleanor
1 *Julia and the hand of God* (1977)
2 *That Julia Redfern* (1982)
3 *Julia's magic* (1984)
4 *Room made of windows* (1971)
5 *Private worlds of Julia Redfern* (1988)

Julia Roper series
Croy, Catherine
see **Julia Arbuthnot series**

Julia series
Gripe, Maria
1 *Night daddy* (1968)
Original edition entitled *Nattpappa*
2 *Julia's house* (1971)
Original edition entitled *Julias hus och Nattpappa*

Julia Tyler series
Revell, Louisa
1 *Bus station murders* (1947)
2 *No pockets in shrouds* (1948)
3 *Silver spade* (1950)
4 *Kindest use a knife* (1952)
5 *Men with three eyes* (1955)
6 *See Rome and die* (1957)
7 *Party for the shooting* (1960)

Julian and Portia series
Enright, Elizabeth
see **Portia and Julian series**

Julian Burroughs series
Murphy, Warren Burton
see **Digger Burroughs series**

Julian Day series
Wheatley, Dennis
1 *Quest of Julian Day* (1939)
2 *Sword of fate* (1941)
3 *Bill for the use of a body* (1964)

Julian Escobar trilogy
O'Dell, Scott
1 *Captive* (1979)
2 *Feathered serpent* (1981)
3 *Amethyst ring* (1983)

Julian Mendoza series
Ronald, James
1 *Cross marks the spot* (1933)
2 *Death croons the blues* (1934)

Julian Morthoe series
Wilson, Philip Whitwell
see **Sir Julian Morthoe series**

Julian Prescot series
Prescot, Julian
see **Case books series**

Julian Quist series
Pentecost, Hugh
1 *Don't drop dead tomorrow* (1971)
2 *Champagne killer* (1972)
3 *Beautiful dead* (1973)
4 *Judas freak* (1974)
5 *Honeymoon with death* (1975)
6 *Die after dark* (1976)
7 *Steel palace* (1977)
8 *Deadly trap* (1978)
9 *Homicidal horse* (1979)
10 *Death mask* (1980)
11 *Sow death, reap death* (1981)
12 *Past, present and murder* (1982)
13 *Murder out of wedlock* (1983)
14 *Substitute victim* (1984)
15 *Party killer* (1985)
16 *Kill and kill again* (1987)

Julian Rivers series
Carnac, Carol
see **Inspector Julian Rivers series**

Julian stories series
Cameron, Ann
1 *Julian stories* (1981)
Stories Julian tells
2 *More stories Julian tells* (1986)

Julian West series
This sequence has two authors
Bellamy, Edward
1 *Looking backward, 2000-1887* (1888)
2 *Equality* (1897)
Reynolds, Mack
3 *Looking backward, from the year 2000* (1973)
4 *Equality, in the year 2000* (1977)

Julie and Jon Howard series
Bracken, Anne
see **Jon and Julie Howard series**

Julie Barden series
Manley-Tucker, Audrie
1 *Julie Barden, district nurse* (1968)
2 *Julie Barden, doctor's wife* (1969)

Julie Gordon series
Grey, Estelle
1 *Julie Gordon and the school fashion contest* (1972)
2 *Julie Gordon and the New Guinea smugglers* (1972)
3 *Julie Gordon and the pony club camp* (1974)

Julie Hayes series
Davis, Dorothy Salisbury
1 *Death in the life* (1976)
2 *Scarlet night* (1980)
3 *Lullaby of murder* (1984)
4 *Habit of fear* (1987)

Julie Jefferson series
Johnson, Pat
1 *Sweet running filly* (1971)
2 *Horse called Bonnie* (1971)

Julie series
Taylor, Cora
1 *Julie* (1985)
2 *Julie's secret* (1991)

Juliet Bravo series
Hardwick, Mollie
Based on a television series
1 *Juliet Bravo, volume 1* (1980)
2 *Juliet Bravo, volume 2* (1980)
3 *Calling Juliet Bravo* (1981)

Juliet Jackson series
Turnbull, Margaret
1 *Madame Judas* (1926)
2 *Rogues' march* (1928)
3 *Return of Jennie Weaver* (1932)
4 *Coast road murder* (1934)

Juliet Jones series
Drake, Stan
Comic strips
1 *Heart of Juliet Jones* (1986)
2 *In big business* (1987)
3 *Eve's new career* (1987)

Juliet Robeson series
Richmond, Grace Smith
1 *Indifference of Juliet* (1902)
2 *With Juliet in England* (1907)

Juliette series
Duche, Jean
1 *I said to my wife* (1951)
Original edition entitled *Elle et lui*
2 *Not at home* (1952)
Original edition entitled *Trois sans toit*

Julio Arceval series
Madariaga, Salvador de
1 *[Arceval y los ingleses]* (1925)
No English edition
2 *Sacred giraffe* (1925)
English edition only

Julius Caesar series
Warner, Rex
see **Caesar series**

Julius Le Vallon series
Blackwood, Algernon
see **Reincarnation series**

Jumbo Collins series
Wood, James
1 *North beat* (1973)
2 *North kill* (1975)

Jumbo Rutherford series
Leslie, Norman
1 *Raid over England* (1938)
2 *Kiwi Club* (1939)

Jumbo Spencer series
Cresswell, Helen
1 *Jumbo Spencer* (1963)
2 *Jumbo back to nature* (1965)
3 *Jumbo afloat* (1966)
4 *Jumbo and the big dig* (1968)

Jungle book series
Kipling, Rudyard
1 *Jungle book* (1894)
2 *Second jungle book* (1895)

Jungle Doctor of Tanganyika series
White, Paul
see **Doctor of Tanganyika series**

Jungle Doctor series
White, Paul
1 *Jungle Doctor* (1942)
Revised edition 1950
2 *Jungle Doctor on safari* (1943)
Revised edition 1950
3 *Jungle Doctor operates* (1944)
Revised edition 1950
4 *Jungle Doctor attacks witchcraft* (1947)
Revised edition 1950
5 *Jungle Doctor's enemies* (1948)
Revised edition 1950
6 *Jungle Doctor meets a lion* (1950)
7 *Jungle Doctor to the rescue* (1951)
8 *Jungle Doctor's case book* (1952)
9 *Jungle Doctor and the whirlwind* (1952)
10 *Eyes of Jungle Doctor* (1953)
11 *Jungle Doctor looks for trouble* (1953)
12 *Jungle Doctor goes west* (1954)
13 *Jungle Doctor stings a scorpion* (1955)
14 *Jungle Doctor hunts big game* (1956)
15 *Jungle Doctor on the hop* (1957)
16 *Jungle Doctor's crooked dealings* (1959)
17 *Jungle Doctor panorama* (1960)
18 *Jungle Doctor spots a leopard* (1963)
19 *Jungle Doctor pulls a leg* (1964)
20 *Jungle Doctor sees red* (1968)
21 *Jungle Doctor's rhino rumblings* (1975)
22 *Jungle Doctor meets mongoose* (1979)
Companion volume: *Alias Jungle Doctor*, an autobiography, 1977

Jungle Doctor's fables series
White, Paul
1 *Jungle Doctor's fables* (1955)
2 *Jungle Doctor's monkey tales* (1957)
3 *Jungle Doctor's tug-of-war* (1958)
4 *Jungle Doctor's hippon happenings* (1966)

Jungle series
Casserly, Gordon
1 *Elephant god* (1920)
2 *Jungle girl* (1921)
3 *Monkey god* (1933)
4 *Tiger girl* (1934)

Jungle series
Traven, B
1 *Carreta* (1931)
Original ed entitled *Die Carreta*; revised German edition entitled *Der Karren*
2 *Government* (1931)
Original edition entitled *Regierung*
3 *March to Caobaland* (1933)
March to the Monteria
Original edition entitled *Der Marsch ins Reich der Caoba*
4 *Trozas* (1936)
Original edition entitled *Trozas*
5 *Rebellion of the hanged* (1936)
Original edition entitled *Die Rebellion der Gehenkten*
6 *General from the jungle* (1940)
Original edition entitled *Ein General kommt aus dem Dschungel*

Junior detective series
Salmon, Michael
see **Who did it series**

Junior High School series
Kenyon, Kate
see **Cedar Grove Junior High School series**

Junior High series
Adorjan, Carol
1 *Eighth grade to the rescue* (1987)
2 *Those craze eighth grade pictures* (1987)
3 *Big date* (1988)
4 *Revolt of the eighth grade* (1988)

Junior listen-hear series
Slepian, Jan
Illustrated by Richard E Martin
1 *Bendemolena* (1967)
Cat who wore a pot on her head
2 *Ding-dong, bing-bong* (1967)
3 *Ear is to hear* (1967)
4 *Hungry thing* (1967)
5 *Silly listening book* (1967)

Junior reporter series
England, Edward Oliver
see **John Rickshaw series**

Junior Trail Blazers series
Gulick, Bill
1 *Abilene or bust* (1946)
2 *Desolation trail* (1946)

Junior transformers find your fate series
This sequence has eight authors
Todd, Casey
1 *Dinobots strike back* (1985)
Siegel, Barbara
2 *Battle drive* (1985)
Beach, Lynn
3 *Attack of the Insecticons* (1985)
Matthews, Ann
4 *Earthquake* (1986)
Razzi, Jim
5 *Desert flight* (1986)
Stamper, Judith Bauer
6 *Decepticon poison* (1986)
7 *Autobot alert!* (1986)

Siegel, Barbara
8 *Project brain drain* (1986)
Sherman, Josepha
9 *Invisibility factor* (1986)

Juno series
Abbott, Jacob
1 *Juno and Georgie* (1870)
2 *Mary Osborn* (1870)
3 *Hubert* (1870)
4 *Juno on a journey* (1870)

Jupiter Jane series
Lavelle, Sheila
1 *Apple pie alien* (1987)
2 *Boggy Bay marathon* (1987)
3 *Topsy-turvy teacher* (1988)
4 *Spots in space* (1988)

Jupiter Jones series
Fuller, Timothy
1 *Harvard has a homicide* (1936)
2 *Three thirds of a ghost* (1941)
3 *Reunion with murder* (1941)
4 *This is murder, Mr Jones* (1943)
5 *Keep cool, Mr Jones* (1950)

Jurnet series
Haymon, Sylvia T
see **Inspector Ben Jurnet series**

Jury series
Grimes, Martha
see **Inspector Richard Jury series**

Just back series
Cole, John Alfred
Memoirs of trips to Germany almost twenty years apart
1 *Just back from Germany* (1938)
2 *My host, Michael* (1955)

Just look at series
Stonehouse, Bernard
1 *Just look at life in the sea* (1984)
2 *Just look at life at the Poles* (1986)

Just look series
Cumming, Robert
1 *Just look* (1980)
A book about paintings
2 *Just imagine* (1982)
Ideas in paintings

Just Mary series
Grannan, Mary
1 *Just Mary* (1941)
2 *Just Mary again* (1941)
Numbers 1 and 2 also published in one volume entitled *Just Mary stories*, 1942, revised edition 1958
3 *New Just Mary stories* (1946)
4 *Happy playtime* (1948)
Numbers 3 and 4 also published in a one volume revised edition entitled *More Just Mary stories*, 1959

Just Men series
Wallace, Edgar
1 *Four Just Men* (1905)
Revised editions 1908 and 1920
2 *Council of justice* (1908)
Numbers 1 and 2 also published in one volume 1920
3 *Just men of Cordova* (1917)
4 *Law of the Four Just Men* (1921)
5 *Three Just Men* (1925)
6 *Again the Three Just Men* (1928)
Again the Three
Law of the Three Just Men

Just north series
Barnes, Michael
1 *Monster from the slimes* (1976)
2 *Chief commanda hi-jack* (1976)
3 *Thunder Bay threat* (1977)
4 *Message to Moosonee* (1977)
5 *Arrest at the Soo* (1977)
6 *Sudbury moon chase* (1977)

Just one more stories series
Tripp, Valerie
1 *Singing dog* (1986)
2 *Baby Koala finds a home* (1987)
3 *Penguins paint* (1987)
4 *Squirrel's Thanksgiving surprise* (1988)
5 *Sillyhen's big surprise* (1989)
6 *Happy, happy Mother's Day* (1989)

Just trilogy
Phelps, Humphrey
Autobiography
1 *Just across the fields* (1976)
2 *Just over yonder* (1977)
3 *Just where we belong* (1978)
Companion volume: *Just around the corner*, 1974

Just William series
Crompton, Richmal
see **William series**

Justa Williams series
Tippette, Giles
1 *Bad news* (1989)
2 *Cross fire* (1990)

Justice Barry College of Technology series
Lewis, Catherine
see **Lisa Thomas series**

Justice Colt series
Allen, Chester
1 *Vengeance trail* (1952)
2 *Marshal of Gunsmoke* (1953)
3 *Badlands showdown* (1953)
4 *Spectre Range* (1954)
5 *Gallows west* (1954)
6 *Blizzard Range* (1955)
7 *Colt heritage* (1956)
8 *Bullet bounty* (1957)

Justice series
Arnett, Jack
see **Book of justice series**

Justice series
Bernhardt, William
1 *Primary justice* (1991)
2 *Blind justice* (1992)
3 *Deadly justice* (1993)
4 *Perfect justice* (1993)

Justice series
Duncan, Francis
see **Peter Justice series**
Forrest, Anthony
see **Captain John Valcourt Justice series**
Longtree, Warren T
see **Ruff Justice series**

Justice trilogy
Hamilton, Virginia
1 *Justice and her brothers* (1978)
2 *Dustland* (1980)
3 *Gathering* (1981)

Justice trilogy
Robinson, Vance
1 *Death at sea* (1981)
2 *Terror at Boulder Dam* (1981)
3 *Killer-stalk* (1982)

Justin Bassett and Scott Gregory series
Stratton, Roy
see **Scott Gregory and Justin Bassett series**

Justin Kelly series
Clevely, Hugh
1 *Justin Kelly* (1959)
2 *Garland of valour* (1963)

Justin March series
Horler, Sydney
see **Ace series**

Justin Peele series
Vaughan, Richard
1 *Moulded in earth* (1951)
2 *Son of Justin* (1955)

Justin Perry series
Revere, John D
1 *Justin Perry, the Assassin* (1983)
2 *Vatican kill* (1983)
3 *Born to kill* (1984)
4 *Death's running mate* (1985)
5 *Stud service* (1985)

Justin Retief series
Doke, Joseph John
see **Karroo series**

Justin Rutherford and Anthea series
Ley, Alice Chetwynd
1 *Reputation dies* (1984)
2 *Fatal assignation* (1987)
3 *Masquerade of vengeance* (1989)

Justine Carmichael series
Chase, Kip
1 *Where there's a will* (1961)
2 *Murder most ingenious* (1962)
3 *Killer be killed* (1963)

Justiss family series
Wisler, Gary Clifton
see **Texas Brazos series**

Justus trilogy
Sadler, Geoffrey
1 *Lash* (1982)
2 *Bloodwater* (1982)
3 *Black vengeance* (1982)

Justus Wise series
Barrett, Alfred Wilson
1 *Justus Wise* (1911)
2 *Tower Hill mystery* (1912)

Justuses series
Rice, Craig
see **John Joseph Malone series**

Juvenile delinquency trilogy
Shulman, Irving
1 *Amboy Dukes* (1947)
2 *Cry tough* (1949)
3 *Big brokers* (1951)

Juvik series
Duun, Ole Julius
see **People of Juvik series**

K

K.F. series
Hall, Aylmer
1 *Admiral's secret* (1953)
2 *K.F. conspiracy* (1955)

K.G.B. series
Andrew, Christopher
1 *K.G.B., the inside story* (1989)
2 *Instruction from the Centre* (1991)
Top secret files on K.G.B. foreign operations, 1975-85
3 *More instruction from the Centre* (1992)
Top secret files on K.G.B. global operations, 1975-85

K series
Kafka, Franz
1 *Castle* (1926)
Original edition entitled *Das Schloss*
2 *Trial* (1925)
Original edition entitled *Der Prozess*

Ka'at series
Norton, Andre
see **Star Ka'at series**

Kable series
Whittaker, June Lovina
see **Henry and Susannah Kable series**

Kabongo series
Baker, Richard Saint Barbe
1 *Kabongo* (1955)
The story of a Kikuyu chief
2 *Kamiti* (1958)
A forester's dream

Kachiah series
Lesley, Craig
see **Danny and Jack Kachiah series**

Kaeldra series
Fletcher, Susan
1 *Flight of the Dragon-kyn* (1993)
2 *Dragon's milk* (1989)

Kaeti series
Roberts, Keith
1 *Kaeti and company* (1986)
2 *Kaeti's apocalypse* (1986)

Kai Lung series
Bramah, Ernest
Short stories
1 *Wallet of Kai Lung* (1900)
Celestial omnibus
Abridged edition entitled *The transmutation of Ling*, 1911
2 *Kai Ling's golden hours* (1922)
3 *Story of Wan and the remarkable shrub* (1927)
Also includes *The story of Ching-Kwei and the destinies*
4 *Kai Lung unrolls his mat* (1928)
Selection entitled *Kin Weng and the miraculous tusk*, 1941; numbers 1, 2 and 4 also published in one volume entitled *The Kai Lung omnibus*, 1936
5 *Moon of much gladness* (1932)
Return of Kai Lung
6 *Kai Lung beneath the mulberry tree* (1941)
7 *Kai Lung, six* (1974)
Uncollected stories from *Punch*

Kailyard School series
Crockett, Samuel Rutherford
see **Stickit minister series**

Kaiser series
Collins, Alan
see **Jacob Kaiser series**

Kalahari series
Van der Post, Laurens
Travels in south-west Africa
1 *Lost world of the Kalahari* (1958)
2 *Heart of the hunter* (1961)

Kalasanda series
Kimenye, Barbara
1 *Kalasanda* (1965)
2 *Kalasanda revisited* (1966)

Kale series
Jon, Montague
see **Stephen Kale series**

Kalevala series
Petaja, Emil
1 *Saga of lost earths* (1966)

2 *Star mill* (1966)
Numbers 1 and 2 also published in one volume 1979
3 *Stolen sun* (1967)
4 *Tramontane* (1967)
Numbers 3 and 4 also published in one volume 1979

Kalinda series
Green, Evan
1 *Dust and glory* (1990)
2 *Kalinda* (1991)

Kalvan series
Piper, Horace Beam
see **Lord Kalvan series**

Kane and Condon series
Jordan, David
see **Tom Kane and Condon series**

Kane and Pendrake series
Spruill, Steven Gregory
1 *Psychopath plague* (1978)
2 *Imperator plot* (1983)
3 *Paradox planet* (1988)

Kane and Rosnovski series
Archer, Jeffrey
see **William Kane and Abel Rosnovski series**

Kane Jackson series
Arden, William
1 *Dark power* (1968)
2 *Deal in violence* (1969)
3 *Goliath scheme* (1971)
4 *Die to a distant dream* (1972)
Murder underground
5 *Deadly legacy* (1973)

Kane Richards series
Frank, Lee
1 *Kane* (1971)
2 *Kane and the goldbar killers* (1973)
3 *Kane and the outlaw's double-cross* (1975)

Kane series
Barrie, Alexander
see **Jonathan Kane series**
Bennett, William Robert
see **Adam Kane series**
Brown, Carter
see **Andy Kane series**
Hill, Eileen
see **Robin Kane series**
Howard, Robert Ervin
see **Solomon Kane series**
Lambert, Janet
see **Candy Kane series**
Marshall, Lovat
see **Sugar Kane series**
Masterson, Louis
see **Morgan Kane series**
Preston, John
see **Mission of Alex Kane series**
Scarlett, Roger
see **Inspector Kane series**
Stone, Nick
see **Ben Kane series**

Kane series
Wagner, Karl Edward
1 *Darkness weaves with many shades* (1970)
Darkness weaves
2 *Death Angel's shadow* (1973)
3 *Bloodstone* (1975)
4 *Dark crusade* (1976)
5 *Night winds* (1978)
6 *Book of Kane* (1985)

Kane trilogy
Bradbury, Edward P
see **Warrior of Mars trilogy**

Kansan series
Mills, Robert E
see **Davy Watson series**

Kantmorie trilogy
Dibell, Ansen
1 *Pursuit of the Screamer* (1978)
2 *Circle, crescent, star* (1981)
3 *Summerfair* (1982)

Kaplan series
Ross, Leonard Q
see **Hyman Kaplan series**

Karabad series
Wren, Percival Christopher
1 *Dew and mildew* (1912)
Semi-detached stories from Karabad, India
2 *Young stagers* (1917)
Further faites and gestes of the Junior Curlton Club of Karabad, India

Karana series
O'Dell, Scott
see **Zia series**

Karate Kommandos series
Weinberg, Larry
see **Chuck Norris and the Karate Kommandos series**

Karate Princess series
Strong, Jeremy
1 *Karate Princess* (1986)
2 *Karate Princess and the cut-throat robbers* (1989)
3 *Karate Princess to the rescue* (1991)

Kar-Chee series
Davidson, Avram
1 *Rogue dragon* (1965)
2 *Kar-Chee reign* (1966)
One volume edition 1979

Karen series
Killilea, Marie
Reminiscences of the author's daughter, a sufferer from cerebral palsy
1 *Karen* (1952)
2 *With love from Karen* (1963)

Karen series
McHugh, Elisabet
1 *Karen's sister* (1983)
2 *Karen and Vicki* (1984)

Karen series
Provensen, Alice
1 *Karen's curiosity* (1963)
2 *Karen's opposites* (1963)

Karl Alberg series
Wright, Laurali R
see **Sergeant Karl Alberg series**

Karl Glogauer series
Moorcock, Michael
1 *Behold the man* (1969)
2 *Breakfast in the ruins* (1972)
A novel of inhumanity

Karlov and Crane series
Hayes, Ralph Eugene
see **Check Force series**

Karlsson series
Gripe, Maria
see **Elvis Karlsson series**

Karlsson-on-the-Roof series
Lindgren, Astrid
1 *Eric and Karlsson-on-the-Roof* (1955)
Karlsson-on-the-Roof
Original edition entitled *Lillebror och Karlsson paa taket*; revised edition 1983
2 *Karlsson flies again* (1962)
Original edition entitled *Karlsson paa taket flyger igen*; Revised edition 1983
3 *[Karlsson paa taket smyger igen]* (1968)
Revised edition 1983; no English edition
4 *[Allt om Karlsson paa taket]* (1972)
No English edition

Karma series
Livingston, Marjorie
1 *Island sonata* (1944)
2 *Muted strings* (1946)
3 *Delphic echo* (1948)

Karns series
DeWeese, Gene
see **Joe Karns series**

Karoleena series
Steiner, Charlotte
1 *Karoleena's red coat* (1960)
2 *Karoleena* (1957)

Karoo series
Smith, Pauline
1 *Little Karoo* (1925)
2 *Beadle* (1926)

Karp series
Tanenbaum, Robert K
see **Assistant District Attorney Butch Karp series**

Karran Kinrade series
Manners, Alexandra
1 *Echoing yesterday* (1981)
2 *Karran Kinrade* (1982)
3 *Red bird* (1984)
4 *Gaming house* (1984)

Karroo series
Doke, Joseph John
1 *Secret city* (1913)
2 *Queen of the secret city* (1916)

Karsten and Rudolph Nilsen series
Griffiths, Ella
see **Rudolph and Karsten Nilson series**

Kaspa series
Stoneham, Charles Thurley
1 *Lion's way* (1931)
King of the jungle
A story of men and lions
2 *Kaspa, the lion man* (1933)

Kate and Ben King series
Smith, Beatrice Schillinger
1 *Case of the lost dogs* (1976)
2 *Case of the missing bills* (1976)
3 *Fish Creek mystery* (1976)
4 *Ghost in the park* (1976)
5 *Mystery of the green gloves* (1976)
6 *Voices from the haunted house* (1976)

Kate and Jim Harris series
Macrae, Travis
see **Jim and Kate Harris series**

Kate and Lynn series
Reid, Meta Mayne
1 *Tinker's summer* (1965)
2 *House at Spaniard's Bay* (1967)

Kate and Mickey Dixon series
Markham, Marion M
see **Dixon twins series**

Kate and Roger Starte series
Williams, Eric Ernest
see **Roger and Kate Starte series**

Kate and Sam series
Cole, Michael
1 *Kate and Sam's tea* (1971)
2 *Kate and Sam's new home* (1971)
3 *Kate and Sam's pet* (1971)
4 *Kate and Sam go out* (1971)

Kate Baeier series
Slovo, Gillian
1 *Morbid symptoms* (1984)
2 *Death by analysis* (1986)
3 *Death comes staccato* (1987)
4 *Betrayal* (1991)
5 *Death comes again* (1994)

Kate Bassett series
Cooper, Gordon
1 *Hour in the morning* (1971)
2 *Time in a city* (1972)
3 *Certain courage* (1975)

Kate Bloomfield and Emily Blair series
Little, Jean
see **Emily Blair and Kate Bloomfield series**

Kate Brannigan series
McDermid, Val
1 *Dead beat* (1992)
2 *Kick back* (1993)
3 *Crackdown* (1994)

Kate Coyle and John Dobie series
Cory, Desmond
see **John Dobie and Kate Coyle series**

Kate Delafield series
Forrest, Katherine V
1 *Amateur city* (1984)
2 *Murder at the Nightwood Bar* (1987)
3 *Beverly Malibu* (1989)

Kate Fansler series
Cross, Amanda
see **Professor Kate Fansler series**

Kate Graham series
Arliss, Joen
1 *Shark Bait affair* (1979)
2 *Lady killer affair* (1980)

Kate Kilgour trilogy
Webster, Jan
1 *Colliers Row* (1977)
2 *Saturday city* (1978)
3 *Beggarman's country* (1979)

Kate Kinsella series
Green, Christine
1 *Deadly errand* (1991)
2 *Deadly admirer* (1992)
3 *Deadly practice* (1994)

Kate Marsh series
Lane, Gret
1 *Curlew Coombe mystery* (1930)
2 *Lantern House affair* (1931)
3 *Hotel Cremona mystery* (1932)
4 *Unknown enemy* (1933)
5 *Death visits the summer house* (1939)
6 *Death in Mermaid Lane* (1940)
7 *Death prowls the cove* (1942)
8 *Guest with the scythe* (1943)

Kate, Reggie and Olivia series
Lehmann, Rosamond
see **Olivia, Kate and Reggie series**

Kate series
Brisson, Pat
1 *Your best friend Kate* (1989)
2 *Kate heads west* (1990)
3 *Kate on the coast* (1992)

Kate series
Chorao, Kay
1 *Kate's car* (1982)
2 *Kate's box* (1982)
3 *Kate's quilt* (1982)

4 *Kate's snowman* (1982)
5 *George told Kate* (1987)

Kate series
Godwin, Catherine Grace
see **Cousin Kate series**

Kate series
Sandberg, Inger
Illustrated by Lasse Sandberg
1 *Kate's Christmas present* (1972)
Original edition entitled *Lilla Annas jul klapp*
2 *Kate's upside down day* (1972)
Original edition entitled *Lilla Annas flytter saker*
3 *Kate's bouncy ball* (1973)
Original edition entitled *Lilla Anna leker med bollar*
4 *Kate, Kate come and help* (1973)
Original edition entitled *Lilla Anna kom och hjalp*
At least three more titles not translated

Kate Theobald series
Black, Lionel
1 *Swinging murder* (1969)
American edition published under the pseudonym Anthony Matthews
2 *Death has green fingers* (1971)
American edition published under the pseudonym Anthony Matthews
3 *Death by hoax* (1974)
4 *Healthy way to die* (1976)
5 *Penny murders* (1979)
6 *Eve of the wedding* (1980)
7 *Rumanian circle* (1981)

Kate Weatherley series
Birmingham, Maisie
1 *You can help me* (1974)
2 *Heat of the sun* (1976)
3 *Sleep in a ditch* (1978)

Katharine of Aragon trilogy
Plaidy, Jean
1 *Katharine, the virgin widow* (1961)
2 *Shadow of the pomegranate* (1962)
3 *King's secret matter* (1962)
One volume edition entitled *Katharine of Aragon*, 1968

Katherine Cornish and Adam Drew series
Hanson, Virginia
see **Adam Drew and Katherine Cornish series**

Katherine Forrester series
L'Engle, Madeleine
1 *Small rain* (1945)
Abridged junior edition entitled *Prelude*, 1968
2 *Severed wasp* (1982)

Katherine Howard trilogy
Ford, Ford Madox
see **Fifth queen trilogy**

Katherine Mortenhoe series
Compton, David Guy
1 *Unsleeping eye* (1974)
Death watch
2 *Windows* (1979)

Katherine Parr series
Evans, Jean
1 *Royal widow* (1971)
Katherine Parr
2 *Katherine, queen dowager* (1973)

Katherine Wentworth series
Stevenson, Dorothy Emily
1 *Katherine Wentworth* (1964)
2 *Katherine's marriage* (1965)
Marriage of Katherine

Katheryn and Gaynor Scarlett series
Maynard, Nan
1 *Wayward flesh* (1969)
2 *Grief ago* (1976)

Kathie series
Douglas, Amanda Minnie
1 *Kathie's three wishes* (1870)
2 *Kathie's Aunt Ruth* (1870)
3 *Kathie's summer at Cedarwood* (1870)
4 *Kathie's soldiers* (1871)
5 *In the ranks* (1872)
6 *Kathie's harvest days* (1872)
7 *Whom Kathie married* (1883)

Kathleen Hartly Taylor and Reed Taylor series
Hart, Catherine
1 *Fire and ice* (1984)
2 *Satin and steel* (1986)
3 *Ashes and ecstasy* (1988)

Kathrine Grey series
Preston, Florence
1 *Harvest of daring* (1957)
2 *Great refusals* (1958)

Kathryn Swinbrooke series
Grace, C L
1 *Shrine of murders* (1993)
2 *Eye of God* (1994)

Kathy Brown series
Paice, Margaret
1 *Lucky fall* (1958)
2 *Secret of Greycliffs* (1961)

Kathy Martin series
James, Josephine
1 *Cap for Cathy* (1959)
2 *Junior nurse* (1960)
3 *Senior nurse* (1960)
4 *Assignment in Alaska* (1961)
5 *Patient in 202* (1961)
6 *Private nurse* (1962)
7 *Search for an island* (1963)
8 *Sierra adventure* (1964)
9 *Courage in crisis* (1964)
10 *Off-duty nurse* (1964)
11 *Affair of the heart* (1965)
12 *Peace Corps nurse* (1965)
13 *African adventure* (1965)

Kathy McNeely series
Charbonneau, Louis
1 *Ice* (1991)
2 *White harvest* (1994)

Kati series
Lindgren, Astrid
1 *Kati in America* (1950)
Original edition entitled *Kati i Amerika*
2 *Kati in Italy* (1952)
Original edition entitled *Kati Kaptensgatan*; revised edition entitled *Kati i Italien*, 1971
3 *Kati in Paris* (1953)
Original edition entitled *Kati i Paris*; revised edition 1972

Katie and Kit series
De Paola, Tomie
1 *Katie and Kit at the beach* (1986)
2 *Pajamas for Kit* (1986)
3 *Katie's good idea* (1986)
4 *Katie, Kit and Cousin Tom* (1986)

Katie and Paige series
Oaks, Tina
see **Stepsisters series**

Katie and Paul Van Riebeck series
Moray, Helga
1 *Untamed* (1951)
2 *Savage earth* (1968)
3 *Harvest burns* (1972)
4 *Blood on the wind* (1973)
5 *Footsteps in the night* (1976)
6 *To make a light* (1978)
7 *Beacon of gold* (1980)

Katie Hooper series
Sorenson, Jane
Katie Hooper is cousin to Jennifer in the **Jennifer series**
1 *Hi, I'm Katie Hooper* (1988)
2 *Home sweet haunted house* (1988)
3 *Happy birth day* (1988)
4 *Honor roll* (1988)
5 *First job* (1989)
6 *Angels on holiday* (1989)
7 *New me* (1989)
8 *Left behind* (1989)

Katie John series
Calhoun, Mary
1 *Katie John* (1960)
2 *Depend on Katie John* (1961)
3 *Honestly, Katie John* (1963)
4 *Katie John and Heathcliff* (1980)

Katie Kusik series
Ryan, Mary Elizabeth
1 *Dance a step closer* (1984)
2 *I'd rather be dancing* (1989)

Katie Morag series
Hedderwick, Mairi
1 *Katie Morag delivers the mail* (1984)
2 *Katie Morag and the two grandmothers* (1985)
3 *Katie Morag and the tiresome Ted* (1986)
4 *Katie Morag and the big boy cousins* (1987)
5 *Katie Morag and the new pier* (1993)

Katie Rose and Stacy Belford series
Weber, Lenora Mattingly
see **Stacy and Katie Rose Belford series**

Katie series
McDaniel, Becky Bring
1 *Katie did it* (1983)
2 *Katie couldn't* (1985)
3 *Katie can* (1987)

Katie series
Tolles, Martha
1 *Too many boys* (1974)
Katie and those boys
2 *Katie for president* (1976)
3 *Katie's babysitting job* (1985)

Katrinka series
Haskell, Helen Eggleston
1 *Katrinka* (1915)
The story of a Russian child
2 *Katrinka grows up* (1932)
3 *Peter, Katrinka's brother* (1933)
4 *Peggy keeps house* (1935)
5 *Nadya makes her bow* (1939)

Katy and Dom series
Oldfield, Pamela
1 *Katy and Dom* (1978)
2 *Katy and Dom and the lost cat* (1979)

Katy series
Coolidge, Susan
1 *What Katy did* (1872)
What Katy did at home
2 *What Katy did at school* (1873)
3 *What Katy did next* (1886)
4 *Clover* (1888)
5 *In the high valley* (1891)

Katy Touchfeather series
Sangster, Jimmy
1 *Touchfeather* (1968)
2 *Touchfeather, too* (1970)
3 *Touch gold* (1970)

Kauffman series
Chastain, Thomas
see **Inspector Max Kauffman series**

Kavanagh series
Stuart, Brian
see **Knock-Out Kavanagh series**

Kavin series
Mason, David
1 *Kavin's world* (1969)
2 *Return of Kavin* (1972)

Kay and Rory series
Clewes, Dorothy
1 *Secret* (1956)
2 *Old pony* (1959)
3 *All the fun of the fair* (1961)

Kay Barth series
Schier, Norma
1 *Death on the slopes* (1978)
2 *Death goes skiing* (1979)
3 *Murder by the book* (1979)
4 *Demon of the opera* (1980)

Kay Cornish and Adam Drew series
Hanson, Virginia
see **Adam Drew and Katherine Cornish series**

Kay Harker series
Masefield, John
1 *Midnight folk* (1927)
2 *Box of delights* (1935)
Alternative title: When the wolves were running

Kay Scarpetta series
Cornwell, Patricia Daniels
see **Doctor Kay Scarpetta series**

Kay series
Walsh, James Morgan
see **Bromley Kay series**

Kay Tracey series
Judd, Frances K
House pseudonym
1 *Secret of the red scarf* (1934)
2 *Strange echo* (1934)
3 *Mystery of the swaying curtains* (1935)
4 *Shadow on the door* (1935)
5 *Six-fingered glove mystery* (1936)
6 *Green cameo mystery* (1936)
7 *Secret of the windmill* (1937)
8 *Beneath the crimson briar bush* (1937)
9 *Message in the sand dunes* (1938)
10 *Murmering portrait* (1938)
11 *When the key turned* (1939)
12 *In the sunken garden* (1939)
13 *Forbidden tower* (1940)
14 *Sacred feather* (1940)
15 *Lone footprint* (1941)
16 *Double disguise* (1942)
17 *Mansion of secrets* (1942)
18 *Mysterious neighbors* (1942)

Kaye series
Waugh, Hillary
see **Simon Kaye series**

Kayla O'Brien series
Stahl, Hilda
1 *Kayla O'Brien and the dangerous journey* (1990)
2 *Kayla O'Brien and the trouble at Bitter Creek Ranch* (1991)
3 *Kayla O'Brien and the runaway orphans* (1991)

Kayle family series
Dwyer, Vera Gladys
1 *War of girls* (1915)
2 *Kayles of Bushy Lodge* (1922)

Kaywana series
Mittelholzer, Edgar
1 *Children of Kaywana* (1952)
2 *Kaywana heritage* (1952)
Children of Kaywana, part 2
3 *Harrowing of Hubertus* (1954)
Kaywana stock
Hubertus
4 *Kaywana blood* (1958)
Old blood

Kaz series
Teilhet, Darwin Le Ora
see **Baron Von Kaz series**

Kazallon series
Verne, Jules
see **J R Kazallon series**

Kazan series
Curwood, James Oliver
1 *Kazan, the wolf-dog* (1914)
2 *Son of Kazan* (1917)
Baree, son of Kazan
3 *Courage of Marge O'Doone* (1918)

Keane series
Faherty, Terence
see **Owen Keane series**

Kearney Associates series
Gores, Joe
see **DKA file series**

Keate and O'Leary series
Eberhart, Mignon Good
see **Sarah Keate and Lance O'Leary series**

Keaton series
Tone, Teona
see **Kyra Keaton series**

Keats and Cotter series
Long, Martin
see **Inspector Keats and Tom Cotter series**

Keats and Leith series
Shore, Viola Brothers
see **Colin Keats and Gwynn Leith series**

Keats series
Gittings, Robert
see **John Keats series**

Kedrigern series
Morressy, John
1 *Voice for Princess* (1986)
2 *Questing of Kedrigern* (1987)
3 *Kedrigern in Wanderland* (1988)
4 *Kedrigern and the charming couple* (1990)
5 *Remembrance for Kedrigern* (1990)

Keeble series
Wood, Andrew
see **Magnus Keeble series**

Keefe series
Wolfe, Michael
see **Michael Keefe series**

Keegan series
Ball, Brian Neville
1 *No-option contract* (1975)
2 *One-way deal* (1976)

Keel series
Schock, T A
see **Daniel Keel series**
Trimnell, Robert L
see **Loner series**

Keeler series
Stong, Philip
see **Ivanhoe Keeler series**

Keen series
Hardy, Lindsay
see **Gregory Keen series**
Lloyd, Hugh
see **Hal Keen series**
Long, Harman
see **Franklyn Keen series**

Keene and Young series
Wood, Eric
see **Arnold Keene and Bernard Young series**

Keene series
Saber, Robert O
see **Max Keene series**
Walsh, James Morgan
see **Oliver Keene series**

Keeper trilogy
King, Bernard
see **Chronicles of the keeper trilogy**

Keeping the faith trilogy
Arnold, Judith
1 *Promises* (1985)
2 *Commitments* (1985)
3 *Dreams* (1986)

Keeps and Hennessy series
Bancroft, Tex
see **Angeltown Keeps and Doc Hennessy series**

Keepsake series
Francis, Dorothy
1 *Right kind of girl* (1987)
2 *Vonnie and Monique* (1987)

Kegan series
Vinter, Michael
see **Barry Kegan series**

Kei series
Ravenswood, Fritzen
1 *Witching* (1980)
2 *Spawning* (1981)

Keill Randor series
Hill, Douglas
see **Last legionary series**

Keith and Sally series
Gree, Alain
1 *Keith and Sally go abroad* (1963)
Original edition entitled *Achille et Bergamote en route*
2 *Keith and Sally at the seaside* (1963)
Original edition entitled *La mer*
3 *[La ville]* (1963)
No English edition
4 *Sally and Billy in the woods* (1964)
Original edition entitled *La foret*
5 *[Les trains]* (1964)
No English edition
6 *Keith and Sally look for oil* (1965)
Original edition entitled *Le petrole*
7 *Sally and Billy look at the ships* (1965)
Original edition entitled *Les navires*
8 *Sally and Billy on the farm* (1965)
Farm
Original edition entitled *La ferme*
9 *Keith and Sally by the river* (1966)
Original edition entitled *La riviere*
10 *Mountains* (1967)
Original edition entitled *La montagne*
11 *Keith and Sally look at television* (1967)
Original edition entitled *La television*
12 *[Sous]* (1967)
No English edition
13 *Sally and billy at the seaside* (1967)
14 *Keith and Sally in the garden* (1968)
Original edition entitled *Au jardin*
15 *[L'automobile]* (1968)
No English edition
16 *[L'electricite]* (1969)
No English edition
17 *[Petit atlas]* (1969)
18 *Keith and Sally' bird book* (1970)
Original edition entitled *Les oiseaux*
19 *Keith and Sally's plant book* (1971)
Original edition entitled *Les plantes*
Six more titles in this sequence not translated into English

Keith Calder series
Hammond, Gerald
1 *Dead game* (1979)
2 *Reward game* (1980)
3 *Revenge game* (1981)
4 *Fair game* (1982)
5 *Game* (1982)
6 *Cousin once removed* (1984)
7 *Sauce for the pigeon* (1984)
8 *Pursuit of arms* (1985)
9 *Silver City scandal* (1986)
10 *Executor* (1986)
11 *Worried widow* (1987)
12 *Adverse report* (1987)
13 *Stray shot* (1988)
14 *Brace of skeet* (1989)
15 *Let us prey* (1990)

Keith County series
Janovy, John
Essays
1 *Keith County journal* (1978)
2 *Back in Keith County* (1981)

Keith series
Carter, Nicholas
see **Harrison Keith series**
Daniels, Norman A
see **Man from A.P.E. series**
Finley, Martha Farquharson
see **Mildred Keith series**
Gleitzman, Morris
see **Misery guts series**

Kek Huuygens series
Fish, Robert Lloyd
1 *Hochmann miniatures* (1967)
2 *Whirligig* (1970)
3 *Tricks of the trade* (1972)
4 *Wager* (1974)
5 *Kek Huuygens, smuggler* (1976)

Kellaway series
Evans, Gwyn
see **Bill Kellaway series**

Keller series
Demille, Nelson
1 *Smack man* (1975)
2 *Cannibal* (1975)
3 *Night of the phoenix* (1975)

Keller trilogy
Kirst, Hans Hellmut
see **Munich trilogy**

Kellerway series
Crauford, William Harold Lane
see **Detective Kellerway series**

Kelleway family series
Bramble, Forbes
1 *Regent Square* (1977)
2 *Iron roads* (1980)

Kelling series
Macleod, Charlotte
see **Sarah Kelling series**

Kellog and Krug series
Weston, Carolyn
see **Casey Kellog and Al Krug series**

Kellogg Brown and Carey Ashton series
Stuart, Becky
1 *Journey's end* (1985)
2 *Someone else* (1985)
3 *Ghost ship* (1986)
4 *Famous last words* (1986)

Kellogg series
Spicer, Bart
see **Benson Kellogg series**

Kells series
Cheyney, Peter
see **Michael Kells series**

Kelly and Carr series
Petievich, Gerald
see **Charles Carr and Jack Kelly series**

Kelly Blake series
Greene, Yvonne
1 *Discovered!* (1986)
2 *Rising star* (1986)
3 *Hard to get* (1986)
4 *Headliners* (1986)
5 *Double trouble* (1986)
6 *Paris nights* (1986)

Kelly Carvel series
Daniels, Norman A
1 *Rape of a town* (1970)
2 *One angry man* (1971)
3 *Licence to kill* (1972)

Kelly Green series
Starr, Leonard
1 *Go-between* (1982)
2 *Blood tapes* (1983)
3 *Million-dollar hit* (1983)
4 *One-two-three die* (1983)

Kelly Maguire trilogy
Hennessy, Max
1 *Lion at sea* (1977)
2 *Dangerous years* (1978)
3 *Back to battle* (1979)

Kelly McCoy series
Buchanan, William
1 *Ghost of Dagger Bay* (1963)
2 *Doctor Anger's island* (1964)
3 *Eagles' Paradise* (1964)

Kelly Robinson and Alexander Scott series
Tiger, John
see **I spy series**

Kelly Ryan series
Dugon, Nora
1 *Lonely summers* (1990)
2 *Clare Street* (1990)

Kelly series
Avery, Robert
see **Joe Kelly series**
Babbin, Jaqueline
see **Clovis Kelly series**
Baker, Nikki
see **Virginia Kelly series**
Bowen, Peter
see **Yellowstone Kelly series**
Burke, Jackson Frederick
see **Samuel Moses Kelly series**
Clevely, Hugh
see **Justin Kelly series**
Dean, S F X
see **Professor Neil Kelly series**

Kelly series
Drake, David
1 *Skyripper* (1983)
2 *Fortress* (1986)

Kelly series
Hildick, Edmund Wallace
see **Lemon Kelly series**
Langton, Jane
see **Homer Kelly series**
Lovelace, Maud Hart
see **Betsy Ray series**

Roth, Holly
see **Lieutenant Kelly series**
Worsley-Gough, Barbara
see **Aloysius Kelly series**

Kelpies series
Hendry, Frances Mary
1 *Quest for a kelpie* (1986)
2 *Quest for a maid* (1988)
3 *Falcon* (1989)
4 *Quest for a babe* (1990)
5 *Lark* (1992)
6 *Jackdaw* (1993)

Kelsey series
Page, Emma
see **Inspector Kelsey series**

Kelso series
White, James Dillon
see **Roger Kelso series**

Kelson trilogy
Kurtz, Katherine
see **Histories of King Kelson trilogy**

Kelston of Kells series
Anderson, Helen M
1 *Kelston of Kells* (1927)
2 *Sons of the forge* (1932)

Keltiad series
Kennealy, Patricia
1 *Copper crown* (1984)
2 *Throne of Scone* (1986)
3 *Silver branch* (1988)

Kelton series
Alexander, Martin
see **Alan Kelton series**

Kemlo series
Eliott, E C
1 *Kemlo and the zones of silence* (1954)
2 *Kemlo and the crazy planet* (1954)
3 *Kemlo and the sky horse* (1954)
4 *Kemlo and the Martian ghosts* (1955)
5 *Kemlo and the craters of the moon* (1955)
6 *Kemlo and the space lanes* (1955)
7 *Kemlo and the star men* (1955)
8 *Kemlo and the gravity rays* (1956)
9 *Kemlo and the purple dawn* (1957)
10 *Kemlo and the end of time* (1957)
11 *Kemlo and the zombie men* (1958)
12 *Kemlo and the space men* (1959)
13 *Kemlo and the satellite builders* (1960)
14 *Kemlo and the space invaders* (1961)
15 *Kemlo and the masters of space* (1963)

Kemp series
Meek, Margaret Reid Duncan
see **Lennox Kemp series**
Woodrooffe, Anne
see **Michael Kemp series**

Ken and Fiona series
Tranter, Nigel Godwin
1 *Spaniards' Isle* (1958)
2 *Border Riding* (1959)
3 *Nestor the monster* (1960)
4 *Birds of a feather* (1961)

Ken, Candy and Co series
Thomas, Millicent Inglis
1 *Ken, Candy and Co* (1939)
2 *Ken, Candy and the hunt for spies* (1948)
3 *Ken, Candy and the castle secret* (1954)

Ken Holt series
Campbell, Bruce
1 *Secret of Skeleton Island* (1949)
2 *Riddle of the stone elephant* (1949)
3 *Black thumb mystery* (1950)
4 *Clue of the marked claw* (1950)
5 *Clue of the coiled cobra* (1951)
6 *Secret of Hangman's Inn* (1951)
7 *Mystery of the iron box* (1952)
8 *Clue of the phantom car* (1953)
9 *Mystery of the galloping horse* (1954)
10 *Mystery of the green flame* (1955)
11 *Mystery of the grinning tiger* (1956)
12 *Mystery of the vanishing magician* (1957)
13 *Mystery of the shattered glass* (1958)
14 *Mystery of the invisible enemy* (1959)
15 *Mystery of Gallows Cliff* (1960)
16 *Clue of the silver scorpion* (1961)
17 *Mystery of the plumed serpent* (1962)
18 *Mystery of the sultan's scimitar* (1963)

Ken Jackson and David Webb series
Fraser, Anthea
see **Inspector David Webb and Sergeant Ken Jackson series**

Ken Malone trilogy
Phillips, Mark
1 *Brain twister* (1962)
2 *Impossibles* (1963)
3 *Supermind* (1963)

Ken series
Miller, Basil
1 *Ken rides the range* (1941)
2 *Ken bails out* (1942)
3 *Ken captures a foreign agent* (1943)
4 *Ken's mercy flight to Australia* (1944)
5 *Ken in Alaska* (1944)
6 *Ken saddles up* (1945)
7 *Ken on the Argentine pampas* (1947)
8 *Ken south of the border* (1947)
9 *Ken on the Navajo trail* (1948)
10 *Ken follows the chuck wagon* (1950)
11 *Ken hits the cowboy trail* (1951)
12 *Ken, range detective* (1952)
13 *Ken and the cattle thieves* (1953)
14 *Ken, range hero* (1954)
15 *Ken and the Navajo treasure map* (1955)
16 *Ken on the Anchor D Ranch* (1956)
17 *Ken and the lost Indian treasure* (1957)

Ken Ward series
Grey, Zane
1 *Young forester* (1910)
2 *Young pitcher* (1911)
3 *Young lion hunter* (1911)
4 *Ken Ward in the jungle* (1912)

Ken Williams series
Barrington, John
1 *Moving finger* (1947)
2 *Murder in White Pit* (1947)

Kencyrath series
Hodgell, Patricia Christine
1 *God stalk* (1982)
2 *Dark of the moon* (1985)
One volume edition entitled *Chronicles of the Kencyrath*, 1988

Kendal Graydon series
Wheeler, H E
1 *Death calls the jester* (1936)
2 *Dead men turn green* (1939)

Kendall and Eisenberg series
Chase, Philip
see **Aaron Eisenberg and William Kendall series**

Kendall series
Baxter, Gillian
see **Angela and Ian Kendall series**
Farjeon, Joseph Jefferson
see **Inspector Kendall series**

Kendall series
Kendall, Carol
1 *Black seven* (1946)
2 *Baby-snatcher* (1952)

Kendall series
Muirden, James
see **Eric Kendall series**

Kendreth series
Chant, Joy
see **Vanderi series**

Kendric and Irissa trilogy
Douglas, Carole Nelson
see **Irissa and Kendric trilogy**

Kendrick family trilogy
Coleman, Lonnie
see **Beulah Land trilogy**

Kendrick series
Mackinnon, Allan
see **Donald Kendrick series**

Kendry series
Chesbro, George Clark
see **Veil Kendry series**

Kenelminster series
Hope-Simpson, Jacynth
see **Bishop of Kenelminster series**

Kenmore trilogy
Leinster, Murray
see **Joe Kenmore trilogy**

Kennedy Middle School series
Cooper, Ilene
see **Kids from Kennedy Middle School series**

Kennedy series
Armstrong, Anthony
see **Patrick Kennedy series**
Charteris, Leslie
see **Bill Kennedy series**
Higgins, George Vincent
see **Jerry Kennedy series**
Kennedy, George
see **George Kennedy series**
Kern, Gregory
see **Cap Kennedy series**
O'Duffy, Eimar
see **Aloysius Kennedy series**
Reeve, Arthur Benjamin
see **Craig Kennedy series**
Venters, Archie
see **Gil Kennedy series**

Kennedys abroad series
This sequence has twelve authors
Someren, Liesje van
1 *Ann and Peter in Holland* (1959)
Callas, Theo
2 *Ann and Peter in southern Spain* (1959)
Einberg, Elizabeth
3 *Ann and Peter in southern Germany* (1959)
Martin, Nancy
4 *Ann and Peter in Denmark* (1959)
Guillemin, Anne
5 *Ann and Peter in Brittany* (1959)
Mannin, Ethel
6 *Ann and Peter in Sweden* (1959)
7 *Ann and Peter in Japan* (1960)
Richards, Phyllis
8 *Ann and Peter in northern Italy* (1960)
Hogg, Garry
9 *Ann and Peter in Norway* (1961)
Richards, Phyllis
10 *Ann and Peter in Yugoslavia* (1962)
Someren, Liesje van
11 *Ann and peter in Belgium* (1962)
Mannin, Ethel
12 *Ann and Peter in Austria* (1962)
Willcox, Kathleen Mary
13 *Ann and Peter in Israel* (1962)
Wilson, Barbara Ker
14 *Ann and Peter in Paris* (1963)
Richards, Phyllis
15 *Ann and Peter in Rome* (1963)
Greenham, Hazel
16 *Ann and Peter in Scotland* (1964)
Willcox, Kathleen Mary
17 *Ann and Peter in Switzerland* (1965)
Wilson, Barbara Ker
18 *Ann and Peter in London* (1965)
Vaughan, Carol
19 *Ann and Peter in Greece* (1966)

Kennet trilogy
Garner, Rolf
1 *Resurgent dust* (1953)
2 *Immortals* (1953)
3 *Indestructible* (1954)

Kenneth Aubrey series
Thomas, Craig
1 *Bear's tears* (1985)
2 *All the grey cats* (1988)

Kenneth Carlisle series
Wells, Carolyn
1 *Sleeping dogs* (1929)
2 *Doorstep murders* (1930)
3 *Skeleton at the feast* (1931)

Kenneth Ducane series
Bingham, John
see **Ducane series**

Kenneth Vandoren series
Bingham, John
see **Ducane series**

Kenney series
Moore, Robin
see **Pat Kenney series**

Kenny Rider series
Hardcastle, Michael
1 *Goals in the air* (1972)
2 *Where the action is* (1976)
3 *Top of the league* (1979)

Kenny series
Dillon, Eilis
see **Inspector Mike Kenny series**

Kensho series
Schmidt, Dennis
1 *Wayfarer* (1978)
2 *Kensho* (1979)
3 *Satori* (1981)
4 *Wanderer* (1985)

Kensington series
Ferguson, Rachel
1 *Passionate Kensington* (1939)
2 *Royal Borough* (1950)

Kent Barstow series
Montgomery, Rutherford George
1 *Jets away* (1957)
2 *Kent Barstow, special agent* (1958)
3 *Missile away* (1959)
4 *Mission intruder* (1960)
5 *Kent Barstow, space man* (1961)
6 *Kent Barstow and the commando flight* (1963)
7 *Kent Barstow on a B-70 mission* (1964)
8 *Kent Barstow aboard the Dyna Soar* (1964)

Kent family series
Jakes, John
1 *Bastard* (1974)
1770-1775
1.1 *Fortune's whirlwind* (1974)
1.2 *To an unknown shore* (1974)
2 *Rebels* (1975)
1775-1781; numbers 1 and 2 also

published in one volume entitled *The patriots*, 1976
3 *Seekers* (1975)
1794-1814
4 *Furies* (1976)
1836-1852; numbers 3 and 4 also published in one volume entitled *The pioneers*, 1976
5 *Titans* (1976)
1860-1862
6 *Warriors* (1977)
1864-1868
7 *Lawless* (1978)
1869-1877
8 *Americans* (1980)
Set in the early twentieth century

Kent Montana trilogy
Fenn, Lionel
1 *Kent Montana and the really ugly thing from Mars* (1990)
2 *Kent Montana and the reasonably invisible man* (1991)
3 *Kent Montana and the once and future thing* (1991)

Kent Murdock series
Coxe, George Harmon
1 *Murder with pictures* (1935)
2 *Barotique mystery* (1936)
Murdock's acid test
3 *Camera clue* (1937)
4 *Four frightened women* (1939)
Frightened women
5 *Glass triangle* (1940)
6 *Mrs Murdock takes a case* (1941)
7 *Charred witness* (1942)
8 *Jade Venus* (1945)
9 *Fifth key* (1947)
10 *Hollow needle* (1948)
11 *Lady killer* (1949)
12 *Eye witness* (1950)
13 *Widow had a gun* (1951)
14 *Crimson clue* (1953)
15 *Focus on murder* (1954)
16 *Murder on their minds* (1957)
17 *Big gamble* (1958)
18 *Last commandment* (1960)
19 *Hidden key* (1963)
20 *Reluctant heiress* (1965)
21 *Easy way to go* (1968)
22 *Fenner* (1971)
23 *Silent witness* (1973)

Kent series
Boswell, John
see **Christopher Kent series**
Cripps, Arthur Shearly
see **John Kent series**
Devon, D G
see **Temple Kent series**
Giles, Guy Elwyn
see **Brice Kent series**
Gunn, John
see **Peter Kent series**
Moorhouse, Hopkins
see **Addison Kent series**
Richards, Milton
see **Dick Kent series**

Kent trilogy
Oldfield, Pamela
1 *Green harvest* (1983)
2 *Summer song* (1984)
3 *Golden tally* (1985)

Kenton and Boone series
Ellis, Edward Sylvester
see **Daniel Boone and Simon Kenton series**

Kenton series
Harvester, Simon
see **Malcolm Kenton series**

Kentucky series
Allen, James Lane
1 *Kentucky cardinal* (1895)
2 *Aftermath* (1896)

Kentucky trilogy
Arnow, Harriette
1 *Mountain path* (1936)
2 *Hunter's horn* (1949)
3 *Dollmaker* (1954)

Kentucky trilogy
Giles, Janice Holt
see **Piney Ridge trilogy**

Kenworthy series
Hilton, John Buxton
see **Superintendent Simon Kenworthy series**

Kenworthys series
Wilson, Margaret
1 *Kenworthys* (1925)
2 *Painted room* (1926)

Kenya childhood series
Huxley, Elspeth
Reminiscences
1 *Flame trees of Thika* (1959)
Memories of an African childhood
2 *Mottled lizard* (1962)
On the edge of the Rift
Memories of Kenya
3 *Love among the daughters* (1968)
Memories of the twenties in England and America
4 *Out in the midday sun* (1985)

Kenya series
Strange, Nora Kathleen
1 *Wife in Kenya* (1925)
2 *Kenya calling* (1928)
3 *Kenya dawn* (1929)
4 *Courtship in Kenya* (1932)
5 *Kenya moon* (1933)
6 *Youth comes to Kenya* (1938)
7 *Jenny* (1947)
8 *Beneath the thorn tree* (1956)
9 *Quiet girl* (1967)

Kenya trilogy
Nicole, Christopher
1 *High country* (1988)
2 *Happy valley* (1989)
3 *Dark sun* (1990)

Kenyatta series
Clark, Al C
Also published under the author's real name Donald Goines
1 *Crime partners* (1974)
2 *Death list* (1974)
3 *Kenyatta's escape* (1974)
4 *Kenyatta's last hit* (1975)

Kenyon series
Crisp, Norman James
see **Inspector Sidney Kenyon series**
Macdonnell, James Edmond
see **Captain Kenyon series**

Keogh series
Lindop, Audrey Erskine
see **Father Keogh series**

Kerby Maxwell series
Corbett, Scott
1 *Lemonade trick* (1960)
2 *Mailbox trick* (1961)
3 *Disappearing dog trick* (1963)
4 *Limerick trick* (1964)
5 *Baseball trick* (1965)
6 *Turnabout trick* (1967)
7 *Hairy horror trick* (1969)
8 *Hateful plateful trick* (1971)
9 *Home run trick* (1973)
10 *Hockey trick* (1974)
11 *Black Mask trick* (1976)
12 *Hangman's ghost trick* (1977)

Kereban the Inflexible series
Verne, Jules
1 *Captain of the Guidara* (1883)
2 *Scarpante, the spy* (1883)
Original one volume edition entitled *Kereban le tetu*

Keremos series
Zaremba, Eve
see **Helen Keremos series**

Kerensky trilogy
Stackpole, Michael
see **Blood of Kerensky trilogy**

Kerinsky series
Ryan, Jim
see **Igor Kerinsky series**

Kerish-lo-Taan's quest series
Harris, Geraldine
see **Seven citadels series**

Kerkhoven trilogy
Wassermann, Jakob
see **Doctor Joseph Kerkhoven trilogy**

Kerr and Fusil series
Alding, Peter
see **C.I.D. Room series**

Kerr series
Orde, Lewis
see **Daniel Kerr series**

Kerrigan series
Gordon, Neil
see **Peter Kerrigan series**
Harrington, Joseph
see **Lieutenant Frank Kerrigan series**

Kerrion Empire series
Morris, Janet Ellen
1 *Dream dancer* (1980)
2 *Cruiser dreams* (1980)
3 *Earth dreams* (1982)

Kerrwood series
Duncan, Allan
see **Major Charles Douglas Kerrwood series**

Kerry series
Ashford, Jeffrey
see **Detective Inspector Don Kerry series**

Kerry series
Leyland, Mal
1 *Kerry's lost dog* (1980)
2 *Gypsy goes to the country* (1981)
Companion volume: *Gypsy's animal alphabet*, 1982

Kerry series
Rohmer, Sax
see **Red Kerry series**

Kershaw series
Shirreffs, Gordon Donald
see **Lee Kershaw series**

Kershaw trilogy
Shirreffs, Gordon Donald
see **Quint Kershaw trilogy**

Kerwood series
Duncan, Allan
see **Major Charles Douglas Kerrwood series**

Kesrick series
Carter, Lin
see **Terra Magica series**

Kessler series
Hutson, Shaun
see **Sergeant Rolf Kessler series**

Kestrels series
Mason, Stanley Weston
1 *Kestrels over the beacon* (1949)
2 *Kestrels jetty* (1950)
3 *Kestrels dare danger* (1951)
4 *Kestrels plot adventure* (1954)

Ketchup series
Stern, Simon
see **Astonishing adventures of Captain Ketchup series**

Ketchup sisters series
Hollands, Judith
Illustrated by Dee De Rosa
1 *Rescue of the red-blooded librarian* (1989)
2 *Deeds of the desperate campers* (1990)
3 *Secret of the haunted doghouse* (1990)

Kettle series
Hyne, Charles John Cutcliffe
see **Captain Owen Kettle series**
White, James Dillon
see **Sebastian Kettle series**

Kettle series
Muir, Marie
1 *Pam, Pot and Kettle* (1964)
2 *Kettle's great adventure* (1965)

Kevin and Sadie series
Lingard, Joan
see **Sadie and Kevin series**

Kevin Corbett series
Hermes, Patricia
1 *Kevin Corbett eats flies* (1986)
2 *Heads, I win* (1989)

Kevin Fikkan series
Shetterly, Will
1 *Cats have no lord* (1985)
2 *Tangled lands* (1989)

Kevin Fitzgerald series
Topor, Tom
1 *Bloodstar* (1978)
2 *Coda* (1984)

Kevin Macinnes series
Bandy, Franklin
1 *Deceit and deadly lies* (1978)
2 *Blackstock affair* (1980)

Keyne series
Wood, Clement
see **Skelton Keyne series**

Keys series
Cooney, Michael
see **Queen's investigator series**

Keys to paradise trilogy
Moran, Daniel Keys
1 *Flame key* (1987)
2 *Skeleton lord's key* (1987)
3 *Key of ice and steel* (1988)
One volume edition entitled *The keys of paradise*, 1986

Keys to the dimensions series
Bulmer, Kenneth
1 *Land beyond the map* (1965)
2 *Key to Irunium* (1967)
3 *Key to Venudine* (1968)
4 *Wizards of Senchuria* (1969)
5 *Ships of Durostorum* (1970)
6 *Hunters of Jundagai* (1971)
7 *Chariots of Ra* (1972)
8 *Diamond contessa* (1983)

Kezzy series
Burns, Patricia
1 *Stacey's flyer* (1985)
2 *Kezzy* (1988)

Khadaji series
Perry, Steve
1 *Ninety seventh step* (1989)
2 *Man who never missed* (1985)

3 *Matadora* (1986)
4 *Macchiavelli interface* (1986)
5 *Omega cage* (1988)
Co-author: Michael Reaves
6 *Albino knife* (1991)
7 *Black steel* (1992)
8 *Brother Death* (1992)

Khairastan series
Wren, Percival Christopher
1 *Man of a ghost* (1937)
Spur of pride
2 *Worth wile* (1937)
To the hilt

Khaki Boys series
Bates, Gordon
1 *Khaki Boys at Camp Sterling* (1918)
Alternative title: Training for the big fight in France
2 *Khaki Boys on the way* (1918)
Alternative title: Doing their bit on land and sea
3 *Khaki Boys at the Front* (1918)
Alternative title: Shoulder to shoulder in the trenches
4 *Khaki Boys over the top* (1919)
Alternative title: Doing and daring for Uncle Sam
5 *Khaki Boys fighting to win* (1919)
Alternative title: Smashing the German lines
6 *Khaki Boys along the Rhine* (1920)
Alternative title: Winning the honors of war

Khaki Girls series
Brooks, Edna
1 *Khaki Girls of the Motor Corps* (1918)
Alternative title: Finding their place in the Big War
2 *Khaki Girls behind the lines* (1918)
Alternative title: Driving with the Ambulance Corps
3 *Khaki Girls at Windsor Barracks* (1919)
Alternative title: Standing to with the Trusty Twenty
4 *Khaki Girls in victory* (1920)
Alternative title: Home with the heroes

Khalindaine series
Burns, Richard
1 *Khalindaine* (1985)
2 *Troubadour* (1988)

Kham series
Foster, Richard
see **Chin Kwang Kham series**

Khan series
Afghan
see **Asaf Khan series**

Kharduni series
Soutar, Andrew
1 *Kharduni* (1933)
2 *Great conspiracy* (1934)
3 *Justice is dome* (1936)

Khassan series
Dawson, Alec John
see **Joseph Khassan series**

Khe Sanh series
Hammel, Eric Maxwell
1 *Siege in the clouds* (1989)
An oral history
2 *Assault on Khe Sanh* (1990)
An oral history
3 *Siege of Khe Sanh* (1990)

Khlit the Cossack series
Lamb, Harold
1 *Curved saber* (1964)
2 *Mighty manslayer* (1969)

Khryse trilogy
Fletcher, Beryl
1 *Word burners* (1991)
2 *Iron mouth* (1993)
Number 3 not yet published

Khyberie series
Enriquez, Colin Metcalfe
1 *Khyberie* (1937)
The story of a pony on the Indian frontier
2 *Khyberie in Burma* (1939)
The adventures of a mountain pony

Kid Breckinridge series
Palmer, Bernard
The original Canadian and the American editions of this sequence differ
1 *Breck's choice* (1981)
2 *Hunted gun* (1984)
Wanted gun
3 *Kid Breckenridge* (1984)
4 *Shoot-out at Buffalo Gulch* (1985)

Kid Collins series
Thompson, Victoria
1 *Texas treasure* (1985)
2 *Texas triumph* (1987)
3 *Angel Heart* (1988)

Kid Curry and Hannibal Hayes series
Fox, Brian
see **Alias Smith and Jones series**

Kid Cyclone series
Gregory, Lester
1 *Trigger Kid* (1947)
2 *Kid Cyclone* (1948)
3 *Cyclone guns* (1952)
4 *Code of the Kid* (1953)

Kid power series
Pfeffer, Susan Beth
1 *Kid power* (1977)
2 *Kid power strikes back* (1984)

Kid series
Culp, John Hewett
see **Martin Cameron series**

Kid-TV series
Adams, Barbara
1 *On the air and off the wall* (1986)
2 *Not-quite-ready-for-prime-time bandits* (1986)
3 *Rock video strikes again* (1986)
4 *Can this telethon be saved?* (1987)

Kidd and Regina series
Dagmar
see **Randy Kidd and Regina series**

Kidd series
Camp, John
1 *Fool's run* (1989)
2 *Empress file* (1991)

Kiddie trilogy
Leighton, Robert
1 *Kiddie of the camp* (1910)
A story of the Western prairies
2 *Kiddie the scout* (1920)
3 *Kiddie, the prairie rider* (1924)

Kidnadze series
Vincent, Kitty
see **Gyp Kidnadze series**

Kids from Kennedy Middle School series
Cooper, Ilene
1 *Queen of the sixth grade* (1988)
2 *Choosing sides* (1990)
3 *Mean streak* (1991)
4 *New, improved Gretchen Hubbard* (1992)

Kids of the Polk Street School series
Giff, Patricia Reilly
1 *Beast in Ms Rooney's room* (1984)
2 *Fish Face* (1984)
3 *Candy corn contest* (1984)
Pop corn contest
4 *December secrets* (1984)
5 *In the dinosaur's paw* (1985)
6 *Valentine star* (1985)
7 *Lazy lions* (1985)
8 *Snaggle doodles* (1985)
9 *Purple climbing days* (1985)
10 *Say cheese* (1985)
11 *Sunny-side up* (1986)
12 *Pickle puss* (1986)
13 *Beast and the Halloween horror* (1990)
Companion volume: *Show time at the Polk Street School, plays you can do yourself*, 1992

Kids on the bus series
Sharmat, Marjorie Weinman
1 *School bus cat* (1990)
2 *Cooking class* (1990)
3 *Haunted bus* (1991)
4 *Bully on the bus* (1991)
5 *Secret notebook* (1991)
6 *Field day mix-up* (1991)

Kids series
Martin, Ann Matthews
1 *Ten kids, no pets* (1988)
2 *Eleven kids, one summer* (1991)

Kids' stuff series
This sequence has three authors
Baker, Denis
1 *Winning is kids' stuff* (1988)
Baker, Ann
2 *Reading is kids' stuff* (1990)
Survival kit for today's parents
3 *Maths is kids' stuff* (1991)

Kids talk series
Arnold, Eric H
1 *Lights out!* (1985)
Kids talk about summer camp
2 *I'm telling!* (1987)
Kids talk about brothers and sisters

Kiel Saint James and Orson Boles series
Chaze, Elliot
1 *Mister Yesterday* (1984)
2 *Little David* (1985)

Kiernan O'Shaughnessy series
Dunlap, Susan
1 *Pious deception* (1989)
2 *Rogue wave* (1991)
3 *High fall* (1994)

Kiet series
Alexander, Gary
see **Superintendent Bamsan Kiet series**

Kiichiro Nire series
Kita, Morio
Translated from the Japanese
1 *House of Nire* (1964)
2 *Fall of the House of Nire* (1964)

Kiki series
Koenig, Lilli
Translated from the German
1 *Gringolo* (1958)
2 *Timba* (1959)

Kiki series
Steiner, Charlotte
1 *Kiki and Muffy* (1943)
2 *Kiki dances* (1949)
3 *Kiki skates* (1950)
4 *Kiki goes to camp* (1953)
5 *Kiki loves music* (1954)
6 *Kiki is an actress* (1958)
7 *Kiki's playhouse* (1962)

Kilakura series
Lister, Stephen
1 *Everything smelt of kippers* (1957)
2 *Tycoon in Eden* (1973)

Kilburn series
Howells, William Dean
see **Annie Kilburn series**

Kilburn series
Victor, Sam
1 *Kilburn* (1974)
2 *Spikebit* (1974)
3 *High hazard* (1975)
4 *Wolf moon* (1975)
5 *Rope law* (1976)
6 *Posse of killers* (1976)

Kilby series
Frazer, Robert Caine
see **Mark Kilby series**
Lenehan, John Christopher
see **Inspector Kilby series**

Kildare junior series
Ackworth, Robert Charles
see **Doctor Kildare junior series**

Kildare series
Brand, Max
see **Doctor Kildare series**

Kilgerrin series
Leonard, Charles L
see **Paul Kilgerrin series**

Kilgour trilogy
Webster, Jan
see **Kate Kilgour trilogy**

Kilkenny series
L'Amour, Louis
see **Lance Kilkenny series**

Kilkhampton series
Croft, Herbert
see **Abbey of kilkhampton series**

Kill Squad series
Cruz, Mark
1 *Kill Squad* (1975)
2 *Voyage of death* (1975)
3 *Dead wrong* (1975)
4 *Dead end* (1975)

Killain series
Marlowe, Dan James
see **Johnny Killain series**

Killashandra series
McCaffrey, Anne
1 *Crystal singer* (1982)
2 *Killashandra* (1985)

Killer instinct series
Boggis, David
1 *Killer instinct* (1980)
2 *Time to betray* (1981)

Killer series
Freedman, Russell
1 *Killer fish* (1982)
2 *Killer snakes* (1982)

Killers series
Netzen, Klaus
American editions published under the name Klaus Nettson
1 *To win and to lose* (1974)
2 *Winston Churchill murder* (1974)
Churchill mission
3 *Night and fog* (1974)
Mission into Auschwitz
4 *Fatal friends* (1975)
5 *Pearl of blood* (1975)

6 *Death village* (1976)
7 *Silent enemy* (1976)

Killinger series
Palmer, P K
see **Jedediah Killinger series**

Killsquad
Cruz, Mark
see **Death Squad series**

Killsquad series
Garrett, Frank
1 *Counter attack* (1986)
2 *Mission revenge* (1986)
3 *Lethal assault* (1986)
4 *Judas soldiers* (1987)
5 *Blood beach* (1987)
6 *Body count* (1987)
7 *Polar assault* (1987)
8 *Slaughter zone* (1987)

Killstar series
Kelly, David J
1 *Baalbak quest* (1980)
2 *Tower of despair* (1980)

Killy series
Quinn, Simon
see **Inquisitor series**

Kilmoonie and Grisman series
Morrell, David
see **Chris Kilmoonie and Saul Grisman series**

Kilsip and Calton series
Hume, Fergus
see **Detective Kilsip and Duncan Calton series**

Kim Aldrich series
McDonnell, Jinny
1 *Miscalculated risk* (1972)
2 *Silent partner* (1972)
3 *Deep six* (1973)
4 *Long shot* (1973)

Kim Locke series
Crossen, Kendell Foster
1 *Tortured path* (1957)
2 *Big dive* (1959)
Sequence continued under the pseudonym Clay Richards
Richards, Clay
3 *Gentle assassin* (1964)

Kim series
This sequence has two authors
Kipling, Rudyard
1 *Kim* (1901)
Murari, Timeri
2 *Imperial agent* (1987)
3 *Last victory* (1988)

Kim Smith series
Boland, John
see **Counterpol series**

Kim the detective series
Holm, Jens K
Translated from the Danish
1 *Kim the detective* (1975)
2 *Kim and the buried treasure* (1975)

Kimball series
Laklan, Carli
see **Nancy Kimball series**

Kincaid and James series
Crombie, Deborah
see **Superintendent Duncan Kincaid and Sergeant Gemma James series**

Kincaid series
Cox, William Robert
see **Tom Kincaid series**
Talbot, Hake
see **Rogan Kincaid series**

Kincaids series
Brady, Taylor
1 *Raging rivers* (1992)
2 *Prairie thunder* (1993)
3 *Mountain fury* (1993)
4 *Westward winds* (1993)

Kind Dog series
Banner, Angela
1 *Ant and Bee and Kind Dog* (1963)
An alphabetical story
2 *Kind Dog on Monday* (1972)
3 *Kind Dog up and down the hill* (1972)

Kind of magic series
Harris, Mollie
Country life in the Cotswolds
1 *Kind of magic* (1969)
2 *Another kind of magic* (1971)

Kinderman series
Blatty, William Peter
see **Lieutenant Bill Kinderman series**

Kindrachill House series
Lyon, Elinor
see **James, Alan and Roslin series**

Kine trilogy
Lloyd, Alan R
1 *Kine* (1982)
Marshworld
2 *Witchwood* (1989)
3 *Dragon pond* (1990)

King Alfred series
Hodges, Cyril Walter
1 *Namesake* (1964)
2 *Marsh king* (1967)

King and Lundberg series
Saunders, Lawrence
see **Wylie King and Nels Lundberg series**

King and queen series
Saddler, Allen
1 *Archery contest* (1982)
2 *King gets fit* (1982)
3 *Fishing competition* (1983)
4 *King and the invisible dwarf* (1983)
5 *King at Christmas* (1984)
6 *Queen's painting* (1984)

King Arthur series
Ashe, Geoffrey
1 *King Arthur's Avalon* (1957)
2 *From Caesar to Arthur* (1960)
3 *Quest for Arthur's Britain* (1968)
4 *Camelot and the vision of Albion* (1971)

King Arthur series
Jones, Courtway
1 *In the shadow of the Oak King* (1991)
2 *Witch of the North* (1992)

King Arthur series
White, Terence Hanbury
see **Once and future king series**

King family series
Colegate, Isabel
1 *Orlando King* (1968)
2 *Orlando at the brazen threshold* (1971)
3 *Agatha* (1973)
The story of Orlando's daughter after his death

King family series
Ehle, John
see **North Carolina series**

King family series
Quigley, John
1 *King's royal* (1975)
2 *Queen's royal* (1977)

King Goblin series
Grimm, Geraldine
1 *King Goblin and his forest friends* (1972)
2 *King Goblin and the golden treasure* (1972)
3 *King Goblin loses his throne* (1973)
5 *King Goblin returns* (1973)

King Goshawk series
O'Duffy, Eimar
1 *King Goshawk and the birds* (1926)
2 *Asses in clover* (1933)

King Jack series
Snowden, James Keighley
1 *King Jack* (1914)
2 *Jack the outlaw* (1926)

King James III series
Aiken, Joan
see **Dido Twite series**

King Kelson trilogy
Kurtz, Katherine
see **Histories of King Kelson trilogy**

King Kong series
This sequence has three authors
Lovelace, Delos
1 *King Kong* (1932)
Wager, Walter
2 *My side* (1976)
Written from the point of view of King Kong
Pascall, Jeremy
3 *King Kong story* (1977)
Companion volumes: *The girl in the hairy paw, King Kong as myth, movie and monster*, by Harry Maurice Geduld and Ronald Gottesman, 1976, *King Kong*, by Ian Thorne, 1977

K'ing Kung-Fu series
Macao, Marshall
1 *Son of the flying tiger* (1973)
2 *Return of the opium wars* (1973)
3 *Rape of Sun Lee Fong* (1975)
4 *Kak-Abdullah conspiracy* (1975)
5 *Red plague in Bolivia* (1974)
6 *New York necromancy* (1974)
7 *Mark of the vulture* (1974)

King of diamonds series
Terry, Carolyn
1 *King of diamonds* (1983)
2 *Fortune seekers* (1985)

King of Kenilwick Castle series
West, Colin
1 *King of Kenilwick* (1986)
2 *King's toothache* (1987)

King of the Commandos series
Johns, William Earl
see **Gimlet series**

King of the Royal Mounted series
Grey, Zane
1 *King of the Royal Mounted* (1936)
Based on a comic strip
2 *King of the Royal Mounted and the northern treasure* (1937)
3 *King of the Royal Mounted and the great jewel mystery* (1937)
4 *King of the Royal mounted in Arctic law* (1937)
5 *King of the Royal Mounted gets his man* (1938)
6 *King of the Royal Mounted in the far north* (1938)
7 *King of the Royal Mounted policing the frozen north* (1938)
8 *King of the Royal Mounted in law of the north* (1939)
9 *King of the Royal Mounted, the long arm of the law* (1942)
10 *King of the Royal Mounted and the ghost guns of Roaring River* (1946)

King of the sticks trilogy
Southall, Ivan
1 *King of the sticks* (1979)
2 *Golden goose* (1981)
3 *Christmas in the tree* (1985)

King of the wind series
Henry, Marguerite
1 *Colt is born* (1988)
2 *Innkeeper's horse* (1988)
3 *Rescue of Sham* (1988)
4 *Battle of the stallions* (1988)
5 *Sultan's gift* (1988)
6 *Sire of champions* (1988)
Original one volume edition entitled *King of the wind*, 1948

King of Ys series
Anderson, Poul
1 *Roma mater* (1986)
2 *Gallicenae* (1987)
Numbers 1 and 2 also published in one volume entitled *The King of Ys*, 1988
3 *Dahut* (1988)
4 *Dog and the wolf* (1988)
Numbers 3 and 4 also published in one volume entitled *The king of Ys*, volume 2

King Olaf Tryggvason series
Sprague, Rosemary
1 *Kingdom to win* (1953)
2 *Heroes of the white shield* (1955)

King Richard II series
Tucker, Terry
1 *Woman into wolf* (1968)
2 *Unravished bride* (1970)

King Rollo series
McKee, David
1 *King Rollo and the birthday* (1979)
2 *King Roll and the bread* (1979)
3 *King Rollo and the new shoes* (1979)
4 *King Rollo and the balloons* (1980)
5 *King Rollo and the tree* (1980)
Numbers 1, 2, 3, 5 also published in one volume entitled *The adventures of King Rollo*, 1983
6 *King Rollo and the dishes* (1980)
7 *King Rollo and the search* (1981)
8 *King Rollo and the bath* (1981)
9 *King Rollo and King Frank* (1981)
Numbers 4, 6, 7, 9 also published in one volume entitled *Further adventures of King Rollo*, 1983
10 *King Rollo and the breakfast* (1982)
11 *King Rollo and the dog* (1982)
12 *King Rollo and the masks* (1982)
13 *King Rollo and the playroom* (1982)
Numbers 10-13 also published in one volume entitled *King Rollo's playroom, and other stories*, 1983
14 *King Rollo and the letter* (1984)
15 *King Rollo's spring* (1986)
16 *King Rollo's autumn* (1986)
17 *King Rollo's summer* (1986)
18 *King Rollo's winter* (1986)
19 *King Rollo's letter, and other stories* (1989)
20 *King Rollo and Santa's beard* (1990)

King series
Banks, Raymond E
see **Sam King series**
Barker, Albert
see **Reefe King series**
Cooper, Natasha
see **Willow King series**
Fisher, Graham
see **Mike King series**

Johns, William Earl
see **Gimlet series**
King, Frank
see **Doctor Frank King series**
Mackenzie, Jake
see **Secret files of Dakota King series**
Miall, Robert
see **Jason King series**
Mundy, Talbot
see **Athelstan King series**
Rosenberger, Joseph
see **Murder Master series**
Scott, Dan
see **Bret King series**
Smith, Beatrice Schillinger
see **Kate and Ben King series**
Stewart, Jane L
see **Camp Fire Girls series**
Thompson, David
see **Nathaniel King series**

King Solomon's mines series
Haggard, Henry Rider
1 *King Solomon's mines* (1885)
2 *Allan Quatermain* (1887)
Allan Quatermain and the lost city of gold
The second title is an edition abridged by Sarah Litvinoff, 1986
3 *Maiwa's revenge* (1888)
4 *Allan's wife* (1887)

King Victor series
Dickinson, Peter
1 *King and joker* (1976)
2 *Skeleton-in-waiting* (1989)

King Wilbur series
Rogerson, James
1 *King Wilbur rebuilds his palace* (1976)
2 *King Wilbur and the bath* (1976)
3 *King Wilbur's birthday present* (1976)
4 *King Wilbur and the bicycle* (1976)

Kingdom of Amber series
Zelazny, Roger
1 *Nine princes in Amber* (1970)
Companion volume: *The black road war, Combat Command in the world of Roger Zelazny's Nine princes in Amber*, by Neil Randall, 1988
2 *Guns of Avalon* (1972)
3 *Sign of the unicorn* (1975)
4 *Hand of Oberon* (1976)
5 *Courts of chaos* (1978)
Numbers 1-5 are also published in one volume entitled *The chronicles of Amber*, 1979
6 *Trumps of doom* (1985)
7 *Blood of Amber* (1986)
8 *Sign of chaos* (1987)
9 *Knight of shadows* (1989)
10 *Prince of chaos* (1991)
Companion volumes: *A rhapsody in Amber*, 1981, also *Seven no-trump, a Crossroads adventure in the world of Roger Zelazny's Amber*, by Neil Randall, 1988, and *Roger Zelazny's visual guide to Castle Amber*, by Neil Randall and Roger Zelazny, 1988

Kingdom of Caledon series
Miller, Margaret Jessy
1 *Queen's music* (1961)
2 *Powers of the Sapphire* (1962)
3 *Doctor Boomer* (1964)

Kingdom of Frome series
Packard, Edward
see **Escape from the Kingdom of Frome series**

Kingdom of Incredibilia series
Hunter, Norman
1 *Larkey legends* (1938)
Dribblesome teapot, and other incredible stories
The second titles is an abridged edition
2 *Home-made dragon, and other incredible stories* (1971)
3 *Frantic phantom, and other incredible stories* (1973)
4 *Dust-up at the Royal Disco* (1975)
5 *Count Bakwerdz on the carpet* (1979)
6 *Sneeze and be slain, and other incredible stories* (1980)

Kingdom of Landover series
Brooks, Terry
see **Magic Kingdom of Landover series**

Kingdom of Leon-Castilla series
Reilly, Bernard F
1 *Kingdom of Leon-Castilla under King Alfonso VI, 1065-1109* (1988)
2 *Kingdom of Leon-Castilla under Queen Urraca, 1109-1126* (1982)

Kingdom of Prydain series
Alexander, Lloyd
see **Prydain series**

Kingdom of sorcery trilogy
Simon, Morris
1 *Sceptre of power* (1986)
2 *Sorcerer's crown* (1986)
3 *Clash of the sorcerers* (1986)

Kingdoms series
Gurney, Gene
Illustrated encyclopaedias of ruling monarchs from ancient times to the present
1 *Kingdoms of Europe* (1982)
2 *Kingdoms of Asia, the Middle East and Africa* (1985)

Kingdoms trilogy
Wells, Angus
1 *Wrath of Ashar* (1988)
2 *Usurper* (1989)
3 *Way beneath* (1990)

Kings Row series
Bellamann, Henry
1 *Kings Row* (1940)
2 *Parris Mitchell of Kings Row* (1948)
Completed by Katherine Bellamann

King's series
Fraser, Christine Marion
1 *King's croft* (1986)
2 *King's acre* (1987)
3 *King's exile* (1989)
4 *King's close* (1991)
5 *King's farewell* (1993)

King's tramp series
De Haven, Tom
see **Chronicles of the king's tramp series**

Kingslake series
E, H F
see **Maud Kingslake series**

Kingsley Toplitt series
Stockwell, Gail
1 *Death by invitation* (1937)
2 *Embarrassed murderer* (1938)
3 *Candy killings* (1940)

Kingston tetralogy
Helwig, David
1 *Glass knight* (1976)
2 *Jennifer* (1979)
3 *Sound like laughter* (1983)
4 *It is always summer* (1982)

Kinky Friedman series
Friedman, Kinky
1 *When the cat's away* (1980)
2 *Greenwich killing time* (1986)
3 *Case of Lone Star* (1987)
Numbers 1-3 also published in one volume entitled *The Kinky Friedman crime club*, 1993
4 *Frequent flyer* (1989)
5 *Musical chairs* (1991)
6 *Elvis, Jesus and Coca Cola* (1993)

Kinnellan series
Mackenzie, Agnes Mure
1 *Lost Kinnellan* (1927)
2 *Falling wind* (1930)
Only published in the one volume edition entitled *Keith o' Kinnellan*, 1930

Kinrade series
Manners, Alexandra
see **Karran Kinrade series**

Kinsella series
Green, Christine
see **Kate Kinsella series**

Kinsey Millhone series
Grafton, Sue
1 *A is for alibi* (1982)
2 *B is for burglar* (1985)
3 *C is for corpse* (1986)
4 *D is for deadbeat* (1987)
5 *E is for evidence* (1988)
6 *F is for fugitive* (1989)
7 *G is for gumshoe* (1990)
8 *H is for homicide* (1991)
9 *I is for innocent* (1992)
10 *J is for judgment* (1993)
11 *K is for killer* (1994)

Kinship series
Cowper, Richard
see **Bird of kinship series**

Kinsman series
Bova, Ben
see **Chet Kinsman series**

Kioga series
Chester, William L
1 *Hawk of the wilderness* (1936)
2 *Kioga of the wilderness* (1976)
3 *One against a wilderness* (1977)
4 *Kioga of the unknown land* (1978)

Kip series
Odaga, Asenath
1 *Kip on the farm* (1972)
2 *Kip at the coast* (1977)
3 *Kip goes to the city* (1977)

Kipper series
Darke, Marjorie
1 *Kipper's turn* (1976)
2 *Kipper skips* (1979)

Kippy Koala series
Morgan, Win
Illustrated by Graham Wade
1 *Kippy Koala and the bushfire* (1985)
2 *Kippy Koala's Christmas present* (1987)

Kirby series
Peters, Elizabeth
see **Jacqueline Kirby series**
Richards, Clay
see **Grant Kirby series**

Kirk series
Blackburn, John
see **General Charles Kirk series**
Burns, Rex
see **Devlin Kirk series**
Hornig, Doug
see **Steven Kirk series**
Patten, Gilbert
see **Don Kirk series**

Kirkbride series
Blamires, Harry
1 *Kirkbride conversations* (1958)
Six dialogues of the Christian faith
2 *Kirkbride and Company* (1959)

Kirke Montgomery series
Mallory, Arthur
see **Doctor Kirke Montgomery series**

Kirlin and Zevich series
Bourgeau, Art
see **Claude Kirlin and F T Zevich series**

Kirsten series
Shaw, Janet
1 *Meet Kirsten, an American girl* (1986)
2 *Kirsten learns a lesson* (1986)
A school story
3 *Kirsten's surprise* (1986)
A Christmas story
4 *Happy birthday, Kirsten!* (1987)
A springtime story
5 *Changes for Kirsten* (1988)
A winter story
6 *Kirsten saves the day* (1988)
A summer story

Kirth Gersen series
Vance, Jack
1 *Star king* (1964)
2 *Killing machine* (1964)
3 *Palace of love* (1967)
4 *Face* (1979)
5 *Book of dreams* (1981)

Kiss Darling and Angus Fane series
Yardley, James
1 *Kiss the boys and make them die* (1970)
2 *Kiss a day keeps the corpses away* (1971)

Kiss series
Sinclair, Heather
1 *Remembered kiss* (1976)
2 *Kiss a stranger* (1976)

Kit Acton series
Bramhall, Marion
1 *Murder solves a problem* (1944)
2 *Button, button* (1944)
3 *Tragedy in blue* (1945)
4 *Murder is an evil business* (1948)
5 *Murder is contagious* (1949)

Kit and Katie series
De Paola, Tomie
see **Katie and Kit series**

Kit and Nita series
Duane, Diane
see **Wizard series**

Kit Carey series
Lounsberry, Lionel
1 *Cadet Kit Carey* (1899)
Alternative title: The young soldier's legacy
2 *Lieutenant Carey's luck* (1899)
3 *Captain Carey of the Gallant Seventh* (1899)
Alternative title: Fighting the Indians at Pine Ridge
4 *Kit Carey's protege* (1899)
Alternative title: The West Point conspiracy

Kit Deleeuw series
Katz, Jon
1 *Death by station wagon* (1993)
2 *Family stalker* (1994)

Kit Fielding series
Francis, Dick
1 *Break in* (1985)
2 *Bolt* (1986)

Kit Hemsworthy series
Courtney, Edith
1 *Price of loving* (1986)
2 *Over the bridge* (1987)

Kit Hunter series
Grey, Peter
1 *Wild One* (1959)
2 *South American mission* (1959)
3 *Rival riders* (1959)
4 *Bush adventure* (1959)
5 *Mystery of the mine* (1960)
6 *Moor Grange mystery* (1960)
7 *Fiesta for Wild One* (1960)
8 *Phantom horse* (1960)
9 *Little Outlaw* (1961)
10 *Last hurdle* (1961)
11 *Royal command* (1961)
12 *Homing trail* (1961)

Kit Quayle series
Aldridge, James
1 *Sporting proposition* (1973)
Ride a wild pony
2 *Untouchable Juli* (1975)

Kit series
Gardam, Jane
1 *Kit* (1983)
2 *Kit in boots* (1986)

Kitchen gadgets series
Barkan, Joanne
see **My first kitchen gadgets series**

Kitchie, Wong and Richard series
Dalton, Clive
see **Malay series**

Kitten board book series
Schongut, Emanuel
1 *Catch kitten* (1983)
2 *Wake kitten* (1983)
3 *Hush kitten* (1983)
4 *Play kitten* (1983)
5 *Look kitten* (1983)

Kitten kids series
De Paola, Tomie
see **Katie and Kit series**

Kitten series
Gover, Robert
1 *One hundred dollar misunderstanding* (1962)
2 *Here goes Kitten* (1964)

Kittiwake Rock series
Westwood, Anne McDougall
1 *Riddle of Kittiwake Rock* (1956)
2 *Trouble at Kittiwake Rock* (1960)

Kitty and Lulu series
Mathews, Joanna Hooe
1 *Touton and pussy* (1872)
2 *Kitty's robins* (1872)
3 *White rabbit* (1872)
4 *Rudie's goat* (1873)
5 *Kitty's visit to grandmamma* (1873)
6 *Kitty's scrapbook* (1873)

Kitty Armitage series
Cobb, Belton
1 *Murder, men only* (1962)
2 *Death of a Peeping Tom* (1963)
3 *No shame for the devil* (1964)
4 *Dead girl's shoes* (1964)
5 *I never miss twice* (1965)
6 *Last drop* (1965)
7 *Some must watch* (1966)
8 *Stone for his head* (1966)
9 *Lost without trace* (1967)
10 *Security secrets sold here* (1967)
11 *Secret enquiry* (1968)
12 *Silence under threat* (1968)
13 *Food for felony* (1969)
14 *Scandal at Scotland Yard* (1969)
15 *Horrible man in Heron's Wood* (1970)
16 *Catch me, if you can* (1970)
17 *Suspicion in triplicate* (1971)
21 *I fell among thieves* (1971)

Kitty Palgrave series
Cobb, Belton
see **Kitty Armitage series**

Kitty series
Delton, Judy
1 *Kitty in the middle* (1979)
2 *Kitty in the summer* (1980)
3 *Kitty in high school* (1984)
4 *Kitty from the start* (1987)

Kitty series
Harris, Robin
see **Hello Kitty series**

Kitty Telfair series
Stevenson, Florence
1 *Witching hour* (1971)
2 *Where Satan dwells* (1971)
3 *Altar of evil* (1973)
4 *Mistress of Devil's Manor* (1973)
5 *Sorcerer of the castle* (1974)
6 *Silent watcher* (1975)

Kitty Villiers series
Gibbs, Lewis
1 *Kitty Villiers* (1942)
2 *Good beauties* (1953)

Kiwi series
Allison, Errol Sampson
Reminiscences of travel
1 *Kiwi at large* (1961)
2 *Kiwi vagabond* (1969)

Klaw series
Fieldhouse, William
1 *Klaw* (1980)
2 *Town of blood* (1981)
3 *Rattler Gang* (1981)

Kleep, space detective series
Nixon, Joan Lowery
1 *Kidnapped on Astarr* (1981)
2 *Mysterious queen of magic* (1981)
3 *Mystery dolls from Planet Urd* (1981)

Klim Samgin series
Gorky, Maxim
see **Life of Klim Samgin series**

Klimova family series
Fedorova, Nina
1 *Family* (1941)
2 *Children* (1942)

Kline series
Martin, Philip
see **John Kline series**

Knave trilogy
Janifer, Laurence Mark
see **Gerald Knave series**

Kneetime animal stories series
Barnum, Richard
1 *Squinty, the comical pig* (1915)
2 *Slicko, the jumping squirrel* (1915)
3 *Mappo, the merry monkey* (1915)
4 *Tum Tum, the jolly elephant* (1915)
5 *Don, a runaway dog* (1915)
6 *Dido, the dancing bear* (1916)
7 *Blackie, a lost cat* (1916)
8 *Flop Ear, the funny rabbit* (1916)
9 *Tinkle the trick pony* (1917)
10 *Lightfoot, the leaping goat* (1917)
11 *Chunky, the happy hippo* (1918)
12 *Sharp Eyes, the silver fox* (1918)
13 *Nero, the circus lion* (1919)
14 *Tamba, the tame tiger* (1919)
15 *Toto, the bustling beaver* (1920)
16 *Shaggo, the mighty buffalo* (1921)
17 *Winkie, the wily woodchuck* (1922)

Knickman series
Eichler, Alfred
see **Inspector Knickman series**

Knight Rider series
Larson, Glen A
1 *Knight Rider* (1983)
2 *Trust doesn't rust* (1984)
3 *Hearts of stone* (1984)
4 *Twenty four carat assassin* (1984)
5 *Mirror image* (1985)

Knight series
Cohler, David Keith
see **Sam Knight series**
King, Frank
see **Clarence Knight series**

Knight series
Oakeshott, Ronald Ewart
1 *Knight and his armour* (1961)
2 *Knight and his horse* (1962)
3 *Knight and his weapons* (1964)
4 *Knight in his castle* (1965)
5 *Knight in battle* (1971)

Knightley series
Horler, Sydney
see **Sir Charles Knightley series**

Knightmare series
This sequence has two authors
Child, Tim
1 *Knightmare* (1988)
Morris, Dave
2 *Labyrinths of fear* (1989)

Knighton series
Morrow, Charlotte
see **Lisa Knighton series**

Knights of wonder series
Rypel, Thadeus Chester
see **Gonji series**

Knights trilogy
Atterton, Julian
1 *Knights of the sacred blade* (1989)
2 *Knights of the lost domain* (1991)

K-Nine series
Von Gunden, Kenneth
1 *K-Nine Corps* (1991)
2 *Under fire* (1991)

Knittle and Threadle series
Meyer, Renate
1 *Story of Little Knittle and Threadle* (1971)
2 *Mister Knitted and the family tree* (1972)

Knock knocks series
Cole, William
Illustrated by Mike Thaler
1 *Knock knocks* (1976)
The most ever
2 *Knock knocks you've never heard before* (1977)
3 *New knock knocks* (1981)
4 *Monster knock knocks* (1982)

Knockabout Club series
This sequence has two authors
Stephens, Charles Asbury
1 *Knockabout Club in the woods* (1881)
The adventures of six young men in the wilds of Maine and Canada
2 *Knockabout Club alongshore* (1882)
The adventures of a party of young men on a trip from Boston to the Land of the Midnight Sun
3 *Knockabout Club in the tropics* (1883)
The adventures of a party of young men in New Mexico, Mexico and Central America
Ober, Frederick Albion
4 *Knockabout Club in the Everglades* (1887)
5 *Knockabout Club in the Antilles and thereabouts* (1888)
6 *Knockabout Club in Spain* (1889)
7 *Knockabout Club in North Africa* (1890)
8 *Knockabout Club on the Spanish Main* (1891)
9 *Knockabout Club in search of treasures* (1892)

Knock-Out Kavanagh series
Stuart, Brian
1 *Knock-Out Kavanagh* (1948)
2 *Affair at Sidi Brahim* (1948)
3 *Silver Phantom murder* (1950)

Knollis series
Vivian, Francis
see **Inspector Gordon Knollis series**

Knowabouts series
Pluckrose, Henry
Photographic illustrations by Chris Fairclough
1 *Counting* (1987)
2 *Numbers* (1987)
3 *Time* (1987)
4 *Weight* (1987)

Knowles series
East, Roger
see **Superintendent Simmonds series**
Holzer, Hans
see **Randy Knowles series**

Knowlton, Ryan and McKay series
Friel, Arthur Olney
see **McKay, Knowlton and Ryan series**

Known Space series
Niven, Larry
1 *World of Ptavvs* (1966)
2 *Gift from earth* (1968)
3 *Neutron star* (1968)
4 *Shape of space* (1969)
5 *Ringworld* (1970)
6 *All the myriad ways* (1971)
7 *Protector* (1973)
8 *Inconstant moon* (1973)
9 *Tales of Known Space* (1975)
10 *Long ARM of Gil Hamilton* (1976)
11 *Convergant series* (1979)
12 *Ringworld engineers* (1980)
13 *Patchwork girl* (1980)
14 *Niven's laws* (1984)
15 *Integral trees* (1984)
16 *Smoke ring* (1987)
17 *Man-Kzin wars* (1988)
co-authors: Poul Anderson and Dean Ing
18 *Man-Kzin wars II* (1988)
Coauthors: Jerry Pournelle, Stephen Michael Stirling and Dean Ing
19 *Man-Kzin wars III* (1990)
Coauthors: Jerry Pournelle, Stephen Michael Stirling and Poul Anderson
20 *N-space* (1990)
21 *Playgrounds of the mind* (1991)
22 *Man-Kzin wars IV* (1991)

Knox series
McDowell, Emmett
see **Jonathan Knox series**

Knute Severson series
Wells, Tobias
see **Detective Knute Severson series**

Koa series
Long, Max
see **Komako Koa series**

Koala Hills Primary Hills series
Flynn, Rachel
Illustrated by Craig Smith; short stories
1 *I hate Fridays* (1990)

2 *It's not fair* (1992)
3 *I can't wait* (1994)

Koala series
De Fossard, Esta
1 *Koala and the bunyip* (1982)
2 *Koala and the billycan* (1982)
3 *Koala and the dragon* (1982)
4 *Koala goes to the rainbow's end* (1983)
5 *Koala catches a thief, almost* (1983)
6 *Koala finds a most peculiar ver strange hole in the ground* (1983)
7 *Koala and Emu and the unexpected box* (1984)
8 *Koala and the Tasmanian devil and the possum hunt* (1984)
9 *Koala's book of poems* (1984)
10 *Koala teaches Emu a lesson* (1986)
11 *Koala and the great comet search* (1986)
12 *Koala has a whole lot of things going on* (1986)

Koala series
Morgan, Win
see **Kippy Koala series**
Richards, Kel
see **Father Koala series**

Kobie and Gretchen series
Ransom, Candice Farris
see **Growing up series**

Koesler series
Kienzle, William Xavier
see **Father Robert Koesler series**

Koharik series
Eshleman, John Morton
see **Lieutenant Larry Koharik series**

Kohler and Saint-Cyr series
Janes, Joseph Robert
see **Jean-Louis Saint-Cyr and Hermann Kohler series**

Kojak series
This sequence has two authors; based on a television series
Mann, Abby
1 *Kojak* (1974)
Miller, Victor Brooke
2 *Siege* (1974)
3 *Requiem for a cop* (1974)
4 *Girl in the river* (1975)
5 *Therapy in dynamite* (1975)
6 *Death is not a passing grade* (1975)
Marked for murder
7 *Very deadly game* (1975)
8 *Take-over* (1975)
9 *Gun business* (1975)
10 *Trade off* (1975)

Koko and Yum Yum series
Braun, Lilian Jackson
see **Jim Qwilleran series**

Kolarova series
Powers, Elizabeth
see **Viera Kolarova series**

Kolchak series
Rice, Jeff
see **Carl Kolchak series**

Kollin series
Hogstrand, Olle
see **Chief Inspector Lars Kollin series**

Komako Koa series
Long, Max
1 *Murder between dark and dark* (1939)
2 *Lava flow murders* (1940)
3 *Death goes native* (1941)

Komantcia series
Keith, Harold
1 *Komantcia* (1965)
Revised edition 1991
2 *Sound of strings* (1992)

Kommandant Van Heerden series
Sharpe, Tom
1 *Riotous assembly* (1971)
2 *Indecent exposure* (1973)

Kommissar Hans Barlach series
Durrenmatt, Friedrich
1 *Judge and his hangman* (1954)
End of the game
Original edition entitled *Der Richter und sein Henker*
2 *Quarry* (1959)
Original edition entitled *Der Verdacht*

Konarr series
Van Arnam, Dave
1 *Players of hell* (1968)
2 *Wizard of storms* (1970)

Konrad Roque series
Morton, Guy
1 *Perrin murder case* (1930)
2 *Scarlet thumb print* (1931)
3 *Ragged robin murders* (1935)

Konrad trilogy
Ferring, David
1 *Konrad* (1990)
2 *Shadowbreed* (1991)
3 *Warblade* (1993)

Konstantin Keller trilogy
Kirst, Hans Hellmut
see **Munich trilogy**

Kootenay series
Howe, Doris
1 *I must go back* (1946)
2 *All vigil ended* (1947)
3 *Eager heart* (1947)
4 *On eagle's wings* (1948)

Kopf series
De Halsalle, Henry
see **Olga von Kopf series**

Korea series
Kim, Richard Eunkook
1 *Martyred* (1964)
2 *Innocent* (1968)

Koregorvsky series
Wood, Andrew
1 *Bright angel* (1933)
2 *Red Square* (1934)

Kori McLeod Price and Peter Brichter series
Pulver, Mary Monica
1 *Unforgiving minutes* (1988)
2 *Murder at the war* (1987)
3 *Ashes to ashes* (1988)
4 *Original sin* (1991)
5 *Show stopper* (1992)

Koronglea series
Stevens, Fae Hewston
1 *Koronglea cobbers* (1961)
2 *Koronglea ponies* (1962)
3 *Koronglea holidays* (1963)
4 *Koronglea adventures* (1965)
5 *Koronglea twins* (1967)

Korotoyev series
Ehrenburg, Ilya
see **Dmitry Korotoyev series**

Kothar series
Fox, Gardner Francis
1 *Kothar, barbarian swordsman* (1969)
2 *Kothar of the magic sword* (1969)
3 *Kothar and the Demon Queen* (1969)
4 *Kothar and the wizard slayer* (1970)
5 *Kothar and the conjuror's curse* (1970)

Kovacks series
De Marco, Gordon
see **Riley Kovacks series**

Kovak series
Cooper, Susan Rogers
see **Milton Kovak series**

Kovakin series
Olcott, Anthony
see **Ivan Kovakin series**

Koval series
Peters, Ron
see **Stash Koval series**

Kowalski and Maguire series
White, Teri
see **Blue Maguire and Spaceman Kowalski series**

Koyama series
Berry, Adrian
1 *Koyama's diamond* (1982)
2 *Labyrinth of lies* (1984)

Koyola series
Beecham, John Charles
1 *Argus pheasant* (1918)
2 *Yellow spider* (1920)

Kozminski series
Downes, Quentin
see **Detective Inspector Abraham Kozminski series**

Krab series
Parry, Edward Abbott
1 *Katawampus, its treatment and cure* (1895)
2 *First book of Krab* (1897)
Christmas stories
Companion volume: *Butterscotia, or, A cheap trip to Fairy Land*, 1896

Krag series
Elvestad, Sven
see **Osborne Crag series**

Krahmer series
Krasney, Samuel A
see **Lieutenant Ben Krahmer series**

Krales series
Gould, Heywood
see **Josh Krales series**

Kramer and Zondi series
McClure, James
see **Lieutenant Kramer and Sergeant Zondi series**

Kramer series
Kruger, Paul
see **Phil Kramer series**
Weidman, Jerome
see **Benny Kramer series**

Krantin series
Coulson, Juanita
1 *Web of wizardry* (1978)
2 *Death god's citadel* (1980)

Krauzes and others trilogy
Naglerowa, Herminia
Originally published in three volumes entitled *Krauzowie i inni*, 1936; only volume 1 translated into English
1 *Loves and ambitions* (1936)
2 *[Krauzowie i inni, tome 2]* (1936)
3 *[Krauzowie i inni, tome 3]* (1936)

Kreutzemark series
Beeding, Francis
see **Professor Kreutzemark series**

Krillet series
Askew, Alice
see **Deborah Krillet series**

Krim series
Cunningham, E V
see **Harvey Krim series**
Marfield, Dwight
see **Major Krim series**

Krip Vorland series
Norton, Andre
1 *Moon of three rings* (1966)
2 *Exiles of the stars* (1971)
3 *Flight in Yiktor* (1986)
4 *Dare to go a-hunting* (1990)

Krishna series
De Camp, Lyon Sprague
1 *Rogue Queen* (1951)
2 *Continent makers, and other tales of the Viagens* (1953)
3 *Cosmic manhunt* (1954)
Planet called Krishna
Queen of Zambia
4 *Hand of Zei* (1963)
4.1 *Search for Zei* (1963)
4.2 *Floating continent* (1963)
5 *Tower of Zanid* (1958)
6 *Virgin of Zesh* (1976)
Numbers 5 and 6 also published in one volume, 1983
7 *Hostage of Zir* (1977)
8 *Prisoner of Zhamanak* (1982)
9 *Bones of Zora* (1983)
Co-author: Catherine Crook de Camp
10 *Swords of Zinjaban* (1991)
Co-author: Catherine Crook de Camp

Krishnamurti series
Lutyens, Mary
1 *Years of awakening* (1975)
2 *Years of fulfilment* (1983)
3 *Open door* (1988)

Krispos series
Turtledove, Harry
see **Tale of Krispos series**

Kristen series
Lindsey, Johanna
1 *Fires of winter* (1980)
2 *Hearts aflame* (1987)

Kristiansson trilogy
Budd, Lillian
1 *April snow* (1952)
2 *Land of strangers* (1953)
3 *April harvest* (1959)

Kristin Lavransdatter trilogy
Undset, Sigrid
1 *Garland* (1920)
Bridal wreath
Original edition entitled *Kransen*
2 *Mistress of Husaby* (1922)
Original edition entitled *Husfrue*
3 *Cross* (1922)
Original edition entitled *Korset*
One volume edition entitled *Kristin Lavransdatter*, 1929

Kristy series
Miller, Olive Thorne
1 *Kristy's queer Christmas* (1904)
2 *Kristy's surprise party* (1905)
3 *Kristy's rainy day picnic* (1906)

Kroy series
Le Guin, Ursula Kroeber
see **Adventures in Kroy series**

Krueger series
Cooper, Jeffrey
see **Nightmare on Elm Street series**

Krug and Kellog series
Weston, Carolyn
see **Casey Kellog and Al Krug series**

Kruger series
Gardner, John Edmund
see **Herbie Kruger series**

Krupnik series
Lowry, Lois
see **Anastasia Krupnik series**

Krustov series
Keast, Francis
see **Darryl Krustov series**

Kung Fu series
This sequence has two authors
Chang, Lee
This pseudonym is used by Joseph Rosenberger for numbers 1-5 and 8 and by Leonard Levinson for number 6
1 *Year of the tiger* (1973)
2 *Year of the snake* (1974)
3 *Year of the rat* (1974)
4 *Year of the dragon* (1974)
5 *Year of the horse* (1975)
6 *Year of the boat* (1975)
Fong, C K
7 *Year of the cock* (1975)
Chang, Lee
8 *Year of the ape* (1975)

Kung Fu series
Lee, Howard
This pseudonym is used by Ron Goulart and Barry Malzburg whose authorship is indicated where it is known
1 *Way of the tiger, the sign of the dragon* (1973)
[Malzburg]
2 *Chains* (1973)
[Goulart]
3 *Superstition* (1973)
[Goulart]
4 *Praying mantis kills* (1974)

Kung Fu western series
Lee, Steve
1 *Man with the iron fists* (1974)
2 *Fistful of hate* (1974)

Kunzer series
Geis, Richard Erwin
see **Roi Kunzer series**

Kuragin series
Heaven, Constance
1 *House of Kuragin* (1972)
2 *Astrov inheritance* (1973)
Astrov legacy
3 *Heir to Kuragin* (1978)

Kurt series
Hudson, Stephen
1 *Richard Kurt* (1919)
2 *Elinore Colhouse* (1921)
3 *Prince Hempseed* (1923)
4 *Tony* (1924)
Numbers 1-4 also published in one volume entitled *A true story*, 1930
5 *Myrtle* (1926)
6 *Richard, Myrtle and I* (1926)

Kurtz series
Curry, Jane Louise
see **Maccubbin family series**

Kusak and Riggs series
Rice, Craig
see **Bingo Riggs and Handsome Kusak series**

Kusik series
Ryan, Mary Elizabeth
see **Ketie Kusik series**

Kuzan family trilogy
Johnson, Susan
1 *Seized by love* (1979)
2 *Love storm* (1981)
3 *Sweet love, survive* (1985)

Kwasi series
Kaye, Geraldine
1 *Kwasi and the parrot, and other stories* (1961)
2 *Kwasi goes to town* (1962)

Kyala series
Easton, Malcolm Coleman
1 *Masters of glass* (1985)
2 *Fisherman's curse* (1987)

Kyd series
Harris, Timothy Hyde
see **Tom Kyd series**

Kyle Brandeis series
Ash, William
1 *Ride a paper tiger* (1968)
2 *Take-off* (1969)

Kyle series
Abshire, Richard
see **Jack Kyle series**
Moore, Robin
see **Pulsar series**

Kylie series
Sheehan, Patti
1 *Kylie's song* (1988)
2 *Kylie's concert* (1993)

Kylie series
Trent, Trisha
1 *Good timing* (1988)
2 *Remember the island* (1991)

Kylix series
Carter, Lin
see **Chronicles of Kylix series**

Kyota series
Thompson, Lloyd S
see **Shimoru Kyota series**

Kyra Keaton series
Tone, Teona
1 *Lady on the line* (1983)
2 *Full cry* (1985)

Kyrannon series
Mayhar, Ardath
1 *How the gods wove in Kyrannon* (1979)
2 *Seekers of Shar-Nuhn* (1980)

Kyreol series
McKillip, Patricia Anne
1 *Moon-Flash* (1984)
2 *Moon and the face* (1985)

Kyrik series
Fox, Gardner Francis
1 *Kyrik, warlock warrior* (1975)
2 *Kyrik fights the demon world* (1975)
3 *Kyrik and the wizard's sword* (1976)
4 *Kyrik and the lost queen* (1976)

Kyyra series
Schmidt, Stanley
1 *Sins of the father* (1976)
2 *Lifeboat Earth* (1978)

L

L.A. quartet
Ellroy, James
see **Los Angeles quartet**

L Division series
Kendall, Ralph Selwood
1 *Benton of the Royal Mounted* (1918)
2 *Luck of the Mounted* (1920)

L F Griddle series
Polsky, Thomas
1 *Curtains for the editor* (1939)
2 *Curtains for the judge* (1939)
3 *Curtains for the copper* (1941)

L Rees Pons series
King, Charles Daly
see **Doctor L Rees Pons series**

L.U.S.T. series
Gray, Rod
see **Lady from L.U.S.T. series**

La-La Land series
Campbell, Robert Wright
see **Whistler series**

La noire series
Fane, Bron
1 *Intruders* (1963)
2 *Somewhere out there* (1963)
3 *Softly by moonlight* (1963)
4 *Unknown destiny* (1964)
5 *Nemesis* (1964)
6 *Suspension* (1964)
7 *Macabre ones!* (1964)
8 *UFO 517* (1966)

Laarmans series
Elsschot, Willem
1 *Soft soap* (1924)
Original edition entitled *Lijmen*
2 *Leg* (1938)
Original edition entitled *Het been*
3 *Will-o'-the-wisp* (1946)
Original edition entitled *Het dwaallicht;* one volume edition 1965
Companion volume *Cheese*, original edition *Kaas*, 1933

LaBas series
Reed, Ishmael
see **Papa LaBas series**

Labrador series
Grenfell, Wilfrid Thomason
1 *Down north on the Labrador* (1911)
2 *Tales of the Labrador* (1916)
3 *Labrador days* (1919)
Tales of the sea toilers
Companion volume: *Labrador doctor*, 1920

Labyrinth series
Scott, Peter Graham
1 *Into the labyrinth* (1981)
2 *Return to the labyrinth* (1982)

Lacaita series
Mackenzie, William Andrew
see **Sir Nigel Lacaita series**

Lace series
Conran, Shirley
1 *Lace* (1982)
2 *Lace 2* (1985)

Lace White series
Nolan, Jeannette Covert
1 *Final appearance* (1943)
2 *I can't die here* (1945)
3 *Sudden squall* (1955)
4 *Fearful way to die* (1956)

Lacebridge ladies series
Gladstone, Maggie
1 *Fortunate belle* (1978)
2 *Love duel* (1978)
3 *Scandalous lady* (1978)
4 *Impudent widow* (1979)

Lacey family series
Settle, Mary Lee
see **Beulah series**

Lacey series
Dart, Dorothy
see **Jo Lacey series**
Stall, Mike
see **Daniel Lacey series**
Tyler, Clarke
see **Clint Lacey series**

Lachlan series
Leith, Mary Charlotte Julia
1 *Black Martinmas* (1912)
2 *Lachlan's widow* (1913)

Lachlann and Alasdair Ban series
McLean, Allan Campbell
see **Alasdair and Lachlann Ban series**

Lacy series
Grey, Zane
see **Nevada Jim Lacy series**

Lad and Lassie
Blanchard, Amy Ella
1 *Kittyboy's Christmas* (1898)
2 *Mabel's mishaps* (1900)
3 *Worth his while* (1901)

Ladbroke series
Campbell, Alice
see **Colin Ladbroke series**

Ladd family series
Roddy, Lee
1 *Secret of the shark pit* (1988)
2 *Legend of fire* (1988)
3 *Mystery of the island jungle* (1989)
4 *Dangerous canoe race* (1990)
5 *Secret of the sunken sub* (1990)
6 *Mystery of the wild surfer* (1990)
7 *Teror at Forbidden Falls* (1993)

Ladd series
Hughes, Dean
see **Lucky Ladd series**

Ladies and gentlemen series
Donaldson, William
1 *Both the ladies and the gentleman* (1975)
2 *Balloons in the black bag* (1978)
Nicknames only
3 *English way of doing things* (1985)

Ladis series
Sanchez-Silva, Jose Maria
1 *Ladis and the ant* (1967)
Original edition entitled *Un gran pequene*
2 *Second summer with Ladis* (1967)
Original edition entitled *El segundo de Ladis*

Lady Addle of Eigg series
Dunn, Mary
1 *Lady Addle remembers* (1936)
2 *Lady Addle at home* (1945)
3 *Memoirs of Mipsie* (1947)
4 *Round the year with Lady Addle* (1948)

Lady Branwen series
Meaney, Dee Morrison
1 *Unkindness of ravens* (1983)
2 *Death of the raven* (1983)

Lady Car series
Oliphant, Margaret Oliphant Wilson
1 *Ladies Lindores* (1883)
2 *Lady Car* (1889)

Lady Catherine Alderly series
Robards, Karen
1 *Island flame* (1987)
2 *Seafire* (1988)

Lady Chatterley series
This sequence has three authors
Lawrence, David Herbert
1 *Lady Chatterley's lover* (1928)
D'Orliac, Jehanne
2 *Lady Chatterley's second husband* (1935)
Robins, Patricia
3 *Lady Chatterley's daughter* (1961)

Lady Cicely Plantagenet trilogy
Wilson, Sandra
1 *Less fortunate than fair* (1973)
2 *Queen's sister* (1974)
3 *Lady Cicely* (1974)

Lady detective series
Hayward, William Stephens
1 *Experiences of a lady detective* (1861)
2 *Revelations of a lady detective* (1864)

Lady Diana trilogy
Dekobra, Maurice
1 *Wings of desire* (1924)
Original edition entitled *Mon coeur au ralenti*
2 *Madonna of the sleeping cars* (1925)
Original edition entitled *Madone des sleepings*
3 *Phantom gondola* (1926)
Thirteenth lover
Original edition entitled *La gondole aux chimeres*

Lady from L.U.S.T. series
Gray, Rod
1 *L.U.S.T. be a lady tonight* (1968)
2 *Lay me odds* (1968)
3 *Sixty-nine pleasures* (1968)
4 *Five beds to Mecca* (1968)
5 *Hot mahatma* (1968)
6 *To Russia with L.U.S.T.* (1969)
7 *Kiss my assassin* (1968)
8 *South of the bordelio* (1968)
9 *Poisoned pussy* (1969)
10 *Big snatch* (1969)
Sock it to me
11 *Lady in heat* (1969)
12 *Laid in the future* (1969)
13 *Blow my mind* (1969)
14 *Copulation explosion* (1970)
15 *Easy ride* (1970)
16 *Lady takes it all off* (1969)
17 *Turned on to L.U.S.T.* (1971)
18 *Skin game dame* (1974)
19 *Lady killer* (1975)
20 *Lady from L.U.S.T.* (1975)

Lady Gay trilogy
Archibald, George, *Mrs*
1 *Lady Gay and her sister* (1891)
2 *Lady Gay* (1898)
The story of a little girl and her friends
3 *Dozen good times that Georgiana and Dolly had* (1898)

Lady Hamilton series
Schumacher, Heinrich
1 *Fair enchantress* (1910)
Original edition entitled *Liebe und Leben der Lady Hamilton*
2 *Nelson's last love* (1915)
Original edition entitled *Lord Nelsons letzte Liebe*

Lady Herbert Somerville series
Yonge, Charlotte Mary
1 *Castle builders* (1854)
2 *Pillars of the house* (1873)
Alternative title: Under wode, under rode

Lady Jennifer, Sandro and Colly series
Drummond, Ivor
1 *Man with the tiny head* (1969)
2 *Priests of the abomination* (1970)
3 *Frog in the moonflower* (1972)
4 *Jaws of the watcdog* (1973)
5 *Power of the bug* (1974)
6 *Tank of sacred eels* (1976)
7 *Necklace of skulls* (1977)
8 *Stench of poppies* (1978)
9 *Diamonds of Loreta* (1980)

Lady Margaret Priam series
Christmas, Joyce
1 *Suddenly in her sorbet* (1988)
2 *Simply to die for* (1989)
3 *Fete worse than death* (1990)
4 *Stunning way to die* (1990)
5 *Friend or foe* (1991)
6 *It's her funeral* (1992)
7 *Perfect day for dying* (1993)

Lady Noggs series
Jepson, Edgar
1 *Lady Noggs, peeress* (1906)
2 *Lady Noggs intervenes* (1908)
3 *Lady Noggs assists* (1924)

Lady of fire series
Mills, Anita
1 *Lady of fire* (1987)
2 *Fire and steel* (1988)
3 *Hearts of fire* (1989)
4 *Follow the heart* (1990)
5 *Fire and the fury* (1991)

Lady of quality series
Burnett, Frances Hodgson
1 *Lady of quality* (1896)
A most curious, hitherto unknown history, as related by Mr Isaac Bickerstaff but not presented to the world of fashion through the pages of the *Tattler* and now for the first time written down
2 *His Grace of Osmond* (1897)
The portions of that nobleman's life omitted in relation of his lady's story presented to the world of fashion under the title of *A lady of quality*

Lady of the decoration series
Little, Frances
1 *Lady of the decoration* (1906)
Originally published anonymously
2 *Little Sister Snow* (1909)
Originally published anonymously
3 *Lady married* (1912)
Lady and Sada San
Originally published anonymously
4 *Jack and I in Lotus Land* (1922)

Lady policeman series
Lock, Joan
Autobiography
1 *Lady policeman* (1968)
2 *Reluctant nightingale* (1970)

Lady series
Brandon, Joyce
1 *Lady and the outlaw* (1985)
2 *Lady and the lawman* (1987)

Lady Susan series
Brady, Cyrus Townsend
1 *Blue ocean's daughter* (1907)
2 *Adventures of Lady Susan* (1908)

Lady Susan series
Cleeve, Lucas
1 *Cardinal and Lady Susan* (1908)
2 *Lady Susan and not the Cardinal* (1910)

Lady Walderhurst series
Burnett, Frances Hodgson
1 *Making of a marchioness* (1901)
2 *Methods of Lady Walderhurst* (1901)

Ladyship and lordship series
Wells, David Dwight
1 *Her ladyship's elephant* (1898)
2 *His lordship's leopard* (1900)

Lafayette O'Leary series
Laumer, Keith
1 *Time bender* (1966)
2 *World shuffler* (1970)
3 *Shape changer* (1972)
4 *Galaxy builder* (1984)

Lafitte series
Ingraham, Joseph Holt
1 *Lafitte, the pirate of the Gulf* (1836)
2 *Theodore* (1844)
Alternative title: The Child of the Sea

Lagrangia series
Reynolds, Mack
1 *Lagrange Five* (1979)
2 *Lagrangists* (1983)
3 *Chaos in Lagrangia* (1984)
4 *Trojan orbit* (1985)
Co-author: Dean Ing

Laidlaw series
Hine, Muriel
see **Clodagh Laidlaw series**
McIlvanney, William
see **Inspector Jack Laidlaw series**

Laidman series
Seaton, Stuart
see **Inspector Martin Laidman series**

Laing series
Laing, Patrick
see **Patrick Laing series**

Laird series
Macleod, Robert
see **Andrew Laird series**

Lake and forest series
Farrar, Charles Alden John
1 *Eastward ho!* (1880)
Alternative title: Adventures at Rangeley Lakes; amusing experiences and startling incidents connected with a trip of a party of Boston boys to the wilds of Maine
2 *Wild woods life* (1884)
Alternative title: A trip to Parmachanee; a realistic story of life in the woods
3 *Down the west branch* (1886)
Alternative title: Camps and tramps around Katahdin
4 *Up the north branch* (1889)
Alternative title: A summer's outing; the record of a camping-out trip up the north branch of the Penobscot and down the Saint John River, through the wilds of Maine and New Brunswick

Lake Jordan series
Foote, Shelby
1 *Tournament* (1949)
2 *Follow me down* (1950)
3 *Love in a dry season* (1951)
4 *Jordan County* (1954)
A landscape in narrative
5 *September September* (1978)

Lake series
Ganpat
see **Harry Lake series**
Singer, Shelley
see **Barrett Lake series**

Lake Shore series
Optic, Oliver
1 *Through by daylight* (1869)
Alternative title: The young engineer of Lake Shore Railroad
2 *Lightning express* (1869)
Alternative title: The rival academies
3 *On time* (1869)
Alternative title: The young captain of the Ucayga steamer
4 *Switch off* (1869)
Alternative title: The war of the students
5 *Brake up* (1869)
Alternative title: The young peacemakers
6 *Bear and forbear* (1869)
Alternative title: The young skipper of Lake Ucayga

Lake Wobegon series
Keillor, Garrison
1 *Lake Wobegon days* (1985)
2 *Leaving home* (1987)
Short stories

Lakeland series
Collingwood, William Gershon
see **Norsemen series**

Lakeport series
Stratemeyer, Edward L
1 *Gun Club boys at Lakeport* (1908)
Alternative title: The island camp; also published as *The island camp, or, The young hunters of Lakeport*, by Ralph Bonehill
2 *Baseball boys of Lakeport* (1908)
Alternative title: The winning run; also published as *The winning run, or, The baseball boys of Lakeport*, by Ralph Bonehill
3 *Boat Club boys of Lakeport* (1908)
Alternative title: The water champions
4 *Football boys of Lakeport* (1909)
Alternative title: More goals than one
5 *Automobile boys of Lakeport* (1910)
Alternative title: A run for fun and fame
6 *Aircraft boys of Lakeport* (1912)
Alternative title: Rivals of the clouds

Lakerim Athletic Club series
Hughes, Rupert
1 *Lakerim Athletic Club* (1898)
2 *Dozen from Lakerim* (1899)
3 *Lakerim cruise* (1910)

Lal Reed series
Wood, Clement
1 *Death in Ankara* (1944)
2 *Death on the pampas* (1944)

Lal series
Hammond, William Alexander
1 *Lal* (1884)
2 *Strong-minded woman* (1885)
Alternative title: Two years after

Lal Singh trilogy
Anand, Mulk Raj
1 *Village* (1939)
2 *Across the black waters* (1940)
3 *Sword and the sickle* (1942)

Lalage and Belinda series
Evans, Cherry
see **Belinda and Lalage series**

Lalu series
Sommerfelt, Aimee
1 *Road to Agra* (1961)
Original edition entitled *Velen til Agra*
2 *White bungalow* (1963)
Original edition entitled *Den huite bungalowen*

Lam and Cool series
Fair, A A
see **Bertha Cool and Donald Lam series**

Lamb series
Donavan, John
see **Sergeant Johnny Lamb series**
Foster, Kingsley
see **Jonathan Lamb series**
Graves, Robert
see **Sergeant Lamb series**
Maynard, Kenneth
see **Lieutenant Lamb series**
Wentworth, Patricia
see **Inspector Ernest Lamb series**

Lambchops series
Brown, Jeff
see **Stanley Lambchops series**

Lambert series
Allan, Joan
see **Valerie Lambert series**
Greene, Bette
see **Beth Lambert series**

Lamia Zacharias series
Williamson, Jerry Neal
1 *Death-coach* (1981)
2 *Death-angel* (1982)
3 *Death-school* (1982)
4 *Death-doctor* (1982)

Lamont Cranston series
Grant, Maxwell
see **Shadow series**

Lampton series
Braine, John
see **Joe Lampton series**

Lan-Kern trilogy
Tremayne, Peter
1 *Fires of Lan-Kern* (1980)
2 *Destroyers of Lan-Kern* (1982)
3 *Buccaneers of Lan-Kern* (1983)

LaNague Federation trilogy
Wilson, Francis Paul
1 *Healer* (1976)
2 *Wheels within wheels* (1978)
3 *Enemy of the state* (1980)

Lanark series
Robertson, Stephen
see **Ryne Lanark series**

Lancashire idylls series
Mather, James Marshall
1 *Lancashire idylls* (1895)
2 *By roaring loom* (1898)

Lancasters series
Bond, Freda Constance
1 *End House* (1943)
2 *Lancasters at Lynford* (1944)
3 *Susan and Priscilla* (1945)

Lance and Nessa series
Hogg, Garry
see **Nessa and Lance series**

Lance Kilkenny series
L'Amour, Louis
1 *Kilkenny* (1954)
2 *Riders of Lost Creek* (1976)
Based on a short story of the same name
Also *A man called Trent*, in *The riders of the Ruby Hills*, 1986

Lance O'Leary and Sarah Keate series
Eberhart, Mignon Good
see **Sarah Keate and Lance O'Leary series**

Lance trilogy
Adams, Hunter
see **Man from Planet X trilogy**

Lancelot Carolus Smith series
Berrow, Norman
see **Inspector Lancelot Carolus Smith series**

Lancelot Priestley series
Rhode, John
see **Doctor Lancelot Priestley series**

Lancelot series
Hewlett, Maurice
see **Mrs Lancelot series**

Lancey series
Frost, Barbara
see **Marka de Lancey series**
Greene, L Patrick
see **Sergeant Lancey series**

Land and overland trilogy
Shaw, Bob
1 *Ragged astronauts* (1986)
2 *Wooden spaceships* (1988)
3 *Fugitive worlds* (1989)

Land and the way series
Waldman, Emerson
1 *Land is large* (1939)
2 *Broad is the way* (1939)

Land and water friends series
Bamford, Mary Ellen
1 *My land and water friends* (1886)
2 *Talks by queer folks* (1893)

Land in need series
Counsel, George
1 *Challenge* (1989)
2 *Make or break* (1990)

Land of Erin trilogy
Scott, Michael
see **Tales from the Land of Erin trilogy**

Land of gold series
Martin, Martha
see **Alaska series**

Land of Ireland series
Marcus, David
1 *Land not theirs* (1986)
2 *Land in flames* (1987)

Land of ten thousand willows trilogy
Grant, Kathryn
1 *Phoenix bells* (1987)
2 *Black jade road* (1989)
3 *Willow garden* (1989)

Land of the giants series
This sequence has three authors; based on a television series
Leinster, Murray
1 *Land of the giants* (1968)
2 *Hot spot* (1969)
3 *Unknown danger* (1969)
Bradwell, James
4 *Mean city* (1969)
Rathjen, Carl Henry
5 *Flight of fear* (1969)

Land of tomorrow series
Maile, Ben
1 *Land of tomorrow* (1990)
2 *Run fox run* (1990)

Land series
Alexander, David
see **Marty Land series**

Land series
Chambers, Robert William
1 *Outdoorland* (1902)
2 *Orchard-land* (1903)
3 *River-land* (1904)
4 *Forest-land* (1905)
Hide and seek in Forest Land
5 *Mountain-land* (1906)
6 *Garden-land* (1907)

Land series
Mackay, Amanda
see **Hannah Land series**

Landlord series
Girtin, Tom
1 *Come landlord* (1957)
2 *Not entirely serious* (1958)

Landlord series
Scott, Walter
see **Tales of my landlord series**

Lando Calrissian trilogy
Smith, Lester Neil
1 *Lando Calrissian and the Mindharp of Sharu* (1983)
2 *Lando Calrissian and the Flamewind of Oseon* (1983)
3 *Lando Calrissian and the Starcave of ThonBoka* (1983)

Landon series
Lewis, Royston
see **Arnold Landon series**
Pattinson, James
see **Harvey Landon series**
Sinstadt, Gerald
see **Geoffrey Landon series**

Landover series
Brooks, Terry
see **Magic Kingdom of Landover series**

Landshark series
Zacharia, Irwin
1 *Landshark* (1982)
2 *Piranha, piranha* (1982)

Lane Parry series
Sarsfield, Maureen
see **Inspector Lane Parry series**

Lane series
Adams, Eustace Lane
see **Andy Lane series**
Hughes, Virginia
see **Peggy Lane series**
Lawrence, Josephine
see **Linda Lane series**
Lockridge, Frances
see **Paul Lane series**
Ross, Barnaby
see **Drury Lane series**
Ryerson, Florence
see **Jimmy Lane series**
Wells, Carolyn
see **Lorimer Lane series**
Zollinger, Norman
see **Corey Lane series**

Langdon series
Smith, Julie
see **Skip Langdon series**

Langham series
Daniel, Roland
see **Inspector Neville Langham series**

Langley series
Meriton, Peter
see **Bill Langley series**
Monmouth, Jack
see **Tom Langley series**

Langry series
Leslie, Francis
see **Jimmy Langry series**

Langston and Coleman family series
Brown, Sandra
see **Coleman family and Jake Langston series**

Langston Hughes series
Rampersad, Arnold
see **Life of Langston Hughes series**

Langton family series
Boyd, Martin
1 *Cardboard crown* (1952)
2 *Difficult young man* (1955)
3 *Outbreak of love* (1947)
4 *When blackbirds sing* (1962)

Lankester family trilogy
Allee, Marjorie Hill
1 *Judith Lankester* (1930)
2 *House of her own* (1934)
3 *Off to Philadelphia* (1936)

Lanky Lawson series
Roe, Harry Mason
1 *Lanky Lawson, the boy from nowhere* (1929)
How he arrived at Beanville, what Beanville did to him and what he did to Beanville
2 *Lanky Lawson with the one-ring circus* (1929)
How he joined the show, what he did to the wild animals, what happened when the circus collapsed
3 *Lanky Lawson and his trained zebra* (1930)
How he happened to get the beast, how the cantankerous animal performed and what happened at the county fair

Lanny Budd series
Sinclair, Upton
see **World's end series**

Lanson series
Bond, J Harvey
see **Mike Lanson series**

Lantree series
Norton, Andre
see **Planet Warlock series**

Lantz and Wright series
Mullen, Clarence
see **Tony Lantz and Eddie Wright series**

Lanyard series
Vance, Louis Joseph
see **Michael Lanyard series**

Laramie Nelson series
This sequence has two authors
Grey, Zane
1 *Raiders of Spanish Peaks* (1938)
Grey, Romer Zane
2 *Last stand at Indigo Flats* (1970)
Based on a character in the short story *Spanish peaks*, by Zane Grey
3 *Other side of the river* (1970)
4 *Lawless land* (1984)

Laredo Garrett and Peter Torres series
Moore, Arthur
see **Bluestar series**

Larey series
Grey, Zane
see **Adam Larey series**

Larges family trilogy
Murphy, Jill
1 *Five minutes' peace* (1986)
2 *All in one piece* (1987)
3 *Piece of cake* (1989)

Largo series
Ard, William
see **Lou Largo series**

Larian series
Murray, Terry
see **Legends of Larian series**

Lark Rise series
Harrison, Sarah
see **Laura from Lark Rise series**

Lark Rise to Candleford series
Thompson, Flora
Based on the author's life in Juniper Hill and Buckingham
1 *Lark Rise* (1939)
2 *Over to Candleford* (1941)
3 *Candleford Green* (1943)
Numbers 1-3 also published in one volume entitled *Lark Rise to Candleford*, 1945
4 *Still glides the stream* (1948)

Lark series
Vipont, Elfrida
see **Haverard family series**

Larkin family series
Bates, Herbert Ernest
1 *Darling buds of May* (1958)
2 *Breath of French air* (1959)
3 *When the green woods laugh* (1960)
Hark, hark, the lark!
4 *Oh to be in England* (1963)
5 *Little of what you fancy* (1970)

Larkin series
Russell, Martin
see **Jim Larkin series**

Larne family trilogy
Bristow, Gwen
see **Louisiana trilogy**

La Rochelle series
Brent-Dyer, Elinor Mary
1 *Gerry goes to school* (1922)
2 *Head girl's difficulties* (1923)
3 *Maids of La Rochelle* (1924)
4 *Heather leaves school* (1929)
5 *Janie of La Rochelle* (1932)
6 *Janie steps in* (1953)

Larose series
Gask, Arthur
see **Gilbert Larose series**

Larren series
Charles, Robert
see **Simon Larren series**

Larrimore and Thompson series
Paull, Jessica
see **Tracy Larrimore and Mike Thompson series**

Larry and Buck baseball series
Dawson, Elmer A
see **Buck and Larry baseball series**

Larry and Nora Blaine series
Davis, Lavinia Riker
see **Nora Hughes and Larry Blaine series**

Larry and Streak series
Grover, Marshall
see **Larry and Stretch series**

Larry and Stretch series
Grover, Marshall
Some titles in this sequence were originally published under the pseudonym Marshall McCoy as indicated
1 *Drift!* (1956)
2 *Arizona wildcat* (1956)
3 *Texans are trouble* (1957)
4 *Trigger trap* (1957)
5 *Tall riders* (1957)
6 *Trail dust* (1958)
7 *Rawhide River ambush* (1958)
8 *Bend of the river* (1958)
9 *Half-cold trail* (1958)
10 *Hell raisers* (1958)
11 *Seventeen guns* (1958)
12 *Ride out, Texans* (1958)
13 *Tall, tough and texture* (1959)
14 *Texas drifters* (1959)
15 *Ride reckless* (1959)
16 *Day of the posse* (1959)
17 *Decoys from hell* (1959)
18 *North of Texas* (1960)
19 *Back in Texas* (1960)
20 *Texans die hard* (1960)
21 *Lone Star hellions* (1960)
22 *Start shooting, Texans* (1961)
23 *Where danger rides* (1961)
24 *Texans never quit* (1961)
25 *Lone Star bodyguards* (1961)
26 *Texans hit hard* (1961)
27 *Saludas, Texans* (1962)
28 *Lone Star Lucky* (1962)
29 *Kid Wichita* (1962)
30 *Texans ride tall* (1962)
31 *Double trouble* (1962)
32 *We're from Texas* (1962)
33 *Lawless miles* (1962)
34 *Bravados from Texas* (1962)
35 *Nomads from Texas* (1963)
36 *Ride wild to glory* (1962)
37 *Ride out shooting* (1963)
38 *Texans walk proud* (1963)
39 *Draw, aim and fire* (1963)
40 *Never prod a Texan* (1963)
41 *Close in for showdown* (1963)
42 *Texas gun-ghost* (1963)
43 *Lone Star valiant* (1963)
44 *Fast right hand* (1963)
45 *Follow the Texans* (1963)
46 *Lone Star fury* (1964)
47 *Colorado pursuit* (1964)
48 *Don't count the odds* (1964)
49 *Face the gun* (1964)
50 *Find Kell Wade* (1964)
51 *Texan in my sights* (1964)
52 *Ride slow, ride wary* (1964)
53 *Feud at Mendoza* (1964)
54 *Born to drift* (1964)
55 *Eyes of Texas* (1964)
56 *Nobody wants Riley* (1964)
57 *Rob a bank in Texas* (1964)
58 *Now, Texan!* (1964)
59 *Lone Star vengeance* (1965)
60 *This range is mine!* (1965)
61 *Emerson challenge* (1965)
62 *Texas rampage* (1965)
63 *Turn and fire* (1965)
64 *All the tall men* (1965)
65 *Trouble is our shadow* (1965)
66 *Freebooters* (1965)
67 *Big dinero* (1965)
68 *Crisis in Babylon* (1965)
69 *Noon stage to Denver* (1965)
70 *Lone Star reckless* (1965)
71 *Defiant Texans* (1965)
72 *Decoys from Texas* (1966)
73 *Border storm* (1966)
74 *Diary of a desperado* (1966)
75 *Lone Star firebrands* (1966)
76 *Noon train to Breslow* (1966)
77 *Cold trail to Kirby* (1966)
78 *Too many Texans* (1966)
79 *Wild trail to Denver* (1966)
80 *Rouge Calibre* (1966)
81 *Wayward kind* (1966)
82 *Lone Star reckoning* (1966)
83 *Gun glory for Texans* (1966)
Also published under the pseudonym Marshall McCoy
84 *Trouble trail yonder* (1967)
Also published under the pseudonym Marshall McCoy
85 *Many a wide mile* (1967)
86 *Two tall strangers* (1967)
87 *Lone Star rowdy* (1967)
88 *Tombstone for a fugitive* (1967)
89 *Texans came shooting* (1967)
90 *Boom town bravados* (1967)
91 *Too rough for San Remo* (1967)
Also published under the pseudonym Marshall McCoy
92 *Legend of Bell Canyon* (1967)
Also published under the pseudonym Marshall McCoy
93 *High Spade* (1968)
Also published under the pseudonym Marshall McCoy
94 *Bar G bunch* (1968)
Also published under the pseudonym Marshall McCoy
95 *Wyoming thunder* (1968)
Also published under the pseudonym Marshall McCoy
96 *Kin to the wild wind* (1968)
Also published under the pseudonym Marshall McCoy
97 *Big day at Blue Creek* (1968)
Also published under the pseudonym Marshall McCoy
98 *Wheels out of Jericho* (1968)
Also published under the pseudonym Marshall McCoy
99 *Hour of jeopardy* (1968)
100 *Amarillo Ridge* (1969)
101 *Glory wagon* (1969)
102 *Calaboose Canyon* (1969)
103 *Garrard heritage* (1969)
Also published under the pseudonym Marshall McCoy
104 *Two for the gallows* (1969)
105 *Hot sky over Paraiso* (1969)
Also published under the pseudonym Marshall McCoy
106 *Three trails to Modoc* (1969)
Also published under the pseudonym Marshall McCoy
107 *Saturday night in Candle Rock* (1970)
108 *Gun fury at sun-up* (1970)
109 *Guns across the Rockies* (1970)
110 *Our kind of love* (1970)
111 *Noose-cheaters* (1970)
112 *They won't forget Sweeney* (1971)
113 *Fast, free and Texan* (1971)
114 *Feuders* (1971)
115 *Four o'clock fracas* (1971)
116 *Seven for Banner Pass* (1971)
117 *Here lies Andy McGraw* (1971)
118 *Rampage at Rico Bend* (1972)
119 *San Saba blockade* (1972)
120 *Montana runaway* (1972)
121 *Hellion breed* (1972)
122 *Hangrope for Beaumont* (1973)
123 *Last ambush* (1973)
124 *Gunsmoke in Utopia* (1973)
125 *War dance at Red Canyon* (1973)
126 *Pursuit trail* (1973)
127 *Mexican jackpot* (1973)
128 *McCracken's marauders* (1973)
129 *Red bandana* (1973)
130 *Get goin', Greeley!* (1973)
131 *Guns for the ladies* (1973)
132 *Cold-Eye Cordell* (1973)
133 *Desperate hours* (1973)
134 *Madigan's day* (1973)
135 *Who killes Rico?* (1973)
136 *Dakota Red* (1974)
137 *Predators* (1974)
138 *Hijacker's moon* (1974)
139 *Odds against O'Shay* (1974)
140 *High country shootout* (1974)
141 *Man on Pulpit Rock* (1974)
142 *Saddletramp justice* (1974)
143 *Doom trail* (1974)
144 *Tin stars for tall Texans* (1974)
145 *They'll hang Billy for sure* (1974)
146 *Devil's dinero* (1974)
147 *Too many enemies* (1975)
148 *First kill* (1975)
149 *Two Jacks and the Joker* (1975)
150 *Rescue party* (1975)
151 *Damn outlaws* (1975)
152 *Last challenge* (1975)
153 *Delaney and the drifters* (1975)
154 *Dollar trail to Ramirez* (1975)
155 *Winners and losers* (1975)
156 *Dawson died twice* (1975)
157 *Follow that train* (1975)
158 *Day of the tornado* (1976)
159 *Kiss the loot goodbye* (1976)
160 *Baxter's last laugh* (1976)
161 *Twenty seven rifles* (1976)
162 *Outcasts of Sabado Creek* (1976)
163 *Colorado Belle* (1976)
164 *Calaboose gang* (1976)
165 *Battle of Blunder Ridge* (1976)
166 *Suddenly a hero* (1976)
167 *Bandit trap* (1976)
168 *Prelude to a showdown* (1976)
169 *Sundown Seven* (1976)
170 *Raid a painted wagon* (1976)
171 *Guns of the valiant* (1976)
172 *Track of the lawless* (1976)
173 *Before he kills again* (1976)
174 *Bullion route* (1977)
175 *Left-Hand Luke* (1977)
176 *Dealer takes three* (1977)
177 *After the payoff* (1977)
178 *Jokers wild* (1977)
179 *Lone Star godfathers* (1977)
180 *Eight ten from Verdugo* (1977)
181 *Royal target* (1977)
182 *Everything happens to Holley* (1977)
183 *Midnight marauders* (1977)
184 *Kansas hex* (1977)
185 *Three days in Davisburg* (1977)
186 *Only bank in town* (1977)
187 *California runaround* (1977)
188 *Ghost of a chance* (1977)
189 *Eight defiant men* (1977)
190 *Troubleshooters die hard* (1977)
191 *Beecher's quest* (1977)
192 *In memory of Marty Malone* (1978)
193 *Nebraska trackdown* (1978)
194 *Double shuffle* (1978)
195 *Gold, guns and the girl* (1978)
196 *Hammer's horde* (1978)
197 *Mark of the star* (1978)
198 *Dinero fever* (1978)
199 *Calaboose express* (1978)
200 *Bullet for a widow* (1978)
201 *Killing of Kirby* (1978)
202 *Last stage to Delarno* (1978)
203 *Rescuers rode west* (1978)
204 *Fogarty's war* (1978)
205 *Wyoming longshot* (1978)
206 *Phantom of Fortuna* (1979)
207 *Doomed of Mesa Rico* (1979)
208 *Baker City breakout* (1979)
209 *Women from Whitlock* (1979)
210 *High stakeout* (1979)
211 *Run from the buzzards* (1979)
212 *Dead man's share* (1979)
213 *Keep Allison alive* (1979)
214 *Pearson County raiders* (1979)
215 *Both sides of Battle Creek* (1979)
216 *Turn the key on Emerson* (1979)
217 *Fort Dillon* (1979)
218 *Wrong name on a tombstone* (1979)
219 *They came to Jurado* (1979)
220 *Seventh guilty man* (1979)
221 *In pursuit of Quincey Budd* (1979)
222 *Posse plus two* (1979)
223 *Brady's back in town* (1979)
224 *Siege of Jericho* (1980)
225 *Wait for the judge* (1980)
226 *El Capitan's enemies* (1980)
227 *Four aces and the knave* (1980)
228 *One more showdown* (1980)
229 *Day of the killers* (1980)
230 *Going straight in Frisbee* (1980)
231 *Prey of the rogue riders* (1980)
232 *Rough night for the guilty* (1980)
233 *Hackett's gold* (1980)
234 *Vengeance in spades* (1980)
235 *Death quest* (1980)
236 *Ride boldly in Dakota* (1980)
237 *Doc Rance of Rambeau* (1980)
238 *He's Valentine, I'm Emerson* (1980)
239 *Kid Lightfingers* (1980)
240 *Lady is a target* (1980)
241 *Gun reckoning at Grundy's grave* (1980)
242 *Twenty-year man* (1980)
243 *Lone Star survivors* (1980)
244 *Deadly dollars* (1981)
245 *We ride for Circle Six* (1981)
246 *Load every rifle* (1981)
247 *Five bullets for Judge Blake* (1981)
248 *Ride out of Paradise* (1981)
249 *Lone Hand Emerson* (1981)
250 *Greel County outcasts* (1981)

251 *Miss Lou and the tall men* (1981)
252 *Little town, big trouble* (1981)
253 *Tin star shadow* (1981)
254 *Bravados of Bandera* (1981)
255 *Wild widow of Wolf Creek* (1981)
256 *For the hell of it* (1981)
257 *Run strong, run free* (1981)
258 *Human target* (1981)
259 *We call him Tex* (1981)
260 *Spanish gold and Texas guns* (1981)
261 *Law always wins* (1981)
262 *Pursuit party* (1981)
263 *Hide in fear* (1982)
264 *Lucky Jake* (1982)
265 *Cormack came back* (1982)
266 *Cedro County crisis* (1982)
267 *Latimer's loot* (1982)
268 *Tame a wild town* (1982)
269 *Forgotten enemy* (1982)
270 *Last witness* (1982)
271 *McEvoy's mountain* (1982)
272 *Emerson's hex* (1982)
273 *Bullet in Mason's back* (1982)
274 *Six-gun wedding* (1982)
275 *Colorado woman* (1982)
276 *Young bucks from Texas* (1982)
277 *Castle on Claw Creek* (1982)
278 *Pledge to a doomed man* (1982)
279 *Greenback trail* (1982)
280 *After-midnight gang* (1982)
281 *Bon chance* (1982)
282 *Two-time winner* (1982)
283 *Cobb Creek bunch* (1982)
284 *Howdy, ladies* (1983)
285 *Debt to a tin star* (1983)
286 *Miracle at Dry Fork* (1983)
287 *Lady Luck and F J Beck* (1983)
288 *Peligro's last hour* (1983)
289 *Beauty and the brigands* (1983)
290 *Wagon number three* (1983)
291 *Wrong side of Glory Mountain* (1983)
292 *Claw Creek crisis* (1983)
293 *Piketown flood* (1983)
294 *Calamity is a woman* (1983)
295 *Tanglefoot* (1983)
296 *Duffy's dollars* (1983)
297 *Saga of Sam Burdew* (1983)
298 *Texas born, Chicago bound* (1983)
299 *Shotgun Sharkey* (1983)
300 *Reunion in Slade City* (1983)
301 *Walking tall, striking fear* (1983)
302 *Stakeout at Council Creek* (1983)
303 *Save a bullet for Kehoe* (1983)
304 *Ventura Pass* (1984)
305 *Dude must die* (1984)
306 *Terror trail to Tortosa* (1984)
307 *Tinhorn murder case* (1984)
308 *Devil's dozen* (1984)
309 *Emerson's hideout* (1984)
310 *Heroes and hellers* (1984)
311 *Dinero train* (1984)
312 *Day of plunderers* (1984)
313 *Ghost-woman of Castillo* (1984)
314 *Kincaid's last ride* (1984)
315 *Defend Beacon Spring* (1984)
316 *Reunion in San Jose* (1984)
317 *Only way is up* (1984)
318 *Meet the McEgans* (1984)
319 *Tandy's legacy* (1984)
320 *Bandit bait* (1984)
321 *Wyoming gun-trap* (1984)
322 *Stay away, Slade!* (1984)
323 *Destination Fort Ross* (1984)
324 *Sound of Seeger's guns* (1985)
325 *Montana mail* (1985)
326 *Five for the shootout* (1985)
327 *Wild night in Widow's Peak* (1985)
328 *Domino man* (1985)
329 *Best and the worst* (1985)
330 *Cannon Mound gang* (1985)
331 *Sonora wildcat* (1985)
332 *Billy Hull, R.I.P.* (1985)
333 *Night of the guns* (1985)
334 *Trigger-fast* (1985)
335 *Who's gunning for Braid?* (1985)
336 *Gollan County gallows* (1985)
337 *Run with the loot* (1985)
338 *President's segundo* (1985)
339 *Truth about Snake Ridge* (1985)
340 *Two works in Wyoming* (1985)
341 *Greenback fever* (1985)
342 *Whiskey Gulch* (1985)
343 *Logantown looters* (1986)
344 *Two gentlemen from Texas* (1986)
345 *Alibi trail* (1986)
346 *Rough route to Rodd County* (1986)
347 *Six guilty men* (1986)
348 *Badge and Tully McGlynn* (1986)
349 *Last big deal* (1986)
350 *Trial of Slow Wolf* (1986)
351 *Jubilo stage* (1986)
352 *Plummer's last posse* (1986)
353 *Bandido hunters* (1987)
354 *Terror's long memory* (1987)
355 *Two graves waiting* (1987)
356 *Fontaine's sidekicks* (1987)
357 *Never cheat a Texan* (1987)
358 *Late Yuma Smith* (1987)
359 *One mean town* (1987)
360 *It had to be Ortega* (1987)
361 *Harrigan's star* (1987)
362 *One ticket to Sun Rock* (1987)
363 *Galatea McGee* (1987)
364 *Seven killers east* (1987)
365 *Dynamite demon* (1988)
366 *Jonah Rock* (1988)
367 *McAllister's victims* (1988)
368 *Queen of Spades* (1988)
369 *Bridegroom's bodyguards* (1988)
370 *Where the money's buried* (1988)
371 *Wyoming war-fever* (1988)
372 *Four-wheeled target* (1988)
373 *Waiting for Wilkie's wagon* (1988)
374 *Go west, Joe Best* (1988)
375 *Battle of Hogan's Hole* (1988)
376 *Feud-breakers* (1988)
377 *Is Glennon guilty?* (1988)
378 *Legend of Coyote Ford* (1988)
379 *Widow from nowhere* (1989)
380 *Second chance man* (1989)
381 *Hostage hunters* (1989)
382 *Alias Ed Dacey* (1989)
383 *Doomsday gun* (1989)
384 *Beeby's big night* (1989)
385 *Langan legacy* (1989)
386 *Hackett's bluff* (1989)
387 *Backtracking Little Red* (1989)
388 *Selina crisis* (1989)
389 *Wells Fargo decoys* (1989)
390 *Wolf Creek or bust* (1989)
391 *Friends of Barney Gregg* (1989)
392 *Runaway Ramsey* (1989)
393 *Battle Alley* (1989)
394 *High card killer* (1989)
395 *Revenge is the spur* (1989)
396 *No name gang* (1989)
397 *Challenge the legend* (1989)
398 *Slow Wolf and Dan Fox* (1989)
399 *Lawman wore black* (1989)
400 *Uneasy money* (1990)
401 *Terror for sale* (1990)
402 *Spencer started something* (1990)
403 *Dakota death-trap* (1990)
404 *Whatever became of Johnny Duke?* (1990)
405 *Once upon a gallows* (1990)
406 *Never say quit* (1990)
407 *Fortune fever* (1990)
408 *Gold movers* (1990)
409 *In cahoots* (1990)
410 *South to Sabine* (1990)
411 *Rough, ready and Texan* (1990)
412 *Banished from Bodie* (1990)
413 *Hold 'em back!* (1990)
414 *One hell of a showdown* (1990)
415 *Ruckus at Gila Wells* (1991)
416 *Woman hunt* (1991)
417 *Wrong victim* (1991)
418 *Bunko trail* (1991)
419 *Bequest to a Texan* (1991)
420 *Rescue a tall Texan* (1991)
421 *Moonlight and gunsmoke* (1991)
422 *Right royal hassle* (1991)
423 *Wrangle Creek* (1991)
424 *Strangers riding by* (1991)
425 *Conways chronicle* (1991)
426 *Vigil on Sundown Ridge* (1992)
427 *Eyes of a killer* (1992)
428 *Wildcat run* (1992)

Larry Baker series
Brown, Carter
1 *Charlie sent me* (1963)
Rewritten from *Swansong for a siren*, 1955 to include Baker
2 *No blonde is an island* (1965)
3 *So what killed the vampire?* (1966)
4 *Had I but groaned* (1968)
Witches
5 *True son of the Beast!* (1970)
6 *Iron maiden* (1975)

Larry Cohen and John Comaday series
Cunningham, E V
see **John Comaday and Larry Cohen series**

Larry Dexter series
Sperry, Raymond
1 *Larry Dexter at the big flood* (1926)
Alternative title: The perils of a reporter; originally published as *From office boy to reporter*, by Howard Roger Garis, 1907
2 *Larry Dexter and the land swindlers* (1926)
Alternative title: Queer adventures in a great city; originally published as *Larry Dexter, the young reporter, by Howard Roger Garis,* 1907
3 *Larry Dexter and the missing millionaire* (1926)
Alternative title: The great search; originally published as *Larry Dexter's great search*, by Howard Roger Garis, 1907
4 *Larry Dexter and the bank mystery* (1926)
Alternative title: Exciting days in Wall Street; originally published as *Larry Dexter and the bank mystery*, by Howard Roger Garis, 1912
5 *Larry Dexter and the stolen boy* (1926)
Alternative title: A chase on the Great Lakes; originally published as *Larry Dexter and the stolen boy*, by Howard Roger Garis, 1915
6 *Larry Dexter at the battle front* (1926)
Alternative title: A war correspondent's double mission; originally published as *Larry Dexter in Belgium*, by Howard Roger Garis, 1915
7 *Larry Dexter and the Ward diamonds* (1927)
Alternative title: The young reporter at Sea Cliff
8 *Larry Dexter's great chase* (1927)
Alternative title: The young reporter across the continent

Larry Grail series
Cousins, Edmund George
1 *Untimely frost* (1953)
2 *To comfort the Signora* (1951)
3 *Moab is my washpot* (1952)
Wine of war

Larry Howe and Berkeley Barnes series
Franklin, Eugene
see **Berkeley Barnes and Larry Howe series**

Larry Koharik series
Eshleman, John Morton
see **Lieutenant Larry Koharik series**

Larry Maver series
Nixon, Alan
1 *Item seven* (1970)
2 *Attack on Vienna* (1971)

Larry Pearson series
Macarthur, David Wilson
1 *Zambesi adventure* (1960)
2 *Valley of hidden gold* (1962)
3 *Guns for Congo* (1963)

Larry Vernon series
Bateson, David
1 *It's murder, Senorita* (1954)
2 *Man from the rock* (1955)
3 *Big tomorrow* (1956)
4 *Soho jungle* (1958)
5 *Night is for violence* (1958)
6 *I'll go anywhere* (1959)
7 *I'll do anything* (1960)

Lars Kollin series
Hogstrand, Olle
see **Chief Inspector Lars Kollin series**

Larson series
Krasney, Samuel A
see **Abe Larson series**

Larssen family series
Unnerstad, Edith
see **Larsson family series**

Larsson family series
Unnerstad, Edith
1 *Saucepan journey* (1949)
Original edition entitled *Kastrullresan*
2 *Pip-Larssons go sailing* (1950)
Peep-Larssons go sailing
Original edition entitled *Nursegler Pip-Larssons*
3 *Pysen* (1952)
Urchin
Original edition entitled *Pysen*
4 *Little O* (1955)
Original edition entitled *Lille O*

Lascaut series
Jones, Lawrence Evelyn
see **Father Lascaut series**

Lash series
Gruber, Frank
see **Simon Lash series**

Lashtrow series
Richmond, Roe
1 *Rio Grande riptide* (1979)
2 *Crusade on the Chisholm* (1980)
3 *Hell on a holiday* (1980)
Carikee crossfire
4 *Guns at Goliad* (1980)
5 *Nevada Queen high* (1980)
6 *Lifeline of Texas* (1981)
7 *Staked plains rendezvous* (1981)
8 *El Paso Del Norte* (1982)

Lassie and Lad series
Blanchard, Amy Ella
see **Lad and Lassie series**

Lassie series
Krulick, Nancy E
1 *Puppy problems* (1989)
2 *Digging up danger* (1989)
3 *Big blow up* (1989)
4 *Water watchdog* (1990)
5 *Skateboard dare* (1990)
6 *Dangerous party* (1990)

Lassie series
This sequence has three authors
Snow, Dorothea Johnston
1 *Lassie and the mystery at Blackberry Bog* (1956)
Verral, Charles Spain
2 *Lassie and the daring rescue* (1957)
3 *Lassie and her day in the sun* (1958)
Snow, Dorothea Johnston
4 *Lassie and the secret of the summer* (1958)
Schroeder, Doris
5 *Forbidden Valley* (1959)

Lassiter series
Grey, Loren Zane
House pseudonym
1 *Lassiter* (1985)
2 *Ambush for Lassiter* (1985)
3 *Lassiter gold* (1986)
4 *Lassiter tough* (1986)
5 *Lassiter luck* (1986)
6 *Grave for Lassiter* (1987)
7 *Mountain manhunt* (1987)
8 *Lassiter on the Texas trail* (1988)
9 *Lassiter and the great horse race* (1989)
10 *Lassiter and the golden dragon* (1989)
11 *Lassiter's showdown* (1990)
12 *Lassiter in the Comanche stronghold* (1990)

Lassiter series
Grey, Zane
see **Mormon series**
Levine, Paul
see **Jake Lassiter series**

Lassiter series
Slade, Jack
1 *Lassiter* (1968)
2 *Man from Yuma* (1968)
3 *Man from Cheyenne* (1968)
4 *Sidewinder* (1968)
5 *Man from Del Rio* (1969)
6 *Funeral Bend* (1970)
7 *Hell of a way to die* (1971)
8 *Guerilla* (1972)
9 *Man from Lordsburg* (1973)
10 *Gunfight at Ringo Junction* (1973)
11 *Gutshot* (1973)
12 *High Lonesome* (1973)
13 *Badlanders* (1973)
14 *Hell at Yuma* (1974)
15 *Man from Tombstone* (1974)
16 *Rimfire* (1974)
17 *Ride into hell* (1974)
18 *Blood river* (1974)
19 *Durango Bill* (1975)
20 *Apache Junction* (1975)
21 *Man from Papago Wells* (1976)
22 *Cattle baron* (1977)
23 *Hangman* (1977)
24 *Lust for gold* (1977)
25 *Wolverine* (1978)
26 *Five graves for Lassiter* (1979)
27 *Canyon kill* (1979)
28 *Blood knife* (1979)
29 *Big Foot's Range* (1979)
30 *Redgate gold* (1981)
31 *Brother Gun* (1985)

Lasson series
Laqueur, Walter
see **Doctor Richard Lasson series**

Last communion trilogy
Yermakov, Nicholas
1 *Last communion* (1981)
2 *Epiphany* (1982)
3 *Jehad* (1984)

Last deadloss vision series
Priest, Christopher
1 *Last deadloss visions* (1987)
2 *Truth shall set you free* (1987)

Last dinosaur series
Murphy, Jim
1 *Last dinosaur* (1988)
2 *Dinosaur for a day* (1992)

Last Herald-Mage trilogy
Lackey, Mercedes
1 *Magic's pawn* (1989)
2 *Magic's promise* (1989)
3 *Magic's price* (1989)
One volume edition entitled *The last Herald-Mage*, 1990

Last legionary series
Hill, Douglas
1 *Young legionary* (1982)
2 *Galactic warlord* (1979)
3 *Deathwing over Veynaa* (1980)
4 *Day of the Starwind* (1980)
5 *Planet of the Warlord* (1981)

Last lion series
Manchester, William
Biography of Winston Spencer Churchill
1 *Visions of glory, 1874-1932* (1983)
2 *Alone, 1932-1940* (1987)

Last love series
Braine, John
1 *One and last love* (1981)
2 *These golden days* (1985)

Last men series
Stapledon, Olaf
1 *Last and first men* (1930)
A story of the near and far future
2 *Last men in London* (1932)
One volume edition 1972
3 *Star maker* (1937)

Last ranger series
Sargent, Craig
1 *Last ranger* (1986)
2 *Savage stronghold* (1986)
3 *Madman's mansion* (1986)
4 *Rabid brigadier* (1987)
5 *War weapons* (1987)
6 *Warlord's revenge* (1988)
7 *Vile village* (1988)
8 *Cutthroat cannibals* (1988)
9 *Damned disciples* (1988)
10 *Is this the end?* (1989)

Last rangers series
David, Jake
1 *High-tech lawmen of the Texas of tomorrow* (1992)
2 *Crime zone* (1993)
3 *Destination Showdown* (1993)

Last summer, first love series
Baker, Carin Greenberg
Created by Jennifer Baker
1 *Time of love* (1994)
2 *Good-bye to love* (1994)

Last Viking trilogy
Anderson, Poul
1 *Golden horn* (1980)
2 *Road of the sea horse* (1980)
3 *Sign of the raven* (1981)

Lastin series
Hougron, Jean
see **Monsieur Lastin series**

Lateral thinking series
De Bono, Edward
1 *Use of lateral thinking* (1967)
New think
2 *Lateral thinking* (1970)
A textbook of creativity
3 *Lateral thinking for management* (1971)
4 *Letters to thinkers* (1987)
5 *Serious creativity* (1992)
Using the power of lateral thinking to create new ideas

Latham series
Ford, Leslie
see **Grace Latham series**

Lathom Dynes series
Robertson, Helen
see **Inspector Lathom Dynes series**

Lathom series
Page, Gertrude
see **Joe Lathom series**

Lathrop family series
Smith, Chard Powers
1 *Artillery of time* (1939)
2 *Ladies' day* (1958)

Latigo series
Owen, Dean
Based on a comic strip by Stan Lynde
1 *Trackdown* (1981)
2 *Vengeance Trail* (1981)
3 *Dead shot* (1981)
4 *Double eagle* (1982)
Companion volume: *Latigo, comic strips*, by Stan Lynde, 1992

Latimer series
Ambler, Eric
see **Charles Latimer series**
Gaite, Francis
see **James and Charles Latimer series**

Latro series
Wolfe, Gene
1 *Soldier of the mist* (1986)
2 *Soldier of Arete* (1989)

Lattimer children series
O'Farrell, Kathleen
1 *Three cheers for Annabelle* (1956)
2 *Off to the sea with Annabelle* (1958)
3 *Cousin Annabelle's Christmas* (1959)

Lauderdale family series
Crawford, Francis Marion
1 *Katherine Lauderdale* (1894)
2 *Ralstons* (1894)

Laughing time series
Smith, William Jay
1 *Laughing time, and other poems* (1969)
2 *Laughing time nonsense poems* (1980)
One volume edition entitled *Laughing time collected nonsense*, 1990

Laughing torso series
Hamnett, Nana
Autobiography
1 *Laughing torso* (1932)
2 *Is she a lady?* (1955)
A problem in autobiography

Launch boys series
Ellis, Edward Sylvester
1 *Launch boys' adventures in northern waters* (1912)
2 *Launch boys' cruise in the Deerfoot* (1912)
Cruise of the Deerfoot

Laura Adler series
Silver, Victoria
1 *Death of a Harvard freshman* (1984)
2 *Death of a Radcliffe roommate* (1986)

Laura and Amy series
Sachs, Marilyn
see **Amy and Laura series**

Laura and Harry series
Eagar, Frances
1 *Little sparrow* (1972)
2 *Tin mine* (1973)
3 *Midnight patrol* (1974)

Laura Brewster series
Eisenberg, Lisa
1 *House of laughs* (1978)
2 *Falling star* (1978)
3 *Killer music* (1978)
4 *Tiger rose* (1978)
5 *Golden idol* (1978)
6 *Fast food king* (1978)

Laura from Lark Rise series
Harrison, Sarah
1 *Laura and old lumber* (1985)
2 *Laura and Edmund* (1985)
3 *Laura and the lady* (1985)
4 *Laura and the squire* (1985)

Laura Ingalls Wilder series
Tedrow, Thomas L
see **Days of Laura Ingalls Wilder series**

Laura Ireland series
Mariz, Linda
1 *Body English* (1992)
2 *Snake dance* (1992)

Laura Scudamore series
Armstrong, Raymond
1 *Sinister Widow* (1951)
2 *Sinister Widow again* (1952)
3 *Sinister Widow returns* (1953)
4 *Widow and the cavalier* (1956)
5 *Sinister Widow comes back* (1957)
6 *Sinister Widow down under* (1958)
7 *Sinister Widow at sea* (1959)

Laura series
Blake, Linda
1 *Ballet for Laura* (1965)
2 *Laura's summer ballet* (1967)

Laura series
Drummond, Violet Hilda
see **Little Laura series**

Laura series
Dumas, Philippe
1 *Laura, Alice's new puppy* (1976)
Original edition entitled *Laura, le Terre-Neuve d'Alice*
2 *Laura and the bandits* (1978)
Original edition entitled *Laura et les bandits*
3 *Laura on the road* (1979)
Original edition entitled *Laura sur la route*
4 *Laura loses her head* (1981)
Original edition entitled *Laura perd la tete*

Laura series
Eliot, Henrietta Robins
1 *Laura's holiday* (1898)
2 *Laura in the mountains* (1905)

Laura series
Lowndes, Marie Belloc
see **Duchess Laura series**

Laura series
Wilder, Laura Ingalls
1 *Little house in the big woods* (1932)
2 *Little house on the prairie* (1935)
3 *On the banks of Plum Creek* (1937)
4 *By the shores of Silver Lake* (1939)
5 *Long winter* (1940)
6 *Little town on the prairie* (1941)
7 *These happy golden years* (1943)
8 *Farmer boy* (1933)
9 *First four years* (1971)
This sequence is followed by **The days of Laura Ingalls Wilder series**, by Thomas L Tedrow

Laurance and Darling series
Hart, Carolyn Gimpel
see **Annie Laurance and Max Darling series**

Laurano series
Scoppettone, Sandra
see **Lauren Laurano series**

Lauren Laurano series
Scoppettone, Sandra
1 *Everything you have is mine* (1991)
2 *I'll be leaving you always* (1993)
3 *My sweet untraceable you* (1994)

Laurence and Carlisle series
Dempster, Guy
see **Guy Laurence and Tony Carlisle series**

Laurence Carroll series
Cronin, Archibald Joseph
1 *Song of sixpence* (1964)
2 *Pocketful of rye* (1969)

Laurie Grant and Stewart Noble series
Mackintosh, May
1 *Appointment in Andalusia* (1972)
2 *King and two queens* (1973)
Assignment in Andorra
3 *Sicilian affair* (1974)
Dark paradise

Laurie Hume series
Duncan, William Murdoch
1 *Murder calls the tune* (1957)
2 *Whispering man* (1959)
3 *Murder man* (1959)

Laurie Jo Hansen series
Pournelle, Jerry
1 *High justice* (1977)
2 *Exiles to glory* (1978)

Laurie series
Cannan, Gilbert
1 *Little brother* (1912)
2 *Round the corner* (1913)
Life and death of Arthur Christopher Folyat
3 *Three pretty men* (1916)
Three sons and a mother
4 *Stucco house* (1918)
5 *Time and eternity* (1919)
A tale of three exiles
6 *Annette and Bennett* (1922)

Laurila series
Low, Ona
see **Arvo Laurila series**

Lavarni family series
Todd, Laura
1 *Place like home* (1987)
Growing up in the School of Industry, 1915-1922
2 *Freshwater, 1922-1928* (1989)

Lavengro series
Borrow, George
see **Gypsy series**

Laverne and Shirley series
Steffanson, Con
Based on a television series
1 *Teamwork* (1976)
2 *Easy money* (1976)
3 *Gold rush* (1976)

Lavette family series
Fast, Howard
1 *Immigrants* (1977)
2 *Second generation* (1978)
3 *Establishment* (1979)
4 *Legacy* (1981)
5 *Immigrant's daughter* (1985)

Lavransdatter trilogy
Undset, Sigrid
see **Kristin Lavransdatter trilogy**

Lavrin family series
Morris, Ira J
1 *Fortune hunter* (1971)
2 *Troika belle* (1967)

Law and order trilogy
Newman, Gordon F
1 *Villain's tale* (1977)
2 *Prisoner's tale* (1977)
3 *Detective's tale* (1977)
One volume edition entitled *Law and order*, 1983

Law at work series
Deming, Richard
1 *Man and society* (1970)
Criminal law at work
2 *Man against man* (1972)
Civil law at work
3 *Man and the world* (1974)
International law at work

Law series
Bear, Greg
1 *Forge of God* (1987)
2 *Anvil of stars* (1992)

Lawe series
Monsarrat, Nicholas
see **Master mariner series**

Lawler series
Cole, Margaret Alice
see **Judy Lawler series**

Lawless series
Bennett, Rolf
see **Commander Lawless series**

Lawless worlds series
Comstock, Jarrod
see **These lawless worlds series**

Lawman series
Newton, Mike
1 *Creed's vengeance* (1981)
2 *Creed's gold* (1982)
3 *Creed's war* (1982)
4 *Creed's kill* (1982)
5 *Creed's treasure* (1982)
6 *Creed's hell* (1982)
7 *Creed's vendetta* (1982)
8 *Creed's ransom* (1982)
9 *Creed's gauntlet* (1982)

Lawmen series
Dancer, J B
This pseudonym is used by John Barton Harvey and Angus Wells as indicated against each title
1 *Evil breed* (1977)
[Harvey]
2 *Kansas, bloody Kansas* (1977)
[Wells]
3 *Judgement day* (1978)
[Harvey]
4 *Vengeance trail* (1978)
[Wells]
5 *Hanged man* (1979)
[Harvey]
6 *One way to die* (1980)
[Wells]

Lawrence and Henderson series
Pritchett, Ron
see **Buck Lawrence and Zeke Henderson series**

Lawrence and Sandy trilogy
Pullein-Thompson, Christine
see **Sandy and Lawrence trilogy**

Lawrence Fenton series
Annesley, Michael
1 *Room fourteen* (1935)
Fenton of the Foreign Office
2 *Spies in the web* (1936)
3 *Spies in action* (1937)
4 *Missing agent* (1938)
5 *Vanished vice-consul* (1939)
6 *Unknown agent* (1940)
7 *Spy against the Reich* (1940)
8 *Suicide spies* (1944)
9 *Agent intervenes* (1944)
10 *Spies abounding* (1945)
11 *Spy, counter spy* (1946)
12 *They won't lie down* (1947)
13 *Spy corner* (1948)
14 *Lights that did not fail* (1949)
15 *Spy island* (1950)

Lawrence Gilmartin series
Barry, Charles
see **Superintendent Lawrence Gilmartin series**

Lawrence Marley series
Walker, Jerry
1 *Mission accomplished* (1947)
2 *Date with destiny* (1949)

Lawrence Maver series
Nixon, Alan
see **Larry Maver series**

Lawrence series
Mackail, Denis
see **David Lawrence series**

Lawrenceville series
Johnson, Owen McMahon
1 *Eternal boy* (1909)
Prodigious Hickey
2 *Varmint* (1910)
3 *Tennessee Shad* (1911)
Chronicling the rise and fall of the firm of Doc Macnooder and the Tennessee Shad
4 *Stover at Yale* (1912)
5 *Skippy Bedelle* (1922)
His sentimental progress from the urchin to the complete man of the world

Lawrie Fenton series
Annesley, Michael
see **Lawrence Fenton series**

Lawson family series
Meredith, Gwen
see **Blue Hills series**

Lawson of the Special Branch series
Bolton, Melvin
1 *Softener* (1984)
2 *Testing* (1987)

Lawson series
Comer, Ralph
see **Robert Lawson series**
Davidson, Helen Beatrice
see **Peter Lawson series**
Dexter, Ross
see **Duke Lawson series**
Leyland, Eric
see **Red Lawson series**
Roe, Harry Mason
see **Lanky Lawson series**
Smith, Joan Mary
see **Loretta Lawson series**
Warfield, Gallatin
see **Gardner Lawson series**

Layne series
Kelton, Elmer
see **Crow Feather series**

Layton series
Roberts, Marion
see **Anne and David layton series**

Lazarus and Decker series
Kellerman, Faye
see **Sergeant Peter Decker and Rina Lazarus series**

Lazarus Long series
Heinlein, Robert Anson
1 *Methuselah's children* (1958)
Selections published as *The past through tomorrow*, 1967
2 *Time enough for love* (1973)
Selections published as *The notebooks of Lazarus Long*, 1978
3 *Cat who walks through walls* (1985)
A comedy of manners
4 *To sail beyond the sunset* (1987)
The life and loves of Maureen Johnson, being the memoirs of a somewhat irregular lady
Companion volume: *The notebooks of Lazarus Long*, 1978

Lazarus series
Berlin, Sven
Autobiography
1 *I am Lazarus* (1961)
2 *Dark monarch* (1962)
A portrait from within

Lazender family series
Kells, Susannah
1 *Crowning mercy* (1983)
2 *Fallen angels* (1984)

Lazy River series
White, William Patterson
1 *Lynch lawyers* (1920)
2 *Hidden trails* (1920)
3 *Paradise Bend* (1920)
4 *Heart of the range* (1921)

Lea Delmas trilogy
Deforges, Regine
1 *Blue bicycle* (1981)
Original edition entitled *La bicyclette bleue*
2 *Lea* (1983)
Original edition entitled *101, Avenue Henri-Martin*
3 *Devil laughs again* (1985)
Original edition entitled *La diable en rit encore*

Leafy series
Lister, Gladys
1 *Grandpuff and Leafy* (1942)
2 *Leafy and Prince Brumby* (1944)
3 *Leafy's seventh wave* (1948)
4 *Tubby, the little round bear* (1949)

Leah Goldfeder series
Goldreich, Gloria
1 *Leah's journey* (1978)
2 *Leah's children* (1985)

Leah Stephenson series
Bernard, Elizabeth
see **Satin slippers series**

Leanne and Sam series
Clark, Margaret
see **Sam and Leanne series**

Leaphorn series
Hillerman, Tony
see **Lieutenant Joe Leaphorn series**

Learn with Moonbird series
Higgs, Mike
1 *Manners* (1984)
2 *Bicycle safety* (1984)
3 *Safety at home* (1984)
4 *Telling the time* (1984)
5 *Moon* (1984)
6 *Safety in the water* (1984)
7 *Safety with fire* (1984)
8 *Weather* (1984)

Learn with Noddy series
Blyton, Enid
1 *Learn to count with Noddy* (1965)
2 *Learn to go shopping with Noddy* (1965)
3 *Learn animal shapes with Noddy* (1965)
Learn to read about animals with Noddy
4 *Learn to tell the time with Noddy* (1965)

Learn with the Munch Bunch series
Reed, Giles
1 *Learn the Alphabet with the Munch Bunch* (1981)
2 *Learn to count with the Munch Bunch* (1981)
3 *Learn the days of the week with the Munch Bunch* (1981)

4 *Learn opposites with the Munch Bunch* (1981)
5 *Learn to tell time with the Munch Bunch* (1981)

Learn with Victoria Plum series
Rippon, Angela
1 *Birds* (1985)
2 *Trees* (1985)
3 *Flowers* (1985)
4 *Woodland animals* (1985)

Learning to read from the Bible primer series
Beers, Victor Gilbert
1 *May I help you?* (1979)
2 *Do you know my friend?* (1979)
3 *Do you love me?* (1979)
4 *Will you come with me?* (1979)

Learning to read from the Bible series
Beers, Victor Gilbert
1 *God is my helper* (1973)
2 *Jesus is my guide* (1973)
3 *Jesus is my teacher* (1973)
4 *God is my friend* (1973)

Lear's daughters series
Kellogg, Marjorie Bradley
1 *Wave and the flame* (1986)
2 *Reign of fire* (1986)
One volume edition entitled *Lear's daughters*, 1987

Leather and lace series
This sequence has three authors
Dixon, Dorothy
1 *Lavender blossom* (1982)
2 *Trembling heart* (1982)
3 *Belle of the Rio Grande* (1982)
4 *Flame of the West* (1982)
5 *Cimarron Rose* (1982)
Armstrong, Carolyn T
6 *Honeysuckle love* (1982)
Dixon, Dorothy
7 *Diamond queen* (1983)
Lee, Tammie
8 *Texas wildflower* (1983)
Dixon, Dorothy
9 *Yellowstone jewel* (1985)

Leather bondage series
Townsend, Larry
1 *Run, little leather boy* (1993)
2 *Run no more* (1993)
3 *Kiss of leather* (1994)
4 *Long leather cord* (1994)

Leather series
Lawrence, David
see **Danny Leather series**

Leatherface Lonergan series
Renwick, Peter
1 *Leatherface Lonergan stakes a claim* (1936)
2 *Black Hogan strikes again* (1937)

Leatherhand series
Wales, Mike
1 *Leatherhand* (1983)
2 *Hangman's legacy* (1983)
3 *Lottery of death* (1984)
4 *Dead wrong* (1984)
5 *Bad day at Bandera* (1984)
6 *Magician* (1985)
7 *Last ride* (1985)
8 *Dark nemesis* (1985)

Leathermouth series
Dawe, Carlton
1 *Leathermouth* (1931)
2 *Sign of the glove* (1932)
3 *Fifteen keys* (1932)
4 *Crumpled lilies* (1933)
5 *Missing treaty* (1934)
6 *Law of the knife* (1934)
7 *Leathermouth's luck* (1934)
8 *Royal alliance* (1935)
9 *Waste lands* (1935)
10 *Tough company* (1936)
11 *Green killer* (1936)

Leathers Auckland series
Chrystie, Edward M
1 *Leathers steps in* (1957)
2 *Leathers again* (1958)
3 *Leathers after big game* (1958)
4 *Leathers in Mozambique* (1959)
5 *Leathers in the wild coast* (1960)

Leatherstocking series
Cooper, James Fenimore
1 *Deerslayer* (1841)
Alternative title: The first war-path
2 *Last of the Mohicans* (1826)
3 *Pathfinder* (1840)
Alternative title: The inland sea
4 *Pioneers* (1823)
Alternative title: The sources of the Susquehanna
5 *Prairie* (1827)
Abridged one volume edition entitled *The Leatherstocking saga*, 1954

LeBeau series
Crafton, Dennis
see **Lobo series**

Le Breton series
Esteven, John
see **Miles Le Breton series**

Lechow family series
Benary, Margot
1 *Ark* (1948)
Original edition entitled *Die Arche Noah*
2 *Rowan Farm* (1949)
Original edition entitled *Die Ebereschenhof*

Lecks and Aleshine series
Stockton, Frank Richard
see **Mrs Lecks and Mrs Aleshine series**

Lecoq series
Gaboriau, Emile
see **Monsieur Lecoq series**

Ledenham School series
Pleydell, Susan
1 *Summer term* (1959)
2 *Young man's fancy* (1962)

Ledermann series
Maxwell, Peter
see **Ralph Ledermann series**

Ledgar Dunstan series
Sheppard, Alfred Tresidder
1 *Rise of Ledgar Dunstan* (1916)
2 *Quest of Ledgar Dunstan* (1917)

Ledger trilogy
Reese, John
see **Jesus on horseback trilogy**

Lee Barcello series
Ransome, Stephen
see **Lieutenant Lee Barcello series**

Lee Beckett series
Crowe, John
see **Buena Costa County series**

Lee Caton series
Mason, Chuck
1 *Gun for hire* (1972)
2 *Hangrope fever* (1973)

Lee Corey series
Williamson, Tony
1 *Connector* (1976)
2 *Doomsday contract* (1977)
3 *Technicians of death* (1978)

Lee Crosley series
Tralins, Sandor Robert
1 *Chic Chic spy* (1966)
2 *Miss from S.I.S.* (1966)
3 *Ring-a-ding UFOs* (1967)

Lee Hayes series
Lacy, Ed
1 *Harlem underground* (1965)
2 *In black and whitey* (1967)

Lee Kershaw series
Shirreffs, Gordon Donald
1 *Showdown in Sonora* (1969)
2 *Manhunter* (1970)
3 *Bowman's kid* (1973)
4 *Renegade's trail* (1974)
5 *Apache hunter* (1976)
6 *Marauders* (1977)

Lee series
Burtis, Thomson
see **Rex Lee series**
Cody, Liza
see **Anna Lee series**
Douglas, George
see **Inspector Bonny Lee series**
Grove, Harriet Pyne
see **Betty Lee series**
Hopkins, Kenneth
see **Gerry Lee series**
Lee, Gypsy Rose
see **Gypsy Rose Lee series**
Lee, Norma
see **Beautiful Gunner series**
Loos, Anita
see **Lorelie Lee and Dorothy series**
Marsh, Richard
see **Judith Lee series**
Optic, Oliver
see **Flora Lee series**
Stewart, William Thomas
see **Gaff Lee series**
Warde, Margaret
see **Nancy Lee series**
White, Robb
see **Midshipman Lee series**

Lee Youngdahl series
Harris, Mark
1 *Wake up, stupid!* (1959)
2 *Lying in bed* (1984)

Leeuwen series
Stendhal
see **Lucien Leeuwen series**

Leffing series
Brennan, Joseph Payne
see **Lucius Leffing series**

Left hand, right hand series
Sitwell, Osbert
Autobiography
1 *Left hand, right hand* (1944)
Cruel month
2 *Scarlet tree* (1946)
3 *Great morning* (1948)
4 *Laughter in the next room* (1949)
5 *Noble essences* (1950)
6 *Tales my father taught me* (1962)

Left right series
Brockway, Fenner
Autobiography
1 *Inside the left* (1942)
2 *Outside the right* (1963)

Left series
Forsyte, Charles
see **Inspector Richard Left series**

Lefty O'Connor series
Shannon, Brad
1 *Lefty O'Connor moves in* (1950)
2 *Lefty cuts loose* (1951)
3 *Bury the guy!* (1951)
4 *Lefty hands it out* (1951)
5 *Lefty takes over* (1952)

Legacy of love trilogy
Harvey, Caroline
1 *Charlotte* (1980)
2 *Alexandra* (1980)
3 *Cara* (1983)
One volume edition entitled *Legacy of love*, 1983

Legacy trilogy
Coulter, Catherine
1 *Wyndham legacy* (1994)
2 *Nightingale legacy* (1994)
Number 3 not yet published

Legend of Ethshar series
Watt-Evans, Lawrence
1 *Misenchanted sword* (1985)
2 *With a single spell* (1987)
3 *Unwilling warlord* (1989)
4 *Blood of a dragon* (1991)
5 *Taking flight* (1993)
6 *Spell of the black dagger* (1993)

Legend of the jade phoenix trilogy
Thurston, Robert
1 *Way of the clans* (1991)
2 *Bloodname* (1991)
3 *Falcon guard* (1991)

Legend series
Gemmell, David A
see **Drenai series**

Legendary castles of Britain series
Alexander, Marc
1 *Legendary castles of the south* (1977)
2 *Legendary castles of the Broder* (1978)

Legendary murders series
Williams, Lawrence
1 *Copper snare* (1980)
2 *Murder triangle* (1982)
3 *Images of death* (1984)

Legendre series
Brush, Katharine
see **Lillian Legendre series**

Legends of Camber of Culdi trilogy
Kurtz, Katherine
The first trilogy in the **World of the Eleven Kingdoms series**
1 *Camber of Culdi* (1976)
2 *Saint Camber* (1978)
3 *Camber the heretic* (1981)

Legends of Eorthe series
Beamer, Charles
1 *Magician's bane* (1980)
2 *Lightning in the bottle* (1981)

Legends of Larian series
Murray, Terry
1 *Shadow's edge* (1992)
2 *Cutting edge* (1993)

Legends of Lone Wolf series
Dever, Joe
1 *Eclipse of the Kai* (1989)
2 *Dark door opens* (1989)
3 *Sword of the sun* (1989)
3.1 *Tides of treachery* (1989)
3 2 *Sword of the sun* (1989)
4 *Hunting Wolf* (1990)
5 *Claws of Helgedad* (1991)
6 *Sacrifice of Ruanon* (1991)

Legends of Skyfall series
Tant, David
1 *Monsters of the marsh* (1985)
2 *Black pyramid* (1985)

Legends of Ulm series
Chetwin, Grace
see **Tales of Gom in the Legends of Ulm series**

Legends series
Everitt, David
1 *Story of Wyatt Earp* (1988)
2 *Story of the Sundance Kid* (1990)
3 *Story of Pat Garrett and Billy the Kid* (1990)

Legends west trilogy
Hall, Oakley
1 *Warlock* (1958)
2 *Bad lands* (1978)
3 *Apaches* (1986)

Legion of Space series
Williamson, Jack
1 *Legion of Space* (1947)
2 *Cometeers* (1950)
3 *One against the Legion* (1967)
Numbers 1-3 also published in one volume entitled *Three from the Legion*, 1979
4 *Queen of the Legion* (1983)
Companion volume: *The Legion of War, Combat Command in the world of Jack Williamson's The Legion of Space, by Andrew Keith*, 1988

Legion of time series
Williamson, Jack
1 *Legion of time* (1961)
2 *After world's end* (1961)
One volume editions entitled *The legion of time*, 1952 and *Two complete novels*, 1963

Legoix series
Benzoni, Juliette
see **Catherine Legoix series**

Le Grande and GENOPS series
Blacker, Irwin Robert
see **General Le Grande and GENOPS series**

Legrange League series
Watkins, William John
1 *Centrifugal rickshaw dancer* (1985)
2 *Going to see the end of the sky* (1986)

Leicester series
Drysdale, Margaret
see **Robert Dudley series**
Jewett, Sarah Orne
see **Betty Leicester series**

Leidl and Miklejohn series
Wilhelm, Kate
see **Charlie Miklejohn and Constance Leidl series**

Leigh family series
Lupton, Joyce
1 *Hill of the Ring* (1960)
2 *Seekers* (1971)

Leigh series
Temple, Richard
see **Simon Leigh series**

Leigh trilogy
Scott, Melissa
see **Silence Leigh trilogy**

Leighton and Harper series
Ernst, Paul
see **Shirley Leighton and Bill Harper series**

Leighton series
Mack, Louise
see **Lennie Leighton series**

Leighton Swift series
Jones, Charles Reed
1 *King murder* (1929)
2 *Torch murder* (1930)
3 *Van Norton murders* (1931)

Leila trilogy
Tytler, Ann Fraser
1 *Leila* (1839)
Alternative title: The island
2 *Leila in England* (1842)
3 *Leila at home* (1852)

Leith and Keats series
Shore, Viola Brothers
see **Colin Keats and Gwynn Leith series**

Leithen series
Buchan, John
see **Sir Edward Leithen series**

Leitmotiv series
Mittelholzer, Edgar
1 *Latticed echoes* (1960)
2 *Thunder returning* (1961)

Leitus series
Monaco, Richard
1 *Runes* (1984)
2 *Broken stone* (1985)

Lek series
Curry, Jane Louise
1 *Wolves of Aam* (1981)
2 *Shadow dancers* (1983)

Leland and Judy Pefley series
Perdue, Tito
1 *New austerities* (1994)
2 *Lee* (1991)

Leland series
Davis, Franklin Milton
see **Quinn Leland series**
Thorp, Roderick
see **Joe Leland series**

Lemanuel Bates and Tobacco Jones series
Floren, Lee
see **Judge Lemanuel Bates and Tobacco Jones series**

Lemmus trilogy
Savarin, Julian Jay
1 *Waiters on the dance* (1972)
2 *Beyond the Outer Mirr* (1976)
3 *Archives of Haven* (1977)

Lemmy Caution series
Cheyney, Peter
1 *This man is dangerous* (1936)
2 *Poison ivy* (1937)
3 *Dames don't care* (1937)
4 *Can ladies kill?* (1938)
5 *Don't get me wrong* (1939)
6 *You'd be surprised* (1940)
7 *Mister Caution, Mister Callaghan* (1941)
Short stories
8 *Your deal, my lovely* (1941)
9 *Never a dull moment* (1942)
10 *You can always duck* (1943)
11 *I'll say she does!* (1945)
12 *Time for Caution* (1946)
Also stories featuring *Caution in G Man at the Yard*, 1953

Lemon Kelly series
Hildick, Edmund Wallace
1 *Meet Lemon Kelly* (1963)
Lemon Kelly
2 *Lemon Kelly digs deep* (1964)
3 *Lemon Kelly and the home-made boy* (1968)

Lemuel Gulliver series
This sequence has ten authors
Swift, Jonathan
1 *Travels into several remote nations of the world* (1726)
Gulliver's travels
Gulliver, Lemuel
2 *Travels into several remote nations of the world, volume III* (1727)
3 *Travels into several remote nations of the world, volume III, part II* (1727)
A voyage to Severambia
Desfontaines, Pierre
4 *Travels of Mister John Gulliver, son to Captain Lemuel Gulliver* (1731)
Perce, Elbert
5 *Gulliver Joi* (1851)
His three voyages, being an account of his marvelous adventures in Kailoo, Hydrogenia and Ejario
Garrison, Wendell Phillips
6 *New Gulliver* (1898)
Anonymous
7 *Laputa* (1905)
Revisited by Gulliver Redivivus in 1905
Herrman, Louis
8 *In the sealed cave* (1935)
A modern commentary on a strange discovery made by Captain Lemuel Gulliver in the year 1721 and now published from manuscript notes recently come to light, a scientific fantasy
Hodgart, Matthew
9 *New voyage to the country of the Houyhnhnms* (1969)
The fifth part of the travels into several remote parts of the world by Lemuel Gilliver, first a surgeon and then a captain of several ships, wherein the author returns and finds a new state of liberal horses and revolting yahoos
Dodderidge, Esme
10 *New Gulliver* (1979)
Alternative title: The adventures of Lemuel Gulliver, Jr. in Capovolta
Brady, John Paul
11 *Voyage to Inshneefa* (1987)
The first-hand account of the fifth voyage of Lemuel Gulliver

Lend-a-hand boys series
Rathborne, Saint George
1 *Lend-a-hand boys team-work* (1931)
2 *Lend-a-hand boys sanitary squad* (1931)
3 *Lend-a-hand boys wild game* (1931)

Lendrick series
Braine, John
see **Clive and Robin Lendrick series**

Lenin series
Cliff, Tony
Biography
1 *Building the Party, 1893-1914* (1975)
2 *All power to the Soviets, 1914-1917* (1976)
3 *Revolution besieged, 1917-1923* (1978)
4 *Bolsheviks and world communism* (1979)
Numbers 3 and 4 also published in one volume entitled *Revolution besieged*, 1980

Lennie Leighton series
Mack, Louise
1 *Teens* (1897)
A story of Australian schoolgirls
2 *Girls together* (1898)
3 *Teens triumphant* (1933)

Lennon series
Meyers, Barlow
see **Janet Lennon series**

Lennox Kemp series
Meek, Margaret Reid Duncan
1 *Sitting ducks* (1984)
2 *Hang the consequences* (1984)
3 *Split second* (1985)
4 *In remembrance of Rose* (1987)
5 *Worm of doubt* (1987)
6 *Mouthful of sand* (1988)
7 *Loose connection* (1989)
8 *This blessed plot* (1990)
9 *Touch and go* (1992)

Lennox series
Ballard, Willis Todhunter
see **Bill Lennox series**
Wainwright, John
see **Chief Inspector Lennox series**

Lenny and Jake series
Townson, Hazel
1 *Great ice-cream crime* (1981)
2 *Siege of Cobb Street School* (1983)
3 *Vanishing Gran* (1983)
4 *Haunted ivy* (1984)
5 *Crimson crescent* (1986)
6 *Staggering snowman* (1987)
7 *Fireworks galore* (1988)
8 *Walnut whirl* (1989)
9 *Lenny and Jake adventures* (1991)
10 *Kidnap report* (1992)
11 *Sign of the crab* (1994)

Lenore and Geoffrey series
Sherwood, Valerie
see **Geoffrey and Lenore series**

Lenore Wahl and Werner Bertin series
Zweig, Arnold
see **Werner Bertin and Lenore Wahl series**

Lens of the world trilogy
Macavoy, Roberta Ann
1 *Lens of the world* (1990)
2 *King of the dead* (1991)
Third volume not yet published

Lensman series
This sequence has three authors
Smith, Edward Elmer
1 *Triplanetary* (1948)
2 *First Lensman* (1950)
3 *Galactic patrol* (1950)
4 *Gray Lensman* (1951)
Grey Lensman
5 *Second stage Lensman* (1953)
6 *Children of the Lens* (1954)
7 *Vortex blaster* (1960)
Masters of the vortex
Ellern, William Bert
8 *New Lensman* (1976)
Kyle, David Ackerman
9 *Dragon Lensman* (1980)
10 *Lensman from Rigel* (1982)
11 *Z-Lensman* (1983)

Leo and Emily series
Brandenberg, Franz
1 *Leo and Emily* (1981)
2 *Leo and Emily's big ideas* (1982)
3 *Leo and Emily and the dragon* (1984)
Companion volume: *Leo and Emily's zoo*, 1988

Leo Bebb tetralogy
Buechner, Frederick
1 *Lion country* (1971)
2 *Open heart* (1972)
3 *Love feast* (1974)
4 *Treasure hunt* (1977)
One volume edition entitled *The book of Bebb*, 1979

Leo Bloodworth and Serendipity Dahlquist series
Lochte, Dick
1 *Sleeping dog* (1985)
2 *Laughing dog* (1988)

Leo Guild series
Gorman, Edward
1 *Guild* (1987)
2 *Death ground* (1988)
3 *Blood game* (1989)
4 *Dark trail* (1990)

Leo Haggerty series
Schutz, Benjamin Merrill
1 *All the old bargains* (1985)
2 *Embrace the wolf* (1985)
3 *Tax in blood* (1987)
4 *Things we do for love* (1989)
5 *Fistful of empty* (1991)
6 *Mexico is forever* (1994)

Leo Haig series
Harrison, Chip
1 *Make out with murder* (1974)
Also published as *Five little rich girls*, under the author's real name Lawrence Block
2 *Topless tulip caper* (1975)
Also published under the author's real name Lawrence Block

Leo Roi series
Lore, Phillips
1 *Who killed the pie man?* (1975)
2 *Murder behind closed doors* (1980)
3 *Looking glass murders* (1980)

Leo the late bloomer series
Kraus, Robert
1 *Leo the late bloomer bakes a cake* (1981)
2 *Leo the late bloomer takes a bath* (1981)

Leo the Lop series
Cosgrove, Stephen Edward
1 *Leo the Lop* (1977)
2 *Leo the Lop, tail two* (1977)
3 *Leo the Lop, tail three* (1977)
Companion volume: *Grampa-Lop*, 1979

Leo, Zack and Emmie series
Ehrlich, Amy
1 *Leo, Zack and Emmie* (1981)
2 *Leo, Zack and Emmie together again* (1987)

Leofwine series
Leslie, Emma
1 *Leofwine the Saxon* (1875)
A story of hopes and struggles, 1052-1066
2 *Elfreda* (1875)
3 *Leofwine the monk* (1882)
Alternative title: The curse of the Ericsons, 1187-1215

Leon and Renee Thornton series
Ashton, Elizabeth
see **Renee and Leon Thornton series**

Leon-Castilla series
Reilly, Bernard F
see **Kingdom of Leon-Castilla series**

Leon Trotsky trilogy
Deutscher, Isaac
1 *Prophet armed, 1879-1921* (1954)
2 *Prophet unarmed, 1921-1929* (1959)
3 *Prophet outcast, 1929-1940* (1963)

Leona series
Havill, Juanita
1 *It always happens to Leona* (1989)
2 *Leona and Ike* (1990)

Leonard Harris and Franklin Perry series
Keverne, Richard
see **Franklin Parry and Leonard Harris series**

Leonard series
Darby, Joan
see **Time machine series**
Wain, John
see **Peter and Brian Leonard series**
Winton, Tim
see **Lockie Leonard series**
Woolley, Catherine
see **Cathy Leonard series**

Leonard Wallace series
Wilson, Alexander
see **Sir Leonard Wallace series**

Leonidas Prike series
Blochman, Lawrence Goldtree
see **Inspector Leonidas Prike series**

Leonidas Witherall series
Tilton, Alice
1 *Beginning with a bash* (1937)
2 *Cut direct* (1938)
3 *Cold steel* (1939)
4 *Left leg* (1940)
5 *Hollow chest* (1941)
6 *File for record* (1943)
7 *Dead Ernest* (1944)
8 *Iron claw* (1947)
Iron hand

Leopard series
Maestro, Giulio
1 *Leopard is sick* (1978)
2 *Leopard and the noisy monkeys* (1979)

Leper series
Mauriac, Francois
1 *Kiss to the leper* (1922)
Original edition entitled *Le baiser au lepreux*
2 *Genetrix* (1923)
Original edition entitled *Genetrix*
One volume editions entitled *The family*, 1930 and, *A kiss for the leper, and, Genetrix*, 1950

Lepski series
Chase, James Hadley
see **Frank Terrell series**

Ler series
Foster, Michael Anthony
1 *Gameplayers of Zan* (1977)
2 *Warriors of dawn* (1975)
3 *Day of the Klesh* (1979)

L'Eree family series
Grange, Peter
1 *King Creole* (1968)
2 *Devil's emissary* (1968)
3 *Tumult at the gate* (1970)
4 *Golden goddess* (1973)

Leric series
Busby, Roger
see **Detective Inspector Leric series**

Le Roux series
Brown, Hosanna
see **Frank Le Roux series**

Leroy Powder series
Lewin, Michael Zinn
see **Lieutenant Leroy Powder series**

Leroy series
Kraft, Eric
see **Peter Leroy series**
Perowne, Barry
see **Rick Leroy series**

Les Ferron series
Keene, Day
1 *Sleep with the devil* (1954)
2 *Notorious* (1954)

Les Girls series
Tomkinson, Constance
Reminiscences of a revue artist
1 *Les Girls* (1956)
2 *African follies* (1959)
3 *What a performance* (1962)

Les Norton series
Barrett, Robert G
1 *You wouldn't be dead for quids* (1985)
2 *Real thing* (1986)
3 *Boys from Binjiwunyawunya* (1987)
4 *Godson* (1989)
5 *Between Devlin and the deep blue sea* (1991)
Les Norton in between the Devlin and the deep blue sea
6 *White shoes, white lines and Blackie* (1992)
7 *Davo's little something* (1992)
8 *And de fun don't done* (1993)
9 *Mele kalimaka, Mr Walker* (1994)

Lesbian series
Hanscombe, Gillian
Poetry
1 *Hecate's charms* (1975)
2 *Sybil, the glide of her tongue* (1992)

Lesley Allan series
Beardmore, George
1 *Lesley's great adventure* (1967)
2 *Islands of Strangers* (1968)
3 *Expedition to Faollen* (1973)
4 *Maid of the Isles* (1974)
5 *Ladies of Spain* (1975)
Treasure of Spanish Bay

Leslie and Russell Stevens series
Davidson, Linda
see **Endless summer series**

Leslie Barnes series
Bradley, Marion Zimmer
1 *Dark Satanic* (1972)
2 *Inheritor* (1984)
3 *Witch hill* (1990)

Leslie Crane series
Jackson, Alison
1 *My brother, the star* (1990)
2 *Crane's rebound* (1991)

Leslie series
Duncan, William Murdoch
see **Superintendent Leslie series**

Leslie Wetzon series
Meyers, Annette
1 *Big killing* (1989)
2 *Tender death* (1990)
3 *Deadliest option* (1991)
4 *Blood on the street* (1992)

Lessinger series
Essex, Richard
1 *Slade of the Yard* (1932)
2 *Slade scores again* (1933)
3 *Lessinger comes back* (1935)
4 *Murder in the bank* (1936)
5 *Marinova of the Secret Service* (1937)
6 *Lessinger laughs last* (1938)
7 *Assisted by Lessinger* (1939)

Lester and Alfred series
Slepian, Jan
see **Alfred and Lester series**

Lester series
Betteridge, Don
see **Tiger Lester series**

Lester series
Blake, Quentin
1 *Lester at the seaside* (1975)
2 *Adventures of Lester* (1978)

Lester series
Finnemore, John
see **Teddy Lester series**
Hichens, Robert
see **Hermione Lester series**

Lesters and Westcotts series
Mantle, Winifred
1 *Hiding place* (1962)
2 *Tinker's Castle* (1963)
3 *Chateau holiday* (1964)
4 *Painted cave* (1965)

Lestrade series
Trow, Meirion James
see **Inspector Sholto Lestrade series**

Lestrange series
Hilton, Alec
see **Doctor Martin Lestrange series**

Letitia Carberry series
Rinehart, Mary Roberts
see **Tish series**

Let's learn about series
Greene, Carla
1 *Where does a letter go?* (1965)
2 *Let's meet the chemist* (1966)
3 *Let's learn about the orchestra* (1967)
4 *Moses, the great lawgiver* (1968)
5 *Let's learn about lighthouses* (1969)

Let's make it series
Fowler, Richard
1 *Let's make it go up and down* (1984)
2 *Let's make it go in and out* (1984)
3 *Let's make it go round and round* (1984)

Let's pretend series
Lloyd, David
Illustrated by Jane Johnson
1 *Explorers* (1985)
2 *Dragon catchers* (1985)
3 *Pirates* (1985)
4 *Treasure hunters* (1985)

Let's series
Macdonald, Amy
1 *Let's do it* (1991)
2 *Let's make a noise* (1991)
3 *Let's play* (1991)
4 *Let's try* (1991)
5 *Let's pretend* (1993)
6 *Let's go* (1993)

Let's talk about series
Berry, Joy
All titles have revised editions published in 1988
1 *Let's talk about being selfish* (1982)
2 *Let's talk about being lazy* (1982)
3 *Let's talk about overdoing it* (1982)
4 *Let's talk about breaking promises* (1982)
5 *Let's talk about disobeying* (1982)
6 *Let's talk about showing off* (1982)
7 *Let's talk about whining* (1982)
8 *Let's talk about throwing tantrums* (1982)
9 *Let's talk about complaining* (1982)
10 *Let's talk about tattling* (1982)
11 *Let's talk about teasing* (1982)
12 *Let's talk about being rude* (1982)
13 *Let's talk about snooping* (1982)
14 *Let's talk about lying* (1982)
15 *Let's talk about cheating* (1982)
16 *Let's talk about stealing* (1982)
17 *Let's talk about being destructive* (1982)
18 *Let's talk about fighting* (1982)
19 *Let's talk about being messy* (1984)
20 *Let's talk about being greedy* (1984)
21 *Let's talk about interrupting* (1984)
22 *Let's talk about gossiping* (1984)
23 *Let's talk about being bullied* (1984)
24 *Let's talk about being bossy* (1984)
25 *Let's talk about being wasteful* (1984)
26 *Let's talk about being careless* (1984)

27 *Let's talk about being forgetful* (1984)
28 *Let's talk about being a bad sport* (1984)
29 *Let's talk about being mean* (1988)

Let's try it out series
Simon, Seymour
1 *Wet and dry* (1969)
2 *Light and dark* (1970)
3 *Finding out with your senses* (1971)
4 *Hot and cold* (1972)
5 *About your heart* (1974)

Let's visit a farm series
Doughty, Sarah
1 *Let's visit a dairy farm* (1989)
2 *Let's visit a poultry farm* (1989)
3 *Let's visit a pig farm* (1989)
4 *Let's visit a fruit farm* (1989)
5 *Let's visit a beef farm* (1989)
6 *Let's visit a fish farm* (1989)
7 *Let's visit a cereal farm* (1990)
8 *Let's visit a sheep farm* (1990)
9 *Let's visit a market garden* (1990)

Letters series
Keane, John Brendan
1 *Letters of a successful T.D.* (1967)
2 *Letters of an Irish parish priest* (1970)
3 *Letters of an Irish parish publican* (1974)
4 *Letters of a love-hungry farmer* (1974)
5 *Letters of a matchmaker* (1975)
6 *Letters of a civic guard* (1976)
7 *Letters of a country postman* (1977)
8 *Letters of an Irish minister of state* (1978)

Letters to a friend series
Alliluyeva, Svetlana
Translated from the Russian; autobiography of Stalin's daughter
1 *Twenty letters to a friend* (1967)
2 *Only one year* (1969)

Letters to a friend series
Macaulay, Rose
1 *Letters to a friend, 1950-1952* (1961)
2 *Last letters to a friend, 1952-1958* (1962)
Companion volume: *Letters to a sister*, 1964

Letters to Timothy series
Gollancz, Victor
Autobiographical letters to his grandson
1 *My dear Timothy* (1952)
2 *More for Timothy* (1953)

Lettie Winterbottom series
Cutter, Leela
1 *Murder after tea-time* (1981)
2 *Who stole Stonehenge?* (1983)
3 *Death of the party* (1985)

Letty series
Griffith, Helen Sherman
1 *Letty and the twins* (1910)
2 *Letty of the circus* (1910)
3 *Letty's new home* (1911)
4 *Letty's sister* (1912)
5 *Letty's treasure* (1913)
6 *Letty's good luck* (1914)
7 *Letty at the conservatory* (1915)
8 *Letty's springtime* (1916)
9 *Letty and Miss Grey* (1917)
10 *Letty Grey, heiress* (1918)

Lev series
Potok, Chaim
see **Asher Lev series**

Le Vallon series
Blackwood, Algernon
see **Reincarnation series**

Level land series
De Jong, Dola
1 *Level land* (1943)
2 *Return to the level land* (1947)

Levert series
Toussant-Samat, Jean
see **Monsieur Levert series**

Levin series
Furst, Alan
see **Roger Levin series**

Levine family series
Nicholson, Celia Anna
1 *Their chosen people* (1923)
2 *First good joy* (1923)

LeVine series
Bergman, Andrew
see **Jack LeVine series**

Levine series
Handler, David
see **Danny Levine series**

Le Vine series
Le Vine, Jack
see **Jack Le Vine series**

Leviston series
Cookson, Catherine
see **Maisie Leviston series**

Levy series
Holding, Elisabeth Sanxay
see **Lieutenant Levy series**

Lew Archer series
Macdonald, Ross
1 *Moving target* (1949)
Harper
Original edition published under the pseudonym John Macdonald
2 *Drowning pool* (1950)
Original edition published under the pseudonym John Ross Macdonald
3 *Way some people die* (1951)
Original edition published under the pseudonym John Ross Macdonald
4 *Ivory grin* (1952)
Marked for murder
Original edition published under the pseudonym John Ross Macdonald
5 *Find a victim* (1954)
Original edition published under the pseudonym John Ross Macdonald
6 *Name is Archer* (1955)
Original edition published under the pseudonym John Ross Macdonald; short stories
7 *Barbarous coast* (1956)
Original edition published under the pseudonym John Ross Macdonald
8 *Doomsters* (1958)
Original edition published under the pseudonym John Ross Macdonald
9 *Galton case* (1959)
Original edition published under the pseudonym John Ross Macdonald
10 *Wycherley woman* (1961)
11 *Zebra-striped hearse* (1962)
Original edition published under the pseudonym John Ross Macdonald
12 *Chill* (1964)
13 *Far side of the dollar* (1965)
14 *Black money* (1966)
15 *Instant enemy* (1968)
16 *Goodbye look* (1969)
17 *Underground man* (1971)
18 *Sleeping beauty* (1973)
19 *Blue hammer* (1976)
21 *Lew Archer, private investigator* (1977)
Short stories

Lew Griffin series
Sallis, James
1 *Long-legged fly* (1992)
2 *Moth* (1993)
3 *Black hornet* (1994)

Lewis and Gilette series
Gresham, Elizabeth
see **Jenny Gilette and Hunter Lewis series**

Lewis and Jones series
Evans, Max
see **Dusty Jones and Wrangler Lewis series**

Lewis Eliot series
Snow, Charles Percy
see **Strangers and brothers series**

Lewis series
Bellairs, John
see **Clock trilogy**
Early, Tom
see **Sons of Texas series**
Frome, David
see **Major Gregory Lewis series**
Kaufelt, David A
see **Wyn Lewis series**
Klein, Dave
see **Butch Lewis series**
Stolz, Mary
see **Polly Lewis series**

Lewis series
Ziefert, Harriet
1 *Lewis the firefighter* (1986)
2 *Good night, Lewis* (1986)
3 *Lewis said, Lewis did* (1987)

Lewisham series
Elias, Eileen
Reminiscences of childhood in London
1 *On Sundays we wore white* (1978)
2 *Straw hats and serge bloomers* (1979)

Lewker series
Styles, Showell
see **Sir Abercrombie Lewker series**

Lewrie series
Lambdin, Dewey
see **Alan Lewrie series**

Lex Cranshaw series
Mason, Dan
1 *Ranger* (1991)
2 *Border bandits* (1991)
3 *Comanche raiders* (1991)
4 *Range war* (1991)
5 *Track down* (1992)
6 *Apache thunder* (1992)
7 *Nueces strip* (1992)
8 *End of the line* (1993)

Lexey Jane Pelazoni series
Head, Lee
1 *Terrarium* (1976)
2 *Crystal clear case* (1977)

Leyden trilogy
Ammers-Kuller, Jo van
1 *Rebel generation* (1925)
Original edition entitled *De opstandigen*
2 *No surrender* (1931)
Original edition entitled *Vrouwen kruistocht*
3 *Apple and Eve* (1932)
Original edition entitled *De appel en Eva*

Leyton series
Becker, Jillian
see **Simon and Josephine Leyton series**

Lhas'kar series
Lukeman, Tim
1 *Rajan* (1979)
2 *Koren* (1981)

Li Kao and Ox series
Hughart, Barry
see **Master Li Kao and Number Ten Ox series**

Li Moh series
Cowdroy, Joan
1 *Watch Mister Moh* (1931)
Flying dagger murder
2 *Murder of Lydia* (1933)
3 *Disappearance* (1934)
4 *Murder unsuspected* (1936)
5 *Death has no tongue* (1938)
6 *Merry-go-round* (1940)

Liam Devlin series
Higgins, Jack
1 *Eagle has landed* (1975)
Revised edition 1982
2 *Touch the devil* (1982)
3 *Confessional* (1985)

Liam series
McKeown, Joseph
1 *Back crack boy* (1978)
2 *Liam at large* (1986)

Liane Crawford and Inspector Hugh Gordon series
Gilruth, Susan
see **Inspector Hugh Gordon and Liane Crawford series**

Liavek series
Shetterly, Will
1 *Liavek* (1985)
2 *Players of luck* (1986)
3 *Wizard's row* (1987)
4 *Spells of binding* (1988)
5 *Festival week* (1990)

Libby series
Woolley, Catherine
1 *Look alive, Libby!* (1962)
2 *Libby looks for a spy* (1965)
3 *Libby shadows a lady* (1974)

Liberation of France series
Aron, Robert
1 *Vichy regime, 1940-44* (1954)
Original edition entitled *Histoire de Vichy, 1940-44*
2 *De Gaulle before Paris* (1959)
The liberation of France, June-August 1944; original edition entitled *Histoire de la liberation de la France*, part 1
3 *De Gaulle triumphant* (1960)
The liberation of France, August 1944-May 1945; original edition entitled *Histoire de la liberation de France*, part 2; numbers 2 and 3 also published in one volume entitled *France reborn, the history of the liberation, June 1944-May 1945*, 1964

Liberator series
Deane, Norman
Revised editions of all titles published under the author's real name, John Creasey, 1974
1 *Return to adventure* (1943)
Revised edition 1974
2 *Gateway to escape* (1944)
3 *Come home to crime* (1945)
Revised edition 1974

Liberia series
Warner, Esther Sietmann
An account of life in Liberia
1 *Seven days to Lomaland* (1954)
Trial by sasswood
2 *Crossing fee* (1968)

Liberty Corps series
Roberts, Mark Kelly
1 *Liberty Corps* (1987)
2 *Maracaibo massacre* (1987)
3 *Canal Zone conquest* (1988)
4 *Korean carnage* (1988)
5 *Poisoned paradise* (1988)
6 *Costa Rican chaos* (1988)

Liddell series
Kane, Frank
see **Johnny Liddell series**

Lieberman series
Kaminsky, Stuart Melvin
see **Abe Lieberman series**

Lieutenant Al Wheeler series
Brown, Carter
1 *Wench is wicked* (1955)
2 *Blonde verdict* (1956)
3 *Booty for a babe* (1956)
4 *Chorine makes a killing* (1957)
5 *Doll for the big house* (1957)
Bombshell
The second title is a revised edition
6 *Eve, it's extortion* (1957)
Victim
Walk softly witch!
The second and third titles are a revised edition
7 *No law against angels* (1957)
Body
The second title is a revised edition
8 *Unorthodox corpse* (1957)
Revised edition 1961
9 *Blonde* (1958)
10 *Death on the downbeat* (1958)
Corpse
The second title is a revised edition
11 *Lover* (1958)
12 *Mistress* (1958)
13 *Dame* (1959)
14 *Desired* (1959)
15 *Passionate* (1959)
16 *Terror comes creeping* (1959)
17 *Wanton* (1959)
18 *Temptress* (1960)
19 *Brazen* (1960)
20 *Lament for a lousy lover* (1960)
21 *Stripper* (1961)
22 *Tigress* (1961)
Wildcat
23 *Exotic* (1961)
24 *Angel!* (1962)
25 *Hellcat* (1962)
26 *Lady is transparent* (1962)
27 *Dum dum murders* (1962)
28 *Girl in a shroud* (1963)
29 *Sinners* (1963)
Girl who was possessed
30 *Lady is not available* (1963)
Lady is available
31 *Dance of death* (1964)
32 *Vixen* (1964)
Velvet vixen
33 *Corpse for Christmas* (1965)
34 *Hammer of Thor* (1965)
35 *Target for their dark desire* (1966)
36 *Plush-lined coffin* (1967)
37 *Until temptation do us part* (1967)
38 *Deep cold green* (1968)
39 *Up-tight blonde* (1969)
40 *Burden of guilt* (1970)
41 *Creative murders* (1971)
42 *W.H.O.R.E.* (1972)
43 *Clown* (1972)
44 *Asceptic murders* (1972)
45 *Born loser* (1973)
46 *Wheeler fortune* (1974)
47 *Night Wheeler* (1975)
48 *Wheeler, dealer* (1975)
49 *Dream merchant* (1976)
50 *Spanking girls* (1979)
51 *Busted Wheeler* (1979)
52 *Model for murder* (1980)
53 *Wicked widow* (1981)
54 *Stab in the dark* (1984)

Lieutenant Al White series
Holden, Genevieve
1 *Killer loose!* (1953)
2 *Sound an alarm* (1954)
3 *Velvet target* (1956)
4 *Something's happened to Kate* (1958)

Lieutenant Al Zimmerman series
George, Theodore
1 *Murders on the square* (1971)
2 *Deadly homecoming* (1972)

Lieutenant Andy Bastian series
Wormser, Richard
1 *Drive east on Sixty Six* (1961)
2 *Nice girl like you* (1963)

Lieutenant Austin Clapp series
Miller, Wade
1 *Deadly weapon* (1946)
2 *Guilty bystander* (1947)
3 *Fatal step* (1948)
4 *Uneasy street* (1948)
5 *Calamity fair* (1950)
6 *Murder charge* (1950)
7 *Shoot to kill* (1951)

Lieutenant Ben Krahmer series
Krasney, Samuel A
1 *Morals Squad* (1959)
2 *Mania for blondes* (1961)

Lieutenant Bill French series
Hale, Christopher
1 *Smoke screen* (1935)
2 *Stormy night* (1937)
3 *Murder on display* (1939)
4 *Witch Wood* (1940)
5 *Dead of winter* (1941)
Going, going, gone
6 *Exit screaming* (1942)
7 *Murder in tow* (1943)
8 *Hangman's tie* (1943)
9 *Rumor hath it* (1945)
10 *Midsummer nightmare* (1945)
11 *Deadly ditto* (1948)
12 *He's late this morning* (1949)

Lieutenant Bill Grady series
Shriber, Ione Sandberg
1 *Head over heels in murder* (1940)
2 *Dark arbor* (1940)
3 *Murder well done* (1941)
4 *Family affair* (1941)
5 *Body for Bill* (1942)
6 *Invitation to murder* (1943)
7 *Pattern for murder* (1944)
8 *Last straw* (1946)

Lieutenant Bill Kinderman series
Blatty, William Peter
1 *Exorcist* (1971)
Parody: *The exerciser*, by Howard Albrecht and Sol Weinstein, 1974
2 *Legion* (1983)
3 *Exorcist III* (1990)
Companion volume: *William Peter Blatty on The exorcist, from novel to film*, 1974

Lieutenant Bunjy Hearne series
Craig, Thurlow
1 *White girls eastward* (1938)
2 *Plague over London* (1939)
3 *Changed face* (1939)

Lieutenant Charles Hillary series
McGrew, Fenn
1 *Taste of death* (1953)
2 *Made for murder* (1954)

Lieutenant Charley Mitchell series
Wolff, William Almon
1 *Manhattan night* (1930)
2 *Murder at Endor* (1933)

Lieutenant Christopher Jensen series
Langley, Lee
1 *Osiris died in autumn* (1964)
Twilight of death
2 *Dead center* (1968)
Dead centre

Lieutenant Clancy series
Pike, Robert L
1 *Mute witness* (1963)
Bullitt
2 *Quarry* (1964)
3 *Police blotter* (1965)

Lieutenant Claude Greenway series
Thompson, Lloyd S
see **Shimoru Kyota series**

Lieutenant Commander Robert Bollinger Badger series
Winton, John
see **Navy series**

Lieutenant Dan Durkin series
Chase, Arthur Minturn
1 *Party at the penthouse* (1932)
2 *Murder of a missing man* (1934)
3 *Twenty minutes to kill* (1938)

Lieutenant Dave Wintino series
Lacy, Ed
1 *Lead with your left* (1957)
2 *Double trouble* (1964)

Lieutenant Diego series
Kelsey, Vera
1 *Owl sang three times* (1941)
2 *Satan has six fingers* (1943)

Lieutenant Favian Markham series
Williams, Jon
see **Privateers and gentlemen series**

Lieutenant Felix Elizalde series
Marshall, William Leonard
see **Battling Mendez series**

Lieutenant Frank Hastings series
Wilcox, Collin
1 *Lonely hunter* (1969)
2 *Disappearance* (1970)
3 *Dead aim* (1971)
4 *Hiding place* (1973)
5 *Long way down* (1974)
6 *Aftershock* (1975)
7 *Third victim* (1976)
8 *Doctor, lawyer* (1977)
9 *Watcher* (1978)
10 *Power plays* (1979)
11 *Mankiller* (1980)
12 *Stalking horse* (1982)
13 *Victims* (1985)
14 *Night games* (1987)
15 *Pariah* (1988)
16 *Death before dying* (1990)
17 *Hire a hangman* (1991)
18 *Switchback* (1993)

Lieutenant Frank Kerrigan series
Harrington, Joseph
1 *Last known address* (1965)
2 *Blind spot* (1966)
3 *Last doorbell* (1969)

Lieutenant George Honegger series
Strange, John Stephen
see **Captain George Honegger series**

Lieutenant Gordon Fuller series
Vaughan, Carter A
1 *Invincibles* (1958)
2 *Wilderness* (1960)

Lieutenant Gray series
Lanham, Edwin
1 *Death of a Corinthian* (1953)
Case of the missing corpse
2 *Death in the wind* (1956)

Lieutenant Jack Stryker series
Gosling, Paula
1 *Monkey puzzle* (1985)
2 *Backlash* (1989)

Lieutenant Jacob Horowitz series
Delman, David
1 *Week to kill* (1972)
2 *Sudden death* (1972)
3 *He who digs a grave* (1973)
4 *One man's murder* (1975)
5 *Nice murderers* (1977)
6 *Murder in the family* (1985)
7 *Death of a nymph* (1985)

Lieutenant Jason Winter series
Gaston, Bill
1 *Winter of the Wildcat* (1977)
2 *Winter and the Wild Witch* (1979)
3 *Winter and the Wild Rover* (1982)
4 *Winter and the widowmakers* (1984)
5 *Winter and the Wanderer* (1986)

Lieutenant Jim Reardon series
Pike, Robert L
1 *Reardon* (1970)
2 *Gremlin's Grampa* (1972)
3 *Bank job* (1974)
4 *Deadline two A.M.* (1976)

Lieutenant Joe Gunther series
Mayor, Archer Huntington
1 *Open season* (1988)
2 *Borderlines* (1990)
3 *Scent of evil* (1992)
4 *Skeleton's knee* (1993)
5 *Fruits of the poisonous tree* (1994)

Lieutenant Joe Leaphorn series
Hillerman, Tony
1 *Blessing way* (1970)
2 *Dance hall of the dead* (1973)
3 *Listening woman* (1978)
4 *Skinwalkers* (1987)
5 *Thief of time* (1988)
6 *Talking God* (1989)
Numbers 1-6 also published in one volume entitled *Joe Leaphorn mysteries*, 1989
7 *Coyote waits* (1990)
8 *Sacred clowns* (1993)

Lieutenant Joe Petrosino series
Nolan, Frederick
1 *NYPD* (1974)
No place to be a cop
2 *Kill Petrosino!* (1975)

Lieutenant John Milton Schwab series
Wheatley, Dennis
1 *Murder off Miami* (1936)
File on Bolitho Blane
2 *Who killed Robert Prentice?* (1937)
File on Robert Prentice
3 *Malinsay massacre* (1938)
4 *Herewith the clues!* (1939)

Lieutenant Joseph Dickerson series
Goldthwaite, Eaton Kenneth
1 *You did it* (1943)
Death springs the trap
Body next door
2 *Scarecrow* (1945)
3 *Cat and mouse* (1946)
Cat and mouse murder
Date with death
4 *Root of evil* (1948)

Lieutenant Joseph Kelly series
Ford, Leslie
1 *Murder in Maryland* (1932)
2 *Clue of the Judas tree* (1933)

Lieutenant Kelly series
Roth, Holly
1 *Content assignment* (1954)
Shocking secret
2 *Button, button* (1966)

Lieutenant Kramer and Sergeant Zondi series
McClure, James
1 *Steam pig* (1971)
2 *Caterpillar cop* (1972)
3 *Gooseberry fool* (1974)
4 *Snake* (1975)
5 *Sunday hangman* (1977)
6 *Blood of an Englishman* (1980)
7 *Artful egg* (1984)
8 *Imago* (1988)
A modern comedy of manners
9 *Song dog* (1991)

Lieutenant Lamb series
Maynard, Kenneth
1 *Lieutenant Lamb* (1984)
2 *First Lieutenant* (1985)
3 *Lamb in command* (1985)
4 *Lamb's mixed fortunes* (1987)

Lieutenant Larry Koharik series
Eshleman, John Morton
1 *Long window* (1953)
Death of a cheat
2 *Long chase* (1954)
Deadly chase

Lieutenant Lee Barcello series
Ransome, Stephen
1 *Night, the woman* (1963)
2 *One-man jury* (1964)
3 *Alias his wife* (1965)
4 *Sin file* (1965)
5 *Hidden hour* (1966)
6 *Trap number six* (1971)

Lieutenant Leroy Powder series
Lewin, Michael Zinn
1 *Night cover* (1976)
2 *Hard line* (1982)
3 *Out of season* (1984)
Out of time
Lieutenant Leroy Powder has a minor role in this title
4 *Late payments* (1986)

Lieutenant Levy series
Holding, Elisabeth Sanxay
1 *Blank wall* (1947)
2 *Too many bottles* (1951)
Party was the pay-off
3 *Widow's mite* (1953)

Lieutenant Luis Mendoza series
Shannon, Dell
1 *Case pending* (1960)
Also published under the author's real name Elizabeth Linington
2 *Ace of Spades* (1961)
Also published under the author's real name Elizabeth Linington
3 *Extra kill* (1962)
Also published under the author's real name Elizabeth Linington
4 *Knave of Hearts* (1962)
Also published under the author's real name Elizabeth Linington
5 *Death of a busybody* (1963)
6 *Double bluff* (1963)
7 *Mark of murder* (1964)
8 *Root of all evil* (1964)
9 *Death-bringers* (1964)
10 *Death by inches* (1965)
11 *Coffin Corner* (1966)
12 *With a vengeance* (1966)
13 *Chance to kill* (1967)
14 *Rain with violence* (1967)
15 *Kill with kindness* (1968)
16 *Schooled to kill* (1969)
17 *Crime on their hands* (1969)
18 *Unexpected death* (1970)
19 *Whim to kill* (1971)
20 *Ringer* (1971)
21 *Murder with love* (1971)
22 *With intent to kill* (1972)
23 *No holiday for crime* (1973)
24 *Spring of violence* (1973)
25 *Crime file* (1974)
26 *Deuces wild* (1975)
27 *Streets of death* (1976)
28 *Appearances of death* (1977)
29 *Cold trail* (1978)
30 *Felony at random* (1979)
31 *Felony file* (1980)
32 *Murder most strange* (1981)
33 *Motive on record* (1982)
34 *Exploits of death* (1983)
35 *Destiny of death* (1984)
36 *Chaos of crime* (1985)
37 *Blood count* (1986)
38 *Murder by the tale* (1987)
Short stories
39 *Dispossessed* (1988)

Lieutenant Madigan series
Lanham, Edwin
1 *Slug it slay* (1946)
Headlined for murder
Headline for murder
2 *Politics is murder* (1947)
3 *One murder too many* (1952)

Lieutenant Marty Walsh series
Cohen, Octavus Roy
1 *My love wears black* (1948)
2 *More beautiful than murder* (1948)
3 *Bullet for my love* (1950)

Lieutenant Max Hunter series
Ballard, Willis Todhunter
1 *Pretty Miss Murder* (1961)
2 *Seven sisters* (1962)
3 *Three for the money* (1963)

Lieutenant Meredith series
Ramsay, Diana
1 *Little murder music* (1972)
2 *Deadly discretion* (1973)
3 *No cause to kill* (1974)
4 *You can't call it murder* (1977)

Lieutenant Michael Fitton series
Styles, Showell
1 *Sword for Mister Fitton* (1975)
2 *Mister Fitton's commission* (1977)
3 *Baltic convoy* (1979)
4 *Gun-brig captain* (1987)
5 *HMS Cracker* (1988)

Lieutenant Mike S Blueberry series
Giraud, Jean
Comic books translated from the French; Giraud drew the stories with text by Jean Michel Charlier
1 *Chuhuahua pearl* (1989)
2 *Ballad for a coffin* (1989)
3 *Angel face* (1989)
4 *Ghost tribe* (1989)
5 *End of the trail* (1989)
6 *Iron horse* (1991)
7 *Steelfingers* (1991)
8 *Trail of the Sioux* (1991)
9 *General Golden Mane* (1991)
10 *Lost Dutchman's Mine* (1991)
11 *Ghost with the golden bullets* (1991)
12 *Marshal Blueberry* (1991)
There are many more French titles not translated into English

Lieutenant Norah Mulcahaney series
O'Donnell, Lillian
see **Detective Norah Mulcahaney series**

Lieutenant Pascal series
Pentecost, Hugh
1 *Lieutenant Pascal's tastes in homicide* (1954)
2 *Obituary Club* (1958)
3 *Lonely target* (1959)
4 *Only the rich die young* (1964)
5 *Creeping hours* (1966)
6 *Dead woman of the year* (1967)

Lieutenant Peter Donnegan series
Quick, Dorothy
1 *Fifth dagger* (1947)
2 *Doctor looks at murder* (1959)

Lieutenant Phelan and Professor Caldwell series
Ozaki, Milton K
see **Professor Caldwell and Lieutenant Phelan series**

Lieutenant Powledge series
Rea, Margaret Lucile Paine
1 *Curtain for crime* (1941)
2 *Compare these dead!* (1941)
3 *Death of an angel* (1943)

Lieutenant Richard Tuck series
Lewis, Lange
1 *Murder among friends* (1942)
Death among friends
2 *Juliet dies twice* (1943)
3 *Meat for murder* (1943)
4 *Birthday murder* (1945)
5 *Passionate victims* (1952)

Lieutenant Romano series
Alexander, David
1 *Most men don't kill* (1951)
Corpse in my bed
2 *Murder in black and white* (1951)
3 *Murder points a finger* (1953)
4 *Shoot a sitting duck* (1955)
5 *Die, little goose* (1956)
6 *Murder of Whistler's brother* (1956)
7 *Hush-a-bye murder* (1957)
8 *Death of Humpty-Dumpty* (1957)
9 *Dead, man, dead* (1959)

Lieutenant Ronnie Gold series
Paulsen, Gary
1 *Sweeper* (1980)
2 *Clutterkill* (1981)

Lieutenant Ryan series
Scherf, Margaret
1 *Owl in the cellar* (1945)
2 *Murder makes me nervous* (1948)

Lieutenant Saint Vincent Halfhyde series
McCutchan, Philip
1 *Beware, beware the Bight of Benin* (1974)
Beware the Bight of Benin
2 *Halfhyde's island* (1975)
3 *Guns of arrest* (1976)
4 *Halfhyde to the narrows* (1977)
5 *Halfhyde for the Queen* (1978)
6 *Halfhyde ordered south* (1979)
7 *Halfhyde and the flag captain* (1980)
8 *Halfhyde on the Yangtse* (1981)
9 *Halfhyde on Zanatu* (1982)
10 *Halfhyde outward bound* (1983)
11 *Halfhyde line* (1984)
12 *Halfhyde and the chain gangs* (1985)
13 *Halfhyde goes to war* (1986)
14 *Halfhyde on the Amazon* (1988)
15 *Halfhyde and the admiral* (1990)
16 *Halfhyde and the fleet review* (1991)

Lieutenant Sandy Ray series
King, Charles
1 *Colonel's daughter* (1883)
Alternative title: Winning his spurs
2 *Marion's faith* (1886)
3 *Captain Blake* (1891)
4 *Garrison triangle* (1896)
5 *Ray's recruit* (1898)
6 *Ray's daughter* (1901)
A story of Manila life
7 *Lieutenant Sandy Ray* (1906)
8 *Captured* (1906)
9 *Further story of Lieutenant Sandy Ray* (1906)

Lieutenant Shomri Shomar series
Klinger, Henry
1 *Wanton for murder* (1961)
2 *Murder off Broadway* (1962)
3 *Essence of murder* (1963)
Lust for murder
One volume edition entitled *Three cases of Shomri Shomar*, 1968

Lieutenant Sigrid Harald series
Maron, Margaret
1 *One coffee with* (1981)
2 *Death of a butterfly* (1984)
3 *Death in blue folders* (1985)
4 *Right Jack* (1987)
5 *Baby doll games* (1988)
6 *Corpus Christmas* (1988)

Lieutenant Stephen Mayhew series
Olsen, D B
1 *Clue in the clay* (1938)
2 *Cat saw murder* (1939)
3 *Ticking heart* (1940)
4 *Cat's claw* (1943)
5 *Catspaw for murder* (1943)
6 *Cat wears a noose* (1944)
7 *Cats don't need coffins* (1946)

Lieutenant Timothy Trant series
Patrick, Q
1 *Death for dear Clara* (1937)
2 *File on Claudia Cragge* (1938)
3 *Death and the maiden* (1939)
Sequence continued under the pseudonym Patrick Quentin
Quentin, Patrick
4 *Black widow* (1953)
5 *My son, the murderer* (1954)
Wife of Ronald Sheldon
6 *Man with two wives* (1955)
7 *Shadow of guilt* (1959)
8 *Family skeletons* (1965)

Lieutenant Valcour series
King, Rufus
1 *Murder by the clock* (1929)
2 *Somewhere in this house* (1929)
Woman is dead
Murderer in this house
The third title is an abridged edition
3 *Murder by latitude* (1930)
4 *Murder in the Willett family* (1931)
5 *Murder on the yacht* (1932)
6 *Valcour meets murder* (1932)
7 *Lesser Antilles case* (1934)
Murder challenges Valcour
8 *Profile of a murder* (1935)
9 *Case of the constant god* (1936)
10 *Crime of violence* (1937)
11 *Murder masks Miami* (1939)

Lieutenant-Colonel James Gore-Bunbury series
Stanford, John Keith
1 *Guns wanted* (1949)
2 *Jimmy Bundobust* (1958)

Life and death of George Proteron series
Stanford, John Keith
1 *Twelfth* (1944)
2 *Full moon at Sweatenham* (1953)

Life and love series
Miller, Henry Russell
1 *Man higher up* (1910)
A story of the fight, which is life and the force, which is love
2 *His rise to power* (1911)

Life and times series
Lang, John Dunmore
1 *Reminiscences of my life and times* (1972)
Covers 1822-1843

2 *Brief sketch of my parliamentary life and times* (1870)
Covers 1843-1869
Companion volume: *John Dunmore Lang, chiefly autobiographical, 1799-1878, 1951*

Life in hell series
Groening, Matt
Comic strips
1 *Love is hell* (1984)
Revised edition 1985
2 *Work is hell* (1986)
3 *School is hell* (1987)
4 *Childhood is hell* (1988)
5 *Akbar and Jeff's guide to life* (1989)
6 *Greetings from hell* (1989)
7 *With love from hell* (1991)
8 *How to go to hell* (1991)
9 *Road to hell* (1992)

Life is a four letter word series
Monsarrat, Nicholas
Autobiography
1 *Breaking in* (1966)
2 *Breaking out* (1970)

Life observed series
Mottram, Ralph Hale
Autobiography
1 *Window seat* (1954)
2 *Another window seat* (1957)

Life of children series
Coles, Robert
1 *Moral life of children* (1986)
2 *Political life of children* (1986)

Life of Jean Robertson series
Sandison, Janet
see **Apology for the life of Jean Robertson series**

Life of Jesus series
Daniel, Rebecca
1 *Jesus, his birth* (1983)
2 *Jesus, his boyhood* (1983)
3 *Jesus, gathering his disciples* (1983)
4 *Jesus, the teacher* (1983)
5 *Jesus, the healer* (1983)
6 *Jesus, the miracle* (1983)
7 *Jesus, his parables* (1983)
8 *Jesus, more parables* (1983)
9 *Jesus, prophecies fulfilled* (1983)
10 *Jesus, his last days* (1983)
11 *Jesus, his last hours* (1983)
12 *Jesus, his resurrection* (1983)

Life of Klim Samgin series
Gorky, Maxim
Translated from the Russian
1 *Bystander* (1927)
2 *Magnet* (1929)
3 *Other fires* (1931)
4 *Spectre* (1936)

Life of Langston Hughes series
Rampersad, Arnold
1 *I, too sing America, 1902-1941* (1986)
2 *I dream a world, 1941-1967* (1988)

Life of one's own series
Brenan, Gerald
Autobiography
1 *Life of one's own* (1962)
Childhood and youth
2 *Personal record, 1920-1972* (1974)

Life of Sherlock Holmes series
Harrison, Michael
1 *In the footsteps of Sherlock Holmes* (1958)
Revised edition 1971
2 *London of Sherlock Holmes* (1972)
3 *World of Sherlock Holmes* (1973)
4 *Theatrical Mister Holmes* (1974)
The world's greatest consulting detective, considered against the background of the contemporary theatre
5 *Immortal sleuth* (1983)
Sherlockian musings and memories
6 *Study in surmise* (1984)
The making of Sherlock Holmes

Life rarely tells trilogy
Lindsay, Jack
Autobiography
1 *Life rarely tells* (1958)
An autobiographical account ending in the year 1921 and set mostly in Brisbane
2 *Roaring twenties* (1960)
Literary life in Sydney in the years 1921-26
3 *Franfolico and after* (1962)
One volume edition entitled *Life rarely tells*, 1982

Life series
Life of a New York family in the early twentieth century
Day, Clarence
1 *Life with father* (1935)
2 *God and my father* (1932)
My father's darkest hour
3 *Life with mother* (1937)

Life series
Ireland, Jill
1 *Life wish* (1987)
2 *Life lines* (1989)

Life series
James, Elizabeth
1 *Life class* (1986)
2 *Life lines* (1988)

Life with Topsy and Tim series
Adamson, Jean
1 *Safety first with Topsy and Tim* (1973)
2 *Topsy and Tim in the kitchen* (1983)
3 *Topsy and Tim's games book* (1983)
4 *Topsy and Tim's music book* (1983)
5 *Topsy and Tim's pet* (1983)
6 *Topsy and Tim tell the time* (1984)
7 *Topsy and Tim's ABC* (1984)
8 *Topsy and Tim's counting book* (1984)
9 *Topsy and Tim's word book* (1984)
Revised edition 1994
10 *Happy birthday, Topsy and Tim* (1986)
11 *Topsy and Tim's safety book* (1990)
12 *Topsy and Tim dressing-up dolls* (1993)
13 *Topsy and Tim's picture dictionary* (1993)

Life without theory series
Stuart-Wortley, Violet
Autobiography
1 *Life without theory* (1946)
2 *Grow old along with me* (1952)

Lifemanship Correspondence College series
Potter, Stephen
Humour
1 *Theory and practice of gamesmanship* (1947)
The art of winning games without actually cheating
2 *Some notes on lifemanship* (1950)
28 studies in advanced lifemanship
3 *One-upmanship* (1952)
Some account of the activities and teaching of the Lifemanship Correspondence College of One-Upness and Gameslifemastery
4 *Supermanship* (1958)
How to stay top without actually falling apart; numbers 1-4 also published in one volume entitled *The complete upmanship*, 1970
5 *Anti-woo* (1965)
6 *Complete golf gamesmanship* (1968)
Golfmanship

Lifeng, Shaofeng and Rose series
Payne, Robert
1 *Love and peace* (1945)
2 *Lovers* (1951)

Liff series
Adams, Douglas Noel
see **Meaning of liff series**

Liffey series
Macgregor, Bill
An account of the troubles in Ireland
1 *Liffey runs black* (1978)
2 *Uncertain trumpet* (1980)

Light fingers series
Morrison, Emmeline
1 *Light fingers* (1927)
2 *Sir Joseph's guests* (1929)

Light of the just series
Troyat, Henri
1 *Brotherhood of the Red Poppy* (1959)
Original edition entitled *Les compagnons do coquelicot*
2 *Baroness* (1960)
Original edition entitled *La Barynia*
3 *[Gloire des vaincus]* (1961)
No English edition
4 *[Dames de Siberie]* (1962)
No English edition
5 *[Sophie, ou, La fin des combats]* (1963)
No English edition

Light on Dumyat series
Fraser, Christine Marion
1 *Light on Dumyat* (1982)
2 *White stag adventure* (1986)
3 *Moving stone* (1994)

Light series
James, Henry
see **Princess Casamassima series**

Light woman series
Gavin, Catherine
1 *Light woman* (1986)
2 *Glory road* (1987)

Lightbringer trilogy
Lee, Samantha
see **Owen Lightbringer trilogy**

Lightfoot trilogy
Sherwood, Valerie
see **Carolina Lightfoot trilogy**

Lighthouse keeper series
Armitage, Ronda
1 *Lighthouse keeper's lunch* (1977)
2 *Lighthouse keeper's catastrophe* (1986)
3 *Lighthouse keeper's rescue* (1989)

Lightnin' Calvert series
Ferguson, William Blair Morton
1 *Lightnin' Calvert* (1931)
2 *Reckoning* (1933)

Lightning conductor series
Williamson, Charles Norris
see **Motoring series**

Lightning Lucy series
Strong, Jeremy
1 *Lightning Lucy* (1981)
2 *Lightning Lucy strikes again* (1985)
3 *Lightning Lucy storms ahead* (1987)

Lightning series
Mason, Miriam Evangeline
1 *Pony called Lightning* (1948)
2 *Broomtail, brother of Lightning* (1952)

Lije Baley series
Asimov, Isaac
see **Elijah Baley series**

Likely lads series
Clement, Dick
Based on a television series
1 *Likely lads* (1967)
2 *What ever happened to the likely lads* (1973)
Adapted by Patrick Tilley

Li'l Abner dailies series
Capp, Al
1 *Li'l Abner dailies, 1934-1935* (1988)
2 *Li'l Abner dailies, 1936* (1988)
3 *Li'l Abner dailies, 1937* (1988)
4 *Li'l Abner dailies, 1938* (1989)
Abner in the orphanage, atrange girl in the swamp
5 *Li'l Abner dailies, 1939* (1989)
6 *Li'l Abner dailies, 1940* (1989)
7 *Li'l Abner dailies, 1941* (1990)
8 *Li'l Abner dailies, 1942* (1990)
9 *Li'l Abner dailies, 1943* (1990)
10 *Li'l Abner dailies, 1944* (1990)
11 *Li'l Abner dailies, 1945* (1991)
12 *Li'l Abner dailies, 1946* (1991)
13 *Li'l Abner dailies, 1947* (1992)
14 *Li'l Abner dailies, 1948* (1992)
15 *Li'l Abner dailies, 1949* (1993)
Kick in the Kiomies
16 *Li'l Abner dailies, 1950* (1993)
In search of the perfect woman
17 *Li'l Abner dailies, 1951* (1993)

Li'l Abner series
Capp, Al
Comic strips
1 *World of Li'l Abner* (1953)
2 *From Dogpatch to Slobovia* (1964)
Selections: *The best of Li'l Abner*, 1978

Lila Fenwick series
McMullan, Kate
1 *Great ideas of Lila Fenwick* (1986)
2 *Great advice of Lila Fenwick* (1988)

Lilburne and Inglis series
Walder, David
see **Charles Lilburne and Rupert Inglis series**

Lilian Singer series
Grenville, Kate
1 *Lilian's story* (1985)
2 *Dark places* (1994)
Albion's story

Lilith and Abel series
Rayner, Claire
see **Performers series**

Lilith series
Southworth, Emma Dorothy Eliza Nevitte
1 *Unloved wife* (1891)
2 *Lilith* (1891)

Lillian Legendre series
Brush, Katharine
1 *Difficult women, and other stories* (1930)
Night-club, and other stories
2 *Red-headed woman* (1931)
3 *Other women* (1933)
Short stories

Lillie of Watts series
Walter, Mildred Pitts
1 *Lillie of Watts, a birthday discovery* (1969)
2 *Lillie of Watts takes a giant step* (1971)

Lillie series
Allan, Luke
see **Tiger Lillie series**

Lilliput series
This sequence has eight authors
Swift, Jonathan
1 *Travels into several remote nations of the world* (1726)
Gulliver's travels
Gulliver, Captain
2 *Memoirs of the court of Lilliput* (1727)
An account of the intrigues and some other particular transactions of that nation, omitted in the two volumes of his travels
Anonymous
3 *Cursory view of the history of Lilliput for these last forty three years* (1727)
Some remarks upon the origin, nature and tendency of the religious and political disputes whic exist amonng the subjects
Arbuthnot, John
4 *Account of the state of learning in the Empire of Lilliput* (1728)
Together with the history and character of Bullum the Emperor's library-keeper, faithfully transcribed out of Captain Lemuel Gulliver's general description of the Empire of Lilliput, mention'd in the 69th page of the first volume of his travels
Gulliver, Lemuel, junior
5 *Lilliput* (1796)
A new journey to that celebrated island, containing a faithful account of the manners, character, customs, religion, laws, politics, revenue, taxes, learning, general progress in arts and sciences, dress amusements and gallantry of those famous little people, from the year 1702, when they were first discovered and visited by Captain Lemuel Gulliver, the father of the compiler of this work, to the present aera, 1796
Wilson, David Alec
6 *Modern Lilliput* (1924)
A history of the recent rediscovery of the Lilliput Archipelago and what has been happening there
White, Terence Hanbury
7 *Mistress Masham's repose* (1946)
Winterfeld, Henry
8 *Castaways in Lilliput* (1960)

Lily series
Webb, Diana
1 *Lily the lollipop lady* (1984)
2 *Lily loses her lollipop* (1986)
3 *Lily's lollipop wand* (1988)

Lily Wu and Janice Cameron series
Sheridan, Juanita
1 *Chinese chop* (1949)
2 *Kahuna killer* (1951)
3 *Mamo murders* (1952)
While the coffin waited
4 *Waikiki widow* (1953)

Lim Quong series
George, Sidney Charles
1 *Wiles of Lim Quong* (1943)
Includes some sketches of Singapore
2 *Bamboo rod* (1951)

Limberlost series
Porter, Gene Stratton
1 *Freckles* (1904)
2 *Girl of the Limberlost* (1909)
Sequence continued by the author's daughter, Jeannette Stratton Porter
Porter, Jeannette Stratton
3 *Freckles comes home* (1929)
Companion volumes: *Moths of the Limberlost*, by Gene Stratton Porter, 1912 and *Birds of the Limberlost*, by Gene Stratton Porter, 1914

Limehouse series
Burke, Thomas
see **London series**

Limpet and Jill series
Willard, Barbara
see **Jill and Limpet series**

Limpie series
Catto, Max
1 *Mister Midas* (1976)
2 *Empty tiger* (1977)

Lin and Sam series
Pullen, Alan
see **Sam and Lin series**

Lincoas series
Curry, Jane Louise
see **Prince Lincoas series**

Lincolm trilogy
Bacheller, Irving
see **Abraham Lincoln trilogy**

Lincoln Blackthorne series
Marsh, Geoffrey
1 *King of Satan's eyes* (1984)
2 *Tail of the Arabian, knight* (1986)
3 *Patch of the Odin soldier* (1987)
4 *Fangs of the hooded demon* (1988)

Lincoln Lions Band series
Giff, Patricia Reilly
1 *Meet the Lincoln Lions Band* (1992)
2 *Yankee Doodle drumsticks* (1992)
3 *Jingle bells jam* (1992)

Lincoln series
Dodge, David
see **John Abraham Lincoln series**
Garth, Ed
see **Matt Lincoln series**
Johnston, William
see **Matt Lincoln series**

Lincoln trilogy
Morrow, Honore Willsie
see **Great Captain trilogy**

Linda and Robin Reismann series
Wolitzer, Hilma
1 *Hearts* (1980)
2 *Tunnel of love* (1994)

Linda Carlton series
Lavell, Edith
1 *Linda Carlton, air pilot* (1931)
2 *Island adventure* (1931)
3 *Linda Carlton's ocean flight* (1931)
4 *Linda Carlton's perilous summer* (1932)
5 *Linda Carlton's Hollywood flight* (1932)

Linda Carroll series
Donald, Winifred
1 *Linda, the schoolgirl detective* (1949)
2 *Linda in Lucerne* (1950)
3 *Linda and the silver greyhounds* (1952)
4 *Linda Cambridge* (1955)
5 *Linda in New York* (1956)

Linda Craig adventures series
Sheldon, Ann
This sequence follows the **Linda Craig series**
1 *Golden secret* (1988)
2 *Star for linda* (1988)
3 *Silver stallion* (1988)
4 *Crystal trail* (1988)
5 *Glimmering ghost* (1989)
6 *Ride to Gold Canyon* (1989)
7 *Horse for Jackie* (1989)
8 *Star in the saddle* (1989)
9 *Riding club* (1989)
10 *Anything for Kelly* (1989)
11 *Everybody's favorite* (1990)
12 *Kathy in charge* (1990)

Linda Craig series
Sheldon, Ann
1 *Linda Craig and the Palomino mystery* (1962)
Palomino mystery
2 *Linda Craig and the clue on the desert trail* (1962)
Clue on the desert trail
3 *Linda Craig and the secret of Rancho del Sol* (1963)
Secret of Rancho del Sol
4 *Linda Craig and the mystery of Horseshoe Canyon* (1963)
Mystery of Horseshoe Canyon
5 *Linda Craig and the ghost town treasure* (1964)
Ghost town treasure
6 *Linda Craig and the mystery in Mexico* (1964)
Mystery in Mexico
7 *Haunted Valley* (1982)
8 *Secret of the Old Sleigh* (1983)
9 *Emperor's pony* (1983)
10 *Phantom of Dark Oaks* (1984)
11 *Search for Scorpio* (1984)
This sequence is followed by the **Linda Craig adventures series**

Linda Lane series
Lawrence, Josephine
1 *Linda Lane* (1925)
2 *Linda Lane helps out* (1925)
3 *Linda Lane's plan* (1926)
4 *Linda Lane's experiments* (1927)
5 *Linda Lane's problem* (1928)
6 *Linda Lane's big sister* (1929)

Linda Lovelace series
Perkins, D M
Based on screenplays
1 *Deep throat* (1973)
2 *Deep throat, part II* (1974)

Linda series
Dudley, Nancy
1 *Linda goes to the hospital* (1953)
2 *Linda travels alone* (1955)
3 *Linda's first flight* (1956)
4 *Linda goes to a TV studio* (1957)
5 *Linda goes on a cruise* (1958)

Linda series
Lewis, Linda
1 *We hate everything but boys* (1985)
2 *Is there life after boys?* (1987)
3 *We love only older boys* (1988)
4 *Two young two go four boys* (1988)
5 *My heart belongs to that boy* (1989)
6 *All for the love of that boy* (1989)
7 *Want to trade two brothers for a cat?* (1989)
8 *Dedicated to that boy I love* (1990)
9 *Loving two is hard to do* (1990)
10 *Tomboy terror in bunk 109* (1991)
11 *Pre-Teen means in between* (1993)

Lindley children series
Wood, Lorna
see **Hag Dowsabel series**

Lindon and Gray series
Whitman, Charles
see **Inspector Lindon and Sergeant Gray series**

Lindsay Gordon series
McDermid, Val
1 *Report for murder* (1987)
2 *Common murder* (1989)
3 *Final edition* (1991)
4 *Union Jack* (1993)

Lindsay series
Cameron, Isabel
see **Doctor Lindsay series**
Finlay, Winifred
see **Gillian Lindsay series**

Lindsey series
Benson, Ben
see **Ralph Lindsey series**

Lindtner series
Michaelis, Karin
see **Elsie Lindtner series**

Lindy Grey series
Cory, Desmond
1 *Begin, murderer!* (1951)
2 *This is Jezebel* (1952)
3 *Lady lost* (1953)
4 *Shaken leaf* (1955)

Liners of time series
Statten, Vargo
1 *Liners of time* (1947)
2 *Zagribud* (1952)
Science Metropolis

Ling Tan series
Buck, Pearl Sydenstricker
1 *Dragon seed* (1942)
2 *Promise* (1943)
Companion volume: *The story of Dragon seed*, 1944

Lingard series
Conrad, Joseph
see **Captain Lingard series**
Smith, Naomi Royde
see **Richard Lingard series**

Lingemann and Connors series
Kelly, Susan
see **Liz Connors and Jack Lingemann series**

Linger-Nots series
Miller, Agnes
1 *Linger-Nots and the mystery house* (1923)
Alternative title: The story of nine adventurous girls
2 *Linger-Nots and the valley feud* (1923)
Alternative title: The great West Point chain
3 *Linger-Nots and their golden quest* (1923)
Alternative title: The log of the Ocean Monarch
4 *Linger-Nots and the whispering charm* (1925)
Alternative title: The secret from old Alaska
5 *Linger-Nots and the secret maze* (1931)
Alternative title: Treasure-trove on Battlefield Hill

Lingham series
Finch, Matthew
see **Dick Lingham series**

Lingua Latina series
Beard, Henry
1 *Latin for all occasions* (1990)
2 *Latin for even more occasions* (1991)

Link series
Binder, Eando
see **Adam Link series**
Vigilant
see **Barry Link series**

Linkum series
Mitgang, Herbert
see **Sam Linkum series**

Linley and Pelham series
Martin, Archibald Edward
see **Pel Pelham and Detective Linley series**

Linn series
Van Vogt, Alfred Elton
see **Clane series**

Linnea series
Bjork, Christina
1 *Linnea in Monet's garden* (1987)
2 *Linnea's windowsill garden* (1988)
3 *Linnea's almanac* (1990)

Linnear series
Lustbader, Eric
see **Ninja series**

Linnett and Hawthorne series
Linscott, Gillian
see **Birdie Linnett and Nimue Hawthorne series**

Linsky series
Averill, Esther
see **Jenny Linsky series**

Lintott series
Stubbs, Jean
see **Inspector John Joseph Lintott series**

Linwoodmuir series
Donald, Henry
1 *Happy story of Wallace the engine* (1955)
2 *Story of Hal 5 and the Haywards* (1955)

Lion and Albert series
Edgar, Marriott
see **Albert and the lion series**

Lion and Lamb series
This sequence has two authors
Hooks, William H
1 *Lion and Lamb* (1989)
Brenner, Barbara
2 *Lion and Lamb step out* (1990)

Lion at sea trilogy
Hennessy, Max
see **Kelly Maguire trilogy**

Lion Jack series
Barnum, Phineas Taylor
1 *Lion Jack* (1875)
A tale of land and sea, being perilous adventures among wild men and the capturing of wild beasts, showing how menageries are made
2 *Jack in the jungle* (1880)
A tale of land and sea

Lion of Macedon series
Gemmell, David A
1 *Lion of Macedon* (1990)
2 *Dark prince* (1991)

Lion series
Hurd, Edith Thatcher
see **Johnny Lion series**

Lion series
Kruse, Max
1 *Lion on the loose* (1965)
Original edition entitled *De Lowe ist los*
2 *Flying lion* (1966)
Original edition entitled *Kommt ein Lowe geflogen*

Lion series
Victor, Sam
see **Talbot Lion series**

Lionel Buckby series
Gloag, John
1 *Ripe for development* (1936)
2 *Unwilling adventurer* (1940)
3 *Mister Buckby is not at home* (1942)
4 *Kind Uncle Buckby* (1946)

Lionel Crane series
Stuart, Donald
1 *White friar* (1934)
2 *Midnight murder* (1935)

Lionel series
Allen, Linda
1 *Lionel's finest hour* (1985)
2 *Lionel and the spy* (1985)
3 *Lionel the lone wolf* (1988)

Lionel series
Krensky, Stephen
1 *Lionel at large* (1986)
2 *Lionel in the fall* (1987)
3 *Lionel in the spring* (1990)
4 *Lionel and Louise* (1992)
5 *Lionel in winter* (1994)

Lioness series
Pierce, Tamora
see **Song of the lioness series**

Liquidator series
Brent, R L
1 *Liquidator* (1974)
2 *Contract for a killing* (1974)
3 *Cocaine connection* (1974)
4 *Invitation to a strangling* (1975)
5 *Exchange* (1978)

Lisa and Emmy and Dodie series
Chastain, Madye Lee
1 *Dark treasure* (1954)
2 *Emmy keeps a promise* (1956)
3 *Magic Island* (1964)

Lisa Clark series
Walden, Amelia
1 *Case of the diamond eye* (1969)
2 *What happened to Candy Carmichael?* (1970)
3 *Valerie Valentine is missing* (1971)
4 *Where was everyone when Sabrina screamed?* (1973)

Lisa Davis series
Waltch, Lilla M
1 *Third victim* (1987)
2 *Fearful symmetry* (1988)

Lisa Knighton series
Morrow, Charlotte
1 *Singing and the gold* (1960)
2 *Noonday thread* (1962)

Lisa Longland series
Burr, Sybil
1 *Life with Lisa* (1958)
2 *Leave it Lisa* (1960)

Lisa series
Peterson, Hans
1 *Liselott and the goloff* (1962)
Original edition entitled *Liselott och garaffen*
2 *Lisa settles in* (1965)
Original edition entitled *Liselott och de andra*
3 *Just Lisa* (1967)
Original edition entitled *Bara Liselott*

Lisa Shelley series
Morrow, Charlotte
see **Lisa Knighton series**

Lisa Thomas series
Lewis, Catherine
1 *Unable by reason of death* (1989)
2 *Not in single spies* (1992)

Lisconnel series
Barlow, Jane
1 *Irish idylls* (1892)
2 *Strangers at Lisconnel* (1895)
3 *From the east unto the west* (1898)

Lisdalia and Mike series
Caswell, Brian
see **Mike and Lisdalia series**

Liselott series
Peterson, Hans
see **Lisa series**

Lisle series
Laurence, Janet
see **Darina Lisle series**

Lissendale series
Horler, Sydney
see **Gerald Lissendale series**

Listener series
Caldwell, Taylor
1 *Listener* (1960)
Man who listens
2 *No one hears but him* (1966)

Listener series
Faulkner, William
1 *Sound and the fury* (1929)
2 *Absalom, Absalom!* (1936)

Listen-hear series
Slepian, Jan
Illustrated by Richard E Martin
1 *Alphie and the dream machine* (1964)
2 *Cock who couldn't crow* (1964)
3 *Lester and the sea monster* (1964)
4 *Magic Arthur and the giant* (1964)
5 *Mister Sipple and the naughty princess* (1964)
6 *Roaring dragon of Redrose* (1964)

Litanies series
Watson, Kathleen
1 *Litanies of life* (1902)
2 *Later litanies* (1914)

Literary reminiscences series
Swinnerton, Frank
see **Background and foreground series**

Little activity series
McGee, Shelagh
1 *Dressing up* (1987)
2 *Pretending* (1987)
3 *Hiding* (1987)
4 *Building* (1987)

Little Agnes series
Leslie, Madeline
1 *Trying to be useful* (1859)
2 *I'll try* (1860)
Alternative title: The young housekeeper
3 *Art and artlessness* (1864)

Little and orphan series
Hesling, Bernard
Humorous reminiscences
1 *Little and orphan* (1954)
2 *Dinkumization and depomification of an artful English immigrant* (1963)
Dinkum Pommie
3 *Stir up this stew* (1966)

Little animal series
Airault, Dominique
1 *Little puppies* (1983)
Original edition entitled *Les petits chiens*
2 *Little pandas* (1983)
Original edition entitled *Les petits pandas*
3 *Little lions* (1983)
4 *Little monkeys* (1984)

Little Bear series
Chapman, Gillian
1 *Little Bear tales* (1987)
2 *More little Bear tales* (1987)
3 *Little Bear's friends* (1987)
4 *Little Bear's food* (1987)
5 *Little Bear's weather* (1987)
6 *Little Bear's colour* (1987)
7 *What's the time, Little Bear?* (1987)

Little Bear series
Clarke, Molly
1 *Big book about Little Bear* (1961)
2 *Another big book about Little Bear* (1961)

Little Bear series
This sequence has two authors
Greaves, Margaret
Illustrated by Francesca Crespi
1 *Little Bear and the Papagini circus* (1986)
Crespi, Francesca
2 *Little Bear and the oompah-pah* (1987)

Little Bear series
Minarik, Else Holmelund
1 *Little Bear* (1957)
2 *Father Bear comes home* (1959)
3 *Little Bear's friend* (1960)
4 *Little Bear's visit* (1961)
Numbers 1, 2, 4 also published in one volume entitled *Little Bear stories*, 1982
5 *Kiss for Little Bear* (1968)

Little Bear trilogy
Davies, Evelyn
1 *Little Bear's feather* (1973)
2 *Little Bear the brave* (1976)
3 *Little Bear's journey* (1979)

Little bedtime books series
Blyton, Enid
1 *Cloud kitten* (1955)
2 *Doll that fell out of the pram* (1955)
3 *Silly Sammy* (1955)
4 *Surprising broom* (1955)
5 *Amanda going away* (1958)
6 *Balloon pipe* (1958)
7 *Golliwog and the wireless* (1958)
8 *Wizard who was really a nuisance* (1958)

Little Black Nickum series
Robertson, Jean
1 *Adventures of Little Black Nickum* (1957)
2 *More adventures of Little Black Nickum* (1958)

Little Black series
Bannerman, Helen
1 *Story of Little Black Sambo* (1899)
2 *Story of Little Black Mingo* (1901)
3 *Story of Little Black Quibba* (1902)
4 *Little Degchie-Head* (1903)
Story of Little Kettle-Head
An awful warning to bad babas
5 *Story of Little Black Quasha* (1908)
6 *Story of Little Black Bobtail* (1909)
7 *Sambo and the twins* (1936)
Story of Sambo and the twins
8 *Story of Little White Squibba* (1966)

Little black waistcoat series
Kiddell-Monroe, Joan
see **In his little black waistcoat series**

Little Blue Engine series
Hourihane, Ursula
1 *Little Blue Engine that wanted a drink* (1953)
2 *Adventures of the Little Blue Engine* (1956)
3 *Little Blue Engine stories* (1956)

Little book series
Burningham, John
1 *Rabbit* (1975)
2 *School* (1975)
3 *Snow* (1975)
4 *Baby* (1975)
5 *Blanket* (1976)
6 *Cupboard* (1976)
7 *Dog* (1976)
8 *Friend* (1976)

Little books series
Blyton, Enid
1 *Brer Rabbit* (1942)
2 *Bed-time stories* (1942)
3 *Jolly tales* (1942)
4 *Ho-Ho and Too Smart* (1942)
5 *Tales of the toys* (1942)
6 *Happy stories* (1942)

Little Brown Bear series
Lebrun, Claude
1 *Little Brown Bear gets dressed* (1979)
Original edition entitled *Petit Ours Brun s'habille*
2 *Little Brown Bear is ill* (1979)
Original edition entitled *Petit Ours Brun est malade*
3 *Little Brown Bear says no* (1979)
Original edition entitled *Petit Ours Brun dit non*
4 *Little Brown Bear takes a bath* (1979)
Original edition entitled *Petit Ours Brun se lave*
5 *Little Brown Bear wakes up* (1982)
Original edition entitled *Petit Ours Brun se reveille*
6 *Little Brown Bear wants a kiss* (1982)
Original edition entitled *Petit Ours Brun veut un baiser*
7 *Little Brown Bear's cold* (1982)
8 *Little Brown Bear is cross* (1982)
9 *Little Brown Bear's story* (1982)
10 *Little Brown Bear's tricycle* (1982)
11 *Little Brown Bear's walk* (1982)
12 *Little Brown Bear won't eat!* (1982)
13 *Little Brown Bear's bad days* (1983)
14 *Little Brown Bear's breakfast egg* (1983)
15 *Little Brown bear can cook!* (1983)
16 *Little Brown Bear is big!* (1983)
17 *Little Brown Bear's playtime* (1983)
18 *Little Brown Bear's snowball* (1983)

Little Brown Mouse series
Uttley, Alison
1 *Snug and Serena meet a queen* (1950)
2 *Snug and Serena pick cowslips* (1950)
3 *Going to the fair* (1951)
4 *Toad's castle* (1951)
5 *Mrs Mouse spring-cleans* (1952)
6 *Christmas at the Rose and Crown* (1952)
7 *Gypsy hedgehogs* (1953)
8 *Snug and the chimney sweeper* (1953)
9 *Flower show* (1955)
10 *Mouse telegram* (1955)
11 *Mister Stoat walks in* (1957)
12 *Snug and the silver spoon* (1957)
13 *Snug and Serena count twelve* (1959)
14 *Snug and Serena go to town* (1961)

Little bunkers series
Hope, Laura Lee
see **Six little bunkers series**

Little Canary series
Osgood, Mary A
1 *Little Canary's Daisy* (1873)
2 *Little Canary* (1873)
3 *Little Canary's cousin Eugene* (1873)
4 *Little Canary's black Cato* (1873)

Little captain series
Biegel, Paul
1 *Little captain* (1971)
Original edition entitled *De kleine kapitein*
2 *Little captain and the seven towers* (1973)
Original edition entitled *De kleine kapitein in het land van waan en wijs*
3 *Little captain and the pirate treasure* (1975)
Original edition entitled *De kleine kapitein en de schat van schrik en vreze*

Little car series
Berg, Leila
1 *Story of the little car* (1955)
Little car
2 *Little car has a day out* (1970)

Little Chick series
Kwitz, Mary DeBall
1 *Little Chick's story* (1978)
2 *Little chick's big day* (1981)
3 *Little Chick's breakfast* (1983)
4 *Little Chick's friend Duckling* (1992)

Little cockalorum series
Simkins, Wallis
1 *Little cockalorum* (1922)
2 *Little cockalorum crows again* (1923)
3 *Little cockalorum on her own* (1924)
4 *Little cockalorum finds romance* (1925)

Little colonel series
Johnston, Annie Fellows
1 *Little colonel* (1896)
2 *Gate of the giant scissors* (1898)
3 *Little colonel's house party* (1900)
4 *Two little knights of Kentucky* (1901)
5 *Little colonel's holidays* (1901)
6 *Little colonel's hero* (1902)
7 *Little colonel at boarding school* (1903)
8 *Little colonel in Arizona* (1904)
9 *Little colonel's Christmas vacation* (1905)
10 *Little colonel, maid of honor* (1906)
11 *Little colonel's knight comes riding* (1907)
12 *Mary Ware, the little colonel's chum* (1908)
13 *Mary Ware in Texas* (1910)
14 *Little colonel's good times book* (1910)
15 *Little colonel's doll book* (1910)
16 *Mary Ware's promised land* (1912)
17 *Mary Ware doll book* (1914)

Little color classics series
Burgess, Thornton Waldo
1 *Little Pete's adventure* (1941)
2 *Little Chuck's adventure* (1941)
3 *Little Red's adventure* (1942)

Little creature series
Piers, Helen
1 *Snail and caterpillar* (1972)
2 *Grasshopper and butterfly* (1975)

Little Creole series
Chambers, Rosemary Mary
1 *Little Creole* (1952)
2 *Losing fight* (1955)

Little disturbances series
Paley, Grace
Short stories
1 *Little disturbances of man* (1959)
2 *Enormous changes at the last minute* (1974)
3 *Later the same day* (1985)

Little dog series
Barr, Jene
1 *Little prairie dog* (1949)
2 *Little circus dog* (1949)

Little donkey series
Blyton, Enid
1 *Neddy the little donkey* (1955)
2 *Clever little donkey* (1956)

Little Dracula series
Waddell, Martin
1 *Little Dracula's first bite* (1986)
2 *Little Dracula's Christmas* (1986)
3 *Little Dracula at school* (1987)
4 *Little Dracula goes to school* (1987)

Little Dragon series
Jungman, Ann
1 *Little Dragon steps out* (1989)
2 *Little Dragon falls out* (1991)
3 *Little Dragon nips out* (1993)

Little drawing books series
Emberley, Ed
see **Ed Emberley's little drawing books series**

Little Ed series
Tully, Tom
1 *Little Ed* (1979)
2 *Little Ed at large* (1980)
3 *Look out, it's Little Ed!* (1981)

Little Elsie series
Dunboyne, Marion Clifford Butler
1 *Little Elsie's summer at Malvern* (1871)
2 *Sunbeam's influence* (1871)
Alternative title: Eight years after

Little Feather series
Palmer, Bernard
1 *Little Feather goes hunting* (1946)
2 *Little Feather at Big Bear Lake* (1947)
3 *Little Feather rides herd* (1947)
4 *Little Feather and the mystery mine* (1948)
5 *Little Feather at Tonak Bay* (1950)
6 *Little Feather and the secret package* (1951)
7 *Little Feather and the river of grass* (1953)

Little Ferret series
Foxall, Raymond
see **Harry Adkins series**

Little Fox series
Radau, Hans
1 *Last chief, Alaskan trapper* (1959)
Original edition entitled *Letster Hauptling, Little Fox*
2 *Little Fox, Alaskan trapper* (1960)
Original edition entitled *Grosser Jager, Little Fox*

Little Frankie series
Leslie, Madeline
1 *Little Frankie at school* (1860)
2 *Little Frankie at his plays* (1860)
3 *Little Frankie on a journey* (1860)
4 *Little Frankie and his father* (1860)
5 *Little Frankie and his mother* (1860)
6 *Little Frankie and his cousin* (1860)

Little girl series
Douglas, Amanda Minnie
1 *Little girl in old New York* (1896)
2 *Hannah Ann* (1896)
3 *Little girl of long ago* (1897)
4 *Little girl in old Boston* (1898)
5 *Little girl in old Philadelphia* (1899)
6 *Little girl in old Washington* (1900)
7 *Little girl in old New Orleans* (1901)
8 *Little girl in old Detroit* (1902)
9 *Little girl in old Saint Louis* (1903)
10 *Little girl in old Chicago* (1904)
11 *Little girl in old San Francisco* (1905)
12 *Little girl in old Quebec* (1906)
13 *Little girl in old Baltimore* (1907)
14 *Little girl in old Salem* (1908)
15 *Little girl in old Pittsburgh* (1909)

Little grey men series
B B
see **Oak Tree House series**

Little Grey Rabbit series
Uttley, Alison
1 *Squirrel, the Hare and the Little Grey Rabbit* (1929)
2 *How Little Grey Rabbit got back his tale* (1930)
3 *Great adventure of Hare* (1931)
4 *Story of Fuzzypeg, the hedgehog* (1932)
5 *Squirrel goes skating* (1934)
6 *Wise Owl's story* (1935)
7 *Little Grey Rabbit's party* (1936)
8 *Knot Squirrel tied* (1937)
9 *Fuzzypeg goes to school* (1938)
10 *Little Grey Rabbit's Christmas* (1939)
11 *Moldy Warp, the mole* (1940)
12 *Little Grey Rabbit's washing day* (1942)
13 *Hare joins the Home Guard* (1942)
14 *Water-Rat's picnic* (1943)
15 *Little Grey Rabbit's birthday* (1944)
16 *Speckledy Hen* (1945)
17 *Little Grey Rabbit and the weasels* (1947)
18 *Grey Rabbit and the wandering hedgehog* (1948)
19 *Little Grey Rabbit makes lace* (1950)
20 *Hare and the Easter eggs* (1952)
21 *Little Grey Rabbit's valentine* (1953)
22 *Little Grey Rabbit goes to sea* (1954)
23 *Hare and Guy Fawkes* (1956)
24 *Little Grey Rabbit's paint-box* (1958)
25 *Grey Rabbit finds a shoe* (1960)
26 *Grey Rabbit and the circus* (1961)
27 *Grey Rabbit's May Day* (1963)
28 *Hare goes shopping* (1965)
29 *Little Grey Rabbit's Pancake Day* (1967)
30 *Little Grey Rabbit goes to the North Pole* (1970)
31 *Fuzzypeg's brother* (1971)
32 *Little Grey Rabbit's spring cleaning party* (1972)
33 *Little Grey Rabbit and the snow-baby* (1973)
34 *Hare and the rainbow* (1975)

Little gymnast series
Haigh, Sheila
1 *Little gymnast* (1982)
2 *Somersaults* (1987)

Little Hippo series
Chagnoux, Christine
1 *Little Hippo* (1967)
Original edition entitled *Petit Potam*
2 *Little Hippo at the circus* (1968)
Original edition entitled *Petit Potam au cirque*

Little Hippo series
Macdonald, Maryann
Illustrated by Anna King
1 *Little Hippo starts school* (1990)
2 *Little Hippo gets glasses* (1991)

Little house series
Wilder, Laura Ingalls
see **Laura series**

Little Indian series
Lewin, Hugh
1 *Good hunting, Little Indian* (1962)
Good hunting, Blue Sky
The second title is a revised edition
2 *Little Indian* (1968)

Little John Rawlings series
Minahan, John
1 *Great hotel robbery* (1982)
2 *Great diamond robbery* (1984)
3 *Great pyramid robbery* (1987)
4 *Great Harvard robbery* (1988)
5 *Great grave robbery* (1989)

Little kids series
Fraser, Mary Ann
1 *Little kids at home* (1989)
2 *Little kids at play* (1989)

3 *Little kids at school* (1989)
4 *Little kids in the neighborhood* (1989)

Little Koala series
Roc, Margaret
Illustrated by Deborah Brown
1 *Little Koala* (1989)
2 *Little Koala paints* (1989)

Little Laura series
Drummond, Violet Hilda
1 *Little Laura's cat* (1960)
2 *Little Laura on the river* (1960)
3 *Little Laura and the lonely ostrich* (1963)
4 *Little Laura and the thief* (1963)
5 *Little Laura and her best friend* (1963)
6 *Anna Truly and the Christmas nights* (1968)

Little Lion series
Godfrey, Jan
Illustrated by Pearl Binder
1 *Little Lion at home* (1986)
2 *Little Lion and friends* (1986)
3 *Little Lion and the butterfly* (1986)
4 *Little Lion and the thunderstorm* (1986)

Little Lucia series
Robinson, Mabel Louise
1 *Doctor Tam O'Shanter* (1921)
2 *Little Lucia* (1922)
3 *Little Lucia and her puppy* (1923)
4 *All by ourselves* (1924)
5 *Little Lucia's island camp* (1924)
6 *Little Lucia's school* (1926)
7 *Sarah's Dakin* (1927)

Little Lulu series
Henderson, Marge
Comic books
1 *Laughs with Little Lulu* (1942)
2 *Fun with Little Lulu* (1944)

Little Mabel series
Cooper, Jilly
1 *Little Mabel* (1980)
2 *Little Mabel's great escape* (1981)
3 *Little Mabel wins* (1982)
4 *Little Mabel saves the day* (1985)

Little magic series
Pulling, Norah Tempe
1 *Little magic for the Browns* (1957)
2 *Little magic for Barbara* (1959)

Little maid series
Curtis, Alice Turner
1 *Little maid of Province Town* (1913)
2 *Little maid of Massachusetts Colony* (1914)
3 *Little maid of Narragansett Bay* (1915)
4 *Little maid of Bunker Hill* (1916)
5 *Little maid of Ticonderoga* (1917)
6 *Little maid of old Connecticut* (1918)
7 *Little maid of old Philadelphia* (1919)
8 *Little maid of old Maine* (1920)
9 *Little maid of old New York* (1921)
10 *Little maid of Virginia* (1922)

Little man series
Kastner, Erich
1 *Little man* (1963)
Original edition entitled *Der kleine Mann*
2 *Little man and the little miss* (1967)
Little man and the big thief
Original edition entitled *Der kleine Mann und die kleine Miss*

Little man series
Velthuijs, Max
1 *Little man finds a home* (1983)
Original edition entitled *Klein Mannchen hat kein Haus*
2 *Little man's lucky day* (1985)
Original edition entitled *Klein Mannchen findet das Gluck*
3 *Little man to the rescue* (1986)
Original edition entitled *Klein Mannchen hilft ein Freund*

Little Miss Cricket trilogy
Jackson, Gabrielle Emilie
1 *Little Miss Cricket* (1905)
2 *Little Miss Cricket at school* (1906)
3 *Little Miss Cricket's new home* (1907)

Little Miss Fales series
Knipe, Emilie Benson
1 *Little Miss Fales* (1910)
2 *Missing pearls* (1911)
Little Miss Fales goes west

Little Miss Pink series
Bennett, Rodney
1 *Little Miss Pink* (1947)
2 *Little Miss Pink at Greytoes* (1948)
3 *Little Miss Pink's school* (1948)
4 *Little Miss Pink at the Great House* (1949)
5 *Little Miss Pink's splendid summer* (1952)
6 *Little Miss Pink's wedding* (1952)

Little monster series
Mayer, Mercer
1 *Little Monster's word book* (1977)
2 *Little Monster at home* (1978)
3 *Little Monster at school* (1978)
4 *Little Monster at work* (1978)
5 *Little Monster's alphabet book* (1978)
6 *Little Monster's you-can-make-it book* (1978)
7 *Little Monster's bedtime book* (1978)
8 *Little Monster's counting book* (1978)
9 *Little Monster's neighborhood* (1978)
10 *Little Monster's Mother Goose* (1979)
11 *Little Monster's scratch and sniff mystery* (1980)

Little Mother series
Lister, Gladys
see **Round series**

Little Mouse series
Cartlidge, Michelle
1 *Little Mouse makes a mobile* (1986)
2 *Little Mouse makes sweets* (1986)
3 *Little Mouse makes cards* (1986)
4 *Little Mouse makes a garden* (1986)
One volume edition entitled *Little mouse makes*, 1991

Little mouse series
Holabird, Katharine
1 *Little mouse ABC* (1983)
2 *Little mouse one two three* (1983)

Little mouse series
Kraus, Robert
1 *Whose mouse are you?* (1970)
2 *Where are you going, Little Mouse?* (1986)
3 *Come out and play, Little Mouse* (1987)

Little Mouse series
Wheeler, Cindy
1 *Merry Christmas Little Mouse* (1986)
2 *New house for Little Mouse* (1987)

Little mouse trapped in a book series
Felix, Monique
1 *Story of a little mouse trapped in a book* (1980)
2 *Another story of a little mouse trapped in a book* (1983)

Little Mushrooms series
Ainsworth, Ruth
Puppet plays
1 *Three little Mushrooms* (1955)
Contains *Here we go round the buttercups, Lob's silver spoon, Hide-and-seek, Hay-making*
2 *More little Mushrooms* (1955)
Contains *Three clever Mushrooms, Tick-tock, Christmas eve, The white stranger*

Little Noddy series
Blyton, Enid
see **Noddy series**

Little nursery rhyme series
McGee, Shelagh
1 *This little piggy* (1987)
2 *Round and round the garden* (1987)
3 *Two little dicky birds* (1987)
4 *One, two, button my shoe* (1987)

Little ones series
Ormerod, Jan
1 *Our Ollie* (1986)
2 *Young Joe* (1986)
3 *Silly goose* (1986)
4 *Just like me* (1986)

Little Orphan Annie series
Gray, Harold
Comic strips
1 *Little Orphan Annie* (1926)
2 *Little Orphan Annie in the circus* (1927)
3 *Little Orphan Annie and the haunted house* (1928)
4 *Little Orphan Annie bucking the world* (1929)
5 *Little Orphan Annie, never say die* (1930)
6 *Little Orphan Annie shipwrecked* (1931)
7 *Little Orphan Annie, willing helper* (1932)
8 *Little Orphan Annie in Cosmic City* (1933)
9 *Little Orphan Annie and Uncle Dan* (1934)
10 *Little Orphan Annie and the Gila Monster Gang* (1944)
11 *Little Orphan Annie and the Gooneyville mystery* (1947)
12 *Little Orphan Annie in the Great Depression* (1979)
Companion volumes: *Arf, the life and hard times of Little Orphan Annie*, 1935-45

Little Owl series
Boyle, Constance
1 *Story of Little Owl* (1985)
2 *Little Owl and the weed* (1985)
3 *Little Owl's favourite uncle* (1985)
4 *Little Owl and the tree house* (1985)

Little Oxford series
Baldwin, Faith
1 *Station wagon set* (1938)
2 *Any village* (1971)
3 *No bed of roses* (1973)
4 *Time and the hour* (1974)
5 *New girl in town* (1975)
6 *Thursday's child* (1976)
7 *Adam's Eden* (1977)

Little Pear series
Lattimore, Eleanor Frances
1 *Little Pear* (1931)
2 *Little Pear and his friends* (1934)
3 *Little Pear and the rabbits* (1956)
4 *More about Little Pear* (1971)

Little people in far off lands series
Rutley, Cecily Marianne
1 *Land of mountains* (1926)
Tyrol
2 *Island home* (1927)
Malta
3 *Africa's garden* (1928)
Abyssinia and its borderlands
4 *Midst moving waters* (1930)
Madagascar
5 *Twixt north and south* (1934)
British Honduras

Little people series
Campbell, Rod
1 *Charlie Clown* (1981)
2 *Nancy Nurse* (1981)
3 *Eddie Engine-driver* (1981)
4 *Freddie Fireman* (1981)
5 *Nigel Knight* (1981)
6 *Gertie Gardener* (1981)
7 *Lots of animals* (1984)
8 *How many hats?* (1984)
9 *Look up at the sky* (1984)
10 *What is colour is that?* (1984)
11 *Big and strong* (1985)
12 *Cars and trucks* (1985)
13 *Road builders* (1985)
14 *Speed!* (1985)

Little people series
Gordon, Elizabeth
see **Loraine series**

Little Peppers series
Sidney, Margaret
see **Five Little Peppers series**

Little pilgrim series
Oliphant, Margaret Oliphant Wilson
see **Stories of the seen and the unseen series**

Little possums series
McGill, Marci
see **Six little possums series**

Little princess series
Higgins, Aileen Cleveland
1 *Little princess of Tenopah* (1909)
2 *Little princess of the Pines* (1910)
3 *Little princess of the patio* (1911)
4 *Little princess of the ranch* (1914)
5 *Little princess of the Stars and Stripes* (1915)

Little Puritan series
Robinson, Edith
1 *Loyal little maid* (1897)
2 *Little Puritan rebel* (1898)
3 *Little daughter of liberty* (1899)
4 *Little Puritan's first Christmas* (1900)
5 *Little Puritan pioneer* (1901)
6 *Puritan knight errant* (1903)
7 *Little Puritan bound-girl* (1904)
Numbers 2, 4, 5, 7 also published in one volume entitled *Little Puritan stories*, 1931
8 *Little Puritan cavalier* (1905)

Little Rabbit series
Wabbes, Marie
Translated from the French
1 *Little Rabbit's garden* (1987)
2 *It's snowing, Little Rabbit* (1987)
3 *Little Rabbit's birthday* (1987)
4 *Goodnight, Little Rabbit* (1987)

Little rabbits series
McCarthy, Ruth
see **Three little rabbits series**

Little raccoon series
Moore, Lilian
1 *Little raccoon and the thing in the pool* (1963)
2 *Little raccoon and the outside world* (1965)
3 *Little raccoon and no trouble at all* (1972)
4 *Little raccoon and poems from the woods* (1975)
5 *Little raccoon takes charge* (1986)
6 *Little raccoon's nighttime adventure* (1986)

Little red engine series
Ross, Diana
1 *Little red engine gets a name* (1942)
2 *Story of the little red engine* (1945)
3 *Little red engine goes to market* (1946)
4 *Little red engine goes to town* (1952)
5 *Little red engine goes travelling* (1955)
6 *Little red engine and the rocket* (1956)
7 *Little red engine goes home* (1958)
8 *Little red engine goes to be mended* (1966)
9 *Little red engine and the Taddlecombe outing* (1968)
10 *Little red engine goes carolling* (1971)

Little Red Fox series
Uttley, Alison
1 *Little Red Fox and the wicked uncle* (1954)
2 *Little Red Fox and Cinderella* (1956)
3 *Little Red Fox and the magic moon* (1958)
4 *Little Red Fox and the unicorn* (1962)
5 *Little Red Fox and the great big tree* (1968)

Little Red House children series
Douglas, Amanda Minnie
1 *Children in the little old Red House* (1912)
2 *Red House children at Grafton* (1913)
3 *Red House Children's vacation* (1914)
4 *Red House Children's year* (1915)
5 *Red House children growing up* (1916)

Little red metro series
Rowlands, Avril
1 *Little red metro for sale* (1984)
2 *Little red metro finds a home* (1984)
3 *Little red metro gets started* (1984)
4 *Little red metro gets cold feet* (1984)

Little red tractor series
Laird, Elizabeth
Illustrated by Colin Reeder
1 *Day Patch stood guard* (1990)
2 *Day Sidney was lost* (1990)
Day Sidney ran off
3 *Day the ducks went skating* (1990)
4 *Day Veronica was nosy* (1990)

Little robins series
Leslie, Madeline
1 *Little robins in the nest* (1860)
2 *Little robins learning to fly* (1860)
3 *Little robins in trouble* (1860)
4 *Little robins love one another* (1860)
5 *Little robins' friends* (1860)

Little runaways series
Curtis, Alice Turner
1 *Little runaways* (1906)
2 *Little runaways at home* (1912)
3 *Little runaways and mother* (1913)
4 *Little runaways at Orchard House* (1914)

Little series
Fowler, Richard
see **Mister Little series**
Parker, Maude
see **Jim Little series**

Little Slimtails series
Chell, Mary
see **Slimtails series**

Little Soup series
Peck, Robert Newton
1 *Little Soup's hayride* (1991)
2 *Little Soup's birthday* (1991)
3 *Little Soup's turkey* (1992)
4 *Little Soup's bunny* (1993)

Little Spook series
Sandberg, Inger
Illustrated by Lasse Sandberg
1 *Little ghost Godfrey* (1965)
Little Spook
Original edition entitled *Lilla spoeket Laban*
2 *Little Spook's grubby day* (1977)
Original edition entitled *Kommer snart, sa Laban och Labolina*
3 *Tiny Spook's guessing game* (1977)
Original edition entitled *Giss vem jag ar i dag?*
4 *Tiny Spook's tumbles* (1977)
Original edition entitled *Labolinas snubbeldag*
5 *Little Spook's baby sister* (1977)
Original edition entitled *Lilla Spoket laban far en lillasyster*
6 *Tiny Spook's tugging game* (1977)
Original edition entitled *Labolenas lina*
7 *Little Spook haunts again* (1978)
Original edition entitled *Pappa ar sjuk, sa Lilla Spoket laban*
8 *Little Spook and the lost doll* (1978)
Original edition entitled *Var ar Labolinas millimina?*

Little stories of life series
Cutting, Mary Stewart
1 *Little stories of courtship* (1905)
2 *Little stories of married life* (1902)
3 *More stories of married life* (1906)
4 *Suburban girls, and other stories of married life* (1907)

Little sunbeams series
Mathews, Joanna Hooe
1 *Belle Power's locket* (1871)
2 *Dora's motto* (1871)
3 *Lily Norris' enemy* (1872)
4 *Jessie's parrot* (1872)
5 *Mamie's watchword* (1872)
6 *Nellie's housekeeping* (1872)

Little talks series
Beers, Victor Gilbert
1 *Little talks about God and you* (1986)
2 *More little talks about God and you* (1987)

Little Tiger series
Janosch
1 *Trip to Panama* (1978)
Original edition entitled *Oh, wie schon ist Panama*
2 *Treasure-hunting trip* (1979)
Original edition entitled *Komm, wir finden einen Schatz*
3 *Letter for Tiger* (1981)
Original edition entitled *Post fur den Tiger*
4 *Little Tiger, get well soon* (1986)
Original edition entitled *Ich mach dich gesund, sagte der Bar*

Little Tom series
Gree, Alain
Translated and adapted by Denise Lebreton, illustrated by Gerard Gree
1 *Little Tom learns about the environment* (1971)
Original edition entitled *Petit Tom protege la nature*
2 *Little Tom and some animal friends* (1972)
Original edition entitled *Petit Tom et les animaux familiers*
3 *Little Tom makes ten discoveries* (1975)
Original edition entitled *Petit Tom fait dix decouvrertes*
4 *Little Tom learns about the time* (1977)
Original edition entitled *Petit Tom sait lire l'heure*
More than 12 more volumes not translated into English

Little Toot series
Gramatky, Hardie
1 *Little Toot* (1939)
2 *Little Toot on the Thames* (1964)
3 *Little Toot on the Grand Canal* (1968)
4 *Little Toot on the Mississippi* (1973)
5 *Little Toot through the Golden Gate* (1975)

Little toy board books series
Peppe, Rodney
1 *Little circus* (1983)
2 *Little dolls* (1983)
3 *Little games* (1983)
4 *Little numbers* (1983)
5 *Little wheels* (1983)

Little tree house series
Blyton, Enid
see **Josie, Click and Bun series**

Little Trulsa series
Ringner-Lundgren, Ester
1 *Little Trulsa* (1961)
Original edition entitled *Lille Trulsa*
2 *Little Trulsa's tea-party* (1962)
Original edition entitled *Lille Trulsas kalas*
3 *Little Trulsa's secret* (1963)
Original edition entitled *Lille Trulsas hemiighet*
4 *Little Trulsa's birthday* (1965)
Original edition entitled *Lille Trulsas namnsdag*

Little vampire series
Sommer-Bodenburg, Angela
1 *Little vampire* (1982)
My friend, the vampire
Original edition entitled *Der kleine Vampir*
2 *Little vampire moves in* (1982)
Vampire moves in
Original edition entitled *De kleine Vampir zieht um*
3 *Little vampire takes a trip* (1984)
Vampire takes a trip
Original edition entitled *Der kleine Vampir verreist*
4 *Little vampire goes on holiday* (1985)
Little vampire on the farm
Vampire on the farm
Original edition entitled *Der kleine Vampir auf dem Bauernhof*
5 *Little vampire in love* (1986)
Vampire in love
Original edition entitled *Der kleine Vampir und die grosse Liebe*
6 *Little vampire in danger* (1985)
Original edition entitled *Der kleine Vampir in Gefahr*
7 *Little vampire in the vale of doom* (1986)
Original edition entitled *Der kleine Vampir im Jammertal*
8 *Little vampire in despair* (1988)
Original edition entitled *Der kleine Vampir liest vor*
9 *Little vampire and the mystery patient* (1989)
Original edition entitled *Der geheimnisvolle Patient*
10 *Little vampire in the lion's den* (1989)
Original edition entitled *In der Hohle des Lowen*
11 *Little vampire learns to be brave* (1989)
Original edition entitled *Das ratselhafte Programm*
12 *Little vampire gets a surprise* (1993)
13 *Little vampire and the wicked plot* (1993)

Little vehicle series
Gay, Michael
Translated from the French
1 *Little truck* (1986)
2 *Little car* (1986)
3 *Little plane* (1986)

Little Washingtons series
This sequence has two authors
Nourse, S Waukley Roy
1 *Little Washingtons* (1918)
Roy, Lillian Elizabeth
2 *Little Washingtons' relative* (1918)
3 *Little Washingtons' travels* (1918)
4 *Little Washingtons at school* (1920)
5 *Little Washingtons' holidays* (1925)
6 *Little Washingtons, farmers* (1926)

Little witch series
Glovach, Linda
1 *Little witch's black magic cookbook* (1972)
2 *Little witch's black magic book of disguises* (1973)
3 *Little witch's black magic book of games* (1973)
4 *Little witch's Christmas book* (1974)
5 *Little witch's Halloween book* (1975)
6 *Little witch's Thanksgiving book* (1976)
7 *Little witch's book of yoga* (1979)
8 *Little witch's birthday book* (1981)
9 *Little witch's carnival book* (1982)
10 *Little witch's spring holiday book* (1983)
11 *Little witch's Valentine book* (1984)
12 *Little witch's dinosaur book* (1984)
13 *Little witch's cat book* (1985)
14 *Little witch's summertime book* (1986)
15 *Little witch's book of toys* (1986)
Companion volume: *The little witch presents a monster joke book*, by Linda Glovach and Charles Keller, 1976

Little Wizard series
Baum, Lyman Frank
1 *Jack Pumpkinhead and the sawhorse* (1913)
2 *Little Dorothy and Toto* (1913)
3 *Ozma and the Little Wizard* (1913)
4 *Cowardly lion and the hungry tiger* (1913)
5 *Scarecrow and the tin woodman* (1913)
6 *Tik-Tok and the nome King* (1913)
One volume edition entitled *Little Wizard stories of Oz*, 1914

Little Wombles series
Beresford, Elisabeth
1 *Snow Womble* (1975)
2 *Orinoco runs away* (1975)
3 *Tomsk and the tired tree* (1975)
4 *Wellington and the blue balloon* (1975)
5 *Bungo knows best* (1976)
6 *MacWomble's pipe band* (1976)
7 *Madame Cholet's picnic party* (1976)
8 *Tobermory's big surprise* (1976)

Little Zip series
Caveney, Sylvia
Illustrated by Sonia Stern
1 *Little Zip's dressing-up book* (1977)
2 *Little Zip's zoo counting book* (1977)
3 *Little Zip's water book* (1978)
4 *Little Zip's night-time book* (1981)

Littlejohn series
Bellairs, George
see **Detective Inspector Thomas Littlejohn series**

Littlenose series
Grant, John
1 *Littlenose* (1968)

2 *Littlenose moves house* (1969)
3 *Littlenose the hero* (1971)
Numbers 1-3 also published in one volume entitled *The adventures of Littlenose*, 1971
4 *Littlenose the hunter* (1972)
5 *Littlenose the fisherman* (1974)
6 *Littlenose to the rescue* (1975)
Numbers 4-6 also published in one volume entitled *More adventures of Littlenose*, 1976
7 *Littlenose the leader* (1977)
8 *Littlenose's birthday* (1979)
9 *Littlenose the marksman* (1982)
10 *Littlenose the joker* (1983)
11 *Littlenose and Two-eyes* (1985)

Littlepage manuscript trilogy
Cooper, James Fenimore
1 *Satanstoe* (1845)
2 *Chainbearer* (1845)
3 *Redskins* (1846)

Littlest angel series
Kidd, Ronald
1 *Littlest angel earns his halo* (1985)
2 *Littlest angel meets the newest angel* (1985)

Littlest series
Tazewell, Charles
1 *Littlest angel* (1946)
2 *Littlest stork* (1953)
3 *Littlest snowman* (1956)

Live Albom series
Albom, Mitch
Selections from sports journalism in various American media
1 *Live Albom* (1988)
2 *Live Albom II* (1990)
3 *Live Albom III* (1992)
Alternative title: Gone to the dogs

Live boys series
Morecamp, Arthur
1 *Live boys* (1879)
Alternative title: Charley and Nasho in Texas; a narrative relating to two boys of fourteen, one a Texan, the other a Mexican
2 *Live boys in the Black Hills* (1879)
Alternative title: The young Texan gold hunters; a narrative in Charley's own language, describing their adventure during a second trip over the great Texas cattle trail

Liverpool series
Whittington-Egan, Richard
1 *Liverpool colonnade* (1955)
2 *Liverpool roundabout* (1957)
3 *Tales of Liverpool* (1967)
Murder, mayhem, mystery
4 *Liverpool characters and eccentrics* (1968)
5 *Liverpool soundings* (1969)
6 *Liverpool, this is my city* (1973)

Lives of the saints series
De Wohl, Louis
1 *Glorious folly* (1957)
Based on the life of Saint Paul
2 *Restless flame* (1951)
Based on the life of Saint Augustine
3 *Citadel of God* (1959)
Based on the life of Saint Benedict
4 *Joyful beggar* (1958)
Based on the life of Saint Francis of Assisi
5 *Quiet life* (1950)
Based on the life of Saint Thomas Aquinas
6 *Lay siege to heaven* (1960)
Based on the life of Saitn Catherine of Siena
7 *Golden thread* (1952)
Based on the life of Saint Ignatius of Loyola
8 *Set all afire* (1953)
Based on the life of Saint Francis Xavier

Living and sleeping series
Lambert, Derek
1 *He must so live* (1956)
2 *No time for sleeping* (1958)

Living dead series
This sequence has three authors
Russo, John
1 *Night of the living dead* (1974)
Based on a screenplay
2 *Return of the living dead* (1978)
Companion volume: *The complete Night of the living dead filmbook*, 1985
Romero, George Andrew
3 *Dawn of the dead* (1978)

Living planet series
Coon, Susan
1 *Rahne* (1980)
2 *Cassilee* (1980)
3 *Virgin* (1981)
4 *Chiy-une* (1982)

Living series
Arnothy, Christine
Reminiscences of a Hungarian refugee to Paris
1 *I am fifteen and I do not want to die* (1955)
Original edition entitled *J'ai quinze ans et je ne veux pas mourir*; set in Hungary during the Second World War
2 *It is not so easy to live* (1957)
Original edition entitled *Il n'est pas si facile de vivre*

Living skills series
Berry, Joy
1 *Every kid's guide to decision making and problem solving* (1987)
2 *Every kid's guide to handling fights with brothers or sisters* (1987)
3 *Every kid's guide to laws that relate to parents and children* (1987)
4 *Every kid's guide to laws that relate to schools and work* (1987)
5 *Every kid's guide to overcoming prejudice and discrimination* (1987)
6 *Every kid's guide to nutrition and health care* (1987)
7 *Every kid's guide to understanding human rights* (1987)
8 *Every kid's guide to understanding parents* (1987)
9 *Every kid's guide to watching TV intelligently* (1987)
10 *Every kid's guide to being a communicator* (1987)
11 *Every kid's guide to family rules and responsibilities* (1987)
12 *Every kid's guide to good manners* (1987)
13 *Every kid's guide to handling disagreements* (1987)
14 *Every kid's guide to laws that relate to kids in the community* (1987)
15 *Every kid's guide to the juvenile justice system* (1987)
16 *Every kid's guide to thinking and learning* (1987)
17 *Every kid's guide to using time wisely* (1987)
18 *Every kid's guide to being special* (1988)
19 *Every kid's guide to handling family arguments* (1988)
20 *Every kid's guide to handling feelings* (1988)
21 *Every kid's guide to making and managing money* (1988)
22 *Every kid's guide to making friends* (1988)
23 *Every kid's guide to responding to danger* (1988)
24 *Every kid's guide to understanding nightmares* (1988)
25 *Every kid's guide to coping with childhood traumas* (1988)
26 *Every kid's guide to handling illness* (1988)
27 *Every kid's guide to intelligent spending* (1988)

Living sword series
Allan, Lennox
1 *And love thee evermore* (1951)
2 *Living sword* (1954)

Living West trilogy
Ellison, Suzanne
1 *Heart of the West* (1990)
2 *Soul of the West* (1990)
3 *Spirit of the West* (1990)

Livingstone series
Allen, Julia
see **Mary Livingstone series**

Liz and Molly series
Macgibbon, Jean
see **Molly and liz series**

Liz and Will series
Resciniti, Angelo G
1 *Liz and Will solve mini-mysteries* (1979)
2 *More mini-mysteries for Liz and Will* (1980)

Liz Archer series
Longley, W B
see **Angel Eyes series**

Liz Connors and Jack Lingemann series
Kelly, Susan
1 *Gemini man* (1985)
2 *Summertime soldiers* (1986)
3 *Chasing the dragon* (1986)
4 *Trail of the dragon* (1988)
5 *Until proven innocent* (1990)
6 *And soon I'll come to kill you* (1991)
7 *Out of the darkness* (1992)

Liz Parrott series
Long, Manning
1 *Here's blood in your eye* (1941)
Modeled in murder
2 *Vicious circle* (1942)
3 *False alarm* (1943)
Invitation to murder
4 *Bury the hatchet* (1944)
5 *Short shrift* (1945)
6 *Dull thud* (1947)
7 *Savage breast* (1948)

Liz Wareham series
Brennan, Carol
1 *Headhunt* (1991)
2 *Full commission* (1993)
3 *In the dark* (1994)

Liza, Bill and Jed series
Parish, Peggy
1 *Key to the treasure* (1966)
2 *Clues in the woods* (1968)
3 *Haunted house* (1971)
4 *Pirate Island adventure* (1975)
5 *Hermit Dan* (1977)

Lizzie and Harold series
Winthrop, Elizabeth
1 *Lizzie and Harold* (1986)
2 *Best Friends Club* (1989)

Lizzie Collins series
Laurie-Long, Ernest
1 *Port of destination* (1933)
2 *Purser's mate* (1938)
3 *Unhappy ship* (1951)

Lizzie Dripping series
Cresswell, Helen
1 *Lizzie Dripping* (1973)
2 *Lizzie Dripping again* (1974)
3 *Lizzie Dripping and the little angel* (1974)
4 *Lizzie Dripping by the sea* (1974)
5 *More Lizzie Dripping* (1974)
6 *Lizzie Dripping and the witch* (1991)

Lizzie Silver series
Singer, Marilyn
1 *Tarantulas on the brain* (1982)
2 *Lizzie Silver of Sherwood Forest* (1986)

Lizzie Thomas and Inspector John Webber series
Oliver, Anthony
1 *Pew group* (1980)
2 *Property of a lady* (1983)
3 *Elburg collection* (1985)
4 *Cover-up* (1987)

Llanwern series
Morgan, Alison
1 *Fish* (1971)
Boy called Fish
2 *Pete* (1972)
3 *Ruth Crane* (1973)
4 *At Willie Tucker's place* (1975)

Llarn series
Fox, Gardner Francis
see **Alan Morgan series**

Llewellyn series
Wodehouse, Pelham Grenville
see **Ivor Llewellyn series**

Llorca series
Ames, Delano
see **Juan Llorca series**

Lloyd Albert and Ancil Witherspoon series
Smith, Doris Buchanan
1 *Last was Lloyd* (1981)
2 *First hard times* (1983)

Lloyd and Hill series
McGown, Jill
see **Chief Inspector Lloyd and Sergeant Judy Hill series**

Lloyd George series
Beaverbrook, William Maxwell Aitken
1 *Politicians and the War, 1914-1916, volume 1* (1928)
2 *Politicians and the War, 1914-1916, volume 2* (1932)
3 *Men and power, 1917-18* (1956)
4 *Decline and fall of Lloyd George, and great was the fall thereof* (1963)

Lloyd Hopkins trilogy
Ellroy, James
see **Sergeant Lloyd Hopkins trilogy**

Lloyd Nicolson series
Wayland, Patrick
1 *Counterstroke* (1964)
2 *Double defector* (1964)
3 *Waiting game* (1965)

Lloyd series
Reed, Wallace
see **Sheriff Bill Lloyd series**

Loams series
Ruyle, John
see **Turlock Loams series**

Lobby Ludd trilogy
Bassett, Ronald
1 *Tinfish run* (1977)
2 *Pierhead jump* (1978)
3 *Neptune landing* (1979)

Lobelia Falls series
Craig, Alisa
see **Osbert Monk series**

Lobo series
Crafton, Dennis
1 *Silver showdown* (1982)
2 *Commanche duel* (1982)

Lochinvar series
Taggart, Marion Ames
see **Miss Lochinvar series**

Locke series
Barnao, Jack
see **John Locke series**
Challis, Mary
see **Jeremy Locke series**
Crossen, Kendell Foster
see **Kim Locke series**
Silliphant, Stirling
see **John Locke series**

Locken series
Rostand, Robert
see **Mike Locken series**

Lockett family series
Atkinson, Mary Evelyn
1 *August adventure* (1936)
2 *Mystery manor* (1937)
3 *Compass points north* (1938)
4 *Smuggler's gap* (1939)
5 *Going gangster* (1940)
6 *Crusoe Island* (1941)
7 *Challenge to adventure* (1942)
8 *Monster of Widgeon Weir* (1943)
9 *Nest of the scarecrow* (1944)
10 *Problem party* (1945)
11 *Chimney cottage* (1947)
12 *House on the moor* (1948)
13 *Thirteenth adventure* (1949)
14 *Steeple folly* (1950)

Lockhart series
Pullman, Philip
see **Sally Lockhart series**

Lockie Leonard series
Winton, Tim
1 *Lockie Leonard, human torpedo* (1990)
2 *Lockie Leonard, scumbuster* (1993)

Lockwood series
Latham, Brad
see **Hook series**

Lodge family series
Street, Pamela
1 *Mill-race* (1983)
2 *Way of the river* (1984)
3 *Many waters* (1985)
4 *Unto the fourth generation* (1985)
One volume edition entitled *Mill-race quartet*, 1988

Lofthouse and Endel series
Marcus, Joanna
see **Romney Marsh series**

Log book series
Seferis, George
1 *Log book I* (1940)
2 *Log book II* (1944)
3 *Log book III* (1955)
One volume edition entitled *Poems*, 1960; also includes *Mythistorema*, 1935

Log cabin series
Ellis, Edward Sylvester
1 *Lost trail!* (1864)
A legend of the far West
2 *Camp-fire and wigwam* (1885)
3 *Footprints in the forest* (1886)

Logan and Sutton series
White, James G
see **Gunslick series**

Logan family series
Taylor, Mildred Davis
1 *Song of the trees* (1975)
2 *Roll of thunder, hear my cry* (1976)
3 *Let the circle be unbroken* (1981)
4 *Road to Memphis* (1990)
Companion volume: *Mississippi bridge*, 1990

Logan series
Chandler, Edna Walker
see **Tom Logan series**
Holt, Henry
see **Mike Logan series**
McCutcheon, Hugh
see **Richard Logan series**

Logan series
Nolan, William Francis
1 *Logan's run* (1967)
Co-author: George Clayton Johnson
2 *Logan's world* (1977)
3 *Logan's search* (1980)
One volume edition entitled *Logan*, 1986

Logan series
Stone, Ned
see **Other Day Logan series**

Logic and order in society series
Wenger, Peter
1 *Rational option* (1989)
2 *Manifesto of the third millenium* (1990)

Logick series
Watts, Isaac
1 *Logick* (1725)
Alternative title: The right use of reason in the enquiry after truth
2 *Improvement of the mind* (1741)
Alternative title: A supplement to the art of logick

Lolami series
Bayliss, Clara Kern
1 *Lolami, the little cliff-dweller* (1901)
2 *Lolami in Tusayan* (1903)
3 *Little cliff-dweller* (1908)

Lollipop lady series
Webb, Diana
see **Lily series**

Lomax brothers series
Bowden, Jim
1 *Renegade riders* (1980)
2 *Gunfight at Elm Creek* (1980)

Lomax family trilogy
Stewart, Desmond
see **Sequence of roles trilogy**

Lomax series
Allegretto, Michael
see **Jacob Lomax series**
Sutcliffe, Halliwell
see **Griff Lomax series**

Lombard family series
Coffman, Virginia
see **Cavalcade series**

London Airport series
Fores, John
1 *Forgotten place* (1956)
2 *Springboard* (1956)

London archaeology series
Harrison, Michael
1 *London beneath the pavement* (1961)
Revised edition 1971
2 *London that was Rome* (1971)
The imperial city receated by the new archaeology

London family series
Hughes, Mary Vivian
1 *London child of the seventies* (1934)
2 *London girl of the eighties* (1936)
3 *London home in the nineties* (1937)
One volume abridged edition entitled *London family chronicle*, 1950; companion volumes: *London at home*, 1931, *London family between the wars*, 1940

London gallery series
Raymond, Ernest
A sequence portraying London life over half a century
1 *We, the accused* (1935)
2 *Marsh* (1937)
3 *Gentle Greaves* (1949)
4 *Witness of Canon Welcome* (1950)
5 *Chorus ending* (1951)
6 *Kilburn tale* (1947)
7 *Child of Norman's End* (1934)
8 *For them that trespass* (1944)
9 *Was there love once* (1942)
10 *Corporal of the guard* (1943)
11 *Song of the tide* (1940)
12 *Chalice and the sword* (1952)
13 *To the wood no more* (1954)
14 *Lord of Wensley* (1956)
15 *Old June weather* (1957)
16 *City and the dream* (1958)
17 *Our late member* (1972)

London Group series
Walpole, Hugh
1 *Fortitude* (1913)
A true and faithful account of the education of an explorer
2 *Duchess of Wrexe* (1914)
Her decline and death
3 *Green mirror* (1917)
4 *Captives* (1920)
5 *Young enchanted* (1921)
6 *Wintersmoon* (1928)
7 *Hans Frost* (1929)
8 *Captain Nicholas* (1934)
9 *Joyful Delaneys* (1938)

London in wartime series
Henrey, Robert
1 *Village in Piccadilly* (1942)
2 *Incredible city* (1944)
3 *Siege of London* (1946)

London Police series
Bruton, Eric
see **City of London Police series**

London quartet
Hastings, Phyllis
1 *Candles of night* (1977)
2 *Feast of the peacock* (1978)
Numbers 3 and 4 not yet published

London series
Burke, Thomas
1 *Limehouse nights* (1916)
Tales of Chinatown
1.1 *Broken blossoms* (1916)
1.2 *In Chinatown* (1916)
2 *Whispering windows* (1921)
More Limehouse nights
Tales of the waterside
3 *East of Mansion House* (1926)
4 *Pleasantries of Old Quong* (1931)
Tea-shop in Limehouse
5 *Dark nights* (1944)

London series
Harris, Wilson
see **Da Silva series**

London transports series
Binchy, Maeve
Short stories
1 *Central Line* (1978)
2 *Victoria Line* (1980)
One volume edition entitled London transports, 1983

London trilogy
Avery, Valerie
Autobiography
1 *London morning* (1980)
2 *London shadows* (1981)
3 *London spring* (1982)

Lone Eagle and Abigail Trent series
Bittner, F Rosanne
see **Savage destiny series**

Lone Hand series
Aiken, Albert W
1 *Lone Hand in Texas* (1888)
Alternative title: The red-gloved raiders of Rio Grande
2 *Lone Hand on the Caddo* (1888)
Alternative title: The bad man of the Big Bayou
3 *Lone Hand, the shadow* (1889)
Alternative title: The master of the Triangle Ranch

Lone Hunter series
Worcester, Donald Emmet
1 *Lone Hunter's gray pony* (1956)
2 *Lone Hunter and the Cheyennes* (1957)
3 *Lone Hunter's first buffalo hunt* (1958)
4 *Lone Hunter and the wild horses* (1959)

Lone Pine Five Club series
Saville, Malcolm
1 *Mystery at Witchend* (1943)
Spy in the hills
2 *Seven white gates* (1944)
3 *Gay Dolphin adventure* (1945)
4 *Secret of Grey Walls* (1947)
5 *Lone Pine Five* (1949)
6 *Elusive Grasshopper* (1951)
7 *Neglected mountain* (1953)
8 *Saucers over the moon* (1955)
9 *Wings over Witchend* (1956)
10 *Lone Pine London* (1957)
11 *Secret of the gorge* (1958)
12 *Mystery mine* (1959)
13 *Sea Witch comes home* (1960)
14 *Not scarlet but gold* (1962)
15 *Treasure at Amorys* (1964)
16 *Man with three fingers* (1966)
17 *Rye Royal* (1969)
18 *Strangers at Witchend* (1970)
19 *Where's my girl?* (1972)
20 *Home to Witchend* (1978)

Lone Ranger series
Striker, Fran
Based on the Lone Ranger adventures created by George Washington Trendle
1 *Lone Ranger* (1936)
2 *Lone Ranger and the mystery ranch* (1938)
3 *Lone Ranger and the gold robbery* (1939)
4 *Lone Ranger and the Texas renegades* (1939)
5 *Lone Ranger and the outlaw stronghold* (1939)
6 *Lone Ranger and Tonto* (1940)
7 *Lone Ranger and the secret of Thunder Mountain* (1940)
8 *Lone Ranger rides* (1941)
9 *Lone Ranger at the Haunted Gulch* (1941)
10 *Lone Ranger traps the smugglers* (1941)
11 *Lone Ranger rides again* (1943)
12 *Lone Ranger rides north* (1946)
13 *Lone Ranger and the silver bullet* (1948)
14 *Lone Ranger on Powderhorn Trail* (1949)
15 *Lone Ranger in Wild Horse Canyon* (1950)
16 *Lone Ranger west of Maverick Pass* (1951)

17 *Lone Ranger's new deputy* (1951)
18 *Lone Ranger on Gunsight Mesa* (1952)
19 *Lone Ranger and the Bitter Spring feud* (1953)
20 *Lone Ranger and the code of the West* (1954)
21 *Lone Ranger, trouble on the Santa Fe* (1955)
Trouble on the Santa Fe
22 *Lone Ranger on the Red Butte Trail* (1956)

Companion volumes: *The Lone Ranger*, by Gaylord Du Bois, based on the famous radio adventure series by Fran Striker, 1936, *The Lone Ranger*, a Little Golden book, by Steffi Fletcher, 1956; *Lone Ranger annual*, 1955-1958, *Lone Ranger adventure stories*, adapted by Richard Lewis from the television series, 1958, *The legend of the Lone Ranger*, by Gary McCarthy, 1981

Lone Rider series
Henderson, Colt
1 *Guns at Lone Star* (1951)
2 *Guns on Eagle Creek* (1952)
3 *Lone Rider* (1954)
4 *Lone Rider's guns* (1955)
5 *Lone Rider's justice* (1955)
6 *Lone Rider's trail* (1956)
7 *Lone Rider's ranch* (1957)
8 *Lone Rider's quest* (1959)
9 *Lone Rider's war* (1959)
10 *Lone Rider's day* (1961)
11 *Lone Rider's law* (1963)
12 *Lone Rider's return* (1965)

Lone Star Kid series
Shane, Steve
1 *Lone Star Kid* (1955)
2 *Trigger trail* (1959)
3 *Guns of Sunset Mesa* (1962)
4 *Shadow riders* (1965)

Lone Star series
Cole, Jackson
see **Jim Hatfield series**

Lone Star series
Ellis, Wesley
1 *Lone Star on the treachery trail* (1982)
2 *Lone Star and the opium rustlers* (1982)
3 *Lone Star and the border bandits* (1982)
4 *Lone Star and the Kansas wolves* (1982)
5 *Lone Star and the Utah Kid* (1982)
6 *Lone Star and the land grabbers* (1982)
7 *Lone Star and the tall timbers* (1983)
Lone Star and the timber pirates
8 *Lone Star and the showdowners* (1983)
9 *Lone Star and the hardrock payoff* (1983)
10 *Lone Star and the renegade Comanches* (1983)
11 *Lone Star on Outlaw Mountain* (1983)
12 *Lone Star and the gold raiders* (1985)
13 *Lone Star and the Denver madam* (1985)
14 *Lone Star and the railroad war* (1985)
15 *Lone Star and the Mexican standoff* (1985)
16 *Lone Star and the badlands war* (1985)
17 *Lone Star and the San Antonio Rais* (1985)
18 *Lone Star and the ghost pirates* (1985)
19 *Lone Star on Owlhoot Trail* (1985)
20 *Lone Star on Devil's Trail* (1985)
21 *Lone Star and the Apache revenge* (1985)
22 *Lone Star and the Texas gambler* (1985)
23 *Lone Star and the hangrope heritage* (1985)
24 *Lone Star and the Montana troubles* (1985)
25 *Lone Star and the mountain man* (1985)
26 *Lone Star and the stockyard showdown* (1985)
27 *Lone Star and the riverboat* (1985)
28 *Lone Star and the Mescalero outlaws* (1985)
29 *Lone Star and the Amarillo rifles* (1985)
30 *Lone Star and the school for outlaws* (1985)
31 *Lone Star on the Treasure River* (1985)
32 *Lone Star and the Moon Trail feud* (1985)
33 *Lone Star and the golden mesa* (1985)
34 *Lone Star and the Rio Grande bandits* (1985)
35 *Lone Star and the buffalo hunters* (1985)
36 *Lone Star and the biggest gun in the West* (1985)
37 *Lone Star and the Apache warrior* (1985)
38 *Lone Star and the gold mine war* (1985)
39 *Lone Star and the California oil war* (1985)
40 *Lone Star and the Alaskan guns* (1985)
41 *Lone Star and the White River curse* (1986)
42 *Lone Star and the tombstone gamble* (1986)
43 *Lone Star and the timberland terror* (1986)
44 *Lone Star in the Cherokee Strip* (1986)
45 *Lone Star and the Oregon rail sabotage* (1986)
46 *Lone Star and the mission war* (1986)
47 *Lone Star and the gunpowder cure* (1986)
48 *Lone Star and the land barons* (1986)
49 *Lone Star and the gulf pirates* (1986)
50 *Lone Star and the Indian rebellion* (1986)
51 *Lone Star and the Nevada mustangs* (1986)
52 *Lone Star and the con man's ransom* (1986)
53 *Lone Star and the stagecoach war* (1987)
54 *Lone Star and the two gun kid* (1987)
55 *Lone Star and the Sierra swindlers* (1987)
56 *Lone Star in the Big Horn Mountains* (1987)
57 *Lone Star and the death train* (1987)
58 *Lone Star and the rustler's ambush* (1987)
59 *Lone Star and the Tong's revenge* (1987)
60 *Lone Star and the outlaw posse* (1987)
61 *Lone Star and the sky warriors* (1987)
62 *Lone Star in a range war* (1987)
63 *Lone Star and the phantom gunmen* (1987)
64 *Lone Star and the Montana land grab* (1987)
65 *Lone Star and the James Gang's loot* (1988)
66 *Lone Star and the master of death* (1988)
67 *Lone Star and the Cheyenne trackdown* (1988)
68 *Lone Star and the lost gold mine* (1988)
69 *Lone Star and the Comancheros* (1988)
70 *Lone Star and Hickok's ghost* (1988)
71 *Lone Star and the deadly stranger* (1988)
72 *Lone Star and the silver bandits* (1988)
73 *Lone Star and the Nevada bloodbath* (1988)
74 *Lone Star in the big thicket* (1988)
75 *Lone Star and the suicide spread* (1988)
76 *Lone Star and the Texas Rangers* (1988)
77 *Lone Star and the death merchants* (1989)
78 *Lone Star and the Comstock crossfire* (1989)
79 *Lone Star and the medicine lodge shoot out* (1989)
80 *Lone Star and the Barbary killers* (1989)
81 *Lone Star and the rogue grizzlies* (1989)
82 *Lone Star in Hell's Canyon* (1989)
83 *Warpath* (1989)
84 *Mountain of gold* (1989)
85 *Lone Star and the diamond swindlers* (1989)
86 *Lone Star and the Texas killers* (1989)
87 *Arizona stranger* (1989)
88 *Shadow catcher* (1989)
89 *Gamble of death* (1990)
90 *Cripple Creek* (1990)
91 *Arizona gunmen* (1990)
92 *Renegade rancher* (1990)
93 *Ripper* (1990)
94 *Italian gold* (1990)
95 *Railroad killers* (1990)
96 *Devil worshipers* (1990)
97 *Bounty hunters* (1990)
98 *Colorado ambush* (1990)
99 *Bank robbers* (1990)
100 *Cheyenne showdown* (1990)
101 *Sierra sabotage* (1991)
102 *Lone Star and the gemstone robbers* (1991)
103 *Oklahoma ambush* (1991)
104 *Lone Star and the Alaskan renegades* (1991)
105 *California gold* (1991)
106 *Lone Star in the Devil's Playground* (1991)
107 *River pirates* (1991)
108 *Lone Star in the Choctaw nation* (1991)
109 *Lone Star and the Yuma Prison break* (1991)
110 *Lone Star and the Oklahoma rustlers* (1991)
111 *Deadly vigilantes* (1991)
112 *Lone Star and the ghost dancers* (1991)
113 *Lone Star and the hellbound pilgrims* (1992)
114 *Lone Star and the trail to Abilene* (1992)
115 *Lone Star and the horse thieves* (1992)
116 *Lone Star and the deep water pirates* (1992)
117 *Lone Star and the Black Bandana Gang* (1992)
118 *Lone Star in Timberlands* (1992)
119 *Mexican muskets* (1992)
120 *Lone Star and the Santa Fe showdown* (1992)
121 *Lone Star and the gunrunners* (1992)
122 *Lone Star and the buccaneers* (1992)
123 *Lone Star and the Aztec treasure* (1992)
124 *Lone Star and the trail of murder* (1992)
125 *Wolf pack* (1993)
126 *Chicago showdown* (1993)
127 *Lone Star and the Brutus Gang* (1993)
128 *Lone Star and the gold mine* (1993)
129 *Lone Star and the San Diego bonanza* (1993)
130 *Lone Star and the ghost ship pirates* (1993)
131 *Lone Star on the hangman's trail* (1993)
132 *Lone Star and the steel rail* (1993)
133 *Lone Star and the bellwether kid* (1993)
134 *Great pilgrim heist* (1993)
135 *River of no return* (1993)
136 *Lone Star and the death mine* (1993)
137 *Lone Star and the Redemption massacre* (1994)
138 *Lone Star and the death chase* (1994)
139 *Lone Star and the slaughter showdown* (1994)
140 *Lone Star and the Montana marauders* (1994)
141 *Lone Star and the trail of blood* (1994)
142 *Lone Star and the deadly vixens* (1994)
143 *Lone Star and a saloon called Hell* (1994)
144 *Lone Star in the Sierra Diablos* (1994)

Lone Tree series
Morris, Wright
1 *Man who was there* (1945)
2 *Home place* (1948)
3 *World in the attic* (1949)
4 *Field of vision* (1956)
5 *Ceremony in Lone Tree* (1960)

Lone Wolf legends series
Dever, Joe
see **Legends of Lone Wolf series**

Lone Wolf series
Barry, Mike
see **Burton Wulff series**

Lone Wolf series
Dever, Joe
1 *Flight from the dark* (1984)
Co-author: Gary Chalk
2 *Fire on the water* (1984)
Co-author: Gary Chalk; numbers 1 and 2 also published in one volume entitled *The Lone Wolf adventures*, 1984
3 *Caverns of Kalte* (1984)
Co-author: Gary Chalk
4 *Chasm of doom* (1985)
Co-author: Gary Chalk
5 *Shadow on the sand* (1985)
Co-author: Gary Chalk
6 *Kingdoms of terror* (1985)
Co-author: Gary Chalk
7 *Castle Death* (1986)
Co-author: Gary Chalk
8 *Jungle of horrors* (1987)
Co-author: Gary Chalk
9 *Cauldron of fear* (1987)
10 *Dungeons of Torgar* (1987)
11 *Prisoners of time* (1987)
12 *Masters of darkness* (1988)

Lone Wolf series
Vance, Louis Joseph
see **Michael Lanyard series**

Lone Wolf's world series
Page, Ian
see **World of Lone Wolf series**

Lonely Londoners trilogy
Selvon, Samuel
1 *Lonely Londoners* (1956)
2 *Moses ascending* (1975)
3 *Moses migrating* (1983)

Loner series
Trimnell, Robert L
1 *Colorado kill* (1974)
2 *New Mexico massacre* (1975)
3 *Winslow's freight* (1975)
4 *Hell on Legg's Hill* (1976)

Lonergan series
Renwick, Peter
see **Leatherface Lonergan series**

Lonesome dove series
McMurtry, Larry
1 *Lonesome dove* (1985)
2 *Streets of Laredo* (1993)

Lonesome River series
Hankins, Robert Maxwell
1 *Lonesome River range* (1941)

Long and Conley series
Fox, James M
see **Jerry Long and Chuck Conley series**

Long and Macnamara series
Macavoy, Roberta Ann
see **Mayland Long and Martha Macnamara series**

Long guns series
Miller, Jim
1 *Mister Henry* (1986)
2 *Big fifty* (1986)
3 *Brass boy* (1987)
4 *Spencer's revenge* (1987)
5 *War clouds* (1987)
6 *That damn single shot* (1988)
7 *Shotgun and sagebrush* (1989)

Long Island aerospace series
Stoff, Joshua
1 *Aerospace heritage of Long Island* (1989)
2 *From airship to spaceship* (1991)
Long Island aviation and space flight

Long John Silver series
This sequence has six authors
Delderfield, Ronald Frederick
Inspired by *Treasure Island*, by Robert Louis Stevenson, 1883
1 *Adventures of Ben Gunn* (1956)
Judd, Denis
2 *Adventures of Long John Silver* (1977)
Stevenson, Robert Louis
3 *Treasure Island* (1883)
Connell, John
4 *Return of Long John Silver* (1949)
Judd, Denis
5 *Return to Treasure Island* (1978)
Leeson, Robert
6 *Silver's revenge* (1978)
Leach, Christopher
7 *Great book raid* (1979)

Long journey trilogy
Originally published as a six volume sequence entitled *Den lange Rejse*, 1909-1922
Jensen, Johannes Vilhelm
1 *Fire and ice* (1922)
Originally published as *Det tabte Land*, 1919, and, *Broen*, 1909 which are volumes 4 and 1 of the original sequence
2 *Cimbrians* (1923)
Originally published as *Cimbernes Tog*, 1922, and, *Norne Goest*, 1919 which are volumes 6 and 3 of the original sequence
3 *Christopher Columbus* (1924)
Original edition entitled *Christofer Columbus*, 1921 which is volume 5 of the original sequence
Volume 2 of the original sequence entitled *Skibet*, 1912 has not been translated into English; one volume edition entitled *The long journey*, 1933

Long Look trilogy
Abbott, Edward
1 *Long Look House* (1877)
2 *Out doors at Long Look* (1878)
3 *Trip eastwards* (1880)

Long Range Desert Group series
Daniels, Norman A
see **Rat Patrol series**

Long Rider series
Dawson, Clay
House pseudonym
1 *Long ride* (1988)
2 *Fast death* (1989)
3 *Gold town* (1989)
4 *Apache dawn* (1989)
5 *Kill Crazy Horse!* (1989)
6 *Shadow war* (1989)
7 *Ghost dancers* (1989)
8 *Hellhole* (1990)
9 *Land bandits* (1990)
10 *Buffalo hunters* (1990)
11 *Santa Fe Ring* (1990)
12 *Killer mustang* (1990)
13 *Vengeance town* (1990)
14 *Comancheros* (1991)
15 *Blood hunt* (1991)
16 *Snaketown* (1991)
17 *Town tamer* (1991)
18 *Texas manhunt* (1992)
19 *Chisholm trail* (1992)
20 *Mountain killer* (1992)
21 *Ranchero* (1992)
22 *Crazy knife* (1993)
23 *Vengeance Valley* (1993)
24 *Dead aim* (1993)
25 *Guns and gold* (1993)
26 *Devil's guns* (1993)
27 *Wanted, dead or alive* (1993)

Long series
Carpenter, Carleton
see **Chester Long series**
Carstairs, Henry
see **Lydford Long series**
Evans, Tabor
see **Longarm series**
Fulman, Al
see **Harry Long series**
Heinlein, Robert Anson
see **Lazarus Long series**
Larson, Glen A
see **Knight Rider series**

Long tall Texan series
Palmer, Diana
1 *Long tall Texan* (1988)
Calhoun
2 *Justin* (1988)
3 *Tyler* (1988)
4 *Donovan* (1992)

Long Tan series
Burstall, Terry
1 *Soldier's story* (1986)
Battle at Xa Long Tan, Vietnam, 18 August 1966
2 *Soldier returns* (1990)
Long Tan veteran discovers the other side of Vietnam

Long Trail Boys series
Wilkins, Dale
1 *Long Trail Boys at Sweet Water Ranch* (1923)
Alternative title: The mystery of the white shadow
2 *Long Trail Boys and the gray cloaks* (1923)
Alternative title: The mystery of the night riders
3 *Long Trail Boys and the scarlet sign* (1925)
4 *Long Trail Boys and the vanishing rider* (1925)
5 *Long Trail Boys and the mystery of the fingerprints* (1928)
6 *Long Trail Boys and the mystery of the unknown messenger* (1928)

Long vacation series
Yonge, Charlotte Mary
1 *Scenes and characters* (1847)
2 *Long vacation* (1895)
3 *Modern broods* (1900)
Alternative title: Developments unlooked for

Long way series
Dutton, Geoffrey
1 *Long way south* (1953)
By car from London to Australia
2 *Africa in black and white* (1956)

Long weekend series
Chapman, Jennifer
1 *Long weekend* (1984)
2 *Regretting it* (1987)

Longarm and Lone Star series
Evans, Tabor
1 *Longarm and the Lone Star legend* (1982)
2 *Longarm and the Lone Star vengeance* (1983)
3 *Longarm and the Lone Star bounty* (1984)
4 *Longarm and the Lone Star rescue* (1985)
5 *Longarm and the Lone Star deliverance* (1986)
6 *Longarm and the Lone Star showdown* (1986)
7 *Longarm and the Lone Star mission* (1987)
8 *Longarm and the Lone Star frame* (1988)
9 *Longarm and the Lone Star rustlers* (1990)
10 *Longarm and the Lone Star captive* (1991)
11 *Longarm and the Lone Star captive* (1991)
12 *Longarm and the San Joaquin war* (1992)
13 *Longarm and the Navaho drums* (1993)
14 *Longarm and the Santee killing grounds* (1994)

Longarm series
Evans, Tabor
This pseudonym is used by several authors including Lou Cameron, William Cecil Knott, Jeffrey Miner Wallmann and Harry Whittington, whose authorship is indicated against those titles where it is known
1 *Longarm* (1978) [Whittington]
2 *Longarm on the border* (1978) [Wallmann; Whittington]
3 *Longarm and the avenging angels* (1978) [Wallmann; Whittington]
4 *Longarm and the Wendigo* (1979) [Wallmann; Whittington]
5 *Longarm in the Indian nation* (1979) [Wallmann; Whittington]
6 *Longarm and the loggers* (1979) [Wallmann; Whittington]
7 *Longarm and the highgraders* (1979) [Wallmann; Whittington]
8 *Longarm and the nesters* (1979) [Wallmann; Whittington]
9 *Longarm and the hatchet men* (1979) [Knott; Whittington]
10 *Longarm and the Molly Maguires* (1979)
11 *Longarm and the Texas Rangers* (1979) [Whittington]
12 *Longarm in Lincoln county* (1979) [Knott; Whittington]
13 *Longarm in the sand hills* (1979)
14 *Longarm in Leadville* (1979)
15 *Longarm on the Devil's Trail* (1979)
16 *Longarm and the Mounties* (1980)
17 *Longarm and the Comancheros* (1980)
18 *Longarm on the Yellowstone* (1980)
19 *Longarm in the four corners* (1980)
20 *Longarm at Robber's Roost* (1980)
21 *Longarm and the shepherders* (1980)
22 *Longarm and the ghost dancers* (1980)
23 *Longarm and the town tamer* (1980)
24 *Longarm and the railroaders* (1980)
25 *Longarm on the Old Mission Trail* (1980)
26 *Longarm and the dragon hunters* (1980) [Knott]
27 *Longarm and the Rurales* (1981)
28 *Longarm on the Humbolt* (1981) [Whittington]
29 *Longarm on the Big Muddy* (1981)
30 *Longarm, south of the Gila* (1981)
31 *Longarm in Northfield* (1981) [Knott]
32 *Longarm and the golden lady* (1981) [Whittington]
33 *Longarm and the Laredo Loop* (1981)
34 *Longarm and the Boot Hillers* (1981) [Knott]
35 *Longarm and the blue norther* (1981) [Whittington]
36 *Longarm on the Santa Fe* (1981)
37 *Longarm and the stalking corpse* (1981)
38 *Longarm and the Comancheros* (1981)
39 *Longarm and the devil's railroad* (1981) [Knott]
40 *Longarm in Silver City* (1982) [Whittington]
41 *Longarm on the Barbary Coast* (1982)
42 *Longarm and the moonshiners* (1982) [Knott]
43 *Longarm in Yuma* (1982)
44 *Longarm in Boulder Canyon* (1982) [Cameron; Whittington]
45 *Longarm in Deadwood* (1982)
46 *Longarm and the Great Train Robbery* (1982)
47 *Longarm in the badlands* (1982)
48 *Longarm in the big thicket* (1982) [Wallmann; Whittington]
49 *Longarm and the eastern dudes* (1982)
50 *Longarm in the Big Bend* (1982) [Wallmann]
51 *Longarm and the snake dancers* (1983)
52 *Longarm on the Great Divide* (1983) [Wallmann]
53 *Longarm and the buckskin rogue* (1983)
54 *Longarm and the Calico Kid* (1983) [Knott]
55 *Longarm and the French actress* (1983)
56 *Longarm and the outlaw lawman* (1983)
57 *Longarm and the bounty hunters* (1983)
58 *Longarm in no man's land* (1984)
59 *Longarm and the big outfit* (1984)
60 *Longarm and the Santa Anna's gold* (1984)
61 *Longarm and the Custer County war* (1984)
62 *Longarm in Virginia City* (1984)
63 *Longarm and the James County war* (1984)
64 *Longarm and the cattle baron* (1984)
65 *Longarm and the steer swindlers* (1984)
66 *Longarm and the hangman's noose* (1984)
67 *Longarm and the Omaha Tinhorns* (1984)
68 *Longarm and the desert duchess* (1984)
69 *Longarm of the painted desert* (1984)
70 *Longarm on the Ogallala Trail* (1984)
71 *Longarm on the Arkansas* (1984)
72 *Longarm and the blindman's vengeance* (1985)
73 *Longarm and the Fort Reno* (1985)
74 *Longarm and the Durango payroll* (1985) [Wallmann]
75 *Longarm, west of the Pecos* (1985) [Wallmann]
76 *Longarm on the Nevada line* (1985) [Wallmann]

77 *Longarm and the Blackfoot guns* (1985) [Wallmann]
78 *Longarm on the Santa Cruz* (1985) [Wallmann]
79 *Longarm and the cowboy revenge* (1985) [Wallmann]
80 *Longarm on the Goodnight Trail* (1985)
81 *Longarm and the frontier duchess* (1985) [Wallmann]
82 *Longarm in the Bitterroots* (1985) [Wallmann]
83 *Longarm and the tenderfoot* (1985) [Wallmann]
84 *Longarm and the stagecoach bandits* (1985) [Wallmann]
85 *Longarm and the big shoot-out* (1986)
86 *Longarm in the Hard Rock country* (1986) [Wallmann]
87 *Longarm in the Texas Panhandle* (1986) [Wallmann]
88 *Longarm and the rancher's showdown* (1986)
89 *Longarm and the island passage* (1986)
90 *Longarm in the Ruby Range* (1986)
91 *Longarm and the great cattle kill* (1986) [Wallmann]
92 *Longarm and the crooked railman* (1986)
Title page has author as Wesley Ellis
93 *Longarm on the Siwash Trail* (1986) [Wallmann]
94 *Longarm and the runaway thieves* (1986)
95 *Longarm and the escape artist* (1986) [Wallmann]; title page has the author as Wesley Ellis
96 *Longarm and the bone skinners* (1986) [Wallmann]
97 *Longarm and the Mexican line-up* (1987) [Wallmann]
98 *Longarm and the trail drive sham* (1987) [Wallmann]
99 *Longarm and the desert spirits* (1987) [Wallmann]
100 *Longarm on Death mountain* (1987) [Wallmann]
101 *Longarm and the cottonwood curse* (1987) [Wallmann]
102 *Longarm and the desperate manhunt* (1987) [Wallmann]
103 *Longarm and the Rocky Mountains chase* (1987) [Wallmann]
104 *Longarm on the overland trail* (1987) [Wallmann]
105 *Longarm and the big posse* (1987) [Wallmann]
106 *Longarm on Deadman's Trail* (1987) [Wallmann]
107 *Longarm in the Bighorn Basin* (1987) [Wallmann]
108 *Longarm and the blood harvest* (1987) [Wallmann]
109 *Longarm and the bloody trackdown* (1988) [Wallmann]
110 *Longarm and the hangman's vengeance* (1988) [Wallmann]
111 *Longarm on the Thunderbird Run* (1988) [Wallmann]
112 *Utah killers* (1988) [Wallmann]
113 *Longarm in the big burnout* (1988) [Wallmann]
114 *Longarm and the quiet guns* (1988) [Wallmann]
115 *Longarm in the Valley of Death* (1988) [Wallmann]
116 *Longarm and the blood bounty* (1988) [Wallmann]
117 *Longarm and the treacherous trail* (1988) [Wallmann]
118 *Longarm and the New Mexico shoot out* (1988) [Wallmann]
119 *Longarm and the renegade sergeant* (1989)
120 *Longarm and the Sierra Madres* (1989) [Wallmann]
121 *Longarm and the medicine wolf* (1989) [Wallmann]
122 *Longarm and the Indian raiders* (1989) [Wallmann]
123 *Longarm in a desert showdown* (1989) [Wallmann]
124 *Longarm and the mad dog killer* (1989) [Wallmann]
125 *Longarm and the hangman's noose* (1989) [Wallmann]
126 *Longarm and the doomed witness* (1989) [Wallmann]
127 *Longarm and the outlaw sheriff* (1989) [Wallmann]
128 *Day of death* (1989) [Wallmann]
129 *Longarm and the rebel killers* (1989) [Wallmann]
130 *Longarm and the hangman's list* (1989) [Wallmann]
131 *Longarm in the Clearwaters* (1989) [Wallmann]
132 *Redwood raiders* (1989) [Wallmann]
133 *Deadly jailbreak* (1990) [Wallmann]
134 *Pawnee kid* (1990) [Wallmann]
135 *Devil's stagecoach* (1990)
136 *Wyoming bloodbath* (1990) [Wallmann]
137 *Red desert* (1990)
138 *Crooked marshal* (1990)
139 *Texas Rangers* (1990)
140 *Vigilantes* (1990)
141 *In the Osage strip* (1990)
142 *Lost mine* (1990)
143 *Longley legend* (1990)
144 *Dead man's badge* (1990)
145 *Longarm and the Chinese puzzle* (1991) [Knott]
146 *Longarm and the Montana massacre* (1991)
147 *Mexican badlands* (1991)
148 *Longarm and the bounty huntress* (1991)
149 *Longarm and the Denver bustout* (1991)
150 *Longarm and the Skull Canyon Gang* (1991)
151 *Longarm and the railroad to Hell* (1991)
152 *Longarm and the river of death* (1991)
153 *Longarm and the gold hunters* (1991)
154 *Longarm and the Colorado gundown* (1991)
155 *Longarm and the grave robbers* (1991)
156 *Longarm and the Arkansas ambush* (1991)
157 *Longarm and the Arizona showdown* (1992)
158 *Longarm and the Ute nation* (1992)
159 *Longarm in the Sierra Oriental* (1992)
160 *Tabor and the gunslicks* (1992)
161 *Longarm and the lady sheriff* (1992)
162 *Longarm on the devil's highway* (1992)
163 *Cimarron City sellout* (1992)
164 *Longarm and the Cheyenne Kid* (1992)
165 *Longarm and the rebel brand* (1992)
166 *Longarm and the double eagles* (1992)
167 *Longarm and the fool killer* (1992)
168 *Longarm and the Shoshoni River* (1992)
169 *Night branders* (1993)
170 *Taos terror* (1993)
171 *Longarm and the Nevada swindle* (1993)
172 *On the Butterfield Spur* (1993)
173 *Longarm and the diamond snatchers* (1993)
174 *Longarm and the border showdown* (1993)
175 *Longarm and the carnival killer* (1993)
176 *Longarm and the captive woman* (1993)
177 *Longarm and the cross fire* (1993)
178 *Golden death* (1993)
179 *Rebel's revenge* (1993)
180 *Longarm and the dead ringers* (1993)
181 *Longarm and the bounty of blood* (1994)
182 *Longarm and the train robbers* (1994)
183 *Longarm on the Fever Coast* (1994)
184 *Longarm and the last man* (1994)
185 *Drifting badge* (1994)
186 *Longarm and the high rollers* (1994)
187 *Longarm and the bounty hunters* (1994)
188 *Longarm and the Gallagher Gang* (1994)

Longchamp series
Andrews, Virginia Cleo
see **Cutler family series**

Longdon-Lorristone family series
Gillespie, Susan
1 *Martyr* (1956)
2 *Grandson* (1957)
3 *Victors* (1959)
4 *Neighbour* (1961)
5 *Summer at home* (1965)
6 *Young green blade* (1963)

Longland series
Burr, Sybil
see **Lisa Longland series**

Longstocking series
Lindgren, Astrid
see **Pippi Longstocking series**

Longtime series
Brinsmead, Hesba Fay
see **Truelance family series**

Lonia Guiu series
Oliver, Maria Antonia
1 *Study in lilac* (1985)
Original edition entitled *Estudi en lila*
2 *Antipodes* (1987)
Original edition entitled *Antipodes*

Lonigan trilogy
Farrell, James Thomas
see **Studs Lonigan trilogy**

Lonny and Wynn racing series
Speed, Eric
see **Wynn and Lonny racing series**

Lonto series
Johnson, Emil Richard
see **Tony Lonto series**

Look about you series
Ainsworth, Ruth
1 *In woods and fields* (1967)
2 *Down the lane* (1967)
3 *Beside the sea* (1967)
4 *By pond and stream* (1969)
5 *In your garden* (1969)
6 *In the park* (1969)

Look ahead series
Rand, Edward Augustus
1 *Making the best of it* (1888)
2 *Up north in a whaler* (1890)
Alternative title: Would he keep his colours flying?
3 *Too late for the tidemill* (1890)
4 *Our clerk from Barkton* (1891)
Alternative title: Right rather than rich

Look and see series
Hands, Hargrave
1 *Duckling sees* (1985)
2 *Puppy sees* (1985)
3 *Little goat sees* (1985)
4 *Little lamb sees* (1985)
5 *Bunny sees* (1985)

Look and see series
Tarsky, Sue
1 *Apple and pear* (1983)
2 *Cup and bowl* (1983)
3 *Doll and drum* (1983)
4 *Table and chair* (1983)

Look back series
Smith, Dodie
Autobiography
1 *Look back with love* (1974)
A Manchester childhood
2 *Look back with mixed feelings* (1978)
3 *Look back with astonishment* (1979)
4 *Look back with gratitude* (1985)

Look series
Gree, Alain
1 *Look goes round* (1968)
Original edition entitled *Qu'est-ce qui tourne?*
2 *Look what smokes* (1968)
Original edition entitled *Qu'est-ce qui fume?*
3 *Look what flies* (1968)
Original edition entitled *Qu'est-ce qui vole?*

Look twice series
Wood, Amanda Jane
Illustrated by Chris Forsey
1 *There's a bear in my bed* (1987)
2 *Elephant came to breakfast* (1987)
3 *There's a panda in the pantry* (1987)
4 *There's a whale in my bath* (1987)

Look-about Club series
Bamford, Mary Ellen
1 *Look-about Club and the curious live things they found* (1887)
2 *Second year of the Look-about Club* (1889)

Looking backward responses series
Edward Bellamy's novel, *Looking backward, 2000-1887*, inspired five books, aimed at refuting his predictions, which are listed here in order of their publication
Morris, Alfred
1 *Looking ahead* (1892)
A tale of adventure, not by the author of *Looking backward*
Roberts, J W
2 *Looking within* (1893)
The misleading tendencies of *Looking backward* made manifest
Bird, Arthur
3 *Looking forward* (1899)
A dream of the United States of the Americas in 1999
West, Julian
4 *My afterdream* (1900)
A sequel to the late Mister Edward Bellamy's *Looking backward*
Yerex, Cuthbert
5 *Christopher Brand* (1934)
Looking forward

Looking backward sequels series
This sequence, by four authors whose works have been inspired by Edward Bellamy's *Looking backward, 2000-1887*, are listed in chronological order of publication
Michaelis, Richard
1 *Looking further forward* (1890)
Stone, C H
2 *One of Berrian's novels* (1890)
Vinton, Arthur Dudley
3 *Looking further backward* (1890)
A series of lectures delivered to the freshman class at Shawmut College by Professor Won Lung Li, successor of Professor Julian West
Geissler, Ludwig A
4 *Looking beyond* (1891)
A sequel to *Looking backward*, by Edward Bellamy and an answer to *Looking further forward*, by Richard Michaelis

Loomis series
Sanders, Leonard
see **Clay Loomis series**

Looney series
Beatty, Jerome
see **Maria Looney series; Matthew Looney series**

Loraine series
Gordon, Elizabeth
1 *Loraine and the little people* (1915)
2 *Loraine and the little people of spring* (1918)
3 *Loraine and the little people of summer* (1920)
4 *Loraine and the little people of the ocean* (1922)

Lord and Lady Dazincourt trilogy
O'Riordan, Conal
see **Stanislaus Priest trilogy**

Lord and Lady Loveland series
Williamson, Charles Norris
1 *Lady Betty across the water* (1906)
2 *Marquis of Loveland* (1908)
3 *Lord Loveland discovers America* (1910)

Lord and Lady Tintagel series
Draco, F
1 *Devil's church* (1951)
2 *Cruise with death* (1952)

Lord Barradine series
Jepson, Edgar
1 *Barradine detects* (1937)
Short stories
2 *Four green fish* (1939)

Lord Blackshirt series
Graeme, Bruce
1 *Son of Blackshirt* (1941)
2 *Lord Blackshirt* (1942)
The son of Blackshirt carries on
3 *Calling Lord Blackshirt* (1943)

Lord Burghley series
Read, Conyers
see **William Cecil series**

Lord Byron series
Quennell, Peter
Biography
1 *Byron, the years of fame* (1935)
2 *Byron in Italy* (1941)
One volume revised edition 1974

Lord Charles Oakshott series
Challoner, Robert
see **Commander Lord Charles Oakshott series**

Lord Chatham trilogy
Sherrard, Owen Aubrey
1 *War minister in the making* (1952)
2 *Pitt and the Seven Years' War* (1955)
3 *Lord Chatham and America* (1958)

Lord Clane Linn series
Van Vogt, Alfred Elton
see **Clane series**

Lord Darcy series
This sequence has two authors
Garrett, Randall
1 *Too many magicians* (1967)
2 *Murder and magic* (1979)
3 *Lord Darcy investigates* (1981)
Short stories; Numbers 1-3 also published in one volume entitled *Lord Darcy*, 1983
Kurland, Michael
4 *Ten little wizards* (1988)
5 *Study in sorcery* (1989)

Lord Edward Fitzgerald series
Bodkin, Matthias McDonnell
1 *Lord Edward Fitzgerald* (1896)
2 *Rebels* (1899)

Lord Grandith series
Farmer, Philip Jose
1 *Feast unknown* (1969)
2 *Lord of the trees* (1970)

Lord Horatio Nelson series
Frye, Pearl
1 *Game for empires* (1950)
Covers the years 1793-1797
2 *Sleeping sword* (1952)
Covers the years 1798-1805

Lord Jim series
Conrad, Joseph
1 *Lord Jim* (1900)
2 *Youth* (1902)
3 *Chance* (1913)

Lord Kalvan series
This sequence has three authors
Piper, Horace Beam
1 *Lord Kalvan of Otherwhen* (1965)
Gunpowder god
Green, Roland James
2 *Great Kings' war* (1985)

Lord Melbourne series
Cecil, David
1 *Young Melbourne and the story of his marriage with Caroline Lamb* (1939)
2 *Lord M* (1954)
The later life of Lord Melbourne
One volume edition entitled *Melbourne*, 1954

Lord Meren series
Robinson, Lynda S
1 *Murder in the place of Anubis* (1994)
2 *Murder at god's gate* (1995)

Lord Nicholas Ramage series
Pope, Dudley
1 *Ramage* (1965)
2 *Ramage and the drumbeat* (1967)
Drumbeat
3 *Ramage and the freebooters* (1969)
Triton brig
4 *Governor Ramage, R.N.* (1973)
5 *Ramage's prize* (1974)
6 *Ramage and the guillotine* (1975)
7 *Ramage's diamond* (1976)
8 *Ramage's mutiny* (1977)
9 *Ramage and the rebels* (1978)
10 *Ramage touch* (1979)
11 *Ramage's signal* (1980)
12 *Ramage and the renegades* (1981)
13 *Ramage's devil* (1982)
14 *Ramage's trial* (1984)
15 *Ramage's challenge* (1985)
16 *Ramage at Trafalgar* (1986)
17 *Ramage and the Saracens* (1988)
18 *Ramage and the Dido* (1989)

Lord of the Rings trilogy
Tolkien, John Ronald Reuel
1 *Fellowship of the Ring* (1954)
Revised edition 1966
2 *Two towers* (1954)
Revised edition 1966
3 *Return of the King* (1955)
Revised edition 1966
One volume edition entitled *The Lord of the Rings*, 1969

Lord of the Unknown series
Carter, Lin
see **Prince Zarkon series**

Lord Peter Wimsey series
Sayers, Dorothy Leigh
1 *Whose body?* (1923)
2 *Clouds of witness* (1926)
3 *Unnatural death* (1927)
Dawson pedigree
4 *Unpleasantness at the Bellona Club* (1928)
5 *Lord Peter views the body* (1928)
Short stories; includes *The man with no face*, 1943 which was published separately
6 *Strong poison* (1930)
7 *Five red herrings* (1931)
Suspicious characters
8 *Have his carcarse* (1932)
9 *Murder must advertise* (1933)
10 *Hangman's holiday* (1933)
Short stories; includes *The image in the mirror*, 1943, and, *The incredible elopement of Lord Peter Wimsey*, 1943 each of which were published separately
11 *Nine tailors* (1934)
Changes rung on an old theme in two short touches and two full peals
12 *Gaudy night* (1935)
13 *Busman's honeymoon* (1937)
14 *In the teeth of the evidence, and other stories* (1939)
15 *Striding folly* (1972)
16 *Abominable history of the man with copper fingers* (1982)
Short stories
Omnibus volume entitled *Lord Peter, a collection of all the Lord Peter Wimsey stories*, 1972

Lord Pig series
Lombard, Nap
see **Lord Winterstone series**

Lord series
Antonius, Soraya
1 *Lord* (1986)
2 *Where the jinn consult* (1987)

Lord series
King, Charles Daly
see **Michael Lord series**

Lord Stranleigh series
Barr, Robert
1 *Young Lord Stranleigh* (1908)
2 *Stranleigh's millions* (1909)
3 *Lord Stranleigh, philanthropist* (1911)
4 *Lord Stranleigh abroad* (1913)

Lord Tedric series
Smith, Edward Elmer
Edited by Gordon Eklund
1 *Lord Tedric* (1978)
Alien worlds
2 *Space pirates* (1979)
3 *Black Knight of the Iron Sphere* (1979)
4 *Alien realms* (1980)
Numbers 1 and 4 also published in one volume 1980

Lord Timothy Dexter series
Marquand, John Phillips
see **Timothy Dexter series**

Lord Winterstone series
Lombard, Nap
1 *Tidy death* (1940)
2 *Murder's a swine* (1943)
Grinning pig

Lords of Dus series
Watt-Evans, Lawrence
1 *Lure of the basilisk* (1980)
2 *Seven altars of Dusarra* (1981)
3 *Sword of Bheleu* (1983)
4 *Book of silence* (1984)

Lorelei Lee and Dorothy series
Loos, Anita
1 *Gentlemen prefer blondes* (1925)
The illuminating diary of a prefessional lady
2 *But gentlemen marry brunettes* (1925)
Short stories
Omnibus volume entitled *Fate keeps on happening, adventures of Lorelie Lee, and other writings*, 1984

Loremasters of Elundium trilogy
Jefferies, Mike
1 *Road to Underfall* (1986)
2 *Palace of kings* (1987)
3 *Shadowlight* (1988)

Loren Mensing series
Nevins, Francis Michael
1 *Publish and perish* (1975)
2 *Corrupt and ensnare* (1978)
3 *One hundred and twenty hour clock* (1986)
4 *Ninety million dollar mouse* (1987)

Loren Swift series
Hornig, Doug
1 *Foul shot* (1984)
2 *Hardball* (1985)
3 *Dark side* (1986)
4 *Deep dive* (1988)

Lorenny family series
Chauncy, Nan
1 *Tiger in the bush* (1957)
2 *Devils' Hill* (1958)
3 *Roaring forty* (1963)

Loretta Lawson series
Smith, Joan Mary
1 *Masculine ending* (1988)
2 *Why aren't they screaming* (1989)
3 *Don't leave me this way* (1991)
4 *What men say* (1993)

Lori Adams series
Palmer, Bernard
1 *Lori Adams and the Old Carter House mystery* (1969)
2 *Lori Adams and the adopted rebel* (1971)
3 *Lori Adams and the river boat mystery* (1971)
4 *Lori Adams and the jungle search* (1974)

Lorimer family series
Melville, Anne
1 *Lorimer line* (1977)
2 *Lorimer legacy* (1979)
Alexa
3 *Lorimers at war* (1980)
4 *Lorimers in love* (1981)
Numbers 3 and 4 also published in one volume entitled *Blaize*, 1981
5 *Last of the Lorimers* (1983)
6 *Lorimer loyalties* (1984)
Numbers 5 and 6 also published in one volume entitled *Family fortunes*, 1984

Lorimer Lane series
Wells, Carolyn
1 *More lives than one* (1924)
2 *Fourteenth key* (1924)

Lorimer series
Standish, Winn
see **Captain Jack Lorimer series**
Stuart, Ian
see **Graham Lorimer series**

Loring series
Doyle, Arthur Conan
see **English bowmen series**
Kincade, Wynn
see **Vicky Loring series**

Lorings series
Courtney, Gwendoline
see **Wild Lorings series**

Lorme family series
Cradock, Fanny
1 *Lormes of Castle Rising* (1975)
2 *Shadows over Castle Rising* (1976)
3 *War comes to Castle Rising* (1977)
4 *Wind of change at Castle Rising* (1978)
5 *Uneasy peace at Castle Rising* (1979)
6 *Thunder over Castle Rising* (1980)
7 *Gathering clouds at Castle Rising* (1981)
8 *Fateful years at Castle Rising* (1982)
9 *Defence of Castle Rising* (1984)
10 *Loneliness of Castle Rising* (1986)

Lorna Donahue series
Hill, Katharine
1 *Dear dead mother-in-law* (1944)
Case of the absent corpse
2 *Case for equity* (1945)

Lorna Doone series
Blackmore, Richard Doddridge
1 *Lorna Doone* (1869)
A romance of Exmoor
2 *Slain by the Doones, and other stories* (1895)
Tales from the telling-house

Lorna Doria and Donna Miro series
Graham, Heather
see **Donna Miro and Lorna Doria series**

Lorna series
Brent-Dyer, Elinor Mary
1 *Lorna at Wynyards* (1947)
2 *Stepsisters for Lorna* (1948)

Lorraine and John series
Zindel, Paul
see **Pigman series**

Lorrington King series
Johns, William Earl
see **Gimlet series**

Lorry series
Hornibrook, Isabel
see **Pemrose Lorry series**

Los Angeles quartet
Ellroy, James
1 *Black dahlia* (1987)
2 *Big nowhere* (1988)
3 *L.A. confidential* (1990)
4 *White jazz* (1992)

Losers and winners series
Miller, Frances Abbott
1 *Aren't you the one who?* (1983)
2 *Losers and winners* (1986)

Loss of Eden trilogy
Masters, John
1 *Now, God be thanked* (1979)
2 *Heart of war* (1980)
3 *By the green of the spring* (1981)

Lost Cabin Mine series
Niven, Frederick
1 *Lost Cabin Mine* (1908)
2 *Hands up!* (1913)

Lost continent series
Tucci, Niccolo
see **Those of the lost continent series**

Lost in space files series
Peel, John
1 *War of the robots* (1986)
2 *Island in the sky* (1987)
3 *Rocket to earth* (1987)
4 *Wild adventure* (1987)
One volume edition entitled *The lost in space files*, 1987; companion volumes: *Lost in space technical manual*, by Richard R Messmann and James Van Hise, 1986, *Lost in space 25th anniversary tribute book*, by James Van Hise, 1990, *Lost in space tribute book*, by James Van Hise, 1990

Lost Island series
Coleman, Clay
1 *Escape from Lost Island* (1990)
2 *Attack!* (1990)
3 *Mutiny!* (1991)
4 *Rediscovered!* (1991)
5 *Revenge!* (1991)
6 *Escape!* (1991)

Lost lands trilogy
Estes, Rose
see **Saga of lost lands trilogy**

Lost paradise series
Chotzinoff, Samuel
Reminiscences
1 *Lost paradise* (1955)
2 *Days at the morn* (1965)

Lost planet series
Macvicar, Angus
see **Jeremy Grant series**

Lost regiment series
Forstchen, William R
1 *Rally cry* (1990)
2 *Union forever* (1991)
3 *Terrible swift sword* (1992)
4 *Fateful lightning* (1993)

Lost series
Larsen, Anita
1 *Lost, and never found* (1984)
2 *Lost, and never found II* (1991)

Lott series
Wade, Henry
see **Inspector Lott series**

Lotus flower series
Morgan de Groot, J
1 *Lotus flower* (1898)
2 *Even if* (1899)

Lou Anderson series
Murray, William Buckley
1 *Tip on a dead crab* (1984)
2 *Hard knocker's luck* (1985)
3 *I'm getting killed right here* (1991)
4 *We're off to see the killer* (1993)
5 *Now you see her, now you don't* (1994)

Lou Largo series
Ard, William
1 *All I can get* (1959)
2 *Like ice she was* (1960)
Numbers 3-5 by John Jakes using the pseudonym William Ard
3 *Make mine Mavis* (1961)
4 *And so to bed* (1962)
5 *Give me this woman* (1962)

Louanne Pig series
Carlson, Nancy
1 *Louanne Pig in the perfect family* (1986)
2 *Louanne Pig in making the team* (1986)
3 *Louanne Pig in Witch Lady* (1986)
4 *Louanne Pig in the talent show* (1986)
5 *Louanne Pig in the mysterious valentine* (1986)

Loudmouth George series
Carlson, Nancy
1 *Loudmouth George and the fishing trip* (1983)
2 *Loudmouth George and the cornet* (1983)
3 *Loudmouth George and the big race* (1983)
4 *Loudmouth George and the new neighbors* (1983)
5 *Loudmouth George and the sixth-grade bully* (1983)

Louie Maude series
Sherman, Helen
1 *Louie Maude* (1924)
2 *Roly Poly family* (1924)
3 *Louie Maude and the caravan* (1925)
4 *Louie Maude and the Mary Ann* (1927)

Louie series
Douglas, Carole Nelson
see **Midnight Louie series**

Louie series
Hildick, Edmund Wallace
1 *Louie's lot* (1965)
2 *Louie's S.O.S.* (1968)
3 *Louie's snowstorm* (1974)
4 *Louie's ransom* (1978)

Louie series
Keats, Ezra Jack
1 *Louie* (1975)
2 *Trip* (1978)
3 *Louie's search* (1980)

Louis Luther King series
Rosenberger, Joseph
see **Murder Master series**

Louis series
Russell, Enid Sherry
see **Ben Louis series**

Louis Solden series
Turner, Bill
see **Detective Inspector Manson series**

Louis XIV series
Lewis, Warren Hamilton
1 *Splendid century* (1953)
Some aspects of French life in the reign of Louis XIV
2 *Sunset of the splendid century* (1955)
The life and times of Louis Auguste de Bourbon, Duc du Maine, 1670-1736

Louis XIV series
Pell, Sylvia
1 *Shadow of the sun* (1978)
Based on the life of Francoise, Marquise of Maintenon
2 *Sun princess* (1979)
Based on the life of Marie-Anne, daughter of Louis XIV

Louis XV trilogy
Plaidy, Jean
1 *Flaunting extravagant queen* (1957)
2 *Louis the Well-Beloved* (1959)
3 *Road to Compiegne* (1959)

Louisa Elliot series
Roberts, Ann Victoria
1 *Louisa Elliot* (1989)
2 *Liam's story* (1991)

Louisa series
Cates, Emily
see **Haunting with Louisa series**

Louise series
Pfanner, Louise
1 *Louise builds a house* (1987)
2 *Louise builds a boat* (1989)

Louise trilogy
Glover, Halcott
1 *Both sides of the blanket* (1945)
2 *Louise and Mister Tudor* (1946)
3 *Louise in London* (1947)

Louise trilogy
Shears, Sarah
1 *Louise* (1976)
2 *Louise's daughters* (1976)
3 *Louise's inheritance* (1977)

Louisiana series
Lowe, Myra
1 *Bayou moon* (1988)
2 *Creole moon* (1988)

Louisiana trilogy
Bristow, Gwen
1 *Deep summer* (1937)
2 *Handsome road* (1938)
3 *This side of glory* (1940)
One volume edition entitled *The plantation trilogy*, 1962

Lourette Hawkins series
Hunter, Kristin
1 *Soul brothers and Sister Lou* (1968)
2 *Lou in the limelight* (1981)

Love among the artists trilogy
Goldring, Douglas
1 *Nobody knows* (1923)
2 *Cuckoo* (1925)
A comedy of adjustments
3 *Facade* (1927)

Love and exile trilogy
Singer, Isaac Bashevis
Autobiography
1 *Little boy in search of God* (1976)
Mysticism in personal light
2 *Young man in search of love* (1978)
3 *Lost in America* (1981)
One volume edition entitled *Love and exile, the early years*, 1984; companion volumes: *In my father's court*, 1956, *A day of pleasure, stories of a boy growing up in Warsaw*, 1976

Love and life series
McGloin, Joseph Thaddeus
1 *Learn a little!* (1961)
Alternative title: What's life all about?
2 *Yearn a little* (1961)
Alternative title: Why did God come up with two sexes?
3 *Burn a little* (1961)
Alternative title: What's love all about?

Love diary series
Wyndham, Joan
1 *Love lessons* (1985)
A wartime diary
2 *Love is blue* (1986)
A wartime diary
3 *Anything once* (1992)

Love Lane series
Snaith, John Collis
1 *Love Lane* (1919)
2 *Council of Seven* (1921)

Love on the Don series
Konsalik, Heinz Gunther
1 *Deep waters* (1970)
Original edition entitled *Liebe am Don*, part 1
2 *Against the tide* (1970)
Original edition entitled *Liebe am Don*, part 2
One volume edition entitled *Love on the Don*, 1980

Love respelt series
Graves, Robert
Poems
1 *Love respelt* (1965)
2 *Colophon to Love respelt* (1967)
3 *Love respelt again* (1969)

Love series
Baxt, George
see **Pharaoh Love series**

Love series
Leasor, James
see **Doctor Jason Love series**
Mann, Mary E
see **Ronald Love series**

Love series
Pascal, Francine
1 *My first love and other disasters* (1979)
2 *Love and betrayal and hold the mayo!* (1985)

Love series
Spencer, Colin
see **Simpson family series**

Love so bold series
Kamada, Annelise
1 *Love so bold* (1978)
2 *Richer than a crown* (1968)

Love trilogy
Galsworthy, John
1 *Dark flower* (1913)
2 *Beyond* (1917)
3 *Saint's progress* (1919)

Love trilogy
Hayes, Alfred
1 *In love* (1953)
2 *My face for the world to see* (1958)
3 *Temptation of Don Volpi* (1960)

Love trilogy
Mitford, Nancy
1 *Pursuit of love* (1945)
2 *Love in a cold climate* (1949)
3 *Don't tell Alfred* (1960)

Love trilogy
Pascal, Francine
1 *Loving* (1986)
2 *Love lost* (1986)
3 *True love* (1986)

Love trilogy
Quick, Larry
1 *Unconditionally yours* (1989)
2 *Listen to me with love* (1989)
3 *Share your heart* (1990)

Lovejoy series
Gash, Jonathan
1 *Judas pair* (1977)
2 *Gold from Gemini* (1978)
Gold by Gemini
3 *Grail Tree* (1979)
4 *Spend game* (1980)
5 *Vatican rip* (1981)
6 *Firefly gadroon* (1982)
7 *Sleepers of Erin* (1983)
8 *Gondola scam* (1983)
9 *Pearlhanger* (1985)
10 *Tartan ringers* (1986)
Tartan sell
11 *Moonspender* (1986)
12 *Jade woman* (1988)
13 *Very last gambado* (1989)
14 *Great California game* (1990)
15 *Lies of fair ladies* (1992)
16 *Paid and loving eyes* (1993)
17 *Sin within her smile* (1993)

Lovel series
Currington, Owen Josiah
see **Jack Lovel series**

Lovelace and Valentine series
Aldyne, Nathan
see **Dan Valentine and Clarissa Lovelace series**

Lovelace series
Perkins, D M
see **Linda Lovelace series**

Loveland series
Williamson, Charles Norris
see **Lord and Lady Loveland series**

Loveleaves series
O'Harris, Pixie
1 *Loveleaves the koala* (1985)
2 *Loveleaves returns to the bush* (1988)

Lovell family series
Palmer, Martin
1 *White Boar* (1968)
2 *Wrong Plantagenet* (1972)

Lovells trilogy
Morrison, Emmeline
1 *Last of the Lovells* (1928)
2 *Countisbury* (1933)
A romance of south Devon
3 *Open secret* (1939)

Lover boy series
Berenstain, Stan
1 *Lover boy* (1958)
2 *Bedside lover boy* (1960)
3 *Office lover boy* (1962)

Lovers of Steadford Abbey series
Allen, Sheila Rosalynd
1 *Reluctant ghost* (1989)
2 *Meddlesome ghost* (1989)
3 *Helpful ghost* (1990)
4 *Passionate ghost* (1991)

Loves of Angela Carlyle series
Du Barry, Michele
see **Angela Carlyle series**

Loves of Carola Mountjoy series
Montague, Jeanne
1 *Brave wild heart* (1987)
2 *Power of love* (1987)
3 *Vengeance is mine* (1987)
4 *Sword of honour* (1987)

Lovesong series
Sherwood, Valerie
1 *Beauty and the English lord* (1987)
2 *Beauty and the buccaneer* (1987)

Lovett series
Arthur, Burt
see **Dan Lovett series**

Lovice Clive series
Morrison, Emmeline
1 *There was a veil* (1923)
2 *There lived a lady* (1925)

Lovick series
Wilson, Gertrude Mary
see **Inspector Lovick series**

Low company series
Benney, Mark
Autobiography
1 *Low company* (1936)
Evolution of a burglar
2 *Scapegoat dances* (1938)
3 *Almost a gentleman* (1966)

Low series
Cecil, Henry
see **Ambrose Low series**

Lowe series
Ormerod, Roger
see **Philipa Lowe series**
Verner, Gerald
see **Trevor Lowe series**

Lowell series
Merritt, Abraham
see **Doctor Lowell series**

Lowenskolds trilogy
Lagerlof, Selma
see **Ring of the Lowenskolds trilogy**

Lower view series
O'Connor, Philip
1 *Memoirs of a public baby* (1958)
2 *Lower view* (1960)
3 *Living in Croesor* (1962)

Lowly Worm series
Scarry, Richard
1 *Richard Scarry's Lowly Worm storybook* (1977)
2 *Richard Scarry's Lowly Worm sniffy book* (1978)
3 *Richard Scarry's Lowly Worm word book* (1981)
4 *Lowly Worm coloring book* (1983)
5 *Lowly Worm cars and trucks book* (1983)
6 *Richard Scarry's Lowly Worm bath book* (1984)
7 *Richard Scarry's Lowly Worm schoolbag* (1987)

Lowry series
Bacon, Josephine Dodge
1 *Luck of Lowry* (1931)
2 *Kathy* (1934)

Lowspeak series
Morton, James
1 *Lowspeak* (1989)
2 *Lowspeak 2* (1991)

Loyalty trilogy
Clifford, Francis
1 *All men are lonely now* (1967)
Set in England
2 *Blind side* (1971)
Set in Biafra
3 *Amigo, amigo* (1973)
Set in Guatemala

Lu Silk series
Chase, James Hadley
1 *Believed violent* (1968)
2 *Whiff of money* (1969)

Luann series
Evans, Greg
Comic strips
1 *Meet Luann* (1986)
2 *Why me?* (1986)
3 *Is it Friday yet?* (1987)
4 *Who invented brothers anyway?* (1989)
5 *School and other problems* (1989)
6 *Homework is ruining my life* (1989)
7 *So many malls* (1990)
8 *Pizza isn't everything but is comes close* (1991)
9 *Dear diary, the following is top secret* (1991)
10 *Will we be tested on this?* (1992)
11 *There's nothing worse than first period P.E.* (1992)
12 *If confusion were a class I'd get an A* (1992)
13 *Schools OK if you can stand the food* (1992)
14 *I'm not always confused, I just look that way* (1993)
15 *My bedroom and other environmental hazards* (1993)

Lucas Davenport series
Sandford, John
1 *Rules of prey* (1989)
2 *Shadow prey* (1990)
3 *Eyes of prey* (1991)
4 *Silent prey* (1992)
5 *Winter prey* (1992)
6 *Night prey* (1994)

Lucas Hallam series
Washburn, Livia Jane
1 *Wild night* (1987)
2 *Dead-stick* (1989)
3 *Dog heavies* (1990)

Luccan series
Morland, Nigel
see **Detective Inspector Rory Luccan series**

Lucia Billson series
This sequence has two authors
Benson, Edward Frederic
1 *Queen Lucia* (1920)
2 *Lucia in London* (1927)
3 *Miss Mapp* (1922)
4 *Male impersonator* (1929)
5 *Mapp and Lucia* (1931)
6 *Lucia's progress* (1935)
Worshipful Lucia
7 *Trouble for Lucia* (1939)
Holt, Tom
8 *Lucia in wartime* (1985)
9 *Lucia triumphant* (1986)

Lucia series
Robinson, Mabel Louise
see **Little Lucia series**

Lucian Carolus series
Ascher, Eugene
1 *There were no asper ladies* (1944)
To kill a corpse
2 *Uncanny adventures* (1944)
Short stories
3 *Grim caretaker* (1944)

Lucias series
Howes, Royce
see **Captain Ben Lucias series**

Lucien Clay series
Gore-Browne, Robert
1 *Murder of an MP* (1927)
2 *Death on delivery* (1929)
By way of confession

Lucien Leeuwen series
Stendhal
Original edition in one volume
1 *Green huntsman* (1894)
2 *Telegraph* (1894)

Lucifer Cove series
Coffman, Virginia
1 *Devil's mistress* (1970)
2 *Priestess of the damned* (1970)
3 *Devil's virgin* (1971)
4 *Masque of Satan* (1971)
5 *Chalet diabolique* (1971)
Chalet of the devil
6 *From Satan, with love* (1971)

Lucifram series
Allonby, Edith
Originally published anonymously
1 *Jewel sowers* (1903)
2 *Marigold* (1905)

Lucija and Rosie series
Ebejer, Francis
1 *Wreath for the innocents* (1958)
Wreath for the Maltese innocents
2 *Wild spell of summer* (1960)
Evil of the king cockroach

Lucilla Eliot trilogy
Goudge, Elizabeth
see **Eliot family trilogy**

Lucille series
Duffield, Elizabeth M
1 *Lucille, the torch bearer* (1915)
2 *Lucille triumphant* (1916)
3 *Lucille, bringer of joy* (1917)
4 *Lucille on the heights* (1918)

Lucinda series
Fry, Rosalie Kingsmill
1 *Lucinda and the painted bell* (1956)
Bell for Ringelblume
2 *Lucinda and the sailor kitten* (1958)
Matelot, little sailor of Brittany
3 *Fly home, Columbina* (1960)

Lucinda Wyman series
Sawyer, Ruth
1 *Roller skates* (1936)
2 *Year of Jubilo* (1940)
Lucinda's year of Jubilo

Lucius Hunt series
Wellard, James
1 *Snake in the grass* (1942)
2 *Moment in time* (1947)
Spotlight on murder

Lucius Leffing series
Brennan, Joseph Payne
Short stories
1 *Casebook of Lucius Leffing* (1973)
2 *Chronicles of Lucius Leffing* (1977)
3 *Act of providence* (1979)
Co-author: Donald M Grant
4 *Adventures of Lucius Leffing* (1990)

Luck and pluck series
Alger, Horatio
1 *Luck and pluck* (1869)
Alternative title: John Oakley's inheritance
2 *Sink or swim* (1870)
Alternative title: Harry Raymond's resolve
3 *Strong and steady* (1871)
Alternative title: Paddle your own canoe
4 *Strive and succeed* (1872)
Alternative title: The progress of Walter Conrad
5 *Try and trust* (1873)
Alternative title: The story of a bound boy
6 *Bound to rise* (1873)
Alternative title: Up the ladder
7 *Risen from the ranks* (1874)
Alternative title: Harry Walton's success
8 *Herbert Carter's legacy* (1875)
Alternative title: The inventor's son

Luck series
Bond, Geoffrey
see **Sergeant Luck series**
Marsh, John
see **Simon Luck series**

Luckett trilogy
Richter, Conrad
see **American pioneer trilogy**

Luckhurst series
Wainwright, John
see **Lucky Luckhurst series**

Luckraft series
Rees, Arthur John
see **Inspector Luckraft series**

Lucky and Rainbow series
Abbott, Jacob
see **Rainbow and Lucky series**

Lucky country series
Horne, Donald
1 *Lucky country* (1964)
Revised edition 1971; social and political studies of Australia
2 *Death of the lucky country* (1976)
3 *Lucky country revisited* (1987)

Lucky dip series
Ainsworth, Ruth
Selections of stories and verses
1 *Lucky dip* (1961)
2 *Another lucky dip* (1973)

Lucky Harry series
Ridgway, Bill
1 *Lucky Harry* (1985)
2 *Lucky Harry takes his time, and other stories* (1985)

Lucky Ladd series
Hughes, Dean
1 *Lucky's crash landing* (1990)
2 *Lucky breaks loose* (1990)
3 *Lucky's gold mine* (1990)
4 *Lucky fights back* (1991)
5 *Lucky's mud festival* (1991)
6 *Lucky's tricks* (1992)
7 *Lucky the detective* (1992)
8 *Lucky's cool club* (1993)
9 *Lucky in love* (1993)

Lucky Luckhurst series
Wainwright, John
1 *Walther P.38* (1976)
2 *Do nothin' till you hear from me* (1977)

Lucky Luke series
Goscinny, Rene
Illustrated by Maurice de Bevere under the pseudonym Morris
1 *Stage coach* (1968)
Original edition entitled *La diligence*
2 *Jesse James* (1968)
Original edition entitled *Jesse James*
3 *Tenderfoot* (1968)
Original edition entitled *Tenderfoot*
4 *Dalton City* (1969)
Original edition entitled *Dalton City*
5 *Western circus* (1970)
Original edition entitled *Western circus*
6 *[L'heritage de Ran Tan Plan]* (1973)
No English edition
7 *Apache Canyon* (1977)
8 *Ma Dalton* (1980)
9 *Curing the Daltons* (1982)
Original edition entitled *Le guerison des Dalton*
10 *Dashing white cowboy* (1982)
Original edition entitled *Le cavalier blanc*

Lucky Starr series
French, Paul
see **David Starr series**

Lucky Terrell series
Cook, Canfield
1 *Spitfire pilot* (1942)
2 *Sky attack* (1942)
3 *Secret mission* (1943)
4 *Lost squadron* (1943)
5 *Springboard to Tokyo* (1943)
6 *Wings over Japan* (1944)
7 *Flying jet* (1945)
8 *Flying wing* (1946)

Lucrezia Borgia series
Plaidy, Jean
1 *Madonna of the Seven Hills* (1958)
2 *Light on Lucrezia* (1958)
One volume edition entitled *Lucrezia Borgia*, 1976

Lucy and Tom series
Hughes, Shirley
1 *Lucy and Tom's day* (1960)
2 *Lucy and Tom go to school* (1973)
3 *Lucy and Tom at the seaside* (1976)
4 *Lucy and Tom's Christmas* (1981)
Companion volumes: *Lucy and Tom's ABC*, 1984, *Lucy and Tom's 1-2-3*, 1987

Lucy Beck series
Conway, Peter
1 *Motive for revenge* (1972)
2 *Padded cell* (1973)
3 *Escape to danger* (1974)

Lucy Fountain and David Dodd series
Reade, Charles
see **David Dodd and Lucy Fountain series**

Lucy Gordon series
Havard, Aline
1 *Captain Lucy and Lieutenant Bob* (1918)
2 *Captain Lucy in France* (1919)
3 *Captain Lucy's flying ace* (1920)
4 *Captain Lucy in the home sector* (1921)

Lucy Hill series
Birch, Claire
1 *Tight spot* (1985)
2 *Collision course* (1985)
3 *Double danger* (1985)
4 *False lead* (1986)

Lucy Ramsdale series
Dolson, Hildegarde
1 *To spite her face* (1971)
2 *Dying fall* (1973)
3 *Please omit funeral* (1975)
4 *Beauty sleep* (1977)

Lucy series
Abbott, Jacob
see **Cousin Lucy series**
Blathwayt, Jean
see **Brownie series**

Lucy series
Jungman, Ann
1 *Lucy and the big bad wolf* (1986)
2 *Lucy and the wolf in sheep's clothing* (1987)
3 *Lucy keeps the wolf from the door* (1989)
Companion volume: *Lucy and the babysitter*, 1983

Lucy series
Storr, Catherine
1 *Lucy* (1961)
2 *Lucy runs away* (1962)

Lucy series
Strong, Jeremy
see **Lightning Lucy series**

Lucy series
Sykes, Pamela
1 *Come back, Lucy* (1973)
2 *Lucy, beware* (1983)

Lucy series
Sypher, Lucy Johnstone
1 *Edge of nowhere* (1972)
2 *Cousins and circuses* (1974)
3 *Spell of the Northern Lights* (1975)
4 *Turnabout year* (1976)

Lucy series
Wood, Joyce
see **Grandmother Lucy series**

Ludd trilogy
Bassett, Ronald
see **Lobby Ludd trilogy**

Ludell Wilson trilogy
Wilkinson, Brenda
1 *Ludell* (1975)
2 *Ludell and Willie* (1977)
3 *Ludell's New York time* (1980)

Ludlow and Montero series
Nash, Simon
see **Inspector Montero and Adam Ludlow series**

Ludovic Fender series
Geddes, Paul
1 *High game* (1968)
2 *November wind* (1970)
3 *State of corruption* (1985)
4 *Goliath* (1986)

Ludovic Saxon series
Cassells, John
1 *Enter the Picaroon* (1954)
2 *Avenging Picaroon* (1955)
3 *Beware, the Picaroon* (1957)
4 *Meet the Picaroon* (1957)
5 *Engaging Picaroon* (1958)
6 *Enterprising Picaroon* (1959)
7 *Salute the Picaroon* (1960)
8 *Picaroon goes west* (1962)
9 *Prey for the Picaroon* (1963)
10 *Challenge for the Picaroon* (1964)
11 *Benevolent Picaroon* (1965)
12 *Plunder for the Picaroon* (1966)
13 *Audacious Picaroon* (1967)
14 *Elusive Picaroon* (1968)
15 *Night of the Picaroon* (1969)
16 *Quest for the Picaroon* (1970)
17 *Picaroon collects* (1970)
18 *Profit for the Picaroon* (1972)
19 *Picaroon laughs last* (1973)
20 *Action for the Picaroon* (1975)
21 *Picaroon gets the run-around* (1976)

Ludovic Travers series
Bush, Christopher
1 *Plumley inheritance* (1926)
2 *Perfect murder case* (1929)
3 *Murder at Fenwold* (1930)
Death of Cosmo Revere
4 *Dead man twice* (1930)
5 *Dancing death* (1931)
6 *Dead man's music* (1931)
7 *Cut throat* (1932)
8 *Case of the unfortunate village* (1932)
9 *Case of the three strange faces* (1933)
Crank in the corner
10 *Case of the April fools* (1933)
11 *Case of the one hundred per cent alibi* (1934)
Kitchen cake murder
12 *Case of the dead shepherd* (1934)
Tea tray murders
13 *Case of the Chinese gong* (1935)
14 *Case of the Monday murders* (1936)
Murder on Mondays
15 *Case of the bonfire body* (1936)
Body in the bonfire
16 *Case of the missing minutes* (1937)
Eight o'clock alibi
17 *Case of the hanging rope* (1937)
Wedding night murder
18 *Case of the Tudor queen* (1938)
19 *Case of the leaning man* (1938)
Leaning man
20 *Case of the flying ass* (1939)
21 *Case of the green felt hat* (1939)
22 *Case of the climbing rat* (1940)
23 *Case of the murdered major* (1941)
24 *Case of the kidnapped colonel* (1942)
25 *Case of the fighting soldier* (1942)
26 *Case of the magic mirror* (1943)
27 *Case of the running mouse* (1944)
28 *Case of the platinum blonde* (1944)
29 *Case of the corporal's leave* (1945)
30 *Case of the missing men* (1946)
31 *Case of the second chance* (1946)
32 *Case of the curious client* (1947)
33 *Case of the Haven Hotel* (1948)
34 *Case of the housekeeper's hair* (1948)
35 *Case of the seven bells* (1949)
36 *Case of the purloined picture* (1949)
37 *Case of the happy warrior* (1950)
Case of the frightened mannequin
38 *Case of the corner cottage* (1951)
39 *Case of the fourth detective* (1951)
40 *Case of the happy medium* (1952)
41 *Case of the counterfeit colonel* (1952)
42 *Case of the burnt Bohemian* (1953)
43 *Case of the silken petticoat* (1953)
44 *Case of the red brunette* (1954)
45 *Case of the three lost letters* (1954)
46 *Case of the benevolent bookie* (1955)
47 *Case of the amateur actor* (1955)
48 *Case of the extra man* (1956)
49 *Case of the flowery corpse* (1956)
50 *Case of the Russian Cross* (1957)
51 *Case of the treble twist* (1958)
Case of the triple twist
52 *Case of the running man* (1958)
53 *Case of the careless thief* (1959)
54 *Case of the sapphire brooch* (1960)
55 *Case of the extra grave* (1961)
56 *Case of the dead man gone* (1961)
57 *Case of the three-ring puzzle* (1962)
58 *Case of the heavenly twin* (1963)
59 *Case of the grand alliance* (1964)
60 *Case of the jumbo sandwich* (1965)
61 *Case of the good employer* (1966)

Ludovic Travers series

62 *Case of the deadly diamonds* (1967)
63 *Case of the prodigal daughter* (1967)

Lugard series
Perham, Margery
see **Frederick Dealtry Lugard series**

Lugh the Harper series
Finney, Patricia
1 *Shadow of gulls* (1977)
2 *Crow goddess* (1978)

Luis Bernal series
Serafin, David
see **Superintendent Luis Bernal series**

Luis Mendoza series
Shannon, Dell
see **Lieutenant Luis Mendoza series**

Luis Montez series
Ramos, Manuel
1 *Ballad of Rocky Ruiz* (1993)
Alternative title: Death of a martyr
2 *Ballad of Gato Guerrero* (1994)

Luke Bradley series
Pentecost, Hugh
1 *Cancelled in red* (1939)
2 *Twenty fourth horse* (1940)
3 *I'll sing at your funeral* (1942)
4 *Brass chills* (1943)
Also one novelette featuring Bradley in *Memory of murder*, 1947

Luke Coldiron series
Parker, F M
1 *Coldiron* (1984)
2 *Shadow of the wolf* (1985)
3 *Shanghaiers* (1987)

Luke Dunlop series
Corris, Peter
1 *Set up* (1992)
2 *Cross off* (1993)

Luke of Winchester trilogy
Christopher, John
see **Prince trilogy**

Luke series
Duncan, Norman
see **Doctor Luke series**
Goscinny, Rene
see **Lucky Luke series**

Luke Skywalker series
This sequence has five authors
Lucas, George
1 *Star wars* (1976)
Foster, Alan Dean
2 *Splinter of the mind's eye* (1978)
Daley, Brian
3 *Han Solo at Stars' End* (1979)
4 *Han Solo's revenge* (1979)
Glut, Donald Frank
5 *Empire strikes back* (1980)
Daley, Brian
6 *Han Solo and the lost legacy* (1980)
Kahn, James
7 *Return of the Jedi* (1983)
Numbers 1, 5, 7 also published in one volume entitled *The star wars trilogy*, 1987
Companion volumes: *The art of The Empire strikes back*, by Vic Bulluck and Valerie Hoffman, 1980, *Star wars, the roleplaying games*, by Greg Costikyan, 1987; parodies: *Space nymph*, by Dustin Lasser, 1980, also published as *Orgy in orbit*, by Traves Tea, *Star wreck, the generation gap, the spacy spoof that dares to boldly go where nobody wanted to go before*, by Leah Rewolinski, 1989

Luke Speare and Schyler Cole series
Davis, Frederick Clyde
see **Schyler Cole and Luke Speare series**

Luke Starbuck series
Braun, Matt
1 *Hangman's Creek* (1979)
2 *Jury of six* (1980)
3 *Tombstone* (1981)
4 *Spoilers* (1981)
5 *Manhunter* (1981)
6 *Deadwood* (1981)
7 *Judas tree* (1982)

Luke Sutton series
Kelley, Leo Patrick
1 *Luke Sutton, outlaw* (1981)
2 *Luke Sutton, gunfighter* (1982)
3 *Luke Sutton, Indian fighter* (1983)
4 *Luke Sutton, avenger* (1983)
5 *Luke Sutton, outrider* (1984)
6 *Luke Sutton, bounty hunter* (1985)
7 *Luke Sutton, hired gun* (1987)
8 *Luke Sutton, lawman* (1989)
9 *Luke Sutton, mustanger* (1990)

Luke Thanet series
Simpson, Dorothy
see **Inspector Luke Thanet series**

Luke Wyatt series
Skinner, Mike
1 *Remington forty four* (1966)
2 *Ride into hell* (1982)
3 *Raiders of Spanish Creek* (1982)
4 *Rough time in Dobie* (1983)

Lulu and Kitty series
Mathews, Joanna Hooe
see **Kitty and Lulu series**

Lulu series
Henderson, Marge
see **Little Lulu series**

Lulu series
O'Connor, Jane
1 *Lulu and the witch baby* (1986)
2 *Lulu goes to witch school* (1987)

Lulu series
Springstubb, Tricia
1 *With a name like Lulu, who needs more trouble?* (1989)
2 *Lulu versus love* (1990)

Lumb and Marsham series
Cross, Laurence
see **Tommy Lumb and Peter Marsham series**

Lumbering trilogy
White, Stewart Edward
1 *Blazed trail* (1902)
2 *Riverman* (1908)
3 *Rules of the game* (1910)
Companion volume: Blazed trail stories, 1904

Lumsden series
Saltmarsh, Max
see **Archie Lumsden series**

Lunar One series
Townsend, John
1 *Rocket-ship saboteurs* (1959)
2 *Warning to earth* (1960)
3 *Secret of Puffin Island* (1962)

Lunatic series
Clouston, Joseph Storer
see **Mister Francis Mandell-Essington series**

Lunch series
Hansen, Derek
1 *Lunch with the generals* (1993)
2 *Lunch with Mussolini* (1994)

Lunchroom series
Hodgman, Ann
1 *Night of a thousand pizzas* (1990)
2 *Frog punch* (1990)
3 *Cokkie caper* (1990)
4 *French fried aliens* (1990)
5 *Rubberband stew* (1990)
6 *Flying popcorn experiment* (1990)
7 *Invasion of the fast food* (1990)
8 *Space food* (1990)
9 *Day of the monster planet* (1991)
10 *Mutant garbage* (1991)

Lund series
Tralins, Sandor Robert
see **Jack Lund series**
Wallis, Ruth Sawtell
see **Eric Lund series**

Lunda series
Saxby, Jessie Margaret Edmonston
see **Shetland series**

Lundberg and King series
Saunders, Lawrence
see **Wylie King and Nels Lundberg series**

Lundstrom and Brandon series
Peters, Bryan
see **Brandon and Lundstrom series**

Lunn series
Cooper, William
see **Scenes from life series**

Lunns of Annerley Junction series
Lunn, Hugh
1 *Over the top with Jim* (1990)
2 *Fred and Olive's blessed lino* (1993)
3 *Head over heels* (1992)
4 *Vietnam, reporter's war* (1985)

Lunt and Dunbar series
Shirreffs, Gordon Donald
see **Bob Dunbar and Gary Lunt series**

Lupin series
Leblanc, Maurice
see **Arsene Lupin series**

Luren series
Lichtenberg, Jacqueline
1 *Those of my blood* (1988)
2 *Dreamspy* (1989)

LUST series
Gray, Rod
see **Lady from L.U.S.T. series**

Lute series
Wood, Bridget
1 *Minstrel's lute* (1987)
2 *Satanic lute* (1987)

Lute trilogy
Macavoy, Roberta Ann
1 *Damiano* (1984)
2 *Damiano's lute* (1984)
3 *Raphael* (1984)
One volume edition entitled *A trio for Lute*, 1985

Luther Bastion series
Holt, Gavin
see **Professor Luther Bastion series**

Luther family series
Cleaver, Vera
1 *Where the lilies bloom* (1969)
2 *Trial valley* (1977)

Luther series
Lanham, Edwin
see **Frank Luther series**

Lutie and Amanda Beagle series
Chanslor, Torrey
1 *Our first murder* (1940)
2 *Our second murder* (1941)

Luvvy Savage series
Carlson, Natalie Savage
1 *Half sisters* (1970)
2 *Luvvy and the girls* (1971)

Luxembourg series
Trevor, Meriol
1 *Fugitives* (1973)
2 *Marked man* (1974)
3 *Enemy at home* (1974)
4 *Forgotten country* (1975)
5 *Treacherous paths* (1976)
6 *Civil prisoners* (1977)
7 *Fortunes of peace* (1978)
8 *Wanton fires* (1979)

Lydford Long series
Carstairs, Henry
1 *Harpinger's hunch* (1943)
2 *Drifting death* (1944)
3 *Black burying* (1945)
4 *Secretary of state for death* (1946)
5 *Cruel dart* (1947)
6 *Blood, m'lud* (1948)
7 *Who lies bleeding?* (1949)
8 *Blackdrop Hall* (1950)
9 *Lying down below* (1951)
10 *Oh, no, you don't* (1952)
11 *When three makes two* (1953)
12 *Death's duet* (1954)
13 *Winston Street mystery* (1955)

Lydie and Jeannot series
Danoen, Emile
see **Jeannot and Lydie series**

Lydis series
Norton, Andre
see **Krip Vorland series**

Lydney series
Fox, Sebastian
see **George Lydney series**

Lyle Curtis and Susan Yates series
Fetta, Emma Lou
1 *Murder in style* (1939)
2 *Murder on the face of it* (1940)

Lyle series
Crabb, Arthur
see **Samuel Lyle series**

Lyle series
Waber, Bernard
1 *House on East Eighty Eighth Street* (1962)
Welcome, Lyle
2 *Lyle, Lyle, crocodile* (1965)
3 *Lyle and the birthday party* (1966)
4 *Lovable Lyle* (1969)
5 *Lyle finds his mother* (1974)

Lyle series
Wainwright, John
see **Inspector Lyle series**

Lynch and Deane series
Vandercook, John Womack
see **Bertram Lynch and Robert Deane series**

Lyndon series
Thackeray, William Makepeace
see **Barry Lyndon series**

Lynette and Jeremy series
Adler, Carole Schwerdtfeger
see **Glits series**

Lynley and Havers series
George, Elizabeth
see **Inspector Thomas Lynley and Sergeant Barbara Havers series**

Lynn and Kate series
Reid, Meta Mayne
see **Kate and lynn series**

Lynn Macdonald series
Strahan, Kay Cleaver
1 *Desert moon mystery* (1928)
2 *Footprints* (1929)
3 *Death traps* (1930)
4 *October House* (1931)
5 *Meriweather* (1932)
6 *Hobgoblin murder* (1934)
7 *Desert lake mystery* (1936)

Lynton Hall series
Mills, Glynn
1 *They came to camp* (1956)
2 *Christmas at Lynton Hall* (1958)

Lynx series
Orde, A J
see **Jason Lynx series**
Vigilant
see **Barry Link series**

Lyon and Bea Wentworth series
Forrest, Richard
1 *Child's garden of death* (1975)
2 *Wizard of death* (1977)
3 *Death through the looking glass* (1978)
4 *Death in the willows* (1979)
5 *Death at Yew Corner* (1981)
6 *Death under the lilacs* (1985)
7 *Death on the Mississippi* (1989)

Lyon series
Winn, Patrick
see **Inspector Lyon series**

Lyonesse series
Swithin, Antony
see **Perilous quest for Lyonesse series**

Lyonesse series
Vance, Jack
1 *Suldrun's garden* (1983)
2 *Green pearl* (1985)
3 *Madouc* (1989)

Lyons series
Anthony, Elizabeth
see **Pauline Lyons series**
Stivers, Dick
see **Able Team series**

Lyra trilogy
Wrede, Patricia Collins
1 *Shadow magic* (1982)
2 *Daughter of witches* (1983)
3 *Caught in crystal* (1987)

Lyson series
Oppenheim, Edward Phillips
see **Major Charles Lyson series**

Lytton Strachey series
Holroyd, Michael
1 *Lytton Strachey, the unknown years, 1880-1910* (1967)
Lytton Strachey
The second title is a revised edition
2 *Lytton Strachey, the years of achievement, 1910-1932* (1968)
Lytton Strachey and the Bloomsbury Group, his work, their influence
The second title is a revised edition

Lyveden series
Yates, Dornford
see **Anthony Lyveden series**

M

M and M series
Ross, Pat
1 *Meet M and M* (1980)
2 *M and M and the haunted house* (1980)
3 *M and M and the big bag* (1981)
4 *M and M and the bad news babies* (1983)
5 *M and M and the mummy mess* (1985)
6 *M and M and the Santa secrets* (1985)
7 *M and M and the superchild afternoon* (1987)

M.A.S.H. series
Hooker, Richard
1 *M.A.S.H.* (1968)
2 *M.A.S.H. goes to Maine* (1971)
3 *M.A.S.H. goes to Paris* (1974)
4 *M.A.S.H. goes to New Orleans* (1975)
5 *M.A.S.H. goes to Morocco* (1975)
6 *M.A.S.H. goes to London* (1975)
7 *M.A.S.H. goes to Las Vegas* (1976)
8 *M.A.S.H. goes to Hollywood* (1976)
9 *M.A.S.H. goes to Vienna* (1976)
10 *M.A.S.H. goes to Miami* (1976)
11 *M.A.S.H. goes to San Francisco* (1976)
12 *M.A.S.H. goes to Texas* (1977)
13 *M.A.S.H. mania* (1977)
14 *M.A.S.H. goes to Moscow* (1977)
15 *M.A.S.H. goes to Montreal* (1977)

M.I.A. Hunter series
Buchanan, Jack
1 *M.I.A. Hunter* (1986)
2 *Cambodian hell-hole* (1986)
3 *Hanoi deathgrip* (1986)
4 *Mountain massacre* (1986)
5 *Exodus from hell* (1986)
6 *Blood storm* (1986)
7 *Saigon slaughter* (1987)
8 *Escape from Nicaragua* (1987)
9 *Invasion U.S.S.R.* (1988)
10 *Miami war zone* (1988)
11 *Crossfire kill* (1989)
12 *Desert death raid* (1989)
13 *L.A. gang war* (1990)
14 *Back to Nam* (1990)
15 *Heavy fire* (1991)
16 *China strike* (1991)

Ma and pa series
Abarbanell, Jacob Ralph
see **Pa and ma series**

Ma and pa series
Lindsay, Rose
Reminiscences
1 *Ma and pa* (1963)
2 *Model wife* (1967)

Maasten series
Sela, Owen
see **Nicholas Maasten series**

Mabel series
Cooper, Jilly
see **Little Mabel series**

Mabinogion series
Walton, Evangeline
1 *Prince of Annwn* (1974)
The first branch
2 *Children of Llyr* (1971)
The second branch
3 *Song of Rhiannon* (1972)
The third branch
4 *Virgin and the swine* (1936)
Island of the mighty
The fourth branch

Mable series
Streeter, Edward
1 *Dere Mable* (1918)
Love letters of a rookie
2 *That's me all over, Mable* (1919)
3 *Same ole Bill, eh, Mable!* (1919)
4 *As you were Bill!* (1920)

Mac Fal series
Taylor, Keith
see **Bard series**

Mac McIntyre series
Corne, Molly E
1 *Death at a masquerade* (1938)
Death is no lady
2 *Death at the manor* (1938)
Death hides a mask
3 *Magnet for murder* (1939)
Jealousy pulls the trigger

Mac series
Barry, Margaret Stuart
see **Tommy Mac series**
Dewey, Thomas Blanchard
see **Private Eye Mac series**
Jungman, Ann
see **Big Mac series**

Mac Slade series
Blumenthal, John
1 *Case of the hardboiled dicks* (1985)
2 *Tinseltown murders* (1985)

Mac Wingate series
Swift, Bryan
1 *Mission code, symbol* (1981)
2 *Mission code, king's pawn* (1981)
3 *Mission code, minotaur* (1981)
4 *Mission code, granite island* (1981)
5 *Mission code, springboard* (1982)
6 *Mission code, snow queen* (1982)
7 *Mission code, Acropolis* (1982)
Co-author: Arthur Wise
8 *Mission code, volcano* (1982)
9 *Mission code, track and destroy* (1982)
10 *Mission code, scorpion* (1982)
11 *Mission code, survival* (1982)

Macadam and West series
Campbell, Alice
see **Geoffrey Macadam and Catherine West series**

Macadam series
Duff, Douglas Valder
see **Adam Macadam series**

McAdden series
Leader, Charles
see **Rick McAdden series**

Macalastair series
Dick, Alexandra
see **Alastair Macalastair series**

MacAlistaire series
Messner-Loebs, William
see **Wolverine MacAlister series**

Macalister children series
Pardoe, Margot
1 *Argle's mist* (1956)
Curtain of mist
2 *Argle's causeway* (1958)
3 *Argle's oracle* (1959)

MacAlister series
Bland, Eleanor Taylor
see **Marti MacAlister series**

Macall series
Fairlie, Gerard
see **Johnny Macall series**

McAllister series
Chisholm, Matt
see **Rem McAllister series**

Macallister series
Coram, Christopher
see **Ross Macallister series**

McAllister series
Hayes, Daniel
see **Tyler McAllister series**

Macallister series
Perry, Ritchie
1 *Macallister* (1984)
2 *Presumed dead* (1987)

McAlpin series
Smithies, Richard Hugo Ripman
see **Inspector William McAlpin series**

McAlpine series
Diment, Adam
see **Philip McAlpine series**

Macandrew and Bull series
Lariar, Lawrence
see **Ham Macandrew and Homer Bull series**

Macandrews Clan series
Zollinger, Norman
1 *Riders to Cibola* (1977)
2 *Passage to Quivera* (1989)

Macaque series
Cloete, Stuart
see **Jean Macaque series**

Mac Art series
Offutt, Andrew Jefferson
see **Cormac Mac Art series**

Macarthur series
Jepson, Selwyn
see **Ian Macarthur series**

Macauley series
Marino, Nick
see **Mike Macauley series**
Thorndike, Russell
see **Mister Macauley series**

McAuslan series
Fraser, George Macdonald
see **Private McAuslan series**

McBain family series
Miller, Hugh
1 *Open city* (1973)
2 *Kingpin* (1974)

McBain series
Robertson, Colin
see **Vicky McBain series**
Stables, Gordon
see **Captain McBain series**

Macbeth series
Beaton, M C
see **Hamish Macbeth series**

McBride series
Adams, Cleve Franklin
see **Rex McBride series**

McBroom series
Fleischman, Sid
1 *McBroom tells the truth* (1966)
2 *McBroom and the big wind* (1967)
3 *NcBroom's ear* (1969)
4 *McBroom's ghost* (1971)
Numbers 1, 2, 4 also published in one volume entitled *McBroom's wonderful one-acre farm*, 1972
5 *McBroom's zoo* (1972)
6 *McBroom the rainmaker* (1973)
7 *McBroom tells a lie* (1976)
Numbers 5-7 also published in one volume entitled *Here comes McBroom*, 1976
8 *McBroom and the beanstalk* (1978)

9 *McBroom and the great race* (1980)
10 *McBroom's almanac* (1983)

McBumby series
McArthur, John
see **Jack McBumby series**

McCabe series
Ford, Sewell
see **Shorty McCabe series**

McCabe trilogy
Cook, Will
see **Guthrie McCabe trilogy**

McCade series
Dietz, William Corey
see **Sam McCade series**
Kester, Ken
see **Steve McCade series**

McCaig series
Rae, Hugh Crauford
see **Superintendent McCaig series**

McCale series
Brown, Gerald
see **Duke McCale series**

McCall and Costaine series
Macneil, Neil
see **Tony Costaine and Bert McCall series**

McCall series
Carrel, Mark
see **Andrew McCall series**
Leader, Charles
see **Mike McCall series**
Queen, Ellery
see **Mike McCall series**

Maccallum series
Mackinnon, Allan
see **Inspector Duncan Maccallum series**

McCann series
McNeill, Janet
see **Specs McCann series**

Maccardle series
Halleran, Tucker
see **Cam Maccardle series**

McCarry series
Boland, John C
see **Donald McCarry series**

McCart series
Martin, David
see **Sean McCart series**

McCarthy series
Brandon, John Gordon
see **Inspector Patrick Aloysius McCarthy series**

McCarty series
Ostrander, Isabel
see **Timothy McCarty series**

McCaskill family trilogy
Doig, Ivan
1 *English Creek* (1984)
2 *Dancing at the Rascal Fair* (1987)
3 *Ride with me, Mariah Montana* (1990)

McChesney series
Ferber, Edna
see **Emma McChesney series**

McClary and Saint James series
Macgregor, T J
see **Quin Saint James and Mike McClary series**

Macclellan series
Dawlish, Peter
see **Sam Macclellan series**

McCleod sisters series
Vandergriff, Aola
see **Daughters series**

McClintock series
Green, Bill
see **Mickey McClintock series**
Oliphant, B J
see **Shirley McClintock series**

McCloud series
Wilcox, Collin
see **Marshal Sam McCloud series**

McClue series
Wickham, Harvey
see **Ferris McClue series**

McClure series
Rudd, Steele
see **Duncan McClure series**

McCone series
Muller, Marcia
see **Sharon McCone series**

Mac Conmara trilogy
Macmanus, Francis
see **Donnacha Mac Conmara trilogy**

McCorkle and Padillo series
Thomas, Ross
1 *Cold war swap* (1966)
Spy in the vodka
2 *Cast a yellow shadow* (1967)
3 *Backup men* (1971)

McCoy giant series
Fletcher, Dirk
see **Spur McCoy giant series**

McCoy series
Bowden, Jim
see **Dan McCoy series**
Buchanan, William
see **Kelly McCoy series**
Fletcher, Dirk
see **Spur McCoy series**
Gluck, Sinclair
see **Ross McCoy series**
Packer, Eleanor
see **Tim McCoy series**
Wolfe, John
see **Johnny McCoy series**

McCoy special series
Fletcher, Dirk
see **Spur McCoy special series**

McCracken series
Land, Jon
see **Blaine McCracken series**

McCrae series
Clarke, Mary Stetson
see **Ross McCrae series**

Maccray series
Jerome, Owen Fox
see **Philip Maccray series**

Maccubbin family series
Curry, Jane Louise
1 *Mindy's mysterious miniature* (1970)
Housenappers
2 *Lost farm* (1974)

McCumhal series
Flint, Kenneth Covey
see **Finn MacCumhal series**

McCunn series
Buchan, John
see **Dickson McCunn series**

McCurtain series
Owens, Louis
see **Cole McCurtain series**

Macdonald series
Lambert, Janet
see **Parri Macdonald series**
Lorac, E C R
see **Inspector Macdonald series**

McDonald series
Smith, Julie
see **Paul McDonald series**

Macdonald series
Strahan, Kay Cleaver
see **Lynn Macdonald series**
Tranter, Nigel Godwin
see **Donald Macdonald series**

MacDougal Duff series
Armstrong, Charlotte
1 *Lay on, Mac Duff!* (1942)
2 *Case of the weird sisters* (1943)
3 *Innocent flower* (1945)
Death filled the glass

McDuff and Pruitt series
Mitchell, Red
see **Doc McDuff and Popcorn Pruitt series**

McDumont series
Garner, Hugh
see **Inspector Walter McDumont series**

Mace series
Chang, Lee
see **Kung Fu series**

Mace series
Grant, James
1 *Mace!* (1984)
2 *Mace's luck* (1985)

Mace series
Keverne, Richard
see **Inspector Mace series**

McFall series
Fulton, Eileen
see **Nina McFall series**

Macfarlane series
Cross, John Keir
see **Albatross series**
Macvicar, Angus
see **Reverend P J Macfarlane series**

McFlannel family series
Pryde, Helen W
1 *First book of the McFlannels* (1947)
2 *McFlannels see it through* (1948)
3 *McFlannels united* (1949)
4 *McFlannel family affairs* (1950)
5 *Maisie McFlannel* (1951)

McFlimsey series
Mariana
see **Miss Flora McFlimsey series**

McFoy series
Shrog, J M
see **Bernard McFoy series**

McGarr series
Gill, Bartholomew
see **Inspector Peter McGarr series**

McGee series
Allen, Pamela
see **Mister McGee series**
Macdonald, John Dann
see **Travis McGee series**
Packard, Edward
see **ESP McGee series**

McGill Feighan series
O'Donnell, Kevin
see **Journeys of McGill Feighan series**

McGill series
Townend, Peter
1 *Man on the end of a rope* (1960)
2 *Road to El Suida* (1961)

Macgillan family series
Jackson, Rosemary Elizabeth
1 *Poltergeist* (1968)
2 *Aunt Eleanor* (1969)
3 *Witch of Castlekerry* (1965)
4 *Street of Mars* (1971)
5 *Wheel of the Finfolk* (1972)

McGillicuddy series
Bateman, Robert
see **Archibald McGillicuddy series**

McGills series
Fidler, Kathleen
1 *McGills at Mystery Farm* (1958)
2 *More adventures of the McGills* (1959)

McGinley series
McNeill, Janet
see **Matt McGonley series**

McGinty series
Hader, Berta
see **Willow Hill series**
Pendower, Jacques
see **Slade McGinty series**

McGlusky series
Hales, Alfred Greenwood
1 *McGlusky* (1902)
The diary of Trooper McWiddy of Remington's Scouts
2 *McGlusky, the reformer* (1910)
3 *McGlusky's great adventure* (1917)
4 *Ginger and McGlusky* (1917)
5 *President McGlusky* (1918)
6 *Adventures of Signor McGlusky* (1919)
7 *McGlusky, the gold seeker* (1920)
8 *McGlusky, the peace maker* (1923)
9 *McGlusky, the sea rover* (1924)
10 *McGlusky, the trail blazer* (1926)
11 *McGlusky o' the Legion* (1927)
12 *McGlusky, the Mormon* (1929)
13 *McGlusky in India* (1931)
14 *McGlusky, the filibuster* (1932)
15 *Snowey and McGlusky* (1933)
16 *McGlusky, M.P.* (1934)
17 *McGlusky, the seal poacher* (1935)
18 *McGlusky abroad* (1936)
19 *McGlusky, empire builder* (1937)

McGlynn and Toda families series
Toland, John
1 *Gods of war* (1985)
2 *Occupation* (1987)

McGonagall series
Milligan, Spike
see **William McGonagall series**

M'Govan series
M'Govan, James
see **James M'Govan series**

McGowan family series
Bell, Robert Vaughn
1 *Valley called Disappointment* (1982)
2 *Feud at Devil's River* (1982)
3 *Stranger in Dodge* (1983)
4 *Platte River crossing* (1983)
5 *To the death* (1984)
6 *Cold trail from Fort Smith* (1986)
7 *Winds blow free* (1988)
8 *Trackdown* (1989)

McGowan series
Aldous, Allan
1 *McGowan climbs a mountain* (1945)

2 *McGowan goes to sea* (1945)
3 *McGowan goes motor racing* (1947)
4 *McGowan goes fishing* (1948)
5 *McGowan goes to Henley* (1949)

McGowan series
Hornsby, Wendy
see **Maggie McGowan series**

McGrath family series
Paige, Frances
1 *Sholtie burn* (1986)
2 *Maeve's daughter* (1987)
3 *Distaff side* (1988)
4 *Men who march away* (1989)
5 *Sholtie flyer* (1990)

McGrath series
Brett, Michael
see **Pete McGrath series**

McGraw series
Champlin, Tim
see **Jay McGraw series**

Macgregor series
Bell, John Joy
see **Wee Macgregor series**

McGregor series
Kane, Henry
see **Inspector McGregor series**

Macgregor series
Mason, Robert
see **Captain James Donald Macgregor series**

Macgregor series
Roberts, Nora
1 *Playing the odds* (1985)
2 *Rempting fate* (1985)
3 *All the possibilities* (1985)
4 *One man's art* (1985)
5 *For now, forever* (1987)

Macgregor series
Scott, Walter
see **Rob Roy Macgregor series**

McGuffin series
Upton, Robert
see **Amos McGuffin series**

M'Guire series
Warren, John Russell
see **Inspector M'Guire series**

McGuire series
Williams, Amanda Kyle
see **Madison McGuire series**

McGurk series
Hildick, Edmund Wallace
1 *Nose knows* (1973)
2 *Dolls in danger* (1974)
Deadline for McGurk
3 *Menaced midget* (1975)
4 *Case of the condemned cat* (1975)
5 *Case of the nervous newsboy* (1976)
6 *Great rabbit robbery* (1976)
Great rabbit rip-off
7 *Case of the invisible dog* (1977)
8 *Case of the secret scribbler* (1978)
9 *Case of the phantom frog* (1979)
10 *Case of the treetop treasure* (1980)
11 *Case of the snowbound spy* (1980)
12 *Case of the bashful bank robber* (1981)
13 *Case of the four flying fingers* (1981)
14 *McGurk gets good and mad* (1982)
15 *Case of the felon's fiddle* (1982)
16 *Case of the slingshot sniper* (1983)
17 *Case of the vanishing ventriloquist* (1985)
18 *Case of the muttering mummy* (1986)
19 *Case of the wandering weathervanes* (1988)
20 *Case of the purloined parrot* (1990)
21 *Case of the dragon in distress* (1991)
22 *Case of the weeping witch* (1992)
23 *Case of the desperate drummer* (1993)
24 *Case of the fantastic footprints* (1994)

McGurk series
Marfield, Dwight
see **Gail McGurk series**
White, Osmar
see **Doctor McGurk series**

Machine gunners trilogy
Westall, Robert
1 *Machine gunners* (1975)
2 *Fathom five* (1979)
3 *Haunting of Chas McGill, and other stories* (1983)

McHugh series
Flynn, Jay
1 *McHugh* (1959)
2 *Viva McHugh* (1960)
3 *Body for McHugh* (1960)
4 *It's murder, McHugh* (1960)
5 *Five faces of murder* (1962)

Macinnes family series
Mackinnon, Charles Roy
see **Scottish chronicle series**

Macinnes series
Bandy, Franklin
see **Kevin Macinnes series**

Macinnes series
Chance, John Newton
1 *Death watch ladies* (1980)
2 *Death importer* (1981)

Macinnes series
Finlay, Campbell Kirkman
see **John Macinnes series**

McIntyre series
Corne, Molly E
see **Mac McIntyre series**

Mack Bolan series
Pendleton, Don
Except for numbers 16 and 26 all titles in this sequence are published under the name Don Pendleton either as a real name or as a house pseudonym used by Tom Arnett, Alan Bomack, E Richard Churchill, Chet Cunningham, Les Danforth, Kent Delaney, Aaron Hill, Tom Jagninski, Steven Krauser, Peter Leslie, Charlie McDade, Mike McQuay, Stephen Mertz, Patrick Neary, Judy A Newton, Mike Newton, Ray Obstfeld, Dan Schmidt, Wiley Slade, Dick Stivers, Saul Wernick where authorship is indicated against the titles
1 *War against the Mafia* (1969)
2 *Death squad* (1969)
3 *Battle mask* (1970)
4 *Miami massacre* (1970)
5 *Continental contract* (1971)
6 *Assault on Soho* (1971)
7 *Nightmare in New York* (1971)
8 *Chicago wipeout* (1971)
9 *Vegas vendetta* (1971)
10 *Caribbean kill* (1972)
11 *California hit* (1972)
12 *Boston blitz* (1972)
13 *Washington IOU* (1972)
14 *San Diego siege* (1972)
15 *Panic in Philly* (1973)
Peterson, Jim
16 *Sicilian slaughter* (1973)
Pendleton, Don
17 *Jersey guns* (1974)
18 *Texas storm* (1974)
19 *Detroit deathwatch* (1974)
20 *New Orleans knockout* (1974)
21 *Firebase Seattle* (1975)
22 *Hawaiian hellground* (1975)
23 *Saint Louis showdown* (1975)
24 *Canadian crisis* (1975)
25 *Colorado kill-zone* (1976)
Peterson, Jim
26 *Death in Acapulco* (1976)
Pendleton, Don
27 *Dixie convoy* (1976)
28 *Savage fire* (1977)
29 *Command strike* (1977) [Mike Newton; Mertz; Pendleton]
30 *Cleveland pipeline* (1977)
31 *Arizona ambush* (1977) [Mike Newton; Pendleton]
32 *Tennessee smash* (1978)
33 *Monday's mob* (1978)
34 *Terrible Tuesday* (1979)
35 *Wednesday's wrath* (1979)
36 *Thermal Thursday* (1979)
37 *Friday's feast* (1979)
38 *Satan's Sabbath* (1980)
39 *New war* (1981) [Wernick]
40 *Double crossfire* (1982) [Krauser]
41 *Violent streets* (1982) [Mike Newton]
42 *Iranian hit* (1982) [Mertz]
43 *Return to Vietnam* (1982) [Mertz]
44 *Terrorist summit* (1982) [Krauser]
45 *Paramilitary plot* (1982) [Mike Newton]
46 *Bloodsport* (1982) [Obstfeld]
47 *Renegade agent* (1982) [Krauser]
48 *Libya connection* (1982) [Mertz]
49 *Doomsday disciples* (1983) [Mike Newton]
50 *Brothers in blood* (1983) [Krauser]
51 *Vulture's vengeance* (1983) [Mertz]
52 *Tuscany terror* (1983) [Neary]
53 *Invisible assassins* (1983) [Bomack]
54 *Mountain rampage* (1983) [Churchill]
55 *Paradine's gauntlet* (1983) [Mike Newton]
56 *Island deathtrap* (1983) [Churchill]
57 *Flesh wounds* (1983) [Obstfeld]
58 *Ambush on Blood River* (1983) [Bomack]
59 *Crude kill* (1983) [Cunningham]
60 *Sold for slaughter* (1983) [Mike Newton]
61 *Tiger war* (1983) [Jagninski]
62 *Day of mourning* (1983) [Mertz]
63 *New war book* (1984) [Hill; Judy A Newton; Slade]
64 *Dead man running* (1984) [Mertz]
65 *Cambodia clash* (1984) [Jagninski]
66 *Orbiting Omega* (1984) [Cunningham]
67 *Beirut payback* (1984) [Mertz]
68 *Prairie fire* (1984) [Mike Newton]
69 *Skysweeper* (1984) [Cunningham]
70 *Ice cold kill* (1984) [Leslie]
71 *Blood dues* (1984) [Mike Newton]
72 *Hellbinder* (1984) [Cunningham]
73 *Appointment in Kabul* (1985) [Mertz]
74 *Savannah swingsaw* (1985) [Obstfeld]
75 *Bone yard* (1985) [Mike Newton]
76 *Teheran wipeout* (1985)
77 *Hollywood hell* (1985) [Mike Newton]
78 *Death games* (1985) [Arnett]
79 *Council of kings* (1985) [Cunningham; Danforth]
80 *Running hot* (1985)
81 *Shock waves* (1985) [Mike Newton]
82 *Hammerhead Reef* (1985) [Bomack]
83 *Missouri deathwatch* (1985) [Mike Newton]
84 *Fastburn* (1985) [Leslie]
85 *Sunscream* (1986) [Leslie]
86 *Hell's gate* (1986) [Arnett]
87 *Hellfire crusade* (1986) [Bomack]
88 *Baltimore trackdown* (1986) [Cunningham]
89 *Defenders and believers* (1986) [Mike Newton]
90 *Blood heat zero* (1986) [Leslie]
91 *Trial* (1986) [Mike Newton]
92 *Moscow massacre* (1986) [Mertz]
93 *Fire eaters* (1986) [Obstfeld]
94 *Save the children* (1986) [Mertz]
95 *Blood and thunder* (1986) [Schmidt]
96 *Death has a name* (1986) [McQuay]
97 *Meltdown* (1987) [McDade]
98 *Black dice* (1987) [Schmidt]
99 *Code of dishonor* (1987) [Mike Newton]
100 *Blood testament* (1987) [Mike Newton]
101 *Eternal triangle* (1987) [Mike Newton]
102 *Split image* (1987) [McDade]
103 *Assault on Rome* (1987) [Mike Newton]
104 *Devil's horn* (1987) [Schmidt]
105 *Countdown to chaos* (1987) [Delaney]
106 *Run to ground* (1987) [Mike Newton]
107 *American nightmare* (1987) [McQuay]
108 *Time to kill* (1988) [Mike Newton]
109 *Hong Kong hit list* (1988) [Leslie]
110 *Trojan horse* (1988) [Schmidt]

Mack Fraser and Elspeth Marriner series
Merwin, Samuel Kimball
see **Elspeth Marriner and Mack Fraser series**

Mack Gerber series
Helm, Eric
see **Scorpion Squad series**

Mack series
Lehrer, Jim
see **One-Eyed Mack series**

Mack trilogy
Hunt, Nan
see **Mrs Millie Mack series**

McKail trilogy
Stringer, Arthur
see **Prairie trilogy**

McKay, Knowlton and Ryan series
Friel, Arthur Olney
1 *Pathless trail* (1922)
2 *Tiger River* (1923)
3 *King of No Man's Land* (1924)
4 *Mountains of mystery* (1925)

Mackay series
Cushing, E Louise
see **Inspector Mackay series**

McKay series
Morris, John
see **Commissioner Robin McKay series**
Strong, Leonard Alfred George
see **Police diversion series**

McKechnie and Collins series
Hitchens, Bert
see **Collins and McKechnie series**

McKee and Joe series
Floren, Lee
see **Buckshot McKee and Tortilla Joe series**

McKee series
Reilly, Helen
see **Inspector Christopher McKee series**

McKeene series
Walker, Rowland
see **Captain Deville McKeene series**

McKellar series
Burch, T R
see **Shane McKellar series**
Peebles, Niles N
see **Ross McKellar series**

McKeller series
McCutcheon, Hugh
see **Inspector McKeller series**

McKelvie series
Harvey, Marion
see **Graydon McKelvie series**

McKenna series
Papazoglou, Orania
see **Patience Campbell McKenna series**

McKenzie series
Humphries, Barry
see **Barry McKenzie series**

Mackenzie series
McNeish, James
1 *Mackenzie* (1970)
2 *Mackenzie affair* (1973)

Mackenzie series
Magowan, Ronald
see **Shane Mackenzie series**

Mackie family series
Livingston, Nancy
1 *Far side of the hill* (1987)
2 *Land of our dreams* (1989)

McKie series
Herbert, Frank
see **Jorj X McKie series**

McKinley quartet
Lingard, Joan
see **Maggie McKinley quartet**

Mackinnon brothers series
Coffman, Elaine
1 *My enemy, my love* (1988)
2 *If my love could hold you* (1989)
3 *Escape not my love* (1990)
4 *Angel in marble* (1991)
5 *For all the right reasons* (1991)
6 *Somewhere along the way* (1992)
7 *So this is love* (1993)
8 *Heaven knows* (1994)

McKinnon series
Macvicar, Angus
see **Jeremy Grant series**
Offord, Lenore Glen
see **Todd McKinnon series**

Mackintosh series
Landon, Lucinda
see **Meg Mackintosh series**

Macklin series
Estleman, Loren D
see **Peter Macklin series**
Ludlow, Ian
see **Vigilante series**

McLaffertys series
Williams, Jude
1 *McLaffertys* (1986)
2 *Desert moon* (1987)

Maclain series
Kendrick, Baynard
see **Captain Duncan Maclain series**

McLane series
Honig, Donald
see **Jed McLane series**

Maclane trilogy
Bonner, Michael
see **Roby Maclane trilogy**

Maclaren family series
Skelton, Clement Lister
1 *Maclarens* (1978)
2 *Sweethearts and wives* (1979)
Regiment
3 *Beloved soldiers* (1985)
A fourth volume announced not yet published

McLaren series
Scott, Bruce
see **Superintendent Steve McLaren series**

Maclary series
Dodd, Lynley
see **Hairy Maclary series**

McLaughlin family series
Wilson, Margaret
1 *Able McLaughlins* (1923)
2 *Law and the McLaughlins* (1936)

McLean series
Corrigan, Mark
see **Mark Corrigan and McLean series**

Maclean series
Gaston, Bill
see **Roy Maclean series**

McLean series
Goodchild, George
see **Inspector McLean series**

Maclean series
McLeave, Hugh
see **Doctor Gregor Maclean series**
Redmayne, John
see **Peter Maclean series**

McLean series
Yates, Margaret Tayler
see **Anne Davenport McLean series**

McLeane's Rangers series
Darby, John
1 *Bourgainville breakout* (1982)
2 *Target Rabaul* (1983)
3 *Hell on Hill 457* (1983)

MacLeod family series
Adair, Denis
1 *Kanata* (1981)
2 *Bitter shield* (1982)
3 *Thundergate* (1982)
4 *Wildfires* (1983)
5 *Victoria* (1983)

Macleod series
McLean, Allan Campbell
see **Inspector Noel Macleod series**

Macleods of Virginia series
Davis, Julia
1 *Cloud on the land* (1952)
2 *Bridle the wind* (1955)
3 *Eagle on the sun* (1957)

McLintock series
Macvicar, Angus
see **Bruce McLintock series**

Maclurg series
Petrie, Rhona
see **Inspector Marcus Maclurg series**

Macmagics series
Dicks, Terrance
1 *Meet the Macmagics* (1990)
2 *My brother the vampire* (1990)
3 *Spell for my sister* (1991)

Macmahon family trilogy
Macken, Walter
1 *Seek the fair land* (1959)
2 *Silent people* (1962)
3 *Scorching wind* (1964)

MacMorgan series
Striker, Randy
see **Dusky MacMorgan series**

McMurdo series
Morland, Nigel
see **Chief Inspector Andrew McMurdo series**

Macnab series
Ferguson, John
see **Francis Macnab series**

McNally series
Sanders, Lawrence
see **Archy McNally series**
Tetlow, L D
see **Brogan McNally series**

Macnamara and Long series
Macavoy, Roberta Ann
see **Mayland Long and Martha Macnamara series**

McNeely series
Charbonneau, Louis
see **Kathy McNeely series**

Macneil series
Jeffers, Harry Paul
see **Harry Macneil series**

McNeill series
Du Bois, Theodora
see **Anne and Jeffrey McNeill series**

Macneill series
Duncan, William Murdoch
see **Superintendent Macneill series**

Macomber series
Knight, Kathleen Moore
see **Elisha Macomber series**

Macondo series
Garçia Marquez, Gabriel
1 *Leaf storm, and other stories* (1955) Original edition entitled *La hojarasca*; includes *Monologue of Isabel watching it rain*, originally entitled *Isabel viendo llover en Macondo*, in *Macondo*, 1967, also, *The handsomest drowned man in the world*, *The last voyage of the ghost ship*, *Nabo*, and, *A very old man with enormous wings*
2 *No one writes to the colonel* (1961) Original edition entitled *El colonel no tiene quien le escriba;* published with *Big Mama's funeral*, originally entitled *Los funerales de la Mama Grande*, 1962
3 *One hundred years of solitude* (1967) Original edition entitled *Cien anos de soledad*

Macpherson series
Derwent, Lavinia
1 *Macpherson* (1961)
2 *Macpherson's funny-bone* (1962)
3 *Macpherson's Highland fling* (1963)
4 *Macpherson in Edinburgh* (1964)
5 *Macpherson in America* (1965)
6 *Macpherson sails the sea* (1966)
7 *Macpherson on the farm* (1967)
8 *Macpherson's caravan* (1968)
9 *Macpherson's skyscraper* (1969)
10 *Macpherson's island* (1970)
11 *Macpherson's winter sports* (1972)
12 *Macpherson's lighthouse adventure* (1977)
13 *Macpherson's mystery adventure* (1982)

Macpherson series
McCrumb, Sharon
see **Elizabeth Macpherson series**

McQuaid series
Rifkin, Shepard
see **Damian McQuaid series**

Macquart series
Zola, Emile
see **Rougon Macquart series**

McQueen family series
Newcomb, Kerry
1 *Guns of liberty* (1991)
2 *Sword of vengeance* (1991)
3 *Only the gallant* (1991)
4 *Warriors of the night* (1991)
Companion volume: Ride the panther, 1992

McQueen series
Litchfield, Michael
see **Superintendent Fergus McQueen series**

McQuint series
Grove, Frederick Philip
see **Dude McQuint series**

Macrae series
Barker, Albert
see **Hawk Macrae series**

Macready series
Holman, Hugh
see **Sheriff Macready series**

McShane series
Hunter, Mollie
see **Bridie McShane series**

McSmithers series
Alderson, Sue Ann
see **Bonnie McSmithers series**

Macsporran series
Hill, Lawrence
see **Inspector Macsporran series**

McSweeney series
Spencer, Thomas Edward
see **Bridget McSweeney series**

Mactaggart series
Walker, David Harry
see **Geordie Mactaggart series**

McTavish series
Brooks, Collin
see **O Swete McTavish series**

Mactavish series
Cheyney, Peter
see **Alonzo Mactavish series**

McTavish series
Dreher, Sarah
see **Stoner McTavish series**

McVeigh series
Emmett, Robert
see **American Avenger series**
Macveigh, Sue
see **Captain Andy and Sue McVeigh series**

McVeys series
Kirkland, Joseph
1 *Zury* (1887)
The meanest man in Spring County
2 *McVeys* (1888)
An episode

Macwhorter series
Keeler, Harry Stephen
see **Angus Macwhorter series**

Macwilliams series
Blizard, Marie
see **Eve Macwilliams series**

Macy Donovan series
Palmer, Vance
1 *Golconda* (1948)
2 *Seedtime* (1957)
3 *Big Fellow* (1959)

Mad doctor series
Thwaites, Frederick Joseph
1 *Mad doctor* (1935)
2 *Mad doctor in Harley Street* (1938)

Mad Max series
This sequence has three authors; based on screenplays
Kaye, Terry
1 *Mad Max* (1979)
Mad Max 1
Ruhen, Carl
2 *Mad Max 2* (1981)
Vinge, Joan Dennison
3 *Mad Max beyond the Thunderdome* (1985)
Companion volume: *Mad Max beyond the Thunderdome*, film script, by Ann Matthews, 1985

Mad Scientists' Club series
Brinley, Bertrand Russell
1 *Mad Scientists' Club* (1964)
2 *New adventures of the Mad Scientists' Club* (1968)

Madame Dominique Aubry series
Travers, Hugh
1 *Madame Aubry and the police* (1966)
2 *Madame Aubry dines with death* (1967)

Madame Midas series
Hume, Fergus
1 *Madame Midas* (1888)
2 *Miss Mephistopheles* (1890)

Madame Rosika Storey series
Footner, Hulbert
1 *Under dogs* (1925)
2 *Madame Storey* (1926)
Short stories
3 *Velvet hand* (1928)
Two of the stories from this collection reprinted in *The viper*, 1930
4 *Doctor who held hands* (1929)
Murderer's challenge
5 *Easy to kill* (1931)
6 *Casual murderer* (1932)
Kidnapping of Madame Storey, and other stories
The second title omits the title story from the first
7 *Almost perfect murder* (1933)
Short stories
8 *Dangerous cargo* (1934)

Madden series
Disney, Doris Miles
see **David Madden series**
Santiago, V J
see **Joseph Madden series**

Maddie series
Winberg, Greta
1 *When someone splits* (1972)
Original edition entitled *Nar nagon bara sticker*
2 *When someone comes along* (1972)
Original edition entitled *Nar narg ot bara hander*

Maddison series
Williamson, Henry
see **Flax of dream series**

Maddison series, number 2
Williamson, Henry
see **Chronicles of ancient sunlight series**

Maddock series
McCaffrey, Anne
see **Yanaba Maddock series**

Maddox series
Linington, Elizabeth
see **Sergeant Ivor Maddox series**

Maddox series
Walker, Martin
1 *Infiltrator* (1978)
2 *Mercenary calling* (1980)
Money soldiers

Maddy and Alex Phillips series
Zimmerman, R D
1 *Death trance* (1992)
2 *Blood trance* (1994)
3 *Red trance* (1994)

Maddy series
Brown, Pamela
see **Blue Door Theatre Company series**

Made in Australia series
Collins, Tom
see **Such is life series**

Madeleine reminiscences series
Henrey, Madeleine
1 *Paloma* (1951)
Memories of Marie Siller, actress
2 *Madeleine's journal* (1953)
3 *Month in Paris* (1954)
4 *Mistress of myself* (1959)
5 *Bloomsbury Fair* (1955)
6 *Milou's daughter* (1955)
Memories of life in Provence
7 *London* (1948)
8 *Virgin of Aldermanbury* (1958)
Rebirth of the City of London
9 *Spring in a Soho street* (1962)
10 *Winter wild* (1966)

Madeleine series
Henrey, Madeleine
Autobiography
1 *Little Madeleine* (1951)
2 *Exile in Soho* (1952)
The life of the author's mother, Etienne Leblanc
3 *Julia* (1971)
A year in the author's life as a London shop girl
4 *Girl at twenty* (1974)
Six months in the life of the author
5 *Madeleine grown up* (1952)
6 *Madeleine young wife* (1954)
7 *Green leaves* (1976)
Life in London in the 1930s and 1940s
8 *London under fire, 1940-45* (1969)
Based on *A village in Piccadilly*, 1942, *The incredible city*, 1944, and, *The siege of London*, 1946, published under the author's pseudonym, Robert Henrey
9 *Her April days* (1963)
10 *Wednesday at four* (1964)
11 *She who pays* (1969)

Madeline Payne series
Lynch, Lawrence L
1 *Madeline Payne, the detective's daughter* (1884)
Detective's daughter
Also published under the author's real name Emma Murdoch Van Deventer
2 *Moina* (1891)
Alternative title: Against the mighty

Madeline series
Bemelmans, Ludwig
Stories in verse
1 *Madeline* (1939)
2 *Madeline's rescue* (1953)
3 *Madeline's Christmas in Texas* (1955)
4 *Madeline and the bad hat* (1956)
5 *Madeline and the gypsies* (1959)
6 *Madeline in London* (1961)
7 *Madeline's Christmas* (1985)
Completed by Madeline and Barbara Bemelmans after the author's death

Madero series
Homes, Geoffrey
see **Jose Manuel Madero series**

Madge Morton series
Chalmers, Amy D V
1 *Madge Morton, captain of the Merry Maid* (1913)
2 *Madge Morton's secret* (1913)
3 *Madge Morton's trust* (1914)
4 *Madge Morton's victory* (1914)

Madge series
Saunders, Marjorie
1 *Madge's sister* (1949)
2 *Leave it to Madge* (1953)

Madge Sterling series
Wirt, Ann
1 *Missing formula* (1932)
2 *Deserted yacht* (1932)
3 *Secret of the sundial* (1932)

Madge Stillworthy series
Marshall, May
see **Sister Madge Stillworthy series**

Madigan series
Cassidy, Bruce
see **Cash Madigan series**

Madison McGuire series
Williams, Amanda Kyle
1 *Club Twelve* (1990)
2 *Providence file* (1991)
3 *Singular spy* (1992)
4 *Spy in question* (1993)

Mado series
Tute, Warren
see **George Mado series**

Madoc Rhys series
Craig, Alisa
see **Inspector Madoc Rhys series**

Madonna series
Dekobra, Maurice
1 *Madonna of the sleeping cars* (1925)
Original edition entitled *La madone des sleepings*
2 *Madonna in Hollywood* (1943)
Original edition entitled *La madone a Hollywood*

Mael family series
Berna, Paul
1 *Vagabonds of the Pacific* (1973)
Original edition entitled *Les Vagabonds du Pacifique*
2 *Vagabonds ashore* (1973)
Original edition entitled *Le Grande rallye de Mirabel*

Mafia series
Davis, John H
1 *Mafia kingfish* (1988)
Carlos Marcello and the assassination of John F Kennedy
2 *Mafia dynasty* (1993)
The rise and fall of the Gambino crime family

Mafia series
Romano, Don
This pseudonym is used by Paul Eiden, Allan Nixon and Robert Turner as indicated against each title
1 *Operation porno* (1973)
[Nixon; Turner]
2 *Operation cocaine* (1974)
[Nixon; Turner]
3 *Operation hijack* (1974)
[Eiden]
4 *Operation hit man* (1974)
[Nixon; Turner]
5 *Operation loan shark* (1974)
[Eiden]

Mag and Simon series
Styles, Showell
see **Simon and Mag series**

Magdah series
Sheldon, Roy
1 *Mammoth man* (1952)
2 *Two days of terror* (1952)

Mage winds series
Lackey, Mercedes
1 *Winds of fate* (1991)
2 *Winds of change* (1992)
3 *Winds of fury* (1993)

Magellan series
McCurtin, Peter
see **Marksman series**

Mages of Garillon trilogy
Harris, Deborah Turner
1 *Burning stone* (1987)
2 *Gauntlet of malice* (1987)
3 *Spiral of fire* (1989)

Maggie Adams series
Dean, Karen Strickler
1 *Maggie Adams, dancer* (1982)
2 *Between dances* (1986)
Maggie Adams' eighteenth summer
3 *Stay on your toes, Maggie Adams* (1986)

Maggie and Devildust series
Alter, Judy
1 *Maggie and a horse named Devildust* (1989)
2 *Maggie and the search for Devildust* (1989)
3 *Maggie and Devildust, ridin' high!* (1990)

Maggie and Iris series
Jukes, Mavis
1 *Getting even* (1988)
2 *Wild Iris blooms* (1991)

Maggie and Jiggs series
McManus, George
Edited by Bill Blackbeard
Comic strips begun in 1913
1 *Bringing up father* (1986)
2 *Jiggs is back* (1986)
Companion volume: *Bringing up father*, edited by Herb Galewitz, 1973

Maggie Bennett series
Stuart, Anne
1 *Darkness before the dawn* (1986)
2 *Escape out of darkness* (1987)
3 *At the edge of the sun* (1987)

Maggie Bradford series
Mathews, Joanna Hooe
1 *Maggie and Bessie and their way to do good* (1868)
2 *Maggie Bradford's club* (1889)
3 *Maggie Bradford's school-mates* (1890)
4 *Maggie bradford's fair* (1892)

Maggie Courtney series
Pearson, Ann
1 *Murder by degrees* (1979)
2 *Stitch in time* (1979)
3 *Cat got your tongue?* (1980)

Maggie Elliott series
Taylor, Elizabeth Atwood
1 *Cable car murder* (1981)
2 *Murder at Vassar* (1987)
3 *Northwest murders* (1992)

Maggie Gumption series
Barry, Margaret Stuart
1 *Maggie Gumption* (1979)
2 *Maggie Gumption flies high* (1981)

Maggie McGowan series
Hornsby, Wendy
1 *Telling lies* (1992)
2 *Midnight baby* (1993)
3 *Bad intent* (1994)

Maggie McKinley quartet
Lingard, Joan
Revised editions 1994
1 *Clearance* (1974)
2 *Resettling* (1975)
3 *Pilgrimage* (1976)
4 *Reunion* (1977)

Maggie Marmelstein series
Sharmat, Marjorie Weinman
1 *Getting something on Maggie Marmelstein* (1971)
2 *Maggie Marmelstein for president* (1975)
3 *Mysteriously yours, Maggie Marmelstein* (1982)

Maggie Muggins series
Grannan, Mary
1 *Maggie Muggins* (1944)
2 *Maggie Muggins stories* (1947)
3 *New Maggie Muggins stories* (1947)
4 *Maggie Muggins in the meadow* (1956)
5 *This is Maggie Muggins* (1959)
6 *More Maggie Muggins* (1959)
7 *Maggie muggins and her animal friends* (1959)
8 *Maggie Muggins bedtime stories* (1959)
9 *Maggie Muggins by the sea* (1959)
10 *Wonderful world of Maggie Muggins* (1959)
11 *Maggie Muggins and the fieldmouse* (1959)
12 *Maggie Muggins and the cottontail* (1960)
13 *Maggie Muggins gives a party* (1961)

Maggie Ryan series
Carlson, Patricia McEvoy
1 *Audition for murder* (1985)
2 *Murder is academic* (1985)
3 *Murder is pathological* (1986)
4 *Rehearsal for murder* (1988)
5 *Murder misread* (1990)
6 *Murder unrenovated* (1990)
7 *Murder in the dog days* (1991)
8 *Bad blood* (1991)
9 *Gravestone* (1993)

Maggie series
Devlin, Wende
see **Cranberryport series**

Maggie series
Hollowood, Jane
1 *Maggie and the chickens* (1967)
2 *Maggie and the roundabout* (1967)
3 *Maggie and the birthday surprise* (1969)
4 *Maggie in the snow* (1969)

Maggie series
Nixon, Joan Lowery
1 *Maggie, too* (1985)
2 *And Maggie makes three* (1986)
3 *Maggie forevermore* (1987)

Maggie Slone series
Stone, Elizabet M
1 *Poison, poker and pistols* (1946)
2 *Murder at the mardi gras* (1947)

Maggody series
Hess, Joan
see **Arly Hanks series**

Magi trilogy
Van der Naillen, Albert
1 *On the heights of Himalay* (1890)
2 *In the sanctuary* (1896)
3 *Balthazer the magus* (1904)

Magic carpet series
Mamlok, Gwyneth
1 *Magic carpet to Animal Rhyme Land* (1964)
2 *Magic carpet to Nursery Rhyme Land* (1964)
3 *Magic carpet to Pudding Pie Land* (1964)
4 *Magic carpet to Story Rhyme Land* (1964)

Magic circle series
Bunting, Eve
1 *Two giants* (1972)
2 *Gift for Lonny* (1973)
3 *Box, Fox, Ox and the peacock* (1974)
4 *Say it fast* (1974)
5 *We need a bigger zoo* (1974)

Magic day series
McKimmie, Christopher
1 *Shape I'm in* (1977)
2 *Magic day* (1977)
3 *One rainy day* (1977)
4 *Caught bird* (1977)

Magic faraway tree series
Blyton, Enid
see **Faraway tree series**

Magic in Ithkar series
Adams, Robert
1 *Magic in Ithkar* (1985)
Magic in Ithkar I
2 *Magic in Ithkar II* (1985)
3 *Magic in Ithkar III* (1986)
4 *Magic in Ithkar IV* (1987)

Magic Kingdom of Landover series
Brooks, Terry
1 *Magic kingdom for sale, sold!* (1987)
2 *Black unicorn* (1987)
3 *Wizard at large* (1988)
4 *Tangle box* (1994)

Magic makers series
Sutton, Margaret
1 *Magic makers and the bramble bush man* (1936)
2 *Magic makers and the golden charm* (1936)
3 *Magic makers in Backwards Land* (1936)

Magic Man series
Bannerman, David
1 *Magic Man* (1983)
2 *Gamov factor* (1983)
3 *Pipeline from hell* (1984)

Magic meadow series
Friskey, Margaret
1 *Mystery of the magic meadow* (1968)
2 *Mystery of Rackety's way* (1969)

Magic micro adventure series
This sequence has five authors
Buckholtz, Eileen
1 *Captain Kid and the pirates* (1985)
Otfinoski, Steven
2 *Superworld* (1985)
Stine, Harlan William
3 *Wizards of wonder* (1985)
Buckholtz, Eileen
4 *Cats of Castle Mountain* (1985)

Magic monsters series
Tester, Sylvia Root
1 *What is a monster?* (1979)
2 *Magic monsters around the year* (1979)
3 *Magic monsters learn about safety* (1979)
4 *Magic monsters' Halloween* (1980)
5 *Magic monsters learn about weather* (1980)

Magic Moscow series
Pinkwater, Daniel Manus
1 *Magic Moscow* (1980)
2 *Attila the pun* (1981)
3 *Slaves of Spiegel* (1982)

Magic mystery series
Levy, Elizabeth
1 *Case of the gobbling squash* (1988)
2 *Case of the mind-reading mommies* (1989)
3 *Case of the tattletale heart* (1990)
4 *Case of the dummy with cold eyes* (1991)

Magic of Xanth series
Anthony, Piers
see **Xanth series**

Magic people series
Softly, Barbara
1 *Magic people* (1966)
2 *More magic people* (1969)
Magic people around the world

Magic plant series
Macdonald, Elizabeth
1 *Incredible magic plant* (1976)
2 *Little weather house* (1978)

Magic roundabout series
Thompson, Eric
see **Dougal series**

Magic school bus series
Cole, Joanna
1 *Magic school bus at the waterworks* (1986)
2 *Magic school bus inside the earth* (1987)
3 *Magic school bus inside the human body* (1989)
4 *Magic school bus lost in the solar system* (1990)

Magic series
Baker, James Webb
1 *Birthday magic* (1988)
2 *Christmas magic* (1988)
3 *Halloween magic* (1988)
4 *Valentine magic* (1988)
5 *April Fool's Day magic* (1989)
6 *New Year's Day magic* (1989)
7 *President's Day magic* (1989)
8 *Thanksgiving magic* (1989)
9 *Saint Patrick's Day magic* (1990)
10 *Arbor Day magic* (1990)
11 *Independence Day magic* (1990)
12 *Columbus Day magic* (1990)

Magic series
Beresford, Elisabeth
1 *Awkward magic* (1964)
Magic world
2 *Travelling magic* (1965)
Vanishing garden
3 *Sea-green magic* (1968)
4 *Vanishing magic* (1970)
5 *Dangerous magic* (1972)
6 *Invisible magic* (1974)
7 *Secret magic* (1978)
8 *Curious magic* (1980)
9 *Strange magic* (1986)

Magic series
Eager, Edward
1 *Half magic* (1954)
2 *Knight's castle* (1956)
3 *Magic by the lake* (1957)
4 *Time garden* (1958)
5 *Magic or not?* (1959)
6 *Well-wishers* (1960)
7 *Seven-day magic* (1962)

Magic series
Morris, Anthony Paschel
see **Mark Magic series**

Magic series
Norton, Andre
1 *Steel magic* (1965)
Gray magic
2 *Octagon magic* (1967)
3 *Fur magic* (1968)
4 *Dragon magic* (1972)
5 *Lavender-green magic* (1974)
6 *Red hart magic* (1976)

Magic series
Severn, Bill
1 *Magic wherever you are* (1957)
2 *Shadow magic* (1959)
3 *Magic with paper* (1962)
4 *Magic in your pockets* (1964)
5 *Magic comedy* (1968)
6 *Magic across the table* (1972)
7 *Bill Severn's magic trunk* (1974)
8 *Bill Severn's magic workshop* (1976)
9 *Magic with coins and bills* (1977)
10 *Bill Severn's big book of close-up magic* (1978)
11 *Bill Severn's` guide to magic as a hobby* (1979)
12 *More magic in your pockets* (1980)
13 *Magic with rope* (1982)
14 *Bill Severn's impromptu magic* (1984)
15 *Bill Severn's Magic in mind* (1993)
16 *Bill Severn's money magic* (1993)
Companion volumes: *Magic and magicians*, 1958, *Magic shows you can give*, 1965, *Magic in mind*, 1974, *Magic fun for everyone*, 1986, *Bill Severn's best magic*, 1990, *Bill Severn's amazing magic*, 1992

Magic trilogy
Coulter, Catherine
see **Victoria Albemarle trilogy**

Magic trilogy
Niven, Larry
1 *Magic goes away* (1978)
2 *Magic may return* (1981)
3 *More magic* (1984)

Magic voyage series
Norton, John
1 *Mission from Vitrium* (1985)
2 *Silicon sabotage* (1985)
3 *Invaders from the lost galaxy* (1985)
4 *Into the sun* (1985)

Magica series
Carter, Lin
see **Terra Magica series**

Magical car series
Fleming, Ian
see **Chitty-Chitty-Bang-Bang series**

Magical tales of Taormin series
Franklin, Cheryl Jean
1 *Fire get* (1987)
2 *Fire lord* (1989)
3 *Fire crossing* (1991)

Magician series
McKee, David
see **Melric the magician series**

Magician trilogy
McGowen, Tom
1 *Magician's apprentice* (1987)
2 *Magician's company* (1988)
3 *Magician's challenge* (1989)

Magician's house trilogy
Corlett, William
1 *Steps up the chimney* (1990)
2 *Door in the tree* (1991)
3 *Tunnel behind the waterfall* (1991)

Magill series
Gardiner, Dorothy
see **Sheriff Moss Magill series**

Magira trilogy
Walker, Hugh
1 *War-gamer's world* (1978)
Original edition entitled *Reiter der Finsternis*
2 *Army of darkness* (1979)
Original edition entitled *Das heer der Finsternis*
3 *Messengers of darkness* (1979)
Original edition entitled *Boten der Finsternis*

Magnificent barb series
Faralla, Dana
1 *Magnificent barb* (1947)
2 *Black renegade* (1954)

Magnus Keeble series
Wood, Andrew
1 *Prom concert murders* (1948)
2 *Big Ben struck twelve* (1948)
3 *Eros is no hangman* (1949)
4 *Murder by the minute* (1955)

Magnus series
Derwent, Lavinia
1 *Sula* (1969)
2 *Return to Sula* (1971)
3 *Boy from Sula* (1973)
4 *Song of Sula* (1976)

Magnus series
Peterson, Hans
1 *Magnus and the squirrel* (1956)
Original edition entitled *Magnus och ekorrungen*
2 *Magnus and the van horse* (1958)
Magnus and the wagon horse
Original edition entitled *Magnus, Mattias och Mari*
3 *Magnus in the harbour* (1958)
Original edition entitled *Magnus i hamn*
4 *Magnus in danger* (1959)
Original edition entitled *Magnus i fara*
5 *Magnus and the ship's mascot* (1961)
Original edition entitled *Magnus och skeppshunden Jack*
6 *Eric and the Christmas horse* (1968)
Original edition entitled *Magnus Lindberg och haesten Mari*

Magnus trilogy
Temple, William Frederick
see **Martin Magnus series**

Maguire and Kowalski series
White, Teri
see **Blue Maguire and Spaceman Kowalski series**

Maguire series
Himmel, Richard
see **Johnny Maguire series**
Radford, John P
see **Illusionist series**

Maguire trilogy
Hennessy, Max
see **Kelly Maguire trilogy**

Magus series
Davidson, Avram
see **Virgil Magus series**

Magwitch series
This sequence has two authors
Dickens, Charles
1 *Great expectations* (1861)
Noonan, Michael
2 *Magwitch* (1982)

Mahogany series
Traven, B
see **Jungle series**

Mahon series
Courtier, Sidney Hobson
see **Ambrose Mahon series**

Mahoney series
Flannery, Sean
see **Wallace and John Mahoney series**

Mahony trilogy
Richardson, Henry Handel
see **Fortunes of Richard Mahony trilogy**

Mahota series
Burgin, George Brown
see **Monastery of Mahota series**

Mahoun series
Smith, Clark
see **Nicky Mahoun series**

Maida series
Irwin, Inez Haynes
1 *Maida's little shop* (1909)
2 *Maida's little house* (1921)
3 *Maida's little school* (1926)
4 *Maida's little island* (1939)
5 *Maida's little camp* (1940)
6 *Maida's little village* (1942)
7 *Maida's little houseboat* (1943)
8 *Maida's little theater* (1946)
9 *Maida's little cabins* (1947)
10 *Maida's little zoo* (1949)
11 *Maida's little lighthouse* (1951)
12 *Maida's little hospital* (1952)
13 *Maida's little farm* (1953)
14 *Maida's little house party* (1954)
15 *Maida's little treasure hunt* (1955)

Maidment series
Cronin, Michael
see **Richard Maidment series**

Maids and mistresses series
Powell, Margaret
1 *Maids and mistresses* (1981)
2 *Housekeeper* (1982)

Maigret series
Simenon, Georges
see **Inspector Jules Maigret series**

Main family trilogy
Jakes, John
see **North and South trilogy**

Maine series
Power, Phyllis Mary
see **Hannah Maine series**

Mainwaring series
Carnegie, Sacha
see **Major Gair Mainwaring series**

Maironi family trilogy
Fogazzaro, Antonio
1 *Patriot* (1895)
Little world of the past
Original edition entitled *Il piccolo mondo antico*
2 *Sinner* (1901)
Man of the world
Original edition entitled *Il piccolo mondo moderno*
3 *Saint* (1906)
Original edition entitled *Il santo*
Companion volume: *Leila*, 1910

Maisie Leviston series
Cookson, Catherine
1 *Hamilton* (1983)
2 *Goodbye Hamilton* (1984)
3 *Harold* (1985)

Maitland and Harding series
Woods, Sara
see **Sir Nicholas Harding and Antony Maitland series**

Maitland series
Ballantyne, Jean
1 *Holiday trench* (1959)
2 *Kidnappers at Coombe* (1960)
3 *No mystery to the Maitlands* (1961)

Maitland series
Daniel, Roland
see **Jim Maitland series**
Oliphant, Margaret Oliphant Wilson
see **Mrs Margaret Maitland series**
Sapper
see **Jim Maitland series**
Severy, Martin
see **George Maitland series**

Maitlands series
Streatfeild, Noel
1 *Meet the Maitlands* (1978)
2 *All change at Cuckly Place* (1979)

Majeika series
Carpenter, Humphrey
see **Mister Majeika series**

Majipoor trilogy
Silverberg, Robert
1 *Lord Valentine's castle* (1980)
Desert of stolen dreams
2 *Majipoor chronicles* (1982)
3 *Valentine Pontifex* (1983)
Companion volume: *Revolt on Majipoor, a Crossroads adventure in the world of Robert Silverberg's Majipoor*, by Matt Costello, 1987

Major Adrian Titterton series
Brown, Edward
1 *Penny to spend* (1966)
2 *Vandersley* (1967)

Major Brains Cunningham series
Thorne, Ernest Pollett
1 *Smile of Cheng Su* (1946)
2 *Face of Inspector Britt* (1947)
3 *Sinister sanctuary* (1949)
4 *Justice is mine* (1950)
5 *Shadow of Doctor Ferrari* (1950)
6 *Moon dance* (1953)
7 *Red bamboo* (1954)
8 *Date with the departed* (1955)
9 *Lady with a gun* (1955)
10 *Bengal spider plan* (1961)
11 *House of the fragrant lotus* (1962)
12 *Chinese poker* (1964)
13 *Zero minus nine* (1964)
14 *Caribbean affair* (1966)
15 *Operation Dragnet* (1966)

Major Charles Douglas Kerrwood series
Duncan, Allan
1 *Official secret* (1937)
2 *Cabinet minister resigns* (1939)

Major Charles Lyson series
Oppenheim, Edward Phillips
Short stories
1 *Pulpit in the grill room* (1938)
2 *Milan grill room* (1940)
Further adventures of Louis, the manager and Major Lyson, the raconteur

Major Dick Burton series
Beckett, Mark
1 *Murder at the flower show* (1933)
2 *Murder of a magnate* (1934)
3 *Dower house mystery* (1935)
4 *Tea time tragedy* (1935)
5 *Escape from Dartmoor* (1936)
6 *Bullet in the cornice* (1937)

Major Faide series
Wade, Henry
1 *No friendly drop* (1931)
2 *High sheriff* (1937)

Major Gair Mainwaring series
Carnegie, Sacha
1 *Noble purpose* (1954)
2 *Sunset in the East* (1955)

Major General Duke James series
Rizzi, Timothy
1 *Nightstalker* (1992)
2 *Strike of the cobra* (1993)
3 *Phalanx dragon* (1994)

Major Gregory Lewis series
Frome, David
1 *Murder of an old man* (1929)
2 *Strange death of Martin Green* (1931)
Murder on the sixth hole

Major Harry Maxim series
Lyall, Gavin
1 *Secret servant* (1980)
2 *Conduct of Major Maxim* (1982)
3 *Crocus list* (1985)
4 *Uncle Target* (1988)

Major Hazelrigg series
Wren, Percival Christopher
1 *Beggars' horses* (1934)
Dark woman
2 *Worth wile* (1937)
To the hilt

Major Holbrooke series
Pullein-Thompson, Josephine
1 *Six ponies* (1946)
2 *Pony club team* (1950)
3 *Radney Riding Club* (1951)
4 *One day event* (1954)
5 *Pony club camp* (1957)

Major Hutton Seary series
Ross, John
1 *Moccasin man* (1936)
2 *Major* (1938)
3 *Major steps out* (1939)

Major John Falconbridge series
Somers, Derek
1 *Falcon, queen's messenger* (1954)
2 *Falcon and the diamond reef* (1955)

Major Krim series
Marfield, Dwight
1 *Mystery of King Cobra* (1933)
2 *Ghost on the balcony* (1939)

Major Maurice Hemyock series
Browne, Douglas Gordon
1 *Uncle William, and other stories* (1930)
2 *Dead won't bite* (1933)
3 *Looking glass murders* (1935)
4 *May week murders* (1937)

Major Mitchell Grant series
Thomas, Craig
see **Firefox series**

Major Mosson series
Cargill, Leslie
1 *Murder in the procession* (1937)
2 *It might have meant murder* (1940)
3 *Missing background* (1942)
4 *Next door to murder* (1948)

Major Peter Blair series
Anderson, John Richard Lane
1 *Reckoning in ice* (1971)
2 *Death on the rocks* (1973)
3 *Death in the Thames* (1974)
4 *Nine-spoked wheel* (1975)
5 *Death in the North Sea* (1975)
6 *Redundancy pay* (1976)
Death in the Channel
7 *Death in the desert* (1976)
8 *Death in the city* (1977)
9 *Death in the Caribbean* (1977)
10 *Death in the greenhouse* (1978)
11 *Death in a high latitude* (1981)
Death in the high latitude

Major Roger Bennion series
Adams, Herbert
1 *Rogues fall out* (1928)
2 *Old Jew mystery* (1936)
3 *Death off the fairway* (1936)
4 *Single hair* (1937)
5 *Bluff* (1938)
6 *Damned spot* (1938)
7 *Black death* (1939)
8 *Nineteenth hole mystery* (1939)
9 *Case of the stolen bridegroom* (1940)
10 *Chief witness* (1940)
11 *Stab in the back* (1941)
12 *Roger Bennion's double* (1941)
13 *Araway oath* (1942)
14 *Signal for invasion* (1942)
15 *Victory song* (1943)
16 *Four winds* (1944)
17 *Writing on the wall* (1945)
18 *Welcome home* (1946)
19 *Diamonds are trumps* (1947)
20 *Crime wave at Little Cornford* (1948)
21 *One to play* (1949)
22 *Dean's daughters* (1950)
23 *Sleeping draught* (1951)
24 *Exit the skeleton* (1952)
25 *Spectre in brown* (1953)
26 *Slippery Dick* (1954)
27 *Judas kiss* (1955)
28 *Death on the first tee* (1957)
29 *Death of a viewer* (1958)

Major series
Greene, L Patrick
see **Aubrey Saint John Major series**

Major Thompson series
Daninos, Pierre
1 *Major Thompson lives in France and discovers the French* (1954)
Notebooks of Major Thompson
Original edition entitled *Les carnets du Major Thompson*
2 *Major Thompson and I* (1956)
Original edition entitled *Le secret du Major Thompson*
3 *Major Thompson goes French* (1968)
Original edition entitled *Le Major Tricolore*

Make it work series
Firmin, Peter
1 *Mills and the big wheels* (1993)
2 *Ships and cranes* (1993)
3 *Racing cars and cycles* (1993)
4 *Flying machines* (1993)

Make me a star series
Pfeffer, Susan Beth
1 *Fantasy summer* (1984)
2 *Take two and rolling* (1985)
3 *Wanting it all* (1985)
4 *Prime time* (1985)
5 *Love scenes* (1986)

Make me laugh series
Roop, Peter
1 *Space out!* (1984)
Jokes about outer space
2 *Go hog wild!* (1984)
Jokes from down on the farm
3 *Out to lunch!* (1984)
Jokes about food
4 *Stick out your tongue!* (1986)
Jokes about doctors and patients
5 *Going buggy!* (1986)
Jokes about insects
6 *Let's celebrate!* (1986)
Jokes about holidays

Make-believe stories series
Hope, Laura Lee
House pseudonym
1 *Story of a sawdust doll* (1920)
2 *Story of a white rocking horse* (1920)
3 *Story of a lamb on wheels* (1920)
4 *Story of a bold tin soldier* (1920)
5 *Story of a candy rabbit* (1920)
6 *Story of a monkey on a stick* (1920)
7 *Story of a calico clown* (1920)
8 *Story of a nodding donkey* (1921)
9 *Story of a china cat* (1921)
10 *Story of a plush bear* (1921)
11 *Story of a stuffed elephant* (1922)
12 *Story of a woolly dog* (1923)

Makepeace and Dempsey series
Carr-Martindale, Jesse
see **Dempsey and Makepeace series**

Makepeace series
Farmer, Penelope
see **Charlotte and Emma Makepeace series**

Maker series
Card, Orson Scott
see **Alvin Maker series**

Makers series
McCollum, Michael
1 *Life PROBE* (1983)
2 *Procyon's promise* (1985)

Making of America, second series
Willoughby, Lee Davis
see **Women who won the West series**

Making of America series
Cameron, Lou
This sequence has many authors including Michael Avallone, Charles Beardsley, Lou Cameron, Ward Davis, William Louis De Andrea, Aaron Fletcher, Georgia Granger, Greg Hunt, Leo Patrick Kelley, Richard Laymon, Ian McMahan, Paula Moore, Karl Myer, Barry Myers, Tad Richards, George Ryan, James Seafidel, Jeanne Sommers, Jane Toombs, Robert Vaughan, Walter Wager, Francis Webb, Elizabeth Zachary; from number 11 all titles were published under the pseudonym Lee Davis Willoughby and the authorship is indicated in those cases where it is known
1 *Wilderness seekers* (1979)
Fletcher, Aaron
2 *Mountain breed* (1979)
Sommers, Jeanne
3 *Conestoga people* (1979)
Toombs, Jane
4 *Forty-niners* (1979)
Moore, Paula
5 *Hearts divide* (1979)
Sommers, Jeanne
6 *Builders* (1979)
Zachary, Elizabeth
7 *Land rushers* (1979)
Granger, Georgia
8 *Wild and the wayward* (1980)
Toombs, Jane
9 *Texans* (1980)
Myers, Barry
10 *Alaskans* (1980)
Willoughby, Lee Davis
11 *Golden Staters* (1980)
12 *River people* (1981) [Hunt]
13 *Landgrabbers* (1981) [Myers]
14 *Ranchers* (1981) [Vaughan]
15 *Homesteaders* (1981)
16 *Frontier healers* (1981) [Fletcher]
17 *Buffalo people* (1981) [Myers]
18 *Border breed* (1981) [Toombs]
19 *Far islanders* (1981) [Vaughan]
20 *Boomers* (1981) [Beardsley]
21 *Wildcatters* (1981)
22 *Gunfighters* (1982) [Avallone]
23 *Cajuns of Willoughby* (1982) [Webb]
24 *Donner people* (1982) [Myers]
25 *Creoles* (1982) [Toombs]
26 *Nightriders* (1982)
27 *Sooners* (1982)
28 *Express riders* (1982)
29 *Vigilantes* (1982) [Davis]
30 *Soldiers of fortune* (1982) [Ryan]
31 *Wranglers* (1982) [Myer]
32 *Baja people* (1983)
33 *Yukon breed* (1983) [Myers]
34 *Smugglers* (1983)
35 *Voyageurs* (1983) [De Andrea]
36 *Barbary Coasters* (1983)
37 *Whalers* (1983)
38 *Canadians* (1983) [Richards]
39 *Prophet's people* (1983) [Kelley]
40 *Lawmen* (1983) [Laymon]
41 *Copper kings* (1983) [Cameron]
42 *Caribbeans* (1983) [Wager]
43 *Trail blazers* (1983)
44 *Gamblers* (1983) [McMahan]
45 *Robber barons* (1983)
46 *Assassins* (1984) [Seafidel]
47 *Bounty hunters* (1984)
48 *Texas Rangers* (1984)
49 *Outlaws* (1984)
50 *Fugitives* (1984)
51 *Frontier detectives* (1984)
52 *Raiders* (1984)
53 *Rough riders* (1984)
54 *Warriors of the code* (1985) [Vaughan]
55 *Scarlet sisters* (1985) [Myers]
56 *Sixgun apostles* (1985) [Avallone]

Making of the cities series
Willoughby, Lee Davis
see **Americana series**

Making out series
Lantz, Francess Lin
1 *Truth about making out* (1990)
2 *Dear Celeste, my life is a mess* (1991)

Making series
Whelpton, Eric
Autobiography
1 *Making of a European* (1974)
2 *Making of an Englishman* (1977)

Malabar series
Bromfield, Louis
Reminiscences of American farm life
1 *Pleasant Valley* (1945)
2 *Malabar Farm* (1948)
3 *Out of the earth* (1950)
4 *From my experience* (1955)
One volume abridged edition entitled *Louis Bromfield at Malabar*, 1988

Malarkey series
Kennedy, William
see **Charley Malarkey series**

Malay series
Dalton, Clive
1 *Malay canoe* (1960)
2 *Malay boy* (1961)
3 *Malay island* (1962)
4 *Malay cruise* (1964)
5 *Malay schooner* (1965)
Mystery of the Malay schooner
6 *Malay treasure* (1967)
7 *Malay pirate* (1972)

Malayan trilogy
Burgess, Anthony
1 *Time for a tiger* (1956)
2 *Enemy in the blanket* (1958)
3 *Beds in the East* (1959)
One volume editions entitled *The Malayan trilogy*, 1964, and *The long day wanes*, 1965

Malcolm Kenton series
Harvester, Simon
1 *Bamboo screen* (1955)
2 *Dragon road* (1956)
3 *Paradise men* (1956)
4 *Golden fear* (1957)
5 *Copper butterfly* (1957)

Malcolm P Muddle series
Mallett, Jerry J
1 *Mystery at Chung's Chinese restaurant* (1987)
2 *Mystery at Madame Darkle's wax museum* (1987)
3 *Mystery at the Hollender Hotel* (1987)
4 *Mystery at the Laff-a-Lott amusement park* (1987)
5 *Mystery at the Seesaw Cinema Company* (1987)

Malcolm Sage series
Jenkins, Herbert
1 *John Dene of Toronto* (1919)
2 *Malcolm Sage, detective* (1920)
One story about Malcolm Sage included in *The Stiffsons, and other stories*, 1928

Malcolm series
Fairlie, Gerard
see **Mister Malcolm series**
Grady, James
see **Condor series**
Graham, Neill
see **Solo Malcolm series**

Malcolm series
Macdonald, George
1 *Malcolm* (1875)
Fisherman's lady
The second title is a revised edition
2 *Marquis of Lossie* (1877)
Marquis' secret
The second title is a revised edition

Malcolm series
Taylor, Jenny
see **Messy Malcolm series**

Malcolm Warren series
Kitchin, Clifford Henry Benn
1 *Death of my aunt* (1929)
2 *Crime at Christmas* (1934)
3 *Death of his uncle* (1939)
4 *Cornish fox* (1949)

Malcome Steele series
Scott, Mansfield
see **Inspector Malcome Steele series**

Maledon and Parker series
Gardner, Jerome
see **Hanging Judge series**

Malgudi series
Narayan, Rasipuram Krishnaswami
1 *Waiting for the Mahatma* (1955)
2 *Financial expert* (1952)
3 *Mister Sampath* (1949)
Printer of Malgudi
4 *English teacher* (1945)
Grateful to life and death
5 *Dark room* (1938)
6 *Bachelor of arts* (1937)
7 *Swami and friends* (1935)
Numbers 6 and 7 also published in one volume 1954
8 *Guide* (1958)
9 *Man-eater of Malgudi* (1961)
10 *Vendor of sweets* (1967)
Sweet-vendor
11 *Horse and two goats, and other stories* (1970)
12 *Painter of signs* (1976)
13 *Malgudi days* (1982)
Malgudi days, 1941 has different contents which are reprinted in other volumes in the sequence
14 *Tiger for Malgudi* (1983)
15 *Under the banyan tree, and other stories* (1985)
16 *Talkative man* (1986)
17 *World of Nagaraj* (1990)
Selections: *Dodu, and other stories*, 1943, *Cyclone, and other stories*, 1944, *An astrologer's day, and other stories*, 1947, *Lawley Road, and other stories*, 1956

Malins, Mornington and Hawkins series
Dix, Maurice Buxton
see **Tommy Malins, Anthony Mornington and George Hawkins series**

Malinson brothers trilogy
Aspinall, Ruth
1 *Yesterday's kingdom* (1961)
2 *Promise of his return* (1962)
3 *Echo sounding* (1965)

Malko Linge series
This sequence includes all the titles which have been translated into English; there are 23 other untranslated titles published between 1966 and 1975
De Villiers, Gerard
1 *S.A.S. versus the C.I.A.* (1965)
Original edition entitled *S.A.S. contre C.I.A.*
2 *Black magic in New York* (1967)
Operation New York
Original edition entitled *Magie noir a New York*
3 *West of Jerusalem* (1967)
Original edition entitled *A l'ouest de Jerusalem*
4 *Death of the River Kwai* (1968)
Original edition entitled *L'or de la Rivier Kwai*
5 *Countess and the spy* (1969)
Original edition entitled *Le bal de la Comtesse Adler*
6 *Operation Apocalypse* (1970)
Original edition entitled *Operation Apocalypse*
7 *Que viva Guevara* (1970)
Original edition entitled *Qui vive Guevara*
8 *Man from Kabul* (1971)
Original edition entitled *L'homme de Kabul*
9 *Angel of vengeance* (1973)
Original edition entitled *L'ange de Montevideo*
10 *Kill Kissinger* (1974)
Original edition entitled *Kill Kissinger*
11 *Belfast connection* (1974)
Original edition entitled *Furie a Belfast*
12 *Checkpoint Charlie* (1974)
Original edition entitled *Rendez-vous a Boris Gleb*
13 *Hostage in Tokyo* (1975)
Original edition entitled *Les otages de Tokyo*
14 *Death in Santiago* (1975)
Original edition entitled *L'ordre regne a Santiago*
15 *Portuguese defection* (1975)
Original edition entitled *Les sorciers du tage*

Mall series
Sloan, Carolyn
1 *Setting up shop* (1989)
2 *Open for business* (1989)
3 *Gangs, ghosts and gypsies* (1989)
4 *Money matters* (1989)

Mallaby series
Norman, Bruce
see **James Mallaby series**

Mallamshire series
Fitzroy, Rosamond
1 *Manor of Brays* (1979)
2 *Widow's might* (1980)
3 *American duchess* (1980)
4 *Ill fares the land* (1987)
5 *Barnaby's charity* (1988)

Mallandine family trilogy
Moore, William
1 *Bayonets in the sun* (1974)
2 *Against the Assegais* (1975)
Bushman!
3 *Storm of steel* (1975)

Mallard series
Quackenbush, Robert Mead
see **Miss Mallard series**
Spiller, Andrew
see **Chief Inspector Duck Mallard series**

Mallare series
Hecht, Ben
see **Fantazius Mallare series**

Mallen family trilogy
Cookson, Catherine
1 *Mallen streak* (1973)
2 *Mallen girl* (1974)
3 *Mallen litter* (1974)
Mallen lot
One volume edition entitled *The Mallen novels*, 1979

Maller series
Gregoire, Jean Albert
see **Auguste Maller series**

Malleson series
Godfrey, William
see **Test cricket series**

Mallett series
Fitt, Mary
see **Superintendent Mallett series**
Hare, Cyril
see **Inspector Mallett series**
Macdonnell, James Edmond
see **Commander William Mallett series**
Orgill, Douglas
see **William Mallett series**
Parrish, Frank
see **Dan Mallett series**

Mallin and Coe series
Ormerod, Roger
see **David Mallin and George Coe series**

Malling-Gaywood family series
Seymour, Beatrice Kean
1 *Buds of May* (1943)
2 *Tumbled house* (1946)
3 *Children grow up* (1949)

Malloreon series
Eddings, David
1 *Guardians of the West* (1987)
2 *King of the Murgos* (1988)
3 *Demon lord of Karanda* (1988)
4 *Sorceress of Darshiva* (1989)
5 *Seeress of Kell* (1991)

Mallory and Duncan series
Asprin, Robert Lynn
see **Duncan and Mallory series**

Mallory children series
Bawden, Nina
1 *Secret passage* (1963)
House of secrets
2 *On the run* (1964)
Three on the run

Mallory family series
Boileau, Ethel
1 *Turnip-tops* (1932)
2 *Ballade in G minor* (1938)

Mallory series
Collins, Max Allan
1 *Baby blue rip-off* (1983)
2 *No cure for death* (1983)
3 *Kill your darlings* (1984)
4 *Shroud for Aquarius* (1985)
5 *Nice weekend for a murder* (1986)

Mallory series
Garrison, Frederick
see **West Point series**
Hoult, Norah
see **Monty Mallory series**
Lindsey, Johanna
see **Anthony Mallory series**
Maclean, Alistair
see **Navarone series**
Sennocke, T J R
see **Sergeant Mallory series**

Mallorys and Medleys series
Willard, Barbara
see **Mantlemass series**

Malloy series
Chase, James Hadley
see **Vic Malloy series**
Hess, Joan
see **Claire Malloy series**

Malloy series
Stoddard, Charles
1 *Trapper of Rat River* (1941)
2 *Malloy of the Royal Mounted* (1944)
3 *Killer at Fort Norman* (1944)
4 *Timber beasts* (1945)
5 *Killer of Sheep River* (1946)
6 *Tundra trail* (1947)
7 *Death rides the rails* (1955)
8 *Golden Arrow* (1956)
9 *Caribou patrol* (1957)

Malone family trilogy
Peters, Maureen
1 *Tansy* (1975)
2 *Kate Alanna* (1975)
3 *Child called Freedom* (1976)

Malone series
Cleary, Jon
see **Scobie Malone series**
Dower, Penn
see **Marshal Bret Malone series**
Dresser, Davis
see **Twister Malone series**
Findley, Ferguson
see **Johnny Malone series**
Hawes, Louise
see **Nelson Malone series**
Herman, Charlotte
see **Max Malone series**
Jacobs, Thomas Curtis Hicks
see **Jim Malone series**
Morland, Nigel
see **Steven Malone series**
Rice, Craig
see **John Joseph Malone series**
Weber, Lenora Mattingly
see **Beany Malone series**

Malone trilogy
Phillips, Mark
see **Ken Malone trilogy**

Malory Towers series
Blyton, Enid
1 *First term at Malory Towers* (1946)
2 *Second form at Malory Towers* (1947)
3 *Third term at Malory Towers* (1948)
4 *Upper Fourth at Malory Towers* (1949)
5 *In the Fifth at Malory Towers* (1950)
6 *Last term at Malory Towers* (1951)

Malter and Saunders series
Potok, Chaim
see **Danny Saunders and reuven Malter series**

Maltravers series
Richardson, Robert
see **Augustus Maltravers series**

Mama and Ike series
Snyder, Carol
see **Ike and Mama series**

Mama and papa series
Saroyan, William
1 *Mama, I love you* (1956)
2 *Papa, you're crazy* (1958)

Mama series
Hopkins, Lee Bennett
1 *Mama* (1977)
2 *Mama and her boys* (1981)

Mame series
Dennis, Patrick
see **Auntie Mame series**

Mamie Stover series
Huie, William Bradford
1 *Revolt of Mamie Stover* (1951)
2 *Americanization of Emily* (1959)
3 *Hotel Mamie Stover* (1962)

Mamur Zapt series
Pearce, Michael
1 *Mamur Zapt and the return of the carpet* (1988)
2 *Mamur Zapt and the night of the dog* (1989)
3 *Mamur Zapt and the donkey-vous* (1990)
4 *Mamur Zapt and the men behind* (1991)
5 *Mamur Zapt and the girl in the Nile* (1991)
6 *Mamur Zapt and the spoils of Egypt* (1992)
7 *Mamur Zapt and the camel of destruction* (1993)

Man alone series
Norwood, Victor George Charles
1 *Man alone* (1956)
2 *Hand full of diamonds* (1960)

Man and mantra trilogy
Anthony, Piers
see **Of man and mantra trilogy**

Man called Black series
Manson, Will
1 *Man called Black* (1967)
2 *Chinese conundrum* (1967)
3 *Dangerous one* (1968)
4 *Very Black deed* (1968)

Man called Horse series
This sequence has two authors
Johnson, Dorothy Marie
1 *Indian country* (1953)
Man called Horse
Wells, Angus
2 *Return of a man called Horse* (1976)
Based on a screenplay

Man-eaters series
Corbett, Jim
1 *Man-eaters of Kumaon* (1946)
2 *Man-eating leopard of Rudraprayag* (1948)
Abridged one volume edition of numbers 1 and 2 published as *Man against man-eaters*, 1954
3 *Temple tiger and more man-eaters of Kumaon* (1954)

Man-eaters series
Ludwig, Charles Shelton
see **Missionary adventure series**

Man from A.P.E. series
Daniels, Norman A
1 *Hunt Club* (1964)
2 *Overkill* (1964)
3 *Spy ghost* (1965)
4 *Operation K* (1965)
5 *Operation N* (1965)
6 *Operation T* (1967)
7 *Operation VC* (1967)
8 *Operation S-L* (1971)

Man from Atlantis series
Woodley, Richard
1 *Man from Atlantis* (1977)
Sea kill
2 *Death scouts* (1977)
3 *Killer spores* (1978)
4 *Ark of doom* (1978)

Man from C.H.A.R.I.S.M.A. series
Mark, Ted
1 *Man from C.H.A.R.I.S.M.A.* (1970)
2 *Right on, Relevant* (1970)
3 *Rip off, Relevant* (1970)

Man from O.R.G.Y. series
Mark, Ted
1 *Man from O.R.G.Y.* (1965)
2 *Nine-month caper* (1965)
3 *Here's your O.R.G.Y.* (1965)
4 *Real gone girls* (1966)
5 *Around the world is no trip* (1966)
6 *Doctor Nyet* (1966)
7 *Hard day's knight* (1966)
Short stories
8 *My son the double agent* (1966)
9 *Unhatched egghead* (1966)
10 *Dial O for O.R.G.Y.* (1967)
11 *Room at the topless* (1967)
12 *Square root of sex* (1967)
13 *I was a teeny-bopper for the CIA* (1967)
14 *Back home at the O.R.G.Y.* (1968)
15 *Come be my O.R.G.Y.* (1968)
16 *Girls from O.R.G.Y.* (1968)
17 *This nude for hire* (1969)
18 *Where's your O.R.G.Y.?* (1969)
19 *Honeymoon in Honolulu* (1970)
20 *Regina Blue* (1972)
21 *Beauty and the bug* (1975)

Man from P.U.S.S.Y. series
Rico, Don
see **Burgess Cardigan series**

Man from Planet X trilogy
Adams, Hunter
1 *She-beast* (1975)
2 *Tiger by the tail* (1975)
3 *Devil to pay* (1977)

Man from S.T.U.D. series
Paul, F W
1 *Three for an orgy* (1968)
2 *Orgy at Madame Dracula's* (1968)
3 *Sock it to me, zombie!* (1968)
4 *Solid gold screw* (1968)
5 *Tool of the trade* (1969)
6 *Rape is a no-no* (1969)
7 *Planned parenthood caper* (1969)
8 *Girl with the polka dot box* (1969)
9 *Lay of the land* (1969)
Numbers 2, 3 and 9 also published in one volume entitled *The man from S.T.U.D. versus the Mafia*, 1972

Man from Snowy River series
This sequence has two authors
Mitchell, Elyne
1 *Man from Snowy River* (1982)
The stirring tale of the boy who became the Man from Snowy River based on the film
Paterson, Andrew Barton
2 *Man from Snowy River, and other verses* (1895)
3 *Rio Grande's last race, and other verses* (1902)

Man from T.O.M.C.A.T. series
Knight, Mallory T
1 *Dozen deadly dragons of joy* (1967)
2 *Million missing maidens* (1967)
3 *Terrible ten* (1967)
4 *Dirty rotten depriving ray* (1967)
5 *Tsimmis in Tangier* (1968)
6 *Malignant metaphysical menace* (1968)
7 *Ominous orgy* (1969)
8 *Peking pornographer* (1969)
9 *Return of Alexander Graham Wang* (1969)
10 *Doom dollies* (1970)
11 *Bra burners' brigade* (1971)

Man from U.N.C.L.E. series
This sequence has ten authors; the English editions of this sequence omit numbers 10-15 and 17 and are numbered in a different order
Avallone, Michael
1 *Man from U.N.C.L.E.* (1965)
Thousand coffins affair
Whittington, Harry
2 *Doomsday affair* (1965)
Oram, John
3 *Copenhagen affair* (1965)
McDaniel, David
4 *Dagger affair* (1965)
Phillifent, John Thomas
5 *Mad scientist affair* (1966)
McDaniel, David
6 *Vampire affair* (1966)
Leslie, Peter
7 *Radioactive camel affair* (1966)
McDaniel, David
8 *Monster wheel affair* (1967)
Leslie, Peter
9 *Diving dames affair* (1967)
Holly, Joan Hunter
10 *Assassination affair* (1967)
Stratton, Thomas
11 *Invisibility affair* (1967)
12 *Mind-twisters affair* (1967)
McDaniel, David
13 *Rainbow affair* (1967)
Davies, Fredric
14 *Cross of gold affair* (1968)
McDaniel, David
15 *Utopia affair* (1968)
Leslie, Peter
16 *Splintered sunglasses affair* (1968)
McDaniel, David
17 *Hollow crown affair* (1969)
Leslie, Peter
18 *Unfair fare affair* (1969)
Phillifent, John Thomas
19 *Power cube affair* (1969)
20 *Corfu affair* (1970)
Bernard, Joel
21 *Thinking machine affair* (1970)
Oram, John
22 *Stone-cold dead in the market affair* (1970)
Leslie, Peter
23 *Finger in the sky affair* (1971)
Holly, Joan Hunter
24 *Wolves and the lambs affair* (1977)
Companion volumes: *The man from U.N.C.L.E. and the affair of the gentle saboteur*, by Brandon Keith, 1966, *The man from U.N.C.L.E. and the affair of the gun-runners' gold*, by Brandon Keith, 1967, *The Calcutta affair*, by George S Elrick, 1967, *The Man from U.N.C.L.E.'s ABCs of espionage*, by John Hill, 1966, *U.N.C.L.E. technical manual*, by Glenn A Magee, 1986

Man in China series
Munro, Donald Jacques
1 *Concept of man in early China* (1969)
2 *Concept of man in contemporary China* (1977)

Man in the gray flannel suit series
Wilson, Sloan
1 *Man in the gray flannel suit* (1955)
Man in the grey flannel suit
2 *Man in the gray flannel suit II* (1984)
Companion volume: *What shall we wear to this party, the man in the gray flannel suit 20 years before and after*, 1976

Man-Kzin wars series
Niven, Larry
1 *Man-Kzin wars* (1988)
Co-authors: Dean Ing and Poul Anderson
2 *Man-Kzin wars II* (1989)
Co-authors: Dean Ing, Jerry Pournelle and Stephen Michael Stirling
3 *Man-Kzin wars III* (1990)
Co-authors: Poul Anderson, Jerry Pournelle and Stephen Michael Stirling
4 *Man-Kzin wars IV* (1991)
5 *Man-Kzin wars V* (1992)
Companion volumes: *Cathouse*, by Dean Ing, 1990, *The children's hour*, by Jerry Pournelle and Stephen Michael Stirling, 1991, *Inconstant star*, by Poul Anderson, 1991

Man of his word series
Duncan, Dave
1 *Magic casement* (1990)
2 *Faery lands forlorn* (1991)
3 *Perilous seas* (1991)
4 *Emperor and clown* (1991)

Man of Justice series
Cafferty, Jake
see **Vic Merritt series**

Man of liberty series
Wibberley, Leonard
1 *Young man from the Piedmont* (1963)
The youth of Thomas Jefferson
2 *Dawn in the trees* (1964)
Thomas Jefferson, the years1776 to 1789
3 *Gales of spring* (1965)
Thomas Jefferson, the years 1789 to 1801
4 *Time of the harvest* (1966)
Thomas Jefferson, the years 1801 to 1826

Man on my back series
Linklater, Eric
Autobiography
1 *Man on my back* (1941)
2 *Year of space* (1953)
Travels in Japan, Korea, New Zealand, Australia, New Guinea and Ceylon
3 *Fanfare for a tin hat* (1970)

Man series
Heller, Keith
see **George Man series**

Man with no name series
Millard, Joseph John
see **Dollar series**

Man without qualities series
Musil, Robert
Original one volume edition entitled Der Mann ohne Eigenschaften
1 *Sort of introduction* (1930)
Also includes *The like of it now happens*, part 1
2 *Like of it now happens, part 2* (1933)
3 *Into the millenium* (1943)
Unfinished at the author's death

Manahoa series
Owen, Roderic
1 *Green heart of heaven* (1955)
2 *Worse than wanton* (1956)

Manatitlans series
Smile, R Elton
1 *Manatitlans* (1877)
Alternative title: A record of recent scientific explorations in the Andean La Plata
2 *Investigations and experiences of M. Shawtinbach at Saar Soong, Sumatra* (1879)
Originally published anonymously

Manawaka series
Laurence, Margaret
1 *Stone angel* (1964)
2 *Jest of God* (1966)
Rachel, Rachel
Now I lay me down
3 *Fire-dwellers* (1969)

4 *Bird in the house* (1970)
Short stories
5 *Diviners* (1974)

Manchenil series
Douglass, Donald McNutt
see **Bolivar Manchenil series**

Manchester series
Spring, Howard
1 *Shabby tiger* (1934)
2 *Rachel Rosing* (1935)

Manciple and Blow series
Hopkins, Kenneth
see **Doctor William Blow and Professor Gideon Manciple series**

Mancuso and Borgneff series
Luckless, John
see **Eddie Mancuso and Vasily Borgneff series**

Mandarin series
Zorro
see **Doctor Death series**

Mandell-Essington series
Clouston, Joseph Storer
see **Mister Francis Mandell-Essington series**

Manderton series
Williams, Valentine
see **Inspector Manderton series**

Mandeville trilogy
Trease, Geoffrey
1 *Mandeville* (1980)
2 *Saraband for shadows* (1982)
3 *Cormorant venture* (1984)

Mandie series
Leppard, Lois Gladys
1 *Mandie and the secret tunnel* (1983)
2 *Mandie and the Cherokee legend* (1983)
3 *Mandie and the ghost bandits* (1984)
4 *Mandie and the forbidden attic* (1985)
5 *Mandie and the trunk's secret* (1985)
6 *Mandie and the medicine man* (1986)
7 *Mandie and the Charleston phantom* (1986)
8 *Mandie and the abandoned mine* (1987)
9 *Mandie and the hidden treasure* (1987)
10 *Mandie and the mysterious bells* (1988)
11 *Mandie and the holiday surprise* (1988)
12 *Mandie and the Washington nightmare* (1989)
13 *Mandie and the midnight journey* (1989)
14 *Mandie and the shipboard mystery* (1990)
15 *Mandie and the foreign spies* (1990)
16 *Mandie and the silent catacombs* (1990)
17 *Mandie and the singing chalet* (1991)
18 *Mandie and the jumping juniper* (1991)
19 *Mandie and the mysterious fisherman* (1992)
20 *Mandie and the windmill's message* (1992)
21 *Mandie and the fiery rescue* (1992)
22 *Mandie and the angel's secret* (1993)
23 *Mandie and the dangerous imposter* (1994)
Companion volume: *Mandie's cookbook*, 1991

Mandrake series
Bonett, John
see **Professor Mandrake series**

Haythorne, John
see **Oliver Mandrake series**

Mandrell series
McAuliffe, Frank
see **Augustus Mandrell series**

Mandy and Michael series
Coles, Alison
see **Michael and Mandy series**

Mandy and Mick series
Schmidt, Annie Maria Geertruida
see **Bob and Jilly series**

Mandy, Mops and Cubby series
Blyton, Enid
1 *Mandy, Mops and Cubby find a house* (1952)
2 *Mandy, Mops and Cubby again* (1952)
3 *Mandy, Mops and Cubby and the whitewash* (1955)

Manfred series
Hilliard, Alec Rowley
see **Judge Manfred series**

Mango season series
Osbourne, Ivor
1 *Mango season* (1979)
2 *Prodigal* (1987)

Manhattan series
Adams Round Table
1 *Missing in Manhattan* (1992)
2 *Justice in Manhattan* (1994)

Manhattan series
Wright, Terrance Michael
1 *Manhattan ghost story* (1984)
2 *Waiting room* (1986)

Manila Bay series
Marshall, William Leonard
see **Battling Mendez series**

Manipulator trilogy
Mark, Jan
1 *Ennead* (1978)
2 *Divide and rule* (1979)
3 *Aquarius* (1982)

Manitou series
Masterton, Graham
1 *Manitou* (1975)
2 *Revenge of the Manitou* (1979)
3 *Burial* (1994)

Mann series
Spillane, Mickey
see **Tiger Mann series**

Mannering series
Morton, Anthony
see **Baron series**
Paternoster, George Sidney
see **Randolph Mannering series**

Manners series
Dutton, Charles Judson
see **Harley Manners series**
Moffatt, James
see **Silas Manners series**

Manning and Grogan series
Neville, Margot
see **Inspector Grogan and Sergeant Manning series**

Manning series
Cobb, Belton
see **Superintendent Manning series**
Dines, Michael
see **Johnny Manning series**

Mannion family series
Dark, Eleanor
1 *Timeless land* (1941)
2 *Storm of time* (1948)
3 *No barrier* (1953)

Mannix series
This sequence has two authors; based on a television series
Avallone, Michael
1 *Mannix* (1968)
Maccargo, J T
2 *Faces of murder* (1975)
3 *Fine day for dying* (1975)
4 *Walk on the blind side* (1975)
5 *Round trip to nowhere* (1975)

Manny De Witt series
Rabe, Peter
1 *Girl in a big brass bed* (1965)
2 *Spy who was three feet tall* (1966)
3 *Code name Gadget* (1967)

Manny Moon series
Deming, Richard
see **Manville Moon series**

Manorfield Stud series
Vaughan, Carol
1 *Missing Matilda* (1964)
2 *Two foals for Matilda* (1965)
3 *Dancing horse* (1966)
4 *Trekker's trail* (1967)
5 *King of the castle* (1968)

Mansart trilogy
Du Bois, William Edward Burghardt
see **Black flame trilogy**

Manse series
Cantrell, Lisa Wright
1 *Manse* (1987)
2 *Torments* (1990)

Mansel series
Yates, Dornford
see **Jonah Mansel series**

Mansell series
Masefield, John
see **Autobiography of a corpse series**

Mansfield Park series
This sequence has three authors
Austen, Jane
1 *Mansfield Park* (1814)
Aiken, Joan
2 *Mansfield revisited* (1984)
Gordon, Victor
3 *Mrs Rushworth* (1989)
Companion volume: *Ladysmead*, by Jane Gillespie, 1982

Man-Shy series
Davison, Frank Dalby
1 *Man-Shy* (1931)
Red heifer
A story of men and cattle
2 *Woman at the mill* (1940)
Short stories

Manson series
Divine, David
see **Mig and Peter Manson series**
Radford, Edwin
see **Doctor Manson series**
Turner, Bill
see **Detective Inspector Manson series**

Mantlemass series
Willard, Barbara
1 *Lark and the laurel* (1970)
Set during the Wars of the Roses
2 *Miller's boy* (1976)
Set in the late 15th century
3 *Sprig of broom* (1971)
Set in the late 15th century
4 *Cold wind blowing* (1972)
Set during the dissolution of the monasteries by Henry VIII
5 *Flight of the swans* (1980)
Set during the Spanish Armada
6 *Iron lily* (1973)
A story of iron-working in the 17th century
7 *Eldest son* (1977)
A story of horse breeding in the 17th century
8 *Harrow and harvest* (1974)
9 *Keys of Mantlemass* (1981)
Short stories
Companion volume: *Queen of the Pharisee's children*, 1983

Manton series
Underwood, Michael
see **Superintendent Simon Manton series**

Manuel and his descendants series
Cabell, James Branch
see **Dom Manuel and his descendants series**

Manville Moon series
Deming, Richard
1 *Gallows in my garden* (1952)
2 *Tweak the devil's nose* (1953)
Hand-picked to die
3 *Whistle past the graveyard* (1955)
Give the girl a gun
4 *Juvenile delinquent* (1958)

Many lives of Underfoot the cat series
Maguire, Jack
1 *Trouble and more trouble* (1990)
2 *Hit the road and strike it rich* (1991)
3 *Surprise and double surprise* (1991)

Many years series
Rubinstein, Arthur
Autobiography
1 *My young years* (1973)
2 *My many years* (1980)

Manyshaped trilogy
Tepper, Sheri S
see **Mavin Manyshaped series**

Maori Wars trilogy
Brathwaite, Errol
1 *Flying fish* (1964)
2 *Needle eye* (1965)
3 *Evil day* (1967)

Maple Hill Farm series
Provensen, Alice
1 *Our animal friends* (1974)
Our animal friends at Maple Hill Farm
2 *Year at Maple Hill Farm* (1978)
3 *Horse and a hound, a goat and a gander* (1979)

Maple Street Five series
Gezi, Kal
1 *Mystery of the missing raccoon* (1978)
2 *Mystery of the live ghosts* (1978)
3 *Mystery of the secret club house* (1978)
4 *Mystery of the missing dogs* (1980)
5 *Mystery of the missing footprints* (1980)
6 *Mystery of the blind writer* (1980)
7 *Mystery of the midget clown* (1980)
8 *Mystery at Midget Falls* (1980)
9 *Mystery at the tree house* (1980)

Maple Street kids series
Roos, Stephen
1 *Dear Santa, make me a star* (1991)
2 *Leave it to Augie* (1991)
3 *Silver secrets* (1991)
4 *My blue tongue* (1991)

Maplechester series
Ford, Elizabeth
1 *Empty heart* (1957)
2 *Cottage at Drimble* (1957)
3 *Butter Market House* (1958)
4 *Heron's Nest* (1960)
5 *Week by the sea* (1962)
6 *Holiday engagement* (1963)
7 *No room for Joanna* (1964)

Mappin series
Footner, Hulbert
see **Amos Lee Mappin series**

Maquis series
Millar, George
Autobiography
1 *Maquis* (1945)
Waiting in the night
2 *Horned pigeon* (1946)

Mara and Sammy series
Van der Meer, Ron
see **Sammy and Mara series**

Maradick series
Walpole, Hugh
1 *Captives* (1920)
2 *Maradick at forty* (1910)
A transition
3 *Fortitude* (1913)
A true and faithful account of the education of an explorer
4 *Portrait of a man with red hair* (1925)
A romantic macabre

Marathon man series
Goldman, William
1 *Marathon man* (1974)
2 *Brothers* (1981)

Marathon trilogy
Smith, David Alexander
1 *Marathon* (1982)
2 *Rendezvous* (1988)
3 *Homecoming* (1990)

Marauders series
McGann, Michael
1 *Marauders* (1989)
2 *Blood kin* (1989)
3 *Liar's dice* (1990)
4 *Convoy strike* (1990)
5 *Ghost warriors* (1990)
6 *Blood and fire* (1991)
7 *Fortress of death* (1991)

Marble foot series
Quennell, Peter
Autobiography
1 *Marble foot* (1976)
1905-1938
2 *Wanton chase* (1980)
From 1939

Marble Mountain series
Gardner, Hugh
1 *Beyond the Marble Mountain* (1948)
2 *Back to the Marble Mountain* (1949)
One volume edition entitled *Tales from the Marble Mountain*, 1967

Marc Brody series
Brody, Marc
1 *Sensation of Sin Street* (1955)
2 *Dame on the deadline* (1955)
3 *Murder, special edition!* (1955)
4 *Stop press standover* (1955)
5 *Page me a pin-up* (1955)
6 *Her column's a killer* (1955)
7 *No copyright on murder* (1955)
8 *Murder in my fashion* (1955)
9 *Blueprints for murder* (1956)
10 *Lay out my lady* (1956)
11 *Bulletin blonde* (1956)
12 *Carbon copy killer* (1956)
13 *Big shot's final edition* (1956)
14 *Death of a scandal sister* (1956)
15 *Sinner, or later* (1956)
16 *Mastermind wears mink* (1956)
17 *Murder, extra special* (1956)
18 *Blackmail in red headlines* (1956)
19 *Strictly corruptible* (1956)
20 *Sweet, svelre and sinful* (1956)
21 *Downtown and dead* (1956)
22 *Syndicate for sin* (1956)
23 *Cover girl cries murder* (1956)
24 *Step swiftly, sinner* (1956)
25 *Maid for the morgue* (1956)
26 *Stand-in for sin* (1956)
27 *Lament for a lovely* (1956)
28 *Set-up for scandal* (1956)
Numbers 25, 26, 28 also published in one volume 1958
29 *My baby was blasted* (1956)
30 *Flame was fatal* (1956)
31 *Dames in his death* (1957)
32 *Sinister sister* (1957)
33 *Bride wore black* (1957)
34 *Last will of a wanton* (1957)
35 *Deadline for a dame* (1957)
36 *Headlines for a hussy* (1957)
37 *Justice for a jinx* (1957)
38 *Libel was a blonde* (1957)
Numbers 33, 35, 38 also published in one volume 1959
39 *Set-up for a sinner* (1957)
40 *Obituary blonde* (1957)
41 *Maid-up for murder* (1957)
42 *Blonde cries blackmail* (1957)
43 *Blackmail was a brunette* (1957)
44 *Her halo in headlines* (1957)
45 *Larceny for a lover* (1957)
46 *Sweetheart, you're a sinner* (1957)
47 *Baby, your racket's busted* (1957)
48 *Big splash for Belinda* (1957)
49 *Killers don't cry* (1957)
50 *Frame for the front page* (1957)
51 *Lady's out of circulation* (1957)
52 *Blonde for my punch-line* (1957)
53 *Move on Miss Mayhem* (1957)
54 *Dame on a death round* (1957)
55 *Blueprints for a blonde* (1958)
56 *Hers is a hearse* (1958)
Numbers 57-82 are numbered 1-26 in the publisher's series
57 *Murder is a maiden's handicap* (1958)
58 *Undercover cutie* (1958)
59 *Baby, your type's murder* (1958)
60 *Stop press in scarlet* (1958)
61 *Red hot and morgue bound* (1958)
62 *Second story sinner* (1958)
63 *Write off the redhead* (1958)
64 *Book her for murder* (1958)
65 *Hot line for a honey* (1958)
66 *Teaser set to kill* (1958)
67 *Late final blonde* (1958)
68 *Brunette on the beam* (1958)
69 *Siren on the skids* (1958)
70 *Penthouse preview* (1958)
71 *Sugar you're a scoop* (1958)
Bullet in a bedroom
72 *Lady, don't shroud me* (1958)
73 *High tide temptress* (1958)
74 *One shot for Sadie* (1958)
75 *Kitten you're a killer* (1958)
76 *Babe bound to kill* (1958)
77 *Hood for a honey* (1959)
78 *Blonde at bay* (1959)
79 *Low dive for Lola* (1959)
80 *Poison pen playgirl* (1959)
81 *Lady you're lethal* (1959)
82 *Rub out the redhead* (1960)

Marc Castleman series
Kutak, Rosemary
see **Doctor Marc Castleman series**

Marc Dean series
Buck, Peter
1 *Thirteen for the kill* (1981)
2 *Secret of San Felipe* (1981)
3 *Deadly birdman* (1981)
4 *Operation Icicle* (1981)
5 *School for slaughter* (1982)
6 *Ready, aim, die* (1982)
7 *Black gold briefing* (1982)
8 *Megadeath option* (1983)
9 *Passport to peril* (1983)

Marc Jordan series
Laurenson, Robert Mark
1 *Railroad murder case* (1948)
2 *Case of the six bullets* (1949)

Marc Savage series
Eden, Matthew
1 *Countdown to crisis* (1968)
2 *Dangerous exchange* (1969)
3 *Flight of hawks* (1969)
4 *Man who fell* (1970)
5 *Gilt-edged traitor* (1972)
6 *Conquest before autumn* (1973)

Marceau case trilogy
Keeler, Harry Stephen
1 *Marceau case* (1936)
2 *X Jones of Scotland Yard* (1936)
X Jones
3 *Wonderful scheme of Mister Christopher Thorne* (1936)
Wonderful scheme

Marcella Boyce series
Ward, Mary Augusta
1 *Marcella* (1894)
2 *Sir George Tressady* (1896)

March family series
Alcott, Louisa May
see **Jo March series**

March series
Bamburg, Lilian
see **Septimus March series**
Chaber, M E
see **Milo March series**
Horler, Sydney
see **Ace series**
Howells, William Dean
see **Mister and Mrs March series**

March series
Jennings, Gary
1 *March of the robots* (1962)
2 *March of the heroes* (1975)
3 *March of the gods* (1976)
4 *March of the demons* (1977)

Marchbanks series
Davies, Robertson
see **Samuel Marchbanks series**

Marco Paul's adventures in pursuit of knowledge series
Abbott, Jacob
1 *City of New York* (1843)
2 *On the Erie Canal* (1843)
3 *Forests of Maine* (1843)
4 *State of Vermont* (1843)
5 *City of Boston* (1843)
6 *Springfield Armory* (1843)

Marco Polo Junior series
Moldoff, Sheldon
1 *By sea to Xanadu* (1972)
2 *By land to Xanadu* (1972)

Marcus Aurelius Farrow series
Ross, Angus
see **Mark Farrow series**

Marcus Cavanaugh series
Carrington, G A
1 *Oushata massacre* (1989)
2 *Cavanaugh's island* (1989)
3 *Battle of Thunderhorse Mesa* (1989)
4 *Comanche war* (1990)
5 *Templeton massacre* (1990)
6 *Battle of Horsetooth Mountain* (1990)

Marcus Didius Falco series
Davis, Lindsey
1 *Silver pigs* (1989)
2 *Shadows in bronze* (1990)
3 *Venus in copper* (1991)
4 *Iron hand of Mars* (1992)
5 *Poseidon's gold* (1993)
6 *Last act in Palmyra* (1994)

Marcus Maclurg series
Petrie, Rhona
see **Inspector Marcus Maclurg series**

Marcus Obadiah series
Tate, Richard
1 *Dead travel fast* (1971)
2 *Emperor on ice* (1973)
3 *Birds of a bloodied feather* (1974)

Marcy Benson series
Ewing, Kathryn
1 *Private matter* (1975)
2 *Things won't be the same* (1980)

Marcy series
Du Jardin, Rosamond
1 *Wait for Marcy* (1950)
2 *Marcy catches up* (1952)
3 *Man for Marcy* (1954)
4 *Senior prom* (1957)

Mardick series
Hartley, Leslie Poles
see **Richard Mardick series**

Mardie series
Lindgren, Astrid
1 *Mardie* (1960)
Original edition entitled *Madicken*
2 *Mardie to the rescue* (1961)
Original edition entitled *Madicken och Junibackens Pims*

Margaret and Babs series
Avery, Elizabeth
see **Babs series**

Margaret Binton series
Barth, Richard
1 *Rag Bag Clan* (1978)
2 *Ragged plot* (1981)
3 *One dollar death* (1982)
4 *Condo kill* (1985)
Co-op kill
5 *Deadly climate* (1988)
6 *Blood doesn't tell* (1989)
7 *Furnished for murder* (1990)
8 *Final shot* (1992)
9 *Deathics* (1993)

Margaret Cottage series
Armstrong, Anthony
Reminiscences
1 *Cottage into house* (1937)
2 *We like the country* (1940)
3 *Village at war* (1941)
4 *We keep going* (1946)
5 *Year at Margarets* (1953)

Margaret Dashwood series
This sequence has two authors
Austen, Jane
1 *Sense and sensibility* (1811)
Brown, Edith Charlotte
2 *Margaret Dashwood* (1929)
Alternative title: Interference
3 *Susan Price* (1930)
Alternative title: Resolution

Margaret Davis and Isobel Quirk trilogy
Wakefield, Tom
1 *Trixie Trash, star ascending* (1977)
2 *Isobel Quirk in orbit* (1978)
3 *Love siege* (1979)

Margaret family series
Bassett, Ronald
1 *Witch-finder general* (1966)
2 *Amorous trooper* (1968)
3 *Rebecca's brat* (1969)
4 *Kill the Stuart* (1970)

Margaret Maitland series
Oliphant, Margaret Oliphant Wilson
see **Mrs Margaret Maitland series**

Margaret Montgomery series
Short, Agnes
1 *Heritors* (1977)
2 *Clatter vengeance* (1978)

Margaret Newman series
Nuttall, Nesta
see **Meri Newman series**

Margaret of Ashbury series
Riley, Judith Merkle
1 *Vision of light* (1989)
2 *In pursuit of the green lion* (1990)

Margaret Priam series
Christmas, Joyce
see **Lady Margaret Priam series**

Margaret series
Porter, Eleanor Hodgman
see **Cross currents series**

Margery series
Holt, Emily Sarah
see **Mistress Margery series**

Margery Stanfield series
Jones, Adrienne
1 *Whistle down a dark lane* (1982)
2 *Matter of spunk* (1983)

Marget Pow trilogy
Slater, Catherine Ponton
1 *Marget Pow in foreign parts* (1912)
2 *Marget Pow comes home* (1914)
3 *Marget Pow looks back* (1920)
One volume edition entitled Marget Pow, 1925

Margetson series
Keate, Edith Murray
see **Superintendent Margetson series**

Margie Carson and Ethel Hardisen series
Tate, Eleanora Elaine
1 *Just an overnight guest* (1980)
2 *Front porch stories of the one-room school* (1992)

Margie series
Rand, Edward Augustus
1 *Her Christmas and her Easter* (1887)
2 *Margie at Harbour Light* (1888)

Margo Franklin and Philip Spence series
Jenkins, Jerry Bruce
1 *Margo* (1979)
2 *Karlyn* (1980)
3 *Hilary* (1980)
4 *Paige* (1981)
5 *Erin* (1981)
6 *Shannon* (1982)
7 *Allyson* (1981)
8 *Meagham* (1983)
9 *Lindsey* (1983)
10 *Janell* (1983)
11 *Courtney* (1983)
12 *Lyssa* (1984)
13 *Margo's reunion* (1984)
14 *Veiled threat* (1985)

Margot Blair series
Knight, Kathleen Moore
1 *Rendezvous with the past* (1940)
2 *Exit a star* (1941)
3 *Terror by twilight* (1942)
4 *Design in diamonds* (1944)

Marguerite Cranleigh series
Wright, Sydney Fowler
1 *Dream* (1931)
Alternative title: The simian maid
2 *Spiders' war* (1954)

Maria and Victor series
Vendrell, Carme Sole
see **Victor and Maria series**

Maria Henniker-Haddon series
Avery, Gillian
1 *Warden's niece* (1957)
Maria escapes
2 *Italian spring* (1964)

Maria Looney series
Beatty, Jerome
1 *Maria Looney on the red planet* (1977)
2 *Maria Looney and the cosmic circus* (1978)
3 *Maria Looney and the remarkable robot* (1979)

Maria series
Blackwood, Algernon
1 *Maria of England in the rain* (1933)
2 *Fruit stoners* (1934)

Maria series
Hellberg, Hans Eric
1 *Maria* (1969)
Original edition entitled *Morfars Maria*
2 *Maria and Martin* (1970)
Original edition entitled *Martins Maria*
3 *I am Maria* (1971)
Original edition entitled *Jag ar Maria jag*

Maria series
Slate, John
see **Black Maria series**

Maria series
Stewart, Maureen
1 *Maria's diary* (1988)
2 *Maria in love* (1990)

Maria trilogy
Lane, Anna
1 *According to Maria* (1910)
2 *Maria again* (1915)
3 *War phases according to Maria* (1917)

Mariah Delany series
Greenwald, Sheila
1 *Mariah Delany lending library disaster* (1977)
2 *Mariah Delany's author of the month club* (1990)

Marianne O'Hara series
Haldeman, Joe
Edited by Anson Richard Barbour
1 *Worlds* (1981)
2 *Worlds apart* (1983)

Marianne series
Benzoni, Juliette
1 *Marianne* (1969)
Original edition entitled *Marianne, une etoile pour Napoleon*
1.1 *Bride of Selton Hall* (1969)
1.2 *Eagle and the Nightingale* (1969)
2 *Marianne and the masked prince* (1970)
Original edition entitled *Marianne et l'inconnu de Toscane*
3 *Marianne and the privateer* (1971)
Original edition entitled *Marianne, Jason des quatre mers*
4 *Marianne and the rebels* (1972)
Original edition entitled Toi Marianne
5 *Marianne and the Lords of the East* (1974)
Original edition entitled *Marianne, les lauriers de flammes*, part 1
6 *Marianne and the crown of fire* (1976)
Crown of fire
Original edition entitled *Marianne, les lauriers de flammes*, part 2

Marianne series
Storr, Catherine
1 *Marianne dreams* (1958)
Magic drawing pencil
Revised edition 1964
2 *Marianne and Mark* (1960)

Marianne trilogy
Tepper, Sheri S
1 *Marianne, the magus and the manticore* (1985)
2 *Marianne, the madame and the momentary gods* (1988)
3 *Marianne, the matchbox and the malachite mouse* (1989)
One volume edition entitled *The Marianne trilogy*, 1990

Marid Audran series
Effinger, George Alec
1 *When gravity fails* (1987)
2 *Fire in the sun* (1989)
3 *Exile kiss* (1991)

Marie Antoinette series
Dumas, Alexandre
1 *Memoirs of a physician* (1848)
Joseph Balsamo
Original edition entitled *Memoires d'un medecin*
2 *Queen's necklace* (1850)
Original edition entitled *Le collier de la reine*
3 *Ange Pitou* (1852)
Taking of the Bastille
Six years later
Original edition entitled *Ange Pitou*
4 *Countess de Charny* (1854)
Original edition entitled *La Comtesse de Charny*
5 *Chevalier de Maison Rouge* (1846)
Original edition entitled *Le Chevalier de Maison Rouge*
5.1 *Andree de Taverney* (1846)
5.2 *Mesmerist's victim* (1846)
5.3 *Reign of Terror* (1846)
5.4 *Chevalier* (1846)
6 *Monsieur de Chauvelin's will* (1861)
Original edition entitled *Le testament de Monsieur Chauvelin*
Companion volume: *The woman with the velvet necklace*, originally published as *La femme au collier de velours*, 1859

Marie Carlsen series
Olsen, Violet
1 *Growing season* (1982)
2 *View from the pighouse roof* (1987)

Marie-Claire series
Audoux, Marguerite
1 *Marie-Claire* (1910)
Original edition entitled *Marie-Claire*
2 *Marie-Claire's workshop* (1920)
Original edition entitled *L'atelier de Marie-Claire*

Marie Louise series
Carlson, Natalie Savage
1 *Marie Louise and Christophe* (1974)
2 *Marie Louise's heyday* (1975)
3 *Runaway Marie Louise* (1977)
4 *Marie Louise and Christophe at the carnival* (1981)

Marie series
Gaillard, Robert
1 *Marie of the Isles* (1948)
Marie, mistress of the islands
Original edition entitled *Marie des Isles*, part 1
2 *Marie, the secret bride* (1949)
Original edition entitled *Marie des Isles*, part 2
3 *Marie, the captain's mistress* (1949)
Original edition entitled *Marie Galante*, part 1
4 *Marie, island in revolt* (1949)
Island in revolt
Original edition entitled *Marie Galante*, part 2
5 *Marie, the dance of death* (1950)
Dance of death
Original edition entitled *Capitaine Le Fort*, part 1
6 *Marie, men of war* (1950)
Men of war
Original edition entitled *Capitaine Le Fort*, part 2
7 *War with the corsairs* (1961)
Original edition entitled *L'heritier des Isles*

Marie series
Grossman, Alfred
1 *Marie beginning* (1964)
2 *Do-gooders* (1968)

Marieanne Payne series
Quinn, Olga
1 *Spies on the roof* (1969)
2 *Spies go running* (1971)

Marietta Danvers series
Wilde, Jennifer
1 *Love's tender fury* (1976)
2 *Love me, Marietta* (1981)

Marigold Cottage trilogy
Thomson, Arthur Alexander
1 *Marigold Cottage* (1927)
2 *Trust Tilty* (1928)
3 *Steeple Thatchby* (1928)

Marigold series
Foster, Edith Francis
1 *Mary 'n' Mary* (1905)
2 *Marigold* (1906)
3 *Marigold's winter* (1908)

Marigold series
Webster, Joanne
1 *Marigold summer* (1984)
2 *Marigold days* (1985)

Marilda series
Bates, Esther
1 *Marilda's house* (1956)
2 *Marilda and the witness tree* (1957)
3 *Marilda and the bird of time* (1960)

Marilyn Ambers series
Saint Clair, Elizabeth
1 *Murder in the act* (1978)
2 *Sandcastle murders* (1979)
3 *Trek or treat* (1980)

Marine Combined Action Platoons series
Sherman, David
see **Night fighters series**

Marino family series
Sloane, Robert C
1 *Nice place to live* (1981)
2 *Vengeance* (1983)

Mario and Giovanna series
De Polnay, Peter
1 *Out of the square* (1950)
2 *Mario* (1961)

Mario Balzic series
Constantine, K C
1 *Rocksburg Railroad murders* (1972)
2 *Man who liked to look at himself* (1973)
3 *Blank page* (1974)
4 *Fix like this* (1975)
5 *Man who liked slow tomatoes* (1982)
6 *Always a body to trade* (1983)
7 *Upon some midnights clear* (1985)
8 *Joey's case* (1988)
9 *Sunshine enemies* (1989)
10 *Bottom liner blues* (1993)
11 *Cranks and shadows* (1995)

Mariposa series
Baerlein, Henry
1 *Mariposa* (1924)
2 *Mariposa on the way* (1927)

Maris series
Moon, Sheila
1 *Knee-deep in thunder* (1967)
2 *Hunt down the prize* (1971)

Marise Duncan series
Carter, Dorothy
1 *Mistress of the air* (1939)
2 *Star of the air* (1940)
3 *Snow-Queen of the air* (1941)
4 *Sword of the air* (1941)
5 *Comrades of the air* (1942)
6 *Marise flies south* (1944)

Marissa and Vi series
Cooney, Caroline B
see **Vi and Marissa series**

Marji Parker series
Benton, John W
1 *Marji* (1980)
2 *Marji and the kidnap plot* (1980)

Marjorie Dean college series
Lester, Pauline
1 *Marjorie Dean, college freshman* (1922)
2 *Marjorie Dean, college sophomore* (1922)
3 *Marjorie Dean, college junior* (1922)
4 *Marjorie Dean, college senior* (1922)

Marjorie Dean high school series
Lester, Pauline
1 *Marjorie Dean, high school freshman* (1917)
2 *Marjorie Dean, high school sophomore* (1917)
3 *Marjorie Dean, high school junior* (1917)
4 *Marjorie Dean, high school senior* (1917)

Marjorie Dean post-graduate series
Lester, Pauline
1 *Marjorie Dean at Hamilton Arms* (1925)
2 *Marjorie Dean, marvelous manager* (1925)
3 *Marjorie Dean, post-graduate* (1925)
4 *Marjorie Dean's romance* (1925)
5 *Marjorie Dean Macy* (1926)
6 *Marjorie Dean Macy's Hamilton colony* (1930)

Marjorie Maynard series
Wells, Carolyn
1 *Marjorie's vacation* (1907)
2 *Marjorie's busy days* (1908)
3 *Marjorie's new friend* (1909)
4 *Marjorie in command* (1910)
5 *Marjorie's Maytime* (1911)
6 *Marjorie at Seacote* (1912)

Marjorie series
Curtis, Alice Turner
1 *Marjorie's way* (1905)
2 *Marjorie's schooldays* (1911)
3 *Marjorie in the sunny South* (1912)
4 *Marjorie on Beacon Hill* (1913)

Marjorie series
Hill, Lorna
1 *Marjorie and Co.* (1948)
2 *Stolen holiday* (1948)
3 *Border Peel* (1950)
4 *So Guy came too* (1954)
5 *No medals for Guy* (1962)

Marjorie series
Lincoln, Jeanie Gould
1 *Marjorie's quest* (1872)
2 *Genuine girl* (1896)

Marjorie series
Paull, Minnie E
1 *Marjorie's doings* (1900)
2 *Marjorie's play days* (1901)
3 *Marjorie darling* (1904)

Mark and Rich series
Bamman, Henry A
see **World of adventure series**

Mark and Wendy series
This sequence has three authors
Egan, Ted
1 *Outback holiday* (1978)
Maymaru, Narritjan
2 *Milky Way* (1978)
As told to Ted Egan
Roughsey, Labamu
3 *Turkey and the emu* (1978)
As told to Ted Egan

Mark Antony series
Curzon, Colin
1 *Body in the barrage balloon* (1941)
Alternative title: Who killed the corpse?
2 *Case of the eighteenth ostrich* (1943)

Mark Appleby series
Trease, Geoffrey
1 *Follow the black plumes* (1963)
2 *Thousand for Sicily* (1964)

Mark Blood series
Morgan, Allan
1 *Blood* (1974)
2 *Spandau warrant* (1974)
3 *Cat Cay warrant* (1974)

Mark Bourke and Carol Ashton series
McNab, Claire
see **Inspector Carol Ashton and Sergeant Mark Bourke series**

Mark Brand series
Connington, John Jervis
1 *Counsellor* (1939)
2 *Four defences* (1940)

Mark Brandon series
Warren, Vernon
1 *Brandon takes over* (1953)
2 *Brandon in New York* (1953)
3 *Brandon returns* (1954)
4 *Blue Mauritius* (1954)
5 *No bouquets for Brandon* (1955)
6 *Bullets for Brandon* (1955)
7 *Runaround* (1958)

Mark Corrigan and McLean series
Corrigan, Mark
1 *Bullets and brown eyes* (1948)
2 *Sinner takes all* (1949)
3 *Lovely lady* (1950)
4 *Wayward blonde* (1950)
5 *Golden angel* (1950)
6 *Shanghai Jezebel* (1951)
7 *Madame Sly* (1951)
8 *Baby face* (1952)
9 *Lady of China Street* (1952)
10 *All brides are beautiful* (1953)
11 *Sweet and deadly* (1953)
12 *I like danger* (1954)
13 *Naked lady* (1954)
14 *Love for sale* (1954)
15 *Madam and Eve* (1955)
16 *Big squeeze* (1955)
17 *Big boys don't cry* (1956)
18 *Sydney for sin* (1956)
19 *Cruel lady* (1957)
20 *Dumb as they come* (1957)
21 *Menace in Siam* (1958)
22 *Honolulu snatch* (1958)
23 *Girl from Moscow* (1959)
24 *Singapore downbeat* (1959)
25 *Sin of Hong Kong* (1960)
26 *Lady from Tokyo* (1960)
27 *Danger's green eyes* (1962)
28 *Riddle of Double Island* (1962)
29 *Why do women?* (1963)
30 *Riddle of the Spanish circus* (1964)

Mark Danby series
Gard, Joyce
1 *Woorroo* (1961)
2 *Dragon of the hill* (1963)

Mark Doone series
Reno, Clint
see **Vigilante series**

Mark East series
Lawrence, Hilda
1 *Blood upon the snow* (1944)
2 *Time to die* (1945)
3 *Death of a doll* (1947)

Mark Farrow series
Ross, Angus
1 *Manchester thing* (1970)
Manchester connection
2 *Huddersfield job* (1971)
3 *London assignment* (1972)
4 *Dunfermline affair* (1973)
5 *Bradford business* (1974)
6 *Amsterdam diversion* (1974)
7 *Leeds fiasco* (1975)
8 *Edinburgh exercise* (1975)
9 *Ampurias exchange* (1976)
10 *Aberdeen conundrum* (1977)
11 *Burgos contract* (1978)
12 *Congleton lark* (1979)
13 *Hamburg switch* (1980)
14 *Menwith tangle* (1982)
15 *Darlington jaunt* (1983)
16 *Bad April* (1984)
17 *Luxembourg run* (1985)
18 *Tyneside ultimatum* (1988)

Mark Fox series
Hardcastle, Michael
1 *First goal* (1976)
2 *Breakaway* (1976)
3 *On the ball* (1977)
4 *Shooting star* (1977)
5 *Goal in Europe* (1978)
6 *Kick off* (1981)
7 *Attack!* (1982)

Mark Gilmore series
Fitzhugh, Percy Keese
1 *Mark Gilmore, Scout of the air* (1930)
2 *Mark Gilmore, speed flyer* (1931)
3 *Mark Gilmore's lucky landing* (1931)

Mark Girland series
Chase, James Hadley
1 *This is for real* (1965)
2 *You have yourself a deal* (1966)
3 *Have this one on me* (1967)
4 *Believed violent* (1968)
5 *Whiff of money* (1969)

Mark Hardin series
Derrick, Lionel
see **Penetrator series**

Mark Harris series
Woodley, Richard
see **Man from Atlantis series**

Mark Holland series
Myers, Paul
1 *Deadly variations* (1985)
2 *Deadly cadenza* (1986)
3 *Deadly aria* (1987)
4 *Deadly sonata* (1987)
5 *Deadly score* (1988)
6 *Deadly crescendo* (1989)

Mark Isen series
Ruggero, Ed
1 *Common defense* (1992)
2 *Fire fall* (1994)

Mark Kilby series
Frazer, Robert Caine
1 *Mark Kilby solves a murder* (1959)
R.I.S.C.
Timid tycoon
2 *Mark Kilby and the secret syndicate* (1960)
Secret syndicate
3 *Mark Kilby and the Miami mob* (1960)
Miami mob
4 *Mark Kilby takes a risk* (1961)
Hollywood hoax
5 *Mark Kilby stands alone* (1962)
Mark Kilby and the Manhattan murders

Mark Kingsley Hood series
Dark, James
1 *Spy from the grave* (1964)
2 *Bamboo bomb* (1965)
3 *Come die with me* (1965)
4 *Assignment Hong Kong* (1966)
5 *Assignment Tokyo* (1966)
6 *Spy from the deep* (1966)
7 *Operation Jackal* (1967)
8 *Sword of Genghis Khan* (1967)
9 *Throne of Satan* (1967)
10 *Operation Scuba* (1967)
11 *Operation Octopus* (1968)
12 *Spying blind* (1968)
13 *Invisibles* (1969)
14 *Operation Ice Cap* (1969)
15 *Reluctant assassin* (1970)
16 *Sea scrape* (1970)

Mark Magic series
Morris, Anthony Paschel
1 *Mark Magic, the detective* (1884)
Alternative title: The story of a beautiful woman's strange career
2 *Head hunter* (1885)
Alternative title: Mark Magic in the mines
3 *Cipher detective* (1886)
Alternative title: Mark Magic on a new trail

Mark Mallory series
Garrison, Frederick
see **West Point series**

Mark Nicolson series
Charles, Robert
see **Counter-terror series**

Mark Preston series
Chambers, Peter
1 *Murder is for keeps* (1961)
2 *Wreath for a redhead* (1962)
3 *Big goodbye* (1962)
4 *Dames can be deadly* (1963)
5 *Down-beat kill* (1963)
6 *Lady, this is murder* (1963)
7 *This'll kill you* (1964)
8 *Nobody lives forever* (1964)
9 *You're better off dead* (1965)
10 *Always take the big ones* (1965)
11 *No gold when you go* (1966)
12 *Don't bother to knock* (1966)
13 *Bad die young* (1967)
14 *Blonde wore black* (1968)
15 *No peace for the wicked* (1968)
16 *Speak ill of the dead* (1968)
17 *They call it murder* (1973)
18 *Somebody has to lose* (1975)
19 *Deader they fall* (1979)
20 *Lady, you're killing me* (1979)
21 *Day of the big dollar* (1979)
22 *Beautiful golden frame* (1980)
23 *Nothing personal* (1980)
24 *Deep blue cradle* (1980)
25 *Long time dead* (1981)
26 *Lady who never was* (1981)
27 *Female, handle with care* (1981)
28 *Murder is its own reward* (1982)
29 *Highly explosive case* (1982)
30 *Miniature murder mystery* (1982)
31 *Jail bait* (1983)

32 *Dragons can be dangerous* (1983)
33 *Bomb-scare flight 147* (1984)
34 *Moving picture writes* (1984)
35 *Vanishing holes murder* (1985)

Mark Raeburn series
Gair, Malcolm
1 *Sapphires on Wednesday* (1957)
2 *Long hard look* (1958)
3 *Burning of Troy* (1958)
4 *Bad dreams* (1960)
5 *Schultz money* (1960)
6 *Snow job* (1962)

Mark Randall series
Eland, Charles
1 *Dossier closed* (1970)
2 *Desperate search* (1971)
3 *Gold hijack* (1973)

Mark Register series
Douglas, Arthur
1 *Special murders* (1974)
2 *Noah's Ark murders* (1974)
3 *Decoy murders* (1975)

Mark Rendle series
Lindsay, Paula
1 *Charity child* (1962)
2 *This bright mantle* (1963)

Mark Rutherford series
White, William Hale
1 *Autobiography of Mark Rutherford* (1881)
2 *Mark Rutherford's deliverance* (1885)

Mark Rutter series
Garnett, Richard
1 *Silver kingdom* (1956)
Undersea treasure
2 *White dragon* (1963)

Mark Savage series
Payne, Laurence
1 *Take the money and run* (1982)
2 *Malice in camera* (1983)
3 *Vienna blood* (1984)
4 *Dead for a ducat* (1986)
5 *Late knight* (1987)
Knight fall

Mark Stone series
Buchanan, Jack
see **M.I.A. Hunter series**

Mark Stoner series
Hayes, Ralph Eugene
1 *Golden god* (1976)
2 *Satan stone* (1976)
3 *All that glitters* (1977)
4 *King's ransom* (1978)

Mark Stratton series
Bickers, Richard Townshend
1 *Hellions* (1965)
2 *Scent of mayhem* (1965)

Mark Stryker series
Cain, Jonathan
see **Saigon commandos series**

Mark Tidd series
Kelland, Clarence Budington
1 *Mark Tidd, his adventures and strategies* (1913)
2 *Mark Tidd in the backwoods* (1914)
3 *Mark Tidd in business* (1915)
4 *Mark Tidd's citadel* (1916)
5 *Mark Tidd, editor* (1917)
6 *Mark Tidd, manufacturer* (1918)
7 *Mark Tidd in Italy* (1925)
8 *Mark Tidd in Egypt* (1926)
9 *Mark Tidd in Sicily* (1928)

Mark Treasure series
Williams, David
1 *Unholy writ* (1976)
2 *Treasure by degrees* (1977)
3 *Treasure up in smoke* (1978)
4 *Murder for Treasure* (1980)
5 *Copper, Gold and Treasure* (1982)
6 *Treasure preserved* (1983)
7 *Advertise for Treasure* (1984)
8 *Wedding Treasure* (1985)
9 *Murder in Advent* (1985)
10 *Treasure in roubles* (1987)
11 *Divided Treasure* (1987)
12 *Treasure in Oxford* (1988)
13 *Holy Treasure!* (1989)
14 *Prescription for murder* (1990)
15 *Treasure by post* (1991)
16 *Planning on murder* (1992)
17 *Banking on murder* (1993)
18 *Last seen breathing* (1994)

Mark Tudor series
Nash, Anne
1 *Said with flowers* (1943)
2 *Death by design* (1944)

Mark Twain Elementary School series
Haynes, Betsy
see **Taffy Sinclair series**

Mark Urgent series
Forde, Nicholas
1 *Urgent enquiry* (1973)
2 *Urgent action* (1974)
3 *Ergent delivery* (1975)
4 *Urgent wedding* (1977)
5 *Urgent trip* (1979)
6 *Urgent conference* (1981)

Marka de Lancey series
Frost, Barbara
1 *Corpse said no* (1949)
2 *Corpse died twice* (1951)
3 *Innocent bystander* (1955)

Markam series
Dewhurst, Eileen
see **Helen Johnson series**

Markand series
Frank, Waldo
see **David Markand series**

Markby and Mitchell series
Granger, Ann
see **Meredith Mitchell and Chief Inspector Alan Markby series**

Marked man series
Ingrid, Charles
1 *Marked man* (1989)
2 *Last recall* (1991)

Marker series
Marriott, Anthony
see **Frank Marker series**

Market place series
Dehan, Richard
1 *Pipers of the market place* (1924)
2 *Lovers of the market place* (1928)

Markham series
Williams, Jon
see **Privateers and gentlemen series**

Marklin series
Steed, Neville
see **Peter Marklin series**

Marks series
Barns, Glenn Miller
see **Jonathan Marks series**

Marksman series
This sequence has two authors
McCurtin, Peter
1 *Vendetta* (1973)
2 *Death hunt* (1973)
Scarpetta, Frank
3 *Kill them all* (1973)
4 *Mafia wipe out* (1973)
5 *Headhunter* (1973)
6 *Death to the Mafia* (1973)
7 *Slaughterhouse* (1973)
8 *Stone killer* (1974)
9 *Body count* (1974)
10 *Open contract* (1974)
11 *Counterattack* (1974)
12 *Mafia massacre* (1974)
13 *Kiss of death* (1974)
14 *Kill!* (1974)
15 *Die killer die* (1975)
16 *This animal must die* (1975)
17 *Killer on the prowl* (1975)
18 *Torture contract* (1975)
19 *Icepick in the spine* (1975)
Also published as *Icepick* under the author's real name Aaron Fletcher
20 *Murder machine* (1975)
21 *Bloody Sunday* (1976)
Also published under the author's real name Aaron Fletcher
22 *Times Square connection* (1976)
Sequence continued under the author's real name Aaron Fletcher
Fletcher, Aaron
23 *Reckoning* (1981)

Marla Trent series
Kane, Henry
1 *Private eyeful* (1959)
2 *Kisses of death* (1962)
Killer's kiss

Marlborough series
Kenyon, Frank Wilson
see **John Churchill, Duke of Marlborough series**

Marle series
Carr, John Dickson
see **Henri Bencolin series**

Marley series
Walker, Jerry
see **Lawrence Marley series**

Marlow Ancestors series
Forest, Antonia
1 *Player's boy* (1970)
2 *Players and the rebels* (1971)

Marlow family series
Forest, Antonia
1 *Autumn term* (1948)
2 *Marlows and the traitor* (1953)
3 *Falconer's lure* (1957)
The story of a summer holiday
4 *End of term* (1959)
5 *Peter's room* (1961)
6 *Thuggery affair* (1965)
7 *Ready-made family* (1967)
8 *Cricket team* (1974)
9 *Attic term* (1976)
10 *Run away home* (1982)

Marlow series
Dickson, Grierson
see **Superintendent Cissie Marlow series**
Fenady, Andrew J
see **Sam Marlow series**
Hone, Joseph
see **Peter Marlow series**

Marlowe family series
Keyes, Frances Parkinson
1 *Senator Marlowe's daughter* (1933)
Christian Marlowe's daughter
2 *Great tradition* (1939)

Marlowe series
Chandler, Raymond
see **Philip Marlowe series**
Marlowe, Greg
see **Greg Marlowe series**

Marlows series
Boden, Hilda
1 *Marlows at Newgate* (1956)
2 *Marlows win a prize* (1957)
3 *Marlows dig for treasure* (1958)
4 *Marlows into danger* (1959)
5 *Marlows at Castle Cliff* (1960)
6 *Marlows and the regatta* (1961)
7 *Marlows' Irish holiday* (1962)
8 *Marlows' pigeon post* (1963)
9 *Marlows in town* (1964)

Marmaduke and Helen series
Monkhouse, Allan
see **Helen and Marmaduke series**

Marmaduke series
Chapman, Elizabeth
1 *Marmaduke the lorry* (1953)
2 *Marmaduke and Joe* (1954)
3 *Riding with Marmaduke* (1954)
4 *Adventures with Marmaduke* (1956)
5 *Merry Marmaduke* (1957)
6 *Marmaduke and his friends* (1958)
7 *Marmaduke and the elephant* (1959)
8 *Marmaduke and the lambs* (1960)
9 *Marmaduke goes to France* (1962)
10 *Marmaduke goes to Holland* (1963)
11 *Marmaduke goes to America* (1965)
12 *Marmaduke goes to Italy* (1970)
13 *Marmaduke goes to Switzerland* (1977)

Marmaduke series
O'Harris, Pixie
1 *Marmaduke the possum* (1942)
Adventures of Marmaduke the possum
2 *Marmaduke and Margaret* (1953)
3 *Marmaduke the possum in the cave of the gnomes* (1977)

Marmalade Atkins series
Davies, Andrew
1 *Marmalade and Rufus* (1979)
Marmalade Atkins' dreadful deeds
2 *Marmalade Atkins in space* (1981)
3 *Educatin g Marmalade* (1983)
4 *Danger, Marmalade at work* (1984)
5 *Marmalade hits the big time* (1984)

Marmalade cat series
Hale, Kathleen
see **Orlando series**

Marmalade Jim series
Sillitoe, Alan
1 *City adventures of Marmalade Jim* (1967)
Revised edition 1977
2 *Marmalade Jim at the farm* (1980)
3 *Marmalade Jim and the fox* (1984)

Marmalade series
Wheeler, Cindy
1 *Marmalade's snowy day* (1982)
2 *Marmalade's yellow leaf* (1982)
3 *Marmalade's nap* (1983)
4 *Marmalade's picnic* (1983)
5 *Marmalade's Christmas present* (1984)

Marmelstein series
Sharmat, Marjorie Weinman
see **Maggie Marmelstein series**

Marne series
Keenan, William
see **Chief Superintendent Charles Miller series**

Maroc series
Lustbader, Eric
see **Jake Maroc series**

Marony series
Kline, Suzy
see **Mary Marony series**

Maroon boy trilogy
Leeson, Robert
see **Matthew Morten trilogy**

Marooned in orbit series
Ballou, Arthur W
1 *Marooned in orbit* (1968)
2 *Bound for Mars* (1970)

Marooners series
Goulding, Francis Robert
1 *Robert and Harold* (1852)
Robert and Harold on the Florida coast
Young marooners
Young marooners on the Florida coast
Revised edition 1866
2 *Marooner's Island* (1868)
Doctor Gordon in search of his children
Companion volume: *Frank Gordon, or, When I was a little boy*, 1869

Marple series
Christie, Agatha
see **Miss Jane Marple series**

Marquess de Brussac series
Gerard, Francis
1 *Flail and the fish* (1949)
2 *Envoy of the Emperor* (1951)

Marquis de Mores series
Davis, Kathryn
see **Dakotas series**

Marquis series
Post, Melville Davisson
see **Sir Henry Marquis series**

Marrakesh series
Diamond, Graham
Edited by Joe Dever
1 *Marrakesh* (1981)
2 *Marrakesh nights* (1984)

Marrell series
Hopkins, Stanley
see **Peter Marrell series**

Marriage of adventure series
Gaboriau, Emile
1 *Chance marriage* (1862)
Marriage at a venture
2 *Promise of marriage* (1862)
Promises of marriage
Original edition entitled *Promesses de mariage*
One volume edition entitled *Marriage of adventure*, 1921, originally published as *Les mariages d'aventure*

Marriage series
Balzac, Honore de
Translated from the French
1 *Physiology of marriage* (1829)
2 *Pinpricks of married life* (1843)

Marriage series
Campbell, Ross
1 *Daddy, are you married?* (1962)
2 *Mummy, who is your husband?* (1964)

Marriage series
Gordon, Giles
see **Edward series**

Marriage series
Musselman, Morris McNeil
1 *I married a redhead* (1949)
2 *Second honeymoon* (1952)
Travels in Europe

Marriner and Fraser series
Merwin, Samuel Kimball
see **Elspeth Marriner and Mack Fraser series**

Marryat series
Leek, Margaret
see **Stephen Marryat series**

Mars series
Brackett, Leigh
1 *Shadow over Mars* (1951)
Nemesis from Terra
2 *Sword of Rhiannon* (1953)
3 *Coming of the Terrans* (1967)

Mars series
Burroughs, Edgar Rice
see **Martian series**

Mars series
Carter, Lin
1 *Man who loved Mars* (1973)
2 *Valley where time stood still* (1974)
3 *City outside the world* (1977)
4 *Down to a sunless sea* (1984)

Mars series
Fearn, John Russell
see **Clayton Drew series**

Mars series
Kline, Otis Adelbert
1 *Swordsman of Mars* (1960)
2 *Outlaws of Mars* (1961)

Mars series
Moore, Patrick
see **Maurice Gray series**

Mars series
Robinson, Kim Stanley
1 *Red Mars* (1993)
2 *Green Mars* (1994)

Mars series
Wollheim, Donald Allen
see **Mike Mars series**

Marsala series
D'Amato, Barbara
see **Cat Marsala series**

Marsden Acton series
Bramhall, Marion
see **Kit Acton series**

Marsden family series
Jacob, Naomi
1 *Time piece* (1936)
2 *Fade out* (1937)

Marsden series
Backhouse, Elizabeth
see **Inspector Christopher Marsden series**
Graham, Anthony
see **Eric Marsden series**

Marsh and Fairbanks series
Dean, Elizabeth
see **Emma Marsh and Hank Fairbanks series**

Marsh series
Adam, Ruth
see **Susan Marsh series**
Chance, John Newton
see **John Marsh series**
Deming, Dorothy
see **Penny Marsh series**
Lane, Gret
see **Kate Marsh series**

Marshal Andrew Anderson series
Sadler, Jeff
1 *Arizona blood trail* (1981)
2 *Sonora lode* (1982)
3 *Tamaulipas guns* (1982)
4 *Severo siege* (1983)
5 *Lobo moon* (1983)
6 *Sierra showdown* (1983)
7 *Throw of a rope* (1984)
8 *Manhunt in Chihuahua* (1985)
9 *Return of Amarillo* (1986)
10 *Montana mine* (1987)
11 *Saltillo Road* (1987)
12 *Long gun war* (1988)
13 *Palomino stud* (1988)
14 *Ghost town guns* (1990)

Marshal Ben Pedley series
Sterling, Stewart
see **Fire Marshal Ben Pedley series**

Marshal Bret Malone series
Dower, Penn
1 *Bret Malone, Texas marshal* (1953)
2 *Gunsmoke over Alba* (1953)
3 *Texas stranger* (1954)
4 *Indian moon* (1954)
5 *Malone rides in* (1955)

Marshal Carl Travis series
Jons, Hal
1 *Guns of justice* (1980)
2 *Travis, U.S. Marshal* (1982)
3 *Guns at Chinooga Peak* (1983)

Marshal Creed Wetherall series
Sutton, Stack
1 *Tumbleweed* (1964)
2 *Leatherwood* (1972)
3 *Marshal's gun* (1978)
4 *End of the tracks* (1981)

Marshal Guarnaccia series
Nabb, Magdalen
1 *Death of an Englishman* (1981)
2 *Death of a Dutchman* (1982)
3 *Death in spingtime* (1983)
4 *Death in autumn* (1985)
5 *Marshal and the murderer* (1987)
6 *Marshal and the madwoman* (1988)
7 *Marshal's own case* (1990)
8 *Marshal makes his report* (1991)
9 *Marshal at the Villa Torrini* (1993)

Marshal Jeremy Six series
Wynne, Brian
1 *Range justice* (1960)
Justice at Spanish Flat
2 *Justice at Spanish Flat* (1960)
3 *Mister Sixgun* (1964)
4 *Night it rained bullets* (1965)
5 *Bravos* (1966)
6 *Proud riders* (1967)
7 *Badge for a badman* (1967)
8 *Brand of the gun* (1968)
9 *Gundown* (1969)
10 *Big country, big men* (1969)

Marshal Jim Sinclair series
Mann, Edward Beverly
see **Whistler series**

Marshal Rusty McCade series
Kester, Ken
see **Steve McCade series**

Marshal Sam McCloud series
This sequence has two authors; based on a television series
Wilcox, Collin
1 *McCloud* (1973)
2 *New Mexico connection* (1974)
Wilson, David
3 *Killing* (1974)
4 *Corpse-maker* (1974)
5 *Dangerous place to die* (1975)
6 *Park Avenue executioner* (1975)

Marshal series
Shappiro, Herbert
see **Mustang Marshal series**
Simpson, Dorothy
see **Janie Marshal series**

Marshall family series
Brooke, Carol
1 *As others see us* (1952)
2 *Changing tide* (1952)
3 *Bitter summer* (1954)
4 *Way of life* (1956)
5 *To each his own* (1958)

Marshall series
Barrington, Pamela
see **Inspector George Marshall series**
Collins, Michelle
see **Megan Marshall series**
Denning, Mark
see **John Marshall series**
Fox, James M
see **John and Suzy Marshall series**
Mitcham, Gilroy
see **Nick Marshall series**
Newman, Bernard
see **Inspector Marshall series**

Marsham and Lumb series
Cross, Laurence
see **Tommy Lumb and Peter Marsham series**

Marsham family series
Harris, Catherine
1 *They rescued a pony* (1956)
2 *Ponies of Cuckoo Mill Farm* (1958)
3 *Riding for ransom* (1960)
4 *To horse and away* (1962)

Marston Baines series
Saville, Malcolm
1 *Three towers in Tuscany* (1963)
2 *Purple valley* (1964)
3 *Dark danger* (1965)
4 *White fire* (1966)
5 *Power of three* (1968)
6 *Dagger and the flame* (1970)
7 *Marston, master spy* (1978)

Marstons series
Gervaise, Mary
1 *Golden Path adventure* (1953)
2 *Secret of the Golden Path* (1956)
3 *Golden Path pets* (1957)
4 *Strangers at Golden Path* (1958)

Marten family series
Lindgren, Astrid
1 *Children on Troublemaker Street* (1958)
Mischievous Martens
Revised edition 1982; original edition entitled *Barnen paa Braakmakargatan*; adapted as *Visst kan Lotta cykla*, 1971 and translated as *Of course Polly can ride a bike*, also entitled *Lotta's bike*
2 *Lotta on Troublemaker Street* (1961)
Lotta leaves home
Revised edition 1983; original edition entitled *Lotta paa Braakmakargatan*; selections entitled *Lotta*
3 *Of course Lotta can do almost everything* (1977)
Lotta's Christmas surprise
Original edition entitled *Visst kan Lotta naastan allting*
4 *Lotta's Easter surprise* (1990)
Original edition entitled *Visst ar Lotta en glad unge*

Marten series
Turley, Charles
see **Godfrey Marten series**

Martha and George series
Marshall, James
see **George and Martha series**

Martha and Martha Washington Parke series
Curtis, Alice Turner
see **Little Washingtons series**

Martha B Rabbit series
Barber, Shirley
1 *Martha B Rabbit and how she became the fairies' cook* (1988)

2 *Martha B Rabbit and the unexpected guests* (1993)
Companion volumes: *Martha B Rabbit address book*, 1989, *Martha B Rabbit birthday book*, 1989

Martha Diver series
Sharp, Margery
1 *Eye of love* (1957)
Martha and the eye of love
2 *Martha in Paris* (1962)
3 *Martha, Eric and George* (1964)

Martha Jane Canary series
Edson, John Thomas
see **Calamity Jane series**

Martha Jane series
Specking, Inez
1 *Western boarding school* (1925)
2 *Martha Jane at college* (1926)
3 *Martha Jane, sophomore* (1929)

Martha Macnamara and Mayland Long series
Macavoy, Roberta Ann
see **Mayland Long and Martha Macnamara series**

Martha series
Dowdall, Mary Frances
1 *Book of Martha* (1913)
2 *Second book of Martha* (1923)

Martha series
Meddaugh, Susan
1 *Martha speaks* (1992)
2 *Martha calling* (1994)

Martha series
Steel, Danielle
1 *Martha's best friend* (1989)
2 *Martha's new daddy* (1989)
3 *Martha's new school* (1989)
4 *Martha's new puppy* (1990)

Martha trilogy
Lippmann, Julie Mathilde
1 *Martha by-the-day* (1912)
2 *Making over Martha* (1913)
3 *Martha and Cupid* (1914)

Martha's Vineyard series
Craig, Philip R
1 *Beautiful place to die* (1989)
2 *Woman who walked into the sea* (1991)
3 *Doubleminded men* (1992)
4 *Cliff hanger* (1993)
5 *Off season* (1994)

Martha's Vineyard series
Hough, Henry Beetle
1 *Country editor* (1940)
2 *Mostly on Martha's Vineyard* (1975)
3 *To the harbor light* (1976)

Marti MacAlister series
Bland, Eleanor Taylor
1 *Dead time* (1992)
2 *Slow burn* (1993)
3 *Gone quiet* (1994)

Martian series
This sequence has two authors
Burroughs, Edgar Rice
1 *Princess of Mars* (1917)
2 *Gods of Mars* (1918)
3 *Warlord of Mars* (1919)
4 *Thuvia, maid of Mars* (1920)
5 *Chessmen of Mars* (1922)
6 *Master mind of Mars* (1928)
7 *Fighting man of Mars* (1931)
8 *Swords of Mars* (1936)
9 *Synthetic men of Mars* (1940)
Numbers 8 and 9 also published in one volume 1975
10 *Llana of Gathol* (1948)
Short stories
11 *John Carter of Mars* (1964)
John Carter and the giant of Mars
Resnick, Mike
12 *Forgotten sea of Mars* (1965)
Short stories
Companion volume: *Lost on Jupiter*, by William Gilmour, 1962

Martian series
Williams, Michael Lindsay
1 *Martian spring* (1986)
2 *FTL* (1987)
Further than life

Martian wars trilogy
Murdock, Melinda Seabrooke
1 *Rebellion 2456* (1989)
2 *Hammer of Mars* (1989)
3 *Armageddon of Vesta* (1989)

Martie twins series
Allen, Alice E
1 *Joe, the circus boy* (1911)
2 *Martie twins* (1913)
3 *Marjory, the circus girl* (1918)
4 *Marjory at the Willows* (1920)
5 *Marjory's house party* (1921)
6 *Marjory's discovery* (1923)

Martin Ainsworth series
Underwood, Michael
1 *Unprofessional spy* (1964)
2 *Shadow game* (1969)

Martin Ames series
Eichler, Alfred
1 *Murder in the radio department* (1943)
2 *Death at the mike* (1946)
3 *Election by murder* (1947)
4 *Death of an ad man* (1954)
Hearse for the boss
5 *Death of an artist* (1955)
6 *Pipeline to death* (1962)

Martin and Richard Fane series
Halliday, Michael
Also published under the author's real name, John Creasey
1 *Take a body* (1951)
Revised edition 1964
2 *Lame dog murder* (1952)
3 *Murder in the stars* (1953)
4 *Man on the run* (1953)

Martin Beck series
Sjowall, Maj
see **Inspector Martin Beck series**

Martin Buell series
Scherf, Margaret
see **Reverend Martin Buell series**

Martin Cameron series
Culp, John Hewett
1 *Born of the sun* (1959)
2 *Restless land* (1962)

Martin Conisby series
Farnol, Jeffery
1 *Black Bartlemy's treasure* (1920)
2 *Martin Conisby's vengeance* (1921)

Martin Corridon series
Marshall, Raymond
see **Brick-Top Corridon series**

Martin Cotterell series
Trench, John
1 *Docken dead* (1953)
2 *Dishonoured bones* (1954)
3 *What rough beast* (1957)

Martin Crow series
Norsworthy, George
1 *House-party mystery* (1935)
2 *Crime at the Villa Gloria* (1936)

Martin Dymoke series
Deeley, Roger
1 *King's man* (1968)
2 *By courtesy of the cardinal* (1971)
3 *Three crowns for the queen* (1972)
4 *Byzantine eagle* (1974)

Martin Falconer series
Harris, John
1 *Fledglings* (1971)
2 *Professionals* (1973)
3 *Victors* (1975)
4 *Interceptors* (1977)
5 *Revolutionaries* (1978)

Martin family series
Warde, Joan
see **Forrester family series**

Martin Hewitt series
Morrison, Arthur
Short stories
1 *Martin Hewitt, investigator* (1894)
2 *Chronicles of Martin Hewitt* (1895)
3 *Adventures of Martin Hewitt* (1896)
4 *Red triangle* (1903)

Martin Huish series
Horler, Sydney
1 *Secret service man* (1929)
2 *Evil messenger* (1938)
Also one story featuring Martin Huish in *The stroke sinister, and other stories*, 1935

Martin Kane series
Kane, Martin
1 *Lady on the lam* (1958)
2 *Racketeer's a redhead* (1958)
3 *Hands off the lovely* (1958)
4 *Damsel not for drowning* (1958)
5 *Dream stuff, you're murder* (1958)
6 *Piracy wears pink* (1958)
7 *Sing baby, Sing Sing* (1958)
8 *Brass for a nude* (1959)
9 *Corpus delicious* (1959)
10 *Fatal frame* (1959)
11 *Limpid lady* (1959)
12 *Margin for murder* (1959)
13 *Kane and Miss Able* (1959)
14 *Shroud for Sharon* (1959)
15 *Adam and evil* (1959)
16 *Model killer* (1959)
17 *Morgue the merrier* (1959)
18 *Murder in striplicate* (1959)
19 *Pay-off for a penny* (1959)
20 *Quit playing dames* (1959)

Martin Laidman series
Seaton, Stuart
see **Inspector Martin Laidman series**

Martin Lestrange series
Hilton, Alec
see **Doctor Martin Lestrange series**

Martin Magnus trilogy
Temple, William Frederick
1 *Martin Magnus, planet rover* (1955)
2 *Martin Magnus on Venus* (1955)
3 *Martin Magnus on Mars* (1956)

Martin Moon series
Malloy, Lester
1 *Jo Jo and the private eye* (1981)
2 *Happiest ghost in town* (1981)
3 *So help me Hannah* (1982)
4 *Beware the yellow Packard* (1982)
5 *Bullet-proof toga* (1984)

Martin Pippin series
Farjeon, Eleanor
1 *Martin Pippin in the apple-orchard* (1921)
2 *Martin Pippin in the daisy-field* (1937)

Martin Ridgway series
Helm, Peter
1 *Dead man's fingers* (1960)
Walk into murder
2 *Death has a thousand entrances* (1962)
3 *Man with no bones* (1966)

Martin Ross series
Allyson, Alan
1 *Don't mess with murder* (1972)
2 *Do you deal in murder?* (1972)
3 *Lady said no* (1972)

Martin Ryott series
Rhodes, Kathlyn
1 *Wild heart of youth* (1923)
2 *Golden flower* (1930)

Martin series
Amberley, Richard
see **Inspector Martin series**
Bardsley, Michael
see **Superintendent Donald Martin series**
Beeding, Francis
see **Inspector George Martin series**
Bunting, Eve
see **Jane Martin series**
Carey, Wymond
see **Monsieur Martin series**
Cooper, John R
see **Mel Martin series**
Fitzhugh, Percy Keese
see **Westy Martin series**
Francis, William
see **Anthony Martin series**
Hubbard, Kin
see **Abe Martin series**
Jackson, Wallace
see **Inspector Clancy Martin series**
James, Josephine
see **Kathy Martin series**
Messmann, Jon
see **Revenger series**
Reinsmith, Richard
see **Bodyguard series**
Sanders, Charles Wesley
see **Mournful Martin series**
Stanton, Ken
see **William Martin series**
Taylor, Mary Ann
see **Emil Martin series**
Winsor, Diana
see **Tavy Martin series**

Martin Speed series
This sequence has three authors
Elliott, George
1 *Case of the missing airmen* (1944)
2 *Mystery of the missing corpses* (1945)
Norman, John
3 *Concert party murders* (1945)
4 *Case of the four pages* (1946)
5 *Express train murder* (1946)
6 *Mystery of the Aztec chain* (1946)
Hugi, Maurice G
7 *Martin Speed versus The Snatcher* (1946)
8 *Convict's hoard* (1947)
9 *Tin bath murder* (1947)

Martin trilogy
Pascal, Francine
see **Victoria Martin trilogy**

Martin Webster series
Wright, Sydney Fowler
1 *Deluge* (1927)
2 *Dawn* (1929)
One volume edition 1975

Martin Zane series
Trimble, Louis
1 *Cargo for the Styx* (1959)
2 *Dead and the deadly* (1963)

Martineau series
Procter, Maurice
see **Chief Inspector Harry Martineau series**

Martini series
Raine, Richard
see **David Martini series**

Martinson series
Clevely, Hugh
see **John Martinson series**
Fitzsimmons, Cortland
see **Arthur Martinson series**

Martinus Harinxma trilogy
De Hartog, Jan
see **Captain Martinus Harinxma trilogy**

Martiny series
Haggard, William
see **Paul Martiny series**

Marty and Eddie series
Slobodkin, Louis
see **Space ship series**

Marty Gold series
Kaye, Marvin
1 *My son, the druggist* (1977)
2 *My brother, the druggist* (1979)

Marty Land series
Alexander, David
1 *Death of Daddy-O* (1960)
2 *Bloodstain* (1961)

Marty Walsh series
Cohen, Octavus Roy
see **Lieutenant Marty Walsh series**

Marty Warren series
Bialk, Elisa
1 *Marty* (1953)
2 *Marty goes to Hollywood* (1954)
3 *Marty on the campus* (1956)

Martyn Cale series
Long, Patrick
1 *Heil Britannia* (1973)
2 *Eagle Six* (1975)

Martyn Finch series
Cleife, Philip
1 *Pinchbeck masterpiece* (1970)
Tour de force
2 *Slick and the dead* (1972)

Marvel superheroes adventure gamebooks series
This sequence has seven authors
Grubb, Jeff
1 *City in darkness* (1986)
Novak, Kate
2 *Rocket's red glare* (1986)
Epperson, Jerry
3 *Night of the wolverine* (1986)
Varney, Allen
4 *Doctor Strange, Through six generations* (1987)
Spector, Warren
5 *Thing, One thing after another* (1987)
Novak, Kate
6 *Uncanny X-men, An X-cellent death* (1987)
David, Peter
7 *Amazing Spiderman, As the world burns* (1987)

Marvel superheroes, new series
This sequence has eight authors
Wein, Len
1 *Amazing Spiderman, Mayhem in Manhattan* (1978)
Silva, Joseph
2 *Incredible Hulk, Stalker from the stars* (1978)
Meyers, Richard S
3 *Cry of the beast* (1979)
Silva, Joseph
4 *Captain America, Holocaust for hire* (1979)
Wolfman, Marv
5 *Fantastic Four, Doomsday* (1979)
Rotsler, William
6 *Iron Man, And call my killer, Modok!* (1979)
7 *Doctor Strange, Nightmare* (1979)
Kupperberg, Paul
8 *Amazing Spiderman, Crime campaign* (1979)
Wein, Len
9 *Marvel superheroes* (1979)
Michelinie, David
10 *Man who stole tomorrow* (1979)
Kupperberg, Paul
11 *Incredible Hulk and Spiderman, Murdermoon* (1979)
Companion volume: *Comics file magazine spotlight on The Fantastic Four files*, by James Van Hise, 1986

Marvel superheroes series
This sequence has two authors
Binder, Otto
1 *Avengers battle the earth-wrecker* (1967)
White, Ted
2 *Captain America, The great gold steal* (1968)

Marvin and Milton series
Modell, Frank B
see **Milton and Marvin series**

Marvin series
Edmunds, Brent
see **Pete Marvin series**
Eyles, Leonora
see **Doctor Joan Marvin series**

Marx series
Kapp, Eleanor
see **Eleanor Marx series**
White, Terence Hanbury
see **Mister Marx series**

Mary and Arnold series
Sinclair, May
1 *Mary Olivier* (1919)
2 *Arnold Waterlow* (1924)

Mary and Florence series
Tytler, Ann Fraser
1 *Mary and Florence* (1835)
Alternative title: Grave and gay
2 *Mary and Florence at sixteen* (1838)

Mary and Jerry Denton series
Hunt, Francis
1 *Messenger dog's secret* (1935)
2 *Mystery of the toy bank* (1935)
3 *Story the parrot told* (1935)
4 *Secret of the missing clown* (1936)
5 *Mystery of the crooked tree* (1937)

Mary and John series
Blyton, Enid
see **John and Mary series**
James, Grace
see **John and Mary series**

Mary and Michael series
Saville, Malcolm
see **Michael and Mary series**

Mary and Nan Cantwell series
Boylan, Clare
see **Nan and Mary Cantwell series**

Mary-Ann series
De Banke, Cecile
see **Tabby series**

Mary Ann Shaughnessy series
Cookson, Catherine
1 *Grand man* (1954)
2 *Lord and Mary Ann* (1956)
3 *Devil and Mary Ann* (1958)
4 *Love and Mary Ann* (1961)
5 *Life and Mary Ann* (1962)
6 *Marriage and Mary Ann* (1964)
7 *Mary Ann's angels* (1965)
8 *Mary Ann and Bill* (1967)
Companion volume: *Fanny McBride*, 1959; omnibus volume: *Mary Ann omnibus*, 1981

Mary, Ben and William series
Furminger, Jo
1 *Spell for Miss Grimscuttle* (1979)
2 *Mrs Boffy's birthday* (1980)
3 *Oh no, Aunt Belladonna!* (1982)
4 *Ghost for Miss Grimscuttle* (1983)
5 *Hurry home, Mrs Boffy!* (1986)
6 *Mrs Boffy's dreadful day* (1987)

Mary Call series
Cleaver, Vera
see **Luther family series**

Mary Carner series
Popkin, Zelda
see **Mary Carner Whittaker series**

Mary Carner Whittaker series
Popkin, Zelda
1 *Death wears a white gardenia* (1938)
2 *Time off for murder* (1940)
3 *Murder in the mist* (1940)
4 *Dead men's gift* (1941)
5 *No crime for a lady* (1942)

Mary Carrick series
Turner, Sheila
Reminiscences of country life
1 *Over the counter* (1960)
A year in a village shop in Wiltshire
2 *Farmer's wife* (1963)
3 *Farm at King's Standing* (1964)
Little place called King's Standing

Mary Cary series
Bosher, Kate Lee Langley
1 *Mary Cary, frequently Martha* (1910)
2 *Miss Gibbie Gault* (1911)

Mary Elizabeth series
Nixon, Joan Lowery
1 *Dark and deadly pool* (1987)
2 *Weekend was murder* (1992)

Mary Ellis series
Newell, Hope
1 *Cap for Mary Ellis* (1953)
2 *Mary Ellis, student nurse* (1958)

Mary Faith Rapple series
Sayers, Valerie
1 *Due East* (1987)
2 *How I got him back* (1989)
Alternative title: Under the cold moon's shine

Mary Fenwick series
Whitby, Beatrice
1 *Awakening of Mary Fenwick* (1889)
2 *Mary Fenwick's daughter* (1894)

Mary Finney series
Head, Matthew
see **Doctor Mary Finney series**

Mary Helen series
O'Marie, Carol Anne
see **Sister Mary Helen series**

Mary Hervey Russell trilogy
Jameson, Storm
see **Triumph of time trilogy**

Mary Hervey series
Jameson, Storm
see **Triumph of time series**

Mary Jane series
Carson, Hilda
1 *Plain Mary Jane* (1957)
2 *Mary Jane and the visitors* (1959)

Mary Jane series
Judson, Clara Ingram
1 *Mary Jane, her book* (1918)
2 *Mary Jane, her visit* (1918)
3 *Mary Jane's kindergarten* (1918)
4 *Mary Jane down South* (1919)
5 *Mary Jane's city home* (1920)
6 *Mary Jane in New England* (1921)
7 *Mary Jane's country home* (1922)
8 *Mary Jane at school* (1923)
9 *Mary Jane in Canada* (1924)
10 *Mary Jane's summer fun* (1925)
11 *Mary Jane's winter sports* (1926)
12 *Mary Jane's vacation* (1927)
13 *Mary Jane in England* (1928)
14 *Mary Jane in Scotland* (1929)
15 *Mary Jane in France* (1930)
16 *Mary Jane in Switzerland* (1931)
17 *Mary Jane in Italy* (1933)
18 *Mary Jane in Spain* (1937)
19 *Mary Jane's friends in Holland* (1939)

Mary Jane series
Sims, George Robert
1 *Mary Jane's memoirs* (1887)
2 *Mary Jane married* (1888)
Tale of a village inn

Mary Kate series
Morgan, Helen
1 *Meet Mary Kate* (1963)
2 *Mary Kate and the Jumble Bear, and other stories* (1967)
3 *Mary Kate and the school bus, and other stories* (1970)
Mary Kate

Mary Livingstone series
Allen, Julia
1 *Mary Livingstone, M.D.* (1956)
2 *Shadows must talk* (1958)

Mary Lou series
Lavell, Edith
1 *Mystery at Dark Cedars* (1935)
2 *Mystery of the fires* (1935)
3 *Mystery of the secret band* (1935)

Mary Louise and Josie O'Gorman series
Van Dyne, Edith
This pseudonym is used by Lyman Frank Baum for the first five titles in the sequence and by Emma Sampson for the remaining five titles
1 *Mary Louise* (1916)
2 *Mary Louise in the country* (1916)
3 *Mary Louise solves a mystery* (1917)
4 *Mary Louise and the Liberty girls* (1918)
5 *Mary Louise adopts a soldier* (1919)
6 *Mary Louise at Dorfield* (1920)
7 *Mary Louise stands the test* (1920)
8 *Mary Louise and Josie O'Gorman* (1922)
9 *Josie O'Gorman* (1923)
Originally published under the author's real name Emma Sampson
10 *Josie O'Gorman and the meddlesome major* (1924)
Originally published under the author's real name Emma Sampson

Mary Marony series
Kline, Suzy
1 *Mary Marony and the snake* (1992)
2 *Mary Marony hides out* (1993)

Mary-Mary series
Robinson, Joan Gale
1 *Mary-Mary* (1957)
2 *More Mary-Mary* (1958)
3 *Madam Mary-Mary* (1960)
One volume selection entitled *Mary-Mary stories*, 1965

Mary Mouse series
Blyton, Enid
1 *Mary Mouse and the doll's house* (1942)
2 *More adventures of Mary Mouse* (1943)
3 *Little Mary Mouse again* (1944)
4 *Hallo, Little Mary Mouse* (1945)
5 *Mary Mouse and her family* (1946)
6 *Here comes Mary Mouse again* (1947)
7 *How do you do, Mary Mouse* (1948)
8 *Hurrah for Mary Mouse* (1949)
9 *We do love Mary Mouse* (1950)
10 *Welcome Mary Mouse* (1950)
11 *Prize for Mary Mouse* (1951)
12 *Mary Mouse and her bicycle* (1952)
13 *Mary Mouse and the Noah's Ark* (1953)
14 *Mary Mouse to the rescue* (1954)
15 *Mary Mouse in Nursery Rhyme Land* (1955)
16 *Day with Mary Mouse* (1956)
17 *Mary Mouse and the garden party* (1957)
18 *Mary Mouse goes to the fair* (1958)
19 *Mary Mouse has a wonderful idea* (1959)
20 *Mary Mouse goes to sea* (1960)
21 *Mary Mouse goes out for the day* (1961)
22 *Fun with Mary Mouse* (1962)
23 *Mary Mouse and the little donkey* (1964)

Mary of England series
Lewis, Hilda
Based on the life of Mary, Queen Consort of Louis XII of France
1 *Rose of England* (1977)
2 *Heart of a rose* (1978)

Mary of Nazareth series
Borden, Mary
1 *Mary of Nazareth* (1933)
2 *King of the Jews* (1935)

Mary Owen series
Spender, Jean Maud
1 *Seven days for hanging* (1958)
2 *Murder on the prowl* (1960)
3 *Death renders account* (1960)

Mary Plain series
Rae, Gwynedd
1 *Mostly Mary* (1930)
2 *All Mary* (1930)
3 *Mary Plain in town* (1935)
4 *Mary Plain on holiday* (1937)
5 *Mary Plain in trouble* (1940)
6 *Mary Plain in wartime* (1942)
Mary Plain lends a paw
7 *Mary Plain's big adventure* (1944)
8 *Mary Plain home again* (1948)
9 *Mary Plain to the rescue* (1950)
10 *Mary Plain and the twins* (1954)
11 *Mary Plain goes bob-a-jobbing* (1954)
12 *Mary Plain goes to America* (1957)
13 *Mary Plain, V.I.P.* (1961)
14 *Mary Plain's whodunit* (1965)

Mary Poppins series
Travers, Pamela Lyndon
1 *Mary Poppins* (1934)
Revised edition 1981
2 *Mary Poppins comes back* (1935)
One volume edition 1937
3 *Mary Poppins opens the door* (1943)
4 *Mary Poppins in the park* (1945)
5 *Mary Poppins from A to Z* (1963)
6 *Mary Poppins in Cherry Tree Lane* (1982)
7 *Mary Poppins and the house next door* (1989)
Companion volume: *Mary Poppins in the kitchen, a cookery book with a story*, 1975

Mary Powell series
Manning, Anne
1 *Maiden and married life of Mary Powell* (1849)
Mary Powell
2 *Deborah's diary* (1859)
One volume edition 1898

Mary, Queen of Scots series
Plaidy, Jean
1 *Royal road to Fotheringay* (1955)
Mary, Queen of Scotland, the triumphant years
2 *Captive Queen of Scots* (1963)

Mary, Queen of Scots series
Scott, Walter
Originally published anonymously
1 *Monastery* (1820)
2 *Abbot* (1820)

Mary Rose Onetree series
Clifford, Eth
1 *Help, I'm a prisoner in the library!* (1979)
2 *Dastardly murder of Dirty Pete* (1981)
3 *Just tell me when we're dead* (1983)

Mary Rose series
Wirries, Mary Mabel
1 *Mary Rose at boarding school* (1924)
2 *Mary Rose keeps house* (1925)
3 *Mary Rose, sophomore* (1925)
4 *Mary Rose, graduate* (1926)
5 *Mary Rose at Rose Gables* (1928)
6 *Mary Rose in Friendville* (1930)
7 *Mary Rose's sister Bess* (1932)

Mary series
Brock, Emma Lillian
1 *Ballet for Mary* (1954)
2 *Mary's secret* (1962)
3 *Mary's camera* (1963)
4 *Mary makes a cake* (1964)
5 *Mary on roller skates* (1967)

Mary series
Delahaye, Gilbert
1 *Nicest day of the year* (1956)
Original edition entitled *Martine au cirque*
2 *Mary's mountain holiday* (1960)
3 *Mary goes camping* (1961)
4 *Mary's happy year* (1963)
Original edition entitled *Martine et les quatre saisons*
5 *Mary's seaside holiday* (1964)
6 *Mary goes to the sea* (1966)
Original edition entitled *Martine a la mer*
7 *Mary goes to the park* (1967)
Original edition entitled *Martine au parc*
8 *Mary learns to ride* (1967)
9 *Mary and Mark* (1968)
Original edition entitled *Martine petite maman*
10 *Mary's birthday party* (1969)
Original edition entitled *Martine fete son anniversaire; numbers* 7, 8, 10 also published in one volume entitled *Mary and her friends*, 1973
11 *Mary and her garden* (1970)
Original edition entitled *Martine embellit son jardin*; numbers 4, 5, 11 also published in one volume entitled *Mary and her family*, 1974
12 *Mary learns to dance* (1972)
Original edition entitled *Martine, petit rat de l'opera*
13 *Mary at the flower festival* (1973)
Original edition entitled *Martine a la fete des fleurs*
14 *Mary learns to cook* (1974)
Original edition entitled *Martine fait la cuisine*
15 *Mary learns to swim* (1975)
Original edition entitled *Martine apprend a nager*
16 *Mary learns to ski* (1975)
Omnibus volumes: *Mary goes travelling*, 1975, *Mary's holidays*, 1975
Other titles not published in English

Mary series
Grannan, Mary
see **Just Mary series**

Mary speaks to the world series
Faricy, Robert Leo
1 *Medjugorje up close* (1986)
2 *Medjugorje journal* (1987)
Companion volume: *Medjugorje retreat*, 1989

Mary Teresa series
Quill, Monica
see **Sister Mary Teresa series**

Mary Tudor series
Churchill, Rosemary
1 *King's daughter* (1969)
2 *Daughter of Henry VIII* (1971)

Mary Tudor trilogy
Lewis, Hilda
1 *I am Mary Tudor* (1971)
2 *Mary the Queen* (1973)
3 *Bloody Mary* (1974)

Marytary series
Creswell, Harry Bulkeley
1 *Marytary* (1928)
2 *Johnny and Marytary* (1936)

Masao Masuto series
Cunningham, E V
1 *Samantha* (1967)
Case of the angry actress
2 *Case of the one-penny orange* (1977)
3 *Case of the Russian diplomat* (1978)
4 *Case of the poisoned eclairs* (1979)
5 *Case of the sliding pool* (1981)
6 *Case of the kidnapped angel* (1982)
7 *Case of the murdered Mackenzie* (1984)

Mascot schoolboy series
Richards, Frank
1 *Top study at Topham* (1947)
2 *Bunny Binks on the war-path* (1947)
3 *Dandy of Topham* (1947)
4 *Sent to Coventry* (1947)

Mascot series
Hardcastle, Michael
1 *Team that wouldn't give in* (1984)
2 *Mascot* (1987)

Masculine ending series
Smith, Joan
1 *Masculaine ending* (1988)
2 *Why aren't they screaming?* (1988)

MASH series
Hooker, Richard
see **M.A.S.H. series**

Masha series
Kay, Mara
1 *Masha* (1968)
2 *Youngest lady in waiting* (1969)

Mask trilogy
Cooke, Catherine
1 *Mask of the wizard* (1985)
2 *Veil of shadow* (1987)
3 *Hidden temple* (1988)

Masked Rider and Blue Hawk series
This sequence has six authors
Hobart, Donald Bayne
1 *Whistling waddy* (1928)
2 *Adventure trail* (1929)
3 *Horseshoe trail* (1952)
Trail of the twisted horseshoes
4 *Ruthless range* (1957)
5 *Dark trail* (1959)
6 *Hardcase guns* (1959)
7 *Arizona outlaw* (1961)
8 *Six-gun empire* (1965)
9 *Iron horse gunsmoke* (1965)
10 *Vulture Valley* (1966)
11 *Guns of the big hills* (1966)
12 *Gallows gold* (1966)
13 *Longhorn trail* (1967)
14 *Red river guns* (1967)
15 *Black stallion mesa* (1967)
16 *Gunsmoke country* (1967)
17 *Ambush at Big Creek* (1967)
18 *Haunted mesa* (1967)
Hopson, William L
19 *Guns of the clan* (1967)
Hobart, Donald Bayne
20 *Desert of doom* (1967)
21 *Guns along the river* (1968)
22 *Warrior range* (1968)
23 *Sinister ranch* (1968)
24 *Desolation Range* (1968)
Harris, Larry
25 *Lobo Trail* (1968)
Curry, Tom
26 *Chaparral marauders* (1968)
Tompkins, Walker Allison
27 *Two rails west* (1969)
30 *Ghost Mine gold* (1969)
Hopson, William L
31 *Boom town guns* (1970)
Harrison, C William
32 *Gun trail to Spanish gold* (1970)
Clancy, Eugene A
33 *Owlhoot justice* (1970)

Mason Brant series
Hopkins, Nevil Monroe
1 *Strange cases of Mason Brent* (1916)
Three stories; *Investigation at Holman Square* published separately, 1935
2 *Racoon Lake mystery* (1917)

Mason series
Armstrong, Raymond
see **Inspector Dick Mason series**
Duncan, Alex
see **Country doctor series**
Gardner, Erle Stanley
see **Perry Mason series**
Gregor, Elmer Russell
see **Jim Mason series**
Leader, Charles
see **Paul Mason series**
Plant, Jack
see **Rusty Mason series**
Post, Melville Davisson
see **Randolph Mason series**
Stahl, Hilda
see **Sendi Lee Mason series**

Massachusetts State Police series
Stratton, Roy
see **Scott Gregory and Justin Bassett series**

Massel series
Golding, Louis
see **Philip Massel series**

Massey series
Van Siller, Hilda
see **Richard Massey series**

Massingham series
Lincoln, Maurice
see **Reginald Massingham series**

Master Christopher series
De la Pasture, Elizabeth
1 *Master Christopher* (1911)
2 *Erica* (1912)
Honourable Mrs Garry

Master Li Kao and Number Ten Ox series
Hughart, Barry
1 *Bridge of birds* (1984)
A novel of an ancient China that never was
2 *Story of the stone* (1988)
3 *Eight skilled gentlemen* (1991)

Master mariner series
Monsarrat, Nicholas
1 *Running proud* (1978)
2 *Darken ship* (1980)
Further volumes were planned but never written

Master of Gray series
Tranter, Nigel Godwin
see **Patrick Gray series**

Master of Hestviken series
Undset, Sigrid
1 *Axe* (1925)
Ax
Original edition entitled *Olav Audunsson i Hestviken*, volume 1
2 *Snake pit* (1925)
Original edition entitled *Olav Audunsson i Hestviken*, volume 2
3 *In the wilderness* (1927)
Original edition entitled *Olav Audunsson hans born*, volume 1
4 *Son avenger* (1927)
Original edition entitled *Olav Audunsson hans born*, volume 2
One volume edition entitled *The Master of Hestviken*, 1942

Master of the stars trilogy
Hoskins, Robert
1 *Master of the stars* (1976)
2 *To control the stars* (1977)
3 *To escape the stars* (1978)

Master series
Brightfield, Richard
1 *Master of kung fu* (1989)
2 *Master of tae kwon do* (1990)
3 *Master of karate* (1990)

Masterdillo series
Wawn, F T
1 *Masterdillo* (1913)
2 *Road to the stars* (1916)

Masterful monk series
Dudley, Owen Francis
see **Problems of human happiness series**

Masters of darkness series
Etchison, Dennis
1 *Masters of darkness* (1986)
2 *Masters of darkness II* (1988)
3 *Masters of darkness III* (1991)
One volume edition entitled *The complete Masters of darkness*, 1991

Masters of space trilogy
Vardeman, Robert Edward
1 *Stellar death plan* (1987)
2 *Alien web* (1987)
3 *Plague in paradise* (1987)
One volume edition entitled *Masters of space*, 1990

Masters series
Clark, Douglas
see **Inspector George Masters series**
Lynch, Lawrence L
see **Carl Masters series**
Rud, Anthony Melville
see **J C K Masters series**

Masterson series
Hawton, Hector
see **Colonel Max Masterson series**

Masterthinker series
De Bono, Edward
1 *Masterthinker* (1988)
2 *Masterthinker II* (1988)
3 *Masterthinker's handbook* (1992)

Masuto series
Cunningham, E V
see **Masao Masuto series**

Mata series
Grayland, Valerie Merle
see **Hoani Mata series**

Match series
Saint Meyer, Ned
1 *Match* (1890)
Alternative title: The golden wedding at Turkey Hollow
2 *Match as a fakir* (1890)
Alternative title: The Pumpkinville County Fair

Mates series
Munroe, Kirk
1 *Dorymates* (1890)
A tale of the fishing banks
2 *Campmates* (1891)
A story of the Plains
3 *Canoemates* (1892)
A story of the Florida Reef and Everglades
4 *Raftmates* (1893)
A story of the great river

Math games series
Anno, Mitsumasa
1 *Anno's math games* (1987)
2 *Anno's math games II* (1989)

Mather series
Graeme, Bruce
see **Detective Sergeant Robert Mather series**

Matheson series
Wright, June
see **Sergeant Matheson series**

Mathew Dilke series
Gutteridge, Lindsay
1 *Cold war in a country garden* (1971)
2 *Killer pine* (1973)
3 *Fratricide is a gas* (1975)

Mathew Swain series
McQuay, Mike
1 *Hot time in old town* (1981)
2 *When trouble beckons* (1981)
3 *Deadliest show in town* (1982)
4 *Odds are murder* (1982)

Matilda and George Mouse series
Buchanan, Heather S
see **Tales of George and Matilda Mouse series**

Matilda Perks series
Woodthorpe, Ralph Carter
1 *Death in a little town* (1935)
2 *Shadow on the Downs* (1935)

Matilda series
Brand, Christianna
see **Nurse Matilda series**

Matilda series
Cleugh, Sophia
1 *Matilda, governess of the English* (1924)
2 *Ernestine Sophie* (1925)
3 *Daisy boy* (1931)
Young Jonathan

Matilda series
Vaughan, Carol
see **Manorfield Stud series**

Matilda Worthing series
Drummond, John Keith
1 *Thy sting, oh death* (1985)
2 *'Tis the season to be dying* (1988)
3 *Mass murder* (1991)

Matravers series
Farnol, Jeffery
see **Oliver Matravers series**

Matriarch series
Stern, Gladys Bronwyn
see **Rakonitz family series**

Matrix principle series
Laura, Ronald S
1 *Matrix principle* (1991)
A revolutionary approach to muscle develeopment
2 *Matrix for muscle gain* (1993)

Matson series
James, Breni
see **Sergeant Gunnar Matson series**

Matt Archer series
Henry, Clay
1 *Welcome home, Lily Glow* (1960)
2 *Devils burn too* (1962)
3 *Nude on the rocks* (1965)

Matt Bishop series
Jeier, Thomas
1 *Return to Conta Lupe* (1983)
2 *Celluloid kid* (1984)

Matt Cobb series
De Andrea, William Louis
1 *Killed in the ratings* (1978)
2 *Killed in the act* (1981)
3 *Killed with a passion* (1983)
4 *Killed on the ice* (1984)
5 *Killed in paradise* (1988)
6 *Killed on the rocks* (1990)

Matt Eberhart series
Sandberg, Berent
1 *Brass diamonds* (1980)
2 *Hobeycomb bid* (1981)
3 *Chinese spur* (1983)

Matt Erridge series
Stein, Aaron Marc
1 *Sitting up dead* (1958)
2 *Never need an enemy* (1958)
3 *Home and murder* (1962)
4 *Blood on the stars* (1964)
5 *I fear the Greeks* (1966)
Executioner's rest
6 *Deadly delight* (1967)
7 *Snare Andalucian* (1968)
Faces of death
8 *Kill is a four-letter word* (1968)
9 *Alp murder* (1970)
10 *Finger* (1973)
11 *Coffin country* (1976)
12 *Lend me your ears* (1977)
13 *Body search* (1978)
14 *Nowhere?* (1978)
15 *Chill factor* (1978)
16 *Rolling heads* (1979)
17 *One dip dead* (1979)
18 *Cheating butcher* (1980)
19 *Nose for it* (1981)
20 *Body for a buddy* (1981)
21 *Hangman's row* (1982)
22 *Bombing run* (1983)
23 *Garbage collector* (1984)

Matt Gabriel series
Gosling, Paula
see **Sheriff Matt Gabriel series**

Matt Hawke series
Cunningham, Chet
1 *Avenger* (1987)
2 *Houston hellground* (1988)
3 *Colombia crackdown* (1988)
4 *Manhattan massacre* (1988)

Matt Helm series
Hamilton, Donald
1 *Death of a citizen* (1960)
2 *Wrecking crew* (1960)
3 *Removers* (1961)
4 *Murderer's row* (1962)
5 *Silencers* (1962)
6 *Ambushers* (1963)
7 *Ravagers* (1964)
8 *Shadowers* (1964)
9 *Devastators* (1965)
10 *Betrayers* (1966)
11 *Menacers* (1968)
12 *Interlopers* (1969)
13 *Poisoners* (1971)
14 *Intriguers* (1972)
15 *Intimidators* (1974)
16 *Terminators* (1975)
17 *Retaliators* (1976)
18 *Terrorizers* (1977)
19 *Revengers* (1982)
20 *Annihilators* (1983)
21 *Infiltrators* (1984)
22 *Detonators* (1985)
23 *Vanishers* (1986)
24 *Demolishers* (1987)
25 *Frighteners* (1989)
26 *Threateners* (1992)
27 *Damagers* (1993)

Matt Hughes series
Martin, Aylwin Lee
1 *Death on a ferris wheel* (1951)
2 *Death for a hussy* (1952)
3 *Crimson frame* (1952)
4 *Fear comes calling* (1952)

Matt Lincoln series
Johnston, William
Based on a television series
1 *Revolutionist* (1970)
2 *Hostage* (1971)

Matt McGinley series
McNeill, Janet
1 *Battle of Saint George Without* (1966)
2 *Goodbye, Dove Square* (1969)

Matt Price series
Newton, Mike
see **Bounty Man series**

Matt Riordan series
Huebner, Frederick D
1 *Joshua sequence* (1986)
2 *Judgement by fire* (1988)
3 *Picture postcard* (1991)
4 *Methods of extinction* (1994)

Matt Rudd series
Deming, Richard
1 *Vice cop* (1961)
2 *Anything but saintly* (1963)
3 *Death of a pusher* (1964)

Matt Savage series
Cooper, Craig
1 *Blackmail is murder* (1968)
2 *Dame in distress* (1968)
3 *What's funny about murder?* (1968)
4 *You'll die laughing* (1968)
5 *Catch and squeeze* (1968)
6 *Who killed Honey Bee?* (1968)

Matt Skinner series
Mulford, Clarence Edward
1 *Rustlers' Valley* (1924)
2 *Hopalong Cassidy and the eagle's brood* (1931)

Matt Sutton and Diana Logan series
White, James G
see **Gunslick series**

Matt Tierney series
Champlin, Tim
1 *Summer of the Sioux* (1982)
2 *Dakota gold* (1982)
3 *Staghorn* (1984)
4 *Shadow catcher* (1985)
5 *Great timber race* (1986)
6 *Iron trail* (1987)
7 *Colt lightning* (1989)
8 *King of the highbinders* (1989)
9 *Flying eagle* (1990)

Matt Winters series
Oellrichs, Inez
1 *Man who didn't answer* (1939)
2 *Kettel Mill mystery* (1939)
3 *Murder comes at night* (1940)
4 *And die she did* (1945)
5 *Murder helps* (1947)
6 *Death of a white witch* (1949)
7 *Death in a chilly corner* (1964)

Matter, space and time series
Cummings, Ray
1 *Girl in the golden atom* (1922)
2 *Princess of the atom* (1929)
3 *Man who mastered time* (1924)
4 *Shadow girl* (1929)
5 *Exile of time* (1931)

Matthew and Moonface series
Prime, Honor
see **Moonface series**

Matthew and Son series
Kenworthy, Christopher
1 *In the dark of the moon* (1981)
2 *Ride a dark tide* (1982)
3 *Storm in the dark* (1983)
4 *Against a dark shore* (1985)

Matthew Coll series
Lewis, Roy Harley
1 *Cracking of spines* (1980)
2 *Manuscript murders* (1981)
3 *Pension for death* (1983)

Matthew Faraday series
Grant, William
1 *Iron horse* (1988)
2 *Collision course* (1988)
3 *Gold train* (1988)
4 *Colorado special* (1988)
5 *Trackwalker* (1989)
6 *Train of glory* (1989)
7 *Avalanche run* (1989)
8 *Owlhoot Express* (1989)

Matthew Furnival series
Phillips, Stella
see **Inspector Matthew Furnival series**

Matthew Gunn series
Muir, James A
see **Breed series**

Matthew Higgins series
Davis, Means
1 *Hospital murders* (1934)
2 *Murder without weapons* (1935)

Matthew Hope series
McBain, Ed
1 *Goldilocks* (1977)
2 *Rumpelstiltskin* (1981)
3 *Beauty and the beast* (1982)
4 *Jack and the beanstalk* (1984)
5 *Snow White and Rose Red* (1985)
6 *Cinderella* (1986)
7 *Puss in Boots* (1987)
8 *House that Jack built* (1988)
9 *Three blind mice* (1990)
10 *Mary, Mary* (1993)
11 *There was a little girl* (1994)

Matthew Jacob series
Klein, Zachary
1 *Still among the living* (1990)
2 *Two way toll* (1991)

Matthew Lawe series
Monsarrat, Nicholas
see **Master mariner series**

Matthew Looney series
Beatty, Jerome
1 *Matthew Looney's voyage to the earth* (1961)
2 *Matthew Looney's invasion of the earth* (1965)
3 *Matthew Looney in the outback* (1969)
4 *Matthew Looney and the space pirates* (1972)

Matthew Morten trilogy
Leeson, Robert
1 *Maroon boy* (1974)
2 *Bess* (1975)
3 *White horse* (1977)

Matthew Ratton series
Knowles, Anne
1 *Matthew Ratton* (1980)
2 *Raven tree* (1981)

Matthew Rogerson series
McInerny, Ralph
1 *Jolly Rogerson* (1967)
2 *Rogerson at bay* (1976)

Matthew Scudder series
Block, Lawrence
1 *When the sacred gin mill closes* (1986)
2 *In the midst of death* (1976)
3 *Sins of the fathers* (1977)
4 *Time to murder and create* (1977)
5 *Stab in the dark* (1981)
6 *Eight million ways to die* (1982)
7 *Out on the cutting edge* (1989)
8 *Ticket to the boneyard* (1990)
9 *Dance at the slaughterhouse* (1991)
10 *Devil knows you're dead* (1993)
11 *Long line of dead men* (1994)
Also short stories in *Sometimes they bite*, 1983 and *Like a lamb to the slaughter*, 1984

Matthew Stock series
Tourney, Leonard
1 *Player's boy is dead* (1980)
2 *Low treason* (1983)
3 *Familiar spirits* (1985)
4 *Bartholomew Fair murders* (1986)
5 *Old Saxon blood* (1988)
6 *Knaves Templar* (1991)
7 *Witness of bones* (1992)
8 *Frobisher's savage* (1994)

Matthew Sumner series
Davey, Norman
see **Pilgrim series**

Matthew Tobin series
Caillou, Alan
see **Colonel Matthew Tobin series**

Matthews and Plante series
Palmer, John
see **Guy Plante and Freya Matthews series**

Matthews and Strong series
Oursler, William
see **Philip Strong and James Matthews series**

Matthews series
Meredith, Doris R
see **Sheriff Charles Timothy Matthews series**
Wright, Harold Bell
see **Dan Matthews series**

Matty Doolin and Joe Darling series
Cookson, Catherine
1 *Matty Doolin* (1965)
2 *Joe and the gladiator* (1968)

Matty series
Robinson, Martha
1 *Matty in films* (1953)
2 *First act* (1955)
3 *Matty in television* (1959)

Matty Sinclair series
Fennelly, Tony
1 *Glory hole murders* (1985)
2 *Closet hanging* (1987)

Matty Trakker series
Dunn, Roger
1 *Matty Trakker and the money men* (1985)
2 *Matty Trakker and the UFO* (1985)

Maturin and Aubrey series
O'Brian, Patrick
see **Jack Aubrey and Stephen Maturin series**

Maud Kingslake series
This sequence has two authors
E, H F
1 *Maud Kinglake's collect* (1882)
Originally published anonymously
Everett-Green, Evelyn
2 *Cuthbert Coningsby* (1884)

Maud Noakes series
Neame, Alan
1 *Adventures of Maud Noakes* (1961)
2 *Maud Noakes, guerrilla* (1965)

Maud Silver series
Wentworth, Patricia
see **Miss Maud Silver series**

Maureen and Jules Wendall trilogy
Oates, Joyce Carol
see **Jules and Maureen Wendall trilogy**

Maureen O'Connor series
Branson, Karen
1 *Potato eaters* (1979)
2 *Streets of gold* (1981)

Maurice Avery and Jenny Pearl series
Mackenzie, Compton
see **Jenny Pearl and Maurice Avery series**

Maurice Gray series
Moore, Patrick
1 *Mission to Mars* (1955)
2 *Domes of Mars* (1956)
3 *Voices of Mars* (1957)
4 *Peril on Mars* (1958)
5 *Raiders of Mars* (1959)

Maurice Hemyock series
Browne, Douglas Gordon
see **Major Maurice Hemyock series**

Maurice Hepburn series
Gorell, Ronald Gorell Barnes
see **Inspector Maurice Hepburn series**

Maurice the moose series
Harris, Leon
1 *Great picture robbery* (1967)
2 *Maurice goes to sea* (1969)

Maurice Wallion series
Regis, Julius
1 *Copper house* (1918)
Original edition entitled *Kopparhuset*
2 *Number thirteen Toroni* (1919)
Original edition entitled *Nr. 13 Toroni*

Maurice Ygrec series
Rippon, Marion
see **Inspector Maurice Ygrec series**

Maurin series
Aicard, Jean
1 *Diverting adventures of Maurin* (1908)
Original edition entitled *Maurin des Maures, comme on rit chez nous*
2 *Maurin the Illustrious* (1908)
Original edition entitled *L'illustre Maurin, suite et fin des memorables aventures de Maurin des Maures*

Maury series
Walsh, James Morgan
see **Tiger Bay series**

Maus series
Spiegelman, Art
see **Survivor's tale series**

Mauser series
Reynolds, Mack
see **Joe Mauser series**

Maushope's Landing series
Richardson, Judith Benet
1 *David's landing* (1985)
2 *Mirrors and lonely* (1992)

Maver series
Nixon, Alan
see **Larry Maver series**

Mavin Manyshaped trilogy
Tepper, Sheri S
1 *Song of Mavin Manyshaped* (1985)
2 *Flight of Mavin Manyshaped* (1985)
3 *Search of Mavin Manyshaped* (1985)
One volume edition entitled The chronicles of *Mavin Manyshaped*, 1986

Mavis Seidlitz series
Brown, Carter
1 *Honey, here's your hearse!* (1955)
2 *Bullet for my baby* (1955)
3 *Good morning, Mavis* (1957)
4 *Loving and the dead* (1959)
5 *None but the lethal heart* (1959)
Fabulous
6 *Tomorrow is murder* (1960)
7 *Lament for a lousy lover* (1960)
8 *Murder wears a mantilla* (1962)
An earlier version of this novel published in 1957 did not include Mavis Seidlitz
9 *Bump and grind murders* (1964)
10 *Seidlitz and the super-spy* (1967)
Super-spy
11 *Murder is so nostalgic* (1972)
12 *And the undead sing* (1974)

Mavor series
Bridie, James
Autobiography
1 *Some talk of Alexander* (1926)
A revue with interludes in the antique mode
2 *One way of living* (1939)

Mavreen trilogy
Lorrimer, Claire
1 *Mavreen* (1976)
2 *Tamarisk* (1978)
3 *Chantal* (1980)

Max and Diana series
Ziefert, Harriet
Illustrated by Lonni Sue Johnson
1 *Max and Diana and the snowy day* (1987)
2 *Max and Diana and the shopping trip* (1987)
3 *Max and Diana and the beach day* (1987)
4 *Max and Diana and the birthday present* (1987)

Max and me series
Greer, Gery
1 *Max and me and the time machine* (1983)
2 *Max and me and the Wild West* (1988)

Max and Scrap series
Leyland, Eric
1 *Mystery of Pig's Nose* (1951)
2 *All hands on deck* (1952)
3 *Villages under the water* (1953)
4 *Danger below* (1954)
5 *Man overboard* (1955)
6 *White Fury* (1956)
7 *Forest feud* (1957)
8 *Wings over the outback* (1958)

Max Blythe and Carole Trevor series
Philips, Judson Pentecost
see **Carole Trevor and Max Blythe series**

Max Brindle series
Fleischman, Sid
1 *Straw donkey case* (1948)
2 *Murder's no accident* (1949)

Max Carrados series
Bramah, Ernest
Short stories
1 *Max Carrados* (1914)
2 *Eyes of Max Carrados* (1923)
3 *Specimen case* (1924)
4 *Max Carrados mysteries* (1927)
5 *Bravo of London* (1934)
Also three stories featuring Carrados in *Short stories*, 1929; omnibus volume: *Best Max Carrados detective stories*, 1972

Max Curfew series
Brunner, John
1 *Plague on both your causes* (1969) *Backlash*
2 *Good men do nothing* (1970)
3 *Honky in the woodpile* (1971)

Max Darling and Annie Laurance series
Hart, Carolyn Gimpel
see **Annie Laurance and Max Darling series**

Max Farne series
Butler, Richard
1 *Where all the girls are sweeter* (1975)
2 *Italian assets* (1976)

Max Flynn series
James, Peter
1 *Dead letter drop* (1981)
2 *Atom bomb angel* (1982)

Max Frend and Petunia Best series
Chetwynd, Bridget
see **Petunia Best and Max Frend series**

Max Gold series
Cohen, Octavus Roy
1 *Danger in paradise* (1945)
2 *Love has no alibi* (1946)
3 *Don't ever love me* (1947)

Max Guttman series
Goldstein, Arthur David
1 *Person shouldn't die like that* (1972)
2 *You're never to old to die* (1974)
3 *Nobody's sorry he got killed* (1976)

Max Hale series
Coxe, George Harmon
1 *Murder for the asking* (1939)
2 *Lady is afraid* (1940)

Max Hale series
Sandford, Ken
1 *Dead reckoning* (1955)
2 *Dead secret* (1957)

Max Heald series
Hossent, Harry
1 *Spies die at dawn* (1958)
2 *No end to fear* (1959)
3 *Memory of treason* (1961)
4 *Spies have no friends* (1963)
5 *Run for your death* (1965)
6 *Fear business* (1967)

Max Hunter series
Ballard, Willis Todhunter
see **Lieutenant Max Hunter series**

Max Kauffman series
Chastain, Thomas
see **Inspector Max Kauffman series**

Max Keene series
Saber, Robert O
1 *Dame called murder* (1955)
2 *Time for murder* (1956)

Max Malone series
Herman, Charlotte
1 *Max Malone and the great cereal rip-off* (1990)
2 *Max Malone makes a million* (1991)
3 *Max Malone, superstar* (1991)

Max Masterson series
Hawton, Hector
see **Colonel Max Masterson series**

Max Moss series
Thompson, Steven Lynn
1 *Recovery* (1980)
2 *Countdown to China* (1982)

Max Roper series
Platt, Kin
1 *Pushbutton butterfly* (1970)
2 *Kissing gourami* (1970)
3 *Princess stakes murder* (1973) *Pride of women*
4 *Giant kill* (1974)
5 *Match point for murder* (1975)
6 *Body beautiful murder* (1976)
7 *Screwball king murder* (1978)

Max Roth series
Arvay, Harry
see **Israeli Security Branch series**

Max series
Dicks, Terrance
see **Cat called Max series**
Kaye, Marilyn
see **Out of this world series**
Kaye, Terry
see **Mad Max series**
Lindgren, Barbro
see **Sam series**
Platt, Kin
see **Big Max series**
Rohmer, Sax
see **Gaston Max series**

Max series
Steel, Danielle
1 *Max and the baby-sitter* (1989)
2 *Max's daddy goes to the hospital* (1989)
3 *Max's new baby* (1989)

Max series
Wells, Rosemary
1 *Max's first word* (1979)
2 *Max's new suit* (1979)
A child's book about sexual abuse
3 *Max's ride* (1979)
4 *Max's toys* (1979)
A counting book
5 *Max's bath* (1985)
6 *Max's bedtime* (1985)
7 *Max's breakfast* (1985)
8 *Max's birthday* (1985)
9 *Hooray for Max* (1986)
10 *Max's Christmas* (1986)
11 *Max's chocolate chicken* (1989)
12 *Max's dragon shirt* (1991)

Max Smart series
Johnston, William
see **Maxwell Smart series**

Max Stafford series
Bagley, Desmond
1 *Flyaway* (1978)
2 *Windfall* (1982)

Max the cat series
Whitmore, Adam
1 *Max leaves home* (1986)
2 *Max in America* (1986)
3 *Max in India* (1986)
4 *Max in Australia* (1986)

Max the Mouse series
Turk, Hanne
1 *Surprise for Max* (1982)
2 *Rope skips Max* (1982)
3 *Max versus the cube* (1982)
4 *Rainy day Max* (1983)
5 *Goodnight, Max* (1983)
6 *Lesson for Max* (1983)
7 *Max the art lover* (1983)
8 *Merry Christmas, Max* (1983)
9 *Raking leaves with Max* (1983)
10 *Happy birthday, Max!* (1984)
11 *Max packs* (1984)
12 *Snapshot Max* (1984)
13 *Butterfly Max* (1984)
14 *Good sport Max* (1984)
15 *Friendship Max* (1985)
16 *Chocolate Max* (1985)
17 *Robinson Max* (1985)

Max Thursday series
Miller, Wade
1 *Guilty bystander* (1947)
2 *Fatal step* (1948)
3 *Uneasy street* (1948)
4 *Calamity fair* (1950)
5 *Murder charge* (1950)
6 *Shoot to kill* (1951)

Max Van Larsen and Sylvia Plotkin series
Baxt, George
see **Sylvia Plotkin and Max Van Larsen series**

Maxie Pichelsteiner series
Kastner, Erich
see **Little man series**

Maxie series
Gardner, Elsie Bell
1 *Maxie, an adorable girl* (1932)
Alternative title: Her adventures in the British West Indies
2 *Maxie in Venezuela* (1932)
Alternative title: The clue to the diamond mine
3 *Maxie searching for her parents* (1934)
Alternative title: The mystery in Australian waters
4 *Maxie at Brinksome Hall* (1936)
Alternative title: Strange adventures with her chums
5 *Maxie and her adventures in Spain* (1937)
Alternative title: The rescue of a Royalist
6 *Maxie in the jungle* (1937)
Alternative title: The temple of the Incas
7 *Maxie and the golden bird* (1939)
Alternative title: The mysterious Council of Seven

Maxim series
Lyall, Gavin
see **Major Harry Maxim series**

Maxim trilogy
Strugatsky, Arkady
Translated from the Russian
1 *Prisoners of power* (1977)
2 *Beetle in the anthill* (1980)
3 *Time wanderers* (1986)

Maxine Dangerfield series
Franklin, Charles
1 *Dangerous ones* (1964)
2 *On the day of the shooting* (1965)
3 *Death in the east* (1967)
4 *Escape* (1968)

Maxine Reynolds series
Grove, Marjorie
1 *You'll die when you hear this* (1978)
2 *You'll die laughing* (1978)
3 *You'll die tomorrow* (1978)
4 *You'll die, darling* (1979)
5 *You'll die tonight* (1979)
6 *You'll die yesterday* (1979)
7 *You'll die today* (1979)

Maxwell and Brill trilogy
Killough, Lee
see **Brill and Maxwell trilogy**

Maxwell and Carrie series
Clewes, Dorothy
see **Carrie and Maxwell series**

Maxwell and Scott series
Macdonald, William Colt
see **Nogales Scott and Caliper Maxwell series**

Maxwell Archer series
Clevely, Hugh
1 *Zero with death* (1937)
2 *Archer plus twenty* (1938)
3 *Three wooden overcoats* (1939)
4 *No peace for Archer* (1947)
5 *More trouble for Archer* (1949)
6 *Not nice people* (1950)
7 *Blood and thunder* (1951)

Maxwell Fenner series
Booth, Louis F
1 *Bank vault mystery* (1933)
2 *Broker's end* (1935)

Maxwell Quayne series
Symonds, Francis Addington
see **Superintendent Maxwell Quayne series**

Maxwell Sanderson series
Chichester, John Jay
1 *Silent cracksman* (1929)
2 *Sanderson, master rogue* (1929)
3 *Rogues of fortune* (1929)
4 *King of diamonds* (1930)
5 *Sanderson's diamond loot* (1935)

Maxwell series
Corbett, Scott
see **Kerby Maxwell series**
Friedman, Mickey
see **Georgia Lee Maxwell series**
Graeme, Bruce
see **Henry Maxwell series**
Sheldon, Charles Monroe
see **Henry Maxwell series**

Maxwell Smart series
Johnston, William
Based on a television series
1 *Get Smart!* (1965)
2 *Sorry, chief* (1966)
3 *Get Smart once again!* (1966)
4 *Max Smart and the perilous pellets* (1966)
5 *Missed by that much!* (1967)

6 *And loving it!* (1967)
7 *Max Smart, the spy who went out to the cold* (1968)
8 *Max Smart loses control* (1968)
9 *Max Smart and the ghastly ghost affair* (1969)

Maxwell Speed series
Starnes, Richard
1 *Requiem in Utopia* (1967)
2 *Flypaper war* (1969)

May family series
Yonge, Charlotte Mary
1 *Daisy chain* (1856)
2 *Trial* (1864)

May Iverson trilogy
Jordan, Elizabeth Garver
1 *May Iverson, her book* (1904)
2 *May Iverson tackles life* (1912)
3 *May Iverson's career* (1914)

May series
Branscum, Robbie
see **Johnny May series**
Kemp, Sarah
see **Doctor Tina May series**
Le Breton, Thomas
see **Mrs May series**
Taylor, Selman
see **Inspector May series**

Maya series
Bonsels, Waldemar
1 *Maya* (1921)
Original edition entitled *Die Biene Maja und ihre Abenteur*
2 *Heaven folk* (1921)
Original edition entitled *Himmelvolk*

Mayberry and Bradley series
Tree, Gregory
see **Bill Bradley and Noel Mayberry series**

Maybonne series
Barry, Lynda
Comic strips
1 *Come over, come over* (1990)
2 *My perfect life* (1992)

Maybridge series
Gill, B M
see **Inspector Tom Maybridge series**

Maybury family series
Weir, Rosemary
1 *Secret journey* (1957)
2 *Secret of Cobbet's Farm* (1957)

Mayfair witches series
Rice, Anne
1 *Witching hour* (1991)
2 *Lasher* (1993)
3 *Taltos* (1994)

Mayfield family series
Price, Reynolds
1 *Surface of earth* (1975)
2 *Source of light* (1981)

Mayhew series
Olsen, D B
see **Lieutenant Stephen Mayhew series**

Mayland Long and Martha Macnamara series
Macavoy, Roberta Ann
1 *Tea with the Black Dragon* (1983)
2 *Twisting the rope* (1986)

Mayli and Ngali series
Trezise, Percy
see **Ngali and Mayli series**

Maynard series
Swiggett, Howard
see **Garrett Maynard series**
Wells, Carolyn
see **Marjorie Maynard series**

Mayo series
Taylor, Phoebe Atwood
see **Asey Mayo series**

Maythorn series
Trease, Geoffrey
see **Mike and Sandra series**

Maztica trilogy
Niles, Douglas
1 *Ironhelm* (1990)
2 *Viperhand* (1990)
3 *Feathered dragon* (1991)

Me and Alice series
Rogers, Paul
1 *Me and Alice go to the museum* (1989)
2 *Me and Alice go to the gallery* (1989)

Me and Gus series
Anthony, Frank Sheldon
see **Gus Tomlins series**

Me and Jill Robinson series
Digby, Anne
1 *Me, Jill Robinson and the television quiz* (1983)
2 *Me, Jill Robinson and the seaside mystery* (1983)
3 *Me, Jill Robinson and the Christmas pantomime* (1983)
4 *Me, Jill Robinson and the school camp adventure* (1983)
5 *Me, Jill Robinson and the Perdou painting* (1984)
6 *Me, Jill Robinson and the stepping stones mystery* (1985)

Me and Mister T series
Graeber, Charlotte Towner
see **Mister T and me series**

Me series
Godfrey, Jan
1 *Me and the doctors* (1985)
2 *Me at the supermarket* (1985)
3 *Me at the playgroup* (1985)
4 *Me on a rainy day* (1985)

Me series
Jacob, Naomi
1 *Me* (1933)
A chronicle about other people
2 *Me again* (1937)
3 *More about me* (1939)
4 *Me in wartime* (1940)
5 *Me and the Mediterranean* (1945)
6 *Me over there* (1947)
7 *Me and mine, you and yours* (1949)
8 *Me, looking back* (1950)
9 *Robert, Nana and me* (1952)
10 *Me, likes and dislikes* (1954)
11 *Me, yesterday and today* (1957)
12 *Me and the swans* (1963)
13 *Me and the stags* (1964)
14 *Me thinking things over* (1964)
Companion volumes: *Me in the kitchen*, 1935, *Just about us*, 1953

Mead series
McGerr, Patricia
see **Selena Mead series**

Meadow-Brook girls series
Aldridge, Janet
1 *Meadow-Brook girls across country* (1913)
Alternative title: The young pathfinders on a summer hike
2 *Meadow-Brook girls under canvas* (1913)
Alternative title: Fun and frolic in the summer camp
3 *Meadow-Brook girls afloat* (1913)
Alternative title: The stormy cruise of the Red Rover
4 *Meadow-Brook girls in the hills* (1914)
Alternative title: The missing pilot of the White Mountains
5 *Meadow-Brook girls by the sea* (1914)
6 *Meadow-Brook girls on the tennis courts* (1914)
Alternative title: Winning out in the big tournament

Meadowlark series
Bower, Bertha Muzzy
1 *Meadowlark Basin* (1925)
2 *White wolves* (1927)

Meaning of liff series
Adams, Douglas Noel
1 *Meaning of liff* (1983)
2 *Deeper meaning of liff* (1990)

Measure of the years series
Colver, Alice Ross
1 *Measure of the years* (1954)
2 *There is a season* (1957)

Meatballs series
Mooser, Stephen
see **All-Star Meatballs series**

Meatyard series
Horler, Sydney
see **Constable Meatyard series**

Meave series
Conyers, Dorothea
1 *Meave* (1915)
2 *Meave must marry* (1933)

Mechanical sky series
Moffitt, Donald
1 *Crescent in the sky* (1990)
2 *Gathering of stars* (1990)

Med Service series
Leinster, Murray
1 *Mutant weapon* (1959)
2 *This world is taboo* (1961)
3 *Doctor to the stars* (1964)
Numbers 1-3 also published in one volume entitled *The Med series*, 1983
4 *S.O.S. from three worlds* (1967)

Medal series
Newcomb, Kerry
see **McQueen family series**

Meddle series
Blyton, Enid
see **Mister Meddle series**

Medenham series
Dale, Norman
1 *Clock that struck fifteen* (1956)
2 *Medenham carnival* (1957)
3 *Pied Piper of Medenham* (1958)
4 *All change for Medenham* (1959)
5 *Medenham secret* (1962)

Medford series
Roth, Holly
see **Inspector Medford series**
Starr, Jimmy
see **Joe Medford series**

Mediaeval France trilogy
Prescott, Hilda Frances Margaret
1 *Unharrying chase* (1925)
2 *Lost fight* (1928)
3 *Son of dust* (1932)

Mediaeval Rhine series
Barr, Robert
1 *Countess Tekla* (1898)
2 *Strong arm* (1900)
Short stories
3 *Swordmaker* (1910)

Mediaeval Wales trilogy
Pargeter, Edith
1 *Heaven tree* (1960)
2 *Green branch* (1962)
3 *Scarlet seed* (1963)

Medical murder mystery series
Duke, Madelaine
see **Doctor Norah North series**

Medical nobody series
Lane, Kenneth
Autobiography
1 *Diary of a medical nobody* (1982)
2 *West Country doctor* (1984)

Medical power series
Seide, Diane
1 *Nurse power* (1986)
2 *Physician power* (1989)

Medici series
Woodhouse, Martin
1 *Medici guns* (1974)
2 *Medici emerald* (1976)
3 *Medici hawks* (1978)

Medici trilogy
Plaidy, Jean
see **Catherine de Medici trilogy**

Medicine Trail series
Wisler, Gary Clifton
1 *Medicine Trail* (1991)
2 *Stone Wolf's vision* (1991)
3 *Buffalo shield* (1992)
4 *Dreaming Wolf* (1992)

Medico series
Rubel, James Lyon
1 *Medico of Painted Springs* (1934)
2 *Medico rides* (1935)
3 *Medico on the trail* (1938)

Meditations series
Hausman, Gerald
1 *Meditations with animals* (1986)
A native American bestiary
2 *Meditations with the Navajo* (1988)

Medjugorje series
Faricy, Robert Leo
see **Mary speaks to the world series**

Medleys and Mallorys series
Willard, Barbara
see **Mantlemass series**

Meehan series
Patchett, Mary Elwyn
see **Joey Meehan series**

Meenie series
Gilbert, Edith Laura
1 *Frolicsome four* (1903)
2 *Making of Meenie* (1904)

Meet the Samuel family series
Watson, Jean
1 *Martha's busy morning* (1980)
2 *Dan the shepherd* (1980)
3 *Martha is afraid of the dark* (1980)
4 *Matthew goes to market* (1980)

Meetings series
This sequence has four authors
Anthony, Mark
1 *Kindred spirits* (1991)
Kirchoff, Mary Lynn
2 *Wanderlust* (1991)

Meg and Mog series
Nicoll, Helen
Illustrated by Jan Pienkowski
1 *Meg and Mog* (1972)
Revised edition 1977
2 *Meg's eggs* (1972)
Revised edition 1977
3 *Meg on the moon* (1973)
4 *Meg at sea* (1973)
Revised edition 1979
5 *Meg's car* (1975)
6 *Meg's castle* (1975)
7 *Meg's veg* (1976)
8 *Mog's mumps* (1976)
9 *Mog at the zoo* (1982)
10 *Mog in the fog* (1984)
11 *Owl at school* (1984)
12 *Mog's box* (1987)
13 *Owl at the vet* (1990)
Companion volumes: *Meg and Mog birthday book*, 1979, *Meg and Mog colour in book*, 1990, *Mog's games*, 1990

Meg Duncan series
Walker, Holly Beth
1 *Disappearing diamonds* (1967)
2 *Secret of the witch's stairway* (1967)
3 *Treasure nobody saw* (1970)
4 *Meg and the ghost of Hidden Springs* (1970)
5 *Mystery of the Black-Magic Cave* (1971)
6 *Mystery in Williamsburg* (1972)

Meg Halloran series
Lapierre, Janet
1 *Cruel mother* (1990)
2 *Grandmother's house* (1991)
3 *Old enemies* (1993)

Meg Mackintosh series
Landon, Lucinda
1 *Meg Mackintosh and the case of the missing Babe Ruth baseball* (1987)
2 *Meg Mackintosh and the case of the curious whale watch* (1987)
3 *Meg Mackintosh and the mystery of the medieval castle* (1989)
4 *Meg Mackintosh and the mystery at C* (1990)
5 *Meg Mackintosh and the mystery in the locked library* (1993)

Meg Murry series
L'Engle, Madeleine
1 *Wrinkle in time* (1962)
2 *Wind in the door* (1973)
3 *Swiftly tilting planet* (1978)
Numbers 1-3 also published in one volume edition entitled *The time trilogy*, 1979
4 *Many waters* (1986)
5 *Acceptable time* (1989)

Meg of Heron's Neck series
Ladd, Elizabeth
1 *Meg of Heron's Neck* (1961)
2 *Mystery for Meg* (1962)
3 *Meg's mysterious island* (1963)
4 *Meg and Melissa* (1964)
5 *Trouble at Heron's Neck* (1966)
6 *Treasure of Heron's Neck* (1967)

Megabot series
Hall, Willis
1 *Making of Megabot* (1986)
2 *Back in time with Megabot* (1986)

Megan Marshall series
Collins, Michelle
1 *Murder at Willow Run* (1979)
2 *Premiere at Willow Run* (1980)

Megan series
Hearne, Betsy Gould
1 *South star* (1977)
2 *Home* (1979)

Megatrends series
Aburdene, Patricia
1 *Megatrends 2000* (1990)
Ten new directions for the 1990s
2 *Megatrends for women* (1992)

Meggs series
Bancks, James Charles
see **Ginger Meggs series**

Mehitabel and Archy series
Marquis, Don
see **Archy and Mehitabel series**

Mehta family series
Mehta, Ved
1 *Daddyji* (1972)
2 *Mamaji* (1979)
3 *Vedi* (1982)
4 *Ledge between the streams* (1984)

Meigs series
Corbett, Elizabeth
see **Mrs Meigs series**

Mel Martin series
Cooper, John R
1 *Mystery of the ball park* (1947)
2 *Southpaw's secret* (1947)
3 *Phantom homer* (1952)
4 *First base jinx* (1952)
5 *College league mystery* (1953)
6 *Fighting shortstop* (1953)

Mel Webb series
Palmer, Bernard
1 *Mel Webb and the border collie* (1964)
2 *Mel Webb on the danger trail* (1964)
3 *Mel Webb and the stolen dog mystery* (1964)

Melanie Brown series
Oldfield, Pamela
1 *Melanie Brown goes to school* (1970)
2 *Melanie Brown climbs a tree* (1972)
3 *Melanie Brown and the jar of sweets* (1974)

Melanie Gaye series
Freed, Artelle
1 *Come, pretty puss!* (1959)
2 *Diamonds and minx* (1960)

Melbourne series
Cecil, David
see **Lord Melbourne series**

Melbourne series
Hibberd, Jack
1 *Memoirs of an old bastard* (1990)
A portrait of a city and Epicurean chronicle, fantasia and search
2 *Perdita* (1992)

Melbourne series
Luscombe, Tom
1 *Priest and the governor* (1970)
2 *Village on the Yarra* (1974)
3 *Bridge over the Yarra* (1980)

Melbury trilogy
Darbyshire, Shirley
1 *Journey to Melbury* (1953)
2 *Years at Melbury* (1953)
3 *High noon at Melbury* (1954)

Melchior and Jakob series
Meynell, Esther
see **Jakob and Melchior series**

Melde series
Babbitt, Lucy Cullyford
1 *Oval amulet* (1985)
2 *Children of the maker* (1988)

Meldon series
Birmingham, George A
see **Reverend J J Meldon series**

Meldrum and Muller series
Glanville, Alec
see **Inspector Dusty Muller and Tiny Meldrum series**

Melendy family series
Enright, Elizabeth
1 *Saturdays* (1941)
2 *Four-Storey Mistake* (1942)
3 *Then there were five* (1944)
Numbers 1-3 also published in one volume entitled *The Melendy family*, 1947
4 *Spiderweb for two* (1951)

Melinda Pink series
Moffat, Gwen
see **Miss Melinda Pink series**

Melinda, Timothy and Ellen series
Storey, Margaret
see **Timothy, Ellen and Melinda series**

Melissa and Tony series
Byers, Irene
see **Tony and Melissa series**

Melissa Craig series
Rowlands, Betty
1 *Little gentle sleuthing* (1990)
2 *Finishing touch* (1991)
3 *Over the edge* (1992)
4 *Exhaustive enquiries* (1993)

Melissa Mouse series
Claret, Maria
1 *Melissa Mouse* (1984)
Original edition entitled *La ratita Blasa*
2 *Chocolate rabbit* (1984)
Original edition entitled *El conejo de chocolate*
3 *Melissa Mouse's birthday surprise* (1986)
Original edition entitled *La sopresa de la ratita Blasa*

Melita Pargeter series
Brett, Simon
see **Mrs Melita Pargeter series**

Melling School series
Biggs, Margaret
1 *Blakes come to Melling* (1951)
2 *New prefect at Melling* (1952)
3 *Last term for Helen* (1953)
4 *Head girl of Melling* (1954)
5 *Susan in the Sixth* (1955)
6 *New girl at Melling* (1956)
7 *Summer term at Melling* (1957)

Melling series
Klein, Robin
1 *All in the blue unclouded weather* (1992)
2 *Dresses of red and gold* (1992)

Melling series
Phillips, Leon
see **Hugh Melling series**

Mellingham series
Oleksiw, Susan
see **Joe Silva series**

Mellonia trilogy
Swann, Thomas Burnett
1 *Queens walk in the dusk* (1977)
2 *Green phoenix* (1972)
3 *Lady of the bees* (1976)

Melodie series
Sabey, Ian
1 *Melodie's year* (1946)
2 *Of the thunder of hooves* (1982)

Melody Lane series
Garis, Lilian C
1 *Forbidden trail* (1933)
2 *Ghost of Melody Lane* (1933)
3 *Tower secret* (1933)
4 *Wild warning* (1934)
5 *Terror at Morning Cliff* (1935)
6 *Dragon of the hills* (1936)
7 *Mystery of Stingyman's Alley* (1938)
8 *Secret of the kashmir shawl* (1939)
9 *Hermit of Proud Hill* (1940)

Melody series
Petersen-Schaefer, Karin
1 *Dawn ride* (1993)
2 *Winning* (1994)

Melody series
Thwaites, Frederick Joseph
1 *Broken melody* (1930)
2 *Melody lingers* (1935)

Melody trilogy
Richards, Laura Elizabeth
1 *Melody* (1893)
2 *Marie* (1894)
3 *Rosin the beau* (1898)

Melric the magician series
McKee, David
1 *Magician who lost his magic* (1970)
2 *Magician and the sorcerer* (1974)
Melric and the sorcerer
3 *Magician and the petnapping* (1976)
4 *Magician and the balloon* (1978)
Melric and the balloon
5 *Magician and the dragon* (1979)
Melric and the dragon
6 *Magician and double trouble* (1981)
7 *Magician's apprentice* (1987)
Melric's apprentice
8 *Magician and the crown* (1988)
Omnibus volume: *Tales of Melric the magician*, 1991

Melrose Place series
This sequence has three authors; based on a television series
Nelson, Peter N
1 *Melrose Place* (1992)
Mills, Bart
2 *Off the record* (1992)
James, Dean
3 *Keeping the faith* (1993)
4 *Three's a crowd* (1993)
Companion volume: *Melrose Place, meet the stars of today's hottest new show*, by Randi Reisfeld, 1992

Melrose series
Mills, Woosnam
see **John Melrose series**

Melville Fairr series
Venning, Michael
1 *Man who slept all day* (1942)
2 *Murder through the looking glass* (1943)
3 *Jethro Hammer* (1944)

Melville series
Edelman, Maurice
see **Geoffrey Melville series**
Smith, Evelyn E
see **Miss Susan Melville series**

Melvin Spitznagle series
Wahl, Jan
1 *Furious flycycle* (1968)
2 *S.O.S. bobomobile!* (1973)

Melvyn series
Franklin, Miles
see **Sybylla Penelope Melvyn series**

Memed series
Kemal, Yashar
see **Slim Memed series**

Memoirs of a physician series
Dumas, Alexandre
1 *Memoirs of a physician* (1846)
Balsamo the magician

Original edition entitled *Memoires d'un medecin*, part 1
2 *Joseph Balsamo* (1848)
Elixir of life
Original edition entitled *Memoires d'un medecin*, part 2
3 *Queen's necklace* (1850)
Original edition entitled *Le collier de la reine*

Memoirs of an accompanist series
Moore, Gerald
Autobiography
1 *Am I too loud?* (1962)
2 *Farewell recital* (1978)
3 *Furthermoore* (1983)
Interludes in an accompanist's life

Memoirs of Ijon Tichy series
Lem, Stanislaw
see **Ijon Tichy series**

Memoirs of the years series
Truman, Harry S
Autobiography
1 *Year of decision, 1945* (1955)
2 *Years of trial and hope, 1946-1953* (1956)

Memories and gardens series
Spring, Marion Howard
Autobiography
1 *Frontispiece* (1969)
Childhood portrait
2 *Memories and gardens* (1964)

Memories and impressions series
Ford, Ford Madox
1 *Ancient lights and certain new reflections* (1911)
Memories and impressions
A study in atmospheres
2 *Thus to revisit* (1921)
3 *Return to yesterday* (1931)
Reminiscences, 1894-1914
4 *It was the nightingale* (1933)

Memories of Ireland and England series
Clarke, Austin
1 *Twice round the black church* (1962)
2 *Penny in the clouds* (1968)

Memories series
Jepson, Edgar
Autobiography
1 *Memories of a Victorian* (1933)
2 *Memories of an Edwardian and neo-Georgian* (1937)
Memories of an Edwardian
The second title is an enlarged edition

Memories series
Mackenzie, Compton
1 *Gallipoli memories* (1929)
2 *First Athenian memories* (1931)
3 *Greek memories* (1939)
4 *Aegean memories* (1940)

Memory in a house series
Boston, Lucy Maria
Autobiography
1 *Perverse and foolish* (1979)
A memoir of childhood and youth
2 *Memory in a house* (1973)

Memory series
Lancaster, Osbert
Autobiography
1 *All done from memory* (1953)
2 *With an eye to the future* (1967)

Memory, sorrow and thorn series
Williams, Tad
1 *Dragonbone chair* (1988)
2 *Stone of farewell* (1990)

Memphis series
Taylor, Peter
1 *Summons to Memphis* (1986)
2 *In the Tennessee country* (1994)

Men and animals series
Morris, Desmond
1 *Men and snakes* (1965)
2 *Men and apes* (1966)
3 *Men and pandas* (1966)
Giant panda
The second title is a revised edition

Men and memories series
Rothenstein, William
Reminiscences
1 *Men and memories, 1872-1900* (1931)
2 *Men and memories, 1900-1922* (1932)
3 *Since fifty* (1939)
1922-1938
One volume abridged edition entitled *Men and memories*, 1978

Men and women series
Dreiser, Theodore
Reminiscences
1 *Twelve men* (1919)
2 *Gallery of women* (1928)

Men and women trilogy
Maxwell, William Babington
1 *Tudor Green* (1935)
2 *Emotional journey* (1936)
3 *Everslade* (1938)

Men and work series
Citrine, Walter McLennan
Autobiography
1 *Men and work* (1964)
2 *Two careers* (1967)

Men at arms series
Sellers, Con
History of the Second World War
1 *Gathering storm* (1991)
2 *Flames of war* (1991)
3 *World ablaze* (1992)
4 *Allied in victory* (1992)

Men at war series
Baldwin, Alex
1 *Last heroes* (1985)
2 *Secret warriors* (1986)
3 *Soldier spies* (1987)
4 *Fighting agents* (1988)

Men in white series
Soubiran, Andre
see **Jean Nerac series**

Men of goodwill series
Romains, Jules
1 *Sixth of October* (1932)
Original edition entitled *Le six October*
2 *Quinette's crime* (1932)
Original edition entitled *Le crime de Quinette*; numbers 1 and 2 also published in one volume entitled *Men of good will*, 1933
3 *Childhood's loves* (1932)
Original edition entitled *Les amours enfantines*
4 *Eros in Paris* (1932)
Original edition entitled *Eros de Paris;* numbers 3 and 4 also published in one volume entitled *Passion's pilgrims*, 1934
5 *Proud* (1933)
Original edition entitled *Les superbes*
6 *Meek* (1933)
Original edition entitled *Les humbles*; 5 and 6 also published in one volume entitled *The proud and the meek*, 1934
7 *Lonely* (1934)
Original edition entitled *Recherche d'une Eglise*
8 *Provincial interlude* (1934)
Original edition entitled *Province*; numbers 7 and 8 also published in one volume entitled *The world from below*, 1935
9 *Flood warning* (1935)
Original edition entitled *Montee des perils*
10 *Powers that be* (1935)
Original edition entitled *Les pouvoirs*; numbers 9 and 10 also published in one volume entitled *The earth trembles*, 1936
11 *To the gutter* (1936)
Original edition entitled *Recours a l'abine*
12 *To the stars* (1936)
Original edition entitled *Les createurs;* numbers 11 and 12 also published in one volume entitled *The depths and the heights*, 1937
13 *Mission to Rome* (1937)
Original edition entitled *Mission a Rome*
14 *Black flag* (1937)
Original edition entitled *Le drapeau noir*; numbers 13 and 14 also published in one volume entitled *Death of a world*, 1938
15 *Prelude* (1938)
Original edition entitled *Prelude a Verdun*
16 *Battle* (1938)
Original edition entitled *Verdun*; numbers 15 and 16 also published in one volume entitled *Verdun*, 1939
17 *Vorge against Quinette* (1939)
Original edition entitled *Vorge contre Quinette*
18 *Sweets of life* (1939)
Original edition entitled *La douceur de la vie*; numbers 17 and 18 also published in one volume entitled *Aftermath*, 1941
19 *Promise of dawn* (1941)
Original edition entitled *Cette grande lueur a l'est*
20 *World is your adventure* (1941)
Original edition entitled *Le monde est ton aventure*; numbers 19 and 20 also published in one volume entitled *The new day*, 1942
21 *Mountain days* (1942)
Original edition entitled *Jeunesse dans la montagne*
22 *Work and play* (1943)
Original edition entitled *Les travaux et les joies*; numbers 21 and 22 also published in one volume entitled *Work and play*, 1944
23 *Gatherings of the gangs* (1944)
Original edition entitled *Naissance de la bande*
24 *Offered in evidence* (1944)
Original edition entitled *Comparutions*; numbers 23 and 24 also published in one volume entitled *The wind is rising*, 1945
25 *Magic carpet* (1946)
Original edition entitled *Le tapis magique*
26 *Francoise* (1946)
Original edition entitled *Francoise;* numbers 25 and 26 also published in one volume entitled *Escape in passion*, 1946
27 *Seventh of October* (1946)
Original edition entitled *Le sett octobre*

Men of mysteries past series
Hooper, Kay
1 *Touch of Max* (1993)
2 *Hunting the Wolfe* (1993)
3 *All for Quinn* (1993)

Men who ruled India series
Woodruff, Philip
1 *Founders* (1953)
2 *Guardians* (1954)

Men, years and life series
Ehrenburg, Ilya
Translated from the Russian
1 *Memoirs of 1891-1917* (1961)
2 *First years of Revolution, 1918-21* (1962)
3 *Truce, 1921-33* (1963)
4 *Eve of war, 1933-1941* (1963)
5 *War, 1941-45* (1964)
6 *Post-war years, 1945-1954* (1966)

Mendez series
Marshall, William Leonard
see **Battling Mendez series**

Mendip Hills series
Raymond, Walter
1 *Two men o' Mendip* (1899)
2 *No soul above money* (1899)

Mendoza series
Ronald, James
see **Julian Mendoza series**
Shannon, Dell
see **Lieutenant Luis Mendoza series**

Menendes series
Blanc, Suzanne
see **Inspector Miguel Menendes series**

Mensing series
Nevins, Francis Michael
see **Loren Mensing series**

Mercedes Quero series
Locke, Gladys Edson
1 *Affair at Portstead Manor* (1914)
2 *Red cavalier* (1922)

Mercenaries series
Hart, Jon
1 *Black blood* (1977)
2 *High slaughter* (1977)
3 *Triangle of death* (1977)
4 *Guerrilla attack* (1977)
5 *Death raid* (1978)

Mercenary doctor series
Flanders, Peter
Autobiography
1 *Doctor, doctor* (1985)
2 *Mercenary doctor* (1987)

Mercenary series
Buck, Peter
see **Marc Dean series**
Kilgore, Axel
see **They call me the Mercenary series**

Mercenary series
Palmer, Diana
1 *Soldier of fortune* (1985)
2 *Tender stranger* (1985)
3 *Enamored* (1988)

Mercer series
Clandon, Henrietta
see **Penny and Vincent Mercer series**

Merchant Navy series
Knight, Frank
see **Clipper ship series**

Merchant Navy trilogy
King, Robin
Autobiography
1 *No paradise* (1955)
2 *Sailor in the East* (1956)
3 *Angry sun* (1959)
Impressions of a lotus-eating island, i.e. Majorca

Merchanter series
Cherryh, Carolyn Janice
1 *Merchanter's luck* (1982)
2 *Heavy time* (1991)
3 *Hellburner* (1992)
4 *Tripoint* (1994)

Mercy of a rude stream series
Roth, Henry
1 *Star shines over Mount Morris Park* (1994)
2 *Diving rock on the Hudson* (1995)

Mercy series
Vanauken, Sheldon
1 *Severe mercy* (1977)
Autobiography and poetry
2 *Under the mercy* (1985)
Essays and biography
3 *Mercies* (1988)
Collected poems

Meredith and Uncle George series
Leyland, Eric
see **Jack Meredith and Uncle George series**

Meredith children series
Dehn, Olive
1 *Caretakers* (1960)
2 *Caretakers and the poacher* (1961)
3 *Caretakers and the gipsy* (1962)
4 *Caretakers and the rescue* (1964)
5 *Caretakers of Wilmhurst* (1967)

Meredith family series
Byers, Irene
1 *Merediths of Mappins* (1964)
2 *House of the speckled browns* (1967)

Meredith family series
Lyon, Elinor
1 *Green grow the rushes* (1964)
2 *Echo Valley* (1965)

Meredith Mitchell and Chief Inspector Alan Markby series
Granger, Ann
1 *Say it with poison* (1991)
2 *Season for murder* (1991)
3 *Cold in the earth* (1992)
4 *Murder among us* (1992)
5 *Where old bones lie* (1993)
6 *Fine place for death* (1994)

Meredith series
Arundel, Honor
see **Janet Meredith series**
Bude, John
see **Inspector Meredith series**
Gerard, Francis
see **Sir John Meredith series**
Ramsay, Diana
see **Lieutenant Meredith series**

Meredith trilogy
Johnston, George Henry
see **David Meredith trilogy**
Lambert, Janet
see **Drai Meredith trilogy**

Meren series
Robinson, Lynda S
see **Lord Meren series**

Merewether series
Meacham, Ellis Kirby
see **Captain Percival Merewether series**

Meri Newman series
Nuttall, Nesta
1 *Severn holiday* (1962)
2 *Mendip holiday* (1963)

Merilyn Forrester series
Grove, Harriet Pyne
1 *Merilyn at Camp Meenahga* (1927)
2 *Merilyn enters Beechwold* (1927)
3 *Merilyn Forrester, co-ed* (1927)
4 *Merilyn's new adventure* (1927)
5 *Merilyn tests loyalty* (1927)
6 *Merry Lynn Mine* (1928)
7 *Merilyn's senior dreams* (1929)
8 *Merilyn's rose garden* (1930)

Merlin and Arthur series
Stewart, Mary
1 *Crystal cave* (1970)
Merlin of the crystal cave
2 *Hollow hills* (1973)
3 *Last enchantment* (1979)
Numbers 1-3 also published in one volume entitled *Mary Stewart's Merlin trilogy*, 1980
4 *Wicked day* (1983)

Merlin Capricorn series
Winslow, Pauline Glen
see **Superintendent Merlin Capricorn series**

Merlin series
Corbett, Scott
see **Doctor Merlin series**
Rotsler, William
see **Mister Merlin series**

Merlin Sorrel series
Clare, Marguerite
1 *Star of the goddess* (1968)
2 *Barefoot witch* (1968)

Merlini series
Rawson, Clayton
see **Great Merlini series**

Merlotti series
Deane, Jim
see **Nick Merlotti series**

Mermaid Madonna series
Myrivilis, Stratis
Translated from the modern Greek
1 *Mermaid Madonna* (1959)
2 *Schoolmistress with the golden eyes* (1964)

Merovingen nights series
Cherryh, Carolyn Janice
1 *Angel with the sword* (1985)
Festival moon
The second title is a revised edition
2 *Fever season* (1987)
3 *Troubled waters* (1988)
4 *Smuggler's gold* (1988)
5 *Divine right* (1989)
6 *Flood tide* (1990)
7 *Endgame* (1991)

Merrick family series
Hill, Deborah
1 *This is the house* (1976)
2 *House of Kingsley Merrick* (1977)

Merridrew series
Fearn, John Russell
see **Jenkinson Talbot Merridrew series**

Merrill and Alex trilogy
Main, Carol
see **Fraser family trilogy**

Merrill series
Deering, Fremont B
see **Border Boys series**

Merrill series
Lounsberry, Lionel
1 *Midshipman Merrill* (1899)
2 *Ensign Merrill* (1899)

Merriman series
Burke, Jonathan
see **Mike Merriman series**

Merrion and Arnold series
Burton, Miles
see **Inspector Arnold and Desmond Merrion series**

Merritales series
Wilhelm, Hans
1 *New home, a new friend* (1985)
2 *Don't give up, Josephine* (1985)
3 *Totally bored Boris* (1986)
4 *Not another day like this* (1988)
5 *Runaway giant* (1989)
6 *Teaming up together* (1989)
7 *Here comes trouble* (1989)
8 *Never lonely again* (1989)
9 *I want more* (1989)
10 *Friends are forever* (1989)
11 *I would never tell a lie* (1989)

Merritt series
Cafferty, Jake
see **Vic Merritt series**
Harewood, Jocelyn
see **Peregrine Merritt series**

Merrivale series
Dickson, Carter
see **Sir Henry Merrivale series**

Merriweather girls series
Edholm, Lizette
1 *Merriweather girls and the mystery of the queen's fan* (1932)
2 *Merriweather girls at good old Rockhill* (1932)
3 *Merriweather girls in quest of treasure* (1932)
4 *Merriweather girls on Campers' Trail* (1932)

Merriwell series
Frederic, Mike
see **Frank Merriwell series**

Merry Arundel series
Mallory, Clare
1 *Merry begins* (1947)
2 *Merry again* (1947)
3 *Merry marches on* (1947)

Merry-go-rhymes series
Manning, Paul
1 *Cook* (1987)
2 *Clown* (1987)
3 *Fisherman* (1987)
4 *Boy* (1987)

Merry Hall trilogy
Nichols, Beverley
1 *Merry Hall* (1951)
2 *Laughter on the stairs* (1953)
3 *Sunlight on the lawn* (1956)

Merry mailman series
Martin, Marcia
1 *Merry mailman* (1953)
2 *Merry mailman around the world* (1955)

Merry Muffin series
This sequence has two authors
Mills, Annette
1 *Muffin and Louise* (1954)
2 *Muffin and Peregrine* (1954)
3 *Muffin's birthday* (1954)
Hogarth, Ann
4 *Muffin climbs high* (1955)
5 *Muffin sings a song* (1955)
6 *Muffin's thinking cap* (1955)

Merry series
Clifford, Martin
see **Tom Merry series**

Merryl Hastings series
Sutton, Phyllis
1 *Continental holiday* (1952)
2 *Spanish holiday* (1952)
3 *Tyrolean holiday* (1954)
4 *Swiss holiday* (1955)
5 *Italian holiday* (1955)
6 *Dalmatian holiday* (1957)

Merrymole series
Dodd, Maurice
1 *Merrymole the magnificent* (1982)
2 *Merrymole the intrepid* (1984)

Merryvale girls series
Burnett, Alice Hale
1 *Beth's garden party* (1916)
2 *Day at the country fair* (1916)
3 *Geraldine's birthday surprise* (1916)
4 *Mary entertains the Sewing Club* (1916)
5 *Merryvale girls at the seaside* (1916)
6 *Merryvale girls in the country* (1916)

Mersey series
Clement, Frank A
see **Superintendent Mersey series**

Mersey series
Forrester, Helen
1 *Twopence to cross the Mersey* (1974)
Liverpool miss
2 *Minerva's stepchild* (1979)
Liverpool Daisy
3 *By the waters of Liverpool* (1981)
4 *Lime Street at two* (1985)

Merston series
Welcome, John
see **Mister Merston series**

Merthyr trilogy
Cordell, Alexander
1 *Fire people* (1972)
2 *This sweet and bitter earth* (1977)
3 *Land of my fathers* (1983)

Merton Heimrich series
Lockridge, Frances
see **Inspector Merton Heimrich series**

Mervyn Mouse series
Creche, Sylvia
1 *Two tales of Mervyn Mouse* (1980)
2 *Mervyn Mouse at the fair* (1982)
3 *Mervyn Mouse joins the sports club* (1982)
4 *Mervyn Mouse goes camping* (1982)
5 *Mervyn Mouse at the zoo* (1982)
Numbers 2-5 also published in one volume entitled *Hooray for Mervyn Mouse*, 1982

Mervyn series
Peguero, Leone
1 *Mervyn's revenge* (1990)
2 *Mervyn's Christmas* (1992)

Meryemdje series
Kemal, Yashar
1 *Wind from the plain* (1960)
Original edition entitled *Ortadirek*
2 *Iron earth, copper sky* (1963)
Original edition entitled *Ver demir, gok bakir*
3 *Undying grass* (1968)
Original edition entitled *Olmez otu*

Mesklin series
Clement, Hal
1 *Mission of gravity* (1954)
2 *Close to critical* (1964)
3 *Star light* (1971)

Mesmerian annals series
Eckert, Allan Wesley
1 *Dark green tunnel* (1984)
2 *Wand* (1985)

Mesquite Jenkins series
Mulford, Clarence Edward
1 *Hopalong Cassidy returns* (1924)

2 *Hopalong Cassidy's protege* (1926)
Hopalong Cassidy's saddle mate
3 *Mesquite Jenkins* (1928)
4 *Mesquite Jenkins, Tumbleweed* (1932)

Mesquite series
Curry, Tom
see **Captain Mesquite series**

Messages from Michael series
Yarbro, Chelsea Quinn
1 *Messages from Michael on the nature of the evolution of the human soul* (1979)
2 *More messages from Michael* (1986)
3 *Michael's people* (1988)

Messenger chronicles series
Kelly, James Patrick
1 *Planet of whispers* (1984)
2 *Look into the sun* (1989)

Messenger series
Dickens, Monica
1 *Messenger* (1985)
2 *Ballad of favour* (1985)
3 *Haunting of Bellamy four* (1986)
4 *Cry of a seagull* (1986)

Messiah series
Caidin, Martin
1 *Messiah stone* (1986)
2 *Dark messiah* (1990)

Messiah series
Dixon, Roger
see **Jesus Christ series**

Messiah trilogy
Storey, Anthony
see **Second Coming trilogy**

Messy Bessey series
McKissack, Patricia Carwell
1 *Messy Bessey* (1987)
2 *Messy Bessey's closet* (1989)
3 *Messy Bessey's garden* (1991)

Messy Malcolm series
Taylor, Jenny
1 *Messy Malcolm* (1972)
2 *Messy Malcolm's birthday* (1978)
3 *Messy Malcolm's dream* (1981)

Metcalfe series
Finkel, George
see **Group Captain Alan Metcalfe series**

Meteorite series
Mason, Anne
see **Dancing meteorite series**

Methodist idylls series
Lindsay, Harry
1 *Methodist idylls* (1897)
2 *More Methodist idylls* (1899)

Methodist people series
Church, Leslie Frederic
History of Methodism in the 18th century
1 *Early Methodist people* (1948)
2 *More about the early Methodist people* (1949)

Methuselah series
Vachell, Horace Annesley
1 *Now came still evening on* (1946)
2 *Twilight grey* (1948)
3 *In sober livery* (1949)
4 *Methuselah's diary* (1950)
5 *More from Methuselah* (1951)
6 *Quests* (1954)

Metropolitan Police series
Carr, John Dickson
1 *Fire, burn!* (1957)
Set in 1829
2 *Scandal at High Chimneys* (1959)
Set in 1865
3 *Witch of the low-tide* (1961)
Set in 1907

Mettle series
Macnell, James
see **Captain Mettle series**

Metzada series
Rosenberg, Joel
1 *Ties of blood and silver* (1984)
2 *Emile and the Dutchman* (1986)
3 *Not for glory* (1988)
4 *Hero* (1990)

Mexican war series
Bonehill, Ralph
This sequence was reissued under the author's real name Edward L Stratemeyer
1 *For the liberty of Texas* (1900)
2 *With Taylor on the Rio Grande* (1901)
3 *Under Scott in Mexico* (1902)

Mexican war series
Candaleria, Nash
1 *Not by the sword* (1982)
2 *Inheritance of strangers* (1984)

Mexico series
Chandos, Dane
Life in a Mexican vilage
1 *Village in the sun* (1948)
2 *House in the sun* (1950)

Meynell series
Baker, Ivon
see **David Meynell series**

Mia series
Beckman, Gunnel
1 *Mia* (1973)
Mia alone
Original edition entitled *Tre vector over tiden*
2 *Loneliness of Mia* (1974)
That early spring
Original edition entitled *Varen da allting hande*

Miami Vice series
Grave, Stephen
Based on a television series
1 *Florida run* (1985)
2 *Vengeance game* (1985)

Micah Truelove series
Rodgers, Sherlaw Johnston
1 *Silver and lead* (1982)
2 *Boracho* (1982)
3 *Rough diamonds* (1983)

Mice series
Peppe, Rodney
1 *Mice who lived in a shoe* (1981)
2 *Kettleship pirates* (1983)
3 *Mice and the flying basket* (1985)
4 *Mice and the clockwork bus* (1986)
5 *Mice on the moon* (1992)
6 *Mice and the travel machine* (1993)

Michael and Mandy series
Coles, Alison
1 *Michael's first day at school* (1984)
2 *Michael in the dark* (1984)
3 *Mandy and the hospital* (1984)
4 *Mandy and the train journey* (1984)
5 *Michael and the sea* (1985)
6 *Mandy and the dentist* (1985)

Michael and Mary series
Saville, Malcolm
1 *Trouble at Townsend* (1945)
2 *Riddle of the painted box* (1947)
3 *Flying fish adventure* (1950)
4 *Secret of the hidden pool* (1953)
5 *Young Johnnie Bimbo* (1956)
6 *Fourth key* (1957)

Michael and Mordecai Lewis series
Early, Tom
see **Sons of Texas series**

Michael and Terry Terence series
Brandon, Gordon
1 *Swell night for murder* (1947)
2 *Here comes the corpse* (1949)
3 *Murder in Maytime* (1950)
4 *Mild case of murder* (1951)
5 *Homicidal holiday* (1954)
6 *Murder and marigold* (1956)

Michael Apafi series
Jokai, Mor
1 *'Midst the wild Carpathians* (1852)
Original edition entitled *Az erdely arany kora*
2 *Slaves of the Padishah* (1853)
Original edition entitled *Torok vilag Magyarerszagon*

Michael Berresford series
Le Grand, Leon
1 *Von Kessel dossier* (1985)
2 *Two-ten conspiracy* (1986)
3 *Whittington pact* (1988)

Michael Brennan series
Zackel, Fred
1 *Cocaine and blue eyes* (1978)
2 *Cinderella after midnight* (1980)

Michael Brent series
McFarlane, Leslie
1 *Streets of shadow* (1930)
2 *Murder tree* (1931)

Michael Brooks series
Rothwell, Henry Talbot
1 *Exit a spy* (1966)
2 *Dive deep for danger* (1966)
3 *Duet for three spies* (1967)
4 *No honour among spies* (1969)
5 *No kisses from the Kremlin* (1969)

Michael Carmichael series
Durst, Paul
1 *Backlash* (1967)
2 *Badge of infamy* (1968)

Michael Carvajel series
Waltari, Mika
1 *Adventurer* (1948)
Michael, the Finn
Original edition entitled *Mikael Karavajalk*
2 *Wanderer* (1949)
Sultan's renegade
Original edition entitled *Mikael Hakin*

Michael Corleone series
Puzo, Mario
see **Godfather series**

Michael Davis series
Lord, Beman
see **Spaceship series**

Michael Dene series
Verner, Gerald
1 *Seven clues* (1936)
2 *Dene of the Secret Service* (1941)
3 *Heel of Achilles* (1946)

Michael Drexel series
Usher, Gray
see **Superintendent Michael Drexel series**

Michael Dundas series
Rath, Virginia
1 *Dark cavalier* (1938)
2 *Murder with a theme song* (1939)
3 *Death of a lucky lady* (1940)
4 *Death breaks the ring* (1941)
5 *Posted for murder* (1942)
6 *Epitaph for Lydia* (1942)
7 *Dirge for her* (1947)
8 *Shroud for Rowena* (1947)

Michael Evans series
Graham, Burton
1 *Spy trap* (1971)
2 *Spy or die* (1972)

Michael Farrant series
Larbalestier, Philip George
see **Inspector Michael Farrant series**

Michael Fitton series
Styles, Showell
see **Lieutenant Michael Fitton series**

Michael Forrester series
Wees, Frances Shelley
1 *Maestro murders* (1931)
2 *Mystery of the creeping man* (1931)

Michael Gaunt series
Braddon, George
1 *Death in the picture* (1951)
2 *Death rings no bell* (1951)
3 *Death doubles death* (1952)
4 *Time off for death* (1952)

Michael Glenn series
Lee, Robert Corwin
1 *Iron arm of Michael Glenn* (1965)
2 *Day it rained forever* (1968)

Michael Grant series
Daniel, Roland
1 *Frightened eyes* (1956)
2 *Dangerous moment* (1957)
3 *All things are dangerous* (1958)
4 *Kidnappers* (1959)
5 *Brunettes are dangerous* (1960)
6 *Red-headed dames and murder* (1960)
7 *Women, dope and murder* (1962)
8 *Death by the lake* (1963)
9 *Murder in Ocean Drive* (1964)

Michael Grant series
Redwood, Alec
1 *Lady is not fooling* (1974)
2 *Mad dogs and Englishmen* (1976)
3 *Day of the redeemer* (1977)

Michael Gray series
Kuttner, Henry
see **Doctor Michael Gray series**

Michael Hawk series
Streib, Dan
1 *Deadly crusader* (1980)
2 *Mind twisters* (1980)
3 *Power barons* (1980)
4 *Predators* (1980)
5 *California shakedown* (1981)
6 *Seeds of evil* (1981)
7 *Death riders* (1981)
8 *Enemy within* (1981)
9 *Down under and dirty* (1981)
10 *Cargo gods* (1981)
11 *Terror merchants* (1981)
12 *Virgin stealers* (1981)
13 *Hawaiian takeover* (1981)
14 *Treasure divers* (1981)

Michael Hornsley series
Salter, Elizabeth
see **Inspector Michael Hornsley series**

Michael Jousse series
Berna, Paul
1 *Threshold of the stars* (1954)
Original edition entitled *La porte des etoiles*
2 *Continent in the sky* (1955)
Original edition entitled *Le continent du ciel*

Michael Joyce series
Cornell, Louis
1 *Poison case number ten* (1931)
2 *Murder case number thirty three* (1932)

Michael Kane trilogy
Bradbury, Edward P
see **Warrior of Mars trilogy**

Michael Keefe series
Wolfe, Michael
1 *Man on a string* (1973)
2 *Two-star pigeon* (1975)
3 *Chinese fire drill* (1976)
4 *Panama paradox* (1977)

Michael Kells series
Cheyney, Peter
1 *Sinister errand* (1945)
Sinister murders
2 *Ladies won't wait* (1951)
Cocktails and the killer

Michael Kemp series
Woodrooffe, Anne
1 *Michael Kemp, the happy farmer's lad* (1819)
A tale of rustic life, illustrative of the spiritual blessings and temporal advantages of early piety
2 *Michael, the married man* (1827)

Michael Lanyard series
Vance, Louis Joseph
1 *Lone Wolf* (1914)
2 *False faces* (1918)
3 *Alias the Lone Wolf* (1921)
4 *Red masquerade* (1921)
5 *Lone Wolf returns* (1923)
6 *Lone Wolf's son* (1931)
7 *Encore the Lone Wolf* (1933)
8 *Lone Wolf's last prowl* (1934)

Michael Long series
Larson, Glen A
see **Knight Rider series**

Michael Lord series
King, Charles Daly
1 *Obelists en route* (1934)
2 *Obslists fly high* (1935)
3 *Careless corpse* (1937)
4 *Arrogant alibi* (1938)
5 *Bermuda burial* (1940)

Michael O'Kelly series
O'Brine, Manning
1 *Killers must eat* (1951)
2 *Corpse to Cairo* (1952)
3 *Dodos don't duck* (1953)
Dead as a dodo
4 *Deadly interlude* (1954)
5 *Passport to treason* (1955)
6 *Hungry killer* (1955)
7 *Dagger before me* (1957)

Michael Perrin series
Bear, Greg
1 *Infinity concerto* (1984)
2 *Serpent mage* (1986)

Michael Regan series
Hale, Edgar
see **Inspector Michael Regan series**

Michael Revel series
Berrow, Norman
1 *Fingers for ransom* (1939)
2 *Murder in the melody* (1940)
3 *Words have wings* (1946)
4 *Singing room* (1948)

Michael series
Rogers, Pamela
1 *Fish and chips* (1970)
2 *Rainy picnic* (1972)
3 *Outing for three* (1974)

Michael series
Yarbro, Chelsea Quinn
see **Messages from Michael series**

Michael Shannon series
Bowman, Gerald
1 *Pattern in poison-ivy* (1948)
2 *Sawdust angel* (1949)
3 *Quick and the wed* (1950)

Michael Shayne series
Halliday, Brett
This pseudonym is used by Davis Dresser up to 1958; from 1958 it is used by several authors including Ryerson Johnson and Robert Terrall whose authorship is indicated against those titles where it is known
1 *Dividend on death* (1939)
2 *Private practice of Michael Shayne* (1940)
3 *Uncomplaining corpse* (1940)
4 *Bodies are where you find them* (1941)
Numbers 1-4 are also published in one volume entitled *Michael Shayne takes over*, 1942
5 *Tickets for death* (1941)
6 *Corpse came calling* (1942)
Numbers 4 and 6 also published in one volume entitled *Michael Shayne investigates*, 1943
7 *Murder wears a mummer's mask* (1943)
8 *Blood on the black market* (1943)
Heads you lose
The second title is a revised edition; numbers 7 and 8 also published in one volume entitled *Michael Shayne takes a hand*, 1944
9 *Michael Shayne's long chance* (1944)
10 *Murder and the married virgin* (1944)
11 *Murder is my business* (1945)
12 *Marked for murder* (1945)
13 *Dead man's diary* (1945)
Also includes Dinner at Dupre's
14 *Blood on Biscayne Bay* (1946)
15 *Counterfeit wife* (1947)
16 *Michael Shayne's triple mystery* (1948)
Contains *Dead man's diary, A taste of cognac, Dinner at Dupre's*; *A taste of cognac* also published separately in 1951, and *Dinner at Dupre's* rewritten as *Date with a dead man*, 1959
17 *Blood on the stars* (1948)
Murder is a habit
18 *Call for Michael Shayne* (1949)
19 *Taste for violence* (1949)
20 *This is it, Michael Shayne* (1950)
21 *Framed in blood* (1951)
22 *When Dorinda dances* (1951)
23 *What really happened* (1952)
24 *One night with Nora* (1953)
Lady came by night
25 *She woke to darkness* (1954)
26 *Death has three lives* (1955)
27 *Stranger in town* (1955)
28 *Blonde cried murder* (1956)
29 *Weep for a blonde* (1957)
30 *Shoot the works* (1957)
31 *Murder and the wanton bride* (1958)
32 *Fit to kill* (1958)
[Terrall]
33 *Date with a dead man* (1959)
Rewritten from *Dead man's diary* originally published in *Michael Shayne's triple mystery*, 1948
34 *Target, Mike Shayne* (1959)
[Terrall]
35 *Die like a dog* (1959)
36 *Murder takes no holiday* (1960)
[Terrall]
37 *Dolls are deadly* (1960)
[Johnson]
38 *Homicidal virgin* (1960)
39 *Killers from the Keys* (1961)
[Johnson]
40 *Murder in haste* (1961)
[Terrall]
41 *Carelss corpse* (1961)
42 *Pay-off in blood* (1962)
43 *Murder by proxy* (1962)
44 *Never kill a client* (1962)
45 *Too friendly, too dead* (1963)
46 *Corpse that never was* (1963)
47 *Body that came back* (1963)
48 *Redhead for Mike Shayne* (1964)
49 *Shoot to kill* (1964)
50 *Michael Shayne's fiftieth case* (1964)
51 *Dangerous dames* (1965)
52 *Nice fillies finish last* (1965)
[Terrall]
53 *Violent world of Michael Shayne* (1965)
[Terrall]
54 *Armed, dangerous* (1966)
[Terrall]
55 *Murder spins the wheel* (1966)
[Terrall]
56 *Mermaid on the rocks* (1967)
[Terrall]
57 *Guilty as hell* (1967)
[Terrall]
58 *Violence is golden* (1968)
[Terrall]
59 *So lush, so deadly* (1968)
[Terrall]
60 *Lady, be bad* (1969)
[Terrall]
61 *Fourth down to death* (1970)
[Terrall]
62 *Six seconds to kill* (1970)
[Terrall]
63 *Count backwards to zero* (1971)
[Terrall]
64 *I come to kill you* (1971)
[Terrall]
65 *Caught dead* (1972)
[Terrall]
66 *Blue murder* (1973)
[Terrall]
67 *Kill all the young girls* (1973)
[Terrall]
68 *At the point of a thirty eight* (1974)
[Terrall]
69 *Last seen hitchhiking* (1974)
[Terrall]
70 *Million dollar handling* (1976)
[Terrall]
71 *Win some, lose some* (1976)
[Terrall]

Michael Shayne stories series
Halliday, Brett
see **Mike Shayne stories series**

Michael Sheriff series
McAdam, Preston
see **Shield series**

Michael Skinner series
Tolan, Stephanie Stein
see **Great Skinner series**

Michael Skye and Jessie Walters series
Hart, Bruce
see **Jessie Walters and Michael Skye series**

Michael Spraggue series
Barnes, Linda
1 *Blood will have blood* (1982)
2 *Bitter finish* (1983)
3 *Dead heat* (1984)
4 *Cities of the dead* (1986)

Michael Tandy series
Shepherd, Neal
see **Chief Inspector Michael Tandy series**

Michael Triggington series
Allum, Tom
see **Captain Michael Triggington series**

Michael Wallace series
Daniel, Roland
1 *Lovely but dangerous* (1960)
2 *Lady was a spy* (1962)
3 *Night club murder* (1963)
4 *Prisoner* (1965)

Michael Wyman series
Cook, Bob
1 *Disorderly elements* (1985)
2 *Questions of identity* (1987)

Michel Ardan series
Verne, Jules
see **From the earth to the moon series**

Michelangelo Buonarotti trilogy
Alexander, Sidney
1 *Michelangelo the Florentine* (1957)
2 *Hand of Michelangelo* (1965)
3 *Nicodemus* (1984)
The Roman years of Michelangelo, 1534-1564

Mici Anhalt series
O'Donnell, Lillian
1 *Aftershock* (1977)
2 *Falling star* (1979)
3 *Wicked designs* (1980)

Mick and Caroline Templeton series
Treadgold, Mary
1 *We couldn't leave Dinah* (1941)
Left till called for
2 *Polly Harris* (1951)
Mystery of the Polly Harris

Mick and Mandy series
Schmidt, Annie Maria Geertruida
see **Bob and Jilly series**

Mick and Muff series
Stiessel, Lena
1 *Mick and Muff* (1977)
Original edition entitled *Agel Gagel och Voffsen Kloffsen*
2 *Mick and Muff in the country* (1977)
Original edition entitled *Agel Gagel och Voffsen Kloffsen pa landet*
3 *Mick and Muff painting* (1979)
Original edition entitled *Agel Gagel och Voffsen Kloffsen malar*
4 *Mick and Muff and the little car* (1979)
Original edition entitled *Agel Gagel och Voffsen Kloffsen och den lilla bilen*

Mick and Rob series
Peyton, K M
1 *Stormcock meets trouble* (1961)
2 *Hard way home* (1962)
Sing a song of ambush
3 *Brownsea silver* (1964)

Mick Axbrewder series
Stephens, Reed
1 *Man who killed his brother* (1980)
2 *Man who risked his partner* (1984)

Mick Cardby series
Hume, David
1 *Bullets bite deep* (1932)
2 *Murders for fours* (1933)
Foursquare murder
3 *Crime unlimited* (1933)
4 *Below the belt* (1934)
5 *Too dangerous to live* (1934)
6 *They called him death* (1934)
7 *Dangerous Mister Dell* (1935)
8 *Gaol gates are open* (1935)
9 *Meet the dragon* (1936)
10 *Bring 'em back dead* (1936)
11 *Halfway to horror* (1937)
12 *Cemetery first stop!* (1937)
13 *Good-bye to life* (1938)
14 *Corpses never argue* (1938)

15 *Heads you lose* (1939)
16 *Death before honour* (1939)
17 *Make way for the mourners* (1939)
18 *Eternity, here I come!* (1940)
19 *Return of Mick Cardby* (1941)
20 *Destiny is my name* (1942)
21 *Get out the cuffs* (1943)
22 *Dishonour among thieves* (1943)
23 *Mick Cardby works overtime* (1944)
24 *Toast to a corpse* (1944)
25 *They never came back* (1945)
26 *Come back for the body* (1945)
27 *Heading for a wreath* (1946)

Mickel Mickelson series
Mattson, Olle
1 *Brig Three Lilies* (1955)
Original edition entitled *Briggen Tre Lilljor*
2 *Mickel seafarer* (1958)
Original edition entitled *Mickel sjofarare*

Mickelson series
Mattson, Olle
see **Mickel Mickelson series**

Mickey and Kate Dixon series
Markham, Marion M
see **Dixon twins series**

Mickey Denton series
Kane, Frank
1 *Juke box king* (1959)
2 *Dead rite* (1962)

Mickey McClintock series
Green, Bill
1 *Police rescue 1* (1992)
2 *Police rescue 2* (1992)

Mickey Turner series
Palmer, Bernard
1 *Fire detectives* (1955)
2 *Trapped on Sugar Loaf Mountain* (1955)
3 *Mickey Turner and the phantom dog* (1955)
4 *Mickey Turner, ranger's son* (1955)

Micklem series
Marshall, Raymond
see **Don Micklem series**

Micky Douglas and Inspector Reeves series
Infante, Anne
1 *Death on a hot summer night* (1989)
2 *Death among the dunes* (1990)
3 *Deathwater* (1991)
4 *Death in green* (1992)

Micky Regan series
Hale, Edgar
see **Inspector Michael Regan series**

Micro adventure series
This sequence has nine authors
Buckholtz, Eileen
1 *Space attack* (1984)
Stine, Megan
2 *Jungle quest* (1984)
West, Chassie L
3 *Million dollar gamble* (1984)
Favors, Jean M
4 *Time trap* (1984)
Buckholtz, Eileen
5 *Mindbenders* (1984)
Kraft, David Anthony
6 *Robot race* (1984)
Glick, Ruth
7 *Doom stalker* (1985)
Favors, Jean M
8 *Big freeze* (1985)
West, Chassie L
9 *Dead ringer* (1985)
Stine, Megan
10 *Spellbound* (1985)

Micronauts series
Williams, Gordon Maclean
1 *Micronauts* (1977)
2 *Microcolony* (1979)
Micronaut world
3 *Revolt of the Micronauts* (1981)

Mida series
Green, Sharon
see **Jalav series**

Midas series
Hume, Fergus
see **Madame Midas series**

Midchester series
Mills, Osmington
see **Midset C.I.D. series**

Mid-City Hospital series
Barclay, Virginia
1 *Emergency* (1981)
2 *High risk* (1981)
3 *Trauma* (1981)
4 *Crisis* (1982)
5 *Double face* (1982)
6 *Life support* (1982)

Middle Ages series
Birt, David
1 *Norman Conquest* (1974)
2 *Mediaeval village* (1974)
3 *Knights and tournaments* (1974)
4 *Stephen and Matilda* (1974)
5 *Murder of Becket* (1974)
6 *First and Third Crusades* (1974)
7 *King John* (1974)
8 *Castle* (1974)
9 *Monastery* (1974)
10 *Edward I* (1974)
11 *Black Prince* (1974)
12 *Black death* (1974)
13 *Peasants' Revolt* (1974)
14 *Battle of Agincourt* (1974)
15 *Joan of Arc* (1974)
16 *Marco Polo* (1974)
17 *Ships and voyages* (1974)
18 *Mediaeval town* (1974)
19 *Wars of the Roses* (1974)
20 *Richard III* (1974)

Middle Border series
Garland, Hamlin
1 *Son of the Middle Border* (1917)
2 *Daughter of the Middle Border* (1921)
3 *Trail-makers of the Middle Border* (1926)
4 *Back-trailers of the Middle Border* (1928)

Middle Earth quest series
This sequence has six authors
Ruemmler, John David
1 *Night of the Nazgul* (1985)
Kubasch, Heike
2 *Legend of Weathertop* (1985)
Lientz, Gerald
3 *Rescue in Mirkwood* (1986)
Barrett, Kevin
4 *Treason at Helms Deep* (1988)
Amthor, Terry K
5 *Spy in Isengard* (1988)

Middle Earth series
Tolkien, John Ronald Reuel
1 *Silmarillion* (1977)
2 *Hobbit* (1937)
Revised editions 1951 and 1966; companion volume: *A Hobbit's travels, being hitherto unpublished travel sketches of Sam Gamgee*, by Michael Green, 1978
3 *Fellowship of the Ring* (1954)
Revised edition 1966
4 *Two towers* (1954)
Revised edition 1966
5 *Return of the King* (1955)
Revised edition 1966; one volume edition of numbers 3-5 entitled *The Lord of the Rings*, 1969
Companion volumes: *Bilbo's last song*, 1974, *Unfinished tales of Numenor and Middle Earth*, 1980, *The history of Middle Earth*, volumes 1-9, edited by Christopher Tolkien, 1983-1992, *Middle Earth, the world of Tolkien* illustrated, by Lin Carter and David Wenzel, 1977, *An introduction to Elvish, and to other tongues and proper names and writing systems of the Third Age of the western lands of Middle Earth, as set forth in the published writings of Professor John Ronald Reuel Tolkien*, edited and compiled by Jim Allan and others, 1978, *The Middle Earth quiz book*, by Suzanne Buchholz, 1979, *The atlas of Middle Earth*, by Karen Wynn Fonstad, 1981, revised edition 1991, *The song of Middle Earth, J R R Tolkien's themes, symbols and myths*, by David Harvey, 1985; parody: *Bored of the rings*, by Henry N Beard and Douglas C Kenney, 1969

Middle East series
Mason, Robert
see **Captain James Donald Macgregor series**

Middle England trilogy
Oakes, Philip
Autobiography
1 *From middle England* (1980)
A memory of the 1930s and 1940s
2 *Dwellers all in time and space* (1981)
A memory of the 1940s
3 *At the Jazz Band Ball* (1983)
A memory of the 1950s

Middles series
Soderback, Marianne
1 *Middles run away* (1967)
Original edition entitled *Mellis rymmer*
2 *Middles and Tessa* (1968)
Original edition entitled *Mellis och Tessa*

Middleton-Brown series
Charles, Kate
see **David Middleton-Brown series**

Midge and Tobey Heydon series
Du Jardin, Rosamond
see **Tobey and Midge Heydon series**

Midget Mouse series
Lindsay, Hilarie
Illustrated by Marenelle
1 *Midget Mouse finds a house* (1978)
2 *Midget Mouse goes to sea* (1989)

Midlanders series
Coxhead, Elizabeth
see **Alney series**

Mid-life crisis series
This sequence has two authors
Conway, Jim
1 *Men in mid-life crisis* (1978)
Conway, Sally
2 *Your husband's mid-life crisis* (1980)
Revised edition 1987
Conway, Jim
3 *Women in mid-life crisis* (1983)
4 *Your marriage can survive mid-life crisis* (1987)

Midnight Avenger series
Dille, Flint
see **Agent thirteen series**

Midnight Louie series
Douglas, Carole Nelson
1 *Catnap* (1992)
2 *Pussyfoot* (1993)
3 *Cat on a blue Monday* (1994)

Midset C.I.D. series
Mills, Osmington
1 *Headlines make murder* (1962)
3 *Dusty death* (1965)
4 *Enemies of the bride* (1966)
5 *Death enters the lists* (1967)
6 *Sundry fell designs* (1968)
7 *Many a slip* (1969)
8 *Ghost of a clue* (1970)
22 *Traitor betrayed* (1964)

Midshipman Lee series
White, Robb
1 *Midshipman Lee* (1938)
2 *Midshipman Lee of the Naval Academy* (1954)

Midshipman Murdock series
Icenhower, Joseph Bryan
see **Mister Midshipman Murdock series**

Midshipman Quinn series
Styles, Showell
1 *Midshipman Quinn* (1956)
2 *Quinn of the Fury* (1958)
3 *Midshipman Quinn wins through* (1961)
Midshipman Quinn and Denise the spy
4 *Quinn at Trafalgar* (1965)

Midshipmen series
Pearson, Parry
see **Jeremy Barton and Samuel Best series**

Midwife series
Courter, Gay
1 *Midwife* (1985)
2 *Midwife's advice* (1992)

Mifflin series
Morley, Christopher
see **Roger and Helen Mifflin series**

Miffy series
Bruna, Dick
1 *Miffy* (1955)
Original edition entitled *Nijntje*; revised edition 1963
2 *Miffy at the zoo* (1955)
Original edition entitled *Nijntje in de dierentuin*; revised edition 1963
3 *Miffy in the snow* (1963)
Original edition entitled *Nijntje in de sneeuw*
4 *Miffy at the seaside* (1963)
Miffy at the beach
Original edition entitled *Nijntje aan see*
5 *Miffy's birthday* (1970)
Original edition entitld *Het feest van Nijntje*
6 *Miffy goes flying* (1970)
Original edition entitled *Nijntje vliegt*
7 *Miffy at the playground* (1975)
Original edition entitled *Nijntje in de speeltuin*
8 *Miffy in hospital* (1975)
Miffy in the hospital
Original edition entitled *Nijntje in het ziekenhuis*; numbers 5, 6, 8 also published in one volume entitled *Miffy books*, 1978
9 *Miffy's dream* (1979)
Original edition entitled *Nijntje's droom*
10 *Miffy's bicycle* (1982)
Original edition entitled *Nijntje op de fiets*
11 *Miffy goes to school* (1984)
Original edition entitled *Nijntje op school*
12 *Miffy and her friend* (1988)
Original edition entitled *Nijntje gaat logeren*
13 *Miffy goes to stay* (1989)

Miffy series

Original edition entitled *Opa en oma pluis*
Companion volume: *Miffy painting book*, 1974

Mig and Peter Manson series
Divine, David
1 *Stolen seasons* (1967)
2 *Key of England* (1968)
3 *Three red flares* (1970)

Migglewade series
Hale, Edgar
see **Montague Migglewade series**

Miguel Menendes series
Blanc, Suzanne
see **Inspector Miguel Menendes series**

Miguel series
Merino, Jose Maria
1 *Gold of dreams* (1992)
2 *Beyond the ancient cities* (1994)

Miguel Urizar series
McCloy, Helen
1 *Goblin market* (1943)
2 *She walks alone* (1948)
Wish you were dead

Mika trilogy
Estes, Rose
1 *Master wolf* (1987)
2 *Price of power* (1987)
3 *Demon hand* (1987)

Mikael Petros series
Anderson, James
1 *Assassin* (1969)
2 *Abolition of death* (1974)

Mike and Ally series
Elfman, Blossom
1 *Love me deadly* (1989)
2 *Tell me no lies* (1989)
3 *Ghost-sitter* (1990)
4 *Curse of the dancing doll* (1991)

Mike and Bill Hendry series
Lee, Benjamin
1 *Paganini strikes again* (1970)
2 *Man in fifteen* (1972)

Mike and Caroline series
Delgado, Alan
1 *Very hot water-bottle* (1962)
Hot-water bottle mystery
2 *Hide the slipper* (1963)
3 *Return ticket* (1965)

Mike and Lisdalia series
Caswell, Brian
1 *Mike* (1993)
2 *Lisdalia* (1994)

Mike and Sandra series
Trease, Geoffrey
1 *Maythorn story* (1960)
2 *Change at Maythorn* (1962)

Mike, Belinda and Ann series
Blyton, Enid
1 *Caravan family* (1945)
2 *Saucy Jane family* (1947)
3 *Pole Star family* (1950)
4 *Seaside family* (1950)
5 *Buttercup Farm family* (1951)
6 *Queen Elizabeth family* (1951)

Mike Benasque series
Caillou, Alan
1 *Plotters* (1960)
2 *Marseilles* (1964)
3 *Who'll buy my evil?* (1966)
4 *Diamonds wild* (1979)

Mike Brent series
Fennell, George
1 *Blood patrol* (1970)
2 *Killer patrol* (1970)

Mike Brett series
Campbell, Keith
1 *Goodbye gorgeous* (1947)
2 *Listen lovely* (1949)
3 *Darling, don't* (1950)
4 *Born beautiful* (1951)
5 *That was no lady* (1952)
6 *Pardon my gun* (1954)

Mike Britton series
Smith, Guy Newman
see **Truckers series**

Mike Brooks series
Rothwell, Henry Talbot
see **Michael Brooks series**

Mike Darroch series
Mackinnon, Allan
1 *Red-winged angel* (1958)
Summons from Baghdad
2 *Assignment in Iraq* (1960)

Mike Daryl series
Wilkinson, Laurence
1 *Turn in, my Lord* (1949)
2 *Touch of Judas* (1952)
3 *Salamander sword* (1953)
4 *Appointment in Tangier* (1955)

Mike Delaney series
Maine, Charles Eric
1 *Isotope man* (1957)
2 *Subterfuge* (1959)
3 *Never let up* (1964)

Mike Dime series
Fantoni, Barry
1 *Mike Dime* (1980)
2 *Stickman* (1982)

Mike Faraday series
Copper, Basil
1 *Dark mirror* (1966)
2 *Night frost* (1966)
3 *No flowers for the general* (1967)
4 *Scratch on the dark* (1967)
5 *Die now, live later* (1968)
6 *Don't bleed on me* (1968)
7 *Marble orchard* (1969)
8 *Dead file* (1970)
9 *No letters from the grave* (1971)
10 *Big chill* (1972)
11 *Strong-arm* (1972)
12 *Great year for dying* (1973)
13 *Shock-wave* (1973)
14 *Breaking point* (1973)
15 *Voice from the dead* (1974)
16 *Feedback* (1974)
17 *Ricochet* (1974)
18 *High wall* (1975)
19 *Impact* (1975)
20 *Good place to die* (1975)
21 *Lonely place* (1976)
22 *Crack in the sidewalk* (1976)
23 *Tight corner* (1976)
24 *Year of the dragon* (1977)
25 *Death squad* (1977)
26 *Murder one* (1977)
27 *Quiet room in hell* (1979)
28 *Big rip-off* (1979)
29 *Caligari complex* (1980)
30 *Flip-side* (1980)
31 *Long rest* (1981)
32 *Empty silence* (1981)
33 *Dark entry* (1981)
34 *Hang loose* (1982)
35 *Shoot-out* (1982)
36 *Far horizon* (1982)
37 *Trigger-man* (1983)
38 *Pressure-point* (1983)
39 *Hard contract* (1983)
40 *Narrow corner* (1983)
41 *Hook* (1984)
42 *You only die once* (1984)
43 *Tuxedo Park* (1985)
44 *Far side of fear* (1985)
45 *Snow-job* (1986)
46 *Jet-lag* (1986)
47 *Blood on the moon* (1986)
48 *Heavy iron* (1987)
49 *Turn down an empty glass* (1987)
50 *Bad scene* (1987)
51 *House-dick* (1988)
52 *Print-out* (1988)

Mike Farrel series
Brown, Carter
1 *Million dollar babe* (1961)
Rewritten from *Cutie cashed his chips*, 1955
2 *Scarlet flush* (1963)

Mike Gannon series
Ballenger, Dean
1 *Blood for breakfast* (1973)
2 *Blood fix* (1974)
3 *Blood beast* (1974)

Mike Garfin series
Brett, Martin
1 *Hot freeze* (1954)
2 *Darker traffic* (1954)
Blondes are my trouble
3 *Dum-dum for the president* (1961)

Mike Haller series
Byrd, Max
1 *California thriller* (1981)
2 *Fly away, Jill* (1981)
3 *Finders weepers* (1983)

Mike Hammer series
Spillane, Mickey
1 *I, the jury* (1947)
2 *Vengeance is mine* (1950)
3 *My gun is quick* (1950)
4 *Big kill* (1951)
5 *One lonely night* (1951)
6 *Kiss me, deadly* (1952)
7 *Deep* (1961)
8 *Girl hunters* (1962)
9 *Snake* (1964)
10 *Twisted thing* (1966)
11 *Body lovers* (1967)
12 *Survival, zero!* (1970)
13 *Killing man* (1989)
Companion volume: *One lonely knight, Mickey Spillane's Mike Hammer*, by Max Allan Collins and James L Traylor, 1984

Mike Harman series
Walsh, James Morgan
1 *Express delivery* (1946)
2 *Walking shadow* (1948)
3 *Time to kill* (1949)

Mike Hazzard series
Bowles, Colin
1 *Flying blind* (1986)
2 *Flying Hazzard* (1987)

Mike Hornsley series
Salter, Elizabeth
see **Inspector Michael Hornsley series**

Mike Hubbard series
Seuffert, Muir
1 *Hand of a killer* (1967)
2 *Trespassers will die* (1968)
3 *Devil at the door* (1972)

Mike Jagger series
Garner, William
1 *Overkill* (1966)
2 *Deep, deep freeze* (1968)
3 *Us or them war* (1969)
4 *Big enough wreath* (1974)

Mike James series
Scott, Denis
1 *Murder makes a villain* (1944)
2 *Beckoning shadow* (1946)

Mike Kenny series
Dillon, Eilis
see **Inspector Mike Kenny series**

Mike King series
Fisher, Graham
1 *Face of danger* (1974)
2 *End of the line* (1975)
3 *Villain of the piece* (1977)

Mike Lanson series
Bond, J Harvey
1 *Bye, bye, baby!* (1958)
2 *Murder isn't funny* (1958)
3 *Kill me with kindness* (1960)
4 *If wishes were hearses* (1961)

Mike Locken series
Rostand, Robert
1 *Killer elite* (1973)
2 *Viper's game* (1974)
3 *Killing in Rome* (1977)

Mike Logan series
Holt, Henry
1 *No lilies* (1947)
2 *Wreath for the lady* (1959)
3 *Don't shoot, darling* (1961)

Mike Macauley series
Marino, Nick
1 *One way street* (1952)
2 *City limits* (1958)
Co-author: Richard Deming

Mike Mars series
Wollheim, Donald Allen
1 *Mike Mars, astronaut* (1961)
2 *Mike Mars flies the X-15* (1961)
3 *Mike Mars at Cape Canaveral* (1961)
Mike Mars at Cape Kennedy
4 *Mike Mars in orbit* (1961)
5 *Mike Mars flies the Dyna-Soar* (1962)
6 *Mike Mars, South Pole spaceman* (1962)
7 *Mike Mars and the mystery satellite* (1963)
8 *Mike Mars around the moon* (1964)

Mike McCall series
Leader, Charles
1 *Double M man* (1969)
2 *Death of a marine* (1970)
3 *Salesman of death* (1971)
4 *Scavengers at war* (1974)

Mike McCall series
Queen, Ellery
1 *Campus murders* (1969)
2 *Black hearts murder* (1970)
3 *Blue movie murders* (1972)

Mike McClary and Quin Saint James series
Macgregor, T J
see **Quin Saint James and Mike McClary series**

Mike McVeigh series
Emmett, Robert
see **American Avenger series**

Mike Merriman series
Burke, Jonathan
1 *Fear by instalments* (1960)
2 *Deadly downbeat* (1962)

Mike Paradise series
Canon, Jack
1 *Angel for Paradise* (1979)
2 *No love for Paradise* (1979)
3 *Hangman for Paradise* (1980)

Mike Ross series
Carr, Kirby
see **Hitman series**

Mike S Blueberry series
Giraud, Jean
see **Lieutenant Mike S Blueberry series**

Mike series
Colwell, Max
1 *Half days and patched pants* (1977)
2 *Full days and pressed pants* (1978)

Mike series
Cresswell, Helen
1 *Bluebirds over Pit Row* (1972)
2 *Roof fall!* (1972)
3 *Short back and sides* (1972)
4 *Long day* (1972)
5 *Key* (1973)
6 *Trap* (1974)
7 *Cheap day return* (1974)
8 *Shady deal* (1974)

Mike Seton series
Jacobs, Thomas Curtis Hicks
1 *Target for terror* (1961)
2 *Elusive Monsieur Drago* (1964)

Mike Shayne series
Halliday, Brett
see **Michael Shayne series**

Mike Shayne stories series
Halliday, Brett
Includes stories by other authors
1 *Murder go round* (1979)
2 *No day for murder* (1979)
3 *Guadaloupe caper* (1979)
4 *Scent of death* (1979)
5 *Widow for killing* (1979)
6 *Mike Shayne mysteries* (1979)
7 *Murder to come* (1980)
8 *Death in Xanadu* (1980)
9 *Deadline for murder* (1980)
10 *Night of the white hunter* (1980)

Mike Strang series
Cagney, Peter
1 *No diamonds for a doll* (1960)
2 *Hear the stripper scream* (1960)
3 *Grave for madam* (1961)

Mike Thompson and Tracy Larrimore series
Paull, Jessica
see **Tracy Larrimore and Mike Thompson series**

Mike Tucker series
Coffey, Brian
1 *Blood risk* (1973)
2 *Surrounded* (1974)
3 *Wall of masks* (1975)

Mike Warlock series
Haggard, Paul
1 *Dead is the door-nail* (1937)
2 *Death talks shop* (1938)
3 *Poison from a wealthy widow* (1938)
4 *Death walks on cat feet* (1938)

Mike Yeadings and Angus Mott series
Curzon, Clare
see **Superintendent Mike Yeadings and Sergeant Angus Mott series**

Miklejohn and Leidl series
Wilhelm, Kate
see **Charlie Miklejohn and Constance Leidl series**

Mikrokid mystery series
This sequence has two authors
Bartholomew, Barbara
1 *Great gradepoint mystery* (1983)
McMahan, Ian
2 *Fox's lair* (1983)
3 *Lake fear* (1985)
4 *Lost forest* (1985)

Milan Jacovich series
Roberts, Les
1 *Pepper Pike* (1988)
2 *Full Cleveland* (1989)
3 *Deep shaker* (1991)
4 *Cleveland connection* (1993)

Milano series
Ellin, Stanley
see **John Milano series**

Milbury series
Jeffery, Gordon
1 *On the ball* (1962)
2 *Up the Town!* (1964)

Mildmay series
Wilkinson, Burke
see **Geoffrey Mildmay series**

Mildred Arkell series
Wood, Ellen
1 *Mildred Arkell* (1865)
2 *Saint Martin's Eve* (1866)

Mildred Hubble series
Murphy, Jill
see **Worst Witch series**

Mildred Keith series
Finley, Martha Farquharson
1 *Mildred and Elsie* (1861)
2 *Mildred Keith* (1878)
3 *Mildred at Roselands* (1879)
4 *Mildred's married life* (1882)
5 *Mildred at home* (1884)
6 *Mildred's boys and girls* (1886)
7 *Mildred's new daughter* (1894)

Miles and Barnaby series
Chan, Melissa
see **Inspector Joe Barnaby and Francesca Miles series**

Miles Bredon series
Knox, Ronald Arbuthnott
1 *Three taps* (1927)
A detective story without a moral
2 *Footsteps at the lock* (1928)
3 *Body in the silo* (1933)
Settled out of court
4 *Still dead* (1934)
5 *Double cross purposes* (1937)

Miles Cabot series
Farley, Ralph Milne
1 *Radio man* (1948)
Earth man on Venus
2 *Radio beasts* (1964)
3 *Radio planet* (1964)

Miles Jacoby series
Randisi, Robert Joseph
1 *Eye in the ring* (1982)
2 *Steinway collection* (1983)
3 *Full contact* (1984)
4 *Separate cases* (1990)

Miles Le Breton series
Esteven, John
1 *By night at Dinsmore* (1935)
2 *While murder waits* (1936)

Miles Naismith Vorkosigan series
Bujold, Lois McMaster
1 *Warrior's apprentice* (1986)
2 *Borders of infinity* (1989)
Short stories
3 *Brothers in arms* (1989)
4 *Vor game* (1990)
Numbers 2 and 4 also published in one volume entitled *Vorkosigan's game*, 1990
5 *Barrayar* (1991)
6 *Spirit ring* (1992)
7 *Mirror dance* (1993)
Companion volumes: *Shards of honor*, 1986 also published as *Shards of honour*, *Ethan of Athos*, 1986

Miles Pennoyer series
Lawrence, Margery
1 *Number seven, Queer Street* (1945)
2 *Master of shadows* (1959)

Miles series
Rosenberger, Joseph
see **C.O.B.R.A. series**

Miles Standish Rice series
Kendrick, Baynard
1 *Eleven of diamonds* (1936)
2 *Iron spiders* (1936)
Iron spiders murder
3 *Death beyond the go-thru* (1938)

Miles trilogy
Canning, Victor
see **Smiler Miles trilogy**

Miles Wallingford series
Cooper, James Fenimore
1 *Afloat and ashore* (1844)
A sea tale
2 *Lucy Hardinge* (1854)
Miles Wallingford

Militant series
Crick, Michael
1 *Militant* (1984)
2 *March of Militant* (1986)

Military balance series
Collins, John Martin
1 *U.S.-Soviet military balance, concepts and capability, 1960-1980* (1980)
2 *U.S.-Soviet military balance, 1980-1985* (1985)

Military life series
Balzac, Honore de
see **Scenes of military life series**

Military techno-thrillers series
Weber, Joe
1 *Defcon one* (1990)
2 *Shadow flight* (1990)
3 *Rules of engagement* (1991)
4 *Targets of opportunity* (1993)

Mill Creek Irregulars series
Derleth, August
1 *Mill Creek Irregulars* (1959)
2 *Irregulars strike again* (1964)

Mill House series
Baker, Denys Val
see **Cornish series**

Mill on the Po series
Bacchelli, Riccardo
1 *Mill on the Po* (1938)
Originally published as *Dio ti salvi, 1812-48*, 1938 and *La miseria viene in barca, 1849-72*, part 1, 1939
2 *Nothing new under the sun* (1939)
Original edition entitled *La miseria viene in barca, 1949-72*, 1939, parts 2 and 3
3 *[Mondo vecchio sempre nuovo, 1873-1918]* (1940)
No English edition

Mill-race quartet
Street, Pamela
see **Lodge family series**

Millais and Effie Gray series
Lutyens, Mary
see **Effie Gray series**

Miller family series
Constant, Alberta Wilson
1 *Those Miller girls* (1965)
2 *Motoring Millers* (1969)
3 *Does anybody care about Lou Emma Miller?* (1979)

Miller series
Dix, Maurice Buxton
see **Inspector James Miller series**
Hunt, Peter
see **Alan miller series**
Keenan, William
see **Chief Superintendent Charles Miller series**
Masters, Edgar Lee
see **Mitch Miller series**
Patterson, Henry
see **Nick Miller series**
Smaridge, Norah
see **Robin Miller series**

Millers series
Merriman, Effie Woodward
1 *Little Millers* (1891)
2 *Mollie Miller* (1895)

Millers series
Pierson, Clara Dillingham
1 *Three little Millers* (1905)
2 *Millers at Pencroft* (1906)
4 *Millers and their playmates* (1908)

Millett series
Bowden, Jim
see **Cap Millett series**

Millhone series
Grafton, Sue
see **Kensey Millhone series**

Millicent Hetherege series
Bernard, Robert
1 *Deadly meeting* (1970)
2 *Illegal entry* (1972)

Millicent Newberry series
Lee, Jennette Barbour Perry
1 *Green jacket* (1917)
2 *Mysterious office* (1922)
3 *Dead right* (1925)

Millie Cooper series
Herman, Charlotte
1 *Millie Cooper* (1985)
2 *Millie Cooper takes a chance* (1988)

Millie Mack trilogy
Hunt, Nan
see **Mrs Millie Mack series**

Milligan letters series
Milligan, Spike
1 *Spike Milligan letters* (1977)
2 *More Milligan letters* (1984)

Milligan series
Buckeridge, Anthony
see **Rex Milligan series**

Millikens series
Cass, Joan Evelyn
see **Molly Millikens series**

Millington series
Hackforth-Jones, Gilbert
see **Submarine Service series**

Million series
Schwartz, David Martin
Illustrated by Steven Kellogg
1 *How much is a million* (1985)
2 *If you made a million* (1989)

Millionaire gangster series
Wallace, John
1 *Millionaire gangster* (1937)
2 *Millionaire gangster again* (1942)

Mills series
O'Brine, Manning
1 *Mills* (1969)
2 *No earth for foxes* (1974)

Millwall series
Sandys, James
see **Inspector Millwall series**

Milly-Molly-Mandy series
Brisley, Joyce Lankester
1 *Milly-Molly-Mandy stories* (1928)
2 *More of Milly-Molly-Mandy* (1929)
3 *Further doings of Milly-Molly-Mandy* (1932)
4 *Milly-Molly-Mandy again* (1948)
5 *Milly-Molly-Mandy and Company* (1955)
6 *Milly-Molly-Mandy and Billy Blunt* (1967)
Companion volume: *Three Milly-Molly-Mandy plays*, 1938

Milly Mouse series
Cass, Joan Evelyn
1 *Milly Mouse* (1974)
2 *Milly Mouse's measles* (1976)

Milnes series
Pope-Hennessy, James
see **Monckton Milnes series**

Milo March series
Chaber, M E
1 *Hangman's harvest* (1952)
Don't get caught
2 *No grave for March* (1953)
All the way down
3 *Man inside* (1954)
Now it's my turn
4 *As old as Cain* (1954)
Take one for murder
5 *Splintered man* (1955)
6 *Lonely walk* (1956)
7 *Gallows garden* (1958)
Lady came to kill
8 *Hearse of another colour* (1958)
9 *So dead the rose* (1959)
10 *Jade for a lady* (1962)
11 *Softly in the night* (1963)
12 *Uneasy lies the dead* (1964)
13 *Six who ran* (1964)
14 *Wanted, dead man* (1965)
15 *Day it rained diamonds* (1966)
16 *Man in the middle* (1967)
17 *Wild midnight falls* (1968)
18 *Flaming man* (1969)
19 *Green grow the graves* (1970)
20 *Bonded dead* (1971)
21 *Born to be hanged* (1973)

Milo Milodragovitch series
Crumley, James
1 *Wrong case* (1975)
2 *Dancing bear* (1983)

Milodragovitch series
Crumley, James
see **Milo Milodragovitch series**

Miltiades Vaiden trilogy
Stribling, Thomas Sigismund
see **Colonel Miltiades Vaiden trilogy**

Milton and Marvin series
Modell, Frank B
1 *Seen any cats?* (1979)
2 *Tooley, Tooley!* (1979)
3 *One zillion valentines* (1981)
4 *Goodbye old year, hello new year* (1984)
5 *Look out, it's April Fool's Day* (1985)
6 *Ice cream soup* (1987)
7 *Skeeter and the computer* (1988)

Milton Hicks series
Hicks, D L
1 *Kwahari* (1988)
2 *Breed's rampage* (1988)

Milton Kovak series
Cooper, Susan Rogers
1 *Man in the green Chevy* (1988)
2 *Houston in the rearview mirror* (1990)
3 *Other people's houses* (1991)
4 *Chasing away the devil* (1991)
5 *Dead moon on the rise* (1994)

Milton series
Henderson, Laurence
see **Sergeant Arthur Milton series**

Milton series
Kraus, Robert
1 *Milton the early riser* (1972)
2 *Milton the early riser takes a trip* (1981)

Mimff series
Kaeser, Hildegarde Johanna
Translated from the German
1 *Mimff* (1939)
The story of a boy who was not afraid
2 *Mimff in charge* (1949)
3 *Mimff takes over* (1954)
4 *Mimff-Robinson* (1958)

Mimi series
Davis, Anne Pence
1 *Mimi at camp* (1935)
2 *Mimi's houseparty* (1936)
3 *Mimi at Sheridan* (1937)

Mimosa series
Saint Albans, Suzanne Marie Adele Beauclerk
Autobiography
1 *Mimosa and the mango* (1974)
2 *Road to Bordeaux* (1976)
3 *Uncertain wings* (1977)

Mimosa Winter series
Mackenzie, Joan
1 *Mimosa Winter* (1971)
2 *Mimosa and her man* (1973)
3 *No halo for Mimosa* (1977)

Minack chronicles series
Tangye, Derek
1 *Gull on the roof* (1961)
2 *Cat in the window* (1962)
3 *Drake at the door* (1963)
4 *Donkey in the meadow* (1965)
5 *Lama* (1966)
6 *Way to Minack* (1968)
7 *Cornish summer* (1970)
8 *Cottage on a cliff* (1972)
9 *Cat affair* (1974)
Abridged one volume edition of numbers 2, 5, 9 published as *Somewhere a cat is waiting*, 1977
10 *Sun on the lintel* (1976)
11 *Winding lane* (1978)
12 *When the winds blow* (1980)
13 *Ambrose rock* (1982)
14 *Quiet year* (1984)
15 *Cherry tree* (1986)

Mind brothers series
Heath, Peter
see **Jason Starr and Adam Cyber series**

Mind master series
Townsend, Larry
1 *Masters' counterpoints* (1991)
2 *One for the master, tow for the fool* (1992)
3 *Mind master* (1994)
Companion volume: *Dream master, and other SM stories*, 1992

Mind Masters series
Rossmann, John F
1 *Mind Masters* (1974)
2 *Shamballah* (1975)
3 *Door* (1975)
Sequence continued under the pseudonym Ian Ross
Ross, Ian
4 *Amazons* (1976)
5 *Recycled souls* (1976)

Mind series
Belden, Wilanne Schneider
1 *Mind-call* (1981)
2 *Mind-hold* (1987)
3 *Mind-find* (1988)

Minden curse series
Roberts, Willo Davis
1 *Minden curse* (1978)
2 *More Minden curses* (1980)

Mindkiller series
Robinson, Spider
1 *Mindkiller* (1982)
2 *Time pressure* (1987)

Mindslip series
Elder, Michael
1 *Mindslip* (1976)
2 *Mindquest* (1978)

Mindy series
Curry, Jane Louise
see **Maccubbin family series**

Mine enemy grows older series
King, Alexander
Autobiography of an artist who was also an editor of *Life magazine* and a drug addict
1 *Mine enemy grows older* (1958)
2 *May this house be safe from tigers* (1960)
3 *I should have kissed her more* (1961)
4 *Is there life after birth?* (1963)

Miners series
Hall, Penny
1 *Paperchaser* (1989)
2 *Catalyst* (1993)

Minerva series
Sampson, Emma
see **Miss Minerva series**

Minervan experiment series
Hogan, James Patrick
1 *Inherit the stars* (1977)
2 *Gentle giants of Ganymede* (1978)
3 *Giants' star* (1981)
Numbers 1-3 also published in one volume editions entitled *The Minervan experiment*, 1981 and *The giant novels*, 1991
4 *Entoverse* (1991)

Ming and Jeremiah series
Jennings, Sharon
see **Jeremiah and Mrs Ming series**

Minikin series
Hillyard, Mary Dorothea
1 *Minikin's visit* (1953)
2 *Minikin's new home* (1954)
3 *Minikin and her friends* (1955)
4 *Timothy, Minikin and all* (1956)
5 *Treat for Minikin* (1958)

Minimal Farm series
Carmichael, Claire
1 *Minimal Farm* (1994)
2 *Trouble at Minimal Farm* (1994)

Minister series
Bexell, Eva
1 *Minister's naughty grandchildren* (1976)
Original edition entitled *Prostens barnbarn*
2 *Christmas with grandfather* (1976)
Original edition entitled *Kalabalik hos morfar prosten*

Ministering children series
Charlesworth, Maria Louisa
1 *Ministering children* (1854)
Also published in four parts
1.1 *Blind man's child* (1854)
1.2 *Rose, the ministering child* (1854)
1.3 *Little Jane, and other tales* (1854)
1.4 *Ruth and Patience* (1854)
2 *Ministering children, a sequel* (1867)
Basket maker's shop

Mink and sables series
Spanier, Ginette
Autobiography
1 *It isn't all mink* (1959)
2 *And now it's sables* (1970)
Companion volume: *Long road to freedom*, 1976

Minka and Curdy series
White, Antonia
1 *Minka and Curdy* (1957)
2 *Living with Minka and Curdy* (1970)

Minnesota girl series
Sterrett, Frances Roberta
see **Rusty series**

Minnett series
Logan, Mark
see **Nicholas Minnett series**

Minnie Ashe series
Kersh, Cyril
1 *Aggravations of Minnie Ashe* (1970)
2 *Minnie Ashe at war* (1979)

Minnie Santangelo series
Mancini, Anthony
1 *Minnie Santangelo's mortal sin* (1975)
2 *Minnie Santangelo and the evil eye* (1977)

Minnie's pets series
Leslie, Madeline
1 *Minnie's pet cat* (1864)
2 *Minnie's pet dog* (1864)
3 *Minnie's pet horse* (1864)
4 *Minnie's pet lamb* (1864)
5 *Minnie's pet monkey* (1864)
6 *Minnie's pet parrot* (1864)

Minnifield series
Williamson, Jerry Neal
1 *Ghost mansion* (1981)
2 *Horror mansion* (1982)

Minnipins series
Kendall, Carol
1 *Gammage cup* (1959)
Minnipins
2 *Whisper of Glocken* (1965)

Minotaur trilogy
Swann, Thomas Burnett
1 *Cry silver bells* (1977)
2 *Forest of forever* (1971)
3 *Day of the minotaur* (1966)

Minsan series
Keyte, John Charles
1 *Daughter of Cathay* (1926)
2 *Minsan series* (1927)

Minstrel Orfeo series
Craig, Brian
1 *Zaragoz* (1989)
2 *Plague demon* (1990)
3 *Storm warriors* (1991)

Mint series
Doherty, Berlie
see **Tilly Mint series**

Minter series
Wallace, Edgar
see **Superintendent Minter series**

Minty Humble series
Seton, Hilary
1 *Beyond the blue hills* (1973)
2 *Lion in the garden* (1974)

Minty series
Goolden, Barbara
see **Tabor family series**

Minute boys series
This sequence has two authors
Stratemeyer, Edward L
1 *Minute boys of Lexington* (1898)
2 *Minute boys of Bunker Hill* (1899)
Otis, James
3 *Minute boys of the Green Mountains* (1904)
4 *Minute boys of the Mohawk Valley* (1905)
5 *Minute boys of the Wyoming Valley* (1906)
6 *Minute boys of South Carolina* (1907)
7 *Minute boys of Long Island* (1908)
8 *Minute boys of New York* (1909)
9 *Minute boys of Boston* (1910)
10 *Minute boys of Philadelphia* (1911)
11 *Minute boys of Yorktown* (1912)

Minute tales series
Blyton, Enid
1 *Five minute tales* (1933)
2 *Ten minute tales* (1934)
3 *Fifteen minute tales* (1936)
4 *Twenty minute tales* (1940)

Mirabelle and Jenny series
Gifford, Griselda
see **Jenny and Mirabelle series**

Miracle series
Martin, Betty
Edited by Evelyn Wells; experiences as a leprosy sufferer
1 *Miracle at Carville* (1952)
2 *No one must ever know* (1959)

Miracleman series
This sequence has four authors
Moore, Alan
1 *Dream of flying* (1988)
2 *Red King syndrome* (1990)
3 *Olympus* (1991)
Co-author: John Totleben
Gaiman, Neil
4 *Golden age* (1992)
Jones, Valerie
5 *Apocrypha* (1993)

Miracles of Jesus series
Blyton, Enid
Stories of miracles reported in the New Testament
1 *Little girl at Capernaum* (1948)
2 *Boy with the loaves and fishes* (1948)

Mirage mysteries series
Dengler, Sandy
1 *Cat killer* (1993)
2 *Mouse trapped* (1993)
3 *Last dinosaur* (1994)
4 *Gila monster* (1994)
5 *Fatal fishes* (1994)

Miranda series
Gervaise, Mary
1 *That imp Miranda* (1930)
2 *Miranda at Merryfield* (1931)
3 *Captain Miranda* (1932)

Miranda series
Winthrop, Elizabeth
1 *Marathon Miranda* (1979)
2 *Miranda in the middle* (1980)

Miranda Welch trilogy
Walden, Amelia
1 *When love speaks* (1961)
2 *So near the heart* (1962)
3 *My world's the stage* (1964)

Mirdath series
McNaughton, Brian
1 *Satan's love child* (1977)
2 *Satan's mistress* (1978)
3 *Satan's seductress* (1980)
4 *Satan's surrogate* (1982)

Miriam Birdseye series
Spain, Nancy
1 *Death goes on skis* (1949)
2 *Poison for teacher* (1949)
3 *Cinderella goes to the morgue* (1950)
Minutes to midnight
4 *R in the month* (1950)
5 *Not wanted on voyage* (1951)
6 *Out damned tot!* (1952)

Miriam Henderson series
Richardson, Dorothy Miller
see **Pilgrimage series**

Miro and Doria series
Graham, Heather
see **Donna Miro and Lorna Doria series**

Miro series
Herron, Shaun
1 *Miro* (1969)
2 *Hound and the fox and the harper* (1970)
Miro papers
3 *Through the dark and hairy wood* (1972)

Mirror in darkness trilogy
Jameson, Storm
1 *Company parade* (1934)
2 *Love in winter* (1935)
3 *None turn back* (1936)
Originally planned as a five volume sequence

Mirrors series
Barlette, Danielle
1 *I'll take Manhattan* (1985)
2 *To London with love* (1985)

Mischief series
Blyton, Enid
1 *Laughing kitten* (1954)
2 *Mischief again* (1955)

Mischief series
Rabinowitz, Sandy
1 *Colt named Mischief* (1979)
2 *How I trained my colt* (1981)

Mischief series
Tilman, Harold William
1 *Mischief in Patagonia* (1957)
2 *Mischief among the penguins* (1961)
3 *Mischief in Greenland* (1964)
Companion volume: *Mostly Mischief*, 1966

Misery guts series
Gleitzman, Morris
1 *Misery guts* (1991)
2 *Worry warts* (1991)
3 *Puppy fat!* (1994)

Mishmash series
Cone, Molly
1 *Mishmash* (1962)
2 *Mishmash and the substitute teacher* (1963)
3 *Mishmash and the sauerkraut mystery* (1965)
4 *Mishmash and Uncle Looey* (1968)
5 *Mishmash and the Venus flytrap* (1976)
6 *Mishmash and the robot* (1981)
7 *Mishmash and the big fat problem* (1982)

Misleading cases series
Herbert, Alan Patrick
1 *Misleading cases in the common law* (1927)
2 *More misleading cases* (1930)
3 *Still more misleading cases* (1933)
Numbers 1-3 also revised and published in one volume entitled *Uncommon law*, 1935
4 *Codd's last case, and other misleading cases* (1952)
5 *Bardot M.P., and other misleading cases* (1964)
Thirty-four cases selected from this sequence entitled *Wigs at work*, 1966

Misquamacus series
Masterton, Graham
see **Manitou series**

Misrule series
Jones, Gareth
1 *Lord of misrule* (1980)
2 *Noble savage* (1985)

Miss Abigail Patience Danforth series
Jackson, Marian J A
1 *Punjat's ruby* (1990)
2 *Arabian pearl* (1990)
3 *Cat's eye* (1991)
4 *Diamond Head* (1992)
5 *Sunken treasure* (1994)

Miss Anna Truly series
Drummond, Violet Hilda
1 *Miss Anna Truly* (1945)
2 *Miss Anna Truly and the Christmas lights* (1968)

Miss Ashton's girls series
Mathews, Joanna Hooe
1 *Fanny's birthday gift* (1874)
2 *New scholars* (1874)
3 *Rosalie's pet* (1875)
4 *Eleanor's visit* (1875)
5 *Mabel Walton's experiment* (1875)
6 *Elsie's Santa Claus* (1876)

Miss Bagshot series
Telscombe, Anne
1 *Miss Bagshot goes to Moscow* (1960)
2 *Miss Bagshot goes to Tibet* (1962)

Miss Bianca series
Sharp, Margery
1 *Rescuers* (1959)
2 *Miss Bianca* (1962)
3 *Turret* (1964)
4 *Miss Bianca in the salt mines* (1966)
5 *Miss Bianca in the Orient* (1970)
6 *Miss Bianca in the Antarctic* (1970)
7 *Miss Bianca and the bridesmaid* (1972)
8 *Bernard the brave* (1976)
9 *Bernard into battle* (1979)
Companion volume: *The rescuers downunder*, 1990

Miss Billy series
Porter, Eleanor Hodgman
1 *Miss Billy* (1911)
2 *Miss Billy's decision* (1912)
3 *Miss Billy, married* (1914)

Miss Blandish series
Chase, James Hadley
see **Carol Blandish series**

Miss Boo series
Runbeck, Margaret Lee
1 *Our Miss Boo* (1942)
2 *Miss Boo is sixteen* (1957)

Miss Buncle series
Stevenson, Dorothy Emily
1 *Miss Buncle's book* (1934)
2 *Miss Buncle married* (1936)
3 *Two Mrs Abbotts* (1943)
One volume edition entitled *Miss Buncle*, 1964

Miss Cricket trilogy
Jackson, Gabrielle Emilie
see **Little Miss Cricket trilogy**

Miss Dinwiddie series
Hassett, Margaret
1 *Educating Elizabeth* (1937)
2 *Beezer's end* (1949)

Miss Emily Seeton series
This sequence has three authors
Carvic, Heron
1 *Picture Miss Seeton* (1968)
2 *Miss Seeton draws the line* (1969)
3 *Miss Seeton bewitched* (1971)
Witch Miss Seeton
4 *Miss Seeton sings* (1973)
5 *Odds on Miss Seeton* (1975)
6 *Witch Miss Seeton* (1988)
Charles, Hampton
7 *Miss Seeton by appointment* (1990)
8 *Advantage Miss Seeton* (1990)
9 *Miss Seeton at the helm* (1990)
Crane, Hamilton
10 *Miss Seeton cracks the case* (1991)
11 *Miss Seeton paints the town* (1991)
12 *Hands up, Miss Seeton* (1992)
13 *Miss Seeton by moonlight* (1992)
14 *Miss Seeton rocks the candle* (1992)
15 *Miss Seeton goes to bat* (1993)
16 *Miss Seeton plants suspicion* (1993)
17 *Starring Miss Seeton* (1994)
18 *Miss Seeton undercover* (1994)
19 *Miss Seeton rules* (1994)

Miss Emily trilogy
Murdoch, Nina
1 *Miss Emily in black lace* (1930)
2 *Portrait of Miss Emily* (1931)
3 *Exit Miss Emily* (1937)

Miss Fales series
Knipe, Emilie Benson
see **Little Miss Fales series**

Miss Flora Hogg series
Lee, Austin
1 *Sheep's clothing* (1955)
2 *Call in Miss Hogg* (1956)
3 *Miss Hogg and the Bronte murders* (1956)
4 *Miss Hogg and the squash club murder* (1957)
5 *Miss Hogg and the dead dean* (1958)
6 *Miss Hogg flies high* (1958)
7 *Miss Hogg and the Covent Garden murders* (1960)
8 *Miss Hogg and the missing sisters* (1961)
9 *Miss Hogg's last case* (1963)

Miss Flora McFlimsey series
Mariana
Based on the character from the poem Miss McFlimsey, or, Nothing to wear, by William Allen Butler, 1857
1 *Miss Flora McFlimsey's Christmas eve* (1949)
2 *Miss Flora McFlimsey's Easter bonnet* (1951)
3 *Miss Flora McFlimsey and the baby new year* (1951)
4 *Miss Flora McFlimsey's birthday* (1952)
5 *Miss Flora McFlimsey and Little Laughing Water* (1954)
6 *Miss Flora McFlimsey and the little red school house* (1957)
7 *Miss Flora McFlimsey's valentine* (1962)
8 *Miss Flora McFlimsey's May Day* (1969)

Miss Flora McFlimsey series

Miss Flora McFlimsey, Queen of the May
9 *Miss Flora McFlimsey's Halloween* (1972)

Miss from S.I.S. series
Tralins, Sandor Robert
see **Lee Crosley series**

Miss Gator series
Kraus, Robert
1 *Good moring, Miss Gator* (1989)
2 *Miss Gator's school house* (1989)

Miss Gregory series
Gibbon, Percival
1 *Adventures of miss Gregory* (1912)
2 *Second class passenger, and other stories* (1913)

Miss Havisham series
This sequence has two authors
Dickens, Charles
1 *Great expectations* (1861)
Roe, Sue
2 *Estella, her expectations* (1982)
Companion volume: *Estella*, by Alanna Knight, 1986

Miss Jane Fairfax series
This sequence has three authors
Austen, Jane
1 *Emma* (1816)
Grey, Charlotte
2 *Journal of Miss Jane Fairfax* (1984)
Aiken, Joan
3 *Jane Fairfax* (1990)

Miss Jane Marple series
Christie, Agatha
1 *Murder at the vicarage* (1930)
2 *Thirteen problems* (1932)
Miss Marple and the thirteen problems
Tuesday Club murders
A selection of these stories published as *The mystery of the blue geranium, and other Tuesday Club murders*, 1940
3 *Body in the library* (1942)
4 *Moving finger* (1942)
5 *Sleeping murder* (1976)
6 *Murder is announced* (1950)
7 *They do it with mirrors* (1952)
Murder with mirrors
8 *Pocket full of rye* (1953)
9 *Four fifty from Paddington* (1957)
Murder she said
What Mrs McGillicuddy saw!
10 *Mirror crack'd from side to side* (1962)
Mirror crack'd
11 *Caribbean mystery* (1964)
12 *At Bertram's Hotel* (1965)
13 *Nemesis* (1971)
14 *Miss Marple's final cases, and two other stories* (1979)
Omnibus volume: *Miss Marple, complete short stories*, 1985; a selection entitled *Thirteen clues for Miss Marple*, 1966; companion volume: *The life and times of Miss Jane Marple*, by Anne Hart, 1985; also stories featuring Miss Marple in *The regatta mystery*, 1939, four stories in *The mousetrap, and other stories*, 1950, one story in *The adventure of the Christmas pudding*, 1960, two stories in *Double sin, and other stories*, 1961

Miss Know It All series
York, Carol Beach
1 *Miss Know It All* (1966)
2 *Christmas dolls* (1967)
3 *Good day mice* (1968)
4 *Good Charlotte* (1969)
5 *Ten O'Clock Club* (1970)
6 *Miss Know It All returns* (1972)
7 *Kate be late* (1987)
8 *Miss Know It All and the wishing lamp* (1987)
9 *Miss Know It All and the three-ring circus* (1988)
10 *Miss Know It All and the magic house* (1989)
11 *Rabbit magic* (1991)
12 *Secret house* (1992)

Miss Lochinvar series
Taggart, Marion Ames
1 *Miss Lochinvar* (1902)
2 *Miss Lochinvar's return* (1906)

Miss Mallard series
Quackenbush, Robert Mead
1 *Express train to trouble* (1981)
2 *Cable car to catastrophe* (1982)
3 *Dig to disaster* (1982)
4 *Gondola to danger* (1983)
5 *Stairway to doom* (1983)
6 *Rickshaw to horror* (1984)
7 *Taxi to intrigue* (1984)
8 *Stage door to terror* (1985)
9 *Bicycle to treachery* (1985)
10 *Surfboard to peril* (1986)
11 *Texas trail to Calamity* (1986)
12 *Dog sled to Dread* (1987)
13 *Danger in Tibet* (1989)
14 *Lost in the Amazon* (1990)
15 *Evil under the sea* (1992)

Miss Maud Silver series
Wentworth, Patricia
1 *Grey mask* (1928)
2 *Case is closed* (1937)
3 *Lonesome road* (1939)
4 *Who pays the piper?* (1940)
Account rendered
5 *In the balance* (1941)
Danger point
6 *Chinese shawl* (1943)
7 *Miss Silver deals with death* (1943)
Miss Silver intervenes
8 *Key* (1944)
9 *Clock strikes twelve* (1944)
10 *She came back* (1945)
Traveller returns
11 *Pilgrim's rest* (1946)
Dark threat
12 *Latter end* (1947)
13 *Wicked uncle* (1947)
Spotlight
14 *Case of William Smith* (1948)
15 *Eternity ring* (1948)
16 *Miss Silver comes to stay* (1949)
17 *Catherine-Wheel* (1949)
18 *Brading collection* (1950)
Mister Brading's collection
19 *Through the wall* (1950)
20 *Anna, where are you?* (1951)
Death at the deep end
21 *Ivory dagger* (1951)
22 *Watersplash* (1951)
23 *Ladies' bane* (1952)
24 *Vanishing point* (1953)
25 *Out of the past* (1953)
26 *Benevent treasure* (1954)
27 *Silent pool* (1954)
28 *Poison in the pen* (1955)
29 *Listening eye* (1955)
30 *Gazebo* (1956)
Summerhouse
31 *Fingerprint* (1956)
32 *Alington inheritance* (1958)
33 *Girl in the cellar* (1961)

Miss Melinda Pink series
Moffat, Gwen
1 *Lady with a cool eye* (1973)
2 *Miss Pink at the edge of the world* (1975)
3 *Over the sea to death* (1976)
4 *Short time to live* (1976)
5 *Persons unknown* (1978)
6 *Die like a dog* (1982)
7 *Last chance country* (1983)
8 *Grizzly trail* (1984)
9 *Snare* (1987)
10 *Stone hawk* (1989)
11 *Rage* (1990)
12 *Raptor zone* (1990)
13 *Veronica's sisters* (1992)
14 *Outside edge* (1993)

Miss Minerva series
Sampson, Emma
1 *Billy and the major* (1918)
2 *Miss Minerva's baby* (1920)
3 *Miss Minerva on the old plantation* (1923)
4 *Miss Minerva broadcasts Billy* (1925)
5 *Miss Minerva's scallywags* (1927)
6 *Miss Minerva's neighbors* (1929)
7 *Miss Minerva goin' places* (1931)
8 *Miss Minerva's mystery* (1933)
9 *Miss Minerva's problem* (1936)
10 *Miss Minerva's vacation* (1939)
Companion volume: *Miss Minerva's cook book*, 1931

Miss Moppet series
King, Louise Wooster
1 *Day we were mostly butterflies* (1963)
2 *Velocipede handicap* (1965)

Miss Nelson series
Allard, Harry
1 *Miss Nelson is missing!* (1977)
2 *Miss Nelson is back* (1982)
3 *Miss nelson has a field day* (1985)

Miss Otis series
Sarto, Ben
1 *Miss Otis throws a come-back* (1947)
2 *Miss Otis comes to Piccadilly* (1947)
3 *Jews Pellegrini* (1947)
4 *Miss Otis goes up* (1947)
5 *Miss Otis has a daughter* (1948)
6 *Miss Otis blows town* (1953)
7 *Miss Otis makes a date* (1953)
8 *Miss Otis moves in* (1953)
9 *Miss Otis takes the rap* (1953)
10 *Miss Otis plays Eve* (1953)
11 *Miss Otis hits back* (1953)
12 *Miss Otis says yes* (1953)
13 *Miss Otis goes French* (1953)
14 *Miss Otis desires* (1954)
15 *Miss Otis makes hay* (1954)
16 *Miss otis plays ball* (1954)
17 *Miss Otis gets fresh* (1954)
18 *Miss Otis relents* (1954)

Miss Pat series
Ginther, Mary Pemberton
1 *Miss Pat and her sisters* (1915)
2 *Miss Pat at school* (1915)
3 *Miss Pat in the Old World* (1915)
4 *Miss Pat and Company, Limited* (1916)
5 *Miss Pat's holidays at Greycroft* (1916)
6 *Miss Pat with the Russian Army* (1916)
7 *Miss Pat at Artemis Lodge* (1916)
8 *Miss Pat's problem* (1917)
9 *Miss Pat in Buenos Ayres* (1917)
10 *Miss Pat's career* (1917)
11 *Miss Pat's great idea* (1917)

Miss Philura trilogy
Kingsley, Florence Morse
1 *Transfiguration of Miss Philura* (1901)
2 *Miss Philura's wedding gown* (1912)
3 *Heart of Philura* (1914)

Miss Phoebe Gray series
Brown, Helen Dawes
see **Anna Lavinia series**

Miss Pickerell series
This sequence has two authors
Macgregor, Ellen
1 *Miss Pickerell goes to Mars* (1951)
Based on a short story, Swept her into space
2 *Miss Pickerell and the geiger counter* (1953)
3 *Miss Pickerell goes undersea* (1953)
4 *Miss Pickerell goes to the Arctic* (1954)
5 *Miss Pickerell on the moon* (1965)
6 *Miss Pickerell goes on a dig* (1966)
7 *Miss Pickerell harvests the sea* (1968)
8 *Miss Pickerell and the weather satellite* (1971)
9 *Miss Pickerell meets Mister H.U.M.* (1974)
10 *Miss Pickerell takes the bull by the horns* (1976)
11 *Miss Pickerell to the earthquake rescue* (1977)
12 *Miss Pickerell and the supertanker* (1978)
13 *Miss Pickerell tackles the energy crisis* (1980)
14 *Miss Pickerell on the trail* (1981)
15 *Miss Pickerell and the blue whales* (1982)
Pantell, Dora
16 *Miss Pickerell and the war of the computers* (1984)
17 *Miss Pickerell and the lost world* (1988)

Miss Pink series
Bennett, Rodney
see **Little Miss Pink series**

Miss Pinkerton series
Rinehart, Mary Roberts
see **Nurse Hilda Adams series**

Miss Price series
Norton, Mary
see **Bed-knob and broomstick series**

Miss Priscilla series
Zabel, Jennifer
Illustrated by Christopher Masters
1 *Miss Priscilla scares 'em stiff* (1981)
2 *Miss Priscilla's secret* (1978)
3 *Miss Priscilla strikes again* (1979)

Miss Pussy series
Ross, Diana
1 *Golden hen, and other stories* (1942)
2 *Wild cherry* (1943)
3 *Enormous apple pie, and other Miss Pussy tales* (1951)
4 *Bran tub* (1954)
5 *Merry-go-round* (1963)

Miss Rosamund series
Rhoades, Nina
1 *Little girl next door* (1902)
2 *Little Miss Rosamund* (1906)

Miss Slimmens series
Victor, Metta Victoria
1 *Miss Slimmens' window, and other papers* (1859)
2 *Miss Slimmens' boarding house* (1882)

Miss Susan Melville series
Smith, Evelyn E
1 *Miss Melville regrets* (1986)
2 *Miss Melville returns* (1987)
3 *Miss Melville's revenge* (1989)
4 *Miss Melville rides a tiger* (1992)
5 *Miss Melville runs for cover* (1994)

Miss Susie Slagle series
Tucker, Augusta
1 *Miss Susie Slagle's* (1939)
2 *Man Miss Susie loved* (1943)

Miss Three Hundred and Eighteen series
Hughes, Rupert
1 *Miss Three Hundred and Eighteen* (1911)
A story in season and out of season

2 *Miss Three Hundred and Eighteen and Mister Thirty Seven* (1912)

Miss Toosie series
Whitaker, Evelyn
1 *Miss Toosie's mission* (1878)
2 *Laddie* (1879)
3 *Lassie* (1901)

Miss Westminster's Fine School for Girls series
Stanley, George Edward
see **Doctor Constance Daniels series**

Miss Winter series
Mackenzie, Kathleen
1 *Thanks to Miss Winter* (1950)
2 *Magpie and Miss Winter* (1952)

Miss Woolfe series
Graham, Winifred
1 *Wolf of the evenings* (1930)
2 *Last laugh* (1930)
3 *Wolf-net* (1931)

Missabella series
Spence, Eleanor
see **Arabella Braithwaite series**

Mission code series
Swift, Bryan
see **Mac Wingate series**

Mission doctor trilogy
Doell, E W
Autobiography
1 *Doctor against witch doctor* (1955)
2 *Hospital in the bush* (1957)
3 *Mission doctor sees the wind of change* (1960)

Mission earth series
Hubbard, Lafayette Ronald
1 *Invaders plan* (1985)
2 *Black genesis, fortress of evil* (1986)
3 *Enemy within* (1986)
4 *Alien affair* (1986)
5 *Fortune of fear* (1986)
6 *Death quest* (1987)
7 *Voyage of vengeance* (1987)
8 *Disaster* (1987)
9 *Villainy victorious* (1987)
10 *Doomed planet* (1987)

Mission impossible series
This sequence has three authors; based on a television series
Tiger, John
1 *Mission impossible* (1967)
Walker, Max
2 *Code name, Judas* (1968)
3 *Code name, Rapier* (1968)
Tiger, John
4 *Code name, Little Ivan* (1969)
Powell, Talmage
5 *Priceless particle* (1969)
6 *Money explosion* (1970)

Mission of Alex Kane series
Preston, John
1 *Sweet dreams* (1984)
2 *Golden years* (1984)
3 *Deadly liars* (1985)
4 *Stolen moments* (1986)
5 *Secret dangers* (1986)
6 *Lethal secrets* (1987)

Mission series
Kurland, Michael
1 *Third force* (1967)
2 *Tank war* (1968)
3 *Police action* (1969)
4 *Sneaky Sam* (1969)
Plague of spies

Mission top secret series
McCarthy, Maureen
1 *Falling star* (1993)
2 *Eagles from the east* (1993)
3 *Mona Lisa mix-up* (1993)
4 *Treasure of Cala Figuera* (1993)
5 *Polish pony puzzle* (1993)
6 *Flight of the Golden Goose* (1993)

Missionary adventure series
Ludwig, Charles Shelton
1 *Man-eaters and Masai spears* (1953)
2 *Man-eaters don't knock* (1953)
3 *Man-eaters don't laugh* (1955)
4 *Man-eater's clauw* (1957)

Missionary mum series
Rosser, Glenda Dawn
Autobiography
1 *Under the shadow of His wings* (1990)
I cried, he comforted
2 *Here am I, but please send my sister!* (1993)
The diary of one very human missionary mum

Missis and Pongo series
Smith, Dodie
see **Pongo and Missis series**

Missouri series
Rayner, William
1 *Bloody affair at Riverside Drive* (1972)
Seth and Belle and Mr Quarles and me
2 *Trail to Bear Paw Mountain* (1974)
3 *Weekend with Captain Jack* (1975)

Mist series
Heimler, Eugene
Autobiography
1 *Night of the mist* (1959)
Life in German concentration camps
2 *Link in the chain* (1962)

Mister and Mrs Bear series
Runyon, Catherine
1 *All wrong, Mrs Bear* (1972)
2 *Too soon, Mister Bear* (1979)

Mister and Mrs Bridge series
Connell, Evan Shelby
see **Bridge series**

Mister and Mrs March series
Howells, William Dean
1 *Their wedding journey* (1871)
Revised edition 1888
2 *Chance acquaintance* (1873)
3 *Hazard of new fortunes* (1889)
4 *Shadow of a dream* (1890)
5 *Open-eyed conspiracy* (1897)
6 *Their silver wedding journey* (1899)
7 *Pair of patient lovers* (1901)

Mister and Mrs North series
Lockridge, Frances
1 *Mister and Mrs North* (1936)
2 *Norths meet murder* (1940)
Mister and Mrs North meet murder
3 *Murder out of turn* (1941)
4 *Pinch of poison* (1941)
5 *Death on the aisle* (1942)
6 *Hanged for a sheep* (1942)
7 *Death takes a bow* (1943)
8 *Killing the goose* (1944)
9 *Payoff for the banker* (1945)
10 *Murder within murder* (1946)
11 *Death of a tall man* (1946)
12 *Untidy murder* (1947)
13 *Murder is served* (1948)
14 *Dishonest murderer* (1949)
15 *Murder in a hurry* (1950)
16 *Murder comes first* (1951)
17 *Dead as a dinosaur* (1952)
18 *Death has a small voice* (1953)
19 *Curtain for a jester* (1953)
20 *Key to death* (1954)
21 *Death of an angel* (1955)
Mister and Mrs North and the poisoned playboy
22 *Voyage into violence* (1956)
23 *Long skeleton* (1958)
24 *Murder is suggested* (1959)
25 *Judge is reversed* (1960)
26 *Murder has its points* (1961)
27 *Ticking clock* (1962)
28 *Murder by the book* (1963)

Mister and Mrs Pig series
Rayner, Mary
1 *Mister and Mrs Pig's evening out* (1976)
2 *Garth Pig and the Ice Cream Lady* (1977)
3 *Mrs Pig's bulk buy* (1981)
4 *Mrs Pig gets cross, and other stories* (1986)

Mister B series
Saro-Wiwa, Ken
1 *Mister B* (1987)
2 *Transistor radio* (1989)
3 *Mister B again* (1989)
4 *Mister B goes to Lagos* (1989)
5 *Mister B is dead* (1991)
6 *Segi finds the radio* (1991)
7 *Shipload of rice* (1991)
8 *Mister B's mattress* (1992)
9 *Mister B goes to the moon* (1992)
10 *Bride for Mister B* (1992)
Companion volume: *Basi and Company*, four television plays, 1989

Mister Bailey-Martin series
White, Percy
1 *Mister Bailey-Martin* (1894)
2 *Mister Bailey-Martin, O.B.E.* (1923)

Mister Barnes series
Gunter, Archibald Clavering
1 *Mister Barnes of New York* (1887)
2 *Mister Barnes, American* (1906)
Shadow of a vendetta

Mister Bear series
Kuratomi, Chizuko
Translated from the Japanese
1 *Remember Mister Bear* (1967)
2 *Mister Bear goes to sea* (1968)
3 *Mister Bear in the air* (1969)
4 *Mister Bear's trumpet* (1970)
5 *Mister Bear and the robbers* (1971)
6 *Mister Bear, station-master* (1972)
7 *Mister Bear and apple jam* (1973)
8 *Mister Bear's Christmas* (1974)
9 *Mister Bear's drawing* (1975)
10 *Mister Bear, babyminder* (1976)
11 *Mister Bear's meal* (1978)
12 *Mister Bear, postman* (1979)
13 *Mister Bear's shadow* (1980)
14 *Mister Bear, baker* (1981)
15 *Mister Bear's winter sleep* (1982)
16 *Mister Bear's journey* (1983)
17 *Mister Bear and the ghost* (1984)
18 *Mister Bear's birthday* (1986)
19 *Mister Bear, shipwrecked* (1986)

Mister Benn series
McKee, David
1 *Mister Benn* (1967)
2 *One two three four five six seven eight nine Benn* (1970)
3 *Big game Benn* (1979)
4 *Big top Benn* (1979)
Companion volume: *Mister Benn annual*, 1972

Mister Bill series
Adams, Georgie
1 *Mister Bill and the runaway sausages* (1983)
2 *Mister Bill and the flying fish* (1985)

Mister Birtley series
Alington, Cyril Augustine
1 *Archdeacons afloat* (1946)
2 *Midnight wireless* (1947)
3 *Gold and gaiters* (1950)

Mister Bits and Pieces series
Lindsay, Frances
1 *Mister Bits and Pieces* (1976)
2 *Bits and Pieces solves a mystery* (1978)
3 *Bits and Pieces and the smugglers* (1984)

Mister Blandings series
Hodgins, Eric
see **Blandings series**

Mister Brent series
Davison, Gilderoy
1 *Mysterious Mister Brent* (1935)
2 *Exit Mister Brent* (1936)

Mister Browser series
Curtis, Philip
1 *Mister Browser and the Brain Sharpeners* (1979)
Invasion of the Brain Sharpeners
2 *Mister Browser meets the Borrowers* (1980)
Invasion from below the earth
3 *Mister Browser and the comet crisis* (1981)
Invasion of the comet people
4 *Revenge of the Brain Sharpeners* (1982)
5 *Beware of the Brain Sharpeners* (1983)
6 *Mister Browser and the mini-meteorites* (1983)
7 *Mister Browser in the space museum* (1985)
8 *Bewitched by the Brain Sharpeners* (1986)
9 *Brain Sharpeners abroad* (1987)
10 *Chaos comes to Chivvy Chase* (1988)
11 *Mister Browser and the space maggots* (1989)
12 *Mister Browser meets the mind shrinkers* (1989)

Mister Bubbus series
Drake, Joan
1 *Mister Bubbus and the apple-green engine* (1971)
2 *Mister Bubbus and the railway smugglers* (1976)

Mister Budge series
Adamson, Gareth
1 *Mister Budge builds a house* (1963)
2 *Mister Budge buys a car* (1965)

Mister Bumblemoose series
Andreus, Hans
1 *Stories of Mister Bumblemoose* (1964)
Original edition entitled *De verhalen van Meester Pompelmoes*
2 *Mister Bumblemoose and the flying boy* (1965)
Original edition entitled *Op avontuur met Meester Pompelmoes*
3 *Mister Bumblemoose and the glad dog* (1965)
Original edition entitled *De nieuwe avonturen van Meester Pompelmoes*
4 *Mister Bumblemoose buys a motor car* (1966)
Original edition entitled *Meester Pompelmoes koopt een auto*
5 *Mister Bumblemoose and the laughing record* (1967)
Original edition entitled *Meester Pompelmoes en de lachplaat*
6 *Mister Bumblemoose and the Mumblepuss* (1968)
Original edition entitled *Meester Pompelmoes en de Mompelpoes*
7 *Mister Bumblemoose and the tiger skin rug* (1969)
Original edition entitled *Meester Pompelmoes en het tijgervel*

Mister Bumblemoose series

8 *Mister Bumblemoose goes to Paris* (1970)
Original edition entitled *Meester Pompelmoes gaat naar Parijs*

Mister Bunting series
Greenwood, Robert
1 *Mister Bunting* (1940)
2 *Mister Bunting at war* (1941)
3 *Mister Bunting in the promised land* (1949)

Mister Cain series
Freeborn, Brian
1 *Good luck, Mister Cain* (1976)
2 *Ten days, Mister Cain?* (1977)

Mister Callaghan series
Cheyney, Peter
see **Slim Callaghan series**

Mister Campion series
Allingham, Margery
see **Albert Campion series**

Mister Chang series
Apple, A E
1 *Mister Chang of Scotland Yard* (1926)
2 *Mister Chang's crime ray* (1928)

Mister Charles Blessington series
Sherwood, John
1 *Disappearance of Doctor Bruderstein* (1949)
Doctor Bruderstein vanishes
2 *Mister Blessington's plot* (1951)
Mister Blessington's imperialist
3 *Ambush for Anatol* (1952)
Murder of a mistress
The second title is an abridged edition
4 *Two died in Singapore* (1954)
5 *Vote against poison* (1956)

Mister Charlie series
Hurd, Edith Thatcher
1 *Mister Charlie's chicken house* (1955)
2 *Mister Charlie's gas station* (1956)
3 *Mister Charlie's camping trip* (1957)
4 *Mister Charlie, the fireman's friend* (1958)
5 *Mister Charlie's pet shop* (1959)
6 *Mister Charlie's farm* (1960)

Mister Chips series
Hilton, James
1 *Goodbye Mister Chips* (1934)
2 *To you, Mister Chips* (1938)

Mister Clackworthy series
Booth, Christopher B
see **Amos Clackworthy series**

Mister Clerihew series
This sequence has two authors
Allen, Herbert Warner
1 *Mister Clerihew, wine merchant* (1933)
Bentley, Edmund Clerihew
2 *Trent's own case* (1936)

Mister Cogg series
Sloan, Carolyn
1 *Mister Cogg and his computer* (1979)
2 *Further inventions of Mister Cogg* (1981)
3 *Mister Cogg and the exploding Easter eggs* (1984)

Mister Colin Andrew Macthrockle Glencannon series
Gilpatric, Guy
1 *Scotch and water* (1931)
2 *Half-seas over* (1932)
3 *Mister Glencannon* (1934)
Numbers 1-3 also published in one volume editions entitled *Glencannon omnibus*, 1938, and First Glencannon omnibus, 1945
4 *Three sheets in the wind* (1936)
5 *Gentleman with the walrus moustache* (1939)
6 *Glencannon afloat* (1941)
Numbers 4-6 also published in one volume entitled *Second Glencannon omnibus*, 1942
7 *Mister Glencannon ignores the war* (1944)
8 *Canny Mister Glencannon* (1948)
Numbers 7 and 8 also published in one volume entitled *Last Glencannon omnibus*, 1953
9 *Glencannon meets Tugboat Annie* (1950)
Serialized as *The Glencannon Tugboat Annie affair*
Selections: *The best of Glencannon*, 1968, *Glencannon, great stories from the Saturday Evening Post*, 1977

Mister Collin series
Heller, Frank
1 *London adventures of Mister Collin* (1924)
Perilous transactions of Mister Collin
Short stories
2 *Mister Collin is ruined* (1925)
3 *Strange adventures of Mister Collin* (1926)
Short stories

Mister Collins and Tony series
This sequence has two authors
Dudley, Christine
1 *Mister Collins and Tony go fishing* (1957)
2 *Mister Collins and Tony visit Heron Wood* (1957)
3 *Mister Collins and Tony go tracking* (1958)
4 *Mister Collins and Tony and the sleeping mouse* (1958)
Elwell, Felicia Rosemary
5 *Mister Collins and Tony by the sea* (1960)
6 *Mister Collins and Tony in London* (1960)

Mister Copplestone series
Avery, Gillian
1 *Warden's niece* (1951)
Maria escapes
2 *Trespassers at Charlcote* (1958)
3 *To tame a sister* (1961)

Mister Craw series
Bell, John Joy
1 *Mister Craw* (1924)
2 *Mister and Mrs Craw* (1926)
3 *Meet Mister Craw* (1929)

Mister Cribbage series
Traill, Peter
1 *Wedding of the jackal* (1943)
2 *Under the plane trees* (1947)
3 *So sits the turtle* (1948)

Mister Crook series
Gilbert, Anthony
see **Arthur Crook series**

Mister Curlon series
Laumer, Keith
1 *Worlds of the Imperium* (1962)
2 *Other side of time* (1965)
3 *Assignment to nowhere* (1968)
Numbers 2 and 3 also published in one volume entitled *Beyond the Imperium*, 1981
4 *Zone yellow* (1990)

Mister Dee series
Cory, Desmond
1 *Stranglehold* (1961)
2 *Name of the game* (1964)

Mister DeHavilland series
Chance, John Newton
1 *Wheels in the forest* (1935)
2 *Maiden possessed* (1937)
3 *Death of an innocent* (1938)
4 *Red knight* (1945)
5 *Knight and the castle* (1946)
6 *Black highway* (1947)
7 *Coven gibbet* (1948)
8 *Brandy pole* (1949)
9 *Night of the full moon* (1950)
10 *Alarm at Black Brake* (1960)
11 *Forest affair* (1963)
12 *Stormlight* (1966)

Mister Dooley series
Dunne, Finley Peter
Satirical colloquies on topics of the day
1 *Mister Dooley in peace and war* (1898)
2 *Mister Dooley in the hearts of his countrymen* (1899)
3 *Mister Dooley's philosophy* (1900)
4 *Mister Dooley's opinions* (1901)
5 *Observations by Mister Dooley* (1902)
6 *Dissertations by Mister Dooley* (1906)
7 *Mister Dooley says* (1910)
8 *Mister Dooley on making a will, and other necessary evils* (1919)

Mister Dormer series
Mottram, Ralph Hale
see **Captain Dormer series**

Mister Durward series
Walpole, Hugh
1 *Dark forest* (1916)
2 *Secret city* (1919)

Mister Dynamite series
Guenter, C H
see **Robert Urban series**

Mister Enderby series
Burgess, Anthony
1 *Inside Mister Enderby* (1963)
Originally published under the pseudonym Joseph Kell
2 *Enderby outside* (1968)
Numbers 1 and 2 also published in one volume entitled *Enderby*, 1968
3 *Clockwork testament* (1974)
Alternative title: Enderby's end; numbers 1-3 also published in one volume entitled *Enderby*, 1982
4 *Enderby's dark lady* (1984)
Alternative title: No end to Enderby

Mister Essington series
Clouston, Joseph Storer
see **Mister Francis Mandell-Essington series**

Mister Fiddle series
Styles, Showell
1 *Mister Fiddle* (1965)
2 *Mister Fiddle's pig* (1966)
3 *Mister Fiddle's band* (1967)
4 *Case for Mister Fiddle* (1969)

Mister Finchley series
Canning, Victor
Short stories
1 *Mister Finchley discovers his England* (1934)
Mister Finchley's holiday
2 *Mister Finchley goes to Paris* (1938)
3 *Mister Finchley takes the road* (1940)

Mister Fitton series
Styles, Showell
see **Lieutenant Michael Fitton series**

Mister Francis Mandell-Essington series
Clouston, Joseph Storer
1 *Lunatic at large* (1899)
2 *Count Bunker* (1906)
3 *Lunatic at large again* (1922)
4 *Lunatic still at large* (1923)
5 *Lunatic in charge* (1926)
6 *Mister Essington in love* (1927)
Lunatic in love
7 *Best story ever* (1932)

Mister Francis Newnes series
Martindale, Cyril Charlie
1 *Jock, Jack and the corporal* (1920)
2 *Mister Francis Newnes* (1921)

Mister Galliano's circus series
Blyton, Enid
1 *Mister Galliano's circus* (1938)
2 *Hurrah for the circus!* (1939)
3 *Circus days again* (1942)
4 *Come to the circus* (1944)

Mister Gilly series
Duncan, William Murdoch
1 *Crime Master* (1963)
2 *Big timer* (1973)
3 *Death and Mister Gilly* (1974)

Mister Gimblet series
Bryce, Charles, *Mrs*
1 *Mrs Vanderstein's jewels* (1914)
2 *Ashiel mystery* (1915)

Mister Glencannon series
Gilpatric, Guy
see **Mister Colin Andrew Macthrockle Glencannon series**

Mister Gosling series
Cunliffe, John Arthur
1 *Mister Gosling and the runaway chair* (1978)
2 *Mister Gosling and the great art robbery* (1979)

Mister Greenleaf series
Yardley, Herbert Osborn
1 *Blonde countess* (1934)
2 *Red sun of Nippon* (1934)

Mister Grimpwinkle series
Drake, Joan
1 *Jiggle woggle bus* (1957)
2 *Mister Grimpwinkle* (1958)
3 *Mister Grimpwinkle's marrow* (1959)
4 *Mister Grimpwinkle, pirate cook* (1960)
5 *Mister Grimpwinkle buys a bus* (1961)
6 *Mister Grimpwinkle's holiday* (1963)
8 *Mister Grimpwinkle's visitor* (1964)

Mister Groode series
Griswold, George
1 *Gambit for Mister Goode* (1952)
2 *Checkmate by the colonel* (1953)
3 *Red pawns* (1954)
4 *Pinned man* (1955)

Mister Guelpa series
Thompson, Vance
1 *Pointed tower* (1922)
2 *Mister Guelpa* (1925)

Mister Gumpy series
Burningham, John
1 *Mister Gumpy's outing* (1970)
2 *Mister Gumpy's motor car* (1973)

Mister Hare series
Holland, Muriel
1 *Mister Hare makes stone soup* (1959)

2 *Mister Hare and the honey bees* (1961)
3 *Mister Hare has a bright idea* (1963)

Mister Harvey Tuke series
Browne, Douglas Gordon
1 *Death wears a mask* (1940)
2 *Too many cousins* (1946)
3 *What beckoning ghost* (1947)
4 *Rustling end* (1948)
5 *Death in perplexity* (1950)
6 *Sergeant Death* (1955)
7 *Death in seven volumes* (1958)

Mister Hero series
Leigh, Roberta
1 *Adventures of Mister Hero* (1961)
2 *Mister Hero and the Raggler children* (1961)

Mister Hodson series
Bidwell, Margaret
1 *Death on the agenda* (1939)
2 *Death and his brother* (1940)

Mister Horatio Green series
Nichols, Beverley
1 *No man's street* (1954)
2 *Moonflower* (1955)
Moonflower murder
3 *Death to slow music* (1956)
4 *Rich die hard* (1957)
5 *Murder by request* (1960)

Mister Hoyland series
Williams, Philip Claxton
1 *Mister Hoyland looks round* (1941)
Short stories
2 *Hoyland intervenes* (1944)
3 *Murder will out* (1945)
4 *Hoyland steps out* (1946)

Mister I series
Keeler, Harry Stephen
see **Mysterious Mister I series**

Mister J G Reeder series
Wallace, Edgar
1 *Room thirteen* (1923)
2 *Mind of Mister J G Reeder* (1925)
Murder book of Mister J G Reeder
3 *Terror Keep* (1927)
4 *Red aces* (1929)
Three novelettes
5 *Guv'nor, and other stories* (1932)
Mister Reeder returns
5.1 *Guv'nor* (1932)
5.2 *Mister J G Reeder returns* (1932)
Mister J G Reeder also appears in *The return of Rapido Clint and Mister J G Reeder*, by John Thomas Edson, 1984

Mister Jasper Shrig of Bow Street series
Farnol, Jeffery
1 *Amateur gentleman* (1913)
2 *Peregrine's progress* (1922)
3 *Loring mystery* (1925)
4 *High adventure* (1926)
5 *Crooked furrow* (1937)
6 *Happy harvest* (1939)
7 *Murder by nail* (1942)
Valley of night
8 *Heritage perilous* (1946)
9 *Ninth earl* (1950)
10 *Waif of the river* (1952)
Also one story featuring Shrig in *A matter of business, and other stories*, 1940

Mister Jellipot series
Fowler, Sydney
1 *Bell Street murders* (1931)
2 *Attic murder* (1936)
3 *Post-mortem evidence* (1936)
4 *Four callers in Razor Street* (1937)
5 *Jordans murder* (1938)
6 *Murder in Bethnal Square* (1938)
7 *Wills of Jane Kanwhistle* (1939)
8 *Dinner in New York* (1943)
9 *Too much for Mister Jellipot* (1945)
10 *With cause enough* (1954)

Mister John Jorrocks series
Surtees, Robert Smith
Originally published anonymously
1 *Jorrocks' jaunts and jollities* (1838)
Mister Jorrocks' jaunts and jollities
Jaunts and jollities of that renowned sporting citizen, Mr John Jorrocks
Revised edition 1869
2 *Handley Cross* (1843)
Alternative title: Mister Jorrocks' hunt; selections: *The Jorrocks' birthday book*, 1897, *Hunts with Jorrocks*, 1908, *The Jorrocks' calendar*, 1910, 1909, *Mister Jorrocks' lectors*, 1910, *Hunting with Jorrocks*, 1956
3 *Hillingdon Hall* (1845)
Alternative title: Cockney squire

Mister Jones series
Matthewman, Phyllis
1 *Thanks to Mister Jones* (1948)
2 *Peter, new girl* (1948)
3 *Mister Jones tips the scales* (1950)
4 *Peter plays sleuth* (1950)

Mister Joseph Jorkens series
Dunsany, Edward John Moreton Drax Plunkett
see **Jorkens series**

Mister Joshua Clunk series
Bailey, Henry Christopher
1 *Garstons* (1930)
Garston murder case
2 *Red castle* (1932)
Red castle mystery
3 *Sullen sky mystery* (1935)
4 *Clunk's claimant* (1937)
Twittering bird mystery
5 *Great game* (1939)
6 *Veron mystery* (1939)
Mister Clunk's text
7 *Little captain* (1941)
Orphan Ann
8 *Dead man's shoes* (1942)
Nobody's vineyard
9 *Slippery Ann* (1944)
Queen of Spades
10 *Wrong man* (1945)
11 *Shrouded death* (1950)

Mister Little series
Fowler, Richard
1 *Mister Little's noisy car* (1985)
2 *Mister Little's noisy boat* (1986)
3 *Mister Little's noisy 123* (1987)
4 *Mister Little's noisy ABC* (1987)
5 *Mister Little's noisy plane* (1988)
6 *Mister Little's noisy truck* (1989)
7 *Mister Little's noisy fire engine* (1990)

Mister Macauley series
Thorndike, Russell
1 *Slype* (1927)
2 *Herod's peal* (1931)
Devil in the belfry

Mister McGee series
Allen, Pamela
1 *Mister McGee* (1989)
2 *Mister McGee goes to sea* (1992)
3 *Mister McGee and the blackberry jam* (1993)

Mister Majeika series
Carpenter, Humphrey
1 *Mister Majeika* (1984)
2 *Mister Majeika and the music teacher* (1986)
3 *Mister Majeika and the haunted hotel* (1987)
4 *Mister Majeika and the dinner lady* (1989)
5 *More T.V. adventures of Mister Majeika* (1990)
6 *Mister Majeika and the school play* (1991)
7 *Mister Majeika and the school book week* (1992)
8 *Mister Majeika and the school inspector* (1993)

Mister Malcolm series
Fairlie, Gerard
1 *Shot in the dark* (1932)
2 *Mister Malcolm presents* (1932)
3 *Men for counters* (1933)

Mister Marx series
White, Terence Hanbury
1 *Earth stopped* (1934)
Alternative title: Mister Marx's sporting tour
2 *Gone to ground* (1935)

Mister Meddle series
Blyton, Enid
1 *Mister Meddle's mischief* (1940)
2 *Mister Meddle's muddles* (1950)
3 *Merry Mister Meddle* (1954)

Mister Merlin series
Rotsler, William
1 *Mister Merlin, episode one* (1981)
2 *Mister Merlin, episode two* (1981)

Mister Merston series
Welcome, John
1 *Mister Merston's money* (1951)
2 *Mister Merston's hounds* (1953)

Mister Midshipman Murdock series
Icenhower, Joseph Bryan
1 *Mister Midshipman Murdock and the Barbary pirates* (1957)
2 *Mister Murdock takes command* (1958)

Mister Montmorency series
Worboise, Emma Jane
1 *Mister Montmorency's money* (1870)
2 *Emilia's inheritance* (1874)

Mister Moses Burdekin series
Campion, Sarah
1 *Mister Burdekin* (1941)
2 *Bonanza* (1942)
3 *Pommy cow* (1944)

Mister Moto series
Marquand, John Phillips
1 *No hero* (1935)
Mister Moto takes a hand
Your turn, Mister Moto
2 *Thank you, Mister Moto* (1936)
3 *Think fast, Mister Moto* (1937)
4 *Mister Moto is so sorry* (1938)
5 *Last laugh, Mister Moto* (1942)
6 *Stopover, Tokyo* (1957)
Last of Mister Moto
Right you are, Mister Moto

Mister Mulliner series
Wodehouse, Pelham Grenville
1 *Meet Mister Mulliner* (1927)
2 *Mister Mulliner speaking* (1929)
3 *Mulliner nights* (1933)
Also five Mulliner stories in *Blandings Castle*, 1935, three in *Young men in spats*, 1936, one in *Lord Emsworth and others*, 1937, one in *Eggs, beans and crumpets*, 1940, one in *A few quick ones*, 1959

Mister Munch series
Owen, Dilys
1 *Milk* (1974)
2 *Cereals* (1974)
3 *Sugar* (1974)
4 *Fish* (1976)
5 *Meat* (1976)
6 *Salt and spices* (1976)

Mister Munday series
Pryor, Bonnie
1 *Mister Munday and the rustlers* (1987)
2 *Mister Munday and the space creatures* (1989)

Mister Muster series
Lobel, Arnold
1 *Zoo for Mister Muster* (1962)
2 *Holiday for Mister Muster* (1963)

Mister Mycroft series
Heard, Henry Fitzgerald
1 *Taste for honey* (1941)
Taste for murder
2 *Reply paid* (1942)
3 *Doppelgangers* (1947)
An episode of the fourth, the psychological revolution, 1997
4 *Notched hairpin* (1949)

Mister Mysterious series
Fleischman, Sid
1 *Mister Mysterious and Company* (1962)
2 *Mister Mysterious's secrets of magic* (1975)

Mister Pendlebury series
Webb, Anthony
1 *Verdict without jury* (1937)
2 *Mister Pendlebury's second case* (1938)
3 *Thank you, Mister Pendlebury* (1939)
4 *Mister Pendlebury makes a catch* (1939)
5 *Mister Pendlebury's hat trick* (1940)
6 *One man saw them die* (1940)
7 *Mister Pendlebury and the Suicide Club* (1941)
8 *Murder in reverse* (1945)
9 *Queer bag of bodies* (1947)

Mister Pengachoosa series
Rush, Caroline
1 *Tales of Mister Pengachoosa* (1965)
2 *Further tales of Mister Pengachoosa* (1967)
One volume edition entitled *Eight tales of Mister Pengachoosa*, 1971

Mister Pennington series
Brandon, John Gordon
see **Arthur Stukeley Pennington series**

Mister Penny series
Ets, Marie Hall
1 *Mister Penny* (1957)
2 *Mister Penny's racehorse* (1958)
3 *Mister Penny's circus* (1961)

Mister Pettigrew series
Clark, Leonard
1 *Mister Pettigrew's harvest festival* (1974)
2 *Mister Pettigrew's train* (1975)
3 *Mister Pettigrew and the bell ringers* (1976)

Mister Pig series
Hoban, Lillian
1 *Mister Pig and Sonny Too* (1977)
2 *Mister Pig and family* (1980)

Mister Pilgrim series
Cory, Desmond
1 *Pilgrim at the gate* (1957)
2 *Pilgrim on the island* (1959)

Mister Pink-Whistle series
Blyton, Enid
1 *Adventures of Mister Pink-Whistle* (1941)
2 *Mister Pink-Whistle interferes* (1950)

3 *Mister Pink-Whistle's party* (1955)
Companion volume: *Mister Pink-Whistle's big book*, 1958

Mister Plum series
Trimby, Elisa
1 *Mister Plum's paradise* (1976)
2 *Mister Plum's oasis* (1981)

Mister Pomander series
Hakansson, Gunvor
see **Pomander series**

Mister Poppleberry series
Lindsay, Hilarie
Illustrated by Gavin Ryan
1 *Mister Poppleberry and the Dog's Own Daily* (1983)
2 *Mister Poppleberry and the milk thieves* (1983)
3 *Mister Poppleberry and Fred the white cockatoo* (1983)
4 *Mister Poppleberry's birthday* (1989)

Mister Popplecorn series
Musson, Margaret
1 *Mister Popplecorn and four little hens* (1946)
2 *Mister Popplecorn, Tasker and Moo* (1948)

Mister Poskitt trilogy
Fletcher, Joseph Smith
1 *Owd Poskitt* (1903)
His opinions on Mr Chamberlain in particular and on English trade in general
2 *Mister Poskitt* (1907)
3 *Mister Poskitt's nightcaps* (1910)
Stories of a Yorkshire farmer

Mister Potter
Foley, Rae
see **Hiram Potter series**

Mister Potter's garden series
Fenwick, Jill
1 *Mister Potter's parsnip* (1978)
2 *Mister Potter and the parrots* (1979)

Mister Pratt series
Lincoln, Joseph Crosby
1 *Mister Pratt* (1906)
2 *Mister Pratt's patients* (1913)

Mister Preed series
Black, Ladbroke
1 *Mister Preed investigates* (1939)
2 *Mister Preed's gangster* (1939)

Mister Prentice trilogy
Traill, Peter
1 *Portly peregrine* (1948)
2 *Wings of to-morrow* (1950)
3 *Rope of sand* (1951)

Mister Puffett series
Catling, Gordon
1 *Mister Puffett's teamboat* (1963)
2 *Mister Puffett's caravan* (1965)

Mister Putter and Tabby series
Rylant, Cynthia
1 *Mister Putter and Tabby pour the tea* (1994)
2 *Mister Putter and Tabby walk the dog* (1994)

Mister Reggie Fortune series
Bailey, Henry Christopher
1 *Call Mister Fortune* (1920)
2 *Mister Fortune's practice* (1923)
3 *Mister Fortune's trials* (1925)
4 *Mister Fortune, please* (1927)
5 *Mister Fortune speaking* (1929)
6 *Mister Fortune explains* (1931)
7 *Case for Mister Fortune* (1932)
8 *Mister Fortune wonders* (1933)
9 *Shadow on the wall* (1934)
10 *Mister Fortune objects* (1935)
11 *Clue for Mister Fortune* (1936)
12 *Black land, white land* (1937)
13 *This is Mister Fortune* (1938)
14 *Great game* (1939)
15 *Mister Fortune here* (1940)
16 *Bishop's crime* (1940)
17 *No murder* (1942)
Apprehensive dog
18 *Mister Fortune finds a pig* (1943)
19 *Cat's whiskers* (1944)
Dead man's effects
20 *Wrong man* (1945)
21 *Life sentence* (1946)
22 *Honour among thieves* (1947)
23 *Saving a rope* (1948)
Save a rope
Selections from this sequence published as *Mister Fortune's casebook*, 1936, *Meet Mister Fortune*, 1942, *The best of Mister Fortune*, 1943

Mister Roberts series
This sequence has two authors; based on screenplays
Heggen, Thomas
1 *Mister Roberts* (1946)
Lederer, William Julius
2 *Ensign O'Toole and me* (1957)

Mister Rose's class series
Ziefert, Harriet
1 *Animal day* (1988)
1 *Pet day* (1987)
2 *Trip day* (1987)
3 *Pond day* (1988)
3 *Worm day* (1987)
4 *Egg-drop day* (1988)
5 *Mystery day* (1988)

Mister Rutherford series
Warner, Susan Bagert
1 *Mister Rutherford's children* (1853)
2 *Christmas stocking* (1853)
Karl Krinken, his Christmas stocking

Mister Sabin series
Oppenheim, Edward Phillips
1 *Mysterious Mister Sabin* (1898)
2 *Yellow crayon* (1903)

Mister Sandyman series
Graham, Neill
1 *Symbol of the Cat* (1948)
2 *Passport murder* (1949)
3 *Murder walks on tiptoe* (1951)
4 *Quest of Mister Sandyman* (1951)
5 *Again, Mister Sandyman* (1952)
6 *Amazing Mister Sandyman* (1952)
7 *Salute Mister Sandyman* (1953)

Mister Saucy Squirrel series
Wyatt, Woodrow Lyle
1 *Exploits of Mister Saucy Squirrel* (1976)
2 *Further exploits of Mister Saucy Squirrel* (1977)

Mister Scotter series
Warriner, Thurman
1 *Method in his murder* (1950)
2 *Ducats in her coffin* (1951)
3 *Death's dateless night* (1952)
4 *Doors of sleep* (1955)
5 *Death's bright angel* (1956)
6 *She died, of course* (1958)
7 *Heavenly bodies* (1960)

Mister Seidman series
Moll, Elick
see **Morris Seidman series**

Mister Slade series
Deeping, Warwick
see **James Slade series**

Mister Springfield series
Sandys, James
1 *Thicker than water* (1941)
2 *Lodestar of death* (1946)
3 *Darkest under the lamp* (1949)
4 *Man who wasn't there* (1953)

Mister T and me series
Graeber, Charlotte Towner
1 *Best bike ever* (1985)
2 *Hand-me-down cup* (1985)
3 *Hard luck mutt* (1985)
4 *My Mister T doll* (1985)
5 *Not-do-great place* (1985)
6 *Phony-Baloney, the counterfeit kid* (1985)
7 *Sidewalk mockers* (1985)
8 *Silver squawk box* (1985)
9 *Somebody kid* (1985)
10 *Tackle block stop* (1985)
11 *I'm so-so, so what?* (1985)
12 *Muscle tussle* (1985)

Mister T B Smith series
Wallace, Edgar
1 *Nine bears* (1910)
Other man
Silinski, master criminal
Cheaters
The second, third and fourth titles are revised editions
2 *Admirable Carfew* (1914)
Short stories
3 *Kate plus ten* (1917)
4 *Secret house* (1917)

Mister Tewkesbury series
Cecil, Henry
1 *Painswick Line* (1951)
2 *Natural causes* (1953)
3 *Much in evidence* (1957)
Long arm
4 *Settled out of court* (1959)

Mister Thake trilogy
Morton, John Bingham
1 *Mister Thake, his life and letters* (1929)
2 *Mister Thake again* (1931)
3 *Mister Thake and the ladies* (1935)

Mister Thimblefinger series
Harris, Joel Chandler
1 *Little Mister Thimblefinger and his queer country* (1894)
What the children saw and heard there
2 *Mister Rabbit at home* (1895)

Mister Toffy's circus series
Ross, Tony
see **Tales from Mister Toffy's circus series**

Mister Tompkins series
Gamow, George
1 *Mister Tompkins in Wonderland* (1939)
2 *Mister Tompkins explores the atom* (1944)
3 *Mister Tompkins learns the facts of life* (1953)
4 *Mister Tompkins inside himself* (1967)
Co-author: Martynas Ycas

Mister Tootleoo series
Darwin, Bernard
1 *Tale of Mister Tootleoo* (1925)
2 *Tootleoo two* (1927)
Numbers 1 and 2 also published in one volume entitled *Mister Tootleoo, one and two*, 1932
3 *Mister Tootleoo and Company* (1935)

Mister Townshend series
Cobban, James Maclaren
1 *Pursued by the law* (1899)
2 *Golden tooth* (1901)

Mister Treadgold series
Williams, Valentine
1 *Dead Man Manor* (1936)
2 *Mister Treadgold cuts in* (1937)
Curiosity of Mister Treadgold
Short stories
3 *Skeleton out of the cupboard* (1946)

Mister Tumpy series
Blyton, Enid
1 *Mister Tumpy and his caravan* (1949)
2 *Mister Tumpy plays a trick on Saucepan* (1952)
3 *Mister Tumpy in the land of wishes* (1953)
4 *Mister Tumpy in the land of boys and girls* (1955)

Mister Twee Deedle series
Gruelle, Johnny
1 *Mister Twee Deedle* (1913)
2 *Mister Twee Deedle's further adventures* (1914)

Mister Twiddle series
Blyton, Enid
1 *Hello Mister Twiddle* (1942)
2 *Don't be silly, Mister Twiddle* (1949)
3 *Well, really, Mister Twiddle!* (1953)

Mister Twink series
Hurt, Freda Mary
1 *Clever Mister Twink* (1953)
2 *Mister Twink takes charge* (1954)
3 *Mister Twink finds out* (1956)
4 *Mister Twink, detective* (1957)
5 *Mister Twink and the kitten mystery* (1958)
6 *Mister Twink and the pirates* (1959)
7 *Mister Twink and the jungle garden* (1960)
8 *Mister Twink finds a family* (1961)
9 *Mister Twink and the cat-thief* (1962)

Mister Twitmeyer series
Moore, Lilian
1 *Terrible Mister Twitmeyer!* (1952)
2 *Mister Twitmeyer and the poodle* (1963)

Mister Verdant Green series
Bede, Cuthbert
1 *Adventures of Mister Verdant Green, an Oxford freshman* (1853)
2 *Further adventures of Mister Verdant Green, an Oxford freshman* (1854)
3 *Mister Verdant Green married and done for* (1857)
Numbers 1-3 also published in one volume entitled *Mister Verdant Green*, 1898
4 *Little Mister Bouncer and his friend, Mister Verdant Green* (1860)
Companion volume: *Tales of college life*, 1856

Mister Verity series
Antony, Peter
1 *Woman in the wardrobe* (1951)
2 *How doth the little crocodile* (1952)
Also published under the authors' real names Anthony and Peter Shaffer

Mister Watson series
Gardiner, Dorothy
1 *Transatlantic ghost* (1933)
2 *Drink for Mister Cherry* (1934)
Mister Watson intervenes

Mister Whisper series
Macrow, Brenda Grace
1 *Amazing Mister Whisper* (1958)
2 *Return of Mister Whisper* (1959)

Mister Wicker series
Dawson, Carley
1 *Mister Wicker's window* (1952)
2 *Sign of the seven seas* (1954)

Mister William Holmes series
Bark, Conrad Voss
1 *Mister Holmes at sea* (1962)
2 *Mister Homes goes to ground* (1963)
3 *Mister Holmes and the fair Armenian* (1964)
4 *Mister Holmesand the love bank* (1964)
5 *Shepherd file* (1966)
6 *See the living crocodiles* (1967)
7 *Second red dragon* (1968)

Mister Winkley series
Rutland, Harriet
1 *Knock, murderer, knock!* (1939)
2 *Bleeding hooks* (1940)
Poison fly murder

Mister Wycherly series
Harker, Lizzie Allen
1 *Miss Esperance and Mycherly* (1908)
2 *Mister Wycherly's wards* (1912)
3 *Montagu Wycherly* (1908)
His first leave
4 *Allegra* (1919)

Mister Yowder series
Rounds, Glen
1 *Mister Yowder and the lion roar capsules* (1976)
2 *Mister Yowder and the steamboat* (1977)
3 *Mister Yowder and the giant bull-snake* (1978)
4 *Mister Yowder, the peripatetic sign painter* (1980)
Three tall tales
5 *Mister Yowder and the train robbers* (1981)
6 *Mister Yowder and the windwagon* (1983)

Misterioso trilogy
Sorrentino, Gilbert
1 *Odd numbers* (1985)
2 *Rose Theatre* (1987)
3 *Misterioso* (1989)

Mistress and wife series
Friedman, Rosemary
1 *Loving mistress* (1983)
2 *Second wife* (1985)

Mistress Margery series
Holt, Emily Sarah
1 *Mistress Margery* (1868)
A tale of the Lollards
2 *Margery's son* (1878)
Alternative title: Until he find it; a fifteenth century tale of the court of Scotland

Mistworld series
Green, Simon
1 *Mistworld* (1992)
2 *Ghostworld* (1993)
3 *Hellworld* (1993)

Misty isle series
Dengler, Sandy
see **Heroes of the misty isle series**

Misty series
Henry, Marguerite
see **Chincoteague series**

Misty Wood series
Joyner, Simon
see **Tales from the Misty Wood series**

Mitch Bushyhead series
Hager, Jean
1 *Grandfather medicine* (1989)
2 *Night walker* (1990)
3 *Ghostland* (1992)

Mitch Miller series
Masters, Edgar Lee
1 *Mitch Miller* (1920)
2 *Skeeters Kirby* (1923)

Mitch series
Sharmat, Marjorie Weinman
see **Rich Mitch series**

Mitch Taylor series
Treat, Lawrence
1 *V as in victim* (1945)
2 *Q as in quicksand* (1947)
Step into quicksand
3 *T as in trapped* (1947)
4 *Big shot* (1951)
5 *Weep for a wanton* (1956)
6 *Lady, drop dead* (1960)
7 *P as in police* (1970)

Mitchell and Ellis series
Lavelle, Sheila
see **Charlie Ellis and Angela Mitchell series**

Mitchell and Markby series
Granger, Ann
see **Meredith Mitchell and Chief Inspector Alan Markby series**

Mitchell computer mystery series
D'Ignazio, Fred
see **Chip Mitchell computer mystery series**

Mitchell family series
Farrell, Anne
1 *Gift-wrapped pony* (1973)
2 *Calf on Shale Hill* (1974)
3 *Eight days at Guara* (1976)

Mitchell Grant series
Thomas, Craig
see **Firefox series**

Mitchell series
Bell, Josephine
see **Inspector Steven Mitchell series**
Bellamann, Henry
see **Kings Row series**
Cooke, Geoffrey Walter
see **Peter Mitchell series**
Harvey, John Barton
see **Scott Mitchell series**
Luckey, William A
see **Blue Mitchell series**
Ottolengui, Rodrigues
see **Robert Leroy Mitchell series**
Wolff, William Almon
see **Lieutenant Charley Mitchell series**
Wrenn, Harold Albert
see **William Mitchell series**

Mitchell Tobin series
Coe, Tucker
1 *Kinds of love, kinds of death* (1966)
2 *Murder among children* (1967)
3 *Wax apple* (1970)
4 *Jade in Aries* (1970)
5 *Don't lie to me* (1972)

Mitchum series
Wrexe, Charles
see **Bill Mitchum series**

Mithgarian series
McKiernan, Dennis L
see **Iron tower trilogy**

Mitya series
Bartos-Hoppner, Barbara
1 *Cossacks* (1959)
Original edition entitled Kosaken gegen Kutschum-Khan
2 *Save the Khan* (1961)
Original edition entitled *Retten den grossen Khan*

Mitzi Mouse series
Bullock, Kathleen
1 *Surprise for Mitzi Mouse* (1989)
2 *Friend for Mitzi Mouse* (1990)

Mitzi series
Williams, Barbara
1 *Mitzi and the terrible tyrannosaurus rex* (1982)
2 *Mitzi's honeymoon with Nana Potts* (1983)
3 *Mitzi and Frederick the Great* (1984)
4 *Mitzi and the elephants* (1985)

Mixed-up Mice series
Kraus, Robert
1 *Mixed-up Mice clean house* (1990)
2 *Mixed-up Mice in the big birthday mix-up* (1990)

Mo Bowdre series
Page, Jake
1 *Stolen gods* (1993)
2 *Deadly caution* (1994)

Moana series
Gorsky, Bernard
1 *Moana* (1956)
Alternative title: Vastness of waters; original edition entitled *Le tour du monde de la chasse sous-marine sur un voilier*
2 *Moana returns* (1957)
Original edition entitled *Expedition Moana*

Mod Squad junior series
Deming, Richard
1 *Assignment, the arranger* (1969)
2 *Assignment, the hideout* (1970)

Mod Squad series
This sequence has two authors; based on a television series
Deming, Richard
1 *Greek god affair* (1968)
2 *Groovy way to die* (1968)
3 *Sock-it-to-em murders* (1969)
4 *Spy-in* (1969)
5 *Hit* (1970)
Johnston, William
6 *Home is where the quick is* (1971)

Mode series
Anthony, Piers
1 *Virtual mode* (1991)
2 *Fractal mode* (1992)
3 *Chaos mode* (1994)

Model-railway men series
Pope, Ray
see **Telford series**

Modern America series
Lindop, Edmund
1 *Dazzling twenties* (1970)
2 *Turbulent thirties* (1970)
Companion volume: An album of the fifties, 1978

Modern comedy series
This sequence has two authors
Galsworthy, John
1 *White monkey* (1924)
2 *Silver spoon* (1926)
3 *Swan song* (1928)
Numbers 1-3 also published in one volume entitled *A modern comedy*, 1929 which also includes two interludes entitled *A silent wooing* and *Passers by*
Dawson, Suleika
4 *Forsytes, the saga continues* (1994)
Announced as *Forsyte reprise*

Modern culture trilogy
Hardison, Osborne Bennett
1 *Entering the maze* (1982)
Identity and change in modern culture
2 *Disappearing through the skylight* (1989)
Culture and technology in the twentieth century
Number three not yet published

Modern East series
Grier, Sydney Carlyon
1 *Advanced guard* (1903)
2 *His Excellency's English governess* (1896)
3 *Peace with honour* (1897)
4 *Warden of the Marshes* (1901)

Modern girl series
Cooke, Kaz
1 *Modern girl's guide to everything* (1987)
2 *Modern girl's guide to safe sex* (1988)
Second edition 1993
Companion volumes: *Modern girl's diary*, 1993 and 1994

Modern Greece trilogy
Vassilikos, Vassilis
Translated from the Greek
1 *Plant* (1961)
2 *Well* (1961)
3 *Angel* (1961)

Modern scene series
Undset, Sigrid
1 *Wild orchid* (1929)
Original edition entitled *Gymnadenia*
2 *Burning bush* (1930)
Original edition entitled *Den broendende busk*

Modern superstars series
Gutman, Bill
1 *Modern baseball superstars* (1973)
2 *Modern football superstars* (1974)
3 *Modern basketball superstars* (1975)
4 *Modern hockey superstars* (1976)
5 *Modern women superstars* (1977)
6 *More modern baseball superstars* (1978)
7 *Modern soccer superstars* (1979)
8 *More modern women superstars* (1979)
9 *Gridiron superstars* (1983)
Companion volumes: *Football superstars of the 70s*, 1975, *Superstars of the sports world*, 1978

Modern youth trilogy
Duke, Madelaine
1 *Sobaka* (1965)
2 *Lethal innocents* (1968)
3 *Because of fear in the night* (1973)

Modesty Blaise comic strip series
O'Donnell, Peter
1 *Black pearl* (1978)
Also includes The Vikings
2 *In the beginning* (1978)
3 *Gabriel set-up* (1984)
4 *Mister Sun* (1985)
5 *Hell-makers* (1986)
6 *Warlords of Phoenix* (1986)
7 *Death of a jester* (1987)
8 *Puppet master* (1987)
9 *Iron god* (1989)

Modesty Blaise series
O'Donnell, Peter
1 *Modesty Blaise* (1965)
2 *Sabre-Tooth* (1966)
3 *I, Lucifer* (1967)
4 *Taste for death* (1969)
5 *Impossible virgin* (1971)
6 *Pieces of Modesty* (1972)
Short stories
7 *Silver mistress* (1973)
8 *Last day in limbo* (1976)
9 *Dragon's claw* (1978)
10 *Xanadu talisman* (1981)
11 *Night of Morningstar* (1982)
12 *Dead man's handle* (1985)

Moffat family series
Estes, Eleanor
1 *Moffats* (1941)
2 *Middle Moffat* (1942)
3 *Rufus M* (1943)

Moffat series
Cousins, Edmund George
see **Captain Moffat series**

Mog and Meg series
Nicoll, Helen
see **Meg and Mog series**

Mog series
Kerr, Judith
1 *Mog, the forgetful cat* (1970)
2 *Mog's Christmas* (1976)
3 *Mog and the baby* (1980)
4 *Mog in the dark* (1983)
5 *Mog and me* (1984)
6 *Mog's family of cats* (1985)
7 *Mog's amazing birthday caper* (1986)

Moh series
Cowdroy, Joan
see **Li Moh series**

Mohawk series
Russo, Richard
1 *Mohawk* (1986)
2 *Risk pool* (1988)

Mohicans of Paris series
Dumas, Alexandre
1 *Mohicans of Paris* (1862)
Original edition entitled *Les Mohicans de Paris*
2 *Salvator* (1863)

Mohune series
Groom, Pelham
see **Peter Mohune series**

Mojo Swoptops series
Black, Cindy
1 *Mojo Swoptops gets all mixed up* (1979)
2 *Mojo Swoptops keeps his cool* (1979)
3 *Mojo Swoptops cleans up* (1979)
4 *Mojo Swoptops goes to the races* (1979)
5 *Mojo Swoptops fights a fire* (1979)
6 *Mojo Swoptops goes to school* (1979)

Mole and Mouse series
Dunbar, Joyce
see **Mouse and Mole series**

Mole and Troll series
Johnston, Tony
1 *Adventures of Mole and Troll* (1972)
2 *Mole and Troll trim the tree* (1974)
3 *Night noises and other Mole and Troll stories* (1977)

Mole series
Quackenbush, Robert Mead
see **Detective Mole series**
Townsend, Sue
see **Adrian Mole series**

Moles series
Horwood, William
see **Duncton chronicles series**

Moleskin Joe series
Macgill, Patrick
Autobiography of a navvy
1 *Children of the dead end* (1914)
2 *Rat-pit* (1915)
3 *Moleskin Joe* (1923)

Molesworth series
Willans, Geoffrey
see **Nigel Molesworth series**

Mollie and the unwisemen series
Bangs, John Kendrick
1 *Mollie and the unwisemen* (1902)
2 *Mollie and the unwisemen abroad* (1910)

Mollie Bourne and Hugh Curtis series
Somers, Paul
see **Hugh Curtis and Mollie Bourne series**

Mollie Fox series
Nelson, Peter N
1 *First to die* (1992)
2 *Double dose* (1992)
3 *Third degree* (1992)
4 *Fourth quarter fix* (1992)
5 *Death threat* (1993)
6 *Six deadly laws* (1993)

Molly and Dolly series
Gordon, Elizabeth
see **Dolly and Molly series**

Molly and Liz series
Macgibbon, Jean
1 *View-finder* (1963)
2 *Liz* (1966)

Molly and Tom series
Costa, Nicoletta
1 *Dressing up* (1984)
2 *Missing cat* (1984)
3 *Friend comes to play* (1984)
4 *Birthday party* (1984)

Molly Brown series
Speed, Nell
1 *Molly Brown's freshman days* (1912)
2 *Molly Brown's sophomore days* (1912)
3 *Molly Brown's junior days* (1912)
4 *Molly Brown's senior days* (1913)
Sequence continued by Emma Sampson using the pseudonym Nell Speed
5 *Molly Brown's post-graduate days* (1914)
6 *Molly Brown's orachard home* (1915)
7 *Molly Brown of Kentucky* (1917)
8 *Molly Brown's college friends* (1921)

Molly Davenant series
Benson, Arthur Christopher
1 *House of Menerdue* (1925)
2 *Canon* (1926)

Molly Fountain series
Wheatley, Dennis
1 *To the devil, a daughter* (1953)
2 *Satanist* (1960)

Molly Hilton series
Lonsdale, Bertha
1 *Molly Hilton, library assistant* (1954)
2 *Molly qualifies as a librarian* (1958)

Molly Millikens series
Cass, Joan Evelyn
1 *Witch of Witchery Wood* (1973)
2 *Witch and the naughty princesses* (1976)
3 *Witches' lost spell book* (1980)
4 *Trouble among the witches* (1983)
5 *Witches' school* (1985)
6 *Witches go on a package holiday* (1986)

Molly Morganthau series
Bonner, Geraldine
1 *Girl at Central* (1915)
2 *Black eagle mystery* (1916)

Molly Owens series
Overholser, Stephen
1 *Molly and the confidence man* (1975)
2 *Molly and the gold baron* (1981)
3 *Molly on the outlaw trail* (1982)
4 *Molly and the Indian agent* (1982)
5 *Molly and the railroad tycoon* (1983)
6 *Molly and the gambler* (1984)

Molly series
Chaikin, Miriam
1 *I should worry, I should care* (1979)
2 *Finders weepers* (1980)
3 *Getting even* (1982)
4 *Lower, higher, you're a liar!* (1984)

Molly series
Chorao, Kay
1 *Molly's Moe* (1976)
2 *Molly's lies* (1979)

Molly series
Storey, Margaret
1 *Smallest doll* (1966)
2 *Smallest bridesmaid* (1966)
3 *Mollyday holiday* (1971)

Molly series
Tripp, Valerie
1 *Meet Molly, an American girl* (1986)
2 *Molly learns a lesson* (1986)
A school story
3 *Molly's surprise* (1986)
A Christmas story
4 *Happy birthday, Molly!* (1987)
A springtime story
5 *Changes for Molly* (1988)
A winter story
6 *Molly saves the day* (1988)
A summer story

Molt brother series
Lichtenberg, Jacqueline
1 *Molt brother* (1982)
2 *City of a million legends* (1985)

Moments in sport series
Weber, Bruce
1 *Weird moments in sport* (1975)
2 *More weird moments in sport* (1983)

Mommies and daddies at work series
Merriam, Frank
1 *Mommies at work* (1961)
2 *Daddies at work* (1989)

Momoko series
Iwasaki, Chihiro
1 *Momoko's lovely day* (1969)
2 *Brother for Momoko* (1970)
3 *Momoko and the pretty bird* (1972)
4 *Momoko's birthday* (1973)

Momolu series
Graham, Lorenz
1 *Tales of Momolu* (1946)
2 *I, Momolu* (1966)

Mona series
Fitzwilliam, Jennifer
1 *Anyway, this particular Sunday* (1975)
2 *How many years was it now?* (1978)

Monach light series
Morrison, J Strang
1 *Wind force seven* (1958)
2 *Monach light* (1961)

Monastery of Mahota series
Burgin, George Brown
1 *Shutters of silence* (1903)
The romance of a Trappist
2 *Within the gates* (1914)

Monckton Milnes series
Pope-Hennessy, James
1 *Years of promise, 1809-1851* (1949)
2 *Flight of youth, 1851-1885* (1951)

Monday series
Bellairs, John
see **Anthony Monday series**

Mondebon trilogy
Davis, Albert Belisle
1 *Leechtime* (1989)
2 *Marquis at bay* (1992)
Number 3 not yet published

Mondo series
De Stefano, Anthony
1 *Mondo* (1975)
2 *Cocaine kill* (1977)
3 *Minute to pray, a second to die* (1977)

Monella trilogy
Aubrey, Frank
1 *Devil-tree of El Dorado* (1897)
A romance of British Guiana
2 *Queen of Atlantis* (1899)
A romance of the Caribbean Sea
3 *King of the dead* (1903)
A weird romance

Money series
James, Elizabeth
1 *Managing your money* (1977)
2 *Understanding money* (1977)
3 *What is money?* (1977)

Mongo series
Chesbro, George Clark
1 *Shadow of a broken man* (1977)
2 *City of whispering stone* (1978)
3 *Affair of sorcerers* (1979)
4 *Beasts of Valhalla* (1985)
5 *Two songs this archangel sings* (1986)
6 *Cold smell of sacred stone* (1988)
7 *Second horseman out of Eden* (1989)
8 *Language of cannibals* (1990)
9 *In the house of secret enemies* (1990)
10 *Fear in yesterday's rings* (1991)

Mongol series
Yan, Vasiliy Grigorievich
Translated from the Russian; set in Asia during the 13th century
1 *Jenghiz-Khan* (1939)
2 *Batu-Khan* (1941)
A third volume has not been translated

Monhegan Island series
Martin, Charles E
1 *Island winter* (1984)
2 *Summer business* (1984)
3 *Island rescue* (1985)
4 *Sam saves the day* (1987)

Monica series
Allum, Nancy
1 *Monica joins the W.R.A.C.* (1961)
2 *Monica takes a commission* (1965)

Monique and Vonnie series
Francis, Dorothy
see **Keepsake series**

Monk series
Craig, Alisa
see **Osbert Monk series**
Moore, Frank Frankfort
see **Raymond Monk series**
Perry, Anne
see **Inspector William Monk series**
Underwood, Michael
see **Richard Monk series**

Monkey Planet series
Boulle, Pierre
see **Planet of the Apes series**

Monmouth series
Morley, Iris
1 *Cry treason* (1940)

2 *We stood for freedom* (1941)
3 *Mighty years* (1943)

Monroe series
Bell, Margaret Elizabeth
see **Florence Monroe series**
Hannah, Barry
see **Harry Monroe series**
Hubel, James Lyon
see **Medico series**
Schultz, James Willard
see **Hugh Monroe series**

Monsieur Blackshirt series
Graeme, David
1 *Monsieur Blackshirt* (1933)
2 *Vengeance of Monsieur Blackshirt* (1934)
3 *Sword of Monsieur Blackshirt* (1936)
4 *Inn of Thirteen Swords* (1938)

Monsieur C Auguste Dupin series
This sequence has two authors
Poe, Edgar Allan
1 *Monsieur Dupin* (1904)
Contains *Murders in the Rue Morgue, The mystery of Marie Roget, The purloined letter, Thou art the man*, the first three of which have been published separately
Harrison, Michael
2 *Exploits of the Chevalier Dupin* (1968)
Murder in the Rue Royale
The first title includes seven stories, the second title includes twelve stories

Monsieur d'Olive series
Chapman, George
Plays
1 *Gentleman usher* (1606)
2 *Monsieur d'Olive* (1606)

Monsieur Dupuy series
Gilbert, Anthony
see **Dupuy series**

Monsieur Lastin series
Hougron, Jean
1 *Reap the whirlwind* (1950)
2 *Blaze of the sun* (1952)

Monsieur Lecoq series
This sequence has two authors
Gaboriau, Emile
1 *Widow Lerouge* (1866)
Lerouge case
Original edition entitled *L'affair Lerouge*
2 *Mystery of Orcival* (1867)
Crime at Orcival
Original edition entitled *Le crime d'Orcival*
3 *Monsieur Lecoq* (1868)
Original edition entitled *Monsieur Lecoq*
3.1 *Detective's dilemma* (1868)
Monsieur Lecoq
Original edition entitled *L'enquete*
3.2 *Detective's triumph* (1868)
Honor of the name
Original edition entitled *L'honneur du nom*
4 *Slaves of Paris* (1868)
Original edition entitled *Les eclaves de Paris*
4.1 *Caught in the net* (1868)
Original edition entitled *Le chantage*
4.2 *Champdoce mystery* (1868)
Original edition entitled *Le secret de Champdoce*
Du Boisgobey, Fortune
5 *Old age of Lecoq, the detective* (1878)
Old age of Monsieur Lecoq
Original edition entitled *La vieillesse de Monsiuer Lecoq*; contains Monsieur Lecoq *in retirement*, and *Monsieur Lecoq in action*
6 *Nabob of Bahour* (1880)

Monsieur Levert series
Toussant-Samat, Jean
1 *Shoes that had walked twice* (1932)
Original edition entitled *L'horrible mort de Miss Gildchrist*
2 *Dead man at the window* (1933)
Original edition entitled *Le mort a la fenetre*

Monsieur Martin series
Carey, Wymond
1 *Monsieur Martin* (1902)
A romance of the great Swedish war
2 *For the White Rose* (1903)

Monsieur Pamplemousse series
Bond, Michael
1 *Monsieur Pamplemousse* (1983)
2 *Monsieur Pamplemousse en fete* (1984)
3 *Monsieur Pamplemousse and the secret mission* (1984)
4 *Monsieur Pamplemousse on the spot* (1986)
5 *Monsieur Pamplemousse takes the cure* (1987)
6 *Monsieur Pamplemousse aloft* (1989)
7 *Monsieur Pamplemousse rests his case* (1990)
8 *Monsieur Pamplemousse stands firm* (1991)
9 *Monsieur Pamplemousse on location* (1992)
10 *Monsieur Pamplemousse takes the train* (1993)

Monsieur Pinaud series
Audemars, Pierre
1 *Two imposters* (1958)
2 *Fire and the clay* (1959)
3 *Turns of time* (1961)
4 *Crown of night* (1962)
5 *Dream and the dead* (1963)
6 *Wings of darkness* (1963)
Street of grass
7 *Fair maids missing* (1964)
8 *Dead with sorrow* (1965)
Woven web
9 *Time of temptation* (1966)
10 *Thorn in the dust* (1967)
11 *Veins of compassion* (1967)
12 *White leaves of death* (1968)
13 *Flame in the mist* (1969)
14 *Host for dying* (1970)
15 *Stolen like magic away* (1971)
16 *Delicate dust of death* (1973)
17 *No tears for the dead* (1974)
18 *Nightmare in rust* (1975)
19 *And one for the dead* (1975)
20 *Healing hands of death* (1977)
21 *Now dead is any man* (1978)
22 *Sad and savage dying* (1978)
23 *Slay me a sinner* (1979)
24 *Gone to her death* (1981)
25 *Bitter path of death* (1982)
26 *Red rust of death* (1983)
27 *Small slain body* (1985)

Monsieur V series
Upward, Allen
1 *Secret history of today* (1904)
Short stories
2 *Phantom torpedo-boats* (1905)
International spy

Monsignor John Blackwood Ryan series
Greeley, Andrew Moran
1 *Virgin and martyr* (1985)
A Christmas legend
2 *Happy are the meek* (1985)
3 *Happy are the clean of heart* (1986)
4 *Rite of spring* (1986)
5 *Happy are those who thirst for justice* (1987)
6 *Saint Valentine's night* (1989)
7 *Happy are the merciful* (1992)
8 *Happy are the peacemakers* (1993)

Monsoon trilogy
Moxon, Oliver
1 *Bitter monsoon* (1955)
Based on the memoirs of a fighter pilot; title page has the author as Stefan James
2 *Last monsoon* (1957)
3 *After the monsoon* (1958)

Monster hunters series
Garden, Nancy
1 *Mystery of the night raiders* (1987)
2 *Mystery of the midnight menace* (1988)
3 *Mystery of the secret marks* (1989)
4 *Mystery of the kidnapped kidnapper* (1994)
5 *Mystery of the watchful witches* (1994)

Monster series
Blance, Ellen
1 *Monster comes to the city* (1973)
2 *Monster looks for a house* (1973)
3 *Monster cleans his house* (1973)
4 *Monster looks for a friend* (1973)
5 *Monster meets Lady Monster* (1973)
6 *Monster and the magic umbrella* (1973)
Numbers 1-6 also published in one volume entitled *The first big Monster book*, 1976
7 *Monster goes to the museum* (1973)
8 *Monster on the bus* (1973)
9 *Monster goes to school* (1973)
Numbers 7-9 also published in one volume entitled *The second big Monster book*, 1976
10 *Monster at school* (1973)
11 *Monster has a party* (1973)
12 *Monster goes to the zoo* (1973)
Numbers 10-12 also published in one volume entitled *The third big Monster book*, 1976
13 *Monster and the mural* (1977)
14 *Lady Monster helps out* (1977)
15 *Lady Monster and the bike ride* (1977)
Numbers 13-15 also published in one volume entitled *The fourth Monster book*, 1978
16 *Monster goes to the circus* (1977)
17 *Monster goes to the hospital* (1977)
18 *Monster goes to the beach* (1977)
Numbers 16-18 also published in one volume entitled *The fifth Monster book*, 1978
19 *Monster gets a job* (1977)
20 *Monster and the surprise cookie* (1977)
21 *Monster goes around the town* (1977)
Numbers 19-21 also published in one volume entitled *The sixth Monster book*, 1978
22 *Monster and the toy sale* (1977)
23 *Monster buys a pet* (1977)
24 *Lady Monster has a plan* (1977)
Numbers 22-24 also published in one volume entitled *The seventh Monster book*, 1978
25 *Monster, Lady Monster and the pet shop* (1987)
26 *Monster flies a kite* (1987)
27 *Monster, Lady Monster and the garden* (1987)
Numbers 25-27 also published in one volume entitled *The eighth Monster book*, 1987
28 *Lady Monster and the great search* (1987)
29 *Monster makes music* (1987)
30 *Monster goes camping* (1987)
Numbers 28-30 also published in one volume entitled *The ninth Monster book*, 1987

Monster series
Bridwell, Norman
1 *How to care for your monster* (1970)
2 *Monster jokes and riddles* (1972)
3 *Monster holidays* (1974)

Monster series
Cole, Joanna
1 *Monster manners* (1986)
2 *Monster movie* (1987)
3 *Monster valentines* (1990)

Monster series
Forsyth, Anne
1 *Monster Monday* (1983)
2 *Wedding-day scramble* (1985)
3 *Mostly magic* (1986)
4 *Monster flower show* (1987)

Monstrous regiment series
Constantine, Storm
1 *Monstrous regiment* (1990)
2 *Aleph* (1991)

Montague Cork series
Hastings, Macdonald
1 *Cork on the water* (1951)
Fish and kill
2 *Cork in bottle* (1953)
3 *Cork and the serpent* (1955)
4 *Cork in the doghouse* (1957)
5 *Cork on telly* (1966)
Cork on location

Montague family series
Lane, Jane
1 *King's critic* (1935)
2 *England for sale* (1943)
3 *Gin and bitters* (1945)
Madame Geneva

Montague Migglewade series
Hale, Edgar
1 *Blue murder* (1948)
2 *Coffee for one* (1949)

Montana Kid series
Evans, Evan
1 *Montana rides!* (1933)
2 *Montana rides again* (1934)
3 *Song of the whip* (1936)

Montana series
Cody, Al
1 *Montana fury* (1967)
2 *Texan from Montana* (1970)
3 *Montana's territory* (1970)
4 *Montana's golden gamble* (1970)
5 *Iron horse country* (1972)
6 *Ranch at Powder River* (1972)
7 *Broken wheels* (1973)
8 *East to Montana* (1974)
9 *Gun song at twilight* (1976)
10 *Tail dies at Sundown* (1976)
11 *Three McMahons* (1977)

Montana trilogy
Fenn, Lionel
see **Kent Montana trilogy**

Montana woman series
Bittner, F Rosanne
1 *Montana woman* (1990)
2 *Embers of the heart* (1990)

Monte Cristo series
Dumas, Alexandre
see **Count of Monte Cristo series**
Robertson, Alexander
see **Irish Monte Cristo series**

Montero and Ludlow series
Nash, Simon
see **Inspector Montero and Adam Ludlow series**

Montero series
Buchanan, Edna
see **Britt Montero series**

Montez series
Ramos, Manuel
see **Luis Montez series**

Montgomerie series
Heaton, Rose Henniker
see **James Montgomerie series**

Montgomery annals series
Deveraux, Jude
1 *Velvet promise* (1981)
2 *Highland velvet* (1982)
3 *Velvet song* (1983)
4 *Velvet angel* (1983)
5 *Temptress* (1986)
6 *Raider* (1987)

Montgomery family series
Sanders, Dorothy Lucie
1 *Six for heaven* (1952)
Also published under the pseudonym Lucy Walker
2 *Shining river* (1954)
Also published under the pseudonym Lucy Walker
3 *Waterfall* (1956)
Also published as *The bell branch*, by Lucy Walker
4 *Ribbons in her hair* (1957)
Also published under the pseudonym Lucy Walker
5 *Pepper Tree Bay* (1959)
Also published under the pseudonym Lucy Walker
6 *Monday in summer* (1961)
Also published under the pseudonym Lucy Walker

Montgomery of Alamein trilogy
Hamilton, Nigel
Biography of Viscount Montgomery of Alamein
1 *Making of a general, 1887-1942* (1981)
2 *Master of the battlefield, 1942-1944* (1983)
3 *Field Marshal, 1944-1976* (1986)
Companion volume: *Monty,the man behind the legend*, 1987

Montgomery series
Mallory, Arthur
see **Doctor Kirke Montgomery series**
Short, Agnes
see **Margaret Montgomery series**
Wetherell, Elizabeth
see **Ellen Montgomery series**

Montigny series
Torgerson, Edwin Dial
see **Pierre Montigny series**

Montmorency series
Worboise, Emma Jane
see **Mister Montmorency series**

Montrose Arbuthnot series
Temple-Ellis, N A
1 *Inconsistent villains* (1929)
2 *Man who was there* (1930)
3 *Quest* (1931)
4 *Dead in no time* (1935)

Montrose series
Tranter, Nigel Godwin
see **James Graham, Earl of Montrose series**

Monty Bodkin series
Wodehouse, Pelham Grenville
1 *Luck of the Bodkins* (1935)
2 *Pearls, girls and Monty Bodkin* (1972)

Monty Mallory series
Hoult, Norah
1 *Father and daughter* (1957)
2 *Husband and wife* (1959)

Monty Nash series
Telfair, Richard
1 *Bloody medallion* (1959)
2 *Corpse that talked* (1959)
3 *Scream bloody murder* (1960)
4 *Good luck, sucker* (1961)
5 *Slavers* (1961)

Monty Python series
Monty Python
Based on television and film scripts
1 *Monty Python's big red book* (1972)
2 *Brand new Monty Python bok* (1973)
Brand new Monty Python paperbok
3 *Monty Python and the Holy Grail* (1977)
4 *Monty Python's life of Brian* (1979)
5 *Monty Python's meaning of life* (1983)
Numbers 1-5 also published in one volume entitled *The complete Monty Python*, 1990; sequence continued by Kim Howard Johnson
Johnson, Kim Howard
6 *First two hundred years of Monty Python* (1989)
7 *And now for something completely trivial* (1991)
Monty Python trivia and quiz book
8 *Life before, and after, Monty Python* (1993)
Solo flights of the Flying Circus

Monty series
West, Colin
1 *Monty, up to his neck in trouble* (1991)
2 *Monty bites back* (1991)
Shape up Monty

Monty trilogy
Hamilton, Nigel
see **Montgomery of Alamein trilogy**

Monty Trio series
Mackinnon, Andrew
1 *Monty Trio's great adventure* (1945)
2 *Further adventures of Monty Trio* (1946)
3 *Monty Trio investigate* (1947)
4 *Monty Trio's fourth adventure* (1948)
5 *Monty Trio explore* (1949)

Monty Woodpig series
B B
1 *Monty Woodpig's caravan* (1957)
2 *Monty Woodpig and his bubblebuzz car* (1958)

Mooch series
Sharmat, Marjorie Weinman
1 *Mooch the messy* (1976)
2 *Mooch the messy meets Prudence the neat* (1979)

Moochers series
Shaw, Jane
1 *Moochers* (1950)
2 *Moochers abroad* (1951)

Moodrow series
Solomita, Stephen
see **Syanley Moodrow series**

Moody series
Chambers, Robert
see **Hank Moody series**
Lester, Edward Castellain
see **Nathaniel Moody series**

Moomin series
Jansson, Tove
1 *Comet in Moominland* (1945)
Original editions entitled *Kometjakten*, and, *Mumintrollet och kometjakt*; revised edition entitled *Kometen komer*
2 *Finn family Moomintroll* (1949)
Happy Moomins
Original edition entitled *Trollkarlens hatt*
3 *Exploits of Moominpappa* (1950)
Original edition entitled *Moominpappans bravader*; revised edition entitled *Muminpappans memoar*
4 *Book about Moomin, Mymble and little My* (1953)
Original edition entitled *Hur gick det sen?*
5 *Moominsummer madness* (1954)
Original edition entitled *Farlig midsommar*
6 *Moominland midwinter* (1957)
Original edition entitled *Trollvinter*
7 *Tales from Moominvalley* (1962)
Original edition entitled *Det osynliga barnet och andra beraettelser*
8 *Moominpappa at sea* (1965)
Original edition entitled *Pappan och havet*
9 *Moominvalley in November* (1970)
Original edition entitled *Sent in November;* numbers 1, 2, 5, 6, 7, 8, 9 also published in one volume entitled *Moomintroll*, 1978
10 *[Skurken i Muminhuset]* (1980)
No English edition
Companion volume: *Who will comfort Toffle*, a picture book originally entitled *Vem ska troesta Knyttet*, 1960\

Moon glows series
VerDorn, Bethea
1 *Moon glows* (1990)
2 *Day breaks* (1992)

Moon magic series
Norton, Andre
see **Krip Vorland series**

Moon series
Burroughs, Edgar Rice
1 *Moon maid* (1962)
2 *Moon men* (1962)
One volume editions entitled *The moon maid*, 1926 and *The moon men*, 1962

Moon series
Darby, Catherine
1 *Whisper down the moon* (1977)
2 *Frost on the moon* (1977)
3 *Flaunting moon* (1977)
4 *Sing me a moon* (1977)
5 *Cobweb across the moon* (1978)
6 *Moon in Pisces* (1978)

Moon series
Deming, Richard
see **Manville Moon series**
Hughes, Shirley
see **Charlie Moon series**
Malloy, Lester
see **Martin Moon series**
Strickland, Brad
see **Jeremy Moon series**

Moon singer series
Norton, Andre
see **Krip Vorland series**

Moon trilogy
Del Rey, Lester
1 *Step to the stars* (1954)
2 *Mission to the moon* (1956)
3 *Moon of mutiny* (1961)

Moonbird series
Higgs, Mike
1 *Moonbird* (1981)
2 *Moonbird to the rescue* (1981)
3 *Moonbird and the unicorn* (1981)
4 *Moonbird and the space pirates* (1981)
5 *Moonbird and the green dog* (1983)
6 *Moonbird and the fire fountain* (1983)
7 *Moonbird and the lonely ghost* (1983)
8 *Moonbird and the fun palace* (1983)

Moon-Calf trilogy
Dell, Floyd
see **Felix Fay trilogy**

Moondance and Mop series
Myers, Walter Dean
see **Mop and Moondance series**

Mooney County trilogy
Reese, John
see **Jesus on horseback trilogy**

Mooney series
Magarshack, David
see **Superintendent Mooney series**
O'Neil, Kerry
see **Jerry Mooney series**

Moonface series
Prime, Honor
1 *Moonface* (1961)
2 *Moonface and Matthew* (1963)
3 *Matthew's car* (1964)

Moonheart series
De Lint, Charles
1 *Moonheart* (1984)
2 *Ascian in rose* (1987)
3 *Westlin wind* (1989)
4 *Ghostwood* (1990)

Moonie and T.G. series
Maschler, Fay
see **T.G. and Moonie series**

Moon's a ballon series
Niven, David
Memoirs
1 *Moon's a balloon* (1971)
2 *Bring on the empty horses* (1975)

Moonshae trilogy
Niles, Douglas
1 *Darkwalker on Moonshae* (1987)
2 *Black wizards* (1988)
3 *Darkwell* (1989)

Moonster series
Johnson, Patricia Irene
Illustrated by Jan Van der Voo
1 *Katie, James and the Moonster* (1986)
2 *Katie, James and the Moonster go to Mars* (1986)

Moor pony series
Pullein-Thompson, Josephine
1 *Star-riders of the moor* (1976)
2 *Fear treks the moor* (1979)
3 *Ride to the rescue* (1979)
4 *Ghost horse on the moor* (1980)
5 *Treasure on the moor* (1981)
6 *Mystery on the moor* (1984)
7 *Suspicion stalks the moor* (1986)

Moore and the Crimefighters series
Hulke, Malcolm
see **Roger Moore and the Crimefighters series**

Moore series
Ingersol, Jared
see **Carl Moore series**
Lacy, Ed
see **Toussaint Moore series**
Logue, John
see **John Moore series**

Moorhouse family trilogy
McCrone, Guy
1 *Wax fruit* (1947)
Red plush
Contains *Antimacassar City*, 1940, also known as *The city, The Philistines, and The Puritans*
2 *Aunt Bel* (1949)
3 *Hayburn family* (1952)

Moorland princess series
Marlitt, E
Original one volume edition entitled *Das Haideprinzesschen*
1 *Princess of the moor* (1872)
2 *Little moorland princess* (1872)

Mop and Moondance series
Myers, Walter Dean
1 *Me, Mop and the Moondance Kid* (1988)
2 *Mop, Moondance and the Nagasaki knights* (1992)

Moppet series
King, Louise Wooster
see **Miss Moppet series**

Moppy series
Asher, Jane
1 *Moppy is angry* (1987)
2 *Moppy is happy* (1987)

Mops, Cubby and Mandy series
Blyton, Enid
see **Mandy, Mops and Cubby series**

Morag series
Hedderwick, Mairi
see **Katie Morag series**

Moraghan family trilogy
Matthews, Clayton
1 *Birthright* (1980)
2 *Disinherited* (1983)
3 *Redeemers* (1984)

Moral Pirates series
Alden, William Livingston
1 *Moral Pirates* (1880)
2 *Cruise of the Ghost* (1882)
3 *Cruise of the Canoe Club* (1883)

Moran series
Beckett, Samuel
see **Jacques Moran series**
Pease, Howard
see **Tod Moran series**
Roeburt, John
see **Jigger Moran series**
Verne, Henry
see **Bob Moran series**

Moran trilogy
Broomall, Robert Walter
see **Jake Moran trilogy**

Morane series
Farrington, Robert
see **Henry Morane series**

Mordant's need series
Donaldson, Stephen Reeder
1 *Mirror of dreams* (1986)
2 *Man rides through* (1987)

Mordecai and Michael Lewis series
Early, Tom
see **Sons of Texas series**

Mordecai Euripides Tremaine series
Duncan, Francis
1 *They'll never find out* (1944)
2 *Murder has a motive* (1947)
3 *Murderer's bluff* (1948)
4 *So pretty a problem* (1950)
5 *In at the death* (1952)
6 *Behold a fair woman* (1954)

More series
Percy, Walker
see **Doctor Tom More series**

Moreau series
Vanardy, Varick
see Crewe series
Wells, Herbert George
see **Doctor Moreau series**

Moreau trilogy
Boissard, Janine
1 *Matter of feeling* (1977)
Original edition entitled *L'esprit de famille*
2 *Christmas lessons* (1979)
Question of happiness
Original edition entitled *Claire et le bonheur*
3 *Time to choose* (1980)
Original edition entitled *Moi, Pauline*

Morel series
Lodi, Maria
see **Charlotte Morel series**

Morelle series
Dudley, Ernest
see **Doctor Morelle series**

Moreno series
Allen, Eric
see **Pepe Moreno series**
Morales, Pablo
see **Pedro Moreno series**

Moreton Shade series
Boyle, Denis
see **Commander Moreton Shade series**

Moretti series
Sherburne, James
see **Paddy Moretti series**

Morey, Wade and Arcot series
Campbell, John Wood
see **Arcot, Morey and Wade series**

Morgaine series
Cherryh, Carolyn Janice
see **Chronicles of Morgaine series**

Morgan and Brandon series
Rogers, Rosemary
see **Ginny Brandon and Steve Morgan series**

Morgan and Ramon series
McQuay, Mike
see **Ramon and Morgan series**

Morgan Bay series
Rambeau, John
1 *Mystery of Morgan Castle* (1962)
2 *Mystery of the marble angel* (1962)
3 *Mystery of the midnight visitor* (1962)
4 *Mystery of the missing Marlin* (1962)
5 *Mystery of the musical ghost* (1965)
6 *Mystery of Monks' Island* (1965)
7 *Mystery of the marauder's gold* (1965)
8 *Mystery of the Myrmidon's journey* (1965)

Morgan Butler series
Anthony, David
1 *Midnight lady and the mourning man* (1969)
2 *Blood on the harvest moon* (1972)
3 *Long hard cure* (1979)

Morgan family series
This sequence has two authors
Morgan, Bill
1 *Behind the steam* (1973)
Life on the Great Western Railway in Wales
Meyrick, Bette
2 *Behind the light* (1975)
Based on the lives of the author's grandfather and father on the Great Western Railway

Morgan Farraday series
Caraker, Mary
see **Seven worlds series**

Morgan Kane series
Masterson, Louis
Translated from the Norwegian
1 *Without mercy* (1971)
Original edition entitled *Unten nade*
2 *Claw of the dragon* (1971)
Original edition entitled *I dragons klar*
3 *Star and the gun* (1971)
4 *Backed by the law* (1971)
5 *Ranger's honour* (1971)
Original edition entitled *En rangers aera*
6 *Marshal and murderer* (1971)
Original edition entitled *Mordor og marshal*
7 *Pistolero* (1971)
8 *Monster from Yuma* (1971)
Original edition entitled *Udyret fra Yuma*
9 *Devil's marshal* (1971)
Original edition entitled *Djevelons marshal*
10 *Gunman's inheritance* (1971)
Original edition entitled *Revolvermanns arv*
11 *Revenge* (1971)
Original edition entitled *Heon*
12 *Storm over Sonora* (1971)
13 *Law of the jungle* (1972)
Original edition entitled *Jungelens lov*
14 *No tears for Morgan Kane* (1972)
Original edition entitled *Ingen tara for Morgan Kane*
15 *Between life and death* (1972)
16 *Return to action* (1972)
17 *Rio Grande* (1972)
18 *Bravado* (1973)
19 *Gallows express* (1973)
20 *Ransom* (1973)
Original edition entitled *De piskede*
21 *Killing for the law* (1973)
Original edition entitled *Drep for loven*
22 *Buthcher from Guerro* (1973)
23 *Duel in Tombstone* (1974)
24 *To the death, Senor Kane* (1974)
25 *Hell below zero* (1974)
Original edition entitled *Helvete under null*
26 *Coyoteros!* (1974)
27 *Day of death* (1975)
Original edition entitled *De dodes dag*
28 *Bloody earth* (1975)
29 *New Orleans gamble* (1975)
Original edition entitled *Hoy spill i New Orleans*
30 *Apache breakout* (1975)
31 *Blood and gold* (1975)
Original edition entitled *Blod og gull*
32 *Southern showdown* (1976)
Original edition entitled *Kanes likenann*
33 *Bell of death* (1976)
34 *Demon of Nicaragua* (1976)
35 *Revenging angels* (1977)
36 *Vulture of Sierra Madre* (1977)
37 *Dead man's shadow* (1978)
38 *El Gringo* (1978)
39 *El Gringo's revenge* (1978)
40 *Harden than steel* (1979)
41 *Killer Kane* (1979)

Morgan series
Chilton, Charles
see **Jet Morgan series**
Coburn, Andrew
see **James Morgan series**

Morgan series
Cosgrove, Stephen Edward
1 *Morgan and me* (1975)
2 *Morgan and yew* (1982)
3 *Morgan mine* (1982)
4 *Morgan morning* (1982)
5 *Misty Morgan* (1987)

Morgan series
Farrar, Stewart
see **Inspector Elwyn Morgan series**
Fox, Gardner Francis
see Alan Morgan series
Giff, Patricia Reilly
see **Ronald Morgan series**
Haig-Brown, Roderic Langmere
see **Don Morgan series**
Hendryx, James Beardsley
see **Connie Morgan series**
Johnson, Duff
see **Gutsy Morgan series**
Lambert, Rosa
see **Glyn Morgan series**
Ledd, Paul
see **Shelter Morgan series**
Llewellyn, Richard
see **Huw Morgan series**
Owen, Richard
see **David Morgan series**
Wambaugh, Joseph
see **Bumper Morgan series**

Morgan Swift find your fate series
This sequence has three authors
Hughes, Sara
1 *Morgan Swift and the kidnapped goddess* (1985)
2 *Morgan Swift and the treasure of Crocodile Key* (1985)
Lesley, Martine
3 *Morgan Swift and the trail of the jaguar* (1985)
Saunders, Susan
4 *Morgan Swift and the lake of diamonds* (1986)

Morgan the Welshman series
Smollett, Tobias
Originally published anonymously
1 *Adventures of Roderick Random* (1745)
Roderick Random
2 *History and adventures of Peregrine Pickle* (1751)
Adventures of Peregrine Pickle
Peregrine Pickle

Morgan trilogy
Jeffers, Harry Paul
1 *Morgan* (1989)
2 *Blood on the Nueces* (1989)
3 *Texas bounty* (1989)

Morgan Wayne series
Blood, Matthew
1 *Avenger* (1952)
2 *Death is a lovely dame* (1954)

Morgana series
DeBolt, Adriana
see **Myra Morgana series**

Morgana Shee series
Smith, Lisa J
see **Solstice series**

Morganthau series
Bonner, Geraldine
see **Molly Morganthau series**

Morgette series
Boyer, Glenn G
see **Dolf Morgette series**

Morgon trilogy
McKillip, Patricia Anne
1 *Riddle-master of Hed* (1976)
2 *Heir of sea and fire* (1978)

Morgon trilogy

3 *Harpist in the wind* (1979)
One volume editions entitled *Riddle of stars*, 1979 and *The chronicles of Morgon, Prince of Hed*, 1981

Moriarty series
Gardner, John Edmund
see **Professor Moriarty series**

Morigu series
Perry, Mark Christopher
1 *Desecration* (1986)
2 *Dead* (1990)

Morini series
Conroy, Al
see **Johnny Morini series**

Moriston series
Laine, Annabel
see **Earl of Moriston series**

Mork and Mindy series
This sequence has two authors
Church, Ralph
1 *Mork and Mindy* (1979)
Wagner, Robin S
2 *Incredible shrinking Mork* (1980)
Companion volume: *Mork and Mindy*, by Paul D Schneck, 1980

Morland family series
Harrod-Eagles, Cynthia
1 *Founding* (1980)
2 *Dark rose* (1981)
3 *Princeling* (1981)
Distant wood
4 *Oak apple* (1982)
Crystal crown
5 *Black pearl* (1982)
6 *Long shadow* (1983)
7 *Chevalier* (1984)
8 *Maiden* (1985)
9 *Flood-tide* (1986)
10 *Tangled thread* (1987)
11 *Emperor* (1988)
12 *Victory* (1989)
13 *Regency* (1990)
14 *Campaigners* (1991)
15 *Reckoning* (1992)
16 *Devil's horse* (1993)

Mormon series
Grey, Zane
1 *Riders of the purple sage* (1912)
2 *Rainbow Trail* (1915)
This sequence is followed by the **Lassiter series**, by Jack Slade and the **Lassiter series**, by Loren Zane Grey

Mormon series
Kennelly, Ardyth
1 *Peacable kingdom* (1949)
2 *Up home* (1955)

Morning glory series
Motley, Mary
1 *Devils in waiting* (1959)
2 *Morning glory* (1961)
3 *Home to Numidia* (1964)

Morning Star series
Haggard, Henry Rider
1 *Morning Star* (1910)
2 *Queen of the dawn* (1925)
3 *Way of the spirit* (1906)

Mornington, Hawkins and Malins series
Dix, Maurice Buxton
see **Tommy Malins, Anthony Mornington and George Hawkins series**

Moro series
Eigl, Kurt
1 *Moro, the little black donkey* (1962)
Original edition entitled *Alle branchen Moro*
2 *Moro at the holiday camp* (1966)
Original edition entitled *Moro auf dem Campingplatz*

Morocco Jones series
Baynes, Jack
1 *Meet Morocco Jones* (1957)
2 *Meet Morocco Jones in the case of the Syndicate Hoods* (1957)
3 *Hand of the Mafia* (1958)
4 *Peeping Tom murders* (1958)
5 *Morocco Jones in the case of the golden angel* (1959)

Moroni Traveler series
Irvine, Robert Ralstone
1 *Baptism for the dead* (1988)
2 *Angel's share* (1989)
3 *Gone to glory* (1990)
4 *Called home* (1991)
5 *Spoken word* (1992)
6 *Great reminder* (1993)
7 *Hosanna shout* (1994)

Morph series
Dowling, Patrick
see **Amazing adventures of Morph series**

Morphodite trilogy
Foster, Michael Anthony
1 *Morphodite* (1981)
2 *Transformer* (1983)
3 *Preserver* (1985)

Morpurgo trilogy
Garner, William
see **John Morpurgo trilogy**

Morris and Scott series
Gulick, Bill
see **Junior Trail Blazers series**

Morris Bird III series
Robertson, Don
1 *Greatest thing since sliced bread* (1965)
2 *Sum and total of now* (1966)
3 *Greatest thing that almost happened* (1970)

Morris Brookside series
Sharmat, Marjorie Weinman
1 *Morris Brookside, a dog* (1973)
2 *Morris Brookside is missing* (1974)

Morris Seidman series
Moll, Elick
1 *Seidman and Son* (1958)
2 *Mister Seidman and the geisha* (1962)
3 *Perilous spring of Morris Seidman* (1972)

Morris series
Stevenson, Dorothy Emily
see **Sarah Morris series**

Morris Zapp and Philip Sparrow series
Lodge, David
see **Rummidge University series**

Morrison series
Fisher, Norman
see **Nigel Morrison series**
Shallit, Joseph
see **Dan Morrison series**
Whittingham, Richard
see **Joe Morrison series**

Morrison Sharpe series
Cargill, Leslie
1 *Death goes by bus* (1936)
2 *Heads you lose* (1938)

Morrison-Burke series
Porter, Joyce
see **Honourable Constance Ethel Morrison-Burke series**

Morro series
Buranelli, Prosper
see **Nick Morro series**

Morrow series
Hoover, Helen Mary
1 *Children of Morrow* (1973)
2 *Treasures of Morrow* (1976)

Morse series
Dexter, Colin
see **Inspector Morse series**

Mort series
Tinniswood, Peter
see **Uncle Mort series**

Mortdecai series
Bonfiglioli, Kyril
see **Charlie Mortdecai series**

Morten trilogy
Leeson, Robert
see **Matthew Morten trilogy**

Mortenhoe series
Compton, David Guy
see **Katherine Mortenhoe series**

Morthoe series
Wilson, Philip Whitwell
see **Sir Julian Morthoe series**

Mortimer and Arabel series
Aiken, Joan
see **Arabel and Mortimer series**

Mortimer Blunt series
Cranston, Maurice
see **Inspector Mortimer Blunt series**

Mortimer Sark series
Hawk, John
1 *Lone Lodge mystery* (1926)
2 *Serpent-headed stick* (1926)
3 *Mid-ocean tragedy* (1927)
4 *Titanic Hotel mystery* (1928)
5 *Murder of a mystery writer* (1929)

Morton and Bragg series
Harrison, Ray
see **Sergeant Joseph Bragg and Constable James Morton series**

Morton series
Bosworth, Frank
see **Earl Morton series**
Chalmers, Amy D V
see **Madge Morton series**
Govan, Margaret
see **Betty Morton series**
Smith, Ford
see **Dark Knight series**
Smith, Mabell Shipple Clarke
see **Ethel Morton series**
Thomas, Gordon
see **David Morton series**

Mortorio series
Burgess, Eric
1 *Mortorio* (1973)
2 *Mortorio two* (1975)

Mortymers series
Cordell, Alexander
1 *This proud and savage land* (1987)
2 *Rape of the fair country* (1959)
3 *Hosts of Rebecca* (1960)
Robe of honor
4 *Song of the earth* (1969)
5 *Fire people* (1972)
6 *This sweet and bitter earth* (1977)
7 *Land of my fathers* (1983)
8 *Beloved exile* (1993)

Morville family series
This sequence has two authors
Yonge, Charlotte Mary
1 *Heir of Redclyffe* (1853)
Hicks Beach, Susan Emily
2 *Amabel and Mary Verena* (1944)

Mosby series
Hogan, Ray
see **John Mosby series**

Moseby series
Sharp, Alan
see **John Moseby series**

Moseley series
Willeford, Charles
see **Hoke Moseley series**

Moses Burdekin series
Campion, Sarah
see **Mister Moses Burdekin series**

Moses series
Golding, Louis
1 *In the steps of Moses the lawgiver* (1937)
2 *In the steps of Moses the conqueror* (1938)

Moses series
Kimenye, Barbara
1 *Moses* (1967)
2 *Moses and Mildred* (1967)
3 *Moses and the kidnappers* (1968)
4 *Moses in trouble* (1968)
5 *Moses in a muddle* (1970)
6 *Moses and the ghost* (1971)
7 *Moses on the move* (1972)
8 *Moses and the pen pal* (1973)
9 *Moses, the camper* (1973)

Moses trilogy
Selvon, Samuel
see **Lonely Londoner trilogy**

Moses Waters series
Armstrong, William
1 *Sounder* (1969)
2 *Sourland* (1971)

Moses Wine series
Simon, Roger Lichtenberg
1 *Big fix* (1973)
2 *Wild turkey* (1974)
3 *Peking duck* (1979)
4 *California roll* (1985)
5 *Straight man* (1986)
6 *Raising the dead* (1988)
7 *Dead meet* (1988)

Mosley series
Greenwood, John
see **Inspector Mosley series**
Mosley, Nicholas
see **Sir Oswald Mosley series**

Moss and Stroheim trilogy
Bantock, Nick
see **Griffin Moss and Sabine Stroheim trilogy**

Moss and Thane series
Knox, Bill
see **Inspector Colin Thane and Phil Moss series**

Moss Magill series
Gardiner, Dorothy
see **Sheriff Moss Magill series**

Moss series
Jackson, Jesse
see **Charley Moss series**
Thompson, Steven Lynn
see **Max Moss series**

Mossdyche series
Porteous, Crichton
1 *Farm by the lake* (1942)
2 *Snow* (1944)
3 *Earth remains* (1945)

Most wanted trilogy
Palmer, Diana
1 *Case of the mesmerizing boss* (1992)
2 *Case of the confirmed bachelor* (1992)
3 *Case of the missing secretary* (1992)

Mostly ghosts series
Anderson, Mary
1 *Haunting of Hillcrest* (1987)
2 *Leipzig vampire* (1987)
3 *Terror under the tent* (1987)
4 *Three spirits of Vandermeer Manor* (1987)

Mostyn series
Hebden, Mark
see **Colonel Mostyn series**

Moth Graham series
Richardson, Jean
1 *First step* (1979)
2 *Dancer in the wings* (1981)
3 *One foot on the ground* (1982)

Mother and Father Goose series
Baum, Lyman Frank
1 *Mother Goose in prose* (1897)
2 *Father Goose, his book* (1899)
Companion volume: *The songs of Father Goose for the home, school and nursery*, 1900

Mother animal series
Hurd, Edith Thatcher
1 *Mother beaver* (1971)
2 *Mother deer* (1972)
3 *Mother whale* (1973)
4 *Mother owl* (1974)
5 *Mother kangaroo* (1976)
6 *Mother chimpanzee* (1978)

Mother earth trilogy
Harrison, Sue
1 *Mother earth, father sky* (1990)
2 *My sister the moon* (1992)
3 *Brother wind* (1994)

Mother Goose library series
Spier, Peter
1 *London Bridge is falling down* (1967)
2 *To market, to market!* (1967)
3 *Hurrah, we're outward bound* (1968)
4 *And so my garden grows* (1969)

Mother Goose series
Hopkins, Lee Bennett
1 *Animals from Mother Goose* (1989)
2 *People from Mother Goose* (1989)

Mother Paul series
Wright, June
1 *Reservation for murder* (1958)
2 *Faculty of murder* (1961)
3 *Make-up for murder* (1966)

Mother sea series
Karlsson, Elis
Reminiscences of sea voyages
1 *Mother sea* (1964)
2 *Pully-haul* (1966)
3 *Cruising off Mozambique* (1969)

Mother series
Daniel, Rebecca
1 *Mother, I'm mad* (1988)
2 *Mother, I'm embarrassed* (1988)
3 *Mother, I'm worried* (1988)
4 *Mother, I'm disappointed* (1988)

Mother West Wind series
Burgess, Thornton Waldo
see **Old Mother West Wind series**

Mother's and Father's Day series
Sharmat, Marjorie Weinman
1 *Hooray for Mother's Day* (1986)
2 *Hooray for Father's Day* (1987)

Mother's bedtime tales series
Paull, Minnie E
1 *Mother's bedtime tales* (1893)
2 *More bedtime tales* (1894)

Moth-kin series
Tapp, Kathy Kennedy
1 *Moth-kin magic* (1983)
2 *Flight of the moth-kin* (1987)
3 *Scorpio ghosts and the Black Hole Gang* (1987)
Ghostmobile

Motion picture chums series
Appleton, Victor
1 *Motion picture chums' first venture* (1913)
Alternative title: Opening a photo playhouse in Fairlands
2 *Motion picture chums at Seaside Park* (1913)
Alternative title: The rival photo theatres of the boardwalk
3 *Motion picture chums on Broadway* (1914)
Alternative title: The mystery of the missing cash box
4 *Motion picture chums' outdoor exhibition* (1914)
Alternative title: The film that solved a mystery
5 *Motion picture chums' new idea* (1914)
Alternative title: The first educational photo playhouse
6 *Motion picture chums at the fair* (1915)
Alternative title: The greatest film ever exhibited
7 *Motion picture chums' war spectacle* (1916)
Alternative title: The film that won the prize

Motion picture comrades series
Barnes, Elmer Tracey
1 *Motion picture comnrades' great venture* (1917)
Alternative title: On the road with the big round-top
2 *Motion picture comrades in African jungles* (1917)
Motion picture comrades through African jungles
Alternative title: The camera boys in wild animal land
3 *Motion picture comrades along the Orinoco* (1917)
Alternative title: Facing perils in the tropics
4 *Motion picture comrades aboard a submarine* (1917)
Alternative title: Searching for treasure under the sea
5 *Motion picture comrades producing a success* (1917)
Alternative title: Featuring a sensation

Motives series
Burke, Kenneth
1 *Grammar of motives* (1945)
2 *Rhetoric of motives* (1950)
One volume edition 1962

Moto series
Marquand, John Phillips
see **Mister Moto series**

Motor boat boys series
Arundel, Louis
1 *Motor boat boys' Mississippi cruise* (1912)
Alternative title: The dash for Dixie
2 *Motor boat boys on the Saint Lawrence* (1912)
Alternative title: Solving the mystery of the thousand islands
3 *Motor boat boys on the Great Lakes* (1912)
Alternative title: Exploring the mystic isle of Mackinac
4 *Motor boat boys down the coast* (1912)
Alternative title: Through storm and stress to Florida
5 *Motor boat boys among the Florida Keys* (1913)
Alternative title: The struggle for the leadership
6 *Motor boat boys' river chase* (1914)
Alternative title: Six chums afloat and ashore
7 *Motor boat boys down the Danube* (1915)
Alternative title: Four chums abroad

Motor Boat Club series
Hancock, Harrie Irving
1 *Motor Boat Club of the Kennebec* (1909)
Alternative title: The secret of Smugler's Island
2 *Motor Boat Club at Nantucket* (1909)
Alternative title: The mystery of the Dunstan heir
3 *Motor Boat Club off Long Island* (1909)
Alternative title: A daring marine game at racing speed
4 *Motor Boat Club and the wireless* (1909)
Alternative title: The dot, dash and dare cruise
5 *Motor Boat Club in Florida* (1909)
Alternative title: Laying the ghost of Alligator Swamp
6 *Motor Boat Club at the Golden Gate* (1909)
Alternative title: A thrilling capture in the great fog
7 *Motor Boat Club on the Great Lakes* (1912)
Alternative title: The Flying Dutchman of the Big Fresh Water

Motor boys series
Young, Clarence
1 *Motor boys* (1906)
Alternative title: Chums through thick and thin
2 *Motor boys overland* (1906)
Alternative title: A long trip for fun and fortune
3 *Motor boys in Mexico* (1906)
Alternative title: The secret of the buried city
4 *Motor boys across the plains* (1907)
Alternative title: The hermit of Lost Lake
5 *Motor boys afloat* (1908)
Alternative title: The stirring cruise of the Dartaway
6 *Motor boys on the Atlantic* (1908)
Alternative title: The mystery of the lighthouse
7 *Motor boys in strange waters* (1909)
Alternative title: Lost in a floating forest
8 *Motor boys on the Pacific* (1909)
Alternative title: The young derelict hunters
9 *Motor boys in the clouds* (1910)
Alternative title: A trip for fame and fortune
10 *Motor boys over the Rockies* (1911)
Alternative title: A mystery of the air
11 *Motor boys over the ocean* (1911)
Alternative title: A marvelous rescue in mid-air
12 *Motor boys on the wing* (1912)
Alternative title: Seeking the airship treasure
13 *Motor boys after a fortune* (1912)
Alternative title: The hut on Snake Island
14 *Motor boys on the border* (1913)
Alternative title: Sixty nuggets of gold
15 *Motor boys under the sea* (1914)
Alternative title: From airship to submarine
16 *Motor boys on road and river* (1915)
Alternative title: Racing to save a life
17 *Ned, Bob and Jerry at Boxwood Hall* (1916)
Motor boys at Boxwood Hall
Alternative titles: The motor boys as freshmen, and Ned, Bob and Jerry as freshmen
18 *Ned, Bob and Jerry on a ranch* (1917)
Motor boys on a ranch
Alternative titles: The motor boys among the cowboys, and Ned, Bob and Jerry among the cowboys
19 *Ned, Bob and Jerry in the army* (1918)
Motor boys in the army
Alternative titles: The motor boys as volunteers, and Ned, Bob and Jerry as volunteers
20 *Ned, Bob and Jerry on the firing line* (1919)
Motor boys on the firing line
Alternative titles: The motor boys fighting for Uncle Sam, and Ned, Bob and Jerry fighting for Uncle Sam
21 *Ned, Bob and Jerry bound for home* (1920)
Motor boys bound for home
Alternative titles: The motor boys on the wrecked troopship, and Ned, Bob and Jerry on the wrecked troopship
22 *Motor boys on Thunder Mountain* (1924)
Alternative title: The treasure chest of Blue Rock

Motor City series
Gilden, Mel
see **Zoomers of Motor City series**

Motor cycle chums series
Payson, Howard
1 *Motor cycle chums around the world* (1912)
2 *Motor cycle chums of the Northwest Patrol* (1912)
3 *Motor cycle chums in the goldfields* (1912)
4 *Motor cycle chums' whirlwind tour* (1913)
5 *Motor cycle chums south of the Equator* (1914)
6 *Motor cycle chums through historic America* (1915)

Motor girls series
Penrose, Margaret
1 *Motor girls* (1910)
Alternative title: A mystery of the road
2 *Motor girls on a tour* (1910)
Alternative title: Keeping a strange promise
3 *Motor girls at Lookout Beach* (1911)
Alternative title: In quest of the runaways
4 *Motor girls through New England* (1911)
Alternative title: Held by the gypsies
5 *Motor girls on Cedar Lake* (1912)
Alternative title: The hermit of Fern Island
6 *Motor girls on the coast* (1913)

Alternative title: The waif from the sea
7 *Motor girls on Crystal Bay* (1914)
Alternative title: The secret of the red oar
8 *Motor girls on waters blue* (1915)
Alternative title: The strange cruise of the Tartar
9 *Motor girls at Camp Surprise* (1916)
Alternative title: The cave in the mountains
10 *Motor girls in the mountains* (1917)
Alternative title: The gysy girl's secret

Motor Maids series
Stokes, Katherine
1 *Motor Maids' school days* (1911)
2 *Motor Maids by palm and pine* (1911)
3 *Motor Maids by rose, shamrock and thistle* (1912)
4 *Motor Maids in fair Japan* (1913)
5 *Motor Maids at Sunrise Camp* (1914)
6 *Motor Maids across the continent* (1917)

Motor pirate series
Paternoster, George Sidney
see **Randolph Mannering series**

Motor power series
Grayson, Donald
see **Bob Steele series**

Motor rally series
Gibson, Michael
1 *Ian Munro's Monte Carlo Rally* (1958)
2 *Le Mans 24 hours* (1962)

Motor Rangers series
West, Marvin
1 *Motor Rangers' lost mine* (1911)
2 *Motor Rangers through the Sierras* (1911)
3 *Motor Rangers on Blue Water* (1911)
4 *Motor Rangers' cloud cruiser* (1912)
5 *Motor Rangers' wireless station* (1913)
6 *Motor Rangers touring for the trophy* (1914)

Motorcycle chums series
Lincoln, Andrew Carey
1 *Motorcycle chums in New England* (1912)
Alternative title: The Mount Holyoke adventure
2 *Motorcycle chums in the land of the sky* (1912)
Alternative title: Thrilling adventures on the Carolina border
3 *Motorcycle chums on the Santa Fe Trail* (1912)
Alternative title: Key to the Indian treasure cave
4 *Motorcycle chums in Yellowstone Park* (1913)
Alternative title: Lending a helping hand
5 *Motorcycle chums in the Adirondacks* (1913)
Alternative title: The search for the lost pacemaker
6 *Motorcycle chums stormbound* (1914)
Alternative title: The strange adventures of a road chase

Motoring series
This sequence has two authors
Williamson, Charles Norris
1 *Lightning conductor* (1902)
Strange adventures of a motor car
2 *Princess passes* (1904)
A romance of a motor car
3 *My friend the chauffeur* (1905)
4 *Botor chaperon* (1907)
Chauffeur and the chaperon
Chaperon
5 *Motor maid* (1909)
6 *Lightning conductress* (1916)
Lightning conductress discovers America
Williamson, Alice Muriel
7 *Lightning conductor comes back* (1933)

Mott and Yeadings series
Curzon, Clare
see **Superintendent Mike Yeardings and Sergeant Angus Mott series**

Mott series
Jones, Jennifer
see **Daisy Jane Mott series**

Motto excelsior series
De Vere, V C
1 *Motto excelsior, book I* (1988)
2 *Motto excelsior, books II-IV* (1988)
3 *Motto excelsior, book V-VIII* (1990)
Also published in two volumes as *The idea*, under the pseudonym Roger Mason

Mottram Park series
Chaney, Jill
1 *Mottram Park* (1971)
2 *Return to Mottram Park* (1974)

Mould series
Wheeler, David
see **Edwin Mould series**

Mount Cedar series
Tannenforst, Ursula
1 *Thistles of Mount Cedar* (1905)
2 *Herines of a schoolroom* (1907)

Mount Royal trilogy
Corbett, Elizabeth
1 *Langworthy family* (1937)
2 *Light of other days* (1938)
3 *Far down* (1939)

Mountain bike series
Van de Plas, Rob
1 *Mountain bike book* (1990)
Choosing, riding and maintaining the off-road bicycle
2 *Mountain bike magic* (1991)
3 *Mountain bike maintenance* (1991)
4 *Mountain bike technology* (1992)

Mountain born series
Yates, Elizabeth
1 *Mountain born* (1943)
2 *Place for Peter* (1953)

Mountain Boys series
Boone, Silas K
see **Phil Bradley series**

Mountain girl series
Fox, Genevieve May
1 *Mountain girl* (1932)
2 *Mountain girl comes home* (1934)
3 *Lona of Hollybush Creek* (1935)

Mountain Jack Pike series
Meek, Joseph
1 *Mountain Jack Pike* (1989)
2 *Rocky Mountain kill* (1989)
3 *Comanche come-on* (1989)
4 *Crow bait* (1989)
5 *Green River hunt* (1990)
6 *Saint Louis fire* (1990)
7 *Russian bear* (1991)
8 *Hard for justice* (1991)
9 *Big gun bushwhacker* (1991)
10 *Bullseye blood* (1992)
11 *Deep canyon kill* (1992)
12 *Fire in the hole* (1993)
13 *High country climax* (1993)
14 *Trail heat* (1993)
15 *Rough trade* (1993)

Mountain journey series
Paton, Alan
Autobiography
1 *Towards the mountain* (1980)
2 *Journey continued* (1988)

Mountain majesty series
Killdeer, John
1 *Wild country* (1992)
2 *Untamed* (1992)
3 *Wilderness rendezvous* (1992)
4 *Blood kin* (1993)
5 *Passage west* (1994)
6 *Far horizon* (1994)

Mountain Man Preacher series
Johnstone, William Wallace
1 *First mountain man* (1991)
2 *Blood on the divide* (1992)

Mountain Man series
Johnstone, William Wallace
1 *Last Mountain Man* (1986)
2 *Return of the Mountain Man* (1986)
3 *Trail of the Mountain Man* (1987)
4 *Revenge of the mountain Man* (1988)
5 *Journey of the Mountain Man* (1989)
6 *Law of the Mountain Man* (1989)
7 *Mountain Man's vengeance* (1989)
8 *War of the Mountain Man* (1990)
9 *Code of the Mountain Man* (1991)
10 *Pursuit of the Mountain Man* (1991)
11 *First Mountain Man* (1991)
12 *Courage of the Mountain Man* (1992)
13 *Blood of the Mountain Man* (1992)
14 *Fury of the Mountain Man* (1993)

Mountain pony series
Larom, Henry V
1 *Mountain pony* (1946)
A story of the Wyoming Rockies
2 *Mountain pony and the pinto colt* (1947)
3 *Mountain pony and the rodeo mystery* (1949)
4 *Mountain pony and the elkhorn mystery* (1950)

Mountain series
Firbank, Thomas
1 *I bought a mountain* (1940)
2 *Bride to the mountain* (1940)
3 *I bought a star* (1951)
4 *Country of memorable honour* (1953)
5 *Log hut* (1954)

Mountain sheriff series
Murray, Earl
see **Dan Sleyter series**

Mountain standard time trilogy
Horgan, Paul
1 *Main line west* (1936)
2 *Far from Cibola* (1938)
3 *Common heart* (1942)
One volume edition entitled *Mountain standard time*, 1962

Mountain west series
Skurzynski, Gloria
1 *Lost in the Devil's Desert* (1982)
2 *Trapped in the Slickrock* (1984)
3 *Caught in the moving mountains* (1984)
4 *Swept in the wave of terror* (1985)

Mountaineering series
Brown, Eric
Reminiscences of a mountaineer
1 *Knave of clubs* (1961)
2 *Out of the bag* (1964)

Mountaineering series
Moffat, Gwen
1 *Space below my feet* (1961)
2 *On my home ground* (1968)
3 *Survival count* (1972)

Mountaineering trilogy
Unsworth, Walter
1 *Matterhorn Man* (1965)
2 *Tiger in the snow* (1967)
The life and adventures of A F Mummery
3 *Because it is there* (1968)
Famous mountaineers, 1840-1940

Mounties series
Dicks, Terrance
1 *Great march west* (1976)
2 *Massacre in the hills* (1976)
3 *War drums of the Blackfoot* (1976)

Mountjoy series
Montague, Jeanne
see **Loves of Carola Mountjoy series**

Mountry series
Hammand, Norman Bentley
see **Sir Nicholas Mountry series**

Moura series
Coffman, Virginia
1 *Moura* (1959)
2 *Devil's vicar* (1966)
Vicar of Moura
The second title is a revised edition
3 *Dark gondola* (1968)
Dark beyond Moura
4 *Vampyre of Moura* (1970)

Mournful Martin series
Sanders, Charles Wesley
1 *Desert ranch* (1932)
2 *Lone fighter* (1933)
Long fighter
Mournful Martin makes his bow
3 *Storm riders* (1935)
4 *Roaring Rocketts* (1935)
5 *Mournful rides again* (1936)
6 *Mournful Martin* (1937)

Mouse and Elephant series
Grambling, Lois Goodwin
see **Elephant and Mouse series**

Mouse and Mole series
Dunbar, Joyce
1 *Mouse and Mole* (1993)
2 *Mouse and Mole have a party* (1993)

Mouse series
Althea
see **Jeremy Mouse series**

Mouse series
Arnosky, Jim
1 *Mouse numbers and letters* (1982)
2 *Mouse writing* (1983)

Mouse series
Brook, Judy
see **Tim Mouse series**

Mouse series
Cartlidge, Michelle
1 *Mouse's diary* (1981)
2 *Mousework* (1982)
Welcome to Mouseville!
3 *Baby mice* (1991)
4 *Mouse's Christmas house* (1991)
5 *Mouse wedding* (1993)

Mouse series
Claret, Maria
see **Melissa Mouse series**
Cleary, Beverly
see **Ralph S Mouse series**
Creche, Sylvia
see **Mervyn Mouse series**

Mouse series
Crump, Fred H
1 *Mouse opera house* (1992)
2 *Mouse ballet* (1993)

Mouse series
Gibson, Gloria
see **Rachel Payne series**

Mouse series
Jennens, Frank
1 *Brown Mouse* (1947)
2 *Brown and white* (1947)

Mouse series
Kraus, Robert
see **Pinchpenny Mouse series**

Mouse series
Lobel, Arnold
1 *Mouse tales* (1972)
2 *Mouse soup* (1977)

Mouse series
Wibberley, Leonard
see **Grand Fenwick series**

Mouse Woman series
Harris, Christie
American Indian legends
1 *Mouse Woman and the vanished princesses* (1976)
2 *Mouse Woman and the mischief-makers* (1977)
3 *Mouse Woman and the muddleheads* (1979)

Mousehaven Manor series
Kwitz, Mary DeBall
1 *Shadow over Mousehaven Manor* (1989)
2 *Bell tolls at Mousehaven Manor* (1991)

Mousehole trilogy
Stolz, Mary
see **Tales at the Mousehole trilogy**

Mousekin series
Miller, Edna
1 *Mousekin's golden house* (1964)
2 *Mousekin finds a friend* (1967)
3 *Mousekin's family* (1969)
4 *Mousekin's ABC's* (1972)
5 *Mousekin's Christmas Eve* (1972)
6 *Mousekin's woodland birthday* (1974)
7 *Mousekin takes a trip* (1976)
8 *Mousekin's woodland sleepers* (1977)
9 *Mousekin's close call* (1978)
10 *Mousekin's birth* (1982)
11 *Mousekin's fables* (1982)
12 *Mousekin's mystery* (1983)
13 *Mousekin's Thanksgiving* (1985)
14 *Mousekin's Easter basket* (1986)
15 *Mousekin's frosty friend* (1990)
16 *Mousekin's lost woodland* (1992)

Mousie series
Golden Gorse
1 *Moorland Mousie* (1929)
2 *Older Mousie* (1932)

Mousme series
Holland, Clive
1 *My Japanese wife* (1895)
A Japanese idyll
2 *Mousme* (1901)

Movie boys series
Appleton, Victor
1 *Movie boys on call* (1926)
Alternative title: Filming the perils of a great city; based on *The moving picture boys*, 1913
2 *Movie boys in the Wild West* (1926)
Alternative title: Stirring days among the cowboys and Indians; based on *The moving picture boys in the West*, 1913
3 *Movie boys and the wreckers* (1926)
Alternative title: Facing the perils of the deep; based on *The moving picture boys on the coast*, 1913
4 *Movie boys in the jungle* (1926)
Alternative title: Lively times among the wild beasts; based on *The moving picture boys in the jungle*, 1913
5 *Movie boys in earthquake land* (1926)
Alternative title: Filming pictures amid strange perils; based on *The moving picture boys in earthquake land*, 1913
6 *Movie boys and the flood* (1926)
Alternative title: Perilous days on the mighty Mississippi; based on *The moving picture boys and the flood*, 1914
7 *Movie boys in peril* (1926)
Alternative title: Strenuous days along the Panama Canal; based on *The moving picture boys at Panama*, 1915
8 *Movie boys under the sea* (1926)
Alternative title: The treasure of the lost ship; based on *The moving picture boys under the sea*, 1916
9 *Movie boys under fire* (1926)
Alternative title: The search for the stolen film; based on *The moving picture boys on the war front*, 1918
10 *Movie boys under Uncle Sam* (1926)
Alternative title: Taking pictures for the army; based on *The moving picture boys on French battlefields*, 1919
11 *Movie boys' first showhouse* (1926)
Alternative title: Fighting for a foothold in Fairlands; based on *The motion picture* chums' first venture, 1913
12 *Movie boys at Seaside Park* (1926)
Alternative title: The rival photo houses of the boardwalk; based on The motion *picture chums at Seaside Park*, 1913
13 *Movie boys on Broadway* (1926)
Alternative title: The mystery of the missing cash box; based on *The motion picture chums on Broadway*, 1914
14 *Movie boys' outdoor exhibition* (1927)
Alternative title: The film that solved a mystery; based on *The motion picture chums' outdoor exhibition*, 1914
15 *Movie boys' new idea* (1927)
Alternative title: Getting the best of their enemies; based on *The motion picture chums' new idea*, 1914
16 *Movie boys at the big fair* (1927)
Alternative title: The greatest filme ever exhibited; based on *The motion picture chums at the fair*, 1915
17 *Movie boys' war spectacle* (1927)
Alternative title: The film that won the prize; based on *The motion picture chums' war spectacle*, 1916

Moving picture boys series
Appleton, Victor
1 *Moving picture boys* (1913)
Alternative title: The perils of a great city depicted
2 *Moving picture boys in the West* (1913)
Alternative title: Taking scenes among the cowboys and Indians
3 *Moving picture boys on the coast* (1913)
Alternative title: Showing the perils of the deep
4 *Moving picture boys in the jungle* (1913)
Alternative title: Stirring times among the wild animals
5 *Moving picture boys in earthquake land* (1913)
Alternative title: Working amid many perils
6 *Moving picture boys and the flood* (1914)
Alternative title: Perilous days on the Mississippi
7 *Moving picture boys at Panama* (1915)
Alternative title: Stirring adventures along the great canal
8 *Moving picture boys under the sea* (1916)
Alternative title: The treasure of the lost ship
9 *Moving picture boys on the war front* (1918)
Alternative title: The hunt for the stolen army film
10 *Moving picture boys on French battlefields* (1919)
Alternative title: Taking pictures for the U.S. Army
11 *Moving picture boys' first showhouse* (1921)
Alternative title: Opening up for business in Fairlands; based on *The motion picture chums' first venture*, 1913
12 *Moving picture boys at Seaside Park* (1921)
Alternative title: The rival photo theatres of the Boardwalk; based on *The motion picture chums at Seaside Park*, 1913
13 *Moving picture boys on Broadway* (1921)
Alternative title: The mystery of the missing cash box; based on *The motion picture chums on Broadway*, 1914
14 *Motion picture boys' outdoor exhibition* (1922)
Alternative title: The film that solved a mystery; based on *The motion picture chums' outdoor exhibition*, 1914
15 *Moving picture boys' new idea* (1922)
Based on *The motion picture chums' new idea*, 1914

Moving picture girls series
Hope, Laura Lee
House pseudonym
1 *Moving picture girls* (1914)
Alternative title: First appearances in photo dramas
2 *Moving picture girls at Oak Farm* (1914)
Alternative title: Queer happenings while taking rural plays
3 *Moving picture girls snowbound* (1914)
Alternative title: The proof on the film
4 *Moving picture girls under the palms* (1914)
Alternative title: Lost in the wilds of Florida
5 *Moving picture girls at Rocky Ranch* (1914)
Alternative title: Great days among the cowboys
6 *Moving picture girls at sea* (1915)
Alternative title: A pictured shipwreck that became real
7 *Moving picture girls in war plays* (1916)
Alternative title: The sham battles at Oak Farm

Mozart series
Weiss, David
see **Wolfgang Amadeus Mozart series**

Mr
see **Mister**

Mrs Aleshine and Mrs Lecks series
Stockton, Frank Richard
see **Mrs Lecks and Mrs Aleshine series**

Mrs and Mister Bear series
Runyon, Catherine
see **Mister and Mrs Bear series**

Mrs Appleyard series
Kent, Louise Andrews
see **Appleyard family series**

Mrs Arbuckle series
Smyth, Gwenda
1 *Pet for Mrs Arbuckle* (1981)
2 *Hobby for Mrs Arbuckle* (1989)

Mrs Ariadne Oliver series
Christie, Agatha
1 *Mister Parker Pyne, detective* (1934)
2 *Cards on the table* (1936)
3 *Mrs McGinty's dead* (1952)
Blood will tell
4 *Dead man's folly* (1956)
5 *Pale horse* (1961)
6 *Third girl* (1966)
7 *Hallowe'en party* (1969)
8 *Elephants can remember* (1972)

Mrs 'Arris series
Poultney, Clifford Blake
1 *Mrs 'Arris* (1923)
2 *More Mrs 'Arris* (1924)
3 *Mrs 'Arris again* (1926)
4 *Still Mrs 'Arris* (1930)
5 *Mrs 'Arris carries on* (1934)

Mrs Babcary series
Goldsmith, John
1 *Mrs Babcary goes to sea* (1980)
2 *Mrs Babcary goes to town* (1980)
3 *Mrs Babcary goes west* (1980)
4 *Mrs Babcary's treat* (1981)
5 *Mrs Babcary's steam car* (1981)
6 *Mrs Babcary's driving machine* (1981)

Mrs Beatrice Bradley series
Mitchell, Gladys
see **Dame Beatrice Bradley series**

Mrs Brown series
Roberts, Cecil
1 *Victoria four-thirty* (1937)
2 *They wanted to live* (1939)

Mrs Butler series
Ahlberg, Allan
Illustrated by Fritz Wegner
Verses
1 *Please Mrs Butler* (1983)
2 *Heard it in the playground* (1989)

Mrs Caroline series
Franzero, Carlo Maria
1 *House of Mrs Caroline* (1942)
2 *Appassionata* (1945)

Mrs Caywood Weston series
Thomas, Eugene
1 *Death rides the dragon* (1932)
2 *Dancing dead* (1933)

Mrs Coverlet series
Nash, Mary
1 *While Mrs Coverlet was away* (1958)
2 *Mrs Coverlet's magicians* (1961)
3 *Mrs Coverlet's detectives* (1965)

Mrs Craggs series
Keating, Henry Reymond Fitzwalter
1 *Death of a fat god* (1963)
2 *Mrs Craggs, crimes cleaned up* (1985)
Short stories

Mrs Dalloway series
Woolf, Virginia
1 *Voyage out* (1915)
2 *Mrs Dalloway* (1925)
3 *Mrs Dalloway's party* (1973)

Mrs Dorothy Cope series
Charlesworth, Maria Louisa
Recollections of service
1 *Old looking-glass* (1878)
2 *Broken looking-glass* (1880)

Mrs Easter series
Drummond, Violet Hilda
1 *Mrs Easter's parasol* (1944)
2 *Mrs Easter and the storks* (1957)
3 *Mrs Easter and the Golden Bounder* (1970)
4 *Mrs Easter's Christmas flight* (1972)

Mrs Edwina Charles series
Warner, Mignon
1 *Nice way to die* (1976)
Medium for murder
2 *Tarot murders* (1978)
3 *Death in time* (1982)
4 *Girl who was clairvoyant* (1982)
5 *Devil's knell* (1983)
6 *Illusion* (1984)
7 *Speak no evil* (1985)

Mrs Elizabeth Warrender series
Cole, George Douglas Howard
1 *Mrs Warrender's profession* (1938)
Short stories
2 *Knife in the dark* (1941)
Also stories featuring Mrs Warrender in *A lesson in crime, and other stories,* 1933

Mrs Emily Pollifax series
Gilman, Dorothy
1 *Unexpected Mrs Pollifax* (1967)
Mrs Pollifax, spy
2 *Amazing Mrs Pollifax* (1970)
3 *Elusive Mrs Pollifax* (1971)
4 *Palm for Mrs Pollifax* (1973)
5 *Mrs Pollifax on safari* (1977)
6 *Mrs Pollifax on the China station* (1983)
7 *Mrs Pollifax and the Hong Kong Buddha* (1985)
8 *Mrs Pollifax and the Golden Triangle* (1988)
9 *Mrs Pollifax and the whirling dervish* (1990)
10 *Mrs Pollifax and the second thief* (1993)
11 *Mrs Pollifax pursued* (1995)

Mrs Eugenia Potter series
Rich, Virginia
1 *Cooking school murders* (1982)
2 *Baked bean supper murders* (1983)
3 *Nantucket diet murders* (1985)
Companion volume: *The twenty seven ingredient chili con carne murders,* by Nancy Pickard, 1993

Mrs Feeley series
Lasswell, Mary
1 *Suds in your eye* (1942)
2 *High time* (1947)
3 *One on the house* (1949)
4 *Wait for the wagon* (1951)
5 *Tooner schooner* (1953)
6 *Let's go for broke* (1962)

Mrs Fluster series
Ogden, Angela
1 *Mrs Fluster and family* (1947)
2 *Mrs Fluster's circus* (1948)

Mrs Gaddy series
Gage, Wilson
1 *Mrs Gaddy and the ghost* (1979)
2 *Crow and Mrs Gaddy* (1984)
3 *Mrs Gaddy and the fast-growing vine* (1985)

Mrs Green series
Rynd, Evelyne Elise
1 *Mrs Green* (1901)
2 *Mrs Green again* (1915)

Mrs Grundy series
James, Charles Thomas Clement
1 *Holy wedlock* (1891)
A story of things as they are
2 *Mrs Grundy at home* (1893)

Mrs Harris series
Gallico, Paul
1 *Flowers for Mrs Harris* (1958)
Mrs 'Arris goes to Paris
2 *Mrs Harris goes to New York* (1960)
Mrs 'Arris goes to New York
3 *Mrs Harris, M.P.* (1965)
Mrs 'Arris goes to Parliament
4 *Mrs Harris goes to Moscow* (1974)
Mrs 'Arris goes to Moscow

Mrs Jim series
Conrad, Stephen
1 *Second Mrs Jim* (1904)
2 *Mrs Jim and Mrs Jimmie* (1905)
Certain town experiences of the second Mrs Jim as related to Jimmie's wife

Mrs Lancelot series
Hewlett, Maurice
1 *Mrs Lancelot* (1912)
A comedy of assumptions
2 *Bendish* (1913)
A study in prodigality

Mrs Lecks and Mrs Aleshine series
Stockton, Frank Richard
1 *Casting away of Mrs Lecks and Mrs Aleshine* (1886)
2 *Dusantes* (1888)

Mrs McNab series
Lockhart, John Gilbert
1 *Mrs McNab and the pirates* (1952)
2 *Mrs McNab goes west* (1954)

Mrs Margaret Maitland series
Oliphant, Margaret Oliphant Wilson
1 *Passages in the life of Mrs Margaret Maitland* (1849)
2 *Lilliesleaf* (1856)

Mrs May series
Le Breton, Thomas
Stories of the life of a charlady
1 *Mrs May* (1921)
2 *Confessions of Mrs May* (1922)
3 *Mister and Mrs May* (1923)
4 *Mrs May's lectures* (1925)
5 *Adventures of Mrs May* (1925)
Co-author: Harold Bevir
6 *Mrs May's latest* (1929)

Mrs Meigs series
Corbett, Elizabeth
1 *She was Carrie Eaton* (1938)
2 *Young Mrs Meigs* (1931)
3 *Nice long evening* (1933)
4 *Mrs Meigs and Mister Cunningham* (1936)
Numbers 2-4 also published as *Our Mrs Meigs,* 1954
5 *Mister and Mrs Meigs* (1940)
6 *Excuse me, Mrs Meigs* (1943)

Mrs Melita Pargeter series
Brett, Simon
1 *Nice class of corpse* (1986)
2 *Mrs, presumed dead* (1988)
3 *Mrs Pargeter's package* (1991)
4 *Mrs Pargeter's pound of flesh* (1993)

Mrs Millie Mack trilogy
Hunt, Nan
Illustrated by Craig Smith
1 *Whistle up the chimney* (1981)
2 *Rain, hail or shine* (1984)
3 *Whistle stop party* (1990)

Mrs Ming and Jeremiah series
Jennings, Sharon
see **Jeremiah and Mrs Ming series**

Mrs Murgatroyd series
Farrington, Liz
1 *And Peter said goodbye* (1993)
Co-author: Jennifer C Weil
2 *Painting the fire* (1993)
Co-author: Jonathan Sherwood
3 *Rainbow fields* (1993)
Co-author: Susan G Rubin
4 *Nightmares in the mist* (1994)
Co-author: Leslie McGuire

Mrs Murphy series
Brown, Rita Mae
1 *Wish you were here* (1990)
2 *Rest in pieces* (1992)
3 *Murder at Monticello* (1994)
Alternative title: Old sins

Mrs Norris and Jasper Tully series
Davis, Dorothy Salisbury
1 *Death of an old sinner* (1957)
2 *Gentleman called* (1958)
3 *Old sinners never die* (1959)
Also one story featuring Mrs Norris in *Tales for a stormy night,* 1984

Mrs Palmyra Pym series
Morland, Nigel
1 *Moon murders* (1935)
2 *Phantom gunman* (1935)
3 *Street of the leopard* (1936)
4 *Clue of the bricklayer's aunt* (1936)
5 *Clue in the mirror* (1937)
6 *Case without a clue* (1938)
7 *Rope for the hanging* (1938)
8 *Knife for the killer* (1939)
Murder at Radio City
9 *Gun for a god* (1940)
Murder in Wardour Street
10 *Clue of the careless hangman* (1940)
Careless hangman
11 *Corpse on the flying trapeze* (1941)
12 *Coffin for the body* (1943)
13 *Mrs Pym of Scotland Yard* (1946)
Short stories
14 *Dressed to kill* (1947)
15 *Lady had a gun* (1951)
16 *Call him early for the murder* (1952)
17 *Sing a song of cyanide* (1953)
18 *Look in any doorway* (1957)
19 *Death and the golden boy* (1958)
20 *Bullet for Midas* (1958)
21 *So quiet a death* (1960)
22 *Concrete maze* (1960)
23 *Dear, dead girls* (1961)
Omnibus volume: *Mrs Pym, and other stories,* 1976

Mrs Paschal series
Hayward, William Stephens
see **Lady detective series**

Mrs Pepperpot series
Proysen, Alf
1 *Little old Mrs Pepperpot, and other stories* (1958)
Original edition entitled *Kjarlighet pa rundpinne*
2 *Mrs Pepperpot again, and other stories* (1959)
Original edition entitled *Teskjekjerringa, pa nye eventyr*
3 *Mrs Pepperpot to the rescue, and other stories* (1960)
Original edition entitled *Teskeilsgummans fodelsedag*
4 *Mrs Pepperpot in the Magic Wood, and other stories* (1965)
Original edition entitled *Teskjekjerringa i eventyrskauen*
5 *Mrs Pepperpot's busy day* (1967)
Original edition entitled *Kjerringa som bue sa lita som ei te-skje*
6 *Mrs Pepperpot's outing, and other stories* (1967)
Original edition entitled *Teskjekjerringa pa camping*
7 *Mrs Pepperpot's year* (1970)
Original edition entitled *Teskjekjerringa pa julehandel*

Mrs Piggle-Wiggle series
Macdonald, Betty
1 *Mrs Piggle-Wiggle* (1947)
2 *Mrs Piggle-Wiggle's magic* (1949)
3 *Mrs Piggle-Wiggle's farm* (1954)
4 *Hello, Mrs Piggle-Wiggle* (1957)

Mrs Pinkerton-Trunks series
Isherwood, Shirley
see **Get up and go series**

Mrs Pinny series
Morgan, Helen
1 *Mrs Pinny and the blowing day* (1968)
2 *Mrs Pinny and the sudden snow* (1969)
3 *Mrs Pinny and the salty sea day* (1972)

Mrs Ross series
Nicolson, Robert
1 *Mrs Ross* (1961)
2 *Flight of steps* (1966)

Mrs Simkin series
Allen, Linda
1 *Mrs Simkin and the very big mushroom* (1986)
2 *Mrs Simkin and the magic wheelbarrow* (1987)
3 *Mrs Simkin and the groovy old gramophone* (1992)
4 *Mrs Simkin and the wishing well* (1993)

Mrs Tim series
Stevenson, Dorothy Emily
1 *Mrs Tim of the Regiment* (1932)
Mrs Tim Christie
Originally published anonymously
2 *Golden days* (1934)
Numbers 1 and 2 also published in one volume entitled *Mrs Tim,* 1941
3 *Mrs Tim carries on* (1941)
4 *Mrs Tim gets a job* (1947)
5 *Mrs Tim flies home* (1952)

Mrs Toggle series
Pulver, Robin
1 *Mrs Toggle's zipper* (1990)
2 *Mrs Toggle and the dinosaur* (1991)
3 *Mrs Toggle's beautiful blue shoe* (1994)

Mrs Tree series
Richards, Laura Elizabeth
1 *Mrs Tree* (1902)
2 *Mrs Tree's will* (1905)

Mrs Tubbs series
Lofting, Hugh
1 *Story of Mrs Tubbs* (1923)
2 *Tommy, Tilly and Mrs Tubbs* (1936)

Mrs Warren series
This sequence has two authors
Shaw, George Bernard
1 *Mrs Warren's profession* (1902)
A play in four acts
Johnston, Harry Hamilton
2 *Mrs Warren's daughter* (1920)
A story of the woman's movement

Mrs Wiggs series
Rice, Alice Hegan
1 *Mrs Wiggs of the Cabbage Patch* (1901)
2 *Lovey Mary* (1903)

Mrs Zimmerman trilogy
Bellairs, John
see **Clock trilogy**

Ms. Squad series
Endfield, Mercedes
1 *Lucky Pierre* (1975)
2 *On the brink* (1975)

Ms. Tree series
Collins, Max Allan
Comic strips illustrated by Terry Beatty
1 *Files of Ms Tree* (1984)
2 *Cold dish* (1985)

Mu series
Churchward, James
1 *Lost continent of Mu* (1926)
2 *Children of Mu* (1931)
3 *Sacred symbols of Mu* (1933)
Revised edition 1960
4 *Cosmic forces as they were taught in Mu* (1934)
Cosmic forces of Mu

Mucker series
Burroughs, Edgar Rice
1 *Mucker* (1921)
2 *Man without a soul* (1922)
Return of the Mucker
One volume edition entitled *The mucker*, 1921

Muckfield series
Pressman, Lee
1 *Muckfield's midnight monster match* (1985)
2 *Muckfield and the muckoid menace* (1987)

Mud larks series
Garstin, Crosbie
1 *Mud larks* (1918)
2 *Mud larks again* (1919)

Muddle-headed wombat series
Park, Ruth
1 *Muddle-headed wombat* (1962)
2 *Muddle-headed wombat on holiday* (1964)
3 *Muddle-headed wombat in the tree-tops* (1965)
4 *Muddle-headed wombat at school* (1966)
Numbers 1-4 also published in one volume entitled *The adventures of the muddle-headed wombat*, 1979
5 *Muddle-headed wombat in the snow* (1966)
6 *Muddle-headed wombat on a rainy day* (1969)
7 *Muddle-headed wombat in the spring-time* (1970)
8 *Muddle-headed wombat on the river* (1971)
Numbers 5-8 also published in one volume entitled *More adventures of the muddle-headed wombat*, 1980
9 *Muddle-headed wombat and the bush band* (1973)
10 *Muddle-headed wombat and the invention* (1975)
11 *Muddle-headed wombat on clean-up day* (1976)
12 *Muddle-headed wombat is very bad* (1981)
13 *Muddle-headed wombat stays at home* (1982)

Muddle series
Mallett, Jerry J
see **Malcolm P Muddle series**

Mudge and Henry series
Rylant, Cynthia
see **Henry and Mudge series**

Mudhen series
Allen, Merritt Parmelee
1 *Mudhen* (1945)
2 *Mudhen and the walrus* (1950)
3 *Mudhen acts naturally* (1955)

Mueller series
Lovelace, Maud Hart
see **Betsy Ray series**

Muff and Mick series
Stiessel, Lena
see **Mick and Muff series**

Muffet series
Fine, Anne
see **Ione Muffet series**

Muffin book series
Hogarth, Ann
1 *Red Muffin book* (1950)
2 *Blue Muffin book* (1951)
3 *Green Muffin book* (1952)
4 *Purple Muffin book* (1953)

Muffin series
Freemantle, Brian
see **Charlie Muffin series**

Muffin series
This sequence has two authors
Mills, Annette
1 *Muffin the mule* (1949)
2 *More about Muffin* (1950)
3 *Muffin and the magic hat* (1951)
4 *Here comes Muffin* (1952)
5 *Muffin at the seaside* (1953)
6 *Muffin's splendid adventure* (1954)
Hogarth, Ann
7 *Meet Muffin the mule* (1954)

Muffkin series
Beers, Victor Gilbert
1 *Mini and Maxi in Muffkinland* (1981)
2 *Muffkins on parade* (1982)

Muffletump series
Wahl, Jan
1 *Muffletumps* (1966)
The story of four dolls
2 *Muffletump storybook* (1975)
3 *Muffletumps' Christmas party* (1975)
4 *Muffletumps' Halloween scare* (1977)

Muggins series
Grannan, Mary
see **Maggie Muggins series**

Muir series
Grierson, Francis Durham
see **Inspector George Muir series**

Mulcahaney series
O'Donnell, Lillian
see **Detective Norah Mulcahaney series**

Mulcahy series
Street, James
see **Eugene Mulcahy series**

Muldoon and Tillman series
Marshall, William Leonard
see **Tillman and Muldoon series**

Muldoon series
Flagg, John
see **Hart Muldoon series**
James, Martin
see **Rick Muldoon series**

Muldrew series
Allan, Luke
see **Blue Pete series; Tiger Lillie series**

Mulheisen series
Jackson, Jon Anthony
see **Sergeant Fang Mulheisen series**

Muller and Meldrum series
Glanville, Alec
see **Inspector Dusty Muller and Tiny Meldrum series**

Muller series
Colbron, Grace Isabel
see **Joe Muller series**
Muller, Paul
see **Paul Muller series**

Mulliner series
Wodehouse, Pelham Grenville
see **Mister Mulliner series**

Mulroney series
Murphy, Rae Allan
see **Brain Mulroney series**

Mulvane series
Heuman, William
see **Grady Mulvane series**

Mumfie series
Tozer, Katharine
1 *Wanderings of Mumfie* (1935)
2 *Here comes Mumfie* (1936)
3 *Mumfie the admiral* (1937)
4 *Mumfie's magic box* (1938)
5 *Mumfie's Uncle Samuel* (1939)
6 *Mumfie marches on* (1942)
Companion volume: *Mumfie's picture book*, 1947

Mummy and daddy series
Harper, Anita
see **Daddy and mummy series**

Mummy series
Kraus, Robert
1 *Mummy know best* (1990)
2 *Mummy vanishes* (1990)

Mummy series
Pond, Roy
1 *Mummy monster game* (1993)
2 *Mummy tomb hunt* (1994)

Munch Bunch character series
Reed, Giles
1 *Olly Onion* (1979)
2 *Tom Tomato* (1979)
3 *Billy Blackberry* (1979)
4 *Pete Pepper* (1979)
5 *Sally Strawberry* (1979)
6 *Lizzie Leek* (1979)
7 *Pipa Pear* (1980)
8 *Wally Walnut* (1980)
9 *Adam Avocado* (1980)
10 *Pedro Orange* (1980)
11 *Emma Apple* (1980)
12 *Lucy Lemon* (1980)
13 *Casper Carrot* (1980)
14 *Scruff Gooseberry* (1980)
15 *Suzie Celery* (1980)
16 *Percy Prune* (1982)
17 *Aubrey Aubergine* (1982)
18 *Penny Parsnip* (1982)
19 *Rory Rhubarb* (1982)
20 *Corky Coconut* (1982)
21 *Chunky Pineapple* (1982)
22 *Nurse Plum* (1982)
23 *Barnabus Beetroot* (1982)
24 *Runner Bean* (1982)
25 *Dick Turnip* (1982)
26 *Merv Marrow* (1982)
27 *Rozzy Raspberry* (1982)

Munch Bunch series
Reed, Giles
Illustrated by Angela Mitson
1 *Munch Bunch* (1979)
2 *Munch Bunch goes camping* (1979)
3 *Munch Bunch at the seaside* (1979)
4 *Munch Bunch have a party* (1979)
5 *Munch Bunch welcomes new friends* (1981)

Munch Bunch story books series
Reed, Giles
1 *Spud and the big red balloon* (1984)
2 *Sally Strawberry and the painted snake* (1984)
3 *Olly Onion's fancy dress party* (1984)
4 *Casper Carrot's new blue jumper* (1984)
5 *Dick Turnip and the crazy clowns* (1984)
6 *Rozzy Raspberry's wallpaper machine* (1984)
7 *Billy Blackberry's secret tunnel* (1984)
8 *Corny-on-the-Cob's not so funny day* (1984)
9 *Rory Rhubarb and the river monster* (1984)
10 *Merv Marrow's new police car* (1984)
11 *Scruff Gooseberry and the wishing well* (1984)
12 *Emma Apple's late birthday party* (1984)

Munch Bunch stretch series
Reed, Giles
Board books
1 *Day on the farm* (1983)
2 *Day at the zoo* (1983)
3 *Day in the park* (1983)
4 *Day at the seaside* (1983)
5 *Day at school* (1983)
6 *Day at the fair* (1983)

Munch Bunch word book series
Reed, Giles
1 *Green Munch Bunch word book* (1985)
2 *Red Munch Bunch word book* (1985)
3 *Blue Munch Bunch word book* (1985)
4 *Yellow Munch Bunch word book* (1985)

Munch series
Owen, Dilys
see **Mister Munch series**

Munchausen series
Mitchell, Adrian
see **New Baron Munchausen series**
Raspe, Rudolf Erich
see **Baron Munchausen series**

Munday series
Pryor, Bonnie
see **Mister Munday series**

Munde series
Odaga, Asenath
1 *Munde and his friends* (1987)
2 *Munde goes to the market* (1987)

Mundy series
Brewer, Gil
see **Al Mundy series**

Munich trilogy
Kirst, Hans Hellmut
1 *Time for scandal* (1971)
Original edition entitled *Verdammt zum Erfolg*
2 *Time for truth* (1972)
Original edition entitled *Veruteilt zum Wahrheit*
3 *Time for payment* (1974)
Original edition entitled *Alles hat seinen Preis*

Munro and Carter series
Higgins, Jack
see **Brigadier Dougal Munro and Captain Jack Carter series**

Munro series
Black, Ian Stuart
see **Peter Munro series**
Campbell, John Wood
see **Aarn Munro series**

Munroe Tallant series
York, Andrew
see **Colonel Munroe Tallant series**

Munsters series
This sequence has two authors; based on a television series
Cooper, Morton
1 *Munsters* (1964)
Johnston, William
2 *Munsters and the great camera caper* (1965)
3 *Last resort* (1966)

Muppets Fraggle Rock series
Muntean, Michaela
see **Fraggle Rock series**

Murder in the Carolinas series
Rhyne, Nancy
1 *Murder in the Carolinas* (1988)
2 *More murder in the Carolinas* (1990)

Murder Island series
Jamieson, Leland
see **Dan Gregory series**

Murder League series
Fish, Robert Lloyd
1 *Murder League* (1968)
2 *Rub-a-dub-dub* (1971)
Death cuts the deck
3 *Gross carriage of justice* (1979)

Murder Master series
Rosenberger, Joseph
1 *Death trap* (1973)
2 *Caribbean caper* (1974)
3 *Hooker-smash operation* (1974)

Murder series
Wilson, Colin
1 *Encyclopaedia of murder* (1964)
2 *Casebook of murder* (1969)
3 *Order of assassins* (1972)
The psychology of murder
4 *Encyclopaedia of modern murder, 1962-82* (1983)

Murder she wrote series
Anderson, James
see **Jessica Fletcher series**

Murdoc Jern series
Norton, Andre
1 *Zero stone* (1968)
2 *Uncharted stars* (1969)

Murdoch series
Deane, Norman
see **Bruce Murdoch series**

Murdock series
Coxe, George Harmon
see **Kent Murdock series**
Estleman, Loren D
see **Page Murdock series**
Icenhower, Joseph Bryan
see **Mister Midshipman Murdock series**
Norton, Andre
see **Time war series**
Olsen, D B
see **Rachel and Jennifer Murdock series**

Murgatroyd series
Farrington, Liz
see **Mrs Murgatroyd series**
Osborne, William Hamilton
see **William Murgatroyd series**

Murmur series
Harvester, Simon
see **Heron Murmur series**

Murphy family series
McKenna, Colleen O'Shaughnessy
1 *Too many Murphys* (1988)
2 *Fourth grade is a jinx* (1989)
3 *Fifth grade, here comes trouble* (1989)
4 *Eenie, meanie, Murphy, no* (1990)
5 *Murphy's island* (1991)
6 *Truth about sixth grade* (1991)
7 *Mother Murphy* (1992)
8 *Camp Murphy* (1992)

Murphy series
Brown, Rita Mae
see **Mrs Murphy series**
Paulsen, Gary
see **Al Murphy series**
Weinberg, Larry
see **Father John Murphy series**

Murphy's mob series
This sequence has two authors; based on a television series
Saunders, Michael
1 *Murphy's mob* (1982)
Masters, Anthony
2 *Murphy and Co.* (1983)

Murray River series
Fatchen, Max
1 *River kings* (1966)
2 *Conquest of the river* (1970)

Murray series
Colin, Aubrey
see **Inspector Bill Murray series**

Murry series
L'Engle, Madeleine
see **Meg Murry series**

Mushroom planet series
Cameron, Eleanor
see **Tyco Bass series**

Music makers series
Nichols, Janet
1 *American music makers* (1990)
2 *Women music makers* (1992)

Music of time series
Powell, Anthony
see **Dance to the music of time series**

Musical diaries series
Rorem, Ned
1 *Paris diary* (1966)
2 *New York diary* (1967)
Numbers 1 and 2 also published in one volume entitled *The Paris and New York diaries, 1951-1961*, 1983
3 *Final diary, 1961-1972* (1974)
Later diaries
4 *Nantucket diary* (1987)

Musket boys series
Warren, George A
1 *Musket boys of old Boston* (1909)
Alternative title: The first blow for liberty
2 *Musket boys under Washington* (1909)
Alternative title: The Tories of old New York
3 *Musket boys on the Delaware* (1910)
Alternative title: A stirring victory at Trenton

Mustang Marshal series
Shappiro, Herbert
1 *Black rider* (1941)
Also published under the pseudonym Burt Arthur
2 *Valley of Death* (1941)
3 *Chenango Pass* (1942)
4 *Mustang Marshal* (1943)
5 *Trouble at Moon Pass* (1943)
6 *Silver City Rangers* (1944)
Also published under the pseudonym Burt Arthur
7 *Gunsmoke over Utah* (1945)
Sequence continued under the pseudonym Burt Arthur
Arthur, Burt
8 *Lead hungry lobos* (1945)
9 *Flaming guns* (1964)

Mustang Terry Simmons series
Lytton, Shel
1 *Mustang on the Matterhorn* (1968)
2 *Mustang nonstop in London* (1969)

Mustard jar series
Suter, Jon Michael
1 *Adventures of the mustard jar* (1976)
2 *Orange knight of Oz* (1976)
3 *Case of the limping librarian* (1978)
4 *Passing of Fu Manchu* (1976)
5 *Blueankle* (1976)
6 *Autocrats of Oz* (1976)
7 *Case of the perpidious president* (1978)
8 *Adventure of the bald bibliophile* (1977)

Mustard seed series
Kile, Joan
see **Musty the mustard seed series**

Mustard series
Daniel, Roland
see **Buddy Mustard series**

Muster series
Lobel, Arnold
see **Mister Muster series**

Mustian family series
Price, Reynolds
1 *Long and happy life* (1962)
2 *Generous man* (1966)
3 *Good hearts* (1988)
Short stories about the Mustian family also published in the collection entitled *The names and faces of the heroes*, 1963

Musty the mustard seed series
Kile, Joan
1 *God's mustard seed* (1993)
2 *God's rugged cross* (1994)
3 *God's fruit tree* (1994)
4 *God's fig tree* (1994)

Mutant series
Haber, Karen
1 *Mutant season* (1989)
Co-author: Robert Silverberg
2 *Mutant prime* (1990)
3 *Mutant star* (1992)
4 *Mutant legacy* (1993)

Mutants amok series
Grant, Mark
This pseudonym is used by David Bischoff, Bruce King and Tim Sullivan as indicated against each title
1 *Mutants amok* (1991)
[Bischoff; Sullivan]
2 *Mutant hell* (1991)
[Bischoff]
3 *Rebel attack* (1991)
[Bischoff]
4 *Holocaust horror* (1991)
[Bischoff]
5 *Christmas slaughter* (1991)
[King]

Mutants series
Haiblum, Isidore
1 *Mutants are coming* (1984)
2 *Out of sync* (1990)

Muvian series
Leighton, Edward
1 *Out of the earth's deep* (1977)
2 *Light from tomorrow* (1977)
3 *Lord of the lightning* (1977)

My adventures series
McLaren, Jack
1 *My odyssey* (1923)
Reminiscences of travel
2 *My crowded solitude* (1926)
3 *Blood on the deck* (1933)
My first voyage
The true record of a deep-sea sailing ship
4 *My South Seas adventures* (1936)
5 *My civilised adventure* (1952)

My book series
Farmer, Lynne
1 *My counting book* (1987)
2 *My colour book* (1987)

My class series
Griffiths, Vivien
This sequence has four authors
Photographic illustrations by Chris Fairclough
1 *My class goes to the library* (1985)
Vivien Griffiths meets Angela Verma
2 *My class goes swimming* (1985)
Vivien Griffiths meets Robin Schaechter
Lee, Vicki
3 *My class looks after pets* (1985)
Vicki Lee meets Martin Cox
4 *My class visits a park* (1985)
Vicki Lee meets Kirsty Lloyd-Hall
Flanders, Jill
5 *My class goes to the seaside* (1986)
Jill Flanders meets Charlie Harris
Thomson, Ruth
6 *My class on sports day* (1986)
Ruth Thomson meets Theo Fisher
7 *My class at Diwali* (1986)
Ruth Thomson meets Samantha Zeglicki
8 *My class at Harvest Festival* (1986)
Ruth Thomson meets David Adams
Lee, Vicki
9 *My class makes music* (1986)
Vicki Lee meets Daniel Thomas
Thomson, Ruth
10 *My class at Christmas* (1986)
Ruth Thomson meets Lola Almudevar
Griffiths, Vivien
11 *My class visits a nature centre* (1987)
Vivien Griffiths meets Jusna Ali
12 *My class visits a museum* (1987)
Vivien Griffiths meets Lorraine Copes
Thomson, Ruth
13 *My class likes dancing* (1987)
Ruth Thomson meets Paul Gadsby
14 *My class enjoys cooking* (1987)
Ruth Thomson meets Philip Jones

My clothes series
Neitzel, Shirley
Illustrated by Nancy Winslow Parker
1 *Jacket I wear in the snow* (1989)
2 *Dress I'll wear to the party* (1992)
3 *Bag I'm taking to grandma's* (1994)

My day series
Coote, Roger
1 *Morning* (1989)
2 *Afternoon* (1989)
3 *Evening* (1989)
4 *Night* (1989)

My days series
Raymond, Ernest
Autobiography
1 *Story of my days* (1968)
Covers 1888-1922
2 *Please you, draw near* (1969)
Covers 1922-1968
3 *Good morning, good people* (1970)
A record of past and present

My diary series
Citrine, Walter McLennan
1 *My Finnish diary* (1940)
2 *My American diary* (1941)

My dog series
Adler, David A
1 *My dog and the key mystery* (1982)
2 *My dog and the knock knock mystery* (1985)
3 *My dog and the green sock mystery* (1986)
4 *My dog and the birthday mystery* (1987)

My family series
Coote, Roger
1 *My little sister* (1989)
2 *My grandparents* (1989)
3 *My parents* (1989)
4 *My big brother* (1989)

My father's moon series
Jolley, Elizabeth
1 *My father's moon* (1989)
2 *Cabin fever* (1990)

My Father's world series
DeJonge, Joanne E
1 *Rustling grass* (1985)
2 *Of skies and seas* (1985)
3 *My listening ears* (1985)
4 *All nature sings* (1985)

My first day series
Smith, Wendy
1 *My first day at playgroup* (1987)
2 *My first day with the babysitter* (1987)
3 *My first day at the swimming pool* (1987)
4 *My first day on an aeroplane* (1987)

My first gardening tools series
Barkan, Joanne
1 *My watering can* (1990)
2 *My rake* (1990)
3 *My trowel* (1990)
4 *My pruning shears* (1990)

My first kitchen gadgets series
Barkan, Joanne
1 *My frying pan* (1989)
2 *My cooking pot* (1989)
3 *My cooking spoon* (1989)
4 *My spatula* (1989)
5 *My measuring cup* (1989)
6 *My rolling pin* (1989)

My first pop-up series
Brown, Graham
1 *My first pop-up book of opposites* (1984)
2 *My first pop-up book of togethers* (1984)

My first series
Allen, Julia
1 *My first dentist visit* (1987)
2 *My first doctor visit* (1987)
3 *My first phone call* (1987)
4 *My first animal ride* (1987)
5 *My first camping trip* (1987)
6 *My first job* (1987)

My first series
De Paola, Tomie
1 *My first Easter* (1991)
2 *My first Passover* (1991)
3 *My first Halloween* (1991)

My friends series
Duncan, Jane
see **Reachfar series**

My journey series
Anno, Mitsumasa
see **Anno's journey series**

My life series
Ayer, Alfred Jules
Memoirs of a philosopher
1 *Part of my life* (1977)
2 *More of my life* (1984)

My life series
Bartlett, Vernon
1 *This is my life* (1937)
2 *And now, tomorrow* (1960)
3 *Tuscan retreat* (1964)
4 *Tuscan harvest* (1971)
5 *I know what I liked* (1974)

My life series
Keller, Helen
1 *Story of my life* (1902)
Autobiography of a blind, deaf and dumb woman
2 *Midstream* (1929)

My life series
Morris, Neil
Illustrated by Kati Teague
1 *My week* (1985)
2 *My year* (1985)
3 *My family* (1987)
4 *My friends* (1987)
5 *My new house* (1988)
6 *My new school* (1988)

My life series
Sumiko
1 *My baby brother Ned* (1981)
2 *My school* (1983)
3 *My holidays* (1985)

My memory series
Terhune, Albert Payson
Autobiography
1 *Now that I'm fifty* (1924)
2 *To the best of my memory* (1940)

My mom series
Delton, Judy
1 *My mom hates me in January* (1977)
2 *Best mom in the world* (1979)
3 *My mother lost her job today* (1980)
Numbers 4-6 illustrated by Lisa McCue
4 *My mom made me go to camp* (1990)
5 *My mom made me go to school* (1991)
6 *My mom made me take piano lessons* (1993)

My name is Paris series
Howard, Elizabeth Howard
1 *Mystery of the Metro* (1987)
2 *Mystery of the magician* (1987)
3 *Scent of mystery* (1987)
4 *Mystery of the deadly diamond* (1987)

My name series
Mazer, Norma Fox
1 *A, my name is Ami* (1986)
2 *B, my name is Bunny* (1987)
3 *C, my name is Cal* (1990)
4 *D, my name is Danita* (1991)
5 *E, my name is Emily* (1991)

My naughty little sister series
Edwards, Dorothy
Based on a radio series
1 *My naughty little sister* (1952)
2 *My naughty little sister and some others* (1957)
3 *My naughty little sister's friends* (1962)
4 *When my naughty little sister was good* (1968)
Numbers 1-4 also published in one volume entitled *All about my naughty little sister*, 1969
5 *My naughty little sister stories* (1970)
6 *My naughty little sister and bad Harry* (1974)
7 *My naughty little sister goes fishing* (1976)
8 *My naughty little sister and Bad Harry's rabbit* (1977)
9 *My naughty little sister at the fair* (1979)
Companion volume: *My naughty little sister's birthday book*, 1982

My own story series
Baruch, Bernard Mannes
Autobiography
1 *My own story* (1957)
2 *Public years* (1960)

My pet series
Taylor, Judy
Illustrated by Reg Cartwright
1 *My dog* (1988)
2 *My cat* (1988)

My place series
Morgan, Sally
Edited by Barbara Ker Wilson
Based on My place, 1987
1 *Sally's story* (1990)
2 *Arthur Corunna's story* (1990)
3 *Mother and daughter* (1990)
The story of Daisy and Gladys Corunna

My political life trilogy
Amery, Leopold Stennett
Autobiography
1 *England before the storm, 1896-1914* (1953)
2 *War and peace, 1914-1929* (1953)
3 *Unforgiving years, 1929-1940* (1955)

My prairie series
Harvey, Brett
1 *My prairie year* (1986)
Based on the diary of Eleanor Plaisted
2 *My prairie Christmas* (1990)

My salvation series
Skidmore, Hubert
1 *I will lift up mine eyes* (1936)
2 *Heaven came so near* (1938)

My school series
Bentley, Diana
1 *School caretaker* (1987)
2 *School secretary* (1987)
3 *Dinner ladies* (1987)
4 *Lollipop lady* (1987)
5 *Class teacher* (1987)
6 *Road safety officer* (1987)
7 *School nurse* (1988)
8 *School outing* (1988)
9 *School fete* (1988)
10 *Harvest festival* (1988)
11 *Librarian* (1988)
12 *Christmas* (1988)
13 *Lollipop man* (1989)

My series
Nakatani, Chiyoko
1 *My teddy bear* (1975)
2 *My day on the farm* (1975)
3 *My treasures* (1975)
4 *My animal friends* (1975)

My series
Young, Ruth
1 *My blanket* (1987)
2 *My babysitter* (1987)
3 *My new baby* (1987)
4 *My potty chair* (1987)

My sister series
Ransom, Candice Farris
1 *My sister the meanie* (1988)
2 *My sister the traitor* (1990)
3 *My sister the creep* (1990)

My teacher series
Coville, Bruce
1 *My teacher is an alien* (1989)
2 *My teacher fried my brains* (1991)
3 *My teacher glows in the dark* (1991)
4 *My teacher flunked the planet* (1992)

My Teddy series
Bawden, Juliet
1 *Naughty Teddy* (1987)
2 *Poor Teddy* (1987)
3 *Good Teddy* (1987)
4 *My Teddy* (1987)

My very first series
Carle, Eric
1 *My very first book of colors* (1974)
2 *My very first book of numbers* (1974)
3 *My very first book of shapes* (1974)
4 *My very first book of words* (1974)
5 *My very first book of growth* (1986)
6 *My very first book of motion* (1986)
7 *My very first book of homes* (1986)
8 *My very first book of touch* (1986)
9 *My very first book of heads and tales* (1986)
10 *My very first book of tools* (1986)
11 *My very first book of food* (1986)
12 *My very first book of sounds* (1986)

My visit series
This sequence has two authors
Bentley, Diana
1 *My visit to the doctor* (1989)
2 *My visit to the seaside* (1989)
3 *My visit to the airport* (1989)
4 *My visit to the swimming pool* (1989)
5 *My visit to the dentist* (1989)
6 *My visit to the supermarket* (1989)
Davies, Sophie
7 *My visit to the zoo* (1989)
8 *My visit to the hospital* (1989)
9 *My visit to the birthday party* (1989)
10 *My visit to the fire station* (1990)
11 *My visit to a museum* (1990)
12 *My visit to the theme park* (1990)

My word series
Muir, Frank
Originally broadcast on BBC Radio
1 *You can't have your kayak and heat it* (1973)
2 *Upon my word!* (1974)
3 *Take my word for it* (1978)
4 *Oh, my word* (1980)
Omnibus: *Complete and utter my word*, 1983

My world series
Coote, Roger
1 *My garden* (1989)
2 *My house* (1989)
3 *My school* (1989)
4 *My street* (1989)

My yesterdays series
Hamilton, Frederic
see **Vanished pomps of yesterday series**

Mycaenean Greece series
Ray, Mary
1 *Standing lions* (1968)
2 *Shout against the wind* (1970)

Mycroft series
Heard, Henry Fitzgerald
see **Mister Mycroft series**

Myles Rusby series
Markham, Virgil
1 *Inspector Rusby's finale* (1933)
2 *Deadly jest* (1935)

Mylor series
Maguire, Michael
1 *Most powerful horse in the world* (1977)
2 *Kidnap* (1978)

Myra Morgana series
DeBolt, Adriana
1 *Crystal of power* (1980)
Sequence continued under the pseudonym Christopher Dane
Dane, Christopher
2 *Galactic arena* (1981)

Myra, Myron series
Vidal, Gore
1 *Myra Breckenridge* (1968)
2 *Myron* (1974)

Myra Savage series
McShane, Mark
1 *Seance* (1961)
Seance on a wet afternoon
2 *Seance for two* (1972)

Myrl series
Bodkin, Matthias McDonnell
see **Dora Myrl series**

Myrtle Albertina series
Pohlmann, Lillian
1 *Myrtle Albertina's secret* (1956)
2 *Myrtle Albertina's song* (1958)

Mysteries of the people series
Sue, Eugene
Originally published in French in the 1840s and 1850s; the dates given are those of the first English editions
1 *Gold sickle* (1904)
Alternative title: Hena, the virgin of the Isle of Sen
2 *Brass bell* (1907)
Alternative title: The chariot of death, a tale of Caesar's Gallic invasion
3 *Iron collar* (1909)
Alternative title: Faustina and Syomara, a tale of slavery under the Romans
4 *Silver cross* (1899)
Alternative title: The carpenter of Nazareth, a tale of Jerusalem
5 *Casque's lark* (1909)
Alternative title: Victoria, the mother of the camps, a tale of the Frankish invasion of Gaul
6 *Poniard's hilt* (1907)
Alternative title: Karadeucq and Ronan, a tale of Bagauders and Vagres
7 *Branding needle* (1908)
Alternative title: The monastery of Charolles, a tale of the first Communal Charter
8 *Abbatical crosier* (1908)
The tale of a medieval abbess
9 *Carlovingian coins* (1908)
Alternative title: The daughters of Charlemagne, a tale of the ninth century
10 *Iron arrow head* (1909)
Alternative title: The Buckler maiden, a tale of the Nortman invasion
11 *Infant's skull* (1904)
Alternative title: The end of the world, a tale of the millenium
12 *Pilgrim's shell* (1904)
Alternative title: Fergan the quarryman, a tale from the feudal times
13 *Iron pincers* (1909)
Alternative title: Mylio and Karvel, a tale of the Albigensian Crusade
14 *Iron trivet* (1906)
Alternative title: Jocelyn the Champion, a tale of the Jacquerie
15 *Executioner's knife* (1910)
Alternative title: Joan of Arc, a tale of the Inquisition
16 *Pocket Bible* (1910)
Alternative title: Christian the printer, a tale of the sixteenth century
17 *Blacksmith's hammer* (1910)
Alternative title: The peasant's code
18 *Sword of honor* (1910)
Alternative title: The foundation of the French Republic, a tale of the French Revolution
19 *Galley slave's ring* (1911)
Alternative title: The family of Lebrenn, a tale of the French Revolution of 1848

Mysteries of the universe series
Branley, Franklyn Mansfield
1 *Mysteries of the universe* (1984)
2 *Mysteries of outer space* (1985)
3 *Mysteries of the satellites* (1986)
4 *Mysteries of life on earth and beyond* (1987)
5 *Mysteries of the planets* (1988)
6 *Mysteries of the planet earth* (1989)

Mysterious Mister I series
Keeler, Harry Stephen
Based on *The mysterious Mister I*, 1937
1 *Mysterious Mister I* (1938)
2 *Chameleon* (1939)

Mystery and adventure series
Norton, Carol
1 *Phantom yacht* (1928)
2 *Bobs, a girl detective* (1928)
3 *Seven Sleuths' Club* (1928)

Mystery cat series
Saunders, Susan
1 *Mystery cat* (1986)
2 *Mystery cat and the chocolate trap* (1986)
3 *Mystery cat and the monkey business* (1986)

Mystery Island series
White, Palmer
1 *Mystery Island* (1930)
2 *Circle of confusion* (1930)

Mystery of series
Christian, Mary Blount
1 *Bigfoot* (1987)
2 *UFOs* (1987)

Mystery Squad series
Waddell, Martin
1 *Mystery Squad and the dead man's message* (1984)
2 *Mystery Squad and the Artful Dodger* (1984)
3 *Mystery Squad and Mr Midnight* (1984)
4 *Mystery Squad and the whistling teeth* (1984)
5 *Mystery Squad and the creeping castle* (1985)
6 *Mystery Squad and the candid camera* (1985)
7 *Mystery Squad and the robot's revenge* (1986)
8 *Mystery Squad and the cannonball kid* (1986)

Mystic rebel series
Syvertsen, Ryder
1 *Mystic rebel* (1988)
2 *Dancing dead* (1988)
3 *Darkness descends* (1988)
4 *Temple of dark destiny* (1989)
5 *Cave of the master* (1990)
6 *Fortress of forbidden destiny* (1991)

Myth series
Asprin, Robert Lynn
see **Skeeve series**

Mythago series
Holdstock, Robert
1 *Mythago Wood* (1984)
2 *Lavondyss* (1988)
Journey to an unknown region
3 *Hollowing* (1994)

Mythology series
Nye, Jody Lynn
1 *Mythology 101* (1990)
2 *Mythology abroad* (1991)

N

Nabokov series
Boyd, Brian
see **Vladimir Nabokov series**

Nada the lily series
Haggard, Henry Rider
see **Zulu series**

Naff series
Bryson, Kit
Humour
1 *Complete Naff guide* (1983)
Co-authors: Selina Fitzherbert and Jean-Luc Legris
2 *Naff sex guide* (1984)
Co-authors: Selina Fitzherbert and Jean-Luc Legris

Naga Teot series
Gladney, Heather
see **Song of Naga Teot series**

Naill Renfro series
Norton, Andre
see **Janus series**

Nairn series
Hartland, Michael
see **David Nairn series**

Najork series
Hoban, Russell
see **Captain Najork series**

Naked civil servant series
Crisp, Quentin
Autobiography
1 *Naked civil servant* (1968)
2 *How to become a virgin* (1981)

Name to conjure with series
Aamodt, Donald
1 *Name to conjure with* (1989)
2 *Troubling along the border* (1991)

Nameless detective series
Pronzini, Bill
see **Private Eye series**

Nameless nobleman series
Austin, Jane Goodwin
1 *Nameless nobleman* (1881)
2 *Doctor Le Baron and his daughters* (1890)
A story of the old colony

Nan and Mary Cantwell series
Boylan, Clare
1 *Holy pictures* (1983)
2 *Home rule* (1992)
Eleven Edward Street

Nan series
Hamlin, Myra Sawyer
1 *Nan at Camp Chicopee* (1896)
Alternative title: Nan's summer with the boys
2 *Nan in the city* (1897)
Alternative title: Nan's winter with the girls
3 *Nan's Chicopee children* (1900)
4 *Catherine's proxy* (1902)
5 *Persis Putnam's treasure* (1908)
Alternative title: Nan's girls at Camp Chicopina

Nan Sherwood series
Carr, Annie Roe
1 *Nan Sherwood at Pine Camp* (1916)
Alternative title: The old lumberman's secret
2 *Nan Sherwood at Lakeview Hall* (1916)
Alternative title: The mystery of the haunted boathouse
3 *Nan Sherwood's winter holidays* (1916)
Alternative title: Rescuing the runaways
4 *Nan Sherwood at Rose Ranch* (1919)
Alternative title: The old Mexican's treasure
5 *Nan Sherwood at Palm Beach* (1921)
Alternative title: Strange adventures among the orange groves
6 *Nan Sherwood's summer holidays* (1937)
7 *Nan Sherwood on the Mexican border* (1937)

Nancarrow series
Brinsmead, Hesba Fay
see **Clippie Nancarrow series**

Nancy and Nick series
Barton, Olive Roberts
1 *Wonderful land of Up* (1918)
2 *Nancy and Nick in Helter-Skelter-Land* (1921)
3 *Nancy and Nick in Scrub-Up-Land* (1921)
4 *Nancy and Nick in the Land-of-Dear-Knows-Where* (1921)
5 *Nancy and Nick in the Land-of-Near-by* (1921)
6 *Nancy and Nick in Topsy-Turvy-Land* (1921)

Nancy Bruce series
Lindquist, Jennie Dorothea
1 *Golden name day* (1955)
2 *Little silver house* (1959)
3 *Crystal tree* (1966)

Nancy Drew and Hardy boys supermystery series
Keene, Carolyn
House pseudonym
1 *Double crossing* (1988)
2 *Crime for Christmas* (1988)
3 *Shock waves* (1989)
4 *Dangerous game* (1989)
5 *Last resort* (1989)
6 *Buried in time* (1990)
7 *Mystery train* (1990)
8 *Paris connection* (1990)
9 *Best of enemies* (1991)
10 *High survival* (1991)
11 *New Year's evil* (1991)
12 *Tour of danger* (1992)
13 *Spies and lies* (1992)
14 *Hits and misses* (1993)
15 *Courting disaster* (1993)
16 *Evil in Amsterdam* (1993)
17 *Desperate measures* (1994)
18 *Passport to danger* (1994)

Nancy Drew and the Hardy boys be a detective mystery series
Keene, Carolyn
House pseudonym
1 *Secret of the knight's sword* (1984)
2 *Danger on ice* (1984)
3 *Feathered serpent* (1984)
4 *Secret cargo* (1984)
5 *Alaskan mystery* (1985)
6 *Missing money mystery* (1985)
7 *Jungle of evil* (1985)
8 *Ticket to intrigue* (1985)
Companion volumes: *Nancy Drew and the Hardy boys super sleuths*, volumes 1-2, 1981-1984, *Nancy Drew and the Hardy boys camp fire stories*, 1984

Nancy Drew files series
Keene, Carolyn
House pseudonym
1 *Secrets can kill* (1986)
2 *Deadly intent* (1986)
3 *Murder on ice* (1986)
4 *Smile and say murder* (1986)
5 *Hit and run holiday* (1986)

6 *White water terror* (1987)
7 *Deadly doubles* (1987)
8 *Two points for murder* (1987)
9 *False moves* (1987)
10 *Buried secrets* (1987)
11 *Heart of danger* (1987)
12 *Fatal ransom* (1987)
13 *Wings of fear* (1987)
14 *This side of evil* (1987)
15 *Trial by fire* (1987)
16 *Never say die* (1987)
17 *Stay tuned for danger* (1987)
18 *Circle of evil* (1987)
19 *Sisters in crime* (1988)
20 *Very deadly yours* (1988)
21 *Recipe for murder* (1988)
22 *Fatal attraction* (1988)
23 *Sinister parade* (1988)
24 *Till death do us part* (1988)
25 *Rich and dangerous* (1988)
26 *Playing with fire* (1988)
27 *Most likely to die* (1988)
28 *Black widow* (1988)
29 *Pure poison* (1988)
30 *Death by design* (1988)
31 *Trouble in Tahiti* (1989)
32 *high marks for malice* (1989)
33 *Danger in disguise* (1989)
34 *Vanishing act* (1989)
35 *Bad medicine* (1989)
36 *Over the edge* (1989)
37 *Last dance* (1989)
38 *Final scene* (1989)
39 *Suspect next door* (1989)
40 *Shadow of a doubt* (1989)
41 *Something to hide* (1989)
42 *Wrong chemistry* (1989)
43 *False impressions* (1990)
44 *Scent of danger* (1990)
45 *Out of bounds* (1990)
46 *Win, place or die* (1990)
47 *Flirting with danger* (1990)
48 *Date with deception* (1990)
49 *Portrait in crime* (1990)
50 *Deep secrets* (1990)
51 *Model crime* (1990)
52 *Danger for hire* (1990)
53 *Trail of lies* (1990)
54 *Cold as ice* (1990)
55 *Don't look twice* (1991)
56 *Make no mistake* (1991)
57 *Into thin air* (1991)
58 *Hot pursuit* (1991)
59 *High risk* (1991)
60 *Poison pen* (1991)
61 *Sweet revenge* (1991)
62 *Easy marks* (1991)
63 *Mixed signals* (1991)
64 *Wrong track* (1991)
65 *Final notes* (1991)
66 *Tall, dark and deadly* (1991)
67 *Nobody's business* (1992)
68 *Crosscurrents* (1992)
69 *Running scared* (1992)
70 *Cutting edge* (1992)
71 *Hot tracks* (1992)
72 *Swiss secrets* (1992)
73 *Rendezvous in Rome* (1992)
74 *Greek odyssey* (1992)
75 *Talent for murder* (1992)
76 *Perfect plot* (1992)
77 *Danger on parade* (1992)
78 *Update in crime* (1992)
79 *No laughing matter* (1993)
80 *Power of suggestion* (1993)
81 *Making waves* (1993)
82 *Dangerous relations* (1993)
83 *Diamond deceit* (1993)
84 *Choosing sides* (1993)
85 *Sea of suspicion* (1993)
86 *Let's talk terror* (1993)
87 *Moving target* (1993)
88 *False pretenses* (1993)
89 *Designs in crime* (1993)
90 *Stage fright* (1993)
91 *If looks could kill* (1994)
92 *My deadly valentine* (1994)
93 *Hotline to danger* (1994)
94 *Illusions of evil* (1994)
95 *Instinct for trouble* (1994)
96 *Runaway bride* (1994)
97 *Squeeze play* (1994)
98 *Island of secrets* (1994)
99 *Cheating heart* (1994)
100 *Dance till you die* (1994)
101 *Picture of guilt* (1994)
102 *Counterfeit Christmas* (1994)

Nancy Drew notebooks series
Keene, Carolyn
House pseudonym
1 *Slumber party secret* (1994)
2 *Lost locket* (1994)

Nancy Drew picture books series
Keene, Carolyn
House pseudonym
1 *Mystery of the lost dogs* (1977)
2 *Secret of the twin puppets* (1977)

Nancy Drew series
Keene, Carolyn
House pseudonym
1 *Secret of the old clock* (1930)
Revised edition 1959
2 *Hidden staircase* (1930)
Revised edition 1959
3 *Bungalow mystery* (1930)
Revised edition 1960
4 *Mystery at Lilac Inn* (1930)
Revised edition 1961
5 *Secret at Shadow Ranch* (1930)
Secret of Shadow Ranch
Revised edition 1965
6 *Secret of Red Gate Farm* (1931)
Revised edition 1961
7 *Clue in the diary* (1932)
Revised edition 1962
8 *Nancy's mysterious letter* (1932)
Revised edition 1968
9 *Sign of the twisted candles* (1933)
Revised edition 1968
10 *Password to Larkspur Lane* (1933)
Revised edition 1966
11 *Clue of the broken locket* (1934)
Revised edition 1965
12 *Message in the hollow oak* (1935)
Revised edition 1972
13 *Mystery of the ivory charm* (1936)
Revised edition 1974
14 *Whispering statue* (1937)
Revised edition 1970
15 *Haunted bridge* (1937)
Revised edition 1972
16 *Clue of the tapping heels* (1939)
Revised edition 1969
17 *Mystery of the brass bound trunk* (1940)
Revised edition 1976
18 *Mystery of the moss-covered mansion* (1941)
Revised edition 1971
19 *Quest of the missing map* (1942)
Revised edition 1969
20 *Clue in the jewel box* (1943)
Revised edition 1972
21 *Secret in the old attic* (1944)
Revised edition 1970
22 *Clue in the crumbling wall* (1945)
Revised edition 1973
23 *Mystery of the tolling bell* (1946)
Revised edition 1973
24 *Clue in the old album* (1947)
Revised edition 1977
25 *Ghost of Blackwood Hall* (1948)
Revised edition 1967
26 *Clue of the leaning chimney* (1949)
Revised edition 1967
27 *Secret of the wooden lady* (1950)
Revised edition 1967
28 *Clue of the black keys* (1951)
Revised edition 1968
29 *Mystery at the ski jump* (1952)
Revised edition 1968
30 *Clue of the velvet mask* (1953)
Revised edition 1969
31 *Ringmaster's secret* (1953)
Revised edition 1974
32 *Scarlet slipper mystery* (1954)
Revised edition 1974
33 *Witch tree symbol* (1955)
Revised edition 1975
34 *Hidden window mystery* (1957)
Revised edition 1975
35 *Haunted showboat* (1957)
36 *Secret of the golden pavilion* (1959)
37 *Clue in the old stagecoach* (1960)
38 *Mystery of the fire dragon* (1961)
39 *Clue of the dancing puppet* (1962)
40 *Moonstone Castle mystery* (1963)
41 *Clue of the whistling bagpipes* (1964)
42 *Phantom of Pine Hill* (1965)
43 *Mystery of the ninety nine steps* (1966)
44 *Clue in the crossword cipher* (1967)
45 *Spider sapphire mystery* (1968)
46 *Invisible intruder* (1969)
47 *Mysterious mannequin* (1970)
48 *Crooked bannister* (1971)
49 *Secret of Mirror Bay* (1972)
50 *Double junk mystery* (1973)
51 *Mystery of the glowing eye* (1974)
52 *Secret of the forgotten city* (1975)
53 *Sky phantom* (1976)
54 *Strange message in the parchment* (1977)
55 *Mystery of Crocodile Island* (1978)
56 *Thirteenth pearl* (1979)
57 *Triple hoax* (1979)
58 *Flying saucer mystery* (1980)
59 *Secret in the old place* (1980)
60 *Greek symbol mystery* (1981)
61 *Swami's ring* (1981)
62 *Kachina doll mystery* (1981)
63 *Twin dilemma* (1981)
64 *Captive witness* (1981)
65 *Mystery of the winged lion* (1982)
66 *Race against time* (1982)
67 *Sinister omen* (1982)
68 *Elusive heiress* (1982)
69 *Clue in the ancient disguise* (1982)
70 *Broken anchor* (1983)
71 *Silver cobweb* (1983)
72 *Haunted carousel* (1983)
73 *Enemy match* (1983)
74 *Mysterious image* (1984)
75 *Emerald-eyed cat mystery* (1984)
76 *Eskimo's secret* (1985)
77 *Bluebeard room* (1985)
78 *Phantom of Venice* (1985)
Ghost in the gondola
79 *Double horrow of Fenley Place* (1987)
80 *Case of the disappearing diamonds* (1987)
81 *Mardi gras mystery* (1988)
82 *Clue in the camera* (1988)
83 *Case of the vanishing veil* (1988)
84 *Joker's revenge* (1988)
85 *Secret of Shady Glen* (1988)
86 *Mystery of Misty Canyon* (1988)
87 *Case of the rising stars* (1989)
88 *Search for Cindy Austin* (1989)
89 *Case of the disappearing deejay* (1898)
90 *Puzzle at Pineview School* (1898)
91 *Girl who couldn't remember* (1898)
92 *Ghost of Craven Cove* (1898)
93 *Case of the safecracker's secret* (1990)
94 *Picture perfect mystery* (1990)
95 *Silent suspect* (1990)
96 *Case of the photo finish* (1990)
97 *Mystery at Magnolia Mansion* (1990)
98 *Haunting of Horse Island* (1990)
99 *Secret at Seven Rocks* (1991)
100 *Secret in time* (1991)
101 *Mystery of the missing millionairess* (1991)
102 *Secret in the dark* (1991)
103 *Stranger in the shadows* (1991)
104 *Mystery of the jade tiger* (1991)
105 *Clue in the antique trunk* (1992)
106 *Case of the artful crime* (1992)
107 *Legend of Miner's Creek* (1992)
108 *Secret of the Tibetan treasure* (1992)
109 *Mystery of the masked rider* (1992)
110 *Nutcracker Ballet mystery* (1992)
111 *Secret at Solaire* (1993)
112 *Crime in the queen's court* (1993)
113 *Secret lost at sea* (1993)
114 *Search for the silver Persian* (1993)
115 *Suspect in smoke* (1993)
116 *Case of the twin teddy bears* (1993)
117 *Mystery on the menu* (1994)
118 *Trouble at Lake Tahoe* (1994)
119 *Mystery of the missing mascot* (1994)
120 *Floating crime* (1994)
121 *Fortune-teller's secret* (1994)
122 *Message in the haunted mansion* (1994)

Companion volumes: *The Nancy Drew cookbook*, 1973, *The Nancy Drew sleuth book*, 1979, *Nancy Drew book of hidden clues*, 1980, *Nancy Drew ghost stories*, 1983, *Nancy Drew ghost stories II*, 1985, *The Hardy boys and Nancy Drew meet Dracula*, by Glen A Larsen and Michael Sloan, 1978

Nancy, Girl Scout series
Large, Jean Henry
1 *Nancy goes Girl Scouting* (1930)
2 *Nancy's lone Girl Scouts* (1930)
3 *Nancy goes camping* (1931)

Nancy Kimball series
Laklan, Carli
1 *Nancy Kimball, nurse's aide* (1962)
2 *Nurse in training* (1965)
3 *Second year nurse* (1967)
Nancy Kimball at City Hospital

Nancy Lee series
Warde, Margaret
1 *Nancy Lee* (1912)
2 *Nancy Lee's spring term* (1913)
3 *Nancy Lee's lookout* (1915)
4 *Nancy Lee's namesake* (1917)

Nancy Naylor series
Lansing, Elizabeth
1 *Nancy Naylor, air pilot* (1941)
2 *Nancy Naylor flies south* (1943)
3 *Nancy Naylor, flight nurse* (1944)
4 *Nancy Naylor, captain of flight nurses* (1946)
5 *Nancy Naylor, visiting nurse* (1947)

Nancy Pembroke series
Van Epps, Margaret T
1 *Nancy Pembroke, college maid* (1930)
2 *Nancy Pembroke's vacation in Canada* (1930)
3 *Nancy Pembroke, sophomore at Roxford* (1930)
4 *Nancy Pembroke in New Orleans* (1930)
5 *Nancy Pembroke, junior* (1930)
6 *Nancy Pembroke in Nova Scotia* (1930)
7 *Nancy Pembroke, senior* (1931)

Nancy Porter series
Taggart, Marion Ames
see **Doctor's little girl series**

Nancy Prentiss series
Wasson, Mildred
1 *Nancy* (1932)
A story of the younger set
2 *Miss Nancy Prentiss* (1934)
3 *Nancy sails* (1936)
4 *Bill and Nancy* (1940)

Nancy series
Brainerd, Eleanor Hoyt
1 *Misdemeanors of Nancy* (1902)
2 *Nancy's country Christmas* (1904)

Nancy series
Bruce, Dorita Fairlie
1 *Girls of Saint Bride's* (1925)
2 *That boarding school girl* (1925)
3 *New girl and Nancy* (1926)
4 *Nancy to the rescue* (1927)
5 *Nancy at Saint Bride's* (1933)
6 *Nancy in the sixth* (1935)
7 *Nancy returns to Saint Bride's* (1938)
8 *Nancy calls the tune* (1944)

Nancy series
Garrard, Phillis
1 *Nancy, Canadian schoolgirl* (1950)
2 *Nancy, young Canadian* (1961)

Nanny and the professor series
Johnston, William
1 *Nanny and the professor* (1970)
2 *What hath Nanny wrought?* (1970)
3 *Nanny's miracle* (1970)

Nanny Noony series
Frascino, Edward
1 *Nanny Noony and the magic spell* (1988)
2 *Nanny Noony and the dust queen* (1990)

Nap and Ted series
Tilsley, Frank
1 *Voice of the crowd* (1954)
2 *Brother Nap* (1954)

Naphar series
Baker, Sharon
1 *Quarreling* (1984)
2 *Journey to Membliar* (1987)
3 *Burning tears of Sassurum* (1988)

Napier family trilogy
Napier, Priscilla
1 *Sword dance* (1971)
Lady Sarah Lennox and the Napiers
2 *Difficult country* (1972)
The Napiers in Scotland
3 *Revolution and the Napier brothers, 1820-1840* (1973)

Napoleon and Josephine series
Chambers, Rosamund Mary
1 *Little Creole* (1952)
2 *Losing fight* (1955)
3 *Strangers at the farm* (1961)

Napoleon Bonaparte series
Austin, Frederick Britten
1 *Road to glory* (1935)
2 *Forty centuries look down* (1937)

Napoleon Bonaparte series
Delderfield, Ronald Frederick
1 *Napoleon in love* (1959)
2 *March of the twenty six* (1962)
Napoleon's marshals
3 *Retreat from Moscow* (1967)
4 *Imperial sunset* (1968)
The fall of Napoleon, 1813-14

Napoleon Bonaparte series
Upfield, Arthur William
1 *Barrakee mystery* (1928)
Lure of the bush
2 *Sands of Windee* (1931)
3 *Wings above the Diamantina* (1936)
Winged mystery
Wings above the claypan
4 *Mister Jelly's business* (1937)
Murder down under
5 *Winds of evil* (1937)
6 *Bone is pointed* (1938)
7 *Mystery of Swordship Reef* (1939)
8 *Bushranger of the skies* (1940)
No footprints in the bush
9 *Death of a swagman* (1945)
10 *Devil's steps* (1946)
11 *Author bites the dust* (1948)
12 *Mountains have a secret* (1948)
13 *Widows of Broome* (1950)
14 *Bachelors of Broken Hill* (1950)
15 *New shoe* (1952)
Clue of the new shoe
16 *Venom House* (1953)
17 *Murder must wait* (1953)
18 *Death of a lake* (1954)
19 *Cake in the hatbox* (1954)
Sinister stones
20 *Battling prophet* (1956)
21 *Man of two tribes* (1956)
22 *Bony buys a woman* (1957)
Bushman who came back
23 *Bony and the mouse* (1959)
Journey to the hangman
24 *Bony and the black virgin* (1959)
25 *Bony and the Kelly Gang* (1960)
Valley of smugglers
26 *Bony and the white savage* (1961)
White savage
27 *Will of the tribe* (1962)
28 *Madman's Bend* (1963)
Body at Madman's Bend
29 *Lake Frome monster* (1966)
Completed by J L Price and Dorothy Strange after the author's death

Also a short story entitled *Wisp of wool and disk of silver* published in *Ellery Queen's crime cruise round the world*, 1981

Napoleon III series
Kenyon, Frank Wilson
see **Emperor Napoleon III series**

Napoleon III trilogy
Neumann, Alfred
1 *New Caesar* (1934)
Original edition entitled *Neuer Caesar*
2 *Man of December* (1936)
Gaudy empire
Original edition entitled *Kaiserreich*
3 *Friends of the people* (1938)
Original edition entitled *Die Volksfreunde*

Napoleon series
Caine, Oliver Vernon
Set in the years 1812-15
1 *Face to face with Napoleon* (1898)
2 *In the year of Waterloo* (1899)

Napoleon series
Dumas, Alexandre
1 *Whites and the Blues* (1868)
First Republic
Original edition entitled *Les blancs et les bleus*
2 *Companions of Jehu* (1857)
Roland montreval
Original edition entitled *Les compagnons de Jehu*
3 *She-wolves of Machecoul* (1859)
La vendee
Original edition entitled *Les louves de Machecoul*
4 *Corsican brothers* (1845)
Original edition entitled *Les freres corses*

Napoleon Solo series
Avallone, Michael
see **Man from U.N.C.L.E. series**

Napoleonic Europe series
Coffman, Virginia
1 *Veronique* (1975)
2 *Marsanne* (1976)
3 *Alpine coach* (1976)
4 *Dark winds* (1985)
5 *Dark desire* (1987)

Napoleonic series
Aminoff, Constance Leonie Caroline
1 *Revolution* (1921)
2 *Love* (1922)
3 *Ambition* (1923)
4 *Success* (1924)
5 *Victory* (1925)
6 *Triumph* (1926)
7 *Glory* (1927)
8 *Arrogance* (1928)
9 *Storm* (1930)
10 *Retreat* (1938)

Companion volume: *Torchlight*, 1921

Napoleonic trilogy
Coryn, Marjorie
1 *Marriage of Josephine* (1945)
2 *Swarm of bees* (1947)
Goodbye my son
3 *Power instead* (1947)
Alone among men

Napoleonic Wars trilogy
Bryant, Arthur
1 *Years of endurance, 1793-1802* (1942)
2 *Years of victory, 1802-1812* (1944)
3 *Age of elegance, 1812-1822* (1950)

Napper series
Waddell, Martin
1 *Napper goes for goal* (1981)
2 *Napper strikes again* (1981)
3 *Napper's golden goals* (1984)

Napper Tandy series
Shepherd, Neal
see **Chief Inspector Michael Tandy series**

Napraxine series
Ouida
see **Princess Napraxine series**

Narayan series
Casberg, Melvin A
see **Captain Prem Narayan series**

NARC series
Hawkes, Robert
1 *NARC* (1973)
2 *Death of a courier* (1974)
3 *Death list* (1974)
4 *Delgado killings* (1974)
5 *Kill the dragon* (1974)
6 *Beauty kill* (1975)
7 *Corsican death* (1975)
8 *Kill for it* (1975)
9 *Death song* (1975)

Narcissa series
Faulkner, William
1 *Sartoris* (1929)
Flags in the dust
The second title is an enlarged edition
2 *Sanctuary* (1931)

Narnia series
Lewis, Clive Staples
1 *Magician's nephew* (1955)
2 *Lion, the witch and the wardrobe* (1950)
3 *Horse and his boy* (1954)
4 *Prince Caspian* (1951)
5 *Voyage of the Dawn Trader* (1952)
Numbers 4 and 5 also published in one volume 1989
6 *Silver chair* (1953)
7 *Last battle* (1956)
Numbers 6 and 7 also published in one volume 1990

Companion volume: *Narnia explored*, by Paul A Karkainen, 1979

Narnia solo games series
This sequence has four authors
Norris, Curtis
1 *Return to Deathwater* (1988)
Schraff, Anne Elaine
2 *Sorceress and the book of spells* (1988)
Norris, Curtis
3 *Leap of the lion* (1988)
Lientz, Gerald
4 *Lost crowns of Cair Paravel* (1988)
Bell, Rob
5 *Return of the white witch* (1988)

Narrow boat series
Finlay, Winifred
see **Susan series**

Narrow street series
Paul, Elliot
Reminiscences
1 *Last time I saw Paris* (1942)
Narrow street
2 *Linden on the Saugus branch* (1947)
3 *Ghost town on the Yellowstone* (1948)
4 *My old Kentucky home* (1949)
5 *Springtime in Paris* (1950)
6 *Desperate scenery* (1954)

Nash regime romance series
Castle, Agnes
see **Beau Nash regime romance series**

Nash series
Butler, Ragan
see **Captain George Nash series**
Davis, Tech
see **Aubrey Nash series**
Telfair, Richard
see **Monty Nash series**
Tucker, Wilson
see **Gilbert Nash series**

Nashville series
Crabb, Alfred Leland
1 *Dinner at Belmont* (1942)
2 *Supper at the Maxwell house* (1943)
3 *Breakfast at the Hermitage* (1945)
4 *Lodging at the Saint Cloud* (1946)
5 *Home to the Hermitage* (1948)

Companion volume: *Journey to Nashville, a story of the founding*, 1957

Nassim Pride series
Petrie, Rhona
see **Doctor Nassim Pride series**

Nat Ridley series
Ridley, Nat
1 *Guilty or not guilty?* (1926)
Alternative title: Nat Ridley's great race track case
2 *Tracked to the west* (1926)
Alternative title: Nat Ridley at the Magnet mine
3 *In the nick of time* (1926)
Alternative title: Nat Ridley saving a life
4 *Crime on the Limited* (1926)
Alternative title: Nat Ridley in the Follies
5 *Daring abduction* (1926)
Alternative title: Nat Ridley's biggest fight
6 *Stolen nugget of gold* (1926)
Alternative title: Nat Ridley on the Yukon
7 *Secret of the stage* (1926)
Alternative title: Nat Ridley and the bouquet of death
8 *Great circle mystery* (1926)
Alternative title: Nat Ridley on a crooked trail
9 *Scream in the dark* (1926)
Alternative title: Nat Ridley's crimson clue
10 *Racetrack crooks* (1926)
Alternative title: Nat Ridley's queerest puzzle
11 *Stolen Liberty Bonds* (1926)
Alternative title: Nat Ridley's circle of clues

12 *In the grip of the kidnappers* (1926)
Alternative title: Nat Ridley in high society
13 *Double dagger* (1926)
Alternative title: Nat Ridley's Mexican trail
14 *Mountain inn mystery* (1927)
Alternative title: Nat Ridley with the Forest Rangers
15 *Western Express robbery* (1927)
Alternative title: Nat Ridley and the mail thieves
16 *Struck down at midnight* (1927)
Alternative title: Nat Ridley and his rivals
17 *Detective against detective* (1927)
Alternative title: Nat Ridley showing his nerve

Nat series
Iwamura, Kazuo
Translated from the Japanese; English text by Kaye Webb
1 *Nat's hat* (1982)
2 *Nat's braces* (1982)

Nat Trevor series
West, Marvin
see **Motor Rangers series**

Natal series
Seed, Jenny
1 *Voice of the great elephant* (1968)
2 *Prince of the bay* (1970)
Vengeance of the Zulu king
3 *Broken spear* (1972)

Nate and Ricky series
Carkeet, David
see **Ricky and Nate series**

Nate Rosen series
Levitsky, Ronald
1 *Love that kills* (1991)
2 *Wisdom of serpents* (1992)
3 *Stone boy* (1993)
4 *Innocence that kills* (1994)

Nate the great series
Sharmat, Marjorie Weinman
Illustrated by Marc Simont
1 *Nate the great* (1972)
2 *Nate the great goes undercover* (1974)
3 *Nate the great and the lost list* (1975)
4 *Nate the great and the phony clue* (1977)
5 *Nate the great and the sticky case* (1978)
6 *Nate the great and the missing key* (1981)
7 *Nate the great and the snowy trail* (1982)
8 *Nate the great and the fishy prize* (1985)
9 *Nate the great stalks Stupidweed* (1986)
10 *Nate the great and the boring beach bag* (1987)
11 *Nate the great goes down in the dumps* (1989)
12 *Nate the great and the Halloween hunt* (1989)
13 *Nate the great and the musical note* (1990)
Co-author: Craig Sharmat
14 *Nate the great and the stolen base* (1992)

Nate Twitchell series
Butterworth, Oliver
1 *Enormous egg* (1956)
2 *Narrow passage* (1973)

Nathalie Page series
Halsey, Rena Isabelle
1 *Blue Robin, the girl pioneer* (1917)
2 *America's daughter* (1918)
3 *Liberty girl* (1919)

Nathan Brazil series
Chalker, Jack Laurence
see **Well world series**

Nathan Heller series
Collins, Max Allan
Set in Chicago in the 1930s introducing many historical characters such as Al Capone and Eliot Ness
1 *True detective* (1983)
2 *True crime* (1985)
3 *Million-dollar wound* (1986)
4 *Neon mirage* (1988)
5 *Dying in the post-war world* (1991)
6 *Carnal hours* (1993)

Nathan Jago series
Thompson, Ernest Victor
1 *Restless sea* (1983)
2 *Polrudden* (1985)

Nathan Mason Stark series
Fisher, Clay
1 *Tall men* (1954)
2 *Big pasture* (1955)

Nathan Shapiro series
The volumes of this sequence are published variously under the real names of the authors, separately or together, and under their pseudonym Francis Richards, in some cases using different names in the English and American editions
Lockridge, Frances
1 *Faceless adversary* (1956)
Case of the murdered redhead
2 *Tangled cord* (1957)
3 *Murder and blueberry pie* (1959)
English edition entitled *Call it coincidence*, published under the pseudonym Francis Richards
4 *Drill is death* (1961)
English edition published under the pseudonym Francis Richards
Lockridge, Richard
5 *Murder can't wait* (1964)
English edition published under the pseudonym Francis Richards
6 *Murder for art's sake* (1967)
English edition published under the pseudonym Francis Richards
7 *Die laughing* (1969)
English edition published under the pseudonym Francis Richards
8 *Preach no more* (1971)
9 *Write murder down* (1972)
10 *Or was he pushed?* (1975)
11 *Streak of light* (1976)
12 *Old die young* (1980)

Nathan Zuckerman series
Roth, Philip
1 *Ghost writer* (1979)
2 *Zuckerman unbound* (1981)
3 *Anatomy lesson* (1983)
Numbers 1-3 also published in one volume editions entitled *Zuckerman bound*, 1985, and *The Prague orgy*; this volume includes an epilogue entitled *The Prague orgy*
4 *Counterlife* (1987)
Companion volume: *My life as a man*, 1974

Nathaniel Bunce series
Curtiss, Elizabeth Mangam
1 *Nine doctors and a madman* (1937)
2 *Dead dogs bite* (1939)

Nathaniel Drinkwater series
Woodman, Richard
1 *Eye of the fleet* (1981)
2 *King's cutter* (1982)
3 *Brig of war* (1983)
4 *Bomb vessel* (1984)
5 *Corvette* (1985)
Arctic treachery
6 *Eighteen hundred and five* (1985)
Decision at Trafalgar
7 *Baltic mission* (1986)
8 *In distant waters* (1988)
9 *Private revenge* (1989)
10 *Wager* (1990)
11 *Under false colours* (1991)
12 *Flying squadron* (1992)

Nathaniel Ironsides Goss series
Willock, Colin Dennistoun
1 *Death at flight* (1956)
2 *Death at the strike* (1957)
3 *Death in covert* (1961)

Nathaniel King series
Thompson, David
1 *King of the mountain* (1990)
2 *Lure of the wild* (1990)
3 *Savage rendezvous* (1991)
4 *Dead man's ride* (1991)
5 *Tomahawk revenge* (1991)
6 *Black powder justice* (1991)
7 *Vengeance trail* (1991)
8 *Death hunt* (1992)
9 *Mountain devil* (1992)
10 *Blackfoot massacre* (1992)
11 *Northwest Passage* (1992)
12 *Apache blood* (1992)
13 *Mountain manhunt* (1993)
14 *Tenderfoot* (1993)
15 *Winterkill* (1993)
16 *Blood truce* (1993)
17 *Trapper's blood* (1994)
18 *Mountain cat* (1994)
19 *Iron warrior* (1994)
20 *Wolf pack* (1995)

Nathaniel Moody series
Lester, Edward Castellain
1 *Guy Fawkes murder* (1936)
2 *Murder of Martin Fotherill* (1937)

Nathaniel series
Arnosky, Jim
1 *Nathaniel* (1978)
2 *Mudtime and more Nathaniel stories* (1979)

National episodes series, epoch 1
Perez Galdos, Benito
1 *Trafalgar* (1873)
Original edition entitled *Trafalgar*
2 *Court of Charles IV* (1873)
Original edition entitled *La corte de Carlos IV*
3 *[Diecinuove de marzo y el dos de mayo]* (1873)
No English edition
4 *[Bailen]* (1873)
No English edition
5 *[Napoleon en Chamartin]* (1874)
No English edition
6 *Saragossa* (1874)
Original edition entitled *Zaragoza*
7 *[Gerona]* (1874)
No English edition
8 *[Cadiz]* (1874)
No English edition
9 *[Juan Martin el Empecinado]* (1874)
No English edition
10 *Battle of Salamanca* (1875)
Original edition entitled *La batalla de los Arapiles*
National episodes series, epochs 2-5, 1875-1912 are not translated into English

National Football League series
Berger, Phil
1 *Championship teams of the NFL* (1968)
2 *More championship teams of the NFL* (1974)

Native dwellings series
Shemie, Bonnie
1 *Houses of snow, skin and bones* (1989)
2 *Houses of bark* (1990)
Tipi, wigwam and longhouse
3 *Houses of hide and earth* (1991)
Tipi and earthlodges
4 *Houses of wood* (1992)
5 *Mounds of earth and shell* (1993)
6 *Houses of stone and adobe* (1994)

Native son series
Baldwin, James Arthur
Autobiography
1 *Notes of a native son* (1955)
2 *Nobody knows my name* (1961)

Native tongue series
Elgin, Suzette Haden
1 *Native tongue* (1984)
2 *Judas rose* (1987)

Natty Bumppo series
Cooper, James Fenimore
see **Leatherstocking series**

Natural and unnatural history series
McHargue, Georgess
1 *Beasts of Never* (1968)
Revised edition 1988; monsters mythological and magical
2 *Impossible people* (1972)
Beings terrible and wonderful

Natural history series
Burgess, Thornton Waldo
1 *Burgess bird book for children* (1919)
2 *Burgess animal book for children* (1920)
3 *Burgess flower book for children* (1923)
4 *Burgess seashore book for children* (1929)

Natural man series
Lloyd, John William
1 *Natural man* (1902)
A romance of the Golden Age
2 *Dwellers in Vale Sunrise* (1904)
How they got together and lived happy ever after

Naturalist series
Chambers, Robert William
see **Tales of a naturalist series**

Naturalized animals series
Lever, Christopher
1 *Naturalized animals of the British Isles* (1977)
2 *Naturalized mammals of the world* (1985)
3 *Naturalized birds of the world* (1988)

Nature and science series
Barclay, Vera Charlesworth
see **Joc and Colette series**

Nature secrets series
Selberg, Ingrid
1 *Secrets of the deep* (1990)
2 *Secrets of the pond* (1991)

Nature stories series
Burgess, Thornton Waldo
1 *On the green meadows* (1944)
2 *At the Smiling Pool* (1945)
3 *Crooked little path* (1946)
4 *Dear old briar-patch* (1947)
5 *Along Laughing Brook* (1949)
6 *At Paddy the Beaver's pond* (1950)

Naughtiest boy in the world series
Dickens, Frank
see **Albert Henry Hawkins series**

Naughtiest girl series
Blyton, Enid
1 *Naughtiest girl in the school* (1940)
2 *Naughtiest girl again* (1942)
3 *Naughtiest girl is a monitor* (1945)

Naughty baby series
McMullen, Nigel
1 *Never mind* (1984)
2 *Oh dear!* (1984)
3 *Night, night!* (1984)
4 *Hello, goodbye!* (1985)

Naughty children series
Blyton, Enid
1 *Book of naughty children* (1944)
2 *Second book of naughty children* (1947)

Naughty little sister series
Edwards, Dorothy
see **My naughty little sister series**

Naughty stories series
Milne, Christopher
1 *Naughty stories for good boys and girls* (1991)
2 *More naughty stories for good boys and girls* (1992)
3 *Even more naughty stories for good boys and girls* (1993)
4 *Naughty stories for good boys and girls, number 4* (1993)
5 *Naughty stories for good boys and girls, number 5* (1993)

Nautical series
Reynolds, Stephen
1 *Poor man's house* (1908)
2 *Alongshore* (1910)
Where man and the sea face one another
3 *Seems so* (1911)
A working class view of politics
4 *How 'twas* (1912)
Short stories and small travels

Naval adventure trilogy
Scott, Ian
1 *Two cadets* (1947)
2 *Two sub-lieutenants* (1950)
3 *Two lieutenants* (1952)

Naval digressions series
Franklin, Gordon
1 *Naval digression* (1916)
Originally published under the pseudonym G.F.
2 *Another naval digression* (1920)
The story of an Orcadian year

Naval life series
Baynham, Henry
1 *From the lower deck* (1969)
The old Navy, 1780-1840
2 *Before the mast* (1971)
Naval ratings of the nineteenth century

Naval occasions series
Bartimeus
1 *Naval occasions and some traits of the sailor-men* (1914)
2 *Tall ship on other naval occasions* (1915)
3 *Long trek* (1917)
Tales of the Navy in the First World War
4 *Awfully big adventure* (1919)
5 *Unreality* (1920)
A romance
6 *Seaways* (1923)
Short stories
7 *Under sealed orders* (1938)
A tale of yesterday
8 *Steady as you go* (1941)
Action stations
Sketches of naval occasions in World War II

Navarone series
Maclean, Alistair
1 *Guns of Navarone* (1957)
2 *Force ten from Navarone* (1968)

Navigator trilogy
Carr, Jayge
1 *Navigator's sindrome* (1983)
2 *Treasure in the heart of the maze* (1985)
3 *Rabelaisian reprise* (1988)

Navigators trilogy
Burton, Anthony
1 *Master idol* (1975)
2 *Navigators* (1976)
3 *Place to stand* (1977)

Navy and army series
Optic, Oliver
see **Army and navy series**

Navy boys of World War I series
Davidson, Halsey
1 *Navy boys after the submarines* (1918)
Alternative title: Protecting the giant convoy
2 *Navy boys chasing a sea raider* (1918)
Alternative title: Landing a million dollar prize
3 *Navy boys behind the big guns* (1919)
Alternative title: Sinking the German U-boats
4 *Navy boys to the rescue* (1919)
Alternative title: Answering the wireless call for help
5 *Navy boys at the big surrender* (1919)
Alternative title: Rounding up the German Fleet
6 *Navy boys on special service* (1920)
Alternative title: Guarding the floating treasury

Navy boys series
This sequence has three authors
Otis, James
1 *Navy boys' cruise with Paul Jones* (1898)
2 *Navy boys in New York Bay* (1898)
Chipman, William Pendleton
3 *Navu boys in the track of the enemy* (1898)
Otis, James
4 *Navy boys at the siege of Havana* (1899)
5 *Navy boys on Long Island Sound* (1901)
Chipman, William Pendleton
6 *Navy boys' daring capture* (1901)
7 *Navy boys' cruise to the Bahamas* (1903)
Ober, Frederick Albion
8 *Navy boys' cruise with Columbus* (1903)
Chipman, William Pendleton
9 *Navy boys in defense of liberty* (1908)
Otis, James
10 *Navy boys on Lake Ontario* (1908)
11 *Navy boys' cruise on the Pickering* (1909)
12 *Navy boys with Grant at Vicksburg* (1910)

Navy Seals series
Reeves, James R
1 *Mekong* (1987)
2 *Covert action* (1987)
Co-author: James C Taylor

Navy series
Winton, John
1 *We joined the Navy* (1959)
2 *We saw the sea* (1960)
3 *Down th hatch* (1961)
4 *Never go to sea* (1963)
5 *All the nice girls* (1964)
6 *Good enough for Nelson* (1977)

Naylor series
Lansing, Elizabeth
see **Nancy Naylor series**

Nazi hunter series
Mandell, Mark
1 *Nazi hunter* (1981)
2 *Slaughter summit* (1982)
3 *Killer instinct* (1982)
4 *Butcher block* (1982)
5 *Hell nest* (1983)

Nazi paratrooper series
Lutz, Gunther
1 *Storm Belgium* (1983)
2 *Crete must fall* (1983)
3 *Cassino corpse factory* (1983)

N'dala series
Young, Francis Brett
1 *Pilgrim's rest* (1922)
2 *Woodsmoke* (1924)

Neal Cotton series
Taylor, Sam S
1 *Sleep no more* (1949)
2 *No head for her pillow* (1952)
3 *So cold, my bed* (1953)

Neal Fargo series
This sequence is by Ben Haas using the pseudonym John Benteen except for number 18 which is by John W Hardin
Benteen, John
1 *Fargo* (1971)
2 *Panama gold* (1969)
3 *Alaska steel* (1969)
4 *Massacre river* (1969)
5 *Wildcatters* (1970)
6 *Apache raiders* (1970)
7 *Wolf's head* (1970)
8 *Valley of skulls* (1970)
9 *Sharpshooters* (1970)
10 *Black bulls* (1971)
11 *Phantom gunman* (1972)
12 *Killing spree* (1972)
13 *Shotgun man* (1973)
14 *Bandolero* (1973)
15 *Border jumpers* (1976)
16 *Hell on wheels* (1976)
17 *Killer's moon* (1976)
Hardin, John W
18 *Sierra silver* (1976)
Benteen, John
19 *Dynamite fever* (1976)
20 *Gringo guns* (1976)
21 *Death Valley gold* (1976)
22 *Dakota badlands* (1977)
23 *Fargo and the Texas rangers* (1977)

Neal Rafferty series
Wiltz, Chris
1 *Killing circle* (1981)
2 *Diamond before you die* (1987)

Near and distant series
Wright, Patrick
1 *I am England* (1987)
2 *That near and distant place* (1988)

Near and far series
Machen, Arthur
Autobiography
1 *Far off things* (1922)
2 *Things near and far* (1923)
One volume edition entitled *The autobiography of Arthur Machen*, 1974

Near-death series
Perry, Paul
Studies of near-death experiences
1 *Light beyond* (1988)
Co-author: Raymond Moody
2 *Close to the light* (1990)
Co-author: Melvin Morse
3 *Coming back* (1991)
Co-author: Raymond Moody
4 *Transformed by the light* (1992)
Co-author: Melvin Morse

Nebraska series
Reynolds, William J
1 *Nebraska quotient* (1984)
2 *Moving targets* (1986)
3 *Money trouble* (1988)
4 *Things invisible* (1989)
5 *Naked eye* (1990)

Nebraska trilogy
Sandoz, Mari
1 *Slogum House* (1937)
2 *Capital city* (1939)
3 *Tom-walker* (1947)

Nebraska trilogy
Winther, Sophus Keith
1 *Take all to Nebraska* (1936)
2 *Mortgage your heart* (1937)
3 *This passion never dies* (1938)

Necessary Smith and Jason Jones series
Crossen, Kendell Foster
see **Jason Jones and Necessary Smith series**

Necroscope series
Lumley, Brian
1 *Necroscope* (1982)
2 *Wamphyri!* (1988)
Vamphyri!
3 *Source* (1989)
4 *Deadspeak* (1990)
5 *Deadspawn* (1991)

Ned and Denise Toodles series
Jackson, Gabrielle Emilie
see **Denise and Ned Toodles series**

Ned, Bill and Jake series
Leyland, Eric
see **Bill, Jake and Ned series**

Ned, Bob and Jerry series
Young, Clarence
see **Motor boys series**

Ned Butler series
Rey, Bret
1 *Hold-up* (1987)
2 *Ned Butler, bounty hunter* (1988)
3 *Railroad robbers* (1988)

Ned Mansell series
Masefield, John
see **Autobiography of a corpse series**

Ned Parker series
Shelynn, Jack
1 *Place called Purgatory* (1978)
2 *Cuoto snatch* (1978)
3 *Night marches* (1979)
4 *For a girl called Isaiah* (1979)
5 *Judas factor* (1980)
6 *Joker in a stacked deck* (1981)

Ned Remington series
Boone, James Calder
1 *West of the Pecos* (1987)
2 *Good day for a hangin'* (1987)
3 *Showdown at Comanche Butte* (1987)
4 *Lawman's justice* (1987)
5 *Wyoming blood* (1987)
6 *Border trouble* (1988)
7 *Red River revenge* (1988)
8 *Six-guns at Spanish Peak* (1988)
9 *Lawless clan* (1988)

Ned series
Ellis, Edward Sylvester
see **Boy pioneer series**
Kroll, Steven
see **Newsman Ned series**
Masefield, John
see **Autobiography of a corpse series**

Ned series
Zinnemann-Hope, Pam
Illustrated by Kady Macdonald Denton
1 *Time for bed, Ned* (1986)

2 *Find your coat, Ned* (1986)
3 *Let's play ball, Ned* (1986)
4 *Let's go shopping, Ned* (1986)

Ned Shackleton series
Crawley, Rayburn
1 *Valley of Creeping Men* (1930)
2 *Chattering gods* (1931)

Ned Yorke series
Pope, Dudley
1 *Convoy* (1979)
2 *Buccaneer* (1981)
3 *Admiral* (1982)
4 *Decoy* (1983)
5 *Galleon* (1986)
6 *Corsair* (1987)

Nedao trilogy
Emerson, Ru
1 *To the haunted mountains* (1987)
2 *In the caves of exile* (1988)
3 *On the seas of destiny* (1989)

Needle series
Clement, Hal
1 *Needle* (1950)
From outer space
2 *Through the eye of a needle* (1978)

Nefertiti trilogy
Hamilton, Alexandra
1 *Beautiful one* (1979)
2 *Lady of grace* (1979)
3 *Devious being* (1980)

Neighbours series
Shears, Sarah
1 *Neighbours* (1982)
2 *Neighbours' children* (1983)

Neil and Swede trilogy
Robertson, Keith
1 *Mystery of Burnt Hill* (1952)
2 *Three stuffed owls* (1954)
3 *Crow and the castle* (1957)

Neil Bathurst series
Lynch, Lawrence L
1 *Shadowed by three* (1879)
2 *Diamond coterie* (1882)
3 *Out of the labyrinth* (1885)

Neil Carter series
Dewhurst, Eileen
see **Inspector Neil Carter series**

Neil Falder series
Ward, Richard Heron
1 *Conspiracy* (1964)
2 *Wilderness* (1958)
3 *Offenders* (1960)

Neil Hamel series
Van Gieson, Judith
1 *North of the border* (1988)
2 *Raptor* (1990)
3 *Other side of death* (1991)
4 *Wolf path* (1992)
5 *Lies that bind* (1993)

Neil Hockaday series
Adcock, Thomas
1 *Dark maze* (1991)
2 *Drown all the dogs* (1994)
3 *Devil's heaven* (1995)

Neil Kelly series
Dean, S F X
see **Professor Neil Kelly series**

Nell Bartlett series
Elias, David
1 *Cause of the screaming* (1953)
2 *Gory details* (1954)
3 *Dress up and die* (1955)

Nell Gwynne trilogy
Sumner, Richard
Based on the life of Nell Gwynne
1 *Mistress of the streets* (1974)
2 *Mistress of the boards* (1976)
3 *Mistress of the King* (1978)

Nell Willard series
Lynch, Miriam
1 *Time to kill* (1979)
2 *You'll be the death of me* (1979)

Nellie Gates series
Boardman, M M
1 *Nellie Gates and the little missionary* (1867)
2 *Mother-in-law* (1867)

Nels Lundberg and Wylie King series
Saunders, Lawrence
see **Wylie King and Nels Lundberg series**

Nelson boys series
Barnes, Michael
1 *Nelson boys and their cobalt adventure* (1973)
Alternative title: The mystery of the old mine
2 *Nelson boys and their Wawa adventure* (1975)
Alternative title: Lake Superior diamond mystery

Nelson in Naples series
Dumas, Alexandre
1 *Neapolitan lovers* (1865)
Original edition entitled *La San-Felice*
2 *Love and liberty* (1865)
Alternative title: Nelson at Naples; original edition entitled *Souvenirs d'une favourite*

Nelson Malone series
Hawes, Louise
1 *Nelson Malone meets the man from Mush-Nut* (1986)
2 *Nelson Malone saves Flight 942* (1988)

Nelson of the Guards series
Kersh, Gerald
see **Brigade of Guards series**

Nelson series
Allard, Harry
see **Miss Nelson series**
Fenisong, Ruth
see **Captain Gridley Nelson series**
Frye, Pearl
see **Lord Horatio Nelson series**
Grey, Romer Zane
see **Laramie Nelson series**
Mulford, Clarence Edward
see **Johnny Nelson series**
Norman, Frank
see **Ed Nelson series**

Nemo series
Verne, Jules
see **Captain Nemo series**

Nerac series
Soubiran, Andre
see **Jean Nerac series**

Nere series
Colette, Sidonie Gabrielle
see **Renee Nere series**

Nero Wolfe and Archie Goodwin series
This sequence has two authors
Stout, Rex
1 *Fer-de-lance* (1934)
Meet Nero Wolfe
2 *League of Frightened Men* (1935)
3 *Rubber band* (1936)
To kill again
4 *Red box* (1937)
Case of the red box
5 *Too many crooks* (1938)
6 *Some buried Caesar* (1938)
Red bull
7 *Over my dead body* (1940)
8 *Where there's a will* (1940)
9 *Black orchids* (1942)
Case of the black orchids
Two novelettes entitled *Cordially invited to meet death*, also published separately, 1945, and, *Black orchids*
10 *Not quite dead enough* (1944)
Two novelettes entitled *Not quite dead enough*, and, *Booby trap*
11 *Silent speaker* (1946)
12 *Too many women* (1947)
13 *And be a villain* (1948)
More deaths than one
14 *Trouble in triplicate* (1949)
Three novelettes entitled *Help wanted, male, Instead of evidence, Before I die*
15 *Second confession* (1949)
Even in the best families
16 *Three doors to death* (1950)
Three novelettes entitled *Man alive, Omit flowers, Door to death*
17 *In the best families* (1950)
Even in the best families
18 *Curtains for three* (1950)
Three novelettes entitled *Bullet for one, The gun with wings, Disguise for murder*
19 *Murder by the book* (1951)
20 *Triple jeopardy* (1952)
Three novelettes entitled *The cop-killer, The squirt and the monkey, Home to roost*
21 *Prisoner's Base* (1952)
Out she goes
22 *Golden spiders* (1953)
23 *Three men out* (1954)
Three novelettes entitled *This won't kill you, Invitation to murder, The zero clue*
24 *Black mountain* (1954)
25 *Before midnight* (1955)
26 *Three witnesses* (1956)
Three novelettes entitled *When a man murders, Die like a dog, The next witnesses*
27 *Might as well be dead* (1956)
28 *Three for the chair* (1956)
Three novelettes entitled *Immune to murder, A window for death, Too many detectives*
29 *If death ever slept* (1957)
30 *Champagne for one* (1958)
31 *And four to go* (1958)
Crime and again
Four novelettes entitled *Christmas party, Easter Parade, Fourth of July picnic, Murder is no joke*
32 *Plot it yourself* (1959)
Murder in style
33 *Three at Wolfe's door* (1960)
Three novelettes entitled *Poison a la carte, Method three for murder, The rodeo murder*
34 *Too many clients* (1960)
35 *Final deduction* (1961)
36 *Homicide trinity* (1962)
Three novelettes entitled *Death of a demon, Eeny meeny murder, Counterfeit for murder*
37 *Gambit* (1962)
38 *Mother hunt* (1963)
39 *Trio for blunt instruments* (1964)
Three novelettes entitled *Kill now, pay later, Murder is corny, Blood will tell*
40 *Right to die* (1964)
41 *Doorbell rang* (1965)
42 *Death of a doxy* (1966)
43 *Father hunt* (1968)
44 *Death of a dude* (1969)
45 *Please pass the guilt* (1973)
46 *Family affair* (1975)
47 *Death times three* (1985)
Three novelettes
Goldsborough, Robert
48 *Murder in E minor* (1986)
49 *Death on deadline* (1987)
50 *Bloodied ivy* (1988)
51 *Last coincidence* (1989)
52 *Fade to black* (1990)
Companion volume: *Nero Wolfe cook book*, by Rex Stout, 1973

Ness series
Collins, Max Allan
see **Eliot Ness series**

Nessa and Lance series
Hogg, Garry
1 *Cross-Channel quest* (1956)
2 *Mystery on the moor* (1957)

Nessa series
Luenn, Nancy
1 *Nessa's fish* (1990)
2 *Nessa's story* (1994)

Nessel series
Blomefield, Mathena
1 *Bulleymung pit* (1946)
2 *Nuts in the rockery* (1946)

Nessie series
Mosley, Francis
1 *Nessie goes to Mars* (1988)
2 *Nessie on holiday* (1988)
3 *Tim and Emily meet Nessie* (1988)
4 *Nessie goes to Hollywood* (1988)

Nestleton series
Adamson, Lydia
see **Alice Nestleton series**

Nethercourt series
Adams, Henry Cadwallader
1 *Chief of the school* (1873)
Alternative title: Schoolboy ambition
2 *Doctor's birthday* (1873)
Alternative title: The force of example
3 *Walter's friend* (1873)
Alternative title: Big boys and little ones
4 *Lost rifle* (1880)
Alternative title: Schoolboy faction

Netta and Paul tetralogy
Hilliard, Noel
1 *Maori girl* (1960)
2 *Power of joy* (1965)
3 *Maori woman* (1974)
4 *Glory and the dream* (1978)

Nettleford series
Saville, Malcolm
1 *All summer through* (1951)
2 *Christmas at Netleford* (1953)
3 *Spring comes to Nettleford* (1954)
4 *Secret of Buzzard Scar* (1955)

Network-Consortium series
Franklin, Cheryl Jean
1 *Light in exile* (1990)
2 *Inquisitor* (1992)

Neuman series
Oster, Jerry
see **Jake neuman series**

Neumiller family series
Woiwode, Larry
1 *Beyond the bedroom wall* (1975)
2 *Born brothers* (1988)

Neuromancer trilogy
Gibson, William
1 *Neuromancer* (1984)
2 *Count Zero* (1986)
3 *Mona Lisa overdrive* (1988)

Neustrian trilogy
Barringer, Leslie
1 *Gerfalcon* (1927)
2 *Joris of the Rock* (1928)
3 *Shy leopardess* (1948)

Nevada Jim Lacy series
This sequence has two authors
Grey, Zane
1 *Nevada* (1928)
Grey, Romer Zane
2 *Beyond the Mogollon Rim* (1980)

Nevada Jim series
Grover, Marshall
Some titles in this sequence were originally published under the pseudonym Marshall McCoy as indicated
1 *Night McLennan died* (1964)
2 *Gun-trapped* (1964)
3 *Meet me in Moredo* (1965)
4 *Gun sinister* (1965)
5 *Killer's noon* (1965)
6 *One man jury* (1965)
7 *Devil's legend* (1965)
8 *No escape trail* (1965)
9 *League of the lawless* (1965)
10 *Valiant die fast* (1965)
11 *One thousand dollar target* (1965)
12 *Hour before disaster* (1965)
13 *Main Street Gallego* (1965)
14 *Saturday wild* (1966)
15 *Wear black for Johnny* (1966)
16 *Man who hunts Jenner* (1966)
17 *Canyon vigil* (1966)
18 *Shadow of a Colt .45* (1966)
19 *They came to plunder* (1966)
20 *Tall man's challenge* (1966)
21 *Bullet is faster* (1966)
22 *Die lonesome* (1966)
23 *Thirty raiders south* (1966)
24 *Satan pulled the trigger* (1966)
25 *Diablo's shadow* (1966)
26 *Kid Daybreak* (1966)
27 *Vengeance rides a black horse* (1966)
McCoy, Marshall
28 *Man called Drago* (1967)
Grover, Marshall
29 *Six rogues riding* (1967)
30 *Fury at Broken Wheel* (1967)
McCoy, Marshall
31 *Big Lobo* (1967)
Grover, Marshall
32 *Challenge the guilty* (1967)
33 *Driscoll* (1967)
McCoy, Marshall
34 *Limbo Pass* (1967)
35 *Seven westbound* (1967)
36 *Justice for Jenner* (1967)
Grover, Marshall
37 *Bury the guilty* (1967)
Also published under the pseudonym Marshall McCoy
McCoy, Marshall
38 *Crisis at Cornerstone* (1967)
39 *No gun is neutral* (1967)
40 *Die brave* (1967)
41 *Killers came at noon* (1967)
42 *Guns of greed* (1968)
43 *Gun flash* (1968)
44 *Killer bait* (1968)
Grover, Marshall
45 *Hangrope fever* (1968)
46 *Spur route* (1968)
47 *Behind a black mask* (1968)
Also published under the pseudonym Marshall McCoy
48 *Requiem for Sam Wade* (1968)
49 *Dead man's bluff* (1968)
50 *Satan's back-trail* (1968)
Also published under the pseudonym Marshall McCoy
51 *Bounty on Wes Durand* (1968)
Also published under the pseudonym Marshall McCoy
52 *Willing target* (1969)
53 *Stand alone* (1969)
54 *Rogue trail* (1969)
55 *Danger rode drag* (1969)
56 *Day of vengeance* (1969)
57 *Carson's bonanza* (1969)
58 *Savage Sunday* (1969)
59 *Name on the bullet* (1969)
60 *Ransom on a redhead* (1969)
61 *Fort Ricks* (1970)
62 *Sundance creek* (1970)
63 *No tomorrow for Tobin* (1970)
64 *Killers wore black* (1971)
65 *Hartigan* (1971)
66 *Gunfight at Doone's Well* (1971)
67 *Hell in High County* (1984)
68 *Ten fast horses* (1984)

Never-Never series
Gunn, Jeannie
1 *Little black princess* (1905)
Little black princess of the Never-Never
2 *We of the Never-Never* (1908)

Never sink nine series
Davis, Gibbs
1 *Lucky socks* (1991)
2 *Major-league Melissa* (1991)
3 *Slugger Mike* (1991)
4 *Pete the Magnificent* (1991)
Number 5 not identified
6 *Christy's magic glove* (1992)
7 *Olympics Otis* (1993)
8 *Katie kicks off* (1994)
9 *Diamond Park dinosaur* (1994)

Nevers series
Glazner, Joseph Mark
see **Billy Nevers series**

Neveryon series
Delany, Samuel Ray
1 *Tales of Neveryon* (1979)
2 *Neveryona* (1983)
Alternative title: The tale of signs and cities
3 *Flight from Neveryon* (1985)
4 *Bridge of lost desire* (1987)
Return to Neveryon

Neville Langham series
Daniel, Roland
see **Inspector Neville Langham series**

Neville series
Irwin, Frances
see **Anne Neville series**

Nevsky series
Gat, Dimitri
see **Yuri Nevsky series**

New age series
Hood, Hugh
1 *Swing in the garden* (1975)
2 *New Athens* (1977)
3 *Reservoir ravine* (1979)
4 *Black and white keys* (1982)
5 *Scenic art* (1984)
6 *Motor boys in Ottowa* (1986)
7 *Tony's book* (1988)
8 *Property and value* (1990)
9 *Be sure to close your eyes* (1994)

New Americans series
Nicole, Christopher
1 *Brothers and enemies* (1982)
2 *Lovers and outlaws* (1982)

New Atalantis series
Manley, Mary de la Riviere
1 *Secret memoirs and manners of several persons of quality* (1709)
Originally published in two volumes
2 *Memoirs of Europe, towards the close of the eighth century* (1710)
Originally published in two volumes under the pseudonym Eginardus
3 *Court intrigues in a collection of original letters* (1711)
4 *Modern Atalantis* (1784)
Alternative title: The devil in an air balloon, containing the characters and secret memoirs of the most conspicuous persons of high quality of both sexes in the island of Libertusia

New Avengers series
This sequence has four authors
Cave, Peter
1 *House of cards* (1976)
Carter, John
2 *Eagle's nest* (1976)
Harris, Walter
3 *To catch a rat* (1977)
Cartwright, Justin
4 *Fighting men* (1977)
Cave, Peter
5 *Last of the Cybernauts* (1977)
6 *Hostage* (1977)

New baby books series
Ormerod, Jan
1 *This little nose* (1987)
2 *Bend and stretch* (1987)
3 *Making friends* (1987)
4 *Mum's home* (1987)

New baby series
Graham, Bob
1 *Waiting for the new baby* (1989)
2 *Visiting the new baby* (1989)
3 *Bringing home the new baby* (1989)
4 *Getting to know the new baby* (1989)

New Baron Munchausen series
Mitchell, Adrian
Illustrated by Patrick Benson
1 *Baron rides out* (1985)
2 *Baron on the Island of Cheese* (1986)
3 *Baron all at sea* (1987)

New Bobbsey twins series
Hope, Laura Lee
House pseudonym
1 *Secret of Jungle Park* (1987)
2 *Case of the runaway money* (1987)
3 *Clue that flew away* (1987)
4 *Secret of the sand castle* (1988)
5 *Case of the close encounter* (1988)
6 *Mystery on the Mississippi* (1988)
7 *Trouble in Toyland* (1988)
8 *Secret of the stolen puppies* (1988)
9 *Clue in the classroom* (1988)
10 *Chocolate-covered clue* (1989)
11 *Case of the crooked contest* (1989)
12 *Secret of the sunken treasure* (1989)
13 *Case of the crying clown* (1989)
14 *Mystery of the missing mummy* (1989)
15 *Secret of the stolen clue* (1989)
16 *Case of the missing dinosaur* (1990)
17 *Case at Creepy Castle* (1990)
18 *Secret at Sleepaway Camp* (1990)
19 *Show and tell mystery* (1990)
20 *Weird science mystery* (1990)
21 *Great skate mystery* (1990)
22 *Super-duper cookie caper* (1991)
23 *Monster mouse mystery* (1991)
24 *Case of the Goofy game show* (1991)
25 *Case of the crazy collections* (1991)
26 *Clue at Casper Creek* (1991)
27 *Big pig puzzle* (1991)
28 *Case of the vanishing video* (1992)
29 *Case of the tricky trickster* (1992)
30 *Mystery of the mixed-up mall* (1992)

New boy trilogy
Horne, Donald
Autobiography
1 *Education of young Donald* (1967)
2 *Confessions of a new boy* (1985)
3 *Portrait of an optimist* (1988)

New breed heroes series
Gutman, Bill
1 *New breed heroes in pro baseball* (1973)
2 *New breed heroes in pro football* (1974)

New Brotherhood series
Ward, Mary Augusta
1 *Robert Elsmore* (1888)
2 *Case of Richard Meynell* (1911)

New Deerfoot series
Ellis, Edward Sylvester
1 *Deerfoot in the forest* (1905)
2 *Deerfoot in the mountains* (1905)
3 *Deerfoot on the prairie* (1905)

New Doctor Who adventures series
Peel, John
see **Timewyrm series**

New Eden series
Roos, Stephen
1 *My horrible secret* (1983)
2 *Terrible truth* (1983)
Secrets of a sixth-grader
3 *My secret admirer* (1984)

New Forest series
Mogridge, Stephen
1 *New Forest adventure* (1953)
2 *New Forest mystery* (1954)
3 *New Forest quest* (1955)
4 *New Forest exploits* (1956)
5 *New Forest discoveries* (1957)
6 *New Forest smugglers* (1958)
7 *New Forest pirates* (1959)
8 *New Forest vagabond* (1960)
9 *New Forest detectives* (1962)
10 *New Forest treasure* (1963)
11 *New Forest spies* (1964)

New Holland series
Weaver, Rix
1 *Behold, New Holland!* (1940)
2 *New Holland heritage* (1941)

New kids at the Polk Street School series
Giff, Patricia Reilly
1 *Watch out, man-eating snake* (1988)
2 *If the shoe fits* (1988)
3 *All about Stacy* (1988)
4 *B-E-S-T friends* (1988)
5 *Spectacular stone soup* (1989)
6 *Stacy says good-bye* (1989)
7 *Stacy says good-bye* (1989)
8 *Spectacular stone soup* (1989)
9 *Beast and the Halloween horror* (1989)

New kids on the block series
Catalano, Grace
1 *New kids on the block* (1989)
2 *New kids on the block scrapbook* (1990)

New lady from L.U.S.T. series
Gray, Rod
1 *Go for broke* (1975)
2 *Have a snort* (1975)
3 *Target for tonight* (1975)
4 *Maracaibo affair* (1975)
5 *Voodoo kill* (1975)
6 *Kill her with love* (1975)

New Mexico trilogy
Eastlake, William
see **Bowman family trilogy**

New Mexico trilogy
Nichols, John
1 *Milagro Beanfield War* (1974)
2 *Magic journey* (1978)
3 *Nirvana blues* (1981)

New series
Peterson, Hans
1 *New house* (1964)
Original edition entitled *Det nya huset*
2 *New road* (1967)
Original edition entitled *Den nya vagen*

3 *New bridge* (1969)
Original edition entitled *Den nya bron*

New South Wales series
Bonner, Terry Nelsen
This pseudonym is used by several authors whose authorship is indicated against those titles where it is known
1 *Rum colony* (1982)
2 *First families* (1982)
3 *Free woman* (1983)
[Laura Ann Castoro]
4 *Pioneers* (1983)
5 *Outback* (1983)
[Chelsea Quinn Yarbro]
6 *Unvanquished* (1983)
7 *Diggers* (1983)
[Steven Mark Krauzer]
8 *Seekers* (1983)
9 *Defiant* (1983)
[Sheila Raeschild]

New springtime series
Silverberg, Robert
1 *At winter's end* (1988)
Winter's end
2 *Queen of springtime* (1989)
New springtime

New Tarzan series
Werper, Barton
1 *Tarzan and the silver globe* (1964)
2 *Tarzan and the cave city* (1964)
3 *Tarzan and the snake people* (1964)
4 *Tarzan and the abominable snowman* (1965)
5 *Tarzan and the winged invaders* (1965)

New theories series
Lampton, Christopher
1 *New theories on the dinosaurs* (1989)
2 *New theories on the origins of the human race* (1989)
3 *New theories on the birth of the universe* (1989)

New time trilogy
Cannan, Gilbert
1 *Pugs and peacocks* (1921)
2 *Sembal* (1922)
3 *House of prophecy* (1924)

New world series
Huxley, Aldous
1 *Brave new world* (1932)
A novel concerning mind control
2 *Brave new world revisited* (1958)
A study of the development of mind control in the twentieth century

New world trilogy
Alger, Horatio
1 *Digging for gold* (1892)
2 *Facing the world* (1893)
Alternative title: The haps and mishaps of Harry Vane
3 *In a new world* (1893)
Alternative title: Among the gold fields of Australia

New world trilogy
Kahn, James
1 *World enough, and time* (1980)
2 *Time's dark laughter* (1982)
3 *Timefall* (1987)

New world trilogy
Madariaga, Salvador de
1 *Christopher Columbus* (1939)
The life of the very magnificent Lord Don Cristobal Colon
2 *Hernan Cortes* (1941)
Conqueror of Mexico
3 *Bolivar* (1951)
Abridged from the two volume Spanish edition

New York detective series
Marshall, William Leonard
see **Tillman and Muldoon series**

New York diaries series
Carroll, Jim
1 *Basketball diaries* (1978)
12 to 15 years old
2 *Forced entries* (1987)
The downtown diaries, 1971-73

New York gang series
Cruz, Nicky
Reminiscences of life in a teenage gang
1 *Run, baby, run* (1968)
2 *Lonely now* (1971)

New York in maps series
George, Jean Craighead
1 *New York in maps, 1972-73* (1974)
2 *New York in flashmaps, 1974-75* (1976)

New York series
Frederic, Harold
1 *Seth's brother's wife* (1886)
A study of life in greater New York
2 *Lawton girl* (1890)

New York series
Gill, Brendan
1 *Here at the New Yorker* (1975)
2 *New York life* (1990)
Of friends and others

New York trilogy
Auster, Paul
1 *City of glass* (1985)
2 *Ghosts* (1986)
3 *Locked room* (1987)
One volume edition entitled *The New York trilogy*, 1987

New York trilogy
Barr, Amelia Edith
1 *Bow or orange ribbons* (1888)
2 *Maid of Maiden Lane* (1900)
3 *Song of a single note* (1905)

New York trilogy
Friesner, Esther Mona
1 *New York by knight* (1986)
2 *Elf defense* (1988)
3 *Sphynxes wild* (1989)

New York trilogy
Sinclair, Upton
1 *Metropolis* (1907)
2 *Moneychangers* (1908)
Revised edition 1923
3 *Machine* (1912)
A play

New York trilogy
Stead, Christina
1 *Letty Fox, her luck* (1946)
2 *Little tea, a little chat* (1948)
3 *People with the dogs* (1952)

New Zealand bush series
Dallas, Ruth
see **Jean, Robbie, Sophie and Helen series**

New Zealand life series
Scott, Mary
1 *Breakfast at six* (1953)
2 *Yours to oblige* (1954)
3 *Dinner doesn't matter* (1957)
4 *Tea and biscuits* (1961)
5 *Change from mutton* (1964)
6 *Turkey at twelve* (1968)
7 *Haven't we met before?* (1970)
8 *If I don't, who will?* (1971)
9 *Shepherd's pie* (1972)
10 *Strangers for tea* (1975)
11 *Board but no breakfast* (1978)

New Zealand revolution series
James, Colin
1 *Quiet revolution* (1986)
New Zealand in transition
2 *New territory* (1993)
Transformation of New Zealand, 1984-1992

New Zealand schoolgirl series
Garrard, Phillis
see **Hilda series**

Newberry series
Lee, Jennette Barbour Perry
see **Millicent Newberry series**

Newcastle-upon-Tyne series
Common, Jack
1 *Kiddar's luck* (1951)
Reminiscences of childhood
2 *Ampersand* (1954)
Autobiographical novel

Neweden trilogy
Leigh, Stephen
1 *Slow fall to dawn* (1981)
2 *Dance of the hag* (1983)
3 *Quiet of stone* (1984)

Newell Paige series
Douglas, Lloyd Cassel
1 *Green light* (1934)
2 *Invitation to live* (1940)

Newhome series
Randall, Marta
1 *Journey* (1978)
2 *Dangerous games* (1980)

Newman and Townley series
Bearshaw, Brian
see **Superintendent Robert Townley and Sergeant Roger Newman series**

Newman series
Nuttall, Nesta
see **Meri Newman series**

Newman, Tweed and Grey series
Forbes, Colin
see **Tweed, Grey and Newman series**

Newnes series
Martindale, Cyril Charlie
see **Mister Francis Newnes series**

News from Korea series
Perry, Jean
1 *Chilgoopie the Glad* (1906)
2 *Man in grey* (1906)
3 *Uncle Mac the missionary* (1906)
Companion volume: *Twenty years a Korean missionary*, 1911

Newsman Ned series
Kroll, Steven
1 *Newsman Ned meets the new family* (1988)
2 *Newsman Ned and the broken rules* (1989)

Newsom series
Stewart, Flora
see **Inspector Newsom series**

Newspaper Children series
De la Mahotiere, Mary
1 *Newspaper Children* (1959)
2 *Round-up on Exmoor* (1961)

Newspaper series
Garis, Howard Roger
see **Great newspaper series**

Newton series
Conway, Peter
see **Inspector Newton series**

Next wave series
This sequence has two authors
Sykes, Sondra Catharine
1 *Red genesis* (1991)
Leigh, Stephen
2 *Alien tongue* (1991)

Neyler family series
Saxton, Judith
1 *Pride* (1981)
2 *Glory* (1982)
3 *Splendour* (1983)
4 *Full circle* (1984)

Ngali and Mayli series
Trezise, Percy
1 *Lasca and her pups* (1990)
2 *Children of the great lake* (1992)

Nghsi-Altai series
Nichols, Robert
see **Daily lives in Nghsi-Altai series**

Ni-lach series
Bennett, Marcia Joanne
1 *Where the Ni-lach* (1983)
2 *Shadow singer* (1984)
3 *Beyond the Draak's teeth* (1986)
4 *Seeking the dream brother* (1989)

Nibs series
Nokes, Ethel
see **Billy Bunker series**

Niccolo Benedetti series
De Andrea, William Louis
1 *Werewolf murders* (1992)
2 *Manx murders* (1994)

Niccolo series
Dunnett, Dorothy
see **House of Niccolo series**

Nicholas and Suzanne series
Ichikawa, Satomi
see **Suzanne and Nicholas series**

Nicholas and Suzette series
Mangin, Marie France
see **Suzette and Nicholas series**

Nicholas Barlow series
Carter, Robert A
1 *Casual slaughters* (1992)
2 *Final edit* (1994)

Nicholas Carter series
Carter, Nicholas
This pseudonym is used by many authors including Andrews, A L Armagnac, Babcock, Ball, William Perry Brown, George Waldo Browne, Buchanan, Frederick Russel Burton, O P Caylor, Stephen Chalmers, Weldon J Cobb, William Wallace Cook, John Russell Coryell, S A D Cox, Frederick William Davis, E C Derby, Frederic Van Rensselaar Dey, Ferguson, Walter Bertram Foster, Charles Witherle Hooke, Howard, William Cadwalader Hudson, George Charles Jenks, Larned, Lincoln, Charles Agnw Maclean, Makee, St George Rathborne, Rich, Russell, Eugene T Sawyer, Vincent Scott, Samuel C Spalding, Splint, Edward L Stratemeyer, Alfred B Tozer, Tyson, R F Walsh, Willard whose authorship is indicated where it is known; this sequence character, Nicholas Carter, is the original Nick Carter, private detective
1 *Titled counterfeiter* (1888)
[Coryell]
2 *American marquis* (1889)
[Coryell]
3 *Old detective's pupil* (1889)
[Coryell]
4 *Wall Street haul* (1889)
[Coryell]

Nicholas Carter series

5 *Woman's hand* (1890) [Coryell]
6 *Victim of circumstance* (1891) [Davis]
7 *Crime of a countess* (1892) [Coryell]
8 *Gambler's syndicate* (1892) [Dey]
9 *Fighting against millions* (1892) [Coryell]
10 *Great enigma* (1892) [Dey]
11 *Piano box mystery* (1892) [Dey]
12 *Stolen identity* (1892) [Dey]
13 *Australian Klondyke* (1897) [Burton; Dey]
14 *Caught in the toils* (1897) [Dey]
15 *Klondike claim* (1897) [Lincoln]
16 *Mysterious mail robbery* (1897) [Dey]
17 *Playing a bold game* (1897) [Dey]
18 *Tracked across the Atlantic* (1897) [Dey]
19 *At odds with Scotland Yard* (1898) [Burton]
20 *Accidental password* (1898) [Burton]
21 *Among the nihilists* (1898) [Burton]
22 *At Thompson's ranch* (1898) [Burton]
23 *Check number 777* (1898) [Burton]
24 *Deposit vault puzzle* (1898) [Dey]
25 *Chance discovery* (1898) [Dey]
26 *Double Shuffle Club* (1898) [Burton]
27 *Evidence by telephone* (1898) [Dey]
28 *Found on the beach* (1898) [Burton]
29 *Fair criminal* (1898) [Burton]
30 *Man from India* (1898) [Burton]
31 *Millionaire partner* (1898) [Burton]
32 *Among the counterfeiters* (1898) [Dey]
33 *Bite of an apple, and other stories* (1899) [Hooke]
34 *Adventures of Harrison Keith, detective* (1899) Short stories
35 *Detective's pretty neighbor, and other stories* (1899)
36 *Dead man's grip* (1899) [Dey]
37 *Clever celestial* (1899) [Burton]
38 *Crescent brotherhood* (1899) [Tozer]
39 *Gideon Drexel's millions, and other stories* (1899) [Dey]
40 *Diamond mine case* (1899) [Burton]
41 *Great money order swindle* (1899) [Dey]
42 *Herald personal, and other stories* (1899) [Hooke]
43 *Man who vanished* (1899) [Burton; Cobb]
44 *Nick Carter's clever protege* (1899) [Burton; Cobb]
45 *Nick Carter and the green goods men* (1899) [Dey]
46 *Sealed orders* (1899) [Dey]
47 *Puzzle of the five pistols, and other stories* (1899) [Hooke]
48 *Sign of the crossed knives* (1899) [Burton]
49 *Stolen racehorse* (1899) [Hooke] Short stories
50 *Twelve wise men* (1899) [Burton]
51 *Twelve tin boxes* (1899) [Cobb]
52 *Stolen pay train, and other stories* (1899) [Hooke]
53 *Two plus two* (1899) [Dey]
54 *Wanted by two clients* (1899) [Burton]
55 *Van Alstine case* (1899) [Burton]
56 *Brought to bay* (1900) [Cobb; Stratemeyer]
57 *Crime of the French cafe, and other stories* (1900) [Hooke]
58 *Crossed wires* (1900) [Cobb]
59 *Elevated railroad mystery, and other stories* (1900) [Hooke]
60 *Game of craft* (1900) [Sawyer; Tozer]
61 *Framework of fate* (1900) [Davis]
62 *Held for trial* (1900) [Davis]
63 *Lady Velvet* (1900)
64 *Nick Carter's clever ruse* (1900) [Davis]
65 *Man who stole millions, and other stories* (1900) [Hooke]
66 *Nick Carter down east* (1900) [Burton]
67 *Nick Carter's girl detective* (1900) [Cobb]
68 *Nick Carter's star pupils* (1900) [Cobb]
69 *Princess of crime* (1900) [Cobb]
70 *Nick Carter's retainer* (1900)
71 *Silent passenger* (1900) [Davis]
72 *Bogus clew* (1901) [Burton]
73 *Blow of a hammer, and other stories* (1901) [Cobb]
74 *Bottle and the black label* (1901) [Cobb]
75 *Desperate chance* (1901) [Davis]
76 *Dumb witness, and other stories* (1901) [Cobb]
77 *Man of mystery* (1901) [Sawyer]
78 *In letters of fire* (1901)
79 *Man from London* (1901) [Cobb]
80 *Man at the window* (1901) [Davis]
81 *Murray Hill mystery* (1901)
82 *Missing cotton king* (1901) [Burton; Dey; Tozer]
83 *Millions at stake, and other stories* (1901) [Cobb; Sawyer; Tozer]
84 *Price of a secret* (1901) [Dey]
85 *Prince of rogues* (1901) [Cobb]
86 *Queen of knaves, and other stories* (1901) [Dey; Tozer]
87 *Seal of silence* (1901) [Cobb]
88 *Scrap of black lace* (1901) [Davis]
89 *Triple crime* (1901) [Cobb]
90 *Steel casket, and other stories* (1901) [Sawyer]
91 *At the knife's point* (1902) [Caylor; Stratemeyer; Tozer]
92 *Behind a mask* (1902) [Dey]
93 *Deal in diamonds* (1902) [Cobb]
94 *Chain of evidence* (1902) [Dey]
95 *Claws of the tiger* (1902) [Davis]
96 *Criminal link* (1902) [Dey]
97 *Double-handed game* (1902) [Dey; Stratemeyer]
98 *Driven from cover* (1902) [Dey]
99 *False combination* (1902)
100 *Hounded to death* (1902) [Hudson]
101 *Man against man* (1902) [Dey]
102 *Man and his price* (1902) [Burton; Cook; Tozer]
103 *Move in the dark* (1902) [Davis]
104 *Nick Carter's death warrant* (1902) [Sawyer; Tozer]
105 *Played to a finish* (1902) [Davis]
106 *Race for ten thousand* (1902) [Davis]
107 *Red signal* (1902) [Davis]
108 *Run to earth* (1902) [Dey]
109 *Trusted rogue* (1902) [Davis]
110 *Stroke of policy* (1902) [Hudson]
111 *Syndicate of rascals* (1902) [Cobb]
112 *Two villains in one* (1902) [Hudson]
113 *Tell-tale photographs* (1902) [Davis]
114 *Toss of a coin* (1902) [Dey; Stratemeyer]
115 *Vial of death* (1902) [Dey; Stratemeyer]
116 *Weaving the web* (1902) [Dey]
117 *Blackmailer's bluff* (1903) [Hooke; Hudson; Walsh]
118 *Blow for vengeance* (1903) [Burton]
119 *Blood-red badge* (1903) [Burton]
120 *Barrel mystery* (1903) [Burton]
121 *Bonded villain* (1903) [Caylor]
122 *Cashier's secret* (1903) [Caylor; Hooke]
123 *Checkmated scoundrel* (1903) [Hudson]
124 *Crown diamond* (1903) [Burton]
125 *Cloak of guilt* (1903) [Burton; Stratemeyer]
126 *Council of death* (1903) [Hudson]
127 *Circumstantial evidence* (1903) [Hudson]
128 *Fatal prescription* (1903) [Hudson]
129 *Guilty governor* (1903) [Burton]
130 *Heard in the dark* (1903) [Hudson]
131 *Great conspiracy* (1903) [Burton]
132 *Hole in the vault* (1903) [Hudson]
133 *Masterpiece of crime* (1903) [Burton]
134 *Mysterious game* (1903)
135 *Paid with death* (1903) [Davis]
136 *Photographer's evidence* (1903) [Burton]
137 *Seal of death* (1903)
138 *Race track gamble* (1903) [Hudson; Stratemeyer]
139 *Sharper's downfall* (1903) [Hudson]
140 *Ring of dust* (1903) [Burton]
141 *Twin mystery* (1903) [Hudson]
142 *Under false colors* (1903) [Burton]
143 *Cab driver's secret* (1904) [Caylor; Tozer]
144 *Against desperate odds* (1904) [Dey]
145 *Bundle of clews* (1904) [Caylor; Sawyer]
146 *Beyond pursuit* (1904) [Hooke; Stratemeyer]
147 *Ahead of the game* (1904) [Cobb; Stratemeyer; Tozer]
148 *Broken trail* (1904) [Tozer]
149 *Certified check* (1904) [Cook, Derby, Tozer]
150 *Following a chance clew* (1904) [Caylor; Hooke; Tozer]
151 *Detective's theory* (1904) [Caylor; Cobb]
152 *In the gloom of night* (1904) [Dey]
153 *Hot air clew* (1904) [Andrews; Stratemeyer]
154 *Ingenious strategem* (1904) [Dey]
155 *Mystic diagram* (1904) [Dey]
156 *Missing man* (1904) [Caylor; Hooke; Sawyer]
157 *Master villain* (1904) [Browne; Hooke; Sawyer]
158 *Mysterious foe* (1904) [Burton; Hudson]
159 *Playing a lone hand* (1904) [Cobb]
160 *Secret panel* (1904) [Hooke; Tozer]
161 *Scientific forger* (1904) [Burton; Dey; Tozer]
162 *Queen of diamonds* (1904) [Caylor; Sawyer]
163 *Ruby pin* (1904) [Burton]
164 *Toss of a penny* (1904) [Caylor; Derby]
165 *Terrible threat* (1904)
166 *Wizard of the cue* (1904) [Caylor; Stratemeyer; Tozer]
167 *Bloodstone terror* (1905) [Dey]
168 *Cigarette clew* (1905) [Cook]
169 *Crime of the camera* (1905) [Dey]
170 *Boulevard mutes* (1905) [Dey]
171 *Baffled oath* (1905) [Cook]
172 *Down and out* (1905) [Dey]
173 *Four-fingered glove* (1905) [Dey]
174 *Diamond trail* (1905) [Burton]
175 *Living mask* (1905)
176 *Key ring clew* (1905) [Armagnac]
177 *Marked hand* (1905)
178 *Plot that failed* (1905)
179 *Nick Carter's double catch* (1905) [Dey]
180 *Playing for a fortune* (1905) [Davis]
181 *Mysterious graft* (1905) [Cook; Davis]
182 *Price of treachery* (1905) [Dey]
183 *Pretty stenographer mystery* (1905) [Makee]
184 *Royal thief* (1905) [Burton; Cook]
185 *Victim of deceit* (1905) [Dey]
186 *Under a black veil* (1905) [Dey]
187 *Trapped in his own net* (1905) [Dey]
188 *Terrible thirteen* (1905) [Dey]

189 *Tangled case* (1905) [Hooke; Stratemeyer; Tozer]
190 *Villainous scheme* (1905) [Burton; Hudson]
191 *Triple identity* (1905) [Dey]
192 *With links of steel* (1905) [Dey]
193 *Broadway cross* (1906) [Dey]
194 *Behind a throne* (1906) [Dey]
195 *Captain Sparkle, private* (1906) [Dey]
196 *Baffled, but not beaten* (1906) [Dey]
197 *Accident or murder?* (1906) [Dey; Howard]
198 *Case without a clue* (1906) [Dey]
199 *Death circle* (1906) [Dey]
200 *From a prison cell* (1906) [Dey]
201 *Doctor Quartz, magician* (1906) [Dey]
202 *Doctor Quartz's quick move* (1906) [Dey]
203 *Limited hold-up* (1906) [Dey]
204 *In the lap of danger* (1906) [Spalding]
205 *Lure of gold* (1906) [Dey]
206 *Man who was cursed* (1906) [Dey]
207 *Marked for death* (1906) [Dey]
208 *Nick Carter's fall* (1906) [Dey]
209 *Out of death's shadow* (1906) [Sawyer]
210 *Nick Carter's masterpiece* (1906) [Dey]
211 *Plot within a plot* (1906) [Dey]
212 *Sign of the dagger* (1906) [Dey]
213 *Unaccountable crook* (1906) [Dey]
214 *Trapped by a woman* (1906) [Dey]
215 *Under the tiger's claw* (1906) [Dey]
216 *Voice from the past* (1906) [Sawyer]
217 *Through the cellar wall* (1906) [Dey]
218 *Amazing scoundrel* (1907) [Dey]
219 *Brotherhood of death* (1907) [Dey]
220 *Chase in the dark* (1907) [Dey; Hooke; Sawyer]
221 *Bank draft puzzle* (1907) [Dey; Tozer]
222 *Carnival of crime* (1907) [Dey]
223 *Bargain in crime* (1907) [Dey; Sawyer]
224 *Chain of clues* (1907) [Dey; Maclean]
225 *Demon's eye* (1907) [Dey; Willard]
226 *Fight for a throne* (1907) [Dey; Tozer]
227 *Dead stranger* (1907)
228 *Done in the dark* (1907) [Dey]
229 *Finger of suspicion* (1907) [Dey]
230 *Cry for help* (1907) [Dey; Willard]
231 *Game of plots* (1907) [Dey; Tozer]
232 *Demons of the night* (1907) [Burton; Dey]
233 *Double plot* (1907) [Dey]
234 *Dynamite trap* (1907) [Browne; Dey]
235 *Harrison Keith's chance clue* (1907) [Lincoln]
236 *Harrison Keith's warning* (1907) [Sawyer]
237 *Harrison Keith's struggle* (1907)
238 *Harrison Keith's dilemma* (1907) [Sawyer]
239 *Harrison Keith's triumph* (1907) [Sawyer]
240 *Harrison Keith's greatest task* (1907) [Foster]
241 *Harrison Keith's oath* (1907) [Lincoln]
242 *Harrison Keith's big stakes* (1907) [Lincoln]
243 *Harrison Keith, sleuth* (1907) [Dey]
244 *Harrison Keith's danger* (1907) [Sawyer]
245 *Human fiend* (1907) [Dey; Sawyer]
246 *Man of iron* (1907) [Dey]
247 *Legacy of hate* (1907) [Caylor; Dey]
248 *Man without a conscience* (1907) [Dey]
249 *Nick Carter's close call* (1907) [Dey; Sawyer]
250 *Nick Carter's Chinese puzzle* (1907) [Dey]
251 *Red League* (1907) [Dey; Sawyer]
252 *Silent guardian* (1907) [Dey; Sawyer]
253 *Worst case on record* (1907) [Stratemeyer]
254 *Woman of evil* (1907) [Dey]
255 *Woman of steel* (1907) [Dey; Sawyer]
256 *Crime and the motive* (1908) [Dey]
257 *Artful schemer* (1908) [Dey]
258 *Game well played* (1908) [Caylor; Dey]
259 *False claimant* (1908) [Dey]
260 *Girl in the case* (1908) [Dey]
261 *From peril to peril* (1908) [Dey; Scott]
262 *Doctor's strategem* (1908) [Davis]
263 *Fight with a fiend* (1908) [Dey]
264 *Hand that won* (1908) [Dey; Lincoln]
265 *Hand to hand* (1908) [Babcock; Dey; Makee]
266 *Harrison Keith's fight for life* (1908) [Foster]
267 *Harrison Keith's drag net* (1908) [Foster]
268 *Harrison Keith's time lock case* (1908) [Foster]
269 *Harrison Keith's double mystery* (1908) [Jenks]
270 *Harrison Keith's weird partner* (1908) [Foster]
271 *Harrison Keith's wireless message* (1908) [Sawyer]
272 *Harrison Keith's queer clue* (1908) [Jenks]
273 *Harrison Keith's crooked trail* (1908) [Foster]
274 *Harrison Keith's tact* (1908) [Foster]
275 *Harrison Keith's chance shot* (1908) [Jenks]
276 *Harrison Keith's strange summons* (1908) [Foster]
277 *Harrison Keith's mystic letter* (1908) [Foster]
278 *Harrison Keith's diamond case* (1908) [Sawyer]
279 *Hunter of men* (1908) [Dey; Hooke]
280 *In death's grip* (1908) [Dey]
281 *Lost Chittendens* (1908) [Dey]
282 *Man to be feared* (1908) [Dey]
283 *Lady of shadows* (1908) [Dey]
284 *Into Nick Carter's web* (1908) [Dey]
285 *Nick Carter's cipher* (1908) [Derby; Dey]
286 *Nabob and knave* (1908) [Cook; Davis]
287 *Nick Carter's promise* (1908) [Dey; Sawyer]
288 *Nick Carter's auto trail* (1908) [Dey]
289 *One step too far* (1908) [Foster]
290 *Plunge into crime* (1908) [Dey]
291 *Snare and the game* (1908) [Davis]
292 *Silent partner* (1908) [Davis; Dey]
293 *Ring of rascals* (1908) [Dey]
294 *Prince of liars* (1908) [Derby; Scott]
295 *Trap of tangled wire* (1908) [Dey; Ferguson]
296 *Strike for freedom* (1908) [Dey; Stratemeyer]
297 *Tangled threads* (1908) [Davis; Dey]
298 *When the trap was sprung* (1908) [Dey]
299 *Without a clue* (1908) [Dey]
300 *At mystery's threshold* (1909) [Davis]
301 *Blindfold mystery* (1909) [Dey]
302 *Death at the feast* (1909) [Dey]
303 *Disciple of Satan* (1909) [Davis]
304 *Harrison Keith's battle of nerve* (1909) [Larned]
305 *Harrison Keith's abduction tangle* (1909) [Larned]
306 *Harrison Keith's dual role* (1909) [Davis]
307 *Harrison, Keith, magician* (1909) [Davis]
308 *Harrison Keith at bay* (1909) [Larned]
309 *Harrison Keith's green diamond* (1909) [Larned]
310 *Harrison Keith and the phantom heiress* (1909) [Larned]
311 *Harrison Keith's haunted client* (1909) [Larned]
312 *Harrison Keith's triple tragedy* (1909) [Davis]
313 *Harrison Keith's death compact* (1909) [Davis]
314 *Harrison Keith's lucky strike* (1909) [Jenks]
315 *Harrison Keith's mummy mystery* (1909) [Larned]
316 *Harrison Keith's close quarters* (1909) [Davis]
317 *Harrison Keith's cameo case* (1909) [Larned]
318 *Harrison Keith's padlock mystery* (1909) [Davis]
319 *Harrison Keith's sparkling trail* (1909) [Larned]
320 *Harrison Keith's river front ruse* (1909) [Larned]
321 *Harrison Keith's double cross* (1909) [Davis]
322 *In search of himself* (1909) [Dey]
323 *Master of deviltry* (1909) [Dey]
324 *Nick Carter's swim to victory* (1909) [Dey]
325 *Plaything of fate* (1909) [Dey]
326 *Out of crime's depth* (1909) [Davis]
327 *Reaping the whirlwind* (1909) [Davis]
328 *Saved by a ruse* (1909) [Dey]
329 *Plot uncovered* (1909) [Dey; Tozer]
330 *Temple of vice* (1909) [Dey]
331 *Great diamond syndicate* (1909) [Tozer]
332 *When the wicked prosper* (1909) [Dey]
333 *Woman at bay* (1909) [Dey]
334 *Behind closed doors* (1910)
335 *Disappearing princess* (1910) [Dey]
336 *Behind the black mask* (1910)
337 *Crystal mystery* (1910) [Dey]
338 *Doom of the Reds* (1910) [Dey]
339 *Harrison Keith's death watch* (1910) [Larned]
340 *Last move in the game* (1910) [Foster]
341 *Harrison Keith's labyrinth* (1910) [Larned]
342 *Harrison Keith's studio crime* (1910) [Larned]
343 *Harrison Keith's wager* (1910) [Larned]
344 *Harrison Keith's perilous contract* (1910) [Cox]
345 *King's prisoner* (1910) [Dey]
346 *Harrison Keith's poison problem* (1910)
347 *Harrison Keith's river mystery* (1910) [Larned]
348 *Harrison Keith, star reporter* (1910) [Larned]
349 *Harrison Keith's cyclone clue* (1910) [Larned]
350 *Nick Carter's convict client* (1910) [Tozer]
351 *Nick Carter's wildest chase* (1910) [Dey]
352 *Nick Carter's persistence* (1910) [Brown]
353 *Nation's peril* (1910) [Dey]
354 *Rajah's ruby* (1910) [Dey]
355 *Scourge of the wizard* (1910)
356 *Talika, the geisha girl* (1910) [Dey]
357 *Trail of the catspaw* (1910)
358 *Elusive knave* (1911) [Dey]
359 *At face value* (1911) [Dey]
360 *Devil's son* (1911) [Spalding]
361 *Fatal margin* (1911) [Dey]
362 *Comrades of the right hand* (1911) [Tozer]
363 *Chase for millions* (1911) [Dey]
364 *Face in the shadow* (1911) [Tozer]
365 *Call on the phone* (1911) [Dey]
366 *Broken on crime's wheel* (1911) [Tozer]
367 *Confidence king* (1911) [Dey]
368 *Fatal falsehood* (1911) [Dey]
369 *For a madman's millions* (1911) [Dey]
370 *Jeweled mummy* (1911) [Foster]
371 *Matter of skill* (1911) [Splint]

Nicholas Carter series

372 *Four hoodoo charms* (1911) [Dey]
373 *Masterly trick* (1911) [Dey]
374 *Man in the auto* (1911) [Foster]
375 *Gift of the gods* (1911) [Splint]
376 *House of doom* (1911) [Rathborne]
377 *House of the yellow door* (1911) [Larned]
378 *Madame Q* (1911) [Larned]
379 *King of the underworld* (1911) [Splint]
380 *Handcuff wizard* (1911) [Larned]
381 *Live wire clue* (1911) [Foster]
382 *Quest of the Lost Hope* (1911) [Tozer]
383 *Room of mirrors* (1911) [Dey]
384 *Plot for an empire* (1911) [Dey]
385 *Question of time* (1911) [Rathborne]
386 *Mysterious castle* (1911) [Dey]
387 *Nick Carter's intuition* (1911) [Larned]
388 *Pauline* (1911) [Dey]
389 *Nick Carter's roundup* (1911) [Larned]
390 *War of brains* (1911) [Foster]
391 *Second Mister Carstairs* (1911) [Rathborne]
392 *Submarine trail* (1911) [Foster]
393 *Senator's plot* (1911) [Dey]
394 *Streaked peril* (1911) [Dey]
395 *Shown on the screen* (1911) [Dey]
396 *Weak-kneed rogue* (1911) [Rathborne]
397 *Triple knock* (1911) [Tozer]
398 *Vanishing emerald* (1911) [Foster]
399 *When a man yields* (1911) [Larned]
400 *Way of the wicked* (1911) [Tozer]
401 *When necessity drives* (1911) [Tyson]
402 *Whirling death* (1911) [Rathborne]
403 *Crime of a century* (1912) [Dey]
404 *Fatal hour* (1912) [Dey]
405 *Connecting link* (1912) [Davis]
406 *Buried secret* (1912) [Dey]
407 *By an unseen hand* (1912) [Spalding]
408 *Call in the night* (1912) [Spalding]
409 *Bandits of the air* (1912) [Hooke]
410 *Crimson flash* (1912) [Davis]
411 *Double mystery* (1912) [Davis]
412 *Case of the two doctors* (1912) [Spalding]
413 *Deadly scarab* (1912) [Spalding]
414 *Dead man's accomplice* (1912) [Dey]
415 *Clew by clew* (1912) [Davis]
416 *Man with a crutch* (1912) [Davis]
417 *On a crimson trail* (1912) [Davis]
418 *Man with a double* (1912)
419 *Nick Carter's subtle foe* (1912) [Dey]
420 *Master criminal* (1912) [Davis]
421 *Nick Carter's menace* (1912) [Spalding]
422 *House of whispers* (1912) [Davis]
423 *In queer quarters* (1912)
424 *Nick Carter's last card* (1912) [Dey]
425 *Nick Carter's Egyptain clew* (1912) [Cook]
426 *In the face of the evidence* (1912) [Rathborne]
427 *Nick Carter's counterplot* (1912) [Dey]
428 *In the Nick of time* (1912)
429 *Million in diamonds* (1912) [Spalding]
430 *Nick Carter's close finish* (1912)
431 *Nick Carter's chance clue* (1912) [Dey]
432 *Mysterious cavern* (1912) [Dey]
433 *Missing deputy chief* (1912) [Spalding]
434 *Play for millions* (1912) [Dey]
435 *Silver hair clue* (1912) [Davis]
436 *Red triangle* (1912) [Dey]
437 *Out for vengeance* (1912) [Davis]
438 *Plot for a warship* (1912)
439 *Seven schemers* (1912) [Dey]
440 *Taxicab riddle* (1912) [Dey]
441 *Stolen name* (1912) [Dey]
442 *Path of the spendthrift* (1912)
443 *Tangled in crime* (1912) [Dey]
444 *Rogue's reach* (1912) [Dey]
445 *Vanishing heiress* (1912) [Dey]
446 *Trail of the Yoshiga* (1912)
447 *Triple knavery* (1912) [Ball]
448 *Woman of mystery* (1912) [Dey]
449 *When jealousy spurs* (1912)
450 *Written in blood* (1912) [Davis]
451 *Vampire's trail* (1912) [Foster]
452 *Tooth and nail* (1912) [Davis]
453 *Vain sacrifice* (1912) [Dey]
454 *Woman in black* (1912) [Browne]
455 *Diamond cut diamond* (1913)
456 *In the shadow of fear* (1913)
457 *Clutch of dread* (1913) [Spalding]
458 *Angel of death* (1913) [Spalding]
459 *In suspicion's shadow* (1913) [Russell]
460 *Babbington case* (1913) [Dey]
461 *Cornered at last* (1913) [Davis]
462 *Doomed to failure* (1913)
463 *House across the street* (1913)
464 *Double identity* (1913) [Dey]
465 *Driven to desperation* (1913)
466 *Duel of brains* (1913) [Spalding]
467 *Brought to the mark* (1913)
468 *Day of reckoning* (1913)
469 *Heart of the underworld* (1913)
470 *For the sake of revenge* (1913)
471 *Finish of a rascal* (1913)
472 *Caught in a whirlpool* (1913)
473 *Mills of the law* (1913) [Spalding]
474 *Riddle of identities* (1913) [Dey]
475 *Repaid in like coin* (1913)
476 *Moving picture mystery* (1913)
477 *Knots in the noose* (1913)
478 *Kregoff necklace* (1913) [Dey]
479 *Purple spot* (1913) [Davis]
480 *Poisons of Exili* (1913) [Davis]
481 *Nick Carter and the red button* (1913) [Dey]
482 *Nick Carter's new assistant* (1913) [Dey]
483 *Nick Carter's treasure chest case* (1913) [Davis]
484 *Points to crime* (1913) [Dey]
485 *Man who fainted* (1913)
486 *Plea for justice* (1913)
487 *International Crook League* (1913) [Davis]
488 *Maze of motives* (1913)
489 *On the eve of triumph* (1913) [Spalding]
490 *Rogue of quality* (1913) [Spalding]
491 *Midnight message* (1913) [Dey]
492 *Millionaire's mania* (1913) [Larned]
493 *Turn of a card* (1913) [Dey]
494 *Toying with fate* (1913)
495 *Whom the gods would destroy* (1913) [Spalding]
496 *While the fetters were forged* (1913)
497 *Spider's parlor* (1913) [Dey]
498 *Unfinished letter* (1913) [Dey]
499 *Sign of the coin* (1913) [Dey]
500 *Tower of strength* (1913)
501 *When clews are hidden* (1913) [Spalding]
502 *When all is staked* (1913)
503 *Sting of the adder* (1913) [Spalding]
504 *When a rogue's in power* (1913) [Spalding]
505 *Thief in the night* (1913)
506 *Weighed in the balance* (1913) [Spalding]
507 *Sway of sin* (1913)
508 *Miscarriage of justice* (1914) [Spalding]
509 *After the verdict* (1914)
510 *Instinct at fault* (1914) [Jenks]
511 *In the toils of fear* (1914) [Jenks]
512 *Microbe of crime* (1914) [Davis]
513 *Birds of prey* (1914) [Davis]
514 *Blind man's daughter* (1914) [Davis]
515 *Heritage of trouble* (1914)
516 *Bolts from blue skies* (1914) [Spalding]
517 *Man who paid* (1914)
518 *Bullion mystery* (1914) [Jenks]
519 *Man who changed faces* (1914) [Armagnac]
520 *Called to account* (1914) [Rich]
521 *Fixed alibi* (1914) [Davis]
522 *Fight for right* (1914)
523 *Door of doubt* (1914)
524 *Dodging the law* (1914)
525 *Knaves in high places* (1914)
526 *Crime in paradise* (1914) [Spalding]
527 *Keeper of the black hounds* (1914) [Jenks]
528 *Crook's blind* (1914) [Davis]
529 *Man of riddles* (1914)
530 *Gloved hand* (1914) [Davis]
531 *Just and the unjust* (1914) [Jenks]
532 *Grafters* (1914) [Spalding]
533 *Deeper game* (1914) [Davis]
534 *Last call* (1914) [Davis]
535 *On the ragged edge* (1914) [Jenks]
536 *Not on the records* (1914)
537 *Spoilers and the spoils* (1914)
538 *Perilous parole* (1914) [Jenks]
539 *With shackles of fire* (1914) [Spalding]
540 *Rascal of quality* (1914) [Jenks]
541 *Spoils of chance* (1914) [Davis]
542 *Red god of tragedy* (1914) [Spalding]
543 *When destruction threatens* (1914) [Davis]
544 *Rogue worth trapping* (1914)
545 *Rope of slender threads* (1914) [Spalding]
546 *Wanted, a clew* (1914) [Davis]
547 *Sandalwood slipper* (1914) [Andrews]
548 *Struggle with destiny* (1914) [Jenks]
549 *Wages of rascality* (1914) [Chalmers]
550 *Unseen foes* (1914) [Davis]
551 *Tangled skein* (1914) [Spalding]
552 *Trail of the fingerprints* (1914) [Spalding]
553 *Thief who was robbed* (1914) [Davis]
554 *Skyline message* (1914) [Davis]
555 *Slave of crime* (1914)
556 *Out with the tide* (1914) [Jenks]
557 *One object in life* (1914) [Jenks]
558 *Wolf within* (1914) [Davis]
559 *As a crook sows* (1915) [Jenks]
560 *Girl prisoner* (1915) [Spalding]
561 *Gargoni girdle* (1915) [Davis]
562 *Middle link* (1915) [Davis]
563 *In record time* (1915) [Armagnac; Derby]
564 *Danger of folly* (1915) [Spalding]
565 *Held in suspense* (1915) [Jenks]
566 *Hate that kills* (1915) [Davis]
567 *Just one slip* (1915) [Jenks]
568 *Too late to talk* (1915)
569 *Where peril beckons* (1915) [Jenks]
570 *When honors pall* (1915) [Armagnac]
571 *Rascals and Company* (1915) [Spalding]
572 *On a million dollar trail* (1915) [Scott]

573 *Test of courage* (1915)
574 *Satan's apt pupil* (1915) [Jenks]
575 *Scoundrels rampant* (1915)
576 *Scourged by fear* (1915) [Spalding]
577 *One shipwreck too many* (1915)
578 *When brave men tremble* (1915) [Jenks]
579 *Soul destroyers* (1915) [Jenks]
580 *Weird treasure* (1915) [Spalding]
581 *To the ends of the earth* (1915) [Jenks]
582 *One hundred thousand dollar kiss* (1915) [Spalding]
583 *Yellow brand* (1915) [Spalding]
584 *Man without a will* (1916) [Spalding]
585 *Red palgue* (1916) [Spalding]
586 *Mixed-up mess* (1916) [Davis]
587 *Broken bars* (1916) [Davis]
588 *Burden of proof* (1916)
589 *Case of many clues* (1916) [Spalding]
590 *Clew against clew* (1916)
591 *Clue from the unknown* (1916) [Spalding]
592 *Conspiracy of rumors* (1916) [Spalding]
593 *When rogues conspire* (1916) [Spalding]
594 *Twelve in a grave* (1916) [Spalding]
595 *Trail of the human tiger* (1916) [Dey]
596 *Evil formula* (1916) [Davis]
597 *Stolen brain* (1916) [Buchanan; Spalding]
598 *Over the edge of the world* (1916) [Spalding]
599 *From clue to clue* (1916)
600 *Great opium case* (1916)
601 *Sealed door* (1916) [Spalding]
602 *In the grip of fate* (1916) [Spalding]
603 *Magic necklace* (1916)
604 *Man of many faces* (1916) [Spalding]
605 *Round the world for a quarter* (1916) [Spalding]
606 *Pressing peril* (1917) [Davis]
607 *Outlaws of the blue* (1917) [Jenks]
608 *Sultan's pearls* (1917) [Jenks]
609 *Paying the price* (1917) [Davis]
610 *Won by magic* (1917) [Jenks]
611 *For a pawned crown* (1917) [Spalding]
612 *Found in the jungle* (1917) [Jenks]
613 *Needy Nine* (1917) [Davis]
614 *Man they held back* (1917) [Jenks]
615 *Adder's brood* (1917) [Spalding]
616 *Blood will tell* (1918) [Davis]
617 *Crook's double* (1918) [Davis]
618 *Crossed needles* (1918) [Jenks]
619 *Amphitheatre plot* (1918) [Spalding]
620 *Death in life* (1918) [Spalding]
621 *Snarled identities* (1918)
622 *Yellow label* (1918) [Jenks; Spalding]
623 *Network of crime* (1918) [Davis]
624 *Partners in peril* (1919)
625 *Broken bond* (1919)
626 *Threefold disappearance* (1919) [Spalding]
627 *Sea Fox* (1919)
628 *Hidden foes* (1919)
629 *Battle for the right* (1919)
630 *Secret of the marble mantle* (1920) [Spalding]
631 *Wildfire* (1920) [Spalding]
632 *Spinner of death* (1920) [Spalding]

Nicholas Cornish series
Mackenzie, Andrew
1 *Always fight back* (1955)
2 *Three hours to hang* (1955)
3 *Grave is waiting* (1957)
4 *Reaching hand* (1957)
5 *Shadow of a spy* (1958)
6 *Man from the past* (1958)
7 *Missile* (1959)

Nicholas de la Haye series
Turner, James Ernest
1 *Crimson moth* (1962)
2 *Long avenue* (1964)
3 *Anna Chevron* (1966)

Nicholas Harding and Antony Maitland series
Woods, Sara
see **Sir Nicholas Harding and Antony Maitland series**

Nicholas Hart series
Glemser, Bernard
1 *Nicholas kept on writing* (1964)
2 *Departing friends* (1979)

Nicholas Howard series
Sims, George
1 *Last best friend* (1967)
2 *Sand dollar* (1969)

Nicholas Irtenyev trilogy
Tolstoi, Leo Nikolaevich
Translated from the Russian; autobiographical novels
1 *Childhood* (1852)
2 *Boyhood* (1854)
3 *Youth* (1857)

Nicholas Linnear series
Lustbader, Eric
see **Ninja series**

Nicholas Maasten series
Sela, Owen
1 *Bearer plot* (1972)
2 *Portuguese fragment* (1973)
3 *Kiriov tapes* (1973)

Nicholas Minnett series
Logan, Mark
1 *Tricolour* (1976)
Captain's woman
2 *Guillotine* (1976)
French kiss
3 *Brumaire* (1978)
December passion

Nicholas Mountry series
Hammand, Norman Bentley
see **Sir Nicholas Mountry series**

Nicholas Pym series
Sanders, John
1 *Firework for Oliver* (1964)
2 *Hat of authority* (1965)
3 *Without trumpet or drum* (1966)
4 *Cromwell's cavalier* (1968)
5 *Roundhead retreat* (1971)

Nicholas Ramage series
Pope, Dudley
see **Lord Nicholas Ramage series**

Nicholas series
Douglas, Felicity
1 *Alarms and excursions* (1952)
2 *Sentimental smuggler* (1953)

Nicholas series
Goscinny, Rene
1 *Young Nicholas* (1960)
Original edition entitled *Le petit Nicolas*
2 *Nicholas and the gang* (1960)
Original edition entitled *Le petit Nicolas et les copains*, part 1
3 *Nicholas and the gang at school* (1960)
Adventures of Nicholas and the gang
Original edition entitled *Le petit Nicolas et les copains*, part 2
4 *Nicholas and the gang again* (1961)
Original edition entitled *Les recres du petit Nicolas*
5 *Nicholas on holiday* (1962)
Original edition entitled *Les vacances du petit Nicolas*
6 *Nicholas at large* (1964)
Original edition entitled *Joachim a des ennuis*

Nicholas series
Sandberg, Inger
Illustrated by Lasse Sandberg
1 *Nicholas' red day* (1964)
Original edition entitled *Niklas roeda dag*
2 *Nicholas' ideal pet* (1967)
Nicholas' favorite pet
Original edition entitled *Niklas oenskedjur*

Nicholas Slade series
Woodthorpe, Ralph Carter
1 *Silence of a purple shirt* (1934)
Death wears a purple shirt
2 *Necessary corpse* (1939)

Nicholas Van Rijn and David Falkeyn series
Anderson, Poul
see **Polesotechnic League series**

Nichols and Burton series
Peters, Geoffrey
see **Inspector Trevor Nichols and Sergeant Tom Burton series**

Nichols series
Clark, Joan
see **Penny Nichols series**

Nicholson series
Barr, Robert
see **Nick Nicholson series**

Nicholson series
Kelly, Mary
1 *Spoilt kill* (1961)
2 *Due to a death* (1962)
Dead of summer

Nick Allard series
Barclay, Bill
This sequence was rewritten as the **Jerry Cornell series** under the author's real name Michael Moorcock
1 *Somewhere in the night* (1966)
2 *Printer's devil* (1966)

Nick and Company series
Croson, Bob
1 *Nick and Company in a fix* (1985)
2 *Nick and Company on holiday* (1986)
3 *Nick and Company to the rescue* (1990)
4 *Nick and Company clean up* (1993)

Nick and Nancy series
Barton, Olive Roberts
see **Nancy and Nick series**

Nick and Tim Diamond series
Horowitz, Anthony
1 *Falcon's Malteser* (1986)
2 *Public enemy number two* (1987)

Nick Attwell series
Underwood, Michael
see **Sergeant Nick Attwell series**

Nick Bailey series
Carter, Bruce
1 *Four wheel drift* (1959)
Revised edition 1973
2 *Fast circuit* (1962)

Nick Caine series
Zochert, Donald
1 *Another weeping woman* (1980)
2 *Man of glass* (1983)

Nick Carter series
Carter, Nick
This pseudonym is used by many authors whose authorship is indicated against those titles where it is known; the series character, Nick Carter, differs from the original character in the **Nicholas Carter series** in that he is portrayed as a spy rather than as a private detective
1 *Run, spy, run* (1964) [Michael Avallone; Valerie Moolman]
2 *China doll* (1964) [Michael Avallone; Valerie Moolman]
3 *Checkmate in Rio* (1964) [Valerie Moolman]
4 *Safari for spies* (1964) [Valerie Moolman]
5 *Fraulein Spy* (1964) [Valerie Moolman]
6 *Saigon* (1964) [Michael Avallone; Valerie Moolman]
7 *Bullet for Fidel* (1965) [Valerie Moolman]
8 *Thirteenth spy* (1965) [Valerie Moolman]
9 *Eyes of the tiger* (1965) [Manning Lee Stokes]
10 *Istanbul* (1965) [Manning Lee Stokes]
11 *Web of spies* (1966) [Manning Lee Stokes]
12 *Spy castle* (1966) [Manning Lee Stokes]
13 *Terrible ones* (1966) [Valerie Moolman]
14 *Dragon flame* (1966) [Manning Lee Stokes]
15 *Hanoi* (1966) [Valerie Moolman]
16 *Danger key* (1966) [Lew Louderback]
17 *Operation Starvation* (1966) [Nicholas Browne]
18 *Mind poisoners* (1966) [Lionel White; Valerie Moolman]
19 *Weapon of night* (1967) [Valerie Moolman]
20 *Golden serpent* (1967) [Manning Lee Stokes]
21 *Red guard* (1967) [Manning Lee Stokes]
22 *Double identity* (1967) [Manning Lee Stokes]
23 *Devil's cockpit* (1967) [Manning Lee Stokes]
24 *Chinese paymaster* (1967) [Nicholas Browne]
25 *Seven against Greece* (1967) [Nicholas Browne]
26 *Korean tiger* (1967) [Manning Lee Stokes]

Nick Carter series

27 *Assignment Israel* (1967) [Manning Lee Stokes]
28 *Mission to Venice* (1967) [Manning Lee Stokes]
29 *Filthy five* (1967) [Manning Lee Stokes]
30 *Bright blue death* (1967) [Nicholas Browne]
31 *Macao* (1968) [Manning Lee Stokes]
32 *Operation Moon Rocket* (1968) [Lew Louderback]
33 *Judas spy* (1968) [William Laurence Rohde]
34 *Hood of death* (1968) [William Laurence Rohde]
35 *Amsterdam* (1968) [William Laurence Rohde]
36 *Temple of fear* (1968) [Manning Lee Stokes]
37 *Fourteen seconds to hell* (1968) [Jon Messmann]
38 *Defector* (1969) [George Snyder]
39 *Carnival for killing* (1969) [Jon Messmann]
40 *Rhodesia* (1968) [William Laurence Rohde]
41 *Red rays* (1969) [Manning Lee Stokes]
42 *Peking* (1969) [Arnold Marmor]; also includes *The tulip affair*
43 *Amazon* (1969) [Jon Messmann]
44 *Sea trap* (1969) [Jon Messmann]
45 *Berlin* (1969) [Jon Messmann]
46 *Human time bomb* (1969) [William Laurence Rohde]
47 *Cobra kill* (1969) [Manning Lee Stokes]
48 *Living death* (1969) [Jon Messmann]
49 *Operation Che Guevara* (1969) [Jon Messmann]
50 *Doomsday formula* (1969) [Jon Messmann]
51 *Operation Snake* (1969) [Jon Messmann]
52 *Casbah killers* (1969) [Jon Messmann]
53 *Arab plague* (1970) *Slavemaster* [Jon Messmann]
54 *Red rebellion* (1970) [Jon Messmann]
55 *Executioners* (1970) [Jon Messmann]
56 *Black death* (1970) [Manning Lee Stokes]
57 *Mind killers* (1970) [Jon Messmann]
58 *Time clock of death* (1970) [George Snyder]
59 *Cambodia* (1970) [George Snyder]
60 *Death strain* (1970) [Jon Messmann]
61 *Moscow* (1970) [George Snyder]
62 *Jewel of doom* (1970) [George Snyder]
63 *Ice bomb zero* (1971) [George Snyder]
64 *Mark of Cosa Nostra* (1971) [George Snyder]
65 *Cairo Mafia* (1972) [Ralph Eugene Hayes]
66 *Inca death squad* (1972) [Martin Cruz Smith]
67 *Assault on England* (1972) [Ralph Eugene Hayes]
68 *Omega terror* (1972) [Ralph Eugene Hayes]
69 *Code name, Werewolf* (1973) [Martin Cruz Smith]
70 *Strike force terror* (1973) [Ralph Eugene Hayes]
71 *Target, Doomsday Island* (1973) [Richard Hubbard]
72 *Night of the avenger* (1973) [Chet Cunningham; Dan Streib]
73 *Butcher of Belgrade* (1973) [Ralph Eugene Hayes; Larry Powell]
74 *Assassination brigade* (1973) [Thomas Chastain]
75 *Liquidator* (1973) [Richard Hubbard]
76 *Devil's dozen* (1973) [Martin Cruz Smith]
77 *Code* (1973) [Larry Powell]
78 *Agent counter agent* (1973) [Ralph Eugene Hayes]
79 *Hour of the wolf* (1973) [Jeffrey Miner Wallmann]
80 *Our agent in Rome is missing* (1973) [Al Hine]
81 *Kremlin file* (1973) [Willis Todhunter Ballard]
82 *Spanish connection* (1973) [Bruce Cassiday]
83 *Death's head conspiracy* (1973) [Robert Colby]
84 *Peking dossier* (1974) [Linda Stewart]
85 *Ice trap terror* (1974) [Jeffrey Miner Wallmann]
86 *Assassin, code name Vulture* (1974) [Ralph Eugene Hayes]
87 *Massacre in Milan* (1974) [Al Hine]
88 *Vatican vendetta* (1974) [Ralph Eugene Hayes; George Snyder]
89 *Sign of the cobra* (1974) [James Fritzhand]
90 *Man who sold death* (1974) [Lawrence Van Gelder]
91 *N three conspiracy* (1974) [Dennis Lynds]
92 *Beirut incident* (1974) [Forrest Perrin]
93 *Death of the Falcon* (1974) [Jim Bowser]
94 *Aztec avenger* (1974) [Saul Wernick]
95 *Jerusalem file* (1975) [Linda Stewart]
96 *Counterfeit agent* (1975) [Douglas Marland]
97 *Six bloody summer days* (1975) [DeWitt Copp]
98 *Doctor Death* (1975) [Craig Nova]
99 *Z document* (1975) [Homer Morris]
100 *Katmandu contract* (1975) [James Fritzhand]
101 *Ultimate code* (1975) [William Odell]
102 *Assignment Intercept* (1976) [Marilyn Granbeck]
103 *Green wolf connection* (1976) [Dennis Lynds]
104 *Death message* (1976) [Dee Stuart; Ansel Chapin]; also includes *Oil seventy four two*
105 *List* (1976) [James Fritzhand]
106 *Fanatics of Al Asad* (1976) [Saul Wernick]
107 *Snake flag conspiracy* (1976) [Saul Wernick]
108 *Turncoat* (1976) [Leon Lazarus]
109 *Sign of the prayer shawl* (1976) [David Hagberg]
110 *Vulcan disaster* (1976) [George Warren]
111 *High yield in death* (1976) [Jim Bowser]
112 *Nichovev plot* (1976) [Craig Nova]
113 *Triple cross* (1976) [Dennis Lynds]
114 *Gallagher plot* (1976) [Saul Wernick]
115 *Plot for the Fourth Reich* (1977) [Bob Latona]
116 *Revenge of the generals* (1978) [Saul Wernick]
117 *Under the wall* (1978) [DeWitt Copp]
118 *Ebony cross* (1978) [Jack Canon]
119 *Deadly doubles* (1978) [Lawrence Van Gelder]
120 *Race of death* (1978) [David Hagberg]
121 *Trouble in paradise* (1978) [Robert Derek Steeley]
122 *Pamplona affair* (1978) [Dee Stuart; Ansel Chapin]
123 *Doomsday spore* (1979) [George Warren]
124 *Asian mantrap* (1978) [William Odell]
125 *Thunderstrike in Syria* (1979) [Joseph Rosenberger]
126 *Redolmo affair* (1979) [Jack Canon]
127 *Jamaican exchange* (1979) [Leon Lazarus]
128 *Tropical deathpact* (1979) [Bob Stokesberry]
129 *Pemex chart* (1979) [Dwight Vreeland Swain]
130 *Hawaii* (1979) [Daniel C Prince]
131 *Satan trap* (1979) [Jack Canon]
132 *Reich Four* (1979) [Frederick Vincent Huber]
133 *Nowhere weapon* (1979) [William Odell]
134 *Strike of the hawk* (1980) [John Lee Gilmore]
135 *Day of the dingo* (1980) [John Stevenson]
136 *And next the king* (1980) [Steve Simmons]
137 *Tarantula strike* (1980) [Dan Reardon]
138 *Ten times dynamite* (1980) [Frank Adduci]
139 *Eight card Stud* (1980) [Robert Edward Vardeman]
140 *Suicide seat* (1980) [George Warren]
141 *Death mission, Havana* (1980) [Ron Felber]
142 *War from the clouds* (1980) [John Lee Gilmore]
143 *Turkish bloodbath* (1980) [Jerry Ahern]
144 *Coyote connection* (1981) [Bill Crider; Jack Davis]
145 *Q-man* (1981) [John Stevenson]
146 *Society of nine* (1981) [Jack Canon]
147 *Ouster conspiracy* (1981) [David Hagberg]
148 *Golden bull* (1981) [John Stevenson]
149 *Dubrovnik massacre* (1981) [Henry Rasof; Stephen Williamson]
150 *Solar menace* (1981) [Robert Edward Vardeman]
151 *Strontium code* (1981) [David Hagberg]
152 *Pleasure Island* (1981) [Robert Joseph Randisi]
153 *Cauldron of Hell* (1981) [Michael Jahn]
154 *Parisian affair* (1981) [H Edward Hunsberger]
155 *Chessmaster* (1982) [Robert Joseph Randisi]
156 *Last Samurai* (1982) [Bruce Algozin]
157 *Puppet master* (1982) [David Hagberg]
158 *Damocles threat* (1982) [David Hagberg]
159 *Dominican affair* (1982) [Bruce Algozin]
160 *Deathlight* (1982) [Jerry Ahern]
161 *Israeli connection* (1982) [Robert Derek Steeley]
162 *Treason game* (1982) [Joseph Lee Gilmore]
163 *Earth shaker* (1982) [Robert Edward Vardeman]
164 *Norwegian typhoon* (1982) [Robert Edward Vardeman]
165 *Hunter* (1982) [David Hagberg]
166 *Operation McMurdo Sound* (1982) [David Hagberg]
167 *Appointment in Haiphong* (1982) [David Hagberg]
168 *Retreat for death* (1982) [David Hagberg]
169 *Mendoza manuscript* (1982) [Robert Joseph Randisi]
170 *Death star affair* (1982) [Jack Canon]
171 *Doctor DNA* (1982) [Robert Edward Vardeman]
172 *Christmas kill* (1983) [Joseph Lee Gilmore]
173 *Greek summit* (1983) [Robert Joseph Randisi]
174 *Outback ghosts* (1983) [Robert Edward Vardeman]
175 *Hide and go die* (1983) [Jack Canon]
176 *Kali death cafe* (1983) [Robert Edward Vardeman]
177 *Operation Vendetta* (1983) [Joseph Lee Gilmore]
178 *Yukon target* (1983) [Robert Edward Vardeman]
179 *Death dealer* (1983) [Jack Canon]
180 *Istanbul decision* (1983) [David Hagberg]
181 *Decoy hit* (1983) [Robert Joseph Randisi]
182 *Earthfire north* (1983) [David Hagberg]
183 *Budapest run* (1983) [Jack Canon]
184 *Caribbean coup* (1983) [Robert Joseph Randisi]
185 *Algarve affair* (1984) [Jack Canon]
186 *Zero hour strike force* (1984) [David Hagberg]
187 *Operation Sharkbite* (1984) [Jack Canon]
188 *Death Island* (1984) [David Hagberg]
189 *Night of the warheads* (1984) [Jack Canon]
190 *Day of the Mahdi* (1984) [Dennis Lynds]
191 *Assignment Rio* (1984) [Jack Canon]
192 *Death hand play* (1984) [David Hagberg]
193 *Kremlin kill* (1984) [Jack Canon]
194 *Mayan connection* (1984) [Dennis Lynds]
195 *San Juan inferno* (1984) [Joseph Lee Gilmore]
196 *Circle of scorpions* (1985) [Jack Canon]
197 *Blue ice affair* (1985) [Ron Felber]
198 *Macao massacre* (1985) [Jack Canon]
199 *Pursuit of the eagle* (1985) [Dennis Lynds]
200 *Vengeance game* (1985) [David Hagberg]
201 *Last flight to Moscow* (1985) [Joseph Lee Gilmore]
202 *Normandy code* (1985) [Jack Canon]
203 *White death* (1985) [Dennis Lynds]
204 *Assassin convention* (1985) [Joseph Lee Gilmore]

205 *Blood of the scimitar* (1985)
[Jack Canon]
206 *Execution exchange* (1985)
[Dennis Lynds]
207 *Tarlov cipher* (1985)
[Jack Canon]
208 *Target red star* (1986)
[Jack Canon]
209 *Killing ground* (1986)
[David Hagberg]
210 *Berlin target* (1986)
[Jack Canon]
211 *Mercenary mountain* (1986)
[Dennis Lynds]
212 *Blood ultimatum* (1986)
[Ron Felber]
213 *Cyclops conspiracy* (1986)
[Dennis Lynds]
214 *Tunnel for traitors* (1986)
[Jack Canon]
215 *Samurai kill* (1986)
[Dennis Lynds]
216 *Terror times two* (1986)
[Jack Canon]
217 *Death orbit* (1986)
[David Hagberg]
218 *Slaughter day* (1986)
[Jack Canon]
219 *Master assassin* (1986)
[Dennis Lynds]
220 *Operation Petrograd* (1986)
[David Hagberg]
221 *Crossfire red* (1987)
[Jack Canon]
222 *Blood of the falcon* (1987)
[Dennis Lynds]
223 *Death squad* (1987)
[Jack Canon]
224 *Terror code* (1987)
[Jack Canon]
225 *Holy war* (1987)
226 *Blood raid* (1987)
[Jack Canon]
227 *East of hell* (1987)
[David Hagberg]
228 *Killing games* (1987)
[Jack Canon]
229 *Terms of vengeance* (1987)
[Jack Canon]
230 *Pressure point* (1987)
231 *Night of the Condor* (1987)
232 *Poseidon target* (1987)
[Jack Canon]
233 *Andropov file* (1988)
234 *Dragonfire* (1988)
235 *Bloodtrail to Mecca* (1988)
236 *Deathstrike* (1988)
237 *Lethal prey* (1988)
238 *Spykiller* (1988)
239 *Bolivian heat* (1988)
240 *Rangoon man* (1988)
241 *Code name Cobra* (1988)
242 *Afghan intercept* (1988)
243 *Countdown to Armageddon* (1988)
244 *Black Sea bloodbath* (1988)
245 *Deadly diva* (1988)
246 *Invitation to death* (1989)
247 *Day of the assassin* (1989)
248 *Korean kill* (1989)
249 *Middle East massacre* (1989)
250 *Sanction to slaughter* (1989)
251 *Hong Kong hit* (1989)
252 *Deep sea death* (1989)
253 *Arms of vengeance* (1989)
254 *Hell-bound express* (1989)
255 *Isle of blood* (1990)
256 *Singapore sling* (1990)
257 *Ruby red death* (1990)
258 *Arctic abduction* (1990)
259 *Dragon slay* (1990)

Nick Chase series
Cort, Ned
see **Boxer Unit SS series**

Nick Cranley series
Storm, Michael
1 *Make mine a harlot* (1949)
2 *Dame in my bed* (1951)
3 *Carmen was a virgin* (1952)
4 *Curtains for Carla* (1952)
5 *This woman is death* (1953)

Nick Duffy series
Kavanagh, Dan
1 *Duffy* (1980)
2 *Fiddle City* (1981)
3 *Putting the boot in* (1985)
4 *Going to the dogs* (1987)

Nick Everard series
Fullerton, Alexander
1 *Blooding of the guns* (1976)
2 *Sixty minutes for Saint George* (1977)
3 *Patrol to the Golden Horn* (1978)
4 *Storm force to Narvik* (1979)
5 *Last lift from Crete* (1980)
6 *All the drowning seas* (1981)
7 *Share of honour* (1982)
8 *Torch bearers* (1983)
9 *Gate-crashers* (1984)

Nick Maasten series
Sela, Owen
see **Nicholas Maasten series**

Nick Marshall series
Mitcham, Gilroy
1 *Full stop* (1957)
2 *Man from Bar Harbour* (1958)
3 *Dead reckoning* (1960)

Nick Merlotti series
Deane, Jim
1 *Great pretender* (1974)
2 *Moon over Miami* (1975)

Nick Miller series
Patterson, Henry
This sequence is also published under the pseudonym Jack Higgins
1 *Graveyard shift* (1965)
2 *Brought in dead* (1967)
3 *Hell is always today* (1968)

Nick Morro series
Buranelli, Prosper
1 *Big Nick* (1931)
2 *News reel murder* (1940)

Nick Nicholson series
Barr, Robert
1 *Dark island* (1972)
2 *Edge of the forest* (1973)

Nick of time series
Effinger, George Alec
1 *Nick of time* (1985)
2 *Bird of time* (1986)

Nick Polo series
Kennealy, Jerry
1 *Polo solo* (1987)
2 *Polo, anyone?* (1988)
3 *Polo's ponies* (1988)
4 *Polo in the rough* (1989)
5 *Polo's wild card* (1990)
6 *Green with envy* (1991)
7 *Special delivery* (1992)
8 *Vintage Polo* (1993)

Nick Ratcliffe series
Dell, Ethel May
1 *Way of an eagle* (1911)
2 *Keeper of the door* (1915)
3 *By request* (1927)
Peggy by request

Nick series
Hayle, Felicity
see **Our brother Nick series**

Nick series
Prince, Alison
1 *Goodbye summer* (1983)
2 *Nick's October* (1986)

Nick Trevellyan and Alison Hope series
Kelly, Susan
see **Alison Hope and Inspector Nick Trevellyan series**

Nick Velvet series
Hoch, Edward Dentinger
Short stories
1 *Spy and the thief* (1971)
2 *Thefts of Nick Velvet* (1978)
Single story published separately: *The quest of the Persian slipper*, 1978

Nicki Holland series
Hunt, Angela Elwell
1 *Case of the mystery mark* (1991)
2 *Case of the phantom friend* (1991)
3 *Case of the teenager terminator* (1991)
4 *Case of the terrified track star* (1992)
5 *Case of the counterfeit cash* (1992)
6 *Case of the haunting of Lowell Lanes* (1992)
7 *Case of the birthday bracelet* (1993)
8 *Secret of Cravenhill Castle* (1993)
9 *Riddle of Baby Rosalind* (1993)

Nickum series
Robertson, Jean
see **Little Black Nickum series**

Nicky and Nigger series
Craigie, Dorothy
1 *Nicky and Nigger join the circus* (1960)
2 *Nicky and Nigger and the pirate* (1960)

Nicky and Simon Carr series
Leyland, Eric
1 *Eagles flew straight* (1965)
2 *Waggon Wheelers on tour* (1967)

Nicky and Sophie series
Ichikawa, Satomi
see **Suzanne and Nicholas series**

Nicky Lee series
Lee, Norma
see **Beautiful Gunner series**

Nicky Mahoun series
Smith, Clark
1 *Speaking eye* (1955)
2 *Deadly reaper* (1956)
3 *Case of torches* (1957)

Nicky series
Ziefert, Harriet
Illustrated by Richard Brown
1 *Nicky's Christmas surprise* (1985)
2 *Let's watch Nicky* (1986)
3 *Nicky's noisy night* (1986)
4 *Nicky's friends* (1986)
5 *Nicky's picnic* (1986)
6 *No, no, Nicky!* (1986)
7 *Where is Nicky's Valentine* (1987)
8 *Nicky upstairs and down* (1987)
9 *Thank you, Nicky!* (1988)

Nicky Weaver series
Weaver, Nicky
1 *Love, blood and tears* (1963)
2 *Love or kill them all* (1963)

Nicola Bruce series
Ure, Jean
1 *Hi there, supermouse* (1983)
Supermouse
2 *Nicola Mimosa* (1985)
Most important thing

Nicole and Cindy series
Cole, Jennifer
see **Cindy and Nicole series**

Nicolette series
Cameron, Margaret Locherbie
1 *Nicolette detects* (1949)
2 *Nicolette finds her* (1953)

Nicolson series
Charles, Robert
see **Counter-terror series**
Wayland, Patrick
see **Lloyd Nicolson series**

Nidor series
Randall, Robert
1 *Shrouded planet* (1957)
2 *Dawning light* (1959)

Nies family series
Fletcher, Grace Nies
1 *In my father's house* (1955)
Biography of Lee Nies
2 *Preacher's kids* (1958)

Nigel Blair and Archibald Beldrum series
Hay, Lindsay Fitzgerald
see **Archibald Beldrum and Nigel Blair series**

Nigel Lacaita series
Mackenzie, William Andrew
see **Sir Nigel Lacaita series**

Nigel Loring series
Doyle, Arthur Conan
see **English bowmen series**

Nigel Molesworth series
This sequence has two authors
Willans, Geoffrey
Illustrated by Ronald Searle
1 *Down with skool* (1953)
2 *How to be topp* (1954)
3 *Whizz for atomms* (1956)
4 *Back in the jug* (1959)
Brett, Simon
5 *Molesworth rites again* (1983)

Nigel Morrison series
Fisher, Norman
1 *Walk at a steady pace* (1970)
2 *Rise at dawn* (1971)
3 *Last assignment* (1972)

Nigel Rix series
Goodchild, George
1 *Quest of Nigel Rix* (1934)
2 *Knock and come in* (1935)

Nigel Strangeways series
Blake, Nicholas
1 *Question of proof* (1935)
2 *Thou shell of death* (1936)
Shell of death
3 *There's trouble brewing* (1937)
4 *Beast must die* (1938)
5 *Smiler with the knife* (1939)
6 *Malice in wonderland* (1940)
Summer camp mystery
Malice with murder
7 *Case of the abominable snowman* (1941)
Corpse in the snowman
8 *Minute for murder* (1947)
9 *Head of a traveller* (1949)
Head of a traveler
10 *Dreadful hollow* (1953)
11 *Whisper in the gloom* (1954)
Catch and kill
12 *End of a chapter* (1957)
13 *Widow's cruise* (1959)
14 *Worm of death* (1961)
15 *Sad variety* (1964)
16 *Morning after death* (1966)

Nigerian series
Ulasi, Adaora Lily
1 *Many things you no understand* (1970)
2 *Many things begin for change* (1971)

Nigger and Nicky series
Craigie, Dorothy
see **Nicky and Nigger series**

Night fighters series
Sherman, David
1 *Knives in the night* (1987)
2 *Main force assault* (1987)
3 *Out of fire* (1988)
4 *Rock and a hard place* (1988)
5 *Nghu night falls* (1989)
6 *Charlie don't live here any more* (1989)
7 *Squad* (1991)

Night light series
Kraus, Robert
1 *Good night, Little One* (1972)
2 *Good night, little ABC* (1972)
3 *Good night, little Richard Rabbit* (1972)

Night monsters series
Howe, James
1 *There's a monster under my bed* (1986)
2 *There's a dragon in my sleeping bag* (1994)

Night series
Straker, Philip
1 *Night date* (1982)
2 *Night lust* (1982)

Night-threads series
Emerson, Ru
1 *Calling of the three* (1990)
2 *Two in hiding* (1991)
3 *One land, one duke* (1992)
4 *Craft of light* (1993)

Night trilogy
Wiesel, Elie
Set in German concentration camps during the Second World War
1 *Night* (1958)
Original edition entitled *La nuit*; based on an earlier work in Yiddish entitled *Un di Velt hot Geshvign*, 1956
2 *Dawn* (1961)
Original edition entitled *L'aube*
3 *Accident* (1962)
Original edition entitled *Le jour*
One volume editions entitled *Night, dawn, day*, 1985, and *Night trilogy*, 1987

Night warriors series
Masterton, Graham
1 *Night warriors* (1986)
2 *Death dream* (1988)
3 *Night plague* (1991)

Night-Watchman series
Jacobs, William Wymark
1 *Many cargoes* (1896)
2 *Sea urchins* (1898)
More cargoes
3 *Light freights* (1901)
4 *Lady of the barge* (1902)
5 *Odd craft* (1903)
6 *Captains all* (1905)
7 *Short cruises* (1907)
8 *Sailor's knots* (1909)
9 *Ship's company* (1911)
10 *Night watches* (1914)
11 *Deep waters* (1919)
12 *Sea whispers* (1926)

Night whistlers series
Trevor, Dan
1 *Night whistlers* (1991)
2 *Penetrate* (1992)
3 *Terminate* (1992)

Night whistlers trilogy
Trevor, Dan
1 *Night whistlers* (1991)
2 *Penetrate* (1992)
3 *Terminate* (1992)

Night wind series
Mountjoy, Roberta Jean
1 *Night wind* (1981)
2 *Black thunder* (1983)

Night wind series
Vanardy, Varick
see **Bingham Harvard series**

Nighthawk series
Horler, Sydney
1 *They called him Nighthawk* (1937)
2 *Return of Nighthawk* (1940)
3 *Nighthawk strikes to kill* (1941)
4 *Nighthawk mops up* (1944)
5 *Ring up Nighthawk* (1947)
6 *Nap on Nighthawk* (1950)
7 *Nighthawk swears vengeance* (1954)

Nighthunter series
Faulcon, Robert
1 *Stalking* (1983)
Nighthunter
2 *Talisman* (1983)
3 *Ghost dance* (1983)
4 *Shrine* (1984)
5 *Hexing* (1984)
6 *Labyrinth* (1987)

Nightingale series
Kelly, Mary
see **Inspector Brett Nightingale series**
Revelli, George
see **Amanda Nightingale series**

Nightmare Hall series
Hoh, Diane
1 *Silent scream* (1993)
2 *Roommate* (1993)
3 *Deadly attraction* (1993)
4 *Wish* (1993)
5 *Scream team* (1993)
6 *Guilty* (1993)

Nightmare on Elm Street series
This sequence has two authors
Cooper, Jeffrey
1 *Nightmares on Elm Street, parts 1, 2, 3* (1987)
The continuing story
Locke, Joseph
2 *Nightmares on Elm Street, parts 4, 5* (1989)
Includes *The dream master*, and *The dream child*
Companion volumes: *The nightmare on Elm Street companion, the official guide to America's favorite fiend*, by Jeffrey Cooper, 1987, *Nightmares on Elm Street, Freddy Krueger's seven sweetest dreams*, edited by Martin Harry Greenberg, 1991

Nightmare trilogy
Cabell, James Branch
1 *Smirt* (1934)
An urbane nightmare
2 *Smith* (1935)
A sylvan interlude
3 *Smire* (1937)
An acceptance in third person
One volume edition entitled *The nightmare has triplets*, 1972; companion volume: *The nightmare has triplets, an author's notes on Smire*, 1937

Nighttime tales series
Blyton, Enid
1 *Tales after tea* (1948)
2 *Tales after supper* (1949)
3 *Tales at bedtime* (1960)

Nightworld series
Bischoff, David
1 *Nightworld* (1979)
2 *Vampires of nightworld* (1981)

Nihilist series
Turgenev, Ivan Sergeevich
Translated from the Russian
1 *Fathers and children* (1862)
Fathers and sons
2 *Virgin soil* (1876)
Companion volume: *Possessed*, by Thedor Mikhailovich Dostoevsky, 1871

Nikki Holden and Roman Cantrell series
Chase, Elaine Raco
see **Roman Cantrell and Nikki Holden series**

Nikola series
Boothby, Guy
see **Doctor Nikola series**

Nile Boyd series
Jackson, Giles
1 *Witch's moon* (1941)
Abridged edition entitled *Blood on the blonde*, under the pseudonym Dana Chambers, 1952
2 *Court of shadows* (1943)

Nils Jarnhan series
Dalmas, John
1 *Yngling* (1971)
Revised edition 1984
2 *Homecoming* (1984)
Numbers 1 and 2 also published in one volume entitled *The Orc wars*, 1992
3 *Yngling in the circle of power* (1992)

Nils series
Lagerlof, Selma
1 *Wonderful adventures of Nils* (1906)
Original edition entitled *Nils Holgerssons underbara resa denoa Sverige*, volume 1
2 *Further adventures of Nils* (1907)
Original edition entitled *Nils Holgerssons underbara resa denoa Sverige*, volume 2

Nilsen series
Griffiths, Ella
see **Rudolph and Karsten Nilson series**
Wilson, Barbara Ellen
see **Pam Nilsen series**

Nils-Frederick Blixen series
Larson, Charles
1 *Someone's death* (1973)
2 *Matthew's hand* (1974)
3 *Muir's blood* (1976)
4 *Portland murders* (1983)

Nim series
Joanny, Andre
1 *Nim and his world* (1973)
Original edition entitled *Jeudi et la nature*
2 *Nim and his money* (1973)
Original edition entitled *Jeudi et la monnaie*
3 *Nim and his food* (1974)
Original edition entitled *Jeudi a bon appetit*
4 *Nim buys and sells* (1974)

Nimbus series
Smith, Jim
1 *Nimbus and the crown jewels* (1981)
2 *Nimbus and the explorer* (1981)

NIMH series
This sequence has two authors
O'Brien, Robert C
1 *Mrs Frisby and the rats of NIMH* (1971)
Secret of NIMH
Conly, Jane Leslie
2 *Rasco and the rats of NIMH* (1986)
3 *RT, Margaret and the rats of NIMH* (1990)

Nimmo trilogy
Cary, Joyce
see **Chester Nimmo trilogy**

Nimrods series
Knox, Thomas Wallace
see **Hunting adventures on land and sea series**

Nimue Hawthorne and Birdie Linnett series
Linscott, Gillian
see **Birdie Linnett and Nimue Hawthorne series**

Nina and Ted series
De Angeli, Marguerite
see **Ted and Nina series**

Nina Cristina series
Matranga, Frances Carfi
1 *Secret behind the blue door* (1981)
2 *Mysterious prowler* (1984)
3 *Forgotten treasure* (1986)
4 *Mystery of the missing will* (1986)
5 *Big top mystery* (1987)

Nina Fischman series
Piesman, Marissa
1 *Unorthodox practices* (1989)
2 *Personal effects* (1991)
3 *Heading uptown* (1993)
4 *Close quarters* (1994)

Nina McFall series
Fulton, Eileen
1 *Death of a golden girl* (1988)
2 *Take one for murder* (1988)
3 *Dying for stardom* (1988)
4 *Lights, camera, death* (1988)
5 *Setting for murder* (1988)
6 *Fatal flashback* (1989)

Nina series
Brandenberg, Franz
see **Aunt Nina series**

Nine series
Prime, Heather
see **Adventurous Nine series**

Nine winds series
Crowley, Carl Campbell
Poems
1 *Nine winds* (1959)
2 *Wings and winged thoughts* (1959)
3 *Bouquet of sonnets* (1959)
4 *Around the year at Alectown* (1959)
5 *Chant of the vanishing race* (1961)
6 *Charitas* (1962)
The more excellent way
7 *Art of living* (1963)

Niner series
Bradman, Tony
see **Tommy Niner series**

Nineteenth century America series
Fisher, Leonard Everett
1 *Factories* (1979)
2 *Railroads* (1979)
3 *Hospitals* (1980)
4 *Sports* (1980)
5 *Newspapers* (1981)
6 *Unions* (1982)
7 *Schools* (1983)

Ninety-nine Fear Street series
Stine, Robert Lawrence
1 *First horror* (1994)
2 *Second horror* (1994)
3 *Third horror* (1994)

Nini series
Lloyd, Errol
1 *Nini at carnival* (1978)
2 *Nini on time* (1981)

Ninja Master series
Barker, Wade
1 *Vengeance is his* (1981)
2 *Mountain of fear* (1981)
3 *Borderland of hell* (1982)
4 *Million-dollar massacre* (1982)
5 *Black magician* (1982)
6 *Death's door* (1982)
7 *Skin swindle* (1983)
8 *Only the good die* (1983)
This sequence is followed by the **Year of the Ninja Master series**

Ninja series
Lustbader, Eric
1 *Ninja* (1980)
2 *Miko* (1984)
3 *White Ninja* (1989)
4 *Kaisho* (1993)
5 *Floating city* (1994)

Nintendo adventure series
This sequence has three authors
Bosco, Clyde
1 *Double trouble* (1991)
2 *Leaping lizards* (1991)
McCay, Bill
3 *Monster mix-up* (1991)
4 *Koopa capers* (1991)
Bosco, Clyde
5 *Pipe down!* (1991)
McCay, Bill
6 *Doors to doom* (1991)
Bosco, Clyde
7 *Dinosaur dilemma* (1991)
Wayne, Matt
8 *Flown the Koopa* (1991)
9 *Crystal trap* (1991)
10 *Shadow prince* (1991)
11 *Unjust desserts* (1991)
12 *Brain drain* (1991)

Nintendo series
Lampton, Christopher
1 *Nintendo action games* (1991)
2 *Nintendo role-playing games* (1991)

Nire series
Kita, Morio
see **Kiichiro Nire series**

Nita and Kit series
Duane, Diane
see **Wizard series**

Nixon series
Ambrose, Stephen Edward
see **Richard Nixon series**
Murray, Lillian
see **Virginia Nixon series**

No lady series
Bloom, Ursula
Reminiscences
1 *Log of no lady* (1940)
The story of a London woman evacuated before the outbreak of war
2 *No lady buys a cot* (1943)
3 *No lady in bed* (1944)
4 *No lady with a pen* (1947)
5 *No lady meets no gentleman* (1947)
6 *No lady in the cart* (1949)
7 *Mum's girl was no lady* (1951)
Reminiscences of the author's mother, Polly Bloom
8 *No lady has a dog's day* (1956)
Companion volume: *Trilogy*, 1954

No regrets series
Carnarvon, Henry
Autobiography
1 *No regrets* (1976)
2 *Ermine tales* (1980)

No starch in my coat series
Delaney, Joyce
Memoirs of an Irish doctor in a mental hospital
1 *No starch in my coat* (1971)
2 *Smile at me, doctor* (1972)
3 *Pass the happy pills* (1978)
4 *It's my nerves, doctor* (1980)

No such things series
Bunting, Eve
1 *Creature of Cranberry Cove* (1976)
2 *Demon* (1976)
3 *Ghost* (1976)
4 *Tongue of the ocean* (1976)

No time to weep series
Godden, Rumer
Autobiography
1 *Two under the Indian sun* (1966)
Co-author: Jon Godden
2 *Time to dance, no time to weep* (1988)
3 *House with four rooms* (1989)

Noah Bradshaw series
Johnston, Madeleine
1 *Comets have long tails* (1938)
2 *Death casts a lure* (1938)

Noah family series
Horrabin, James Francis
1 *Some adventures of the Noah family, including Japhet* (1920)
2 *Noahs on holiday, with Japhet* (1921)
3 *Japhet and Fido* (1921)
4 *Mister Noah* (1921)
5 *More about the Noahs, and Tim Tosset* (1922)
6 *Japhet book* (1924)
A record of the doings of the Noah family, The Ark, Ararat Avenue
7 *About Japhet and the rest of the Noah family* (1926)
8 *Japhet and Company, including Happy* (1927)
9 *Japhet and the Arkubs of the The Ark, Ararat Avenue, S.W.* (1928)
10 *Japhet and the Arkubs at sea* (1929)
11 *Japhet and Company on Arkub Island* (1930)
Companion volumes: *Japhet and Happy book*, 1931-1932, *Japhet and Happy annual*, 1933-1944, *Japhet holiday book*, 1937-1941, *Japhet and Happy painting book*, 1949

Noah Green series
Hentoff, Nat
1 *Blues for Charlie Darwin* (1982)
2 *Man from Internal Affairs* (1985)

Noah Pandre series
Schneour, Salman
Translated from the Yiddish
1 *Noah Pandre* (1936)
2 *Noah Pandre's village* (1938)

Noah series
Brook, Judy
1 *Noah's ark* (1972)
2 *Mrs Noah and the animals* (1977)
3 *Mrs Noah's ABC 123* (1979)

Noah series
Greenfeld, Josh
1 *Child called Noah* (1972)
2 *Place for Noah* (1978)
3 *Client called Noah* (1986)

Noah series
Topek, Susan Remick
1 *Holiday for Noah* (1990)
2 *Turn for Noah* (1992)
3 *Taste for Noah* (1993)

Noakes series
Neame, Alan
see **Maud Noakes series**

Nobby Clark and Snowy White series
Andrews, Stephen
1 *Cubs with a difference* (1974)
2 *Cubs away* (1975)
3 *Cubs on Saturday* (1976)
4 *Cubs at play* (1977)

Nobel Prize winners series
Aaseng, Nathan
1 *Disease fighters* (1987)
The Nobel Prize in medicine
2 *Inventors* (1987)
Nobel Prizes in chemistry, physics and medicine
3 *Peace seekers* (1987)
The Nobel Peace Prize

Noble and Grant series
Mackintosh, May
see **Laurie Grant and Stewart Noble series**

Noble series
Martin, A Richard
see **Branders Noble series**

Nobody series
This sequence has two authors
Grossmith, George
1 *Diary of a nobody* (1894)
Waterhouse, Keith
2 *Mrs Pooter's diary* (1983)
3 *Collected letters of a nobody* (1986)
Including *Mister Pooter's advice to his son*

Nobody somebody series
Williams, Donna
1 *Nobody nowhere* (1992)
The extraordinary autobiography of an autistic
2 *Somebody somewhere* (1994)

Nobody's horse trilogy
Webster, Joanne
1 *Nobody's horse* (1975)
2 *Horse on a hilltop* (1976)
3 *Horses is like people* (1979)

Nodd's Ridge series
King, Tabitha
1 *Small world* (1981)
2 *Caretakers* (1983)
3 *Trap* (1985)
4 *One on one* (1993)
5 *Book of Reuben* (1994)

Noddy picture books series
Blyton, Enid
1 *Noddy and Big Ears* (1952)
2 *Day with Noddy* (1956)
3 *My Noddy picture book* (1958)
4 *Noddy's car picture book* (1959)
5 *Noddy's Toyland train picture book* (1961)
6 *Day at school with Noddy* (1962)
7 *Noddy and his friends* (1965)
8 *Noddy and the Noah's Ark adventure picture book* (1967)
9 *Noddy in Toyland picture book* (1967)
10 *Noddy Toyland ABC picture book* (1967)
Noddy's Toyland ABC
11 *Noddy's aeroplane picture book* (1967)
12 *Noddy goes to sea* (1969)
Companion volumes: *Noddy's own nursery rhymes*, 1958, *ABC with Noddy*, 1959, *Noddy's one, two, three book*, 1961

Noddy pop-up books series
Blyton, Enid
1 *Noddy goes to the fair* (1954)
2 *Noddy and his friends* (1956)
3 *Noddy's chimney pot* (1969)

Noddy series
Blyton, Enid
1 *Little Noddy goes to Toyland* (1949)
Noddy goes to Toyland
2 *Hurrah for little Noddy* (1950)
3 *Noddy and his car* (1951)
4 *Here comes Noddy again* (1951)
5 *Well done, Noddy* (1952)
6 *Noddy goes to school* (1952)
7 *Noddy at the seaside* (1953)
8 *Noddy gets into trouble* (1954)
9 *Noddy and the magic rubber* (1954)
10 *You funny little Noddy!* (1955)
11 *Noddy meets Father Christmas* (1955)
12 *Noddy and Tessie Bear* (1956)
13 *Be brave, little Noddy!* (1956)
14 *Noddy and the bumpy dog* (1957)
15 *Do look out, Noddy!* (1957)
16 *You're a good friend, Noddy!* (1958)
17 *Noddy has an adventure* (1958)
18 *Noddy goes to sea* (1959)
19 *Noddy and the bunkey* (1959)
20 *Cheer up, little Noddy!* (1960)
21 *Noddy goes to the fair* (1960)
22 *Mister Plod and little Noddy* (1961)
23 *Noddy and the Tootles* (1962)
24 *Noddy and the aeroplane* (1964)
Companion volumes: *The big Noddy book*, 1951-1973, *Noddy painting book*, 1951-1957, *Noddy song book*, 1952, *Noddy cut-out model book*, 1953, *Noddy giant painting book*, 1954, *Noddy play day painting book*, 1956, *Noddy in Toyland, musical play*, 1956, *Noddy nursery rhymes*, 1956, *Noddy's own nursery rhymes*, 1958; *My Big-Ears picture book*, 1958

Noddy stories series
Blyton, Enid
1 *Noddy and Big Ears have a picnic* (1951)
2 *Noddy has a shock* (1951)
3 *Noddy has more adventures* (1951)
4 *Noddy goes to the seaside* (1951)
5 *Noddy off to Rocking Horse Land* (1951)
6 *Tale of little Noddy* (1951)
7 *Noddy and the witch's wand* (1952)
8 *Noddy's car gets a squeak* (1952)
9 *Noddy's penny wheel car* (1952)
10 *Noddy and the cuckoo's nest* (1953)
11 *Noddy gets captured* (1953)
12 *Noddy is very silly* (1953)
13 *Three cheers for Noddy* (1961)
14 *Noddy be careful* (1962)
15 *Noddy's grand adventure* (1964)
16 *Noddy and his passengers* (1967)
Selections from this sequence in *Tales of Toyland*, 1952 and *Noddy in Toyland*, 1955

Noddy tall colour series
Blyton, Enid
1 *Noddy tall blue book* (1960)
2 *Noddy tall green book* (1960)
3 *Noddy tall orange book* (1960)
4 *Noddy tall pink book* (1960)
5 *Noddy tall red book* (1960)
6 *Noddy tall yellow book* (1960)

Noddy tiny strip books series
Blyton, Enid
1 *Noddy goes dancing* (1953)
2 *Noddy the cry-baby* (1953)
3 *Noddy and the snow house* (1954)
4 *How funny you are, Noddy* (1954)
5 *Noddy and the bear who lost his growl* (1957)
6 *Noddy and the tricky teddy* (1957)
7 *Noddy tricks Mr Sly* (1957)
8 *Noddy and the runaway wheel* (1960)
9 *Noddy's bag of money* (1960)
10 *Noddy's car gets into trouble* (1960)
Companion volumes: *Noddy colour strip book*, 1952 *New Noddy colour strip book*, 1953

Noel Gray series
Mace, Helen
see **Noel Vickery series**

Noel Macleod series
McLean, Allan Campbell
see **Inspector Noel Macleod series**

Noel Mayberry and Bill Bradley series
Tree, Gregory
see **Bill Bradley and Noel Mayberry series**

Noel series
Boden, Hilda
1 *Noel and the donkeys* (1960)
2 *Noel's happy day* (1961)
3 *Noel's Christmas holiday* (1962)
4 *Noel the brave* (1963)
5 *Noel the explorer* (1965)
6 *Job for Noel* (1966)

Noel Tracy series
Fraser, Alex
see **Inspector Noel Tracy series**

Noel Vickery series
Mace, Helen
1 *Murder among those present* (1957)
2 *House of hate* (1958)
3 *And death came too* (1961)

Nogales Scott and Caliper Maxwell series
Macdonald, William Colt
1 *Punchers of Phantom Pass* (1939)
2 *Riddle of Ramrod Ridge* (1942)

Noggin series
Postgate, Oliver
Illustrated by Peter Firmin
1 *Noggin and the whale* (1965)
2 *Noggin the king* (1965)
3 *Noggin and the dragon* (1966)
4 *Nogbad comes back* (1966)
5 *Noggin and the moon mouse* (1967)
6 *Nogbad and the elephant* (1967)
7 *Noggin and the money* (1973)
8 *Noggin and the storks* (1973)

Noggin the Nog series
Postgate, Oliver
see **Saga of Noggin the Nog series**

Noggs series
Jepson, Edgar
see **Lady Noggs series**

Noibla series
Lunatic, Humphry
An account of the island of Noibla, its inhabitants, religious and political customs, &c.
1 *Trip to the moon* (1764)
2 *Trip to the moon, volume II* (1765)

Noisy book series
Brown, Margaret Wise
1 *Noisy book* (1939)
2 *Country noisy book* (1940)
3 *Seashore noisy book* (1941)
4 *Indoor noisy book* (1942)
5 *Noisy bird book* (1943)
6 *Winter noisy book* (1947)
7 *Quiet noisy book* (1950)
8 *Summer noisy book* (1951)

Noisy Village series
Lindgren, Astrid
see **Bullerby series**

Noisy words series
Burningham, John
see **First words series**

Nolan series
Collins, Max Allan
1 *Bait money* (1973)
Revised edition 1981
2 *Blood money* (1973)
Revised edition 1981
3 *Fly paper* (1981)
4 *Hush money* (1981)
5 *Hard cash* (1981)
6 *Scratch fever* (1982)
7 *Spree* (1987)

Nolan series
McElfresh, Adeline
see **Jill Nolan series**
Nicolai, Charles
see **John Nolan series**

Nomad of time series
Moorcock, Michael
see **Oswald Bastable series**

Nomad series
Ellison, Norman
1 *Wandering with Nomad* (1946)
2 *Out of doors with Nomad* (1947)
3 *Over the hills with Nomad* (1948)
4 *Roving with Nomad* (1949)
5 *Adventuring with Nomad* (1950)
6 *Northwards with Nomad* (1951)
Companion volume: *Down nature's byways*, 1938

Nomes trilogy
Pratchett, Terry
see **Book of the Nomes trilogy**

Nona Fell series
Godden, Rumer
1 *Miss Happiness and Miss Flower* (1961)
2 *Little Plum* (1963)

Nonage series
Shaw, George Bernard
1 *Unsocial socialist* (1887)
2 *Irrational knot* (1905)
3 *Love among the artists* (1889)
4 *Cashel Byron's profession* (1886)
Also includes *The honourable Bashville* and an essay on modern prize-fighting

Nonconformist history of our times series
Stone, Isidor Feinstein
1 *War years, 1939-1945* (1988)
2 *Truman era, 1945-1952* (1988)
3 *Hidden history of the Korean War, 1950-1951* (1988)
4 *Haunted fifties, 1953-1963* (1989)
5 *In a time of torment* (1989)
6 *Polemics and prophecies, 1967-1970* (1989)

Nonsense novels series
Leacock, Stephen
1 *Nonsense novels* (1911)
2 *Winsome Winnie, and other new nonsense novels* (1920)

Nonsense series
Evans, Bergen Baldwin
1 *Natural history of nonsense* (1947)
2 *Spoor of spooks, and other nonsense* (1955)

Noodleman trilogy
Manes, Stephen
see **Oscar Noodleman trilogy**

Noodles series
Mackail, Denis
1 *Another part of the wood* (1929)
2 *Summer leaves* (1934)

Noomas series
Nuetzel, Charles
1 *Warriors of Noomas* (1969)
2 *Raiders of Noomas* (1969)

Noon series
Avallone, Michael
see **Ed Noon series**

Noony series
Frascino, Edward
see **Nanny Noony series**

Noose series
Cullen, Seamus
1 *Noose of light* (1986)
2 *Sultan's turret* (1986)

Nop series
McCaig, Donald
1 *Nop's hope* (1984)
2 *Nop's hope* (1994)

Nora and Larry Blaine series
Davis, Lavinia Riker
see **Nora Hughes and Larry Blaine series**

Nora and Teddy series
Hurwitz, Johanna
1 *Busybody Nora* (1976)
2 *Nora and Mrs Mind-Your-Own-Business* (1977)
3 *New neighbors for Nora* (1979)
4 *Superduper Teddy* (1980)
5 *Rip-Roaring Russell* (1983)

Nora Helmer series
This sequence has two authors
Ibsen, Henrik
1 *Doll's house* (1879)
Original edition entitled *Et dukkehjem;* a four act play
Cheney, Ednah Dow
2 *Nora's return* (1890)

Nora Hughes and Larry Blaine series
Davis, Lavinia Riker
1 *Evidence unseen* (1945)
2 *Taste of vengeance* (1947)

Nora series
Ichikawa, Satomi
Translated from the Japanese
1 *Nora's castle* (1986)
2 *Nora's stars* (1989)
3 *Nora's duck* (1991)
4 *Nora's roses* (1993)
5 *Nora's surprise* (1994)

Norah and Gavin trilogy
Pearson, Kit
see **Evacuee trilogy**

Norah Mulcahaney series
O'Donnell, Lillian
see **Detective Norah Mulcahaney series**

Norah North series
Duke, Madelaine
see **Doctor Norah North series**

Norah series
Swindells, Robert
1 *Norah's ark* (1979)
2 *Norah's shark* (1979)
3 *Norah to the rescue* (1981)
4 *Norah and the whale* (1981)

Norah the snorer series
Palfrey, Heather Mary
1 *Foxer gets smart* (1992)
2 *Norah the snorer* (1993)
3 *Finding a mate* (1994)

Nora's friends series
Leith, Mary Charlotte Julia
1 *Nora's friends* (1889)
Alternative title: A girl's influence
2 *Under cliff* (1890)

Norby series
Asimov, Isaac
1 *Norby, the mixed-up robot* (1983)
2 *Norby's other secret* (1984)
Numbers 1 and 2 also published in one volume entitled *The Norby chronicles*, 1986
3 *Norby and the lost princess* (1985)
4 *Norby and the invaders* (1985)
Numbers 3 and 4 also published in one volume entitled *Norby, robot for hire*, 1987
5 *Norby and the queen's necklace* (1986)
6 *Norby finds a villain* (1987)
Numbers 5 and 6 also published in one volume entitled *Norby through space and time*, 1988
7 *Norby down to earth* (1989)
8 *Norby and Yobo's great adventure* (1989)
9 *Norby and the oldest dragon* (1990)
10 *Norby and the court jester* (1991)

Nordejoong series
McKernan, Victoria
see **Chicago Nordejoong series**

Noreen and Aunt Joan series
Dawson, Helen
1 *Noreen's first case* (1957)
2 *House in Haven Street* (1960)
3 *Noreen and the Barclay affair* (1963)
4 *Noreen and the missing schoolgirl* (1963)
5 *Noreen and the Henry affair* (1964)
6 *Noreen and the mystery hero* (1965)

Noren series
Engdahl, Sylvia Louise
1 *This star shall abide* (1972)
Heritage of the star
2 *Beyond the tomorrow mountains* (1973)
3 *Doors of the universe* (1981)

Norfolk life series
Haggard, Lilias Rider
1 *Norfolk life* (1943)
Co-author: Henry Williamson
2 *Norfolk notebook* (1946)
3 *Country scrap book* (1946)

Norfolk village series
Douglas, Peter
1 *Down the village street* (1978)
2 *About this village* (1980)
3 *Village life* (1981)

Norgil series
Gibson, Walter Brown
1 *Norgil the magician* (1976)
2 *More tales of prestidigitection* (1979)

Norma and Alexander Magnus Gold series
Resnicow, Herbert
see **Alexander Magnus and Norma Gold series**

Norma Lee series
Lee, Norma
see **Beautiful Gunner series**

Norman and Henry Bones series
Wilson, Anthony Clifford
1 *Norman Bones, detective* (1949)
2 *Norman and Henry Bones* (1952)
3 *Norman and Henry Bones investigate* (1953)
4 *Four mysteries solved by Norman and Henry Bones* (1957)
5 *Norman and Henry solve the problem* (1957)
6 *Norman and Henry follow the trail* (1959)

Norman Bates series
Bloch, Robert
see **Psycho series**

Norman Conquest series
Gray, Berkeley
1 *Mister Mortimer gets the jitters* (1938)

2 *Vultures Ltd.* (1938)
3 *Miss Dynamite* (1939)
4 *Conquest marches on* (1939)
5 *Leave it to Conquest* (1939)
6 *Conquest takes all* (1940)
7 *Meet the Don* (1940)
8 *Six to kill* (1940)
9 *Convict 1066* (1940)
10 *Thank you, Mister Conquest* (1941)
11 *Six feet of dynamite* (1941)
12 *Blonde for danger* (1943)
13 *Gay desperado* (1944)
14 *Cavalier Conquest* (1944)
15 *Alias Norman Conquest* (1945)
16 *Mister Ball of Fire* (1946)
17 *Killer Conquest* (1947)
18 *Conquest touch* (1948)
19 *Spot marked X* (1948)
20 *Duel murder* (1949)
21 *Dare-Devil Conquest* (1950)
22 *Seven dawns to death* (1950)
23 *Operation Conquest* (1951)
24 *Conquest in Scotland* (1951)
25 *Lady is poison* (1952)
26 *Half-open door* (1953)
27 *Target for Conquest* (1953)
28 *Follow the lady* (1954)
29 *Conquest goes west* (1954)
30 *Turn left for danger* (1955)
31 *House of the lost* (1956)
32 *Conquest in command* (1956)
33 *Conquest after midnight* (1957)
34 *Conquest goes home* (1957)
35 *Conquest in California* (1958)
36 *Death on the Hit Parade* (1958)
37 *Big brain* (1959)
38 *Murder and Co.* (1959)
39 *Nightmare house* (1960)
40 *Conquest on the run* (1960)
41 *Get ready to die* (1961)
42 *Call Conquest for danger* (1961)
43 *Conquest in the underworld* (1962)
44 *Count down for Conquest* (1963)
45 *Castle Conquest* (1964)
46 *Conquest overboard* (1964)
47 *Calamity Conquest* (1965)
48 *Conquest likes it hot* (1965)
49 *Curtains for Conquest?* (1966)
50 *Conquest calls the tune* (1968)
Written by Mrs F Brooks and Lionel Brooks on an outline by Berkeley Gray
51 *Conquest in Ireland* (1969)
Written by Mrs F Brooks and Lionel Brooks on an outline by Berkeley Gray

Norman Pink series
McShane, Mark
see **Sergeant Norman Pink series**

Norman series
Thorndyke, Helen Louise
see **Honey Bunch series**

Norman Shotover series
Wilson, Andrew Norman
1 *Unguarded hours* (1978)
2 *Kindly light* (1979)

Norman trilogy
Anand, Valerie
1 *Gildenford* (1978)
2 *Norman pretender* (1979)
3 *Disputed crown* (1982)

Norman trilogy
Dymoke, Juliet
see **Henry I trilogy**

Norman trilogy
Plaidy, Jean
1 *Bastard king* (1974)
2 *Lion of Justice* (1975)
3 *Passionate enemies* (1976)

Normandy Campaign trilogy
Ryan, Cornelius
1 *Longest day* (1960)
The story of VE Day
2 *Last battle* (1966)
3 *Bridge too far* (1974)

Normandy Farm series
Henrey, Robert
Reminiscences
1 *Farm in Normandy* (1941)
2 *Return to the farm* (1947)
3 *Matilda and the chickens* (1950)

Norrington, Di Ganzarello and Tucker series
Drummond, Ivor
see **Lady Jennifer, Sandro and Colly series**

Norris and the Karate Kommandos series
Weinberg, Larry
see **Chuck Norris and the Karate Kommandos series**

Norris and Tully series
Davis, Dorothy Salisbury
see **Mrs Norris and Jasper Tully series**

Norris series
Elliott, Richard
see **John Norris series**
Runyan, John
see **Biff Norris series**

Norroy series
Bronson-Howard, George
see **Yorke Norroy series**

Norse series
Esteven, John
see **Inspector Rae Norse series**

Norsemen series
Collingwood, William Gershon
A saga of Northmen in Lakeland
1 *Thorstein of the Mere* (1895)
2 *Bondwoman* (1896)

North against South series
Verne, Jules
1 *Burbank the northerner* (1887)
Original edition entitled *Nord contre Sud*, part 1
2 *Texar the southerner* (1887)
Original edition entitled *Nord contre Sud*, part 2

North American Confederacy trilogy
Smith, Lester Neil
1 *Tom Paine Maru* (1984)
2 *Gallatin divergence* (1985)
3 *Brightsuit MacBear* (1988)

North American wildlife series
Kalman, Bobbie
Illustrated by Glen Loates
1 *Animal babies* (1987)
2 *Birds at my feeder* (1987)
3 *Forest mammals* (1987)
4 *Owls* (1987)

North and Redmayne series
Moore, Patrick
see **Robin North and Rex Redmayne series**

North and South trilogy
Jakes, John
1 *North and South* (1982)
1842-1861
2 *Love and war* (1984)
1861-1865
3 *Heaven and hell* (1987)
1865-1876

North Carolina series
Ehle, John
1 *Land breakers* (1964)
2 *Journey of August King* (1971)
3 *Time of drums* (1970)
4 *Road* (1967)
5 *Last one home* (1984)
6 *Lion on the hearth* (1961)
7 *Winter people* (1982)

North Dakota series
Erdrich, Louise
see **Argus series**

North series
Duke, Madelaine
see **Doctor Norah North series**
Lockridge, Frances
see **Mister and Mrs North series**
Mason, Francis Van Wyck
see **Colonel Hugh North series**
Mitchell, Silas Weir
see **Doctor North series**
North, Gerry
see **Gerry North series**
Robertson, Colin
see **Edward North series**

North star series
Eaton, Evelyn
Autobiography
1 *Every month was May* (1947)
2 *North star is nearer* (1949)

North-West Mounted Police series
Connor, Ralph
1 *Corporal Cameron* (1909)
Tale of the North-West Mounted Police
2 *Patrol of the Sun Dance Trail* (1914)

Northanger Abbey series
This sequence has two authors
Austen, Jane
1 *Northanger Abbey* (1818)
Gillespie, Jane
2 *Uninvited guests* (1994)

Northeast series
Cannan, Joanna
see **Inspector Guy Northeast series**

Northern Ireland trilogy
Sefton, Catherine
1 *Starry night* (1986)
2 *Frankie's story* (1988)
3 *Beat of the drum* (1989)

Northern Police series
Wainwright, John
1 *Death in a sleeping city* (1965)
2 *Ten steps to the gallows* (1965)
3 *Evil intent* (1966)
4 *Crystallised carbon pig* (1966)
5 *Talent for murder* (1967)
6 *Worms must wait* (1967)
7 *Web of silence* (1968)
8 *Edge of extinction* (1968)
9 *Darkening glass* (1968)
10 *Take-over man* (1969)
11 *Big tickle* (1969)
12 *Prynter's devil* (1970)
13 *Freeze thy blood less coldly* (1970)
14 *Last buccaneer* (1971)
15 *Dig the grave and let him lie* (1971)
16 *Night is the time to die* (1972)
17 *Requiem for a loser* (1972)
18 *Pride of pigs* (1973)
19 *High-class kill* (1973)
20 *Touch of malice* (1973)
21 *Evidence I shall give* (1974)
22 *Cause for a killing* (1974)
23 *Kill the girls and make them cry* (1974)
24 *Hard hit* (1974)
25 *Square dance* (1975)
26 *Death of a big man* (1975)
27 *Landscape with violence* (1975)
28 *Coppers don't cry* (1975)
29 *Walther P.38* (1976)
30 *Acquittal* (1976)
31 *Who goes next?* (1976)
32 *Bastard* (1976)
33 *Pool of tears* (1977)
34 *Nest of rats* (1977)
35 *Day of the peppercorn kill* (1977)
36 *Jury people* (1978)
37 *Thief of time* (1978)
38 *Death certificate* (1978)
39 *Ripple of murders* (1978)
40 *Brainwash* (1979)
41 *Tension* (1979)
42 *Duty elsewhere* (1979)
43 *Take murder* (1979)
44 *Eye of the beholder* (1980)
45 *Venus fly-trap* (1980)
46 *Dominoes* (1980)
47 *Kill of consequence* (1980)
48 *Tainted man* (1980)
49 *All on a summer's day* (1981)
50 *Urge for justice* (1981)
51 *Blayde R.I.P.* (1982)
52 *Anatomy of a riot* (1982)
53 *Distaff factor* (1982)
54 *Their evil ways* (1983)
55 *Spiral staircase* (1983)
56 *Clouds of guilt* (1985)
57 *All through the night* (1985)
58 *Forgotten murders* (1987)
59 *Very parochial murder* (1988)
60 *Man who wasn't there* (1989)

Northern Territory recollections series
Priest, Charles Ashley Vincent
1 *Earlier Northern Territory recollections* (1986)
2 *Northern Territory recollections* (1986)
3 *Further Northern Territory recollections* (1986)
4 *Still further Northern Territory recollections* (1986)
5 *Recollections of Alice Springs* (1987)
6 *Tennant Creek recollections* (1987)
With a South Australian interlude
Companion volume: *Glimpses of bygone days*, 1989

Northmen series
Collingwood, William Gershon
see **Norsemen series**

Northwest destiny trilogy
Gulick, Bill
1 *Distant trails, 1805-1836* (1988)
2 *Gathering storm, 1837-1868* (1988)
3 *Lost Wallowa, 1869-1879* (1988)

Northwest series
Ellis, Edward Sylvester
1 *Strange craft and its wonderful voyage* (1897)
2 *Cowmen and rustlers* (1898)
3 *Two boys in Wyoming* (1898)

Northwest stories series
This sequence has three authors
Snell, Leroy
1 *Lead disk* (1934)
2 *Shadow patrol* (1934)
3 *Wolf cry* (1934)
4 *Spirit of the north* (1935)
5 *Challenge of the yukon* (1935)
6 *Phantom of the rivers* (1936)
Rowe, John Gabriel
7 *Sergeant Dick* (1929)
8 *Carcajou* (1931)
Bennett, Billy L
9 *Danger trails north* (1936)

Northwest Territory series
Payne, Oliver
1 *Warpath* (1982)
2 *Conquest* (1982)
3 *Defiance* (1984)
4 *Conflict* (1984)
5 *Rebellion* (1984)
6 *Triumph* (1985)
7 *Betrayal* (1986)
8 *Honor* (1987)

Northworld series
Drake, David
1 *Northworld* (1990)
2 *Vengeance* (1991)
3 *Justice* (1992)

Norton series
Barrett, Robert G
see **Les Norton series**
Finlay, Winifred
see **Judith Norton series**
Malloch, Peter
see **Inspector Dave Norton series**
Palmer, Bernard
see **Dell Norton series**

Norwich series
Blake, M M
1 *Siege of Norwich Castle* (1893)
2 *Glory and sorrow of Norwich* (1899)

Nosegay series
Biegel, Paul
see **Virgil Nosegay series**

Nosey and Henrietta series
Pizer, Abigail
see **Henrietta and Nosey series**

Nostradamus trilogy
Laurance, Andrew
1 *Premonitions of an inherited mind* (1979)
Premonition
2 *Link* (1980)
Blood of Nostradamus
3 *Embryo* (1980)
Unborn

Not in our stars series
Maurice, Michael
1 *Not in our stars* (1923)
2 *But in ourselves* (1928)

Not quite human series
McEvoy, Seth
1 *Batteries not included* (1985)
2 *All geared up* (1985)
3 *Bug in the system* (1985)
4 *Reckless robot* (1986)
5 *Terror at play* (1986)
6 *Killer robot* (1986)

Not such dumb questions series
Cobb, Vicki
1 *Why can't you unscramble an egg?* (1989)
Questions about matter
2 *Why doesn't the sun burn out?* (1990)
Questions about energy

Notebook series
Charters, Samuel
Poetry
1 *From a Swedish notebook* (1972)
2 *From a London notebook* (1973)

Notebooks series
Picard, Sam
see **John Scott series**

Notes and sketches series
Meredith, Louisa Anne
1 *Notes and sketches of New South Wales* (1844)
Covers 1839-1840
2 *My home in Tasmania, during a residence of nine years* (1852)
Covers 1840-1848

Nothing and something series
Macgregor, Reginald James
One act plays
1 *Nothing ever happens* (1938)
2 *Something always happens* (1940)

Nothing but money series
Arthur, Timothy Shay
1 *Nothing but money* (1865)
2 *What came afterwards* (1865)

Nothing to lose series
Priest, Charles Ashley Vincent
Autobiography
1 *Nothing to lose* (1987)
2 *Free as the breeze* (1987)
3 *Toiling, rejoicing, sorrowing* (1987)

Notice me series
Sharmat, Marjorie Weinman
1 *He noticed I'm alive, and other hopeful signs* (1984)
2 *Two guys noticed me, and other miracles* (1985)

Nott series
Judd, Alfred
see **Toddy Nott series**

Nouveau siecle series
Hood, Hugh
see **New age series**

Nova trilogy
Burroughs, William Seward
see **Tangier trilogy**

Novak series
Hunt, Everette Howard
see **Jack Novak series**

Novaria series
De Camp, Lyon Sprague
see **Jorian series**

Novelas espanolas contemporaneas
Perez Galdos, Benito
see **Contemporary novels of Spain series**

Novels of character and environment series
Hardy, Thomas
1 *Tess of the D'Urbevilles* (1891)
2 *Far from the madding crowd* (1874)
3 *Jude the obscure* (1895)
4 *Return of the native* (1878)
5 *Life and death of the Mayor of Casterbridge* (1886)
6 *Woodlanders* (1887)
7 *Under the greenwood tree* (1872)
8 *Life's little ironies* (1894)
9 *Wessex tales* (1888)

Novels of ingenuity series
Hardy, Thomas
1 *Desperate remedies* (1871)
2 *Hand of Ethelberta* (1876)
3 *Laodicean* (1881)

November Man series
Granger, Bill
1 *November Man* (1979)
2 *Public murders* (1980)
3 *Schism* (1981)
4 *Shattered eye* (1982)
5 *British Cross* (1983)
6 *Zurich numbers* (1984)
7 *Hemingway's notebook* (1986)
8 *There are no spies* (1986)
9 *Infant of Prague* (1987)
10 *Henry McGee is not dead* (1988)
11 *Man who heard too much* (1989)

November 1918 series
Doblin, Alfred
see **German revolution series**

Now I see series
Lunn, Arnold
Memoirs of spiritual life
1 *Now I see* (1933)
2 *Come what may* (1940)
3 *And yet so new* (1958)
Companion volume: *Memory to memory*, 1956

Nowell family series
Wall, Robert Emmet
1 *Blackrobe* (1981)
2 *Bloodbrothers* (1981)
3 *Birthright* (1982)
4 *Patriots* (1982)
5 *Inheritors* (1983)
6 *Dominion* (1984)
7 *Acadians* (1984)
8 *Brotherhood* (1985)

Noziere series
France, Anatole
see **Pierre Noziere series**

Nuala series
Kimbriel, Katharine Eliska
1 *Fire sanctuary* (1986)
2 *Fires of Nuala* (1988)
3 *Hidden fires* (1991)

Nuclear trilogy
Wongar, B
1 *Walg* (1983)
2 *Karan* (1985)
3 *Gabo Djara* (1987)

Nuda veritas series
Sheridan, Clare
1 *Nuda veritas* (1927)
2 *Arab interlude* (1936)

Nudger series
Lutz, John
see **Alo Nudger series**

Nugan series
Turner, George Reginald
1 *Destiny makers* (1993)
2 *Genetic soldier* (1994)

Nugent family series
Burton, Betty
1 *Jude* (1986)
2 *Jaen* (1987)
3 *Women of no account* (1988)

Null-A series
Van Vogt, Alfred Elton
1 *World of A* (1948)
World of Null-A
2 *Pawns of Null-A* (1956)
Players of Null-A
3 *Null-A three* (1985)

Number One Area Crime Squad series
Keenan, William
see **Chief Superintendent Charles Miller series**

Number one boy series
Ward, Edward
Autobiography
1 *Number one boy* (1969)
2 *I've lived like a lord* (1970)

Number play series
Burningham, John
1 *Count up* (1983)
Learning sets
2 *Five down!* (1983)
Numbers as signs
3 *Just cars* (1983)
Learning groups
4 *Pigs plus* (1983)
Learning addition
5 *Read one* ()
Numbers as words
6 *Ride off* ()
Learning subtraction

Number Ten Ox and Master Li Kao series
Hughart, Barry
see **Master Li Kao and Number Ten Ox series**

Nungu series
Cole, Babette
1 *Nungu and the crocodile* (1978)
2 *Nungu and the hippopotamus* (1978)
3 *Nungu and the elephant* (1980)

Nuns series
Routh, Jonathan
1 *Nuns go to Penguin Island* (1971)
2 *Nuns go to Africa* (1971)
3 *Nuns go east* (1972)
4 *Nuns go west* (1972)
5 *Nuns go car racing* (1973)

Nur Bey series
Rathbone, Julian
see **Colonel Nur Bey series**

Nuranian series
Jenkins, Robin
1 *Dust on the paw* (1961)
2 *Tiger of gold* (1962)

Nuri Iskirlak series
Fleming, Joan
1 *When I grow rich* (1962)
2 *Nothing is the number when you die* (1965)

Nurlingas series
Bailey, Gerald Earl
1 *Madame Trinh* (1966)
2 *Winnowing winds* (1967)
3 *House of a stranger* (1979)
4 *Sword of the Nurlingas* (1979)
5 *Sword of Poyana* (1979)

Nurse Agnes Carmichael series
Cohen, Anthea
1 *Angel without mercy* (1982)
2 *Angel of vengeance* (1983)
3 *Angel of death* (1983)
4 *Fallen Angel* (1984)
5 *Guardian Angel* (1985)
6 *Hell's Angel* (1986)
7 *Ministering Angel* (1987)
8 *Destroying Angel* (1988)
9 *Angel dust* (1989)
10 *Recording Angel* (1991)
11 *Angel in action* (1992)
12 *Angel in love* (1993)

Nurse Carter series
Darbyshire, Shirley
1 *Young Nurse Carter* (1954)
2 *Nurse Carter married* (1955)
Sequence continued by the author's husband, Laurence Walter Meynell
Meynell, Laurence Walter
3 *District Nurse Carter* (1958)

Nurse Hilda Adams series
Rinehart, Mary Roberts
1 *Miss Pinkerton* (1932)
Double alibi
2 *Mary Roberts Rinehart's crime book* (1933)
Includes two novelettes entitled *The buckled bag* and *Locked doors*
3 *Haunted lady* (1942)

Nurse Jane Taylor series
Ridley, Sheila
1 *Nurse in danger* (1862)
2 *Nurse in doubt* (1964)
3 *Nurse in the South Seas* (1965)
4 *Nurses and ladies* (1967)
5 *Nurse in the Mutiny* (1970)

Nurse Jones series
Jones, Joanna
Reminiscences
1 *Nurse is a neighbour* (1958)
2 *Nurse on the district* (1959)

Nurse Kathy Martin series
James, Josephine
see **Kathy Martin series**

Nurse Matilda series
Brand, Christianna
1 *Nurse Matilda* (1964)
2 *Nurse Matilda goes to town* (1967)
3 *Nurse Matilda goes to hospital* (1974)

Nurse Ross series
Meynell, Laurence Walter
1 *Nurse Ross takes over* (1958)
2 *Nurse Ross shows the way* (1959)
3 *Nurse Ross saves the day* (1960)
4 *Nurse Ross and the doctor* (1962)
5 *Good luck, Nurse Ross* (1963)

Nurse series
Deal, Paula
Reminiscences
1 *Nurse, nurse, nurse!* (1959)
2 *Forward, staff nurse* (1960)
3 *Nurse at Butlins* (1961)
4 *Surgery nurse* (1962)
5 *Factory nurse* (1963)
6 *Village nurse* (1964)

Nurse series
Grant, Jane
Reminiscences
1 *Come hither, nurse* (1957)
2 *Come again, nurse* (1960)
3 *Sisters under their skins* (1965)
4 *Round-the-clock nurse* (1968)

Nurse series
Prentis, Evelyn
Autobiography
1 *Nurse in time* (1977)
2 *Nurse in action* (1978)
3 *Nurse in parts* (1980)
4 *Nurse near by* (1981)
5 *Turn for the nurse* (1982)

Nurse series
Treger, Anne
Reminiscences
1 *Probationer nurse* (1958)
2 *Maternity nurse* (1960)

Nurse Sue Barton series
Boylston, Helen Dore
see **Sue Barton series**

Nurse Verena Frodesley series
Lance, Leslie
1 *Nurse in the woods* (1969)
2 *Nurse Verena at Weirwater* (1970)
3 *Nurse on the moors* (1970)

Nursery Rhyme Land series
Blyton, Enid
1 *Twins go to Nursery Rhyme Land* (1945)
2 *Mary Mouse in Nursery Rhyme Land* (1955)

Nursery series
Hughes, Shirley
1 *When we went to the park* (1985)
2 *Noisy* (1985)
3 *Bathwater's hot* (1985)
4 *All shapes and sizes* (1986)
5 *Colours* (1986)
6 *Two shoes, new shoes* (1986)

Nursery tales series
De Paola, Tomie
1 *Tomie De Paola's Mother Goose* (1986)
2 *Tomie De Paola's Favourite nursery tales* (1987)

Nurses three series
Kirby, Jean
see **Scott sisters series**

Nursing howlers series
Brook, Roger
Howlers taken from examination papers of many great hospitals
1 *Really, nurse* (1960)
2 *Wake up, nurse* (1963)

Nursing trilogy
Bright, Pamela
Autobiography
1 *Life in our hands* (1955)
2 *Breakfast at night* (1956)
3 *Day's end* (1959)

Nutsell series
Hughes, Dean
see **Nutty Nutsell series**

Nutty Nutsell series
Hughes, Dean
1 *Nutty for president* (1981)
2 *Nutty and the case of the mastermind thief* (1985)
3 *Nutty and the case of the ski-slope spy* (1985)
4 *Nutty can't miss* (1987)
5 *Nutty knows all* (1988)
6 *Nutty the movie star* (1989)
7 *Nutty's ghost* (1993)
8 *Re-elect Nutty!* (1994)

Nydia and Sam Balon series
Johnstone, William Wallace
see **Beasts series**

Nyla Wade series
McConnell, Vicki P
1 *Burnton widows* (1984)
2 *Mrs Porter's letter* (1986)
3 *Double daughter* (1988)

O

O Gang series
Edwards, Hazel
1 *O Gang* (1985)
2 *O Gang again* (1991)

O.R.G.Y. series
Mark, Ted
see **Man from O.R.G.Y. series**

O.S.S.117 series
Bruce, Jean
see **Secret Agent O.S.S.117 series**

O series
Reage, Pauline
1 *Story of O* (1954)
Original edition entitled *Histoire d'O*
2 *Return to the chateau* (1969)
Original edition entitled *Retour a Loissy*

O Swete McTavish series
Brooks, Collin
1 *Found dead* (1930)
2 *Three yards of cord* (1931)

Oak Tree House series
B B
1 *Little grey men* (1942)
A story for the young in heart
2 *Down the bright stream* (1948)
Little grey men go down the bright stream

Oakalla series
Riggs, John Raymond
see **Garth Ryland series**

Oakapple Wood series
Partridge, Jenny
1 *Mister Squint* (1980)
2 *Colonel Grunt* (1980)
3 *Hopfellow* (1980)
4 *Peterkin Pollensnuff* (1980)
Numbers 1-4 also published in one volume entitled *Oakapple Wood treasury*, 1982
5 *Dominic Sly* (1981)
6 *Grandma Snuffles* (1981)
7 *Lop-ear* (1981)
8 *Harriet Plume* (1981)
Numbers 5-8 also published in one volume entitled *Four friends in Oakapple Wood*, 1984
9 *Tale of Oakapple Wood* (1983)
10 *Rifkins* (1986)
11 *Jack Flax* (1986)
12 *Rafferty* (1986)
13 *Clara Quince* (1986)

Oakes series
Buckley, William Frank
see **Blackford Oakes series**
Gardner, John Edmund
see **Boysie L Oakes series**
Jackson, Charles Ross
see **Quintus Oakes series**

Oakhurst series
Johnson, Walter Reed
1 *Oakhurst* (1978)
2 *Mistress of Oakhurst* (1978)
3 *Lions of Oakhurst* (1979)
4 *Fires of Oakhurst* (1980)

Oakleigh Farm series
Layberry, Layton George Joseph
1 *Hayseed* (1980)
2 *Gleanings* (1981)
A farming love story
3 *To be a farmer's girl* (1982)
4 *Pocket full of rye* (1983)
5 *Last mophrey* (1986)
6 *As long as the fields are green* (1987)
7 *New earth* (1988)

Oakley series
Schroeder, Doris
see **Annie Oakley series**

Oakshott series
Challoner, Robert
see **Commander Lord Charles Oakshott series**

Oakwood family series
Pearsall, Ronald
1 *Tides of war* (1978)
2 *Iron sleep* (1979)

Oath series
Durrant, Digby
see **Hamish Oath series**

Obadiah series
Tate, Richard
see **Marcus Obadiah series**

Obadiah series
Turkle, Brinton
1 *Obadiah the Bold* (1965)
2 *Thy friend, Obadiah* (1969)
3 *Adventures of Obadiah* (1972)
4 *Rachel and Obadiah* (1978)

Obedience series
Gage, Joy Pennock
1 *Heart for obedience* (1987)
2 *Wrestling with obedience* (1991)

Obedient servant series
Scott, Harold
Reminiscences of the Commissioner of the Metropolitan Police, London
1 *Your obedient servant* (1959)
2 *From inside Scotland Yard* (1963)
Co-author: Philippa Pearce

Obernewtyn chronicles series
Carmody, Isobelle
1 *Obernewtyn* (1987)
2 *Farseekers* (1990)
3 *Scatterlings* (1991)

O'Blivion series
Scott, Jody
see **Sterling O'Blivion series**

O'Breen series
Boucher, Anthony
see **Fergus O'Breen series**

O'Brien, Buffalo Hunter series
Hayes, Ralph Eugene
1 *Secret of Sulphur Creek* (1970)
Gunslammer
2 *Four ugly guns* (1970)
Vengeance is mine
3 *Hunter's moon* (1972)
4 *Name is O'Brien* (1972)
Hellhole
5 *Revenge of the Buffalo Hunter* (1992)

O'Brien series
Bridges, Ben
see **Carter O'Brien series**
Marlett, Melba
see **Sarah O'Brien series**
Poploff, Michelle
see **Busy O'Brien series**
Stahl, Hilda
see **Kayla O'Brien series**

Occupied Germany series
Habe, Hans
Translated from the German manuscripts
1 *Aftermath* (1947)
2 *Walk in darkness* (1948)

Ocean critterland series
Reese, Bob
1 *Dale the whale* (1983)
2 *Spongee sponge* (1983)
3 *Ocean fish school* (1983)
4 *Oola Oyster* (1983)
5 *Wellington Pelican* (1983)
6 *Coral reef* (1983)

Ocean series
Benford, Gregory
1 *In the ocean of night* (1977)
2 *Across the sea of suns* (1984)
Revised edition 1987
3 *Deeper than the darkness* (1970)
Stars in shroud
The second title is a revised edition, 1978

Ocean series
Stafford-Deitsch, Jeremy
1 *Shark* (1987)
A photographer's story
2 *Reef* (1991)
A safari through the coral world

Ocean waifs series
Reid, Mayne
Autobiography
1 *Ran away to sea* (1858)
2 *Ocean waifs* (1871)

Ocean Wireless Boys series
Lawton, Wilbur
1 *Ocean Wireless Boys on the Atlantic* (1914)
2 *Ocean Wireless Boys and the lost liner* (1914)
3 *Ocean Wireless Boys of the Iceberg Patrol* (1915)
4 *Ocean Wireless Boys and the navy code* (1915)
5 *Ocean Wireless Boys on the Pacific* (1916)
6 *Ocean Wireless Boys on warswept seas* (1917)

Oceola Archer series
Carr, Joseph Baker
1 *Death whispers* (1933)
2 *Man with bated breath* (1934)

O'Connor series
Branson, Karen
see **Maureen O'Connor series**
Shannon, Brad
see **Lefty O'Connor series**

Octave trilogy
Marston, Jeffery
1 *Octave* (1925)
2 *Summer storm* (1932)
3 *No middle way* (1938)

Octavius Fanks series
Hume, Fergus
1 *Monsieur Judas* (1891)
2 *Chinese jar* (1893)
3 *Carbuncle clue* (1896)

Octopus series
Craig, Randolph
1 *City condemned to hell* (1975)
2 *Satan's incubator* (1976)

Odan the half-god trilogy
Norvil, Manning
1 *Dream chariots* (1977)
2 *Whetted bronze* (1977)
3 *Crown of the sword god* (1980)

O'Dare series
Buncher, Walter
see **Donald O'Dare series**

O'Day series
Gaines, Audrey
see **Chauncey O'Day series**

Odd and Elsewhere series
Roose-Evans, James
1 *Adventures of Odd and Elsewhere* (1971)
2 *Secret of the seven bright shiners* (1972)
3 *Odd and the Great Bear* (1973)
4 *Elsewhere and the gathering of the clowns* (1974)
5 *Return of the Great Bear* (1975)
Odd to the rescue
6 *Secret of Tippety-Witchet* (1975)
7 *Lost treasure of Wales* (1977)

Odd jobs series
Goulart, Ron
1 *Odd jobs number one hundred and one, and other future crimes and intrigues* (1971)
Short stories
2 *Calling Doctor Patchwork* (1978)
3 *Big bang* (1982)
4 *Brainz, Inc.* (1985)

Odd jobs series
Johnston, Tony
1 *Odd jobs* (1977)
2 *Odd jobs and friends* (1982)

Odd series
Le Feuvre, Amy
1 *Odd one* (1897)
2 *Odd made even* (1902)
One volume edition entitled *Odd*, 1904

Oddly series
Blake, Jon
1 *Oddly* (1989)
2 *Melody of Oddly* (1992)

Oddly series
Jennings, Paul Francis
1 *Oddly enough* (1950)
2 *Even oddlier* (1952)
3 *Oddly Bodlikins* (1953)
4 *Next to oddliness* (1955)
5 *Model oddlies* (1956)
6 *Gladly Oddly* (1958)
7 *Idly Oddly* (1959)
8 *I said Oddly, diddle I?* (1961)
9 *Oodles of oddlies* (1963)
10 *Oddly ad lib* (1965)

O'Dea series
Coburn, Andrew
see **Rita Gardella O'Dea series**

O'Dell series
Chipperfield, Robert Orr
see **Barry O'Dell series**

Odell series
Lory, Robert
see **Shamryke Odell series**
Powell, Lester
see **Philip Odell series**

Odin series
Bethancourt, Tomas Ernesto
1 *Mortal instruments* (1977)
2 *Instruments of darkness* (1977)

Odin series
Kelleam, Joseph Everidge
see **Jack Odin series**

Odious child series
Zinkin, Taya
Autobiography
1 *Odious child* (1971)
2 *Weeds grow fast* (1973)

Odom series
Boniface, Marjorie
see **Sheriff Hiram Odom series**

O'Donnell series
Eyre, Donald Cuthbert
see **Captain O'Donnell series**

O'Dowda series
Finch, Matthew
see **Stevie O'Dowda series**

O'Driscoll series
Doyle, Brian
see **Hubbo O'Driscoll series**

Odysseus series
Homer
see **Trojan war series**

Odyssey of the Irish trilogy
Llywelyn, Morgan
1 *Lion of Ireland* (1980)
2 *Horse goddess* (1983)
3 *Bard* (1984)

Oedipus series
Sophocles
Plays translated from the ancient Greek
1 *Oedipus Rex* (-420)
Oedipus Tyrannus
2 *Oedipus at Colonnus* (-410)

Of man and mantra trilogy
Anthony, Piers
1 *Omnivore* (1968)
2 *Orn* (1971)
3 *Ox* (1976)
One volume edition entitled *Of man and mantra*, 1986

Of time series
Johnston, Norma
1 *Of time and of seasons* (1975)
2 *Striving after wind* (1976)

Off season series
Ketchum, Jack
1 *Off season* (1980)
2 *Offspring* (1991)

Off the leash series
Park, William Bryan
Cartoons
1 *Off the leash* (1987)
2 *Far off the leash* (1989)

Officer and gentleman series
Fetterless, Arthur
1 *Gog* (1916)
2 *Battle days* (1918)

O'Friel trilogy
Macmanus, Seumas
1 *Bend of the road* (1898)
2 *Lad of the O'Friel's* (1903)
3 *Yourself and the neighbours* (1914)

Og series
Crump, James Irving
1 *Og, son of fire* (1922)
2 *Og, boy of battle* (1925)
3 *Og of the cave people* (1935)
4 *Og, son of Og* (1965)

Oggy series
Lawrence, Ann
1 *Travels of Oggy* (1973)
2 *Oggy at home* (1977)
3 *Oggy and the holiday* (1979)

Ogilvie series
Macneil, Duncan
see **James Ogilvie series**

Ogle-Oxley series
French, Fergus
see **General Ogle-Oxley series**

O'Gorman and Mary Louise series
Van Dyne, Edith
see **Mary Louise and Josie O'Gorman series**

O'Grady series
Maurois, Andre
see **Doctor O'Grady series**
Sharpe, Jon
see **Canyon O'Grady series**

O'Hannay and East series
Rushton, Charles
see **James O'Hannay and Floyd East series**

O'Hara dynasty trilogy
Cannon, Mary
1 *Defiant* (1981)
2 *Survivors* (1982)
3 *Renegade* (1982)

O'Hara series
Costello, Paul
see **Terence O'Hara series**
Haldeman, Joe
see **Marianne O'Hara series**
Mitchell, Margaret
see **Scarlett O'Hara series**

O'Hara trilogy
Gagnon, Maurice
see **Deirdre O'Hara trilogy**

Ohio frontier trilogy
Ellis, William Donohue
1 *Bounty lands* (1952)
2 *Jonathan Blair, bounty lands lawyer* (1954)
3 *Brooks legend* (1958)

O'Hurley trilogy
Roberts, Nora
1 *Last honest woman* (1988)
2 *Dance to the piper* (1988)
3 *Skin deep* (1988)

Oil-seeker series
Elder, Michael
1 *Oil-seeker* (1977)
2 *Oil-planet* (1978)

Oink and Pearl series
Chorao, Kay
1 *Oink and Pearl* (1981)
2 *Ups and downs woth Oink and Pearl* (1985)

O'Keefe series
L'Engle, Madeleine
see **Poly and Charles O'Keefe series**

O'Kelly series
O'Brine, Manning
see **Michael O'Kelly series**

Okewood series
Williams, Valentine
see **Clubfoot series**

Okkie series
Roggeveen, Leonard
1 *Okkie Gingernut* (1934)
Original edition entitled *Okkie Pepernoot*
2 *Okkie and his little friends* (1934)
Original edition entitled *Okkie en zijn vriendjes*
3 *Okkie knows what to do!* (1934)
Original edition entitled *Okkie weet raad!*
4 *Okkie in the cold* (1934)
Original edition entitled *Okkie in de kou*
Eight more titles in this sequence published between 1940 and 1959 have not been translated

Ola series
D'Aulaire, Ingri
1 *Ola* (1932)
2 *Ola and Blakken and Line, Sine, Trine* (1933)
Terrible troll bird
The second title is a revised edition

Olaf series
Lexau, Joan M
1 *Olaf reads* (1961)
2 *Olaf is late* (1963)

Olaf the Viking series
Laird, Elizabeth
1 *Long house in danger* (1986)
2 *Dark forest* (1986)

Olaf Tryggvason series
Sprague, Rosemary
see **King Olaf Tryggvason series**

Olav Audunsson series
Undset, Sigrid
see **Master of Hestviken series**

Old Bear series
Hissey, Jane
1 *Old Bear* (1986)
2 *Old Bear tales* (1988)

Old Bill series
Bairnsfather, Bruce
1 *Bystander's fragments of France* (1916)
2 *More fragments from France* (1916)
3 *Still more from Bystander* (1917)
4 *Bullets and billets* (1917)
5 *Bystander's fragments from France, volume 5* (1918)
6 *Bystander's fragments from France, volume 6* (1918)
7 *From mud to mufti* (1919)
8 *Fragments away from France* (1920)
9 *Laughing through the Orient* (1933)
10 *Old Bill stands by* (1939)
11 *Old Bill does it again* (1940)
A memoir of pre-blitz France
12 *Old Bill and son* (1940)
Co-author: Ian Dalrymple

Old Chester series
Deland, Margaret
1 *Philip and his wife* (1894)
2 *Old Chester tales* (1899)
Includes *Good for the soul*, also published separately, 1899
3 *Doctor Lavendar's people* (1903)
4 *Around old Chester* (1915)
Short stories
5 *Old Chester secret* (1920)
6 *New friends in old Chester* (1924)
Includes *An old Chester secret*, 1920
Selections from this sequence published as *Old Chester days*, 1937

Old Chicago series
Bradley, Mary Hastings
1 *Fort* (1933)
2 *Duel* (1933)
3 *Debt of honor* (1933)
4 *Metropolis* (1933)

Old England series
Gilbert, Bernard
1 *Old England* (1921)
A God's eye view of a village
2 *King Lear at Hordle* (1922)
3 *Tyler of Barnet* (1922)
4 *Rural scene* (1923)

Old Ernie series
Mallett, Jerry J
see **Ernie series**

Old farm series
Ober, Frederick Albion
1 *When life was young at the old farm* (1912)
2 *Great year of our lives at the old squire's* (1912)
3 *Busy year at the old squire's* (1922)
4 *Haps and mishaps at the old farm* (1925)
Companion volumes: *Stories of my home folks*, 1926, *My folks in Maine*, 1934

Old fashioned stories from the DreamMaker series
Cosgrove, Stephen Edward
see **DreamMaker series**

Old Glory series
Stratemeyer, Edward L
1 *Under Dewey at Manila* (1898)
Alternative title: The war fortunes of a castaway
2 *Young volunteer in Cuba* (1898)
Alternative title: Fighting for the single star
3 *Fighting in Cuban waters* (1899)
Alternative title: Under Schley on the Brooklyn
4 *Under Otis in the Philippines* (1899)
Alternative title: Young officer in the tropics
5 *Campaign of the jungle* (1900)
Alternative title: Under Lawton through Luzon
6 *Under Macarthur in Luzon* (1901)
Alternative title: Last battles in the Philippines

Old Growler trilogy
Deegan, Jon J
1 *Amateurs in alchemy* (1952)
2 *Antro, the life-giver* (1953)
3 *Great ones* (1953)

Old Hector and young Art series
Gunn, Neil Miller
see **Young Art and old Hector series**

Old Ireland Yard series
Butler, William Vivian
1 *Scare power* (1969)
2 *Lie witnesses* (1971)
3 *Clampdown* (1971)

Old London series
Benson, Edward Frederic
1 *Portrait of an English nobleman* (1937)
Life in Georgian London
2 *Janet* (1937)
Set in early Victorian London
3 *Friend of the rich* (1937)
Set in mid-Victorian London
4 *Unwanted* (1937)
Set in Edwardian London

Old man in the corner series
Orczy, Emmuska
1 *Case of Miss Elliott* (1905)
Short stories
2 *Old man in the corner* (1909)
Man in the corner
Augmented edition 1980
3 *Mystery of the khaki tunic* (1923)
4 *Mystery of the pearl necklace and the tragedy in Bishop's Road* (1924)
5 *Mystery of the Russian prince and of Dog's Tooth Cliff* (1924)
6 *Mystery of the white carnation and the Montmartre hat* (1925)
7 *Mystery of the Fulton Gardens and the moorland tragedy* (1925)
8 *Unravelled knots* (1924)

Old man series
Ruark, Robert
1 *Old man and the boy* (1957)
2 *Old man's boy grows older* (1961)

Old Melbourne series
Cannon, Michael
1 *Old Melbourne town before the gold rush* (1991)
2 *Melbourne after the gold rush* (1993)

Old Mother West Wind series
Burgess, Thornton Waldo
1 *Old Mother West Wind* (1910)
Adventures of Old Mother West Wind
2 *Mother West Wind's children* (1911)
Adventures of Mother West Wind's children
3 *Mother West Wind's animal friends* (1912)
Adventures of Mother West Wind's animal friends
4 *Mother West Wind's neighbors* (1913)
Adventures of Mother West Wind's neighbours
5 *Mother West Wind why stories* (1915)
6 *Mother West Wind how stories* (1916)
7 *Mother West Wind when stories* (1917)
8 *Mother West Wind where stories* (1918)

Old New Orleans quartet
Tinker, Frances
1 *Widows only* (1931)
1860s
2 *Strife* (1931)
1870s
3 *Closed shutters* (1931)
1880s
4 *Mardi gras masks* (1931)
1890s

Old New York quartet
Wharton, Edith
1 *False dawn* (1924)
2 *Old maid* (1924)
3 *Spark* (1924)
4 *New Year's Day* (1924)
One volume edition entitled *Old New York*, 1952

Old ones trilogy
Horowitz, Anthony
1 *Devil's door-bell* (1983)
2 *Night of the scorpion* (1984)
3 *Silver citadel* (1986)

Old Paris series
Stacpoole, Henry de Vere
1 *Order of release* (1912)
2 *Monsieur de Rochefort* (1914)

Old peoples' home trilogy
Brindley, Louise
1 *They must have seen me coming* (1978)
2 *There's one born every minute* (1982)
3 *Vicky and I* (1984)

Old Philadelphia series
Gibbs, George
1 *Loyal rebel* (1931)
The 1770s
2 *Supercargo* (1931)
The 1790s
3 *Autumn* (1931)
The 1830s
4 *North Star* (1931)
The 1850s

Old plantation series
Harris, Joel Chandler
see **Uncle Remus series**

Old Possum series
Eliot, Thomas Stearns
1 *Old Possum's book of practical cats* (1939)
2 *Practical Possum* (1947)

Old Pull'n Push series
Weir, Rosemary
see **Tempest family series**

Old Quong series
Burke, Thomas
see **London series**

Old San Francisco series
Mitchell Ruth Comfort
1 *Blue for true love* (1933)
The 1840s
2 *Fire!* (1933)
The 1850s
3 *Curtain!* (1933)
The 1860s
4 *Tell your fortune* (1933)
The 1870s

Old squire's series
Ober, Frederick Albion
see **Old farm series**

Old Swithinford series
Marshall, Sybil
1 *Nest of magpies* (1993)
2 *Sharp through the hawthorn* (1994)

Old-timers series
Miller, Jim
1 *Old-timers of Gun Shy* (1987)
2 *Old-timers in the Sangre de Cristos* (1988)
3 *Old-timers on the open range* (1988)

Old Witch series
Devlin, Wende
Illustrated by Harry Devlin
1 *Old Black Witch* (1963)
2 *Old Witch and the polka dot ribbon* (1970)
3 *Old Witch rescues Halloween* (1973)

Old Yeller series
Gipson, Fred
1 *Old Yeller* (1956)
2 *Savage Sam* (1962)

Oldcastle series
Lindsay, Philip
see **Sir John Oldcastle series**

Olden times series
Deal, Borden
1 *Least one* (1967)
2 *Other room* (1974)

Oldest member series
Wodehouse, Pelham Grenville
1 *Clicking of Cuthbert* (1922)
2 *Heart of a goof* (1926)
3 *Nothing serious* (1950)

Oldroyd family series
Bentley, Phyllis
1 *Inheritance* (1932)
2 *Rise of Henry Morcar* (1946)
3 *Man in his times* (1966)
4 *Ring in the new* (1969)

Oldtown series
Stowe, Harriet Beecher
1 *Oldtown folks* (1869)
2 *Sam Lawson's Oldtown fireside stories* (1872)

Ole Devil Hardin series
Edson, John Thomas
1 *Young Ole Devil* (1975)
2 *Ole Devil and the Caplocks* (1976)
3 *Ole Devil and the mule train* (1976)
4 *Ole Devil at San Jacinto* (1977)
5 *Get Urrea* (1975)
6 *Ole Devil's hands and feet* (1983)

Oleandre series
Fretland, Donald John
1 *Persimmon sequence* (1971)
2 *Winds of the Heliopolis* (1972)
Originally announced as a trilogy

O'Leary and Keate series
Eberhart, Mignon Good
see **Sarah Keate and Lance O'Leary series**

O'Leary series
Laumer, Keith
see **Lafayette O'Leary series**
Scoggins, Charles Elbert
see **Colin O'Leary series**

Oleg series
Brisville, Jean Claude
1 *Oleg the snow leopard* (1978)
Original edition entitled *Oleg le leopard des neiges*
2 *King Oleg* (1982)
Original edition entitled *Oleg retrouve son royaume*

Olga da Polga picture books series
Bond, Michael
Based on *The tales of Olga da Polga*, 1971
1 *Olga counts her blessings* (1975)
2 *Olga makes a friend* (1975)
3 *Olga makes a wish* (1975)
4 *Olga makes her mark* (1975)
5 *Olga takes a bite* (1975)
6 *Olga's new home* (1975)
7 *Olga's second house* (1975)
8 *Olga's special day* (1975)

Olga da Polga series
Bond, Michael
1 *Tales of Olga da Polga* (1971)
1.1 *First big Olga da polga book* (1971)
1.2 *Second big Olga da polga book* (1971)
2 *Olga meets her match* (1973)
3 *Olga carries on* (1976)
4 *Olga takes charge* (1982)
One volume edition entitled *The complete adventures of Olga da Polga*, 1983

Olga von Kopf series
De Halsalle, Henry
1 *Secret service woman* (1917)
2 *Woman spy* (1918)

Oliphant series
Blake, George
1 *Constant star* (1945)
2 *Westering sun* (1946)

Oliphant series
Newby, Percy Howard
see **Hesketh and Jane Oliphant series**

Oliver and company series
This sequence has three authors
McBrier, Page
Illustrated by Blanche Sims
1 *Oliver and the lucky duck* (1986)

Oliver and company series

2 *Oliver's lucky day* (1986)
McBrier, Michael
3 *Oliver and the runaway alligator* (1987)
4 *Oliver's back-yard circus* (1987)
5 *Oliver's high-flying adventure* (1987)
6 *Getting Oliver's ghost* (1988)
7 *Oliver and the amazing spy* (1988)
8 *Oliver smells trouble* (1988)
9 *Oliver's barnyard blues* (1988)
Korman, Justine
10 *Oliver finds a home* (1988)
11 *More the merrier* (1988)
Companion volume: *Disney's Oliver and company movie storybook*, 1988

Oliver and Jenny series
Segal, Erich
1 *Love story* (1970)
2 *Oliver's story* (1977)

Oliver Armiston series
Anderson, Frederick Irving
1 *Adventures of the infallible Godahl* (1914)
Short stories
2 *Notorious Sophie Lang* (1925)
Short stories
3 *Book of murder* (1930)
Short stories

Oliver Aylsham series
Heaven, Constance
1 *Lord of Ravensley* (1978)
2 *Ravensley touch* (1982)

Oliver Bubb series
Craig, George
see **Sir Oliver Bubb series**

Oliver Colfax series
Conley, Robert Jackson
1 *Killing time* (1988)
2 *Colfax* (1989)
3 *Quitting time* (1989)

Oliver, Colin and Prill series
Cheetham, Ann
see **Black harvest series**

Oliver Crowe series
Daniell, David Scott
see **Drummer Oliver Crowe series**

Oliver Cutter series
Haugaard, Erik Christian
1 *Messenger for Parliament* (1976)
2 *Cromwell's boy* (1978)

Oliver Galt and Hugo Tower series
France, Victor
1 *Carved emerald* (1926)
2 *Naked five* (1927)

Oliver Huffam series
Mackenzie, Compton
1 *Red tapeworm* (1941)
2 *Paper lives* (1966)

Oliver Keene series
Walsh, James Morgan
1 *Island of spies* (1937)
2 *Black dragon* (1938)
3 *Dial nine nine nine* (1938)
4 *Bullets for breakfast* (1939)
5 *King's enemies* (1939)
6 *Secret weapons* (1940)
7 *Spies from the skies* (1941)
8 *Death at his elbow* (1941)
9 *Face value* (1941)
10 *Danger zone* (1942)
11 *Island alert* (1943)
12 *Whispers in the dark* (1945)

Oliver Mandrake series
Haythorne, John
1 *None of us cared for Kate* (1968)
2 *Strelsau dimension* (1981)
3 *Mandrake in Granada* (1984)
4 *Mandrake in the monastery* (1985)

Oliver Matravers series
Farnol, Jeffery
1 *Crooked furrow* (1937)
2 *Happy harvest* (1939)

Oliver Pig series
Van Leeuwen, Jean
1 *Tales of Oliver Pig* (1979)
2 *More tales of Oliver Pig* (1981)

Oliver series
Chappell, Audrey
1 *Surprise fo Oliver* (1989)
2 *Outing for Oliver* (1990)

Oliver series
Christie, Agatha
see **Mrs Ariadne Oliver series**
Dicks, Terrance
see **Ask Oliver series**
Elkins, Aaron J
see **Professor Gideon Oliver series**

Oliver series
Gibbs, Philip
1 *Street of adventure* (1909)
2 *Oliver's kind women* (1911)

Oliver series
Tomalin, Ruth
see **Ralph Oliver series**

Oliver series
Van Dyke, Henry
1 *Ladies of the Rachmaninoff eyes* (1965)
2 *Blood of strawberries* (1969)

Oliver series
Wiggin, Kate Douglas
see **Polly Oliver series**

Oliver Slater Fijiian series
Foreman, Russell
1 *Long pig* (1958)
2 *Sandalwood Island* (1961)

Oliver Smaile series
Adye, John
1 *At the house of the priest* (1925)
2 *Golden scarab* (1926)
3 *Flash of lightning* (1927)

Oliveres series
Foster, David
see **D'Arcy Oliveres series**

Olivia, Kate and Reggie series
Lehmann, Rosamond
1 *Invitation to the waltz* (1932)
2 *Weather in the streets* (1936)

Olivia Sharp series
Sharmat, Marjorie Weinman
1 *Pizza monster* (1989)
2 *Princess of the Fillimore Street School* (1989)
3 *Sly spy* (1990)
4 *Green Toenails Gang* (1991)

Olivier Chateauneuf series
Sabatier, Robert
1 *Safety matches* (1969)
Match boy
Original edition entitled *Les allumettes suedoises*
2 *Three mint lollipops* (1972)
Original edition entitled *Trois sucettes a la menthe*

Olivirez series
Muller, Marcia
see **Elena Olivirez series**

Ollafubs series
Lethbridge, Katharine Greville
1 *Rout of the Ollafubs* (1964)
2 *In search of Thunder* (1966)

Ollie series
Solomon, Helen
1 *Ollie's trolley* (1983)
2 *Ollie's family* (1984)

Olly sees it through series
Gydal, Monica
1 *When Olly went to hospital* (1976)
2 *When Olly had a little brother* (1976)
3 *When Gemma's parents got divorced* (1976)
4 *When Olly's grandad died* (1976)
5 *When Olly saw an accident* (1977)
6 *When Olly moved house* (1977)

Olmeg series
Jordan, William Johnston
1 *Olmeg's lucky escape* (1988)
2 *Olmeg's eventful morning* (1989)
3 *Olmeg's tiring journey* (1991)

Olof tetralogy
Johnson, Eyvind
1 *Nineteen fourteen* (1934)
Original edition entitled *Nu var det*, 1914
2 *Return to Ithaca* (1946)
The Odyssey retold as a modern novel; original edition entitled *Straandernas svall*
3 *Dreams of roses and fire* (1949)
Original edition entitled *Droemmer om rosor och eld*
4 *Days of his grace* (1960)
Original edition entitled *Hans naades tid*

Olympic High School series
Chandler, A C
see **Going for it series**

Oma series
Kleberger, Ilse
see **Grandmother Oma series**

O'Malley series
Daniel, Roland
see **Brian O'Malley series**
Kenyon, Michael
see **Superintendent O'Malley series**
Lysaght, Brian
see **Ben O'Malley series**
Ross, Gene
see **Shaun O'Malley series**
Small, Beatrice
see **Skye O'Malley series**

O'Mara series
Cheyney, Peter
see **Shaun O'Mara series**

Omaran series
Cole, Adrian
1 *Place among the fallen* (1986)
2 *Throne of fools* (1987)
3 *King of light and shadows* (1988)
4 *Gods in anger* (1988)

O'Meara series
Bannerman, David
see **Magic Man series**

Omega Point trilogy
Zebrowski, George
1 *Ashes and stars* (1977)
2 *Omega Point* (1983)
Numbers 2 and 3 only published in the one volume edition
3 *Mirror of minds* (1983)
One volume edition entitled *The Omega Point trilogy*, 1983

Omega series
Carter, Lin
see **Prince Zarkon series**

Omega sub series
Cameron, J D
This pseudonym is used by Michael Jahn and David Robbins as indicated against each title
1 *Omega sub* (1991)
[Jahn]
2 *Command decision* (1991)
[Robbins]
3 *City of fear* (1991)
[Jahn]
4 *Blood tide* (1991)
[Robbins]

Omen series
This sequence has three authors
Seltzer, David
1 *Omen* (1976)
Howard, Joseph
2 *Damien* (1978)
McGill, Gordon
3 *Final conflict* (1980)
4 *Armageddon 2000* (1982)
5 *Abomination* (1985)

Omina series
Starr, Roland
1 *Operation Omina* (1970)
2 *Omina uncharted* (1974)
3 *Time factor* (1975)
4 *Return from Omina* (1976)

Ommony series
Mundy, Talbot
see **Cotswold Ommony series**

Omni odysseys trilogy
This sequence has three authors
Mixon, Laura J
1 *Astropilots* (1987)
Astro pilots
Coville, Bruce
2 *Space Station ICE-three* (1987)
Murder in orbit
Kruchten, Marcia
3 *Skyborn* (1988)
Skytorn

Omnivore trilogy
Anthony, Piers
see **Of man and mantra trilogy**

Omri series
Banks, Lynne Reid
1 *Indian in the cupboard* (1980)
2 *Return of the Indian* (1986)
3 *Secret of the Indian* (1989)
4 *Mystery of the cupboard* (1993)

On foot series
Fermor, Patrick Leigh
1 *Time of gifts* (1977)
On foot to Constantinople, from the Hook of Holland to the middle Danube
2 *Between the woods and the water* (1986)
On foot to Constantinople from the Hook of Holland, the middle Danube to the Iron Gates

On language series
Safire, William
1 *On language* (1980)
2 *What's the good word* (1982)
3 *I stand corrected* (1984)
4 *Take my word for it* (1986)
5 *You could look it up* (1988)
6 *Language maven strikes again* (1990)
7 *Quoth the maven* (1993)

On my nose series
Burke, Billie
Autobiography
1 *With a feather on my nose* (1950)
2 *With powder on my nose* (1959)

On my own series
Roosevelt, Eleanor
Autobiography
1 *On my own* (1959)
2 *You learn by living* (1960)

On our own series
Quin-Harkin, Janet
see **Toni Redmond and Jill Gardner series**

On our way series
Ziefert, Harriet
Board books
1 *On our way to the zoo* (1985)
2 *On our way to the barn* (1985)
3 *On our way to the forest* (1985)
4 *On our way to the water* (1985)

On series
Belloc, Hilaire
Essays
1 *On nothing and kindred subjects* (1908)
2 *On everything* (1909)
3 *On anything* (1910)
4 *On something* (1910)
5 *On* (1923)
A book of lads and poets, Pyrenean springs, ambitions and loves of Eastern kings, the eternal sea and several other things

On the shore trilogy
Vercors
1 *[Le periple]* (1958)
No English edition
2 *Monsieur Prousthe* (1958)
Original edition entitled *Monsieur Prousthe*
3 *Freedom in December* (1960)
Paths of love
Original edition entitled *La liberte de Decembre, et, Clementine*

Once and future king series
White, Terence Hanbury
1 *Sword in the stone* (1938)
2 *Witch in the wood* (1939)
Queen of air and darkness
3 *Ill-made knight* (1940)
Revised edition of numbers 1-3 and *Candle in the wind* published in one volume entitled *The once and future king*, 1958
4 *Book of Merlyn* (1977)

Once in England trilogy
Raymond, Ernest
1 *Family that was* (1929)
2 *Jesting army* (1930)
3 *Mary Leith* (1931)

Once upon a time series
Hooper, Kay
1 *Golden threads* (1989)
2 *Glass shoe* (1989)
3 *What dreams may come* (1990)
4 *Through the looking glass* (1990)
5 *Lady and the lion* (1990)

Once-upon-a-time-in-America series
Coatsworth, Elizabeth
Stories of American history, 1620-1945
1 *First adventure* (1950)
2 *Wishing pear* (1951)
3 *Boston bells* (1952)
4 *Aunt Flora* (1953)
5 *Old Whirlwind* (1953)
A story of Davy Crockett
6 *Sod house* (1954)
7 *Cherry Ann and the dragon horse* (1955)

Once upon a time series
Taulbert, Clifton Lemoure
1 *Once upon a time when we were colored* (1989)
2 *Last train north* (1992)

One day series
George, Jean Craighead
1 *One day in the desert* (1983)
2 *One day in the alpine tundra* (1984)
3 *One day in the prairie* (1986)
4 *One day in the woods* (1988)
5 *One day in the tropical rain forest* (1990)

One day series
Kirtland, G B
1 *One day in ancient Rome* (1961)
2 *One day in Elizabethan England* (1962)
3 *One day in Aztec Mexico* (1963)

One End Street series
Garnett, Eve
see **Ruggles family series**

One-Eye trilogy
Gordon, Stuart
see **Eyes trilogy**

One-Eyed Mack series
Lehrer, Jim
1 *Kick the can* (1988)
2 *Crown Oklahoma* (1989)
3 *Sooner spy* (1990)
4 *Lost and found* (1991)
5 *Short list* (1992)
6 *Blue hearts* (1993)
7 *Fine lines* (1994)

One man series
Gibson, Morris
Autobiography
1 *One man's medicine* (1981)
2 *Doctor in the west* (1983)

One of us series
Frankau, Gilbert
Novels in verse
1 *One of us* (1912)
Jack, one of us
2 *More of us* (1937)
Companion volume: *One of them*, 1918

One pair series
Dickens, Monica
Autobiography
1 *One pair of hands* (1939)
2 *One pair of feet* (1942)
3 *My turn to make the tea* (1951)

One Week Wimble series
Burnham, Helen
1 *Murder of Lalla Lee* (1931)
2 *Telltale telegram* (1932)

One writer's trilogy
Yates, Elizabeth
Autobiography
1 *My diary, my world* (1981)
2 *My widening world* (1983)
3 *One writer's way* (1984)

O'Neal and Teetoncey trilogy
Taylor, Theodore
see **Teetoncey and Ben O'Neal trilogy**

Onedin Line series
Abraham, Cyril
1 *Shipmaster* (1972)
2 *Iron ships* (1974)
3 *High seas* (1975)
4 *Trade winds* (1977)
5 *White ships* (1979)

O'Neil and the Baker Street Sports Club series
Jenkins, Jerry Bruce
see **Dallas O'Neil and the Baker Street Sports Club series**

O'Neil mysteries series
Jenkins, Jerry Bruce
see **Dallas O'Neil mysteries series**

O'Neill series
Farrell, James Thomas
see **Danny O'Neill series**

Onetree series
Clifford, Eth
see **Mary Rose Onetree series**

Onlookers series
Avery, Gillian
1 *Lost railway* (1980)
2 *Onlookers* (1983)

Only child series
Kirkup, James
1 *Only child* (1957)
2 *Sorrows, passions and alarms* (1959)
3 *I, of all people* (1988)

Only child series
Klein, Norma
1 *Confessions of an only child* (1974)
2 *Tomboy* (1978)

Only child series
O'Connor, Frank
1 *Only child* (1961)
2 *My father's son* (1968)

Only mouse series
Smith, Wendy
1 *Lonely only mouse* (1986)
2 *Twice mice* (1987)

Onward and upward series
Optic, Oliver
1 *Field and forest* (1871)
Alternative title: The fortunes of a farmer
2 *Plane and plank* (1871)
Alternative title: The mishaps of a mechanic
3 *Desk and debit* (1871)
Alternative title: The catastrophes of a clerk
4 *Cringle and cross-tree* (1871)
Alternative title: The sea swashes of a sailor
5 *Bivouac and battle* (1871)
Alternative title: The struggles of a soldier
6 *Sea and shore* (1872)
Alternative title: The tramps of a traveller

Oonaderra Station series
Roy, Thomas Albert
see **Jimmy Brent series**

Opar series
This sequence has two authors
Farmer, Philip Jose
1 *Hadon of ancient Opar* (1974)
Burroughs, Edgar Rice
2 *Tarzan and the jewel of Opar* (1918)
Farmer, Philip Jose
3 *Flight to Opar* (1976)
Companion volume: *Time's last gift*, 1972

Opara series
Uhnak, Dorothy
see **Christie Opara series**

Open garden series
Nichols, Beverley
1 *Garden open today* (1963)
2 *Garden open tomorrow* (1968)

Open road quartet
Macdonald, Peter G
1 *Hope of glory* (1980)
2 *Wide horizon* (1980)
3 *One way street* (1981)
4 *Exit* (1982)

Opening bars series
Hughes, Spike
Autobiography
1 *Opening bars* (1946)
2 *Second movement* (1951)

Operation Hang Ten series
Morgan, Patrick
1 *Hang dead Hawaiian style* (1969)
2 *Too mini murders* (1969)
3 *Deadly group down under* (1970)
4 *Cute and deadly surf twins* (1970)
5 *Scarlet surf at Makaha* (1970)
6 *Girl in the telltale bikini* (1971)
7 *Topless dancer hangup* (1971)
8 *Beach queen blowout* (1971)
9 *Death car surfside* (1972)
10 *Freaked out stranger* (1973)

Operation series
Price, Edgar Hoffmann
1 *Operation misfit* (1980)
2 *Operation longlife* (1983)
3 *Operation exile* (1986)
4 *Operation Isis* (1987)

Operation Star Hawks series
Dalton, Sean
1 *Space Hawks* (1990)
2 *Code name Peregrine* (1990)
3 *Beyond the void* (1991)
4 *Rostma lure* (1991)
5 *Destination mutiny* (1991)

Operation Titan series
Horvat, Dilwyn
1 *Operation Titan* (1983)
2 *Assault on Omega Four* (1986)

Operator Five series
Steele, Curtis
see **James Christopher series**

Opium war trilogy
Gaan, Margaret
see **Red barbarian trilogy**

Oppidan trilogy
Leslie, Shane
1 *Oppidan* (1922)
2 *Cantab* (1926)
3 *Anglo-Catholic* (1929)

Opportunities series
Warner, Susan Bagert
1 *What she could* (1870)
2 *Opportunities* (1871)
3 *House in town* (1871)
4 *Trading* (1872)

Opposing viewpoints series
Roop, Peter
see **Great mysteries series**

Oracle trilogy
Resnick, Mike
1 *Soothsayer* (1991)
2 *Oracle* (1992)
3 *Prophet* (1993)

Oral histories of slaves series
Hurmence, Belinda
1 *My folks don't want me to talk about slavery* (1984)
Former North Carolina slaves
2 *Before freedom, when I just can't remember* (1989)
Former South Carolina slaves; numbers 1 and 2 also published in one volume entitled *Before freedom*, 1990
3 *We lived in a little cabin in the yard* (1994)
Former Virginia slaves

Orange County trilogy
Robinson, Kim Stanley
1 *Wild shore* (1984)

Orange County trilogy

2 *Gold coast* (1988)
3 *Pacific edge* (1990)

Orange series
Hobbes, John Oliver
see **Robert Orange series**

Orange Street series
Arnold, Ralph
Autobiography
1 *Very quiet war* (1962)
2 *Orange Street and Brickhole Lane* (1963)

Orbital decay series
Steele, Allen
1 *Orbital decay* (1989)
2 *Lunar descent* (1991)

Orbitsville trilogy
Shaw, Bob
1 *Orbitsville* (1975)
2 *Orbitsville departure* (1983)
3 *Orbitsville judgement* (1991)

Orchid series
Chase, James Hadley
see **Carol Blandish series**

Orchid trilogy
Brooke, Jocelyn
1 *Military orchid* (1948)
2 *Mine of serpents* (1949)
3 *Goose cathedral* (1950)
One volume edition entitled *The orchid trilogy*, 1981

Orcutt girls series
Vaile, Carlotte Marion
1 *Orcutt girls* (1896)
Alternative title: One term at the academy
2 *Sue Orcutt* (1897)

Ord series
Allen, Austen
see **Inspector Ord series**

Orde family series
White, Stewart Edward
1 *Blazed trail* (1902)
2 *Riverman* (1908)
3 *Rules of the game* (1910)
4 *Adventures of Bobby Orde* (1911)
Bobby Orde
5 *Gold* (1913)
A tale of the forty-niners
6 *Gray dawn* (1915)
Grey dawn

Ordeal trilogy
Tolstoi, Aleksei Nikolaevich
Translated from the Russian
1 *Sisters* (1921)
2 *Nineteen eighteen* (1928)
Partial translation of numbers 1 and 2 entitled *Darkness and dawn*, 1935
3 *Bleak morning* (1941)
One volume editions entitled *The road to Calvary*, 1946, *Ordeal*, 1953

Order of Sion series
Baigent, Michael
1 *Holy Blood and the Holy Grail* (1982)
Co-authors: Richard Leigh and Henry Lincoln
2 *Messianic legacy* (1986)
Co-authors: Richard Leigh and Henry Lincoln

Orderly man series
Bogarde, Dirk
Autobiography
1 *Postillion struck* (1977)
2 *Snakes and ladders* (1978)
3 *Orderly man* (1983)
4 *Backcloth* (1986)
One volume edition entitled *Dirk Bogarde, the complete autobiography*, 1988

O'Reilly series
Agry, Ed
1 *Assault force* (1981)
2 *Blowtorch* (1982)

O'Reilly series
Hawk, Alex
see **Elfego O'Reilly series**

Orestes Bignon series
Didelot, Francis
see **Commissaire Orestes Bignon series**

Organic future series
Easton, Thomas Atwood
see **Sparrowhawk series**

Orient series
Lauria, Frank
see **Doctor Owen Orient series**

Origin of Dragonrealm series
Knaak, Richard Allen
1 *Shrouded realm* (1991)
2 *Children of the drake* (1991)
This sequence is followed by the **Dragonrealm series**

Orin Boyd series
Westermann, John
1 *Exit wounds* (1990)
2 *Honor Farm* (1994)

Oriole series
Marlowe, Amy Bell
1 *When Oriole came to Harbor Light* (1920)
2 *When Oriole travelled westward* (1921)
3 *When Oriole went to boarding school* (1927)
One volume edition, also including *The girls of Rivercliff School*, 1916, entitled *Oriole's adventures*, 1933

Orion series
Bova, Ben
1 *Orion* (1984)
2 *Vengeance of Orion* (1988)
3 *Orion in the dying time* (1990)

Orion series
Harris, Rosemary
1 *Quest for Orion* (1978)
2 *Tower of the stars* (1980)

Orlando King series
Colegate, Isabel
see **King family series**

Orlando series
Hale, Kathleen
1 *Orlando, the marmalade cat, a camping holiday* (1938)
Orlando's camping holiday
2 *Orlando, the marmalade cat, a trip abroad* (1939)
Orlando's trip abroad
3 *Orlando's evening out* (1941)
4 *Orlando's home life* (1942)
5 *Orlando, the marmalade cat, buys a farm* (1942)
6 *Orlando, the marmalade cat, becomes a doctor* (1944)
7 *Orlando, the marmalade cat, his silver wedding* (1944)
Orlando's silver wedding
8 *Orlando's invisible pyjamas* (1947)
9 *Orlando, the marmalade cat, keeps a dog* (1949)
10 *Orlando the judge* (1950)
11 *Orlando, the marmalade cat, a seaside holiday* (1952)
Orlando's seaside holiday
12 *Orlando's zoo* (1954)
13 *Orlando, the marmalade cat, the frisky housewife* (1956)
14 *Orlando's magic carpet* (1958)
15 *Orlando, the marmalade cat, buys a cottage* (1963)
16 *Orlando and the three Graces* (1965)
17 *Orlando, the marmalade cat, goes to the moon* (1968)
18 *Orlando, the marmalade cat, and the water cats* (1972)
Companion volume: *Orlando's country life, a peep-show book*, 1951

Orlis series
Palmer, Bernard
see **Danny Orlis series**

Orlis twins series
Palmer, Bernard
1 *Orlis twins and the secret of the mountain* (1959)
2 *Orlis twins and the High School Gang* (1959)
3 *Orlis twins live for Christ* (1959)
4 *Orlis twins and the new coach* (1960)
5 *Orlis twins and Mike's last chance* (1960)
6 *Orlis twins and Ron's big problem* (1961)
7 *Orlis twins and Jim Morgan's ordeal* (1962)
8 *Orlis twins and Roxie's triumph* (1963)

Ormiston series
Walsh, James Morgan
see **Colonel Ormiston series**

Ormond series
Barrington, E
1 *Ninth vibration, and other stories* (1922)
2 *House of fulfilment* (1927)
The romance of a soul

Ormsberry series
Strange, John Stephen
see **Van Dusen Ormsberry series**

Orn trilogy
Anthony, Piers
see **Of man and mantra trilogy**

O'Roarke and Gerard series
Dentinger, Jane
see **Jocelyn O'Roarke and Phillip Gerard series**

Oron series
Smith, David Claude
1 *Mosultha's magic* (1982)
2 *Valley of Ogrum* (1982)
3 *Ghost army* (1983)
4 *Oron* (1978)
5 *Sorcerer's shadow* (1978)

O'Rourke series
Sherry, Sylvia
see **Rocky O'Rourke series**
Vance, Louis Joseph
see **Terence O'Rourke series**

Orp series
Kline, Suzy
1 *Orp* (1989)
2 *Orp and the chop suey burgers* (1990)
3 *Orp goes to the hoop* (1991)
4 *Who's Orp's girlfriend?* (1992)

Orphan Annie series
Gray, Harold
see **Little Orphan Annie series**

Orphan family series
Grahame, Kenneth
see **Smith family series**

Orphan series
Morgan, Geoffrey
1 *Small piece of paradise* (1967)
2 *Touch of magic* (1968)
3 *Window of sky* (1969)

Orphan train quintet
Nixon, Joan Lowery
1 *Family apart* (1987)
2 *Caught in the act* (1988)
3 *In the face of danger* (1988)
4 *Place to belong* (1989)
5 *Dangerous promise* (1994)
Companion volume: *The dark and deadly pool*, 1987

Orphans' home series
Foote, Horton
Plays; the dates are those of the first production rather of publication since not all of these plays have been published individually
1 *Roots in a parched ground* (1960)
Also known as The night of the storm
2 *On Valentine's Day* (1980)
3 *Nineteen eighteen* (1982)
4 *Convicts* (1983)
5 *Courtship* (1984)
Numbers 2, 3 and 5 published in one volume as *Three plays from the Orphans' home cycle*, 1987
6 *Cousins* (1984)
7 *Lily Dale* (1986)
8 *Widow Claire* (1986)
Numbers, 1, 4, 7 and 8 published in one volume, 1988
9 *Death of papa* (1989)
Numbers 6 and 9 published in one volume entitled *Two plays from the Orphans' home*, 1989

Orphelines series
Carlson, Natalie Savage
1 *Happy Orpheline* (1957)
2 *Brother for the Orphelines* (1959)
3 *Pet for the Orphelines* (1962)
4 *Orphelines in the enchanted castle* (1964)
5 *Grandmother for the Orphelines* (1980)

Orsini series
Kenyon, Paul
see **Baroness Penelope Saint-John Orsini series**

Orthe series
Gentle, Mary
1 *Golden witchbread* (1983)
2 *Ancient light* (1987)

Ortiz series
Stern, Richard Martin
see **Johnny Ortiz series**

Orwell series
Hays, Lee
see **Harry Orwell series**
Stansky, Peter
see **George Orwell series**

Osbert Monk series
Craig, Alisa
1 *Grub-and-Stakers move a mountain* (1981)
2 *Grub-and-Stakers quilt a bee* (1985)
3 *Grub-and-Stakers pinch a poke* (1988)
4 *Grub-and-Stakers spin a yarn* (1990)
5 *Grub-and-Stakers house a haunt* (1993)

Osborn series
Beach, Edward Latimer, senior
see **Ralph Osborn series**

Osborne Crag series
Elvestad, Sven
Original editions published under the pseudonym Stein Riverton
1 *Man who plundered the city* (1915)
Original edition entitled *Manden som vilde Plyndre Kristiania*
2 *Mystery of the Abbe Montrose* (1917)
Original edition entitled *Montrose*

Oscar Noodleman trilogy
Manes, Stephen
1 *That game from outer space* (1983)
2 *Oscar J Noodleman television network* (1984)
3 *Chicken trek* (1987)

Oscar Sallis and Amanda Curzon series
Usher, Frank
see **Amanda Curzon and Oscar Sallis series**

O'Shane series
Knight, Mallory T
see **Man from T.O.M.C.A.T. series**

O'Shaughnessy series
Dunlap, Susan
see **Kiernan O'Shaughnessy series**
Vaizey, Jessie Bell
see **Pixie O'Shaughnessy series**

O'Shaunnessey and Gregory Pavlov series
Ryan, Jessica
see **Gregory Pavlov and O'Shaughnessey series**

O'Shay series
Lynde, Stan
see **Rick O'Shay series**

O'Shea series
Clinton, Jeff
see **Wildcat O'Shea series**
Yates, Renate
see **Inspector Ereache O'Shea series**

Ossie series
Davies, Hunter
1 *Come on Ossie!* (1985)
2 *Ossie goes supersonic* (1986)
3 *Ossie the millionaire* (1987)

Oswald Bastable series
Moorcock, Michael
1 *Warlord of the air* (1971)
2 *Land leviathan* (1974)
3 *Steel tsar* (1981)
One volume edition entitled *The nomad of time*, 1984

Oswald Mosley series
Mosley, Nicholas
see **Sir Oswald Mosley series**

Otani series
Melville, James
see **Superintendent Tetsuo Otani series**

Other Day Logan series
Stone, Ned
1 *Breed* (1990)
2 *Mountain massacre* (1990)
3 *Blood on the rails* (1990)
4 *One-man jury* (1991)

Other day series
Whipple, Dorothy
1 *Other day* (1936)
2 *Random commentary* (1966)

Other Edens series
Evans, Chris
1 *Other Edens* (1987)
2 *Other Edens II* (1988)
3 *Other Edens III* (1989)

Others trilogy
Bonanno, Margaret Wander
1 *Others* (1990)
2 *OtherWhere* (1991)
3 *OtherWise* (1993)

Otho Belleme series
Wren, Percival Christopher
1 *Soldiers of misfortune* (1929)
2 *Valiant dust* (1932)

Otis Beagle series
Gruber, Frank
1 *Silver jackass* (1941)
Originally published under the pseudonym Charles K Boston
2 *Beagle scented murder* (1946)
Market for murder
3 *Lonesome badger* (1954)
Mood for murder

Otis series
Sarto, Ben
see **Miss Otis series**

Otley quartet
Waddell, Martin
see **Gerald Otley quartet**

O'Toole and Garnish series
McConnell, Frank
see **Harry Garnish and Bridget O'Toole series**

O'Toole series
Thurston, Robert
see **Rugger series**

Otter Patrol series
Martin, Edward Le Breton
1 *Boys of the Otter Patrol* (1909)
2 *Otters to the rescue* (1910)

Ottley trilogy
Leverson, Ada
see **Edith Ottley trilogy**

Otto series
Pene du Bois, William
1 *Giant Otto* (1936)
Otto in Africa
The second title is a revised edition
2 *Otto at sea* (1936)
Revised edition 1958
3 *Otto in Texas* (1959)
4 *Otto and the magic potatoes* (1970)

Otto Stahl series
Kessler, Leo
1 *Otto's phoney war* (1981)
2 *Otto's blitzkrieg* (1982)
3 *Otto and the Reds* (1982)
4 *Otto and the Yanks* (1983)
5 *Otto and the SS* (1983)
6 *Otto and the Himmler love letters* (1984)

Otto von Heynitz series
Le Queux, William
1 *Hushed up at German Headquarters* (1917)
Startling revelations of the Crown Prince's shameful actions
2 *Behind the German lines* (1918)
Amazing confessions

Ottoline series
Morrell, Ottoline
Edited by Robert Gathorne-Hardy
1 *Ottoline* (1963)
Early memoirs
2 *Ottoline at Garsington* (1974)
Memoirs, 1915-1918

Our baby series
Hessell, Jenny
1 *Our baby helps* (1988)
2 *Our baby doesn't* (1988)
3 *Our baby gets dressed* (1988)

Our brother Nick series
Hayle, Felicity
1 *Our brother Nick and the tolling bell* (1958)
2 *Our brother Nick and the old quarry* (1958)
3 *Our brother Nick and the tattooed gardener* (1958)
4 *Our brother Nick and the African drums* (1958)
5 *Our brother Nick and the ugly idol* (1961)
6 *Our brother Nick and the hole in the dyke* (1961)

Our cat and puppy series
Brown, Ruth
1 *Out cat Flossie* (1986)
2 *Our puppy's holiday* (1987)

Our endangered planet series
Hoff, Mary
1 *Groundwater* (1991)
2 *Rivers and lakes* (1991)
3 *Oceans* (1991)
4 *Population growth* (1991)
5 *Tropical rain forests* (1991)
6 *Life on land* (1992)
7 *Life in the sea* (1993)

Our greatest heritage series
Daniel, Rebecca
1 *Adam and Eve* (1983)
2 *Noah* (1983)
3 *Abraham* (1983)
4 *Joseph* (1983)
5 *Moses* (1983)
6 *Joshua* (1983)
7 *Samson* (1983)
8 *David* (1983)
9 *Solomon* (1983)
10 *Daniel* (1983)
11 *Jonah* (1983)
12 *Women of the Old Testament* (1983)

Our hearts series
This sequence has two authors; humorous reminiscences
Skinner, Cornelia Otis
1 *Our hearts were young and gay* (1942)
Kimbrough, Emily
2 *We followed our hearts to Hollywood* (1943)

Our life series
Rockwell, Anne
1 *First comes spring* (1985)
2 *In our house* (1985)
3 *Come to town* (1987)

Our mutual friend series
This sequence has two authors
Dickens, Charles
1 *Our mutual friend* (1865)
Johnston, Harry Hamilton
2 *Veneerings* (1922)

Our services series
Crump, James Irving
1 *Our police* (1935)
Co-author: John W Newton
2 *Our airmen* (1936)
Co-author: John W Newton
3 *Our G-men* (1937)
Co-author: John W Newton
4 *Our firemen* (1938)
5 *Our airliners* (1938)
Co-author: Norman Maul
6 *Our movie makers* (1940)
7 *Our United States secret service* (1942)
8 *Our marines* (1944)
9 *Our oil hunters* (1948)
10 *Our tanker fleet* (1952)
11 *Our army engineers* (1954)
12 *Our state police* (1955)
13 *Our Merchant Marine Academy, Kings Point* (1958)
14 *Our United States Coast Guard Academy* (1961)

Our vow series
Haverfield, Eleanor Luisa
1 *Our vow* (1899)
2 *Blind loyalty* (1900)

Out and about series
Border, Rosemary
1 *Lucy helps in the garden* (1985)
2 *Sam's visit to the zoo* (1985)
3 *Sam goes shopping* (1985)
4 *Ben's birthday party* (1985)
5 *Katy goes to the seaside* (1985)
6 *Lucy goes to playgroup* (1985)

Out of the ark series
Beaman, Sydney George Hulme
1 *Teddy's new job* (1927)
2 *Wally the kangaroo* (1927)
3 *Grunty the pig* (1927)
4 *Jimmy the baby elephent* (1927)
5 *Ham and the egg* (1927)
6 *Jenny the giraffe* (1927)

Out of the smoke series
Parkin, Ray
1 *Out of the smoke* (1960)
2 *Into the smother* (1963)
3 *Sword and the blossom* (1968)

Out of this world series
Kaye, Marilyn
1 *Max on earth* (1986)
2 *Max in love* (1986)
3 *Max on fire* (1986)
4 *Max flips out* (1986)
5 *Max goes bad* (1989)
6 *Max all over* (1989)

Outback tales series
Garvey, Keith
1 *Tales of my Uncle Harry* (1978)
Broadcast on ABC radio as My Uncle Harry
2 *Funny bugger, and other tales* (1978)
3 *Shout for the adder, and other bush yarns* (1980)
4 *Uncle Harry rides again* (1981)
Numbers 2-4 also published in one volume entitled *The Keith Garvey omnibus*, 1982
5 *Slowly sweats the gun, and other tales of an earlier outback Australia* (1981)

Outdoor chums series
Allen, Quincy
1 *Outdoor chums* (1911)
Alternative title: The first tour of the Rod, Gun and Camera Club
2 *Outdoor chums on the lake* (1911)
Alternative title: Lively adventures on Wildcat Island
3 *Outdoor chums in the forest* (1911)
Alternative title: Laying the ghost of Oak Ridge
4 *Outdoor chums on the gulf* (1911)
Alternative title: Rescuing the lost balloonists
5 *Outdoor chums after big game* (1911)
Alternative title: Perilous adventures in the wilderness
6 *Outdoor chums on a houseboat* (1913)
Alternative title: The rivals of the Mississippi
7 *Outdoor chums in the big woods* (1915)
Alternative title: The rival hunters of Lumber Run

8 *Outdoor chums at Cabin Point* (1916)
Alternative title: The golden cup mystery

Outdoor girls series
Hope, Laura Lee
House pseudonym
1 *Outdoor girls of Deepdale* (1913)
Alternative title: Camping and tramping for fun and health
2 *Outdoor girls at Rainbow lake* (1913)
Alternative title: The stirring cruise of the motor boat Gem
3 *Outdoor girls in a motor car* (1913)
Alternative title: The haunted mansion of Shadow Valley
4 *Outdoor girls in a winter camp* (1913)
Alternative title: Glorious days on skates and iceboats
5 *Outdoor girls in Florida* (1913)
Alternative title: Wintering in the sunny South
6 *Outdoor girls at Ocean View* (1915)
Alternative title: The box that was found in the sand
7 *Outdoor girls on Pine Island* (1916)
Alternative title: A cave and what it contained
8 *Outdoot girls in army service* (1918)
Alternative title: Doing their bit for the soldier boys
9 *Outdoor girls at the Hostess House* (1919)
Alternative title: Doing their best for the soldiers
10 *Outdoor girls at Bluff Point* (1920)
Alternative title: A wreck and a rescue
11 *Outdoor girls at Wild Rose Lodge* (1921)
Alternative title: The hermit of Moonlight Falls
12 *Outdoor girls in the saddle* (1922)
Alternative title: The girl miner of Gold Run
13 *Outdoor girls around the campfire* (1923)
Alternative title: The old maid of the mountains
14 *Outdoor girls at Cape Cod* (1924)
Alternative title: Sally Ann of Lighthouse Rock
15 *Outdoor girls at Foaming Falls* (1925)
Alternative title: Robina of Red Kennels
16 *Outdoor girls along the coast* (1926)
Alternative title: The cruise of the motor boat Liberty
17 *Outdoor girls at Spring Hill Farm* (1927)
Alternative title: The ghost of the Old Milk House
18 *Outdoor girls at New Moon Ranch* (1928)
Alternative title: Riding with the cowboys
19 *Outdoor girls on a hike* (1929)
Alternative title: The mystery of the deserted airplane
20 *Outdoor girls on a canoe trip* (1930)
Alternative title: The secret of the Brown Mill
21 *Outdoor girls at Cedar Ridge* (1931)
Alternative title: The mystery of the old windmill
22 *Outdoor girls in the air* (1932)
Alternative title: Saving the stolen invention
23 *Outdoor girls in Desert Valley* (1933)
Alternative title: Strange happenings in a cowboy camp

Outhouse series
Hillier, Fred
1 *Down the back* (1983)
Era of the outhouse
2 *Further down the back* (1993)
A celebration of the great Australian dunny

Outings series
Coote, Roger
1 *Day in the city* (1989)
2 *Day in the country* (1989)
3 *Day in the mountains* (1989)
4 *Day at the seaside* (1989)

Outlander series
Coblentz, Stanton Arthur
1 *Moon people* (1964)
2 *Crimson capsule* (1967)
Animal people
3 *Island people* (1971)

Outlander series
Gabaldon, Diana
1 *Outlander* (1991)
Cross stitch
2 *Dragonfly in amber* (1992)
3 *Voyager* (1994)

Outlaws series
Cunningham, Chet
1 *Ride tall or hang high* (1989)
2 *Six guns* (1989)
3 *Dead man's hand* (1989)
4 *Avengers* (1990)
5 *Rio Grande revenge* (1990)
6 *Flagstaff showdown* (1991)

Outrider series
Harding, Richard
1 *Outrider* (1984)
2 *Fire and ice* (1984)
3 *Blood highway* (1984)
4 *Bay City burnout* (1985)
5 *Built to kill* (1985)

Outsider series
Wilson, Colin
1 *Outsider* (1956)
2 *Beyond the outsider* (1965)
The philosophy of the future
3 *Musician as outsider* (1987)
4 *Misfits* (1988)
A study of sexual outsiders

Outskirts series
Clifford, Hugh
1 *Sally, and other tales of the outskirts* (1904)
2 *Saleh* (1908)

Outtakes series
Sanders, Bill
1 *Outtakes for guys* (1988)
2 *Outtakes for girls* (1988)

Over the bridge series
Church, Richard
Autobiography
1 *Over the bridge* (1955)
2 *Golden sovereign* (1957)
3 *Voyage home* (1964)

Over-the-hill series
Calif, Ruth
1 *Over-the-hill ghost* (1988)
2 *Over-the-hill witch* (1990)

Overland Riders series
Flower, Jessie Graham
see **Grace Harlowe's Overland Riders series**

Overland series
Ellis, Edward Sylvester
1 *Alden, the pony express rider* (1909)
Alternative title: Racing for life
2 *Alden among the Indians* (1909)
Alternative title: The search for the missing pony express rider

Overload series
Ham, Bob
1 *Personal war* (1989)
2 *Wrath* (1989)
3 *Highway warriors* (1989)
4 *Tennessee terror* (1989)
5 *Atlanta burn* (1990)
6 *Nebraska nightmare* (1990)
7 *Rolling vengeance* (1990)
8 *Ozark payback* (1991)
9 *Huntsville horror* (1991)
10 *Michigan madness* (1991)
11 *Alabama bloodbath* (1991)
12 *Vegas gamble* (1991)

Overmantel family series
Norton, Mary
see **Borrowers series**

Overnight Sensation series
Lantz, Francess Lin
1 *Can't stop us now* (1986)
2 *Making it on our own* (1986)

Oversoul Seven series
Roberts, Jane
1 *Education of Oversoul Seven* (1973)
2 *Further education of Oversoul Seven* (1979)
3 *Oversoul Seven and the museum of time* (1984)

Overton College series
Flower, Jessie Graham
see **Grace Harlowe at college series**

Owen Keane series
Faherty, Terence
1 *Lost Keats* (1993)
2 *Deadstick* (1991)
3 *Die dreaming* (1994)

Owen Kettle series
Hyne, Charles John Cutcliffe
see **Captain Owen Kettle series**

Owen Lightbringer trilogy
Lee, Samantha
1 *Quest for the sword of infinity* (1979)
2 *Land where serpents rule* (1980)
3 *Path through the circle of time* (1980)

Owen Orient series
Lauria, Frank
see **Doctor Owen Orient series**

Owen series
Madison, Lucy Foster
see **Peggy Owen series**
Orczy, Emmuska
see **Old man in the corner series**
Punshon, Ernest Robertson
see **Bobby Owen series**
Sharp, Marilyn
see **Richard Owen series**
Spender, Jean Maud
see **Mary Owen series**
Wells, Anna Mary
see **Doctor Hillis Owen series**

Owen Smith series
Barnett, James
see **Superintendent Owen Smith series**

Owen Tudor series
Beamish, Noel de Vic
1 *Grafting of the Rose* (1954)
2 *Blooming of the Rose* (1962)

Owens series
Overholser, Stephen
see **Molly Owens series**

Owl and Billy series
Waddell, Martin
1 *Owl and Billy* (1986)
2 *Owl and Billy and the space days* (1988)

Owl Pen series
Wells, Kenneth McNeil
1 *Owl Pen* (1947)
Revised edition 1955
2 *By Moonstone Creek* (1949)
3 *Up Medonte way* (1951)
4 *By Jumping Cat Bridge* (1956)

Owl series
Forward, Robert Dodson
1 *Owl* (1984)
2 *Scarlet serenade* (1990)

Owl series
Rodney, Bryan
see **Francis Villiers series**

Owlglass series
Nickless, Will
see **Rotherside series**

Owliver series
Kraus, Robert
1 *Owliver* (1974)
2 *Owliver the actor takes a bow* (1981)

Owning up series
Melly, George
Autobiography of a jazz singer
1 *Scouse Mouse* (1984)
Alternative title: I never got over it; growing up in the 1930s
2 *Rum, bum and concertina* (1977)
Life in the Royal Navy in the 1940s
3 *Owning up* (1965)
4 *Mellymobile, 1970-1981* (1982)

O'Wynn series
Atkey, Bertram
see **Winnie O'Wynn series**

Ox and Li Kao series
Hughart, Barry
see **Master Li Kao and Number Ten Ox series**

Oxford conferences series
Knox, Ronald Arbuthnott
1 *In soft garments* (1942)
2 *Hidden stream* (1952)

Oxford freshman series
Bede, Cuthbert
see **Mister Verdant Green series**

Oxford lectures on poetry series
Fuller, Roy
1 *Owls and artificers* (1971)
2 *Professors and gods* (1973)

Oxford life series
Balsdon, Dacre
1 *Oxford life* (1957)
2 *Oxford now and then* (1970)

Oxford Ox trilogy
Williams, Ferelith Eccles
1 *One old Oxford ox* (1976)
2 *Oxford Ox's alphabet* (1977)
3 *Oxford Ox's calendar* (1980)

Oxford series
Stewart, John Innes Mackintosh
see **Duncan Pattullo series**

Oxrun Station series
Grant, Charles Lewis
1 *Hour of the Oxrun dead* (1977)
2 *Sound of midnight* (1978)
3 *Last call of mourning* (1979)
4 *Grave* (1981)
5 *Nightmare seasons* (1982)
6 *Bloodwind* (1982)
7 *Soft whisper of the dead* (1982)
8 *Dark cry of the moon* (1985)
9 *Long night of the grave* (1986)
10 *Orchard* (1986)

Oxus series
Hull, Katharine
1 *Far-distant Oxus* (1937)
2 *Escape to Persia* (1938)
3 *Oxus in summer* (1939)

Oy-oy-seven series
Weinstein, Sol
see **Israel Bond series**

Oz-man tales series
Baum, Lyman Frank
see **Snuggle tales series**

Oz series
This sequence has thirteen authors
Baum, Lyman Frank
1 *Wonderful wizard of Oz* (1900)
Wizard of Oz
New wizard of Oz
2 *Marvelous land of Oz* (1904)
Land of Oz
3 *Ozma of Oz* (1907)
Princess Ozma of Oz
4 *Dorothy and the wizard of Oz* (1908)
5 *Road to Oz* (1909)
6 *Emerald City of Oz* (1910)
7 *Patchwork Girl of Oz* (1913)
8 *Tik-Tok of Oz* (1914)
9 *Scarecrow of Oz* (1915)
10 *Rinkitink in Oz* (1916)
11 *Lost princess of Oz* (1917)
12 *Tin Woodman of Oz* (1918)
13 *Magic of Oz* (1919)
14 *Glinda of Oz* (1920)
Companion volume: *The visitors from Oz*, 1960
Thompson, Ruth Plumly
The titles by this author were published anonymously with the credit line "founded on and continuing the famous Oz stories by L Frank Baum"
15 *Royal book of Oz* (1921)
Kabumpo in Oz
16 *Cowardly lion of Oz* (1923)
17 *Grampa in Oz* (1924)
18 *Lost king of Oz* (1925)
19 *Hungry tiger in Oz* (1926)
20 *Gnome king of Oz* (1927)
21 *Giant horse of Oz* (1928)
22 *Jack Pumpkinhead of Oz* (1929)
23 *Yellow knight of Oz* (1930)
24 *Pirates in Oz* (1931)
25 *Purple prince of Oz* (1932)
26 *Ojo in Oz* (1933)
27 *Speedy in Oz* (1934)
28 *Wishing horse of Oz* (1935)
29 *Captain Salt in Oz* (1936)
30 *Handy Mandy in Oz* (1937)
31 *Silver princess in Oz* (1938)
32 *Ozoplaning with the Wizard of Oz* (1939)
Numbers 33-50 are by ten authors
Neill, John Rea
33 *Wonder city of Oz* (1940)
34 *Scalawagons of Oz* (1941)
35 *Lucky Bucky in Oz* (1942)
Snow, Jack
36 *Magical mimics* (1946)
37 *Shaggy man of Oz* (1949)
Cosgrove, Rachel
38 *Hidden valley of Oz* (1951)
McGraw, Eloise Jervis
39 *Merry go round in Oz* (1963)
Thompson, Ruth Plumly
40 *Yankee in Oz* (1972)
41 *Enchanted island of Oz* (1976)
Suter, Jon Michael
42 *Autocrats of Oz* (1976)
43 *Orange knight of Oz* (1976)
McGraw, Eloise Jervis
44 *Forbidden fountain of Oz* (1980)
Farmer, Philip Jose
45 *Barnstormer in Oz* (1982)
Alternative title: A rationalization and extrapolation of the split-level continuum
Vinge, Joan Dennison
46 *Return to Oz* (1982)
Howe, James
47 *Mister Tinker of Oz* (1985)
Saunders, Susan
48 *Dorothy and the magic belt* (1985)
Baum, Roger S
49 *Dorothy of Oz* (1989)
50 *Rewolf of Oz* (1990)
51 *SillyOZbuls of Oz* (1991)
Companion volumes: *The woggle-bug book*, by Lyman Frank Baum, 1905, *Little wizard stories of Oz*, by Lyman Frank Baum, 6 volumes, 1913, *The laughing dragon of Oz*, by Frank Joslyn Baum, 1934; parodies: *Dorothy and the lizard of Oz*, by Richard A Gardner, 1980, *Somewhere over the orgy*, by Maggie Kaye, 1981

Ozark fantasy trilogy
Elgin, Suzette Haden
1 *Twelve fair kingdoms* (1981)
2 *Grand jubilee* (1981)
3 *And then there'll be fireworks* (1981)
One volume edition entitled *The Ozark trilogy*, 1982

Ozark series
Hess, Joan
see **Arly Hanks series**

Ozmar series
Hulme-Beaman, Emeric
1 *Ozmar the mystic* (1896)
2 *Prince's diamond* (1898)

P

P.C.Richardson series
Thomson, Basil
see **Superintendent Richardson series**

P Division series
Turnbull, Peter
1 *Deep and crisp and even* (1981)
2 *Dead knock* (1982)
3 *Fair Friday* (1983)
4 *Big money* (1984)
5 *Two way cut* (1988)
6 *Condition purple* (1989)
7 *And did murder him* (1991)
8 *Long day Monday* (1992)

P J Davenant series
Hamilton, Frederic
Short stories
1 *Holiday adventures of Mister P J Davenant* (1915)
Nine holiday adventures of Mister P J Davenant in the year 1915
The second title is a revised edition
2 *Some further adventures of Mister P J Davenant* (1915)
3 *Education of Mister P J Davenant* (1916)
4 *Beginnings of Mister P J Davenant* (1917)
5 *P J, the secret service boy* (1922)
6 *More about P J< the secret service boy* (1923)

P J Macfarlane series
Macvicar, Angus
see **Reverend P J Macfarlane series**

P.O.W. series
Goodwin, Ralph
see **Prisoner of war series**

P.U.S.S.Y. series
Rico, Don
see **Burgess Cardigan series**

P.U.S.S.Y.C.A.T. series
Mark, Ted
see **Girl from P.U.S.S.Y.C.A.T. series**

Pa and ma series
Abarbanell, Jacob Ralph
1 *Pa* (1887)
A history of comical adventures
2 *Ma* (1887)

Pace series
Bell, Adrian
see **Roland Pace series**
Denbie, Roger
see **Doctor Quentin Pace series**

Pacific coast series
Munroe, Kirk
1 *Fur-seal's tooth* (1894)
A story of Alaskan adventure
2 *Snow-shoes and sledges* (1895)
3 *Rick Dale* (1896)
A story of the northwest coast
4 *Painted desert* (1897)
A story of northern Arizona

Pacific Northwest trilogy
McQuinn, Donald E
1 *Warrior* (1990)
2 *Wanderer* (1993)
3 *Witch* (1994)

Pacific series
Alger, Horatio
1 *Young adventurer* (1878)
Alternative title: Tom's trip across the plains
2 *Young miner* (1879)
Alternative title: Tom Nelson in California
3 *Young explorer* (1880)
Alternative title: Among the sierra
4 *Ben's nugget* (1882)
Alternative title: A boy's search for fortune

Pacific shipwreck series
Houston, Edwin James
1 *Five months on a derelict* (1903)
Alternative title: Adventures on a floating wreck in the Pacific
2 *Wrecked on a coral island* (1908)
3 *In captivity in the Pacific* (1909)
Alternative title: In the land of the bread fruit tree
4 *At school in the Cannibal Islands* (1909)

Pacifist series
Partridge, Frances
Autobiography
1 *Pacifist's war* (1978)
2 *Everything to lose* (1985)
Diaries, 1945-1960

Pack and follow series
Packer, Joy
Autobiography
1 *Pack and follow* (1945)
2 *Grey mistress* (1949)
3 *Apes and ivory* (1953)
4 *Home from sea* (1963)

Pack Rat series
Quackenbush, Robert Mead
see **Pete Pack Rat series**

Packard series
Galway, Robert Conington
see **James Packard series**

Packet series
Enright, Dennis Joseph
1 *Academic year* (1955)
2 *Heaven knows where* (1957)

Paddington learning and activity series
Bond, Michael
1 *Paddington's loose end book* (1976)
An ABC of things to do
2 *Paddington's party book* (1976)
3 *Fun and games with Paddington* (1977)
4 *Paddington's birthday party* (1977)
5 *Paddington carpenter* (1977)
6 *Paddington conjurer* (1977)
7 *Paddington cook* (1977)
8 *Paddington golfer* (1977)
Companion volumes: *Paddington colouring book*, 1989, *Paddington sticker book*, 1989, *Paddington activity book*, 1989, *Please look after this bear*, 1989

Paddington pastime series
Bond, Michael
1 *Paddington's first book* (1977)
An object recognition book with pictures to colour
2 *Paddington's first counting book* (1977)
Learn the numbers, colour the pictures
3 *Paddington's first word book* (1977)
Words to copy, pictures to colour
4 *Paddington's first play book* (1977)
Things to make, games to play, pictures to colour

Paddington picture book series
Bond, Michael
1 *Paddington Bear* (1972)
2 *Paddington's garden* (1972)
3 *Paddington at the circus* (1973)
4 *Paddington goes shopping* (1973)
Paddington's lucky day
5 *Paddington at the Tower* (1975)
6 *Paddington at the seaside* (1975)
Numbers 1-6 also published in one volume editions entitled *The great big Paddington book*, 1976, *The great big Paddington Bear picture book*, 1977, and *Paddington's picture book*, 1978
7 *Paddington takes a bath* (1976)
8 *Paddington goes to the sales* (1976)
9 *Paddington's new room* (1976)
10 *Paddington at the station* (1976)
11 *Paddington hits out* (1977)
12 *Paddington does it himself* (1977)
13 *Paddington in the kitchen* (1977)
14 *Paddington goes out* (1980)
15 *Paddington weighs in* (1980)
16 *Paddington at home* (1980)
17 *Paddington and Auny Lucy* (1980)
18 *Paddington in touch* (1980)
19 *Paddington has fun* (1982)
20 *Paddington works hard* (1982)
21 *Paddington on the river* (1983)
22 *Paddington at the zoo* (1984)
23 *Paddington and the knicker-bocker rainbow* (1984)
24 *Paddington's painting exhibition* (1985)
Paddington's art exhibition
25 *Paddington at the fair* (1985)
26 *Paddington at the palace* (1986)
27 *Paddington minds the house* (1986)
28 *Paddington spring cleans* (1986)
29 *Paddington cleans up* (1986)
30 *Paddington's busy day* (1987)
31 *Paddington and the marmalade maze* (1987)
32 *Paddington's magical Christmas* (1988)
Companion volume: *Paddington's cartoon book*, 1979; omnibus volume: *Paddington's storybook*, 1983

Paddington play and learn series
Bond, Michael
1 *Paddington's numbers* (1987)
2 *Paddington's colours* (1987)
Companion volumes: *Paddington's first puzzle book*, 1987, *Paddington's second puzzle book*, 1987

Paddington pop-up series
Bond, Michael
1 *Paddington's pop-up book* (1977)

Paddington pop-up series

2 *Paddington at the launderette* (1981)
3 *Paddington's birthday treat* (1981)
4 *Paddington's shopping adventure* (1981)
5 *Paddington and the snowbear* (1981)

Paddington series

Bond, Michael
1 *Bear called Paddington* (1958)
2 *More about Paddington* (1959)
Numbers 1 and 2 also published in one volume entitled *The adventures of Paddington*, 1965
3 *Paddington helps out* (1960)
4 *Paddington abroad* (1961)
5 *Paddington at large* (1962)
6 *Paddington marches on* (1964)
Numbers 1, 2, 3, 5, 6 also published in one volume entitled *A bear called Paddington*, 1985
7 *Paddington at work* (1966)
Numbers 1, 2, 3, 5, 7 also published in one volume entitled *The hilarious adventures of Paddington*, 1986
8 *Paddington goes to town* (1968)
9 *Paddington takes the air* (1970)
10 *Paddington on top* (1974)
11 *Paddington takes the test* (1979)
Plays based on the Paddington series: *The adventures of a bear called Paddington*, 1974, *Paddington on stage*, 1974
Companion volume: *The life and times of Paddington Bear*, by Russell Ash with Michael Bond, 1988; selections: *A disappearing trick, and other stories*, 1979

Paddington slot book series

Bond, Michael
1 *Paddington at the airport* (1986)
2 *Paddington posts a letter* (1986)
Paddington mails a letter
3 *Paddington's clock book* (1986)
4 *Paddington's London, on four wheels* (1986)
5 *Paddington's bus ride* (1986)

Paddington's Blue Peter story series

Bond, Michael
Selections from the *Blue Peter annuals*
1 *Paddington's Blue Peter story book* (1973)
Paddington takes to TV
2 *Paddington on screen* (1981)

Paddle your own canoe trilogy

Ellis, Edward Sylvester
1 *Forest messengers* (1907)
2 *Mountain star* (1907)
3 *Queen of the clouds* (1907)

Paddy Joe series

Stranger, Joyce
1 *Paddy Joe* (1971)
2 *Trouble for Paddy Joe* (1973)
3 *Paddy Joe at Deep Hollow Farm* (1975)
4 *Paddy Joe and Tomkin's folly* (1979)

Paddy Moretti series

Sherburne, James
1 *Death's pale horse* (1980)
2 *Death's gray angel* (1981)
3 *Death's clenched fist* (1982)

Paddy Pork series

Goodall, John Strickland
1 *Adventures of Paddy Pork* (1968)
Second edition 1980
2 *Ballooning adventures of Paddy Pork* (1969)
Second edition 1980
3 *Shrewbettina's birthday* (1970)
4 *Jacko* (1971)
5 *Midnight adventures of Kelly, Dot and Esmeralda* (1972)
Kelly, Dot and Esmeralda
6 *Paddy's evening out* (1973)
7 *Naughty Nancy, the bad bridesmaid* (1975)
8 *Creepy Castle* (1975)
9 *Paddy Pork's holiday* (1976)
10 *Surprise picnic* (1977)
11 *Paddy's new hat* (1980)
12 *Escapade* (1980)
13 *Paddy goes traveling* (1982)
14 *Paddy under water* (1984)
15 *Paddy Pork, odd jobs* (1982)
16 *Paddy Pork to the rescue* (1985)
17 *Naughty Nancy goes to school* (1985)
Companion volumes: *Paddy finds a job*, 1981, *Shrewbettina goes to work*, 1981, *Lavinia's cottage*, 1982

Paddy the beaver series

Burgess, Thornton Waldo
1 *Paddy's surprise visitor* (1940)
Paddy the beaver's visitor
2 *At Paddy the beaver's pond* (1950)

Padillo and McCorkle series

Thomas, Ross
see **McCorkle and Padillo series**

Padre series

Goyne, Richard
1 *Crime philosopher* (1945)
2 *Savarin's shadow* (1947)
3 *Traitor's tide* (1948)
4 *Dark mind* (1948)
5 *Courtway case* (1951)

Pagan series

Armstrong, Campbell
see **Detective Frank Pagan series**

Pagan series

Benedict, Dorothy
1 *Pagan the black* (1960)
2 *Fabulous* (1961)
3 *Bandoleer* (1963)

Pagans series

Bates, Arlo
1 *Pagans* (1884)
2 *Philistines* (1889)

Pagans trilogy

Herley, Richard
1 *Stone arrow* (1978)
2 *Flint lord* (1981)
3 *Earth goddess* (1984)
One volume edition entitled *The pagans*, 1986

Page Murdock series

Estleman, Loren D
1 *High rocks* (1979)
2 *Stamping ground* (1980)
3 *Murdock's law* (1982)
4 *Stranglers* (1984)

Page series

Boylston, Helen Dore
see **Carol Page series**
Forrester, Izola Louise
see **Polly Page series**
Halsey, Rena Isabelle
see **Nathalie Page series**
Stockley, Grif
see **Gideon Page series**

Pageant of England tetralogy

Costain, Thomas Bertram
see **History of the Plantagenets tetralogy**

Pagett series

Drury, William Price
1 *Peradventures or Private Pagett* (1904)
2 *Pagett calling* (1930)
Short stories

Paige and Katie series

Oaks, Tina
see **Stepsisters series**

Paige series

Douglas, Lloyd Cassel
see **Newell Paige series**

Paine series

Batchelor, John Calvin
see **Gordon Liddy is my muse series**

Painted Post series

Gunn, Tom
see **Sheriff Blue Steele series**

Paisley series

Hood, Evelyn
1 *Stranger to the town* (1985)
2 *Silken thread* (1986)

Pajama party series

Hest, Amy
1 *Pajama party* (1992)
2 *Nannies for hire* (1994)

Paksenarrion series

Moon, Elizabeth
see **Deed of Paksenarrion series**

Palace plays series

Housman, Laurence
Plays on the life of Queen Victoria
1 *Palace plays* (1930)
Contains *The revolting daughter*, and *The wicked uncles*
2 *Queen's progress* (1932)
Contains *Poor mamma, Woman proposes, Leading-strings, The intruder, Royal favour, The blue ribbon, Promotion cometh, A great relief, Happy and glorious*
3 *Victoria and Albert* (1933)
Contains *Enter Prince, Morning glory, A good lesson, Under fire, A fall from power, Amende Honorable,* also known as *The rose and the thorn, The go-between, Intervention, Death and the doctors, Bereavement, We are not amused, Religious difficulties, Painful necessity*; selections from numbers 1-3 published in *Victoria Regina*, 1934, with *The Queen, God bless her,* and *His favourite flower*, from *Angels and ministers*, 1921, and *Morning glory*, and *Aims and objects*
4 *Palace scenes* (1937)
Contains *The bed-chamber plot, The court circle, The first-born, Forward but not too fast, The family portrait, The anniversary, Stable government, A star from the east, Please to look pleasant, Royal table manners, The primrose way, Ashes to ashes;* also published in *The golden sovereign*, 1937; numbers 2 and 3 also published in *Happy and glorious*, 1943, with selections from number 4 and *A heavy change, The bell, The popular voice, Extremes meet, This is the heir, Life in the Highlands, A domestic difference, A visit to Birmingham, Ruling powers, The superlative relative,* and *Recollections*

Palaces trilogy

Miller, Ron
see **Bronwyn trilogy**

Palestine home series

Harthern, Ernest
1 *Going home* (1936)
Original edition entitled *Heimkehr*; a modern Jew returns to Palestine
2 *Home at last* (1937)
Original edition entitled *Das Land das seine Menschen*

Palfrey series

Creasey, John
see **Doctor Palfrey series**

Palgrave series

Cobb, Belton
see **Kitty Armitage series**

Palliser novels series

Trollope, Anthony
1 *Can you forgive her?* (1864)
2 *Phineas Finn* (1869)
3 *Eustace diamonds* (1872)
4 *Phineas redux* (1873)
5 *Prime Minister* (1876)
6 *Duke's children* (1880)

Palmer series

Deighton, Len
see **Secret file series**
Waller, Leslie
see **Woods Palmer series**
Woolley, Lazelle Thayer
see **Faith Palmer series**

Palmyra Pym series

Morland, Nigel
see **Mrs Palmyra Pym series**

Pam and Jerry North series

Lockridge, Frances
see **Mister and Mrs North series**

Pam and Penny series

Du Jardin, Rosamond
1 *Double date* (1952)
2 *Double feature* (1953)
3 *Showboat summer* (1955)
4 *Double wedding* (1959)

Pam Nilsen series

Wilson, Barbara Ellen
1 *Murder in the collective* (1984)
2 *Sisters of the road* (1986)
3 *Dog collar murders* (1989)

Pam series

Hutten zum Stolzenberg, Bettina Riddle
1 *Pam* (1905)
2 *What became of Pam* (1906)
Pam decides
3 *Halo* (1907)
4 *Kingsmead* (1909)
5 *Pam at fifty* (1923)
6 *Pam's own story* (1930)

Pamela series

Hadath, Florence Gunby
1 *Pamela* (1939)
A story for girls and their aunts and uncles
2 *Pamela Calling* (1940)

Pamela series

Roberts, Cecil
1 *Pamela's spring song* (1929)
2 *Spears against us* (1932)

Pamela series

Taggart, Marion Ames
1 *Dearest girl* (1924)
2 *Pamela's legacy* (1925)

Pamplemousse series

Bond, Michael
see **Monsieur Pamplemousse series**

Pamra Don series

Tepper, Sheri S
see **Awakeners series**

Pan Sagittarius series

Wallace, Ian
1 *Deathstar voyage* (1969)
2 *Pan Sagittarius* (1973)
3 *Voyage to Dari* (1974)
4 *World asunder* (1976)

Panama series

Verrill, Alpheus Hyatt
1 *Panama, past and present* (1921)
2 *Panama of today* (1927)

Pan-American series
Stratemeyer, Edward L
1 *Lost on the Orinoco* (1902)
Alternative title: American boys in Venezuela
2 *Young volcano explorers* (1902)
Alternative title: American boys in the West Indies
3 *Young explorers of the Isthmus* (1903)
Alternative title: American boys in Central America
4 *Young explorers of the Amazon* (1904)
Alternative title: American boys in Brazil
5 *Treasure seekers of the Andes* (1907)
Alternative title: American boys in Peru
6 *Chased across the Pampas* (1911)
Alternative title: American boys in Argentina and homeward bound

Pancho series
Buckingham, Bruce
see **Don Pancho series**

Panda One series
Walker, Peter Norman
1 *Panda One on duty* (1971)
2 *Panda One investigates* (1973)
3 *Witchcraft for Panda One* (1978)
4 *Siege for Panda One* (1981)

Panda series
Berenstain, Michael
1 *Panda's Club tree house* (1989)
2 *Panda's new pet* (1990)

Panda series
Foreman, Michael
1 *Panda's puzzle and his voyage of discovery* (1977)
2 *Panda and the odd lion* (1979)
3 *Panda and the bunyips* (1984)
4 *Panda and the bushfire* (1986)

Panda series
Taro, Oda
1 *Panda the train driver* (1981)
2 *Panda the doctor* (1981)
3 *Panda the explorer* (1981)
4 *Panda the racing driver* (1981)
5 *Panda the soldier* (1981)
6 *Panda the wizard* (1981)
7 *Panda the builder* (1982)
8 *Panda and the sparrow* (1982)
9 *Panda and the circus* (1982)
10 *Panda and the snow* (1982)
11 *Panda at the seaside* (1982)
12 *Panda and the ball* (1982)
Companion volumes: *Panda's alphabet book*, 1983, *Panda's book of colours*, 1983, *Panda's book of numbers*, 1983

Pandervil series
Bullett, Gerald
see **History of Pandervil series**

Pandora series
Herbert, Frank
1 *Destination, void* (1966)
Revised edition 1978
2 *Jesus incident* (1979)
Co-author: Bill Ransom
3 *Lazarus effect* (1983)
Co-author: Bill Ransom
4 *Ascension factor* (1988)
Co-author: Bill Ransom

Pandora series
Lance, Kathryn
1 *Pandora's genes* (1985)
2 *Pandora's children* (1986)

Pandre series
Schneour, Salman
see **Noah Pandre series**

Pangaia trilogy
Frith, Nigel
1 *Jormundgand* (1986)
2 *Dragon* (1987)
3 *Olympiad* (1988)

Pangers series
Wood, Lorna
1 *Dogs of Pangers* (1970)
2 *Pangers' pup* (1972)

Pangur Ban series
Sampson, Fay
1 *Pangur Ban the white cat* (1983)
2 *Finnglas of the horses* (1985)
3 *Finnglas and the stones of choosing* (1986)
4 *Shape-shifter, the naming of Pangur Ban* (1988)
5 *Serpent of Senargad* (1989)
6 *White horse is running* (1990)

Panhasard series
Hine, Muriel
see **April Panhasard series**

Panjandrum series
Farrow, George Edward
1 *Little Panjandrum's dodo* (1898)
2 *New Panjandrum* (1901)
3 *Adventures of a dodo* (1907)

Panky series
Saxon, Nancy
1 *Panky and William* (1983)
2 *Panky and the saddle* (1984)

Panorama of the old West series
Gentry, Georgina
1 *Cheyenne captive* (1987)
2 *Cheyenne princess* (1987)
3 *Comanche cowboy* (1988)
4 *Bandit's embrace* (1989)
5 *Nevada nights* (1989)
6 *Cheyenne caress* (1990)
7 *Quicksilver passion* (1990)
8 *Apache caress* (1991)
9 *Sioux slave* (1992)
10 *Half breed's bride* (1993)
11 *Nevada dawn* (1993)
12 *Cheyenne splendor* (1994)

Pansy and Atalanta series
Symons, Geraldine
see **Atalanta and Pansy series**

Pantaloon series
Toynbee, Philip
see **Valediction of Pantaloon series**

Pantomime ponies series
Baxter, Gillian
see **Angela and Ian Kendall series**

Panton series
Purser, Philip
see **Colin Panton series**

Pantouflia series
Lang, Andrew
1 *Prince Prigio* (1889)
2 *Prince Ricardo of Pantouflia* (1893)
The adventures of Prince Prigio's son
One volume edition entitled *My own fairy book, namely certain chronicles of Pantouflia, as notably the adventures of Prigio, prince of that country and of his son Ricardo, with an excerpt from the Annals of Scotland as touching Ker of Fairnilee, his sojourn with the Queen of Faery*, 1895

Pants series
Colwell, Max
see **Mike series**

Panuck and Andy series
Machetanz, Frederick
see **Andy and Panuck series**

Panzer Platoon series
Lutz, Gunther
1 *Blitzkrieg!* (1977)
2 *Invade Russia!* (1977)
3 *Blood and ice* (1978)
4 *Support Rommel* (1979)
5 *Death ride* (1980)
6 *Attack Anzio* (1980)

Paola and Francesca series
Fleetwood, Frances
see **Concordia series**

Paola and George series
Sampson, George
1 *Drug on the market* (1967)
2 *Playing with fire* (1968)

Papa and mama series
Saroyan, William
see **Mama and papa series**

Papa LaBas series
Reed, Ishmael
1 *Mumbo jumbo* (1972)
2 *Last days of Louisiana Red* (1974)

Papa Pontivy series
Newman, Bernard
1 *Death to the spy* (1939)
2 *Maginot Line murder* (1939)
Papa Pontivy and the Maginot Line
3 *Siegfried spy* (1940)
4 *Secret weapon* (1941)
5 *Death to the Fifth Column* (1941)
6 *Black market* (1942)
7 *Second Front, first spy* (1944)
8 *Spy in the Brown Derby* (1945)
9 *Dead man murder* (1946)
10 *Moscow murder* (1948)
11 *Double menace* (1954)
12 *Operation Barbarossa* (1956)
13 *Otan plot* (1957)
14 *This is your life* (1963)
15 *Spy at Number Ten* (1965)
Also four Papa Pontivy stories in *The spy catchers*, 1945

Papa Schimmelhorn series
Bretnor, Reginald
1 *Schimmelhorn file* (1979)
Memoirs of a dirty old genius
2 *Schimmelhorn's gold* (1986)

Paper chase series
Bayer, Oliver Weld
1 *Paper chase* (1943)
2 *No little enemy* (1944)

Paper tearing series
Westphail, Arnold Carl
1 *Paper tearing trick talks* (1967)
2 *Fold 'n' cut surprise sermonettes* (1968)
3 *Paper tearing Gospel illustrations* (1969)
4 *Paper tearing Bible talks* (1970)
5 *Paper and scissors truth talks* (1971)
6 *Fold 'n' cut story sermonettes* (1973)
7 *Fold 'n' snip Bible bits* (1974)
8 *Paper tearing evangels* (1975)
9 *Surprise paper tearing talks* (1976)
10 *Trick paper tears with Gospel truth* (1977)
11 *Gospel paper tears with surprise climax* (1983)
12 *Voyag of life on a paper boat* (1983)
13 *Gospel surprise paper tears* (1986)
14 *Paper tears with a Gospel message* (1990)

Papers series
Livingston, Kenneth
1 *Dodd papers* (1933)
2 *Cloze papers* (1936)

Papillon series
Charriere, Henri
Translated from the French
1 *Papillon* (1969)
2 *Banco* (1972)

Parables series
Capon, Robert
1 *Parables of the Kingdom* (1985)
2 *Parables of grace* (1988)
3 *Parables of judgment* (1989)

Parade's end series
Ford, Ford Madox
1 *Some do not* (1924)
2 *No more parades* (1925)
3 *Man could stand up* (1926)
4 *Last post* (1928)
One volume edition entitled *Parade's end*, 1950

Paradise series
Couper, Stephen
1 *Dying of paradise* (1982)
Based on *The last rose of summer*, published under the author's real name Stephen Gallagher, 1978
2 *Ice belt* (1983)

Paradise series
Tempski, Armine von
1 *Born in paradise* (1945)
2 *Aloha* (1950)
My love to you

Paradys series
Lee, Tanith
see **Secret books of Paradys series**

Paralyzing ray trilogy
Nizzi, Guido
1 *Victor* (1946)
2 *Paralyzing ray versus the nuclears* (1964)
3 *Daring trip to the moon* (1968)

Paratime police series
This sequence has three authors
Piper, Horace Beam
1 *Lord Kalvan of Otherwhen* (1965)
Gunpowder god
2 *Paratime* (1981)
Green, Roland James
3 *Great King's war* (1985)

Paratwa trilogy
Hinz, Christopher
1 *Liege-killer* (1987)
2 *Ash Ock* (1989)
3 *Paratwa* (1991)

Parbitter series
Hammond, Gerald
see **Simon Parbitter series**

Pardners series
Lynde, Stan
Picture book format
1 *Bonding* (1991)
2 *Legacy* (1991)

Pardoe series
Bowers, Dorothy
see **Inspector Pardoe series**

Parew and Carpenter series
Eldredge, Gilbert
see **Thibault Parew and Chips Carpenter series**

Pargeter series
Brett, Simon
see **Mrs Melita Pargeter series**

Paris Opera trilogy
Crawford, Francis Marion
1 *Soprano* (1905)
2 *Prima-donna* (1908)
3 *Diva's ruby* (1908)
Fair Margaret

Paris series
Benson, Ben
see **Inspector Wade Paris series**
Brett, Simon
see **Charles Paris series**
Howard, Elizabeth Howard
see **My name is Paris series**

Paris series
Oldenbourg, Zoe
1 *Awakened* (1956)
Original edition entitled *Reveilles de la vie*
2 *Chains of love* (1958)
Original edition entitled *Les irreductibles*

Paris trilogy
Flanner, Janet
Extracts from Letters from Paris columns published in the *New Yorker* under the pseudonym Genet
1 *Paris was yesterday, 1925-39* (1973)
2 *Paris journal, 1944-65* (1966)
3 *Paris journal, 1965-1971* (1971)
Companion volume: An American in Paris, profile of an interlude between two *wars*, 1940

Parisian life series
Balzac, Honore de
see **Scenes of Parisian life series**

Parisian series
Merrick, Leonard
1 *Man who understood women, and other stories* (1908)
2 *All the world wondered* (1911)
3 *While Paris laughed* (1918)
4 *Chair of the boulevard* (1920)
5 *To tell you the truth* (1922)
6 *Little dog laughed* (1930)

Park series
Aska, Warabe
1 *Who goes to the park?* (1984)
2 *Who hides in the park?* (1986)

Parke series
Curtis, Alice Turner
see **Little Washingtons series**

Parker and Maledon series
Gardner, Jerome
see **Hanging Judge series**

Parker and Willows series
Gough, Laurence
see **Willows and Parker series**

Parker Rowe series
Maner, William
1 *Image killer* (1968)
2 *There goes the bride* (1973)

Parker series
Austwick, John
see **Inspector Parker series**
Benton, John W
see **Marji Parker series**
Martin, Marcia
see **Donna Parker series**
Mogridge, Stephen
see **Barry Parker series**
Shelynn, Jack
see **Ned Parker series**

Parker series
Stark, Richard
1 *Hunter* (1962)
Point blank
2 *Man with the getaway face* (1963)
Steel hilt
3 *Outfit* (1963)
4 *Mourner* (1963)
5 *Score* (1964)
Killtown
6 *Jugger* (1965)
7 *Seventh* (1966)
Split
8 *Handle* (1966)
Run lethal
9 *Rare coin score* (1967)
10 *Green eagle score* (1967)
11 *Black ice score* (1968)
12 *Sour lemon score* (1969)
13 *Deadly edge* (1971)
14 *Slayground* (1971)
15 *Plunder squad* (1972)
16 *Butcher's moon* (1974)

Parker series
Wirt, Mildred Augustine
see **Penny Parker series**
Zimmerman, Bruce
see **Quinn Parker series**

Parkin series
Burton, Hester
see **Stephen Parkin series**

Parkman series
Hunt, Greg
see **Ridge Parkman series**

Parks series
Richards, Laura Elizabeth
see **Calvin Parks series**

Parliament series
Hyland, Stanley
1 *Who goes hang?* (1958)
2 *Green grow the tresses-O* (1965)
3 *Top bloody secret* (1969)

Parliamentary novels series
Trollope, Anthony
see **Palliser novels series**

Parlicoot series
Macleod, Alex W
1 *Parlicoot, and how he sets out to find a playmate* (1845)
2 *Parlicoot's house* (1947)
Parlicoot and playmate find a home

Parnell series
Smith, Don
see **Tim Parnell series**

Parodies series
Vallins, George Henry
Parodies in verse
1 *Sincere flattery* (1954)
2 *After a manner* (1956)

Parr series
Anderson, Frederick Irving
see **Deputy Parr series**

Parren series
Hildick, Edmund Wallace
1 *Here comes Parren* (1968)
2 *Back with Parren* (1968)

Parri Macdonald series
Lambert, Janet
1 *Introducing Parri* (1962)
2 *That's my girl* (1964)
3 *Stagestruck* (1966)
4 *My Davy* (1968)

Parric family trilogy
Grant, Charles Lewis
1 *Shadows of Alpha* (1976)
2 *Ascension* (1977)
3 *Legion* (1979)

Parris Mitchell series
Bellamann, Henry
see **Kings Row series**

Parrish Darby series
Aresbys
1 *Who killed Coralie?* (1927)
2 *Mark of the dead* (1929)

Parrish series
Lambert, Janet
see **Penny Parrish series; Tippy Parrish series**

Parrot in the house series
Allen, Linda
1 *Parrot in the house* (1988)
2 *When grandfather's parrot inherited Kennington Court* (1992)

Parrott series
Long, Manning
see **Liz Parrott series**

Parry and Harris series
Keverne, Richard
see **Franklin Parry and Leonard Harris series**

Parry series
Humphreys, Emyr
see **Amy Parry series**
Sarsfield, Maureen
see **Inspector Lane Parry series**

Parsina series
Goldin, Stephen
1 *Shrine of the desert mage* (1988)
2 *Storyteller and the Jann* (1988)
3 *Crystals of air and water* (1989)

Parsival series
Monaco, Richard
1 *Parsival* (1977)
Alternate title: A knight's tale
2 *Grail war* (1979)
3 *Final quest* (1980)
4 *Blood and dreams* (1985)

Parsley series
Bond, Michael
1 *Parslay's tail* (1969)
2 *Parsley's good deed* (1969)
3 *Parsley's last stand* (1970)
4 *Parsley's problem present* (1970)
5 *Parsley's parade* (1972)
6 *Parsley the lion* (1972)
7 *Parsley and the herbs* (1976)

Parson Carnaby series
Emerson, David
1 *Pride of Parson Carnaby* (1953)
2 *Trouble at Shaplinch* (1959)

Parsonage series
Spence, Hartzell
Reminiscences of life in a Methodist parsonage
1 *One foot in heaven* (1940)
2 *Get thee behind me* (1942)

Parson's daughter series
Newbery, Esylt
Autobiography
1 *Parson's daughter* (1958)
2 *Parson's daughter again* (1960)

Parsons series
Peyton, K M
see **Flambards series**
Scott, Jack S
see **Chief Inspector Peter Parsons series**

Parsons trilogy
Shears, Sarah
see **Annie Parsons trilogy**

Partanna series
Condon, Richard
see **Prizzi family series**

Partial view trilogy
Maugham, William Somerset
see **Summing up trilogy**

Particulars series
Rolph, C H
Autobiography
1 *London particulars* (1980)
2 *Further particulars* (1987)

Partnership series
Webb, Beatrice
Autobiography
1 *My apprenticeship* (1926)
2 *Our partnership* (1948)

Parton series
Evans, John
see **Habbakuk Parton series**

Partridge family series
Avallone, Michael
1 *Partridge family* (1970)
2 *Haunted hall* (1970)
3 *Keith, the hero* (1970)
Sequence continued under the pseudonym Vance Stanton
Stanton, Vance
4 *Keith Partridge, master spy* (1971)
5 *Fat and skinny murder mystery* (1972)
6 *Walking fingers* (1972)
7 *Who's that laughing in the grave?* (1972)
8 *Love comes to Keith Partridge* (1973)

Pascal series
Pentecost, Hugh
see **Lieutenant Pascal series**

Pascalet and Aunt Martine series
Bosco, Henri
1 *Boy and the river* (1945)
Original edition entitled *L'enfant et la riviere*
2 *Fox in the island* (1956)
Original edition entitled *Le renard dans l'ile*
3 *Barboche* (1957)
Original edition entitled *Barboche*

Pascalian series
Maeterlinck, Maurice
1 *Beyond the great silence* (1934)
Original edition entitled *Avant le grand silence*
2 *Hourglass* (1935)
Original edition entitled *Le sablier*
3 *[L'ombre des ailes]* (1936)
No English edition
4 *[Devant dieu]* (1937)
No English edition
5 *[Le grand porte]* (1938)
No English edition
6 *Great beyond* (1942)
Original edition entitled *L'autre monde*

Paschal series
Hayward, William Stephens
see **Lady detective series**

Pascoe and Dalziel series
Hill, Reginald
see **Superintendent Andrew Dalziel and Sergeant Pascoe series**

Pasquier series
Duhamel, Georges
1 *News from Havre* (1933)
Papa Pasquier
Original edition entitled *Le notaire du Havre*

2 *Young Pasquier* (1934)
Caged beasts
Original edition entitled *Le jardin des betes sauvages*
3 *In sight of the promised land* (1934)
Original edition entitled *Vue de la terre promise*
4 *Saint John's Eve* (1935)
Original edition entitled *Le nuit de la Saint-Jean*
5 *House in the desert* (1937)
Original edition entitled *Le desert de bievres*; numbers 1-5 published in one volume entitled *The Pasquier chronicles*, 1937
6 *Pastors and masters* (1937)
Original edition entitled *Les maitres*
7 *Cecile* (1938)
Original edition entitled *Cecile parmi nous*
8 *Fight against the shadows* (1939)
Original edition entitled *Le combat contre les ombres*; numbers 6-8 published in one volume entitled *Cecile among the Pasquiers*, 1940
9 *Suzanne and the young men* (1941)
Original edition entitled *Suzanne et les jeunes hommes*
10 *Passion of Joseph Pasquier* (1942)
Original edition entitled *Le passion du Joseph Pasquier*; numbers 9 and 10 published in one volume entitled *Suzanne and Joseph Pasquier*, 1946

Passenger to London series
Fay, Gerard
Autobiography
1 *Passenger to London* (1961)
2 *Fay's third book* (1964)

Passing bells trilogy
Rock, Phillip
see **Greville family trilogy**

Passing of the Plantagenets series
Williamson, Hugh Ross
1 *Butt of Malmsey* (1967)
2 *Marriage made in blood* (1968)
3 *Matter of martyrdom* (1969)
4 *Cardinal in exile* (1969)
5 *Cardinal in England* (1970)

Passion Flowers series
Erskine, Rosalind
1 *Passion Flower Hotel* (1962)
2 *Passion Flowers in Italy* (1963)
3 *Passion Flowers in business* (1965)

Passion for romance series
Jepson, Edgar
1 *Passion for romance* (1896)
2 *Keepers of the people* (1898)

Passion trilogy
Copeland, Lori
1 *Avenging angel* (1987)
2 *Passion's captive* (1988)
3 *Sweet talkin' stranger* (1989)

Passover trilogy
Greeley, Andrew Moran
1 *Thy brother's wife* (1982)
2 *Ascent into hell* (1983)
3 *Lord of the dance* (1984)

Passport series
Bagot, Richard
1 *Passport* (1905)
2 *Darneley Place* (1912)

Passport to danger series
Paull, Jessica
1 *Passport to danger* (1968)
2 *Destination Terror* (1968)
3 *Rendezvous with death* (1969)

Passport to romance trilogy
Keene, Carolyn
House pseudonym
1 *Swiss secrets* (1992)
2 *Rendezvous in Rome* (1992)
3 *Greek odyssey* (1992)

Past and future series
Bielenberg, Christabel
Autobiography
1 *Past is myself* (1968)
2 *Road ahead* (1993)

Past forgetting series
Cushing, Peter
Autobiography
1 *Peter Cushing* (1986)
2 *Past forgetting* (1988)
Memoirs of the Hammer years

Past imperfect series
Chase, Ilka
Autobiography
1 *Past imperfect* (1942)
2 *Free admission* (1948)
3 *Always in Vogue* (1954)
Co-author: Edna Woolman Chase
4 *Carthaginian rose* (1961)

Past through tomorrow series
Heinlein, Robert Anson
see **Future history series**

Pastor Pontus Franzon series
Bjorn, Thyra Ferre
1 *Papa's wife* (1955)
2 *Papa's daughter* (1958)
3 *Mama's way* (1959)
Numbers 1-3 also published in one volume, 1961
4 *Dear papa* (1963)

Pastor's son trilogy
Walter, William Wilfred
1 *Pastor's son* (1907)
2 *Doctor's daughter* (1909)
3 *Arbiter of your fate* (1911)

Pat and David series
Pullein-Thompson, Christine
see **David and Pat series**

Pat and Jean Abbott series
Crane, Frances
1 *Turquoise shop* (1941)
2 *Golden box* (1942)
3 *Yellow violet* (1942)
4 *Pink umbrella* (1943)
Pink umbrella murder
5 *Applegreen cat* (1943)
6 *Amethyst spectacles* (1944)
7 *Indigo necklace* (1945)
Indigo necklace murders
8 *Shocking pink hat* (1946)
9 *Cinnamon murder* (1946)
10 *Murder on the purple water* (1947)
11 *Black cypress* (1948)
12 *Flying red horse* (1950)
13 *Daffodil blonde* (1951)
14 *Polkadot murder* (1951)
15 *Murder in Blue Street* (1951)
Death in the blue hour
16 *Thirteen white tulips* (1953)
17 *Murder in bright red* (1953)
18 *Coral princess murders* (1954)
19 *Death in lilac time* (1955)
20 *Horror on the Ruby X* (1956)
21 *Ultraviolet widow* (1956)
22 *Man in gray* (1958)
Grey stranger
23 *Buttercup case* (1958)
24 *Death-wish green* (1960)
25 *Amber eyes* (1962)
26 *Body beneath a mandarin tree* (1965)

Pat and Tony Pratt series
Lee, Bernie
see **Tony and Pat Pratt series**

Pat Campbell series
Colter, Eli
1 *Gull Cove murders* (1946)
2 *Cheer for the dead* (1947)
3 *Rehearsal for the funeral* (1953)

Pat Collins series
Palmer, Bernard
1 *Pat Collins and the peculiar Doctor Brockton* (1957)
2 *Pat Collins and the secret engine* (1957)
3 *Pat Collins and the hidden treasure* (1957)
4 *Pat Collins and the wingless plane* (1957)
5 *Pat Collins and the mysterious orbiting rocket* (1958)
6 *Pat Collins and the captive scientist* (1958)

Pat Kenney series
Moore, Robin
1 *French connection* (1969)
An account of the world's most crucial narcotics investigation
2 *Fifth estate* (1973)

Pat series
Ginther, Mary Pemberton
see **Miss Pat series**
Montgomery, Lucy Maud
see **Silver Bush series**

Pat Stockton series
Joyce, Cyril
see **Chief Superintendent Pat Stockton series**

Pat Thompson series
Dean, Robert George
1 *Sutton Place murders* (1936)
2 *What gentleman strangles a lady?* (1936)
3 *Three lights went out* (1937)
4 *Murder on margin* (1937)

Patch series
Bracken, Anne
1 *Tale, or, tale, of Patch the puppy* (1944)
2 *Patch and his friend Pom-Pom* (1947)

Patch series
Oxenham, Elsie J
1 *Patch and a pawn* (1940)
2 *Secrets of Vairy* (1947)
3 *Song of the Abbey* (1954)

Patchkin series
Morgan, Helen
see **Satchkin Patchkin series**

Patchogue series
McGonigle, Thomas
1 *In Patchogue* (1984)
2 *Going to Patchogue* (1992)

Patchwork child series
Astor, Brooke
Autobiography
1 *Patchwork child* (1962)
2 *Footprints* (1980)

Paternoster series
Inchbald, Ralph
see **Colonel Paternoster series**

Paterson series
Field, Katherine
see **Inspector Ross Paterson series**

Paths of the blind trilogy
Neuman, Berman Paul
1 *Greatness of Josiah Porlick* (1904)
Originally published anonymously
2 *Spoils of victory* (1906)
3 *Dominy's dollars* (1908)

Patience Campbell McKenna series
Papazoglou, Orania
1 *Sweet, savage death* (1984)
2 *Wicked, loving murder* (1985)
3 *Death's savage passion* (1986)
4 *Rich, radiant slaughter* (1988)
5 *Once and always murder* (1990)

Patience series
Hill, Lorna
1 *They called her Patience* (1951)
2 *It was all through Patience* (1952)
3 *Castle in Northumbria* (1953)
4 *So Guy came too* (1954)
5 *Five shilling holiday* (1955)

Paton series
Draper, Alfred
see **Crispin Paton series**

Patras series
Grierson, Francis Durham
see **Commissaire Patras series**

Patricia and Colin series
Rutley, Cecil Bernard
see **Colin and Patricia series**

Patricia trilogy
Murphy, Marguerite
1 *Patricia from New York* (1925)
2 *Patricia and the other girls* (1926)
3 *Patricia's problem* (1927)

Patrick Aloysius McCarthy series
Brandon, John Gordon
see **Inspector Patrick Aloysius McCarthy series**

Patrick Butler series
Carr, John Dickson
1 *Below suspicion* (1949)
2 *Patrick Butler for the defence* (1956)

Patrick Cory series
Siodmak, Curt
see **Doctor Patrick Cory series**

Patrick Costello series
Hall, Richard
1 *Costello* (1989)
2 *Noumea* (1990)

Patrick Dawlish series
Ashe, Gordon
1 *Speaker* (1939)
Croaker
2 *Death on demand* (1939)
3 *Who was the jester?* (1940)
Masked gunman
4 *Terror by day* (1940)
5 *Secret murder* (1940)
6 *'Ware danger* (1941)
7 *Murder most foul* (1942)
Revised edition 1973
8 *There goes death* (1942)
Revised edition 1973
9 *Death in high places* (1942)
10 *Death in flames* (1943)
11 *Two men missing* (1943)
Revised edition 1971
12 *Rogues rampant* (1944)
Revised edition 1973
13 *Death on the move* (1945)
14 *Invitation to adventure* (1945)
15 *Here is danger!* (1946)
16 *Give me murder* (1947)
17 *Murder too late* (1947)
18 *Engagement with death* (1948)
19 *Dark mystery* (1948)
20 *Puzzle in pearls* (1949)
Revised edition 1971
21 *Kill or be killed* (1949)
22 *Dark circle* (1950)
23 *Murder with mushrooms* (1950)
Revised edition 1971
24 *Death in diamonds* (1951)

Patrick Dawlish series

25 *Missing or dead?* (1951)
26 *Death in a hurry* (1952)
27 *Sleepy death* (1953)
28 *Long search* (1953)
Drop dead
29 *Death in the trees* (1954)
30 *Double for death* (1954)
31 *Kidnapped child* (1955)
Kidnaped child
Snatch
32 *Day of fear* (1956)
33 *Wait for death* (1957)
34 *Come home to death* (1958)
Pack of lies
35 *Elope to death* (1959)
36 *Don't let him kill* (1960)
Man who laughed at murder
37 *Crime Haters* (1960)
The Crime Haters feature in numbers 37-42
38 *Rogue's ransom* (1961)
39 *Death from below* (1963)
40 *Big call* (1964)
41 *Promise of diamonds* (1964)
42 *Taste of treasure* (1966)
43 *Clutch of coppers* (1967)
44 *Shadow of death* (1968)
45 *Scream of murder* (1969)
46 *Nest of traitors* (1970)
47 *Rabble of rebels* (1971)
48 *Life for a death* (1973)
49 *Herald of doom* (1974)
50 *Blast of trumpets* (1975)
51 *Plague of demons* (1976)

Patrick Faraday series
Pertwee, Roland
1 *Islanders* (1950)
2 *Rough water* (1951)
3 *Actor's life for me* (1953)
4 *Operation Wild Goose* (1955)

Patrick Gillard series
Duffy, Margaret
1 *Murder of crows* (1987)
2 *Death of a raven* (1988)
3 *Brass eagle* (1988)
4 *Who killed Cock Robin?* (1990)
5 *Rook-shoot* (1988)
6 *Gallows-bird* (1993)

Patrick Grant series
Yorke, Margaret
see **Doctor Patrick Grant series**

Patrick Gray series
Tranter, Nigel Godwin
1 *Master of Gray* (1961)
Lord and master
2 *Courtesan* (1963)
3 *Past Master* (1965)
4 *Mail royal* (1989)

Patrick Hardy series
Meyers, Martin
1 *Kiss and kill* (1975)
2 *Hung up to die* (1976)
3 *Red is for murder* (1975)
4 *Reunion for death* (1975)
5 *Spy and die* (1975)

Patrick Heron series
Brogan, Colm
1 *Ghost walks* (1932)
2 *Plunge* (1933)

Patrick Kennedy series
Armstrong, Anthony
1 *Patrick, undergraduate* (1926)
2 *Patrick engaged* (1927)
3 *Patrick helps* (1928)

Patrick Laing series
Laing, Patrick
1 *If I should murder* (1945)
2 *Stone dead* (1945)
3 *Murder for the mind* (1946)
4 *Brief case of murder* (1949)
5 *Lady is dead* (1951)
6 *Shadow of murder* (1957)

Patrick McLanahan series
Brown, Dale
1 *Flight of the Old Dog* (1987)
2 *Day of the cheetah* (1989)
3 *Sky masters* (1991)

Patrick Michael Doyle series
Newell, Audrey
1 *Who killed Cavelotti?* (1930)
2 *Murder is not mute* (1940)

Patrick O'Brien series
Irwin, Inez Haynes
1 *Murder masquerade* (1935)
Murder in fancy dress
2 *Poison cross mystery* (1936)
3 *Body rolled downstairs* (1938)
4 *Many murders* (1941)
5 *Women swore revenge* (1946)

Patrick Pennington series
Peyton, K M
1 *Pennington's seventeenth summer* (1970)
Pennington's last term
2 *Beethoven Medal* (1971)
3 *Pennington's heir* (1973)
4 *Marion's angels* (1979)
Fallen angel
This sequence is a companion to the **Ruth Hollis series**

Patrick Petrella series
Gilbert, Michael Francis
1 *Blood and judgement* (1959)
2 *Petrella at Q* (1977)
Short stories
3 *Young Petrella* (1988)
4 *Anything for a quiet life* (1990)
Short stories
5 *Roller coaster* (1993)
Also four stories featuring Petrella in *Amateur in violence*, 1973

Patrick Pyrton series
Clark, William
1 *Number Ten* (1966)
2 *Special relationship* (1968)

Patrick series
Daly, Maureen
1 *Patrick visits the farm* (1959)
2 *Patrick takes a trip* (1960)
3 *Patrick visits the library* (1961)
4 *Patrick visits the zoo* (1963)

Patrick series
Lofgren, Ulf
1 Adapted by Patricia Crampton
Patrick's aeroplane (1967)
Original edition entitled *Patrik och flygmaskinen*
2 *Patrick's workshop* (1969)
Original edition entitled *Patriks snabbverkstad*
3 *Patrick's circus* (1971)
Original edition entitled *Patriks cirkus*

Patrick Shannon series
Quinn, Jake
1 *Undertaker* (1974)
2 *Shallow grave* (1974)
3 *Mindbenders* (1975)

Patrick Shirley and Rip Irving series
Mills, Osmington
see **Sergeant Patrick Shirley and Inspector Rip Irving series**

Patrick Standish series
Amis, Kingsley
1 *Take a girl like you* (1960)
2 *Difficulties with girls* (1988)

Patrick's dinosaurs series
Carrick, Carol
1 *Patrick's dinosaurs* (1983)
2 *What happened to Patrick's dinosaurs?* (1986)

Patriots series
Rutledge, Adam
1 *Sons of liberty* (1992)
2 *Rebel guns* (1992)
3 *Turncoat* (1993)
4 *Life and liberty* (1993)

Patsy Carroll series
Gordon, Grace
1 *Patsy Carroll at Wilderness Lodge* (1917)
2 *Patsy Carroll under southern skies* (1918)
3 *Patsy Carroll in the Golden West* (1920)
4 *Patsy Carroll in old New England* (1921)

Patten series
Randall, Anthony Asheton
see **Roger Patten series**

Patten trilogy
Callow, Philip
see **Colin Patten trilogy**

Patteran trilogy
Wendorf, Patricia
1 *Larksleve* (1985)
2 *Blanche* (1986)
3 *Bye bye blackbird* (1987)

Patternists series
Butler, Octavia Estelle
1 *Patternmaster* (1976)
2 *Mind of my mind* (1977)
3 *Survivor* (1978)
4 *Wild seed* (1980)
5 *Clay's ark* (1984)

Patterns of chaos series
Ingrid, Charles
1 *Radius of doubt* (1991)
2 *Path of fire* (1992)

Patterson family series
Wees, Frances Shelley
1 *Treasure of Echo Valley* (1964)
2 *Mystery in Newfoundland* (1965)

Patterson series
Walker, Peter Norman
see **Panda One series**

Patterson trilogy
Stirling, Jessica
see **Elspeth and Anna Patterson trilogy**

Patton series
Ormerod, Roger
see **Richard Patton series**

Pattullo series
Stewart, John Innes Mackintosh
see **Duncan Pattullo series**

Patty and Ginger series
Lambert, Janet
1 *We're going steady* (1958)
2 *Boy wanted* (1959)
3 *Spring fever* (1960)
4 *Summer madness* (1962)
5 *Extra special* (1963)
6 *On her own* (1964)

Patty Bergen series
Greene, Bette
1 *Summer of my German soldier* (1973)
2 *Morning is a long time coming* (1978)

Patty Fairfield series
Wells, Carolyn
1 *Patty Fairfield* (1901)
2 *Patty at home* (1904)
3 *Patty in the city* (1905)
4 *Patty in Paris* (1907)
5 *Patty's friends* (1908)
6 *Patty's summer days* (1908)
7 *Patty's pleasure trip* (1909)
8 *Patty's success* (1910)
9 *Patty's motor car* (1911)
10 *Patty's butterfly days* (1912)
11 *Patty's social season* (1913)
12 *Patty's suitors* (1914)
13 *Patty's romance* (1915)
14 *Patty's fortune* (1916)
15 *Patty Blossom* (1917)
16 *Patty-bride* (1918)
17 *Patty and Azalea* (1919)

Patty Lou series
Miller, Basil
1 *Patty Lou of the Golden West* (1942)
2 *Patty Lou and the White Gold Ranch* (1943)
3 *Patty Lou's pot of gold* (1943)
4 *Patty Lou in the Coast Guard* (1944)
5 *Patty Lou, the flying nurse* (1945)
6 *Patty Lou, the girl forester* (1947)
7 *Patty Lou, flying missionary* (1948)
8 *Patty Lou in the wilds* (1949)
9 *Patty Lou under Western skies* (1950)
10 *Patty Lou home on the range* (1951)
11 *Patty Lou at Sunset Pass* (1952)
12 *Patty Lou lost in the jungle* (1953)
13 *Patty Lou, range nurse* (1954)
14 *Patty Lou and the Seminole Indians* (1955)

Patty series
Treadgold, Mary
1 *Elegant Patty* (1967)
2 *Poor Patty* (1968)

Patty series
Webster, Jean
1 *When Patty went to college* (1903)
Patty and Priscilla
2 *Just Patty* (1911)

Patuffa series
Harraden, Beatrice
1 *Spring shall plant* (1920)
2 *Patuffa* (1923)

Paul and Ann series
Marokvia, Mireille
see **Ann and Paul series**

Paul and Arthur series
Rockwell, Anne Foote
1 *Paul and Arthur search for the egg* (1964)
2 *Paul and Arthur and the little explorer* (1972)

Paul and Fritzi's year series
Best, Jacqueline
Adapted by Marion Koenig
1 *Spring* (1973)
2 *Summer* (1973)
3 *Autumn* (1973)
4 *Winter* (1973)

Paul and Katie Van Riebeck series
Moray, Helga
see **Katie and Paul Van Riebeck series**

Paul and Netta tetralogy
Hilliard, Noel
see **Netta and Paul tetralogy**

Paul and Peggy series
Scott, Florence E
1 *Here and there with Paul and Peggy* (1914)

2 *Across the continent with Paul and Peggy* (1915)
3 *Through the Yellowstone with Paul and Peggy* (1916)

Paul and Peter Selbon series
McCulley, Johnston
see **Avenging Twins series**

Paul and Sally series
Iseborg, Harry
Adapted by Irene Dagny Morris
1 *Paul, Sally and the fox cub* (1965)
Original edition entitled *Eaven leker med Bobo och Clarina*
2 *Paul, Sally and Little Grey* (1968)
Original edition entitled Bobo och Clarina och Lille Gra
3 *Paul and Sally at Christmas* (1968)
Original edition entitled *Glad Jul med Bobo och Clarina*
4 *Paul, Sally and the wash-tub* (1969)
Original edition entitled *Balljan rullar med Bobo och Clarina*

Paul Atreides trilogy
Herbert, Frank
1 *Dune* (1965)
Illustrated Dune
2 *Dune messiah* (1969)
3 *Children of Dune* (1976)

Paul Baker series
Norman, Barry
1 *Matter of Mandrake* (1967)
2 *Hounds of Sparta* (1968)

Paul Beck series
Bodkin, Matthias McDonnell
1 *Paul Beck, the rule of thumb detective* (1898)
Short stories
2 *Quest of Paul Beck* (1908)
3 *Capture of Paul Beck* (1909)
4 *Young Beck* (1911)
Short stories
5 *Pigeon blood rubies* (1915)
6 *Paul Beck, detective* (1929)
Short stories

Paul Benjamin series
Garfield, Brian Wynne
1 *Death wish* (1972)
2 *Death sentence* (1975)
3 *Recoil* (1977)

Paul Bernard series
Gluck, Sinclair
1 *Last trap* (1928)
2 *Shadow in the house* (1929)
Death comes to dinner

Paul Bunyan series
McCormick, Dell J
1 *Paul Bunyan swings his axe* (1936)
2 *Tall timber tales* (1939)

Paul Cameron series
Wright, Wade
1 *Shadows don't bleed* (1967)
2 *Sharp edge* (1968)
3 *No haloes in hell* (1969)
4 *Hades hello* (1973)

Paul Campenhaye series
Fletcher, Joseph Smith
1 *Secret cargo* (1913)
2 *Paul Campenhaye, specialist in criminology* (1918)
Clue of the artificial eye
Short stories
Also two stories featuring Campenhaye in *The Massingham butterfly, and other stories*, 1926

Paul Chavasse series
Fallon, Martin
This sequence also published under the pseudonym Jack Higgins
1 *Testament of Casper Schultz* (1962)
2 *Year of the tiger* (1963)
3 *Keys of hell* (1965)
4 *Midnight never comes* (1966)
5 *Dark side of the street* (1967)
6 *Fine night for dying* (1969)

Paul Chisholm series
Eyles, Alfred W
1 *Murder in hospital* (1944)
2 *Mirrored murder* (1945)
3 *Murder brewing* (1947)
4 *Murder at out-patients* (1948)

Paul Christopher series
McCarry, Charles
1 *Miernik dossier* (1973)
2 *Tears of autumn* (1975)
3 *Secret lovers* (1977)
4 *Last supper* (1983)
5 *Second sight* (1991)
The story of the ancestors of Paul Christopher in the 17th century
Companion volume: *Bride of the wilderness*, 1988

Paul Coquenil series
Moffett, Cleveland
1 *Through the wall* (1909)
2 *Master mind* (1927)

Paul Craine series
Healy, Eugene P
1 *Craine's first case* (1939)
2 *Mister Sandman loses his life* (1940)

Paul Crane series
Curtis, Wade
1 *Red heroin* (1969)
2 *Red dragon* (1971)

Paul Crook series
West, Charles
1 *Stonefish* (1990)
2 *Little Ripper* (1991)

Paul Dean series
Francis, Basil
see **Sergeant Paul Dean series**

Paul Decker series
Albert, Andrew I
1 *Maori murder case* (1944)
2 *Murder for a hollow shell* (1945)

Paul Dexter series
Hackforth-Jones, Gilbert
1 *Chinese poison* (1969)
2 *All stations to Malta* (1971)
3 *Explosive situation* (1972)
4 *Shadow of the Rock* (1973)
5 *Second-in-command* (1974)
6 *Redoubtable Dexter* (1975)
7 *Dexter at war* (1976)

Paul Donavan series
Brown, Carter
1 *Donavan* (1974)
2 *Donavan's day* (1975)
3 *Chinese Donavan* (1976)
4 *Donavan's delight* (1979)

Paul Ferroll series
Clive, Caroline
1 *Paul Ferroll* (1855)
2 *Why Paul Ferroll killed his wife* (1860)

Paul Fox series
Mounce, David R
1 *Shield Project* (1971)
2 *Operation Cuttlefish* (1972)

Paul Gallant series
Suthren, Victor
1 *Black cockade* (1977)
Paul Gallant's Louisbourg command
2 *King's ransom* (1980)
3 *In perilous seas* (1984)
4 *Royal Yankee* (1987)

Paul Gane series
Woodman, Michael
1 *Medusa kiss* (1970)
2 *Bullion* (1971)

Paul Grainger series
Sinclair, Fiona
see **Inspector Paul Grainger series**

Paul Griggs series
Crawford, Francis Marion
1 *Mister Isaacs* (1882)
2 *Paul Patoff* (1887)
3 *Katherine Lauderdale* (1894)
4 *Ralstons* (1894)
5 *Casa Braccio* (1895)
6 *Prima-donna* (1908)

Paul Harley series
Rohmer, Sax
1 *Bat-Wing* (1921)
2 *Fire-Tongue* (1922)
Stories about Paul Harley also in *Tales of Chinatown*, 1922, *Tales of East and West*, 1932, *Salute to Bazarada, and other stories*, 1939

Paul Harris series
Black, Gavin
1 *Suddenly, at Singapore* (1961)
2 *Dead man calling* (1962)
3 *Dragon for Christmas* (1963)
4 *Eyes around me* (1964)
5 *You want to die, Johnny?* (1966)
6 *Wind of death* (1967)
7 *Cold jungle* (1969)
8 *Time for pirates* (1971)
9 *Bitter tea* (1972)
10 *Golden cockatrice* (1974)
11 *Big wind for summer* (1975)
Gale force
12 *Moon for killers* (1976)
Killer moon
13 *Night run from Java* (1979)

Paul Harvard series
Gibbs-Smith, Charles Harvard
1 *Operation Caroline* (1953)
Caroline affair
2 *Escape and be secret* (1957)

Paul Hatfield series
Rogers, Samuel
see **Professor Paul Hatfield series**

Paul Hedley series
Healey, Ben
1 *Waiting for a tiger* (1965)
2 *Millstone men* (1966)
3 *Death in three masks* (1967)
Terrible pictures
4 *Murder without crime* (1968)
5 *Trouble with Penelope* (1972)
6 *Blanket of the dark* (1976)
7 *Snapdragon murders* (1978)
8 *Last ferry from the Lido* (1981)
Midnight ferry to Venice

Paul Holton series
Hunt, Charlotte
see **Doctor Paul Holton series**

Paul Irving series
Grex, Leo
1 *Tragedy at Draythorpe* (1931)
2 *Lonely Inn mystery* (1933)
3 *Madison murder* (1933)
4 *Murder in the sanctuary* (1934)
5 *Stolen death* (1936)
6 *Carlent Manor crime* (1939)
Also published under the author's real name Leonard Reginald Gribble
7 *Ace of danger* (1952)

Paul Jones series
This sequence has three authors
Cooper, James Fenimore
1 *Pilot* (1819)
Dumas, Alexandre
2 *Paul Jones* (1838)
A drama in 5 acts; original edition entitled *Le Capitaine Paul*

Paul Kilgerrin series
Leonard, Charles L
1 *Deadline for destruction* (1942)
2 *Stolen squadron* (1942)
3 *Fanatic of Fez* (1943)
Assignment to death
4 *Secret of the spa* (1944)
5 *Expert in murder* (1945)
6 *Pursuit in Peru* (1946)
7 *Search for a scientist* (1947)
8 *Fourth funeral* (1948)
9 *Sinister shelter* (1949)
10 *Secrets for sale* (1950)
11 *Treachery in Trieste* (1951)

Paul Lane series
Lockridge, Frances
1 *Night of shadows* (1962)
English edition published under the pseudonym Francis Richards
2 *Quest for the bogeyman* (1964)

Paul Martiny series
Haggard, William
1 *Protectors* (1972)
2 *Kinsmen* (1974)

Paul Mason series
Leader, Charles
1 *Frontier of violence* (1966)
2 *Strangler's moon* (1968)

Paul McDonald series
Smith, Julie
1 *True-life adventure* (1985)
2 *Huckleberry fiend* (1987)

Paul Muller series
Muller, Paul
1 *You kill me!* (1967)
2 *Make mine mayhem* (1967)
3 *Lady is lethal* (1968)
4 *Finders, losers* (1968)
5 *Danger, dame at work* (1968)
6 *Hasty heiress* (1968)
7 *Slay time* (1968)
8 *Good-bye, Shirley* (1969)
9 *Why pick on me* (1969)
10 *Don't push your luck* (1970)
11 *Some dames don't* (1970)
12 *Wistful wanton* (1971)
13 *This is murder* (1971)
14 *Friendly fiends* (1972)
15 *Viper in her bosom* (1975)

Paul Pine series
This sequence has two authors
Evans, John
1 *Halo in blood* (1946)
2 *Halo for Satan* (1948)
3 *Halo in brass* (1949)
Browne, Howard
4 *Taste of ashes* (1957)
5 *Paper gun* (1985)

Paul Plush series
Keystone, Oliver
1 *Major crime* (1948)
2 *Deep as the grave* (1950)
3 *Arsenic for the teacher* (1950)

Paul Prye series
Millar, Margaret
see **Doctor Paul Prye series**

Paul Reeder series
Dennis, Robert C
1 *Sweat of fear* (1973)
2 *Conversations with a corpse* (1974)

Paul Rivington series
Verner, Gerald
1 *Con man* (1934)
2 *White wig* (1935)

Paul Ross and Susan Campbell series
Henneker, Philip
see **Susan Campbell and Paul Ross series**

Paul Savoy series
Gregory, Jackson
1 *House of the opal* (1932)
First case of Mister Paul Savoy
2 *Case for Mister Paul Savoy* (1933)
Second case of Mister Paul Savoy
3 *Emerald murder trap* (1934)
Third case of Mister Paul Savoy

Paul Scarf series
Boyd, Raymond
1 *Death joins the party* (1944)
2 *Fetch me a rope* (1947)
3 *Murder is a furtive thing* (1950)

Paul series
Berstl, Julius
see **Saint Paul series**
Blackwood, Algernon
see **Uncle Paul series**
Blyton, Enid
see **Prince Paul series**

Paul Shaw series
Sadler, Mark
1 *Falling man* (1970)
2 *Here to die* (1971)
3 *Mirror image* (1972)
4 *Circle of fire* (1973)
5 *Touch of death* (1983)
6 *Deadly innocents* (1986)

Paul Temple series
Durbridge, Francis
Based on a radio series
1 *Send for Paul Temple* (1938)
Co-author: John Thewes
2 *Paul Temple and the front page men* (1939)
Co-author: Charles Hatton
3 *News of Paul Temple* (1940)
Co-author: Charles Hatton
4 *Paul Temple intervenes* (1944)
Co-author: Charles Hatton
5 *Send for Paul Temple again!* (1948)
Co-author: Charles Hatton
6 *Tyler mystery* (1957)
Co-author: Douglas Rutherford; originally published under the pseudonym Paul Temple
7 *East of Algiers* (1959)
Co-author: Douglas Rutherford; originally published under the pseudonym Paul Temple
8 *Paul Temple and the Harkdale robbery* (1970)
9 *Paul Temple and the Kelby affair* (1970)
10 *Geneva mystery* (1971)
11 *Curzon case* (1972)
12 *Paul Temple and the Margo mystery* (1986)
13 *Paul Temple and the Madison case* (1988)

Paul Templeton series
Goyne, Richard
1 *Strange motives* (1934)
2 *Produce the body* (1935)
3 *Murder at the inn* (1935)
4 *Death by desire* (1936)
5 *Hanged I'll be* (1936)
6 *Death in harbour* (1937)
7 *Seven were suspect* (1938)
8 *Merrylees mystery* (1939)
9 *Who kills my wife* (1940)
10 *Five Roads Inn* (1944)
11 *Murder made easy* (1944)
12 *Fear haunts the fells* (1944)
13 *Murderer's moon* (1949)

Paul, Tommycat and Anna series
Girard, Nicole
see **Anna, Paul and Tommycat series**

Paul Venneker series
Geddes, Paul
1 *High game* (1968)
2 *November wind* (1970)
3 *Ottawa allegation* (1973)
4 *State of corruption* (1985)

Paul Vivanti series
Horler, Sydney
1 *Mystery of number one* (1925)
Order of the octopus
2 *Vivanti* (1927)
3 *Worst man in the world* (1929)
Short stories
4 *Vivanti returns* (1931)
5 *Lord of terror* (1935)
6 *Virus X* (1945)

Paul Whelan series
Raleigh, Michael
1 *Death in uptown* (1991)
2 *Body in Belmont Harbor* (1993)

Paul Williams series
Macdonald, Hugh Chisholm
1 *Hour of the Blue Fox* (1975)
2 *Five signs from Ruby* (1976)
3 *Letter from Kiev* (1977)

Paula Grey series
Forbes, Colin
see **Tweed, Grey and Newman series**

Paulding series
Beach, Edward Latimer, senior
see **Roger Paulding series**

Pauline Lyons series
Anthony, Elizabeth
1 *Ballet of death* (1979)
2 *Ballet of fear* (1979)

Paulus series
Dulieu, Jean
1 *[Winterboek van Paulus]* (1948)
No English edition
2 *[Paulus en Priegeltje]* (1957)
No English edition
3 *[Paulus de hulpsinterklaas]* (1962)
No English edition
4 *[Paulus en Eucalypta]* (1962)
No English edition
5 *[Paulus en het levenswater]* (1962)
No English edition
6 *[Paulus en Joris het vispaard]* (1962)
No English edition
7 *Paulus and mole* (1962)
Original edition entitled *Paulus en Mol*
8 *[Paulus en Wawwa]* (1962)
No English edition
9 *Paulus and the three robbers* (1963)
Original edition entitled *Paulus en de drie rovers*
10 *[Paulus en Pieter]* (1963)
No English edition
11 *Paulus and Solomon* (1963)
Original edition entitled *Paulus en Salomon*
12 *Paulus and the dragon* (1964)
Original edition entitled Paulus en het draakje
13 *[Paulus en schipper Makreel]* (1964)
No English edition
14 *Paulus and the acornmen* (1965)
Original edition entitled *Paulus en de eikelmannetjes*
15 *[De zeurboom, en andere verhalen van Paulus de boskebouter]* (1978)
No English edition
16 *[Paulus en de insekten]* (1981)
No English edition
17 *[Paulus en het beest van Ploemariac]* (1982)
No English edition
18 *[Paulus en het toverhoes]* (1983)
No English edition

Pavlov and O'Shaughnessey series
Ryan, Jessica
see **Gregory Pavlov and O'Shaughnessey series**

Paws series
Bisset, Donald
1 *Paws with shapes* (1976)
2 *Paws with numbers* (1976)
Co-author: Michael Morris

Paxton women series
Carroll, Shana
1 *Paxton pride* (1976)
2 *Raven* (1978)
3 *Yellow rose* (1982)
4 *Live for love* (1985)

Payling Green series
Alington, Adrian
1 *These, our strangers* (1940)
2 *Those kids from town again* (1943)

Payne series
Gibson, Gloria
see **Rachel Payne series**
Lynch, Lawrence L
see **Madeline Payne series**
Quinn, Olga
see **Marieanne Payne series**
Secrist, Kelliher
see **Sham Payne series**

Payo series
Salmon, Ross
1 *High jungle* (1956)
2 *Mountain trek* (1958)

Payran series
Nisot, Elizabeth
see **Commissaire Payran series**

Payson series
Sampson, Emma
see **Priscilla Payson series**

Payton series
Whitehill, Dorothy
see **Joy Payton series**

PB series
Rose, Gerald
Picture books
1 *PB takes a holiday* (1980)
2 *PB on ice* (1982)

Peabody series
Peters, Elizabeth
see **Amelia Peabody Emerson series**
Thomson, Ruth
see **Detective Peabody series**

Peacable kingdom series
Kelland, Clarence Budington
1 *Peacable kingdom* (1949)
2 *Up home* (1955)

Peace and war series
Milne, Alan Alexander
1 *Peace with honour* (1934)
An enquiry into the War Convention; revised edition 1935
2 *War with honour* (1940)

Peace Company trilogy
Green, Roland James
1 *Peace Company* (1985)
2 *These green foreign hills* (1987)
3 *Mountain walks* (1989)

Peace Greenfield series
Brown, Ruth Alberta
1 *At the little brown house* (1913)
2 *Lilac lady* (1914)
3 *Heart of gold* (1915)

Peace series
Barnard, Robert
see **Charlie Peace series**
Jenkins, Geoffrey
see **Commander Geoffrey Peace series**

Peace series
Murphy, Jill
1 *Peace at last* (1980)
2 *Whatever next* (1983)

Peace series
Shaw, Bob
see **Warren Peace series**

Peaceable kingdom series
De Hartog, Jan
1 *Children of the light* (1972)
2 *Holy experiment* (1972)
One volume edition entitled *The peaceable kingdom*, 1972

Peacemaker series
Brady, William S
This pseudonym is used by John Barton Harvey and Angus Wells as indicated against each title
1 *Comanche!* (1981)
[Wells]
2 *Outlaws* (1981)
[Wells]
3 *Whiplash* (1981)
[Harvey]
4 *Lynch law* (1981)
[Wells]
5 *Blood run* (1982)
[Wells]
6 *War party* (1983)
[Harvey]
7 *One thousand dollar death* (1983)
[Harvey]
8 *Lost* (1984)
[Wells]
9 *Shootout!* (1984)
[Wells]

Peacemaker series
Hamilton, Adam
1 *Zaharan pursuit* (1974)
2 *Yashar pursuit* (1974)
3 *Xander pursuit* (1974)
4 *Wyss pursuit* (1975)

Peacemakers series
Faucette, John Matthew
1 *Warriors of Terra* (1970)
2 *Siege of earth* (1971)

Peach series
Saint John, Mabel
see **Daisy Peach series**

Peachy and Forge series
Starnes, Richard
see **Barney Forge and Doctor Saint George Peachy series**

Peacock and Arrow series
Mantell, Laurie
see **Sergeant Steve Arrow and Chief Inspector Peacock series**

Peacock family series
Bullett, Gerald
1 *Daughters of Mrs Peacock* (1957)
2 *Peacock brides* (1958)

Peacock series
Fitzsimmons, Cortland
see **Percy Peacock series**

Peacock series
Gordon, Katharine
1 *Emerald Peacock* (1978)
2 *Peacock in flight* (1979)

3 *In the shadow of the Peacock* (1980)
4 *Peacock ring* (1981)
5 *Peacock in jeopardy* (1982)

Peanut Butter and Jilly series
Haas, Dorothy
1 *New friends* (1988)
2 *Peanut and Jilly forever* (1988)
3 *Haunted house* (1988)
4 *Trouble at Alcott School* (1989)
5 *Not starring Jilly!* (1989)
6 *Peanut in charge* (1989)
7 *Friendship test* (1990)
8 *Two friends too many* (1990)
9 *Alcott Library is falling down* (1991)

Pearce and Hart series
Gardner, Jerome
see **Dripspring series**

Pearl and Avery series
Mackenzie, Compton
see **Jenny Pearl and Maurice Avery series**

Pearl series
Asch, Frank
1 *Pearl's promise* (1984)
2 *Pearl's pirates* (1987)\

Pearl series
Bailey, Pearl
1 *Raw Pearl* (1968)
2 *Talking to myself* (1971)

Pearson series
Daniel, Roland
see **Inspector Jack Pearson series**
Macarthur, David Wilson
see **Larry Pearson series**
Shepherd, Eric
see **Superintendent Andrew Pearson series**

Peart and Bowman series
Burrows, Julie
see **Superintendent Bowman and Sergeant Peart series**

Peasant series
Erckmann, Emile
see **Story of a peasant series**

Peat Moss and Ivy series
Berenstain, Michael
1 *Peat Moss and Ivy's backyard adventure* (1986)
2 *Peat Moss and ivy and the birthday present* (1986)
3 *Peat Moss and Ivy meet Santa Claws* (1987)

Pebbles series
Cooper, Michael
1 *Meet the Pebbles* (1973)
2 *Pebbles go to town* (1975)
3 *Pebbles in the country* (1975)
4 *Pebbles' night adventure* (1976)
5 *Pebbles go to sea* (1976)

Peck series
Derleth, August
see **Judge Ephraim Peck series**

Peckover series
Kenyon, Michael
see **Inspector Henry Peckover series**

Peck's bad boy series
Peck, George Wilbur
1 *Peck's bad boy and his pa* (1883)
A play with the same title based on this work by Charles George was published in 1938
2 *Groceryman and Peck's bad boy* (1883)
Peck's bad boy and the groceryman
3 *Peck's Irish friend* (1887)
4 *Peck's Uncle Ike and the red headed boy* (1899)
5 *Peck's red-headed boy* (1901)
6 *Peck's bad boy abroad* (1904)
7 *Peck's bad boy with the circus* (1906)
8 *Peck's bad boy with the cowboys* (1907)
9 *Peck's bad boy in an airship* (1908)
Companion volumes: *Peck's fun*, 1879, *Peck's sunshine book*, 1884, *How Private George W Peck put down the rebellion*, 1887, *Sunbeams*, 1900

Pecos Appleby series
Koehler, Robert Portner
1 *Sing a song of murder* (1941)
2 *Murder in the green sedan* (1942)
Murder wore green
3 *Here come the dead* (1942)

Pecos Gang series
Benedict, Rex
1 *Good Luck Arizona Man* (1972)
2 *Goodbye to the purple sage* (1973)
Last ride of Sheriff of Medicine Creek
3 *Last stand at Goodbye Gulch* (1974)
4 *Ballad of Cactus Jack* (1975)

Pecos Kid series
Bodine, J D
1 *Beginner's luck* (1992)
2 *Reckoning* (1993)
3 *Apache moon* (1993)
4 *Outlaw hell* (1993)

Peculiar treasure series
Ferber, Edna
Autobiography
1 *Peculiar treasure* (1939)
2 *Kind of magic* (1963)

Pedley series
Sterling, Stewart
see **Ben Pedley series; Fire Marshal Ben Pedley series**

Pedlock family series
Longstreet, Stephen
1 *Pedlocks* (1951)
2 *God and Sarah Pedlock* (1976)
Strange ordeal of Sarah Pedlock
3 *Pedlock and Sons* (1966)
4 *Pedlock saint, Pedlock sinner* (1969)
5 *Pedlock inheritance* (1972)
6 *Pedlocks in love* (1978)

Pedro Moreno series
Morales, Pablo
1 *Victim for hire* (1979)
2 *Big deal in Veragua* (1979)

Pedro the fisherman series
Du Soe, Robert C
1 *Three without fear* (1947)
2 *Sea boots* (1949)

Pee-Wee Harris series
Fitzhugh, Percy Keese
1 *Pee-Wee Harris* (1922)
2 *Pee-Wee Harris on the trail* (1922)
3 *Pee-Wee Harris in camp* (1922)
4 *Pee-Wee Harris in luck* (1922)
5 *Pee-Wee Harris adrift* (1922)
6 *Pee-Wee Harris, F.O.B. Bridgeboro* (1923)
7 *Pee-Wee Harris fixer* (1924)
8 *Pee-Wee Harris, as good as his word* (1925)
9 *Pee-Wee Harris, mayor for a day* (1926)
10 *Pee-Wee Harris and the sunken treasure* (1927)
11 *Pee-Wee Harris on the briny deep* (1928)
12 *Pee-Wee Harris in darkest Africa* (1929)
13 *Pee-Wee Harris turns detective* (1930)

Pee wee scout series
Delton, Judy
Illustrated by Alan Tiegreen
1 *Cookies and crutches* (1988)
2 *Camp Ghost-Away* (1988)
3 *Lucky dog days* (1988)
4 *Blue skies, French fries* (1988)
5 *Grumpy pumpkins* (1988)
6 *Peanut-butter pilgrims* (1988)
7 *Pee wee Christmas* (1988)
8 *That mushy stuff* (1989)
9 *Spring sprouts* (1989)
10 *Pooped troop* (1989)
11 *Pee wee jubilee* (1989)
12 *Bad, brown bunnies* (1990)
13 *Rosy noses, freezing toes* (1990)
14 *Sonny's secret* (1990)
15 *Sky babies* (1990)
16 *Trash bash* (1990)
17 *Pee wees on parade* (1992)
18 *Lights, action, land-ho!* (1992)
19 *Piles on pets* (1993)
20 *Fishey wishes* (1993)
21 *Pee wees on skis* (1993)

Peebles series
Hedderwick, Mairi
see **Peedie Peebles series**

Peedie Peebles series
Hedderwick, Mairi
1 *Peedie Peebles' summer or winter book* (1989)
P.D.Peebles' summer or winter book
2 *Peedie Peebles colour book* (1994)

Peek-a-book series
Hill, Eric
1 *Nursery rhymes* (1982)
2 *Opposites* (1982)
3 *Animals* (1982)
4 *Who does what?* (1982)
5 *Baby animals* (1984)
6 *More opposites* (1985)
7 *Fairy tales* (1985)
8 *What's inside?* (1985)

Peekay series
Courtenay, Bryce
1 *Power of one* (1989)
2 *Tandia* (1991)

Peel series
Gash, Norman
see **Sir Robert Peel series**

Peele series
Vaughan, Richard
see **Justin Peele series**

Peep-Larsson family series
Unnerstad, Edith
see **Larsson family series**

Peep series
Astrop, John
1 *Peep's diary* (1986)
2 *Peep in the dark* (1986)
3 *Peep's bath* (1986)
4 *Peep's pals* (1986)

Peer Holm series
Bojer, Johan
1 *Great hunger* (1916)
Original edition entitled *Den store hunger*
2 *New temple* (1927)
Original edition entitled *Det nye tempel*

Peewee Clinton series
Stevens, William Oliver
1 *Peewee Clinton, plebe* (1912)
A story of Annapolis
2 *Messmates* (1913)
Midshipman Peewee Clinton's first cruise

Pefley series
Perdue, Tito
see **Leland and Judy Pefley series**

Peg and James series
Batchelor, Mary
1 *Peg and James go to market* (1977)
2 *Peg and James and the new baby* (1977)
3 *Peg and james plant some bulbs* (1977)
4 *Peg and James go to the park* (1977)

Peg-Leg series
Dawlish, Peter
see **Captain Peg-Leg series**

Peg series
Hann, Dorothy Owen
1 *Peg's patrol* (1924)
2 *Peg, lieutenant* (1927)
3 *Captain Peg* (1928)
4 *Peg and her company* (1929)
5 *Peg's babies* (1930)
6 *Peg, junior* (1931)
7 *What happened to Peg* (1932)

Pegana series
Dunsany, Edward John Moreton Drax Plunkett
see **Gods of Pegana series**

Pegasus series
McCaffrey, Anne
1 *To ride Pegasus* (1973)
2 *Pegasus in flight* (1990
One volume entitled *The wings of Pegasus*, 1991

Peggy Fairfield series
Liddon, Eloise
1 *Riddle of the Russian princess* (1934)
2 *Riddle of the Florentine folio* (1935)

Peggy Lane series
Hughes, Virginia
1 *Peggy finds the theater* (1962)
2 *Peggy plays off-Broadway* (1962)
3 *Peggy goes straw hat* (1963)
4 *Peggy on the road* (1963)
5 *Peggy goes Hollywood* (1964)
6 *Peggy's London debut* (1964)
7 *Peggy plays Paris* (1965)
8 *Peggy's Roman holiday* (1965)

Peggy Owen series
Madison, Lucy Foster
1 *Peggy Owen* (1908)
2 *Peggy Owen, patriot* (1910)
3 *Peggy Owen at Yorktown* (1911)
4 *Peggy Owen and liberty* (1912)

Peggy Raymond series
Smith, Harriet Lummis
see **Friendly Terrace series**

Peggy Saville series
Vaizey, Jessie Bell
1 *About Peggy Saville* (1900)
2 *More about Peggy* (1903)

Peggy series
Bugbee, Emma
1 *Peggy covers the news* (1936)
2 *Peggy covers Washington* (1937)
3 *Peggy covers London* (1939)
4 *Peggy covers the clipper* (1941)
5 *Peggy goes overseas* (1945)

Peggy series
Hillyard, Mary Dorothea
1 *Peggy's giant* (1920)
2 *Peggy and the giant's aunt* (1921)

Peggy series
Sewell, Helen
1 *Peggy and the pony* (1940)
2 *Peggy and the pup* (1941)

Peggy Stewart series
Jackson, Gabrielle Emilie
1 *Peggy Stewart* (1911)
2 *Peggy Stewart at home* (1912)
3 *Peggy Stewart at school* (1912)
4 *Peggy Stewart, navy girl* (1920)

Pegmen series
McFadyen, Ella
1 *Pegmen tales* (1946)
2 *Pegmen go walkabout* (1947)
One volume edition entitled *The big book of Pegmen tales*, 1959

Pel Pelham and Detective Linley series
Martin, Archibald Edward
1 *Common people* (1944)
Outsiders
Murder in Sideshow Alley
2 *Bridal bed murders* (1954)
Chinese bed mysteries

Pel series
Hebden, Mark
see **Inspector Clovis Pel series**

Pelazoni series
Head, Lee
see **Lexey Jane Pelazoni series**

Pelbar series
Williams, Paul Osborne
1 *Breaking of Northwall* (1981)
2 *Ends of the circle* (1981)
3 *Dome in the forest* (1981)
4 *Fall in the shell* (1982)
5 *Ambush of shadows* (1983)
6 *Song of the axe* (1984)
7 *Sword of forbearance* (1985)

Pelham and Linley series
Martin, Archibald Edward
see **Pel Pelham and Detective Linley series**

Pelham family series
Sinopy, Hilda
1 *Family gold rush* (1959)
2 *Both sides of the medal* (1960)

Pelle Jansson series
Peterson, Hans
1 *Pelle Jansson* (1970)
Original edition entitled *Pelle Jansson, en kille med tur*
2 *Pelle in the big city* (1971)
Original edition entitled *Pelle Jansson, en kille mit i stan*
3 *Pelle in trouble* (1972)
Original edition entitled *Pelle Jansson en kille son inte ger sig*

Pelle the conqueror series
Nexo, Martin Andersen
Original one volume edition entitled *Pelle Erorbreren*
1 *Boyhood* (1906)
2 *Apprenticeship* (1907)
3 *Great struggle* (1908)
4 *Daybreak* (1910)

Pellew and Clymping series
Gielgud, Val
see **Inspector Gregory Pellew and Viscount Clymping series**

Pellucidar series
This sequence has two authors
Burroughs, Edgar Rice
1 *At the earth's core* (1922)
2 *Pellucidar* (1923)
3 *Tanar of Pellucidar* (1930)
Numbers 1-3 also published in one volume, 1963
4 *Tarzan at the earth's core* (1930)
5 *Back to the stone age* (1937)
6 *Land of terror* (1944)
7 *Savage Pellucidar* (1963)
Holmes, John Eric
8 *Mahars of Pellucidar* (1976)

Pelmen trilogy
Hughes, Robert Don
1 *Prophet of Lamath* (1979)
2 *Wizard in waiting* (1982)
3 *Power and the prophet* (1985)

Pemberty series
Conde, Phillip
see **Dick Pemberty series**

Pembroke series
Shelby, Graham
see **William Marshal series**
Van Epps, Margaret T
see **Nancy Pembroke series**

Pembrokeshire family series
Morgan, Bill
see **Morgan family series**

Pemrose Lorry series
Hornibrook, Isabel
1 *Pemrose Lorry, camp fire girl* (1921)
2 *Pemrose Lorry, radio amateur* (1923)
3 *Pemrose Lorry, sky sailor* (1924)
4 *Pemrose Lorry, torchbearer* (1926)

Penaluna trilogy
Harris, John
see **Ira Penaluna trilogy**

Pencarrow family series
Scanlan, Nelle Margaret
1 *Pencarrow* (1932)
2 *Tides of youth* (1933)
3 *Winds of heaven* (1934)
4 *Kelly Pencarrow* (1939)

Pencroft series
Pierson, Clara Dillingham
see **Millers series**

Pendennis series
Thackeray, William Makepeace
see **Arthur Pendennis series**

Pendexter series
Cole, George Douglas Howard
see **Doctor Benjamin Tancred series**

Pendlebury series
Webb, Anthony
see **Mister Pendlebury series**

Pendleton series
Harding, Dolores Charlotte Frederica
1 *Pendleton fortune* (1937)
2 *Pendleton harvest* (1941)

Pendletons trilogy
Jameson, E M
1 *Pendletons* (1904)
2 *Peggy Pendleton* (1906)
Peggy Pendleton's plan
3 *Pendleton twins* (1908)

Pendragon series
Trevelyan, Robert
1 *Pendragon, late of Prince Albert's Own* (1975)
2 *His Highness commands Pendragon* (1976)
3 *Montenegran plot* (1977)
4 *Seeds of mutiny* (1979)

Pendragon trilogy
Lawhead, Stephen
1 *Taliesen* (1987)
2 *Merlin* (1988)
3 *Arthur* (1989)

Pendrake and Kane series
Spruill, Steven Gregory
see **Kane and Pendrake series**

Penelope and Guillaume series
Baron, Nicole de
1 *Sahara boom-de-ay* (1956)
Original edition entitled *Drole de Sahara*
2 *To the gondolas* (1957)
Original edition entitled *Et vogue la gondole*
3 *Say I'm in conference* (1958)
Original edition entitled *Les pieds sur le bureau*

Penelope and Guillaume trilogy
Buron, Nicole de
1 *Sahara boom-de-ay* (1956)
Original edition entitled *Drole de Sahara*
2 *To the gondolas* (1957)
Bride and the Bugatti
Original edition entitled *Et vogue la gondole*
3 *Say I'm in conference* (1958)
Original edition entitled *Les pieds sur le bureau*

Penelope Hamilton series
Wiggin, Kate Douglas
1 *Penelope's English experience* (1893)
Originally published in *A cathedral courtship*, and, *Penelope's English experiences*
2 *Penelope's progress* (1898)
Penelope's experiences in Scotland
3 *Penelope's Irish experiences* (1901)
4 *Penelope's postscripts* (1915)
Switzerland, Venice, Wales, Devon, home

Penelope Saint-John Orsini series
Kenyon, Paul
see **Baroness Penelope Saint-John Orsini series**

Penelope series
Anderson, William Charles
1 *Penelope* (1963)
2 *Penelope, the damp detective* (1964)

Penelope series
Bullingham, Ann
1 *Penelope* (1953)
2 *Penelope and Curlew* (1957)
3 *Summer on the hills* (1960)

Penelope series
Castelhun, Dorothea
1 *Penelope's problems* (1922)
2 *Penelope and the Golden Orchard* (1924)
3 *House in the Golden Orchard* (1925)
4 *Penelope in California* (1926)

Penelope Spring and Sir Tobias Glendower series
Arnold, Margot
1 *Exit actors, dying* (1979)
2 *Cape Cod caper* (1980)
3 *Zadok's treasure* (1980)
4 *Death of a voodoo doll* (1982)
5 *Death on the dragon's tongue* (1982)
6 *Menehune murders* (1989)
7 *Toby's folly* (1990)
8 *Catacomb conspiracy* (1992)
9 *Cape Cod conundrum* (1993)
10 *Dirge for a Dorset druid* (1994)

Penetrator series
Derrick, Lionel
This pseudonym is used by Mark Kelly Roberts who wrote the odd-numbered titles in this sequence and Chet Cunningham who wrote the even-numbered titles
1 *Target is H* (1973)
2 *Blood on the strip* (1973)
3 *Capitol hell* (1974)
4 *Hijacking Manhattan* (1974)
5 *Mardi gras massacre* (1974)
6 *Tokyo purple* (1974)
7 *Baja bandidos* (1974)
8 *Northwest contract* (1975)
9 *Dodge City bombers* (1975)
10 *Hellbomb flight* (1975)
11 *Terror in Taos* (1975)
12 *Bloody Boston* (1976)
13 *Dixie death squad* (1976)
14 *Mankill sport* (1976)
15 *Quebec connection* (1976)
16 *Deepsea shootout* (1976)
17 *Demented empire* (1976)
18 *Countdown to terror* (1977)
19 *Panama power play* (1977)
20 *Radiation hit* (1977)
21 *Supergun mission* (1977)
22 *High disaster* (1977)
23 *Divine death* (1977)
24 *Cryogenic nightmare* (1978)
25 *Floating death* (1978)
26 *Mexican brown death* (1978)
27 *Animal game* (1978)
28 *Skyhigh betrayers* (1978)
29 *Aryan onslaught* (1979)
30 *Computer kill* (1979)
31 *Oklahoma firefight* (1979)
32 *Showbiz wipeout* (1979)
33 *Satellite slaughter* (1979)
34 *Death ray terror* (1979)
35 *Black massacre* (1980)
36 *Deadly silence* (1980)
37 *Candidate's blood* (1980)
38 *Hawaiian trackdown* (1980)
39 *Cruise into chaos* (1980)
40 *Assassination factor* (1981)
41 *Hell's hostages* (1981)
42 *Inca gold hijack* (1981)
43 *Rampage in Rio* (1981)
44 *Deep cover blast-off* (1981)
45 *Quaking terror* (1982)
46 *Terrorist torment* (1982)
47 *Orphan army* (1982)
48 *Jungle blitz* (1982)
49 *Satan's swarm* (1983)
50 *Brotherhood of blood* (1983)
51 *Neutron nightmare* (1983)
52 *Plundered paradise* (1983)
53 *City of the dead* (1983)

Pengachoosa series
Rush, Caroline
see **Mister Pengachoosa series**

Penguin Pete series
Pfister, Marcus
Translated from the German
1 *Penguin Pete* (1988)
2 *Penguin Pete's new friends* (1988)
3 *Penguin Pete and Pat* (1989)
4 *Penguin Pete ahoy!* (1993)

Penguin series
Abrahams, Anthony
see **Polonius Penguin series**

Penhales trilogy
Garstin, Crosbie
1 *Owl's House* (1923)
2 *High noon* (1925)
3 *West wind* (1926)

Penhaligon trilogy
White, Simon
1 *English Captain* (1977)
2 *Clear for action* (1977)
3 *His Majesty's frigate* (1979)

Peninsular War series
Henty, George Alfred
1 *With Moore at Corunna* (1897)
2 *Under Wellington's command* (1898)

Peninsular War series
Styles, Showell
see **Ensign Peter Byrd series**

Penk series
Gore, William
see **Inspector Penk series**

Pennington series
Brandon, John Gordon
see **Arthur Stukeley Pennington series**
Peyton, K M
see **Patrick Pennington series**
Snell, Edmund
see **Peter Pennington series**

Pennington Wise series
Wells, Carolyn
1 *Man who fell through the earth* (1919)
2 *In the onyx lobby* (1920)
3 *Come back* (1921)
4 *Luminous face* (1921)
5 *Vanishing of Betty Varian* (1922)
6 *Affair at Flower Acres* (1923)
7 *Wheels within wheels* (1923)

Pennithorne and Snail series
Willard, Barbara
see **Snail and Pennithorne series**

Pennoyer series
Lawrence, Margery
see **Miles Pennoyer series**

Penny and Baby series
Mazzetti, Lorenza
1 *Sky falls* (1961)
Original edition entitled *Il cielo cade*
2 *Rage* (1963)
Original edition entitled *Con rabbia*

Penny and Dorabella series
Bracken, Anne
1 *Penny and Dorabella at the beach* (1947)
2 *Penny and Dorabella at the circus* (1947)

Penny and Gillian series
Byers, Irene
1 *Adventure at Fairborough's Farm* (1955)
2 *Adventure at Dillingdon Dene* (1956)
3 *Adventure at the Blue Cockatoo* (1958)

Penny and Pam series
Du Jardin, Rosamond
see **Pam and Penny series**

Penny and Pete series
Johnston, Dorothy Grunbock
see **Pete and Penny series**

Penny and Vincent Mercer series
Clandon, Henrietta
1 *Rope by arrangement* (1925)
2 *This delicate murder* (1936)
3 *Power on the scent* (1937)
4 *Fog off Weymouth* (1938)

Penny Dawson series
Milligan, Elsie
1 *Penny goes a-sailing* (1958)
2 *Penny goes exploring* (1959)
3 *Penny goes to Rhodesia* (1960)
4 *Penny goes a-flying* (1961)
5 *Penny goes a-camping* (1962)
6 *Penny goes home again* (1964)

Penny Marsh series
Deming, Dorothy
1 *Penny Marsh, public health nurse* (1938)
2 *Penny Marsh, supervisor of public health nurses* (1939)
3 *Penny Marsh finds adventure in public health nursing* (1940)
4 *Ginger Lee, war nurse* (1942)
5 *Penny Marsh and Ginger Lee, wartime nurses* (1943)
6 *Penny and pam, nurse and cadet* (1944)
7 *Pam Wilson, registered nurse* (1946)
8 *Penny Marsh, R.N., director of nurses* (1960)

Penny Nichols series
Clark, Joan
1 *Penny Nichols finds a clue* (1936)
2 *Penny Nichols and the mystery of the lost key* (1936)
3 *Penny Nichols and the black imp* (1936)
4 *Penny Nichols and the Knob Hill mystery* (1939)

Penny Parker series
Wirt, Mildred Augustine
1 *Tale of the witch doll* (1939)
2 *Vanishing houseboat* (1939)
3 *Danger at the drawbridge* (1940)
4 *Behind the green door* (1940)
5 *Clue of the silken ladder* (1941)
6 *Secret pact* (1941)
7 *Clock strikes thirteen* (1942)
8 *Wishing well* (1942)
9 *Ghost beyond the gate* (1943)
10 *Saboteurs on the river* (1943)
11 *Hoofbeats on the turnpike* (1944)
12 *Voice from the cave* (1944)
13 *Guilt of the brass thieves* (1945)
14 *Signal in the dark* (1946)
15 *Whispering walls* (1946)
16 *Swamp Island* (1947)
17 *Cry at midnight* (1947)

Penny Parrish series
Lambert, Janet
1 *Star spangled summer* (1941)
2 *Dreams of glory* (1942)
3 *Glory be!* (1943)
4 *Up goes the curtain* (1946)
5 *Practically perfect* (1947)
6 *Reluctant heart* (1950)

Penny Pollard series
Klein, Robin
1 *Penny Pollard's diary* (1983)
2 *Penny Pollard's letters* (1984)
3 *Penny Pollard in print* (1986)
4 *Penny Pollard's passport* (1988)
5 *Penny Pollard's guide to modern manners* (1989)

Penny Scott series
Kirby, Jean
see **Scott sisters series**

Penny series
Bliss, Adam
see **Alice Penny series**

Penny series
Clewes, Dorothy
1 *Runaway* (1957)
2 *Happiest day* (1958)
3 *Hide and seek* (1959)
4 *Birthday* (1962)
5 *Holiday* (1964)

Penny series
Ets, Marie Hall
see **Mister Penny series**

Penny series
Haynes, Ambrose
1 *Inquisitive Penny* (1959)
2 *Helpful Penny* (1962)

Penny series
Haywood, Carolyn
1 *Here's Penny* (1944)
2 *Penny and Peter* (1946)
3 *Penny goes to camp* (1948)

Penny series
Jackson, Wallace
see **Archibald Penny series**
Joseph, Marie
see **Daisy Penny series**

Penny series
Ramstedt, Viveka
1 *Pickle and Penny* (1979)
Original edition entitled *Stella och Stina*
2 *Penny and Sue* (1980)
Original edition entitled *Stina och Lena*

Penny series
Shaw, Jane
1 *Penny foolish* (1953)
2 *Twopence coloured* (1954)
3 *Threepenny bit* (1955)
4 *Fourpenny fair* (1956)
5 *Fivepenny mystery* (1958)

Penny series
Tring, A Stephen
1 *Penny dreadful* (1949)
2 *Penny triumphant* (1953)
3 *Penny penitent* (1949)
4 *Penny puzzled* (1955)
5 *Penny dramatic* (1956)
6 *Penny in Italy* (1957)
7 *Penny and the pageant* (1959)
8 *Penny says goodbye* (1961)

Penny Wanawake series
Moody, Susan
1 *Penny black* (1984)
2 *Penny dreadful* (1984)
3 *Penny post* (1985)
4 *Penny royal* (1986)
5 *Penny wise* (1988)
6 *Penny pinching* (1989)
7 *Penny saving* (1990)

Pennycress series
Toms, Patricia
see **Chronicles of Pennycress series**

Pennyfeather series
Olsen, D B
see **Professor A Pennyfeather series**

Pennyfoot Hotel series
Kingsbury, Kate
1 *Room with a clue* (1993)
2 *Do not disturb* (1994)
3 *Service for two* (1994)

Pennylove series
Martin, Robert
see **Ginger Pennylove series**

Pennypackers series
Swett, Sophia Miriam
1 *Six little Pennypackers* (1911)
Alternative title: From Little Bear Lighthouse to London
2 *How the Pennypackers kept the light* (1912)

Penrod series
Christian, Mary Blount
1 *Penrod's pants* (1986)
2 *Penrod again* (1987)
3 *Penrod's party* (1990)
4 *Penrod's picture* (1991)

Penrod trilogy
Tarkington, Booth
1 *Penrod* (1914)
2 *Penrod and Sam* (1916)
3 *Penrod Jashber* (1929)
One volume edition entitled *Penrod, his complete story*, 1931

Pentecost family series
Malpass, Eric Lawson
see **Gaylord series**

Pentecost trilogy
Corbett, William Jesse
1 *Song of Pentecost* (1982)
2 *Pentecost and the chosen one* (1984)
3 *Pentecost of Lickey Top* (1987)

Pentire family series
Mackenzie, Kathleen
1 *Four Pentires and Jimmy* (1947)
2 *We four and Sandy* (1947)
3 *Green fox* (1949)
4 *Vicky and the Pentires* (1951)

People in a diary series
Behrman, Samuel Nathaniel
Reminiscences
1 *Worcester account* (1954)
2 *People in a diary* (1972)
Tribulations and laughter

People in the picture series
Middleton, Haydn
1 *People in the picture* (1987)
2 *Collapsing castle* (1990)

People like ourselves series
Douglas, O
see **Priorsford series**

People like us series
Bye, Beryl
Reminiscences of missionary life
1 *People like us* (1971)
2 *More people like us* (1972)

People of Juvik series
Duun, Ole Julius
1 *Trough of the wave* (1920)
Original edition entitled Juvikingar
2 *Blind man* (1920)
Original edition entitled *I blinda*
3 *Big wedding* (1921)
Original edition entitled *Storbryllope*
4 *Odin in fairyland* (1921)
Original edition entitled *I eventyre*
5 *Odin grows up* (1922)
Original edition entitled I ungdommen
6 *Storm* (1923)
Original edition entitled *I stormen*

People of the forces trilogy
Barker, Dennis
1 *Soldiering on* (1981)
An unofficial portrait of the British Army
2 *Ruling the waves* (1986)
An unofficial portrait of the British Navy
3 *Guarding the skies* (1989)
An unofficial portrait of the Royal Air Force

People series
Gear, William Michael
1 *People of the wolf* (1990)
2 *People of the fire* (1991)
3 *People of the earth* (1992)
4 *People of the river* (1992)
5 *People of the sea* (1993)

People series
Henderson, Zenna
1 *Pilgrimage* (1961)
Alternative title: The book of the people
2 *People* (1966)
Alternative title: No different flesh
One volume edition entitled *The people collection*, 1991, which also includes four short stories

People series
Judson, Clara Ingram
1 *People who come to our house* (1940)
2 *People who work near our house* (1942)
3 *Pople who work in the country and the city* (1943)

Pepe and Ronnie series
Knight, Clayton
1 *Quest of the Golden Condor* (1952)
2 *Secret of the buried tomb* (1954)
3 *Skyroad to mystery* (1954)

Pepe Moreno series
Allen, Eric
1 *Pepe Moreno* (1955)
2 *Pepe Moreno and the roller skates* (1958)
3 *Pepe on the run* (1959)

4 *Pepe Moreno and the dilapidated donkey* (1960)
5 *Pepe Moreno's Quixotic adventure* (1963)

Pepper Anderson series
Trevor, Leslie
see **Policewoman series**

Pepper family series
Sidney, Margaret
see **Five Little Peppers series**

Pepper series
Packer, Jo
1 *No pony like Pepper* (1957)
2 *Gymkhana trek* (1959)
3 *Pepper leads the string* (1965)

Pepper series
Roberts, Gillian
see **Amanda Pepper series**
Smith, Frank Allan
see **Superintendent Pepper series**

Pepper Street series
Smith, Joan Mary
1 *We three kings from Pepper Street Prime* (1985)
2 *Pepper Street papers* (1987)
3 *Pepper Street hero* (1992)

Pepper Tree Bay series
Sanders, Dorothy Lucie
see **Montgomery family series**

Pepperoni Hero series
Kelly, Bill
1 *Sandwiches are not my business* (1975)
2 *Peanut butter and jelly is not for kids* (1975)
3 *Tuna is not for eating* (1975)

Pepperpot series
Proysen, Alf
see **Mrs Pepperpot series**

Pepys series
Hammond, Gerald
see **Beau Pepys series**

Per Eilevson Bufast series
Vesaas, Tarjei
1 *Great cycle* (1934)
Original edition entitled *Det store spelet*
2 *Women call, come home* (1935)
Original edition entitled *Kvinnor ropar heim*

Per Hansa trilogy
Rolvaag, Ole Edvart
Translated from the Norwegian
1 *Giants in the earth* (1925)
A saga of the prairie; original edition in two volumes entitled *I de dage*, 1924 and *Riket grundlaegges*, 1925
2 *Peder victorious* (1927)
A tale of the pioneers 20 years later; original edition entitled *Peder seier*
3 *Their father's god* (1931)
Original edition entitled *Den signede dage*

Percival Merewether series
Meacham, Ellis Kirby
see **Captain Percival Merewether series**

Percival series
Armstrong, Anthony
1 *Percival and I* (1927)
2 *Percival at play* (1929)
3 *Apple and Percival* (1931)

Percival Soames series
Behrens, Margaret
1 *In masquerade* (1930)
2 *Puck in petticoats* (1931)

Percy Aloysius Huff series
Edwards, Charman
1 *Terror ship* (1935)
2 *Blue macaw* (1935)
3 *Ten thirteen* (1936)
4 *Fear haunts the roses* (1936)
5 *Confetti for a killing* (1937)

Percy Blakeney series
Orczy, Emmuska
see **Scarlet Pimpernel series**

Percy Darrow series
White, Stewart Edward
1 *Mystery* (1907)
Co-author: Samuel Hopkins Adams
2 *Sign at Six* (1912)

Percy Peacock series
Fitzsimmons, Cortland
1 *Death rings a bell* (1942)
2 *Tied for murder* (1943)

Percy Pig series
Bennett, Rodney
1 *Marvellous adventures of Percy Pig* (1937)
2 *Percy Pig ahoy!* (1949)
3 *Percy Pig goes to town* (1950)

Percy series
Allen, Joy
1 *Percy goes on holiday* (1991)
2 *Percy goes to Spain* (1993)

Percy series
Hitchcock, Raymond
1 *Percy* (1969)
2 *Percy's progress* (1972)
Based on a screenplay

Percy trilogy
Wensby-Scott, Carol
1 *Lion of Alnwick* (1980)
2 *Lion dormant* (1983)
3 *Lion invincible* (1984)

Perdita series
Todd, Barbara Euphan
1 *Box in the attic* (1970)
2 *Wand from France* (1972)

Perdition series
Carter, Nevada
1 *Perdition Wells* (1964)
2 *Perdition Range* (1964)

Peregrine and Petronella Pig series
Hauptmann, Tatjana
see **Petronella and Peregrine Pig series**

Peregrine connection trilogy
York, Rebecca
1 *Tales of the falcon* (1986)
2 *Flight of the raven* (1986)
3 *In search of the dove* (1986)

Peregrine Merritt series
Harewood, Jocelyn
1 *Voices in the washhouse* (1990)
2 *Movement on the sofa* (1991)

Peregrine Piecrust series
Savage, Deborah
1 *Bubble trouble* (1986)
2 *Bird's nest* (1986)
3 *Square eyes* (1986)
4 *Big ears* (1986)
5 *Funny face* (1986)
6 *Big mouth* (1986)

Peregrine series
Davidson, Avram
1 *Peregrine primus* (1971)
2 *Peregrine secundus* (1981)

Peregrine White series
Spicer, Bart
see **Colonel Peregrine White series**

Perelandra trilogy
Lewis, Clive Staples
see **Space trilogy**

Perfect series
Heaton, Rose Henniker
1 *Perfect hostess* (1931)
2 *Perfect schoolgirl* (1931)
3 *Perfect Christmas* (1932)
4 *Perfect cruise and other holidays* (1935)
5 *Perfect address book* (1936)

Perfect series
Noel, Jeffrey
see **Johnny Perfect series**

Perfect wife series
Bradford, Barbara Taylor
see **How to be the perfect wife series**

Performers series
Rayner, Claire
1 *Gower Street* (1973)
2 *Haymarket* (1974)
3 *Paddington Green* (1975)
4 *Soho Square* (1976)
5 *Bedford Row* (1977)
6 *Long Acre* (1978)
Covent Garden
7 *Charing Cross* (1979)
Trafalgar Square
8 *Strand* (1980)
9 *Chelsea Reach* (1982)
10 *Shaftesbury Avenue* (1983)
11 *Piccadilly* (1985)
12 *Seven Dials* (1987)

Performing flea series
Wodehouse, Pelham Grenville
1 *Performing flea* (1953)
A self-portrait in letters
2 *Over seventy* (1957)
An autobiography with digressions

Peril series
Kennett, John
see **Black Circle Gang series**

Peril trilogy
Kline, Otis Adelbert
see **Grandon trilogy**

Perilous quest for Lyonesse series
Swithin, Antony
1 *Princes of Sandastre* (1990)
2 *Lords of the Stoney Mountains* (1991)

Periscope series
Clark, Halsey
House pseudonym
1 *Pacific standoff* (1983)
2 *Deepwater showdown* (1983)
3 *Depths of danger* (1983)
4 *Grand finale* (1983)
5 *Supersub* (1983)

Perkins and Tate series
Babson, Marian
see **Douglas Perkins and Gerry Tate series**

Perkins series
Garnett, Roger
see **R I Perkins series**
Hunt, Angela Elwell
see **Cassie Perkins series**
Lilly, Jean
see **Bruce Perkins series**

Perks series
Woodthorpe, Ralph Carter
see **Matilda Perks series**

Pern and the Red Planet series
McCaffrey, Anne
Numbers 1-3 cover events relating to the origins of the Pern settlements
1 *Dragonsdawn* (1988)
2 *Moreta, dragonlady of Pern* (1983)
3 *Nerilka's story* (1986)
4 *Dragonflight* (1968)
5 *Dragonquest* (1971)
6 *White dragon* (1978)
Includes *A time when, being a tale of young Lord Jaxom, his white dragon Ruth and various fire-lizards*, 1975; numbers 4-6 also published in one volume as *The dragon riders of Pern*, 1978 and as *The Harper Hall of Pern*, 1984
7 *Dragonsong* (1976)
8 *Dragonsinger* (1977)
9 *Dragondrums* (1979)
10 *Renegades of Pern* (1989)
11 *All the weyrs of Pern* (1991)
12 *Dolphins of Pern* (1994)
Companion volumes: *The girl who heard dragons*, 1985, *Rescue run*, 1991, *Dragonharper*, by Jody Lynn Nye, 1987, *Dragonfire*, by Jody Lynn Nye, 1988, *Dragonlover's guide to Pern*, by Jody Lynn Nye and Ann McCaffrey, 1989, *The atlas of Pern*, by Karen Wynn Fonstad, 1984

Peroni series
Holme, Timothy
see **Inspector Achille Peroni series**

Perrin series
Bear, Greg
see **Michael Perrin series**
Nobbs, David
see **Reginald Perrin series**
Waye, Cecil
see **Christopher Perrin series**

Perrine and Remi series
Malot, Hector
see **Remi and Perrine series**

Perry family series
Turner, Lilian
1 *Paradise and the Perrys* (1908)
2 *Perry girls* (1909)

Perry Mason series
This sequence has two authors
Gardner, Erle Stanley
1 *Case of the velvet claws* (1933)
2 *Case of the sulky girl* (1933)
3 *Case of the lucky legs* (1934)
4 *Case of the howling dog* (1934)
5 *Case of the curious bride* (1934)
6 *Case of the counterfeit eye* (1935)
7 *Case of the caretaker's cat* (1935)
8 *Case of the sleepwalker's niece* (1936)
9 *Case of the stuttering bishop* (1936)
10 *Case of the dangerous dowager* (1937)
11 *Case of the lame canary* (1937)
12 *Case of the substitute face* (1938)
13 *Case of the shoplifter's shoe* (1938)
14 *Case of the perjured parrot* (1939)
15 *Case of the rolling bones* (1939)
16 *Case of the baited hook* (1940)
17 *Case of the silent partner* (1940)
18 *Case of the empty tin* (1941)
19 *Case of the haunted husband* (1941)
20 *Case of the drowning duck* (1942)
21 *Case of the careless kitten* (1942)
22 *Case of the buried clock* (1943)
23 *Case of the drowsy mosquito* (1943)
24 *Case of the crooked candle* (1944)
25 *Case of the black-eyed blonde* (1944)
26 *Case of the gold-digger's purse* (1945)
27 *Case of the half-wakened wife* (1945)
28 *Case of the borrowed brunette* (1946)
29 *Case of the fan-dancer's horse* (1947)
30 *Case of the lazy lover* (1947)
31 *Case of the vagabond virgin* (1948)
32 *Case of the lonely heiress* (1948)
33 *Case of the dubious bridegroom* (1949)

34 *Case of the cautious coquette* (1949)
35 *Case of the negligent nymph* (1949)
36 *Case of the one-eyed witness* (1950)
37 *Case of the angry mourner* (1951)
38 *Case of the fiery fingers* (1951)
39 *Case of the grinning gorilla* (1952)
40 *Case of the moth-eaten mink* (1952)
41 *Case of the green-eyed sister* (1953)
42 *Case of the hesitant hostess* (1953)
43 *Case of the fugitive nurse* (1953)
44 *Case of the runaway corpse* (1954)
45 *Case of the restless redhead* (1954)
46 *Case of the glamorous ghost* (1955)
47 *Case of the sunbather's diary* (1955)
48 *Case of the nervous accomplice* (1955)
49 *Case of the terrified typist* (1956)
50 *Case of the gilded lily* (1956)
51 *Case of the demure defendant* (1956)
Case of the missing poison
52 *Case of the lucky loser* (1957)
53 *Case of the screaming woman* (1957)
54 *Case of the daring decoy* (1957)
55 *Case of the long-legged models* (1958)
Case of the dead man's daughters
56 *Case of the foot-loose doll* (1958)
57 *Case of the calendar girl* (1958)
58 *Case of the deadly toy* (1959)
Case of the greedy grandpa
59 *Case of the mythical monkeys* (1959)
60 *Case of the singing skirt* (1959)
61 *Case of the waylaid wolf* (1960)
62 *Case of the duplicate daughter* (1960)
63 *Case of the shapely shadow* (1960)
64 *Case of the spurious spinster* (1961)
65 *Case of the bigamous spouse* (1961)
66 *Case of the reluctant model* (1962)
67 *Case of the blonde bonanza* (1962)
68 *Case of the ice-cold hands* (1962)
69 *Case of the mischievous doll* (1963)
70 *Case of the stepdaughter's secret* (1963)
71 *Case of the amorous aunt* (1963)
72 *Case of the daring divorcee* (1964)
73 *Case of the phantom fortune* (1964)
74 *Case of the horrified heirs* (1964)
75 *Case of the troubled trustee* (1965)
76 *Case of the beautiful beggar* (1965)
77 *Case of the worried waitress* (1966)
78 *Case of the queenly contestant* (1967)
79 *Case of the careless Cupid* (1968)
80 *Case of the fabulous fake* (1969)
81 *Case of the fenced-in woman* (1972)
82 *Case of the postponed murder* (1973)
Also one story each in *The case of the crimson kiss*, 1971, *The case of the crying swallow*, 1971, *The case of the irate witness*, 1972

Chastain, Thomas
83 *Case of too many murders* (1989)
84 *Case of the burning bequest* (1990)

Companion volume: *A case for Mason*, a two-act play, by William McCleery, 1967

Perry Pierce series

Locke, Clinton W
1 *Who closed the door?* (1931)
Alternative title: Perry Pierce and the old storehouse mystery
2 *Who opened the safe?* (1931)
Alternative title: Perry Pierce and the secret cipher mystery
3 *Who hid the key?* (1932)
Alternative title: Perry Pierce tracing the counterfeit money
4 *Who took the papers?* (1934)
Alternative title: Perry Pierce gathering the printed clues

Perry Rhodan series

This sequence has seven authors; translated from the German

Scheer, Karl Herbert
1 *Enterprise Stardust* (1969)
2 *Radiant dome* (1969)

Mahr, Kurt
3 *Galactic alarm* (1970)

Ernsting, Walter
4 *Invasion from space* (1970)

Scheer, Karl Herbert
5 *Vega Sector* (1970)

Darlton, Clark
6 *Secret of the time vault* (1971)

Scheer, Karl Herbert
7 *Fortress of the six moons* (1971)

Darlton, Clark
8 *Galactic riddle* (1971)
9 *Quest through space and time* (1971)

Mahr, Kurt
10 *Ghosts of Gol* (1971)
11 *Planet of the dying man* (1972)

Darlton, Clark
12 *Rebels of Tuglan* (1972)

Scheer, Karl Herbert
13 *Peacelord of the universe* (1972)

Mahr, Kurt
14 *Venus in danger* (1972)

Darlton, Clark
15 *Escape to Venus* (1972)

Shols, W W
16 *Secret barrier X* (1972)

Mahr, Kurt
17 *Venus trap* (1972)
18 *Menace of the mutant master* (1972)

Darlton, Clark
19 *Mutants versus mutants* (1972)
20 *Thrall of Hypno* (1972)

Scheer, Karl Herbert
21 *Cosmic decoy* (1973)

Mahr, Kurt
22 *Fleet of the springers* (1973)
23 *Peril on Ice Planet* (1973)

Darlton, Clark
24 *Infinity flight* (1973)
Flight into infinity
25 *Snowman in flames* (1973)
26 *Cosmic traitor* (1973)

Mahr, Kurt
27 *Planet of the gods* (1973)

Darlton, Clark
28 *Plague of oblivion* (1973)
29 *World gone mad* (1973)
30 *To Arkon!* (1973)

Scheer, Karl Herbert
31 *Realm of the tri-planets* (1973)

Darlton, Clark
32 *Challenge of the unknown* (1973)
33 *Giant's partner* (1973)

Brand, Kurt
34 *S.O.S. Spaceship Titan* (1973)

Mahr, Kurt
35 *Beware the microbats* (1973)

Scheer, Karl Herbert
36 *Man and monster* (1973)

Darlton, Clark
37 *Epidemic Center, Aralon* (1974)

Brand, Kurt
38 *Project Earthsave* (1974)

Mahr, Kurt
39 *Silence of Gom* (1974)

Darlton, Clark
40 *Red eye of Betelgeuse* (1974)
41 *Earth dies* (1974)

Scheer, Karl Herbert
42 *Time's lonely one* (1974)

Brand, Kurt
43 *Life hunt* (1974)

Darlton, Clark
44 *Pseudo one* (1974)

Mahr, Kurt
45 *Unknown sector, Milky Way* (1974)

Scheer, Karl Herbert
46 *Again Atlan* (1974)

Brand, Kurt
47 *Shadow of the mutant master* (1974)

Darlton, Clark
48 *Dead alive* (1974)

Mahr, Kurt
49 *Solar assassins* (1974)

Darlton, Clark
50 *Attack from the unseen* (1974)

Mahr, Kurt
51 *Return from the void* (1974)

Scheer, Karl Herbert
52 *Fortress Atlantis* (1974)

Darlton, Clark
53 *Spybot* (1974)

Mahr, Kurt
54 *Blue dwarfs* (1974)

Darlton, Clark
55 *Micro-techs* (1974)
56 *Prisoner of time* (1974)
57 *Touch of eternity* (1974)

Mahr, Kurt
58 *Guardians* (1974)

Brand, Kurt
59 *Interlude Silko Five* (1974)

Mahr, Kurt
60 *Dimension search* (1974)
61 *Death waits in semispace* (1975)

Scheer, Karl Herbert
62 *Last days of Atlantis* (1975)

Brand, Kurt
63 *Tigris leaps* (1975)

Mahr, Kurt
64 *Ambassadors from Aurigel* (1975)
65 *Renegades of the future* (1975)

Voltz, William
66 *Horror* (1975)

Scheer, Karl Herbert
67 *Crimson universe* (1975)

Darlton, Clark
68 *Under the stars of Druufon* (1975)
69 *Bonds of eternity* (1975)

Brand, Kurt
70 *Thora's sacrifice* (1975)

Mahr, Kurt
71 *Atom hell of Grautier* (1975)
72 *Caves of the Druufs* (1975)

Darlton, Clark
73 *Spaceship of ancestors* (1975)

Mahr, Kurt
74 *Checkmate universe* (1975)

Brand, Kurt
75 *Planet Toride, please reply!* (1975)

Darlton, Clark
76 *Recruits for Arkon* (1975)
77 *Conflict center Naator* (1975)

Scheer, Karl Herbert
78 *Power key* (1975)

Voltz, William
79 *Sleepers* (1975)

Scheer, Karl Herbert
80 *Columbus affair* (1975)

Brand, Kurt
81 *Pucky's greatest hour* (1975)
82 *Atlan in danger* (1975)

Darlton, Clark
83 *Ernst Ellert returns!* (1975)

Voltz, William
84 *Secret mission, Moluk* (1975)

Mahr, Kurt
85 *Enemy in the dark* (1975)

Darlton, Clark
86 *Blazing sun* (1976)
87 *Starless realm* (1976)

Scheer, Karl Herbert
88 *Mystery of the Anti* (1976)

Brand, Kurt
89 *Power's price* (1976)
90 *Unleashed powers* (1976)

Voltz, William
91 *Friend to mankind* (1976)

Scheer, Karl Herbert
92 *Target star* (1976)

Darlton, Clark
93 *Vagabond of space* (1976)

Mahr, Kurt
94 *Action, Division Three* (1976)
95 *Plasma monster* (1976)

Voltz, William
96 *Horn Green* (1976)

Darlton, Clark
97 *Phantom fleet* (1976)

Mahr, Kurt
98 *Idol from Pasha* (1976)

Scheer, Karl Herbert
99 *Blue system* (1976)

Mahr, Kurt
100 *Desert of death's domain* (1976)

Brand, Kurt
101 *Blockade Lepso* (1976)

Voltz, William
102 *Spoor of the Antis* (1976)

Darlton, Clark
103 *False front* (1976)

Brand, Kurt
104 *Man with two faces* (1976)

Mahr, Kurt
105 *Wonderflower of Utik* (1976)

Brand, Kurt
106 *Caller from eternity* (1976)

Voltz, William
107 *Emperor and the monster* (1977)

Scheer, Karl Herbert
108 *Duel under the double sun* (1977)

Darlton, Clark
109 *Stolen spacefleet* (1977)

Mahr, Kurt
110 *Sergeant Robot* (1977)

Voltz, William
111 *Seeds of ruin* (1977)

Scheer, Karl Herbert
112 *Planet Mechanica* (1977)

Darlton, Clark
113 *Heritage of the lizard people* (1977)

Mahr, Kurt
114 *Death's demand* (1977)

Brand, Kurt
115 *Saboteurs in A-1* (1977)

Voltz, William
116 *Psycho deal* (1977)

Scheer, Karl Herbert
117 *Savior of the Empire* (1977)

Darlton, Clark
118 *Shadows attack* (1977)

Mahr, Kurt
119 *Between the galaxies* (1978)
Original edition entitled *Zwischen den Milchstrassen*

Voltz, William
120 *Killers from hyperspace* (1978)
Original edition entitled *Morder aus dem Hyperraum*

Darlton, Clark
121 *Atom fire on Mechanica* (1978)
Original edition entitled *Atombrand auf Mechanica*

Brand, Kurt
122 *Volunteers for Frago* (1978)
Original edition entitled *Freiwillige fur Frago*

Mahr, Kurt
123 *Fortress in time* (1978)
Original edition entitled *Das Versteck in der Zukunft*

Brand, Kurt
124 *Sinister power* (1978)
Original edition entitled *Die Macht der Unheimlichen*

Voltz, William
125 *Robots, bombs and mutants* (1979)
Original edition entitled *Roboter, Bomben un Mutanten*

Scheer, Karl Herbert
126 *Guns of Everblack* (1979)
Original edition entitled *Die Kanonen von Everblack*

Darlton, Clark
127 *Sentinels of solitude* (1979)
Original edition entitled *Wachter in der Einsamkeit*

Mahr, Kurt
128 *Beasts below* (1979)
Original edition entitled *Bestien der Unterwelt*

Brand, Kurt
129 *Blitzkrieg galactica* (1979)
Original edition entitled *Sturm auf die Galaxis*
130 *Peril unlimited* (1979)
Original edition entitled *Ridiko unendlich gross*

Voltz, William
131 *World without mercy* (1979)
Original edition entitled *Die Laurins kommen!*

Darlton, Clark
132 *Deadmen shouldn't die* (1979)
Original edition entitled *Ein Toter soll nicht sterben*

Perry Rhodan series

Mahr, Kurt
133 *Station of the invisibles* (1979)
Original edition entitled *Station der Unsichtbaren*
Brand, Kurt
134 *Agents of destruction* (1979)
Original edition entitled *Agenten der Vernichtung*
Voltz, William
135 *Humans keep out!* (1979)
Original edition entitled *Fur Menschen verboten!*
Scheer, Karl Herbert
136 *Robot invitation* (1979)
Original edition entitled *Roboter lassen bitten*
Darlton, Clark
137 *Phantom horde* (1979)
Companion volumes: *Menace of atomigeddon*, by Kurt Mahr, 1977, *Robot threat, New York*, by W W Shols, 1977, *The wasp men attack*, by W W Shols, 1977, *In the center of the galaxy*, by Clark Darlton, 1978

Perry series
Campbell, Michael
see **Peter Perry series**
Revere, John D
see **Justin Perry series**
Sedgwick, Modwena
see **Jan Perry series**

Perry Trethowan series
Barnard, Robert
see **Superintendent Perry Trethowan series**

Persia trilogy
Najafi, Najmeli
As told to Helen Hinckley; autobiography
1 *Persia is my heart* (1953)
2 *Reveille for a Persian village* (1959)
3 *Wall and three willows* (1967)

Persis Willum series
Watson, Clarissa
1 *Fourth stage of Gainsborough Brown* (1977)
2 *Bishop in the back seat* (1980)
3 *Runaway* (1985)
4 *Last plane from Nice* (1987)
5 *Somebody killed the messenger* (1988)

Personal recording series
Inchfawn, Fay
Autobiography
1 *Those remembered days!* (1963)
2 *Something more to say* (1965)
3 *Not the final word* (1969)
Alternative title: A joyful tribute

Personality quartet
Harris, Wilson
see **Agent of personality quartet**

Persons and places trilogy
Santayana, George
Autobiography
1 *Persons and places* (1944)
2 *Middle span* (1945)
3 *My host the world* (1953)

Persson series
Moorcock, Michael
see **Una Persson series**

Persuaders series
Smith, Frederick Escreet
Based on a television series
1 *Persuaders* (1972)
2 *Persuaders, book two* (1972)
Persuaders again
3 *Persuaders, book three* (1973)
Persuaders at large

Pet lamb series
Warren, Rebecca
1 *Where no mains flow* (1959)
2 *Lamb in the lounge* (1959)

Pet Lovers Club series
Roos, Stephen
1 *Love me, love my werewolf* (1991)
2 *Cottontail caper* (1992)
3 *Crocodile Christmas* (1992)

Petaybee series
McCaffrey, Anne
see **Yanaba Maddock series**

Pete and Bill series
De Paola, Tomie
see **Bill and Pete series**

Pete and Penny series
Johnston, Dorothy Grunbock
1 *Pete and Penny play and pray* (1954)
2 *Pete and Penny know and grow* (1957)
3 *Pete and Penny live and learn* (1963)
4 *Pete and Penny think and thank* (1972)

Pete and Rick Clayton series
Marsh, Jean Evelyn
see **Rick and Pete Clayton series**

Pete Draco series
Foster, Richard
1 *Bier for a chaser* (1959)
2 *Too late for morning* (1960)

Pete Fry series
Fry, Pete
1 *Long overcoat* (1957)
2 *Scarlet cloak* (1968)
3 *Grey sombrero* (1968)
4 *Black beret* (1959)
5 *Purple dressing gown* (1960)
6 *Green scarf* (1961)
7 *Red stockings* (1962)
8 *Yellow trousers* (1963)
9 *Thick blue sweater* (1964)
10 *Paint-stained flannels* (1965)
11 *Orange necktie* (1966)
12 *bright green waistcoat* (1967)
13 *Brown suede jacket* (1968)
14 *White crash helmet* (1969)
15 *Black cotton gloves* (1970)

Pete Hacker series
Bartlett, James Y
1 *Death is a two stroke penalty* (1991)
2 *Death from the ladies tee* (1992)

Pete Heysen series
Hamilton, Ian Sydney
1 *Persecutor* (1965)
2 *Man with the brown paper face* (1967)
Creeping vicar
3 *Never die in Honolulu* (1969)
4 *Thrill machine* (1972)

Pete Hunter series
Marcus, Arthur A
1 *Widow Gay* (1948)
Post-mark homicide
2 *Walk the bloody boulevard* (1951)
3 *Make way for murder* (1955)

Pete Marvin series
Edmunds, Brent
1 *Gun in my back* (1955)
2 *Ride a dead horse* (1955)
3 *Beware the crimson cord!* (1956)
4 *Spiders in the night* (1956)

Pete McGrath series
Brett, Michael
1 *Kill him quickly, it's raining* (1966)
2 *Dead upstairs in the tub* (1967)
3 *Ear for murder* (1967)
4 *Flight of the stiff* (1967)
5 *Turn blue, you murderers* (1967)
6 *We, the killers* (1967)
7 *Another day, another stiff* (1968)
8 *Death of a hippie* (1968)
9 *Slit my throat* (1968)
10 *Lie a little, die a little* (1968)
Cry uncle!

Pete Pack Rat series
Quackenbush, Robert Mead
1 *Pete Pack Rat* (1976)
2 *Pete Pack Rat and the Gila Monster Gang* (1978)
3 *Pete Pack Rat and the Christmas Eve surprise* (1981)

Pete Rector series
Van Siller, Hilda
1 *Good night, ladies* (1943)
2 *Under a cloud* (1944)

Pete Riley series
Quinn, Patrick
1 *Once upon a private eye* (1968)
2 *Twice upon a crime* (1969)
3 *Thrice upon a killing spree* (1970)
4 *Fatal complaint* (1970)

Pete Schofield series
Dewey, Thomas Blanchard
1 *And where she stops* (1957)
I.O.U. murder
2 *Go to sleep, Jeannie* (1959)
3 *Too hot for Hawaii* (1960)
4 *Golden hooligan* (1961)
Mexican slay ride
5 *Go, Honeylou* (1962)
6 *Girl with the sweet plump knees* (1963)
7 *Only on Tuesdays* (1964)
8 *Girl in the punchbowl* (1964)
9 *Nude in Nevada* (1965)

Pete Selby series
Craig, Jonathan
1 *Dead darling* (1955)
2 *Morgue for Venus* (1956)
3 *Case of the cold coquette* (1957)
4 *Case of the beautiful body* (1957)
5 *Case of the petticoat murder* (1958)
6 *Case of the nervous nude* (1959)
7 *Case of the village tramp* (1959)
8 *Case of the laughing virgin* (1960)
9 *Case of the silent stranger* (1964)
10 *Case of the brazen beauty* (1966)

Pete series
Dixon, Rex
1 *Pete and the prairie people* (1954)
2 *Pete and the Wild Grass Country* (1954)

Pete series
Pfister, Marcus
see **Penguin Pete series**

Pete Taylor series
Abrahams, Robert
1 *Death after lunch* (1941)
2 *Death in one-two-three* (1942)

Peter Allen series
Anson, Lindsay
1 *Such natural deaths* (1939)
Even doctors die
2 *I don't like cats* (1940)

Peter and Ann series
Someren, Liesje van
see **Kennedys abroad series**

Peter and Brian Leonard series
Wain, John
1 *Where the rivers meet* (1988)
2 *Comedies* (1990)
3 *Hungry generations* (1994)

Peter and Carol Garret series
Smythe, Pat
1 *Swiss adventure* (1970)
2 *Spanish adventure* (1971)
3 *Cotswold adventure* (1973)

Peter and Ginger series
Dale, Norman
1 *Secret service* (1943)
2 *Dangerous treasure* (1944)
3 *Best adventure* (1945)

Peter and Janet Barron series
Darby, Ruth
1 *Death boards the Lazy Lady* (1939)
2 *Death conducts a tour* (1940)
3 *If this be murder* (1941)
4 *Beauty sleep* (1942)
5 *Murder with orange blossoms* (1943)

Peter and Lotta series
Beskow, Elsa
1 *Aunt Green, Aunt Brown and Aunt Lavender* (1918)
Original edition entitled *Tan Groen, Tant Brun och Tant Gredelin*
2 *Aunt Brown's birthday* (1925)
Original edition entitled *Tant Bruns fodelsdag*
3 *Adventures of Peter and Lotta* (1931)
Original edition entitled *Petter och Lotta paa aventyr*
4 *[Petters och Lottas jul]* (1947)
No English edition
5 *Mister Peter* (1949)
Companion volume: *Peter's voyage, verse*, 1921

Peter and Mig Manson series
Divine, David
see **Mig and Peter Manson series**

Peter and Paul Selbon series
McCulley, Johnston
see **Avenging Twins series**

Peter and Polly series
Lucia, Rose
1 *Peter and Polly in summer* (1912)
2 *Peter and Polly in winter* (1914)
3 *Peter and Polly in spring* (1915)
4 *Peter and Polly in autumn* (1918)

Peter and Rusty series
Barrington, G W
see **Rusty and Peter series**

Peter and Tim series
Brown, T Burton
1 *Adventures of Peter and Tim* (1943)
2 *Peter and Tim on the trail* (1945)
3 *Peter and Tim's schooldays* (1949)

Peter and Veronica series
Beech, Margaret
1 *Peter and Veronica* (1928)
Springtime lessons in an old garden
2 *Peter and Cub* (1928)
3 *Peter and Veronica growing up* (1935)
A book for readers of 15 to 17

Peter Ashton series
Egleton, Clive
1 *Hostile intent* (1993)
2 *Killing in Moscow* (1994)

Peter Aswell series
Brown, Wenzell
1 *Murder seeks an agent* (1945)
2 *Rum and Coca-Cola murders* (1960)
Also includes *Calypsonian*, by Samuel Selvon

Peter Bartholomew series
Gunning, Sally
1 *Hot water* (1990)
2 *Under water* (1992)

3 *Ice water* (1993)
4 *Troubled water* (1993)

Peter Bentley series
Macdonnell, James Edmond
see **Captain Peter Bentley series**

Peter Blair series
Anderson, John Richard Lane
see **Major Peter Blair series**

Peter Blood series
Sabatini, Rafael
see **Captain Blood series**

Peter Bounty series
Downing, Todd
1 *Murder on the tropic train* (1935)
2 *Death under the moonflower* (1938)
3 *Lazy Lawrence murders* (1941)

Peter Bradfield series
Witting, Clifford
see **Inspector Peter Bradfield series**

Peter Bragg series
Lynch, Jack
1 *Bragg's Bunch* (1982)
2 *Missing and the dead* (1982)
3 *Pieces of death* (1982)
4 *Sausalito* (1984)
5 *San Quentin* (1984)
6 *Monterey* (1985)
7 *Seattle* (1985)

Peter Brichter and Kori McLeod Price series
Pulver, Mary Monica
see **Kori McLeod Price and Peter Brichter series**

Peter Burgoyne series
Burgoyne, Peter
1 *School mystery* (1954)
2 *Fighting formula* (1956)
3 *Schoolmaster spy* (1958)
4 *Contrband castle* (1960)

Peter Byrd series
Styles, Showell
see **Ensign Peter Byrd series**

Peter Cardigan series
Barrett, Monte
1 *Pelham murder case* (1930)
2 *Murder off stage* (1931)
Knotted silk
3 *Wedding march murder* (1933)

Peter Cardiman and Quong series
De Fraga, Geoff
1 *Murder at the cookout* (1968)
2 *Murder by wash of light* (1970)

Peter Carr series
Bratby, John
1 *Breakfast and elevenses* (1961)
2 *Brake-pedal down* (1962)

Peter Casey series
Mead, Russell
see **Doctor Peter Casey series**

Peter Castle series
Davison, Gilderoy
1 *Man with the Twisted Face* (1931)
2 *Prince of spies* (1932)
3 *Mystery of the red-haired valet* (1934)
4 *Exit Mister Brent* (1936)
5 *Man with half a face* (1936)
6 *Dog fight with death* (1940)

Peter Chambers series
Kane, Henry
1 *Halo for nobody* (1947)
Martinis and murder
2 *Armchair in hell* (1948)
3 *Hang by your neck* (1949)
4 *Report for a corpse* (1950)
Murder of the Park Avenue playgirl
Six stories and novelettes
5 *Corpse for Christmas* (1951)
Homicide at Yuletide
Deadly doll
6 *Until you are dead* (1951)
7 *My business is murder* (1954)
Includes *Big touch*, and, *Loose end*
8 *Trinity in violence* (1955)
American edition includes *Far cry*, *Slaughter on Sunday*, and, *Skip a beat*; British edition includes *Big touch*, *Loose end*, and, *Far cry*; *Trilogy in jeopardy*, 1955 includes *Skip a beat*, and, *Slaughter on Sunday*
9 *Case of the murdered madame* (1955)
Triple terror
Three novelettes
10 *Too French and too deadly* (1955)
Narrowing lust
11 *Who killed Sweet Sue?* (1956)
Sweet Charlie
12 *Death on the double* (1957)
13 *Fistful of death* (1958)
Dangling man
14 *Death is the last lover* (1959)
Nirvana can also mean death
15 *Death of a flack* (1961)
16 *Dead in bed* (1961)
17 *Death of a hooker* (1961)
18 *Kisses of death* (1962)
Killer's kiss
19 *Death of a dastard* (1962)
20 *Never give a millionaire an even break* (1963)
Murder for the millions
21 *Nobody loves a loser* (1963)
Who dies there?
22 *Snatch an eye* (1963)
23 *Devil to pay* (1966)
Unholy trio
Better wed than dead
24 *Don't call me madame* (1969)
25 *Schack job* (1969)
26 *Bomb job* (1970)
27 *Don't go away dead* (1970)
28 *Glow job* (1971)
29 *Tail job* (1971)
30 *Come kill with me* (1972)
31 *Escort job* (1972)
32 *Kill for the millions* (1972)
Selections from various volumes of short stories and novelettes: *The name is Chambers*, 1957, and, *Kiss, kiss, kill, kill*, 1970

Peter Chard series
Verner, Gerald
1 *Thirsty evil* (1946)
2 *They walk in darkness* (1947)

Peter Clancy series
Thayer, Lee
1 *Mystery of the thirteenth floor* (1919)
2 *Unlatched door* (1920)
3 *That affair at the Cedars* (1921)
4 *Q.E.D.* (1922)
Puzzle
5 *Sinister mark* (1923)
6 *Key* (1924)
7 *Poison* (1926)
8 *Alias Doctor Ely* (1927)
9 *Darkest spot* (1928)
10 *Dead men's shoes* (1929)
11 *They tell no tales* (1930)
12 *Last shot* (1931)
13 *Set a thief* (1931)
To catch a thief
14 *Glass knife* (1932)
15 *Scrimshaw millions* (1932)
16 *Counterfeit* (1933)
Counterfeit bill
17 *Hell-gate tides* (1933)
18 *Second bullet* (1934)
Second shot
19 *Dead storage* (1935)
Death weed
20 *Sudden death* (1935)
Red-handed
21 *Dark of the moon* (1936)
Death in the gorge
22 *Dead end street, no outlet* (1936)
Murder in the mirror
23 *Last trump* (1937)
24 *Man's enemies* (1937)
This man's doom
25 *Ransom racket* (1938)
26 *That strange Sylvester affair* (1938)
27 *Lightning strikes twice* (1939)
28 *Stark murder* (1939)
29 *Guilty!* (1940)
30 *X marks the spot* (1940)
31 *Hallowe'en homicide* (1941)
32 *Persons unknown* (1941)
33 *Murder is out* (1942)
34 *Murder on location* (1942)
35 *Accessory after the fact* (1943)
36 *Hanging's too good* (1943)
37 *Plain case of murder* (1944)
38 *Five bullets* (1944)
39 *Accident, manslaughter or murder?* (1945)
40 *Hair's breadth* (1946)
41 *Jaws of death* (1946)
42 *Murder stalks the circle* (1947)
43 *Out, brief candle!* (1948)
44 *Pig in a poke* (1948)
Clue for Clancy
45 *Evil root* (1949)
46 *Within the vault* (1950)
Death within the vault
47 *Too long endured* (1950)
48 *Do not disturb* (1951)
Clancy's secret mission
49 *Guilt-edged* (1951)
Guilt-edged murder
50 *Blood on the knight* (1952)
51 *Prisoner pleads not guilty* (1953)
52 *Dead reckoning* (1954)
Murder on the Pacific
53 *No holiday for death* (1954)
54 *Who benefits?* (1955)
Fatal alibi
55 *Guilt is where you find it* (1957)
56 *Still no answer* (1958)
Web of hate
57 *Two ways to die* (1959)
58 *Dead on arrival* (1960)
59 *And one cried murder* (1961)
60 *Dusty death* (1966)
Death walks in shadow

Peter Cottontail series
Burgess, Thornton Waldo
see **Peter Rabbit series**

Peter Craig series
Benton, Kenneth
1 *Twenty-fourth level* (1969)
2 *Sole agent* (1970)
3 *Spy in Chancery* (1972)
4 *Craig and the Jaguar* (1973)
5 *Craig and the Tunisian tangle* (1974)
6 *Craig and the Midas touch* (1975)
7 *Single monstrous act* (1976)

Peter Creighton series
Livingston, Armstrong
1 *On the right wrists* (1925)
2 *Light fingered ladies* (1927)
3 *Monk of Hambledon* (1928)
4 *Guilty accuser* (1928)
5 *Trackless death* (1930)

Peter Curwen and Hugh Stanton series
Vickers, Roy
see **Inspector Peter Curwen and Hugh Stanton series**

Peter Cutler Sergeant series
Box, Edgar
1 *Death in the fifth position* (1952)
2 *Death before bedtime* (1953)
3 *Death likes it hot* (1954)
One volume edition entitled Three by Box, 1978

Peter Decker and Rina Lazarus series
Kellerman, Faye
see **Sergeant Peter Decker and Rina Lazarus series**

Peter Devlin series
Buddee, Paul
1 *Peter Devlin fights for survival* (1974)
2 *Peter Devlin, range rider* (1974)
3 *Peter Devlin, buffalo hunter* (1974)
4 *Peter Devlin and the road bandits* (1974)

Peter Donnegan series
Quick, Dorothy
see **Lieutenant Peter Donnegan series**

Peter Duluth series
Quentin, Patrick
1 *Puzzle for fools* (1936)
2 *Puzzle for players* (1938)
3 *Puzzle for puppets* (1944)
4 *Puzzle for wantons* (1945)
Slay the loose ladies
5 *Puzzle for fiends* (1947)
Love is a deadly weapon
6 *Puzzle for pilgrims* (1948)
Fate of the immodest blonde
7 *Run to death* (1948)
8 *Black widow* (1952)
Fatal woman

Peter Feltham series
Mather, Berkely
1 *Achilles affair* (1959)
2 *With extreme prejudice* (1975)

Peter Finley series
Lupica, Mike
1 *Dead air* (1986)
2 *Extra credits* (1988)
3 *Limited partner* (1990)

Peter Fleck series
Clapperton, Richard
1 *No news on Monday* (1968)
You're a long time dead
2 *Victims unknown* (1970)
3 *Sentimental kill* (1976)

Peter Gale series
Craig, David
1 *Albion case* (1975)
2 *Faith, hope and death* (1976)

Peter Graham series
Keable, Robert
1 *Simon called Peter* (1921)
2 *Recompense* (1923)
3 *Lighten our darkness* (1927)

Peter Graham series
Thomson, Basil
1 *Metal flask* (1929)
2 *Kidnapper* (1933)

Peter Grayleigh series
Robertson, Colin
1 *Temple of dawn* (1939)
2 *Stalking stranger* (1939)
3 *Amazing corpse* (1942)
4 *Zero hour* (1942)
5 *Alibi in black* (1944)
6 *Explosion!* (1945)
7 *Two must die* (1946)
8 *Dark knight* (1946)
9 *Devil's lady* (1947)
10 *Knave's castle* (1948)
11 *Calling Peter Gayleigh* (1948)
12 *Sweet justice* (1949)
13 *Death wears red shoes* (1949)
14 *Peter Gayleigh flies high* (1951)

Peter Grayleigh series
15 *Demon's moon* (1951)
16 *Smugglers' moon* (1954)
17 *Lonely place to die* (1969)

Peter Hatcher series
Blume, Judy
1 *Tales of a Fourth Grade nothing* (1972)
2 *Otherwise known as Sheila the Great* (1972)
3 *Superfudge* (1980)
4 *Fudge-a-mania* (1990)

Peter Hill series
Walters, Hugh
1 *Boy astronaut* (1977)
2 *First family on the moon* (1979)

Peter Hovden series
Hamre, Leif
1 *Otter Three Two calling* (1958)
Original edition entitled *Otter Tre To kaller*
2 *Blue Two, bale-out* (1958)
Original edition entitled *Bla To, hopp ut*
3 *Ready for take-off* (1959)
Original edition entitled *Klart fly*

Peter Howard series
Williams, Eric Ernest
Account of an escape from a German prison camp
1 *Tunnel* (1951)
2 *Wooden horse* (1949)

Peter Jackson series
Frankau, Gilbert
1 *Woman of the horizon* (1917)
A romance of nineteen-thirteen
2 *Peter Jackson, cigar merchant* (1919)
Peter Jameson
A romance of married life
3 *Men, maids and mustard-pot* (1923)
A collection of tales
4 *Concerning Peter Jackson and others* (1931)

Peter Jensen series
Wahloo, Per
see **Chief Inspector Peter Jensen series**

Peter, Jeremy and Algy series
Scott, Philip
see **Algy, Peter and Jeremy series**

Peter Jerningham series
Myers, Isabel Briggs
1 *Murder yet to come* (1930)
2 *Give me death* (1934)

Peter Johnson series
Peterson, Hans
1 *Peter Johnson and his guitar* (1959)
Original edition entitled *Petter Joensson hade en gitarr*
2 *Here comes Peter* (1963)
Original edition entitled *Har kommer Petter*
3 *Peter comes back* (1964)
Original edition entitled *Petter kommer igen*
4 *Peter makes his way* (1966)
Original edition entitled *Petter klarar allt*
5 *When Peter was lost in the forest* (1969)
Original edition entitled *Naer Per gick vilse i skogen*

Peter Jumping Horse series
Hall, Gordon Langley
1 *Peter Jumping Horse* (1959)
2 *Peter at the stampede* (1961)

Peter Justice series
Duncan, Francis
1 *Sword of Justice* (1937)
2 *League of Justice* (1937)
3 *Justice returns* (1940)
4 *Justice limited* (1941)
5 *Hand of Justice* (1945)

Peter Kent series
Gunn, John
1 *Barrier Reef espionage* (1955)
2 *Battle in the ice* (1956)
3 *Gibraltar sabotage* (1957)
4 *Submarine island* (1958)
5 *Peter Kent's command* (1960)
6 *City in danger* (1962)

Peter Kerrigan series
Gordon, Neil
1 *Murder in Earl's Court* (1931)
2 *Shakespeare murders* (1933)

Peter Lance trilogy
Adams, Hunter
see **Man from Planet X trilogy**

Peter Lawson series
Davidson, Helen Beatrice
1 *Peter Lawson, wolf-cub* (1926)
Alternate title: The mystery of Redcroft Farm
2 *Peter Lawson, camper* (1930)

Peter Leroy series
Kraft, Eric
1 *Little follies* (1992)
2 *Where do you stop?* (1992)
3 *What a piece of work I am* (1994)

Peter Macklin series
Estleman, Loren D
1 *Kill zone* (1984)
2 *Roses are dead* (1985)
3 *Any man's death* (1986)

Peter Maclean series
Redmayne, John
1 *Redcoat spy* (1964)
2 *Substitute general* (1965)
3 *Night riders* (1967)

Peter Marklin series
Steed, Neville
1 *Tin-plate* (1986)
2 *Die-cast* (1987)
3 *Chipped* (1988)
4 *Clockwork* (1989)
5 *Wind up* (1990)
6 *Boxed in* (1991)

Peter Marlow series
Hone, Joseph
1 *Private sector* (1971)
2 *Sixth directorate* (1975)
3 *Flowers of the forest* (1980)
Oxford gambit
4 *Valley of the fox* (1982)

Peter Marrell series
Hopkins, Stanley
1 *Murder by inches* (1943)
2 *Parchment key* (1944)

Peter Marshall series
Marshall, Catherine
1 *Man called Peter* (1951)
Biography of the author's husband
2 *To live again* (1957)
The author's life after her husband's death

Peter Marsham and Tommy Lumb series
Cross, Laurence
see **Tommy Lumb and Peter Marsham series**

Peter McGarr series
Gill, Bartholomew
see **Inspector Peter McGarr series**

Peter Mitchell series
Cooke, Geoffrey Walter
1 *Death can wait* (1957)
2 *Death takes a dive* (1962)
3 *Death is the end* (1965)

Peter Mohune series
Groom, Pelham
1 *Sabotage unlimited* (1938)
2 *What are your angels now?* (1943)
Mohune's nine lives
3 *Little hanging men* (1946)
4 *Fourth seal* (1948)
5 *Purple twilight* (1948)

Peter Munro series
Black, Ian Stuart
1 *Man on the bridge* (1975)
2 *Journey to a safe place* (1979)

Peter Pan series
This sequence has three authors
Barrie, James Matthew
1 *Peter and Wendy* (1911)
Peter Pan and Wendy
Alternative title: The boy who would not grow up; based on the play, *Peter Pan* originally produced in 1904
2 *Peter Pan in Kensington Gardens* (1906)
Based on *The little white bird, or, Adventures in Kensington Gardens*, 1902
3 *When Wendy grew up* (1957)
An afterthought; based on the play *Peter Pan, an afterthought*, first produced in 1908
Adair, Gilbert
4 *Peter Pan and the only children* (1987)
Korman, Justine
5 *Peter Pan saves the day* (1988)

Peter Parsons series
Scott, Jack S
see **Chief Inspector Peter Parsons series**

Peter Pennington series
Snell, Edmund
1 *Yellow seven* (1923)
2 *Yellow Jacket* (1936)

Peter Perry series
Campbell, Michael
1 *Peter Perry* (1956)
2 *Nothing doing* (1970)

Peter Pig series
Wada, Yoshiomi
Translated from the Japanese
1 *Peter Pig's telephone book* (1985)
2 *Peter Pig's number play book* (1986)

Peter Piper series
Long, Amelia Reynolds
1 *Corpse at the Quill Club* (1940)
2 *Four feet in the grave* (1941)
3 *Murder goes south* (1942)
4 *Murder by scripture* (1942)
5 *Death looks down* (1945)
6 *It's death, my darling* (1948)
7 *Lady saw red* (1951)

Peter Piper series
Mavity, Nancy Barr
1 *Tule Marsh murder* (1929)
2 *Body on the floor* (1929)
3 *Case of the missing sandals* (1930)
4 *Other bullet* (1930)
5 *Man who didn't mind hanging* (1932)
He didn't mind hanging

Peter Pipers series
Moss, Elaine
1 *Peter Pipers go to the fair* (1983)
2 *Peter Pipers in the garden* (1983)
3 *Peter Pipers at the wildlife park* (1983)
4 *Peter Pipers' birthday party* (1983)

Peter Ponsonby series
Leslie, Jean
1 *One cried murder* (1945)
2 *Two faced murder* (1946)
3 *Three-cornered murder* (1947)

Peter Possum series
Hibberd, Jean
1 *Adventures of Peter Possum and his friends* (1986)
2 *Further adventures of Peter Possum and his friends* (1988)

Peter Proud series
Ehrlich, Max
1 *Reincarnation of Peter Proud* (1974)
2 *Reincarnation in Venice* (1979)
Bond

Peter Quayle series
Trent, Paul
1 *Quayle of the Yard* (1935)
2 *Quayle's first case* (1936)

Peter Quentin series
Quest, Rodney
1 *Cerberus murders* (1969)
2 *Murder with a vengeance* (1971)
3 *Death of a sinner* (1971)

Peter Quint series
Austin, Hugh
1 *It couldn't be murder* (1935)
2 *Murder in triplicate* (1935)
3 *Murder of a matriarch* (1936)
4 *Upside down murders* (1937)
5 *Cock's tail murder* (1938)

Peter Rabbit series
Burgess, Thornton Waldo
1 *Peter Rabbit's carrots* (1933)
2 *Peter Rabbit proves a friend* (1940)
Peter Rabbit goes scouting
3 *Peter Rabbit and Reddy Fox* (1954)
Peter Cottontail and Reddy Fox
4 *Little Peter Cottontail* (1956)
Companion volumes: *Peter Cottontail's own paint book*, 1925, *Peter Rabbit's gardening book*, by Sarah Garland, 1983

Peter Rabbit series
Potter, Beatrix
1 *Tale of Peter Rabbit* (1901)
Revised edition 1902
2 *Tailor of Gloucester* (1902)
Revised edition 1903
3 *Tale of Squirrel Nutkin* (1903)
4 *Tale of Benjamin Bunny* (1904)
5 *Tale of two bad mice* (1904)
6 *Tale of Mrs Tiggy-Winkle* (1905)
7 *Pie and the patty-pan* (1905)
Tale of the pie and the patty-pan
8 *Tale of Mister Jeremy Fisher* (1906)
9 *Story of a fierce bad rabbit* (1906)
10 *Story of Miss Moppet* (1906)
11 *Tale of Tom Kitten* (1907)
12 *Tale of Jemima Puddle-Duck* (1908)
13 *Roly-poly pudding* (1908)
Tale of Samuel Whiskers
14 *Tale of the flopsy bunnies* (1909)
15 *Ginger and Pickles* (1909)
16 *Tale of Mrs Tittlemouse* (1910)
17 *Tale of Timmy Tiptoes* (1911)
18 *Tale of Mister Tod* (1912)
19 *Tale of Pigling Bland* (1913)
20 *Tale of Johnny Town-Mouse* (1918)
21 *Tale of Little Pig Robinson* (1930)
Companion volumes: *Peter Rabbit's painting book*, 1911, *Tom Kitten's painting book*, 1917, *Jemima Puddle-Duck's paint-*

ing book, 1925, *Jeremy Fisher's painting book*, 1954, *Peter Rabbit's almanac for 1929*, 1928, *Yours affectionately, Peter Rabbit, miniature letters*, edited by Anne Emerson, 1983

Peter Rabbit verse series
Potter, Beatrix
1 *Appley Dapply's nursery rhymes* (1917)
2 *Cecily Parsley's nursery rhymes* (1922)
One volume edition entitled *Beatrix Potter's nursery rhyme book*, 1984

Peter Robin, Alistair and Elizabeth series
Fitzgerald, Hilary
see **Alastair, Elizabeth and Peter Robin series**

Peter Rourke series
Cooke, David Coxe
1 *C/o American Embassy* (1967)
2 *Fourteenth agent* (1967)
3 *Sleep with nightmares* (1969)

Peter Ruff series
Oppenheim, Edward Phillips
Short stories
1 *Double four* (1911)
Peter Ruff and the double four
2 *Peter Ruff* (1912)

Peter, Sandy and David series
Hunter, Evan
see **David, Peter and Sandy series**

Peter Scarlett series
Horler, Sydney
1 *Scarlett, Special Branch* (1950)
2 *Scarlett gets the kidnapper* (1951)

Peter Schlemihl series
This sequence has two authors
Chamisso, Adalbert von
1 *Shadowless man* (1814)
Peter Schlemihl
Original edition entitled *Peter Schlemihls wundersame Geschichte*
Wood, George
2 *Peter Schlemihl in America* (1848)
Originally published anonymously
3 *Future life* (1858)
Gates wide open
Alternative title: Scenes in another world

Peter series
Baxter, Biddy
see **Blue Peter series**
Borie, Lysbeth Boyd
see **Poems for Peter series**

Peter series
Bruce, Mary Grant
1 *Told by Peter* (1938)
2 *Peter and Company* (1940)

Peter series
Conyers, Dorothea
1 *Peter's pedigree* (1904)
2 *Aunt Jane and Uncle James* (1908)

Peter series
Corson, Hazel Wyman
1 *Peter and the rocket ship* (1955)
2 *Peter and the two-hour moon* (1956)
3 *Peter and the moon trip* (1957)
4 *Peter and the unlucky rocket* (1959)
5 *Peter and the big balloon* (1959)
6 *Peter, the rocket sitter* (1964)
7 *Peter and the rocket fishing trip* (1964)

Peter series
Douglas, Lloyd Cassel
see **Apostle Peter series**

Peter series
Haynes, Ambrose
1 *Peter's adventurous holiday* (1953)
2 *Peter's return* (1955)

Peter series
Keats, Ezra Jack
1 *Snowy day* (1962)
2 *Whistle for Willie* (1964)
3 *Peter's chair* (1967)
4 *Letter to Amy* (1968)
5 *Goggles!* (1969)
6 *Hi, Cat!* (1970)
7 *Pet show!* (1972)

Peter series
Kingman, Lee
1 *Peter's long walk* (1953)
2 *Peter's pony* (1963)

Peter series
Mogridge, Stephen
1 *Peter and the flying saucers* (1954)
2 *Peter and the atomic valley* (1955)
3 *Peter and the moon bomb* (1956)
4 *Peter and the flying submarine* (1957)
5 *Peter's Denmark adventure* (1958)

Peter series
Peter, Laurence Johnston
1 *Peter principle* (1969)
Why things always go wrong; co-author, Raymond Hull
2 *Peter prescription* (1972)
How to make things go right
3 *Peter plan* (1975)
A proposal for survival
4 *Peter's quotations* (1977)
Ideas for our times
5 *Peter's people and their marvelous ideas* (1979)
6 *Peter's almanac* (1982)
7 *Why things go wrong* (1984)
The Peter principle revisited
8 *Peter pyramid* (1987)

Peter series
Schermele, Willy
1 *Peter and his magic pebble* (1953)
2 *Peter and his pets* (1965)
3 *Peter and his playmates* (1965)
4 *Peter and his pony* (1965)
5 *Peter and his puppy* (1965)

Peter Shandy series
Macleod, Charlotte
see **Professor Peter Shandy series**

Peter Shane series
Bonnamy, Francis
1 *Death by appointment* (1931)
2 *Death on a dude ranch* (1937)
3 *Dead reckoning* (1943)
4 *Rope of sand* (1944)
5 *King is dead on Queen Street* (1945)
6 *Portrait of the artist as a dead man* (1947)
Self-portrait of murder
Murder as a fine art
7 *Blood and thirsty* (1949)
8 *Man in the mist* (1951)

Peter Slavine series
Sava, George
1 *Boy in Samarkand* (1950)
2 *Caught by revolution* (1952)
3 *Flight from the palace* (1953)
4 *Pursuit in the desert* (1955)

Peter Strangely series
Black, Elizabeth Best
1 *Revenelle riddle* (1933)
2 *Crime of the chromium bowl* (1934)

Peter Styles series
Philips, Judson Pentecost
1 *Laughter trap* (1964)
2 *Black glass city* (1964)
3 *Twisted people* (1965)
4 *Wings of madness* (1966)
5 *Thursday's follow* (1967)
6 *Hot summer killing* (1968)
7 *Nightmare at dawn* (1970)
8 *Escape a killer* (1971)
9 *Vanishing senator* (1972)
10 *Larkspur conspiracy* (1973)
11 *Power killers* (1974)
12 *Walk a crooked mile* (1975)
13 *Backlash* (1976)
14 *Five roads to death* (1977)
15 *Murder arranged* (1977)
16 *Why murder?* (1979)
17 *Death is a dirty trick* (1980)
18 *Murder as the curtain rises* (1981)
19 *Target for tragedy* (1982)

Peter Tangent series
Sanders, Lawrence
1 *Tangent objective* (1976)
2 *Tangent factor* (1978)

Peter Thorne series
Vardeman, Robert Edward
1 *Screaming knife* (1990)
2 *Resonance of blood* (1992)

Peter Torres and Laredo Garrett series
Moore, Arthur
see **Bluestar series**

Peter Trant series
Kenyon, James William
1 *Peter Trant, cricketer-detective* (1944)
2 *Peter Trant, heavyweight champion* (1946)
3 *Peter Trant, speed king* (1949)

Peter Trees series
Q, John
1 *Bunnies* (1965)
2 *Survivor* (1965)
3 *Tournament* (1966)

Peter trilogy
Cheesman, Lilian
1 *Peter* (1916)
Daddy's boy and mother's little man
2 *Big Peter's little Peter* (1918)
3 *That curly headed rogue* (1920)

Peter trilogy
Tepper, Sheri S
see **True game trilogy**

Peter Ward series
Saint John, David
1 *On hazardous duty* (1965)
Hazardous duty
2 *Return from Vorkuta* (1965)
3 *Towers of silence* (1966)
Also published under the author's real name Everette Howard Hunt
4 *Festival for spies* (1966)
5 *Venus probe* (1966)
6 *One of our agents is missing* (1967)
7 *Mongol mask* (1968)
8 *Sorcerers* (1969)
Also published under the author's real name Everette Howard Hunt
9 *Diabolus* (1971)
10 *Coven* (1972)

Peter Wells series
Whitelaw, David
1 *Little hour of Peter Wells* (1913)
2 *Wolf's Crag* (1936)
The little hour of Peter Wells, junior

Peter Westcott series
Walpole, Hugh
1 *Fortitude* (1913)
A true and faithful account of the education of an explorer
2 *Young enchanted* (1921)
3 *Duchess of Wrexe* (1914)
Her decline and death
4 *Hans Frost* (1929)
5 *Captain Nicholas* (1934)

Peter Wimsey series
Sayers, Dorothy Leigh
see **Lord Peter Wimsey series**

Peter Winston series
Winston, Peter
see **Adjusters series**

Peterkin series
Boon, Emilie
1 *Peterkin meets a star* (1983)
2 *Peterkin's wet walk* (1983)
3 *It's spring, Peterkin* (1986)

Peterkin series
Hale, Lucretia Peabody
1 *Peterkin papers* (1880)
2 *Last of the Peterkins* (1886)
One volume edition entitled *The complete Peterkin papers*, 1960; selections published as *Stories from the Peterkin papers*, 1984

Peterloo trilogy
Blake, M Glaiser
see **Ayesthorpe trilogy**

Peters series
Bosworth, Ellen
see **Shelley Peters series**
Kaminsky, Stuart Melvin
see **Toby Peters series**
Law, Janice
see **Anna Peters series**
Moore, Harry F S
see **Casey Peters series**
Neels, Betty
see **Adelaide Peters series**

Peterson series
Cody, James P
see **Brian Peterson series**

Pethi and Tini series
Macdonald, Shelagh
1 *Circle of stones* (1973)
2 *Five from me, five from you* (1974)

Petland photo tales series
Frees, Harry Whittier
1 *Mister Bunny and the magic pool* (1932)
2 *Pot of gold at rainbow's end* (1932)
3 *King who never smiled* (1932)
4 *Circus day at Catnip Center* (1932)
5 *Kitty's first day at Catnip School* (1932)

Petrella series
Gilbert, Michael Francis
see **Patrick Petrella series**

Petrie series
Turner, John Victor
see **Amos Petrie series**

Petronella and Peregrine Pig series
Hauptmann, Tatjana
1 *Day in the life of Petronella Pig* (1978)
Original edition entitled *Ein Tag in Leben der Dorothea Wutz*
2 *Hurray for Peregrine Pig* (1979)
Original edition entitled *Hurra, Eberhard Wutz ist wieder da*

Petros series
Anderson, James
see **Mikael Petros series**

Pets, Inc. series
Armstrong, Jennifer
1 *Puppy ptoject* (1990)

2 *Too many pets* (1990)
3 *Hillary to the rescue* (1990)
4 *That champion chimp* (1990)

Pets series
Herriot, James
1 *Moses, the kitten* (1984)
2 *Only one woof* (1985)
3 *Christmas Day kitten* (1986)
4 *Bonny's big day* (1987)

Pettengill series
Rowe, Anne
see **Inspector Pettengill series**

Pettigrew series
Clark, Leonard
see **Mister Pettigrew series**
Hare, Cyril
see **Francis Pettigrew series**

Petunia Best and Max Frend series
Chetwynd, Bridget
1 *Death has ten thousand doors* (1951)
2 *Rubies, emeralds and diamonds* (1952)

Petunia series
Duvoisin, Roger
1 *Petunia* (1950)
2 *Petunia and the song* (1951)
3 *Petunia's Christmas* (1952)
4 *Petunia takes a trip* (1953)
5 *Petunia, beware!* (1958)
6 *Petunia, I love you* (1965)
7 *Petunia's treasure* (1975)

Petworth series
Aiken, Joan
1 *Smile of the stranger* (1978)
2 *Lightning tree* (1980)
Weeping ash

Peverills and Folletts series
Leslie, Doris
see **Folletts and Peverills series**

Pewit's nest series
Finley, Martha Farquharson
1 *Pewit's nest* (1876)
2 *Harry's fourth of July* (1876)
3 *Harry's ride* (1876)
4 *Harry's walks* (1876)
5 *Harry's little sister* (1876)
6 *Harry's Christmas* (1876)
7 *Harry and his chickens* (1876)
8 *Aunt Kitty's fowls* (1876)
9 *Harry's grandma* (1876)
10 *Rose and Robbie* (1876)
11 *Harry at Aunt Jane's* (1876)
12 *Harry and his cousins* (1876)

Pewter series
Wainwright, John
1 *Crystallised carbon pig* (1966)
2 *Web of silence* (1968)
3 *Take-over man* (1969)
4 *Prynter's devil* (1970)
5 *Cause for a killing* (1974)

Peyton children series
Reid, Meta Mayne
1 *All because of Dawks* (1955)
2 *Dawks does it again* (1956)
3 *Dawks on Robbers' Mountain* (1957)
4 *Dawks and the duchess* (1958)

Peyton Place series
This sequence has two authors
Metalious, Grace
1 *Peyton Place* (1957)
2 *Return to Peyton Place* (1959)
Fuller, Roger
3 *Again Peyton Place* (1967)
4 *Carnival at Peyton Place* (1968)
5 *Pleasures of Peyton Place* (1968)
6 *Secrets of Peyton Place* (1968)
7 *Evils of Peyton Place* (1969)
8 *Hero in Peyton Place* (1969)

Phaid the Gambler series
Farren, Mick
see **Song of Phaid the Gambler series**

Phantom battleship series
Chesterton, Rupert
1 *Phantom battleship* (1909)
2 *Captain of the Phantom* (1921)

Phantom Detective series
Wallace, Robert
House pseudonym; the dates of titles in this sequence are those of their original magazine publication
1 *Scarlet menace* (1933)
2 *Jewels of doom* (1933)
3 *Milestones of murder* (1934)
4 *Crimson killer* (1934)
5 *Prince of murder* (1935)
6 *Specter of death* (1936)
7 *Sign of the scar* (1936)
8 *Dancing doll murders* (1937)
9 *Beast-king murders* (1937)
10 *Corpse parade* (1937)
11 *Fangs of murder* (1938)
12 *Tycoon of crime* (1938)
13 *Yello shadows of death* (1938)
14 *Broadway murders* (1938)
15 *Counterfeit killers* (1938)
16 *Death glow* (1938)
17 *Forty thieves* (1939)
18 *Death under contract* (1939)
19 *Money mad murders* (1939)
20 *Phantom's gamble with death* (1940)
21 *Murder trail* (1940)
Originally published as *The Phantom's murder trail*
22 *Daggers of Kali* (1940)
Originally published as *The Phantom and the daggers of Kali*
23 *Uniformed killers* (1940)
Originally published as *The Phantom and the uniformed killers*
24 *Vampire murders* (1940)
Originally published as *The Phantom and the vampire murders*
25 *Melody murders* (1940)
Originally published as *The Phantom and the melody murders*
26 *Green glare murders* (1940)
Originally published as *The Phantom and the green glare murders*
27 *Television murders* (1940)
28 *Curio murders* (1941)
Originally published as *The Phantom and the curio murders*
29 *Trail to death* (1941)
30 *Murder stalks a billion* (1941)
31 *Arsenal of death* (1942)
32 *Murder makes a movie* (1942)
33 *Murder cuts diamonds* (1942)
34 *Stones of Satan* (1943)
35 *Murder money* (1943)
36 *Murder under the big top* (1943)

Phantom horse series
Pullein-Thompson, Christine
1 *Phantom horse* (1955)
2 *Phantom horse comes home* (1970)
3 *Phantom horse goes to Ireland* (1972)
4 *Phantom horse in danger* (1980)
5 *Phantom horse goes to Scotland* (1981)

Phantom Lobster series
Walmsley, Leo
1 *Foreigners* (1935)
2 *Three fevers* (1932)
3 *Sally Lunn* (1937)
4 *Phantom Lobster* (1933)
5 *Love in the sun* (1939)
6 *Golden waterwheel* (1954)
7 *Happy ending* (1957)
8 *Paradise Creek* (1963)

Phantom series
Ainsworth, Ruth
see **Ghostly tales series**

Phantom series
Falk, Lee
1 *Story of the Phantom* (1972)
2 *Phantom and the slave market of Macar* (1972)
Co-author: Basil Copper
3 *Phantom and the Scorpia menace* (1972)
Co-author: Basil Copper
4 *Veiled lady* (1973)
Co-author: Frank S Shawn
5 *Golden circle* (1973)
Co-author: Frank S Shawn
6 *Mysterious ambassador* (1973)
7 *Mystery of the sea horse* (1973)
Co-author: Frank S Shawn
8 *Hydra monster* (1973)
Co-author: Frank S Shawn
9 *Killer's town* (1973)
10 *Goggle-eyed pirates* (1974)
Co-author: Frank S Shawn
11 *Swamp rats* (1974)
Co-author: Frank S Shawn
12 *Vampires and the witch* (1974)
13 *Island of dogs* (1975)
Co-author: Warren Shanahan
14 *Assassins* (1975)
Co-author: Warren Shanahan
15 *Curse of the two-headed bull* (1975)
Co-author: Warren Shanahan

Phantom Valley series
Beach, Lynn
1 *Evil one* (1991)
2 *Dark* (1991)
3 *Scream of the cat* (1992)
4 *Stranger in the mirror* (1992)
5 *Spell* (1992)
6 *Dead man's secret* (1992)
7 *In the mummy's tomb* (1992)
8 *Headless ghost* (1992)
9 *Curse of the claw* (1993)

Phantoms series
Dunn, Pauline
Based on *Phantoms*, by Dean Ray Koontz, 1983
1 *Demonic color* (1990)
2 *Crawling dark* (1991)

Phantoms series
Ross, Marilyn
1 *Phantom of Fog Island* (1971)
2 *Phantom of the swamp* (1972)
3 *Night of the phantom* (1972)
4 *Phantom of the thirteenth floor* (1975)
5 *Phantom wedding* (1976)
6 *Phantom of the snow* (1977)

Pharamaul series
Monsarrat, Nicholas
1 *Tribe that lost its head* (1956)
2 *Richer than all his tribe* (1968)

Pharaoh Love series
Baxt, George
1 *Queer kind of death* (1966)
2 *Swing low, sweet Harriet* (1967)
3 *Topsy and evil* (1968)
4 *Queer kind of love* (1994)

Phelan and Caldwell series
Ozaki, Milton K
see **Professor Caldwell and Lieutenant Phelan series**

Phelan family series
Kennedy, William
1 *Billy Phelan's greatest game* (1978)
2 *Ironweed* (1983)

Phelan series
Duff, James P
see **Johnny Phelan series**
Kyd, Thomas
see **Sam Phelan series**

Phelps series
Childerness, George
see **Chet Phelps series**

Phenwick women series
Kimbrough, Katheryn
1 *Augusta, the first* (1975)
2 *Jane, the courageous* (1975)
3 *Margaret, the faithful* (1975)
4 *Patricia, the beautiful* (1975)
5 *Rachel, the possessed* (1975)
6 *Susannah, the righteous* (1975)
7 *Rebecca, the mysterious* (1975)
8 *Joanne, the unpredictable* (1976)
9 *Olivia, the tormented* (1976)
10 *Harriet, the haunted* (1976)
11 *Nancy, the daring* (1976)
12 *Marcia, the innocent* (1977)
13 *Kate, the curious* (1976)
14 *Ilene, the superstitious* (1977)
15 *Millijoy, the determined* (1977)
16 *Barbara, the valiant* (1977)
17 *Ruth, the unsuspecting* (1977)
18 *Ophelia, the anxious* (1977)
19 *Dorothy, the terrified* (1977)
20 *Ann, the gentle* (1978)
21 *Nellie, the obvious* (1978)
22 *Isabelle, the frantic* (1978)
23 *Evelyn, the ambitious* (1978)
24 *Louise, the restless* (1978)
25 *Polly, the worried* (1979)
26 *Yvonne, the confident* (1979)
27 *Joyce, the beloved* (1979)
28 *Augusta, the second* (1979)
29 *Carol, the pursued* (1979)
30 *Katherine, the returned* (1980)
31 *Peggy, the concerned* (1980)
32 *Olga, the disillusioned* (1980)
33 *Phyllis, the cautious* (1980)
34 *Ursula, the proud* (1980)
35 *Letitia, the dreamer* (1981)
36 *Alexandria, the ambivalent* (1981)
37 *Romula, the dedicated* (1981)
38 *Laura, the imperiled* (1981)
39 *Iris, the bewitched* (1982)
40 *Belinda, the impatient* (1982)

Phibes series
Goldstein, William
see **Doctor Phibes series**

Phil Bradley series
Boone, Silas K
1 *Phil Bradley's Mountain Boys* (1915)
Alternative title: The Birch Bark Lodge
2 *Phil Bradley at the wheel* (1915)
Alternative title: The Mountain Boys' mad auto dash
3 *Phil Bradley's shooting box* (1915)
Alternative title: The Mountain Boys on Currituck Sound
4 *Phil Bradley's snowshoe trail* (1915)
Alternative title: The Mountain Boys in the Canadian wilds
5 *Phil Bradley's winning* (1917)
6 *Phil Bradley's big exploit* (1919)

Phil Kramer series
Kruger, Paul
1 *Weep for Willow Green* (1966)
2 *Weave a wicked web* (1967)
3 *If the shroud fits* (1969)
4 *Bronze claws* (1972)
5 *Cold ones* (1972)

Phil Moss and Inspector Colin Thane series
Knox, Bill
see **Inspector Colin Thane and Phil Moss series**

Phil Sanderson series
Grex, Leo
1 *Violent keepsake* (1967)
2 *Hard kill* (1969)

Phil Sherman series
Smith, Don
see **Secret mission series**

Phil, the showman series
Norris, Stanley
1 *Phil, the showman* (1902)
Alternative title: Life in the sawdust ring
2 *Young showman's rivals* (1903)
Ups and downs of the road
3 *Young showman's pluck* (1903)
Alternative title: An unknown rider in the ring
4 *Young showman's triumph* (1903)
Alternative title: A grand tour on the road

Phileas Fogg series
This sequence has two authors
Verne, Jules
1 *Tour of the world in eighty days* (1872)
Around the world in eighty days
Round the world in eighty days
Original edition entitled *Le tour du monde en quatre-vingt jours*
Farmer, Philip Jose
2 *Other log of Phileas Fogg* (1973)

Philip Cabot series
McDougald, Roman
1 *Deaths of Lora Karen* (1944)
2 *Whistling legs* (1945)
3 *Blushing monkey* (1953)

Philip Embree series
Bosse, Malcolm Joseph
1 *Warlords* (1983)
2 *Fire in heaven* (1986)

Philip Hazard series
Stuart, Vivian
see **Commander Philip Hazard series**

Philip Holt series
Durbridge, Francis
1 *Desperate people* (1966)
2 *Dead to the world* (1967)

Philip Hunter series
Procter, Maurice
see **Superintendent Philip Hunter series**

Philip Jose Farmer's The dungeon series
Lupoff, Richard Allen
see **Dungeon series**

Philip Maccray series
Jerome, Owen Fox
1 *Hand of horror* (1927)
2 *Red kite clue* (1928)
3 *Murder at Avalon Arms* (1930)
4 *Five assassins* (1958)
5 *Leave eveything to me* (1959)

Philip Marlowe series
Chandler, Raymond
1 *Big sleep* (1939)
2 *Farewell, my lovely* (1940)
3 *High window* (1942)
4 *Lady in the lake* (1943)
Numbers 1-4 also published in one volume entitled *The Raymond Chandler omnibus*, 1964
5 *Little sister* (1949)
Marlowe
6 *Simple art of murder* (1950)
Also published in three volumes entitled *Trouble is my business*, 1951, *Pick-up on Noon Street*, 1952, *The simple art of murder*, 1953
7 *Long goodbye* (1953)
8 *Playback* (1958)
9 *Poodle Springs* (1989)
Completed by Robert Brown Parker
Companion volume: *Raymond Chandler's Philip Marlowe, a centennial celebration*, edited by Byron Preiss, 1988

Philip Massel series
Golding, Louis
1 *Forward from Babylon* (1920)
2 *Give up your lovers* (1930)
Companion volume: *Day of Atonement*, 1925

Philip McAlpine series
Diment, Adam
1 *Dolly dolly spy* (1967)
2 *Great spy race* (1968)
3 *Bang bang birds* (1968)
4 *Think Inc.* (1971)

Philip Odell series
Powell, Lester
1 *Count of six* (1948)
2 *Shadow play* (1949)
3 *Spot the lady* (1950)
4 *Still of night* (1952)
5 *Black casket* (1953)

Philip Quest series
Townend, Peter
1 *Out of focus* (1971)
2 *Zoom!* (1972)
3 *Fisheye* (1974)
4 *Triple exposure* (1977)

Philip Saint George series
Avallone, Michael
see **Satan Sleuth series**

Philip Saint Ives series
Bleeck, Oliver
1 *Brass go-between* (1969)
2 *Protocol for a kidnapping* (1971)
3 *Procane chronicle* (1971)
Thief who painted sunlight
Saint Ives
4 *Highbinders* (1973)
5 *No questions asked* (1976)

Philip Scott series
Howard, Hartley
1 *Department K* (1964)
Assignment K
2 *Eye of the hurricane* (1968)

Philip series
Pickering, Robert Easton
see **Dick Philip series**

Philip Sparrow and Morris Zapp series
Lodge, David
see **Rummidge University series**

Philip Spence and Margot Franklin series
Jenkins, Jerry Bruce
see **Margo Franklin and Philip Spence series**

Philip Stevenson series
Elder, Michael
see **Mindslip series**

Philip Strong and James Matthews series
Oursler, William
1 *Trial of Vincent Doon* (1941)
2 *Folio on Florence White* (1942)

Philip Tolefree series
Walling, Robert Alfred John
1 *Fatal five minutes* (1932)
2 *Behind the yellow blind* (1932)
Murder at midnight
3 *Follow the blue car* (1933)
In time for murder
4 *Tolliver case* (1933)
Prove it, Mr Tolliver
5 *Eight to nine* (1934)
Bachelor flat mystery
6 *Legacy of death* (1934)
Five suspects
7 *Cat and the corpse* (1935)
Corpse in the green pajamas
8 *Corpse in the coppice* (1935)
Mister Tolefree's reluctant witnesses
9 *Corpse in the crimson slippers* (1936)
10 *Corpse with the floating foot* (1936)
Mystery of Mister Mock
11 *Corpse with the dirty face* (1936)
Crime in Cumberland Court
12 *Bury him deeper* (1937)
Marooned with murder
13 *Coroner doubts* (1938)
Corpse with the blue cravat
14 *More than one serpent* (1938)
Corpse with the grimy glove
15 *Dust in the vault* (1939)
Corpse with the blistered hand
16 *They liked Entwistle* (1939)
Corpse with the red-headed friend
17 *Why did Trethewy die?* (1940)
Spider and the fly
18 *By hook or by crook* (1941)
By hook or crook
19 *Castle Dinas* (1942)
Corpse with the eerie eye
20 *Doodled asterisk* (1943)
21 *Corpse without a clue* (1944)
22 *Late unlamented* (1948)
23 *Corpse with the missing watch* (1949)

Philip Tracy series
Ashbrook, Harriette
1 *Murder of Cecily Thane* (1930)
2 *Murder of Steven Kester* (1931)
3 *Murder of Sigurd Sharon* (1933)
4 *Most immoral murder* (1935)
5 *Murder makes murder* (1937)
6 *Murder comes back* (1940)
7 *Purple onion mystery* (1941)
Murder on Friday

Philip Trent series
Bentley, Edmund Clerihew
1 *Trent's last case* (1913)
Woman in black
Revised edition 1929
2 *Trent's own case* (1936)
3 *Trent intervenes* (1938)
Short stories

Philipa Lowe series
Ormerod, Roger
1 *Hung in the balance* (1990)
2 *When the old man died* (1991)
3 *Bury him darkly* (1991)
4 *Key to the case* (1992)
5 *Third time fatal* (1992)
6 *Shot at nothing* (1993)
7 *Mask of innocence* (1994)
8 *And hope to die* (1994)

Philippa trilogy
Gerry, Margarita Spalding
1 *Philippa's fortune* (1921)
2 *Philippa at the chateau* (1922)
3 *Philippa's experiments* (1923)

Philips trilogy
Ulyatt, Kenneth
see **Portugee Philips trilogy**

Philis series
Perry, Ritchie
1 *Fall guy* (1972)
2 *Nowhere man* (1973)
Hard man to kill
3 *Ticket to ride* (1973)
4 *Holiday with a vengeance* (1974)
5 *Your money and your wife* (1975)
6 *One good death deserves another* (1976)
7 *Dead end* (1977)
8 *Dutch courage* (1978)
9 *Bishop's pawn* (1979)
10 *Grand slam* (1980)
11 *Fool's mate* (1981)
12 *Foul up* (1982)
13 *Kolwezi* (1985)
14 *Creepy tale* (1989)

Phillip Gerard and Jocelyn O'Roarke series
Dentinger, Jane
see **Jocelyn O'Roarke and Phillip Gerard series**

Phillip Maddison series
Williamson, Henry
see **Chronicles of ancient sunlight series**

Phillip Magellan series
McCurtin, Peter
see **Marksman series**

Phillips series
Zimmerman, R D
see **Maddy and Alex Phillips series**

Philo Vance series
Van Dine, S S
1 *Benson murder case* (1926)
2 *Canary murder case* (1927)
3 *Greene murder case* (1928)
4 *Bishop murder case* (1929)
5 *Scarab murder case* (1930)
6 *Kennel murder case* (1933)
7 *Dragon murder case* (1933)
8 *Casino murder case* (1934)
9 *Garden murder case* (1935)
10 *Kidnap murder case* (1936)
11 *Gracie Allen murder case* (1938)
Smell of murder
12 *Winter murder case* (1939)

Philosophic studies series
Balzac, Honore de
1 *Wild ass's skin* (1831)
Fatal skin
Original edition entitled *La peau de chagrin*
2 *Christ in Flanders* (1831)
Jesus Christ in Flanders
Original edition entitled *Jesus-Christ en Flandre*
3 *Melmoth reconciled* (1835)
Original edition entitled *Melmoth reconcilie*
4 *Massimilla Doni* (1839)
5 *Unknown masterpiece* (1831)
Original edition entitled *Le chef d'ouevre inconnu*
6 *Gambara* (1839)
7 *Quest of the absolute* (1834)
Original edition entitled *La recherche de l'absolu*
8 *Child accursed* (1831)
Father's curse
Original edition entitled *L'enfant maudit*
9 *Adieu* (1830)
Farewell
Original edition entitled *Adieu*
10 *Maranas* (1832)
Original edition entitled *Les Marana*
11 *Conscript* (1831)
Original edition entitled *Le requisitionnaire*
12 *Executioner* (1831)
Original edition entitled *El verdugo*
13 *Seaside tragedy* (1834)
Seashore drama
Original edition entitled *Un drame au bord de la mer*
14 *Master Cornelius* (1832)
Original edition entitled *Maitre Cornelius*
15 *Red House* (1831)
Red Inn
Original edition entitled *L'Auberge Rouge*
16 *About Catherine de Medici* (1843)
Original edition entitled *Sur Catherine de Medici*
16.1 *Calvinist martyr* (1843)
16.2 *Confession of Ruggieri* (1843)
16.3 *Two dreams* (1843)

Philosophic studies series

17 *Elixir of long life* (1831)
Original edition entitled *L'elixir de longue vie*
18 *Exiles* (1831)
Original edition entitled *Les proscrits*
19 *Louis Lambert* (1832)
20 *Seraphita* (1835)

Philpotts series
Caldwell, Alfred Betts
see **Freddy Philpotts series**

Philura trilogy
Kingsley, Florence Morse
see **Miss Philura trilogy**

Phin series
Sladek, John Thomas
see **Thackeray Phin series**

Phineas Spinnet series
Soutar, Andrew
1 *Hanging sword!* (1933)
2 *Night of horror* (1934)
3 *Eight three five* (1935)
4 *Facing east* (1936)
5 *Museum mystery* (1936)
6 *Black spot mystery* (1938)
7 *Silent accuser* (1938)
8 *One page missing* (1938)
9 *Chain murder* (1939)
10 *Stranger came to dinner* (1939)
11 *Wolves and the lamb* (1940)
12 *Strange case of Sir Merton Quest* (1940)
13 *Motive for the crime* (1941)
14 *Study in suspense* (1941)

Phipps and Walsh series
Hunt, Richard
see **Chief Inspector Walsh and Constable Brenda Phipps series**

Phipps-Mangot series
Hackforth-Jones, Gilbert
see **Commander Wally Phipps-Mangot series**

Phoebe and Ernest series
Gillmore, Inez Haynes
1 *Phoebe and Ernest* (1910)
2 *Phoebe, Ernest and Cupid* (1912)

Phoebe Gray series
Brown, Helen Dawes
see **Anna Lavinia series**

Phoebe Siegel series
Prowell, Sandra West
1 *By evil means* (1993)
2 *Killing of Monday Brown* (1994)

Phoenix Force series
Pendleton, Don
Numbers 1-3 of this sequence are published under the joint authorship od Don Pendleton with Gar Wilson which is a house pseudonym
1 *Argentine deadline* (1982)
2 *Guerilla games* (1982)
3 *Atlantic scramble* (1982)
Wilson, Gar
From number 4 this sequence is published under the house pseudonym Gar Wilson alone which is used by several authors including William Fieldhouse, Robert Hoskins, Paul Glen Newman, Thomas P Ramirez, Rex Swenson whose authorship is indicated against those titles where it is known
4 *Tigers of justice* (1983)
[Fieldhouse]
5 *Fury bombs* (1983)
[Hoskins]
6 *White hell* (1983)
[Ramirez]
7 *Dragon's kill* (1983)
[Fieldhouse]
8 *Asian hellbox* (1983)
[Ramirez; Swenson]
9 *Ultimate terror* (1984)
[Fieldhouse]
10 *Korean killground* (1984)
[Ramirez]
11 *Return to Armageddon* (1984)
[Fieldhouse]
12 *Black alchemists* (1984)
[Fieldhouse]
13 *Harvest hell* (1984)
[Fieldhouse]
14 *Phoenix in flames* (1984)
[Fieldhouse]
15 *Viper factor* (1984)
[Fieldhouse]
16 *No rules, no referee* (1985)
[Fieldhouse]
17 *Welcome to the feast* (1985)
[Fieldhouse]
18 *Night of the thuggie* (1985)
[Fieldhouse]
19 *Sea of savages* (1985)
[Fieldhouse]
20 *Tooth and claw* (1985)
[Fieldhouse]
21 *Twisted cross* (1985)
[Fieldhouse; Newman]
22 *Time bomb* (1986)
[Fieldhouse]
23 *Chip off the bloc* (1986)
[Newman]
24 *Doomsday syndrome* (1986)
[Fieldhouse]
25 *Down under thunder* (1986)
[Newman]
26 *Hostaged Vatican* (1986)
[Fieldhouse]
27 *Weep, Moscow, weep* (1986)
[Fieldhouse]
28 *Slow death* (1987)
[Newman]
29 *Nightmare merchants* (1987)
[Fieldhouse]
30 *Bonn blitz* (1987)
[Newman]
31 *Terror in the dark* (1987)
[Fieldhouse]
32 *Fair game* (1987)
[Newman]
33 *Ninja blood* (1988)
[Fieldhouse]
34 *Tigers of justice* (1988)
35 *Kingston carnage* (1988)
36 *Belgrade deception* (1988)
37 *Show of force* (1988)
38 *Missile menace* (1988)
39 *Jungle sweep* (1989)
40 *Rim of fire* (1989)
41 *Amazon strike* (1989)
42 *China command* (1989)
43 *Gulf of fire* (1989)
44 *Main offensive* (1989)
45 *African burn* (1990)
46 *Iron Claymore* (1990)
47 *Terror in Guyana* (1990)
48 *Barracuda run* (1990)
Number 49 not identified
50 *Extreme prejudice* (1990)
51 *Savage world* (1991)

Phoenix Force super series
Wilson, Gar
House pseudonym
1 *Fire storm* (1988)
2 *Search and destroy* (1989)
3 *Cold dead* (1990)
4 *Wall of flame* (1991)

Phoenix legacy trilogy
Wren, M K
1 *Sword of the Lamb* (1981)
2 *Shadow of the swan* (1981)
3 *House of the wolf* (1981)

Phoenix series
Alexander, David
1 *Dark messiah* (1987)
2 *Ground zero* (1987)
3 *Death quest* (1988)
4 *Metal storm* (1988)
5 *Whirlwind* (1988)

Photinus the Greek series
James, John
1 *Votan* (1966)
2 *Not for all the gold in Ireland* (1968)
3 *Men went to Cattraeth* (1969)

Photo history of two world wars series
Forty, George
1 *Photo history of tanks in two world wars* (1984)
2 *Photo history of armoured cars in two world wars* (1984)

Photon series
Peters, David
1 *For the glory* (1987)
Based on a game
2 *High stakes* (1987)
3 *In search of MOM* (1987)
4 *This is your life, Bhodi Li* (1987)
5 *Exile* (1987)
6 *Skin deep* (1988)
Companion volume: *Thieves of light*, by Michael Hudson, 1987

Photon series
Teitelbaum, Michael
1 *Darkness missiles* (1987)
2 *Prisoners of evil* (1987)

Phryne Fisher series
Greenwood, Kerry
1 *Cocaine blues* (1989)
Death by misadventure
2 *Flying too high* (1990)
3 *Murder on the Ballarat train* (1991)
4 *Death at Victoria Dock* (1992)
5 *Green Mill murder* (1993)
6 *Blood and circuses* (1994)

Phrynette series
Troly-Curtin, Marthe
1 *Phrynette and London* (1911)
2 *Phrynette married* (1912)

Phule series
Asprin, Robert Lynn
1 *Phule's company* (1990)
2 *Phule's paradise* (1992)

Phyllis and Janet series
Whitehill, Dorothy
see **Janet and Phyllis series**

Pibble series
Dickinson, Peter
see **Superintendent James Pibble series**

Pic series
Langford, George
1 *Pic, the weapon-maker* (1920)
2 *Kutnar, son of Pic* (1921)

Picaroon series
Cassells, John
see **Ludovic Saxon series**

Picaroon series
Landon, Herman
1 *Elusive Picaroon* (1932)
Short stories
2 *Green shadow* (1928)
3 *Picaroon does justice* (1928)
Short stories
4 *Buy my silence* (1929)
Short stories
5 *Trailing of the Picaroon* (1930)
Short stories
6 *Picaroon resumes practice* (1931)
Short stories
7 *Picaroon in pursuit* (1932)
8 *Picaroon, knight errant* (1933)
Short stories
9 *Picaroon and the burglar tools* (1944)

Piccardi series
Coccioli, Carlo
see **Ardito Piccardi series**

Piccolo series
Hewett, Anita
1 *Piccolo* (1960)
2 *Piccolo and Maria* (1962)

Pichelsteiner series
Kastner, Erich
see **Little man series**

Pick-a-path series
This sequence has eleven authors
O'Connor, Jane
1 *Dandee diamond mystery* (1982)
Manushkin, Fran
2 *Roller coaster ghost* (1983)
Wenk, Richard
3 *Great baseball championship* (1983)
O'Connor, Jane
4 *Amazing bubblegum caper* (1983)
Wenk, Richard
5 *Super trail bike* (1983)
Pascal, Laurie
6 *Mystery at Mockingbird Manor* (1983)
Hiller, Barbara B
7 *Fantastic journey of the space shuttle* (1984)
O'Connor, Jane
8 *Magic top mystery* (1984)
Logan, Nora
9 *Jungle adventure* (1984)
McMullan, Kate
10 *Mystery of the missing money* (1984)
Logan, Nora
11 *Dinosaur adventure* (1984)
Pascal, Jamie
12 *Ballerina mystery* (1984)
Hiller, Barbara B
13 *Secret of thirteen* (1984)
Logan, Nora
14 *RIM, the rebel robot* (1984)
Hiller, Barbara B
15 *Hot Dog Gang caper* (1985)

Pickerell series
Macgregor, Ellen
see **Miss Pickerell series**

Pickering series
Ketchum, Philip
see **Elijah Cabot Pickering series**

Pickle series
Lang, Andrew
1 *Pickle the spy* (1897)
Alternative title: The incognito of Prince Charles
2 *Companions of Pickle* (1898)

Picklock Holes series
Lehmann, Rudolf Chambers
Satires on the character of Sherlock Holmes
1 *Adventures of Picklock Holes* (1901)
Short stories
2 *Return of Picklock Holes* (1980)

Pickwick series
This sequence has three authors
Dickens, Charles
1 *Posthumous papers of the Pickwick Club* (1837)
Pickwick papers
Reynolds, George Macarthur
2 *Pickwick abroad* (1839)
Alternative title: The tour in France
Harper, Charles George
3 *Mister Pickwick's second time on earth* (1927)

Picture book of Jewish holidays series
Adler, David A
1 *Picture book of Jewish holidays* (1981)

2 *Picture book of Passover* (1982)
3 *Picture book of Hannukah* (1982)

Picture of life series
Mersey, Charles Clive
Autobiography
1 *Picture of life, 1872-1940* (1941)
2 *Journal and memories* (1952)

Pictures to stretch the imagination series
Anno, Mitsumasa
Translated from the Japanese
1 *Topsy-turvies* (1968)
2 *Upside-downers* (1969)

Pictures to talk about
Lionni, Leon
1 *Who?* (1983)
2 *What?* (1983)
3 *Where?* (1983)
4 *When?* (1983)

Piecrust series
Savage, Deborah
see **Peregrine Piecrust series**

Pierce family series
Erdman, Loula Grace
1 *Wind blows free* (1952)
2 *Wide horizon* (1956)
3 *Good land* (1959)

Pierce series
Locke, Clinton W
see **Perry Pierce series**

Pierre Allain and William Stevens series
Graeme, Bruce
see **Superintendent William Stevens and Inspector Pierre Allain series**

Pierre-Ange Sawyer series
Albert, Marvin Hubert
1 *Stone angel* (1986)
2 *Back in the real world* (1986)
3 *Get off at Babylon* (1987)
4 *Long teeth* (1987)
5 *Last smile* (1988)
6 *Midnight sister* (1989)
7 *Bimbo heaven* (1990)

Pierre Chambrun series
Pentecost, Hugh
1 *Cannibal who overate* (1962)
2 *Shape of fear* (1963)
3 *Evil that men do* (1966)
4 *Golden trap* (1967)
5 *Gilded nightmare* (1968)
6 *Girl watcher's funeral* (1969)
7 *Deadly joke* (1971)
8 *Birthday, deathday* (1972)
9 *Walking dead man* (1973)
10 *Bargain with death* (1974)
11 *Time of terror* (1975)
12 *Fourteen dilemma* (1976)
13 *Death after breakfast* (1978)
14 *Random killer* (1979)
15 *Beware young lovers* (1980)
16 *Murder in luxury* (1981)
17 *With intent to kill* (1982)
18 *Murder in high places* (1983)
19 *Remember to kill me* (1984)
20 *Murder round the clock* (1985)
Short stories
21 *Nightmare time* (1986)
22 *Murder goes round and round* (1988)

Pierre Fremont trilogy
Zola, Emile
see **Abbe Pierre Fremont trilogy**

Pierre Montigny series
Torgerson, Edwin Dial
1 *Murderer returns* (1930)
2 *Cold finger curse* (1933)

Pierre Noziere series
France, Anatole
1 *My friend's book* (1885)
Original edition entitled *Le livre de mon ami*
2 *Pierre Noziere* (1899)
Original edition entitled *Pierre Noziere*
3 *Little Pierre* (1918)
Original edition entitled *Le petir Pierre*
4 *Bloom of life* (1922)
Original edition entitled *La vie en fleurs*

Pierre series
Hudson, Jay William
see **Abbe Pierre series**
Parker, Gilbert
see **Pretty Pierre series**

Pierre the clown series
Cooper, Elizabeth
1 *My day begins with Pierre the clown* (1980)
2 *My morning with Pierre the clown* (1980)
3 *My afternoon with Pierre the clown* (1980)
4 *My bedtime with Pierre the clown* (1980)

Piers Roper series
Follett, Ken
1 *Shakeout* (1975)
2 *Bear raid* (1976)

Piet Deventer series
Anderson, John Richard Lane
see **Inspector Piet Deventer series**

Piet Potter series
Quackenbush, Robert Mead
1 *Piet Potter's first case* (1980)
2 *Piet Potter returns* (1980)
3 *Piet Potter strikes again* (1981)
4 *Piet Potter to the rescue* (1981)
5 *Piet Potter on the run* (1982)
6 *Piet Potter's hot clue* (1982)

Pieter Tonneman series
Meyers, Maan
1 *Dutchman* (1992)
2 *Kingsbridge plot* (1993)
3 *High constable* (1994)

Pietro Spina series
Silone, Ignazio
1 *Bread and wine* (1936)
Original edition entitled *Pane e vino*; revised edition 1962
2 *Seed beneath the snow* (1940)
Original edition entitled *Il seme sottot la neve*

Pietro Tonelli series
Williams, Alexander
see **Detective Sergeant Pietro Tonelli series**

Pig farming trilogy
Drysdale, Ann
Autobiography
1 *Faint heart never kissed a pig* (1982)
2 *Sows ears and silk purses* (1984)
3 *Pearls before swine* (1985)

Pig Pig series
McPhail, David Michael
1 *Pig Pig grows up* (1980)
2 *Pig Pig rides* (1982)
3 *Pig Pig goes to camp* (1983)
4 *Pig Pig and the magic photo album* (1986)
5 *Pig Pig gets a job* (1990)

Pig Plantagenet series
Andrews, Allen
1 *Pig Plantagenet* (1980)
2 *Castle Crespin* (1982)

Pig series
Bennett, Rodney
see **Percy Pig series**

Pig series
Brush, Karen Alexandra
1 *Pig, the prince and the unicorn* (1987)
2 *Demon pig* (1991)

Pig series
Hauptmann, Tatjana
see **Petronella and Peregrine Pig series**
Hoban, Lillian
see **Mister Pig series**

Pig series
Lobe, Mira
1 *Pig in a muddle* (1983)
Original edition entitled *Quiekfidele Berstentier*
2 *Pig on the run* (1986)
Original edition entitled *Schweinchen Knut mit dem Hut*

Pig series
Rayner, Mary
see **Mister and Mrs Pig series**
Van Leeuwen, Jean
see **Oliver Pig series**
Wada, Yoshiomi
see **Peter Pig series**

Pigeon Camp series
James, Martha
1 *Jimmie Suter and the boys of Pigeon Camp* (1906)
2 *Boys of Pigeon Camp, their luck and fun* (1907)
3 *Hero of Pigeon Camp* (1908)
Alternative title: How Lucci made good

Pigeon Hoo series
Lushington, Franklin
1 *Pigeon Hoo* (1935)
2 *Pennybridge* (1937)

Pigeon Street series
Cole, Michael
1 *Flood* (1982)
2 *Gerald kicks off* (1982)
3 *Light in the sky* (1982)
4 *Pigeon at sea* (1982)

Piggins series
Yolen, Jane
1 *Piggins* (1988)
2 *Picnic with Piggins* (1988)
3 *Piggins and the royal wedding* (1989)

Piggle-Wiggle series
Macdonald, Betty
see **Mrs Piggle-Wiggle series**

Piggy Grunter series
Shelley, Noreen
1 *Piggy Grunter at the circus* (1944)
2 *Piggy Grunter and the town hall fire* (1944)
3 *Piggy Grunter's red umbrella* (1944)
4 *Three cheers for Piggy Grunter* (1959)

Piglet series
Milne, Alan Alexander
Stories originally published in *Winnie-the-Pooh*, 1926
1 *Winnie-the-Pooh and some bees* (1975)
2 *Pooh goes visiting* (1975)
Also includes *Pooh and Piglet nearly catch a woozle*
3 *Piglet meets a heffalump* (1975)
4 *Eeyore has a birthday* (1975)
5 *Kanga and the Baby Roo come to the forest* (1975)
6 *Exposition to the North Pole* (1975)

Pigman series
Zindel, Paul
1 *Pigman* (1968)
2 *Pigman's legacy* (1980)

Pigs series
Dubanevich, Arlene
1 *Pigs in hiding* (1983)
2 *Pig William* (1985)
3 *Pigs at Christmas* (1986)
4 *Piggest show on earth* (1989)

Pigwig series
Dyke, John
1 *Pigwig* (1978)
2 *Pigwig and the pirates* (1979)

Pike series
Javor, Frank A
see **Eli Pike series**
Meek, Joseph
see **Mountain Jack Pike series**

Pike's Peak trilogy
Waters, Frank
1 *Wild earth's nobility* (1935)
2 *Below grass roots* (1937)
3 *Dust within the rock* (1940)
One volume revised edition entitled *Pike's Peak*, 1971

Pikey's Steep series
This sequence has two authors
Roberts, Gruffydd Dewi
1 *House that was forgotten* (1935)
2 *Heron's Island* (1937)
Roberts, Constance Evelyn
3 *Herons of Pikey's Steep* (1945)
4 *Winter at Piukey's Steep* (1949)

Pikolo series
Filion, Pierre
Illustrated by Gilles Tibo
1 *Paper nights* (1992)
Original edition entitled *Le secret du garde-robe*
2 *Pikolo's night voyage* (1994)

Pilgrim Cottage series
Roberts, Cecil
1 *Pilgrim Cottage* (1933)
2 *Guests arrive* (1934)
3 *Volcano* (1935)

Pilgrim series
Brittain, Harry Ernest
1 *Pilgrims and partners* (1946)
2 *Happy pilgrimage* (1949)
Companion volume: *Pilgrim partners*, 1942

Pilgrim series
Cory, Desmond
see **Mister Pilgrim series**
Cronin, Michael
see **Richard Maidment series**

Pilgrim series
Davey, Norman
1 *Pilgrim of a smile* (1922)
2 *Penultimate adventure* (1924)
One volume edition entitled *The pilgrim of a smile*, 1933

Pilgrim series
Potter, Jay Hill
1 *Call me Pilgrim* (1981)
2 *Pilgrim's trail* (1982)
3 *Young Joe Pilgrim* (1982)
4 *Pilgrim's blood* (1982)
5 *Bounty for Pilgrim* (1983)
6 *Requiem for Pilgrim* (1983)
7 *Pilgrim raid* (1983)
8 *Coffin for Pilgrim* (1986)

Pilgrim series

9 *Pilgrim kill* (1985)
10 *Pilgrim's revenge* (1990)
11 *Hills of the dead* (1991)

Pilgrim series

Saberhagen, Fred
1 *Pyramids* (1987)
2 *After the fact* (1988)

Pilgrimage series

Richardson, Dorothy Miller
1 *Pointed roofs* (1915)
2 *Backwater* (1916)
3 *Honeycomb* (1917)
Numbers 1-3 also published in one volume entitled *Pilgrimage,* volume 1, 1938
4 *Tunnel* (1919)
5 *Interim* (1919)
Numbers 4 and 5 also published in one volume entitled *Pilgrimage,* volume 2, 1938
6 *Deadlock* (1921)
7 *Revolving lights* (1923)
8 *Trap* (1925)
Numbers 6-8 also published in one volume entitled *Pilgrimage,* volume 3, 1938
9 *Oberland* (1928)
10 *Dawn's left hand* (1931)
11 *Clear horizon* (1935)
12 *Dimple Hill* (1938)
Numbers 9-12 also published in one volume entitled *Pilgrimage,* volume 4, 1938
13 *March moonlight* (1967)
Numbers 9-13 also published in one volume entitled *Pilgrimage,* volume 4, 1967

Pilgrims and sailors series

McFee, William
1 *Pilgrim of adversity* (1928)
2 *Sailors of fortune* (1930)

Pilgrims of Plymouth series

Austin, Jane Goodwin
1 *Standish of Standish* (1890)
2 *Betty Alden, the first-born daughter of the Pilgrims* (1891)
3 *David Alden's daughters, and other stories of colonial times* (1892)

Pillar to post series

Mehdevi, Anne Sinclair
Reminiscences of travel
1 *From pillar to post* (1956)
2 *Persian adventure* (1953)
3 *Persia revisited* (1965)

Pillars of the house series

Yonge, Charlotte Mary
1 *Daisy chain* (1856)
2 *Hopes and fears* (1860)
3 *Countess Kate* (1862)
4 *Trial* (1864)
5 *Pillars of the house* (1873)
Alternative title: Under wode, under rode

Pilot series

Peel, Hazel Mary
1 *Pilot the hunter* (1962)
2 *Pilot the chaser* (1964)

Pilpali Sahab series

Anand, Mulk Raj
Autobiography
1 *Story of a childhood under the Raj* (1985)
2 *Story of a big ego in a small body* (1990)

Pimpernel series

Walker, David Esdaile
1 *Fat cat Pimpernel* (1958)
2 *Pimpernel and the poodle* (1959)

Pin a rose on me series

Blumenfeld, Josephine
Reminiscences
1 *Pin a rose on me* (1958)
2 *See me dance the polka* (1962)

Pinaud series

Audemars, Pierre
see **Monsieur Pinaud series**

Pinch series

Green, Edith
see **Dearborn V Pinch series**

Pinchpenny Mouse series

Kraus, Robert
1 *Pinchpenny Mouse* (1974)
2 *Gondolier of Venice* (1976)

Pincus series

Rosten, Leo
see **Silky Pincus series**

Pine cone series

Allen, Willis Boyd
1 *Pine cones* (1885)
2 *Silver rages* (1886)
3 *Northern Cross* (1887)
4 *Kelp* (1888)
5 *Cloud and cliff* (1889)
6 *Gulf and glacier* (1892)

Pine series

Evans, John
see **Paul Pine series**

Pine Street series

Allan, Mabel Esther
1 *Pine Street pageant* (1978)
2 *Pine Street goes camping* (1980)
3 *Pine Street problem* (1981)
4 *Goodbye to Pine Street* (1982)
5 *Alone at Pine Street* (1983)
6 *Friends at Pine Street* (1984)
7 *Pride of Pine Street* (1985)

Pineapple Place series

Lindbergh, Anne Morrow
1 *People in Pineapple Place* (1982)
2 *Prisoner of Pineapple Place* (1988)

Pinetops series

Hurt, Freda Mary
1 *Wonderful birthday* (1953)
2 *Fun next door* (1954)
3 *Two to make friends* (1955)
4 *Exciting summer* (1956)
5 *Thirteen for luck* (1958)
6 *Intruders at Pinetops* (1958)

Piney Ridge trilogy

Giles, Janice Holt
1 *Enduring hills* (1950)
2 *Miss Willie* (1951)
3 *Tara's healing* (1951)

Pingwings series

Postgate, Oliver
Illustrated by Babette Cole
1 *Narrow boat* (1978)
2 *Flying bird* (1978)

Pink Panther series

Albert, Marvin Hubert
see **Inspector Clouseau series**

Pink Pig series

Adler, Carole Schwerdtfeger
1 *Good-bye, Pink Pig* (1986)
2 *Help, Pink Pig!* (1990)

Pink series

Bennett, Rodney
see **Little Miss Pink series**
McShane, Mark
see **Sergeant Norman Pink series**
Moffat, Gwen
see **Miss Melinda Pink series**

Pink-Whistle series

Blyton, Enid
see **Mister Pink-Whistle series**

Pinkerton family series

Kibbe, Pat
1 *Hocus-pocus dilemma* (1979)
2 *My mother, the mayor, maybe* (1981)

Pinkerton series

Baker, William Howard
4 *Blood trail* (1966)

Pinkerton series

Frome, David
see **Evan Pinkerton series**

Pinkerton series

Kellogg, Steven
1 *Pinkerton, behave!* (1979)
2 *Rose for Pinkerton* (1981)
3 *Tallyho, Pinkerton!* (1982)
4 *Prehistoric Pinkerton* (1987)

Pinkerton series

Reid, Desmond
1 *Babcock boys* (1966)
2 *Death waits in Tucson* (1966)
3 *Man from Pecos* (1966)

Pinkerton series

Rinehart, Mary Roberts
see **Nurse Hilda Adams series**

Pinkerton-Trunks series

Isherwood, Shirley
see **Get up and go series**

Pinkie series

Ruff, Agnes
1 *Adventures of Pinkie* (1955)
2 *More adventures of Pinkie* (1959)

Pinkney series

Wills, Cecil Melville
see **Sylvester Horatio Pinkney series**

Pinky and Rex series

Howe, James
Illustrated by Melissa Sweet
1 *Pinky and Rex* (1990)
2 *Pinky and Rex get married* (1990)
3 *Pinky and rex and the spelling bee* (1991)
4 *Pinky and Rex and the mean old witch* (1991)
5 *Pinky and Rex go to camp* (1992)
6 *Pinky and Rex and the new baby* (1993)

Pinner series

Kaye, Mollie
see **Potter Pinner series**

Pinny series

Firmin, Peter
1 *Pinny and the bird* (1985)
2 *Pinny finds a house* (1985)
3 *Pinny in the snow* (1985)
4 *Pinny's party* (1986)
5 *Pinny and the floppy dog* (1986)

Pinny series

Morgan, Helen
see **Mrs Pinny series**

Pinocchio series

This sequence has three authors
Collodi, Carlo
1 *Adventures of Pinocchio* (1882)
Story of a puppet
Pinocchio
Original edition entitled *La avventure di Pinocchio*
Parsons, Virginia
2 *Pinocchio goes on the stage* (1977)
3 *Pinocchio and Geppetto* (1977)
4 *Pinocchio and the money tree* (1978)
5 *Pinocchio plays truant* (1978)
Coover, Robert
6 *Pinocchio in Venice* (1991)

Pioneer boys series

Adams, Harrison
1 *Pioneer boys of the Ohio* (1912)
Alternative title: Clearing the wilderness
2 *Pioneer boys on the Great Lakes* (1912)
Alternative title: On the trail of the Iriquois
3 *Pioneer boys of the Mississippi* (1913)
Alternative title: The homestead in the wilderness
4 *Pioneer boys of the Missouri* (1914)
Alternative title: In the country of the Sioux
5 *Pioneer boys of the Yellowstone* (1915)
Alternative title: Lost in the land of wonders
6 *Pioneer boys of the Columbia* (1916)
Alternative title: In the wilderness of the great Northwest
7 *Pioneer boys of the Colorado* (1926)
Alternative title: Braving the perils of the Grand Canyon country
8 *Pioneer boys of Kansas* (1928)
Alternative title: A prairie home in Buffalo land

Pioneer children series

Richter, Conrad
1 *Light in the forest* (1953)
2 *Country of strangers* (1966)

Pioneer family series

Dengler, Sandy
1 *Summer of the wild pig* (1979)
2 *Horse who loved picnics* (1980)
3 *Arizona Longhorn adventure* (1980)
4 *Melon hound* (1980)
5 *Rescue in the desert* (1981)
6 *Mystery at McGeehan Ranch* (1982)

Pioneer girls series

Palmer, Bernard
1 *Pioneer girls and the mystery of Oak Ridge Manor* (1959)
2 *Pioneer girls and the mystery of missing cocker* (1959)
3 *Pioneer girls and the strange adventures on Tomahawk Hill* (1959)
4 *Pioneer girls at Caribou Flats* (1959)
5 *Pioneer girls and the secret of the jungle* (1962)
6 *Pioneer girls and the mysterious bedouin cave* (1963)
7 *Pioneer girls and the Dutch mill mystery* (1968)

Pioneer scout series

Tomlinson, Everett Titsworth
1 *Scouting with Daniel Boone* (1914)
2 *Scouting with Kit Carson* (1916)
3 *Scouting with General Funston* (1917)
4 *Scouting with General Pershing* (1918)

Pioneer series

Otis, James
1 *Hannah of Kentucky* (1912)
A story of the Wilderness Road
2 *Benjamin of Ohio* (1912)
A story of the settlement of Marietta
3 *Seth of Colorado* (1912)
A story of the settlement of Denver
4 *Antoine of Oregon* (1912)
A story of the Oregon Trail
5 *Martha of California* (1913)
A story of the Californai Trail

6 *Philip of Texas* (1913)
A story of sheep raising in Texas

Pip and Andrew series
Wilson, Keane
1 *Pip of Pynalong* (1949)
2 *Pip and Andrew, schoolmates* (1949)
3 *Pip and Andrew in danger* (1950)

Pip-Larsson family series
Unnerstad, Edith
see **Larsson family series**

Pip series
Blyton, Enid
1 *Adventures of Pip* (1948)
2 *More adventures of Pip* (1948)

Piper and Quinn series
Carmichael, Harry
see **John Piper and Quinn series**

Piper series
Long, Amelia Reynolds
see **Peter Piper series**
Mavity, Nancy Barr
see **Peter Piper series**

Pipers series
Moss, Elaine
see **Peter Pipers series**

Pipers series
Parker, Richard
1 *Valley full of Pipers* (1962)
2 *Perversity of Pipers* (1964)
3 *Beyond the back gate* (1975)

Pipkins series
Wahl, Jan
1 *Pipkins go camping* (1982)
2 *More room for the Pipkins* (1983)

Pippa Mouse series
Boegehold, Betty
1 *Pippa Mouse* (1973)
2 *Here's Pippa again* (1975)
3 *Pippa pops out!* (1979)
4 *Hooray for Pippa!* (1980)

Pippa series
Berrisford, Judith Mary
1 *Pony-trekkers, go home!* (1981)
2 *Sabotage at Stableways* (1982)
3 *Pippa's mystery horse* (1983)

Pippa series
Ohlson, Edith Emilie
1 *Pippa at home* (1953)
2 *Pippa in Switzerland* (1955)
3 *Pippa at Brighton* (1956)
4 *Pippa and James* (1943)

Pippi Longstocking series
Lindgren, Astrid
1 *Pippi Longstocking* (1945)
Original edition entitled *Pippi Langstrump*
2 *Pippi goes aboard* (1946)
Pippi goes on board
Original edition entitled *Pippi Langstrump gaar ombord*
3 *Pippi in the South Seas* (1948)
Original edition entitled *Pippi Langstrump i Soderhavet*
4 *[Boken om Pippi Langstrump]* (1952)
No English edition
Companion volumes: *Pippi on the run*, picture book, originally published as *Paa rymmen ged Pippi Langstrump*, 1971, *The new adventures of Pippi Longstocking*, 1988

Pippin series
Farjeon, Eleanor
see **Martin Pippin series**

Pippins series
Gissing, Vera
1 *Peacock duck* (1987)
Retold from a story by Roselyne Morel
2 *Little Sally Shrimp* (1987)
Retold from a story by Marie-France Mangin
3 *Brave white rabbit* (1987)
Retold from a story by Roselyne Morel
4 *New neighbours* (1987)
Retold from a story by Anne-Marie Dalmais
5 *Dragon at school* (1987)
Retold from a story by Marie Tenaille
6 *Music master* (1987)
Retold from a story by Alain Thomas

Pirates series
Taffrail
1 *Pirates* (1929)
2 *Lonely bungalow* (1931)

Pirates series
Townsend, Tom
1 *Where the pirates are* (1985)
2 *Powderhorn passage* (1988)

Piro series
Baumann, Kurt
1 *Piro and the fire brigade* (1981)
Original edition entitled *Piro und die Feuerwehr*
2 *Piro and the treasure hunt* (1986)
Original edition entitled *Piro auf Schatzsuche*
3 *Piro and the runaway train* (1987)
Original edition entitled *Piro und die Dampflok*
4 *Piro and the digger* (1988)
Original edition entitled *Piro und der Bagger*
5 *Piro the pilot* (1989)

Piron series
McGirr, Edmund
see **Jim Piron series**

Pirx series
Lem, Stanislaw
1 *Tales of Pirx the pilot* (1968)
Original edition entitled *Opowiesci o pilocie Pirxie*, part 1
2 *More tales of Pirx the pilot* (1968)
Original edition entitled *Opowiesci o pilocie Pirxie*, part 2

Pisistratus Caxton trilogy
Lytton, Edward George Earle Lytton Bulwer-Lytton
see **Real and the ideal trilogy**

Pistol and Tim series
Garfield, Leon
see **Tim and Pistol series**

Pit dragons trilogy
Yolen, Jane
1 *Dragon's blood* (1982)
2 *Heart's blood* (1984)
3 *Sending of dragons* (1987)

Pitamaken series
Schultz, James Willard
1 *Sinopah, the Indian boy* (1913)
2 *With the Indians in the Rockies* (1912)
Boy trappers in the Rockies
The second title is an expanded edition
3 *Quest of the dog-fish skin* (1913)
4 *On the warpath* (1914)
5 *War-trail fort* (1921)

Pitt series
Cussler, Clive
see **Dirk Pitt series**
Maughan, Anne Margery
see **Young Pitt series**
Perry, Anne
see **Charlotte Ellison Pitt and Inspector Thomas Pitt series**
Straker, John Foster
see **Inspector Pitt series**

Pitt the Elder trilogy
Sherrard, Owen Aubrey
see **Lord Chatham trilogy**

Pivar series
Black, William
see **Bella Pivar series**

Pixie O'Shaughnessy series
Vaizey, Jessie Bell
1 *Pixie O'Shaughnessy* (1903)
2 *More about Pixie* (1903)
3 *Love affairs of Pixie* (1914)

Plain series
Rae, Gwynedd
see **Mary Plain series**

Plainsmen series
Johnston, Terry Conrad
1 *Sioux dawn* (1990)
Fetterman massacre, 1866
2 *Red Cloud's revenge* (1990)
Hammett
Showdown on the northern plains, 1867
3 *Stalkers* (1990)
The battle of Beecher Island, 1868
4 *Black sun* (1991)
The battle of Summit Springs, 1869
5 *Devil's backbone* (1991)
The Modoc war, 1872-3
6 *Shadow riders* (1991)
The southern plains uprising, 1873
7 *Dying thunder* (1992)
The fight at Adobe Wells and the battle of Palo Duro Canyon, 1874-1875

Plaintext series
Mairs, Nancy
Autobiographical essays
1 *Plaintext* (1986)
2 *Remembering the bone-house* (1989)
3 *Carnal acts* (1990)
Also includes some fiction

Plan of man trilogy
Pohl, Frederik
1 *Reefs of space* (1964)
2 *Starchild* (1965)
3 *Rogue star* (1969)
One volume edition entitled *Starchild trilogy*, 1977

Plando series
Bryce, Charles
1 *Plando the mouse deer* (1962)
2 *Plando and the nightingale* (1963)

Planet Arzor series
Norton, Andre
see **Arzor series**

Planet builders series
Tallis, Robyn
This pseudonym is used by Bruce Coville, Debra Doyle, James Douglas Macdonald, Jymn Magon, Sherwood Smith and Mary Frances Zambreno as indicated against each title
1 *Mountain of stolen dreams* (1988)
[Coville]
2 *Night of ghosts and lightning* (1989)
[Doyle; Macdonald]
3 *Rebel from Alphorion* (1989)
[Smith]
4 *Visions from the sea* (1989)
[Smith]
5 *Zero-sum games* (1989)
[Doyle; Macdonald]
6 *Night of two new moons* (1989)
[Coville]
7 *Children of the storm* (1989)
[Zambreno]
8 *Horrorvid* (1989)
[Magon]
9 *Giants of Elenna* (1989)
[Smith]
10 *Fire in the sky* (1989)
[Smith]

Planet dweller series
Palmer, Jane
1 *Planet dweller* (1985)
2 *Moving moosevan* (1990)

Planet Five series
Lessing, Doris
see **Canopus in Argus archives series**

Planet of adventure series
Vance, Jack
see **Tschai series**

Planet of the Apes series
This sequence has six authors
Boulle, Pierre
1 *Planet of the Apes* (1963)
Monkey Planet
Original edition entitled *La Planete des Singes*; numbers 1-5 are based on screenplays
Avallone, Michael
2 *Beneath the Planet of the Apes* (1970)
Pournelle, Jerry
3 *Escape from the Planet of the Apes* (1974)
Jakes, John
4 *Conquest of the Planet of the Apes* (1974)
Gerrold, David
5 *Battle for the Planet of the Apes* (1973)
Effinger, George Alec
6 *Man, the fugitive* (1974)
Numbers 6-9 are based on the television series
7 *Escape to tomorrow* (1975)
8 *Journey into terror* (1975)
9 *Lord of the apes* (1976)
Continued by **Return to the Planet of the Apes series**

Planet of the monsters series
May, Stephen
1 *Planet of the monsters* (1985)
2 *Monsters on earth* (1987)

Planet pirates series
McCaffrey, Anne
1 *Sassinak* (1990)
Co-author: Elizabeth Moon
2 *Death of sleep* (1990)
Co-author: Jody Lynn Nye
3 *Generation warriors* (1991)
Co-author: Elizabeth Moon

Planet Warlock series
Norton, Andre
1 *Storm over Warlock* (1960)
2 *Ordeal in otherwise* (1964)
3 *Forerunner foray* (1973)
4 *Forerunner* (1981)
5 *Forerunner, the second venture* (1985)

Planet X trilogy
Adams, Hunter
see **Man from Planet X trilogy**

Planetary Agent series
Reynolds, Mack
1 *Planetary Agent X* (1965)
2 *Amazon planet* (1975)
3 *Dawnsman planet* (1966)
4 *Rival Regellians* (1967)
Numbers 1 and 4 also published in one volume 1974

Planetary Agent series

5 *Code duello* (1968)
6 *Section G, United Planets* (1976)

Planetfall series
Cover, Arthur Byron
1 *Planetfall* (1988)
2 *Stationfall* (1989)

Plant that ate dirty socks series
McArthur, Nancy
1 *Plant that ate dirty socks* (1988)
2 *Return of the plant that ate dirty socks* (1990)

Plant trilogy
King, Stephen
1 *Plant* (1982)
The opening segment of an ongoing work
2 *Plant, part 2* (1983)
3 *Plant, part 3* (1985)

Plantagenet series
Farely, Alison
1 *Leopard from Anjou* (1970)
2 *Crown of splendour* (1968)
3 *Devils Royal* (1968)
4 *Lion and the Wolf* (1969)
5 *Last roar of the Lion* (1969)
6 *King Wolf* (1974)
7 *kingdom under tyranny* (1974)
8 *Last howl of the Wolf* (1975)

Plantagenet series
Plaidy, Jean
1 *Plantagenet prelude* (1976)
The story of Eleanor and Henry II
2 *Revolt of the eaglets* (1977)
The story of the old age of Henry II
3 *Heart of the Lion* (1977)
Based on the life of Richard I
4 *Prince of darkness* (1978)
Based on the life of King John
5 *Battle of the queens* (1978)
The story of the feud between Isabella, King John's widow and Queen Blanche of Castille
6 *Queen from Provence* (1979)
Based on the lives of Henry III and his wife, Eleanor of Provence
7 *Edward Longshanks* (1979)
Hammer of the Scots
The story of the reign of Edward I
8 *Follies of the King* (1980)
Based on the lives of Edward II and Queen Isabella
9 *Vow on the heron* (1980)
The story of the reign of Edward III
10 *Passage to Pontefract* (1981)
The story of the rivalry between Edward the Black Prince and John of Gaunt
11 *Star of Lancaster* (1981)
The lives of Henry IV and Henry V
12 *Epitaph for three women* (1981)
Based on the lives of Queen Katherine of Valois, Joan of Arc and Eleanor of Gloucester
13 *Red rose of Anjou* (1982)
The story of Queen Margaret of Anjou, wife of Henry VI
14 *Sun in splendour* (1982)
Set during the reign of Edward IV during the Wars of the Roses
15 *Uneasy lies the head* (1982)
Based on the life of Henry VII

Plantagenet trilogy
Wilson, Sandra
see **Lady Cicely Plantagenet trilogy**

Plantagenets series
Dymoke, Juliet
1 *Pride of kings* (1978)
2 *Royal griffin* (1978)
3 *Lion of Mortimer* (1979)
4 *Lady of the Garter* (1979)
5 *Lord of Greenwich* (1980)
6 *Sun in splendour* (1980)
7 *Border knight* (1987)

Plantagenets series
Williamson, Hugh Ross
see **Passing of the Plantagenets series**

Plantagenets tetralogy
Costain, Thomas Bertram
see **History of the Plantagenets tetralogy**

Plantaine trilogy
Mosco, Maisie
see **Between two worlds trilogy**

Plantation series
Johnson, Barbara Ferry
1 *Delta blood* (1977)
2 *Homeward winds the river* (1979)

Plantation trilogy
Bristow, Gwen
see **Louisiana trilogy**

Plante and Matthews series
Palmer, John
see **Guy Plante and Freya Matthews series**

Platinum series
Storey, Anthony
1 *Platinum Jag* (1972)
2 *Platinum ass* (1975)

Play and learn series
Burningham, John
1 *Alphabet book* (1985)
John Burningham's ABC
2 *John Burningham's colours* (1985)
John Burningham's colors
3 *John Burningham's one two three* (1985)
4 *John Burningham's opposites* (1985)

Play and study series
Leslie, Madeline
1 *Motherless children* (1858)
2 *Howard and his teacher* (1859)
Also includes *The sister's influence, and other stories*
3 *Jack, the clumsy sweeper, and other stories for children* (1859)
4 *Play and study* (1859)

Pleasance series
Elsna, Hebe
1 *House called Pleasance* (1963)
Also published under the pseudonym Laura Conway
2 *Too well beloved* (1964)
Revised edition published under the pseudonym Laura Conway, 1978
3 *Undying past* (1964)
Also published under the pseudonym Laura Conway

Pleasant Cove series
Kellogg, Elijah
1 *Arthur Brown, young captain* (1870)
2 *Young deliverers of Pleasant Cove* (1871)
3 *Cruise of the Casco* (1871)
4 *Child of the island glen* (1872)
5 *John Godsoe's legacy* (1873)
6 *Fisher boys of Pleasant Cove* (1874)

Pleasant Fieldmouse series
Wahl, Jan
1 *Pleasant Fieldmouse* (1964)
2 *Pleasant Fieldmouse's Halloween party* (1974)
3 *Pleasant Fieldmouse storybook* (1977)
4 *Pleasant Fieldmouse Valentine trick* (1977)

Pleasant places series
Grenfell, Joyce
Autobiography
1 *Joyce Grenfell requests the pleasure* (1976)
2 *In pleasant places* (1979)

Pleasant Valley series
Bromfield, Louis
see **Malabar series**

Pleasure garden series
Sandys, Oliver
1 *Pleasure garden* (1923)
2 *Old roses* (1923)

Pleistocene mammals series
Kurten, Bjorn
1 *Pleistocene mammals of Europe* (1968)
2 *Pleistocene mammals of North America* (1980)
Co-author: Elaine Anderson

Pleydell series
Yates, Dornford
see **Berry series**

Pliocene exile series
May, Julian
1 *Intervention* (1987)
A root tale to the galactic milieu and a vinculum between it and the Saga of Pliocene exile
1.1 *Surveillance* (1987)
1.2 *Metaconcert* (1987)
2 *Many-colored land* (1981)
3 *Golden torc* (1981)
Numbers 2 and 3 also published in one volume 1982
4 *Nonborn king* (1983)
5 *Adversary* (1984)
Numbers 4 and 5 also published in one volume 1984
Companion volumes: *Brede's tale*, 1982, *A Pliocene companion*, 1984

Plot-it-yourself horror stories series
Milton, Hilary
see **Plot your own horror stories series**

Plot your own horror stories series
Milton, Hilary
1 *Craven house horrors* (1982)
Horror house
2 *Nightmare store* (1982)
3 *Space age terrors!* (1983)
4 *Horror hotel!* (1983)
Grand hotel of horror
5 *Escape from high doom* (1984)
6 *Fun house terrors!* (1984)
7 *Museum of the living dead* (1985)
Dining with dinosaurs
8 *Dungeon demons* (1985)

Plotkin and Van Larsen series
Baxt, George
see **Sylvia Plotkin and Max Van Larsen series**

Ploughman of heaven series
Service, Robert William
1 *Ploughman of heaven* (1946)
2 *Harper of heaven* (1948)

Plowing series
North, Sterling
1 *Plowing on Sunday* (1934)
2 *Night outlasts the whipporwill* (1936)

Pluckrose series
Fearon, Ethelind
1 *Sheepdog adventure* (1953)
2 *Pluckrose's horse* (1955)
3 *Secret of the chateau* (1955)

Plum Daffy series
Coatsworth, Elizabeth
1 *Littlest house* (1940)
2 *Plum Daffy adventure* (1947)

Plum series
King, Kay
see **Cornelius Plum series**

Rippon, Angela
see **Victoria Plum series**
Trimby, Elisa
see **Mister Plum series**

Plumb series
Szudek, Agnes Susan Philomena
see **Victoria Plumb series**

Plumb trilogy
Gee, Maurice
1 *Plumb* (1978)
2 *Meg* (1981)
3 *Sole survivor* (1983)

Plummer children series
Govan, Christine Noble
1 *Those Plummer children* (1934)
2 *Five at Ashefield* (1935)
3 *Judy and Chris* (1936)
4 *Narcissus an' de chillun* (1938)

Plummer series
Lees, Dan
see **Jeff Plummer series**

Plush series
Keystone, Oliver
see **Paul Plush series**

Pocket wheels series
Campbell, Rod
1 *Big and strong* (1985)
2 *Cars and trucks* (1985)
3 *Road builders* (1985)
4 *Speed!* (1985)

Pockets series
Sundown, Will
1 *Pockets of resistance* (1990)
2 *Hellbound train* (1990)

Pocomoto series
Dixon, Rex
1 *Pocomoto, pony express rider* (1953)
2 *Pocomoto, tenderfoot* (1953)
3 *Pocomoto and the night riders* (1953)
4 *Pocomoto, bronco buster* (1953)
5 *Pocomoto and the canyon treasure* (1954)
6 *Pocomoto, brush popper* (1954)
7 *Pocomoto and the l'il fella* (1954)
8 *Pocomoto, buffalo hunter* (1954)
9 *Pocomoto, cowboy cavalier* (1955)
10 *Pocomoto and the lazy river* (1955)
11 *Pocomoto and the snow wolf* (1955)
12 *Pocomoto and the Indian trails* (1956)
13 *Pocomoto and the robbers' trail* (1956)
14 *Pocomoto and the Spanish steed* (1957)
15 *Pocomoto and the desert gold* (1957)
16 *Pocomoto and the circus folk* (1957)
17 *Pocomoto and the Texas pioneers* (1958)
18 *Pocomoto and the lazy sheriff* (1958)
19 *Pocomoto and the lost hunters* (1959)
20 *Pocomoto and the Texas ranger* (1960)
21 *Pocomoto and the golden herd* (1960)
22 *Pocomoto and the warrior braves* (1961)
23 *Pocomoto and the Mexican bandits* (1963)

Poddy series
Judd, Alfred
1 *Poddy's progress* (1928)
2 *Poddy the winner* (1930)

Poe series
Steward, Barbara
see **Edgar Allan Poe series**

Poems for Peter series
Borie, Lysbeth Boyd
1 *Poems for Peter* (1928)
2 *More poems for Peter* (1931)

Poems for pictures series
Ford, Ford Madox
1 *Poems for pictures and for notes of music* (1900)
2 *Face of the night* (1904)

Poems to solve series
Swenson, May
1 *Poems to solve* (1966)
2 *More poems to solve* (1971)

Poems to trouble your sleep series
Prelutsky, Jack
1 *Nightmares* (1976)
2 *Headless horseman rides tonight* (1980)

Poet in the family series
Abse, Dannie
Autobiography
1 *Ash on a youg man's sleeve* (1954)
Revised edition 1969
2 *Poet in the family* (1974)
3 *Strong dose of myself* (1983)

Poggioli series
Stribling, Thomas Sigismund
see **Professor Henry Poggioli series**

Pogy Rogers and Beau Smith series
Ross, Zola Helen
see **Beau Smith and Pogy Rogers series**

Poictesme trilogy
Cabell, James Branch
1 *Figures of earth* (1921)
A comedy of appearances
2 *Silver stallion* (1926)
A comedy of redemption
3 *Jurgen* (1919)
Revised edition 1921; a comedy of justice

Point of departure series
Cameron, James
Autobiography
1 *Point of departure* (1967)
2 *Indian summer* (1974)

Point Team series
Hadley, J B
1 *Point Team* (1984)
2 *Viper Squad* (1985)
3 *Cobra strike* (1986)

Point thirty eight series
Copper, Basil
see **Mike Faraday series**

Pointer series
Fielding, A
see **Inspector Pointer series**

Poirot series
Christie, Agatha
see **Hercule Poirot series**

Pokerface series
Corris, Peter
1 *Pokerface* (1985)
2 *Baltic business* (1988)
3 *Kimberley killing* (1988)
Based on a story outline by Bill Garner
4 *Cargo Club* (1990)
5 *Azanian action* (1991)
6 *Japanese job* (1992)
7 *Time trap* (1994)

Pol Blancanales series
Stivers, Dick
see **Able Team series**

Polack Annie series
Lait, Jack
1 *Put on the spot* (1930)
2 *Gangster girl* (1930)

Polaris trilogy
Stilson, Charles Billings
1 *Polaris, of the snows* (1965)
2 *Minos of Sardanes* (1966)
3 *Polaris and the immortals* (1968)

Poldark series
Graham, Winston
Set in Cornwall during the period of the French Revolution and First Empire
1 *Ross Poldark* (1945)
Renegade
1783-1787
2 *Demelza* (1946)
Elizabeth's story
1788-1790
3 *Jeremy Poldark* (1950)
Venture once more
1790-1791
4 *Warleggan* (1953)
Last gamble
1792-1793
5 *Black moon* (1973)
1794-1795
6 *Four swans* (1976)
1795-1797
7 *Angry tide* (1977)
1798-1799
8 *Stranger from the sea* (1981)
1810-1811
9 *Miller's dance* (1982)
1812-1813
10 *Loving cup* (1984)
1813-1815
11 *Twisted sword* (1990)
1815-1816
Companion volume: *Poldark's Cornwall*, 1983

Polesotechnic League series
Anderson, Poul
1 *Let the spacemen beware!* (1963)
Night face
2 *People of the wind* (1973)
3 *Satan's world* (1969)
4 *Trader to the stars* (1964)
Short stories
5 *War of the wing-men* (1958)
Man who counts
6 *Mirkheim* (1977)
7 *Earth book of Stormgate* (1978)
8 *Long night* (1983)

Polga series
Bond, Michael
see **Olga da Polga series**

Police diversion series
Strong, Leonard Alfred George
1 *All fall down* (1944)
2 *Othello's occupation* (1945)
Murder plays and ugly scene
3 *Which I never* (1950)
4 *Treason in the egg* (1958)

Police series
Jeffries, Roderic Graeme
1 *Police and detection* (1962)
Against time!
2 *Police dog* (1965)
3 *Police car* (1967)
Patrol car

Police Special Branch series
Lilley, Tom
1 *Projects Section* (1970)
Officer from Special Branch
2 *K Section* (1972)

Policeman series
Farmer, Bernard James
see **Tom Ward series**

Policeman's life series
Cole, Harry
Reminiscences
1 *Policeman's progress* (1980)
2 *Policeman's lot* (1981)
3 *Policeman's patch* (1982)
4 *Policeman's patrol* (1983)
5 *Policeman's prelude* (1984)
6 *Policeman's story* (1985)
7 *Policeman's gazette* (1987)

Policewoman series
Trevor, Leslie
Based on a television series
1 *Rape* (1975)
2 *Code one thousand and thirteen* (1975)
3 *Death of a call girl* (1975)

Polish history trilogy
Sienkiewicz, Henryk
Covers the years 1647 to 1674
1 *With fire and sword* (1886)
Original edition entitled *Ogniem i mieczem*
2 *Deluge* (1888)
Original edition entitled *Potop*
3 *Pan Michael* (1893)
Fire in the steppe
Original edition entitled *Pan woiodyjowski*

Polish war trilogy
Kuniczak, Wieslaw Stanislaw
1 *Thousand hour day* (1969)
Sempinski affair
2 *March* (1979)
3 *Valedictory* (1983)

Polished ebony series
Cohen, Octavus Roy
1 *Polished ebony* (1919)
2 *Come seven* (1920)

Political life series
Balzac, Honore de
see **Scenes of political life series**

Political police officer series
Brust, Harold
Memoirs of a political police officer
1 *I guarded kings* (1935)
2 *In plain clothes* (1937)

Polk Street School series
Giff, Patricia Reilly
see **Kids of the Polk Street School series**

Polka Dot series
Giff, Patricia Reilly
1 *Mystery of the blue ring* (1987)
2 *Ring of the red purse* (1987)
3 *Secret at the Polk Street School* (1987)
4 *Powder puff puzzle* (1987)
5 *Case of the Cool-Itch Kid* (1989)
6 *Garbage juice for breakfast* (1989)
7 *Trail of the screaming teenager* (1990)
Co-author: Blanche Sims
8 *Clue at the zoo* (1990)

Pollard series
Klein, Robin
see **Penny Pollard series**
Lemarchand, Elizabeth
see **Superintendent Tom Pollard series**

Pollie Green series
Saint John, Mabel
1 *Pollie Green* (1909)
2 *Pollie Green at Coosha* (1909)
3 *Pollie Green at Cambridge* (1909)
4 *Pollie Green in society* (1910)
5 *Pollie Green, engaged* (1910)
6 *Pollie Green at twenty-one* (1911)

Pollifax series
Gilman, Dorothy
see **Mrs Emily Pollifax series**

Pollitt family series
Free, Colin
1 *Vinegar Hill* (1978)
2 *Bay of Shadows* (1980)
3 *Brannon* (1981)

Polly and Oliver series
Daniell, David Scott
see **Drummer Oliver Crowe series**

Polly and Peter series
Lucia, Rose
see **Peter and Polly series**

Polly and the wolf series
Storr, Catherine
1 *Clever Polly, and other stories* (1952)
2 *Clever Polly and the stupid wolf* (1955)
3 *Polly, the giant's bride* (1956)
4 *Adventures of Polly and the wolf* (1957)
Polly and the wolf again
5 *Tales of Polly and the hungry wolf* (1980)

Polly Brewster series
Roy, Lillian Elizabeth
1 *Polly of Pebbly Pit* (1922)
2 *Polly and Eleanor* (1922)
3 *Polly in New York* (1922)
4 *Polly and her friends abroad* (1922)
5 *Polly's business venture* (1922)
6 *Polly's southern cruise* (1923)
7 *Polly in South America* (1924)
8 *Polly in the Southwest* (1925)
9 *Polly in Alaska* (1926)
10 *Polly in the Orient* (1927)
11 *Polly in Egypt* (1928)
12 *Polly's new friends* (1929)
13 *Polly and Carola* (1930)
14 *Polly and Carola at Ravenswood* (1931)
15 *Polly learns to fly* (1932)
16 *Polly learns to play* (1932)

Polly Burton series
Orczy, Emmuska
see **Old man in the corner series**

Polly-Dear, Rod and Small series
Goode, Evelyn
1 *Days that speak* (1908)
A story of Australian child life
2 *Childhood of Helen* (1913)

Polly Devenish series
Sudbery, Rodie
1 *House in the wood* (1968)
Sound of crying
2 *Cowls* (1969)
3 *Rich and famous and bad* (1970)
4 *Warts and all* (1972)
5 *Ducks and drakes* (1975)

Polly French series
Lewis, Francine
1 *Polly French of Whitford High* (1952)
2 *Polly finds out* (1953)
3 *Polly takes charge* (1954)
4 *Polly and the surprising stranger* (1955)

Polly Lewis series
Stolz, Mary
1 *Ferris wheel* (1977)
2 *Cider days* (1978)

Polly Oliver series
Wiggin, Kate Douglas
1 *Summer in a canon* (1890)
A California story
2 *Polly Oliver's problem* (1893)

Polly Page series
Forrester, Izola Louise
1 *Polly Page Yacht Club* (1910)
2 *Polly Page Ranch Club* (1911)
3 *Polly Page Motor Club* (1913)
4 *Polly Page Camping Club* (1915)

Polly Prentiss series
Gould, Elizabeth Lincoln
1 *Little Polly Prentiss* (1902)
2 *Polly Prentiss goes to school* (1912)
3 *Polly Prentiss goes a-visiting* (1913)
4 *Polly Prentiss keeps a promise* (1914)

Polly series
Bailey, Hilary
1 *Polly put the kettle on* (1975)
2 *As time goes by* (1988)

Polly series
Brooks, Amy
see **Princess Polly series**

Polly series
Dowd, Emma C
1 *Polly of the hospital staff* (1912)
2 *Polly of Lady Gay Cottage* (1913)
3 *Doodles, the sunshine boy* (1915)
4 *Polly and the princess* (1917)
5 *When Polly was eighteen* (1921)

Polly series
Jackson, Gabrielle Emilie
see **Captain Polly series**

Polly series
Whitehill, Dorothy
1 *Polly's first year at boarding school* (1916)
2 *Polly's summer vacation* (1917)
3 *Polly's senior year at boarding school* (1917)
4 *Polly sees the world at war* (1918)
5 *Polly and Lois* (1920)
6 *Polly and Bob* (1922)
7 *Polly's reunion* (1924)
8 *Polly's Polly* (1925)
9 *Polly at Pixie's Haunt* (1926)
10 *Polly's house party* (1927)
11 *Polly's Polly at boarding school* (1928)
12 *Joyful adventures of Polly* (1929)
13 *Polly's Polly and Priscilla* (1932)

Polly Wog and Tommy Tad series
Trick, Edgar Harold
see **Tommy Tad and Polly Wog series**

Pollyanna series
This sequence has five authors
Porter, Eleanor Hodgman
1 *Pollyanna* (1913)
2 *Pollyanna grows up* (1915)
Smith, Harriet Lummis
3 *Pollyanna of the orange blossoms* (1924)
4 *Pollyanna's jewels* (1926)
5 *Pollyanna's debt of honor* (1927)
6 *Pollyanna's western adventure* (1930)
De Trevino, Elizabeth Borton
7 *Pollyanna in Hollywood* (1931)
8 *Pollyanna's castle in Mexico* (1934)
9 *Pollyanna's door to happiness* (1936)
10 *Pollyanna's golden horseshoe* (1939)
Chalmers, Margaret Piper
11 *Polyanna's protege* (1947)
Moffitt, Virginia May
12 *Pollyanna at Six Star Ranch* (1947)
13 *Pollyanna of Magic Valley* (1949)
De Trevino, Elizabeth Borton
14 *Pollyanna and the secret mission* (1951)

Pollyooly series
Jepson, Edgar
1 *Pollyooly* (1911)
2 *Second Pollyooly book* (1914)
3 *Pollyooly dances* (1920)

Polo series
Kennealy, Jerry
see **Nick Polo series**

Polonius Penguin series
Abrahams, Anthony
1 *Polonius Penguin comes to town* (1963)
2 *Polonius Penguin and the flying doctor* (1966)

Polonsky family series
Angoff, Charles
1 *Journey to the dawn* (1951)
2 *In the morning light* (1952)
3 *Sun at noon* (1955)
4 *Between day and dark* (1959)
5 *Bitter spring* (1961)
6 *Summer storm* (1963)
7 *Memory of autumn* (1968)
8 *Winter twilight* (1970)
9 *Season of mists* (1971)
10 *Mid-century* (1973)
11 *Toward the horizon* (1978)

Polson series
Bond, Michael
see **J D Polson series**

Poltergeist series
Kahn, James
1 *Poltergeist* (1982)
2 *Other side* (1986)

Poly and Charles O'Keefe series
L'Engle, Madeleine
1 *Arm of the starfish* (1965)
2 *Young unicorns* (1968)
3 *Dragons in the waters* (1976)
4 *House like a lotus* (1984)

Pomander series
Hakansson, Gunvor
1 *Mister Pomander* (1958)
Original edition entitled *Herr Pomander, Malare*
2 *Pomanders of Little Chipping* (1960)
Original edition entitled *Pomanders i lillkoping*

Pomeroy series
Williams, Gordon Maclean
1 *Pomeroy* (1981)
2 *Pomeroy unleashed* (1983)

Pompey's Head series
Basso, Hamilton
1 *Light Infantry ball* (1959)
2 *View from Pompey's Head* (1954)
Pompey's Head

Pond Hall series
Freeman, Harold Webber
1 *Fathers of their people* (1932)
2 *Pond Hall's progress* (1933)

Ponder and William series
Softly, Barbara
1 *Ponder and William* (1966)
2 *Ponder and William on holiday* (1968)
3 *Ponder and William at home* (1972)
4 *Ponder and William at the weekend* (1974)

Ponders series
Hoban, Russell
Illustrated by Martin Baynton
1 *Jim Frog* (1983)
2 *Big John Turkle* (1983)
3 *Charlie Meadows* (1984)
4 *Lavinia Bat* (1984)

Pongo and Missis series
This sequence has two authors
Smith, Dodie
1 *Hundred and one dalmatians* (1956)
2 *Starlight barking* (1967)
Korman, Justine
3 *Hundred and one dalmatians escape from danger* (1988)
Companion volume: *Hundred and one dalmatians movie storybook*, 1991

Ponies series
Campbell, Judith
1 *Four ponies* (1959)
2 *Merrow ponies* (1960)

Pons series
Derleth, August
see **Solar Pons series**
King, Charles Daly
see **Doctor L Rees Pons series**

Ponsonby series
Leslie, Jean
see **Peter Ponsonby series**

Pont Clery series
Sandstrom, Flora
1 *Midwife of Pont Clery* (1954)
2 *Virtuous women of Pont Clery* (1956)

Ponting series
Bolt, Ben
see **Bob Ponting series**

Pontivy series
Newman, Bernard
see **Papa Pontivy series**

Pontus Franzon series
Bjorn, Thyra Ferre
see **Pastor Pontus Franzon series**

Pony and bear series
Heuck, Sigrid
1 *Pony, the bear and the stolen apples* (1977)
Original edition entitled *Die Pony-Baren-Apfel-Geschichte*
2 *Pony, the bear and the parrot* (1977)
Original edition entitled *Pony, Bar und Papugei*

Pony Club series
Lengstrand, Rof
1 *Long Pony race* (1963)
Original edition entitled *Det Stora Ponny-Lopet*, part 1
2 *Pony Club through smoke and fire* (1963)
Original edition entitled *Det Stora Ponny-Lopet*, part 2

Pony George series
Colt, Clem
1 *Gun-smoke* (1938)
Also published under the author's real name Nelson Coral Nye
2 *Shootin' sheriff* (1938)

Pony patrol series
Pullein-Thompson, Christine
1 *Pony patrol* (1977)
2 *Pony patrol S.O.S.* (1977)
3 *Pony patrol fights back* (1977)
4 *Pony patrol and the mystery horse* (1980)

Pony Rider Boys series
Patchin, Frank Gee
1 *Pony Rider Boys in the Rockies* (1909)
Alternative title: The secret of the lost claim
2 *Pony Rider Boys in Texas* (1910)
Alternative title: The veiled riddle of the Plains
3 *Pony Rider Boys in Montana* (1910)
Alternative title: The mystery of the old Custer trail
4 *Pony Rider Boys in the Ozarks* (1910)
Alternative title: The secret of Ruby Mountain
5 *Pony Rider Boys in the Alkali* (1910)
Alternative title: Finding the key to the desert
6 *Pony Rider Boys in New Mexico* (1910)
Alternative title: The end of the silver trail
7 *Pony Rider Boys in the Grand Canyon* (1912)
Alternative title: The mystery of Bright Angel
8 *Pony Rider Boys with the Texas Rangers* (1920)
Alternative title: On the trail of the border bandits
9 *Pony Rider Boys on the Blue Ridge* (1924)
Alternative title: A lucky find in the Carolina mountains
10 *Pony Rider Boys in New England* (1924)
Alternative title: An exciting quest in the Maine wilderness
11 *Pony Rider Boys in Louisiana* (1924)
Alternative title: Following the game trails in the Canebreak
12 *Pony Rider Boys in Alaska* (1924)
Alternative title: The gold diggers of Taku Pass

Pony seekers series
Pullein-Thompson, Diana
1 *Ponies in the valley* (1976)
2 *Ponies on the trail* (1978)
3 *Ponies in peril* (1979)
4 *Foal for Candy* (1981)
5 *Pony found* (1983)

Pony series
Doty, Jean Slaughter
1 *Winter pony* (1973)
2 *Summer pony* (1975)
3 *Valley of the ponies* (1982)

Pony soldiers series
Cunningham, Chet
1 *Slaughter at Buffalo Creek* (1987)
2 *Comanche massacre* (1987)
3 *Comanche moon* (1988)
4 *Cheyenne blood storm* (1988)
5 *Sioux showdown* (1988)
6 *Sioux slaughter* (1988)
7 *Boots and saddles* (1988)
8 *Renegade army* (1988)
9 *Battle cry* (1989)
10 *Fort Blood* (1989)

Pooh series
Milne, Alan Alexander
1 *Winnie-the-Pooh* (1926)
2 *House at Pooh Corner* (1928)
Revised edition 1961

Pook series
Pook, Peter
1 *Banking on form* (1962)
2 *Pook in boots* (1963)
3 *Pook in business* (1963)
4 *Pook Sahib* (1965)
A light satire on all things Eastern, including the English who go there
5 *Bwana Pook* (1965)
The big white dowry hunter
6 *Professor Pook* (1966)
The schoolmistress's companion; numbers 2, 3, 6 also published as *Pook*, 1976
7 *Banker Pook confesses* (1967)
Exposing the promotion rat-race in banking, including the author's early struggles to wed the chairman's daughter
8 *Pook at college* (1968)
Britain's answer to the brain drain

9 *Pook's tender years* (1969)
Recalling his first childhod before the onet of his second
10 *Pook and partners* (1969)
Secrets of an international agent and rent collector
11 *Playboy Pook* (1970)
12 *Pook's class war* (1971)
Pook finds teaching and warfare almost inseparable
13 *Pook's tale of woo* (1972)
A simple story of passion, intrigue and blackmail
14 *Pook's Eastern promise* (1972)
Three years behind the mast
15 *Beau Pook proposes* (1973)
16 *Pook's tours* (1974)
You too can love dangerously
17 *Teacher's hand-Pook* (1975)
An introduction to children for teachers, parents and education experts
18 *Gigolo Pook* (1975)
Dance your way into her purse
19 *Pook's love nest* (1976)
20 *Pook's china doll* (1977)
21 *Pook's curiosity shop* (1977)
22 *Marine Pook, Esquire* (1978)
23 *Pook's Viking virgins* (1979)

Pookie series
Wallace, Ivy Lilian
1 *Pookie* (1946)
Revised edition 1963
2 *Pookie and the gypsies* (1947)
3 *Pookie puts the world right* (1949)
4 *Pookie in search of a home* (1951)
Numbers 1-4 also published in one volume entitled *The story of Pookie*, 1953
5 *Pookie at the seaside* (1956)
6 *Pookie's big day* (1958)
7 *Pookie and the swallows* (1961)
8 *Pookie in Wonderland* (1963)
9 *Pookie believes in Santa Claus* (1965)
10 *Pookie and his shop* (1967)

Poole series
Brent of Bin Bin
see **Bert Poole series**
Wade, Henry
see **Inspector Poole series**

Poop series
Locklin, Gerald
1 *Poop, and other poems* (1973)
2 *Son of Poop* (1974)

Poor girl series
Van der Meersch, Maxence
1 *Poor girl* (1948)
Original edition entitled *La fille pauvre*
2 *Hour of love* (1955)
Original edition entitled *La compagnie*

Poor relation series
Chesney, Marion
1 *Lady Fortescue steps out* (1992)
2 *Miss Tonks turns to crime* (1993)
3 *Mrs Budley falls from grace* (1993)
4 *Sir Philip's folly* (1993)
5 *Colonel Sandhurst to the rescue* (1994)

Poor relations series
Balzac, Honore de
1 *Cousin Bette* (1846)
Cousin Betty
Original edition entitled *La cousine Bette*
2 *Cousin Pons* (1847)
Original edition entitled *Le cousin Pons*

Popcorn Pruitt and Doc McDuff series
Mitchell, Red
see **Doc McDuff and Popcorn Pruitt series**

Popeye series
Verral, Charles Spain
1 *Popeye goes fishing* (1980)
2 *Popeye and the haunted house* (1980)
3 *Popeye climbs a mountain* (1980)

Popeye the Sailor series
Segar, Elzie Crisler
1 *Popeye the Sailor* (1931)
Thimble Theatre starring Popeye
2 *Popeye among the savages* (1934)
Includes pop-up picture
3 *Popeye, the sailor man* (1937)
4 *Popeye and the pirates* (1945)
Companion volume: *Popeye, the cartoon book*, 1934

Poplar series
Lax, William Henry
Reminiscences
1 *Lax of Poplar* (1927)
2 *Let's go to Poplar* (1929)
3 *Adventure in Poplar* (1933)
4 *Mrs Benger carries on* (1935)

Poppies series
Middleton, Ivy Florence Emily
1 *Chris Temple, patrol leader* (1964)
2 *Challenge for the Poppies* (1965)
3 *Poppies and Mandy* (1966)

Poppins series
Travers, Pamela Lyndon
see **Mary Poppins series**

Poppleberry series
Lindsay, Hilarie
see **Mister Poppleberry series**

Popplecorn series
Musson, Margaret
see **Mister Popplecorn series**

Poppy Pig series
Bruna, Dick
1 *Poppy Pig* (1977)
Original edition entitled *Betje Big*
2 *Poppy Pig's garden* (1977)
Original edition entitled *De tuin van Betje Big*
3 *Poppy Pig goes to market* (1980)
Original edition entitled *Betje Big gaat naar de markt*
4 *Poppy Pig's birthday* (1986)
Original edition entitled *De verjaardag van Betje Big*

Poppy series
Rayner, Claire
1 *Jubilee* (1987)
2 *Flanders* (1988)

Poppy Treloar series
O'Harris, Pixie
1 *Fortunes of Poppy Treloar* (1941)
2 *Poppy and the gems* (1944)
3 *Poppy faces the world* (1947)

Porfiry Petrovich Rostnikov series
Kaminsky, Stuart Melvin
see **Inspector Porfiry Petrovich Rostnikov series**

Pork series
Goodall, John Strickland
see **Paddy Pork series**

Porridge series
This sequence has three authors; based on a television series
Marshall, Jonathan
1 *Porridge* (1975)
Victor, Paul
2 *Another stretch of Porridge* (1976)
Short stories
3 *Further stir of Porridge* (1977)
4 *Going straight* (1978)
Ableman, Paul
5 *Porridge, the inside story* (1979)

Port series
Rabe, Peter
see **Daniel Port series**

Porter series
Lovell, Marc
see **Appleton Porter series**
Naha, Ed
see **Harry Porter series**
Stratemeyer, Edward L
see **Dave Porter series**
Taggart, Marion Ames
see **Doctor's little girl series**
Travis, Elizabeth
see **Ben and Carrie Porter series**

Portia and Julian series
Enright, Elizabeth
1 *Gone-Away Lake* (1957)
2 *Return to Gone-Away* (1961)

Portrait of a psychiatrist series
Viscott, David Steven
Autobiography
1 *Dorchester boy* (1973)
2 *Making of a psychiatrist* (1973)

Portugee Philips trilogy
Ulyatt, Kenneth
1 *North against the sioux* (1965)
2 *Longhorn trail* (1967)
The story of a cattle drive from Texas to Wyoming in the 1860s
3 *Custer's gold* (1971)
A story of the American West at the time of the Battle of Little Big Horn

Poseidon series
Gallico, Paul
1 *Poseidon adventure* (1969)
2 *Beyond the Poseidon adventure* (1978)

Poskitt trilogy
Fletcher, Joseph Smith
see **Mister Poskitt trilogy**

Posse series
Alington, Adrian
see **Inspector Posse series**

Possessed series
Powe, Ronald
1 *Possessed* (1989)
2 *Possessed II* (1990)

Possessors self-possessed series
O'Neill, Eugene
Originally planned as a cycle of six of which only two survive
1 *Touch of the poet* (1957)
A play in four acts
2 *More stately mansions* (1964)
A play in three acts

Possibility wars series
Slavicsek, Bill
see **Torg series**

Possum series
Eliot, Thomas Stearns
see **Old Possum series**
Hibberd, Jean
see **Peter Possum series**

Possums series
McGill, Marci
see **Six little possums series**

Post series
Irving, Alexander
see **Doctor Anthony Post series**

Posthumous works of Julio Arceval series
Madariaga, Salvador de
see **Julio Arceval series**

Postman Pat readers series
Cunliffe, John Arthur
1 *Postman Pat's safari* (1986)
2 *Postman Pat plays for Greendale* (1986)
3 *Postman Pat's messy day* (1986)
4 *Postman Pat's wet day* (1986)
5 *Postman Pat makes a splash* (1987)
6 *Postman Pat's day in bed* (1987)
7 *Postman Pat and the Greendale ghost* (1987)
8 *Postman Pat and the Christmas puddings* (1987)
9 *Postman Pat and the cleaning day* (1988)
10 *Postman Pat and the dinosaur bone* (1988)
11 *Postman Pat and the pet show* (1988)
12 *Postman Pat's washing day* (1988)
13 *Postman Pat's sore tooth* (1989)
14 *Postman Pat and the bees* (1989)

Postman Pat series
Cunliffe, John Arthur
1 *Postman Pat's treasure hunt* (1981)
2 *Postman Pat and the mystery thief* (1981)
3 *Postman Pat's secret* (1982)
4 *Postman Pat's rainy day* (1982)
5 *Postman Pat's foggy day* (1982)
6 *Postman Pat's difficult day* (1982)
7 *Postman Pat's tractor express* (1983)
8 *Postman Pat takes a message* (1983)
9 *Postman Pat's thirsty day* (1984)
10 *Postman Pat goes sledging* (1984)
11 *Postman Pat and his village* (1984)
12 *Postman Pat's breezy day* (1985)
13 *Postman Pat's letters on ice* (1985)
14 *Postman Pat to the rescue* (1986)
15 *Postman Pat's market day* (1988)
16 *Postman Pat and the harvest parcel* (1988)
17 *Postman Pat goes to town* (1988)
18 *Postman Pat's cat-up-a-tree party* (1988)
19 *Postman Pat gets a pet* (1988)
20 *Postman Pat and the letter puzzle* (1988)
21 *Postman Pat's discovery* (1989)
22 *Postman Pat's Christmas surprise* (1989)
23 *Postman Pat's Christmas tree* (1989)
24 *Postman Pat and the puzzle parcels* (1990)
25 *Postman Pat's lost hat* (1990)
26 *Postman Pat wins a psize* (1991)
27 *Postman Pat's sleepy day* (1991)
28 *Postman Pat and the toy soldiers* (1991)
29 *Postman Pat makes a present* (1992)
30 *Postman Pat takes the bus* (1992)
31 *Postman Pat's wild cat chase* (1992)
32 *Postman Pat, plant-sitter* (1993)
33 *Postman Pat and the flood* (1994)
34 *Postman Pat and the tuba* (1994)
35 *Postman Pat and the barometer* (1994)
Companion volumes: *The Postman Pat fun book*, 1987, *Fun and games with Postman Pat*, an activity book, by John Arthur Cunliffe and Ivor Wood, 1983

Postman Pat's storybook series
Cunliffe, John Arthur
1 *Postman Pat's winter storybook* (1987)
2 *Postman Pat's summer storybook* (1987)
3 *Postman Pat's zodiac storybook* (1989)
4 *Postman Pat's Greendale storybook* (1990)

Post-war Britain series
Target, George William
1 *Evangelists* (1958)
2 *Teachers* (1960)

Post-war Britain series

3 *Missionaries* (1961)
4 *Shop stewards* (1962)
5 *Americans* (1964)
6 *Scientists* (1966)
7 *Young lovers* (1970)
8 *Patriots* (1974)
9 *Strike the strikers* (1975)

Post-war trilogy
Mathew, David
1 *Mango on the mango tree* (1950)
2 *In Valombrosa* (1952)
3 *Prince of Wales's Feathers* (1953)

Posy Bates series
Cresswell, Helen
1 *Meet Posy Bates* (1990)
2 *Posy Bates, again!* (1991)
3 *Posy Bates and the bag lady* (1993)

Potash series
Glass, Montague
1 *Potash and Perlmutter, their co-partnership, ventures and adventures* (1914)
2 *Abe and Mawruss* (1914)
3 *Potash and Perlmutter in society* (1917)
4 *Y' understand* (1925)
5 *Lucky numbers* (1927)

Potato Head series
Slier, Debby
1 *Mister Potato Head's new tool set* (1985)
2 *Mrs Potato Head's new hat* (1985)

Potato man series
McDonald, Megan
1 *Potato man* (1991)
2 *Great pumpkin switch* (1992)

Potomac Army trilogy
Catton, Bruce
1 *Mister Lincoln's army* (1951)
2 *Glory Road* (1952)
The bloody route from Fredericksburg to Gettysburg
3 *Stillness at Appomattox* (1953)

Potted stories series
Barclay, Vera Charlesworth
1 *Potted stories to tell Scouts and Cubs* (1926)
2 *More potted stories to tell Scouts and Cubs* (1936)

Potter boys series
Cobb, Frank
see **Stars and Stripes series**

Potter Pinner series
This sequence has two authors
Kaye, Mollie
1 *Potter Pinner Meadow* (1937)
2 *Black Bramble Wood* (1938)
Tempest, Margaret
3 *Willow Witches Brook* (1945)
4 *Gold Gorse Common* (1946)

Potter series
Foley, Rae
see **Hiram Potter series**
Korman, Gordon
see **Bugs Potter series**
Maling, Arthur
see **Brock Potter series**
Quackenbush, Robert Mead
see **Piet Potter series**
Rich, Virginia
see **Mrs Eugenia Potter series**

Potter trilogy
Bacheller, Irving
see **Socrates Potter trilogy**

Potter's garden series
Fenwick, Jill
see **Mister Potter's garden series**

Pottinger series
Diver, Maud
see **Eldred Pottinger series**

Pottleton series
Tuite, Hugh
1 *Mrs Pottleton's bridge parties* (1926)
2 *Pottleton bridge club* (1929)

Potts series
Spence, Peter
see **Professor Potts series**

Pound puppies series
Korman, Justine
1 *Pound puppies, problem puppies* (1986)
2 *Pound puppies in public nuisance* (1988)

Povin series
Trenhaile, John
see **General Povin series**

Pow trilogy
Slater, Catherine Ponton
see **Marget Pow trilogy**

Powder Valley series
Field, Peter
This pseudonym is used by S Lancer Cheney, Harry Sinclair Drago, Davis Dresser, Fred East, Lucien Waldo Emerson, Francis Thayer Hobson, Robert Jasper Hogan, Edward Beverly Mann, Samuel Mines, Ed Earl Repp, Tom West as indicated against each title
1 *Outlaws three* (1933) [Hobson]
2 *Dry-Gulch Adams* (1934) [Hobson]
3 *Gringo guns* (1935) [Hobson]
4 *Boss of the Lazy 9* (1936) [Mann]
5 *Coyote Gulch* (1936) [Mines]
6 *Mustang Mesa* (1937) [Repp]
7 *Canyon of death* (1938) [Drago]
8 *Outlaw of Eagle Nest* (1938) [Cheney]
9 *Tenderfoot Kid* (1939) [Drago]
10 *Doctor Two Guns* (1939) [Drago]
11 *Man from Thief River* (1940) [Drago]
12 *Law badge* (1940) [Drago]
13 *Guns from Powder Valley* (1941) [Dresser]
14 *Powder Valley pay-off* (1941) [Dresser]
15 *Trail south from Powder Valley* (1942) [Dresser]
16 *Law man of Powder Valley* (1942) [Dresser]
17 *Fight for Powder Valley* (1942) [Dresser]
18 *Powder Valley vengeance* (1943) [Dresser]
19 *Sheriff on the spot* (1943) [Dresser]
20 *Smoking iron* (1944) [Dresser]
21 *Maverick's return* (1944) [West]
22 *Midnight roundup* (1944) [Dresser]
23 *Death rides the night* (1944) [Dresser]
24 *End of the trail* (1945) [Dresser]
25 *Road to Laramie* (1945) [Dresser]
26 *Gambler's gold* (1946) [East]
27 *Powder Valley showdown* (1945) [Dresser]
28 *Ravaged range* (1946) [East]
29 *Trail from Needle Rock* (1946) [East]
30 *Return to Powder Valley* (1948) [Hogan]
31 *Outlaw Valley* (1949) [Hogan]
32 *Sheriff wanted* (1949) [Hogan]
33 *Blacksnake Trail* (1950) [Hogan]
34 *Powder Valley ambush* (1950) [Emerson]
35 *Back trail to danger* (1951) [Emerson]
36 *Canyon hideout* (1951) [Emerson]
37 *Marauders at the Lazy Mare* (1951) [Emerson]
38 *Guns in the saddle* (1952) [Emerson]
39 *Powder Valley hold-up* (1952) [Emerson]
40 *Riders of the outlaw trail* (1952) [Emerson]
41 *Three guns from Colorado* (1952) [Emerson]
42 *Dig the spurs deep* (1953) [Emerson]
43 *Guns roaring west* (1953) [Emerson]
44 *Montana maverick* (1952) [Emerson]
45 *Powder Valley deadlock* (1954) [Emerson]
46 *Powder Valley stampede* (1954) [Emerson]
47 *Ride for Trinidad* (1954) [Emerson]
48 *War in the painted buttes* (1954) [Emerson]
49 *Breakneck Pass* (1955) [Emerson]
50 *Outlaw of Castle Canyon* (1954) [Emerson]
51 *Rawhide rider* (1955) [Emerson]
52 *Saddles to Santa Fe!* (1955) [Emerson]
53 *Powder Valley renegade* (1955) [Emerson]
54 *Strike for Tomahawk* (1956) [Emerson]
55 *Wild horse lightning* (1956) [Emerson]
56 *Guns for Grizzly Flat* (1957) [Emerson]
57 *Man from Robber's Roost* (1957) [Emerson]
58 *Powder Valley manhunt* (1957) [Emerson]
59 *Raiders at Medicine Bow* (1957) [Emerson]
60 *Hangman's trail* (1958) [Emerson]
61 *Rustler's rock* (1958) [Emerson]
62 *Sagebrush swindle* (1958) [Emerson]
63 *Drive for Devil's River* (1959) [Emerson]
64 *Outlaw express* (1959) [Emerson]
65 *Trail to Troublesome* (1959) [Emerson]
66 *Double-Cross Canyon* (1960) [Emerson]
67 *Powder Valley plunder* (1960) [Emerson]
68 *Battlesnake Range* (1961) [Emerson]
69 *Rimrock riders* (1961) [Emerson]
70 *Wolfpack trail* (1961) [Emerson]
71 *Cougar Canyon* (1962) [Emerson]
72 *Outlaw herd* (1962) [Emerson]
73 *Powder Valley ransom* (1962) [Emerson]
74 *Outlaw deputy* (1963) [Emerson]
75 *Powder Valley getaway* (1963) [Emerson]
76 *Trail through Tascosa* (1963) [Emerson]
77 *Rustler's empire* (1964) [Emerson]
78 *Feud at Silvermine* (1965) [Emerson]

Powdersmoke series
Westland, Lynn
1 *Powdersmoke Pass* (1937)
2 *Powdersmoke payoff* (1963)
Also published under the pseudonym Al Cody
3 *Heritage in Powdersmoke* (1967)

Powell family series
Palmer, Bernard
1 *Rebel of the Lazy H Ranch* (1980)
2 *Case of the missing dinosaur* (1981)
3 *Clue of the old sea chest* (1981)
4 *Mystery at Poor Boy's Folly* (1981)

Powell series
Fowles, Anthony
see **Richard Powell series**
Sperry, Armstrong
see **Chad Powell series**

Powell's army series
Duncan, Terence
1 *Unchained lightning* (1987)
2 *Apache raiders* (1987)
3 *Mustang warriors* (1987)
4 *Robert's roost* (1988)
5 *Rocky Mountains showdown* (1988)
6 *Red River desperadoes* (1988)
7 *Missouri woodhawks* (1989)
8 *Rio renegades* (1989)

Power boys series
Lyle, Mel
1 *Mystery of the haunted skyscraper* (1964)
2 *Mystery of the flying skeleton* (1964)
3 *Mystery of the burning ocean* (1965)
4 *Mystery of the million-dollar penny* (1965)
5 *Mystery of the double kidnapping* (1966)
6 *Mystery of the vanishing lady* (1967)

Power of the night trilogy
Horowitz, Anthony
see **Old ones trilogy**

Power series
Clandon, Henrietta
see **William Power series**
Gray, Juliet
see **Stephen Power series**

Powers of light series
O'Neal, Kathleen M
1 *Abyss of light* (1990)
2 *Treasure of light* (1990)
3 *Redemption of light* (1991)

Powers series
Rayter, Joe
see **Johnny Powers series**
Zacharia, Irwin
see **Vendetta series**

Powers trilogy
Wink, Walter Philip
1 *Naming the powers* (1984)
2 *Unmasking the powers* (1985)
3 *Engaging the powers* (1992)

Powledge series
Rea, Margaret Lucile Paine
see **Lieutenant Powledge series**

Powlett-Jones series
Delderfield, Ronald Frederick
see **To serve them all my days series**

Powranna series
Lyne, Nairda
1 *Tasmanian tales* (1965)
2 *Adventures at Powranna* (1969)

Poynings series
Burt, Michael
see **Roger Poynings series**

Practice trilogy
Vernon, Edward
Medical reminiscences
1 *Practice makes perfect* (1977)
2 *Practise what you preach* (1978)
3 *Getting into practice* (1979)

Prairie children series
Allen, Gina
1 *Prairie children* (1941)
2 *On the Oregon trail* (1942)

Prairie romance series
Oke, Janette
see **Davis family series**

Prairie series
Stahl, Hilda
1 *Blossoming love* (1991)
2 *Stranger's wife* (1992)
3 *Makeshift husband* (1993)

Prairie trilogy
Stringer, Arthur
1 *Prairie wife* (1915)
2 *Prairie mother* (1920)
3 *Prairie child* (1922)

Prairies series
Hunkins, Ralph Valentine
see **Tales of the prairies series**

Prank series
Older, Jules
see **Hank Prank series**

Pratt portraits series
Fuller, Anna
Sketched in a New England suburb
1 *Pratt portraits* (1892)
2 *Later Pratt portraits* (1911)

Pratt series
Blair, Cynthia
see **Susan and Christine Pratt series**
Grand, Sarah
see **Adnam Pratt series**
Lee, Bernie
see **Tony and Pat Pratt series**
Leslie, David Stuart
see **Ernie Pratt series**
Lincoln, Joseph Crosby
see **Mister Pratt series**
Nobbs, David
see **Henry Pratt series**

Prayers series
L'Engle, Madeleine
1 *Everyday prayers* (1974)
2 *Prayers for Sunday* (1974)

Preacher series
Johnstone, William Wallace
see **Mountain Man Preacher series**

Preacher's law series
This sequence has two authors
McElwain, Dean L
1 *Widow maker* (1987)
2 *Trail of death* (1987)
3 *Gavel and the gun* (1987)
4 *Last gunfight* (1988)
5 *Slaughter at Ten Sleep* (1988)
Myers, Barry
6 *Rebel* (1988)
7 *Raiders* (1989)

Precious moments series
Beers, Victor Gilbert
1 *Precious moment through the year* (1990)
2 *Precious moment through the day* (1991)

Pre-Columbian trilogy
Peters, Daniel
1 *Luck of Huemac* (1981)
A novel about the Aztecs
2 *Tikal* (1983)
A novel about the Maya
3 *Four quarters* (1991)
A novel about the Incas

Predator series
This sequence has two authors
Monette, Paul
1 *Predator* (1987)
Hawke, Simon
2 *Predator two* (1990)

Preed series
Black, Ladbroke
see **Mister Preed series**

Preep series
Shulman, Milton
1 *Preep, the little pigeon of Trafalgar Square* (1964)
2 *Preep in Paris* (1967)
3 *Preep and the Queen* (1970)

Prefabulous animiles series
Reeves, James
see **Animiles series**

Prehistoric adventure series
Denzel, Justin Francis
1 *Boy of the painted cave* (1988)
2 *Hunt for the last cat* (1991)
3 *Land of the thundering herds* (1993)

Preleshnik series
Ka-tzetnik 135633
see **Harry Preleshnik series**

Prem Narayan series
Casberg, Melvin A
see **Captain Prem Narayan series**

Prentice series
Sea-Lion
see **John Prentice series**

Prentice trilogy
Traill, Peter
see **Mister Prentice trilogy**

Prentis series
Backhouse, Elizabeth
see **Inspector Prentis series**

Prentiss series
Gould, Elizabeth Lincoln
see **Polly Prentiss series**
Wasson, Mildred
see **Nancy Prentiss series**

Pre-Raphaelite Brotherhood series
Fleming, Gordon Howard
1 *Rossetti and the Pre-Raphaelite Brotherhood* (1967)
2 *That ne'er shall meet again* (1971)
Rossetti, Millais, Hunt

Prescot series
Akers, Alan Burt
see **Dray Prescot series**
Prescot, Julian
see **Case books series**

Prescott series
Hendricksen, Louise
see **Doctor Amy Prescott series**
Wisler, Gary Clifton
see **Darby Prescott series**

Present and future series
Coward, Noel
Autobiography
1 *Present indicative* (1937)
2 *Past conditional* (1986)
3 *Future indefinite* (1954)

Presidential trilogy
Hawkey, Raymond
1 *Wild card* (1974)
Co-author: Roger Bingham; revised edition 1988
2 *Side-effect* (1979)
3 *It* (1983)
End stage

President's daughter series
White, Ellen Emerson
1 *President's daughter* (1984)
2 *White House autumn* (1985)

Press and play series
Cartlidge, Michelle
1 *Birthday bunnies* (1987)
2 *Toyshop bunnies* (1987)
3 *Playground bunnies* (1988)
4 *Seaside bunnies* (1988)

Press Gang series
Moffat, Bill
1 *First edition* (1994)
2 *Public exposure* (1994)
3 *Checkmate* (1994)
4 *Date* (1994)

Prester John series
Page, Norvell W
1 *Flame winds* (1969)
2 *Sons of the Bear-God* (1969)

Prester series
Dengler, Sandy
see **Jack Prester series**

Preston series
Chambers, Peter
see **Mark Preston series**
Chester, Peter
see **Johnny Preston series**
Resnick, Sylvia
see **Debbie Preston, teenage reporter series**

Presumption series
This sequence has two authors
Austen, Jane
1 *Pride and prejudice* (1813)
Barrett, Julia
2 *Presumption* (1994)
An entertainment

Pretty Pierre series
Parker, Gilbert
1 *Pierre and his people* (1892)
2 *Adventure of the north* (1895)
3 *Romany of the snows* (1898)

Pretzel series
Rey, Margret
Illustrated by Hans Augusto Rey
1 *Pretzel* (1944)
2 *Pretzel and the puppies* (1946)

Prey series
Goddard, Kenneth
1 *Prey* (1992)
2 *Wildfire* (1994)

Prey series
Sandford, John
see **Lucas Davenport series**

Priam series
Christmas, Joyce
see **Lady Margaret Priam series**

Price and Brichter series
Pulver, Mary Monica
see **Kori McLeod Price and Peter Brichter series**

Price family series
Pye, Virginia
1 *Red letter holiday* (1940)
2 *Snow bird* (1941)
3 *Primrose Polly* (1942)
4 *Half-term holiday* (1943)
5 *Prices return* (1946)
6 *Stolen jewels* (1948)
7 *Johanna and the Prices* (1951)
8 *Holiday exchange* (1953)

Price series
Cannan, Joanna
see **Inspector Ronald Price series**
Chichester, John Jay
see **Jimmy Price series**
Kelly, Vince
see **Detective Inspector Price series**
Morice, Anne
see **Tessa Crichton Price series**
Newton, Mike
see **Bounty Man series**
Norton, Mary
see **Bed-knob and broomstick series**

Prickle Farm series
Hayes, Mike
1 *Prickle Farm* (1983)
2 *Prickle Farm round two* (1985)
3 *Prickle Farm greener pastures* (1987)
4 *Tussock Flat tales* (1991)

Prickles series
Adams, Georgie
see **Great Uncle Prickles series**

Pride and prejudice series
This sequence has two authors
Austen, Jane
1 *Pride and prejudice* (1813)
Tennant, Emma
2 *Pemberley* (1993)
3 *Unequal marriage* (1994)
Alternative title: Pride and prejudice twenty years later

Pride series
Frazer, Andrew
see **Duncan Pride series**
O'Neill, Archie
see **Jeff Pride series**
Petrie, Rhona
see **Doctor Nassim Pride series**

Priest series
Cobb, Irwin Shrewsbury
see **Judge priest series**

Priest trilogy
O'Riordan, Conal
see **Stanislaus Priest trilogy**

Priestley series
Rhode, John
see **Doctor Lancelot Priestley series**

Prike series
Blochman, Lawrence Goldtree
see **Inspector Leonidas Prike series**

Prill, Oliver and Colin series
Cheetham, Ann
see **Black harvest series**

Primal land series
Lumley, Brian
see **Tales of the primal land series**

Primeval forest series
Schweitzer, Albert
Translated from the German
1 *On the edge of the primeval forest* (1922)
Experiences and observations of a doctor in Equatorial Africa
2 *More from the primeval forest* (1931)
One volume edition 1948

Primitive series
Bennet, Robert Ames
1 *Into the primitive* (1908)
2 *Out of the primitive* (1911)

Primrose series
Ford, Leslie
see **Colonel John Primrose series**

Prince Albert series
Lovesey, Peter
see **Bertie series**

Prince and Jill series
Dickins, Joan
see **Jill and Prince series**

Prince Charles series
Lang, Andrew
see **Pickle series**

Prince Corum and the silver hand trilogy
Moorcock, Michael
see **Chronicle of Prince Corum and the silver hand trilogy**

Prince Corum series
Moorcock, Michael
see **Corum series**

Prince Dimple trilogy
Paull, Minnie E
1 *Prince Dimple and his everyday doings* (1890)
2 *Prince Dimple's further doings* (1891)
3 *Prince Dimple on his travels* (1892)

Prince Jali series
Myers, Leopold Hamilton
1 *Near and the far* (1929)
2 *Prince Jali* (1931)
3 *Rajah Amar* (1935)
Only published in *The root and the flower*, 1935 which also includes numbers 1 and 2
4 *Pool of Vishnu* (1940)
Omnibus volume entitled *The root and the flower*, 1940

Prince Lincoas series
Curry, Jane Louise
1 *Daybreakers* (1970)
2 *Over the sea's edge* (1971)

Prince of Hed trilogy
McKillip, Patricia Anne
see **Morgon trilogy**

Prince of shadows series
Chalk, Gary
Fantasy role-playing games stories
1 *Mean streets* (1988)
2 *Creatures from the depths* (1989)

Prince of Stars in the Cavern of Time series
Dennis, Ian
1 *Bagdad* (1985)
2 *Prince of Stars* (1987)
One volume edition entitled *The Prince of Stars in the Cavern of Time*, 1989

Prince Paul series
Blyton, Enid
1 *Secret island* (1938)
2 *Secret of Spiggy Holes* (1940)
3 *Secret mountain* (1941)
4 *Secret of Killimooin* (1943)
5 *Secret of moon Castle* (1953)

Prince Rupert series
D'Oyley, Elizabeth
1 *English march* (1953)
2 *Prince Rupert's daughter* (1954)

Prince series
Gregg, Cecil Freeman
see **Henry Prince series**

Prince trilogy
Christopher, John
1 *Prince in waiting* (1970)
2 *Beyond the burning lands* (1971)
3 *Sword of the spirits* (1972)
One volume editions entitled *The sword of the spirits trilogy*, 1980, *The prince in waiting trilogy*, 1983

Prince Zarkon series
Carter, Lin
1 *Nemesis of evil* (1975)
2 *Invisible death* (1975)
3 *Volcano ogre* (1976)
4 *Earth-shaker* (1982)
5 *Horror wears blue* (1987)

Princes of Gwynedd trilogy
Penman, Sharon Kay
1 *Here be dragons* (1985)
2 *Falls the shadow* (1988)
3 *Reckoning* (1991)

Princess Alysa series
Taylor, Janelle
1 *Wild is my love* (1987)
2 *Wild sweet promise* (1989)

Princess Beatrice Hospital series
Cooper, Lisa
1 *Rose for the surgeon* (1979)
2 *Nurse on Ward Nine* (1980)
3 *Angels in red* (1980)
4 *Over the green mask* (1981)
5 *Doctor in plaster* (1981)
6 *New pupil midwife* (1982)
7 *Love comes by ambulance* (1982)
8 *Talisman for a surgeon* (1982)
9 *Hospital across the bridge* (1982)
10 *Flyaway sister* (1983)
11 *Return of Doctor Boris* (1983)

Princess Casamassima series
James, Henry
1 *Roderick Hudson* (1875)
2 *Princess Casamassima* (1886)

Princess Napraxine series
Ouida
1 *Princess Napraxine* (1884)
2 *Othmar* (1885)

Princess of Paris series
Gunter, Archibald Clavering
1 *Princess of Paris* (1894)
2 *King's stockbroker* (1894)

Princess Polly series
Brooks, Amy
1 *Princess Polly* (1910)
2 *Princess Polly's playmates* (1911)
3 *Princess Polly at school* (1912)
4 *Princess Polly by the sea* (1913)
5 *Princess Polly's gay winter* (1914)
6 *Princess Polly at play* (1915)
7 *Princess Polly at Cliffmore* (1925)

Princess series
Grier, Sydney Carlyon
1 *Royal marriage* (1914)
2 *Princess's tragedy* (1918)
3 *Strong hand* (1920)
4 *Out of prison* (1922)
Companion volume: *A brother of girls, some experiences of Major William Barnes*, 1925

Princess series
Oldmeadow, Katharine Louise
1 *Princess Candida* (1922)
2 *Princess Charming* (1923)
3 *Princess Pat* (1924)
4 *Princess Anne* (1925)
5 *Princess Elizabeth* (1926)
6 *Princess Prunella* (1928)

Princess Smartypants series
Cole, Babette
1 *Princess Smartypants* (1978)
2 *Prince Cinders* (1987)
3 *King Change-a-Lot* (1988)

Princess Susan series
Russell, Ivy
1 *Princess Susan* (1954)
2 *Rival clubs* (1958)

Princess Victoria Babenberg series
Cost, March
1 *Hour awaits* (1952)
2 *Invitation from Minerva* (1954)

Princeton boy series
Tomlinson, Paul Greene
1 *Princeton boy under the King* (1921)
2 *Princeton boy in the Revolution* (1922)

Princeton series
Williams, Jesse Lynch
1 *Princeton stories* (1895)
2 *Adventures of a freshman* (1899)

Prine series
Garrisen, Paul
see **Dirk Prine series**

Pringle series
Ashdown, Clifford
see **Romney Pringle series**
Livingston, Nancy
see **G D H Pringle series**
Manning, Olivia
see **Guy and Harriet Pringle series**

Prior Report trilogy
Gibbs, Henry
1 *Not to the swift* (1944)
2 *Blue days and fair* (1946)
3 *Withered garland* (1950)

Prior series
Barker, Pat
see **Billy Prior series**

Priorsford series
Douglas, O
1 *Penny plain* (1920)
2 *Pink sugar* (1924)
3 *Day of small things* (1930)
4 *Priorsford* (1932)
5 *House that is our own* (1940)
6 *Farewell to Priorsford* (1950)

Priory House series
Gee, Herbert Leslie
Religious meditations
1 *Do you agree?* (1960)
2 *It seems to me* (1962)

Priory series
Matthewman, Phyllis
1 *Because of Vivian* (1951)
2 *Turbulence of Tony* (1951)
3 *Coming of Lys* (1951)
4 *Amateur prefects* (1951)

Priscilla Payson series
Sampson, Emma
1 *Priscilla Payson* (1931)
2 *Priscilla at Hunting Hill* (1932)

Priscilla series
Zabel, Jennifer
see **Miss Priscilla series**

Prism pentad series
Denning, Troy
1 *Verdant passage* (1991)
2 *Crimson legion* (1992)
3 *Amber enchantress* (1992)
4 *Obsidian oracle* (1993)
5 *Cerulean storm* (1993)

Prison diaries series
Boyle, Jimmy
1 *Sense of freedom* (1977)
2 *Pain of confinement* (1984)

Prison diary series
Berrigan, Daniel
1 *Go from here* (1968)
2 *Lights on in the house of the dead* (1974)

Prison series
Sahgal, Nayantara
Autobiography
1 *Prison and chocolate cake* (1954)
2 *From fear set free* (1962)

Prisoner, Cell Block H series
Sinclair, Murray
see **Caged women series**

Prisoner of dreams series
Ripley, Karen
1 *Prisoner of dreams* (1989)
2 *Tenth class* (1991)

Prisoner of war series
Goodwin, Ralph
1 *Hongkong escape* (1953)
2 *Passport to eternity* (1956)

Prisoner series
This sequence has three authors; based on a television series
Disch, Thomas Michael
1 *Prisoner* (1969)
McDaniel, David
2 *Prisoner 2* (1969)
Who is number two?
Stine, Hank
3 *Day in the life* (1970)
McDaniel, David
4 *Prisoner 3* (1981)
Companion volumes: *The prisoner files*, volumes 1-6, 1985-86

Private Badger Coe and Sergeant Blizzard Wilson series
Cameron, Caddo
1 *It's hell to be a ranger* (1937)
2 *Rangers is powerful hard to kill* (1937)
3 *At the end of a Texas rope* (1938)
4 *Ghosts on the range to-night* (1941)

Private education series
Mason, Peter
1 *Private education in the EEC* (1983)
2 *Private education in North America* (1984)
3 *Private education in Australia and New Zealand* (1987)
4 *Independent education in southern Africa* (1990)

Private Eye Mac series
Dewey, Thomas Blanchard
1 *Draw the curtain close* (1947)
Dame in danger
2 *Every bet's a sure thing* (1953)
3 *Prey for me* (1954)
Case of the murdered model
4 *Mean streets* (1955)
5 *Brave, bad girls* (1956)
6 *You've got him cold* (1958)
7 *Case of the chased and the unchaste* (1959)
8 *Girl who wasn't there* (1960)
Girl who never was
9 *How hard to kill* (1962)

10 *Sad song for singing* (1963)
11 *Don't cry for long* (1964)
12 *Portrait of a dead heiress* (1965)
13 *Deadline* (1966)
14 *Death and taxes* (1967)
15 *King-killers* (1968)
Death turns right
16 *Love-death thing* (1969)
17 *Taurus trip* (1970)

Private Eye series
Marriott, Anthony
see **Frank Marker series**

Private Eye series
Pronzini, Bill
1 *Snatch* (1971)
2 *Vanished* (1973)
3 *Undercurrent* (1973)
4 *Blowback* (1977)
5 *Twospot* (1978)
Co-author: Colin Willcox
6 *Labyrinth* (1980)
7 *Hoodwink* (1981)
8 *Scattershot* (1982)
9 *Dragonfire* (1983)
10 *Cat's paw* (1983)
Short stories
11 *Bindlestiff* (1983)
12 *Quicksilver* (1984)
13 *Nightshades* (1984)
14 *Double* (1984)
Co-author: Marcia Miller
15 *Bones* (1985)
16 *Deadfall* (1986)
17 *Shackles* (1988)
18 *Jackpot* (1990)
19 *Breakdown* (1991)
20 *Quarry* (1992)
21 *Epitaphs* (1992)
22 *Demons* (1993)
Companion volume: *A killing in Xanadu*, 1980; selections: *Casefile, the best of the Nameless Detective stories*, 1983, also three stories featuring the Nameless Detective in *Graveyard plots*, 1985

Private eyes series
Winfield, Julia
1 *Partners in crime* (1989)
2 *Tug of hearts* (1989)
3 *On Dangerous* (1989)

Private hells trilogy
Gibson, Patricia Jeann
Sketches in reality in one act plays
1 *You must die before my eyes as I have before yours* (1981)
2 *But I feed the pigeons, well I watch the sun* (1981)
3 *Can you tell me who they is?* (1981)

Private Ivan Chonkin series
Voinovich, Vladimir Nikolaevich
Translated from the Russian
1 *Life and extraordinary adventures of Private Ivan Chonkin* (1969)
2 *Pretender to the throne* (1979)

Private Johnny Jackson series
Rigby, Ray
1 *Jackson's war* (1967)
2 *Jackson's peace* (1974)
3 *Jackson's England* (1979)

Private, keep out series
Grant, Gwen
1 *Private, keep out* (1978)
2 *Knock and wait* (1979)
3 *One way only* (1983)

Private life series
Balzac, Honore de
see **Scenes of private life series**

Private McAuslan series
Fraser, George Macdonald
1 *General danced at dawn* (1970)
2 *McAuslan in the rough, and other stories* (1974)
3 *Sheikh and the dustbin, and other McAuslan stories* (1988)

Private pilot's series
Gurney, Gene
1 *Private pilot's handbook of weather* (1964)
Co-author: Joseph A Skiera; second edition 1974
2 *Private pilot's handbook of navigation* (1967)
Co-author: James C Elliott

Private school series
Charles, Steven
1 *Nightmare session* (1986)
2 *Academy of terror* (1986)
3 *Witch's eye* (1986)
4 *Skeleton key* (1986)
5 *Enemy within* (1987)
6 *Last alien* (1987)

Private Takeo series
Tasaki, Hanama
1 *Long the imperial way* (1949)
2 *Mountains remain* (1952)

Privateers and gentlemen series
Williams, Jon
1 *Privateer* (1981)
2 *Yankee* (1981)
3 *Raider* (1981)
4 *Macedonia* (1984)
5 *Cat Island* (1984)

Privateersman series
Ingraham, Joseph Holt
see **Freemantle series**

Prizzi family series
Condon, Richard
1 *Prizzi's family* (1986)
2 *Prizzi's honor* (1982)
Prizzi's honour
3 *Prizzi's glory* (1988)
4 *Prizzi's money* (1994)

Pro series
Curtis, Richard
see **Dave Bolt series**

Probability series
Ball, Brian Neville
1 *Probability man* (1973)
2 *Planet Probability* (1973)

Probe series
Douglas, Carole Nelson
1 *Probe* (1985)
2 *Counterprobe* (1988)

Problems and chronicles series
Borges, Jorge Luis
1 *Six problems for Don Isidro Parodi* (1978)
Original edition entitled *Seis problemas para don Isidro Parodi*
2 *Chronicles of Bustos Domecq* (1979)
Original edition entitled *Cronicas de Bustos Domecq*

Problems of human happiness series
Dudley, Owen Francis
1 *Will men be like gods?* (1924)
2 *Shadow on the earth* (1926)
3 *Masterful monk* (1929)
4 *Pageant of life* (1932)
5 *Coming of the monster* (1936)
6 *Tremaynes and the masterful monk* (1940)
7 *Michael, the masterful monk* (1948)
8 *Last crescendo* (1954)

Probyn series
Bridge, Ann
see **Julia Probyn series**

Procurator trilogy
Mitchell, Kirk
1 *Procurator* (1984)
2 *New barbarians* (1986)
3 *Cry republic* (1989)

Professionals series
Blake, Ken
Based on a television series
1 *Where the jungle ends* (1978)
Also published under the author's real name, Kenneth Bulmer
2 *Long shot* (1978)
Also published under the author's real name, Kenneth Bulmer
3 *Stake out* (1978)
4 *Hunter hunted* (1978)
5 *Blind run* (1979)
Also published under the author's real name, Kenneth Bulmer
6 *Fall girl* (1979)
Also published under the author's real name, Kenneth Bulmer
7 *Hiding to nothing* (1980)
8 *Dead reckoning* (1980)
9 *No stone* (1981)
10 *Cry wolf* (1981)
11 *Spy probe* (1981)
12 *Assassin!* (1982)
13 *Foxhole* (1982)
14 *Untouchables* (1982)
15 *Operation Susie* (1982)
16 *You'll be all right* (1982)
Also published under the author's real name, Kenneth Bulmer

Professor A Pennyfeather series
Olsen, D B
1 *Bring the bride a shroud* (1945)
2 *Gallows for the groom* (1947)
3 *Devious design* (1948)
4 *Something about midnight* (1950)
5 *Love me in death* (1951)
6 *Enrollment cancelled* (1952)
Dead babes in the wood

Professor Adrian Criddle series
Strong, Ben
1 *Track of the slayer* (1925)
2 *Secret of Gnome Head* (1928)

Professor and Nanny series
Johnston, William
see **Nanny and the professor series**

Professor Arnold Rhymer series
Key, Uel
1 *Broken fang, and other experiences of a specialist in spooks* (1920)
Short stories
2 *Yellow death* (1921)
A tale of occult mysteries

Professor Augustus S F X Van Dusen series
Futrelle, Jacques
1 *Chase of the golden plate* (1906)
2 *Thinking Machine* (1907)
Problem of Cell 13
Short stories
3 *Thinking Machine on the case* (1908)
Professor on the case
Short stories
Also *The haunted bell* in *The diamond master*, 1909; omnibus volumes: *Best Thinking Machine detective stories*, 1973, *Great cases of the Thinking Machine*, 1976

Professor Blinkwell series
Fowler, Sydney
1 *Bell Street murders* (1931)
2 *Secret of the screen* (1933)
3 *Who murdered Reynard?* (1947)

Professor Boffin series
Alexander, Louis George
1 *Professor Boffin's robot* (1969)
2 *Professor Boffin's umbrella* (1971)

Professor Branestawm series
Hunter, Norman
1 *Incredible adventures of Professor Branetawm* (1933)
2 *Professor Branestawm's treasure hunt, and other incredible adventures* (1937)
3 *Stories of Professor Branestawm* (1939)
4 *Peculiar triumph of Professor Branestawm* (1970)
5 *Professor Branestawm up the pole* (1972)
6 *Professor Branestawm's great revolution* (1974)
7 *Professor Branestawm round the bend* (1977)
8 *Professor Branestawm's perilous pudding* (1979)
9 *Professor Branestawm and the wild letters* (1981)
10 *Professor Branestawm's pocket motor car* (1981)
11 *Professor Branestawm's building bust-up* (1982)
12 *Professor Branestawm's mouse war* (1982)
13 *Professor Branestawm's crunchy crockery* (1983)
14 *Professor Branestawm's hair-raising idea* (1983)
Companion volumes: *Professor Branestawm's dictionary*, 1973, *Professor Branestawm's compendium of conundrums, riddles, puzzles, brain twiddlers and dotty descriptions*, 1975, *Professor Branestawm's do-it-yourself handbook*, 1976

Professor Caldwell and Lieutenant Phelan series
Ozaki, Milton K
1 *Cuckoo clock* (1946)
Too many women
2 *Fiend in need* (1947)
3 *Dummy murder case* (1951)

Professor Challenger series
This sequence has two authors
Doyle, Arthur Conan
1 *Lost world* (1912)
2 *Poison belt* (1913)
3 *Land of mist* (1925)
4 *When the world screamed, and other stories* (1968)
One volume edition, also including *The disintegration machine*, entitled The *Professor Challenger stories*, 1952; also two Challenger stories in *The Maracot Deep, and other stories*, 1929
Nye, Nicholas
5 *Return to the lost world* (1991)

Professor Christopher Fenton series
Mackenzie, Nigel
1 *Day of judgment* (1956)
2 *Wrath to come* (1957)

Professor Clifford Wells series
Bortner, Norman Stanley
1 *Bond Grayson murdered!* (1936)
2 *Death of a merchant of death* (1937)

Professor Cyrus Hatch series
Davis, Frederick Clyde
1 *Coffins for three* (1938)
Also published as *One murder too many*, under the pseudonym Stephen Ransome
2 *He wouldn't stay dead* (1939)
Also published under the pseudonym Stephen Ransome
3 *Poor, poor Yorick* (1939)
Also published as *Murder doesn't always out*, under the pseudonym Stephen Ransome

Professor Cyrus Hatch series
4 *Graveyard never closes* (1940)
Also published under the pseudonym Stephen Ransome
5 *Let the skeletons rattle* (1944)
Also published under the pseudonym Stephen Ransome
6 *Detour to oblivion* (1947)
Also published under the pseudonym Stephen Ransome
7 *Thursday's blade* (1947)
Also published under the pseudonym Stephen Ransome
8 *Gone tomorrow* (1948)
Also published under the pseudonym Stephen Ransome

Professor David Connell series
Weatherhead, John
1 *Force of innocence* (1966)
2 *Sacred shaft* (1967)

Professor Dennis Barrie series
Reynolds, Adrian
1 *Formula for murder* (1947)
2 *Leprechaun murders* (1950)
3 *Round table murders* (1952)

Professor Gideon Manciple and Doctor William Blow series
Hopkins, Kenneth
see **Doctor William Blow and Professor Gideon Manciple series**

Professor Gideon Oliver series
Elkins, Aaron J
1 *Fellowship of fear* (1982)
2 *Dark place* (1983)
3 *Murder in the Queen's Armes* (1985)
4 *Old bones* (1987)
5 *Curses!* (1989)
6 *Icy clutches* (1990)
7 *Make no bones* (1991)
8 *Dead men's hearts* (1994)

Professor Harding series
Stanners, Harold H
1 *Murder at Markenden Court* (1936)
2 *At the tenth clue* (1937)
3 *Crowning murder* (1938)

Professor Henry Arthur Fielding series
Sharp, David
1 *When no man pursueth* (1930)
2 *My particular murder* (1931)
3 *None of my business* (1931)
Code-letter mystery
4 *I, the criminal* (1932)
5 *Inconvenient corpse* (1933)
6 *Marriage and murder* (1934)
7 *Disputed quarry* (1938)
8 *Frightened sailor* (1939)
9 *Everybody suspect* (1939)

Professor Henry Poggioli series
Stribling, Thomas Sigismund
1 *Clues of the Caribbees* (1929)
2 *Best Doctor Poggioli detective stories* (1975)

Professor Herman Brierly series
Levinrew, Will
1 *Poison plague* (1929)
2 *Murder on the Palisades* (1930)
Wheelchair corpse
3 *Murder from the grave* (1930)
4 *Death points a finger* (1933)

Professor Hilary Tamar series
Caudwell, Sarah
1 *Thus was Adonis murdered* (1981)
2 *Shortest way to Hades* (1984)
3 *Sirens song of murder* (1989)

Professor Jameson series
Jones, Neil Ronald
1 *Planet of the double sun* (1967)
2 *Sunless world* (1967)
3 *Space war* (1967)
4 *Twin worlds* (1967)
5 *Doomsday on Ajiat* (1968)
Many uncollected stories featuring Professor Jameson in *Astonishing Science Fiction* and *Super Science*

Professor John Stubbs series
Campbell, R T
1 *Unholy dying* (1945)
2 *Bodies in a bookshop* (1946)
3 *Take thee a sharp knife* (1946)
4 *Death for Madame* (1946)
5 *Adventure with a goat* (1946)
Two stories
6 *Death cap* (1946)
7 *Swing low, sweet death* (1946)
Numbers 6 and 7 also published in one volume 1947

Professor Kate Fansler series
Cross, Amanda
1 *In the last analysis* (1964)
2 *James Joyce murder* (1967)
3 *Poetic justice* (1970)
4 *Theban mysteries* (1971)
5 *Question of Max* (1976)
6 *Death in the faculty* (1981)
Death in a tenured position
7 *Sweet death, kind death* (1984)
8 *No word from Winifred* (1986)
9 *Trap for fools* (1989)
10 *Players come again* (1990)
11 *Imperfect spy* (1995)

Professor Kreutzemark series
Beeding, Francis
1 *Seven sleepers* (1925)
2 *Hidden kingdom* (1927)

Professor Kurtz series
Curry, Jane Louise
see **Maccubbin family series**

Professor Lancelot Priestley series
Rhode, John
see **Doctor Lancelot Priestley series**

Professor Luther Bastion series
Holt, Gavin
1 *Six minutes past twelve* (1928)
2 *White-faced man* (1929)
Praying monkey
3 *Green talons* (1930)
4 *Murder at Marble Arch* (1931)
5 *Garden of silent beasts* (1931)
6 *Trail of the skull* (1931)
7 *Valse caprice* (1932)
8 *Red eagle* (1932)
9 *Drum beats at night* (1932)
10 *Mark of the paw* (1933)
11 *Golden witch* (1933)
12 *Dark lady* (1933)
13 *Death takes the stage* (1934)
14 *Trafalgar Square* (1934)
15 *Black bullets* (1935)
16 *Emerald spider* (1935)
17 *Steel shutters* (1936)

Professor Mandrake series
Bonett, John
1 *Dead lion* (1949)
2 *Banner for Pegasus* (1951)
Not in the script
3 *No grave for a lady* (1959)

Professor Moriarty series
Gardner, John Edmund
Based on the character from the Sherlock Holmes stories of Sir Arthur Conan Doyle
1 *Return of Moriarty* (1974)
Moriarty
2 *Revenge of Moriarty* (1975)

Professor Neil Kelly series
Dean, S F X
1 *By frequent anguish* (1982)
2 *Such pretty toys* (1982)
3 *It can't be my grave* (1983)
4 *Ceremony of innocence* (1984)
5 *Death and the mad heroine* (1985)
6 *Nantucket soap opera* (1987)

Professor Paul Hatfield series
Rogers, Samuel
1 *Don't look behind you!* (1944)
2 *You'll be sorry!* (1945)
Murder is grim
3 *You leave me cold!* (1946)

Professor Paula Glenning series
Clarke, Anna
1 *Last judgement* (1985)
2 *Cabin 3033* (1986)
3 *Mystery lady* (1986)
4 *Last seen in London* (1987)
5 *Murder in writing* (1988)
6 *Whitelands affair* (1989)
7 *Case of the paranoid patient* (1991)

Professor Peter Shandy series
Macleod, Charlotte
1 *Rest you merry* (1978)
2 *Luck runs out* (1979)
3 *Wrack and rune* (1982)
4 *Something the cat dragged in* (1983)
5 *Curse of the giant hogweed* (1985)
6 *Corpse in Oozak's Pond* (1986)
7 *Vane pursuit* (1989)
8 *Owl too many* (1991)

Professor Potts series
Spence, Peter
Illustrated by Gillian Chapman
1 *Professor Potts meets the animals in Africa* (1981)
2 *Professor Potts meets the animals in North America* (1981)
3 *Professor Potts meets the animals in Asia* (1981)

Professor Robert Harmon series
Elman, Richard Martin
1 *Breadfruit lotteries* (1980)
2 *Menu cypher* (1982)

Professor Ronald Challis series
Martin, Shane
1 *Twelve girls in the garden* (1957)
2 *Saracen shadow* (1957)
3 *Man made of tin* (1958)
4 *Myth is murder* (1959)
Third statue
5 *Wake for mourning* (1962)
Mourner's voyage

Professor Wells and Inspector Sims series
Grierson, Francis Durham
see **Inspector Sims and Professor Wells series**

Professor Wormbog series
Mayer, Mercer
1 *Professor Wormbog in search of the zippercrump-a-zoo* (1976)
2 *Professor Wormbog's gloomy kerploppus* (1977)
Book of great smells and a heart-warming story, besides
3 *Professor Wormbog's cut it, glue it, tape it, do-it book* (1980)
4 *Professor Wormbog's crazy cut-ups* (1980)

Projekt Saucer series
Harbinson, William Allen
1 *Inception* (1991)
2 *Genesis* (1980)

Prom series
Aks, Patricia
1 *Junior prom* (1982)
2 *Senior prom* (1985)

Promise keeper series
Leeson, Muriel
1 *Oranges and UFOs* (1975)
Promise keeper
2 *Path of the promise keeper* (1984)

Promise me series
Copeland, Lori
1 *Promise me today* (1992)
2 *Promise me tomorrow* (1993)
3 *Promise me forever* (1994)

Promise series
Cole, Babette
1 *Promise solves the problem* (1976)
2 *Promise and the monster* (1981)

Promise trilogy
Pascal, Francine
1 *Tender promises* (1986)
2 *Promises broken* (1986)
3 *New promise* (1987)

Pronoun series
Anonymous
1 *Her* (1970)
2 *Him* (1972)
3 *Us* (1973)
4 *You* (1975)
5 *Me* (1976)
6 *Them* (1978)
7 *I* (1980)
8 *Two* (1982)
9 *Woman* (1983)

Prophet series
Green, Russell
1 *Prophet without honour* (1934)
2 *Wilderness blossoms* (1936)

Prophet trilogy
Weis, Margaret
see **Rose of the prophet trilogy**

Proposed series
Willard, Barbara
1 *Proposed and seconded* (1951)
2 *Echo answers* (1952)

Prospects series
Raymond, John
Based on screenplays
1 *Partners in brine* (1986)
2 *Dirty weekend* (1986)

Prospero Group series
Jewell, Derek
1 *Come in, number one, your time is up* (1971)
2 *Sellout* (1973)

Protection Limited series
Harman, Neal
1 *Case of the wounded mastiff* (1947)
2 *Death and the archdeacon* (1949)

Protector series
Rainey, Rich
see **Alex Dartanian series**
Zacharia, Irwin
see **Irving Martin Reddy series**

Protectors series
Blue, Zachary
1 *Petrova twist* (1987)
2 *Jet fighter trap* (1987)

Proteron series
Stanford, John Keith
see **Life and death of George Proteron series**

Proteus series
Sheffield, Charles
1 *Sight of Proteus* (1978)
2 *Proteus unbound* (1989)
One volume edition entitled *Proteus manifest*, 1989

Prothero quartet
Swinnerton, Frank
1 *Woman from Sicily* (1957)
2 *Tigress in Prothero* (1959)
Tigress in the village
3 *Grace divorce* (1960)
4 *Quadrille* (1965)

Proud waters series
Brookes, Ewart
1 *Proud waters* (1954)
2 *Glass years* (1957)

Prouse series
McCulley, Johnston
see **Crimson Clown series**

Provencal Hills series
Wylie, Ida Alexa Ross
1 *Undefeated* (1957)
2 *Home are the hunted* (1959)

Provence series
Fortescue, Winifred
Reminiscences of life in Provence
1 *Perfume from Provence* (1935)
2 *Sunset House* (1937)
3 *There's rosemary, there's rue* (1939)
4 *Trampled lilies* (1941)
5 *Mountain madness* (1943)
6 *Beauty for ashes* (1948)
7 *Laughter in Provence* (1950)

Provence series
Mayle, Peter
1 *Year in Provence* (1989)
2 *Toujours Provence* (1991)

Provence trilogy
Clayton, John
1 *Gold of Toulouse* (1932)
2 *Dew in April* (1934)
3 *Anger of the north* (1936)

Proverb trilogy
Bradley, Mary Emily Neely
1 *Birds of a feather* (1869)
2 *Handsome is that handsome does* (1869)
3 *Wrong confessed* (1871)

Provincial group series
Walpole, Hugh
1 *Cathedral* (1922)
2 *Harmer John* (1926)
3 *Old ladies* (1924)
4 *Inquisitor* (1935)

Provincial lady series
Delafield, E M
1 *Diary of a provincial lady* (1930)
2 *Provincial lady goes further* (1932)
Provincial lady in London
3 *Provincial lady in America* (1934)
4 *Straw without bricks* (1937)
I visit the Soviets
Alternative titles: I visit Soviet Russia, and The provincial lady looks at Russia
5 *Provincial lady in war-time* (1940)
Companion volumes: *Provincial daughter*, by Fosamund Margaret Dashwood, 1951, *The life of a provincial lady*, by Violet Powell, 1988

Provincial life series
Balzac, Honore de
see **Scenes of provincial life series**

Prudence and Hector series
Koscielniak, Bruce
see **Hector and Prudence series**

Prudence series
Hueston, Ethel
1 *Prudence of the parsonage* (1915)
2 *Prudence stays so* (1916)
3 *Sunny slopes* (1917)
Prudence's sisters
4 *Prudence's daughter* (1924)
One volume edition entitled *Prudence's omnibus*, 1936

Prue Foster series
Buzo, Alexander
1 *Search for Harry Allway* (1991)
2 *Prue flies north* (1991)

Prue series
Brooks, Amy
1 *Little sister Prue* (1908)
2 *Prue at school* (1909)
3 *Prue's playmates* (1910)
4 *Prue's merry times* (1911)
5 *Prue's little friends* (1912)
6 *Prue's jolly winter* (1913)

Pruitt and McDuff series
Mitchell, Red
see **Doc McDuff and Popcorn Pruitt series**

Prus trilogy
Kuniczak, Wieslaw Stanislaw
see **Polish war trilogy**

Prussian series
Spielhagen, Friedrich
1 *Problematic characters* (1860)
Original edition entitled *Problematische Naturen*
2 *Through night to light* (1861)
Original edition entitled *Durch Nacht zum Lichte*

Pry series
Large, Ernest Charles
see **Charles Pry series**

Prydain series
Alexander, Lloyd
1 *Book of three* (1964)
2 *Black cauldron* (1965)
3 *Castle of Llyr* (1966)
Numbers 1-3 also published in one volume entitled *The first chronicles of Prydain*, 1986
4 *Taran Wanderer* (1967)
5 *High King* (1968)
Numbers 4 and 5 also published in one volume entitled *The second chronicles of Prydain*, 1986
6 *Foundling, and other tales of Prydain* (1973)
One volume edition entitled *The Prydain chronicles*, 1991; companion volumes: *Coll and his white pig*, 1965, *The truthful harp*, 1967

Pryderi series
Walton, Evangeline
see **Mabinogion series**

Prye series
Millar, Margaret
see **Doctor Paul Prye series**

Prynne series
Bigsby, Christopher
see **Hester Prynne series**

Psammaed series
Nesbit, Edith
see **Five children series**

Psi-Man series
Peters, David
1 *Psi-Man* (1990)
2 *Deathscape* (1991)
3 *Main Street D.O.A.* (1991)
4 *Chaos kid* (1991)
5 *Stalker* (1991)

Psi Patrol trilogy
This sequence is by Betty Anne Crawford using three pseudonyms
Liquori, Sal
1 *Sal's book* (1985)
Benoit, Hendra
2 *Hendra's book* (1985)
Hurley, Maxwell
3 *Max's book* (1985)

Psion series
Vinge, Joan Dennison
1 *Psion* (1982)
2 *Catspaw* (1988)
Cats paw
One volume edition entitled *Alien blood*, 1988

Psmith series
Wodehouse, Pelham Grenville
1 *Mike* (1909)
1.1 *Mike at Wrykyn* (1909)
1.2 *Mike and Psmith* (1909)
Enter Psmith
2 *Psmith in the city* (1910)
3 *Psmith, journalist* (1915)
4 *Leave it to Psmith* (1923)

Psych trilogy
Lumley, Brian
1 *Psychomech* (1984)
2 *Psychosphere* (1984)
3 *Psychamok* (1985)

Psychic detective series
Holzer, Hans
see **Randy Knowles series**

Psychic series
Pluis, Bridget
1 *ABC of ESP* (1985)
Bridget's guide to developing your psychic ability
2 *Bridget's cosmic connections* (1988)
3 *Let Bridget be your guide* (1993)

Psycho series
Bloch, Robert
1 *Psycho* (1959)
2 *Psycho II* (1982)
3 *Psycho-house* (1990)

Psychodrome series
Hawke, Simon
1 *Psychodrome* (1987)
2 *Shapechanger scenario* (1988)

Psychotechnic League series
Anderson, Poul
1 *Psychotechnic League* (1981)
2 *Cold victory* (1982)
3 *Star ship* (1982)

Publisher presents himself series
Johnson, Donald McIntosh
1 *Doctor regrets* (1949)
2 *Bars and barricades* (1952)
3 *Doctor returns* (1956)
4 *Doctor in Parliament* (1958)
5 *Cassandra in Westminster* (1967)
6 *Doctor reflects* (1975)
Miracles and mirages

Publishing series
Warburg, Fredric
Autobiography
1 *Occupation for gentlemen* (1959)
2 *All authors are equal* (1973)

Puck Bure series
Lang, Maria
see **Christer Wick series**

Puck series
Kipling, Rudyard
see **Rewards and fairies series**

Puckett series
Jenkins, Dan
see **Billy Clyde Puckett series**

Pudgy series
Shine, Deborah
1 *Pudgy I love you book* (1988)
2 *Pudgy noisy book* (1988)

Puff trilogy
Shepherd, Jo
1 *Puff to the rescue* (1977)
2 *Huff and Puff* (1978)
3 *Puff in Canada* (1979)

Puffett series
Catling, Gordon
see **Mister Puffett series**

Puffin, Twink and Waggle series
Bennett, Rodney
1 *Puffin, Twink and Waggle at home* (1943)
2 *Puffin, Twink and Waggle at the zoo* (1943)
3 *Puffin, Twink and Waggle at the fair* (1944)
4 *Puffin, Twink and Waggle at the seaside* (1944)

Pug Henry series
Wouk, Herman
see **Commander Pug Henry series**

Pugwall series
Clark, Margaret Dianne
1 *Pugwall* (1989)
2 *Pugwall's summer* (1989)

Pull'n Push series
Weir, Rosemary
see **Tempest family series**

Pulsar series
Moore, Robin
1 *London switch* (1974)
London connection
2 *Italian connection* (1975)

Puma series
Scott, Roney
see **Joe Puma series**

Pumpkin Hill fact series
Davis, Anne
1 *Lists, lists, lists!* (1993)
2 *Find it!* (1993)
3 *Pumpkins for the pot* (1993)
4 *Snakes alive!* (1993)
5 *Tricky tracks* (1993)

Pumpkin Hollow series
Davis, Anne
1 *Pumpkin Hollow countdown* (1993)
2 *On the way* (1993)
3 *Bad bungle!* (1993)
4 *Scrub-a-dub-dub* (1993)
5 *Mystery animals?* (1993)

Punchbowl Farm series
Edwards, Monica
1 *No mistaking Corker* (1947)
2 *Black hunting whip* (1950)
3 *Punchbowl midnight* (1951)
4 *Spirit of Punchbowl Farm* (1952)
5 *Wanderer* (1953)
6 *Punchbowl harvest* (1954)
7 *Frenchman's secret* (1956)
8 *Cownappers* (1958)
9 *Outsider* (1961)
10 *Fire in the Punchbowl* (1965)
11 *Wild one* (1967)

Punishment battalion series
Kostov, K N
1 *Baptism of blood* (1980)
2 *Gulag rats* (1981)
3 *Blood on the Baltic* (1981)
4 *Steppe wolves* (1981)

Punkin series
Stahl, Hilda
see **Daisy Punkin series**

Punky Brewster series
Matthews, Ann
1 *Starring Punky Brewster* (1986)
2 *Punky Brewster at Camp Chipmunk* (1986)

Punography series
McMillan, Bruce
Humorous photography
1 *Punography* (1978)
2 *Punography too* (1980)

Puppets series
Bussell, Jan
Memoirs of a puppeteer
1 *Puppets and I* (1950)
2 *Puppet's progress* (1953)

Puppets series
Wilkinson, Walter
1 *Peep show* (1927)
2 *Vagabonds and puppets* (1930)
3 *Puppets in Yorkshire* (1931)
4 *Sussex peep-show* (1934)
5 *Puppets into Scotland* (1935)
6 *Puppets through Lancashire* (1936)
7 *Puppets through America* (1938)
8 *Puppets in Wales* (1948)

Puppy series
Szekeres, Cyndy
1 *Nothing-to-do puppy* (1985)
2 *Puppy lost* (1986)
3 *Puppy learns to share* (1990)

Purbright series
Watson, Colin
see **Inspector Purbright series**

Purcell sisters quartet
Harris, Ruth Elwin
see **Quantocks quartet**

Purchis family series
Hodge, Jane Aiken
1 *Judas flowering* (1976)
2 *Wide is the water* (1981)
3 *Runaway bride* (1975)
4 *Savannah purchase* (1971)

Purdue series
Spencer, Ross Harrison
see **Chance Purdue series**

Purim series
Simon, Norma
1 *Happy Purim night* (1959)
2 *Purim party* (1959)

Purity series
Seymour, Janette
1 *Purity's passion* (1977)
2 *Purity's ecstasy* (1978)
3 *Purity's shame* (1978)

Purple dress series
Wayne, Jenifer
Autobiography
1 *Brown bread and butter* (1973)
Childhood in the twenties
2 *Purple dress* (1979)
Growing up in the thirties

Purple Pennant trilogy
Barbour, Ralph Henry
1 *Lucky seventh* (1915)
2 *Secret play* (1915)
3 *Purple Pennant* (1916)

Purslane series
Harris, Bernice
1 *Purslane* (1939)
2 *Portulaca* (1941)

Pursuit series
Will, George Frederick
Essays
1 *Pursuit of happiness, and other sobering thoughts* (1978)
2 *Pursuit of virtue, and other Tory notions* (1982)

Puss in Boots series
Gray, Nicholas Stuart
1 *Marvellous story of Puss in Boots* (1955)
Musical play
2 *Further adventures of Puss in Boots* (1971)
Stories

Pusser series
Morris, W R
see **Sheriff Buford Pusser series**

Pussy series
Ross, Diana
see **Miss Pussy series**

PUSSYCAT series
Mark, Ted
see **Girl from P.U.S.S.Y.C.A.T. series**

Putnam Hall series
Winfield, Arthur M
1 *Putnam Hall cadets* (1901)
Cadets of putnam Hall
Alternative title: Good times in school and out
2 *Putnam Hall rivals* (1906)
Rivals of Putnam Hall
Alternative title: Fun and sport afloat and ashore
3 *Putnam Hall champions* (1908)
Champions of Putnam Hall
Alternative title: Bound to win out
4 *Putnam Hall rebellion* (1909)
Rebellion at Putnam Hall
Alternative title: The rival runaways
5 *Putnam Hall encampment* (1910)
Camping out days at Putnam Hall
Alternative title: The secret of the old mill
6 *Putnam Hall mystery* (1911)
Mystery at Putnam Hall
Alternative title: The school chums' strange discovery

Pyanfar series
Cherryh, Carolyn Janice
see **Chanur series**

Pyat series
Moorcock, Michael
see **Colonel Pyat series**

Pye family series
Estes, Eleanor
1 *Ginger Pye* (1951)
2 *Pinky Pye* (1958)

Pyford Hall series
Fisher, Douglas George
see **Jeff Tellford series**

Pym family series
Miller, Rosalind
1 *Adventures of Margery Pym* (1939)
2 *Pyms of Yarrambeat* (1940)

Pym series
Burley, William John
see **Doctor Henry Pym series**
Morland, Nigel
see **Mrs Palmyra Pym series**
Poe, Edgar Allan
see **Arthur Gordon Pym series**
Sanders, John
see **Nicholas Pym series**

Pynchon and Tyson-Tyree series
Pedneau, Dave
see **Whit Pynchon and Annie Tyson-Tyree series**

Pyrton series
Clark, William
see **Patrick Pyrton series**

Q

Q annual series
Milligan, Spike
1 *Q annual* (1979)
2 *Get in the Q annual* (1980)

Q challenge quiz series
Cranfield, Ingrid
1 *Know it all* (1988)
2 *Word wise* (1988)
3 *Trivia I* (1988)
4 *Trivia II* (1988)

Q.E.D. series
Thorne, Ernest Pollett
see **Quentin Eady series**

Q series
Hoyle, Trevor
see **Christian Queghan series**
Prichard, Katherine
see **Don Q series**

Qanar series
White, Ted
1 *Phoenix prime* (1966)
2 *Sorceress of Qar* (1966)
3 *Star wolf!* (1971)

Qantas series
Fysh, Hudson
History of the Australian airline
1 *Qantas rising* (1966)
Autobiography of the flying Fysh
2 *Qantas at war* (1968)

QFWFQ series
Calvino, Italo
1 *Cosmicomics* (1965)
Original edition entitled *Le cosmicouche*
2 *T zero* (1967)
Time and the hunter
Original edition entitled *Ti con zero*

Qhe series
W, W
1 *Taming power* (1974)
2 *White fire* (1974)
3 *Riches* (1975)
4 *Prophet of evil* (1976)

Qsaprinel trilogy
Gotlieb, Phyllis
1 *Judgement of dragons* (1980)
2 *Emperor, swords, pentacles* (1982)
3 *Kingdom of the cats* (1985)

Quadroon trilogy
Gray, Harriet
1 *Gold for the gay masters* (1954)
2 *Bride of doom* (1956)
Bride of violence
3 *Flame and the frost* (1957)
Also published in *Fauna*, by Denise Robins, 1978

Quaile series
Walsh, James Morgan
see **Inspector Quaile series**

Quaker tales series
Robinson, Maude
1 *Time of her life, and other stories* (1919)
2 *Nicholas the weaver, and other Quaker stories* (1922)
3 *Wedded in prison, and other Quaker stories* (1925)

Quality Chase series
Tiltman, Marjorie Hessell
1 *Quality Chase* (1939)
2 *Quality Chase's daughter* (1955)

Quality of hurt series
Himes, Chester
Autobiography
1 *Quality of hurt* (1972)
2 *My life of absurdity* (1976)

Quan series
Begbie, Garstin
see **Superintendent Samuel Quan series**

Quane series
Kilvington, Edwin
see **Crispin Quane series**

Quantocks quartet
Harris, Ruth Elwin
1 *Silent shore* (1986)
2 *Beckoning hills* (1987)
3 *Dividing sea* (1989)
4 *Secluded garden* (1994)

Quantrell series
Gruber, Frank
see **William Clarke Quantrell series**

Quantrill series
Radley, Sheila
see **Chief Inspector Douglas Quantrill series**

Quantrill trilogy
Ing, Dean
see **Ted Quantrill trilogy**

Quantum leap series
McConnell, Ashley
1 *Quantum leap* (1992)
2 *Too close for comfort* (1993)
3 *Wall* (1994)
4 *Prelude* (1994)

Quantum leap series
Robitaille, Julie
1 *Beginning* (1990)
2 *Ghost and the gumshoe* (1990)

Quantum series
Zohar, Danah
1 *Quantum self* (1990)
A revolutionary view of human nature and consciousness rooted in the new physics
2 *Quantum society* (1993)

Quare women trilogy
Furman, Lucy
1 *Quare women* (1923)
A story of the Kentucky mountains
2 *Glass window* (1925)
3 *Lonesome road* (1927)

Quarles series
Brebner, Percy
see **Christopher Quarles series**
Symons, Julian
see **Francis Quarles series**

Quarrel and Ames series
Krentz, Jayne Ann
see **Verity Ames and Jonas Quarrel series**

Quarry series
Collins, Max Allan
1 *Broker* (1976)
Quarry
2 *Broker's wife* (1976)
Quarry's list
3 *Dealer* (1976)
Quarry's deal
4 *Slasher* (1977)
Quarry's cut
5 *Primary target* (1987)

Quarry series
Hunter, Robin
see **Simon Quarry series**

Quarshie series
Wyllie, John
see **Doctor Quarshie series**

Quartz series
Carter, Nicholas
see **Doctor Quartz series**

Quatermain series
Haggard, Henry Rider
see **Allan Quatermain series**

Quatermass series
Kneale, Nigel
Television plays
1 *Quatermass experiment* (1959)
Creeping unknown
2 *Quatermass II* (1960)
Enemy from space
3 *Quatermass and the pit* (1960)
Five million years to earth
Companion volume: *Quatermass, a novelization*, 1979

Quayle series
Aldridge, James
see **Kit Quayle series**
Caillou, Alan
see **Ian Quayle series**
Cheyney, Peter
see **Everard Peter Quayle series**
Kaye, Marvin
see **Hilary Quayle series**
Trent, Paul
see **Peter Quayle series**

Quayne series
Symonds, Francis Addington
see **Superintendent Maxwell Quayne series**

Quebec series
Curwood, James Oliver
1 *Black hunter* (1926)
A novel of old Quebec
2 *Plains of Abraham* (1928)

Queen Anne's England trilogy
Trevelyan, George Macaulay
1 *Blenheim* (1930)
2 *Ramillies and the union with Scotland* (1932)
3 *Peace and the Protestant succession* (1934)

Queen Hildegarde series
Richards, Laura Elizabeth
see **Hildegarde series**

Queen series
Queen, Ellery
see **Ellery Queen series**
Queen, Ellery, Junior
see **Gulliver Queen series**

Queen Victoria series
Plaidy, Jean
1 *Captive of Kensington Palace* (1972)
2 *Victoria in the wings* (1972)
3 *Queen and Lord M* (1973)
4 *Queen's husband* (1973)
5 *Widow of Windsor* (1974)

Queen Victoria trilogy
Whittle, Tyler
1 *Young Victoria* (1971)
2 *Albert's Victoria* (1972)
3 *Widow of Windsor* (1973)

Queen Yesno series
Tozer, Mary
1 *Queen Yesno* (1981)
2 *Isabella Bella rides again* (1983)

Queen's Chantry series
Little Sylvia
1 *Trouble at Queen's Chantry* (1950)
2 *Christmas term at Queen's Chantry* (1951)

Queen's investigator series
Cooney, Michael
1 *Doomsday England* (1967)
2 *Ten days to oblivion* (1968)

Queens of England series
Plaidy, Jean
1 *Myself, my enemy* (1983)
2 *Queen of the realm* (1984)
3 *Victoria victorious* (1985)
4 *Lady in the Tower* (1986)
5 *Courts of love* (1987)
6 *In the shadow of the crown* (1988)

Queen's quarter series
Snyder, Midori
1 *New moon* (1989)
2 *Sadar's keep* (1990)

Queens series
Manning, Val
1 *Falcon Queen* (1979)
2 *Fertility Queen* (1980)

Queensland series
Thorne, Sandy
Humour
1 *I've met some bloody wags!* (1980)
2 *Tickel a bushie's fancy* (1982)

Queer series
Colbeck, Maurice
1 *Queer folk* (1977)
2 *Queer goings on* (1979)

Queghan series
Hoyle, Trevor
see **Christian Queghan series**

Quentin and Winfield series
Peterson, Audrey
see **Jane Winfield and Andrew Quentin series**

Quentin Drex series
Evans, Gwyn
1 *His majesty, the crook* (1935)
2 *Rogue royal* (1936)

Quentin Eady series
Thorne, Ernest Pollett
1 *Seven red herrings* (1956)
2 *Devil's chapel* (1957)
3 *Evil in the cup* (1958)
4 *Gallows Inn* (1958)
5 *Die wearing a rose* (1959)
6 *Expect no mercy* (1962)

Quentin Gourlay series
Ronald, James
1 *Man born of woman* (1951)
Young quentin
2 *Sparks fly upward* (1952)

Quentin Jacoby series
Smith, J C S
1 *Jacoby's first case* (1980)
2 *Nightcap* (1984)

Quentin Pace series
Denbie, Roger
see **Doctor Quentin Pace series**

Quentin series
Faulkner, William
see **Listener series**
Quest, Rodney
see **Peter Quentin series**

Quentin Toby series
Schley, Sturges Mason
see **Doctor Quentin Toby series**

Quero series
Locke, Gladys Edson
see **Mercedes Quero series**

Quest for a queen series
Hendry, Frances Mary
1 *Falcon* (1989)
2 *Lark* (1992)
3 *Jackdaw* (1993)

Quest for the white duck trilogy
Fenn, Lionel
1 *Blood river down* (1986)
2 *Web of defeat* (1987)
3 *Agnes day* (1987)

Quest of the serpent series
Warrington, Freda
1 *Blackbird in silver* (1985)
2 *Blackbird in darkness* (1986)
3 *Blackbird in amber* (1987)
4 *Blackbird in twilight* (1988)

Quest series
Andrews, Roy Chapman
1 *Quest in the desert* (1952)
2 *Quest of the snow leopard* (1955)

Quest series
Moore, Patrick
see **Gregory Quest series**
Striker, Fran
see **Tom Quest series**
Townend, Peter
see **Philip Quest series**

Questers series
Hildick, Edmund Wallace
1 *Questers* (1966)
2 *Calling Questers four* (1967)
3 *Questers and the whispering spy* (1967)

Questioner trilogy
Schmidt, Dennis
1 *Labyrinth* (1989)
2 *City of crystal shadow* (1990)
3 *Dark paradise* (1990)

Questions series
Wood, Barry
1 *Questions new Christians ask* (1979)
2 *Questions non-Christians ask* (1980)
3 *Questions teenagers ask about dating and sex* (1981)
4 *Questions Christians ask about prayer and intercession* (1984)

Quick and the dead series
Sitwell, Sacheverell
Reminiscences
1 *Dance of the quick and the dead* (1936)
2 *Sacred and profane love* (1940)
3 *Splendours and miseries* (1943)
4 *Hunters and the hunted* (1947)
5 *Cupid and the jacaranda* (1952)

Quickshott series
Church, Richard
see **John Quickshott series**

Quicksilver series
Carter, Lin
see **Hautley Quicksilver series**
Daniel, Roland
see **John Quicksilver series**

Quicksilver series
Moore, Amos
1 *Quicksilver* (1929)
Quicksilver rides
2 *Quicksilver justice* (1930)

Quiet are the mountains series
Yeh, Chun-Chan
Translated from the Chinese
1 *Mountain village* (1947)
2 *Open fields* (1988)
3 *Distant journey* (1989)

Quiet Don series
Sholokhov, Mikhail
see **Don series**

Quiet moment series
Sorenson, Jane
1 *Quiet moments with young children* (1988)
2 *Quiet moments with older children* (1988)

Quiet neighbourhood series
Macdonald, George
1 *Annals of a quiet neighbourhood* (1867)
Quiet neighborhood
The second title is an abridged edition
2 *Seaboard parish* (1868)
3 *Vicar's daughter* (1872)

Quigly series
Van Slyke, Helen
see **Elizabeth Quigly series**

Quill and Glover series
Lamb, Lynton
see **Superintendent Quill and Inspector Glover series**

Quill series
Brahms, Caryl
see **Inspector Adam Quill series**
Morgan, Damian
see **Andrea Quill series**

Quiller series
Hall, Adam
1 *Berlin memorandum* (1965)
Quiller memorandum
2 *Ninth directive* (1966)
3 *Striker portfolio* (1969)
4 *Warsaw document* (1971)
5 *Tango briefing* (1973)
6 *Mandarin cypher* (1975)
7 *Kobra manifesto* (1976)
8 *Sinkiang executive* (1978)
9 *Scorpion signal* (1979)
10 *Sibling* (1979)
English edition published under the pseudonym Elleston Trevor
11 *Pekin target* (1981)
Peking target
12 *Northlight* (1985)
Quiller
13 *Quiller's run* (1988)
14 *Quiller, KGB* (1989)
15 *Quiller barracuda* (1990)
16 *Quiller bamboo* (1991)
17 *Quiller solitaire* (1992)
18 *Quiller meridian* (1993)
19 *Quiller salamander* (1994)

Quimby series
Cleary, Beverly
see **Ramona Quimby series**

Quin Saint James and Mike McClary series
Macgregor, T J
1 *Kill flash* (1987)
2 *Dark fields* (1987)
3 *Death sweet* (1988)
4 *On ice* (1989)
5 *Kin dread* (1990)
6 *Death flats* (1991)
7 *Spree* (1992)

Quin series
Horler, Sydney
see **Sebastian Quin series**

Quincannon series
Pronzini, Bill
1 *Quincannon* (1985)

2 *Beyond the grave* (1986)
Co-author: Marcia Muller

Quincas Borba series
Machado de Assis, Joachim Maria
1 *Epitaph of a small winner* (1880)
Original edition entitled *Memorias posthumas de Braz Cubas*
2 *Heritage of Quincas Borba* (1891)
Original edition entitled *Quincas Borba*

Quincy Adams Sawyer series
Pidgin, Charles Felton
1 *Quincy Adams Sawyer and Mason's corner folks* (1900)
A picture of New England home life
2 *Further adventures of Quincy Adams Sawyer* (1909)
3 *Chronicles of Quincy Adams Sawyer* (1912)

Quincy Durant and Artie Wu series
Thomas, Ross
see **Artie Wu and Quincy Durant series**

Quinn and Piper series
Carmichael, Harry
see **John Piper and Quinn series**

Quinn Leland series
Davis, Franklin Milton
1 *Kiss the tiger* (1961)
2 *Secret* (1962)

Quinn Parker series
Zimmerman, Bruce
1 *Blood under the bridge* (1989)
2 *Thicker than water* (1991)
3 *Full-bodied red* (1993)
4 *Crimson green* (1994)

Quinn series
Jones, G Wayman
see **Black Bat series**

Quinn series
Scanlon, Noel
1 *Quinn* (1973)
2 *Quinn and the desert oil* (1975)

Quinn series
Styles, Showell
see **Midshipman Quinn series**
Williams, Alan
see **Rupert Quinn series**

Quinney series
Vachell, Horace Annesley
see **Joe Quinney series**

Quinney trilogy
Hennessy, Max
see **Dicken Quinney trilogy**

Quinn's Raiders series
Bodine, J D
1 *Diablo double cross* (1988)
2 *Blood money* (1988)
3 *Desert guns* (1988)
4 *Outlaw gold* (1989)
5 *Whitewater death* (1989)
6 *Red Bluff revenge* (1989)

Quinny Hite series
Burke, Richard
1 *Dead take no bows* (1941)
2 *Here lies the body* (1942)
3 *Chinese red* (1942)
4 *Fourth star* (1946)
5 *Sinister Street* (1948)

Quint Kershaw trilogy
Shirreffs, Gordon Donald
1 *Now he is legend* (1979)
2 *Untamed breed* (1981)
3 *Bold legend* (1982)

Quint series
Austin, Hugh
see **Peter Quint series**

Quintain series
Baker, William Howard
see **Richard Quintain series**

Quintara Marathon series
Chalker, Jack Laurence
1 *Demons at Rainbow Bridge* (1989)
2 *Run to Chaos Keep* (1991)
3 *Ninety trillion Fausts* (1991)

Quintilian series
Hatfield, John
1 *Quintilian* (1968)
2 *Quintilian and the curious weather shop* (1969)
3 *Quintilian meets Mr Punch* (1970)

Quinto series
Norman, James
see **Gimiendo Hernandez Quinto series**

Quints series
Pevsner, Stella
1 *Sister of the quints* (1987)
2 *I'm Emma, I'm a quint* (1994)

Quintus Oakes series
Jackson, Charles Ross
1 *Third degree* (1903)
2 *Quintus Oakes* (1904)

Quirk and Davis trilogy
Wakefield, Tom
see **Margaret Davis and Isobel Quirk trilogy**

Quirke series
Gribdan, Volsted
see **Adam Quirke series**

Quist series
Macdonald, William Colt
see **Gregory Quist series**
Pentecost, Hugh
see **Julian Quist series**

Quong and Peter Cardiman series
De Fraga, Geoff
see **Peter Cardiman and Quong series**

Quong Lee series
Burke, Thomas
see **London series**

Quong series
George, Sidney Charles
see **Lim Quong series**

Quote series
Lambert, Derek
1 *Don't quote me, but* (1979)
2 *And I quote* (1980)
3 *Unquote* (1981)

Qwilleran series
Braun, Lilian Jackson
see **Jim Qwilleran series**

R

R.A.F. trilogy
Hennessy, Max
see **Dicken Quinney trilogy**

R.Dragon and Susan series
Manning, Rosemary
see **Susan and R.Dragon series**

R I Perkins series
Garnett, Roger
1 *Starr Bedford dies* (1937)
2 *Killing of Paris Norton* (1938)

Ra-ab Hotep series
Grant, Joan
Based on the author's recollections of previous lives
1 *Eyes of Horus* (1942)
2 *Lord of the horizon* (1943)

Rab Hewison series
Douglas, G A H
1 *Rab Hewison's visit to Edinburgh* (1910)
With views of some of its historical buildings
2 *Further adventures of Rab Hewison* (1921)

Rabbi Daniel Winter series
Telushkin, Joseph
1 *Unorthodox murder of Rabbi Moss* (1986)
2 *Final analysis of Doctor Stark* (1988)

Rabbi David Small series
Kemelman, Harry
1 *Friday the Rabbi slept late* (1964)
2 *Saturday the Rabbi went hungry* (1966)
3 *Sunday the Rabbi stayed home* (1969)
4 *Monday the Rabbi took off* (1972)
5 *Tuesday the Rabbi saw red* (1973)
6 *Wednesday the Rabbi got wet* (1976)
7 *Thursday the Rabbi walked out* (1978)
8 *Someday the Rabbi will leave* (1985)
9 *One fine day the Rabbi bought a cross* (1987)
Companion volume: *Conversations with Rabbi Small*, 1981

Rabbit and Chicken series
Landa, Norbert
Illustrated by Hanne Turk
1 *Rabbit and Chicken count eggs* (1992)
2 *Rabbit and Chicken find the right box* (1992)
3 *Rabbit and Chicken look at colors* (1992)
4 *Rabbit and chicken play hide and seek* (1992)

Rabbit Angstrom series
Updike, John
1 *Rabbit, run* (1960)
2 *Rabbit redux* (1971)
3 *Rabbit is rich* (1981)
Numbers 1-3 also published in one volume 1981
4 *Rabbit at rest* (1990)

Rabbit Hill series
Lawson, Robert
1 *Rabbit Hill* (1944)
2 *Tough winter* (1954)

Rabbit series
Barber, Shirley
see **Martha B Rabbit series**
Billam, Rosemary
see **Alpaca series**

Rabbit series
Delton, Judy
1 *Rabbit finds a way* (1975)
2 *Rabbit's new run* (1979)
3 *Rabbit goes to night school* (1986)
4 *Hired help for Rabbit* (1988)

Rabbit series
Flynn, Mary
see **Cornelius Rabbit series**
Gackenbach, Dick
see **Hattie Rabbit series**
Korman, Justine
see **Roger Rabbit series**

Rabbit series
Manning-Sanders, Ruth
1 *Boastful Rabbit* (1978)
2 *Oh really, Rabbit!* (1980)

Rabbit series
Uttley, Alison
see **Timothy Rabbit series**
Wahl, Jan
see **Doctor Rabbit series**

Rabbits series
McCarthy, Ruth
see **Three little rabbits series**

Rabbitte family trilogy
Doyle, Roddy
see **Barrytown trilogy**

Raccoon series
Moore, Lilian
see **Little raccoon series**

Race against time series
Fortune, J J
1 *Revenge in the silent tomb* (1984)
2 *Escape from Raven Castle* (1984)
3 *Pursuit of the deadly diamonds* (1984)
4 *Search for Mad Jack's crown* (1984)
5 *Duel for the Samurai sword* (1984)
6 *Evil in paradise* (1984)
7 *Secret of the third watch* (1984)
8 *Trapped in the U.S.S.R.* (1984)
9 *Journey to Atlantis* (1985)
10 *Danger due north* (1985)

Race series
Christie, Agatha
see **Colonel Race series**
Tyler, Charles Waller
see **Blue Jean Billy Race series**

Race Williams series
Daly, Carroll John
1 *Snarl of the beast* (1926)
2 *Hidden hand* (1929)
3 *Tag murders* (1930)
4 *Tainted power* (1931)
5 *Third murderer* (1931)
6 *Amateur murderer* (1933)
7 *Murder from the east* (1935)
8 *Better corpses* (1940)
9 *Adventures of Race Williams* (1987)
Short stories

Racer boys series
Young, Clarence
1 *Racer boys* (1912)
Alternative title: The mystery of the wreck; also published as *Frank and Andy afloat, or, The cave on the island*, under the pseudonym Vance Barnum
2 *Racer boys at boarding school* (1912)
Alternative title: Striving for the championship; also published as *Frank and Andy at boarding school, or, Rivals for many honors*, under the pseudonym Vance Barnum
3 *Racer boys to the rescue* (1912)
Alternative title: Stirring days in a winter camp; also published as *Frank and Andy in a winter camp, or, The young hunters' strange discovery*, under the pseudonym Vance Barnum
4 *Racer boys on the prairies* (1913)
Alternative title: The treasure of Golden Peak
5 *Racer boys on guard* (1913)
Alternative title: The rebellion at Riverview Hall

6 *Racer boys forging ahead* (1914)
Alternative title: The rivals of the school league

Rachel and Damaris series
Oxenham, Elsie J
1 *Biddy's secret* (1932)
2 *Maidlin to the rescue* (1934)
3 *Damaris at Dorothy's* (1937)
4 *Maidlin bears the torch* (1937)
5 *Damaris dances* (1940)
6 *Rachel in the Abbey* (1952)

Rachel and Jennifer Murdock series
Olsen, D B
1 *Cat saw murder* (1939)
2 *Alarm of the black cat* (1942)
3 *Catspaw for murder* (1943)
4 *Cat's claw* (1943)
5 *Cat wears a noose* (1944)
6 *Cats don't smile* (1945)
7 *Cats don't need coffins* (1946)
8 *Cats have tall shadows* (1948)
9 *Cat wears a mask* (1949)
10 *Death wears cat's eyes* (1950)
11 *Cat and Capricorn* (1951)
12 *Cat walk* (1953)
13 *Death walks on cat feet* (1956)

Rachel Fairfax series
Norris, Kathleen
1 *Heart of Rachel* (1916)
2 *Martie the unconquered* (1917)

Rachel Gold series
Kahn, Michael A
1 *Canaan legacy* (1988)
Grave designs
2 *Death benefits* (1992)
3 *Firm ambitions* (1994)

Rachel Hennings series
Breen, Jon Linn
1 *Gathering place* (1984)
2 *Touch of the past* (1988)

Rachel Payne series
Gibson, Gloria
1 *Mouse in the attic* (1980)
2 *Mouse in school* (1982)

Rachel Rosing series
Spring, Howard
see **Manchester series**

Rachel series
Gross, Joel
1 *Lives of Rachel* (1984)
2 *Books of Rachel* (1979)

Racina series
Keyes, Frances Parkinson
see **Joe and Judith Racina series**

Racing series
Hardcastle, Michael
1 *Roar to victory* (1982)
2 *Fast from the gate* (1983)

Racing wheels series
Dean, Anabel
1 *Hot rod* (1972)
2 *Drag race* (1972)
3 *Destruction Derby* (1972)
4 *Stock car race* (1972)
5 *Road race* (1972)
6 *Indy Five Hundred* (1972)

Rack series
James, Laurence
see **Simon Rack series**

Rack the Healer series
Hughes, Zach
1 *Book of Rack the Healer* (1973)
2 *Thunderworld* (1982)

Rackstraw series
Hardwick, Michael
see **Thomas Rodolfo Rackstraw series**

Radcliff series
Mallory, Roosevelt
1 *Harlem hit* (1973)
2 *San Francisco vendetta* (1974)
3 *Double trouble* (1975)
4 *New Jersey showdown* (1976)

Radcliffe reunion series
Jaffe, Rona
see **Reunion series**

Radetzky series
Roth, Joseph
1 *Radetzky march* (1932)
Original edition entitled *Radetzkymarsch*
2 *Emperor's tomb* (1938)
Original edition entitled *Die Kapuzinergruft*

Radford series
Robb, John
see **Red Radford series**
White, Paul
see **Ranford series**

Radiant way trilogy
Drabble, Margaret
1 *Radiant way* (1987)
2 *Natural curiosity* (1989)
3 *Gates of ivory* (1991)

Radio boys series
Breckenridge, Gerald
1 *Radio boys on Secret Service duty* (1922)
2 *Radio boys on the Mexican border* (1922)
3 *Radio boys search for the Incas treasure* (1922)
4 *Radio boys with the Revenue Guards* (1922)
5 *Radio boys seek the lost Atlantis* (1923)
6 *Radio boys with the border patrol* (1924)

Radio boys series
Chapman, Allen
1 *Radio boys' first wireless* (1922)
Alternative title: Winning the Ferberton Prize
2 *Radio boys at Ocean Point* (1922)
Alternative title: The message that saved the ship
3 *Radio boys at the sending station* (1922)
Alternative title: Making good in the wireless room
4 *Radio boys at Mountain Pass* (1922)
Alternative title: The midnight call for assistance
5 *Radio boys trailing a voice* (1922)
Alternative title: Solving a wireless mystery
6 *Radio boys with the forest rangers* (1923)
Alternative title: The great fire on Spruce Mountain
7 *Radio boys with the Iceberg Patrol* (1924)
Alternative title: Making safe the ocean lanes
8 *Radio boys with the flood fighters* (1925)
Alternative title: Saving the city in the valley
9 *Radio boys on Signal Island* (1926)
Alternative title: Watching for the ships of mystery
10 *Radio boys in Gold Valley* (1927)
Alternative title: The mystery of the deserted mining camp
11 *Radio boys aiding the snowbound* (1928)
Alternative title: Starvation days at Lumber Run
12 *Radio boys on the Pacific* (1929)
Alternative title: Shipwrecked on an unknown island
13 *Radio boys to the rescue* (1930)
Alternative title: The search for the Barmore twins

Radio detectives series
Verrill, Alpheus Hyatt
1 *Radio detectives* (1922)
2 *Radio detectives under the sea* (1922)
3 *Radio detectives southward bound* (1922)
4 *Radio detectives in the jungle* (1922)

Radio girls series
Penrose, Margaret
1 *Radio girls of Roselawn* (1922)
Alternative title: A strange message from the air; reissued as *The campfire girls of Roselawn*, 1930
2 *Radio girls on the program* (1922)
Alternative title: Singing and reciting at the sending station; reissued as *The campfire girls on the program*, 1930
3 *Radio girls on Station Island* (1922)
Alternative title: The wireless from the steam yacht; reissued as *The campfire girls on Station Island*, 1930
4 *Radio girls at Forest Lodge* (1924)
Alternative title: The strange hut in the swamp; reissued as *The campfire girls at Forest Lodge*, 1930

Radio pals series
Ludwig, Charles Shelton
1 *Radio pals marooned* (1952)
2 *Radio pals fight the flood* (1953)
3 *Radio pals on Bar T Ranch* (1953)
4 *Radio pals in the hands of the Mau Mau* (1955)
5 *Radio pals in the flaming forest* (1955)

Radio series
Escott, John
1 *Radio alert* (1984)
2 *Radio detective* (1985)
3 *Radio reporters* (1986)
4 *Radio trap* (1987)
5 *Radio reporters* (1988)
6 *Radio rescue* (1990)

Radix Tetrad series
Attanasio, A A
1 *Radix* (1981)
2 *In other worlds* (1984)
3 *Arc of the dream* (1986)
4 *Last legends of earth* (1989)

Radnitz series
Chase, James Hadley
see **Herman Radnitz series**

Rae Norse series
Esteven, John
see **Inspector Rae Norse series**

Raeburn series
Gair, Malcolm
see **Mark Raeburn series**

Raeburn Steel series
Brooks, Collin
1 *Mister X* (1927)
2 *Body snatchers* (1927)
3 *Ghost hunters* (1928)

Rafferty series
Wiltz, Chris
see **Neal Rafferty series**

Rafferty series
Woodberry, Joan
1 *Rafferty takes to fishing* (1959)
2 *Floodtide for Rafferty* (1960)
3 *Rafferty rides a winner* (1961)
4 *Rafferty makes a landfall* (1962)

Raffi songs to read series
Raffi
1 *Down by the bay* (1987)
2 *Shake my sillies out* (1987)
3 *One light, one sun* (1988)
4 *Wheels on the bus* (1988)
5 *Tingalayo* (1989)
6 *Five little ducks* (1989)
7 *Everything grows* (1989)
8 *Baby Beluga* (1990)

Raffles series
This sequence has four authors
Hornung, Ernest William
1 *Amateur Cracksman* (1899)
Raffles, the Amateur Cracksman
Dramatized as *Raffles, the Amateur Cracksman*, by Ernest William Hornung and Eugene W Presbrey, 1903
2 *Black mask* (1901)
Further adventures of the Amateur Cracksman
3 *Thief in the night* (1905)
4 *Mister Justice Raffles* (1909)
Perowne, Barry
5 *Raffles after dark* (1933)
Return of Raffles
Short stories; the second title is a revised edition
6 *Raffles in pursuit* (1934)
Four novelettes
7 *Raffles under sentence* (1936)
Four novelettes
8 *She married Raffles* (1936)
9 *Raffles' crime in Gibraltar* (1937)
They hang them in Gibraltar
10 *Raffles versus Sexton Blake* (1937)
11 *A.R.P. mystery* (1939)
12 *Whispering Cracksman* (1940)
Ten words of poison
13 *Raffles and the key man* (1940)
14 *Raffles revisited* (1974)
Short stories
15 *Raffles of the Albany* (1976)
Short stories
Fletcher, David
16 *Raffles* (1977)
Short stories
Perowne, Barry
17 *Raffles of the M.C.C.* (1979)
Tremayne, Peter
18 *Return of Raffles* (1981)
Companion volumes: *A visit from Raffles*, a play, by Ernest William Hornung and Charles Sansom, 1909, *The return of A.J.Raffles*, a play, by Graham Greene, 1975; omnibus volume: *The complete short stories of Raffles, the Amateur Cracksman*, by Ernest William Hornung, edited by Peter Haining, 1984

Rag Bag Clan series
Barth, Richard
see **Margaret Binton series**

Rag woman, rich woman series
Davis, Margaret Thomson
1 *Rag woman, rich woman* (1987)
2 *Daughters and mothers* (1988)

Ragbag chronicles series
Stern, Gladys Bronwyn
1 *Monogram* (1936)
2 *Another part of the forest* (1941)
3 *Trumpet voluntary* (1944)
4 *Benefits forgot* (1949)
5 *Name to conjure with* (1953)
6 *All in good time* (1954)
7 *Way it worked out* (1956)

Ragdolly Anna series
Kenward, Jean
1 *Ragdolly Anna stories* (1979)
2 *Ragdolly Anna* (1979)

Ragdolly Anna series

3 *Ragdolly Anna goes to the fair* (1979)
4 *Ragdolly Anna and the river picnic* (1979)
5 *Three cheers for Ragdolly Anna* (1985)
6 *Ragdolly Anna's circus* (1987)
7 *Ragdolly Anna's treasure hunt* (1989)

Ragged Dick series

Alger, Horatio
1 *Ragged Dick* (1868)
Alternative title: Street life in New York
2 *Fame and fortune* (1868)
Alternative title: The progress of Richard Hunter
3 *Mark, the match boy* (1869)
Alternative title: Richard Hunter's ward
4 *Rough and Ready* (1869)
Alternative title: Life among the New York newsboys
5 *Ben, the luggage boy* (1870)
Alternative title: Among the wharves
6 *Rufus and Rose* (1870)
Alternative title: The fortunes of Rough and Ready

Raggedy Ann series

Gruelle, Johnny
1 *Raggedy Ann stories* (1918)
2 *Raggedy Andy stories* (1920)
Introducing the little rag brother of Raggedy Ann
3 *Raggedy Ann and Andy and the camel with wrinkled knees* (1924)
Camel with wrinkled knees
4 *Raggedy Ann and Andy's sunny stories* (1925)
5 *Raggedy Ann and Andy's animal friends* (1925)
6 *Raggedy Ann and Andy's merry adventures* (1925)
7 *Raggedy Ann's wishing pebble* (1925)
8 *Raggedy Ann and the paper dragon* (1926)
Paper dragon
9 *Raggedy Ann's magical wishes* (1928)
10 *Raggedy Ann in the deep, deep woods* (1930)
11 *Raggedy Ann in Cookie Land* (1931)
12 *Raggedy Ann's lucky pennies* (1932)
13 *Raggedy Ann and the left-handed safety pin* (1935)
14 *Raggedy Ann and the golden pebble* (1935)
15 *Raggedy Ann in the magic book* (1939)
16 *Raggedy Ann and the golden butterfly* (1940)
17 *Raggedy Ann and the hoppy toad* (1940)
18 *Raggedy Ann and the laughing brook* (1940)
19 *Raggedy Ann helps Grandpa Hoppergrass* (1940)
20 *Raggedy Ann in the garden* (1940)
21 *Raggedy Ann goes sailing* (1941)
22 *Raggedy Ann and Andy and the nice fat policeman* (1942)
23 *Raggedy Ann and Betsy Bonnet String* (1943)
24 *Raggedy Ann and Andy* (1944)
25 *Raggedy Ann in the Snow White castle* (1946)
26 *Raggedy Ann and the slippery slide* (1947)
27 *Raggedy Ann's mystery* (1947)
28 *Raggedy Ann's adventure* (1947)
29 *Raggedy Ann at the end of the rainbow* (1947)
30 *Raggedy Ann's merriest Christmas* (1952)
31 *Raggedy Ann and Marcella's frist day at school* (1952)
32 *Raggedy Andy's surprise* (1953)
33 *Raggedy Ann's tea party* (1954)
34 *Raggedy Ann and the wonderful witch* (1961)
35 *Raggedy Ann and the happy meadow* (1961)
36 *Raggedy Ann and the golden ring* (1961)
37 *Raggedy Ann and the hobby horse* (1961)
From number 38 this sequence is by several authors
Hazen, Barbara Shook
38 *Raggedy Ann and Fido* (1969)
Fulton, Janet
39 *Raggedy Ann* (1969)
Whalley, Dean
40 *Raggedy Ann and the daffy taffy pull* (1972)
Carey, Mary Virginia
41 *Raggedy Ann and the sad and glad days* (1972)
Hazen, Barbara Shook
42 *Raggedy Ann and the cookie snatcher* (1972)
43 *Raggedy Ann and Andy and the rainy day circus* (1973)
Sukus, Jan
44 *Raggedy Ann and Raggedy Andy book* (1973)
Gruelle, Johnny
45 *Raggedy Ann and Andy and the kindly rag man* (1975)
46 *Raggedy Ann and Andy and Witchie Kissabye* (1977)
Thackray, Patricia
48 *Raggedy Ann at the carnival* (1977)
Daly, Kathleen N
49 *Raggedy Ann and Andy* (1977)
Based on a moving picture
Companion volumes: *Raggedy Ann's alphabet book*, by Johnny Gruelle, 1925, *Raggedy Ann's number book*, by Johnny Gruelle, 1928, *A thank you please and I love you book*, by Nora Smaridge, 1970, *The I can do it, you can do it book*, by Nora Smaridge, 1973

Raggedy Ann's household series

This sequence has three authors
Hazelton, Nika
1 *Raggedy Ann and Andy's cookbook* (1975)
Nelson, Alix R
2 *Raggedy Ann and Andy's green thumb book* (1975)
Thackray, Patricia
3 *Raggedy Ann's sweet and dandy sugar candy fragrance bok* (1976)

Raggedy Ann's songs series

Gruelle, Johnny
1 *Raggedy Ann's sunny songs* (1930)
2 *Raggedy Ann's joyful songs* (1937)

Ragnarok series

Godwin, Tom
1 *Survivors* (1958)
Space prison
2 *Space barbarians* (1964)

Ragoczy Saint-Germain series

Yarbro, Chelsea Quinn
see **Count Ragoczy Saint-Germain series**

Ragpickers series

Simon, Boris
1 *Abbe Pierre and the ragpickers* (1954)
Original edition entitled *Les chifonieres d'Emmaus*
2 *Ragman's city* (1956)
Original edition entitled *Les poids des autres*

Rags series

Dutton, Lewis
1 *Rags, M.D.* (1933)
2 *Rags, Tatters and Bill* (1934)
3 *Again Rags* (1935)
4 *Rags and Buttons* (1936)
5 *Rags and Tuppence* (1937)

Raider and Doc series

Hardin, J D
1 *Blood, sweat and gold* (1979)
2 *Good, the bad and the deadly* (1979)
3 *Slick and the dead* (1979)
4 *Bullets, buzzards, boxes of pine* (1980)
5 *Face down in a coffin* (1980)
6 *Man who bit snakes* (1980)
7 *Spirit and the flesh* (1980)
8 *Bloody sands* (1980)
9 *Raider's hell* (1980)
10 *Raider's revenge* (1981)
11 *Hard chains, soft women* (1981)
12 *Raider's gold* (1981)
13 *Silver tombstones* (1981)
14 *Death lode* (1981)
15 *Coldhearted lady* (1981)
16 *Gunfire at Spanish Rock* (1982)
17 *Sons and sinners* (1982)
18 *Death flotilla* (1982)
19 *Sbake River rescue* (1982)
20 *Lone Star massacre* (1982)
21 *Bobbies, baubles and blood* (1982)
22 *Bibles, bullets and brides* (1983)
23 *Hellfire hideaway* (1983)
24 *Apache gold* (1983)
25 *Saskatchewan rising* (1983)
26 *Hangman's noose* (1983)
27 *Bloody time in Blacktower* (1983)
28 *Man with no face* (1983)
29 *Firebrands* (1983)
30 *Downriver to hell* (1983)
31 *Bounty hunter* (1983)
32 *Queens over deuces* (1983)
33 *Carnival of death* (1984)
34 *Satan's bargain* (1984)
35 *Wyoming special* (1984)
36 *Lead-lined coffins* (1984)
37 *San Juan shoot-out* (1984)
38 *Pecos dollars* (1984)
39 *Vengeance Valley* (1984)
40 *Outlaw trail* (1984)
41 *Homesteader's revenge* (1984)
42 *Tombstone in Deadwood* (1984)
43 *Ozark outlaws* (1984)
44 *Colorado silver queen* (1984)
45 *Buffalo soldier* (1985)
46 *Great jewel robbery* (1985)
47 *Cochise County war* (1985)
48 *Apache trail* (1985)
49 *In the heart of Texas* (1985)
50 *Colorado sting* (1985)
51 *Hell's belle* (1985)
52 *Cattletown war* (1985)
53 *Ghost mine* (1985)
54 *Maximilian's gold* (1985)
55 *Tincup railroad war* (1985)
56 *Carson City colt* (1986)
57 *Guns at Buzzard Bend* (1986)
58 *Runaway rancher* (1986)
59 *Longest manhunt* (1986)
60 *Northland marauders* (1986)
61 *Blood in the big hatchets* (1986)
62 *Gentleman brawler* (1986)
63 *Murder on the rails* (1986)
64 *Iron trail to death* (1986)
65 *Hell in the Palo Duro* (1986)
66 *Alamo treasure* (1986)
67 *Brewer's war* (1986)
68 *Swindler's trail* (1987)
69 *Black Hills showdown* (1987)
70 *Savage revenge* (1987)
71 *Train ride to hell* (1987)
72 *Thunder Mountain massacre* (1987)
73 *Hell on the Powder River* (1987)

Raider series

Hardin, J D
1 *Raider* (1987)
2 *Sixgun circus* (1987)
3 *Yuma roundup* (1987)
4 *Guns of El Dorado* (1987)
5 *Thirst for vengeance* (1987)
6 *Death's deal* (1987)
7 *Vengeance ride* (1988)
8 *Cheyenne fraud* (1988)
9 *Gulf pirates* (1988)
10 *Timber war* (1988)
11 *Silver City ambush* (1988)
12 *Northwest railroad* (1988)
13 *Madman's blade* (1988)
14 *Wolf Creek feud* (1988)
15 *Baja diablo* (1988)
16 *Stagecoach ransom* (1988)
17 *Riverboat gold* (1988)
18 *Wilderness manhunt* (1988)
19 *Sins of the gunslinger* (1989)
20 *Black Hills trackdown* (1989)
21 *Gunfighter's showdown* (1989)
22 *Anderson Valley shootout* (1989)
23 *Badlands patrol* (1989)
24 *Yellowstone thieves* (1989)
25 *Arizona hellride* (1989)
26 *Border war* (1989)
27 *East Texas deception* (1989)
28 *Deadly avengers* (1989)
29 *Highway of death* (1989)
30 *Pinkerton killers* (1989)
31 *Tombstone territory* (1990)
32 *Mexican showdown* (1990)
33 *California Kid* (1990)
34 *Border law* (1990)
35 *Hangman's law* (1990)
36 *Fast death* (1990)
37 *Desert death trap* (1990)
38 *Wyoming ambush* (1990)
39 *Killer's moon* (1990)
40 *Ambush Valley* (1990)
41 *Utah double cross* (1990)
42 *End of the trail* (1990)

Raiders series

Crockett, Samuel Rutherford
Tales of the Scottish Borders in the early 18th century
1 *Raiders* (1894)
2 *Dark of the moon* (1902)

Rail and water series

Munroe, Kirk
1 *Under orders* (1890)
A story of a young reporter
2 *Prince Dusty* (1891)
A story of the oil regions
3 *Cab and caboose* (1892)
The story of a railroad boy
4 *Coral ship* (1893)
A story of the Florida Reef

Railroad series

Stevenson, Burton Egbert
see **Boys' story of the railroad series**

Railroad stories series

Spearman, Frank Hamilton
1 *Nerve of Foley, and other railroad stories* (1900)
2 *Held for orders* (1901)

Railton family trilogy

Gardner, John Edmund
see **Secret generations trilogy**

Railway Cat series

Arkle, Phyllis
1 *Railway Cat* (1983)
2 *Railway Cat and Digby* (1984)
3 *Railway Cat's secret* (1985)
4 *Railway Cat and the horse* (1987)

Railway series

This sequence has two authors who are father and son
Awdry, Wilbert
1 *Three railway engines* (1945)
2 *Thomas, the tank engine* (1946)
3 *James, the red engine* (1948)
4 *Tank-engine Thomas again* (1949)
5 *Troublesome engines* (1950)
6 *Henry, the green engine* (1951)
7 *Toby, the tram engine* (1952)
8 *Gordon, the big engine* (1953)

9 *Edward, the blue engine* (1954)
10 *Four little engines* (1955)
11 *Percy, the small engine* (1956)
12 *Eight famous engines* (1957)
13 *Duck and the diesel engine* (1958)
14 *Little old engine* (1959)
15 *Twin engines* (1960)
16 *Branch line engines* (1961)
17 *Gallant old engine* (1962)
18 *Stepney, the Bluebell engine* (1963)
19 *Mountain engines* (1964)
20 *Very old engines* (1965)
21 *Main line engines* (1966)
22 *Small railway engines* (1967)
23 *Enterprising engines* (1968)
24 *Oliver, the western engine* (1969)
25 *Duke, the lost engine* (1970)
26 *Tramway engines* (1972)
Awdry, Christopher
27 *Really useful engines* (1983)
28 *James and the diesel engines* (1984)
29 *Great little engines* (1985)
30 *More about Thomas the tank engine* (1986)
31 *Gordon, the high-speed engine* (1987)
32 *Toby, trucks and trouble* (1988)
33 *Thomas and the twins* (1989)
34 *Thomas and the dinosaur* (1992)
35 *Percy and the kite* (1992)
36 *Thomas comes home* (1992)
37 *Henry and the express* (1993)
Companion volumes: *Thomas's Christmas party*, by Wilbert Awdry, 1984, *Thomas comes to breakfast*, by Wilbert Awdry, 1985, *Thomas' A.B.C.*, by Wilbert Awdry, 1987, *Thomas' counting book*, by Wilbert Awdry, 1987

Raimann series
Buckley, Eunice
see **Sandor Raimann series**

Rain Morgan series
Grant-Adamson, Lesley
1 *Patterns in the dust* (1985)
Death on Widow's Walk
2 *Face of death* (1985)
3 *Guilty knowledge* (1986)
4 *Wild justice* (1987)
5 *Curse the darkness* (1990)

Rain unravelled tales series
Heylin, Clinton
1 *Rain unravelled tales* (1982)
2 *More rain unravelled tales* (1984)

Rainbow and Lucky series
Abbott, Jacob
1 *Handie* (1860)
2 *Rainbow's journey* (1860)
3 *Three pines* (1860)
4 *Selling Lucky* (1860)
5 *Up the river* (1861)

Rainbow Brite series
Lewis, Jean
1 *Starlight saves the day* (1985)
2 *Twink's magic carpet ride* (1985)

Rainbow chasers series
Hoag, Tami
1 *Heart of gold* (1990)
2 *Keeping company* (1990)
3 *Reilly's return* (1990)

Rainbow Hills series
Garrett, Sally
1 *Until forever* (1987)
2 *Visions* (1987)

Rainbow Ripley series
Lomax, Bliss
1 *Saddle hawks* (1944)
2 *Lost buckaroo* (1949)
3 *Law busters* (1950)

Rainbow season series
Gregory, Lisa
1 *Rainbow season* (1984)
2 *Rainbow promise* (1989)

Rainbow series
Cooper, Diana Olivia Winifred Maud
1 *Rainbow comes and goes* (1958)
2 *Light of common day* (1959)
3 *Trumpets from the steep* (1960)
One volume edition entitled *The autobiography of Diana Cooper*, 1979

Rainbow series
Thwaites, Frederick Joseph
see **Doctor Joszef Venesz series**

Raine and Wincourt series
Hodge, Charles
see **Jim Raine and Bob Wincourt series**

Raines of Rayleigh series
Heath-Miller, Mavis
1 *Never go back* (1968)
2 *No exit* (1969)
3 *Give me tomorrow* (1970)
4 *Bitter herb* (1973)
5 *Narrow stair* (1974)

Rainey series
McCurtin, Peter
see **Jim Rainey series**

Rainton series
Craddock, Mary
Autobiography
1 *North Country maid* (1962)
2 *Return to Rainton* (1963)

Rainwood family series
Bromige, Iris
1 *Stepdaughter* (1966)
2 *Quiet hills* (1967)
3 *April girl* (1967)
4 *Tangled wood* (1969)
5 *Sheltering tree* (1970)
6 *Magic place* (1971)
7 *Bend in the river* (1975)
8 *Distant song* (1977)
9 *Happy fortress* (1978)
10 *One day, my love* (1980)

Rainy day playbooks series
Phillpotts, Beatrice
1 *Our boat* (1987)
2 *Our plane* (1987)
3 *Our submarine* (1987)
4 *Our train* (1987)

Raisin series
Beaton, M C
see **Agatha Raisin series**

Raising a riot series
Toombs, Alfred
Humorous reminiscences
1 *Raising a riot* (1949)
2 *Honeymoon for seven* (1951)

Raising sons and daughters series
Elium, Don
1 *Raising a son* (1992)
Parents and the making of a healthy man
2 *Raising a daughter* (1993)
The awakening of a healthy woman

Raj quartet
Scott, Paul
see **British India quartet**

Rajan series
Lukeman, Tim
see **Lhas'kar series**

Rakehell dynasty series
Scott, Michael William
1 *Rakehell dynasty* (1980)
2 *China bride* (1981)
3 *Orient affair* (1982)
4 *Mission to Cathay* (1984)

Rakehell series
Hammand, Norman Bentley
see **Sir Nicholas Mountry series**

Raker series
Scott, Don
1 *Raker* (1982)
2 *Tijuana traffic* (1982)

Rakonitz family series
Stern, Gladys Bronwyn
1 *Tents of Israel* (1924)
Matriarch
Revised edition 1936
2 *Deputy was king* (1926)
3 *Mosaic* (1930)
4 *Shining and free* (1935)
A day in the life of a matriarch
5 *Young matriarch* (1942)

Ralegh family trilogy
Fecher, Constance
1 *Queen's delight* (1966)
Queen's favorite
2 *Traitor's son* (1967)
3 *King's legacy* (1967)
Companion volume: *Player queen*, 1968, also published as *The lovely wanton*

Rali series
Cole, Allan
1 *Far kingdom* (1994)
2 *Warrior's tale* (1994)

Ralph Brand series
Hinxman, Margaret
see **Detective Inspector Ralph Brand series**

Ralph Coates series
Rey, Bret
1 *Birth of a gunman* (1985)
2 *Stranger in town* (1987)

Ralph Cole series
Cawley, Winifred
1 *Down the long stairs* (1964)
2 *Feast of the serpent* (1969)

Ralph Conway series
Jennings, D K
see **Doctor Ralph Conway series**

Ralph de Giret trilogy
Morgan, Denise
1 *Second son* (1980)
2 *Kingmaker's knight* (1981)
3 *Sons and roses* (1981)

Ralph Delchard and Gervase Bret series
Marston, Edward
see **Gervase Bret and Ralph Delchard series**

Ralph Fairbanks of the railroad series
Chapman, Allen
1 *Ralph of the roundhouse* (1906)
Alternative title: Bound to become a railroad man
2 *Ralph in the switch tower* (1907)
Alternative title: Clearing the track
3 *Ralph on the engine* (1909)
Alternative title: The young fireman of the Limited Mail
4 *Ralph on the Overland Express* (1910)
Alternative title: The trials and triumphs of a young engineer; numbers 1-4 also published in one volume entitled *Ralph on the railroad*, 1933
5 *Ralph, the train dispatcher* (1911)
Alternative title: The mystery of the pay car
6 *Ralph on the army train* (1918)
Alternative title: The young railroader's most daring exploit
7 *Ralph on the Midnight Flyer* (1923)
Alternative title: The wreck at Shadow Valley
8 *Ralph and the missing mail pouch* (1924)
Alternative title: The stolen government bonds
9 *Ralph on the Mountain Division* (1927)
Alternative title: Fighting both flames and flood
10 *Ralph and the train wreckers* (1928)
Alternative title: The secret of the blue freight cars

Ralph Hannon series
Law, Winifred
1 *Through space to the planets* (1944)
2 *Rangers of the Universe* (1945)

Ralph Ledermann series
Maxwell, Peter
1 *Insanity machine* (1978)
2 *Killfactor five* (1979)

Ralph Lindsey series
Benson, Ben
1 *Venus death* (1953)
2 *Girl in the cage* (1954)
3 *Silver cobweb* (1955)
4 *Broken shield* (1955)
5 *Running man* (1957)
6 *End of violence* (1959)
7 *Seven steps east* (1959)

Ralph Oliver series
Tomalin, Ruth
1 *Garden house* (1964)
2 *Spring house* (1968)
3 *Away to the west* (1972)

Ralph Osborn series
Beach, Edward Latimer, senior
1 *Ralph Osborn, midshipman at Annapolis* (1909)
A story of life at the US Naval Academy
2 *Midshipman Ralph Osborn at sea* (1910)
A story of the US Navy
3 *Ensign Ralph Osborn* (1911)
The story of the trials and triumphs in a battleship engine rooms
4 *Lieutenant Ralph Osborn* (1912)
The story of how Ralph Osborn became a lieutenant and of his cruise in an American torpedo boat destroyer in West Indian waters

Ralph S Mouse series
Cleary, Beverly
1 *Mouse and the motorcycle* (1965)
2 *Runaway Ralph* (1970)
3 *Ralph S Mouse* (1982)

Ralph series
Gantos, Jack
see **Rotten Ralph series**

Ralph series
Moody, Ralph
1 *Little Britches* (1950)
2 *Man of the family* (1951)
3 *Fields of home* (1953)
4 *Home ranch* (1956)
5 *Mary Emma and Company* (1956)
6 *Shaking the nickel bush* (1962)

Ralph Simmons series
Gillespie, Robert Byrne
1 *Print-out* (1983)
2 *Heads you lose* (1985)

Ralph Whitgift series
Kirsten, Angela
1 *Young Lucifer* (1984)
2 *Satan's child* (1985)

Rama series
Clarke, Arthur Charles
1 *Rendezvous with Rama* (1973)
Abridged version by David Fickling, 1979
2 *Rama II* (1989)
Co-author: Gentry Lee
3 *Garden of Rama* (1991)
Co-author: Gentry Lee

Ramage series
Pope, Dudley
see **Lord Nicholas Ramage series**

Rambo series
Morrell, David
see **John Rambo series**

Ramon and Morgan series
McQuay, Mike
1 *Pure blood* (1985)
2 *Mother Earth* (1985)

Ramona Quimby series
Cleary, Beverly
1 *Beezus and Ramona* (1955)
Companion volume: *Beezus and Ramona diary*, 1986
2 *Ramona the pest* (1968)
3 *Ramona the brave* (1975)
4 *Ramona and her father* (1977)
5 *Ramona and her mother* (1979)
6 *Ramona Quimby, age 8* (1981)
7 *Ramona forever* (1984)
Companion volumes: *Cutting up with Ramona*, 1983, *Ramona Quimby diary*, 1984 and 1988; numbers 2, 4, 5, 6, 7 also published in one volume entitled *Meet Ramona Quimby*, 1989

Rampion Savage series
Turner, James Ernest
1 *Murder at Landred Hall* (1954)
2 *Death by the sea* (1955)
3 *Strange little snakes* (1956)
4 *Frontiers of death* (1957)
5 *Crystal wave* (1957)
6 *Dark index* (1959)
7 *Glass interval* (1961)
8 *Nettle shade* (1963)
9 *Slate landscape* (1964)
10 *Blue mirror* (1965)
11 *Requiem for two sisters* (1968)
12 *Stone dormitory* (1969)

Rampole family series
Holt, Isabella
1 *Rampole Place* (1952)
2 *Midpoint* (1955)

Ramsay and Reid series
Matschat, Cecile Hulse
see **Andrea Reid and David Ramsay series**

Ramsay series
Cleeves, Ann
see **Inspector Stephen Ramsay series**
Wallace, C H
see **Steve Ramsay series**
Wallace, Kathleen
see **Veronica Ramsay series**

Ramsdale series
Dolson, Hildegarde
see **Lucy Ramsdale series**

Ramsey series
Owen, Dean
see **Hec Ramsey series**

Ramseys series
McLennan, Will
1 *Ramseys* (1989)
2 *Ramsey's luck* (1989)
3 *Matt Ramsey* (1989)
4 *Blood money* (1990)
5 *Ramsey's gold* (1990)
6 *Death trail* (1990)
7 *Ramsey's badge* (1990)
8 *Deadly stranger* (1990)
9 *Comanche* (1990)
10 *Bad blood* (1991)
11 *Death hunt* (1991)
12 *Gundown* (1991)
13 *Ramsey's law* (1991)
14 *Blood storm* (1991)
15 *Ramsey's revenge* (1991)
16 *Blood oath* (1992)
17 *Range war* (1992)
18 *Plains war* (1992)

Rance Mandarin series
Zorro
see **Doctor Death series**

Ranch and range series
Rathborne, Saint George
1 *Sunset Ranch* (1902)
2 *Chums of the prairie* (1902)
3 *Young range riders* (1902)

Ranch Girls series
Vandercook, Margaret
1 *Ranch Girls at Rainbow Lodge* (1911)
2 *Ranch Girls' pot of gold* (1912)
3 *Ranch Girls at boarding school* (1913)
4 *Ranch Girls in Europe* (1913)
5 *Ranch Girls at home again* (1915)
6 *Ranch Girls and their great adventure* (1917)
7 *Ranch Girls and their heart's desire* (1920)
8 *Ranch Girls and the silver arrow* (1921)
9 *Ranch Girls and the mystery of the three roads* (1924)

Rancher series
Hobson, Richmond Pearson
Autobiography
1 *Grass beyond the mountains* (1951)
2 *Nothing too good for a cowboy* (1953)
3 *Rancher takes a wife* (1961)

Rancho Bravo series
Douglas, Thorne
1 *Calhoon* (1973)
2 *Big drive* (1973)
3 *Killraine* (1975)
4 *Night riders* (1975)
5 *Mustang men* (1977)

Rand series
Grover, Marshall
see **Nevada Jim series**

Rand series
Thompson, Neil
1 *Shadow on the sea* (1965)
2 *Ride the hurricane in* (1966)
3 *Storm north* (1967)
4 *Ask the wind, ask the sea* (1967)
5 *Southern backwash* (1968)

Rand Stannard series
Hershatter, Richard Lawrence
1 *Spy who hated licorice* (1966)
2 *Fallout for a spy* (1969)
3 *Spy who hated fudge* (1970)

Randall Gatsby Sierra series
Hill, Richard
1 *What rough beast?* (1992)
2 *Shoot the piper* (1994)

Randall Roberts series
Brown, Carter
see **Randy Roberts series**

Randall series
Bowen, Robert Sidney
see **Red Randall series**
Eland, Charles
see **Mark Randall series**
Gordons
see **Undercover Cat series**
Leyland, Eric
see **Rip Randall series**

Randel series
Wuamett, Victor
see **Chase Randel series**

Randollph series
Smith, Charles Merrill
see **Reverend Randollph series**

Randolph Cranstone series
Bullock, Michael
1 *Randolph Cranstone and the pursuing river* (1974)
Randolph Cranstone and the glass thimble
A parabolic fiction
2 *Randolph Cranstone and the veil of Maya* (1986)
3 *Randolph Cranstone takes the inward path* (1988)

Randolph Mannering series
Paternoster, George Sidney
1 *Motor pirate* (1903)
2 *Cruise of the motor-boat conqueror* (1906)

Randolph Mason series
Post, Melville Davisson
1 *Strange schemes of Randolph Mason* (1896)
2 *Man of last resort* (1897)
Alternative title: The clients of Randolph Mason
3 *Corrector of destinies* (1908)

Randolph trilogy
Wells, Marian
see **Amy Randolph trilogy**

Random reminiscences series
Binstead, Arthur Morris
Random reminiscences, sporting and otherwise, of Arthur M Binstead and Ernest Wells
1 *Pink 'un and a pelican* (1898)
2 *Pitcher in paradise* (1903)

Random series
Anderson, Oliver
see **Guy Random series**

Randor series
Hill, Douglas
see **Last legionary series**

Randy Kidd and Regina series
Dagmar
1 *Spy who came in from the Copa* (1967)
2 *Spy with the blue kazoo* (1967)

Randy Knowles series
Holzer, Hans
1 *Red Chindvit conspiracy* (1970)
2 *Alchemy deception* (1973)
3 *Unicorn* (1976)

Randy Roberts series
Brown, Carter
1 *Murder in the family* (1971)
2 *Angry Amazons* (1972)
3 *Seven sirens* (1972)
4 *Murder on high* (1973)
5 *Sex trap* (1975)

Randy Starr series
Martin, Eugene
1 *Randy Starr after an air prize* (1931)
Alternative title: The Sky Flyers in a dash down the States
2 *Randy Starr above stormy seas* (1931)
Alternative title: The Sky Flyers on a perilous journey
3 *Randy Starr leading the air circus* (1932)
Alternative title: The Sky Flyers in a daring stunt
4 *Randy Starr tracing the air spy* (1933)
Alternative title: The Sky Flyers seeking the stolen plane

Rane Falconer and Alexandria Thaine trilogy
De Blasis, Celeste
see **Wild Swan trilogy**

Raneleigh series
Luther, Mark Lee
see **Arthur Raneleigh series**

Ranford series
White, Paul
1 *Ranford mystery miler* (1960)
Radford's big race
The second title is a revised edition
2 *Ructions at Ranford* (1961)
Uproar at Radford
3 *Ranford goes fishing* (1962)
4 *Ranford in flames* (1965)

Range and Grange Hustlers series
Patchin, Frank Gee
1 *Range and Grange Hustlers on the ranch* (1912)
Alternative title: The boy shepherds of the Great Divide
2 *Range and Grange Hustlers' greatest roundup* (1912)
Alternative title: Putting their wits against a packer's combine
3 *Range and Grange Hustlers on the Plains* (1913)
Alternative title: Following the steam plows across the prairies
4 *Range and Grange Hustlers at Chicago* (1913)
Alternative title: The conspiracy of the wheat pit

Ranger Boys series
Labelle, Claude A
1 *Ranger Boys and the border smugglers* (1922)
2 *Ranger Boys and their reward* (1922)
3 *Ranger Boys find the hermit* (1922)
4 *Ranger Boys outwit the timber thieves* (1922)
5 *Ranger Boys to the rescue* (1922)

Ranger Jim Hatfield series
Cole, Jackson
see **Jim Hatfield series**

Ranger series
Cameron, Caddo
see **Private Badger Coe and Sergeant Blizzard Wilson series**
Lounsberry, Lionel
see **Rob Ranger series**
Mason, Dan
see **Lex Cranshaw series**

Ranger series
Moore, Amos
1 *Ranger rides alone* (1936)
2 *Ranger's round-up* (1940)

Ranger series
Strong, Charles Stanley
1 *Ranger, sea dog of the Royal Canadian Mounted Police* (1948)
2 *Ranger's Arctic patrol* (1952)

Ranger series
Young, Clarence
see **Jack Ranger series**

Ranjha series
Sharma, Partap
1 *Dog detective Ranjha* (1978)
2 *Top dog* (1985)

Rankin series
Buddee, Paul
see **Ann Rankin series**
Grady, James
see **James Rankin series**
Propper, Milton
see **Tommy Rankin series**

Rannoch series
Vanner, Lyn
1 *Rannoch Chase* (1985)
2 *Guardian of Rannoch* (1986)

Ransom trilogy
Lewis, Clive Staples
see **Space trilogy**

Ransome Dragoon and Vicky Gaines series
Diamond, Frank
1 *Murder in five columns* (1944)
2 *Murder rides a rocket* (1946)

Ransome series
Morgan, Dean
see **Rogue Ransome series**
Ransome, Stephen
see **Steve Ransome series**
Sea-Lion
see **Tiger Ransome series**

Rant series
Wheeler, H E
see **Stephen Rant series**

Raoul de Rohan series
Graeme, David
see **Monsieur Blackshirt series**

Raphael Drale series
Aronin, Ben
1 *Lost tribe* (1934)
2 *Cavern of destiny* (1943)

Raphael trilogy
Macavoy, Roberta Ann
see **Lute trilogy**

Rapid fire detective series
Ridley, Nat
see **Nat Ridley series**

Rappaport series
Lurie, Morris
1 *Rappaport* (1966)
2 *Rappaport's revenge* (1973)

Rapple series
Sayers, Valerie
see **Mary Faith Rapple series**

Rapstoff series
Pullen, Alan
see **Sam and Lin series**

Rasmus series
Lindgren, Astrid
1 *Rasmus and the vagabond* (1956)
Rasmus and the tramp
Original edition entitled *Rasmus paa luffen*
2 *[Rasmus, Pontus och Toker]* (1957)
No English edition

Rason series
Vickers, Roy
see **Inspector George Rason series; Inspector J Rason series**

Rasselas series
This sequence has two authors
Johnson, Samuel
1 *Rasselas* (1759)
Prince of Abyssinia
Knight, Ellis Cornelia
2 *Dinarbas* (1790)

Rassendyl series
Hope, Anthony
see **Rudolf Rassendyl series**

Rat Bastards series
Mackie, John
House pseudonym
1 *Hit the beach!* (1983)
2 *Death squad* (1983)
3 *River of blood* (1983)
4 *Meat Grinder Hill* (1984)
5 *Down and dirty* (1984)
6 *Green hell* (1984)
7 *Too mean to die* (1984)
8 *Hot lead and cold steel* (1984)
9 *Do or die* (1984)
10 *Kill crazy* (1985)
11 *Nightmare Alley* (1985)
12 *Go for broke* (1985)
13 *Tough guys die hard* (1985)
14 *Suicide River* (1985)
15 *Satan's cage* (1985)
16 *Go down fighting* (1986)

Rat Patrol series
This sequence has two authors; based on a television series
Daniels, Norman A
1 *Rat Patrol* (1966)
King, David
2 *Desert danger* (1967)
3 *Trojan tank* (1967)
4 *Two-faced enemy* (1967)
5 *Target for tonight* (1968)
6 *Desert masquerade* (1968)
Companion volume: *The iron monster raid*, by Ivy Gordon Edmonds, 1967

Rat series
This sequence has two authors
Bottome, Phyllis
1 *Rat* (1927)
Based on a play by Ivor Novello and Constance Collier
Robins, Denise
2 *Triumph of the Rat* (1927)
Based on a screenplay

Rat series
Claridge, David
see **Roland Rat series**
Forster, Michelanne
see **Rodney Rat series**

Ratcliffe series
Dell, Ethel May
see **Nick Ratcliffe series**

Ratha series
Bell, Clare
1 *Ratha's creature* (1983)
2 *Clan ground* (1984)
3 *Ratha and Thistle-Chaser* (1990)

Rathcapple series
Reid, Meta Mayne
1 *McNeils at Rathcapple* (1959)
2 *Sandy and the hollow book* (1961)
3 *With Angus in the forest* (1963)

Ratlin series
Roffman, Jan
see **Sergeant Ratlin series**

Rats of NIMH series
O'Brien, Robert C
see **NIMH series**

Rats series
Glassop, Lawson
1 *We were the Rats* (1944)
Based on experiences in Tobruk during World War 2
2 *Rats in New Guinea* (1963)

Rats series
Marshall, James
1 *Rats on the roof, and other stories* (1991)
2 *Rats on the range, and other stories* (1993)

Rats trilogy
Herbert, James
1 *Rats* (1974)
Deadly eyes
2 *Lair* (1979)
3 *Domain* (1984)

Ratton series
Knowles, Anne
see **Matthew Ratton series**

Raum series
Sherrell, Carl
1 *Raum* (1977)
2 *Skraelings* (1987)

Ravel series
Jones, Bradshaw
see **Claude Ravel series**

Raven Hunter and Runs-in-Light series
Gear, William Michael
see **People series**

Raven series
Boucher, Alan Estcourt
see **Halli Thordason series**
Griffin, John
see **Richard Raven series**

Raven series
Kirk, Richard
This pseudonym is used by Robert Holdstock and Angus Wells as indicated against each title
1 *Raven, swordsmistress of chaos* (1978)
[Holdstock; Wells]
2 *Time of ghosts* (1978)
[Holdstock]
3 *Frozen god* (1978)
[Wells]
4 *Lord of the shadows* (1979)
[Holdstock]
5 *Time of dying* (1979)
[Wells]

Raven series
Mackenzie, Donald
see **Johnny Raven series**
Meaney, Dee Morrison
see **Lady Branwen series**

Raven series
Quartermain, James
1 *Diamond hook* (1970)
2 *Man who walked on diamonds* (1970)
3 *Rock of diamond* (1972)
4 *Diamond hostage* (1975)

Ravenhill series
Foster, Reginald Francis
see **Anthony Ravenhill series**

Ravenloft series
This sequence has two authors
Golden, Christie
1 *Vampire of the mists* (1991)
Lowder, James
2 *Knight of the black rose* (1991)

Ravensgill series
Livings, Henry
1 *Pennine tales* (1983)
2 *Flying eggs and things* (1986)

Ravensley series
Heaven, Constance
see **Oliver Aylsham series**

Ravensmith series
Frost, Jason
see **Warlord series**

Ravenswyke series
White, Alan
1 *Ravenswyke* (1980)
2 *Homeward tide* (1981)

Raw Pearl series
Bailey, Pearl
Autobiography
1 *Raw Pearl* (1968)
2 *Talking to myself* (1971)
3 *Between you and me* (1989)
A heartfelt memoir on learning, loving and living

Rawhide Rawlins series
Russell, Charles Marion
1 *Rawhide Rawlins stories* (1921)
2 *More Rawhides* (1925)
3 *Trail plowed under* (1927)
Omnibus volume: *Rawhide Rawlins rides again, or, Behind the swinging doors*, 1948 which includes eight previously unpublished stories

Rawlings series
Minahan, John
see **Little John Rawlings series**

Rawlins series
Mosley, Walter
see **Ezekiel Rawlins series**
Russell, Charles Marion
see **Rawhide Rawlins series**

Rawson series
Dorrance, Ethel Smith
see **Sergeant Alfred Rawson series**

Ray Crawley series
Corris, Peter
see **Pokerface series**

Ray Decker series
Graber, Richard
1 *Little breathing room* (1978)
2 *Pay your respects* (1979)
3 *Black cow summer* (1980)

Ray family series
Lovelace, Maud Hart
see **Betsy Ray series**

Ray Felton series
Marsh, John
1 *Murderer's maze* (1957)
2 *Operation Snatch* (1958)
3 *City of fear* (1958)
4 *Small and deadly* (1960)

Ray Guinness series
Guild, Nicholas
1 *Summer soldier* (1978)
2 *Old acquaintance* (1979)
3 *Favor* (1981)

Ray Martin series
Reinsmith, Richard
see **Bodyguard series**

Ray of darkness series
Evans, Margiad
1 *Autobiography* (1943)
2 *Ray of darkness* (1952)

Ray series
King, Charles
see **Lieutenant Sandy Ray series**
Roderus, Frank
see **Billy Ray series**

Raymond and Bradley series
Longmate, Norman
see **Inspector Bradley and Sergeant Raymond series**

Raymond Ingelram series
Household, Geoffrey
1 *Rogue male* (1939)
Man hunt
2 *Rogue justice* (1982)

Raymond Monk series
Moore, Frank Frankfort
1 *Rise of Raymond* (1916)
2 *Fall of Raymond* (1917)

Raymond series
Smith, Harriet Lummis
see **Friendly Terrace series**
Thwaites, Frederick Joseph
see **Mad doctor series**

Rayne series
Coke, Peter
see **Brigadier Rayne series**

Razoni and Jackson series
Murphy, Warren Burton
see **Edward Razoni and William Jackson series**

Reachfar series
Duncan, Jane
1 *My friends the Miss Boyds* (1959)
2 *My friend Muriel* (1959)
3 *My friend Monica* (1960)
4 *My friend Annie* (1961)
5 *My friend Sandy* (1961)
6 *My friend Martha's aunt* (1962)
7 *My friend Flora* (1962)
8 *My friend Madame Zora* (1963)
9 *My friend Rose* (1964)
10 *My friend Cousin Emmie* (1964)
11 *My friends the Miss Millers* (1965)
12 *My friends from Cairnton* (1966)
13 *My friend my father* (1966)
14 *My friends the Macleans* (1967)
15 *My friends the hungry generation* (1968)
16 *My friend the swallow* (1970)
17 *My friend Sashie* (1972)
18 *My friends the Misses Kindness* (1974)
19 *My friends George and Tom* (1976)
This sequence is a companion to the **Janet Reachfar series**

Read series
Toye, Stanley
see **Anthony Read series**

Ready-set-grow series
Berry, Joy
1 *Mine and yours* (1978)
2 *Needing each other* (1978)
3 *Keeping your body alive and well* (1978)
4 *Saying what you mean* (1978)
5 *Surviving fights with your brothers and sisters* (1978)
6 *Nitty-gritty of family life* (1978)
7 *Kid's guide to making friends* (1978)
8 *Making up your own mind* (1978)
9 *Handling your ups and downs* (1979)
10 *Using your head* (1979)
11 *May I, please, thank you!* (1979)
12 *Danger* (1979)
13 *You're all right* (1979)
14 *You're one of a kind* (1979)
15 *Kid's TV guide* (1979)
16 *Kid's guide to managing time* (1979)
17 *Kid's guide to managing money* (1979)
18 *Consumer's guide for kids* (1979)
19 *You can do it* (1980)
20 *You're either one or the other* (1980)
21 *Handling your disagreements* (1980)
22 *Kid's guide to understanding parents* (1980)
23 *Checking 'em out and sizing 'em up* (1980)
24 *Tuff stuff* (1980)

Real and the ideal trilogy
Lytton, Edward George Earle Lytton Bulwer-Lytton
1 *Caxtons* (1849)
2 *My novel* (1853)
Alternative title: Varieties of English life
3 *What will he do with it?* (1858)

Real life criminals series
Phelan, Jim
1 *Criminals in real life* (1956)
2 *Fetters for twenty* (1957)

Real people series
Conley, Robert Jackson
1 *Way of the priests* (1992)
2 *Dark way* (1993)
3 *White path* (1993)
4 *Way south* (1994)
5 *Long way home* (1994)

Real world series
Aragon, Louis
1 *Bells of Basel* (1934)
Original edition entitled *Les cloches de Bale*
2 *Residential quarters* (1936)
Original edition entitled *Les beaux quartiers*
3 *Passengers of destiny* (1947)
Original edition entitled *Les voyageurs de l'Imperial*
4 *Aurelien* (1944)
Original edition entitled *Aurelien*

Realists trilogy
McKenna, Stephen
1 *Saviours of society* (1926)
2 *Secretary of state* (1927)
3 *Due reckoning* (1927)

Realtime series
Vinge, Vernor
1 *Peace war* (1986)
2 *Marooned in realtime* (1986)
One volume edition entitled *Across realtime*, 1986

Reamer series
Duncan, William Murdoch
see **Superintendent Donald Reamer series**

Reaper series
Holmes, Bryan John
1 *Guns of the Reaper* (1983)
2 *Dollars for the Reaper* (1990)

Reardon series
Pike, Robert L
see **Lieutenant Jim Reardon series**

Rebaumont series
Yonge, Charlotte Mary
1 *Chaplet of pearls* (1868)
Alternative title: White and black Rebaumont
2 *Stray pearls* (1883)
Memoirs of Margaret de Rebaumont, Viscountess of Bellaise

Rebecca Caldwell series
Hunter, E J
see **White Squaw series**

Rebecca De Winter series
This sequence has two authors
Du Maurier, Daphne
1 *Rebecca* (1938)
Companion volume: *The Rebecca notebook, and other memories*, 1981
Hill, Susan
2 *Mrs De Winter* (1993)

Rebecca Schwartz series
Smith, Julie
1 *Death turns a trick* (1982)
2 *Sourdough wars* (1984)
3 *Tourist trap* (1986)
4 *Dead in the water* (1991)

Rebecca series
Wiggin, Kate Douglas
1 *Rebecca of Sunnybrook Farm* (1903)
Dramatized as *Rebecca of Sunnybrook Farm*, 1932
2 *New chronicles of Rebecca of Sunnybrook Farm* (1907)
More about Rebecca of Sunnybrook Farm
Selections: *The flag-raising*, 1907

Rebel angels trilogy
Davies, Robertson
see **Francis Cornish trilogy**

Rebel dynasty series
Busby, Francis Marion
see **Bran Tregare series**

Rebel series
Kessler, Leo
1 *Cannon fodder* (1986)
2 *Die-hards* (1987)
3 *Death match* (1988)
4 *Breakout* (1988)

Rebels in the New World series
Montgomery, Raymond A
1 *Traitors from within* (1990)
2 *Crossing enemy lines* (1990)
3 *Almost lost* (1990)
4 *Hidden evil* (1990)
5 *Escape from China* (1990)
6 *Deadly encounter* (1990)

Rebus series
Adler, David A
see **Happy Rebus series**

Reckoning series
Eden, Anthony
Memoirs
1 *Another world, 1897-1917* (1976)
2 *Facing the dictators* (1962)
3 *Reckoning* (1965)
Covers the period 1938-1945
4 *Full circle, 1951-1957* (1960)

Recollections of royalty series
Peeress
1 *Shadow on the purple* (1911)
Recollections of an ex-attache
2 *Searchlight on the throne* (1912)
Reminiscences of an ex-ambassador

Recon series
Frost, Graham H
1 *Recon* (1987)
2 *Recon strike* (1987)

Reconstruction series
Dixon, Thomas
see **American Reconstruction series**

Recovered pearl series
May, Carrie L
1 *Brownie Sandford* (1866)
Alternative title: The recovered pearl
2 *Nellie Milton's house keeping* (1867)
Alternative title: Sweet clover
3 *Sylvia's burden* (1867)
4 *Ruth Lovell* (1868)
Alternative title: Holidays at home

Rector series
Van Siller, Hilda
see **Pete Rector series**

Red barbarian trilogy
Gaan, Margaret
1 *Red barbarian* (1984)
2 *White poppy* (1985)
3 *Blue mountain* (1987)

Red Baron series
Innes, Brian
1 *Red Baron lives!* (1981)
2 *Red Red Baron* (1983)

Red Blake series
Lee, Edward
1 *Needle's eye* (1941)
2 *Fish for murder* (1944)
Lust to kill
Death goes fishing
The third title is an abridged edition

Red Canavan series
Arthur, Burt
see **Johnny Canavan series**

Red cap series
Crockett, Samuel Rutherford
Tales stolen from the treasure chest of Wizard of the North
1 *Red cap tales* (1904)
2 *Red cap adventures* (1908)

Red China series
Snow, Edgar
1 *Red star over China* (1938)
Revised edition 1968
2 *Other side of the river* (1962)
Companion volume: *Edgar Snow's China*, 1981

Red Clark series
Young, Gordon Ray
1 *Red Clark o' Tulluco* (1933)
Roaring guns
2 *Red Clark rides alone* (1933)
Fast on the draw
3 *Red Clark of the Arrowhead* (1935)
Guns of the Arrowhead
4 *Red Clark on the border* (1937)
Trouble on the border
5 *Red Clark, range boss* (1938)
Red Clark, boss!
Range boss
6 *Red Clark, two-gun man* (1939)
Two-gun man
7 *Red Clark for luck* (1940)
8 *Red Clark takes a hand* (1941)
9 *Red Clark at the Showdown* (1947)
10 *Red Clark in Paradise* (1947)
Holster law
11 *Gunman from Tulluco* (1948)
12 *Red Clark to the rescue* (1948)
Hot Lead Trail
13 *Fighting blood* (1949)

Red Clay trilogy
Ore, Rebecca
see **Tom Red Clay trilogy**

Red Cross girls series
Vandercook, Margaret
1 *Red Cross girls in Belgium* (1916)
2 *Red Cross girls in the British trenches* (1916)
3 *Red Cross girls on the French firing line* (1916)
4 *Red Cross girls with the Russian Army* (1916)
5 *Red Cross girls with the Italian Army* (1917)

6 *Red Cross girls with the Stars and Stripes* (1918)
7 *Red Cross girls afloat with the flag* (1918)
8 *Red Cross girls with Pershing to victory* (1919)
9 *Red Cross girls with the U.S. Marines* (1919)
10 *Red Cross girls in the national Capitol* (1920)

Red Cross series
Martin, Nancy
1 *Teresa joins the Red Cross* (1968)
2 *Red Cross challenge* (1970)

Red Diamond series
Schorr, Mark
1 *Red Diamond, private eye* (1983)
2 *Ace of Diamonds* (1984)
3 *Diamond Rock* (1985)

Red Dwarf series
Naylor, Grant
Based on a television series
1 *Red Dwarf* (1989)
2 *Better than life* (1990)
Numbers 1 and 2 also published in one volume entitled *Red Dwarf omnibus*, 1992
3 *Last human* (1994)
Companion volumes: *Red Dwarf scripts*, 1993, *Making of Red Dwarf*, 1994

Red engine series
Ross, Diana
see **Little red engine series**

Red Fox series
Uttley, Alison
see **Little Red Fox series**

Red Gap series
Wilson, Harry Leon
1 *Ruggles of Red Gap* (1915)
2 *Somewhere in Red Gap* (1916)
Short stories
3 *Ma Pettengill* (1919)
Short stories
4 *Ma Pettengill talks* (1925)

Red Hanlon series
Merrick, Mollie
1 *Upper case* (1936)
2 *Mysterious Mister Frame* (1938)

Red Hawk series
Baxter, George Owen
Also published under the pseudonym Max Brand
1 *War party* (1934)
2 *Frontier feud* (1935)
3 *Cheyenne gold* (1976)

Red House children series
Douglas, Amanda Minnie
see **Little Red House children series**

Red Hussars series
Scott, John Reed
1 *Colonel of the Red Hussars* (1906)
2 *Princess Dehra* (1907)

Red Indian series
Risteen, H L
1 *Chippeway captive* (1948)
2 *Indian silver* (1948)
3 *Tomahawk trail* (1948)
4 *Black Hawk's warpath* (1950)
5 *Redskin raiders* (1951)
6 *Montana gold* (1951)

Red Indian trilogy
Goble, Paul
1 *Red Hawk's account of Custer's last battle* (1969)
2 *Hundred in the hands* (1972)
3 *Lone Bull's horse raid* (1973)

Red Kerry series
Rohmer, Sax
1 *Dope* (1919)
2 *Yellow shadows* (1925)
Also stories featuring Kerry in *Tales of Chinatown*, 1922

Red Lattice series
Dodd, Catherine Isabel
1 *Lords of the Red Lattice* (1930)
2 *Paul and Perdita* (1932)

Red Lawson series
Leyland, Eric
1 *Versus the Shadow* (1950)
2 *No quarter* (1951)
3 *Case for Red Lawson* (1951)
4 *Calling Red Lawson* (1952)
5 *Red Lawsons and the sons of the desert* (1955)

Red moon series
Bradley, Marion Zimmer
1 *Hunters of the red moon* (1973)
2 *Survivors* (1979)

Red nose readers series
Ahlberg, Allan
1 *Help!* (1985)
2 *Big bad pig* (1985)
3 *Make a face* (1985)
4 *So can I* (1985)
5 *Jumping* (1985)
6 *Bear's birthday* (1985)
7 *Happy worm* (1985)
8 *Fee fi fo fum* (1985)
9 *Push the dog* (1986)
10 *Crash, bang, wallop!* (1986)
11 *Me and my friend* (1986)
12 *Shirley shops* (1986)
13 *One two flea!* (1986)
14 *Look out for the seals!* (1986)
15 *Blow me down* (1986)
16 *Tell us a story* (1986)

Red Patrol series
Leighton, Robert
1 *Gildersley's tenderfoot* (1909)
A story of Redskin and prairie
2 *Red Patrol* (1915)
A story of the North West Mounted Police

Red Pepper Burns series
Richmond, Grace Smith
1 *Red Pepper Burns* (1910)
2 *Mrs Red Pepper* (1913)
3 *Red Pepper's patients* (1917)
4 *Red and black* (1920)
5 *Red of the Redfields* (1924)
Redfields
6 *Red Pepper returns* (1931)

Red Planet series
McCaffrey, Anne
see **Pern and the Red Planet series**

Red Plume series
Williams, Edward Huntington
1 *Red Plume* (1925)
2 *Red Plume returns* (1927)
3 *Red Plume with the Royal Northwest Mounted* (1927)

Red Radford series
Robb, John
1 *Red Radford and the Black Legion* (1960)
2 *Red Radford and Operation Kidnap* (1961)
3 *Red Radford and the Iron Guard* (1961)

Red Randall series
Bowen, Robert Sidney
1 *Red Randall at Midway* (1944)
2 *Red Randall on New Guinea* (1944)
3 *Red Randall at Pearl Harbor* (1944)
4 *Red Randall in Burma* (1945)
5 *Red Randall in the Aleutians* (1945)
6 *Red Randall's one-man war* (1946)

Red River County trilogy
Humphrey, William
1 *Home from the hill* (1958)
2 *Ordways* (1965)
3 *Proud flesh* (1973)
Companion volumes: *The last husband, and other stories*, 1953, *A time and a place*, 1968, *Farther off from heaven*, 1977

Red River trilogy
Silver, Alfred
1 *Red River story* (1986)
2 *Lord of the plains* (1990)
3 *When the ghost horse returns* (1991)

Red Ryder series
This sequence has five authors; based on comic strips and moving pictures
Winterbotham, Russell Robert
1 *Red Ryder and the mystery of the whispering walls* (1941)
Stevens, S S
2 *Red Ryder and the secret of Wolf Canyon* (1941)
Thomas, H C
3 *Red Ryder and the adventure of Chimney Rock* (1946)
Smith, Carl W
4 *Red Ryder and the secret of the Lucky Mine* (1947)
McGill, Jerry
5 *Red Ryder and the riddle of Roaring Range* (1951)
6 *Red Ryder and the Gun-Smoke gold* (1954)
7 *Red Ryder and the Thunder Trail* (1956)

Red Saunders series
Phillips, Henry Wallace
1 *Red Saunders, his adventures west and east* (1902)
2 *Plain Mary Smith* (1905)
3 *Mister Scraggs, introduced by Red Saunders* (1906)
4 *Red Saunders' pets and other critters* (1907)

Red series
Kjelgaard, Jim
1 *Big Red* (1945)
2 *Irish Red, son of Big Red* (1951)
3 *Outlaw Red, son of Big Red* (1953)

Red Six series
Styles, Showell
1 *Red for adventure* (1965)
2 *Wolf Cub Island* (1966)
3 *Sea cub* (1967)

Red Sonja series
Smith, David Claude
1 *Ring of Ikribu* (1981)
2 *Demon night* (1982)
3 *When hell laughs* (1982)
4 *Endithor's daughter* (1982)
5 *Against the prince of hell* (1983)
6 *Star of doom* (1983)

Red stain series
Abdullah, Achmed
1 *Red stain* (1915)
2 *Blue-eyed Manchu* (1917)

Redder series
Neuman, Fredric
see **Captain Redder series**

Reddman series
Downing, Warwick
see **Joe Reddman series**

Reddy Fox series
Burgess, Thornton Waldo
1 *Reddy Fox's sudden engagement* (1940)
Reddy Fox leaves in a hurry
2 *Peter Rabbit and Reddy Fox* (1954)
Peter Cottontail and Reddy Fox

Reddy series
Zacharia, Irwin
see **Irving Martin Reddy series**

Redfern series
Cameron, Eleanor
see **Julia Redfern series**

Redheads series
Mathews, M E
see **Cloud family series**

Redheap trilogy
Lindsay, Norman
1 *Redheap* (1930)
Every mother's son
2 *Saturdee* (1933)
3 *Halfway to anywhere* (1947)

Redmayne and North series
Moore, Patrick
see **Robin North and Rex Redmayne series**

Redmayne series
Darke, Marjorie
see **Francis Redmayne series**

Redmond and Gardner series
Quin-Harkin, Janet
see **Toni Redmond and Jill Gardner series**

Redstone Farm series
Lunt, Alice
1 *Eileen at Redstone Farm* (1964)
2 *Mystery at Redstone Farm* (1970)

Redwall series
Jacques, Brian
1 *Martin the warrior* (1993)
2 *Mossflower* (1988)
3 *Redwall* (1986)
4 *Mattimeo* (1989)
Numbers 2-4 also published in one volume entitled *The Redwall trilogy*, 1991
5 *Mariel of Redwall* (1991)
6 *Salamandastron* (1992)

Redwood Primary School series
Pinto, Jacqueline
1 *School dinner disaster* (1983)
2 *School gala disaster* (1985)
3 *School library disaster* (1986)
4 *School outing disaster* (1987)
5 *School donkey disaster* (1988)

Reece series
Douglas, Lauren Wright
see **Caitlin Reece series**

Reed series
Drummond, Charles
see **Sergeant Reed series**
Robertson, Keith
see **Henry Reed series**
Wood, Clement
see **Lal Reed series**

Reeder series
Dennis, Robert C
see **Paul Reeder series**
Wallace, Edgar
see **Mr J G Reeder series**

Reeds series
Carthew, Heather Jean
1 *Twisted reeds* (1986)
2 *Reeds in the wind* (1993)

Reefe King series
Barker, Albert
1 *Gift from Berlin* (1969)
2 *Apollo legacy* (1970)

Rees Pons series
King, Charles Daly
see **Doctor L Rees Pons series**

Rees series
Mather, Berkely
see **Idwal Rees series**

Reeves and Douglas series
Infante, Anne
see **Micky Douglas and inspector Reeves series**

Reflections and excursions series
Fleming, Peter
Reminiscences of travel
1 *My aunt's rhinoceros, and other reflections* (1956)
2 *With the Guards to Mexico, and other excursions* (1957)

Regan series
Brown, Roy Frederick
see **Chips Regan series**
Hale, Edgar
see **Inspector Michael Regan series**
Martin, Ian Kennedy
see **Sweeney series**

Regan trilogy
Cordell, Alexander
see **John Regan trilogy**

Regency series
Hardwick, Michael
see **Thomas Rodolfo Rackstraw series**

Regency series
Mansfield, Elizabeth
1 *Regency sting* (1980)
2 *Regency match* (1980)
3 *Regency charade* (1981)
4 *Regency wager* (1981)

Regency series
Veryan, Patricia
see **Age of Elegance series**

Regency trilogy
Dumas, Alexandre
1 *Conspirators* (1843)
Chevalier d'Harmental
2 *Regent's daughter* (1845)
Original edition entitled *Un fille du regent*
3 *Olympe de Cleves* (1852)
Original edition entitled *Olympe de Cleves*

Reggie Brooks series
Macpherson, Donald
1 *Go home, unicorn* (1935)
2 *Men are like animals* (1937)

Reggie Faulkner series
Snell, Edmund
1 *Z ray* (1932)
2 *Red spinner* (1937)
3 *Murder in Switzerland* (1938)

Reggie Fortune series
Bailey, Henry Christopher
see **Mister Reggie Fortune series**

Reggie, Olivia and Kate series
Lehmann, Rosamond
see **Olivia, Kate and Reggie series**

Regiment series
Dalmas, John
1 *Regiment* (1987)
2 *White regiment* (1990)
3 *Kalif's war* (1991)
4 *Regiment's war* (1993)

Regina and Randy Kidd series
Dagmar
see **Randy Kidd and Regina series**

Regina series
Mastin, John
1 *Stolen planet* (1905)
A scientific romance
2 *Through the sun in an airship* (1909)

Reginald Brett series
Tracy, Louis
1 *Stowmarket mystery* (1904)
Alternative title: A legacy of hate
2 *Albert Gate affair* (1904)
Albert Gate mystery

Reginald Drake Biffin series
Graham, Harry
1 *Bolster book* (1910)
A book for the bedside
2 *Perfect gentleman* (1912)
A guide to social aspirants
3 *Complete sportsman* (1914)
4 *Biffin and his circle* (1919)
5 *Last of the Biffins* (1925)
6 *Biffin papers* (1933)

Reginald Massingham series
Lincoln, Maurice
1 *I, said the sparrow* (1925)
2 *Nothing ever happens* (1927)

Reginald Perrin series
Nobbs, David
1 *Death of Reginald Perrin* (1975)
Fall and rise of Reginald Perrin
2 *Return of Reginald Perrin* (1977)
3 *Better world of Reginald Perrin* (1978)
One volume edition entitled *The complete Reginald Perrin*, 1990

Reginald series
Saki
1 *Reginald* (1904)
2 *Reginald in Russia* (1910)
One volume edition 1926

Reginald Wexford series
Rendell, Ruth
see **Chief Inspector Reginald Wexford series**

Region series
Benet, Juan
1 *[Nunca ilegaras a nada]* (1961)
No English edition
2 *Return to the Region* (1968)
Original edition entitled *Volveras a Region*
3 *Meditation* (1969)
Original edition entitled *Una meditacion*
Numbers 4-7 not translated

Regional series
Lenski, Lois
1 *Bayou Suzette* (1943)
2 *Strawberry girl* (1945)
3 *Blue Ridge Billy* (1946)
4 *Judy's journey* (1947)
5 *Boom town boy* (1948)
6 *Cotton in my sack* (1949)
7 *Texas tomboy* (1950)
8 *Prairie school* (1951)
9 *Mama Hattie's girl* (1953)
10 *Corn-fed boy* (1954)
11 *San Francisco boy* (1955)
12 *Houseboat girl* (1957)
13 *Coal camp girl* (1959)
14 *Shoo-fly girl* (1963)
15 *Deer Valley girl* (1968)

Register series
Douglas, Arthur
see **Mark Register series**

Regulator series
Colter, Dale
1 *Regulator* (1990)
2 *Diablo at daybreak* (1991)
3 *Deadly justice* (1991)
4 *Dead man's ride* (1991)
5 *Gravedancer* (1991)
6 *Scalp hunters* (1992)
7 *Paradise Mountain* (1992)
8 *Desert pursuit* (1992)
9 *Montana showdown* (1993)
10 *Payback* (1993)
11 *Trail of death* (1994)
12 *Slaughter at Paxico* (1994)

Rehm series
Herber, William
see **Jimmy Rehm series**

Rehumanization of Jade Darcy series
Goldin, Stephen
1 *Jade Darcy and the affair of honor* (1988)
2 *Jade Darcy and the Zen pirates* (1990)

Reid and Ramsay series
Matschat, Cecile Hulse
see **Andrea Reid and David Ramsay series**

Reid Bennett series
Wood, Ted
1 *Dead in the water* (1983)
2 *Murder on ice* (1984)
Killing cold
3 *Live bait* (1985)
Dead centre
4 *Fool's gold* (1986)
5 *Corkscrew* (1987)
6 *When the killing starts* (1989)
7 *On the inside* (1990)
8 *Flashback* (1992)
9 *Snowjob* (1993)

Reid series
Howard, Tom
see **Jack Reid series**
Pansy
see **Ester Ried series**

Reign of Herod Antipas trilogy
Mann, Deborah
1 *Now Barabbas was a robber* (1968)
2 *Pilate's wife* (1976)
3 *Song of Salome* (1969)
Companion volume: *The woman called Mary*, 1960

Reilly series
Corbin, Gary
see **Harry Reilly series**

Reilly series
Lockhart, Robin Bruce
1 *Reilly, ace of spies* (1967)
2 *Reilly, the first man* (1987)

Reilly series
Wilson, Barbara Ellen
see **Cassandra Reilly series**

Reincarnation series
Blackwood, Algernon
1 *Julius Le Vallon* (1916)
2 *Bright messenger* (1921)

Reincarnation series
Livingston, Marjorie
see **Karma series**

Reindeer moon series
Thomas, Elizabeth Marshall
1 *Reindeer moon* (1987)
2 *Animal wife* (1990)

Reindeer people series
Lindholm, Megan
1 *Reindeer people* (1988)
2 *Wolf's brother* (1988)
One volume edition entitled *A saga of the reindeer people*, 1988

Reinhart series
Berger, Thomas
see **Carlo Reinhart series**

Reisman series
Nathanson, E M
see **John Reisman series**

Reismann series
Wolitzer, Hilma
see **Linda and Robin Reismann series**

Relations series
Liddell, Robert
1 *Kind relations* (1939)
2 *Stepsons* (1969)

Relentless marriage series
Lambert, Mortan
1 *Relentless marriage* (1951)
2 *Thaxford's wife* (1953)

Religious life series
Hinnebusch, Paul
1 *Religious life* (1965)
A living liturgy
2 *Salvation history and the religious life* (1966)
3 *Signs of the times and the religious life* (1967)

Religious movements series
Hocking, Joseph
1 *Sword of the Lord* (1909)
A novel of the Reformation, Henry VIII and Martin Luther
2 *Lest we forget* (1901)
3 *Flame of fire* (1903)
Set during the Spanish Inquisition
4 *Follow the gleam* (1903)
Set during the Battle of Marston Moor
5 *Coming of the king* (1904)
6 *Chariots of the Lord* (1905)
Set in the late 17th century

Religious questions series
Hocking, Joseph
1 *Scarlet Woman* (1899)
2 *Purple robe* (1900)
3 *Woman of Babylon* (1906)
4 *Soul of Dominic Wildthorne* (1908)

Religious wars trilogy
Drummond, Hamilton
1 *For the religion* (1898)
Records of Blaise de Bernauld
2 *Man of his age* (1899)
3 *King's pawn* (1900)

Reluctant vampire series
Morecambe, Eric
1 *Reluctant vampire* (1982)
2 *Vampire's revenge* (1983)

Rem McAllister series
Chisholm, Matt
1 *McAllister* (1963)
2 *Hard men* (1963)
3 *Death at noon* (1963)
4 *Hangman rides tall* (1963)
5 *Kiowa* (1967)
6 *Death trail* (1967)
7 *Tough to kill* (1968)
8 *McAllister rides* (1969)
9 *Kill McAllister* (1969)
10 *McAllister makes war* (1969)
11 *McAllister strikes* (1969)
12 *McAllister's fury* (1969)
13 *McAllister fights* (1969)
14 *Rage of McAllister* (1969)

15 *McAllister justice* (1969)
Rewritten from *My gun is justice*, by Cy James, 1966
16 *Gunsmoke for McAllister* (1969)
17 *Hell for McAllister* (1969)
Rewritten from *The violent hills*, by Cy James, 1961
18 *Blood on McAllister* (1969)
19 *McAllister says no* (1970)
20 *Danger for McAllister* (1970)
21 *McAllister gambles* (1970)
22 *Hang McAllister* (1970)
23 *Shoot McAllister* (1970)
24 *Trail of McAllister* (1970)
25 *McAllister runs wild* (1972)
26 *Battle for McAllister* (1972)
27 *Brand McAllister* (1972)
28 *Vengeance of McAllister* (1973)
29 *McAllister trapped* (1973)
30 *McAllister must die* (1974)
31 *McAllister legend* (1974)
32 *McAllister on the Comanche crossing* (1981)
33 *McAllister never surrenders* (1981)
34 *McAllister and the Spanish gold* (1981)
35 *McAllister and Cheyenne death* (1981)
36 *McAllister and quarry* (1981)
37 *McAllister in Die-Hard* (1982)
38 *McAllister in Wolf-Bait* (1983)
39 *McAllister in Fire-Brand* (1983)

Rem Remington series
Ladline, Robert
see **J A Remington series**

Remember series
Asquith, Cynthia
Reminiscences
1 *Haply I may remember* (1950)
2 *Remember and be glad* (1952)

Remember trilogy
Randle, Kevin
1 *Remember the Alamo!* (1980)
2 *Remember Gettysburg!* (1988)
3 *Remember the Little Bighorn!* (1990)

Remembrance of things past series
Proust, Marcel
1 *Swann's way, part one* (1913)
Original edition entitled *Du cote de chez Swann*, part 1
2 *Swann's way, part two* (1913)
Original edition entitled *Du cote de chez Swann*, part 2
3 *Within a budding grove, part one* (1918)
Original edition entitled *L'ombre des jeunes filles en fleurs*, part 1
4 *Within a budding grove, part two* (1918)
Original edition entitled *L'ombre des jeunes filles en fleurs*, part 2
5 *Guermantes way, part one* (1920)
Original edition entitled *Le cote de Guermantes*, part 1
6 *Guermantes way, part two* (1921)
Original edition entitled *Le cote de Guermantes*, part 2
7 *Cities of the plain, part one* (1921)
Original edition entitled *Sodome et Gomorrhe*, part 1
8 *Cities of the plain, part two* (1922)
Original edition entitled *Sodome et Gomorrhe*, part 2
9 *Captive, part one* (1923)
Original edition entitled *La prisonniere*, part 1
10 *Captive, part two* (1923)
Original edition entitled *La prisonniere*, part 2
11 *Sweet sheat gone* (1925)
Fugitive
Albertine gone
Original edition entitled *Albertine disparue*
12 *Time regained* (1927)
Past recaptured
Original edition entitled *Le temps retrouve*

Remembrances of childhood series
Pagnol, Marcel
1 *Days were too short* (1957)
Original French edition published in two volumes
1.1 *My father's glory* (1957)
Original edition entitled *La gloire de mon pere*
1.2 *My mother's castle* (1957)
Original edition entitled *Le chateau de ma pere*
2 *Time of secrets* (1960)
Original edition entitled *Le temps des secrets*
3 *Time of love* (1977)
Original edition entitled *Le temps des amours*

Remfrey series
Thompson, Edward
see **Warren Remfrey series**

Remi and Perrine series
Malot, Hector
1 *No relations* (1879)
Nobody's boy
Adventures of Remi
Remi
Original edition entitled *Sans famille*
2 *Nobody's girl* (1894)
Adventures of Perrine
Original edition entitled *En famille*

Remington series
Boone, James Calder
see **Ned Remington series**
Ladline, Robert
see **J A Remington series**

Remo Williams series
Murphy, Warren Burton
see **Destroyer series**

Remover series
Daniel, Roland
1 *Remover* (1933)
2 *Blackmailer* (1934)
3 *Remover returns* (1935)
4 *Again the Remover* (1939)

Remsen series
Montross, David
1 *Traitor's wife* (1962)
2 *Troika* (1963)
Who is Elissa Sheldon?
3 *Fellow-traveler* (1965)

Remus series
Harris, Joel Chandler
see **Uncle Remus series**

Renaissance trilogy
Bowen, Marjorie
1 *Golden roof* (1928)
2 *Triumphant beast* (1934)
3 *Trumpets at Rome* (1936)

Renard series
Audemars, Pierre
see **Hercule Renard series**

Rendal series
Portman, Lionel
see **Hugh Rendal series**

Rendle series
Lindsay, Paula
see **Mark Rendle series**

Renee and Leon Thornton series
Ashton, Elizabeth
1 *Parisian adventure* (1970)
2 *Parade of peacocks* (1972)

Renee Nere series
Colette, Sidonie Gabrielle
1 *Vagabond* (1910)
Vagrant
Renee Nere
Original edition entitled *La vagabonde*; the third title is a revised edition
2 *Shackle* (1913)
Captive
Recaptured
Original edition entitled *L'entrave*

Renegade legion series
Rice, Peter
1 *Interceptor* (1988)
2 *Centurion* (1988)
Revised edition 1991
3 *Leviathan* (1989)
4 *Legionnaire* (1989)
5 *Damned if we do* (1990)
6 *Frost death* (1991)

Renegade Roe series
Roper, Lester V
see **Jerry Roe series**

Renegade series
Thorne, Ramsay
see **Captain Gringo series**

Renfrew series
Erskine, Laurie York
see **Douglas Renfrew series**

Renfro series
Norton, Andre
see **Janus series**

Renko series
Smith, Martin Cruz
see **Arkady Renko series**

Renn series
Jameson, Storm
1 *Before the crossing* (1947)
2 *Black laurel* (1947)

Rennert series
Downing, Todd
see **Hugh Rennert series**

Renny series
Richmond, Philip
see **Duke Renny series**

Reno series
Morris, Gilbert
see **Jim Reno series**

Rentaghost trilogy
Morgan, Hugh
Based on a television series
1 *Rentaghost unlimited* (1982)
2 *Rentaghost enterprises* (1984)
3 *Rentaghost rules* (1985)

Renwick series
Macinnes, Helen
see **Robert Renwick series**

Reporter series
Lambert, Derek
1 *Sheltered days* (1965)
Growing up in the War
2 *Just like the Blitz* (1987)
A reporter's notebook

Repositors series
Cooper, John R
1 *Lord falcon* (1991)
Making of a legend
2 *Azon the youth* (1991)

Rescue series
Gorelick, Molly Chernow
1 *Fire on Sun Mountain* (1967)
2 *Flood at Dry Creek* (1967)
3 *Storm at Sandy Point* (1967)
4 *Fog over Sun City* (1968)
5 *Snowstorm at Green Valley* (1968)

Resistance series
Saint Germain, Gregory
1 *Night and fog* (1982)
2 *Magyar massacre* (1982)
3 *Shadows of death* (1983)
4 *Road of iron* (1983)
5 *Target Sahara* (1983)

Resistance trilogy
Serge, Victor
1 *Midnight in the century* (1939)
Original edition entitled *S'il est minuit dans le siecle*
2 *Case of Comrade Tulayev* (1948)
Original edition entitled *L'affaire Toulaev*
3 *Long dusk* (1946)
Original edition entitled *Les derniers temps*

Resnick series
Harvey, John Barton
see **Inspector Charlie Resnick series**

Retallick family series
Thompson, Ernest Victor
1 *Chase the wind* (1977)
2 *Harvest of the sun* (1978)
3 *Ben Retallick* (1980)
4 *Singing spears* (1982)
5 *Stricken land* (1986)
6 *Lottie Trago* (1990)

Retief series
Doke, Joseph John
see **Karroo series**

Retief series
Laumer, Keith
1 *Envoy to new worlds* (1963)
Retief, envoy to new worlds
2 *Galactic diplomat* (1965)
Nine incidents of the Corps Diplomatique Terrestrienne
3 *Retief's war* (1966)
4 *Retief and the warlords* (1968)
5 *Retief, ambassador to space* (1969)
Seven incidents of the Corps Diplomatique Terrestrienne
6 *Retief's ransom* (1971)
Retief and the Pangalactic Pageant of Pulchritude
Numbers 1 and 6 also published as *Retief unbound*, 1979
7 *Retief of the CDT* (1971)
8 *Retief, emissary to the stars* (1975)
Revised edition 1979
9 *Retief, diplomat at arms* (1982)
10 *Retief to the rescue* (1983)
11 *Return of Retief* (1984)
12 *Retief in the ruins* (1986)
13 *Reward for Retief* (1989)
Companion volume: *Retief at large*, 1978

Retreat series
Frankland, Edward
1 *Retreat* (1926)
2 *Reform* (1928)

Return Kingdom series
Braden, James Andrew
see **John Jerome and Return Kingdom series**

Return of Dracula series
Lory, Robert
see **Dracula horror series**

Return to the Planet of the Apes series
Arrow, William
This pseudonym is used by Donald J Pfeil and William Rotsler as indicated against each title; based on a television series

Return to the Planet of the Apes series

1 *Visions from nowhere* (1976) [Rotsler]
2 *Escape from Terror* (1976) [Pfeil]
3 *Man, the hunted animal* (1976) [Rotsler]

Reuben Brown series
Winstan, Matt
1 *Big herd* (1957)
2 *Gunslick gambler* (1958)
3 *Vengeance rode west* (1959)
4 *One-gun justice* (1959)
5 *New trails blaze west* (1960)
6 *Gunsmoke on the iron trail* (1961)
7 *Pay off in lead* (1961)
8 *Bandit trail* (1962)
9 *Trail to Boot Hill* (1962)
10 *No branding fire* (1963)
11 *Drive to Dodge City* (1963)
12 *Guns at Salt Flats* (1964)
13 *Gold-lust city* (1965)

Reuben Cogburn series
Portis, Charles
see **Rooster Cogburn series**

Reuben trilogy
Harris, Rosemary
see **Egyptian trilogy**

Reunion series
Jaffe, Rona
1 *Class reunion* (1979)
2 *After the reunion* (1985)

Reuven Malter and Danny Saunders series
Potok, Chaim
see **Danny Saunders and reuven Malter series**

Revel series
Berrow, Norman
see **Michael Revel series**

Revenger series
Hedges, Joseph
see **John Stark series**

Revenger series
Messmann, Jon
1 *Revenger* (1973)
2 *Fire in the streets* (1974)
3 *Vendetta contract* (1974)
4 *Stiletto signature* (1974)
5 *City for sale* (1975)
6 *Promise for death* (1975)

Reverend J J Meldon series
Birmingham, George A
1 *Spanish gold* (1908)
2 *Simpkins plot* (1911)
3 *Major's niece* (1911)
4 *Major's candlesticks* (1929)
5 *Sea battle* (1948)

Reverend Jabal Jarrett series
Bream, Freda
1 *Island of fear* (1982)
2 *Vicar done it* (1983)
3 *Vicar investigates* (1983)
4 *Sealed and despatched* (1984)
5 *With murder in mind* (1985)
6 *Problem at Piha* (1986)

Reverend Martin Buell series
Scherf, Margaret
1 *Gilbert's last toothache* (1949)
For the love of murder
2 *Curious custard pie* (1950)
Divine and deadly
3 *Elk and the evidence* (1952)
4 *Cautious overshoes* (1956)
5 *Never turn your back* (1959)
6 *Corpse in the flannel nightgown* (1965)

Reverend P J Macfarlane series
Macvicar, Angus
1 *Temple falls* (1935)
2 *Crouching spy* (1941)

Reverend Randollph series
Smith, Charles Merrill
1 *Reverend Randollph and the wages of sin* (1974)
2 *Reverend Randollph and the avenging angel* (1977)
3 *Reverend Randollph and the fall from Grace, Inc.* (1978)
4 *Reverend Randollph and the holy terror* (1980)
5 *Reverend Randollph and the unholy Bible* (1983)
6 *Reverend Randollph and the splendid Samaritan* (1986)
Completed by the author's son, Terrence Lore Smith

Reverend Septimus Treloar series
Chance, Stephen
see **Septimus Treloar series**

Reversible giant series
Leeson, Robert
1 *Reversible giant* (1986)
2 *Right royal kidnap* (1990)

Revill-Gordon series
Dyson, Elizabeth
1 *With swords in their lips* (1956)
2 *Proud suitor* (1959)

Revolt of Aphrodite series
Durrell, Lawrence
1 *Tunc* (1968)
2 *Nunquam* (1970)
One volume edition entitled *The revolt of Aphrodite*, 1974

Revolution series
Adler, Mortimer Jerome
1 *Democratic revolution* (1956)
2 *Capitalistic revolution* (1957)

Revolution series
True, John Preston
1 *Scouting for Washington* (1900)
A story of the days of Sumter and Tarleton
2 *Morgan's men* (1901)
Adventures of Stuart Schuyler, captain of cavalry during the Revolution
3 *On guard, against Tory and Tarleton* (1902)
Adventures of Stuart Schuyler, major of cavalry during the Revolution
4 *Scouting for Light Horse Harry* (1911)
Adventures of Thomas Ludlow, captain of cavalry during the Revolution, including certain experiences from Bunker Hill to Hookirk's Hill

Revolution trilogy
Serge, Victor
1 *Men in prison* (1930)
Original edition entitled *Les hommes dans la prison*
2 *Birth of our power* (1931)
Original edition entitled *Naissance de notre force*

Revolutionary series
Stoddard, William Osborn
1 *Dan Monroe* (1905)
A story of Bunker Hill
2 *Two cadets with Washington* (1906)

Revolutionary War series
Blanchard, Amy Ella
1 *Girl of '76* (1898)
2 *Revolutionary maid* (1899)
A story of the middle period of the War for Independence
3 *Daughter of freedom* (1900)
A story of the later period of the War for Independence
4 *Heroine of 1812* (1901)
A Maryland romance
5 *Loyal lass* (1902)
A story of the Niagara campaign of 1814
6 *Gentle pioneer* (1903)
The story of the early days in the new West

Rewards and fairies series
Kipling, Rudyard
1 *Puck of Pook's Hill* (1906)
2 *Rewards and fairies* (1910)
For a guide to the recurring characters in Kipling's short stories see *A Kipling dictionary*, by William Arthur Young, revised by John H McGivering, 1967

Rex Anderson series
Buckley, Eunice
1 *Wonder-worker* (1975)
2 *Half of my kingdom* (1976)

Rex Bader series
Reynolds, Mack
1 *Five way secret agent* (1975)
2 *Satellite city* (1975)
3 *Lagrange Five* (1979)
4 *Lagrangists* (1983)
5 *Chaos in Lagrangia* (1984)

Rex Banner series
Chapman, Robert
1 *One jump ahead* (1951)
2 *Crime on my hands* (1952)
3 *Winter wears a shroud* (1952)
4 *Murder for the million* (1953)
5 *Behind the headlines* (1955)
6 *Frozen stiff* (1956)
7 *Downward path* (1959)
8 *Wish you were dead* (1960)

Rex Carver series
Canning, Victor
1 *Whip hand* (1965)
2 *Doubled in diamonds* (1966)
3 *Python project* (1967)
4 *Melting man* (1968)

Rex Clinton series
Johns, William Earl
Stories of interplanetary exploration
1 *Kings of space* (1954)
2 *Return to Mars* (1955)
3 *Now to the stars* (1956)
4 *To outer space* (1957)
5 *Edge of beyond* (1958)
6 *Death rays of Ardilla* (1959)
7 *To worlds unknown* (1960)
8 *Quest for the perfect planet* (1961)
9 *Worlds of wonder* (1962)
10 *Man who vanished into space* (1963)

Rex Coulson series
Mann, Jack
1 *Reckless Coulson* (1933)
2 *Coulson goes south* (1933)
3 *Egyptian nights* (1934)
4 *Dead man's chest* (1934)
5 *Coulson alone* (1936)
6 *Detective Coulson* (1936)

Rex Lee series
Burtis, Thomson
1 *Rex Lee, gypsy flyer* (1928)
2 *Rex Lee on the Border Patrol* (1928)
3 *Rex Lee, ranger of the sky* (1928)
4 *Rex Lee, sky trailer* (1929)
5 *Rex Lee, ace of the Air Mail* (1929)
6 *Rex Lee, night flyer* (1929)
7 *Rex Lee's mysterious flight* (1930)
8 *Rex Lee, rough rider* (1930)
9 *Rex Lee, aerial acrobat* (1930)
10 *Rex Lee, trailing air bandits* (1931)
11 *Rex Lee, flying detective* (1932)

Rex McBride series
Adams, Cleve Franklin
1 *And sudden death* (1940)
2 *Sabotage* (1940)
Death before breakfast
Death at the dam
3 *Decoy* (1941)
4 *Up jumped the devil* (1943)
Murder all over
5 *Crooking finger* (1944)
6 *Shady lady* (1955)

Rex Milligan series
Buckeridge, Anthony
1 *Rex Milligan's busy term* (1953)
2 *Rex Milligan raises the roof* (1955)
3 *Rex Milligan holds forth* (1957)
4 *Rex Milligan reporting* (1961)

Rex Redmayne and Robin North series
Moore, Patrick
see **Robin North and Rex Redmayne series**

Reynold Frame series
Brean, Herbert
1 *Wilders walk away* (1948)
2 *Darker the night* (1949)
3 *Hardly a man is now alive* (1950)
Murder now and then
4 *Clock strikes thirteen* (1952)

Reynolds and Texas Joe series
Martin, Charles Morris
see **Roaming Reynolds and Texas Joe series**

Reynolds series
Grove, Marjorie
see **Maxine Reynolds series**
Hamilton, Elaine
see **Inspector Reynolds series**

Rezaire series
Armstrong, Anthony
see **Jimmie Rezaire series**

Rhada series
Gilman, Robert Cham
1 *Warlock of Rhada* (1985)
2 *Rebel of Rhada* (1968)
3 *Navigator of Rhada* (1969)
4 *Starkahn of Rhada* (1970)

Rhanna series
Fraser, Christine Marion
1 *Rhanna* (1978)
2 *Rhanna at war* (1979)
3 *Children of Rhanna* (1983)
4 *Return to Rhanna* (1984)
5 *Song of Rhanna* (1985)
6 *Storm over Rhanna* (1988)
7 *Stranger on Rhanna* (1992)

Rhea Buerklin series
Dunham, Mikel
1 *Stilled life* (1989)
2 *Casting for murder* (1992)

Rhine series
Barr, Robert
see **Mediaeval Rhine series**

Rhineland heritage series
Schickele, Rene
1 *Maria Capponi* (1925)
Original edition entitled *Maria Capponi*
2 *Heart of Alsace* (1927)
Original edition entitled *Blick auf die Vogesen*

Rhoda series
Oxenham, Elsie J
1 *Rosamund's tuck-shop* (1937)
2 *Patch and a pawn* (1940)

Rhodan series
Scheer, Karl Herbert
see **Perry Rhodan series**

Rhoden series
Walker, Ira
see **Steve Rhoden series**

Rhodenbarr series
Block, Lawrence
see **Bernie Rhodenbarr series**

Rhodes series
Aikman, Anthony
see **Boyet Rhodes series**
Gober, Don
see **James Rhodes series**

Rhodesia series
Macdonald, Sheila
1 *Sally in Rhodesia* (1926)
2 *My African garden* (1928)

Rhodesian history series
Gann, Lewis Henry
see **History of Rhodesia series**

Rhodesian series
Brown, Robin
1 *When the woods became the trees* (1965)
2 *Forest is a long time growing* (1967)

Rhodesian series
Stonier, George Walter
1 *Off the rails* (1967)
2 *Rhodesian spring* (1968)

Rhodry series
Kerr, Katharine
1 *Time of exile* (1991)
2 *Time of omens* (1992)
3 *Time of war* (1993)
4 *Time of justice* (1994)

Rhyme-fingerplay-puppet series
Young, Ruth
1 *Turtle magic* (1990)
2 *Spider magic* (1990)

Rhymes of the never was an always is series
McCord, David
Poems
1 *Far and few* (1952)
2 *Take sky* (1962)
3 *All day long* (1966)
Selections from numbers 1-3 published as *Every time I climb a tree*, 1967
4 *For me to say* (1970)
5 *Away and ago* (1975)
6 *Speak up* (1980)

Rhymes with me series
Bradman, Tony
1 *Hide and seek* (1985)
2 *Play time* (1985)
3 *At the park* (1985)
4 *Let's pretend* (1985)

Rhys series
Craig, Alisa
see **Inspector Madoc Rhys series**

Riam series
Woodbury, David Oakes
see **George Riam series**

Ribsy series
Cleary, Beverly
1 *Henry and Ribsy* (1954)
2 *Ribsy* (1964)

Rice series
Kendrick, Baynard
see **Miles Standish Rice series**
Stand, Marguerite
see **Bill Rice series**

Rich and Mark series
Bamman, Henry A
see **World of adventure series**

Rich and poor series
Whiteing, Richard
1 *Island* (1888)
Alternative title: An adventure of a person of quality
2 *Number five John Street* (1899)

Rich man, poor man trilogy
Fairbank, Janet Ayer
1 *Cortlandts of Washington Square* (1922)
2 *Smiths* (1925)
3 *Rich man, poor man* (1936)

Rich Mitch series
Sharmat, Marjorie Weinman
1 *Rich Mitch* (1983)
2 *Get rich Mitch!* (1985)

Rich Richardson series
Beach, Edward Latimer, junior
1 *Run silent, run deep* (1955)
2 *Dust on the sea* (1972)
3 *Cold is the sea* (1978)

Richard and Martin Fane series
Halliday, Michael
see **Martin and Richard Fane series**

Richard and Valerie series
Held, Jacqueline
English text by Marion Koenig, illustrated by Anne Marie Constant
1 *Richard and Valerie on the farm* (1970)
2 *Richard and Valerie in the garden* (1970)
3 *Richard and Valerie in the mountains* (1970)

Richard Barne series
Cousins, Edmund George
see **Colonel Richard Barne series**

Richard Blade series
Lord, Jeffrey
This pseudonym is used by Roland Green, Ray Faraday Nelson and Manning Lee Stokes whose authorship indicated against the titles
1 *Bronze axe* (1969)
[Stokes]
2 *Jade warrior* (1969)
[Stokes]
3 *Jewel of Tharn* (1969)
[Stokes]
4 *Slave of Sarma* (1969)
[Stokes]
5 *Liberator of Jedd* (1971)
[Stokes]
6 *Monster of the maze* (1972)
[Stokes]
7 *Pearl of Patmos* (1973)
[Stokes]
8 *Undying world* (1972)
[Stokes]
9 *Kingdom of Royth* (1974)
[Green]
10 *Ice dragon* (1974)
[Green]
11 *Dimension of dreams* (1974)
[Green]
12 *King of Zunga* (1975)
[Green]
13 *Golden steed* (1975)
[Green]
14 *Temples of Ayocan* (1975)
[Green]
15 *Towers of Melnon* (1975)
[Green]
16 *Crystal seas* (1975)
[Green]
17 *Mountains of Brega* (1976)
[Green]
18 *Warlords of Gaikon* (1976)
[Green]
19 *Looters of Tharn* (1976)
[Green]
20 *Guardians of the coral throne* (1976)
[Green]
21 *Champions of the gods* (1976)
[Green]
22 *Forests of Gleor* (1977)
[Green]
23 *Empire of blood* (1977)
[Green]
24 *Dragons of Englor* (1977)
[Green]
25 *Torian pearls* (1977)
[Green]
26 *City of the living dead* (1978)
[Green]
27 *Master of the Hashomi* (1978)
[Green]
28 *Wizard of Rentoro* (1978)
[Green]
29 *Treasure of the stars* (1978)
[Green]
30 *Dimension of horror* (1979)
[Nelson]
31 *Gladiators of Hapana* (1979)
[Green]
32 *Pirates of Gohar* (1979)
[Green]
33 *Killer plants of Binaark* (1980)
[Green]
34 *Ruins of Kaldak* (1981)
[Green]
35 *Lords of the Crimson River* (1981)
[Green]
36 *Return to Kaldak* (1983)
[Green]
37 *Warriors of Latan* (1984)
[Green]

Richard Bolitho series
Kent, Alexander
see **Captain Richard Bolitho series**

Richard Bronson series
Rawls, Philip
Based on a television series
1 *Blind rage* (1975)
2 *Streets of blood* (1975)
Also published under the author's real name, Leonard Levinson
3 *Switchblade* (1975)

Richard Browning series
Corris, Peter
1 *Box office Browning* (1987)
2 *Beverly Hills Browning* (1987)
3 *Browning takes off* (1989)
4 *Browning in buckskin* (1991)
5 *Browning, P.I.* (1992)
6 *Browning battles on* (1993)
7 *Browning Sahib* (1994)
A Browning adventure in old Ceylon

Richard Camellion series
Rosenberger, Joseph
see **Death Merchant series**

Richard Chandos series
Yates, Dornford
1 *Blind corner* (1927)
2 *Perishable goods* (1928)
3 *Blood royal* (1929)
4 *Fire below* (1930)
By royal command
5 *She fell among thieves* (1935)
6 *Gale warning* (1939)
7 *Eye for a tooth* (1943)
8 *Red in the morning* (1946)
Were death denied
9 *Cost price* (1949)
Laughing bacchante
10 *Ne'er-do-well* (1954)

Richard Chatterton series
Ayres, Ruby Mildred
1 *Richard Chatterton, V.C.* (1915)
2 *Long lane to happiness* (1915)
3 *Road that bends* (1916)

Richard Cherrington series
Daniel, Glyn
see **Sir Richard Cherrington series**

Richard Dartley series
Barclay, Ian
1 *Crime minister* (1984)
2 *Reprisal* (1985)
3 *Rebound* (1986)
4 *Reckoning* (1987)

Richard De Brun series
Campbell, Marion
1 *Wide blue road* (1957)
2 *Lances and longships* (1963)
3 *Squire of Val* (1964)

Richard Delancey series
Parkinson, Cyril Northcote
1 *Devil to pay* (1973)
2 *Fireship* (1975)
3 *Touch and go* (1977)
4 *So near, so far* (1981)
5 *Dead reckoning* (1978)
6 *Guernsey man* (1982)

Richard Deutsch series
Christian, John
1 *Five gates to Armageddon* (1975)
2 *Persian death-trap* (1976)

Richard Duvall series
Fredericks, Arnold
1 *Ivory snuff box* (1912)
2 *One million francs* (1912)
3 *Blue lights* (1915)
4 *Little fortune* (1915)
5 *Film of fear* (1917)

Richard Emmis series
Burgess, Anthony
1 *Time for a tiger* (1956)
2 *Enemy in the blanket* (1958)
3 *Beds in the east* (1959)
4 *Worm and the ring* (1961)
Revised edition 1970
5 *Vision of battlements* (1965)

Richard Falcon series
Yates, Dornford
see **Superintendent Richard Falcon series**

Richard Furling series
Grierson, Francis Durham
1 *Murder in Mortimer Square* (1932)
2 *Mystery of the golden angel* (1933)
3 *Monkhurst murder* (1933)

Richard Furlong series
Thurston, Ernest Temple
1 *Antagonists* (1912)
2 *Richard Furlong* (1913)
3 *Achievement* (1914)
Achievement of Richard Furlong

Richard Goulburn series
Fletcher, Joseph Smith
1 *Mantle of Ishmael* (1909)
2 *Million-dollar diamond* (1923)
Black house in Harley Street

Richard Graham series
Welcome, John
1 *Run for cover* (1958)
2 *Hard to handle* (1964)
3 *Wanted for killing* (1965)
4 *Hell is where you find it* (1968)
5 *On the stretch* (1969)
6 *Go for broke* (1972)

Richard Hannay series
This sequence has two authors
Buchan, John
1 *Thirty-nine steps* (1915)
2 *Greenmantle* (1916)
3 *Mister Standfast* (1919)
4 *Three hostages* (1924)
5 *Courts of the morning* (1929)
6 *Island of Sheep* (1936)
Man from the Norlands
Also one story featuring Richard Hannay in *The Runagates Club*, 1928
Smithers, Jack
7 *Combined forces* (1983)
The latter-day adventures of Maj. Gen. Sir Richard Hannay, Captain Hugh, Bulldog, Drummond and Berry and Co.

Richard Haven series
Lucas, Edward Verrall
1 *Vermilion box* (1916)
2 *Verena in the midst* (1920)

Richard Herrivell series
Bentley, John
see **Sir Richard Herrivell series**

Richard I series
Kaufman, Pamela
1 *Shield of three lions* (1983)
2 *Banners of gold* (1986)

Richard II series
Tucker, Terry
see **King Richard II series**

Richard III series
Jarman, Rosemary Hawley
1 *We speak no treason* (1971)
2 *King's grey mare* (1973)
Crown of glory
3 *Crown in candlelight* (1978)
4 *Courts of illusion* (1983)

Richard III series
Viney, Jayne
1 *King Richard's friend* (1975)
2 *White Rose dying* (1973)

Richard Jury series
Grimes, Martha
see **Inspector Richard Jury series**

Richard, Kitchie and Wong series
Dalton, Clive
see **Malay series**

Richard Lasson series
Laqueur, Walter
see **Doctor Richard Lasson series**

Richard Left series
Forsyte, Charles
see **Inspector Richard Left series**

Richard Lingard series
Smith, Naomi Royde
1 *Jake* (1935)
2 *How white is my sepulchre* (1958)

Richard Logan series
McCutcheon, Hugh
1 *To dusty death* (1960)
2 *Suddenly in Vienna* (1963)

Richard Mahony trilogy
Richardson, Henry Handel
see **Fortunes of Richard Mahony trilogy**

Richard Maidment series
Cronin, Michael
1 *Paid in full* (1953)
2 *I can cope* (1955)
3 *Climb the wall* (1956)
4 *Sweet water* (1957)
5 *Begin with a gun* (1960)
6 *Curtain wall* (1961)

Richard Malcolm series
Grady, James
see **Condor series**

Richard Mardick series
Hartley, Leslie Poles
1 *Brickfield* (1964)
2 *Betrayal* (1966)

Richard Massey series
Van Siller, Hilda
1 *Echo of a bomb* (1943)
2 *Curtain between* (1947)
Fatal bride

Richard Monk series
Underwood, Michael
1 *Man who died on Friday* (1967)
2 *Man who killed too soon* (1968)

Richard Nixon series
Ambrose, Stephen Edward
1 *Nixon, the education of a politician, 1913-1962* (1987)
2 *Nixon, the triumph of a politician, 1962-1972* (1989)
3 *Nixon, ruin and recovery, 1973-1990* (1991)

Richard Owen series
Sharp, Marilyn
1 *Sunflower* (1979)
2 *Masterstroke* (1981)
3 *Falseface* (1984)

Richard Patton series
Ormerod, Roger
1 *Face value* (1983)
Hanging doll murder
2 *Dead ringer* (1986)
3 *Still life with pistol* (1986)
4 *Alibi too soon* (1987)
5 *Open window* (1988)
6 *Guilt on the lily* (1989)
7 *Death of an innocent* (1989)
8 *No sign of life* (1990)

Richard Powell series
Fowles, Anthony
1 *Dupe negative* (1970)
2 *Double feature* (1972)

Richard Quintain series
Baker, William Howard
1 *Unfriendly persuasion* (1964)
Originally published under the pseudonym W A Ballinger
2 *Take death for a lover* (1965)
3 *Strike north* (1965)
4 *No place for strangers* (1965)
5 *Rape of Berlin* (1965)
Girl, the city and the soldier
6 *Destination Dieppe* (1965)
7 *Dogs of war* (1966)
8 *Inexpendable* (1966)
9 *Drums of the dark gods* (1966)
Originally published under the pseudonym W A Ballinger
10 *Guardians* (1967)
Dirty game
11 *Girl in asses' milk* (1967)
12 *Dead and the damned* (1967)
13 *Night of the Wolf* (1967)
14 *Traitor!* (1967)
Treasure hunters
15 *Charge is treason* (1968)
16 *Judas diary* (1969)

Richard Raven series
Griffin, John
1 *Midas operation* (1976)
2 *Standing into danger* (1976)
3 *Circle of darkness* (1976)
4 *Seeds of destruction* (1977)
5 *Anarchists' moon* (1977)
6 *Ring of Kerry* (1978)
7 *Saint Catherine's wheel* (1978)
8 *Antarctic convergence* (1979)
9 *Florentine Madonna* (1979)
10 *Camelot conundrum* (1979)
11 *Flame of Persepolis* (1981)

Richard Ringwood series
Farrer, Katharine
see **Inspector Richard Ringwood series**

Richard Rollison series
Creasey, John
see **Toff series**

Richard Sarel series
Bryan, John
1 *Difference to me* (1957)
2 *Contessa came too* (1957)
3 *Man who came back* (1958)

Richard series
Lucas, Edward Verrall
1 *Windfall's eve* (1929)
2 *Down the sky* (1930)
3 *Barber's clock* (1931)

Richard Sharpe series
Cornwell, Bernard
1 *Sharpe's rifles* (1988)
Richard Sharpe and the French invasion of Galicia, January 1809
2 *Sharpe's eagle* (1981)
Richard Sharpe and the Talavera Campaign, July 1809
3 *Sharpe's gold* (1981)
Richard Sharpe and the destruction of the Almeida, August 1810
4 *Sharpe's company* (1982)
Richard Sharpe and the Siege of Badajoz, January to April 1812
5 *Sharpe's sword* (1983)
Richard Sharpe and the Salamanca Campaign, June and July 1812
6 *Sharpe's enemy* (1984)
Richard Sharpe and the Defence of Portugal, Christmas 1812
7 *Sharpe's honour* (1985)
Richard Sharpe and the Vitoria Campaign, February to June 1813
8 *Sharpe's regiment* (1986)
Richard Sharpe and the invasion of France, June to November 1813
9 *Sharpe's siege* (1987)
Richard Sharpe and the Winter Campaign, 1814
10 *Sharpe's revenge* (1989)
Richard Sharpe and the peace of 1814
11 *Sharpe's Waterloo* (1990)
The Waterloo Campaign, 15 June to 18 June 1815
12 *Sharpe's devil* (1992)
Richard Sharpe and the Emperor, 1820-1821

Richard Spade series
Johnson, B B
see **Superspade series**

Richard Trenton series
Burton, Anne
1 *Dear departed* (1980)
2 *Where there's a will* (1980)
3 *Worse than a crime* (1981)

Richard trilogy
Horgan, Paul
1 *Things as they are* (1964)
2 *Everything to live for* (1968)
3 *Thin mountain air* (1977)
One volume edition entitled *The Richard trilogy*, 1990

Richard Tuck series
Lewis, Lange
see **Lieutenant Richard Tuck series**

Richard Vaness series
Black, Mansell
1 *Dead on course* (1951)
Also published under the pseudonym Elleston Trevor
2 *Sinister cargo* (1951)
3 *Shadow of evil* (1953)
4 *Steps in the dark* (1954)

Richard Verrell series
Graeme, Bruce
see **Blackshirt series**
Graeme, Roderic
see **Blackshirt series**

Richard Wentworth series
This sequence has two authors; reprinted from 1930s pulp magazines
Scott, Reginald Thomas Maitland
1 *Spider strikes* (1969)
2 *Wheel of death* (1969)
Stockbridge, Grant
This is a pseudonym of Norvell W Page except in number 16 where it is used by Emile C Tepperman
3 *Wings of the black death* (1969)
4 *City of flaming shadows* (1970)
5 *Death reign of the Vampire King* (1975)
6 *Hordes of the Red Butcher* (1975)
7 *City destroyer* (1975)
8 *Death and the Spider* (1975)
9 *Builder of the Black Empire* (1980)
10 *Master of the death madness* (1980)
11 *Overlord of the damned* (1980)
12 *Satan's death blast* (1984)
13 *Corpse cargo* (1985)
14 *Prince of evil* (1985)
15 *Spider, master of men, volume 1* (1991)
Includes *Secret city of crime*, and *The Spider and the Pain Master*
16 *Spider, master of men, volume 2* (1991)
Includes *Dictator of the damned*, and *The mill-town massacres*

Richard York series
Williamson, Audrey
see **Superintendent Richard York series**

Richards series
Frank, Lee
see **Kane Richards series**

Richardson series
Beach, Edward Latimer, junior
see **Rich Richardson series**
Thomson, Basil
see **Superintendent Richardson series**

Richelieu series
Wheatley, Dennis
see **Duc de Richelieu series**

Richmond series
Graham, Anthony
see **Frank Richmond series**

Richmond series
Fritch, Elizabeth
1 *Flame* (1980)
2 *Fire* (1980)
3 *Embers* (1980)
4 *Sparks* (1982)
5 *Blaze* (1982)

Richmond, Virginia series
Dowdey, Clifford
1 *Gamble's hundred* (1939)
Set in the 1730s
2 *Tidewater* (1943)
Set in the 1830s
3 *Where bugles blow no more* (1937)
Set during the American Civil War
4 *Where my love sleeps* (1945)
Set during the American Civil War
5 *Sing for a penny* (1941)
Set in the 1880s

Rick and Pete Clayton series
Marsh, Jean Evelyn
1 *On the trail of the Albatross* (1950)
2 *Secret of the Pygmy herd* (1951)

Rick Brant series
Blaine, John
1 *Rocket's shadow* (1947)
2 *Lost city* (1947)
3 *Sea gold* (1947)
4 *One hundred fathoms under* (1947)
5 *Whispering box mystery* (1948)
6 *Phantom shark* (1949)
7 *Smugglers' Reef* (1950)
8 *Caves of fear* (1951)
9 *Stairway to danger* (1952)
10 *Golden skull* (1954)
11 *Wailing octopus* (1956)
12 *Electronic mind reader* (1957)
13 *Scarlet Lake mystery* (1958)
14 *Pirates of Shan* (1958)
15 *Blue ghost mystery* (1960)
16 *Egyptian cat mystery* (1961)
17 *Flaming mountain* (1962)
18 *Flying stingaree* (1963)
19 *Ruby ray mystery* (1964)
20 *Veiled raiders* (1965)
21 *Rocket jumper* (1966)
22 *Deadly Dutchman* (1967)
23 *Danger below!* (1968)
24 *Magic talisman* (1990)

Rick Holman series
Brown, Carter
1 *Death of a doll* (1956)
Ever-loving blues
The second title is a revised edition; original edition published under the pseudonym Peter Carter Brown
2 *Zelda* (1961)
3 *Murder in the Harem Club* (1962)
Murder in the Key Club
4 *Murderer among us* (1962)
5 *Blonde on the rocks* (1963)
6 *Jade-eyed jinx* (1963)
Jade-eyed jungle
7 *Ballad of loving Jenny* (1963)
White bikini
8 *Wind-up doll* (1963)
9 *Never-was girl* (1964)
10 *Murder is a package deal* (1964)
11 *Who killed Doctor Sex?* (1964)
12 *Nude with a view* (1965)
13 *Girl from outer space* (1965)
14 *Blonde on a broomstick* (1966)
15 *Play now, kill later* (1966)
16 *No tears from the widow* (1966)
17 *Deadly kitten* (1967)
18 *Long time no Leela* (1967)
19 *Die anytime after Tuesday* (1969)
20 *Flagellator* (1969)
21 *Streaked-blonde slave* (1969)
22 *Good year for dwarfs* (1970)
23 *Hang-up kid* (1970)
24 *Where did Charity go?* (1970)
25 *Coven* (1971)
26 *Invisible Flamini* (1971)
27 *Pornbroker* (1972)
28 *Master* (1973)
29 *Negative in blue* (1974)
30 *Star-crossed lover* (1974)
31 *Phreak-out!* (1974)
32 *Ride the roller coaster* (1974)
33 *Remember Maybelle?* (1976)
34 *See it again, Sam* (1979)
35 *Phantom lady* (1980)
36 *Swingers* (1980)
37 *Blonde avalanche* (1984)

Rick Leroy series
Perowne, Barry
1 *Arrest these men!* (1932)
2 *I'm no murderer* (1938)
3 *They hang them in Gibraltar* (1939)
English edition entitled *Raffles' crime in Gibraltar*, 1937 does not include Leroy
4 *Raffles and the key man* (1940)

Rick McAdden series
Leader, Charles
1 *Golden lure* (1967)
2 *Cargo to Saigon* (1969)

Rick Muldoon series
James, Martin
1 *Night train* (1989)
2 *Tomb of Zwaab* (1991)

Rick O'Shay series
Lynde, Stan
Comic strips
1 *Rick O'Shay and Hipshot* (1976)
2 *Month of Sundays* (1985)
3 *Rick O'Shay, Hipshot and me* (1990)
4 *Price of fame* (1992)

Rick series
Walker, David Gordon
1 *Rick goes to Little League* (1982)
2 *Rick heads for soccer* (1982)
3 *Rick tees off* (1985)

Rick Train series
Fischer, Bruno
1 *Hornet's nest* (1944)
2 *Kill to fit* (1946)

Rickman trilogy
Craig, David
see **Roy Rickman trilogy**
White, Jon Manchip
see **Colonel Rickman trilogy**

Ricks series
Kyne, Peter Bernard
see **Cappy Ricks series**

Rickshaw series
England, Edward Oliver
see **John Rickshaw series**

Ricky and Nate series
Carkeet, David
1 *Silent treatment* (1988)
2 *Quiver river* (1991)

Ricky, Rocky and Ringo series
Kunnas, Mauri
Translated from the Finnish
1 *Ricky, Rocky and Ringo count on pizza* (1987)
2 *Ricky, Rocky and Ringo's colourful day* (1987)
Ricky, Rocky and Ringo's colorful day
3 *Ricky, Rocky and Ringo go to the moon* (1987)
4 *Ricky, Rocky and Ringo on TV* (1987)

Ricky series
Lofgren, Ulf
1 *Ricky* (1985)
Original edition entitled *Ludde*
2 *Ricky and someone* (1985)
Original edition entitled *Ludde och nagon*
3 *King Ricky* (1985)
Original edition entitled *Kung Ludde*

Ricky Straight series
Morgan, Geoffrey
1 *No crest for the wicked* (1952)
2 *Heavenly body* (1953)

Ricky Wilson series
Palfrey, Heather Mary
1 *Great egg flap* (1987)
2 *Ricky races to the rescue* (1987)

Riddle Club series
Hardy, Alice Dale
1 *Riddle Club at home* (1924)
How the club was formed, what riddles were asked and how the members solved a mystery
2 *Riddle Club in camp* (1924)
How they journeyed to the lake, what happened around the campfire and how a forgotten name was recalled
3 *Riddle Vlub through the holidays* (1924)
The Club and its doings, how the riddles were solved and what the snowman revealed
4 *Riddle Club at Sunrise Beach* (1925)
How they toured to the shore, what happened on the sand and how they solved the mystery of Rattlesnake Island
5 *Riddle Club at Shadowbrook* (1926)
Why they went there, what happened on the way and what occurred during their absence from home
6 *Riddle Club at Rocky Falls* (1929)
How they went up the river, what adventures they had in the woods and how they solved the mystery of the deserted hotel

Riddle King mini series
Thaler, Mike
1 *Riddle King's pet riddles* (1989)
2 *Riddle King's camp riddles* (1989)
3 *Riddle King's school riddles* (1989)
4 *Riddle King's food riddles* (1989)

Riddle King series
Thaler, Mike
1 *Riddle King's giant book of jokes, riddles and activities* (1987)
2 *Riddle King's jumbo book of jokes, riddles and activities* (1987)
3 *Riddle King's super book of jokes, riddles and activities* (1987)
4 *Riddle King's book of jokes, riddles and activities* (1988)

Riddle series
Rayner, William
see **Missouri series**

Rider series
Hardcastle, Michael
see **Kenny Rider series**
Maguire, Gregory
see **Daniel Rider series**

Ridge Parkman series
Hunt, Greg
1 *Ride to Vengeance* (1980)
2 *De Witt's strike* (1980)
3 *When legends die* (1982)
4 *Havens raid* (1982)
5 *Mission to darkness* (1983)

Ridgway series
Helm, Peter
see **Martin Ridgway series**

Riding series
Selby, Bettina
Record of bicycle trips
1 *Riding the mountains down* (1984)
Riding the Himalayas from Karachi to Kathmandu
2 *Riding to Jerusalem* (1985)
3 *Riding the desert trail* (1988)
Riding in the Sind desert
4 *Riding north one summer* (1990)

Ridingdale series
Bearne, David
1 *Ridingdale boys* (1904)
2 *Lance and his friends* (1905)
3 *Ridingdale year* (1905)
4 *Tommie and his mates* (1907)

Ridings series
Moorman, Frederic William
see **Tales of the Ridings series**

Ridley family series
Baker, Margaret Joyce
1 *Castaway Christmas* (1963)
2 *Cut off from crumpets* (1964)
3 *Send in our shoes* (1976)

Ridley series
Ridley, Nat
see **Nat Ridley series**

Riebeck series
Moray, Helga
see **Katie and Paul Van Riebeck series**

Ried series
Pansy
see **Ester Ried series**

Rififi series
Le Breton, Auguste
1 *Rififi* (1947)
Original edition entitled *Rififi*
2 *Rififi in New York* (1967)
Original edition entitled *Rififi a New York*
This sequence has many other titles which have not been translated into English; companion volume: *Monsieur Rififi, autobiography*, 1976

Rifka series
Burstein, Chaya Malamud
1 *Rifka bangs the teakettle* (1970)
2 *Rifka grows up* (1976)

Rifkind series
Abbey, Lynn
1 *Daughter of the bright moon* (1979)
2 *Black flame* (1980)
Companion volume: *Warhorn, a Crossroads adventure in the world of Lynn Abbey's Rifkind, daughter of the bright moon*, by Dana Kramer, 1987

Riftwar series
Feist, Raymond Elias
1 *Magician* (1982)
1.1 *Magician apprentice* (1982)
1.2 *Magician master* (1982)
2 *Silverthorn* (1985)
3 *Darkness at Sethanon* (1986)
4 *Prince of the blood* (1989)
5 *King's buccaneer* (1992)
6 *Shadow of a dark queen* (1994)

Rig warrior series
Johnstone, William Wallace
1 *Rig warrior* (1987)
2 *Wheels of death* (1988)
3 *Eighteen wheel adventure* (1988)

Riggs and Kusak series
Rice, Craig
see **Bingo Riggs and Handsome Kusak series**

Right to left trilogy
Pritt, Denis Nowell
Autobiography
1 *From right to left, 1887-1941* (1965)
2 *Brasshats and beueaucrats, 1941-1950* (1966)
3 *Defence accuses* (1966)

Riley Blackwood series
Starrett, Vincent
1 *Great hotel murder* (1935)
2 *Midnight and Percy Jones* (1936)

Riley Kovacks series
De Marco, Gordon
1 *October heat* (1979)
2 *Canvas prison* (1984)

Riley series
Quinn, Patrick
see **Pete Riley series**

Rillington series
Orde-Powlett, Nigel
see **Anthony Rillington series**

Rim-Fire series
Ballew, Charles
1 *Bandit of Paloduro* (1934)
2 *Rim-Fire rides* (1935)
3 *Rim-Fire, sheriff* (1936)
4 *Rim-Fire, detective* (1936)
5 *Rim-Fire of the Range* (1936)
6 *Rim-Fire Six Guns* (1936)
7 *Rim-Fire roams* (1937)
8 *Rim-Fire, ranchero* (1937)
9 *Rim-Fire fights* (1937)
10 *Rim-Fire horns in* (1937)
11 *Rim-Fire and Slats* (1938)
12 *Rim-Fire on the desert* (1938)
13 *Rim-Fire slips* (1938)
14 *Rim-Fire presides* (1939)
15 *Rim-Fire in Mexico* (1939)
16 *Rim-Fire gets 'em* (1942)
17 *Rim-Fire runs* (1942)
18 *Rim-Fire returns* (1944)
19 *Rim-Fire on the prod* (1944)
20 *Rim-Fire skunked* (1947)
21 *Rim-Fire and the bear* (1950)
22 *Rim-Fire abstains* (1953)

Rim runners series
Chandler, Arthur Bertram
see **John Grimes series**

Rim series
Chandler, Arthur Bertram
1 *Road to Rim* (1967)
2 *To prime the pump* (1971)
3 *Hard way up* (1972)
Short stories
4 *False fatherland* (1968)
Spartan planet
5 *Inheritors* (1972)
6 *Broken cycle* (1975)
7 *Big black mark* (1975)
8 *Catch the star winds* (1969)
9 *Into the alternate universe* (1964)
10 *Contraband from other space* (1967)
11 *Rim gods* (1969)
Short stories
12 *Alternate orbits* (1971)
Commodore at sea
13 *Nebula alert* (1967)
14 *Gateway to never* (1972)
15 *Dark dimensions* (1971)
Companion volumes: *The Rim of space*, 1961, *Bring back yesterday*, 1961, *Rendezvous on a lost world*, 1961, also published as *When the dream dies*, *Beyond the galactic Rim*, 1963, *The ship from outside*, 1963, *The deep reaches of space*, 1964

Rina Lazarus and Sergeant Peter Decker series
Kellerman, Faye
see **Sergeant Peter Decker and Rina Lazarus series**

Rinehart series
Knudson, Rozanne Ruth
1 *Rinehart lifts* (1980)
2 *Rinehart shouts* (1987)

Ring of fire series
Dodd, Edward Howard
1 *Polynesian art* (1967)
2 *Polynesian seafaring* (1972)
3 *Polynesia's sacred isle* (1976)
4 *Rape of Tahiti* (1983)

Ring of spears series
Goodwin, Tim
1 *Ring of spears* (1979)
2 *Silver hoard* (1980)

Ring of the Lowenskolds trilogy
Lagerlof, Selma
1 *General's ring* (1925)
Original edition entitled *Lowenskoldska ringen*
2 *Charlotte Lowenskold* (1925)
Original edition entitled *Charlotte Lowenskold*
3 *Anna Svard* (1928)
Original edition entitled *Anna Svard*

Ringer series
Wallace, Edgar
1 *Gaunt stranger* (1925)
Ringer
Dramatized as *The Ringer*, 1929
2 *Again the Ringer* (1929)
Ringer returns
Short stories

Ringo, Ricky and Rocky series
Kunnas, Mauri
see **Ricky, Rocky and Ringo series**

Ringrose series
Phillpotts, Eden
see **John Ringrose series**

Rings of the master series
Chalker, Jack Laurence
1 *Lords of the middle dark* (1986)
2 *Pirates of the thunder* (1987)
3 *Warriors of the storm* (1987)
4 *Masks of the martyrs* (1988)

Rings trilogy
Tolkien, John Ronald Reuel
see **Lord of the Rings trilogy**

Ringway series
Lott, Stanley Makepeace
see **Stephen Ringway series**

Ringwood series
Farrer, Katharine
see **Inspector Richard Ringwood series**

Ringworld series
Niven, Larry
1 *Ringworld* (1970)
2 *Ringworld engineers* (1979)

Rinko trilogy
Uchida, Yoshiko
1 *Jar of dreams* (1981)
2 *Best bad thing* (1983)
3 *Happiest ending* (1985)

Rin-Tin-Tin series
This sequence has two authors
Verral, Charles Spain
1 *Rin-Tin-Tin and the outlaw* (1957)
Fannin, Cole
2 *Rin-Tin-Tin and the ghost wagon train* (1958)
Verral, Charles Spain
3 *Rin-Tin-Tin and the hidden treasure* (1959)

Rio Kid series
This sequence has two authors
Roan, Tom
1 *Rio Kid* (1935)
Davis, Don
2 *Return of the Rio Kid* (1940)
3 *Death of Treasure Trail* (1940)
4 *Rio Kid justice* (1941)
5 *Two-Gun Rio Kid* (1941)

Rio series
Wildey, Doug
1 *Rio* (1987)
2 *Rio rides again* (1990)

Riordan series
Huebner, Frederick D
see **Matt Riordan series**

Rip Irving and Patrick Shirley series
Mills, Osmington
see **Sergeant Patrick Shirley and Inspector Rip Irving series**

Rip Randall series
Leyland, Eric
1 *Challenge!* (1952)
2 *Sabotage* (1953)
3 *Counter-attack* (1953)
4 *Madman's Peak* (1954)
5 *Rip Randall and the pharaoh's tomb* (1956)

Ripley series
Gordons
see **John Ripley series**
Highsmith, Patricia
see **Tom Ripley series**
Lomax, Bliss
see **Rainbow Ripley series**
Wainwright, John
see **Superintendent Charles Ripley series**

Ripping yarns series
Palin, Michael
Based on a television series
1 *Ripping yarns* (1978)
2 *More ripping yarns* (1980)

Rise in life series
Alger, Horatio
1 *Out for business* (1900)
Alternative title: Robert Frost's strange career
2 *Falling in with fortune* (1900)
Alternative title: The experiences of a young secretary
3 *Young Captain Jack* (1901)
Alternative title: The son of a soldier
4 *Nelson the newsboy* (1901)
Alternative title: Afloat in new York
5 *Jerry the backwoods boy* (1904)
Alternative title: The Parkhurst treasure
6 *Lost at sea* (1904)
Alternative title: Robert Roscoe's strange cruise
7 *From farm to fortune* (1905)
Alternative title: Nat Nason's strange experience
8 *Young book agent* (1905)
Alternative title: Frank Hardy's road to success
9 *Randy of the river* (1906)
Alternative title: The adventures of a young deck hand
10 *Joe, the hotel boy* (1912)
Alternative title: Winning out by Pluck
11 *Ben Logan's triumph* (1912)
Alternative title: The boys of Boxwood Academy

Rishi series
Zinkin, Taya
1 *Rishi* (1960)
2 *Rishi returns* (1961)

Rising family series
Sallis, Susan
1 *Scattering of daisies* (1984)
April Rising
2 *Daffodils of Newent* (1985)
3 *Bluebell windows* (1987)
4 *Rosemary for remembrance* (1987)

Rissa Kerguelen series
Busby, Francis Marion
1 *Rissa Kerguelen* (1976)
2 *Long view* (1976)
One volume edition entitled *Rissa Kerguelen*, 1977; also published in three volumes
2.1 *Young Rissa* (1976)
2.2 *Rissa and Tregare* (1976)
2.3 *Long view* (1976)
This sequence is followed by the **Bran Tregare series**

Rita Gardella O'Dea series
Coburn, Andrew
1 *Sweetheart* (1985)
2 *Love nest* (1987)
3 *Goldilocks* (1989)

Ritchie series
Deland, Margaret
see **Helen Ritchie series**

Rival campers series
Smith, Ruel Perley
1 *Rival campers* (1905)
The adventures of Henry Burns
2 *Rival campers afloat* (1906)
Alternative title: The prize yacht Viking
3 *Rival campers ashore* (1907)
Alternative title: The mystery of the mill
4 *Jack Harvey's adventures* (1908)
Alternative title: The rival campers among the oyster pirates

River and wilderness trilogy
Ellis, Edward Sylvester
1 *River fugitives* (1893)
2 *Wilderness fugitives* (1893)
3 *Lena Wingo, the Mohawk* (1893)

River boy trilogy
Chapman, James
1 *River boy* (1980)
Life along the St. John
2 *River boy returns* (1983)
3 *River boy at war* (1985)

River diary series
Eastwood, Dorothea
Reminiscences of travel in Wales
1 *River diary* (1950)
On the River Usk
2 *Valleys of springs* (1956)

River Heights series
Keene, Carolyn
House pseudonym
1 *Love times three* (1989)
2 *Guilty secrets* (1989)
3 *Going too far* (1990)
4 *Stolen kisses* (1990)
5 *Between the lines* (1990)
6 *Lessons in love* (1990)
7 *Cheating hearts* (1990)
8 *Trouble with love* (1990)
9 *Lies and whispers* (1991)
10 *Mixed emotions* (1991)
11 *Broken hearts* (1991)
12 *Hard to handle* (1991)
13 *Mind of her own* (1991)
14 *Love and games* (1992)

River motor-boat boys series
Gordon, Harry
1 *River motor-boat boys on the Amazon* (1913)
Alternative title: The secret of Cloud Island
2 *River motor-boat boys on the Columbia* (1913)
Alternative title: The confession of a photograph
3 *River motor-boat boys on the Colorado* (1913)
Alternative title: The clue in the rocks
4 *River motor-boat boys on the Mississippi* (1913)
Alternative title: The trail to the Gulf
5 *River motor-boat boys on the Saint Lawrence* (1913)
Alternative title: The lost channel
6 *River motor-boat boys on the Ohio* (1913)
Alternative title: The three blue lights
7 *River motor-boat boys on the Yukon* (1914)
Alternative title: The lost mine of Rainbow Bend
8 *River motor-boat boys on the Rio Grande* (1915)
Alternative title: In defense of the Rambler

River of fortune trilogy
Moore, Arthur
1 *Passions* (1979)
2 *Pagans* (1980)
3 *Proud* (1980)

River Oxus series
Hull, Katharine
see **Oxus series**

River to rivet trilogy
Messerli, Douglas
Poetry
1 *Dinner on the lawn* (1979)
2 *Some distance* (1982)
3 *Manifesto* (1984)
One volume edition entitled *River to rivet*, 1984

Riverbank series
Lawhead, Stephen
1 *Tale of Jeremy Vole* (1990)
2 *Tale of Timothy Mallard* (1990)
3 *Tale of Anabelle Hedgehog* (1990)

Riverbend and Wildwood tales series
Trueman, Brian
Based on characters from Wind in the willows, by Kenneth Grahame, 1908
1 *Badger and the buried treasure* (1984)
2 *Toad enters a show* (1984)
3 *Mole's cousin* (1984)
4 *Kidnapping of Toad* (1984)

Riverboat Bill series
Green, Cliff
1 *Incredible steam-driven adventures of Riverboat Bill* (1975)
2 *Further adventures of Riverboat Bill* (1981)
3 *Riverboat Bill steams again* (1985)

Riverdale series
Optic, Oliver
1 *Little merchant* (1863)
2 *Young voyagers* (1863)
3 *Christmas gift* (1863)
4 *Dolly and I* (1863)
5 *Uncle Ben* (1863)
6 *Birthday party* (1863)
7 *Proud and lazy* (1863)
8 *Careless Kate* (1863)
9 *Robinson Crusoe, junior* (1863)
10 *Picnic party* (1863)
11 *Gold thimble* (1863)
12 *Do-Somethings* (1863)

Riverita series
Palacio Valdes, Armando
Translated from the Spanish
1 *Riverita* (1886)
2 *Maximina* (1887)

Riverman series
Kelsall, Ernest Michael
1 *Riverman's story* (1986)
2 *In the smoke* (1989)
Riverman moves to the city

Riverport School series
Chapman, Allen
see **Fred Fenton series**

Rivers series
Carnac, Carol
see **Inspector Julian Rivers series**
Powell, Talmage
see **Ed Rivers series**

Rivers west series
This sequence has five authors
Blevins, Winfred
1 *Yellowstone* (1988)
Coldsmith, Don
2 *Smoky Hill* (1989)
McCarthy, Gary
3 *Colorado* (1989)
Blevins, Winfred
4 *Powder River* (1990)
McCarthy, Gary
5 *Russian River* (1990)
Sherman, Jory
6 *Arkansas River* (1991)
McCarthy, Gary
7 *American River* (1992)
8 *Gila River* (1993)
Wheeler, Richard Seabrook
9 *Two Medicine Rivers* (1993)
Companion volume: *The Snake River*, by Win Blevins, 1992

Riverside Theatre series
Ure, Jean
1 *Early stages* (1977)
2 *All in a summer season* (1977)
3 *Dress rehearsal* (1978)
4 *Bid time return* (1978)
5 *Curtain fall* (1978)

Riverview series
Hawkins, Laura
1 *Figment, your dog, speaking* (1991)
2 *Cat that could spell Mississippi* (1992)
3 *Valentine to a flying mouse* (1993)

Riverview trilogy
Fuller, Kathleen
1 *Bitter legacy* (1988)
2 *Lion's share* (1988)
3 *Pride of place* (1989)

Riverworld series
Farmer, Philip Jose
1 *To your scattered bodies go* (1971)
2 *Fabulous riverboat* (1971)
3 *Dark design* (1977)
4 *Magic labyrinth* (1980)
5 *Gods of Riverworld* (1983)
Companion volumes: *Riverworld war*, the suppressed fiction of Philip Jose Farmer, 1980, *River of eternity*, 1983

Rivington series
Verner, Gerald
see **Paul Rivington series**

Rivington Street series
Tax, Meredith
1 *Rivington Street* (1982)
2 *Union Square* (1988)

Rix series
Goodchild, George
see **Nigel Rix series**

Rizzi series
Sterling, Thomas
see **Captain Rizzi series**

Ro-Lan series
Sirota, Mike
1 *Master of Boranga* (1980)
2 *Shrouded walls of Boranga* (1980)
3 *Journey to Mesharra* (1980)
4 *Demons of Zammar* (1981)

Road series
Harvester, Simon
see **Dorian Silk series**

Road to Calvary trilogy
Tolstoi, Aleksei Nikolaevich
see **Ordeal trilogy**

Road to Gundagai series
McInnes, Graham
Autobiography
1 *Road to Gundagai* (1965)
2 *Humping my bluey* (1966)
3 *Finding a father* (1967)
4 *Goodbye, Melbourne town* (1968)

Roadblaster trilogy
Hofrichter, Paul
1 *Hell ride* (1987)
2 *Death ride* (1988)
3 *Blood fire* (1988)

Roads to freedom trilogy
Sartre, Jean Paul
1 *Age of reason* (1945)
Original edition entitled *L'age de raison*
2 *Reprieve* (1945)
Original edition entitled *Le sursis*
3 *Iron in the soul* (1949)
Troubled sleep
Original edition entitled *La mort dans l'ame*
Incomplete fourth volume entitled *The last chance*, 1949, original edition entitled *La derniere chance*

Roag's Syndicate series
Davis, George
1 *Roag's Syndicate* (1960)
2 *Toledano* (1962)
3 *Friday before Bank Holiday* (1964)
4 *Crime in Threadneedle Street* (1968)
5 *Killer grew tired* (1971)
6 *Death of a fire-raiser* (1974)

Roaming Reynolds and Texas Joe series
Martin, Charles Morris
1 *Gun Boss Reynolds* (1937)
2 *Deuce of Diamonds* (1937)
3 *Double or nothing* (1939)

Roath and Bellecroix series
Craig, David
see **Stephen Bellecroix and Sheila Roath series**

Rob and Mick series
Peyton, K M
see **Mick and Rob series**

Rob Ranger series
Lounsberry, Lionel
1 *Rob Ranger's mine* (1903)
Alternative title: The boy who got there
2 *Rob Ranger, the young ranchman* (1903)
Alternative title: Going it alone at Lost River
3 *Rob Ranger's cowboy days* (1903)
Alternative title: The young hunter of the Big Horn

Rob Roy Macgregor series
This sequence has two authors
Scott, Walter
1 *Rob Roy* (1817)
Tranter, Nigel Godwin
2 *Macgregor's gathering* (1957)
3 *Clansman* (1959)

Robak series
Hensley, Joe Louis
see Donald Robak series

Robber Hotzenplotz series
Preussler, Otfried
1 *Robber Hotzenplotz* (1962)
Original edition entitled *Der Rauber Hotzenplatz*
2 *Further adventures of the Robber Hotzenplotz* (1969)
Original edition entitled *Neues vom Rauber Hotzenplotz*
3 *Final adventures of the Robber Hotzenplotz* (1973)
Original edition entitled *Kasper-geschichte*

Robbie Doo series
Waugh, Joseph Laing
1 *Robbie Doo, his reminiscences* (1913)
2 *Cracks wi' Robbie Doo* (1914)

Robbie Jardino series
Singer, Norman
1 *Shakedown kid* (1975)
2 *Diamond stud* (1976)

Robbie, Sophie, Helen and Jean series
Dallas, Ruth
see **Jean, Robbie, Sophie and Helen series**

Robby Hoenig trilogy
Dickson, Gordon Rupert
1 *Secret under the sea* (1960)
2 *Secret under Antarctica* (1963)
3 *Secret under the Caribbean* (1964)
One volume edition entitled *Secrets of the deep*, 1985

Robert Amiss series
Edwards, Ruth Dudley
1 *Corridors of death* (1982)
2 *Saint Valentine's Day murders* (1984)

Robert Andrew series
Clark, Leonard
1 *Robert Andrew tells a story* (1965)
2 *Robert Andrew and Tiffy* (1965)
3 *Robert Andrew and the holy family* (1965)
4 *Robert Andrew by the sea* (1965)
5 *Robert Andrew and the Red Indian chief* (1966)
6 *Robert Andrew in the country* (1966)
7 *Robert Andrew and Skippy* (1966)

Robert Belcourt series
Rougvie, Cameron
1 *Medal from Paploma* (1964)
2 *Tangier assignment* (1965)
3 *Gredos reckoning* (1966)
4 *When Johnny died* (1967)

Robert Bollinger Badger series
Winton, John
see **Navy series**

Robert Briganti series
McCurtin, Peter
see **Assassins series**

Robert Budd series
Verner, Gerald
see **Superintendent Robert Budd series**

Robert Burns series
Barke, James
see **Immortal memory series**

Robert Christopher series
Irvine, Robert Ralstone
1 *Jump cut* (1974)
2 *Freeze frame* (1976)
3 *Horizontal hold* (1978)
4 *Ratings are murder* (1985)

Robert Crane trilogy
Glemser, Bernard
1 *High moon* (1949)
2 *Strangers in Florida* (1950)
3 *Dove on his shoulder* (1953)

Robert Deane and Bertram Lynch series
Vandercook, John Womack
see **Bertram Lynch and Robert Deane series**

Robert Dudley series
Drysdale, Margaret
1 *Quest for a crown* (1982)
2 *Heir for the Earl* (1983)
Originally announced as a trilogy

Robert Dudley series
Wilson, Derek
1 *Bear's whelp* (1978)
2 *Bear rampant* (1981)

Robert Eddison and Dave Cannon series
Delving, Michael
see **Dave Cannon and Robert Eddison series**

Robert Erskine series
Hamilton, Mary
Biography of an Irish soldier
1 *Green and gold* (1948)
2 *Silver road* (1951)

Robert Ervin Howard series
Ellis, Novalyne Price
1 *One who walked alone* (1986)
Robert E Howard, the final years
2 *Day of the stranger* (1989)
Further memories; edited by Rusty Burke

Robert Flick series
Ehrlich, Jack
1 *Parole* (1960)
2 *Slow burn* (1961)
3 *Cry, Baby* (1962)
4 *Girl cage* (1967)

Robert Forsythe and Abigail Sanderson series
Giroux, E X
1 *Death for Adonis* (1984)
2 *Death for a darling* (1985)
3 *Death for a dancer* (1985)
Also published under the author's real name Doris Shannon
4 *Death for a doctor* (1986)
Also published under the author's real name Doris Shannon
5 *Death for a dilettante* (1987)
6 *Death for a dietician* (1988)
7 *Death for a dreamer* (1989)
8 *Death for a double* (1990)
9 *Death for a dancing doll* (1991)
10 *Death for a dodo* (1993)

Robert Fossett trilogy
Hollis, Christopher
Letters
1 *Death of a gentleman* (1943)
2 *Fossett's memory* (1944)
3 *Letters to a sister* (1947)

Robert Frederickson series
Chesbro, George Clark
see **Mongo series**

Robert Fusil and Constable Kerr series
Alding, Peter
see **C.I.D. Room series**

Robert Harmon series
Elman, Richard Martin
see **Professor Robert Harmon series**

Robert Hockney series
De Borchgrave, Arnaud
1 *Spike* (1980)
2 *Monimbo* (1983)

Robert James series
Rooke, Anne
1 *When Robert went to playgroup* (1984)
2 *Robert's playgroup friends* (1985)
3 *Robert and Great Granny* (1986)
4 *When Robert went to stay* (1987)

Robert Koesler series
Kienzle, William Xavier
see **Father Robert Koesler series**

Robert Lawson series
Comer, Ralph
1 *Witchfinders* (1968)
2 *Mirror of Dionysos* (1969)
To dream of evil

Robert Lee Ashley series
Steele, Chester K
see **Colonel Robert Lee Ashley series**

Robert Lee Hunter series
Sauter, Eric
1 *Hunter* (1983)
2 *Hunter and the ikon* (1984)
3 *Hunter and Raven* (1984)
4 *Predators* (1987)
5 *Skeletons* (1990)
6 *Backfire* (1992)

Robert Leroy Mitchell series
Ottolengui, Rodrigues
1 *Artist in crime* (1892)
2 *Conflict of evidence* (1893)
3 *Crime of the century* (1896)
4 *Final proof* (1898)
Alternative title: The value of evidence

Robert Mather series
Graeme, Bruce
see **Detective Sergeant Robert Mather series**

Robert Orange series
Hobbes, John Oliver
1 *School for saints* (1896)
A drama in three acts and in prose
2 *Robert Orange* (1900)

Robert Peel series
Gash, Norman
see **Sir Robert Peel series**

Robert Renwick series
Macinnes, Helen
1 *Hidden target* (1980)
2 *Cloak of darkness* (1982)

Robert Sand series
Olden, Marc
1 *Black Samurai* (1974)
2 *Golden kill* (1974)
3 *Killer warrior* (1974)
4 *Deadly peril* (1974)
5 *Inquisition* (1974)
6 *Warlock* (1975)
7 *Sword of Allah* (1975)
8 *Katana* (1975)

Robert series
Dupasquier, Philippe
Translated from the French
1 *Robert the great* (1985)
2 *Robert and the red balloon* (1985)
3 *Robert and the pilot* (1986)

Robert series
Rooke, Anne
1 *When Robert went to play group* (1984)
2 *Robert's playgroup friends* (1985)
3 *Robert and great nanny* (1986)
4 *When Robert went to stay* (1987)

Robert Shannon series
Cronin, Archibald Joseph
1 *Green years* (1944)
2 *Shannon's way* (1948)

Robert Silverberg's Time tours series
Wu, William Franking
see **Time tours series**

Robert Spicer series
Danvers, Milton
1 *Doctor's crime* (1891)
Alternative title: Simply horrible!
2 *Desperate dilemma* (1892)
Alternative title: An unheard of crime
3 *Grantham mystery* (1893)
Alternative title: Confidence and crime
4 *Detective's honeymoon* (1894)
Alternative title: The doctor of the Pinjarrah
5 *Mysterious disappearance of a bride* (1895)
Alternative title: Who was she?
6 *Fatal finger mark* (1895)
Alternative title: Rose Courtenay's first case

Robert Stairey series
Dick, Kay
1 *By the lake* (1949)
2 *Young man* (1951)

Robert Staunton series
Hill, Peter
see **Inspector Robert Staunton series**

Robert Strong series
Robertson, Colin
see **Inspector Robert Strong series**

Robert the Bruce trilogy
Tranter, Nigel Godwin
1 *Steps to the empty throne* (1969)
2 *Path of the hero king* (1970)
3 *Price of the King's peace* (1971)
One volume edition entitled *Robert the Bruce trilogy*, 1985

Robert Townley and Roger Newman series
Bearshaw, Brian
see **Superintendent Robert Townley and Sergeant Roger Newman series**

Robert Urban series
Guenter, C H
Translated from the German
1 *Hunter of men* (1975)
2 *To know is to die* (1977)
3 *Web of silence* (1977)
4 *Dead drop in Havana* (1978)
5 *Dead in Aqaba* (1978)
6 *Swindler named Zefano* (1979)
7 *Days of vengeance* (1979)

Robert Walpole series
Plumb, John Harold
see **Sir Robert Walpole series**

Robert Waring series
Ebel, Suzanne
see **Sir Robert Waring series**

Robert Wynnton series
Horler, Sydney
1 *Man in the cloak* (1951)
2 *Man who used perfume* (1952)

Roberta series
Baxter, Gillian
1 *Jump to the stars* (1957)
2 *Difficult summer* (1959)
3 *Perfect horse* (1963)

Roberts family series
Wilson, Phillip
1 *Outcasts* (1965)
2 *New Zealand Jack* (1965)

Roberts series
Brown, Carter
see **Randy Roberts series**
Heggen, Thomas
see **Mister Roberts series**
Johnson, Pamela Hansford
see **Toby Roberts series**
Parker, Roger
see **Inspector Taff Roberts series**
Symons, Maurice
see **George Roberts series**

Robertson family series
Frewer, Glyn
1 *Adventure in Forgotten Valley* (1962)
2 *Adventure in the barren lands* (1964)

Robertson series
Sandison, Janet
see **Apology for the life of Jean Robertson series**

Robeson series
Richmond, Grace Smith
see **Juliet Robeson series**

Robicheaux series
Burke, James Lee
see **Dave Robicheaux series**

Robin and Clive Lendrick series
Braine, John
see **Clive and Robin Lendrick series**

Robin and Linda Reismann series
Wolitzer, Hilma
see **Linda and robin Reismann series**

Robin Bishop series
Homes, Geoffrey
1 *Doctor died at dusk* (1936)
2 *Man who murdered himself* (1936)
3 *Man who didn't exist* (1937)
4 *Man who murdered Goliath* (1938)
5 *Then there were three* (1938)

Robin Brent series
Oxenham, Elsie J
1 *Girl who wouldn't make friends* (1909)
2 *Rosamund's tuck-shop* (1937)
3 *Robins in the Abbey* (1947)
4 *New girls at Wood End* (1957)

Robin Hood series
Atterton, Julian
1 *Robin Hood and Little John* (1987)
2 *Robin Hood and the miller's son* (1987)

Robin Hood series
Dumas, Alexandre
1 *Prince of thieves* (1873)
Original edition entitled *Le prince des voleurs*
2 *Robin Hood, prince of outlaws* (1873)
Original edition entitled *Robin Hood, le proscrit*

Robin Hood series
Gilliat, Edward
1 *In Lincoln Green* (1897)
A merrie tale of Robin Hood
2 *Wolf's Head* (1898)
A story of the prince of outlaws

Robin Hood series
Manning-Sanders, Ruth
1 *Robin Hood and Little John* (1977)
2 *Robin Hood and the gold arrow* (1979)
Companion volumes: *Tales of Robin Hood*, by Clayton Emery, 1988, *Robin Hood, prince of thieves*, by Simon Green, 1991

Robin Hood series
Serraillier, Ian
1 *Robin in the greenwood* (1967)
2 *Robin Hood and his merry men* (1969)

Robin Hood series
Suddaby, Donald
1 *New tales of Robin Hood* (1950)
2 *Fresh news from Sherwood* (1959)
3 *Robin Hood's master stroke* (1965)

Robin Kane series
Hill, Eileen
1 *Mystery of the blue pelican* (1966)
2 *Mystery of the phantom* (1966)
3 *Mystery of Glengary Castle* (1966)
4 *Candle shop mystery* (1971)
5 *Mystery in the clouds* (1971)
6 *Monster at Wolf Point* (1971)

Robin McKay series
Morris, John
see **Commissioner Robin McKay series**

Robin Miller series
Smaridge, Norah
1 *Secret of the brownstone house* (1977)
2 *Mystery at Greystone Hall* (1979)

Robin North and Rex Redmayne series
Moore, Patrick
1 *Captives of the moon* (1960)
2 *Wanderer in space* (1961)
3 *Crater of fear* (1962)
4 *Invader from space* (1963)
5 *Caverns of the moon* (1964)

Robin of Sherwood series
This sequence has four authors; based on a television series
May, Robin
1 *Robin of Sherwood and the hounds of Lucifer* (1985)
Horowitz, Anthony
2 *Hooded man* (1986)
Carpenter, Richard
3 *Sword of the Templar* (1987)
Mason, Paul
4 *Time of the wolf* (1988)

Robin Weston series
Meynell, Laurence Walter
1 *Scoop* (1964)
2 *Suspect scientist* (1966)
3 *Shadow in the sun* (1966)

Robins family series
Chastain, Thomas
1 *Who killed the Robins family, & where & when & why did they die?* (1983)
2 *Revenge of the Robins family* (1984)
3 *Picture-perfect murders* (1987)

Robins series
Leslie, Madeline
see **Little robins series**

Robinson and me series
Digby, Anne
see **Me and Jill Robinson series**

Robinson and Scott series
Tiger, John
see **I spy series**

Robinson Crusoe series
This sequence has two authors
Defoe, Daniel
1 *Life and adventures of Robinson Crusoe* (1719)
Robinson Crusoe
Originally published anonymously in three volumes entitled *The life and strange surprising adventures of Robinson Crusoe, The further adventures of Robinson Crusoe, and Serious reflections during the life and surprising adventures of Robinson Crusoe*
Treece, Henry
2 *Return of Robinson Crusoe* (1958)
Further adventures of Robinson Crusoe

Robinson family series
Fowler, Thurley
1 *Green wind* (1985)
2 *Wind is silver* (1991)

Robinson family series
Mather, Bertrand
1 *Through the mill* (1962)
2 *Left foot forward* (1963)

Robinson family series
Wyss, Johann Rudolf
see **Swiss family Robinson series**

Robinson series
Casement, Christina
1 *Wandering Robinson* (1969)
2 *Ringing Robinson* (1971)
3 *Robinson and Slyboots* (1974)

Robinson series
Robinson, Joan Gale
see **Teddy Robinson series**

Robinsons of Guiana series
Boussenard, Louis
1 *Crusoes of Guiana* (1885)
White tiger
Original edition entitled *Le tigre blanc*
2 *Gold seekers* (1885)
Original edition entitled *Le secret de l'or*
3 *[Les mysteres de la foret vierge]* (1885)
No English edition

Robocop series
Naha, Ed
Based on screenplays
1 *Robocop* (1987)
2 *Robocop 2* (1990)

Roboskool series
Blake, Jon
1 *Roboskool* (1990)
2 *Revenge* (1991)

Robot city series
This sequence has five authors
Kube-McDowell, Michael Paul
1 *Odyssey* (1987)
McQuay, Mike
2 *Suspicion* (1987)
Wu, William Franking
3 *Cyborg* (1987)
Cover, Arthur Byron
4 *Prodigy* (1988)
Chilson, Rob
5 *Refuge* (1988)
Wu, William Franking
6 *Perihelion* (1988)

Robot series
Asimov, Isaac
1 *I, robot* (1950)
Short stories
2 *Caves of steel* (1954)
3 *Naked sun* (1957)
Numbers 2 and 3 also published as *The robot novels*, 1957
4 *Eight stories from The rest of the robots* (1966)
Numbers 2-4 also published in one volume entitled *The rest of the robots*, 1964
5 *Complete robot* (1982)
Short stories; numbers 2, 3, 5 also published in one volume entitled *The robot collection*, 1983
6 *Robots of dawn* (1983)
Numbers 2, 3, 6 also published in one volume entitled *The robot novels*, 1988
7 *Robots and Empire* (1985)
Companion volumes: *Robot dreams*, 1986, *Robot visions*, 1990

Robot series
Cook, Ann
1 *Robot comes to stay* (1982)
2 *Robot in danger* (1982)
3 *Robot goes collecting* (1982)
4 *Robot saves the day* (1982)
5 *Robot and the flea market* (1982)
6 *Robot visits school* (1982)

Robot series
Hoban, Lillian
1 *Ready, set, robot!* (1982)
2 *Laziest robot in Zone One* (1983)

Robot series
Leroe, Ellen Whitney
see **Bixby Wyler series**

Robotech series
McKinney, Jack
1 *Genesis* (1987)
2 *Battle cry* (1987)
3 *Homecoming* (1987)
4 *Battlehymn* (1987)
5 *Force of arms* (1987)
6 *Doomsday* (1987)
7 *Southern Cross* (1987)
8 *Metal fire* (1987)
9 *Final nightmare* (1987)
10 *Invid invasion* (1987)
11 *Metamorphosis* (1987)
12 *Symphony of light* (1987)
13 *End of the circle* (1990)

Robots and aliens series
This sequence has five authors
Leigh, Stephen
1 *Changeling* (1989)
Scotten, Cordell
2 *Renegade* (1989)
Thurston, Robert
3 *Intruder* (1990)
Oltion, Jerry
4 *Alliance* (1990)
Bethke, Bruce
5 *Maverick* (1990)
Oltion, Jerry
6 *Humanity* (1990)

Robots series
Asimov, Isaac
see **Elijah Baley series**

Robur series
Verne, Jules
1 *Master of the world* (1904)
A tale of mystery and marvel; original edition entitled *Maitre du monde*
2 *Robur the conqueror* (1886)
Clipper of the clouds
Alternative title: A trip around the world in a flying machine; original edition entitled *Robur le conquerant*
One volume edition 1951

Roby Maclane trilogy
Bonner, Michael
1 *Iron noose* (1961)
2 *Shadow of a hawk* (1963)
3 *Disturbing death of Jenkin Delaney* (1966)

Rochester series
This sequence has two authors
Rhys, Jean
1 *Wide Sargasso sea* (1966)
The story of Rochester's first wife
Bronte, Charlotte
2 *Jane Eyre* (1847)

Rochford trilogy
Lorrimer, Claire
1 *Chatelaine* (1981)
2 *Wilderling* (1982)
3 *Fool's curtain* (1994)

Rock Callahan series
Gault, William Campbell
see **Brock Callahan series**

Rock series
Rossi, Bruno
see **Sharpshooter series**

Rock stars series
Tremlett, George
1 *Osmond story* (1974)
2 *David Essex story* (1974)
3 *Gary Glitter story* (1974)
4 *Rolling Stones story* (1974)
5 *Marc Bolan story* (1975)
6 *Who* (1975)
7 *Slade story* (1975)
8 *Paul McCartney story* (1975)
9 *Cliff Richard story* (1975)
10 *David Bowie story* (1975)
11 *Slik* (1976)
12 *Alvin Stardust story* (1976)
13 *Rod Stewart story* (1976)

Rock trilogy
Lightner, Alice Martha
1 *Rock of three planets* (1963)
2 *Planet poachers* (1965)
3 *Space ark* (1968)

Rockabye County series
Edson, John Thomas
1 *Sixteen-dollar shooter* (1974)
2 *Lawmen of Rockabye County* (1989)
3 *Sheriff of Rockabye County* (1981)
4 *Professional killers* (1968)
5 *Quarter second draw* (1969)
6 *Deputies* (1969)
7 *Point of contact* (1970)
8 *Owlhoot* (1970)
9 *Run for the border* (1971)
10 *Bad hombre* (1971)

Rocket Riders series
Garis, Howard Roger
1 *Rocket Riders across the ice* (1933)
Alternative title: Racing against time
2 *Rocket Riders over the desert* (1933)
Alternative title: Seeking the lost city
3 *Rocket Riders in stormy seas* (1933)
Alternative title: Trailing the treasure divers
4 *Rocket Riders in the air* (1934)
Alternative title: A chase in the clouds

Rockets series
Bergaust, Erik
1 *Rockets and missiles* (1957)
2 *Rockets around the world* (1958)
3 *Rockets of the Navy* (1959)
4 *Rockets of the Air Force* (1960)
5 *Rockets of the Army* (1960)
6 *Birth of a rocket* (1961)
7 *Rocket aircraft, USA* (1961)
8 *Rockets to the moon* (1961)
9 *Rockets to the planets* (1961)
10 *Rocket power* (1962)
11 *Rockets of the armed forces* (1966)

Rockford series
Woolfolk, Dorothy
see **Donna Rockford series**

Rocking-chair series
Atkinson, Alex
Illustrated by Ronald Searle
1 *U.S.A. for beginners* (1959)
2 *Russia for beginners* (1960)
Companion volume: *Escape from the Amazon*, 1964

Rockingham Stone series
Armstrong, Raymond
see **J Rockingham Stone series**

Rocklands School trilogy
Oxenham, Elsie J
1 *Girls of Rocklands School* (1929)
2 *Second term at Rocklands School* (1930)
3 *Third term at Rocklands School* (1931)

Rockmouth and Rockhead township trilogy
Smith, Naomi Royde
1 *Children in the wood* (1928)
2 *Summer holiday* (1929)
3 *Island* (1930)

Rocksburg Police series
Constantine, K C
see **Mario Balzic series**

Rockson series
Stacy, Ryder
see **Doomsday warrior series**

Rockwell and Saber series
Linzee, David
see **Sarah Saber and Chris Rockwell series**

Rockwell series
Iams, Jack
see **Rocky Rockwell series**

Rocky Allan series
Rath, Virginia
1 *Death at Dayton's Folly* (1935)
2 *Murder on the day of judgment* (1936)
3 *Ferryman, take him across!* (1936)
4 *Excellent night for a murder* (1937)
5 *Anger of the bells* (1937)
6 *Murder with a theme song* (1939)

Rocky Mountain Company series
Wheeler, Richard Seabrook
1 *Fitzhug* (1991)
2 *Fort Dance* (1991)
3 *Cheyenne winter* (1992)

Rocky O'Rourke series
Sherry, Sylvia
1 *Pair of Jesus-boots* (1969)
Liverpool cats
2 *Pair of desert wellies* (1985)
3 *Rocky and the ratman* (1988)
4 *Rocky and the black eye mystery* (1992)

Rocky, Ringo and Ricky series
Kunnas, Mauri
see **Ricky, Rocky and Ringo series**

Rocky Rockwell series
Iams, Jack
1 *Do not murder before Christmas* (1949)
2 *What rhymes with murder?* (1950)
3 *Shot of murder* (1950)

Rocky Steele series
West, John B
1 *Cobra venom* (1959)
2 *Eye for an eye* (1959)
3 *Bullets are my business* (1960)
4 *Taste for blood* (1960)
5 *Death on the rocks* (1961)
6 *Never kill a cop* (1961)

Rod Damon series
Conway, Troy
see **Coxeman series**

Rod Gallowglass series
Stasheff, Christopher
see **Gramarye series**

Rod Gavin series
Quinn, John
1 *Mercenary kill* (1982)
2 *Silicon Valley slaughter* (1983)
3 *Kill squad* (1983)
4 *Crystal kill* (1984)
5 *Chameleon kill* (1984)
6 *Checkmate kill* (1985)

Rod, Helen and Polly-Dear series
Goode, Evelyn
see **Polly-Dear, Rod and Small series**

Roddy series
Arkle, Phyllis
1 *Roddy the roadman* (1970)
2 *Roddy and the rustlers* (1972)
3 *Roddy on the motorway* (1974)
4 *Roddy on the canal* (1975)
5 *Roddy and the puma* (1979)
6 *Roddy and the miniature railway* (1980)

Roddy series
Johnson, Helen Kendrick
1 *Roddy's romance* (1874)
2 *Roddy's reality* (1875)
3 *Roddy's ideal* (1876)

Roden series
Cunningham, Albert Benjamin
see **Sheriff Jess Roden series**

Rodeo series
Mitchell, Red
see **Doc McDuff and Popcorn Pruitt series**

Roderick Alleyn series
Marsh, Ngaio
see **Inspector Roderick Alleyn series**

Roderick series
Campbell, Alice
see **Helen Roderick series**

Roderick series
Sladek, John Thomas
1 *Roderick* (1980)
Alternative title: The education of a young machine
2 *Roderick at random* (1983)
Alternative title: Further education of a young machine

Rodney D'Armond series
Stasheff, Christopher
see **Gramarye series**

Rodney Rat series
Forster, Michelanne
1 *Rodney Rat and the sunken treasure* (1983)
2 *Rodney Rat and the Sneaky Weasel Gang* (1986)
3 *Rodney Rat and the space creatures* (1989)

Rodney series
Mannin, Ethel
see **Elspeth Rodney series**

Rodney Wayne series
Cromwell, A G E
1 *Murder in Flat Fourteen* (1939)
2 *Death in the copse* (1940)

Rodway series
Ryland, John Knox
see **Inspector Rodway series**

Roe series
Roper, Lester V
see **Jerry Roe series**

Roersch series
Kastle, Herbert David
see **Sergeant Edmund Roersch series**

Rogan Kincaid series
Talbot, Hake
1 *Hangman's handyman* (1942)
2 *Rim of the pit* (1944)

Rogan series
Dutton, Charles Judson
see **Harley Manners series**

Roger and Hal Hunt series
Price, Willard
see **Hal and Roger Hunt series**

Roger and Helen Mifflin series
Morley, Christopher
1 *Parnassus on wheels* (1917)
2 *Haunted bookshop* (1919)

Roger and Kate Starte series
Williams, Eric Ernest
1 *Dragoman Pass* (1959)
2 *Borders of barbarism* (1961)

Roger Bennion series
Adams, Herbert
see **Major Roger Bennion series**

Roger Brook series
Wheatley, Dennis
1 *Launching of Roger Brook* (1947)
2 *Shadow of Tyburn tree* (1948)
3 *Rising storm* (1949)
4 *Man who killed the king* (1951)
5 *Dark secret of Josephine* (1955)
6 *Rape of Venice* (1959)
7 *Sultan's daughter* (1963)
8 *Wanton princess* (1966)
9 *Evil in a mask* (1969)
10 *Ravishing of Lady Mary Ware* (1971)
11 *Irish witch* (1973)
12 *Desperate measures* (1974)

Roger Chapman series
Sedley, Kate
1 *Death and the Chapman* (1991)
2 *Plymouth cloak* (1993)
3 *Weaver's tale* (1994)

Roger Crammond series
Muir, Thomas
1 *Death in reserve* (1948)
2 *Death in the trooper* (1948)
3 *Death in the lock* (1949)
4 *Death below zero* (1950)
5 *Death without question* (1951)
6 *Death under Virgo* (1952)
7 *Death on the agenda* (1953)
8 *Death in Soundings* (1955)

Roger Dowling series
McInerny, Ralph
see **Father Roger Dowling series**

Roger Ellerdine and Cherry Blossom series
Wills, Cecil Melville
see **Superintendent Roger Ellerdine and Sergeant Cherry Blossom series**

Roger Fleming series
Harvester, Simon
1 *Let them prey* (1942)
2 *Epitaph for Lemmings* (1943)
3 *Maybe a trumpet* (1945)
4 *Breastplate for Aaron* (1949)
5 *Sheep may safely graze* (1950)
6 *Obols for Charon* (1951)
7 *Vessel may carry explosives* (1951)

Roger Garrison series
Rovin, Jeff
1 *Garrison* (1975)
2 *Wolf* (1975)

Roger Hartley series
Ellinger, Geoffrey
1 *Trap in the tunnel* (1931)
2 *Return of Cardannesley* (1934)

Roger Kelso series
White, James Dillon
1 *Young Mister Kelso* (1963)
2 *Brave Captain Kelso* (1959)
3 *Kelso of the Paragon* (1969)
4 *Captain of marine* (1960)
5 *Princess of Persia* (1961)
6 *Commodore Kelso* (1967)
7 *Wind in the rigging* (1973)
8 *Spread of sail* (1975)

Roger Levin series
Furst, Alan
1 *Your day in the barrel* (1976)
2 *Paris drop* (1980)
3 *Caribbean account* (1981)
4 *Shadow trade* (1983)

Roger Moore and the Crimefighters series
This sequence has six authors
Hulke, Malcolm
1 *Siege* (1977)
Smyth, Robin
2 *One thousand and one shoplifters* (1977)
Hughes, Gwilym Fielden
3 *Crook ahoy* (1977)
Gray, Dulcie
4 *Death in denims* (1977)
Holt, Deben
5 *Secrets man* (1977)
Wall, Anthony
6 *Anchor trick* (1977)

Roger Newman and Robert Townley series
Bearshaw, Brian
see **Superintendent Robert Townley and Sergeant Roger Newman series**

Roger Patten series
Randall, Anthony Asheton
1 *Ride a tiger* (1965)
2 *Flashpoint* (1966)

Roger Paulding series
Beach, Edward Latimer, senior
1 *Roger Paulding, apprentice seaman* (1911)
2 *Roger Paulding, gunner's mate* (1912)
3 *Roger Paulding, gunner* (1913)
4 *Roger Paulding, ensign* (1914)

Roger Poynings series
Burt, Michael
1 *Case of the fast young lady* (1942)
2 *Case of the angel's trumpets* (1947)
3 *Case of the laughing Jesuit* (1948)

Roger Rabbit series
Korman, Justine
1 *Different hero* (1988)
2 *Make the world laugh* (1988)
Companion volume: *Who framed Roger Rabbit storybook*, 1988

Roger series
Gretz, Susanna
1 *It's your turn, Roger* (1985)
2 *Roger takes charge* (1987)

Roger series
Leyland, Eric
see **Jolly Roger series**

Roger Sheringham series
Berkeley, Anthony
1 *Layton Court mystery* (1925)
Originally published anonymously
2 *Wychford poisoning case* (1926)
3 *Roger Sheringham and the Vane mystery* (1927)
Vane mystery
Mystery at Lovers' Cave
4 *Silk stocking murders* (1928)
5 *Poisoned chocolates case* (1929)
6 *Second shot* (1930)
7 *Top storey murder* (1931)
Top story murder
8 *Murder in the basement* (1932)
9 *Jumping Jenny* (1933)
Dead Mrs Stratton
10 *Panic party* (1934)
Mister Pigeon's island

Roger Taine series
Household, Geoffrey
1 *Rough shoot* (1951)
2 *Time to kill* (1952)

Roger Tallis series
Rossiter, John
1 *Murder makers* (1969)
2 *Deadly green* (1970)
3 *Rope for General Dietz* (1972)
4 *Golden virgin* (1975)
Deadly gold

Roger Tearle series
Corbett, Scott
see **Inspector Roger Tearle series**

Roger Thursby series
Cecil, Henry
1 *Brothers in law* (1955)
2 *Friends at court* (1956)
3 *Sober as a judge* (1958)

Roger Turnbull series
Tyndall, John
1 *Death in the Jordan* (1970)
2 *Death in the Lebanon* (1971)

Roger Vellacott series
Knight, Peter
1 *Gold of the snow goose* (1959)
2 *Assassin's castle* (1962)

Roger Waterlow series
Mackenzie, Compton
see **Commander Roger Waterlow series**

Roger West series
Creasey, John
see **Inspector Roger West series**

Roger Zelazny's Alien speedway series
This sequence has two authors
Carver, Jeffrey Allan
1 *Clypsis* (1987)
Wylde, Thomas
2 *Pitfall* (1988)
3 *Web* (1988)

Rogers and Smith series
Ross, Zola Helen
see **Beau Smith and Pogy Rogers series**

Rogers family series
Idell, Albert Edward
1 *Rogers' folly* (1957)
2 *Centennial summer* (1943)
3 *Bridge to Brooklyn* (1944)
4 *Great blizzard* (1948)

Rogers series
Brede, Arnold
see **Bull Rogers series**
Crisp, Frank
see **Dirk Rogers series**
Knight, Clifford
see **Huntoon Rogers series**
Middleton, Don
see **Roy Rogers series**
Nowlan, Philip Francis
see **Buck Rogers series**
Ross, Jonathan
see **Superintendent George Rogers series**

Rogers teleplay series
Steele, Addison E
see **Buck Rogers teleplay series**

Rogerson series
McInerny, Ralph
see **Matthew Rogerson series**

Rogue Bishop series
Foreman, Leonard London
1 *Spanish grant* (1962)
2 *Mustang trail* (1965)
3 *Silver flame* (1966)
4 *Rogue's legacy* (1968)

Rogue Ransome series
Morgan, Dean
1 *Rogue Ransome, racketbuster* (1950)
2 *Rogue Ransome, manhunter* (1951)
3 *Rogue Ransome, triggerman* (1951)

Rogue series
Household, Geoffrey
see **Raymond Ingelram series**

Rohan series
Graeme, David
see **Monsieur Blackshirt series**

Roi Kunzer series
Geis, Richard Erwin
1 *Sex machine* (1967)
2 *Endless orgy* (1968)

Roi series
Lore, Phillips
see **Leo Roi series**

Roland Blake series
Mitchell, Silas Weir
1 *Roland Blake* (1886)
2 *Westways* (1913)
A village chronicle

Roland Pace series
Bell, Adrian
1 *Balcony* (1934)
2 *Young man's fancy* (1955)
3 *Mill house* (1958)

Roland Rat series
Claridge, David
Illustrated by Steve Cox
1 *Roland Rat and friends at the seaside* (1986)
2 *Roland Rat and friends in the park* (1986)
3 *Roland Rat and friends on the farm* (1986)
4 *Roland Rat and friends at the shop* (1986)

Roles trilogy
Stewart, Desmond
see **Sequence of roles trilogy**

Rolf Kessler series
Hutson, Shaun
see **Sergeant Rolf Kessler series**

Rolf Ledger trilogy
Reese, John
see **Jesus on horseback trilogy**

Rolfe series
Bonney, Joseph L
see **Simon Rolfe series**
Chase, James Hadley
see **Helga Rolfe series**
Lamb, J J
see **Zack Rolfe series**

Rolling Stone series
Bannister, S F
1 *Tossed and blown* (1953)
2 *God's own country* (1953)

Rolling Stone series
Laing, Kenneth
1 *Malignant showman* (1950)
2 *No man's laughter* (1950)
3 *Midnight walkers* (1951)
4 *Shadow people* (1952)

Rolling stones series
Stockton, Frank Richard
1 *Captain Chap* (1897)
Alternative title: The rolling stones
2 *Young master of Hyson Hall* (1899)
Serialized as *Philip Berkeley, or, The master's gun*

Rollison series
Creasey, John
see **Toff series**

Rollo series
Abbott, Jacob
1 *Rollo learning to talk* (1835)
2 *Rollo learning to read* (1835)
Alternative title: Easy stories for young children
3 *Rollo at work* (1838)
4 *Rollo at play* (1838)
5 *Rollo at school* (1839)
6 *Rollo's vacation* (1839)
7 *Rollo's experiments* (1839)
8 *Rollo's museum* (1839)
9 *Rollo's travels* (1840)
10 *Rollo's correspondence* (1840)
11 *Rollo's philosophy, water* (1841)
12 *Rollo's philosophy, air* (1841)
13 *Rollo's philosophy, fire* (1842)
14 *Rollo's philosophy, sky* (1842)
Companion volumes: *Rollo's code of morals, or, The rules of duty for children*, 1841, *Rollo's garden*, 1864, *Rollo's in the woods*, 1871

Rollo series
Bushby, John
see **Captain James Rollo series**

Rollo's tour in Europe series
Abbott, Jacob
1 *Rollo on the Atlantic* (1853)
2 *Rollo in Paris* (1854)
3 *Rollo in Switzerland* (1855)
4 *Rollo in London* (1855)
5 *Rollo on the Rhine* (1855)
6 *Rollo in Sctland* (1856)
7 *Rollo in Geneva* (1857)
8 *Rollo in Holland* (1857)
9 *Rollo in Naples* (1858)
10 *Rollo in Rome* (1858)
Companion volume: *Rollo's journey to Cambridge*, 1880

Roly Poly series
Brook, Sally
Illustrated by Stephen Cartwright
1 *Roly Poly Bear in the winter* (1986)
2 *Roly Poly Hippo in the bath* (1986)
3 *Roly Poly Panda in the sunshine* (1986)
4 *Roly Poly Pigs at the party* (1986)

Roma sub rosa series
Saylor, Steven
Set in the last years of the Roman Republic
1 *Roman blood* (1991)
2 *Arms of Nemesis* (1992)
3 *Catilini's riddle* (1993)

Roman Britain series
Birt, David
1 *Roman conquest of Britain* (1976)
2 *Roman soldier in Britain* (1976)
3 *Hadrian's Wall* (1976)
4 *Travel and trade* (1976)
5 *Roman villa* (1976)
6 *Roman town* (1976)
7 *Religion in Roman Britain* (1976)
8 *Legions of leave* (1976)
9 *Everyday life in Roman Britain* (1976)
11 *Britain before the Romans* (1976)
12 *Attacking the wall* (1976)
13 *Roman mosaics* (1976)
14 *Boudicca's revolt* (1976)
15 *Investigating the druids* (1976)
16 *Roman ships* (1976)
17 *Gladiators* (1976)
18 *Investigating King Arthur* (1976)
19 *Pottery in Roman Britain* (1976)
20 *Siege machines* (1976)
Companion volumes edited by David Birt: *Gods, myths and legends*, 1986, *The Roman army*, 1986, *Roman pottery*, 1986, *Coins and treasure trove*, 1986

Roman Britain series
Gloag, John
1 *Caesar of the narrow seas* (1969)
2 *Eagles depart* (1973)
3 *Artorius Rex* (1977)

Roman Britain series
Treece, Henry
1 *Legions of the eagle* (1954)
2 *Eagles have flown* (1954)

Roman Britain trilogy
Sutcliff, Rosemary
1 *Eagle of the Ninth* (1954)
2 *Silver branch* (1957)
3 *Lantern bearers* (1959)
Revised edition 1965
One volume edition entitled *Three legions*, 1980

Roman Cantrell and Nikki Holden series
Chase, Elaine Raco
1 *Dangerous places* (1987)
2 *Dark corners* (1988)
3 *Rough edges* (1992)

Roman Catholic Church in Spain series
Blasco Ibanez, Vicente
1 *Shadow of the cathedral* (1903)
Original edition entitled *La cathedral*
2 *Intruder* (1904)
Original edition entitled *El intruso*
3 *Fruit of the vine* (1905)
La Bodega
Original edition entitled La Bodega
4 *Horde* (1905)
Mob
Original edition entitled *La horda*

Roman emperors quartet
Massie, Allan
1 *Augustus* (1986)
The memoirs of the Emperor
2 *Tiberius* (1991)
3 *Caesar* (1993)
Number 4 not yet published

Roman Grey series
Smith, Martin Cruz
1 *Gypsy in amber* (1971)
2 *Canto for a gypsy* (1972)
One volume edition 1984

Roman Republic trilogy
Lindsay, Jack
1 *Rome for sale* (1934)
2 *Caesar is dead* (1934)
3 *Last days with Cleopatra* (1935)

Roman society series
Crawford, Francis Marion
1 *Saracinesca* (1887)
2 *Sant' Ilario* (1889)
3 *Don Orsino* (1892)
4 *Corleone* (1898)
5 *Taquisara* (1896)
6 *White sister* (1909)

Roman trilogy
Hardy, William George
1 *City of libertines* (1957)
2 *Scarlet mantle* (1978)
3 *Bloodied toga* (1979)

Roman world series
Forest, Dael
1 *Barba, the slaver* (1975)
2 *Haesel, the slave* (1975)
3 *Brotan, the breeder* (1975)
4 *Gracus, the centurion* (1975)
5 *Carissa, the vestal virgin* (1976)

Romances and fantasies series
Hardy, Thomas
1 *Pair of blue eyes* (1873)
2 *Trumpet-major* (1880)

3 *Tow on a tower* (1882)
4 *Well-beloved* (1897)
5 *Group of noble dames* (1891)

Romances of the rose trilogy
Annunzio, Gabriele d'
1 *Triumph of death* (1894)
Original edition entitled *Il trionfo della morte*
2 *Child of pleasure* (1889)
Original edition entitled *Il piacere*
3 *Victim* (1892)
Intruder
Original edition entitled *L'innocente*

Romancing the stone series
Wilder, Joan
Based on moving pictures
1 *Romancing the stone* (1984)
2 *Jewel of the Nile* (1985)

Romano series
Alexander, David
see **Lieutenant Romano series**
Hunt, Mabel Leigh
see **Cristy Romano series**

Romano series
Motley, Willard
1 *Knock on any door* (1948)
2 *Let no man write my epitaph* (1958)

Romanoff series
Griffith, George Chetwynd
1 *Angel of the revolution* (1893)
A tale of the coming terror
2 *Olga Romanoff* (1894)
Alternative title: The syren of the skies

Romans series
Burrell, Roy Eric Charles
1 *Romans and their world* (1970)
2 *Romans in Britain* (1971)

Romany Rat trilogy
Williamson, Roger
1 *Cheesemaker mice and the giant* (1983)
2 *Romany Rat* (1985)
3 *Stolen harvest* (1986)

Romany readers series
Evens, George Bramwell
1 *Hotchi the hedgehog* (1946)
2 *Smut the hare* (1946)
3 *Flash the fox* (1948)
4 *Snook the barn owl* (1948)
5 *Pete and Prue the partridges* (1951)
6 *Billy the squirrel* (1951)
7 *Nick the weasel* (1951)
8 *Sleek the otter* (1951)

Romany series
This sequence has two authors
Evens, George Bramwell
1 *Romany in the fields* (1929)
2 *Romany and Raq* (1930)
3 *Romany in the country* (1932)
4 *Romany on the trail* (1934)
5 *Out with Romany* (1937)
6 *Out with Romany again* (1938)
7 *Walks with Romany* (1939)
8 *Out with Romany once more* (1940)
9 *Out with Romany by the sea* (1941)
10 *Out with Romany by moor and dale* (1944)
11 *Out with Romany by meadow and stream* (1944)
Evens, Glyn Kinnaird
12 *Romany turns detective* (1949)
13 *Romany on the farm* (1952)
14 *Romany's caravan returns* (1953)
Companion volume: *Romany, Muriel and Doris*, 1939

Rome series
McCullough, Colleen
1 *First man in Rome* (1990)
Based on the life of Caius Marius
2 *Grass crown* (1991)
Based on the life of Lucius Cornelius Sulla
3 *Fortune's favourites* (1993)
Based on the life of Pompey

Rome series
Rome, Anthony
see **Tony Rome series**

Rome trilogy
Fogazzaro, Antonio
see **Maironi family trilogy**

Romeo series
Gree, Alain
1 *Romeo looks for a job* (1966)
Original edition entitled *Romeo cherche un emploi*
2 *[Romeo, champion de la neige]* (1967)
No English edition
3 *Romeo flies a plane* (1967)
Original edition entitled *Romeo pilote un avion*
4 *Romeo seeks a fortune* (1967)
Original edition entitled *Romeo veut faire fortune*
5 *Romeo becomes a musician* (1968)
Original edition entitled *Romeo apprend la musique*
Two more titles in this sequence not translated into English

Romilly Street series
Denison, Mary
1 *Romilly Street* (1976)
2 *Ballet in Romilly Street* (1977)

Rommel series
Kessler, Leo
1 *Ghost division* (1978)
2 *Massacre* (1979)

Romney Marsh series
Edwards, Monica
1 *Wish for a pony* (1947)
2 *Summer of the great secret* (1948)
3 *Midnight horse* (1949)
4 *White riders* (1950)
5 *Cargo of horses* (1951)
6 *Hidden in a dream* (1952)
7 *Storm ahead* (1953)
8 *No entry* (1954)
9 *Nightbird* (1955)
10 *Operation Seabird* (1957)
11 *Strangers to the Marsh* (1957)
12 *Killer dog* (1959)
13 *No going back* (1960)
14 *Hoodwinkers* (1962)
15 *Dolphin summer* (1963)
16 *Wind is blowing* (1969)

Romney Marsh series
Marcus, Joanna
1 *Few days in Endel* (1968)
Originally published under the pseudonym Diana Gordon
2 *Marsh blood* (1980)

Romney Pringle series
Ashdown, Clifford
1 *Adventures of Romney Pringle* (1902)
2 *Further adventures of Romney Pringle* (1970)

Ron Barron series
Jones, Raymond F
1 *Son of the stars* (1952)
2 *Planet of night* (1953)

Ron Hogget series
Mitchell, James
1 *Sometimes you could die* (1985)
2 *Dead Ernest* (1986)
3 *Dying day* (1988)

Ronald Anglesea series
Milner, George
1 *Stately homicide* (1953)
2 *Shark among herrings* (1954)

Ronald Briercliffe series
Beeding, Francis
1 *Three fishers* (1931)
2 *Two undertakers* (1933)

Ronald Camberwell series
Fletcher, Joseph Smith
1 *Murder at Wrides Park* (1931)
2 *Murder in four degrees* (1931)
3 *Murder in the squire's pew* (1932)
4 *Murder of the Ninth Baronet* (1932)
5 *Who killed Alfred Crowe?* (1933)
Murder of the lawyer's clerk
6 *Murder of the only witness* (1933)
7 *Mystery of the London banker* (1933)
Murder of a banker
8 *Murder of the secret agent* (1934)
9 *Ebony box* (1934)
10 *Eleventh hour* (1935)
11 *Todmanhawe Grange* (1937)
Mill House murder
Completed by Edward Powys Mathers under the pseudonym Torquemada

Ronald Challis series
Martin, Shane
see **Professor Ronald Challis series**

Ronald Love series
Mann, Mary E
1 *Memories of Ronald Love* (1907)
2 *Avenging children* (1909)

Ronald Morgan series
Giff, Patricia Reilly
1 *Watch out, Ronald Morgan* (1985)
2 *Happy birthday, Ronald Morgan* (1986)
3 *Ronald Morgan goes to bat* (1988)

Ronald Price series
Cannan, Joanna
see **Inspector Ronald Price series**

Ronald Standish series
Sapper
American editions published under the author's real name Herman Cyril McNeile
1 *Tiny Carteret* (1930)
2 *Knock-out* (1933)
Bulldog Drummond strikes back
3 *Ronald Standish* (1933)
Short stories
4 *Bulldog Drummond at bay* (1935)
5 *Ask for Ronald Standish* (1936)
Short stories
6 *Challenge* (1937)

Ronicky Doone series
Manning, David
1 *Ronicky Doone* (1926)
2 *Ronicky Doone's treasure* (1926)

Ronnie and Pepe series
Knight, Clayton
see **Pepe and Ronnie series**

Ronnie Drew series
Vivian, Francis
see **Sergeant Ronnie Drew series**

Ronnie Gold series
Paulsen, Gary
see **Lieutenant Ronnie Gold series**

Ronnie series
Antrobus, John
1 *Ronnie and the haunted Rolls-Royce* (1982)
2 *Ronnie and the great knitted robbery* (1982)
3 *Ronnie and the high rise* (1992)
4 *Ronnie and the flying fitted carpet* (1992)

Ronnie series
Hann, Dorothy Owen
1 *Ronnie and the Creed* (1940)
2 *Ronnie and the Lord's Prayer* (1941)
3 *Ronnie and the Commandments* (1944)
4 *Ronnie and the sacraments* (1947)
5 *Ronnie and the parish church* (1954)
6 *Ronnie and the catechism* (1954)
7 *Ronnie and the collects* (1959)
8 *Ronnie and the saints* (1960)

Ronnie Smithers series
Hale, Susan
1 *Painter's mate* (1964)
2 *Mystery boxes* (1965)

Roobarb series
Calveley, Grange
1 *When Roobarb wasn't as pleased as Punch* (1975)
2 *When Roobarb didn't find treasure* (1975)
3 *Adventures of Roobarb when there was a TV show* (1977)

Rook series
Palmer, Stuart
see **Howie Rook series**

Rooke and Twotoes series
Alexander, David
see **Tommy Twotoes and Terry Rooke series**

Room 222 series
Johnston, William
Based on a television series
1 *Whatever happened to Mavis Rooster?* (1970)
2 *Monday morning father* (1970)
3 *Love is a three-letter word* (1970)
4 *Have you heard about Kelly?* (1973)

Roommates series
Galbraith, Kathryn O
Illustrated by Mark Graham
1 *Roommates* (1990)
2 *Roommates and Rachel* (1991)
3 *Rommates again* (1994)

Roosevelt family series
Roosevelt, Elliott
1 *Untold story* (1973)
The Roosevelts of Hyde Park
2 *Rendezvous with destiny* (1975)
The Roosevelts of the White House

Roosevelt series
Lash, Joseph P
see **Eleanor Roosevelt series**
Roosevelt, Elliott
see **Eleanor Roosevelt series**

Rooster Cogburn series
This sequence has two authors
Portis, Charles
1 *True grit* (1966)
Julien, Martin
2 *Rooster Cogburn* (1975)
Based on a screenplay

Root and the flower series
Myers, Leopold Hamilton
see **Prince Jali series**

Rootabaga series
Sandburg, Carl
1 *Rootabaga stories* (1922)
2 *Rootabaga pigeons* (1923)
Selections entitled *Rootabaga country*, 1929

Roots and stars series
Vyvyan, Clara Coltman
Autobiography
1 *Roots and stars* (1962)
2 *Journey up the years* (1966)

Roots series
Haley, Alex
1 *Roots* (1976)
2 *Alex Haley's queen* (1993)
Co-author: David Stevens

Roper series
Croy, Catherine
see **Julia Arbuthnot series**
Follett, Ken
see **Piers Roper series**
Hart, Roy
see **Detective Superintendent Roper series**
Platt, Kin
see **Max Roper series**

Roque series
Morton, Guy
see **Konrad Roque series**

Rorke series
Hine, Muriel
see **Jenny Rorke series**

Rorvik series
Couper, Stephen
see **Paradise series**

Rory and Kay series
Clewes, Dorothy
see **Kay and Rory series**

Rory Luccan series
Morland, Nigel
see **Detective Inspector Rory Luccan series**

Rosa Epton series
Underwood, Michael
1 *Pinch of snuff* (1974)
2 *Menaces, menaces* (1976)
3 *Crime upon crime* (1980)
4 *Double jeopardy* (1981)
5 *Goddess of death* (1982)
6 *Party to murder* (1983)
7 *Death in camera* (1984)
8 *Hidden man* (1985)
9 *Death at Deepwood Grange* (1986)
10 *Uninvited corpse* (1987)
11 *Injudicious judge* (1987)
12 *Dual enigma* (1988)
13 *Compelling case* (1989)
14 *Rosa's dilemma* (1990)
15 *Dangerous business* (1991)
16 *Seeds of murder* (1991)
17 *Guilty conscience* (1992)

Rosa series
Barratt, Isabel
1 *Adventures of Rosa* (1979)
2 *Bardolph the beastly beagle* (1979)

Rosalie Dare series
Brooks, Amy
1 *Rosalie Dare* (1924)
2 *Rosalie Dare's test* (1925)
3 *What Rosalie Dare won* (1926)

Rosalind and Zero series
Buckley, Eunice
see **Zero and Rosalind series**

Rosalind series
Nicholson, Meredith
1 *House of a thousand candles* (1905)
2 *Rosalind at Red Gate* (1907)

Rosamund series
Rhoades, Nina
see **Miss Rosamund series**

Rosanna series
Galt, Katherine Keene
1 *Girl Scouts at home* (1921)
Alternative title: Rosanna's beautiful day
2 *Girl Scouts rally* (1921)
Alternative title: Rosanna wins
3 *Girl Scouts triumph* (1921)
Alternative title: Rosanna's sacrifice

Rose Campbell series
Alcott, Louisa May
1 *Eight cousins* (1874)
Alternative title: The aunt hill
2 *Rose in bloom* (1876)

Rose Cottingham series
Syrett, Netta
1 *Victorians* (1915)
2 *Rose Cottingham married* (1916)

Rose Endel and David Lofthouse series
Marcus, Joanna
see **Romney Marsh series**

Rose-garden series
Widdemer, Margaret
1 *Rose-garden husband* (1915)
2 *Wishing-ring man* (1917)

Rose in the sea series
Simpson, Alyse
Autobiography
1 *I threw a rose into the sea* (1955)
2 *Red dust of Africa* (1952)

Rose, Lifeng and Shaofeng series
Payne, Robert
see **Lifeng, Shaofeng and Rose series**

Rose of the prophet trilogy
Weis, Margaret
1 *Will of the wanderer* (1989)
2 *Paladin of the night* (1989)
3 *Prophet of Akhran* (1989)

Rose series
Caggiano, Phyllis
1 *Love's fragile flame* (1984)
2 *Love's pilgrimage* (1986)

Rose series
Eco, Umberto
1 *Name of the rose* (1984)
Original edition entitled *Il nome della rosa*
2 *Postscript to The name of the rose* (1984)

Rose series
Fairburn, Eleanor
see **Wars of the Roses series**

Rose series
Garland, Sarah
1 *Rose and her bath* (1970)
2 *Rose, the bath and the mer boy* (1972)

Rose series
Harrison, Rosina
1 *Rose* (1975)
My life in service
2 *Gentlemen's gentlemen* (1976)
My friends in service

Rose series
Hughes, Shirley
see **Alfie Rose series**

Rose series
Paget, Guy
1 *Rose of Raby* (1937)
Life of Cecily Nevile, Duchess of York
2 *Rose of Rouen* (1940)
3 *Rose of London* (1934)
The life, career and character of Jane Shore, the mistress of King Edward the Fourth

Rose trilogy
Annunzio, Gabriele d'
see **Romances of the rose trilogy**

Rose trilogy
Sayer, Mandy
1 *Mood indigo* (1989)
2 *Blind luck* (1993)
Number 3 not yet published

Roselands series
Finley, Martha Farquharson
1 *Elsie's holiday and Roselands* (1868)
Holiday at Roselands
2 *Mildred at Roselands* (1879)

Roselynde chronicles series
Gellis, Roberta
1 *Roselynde* (1978)
2 *Alinor* (1978)
3 *Joanna* (1978)
4 *Gilliane* (1979)
5 *Rhiannon* (1981)
6 *Sybelle* (1983)

Rosemary series
Bloom, Ursula
1 *Rosemary for Stratford-on-Avon* (1966)
2 *Rosemary for Frinton* (1970)
3 *Rosemary for Chelsea* (1971)

Rosemary series
Curry, Jane Louise
1 *Parsley, sage, rosemary and time* (1975)
2 *Magical cupboard* (1976)

Rosen series
Levitsky, Ronald
see **Nate Rosen series**

Rosencrantz family series
Goodwin, Ben
1 *Down our street* (1952)
2 *How's by you* (1952)
Short stories

Rose's class series
Ziefert, Harriet
see **Mister Rose's class series**

Roses series
Keyes, Frances Parkinson
Autobiography
1 *Roses in December* (1960)
Revised edition 1966
2 *All flags flying* (1972)
Companion volume: *The cost of a best seller*, 1950

Rosher series
Scott, Jack S
see **Detective Inspector Alfred Stanley Rosher series**

Rosie and Adam series
Thwaites, Lyndsay
see **Super Adam and Rosie Wonder series**

Rosie and Jim series
Cunliffe, John Arthur
1 *Rosie and Jim and the water wizard* (1991)
2 *Rosie and Jim and the rainbow* (1991)
3 *Rosie and Jim* (1992)
Fifty one minute stories
4 *Rosie and Jim and the man in the wind* (1992)
5 *Rosie and Jim and the drink of milk* (1992)
6 *Rosie and Jim and Ragdoll* (1992)
Companion volume: Rosie and Jim special, 1991
7 *Rosie and Jim and the glassblowers* (1993)
8 *Rosie and Jim and the magic sausages* (1994)
Companion volumes: *Rosie and Jim special*, 1991, *Rosie and Jim, apple, banana, carrot alphabet book*, 1993, *Round the year with Rosie and Jim*, two volumes, 1993-94

Rosie and Lucija series
Ebejer, Francis
see **Lucija and Rosie series**

Rosie Bright series
Ruegg, Alfred Henry
1 *John Clutterbuck* (1923)
2 *David Betterton* (1931)

Rosie Carr series
Willis, Ted
1 *Spring at the Winged Horse* (1983)
2 *Green leaves of summer* (1988)
3 *Bells of autumn* (1990)

Rosie Darling series
Swale, Rosie
Reminiscences of travel
1 *Rosie Darling* (1973)
2 *Children of Cape Horn* (1974)
3 *Libras don't say no* (1980)
4 *Back to Cape Horn* (1986)

Rosie Dawes series
Greenwood, Robert
1 *Good angel slept* (1953)
2 *O mistress mine* (1955)

Rosie series
Harris, Robie H
1 *Rosie's double dare* (1980)
2 *Rosie's razzle dazzle deal* (1982)
3 *Rosie's rock 'n' roll riot* (1990)
4 *Rosie's secret spell* (1991)

Rosie series
Macdonald, Maryann
Illustrated by Melissa Sweet
1 *Rosie runs away* (1990)
2 *Rosie's baby tooth* (1991)

Rosie Swanson series
Park, Barbara
1 *Maxie, Rosie and Earl, partners in grime* (1990)
2 *Rosie Swanson, fourth grade geek for president* (1991)

Rosie Vincente and Jake Samson series
Singer, Shelley
see **Jake Samson and Rosie Vincente series**

Rosie Wonder and Super Adam series
Thwaites, Lyndsay
see **Super Adam and Rosie Wonder series**

Rosika Storey series
Footner, Hulbert
see **Madame Rosika Storey series**

Rosina series
Barne, Kitty
1 *Rosina Copper, the mystery mare* (1954)
2 *Rosina and son* (1956)

Rosina series
Farrell, Sally
1 *Rosina and her calf* (1983)
2 *Rosina and the show* (1985)

Rosinante trilogy
Gilliland, Alexis Arnaldus
1 *Revolution from Rosinante* (1981)
2 *Long shot for Rosinante* (1981)
3 *Pirates of Rosinante* (1982)

Rosing series
Spring, Howard
see **Manchester series**

Roslin, James and Alan series
Lyon, Elinor
see **James, Alan and Roslin series**

Rosnovski and Kane series
Archer, Jeffrey
see **William Kane and Abel Rosnovski series**

Ross and Campbell series
Henneker, Philip
see **Susan Campbell and Paul Ross series**

Ross Chesnut trilogy
McDonald, Kay L
1 *Vision of the Eagle* (1977)
2 *Brightwood Expedition* (1976)
3 *Vision is fulfilled* (1983)

Ross family series
Ross, James Davidson
Account of members of the author's family suffering from cancer
1 *Margaret* (1957)
2 *Clare* (1965)

Ross Grant series
Garland, John
1 *Ross Grant, tenderfoot* (1915)
2 *Ross Grant, gold hunter* (1916)
3 *Ross Grant on the trail* (1917)
4 *Ross Grant in Miner's Camp* (1918)

Ross Macallister series
Coram, Christopher
1 *Call to danger* (1968)
2 *Call to die* (1969)
3 *Death in Ptarmigan Forest* (1970)
4 *Death on the motorway* (1973)
5 *Murder by the lake* (1975)
6 *Murder beneath the trees* (1977)

Ross McCoy series
Gluck, Sinclair
1 *Man who never blundered* (1928)
2 *Blind fury* (1930)

Ross McCrae series
Clarke, Mary Stetson
1 *Iron peacock* (1966)
2 *Piper to the clan* (1970)

Ross McKellar series
Peebles, Niles N
1 *See the red blood run* (1968)
2 *Blood brother, blood brother* (1969)

Ross Murdock series
Norton, Andre
see **Time war series**

Ross Paterson series
Field, Katherine
see **Inspector Ross Paterson series**

Ross series
Allyson, Alan
see **Martin Ross series**
Bickham, Jack Miles
see **Charity Ross series**
Carr, Kirby
see **Hitman series**
Connington, John Jervis
see **Superintendent Ross series**
Dwyer-Joyce, Alice
see **Doctor Esmond Ross series**
Gorell, Ronald Gorell Barnes
see **Inspector Gordon Ross series**
Meynell, Laurence Walter
see **Nurse Ross series**
Nicolson, Robert
see **Mrs Ross series**
Waldo, Dale
see **Johnny Ross series**
Wood, James
see **Ian Ross series**

Rostetter series
Campbell, Alice
see **Tommy Rostetter series**

Rostnikov series
Kaminsky, Stuart Melvin
see **Inspector Porfiry Petrovich Rostnikov series**

Rostron Outfit series
Morgan, Dean
1 *Rostron Outfit* (1951)
2 *Rostron Outfit in Rio* (1951)
3 *Rostron Outfit, undercover agents* (1951)
4 *Rostron Outfit in Chicago* (1952)
5 *Rostron Outfit in Mexico* (1952)
6 *Rostron Outfit in Texas* (1952)

Rosy Cole series
Greenwald, Sheila
1 *Give us a great big smile, Rosy Cole* (1981)
2 *Valentine Rosy* (1984)
3 *Rosy Cole's great American guilt club* (1985)
4 *Write on Rosy* (1988)
5 *Rosy's romance* (1989)
6 *Here's Hermione* (1991)

Rosy crucifixion trilogy
Miller, Henry
1 *Sexus* (1949)
Originally published in two volumes
2 *Plexus* (1953)
Originally published in two volumes in French
3 *Nexus* (1960)
Second volume of this title was planned but never written

Roth series
Arvay, Harry
see **Israeli Security Branch series**

Rotherside series
Nickless, Will
1 *Owlglass* (1964)
2 *Nitehood* (1966)
3 *Molepie* (1967)
4 *Dotted lines* (1968)

Rotten Ralph series
Gantos, Jack
1 *Rotten Ralph* (1976)
2 *Worse than Rotten Ralph* (1982)
3 *Rotten Ralph's rotten Christmas* (1984)
4 *Rotten Ralph's trick or treat* (1986)
5 *Rotten Ralph's show and tell* (1989)
6 *Happy birthday, Rotten Ralph* (1990)
7 *Not so Rotten Ralph* (1994)

Rougon Macquart series
Zola, Emile
1 *Fortune of the Rougons* (1871)
Rougon-Macquart family
Original edition entitled *La fortune des Rougon*
2 *In the swim* (1871)
Rush for the spoils
In the whirlpool
Venus of the counting house
Original edition entitled *La curee*
3 *Savage Paris* (1873)
Fat and the thin
Markets of Paris
Flower and market girls of Paris
Original edition entitled *La ventre de Paris*; alternative titles La belle Lisa, Paris market girls
4 *Conquest of Plassans* (1874)
Priest in the house
Mad love
Original edition entitled *La conquete de Plassans*; alternative title: The Abbe and his court
5 *Abbe Mouret's transgression* (1875)
Abbe Mouret's sin
Sin of the Abbe Mouret
Sinful priest
Original edition entitled *La faute de l'abbe Mouret*; alternative titles: The Abbe's temptation, The sin of Father Mouret
6 *His Excellency* (1876)
Zola's court of Napoleon III
Mysteries of the court of Louis Napoleon
Mysteries of Louis Napoleon's court
Original edition entitled *Son Excellence Eugene Rougon*; alternative titles: Clorinda,The rise and reign of His Excellency Eugene Rougon, and His Excellency Eugene Rougon
7 *Dram-shop* (1877)
Drunkard
Drink
Gin palace
Original edition entitled *L'assommier*; alternative titles: Nana's mother, Gervaise
8 *Love episode* (1878)
Love affair
Helene
Original edition entitled *Une page d'amour*
9 *Nana* (1880)
Original edition entitled *Nana*
10 *Piping hot* (1882)
Restless house
Lesson in love
Original edition entitled *Pot-bouille*
11 *Ladies' paradise* (1883)
Ladies' delight
Original edition entitled *Au bonheur des dames*; alternative title: The shop girls of Paris
12 *How jolly life is!* (1884)
Zest for life
Life's joy
Joy of life
Original edition entitled *La joie de vivre*
13 *Germinal* (1885)
Original edition entitled *Germinal*; alternative title: Master and man
14 *His masterpiece?* (1886)
Masterpiece
Original edition entitled *L'oeuvre*; alternative title: Claude Lantier's struggle for fame
15 *Soil* (1887)
Earth
Original edition entitled *La terre*
16 *Dream* (1888)
Dream of love
Original edition entitled *Le reve*
17 *Human beast* (1890)
Beast in man
Monomaniac
Human animal
Original edition entitled *La bete humaine*; alternative title: The human brutes
18 *Money* (1891)
Original edition entitled *L'argent*
19 *Downfall* (1892)
Debacle
Original edition entitled *La debacle*
20 *Doctor Pascal* (1893)
Original edition entitled *Docteur Pascal*; alternative title: Life and heredity

Rouletabille series
Leroux, Gaston
see **Joseph Rouletabille series**

Round River series
Leopold, Aldo
see **Sand County series**

Round series
Lister, Gladys
1 *Little round garden* (1938)
2 *Little round house* (1939)
3 *House that beckons* (1940)
4 *Little round stairway* (1946)
5 *Little round world* (1955)
Companion volume: *Tubby, the little round bear*, 1949

Round stories series
Haley, Gail Einhart
1 *Round stories about things that live on land* (1966)
2 *Round stories about things that live in water* (1966)
3 *Round stories about things that grow* (1966)
4 *Round stories about our world* (1966)

Round Table series
Lawrence, Margery
see **Club of the Round Table series**

Round the corner trilogy
Cannan, Gilbert
1 *Round the corner* (1913)
Life and death of Arthur Christopher Folyat
2 *Sembal* (1922)
3 *House of prophecy* (1924)

Round the twist series
Jennings, Paul Arthur
1 *Unreal!* (1985)
2 *Unbelievable!* (1987)
3 *Uncanny!* (1988)
4 *Unbearable!* (1990)
Includes *Grandad's gifts*, published separately in 1992
5 *Unmentionable!* (1991)
6 *Undone!* (1993)
Companion volume: *Round the twist*, 1990

Round the year series
Blyton, Enid
1 *Spring* (1934)
2 *Summer* (1934)
3 *Autumn* (1934)
4 *Winter* (1934)

Roundabout America series
Lenski, Lois
1 *We live in the South* (1952)
2 *Peanuts for Billy Ben* (1952)
3 *We live in the city* (1954)
4 *Project boy* (1954)
5 *Berries in the scoop* (1956)
6 *We live by the river* (1956)
7 *We live in the country* (1960)
8 *We live in the Southwest* (1962)
9 *We live in the North* (1965)

Roundabout series
Daly, Maureen
Memoirs of travel
1 *Twelve around the world* (1957)
2 *Spanish roundabout* (1960)
3 *Moroccan roundabout* (1961)

Rounders series
Evans, Max
see **Dusty Jones and Wrangler Lewis series**

Rounds series
Butler, Peter
1 *Hickety pickety* (1991)
2 *Jingle with a ball* (1992)

Roundtree women series
Lewerth, Margaret
1 *Roundtree women* (1979)

2 *Claudia* (1979)
3 *Hester* (1979)
4 *Lilith* (1981)

Rourke series
Cooke, David Coxe
see **Peter Rourke series**
Wolf, Jack
see **Timothy Rourke series**

Rousseau series
Duplechan, Larry
see **Johnnie Ray Rousseau series**

Roux series
Chamson, Andre
1 *Roux the bandit* (1925)
Original edition entitled *Roux le bandit*
2 *Road* (1927)
Original edition entitled *Les hommes de la route*
3 *Crime of the just* (1928)
Original edition entitled *Le crime des justes*

Rover boys series
Winfield, Arthur M
1 *Rover boys at school* (1899)
Alternative title: The cadets of Putnam Hall
2 *Rover boys on the ocean* (1899)
Alternative title: A chase for fortune
3 *Rover boys in the jungle* (1899)
Alternative title: Stirring adventures in Africa
4 *Rover boys out West* (1900)
Alternative title: The search for a lost mine
5 *Rover boys on the Great Lakes* (1901)
Alternative title: The secret of the island cave
6 *Rover boys in the mountains* (1902)
Alternative title: A hunt for fun and fortune
7 *Rover boys on land and sea* (1903)
Alternative title: The Crusoes of seven islands
8 *Rover boys in camp* (1904)
Alternative title: The rivals of Pine Island
9 *Rover boys on the river* (1905)
Alternative title: The search for the missing houseboat
10 *Rover boys on the plains* (1906)
Alternative title: The mystery of Red Rock
11 *Rover boys in Southern waters* (1907)
Alternative title: The deserted steam yacht
12 *Rover boys on the farm* (1908)
Alternative title: Last days at Putnam Hall
13 *Rover boys on Treasure Isle* (1909)
Alternative title: The strange cruise of the steam yacht
14 *Rover boys at college* (1910)
Alternative title: The right road and the wrong
15 *Rover boys down East* (1911)
Alternative title: The struggle for the Stanhope fortune
16 *Rover boys in the air* (1912)
Alternative title: From college campus to clouds
17 *Rover boys in New York* (1913)
Alternative title: Saving their father's honor
18 *Rover boys in Alaska* (1914)
Alternative title: Lost in the fields of ice
19 *Rover boys in business* (1915)
Alternative title: The search for the missing bonds
20 *Rover boys on a tour* (1916)
Alternative title: Last days at Brill College; titles from number 21 originally known as **Second Rover boys series**
21 *Rover boys at Colby Hall* (1917)
Alternative title: The struggles of the young cadets
22 *Rover boys on Snowshoe Island* (1918)
Alternative title: The old lumberman's treasure box
23 *Rover boys under canvas* (1919)
Alternative title: The mystery of the wrecked submarine
24 *Rover boys on a hunt* (1920)
Alternative title: The mysterious house in the woods
25 *Rover boys in the land of luck* (1921)
Alternative title: Stirring adventures in the oilfields
26 *Rover boys at Big Horn Ranch* (1922)
Alternative title: The cowboys" double roundup
27 *Rover boys at Big Bear Lake* (1923)
Alternative title: The camps of the rival cadets
28 *Rover boys shipwrecked* (1924)
Alternative title: A thrilling hunt for pirates" gold
29 *Rover boys on Sunset Trail* (1925)
Alternative title: Old miner's mysterious message
30 *Rover boys winning a fortune* (1926)
Alternative title: Strenuous days afloat and ashore

Rowan family series
Darby, Catherine
1 *Rowan Garth* (1982)
2 *Rowan for a queen* (1983)
3 *Scent of Rowan* (1983)
4 *Circle of Rowan* (1983)
5 *Rowan maid* (1984)
6 *Song of a Rowan* (1984)

Rowan series
McCaffrey, Anne
1 *Rowan* (1990)
2 *Lyon's pride* (1994)

Rowe series
Maner, William
see **Parker Rowe series**

Rowena Batts series
Gleitzman, Morris
1 *Blabber mouth* (1992)
2 *Sticky beak* (1993)

Roweny series
Pool, Maria Louise
1 *Roweny in Boston* (1892)
2 *Mrs Keats Bradford* (1892)

Rowlands series
Lucas, Norman
see **Superintendent Bill Rowlands series**

Roxana trilogy
Moray, Helga
1 *I, Roxana* (1965)
2 *Roxana and Alexander* (1971)
3 *Son for Roxana* (1971)

Roxton series
Maddock, Reginald Bertram
see **Jimmy Roxton series**

Roy Blakeley series
Fitzhugh, Percy Keese
1 *Roy Blakeley* (1920)
2 *Roy Blakeley's adventures in camp* (1920)
3 *Roy Blakeley's camp on wheels* (1920)
4 *Roy Blakeley, pathfinder* (1920)
5 *Roy Blakeley's Silver Fox Patrol* (1920)
6 *Roy Blakeley's motor caravan* (1921)
7 *Roy Blakeley, lost, strayed or stolen* (1921)
8 *Roy Blakeley's bee-line hike* (1922)
9 *Roy Blakeley at the haunted camp* (1922)
10 *Roy Blakeley's funny bone hike* (1923)
11 *Roy Blakeley's tangled trail* (1924)
12 *Roy Blakeley on the Mohawk Trail* (1925)
13 *Roy Blakeley's elastic hike* (1926)
14 *Roy Blakeley's roundabout hike* (1927)
15 *Roy Blakeley's happy-go-lucky hike* (1928)
16 *Roy Blakeley's go-as-you-please hike* (1929)
17 *Roy Blakeley's wild goose chase* (1930)
18 *Roy Blakeley up in the air* (1931)

Roy Maclean series
Gaston, Bill
1 *Deep green death* (1963)
2 *Drifting death* (1964)
3 *Death Crag* (1965)
4 *Death dealers* (1966)

Roy Rickman trilogy
Craig, David
1 *Alias man* (1968)
2 *Message ends* (1969)
3 *Contact lost* (1970)

Roy Rogers series
This sequence has seven authors
Middleton, Don
1 *Roy Rogers and the Gopher Creek gunman* (1945)
Miller, Snowden
2 *Roy Rogers and the raiders of Sawtooth Ridge* (1946)
Tompkins, Walker Allison
3 *Roy Rogers and the ghost of Mystery Rancho* (1950)
Miller, Snowden
4 *Roy Rogers and the outlaws of Sundown Valley* (1950)
5 *Roy Rogers and the Rimrock renegades* (1950)
Beecher, Elizabeth
6 *Roy Rogers on the Double-R Ranch* (1951)
Rivers, Jim
7 *Roy Rogers and the enchanted canyon* (1954)
Beecher, Elizabeth
8 *Roy Rogers and the sure 'nough cowpoke* (1954)
Bedford, Annie North
9 *Roy Rogers and the new cowboy* (1954)
Fannin, Cole
10 *Roy Rogers, king of the cowboys* (1956)
11 *River of Peril* (1957)
Companion volumes: *Roy Rogers and the Lane ranch*, anonymous, 1953, *Roy Rogers and the Brasada bandit*, anonymous, 1953, *Roy Rogers' Trigger to the rescue*, anonymous, 1954, *Roy Rogers and the trail of zeroes*, anonymous, 1956

Roy series
Gilroy, Beryl
see **Young Roy series**

Roy Stover series
Bartlett, Philip A
1 *Lakeport Bank mystery* (1929)
2 *Mystery of the snowbound express* (1929)
3 *Cliff Island mystery* (1930)
4 *Mystery of the circle of fire* (1934)

Roy Tucker series
Kennedy, Adam
1 *Domino principle* (1975)
2 *Domino vendetta* (1982)

Roy Tucker series
Tunis, John Roberts
1 *Kid from Tomkinsville* (1940)
2 *World Series* (1941)
3 *Rookie of the year* (1944)
4 *Kid comes back* (1946)

Royal adventures series
Halliburton, Richard
1 *Royal road to romance* (1925)
2 *Glorious adventure* (1927)
3 *New worlds to conquer* (1929)
One volume edition entitled *The royal adventures of Richard Halliburton*, 1947

Royal Air Force series
Graves, Charles
1 *Thin blue line* (1941)
2 *Avengers* (1942)
3 *Seven pilots* (1943)

Royal Air Force trilogy
Hennessy, Max
see **Dicken Quinney trilogy**

Royal Air Force trilogy
Kingston, Guy
1 *Main force* (1978)
2 *Wing and a prayer* (1980)
3 *Boys of Coastal* (1982)

Royal Canadian Mounted Police series
Longstreth, Thomas Morris
1 *Scarlet Force* (1953)
The making of the Mounted Police
2 *Force carries on* (1954)

Royal dynasty series
Gellis, Roberta
1 *Siren song* (1980)
2 *Winter song* (1982)
3 *Fire song* (1984)
4 *Silver mirror* (1989)

Royal Murdoch series
Harlow, Robert
1 *Royal Murdoch* (1964)
2 *Gift of echoes* (1965)

Royal Navy series
Mars, Alastair
Reminiscences of the Second World War
1 *Unbroken* (1953)
The story of a submarine
2 *H.M.S. Thule intercepts* (1956)

Royal Navy series
Taffrail
1 *Pincher Martin* (1916)
2 *Oh, Joshua* (1920)

Royal taxation in fourteenth century France series
Henneman, John Bell
1 *Development of war financing, 1322-1356* (1971)
2 *Captivity and ransom of John II, 1356-1370* (1976)

Royce series
Aldridge, James
see **Rupert Royce series**

Royston Frere series
Elliott, William James
1 *Dope devils* (1942)
2 *Running killer* (1946)

Roz Howard series
Kenney, Susan
1 *Garden of malice* (1983)
2 *Graves in Academe* (1985)

Rozanov quartet
Thomas, Donald Michael
see **Russian quartet**

Rubaiyat series
Wells, Carolyn
Poetry
1 *Rubaiyat of a motor car* (1906)
2 *Rubaiyat of a bridge* (1909)

Ruby and Ruthy series
Paull, Minnie E
1 *Ruby and Ruthy* (1892)
2 *Ruby's ups and downs* (1893)
3 *Ruby at school* (1894)
4 *Ruby's vacation* (1895)

Ruby series
Aitken, Amy
1 *Ruby!* (1979)
2 *Ruby, the red knight* (1983)

Rudd family series
Rudd, Steele
1 *On our selection* (1899)
1.1 *On our selection* (1899)
Chapters 1-16
1.2 *Stocking our selection* (1899)
Chapters 17-26
2 *Our new selection* (1903)
3 *Sandy's selection* (1904)
4 *Back at our selection* (1906)
5 *Dad in politics, and other stories* (1908)
Includes *For life, and other stories*, 1908
6 *From selection to city* (1909)
7 *Book of Dan* (1911)
8 *Grandpa's selection, and other stories* (1916)
9 *Me an' th' son* (1924)
10 *Rudd family* (1926)
Companion volume: *On Emu Creek*, 1923

Rudd series
Davis, Howard Charles
see **Hugh Rudd series**
Thomson, June
see **Inspector Finch series**

Rudder Grange series
Stockton, Frank Richard
1 *Rudder Grange* (1879)
2 *Rudder Grangers abroad, and other stories* (1891)
3 *Pomona's travels* (1894)

Rudi series
Williams, Ursula Moray
see **Toymakers series**

Rudolf Rassendyl series
Hope, Anthony
1 *Prisoner of Zenda* (1894)
2 *Rupert of Hentzau* (1898)
3 *Sophy of Kravonia* (1906)

Rudolph and Karsten Nilsen series
Griffiths, Ella
Translated from the Norwegian
1 *Murder on page three* (1984)
Original edition entitled *Mord pa side 3*
2 *Water widow* (1986)

Ruff Justice series
Longtree, Warren T
1 *Sudden thunder* (1981)
2 *Night of the Apache* (1981)
3 *Blood on the moon* (1981)
4 *Widow Creek* (1982)
5 *Valley of golden tombs* (1982)
6 *Spirit woman war* (1982)
7 *Dark angel riding* (1982)
8 *Death of Iron Horse* (1983)
9 *Windwolf* (1983)
10 *Shoshone run* (1983)
11 *Comanche peak* (1983)
12 *Petticoat express* (1984)
13 *Power pole* (1984)
14 *Stone warriors* (1984)
15 *Cheyenne moon* (1984)
16 *High vengeance* (1984)
17 *Drum roll* (1984)
18 *Riverboat queen* (1985)
19 *Frenchman's Pass* (1985)
20 *Sonora badman* (1985)
21 *Denver duchess* (1985)
22 *Opium queen* (1985)
23 *Death hunters* (1985)
24 *Flame river* (1986)
25 *Jack of diamonds* (1986)
26 *Twisted arrow* (1986)
27 *Thunder riders* (1986)
28 *Lady was an outlaw* (1986)

Ruff series
Oppenheim, Edward Phillips
see **Peter Ruff series**

Rufty Tufty series
Ainsworth, Ruth
1 *Rufty Tufty the golliwog* (1952)
2 *Rufty Tufty at the seaside* (1954)
3 *Rufty Tufty goes camping* (1956)
4 *Rufty Tufty runs away* (1957)
5 *Rufty Tufty flies high* (1959)
6 *Rufty Tufty's island* (1960)
7 *Rufty Tufty and Hattie* (1962)
8 *Rufty Tufty makes a house* (1965)

Rufus and Christopher series
Hastings, Ian
1 *Rufus and Christopher and the box of laughter* (1972)
2 *Rufus and Christopher in the land of lies* (1972)
3 *Rufus and Christopher and the magic bubble* (1973)
Co-author: Eileen Hastings

Rufus Deville series
Noy, John
1 *Red Devil of the Air Police* (1937)
2 *Great airways plot* (1938)
3 *Gangsters of the air* (1938)
4 *Mystery of the Crested Falcon* (1939)

Rufus series
Herbert, Roy
1 *Rufus Tractor* (1961)
2 *Rufus rolls on* (1964)

Rug series
Cresswell, Helen
Illustrated by Susanna Gretz
1 *Rug is a bear* (1968)
2 *Rug plays tricks* (1968)
3 *Rug plays ball* (1969)
4 *Rug and a picnic* (1969)

Rugger series
Thurston, Robert
1 *For the silvership* (1985)
2 *In justice's prison* (1985)

Ruggles family series
Garnett, Eve
1 *Family from One End Street* (1937)
2 *Further adventures of the family from One End Street* (1956)
3 *Holiday at Dew-Drop Inn* (1962)

Ruggles series
Tufts, Warren
see **Casey Ruggles series**

Rulers of Africa series
Gann, Lewis Henry
1 *Rulers of German Africa, 1884-1914* (1977)
2 *Rulers of British Africa, 1870-1914* (1978)
3 *Rulers of Belgian Africa, 1884-1914* (1979)

Rulers of Hylor trilogy
Wilder, Cherry
1 *Princess of the Chameln* (1984)
2 *Yorath the wolf* (1984)
3 *Summer's king* (1986)

Rummidge University series
Lodge, David
1 *Changing places* (1975)
2 *Small world* (1985)
3 *Nice work* (1989)

Rumpole series
Mortimer, John
see **Horace Rumpole series**

Runaway series
Irvine, Lucy
1 *Runaway* (1986)
2 *Castaway* (1983)

Runestaff series
Moorcock, Michael
see **History of Runestaff series**

Runesword series
This sequence has six authors
Emery, Clayton
1 *Outcasts* (1990)
Estes, Rose
2 *Skryling's blade* (1990)
Rivkin, J F
3 *Dreamstone* (1991)
Billias, Stephen
4 *Horrible humes* (1991)
Acres, Mark
5 *Dark divide* (1991)

Running out series
Levy, Elizabeth
1 *Running out of time* (1980)
2 *Running out of magic, with Houdini* (1981)

Running series
Lane, Maxie
1 *Running!* (1977)
2 *Sea-running* (1978)

Running tide series
Roberts, Cynthia S
1 *Running tide* (1988)
2 *Upon stormy downs* (1988)

Runs-in-Light and Raven Hunter series
Gear, William Michael
see **People series**

Runs in the sun series
Parks, Jim
Memoirs of cricket
1 *Runs in the sun* (1961)
2 *Time to hit out* (1967)

Rupert Bear series
This sequence has four authors
Tourtel, Mary
1 *Adventures of Rupert the Little Lost Bear* (1921)
2 *Little Bear and the fairy child* (1921)
3 *Margot the midget* (1922)
Also contains *The Little Bear's Christmas*
4 *Little Bear and the ogres* (1922)
5 *Rupert Little Bear's adventures, volume 1* (1924)
Contains *Rupert and the magic toy man, Rupert and the princess, Rupert at school, Rupert and the old miser*
6 *Rupert Little Bear's adventures, volume 2* (1924)
Contains *Rupert and the magic key, Rupert and the brigands, Rupert and Reynard Fox, Rupert in Dreamland*
7 *Rupert Little Bear's adventures, volume 3* (1925)
Contains *Rupert and the robber wolf, Rupert and the dragon, Rupert and the snowman, Rupert at the seaside*
8 *Rupert and the enchanted princess* (1928)
9 *Rupert and the black dwarf* (1928)
10 *Rupert and his pet monkey* (1928)
11 *Rupert and his friend Margot* (1928)
Also contains *Rupert, Margot and the fairies*
12 *Rupert in the wood of mystery* (1929)
13 *Further adventures of Rupert and his pet monkey* (1929)
Also contains *Rupert and the stolen apples*
14 *Rupert and the three robbers* (1929)
15 *Rupert, the knight and the lady* (1929)
Also contains *Rupert and the wise goat's birthday cake*
16 *Rupert and the circus clown* (1929)
17 *Rupert and the magic hat* (1929)
18 *Rupert and the little prince* (1930)
19 *Rupert and King Pippin* (1930)
20 *Rupert and the wilful princess* (1930)
21 *Rupert's mysterious flight* (1930)
22 *Rupert in trouble again* (1930)
Also contains *Rupert and the fancy dress party*
23 *Rupert and the wooden soldiers* (1930)
Also contains *Rupert's Christmas adventure*
24 *Rupert and the old man of the sea* (1931)
25 *Rupert and Algy at Hawthorne Farm* (1931)
26 *Rupert and the magic whistle* (1931)
27 *Rupert gets stolen* (1931)
28 *Rupert and the wonderful boots* (1931)
29 *Rupert and the Christmas tree fairies* (1931)
Also contains *Rupert and Bill Badger's picnic party*
30 *Rupert and his pet monkey again* (1932)
Also contains Beppo back with Rupert
31 *Rupert's latest adventure* (1932)
32 *Rupert and Prince Humpty-Dumpty* (1932)
33 *Rupert's holiday adventure* (1932)
Also includes *Rupert's message to Father Christmas, and Rupert's New Year's Eve party*
34 *Rupert's Christmas tree* (1932)
Also contains *Rupert's picnic party*
35 *Rupert, the witch and Tabitha* (1933)
36 *Rupert goes hiking* (1933)
37 *Rupert and Wily Wispe* (1933)
38 *Rupert, Margot and the bandits* (1933)
39 *Rupert and Bill keep shop* (1933)
Also contains *Rupert's Christmas thrills*
40 *Rupert and Algernon* (1934)
Also contains *Rupert and the white dove*
41 *Rupert and Dapple* (1934)
42 *Rupert and Bill's aeroplane adventure* (1934)
43 *Rupert and the magician's umbrella* (1934)
44 *Rupert and Bill and the pirates* (1935)
45 *Rupert at the seaside* (1935)
Also contains *Rupert and Bingo*
46 *Rupert gets captured* (1935)
Also contains *Rupert and the snow babe's Christmas*
47 *Rupert, the manikin and the black knight* (1935)
48 *Rupert and the greedy princess* (1935)
49 *Rupert and Bill's seaside holiday* (1936)
Also contains *Rupert and the twins' birthday*
50 *Rupert and Edward and the circus* (1936)

51 *Rupert story book* (1938)
52 *Rupert again* (1940)
53 *Rupert Little Bear, more stories* (1945)
54 *Rupert and the wonderful boots* (1946)
Bestall, Alfred
55 *Rupert and Uncle Bruno* (1949)
56 *Rupert and Rollo* (1949)
57 *Rupert and the wrong presents* (1950)
58 *Rupert and the black moth* (1950)
59 *Rupert and the little plane* (1950)
60 *Rupert and the snow man* (1950)
61 *Rupert and the wicked uncle* (1951)
62 *Rupert and the new rose* (1951)
63 *Rupert and the stray puppy* (1951)
64 *Rupert and the little tree* (1952)
65 *Rupert and Neddy* (1952)
66 *Rupert and the Swan Lake* (1952)
67 *Rupert in the tree tops* (1952)
68 *Rupert and the rocking horse* (1953)
69 *Rupert and the boy pirate* (1953)
70 *Rupert and the double dream* (1953)
71 *Rupert and the seaside holiday* (1953)
72 *Rupert and the space ship* (1954)
73 *Rupert and the wild goose chase* (1954)
74 *Rupert and the lost railway* (1954)
75 *Rupert and the holiday ship* (1954)
76 *Rupert and the snow sports* (1955)
77 *Rupert and the birthday surprise* (1955)
78 *Rupert and the French poodles* (1955)
79 *Rupert and the seaside mystery* (1955)
80 *Rupert and the happy wish* (1956)
81 *Rupert and the bottled moonbeams* (1956)
82 *Rupert and the giant's castle* (1956)
83 *Rupert and the snow pranks* (1957)
84 *Rupert's summer adventure* (1957)
85 *Rupert's winter adventure* (1957)
86 *Rupert and Dickory Dock* (1960)
87 *Rupert and the pink kitten* (1960)
88 *Rupert and the flying chariot* (1971)
89 *Rupert and Raggerty* (1971)
90 *Rupert and the pirates* (1972)
91 *Rupert and the carved stick* (1976)
92 *Rupert and the black moth* (1976)
93 *Rupert and the blue mountain* (1976)
94 *Rupert and the jumping fish* (1976)
95 *Rupert and the young dragon* (1976)
96 *Rupert and the mystery voice* (1976)
Chaplain, Frederick
97 *Rupert and the muddled magic* (1977)
98 *Rupert and Podgy's picnic day* (1977)
99 *Rupert and the hidden lake* (1977)
100 *Rupert and the swift journey* (1977)
101 *Rupert and the strange kingdom* (1977)
102 *Rupert and the lonely bird* (1977)
Collis, Len
103 *Rupert and the Nutwood well* (1986)
104 *Rupert and the wobbly witch* (1986)
105 *Rupert and the trouble with Big Ben* (1986)
106 *Rupert and the Christmas crackers* (1986)
107 *Rupert and the bit of magic* (1986)
108 *Rupert and the yellow elephant* (1986)
109 *Rupert and the funny joke man* (1986)
110 *Rupert and the Chocolate Buttons Gang* (1986)
111 *Rupert and the Nutwood stage* (1986)
112 *Rupert and the smugglers' gold* (1986)
113 *Rupert and the miser's hoard* (1986)
114 *Rupert and the haunted house* (1986)
115 *Rupert and the pirates' den* (1986)
116 *Rupert and the seven keys* (1986)
117 *Rupert and the secret trail* (1986)
118 *Rupert and the mystery moor* (1986)
119 *Rupert and the secret treasure* (1986)

Rupert Bradley series
Ronald, E B
1 *Cat and Fiddle murders* (1954)
2 *Death by proxy* (1956)
3 *Sort of madness* (1958)

Rupert Campbell-Black series
Cooper, Jilly
1 *Riders* (1985)
2 *Rivals* (1988)
Players

Rupert Conway series
Leather, Edwin
1 *Vienna elephant* (1977)
2 *Mozart score* (1977)
3 *Duveen letter* (1980)

Rupert Hambledon series
Dellbridge, John
1 *Searchlight on Hambledon* (1947)
2 *Lady in the wood* (1950)

Rupert Inglis and Charles Lilburne series
Walder, David
see **Charles Lilburne and Rupert Inglis series**

Rupert of the Rhine series
Hunter, Joan
1 *Rupert the devil* (1976)
Cavalier woman
2 *Cavalier* (1977)

Rupert Quinn series
Williams, Alan
1 *Long run south* (1962)
2 *Barbouze* (1963)
False beards

Rupert Royce series
Aldridge, James
1 *Captive in the land* (1962)
2 *Statesman's game* (1966)

Rupert series
D'Oyley, Elizabeth
see **Prince Rupert series**

Rupert TV playbook series
Wells, Mick
1 *Rupert and the postman* (1975)
2 *Rupert goes to the moon* (1975)
3 *Rupert and the magician's hat* (1975)
4 *Rupert and the blue mist* (1975)
5 *Rupert's Christmas cards* (1975)

Rural rides series
Day, James Wentworth
1 *Farming adventure* (1943)
2 *Harvest adventure* (1946)
3 *Coastal adventure* (1949)
4 *Marshland adventure* (1950)
5 *Broadland adventure* (1951)

Rusalka series
Cherryh, Carolyn Janice
1 *Rusalka* (1989)
2 *Chernevog* (1990)
3 *Yvgenie* (1991)

Rusby series
Markham, Virgil
see **Myles Rusby series**

Rush Henry series
Barry, Joe
1 *Third degree* (1943)
2 *Fall guy* (1945)
3 *Triple cross* (1946)
4 *Clean up* (1947)
5 *Pay-off* (1953)

Rush series
Grant-Adamson, Lesley
see **Jim Rush series**

Rushton boys series
Davenport, Spencer
1 *Rushton boys at Rally Hall* (1916)
Alternative title: Great days in school and out
2 *Rushton boys at Treasure Cove* (1916)
Alternative title: The missing oaken chest
3 *Rushton boys in the saddle* (1916)
Alternative title: The ghost of the plains

Rushton series
Russell, Robert
see **Doctor Steven Rushton series**
Teed, George Hamilton
see **Grant Rushton series**

Ruskin and Effie Gray series
Lutyens, Mary
see **Effie Gray series**

Russ Tobin series
Morgan, Stanley
1 *Sewing machine man* (1968)
2 *Debt collector* (1970)
3 *Courier* (1971)
4 *Come again courier* (1972)
5 *Tobin takes off* (1973)
6 *Tobin on safari* (1973)
7 *Tobin in paradise* (1974)
8 *Tobin in trouble* (1974)
9 *Tobin for hire* (1975)
10 *Tobin in Las Vegas* (1975)
11 *Tobin in Tahiti* (1976)
12 *Tobin down under* (1976)
13 *Here comes Tobin* (1977)
14 *Russ Tobin up tight* (1977)
15 *Russ Tobin in Hollywood* (1978)
Companion volume: *The Russ Tobin bedside guide to smoother seduction*, 1977

Russel Wren series
Berger, Thomas
1 *Who is Teddy Villanova?* (1977)
2 *Nowhere* (1985)

Russell and Leslie Stevens series
Davidson, Linda
see **Endless summer series**

Russell Cavendish series
Cooper, Charles
1 *Reflected glory* (1934)
2 *Hong Kong mystery* (1938)

Russell Jones series
Mundy, Max
1 *Pagan pagoda* (1965)
2 *Death cries ole* (1966)

Russell series
Baker, Richard Merriam
see **Franklin Russell series**
Fitzgerald, Nigel
see **Alan Russell series**
Haggard, William
see **Colonel Charles Russell series**

Russell series
Hurwitz, Johanna
1 *Rip-Roaring Russell* (1983)
2 *Russell rides again* (1985)
3 *Russell sprouts* (1987)
4 *Russell and Elisa* (1989)

Russell series
Jameson, Storm
see **Hervey Russell series**
Tunis, John Roberts
see **Spike Russell series**
Yarbro, Chelsea Quinn
see **Sheriff Jason Russell series**

Russell Teed series
Montrose, David
1 *Crime on Cote des Nieges* (1951)
2 *Murder over Dorval* (1952)

Russell trilogy
Jameson, Storm
see **Triumph of time trilogy**

Russell V Chillders series
Sherman, Jory
see **Doctor Russell V Chillders series**

Russia series
Fen, Elisaveta
1 *Russian childhood* (1961)
2 *Girl grew up in Russia* (1970)
3 *Remember Russia, 1915-1925* (1973)

Russian family chronicle series
Aksakov, Sergei Timofeevich
Translated from the Russian
1 *Years of childhood* (1856)
2 *Russian schoolboy* (1858)
3 *Russian gentleman* (1856)

Russian history series
Orenburgsky, Sergei Gussiev
Translated from the Russian
1 *Land of the fathers* (1925)
2 *Land of the children* (1928)

Russian quartet
Thomas, Donald Michael
1 *Ararat* (1983)
2 *Swallow* (1984)
3 *Sphinx* (1986)
4 *Summit* (1987)

Russian Revolution series
Plowman, Stephanie
see **Alexei Hamilton series**

Russian Revolution series
Solzhenitsyn, Alexander
1 *August 1914* (1971)
2 *Lenin in Zurich* (1975)

Russian series
Konrad, Klaus
1 *First blood* (1980)
2 *March on Moscow* (1980)
3 *Front swine* (1982)

Russian tragedy series
Piccard, Eulalie
see **Episodes of the great Russian tragedy series**

Russian wife series
Matthews, Tanya
Autobiography
Russian child and Russian wife (1949)
Journey between freedoms
2 *Russian wife goes west* (1955)

Russo-Japanese War series
Strang, Herbert
1 *Kobo* (1904)
2 *Brown of Moukden* (1905)
Jack Brown in China
Jack Brown, the hero

Rustic series
Roberts, Cecil
Reminiscences of English life and country wanderings
1 *Gone rustic* (1934)
2 *Gone rambling* (1935)
3 *Gone afield* (1936)
4 *Gone sunwards* (1936)

Rusty and Peter series
Barrington, G W
1 *Broken voyage* (1958)
2 *Desert ghost* (1959)

Rusty Hines series
Nickson, Arthur
1 *No star for the deputy* (1957)
2 *Rusty Hines hits the trail* (1958)
3 *Rusty Hines, troubleshooter* (1959)

Rusty Hines series

4 *Dust was his shroud* (1960)
5 *Guns blaze at noon* (1960)
6 *Bounty hunter's trail* (1961)
7 *Lone killer* (1961)
8 *Arizona gun feud* (1962)
9 *Two deputies came riding* (1963)
10 *Gunfight at Nolan's Canyon* (1963)
11 *Arizona hideout* (1964)
12 *Gun trail* (1964)

Rusty McCade series
Kester, Ken
see **Steve McCade series**

Rusty Mason series
Plant, Jack
1 *Spy trail to danger* (1962)
2 *League of the Purple Dagger* (1963)

Rusty series
Sterrett, Frances Roberta
1 *Rusty of the tall pines* (1928)
2 *Rusty of the high towers* (1929)
3 *Rusty of the mountain peaks* (1930)
4 *Rusty of the meadow lands* (1931)

Ruth Darrow series
Wirt, Mildred Augustine
1 *Ruth Darrow in the Air Derby* (1930)
Alternative title: Recovering the silver trophy
2 *Ruth Darrow in the fire patrol* (1930)
Alternative title: Capturing the Redwood thieves
3 *Ruth Darrow in Yucatan* (1931)
4 *Ruth Darrow in the coast guard* (1931)

Ruth Erskine series
Pansy
1 *Ruth Erskine's crosses* (1879)
2 *Judge Burnham's daughters* (1888)
3 *Ruth Erskine's son* (1907)

Ruth Fielding series
Emerson, Alice B
1 *Ruth Fielding of the Red Mill* (1913)
Alternative title: Jasper Parloe's secret
2 *Ruth Fielding at Briarwood Hall* (1913)
Alternative title: Solving the campus mystery
3 *Ruth Fielding at snow camp* (1913)
Alternative title: Lost in the backwoods
4 *Ruth Fielding at Lighthouse Point* (1913)
Alternative title: Nita, the girl castaway
5 *Ruth Fielding at Silver Ranch* (1913)
Alternative title: Schoolgirls among the cowboys
6 *Ruth Fielding on Cliff Island* (1915)
Alternative title: The old hunter's treasure box
7 *Ruth Fielding at Sunrise farm* (1915)
Alternative title: What became of the Ruby orphans?
8 *Ruth Fielding and the gypsies* (1915)
Alternative title: The missing pearl necklace
9 *Ruth Fielding in moving pictures* (1916)
Alternative title: Gelping the dormitory fund
10 *Ruth Fielding down in Dixie* (1916)
Alternative title: Great days in the land of cotton
11 *Ruth Fielding at college* (1917)
Alternative title: The missing examination papers
12 *Ruth Fielding in the saddle* (1917)
Alternative title: College girls in the land of gold
13 *Ruth Fielding in the Red Cross* (1918)
Alternative title: Doing her best for uncle Sam
14 *Ruth Fielding at the War Front* (1918)
Alternative title: The hunt for the lost soldier
15 *Ruth Fielding homeward bound* (1919)
Alternative title: A Red Cross worker's ocean perils
16 *Ruth Fielding down East* (1920)
Alternative title: The hermit of Beach Plum Point
17 *Ruth Fielding in the great Northwest* (1921)
Alternative title: The Indian girl star of the movies
18 *Ruth Fielding on the Saint Lawrwnce* (1922)
Alternative title: The queer old man of the Thousand Islands
19 *Ruth Fielding treasure hunting* (1923)
Alternative title: A moving picture that became real
20 *Ruth Fielding in the Far North* (1924)
Alternative title: The lost motion picture company
21 *Ruth Fielding at Golden Pass* (1925)
Alternative title: The perils of an artificial avalanche
22 *Ruth Fielding in Alaska* (1926)
Alternative title: The miners of Snow Mountain
23 *Ruth Fielding and her great scenario* (1927)
Alternative title: Striving for the motion picture prize
24 *Ruth Fielding at Cameron Hall* (1928)
Alternative title: A mysterious disappearance
25 *Ruth Fielding clearing her name* (1929)
Alternative title: The rivals of Hollywood
26 *Ruth Fielding in talking pictures* (1930)
Alternative title: The prisoners of the Tower
27 *Ruth Fielding and Baby Jane* (1931)
28 *Ruth Fielding and her double* (1932)
29 *Ruth Fielding and her greatest triumph* (1933)
Alternative title: Saving her company from disaster
30 *Ruth Fielding and her crowning victory* (1934)
Alternative title: Winning honors abroad

Ruth Hollis series
Peyton, K M
1 *Fly-by-Night* (1968)
2 *Team* (1975)

Ruth series
Calisher, Hortense
1 *False entry* (1961)
2 *New Yorkers* (1969)

Ruth series
Newte, Horace Wykeham Can
1 *Ruth, the woman who loved* (1916)
2 *He whom I follow* (1917)

Ruth series
Vander Els, Betty
1 *Bombers moon* (1985)
2 *Leaving point* (1987)

Rutherford and Anthea series
Ley, Alice Chetwynd
see **Justin Rutherford and Anthea series**

Rutherford series
De Selincourt, Aubrey
1 *Family afloat* (1940)
2 *Three green bottles* (1941)
3 *One good Tern* (1943)
4 *One more summer* (1944)
5 *Calicut lends a hand* (1946)

Rutherford series
Leslie, Norman
see **Jumbo Rutherford series**
Mathews, Joanna Hooe
see **Uncle Rutherford series**
Warner, Susan Bagert
see **Mister Rutherford series**
White, William Hale
see **Mark Rutherford series**

Ruthy and Ruby series
Paull, Minnie E
see **Ruby and Ruthy series**

Rutter series
Garnett, Richard
see **Mark Rutter series**

Ruyland family series
Adams, Samuel Hopkins
1 *Siege* (1924)
2 *Piper's fee* (1926)

Ryan, McKay and Knowlton series
Friel, Arthur Olney
see **McKay, Knowlton and Ryan series**

Ryan series
Bower, Bertha Muzzy
see **Casey Ryan series**
Carlson, Patricia McEvoy
see **Maggie Ryan series**
Clancy, Tom
see **Jack Ryan series**
Cleeve, Brian
see **Sean Ryan series**
Dugon, Nora
see **Kelly Ryan series**
Ernst, Paul
see **Jim Ryan series**
Greeley, Andrew Moran
see **Monsignor John Blackwood Ryan series**
Lenehan, John Christopher
see **Charlie Ryan series**
Leonard, Elmore
see **Frank Ryan series**
Martin, Larry Jay
see **John Clinton Ryan series**
Morgan, Michael
see **Bill Ryan series**
Scherf, Margaret
see **Lieutenant Ryan series**

Ryddelton series
Stevenson, Dorothy Emily
1 *Celia's house* (1943)
2 *Listening valley* (1944)

Ryder Hook series
Zetford, Tully
1 *Whirlpool of stars* (1974)
2 *Boosted man* (1974)
3 *Star city* (1974)
4 *Virility gene* (1975)

Ryder series
Boyles, William
see **Bounty Hunter series**
Footman, Robert
see **Harry Ryder series**
McGill, Jerry
see **Red Ryder series**
Rutherford, Douglas
see **Chequered flag series**
Watson, Henry Brereton Marriott
see **Dick Ryder series**
Weston, Cole
see **Andrew Ryder series**

Ryderbeit series
Johns, Larry
see **Jacky Ryderbeit series**

Rye series
Hogan, Ray
see **Doomsday Marshal series**
Spain, John
see **Bill Rye series**

Rye Town series
Rawson, Maud Stepney
1 *Tales of Rye Town* (1905)
2 *Adventures at Rye Town* (1925)

Ryeminster Hospital series
Ferrari, Ivy
1 *Sister at Ryeminster* (1963)
2 *Nurse at Ryeminster* (1964)
3 *Doctor at Ryeminster* (1964)
4 *Almoner at Ryeminster* (1965)

Ryker series
Demille, Nelson
see **Joe Ryker series**

Ryland series
Riggs, John Raymond
see **Garth Ryland series**

Ryne Lanark series
Robertson, Stephen
1 *Decoy* (1989)
2 *Blood tells* (1989)
3 *Blood ties* (1990)
4 *Handyman* (1990)

Ryng series
Taylor, Charles Doonan
see **Bernie Ryng series**

Ryott series
Rhodes, Kathlyn
see **Martin Ryott series**

Ryvet series
Carnac, Carol
see **Inspector Ryvet series**

S

S.A.S. series
Albany, James
1 *Warrior caste* (1982)
2 *Mailed fist* (1982)
3 *Deacon's dagger* (1982)
4 *Close combat* (1983)
5 *Marching fire* (1983)
6 *Last bastion* (1984)
7 *Borneo story* (1984)

S-Com series
White, Steve
1 *Terror in Turin* (1981)
2 *Stars and swastikas* (1981)
3 *Battle in Botswana* (1982)
4 *Fighting Irish* (1982)
5 *King of Kingston* (1982)
6 *Sierra death dealers* (1982)

S.O.E. series
Crisp, Jack H
see **Special Operations Executive series**

S.T.U.D. series
Paul, F W
see **Man from S.T.U.D. series**

Sabat series
Smith, Guy Newman
1 *Graveyard vultures* (1982)
2 *Blood merchants* (1982)
3 *Cannibal cult* (1982)
4 *Druid connection* (1983)

Sabata series
Fox, Brian
1 *Sabata* (1970)
2 *Return of Sabata* (1972)

Sabazel trilogy
Carl, Lillian Stewart
1 *Sabazel* (1985)
2 *Winter king* (1986)
3 *Shadow dancers* (1987)

Saber and Rockwell series
Linzee, David
see **Sarah Saber and Chris Rockwell series**

Saber series
Holt, Gavin
see **Inspector Joel Saber series**

Sabin series
Oppenheim, Edward Phillips
see **Mister Sabin series**

Sabine Stroheim and Griffin Moss trilogy
Bantock, Nick
see **Griffin Moss and Sabine Stroheim trilogy**

Sable ivory series
Rockman, Clint
1 *Black queen* (1971)
2 *Black slaver* (1972)
3 *Black ivory* (1972)
4 *Sable Diana* (1973)
5 *Sable adventure* (1974)
6 *Sable mistress* (1974)

Sabo series
Lewis, E W
Originally broadcast on 2LO
1 *Adventures of Sabo* (1924)
2 *More Sabo stories* (1924)

Sabotage series
Finkel, George
1 *Stranded duck* (1973)
2 *Operation Aladdin* (1976)

Sabre family series
Darby, Catherine
1 *Sabre* (1985)
2 *Sabre's child* (1985)
3 *Silken sabre* (1985)
4 *House of Sabre* (1986)
5 *Breed of Sabre* (1987)
6 *Morning of a Sabre* (1987)
7 *Fruit of the Sabre* (1987)
8 *Gentle Sabre* (1988)

Sabrehill series
Giles, Raymond
1 *Sabrehill* (1974)
2 *Slaves of Sabrehill* (1975)
3 *Rebels of Sabrehill* (1976)
4 *Storm over Sabrehill* (1978)
5 *Hellcat of Sabrehill* (1983)

Sabrina Verrick series
McBain, Laurie
1 *Moonstruck madness* (1977)
2 *Chance the winds of fortune* (1980)

Sac Prairie series
Derleth, August
1 *Place of hawks* (1935)
Short stories
2 *Still is the summer night* (1937)
3 *Wind over Wisconsin* (1938)
4 *Any day now* (1938)
Short stories
5 *Restless is the river* (1939)
6 *Evening in spring* (1941)
7 *Village year* (1941)
A Sac Prairie journal
8 *Sweet Genevieve* (1942)
9 *Shadow of night* (1943)
10 *Shield of the valiant* (1945)
11 *Village daybook* (1947)
A Sac Prairie journal; numbers 1, 7, 9, 11 also published in one volume entitled *Wisconsin earth*, 1948
12 *Sac Prairie people* (1948)
Short stories
13 *House of moonlight* (1953)
Short stories
14 *Wisconsin in their bones* (1961)
Short stories
15 *Countryman's journal* (1963)
16 *Wisconsin country* (1965)
A Sac Prairie journal

Sackett family series
L'Amour, Louis
1 *Sackett's land* (1974)
2 *To the far blue mountains* (1976)
3 *Warrior's path* (1980)
4 *Jubal Sackett* (1985)
5 *Ride the river* (1983)
6 *Daybreakers* (1960)
7 *Sackett* (1961)
8 *Lando* (1962)
Numbers 6-8 also published in one volume entitled *The Sacketts, beginning of a dynasty*, 1976
9 *Mojave Crossing* (1964)
10 *Sackett brand* (1965)
11 *Lonely men* (1969)
12 *Treasure Mountain* (1972)
13 *Mustang man* (1966)
14 *Galloway* (1970)
15 *Sky-liners* (1967)
16 *Man from Broken Hills* (1975)
17 *Ride the dark trail* (1972)
18 *Lonely on the mountain* (1980)
Also a short story *Booty from a badman*, in *War party*, 1975

Sackville Street series
Gogarty, Oliver St John
1 *As I was going down Sackville Street* (1937)
A phantasy in fact
2 *Tumbling in the hay* (1939)
3 *Going native* (1941)
4 *Rolling down the lea* (1950)
5 *It isn't this time of year at all!* (1954)
An unpremeditated autobiography

Sacred journey series
Buechner, Frederick
Autobiography
1 *Sacred journey* (1982)
2 *Now and then* (1983)

Sacred stones series
Caldecott, Moyra
1 *Tall stones* (1977)
2 *Temple of the sun* (1977)
3 *Shadow on the stones* (1978)
Numbers 1-3 also published in one volume entitled *Guardians of the tall stones*, 1986
4 *Silver vortex* (1987)

Sad Sontag series
Tuttle, Wilbur Coleman
1 *Sad Sontag plays his hunch* (1926)
Sontag of Sundown
2 *Sontag of Sundown* (1929)
3 *Wild Horse Valley* (1938)
4 *Gold at K-bar-T* (1961)
5 *Galloping gold* (1961)

Saddle boys series
Carson, James
1 *Saddle boys of the Rockies* (1913)
Alternative title: Lost on Thunder Mountain
2 *Saddle boys in the Grand Canyon* (1913)
Alternative title: The hermit of the cave
3 *Saddle boys on the plains* (1913)
Alternative title: After a treasure of gold
4 *Saddle boys at Circle Ranch* (1913)
Alternative title: In at the grand round-up
5 *Saddle boys on Mexican trails* (1915)
Alternative title: In the hands of the enemy

Saddle Club series
Bryant, Bonnie
1 *Horse crazy* (1988)
2 *Horse shy* (1988)
3 *Horse sense* (1989)
Number 4 not identified
5 *Trail mates* (1989)
6 *Dude ranch* (1989)
7 *Horse play* (1989)
8 *Horse show* (1989)
9 *Hoofbeat* (1990)
10 *Riding camp* (1990)
11 *Horse wise* (1990)
12 *Rodeo rider* (1990)
13 *Starlight Christmas* (1990)
14 *Sea horse* (1991)
15 *Team play* (1991)
16 *Horse games* (1991)
17 *Horsenapped!* (1991)
18 *Pack trip* (1991)
19 *Star rider* (1991)
20 *Snow ride* (1992)
Number 21 not identified
22 *Fox hunt* (1992)
23 *Horse trouble* (1992)
24 *Ghost rider* (1992)
25 *Show horse* (1992)
26 *Beach ride* (1993)
27 *Bridle path* (1993)
28 *Stable manners* (1993)
29 *Ranch hands* (1993)
30 *Autumn trail* (1993)
31 *Hayride* (1993)
32 *Chocolate horse* (1994)
33 *High horse* (1994)
34 *Hay fever* (1994)
35 *Horse tale* (1994)
36 *Riding lesson* (1994)
37 *Stage coach* (1994)
38 *Horse trade* (1994)
39 *Pure bred* (1994)

Saddle up series
Dubrovin, Vivian
1 *Better bit and bridle* (1975)
2 *Chance to win* (1975)
3 *Trailering troubles* (1975)
4 *Open the gate* (1975)

Saddler series
Curry, Gene
see **Jim Saddler series**

Saddletramp series
Hawkins, Clint
1 *Saddletramp* (1992)
2 *Captive* (1992)
3 *Gunpowder trail* (1992)
4 *Gold and lead* (1993)
5 *Bandit's blood* (1993)
6 *Sioux trail* (1993)
Number 7 not identified
8 *Death rides in Texas* (1994)

Sader series
Hitchens, Dolores
see **Jim Sader series**

Sadie and Kevin series
Lingard, Joan
1 *Twelfth day of July* (1970)
2 *Across the barricades* (1972)
3 *Into exile* (1973)
4 *Proper place* (1975)
5 *Hostages to fortune* (1976)

Sadie Rose series
Stahl, Hilda
1 *Sadie Rose and the daring escape* (1988)
2 *Sadie Rose and the Cottonwood Creek orphan* (1989)
3 *Sadie Rose and the outlaw rustlers* (1989)
4 *Sadie Rose and the double secret* (1990)
5 *Sadie Rose and the mad fortune hunters* (1991)
6 *Sadie Rose and the phantom warrior* (1991)
7 *Sadie Rose and the champion sharpshooter* (1991)
8 *Sadie Rose and the secret romance* (1992)
9 *Sadie Rose and the impossible birthday wish* (1992)
10 *Sadie Rose and the dangerous search* (1993)
11 *Sadie Rose and the mysterious stranger* (1993)

Sadie Shapiro series
Smith, Robert Kimmel
1 *Sadie Shapiro's knitting book* (1973)
2 *Sadie Shapiro in Miami* (1977)
3 *Sadie Shapiro, matchmaker* (1979)

Sadie Spider series
Edwards, Pat
1 *Sadie Spider* (1987)
2 *Sadie Spider strikes again* (1987)
3 *Sadie Spider moves in* (1990)
4 *Sadie Spider goes to school* (1990)

Sadler's Wells series
Hill, Lorna
1 *Dream of Sadler's Wells* (1950)
2 *Veronica at the Wells* (1951)
Veronica at Sadler's Wells
3 *Masquerade at the Wells* (1952)
Masquerade at the ballet
4 *No castanets at the Wells* (1953)
Castanets for Caroline
5 *Jane leaves the Wells* (1953)
6 *Ella at the Wells* (1954)
7 *Return to the Wells* (1955)
8 *Rosanna joins the Wells* (1956)
9 *Principal role* (1957)
10 *Swan feather* (1958)
11 *Dress rehearsal* (1959)
12 *Back-stage* (1960)
13 *Vicki in Venice* (1962)
14 *Secret* (1964)

Sado-masochism series
Townsend, Larry
1 *Leather Ad-M* (1969)
2 *Leather Ad-S* (1969)

Safety series
Jackson, Ellen B
1 *Earthquake safety* (1991)
2 *Household safety* (1991)
3 *Stranger danger* (1991)

Safford series
Dominic, R B
see **Congressman Ben Safford series**

Saffron series
Smith, Frederick Escreet
1 *Saffron's war* (1975)
2 *Saffron's army* (1976)

Saga of California series
Easton, Robert
1 *This promised land* (1982)
2 *Power and glory* (1989)

Saga of Cuckoo series
Pohl, Frederik
see **Cuckoo's saga series**

Saga of lost lands trilogy
Estes, Rose
1 *Blood of the tiger* (1987)
2 *Brother to the lion* (1988)
3 *Spirit of the hawk* (1988)

Saga of Noggin the Nog series
Postgate, Oliver
1 *King of the Nogs* (1968)

Saga of Noggin the Nog series

2 *Ice dragon* (1968)
3 *Flying machine* (1968)
4 *Omruds* (1969)
5 *Island* (1969)
Noggin and the island
6 *Firecake* (1969)
7 *Flowers* (1971)
Noggin and the flowers
8 *Pie* (1971)
9 *Game* (1972)
10 *Monster* (1969)
11 *Blackwash* (1975)
12 *Icebergs* (1975)
13 *Nogmania* (1977)

Saga of Pliocene exile series
May, Julian
see **Pliocene exile series**

Saga of the exiles series
May, Julian
see **Pliocene exile series**

Saga of the Sierras series
Thoeme, Brock
1 *Gold rush prodigal* (1990)
2 *Men from Shadow Ridge* (1991)
3 *Sequoia scout* (1991)
4 *Cannons of the Comstock* (1992)

Saga of Thorgrim series
Bailey, Gerald Earl
1 *Sword of the Nurlingas* (1979)
2 *Sword of Poyana* (1979)

Saga the Dane trilogy
Creswick, Paul
1 *In Alfred's days* (1900)
2 *Under the black raven* (1901)
3 *Hastings, the pirate* (1902)

Sagamore series
Dalkey, Kara
1 *Curse of Sagamore* (1986)
2 *Sword of Sagamore* (1989)

Sagard the Barbarian series
Gygax, Gary
1 *Ice dragon* (1985)
2 *Green hydra* (1985)
3 *Crimson sea* (1985)
4 *Fire demon* (1986)

Sagas of the Demonspawn series
Brennan, James Herbert
1 *Fire Wolf* (1984)
2 *Crypts of terror* (1984)
3 *Ancient evil* (1985)
4 *Demonstration* (1985)

Sagas retold series
Hewlett, Maurice
1 *Lover's tale* (1915)
2 *Frey and his wife* (1916)
3 *Thorgils of Treadholt* (1917)
4 *Gudrid the Fair* (1918)
5 *Outlaw* (1919)
6 *Light heart* (1920)

Sage series
Jenkins, Herbert
see **Malcolm Sage series**

Saigon commandos series
Cain, Jonathan
1 *Saigon commandos* (1983)
2 *Code zero, shots fired* (1984)
3 *Dinky-dau death* (1984)
4 *Cherry-boy body bag* (1984)
5 *Boonie-rat body burning* (1984)
6 *Di Di Mau or die* (1984)
7 *Sac Mau, Victor Charlie* (1985)
8 *You die, Du Ma!* (1985)
9 *Mad minute* (1985)
10 *Torturers of Tet* (1986)
11 *Hollowpoint hell* (1986)
12 *Suicide squad* (1986)

Sailing series
Calahan, Harold Augustin
1 *Learning to sail* (1932)
2 *Learning to race* (1934)
3 *Learning to cruise* (1935)

Sailor Jack series
Wassermann, Selma
1 *Sailor Jack* (1960)
2 *Sailor Jack and Bluebell* (1960)
3 *Sailor Jack's new friend* (1960)
4 *Sailor Jack and the target ship* (1960)
5 *Sailor Jack goes north* (1961)
6 *Sailor Jack and Homer Pots* (1961)
7 *Sailor Jack and Eddy* (1961)
8 *Sailor Jack and Bluebell's dive* (1961)
9 *Sailor Jack and the jet plane* (1962)
10 *Sailor Jack and the ball game* (1962)

Sailor series
Duff, Reginald Eustace Bluett
see **Hornett family series**

Sailor series
Harling, Robert
1 *Amateur sailor* (1944)
Originally published under the pseudonym Nicholas Drew
2 *Steep Atlantick stream* (1946)

Sainsbury series
Macdonnell, James Edmond
see **Commander Sainsbury series**

Saint Amand series
Teilhet, Darwin Le Ora
see **Jean Henri Saint Amand series**

Saint Angela's Hospital series
Milne, Paula
see **Angels series**

Saint Barnabas' Hospital series
Andrews, Lucilla
1 *Young doctors downstairs* (1963)
2 *New Sister Theatre* (1964)
3 *House for Sister Mary* (1966)

Saint Bernard's series
Scalpel, Aesculapius
1 *Saint Bernard's* (1887)
The romance of a medical student
2 *Dying scientifically* (1888)

Saint Camber trilogy
Kurtz, Katherine
see **Heirs of Saint Camber trilogy**

Saint Clair series
Luigi, Belli
see **Inspector Saint Clair series**

Saint Clare's series
Blyton, Enid
1 *Twins at Saint Clare's* (1941)
2 *O'Sullivan twins* (1942)
3 *Summer term at Saint Clare's* (1943)
4 *Second form at Saint Clare's* (1944)
5 *Claudine at Saint Clare's* (1944)
6 *Fifth formers at Saint Clare's* (1945)
Fifth form of Saint Clare's

Saint Cuthbert's series
Copus, John Edwin
1 *Saint Cuthbert's* (1903)
2 *Shadows lifted* (1904)

Saint-Cyr and Kohler series
Janes, Joseph Robert
see **Jean-Louis Saint-Cyr and Hermann Kohler series**

Saint Cyr series
Wallace, Ian
see **Claudine Saint Cyr series**

Saint Dunstan series
Eldred, Warren L
1 *Crimson ramblers* (1910)
2 *Camp Saint Dunstan* (1911)
3 *Classroom and campus* (1912)
4 *Saint Dunstan Boy Scouts* (1913)

Saint George Peachy and Barney Forge series
Starnes, Richard
see **Barney Forge and Doctor Saint George Peachy series**

Saint George series
Avallone, Michael
see **Satan Sleuth series**

Saint-Germain series
Yarbro, Chelsea Quinn
see **Count Ragoczy Saint-Germain series**

Saint Helen's series
Aldridge, James
see **Kit Quayle series**

Saint Ives series
Bleeck, Oliver
see **Philip Saint Ives series**

Saint James and McClary series
Macgregor, T J
see **Quin Saint James and Mike McClary series**

Saint Jim's series
Clifford, Martin
see **Tom Merry series**

Saint John series
Babula, William
1 *Saint John's Baptism* (1988)
2 *According to Saint John* (1989)
3 *Saint John and the seven veils* (1991)
4 *Saint John's bestiary* (1994)

Saint Kelvern's Bury School series
Pearce, Carol Ann
1 *We're in the sixth!* (1960)
2 *Saint Kelvern's launches out* (1962)

Saint Lawrence's Hospital series
Linton, Cathy
1 *Casualty at Saint Lawrence's* (1975)
2 *Such devoted sisters* (1975)
3 *Too many doctors* (1975)
4 *Reluctant nurse* (1975)
5 *Sister in waiting* (1976)
6 *Silver rose bowl* (1977)
7 *Sister Jackie* (1978)
8 *Houseman's wager* (1980)

Saint Mark's Hospital series
Harrison, Elizabeth
see **Central London Hospital series**

Saint Mark's Hospital series
White, Constance Mary
1 *Cadet nurse at Saint Mark's* (1958)
2 *Junior nurse at Saint Mark's* (1961)
3 *Nurse at Saint Mark's* (1963)
4 *Staff nurse at Saint Mark's* (1966)
5 *Suspect at Saint Mark's* (1972)

Saint Martha's Hospital series
Andrews, Lucilla
1 *My friend the professor* (1960)
2 *Light in the ward* (1965)
3 *Highland interlude* (1968)
4 *Healing time* (1969)
5 *Edinburgh excursion* (1970)
6 *Ring o' roses* (1972)
7 *Silent song* (1973)
8 *In storm and calm* (1975)
9 *Busman's holiday* (1977)
10 *Crystal gull* (1978)
11 *One night in London* (1979)
12 *Weekend in The Garden* (1981)
13 *In an Edinburgh drawing room* (1983)
14 *After a famous victory* (1984)
15 *Lights of London* (1985)

Saint Paul series
Berstl, Julius
1 *Tentmaker* (1951)
Original edition entitled *Paulus von Tarsus, ein Mannin zwei Welten*, part 1
2 *Cross and the eagle* (1954)
Original edition entitled *Paulus von Tarsus, ein Mannin zwei Welten*, part 2

Saint Peter series
Douglas, Lloyd Cassel
see **Apostle Peter series**

Saint Peter's Hospital series
Andrews, Jane
1 *File on Saint Peter's* (1976)
2 *Focus on Saint Peter's* (1977)
3 *Spotlight on Saint Peter's* (1978)
4 *Tension at Saint Peter's* (1979)
5 *Problem at Saint Peter's* (1980)

Saint series
This sequence has five authors
Charteris, Leslie
1 *Meet the tiger* (1928)
Saint meets the tiger
2 *Enter the Saint* (1930)
Three novelettes
3 *Last hero* (1930)
Saint closes the case
Saint and the last hero
4 *Knight Templar* (1930)
Avenging Saint
5 *Featuring the Saint* (1931)
Three novelettes
6 *Alias the Saint* (1931)
Three novelettes; Numbers 5 and 6 also published in one volume entitled *Wanted for murder*, 1931; selections: *Paging the Saint*, 1945
7 *She was a lady* (1931)
Saint meets his match
Angels of doom
8 *Holy terror* (1932)
Saint versus Scotland Yard
Three novelettes
9 *Getaway* (1932)
Saint's getaway
10 *Once more the Saint* (1933)
Saint and Mister Teal
Three novelettes entitled *The gold standard, The man from Saint Louis, The death penalty*
11 *Brighter buccaneer* (1933)
Short stories
12 *Misfortunes of Mister Teal* (1934)
Saint in London
Saint in England
13 *Boodle* (1934)
Saint intervenes
14 *Saint goes on* (1934)
Three novelettes entitled *The high fence, The elusive Ellshaw, The case of the frightened innkeeper*
15 *Saint in New York* (1935)
16 *Saint overboard* (1936)
Pirate Saint
17 *Ace of Knaves* (1937)
Saint in action
Three novelettes
18 *Thieves' picnic* (1937)
Saint bids diamonds
Saint at a thieves' picnic
19 *Prelude for war* (1938)
Saint plays with fire
20 *Follow the Saint* (1939)
Three novelettes

21 *Happy highwayman* (1939)
Selections from numbers 11, 13, 21 published as *The Saint at large*, 1943; Numbers 17 and 21 also published in one volume entitled *The Saint, two in one*, 1942
22 *Saint in Miami* (1940)
23 *Saint goes west* (1942)
Three novelettes
24 *Saint steps in* (1943)
25 *Saint on guard* (1945)
Two novelettes, including *The Saint and the sizzling saboteur*, published separately in 1956
26 *Saint sees it through* (1946)
Two novelettes, including *The Saint and the sizzling saboteur*, 1956
27 *Call for the Saint* (1948)
Two novelettes
28 *Saint errant* (1948)
Nine short stories
29 *Saint in Europe* (1953)
Seven short stories
30 *Saint on the Spanish Main* (1955)
Six short stories
31 *Saint around the world* (1956)
Six short stories
32 *Thanks to the Saint* (1957)
Six short stories
33 *Senor Saint* (1958)
Short stories
34 *Saint to the rescue* (1959)
Six short stories
35 *Trust the Saint* (1962)
Short stories
36 *Saint in the sun* (1963)
Short stories
37 *Vendetta for the Saint* (1964)
38 *Saint on TV* (1968)
Two novelettes, adapted by Fleming Lee, entitled *The death game, The power artist*
39 *Saint returns* (1968)
Two novelettes, adapted by Fleming Lee, entitled *The dizzy daughter, The gadget lovers*
40 *Saint and the fiction makers* (1969)
Two novelettes, adapted by Fleming Lee
41 *Saint abroad* (1969)
Two novelettes, adapted by Fleming Lee
42 *Saint in pursuit* (1970)
Based on a comic strip
43 *Saint and the people importers* (1971)
Adapted by Fleming Lee
44 *Saints alive* (1974)

Lee, Fleming
45 *Catch the Saint* (1975)
Two novelettes entitled *The masterpiece merchant, The adoring socialite*

Short, Christopher
46 *Saint and the Hapsburg necklace* (1976)

Bloxsom, Peter
47 *Send for the Saint* (1977)
Two novelettes

Weaver, Graham
48 *Saint in trouble* (1978)
Two novelettes entitled *The imprudent professor, The red sabbath*
49 *Saint and the Templar treasure* (1979)
50 *Count on the Saint* (1980)

Bloxsom, Peter
51 *Salvage for the Saint* (1983)

Omnibus volumes: *The first Saint omnibus*, 1939, also known as *Arrest the Saint*, 1951, *The second Saint omnibus*, 1951; selections: *Concerning the Saint*, 1958, *The Saint cleans up*, 1959, *The fantastic Saint*, 1982

Saint Simons trilogy
Price, Eugenia
1 *Lighthouse* (1971)
2 *New moon rising* (1969)
3 *Beloved invader* (1965)

Saint Timothy's School series
Pier, Arthur Stanwood
1 *Boys of Saint Timothy's* (1904)
2 *Harding of Saint Timothy's* (1906)
Originally serialized as *Harry Harding's last year*
3 *New boy* (1908)
4 *Jester of Saint Timothy's* (1911)
5 *Grannis of the Fifth* (1914)
Includes *His father's son*
6 *Dormitory days* (1919)
7 *David Ives* (1922)
8 *Friends and rivals* (1925)
9 *Boy from the West* (1930)

Saint Urbain's Street series
Richler, Mordecai
1 *Street* (1969)
2 *Saint Urbain's Horseman* (1971)

Saint Vincent Halfhyde series
McCutchan, Philip
see **Lieutenant Saint Vincent Halfhyde series**

Saint Vincent series
Rossmann, John F
see **Mind Masters series**

Sainte Monique series
Lister, Stephen
1 *Mistral Hotel* (1940)
2 *Sunset over France* (1942)
3 *Peace comes to Sainte monique* (1947)
4 *Marise* (1950)
5 *Miss Sainte Monique* (1953)
6 *Delorme in deep water* (1958)
7 *Sainte Monique roundabout* (1967)
8 *Sainte Monique unlimited* (1968)
9 *Broom* (1969)
10 *Empty valley* (1971)
11 *Hungarian roulette* (1972)
12 *Tycoon in Eden* (1973)
13 *Smell of brimstone* (1974)
14 *Dog that never was* (1975)
15 *Becky* (1976)
16 *Abominable goat* (1977)

Saintly Billy trilogy
Naughton, Bill
Autobiography based on the author's journals
1 *Saintly Billy* (1988)
A Catholic boyhood
2 *On the pig's back* (1987)
Companion volume: *A roof over your head*, 1945, revised 1967

Saints series
Barclay, Vera Charlesworth
1 *Stories of saints by candlelight* (1922)
2 *Saints by firelight* (1931)
Stories for Guides and Rangers
3 *Saints of these islands* (1931)
4 *Saints and adventurers* (1938)

Saints series
De Wohl, Louis
see **Lives of the saints series**

Saints series
Marbach, Ethel
1 *Saints in waiting* (1983)
2 *Saints for the journey* (1984)
3 *Saints for the harvest* (1985)
4 *Saints for the seasons* (1986)
One volume edition 1990

Sakaeland series
Ganpat
see **Harry Lake series**

Sal series
McCloskey, Robert
1 *Blueberries for Sal* (1948)
2 *One morning in Maine* (1952)

Salathiel Albine series
Allen, Hervey
see **Disinherited series**

Salavin series
Duhamel, Georges
1 *Confessions at midnight* (1920)
Original edition entitled *Confession de minuit*
2 *[Deux hommes]* (1927)
No English edition
3 *Salavin's journal* (1927)
Original edition entitled *Journal de Salavin*
4 *Lyonnais Club* (1929)
Original edition entitled *Club de Lyonnais*
5 *End of illusion* (1932)
Original edition entitled *Tel qu'en lui-meme*
One volume edition entitled *Salavin*, 1936

Salem quartet
Cohen, Matt
1 *Disinherited* (1974)
2 *Colours of war* (1977)
Colors of war
3 *Sweet second summer of Kitty Malone* (1979)
4 *Flowers of darkness* (1981)

Salis series
Greener, William Oliver
see **Jo Salis series**

Salisbury and Shearer series
Crawford, Robert
see **Arthur Salisbury and Frank Shearer series**

Sallis and Curzon series
Usher, Frank
see **Amanda Curzon and Oscar Sallis series**

Sallust series
Wheatley, Dennis
see **Gregory Sallust series**

Sally and Billy series
Gree, Alain
see **Keith and Sally series**

Sally and Howard Digburn series
Sanders, Bruce
see **Howard Digburn series**

Sally and Jake series
Cosgrove, Brian
Based on a television series
1 *Sally and Jake and a tortoise* (1974)
2 *Sally and Jake go to the fair* (1974)
3 *Sally and Jake on the farm* (1974)
4 *Sally and Jake play bowls* (1974)

Sally and John Heldar series
Hamilton, Henrietta
see **Johnny and Sally Heldar series**

Sally and John Strang series
Brinton, Henry
see **John and Sally Strang series**

Sally and Paul series
Iseborg, Harry
see **Paul and Sally series**

Sally and Simon series
Dicks, Terrance
see **Simon and Sally series**

Sally and Tom series
Lynam, Terence
1 *Sally and Tom and the helicopter* (1984)
2 *Sally and Tom and the digger* (1984)
3 *Sally and Tom and the tractor* (1984)
4 *Sally and Tom and the road roller* (1984)

Sally-Ann series
Breinburg, Petronella
1 *Sally-Ann's umbrella* (1976)
2 *Sally-Ann in the snow* (1977)
3 *Sally-Ann's skateboard* (1979)

Sally Ann series
Dicks, Terrance
1 *Sally Ann on her own* (1987)
2 *Sally Ann's school play* (1988)
3 *Sally Ann's picnic* (1988)
4 *Sally Ann goes to hospital* (1988)
5 *Sally Ann at the ballet* (1989)
6 *Pony* (1990)

Sally Baxter series
Edwards, Sylvia
1 *Sally Baxter, girl reporter, in Canada* (1958)
2 *Sally Baxter, girl reporter, and the mystery heiress* (1958)
3 *Sally Baxter, girl reporter, and the runaway princess* (1958)
4 *Sally Baxter, girl reporter, on location* (1958)
5 *African alibi* (1959)
6 *Holiday family* (1959)
7 *Sally Baxter, girl reporter, in Australia* (1959)
8 *Sally Baxter, girl reporter, and the underwater adventure* (1959)
9 *Festival holiday* (1960)
10 *Greek goddess* (1960)
11 *Hong Kong deadline* (1960)
12 *Lost ballerina* (1960)
13 *Sally Baxter, girl reporter, and the golden yacht* (1961)
14 *Secret island* (1961)
15 *Sally Baxter, girl reporter, on the shamrock mystery* (1961)
16 *Strangers in Fleet Street* (1961)

Sally Brimmer series
McHugh, Arona
1 *Banner with a strange device* (1964)
2 *Seacoast of Bohemia* (1965)

Sally Deenes series
Christian, Petra
1 *Hitch-hiker* (1971)
2 *New driftage* (1972)
3 *Holiday campers* (1973)
4 *Girls of the night* (1973)
5 *Sexploiters* (1973)
6 *Bust-up* (1974)
7 *Hello sailor!* (1975)
8 *In the club* (1975)

Sally Dunn trilogy
Seymour, Beatrice Kean
1 *Maids and mistresses* (1932)
2 *Interlude for Sally* (1934)
3 *Summer of life* (1936)

Sally Gopher series
Quackenbush, Robert Mead
see **Sheriff Sally Gopher series**

Sally Lockhart series
Pullman, Philip
1 *Ruby in the smoke* (1985)
2 *Shadow in the plate* (1987)
Shadow in the north
3 *Tiger in the well* (1990)
4 *Tin princess* (1994)

Sally Scatterbrain series
Bruce, Dorita Fairlie
1 *Sally Scatterbrain* (1956)
2 *Sally again* (1959)
3 *Sally's summer term* (1961)

Sally series
Carruth, Jean
see **Fun with Sally series**

Sally series
Christian, Catherine Mary
1 *Sally and the sixpenny pig* (1960)
2 *Sally joins the patrol* (1966)

Sally series
Tierney, Frank M
see **Silly Sally series**

Sally Smith series
Coatsworth, Elizabeth
1 *Away goes Sally* (1934)
2 *Five Bushel Farm* (1939)
3 *Fair American* (1940)
4 *White horse* (1942)
White horse of Morocco
5 *Wonderful day* (1946)

Sally the Sleuth series
Barreaux
Based on a comic book character
1 *What a gal, Sally the Sleuth!* (1986)
2 *Kali-flowers, Sally the Sleuth!* (1987)

Salmond series
Dundas, Lawrence
see **Andrew Salmond series**

Salomes series
Pool, Maria Louise
1 *Two Salomes* (1893)
2 *Out of step* (1894)

Salt series
Salt, Jonathan
see **Jonathan Salt series**

Salter series
Wright, Eric
see **Inspector Charlie Salter series**

Salterton trilogy
Davies, Robertson
1 *Tempest-tost* (1952)
2 *Leaven of malice* (1954)
3 *Mixture of frailties* (1958)
One volume edition entitled *The Salterton trilogy*, 1986

Saltfleet series
Wilson, Colin
see **Chief Inspector Gregory Saltfleet series**

Salty series
Westron, Charles
1 *Salty* (1919)
2 *More Salty* (1924)
3 *Salty ashore* (1929)
Companion volume: *Coombe Hamlet*, 1923

Salvation Army series
Haggard, Henry Rider
1 *Report on the Salvation Army colonies* (1905)
Poor and the land
2 *Regeneration* (1910)
An account of the social work of the Salvation Army in Great Britain

Sam and Dave series
Singer, Marilyn
1 *Leroy is missing* (1984)
2 *Case of the sabotaged school play* (1984)
3 *Clue in code* (1985)
4 *Case of the cackling car* (1985)
5 *Case of the fixed location* (1989)
6 *Hoax on you* (1989)

Sam and Kate series
Cole, Michael
see **Kate and Sam series**

Sam and Leanne series
Clark, Margaret Dianne
1 *Hold my hand, or else* (1993)
2 *Living with Leanne* (1994)

Sam and Lin series
Pullen, Alan
1 *Old house* (1965)
2 *Thing on the line* (1965)
3 *Man in the train* (1965)
4 *Black pigeon* (1965)
5 *Night in town* (1966)
6 *On the hook* (1966)
7 *Spoke in the wheel* (1966)
8 *Last straw* (1966)
9 *Over the wall* (1967)
10 *Fox Fair* (1967)
11 *River cats* (1968)
12 *Devil's Dump* (1968)

Sam and Nydia Balon series
Johnstone, William Wallace
see **Beasts series**

Sam and Tom series
Hutchins, Pat
see **Tom and Sam series**

Sam and Tripper series
Robinson, Nancy Konheim
see **Tripper and Sam series**

Sam Bawtrey series
Enefer, Douglas
1 *Pierhead 627* (1968)
2 *Thirteen steps to Lime Street* (1969)
3 *Riverside ninety* (1970)
4 *Girl in a million* (1970)
5 *Long way to Pitt Street* (1972)
6 *Girl on the M6* (1973)
7 *Lakeside zero* (1973)
8 *Jade green judy* (1974)
9 *Last train to Rock Ferry* (1975)
10 *Sixth raid* (1979)
11 *Deadly streak* (1982)
12 *Last leap* (1983)

Sam Benedict series
This sequence has four authors; based on a television series
Lee, Elsie
1 *Cast the first stone* (1963)
Oleck, Howard Leoner
2 *Singular fury* (1968)
Williams, Brad
3 *Conflict of interest* (1971)
4 *Matter of confidence* (1973)

Sam Birge series
Krasner, William
1 *Walk the dark streets* (1949)
2 *Gambler* (1950)
3 *North of Welfare* (1954)
4 *Stag party* (1957)
5 *Death of a minor poet* (1984)
6 *Resort to murder* (1985)

Sam Birkett series
Payne, Laurence
see **Chief Inspector Sam Birkett series**

Sam Boggs series
Washburn, Mark
1 *Armageddon game* (1977)
2 *Omega threat* (1980)

Sam Briggs series
Marsh, Richard
1 *Sam Briggs, his book* (1912)
Short stories
2 *Sam Briggs, VC* (1915)

Sam Briscoe series
Hamill, Pete
1 *Dirty laundry* (1979)
2 *Deadly piece* (1979)

Sam Carroll series
Leigh, Robert
1 *Cheap dream* (1982)
2 *Girl with the bright head* (1982)

Sam Clayton trilogy
Shelynn, Jack
1 *Affair at Cralla Voe* (1978)
2 *Fall of snow* (1980)
3 *Epilogue for Selena* (1980)

Sam Cragg and Johnny Fletcher series
Gruber, Frank
see **Johnny Fletcher and Sam Cragg series**

Sam Crombie series
Coxe, George Harmon
1 *Frightened fiancee* (1950)
2 *Impetuous mistress* (1958)

Sam Dakkers series
Brett, Mike
1 *Guilty bystander* (1959)
2 *Scream Street* (1959)

Sam Durell series
This sequence has two authors
Aarons, Edward Sidney
1 *Assignment to disaster* (1955)
2 *Assignment suicide* (1956)
3 *Assignment treason* (1956)
4 *Assignment Budapest* (1957)
5 *Assignment Stella Marni* (1957)
6 *Assignment Angelina* (1958)
7 *Assignment Madeleine* (1958)
8 *Assignment Carlotta Cortez* (1959)
9 *Assignment Helene* (1959)
10 *Assignment Lili Lamaris* (1959)
11 *Assignment Mara Tirana* (1960)
12 *Assignment Zoraya* (1960)
13 *Assignment Ankara* (1961)
14 *Assignment Lowlands* (1961)
15 *Assignment Burma girl* (1961)
16 *Assignment Karachi* (1962)
17 *Assignment Sorrento siren* (1963)
18 *Assignment Manchurian doll* (1963)
19 *Assignment Sulu Sea* (1964)
20 *Assignment the girl in the gondola* (1964)
21 *Assignment the Cairo dancers* (1965)
22 *Assignment Palermo* (1965)
23 *Assignment Cong Hai kill* (1966)
24 *Assignment school for spies* (1966)
25 *Assignment black Viking* (1967)
26 *Assignment moon girl* (1968)
27 *Assignment nuclear nude* (1968)
28 *Assignment Peking* (1969)
29 *Assignment star stealers* (1970)
30 *Assignment white rajah* (1970)
31 *Assignment Tokyo* (1971)
32 *Assignment Bangkok* (1972)
33 *Assignment golden girl* (1972)
34 *Assignment Maltese maiden* (1972)
35 *Assignment Ceylon* (1973)
36 *Assignment silver scorpion* (1973)
37 *Assignment Amazon queen* (1974)
38 *Assignment Sumatra* (1974)
39 *Assignment black gold* (1975)
40 *Assignment Quayle question* (1975)
41 *Assignment Afghan dragon* (1976)
42 *Assignment unicorn* (1976)
Aarons, Will B
43 *Assignment Sheba* (1976)
44 *Assignment tiger devil* (1977)
45 *Assignment thirteenth princess* (1977)
46 *Assignment mermaid* (1979)
47 *Assignment tyrant's bride* (1980)
48 *Assignment death ship* (1983)

Sam Gross series
Wohl, James Paul
1 *Nirvana contracts* (1977)
2 *Blind trust kills* (1978)

Sam Harris series
Cronin, Michael
1 *By his own hand* (1969)
2 *Proper carve-up* (1970)
3 *Black leather case* (1971)
4 *Con game* (1972)
5 *Nobody needs a corpse* (1972)
6 *Big tickle* (1974)
7 *Killing easy* (1975)
8 *Strictly private business* (1975)
9 *Final instalments* (1976)
10 *Pair of knaves* (1977)
11 *Unfinished business* (1977)
12 *Epitaph for a lady* (1980)

Sam Hilton series
Coryell, Jubert V
1 *Indian brothers* (1935)
2 *Scalp hunters* (1936)

Sam Hook series
Teilhet, Hildegarde Tolman
1 *Hero by proxy* (1942)
English edition published as by Darwin Le Ora Teilhet
2 *Double agent* (1945)
3 *Assassins* (1946)

Sam Hoskins series
Dacre, Richard
1 *Blood runs hot* (1988)
2 *Scream blue murder* (1988)

Sam Houston series
De Puy, Edward Spence
1 *Long knife* (1936)
2 *Hospital homicides* (1937)

Sam Hunter series
Morse, Larry Alan
1 *Big enchilada* (1982)
2 *Sleaze* (1985)

Sam King series
Banks, Raymond E
1 *Computer kill* (1961)
2 *Meet me in darkness* (1961)

Sam Knight series
Cohler, David Keith
1 *Gamemaker* (1980)
Blood sport
2 *Freemartin* (1981)

Sam Linkum series
Mitgang, Herbert
1 *Montauk fault* (1981)
2 *Kings in the counting house* (1983)

Sam Macclellan series
Dawlish, Peter
1 *Macclellan's lake* (1951)
2 *Bagodia episode* (1953)

Sam Marlow series
Fenady, Andrew J
1 *Man with Bogart's face* (1977)
2 *Secret of Sam Marlow* (1980)

Sam McCade series
Dietz, William Corey
1 *War world* (1986)
2 *Imperial bounty* (1988)
3 *Alien bounty* (1990)
4 *McCade's bounty* (1990)

Sam McCloud series
Wilcox, Collin
see **Marshal Sam McCloud series**

Sam Phelan series
Kyd, Thomas
1 *Blood is a beggar* (1946)
2 *Blood of vintage* (1947)
3 *Blood on the bosom devine* (1948)

Sam Pig series
Uttley, Alison
1 *Adventures of Sam Pig* (1940)
2 *Sam Pig goes to market* (1941)
3 *Six tales of Sam Pig* (1941)
4 *Sam Pig and Sally* (1942)
5 *Sam Pig at the circus* (1943)
6 *Sam Pig in trouble* (1948)
7 *Yours ever, Sam Pig* (1951)
8 *Sam Pig and the singing gate* (1955)
9 *Sam Pig goes to the seaside* (1960)
Omnibus volume entitled *The Sam Pig storybook*, 1965

Sam series
Chandler, Edna Walker
see **Cowboy Sam series**

Sam series
Eadington, Joan
1 *Sam the silver bus* (1985)
2 *Sam's wonderful week* (1987)

Sam series
Faulkner, Keith
1 *Sam at the seaside* (1987)
2 *Sam helps out* (1987)

Sam series
Garland, Sarah
1 *Sam's the name* (1987)
2 *Sam's cat* (1987)
3 *Super Sam* (1987)
4 *Sam and Joe* (1987)

Sam series
Henderson, Kathy
1 *Sam and the big machines* (1985)
2 *Sam and the box* (1987)
3 *Sam, Lizzie and the bonfire* (1989)

Sam series
Lambert, Thelma
1 *No swimming for Sam* (1985)
2 *No prize for Sam* (1986)
3 *No presents for Sam* (1986)

Sam series
Lindgren, Barbro
1 *Sam's Teddy bear* (1981)
Sam's Teddy
Original edition entitled *Max nalle*
2 *Sam's car* (1981)
Original edition entitled *Max bil*
3 *Sam's cookie* (1981)
Sam's biscuit
Original edition entitled *Max kaka*
4 *Sam's ball* (1982)
Original edition entitled *Max boll*
5 *Sam's lamp* (1982)
Bad Sam!
Original edition entitled *Max lampa*
6 *Sam's bath* (1982)
Original edition entitled *Max balja*
7 *Sam's potty* (1986)
Original edition entitled *Max potta*
8 *Sam's wagon* (1986)
Sam's cart
Original edition entitled *Max dockvagn*

Sam series
Lowry, Lois
1 *All about Sam* (1988)
2 *Attaboy, Sam!* (1992)

Sam series
Rosenberg, Amye
1 *Sam the detective and the Alef Bet mystery* (1980)
2 *Sam's reading rediness* (1982)

Sam series
Wood, Ted
see **Reid Bennett series**

Sam Shank series
Harrell, Andrew
1 *Twin bridges murder* (1982)
2 *Trailersnatch* (1983)
3 *Rivermist* (1983)
4 *Kickback* (1984)
5 *Touch of jade* (1985)

Sam Sholto series
Hart-Davis, Duff
1 *Gold of Saint Matthew* (1970)
Gold trackers
2 *Spider in the morning* (1972)

Sam Slater series
Colter, Dale
see **Regulator series**

Sam Slick series
Haliburton, Thomas Chandler
1 *Clockmaker, 1st series* (1836)
Sam Slick, the clockmaker
Yankee stories, 1st series
Sayings and doings of Samuel Slick of Slickville
2 *Clockmaker, 2nd series* (1837)
Yankee stories, 2nd series
3 *Clockmaker, 3rd series* (1838)
Yankee stories 3rd series
Numbers 1-3 revised and abridged in one volume entitled *Sam Slick in search of a wife, or, Wise saws, the sayings and doings of Samuel Slick, esq., together with his opinion on matrimony*, 1855
4 *Letter-bag of the Great Western* (1839)
Letters of Sam Slick
Alternative titles: Life in a steamer, and Life in a steamer for the letter-bag of the Great Western
5 *Attache* (1843)
Alternative title: Sam Slick in England
6 *Attache, 2nd series* (1846)
7 *Old judge* (1849)
Alternative title: Life in a colony
8 *Sam Slick's wise saws and modern instances* (1853)
Alternative title: What he said, did or invented
9 *Nature and human nature* (1855)
10 *Season-ticket* (1860)
One volume edition entitled *Sam Slick*, 1923
Companion volume: *The courtship and adventures of Jonathan Home Bred, or, The scrapes and escapes of a live Yankee*, 1860

Sam Small series
Knight, Eric
1 *Flying Yorkshireman* (1938)
2 *Sam Small flies again* (1942)
One volume abridged edition entitled *Sam Small, the flying Yorkshireman*, 1957

Sam Snout series
Lemieux, Anne
see **Super Sam Snout series**

Sam Space series
Nolan, William Francis
1 *Space for hire* (1971)
2 *Look out for space* (1985)

Sam Spade series
Hammett, Dashiell
1 *Maltese Falcon* (1930)
2 *Adventures of Sam Spade, and other stories* (1944)
They can only hang you once
Not all the stories in this volume contain Sam Spade
3 *Man called Spade* (1945)
Not all the stories in this volume contain Sam Spade

Sam Spur series
James, Cy
1 *Cimmaron Kid* (1969)
2 *Longhorn* (1970)
3 *Trail west* (1970)
4 *Gun* (1971)
5 *Brave ride tall* (1971)
6 *Blood at sunset* (1971)

Sam Steele series
Fitzgerald, Hugh
1 *Sam Steele's adventures on land and sea* (1906)
2 *Sam Steele's adventures in Panama* (1907)

Sam, the girl detective series
Bradman, Tony
1 *Sam, the girl detective* (1989)
2 *Cashbox caper* (1990)
3 *Case of the missing mummy* (1990)
4 *Secret of the seventh candle* (1992)

Sam Tucker series
Potter, Jerry Allen
1 *Talent for dying* (1980)
2 *If I should die before I wake* (1981)

Sam Watchman series
Garfield, Brian Wynne
1 *Relentless* (1972)
2 *Threepersons hunt* (1974)

Sam Welpton series
Saxon, John A
1 *Liability limited* (1947)
This was no accident
2 *Half-past mortem* (1947)
Co-author: Robert Leslie Bellem

Sam Wharton series
Buckingham, David
1 *Wind tunnel* (1959)
2 *Cliff face* (1960)

Sam Wilson series
This sequence has two authors
Powell, Jonathan
1 *Sam* (1973)
Sands, Leslie
2 *Stay single and live forever* (1974)
3 *Up in the world* (1975)

Samantha Adams series
Storey, Alice
1 *First kill all the lawyers* (1988)
2 *Then hang all the liars* (1989)

Samantha and Josiah Allen series
Holley, Marietta
1 *Josiah Allen's wife as a P.A. and P.I.* (1877)
Samantha at the Centennial
2 *My wayward pardner* (1880)
Alternative title: My trials with Josiah, America, the Widow Bump and etectery
3 *Sweet Cicely* (1885)
Alternative title: Josiah Allen as a politician
4 *Samantha at Saratoga* (1887)
Alternative titles: Flirtin' with fashion, and Racin' after fashion
5 *Samantha among the brethren* (1890)
6 *Samantha on the race problem* (1892)
Samantha among the colored folks
7 *Samantha at the World's Fair* (1893)
8 *Josiah's alarm and Abel Perry's funeral* (1895)
9 *Samantha in Europe* (1896)
10 *Samantha at the Saint Louis Exposition* (1904)
11 *Around the world with Josiah Allen's wife* (1905)
12 *Samantha versus Josiah* (1906)
The story of a borrowed automobile and what came of it
13 *Samantha on children's rights* (1909)
14 *Samantha at Coney Island and a thousand other islands* (1911)
15 *Samantha on the woman question* (1913)
16 *Josiah Allen on the woman question* (1914)
Companion volume: *Josiah's secret, a play*, 1910

Samantha series
Tripp, Valerie
1 *Meet Samantha, an American girl* (1988)
2 *Samantha learns a lesson* (1988)
A school story
3 *Samantha's surprise* (1988)
A Christmas story
4 *Happy birthday, Samantha!* (1987)
A springtime story
5 *Changes for Samantha* (1988)
A winter story
6 *Samantha saves the day* (1988)
A summer story

Samantha Slade series
Smith, Susan
1 *Samantha Slade, monster-sitter* (1987)
Monster-sitter
2 *Confessions of a teenage frog* (1987)
3 *Our friend, public nuisance number one* (1987)
4 *Terrors of rock and roll* (1988)

Samantha Spayed series
Singer, Marilyn
1 *Fido frame-up* (1983)
2 *Nose for trouble* (1985)
3 *Where there's a will, there's a wag* (1986)

Samantha Wade series
Lorin, Amii
1 *Morgan Wade's woman* (1981)
2 *Night striker* (1985)

Samarkand series
Diamond, Graham
1 *Samarkand* (1980)
2 *Samarkand dawn* (1981)

Samgin series
Gorky, Maxim
see **Life of Klim Samgin series**

Sammy and Mara series
Van der Meer, Ron
1 *My brother Sammy* (1978)
2 *Sammy and Mara* (1978)
3 *Sammy and the cat party* (1979)
4 *Naughty Sammy* (1979)

Sammy day and night series
Szekeres, Cyndy
1 *Good night, Sammy* (1986)
2 *Sammy's special day* (1986)

Sammy Golden and Father Joseph Shanley series
Webb, Jack
see **Father Joseph Shanley and Sammy Golden series**

Sammy series
Elliott, Odette
Illustrated by Amanda Welch
1 *Under Sammy's bed* (1989)
2 *Sammy goes flying* (1990)
3 *Sammy and the telly* (1991)
4 *Sammy's Christmas workshop* (1992)

Sammy's super T-shirt series
Robertson, H Macleod
1 *Sammy's super T-shirt* (1981)
2 *Wanted, Sammy's super T-shirt!* (1986)

Samothrace trilogy
Mundy, Talbot
see **Tros of Samothrace trilogy**

Samson and Vincente series
Singer, Shelley
see **Jake Samson and Rosie Vincente series**

Samson series
Deighton, Len
see **Bernard Samson series**
Douglas, Gavin
see **Captain Samson series**

Samson series

Lewin, Michael Zinn
see **Albert Samson series**
Tripp, Miles
see **John Samson series**

Samuel and David series

Jenkins, Gwyn
1 *Last judge* (1964)
2 *Son of Jesse* (1961)

Samuel Best and Jeremy Barton series

Pearson, Parry
see **Jeremy Barton and Samuel Best series**

Samuel Cutting series

Westbrook, Perry Dickie
see **Doctor Samuel Cutting series**

Samuel family series

Watson, Jean
see **Meet the Samuel family series**

Samuel G Abbott series

Langham, James R
1 *Sing a song of homicide* (1940)
Sing a song of murder
2 *Pocket full of clues* (1941)
Pocketful of clues

Samuel Johnson series

Clifford, James Lowry
1 *Young Sam Johnson* (1955)
2 *Dictionary Johnson* (1979)
Samuel Johnson's middle years

Samuel Johnson series

Moore, Frank Frankfort
see **Doctor Samuel Johnson series**

Samuel Lyle series

Crabb, Arthur
1 *Samuel Lyle, criminologist* (1920)
Short stories
2 *Ghosts* (1921)
Mrs Brown's pearls

Samuel Marchbanks series

Davies, Robertson
1 *Diary of Samuel Marchbanks* (1947)
2 *Table talk of Samuel Marchbanks* (1949)
3 *Samuel Marchbanks' almanack* (1967)
Abridged one volume edition entitled *The papers of Samuel Marchbanks*, 1985

Samuel Miles trilogy

Canning, Victor
see **Smiler Miles trilogy**

Samuel Moses Kelly series

Burke, Jackson Frederick
1 *Location shots* (1974)
2 *Death trick* (1975)
3 *Kelly among the nightingales* (1979)

Samuel Pepys series

Bryant, Arthur
1 *Man in the making* (1933)
2 *Years of peril* (1935)
3 *Saviour of the Navy* (1938)
Revised edition 1970
Companion volume: *Pepys and the Revolution* 1979

Samuel Quan series

Begbie, Garstin
see **Superintendent Samuel Quan series**

Samuel Slick series

Haliburton, Thomas Chandler
see **Sam Slick series**

Samuel Walton series

Green, Roger James
1 *Fear of Samuel Walton* (1984)
2 *Lengthening shadow* (1986)
3 *Devil finds work* (1987)

Samurai Cat series

Rogers, Mark Earl
1 *Adventures of Samurai Cat* (1984)
2 *More adventures of Samurai Cat* (1986)
3 *Samurai Cat in the real world* (1989)
4 *Sword of Samurai Cat* (1991)

San Antonio series

San Antonio
This sequence of 10 titles represent those titles which have been translated into English of the around 65 titles published in French
1 *Stone dead* (1954)
Original edition entitled *C'est mort et ca ne sait pas*
2 *Tough justice* (1955)
Original edition entitled *Messieurs les hommes*
3 *Sub killers* (1958)
Original edition entitled *La rate au Court Bouillon*
4 *Thugs and bottles* (1960)
Original edition entitled *Du brut pour les brutes*
5 *Hatchet man* (1960)
Original edition entitled *Vas-y Beru*
6 *Strangler* (1961)
Original edition entitled *La fin des haricots*
7 *From A to Z* (1961)
Original edition entitled *De l'A jusqu'a Z*
8 *Crooks' Hill* (1963)
Puck of Crooks' Hill
Original edition entitled *Le gala des emplumes*
9 *Knights of Arabia* (1964)
Original edition entitled *Berurier au serail*
10 *Alien archipelago* (1969)
Original edition entitled *L'archipel des malotrus*

San Cristobal series

Lamming, George
1 *Of age and innocence* (1958)
2 *Season of adventure* (1960)

San Diego Zoo series

Irvine, Georgeanne
see **Zoo world series**

San Francisco series

Busch, Niven
1 *California Street* (1959)
2 *San Franciscans* (1962)

San Miguel series

Burnett, William Riley
1 *Adobe walls* (1953)
2 *Pale moon* (1956)

Sanchez family series

Lewis, Oscar
Biography of a Mexican family
1 *Children of Sanchez* (1961)
2 *Death in the Sanchez family* (1969)

Sanchez series

Dunnahoo, Terry
see **Espie Sanchez series**

Sanchia and John Maxwell Senhouse series

Hewlett, Maurice
1 *Halfway house* (1908)
A comedy of degrees
2 *Open country* (1909)
A comedy with a sting
3 *Rest Harrow* (1910)
A comedy of resolution
Companion volume: *Letters to Sanchia upon things as they are, extracted from the correspondence of Mr John Maxwell Senhouse*, 1910

Sanctuary series

This sequence has two authors
Asprin, Robert Lynn
1 *Thieves' world* (1979)
2 *Tales from the Vulgar Unicorn* (1980)
3 *Shadows of sanctuary* (1981)
Numbers 1-3 also published in one volume entitled *Sanctuary*, 1982
4 *Storm season* (1982)
5 *Face of chaos* (1983)
6 *Wings of omen* (1984)
Numbers 4-6 also published in one volume entitled *Cross-currents*, 1984
7 *Dead of winter* (1985)
8 *Soul of the city* (1986)
9 *Blood ties* (1986)
Numbers 7-9 also published in one volume entitled *The shattered sphere*, 1986
10 *Aftermath* (1987)
11 *Uneasy alliances* (1988)
12 *Stealers' sky* (1989)
Numbers 10-12 also published in one volume entitled *The price of victory*, 1990
Companion volumes: *Jamie the Red*, by Gordon Rupert Dickson and Roland Green, 1984, *Beyond sanctuary*, by Janet Ellen Morris, 1985, *Lythande*, by Marion Zimmer Bradley, 1986, *Shadowspawn*, by Andrew Jefferson Offutt, 1987, Dagger, by David Drake, 1988

Sand child series

Ben Jelloun, Tahar
1 *Sand child* (1987)
Original edition entitled *L'enfant de sable*
2 *Sacred night* (1989)
Original edition entitled *La nuit sacree*

Sand County series

Leopold, Aldo
1 *Sand County almanac, and sketches here and there* (1949)
Sand County almanac illustrated
2 *Sand County almanac, with other essays on conservation from Round River* (1966)
Companion volume: *Round River*, 1953

Sand series

Ezell, Marilyn
see **Susan Sand series**
Olden, Marc
see **Robert Sand series**

Sand wars series

Ingrid, Charles
1 *Solar kill* (1987)
2 *Lasertown blues* (1988)
3 *Celestial hit list* (1988)
4 *Alien salute* (1989)
5 *Return fire* (1989)
6 *Challenge met* (1990)

Sandberg family trilogy

Mosco, Maisie
see **Almonds and raisins trilogy**

Sanders and Jeffries series

Sale, Medora
see **Inspector John Sanders and Harriet Jeffries series**

Sanders series

Mulford, Clarence Edward
see **Dave Sanders series**
Wallace, Edgar
see **Commissioner Sanders series**

Sanderson and Forsythe series

Giroux, E X
see **Robert Forsythe and Abigail Sanderson series**

Sanderson series

Chichester, John Jay
see **Maxwell Sanderson series**
Grex, Leo
see **Phil Sanderson series**
Hume, David
see **Inspector Sanderson series**

Sandford series

Childs, Rob
1 *Soccer at Sandford* (1980)
2 *Sandford on the run* (1981)
3 *Sandford on tour* (1983)
4 *Sandford in to bat* (1985)

Sandman series

Dodge, Louis
Stories for large persons to relate to small persons
1 *Sandman's forest* (1918)
2 *Sandman's mountain* (1920)

Sandman series

Frees, Harry Whittier
1 *Sandman, his animal stories* (1916)
2 *Sandman, his kittycat stories* (1917)
3 *Sandman, his bunny stories* (1918)
4 *Sandman, his puppy stories* (1920)

Sandman series

Gaiman, Neil
1 *Doll's house* (1990)
2 *Preludes and nocturnes* (1991)
3 *Dream country* (1991)
4 *Season of mists* (1992)
5 *Game of you* (1993)

Sandman series

Hopkins, William John
1 *Sandman, his stories* (1903)
2 *Sandman, more stories* (1904)
3 *Sandman, his ship stories* (1907)
4 *Sandman, his sea stories* (1908)

Sandman series

Walker, Abbie Phillips
1 *Told by the Sandman* (1916)
2 *Sandman tales* (1917)
3 *Sandman's hour* (1917)
4 *Sandman twilight tales* (1918)
5 *Sandman Christmas stories* (1918)
6 *Sandman's rainy day stories* (1919)
7 *Sandman's stories of Drusilla doll* (1919)
8 *Sandman's goodnight stories* (1921)
9 *Sandman's fairy stories* (1922)
10 *Sandman's might-be-so stories* (1922)
11 *Sandman's stories of Snowed-In Hut* (1923)
12 *Sandman's stories of Twinkle-Eyes* (1923)
13 *Sandman's once-upon-a-time stories* (1925)
14 *Sandman's three-minute stories* (1925)

Sandmen series

Neville, Malcolm
1 *Meet the sandman* (1973)
2 *Sandmen in danger* (1974)

Sandor Raimann series

Buckley, Eunice
1 *They walk on earth* (1966)
2 *Man on the rope* (1967)
3 *Diamonds in the family* (1968)
4 *Flaming sword* (1969)

Sandra and Mike series

Trease, Geoffrey
see **Mike and Sandra series**

Sandra Belloni series
Meredith, George
1 *Emilia in England* (1864)
Sandra Belloni
2 *Vittoria* (1866)

Sandro, Colly and Lady Jennifer series
Drummond, Ivor
see **Lady Jennifer, Sandro and Colly series**

Sands series
Casey, Robert J
see **Jim Sands series**
Millar, Margaret
see **Inspector Sands series**

Sandsy series
Hunting, Henry Gardner
1 *Sandsy's pal* (1915)
Alternative title: How fire forged a friendship
2 *Sandsy himself, together with three other boys* (1918)
3 *Sandsy puts it over* (1924)

Sandwich Street series
Huddy, Delia
1 *Sandwich Street blue* (1974)
2 *Sandwich Street safari* (1977)
3 *Creaky knees* (1978)

Sandwriter series
Hughes, Monica
1 *Sandwriter* (1985)
2 *Promise* (1989)

Sandy and Lawrence trilogy
Pullein-Thompson, Christine
1 *We hunted hounds* (1949)
2 *I carried the horn* (1951)
3 *Goodbye to the hounds* (1952)

Sandy Blunt series
Yates, Peter
1 *Dress cirlcle murders* (1945)
2 *Death in the hands of talent* (1946)

Sandy, David and Peter series
Hunter, Evan
see **David, Peter and Sandy series**

Sandy, Jane and Stephen series
Macgibbon, Jean
1 *Great great rescuer's* (1967)
2 *Tall ship* (1967)
3 *Sandy in Hollow Tree House* (1967)

Sandy Ray series
King, Charles
see **Lieutenant Sandy Ray series**

Sandy series
Conyers, Dorothea
1 *Strayings of Sandy* (1906)
2 *Sandy married* (1913)
3 *Sandy and others* (1925)

Sandy Steele series
Barlow, Roger
1 *Black treasure* (1959)
2 *Danger at Mormon Crossing* (1959)
3 *Stormy voyage* (1959)
4 *Fire at Red Lake* (1959)
5 *Secret mission to Alaska* (1959)
6 *Troubled waters* (1959)
7 *Land of the ten thousand smokes* (1959)

Sandy Stern series
Turow, Scott
The series character is minor in number 1 and central in numbers 2 and 3
1 *Presumed innocent* (1987)
2 *Burden of proof* (1990)
3 *Pleading guilty* (1993)

Sandyman series
Graham, Neill
see **Mister Sandyman series**

Sanford High School series
Lester, Pauline
see **Marjorie Dean high school series**

Sanford series
Proud, Franklin M
see **Joe Sanford series**

Sanger family series
Kennedy, Margaret
1 *Constant nymph* (1924)
2 *Fool in the family* (1930)
Dramatized as *Escape me never*, 1933

Sanguinet series
Veryan, Patricia
1 *Nanette* (1981)
2 *Feather castles* (1982)
3 *Married past redemption* (1983)
4 *Noblest family* (1983)
5 *Sanguinet's crown* (1985)
6 *Give all to love* (1987)

Sansevero series
Giovene, Andrea
see **Giuliano Sansevero series**

Santa Anna trilogy
Metcalfe, Thomas Washington
1 *One night in Santa Anna* (1931)
2 *Life and adventures of Alousius O'Callaghan* (1932)
3 *Fare you well, my shining city* (1933)

Santa Barbara series
Masefield, John
see **Sard Harker series**

Santa Claus series
Baum, Lyman Frank
1 *Life and adventures of Santa Claus* (1902)
2 *Kidnapped Santa Claus* (1969)
Originally published in the *Delineator*, 1896

Santa Claus series
Haywood, Carolyn
1 *Santa Claus forever* (1982)
2 *How the reindeer saved Santa Claus* (1986)

Santa Claus series
Nash, Ogden
1 *Untold adventures of Santa Claus* (1964)
2 *Santa go home* (1967)
A case history for parents

Santa Fe Trail trilogy
Fergusson, Harry
1 *Blood of the conquerors* (1921)
2 *Wolf song* (1927)
3 *In those days* (1929)
An impression of change
One volume editions entitled *Followers of the sun*, 1936, and *Santa Fe omnibus*, 1938

Santana series
Truman, Timothy
see **Emanuel Santana series**

Santangelo family series
Collins, Jackie
1 *Chances* (1981)
2 *Lucky* (1985)

Santangelo series
Mancini, Anthony
see **Minnie Santangelo series**

Santee series
Green, Sharon
see **Diana Santee series**

Santiago Toole series
Wheeler, Richard Seabrook
see **Sheriff Santiago Toole series**

Santos series
Bannerman, W B
see **Domingo Santos series**

Sappers series
Smith, Vian Crocker
1 *Song of the unsung* (1945)
2 *Candles to the dawn* (1946)

Sara Alelia trilogy
Dixelius, Hildur
1 *Minister's daughter* (1920)
Original edition entitled *Prastdottern*
2 *Son* (1921)
Original edition entitled *Prastdotterns son*
3 *Grandson* (1922)
Original edition entitled *Sonsonen*

Sara and Caroline series
Shaw, Jane
see **Caroline and Sara series**

Sara and Hoppity series
Leigh, Roberta
1 *Sara and Hoppity* (1960)
2 *Sara and Hoppity make new friends* (1960)
3 *Sara and hoppity get lost* (1961)
4 *Sara and Hoppity find a cat* (1961)

Sara Crewe series
Burnett, Frances Hodgson
1 *Sara Crewe* (1888)
Alternative title: What happened at Miss Minchin's
2 *Editha's burglar* (1888)
3 *Little princess* (1905)
The whole story of Sara Crewe

Sara Joslyn series
Westlake, Donald Edwin
1 *Trust me on this* (1988)
2 *Baby, would I lie?* (1994)

Sara series
Peterson, Hans
1 *Sara and the blue tit* (1966)
Original edition entitled *Sara och blamesen*
2 *Sara in summertime* (1967)
Original edition entitled *Sara och sommerhuset*
3 *I don't want to, said Sara* (1968)
Original edition entitled *Jag vil inte, sa Sara*
4 *Sara and her brother* (1970)
Original edition entitled *Sara och lillebror*

Saracinesca family series
Crawford, Francis Marion
1 *Saracinesca* (1887)
2 *Pietro Ghisleri* (1893)

Saragossa manuscript series
Potocki, Jan
1 *Saragossa manuscript* (1960)
2 *New Decameron* (1967)
Original one volume edition entitled *Rekopis znaleziony w Saragossie*, published about 1800

Sarah and Alastair series
Willson, Robina Beckles
1 *Leopards on the Loire* (1961)
2 *Seraph in a box* (1963)
3 *Pineapple Palace* (1964)

Sarah, Ben and Sophie series
Barrett, Peter
see **Sophie, Sarah and Ben series**

Sarah Capshaw series
Stevenson, Drew
1 *One ghost too many* (1991)
2 *Toying with danger* (1993)

Sarah Deane and Alex Mackenzie series
Borthwick, J S
1 *Case of the hook-billed kites* (1982)
2 *Down east murders* (1985)
3 *Student body* (1986)
4 *Bodies of water* (1990)

Sarah Fortune series
Fyfield, Frances
1 *Shadows on the mirror* (1989)
2 *Deep sleep* (1991)
3 *Shadow play* (1993)
4 *Perfectly pure and good* (1994)

Sarah Jane Smith series
Dicks, Terrance
1 *Doctor Who and the planet of the spiders* (1975)
Planet of the spiders
2 *Doctor Who and the giant robot* (1974)
Giant robot
3 *Doctor Who and the genesis of the Daleks* (1976)
Genesis of the Daleks
4 *Doctor Who and the revenge of the Cybermen* (1976)
Revenge of the Cybermen
5 *Doctor Who and the Loch Ness Monster* (1976)
Hulke, Malcolm
6 *Doctor Who and the dinosaur invasion* (1976)
Dicks, Terrance
7 *Doctor Who and the pyramids of Mars* (1976)
8 *Doctor Who and the planet of evil* (1977)
Marter, Ian
9 *Doctor Who and the ark in space* (1977)
Ark in space
Dicks, Terrance
10 *Doctor Who and the brain of Morbius* (1977)
Brain of Morbius
Hinchcliffe, Philip
11 *Doctor Who and the seeds of doom* (1977)
12 *Doctor Who and the masque of Mandragora* (1978)
Marter, Ian
13 *Doctor Who and the Sontaron experiment* (1978)
Dicks, Terrance
14 *Doctor Who and death to the Daleks* (1978)
Death to the Daleks
15 *Doctor Who and the android invasion* (1978)
16 *Doctor Who and the time warrior* (1978)
17 *Doctor Who and the hand of fear* (1979)
18 *Doctor Who and the monster of Peladon* (1980)

Sarah Keate and Lance O'Leary series
Eberhart, Mignon Good
1 *Patient in Room 18* (1929)
2 *While the patient slept* (1930)
3 *Mystery of Hunting's End* (1930)
4 *From this dark stairway* (1931)
5 *Murder by an aristocrat* (1932)
Murder of my patient
6 *Dark garden* (1933)
Death in the fog
7 *Wolf in man's clothing* (1942)
This title features Sarah Keate only
8 *Man missing* (1954)
This title features Sarah Keate only

Sarah Kelling series
Macleod, Charlotte
1 *Family vault* (1979)
2 *Withdrawing room* (1980)
3 *Palace guard* (1981)
4 *Bilbao looking glass* (1983)
5 *Convivial codfish* (1984)
6 *Plain old man* (1985)
7 *Recycled citizen* (1987)
8 *Silver ghost* (1987)
9 *Gladstone bag* (1989)
10 *Resurrection man* (1992)

Sarah Morris series
Stevenson, Dorothy Emily
1 *Sarah Morris remembers* (1967)
2 *Sarah's cottage* (1968)

Sarah O'Brien series
Marlett, Melba
1 *Death has a thousand doors* (1941)
2 *Another day toward dying* (1943)
Witness in peril

Sarah Saber and Chris Rockwell series
Linzee, David
1 *Discretion* (1978)
2 *Belgravia* (1979)

Sarah series
Christie, Robert Stuart
see **Book of Sarah series**

Sarah series
Coville, Bruce
1 *Sarah's unicorn* (1979)
2 *Sarah and the dragon* (1984)

Sarah series
Singmaster, Elsie
1 *When Sarah saved the dog* (1909)
2 *When Sarah went to school* (1910)

Sarah series
Taylor, Sydney
see **All-of-a-kind family series**

Sarah Tuldon series
Agnus, Orme
1 *Sarah Tuldon* (1903)
2 *Sarah Tuldon's lovers* (1909)

Sarah Vanessa series
Storm, Joan
1 *Dark emerald* (1951)
2 *Bitter rubies* (1952)
3 *Deadly diamond* (1953)

Saratoga Springs series
Dobyns, Stephen
see **Charlie Bradshaw series**

Sard Harker series
Masefield, John
1 *Sard Harker* (1924)
2 *Odtaa* (1926)
3 *Taking of the Gry* (1934)

Sarel series
Bryan, John
see **Richard Sarel series**

Sargasso Sea series
McPherson, William
1 *Testing the current* (1984)
2 *To the Sargasso Sea* (1987)

Sark series
Hawk, John
see **Mortimer Sark series**

Sarrasri series
Pierce, Tamora
see **Daine series**

Sasha series
Wood, Andrew
1 *Red Square* (1934)
2 *King Vagabond* (1936)

Satan Hall series
Daly, Carroll John
1 *Death's juggler* (1935)
Mystery of the smoking gun
2 *Ready to burn* (1951)
3 *Adventures of Satan Hall* (1988)
Short stories

Satan series
McNaughton, Brian
see **Mirdath series**

Satan Sleuth series
Avallone, Michael
1 *Fallen angel* (1974)
2 *Werewolf walks* (1974)
3 *Devil, devil* (1975)

Satchelmouse series
Barber, Antonia
1 *Satchelmouse and the dinosaurs* (1987)
2 *Satchelmouse and the doll's house* (1987)

Satchkin Patchkin series
Morgan, Helen
1 *Satchkin Patchkin* (1966)
2 *Mother Farthing's luck* (1971)

Satin slippers series
Bernard, Elizabeth
1 *To be a dancer* (1987)
2 *Center stage* (1987)
3 *Stars in her eyes* (1987)
4 *Changing partners* (1987)
5 *Second best* (1988)
6 *Curtain call* (1988)
7 *Temptations* (1988)
8 *Stepping out* (1988)
9 *Chance to love* (1989)
10 *Rising star* (1989)
11 *Starting over* (1989)
12 *Summer dance* (1989)

Saturday night fever series
This sequence has two authors; based on screenplays
Gilmour, H B
1 *Saturday night fever* (1980)
Fleischer, Leonore
2 *Staying alive* (1983)

Saturday series
Goldman, Lawrence Louis
see **Johnny Saturday series**

Saturnalia series
Callin, Grant
1 *Saturnalia* (1986)
2 *Lion on Tharthee* (1987)

Saturnin Dax series
Cumberland, Marten
1 *Someone must die* (1940)
2 *Questionable shape* (1941)
3 *Quislings over Paris* (1942)
4 *Knife will fall* (1943)
5 *Steps in the dark* (1945)
6 *Not expected to live* (1945)
7 *Lovely corpse* (1946)
8 *Hearse in death* (1947)
Dilemma for Dax
9 *And worms have eaten them* (1948)
Hate will find a way
10 *And then came fear* (1948)
11 *Policeman's nightmare* (1949)
12 *Man who covered mirrors* (1949)
13 *On the danger list* (1950)
14 *Confetti can be red* (1950)
House in the forest
15 *One foot in the grave* (1952)
16 *Booked for death* (1952)
Grave consequences
17 *Fade out the stars* (1952)
18 *Which of us is safe?* (1953)
Nobody is safe
19 *Etched in violence* (1953)
20 *Charge is murder* (1953)
21 *Frightened brides* (1954)
22 *Unto death utterly* (1954)
23 *Lying at death's door* (1956)
24 *Far better dead* (1957)
25 *Hate for sale* (1957)
26 *Out of this world* (1958)
27 *Murmurs in the Rue Morgue* (1959)
28 *Remain to be seen* (1960)
29 *There must be victims* (1961)
30 *Attention, Saturnin Dax!* (1962)
31 *Postscript to a death* (1963)
32 *Hate finds a way* (1964)
33 *Dice were loaded* (1965)
34 *No sentiment in murder* (1966)

Saucer series
Binder, Eando
1 *Menace of the saucers* (1969)
2 *Night of the saucers* (1971)

Saucy Squirrel series
Wyatt, Woodrow Lyle
see **Mister Saucy Squirrel series**

Saul Grisman and Chris Kilmoonie series
Morrell, David
see **Chris Kilmoonie and Saul Grisman series**

Saul Weir series
Durrant, Valentine
1 *Modern minister* (1877)
2 *Saul Weir* (1879)

Saumerez series
Dane, Clemence
see **Sir John Saumerez series**

Saunders and Malter series
Potok, Chaim
see **Danny Saunders and reuven Malter series**

Saunders series
Bar-Zohar, Michael
see **Jeff Saunders series**
Moore, Patrick
see **Scott Saunders series**
Phillips, Henry Wallace
see **Red Saunders series**
Steele, V M
see **Chief Inspector Saunders series**

Savage destiny series
Bittner, F Rosanne
1 *Sweet prairie passion* (1983)
2 *Ride the free wind* (1984)
3 *River of love* (1984)
4 *Embrace the wild land* (1985)
5 *Climb the highest mountain* (1985)
6 *Meet the new dawn* (1986)

Savage Empire series
Lorrah, Jean
1 *Savage Empire* (1981)
2 *Dragon Lord of the Savage Empire* (1982)
3 *Captives of the Savage Empire* (1984)
4 *Flight to the Savage Empire* (1986)
Co-author: Winston A Howlett
5 *Sorcerers of the frozen isles* (1986)
6 *Wulfston's odyssey* (1987)
Co-author: Winston A Howlett
7 *Empress unborn* (1988)

Savage family series
Masters, John
1 *Coromandel* (1955)
2 *Deceivers* (1952)
3 *Nightrunners of Bengal* (1951)
4 *Lotus and the wind* (1953)
5 *Far, far the mountain peak* (1957)
6 *Bhowani Junction* (1954)
7 *To the coral strand* (1962)

Savage report series
Rheingold, Howard
1 *Jack Anderson against Doctor Tek!* (1974)
2 *War of the gurus* (1974)

Savage series
Carlson, Natalie Savage
see **Luvvy Savage series**
Cliff, Michelle
see **Clare Savage series**
Cooper, Craig
see **Matt Savage series**
Eden, Matthew
see **Marc Savage series**

Savage series
Edwards, Cassie
1 *Savage heart* (1985)
2 *Savage obsession* (1985)
3 *Savage surrender* (1987)
4 *Savage paradise* (1987)
5 *Savage Eden* (1988)
6 *Savage splendor* (1988)
7 *Savage whispers* (1989)
8 *Savage bliss* (1990)
9 *Savage dream* (1990)
10 *Savage dance* (1991)
11 *Savage persuasion* (1991)
12 *Savage promise* (1992)
13 *Savage mists* (1992)
14 *Savage sunrise* (1993)
15 *Savage illusion* (1993)
16 *Savage embers* (1994)
17 *Savage spirit* (1994)
18 *Savage pride* (1995)

Savage series
Lewis, David
see **Steve Savage series**
McShane, Mark
see **Myra Savage series**
Robeson, Kenneth
see **Doc Savage series**
Theroux, Paul
see **Spencer Monroe Savage series**
Trevor, James
see **John Savage series**
Turner, James Ernest
see **Rampion Savage series**
Wright, June
see **Inspector Savage series**

Savages series
Jackson, Shirley
Humorous reminiscences
1 *Life among the savages* (1953)
2 *Raising demons* (1957)

Savannah quartet
Price, Eugenia
1 *Savannah* (1983)
2 *To see your face again* (1985)
3 *Before the darkness falls* (1987)
4 *Stranger in Savannah* (1989)

Saveman series
Petersen, Paul
see **Smugglers series**

Saville series
Daniel, Roland
see **Bill Saville series**
Vaizey, Jessie Bell
see **Peggy Saville series**

Savoy series
Britton, David
1 *Savoy book* (1978)
2 *Savoy dreams* (1984)

Savoy series
Gregory, Jackson
see **Paul Savoy series**

Savta Simcha series
Gavta, Yaffa
1 *Savta Simcha and the incredible shabbos bag* (1988)
2 *Savta Simcha and the seven splendid gifts* (1988)
3 *Savta Simcha and the cinnamon tree* (1984)

Sawyer series
Albert, Marvin Hubert
see **Pierre-Ange Sawyer series**
Pidgin, Charles Felton
see **Quincy Adams Sawyer series**
Twain, Mark
see **Tom Sawyer series**

Sax series
Bittner, F Rosanne
see **Caleb Sax series**
Franzen, Nils Olof
see **Agaton Sax series**

Saxe series
Shane, Susannah
see **Christopher Saxe series**

Saxon Ashe series
Ashe, Saxon
1 *I am Saxon Ashe* (1940)
2 *Saxon Ashe, secret agent* (1941)

Saxon series
Bogart, William
see **Johnny Saxon series**
Cassells, John
see **Ludovic Saxon series**

Saxon series
Roberts, Les
1 *Infinite number of monkeys* (1987)
2 *Not enough horses* (1988)
3 *Carrot for the donkey* (1989)
4 *Snake oil* (1990)
5 *Seeing the elephant* (1992)

Saxon trilogy
Duggan, Alfred
1 *Conscience of the King* (1951)
2 *Cunning of the dove* (1960)
3 *King of Athelney* (1961)
Right line of Cedric

Saxonhill series
Duncan, Kathleen Mary
1 *Secrets at Saxonhill* (1962)
2 *Lordly isle* (1963)

Saxons and Vikings series
Birt, David
1 *Saxon invasions* (1977)
2 *Coming of Christianity* (1977)
3 *Celtic realms* (1977)
4 *Cross and the Crescent* (1977)
5 *Viking ships* (1977)
6 *Vikings in England* (1977)
7 *King Alfred* (1977)
8 *Viking voyages* (1977)
9 *Viking life* (1977)
10 *Life in Anglo-Saxon England* (1977)
11 *Saxon home* (1977)
12 *King Offa of Mercia* (1977)
13 *Celtic knotwork* (1977)
14 *Trade and traders* (1977)
15 *Longship* (1977)
16 *Battle of Maldon* (1977)
17 *Schools and education* (1977)
18 *Sea routes* (1977)
A game
19 *Iceland settlement* (1977)
20 *Crime and punishment* (1977)

Saxton series
Miles, Keith
see **Alan Saxton series**

Sayward Luckett trilogy
Richter, Conrad
see **American pioneer trilogy**

SBS series
Kerrigan, John
1 *Fireball* (1983)
2 *Bluebeard* (1984)
3 *Watchdog* (1984)

SBS trilogy
Fullerton, Alexander
see **Special Boat Service trilogy**

Scallywags series
Treacy, Sean
1 *Shay Scally and Manny Wagstaff* (1976)
2 *Scallywags* (1979)

Scamp series
Blyton, Enid
1 *Adventures of Scamp* (1943)
Originally published under the pseudonym Mary Pollock
2 *Scamp* (1953)
3 *Scamp goes on holiday* (1954)
4 *Scamp and Caroline* (1954)
5 *Christmas with Scamp and Bimbo* (1955)
6 *Scamp at school* (1956)

Scamp series
Foxall, Peter Augustus
see **Detective Sergeant Scamp series**

Scandal series
Hamilton, Cosmo
1 *Scandal* (1918)
2 *Another scandal* (1923)

Scandal series
White, Terence Hanbury
1 *Age of scandal* (1950)
An excursion through a minor period
2 *Scandalmonger* (1952)

Scanners series
This sequence has two authors
Whiteson, Leon
1 *Scanners* (1981)
David Cronenberg's Scanners
Kimball, Janus
2 *New order* (1991)

Scant series
Knight, Leonard Alfred
see **Jerry Scant series**

Scaramouche series
Sabatini, Rafael
1 *Scaramouche* (1921)
A romance of the French Revolution
2 *Scaramouche, the kingmaker* (1931)

Scared to death trilogy
Pickford, Ted
1 *Bobby's watching* (1993)
2 *Bobby's back* (1994)
3 *Bridesmaids in black* (1994)

Scaredy monsters series
Salmon, Michael
1 *Basil, the monster who was scared of water* (1984)
2 *Grunt, the monster who wouldn't eat his vegetables* (1984)
3 *Scroggy, the monster who was scared of the dark* (1984)
4 *Byron, the monster who didn't want to be alone* (1984)
5 *Grunt goes to school* (1988)

Scarf Jack series
Kavanagh, Patrick Joseph
1 *Scarf Jack* (1978)
Irish captain
2 *Rebel for good* (1980)

Scarf series
Boyd, Raymond
see **Paul Scarf series**

Scarfe series
Goodwin, John
see **Superintendent Scarfe series**

Scarlet Pimpernel series
Orczy, Emmuska
1 *First Sir Percy* (1920)
An adventure of the Laughing Cavalier
2 *Scarlet Pimpernel* (1905)
3 *Way of the Scarlet Pimpernel* (1933)
4 *Sir Percy leads the band* (1936)
5 *Sir Percy hits back* (1927)
6 *I will repay* (1906)
7 *Elusive Pimpernel* (1908)
8 *Lord Tony's wife* (1917)
9 *Eldorado* (1913)
10 *Mam'zelle Guillotine* (1940)
11 *Triumph of the Scarlet Pimpernel* (1922)
12 *League of the Scarlet Pimpernel* (1919)
Short stories
13 *Adventures of the Scarlet Pimpernel* (1929)
Short stories
14 *Pimpernel and Rosemary* (1924)
Companion volumes: *The Scarlet Pimpernel looks at the world*, essays, 1933, *A gay adventurer, being the biography of Sir Percy Blakeney, Bart., known as the Scarlet Pimpernel*, by John Blakeney, i.e. John Montagu Orczy Barstow, 1935; Lady Blakeney's story is followed in the **Blakeney papers series,** by Colin Guy Clayton

Scarlet riders series
Anderson, Ian
1 *Corporal Cavannagh* (1985)
2 *Return of Cavannagh* (1986)
3 *Beyond the stone heaps* (1986)
4 *Sergeant O'Reilly* (1987)
5 *Fort Terror* (1987)
6 *Flying patrol* (1988)
7 *Dead or alive* (1988)

Scarlet series
Theydon, John
see **Captain Scarlet series**

Scarlett O'Hara series
This sequence has two authors
Mitchell, Margaret
1 *Gone with the wind* (1936)
Ripley, Alexandra
2 *Scarlett* (1991)

Scarlett series
Horler, Sydney
see **Peter Scarlett series**
Laing, Alexander
see **Doctor Scarlett series**
Mackenzie, Compton
see **Sylvia Scarlett series**
Maynard, Nan
see **Katheryn and Gaynor Scarlett series**

Scarpetta series
Cornwell, Patricia Daniels
see **Doctor Kay Scarpetta series**

Scarsborough series
Waldy, Frances Helen
1 *Bonnie Edith Copplestone* (1886)
2 *Frolic* (1886)

Scarsdale Waring series
King, T Stanleyan
1 *Black magic* (1934)
2 *Call of death* (1934)
3 *Vampire City* (1935)

Scatterbrain series
Bruce, Dorita Fairlie
see **Sally Scatterbrain series**

Scatterbrook Farm series
Todd, Barbara Euphan
see **Worzel Gummidge series**

Scattergood Baines series
Kelland, Clarence Budington
1 *Scattergood Baines* (1921)
2 *Scattergood returns* (1938)
Short stories
3 *Scattergood Baines pulls the strings* (1939)
Short stories

Scenes and portraits series
Brooks, Van Wyck
Memoirs
1 *Scenes and portraits* (1954)
Memoirs of childhood and youth
2 *Days of the phoenix* (1957)
The 1920s I remember
3 *From the shadow of the mountain* (1961)
My post-meridian years

Scenes from life series
Cooper, William
1 *Scenes from provincial life* (1950)
2 *Scenes from metropolitan life* (1982)
Numbers 1 and 2 also published in one volume 1983
3 *Scenes from married life* (1961)
Numbers 1 and 3 also published in one volume entitled *Scenes from life*, 1961
4 *Scenes from later life* (1983)
Numbers 3 and 4 also published in one volume 1984

Scenes of country life series
Balzac, Honore de
1 *Peasants* (1844)
Peasantry
Original edition entitled *Les paysans*
2 *Country doctor* (1833)
Original edition entitled *Le medecin campagne*
3 *Village cure* (1839)
Country parson
Original edition entitled *Le cure de village*

Scenes of military life series
Balzac, Honore de
1 *Chouans* (1829)
Original edition entitled *Les Chouans, our, Le Bretagne en 1799*
2 *Passion in the desert* (1830)
Original edition entitld *Une passion dans le desert*

Scenes of Parisian life series
Balzac, Honore de
1 *History of the thirteen* (1835)
Original edition entitled *Histories des treize*
1.1 *Ferragus* (1833)
Original edition entitled *Ferragus*
1.2 *Duchess of Langeais* (1834)
Original edition entitled *La Duchesse de Langeais*
1.3 *Girl with the golden eyes* (1835)
Original edition entitled *La fille aux yeux d'or*
2 *Employees* (1838)
Original edition entitled *Les employees*
3 *Sarrasine* (1838)
Original edition entitled *Sarrasine*

Scenes of Parisian life series

4 *Rise and fall of Cesar Birotteau* (1837)
Grandeur and downfall of Cesar Birotteau
Original edition entitled *Histoire de la grandeur et de la decadence de Cesar Birotteau*
5 *House of Nucingen* (1846)
Firm of Nucingen
Original edition entitled *La maison Nucingen*
6 *Facino Cane* (1846)
Original edition entitled *Facino Cane*
7 *Secrets of the Princess of Cadignan* (1838)
Princess's secrets
Original edition entitled *Les secrets de la princesses de Cadignan*
8 *Harlot's progress* (1847)
Splendours and miseries of courtesans
Original edition entitled *Splendeurs et miseres des courtisanes*
8.1 *How harlots love* (1838)
8.2 *What love costs an old man* (1847)
How much love costs an old man
Original edition entitled *Combien l'amour revient aux vieillards*
8.3 *End of evil ways* (1847)
End of bad roads
Original edition entitled *Ou menent les mauvais chemins*
8.4 *Last incarnation of Vautrin* (1847)
Vautrin's last avatar
Original edition entitled *La derniere incarnation de Vautrin*
9 *Prince of Bohemia* (1840)
Original edition entitled *Un prince de la Boheme*
10 *Involuntary comedians* (1846)
Unconscious mummers
Original edition entitled *Les comediens sans le savoir*
11 *Sample of French familiar conversation* (1845)
12 *Petty bourgeois* (1856)
Middle classes
Original edition entitled *Les petits bourgeois*
13 *Seamy side of history* (1848)
Seamy side of contemporary history
Brothers of consolation
Original edition entitled *L'envers de l'histoire contemporaine*
14 *Cousin Pons* (1847)
Original edition entitled *Le cousin Pons*
15 *Cousin Bette* (1846)
Cousin Betty
Original edition entitled *La cousine Bette*

Scenes of political life series

Balzac, Honore de
1 *Episode under the Terror* (1831)
Episode of the Terror
Original edition entitled *Un episode sur le Terreur*
2 *Dark affair* (1841)
Gondreville mystery
Original edition entitled *Une tenebreuse affaire*
3 *Deputy of Arcis* (1847)
Member for Arcis
Original edition entitled *Le depute d'Arcis*
4 *Z Marcus* (1840)

Scenes of private life series

Balzac, Honore de
1 *At the sign of the Cat and Racket* (1830)
Original edition entitled *La maison du Chat-qui-Pelote*
2 *Dance of Sceaux* (1830)
Sceaux ball
Alternative title: The peer of France; original edition entitled *Le bal de Sceaux*
3 *Recollections of two young brides* (1842)
Two young brides
Letters of two brides
Original edition entitled *Memoires de deux jeunes mariees*
4 *Purse* (1832)
Original edition entitled *La bourse*
5 *Modeste Mignon* (1844)
6 *Start in life* (1844)
Original edition entitled *Un debut dans la vie*
7 *Albert Savarus* (1842)
8 *Vendetta* (1830)
Original edition entitled *La vendetta*
9 *Double family* (1830)
Second home
Original edition entitled *Une double famille*
10 *Peace of the household* (1842)
Peace in the house
Original edition entitled *La paix du menage*
11 *Madame Firmiani* (1832)
12 *Study of woman* (1831)
Original edition entitled *Etude de femme*
13 *Pretended mistress* (1842)
Imaginary mistress
Original edition entitled *La fausse maitresse*
14 *Daughter of Eve* (1838)
Original edition entitled *Une fille d'Eve*
15 *Colonel Chabert* (1832)
Original edition entitled *Le Colonel Chabert*
16 *Message* (1832)
Original edition entitled *Le message*
17 *Grenadiere* (1832)
Original edition entitled *La Grenadiere*
18 *Forsaken woman* (1832)
Forsaken lady
Original edition entitled *La femme abandonnee*
19 *Honorine* (1844)
20 *Beatrix* (1844)
21 *Gobseck* (1830)
22 *Woman of thirty* (1831)
Original edition entitled *Le femme de trente ans*
23 *Old Goriot* (1835)
Original edition entitled *Le pere Goriot*
24 *Pierre Grassou* (1841)
25 *Atheist's mass* (1836)
Original edition entitled *La messe de l'athee*
26 *Interdiction* (1836)
Original edition entitled *L'interdiction*
27 *Marriage contract* (1835)
Marriage settlement
Original edition entitled *Le contrat de mariage*
28 *Another study of woman* (1831)
Original edition entitled *Autre etude de femme*

Scenes of provincial life series

Balzac, Honore de
1 *Lily of the valley* (1835)
Original edition entitled *Le lys dans la vallee*
2 *Ursule Mirouet* (1841)
Original edition entitled *Ursule Mirouet*
3 *Eugenie Grandet* (1833)
Original edition entitled *Eugenie Grandet*
4 *Celibates* (1842)
Original edition entitled *Les celibataires*
4.1 *Pierrette* (1840)
Original edition entitled *Pierrette*
4.2 *Vicar of Tours* (1832)
Original edition entitled *Le cure de Tours*
4.3 *Bachelor's establishment* (1842)
Original edition entitled *Un menage de garcon en province*
5 *Parisians in provincial France* (1843)
Original edition entitled *Les Parisiens en province*
5.1 *Gaudissart the Great* (1833)
Original edition entitled *L'illustre Gaudissart*
5.2 *Wrinkled people* (1833)
5.3 *Muse of the department* (1843)
Original edition entitled *La muse du departement*
5.4 *Actress abroad* (1843)
6 *Superior woman* (1833)
7 *Rivalries* (1836)
Old maid
Original edition entitled *Les rivalites, ou La vieille fille*
8 *Provincials in Paris* (1839)
Cabinet of Antiques
Collection of antiquities
Original edition entitled *Les provinciaux, ou Le cabinet des antiques*
9 *Lost illusions* (1837)
Original edition entitled *Illusions perdues*
9.1 *Two poets* (1837)
Original edition entitled *Les deux poetes*
9.2 *Provincial great man in Paris* (1837)
Distinguished provincial in Paris
Original edition entitled *Un grand homme de province a Paris*
9.3 *Investor's sufferings* (1837)
Investor's tribulations

Sceptres and crowns series

Warner, Susan Bagert
1 *Sceptres and crowns* (1874)
2 *Flag of truce* (1875)

Schaefer series

Estow, Daniel
see **William Schaefer series**

Schimmelhorn series

Bretnor, Reginald
see **Papa Schimmelhorn series**

Schlemihl series

Chamisso, Adalbert von
see **Peter Schlemihl series**

Schlock Homes series

Fish, Robert Lloyd
Parodies on the Sherlock Holmes stories
1 *Incredible Schlock Homes* (1966)
2 *Memoirs of Schlock Homes* (1974)

Schmidt series

Bagby, George
see **Inspector Schmidt series**

Schmitty series

Bagby, George
see **Inspector Schmidt series**

Schofield series

Dewey, Thomas Blanchard
see **Pete Schofield series**

School and camp series

Rand, Edward Augustus
1 *Pushing ahead* (1880)
Alternative title: Big brother Dave
2 *Roy's dory at the sea-shore* (1880)

School life series

Benson, Edward Frederic
see **David Blaize series**

School life trilogy

Kelly, Myra
1 *Little citizens* (1904)
2 *Wards of liberty* (1907)
3 *Little aliens* (1910)

School of manners series

Chesney, Marion
1 *Refining Felicity* (1988)
2 *Perfecting Fiona* (1989)
3 *Enlightening Delilah* (1989)
4 *Finessing Clarissa* (1989)
5 *Animating Maria* (1990)
6 *Marrying Harriet* (1991)

Schoolboy series

Richards, Frank
1 *Secret of the school* (1946)
2 *Black sheep of Sparshott* (1946)
3 *First man in* (1946)
4 *Looking after Lamb* (1946)
5 *Heor of Sparshott* (1946)
6 *Pluck will tell* (1946)

Schoolhouse trilogy

Treneer, Anne
1 *Schoolhouse in the wind* (1944)
2 *Cornish years* (1949)
3 *Stranger in the Midlands* (1950)

Schoolmaster series

Blishen, Edward
Reminiscences of life as a teacher; some volumes are autobiographical and some are fictionalized
1 *Roaring boys* (1955)
A schoolmaster's agony
2 *This right soft lot* (1969)
3 *Cack-handed war* (1972)
An account of experiences during the Second World War as a conscientious objector
4 *Uncommon entrance* (1974)
Fictionalized autobiography
5 *Sorry, dad* (1978)
6 *Nest of teachers* (1980)
7 *Shaky relations* (1981)
8 *Lizzie Pye* (1982)
Memories of the author's mother
9 *Donkey work* (1983)
10 *Second skin* (1984)
11 *Outside contributor* (1986)
12 *Disturbance fee* (1988)

Schrodinger's cat trilogy

Wilson, Robert Anton
1 *Universe next door* (1979)
2 *Trick top hat* (1981)
3 *Homing pigeons* (1981)
One volume edition entitled *The Schrodinger's cat trilogy*, 1988

Schroeder family series

Dane, Eva
1 *Shadows in the fire* (1975)
2 *Lion by the mane* (1977)
3 *Vaaldorp diamond* (1978)

Schultz series

Donleavy, James Patrick
see **Sigmund Schultz series**

Schuyler Townsend series

Gordon, Fritz
1 *Flight of the bamboo saucer* (1967)
2 *Tonight they die to Mendelssohn* (1968)

Schwab series

Wheatley, Dennis
see **Lieutenant John Milton Schwab series**

Schwartz series

Smith, Julie
see **Rebecca Schwartz series**
Stivers, Dick
see **Able Team series**

Schweik series

This sequence has two authors
Hasek, Jaroslav
1 *Good soldier Schweik* (1923)
Original edition entitled *Osudy dobrebo vojuka Svejka*
2 *Red commissar* (1981)
Short stories

Putz, Helmut
3 *Adventures of good comrade Schweik* (1965)
Original edition entitled *Die Abenteuer des braven Kommunisten Schwejk*

Schyler Cole and Luke Speare series
Davis, Frederick Clyde
This sequence is also published under the pseudonym Stephen Ransome
1 *Deadly Miss Ashley* (1950)
2 *Lilies in her garden grew* (1951)
3 *Tread lightly, Angel* (1952)
4 *Drag the dark* (1953)
5 *Another morgue heard from* (1954)
Deadly bedfellows
6 *Night drop* (1955)

Science and natural history series
Greene, Carla
1 *How to know dinosaurs* (1966)
2 *After the dinosaurs* (1968)
3 *Before the dinosaurs* (1970)
4 *How man began* (1972)
5 *Our living earth, its origins and ecology of our planet* (1974)
6 *Man and ancient civilizations* (1977)

Science and religion series
Birch, Louis Charles
1 *On purpose* (1990)
2 *Regaining compassion for humanity and nature* (1993)

Science fiction film series
This sequence has three authors
Menville, Douglas
1 *Things to come* (1977)
An illustrated history of the science fiction film
Reginald, Robert
2 *Futurevisions* (1985)
The new golden age of the science fiction film; co-authors: Douglas Menville and Mary Alice Burgess

Scilly series
Sampson, Emma
see **Priscilla Payson series**

Scipio series
Gates, Tudor
see **Vendetta series**

Scissors grinder series
Leslie, Madeline
see **Tim the scissors grinder series**

Scobee Trent series
Owen, Frank
1 *Rare earth* (1931)
2 *House mother* (1929)

Scobie Malone series
Cleary, Jon
1 *High Commissioner* (1966)
2 *Helga's web* (1970)
3 *Ransom* (1973)
4 *Dragons at the party* (1987)
5 *Now and then, amen* (1988)
6 *Babylon South* (1989)
7 *Murder song* (1990)
8 *Pride's harvest* (1991)
9 *Dark summer* (1993)
10 *Bleak spring* (1993)

Scooby Doo series
This sequence has two authors
Lewis, Jean
1 *Scooby Doo and the pirate treasure* (1974)
2 *Scooby Doo and the haunted dog house* (1975)
3 *Scooby Doo and the mystery monster* (1975)
Brown, Fern Goldberg
4 *Scooby Doo and the headless horseman* (1976)
5 *Scooby Doo and the counterfeit money* (1976)
6 *Scooby Doo and the Santa Claus mystery* (1977)

Scoop Griddle series
Polsky, Thomas
see **L F Griddle series**

Scorpio series
Akers, Alan Burt
see **Dray Prescot series**

Scorpio series
McDonough, Alex
1 *Scorpio* (1990)
2 *Scorpio rising* (1990)
3 *Scorpio descending* (1991)
4 *Dragon's blood* (1991)

Scorpion series
Linaker, Michael R
1 *Scorpion* (1981)
Touch of hell
2 *Second generation* (1982)

Scorpion Squad series
Helm, Eric
1 *Body count* (1984)
2 *Nhu sting* (1984)
3 *Chopper command* (1985)
4 *River raid* (1985)

Scorton Rovers series
Hardcastle, Michael
1 *Soccer is also a game* (1966)
2 *Shoot on sight* (1967)

Scot series
Scott, Alastair
1 *Scot free* (1986)
A journey from the Arctic to New Mexico
2 *Scot goes south* (1988)
A journey from Mexico to Ayers Rock
3 *Scot returns* (1989)
A journey from Bali to Skye
Companion volume: *Tracks across Alaska*, 1990

Scots Quair trilogy
Gibbon, Lewis Grassic
1 *Sunset song* (1932)
2 *Cloud Howe* (1933)
3 *Grey granite* (1934)
One volume edition entitled *A Scots quair*, 1977

Scott and Maxwell series
Macdonald, William Colt
see **Nogales Scott and Caliper Maxwell series**

Scott and Morris series
Gulick, Bill
see **Junior Trail Blazers series**

Scott and Robinson series
Tiger, John
see **I spy series**

Scott Egerton series
Gilbert, Anthony
1 *Tragedy at Freyne* (1927)
2 *Murder of Mrs Davenport* (1928)
3 *Death at Four Corners* (1929)
4 *Mystery of the open window* (1929)
5 *Night of the fog* (1930)
6 *Body on the beam* (1932)
7 *Long shadow* (1932)
8 *Musical comedy crime* (1933)
9 *Old lady dies* (1934)
10 *Man who was too clever* (1935)

Scott flying series
Dixon, Franklin W
see **Ted Scott flying stories**

Scott Gregory and Justin Bassett series
Stratton, Roy
1 *Decorated corpse* (1962)
2 *One among none* (1965)

Scott Jordan series
Masur, Harold Q
1 *Bury me deep* (1947)
2 *Suddenly a corpse* (1949)
3 *You can't live forever* (1950)
4 *So rich, so lovely and so dead* (1952)
5 *Big money* (1954)
6 *Tall, dark and deadly* (1956)
7 *Last gamble* (1958)
Last breath
Murder on Broadway
8 *Send another hearse* (1960)
9 *Name is Jordan* (1962)
Short stories
10 *Make a killing* (1964)
11 *Legacy lenders* (1967)
12 *Mourning after* (1981)

Scott Mitchell series
Harvey, John Barton
1 *Amphetamines and pearls* (1976)
2 *Geranium kiss* (1976)
3 *Junkyard angel* (1977)
4 *Neon madman* (1977)

Scott Saunders series
Moore, Patrick
1 *Spy in space* (1977)
2 *Planet of fear* (1977)
3 *Moon raiders* (1978)
4 *Killer comet* (1978)
5 *Terror star* (1979)
6 *Secret of the black hole* (1980)

Scott series
Gaye, Carol
see **Jane Scott series**
Howard, Hartley
see **Philip Scott series**
Picard, Sam
see **John Scott series**
Prather, Richard Scott
see **Shell Scott series**
Royce, Kenneth
see **Spider Scott series**

Scott sisters series
Kirby, Jean
1 *Career for Kelly* (1962)
2 *Nurses three, first assignment* (1963)
3 *On call for trouble* (1964)
4 *Olympic duty* (1965)
5 *Tracy's little people* (1965)

Scott Stuart series
Coffin, Geoffrey
see **Inspector Scott Stuart series**

Scotter series
Warriner, Thurman
see **Mister Scotter series**

Scottish chronicle series
Mackinnon, Charles Roy
1 *House at war* (1973)
2 *Years beyond* (1974)
3 *To whom the glory?* (1974)
4 *House remains* (1977)

Scottish farm life series
Cameron, David Kerr
1 *Ballad and the plough* (1978)
Portrait of the life of old Scottish farmtouns
2 *Willie Gavin, crofter man* (1980)
Portrait of a vanished lifestyle
3 *Cornkister days* (1984)
Portrait of a land and its rituals

Scottish historical trilogy
Davis, Margaret Thomson
1 *Prince and the tobacco lords* (1976)
2 *Roots of bondage* (1977)
3 *Scorpion in the fire* (1977)

Scottish history series
Tranter, Nigel Godwin
1 *Macbeth the king* (1978)
2 *Margaret the queen* (1979)
3 *David the prince* (1980)
4 *True Thomas* (1981)
5 *Wallace* (1975)
This sequence is followed by the **Robert the Bruce trilogy**

Scotty series
Swinford, Betty
1 *Scotty and the horse that wouldn't die* (1963)
2 *Scotty and the mysterious message* (1965)
3 *Scotty and the lost Dutchman Mine* (1969)
4 *Scotty and the hijackers* (1971)
5 *Scotty and the phantom monster* (1972)
6 *Scotty and the mysterious Mister J* (1973)
7 *Scotty and the mystery of the dark angel* (1973)

Scout Grey series
Bellamy, Robert Lowe
1 *Adventures of Scout Grey* (1924)
2 *Scout Grey, detective* (1927)

Scout series
Gentry, Buck
see **Eli Holten series**
Truman, Timothy
see **Emanuel Santana series**

Scouting series
Tomlinson, Everett Titsworth
see **American scouting series**

Scranton High series
Ferguson, Donald
see **Chums of Scranton High series**

Scrap and Max series
Leyland, Eric
see **Max and Scrap series**

Scrapper John series
Bagdon, Paul
1 *Valley of the spotted horse* (1992)
2 *Showdown at Burnt Rock* (1992)
3 *Rendezvous at Skull Mountain* (1992)

Scratch and Company series
Lefebure, Molly
1 *Scratch and Company* (1968)
2 *Hunting of Wilberforce Pike* (1970)

Scratch Flat series
Mitchell, John Hanson
Study of history and prehistory through observations of a small area of land in Massachusetts
1 *Ceremonial time* (1984)
Fifteen thousand years on one square mile
2 *Living at the end of time* (1990)

Screaming series
Blakeston, Oswell
1 *And then the screaming started* (1968)
2 *For crying out shroud* (1969)

Screwtape series
Lewis, Clive Staples
1 *Screwtape letters* (1942)

Screwtape series

2 *Screwtape proposes a toast* (1961)
Published with *The Screwtape letters*; later edition entitled *Screwtape proposes a toast, and other pieces*, 1965

Scruggs series
Conroy, Richard Timothy
see **Henry Scruggs series**

Scruples scruples
Krantz, Judith
1 *Scruples* (1978)
2 *Scruples two* (1992)

Scudamore series
Armstrong, Raymond
see **Laura Scudamore series**

Scudder series
Block, Lawrence
see **Matthew Scudder series**

Scully series
Bleasdale, Alan
see **Franny Scully series**
Laverty, Maura
see **Delia Scully series**

Sea Devil series
Luckner, Felix von
1 *Count Luckner, the Sea Devil* (1927)
Sea Devil
The story of the German war raider as told to Lowell Thomas
2 *Sea Devil's fo'c'sle* (1929)
As told to Lowell Thomas
3 *Out of an old sea chest* (1955)
Original edition entitled *Aus siebzig Lebensjahren*

Sea Devil trilogy
Llewellyn, Sam
see **George Le Fanu Gurney trilogy**

Sea fever trilogy
Rasmussen, Albert Henry
Reminiscences of sea travel
1 *Sea fever* (1952)
2 *China trader* (1954)
3 *Return to the sea* (1956)

Sea journeys series
Innes, Hammond
Reminiscences of travel
1 *Harvest of journeys* (1960)
2 *Sea and islands* (1967)

Sea king trilogy
Springer, Nancy
1 *Madbond* (1987)
2 *Mindbond* (1987)
3 *Godbond* (1988)

Sea of fertiligy quartet
Mishima, Yukio
1 *Spring snow* (1968)
Original edition entitled *Haru no Yuki*
2 *Runaway horses* (1969)
Original edition entitled *Homba*
3 *Temple of dawn* (1970)
Original edition entitled *Akatsuki no Tera*
4 *Decay of the angel* (1971)
Original edition entitled *Tennin gosui*

Sea people series
Dickson, Gordon Rupert
1 *Home from the shore* (1978)
2 *Space swimmers* (1967)

Sea Scouts series
Westerman, Percy Francis
1 *Sea Scouts of the Petrel* (1914)
2 *Sea Scouts all* (1920)
3 *Sea Scouts abroad* (1921)
4 *Sea Scouts up-channel* (1922)
5 *Sea Scouts of the Kestrel* (1926)
6 *Sea Scouts at Dunkirk* (1941)
7 *Sea Scouts alert!* (1955)

Sea series
Baines, Frank
Autobiography
1 *Look towards the sea* (1958)
Reminiscences of childhood
2 *In deep* (1959)
From London to Australia on a four-masted barque

Sea series
Carson, Rachel Louise
1 *Sea around us* (1951)
Second edition 1955
2 *Edge of the sea* (1955)

Sea series
Cresswell, Helen
1 *White sea horse* (1964)
2 *Tide for the captain* (1967)
3 *Sea piper* (1968)
One volume edition entitled *The white sea horse, and other stories from the sea*, 1972

Sea treasure series
Rockwood, Roy
see **Deep sea series**

Sea trilogy
Golding, William
1 *Rites of passage* (1980)
2 *Close quarters* (1987)
3 *Fire down below* (1989)

Sea Urchin series
Stanhope, Douglas
1 *Sea Urchin's first charter* (1947)
2 *Sea Urchin's second charter* (1948)
3 *Sea Urchin's third charter* (1949)
4 *Sea Urchin's last charter* (1951)

Sea Witch series
Edwards, Hugh
1 *Tiger shark* (1976)
2 *Pearl pirates* (1977)
3 *Sea Lion Island* (1977)
4 *Crocodile god* (1982)

Sea Wolf series
Krauss, Bruno
Later editions published under the author's real name Kenneth Bulmer
1 *Steel shark* (1978)
2 *Shark north* (1978)
3 *Shark pack* (1978)
4 *Shark hunt* (1980)
5 *Shark Africa* (1980)
6 *Shark raid* (1982)
7 *Shark America* (1982)
8 *Shark trap* (1982)

Sea Wolves series
Kessler, Leo
1 *Sink the Scharnhorst!* (1981)
2 *Death to the Deutschland* (1982)

Seafaring series
Armstrong, Richard
see **History of seafaring series**

Seal morning series
Farre, Rowena
Autobiography
1 *Seal morning* (1957)
Childhood in Scotland
2 *Time from the world* (1962)
3 *Beckoning land* (1969)

Seal series
Waugh, Evelyn
see **Basil Seal series**

Seals series
Mackenzie, Steve
1 *Ambush!* (1987)
2 *Blackbird* (1987)
3 *Rescue!* (1987)
4 *Target* (1987)
5 *Defection!* (1987)
6 *Desert rain* (1988)
7 *Recon* (1988)
8 *Infiltrate* (1988)
9 *Assault!* (1988)
10 *Sniper* (1988)
11 *Attack* (1989)
12 *Strongheld* (1989)
13 *Crisis!* (1989)
14 *Treasure* (1989)

Sean Courtney series
Smith, Wilbur Addison
1 *When the lion feeds* (1964)
2 *Sound of thunder* (1966)
3 *Sparrow falls* (1977)
This sequence is followed by the **Courtney family series**

Sean Dillon series
Higgins, Jack
1 *Thunder Point* (1993)
2 *On dangerous ground* (1994)

Sean McCart series
Martin, David
1 *Task* (1975)
2 *Ceremony of innocence* (1977)

Sean Ryan series
Cleeve, Brian
1 *Vote X for treason* (1964)
Counterspy
2 *Dark blood, dark terror* (1965)
3 *Judas goat* (1966)
Vice isn't private
4 *Violent death of a bitter Englishman* (1967)

Sean series
Breinburg, Petronella
1 *My brother Sean* (1973)
Shawn goes to school
2 *Doctor Sean* (1974)
Doctor Shawn
3 *Sean's red bike* (1975)
Shawn's red bike

Seance series
McShane, Mark
see **Myra Savage series**

SeaQuest series
This sequence has four authors
Duane, Diane
1 *SeaQuest* (1993)
Costello, Matthew John
2 *Fire below* (1994)
Bischoff, David
3 *Ancient* (1994)

Search series
Weverka, Robert
Based on a television series
1 *Search* (1973)
2 *Moonrock* (1973)

Search trilogy
Bottome, Phyllis
Autobiography
1 *Search for a soul* (1947)
2 *Challenge* (1952)
3 *Goal* (1962)

Searcher series
Edwards, Josh
see **John Stone series**

Seary series
Ross, John
see **Major Hutton Seary series**

Seashore School of Equitation series
Pullein-Thompson, Christine
1 *Empty field* (1961)
2 *Open gate* (1962)
3 *Doping affair* (1963)
Pony dopers

Season of mists series
Woodhouse, Sarah
1 *Season of mists* (1984)
2 *Peacock's feather* (1988)

Seasons series
Lenski, Lois
Poems
1 *Spring is here* (1945)
2 *Now it's fall* (1948)
3 *I like winter* (1950)
4 *On a summer day* (1953)

Seasons trilogy
Miller, Connie
Autobiography, the first volume in the form of a novel
1 *After summer merrily* (1980)
2 *Season of learning* (1983)
3 *Memory be green* (1986)

Sebald Craft series
Patterson, Innis
1 *Eppworth case* (1930)
2 *Standish Gaunt case* (1931)

Sebastian Barth series
Howe, James
1 *What Eric knew* (1985)
2 *Stage fright* (1986)
3 *Eat your poison, dear* (1986)
4 *Dew drop dead* (1990)

Sebastian Blayne series
Blayne, Sebastian
1 *Gay ghastly holiday* (1951)
2 *Terror in the night* (1953)

Sebastian Griffin series
Charles, Wyndham
see **Chief Superintendent Sebastian Griffin series**

Sebastian Kettle series
White, James Dillon
1 *Leipzig affair* (1974)
2 *Salzburg affair* (1977)
3 *Brandenburg affair* (1979)

Sebastian Kitten series
Julian-Ottie, Vanessa
1 *Sebastian* (1988)
2 *Sebastian explores* (1990)

Sebastian Quin series
Horler, Sydney
1 *Evil messenger* (1938)
2 *Fear walked behind* (1942)
Also stories featuring Sebastian Quin in *The screaming skull, and other stories*, 1930, *The house on Greek Street*, 1935 and *Knave and Company*, 1938

Sebastian series
Johnson, James Leonard
see **Code name Sebastian series**

Sebastian series
Plait, Dominique
1 *Sebastian and the wicked water queen* (1985)
2 *Sebastian and the space pirates* (1985)

Sebastian sisters quintet
Pfeffer, Susan Beth
1 *Evvie at sixteen* (1988)
2 *Thea at sixteen* (1988)
3 *Claire at sixteen* (1989)

4 *Sybil at sixteen* (1989)
5 *Meg at sixteen* (1990)

Sebastian Stole series
Wogan, Charles
1 *Hangman's hands* (1947)
2 *Horror at Wardens Hall* (1948)
3 *Cyanide for the chorister* (1950)

Sebastian Super Sleuth series
Christian, Mary Blount
Illustrated by Lisa McCue
1 *Sebastian Super Sleuth* (1974)
2 *Sebastian Super Sleuth and the hair of the dog mystery* (1983)
3 *Sebastian Super Sleuth and the crummy yummies caper* (1983)
4 *Sebastian Super Sleuth and the bone to pick mystery* (1983)
5 *Sebastian Super Sleuth and the Santa Claus caper* (1984)
6 *Sebastian Super Sleuth and the secret of the skewered skier* (1984)
7 *Sebastian Super Sleuth and the clumsy cowboy* (1985)
8 *Sebastian Super Sleuth and the purloined surloin* (1986)
9 *Sebastian Super Sleuth and the stars-in-his-eyes mystery* (1987)
10 *Sebastian Super Sleuth and the Egyptian connection* (1988)
11 *Sebastian Super Sleuth and the time capsule caper* (1989)
12 *Sebastian Super Sleuth and the baffling bigfoot* (1990)
13 *Sebastian Super Sleuth and the mystery patient* (1991)
14 *Sebastian Super Sleuth and the impossible crime* (1992)
15 *Sebastian Super Sleuth and the copycat crime* (1993)

Sebastian, the incredible drawing dog series
Myers, David
1 *Man who made custard* (1987)
2 *Barking cat* (1987)
3 *Shyest man in the world* (1987)
4 *Man with the big ideas* (1987)

Sebastian Zambra series
Hill, Headon
1 *Clues from a detective's camera* (1893)
Short stories
2 *Zambra the detective, some clues from his notebook* (1894)
Short stories
3 *Divinations of Kala Persad, and other stories* (1895)
Short stories
4 *Narrowing circle* (1924)

Sebastien series
Daniels, Les
see **Don Sebastien series**

Sebrill trilogy
Upward, Edward
see **Alan Sebrill trilogy**

Second Bureau series
Dumas, Charles Robert
1 *Second Bureau* (1939)
2 *Spies against them* (1940)

Second chance series
Lewin, Hugh
1 *Bamboo in the wind* (1989)
2 *Flower in the forest* (1989)
3 *Shell on the beach* (1989)
4 *Well in the desert* (1989)

Second chronicles of Thomas Covenant series
Donaldson, Stephen Reeder
1 *Wounded land* (1980)
2 *One tree* (1982)
3 *White gold wielder* (1983)
Companion volume: *Gilden fire*, 1981

Second Coming series
Watson, Sydney
1 *In the twinkling of an eye* (1910)
2 *Mark of the Beast* (1911)

Second Coming trilogy
Storey, Anthony
1 *Rector* (1970)
2 *Centre holds* (1973)
3 *Saviour* (1978)

Second Empire quartet
Gavin, Catherine
1 *Fortress* (1964)
2 *Moon into blood* (1966)
3 *Cactus and the crown* (1962)
4 *Madeleine* (1957)
Companion volume: *Give me the daggers*, 1972

Second from last series
Pratt, Henry
Autobiography
1 *Second from last in the sack race* (1983)
2 *Pratt of the Argus* (1988)

Second sight series
Emerson, Sally
1 *Second sight* (1980)
2 *Listeners* (1983)

Second star series
Stabenow, Dana
1 *Second star* (1991)
2 *Handful of stars* (1991)

Second World War series
Bryant, Arthur
Based on the diaries and autobiographical notes of Field Marshal the Viscount Alanbrooke
1 *Turn of the tide, 1939-1943* (1957)
2 *Triumph in the west, 1943-1946* (1959)

Second World War series
Gibbs, Philip
1 *Sons of the others* (1940)
2 *Amazing summer* (1941)
3 *Long alert* (1941)
4 *Battle within* (1944)
5 *Through the storm* (1945)
6 *Hopeful heart* (1947)
7 *Behind the curtain* (1948)
8 *Both your houses* (1949)

Secret Agent Dangerman series
Baker, William Howard
see **Dangerman series**

Secret Agent O.S.S.117 series
Bruce, Jean
1 *Pole reaction* (1953)
Original edition entitled *O.S.S.117 repond toujours*
2 *Top secret* (1953)
Original edition entitled *O.S.S.117 top secret*
3 *Short wave* (1954)
Original edition entitled *Affaire no. 1*
4 *Shock tactics* (1954)
Original edition entitled *Ombres sur la Bosphore*
5 *Live wire* (1955)
Last quarter hour
Original edition entitled *Le dernier quart d'heure*
6 *Soft sell* (1957)
Original edition entitled *Plan de bataille pour O.S.S.117*
7 *Cold spell* (1957)
Original edition entitled *Cinq gars pour Singapore*
8 *Flash point* (1958)
Original edition entitled *Moche coup a Moscou*
9 *Hot line* (1958)
Trouble in Tokyo
Original edition entitled *A tout couer a Tokie*
10 *Deep freeze* (1960)
Original edition entitled *Tactique arctique*
11 *Double take* (1961)
Original edition entitled *Rentre dans la danse*
12 *Photo finish* (1961)
Original edition entitled *O.S.S.117 a l'ecole*
13 *Strip tease* (1962)
Original edition entitled *Strip tease pour O.S.S.117*
14 *High treason* (1962)
Original edition entitled *Trahison*
15 *Dead silence* (1967)
Translated from the French
There are other untranslated volumes in this sequence

Secret Agent X series
House, Brant
This pseudonym is used by several authors including Paul Chadwick, G T Fleming-Roberts, Emile C Tepperman and Leo Zagat whose authorship is indicated against those titles where it is known; the dates of the titles in this sequence are those of their original magazine publication
1 *Torture trust* (1934)
[Chadwick]
2 *Death torch terror* (1934)
[Chadwick]
3 *City of the living dead* (1934)
[Chadwick]
4 *Octopus of crime* (1934)
[Chadwick]
5 *Hooded hordes* (1934)
6 *Servants of the skull* (1934)
[Chadwick]
7 *Sinister scourge* (1935)
[Chadwick]
8 *Corpse cavalcade* (1935)
9 *Legion of the living dead* (1935)
10 *Ringmaster of doom* (1935)
11 *Brand of the metal maiden* (1936)
[Fleming-Roberts]
12 *Dividends of doom* (1936)
13 *Fear merchants* (1936)
14 *Faceless fury* (1936)
15 *City of madness* (1936)
16 *Slaves of the scorpion* (1937)
17 *Curse of the mandarin's fan* (1938)
[Zagat]
18 *Claws of the corpse* (1938)
19 *Corpse that murdered* (1938)
20 *Curse of the crimson horde* (1938)
21 *Corpse contraband* (1938)

Secret Agent X-9 series
Hammett, Dashiell
1 *Secret Agent X-9* (1934)
2 *Secret Agent X-9, book two* (1934)

Secret army series
Brason, John
Based on a television series
1 *Secret army* (1977)
2 *Secret army dossier* (1978)
3 *End of the line* (1979)
4 *Kessler* (1981)

Secret army series
Hayes, Richard
1 *Secret army* (1977)
2 *Xenon file* (1980)

Secret books of Paradys series
Lee, Tanith
1 *Book of the damned* (1988)
2 *Book of the beast* (1988)
Numbers 1 and 2 also published in one volume entitled *The secret Books of Paradys I and II*, 1991
3 *Book of the dead* (1991)

Secret circle series
Null, Gary
1 *Cuban expedition* (1974)
2 *Operation Royal Family* (1975)

Secret circle series
Smith, Lisa J
1 *Initiation* (1992)
2 *Captive* (1992)
3 *Power* (1992)

Secret country series
Dean, Pamela
1 *Secret country* (1985)
2 *Hidden land* (1986)
3 *Whim of the dragon* (1989)

Secret diary series
Byrd, William
1 *Secret diary* (1941)
Edited by Marion Tinling and Louis B Wright
2 *Another secret diary* (1942)
Edited by Marion Tinling and Maude Woodfin
3 *London diary* (1958)
Edited by Marion Tinling and Louis B Wright
Companion volumes: *The correspondence of the three William Byrds of Westover, Virginia*, edited by Marion Tinling, 1977

Secret file series
Deighton, Len
The central character is not named in these books, but is named Harry Palmer in the film version
1 *Ipcress file* (1962)
2 *Horse under water* (1963)
3 *Funeral in Berlin* (1964)
4 *Billion-dollar brain* (1966)
5 *Expensive place to die* (1967)
6 *Spy story* (1974)
7 *Twinkle, twinkle, little spy* (1976)
Catch a falling spy

Secret files of Dakota King series
Mackenzie, Jake
1 *Operation Black Fang* (1987)
2 *Haunted city of gold* (1987)
3 *Two-wheeled terror* (1988)
4 *Ghost of the lost mine* (1988)

Secret generations trilogy
Gardner, John Edmund
1 *Secret generations* (1985)
Set between 1909 and 1935
2 *Secret houses* (1987)
Set in the late 1940s
3 *Secret families* (1989)
Set in the 1960s

Secret Guardians series
Boshell, Gordon
1 *Black Mercedes* (1974)
2 *Million pound ransom* (1975)
3 *Mendip money-makers* (1976)

Secret life series
Cobb, Vicki
1 *Secret life of school supplies* (1981)
2 *Secret life of hardware* (1982)
A science experiment book
3 *Secret life of cosmetics* (1985)

Secret mission series
Smith, Don
1 *Secret mission, Peking* (1968)
2 *Secret mission, Prague* (1968)
3 *Secret mission, Corsica* (1968)
4 *Secret mission, Morocco* (1968)
5 *Secret mission, Istanbul* (1969)
6 *Secret mission, Tibet* (1969)
7 *Secret mission, Cairo* (1970)
8 *Secret mission, North Korea* (1970)
9 *Secret mission, Angola* (1970)
10 *Secret mission, Munich* (1970)
11 *Secret mission, Athens* (1971)

Secret mission series

12 *Secret mission, the Kremlin plan* (1971)
13 *Death stalks in Spain* (1972)
14 *Marseilles enforcer* (1972)
15 *Night of the assassin* (1972)
16 *Haitian vendetta* (1973)
17 *Libyan contract* (1974)
18 *Peking connection* (1975)
19 *Dalmatian tapes* (1976)
20 *Bavarian connection* (1978)
21 *Strausser transfer* (1978)

Secret of the Unicorn Queen series
This sequence has four authors
Sherman, Josepha
1 *Swept away!* (1988)
Hansen, Gwen
2 *Sun blind* (1988)
Perlman, Dory
3 *Final test* (1988)
Weyn, Suzanne
4 *Into the dream* (1988)
Sherman, Josepha
5 *Dark gods* (1988)
Hansen, Gwen
6 *Moonspell* (1988)

Secret room series
Eames, Marion
1 *Secret room* (1969)
Original edition entitled *Y stafell ddirgel*
2 *Fair wilderness* (1976)
Original edition entitled *Y rhandir mwyn*

Secret series
Blyton, Enid
see **Prince Paul series**

Secret service series
Cheyney, Peter
1 *Dark duet* (1942)
Counter-spy murders
2 *Stars are dark* (1943)
London spy murders
3 *Dark street* (1944)
Dark street murders
4 *Dark hero* (1946)
Case of the dark hero
5 *Dark interlude* (1947)
Terrible night
6 *Dark wanton* (1948)
Case of the dark wanton
7 *Dark Bahama* (1950)
I'll bring her back

Secret service series
Deacon, Richard
1 *History of the British secret service* (1969)
2 *History of the Russian secret service* (1972)
3 *History of the Chinese secret service* (1974)
Chinese secret service
4 *Israeli secret service* (1977)
5 *History of the Japanese secret service* (1982)
Kempei Tai

Secret service series
Frost, Frederick
1 *Secret Agent Number One* (1936)
2 *Spy meets spy* (1937)
3 *Bamboo whistle* (1937)

Secret Seven series
This sequence has two authors
Blyton, Enid
1 *Secret Seven* (1949)
Secret Seven and the mystery of the empty house
2 *Secret Seven adventure* (1950)
Secret Seven and the circus adventure
3 *Well done, Secret Seven* (1951)
Secret Seven and the tree house adventure
4 *Secret Seven on the trail* (1952)
Secret Seven and the railroad mystery
5 *Go ahead Secret Seven* (1953)
Secret Seven get their man
6 *Good work Secret Seven* (1954)
Secret Seven and the case of the stolen car
7 *Secret Seven win through* (1955)
Secret Seven and the hidden cave adventure
8 *Three cheers Secret Seven* (1956)
Secret Seven and the grim secret
9 *Secret Seven mystery* (1957)
Secret Seven and the missing girl mystery
10 *Puzzle for the Secret Seven* (1958)
Secret Seven and the case of the music lover
11 *Secret Seven fireworks* (1959)
Secret Seven and the bonfire adventure
12 *Good old Secret Seven* (1960)
Secret Seven and the old fort adventure
13 *Shock for the Secret Seven* (1961)
Secret Seven and the case of the dog lover
14 *Look out Secret Seven* (1962)
Secret Seven and the case of the missing medals
15 *Fun for the Secret Seven* (1963)
Secret Seven and the case of the old horse
Lallemand, Evelyne
16 *Seven and the lion hunt* (1983)
Original edition entitled *Les Sept a la chasse au lion*
17 *Seven and the magician* (1984)
Original edition entitled *Les Sept et le magicien*
18 *Seven go haunting* (1984)
Original edition entitled *Les Sept sont dans les beaux draps*
19 *Seven strike gold* (1985)
Original edition entitled *Les Sept et la deesse d'or*
20 *Seven to the rescue* (1985)
Original edition entitled *Les Sept et les bulldozers*
21 *Seven on screen* (1986)
Original edition entitled Les Sept font du cinema
22 *Seven and the UFOs* (1986)
Original edition entitled *Les Sept et les soucoupes volantes*
23 *Seven and Father Christmas* (1986)
Original edition entitled *Les Sept ne croient pas au Pere Noel*
24 *Seven and the racing driver* (1987)
Original edition entitled *Les Sept a 200 a l'heure*

Secret Six series
Hogan, Robert Jasper
1 *Red Shadow* (1977)
2 *House of walking corpses* (1987)

Secret window series
Wright, Betty Ren
1 *Secret window* (1982)
2 *Ghost in the window* (1987)

Secrets of power series
This sequence has two authors
Charrette, Robert N
1 *Never deal with a dragon* (1990)
2 *Choose your enemies carefully* (1991)
3 *Find your own truth* (1991)
Findley, Nigel
4 *Two X S* (1992)

Secrets of the deep trilogy
Dickson, Gordon Rupert
see **Robby Hoenig trilogy**

Sector General series
White, James
1 *Hospital station* (1962)
2 *Star surgeon* (1963)
3 *Major operation* (1971)
4 *Ambulance ship* (1979)
5 *Futures past* (1982)
6 *Sector General* (1983)
7 *Star healer* (1985)
8 *Code blue, emergency* (1987)
Also stories concerning Sector General in *The aliens among us*, 1969

See and say series
Frasconi, Antonio
Picture books in four languages
1 *See and say* (1955)
2 *See again, say again* (1964)

Seed and the fruit series
Troyat, Henri
1 *Amelie in love* (1953)
Original edition entitled *Les semailles ettes moissons*
2 *Amelie and Pierre* (1955)
Original edition entitled *Amelie*
3 *Elizabeth* (1956)
Original edition entitled *La grive*
4 *Tender and violent Elizabeth* (1957)
Original edition entitled *Tendre et violente Elizabeth*
5 *Encounter* (1958)
Original edition entitled *La recontre*

Seed and the sower trilogy
Van der Post, Laurens
1 *Bar of shadow* (1954)
2 *Seed and the sower* (1963)
Short stories
3 *Sword and the doll* (1963)
Published in the one volume edition entitled *A Christmas trilogy*, 1963, which also includes the interludes *Christmas Eve*, *Christmas morning*, and *Christmas night*

Seed series
Lawrence, Lars
1 *Morning, noon and night* (1954)
Also known as part 1, volume 1
2 *Out of the dust* (1956)
Also known as part 1, volume 2
3 *Old Father Antic* (1961)
Also known as part 2, volume 1
4 *Hoax* (1961)
Also known as part 2, volume 2
Originally announced as having 3 parts

Seed series
Plante, Edward
1 *Seed of evil* (1988)
2 *Garden of evil* (1988)

Seedbearers trilogy
Timlett, Peter Valentine
see **Atlantis trilogy**

Seeds of war trilogy
Randle, Kevin
1 *Seeds of war* (1986)
2 *Aldebaran campaign* (1988)
3 *Aquarian attack* (1989)

Seeking sword series
Kangilaski, Jaan
1 *Seeking sword* (1977)
2 *Hands of glory* (1981)

Seen and the unseen series
Oliphant, Margaret Oliphant Wilson
see **Stories of the seen and the unseen series**

Seetee series
Williamson, Jack
1 *Seetee ship* (1951)
2 *Seetee shock* (1950)
One volume edition entitled Seetee, 1979

Seeton series
Carvic, Heron
see **Miss Emily Seeton series**

Segelfoss Town series
Hamsun, Knut
1 *Children of the age* (1913)
Original edition entitled *Born av tiden*
2 *Segelfoss Town* (1915)
Original edition entitled *Segelfoss by*

Segrove series
Vickers, Roy
see **James Segrove series**

Seidlitz series
Brown, Carter
see **Mavis Seidlitz series**

Seidman series
Moll, Elick
see **Morris Seidman seeries**

Selbon series
McCulley, Johnston
see **Avenging Twins series**

Selby series
Ball, Duncan
1 *Selby's secret* (1985)
2 *Selby speaks* (1988)
3 *Selby screams* (1989)

Selby series
Craig, Jonathan
see **Pete Selby series**

Selby series
Gardner, Erle Stanley
see **District Attorney series**

Seldon series
Masterman, Walter Sidney
see **Dick Seldon series**

Selena Mead series
McGerr, Patricia
1 *Is there a traitor in the house?* (1964)
2 *Legacy of danger* (1970)

Selfish man series
Hayes, Douglas
see **History of a selfish man series**

Self-made merchant series
Lorimer, George Horace
see **John Graham series**

Self-portrait series
Clark, Kenneth Mackenzie
Autobiography
1 *Another part of the wood* (1974)
2 *Other half* (1977)

Selina series
Kaye-Smith, Sheila
1 *Children's summer* (1932)
Summer holiday
2 *Selina is older* (1935)
Selina

Sellers series
Denton, Derek
see **Harry Sellers series**
Twain, Mark
see **Colonel Sellers series**

Semi series
Eden, Emily
1 *Semi-attached couple* (1860)
2 *Semi-detached house* (1860)
One volume edition 1947

Semlake series
Varnam, John
see **Inspector Semlake series**

Semolina Silkpaws series
Williams, Gladys
1 *Semolina Silkpaws comes to Catstown* (1962)
2 *Fireworks for Semolina Silkpaws* (1964)
3 *Semolina Silkpaws' motor-car* (1968)
One volume edition, including *Semolina Silkpaws takes a holiday abroad*, entitled *All about Semolina Silkpaws*, 1972

Sen family series
Miln, Louise Jordan
1 *Mister and Mrs Sen* (1923)
2 *Ruben and Ivy Sen* (1925)

Sendi Lee Mason series
Stahl, Hilda
1 *Sendi Lee Mason and the milk carton kids* (1990)
2 *Sendi Lee Mason and the stray striped cat* (1990)
3 *Sendi Lee Mason and the big mistake* (1991)
4 *Sendi Lee Mason and the great crusade* (1991)

Sengler's Circus series
Brandon, Grania
1 *Sengler's Circus* (1948)
2 *Sengler's sawdust ring* (1951)
3 *Sengler's rising star* (1952)
4 *Sengler's comes to town* (1953)
5 *Sengler's buys Babette* (1954)

Senhouse and Sanchia series
Hewlett, Maurice
see **Sanchia and John Maxwell Senhouse series**

Senior citizens series
Sawyer, Corinne Holt
1 *J Alfred Prufrock murders* (1988)
2 *Murder in gray and white* (1989)
3 *Murder by owl light* (1992)
4 *Peanut butter murders* (1993)
5 *Murder has no calories* (1994)

Seniors series
Goudge, Eileen
1 *Too much too soon* (1984)
2 *Smart enough to know* (1984)
3 *Winner all the way* (1984)
4 *Afraid to love* (1984)
5 *Before it's too late* (1985)
6 *Too hot to handle* (1985)
7 *Hands of, he's mine* (1985)
8 *Forbidden kisses* (1985)
9 *Touch of ginger* (1985)
10 *Presenting Superhunk* (1985)
11 *Bad girl* (1985)
12 *Don't say good-bye* (1985)
13 *Kiss and make up* (1986)
14 *Looking for love* (1986)
15 *Sweet talk* (1986)
16 *Heart for sale* (1986)
17 *Life of the party* (1986)
18 *Night after night* (1986)
19 *Treat me right* (1986)
20 *Against the rules* (1986)

Sennacherib series
Delderfield, Ronald Frederick
1 *There was a fair maid dwelling* (1960)
Diana
2 *Unjust skies* (1962)

Sensationalists trilogy
McKenna, Stephen
1 *Lady Lilith* (1920)
2 *Education of Eric Lane* (1921)
3 *Secret victory* (1921)

Sensations and accidents series
Rees, Goronwy
Autobiography
1 *Bundle of sensations* (1960)
2 *Chapter of accidents* (1972)

Senses series
Isadora, Rachel
1 *I hear* (1985)
2 *I see* (1985)
3 *I touch* (1985)

Sensitives series
Burkholz, Herbert
1 *Sensitives* (1987)
2 *Strange bedfellows* (1988)
3 *Brain damage* (1992)

Sensual life series
Croft-Cooke, Rupert
1 *Gardens of Camelot* (1958)
2 *Altar in the loft* (1960)
3 *Drums of morning* (1961)
4 *Glittering pastures* (1962)
5 *Numbers came* (1963)
6 *Last of spring* (1964)
7 *Purple streak* (1966)
8 *Wild hills* (1966)
9 *Happy highways* (1967)
10 *Sound of revelry* (1969)
11 *Moon in my pocket* (1948)
Life with the Romanys
12 *Licentious soldiery* (1971)
13 *Blood red island* (1953)
14 *Gorgeous East* (1965)
One man's India
15 *Dogs of peace* (1973)
16 *Life for me* (1952)
17 *Verdict of you all* (1955)
18 *Tangerine house* (1956)
19 *Quest for Quixote* (1959)
Through Spain with Don Quixote
20 *Wintry sea* (1964)
21 *Ghost of June* (1968)
A return to England and the West
22 *Caves of Hercules* (1974)
23 *Long way home* (1974)
24 *Green, green grass* (1977)
25 *World is young* (1937)
Escape to the Andes
26 *Man in Europe Street* (1938)
27 *Circus has no home* (1941)
Revised edition 1950; numbers 25-27 are in the form of a supplement to the sequence

Sensual life series
Mallet-Joris, Francoise
see **Helene series**

Sentience series
Adams, Terry A
1 *Sentience* (1986)
A novel of first contact
2 *Master of chaos* (1989)

Sentimental bloke series
Dennis, Clarence James
Poetry
1 *Songs of a sentimental bloke* (1915)
Doreen and the sentimental bloke
2 *Moods of Ginger Mick* (1916)
3 *Battle of the Wazzir* (1916)
4 *Doreen* (1917)
5 *Digger Smith* (1918)
6 *Rose of Spadgers* (1924)

Sentimental Tommy series
Barrie, James Matthew
see **Tommy series**

Sentinel series
Konvitz, Jeffrey
1 *Sentinel* (1974)
2 *Guardian* (1979)
Apocalypse

Sentinels series
McKinney, Jack
1 *Devil's hand* (1988)
2 *Dark powers* (1988)
3 *Death dance* (1988)
4 *World killers* (1988)
5 *Rubicon* (1988)

Separation trilogy
Rohmer, Richard
1 *Exodus, UK* (1975)
2 *Separation* (1976)
3 *Separation two* (1981)

Septimouse series
Jungman, Ann
1 *Septimouse, supermouse* (1991)
2 *Septimouse, big cheese!* (1994)

Septimus Dodds series
Scott, Sutherland
see **Doctor Septimus Dodds series**

Septimus Finch series
Erskine, Margaret
see **Inspector Septimus Finch series**

Septimus March series
Bamburg, Lilian
1 *Beads of silence* (1926)
2 *Rays of darkness* (1927)

Septimus Treloar series
Chance, Stephen
1 *Septimus and the Danedyke mystery* (1971)
2 *Septimus and the minster ghost* (1972)
Septimus and the minster ghost mystery
3 *Septimus and the stone offering* (1976)
Stone offering
4 *Septimus and the spy ring* (1979)

Sequence of roles trilogy
Stewart, Desmond
1 *Round mosaic* (1965)
2 *Pyramid inch* (1966)
3 *Mamelukes* (1968)

Serafina series
Brunhoff, Laurent de
1 *Serafina the giraffe* (1960)
Original edition entitled *Serafina le girafe*
2 *Serafina's lucky find* (1962)
3 *Captain Serafina* (1963)

Serbian series
Cosic, Dobrica
see **This land, this time series**

Serendipity Dahlquist and Leo Bloodworth series
Lochte, Dick
see **Leo Bloodworth and Serendipity Dahlquist series**

Serge Gorodish series
Delacorta
Translated from the French
1 *Nana* (1984)
2 *Diva* (1984)
3 *Luna* (1984)
4 *Lola* (1984)
5 *Vida* (1985)
6 *Alba* (1989)

Sergeant Alfred Rawson series
Dorrance, Ethel Smith
1 *Get your man* (1921)
2 *Back of beyond* (1925)

Sergeant Allan Cameron series
Connor, Ralph
see **North-West Mounted Police series**

Sergeant Angus Mott and Superintendent Mike Yeadings series
Curzon, Clare
see **Superintendent Mike Yeardings and Sergeant Angus Mott series**

Sergeant Arthur Milton series
Henderson, Laurence
1 *With intent* (1968)
2 *Sitting target* (1970)
3 *Cage until tame* (1972)
4 *Major enquiry* (1976)

Sergeant Barbara Havers and Inspector Thomas Lynley series
George, Elizabeth
see **Inspector Thomas Lynley and Sergeant Barbara Havers series**

Sergeant Beddoes and Inspector Evans series
Jones, Roger William
see **Inspector Evans and Sergeant Beddoes series**

Sergeant Bill Abbot and Inspector George Thorne series
Penn, John
see **Inspector George Thorne and Sergeant Bill Abbot series**

Sergeant Blizzard Wilson and Private Badger Coe series
Cameron, Caddo
see **Private Badger Coe and Sergeant Blizzard Wilson series**

Sergeant Bob Christie series
Preston, James
1 *Valley of no escape* (1961)
2 *Axes of hate* (1963)
3 *Shattered steel* (1964)

Sergeant Caleb Cluff series
North, Gil
1 *Sergeant Cluff stands firm* (1960)
2 *Methods of Sergeant Cluff* (1961)
3 *Sergeant Cluff goes fishing* (1962)
4 *More deaths for Sergeant Cluff* (1963)
5 *Sergeant Cluff and the madmen* (1964)
Two novelettes entitled *The blindness of Sergeant Cluff*, and, *Sergeant Cluff laughs last*
6 *Sergeant Cluff and the price of pity* (1965)
7 *Confounding of Sergeant Cluff* (1966)
8 *Sergeant Cluff and the day of reckoning* (1967)
9 *Procrastination of Sergeant Cluff* (1969)
10 *No choice for Sergeant Cluff* (1971)
11 *Sergeant Cluff rings true* (1972)

Sergeant Cass Harty series
Dane, Joel Y
1 *Murder cum laude* (1935)
Murder in college
2 *Cabana murders* (1937)
3 *Christmas tree murders* (1938)
4 *Grasp at straws* (1938)

Sergeant Charlesworth series
Fletcher, Joseph Smith
1 *Borgia cabinet* (1930)
2 *Burma ruby* (1930)

Sergeant Charley Mitchell series
Wolff, William Almon
see **Lieutenant Charley Mitchell series**

Sergeant Charmian Daniels series
Melville, Jennie
1 *Come home and be killed* (1962)
2 *Burning is a substitute for loving* (1963)
3 *Murderers' houses* (1964)
4 *There lies your love* (1965)
5 *Nell alone* (1966)
6 *Different kind of summer* (1967)

Sergeant Charmian Daniels series

7 *New kind of killer, an old kind of death* (1970)
New kind of killer
8 *Murder has a pretty face* (1981)
9 *Windsor red* (1988)
10 *Cure for dying* (1989)
11 *Making good blood* (1990)

Sergeant Cherry Blossom and Superintendent Roger Ellerdine series
Wills, Cecil Melville
see **Superintendent Roger Ellerdine and Sergeant Cherry Blossom series**

Sergeant Cork series
Swinson, Arthur
Based on a television series
1 *Sergeant Cork's casebook* (1965)
2 *Sergeant Cork's second casebook* (1966)

Sergeant Craig series
Jefferies, Ian
1 *Thirteen days* (1959)
2 *Dignity and purity* (1960)
3 *It wasn't me!* (1961)

Sergeant Cribb and Constable Thackeray series
Lovesey, Peter
1 *Wobble to death* (1970)
2 *Detective wore silk drawers* (1971)
3 *Abracadaver* (1972)
4 *Mad hatter's holiday* (1973)
A novel of murder in Victorian Brighton
5 *Invitation to a dynamite party* (1974)
Tick of death
6 *Case of spirits* (1975)
7 *Swing, swing together* (1976)
8 *Waxwork* (1978)
9 *Bertie and the Tinman* (1987)
From the detective memoirs of King Edward VII

Sergeant De Gier and Adjutant Grijpstra series
Van de Wetering, Janwillem
see **De Gier and Grijpstra series**

Sergeant Demosthenes H de Goede trilogy
Leroux, Etienne
see **Welgevonden trilogy**

Sergeant Dick series
Rowe, John Gabriel
1 *Sergeant Dick of the Royal Mounted Police* (1925)
2 *Carcajou* (1931)

Sergeant Dudley series
Kendall, Ralph Selwood
see **L Division series**

Sergeant Duff and Inspector Cherry series
Van Greenaway, Peter
see **Inspector Cherry and Sergeant Duff series**

Sergeant Edmund Roersch series
Kastle, Herbert David
1 *Cross-country* (1975)
2 *Gang* (1976)
3 *Death squad* (1977)
Hit squad

Sergeant Fang Mulheisen series
Jackson, Jon Anthony
1 *Diehard* (1977)
2 *Blind pig* (1979)
3 *Grootka* (1990)
4 *Hit on the house* (1993)
5 *Deadman* (1994)

Sergeant Fenwick series
Batchelor, Reg
1 *Murder game* (1970)
2 *Murderer's row* (1970)

Sergeant Fuller series
Wallace, John
see **Detective Sergeant Fuller series**

Sergeant Gemma James and Superintendent Duncan Kincaid series
Crombie, Deborah
see **Superintendent Duncan Kincaid and Sergeant Gemma James series**

Sergeant Gray and Inspector Lindon series
Whitman, Charles
see **Inspector Lindon and Sergeant Gray series**

Sergeant Gunnar Matson series
James, Breni
1 *Night of the kill* (1961)
2 *Shake-up* (1964)

Sergeant Hawk series
Clay, Patrick
1 *Sergeant Hawk* (1979)
2 *Return of Sergeant Hawk* (1980)
3 *Under attack* (1981)
4 *Tiger Island* (1982)
5 *Firebolt* (1982)

Sergeant Hobbs series
Lewis, Michael
1 *Brand of the beast* (1925)
2 *Island of disaster* (1926)

Sergeant Honeybody and Inspector Harry James series
Giles, Kenneth
see **Inspector Harry James and Sergeant Honeybody series**

Sergeant Hopkins and Inspector Downes series
Sampson, Victor
see **Inspector Downes and Sergeant Hopkins series**

Sergeant Ivor Maddox series
Linington, Elizabeth
English editions of this sequence published under the pseudonym Anne Blaisdell
1 *Greenmask!* (1964)
2 *No evil angel* (1964)
3 *Date with death* (1966)
4 *Something wrong* (1967)
5 *Policeman's lot* (1968)
6 *Practice to deceive* (1971)
7 *Crime by chance* (1973)
8 *Perchance of death* (1977)
9 *No villain need be* (1979)
10 *Consequence of crime* (1980)
11 *Skeletons in the closet* (1982)
12 *Felony report* (1984)
13 *Strange felony* (1986)
14 *Alter ego* (1987)

Sergeant Jack Wigan series
Farmer, Bernard James
1 *Death at the cascades* (1953)
2 *Death of a bookseller* (1956)
3 *Once, and then the funeral* (1958)
4 *Murder next year* (1959)

Sergeant Jim Chee series
Hillerman, Tony
1 *People of darkness* (1980)
2 *Dark wind* (1982)
3 *Ghost way* (1984)
Numbers 1-3 also published in one volume entitled *The Jim Chee mysteries*, 1990
4 *Skinwalkers* (1987)
5 *Thief of time* (1988)
6 *Talking God* (1989)
7 *Coyote waits* (1990)
8 *Sacred clowns* (1993)

Sergeant Joe Church trilogy
Peters, Lance
see **Detective Sergeant Joe Church trilogy**

Sergeant Joe Dixon series
Wormser, Richard
1 *Man with the wax face* (1934)
2 *Communist's corpse* (1935)

Sergeant John Stryker series
Barnes, Dallas
1 *See the woman* (1973)
2 *Badge of honour* (1974)

Sergeant Johnny Lamb series
Donavan, John
1 *Case of the rusted room* (1937)
2 *Case of the beckoning dead* (1938)
3 *Case of the talking dust* (1938)
4 *Case of the coloured wind* (1939)
Case of the violet smoke
5 *Case of the plastic man* (1940)
Case of the plastic mask

Sergeant Joseph Bragg and Constable James Morton series
Harrison, Ray
1 *French ordinary murder* (1983)
Why kill Arthur Potter?
2 *Death of an Honourable Member* (1984)
3 *Deathwatch* (1985)
4 *Death of a dancing lady* (1985)
5 *Counterfeit of murder* (1986)
6 *Season for death* (1987)
7 *Harvest of death* (1988)
8 *Tincture of death* (1989)

Sergeant Judy Hill and Chief Inspector Lloyd series
McGown, Jill
see **Chief Inspector Lloyd and Sergeant Judy Hill series**

Sergeant Karl Alberg series
Wright, Laurali R
1 *Suspect* (1985)
2 *Sleep while I sing* (1986)
3 *Love in the temperate zone* (1988)
4 *Chill rain in January* (1989)
5 *Fall from grace* (1991)

Sergeant Ken Jackson and Inspector David Webb series
Fraser, Anthea
see **Inspector David Webb and Sergeant Ken Jackson series**

Sergeant Kitty Armitage series
Cobb, Belton
see **Kitty Armitage series**

Sergeant Lamb series
Graves, Robert
1 *Sergeant Lamb of the Ninth* (1940)
Sergeant Lamb's America
2 *Proceed, Sergeant Lamb* (1941)

Sergeant Lancey series
Greene, L Patrick
1 *Sergeant Lancey reports* (1931)
2 *Sergeant Lancey carries on* (1933)
3 *Point of a thousand spears* (1934)
4 *Sergeant Lancey tells the tale* (1947)

Sergeant Lloyd Hopkins trilogy
Ellroy, James
1 *Blood on the moon* (1984)
2 *Because of the night* (1985)
3 *Suicide Hill* (1986)

Sergeant Luck series
Bond, Geoffrey
1 *Luck of the Legion* (1953)
2 *Sergeant Luck takes over* (1954)
3 *Carry on, Sergeant Luck* (1956)
4 *Sergeant Luck's secret mission* (1956)
Cover title: *Luck of the Legion's secret mission*
5 *Luck of the Legion's desert adventure* (1958)
6 *Return of Sergeant Luck* (1964)

Sergeant Mallory series
Sennocke, T J R
1 *Inquest on a lady* (1941)
2 *Inquest on a mistress* (1943)
3 *Inquest betraying* (1943)
4 *Inquests by jury* (1944)
5 *Inquests on the deceased* (1944)

Sergeant Manning and Inspector Grogan series
Neville, Margot
see **Inspector Grogan and Sergeant Manning series**

Sergeant Margetson series
Keate, Edith Murray
see **Superintendent Margetson series**

Sergeant Mark Bourke and Inspector Carol Ashton series
McNab, Claire
see **Inspector Carol Ashton and Sergeant Mark Bourke series**

Sergeant Mark Stryker series
Cain, Jonathan
see **Saigon commandos series**

Sergeant Marshall series
Newman, Bernard
see **Inspector Marshall series**

Sergeant Matheson series
Wright, June
1 *Murder in the telephone exchange* (1948)
2 *So bad a death* (1949)

Sergeant Nelson of the Guards series
Kersh, Gerald
see **Brigade of Guards series**

Sergeant Nick Attwell series
Underwood, Michael
1 *Juror* (1975)
2 *Menaces, menaces* (1976)
3 *Murder with malice* (1977)
4 *Fatal trip* (1977)
5 *Crooked wood* (1978)

Sergeant Norman Pink series
McShane, Mark
1 *Girl nobody knows* (1965)
2 *Night's evil* (1966)
3 *Way to nowhere* (1967)

Sergeant Pascoe and Superintendent Andrew Dalziel series
Hill, Reginald
see **Superintendent Andrew Dalziel and Sergeant Pascoe series**

Sergeant Patrick Shirley and Inspector Rip Irving series
Mills, Osmington
1 *Dusty death* (1965)
2 *Enemies of the bride* (1966)
3 *Death enters the lists* (1967)
4 *Sundry fell designs* (1968)
5 *Many a slip* (1969)
6 *Ghost of a clue* (1970)

Sergeant Paul Dean series
Francis, Basil
1 *Death at the bank* (1938)
2 *Slender margin* (1938)
3 *Holiday camp murder* (1939)
4 *Death for safe custody* (1944)
5 *Death on the roof* (1946)

Sergeant Peart and Superintendent Bowman series
Burrows, Julie
see **Superintendent Bowman and Sergeant Peart series**

Sergeant Peter Bradfield series
Witting, Clifford
see **Inspector Peter Bradfield series**

Sergeant Peter Decker and Rina Lazarus series
Kellerman, Faye
1 *Ritual bath* (1985)
2 *Sacred and profane* (1987)
3 *Milk and honey* (1990)
4 *Day of atonement* (1991)
5 *False prophet* (1992)
6 *Grievous sin* (1993)
7 *Sanctuary* (1994)

Sergeant Ratlin series
Roffman, Jan
1 *Hanging woman* (1965)
Ashes in an urn
2 *Penny for the guy* (1965)
Mask of words

Sergeant Raymond and Inspector Bradley series
Longmate, Norman
see **Inspector Bradley and Sergeant Raymond series**

Sergeant Reed series
Drummond, Charles
1 *Death at the furlong post* (1967)
2 *Death and the leaping ladies* (1968)
3 *Odds on death* (1969)
4 *Stab in the back* (1970)
5 *Death at the bar* (1972)

Sergeant Roger Newman and Superintendent Robert Townley series
Bearshaw, Brian
see **Superintendent Robert Townley and Sergeant Roger Newman series**

Sergeant Rolf Kessler series
Hutson, Shaun
1 *Sledgehammer* (1982)
2 *Kessler's raid* (1982)
3 *Convoy of steel* (1982)
4 *Slaughterhouse* (1983)
5 *Men of blood* (1984)
6 *No survivors* (1985)
7 *Taken by force* (1987)

Sergeant Ronnie Drew series
Vivian, Francis
1 *Arrow of death* (1938)
2 *Dark moon* (1939)
3 *Frog was yellow* (1940)

Sergeant series
Box, Edgar
see **Peter Cutler Sergeant series**
Da Cruz, Daniel
see **Jock Sergeant series**

Sergeant series
Davis, Gordon
1 *Death train* (1980)
2 *Hell Harbor* (1980)
3 *Bloody bush* (1980)
4 *Liberation of Paris* (1981)
5 *Doom River* (1981)
6 *Slaughter City* (1981)
7 *Bullet Bridge* (1981)
8 *Bloody Bastogne* (1981)
9 *Hammerhead* (1982)

Sergeant Silk series
Leighton, Robert
1 *Sergeant Silk, the prairie scout* (1928)
2 *Ratlesnake Ranch* (1912)

Sergeant Spratt and Inspector Hallam series
Douglas, George
see **Inspector Hallam and Sergeant Spratt series**

Sergeant Steve Arrow and Chief Inspector Peacock series
Mantell, Laurie
1 *Murder in fancy dress* (1978)
2 *Murder or three* (1980)
3 *Murder and chips* (1980)
4 *Murder to burn* (1983)
5 *Murder in vain* (1984)

Sergeant Thomas Brunt series
Hilton, John Buxton
see **Inspector Thomas Brunt series**

Sergeant Tom Burton and Inspector Trevor Nichols series
Peters, Geoffrey
see **Inspector Trevor Nichols and Sergeant Tom Burton series**

Sergeant Tom Howard series
Howard, Tom
This sequence has been given various numberings by the author in successive volumes and at least four other titles have been announced but not published; the Jack Reid series is related to this sequence in that John Howard Thomas Reid is the author's real name
1 *Way of life* (1988)
Set at the end of World War II
2 *All possible avenues* (1986)
3 *Health-farm murders* (1984)
4 *Beach-front murders* (1984)
5 *Rim of heaven* (1985)
6 *Last generation* (1986)
Sixteen connected stories
7 *Howard's price* (1987)
8 *Beyond vengeance* (1991)

Sergeant Trevor Dene series
Williams, Valentine
1 *Eye in attendance* (1927)
2 *Death answers the bell* (1931)
3 *Clock ticks on* (1933)
4 *Masks off at midnight* (1934)
5 *Clue of the rising moon* (1935)

Sergeant Venn series
Brock, Lynn
1 *Silver sickle case* (1938)
2 *Fourfingers* (1939)
3 *Riddle of the roost* (1939)

Sergeant William Beef series
Bruce, Leo
1 *Case for three detectives* (1936)
2 *Case without a corpse* (1937)
3 *Case with no conclusion* (1939)
4 *Case with four clowns* (1939)
5 *Case with ropes and rings* (1940)
6 *Case for Sergeant Beef* (1947)
7 *Neck and neck* (1951)
8 *Cold blood* (1952)

Sergeant William Verity series
Selwyn, Francis
1 *Cracksman on velvet* (1974)
Sergeant Verity and the Cracksman
2 *Sergeant Verity and the imperial diamond* (1975)
3 *Sergeant Verity presents his compliments* (1976)
4 *Sergeant Verity and the blood royal* (1979)
5 *Sergeant Verity and the swell mob* (1980)

Sergeant Wittler series
McGuire, Paul
see **Inspector Wittler series**

Sergeant Zondi and Lieutenant Kramer series
McClure, James
see **Lieutenant Kramer and Sergeant Zondi series**

Sergei Rozanov quartet
Thomas, Donald Michael
see **Russian quartet**

Serpent Land trilogy
Connell, Alan
1 *Lords of Serpent Land* (1945)
2 *Prisoners in Serpent Land* (1945)
3 *Warriors of Serpent Land* (1945)

Servadac series
Verne, Jules
see **Hector Servadac series**

Servadec series
Verne, Jules
see **Hector Servadac series**

Servants of Ark trilogy
Wylie, Jonathan
1 *First named* (1987)
2 *Centre of the circle* (1987)
Center of the circle
3 *Mage-born child* (1988)

Servosse series
Tourgee, Albion Winegar
see **Comfort Servosse series**

Sesame Street people series
Moss, Jeffrey
1 *People in your neighborhood* (1983)
2 *People in my family* (1983)

Sesame Street series
Moss, Jeffrey
1 *Songs of Sesame Street in poems and pictures* (1983)
Co-author: David Axelrod
2 *Sesame Street book of poetry* (1991)
3 *Sesame Street songbook* (1992)

Sessions series
Waugh, Hillary
see **Detective Frank Sessions series**

Seth Strummar series
Fackler, Elizabeth
1 *Blood kin* (1992)
2 *Backtrail* (1993)
3 *Road from betrayal* (1994)

Seton series
Jacobs, Thomas Curtis Hicks
see **Mike Seton series**

Setting out series
Breese, Andrea
1 *Setting out* (1981)
2 *Loving imprint* (1982)

Settlement of the American West series
Guthrie, Alfred Bertram
1 *Big sky* (1947)
2 *Way west* (1949)
3 *Fair land, fair land* (1982)
4 *These thousand hills* (1956)
5 *Arfive* (1971)
6 *Last valley* (1975)

Seven ages of man series
Anand, Mulk Raj
1 *Seven summers* (1951)
The story of an Indian childhood
2 *Morning face* (1968)
3 *Confessions of a lover* (1984)
4 *Bubble* (1984)
Three more volumes entitled *And so he plays his part, A world too wide, Last scene*, announced but not published to date

Seven ages series
Dean, Basil
Autobiography
1 *Seven ages* (1970)
1888-1927
2 *Mind's eye* (1973)
1927-1972

Seven citadels series
Harris, Geraldine
1 *Prince of the Godborn* (1982)
2 *Children of the wind* (1982)
3 *Dead kingdom* (1983)
4 *Seventh gate* (1983)

Seven dreams series
Vollman, William T
Books of North American landscapes
1 *Ice-shirt* (1990)
2 *Fathers and crows* (1992)
Numbers 3-5 not yet published
6 *Rifles* (1994)
Number seven not yet published

Seven hundred and twenty nine series
Oxenbury, Helen
1 *Seven hundred and twenty nine animal allsorts* (1980)
Animal allsorts
Merry mix-ups
2 *Seven hundred and twenty nine puzzle people* (1980)
Puzzle people
3 *Seven hundred and twenty nine curious creatures* (1980)
Curious creatures

Seven little sisters series
Andrews, Jane
1 *Seven little sisters who live on the round ball that floats in the air* (1861)
2 *Each and all* (1877)
Seven little sisters prove their sisterhood
3 *Ten boys who lived on the road from long ago to now* (1885)

Seven Scamps series
Steer, Mary
1 *Seven Scamps* (1959)
2 *Seven Scamps solve a mystery* (1962)

Seven series
Blyton, Enid
see **Secret Seven series**

Seven winters series
Bowen, Elizabeth
Memoirs
1 *Seven winters* (1942)
Memories of a Dublin childhood
2 *Pictures and conversations* (1975)

Seven worlds series
Caraker, Mary
1 *Seven worlds* (1986)
2 *Snows of Jaspre* (1989)

Seventeen series
Soya, Carl Erik
Original edition in three volumes entitled Sytten
1 *Seventeen, part 1* (1956)
2 *Seventeen, parts 2 and 3* (1961)

Seventeenth century series
Irwin, Margaret
see **Stuart series**

Seventh Carrier series
Albano, Peter
1 *Seventh Carrier* (1983)
2 *Second voyage of the Seventh Carrier* (1986)
3 *Return of the Seventh Carrier* (1987)
4 *Quest of the Seventh Carrier* (1989)
5 *Attack of the Seventh Carrier* (1989)
6 *Trial of the Seventh Carrier* (1990)
7 *Revenge of the Seventh Carrier* (1992)
8 *Ordeal of the Seventh Carrier* (1992)
9 *Challenge of the Seventh Carrier* (1993)
10 *Super carrier* (1994)

Seventh child series
Gage, Joy Pennock
1 *Land of heart's desire* (1991)
2 *Lee Williams's quest* (1991)
3 *Waiting legacy* (1991)

Seventh sword trilogy
Duncan, Dave
1 *Reluctant swordsman* (1988)
2 *Coming of wisdom* (1988)
3 *Destiny of the sword* (1988)

Several worlds series
Buck, Pearl Sydenstricker
Autobiography
1 *My several worlds* (1954)
2 *Bridge for passing* (1962)

Severance series
Scherf, Margaret
see **Grace Severance series**

Severn series
Bromley, Gordon
see **Inspector Severn series**

Severson series
Wells, Tobias
see **Detective Knute Severson series**

Sevrel series
Worth, Cedric
see **Inspector Sevrel series**

Sex research series
Catling, Patrick Skene
1 *Experiment* (1967)
2 *Surrogate* (1972)

Sexecutioner series
Chase, Glen
see **Cherry Delight series**

Sexton Blake series
This sequence has one hundred and nineteen authors; it includes all Sexton Blake titles identified to date which, for convenience, are listed in order of publication
Bobin, John William
1 *Shadow of his crime* (1915)
Murray, Andrew
2 *Rajah's revenge* (1915)
3 *Ill gotten gains* (1915)
Teed, George Hamilton
4 *Yellow tiger* (1915)
Alais, Ernest W
5 *Lease of Convict 308* (1916)
Bobin, John William
6 *Banker's trust* (1916)
7 *Grip of the law* (1916)
8 *Merchant's secret* (1916)
9 *Payment in full* (1916)
Brooks, Edwy Searles
10 *Midst Balkan perils* (1916)
11 *Red spider* (1916)
12 *Case of the twin detectives* (1916)
13 *Peril of the prince!* (1916)
Graydon, William Murray
14 *Case of the suppressed will* (1916)
15 *Case of the cashiered officer* (1916)
16 *Their great adventure* (1916)
17 *In triple disguise* (1916)
Murray, Andrew
18 *Black chrysanthemum* (1916)
19 *Victims of villainy* (1916)
20 *His Excellency's secret* (1916)
21 *Golden belts* (1916)
Teed, George Hamilton
22 *Two mysteries* (1916)
Alais, Ernest W
23 *Case of blackmail* (1917)
Bayfield, William John
24 *When conscience sleeps* (1917)
Bobin, John William
25 *Ten years after* (1917)
26 *Case of the international adventurer* (1917)
27 *Sexton Blake, special constable* (1917)
Also published under the pseudonym Mark Osborne
28 *Legacy of shame* (1917)
Brooks, Edwy Searles
29 *House with the double moat* (1917)
Graydon, William Murray
30 *Three trails* (1917)
31 *Perils of Petrograd* (1917)
Goddard, Norman
32 *Man with the green eyes* (1917)
Graydon, Robert Murray
33 *Mysterious Mister Reece* (1917)
Hardy, Arthur Steffens
34 *Traitor and spy* (1917)
Graydon, William Murray
35 *Craft and cunning* (1917)
36 *Blockade runners* (1917)
37 *Embassy detective* (1917)
38 *Where the trail ended* (1917)
39 *Secret of the past* (1917)
Murray, Andrew
40 *Half-caste* (1917)
41 *Barrier Reef mystery* (1917)
42 *Black bat* (1917)
43 *Catspaw* (1917)
44 *Secret of Draker's Folly* (1917)
45 *Vengeance* (1917)
Teed, George Hamilton
46 *Diamond sunburst* (1917)
Graydon, William Murray
47 *Reformation of Royce Remington* (1918)
48 *Ordeal of Alick Hillersdon* (1918)
49 *Tern day's leave* (1918)
Bayfield, William John
50 *Matter of millions* (1918)
Bobin, John William
51 *Case of the two bankers* (1918)
52 *Stolen crown* (1918)
53 *In the shadow of the guillotine* (1918)
54 *Case of the girl reporter* (1918)
Hardy, Arthur Steffens
55 *Sexton Blake's vow* (1918)
Graydon, William Murray
56 *Great abduction mystery* (1918)
Murray, Andrew
57 *Missing ships* (1918)
58 *Luck of the Darrells* (1918)
59 *Mosque of the Mahdi* (1918)
60 *Case of the two brothers* (1918)
61 *Secret of the hulk* (1918)
Bayfield, William John
62 *Whose was the hand?* (1918)
Graydon, William Murray
63 *Salvage of the sea* (1919)
64 *Record of the case* (1919)
Murray, Andrew
65 *Loot!* (1919)
Graydon, William Murray
66 *Sheep in wolf's clothing* (1919)
Bayfield, William John
67 *Affair of the demobilized soldier* (1919)
68 *Bungalow tragedy* (1919)
69 *Fourth theory* (1919)
70 *Clue of the charred diary* (1919)
Bobin, John William
71 *Stolen partnership papers* (1919)
72 *Riddle of Riverdale* (1919)
73 *Mystery of the grey car* (1919)
74 *Mystery of the Agony* (1919)
75 *Matador's fortune* (1919)
76 *Problem of the Derby favorite* (1919)
77 *Island mystery* (1919)
78 *Boy without a memory* (1919)
79 *Hidden menace!* (1919)
80 *Daylight robbery* (1919)
Graydon, Robert Murray
81 *Masquerader* (1919)
Hardy, Arthur Steffens
82 *Secret of the mine* (1919)
83 *Crimson mask* (1919)
Graydon, William Murray
84 *Case of the mysterious jockey* (1919)
85 *Five diamonds* (1919)
86 *Dark secrets* (1919)
87 *Five years after* (1919)
Lewis, Jack
88 *Red heart of the Incas* (1919)
Murray, Andrew
89 *Across the divide* (1919)
Merland, Oliver
90 *Branded spy* (1919)
Lewis, Jack
91 *Kestrel Syndicate* (1919)
92 *Chink in the armour* (1919)
93 *Case of the transatlantic fliers* (1919)
Murray, Andrew
94 *Tinker's lone hand* (1919)
95 *Station master's secret* (1919)
96 *Bathchair mystery* (1919)
97 *Settler or slaver* (1919)
98 *Red crescent* (1919)
99 *Mandarin's seal* (1919)
100 *Outcasts* (1919)
101 *Case of the seaside crooks* (1919)
102 *Broken trail* (1919)
103 *First-born son* (1919)
104 *Case of the Burmese dagger* (1919)
105 *Ex-soldier employment swindle* (1919)
106 *Convict by proxy* (1919)
Poole, Reginald Heber
107 *Unjustly branded* (1919)
Alais, Ernest W
108 *Camuflage* (1919)
Bayfield, William John
109 *Case of the bogus ingots* (1920)
110 *Home of his children* (1920)
111 *Lincoln's Inn tragedy* (1920)
Also published under the pseudonym Allan Blair
112 *Marble Arch mystery* (1920)
113 *Twist in the tail* (1920)
Brooks, Leonard Harold
114 *Affair of the Blackfriars financier* (1920)
115 *Avenging seven* (1920)
Bobin, John William
116 *Great diamond bluff* (1920)
117 *His son's honour* (1920)
118 *Link by link* (1920)
119 *Only son* (1920)
120 *Out of the reach of the law* (1920)
121 *Twice wronged!* (1920)
Graydon, William Murray
122 *African gold* (1920)
123 *Black streak* (1920)
124 *By the terms of the will* (1920)
125 *Hand that hid in darkness* (1920)
126 *Shadowed lives* (1920)
127 *Vengeance of three* (1920)
Lewis, Jack
128 *Affair of the Oriental doctor* (1920)
129 *Affair of the world's champion* (1920)
130 *False alibi* (1920)
131 *Jewels of Wu Ling* (1920)
132 *Kestrel's claw* (1920)
133 *Mystery of X04* (1920)
Merland, Oliver
134 *Case of the nameless man* (1920)
Murray, Andrew
135 *Admiral's secret* (1920)
136 *Beachcomber* (1920)
137 *Blood-Brotherhood* (1920)
138 *Changeling* (1920)
139 *Head hunter's secret* (1920)
140 *In the midnight express* (1920)
141 *Man from Kura-Kura* (1920)
142 *Mystery of the thousand peaks* (1920)
143 *Palzer experiment* (1920)
144 *Secret of the glacier* (1920)
145 *Secret of the hunger desert* (1920)
146 *Sheikh's son* (1920)
Poole, Reginald Heber
147 *King's secret* (1920)
148 *Prison breakers* (1920)
149 *Trail under the sea* (1920)
Wignall, Trevor C
150 *Case of the Japanese detective* (1920)
151 *House with the red blinds* (1920)
Sayer, Walter William
152 *Case of the king's spy* (1920)
Missing spy
153 *Case of the strange wireless message* (1920)
154 *Mystery of the living shadow* (1920)
Living shadow
155 *Mystery of the Turkish agreement* (1920)
156 *Mystery box* (1920)
Armour, R Coutts
157 *Leopard man* (1921)
158 *Man who forgot* (1921)
159 *Terror Island* (1921)
160 *Through fire and water* (1921)
Bayfield, William John
161 *Affair of the family diamonds* (1921)
162 *Architect's secret* (1921)
163 *Case of the deserted wife* (1921)
164 *Case of the double tangle* (1921)
165 *False scents* (1921)
Brooks, Leonard Harold
166 *Gnat* (1921)
Bobin, John William
167 *Case of the island trader* (1921)
168 *Payment suspended* (1921)
Hill, Harry Egbert
169 *Idol's eye* (1921)
Home-Gall, William Benjamin
170 *State secrets* (1921)
Graydon, William Murray
171 *At the shrine of the Buddha* (1921)
172 *Brach of trust* (1921)
173 *Case for the prosecution* (1921)
174 *Case of the five merchants* (1921)
175 *Case of the mill owner's son* (1921)
176 *Four trails* (1921)
177 *Gipsy or gentleman?* (1921)
178 *Green turban* (1921)
179 *One of the Flying Squad* (1921)
180 *Sign of the serpent* (1921)
181 *Thirty years after* (1921)
182 *Within fourteen days* (1921)
183 *Yellow face* (1921)
Lewis, Jack
184 *Kestrel's conspiracy* (1921)
185 *Lady of Ravensedge* (1921)
Murray, Andrew
186 *Ambergris!* (1921)
187 *Black opal mine* (1921)
188 *Case of the cinema star* (1921)
189 *Case of the mystery millionaire* (1921)
190 *Case of the undischarged bankrupt* (1921)
191 *City of apes* (1921)
192 *Hidden message* (1921)
193 *Man in the grey cowl* (1921)
194 *Marooned!* (1921)
195 *Mystery of the hundred chests* (1921)
Murray, Edgar Joyce
196 *Pride of the stable* (1921)
Poole, Reginald Heber
197 *Case of the Russian crown jewels* (1921)

Symonds, Francis Addington
198 *Golden casket* (1921)
199 *Iron claw* (1921)
200 *Valley of fear* (1921)
Philips, George Norman
201 *Roumanian envoy* (1921)
Sayer, Walter William
202 *Sacred city* (1921)
203 *Secret of the frozen north* (1921)
204 *Secret of the red mountain* (1921)
Red mountain
205 *Secret of the six black dots* (1921)
Mystery of the missing aviator
Alais, Ernest W
206 *Doctor's double* (1921)
Armour, R Coutts
207 *Episode of the stolen voice* (1921)
208 *By the skin of his teeth* (1922)
209 *Diamond flood* (1922)
210 *Lighthouse mystery* (1922)
211 *Mystery of the sunken road* (1922)
212 *Studio mystery* (1922)
213 *Werewolf of Elphinstone* (1922)
214 *White refugees* (1922)
Bayfield, William John
215 *Case of the vanished husband* (1922)
216 *Mystery of the missing journalist* (1922)
Brooks, Leonard Harold
217 *Fingerprints of fate!* (1922)
218 *House of ghosts* (1922)
Edgar, Alfred
219 *Lawless justice* (1922)
220 *Power of the unknown* (1922)
221 *Sign in the sky* (1922)
Also published as *The secret of the Tong*, under the pseudonym H Gregory
Bobin, John William
222 *Case of the bogus laird* (1922)
223 *Case of the cultured pearls* (1922)
224 *Case of the trade secret* (1922)
225 *Hoodd riders* (1922)
226 *In the grip of the Tong* (1922)
Brooks, Edwy Searles
227 *On the bed of the ocean* (1922)
Hill, Harry Egbert
228 *Case of the rajah's son* (1922)
229 *Golden goddess* (1922)
230 *Mill pond mystery* (1922)
231 *Rajah of Ghanapore* (1922)
Graydon, William Murray
232 *Brigand's secret* (1922)
233 *Derelicts* (1922)
234 *Earl's return* (1922)
235 *Lady Sharlow's secret* (1922)
236 *Lama's secret* (1922)
237 *Lost in Cambodia* (1922)
238 *Mystery of the swamp* (1922)
239 *Sexton Blake inb Silesia* (1922)
240 *Taming of Neville Ibbetson* (1922)
241 *Trader's daughter* (1922)
Lewis, Jack
242 *Case of the Bendigo heirlooms* (1922)
243 *Fallen star* (1922)
Murray, Andrew
244 *Beyond the law* (1922)
245 *Case of the paralyzed man* (1922)
246 *Case of the uncut gems* (1922)
247 *Case of the un-named film* (1922)
248 *Case of the woman in black* (1922)
249 *Great explosion* (1922)
250 *Motor coach mystery* (1922)
251 *Mystery of the clock* (1922)
252 *Prisoner of the Kremlin* (1922)
Murray, Edgar Joyce
253 *Case of the crimson wizard* (1922)
Symonds, Francis Addington
254 *Case of the twisted trail* (1922)
255 *Red dwarf* (1922)
Philips, George Norman
256 *Albino's double* (1922)
Sayer, Walter William
257 *Crimson domino* (1922)
Red domino
258 *Phantom of the Pacific* (1922)
259 *Riders of the sands* (1922)
260 *Secret of the oblong chest* (1922)
Teed, George Hamilton
261 *Case of the Courtlandt jewels* (1922)
262 *Diamond dragon* (1922)
263 *Ivory screen* (1922)
264 *Spirit smuggler* (1922)
Alais, Ernest W
265 *In the shadow of night* (1922)
Armour, R Coutts
266 *Baboon's paw* (1922)
267 *Case of the island princess* (1923)
268 *Case of the mysterious germs* (1923)
269 *Desert trail* (1923)
270 *In savage Hayti* (1923)
271 *Secret of the lagoon* (1923)
272 *Sun god* (1923)
Bayfield, William John
273 *Affair of the seven mummy cases* (1923)
274 *Doctor's secret* (1923)
275 *Last clue* (1923)
Brooks, Leonard Harold
276 *Mystery of Glyn Castle* (1923)
277 *Secret of Thurlston Towers* (1923)
Edgar, Alfred
278 *Secret of the safe* (1923)
Bobin, John William
279 *Legacy of vengeance* (1923)
280 *Mystery mandarin* (1923)
Brooks, Edwy Searles
281 *Green eyes* (1923)
282 *House at Waterloo* (1923)
Hill, Harry Egbert
283 *Actor's secret* (1923)
284 *In darkest Madras* (1923)
Gibbons, Harry Hornaby Clifford
285 *Great revue mystery* (1923)
286 *Solved in thirty-six hours!* (1923)
Graydon, William Murray
287 *Arctic trail* (1923)
288 *Case of the adopted daughter* (1923)
289 *Case of the four barons* (1923)
290 *Down east* (1923)
291 *Mystery of the Dover Road* (1923)
292 *Path of fear* (1923)
293 *Shield of the law* (1923)
Lewis, Jack
294 *House of fear* (1923)
Merland, Oliver
295 *Case of the man in black* (1923)
296 *Face in the film* (1923)
Murray, Andrew
297 *Case of the amber crown* (1923)
298 *Case of the cotton beetle* (1923)
299 *Case of the master organizer* (1923)
300 *Crook's double* (1923)
301 *Man behind the curtain* (1923)
302 *North of fifty five degrees* (1923)
303 *Oyster-bed mystery* (1923)
Murray, Edgar Joyce
304 *Mansion of shadows* (1923)
Sayer, Walter William
305 *Case of the cabaret girl* (1923)
306 *Case of the five dummy books* (1923)
307 *Lost expedition* (1923)
308 *Outlaws of Yugo-Slavia* (1923)
Teed, George Hamilton
309 *Crimson belt* (1923)
310 *Eight-pointed star* (1923)
311 *Orloff diamond* (1923)
312 *Secret emerald mines* (1923)
Armour, R Coutts
313 *Adventure of the oil pirates* (1924)
314 *Case of the eccentric will* (1924)
315 *Case of the kidnapped legatee* (1924)
Also published as *The secret of the gold locket*, under the pseudonym Pierre Quiroule
316 *Case of the millionaire newspaper owner* (1924)
317 *Certified insane* (1924)
318 *Platinum smugglers* (1924)
319 *Trail of the Tiger* (1924)
Bayfield, William John
320 *Case of the income-tax frauds* (1924)
321 *Case of the millionaire's blackmail* (1924)
322 *Farrowshot Park affair* (1924)
323 *Flat Number 4* (1924)
324 *Old Tollgate mystery* (1924)
325 *Strange case of Habberton's Mile* (1924)
Bobin, John William
326 *Case of the head dispenser* (1924)
Brooks, Edwy Searles
327 *Boarding-house mystery* (1924)
328 *Brixham Manor mystery* (1924)
329 *Case of the sleeping partner* (1924)
330 *Human bloodhound* (1924)
331 *Mystery of Rodney's Cove* (1924)
Hill, Harry Egbert
332 *Great museum mystery* (1924)
333 *Loot of Nana Sahib* (1924)
334 *Shrine of Kali* (1924)
Also published as *The curse of Kali*, under the pseudonym Hylton Gregory
Jones, J G
335 *Secret of the bucket shop* (1924)
Gibbons, Harry Hornaby Clifford
336 *Affair of the country club* (1924)
337 *King's secret* (1924)
338 *Secret millionaire* (1924)
339 *Secret of the Carpathians* (1924)
340 *Secret people* (1924)
341 *Third key* (1924)
Graydon, William Murray
342 *Affair of the three gunmen* (1924)
343 *Amateur in crime* (1924)
344 *Case of the two guardians* (1924)
345 *Curious case of the crook's memoirs* (1924)
346 *Game keeper's secret* (1924)
347 *In double disguise* (1924)
348 *In the hand of the Riffs* (1924)
349 *Mystery of the abandoned cttage* (1924)
350 *Next o' kin* (1924)
351 *Prisoner of Ellis Island* (1924)
Merland, Oliver
352 *Case of Larachi the Lascar* (1924)
Miln, H Crichton
353 *Case of the rival race gangs* (1924)
Murray, Edgar Joyce
354 *Great circus mystery* (1924)
Sayer, Walter William
355 *Forest of fortune* (1924)
356 *Mystery of the lost battle-ship* (1924)
Havana mystery
357 *Secret of the black wallet* (1924)
Man with the black wallet
358 *Vanished million* (1924)
Teed, George Hamilton
359 *Case of the clairvoyant's ruse* (1924)
360 *Case of the jade-handled knife* (1924)
361 *Great ivory swindle* (1924)
Armour, R Coutts
362 *Clue of the cloakroom ticket* (1925)
Bayfield, William John
363 *Case of the deported aliens* (1925)
364 *Case of the press photographer* (1925)
365 *Crumblerock crime!* (1925)
366 *Mystery of the Pot-bank* (1925)
367 *Secret of the mansions* (1925)
Brooks, Edwy Searles
368 *In the night watch* (1925)
Hardy, Arthur Steffens
369 *Trainer's secret* (1925)
Hill, Harry Egbert
370 *Hunchback of Hatton Garden!* (1925)
Evans, Gwyn
371 *Barton Manor mystery* (1925)
Curse of the Santyres
372 *Man who never slept!* (1925)
Case of the man who never slept
Gibbons, Harry Hornaby Clifford
373 *Affair of the diamond star* (1925)
374 *Case of the bogus bride!* (1925)
375 *Case of the red Crimona's* (1925)
376 *Crook of Mayfair* (1925)
377 *Limited liability* (1925)
378 *On the night express* (1925)
379 *Riddle of the registry office* (1925)
380 *Yellow cat* (1925)
Graydon, William Murray
381 *Adventure of the Annamese prince* (1925)
382 *Black cargo* (1925)
383 *By order of the king!* (1925)
384 *Case of the nabob's son* (1925)
385 *Case of the society blackmailer* (1925)
386 *Case of the two scapegraces* (1925)
387 *Held in trust!* (1925)
388 *His father's crime* (1925)
389 *Priest's secret* (1925)
Murray, Edgar Joyce
390 *Affair of the phantom car* (1925)
391 *Legacy of doom* (1925)
Pentelow, John Nix
392 *Missing in Mexico* (1925)
Symonds, Francis Addington
393 *By order of the Soviet* (1925)
394 *Case of the golden stool* (1925)
Philips, George Norman
395 *Amazing affair of the renegade prince* (1925)
396 *Mystery of the Swanley Viaduct* (1925)
Also published under the pseudonym Anthony Skene
Sayer, Walter William
397 *Adventure of the Albanian avenger* (1925)
Mystery of the Albanian avenger
398 *Mystery of the platinum nugget!* (1925)
Soho Cafe crime
Teed, George Hamilton
399 *Black eagle* (1925)
400 *Case of the Chinese puzzle* (1925)
401 *Case of the ten diamonds* (1925)
402 *Clue of the four wigs* (1925)
403 *Great Canal plot* (1925)
404 *Mystery of the Seine* (1925)
405 *Secret of the coconut groves* (1925)
406 *Under the eagle's wing* (1925)
Armour, R Coutts
407 *Adventure of the Egyptian student* (1925)
408 *Adventure of the silk smugglers* (1926)
409 *Affair of the trade rivals* (1926)
410 *Mystery of Bullen Point* (1926)
411 *Riddle of the lost emigrant* (1926)
412 *Secret of Torre Island* (1926)
413 *Treasure of the Manchus* (1926)
Bayfield, William John
414 *Adventure of the red-headed man* (1926)
415 *Council of crooks* (1926)
416 *Crook's double* (1926)
417 *Death duty swindle* (1926)
418 *Mystery of Hanging Sword Alley* (1926)
419 *Mystery of the seaside hotel* (1926)
Brooks, Leonard Harold
420 *Riddle of the Lascar's Head* (1926)
Bobin, John William
421 *Case of the bookmaker baronet* (1926)
422 *Case of the long-firm frauds* (1926)
Also published under the pseudonym Mark Osborne
Brooks, Edwy Searles
423 *Impersonators* (1926)
Hardy, Arthur Steffens
424 *Mystery of the championship belt* (1926)
Hill, Harry Egbert
425 *Blackmailed baronet* (1926)
Also published as *The mystery of the blackmailed baronet*, under the pseudonym Hylton Gregory
Evans, Gwyn
426 *Crook of Fleet Street* (1926)
Gibbons, Harry Hornaby Clifford
427 *Affair of the cross-roads* (1926)
428 *Case of the old oak chest* (1926)
429 *Case of the silent safe-cutters* (1926)

430 *Excavator's secret* (1926)
Also published under the pseudonym Gilbert Chester
431 *South Coast mystery* (1926)
Graydon, William Murray
432 *Affair of the missing witness* (1926)
433 *Behind the walls* (1926)
434 *Blackshirt mystery* (1926)
435 *Bloodhound's revenge* (1926)
436 *Case of the bogus treasure hunt* (1926)
437 *Case of the theatrical profiteer* (1926)
438 *Clause in the will* (1926)
439 *Prisoner of the mountains* (1926)
440 *White death* (1926)
441 *Yacht of mystery* (1926)
Murray, Edgar Joyce
442 *Calcroft case* (1926)
443 *Case of the lone plantation* (1926)
444 *City of masks* (1926)
445 *Menace of the silent death* (1926)
446 *Tangle of terror* (1926)
Symonds, Francis Addington
447 *Out of the fog* (1926)
Philips, George Norman
448 *Affair of the seven warnings* (1926)
Sayer, Walter William
449 *Black limousine* (1926)
One hundred thousand pound insurance swindle
450 *Ethiopian's secret* (1926)
Teed, George Hamilton
451 *Black emperor* (1926)
452 *Case of the mummified hand* (1926)
453 *Island of the guilty* (1926)
454 *Riddle of the Russian gold* (1926)
Graydon, William Murray
455 *Shipwrecked detective* (1926)
Armour, R Coutts
456 *Dead man's shoes* (1927)
457 *Movie mystery* (1927)
458 *Pirates of the air way* (1927)
459 *Prisoner of the Buddha* (1927)
Bayfield, William John
460 *All suspected* (1927)
461 *City of horrors* (1927)
462 *Oath of fear* (1927)
463 *Secret of the tomb* (1927)
464 *Trail of the old lag* (1927)
Bidston, Lester
465 *Phantom of the mill* (1927)
Edgar, Alfred
466 *Cup Final mystery* (1927)
Bobin, John William
467 *Fatal pit* (1927)
Also published under the pseudonym Mark Osborne
468 *Tour of terror* (1927)
Also published under the pseudonym Mark Osborne
Brandon, John Gordon
469 *Joy ride* (1927)
Hardy, Arthur Steffens
470 *Team of crooks* (1927)
Hill, Harry Egbert
471 *Riddle of the amber room* (1927)
Also published as *The sign of the black feather*, under the pseudonym Hylton Gregory
Evans, Gwyn
472 *Case of the poisoned pen* (1927)
473 *Prisoners of Peru* (1927)
Gibbons, Harry Hornaby Clifford
474 *Affair of the kidnapped crook* (1927)
475 *Great salvage swindle* (1927)
476 *Mystery of the four rooms* (1927)
477 *Mystery of the mansion fire* (1927)
478 *Secret of the snows* (1927)
Also published under the pseudonym Gilbert Chester
479 *Who killed Carson?* (1927)
Graydon, William Murray
480 *Adventure of the rogue's apprentice* (1927)
481 *Burglar of White Birches* (1927)
482 *Case of the human ape* (1927)
483 *Crime in the wood* (1927)
484 *Crook of Chinatown* (1927)
485 *Man who drove on* (1927)
486 *Masked dictator* (1927)
487 *Rogues of the desert* (1927)
488 *Trail of death* (1927)
489 *Wanted* (1927)
Murray, Edgar Joyce
490 *Palace of terror* (1927)
491 *Riddle of the golden fingers* (1927)
Pentelow, John Nix
492 *Cleopatra Needle mystery* (1927)
493 *Three masked men* (1927)
Poole, Reginald Heber
494 *Great trunk mystery* (1927)
Also published under the pseudonym H Gregory
Symonds, Francis Addington
495 *Case of the hold-up king* (1927)
Townley, Houghton
496 *Case of the human mole* (1927)
Verner, Gerald
497 *Clue of the second tooth* (1927)
Philips, George Norman
498 *Giant city swindle* (1927)
Also published under the pseudonym Anthony Skene
Teed, George Hamilton
499 *Case of the disguised Apache* (1927)
500 *Mystery of the film city* (1927)
501 *Night-club mystery* (1927)
502 *Rogues' republic* (1927)
503 *Terror of Tangier* (1927)
504 *Tiger of Canton* (1927)
Armour, R Coutts
505 *Affair of the crook explorer* (1928)
506 *Mystery of the Isle of Fortune* (1928)
507 *Trail of doom* (1928)
Bayfield, William John
508 *Adventure of the man on bail* (1928)
509 *Flying Squad tragedy* (1928)
510 *Riddle of the million pound bet* (1928)
Carlton, Lewis
511 *Monomark mystery* (1928)
Graydon, Robert Murray
512 *Mystery of the mandarin's idol* (1928)
Hardy, Arthur Steffens
513 *Case of the mystery champion* (1928)
Evans, Gwyn
514 *Case of the crimson conjuror* (1928)
515 *Case of the Jack of Clubs* (1928)
516 *King of the underworld* (1928)
517 *Mystery of Mitcham Common* (1928)
Gibbons, Harry Hornaby Clifford
518 *Fur raiders* (1928)
Also published under the pseudonym Gilbert Chester
519 *Riddle of the garage* (1928)
520 *Riddle of the runaway cat* (1928)
521 *Riddle of the West End hairdresser* (1928)
Also published under the pseudonym Gilbert Chester
Graydon, William Murray
522 *Case of the fatal taxi cab* (1928)
523 *Deserter of the Foreign Legion* (1928)
524 *Doctor who wouldn't tell* (1928)
525 *Mystery of Monte Carlo* (1928)
526 *Mystery of the golden chalice* (1928)
527 *Riddle of Crocodile Creek* (1928)
528 *Rogue of Afghanistan* (1928)
529 *Secret of the Russian refugees* (1928)
530 *Secret of the two blackmailed men* (1928)
Murray, Andrew
531 *Adventure of the speed mad Camden* (1928)
532 *Secret of the green lagoon* (1928)
Shaw, Stanley Gordon
533 *Secret of the monastery* (1928)
Shute, Walter
534 *Affair of the rival cinema kings* (1928)
Symonds, Francis Addington
535 *Man from Australia* (1928)
Verner, Gerald
536 *Box of doom* (1928)
537 *Mystery of Sherwood Towers* (1928)
Also published under the author's real name Donald Stuart
538 *Mystery of the phantom blackmailer* (1928)
539 *Riddle of the phantom plague* (1928)
Philips, George Norman
540 *Case of the rejuvenated millionaire* (1928)
Also published under the pseudonym Anthony Skene
541 *Mystery of the shot P.C.* (1928)
Also published under the pseudonym Anthony Skene
Teed, George Hamilton
542 *Adventure of the bogus sheik* (1928)
543 *Adventure of the voodoo queen* (1928)
544 *Case of the bogus monk* (1928)
545 *Case of the Portuguese giantess* (1928)
546 *Crooks in clover* (1928)
547 *Eighth millionaire* (1928)
548 *Rubber smugglers* (1928)
549 *Terror of Gold-Digger Creek* (1928)
550 *Victim of black magic* (1928)
Armour, R Coutts
551 *Affair of the Atlantic mail robbery* (1929)
552 *Bootlegger's victim* (1929)
553 *Riddle of the dead man's pit* (1929)
554 *Riddle of the Great Art Exhibition* (1929)
555 *Secret of the cask* (1929)
Bayfield, William John
556 *Black Maria mystery* (1929)
557 *Covent Garden mystery* (1929)
558 *Death of Duboyne* (1929)
559 *Down and out* (1929)
560 *Masked forgers* (1929)
561 *Mint mystery* (1929)
Bidston, Lester
562 *Crooks Limited* (1929)
Blake, Stacey
563 *Prisoners of the desert* (1929)
Bobin, John William
564 *Great Tote fraud* (1929)
565 *Secret of the surgery* (1929)
Foster, Reginald Francis
566 *Secret of the white thug* (1929)
Gibbons, Harry Hornaby Clifford
567 *Ballot box mystery* (1929)
568 *Flaming belt* (1929)
569 *Motor show mystery* (1929)
Graydon, William Murray
570 *Bogus tourist-agency* (1929)
571 *Case of the murdered mahout* (1929)
572 *Man who came back* (1929)
Teed, George Hamilton
573 *Secret of the President's daughter* (1929)
Graydon, William Murray
574 *Mystery of the docks* (1929)
575 *Secret of the flames* (1929)
576 *Secret of the vampire actress* (1929)
577 *Sixth victim* (1929)
578 *Vanishing death* (1929)
Hardinge, Rex
579 *Midnight mystery* (1929)
Shute, Walter
580 *Case of the discharged P.C.* (1929)
581 *Fatal number* (1929)
582 *Mystery of Merlyn Mansions* (1929)
583 *Mystery of the uninvited guest* (1929)
Stanton-Hope, William Edward
584 *Dead man's sands* (1929)
Verner, Gerald
585 *Black skull* (1929)
586 *Fatal manuscript* (1929)
587 *Silent slayer* (1929)
Philips, George Norman
588 *Case of the crook M.P.* (1929)
589 *Man who squealed* (1929)
590 *Radium profiteer* (1929)
591 *Victim of the waterway* (1929)
Teed, George Hamilton
592 *Cabaret crime* (1929)
593 *Gunners* (1929)
594 *Mystery of the man from Rio* (1929)
595 *Pearls of doom* (1929)
596 *Prisoner of the chateau* (1929)
Blair, Allan
597 *Law courts mystery* (1930)
Armour, R Coutts
598 *Masked raiders* (1930)
Bayfield, William John
599 *Masked dancer* (1930)
Bidston, Lester
600 *Mystery of Oldham* (1930)
Black, Ladbroke
601 *Case of the crooked banker* (1930)
602 *Informer* (1930)
Blake, Stacey
603 *City of crooks* (1930)
Douthwaite, Louis Charles
604 *Horror house* (1930)
Drew, Sidney
605 *Gangster's deputy* (1930)
Blair, Allan
606 *Lombard Street mystery* (1930)
607 *Murder of Constable Cartwright* (1930)
608 *Mystery of the monument* (1930)
Brisbane, Coutts
609 *Gang's deserter* (1930)
610 *Trapper's victim* (1930)
Chester, Gilbert
611 *Green room crime* (1930)
Elliott, Robert Cowell
612 *Phantom bat* (1930)
Essex, Louis
613 *Crook of Crauford Court* (1930)
Graydon, Robert Murray
614 *Masked marauder* (1930)
Hardy, Arthur Steffens
615 *Who killed Trainer Lincoln?* (1930)
Hincks, Cyril Malcolm
616 *Throne of peril* (1930)
Evans, Gwyn
617 *Mission of doom* (1930)
618 *Silent jury* (1930)
Graydon, William Murray
619 *Crime of Convict 13* (1930)
620 *Desert of doom* (1930)
621 *Feud of fear* (1930)
Hardinge, Rex
622 *Fatal car* (1930)
623 *Mission of menace* (1930)
Poole, Michael
624 *Gang's orders* (1930)
Shute, Walter
625 *Talkie murder mystery* (1930)
Verner, Gerald
626 *Crime of four* (1930)
627 *Secret of the vault* (1930)
Philips, George Norman
628 *Gangster's revenge* (1930)
629 *Riddle of the three marked men* (1930)
Skene, Anthony
630 *Crook's accomplice* (1930)
631 *Death trap* (1930)
632 *Night raiders* (1930)
Stuart, Donald
633 *Death road* (1930)
634 *Fence's victim* (1930)
Teed, George Hamilton
635 *Cassidy the con man* (1930)
636 *Crook of Canada* (1930)
637 *Crook of Marsden Manor* (1930)
638 *Crook of Paris* (1930)
639 *House of silence* (1930)
640 *Masked killer* (1930)
641 *Secret of the strong room* (1930)
642 *Secret of the thieves' kitchen* (1930)
643 *Victim of the gang* (1930)
Ascott, John
644 *Great shipyard mystery* (1931)
Bidston, Lester
645 *Fatal alibi* (1931)
646 *Gang's prisoners* (1931)
647 *Silent syndicate* (1931)

Drew, Sidney
648 *Fortnight* (1931)
649 *Mansion House mystery* (1931)
Edwards, Walter
650 *Ambush* (1931)
Brisbane, Coutts
651 *Death house* (1931)
652 *Secret of the sanatorium* (1931)
Chester, Gilbert
653 *Murder on the marshes* (1931)
654 *Mystery gangster* (1931)
Hardy, Arthur Steffens
655 *Crook of Newmarket* (1931)
Hood, Stephen
656 *Crook from Chicago* (1931)
Hope, Stanton
657 *Death ship* (1931)
658 *Victim of the red mask* (1931)
Red mask
Evans, Gwyn
659 *Abandoned car crime* (1931)
660 *Crystal cell* (1931)
661 *Death sign* (1931)
662 *Riddle of the Turkish baths* (1931)
663 *Steel Face* (1931)
Hardinge, Rex
664 *Mission of vengeance* (1931)
665 *Radio crook* (1931)
Osborne, Mark
666 *Boarding house mystery* (1931)
Skene, Anthony
667 *Death gang* (1931)
668 *Death of four* (1930)
669 *Legacy of fear* (1931)
670 *Nameless five* (1931)
671 *Night-club crime* (1931)
672 *One million pound plot* (1931)
673 *Vault of doom* (1931)
Stuart, Donald
674 *Garden city crime* (1931)
675 *Hooded raider* (1931)
676 *Next victim* (1931)
677 *Terror of Lonely Tor* (1931)
Teed, George Hamilton
678 *Crime of the catacombs* (1931)
679 *Crime on Gallows Hill* (1931)
680 *Crook of Costab Blanca* (1931)
681 *Cross-Channel crime* (1931)
682 *Gang war* (1931)
683 *House of curtains* (1931)
684 *Yellow skull* (1931)
Urquhart, Paul
685 *Gun rule* (1931)
686 *Mystery of the thirteenth chest* (1931)
Bidston, Lester
687 *Cup Final crime* (1932)
688 *Mill of fear* (1932)
Carlton, Lewis
689 *Night safe mystery* (1932)
Douthwaite, Louis Charles
690 *Ghost trail* (1932)
Riddle of the Yukon
Edwards, Walter
691 *Murder on the moor* (1932)
Blair, Allan
692 *Policeboat mystery* (1932)
693 *Town hall crime* (1932)
694 *Waiting room mystery* (1932)
Brisbane, Coutts
695 *Fatal talisman* (1932)
696 *Murder in the air* (1932)
697 *Trafalgar Square mystery* (1932)
Chester, Gilbert
698 *Doctor Duvene's crime* (1932)
699 *Murder on the Broads* (1932)
700 *Palais de Danse tragedy* (1932)
701 *Secret of the farm* (1932)
702 *Studio crime* (1932)
Hope, Stanton
703 *Cruise of terror* (1932)
Evans, Gwyn
704 *Great waxworks crime* (1932)
705 *Man from Dartmoor* (1932)
706 *Sinister Castle* (1932)
Hardinge, Rex
707 *Masked slayer* (1932)
708 *Mystery of the reunion dinner* (1932)
709 *Secret of the African trader* (1932)
Jardine, Warwick
710 *Crook's loot* (1932)
711 *Doomed men* (1932)
Revised edition 1940
712 *Great dumping mystery* (1932)
Osborne, Mark
713 *Consulting room crime* (1932)
Consulting room mystery
The second title is a revised edition
714 *Dead Man's Bay* (1932)
715 *Kennels crime* (1932)
Vickery, William
716 *Racketeer's will* (1932)
Skene, Anthony
717 *Crook town* (1932)
718 *Fatal mascot* (1932)
719 *Green mask* (1932)
720 *Red stilleto* (1932)
Stuart, Donald
721 *Case of the missing estate agent* (1932)
722 *Dead man's secret* (1932)
723 *Embankment crime* (1932)
724 *Secret of seven* (1932)
725 *Squealer's secret* (1932)
Teed, George Hamilton
726 *China town mystery* (1932)
727 *Crook of Monte Carlo* (1932)
728 *Crook of Shanghai* (1932)
729 *House of cellars* (1932)
730 *Phantom of the creek* (1932)
Urquhart, Paul
731 *Brooklands mystery* (1932)
732 *Bungalow crime* (1932)
733 *Mystery of the rajah's jewels* (1932)
734 *Presumed dead* (1932)
Blair, Allan
735 *Artificial road murder* (1933)
Bidston, Lester
736 *Motor coach murder* (1933)
Blake, Stacey
737 *On ticket of leave* (1933)
Carlton, Lewis
738 *Case of the stranded touring company* (1933)
Edwards, Walter
739 *Great stores crime* (1933)
740 *Hiker's secret* (1933)
Blair, Allan
741 *Lord Mayor's Show mystery* (1933)
742 *Man from Dublin* (1933)
Andrews, John
743 *Sexton Blake at the Varsity* (1933)
Brandon, John Gordon
744 *Survivor's secret* (1933)
745 *Taxi-cab murder* (1933)
746 *Tragedy of the West End actress* (1933)
Brisbane, Coutts
747 *Dead man's peak* (1933)
748 *Doctor Ferraro's frame-up* (1933)
749 *Mystery of the tramp steamer* (1933)
750 *Secret of the loch* (1933)
Brooks, Edwy Searles
751 *Black dagger* (1933)
Chester, Gilbert
752 *Case of the bogus prince* (1933)
753 *Crime on the Clyde* (1933)
754 *Murder to music* (1933)
Goyne, Richard
755 *Cinema crime* (1933)
Evans, Gwyn
756 *Death in the jungle* (1933)
757 *Doctor Sinister* (1933)
758 *Fatal friendship* (1933)
Hardinge, Rex
759 *Black-Hill murder case* (1933)
760 *Ivory tusk* (1933)
Jardine, Warwick
761 *Crime in Park Lane* (1933)
762 *Hailey Street murder* (1933)
763 *Man from Tokyo* (1933)
764 *Mystery of the unknown victim* (1933)
765 *Pleasure cruise murder* (1933)
766 *Secret of the Sudan* (1933)
Osborne, Mark
767 *Mystery of the lost legionnaire* (1933)
768 *Stables crime* (1933)
Skene, Anthony
769 *Circus crime* (1933)
770 *Derelict house* (1933)
771 *Road house murder* (1933)
772 *Silent menace* (1933)
Stuart, Donald
773 *Empty house murder* (1933)
774 *Guilty, but insane* (1933)
775 *One million pound film murder* (1933)
Teed, George Hamilton
776 *Crook's decoy* (1933)
777 *Isle of horror* (1933)
778 *Mystery of the old age pensioner* (1933)
779 *Rogues of ransom* (1933)
Urquhart, Paul
780 *Double cross* (1933)
781 *Mister Kilmer sees red* (1933)
782 *Victim of Devil's Alley* (1933)
783 *Yellow vengeance* (1933)
Blair, Allan
784 *Blazing garage crime* (1934)
785 *Crime at the seaside hotel* (1934)
Edwards, Walter
786 *Fatal memoirs* (1934)
Brandon, John Gordon
787 *Case of the gangster's moll* (1934)
788 *Championship crime* (1934)
789 *Chink's victim* (1934)
790 *Glass dagger* (1934)
791 *Murder on the stage* (1934)
792 *Mystery of the three city's* (1934)
793 *On the midnight beat* (1934)
794 *Under police protection* (1934)
Brisbane, Coutts
795 *Secret temple* (1934)
Chester, Gilbert
796 *Caravan crime* (1934)
797 *Case of the deportee* (1934)
798 *Savage pirates* (1934)
Goyne, Richard
799 *Kidnapper's victim* (1934)
Evans, Gwyn
800 *Black cap* (1934)
Hardinge, Rex
801 *Blazing launch murder* (1934)
802 *Man from Holland* (1934)
803 *Mystery of the murdered chef* (1934)
Jardine, Warwick
804 *British Museum mystery* (1934)
805 *Cloakroom murder* (1934)
Osborne, Mark
806 *Case of the crook iron master* (1934)
807 *Dog track murder* (1934)
808 *Great art gallery crime* (1934)
Quiroule, Pierre
809 *Secret of the woods* (1934)
810 *Slaver's secret* (1934)
Skene, Anthony
811 *Missing men* (1934)
812 *Riverside Club murder* (1934)
Stuart, Donald
813 *Motor bus murder* (1934)
814 *Village of fear* (1934)
Teed, George Hamilton
815 *Fatal amulet* (1934)
816 *Murder in Manchuria* (1934)
817 *Mystery of Cell Thirteen* (1934)
Urquhart, Paul
818 *Building estate murder* (1934)
819 *Crime at the crossroads* (1934)
820 *Murder by mistake* (1934)
Hunter, John
821 *Three die at midnight* (1934)
Blair, Allan
822 *Bathing pool mystery* (1935)
823 *Case of the crook councillor* (1935)
824 *Case of the murdered taxi driver* (1935)
Bridges, Thomas Charles
825 *Crime on the moor* (1935)
Edwards, Walter
826 *Case of the murdered pawn broker* (1935)
827 *Man in brown* (1935)
Blair, Allan
828 *Mystery of Becker's Brook* (1935)
829 *Secret inquest* (1935)
Brandon, John Gordon
830 *By order of the Tong* (1935)
831 *Case of the murdered commissionaire* (1935)
832 *Downing Street discovery* (1935)
833 *Murder in Y Division* (1935)
834 *Red boomerang* (1935)
835 *Yellow mask* (1935)
Brisbane, Coutts
836 *Mystery of the rajah's son* (1935)
837 *Nursing home crime* (1935)
838 *Secret of the glen* (1935)
Chester, Gilbert
839 *Abyssinian mystery* (1935)
840 *Beauty parlour mystery* (1935)
841 *Murder on the pier* (1935)
842 *Tithe war mystery* (1935)
Hardy, Arthur Steffens
843 *Bookmaker's crime* (1935)
844 *Touring company crime* (1935)
Hope, Stanton
845 *Case of the missing ships* (1935)
Hardinge, Rex
846 *Case of the black magician* (1935)
847 *Crime in Carson's Shack* (1935)
848 *Secret of the smuggler's cove* (1935)
Jardine, Warwick
849 *Secret of the glacier* (1935)
850 *Stolen test-tube* (1935)
Quiroule, Pierre
851 *Secret of the armaments king* (1935)
Skene, Anthony
852 *Rush hour crime* (1935)
Stuart, Donald
853 *Cottage of terror* (1935)
854 *Secret of the sealed room* (1935)
855 *Truth about Lord Tench* (1935)
Teed, George Hamilton
856 *Martello Tower mystery* (1935)
857 *Mystery of the cashiered officer* (1935)
Urquhart, Paul
858 *Crime of Count Dureen* (1935)
Hunter, John
859 *Case of the fatal film* (1935)
Blair, Allan
860 *Crime at the quay* (1936)
Dix, Maurice Buxton
861 *Victim of the girl spy* (1936)
Edwards, Walter
862 *Barber's shop crime* (1936)
863 *Secret of the identification parade* (1936)
Blair, Allan
864 *Man with the glaring eyes* (1936)
865 *Old Bailey mystery* (1936)
Brandon, John Gordon
866 *Case of the night club queen* (1936)
867 *Dead man's evidence* (1936)
868 *Girl who knew too much* (1936)
869 *Murder on the fourth floor* (1936)
870 *Mystery of the murdered blonde* (1936)
871 *Mystery of the three acrobats* (1936)
872 *Victim of the thieves' den* (1936)
Brisbane, Coutts
873 *Blind man's secret* (1936)
874 *Case of the three absconding swindlers* (1936)
875 *Crime of Gunga Das* (1936)
876 *Secret of the Balkan heiress* (1936)
877 *Trail of the white turban* (1936)
Chester, Gilbert
878 *Case of the brass-bound chest* (1936)
879 *Mystery of the Greek exile* (1936)
880 *Mystery of the Old Curiosity Shop* (1936)
881 *Secret of the steps* (1936)
882 *Stage door crime* (1936)
883 *Taxi man's quest* (1936)
Frazer, Martin
884 *Crime at Crown Inn* (1936)
Hope, Stanton
885 *Dockyard mystery* (1936)
886 *Terror of Thunder Creek* (1936)

Sexton Blake series

Hardinge, Rex
887 *Ex-serviceman's secret* (1936)
888 *Motor show mystery* (1936)
889 *Murder at Hermit's Cottage* (1936)
890 *Murder on the boat express* (1936)
891 *Mystery of the African mine* (1936)
892 *Secret of the sale room* (1936)
Jardine, Warwick
893 *Case of the murdered wedding guest* (1936)
894 *Seaside cafe crime* (1936)
895 *Seaside crime* (1936)
Maxwell, Allan
896 *Priest's secret* (1936)
Quiroule, Pierre
897 *Mystery of number thirteen Cavendish Square* (1936)
Stuart, Donald
898 *Bells of doom* (1936)
Teed, George Hamilton
899 *Dictator's secret* (1936)
Hunter, John
900 *Crook cargo* (1936)
901 *Trail of the dope chief* (1936)
Blair, Allan
902 *Case of the blackmailed banker* (1937)
Bowman, Gerald
903 *Devil's old* (1937)
904 *Hunchback of Hatton Garden* (1937)
Creasey, John
905 *Case of the murdered financier* (1937)
Dilnot, George
906 *Crime reporter's secret* (1937)
Dix, Maurice Buxton
907 *Secret of the dead convict* (1937)
Edwards, Walter
908 *Mystery of the marchers* (1937)
Blair, Allan
909 *Riddle of Five Needle Creek* (1937)
Brandon, John Gordon
910 *Crime in the kiosk* (1937)
911 *Diamond of Ti Lingo* (1937)
912 *Man from Italy* (1937)
913 *Melbourne mystery* (1937)
914 *Mystery of the murdered sentry* (1937)
915 *Mystery of X20* (1937)
916 *Spy from Spain* (1937)
917 *Tattooed triangle* (1937)
918 *Victim of the secret service* (1937)
919 *Bond Street raiders* (1937)
Brisbane, Coutts
920 *Masked man of the desert* (1937)
Brooks, Edwy Searles
921 *Midnight lorry crime* (1937)
Chester, Gilbert
922 *Charity fund mystery* (1937)
923 *Coronation mystery* (1937)
924 *House on the cliffs* (1937)
925 *Man from Moscow* (1937)
Frazer, Martin
926 *Riddle of Dead Man's Mine* (1937)
Frost, C Vernon
927 *Crime on the heath* (1937)
Hope, Stanton
928 *Stolen submarine* (1937)
Hardinge, Rex
929 *Body on the beach* (1937)
930 *Man they could not convict* (1937)
931 *Mystery of the African expedition* (1937)
932 *Secret of the dental surgeon* (1937)
Jardine, Warwick
933 *Pavement artist mystery* (1937)
934 *Victim of the cult* (1937)
Perowne, Barry
935 *Raffles' crime in Gibraltar* (1937) American edition entitled *They hang them in Gibraltar* does not include Raffles
936 *Raffles versus Sexton Blake* (1937)
Quiroule, Pierre
937 *Three lepers' heads* (1937)
Parsons, Anthony
938 *Secret of the ten bales* (1937)
Skene, Anthony
939 *Terror of the tenaments* (1937)
Stuart, Donald
940 *Riddle of the sunken garden* (1937)
941 *Unknown menace* (1937)
Urquhart, Paul
942 *Boro Council ramp* (1937)
Hunter, John
943 *Crime on the promenade* (1937)
944 *Prisoner of Lost Island* (1937)
Blair, Allan
945 *Crooks' convoy* (1938)
Dilnot, George
946 *Black ace* (1938)
947 *Case of the missing bridegroom* (1938)
Edwards, Walter
948 *Newspaper seller's secret* (1938)
Blair, Allan
949 *Mystery of the missing constable* (1938)
Brandon, John Gordon
950 *Mystery of the ice-cream man* (1938)
951 *Clue of the tattooed man* (1938)
952 *False alibi* (1938)
953 *Murder on the high seas* (1938)
954 *Mystery of the dead man's wallet* (1938)
955 *Mystery of the murdered ice cream man* (1938)
956 *Mystery of the street musician* (1938)
957 *Pigeon loft crime* (1938)
958 *Roadhouse mystery* (1938)
Brisbane, Coutts
959 *Mystery of the missing doctor* (1938)
Chester, Gilbert
960 *Hire purchase crime* (1938)
961 *Secret of the sunken ships* (1938)
Gray, Berkeley
962 *Three frightened men* (1938)
Hope, Stanton
963 *Secret of sixty-six fathoms* (1938)
Hardinge, Rex
964 *Case of the kidnapped specialist* (1938)
965 *Case of the murdered postman* (1938)
966 *Dangerous gambler* (1938)
Jardine, Warwick
967 *Lift shaft crime* (1938)
Quiroule, Pierre
968 *Hated eight* (1938)
969 *Mystery of number seven Bitton Court* (1938)
Scott, Hedley
970 *Suspected six* (1938)
Parsons, Anthony
971 *Allah's Eye conspiracy* (1938)
972 *Riddle of Big Ben* (1938)
Stuart, Donald
973 *Danger at Westway's* (1938)
974 *Secret of the Moor House* (1938)
975 *Three who paid* (1938)
976 *Time of the crime* (1938)
Teed, George Hamilton
977 *Bailiff's secret* (1938)
Urquhart, Paul
978 *Man on the dole* (1938)
979 *Secret of the dead man* (1938)
Hunter, John
980 *Man who turned king's evidence* (1938)
981 *Secret of the hold* (1938)
Blair, Allan
982 *Case of the kidnapped prisoner* (1939)
983 *Case of the stolen police dossier* (1939)
Creasey, John
984 *Great air swindle* (1939)
Dix, Maurice Buxton
985 *Great hush-hush mystery* (1939)
Edwards, Walter
986 *Secret of the cellar* (1939)
Brandon, John Gordon
987 *Fatal forgery* (1939)
988 *Great taxi-cab ramp* (1939)
989 *Gunboat mystery* (1939)
990 *In the hands of spies* (1939)
991 *Man from Singapore* (1939)
992 *Man with jitters* (1939)
993 *Murder on the ice rink* (1939)
994 *Mystery of the green bottle* (1939)
Brisbane, Coutts
995 *Middle of the negro's head* (1939)
Chester, Gilbert
996 *Depository mystery* (1939)
997 *Monastery mystery* (1939)
998 *Mystery of the condemned cottage* (1939)
Hardinge, Rex
999 *Case of the missing musician* (1939)
1000 *Mystery of the African farm* (1939)
1001 *Police station mystery* (1939)
Jardine, Warwick
1002 *Riddle of the ranch* (1939)
1003 *Secret of the surgery* (1939)
1004 *Thirteenth code* (1939)
Quiroule, Pierre
1005 *Mystery of the missing envoy* (1939)
1006 *Riddle of the evil eye* (1939)
1007 *Riddle of the ugly face* (1939)
Scott, Hedley
1008 *Mystery of the missing refugee* (1939)
Parsons, Anthony
1009 *Case of the crook rajah* (1939)
1010 *Harem mystery* (1939)
1011 *Secret of the golden horse* (1939)
Stuart, Donald
1012 *Burmese dagger* (1939)
1013 *Hidden menace* (1939)
1014 *Third victim* (1939)
Urquhart, Paul
1015 *Mystery of the lorry driver* (1939)
Hunter, John
1016 *Riddle of the lost ship* (1939)
Blair, Allan
1017 *Case of the dictator's double* (1940)
Black, Ladbroke
1018 *Mystery miliataman* (1940)
Creasey, John
1019 *Man from Fleet Street* (1940)
Dix, Maurice Buxton
1020 *Secret of the Siegfried Line* (1940)
Edwards, Walter
1021 *Great stores mystery* (1940)
Brandon, John Gordon
1022 *Black swastika* (1940)
1023 *Crooks' cargo* (1940)
1024 *On ticket of leave* (1940)
1025 *Riddle of the dead man's bay* (1940)
1026 *Riddle of the Greek financier* (1940)
1027 *Terror of the Pacific* (1940)
Brisbane, Coutts
1028 *Mystery of the red tower* (1940)
Chester, Gilbert
1029 *Black-out crime* (1940)
1030 *Case of the man on leave* (1940)
1031 *Riddle of the gas meter* (1940)
1032 *Riddle of the murdered fisherman* (1940)
Frazer, Martin
1033 *Mystery of the German prisoner* (1940)
Gates, Clifford
1034 *Case of the murdered caretaker* (1940)
Hope, Stanton
1035 *Amazing affair of the shipyard sabotage* (1940)
1036 *In the grip of the Gestapo* (1940)
Hardinge, Rex
1037 *Man from the jungle* (1940)
1038 *Observer Corps mystery* (1940)
Parsons, Anthony
1039 *Case of the missing major* (1940)
1040 *Man from China* (1940)
1041 *Mystery of the free Frenchmen* (1940)
1042 *Secret of Oil Creek* (1940)
Stuart, Donald
1043 *Secret of the hulk* (1940)
1044 *Twenty years of hate* (1940)
Urquhart, Paul
1045 *Secret of the evacuee* (1940)
Hunter, John
1046 *House of darkness* (1940)
1047 *Mysterious Mister Maynard* (1940)
Brandon, John Gordon
1048 *Under secret orders* (1941)
Brooks, Edwy Searles
1049 *Riddle of the body on the road* (1941)
Chester, Gilbert
1050 *Crime of Corporal Sherwood* (1941)
1051 *Man from Norway* (1941)
1052 *Mystery of the hush-hush factory* (1941)
1053 *Riddle of the missing fire watcher* (1941)
Frazer, Martin
1054 *Case of the shot looter* (1941)
Hardinge, Rex
1055 *One of seven* (1941)
Parsons, Anthony
1056 *Clue of the stolen rupees* (1941)
1057 *Man from occupied France* (1941)
1058 *On the stroke of nine* (1941)
Skene, Anthony
1059 *Haunted hotel mystery* (1941)
Hunter, John
1060 *Raiders passed!* (1941)
1061 *Riddle of the black racketeers* (1941)
1062 *Secret of the grave* (1941)
Ames, Delano
1063 *Cornish coast conspiracy* (1942)
Creasey, John
1064 *Case of the mad inventor* (1942)
Chester, Gilbert
1065 *Man who bailed out* (1942)
1066 *Mystery of the underground factory* (1942)
1067 *Paper salvage crime* (1942)
1068 *Silk stocking murders* (1942)
1069 *Victim of the combine* (1942)
Frazer, Martin
1070 *Fatal V sign* (1942)
Hope, Stanton
1071 *Sign of the blue triangle* (1942)
Jackson, Lewis
1072 *Case of John Muir of Merchant Navy* (1942)
1073 *Case of the missing stoker* (1942)
Parsons, Anthony
1074 *House with steel shutters* (1942)
1075 *Mystery of the stolen despatches* (1942)
1076 *Plot of the yellow emperor* (1942)
1077 *Riddle of the captured quisling* (1942)
1078 *Secret of the Burma Road* (1942)
1079 *Stowaway of the S.S. Wanderer* (1942)
Skene, Anthony
1080 *Mystery of the bombed hotel* (1942)
Hunter, John
1081 *Case of the bronze statue* (1942)
1082 *Case of the French raiders* (1942)
1083 *Riddle of the uncensored letter* (1942)
1084 *Secret of the demolition worker* (1942)
Creasey, John
1085 *Private Carter's crime* (1943)
Dix, Maurice Buxton
1086 *Affair of the smuggled millions* (1943)
Douthwaite, Louis Charles
1087 *Army defaulter's secret* (1943)
Chester, Gilbert
1088 *Case of the repatriated prisoner* (1943)
1089 *Doctor Sinister* (1943)
1090 *Mystery of the kidnapped munition worker* (1943)
1091 *Secret of Stillwater Mere* (1943)
1092 *Soldier who came back* (1943)

Jackson, Lewis
1093 *Case of the suspect watchmaker* (1943)
Meriton, Peter
1094 *Man from Madrid* (1943)
Purley, John
1095 *Mansion on the moor* (1943)
Stamper, Joseph
1096 *Shipyard menace* (1943)
Sylvester, John
1097 *Terror of Tregarwith* (1943)
Parsons, Anthony
1098 *Calling Whitehall 1212* (1943)
1099 *Case of the missing DFC* (1943)
1100 *Case of the secret road* (1943)
1101 *Crime of the cashiered major* (1943)
1102 *Riddle of Cubicle 7* (1943)
1103 *Riddle of the disguised crook* (1943)
Skene, Anthony
1104 *Affair of the bronzed basilisk* (1943)
Tyrer, Walter
1105 *Curse of the Carrington's* (1943)
1106 *Mystery of Squadron X* (1943)
Hunter, John
1107 *Devil of Danehurst* (1943)
1108 *Monopoly menace* (1943)
Chester, Gilbert
1109 *Man they couldn't buy* (1944)
1110 *Man who wouldn't out* (1944)
1111 *Mystery of the demobilized soldier* (1944)
1112 *Previously reported missing, now?* (1944)
1113 *Riddle of the kidnapped pensioner* (1944)
1114 *Strange case of the footman's crime* (1944)
Drummond, J
1115 *Essex Road crime* (1944)
1116 *Manor house menace* (1944)
1117 *Painted dagger* (1944)
1118 *Riddle of the leather bottle* (1944)
1119 *Tragic case of the station master's legacy* (1944)
Jackson, Lewis
1120 *Case of the Biscay pirate* (1944)
1121 *Case of the five fugitives* (1944)
1122 *Riddle of the ruins* (1944)
Parsons, Anthony
1123 *Case of the Indian millionaire* (1944)
1124 *Case of the renegade naval officer* (1944)
1125 *Mystery of the bombed monastery* (1944)
1126 *Mystery of the Cairo express* (1944)
1127 *Mystery of the Indian relic* (1944)
Tyrer, Walter
1128 *Case of the conscript miner* (1944)
Hunter, John
1129 *Barred from the West End* (1944)
1130 *Man from the Far East* (1944)
1131 *Riddle of the Italian prisoner* (1944)
Chester, Gilbert
1132 *House in the wood* (1945)
1133 *Mystery of the confiscated ship* (1945)
1134 *Sword of vengeance* (1945)
1135 *Under police observation* (1945)
Drummond, J
1136 *At sixty miles per hour* (1945)
1137 *House on the hill* (1945)
1138 *Riddle of the mummy case* (1945)
Hope, Stanton
1139 *Case of the Monta Grandee diamonds* (1945)
Jackson, Lewis
1140 *Case of the five red herrings* (1945)
1141 *Man from Arnheim* (1945)
1142 *On compassionate leave* (1945)
1143 *Riddle of the workman squire* (1945)
1144 *Tallyman's fate* (1945)
Parsons, Anthony
1145 *Blackmailed refugee* (1945)
1146 *Case of the stolen evidence* (1945)
1147 *Loot of France* (1945)
1148 *Riddle of the gambling den* (1945)
Tyrer, Walter
1149 *Secret of the sands* (1945)
Hunter, John
1150 *Case of the deserted war bride* (1945)
1151 *Great airport racket* (1945)
1152 *Mystery of the red chateau* (1945)
1153 *Sergeant Gray's victim* (1945)
Chester, Gilbert
1154 *Mystery of the double burglary* (1946)
1155 *Red van mystery* (1946)
Hardinge, Rex
1156 *Man from Chun King* (1946)
Jackson, Lewis
1157 *Case of the fatal souvenir* (1946)
1158 *Case of the night lorry driver* (1946)
1159 *Down East!* (1946)
1160 *Tenant of Number Thirteen* (1946)
1161 *Woman with a record* (1946)
Long, Derek
1162 *Case of Lord Greyburn's son* (1946)
Meriton, Peter
1163 *Affair of the fraternizing soldier* (1946)
Reynolds, Warwick
1164 *Mawpath millions* (1946)
Parsons, Anthony
1165 *Case of the missing G.I. bride* (1946)
1166 *Case of the prince's prisoners* (1946)
1167 *Case of the swindler's stooge* (1946)
1168 *man who had to quit* (1946)
1169 *Mystery of the bankrupt estate* (1946)
1170 *Mystery of the two hundred and fifty thousand rupees* (1946)
1171 *Riddle of the Indian alibi* (1946)
Tyrer, Walter
1172 *Crime on the moors* (1946)
Hunter, John
1173 *Case of the defaulting sailor* (1946)
1174 *Fourteen years after!* (1946)
1175 *Mystery of Moat Farm* (1946)
1176 *Mystery of the American envoy* (1946)
1177 *Wimbledon Common trap* (1946)
Chester, Gilbert
1178 *Date with danger* (1947)
1179 *Great currency racket* (1947)
1180 *Mystery of the crashed air liner* (1947)
Hardinge, Rex
1181 *Case of the chinese courier* (1947)
1182 *Man from Mongolia* (1947)
1183 *Secret of the jungle* (1947)
1184 *Secret of the veld* (1947)
1185 *Yellow terror* (1947)
Jackson, Lewis
1186 *According to plan* (1947)
1187 *Case of the fighting padre* (1947)
1188 *Crime on the cliff* (1947)
1189 *Night of the twenty third* (1947)
1190 *Riddle of the film star's jewels* (1947)
Parsons, Anthony
1191 *Affair of the missing parachutist* (1947)
1192 *Euston Road mystery* (1947)
1193 *Man from Kenya* (1947)
1194 *Mystery of the Whitehall bomb* (1947)
1195 *Riddle of the Burmese curse* (1947)
1196 *Riddle of the escaped P.O.W.* (1947)
Skene, Anthony
1197 *Man who lost his memory* (1947)
Tyrer, Walter
1198 *Holiday camp mystery* (1947)
Hunter, John
1199 *Case of the double event* (1947)
1200 *Riddle of the smiling man* (1947)
1201 *Warned off!* (1947)
Drummond, J
1202 *Mystery of the deserted camp* (1948)
1203 *Town of shadows* (1948)
Frazer, Martin
1204 *Mystery of the shadowed footballer* (1948)
Hardinge, Rex
1205 *Case of the African elephant* (1948)
1206 *Case of the stolen mine* (1948)
1207 *Gargoyle of Polgelly* (1948)
1208 *Riddle of the highwayman's stone* (1948)
1209 *Riddle of the sealed room* (1948)
1210 *Secret of the African settler* (1948)
Jackson, Lewis
1211 *Case of the doped heavyweight* (1948)
1212 *Man who went wrong* (1948)
Jardine, Warwick
1213 *Man from Algiers* (1948)
Parsons, Anthony
1214 *Income tax conspiracy* (1948)
1215 *Loot of Pakistan* (1948)
1216 *Man who backed out!* (1948)
1217 *Mystery of Avenue Road* (1948)
1218 *Mystery of the one-day alibi* (1948)
1219 *Mystery of the red cockatoo* (1948)
1220 *Riddle of the Russian bride* (1948)
1221 *Terror at Tree Tops* (1948)
Saxon, Peter
1222 *Voodoo drum* (1948)
Tyrer, Walter
1223 *Case against Doctor Ripon* (1948)
1224 *Motor coach mystery* (1948)
1225 *Mystery of the woman overboard* (1948)
Hunter, John
1226 *Affair of the spiv's secret* (1948)
1227 *Case of the American tourists* (1948)
1228 *Curse of the track* (1948)
Chester, Gilbert
1229 *Riddle of the night garage* (1949)
Drummond, J
1230 *Case of the dead spy* (1949)
1231 *Riddle of the receiver's hoard* (1949)
1232 *Secret of the living skeleton* (1949)
1233 *South Coast mystery* (1949)
Hardinge, Rex
1234 *Case of the African trader* (1949)
1235 *Case of the crime reporter* (1949)
1236 *Case of the secret agent* (1949)
1237 *Legacy of hate* (1949)
1238 *Mystery of the devil mask* (1949)
Consider your verdict
The second title is a revised edition
1239 *Tragedy of the Bromleigh's* (1949)
Jackson, Lewis
1240 *Case of the discharged policeman* (1949)
1241 *Death of Mrs Preedy* (1949)
1242 *Man who left home* (1949)
Jardine, Warwick
1243 *Madman of the marshes* (1949)
Parsons, Anthony
1244 *Case of the Dangra millions* (1949)
1245 *Case of the missing surgeon* (1949)
1246 *Riddle of the rajah's curios* (1949)
Tyrer, Walter
1247 *Affair of the Hollywood contract* (1949)
1248 *Mystery of the missing angler* (1949)
1249 *One of the eleven* (1949)
Drummond, J
1250 *Case of L.A.C. Dickson* (1950)
1251 *House in the woods* (1950)
1252 *Mystery of the haunted square* (1950)
1253 *Secret of the sixty steps* (1950)
Hardinge, Rex
1254 *Mystery of the forbidden territory* (1950)
1255 *Tragedy of Windyridge* (1950)
1256 *With criminal instinct* (1950)
Jardine, Warwick
1257 *Case for M.I.5* (1950)
1258 *Old man of the moors* (1950)
1259 *Secret of Capri* (1950)
Long, Derek
1260 *Mystery of the Italian ruins* (1950)
Parsons, Anthony
1261 *Case of the spiv's secret* (1950)
1262 *Great dollar fraud* (1950)
1263 *Living in fear* (1950)
1264 *Mystery of the crooked gift* (1950)
1265 *Riddle of the prince's stooge* (1950)
1266 *Those on the list* (1950)
Tyrer, Walter
1267 *Affair of Danny the Dip* (1950)
1268 *Case of the cottage crime* (1950)
1269 *Case of the naval defaulter* (1950)
1270 *Evil spell* (1950)
1271 *Mystery of the Rio Star* (1950)
Hunter, John
1272 *When the jury disagreed* (1950)
1273 *Witness to the crime* (1950)
Blakesley, Stephen
1274 *Riddle of the blazing bungalow* (1951)
Drummond, J
1275 *Case of the man with no name* (1951)
1276 *Hated by all!* (1951)
1277 *Mystery of the sabotaged jet* (1951)
King, Hilary
1278 *Mystery of the lost loot* (1951)
1279 *On the eleven forty down* (1951)
1280 *Partners in crime* (1951)
Hardinge, Rex
1281 *Case of the frightened girl* (1951)
1282 *Case of the green caravan* (1951)
1283 *Headmaster's secret* (1951)
1284 *Secret of the desert* (1951)
Jackson, Lewis
1285 *Man from Persia* (1951)
Jardine, Warwick
1286 *Top secret number one* (1951)
Parsons, Anthony
1287 *Bad man of Cairo* (1951)
1288 *Case of the Indian dancer* (1951)
1289 *Millionaire's nest egg* (1951)
1290 *Mystery of the blitzed tower* (1951)
1291 *Mystery of the girl in green* (1951)
1292 *Retired from the Yard* (1951)
Tyrer, Walter
1293 *Case of the two crooked baronets* (1951)
1294 *Crimes at Fenton Towers* (1951)
Hunter, John
1295 *Case of the crooked skipper* (1951)
1296 *It happened in Melgrove Square* (1951)
1297 *Mystery of the new tenant* (1951)
Blakesley, Stephen
1298 *Man with a number* (1952)
1299 *Trail of Raider Number One* (1952)
Clevely, Hugh
1300 *Calling Whitehall 1212* (1952)
Drummond, J
1301 *House on the river* (1952)
Frazer, Martin
1302 *Case of the dope dealers* (1952)
King, Hilary
1303 *Man from Dieppe* (1952)
Hardinge, Rex
1304 *Man from space* (1952)
1305 *Prisoner of the manor* (1952)
1306 *Riddle of the crooked gambler* (1952)
Jardine, Warwick
1307 *Man with a grievance* (1952)
Parsons, Anthony
1308 *Case of the banned film* (1952)
1309 *Case of the blackmailed prince* (1952)
1310 *Case of the Japanese contract* (1952)
1311 *Case of the missing scientist* (1952)
1312 *Man without a passport* (1952)
1313 *Mystery of the mason's arms* (1952)
Tyrer, Walter
1314 *Case of the bogus baron* (1952)
1315 *Dilemma of Doctor Hiley* (1952)

1316 *Hire-purchase fraud* (1952)
1317 *Scrap-metal mystery* (1952)
Hunter, John
1318 *Case of the doped favourite* (1952)
1319 *Case of the girl on remand* (1952)
1320 *Spiv's mistake* (1952)
1321 *Victim of the crooked hypnotist* (1952)
Clevely, Hugh
1322 *Case of the smuggled currency* (1953)
1323 *Girl from Toronto* (1953)
1324 *Nightclub mystery* (1953)
King, Hilary
1325 *Big circus mystery* (1953)
1326 *Crime at the fair* (1953)
Hardinge, Rex
1327 *Case of the African hoodoo* (1953)
1328 *Mystery of the body on the cliff* (1953)
1329 *Secret of the fated family* (1953)
Jardine, Warwick
1330 *Mystery of the Arab agent* (1953)
Passingham, William John
1331 *Case of the ace accomplice* (1953)
1332 *World championship mystery* (1953)
Rees, George
1333 *Secret of the jungle* (1953)
Parsons, Anthony
1334 *Case of the nameless millionaire* (1953)
1335 *Case of the prince's diary* (1953)
1336 *Case of the unknown heir* (1953)
1337 *Crook's deputy* (1953)
1338 *Secret of the Indian lawyer* (1953)
Tyrer, Walter
1339 *case of the missing Nazi* (1953)
1340 *Case of the naval stores bucket* (1953)
1341 *Mystery of the swindler's stooge* (1953)
1342 *Secret of the snows* (1953)
Hunter, John
1343 *Destination unknown* (1953)
1344 *Thieves of Alexandria* (1953)
1345 *Woman on the spot* (1953)
Clevely, Hugh
1346 *Case of the criminal's daughter* (1954)
1347 *Case of the three survivors* (1954)
1348 *Crime at Three A.M.* (1954)
1349 *Heir of Tower House* (1954)
Drummond, J
1350 *Mystery of the five guilty men* (1954)
Hope, Stanton
1351 *Mystery of the engraved skull* (1954)
Hardinge, Rex
1352 *Lodging-house mystery* (1954)
1353 *Riddle of the invisible menace* (1954)
1354 *Victim of the Devil's Bowl* (1954)
1355 *Voyage of fear* (1954)
Rees, George
1356 *Secret of the Suez Canal* (1954)
Parsons, Anthony
1357 *Car park mystery* (1954)
1358 *Case of the second crime* (1954)
1359 *Case of the sinister farm* (1954)
1360 *Case of the Spanish legatee* (1954)
1361 *Case of the wicked three* (1954)
1362 *Man from Maybrick Road* (1954)
1363 *Secret of the castle ruins* (1954)
1364 *Secret of the Moroccan bazaar* (1954)
Tyrer, Walter
1365 *Case of the council swindle* (1954)
1366 *Case of the swindled guarantor* (1954)
1367 *Crime in Room Twenty Seven* (1954)
1368 *Riddle of the French alibi* (1954)
Hunter, John
1369 *Case of the stolen ransom* (1954)
1370 *Crime on the French frontier* (1954)
Baker, William Howard
1371 *Man who knew too much* (1955)
1372 *Without warning* (1955)
Clevely, Hugh
1373 *Case of the legion deserter* (1955)
1374 *House of evil* (1955)
1375 *Strange affair of the widow's diamonds* (1955)
Drummond, J
1376 *Case of the two-faced swindler* (1955)
1377 *Teddy-boy mystery* (1955)
Hardinge, Rex
1378 *Man with five enemies* (1955)
1379 *Mystery of the outlawed black* (1955)
1380 *Secret of the man who died* (1955)
Jardine, Warwick
1381 *Riddle of the green cylinder* (1955)
Parsons, Anthony
1382 *Case of the frightened man* (1955)
1383 *Case of the Indian watcher* (1955)
1384 *Case of the six o'clock scream* (1955)
1385 *Crooks of Tunis* (1955)
1386 *Prisoner in the hold* (1955)
1387 *Secret of the Roman temple* (1955)
1388 *Trail of the missing scientist* (1955)
Tyrer, Walter
1389 *Case of the forbidden island* (1955)
1390 *Case of the returning soldier* (1955)
1391 *Mystery of the mad millionaires* (1955)
1392 *Strange affair of the shot gun sniper* (1955)
Hunter, John
1393 *Murder in the air* (1955)
1394 *Mystery of the vanished trainer* (1955)
Baker, William Howard
1395 *Battle song* (1956)
1396 *Dark mambo* (1956)
1397 *Devil's can-can* (1956)
1398 *Frightened lady* (1956)
Fugitive
The second title is a revised edition
1399 *It happened in Hamburg* (1956)
1400 *Requiem for redheads* (1956)
Kent, Arthur
1401 *Inclining to crime* (1956)
Hardinge, Rex
1402 *By whose hand?* (1956)
Maclean, Arthur
1403 *Broken toy* (1956)
1404 *Canvas jungle* (1956)
1405 *Dark frontier* (1956)
1406 *Night beat* (1956)
Stagg, James
1407 *Assignment in Beirut* (1956)
Parsons, Anthony
1408 *Hotel homicide* (1956)
Saxon, Peter
1409 *Danger ahead* (1956)
1410 *Decoy for murder* (1956)
1411 *Flight into fear* (1956)
1412 *Front page woman* (1956)
Story, Jack Trevor
1413 *Murder, with love* (1956)
Tyrer, Walter
1414 *Clue of the pin-up girl* (1956)
1415 *Mystery of the three demobbed men* (1956)
Hunter, John
1416 *Gangster's girl* (1956)
Arthur, William
1417 *Murder with variety* (1957)
Baker, William Howard
1418 *Walk in fear* (1957)
Every man an enemy
The second title is a revised edition
Burke, Jonathan
1419 *Corpse to Copenhagen* (1957)
Kent, Arthur
1420 *Special edition, murder* (1957)
Maclean, Arthur
1421 *Deadline for danger* (1957)
1422 *Find me a killer!* (1957)
Slaying on the sixteenth floor
1423 *Mask of fury* (1957)
Stagg, James
1424 *Nightmare in Naples* (1957)
1425 *Panic in the night* (1957)
1426 *Passport to danger* (1957)
Reid, Desmond
1427 *Flashpoint for treason* (1957)
1428 *Homicide blues* (1957)
1429 *Roadhouse girl* (1957)
1430 *Stand-in for murder* (1957)
1431 *Victim unknown* (1957)
Saxon, Peter
1432 *Act of violence* (1957)
1433 *Cry in the night* (1957)
1434 *Last days of Berlin* (1957)
1435 *Violent hours* (1957)
Story, Jack Trevor
1436 *Blonde and the boodle* (1957)
1437 *Season of the skylark* (1957)
1438 *Vacation with fear* (1957)
Thomas, Martin
1439 *Copy-cat killings* (1957)
Hunter, John
1440 *Silent witness* (1957)
Baker, William Howard
1441 *Appointed with danger* (1958)
1442 *Crime is my business* (1958)
1443 *Murder most intimate* (1958)
1444 *No time to live* (1958)
1445 *Shoot when ready* (1958)
Harrison, Edwin
1446 *Diamonds can be trouble* (1958)
1447 *Fatal hour* (1958)
Kent, Arthur
1448 *Stairway to murder* (1958)
1449 *Wake up screaming!* (1958)
Maclean, Arthur
1450 *Fatal curtain* (1958)
1451 *House on the bay* (1958)
1452 *Redhead for danger* (1958)
Man who killed me
Stagg, James
1453 *Crime of violence* (1958)
1454 *Murder down below* (1958)
Reid, Desmond
1455 *High heels and homicide* (1958)
Saxon, Peter
1456 *Naked blade* (1958)
1457 *Sea tigers* (1958)
Story, Jack Trevor
1458 *Collapse of stout party* (1958)
1459 *Frightened people* (1958)
1460 *Murder in the sun* (1958)
1461 *Nine o'clock shadow* (1958)
1462 *She ain't got no body* (1958)
Thomas, Martin
1463 *Evil eye* (1958)
1464 *Lady in distress* (1958)
Baker, William Howard
1465 *Expresso jungle* (1959)
1466 *Passport into fear* (1959)
Dolphin, Rex
1467 *Guilty party* (1959)
1468 *Stop press, homicide!* (1959)
1469 *Walk in the shadows* (1959)
Harrison, Edwin
1470 *Killer's playground* (1959)
1471 *Witness to murder* (1959)
Hyde, D Herbert
1472 *Dressed to kill* (1959)
Hardinge, Rex
1473 *Safari with fear!* (1959)
Tubb, Edwin Charles
1474 *Touch of evil* (1959)
Revised by Arthur Maclean
Stagg, James
1475 *Time for murder* (1959)
Reid, Desmond
1476 *Showdown in Sydney* (1959)
Saxon, Peter
1477 *Violent ones* (1959)
Story, Jack Trevor
1478 *Courier for crime* (1959)
1479 *Home sweet homicide* (1959)
1480 *Invitation to a murder* (1959)
Thomas, Martin
1481 *Catch a tiger* (1959)
1482 *Cold night for murder* (1959)
1483 *Fear is my shadow* (1959)
1484 *Shadow of a gun* (1959)
Baker, William Howard
1485 *Angry night* (1960)
Fire over India
The second title is a revised edition
Ballinger, W A
1486 *Epitaph to treason* (1960)
1487 *This man must die!* (1960)
Chambers, Philip
1488 *Bullets to Baghdad* (1960)
Dolphin, Rex
1489 *Some died laughing* (1960)
Fawcett, Frank Dubrez
1490 *Journey to Genoa* (1960)
Kirby, Arthur
1491 *Man on the run!* (1960)
Maclean, Arthur
1492 *Mission to Mexico* (1960)
Stagg, James
1493 *Desert intrigue* (1960)
Williams, Richard
1494 *Hurricane warning!* (1960)
1495 *Large type killer* (1960)
Reid, Desmond
1496 *Conflict within* (1960)
1497 *Contract for a killer* (1960)
1498 *Murder comes calling* (1960)
1499 *Murder made easy* (1960)
1500 *Witch-hunt!* (1960)
1501 *World-shakers* (1960)
Story, Jack Trevor
1502 *Big steal* (1960)
1503 *Danger on the flip side* (1960)
1504 *Violence in quiet places* (1960)
Thomas, Martin
1505 *Bred to kill* (1960)
1506 *Date with danger!* (1960)
1507 *Dead man's destiny* (1960)
1508 *Design for vengeance* (1960)
Ballinger, W A
1509 *Television murders* (1961)
Chambers, Philip
1510 *Keep it a secret* (1961)
1511 *Lotus leaves and larceny* (1961)
1512 *Shot from the dark* (1961)
Dolphin, Rex
1513 *Devil to pay* (1961)
1514 *Trouble is my name* (1961)
Johns, Gilbert
1515 *Thief of clubs* (1961)
1516 *Vote for violence* (1961)
Jardine, Warwick
1517 *Death her destination* (1961)
Maclean, Arthur
1518 *Pursuit to Algeria* (1961)
Williams, Richard
1519 *Vendetta!* (1961)
Reid, Desmond
1520 *Bullets are trumps* (1961)
1521 *Corpse came too* (1961)
1522 *Deadly persuasion* (1961)
1523 *Hunt the lady!* (1961)
1524 *Murder by moonlight* (1961)
1525 *Murder's Rock* (1961)
1526 *State of fear* (1961)
Saxon, Peter
1527 *Lovely, but lethal!* (1961)
Story, Jack Trevor
1528 *Assault and pepper* (1961)
1529 *Danger's child* (1961)
1530 *Rogue's harbour* (1961)
1531 *Suddenly it's murder* (1961)
Thomas, Martin
1532 *Assignment Doomsday* (1961)
Baker, William Howard
1533 *Big smear* (1962)
1534 *Reluctant gunman* (1962)
Ballinger, W A
1535 *Corpse for Christmas* (1962)
1536 *Murder in camera* (1962)
1537 *Savage venture* (1962)
1538 *Studio One murder* (1962)
Chambers, Philip
1539 *Dangerous playmate* (1962)
1540 *Moscow manhunt* (1962)
Hanson, Victor Joseph
1541 *Death and Little Girl Blue* (1962)
Kent, Arthur
1542 *Weak and the strong* (1962)
Kirby, Arthur

1543 *High summer homicide* (1962)
Maclean, Arthur
1544 *Bargain in blood* (1962)
McNeilly, Wilfred
1545 *Come dark, come evil* (1962)
1546 *Killer pack* (1962)
1547 *Terror Loch* (1962)
Sydney, George
1548 *Countdown for murder* (1962)
Williams, Richard
1549 *Somebody wants me dead* (1962)
1550 *Torment was a redhead* (1962)
Reid, Desmond
1551 *Caribbean crisis* (1962)
Revised by Philip Chambers
1552 *Dead on cue* (1962)
1553 *Death in dockland* (1962)
1554 *Death on a high note* (1962)
Saxon, Peter
1555 *White mercenary* (1962)
Thomas, Martin
1556 *Spotlight on murder* (1962)
Baker, William Howard
1557 *Imposter* (1963)
Co-author: Peter Chambers
Ballinger, W A
1558 *Last tiger* (1963)
Williams, Richard
1559 *Murder by proxy* (1963)
1560 *Slaying of Julian Summers* (1963)
1561 *Speak ill of the dead* (1963)
Reid, Desmond
1562 *Anger at World's End* (1963)
Revised by William Howard Baker and Arthur Maclean
1563 *Cult of darkness* (1963)
1564 *Girl who saw too much* (1963)
Thomas, Martin
1565 *Death in small doses* (1963)
1566 *Sound of murder* (1963)
Ballinger, W A
1567 *Murderer at large* (1965)
1568 *Strange face of murder* (1965)
1569 *Witches of Notting Hill* (1965)
Maclean, Arthur
1570 *Savage squeeze* (1965)
McNeilly, Wilfred
1571 *Break out* (1965)
1572 *Case of the stag at bay* (1965)
1573 *Death in the top twenty* (1965)
1574 *Wanted for questioning* (1965)
Williams, Richard
1575 *Man with the iron chest* (1965)
1576 *Sniper* (1965)
Reid, Desmond
1577 *Let my people be* (1965)
Saxon, Peter
1578 *Vengeance is ours!* (1965)
Story, Jack Trevor
1579 *Company of bandits* (1965)
Thomas, Martin
1580 *Laird of evil* (1965)
1581 *Mind killers* (1965)
1582 *Such men are dangerous* (1965)
Reid, Desmond
1583 *Beat on an orange drum* (1965)
Ballinger, W A
1584 *Starlet for a penny* (1966)
Dolphin, Rex
1585 *Murder goes nap* (1966)
Kent, Arthur
1586 *Corpse to Cuba* (1966)
McNeilly, Wilfred
1587 *Case of the muckrakers* (1966)
Richards, Ross
1588 *Murder on the Monte* (1966)
Reid, Desmond
1589 *Deadlier of the species* (1966)
1590 *Death on the spike* (1966)
1591 *Frenzy in the flesh* (1966)
1592 *Snowman cometh* (1966)
1593 *Something to kill about* (1966)
Thomas, Martin
1594 *Sorcerers of Set* (1966)
Quiroule, Pierre
1595 *Case of the Bismarck memoirs* (1966)
Baker, William Howard
1596 *Treason remembered* (1967)
Ballinger, W A
1597 *I, the hangman* (1967)
Christie, Stephen
1598 *Crash and carry* (1967)
Dolphin, Rex
1599 *Trial of the golden girl* (1967)
Mead, Matt
1600 *Star crossed* (1967)
Reid, Desmond
1601 *Dead respectable* (1967)
1602 *Slave brain* (1967)
Saxon, Peter
1603 *This spy must die* (1967)
Thomas, Martin
1604 *Event called murder* (1967)
Ballinger, W A
1605 *Down among the ad men* (1968)
Reid, Desmond
1606 *Abductors* (1968)
1607 *Case of the renegade agent* (1968)
Saxon, Peter
1608 *Black honey* (1968)
1609 *Woman of Saigon* (1968)
Thomas, Martin
1610 *Brainwashed* (1968)
Christie, Stephen
1611 *Slaughter in the sun* (1969)
Dolphin, Rex
1612 *Driven to kill* (1969)
Thomas, Martin
1613 *Mini-skirt murders* (1969)
Gordon, Peter
1614 *Case of the missing bullion* (1969)
Garforth, John
1615 *Sexton Blake and the demon god* (1978)
Based on a television series

Sexual life series
Pendleton, Don
1 *Hypnosis and the sexual life* (1968)
2 *Religion and the sexual life* (1968)
3 *Society and the sexual life* (1968)

Seyrac family series
Masson, Sophie
1 *Opera club* (1993)
2 *Cousin from France* (1993)
3 *Winter in France* (1994)

Shackleford legacy trilogy
Riefe, Barbara
1 *Olivia* (1981)
2 *Julia* (1983)
3 *Lucretia* (1983)

Shackleton series
Crawley, Rayburn
see **Ned Shackleton series**

Shaddrock and Cougar series
Fieldhouse, William
1 *Gun lust* (1982)
2 *Comanchero kill* (1983)

Shade series
Boyle, Denis
see **Commander Moreton Shade series**

Shadith's quest series
Clayton, Jo
1 *Shadowplay* (1990)
2 *Shadowspeer* (1990)
3 *Shadowkill* (1991)

Shadow of the elephant series
Georgeson, Valerie
1 *Seeds of love* (1986)
2 *Whispering roots* (1987)

Shadow series
Grant, Maxwell
House pseudonym
1 *Living Shadow* (1931)
2 *Eyes of the Shadow* (1931)
3 *Shadow laughs* (1931)
4 *Red menace* (1932)
5 *Gangdom's doom* (1932)
6 *Death tower* (1932)
7 *Silent Seven* (1932)
8 *Black master* (1932)
9 *Mobsmen on the spot* (1932)
10 *Hands in the dark* (1932)
11 *Double Z* (1932)
12 *Crime cult* (1932)
13 *Blackmail ring* (1932)
14 *Hidden death* (1932)
15 *Green Eyes* (1932)
16 *Ghost makers* (1932)
17 *Five chameleons* (1932)
18 *Dead man live* (1932)
19 *Romanoff jewels* (1932)
20 *Kings of crime* (1932)
21 *Shadowed millions* (1933)
22 *Creeping death* (1933)
23 *Shadow's shadow* (1933)
24 *Six men of evil* (1933)
25 *Fingers of death* (1933)
26 *Murder trail* (1933)
27 *Silent death* (1933)
28 *Shadow's justice* (1933)
29 *Golden grotto* (1933)
30 *Death giver* (1933)
31 *Red blot* (1933)
32 *Ghost of the manor* (1933)
33 *Living joss* (1933)
34 *Silver scourge* (1933)
35 *Black hush* (1933)
36 *Isle of doubt* (1933)
37 *Grove of doom* (1933)
38 *Master of death* (1933)
39 *Road of crime* (1933)
40 *Death triangle* (1933)
41 *Killer* (1933)
42 *Mox* (1933)
43 *Crime clinic* (1933)
44 *Treasures of death* (1934)
45 *Embassy murders* (1934)
46 *Wealth seeker* (1934)
47 *Black falcon* (1934)
48 *Gray Fist* (1934)
49 *Circle of death* (1934)
50 *Green box* (1934)
51 *Cobra* (1934)
52 *Crime circus* (1934)
53 *Tower of death* (1934)
54 *Death clew* (1934)
55 *Key* (1934)
56 *Crime crypt* (1934)
57 *Charg, monster* (1934)
58 *Chain of death* (1934)
59 *Crime master* (1934)
60 *Gypsy vengeance* (1934)
61 *Spoils of the Shadow* (1934)
62 *Garaucan swindle* (1934)
63 *Murder marsh* (1934)
64 *Death sleep* (1934)
65 *Chinese disks* (1934)
66 *Doom on the hill* (1934)
67 *Unseen killer* (1934)
68 *Cyro* (1934)
69 *Four signets* (1934)
70 *Blue sphinx* (1935)
71 *Plot master* (1935)
72 *Dark death* (1935)
73 *Crooks go straight* (1935)
74 *Bells of doom* (1935)
75 *Lingo* (1935)
76 *Triple trail* (1935)
77 *Golden quest* (1935)
78 *Third skull* (1935)
79 *Murder every hour* (1935)
80 *Condor* (1935)
81 *Fate joss* (1935)
82 *Atoms of death* (1935)
83 *Man from Scotland Yard* (1935)
84 *Creeper* (1935)
85 *Mardi gras mystery* (1935)
86 *London crimes* (1935)
87 *Ribbon clues* (1935)
88 *House that vanished* (1935)
89 *Chinese tapestry* (1935)
90 *Python* (1935)
91 *Zemba* (1935)
92 *Case of Congressman Coyd* (1935)
93 *Ghost murders* (1936)
94 *Castle of doom* (1936)
95 *Death rides the skyway* (1936)
96 *North Woods mystery* (1936)
97 *Voodoo master* (1936)
98 *Third shadow* (1936)
99 *Salamanders* (1936)
100 *Man from Shanghai* (1936)
101 *Gray ghost* (1936)
102 *City of doom* (1936)
103 *Crime oracle* (1936)
104 *Murder town* (1936)
105 *Yellow door* (1936)
106 *Broken napoleons* (1936)
107 *Sledge hammer crimes* (1936)
108 *Terror Island* (1936)
109 *Golden masks* (1936)
110 *Jibaro death* (1936)
111 *City of crime* (1936)
112 *Death by proxy* (1936)
113 *Strange disappearance of Joe Cardona* (1936)
114 *Seven drops of blood* (1936)
115 *Intimidation, Inc.* (1936)
116 *Vengeance is mine* (1937)
117 *Loot of death* (1937)
118 *Quetzal* (1937)
119 *Death token* (1937)
120 *Murder house* (1937)
121 *Washington crime* (1937)
122 *Masked headsman* (1937)
123 *Treasure trail* (1937)
124 *Brothers of doom* (1937)
125 *Shadow's rival* (1937)
126 *Crime insured* (1937)
127 *House of silence* (1937)
128 *Shadow unmasks* (1937)
129 *Yellow band* (1937)
130 *Buried evidence* (1937)
131 *Radium murders* (1937)
132 *Keeper's gold* (1937)
133 *Death turrets* (1937)
134 *Teeth of the dragon* (1937)
Numbers 103 and 134 also published in one volume, 1975
135 *Sealed box* (1937)
136 *Racket town* (1937)
137 *Crystal Buddha* (1938)
138 *Hills of death* (1938)
139 *Murder master* (1938)
140 *Golden pagoda* (1938)
141 *Face of doom* (1938)
142 *Serpents of Siva* (1938)
143 *Cards of death* (1938)
144 *Hand* (1938)
145 *Voodoo trail* (1938)
146 *Racket king* (1938)
147 *Murder for sale* (1938)
148 *Golden vulture* (1938)
149 *Death jewels* (1938)
150 *Green hoods* (1938)
151 *Crime over Boston* (1938)
152 *Dead who lived* (1938)
153 *Vanished treasure* (1938)
154 *Voice* (1938)
155 *Chicago crime* (1938)
156 *Shadow over Alcatraz* (1938)
157 *Silver skull* (1939)
158 *Crime rides the sea* (1939)
159 *Realm of doom* (1939)
160 *Lone tiger* (1939)
161 *Vindicator* (1939)
162 *Death ship* (1939)
163 *Battle of greed* (1939)
164 *Three brothers* (1939)
165 *Smugglers of death* (1939)
166 *City of shadows* (1939)
167 *Death from nowhere* (1939)
168 *Isle of gold* (1939)
169 *Wizard of crime* (1939)
170 *Crime ray* (1939)
171 *Golden master* (1939)
172 *Castle of crime* (1939)
173 *Masked lady* (1939)
174 *Ships of doom* (1939)
175 *City of ghosts* (1939)
176 *Shiwan Khan returns* (1939)
Numbers 171 and 176 also published in one volume entitled *The Shadow and the golden master*, 1984
177 *House of shadows* (1939)

178 *Death's premium* (1940)
179 *Hooded circle* (1940)
180 *Getaway ring* (1940)
181 *Voice of death* (1940)
182 *Invincible Shiwan Khan* (1940)
183 *Veiled prophet* (1940)
184 *Spy ring* (1940)
185 *Death in the stars* (1940)
186 *Masters of death* (1940)
187 *Scent of death* (1940)
188 *Q* (1940)
189 *Gems of doom* (1940)
190 *Crime at Seven Oaks* (1940)
191 *Fifth face* (1940)
192 *Crime county* (1940)
193 *Wasp* (1940)
194 *Crime over Miami* (1940)
195 *Xitli, god of fire* (1940)
196 *Shadow, the Hawk and the Skull* (1940)
197 *Forgotten gold* (1941)
198 *Wasp returns* (1941)
199 *Chinese primrose* (1941)
200 *Mansion of crime* (1941)
201 *Time master* (1941)
202 *House on the ledge* (1941)
203 *League of death* (1941)
204 *Crime under cover* (1941)
205 *Thunder king* (1941)
206 *Star of Delhi* (1941)
207 *Blur* (1941)
208 *Shadow meets the Mask* (1941)
209 *Devil-master* (1941)
210 *Garden of death* (1941)
211 *Dictator of crime* (1941)
212 *Blackmail king* (1941)
213 *Temple of crime* (1941)
214 *Murder mansion* (1941)
215 *Crime's stronghold* (1941)
216 *Alibi trail* (1942)
217 *Book of death* (1942)
218 *Death diamonds* (1942)
219 *Vengeance Bay* (1942)
220 *Formula for crime* (1942)
221 *Room of doom* (1942)
222 *Jade dragon* (1942)
223 *Southdale mystery* (1942)
224 *Twins of crime* (1942)
225 *Devil's feud* (1942)
226 *Five ivory boxes* (1942)
227 *Death about town* (1942)
228 *Legacy of death* (1942)
229 *Judge Lawless* (1942)
230 *Vampire murders* (1942)
231 *Clue for clue* (1942)
232 *Trail of vengeance* (1942)
233 *Murdering ghost* (1942)
234 *Hydra* (1942)
235 *Money master* (1942)
236 *Museum murders* (1943)
237 *Death's masquerade* (1943)
238 *Devil monsters* (1943)
239 *Black dragon* (1943)
240 *Robot master* (1943)
241 *Murder lake* (1943)
242 *Messenger of death* (1943)
243 *House of ghosts* (1943)
Numbers 222 and 243 also published in one volume 1981
244 *King of the black market* (1943)
245 *Muggers* (1943)
246 *Murder by moonlight* (1943)
247 *Crystal skull* (1944)
248 *Syndicate of death* (1944)
249 *Toll of death* (1944)
250 *Crime caravan* (1944)
251 *Freak show murders* (1944)
252 *Voodoo death* (1944)
Numbers 37, 246 and 252 also published in one volume entitled *The weird adventures of the Shadow*, 1966
253 *Town of hate* (1944)
254 *Death in the crystal* (1944)
255 *Chest of Chu Chan* (1944)
256 *Fountain of death* (1944)
257 *No time for murder* (1944)
258 *Guardian of death* (1945)
259 *Merry Mrs Macbeth* (1945)
260 *Five keys to crime* (1945)
261 *Death has gray eyes* (1945)
262 *Teardrops of Buddha* (1945)
263 *Three stamps of death* (1945)
264 *Mask of Mephisto* (1945)
265 *Murder by magic* (1945)
Numbers 264 and 265 also published in one volume 1975
266 *Taiwan joss* (1945)
267 *Quarter of eight* (1945)
Numbers 257 and 267 also published in one volume 1978
268 *White skulls* (1945)
269 *Stars promise death* (1945)
270 *Shadow and the voice of murder* (1945)
271 *Banshee murders* (1946)
272 *Crime out of mind* (1946)
273 *Mother Goose murders* (1946)
274 *Crime over Casco* (1946)
Numbers 273 and 274 also published in one volume 1979
275 *Curse of Thoth* (1946)
276 *Malmordo* (1946)
277 *Dead man's chest* (1948)
278 *Magigals murder* (1949)
279 *Black circle* (1949)
280 *Whispering eyes* (1949)
281 *Return of the Shadow* (1963)
282 *Shadow strikes* (1964)
283 *Shadow beware* (1965)
284 *Cry Shadow* (1965)
285 *Shadow's revenge* (1965)
286 *Mark of the Shadow* (1966)
287 *Shadow, go mad!* (1966)
288 *Night of the Shadow* (1966)
289 *Destination moon* (1967)

Shadowers Inc. series
Fox, David
English editions published under the pseudonym Robert Orr Chipperfield
1 *Man who convicted himself* (1920)
2 *Ethel opens the door* (1922)
3 *Doom dealer* (1923)
4 *Handwriting on the wall* (1924)

Shadowrun series
Charrette, Robert N
see **Secrets of power series**

Shaft series
Tidyman, Ernest
see **John Shaft series**

Shafto series
Feist, Aubrey
see **Jeremy Shafto series**

Shags series
Fujikawa, Gyo
1 *Shags has a dream* (1981)
2 *Shags finds a kitten* (1983)

Shah Jahan series
Payne, Robert
see **Emperor Shah Jahan series**

Shai series
Walther, Daniel
1 *Book of Shai* (1984)
Original edition entitled *Le livre de Swa*
2 *Shai's destiny* (1985)
Original edition entitled *Le destin de Swa*

Shakespeare trilogy
Malpass, Eric Lawson
see **William Shakespeare trilogy**

Shakespearean festival in Canada series
Guthrie, Tyrone
1 *Renown at Stratford* (1953)
2 *Twice have the trumpets sounded* (1954)
Sequence continued by Robertson Davies with others
Davies, Robertson
3 *Thrice the brinded cat hath mew'd* (1955)

Shalimar series
Frost, Kelman Dalgety
see **Captain John Walton series**

Shallowford to Norfolk series
Williamson, Henry
Autobiography
1 *Clear water stream* (1958)
Revised edition 1975
2 *Children of Shallowford* (1939)
Revised edition 1959
3 *Story of a Norfolk farm* (1941)
Companion volume: *The wet Flanders plain*, 1929

Shalom series
Dyck, Peter J
1 *Great Shalom* (1990)
2 *Shalom at last* (1992)

Sham Payne series
Secrist, Kelliher
1 *Murder melody* (1939)
She screamed blue murder
2 *Murder makes by-lines* (1941)

Shamashazir series
Fyson, Jenny Grace
1 *Three brothers of Ur* (1964)
2 *Journey of the eldest brother* (1965)

Shame and glory series
Corder, Eric
1 *Slave* (1967)
2 *Long tattoo* (1968)
3 *Slave ship* (1969)
4 *Hellbottom* (1972)
5 *Savage rite* (1976)

Shamrayev series
Topol, Edward
Translated from the Russian
1 *Red Square* (1983)
2 *Deadly games* (1984)

Shamrock trilogy
This sequence has three authors
Johansen, Iris
1 *York, the renegade* (1986)
Preston, Fayrene
2 *Burke, the kingpin* (1986)
Hooper, Kay
3 *Rafe, the maverick* (1986)

Shamryke Odell series
Lory, Robert
1 *Masters of the lamp* (1970)
2 *Veiled world* (1972)

Shamus Burke series
Webster, H M
1 *Ballycubin mystery* (1947)
2 *Secret of Baron's Folly* (1949)
3 *Tontine treasure* (1951)

Shanahan series
Tierney, Ronald
see **Deets Shanahan series**

Shand series
Enefer, Douglas
see **Dale Shand series**

Shandy series
Macleod, Charlotte
see **Professor Peter Shandy series**

Shane Mackenzie series
Magowan, Ronald
1 *Monopoly to murder* (1970)
2 *Funeral for a commissar* (1970)
3 *Barracuda* (1972)
4 *Fox in the sea* (1975)

Shane McKellar series
Burch, T R
1 *Shane McKellar and the face at the window* (1979)
2 *Shane McKellar and the treasure hunt* (1979)

Shane series
Bonnamy, Francis
see **Peter Shane series**

Shaner series
Greth, Roma
see **Hana Shaner series**

Shank series
Harrell, Andrew
see **Sam Shank series**

Shanley and Golden series
Webb, Jack
see **Father Joseph Shanley and Sammy Golden series**

Shann Lantree series
Norton, Andre
see **Planet Warlock series**

Shannara series
Brooks, Terry
1 *Sword of Shannara* (1977)
2 *Elfstones of Shannara* (1982)
3 *Wishsong of Shannara* (1985)
This sequence is followed by the **Heritage of Shannara series**

Shannon series
Adams, Cleve Franklin
see **John J Shannon series**
Cronin, Archibald Joseph
see **Robert Shannon series**
Heberden, Mary Violet
see **Desmond Shannon series**
Quinn, Jake
see **Patrick Shannon series**
Roberts, Lee
see **Doctor Clinton Shannon series**
Ryland, Clive
see **Superintendent Shannon series**

Shaofeng, Rose and Lifeng series
Payne, Robert
see **Lifeng, Shaofeng and Rose series**

Shaper exile series
Finch, Sheila
1 *Garden of the shaped* (1987)
Revised edition 1988
2 *Shaper's legacy* (1989)
3 *Shaping the dawn* (1989)

Shapes and stories series
Grigson, Geoffrey
Books about pictures
1 *Shapes and stories* (1964)
2 *Shapes and adventures* (1967)
More shapes and stories

Shapiro series
Lockridge, Richard
see **Nathan Shapiro series**
Smith, Robert Kimmel
see **Sadie Shapiro series**

Shard series
McCutchan, Philip
see **Superintendent Simon Shard series**

Share-a-story series
Thomson, Pat
1 *Treasure sock* (1986)
2 *One of these days* (1986)
3 *Can you hear me, Grandad?* (1986)
4 *My friend, Mister Morris* (1987)
5 *Thank you for the tadpole* (1987)
6 *Good girl granny* (1987)
7 *Dial D for disaster* (1990)

8 *No trouble at all* (1990)
9 *Best pest* (1990)
10 *Best thing of all* (1990)

Shark Gotch series
Wetjen, Albert Richard
1 *Shark Gotch of the islands* (1936)
2 *Chronicles of Shark Gotch* (1937)
3 *Shark Gotch shoots it out* (1938)
4 *Shark Gotch and Typhoon Bradley* (1939)
5 *In the wake of Shark Gotch* (1941)

Shark series
Silver, Richard
see **Captain Shark series**

Sharon McCone series
Muller, Marcia
1 *Edwin of the iron shoes* (1977)
2 *Ask the cards a question* (1982)
3 *Cheshire cat's eye* (1983)
4 *Leave a message for Willie* (1984)
5 *Games to keep the dark away* (1984)
6 *Double* (1984)
Co-author: Bill Pronzini
7 *There's nothing to be afraid of* (1985)
8 *Eye of the storm* (1988)
Co-author: Bill Pronzini
9 *There's something in a Sunday* (1989)
10 *Shape of dread* (1989)
11 *Trophies and dead things* (1990)
12 *Where echoes live* (1991)
13 *Pennies on a dead woman's eyes* (1992)
14 *Wolf in the shadows* (1993)
15 *Till the butchers cut him down* (1994)

Sharp family trilogy
Hohl, Joan
1 *Texas gold* (1986)
2 *California copper* (1986)
3 *Nevada silver* (1987)

Sharp series
Sharmat, Marjorie Weinman
see **Olivia Sharp series**
Travers, J M
see **Jack Sharpe series**

Sharpe series
Cargill, Leslie
see **Morrison Sharpe series**
Cornwell, Bernard
see **Richard Sharpe series**
Tanner, Clay
see **Chance Sharpe series**

Sharpshooter series
Rossi, Bruno
This pseudonym is used by several authors including Paul Hofrichter, Leonard Levinson, Russell Smith and John Stevenson whose authorship is indicated against those titles where it is known
1 *Killing machine* (1973)
2 *Blood oath* (1974)
3 *Blood bath* (1974)
4 *Worst way to die* (1974)
[Levinson]
5 *Night of the assassins* (1974)
[Levinson]
6 *Muzzle blast* (1974)
7 *Head crusher* (1974)
[Levinson]
8 *No quarter given* (1974)
9 *Stiletto* (1974)
10 *Hit man* (1974)
[Stevenson]
11 *Triggerman* (1975)
[Smith]
12 *Scarfaced killer* (1975)
[Hofrichter]
13 *Savage slaughter* (1975)
[Hofrichter]
14 *Las Vegas vengeance* (1975)
[Stevenson]
15 *Dirty way to die* (1975)
16 *Mafia death watch* (1975)

Shattered glass series
Bergstrom, Elaine
1 *Shattered glass* (1989)
2 *Blood alone* (1990)
3 *Blood rites* (1991)

Shattered series
Green, Kate
1 *Shattered moon* (1986)
2 *Night angel* (1989)

Shattered series
Reaves, Michael
1 *Shattered moon* (1986)
2 *Night angel* (1988)

Shaughnessy series
Cookson, Catherine
see **Mary Ann Shaughnessy series**

Shaun O'Malley series
Ross, Gene
1 *Two smart dames* (1949)
2 *Lady, throw me a curve* (1950)

Shaun O'Mara series
Cheyney, Peter
1 *Dark street* (1944)
Dark street murders
2 *Dark interlude* (1947)
Terrible night
3 *Dark Bahama* (1950)
I'll bring her back

Shauna Bishop series
Montague, J J
see **Black Swan series**

Shaw family series
Carroll, Gladys Hasty
1 *As the earth turns* (1933)
2 *Dunnybrook* (1943)
Revised edition 1978

Shaw series
Holroyd, Michael
see **Bernard Shaw series**
McCutchan, Philip
see **Commander Esmonde Shaw series**
Ormondroyd, Edward
see **Susan Shaw series**
Sadler, Mark
see **Paul Shaw series**

Shawn series
Breinburg, Petronella
see **Sean series**

Shawn Starbuck series
Hogan, Ray
1 *Rimrocker* (1970)
2 *Outlawed* (1970)
3 *Three cross* (1970)
4 *Deputy of violence* (1971)
5 *Bullet for Mister Texas* (1971)
6 *Marshal of Babylon* (1971)
7 *Brandon's posse* (1971)
8 *Devil's gunhand* (1972)
9 *Passage to Dodge City* (1972)
10 *Hell merchant* (1972)
11 *Lawman for Slaughter Valley* (1972)
Lawman for the slaughter
12 *Guns of Stingaree* (1973)
13 *Highroller's man* (1973)
14 *Skull gold* (1973)
15 *Texas brigade* (1974)
16 *Jenner guns* (1974)
17 *Scorpion killers* (1974)
18 *Tombstone trail* (1974)
19 *Day of the hangman* (1975)
20 *Last Comanchero* (1975)
21 *High green gun* (1976)
22 *Shotgun rider* (1976)
23 *Bounty hunter's moon* (1977)
24 *Guns for Silver Rose* (1977)

Shayne series
Halliday, Brett
see **Michael Shayne series**

Shayne stories series
Halliday, Brett
see **Mike Shayne stories series**

She series
This sequence has six authors
Haggard, Henry Rider
1 *Wisdom's daughter* (1923)
2 *She and Allan* (1921)
3 *She* (1886)
Annotated She
The second title is a critical edition edited by Norman Etherington, 1991; parodies: *He, a companion to She, being a history of the adventures of J Theodosius Aristophano on the island of Rapa Nui in search of his immortal ancestor*, by John De Morgan, 1887, *It, wild, weird history of marvelous, miraculous, phantasmagorical adventures in search of He, She and Jess and leading to the finding of It, a Haggard conclusion*, by John De Morgan, 1887, *He*, by Andrew Lang and Walter Pollock, 1887, *Her*, by J X Williams, 1967
4 *Ayesha* (1905)
The return of She
5 *Allan and the ice gods* (1927)
Marshall, Sidney John
6 *King of Kor* (1903)
Alternative title: She's promise kept
Tremayne, Peter
7 *Vengeance of She* (1978)
Monaco, Richard
8 *Journey to the flame* (1985)
Miller, Thomas Kent
9 *Sherlock Holmes on the roof of the world* (1987)

She, the adventuress series
Crayder, Dorothy
1 *She, the adventuress* (1973)
2 *She and the dubious three* (1974)

Shea series
De Camp, Lyon Sprague
see **Harold Shea series**

Shearer and Salisbury series
Crawford, Robert
see **Arthur Salisbury and Frank Shearer series**

Sheba series
Rita
1 *Sheba* (1889)
A study of girlhood
2 *Countess Pharamond* (1893)

Shee series
Smith, Lisa J
see **Solstice series**

Sheep series
Shaw, Nancy
Illustrated by Margot Apple
1 *Sheep in a jeep* (1986)
2 *Sheep on a ship* (1989)
3 *Sheep in a shop* (1991)
4 *Sheep out to eat* (1992)
5 *Sheep take a hike* (1994)

Sheepfold Farm series
Williams, Susan
1 *Lambing at Sheepfold Farm* (1982)
2 *Summer at Sheepfold Farm* (1983)
3 *Winter at Sheepfold Farm* (1984)

Sheik Ahmed ben Hassan series
Hull, Edith Maude
1 *Sheik* (1919)
2 *Sons of the Sheik* (1925)

Sheila Chester series
Pyke, Lillian Maxwell
1 *Sheila at Happy Hills* (1922)
2 *Sheila, the prefect* (1923)

Sheila Roath and Stephen Bellecroix series
Craig, David
see **Stephen Bellecroix and Sheila Roath series**

Sheila series
Hayter, Adrian
1 *Sheila in the wind* (1959)
A story of a lone voyage
2 *Second step* (1962)
Experiences in the Indian army

Shelby series
Robb, John
1 *Sioux arrow* (1956)
2 *Traitors' territory* (1957)

Sheldon series
Smyth, John George
see **Ann Sheldon series**
Wilson, John Fleming
see **Tad Sheldon series**

Sheldon Six series
Remick, Grace May
1 *Anne* (1920)
2 *Rose* (1921)
3 *Connie* (1923)
4 *Susan* (1924)

Shell Scott series
Prather, Richard Scott
1 *Case of the vanishing beauty* (1950)
Vanishing beauty
2 *Bodies in bedlam* (1951)
3 *Everybody had a gun* (1951)
4 *Find this woman* (1951)
5 *Way of a wanton* (1952)
6 *Darling, it's death* (1952)
7 *Lie down, killer* (1952)
8 *Dagger of flesh* (1952)
9 *Ride a high horse* (1953)
Too many crooks
10 *Always leave 'em dying* (1954)
11 *Strip for murder* (1955)
12 *Wailing frail* (1956)
13 *Have gat, will travel* (1957)
Short stories
14 *Three's a shroud* (1957)
Three novelettes
15 *Slab happy* (1958)
16 *Scrambled yeggs* (1958)
Original edition, not including Shell Scott, published under the pseudonym David Knight entitled *Pattern for murder*, 1952
17 *Take a murder, darling* (1958)
18 *Over her dead body* (1959)
19 *Double in trouble* (1959)
Co-author; Stephen Marlowe
20 *Dance with the dead* (1960)
21 *Pattern for panic* (1961)
Original edition, not including Shell Scott, published in 1954
22 *Shell Scott's seven slaughters* (1961)
Short stories
23 *Dig that crazy grave* (1961)
24 *Kill the clown* (1962)
25 *Dead heat* (1963)
26 *Joker in the deck* (1964)
27 *Cockeyed corpse* (1964)
28 *Trojan horse* (1964)
29 *Kill him twice* (1965)
30 *Dead man's walk* (1965)
31 *Meandering corpse* (1965)
32 *Kubla Khan caper* (1966)
33 *Gat heat* (1967)
34 *Cheim manuscript* (1969)
35 *Kill me tomorrow* (1969)
36 *Dead-bang* (1971)
37 *Sweet ride* (1972)
38 *Sure thing* (1975)

Shell Scott series
39 *Amber effect* (1986)
40 *Shellshock* (1987)
Omnibus volumes: *Shell Scott sampler*, 1969, *Shell Scott's murder mix*, 1970

Shellback series
Duff, Douglas Valder
see **Yarns of a shellback series**

Shelley Peters series
Bosworth, Ellen
1 *Shelley and the bushfire mystery* (1972)
Shelley Peters and the bushfire mystery
2 *Shelley and the pony of the year* (1972)
Shelley Peters and the pony of the year
3 *Shelley and the problem pony* (1974)
Shelley Peters and the problem pony

Shelley series
Morrow, Charlotte
see **Lisa Knighton series**
Rowland, John
see **Inspector Shelley series**

Shellover series
Ainsworth, Ruth
1 *Ten tales of Shellover* (1963)
2 *More tales of Shellover* (1968)

Shelter Morgan series
Ledd, Paul
1 *Prisoner of revenge* (1980)
2 *Hanging moon* (1980)
3 *Chain gang kill* (1980)
4 *China doll* (1980)
5 *Lazarus guns* (1980)
6 *Circus of death* (1981)
7 *Lookout Mountain* (1981)
8 *Bandit queen* (1981)
9 *Apache trail* (1982)
10 *Massacre mountain* (1982)
11 *Rio rampage* (1982)
12 *Blood mesa* (1983)
13 *Comanchero blood* (1983)
14 *Golden shaft* (1983)
15 *Savage night* (1983)
16 *Wichita gunman* (1984)
17 *Naked outpost* (1984)
18 *Taboo territory* (1984)
19 *Hard men* (1984)
20 *Saddle tramp* (1984)
21 *Shotgun Sugar* (1985)
22 *Fast-draw filly* (1985)
23 *Wanted woman* (1985)
24 *Tongue-tied Texan* (1986)
25 *Slave queen* (1986)
26 *Treasure chest* (1986)
27 *Heavenly hands* (1987)
28 *Lay of the land* (1987)
29 *Bang-up showman* (1987)
30 *Whistlestop wench* (1988)
31 *Hot and spicy* (1988)
32 *Tattle-tail* (1989)
33 *Wyoming wench* (1989)

Shelton family series
Friedman, Rosemary
1 *Proofs of affection* (1982)
2 *Rose of Jericho* (1984)
3 *To live in peace* (1987)

Shema series
Cone, Molly
1 *First I say the Shema* (1971)
2 *About belonging* (1972)
3 *About learning* (1972)
4 *About God* (1973)
5 *Mystery of being Jewish* (1989)

Shen series
Bell, Frank
1 *Wild dog* (1978)
2 *Lioness* (1979)
3 *Trapped* (1980)

Shenandoah series
Reeder, Carolyn
1 *Shenandoah heritage* (1978)
The story of the people before the park
2 *Shenandoah vestiges* (1980)
What the mountain people left behind
3 *Shenandoah secrets* (1991)
The story of the park's hidden past

Shenstone series
Barclay, Florence Louisa
1 *Rosary* (1909)
2 *Mistress of Shenstone* (1910)
3 *Following of the star* (1911)

Shep Stone series
Jacks, Jeff
1 *Murder on the wild side* (1972)
2 *Find the don's daughter* (1974)

Shepton children trilogy
Adams, Agnes
1 *Our Lil* (1923)
2 *That Barbara Moore* (1924)
3 *Ella of Berry Farm* (1927)
One volume edition entitled *Those Shepton children*, 1928

Sherburne series
Douglas, Amanda Minnie
1 *Sherburne House* (1892)
2 *Lyndell Sherburne* (1893)
3 *Sherburne cousins* (1894)
4 *Sherburne romance* (1895)
5 *Mistress of Sherburne* (1896)
6 *Children at Sherburne House* (1897)
7 *Sherburne girls* (1898)
8 *Heir of Sherburne* (1899)
9 *Sherburne inheritance* (1901)
10 *Sherburne quest* (1902)
11 *Honor Sherburne* (1904)
12 *In the Sherburne line* (1907)

Sheridan Doome series
Gould, Stephen
1 *Murder of the admiral* (1936)
Sequence continued under the author's real name Steve Fisher
Fisher, Steve
2 *Murder of the pigboat skipper* (1937)
Murder on the S-23

Sheridan family series
Darrell, Elizabeth
1 *At the going down of the sun* (1984)
2 *And in the morning* (1986)

Sheridan Haynes series
Symons, Julian
1 *Three-pipe problem* (1975)
2 *Blackheath poisonings* (1978)
3 *Sweet Adelaide* (1980)
4 *Detling murders* (1982)
Detling secret
5 *Kentish Manor murders* (1988)

Sheridan series
Davy, Colin
see **David Sheridan series**
Stuart, Vivian
see **Captain Alexander Sheridan series**
Torrio, Vincente
see **Hoods series**
Wilcox, Stephen F
see **T S W Sheridan series**

Sheridan Township series
Paine, Lauran
1 *Guns of summer* (1988)
2 *Sheridan Stage* (1989)
3 *Catch colt* (1989)
4 *Young marauders* (1990)
5 *Bandoleros* (1990)

Sheridan Wesley series
Waugh, Hillary
1 *Madam will not dine tonight* (1947)
If I live to dine
2 *Hope to die* (1948)
3 *Odds run out* (1949)

Sheriff Bill Davies series
Mason, Sara Elizabeth
1 *Murder rents a room* (1943)
2 *Crimson feather* (1946)

Sheriff Bill Lloyd series
Reed, Wallace
1 *Time to kill* (1940)
2 *Marked for murder* (1941)
3 *No sign of murder* (1950)

Sheriff Blue Steele series
Gunn, Tom
1 *Painted post outlaws* (1949)
2 *Sheriff of Painted Post* (1951)
3 *Painted Post law* (1952)
4 *Painted Post range* (1953)
5 *Painted Post gunplay* (1954)

Sheriff Buford Pusser series
This sequence has three authors
Based on screenplays
Warren, Doug
1 *Walking tall* (1973)
Morris, W R
2 *Twelfth of August* (1974)
Carey, Webster
3 *Walking tall, part 2* (1975)

Sheriff Charles Timothy Matthews series
Meredith, Doris R
1 *Sheriff and the Panhandle murders* (1984)
2 *Sheriff and the branding iron murders* (1985)
3 *Sheriff and the Folsom man murders* (1987)
4 *Sheriff and the pheasant hunt murders* (1993)

Sheriff Chick Charleston and Jason Beard series
Guthrie, Alfred Bertram
1 *Wild pitch* (1973)
2 *Genuine article* (1977)
3 *No second wind* (1980)
4 *Playing catch-up* (1985)
5 *Murder in the Cotswolds* (1989)

Sheriff Emil Whippletree series
Hinkemeyer, Michael Thomas
1 *Fields of Eden* (1977)
2 *Time to reap* (1984)
3 *Fourth down, death* (1985)

Sheriff family trilogy
Sidgwick, Ethel
1 *Laura* (1924)
A cautionary story
2 *Bells of Shoreditch* (1928)
When I grow rich
3 *Dorothy's wedding* (1931)
Tale of two villages

Sheriff George White series
Mannon, M M
1 *Here lies blood* (1942)
2 *Murder on the program* (1944)

Sheriff Hiram Odom series
Boniface, Marjorie
1 *Murder as an ornament* (1940)
2 *Venom in Eden* (1942)
3 *Wings of death* (1946)

Sheriff Jack Thompson series
Cameron, Evelyn
1 *Dead man's shoes* (1939)
2 *Malice domestic* (1940)

Sheriff Jason Russell series
Yarbro, Chelsea Quinn
1 *Law in Charity* (1989)
2 *Charity, Colorado* (1993)

Sheriff Jess Roden series
Cunningham, Albert Benjamin
1 *Murder at Deer Lick* (1939)
2 *Murder at the schoolhouse* (1940)
3 *Strange death of Manny Square* (1941)
4 *Death at The Bottoms* (1942)
5 *Bancock murder case* (1942)
6 *Affair at the boat landing* (1943)
7 *Great Yant mystery* (1943)
8 *Cane-patch mystery* (1944)
9 *Death visits the Apple Hole* (1945)
10 *Murder before midnight* (1945)
11 *Death rides a sorrel horse* (1946)
12 *One must die* (1946)
13 *Death of a bullionaire* (1947)
14 *Death of a worldly woman* (1948)
15 *Death haunts the dark lane* (1948)
16 *Murder without weapons* (1949)
17 *Hunter is the hunted* (1950)
Blood runs cold
18 *Killer watches the manhunt* (1950)
19 *Skeleton in the closet* (1951)
20 *Who killed pretty Becky Low?* (1951)
21 *Strange return* (1952)

Sheriff Joe Bain series
Vance, John Holbrook
1 *Fox Valley murders* (1966)
2 *Pleasant Grove murders* (1967)

Sheriff Jug Watson series
Zachary, Hugh
1 *Bloodrush* (1981)
2 *Murder in white* (1981)

Sheriff Macready series
Holman, Hugh
1 *Trout in the milk* (1945)
2 *Slay the murderer* (1946)
3 *Up this crooked way* (1946)
4 *Another man's poison* (1947)

Sheriff Matt Gabriel series
Gosling, Paula
1 *Body in Blackwater Bay* (1992)
2 *Few dying words* (1994)

Sheriff Moss Magill series
Gardiner, Dorothy
1 *What crime is it?* (1956)
Case of the hula clock
2 *Seventh mourner* (1958)
3 *Lion in wait* (1963)
Lion, or murder?

Sheriff Sally Gopher series
Quackenbush, Robert Mead
1 *Sheriff Sally Gopher and the haunted dance hall* (1977)
2 *Sheriff Sally Gopher and the Thanksgiving caper* (1982)

Sheriff Santiago Toole series
Wheeler, Richard Seabrook
1 *Incident at Fort Keogh* (1990)
2 *Final tally* (1991)
3 *Fate* (1992)

Sheriff series
McAdam, Preston
see **Shield series**

Sheringham series
Berkeley, Anthony
see **Roger Sheringham series**

Sherlock Chick series
Quackenbush, Robert Mead
1 *Sherlock Chick's first case* (1986)
2 *Sherlock Chick and the peekaboo mystery* (1987)

3 *Sherlock Chick and the giant egg mystery* (1988)
4 *Sherlock Chick and the noisy shed mystery* (1990)

Sherlock Holmes drama series
The following is a list of dramatic works which include Sherlock Holmes as a central character and, for convenience, are numbered in order of publication
Gillette, William
1 *Sherlock Holmes* (1922)
Two-act play
Hershey, John
2 *Sign of the four* (1937)
One-act play
Gillette, William
3 *Painful predicament of Sherlock Holmes* (1955)
Hardwick, Michael
4 *Four Sherlock Holmes plays* (1964)
5 *Game's afoot* (1969)
Kelly, Tim J
6 *If Sherlock Holmes were a woman* (1970)
one-act play
7 *Last of Sherlock Holmes* (1970)
One-act play
Hardwick, Michael
8 *Four more Sherlock Holmes plays* (1973)
Rosa, Dennis
9 *Sherlock Holmes and the curse of the sign of four* (1975)
Alternative title: The mark of Timber Toe
Kelly, Tim J
10 *Sherlock Holmes meets the Phantom* (1975)
One-act play
11 *Hound of the Baskervilles* (1976)
Two-act play
12 *Sherlock Holmes' first case* (1976)
Two-act play
Leslie, Frederic Andrew
13 *Hound of the Baskervilles* (1977)
Two-act play
Kelly, Tim J
14 *Sherlock Holmes* (1977)
Two-act play adapted from the 1922 play by William Gillette
Nowlan, Alden
15 *Incredible murder of Cardinal Tosca* (1979)
Three-act play
Giovanni, Paul
16 *Crucifer of blood* (1979)
Three-act play based on *The sign of four*, by Sir Arthur Conan Doyle
Stokes, Arthur M
17 *Checkmate!* (1980)
A Sherlock Holmes burlesque
Haubold, Cleve
18 *Sherlock Holmes and the curious adventure of the clockwork prince* (1980)
A Victorian romp in one act, with music by James Alfred Hitt; set in London in 1899
Nassivera, John
19 *Penultimate problem of Sherlock Holmes* (1980)
Two-act play
Kelly, Tim J
20 *Speckled band* (1981)
Two-act play based on a short story
21 *Adventure of the speckled band* (1981)
Two-act play based on a short story
Hardwick, Michael
22 *Hound of the Baskervilles, and other Sherlock Holmes plays* (1982)
Kelly, Tim J
23 *Beast of the Baskervilles* (1984)
One-act play

Sherlock Holmes' life series
Harrison, Michael
see **Life of Sherlock Holmes series**

Sherlock Holmes literary studies series
Hall, Trevor Henry
1 *Sherlock Holmes* (1969)
Ten literary studies
2 *Late Mister Sherlock Homes, and other literary studies* (1971)

Sherlock Holmes' London series
Harrison, Michael
see **Life of Sherlock Holmes series**

Sherlock Holmes sequels series
The following is a list of works which include Sherlock Holmes as a central character and, for convenience, are numbered in order of publication
Richardson, Frank
1 *Secret kingdom* (1905)
Starrett, Vincent
2 *Unique Hamlet* (1920)
Muusmann, Carl
3 *Sherlock Holmes at Elsinore* (1935)
Roberts, Sidney Castle
4 *Christmas Eve* (1936)
Roberts, E C
5 *Strange case of the Megatherium thefts* (1945)
Doyle, Adrian Conan
6 *Exploits of Sherlock Holmes* (1954)
Also published in two volumes entitled *The exploits of Sherlock Holmes*, and, *More exploits of Sherlock Holmes*
Fisher, Charles
7 *Some unaccountable exploits of Sherlock Holmes* (1956)
Short stories
Morgan, Roberts
8 *Spotlight on a simple case* (1959)
Alternative title: Who was that horse I saw you with last night?
Iraldi, James C
9 *Problem of the purple maculas* (1968)
Wincor, Richard
10 *Sherlock Holmes in Tibet* (1968)
Hardwick, Michael
11 *Private life of Sherlock Holmes* (1970)
Based on a screenplay
Sherrod, Floyd
12 *Secret adventure of the thoroughbred ghost* (1972)
Pearson, Edmund
13 *Sherlock Holmes and the Drood mystery* (1973)
Jaffee, Mary
14 *Beyond Baker Street* (1973)
Short stories
Palmer, Stuart
15 *Adventure of the marked man, and one other* (1973)
Two stories set in the 1890s
Meyer, Nicholas
16 *Seven-per-cent solution* (1974)
Set around 1890
Wellman, Manly Wade
17 *Sherlock Holmes's war of the worlds* (1975)
Set in 1902
Meyer, Nicholas
18 *West End horror* (1976)
A posthumous memoir of John H Watson, M.D. set around 1890
Boyer, Richard Lewis
19 *Giant rat of Sumatra* (1976)
Set in 1893
Mitchelson, Austin
20 *Earthquake machine* (1976)
Set in 1906
21 *Hellbirds* (1976)
Set in 1905
Bensen, Donald R
22 *Sherlock Holmes in New York* (1976)
Based on a television film
Pearlman, Gilbert
23 *Adventures of Sherlock Holmes' smarter brother* (1976)
Based on a moving picture
Smith, George Henry
24 *Second war of the worlds* (1976)
Set in the future
Utechin, Nicholas
25 *Sherlock Holmes at Oxford* (1977)
Harrison, Michael
26 *I, Sherlock Holmes* (1977)
Memoirs of Mister Sherlock Holmes, OM, sometime consulting detective-in-ordinary to Their Majesties Queen Victoria, King Edward VII and King George V
Hall, Robert Lee
27 *Exit Sherlock Holmes* (1977)
Set in 1903
Estleman, Loren D
28 *Sherlock Holmes versus Dracula* (1978)
Alternative title: The adventures of the sanguinary count; set in the 1890s
Dibdin, Michael
29 *Last Sherlock Holmes story* (1978)
Set in 1888
Jeffers, Harry Paul
30 *Adventure of the stalwart companions* (1978)
Heretofore unpublished letters and papers concerning a singular collaboration between Theodore Roosevelt and Sherlock Holmes
Collins, Randall
31 *Case of the philosopher's ring* (1978)
Saberhagen, Fred
32 *Holmes-Dracula file* (1978)
Set in 1897
Newman, Robert
33 *Case of the Baker Street Irregular* (1978)
Puzzle for Sherlock Holmes
Fischer, Cindy
34 *Adventure of the copper beeches* (1978)
Kurland, Michael
35 *Infernal device* (1978)
Set around 1890
Estleman, Loren D
36 *Doctor Jekyll and Mister Holmes* (1979)
Set in the 1890s
Hodel, Michael P
37 *Enter the lion* (1979)
A posthumous memoir of Mycroft Holmes set in 1875
Weverka, Robert
38 *Murder by decree* (1979)
Based on a moving picture
Gravatt, Glenn
39 *Adventure of the mysterious lodger* (1979)
Hardwick, Michael
40 *Prisoner of the devil* (1979)
Set in 1895
Andrews, Val
41 *Sherlock Holmes and the arthritic clergyman* (1980)
42 *Mystery of the sealed room* (1980)
Thomas, Frank
43 *Sherlock Holmes and the golden bird* (1980)
Set in the 1890s
44 *Sherlock Holmes and the sacred sword* (1980)
Set in the 1890s
Andrews, Val
45 *Sherlock Holmes and a theatrical mystery* (1980)
46 *Case of the chief rabbi's problem* (1980)
Aubrey, Edmund
47 *Sherlock Holmes in Dallas* (1980)
Dworkin, Ira Bernard
48 *Sherlock Holmes in modern times* (1980)
Short stories
Newman, Robert
49 *Case of the vanishing corpse* (1980)
D'Agneau, Marcel
50 *Curse of the Nibelungen* (1981)
The last case of Lord Holmes of Baker Street and Sir John Watson
Matthias, Lee A
51 *Pandora plague* (1981)
Set in 1902
Newman, Robert
52 *Case of the Somerville secret* (1981)
Bensen, Donald R
53 *Irene, good night* (1982)
Kurland, Michael
54 *Death by gaslight* (1982)
Set around 1890
Smith, Dennis O
55 *Adventure of the purple hand* (1982)
Ward, Alfred C
56 *Sherlock Holmes versus John Thorndyke and Reginald Fortune* (1982)
Newman, Robert
57 *Case of the threatened king* (1982)
Andrews, Val
58 *Beekeeper* (1983)
59 *Carriage clock* (1983)
60 *Fair* (1983)
61 *Fowlhaven werewolf* (1983)
62 *Last reunion* (1983)
Dudley, William E
63 *Untold Sherlock Holmes* (1983)
Short stories
Dvorkin, David
64 *Time for Sherlock Holmes* (1983)
Feuer, Lewis
65 *Case of the revolutionist's daughter* (1983)
Garland, Lawrence
66 *Affair of the unprincipled publisher* (1983)
Smith, Dennis O
67 *Adventure of the unseen traveler* (1983)
Hardwick, Michael
68 *Private life of Doctor Watson* (1983)
Newman, Robert
69 *Case of the Etruscan treasure* (1983)
Clouston, Joseph Storer
70 *Truthful lady* (1984)
Hardwick, Michael
71 *Sherlock Holmes, my life and crimes* (1984)
Smith, Dennis O
72 *Adventure of the zodiac plate* (1984)
Van Ash, Cay
73 *Ten years beyond Baker Street* (1984)
Sherlock Holmes matches wits with the diabolical Dr Fu Manchu
Halliwell, Leslie
74 *Ghost of Sherlock Holmes* (1984)
Newman, Robert
75 *Case of the frightened friend* (1984)
Arnold, Allan
76 *Young Sherlock Holmes* (1985)
Based on a moving picture
Lane, W
77 *Sherlock Holmes and the Wood Green Empire mystery* (1985)
Smith, Dennis O
78 *Secret of Shoreswood Hall* (1985)
79 *Adventure of the Christmas visitor* (1985)
Stashower, Daniel
80 *Adventures of the ectoplasmic man* (1985)
Set in 1910
Thomas, Frank
81 *Sherlock Holmes and the treasure train* (1985)
Walsh, Ray
82 *Mycroft memoranda* (1985)
Set in 1888
Shaw, Stanley
83 *Sherlock Holmes at the 1902 Fifth Test* (1985)

Newman, Robert
84 *Case of the murdered players* (1985)
Shaw, Stanley
85 *Sherlock Holmes meets Annie Oakley* (1986)
Thomas, Frank
86 *Sherlock Holmes and the masquerade murders* (1986)
Biggle, Lloyd
87 *Quallsford inheritance* (1986)
Newman, Robert
88 *Case of the Indian curse* (1986)
Miller, Thomas Kent
89 *Sherlock Holmes on the roof of the world* (1987)
Newman, Robert
90 *Case of the watching boy* (1987)
Piercy, Rohase
91 *My dearest Holmes* (1988)
Symons, Julian
92 *Kentish manor murders* (1988)
Andrews, Val
93 *Sherlock Holmes and the eminent thespian* (1988)
Hardwick, Michael
94 *Revenge of the hound* (1988)
Biggle, Lloyd
95 *Glendower conspiracy* (1990)
Vaughan, Ralph E
96 *Sherlock Holmes in the adventure of the ancient gods* (1990)
Methold, Ken
97 *Sherlock Holmes in Australia* (1991)
The adventure of the kidnapped Kanakas; concerns the disappearance of Irene Norton, nee Adler who originally featured in *A scandal in Bohemia* in *The adventures of Sherlock Holmes*, 1892
King, Laurie R
98 *Beekeeper's apprentice* (1994)
On the segregation of the Queen; set in the first years of World War I
Bailey, Hilary
99 *Adventures of Charlotte Holmes* (1994)
Cases investigated by Sherlock Holmes's sister
Siciliano, Sam
100 *Angel of the opera* (1994)
Sherlock Holmes meets the Phantom of the Opera; set in 1890
Saberhagen, Fred
101 *Seance for a vampire* (1994)
Set in 1903
See also **Baker Street Irregulars series,** by Terrance Dicks, **Inspector Sholto Lestrade series,** by Meirion James Trow, **Professor Moriarty series**, by John Edmund Gardner, **Young Sherlock Holmes series,** by Gerald Frow

Sherlock Holmes series
Doyle, Arthur Conan
1 *Study in scarlet* (1887)
2 *Sign of four* (1890)
3 *Adventures of Sherlock Holmes* (1892)
Short stories; another volume with the same title, published in 1976, is a facsimile of magazine stories, also published as *The Sherlock Holmes illustrated omnibus*, 1978
4 *Hound of the Baskervilles* (1902)
5 *Memoirs of Sherlock Holmes* (1893)
Short stories
6 *Return of Sherlock Holmes* (1905)
Short stories
7 *Valley of fear* (1915)
8 *His last bow* (1917)
Short stories
9 *Case-book of Sherlock Holmes* (1927)
Short stories
10 *Final adventures of Sherlock Holmes* (1981)
Short stories
Omnibus volume: *The annotated Sherlock Holmes*, 1967; companion volumes: *Sherlock Holmes and Doctor Watson, a chronology of their adventures*, by Harold Wilmerding Bell, 1932, revised edition 1953, *Sherlock Holmes scrapbook*, edited by Peter Haining, 1974, *Sherlock Holmes, the published apocrypha*, by Sir Arthur Conan Doyle and Jack Tracy, 1980, *Arthur Conan Doyle on Sherlock Holmes*, 1981, *The world bibliography of Sherlock Holmes and Doctor Watson*, by Ronald Burt De Waal, 1983; parodies: *Misadventures of Sherlock Holmes*, edited by Ellery Queen, 1944, *The execution of Newcome Bowles*, by Alan Durward Mickle, 1948, *The sexual adventures of Sherlock Holmes*, by John H Watson, 1971, *The adventures of Herlock Sholmes*, by Charles Hamilton, 1976, also two parodies in *The door to doom, and other detections*, by John Dickson Carr, 1980, and see also the **Turlock Loames series**, by John Ruyle; junior puzzles based on Sherlock Holmes stories: *Match wits with Sherlock Holmes*,1-8, by Murray Shaw, 1990-1993

Sherlock Holmes' youth series
Frow, Gerald
see **Young Sherlock Holmes series**

Sherlock Hound series
Sivers, Brenda
1 *Hound in the Highlands* (1980)
2 *Hound and the witching affair* (1980)
3 *Case of the baffling burglary* (1980)
4 *Count Dobermann Pinscher* (1981)
5 *Hound and the Perilous Pekes* (1981)
6 *Hound and the curse of Kali* (1982)

Sherlock Street detectives series
Christian, Mary Blount
1 *Mystery of the missing scarf* (1989)
2 *North Pole mystery* (1989)
3 *UFO mystery* (1989)
4 *Pet day mystery* (1989)
5 *Mystery of the midnight raider* (1991)
6 *Mystery of the missing red wagon* (1991)
7 *Mystery of the unsigned valentine* (1991)
8 *Mystery of the fallen tree* (1991)
9 *Mystery of the message from the sky* (1991)
10 *Mystery of the polluted stream* (1991)

Sherman series
Smith, Don
see **Secret mission series**

Sherret York series
Holt, Gavin
1 *Murder train* (1936)
2 *Ivory ladies* (1937)

Sherston trilogy
Sassoon, Siegfried
Fictionalized autobiography
1 *Memoirs of a fox-hunting man* (1928)
Originally published anonymously
2 *Memoirs of an infantry officer* (1930)
Originally published anonymously
3 *Sherston's progress* (1936)
One volume edition entitled *The complete memoirs of George Sherston*, 1937, also published as *The memoirs of George Sherston*

Sherwood Forest series
Palmer, Geoffrey
1 *Mystery at Sherwood* (1962)
2 *Greenwooders* (1963)
3 *Greenwooders' triumph* (1964)

Sherwood series
Bude, John
see **Inspector Sherwood series**
Carr, Annie Roe
see **Nan Sherwood series**

Shetland series
Barr, Amelia Edith
1 *Jan Vedder's wife* (1885)
2 *Sheila Vedder* (1912)

Shetland series
Saxby, Jessie Margaret Edmonston
1 *Lads of Lunda* (1887)
2 *Yarl's yacht* (1889)
3 *Viking boys* (1892)
4 *Saga-book of Lunda* (1896)

Shield series
McAdam, Preston
1 *African assignment* (1985)
2 *Arabian assault* (1985)
3 *Island intrigue* (1985)

Shield series
Yonge, Charlotte Mary
1 *Scenes and characters* (1847)
2 *Stokesley secret* (1861)
3 *Two sides of the shield* (1885)

Shields series
Carlon, Patricia
see **Jefferson Shields series**

Shifty Anderson series
Murray, William Buckley
see **Lou Anderson series**

Shike series
Shea, Robert
1 *Time of the dragons* (1981)
2 *Last of the Zinja* (1981)

Shiloh series
Walker, Dalton
1 *Shiloh* (1990)
2 *Desert hell* (1991)
3 *Blood rival* (1991)
4 *Hunted* (1991)
5 *Hell town* (1991)
6 *Sidewinder* (1992)
7 *Vengeance trail* (1992)
8 *Blood bounty* (1992)

Shimmer and Thorn series
Yep, Laurence Michael
1 *Dragon of the lost sea* (1982)
2 *Dragon steel* (1985)
3 *Dragon cauldron* (1991)

Shimoni series
Hesky, Olga
see **Inspector Tami Shimoni series**

Shimoru Kyota series
Thompson, Lloyd S
1 *Death stops the show* (1946)
2 *Hear not my steps* (1953)

Shiner Slattery series
Lee, John Alexander
1 *Shining with the Shiner* (1945)
Short stories
2 *Shiner Slattery* (1964)

Shiny spear series
Sheldon, Roy
1 *Atoms in action* (1953)
2 *House of entropy* (1953)

Ship and shore series
Stratemeyer, Edward L
1 *Last cruise of the Spitfire* (1894)
Alternative title: Luke Foster's strange voyage
2 *Reuben Stone's discovery* (1895)
Alternative title: The young miller of Torrent Bend
3 *True to himself* (1900)
Alternative title: Roger Strong's struggle for place

Ship insurance series
Ledwith, Frank
Autobiography
1 *Best of all possible worlds* (1987)
2 *Ships that go bump in the night* (1974)
3 *Ships afloat in the city* (1977)

Ship of Law series
Bear, Greg
see **Law series**

Ship trilogy
Elsschot, Willem
1 *[Tsjip]* (1934)
No English edition
2 *Lion-tamer* (1940)
Original edition entitled *De leeuwentemmer*
3 *Tank ship* (1942)
Original edition entitled *Het tankschip*

Shipmates series
Lawson, Robert Neale
1 *Beloved shipmates* (1924)
2 *Happy anchorage* (1925)

Ships in the sky series
Gunnarsson, Gunar
Translated from the Danish
1 *Ships in the sky* (1938)
2 *Night and the dream* (1938)

Shipwreck series
Lane, Margaret
1 *Night at sea* (1964)
2 *Smell of burning* (1965)

Shirley and Bill Harper series
Ernst, Paul
see **Shirley Leighton and Bill Harper series**

Shirley and Claude series
Nixon, Joan Lowery
1 *Dark and deadly pool* (1987)
2 *Orphan train quartet* (1987)

Shirley and Irving series
Mills, Osmington
see **Sergeant Patrick Shirley and Inspector Rip Irving series**

Shirley and Laverne series
Steffanson, Con
see **Laverne and shirley series**

Shirley Flight series
This sequence has two authors
Dale, Judith
1 *Shirley Flight, air hostess* (1958)
2 *Shirley Flight, air hostess and the diamond smugglers* (1958)
3 *Desert adventure* (1958)
4 *Shirley Flight, air hostess in Hollywood* (1958)
5 *Shirley Flight, air hostess and the flying doctor* (1959)
6 *Shirley Flight, ait hostess and the rajah's daughter* (1960)
7 *Shirley Flight, air hostess in Congo rescue* (1960)
8 *Great bullion mystery* (1960)
9 *Fjord adventure* (1960)
10 *Pacific castaways* (1960)
Arlen, Trudi
11 *Hawaiian mystery* (1960)
12 *Shirley Flight, air hostess in Spain* (1960)
Dale, Judith
13 *Shirley Flight, air hostess and the Chinese puzzle* (1961)
14 *Flying jet* (1961)
15 *Shirley Flight, air hostess in Canadian capers* (1961)
16 *Storm warning* (1961)

Shirley Leighton and Bill Harper series
Ernst, Paul
1 *Hangman's hat* (1951)
2 *Lady, get your gun* (1955)
Rose from the dead

Shirley McClintock series
Oliphant, B J
1 *Dead in the scrub* (1990)
2 *Unexpected corpse* (1990)
3 *Deservedly dead* (1992)

Shirley series
Burningham, John
1 *Come away from the water, Shirley* (1977)
2 *Time to get out of the bath, Shirley* (1978)

Shirley series
Lewis, Lorna
1 *Shirley goes travelling* (1959)
2 *Shirley goes to America* (1961)

Shirley series
Montgomery, Lucy Maud
see **Avonlea series**

Shiva series
Brennan, James Herbert
1 *Shiva* (1989)
2 *Crone* (1990)
Shiva accused

Shmoo series
Capp, Al
Comic strips
1 *Life and times of the Shmoo* (1948)
2 *Return of the Shmoo* (1959)

Shock and Tucker series
Buchanan, Patrick
see **Ben Shock and Charity Tucker series**

Shoeless Joe Jackson series
Kinsella, William Patrick
1 *Shoeless Joe Jackson comes to Iowa* (1980)
Short stories
2 *Shoeless Joe* (1982)
Based on a story in *Shoeless Joe Jackson comes to Iowa*, 1980

Shoes series
Streatfeild, Noel
1 *Ballet shoes* (1936)
2 *Tennis shoes* (1937)
3 *Circus is coming* (1938)
Circus shoes
Revised edition 1948
4 *Curtain up* (1944)
Theater shoes
Alternative title: Other people's shoes
5 *Party frock* (1946)
Party shoes
6 *Painted garden* (1949)
Movie shoes
7 *White boots* (1951)
Skating shoes
8 *Bell family* (1954)
Family shoes
9 *Wintle's Wonders* (1957)
Dancing shoes
10 *New Town* (1960)
New shoes
11 *Apple Bough* (1962)
Traveling shoes
13 *Ballet shoes for Anna* (1976)

Shoestring series
Ableman, Paul
see **Eddie Shoestring series**

Shoestring trilogy
Pinkerton, Kathrene
Reminiscences
1 *Wilderness wife* (1939)
Life in the Canadian woods
2 *Three's a crew* (1940)
Cruising on the coast of British Columbia and Alaska
3 *Two ends to my shoestring* (1942)

Shogun series
Silverman, Deborah
1 *Fall of the Shogun* (1987)
2 *Black dragon* (1988)

Sholto Lestrade series
Trow, Meirion James
see **Inspector Sholto Lestrade series**

Sholto series
Hart-Davis, Duff
see **Sam Sholto series**

Shomar series
Klinger, Henry
see **Lieutenant Shomri Shomar series**

Shomri Shomar series
Klinger, Henry
see **Lieutenant Shomri Shomar series**

Shore series
Fraser, Antonia
see **Jemima Shore series**

Short sixes series
Bunner, Henry Cuyler
Stories to be read while the candle burns
1 *Short sixes* (1891)
2 *More short sixes* (1894)

Shorty McCabe series
Ford, Sewell
1 *Shorty McCabe* (1906)
2 *Side-stepping with Shorty* (1908)
3 *Odd numbers* (1912)
4 *Shorty McCabe on the job* (1915)
5 *Shorty McCabe looks 'em over* (1918)
6 *Shorty McCabe gets the hail* (1919)
7 *Meet 'em with Shorty McCabe* (1920)

Shorty series
Nye, Nelson Coral
see **Wild Horse Shorty series**

Shorty series
Webster, James
1 *Shorty the hero* (1967)
2 *Shorty and Tom Rabbit* (1967)
3 *Shorty and the bank robbers* (1967)
4 *Shorty again* (1969)
Companion volumes: *Young Shorty books*, 1978, *More young Shorty books*, 1980, *Young Shorty again*, 1981 - 12 readers and 2 workbooks in each series - and Shorty *activity books*, 1985 - 2 books

Shotover series
Wilson, Andrew Norman
see **Norman Shotover series**

Show girl series
McEvoy, Joseph Patrick
1 *Show girl* (1928)
2 *Hollywood girl* (1929)

Show jumping series
Smythe, Pat
Reminiscences
1 *Jump for joy* (1954)
2 *One jump ahead* (1956)
3 *Jumping round the world* (1962)

Show off series
Curtin, Patricia Romero
1 *Michael shows off Baltimore* (1982)
2 *Tippet shows off Washington* (1983)

Showman series
Norris, Stanley
see **Phil, the showman series**

Shrew series
Augarde, Steve
see **Barnaby Shrew series**

Shrig of Bow Street series
Farnol, Jeffery
see **Mister Jasper Shrig of Bow Street series**

Shrublands Estate series
Ure, Jean
1 *Megastar* (1985)
2 *Swings and roundabouts* (1986)

Shukru series
Kubinyi, Laszlo
1 *Zeki and the talking cat Shukru* (1970)
2 *Cat and the flying machine* (1970)

Shulamite series
Askew, Alice
see **Deborah Krillet series**

Shuna series
King, John
1 *Shuna, white queen of the jungle* (1951)
2 *Shuna and the lost tribe* (1951)

Shy stegosaurus series
Lampman, Evelyn Sibley
1 *Shy stegosaurus of Cricket Creek* (1955)
2 *Shy stegosaurus of Indian Springs* (1962)

Siamese cats series
Chetham-Strode, Warren
1 *Three men and a girl* (1958)
2 *Top off the milk* (1959)
3 *Cat called Tootoo* (1966)
4 *Tootoo's friends at the farm* (1967)
5 *Tootoo, the travelling cat* (1968)

Siberian series
Harper, Theodore Acland
1 *Siberian gold* (1927)
2 *Kubrik the outlaw* (1928)
3 *His Excellency and Peter* (1930)
4 *Red sky* (1935)

Sibyl series
Baldwin, Mary
1 *Popular girl* (1901)
A tale of school life in Germany
2 *Sibyl* (1903)
Alternative title: Old school friends

Sibyl Sue Blue series
Brown, Rosel George
1 *Sibyl Sue Blue* (1966)
Galactic Sibyl Sue Blue
2 *Waters of Centaurus* (1970)

Sicilian inquiry series
Dolci, Danilo
1 *Outlaws of Partinico* (1955)
Original edition entitled *Banditi a Partinico*
2 *To feed the hungry* (1956)
Original edition entitled *Inchiesta a Palermo*
3 *Waste* (1960)
Original edition entitled *Spreco*

Sid Ames series
Roden, Henry Wisdom
1 *You only hang once* (1946)
2 *Too busy to die* (1947)
3 *One angel less* (1949)
4 *Wake for a lady* (1950)

Sid Halley series
Francis, Dick
1 *Odds against* (1965)
2 *Whip hand* (1979)

Sidel series
Charyn, Jerome
see **Isaac Sidel series**

Sidhe Lugh series
Flint, Kenneth Covey
1 *Riders of the Sidhe* (1984)
2 *Champions of the Sidhe* (1984)
3 *Master of the Sidhe* (1985)
Companion volume: *The hound of Culain*, 1986

Sidney and Janet series
Ray, Anna Chapin
1 *Sidney, her summer on the Saint Lawrence* (1905)
2 *Janet, her winter in Quebec* (1906)
3 *Day, her year in New York* (1907)
4 *Sidney at college* (1908)
5 *Janet at odds* (1909)
6 *Sidney, her senior year* (1910)

Sidney Kenyon series
Crisp, Norman James
see **Inspector Sidney Kenyon series**

Sidney series
Herbert, Brian
1 *Sidney's comet* (1983)
An account of the remarkable events which occurred during the approach of the Great Garbage Comet
2 *Garbage chronicles* (1985)
An account of the adventures of Tom Javik and Wizzy Malloy in the far-away land of catapulted garbage

Siege of Boston series
Allen, Willis Boyd
1 *Son of liberty* (1896)
2 *Called to the front* (1897)

Siege of Malta series
Wright, Sydney Fowler
1 *Saint Elmo* (1942)
2 *Saint Angelo* (1942)

Siegel series
Prowell, Sandra West
see **Phoebe Siegel series**

Siegfried series
Sassoon, Siegfried
Autobiography
1 *Old country and seven more years* (1938)
2 *Weald of youth* (1942)
3 *Siegfried's journey, 1916-1920* (1945)

Sierra series
Hill, Richard
see **Randall Gatsby Sierra series**

Sierras series
Thoeme, Brock
see **Saga of the Sierras series**

Sigbjorn Wilderness series
Lowry, Malcolm
see **Voyage that never ends series**

Sigmund Schultz series
Donleavy, James Patrick
1 *Schultz* (1979)
2 *Are you listening Rabbi Low* (1987)

Signalman trilogy
Vaughan, Adrian
Autobiography
1 *Signalman's morning* (1981)

Signalman trilogy

2 *Signalman's twilight* (1983)
3 *Signalman's nightmare* (1987)

Signs of the times series
Monsarrat, Nicholas
1 *Time before this* (1962)
2 *Smith and Jones* (1963)
3 *Fair day's work* (1964)
4 *Something to hide* (1965)

Sigrid Harald series
Maron, Margaret
see **Lieutenant Sigrid Harald series**

Sikanska series
Gowland, John Stafford
Reminiscences of a Canadian forest ranger
1 *Smoke over Sikanska* (1955)
2 *Sikanska trail* (1956)

Sikh series
Mundy, Talbot
1 *Winds of the world* (1916)
2 *King, of the Khybers* (1916)
King of the Khyber Rifles
3 *Hira Singh's tale* (1918)

Silas Booth series
Linklater, Joseph Lane
1 *Shadow for a lady* (1947)
2 *Black opal* (1947)
3 *Bishop's cap* (1948)
Bishop's cap murder
4 *And she had a little knife* (1949)
She had a little knife
5 *Odd woman out* (1955)
6 *Tisket, a casket* (1959)

Silas Ermineskin series
Kinsella, William Patrick
Short stories
1 *Dance me outside* (1977)
2 *Scars* (1978)
3 *Born Indian* (1981)
4 *Moccasin telegraph* (1983)
5 *Fencepost chronicles* (1986)

Silas Manners series
Moffatt, James
1 *Sleeping bomb* (1970)
Cambri plot
2 *Justice for a dead spy* (1971)

Silas series
Bates, Herbert Ernest
see **Uncle Silas series**

Silas Wortenheimer series
Learmonth, David
1 *Tainted turf* (1927)
2 *Red mammon* (1928)
Checkmate and stalemate

Silber series
Johnston, Gunnar
1 *Claws of the scorpions* (1935)
2 *Two kings* (1936)

Silence Leigh trilogy
Scott, Melissa
1 *Five-twelfths of heaven* (1985)
2 *Silence in solitude* (1986)
3 *Empress of earth* (1987)
One volume edition entitled *The roads of heaven*, 1988

Silence series
Blackwood, Algernon
see **John Silence series**

Silent company trilogy
Remy
Translated from the French
1 *Memoirs of a secret agent of Free France* (1948)
2 *Courage and fear* (1950)
3 *Portrait of a spy* (1953)
Original edition entitled *Profil d'un espion*

Silent Don series
Sholokhov, Mikhail
see **Don series**

Silent service series
Jones, J Farragut
1 *Waters dark and deep* (1981)
2 *Scourge of Scapa Flow* (1981)
3 *Forty fathoms down* (1981)
4 *Pearl Harbor periscopes* (1981)
5 *Tracking the wolfpack* (1981)
6 *Pacific standoff* (1982)
7 *Deepwater showdown* (1982)
8 *Depths of danger* (1982)

Silent Slade series
Tuttle, Gene
1 *Slade* (1971)
2 *Range guardian* (1972)
3 *Slade, range detective* (1973)

Silent spring series
Carson, Rachel Louise
1 *Silent spring* (1962)
2 *Since silent spring* (1970)
3 *Silent spring revisited* (1987)

Silistra series
Morris, Janet Ellen
1 *High couch of Silistra* (1977)
Returning creation
2 *Golden sword* (1977)
3 *Wind from the abyss* (1978)
4 *Carnelian throne* (1979)

Silk maker series
Legat, Michael
1 *Silk maker* (1985)
2 *Cast iron man* (1987)

Silk series
Chase, James Hadley
see **Lu Silk series**
Harvester, Simon
see **Dorian Silk series**
Leighton, Robert
see **Sergeant Silk series**
O'Sullivan, James Brendan
see **Steve Silk series**

Silken dalliance series
Bruce, Henry James
1 *Silken dalliance* (1947)
2 *Thirty dozen moons* (1949)

Silkpaws series
Williams, Gladys
see **Semolina Silkpaws series**

Silky Pincus series
Rosten, Leo
1 *Silky!* (1979)
2 *King Silky!* (1980)

Silly Sally series
Tierney, Frank M
1 *Silly Sally and the picnic with the porpoises* (1973)
2 *Silly Sally and the snowman* (1975)
3 *Silly Sally and the golden pail* (1977)
4 *Silly Sally and the little pumpkin* (1978)
5 *Silly Sally and the tire and Mrs Corrigan* (1979)
6 *Silly Sally and the moon-baker* (1981)
7 *Silly Sally and Captain G Rumpy* (1988)

Silly Tilly series
Hoban, Lillian
1 *Silly Tilly and the Easter bunny* (1987)
2 *Silly Tilly's Thanksgiving dinner* (1990)

Silva d'Croy series
Williamson, Geoffrey
1 *Lovable outlaw* (1930)
2 *Grand trunk knight* (1933)

Silva series
Oleksiw, Susan
see **Joe Silva series**

Silveira series
Cripps, Arthur Shearly
see **John Kent series**

Silver blades series
Lowell, Melissa
1 *Breaking the ice* (1993)
2 *In the spotlight* (1993)
3 *Competition* (1994)
4 *Going for the gold* (1994)
5 *Perfect pair* (1994)
6 *Skating camp* (1994)

Silver Brumby series
Mitchell, Elyne
1 *Silver Brumby* (1958)
2 *Silver Brumby's daughter* (1960)
3 *Silver brumbies of the south* (1965)
4 *Silver Brumby kingdom* (1966)
5 *Moon filly* (1968)
6 *Silver Brumby whirlwind* (1973)
7 *Son of the whirlwind* (1976)
8 *Colt from Snowy River* (1979)
9 *Snowy River brumby* (1980)
10 *Brumby racer* (1981)
Companion volume: *The man from Snowy River*, 1982, based on the moving picture

Silver Bush series
Montgomery, Lucy Maud
1 *Pat of Silver Bush* (1933)
2 *Mistress Pat* (1935)

Silver call series
McKiernan, Dennis L
1 *Trek to Kraggen-Cor* (1986)
2 *Drega path* (1986)
Companion volume: *Tales of Mithgar*, 1994

Silver Chief series
This sequence has two authors
O'Brien, Jack
1 *Silver Chief, dog of the north* (1933)
2 *Silver Chief to the rescue* (1937)
3 *Return of Silver Chief* (1943)
4 *Royal Red* (1951)
5 *Silver Chief's revenge* (1954)
Miller, Albert Griffith
6 *Silver Chief's big game trail* (1961)

Silver Eagle series
Cumming, Primrose
1 *Silver Eagle Riding School* (1938)
2 *Silver Eagle carries on* (1940)
3 *Rivals to Silver Eagle* (1954)

Silver falcon trilogy
Fisher, Edward
1 *Shakespeare and son* (1962)
2 *Love's labour's won* (1963)
A novel about Shakespeare's lost years
3 *Best house in Stratford* (1965)

Silver Fox Patrol series
Carter, Herbert
see **Boy Scout series**

Silver hand trilogy
Moorcock, Michael
see **Chronicle of Prince Corum and the silver hand trilogy**

Silver John series
Wellman, Manly Wade
1 *Who fears the devil?* (1963)
John the balladeer
The second title is an expanded edition
2 *Old gods waken* (1979)
3 *After dark* (1980)
4 *Lost and the lurking* (1981)
5 *Hanging stones* (1982)
6 *Voice of the mountain* (1984)
Also two Silver John stories in *Worse things waiting*, 1973

Silver medal series
Trowbridge, John Townsend
1 *His own master* (1877)
2 *Bound in honor* (1877)
Alternative title: A harvest of wild oats
3 *Young Joe, and other boys* (1879)
4 *Silver medal* (1880)
5 *Pocket-rifle* (1881)
6 *Jolly rover* (1882)

Silver pencil series
Dalgliesh, Alice
1 *Silver pencil* (1944)
2 *Along Janet's road* (1946)

Silver Ridge series
O'Conner, Elizabeth
1 *Steak for breakfast* (1958)
2 *Second helping* (1969)

Silver series
Delderfield, Ronald Frederick
see **Long John Silver series**
Golding, Louis
see **Elsie Silver series**
Hightower, Lynn S
see **David Silver series**
Holt, Henry
see **Inspector Silver series**
Singer, Marilyn
see **Lizzie Silver series**
Wentworth, Patricia
see **Miss Maud Silver series**

Silver sword series
Du Bois, Mary Constance
1 *Lass of the silver sword* (1909)
2 *League of the Signet Ring* (1910)

Silverface series
Long, Harman
1 *Silverface* (1948)
2 *Silverface surrenders* (1949)

Silverglass series
Rivkin, J F
1 *Silverglass* (1986)
2 *Web of wind* (1987)
3 *Witch of Rhostshyl* (1989)
4 *Mistress of ambiguities* (1991)

Silverlock series
Myers, John Myers
1 *Silverlock* (1949)
2 *Moon's fire-eating daughter* (1981)

Silverthorn and Bendelbinder families series
Longstreet, Stephen
see **Dream seekers series**

Silvertip series
Brand, Max
1 *Valley thieves* (1933)
2 *False rider* (1933)
3 *Silvertip* (1942)
4 *Man from Mustang* (1942)
5 *Silvertip's strike* (1942)
6 *Silvertip's roundup* (1943)
7 *Silvertip's trap* (1943)
8 *Fighting four* (1944)
9 *Silvertip's chase* (1944)
10 *Silvertip's search* (1945)
11 *Stolen stallion* (1945)
12 *Mountain riders* (1946)
13 *Valley of vanishing men* (1947)

Silvestri series
Rennert, Maggie
see **Guy Silvestri series**

Simba series
White, Stewart Edward
1 *Leopard Woman* (1916)
2 *Simba* (1918)
Short stories
3 *Back of beyond* (1927)

Simcha series
Gavta, Yaffa
see **Savta Simcha series**

Sime-Gen series
This sequence has two authors who are responsible for volumes individually and together
Lichtenberg, Jacqueline
1 *House of Zeor* (1974)
2 *Unto Zeor, forever* (1978)
Lorrah, Jean
3 *First channel* (1980)
Lichtenberg, Jacqueline
4 *Mahogany trimrose* (1981)
Lorrah, Jean
5 *Channel's destiny* (1982)
Lichtenberg, Jacqueline
6 *Rene Sime* (1984)
Lorrah, Jean
7 *Ambroo Keon* (1986)
Lichtenberg, Jacqueline
8 *Zelerod's doom* (1986)

Simeon series
Tate, Peter
1 *Thinking seat* (1969)
2 *Moon on an iron meadow* (1974)
3 *Faces in the flames* (1976)

Simkin series
Allen, Linda
see **Mrs Simkin series**

Simmonds series
East, Roger
see **Superintendent Simmonds series**

Simmons series
Gillespie, Robert Byrne
see **Ralph Simmons series**
Lockridge, Frances
see **Assistant District Attorney Bernie Simmons series**
Lytton, Shel
see **Mustang Terry Simmons series**

Simon and Benjie series
Ballard, Martin
see **Benjie and Simon series**

Simon and Jenny series
Jones, Olive
see **Barfield series**

Simon and Josephine Leyton series
Becker, Jillian
1 *Keep* (1967)
2 *Union* (1971)

Simon and Mag series
Styles, Showell
1 *Shop in the mountain* (1961)
2 *Ladder of snow* (1962)
3 *Necklace of glaciers* (1963)
4 *Pass of morning* (1966)

Simon and Nicky Carr series
Leyland, Eric
see **Nicky and Simon Carr series**

Simon and Sally series
Dicks, Terrance
1 *Cry vampire!* (1981)
2 *War of the witches* (1983)

Simon and the witch series
Barry, Margaret Stuart
1 *Simon and the witch* (1976)
2 *Return of the witch* (1978)
3 *Witch of Monopoly Manor* (1979)
4 *Witch on holiday* (1983)
5 *Witch VIP* (1987)
6 *Simon and the witch in school* (1987)
7 *Witch's holiday club* (1988)

Simon Ark series
Hoch, Edward Dentinger
1 *Judges of Hades, and other Simon Ark stories* (1971)
2 *City of brass, and other Simon Ark stories* (1971)
3 *Quests of Simon Ark* (1984)

Simon Artifex series
Keverne, Richard
1 *Artifex intervenes* (1934)
Three novelettes
2 *Crook stuff* (1935)
Short stories including some which do not feature Artifex

Simon Ashton series
Antill, Elizabeth
see **Inspector Simon Ashton series**

Simon Bede and Helen Bullock series
Byfield, Barbara
1 *Solemn high murder* (1975)
Co-author: Frank L Tedeschi
2 *Forever wilt thou die* (1976)
3 *Harder thing than triumph* (1977)
4 *Parcel of their fortunes* (1979)

Simon Black series
Southall, Ivan
1 *Meet Simon Black* (1950)
2 *Simon Black in peril* (1951)
3 *Simon Black in space* (1952)
4 *Simon Black in Coastal Command* (1953)
5 *Simon Black in China* (1954)
6 *Simon Black and the spacemen* (1955)
Simon Black on Venus
7 *Simon Black in the Antarctic* (1956)
8 *Simon Black takes over* (1959)
9 *Simon Black at sea* (1961)

Simon Bognor series
Heald, Tim
1 *Unbecoming habits* (1973)
2 *Blue blood will out* (1974)
3 *Deadline* (1975)
4 *Let sleeping dogs lie* (1976)
5 *Just desserts* (1977)
6 *Murder at Moose Jaw* (1981)
7 *Masterstroke* (1982)
Small masterpiece
8 *Red herrings* (1986)
9 *Brought to book* (1988)
10 *Business unusual* (1989)

Simon Boom series
Suhl, Yuri
1 *Simon Boom gives a wedding* (1972)
2 *Simon Boom gets a letter* (1976)

Simon Brade series
Campbell, Harriette Russell
1 *String glove mystery* (1936)
2 *Porcelain fish mystery* (1937)
Porcelain fish
3 *Moor fires mystery* (1938)
4 *Three names for murder* (1940)
5 *Murder set to music* (1941)
6 *Magic makes murder* (1943)
8 *Crime in crystal* (1946)

Simon Broadstrop series
Kee, Robert
1 *Sign of the times* (1955)
2 *Broadstrop in season* (1959)

Simon Bullion series
Dix, Maurice Buxton
see **Superintendent Simon Bullion series**

Simon Carter series
Friend, Oscar
1 *Buzzard meat* (1953)
2 *Lobo brand* (1954)
3 *Deputies of death* (1954)
4 *Gun-runner* (1956)

Simon Chard series
Malim, Barbara
1 *Murder on holiday* (1937)
2 *Seven looked on* (1939)

Simon Crisp series
Matthew, Christopher
1 *Diary of a somebody* (1978)
2 *Loosely engaged* (1980)
3 *Crisp report* (1981)
4 *Family matters* (1986)

Simon Crole series
Leitfred, Robert H
1 *Corpse that spoke* (1936)
2 *Man who was murdered twice* (1937)
3 *Death cancels the evidence* (1938)
Murder is my racket

Simon Drake series
Maguire, Michael
1 *Shot silk* (1975)
2 *Slaughter horse* (1975)
3 *Scratchproof* (1976)

Simon Drake series
Nielsen, Helen
1 *Gold Coast nocturne* (1951)
Murder by proxy
Dead on the level
2 *After midnight* (1966)
3 *Killer in the street* (1967)
4 *Darkest hour* (1969)
5 *Severed key* (1973)
6 *Brink of murder* (1976)

Simon Gale series
Verner, Gerald
1 *Noose for a lady* (1952)
Based on a radio series
2 *Sorcerer's house* (1956)

Simon Girty series
Truman, Timothy
1 *Borderland* (1989)
2 *Bloody ground* (1990)

Simon Good series
Davis, George
see **Roag's Syndicate series**

Simon Herald series
Welcome, John
1 *Stop at nothing* (1959)
2 *Wanted for killing* (1965)

Simon Ire series
Crow, Duncan
1 *First summer* (1967)
2 *Crimson petal* (1969)
Originally announced as a quartet

Simon Jaffe series
Schorr, Mark
see **Red Diamond series**

Simon Kaye series
Waugh, Hillary
1 *Glenna Powers case* (1980)
2 *Doria Rafe case* (1980)
3 *Billy Cantrell case* (1981)
4 *Nerissa Claire case* (1983)
5 *Veronica Dean case* (1984)
6 *Priscilla Copperwaite case* (1986)

Simon Kelston series
Anderson, Helen M
see **Kelston of Kells series**

Simon Kenton and Daniel Boone series
Ellis, Edward Sylvester
see **Daniel Boone and Simon Kenton series**

Simon Kenworthy series
Hilton, John Buxton
see **Superintendent Simon Kenworthy series**

Simon Larren series
Charles, Robert
1 *Nothing to lose* (1963)
2 *One must survive* (1964)
3 *Dark vendetta* (1964)
4 *Mission of murder* (1965)
5 *Arctic assignment* (1966)
6 *Fourth shadow* (1966)
7 *Assassins for peace* (1967)
8 *Stamboul intrigue* (1968)
9 *Big fish* (1969)
10 *Strikefast* (1969)

Simon Lash series
Gruber, Frank
1 *Simon Lash, private detective* (1941)
Simon Lash, detective
2 *Buffalo box* (1942)
3 *Murder ninety seven* (1948)
Long arm of murder

Simon Leigh series
Temple, Richard
1 *Spy is a dirty word* (1970)
2 *Schulsinger affair* (1971)

Simon Luck series
Marsh, John
1 *Reluctant executioner* (1959)
2 *Girl in a net* (1962)

Simon Manton series
Underwood, Michael
see **Superintendent Simon Manton series**

Simon Parbitter series
Hammond, Gerald
1 *Adverse report* (1987)
2 *Stray shot* (1988)

Simon Quarry series
Hunter, Robin
1 *Fourth angel* (1985)
2 *Quarry's contract* (1987)

Simon Rack series
James, Laurence
1 *Earth lies sleeping* (1974)
2 *Starcross* (1974)
War on Aleph
3 *Backflash* (1975)
4 *Planet of the blind* (1975)
5 *New life for old* (1975)

Simon Rolfe series
Bonney, Joseph L
1 *Death by dynamite* (1940)
2 *Murder without clues* (1940)
No man's fund

Simon series
Dean, Gregory
see **Deputy Commissioner Benjamin Simon series**

Simon series
McLachlan, Edward
1 *Simon and the land of chalk drawings* (1969)
2 *Simon and the chalk drawing army* (1971)
3 *Simon and the moon rocket* (1972)
4 *Simon and the dinosaur* (1973)

Simon series
Pentecost, Hugh
see **Grant Simon series**

Simon series
Salisbury, Ray
1 *Close the door behind you* (1982)
2 *When the boys came out to play* (1984)
3 *Birds of the air* (1988)
4 *Sweet Thursday* (1990)

Simon series
Saville, Malcolm
1 *Three towers in Tuscany* (1963)
2 *Purple valley* (1964)
3 *Dark danger* (1965)
4 *White fire* (1966)

Simon series
Tibo, Gilles
1 *Simon and the snowflakes* (1988)
Original edition entitled *Simon et les flocons de neige*
2 *Simon and the wind* (1989)
Original edition entitled *Simon et le vent d'automne*
3 *Simon welcomes spring* (1990)
Original edition entitled *Simon fete le printemps*
4 *Simon in summer* (1991)
Original edition entitled *Simon et le soleil d'ete*
5 *Simon and the boxes* (1992)
6 *Simon in the moonlight* (1993)
Original edition entitled *Simon au clair de lune*
Simon finds a feather (1994)
Original edition entitled *Simon et la petite plume cassee*

Simon Shard series
McCutchan, Philip
see **Superintendent Simon Shard series**

Simon Sokki series
Frison-Roche, Roger
1 *Raid* (1962)
2 *Last migration* (1964)

Simon Spears series
Gielgud, Val
see **Inspector Simon Spears series**

Simon Templar series
Charteris, Leslie
see **Saint series**

Simon Young series
Trenhaile, John
1 *Mah-Jongg spies* (1986)
2 *Gates of Exquisite View* (1987)
3 *Scroll of Benevolence* (1988)

Simpey series
Roberts, Elisabeth
1 *Simpey and his grandmother* (1967)
2 *Simpey comes to stay* (1968)
Also published in one volume entitled *All about Simpey and his grandmother*, 1973

Simple folk series
Cosgrove, Stephen Edward
1 *Picnic* (1988)
2 *Kind and gentle ladies* (1988)
3 *Chores* (1988)
4 *Nosey birds* (1988)

Simple life series
West, Elizabeth
see **Hafod Garden series**

Simple machines series
Lampton, Christopher
1 *Bathtubs, slides, roller coaster rails* (1991)
Simple machines that are really inclined planes
2 *Marbles, roller skates, doorknobs* (1991)
Simple machines that are really wheels
3 *Seesaws, nutcrackers, brooms* (1991)
Simple machines that are really levers
4 *Simple machines that are really pulleys* (1991)

Simple series
Hughes, Langston
1 *Simple speaks his mind* (1950)
2 *Simple takes a wife* (1953)
3 *Simple stakes a claim* (1957)
4 *Simple's Uncle Sam* (1965)

Simple stories series
Marshall, Archibald
1 *Simple stories* (1927)
2 *Simple people* (1928)
One volume edition entitled *Simple stories from Punch*, 1930

Simpson family series
Spencer, Colin
1 *Anarchists in love* (1963)
Anarchy of love
2 *Tyranny of love* (1967)
3 *Lovers in war* (1969)
4 *Victims of love* (1978)

Simpson series
Ambler, Eric
see **Arthur Abdel Simpson series**

Simpson series
Laurie-Long, Ernest
1 *Seconds and thirds* (1936)
2 *Trials of the Phidias* (1944)

Simpson series
Malcolm, John
see **Tim Simpson series**

Sims and Wells series
Grierson, Francis Durham
see **Inspector Sims and Professor Wells series**

Sin and acquittal series
Mathers, Helen
1 *Story of a sin* (1882)
2 *Eyre's acquittal* (1884)

Sin and salvation series
Faulkner, William
1 *Sartoris* (1929)
2 *Sound and the fury* (1929)
3 *As I lay dying* (1930)
4 *Sanctuary* (1931)
5 *Light in August* (1933)
6 *Absalom, Absalom!* (1936)
7 *Hamlet* (1940)
8 *Requiem for a nun* (1951)
9 *Town* (1957)
10 *Mansion* (1959)

Sin bin series
Miles, Keith
1 *Iggy* (1988)
2 *Melanie* (1988)
3 *Tariq* (1989)
4 *Bev* (1989)

Sinbad Dysart series
Wren, Percival Christopher
1 *Action and passion* (1933)
2 *Sinbad the soldier* (1935)
3 *Fort in the jungle* (1936)

Sinbad trilogy
Gardner, Craig Shaw
see **Arabian Nights trilogy**

Sinbad trilogy
Platt, Kin
1 *Sinbad and me* (1966)
2 *Mystery of the witch who wouldn't* (1969)
3 *Ghost of Hellsfire Street* (1980)

Sinclair and Dolan series
Babson, Marian
see **Trixie Dolan and Evangeline Sinclair series**

Sinclair family series
Potter, Margaret Newman
1 *Touch-and-go year* (1968)
2 *Blow-and-grow year* (1970)

Sinclair series
Decker, Jake
see **Steve Sinclair series**

Sinclair series
Diver, Maud
1 *Lilimani* (1911)
Awakening
2 *Far to seek* (1921)
3 *Singer passes* (1934)
4 *Dream prevails* (1938)

Sinclair series
Fennelly, Tony
see **Matty Sinclair series**
Haynes, Betsy
see **Taffy Sinclair series**
Macarthur, David Wilson
see **Alec Sinclair series**
Mann, Edward Beverly
see **Whistler series**
Masterman, Walter Sidney
see **Sir Arthur Sinclair series**

Sinclair series
Westerman, Percy Francis
1 *Mystery of Stockmere School* (1924)
2 *Sinclair's luck* (1924)
A story of adventure in East Africa

Sinclair series
Wingate, John
see **Submariner Sinclair series**

Singapore series
Gilmour, Oswald Wellington
1 *Singapore to freedom* (1943)
2 *With freedom to Singapore* (1950)

Singer Batts series
Dewey, Thomas Blanchard
1 *Hue and cry* (1944)
Murder of Marion Mason
Room for murder
2 *As good as dead* (1946)
3 *Mourning after* (1950)
4 *Handle with fear* (1951)

Singer series
Grenville, Kate
see **Lilian Singer series**

Singermann family series
Brinig, Myron
1 *Singermann* (1929)
2 *This man is my brother* (1932)
Sons of Singermann

Single life series
Blunt, Wilfrid
Autobiography
1 *Married to a single life* (1983)
1901-1938
2 *Slow on the feather* (1986)
1938-1959

Singleton family series
Burress, John
1 *Little mule* (1952)
2 *Apple on a pear tree* (1953)

Singreale trilogy
Miller, Calvin
1 *Guardians of the Singreale* (1982)
2 *Star riders of Ren* (1983)
3 *War of the Moonrhymes* (1984)

Sinhala series
De Silva, Colin
1 *Winds of Sinhala* (1982)
2 *Founts of Sinhala* (1984)
3 *Fires of Sinhala* (1986)
4 *Last Sinhala lions* (1987)

Sinister Street series
Mackenzie, Compton
1 *Sinister Street* (1913)
1.1 *Youth's encounter* (1913)
1.2 *Sinister Street* (1913)
2 *Guy and Pauline* (1915)
Plasher's Mead
3 *Early adventures of Sylvia Scarlett* (1918)
Early life and adventures of Sylvia Scarlett
Sylvia Scarlett
3.1 *Sylvia Scarlett* (1918)
3.2 *Sylvia and Arthur* (1918)
4 *Sylvia and Michael* (1919)
Numbers 3 and 4 also published in one volume entitled *The adventures of Sylvia Scarlett*, 1950

Sinister Widow series
Armstrong, Raymond
see **Inspector Dick Mason series**

Sioux series
Hanson, Joseph Mills
see **Among the Sioux series**

Sioux series
Taylor, Janelle
1 *Savage ecstasy* (1981)
2 *Defiant ecstasy* (1982)
3 *Forbidden ecstasy* (1982)
4 *Brazen ecstasy* (1983)
5 *Tender ecstasy* (1983)
6 *Savage conquest* (1985)
7 *Stolen ecstasy* (1985)
8 *Bittersweet ecstasy* (1987)
9 *Forever ecstasy* (1991)

Sipstrassi tales series
Gemmell, David A
1 *Wolf in shadow* (1987)
Jerusalem man
2 *Ghost king* (1988)
3 *Last sword of power* (1988)
4 *Last guardian* (1989)

Sir Abercrombie Lewker series
Styles, Showell
1 *Traitor's Mountain* (1945)
2 *Kidnap Castle* (1947)
3 *Hammer Island* (1947)
Sequence continued under the pseudonym Glyn Carr
Carr, Glyn
4 *Death on Milestone Buttress* (1951)
5 *Murder on the Matterhorn* (1951)
6 *Youth hostel murders* (1952)
7 *Corpse in the crevasse* (1952)
8 *Death under Snowden* (1952)
9 *Corpse at Camp Two* (1954)
10 *Murder of an owl* (1956)
11 *Ice axe murders* (1958)
12 *Swing away, climber* (1959)
13 *Holiday with murder* (1960)
14 *Death finds a foothold* (1961)
15 *Lewker in Norway* (1963)
16 *Death of a weirdy* (1965)
17 *Lewker in Tirol* (1967)
18 *Fat Man's Agony* (1969)

Sir Arthur Sinclair series
Masterman, Walter Sidney
1 *Wrong letter* (1926)
2 *Curse of the Reckaviles* (1927)
Crime of the Reckaviles
3 *Two LO* (1928)
Blood on the floor
4 *Yellow mistletoe* (1930)

5 *Mystery of fifty-two* (1931)
6 *Flying beast* (1932)
7 *Nameless crime* (1932)
8 *Baddington horror* (1934)
9 *Rose of death* (1934)
10 *Death turns traitor* (1935)
11 *Avenger strikes* (1936)
12 *Wrong verdict* (1937)
13 *Hunted man* (1938)
14 *Secret of the Downs* (1938)
15 *Hooded monster* (1939)
16 *Curse of Cantire* (1939)
17 *Death coins* (1940)
18 *Back from the grave* (1940)
19 *Silver leopard* (1941)

Sir Brian Dinsmore Conway series
Stone, Simon
1 *Knight missing* (1945)
2 *Conway, K.C.* (1945)
3 *Bookmaker's body* (1947)
4 *Murder gone mad* (1951)

Sir Brian Fordinghame series
Horler, Sydney
1 *False-face* (1926)
2 *Murder mask* (1930)
3 *High stakes* (1932)
4 *Prince of Plunder* (1934)

Sir Charles Knightley series
Horler, Sydney
1 *Man who shook the earth* (1933)
Short stories
2 *Death at court lady* (1936)
Also one story featuring Sir Charles Knightley in *The man who shook earth*, 1933

Sir Clinton Driffield series
Connington, John Jervis
1 *Murder in the maze* (1927)
2 *Tragedy at Ravensthorpe* (1927)
3 *Mystery at Lynden Sands* (1928)
4 *Case with nine solutions* (1928)
5 *Nemesis at Raynham Parva* (1929)
Grim vengeance
6 *Boat-house riddle* (1931)
7 *Sweepstake murders* (1931)
8 *Castleford conundrum* (1932)
9 *Ha-ha case* (1934)
Brandon case
10 *In whose dim shadow* (1935)
Tau Cross mystery
11 *Minor operation* (1937)
12 *Truth comes limping* (1938)
13 *For murder will speak* (1938)
Murder will speak
14 *Twenty-one clues* (1941)
15 *No past is dead* (1942)
16 *Jack-in-the-box* (1944)
17 *Common sense is all you need* (1947)

Sir Dominic Flandry series
Anderson, Poul
1 *We claim these stars!* (1959)
2 *Earthman, go home* (1960)
3 *Mayday orbit* (1961)
Numbers 1-3 also published in one volume entitled *Flandry of Terra*, 1965
4 *Agent of the Terran Empire* (1965)
Includes *We claim these stars!*
5 *Ensign Flandry* (1966)
6 *Rebel worlds* (1969)
Commander Flandry
7 *Circus of hells* (1970)
8 *Knight of ghost and shadows* (1974)
Knight Flandry
9 *Stone in heaven* (1979)
10 *Game of empire* (1985)

Sir Edgar Ewart series
Walter, Alexia E
1 *Patriot* (1928)
2 *Betrayal* (1929)

Sir Edward Leithen series
Buchan, John
1 *Power house* (1916)
2 *John Macnab* (1925)
3 *Dancing floor* (1926)
4 *Gap in the curtain* (1932)
Short stories
5 *Runagates Club* (1928)
Short stories
6 *Sick Heart River* (1941)
Mountain meadow
Also one story featuring Leithen in *The moon endureth*, 1912

Sir Francis Drake series
Turner, Judy
1 *Queen's corsair* (1976)
2 *My master mariner* (1974)

Sir George Bull series
Kennedy, Milward
1 *Bull's eye* (1933)
2 *Corpse in cold storage* (1934)

Sir Gibbie series
Macdonald, George
1 *Sir Gibbie* (1879)
Baronet's song
Wee Sir Gibbie of the Highlands
The second and third titles are revised editions
2 *Donal Grant* (1884)
Shepherd's castle
The second title is a revised edition

Sir Giles Tumulty series
Williams, Charles Walter Stansby
1 *War in heaven* (1930)
2 *Many dimensions* (1931)

Sir Godfrey Tallboys series
Lofts, Norah
1 *Knight's Acre* (1975)
2 *Homecoming* (1975)
3 *Lonely furrow* (1976)

Sir Guyon series
Madden, M S
1 *Sir Guyon, the interloper* (1913)
2 *Sir Guyon in snowland* (1915)

Sir Harker Bellamy series
Horler, Sydney
1 *My lady dangerous* (1932)
2 *Tiger Standish* (1932)
3 *Tiger Standish comes back* (1934)
4 *Mystery of the seven cafes* (1935)
Based on a radio play
5 *Grim game* (1936)
6 *Destroyer* (1938)
Also includes The red-haired death
7 *Tiger Standish takes the field* (1939)
8 *Tiger Standish steps on it* (1940)
9 *Lady with the limp* (1944)
Also stories featuring Sir Harker Bellamy in *The screaming skull, and other stories*, 1930 and *The house in Greek Street*, 1935

Sir Harry Barnaby series
Neill, Robert
1 *Crown and mitre* (1970)
2 *Golden days* (1972)
3 *Lillibulero* (1975)

Sir Henry Marquis series
Post, Melville Davisson
1 *Sleuth of Saint James's Square* (1920)
2 *Bradmoor murder* (1929)
Garden in Asia

Sir Henry Merrivale series
Dickson, Carter
1 *Bowstring murders* (1933)
Originally published under the pseudonym Carr Dickson
2 *Plague Court murders* (1934)
3 *White Priory murders* (1934)
4 *Red widow murders* (1935)
5 *Unicorn murders* (1935)
6 *Magic-lantern murders* (1936)
Punch and judy murders
7 *Peacock feather murders* (1937)
Ten teacups
8 *Judas window* (1938)
Crossbow murder
9 *Death in five boxes* (1938)
10 *Reader is warned* (1939)
11 *Nine and death make ten* (1940)
Murder in the submarine zone
Murder in the Atlantic
12 *And so to murder* (1940)
13 *Seeing is believing* (1941)
Cross of murder
14 *Gilded man* (1942)
Death and the gilded man
15 *She died a lady* (1943)
16 *He wouldn't kill Patience* (1944)
17 *Curse of the bronze lamp* (1945)
Lord of the sorcerors
18 *My late wives* (1946)
19 *Skeleton in the clock* (1948)
20 *Graveyard to let* (1949)
21 *Night at the Mocking Widow* (1950)
22 *Behind the crimson blind* (1952)
23 *Cavalier's cup* (1953)
Short stories featuring Sir Henry Merrivale also in *The third bullet, and other stories*, by John Dickson Carr, 1954 and *The men who explained miracles*, by John Dickson Carr, 1963

Sir John Appleby series
Innes, Michael
1 *Death at the president's lodging* (1936)
Seven suspects
2 *Hamlet, revenge!* (1937)
3 *Lament for a maker* (1938)
4 *Stop press* (1939)
Spider strikes
5 *There came both mist and snow* (1940)
Comedy of terrors
6 *Secret vanguard* (1940)
7 *Appleby on Ararat* (1941)
8 *Daffodil affair* (1942)
9 *Weight of the evidence* (1943)
10 *Appleby's end* (1945)
11 *Night of errors* (1947)
12 *Operation Pax* (1951)
Paper thunderbolt
13 *Private view* (1952)
One-man show
Murder is an art
14 *Appleby talking* (1954)
Dead man's shoes
Short stories
15 *Appleby talks again* (1956)
Short stories
16 *Appleby plays chicken* (1957)
Death on a quiet day
17 *Long farewell* (1958)
18 *Hare sitting up* (1959)
19 *Silence observed* (1961)
20 *Connoisseur's case* (1962)
Crabtree affair
21 *Bloody wood* (1966)
22 *Appleby at Allington* (1968)
Death by water
23 *Family affair* (1969)
Picture of guilt
24 *Death at the chase* (1970)
25 *Awkward lie* (1971)
26 *Open house* (1972)
27 *Appleby's answer* (1973)
28 *Appleby's other story* (1974)
29 *Appleby file* (1975)
Short stories
30 *Gay phoenix* (1976)
31 *Ampersand papers* (1978)
32 *Sheiks and adders* (1982)
33 *Appleby and Honeybath* (1983)
34 *Carson's conspiracy* (1984)
35 *Appleby and the ospreys* (1987)

Sir John Hawkwood series
Cole, Hubert
1 *Hawkwood* (1967)
2 *Hawkwood in Paris* (1969)
3 *Hawkwood and the towers of Pisa* (1973)

Sir John Howden series
Mills, Woosnam
1 *Shadow crusade* (1941)
2 *French hazard* (1942)
3 *Blind reckoning* (1951)
4 *Tarnished gold* (1951)
5 *Dusty coinage* (1953)

Sir John Meredith series
Gerard, Francis
1 *Concrete castle* (1936)
Concrete castle murders
2 *Number one two three* (1936)
One two three murders
3 *Black emperor* (1936)
4 *Dictatorship of the dove* (1936)
5 *Red rope* (1937)
6 *Fatal Friday* (1937)
7 *Secret sceptre* (1937)
8 *Price of paradise* (1938)
9 *Golden guilt* (1938)
10 *Wotan's wedge* (1939)
11 *Emerald embassy* (1939)
12 *Mind of John Meredith* (1946)
13 *Sorcerer's shaft* (1947)
14 *Prisoner of the pyramid* (1948)
15 *Flight with fear* (1948)
16 *Transparent traitor* (1950)
17 *Promise of the phoenix* (1950)

Sir John Oldcastle series
Lindsay, Philip
1 *He rides in triumph* (1945)
2 *Whither shall I wander?* (1947)

Sir John Saumerez series
Dane, Clemence
1 *Enter Sir John* (1929)
2 *Printer's devil* (1930)
Author unknown
3 *Re-enter Sir John* (1932)

Sir Julian Morthoe series
Wilson, Philip Whitwell
1 *Bride's castle* (1944)
2 *Black tarn* (1945)
3 *Old mill* (1946)

Sir Leonard Wallace series
Wilson, Alexander
1 *Mystery of Tunnel 51* (1928)
2 *Murder Mansion* (1929)
3 *Wallace of the Secret Service* (1933)
Short stories
4 *Get Wallace!* (1934)
5 *His Excellency, Governor Wallace* (1936)
6 *Microbes of power* (1937)
7 *Wallace at bay* (1938)
8 *Wallace intervenes* (1939)
9 *Chronicles of the Secret Service* (1940)

Sir Lewis Eliot series
Snow, Charles Percy
see **Strangers and brothers series**

Sir Nicholas Harding and Antony Maitland series
Woods, Sara
1 *They love not poison* (1972)
2 *Bloody instructions* (1962)
3 *Malice domestic* (1962)
4 *Taste of fears* (1963)
Third encounter
5 *Error of the moon* (1963)
6 *Trusted like the fox* (1964)
7 *This little measure* (1964)
8 *Windy side of the law* (1965)
9 *Though I know she lies* (1965)
10 *Enter certain murderers* (1966)
11 *Let's choose executioners* (1966)
12 *Case is altered* (1967)
13 *And shame the devil* (1967)

14 *Knives have edges* (1968)
15 *Past praying for* (1968)
16 *Tarry and be hanged* (1969)
17 *Improbable fiction* (1970)
18 *Serpent's tooth* (1971)
19 *Knavish crows* (1971)
20 *Yet she must die* (1973)
21 *Enter the corpse* (1973)
22 *Done to death* (1974)
23 *Show of violence* (1975)
24 *My life is done* (1976)
25 *Law's delay* (1977)
26 *Thief or two* (1977)
27 *Exit murderer* (1978)
28 *This fatal writ* (1979)
29 *Proceed to judgement* (1979)
30 *They stay for death* (1980)
31 *Weep for her* (1980)
32 *Cry guilty* (1981)
33 *Dearest enemy* (1981)
34 *Enter a gentlewoman* (1982)
35 *Villains by necessity* (1982)
36 *Most grievous murder* (1982)
37 *Call back yesterday* (1983)
38 *Lie direct* (1983)
39 *Where should he die?* (1983)
40 *Bloody book of law* (1984)
41 *Murder's out of tune* (1984)
42 *Defy the devil* (1984)
43 *Obscure grave* (1985)
44 *Away with them to prison* (1985)
45 *Put out the light* (1985)
46 *Most deadly hate* (1986)
47 *Nor live so long* (1986)
48 *Naked villainy* (1987)

Sir Nicholas Mountry series
Hammand, Norman Bentley
1 *Rakehell Mountry* (1972)
2 *Rakehell's progress* (1973)

Sir Nigel Lacaita series
Mackenzie, William Andrew
1 *His Majesty's peacock* (1904)
2 *Drexel dream* (1904)
3 *Black butterfly* (1907)
4 *Bite of the leech* (1914)

Sir Nigel Loring series
Doyle, Arthur Conan
see **English bowmen series**

Sir Oliver Bubb series
Craig, George
1 *Sir Oliver Bubb and the Red Knight* (1978)
2 *Sir Oliver Bubb and the wolf* (1979)

Sir Oswald Mosley series
Mosley, Nicholas
1 *Rules of the game* (1982)
Sir Oswald and Lady Cynthia Mosley, 1896-1933
2 *Beyond the pale* (1983)
Sir Oswald Mosley and family, 1933-1980; one volume edition 1991

Sir Percy Blakeney series
Orczy, Emmuska
see **Scarlet Pimpernel series**

Sir Richard Cherrington series
Daniel, Glyn
1 *Cambridge murders* (1945)
Originally published under the pseudonym Dilwyn Rees
2 *Welcome death* (1954)

Sir Richard Herrivell series
Bentley, John
1 *Berg case* (1934)
Eyes of death
2 *Griffith case* (1935)
3 *L'Estrange case* (1935)
4 *Opperman case* (1936)
5 *Fairbairn case* (1936)
6 *Landor case* (1937)
7 *Whitney case* (1937)
8 *Radcliffe case* (1938)
9 *Hartland case* (1939)

Sir Robert Peel series
Gash, Norman
1 *Mister Secretary Peel* (1961)
The life of Sir Robert Peel to 1830
2 *Sir Robert Peel* (1972)
The life of Sir Robert Peel after 1830

Sir Robert Walpole series
Plumb, John Harold
1 *Making of a statesman* (1956)
2 *King's minister* (1961)

Sir Robert Waring series
Ebel, Suzanne
1 *Name in lights* (1968)
2 *Most suspicious star* (1969)
Sir's daughter
3 *To seek a star* (1973)

Sir series
Braithwaite, Edward Ricardo
Memoirs of a Negro teacher in a London East End school
1 *To Sir, with love* (1959)
2 *Paid servant* (1962)

Sir Toady series
Crockett, Samuel Rutherford
1 *Surprising adventures of Sir Toady Lion* (1897)
2 *Sir Toady Crusoe* (1905)

Sir Tobias Glendower and Penelope Spring series
Arnold, Margot
see **Penelope Spring and Sir Tobias Glendower series**

Sir William Burrill series
Macleod, Adam Gordon
1 *Marloe Mansions murder* (1928)
2 *Case of Matthew Crake* (1932)
3 *Death stalked the fells* (1937)

Siri Ram series
Candler, Edmund
1 *Siri Ram, revolutionist* (1912)
Originally published anonymously; a transcript from life, 1907-1910
2 *Abdication* (1922)

Siscoe and Block series
Haiblum, Isidore
1 *Identity plunderers* (1984)
2 *Hand of Ganz* (1985)

Sister and brother series
Lawrence, Josephine
see **Brother and sister series**

Sister Beatrice series
Anderson, Catherine Corley
1 *Sister Beatrice goes to bat* (1958)
2 *Sister Beatrice goes west* (1961)
3 *Sister Beatrice and the mission mystery* (1963)

Sister Joan series
Black, Veronica
1 *Vow of silence* (1990)
2 *Vow of chastity* (1991)
3 *Vow of sanctity* (1993)
4 *Vow of obedience* (1993)
5 *Vow of penance* (1994)

Sister Madge Stillworthy series
Marshall, May
1 *Mulberry leaf* (1954)
2 *Youth storms in* (1956)

Sister Mary Helen series
O'Marie, Carol Anne
1 *Novena for murder* (1984)
2 *Advent of dying* (1986)
3 *Missing Madonna* (1989)
4 *Murder in ordinary time* (1991)
5 *Murder makes a pilgrimage* (1993)

Sister Mary Teresa series
Quill, Monica
1 *Not a blessed thing!* (1981)
2 *Let us prey* (1982)
3 *And then there was nun* (1984)
4 *Nun of the above* (1985)
5 *Sine qua nun* (1986)
6 *Veil of ignorance* (1988)

Sister series
Du Maurier, Angela
Autobiography
1 *It's only the sister* (1951)
2 *Old maids remember* (1966)

Sister Svenska series
Ghose, Sudhindra Nath
1 *And gazelles leaping* (1949)
2 *Cradle of the clouds* (1951)

Sister Ursula series
Holmes, H H
This sequence is also published under the pseudonym Anthony Boucher
1 *Nine times nine* (1940)
2 *Rockets to the morgue* (1942)

Sisterhood trilogy
Rheingold, Howard
1 *Mama Liz drinks deep* (1973)
2 *Mama Liz tastes flesh* (1973)
3 *Secret sisterhood* (1973)

Sisters impossible series
Landis, James David
1 *Sisters impossible* (1979)
2 *Love's detective* (1984)

Sisters of the Lone Star trilogy
Johnston, Joan
1 *Frontier woman* (1988)
2 *Comanche woman* (1989)
3 *Texas woman* (1989)

Sisters series
Adler, Carole Schwerdtfeger
1 *Split sisters* (1986)
2 *One sister too many* (1989)

Sisters series
Cole, Jennifer
see **Cindy and Nicole series**

Sisters series
Kaye, Marilyn
1 *Phoebe* (1987)
2 *Daphne* (1987)
3 *Cassie* (1987)
4 *Lydia* (1987)
5 *Friend like Phoebe* (1989)

Six cousins series
Blyton, Enid
1 *Six cousins at Mistletoe Farm* (1948)
2 *Six cousins again* (1950)

Six girls series
Taggart, Marion Ames
1 *Six girls and Bob* (1906)
2 *Six girls and the teatoom* (1907)
3 *Six girls growing older* (1908)
4 *Six girls and the seventh one* (1909)
5 *Betty Gaston, the seventh girl* (1910)
6 *Six girls and Betty* (1911)
7 *Six girls grown up* (1912)
8 *Her daughter Jean* (1913)

Six Gun Gauntlet series
Leyland, Eric
1 *Six Gun Gauntlet strikes the trail* (1957)
2 *Six Gun Gauntlet rides again* (1957)
3 *Six Gun Gauntlet gets his man* (1957)
4 *Six Gun Gauntlet hits back* (1959)
5 *Six Gun Gauntlet wins through* (1960)

Six-Gun Samurai series
Lee, Patrick
1 *Six-Gun Samurai* (1981)
2 *Bushido vengeance* (1981)
3 *Gundown at Golden Gate* (1981)
4 *Kamikaze justice* (1981)
5 *Devil's bowman* (1981)
6 *Bushido lawman* (1982)
7 *Prairie Caesar* (1982)
8 *Apache messiah* (1983)

Six-gun series
Langley, John
see **Walt Warren series**

Six kingdoms series
Fergusson, Bruce
1 *Shadow of his wings* (1987)
2 *Mace of souls* (1989)

Six little bunkers series
Hope, Laura Lee
House pseudonym
1 *Six little bunkers at Grandma Bell's* (1918)
2 *Six little bunkers at Aunt Jo's* (1918)
3 *Six little bunkers at Cousin Tom's* (1918)
4 *Six little bunkers at Grandpa Ford's* (1918)
5 *Six little bunkers at Uncle Fred's* (1918)
6 *Six little bunkers at Captain Ben's* (1920)
7 *Six little bunkers at Cowboy Jack's* (1921)
8 *Six little bunkers at Mammy June's* (1922)
9 *Six little bunkers at Farmer Joel's* (1923)
10 *Six little bunkers at Miller Ned's* (1924)
11 *Six little bunkers at Indian John's* (1925)
12 *Six little bunkers at Happy Jim's* (1928)
13 *Six little bunkers at Skipper Bob's* (1929)
14 *Six little bunkers at Lighthouse Nell's* (1930)
Omnibus volume: *Six little bunkers*, 1933

Six little possums series
McGill, Marci
1 *Six little possums* (1982)
2 *Six little possums at home* (1982)
3 *Pepper's good and bad day* (1982)
4 *Six little possums and the baby-sitter* (1982)

Six Million Dollar Man series
This sequence has four authors; based on a television series
Caidin, Martin
1 *Mendelov conspiracy* (1969)
Encounter three
2 *Cyborg* (1972)
3 *Operation Nuke* (1973)
Cyborg II
4 *High crystal* (1974)
5 *Cyborg IV* (1975)
Jahn, Mike
6 *Wine, women and war* (1975)
Richards, Evan
7 *Solid gold kidnapping* (1975)
Barbree, Jay
8 *Pilot error* (1975)
Jahn, Mike
9 *Rescue of Athena One* (1975)
10 *Secret of Bigfoot Pass* (1976)
11 *International incidents* (1977)

Six river motor-boat boys series
Gordon, Harry
see **River motor-boat boys series**

Six series
Cuthbert, Derrick
1 *Six and a secret* (1948)
2 *Six in a castle* (1949)

Six series
Wynne, Brian
see **Marshal Jeremy Six series**

Six sisters series
Chesney, Marion
1 *Minerva* (1982)
2 *Taming of Annabelle* (1983)
3 *Deidre and desire* (1983)
4 *Daphne* (1984)
5 *Diana the huntress* (1985)
6 *Frederica in fashion* (1985)

Six Three Three Squadron series
Smith, Frederick Escreet
1 *Six Three Three Squadron* (1956)
2 *Operation Rhine Maiden* (1975)
3 *Operation Crucible* (1977)
4 *Operation Valkyrie* (1978)
5 *Operation Cobra* (1981)
6 *Operation Titan* (1982)

Six worlds series
Baldry, Cherith
see **Stories of six worlds series**

Sixth perception series
Morgan, Dan
1 *New minds* (1967)
2 *Several minds* (1969)
3 *Mind trap* (1970)
4 *Country of the mind* (1975)

Size spies series
Needle, Jan
1 *Size spies* (1978)
2 *Another fine mess* (1981)

Skane series
Marfield, Dwight
see **Inspector Skane series**

Skarratt series
Fletcher, Joseph Smith
see **Inspector Skarratt series**

Skate Patrol series
Bunting, Eve
1 *Skate Patrol* (1980)
2 *Skate Patrol rides again* (1981)
3 *Skate Patrol and the mystery writer* (1982)

Skeen trilogy
Clayton, Jo
1 *Skeen's leap* (1986)
2 *Skeen's return* (1987)
3 *Skeen's search* (1987)

Skeeve series
Asprin, Robert Lynn
1 *Another fine myth* (1978)
2 *Myth conceptions* (1980)
3 *Myth directions* (1982)
4 *Hit or myth* (1983)
Numbers 1-4 also published in one volume entitled *Myth adventures*, 1984
5 *Myth-ing persons* (1984)
6 *Little myth maker* (1985)
7 *M.Y.T.H. Inc. link* (1986)
Numbers 5-7 also published in one volume entitled *Myth alliances*, 1987
8 *Myth-nomers and im-pervections* (1987)
9 *M.Y.T.H. Inc. in action* (1990)

Skelligs series
Ingelow, Jean
1 *Off the Skelligs* (1872)
2 *Fated to be free* (1875)

Skelton Hall series
Brent-Dyer, Elinor Mary
1 *School at Skelton Hall* (1962)
2 *Trouble at Skelton Hall* (1963)

Skelton Keyne series
Wood, Clement
1 *Corpse in the guest room* (1945)
2 *Double jeopardy* (1947)

Skene series
Mottram, Ralph Hale
see **Geoffrey Skene series**

Sketching outdoors series
Arnosky, Jim
1 *Sketching ourdoors in spring* (1987)
2 *Sketching ourdoors in summer* (1988)
3 *Sketching ourdoors in autumn* (1988)
4 *Sketching ourdoors in winter* (1988)

Skiffy series
Mayne, William
1 *Skiffy* (1972)
2 *Skiffy and the twin planets* (1982)

Skinner series
Dodge, Henry Irving
1 *Skinner's dress suit* (1916)
2 *Skinner's baby* (1917)
3 *Skinner's big idea* (1918)
4 *Skinner makes it fashionable* (1920)

Skinner series
Mulford, Clarence Edward
see **Matt Skinner series**
Tolan, Stephanie Stein
see **Great Skinner series**

Skinny series
Leyland, Eric
1 *Well done, Skinny* (1955)
2 *Skinny on the warpath* (1956)
3 *Skinny's Christmas Eve* (1957)

Skinny series
Smith, Helen Zenna
1 *Not so quiet* (1931)
2 *Luxury ladies* (1933)

Skip Langdon series
Smith, Julie
1 *New Orleans mourning* (1990)
2 *Axeman's jazz* (1991)
3 *Jazz funeral* (1993)
4 *New Orleans beat* (1994)

Skipjack series
Lang, Simon
1 *All the gods of Eiseron* (1973)
2 *Elluvon gift* (1975)

Skipper Gould series
Kalish, Robert
1 *Bloodrun* (1984)
2 *Bloodtide* (1985)
3 *Bloodmoon* (1985)
4 *Buddha's retreat* (1985)

Skipper series
Berrisford, Judith Mary
1 *Skipper, the dog from the sea* (1955)
2 *Skipper and the Headland four* (1957)
Skipper to the rescue
3 *Skipper's exciting summer* (1959)
4 *Skipper and the runaway boy* (1960)
5 *Skipper and son* (1961)

Skipper series
Cox, John Roberts
1 *Dangerous waters* (1954)
2 *Calamity Camp* (1956)

Skipper series
Dixon, Paige
1 *May I cross your golden river* (1975)
2 *Skipper* (1979)

Skippy Dare series
Lloyd, Hugh
1 *Among the river pirates* (1934)
2 *Held for ransom* (1934)
3 *Prisoner's in Devil's Bog* (1934)

Skippy series
Odgers, Sally Farrell
see **Adventures of Skippy series**

Skipton trilogy
Johnson, Pamela Hansford
see **Daniel Skipton trilogy**

Skookum Chuck series
White, Stewart Edward
1 *Skookum Chuck* (1925)
2 *Secret harbour* (1926)

Skrene series
Richardson, Frank
see **Vincent Skrene series**

Skul and Debbie Miles series
Rosenberger, Joseph
see **C.O.B.R.A. series**

Skull Mystery Club series
Locke, Clinton W
see **Perry Pierce series**

Skull series
Craig, Randolph
see **Octopus series**

Skull-Face series
Howard, Robert Ervin
1 *Skull-Face, and others* (1946)
Skull-Face omnibus
1.1 *Skull-Face, and others* (1946)
1.2 *Valley of the worms, and others* (1946)
2 *Return of Skull-Face* (1977)
Co-author: Richard Allen Lupoff

Sky all over series
Smith, David
Autobiography
1 *No rain in these clouds* (1943)
2 *Same sky all over* (1948)

Sky buddies series
Craine, Edith Janice
see **Airplane Boys series**

Sky Flyers series
Martin, Eugene
see **Randy Starr series**

Sky lords series
Brosnan, John
1 *Sky lords* (1988)
2 *War of the sky lords* (1989)
3 *Fall of the sky lords* (1991)

Sky Pilot series
Connor, Ralph
1 *Sky Pilot* (1899)
A tale of the foothills
2 *Pilot at Swan Creek* (1905)
Short stories
3 *Sky Pilot of No Man's Land* (1919)

Skye and Walters series
Hart, Bruce
see **Jessie Walters and Michael Skye series**

Skye Fargo series
Sharpe, Jon
see **Trailsman series**

Skye O'Malley series
Small, Beatrice
1 *Skye O'Malley* (1980)
2 *All the sweet tomorrows* (1984)
3 *This heart of mine* (1985)
4 *Love for all time* (1986)
5 *Lost love found* (1989)

Skye series
Wheeler, Richard Seabrook
see **Skye's West series**

Skye's West series
Wheeler, Richard Seabrook
1 *Sun River* (1989)
2 *Bannack* (1989)
3 *Far tribes* (1990)
4 *Yellowstone* (1990)
5 *Bitterroot* (1991)
6 *Sundance* (1992)
7 *Badlands* (1992)

Skyfall series
Tant, David
see **Legends of Skyfall series**

Skylark series
Smith, Edward Elmer
1 *Skylark of space* (1946)
Originally serialized 1928; revised edition 1958
2 *Skylark Three* (1948)
Originally serialized 1930
3 *Skylark of Valeron* (1949)
Originally serialized 1934-35
4 *Skylark DuQuesne* (1966)

Skyrider series
Bower, Bertha Muzzy
1 *Skyrider* (1918)
2 *Thunder bird* (1919)

Skyrider series
Michaels, Melisa C
1 *Skirmish* (1985)
2 *First battle* (1985)
3 *Last war* (1986)
4 *Pirate prince* (1987)
5 *Floater factor* (1988)

Skyrocket Steele series
Goulart, Ron
1 *Skyrocket Steele* (1980)
2 *Skyrocket Steele conquers the universe, and other media tales* (1990)

Skywalker series
Lucas, George
see **Luke Skywalker series**

Skyway trilogy
De Chancie, John
1 *Starrigger* (1983)
2 *Red limit freeway* (1984)
3 *Paradox Alley* (1986)

Slade McGinty series
Pendower, Jacques
1 *Perfect wife* (1962)
2 *Operation Carlo* (1963)
3 *Sinister talent* (1964)
4 *Master spy* (1964)
5 *Traitor's island* (1967)

Slade series
Bagley, Desmond
1 *Running blind* (1970)
2 *Freedom trap* (1971)
Mackintosh man
The second title is a revised edition

Slade series
Blumenthal, John
see **Mac Slade series**
Deeping, Warwick
see **James Slade series**
Drake, David
see **Hammer's Slammers series**
Essex, Richard
see **John Slade series**
Fitzhugh, Percy Keese
see **Tom Slade series**
Gribble, Leonard Reginald
see **Superintendent Anthony Slade series**
Lester, Frank
see **Geoffrey Slade series**

Slade series

Pennington, Link
see **Frank Slade series**
Scott, Bradford
see **Walt Slade**
Smith, Susan
see **Samantha Slade series**
Tuttle, Gene
see **Silent Slade series**
Woodthorpe, Ralph Carter
see **Nicholas Slade series**

Slagle series
Tucker, Augusta
see **Miss Susie Slagle series**

Slaker series
Redmond, Anton Edward
see **Bill Slaker series**

Slane series
Maddock, Stephen
see **Inspector Slane series**

Slapdash series
Barkin, Carol
1 *Slapdash sewing* (1975)
2 *Slapdash cooking* (1976)
3 *Slapdash alterations* (1977)
How to recycle your wardrobe
4 *Slapdash decorating* (1977)

Slappey series
Cohen, Octavus Roy
see **Florian Slappey series**

Slate Creed series
Harte, Bryce
1 *Creed* (1991)
2 *Wanted* (1991)
3 *Powder keg* (1991)
4 *Creed's war* (1991)
5 *Missouri guns* (1992)
6 *Texan's honor* (1992)
7 *Betrayed* (1992)
8 *Colorado prey* (1992)
9 *Cheyenne justice* (1993)
10 *Arkansas raiders* (1993)

Slate series
Crews, Lary
see **Veronica Slate series**

Slater Fijiian series
Foreman, Russell
see **Oliver Slater Fijiian series**

Slater series
Colter, Dale
see **Regulator series**

Slattery series
Lawrence, Steven C
see **Tom Slattery series**
Lee, John Alexander
see **Shiner Slattery series**

Slaughter and Son series
Majors, E B
1 *Slaughter and Son* (1985)
2 *Nightmare trail* (1985)
3 *Hair trigger kill* (1985)
4 *Death in Durango* (1986)

Slaughter series
This sequence has two authors; based on screenplays
Clement, Henry
1 *Slaughter* (1972)
Kane, Abel
2 *Slaughter's big rip-off* (1973)

Slave series
Fitzgerald, Julia
1 *Royal slave* (1978)
2 *Slave lady* (1980)

Slavery series
Ballard, Martin
see **Benjie and Simon series**

Slaves of Allah series
Burgin, George Brown
1 *Slaves of Allah* (1909)
2 *Diana of dreams* (1910)

Slaves without masters trilogy
Gilchrist, Rupert
1 *House at three o'clock* (1982)
2 *Girl called Friday Night* (1983)
3 *Wrong side of town* (1985)

Slavine series
Sava, George
see **Peter Slavine series**

Slayton series
Sanders, Buck
see **Ben Slayton series**

Sleep out series
Carrick, Carol
1 *Sleep out* (1974)
2 *Lost in the storm* (1976)

Sleepers in moon-crowned valleys series
Purdy, James
1 *Jeremy's version* (1970)
2 *House of the solitary maggot* (1974)
Originally announced as a trilogy

Sleeping Beauty series
Roquelaure, A N
1 *Claiming of Sleeping Beauty* (1983)
An erotic novel of tenderness and cruelty for the enjoyment of men and women
2 *Beauty's punishment* (1984)
3 *Beauty's release* (1985)
The continued erotic adventures of Sleeping Beauty

Sleepover friends series
Saunders, Susan
1 *Patti's luck* (1987)
2 *Starring Stephanie* (1987)
3 *Kate's surprise* (1987)
4 *Patti's new look* (1988)
5 *Lauren's big mixup* (1988)
6 *Kate's campout* (1988)
7 *Stephanie strikes back* (1988)
8 *Lauren's treasure* (1988)
9 *Patti's last sleepover* (1988)
10 *Lauren's sleepover exchange* (1989)
11 *Stephanie's family secret* (1989)
12 *Kate's sleepover disaster* (1989)
13 *Patti's secret wish* (1989)
14 *Sleepover friends* (1989)
15 *Stephanie's big story* (1989)
16 *Kate's crush* (1989)
17 *Patti* (1989)
18 *Stephanie* (1989)
19 *Great Kate* (1989)
20 *Lauren I* (1990)
21 *Starstruck* (1990)
22 *Trouble with Patti* (1990)
23 *Kate's surprise visitor* (1990)
24 *Lauren's new friend* (1990)
25 *Stephanie and the wedding* (1990)
26 *New Kate* (1990)
27 *Where's Patti?* (1990)
28 *Lauren's new address* (1990)
29 *Kate the boss* (1990)
30 *Big sister Stephanie* (1990)
31 *Lauren's afterschool job* (1990)
32 *Valentine for Patti* (1991)
33 *Lauren's double disaster* (1991)
34 *Kate the winner* (1991)
35 *New Stephanie* (1991)
36 *Presenting Patti* (1991)
37 *Lauren saves the day* (1991)
38 *Patti's city adventure* (1991)

Sleepwalkers trilogy
Broch, Hermann
1 *Romantic* (1931)
Original edition entitled *Pasenow oder die Romantik, 1888,* 1931
2 *Anarchist* (1931)
Original edition entitled *Esch oder die Anarchie, 1903,* 1931
3 *Realist* (1932)
Original edition entitled *Huguenau oder die Sachlichkeit, 1918,* 1932
One volume edition entitled *The sleepwalkers,* 1932

Sleepy series
Morris, Ann
1 *Cuddle up* (1986)
2 *Kiss time* (1986)
3 *Night counting* (1986)
4 *Sleepy, sleepy* (1986)

Sleepy Stevens and Hashknife Hartley series
Tuttle, Wilbur Coleman
see **Hashknife Hartley and Sleepy Stevens series**

Sleepy time tales series
Hodgetts, Sheila
1 *Sleepy time tales of Apricot Farm* (1951)
2 *Sleepy time tales of Cherub Village* (1951)
Sleepy time tales of the little cherubs
3 *Sleepy time tales of Playtown* (1951)
Sleepy time tales of Playtime Village
4 *Sleepy time tales of Puddletown* (1951)
Omnibus volumes: *The big sleepy time book,* 1957, *The new big sleepy time annual,* 1958, *The new big sleepy time book,* 1959

Sleuth series
Avallone, Michael
see **Satan Sleuth series**

Sleyter series
Murray, Earl
see **Dan Sleyter series**

Slick series
Haliburton, Thomas Chandler
see **Sam Slick series**

Slievelea series
Lyons, Genevieve
1 *Slievelea* (1986)
2 *Green years* (1987)

Slim Callaghan series
Cheyney, Peter
1 *Urgent hangman* (1938)
2 *Dangerous curves* (1939)
Callaghan
3 *You can't keep the change* (1940)
4 *It couldn't matter less* (1941)
Set-up for murder
5 *Mister Caution, Mister Callaghan* (1941)
Short stories
6 *Never a dull moment* (1942)
7 *Sorry you've been troubled* (1942)
Farewell to the admiral
8 *Unscrupulous Mister Callaghan* (1943)
9 *They never say when* (1944)
10 *Uneasy terms* (1946)
11 *Calling Mister Callaghan* (1953)
Also some stories featuring Callaghan in *G Man at the Yard,* 1953

Slim Goodbody series
Burstein, John
1 *Mister Slim Goodbody presents the inside story* (1977)
2 *Your body health and feelings* (1978)
3 *What can go wrong and how to be strong* (1978)
4 *Slim Goodbody's health days diary* (1983)
Activity book

Slim Memed series
Kemal, Yashar
1 *Memed, my hawk* (1958)
Original edition entitled *Ince Memed,* part 1
2 *They burn the thistles* (1969)
Original edition entitled *Ince Memed,* part 2

Slim Tyler series
Stone, Richard H
1 *Sky riders of the Atlantic* (1930)
Alternative title: Slim Tyler's first trip in the clouds
2 *Lost over Greenland* (1930)
Alternative title: Slim Tyler's search for Dave Boyd
3 *Air cargo of gold* (1930)
Alternative title: Slim Tyler, special bank messenger
4 *Adrift over Hudson Bay* (1931)
Alternative title: Slim Tyler in the land of ice; Numbers 1-4 also published in one volume entitled *Aviation stories for boys,* 1936
5 *Airplane mystery* (1931)
Alternative title: Slim Tyler on the trail
6 *Secret sky express* (1932)
Alternative title: Slim Tyler saving a fortune

Slimmens series
Victor, Metta Victoria
see **Miss Slimmens series**

Slimtails series
Chell, Mary
1 *Slimtails* (1937)
2 *More Slimtails* (1937)
3 *Merry Slimtails* (1938)
4 *Slimtails' friends* (1940)
5 *Slimtails' triplets* (1943)
6 *Slimtails' new house* (1949)
7 *Mrs Slimtails goes shopping* (1949)
8 *Edwin's adventures* (1949)
9 *Slimtails' picnic* (1949)
10 *Slimtails at home* (1956)

Slippery Jim Di Griz series
Harrison, Harry
see **Jim Di Griz series**

Slither trilogy
Halkin, John
1 *Slither* (1980)
2 *Slime* (1984)
3 *Squelch* (1985)

Sloan series
Aird, Catherine
see **Inspector C D Sloan series**

Sloane series
Lee, Steve
see **Kung Fu western series**

Slocum giant series
Logan, Jake
House pseudonym
1 *Slocum's bust out* (1990)
2 *Slocum's war* (1992)

Slocum series
Logan, Jake
see **John Slocum series**

Slone series
Stone, Elizabet M
see **Maggie Slone series**

Slow boats series
Young, Gavin
1 *Slow boats to China* (1981)
Halfway around the world
An improbable journey
2 *Slow boats home* (1986)

Slow motion series
Knox, Ronald Arbuthnott
Sermons
1 *Mass in slow motion* (1948)
2 *Creed in slow motion* (1949)
3 *Gospel in slow motion* (1950)

Slow Street School series
Waddell, Martin
see **Harriet the Troublemaker series**

Slug series
Rudowsky, Colby
1 *Evy-Ivy-Over* (1978)
2 *Julie's daughter* (1985)
Companion volume: *H, my name is Henley*, 1982

Slugs series
Hutson, Shaun
1 *Slugs* (1982)
2 *Breeding ground* (1985)

Smaile series
Adye, John
see **Oliver Smaile series**

Small boat series
Bailey, Maurice
1 *One hundred and seventeen days adrift* (1974)
Staying alive!
Saga of a couple who survived at sea longer than anyone before them
2 *Second chance* (1977)
Voyage to Patagonia

Small boat series
Pilkington, Roger
1 *Small boat through Belgium* (1957)
2 *Small boat through Holland* (1958)
3 *Small boat to the Skagerrak* (1960)
4 *Small boat through Sweden* (1961)
5 *Small boat to Alsace* (1961)
6 *Small boat to Bavaria* (1962)
7 *Small boat through Germany* (1963)
8 *Small boat through France* (1964)
9 *Small boat in southern France* (1965)
10 *Small boat on the Thames* (1966)
11 *Small boat on the Meuse* (1967)
12 *Small boa to Luxembourg* (1967)
13 *Small boat on the Moselle* (1968)
14 *Small boat to Elsinore* (1969)
15 *Small boat to northern Germany* (1970)
16 *Small boat on the Lower Rhine* (1971)
17 *Small boat on the Upper Rhine* (1971)
Companion volume: *Waterways in Europe, guide to inland cruising*, 1972, revised edition 1974

Small family series
Lenski, Lois
1 *Little family* (1932)
2 *Little auto* (1934)
Baby car
3 *Little sail boat* (1937)
Little sailing boat
4 *Little airplane* (1938)
Little aeroplane
Numbers 2, 3, 4 also published in one volume entitled *More Mister Small*, 1979
5 *Little train* (1940)
6 *Little farm* (1942)
7 *Little fire engine* (1946)
8 *Cowboy Small* (1949)
9 *Papa Small* (1951)
10 *Policeman Small* (1962)
Numbers 6, 8, 10 also published in one volume entitled *The big book of Mister Small*, 1979
Companion volume: *Songs of Mister Small*, 1954

Small poems series
Worth, Valerie
Illustrated by Natalie Babbitt
1 *Small poems* (1972)
2 *More small poems* (1976)
3 *Still more small poems* (1978)
4 *Small poems again* (1985)
5 *Other small poems again* (1986)
Omnibus volume: *All the small poems*, 1987

Small Potatoes series
Ziefert, Harriet
Illustrated by Richard Brown
1 *Small Potatoes Club* (1984)
2 *Small Potatoes and the magic show* (1984)
3 *Small Potatoes and the sleep-over* (1985)
4 *Small Potatoes and the birthday party* (1986)
Co-author: Jon Ziefert

Small series
Kemelman, Harry
see **Rabbi David Small series**

Small souls quartet
Couperus, Louis
see **Book of small souls quartet**

Small talk series
Mitchison, Naomi
Autobiography
1 *Small talk* (1973)
Memories of an Edwardian childhood
2 *All change her* (1975)
Girlhood and marriage
3 *You may well ask* (1979)
A memoir, 1920-1940
4 *Among you, taking notes* (1985)
Wartime diary
Companion volumes: *Return to Fairy Hill*, 1966, *Mucking around five continents over fifty years*, 1981, *Naomi Mitchison*, 1986

Small world series
Berg, Leila
1 *Dogs* (1983)
2 *Blood and plasters* (1983)
3 *Worms* (1983)
4 *Bees* (1983)
5 *Rainbows* (1985)
6 *Vacuum cleaners* (1985)
7 *Cars* (1985)
8 *Ducks* (1985)

Smallest pop-up book ever series
Scarry, Richard
1 *Bananas gorilla* (1992)
2 *Mister Fix-It* (1992)
3 *Mister Fumble* (1992)

Smarles series
Urquhart, Macgregor
see **Chief Inspector Joshua Smarles series**

Smart series
Johnston, William
see **Maxwell Smart series**

Smartypants series
Cole, Babette
see **Princess Smartypants series**

Smashers series
Gree, Alain
Illustrated by Luis Camps
1 *Smashers at school* (1973)
At school
Original edition entitled *Les farfeluches a l'ecole*; the second title is a bilingual English-Spanish edition
2 *Smashers go to market* (1973)
Original edition entitled *Les farfeluches au marche*
3 *Smashers by the sea* (1973)
Original edition entitled *Les farfeluches au bord de la mer*
4 *Smashers in the country* (1973)
In the country
Original edition entitled *Les farfeluches a la campagne*; the second title is a bilingual English-Spanish edition
5 *At home* (1973)
Original edition entitled *Les farfeluches a la maison*; bilingual English-Spanish edition
6 *Animal fun* (1979)
Original edition entitled *Les farfeluches aiment les animaux*; bilingual English-Spanish edition
Fifteen other titles in this sequence not translated into English

Smiler Bunn series
Atkey, Bertram
1 *Amazing Mister Bunn* (1911)
2 *Smiler Bunn brigade* (1916)
3 *Smiler Bunn, gentleman crook* (1920)
Smiler Bunn, gentleman adventurer
4 *Smiler Bunn, manhunter* (1920)
5 *Man with the yellow eyes* (1923)
6 *Smiler Bunn, byewayman* (1925)
7 *Mystery of the glass bullet* (1931)
8 *Arsenic and gold* (1939)
9 *House of Clystevill* (1940)
Omnibus volume: *Smiler Bunn, crook*, 1929

Smiler Miles trilogy
Canning, Victor
1 *Runaways* (1972)
2 *Flight of the grey goose* (1973)
3 *Painted tent* (1974)

Smiley Adams series
Burrough, Reath J
1 *Smiley Adams* (1931)
2 *Mystery house* (1933)

Smiley series
Le Carre, John
see **George Smiley series**

Smiley series
Raymond, Moore
1 *Smiley* (1945)
2 *Smiley gets a gun* (1947)
3 *Smiley roams the road* (1959)

Smiling pass series
Robinson, Eliot Harlow
1 *Smiles* (1920)
A rose for the Cumberlands
2 *Smiling pass* (1921)

Smiling Pool series
Burgess, Thornton Waldo
1 *Billy Mink* (1924)
Adventures of Billy Mink
2 *Little Joe Otter* (1925)
Adventures of Little Joe Otter
3 *Jerry Muskrat at home* (1926)
Adventures of Jerry Muskrat at home
4 *Longlegs the heron* (1927)
Adventures of Longlegs the heron

Smiricky series
Skvorecky, Josef
see **Danny Smiricky series**

Smith and Bevan series
Forster, Peter
see **Alex Smith and Tony Bevan series**

Smith and Garratt series
Wentworth, Patricia
see **Benbow Smith and Frank Garratt series**

Smith and Jones series
Crossen, Kendell Foster
see **Jason Jones and Necessary Smith series**

Smith and Rogers series
Ross, Zola Helen
see **Beau Smith and Pogy Rogers series**

Smith family series
Avery, Gillian
1 *Warden's niece* (1957)
Maria escapes
2 *Trespassers at Charlcote* (1958)
3 *James without Thomas* (1959)
4 *Elephant War* (1960)

Smith family series
Blyton, Enid
1 *Smith family at home* (1947)
2 *Smith family at the zoo* (1947)
3 *Smith family at the circus* (1947)

Smith family series
Grahame, Kenneth
1 *Golden age* (1895)
Contains *A holiday, Alarums and excursions, The whitewashed uncle*
2 *Dream days* (1898)
Revised edition 1899; contains *The reluctant dragon*, also published separately, 1938, *The magic ring, The saga of the seas*

Smith Minor series
Hardy, Philip
1 *Buried country* (1945)
2 *Smith Minor on the moon* (1945)

Smith series
Ahlswede, Ann
see **Doctor Cicero Smith series**
Barnett, James
see **Superintendent Owen Smith series**
Berrow, Norman
see **Inspector Lancelot Carolus Smith series**
Bickham, Jack Miles
see **Brad Smith series**
Boland, John
see **Counterpol series**
Brooks, Jeremy
see **Bernard Smith series**
Coatsworth, Elizabeth
see **Sally Smith series**
Crider, Bill
see **Truman Smith series**
Dicks, Terrance
see **Sarah Jane Smith series**
Edson, John Thomas
see **Waxahachie Smith series**
Haggard, William
see **William Wilberforce Smith series**
Nabb, Magdalen
see **Josie Smith series**
Pentecost, Hugh
see **Doctor John Smith series**
Plum, Mary
see **John Smith series**
Reeves, Robert
see **Cellini Smith series**
Sainsbury, Noel
see **Billy Smith series**
Sangster, Jimmy
see **John Smith series**
Scott, Reginald Thomas Maitland
see **Aurelius Smith series**
Smee, Donald
see **Jeremy Smith series**

Smith series
Strong, J J
1 *Smith's tail* (1978)
2 *Smith takes a bath* (1980)

Smith series
Troy, Simon
see **Inspector Smith series**
Usher, Frank
see **Daye Smith series**
Wallace, Edgar
see **Mister T B Smith series**
Zachary, Hugh
see **Tusk Smith series**

Smithers series
Hale, Susan
see **Ronnie Smithers series**

Smiths trilogy
Howard, Keble
1 *Smiths of Surbiton* (1906)
A comedy without a plot
2 *Smiths of Valley View* (1909)
3 *Smiths in war-time* (1917)

Smith-Smith series
Nelson, Peter N
see **Sylvia Smith-Smith series**

Smithsonian Institution series
Conroy, Richard Timothy
see **Henry Scruggs series**

Smithy series
Wallace, Edgar
1 *Smithy* (1905)
Smithy, not to mention Nobby Clark and Spud Murphy
Short stories; the second title is a revised edition
2 *Smithy abroad* (1909)
Barrack room sketches
3 *Smithy's friend Nobby* (1914)
Nobby
4 *Smithy and the Hun* (1915)

Smitty series
Gutman, Bill
1 *Smitty* (1988)
2 *Olympics* (1990)

Smitty series
Sutton-Smith, Brian
1 *Our street* (1952)
2 *Smitty does a bunk* (1961)

Smocker series
Lumbers, Eugene
1 *I, Smocker* (1971)
2 *Smocker takes off* (1972)

Smoke series
Barling, Tom
1 *Smoke* (1986)
2 *Smoke dragon* (1988)

Smoke Wade series
Hogan, Robert Jasper
1 *Challenge of Smoke Wade* (1951)
2 *Stampede Canyon* (1952)

Smokeover series
Jacks, Lawrence Pearsall
1 *Legends of Smokeover* (1921)
2 *Heroes of Smokeover* (1926)
3 *Last legend of Smokeover* (1939)

Smoker series
Comfort, Mildred Houghton
see **Dustin family series**

Smoky Joe series
Meynell, Laurence Walter
1 *Smoky Joe* (1952)
2 *Smoky Joe in trouble* (1953)
3 *Smoky Joe goes to school* (1956)

Smoky sea series
Nutchuk
1 *Son of the smoky sea* (1941)
2 *Back to the smoky sea* (1946)

Smoky the bear series
Verral, Charles Spain
1 *Smoky the bear* (1958)
2 *Smoky the bear and his animal friends* (1960)

Smudge and Dusty series
Schmidt, Annie Maria Geertruida
see **Dusty and Smudge series**

Smudger series
Saddler, Allen
1 *Smudger's seaside spectacular* (1986)
2 *Smudger's Saturday special* (1988)

Smugglers' Castle series
Carus, Zena M
1 *Smugglers' Castle* (1980)
2 *Spy in the school* (1983)

Smugglers series
Petersen, Paul
1 *Smugglers* (1974)
2 *Fools of the trade* (1974)
3 *Murder in blue* (1974)
4 *Mother Luck* (1974)
5 *Crystal fortress* (1975)
6 *Death benefit* (1975)
7 *Welcome to oblivion* (1975)

Smurf series
Peyo
Comic strips translated from the French
1 *King Smurf* (1978)
2 *Smurfette* (1978)
3 *Smurphony in C* (1978)
Also contains *The flying Smurf*
4 *Smurfs and the egg* (1978)
Also contains *The hundredth Smurf*
5 *Astrosmurf* (1979)
6 *Romeo and Smurfette* (1979)
7 *Smurf's apprentice* (1979)
Also contains *Smurftraps*
8 *Weather-smurfing machine* (1979)
Also contains Smurf stories
9 *Smurfic games* (1980)
Also contains *Smurf of one and Smurf a dozen of the other*
10 *Smurfs and the howlibird* (1980)
Companion volumes: *The Smurfs and the magic flute*, 1979, *What do Smurfs do all day*, 1983

Smyth series
Boyd, Eunice Mays
see **F Millard Smyth series**

Smyth versus Smith series
Zach, Cheryl
1 *Oh, brother* (1988)
2 *Stealing the scene* (1988)
3 *Tug of war* (1988)
4 *More than friends* (1989)
5 *Surprise, surprise* (1989)
6 *Growing pains* (1989)

Snail and Pennithorne series
Willard, Barbara
1 *Snail and the Pennithornes* (1957)
2 *Snail and the Pennithornes next time* (1958)
3 *Snail and the Pennithornes and the princess* (1960)

Snake Kirlin and F T Zevich series
Bourgeau, Art
see **Claude Kirlin and F T Zevich series**

Snake oil wars series
Godwin, Parke
1 *Waiting for the galactic bus* (1988)
2 *Snake oil wars* (1989)
Alternative title: Scheherazade Ginsberg strikes again

Snakes series
Polisar, Barry Louis
1 *Snakes and the boy who was afraid of them* (1988)
2 *Snake who was afraid of people* (1988)

Snall, Polly-Dear and Rod series
Goode, Evelyn
see **Polly-Dear, Rod and Small series**

Snappy answers to stupid questions series
Jaffee, Al
1 *Mad's Al Jaffee spews out snappy answers to stupid questions* (1968)
2 *Mad's Al Jaffee spews out still more snappy answers to stupid questions* (1976)
3 *More snappy answers to stupid questions* (1979)
4 *Good Lord, not another book of snappy answers to stupid questions!* (1980)
5 *Snappy answers to stupid questions, number five* (1984)
6 *Once again Mad's Al Jaffee spews out snappy answers to stupid questions* (1987)
7 *Snappy answers to stupid questions, number seven* (1989)
9 *Overblown collection* (1990)

Snaps series
Berg, Leila
1 *Presents* (1977)
2 *Looking for elephants* (1977)
3 *Birthday races* (1977)
4 *Waiting for the dark* (1977)

Snapshot series
Taylor, John Robert
1 *Snapshot* (1989)
2 *Double exposure* (1990)

Snarkout boys series
Pinkwater, Daniel Manus
1 *Snarkout boys and the avocado of death* (1982)
2 *Snarkout boys and the Baconbury horror* (1984)

Sneed series
Newman, Gordon F
see **Inspector Terry Sneed series**

Sniper series
Acres, Mark
1 *Viet rampage* (1987)
2 *Blast out in Lebanon* (1987)
3 *Into China* (1987)
4 *KGB doublecross* (1987)
5 *Ultra deadly* (1987)
6 *Libya strike* (1987)

Snopes family trilogy
Faulkner, William
1 *Hamlet* (1940)
2 *Town* (1957)
3 *Mansion* (1959)
One volume edition entitled *Snopes*, 1965

Snoqualmie Valley series
Paul, Charlotte
1 *Gold Mountain* (1953)
2 *Cup of strength* (1958)
Wild valley

Snow-Eyes series
Smith, Stephanie Ann
1 *Snow-Eyes* (1985)
2 *Boy who was thrown away* (1987)

Snow Queen series
Vinge, Joan Dennison
1 *Snow Queen* (1980)
2 *World's End* (1984)
3 *Summer Queen* (1991)

Snow series
Sawkins, Raymond
see **Superintendent John Snow series**

Snow spider trilogy
Nimmo, Jenny
1 *Snow spider* (1986)
2 *Emlyn's moon* (1987)
Orchard of the crescent moon
3 *Chestnut spider* (1989)
One volume edition entitled *Snow spider trilogy*, 1993

Snowbird series
Stables, Gordon
see **Captain McBain series**

Snowblind moon trilogy
Cooke, John Byrne
1 *Snowblind moon* (1985)
Between the worlds
2 *Pipe carriers* (1986)
3 *Hoop of the nation* (1984)

Snowman series
Briggs, Raymond
1 *Snowman* (1978)
2 *Party* (1985)
3 *Walking in the air* (1985)
4 *Dressing up* (1985)
5 *Building the snowman* (1985)
Numbers 2-5 are based on the film which is based on number one

Snowy White and Nobby Clark series
Andrews, Stephen
see **Nobby Clark and Snowy White series**

Snuffin chronicles series
Cosgrove, Stephen Edward
1 *Snarly Snuffins* (1988)
2 *Rooty Tooty Snooty* (1988)
3 *Snively Snuffin* (1988)
4 *Gruffins* (1988)

Snuffy series
Bruna, Dick
1 *Snuffy* (1969)
Original edition entitled *Snuffie*
2 *Snuffy and the fire* (1969)
Original edition entitled *Snuffie en de brand*
3 *Snuffy's puppies* (1986)
Original edition entitled *De puppies van Snuffie*

Snuggle tales series
Baum, Lyman Frank
1 *Little Bun Rabbit* (1916)
2 *Once upon a time* (1916)
3 *Yellow hen* (1916)
4 *Magic cloak* (1916)
5 *Ginger-bread man* (1917)
6 *Jack Pumpkinhead* (1917)

So Hi series
Beaton-Jones, Cynon
1 *Adventures of the So Hi* (1951)
2 *So Hi and the white horses of Fu* (1952)

Soames series
Behrens, Margaret
see **Percival Soames series**

Soapy series
Lillington, Kenneth
1 *Conjuror's alibi* (1960)
2 *Man called Hughes* (1962)

Soapy Smith series
Strong, Charles Stanley
1 *Trail of Soapy Smith* (1953)
2 *Soapy Smith heads north* (1953)
3 *Ghost of Soapy Smith* (1955)

SOBS series
Hild, Jack
House pseudonym
1 *Barrabas run* (1983)
2 *Plains of fire* (1984)
3 *Butchers of Eden* (1984)
4 *Show no mercy* (1985)
5 *Gulag war* (1985)
6 *Red hammer down* (1985)

7 *Rivers of flesh* (1985)
8 *Eye of the fire* (1985)
9 *Some choose hell* (1985)
10 *Vultures of the horn* (1986)
11 *Agile retrieval* (1986)
12 *Jihad* (1986)
13 *No sanctuary* (1986)
14 *Red vengeance* (1986)
15 *Death deal* (1986)
16 *Firestorm USA* (1987)
17 *Point blank* (1987)
18 *Sakhalin breakout* (1987)
19 *Skylark* (1987)
20 *Alaska deception* (1987)
21 *No safe place* (1987)
22 *Kremlin devils* (1988)
23 *Barrabas strike* (1988)
24 *Barrabas creed* (1988)
25 *Barrabas raid* (1988)
26 *Barrabas edge* (1988)
27 *Barrabas fix* (1988)
28 *Barrabas fallout* (1989)
29 *Barrabas hit* (1989)
30 *Jeweled mountain* (1989)
31 *Barrabas thrust* (1989)
32 *Barrabas fire* (1989)
33 *Barrabas kill* (1989)

Soccer series
Greaves, Jimmy
1 *Final* (1979)
2 *Ball game* (1980)
3 *Boss* (1981)
4 *Second half* (1981)

Socialist trilogy
Sand, George
1 *Master mosaic workers* (1838)
Original edition entitled *Les maitres mosaistes*
2 *Journeyman joiner* (1840)
Alternative title: The companion of the tour of France; original edition entitled *Le compagnon du tour de France*
3 *Miller of Angibault* (1846)
Original edition entitled *Le meunier d'Angibault*

Society of the Crooked Snake series
Wrightson, Patricia
1 *Crooked Snake* (1955)
2 *Bunyip hole* (1958)

Socioland series
Chavannes, Albert
1 *Future commonwealth* (1892)
Alternative title: What Samuel Balcom saw in Socioland
2 *In brighter climes* (1895)
Alternative title: Life in Socioland

Socrates Potter trilogy
Bacheller, Irving
1 *Keeping up with Lizzie* (1911)
2 *Charge it* (1912)
Alternative title: Keeping up with Harry; a story of fashionable extravagance and of the successful efforts to retsrain it made by the Honorable Socrates Potter, the genial friend of Lizzie
3 *Marryers* (1914)
A history gathered from a brief of the Honorable Socrates Potter

Socrates series
Kreeft, Peter
Philosophical discourses
1 *Unaborted Socrates* (1983)
2 *Socrates meets Jesus* (1987)

Sodor series
Awdry, Wilbert
1 *Railway map of the island of Sodor* (1958)
Revised edition 1971
2 *Island of Sodor, its people, history and railways* (1987)

Soeur Angele series
Catalan, Henri
1 *Soeur Angele and the embarrassed ladies* (1953)
Embarrassed ladies affair
Original edition entitled *Le cas de Soeur Angele*
2 *Soeur Angele and the ghosts of Chambord* (1953)
Ghosts of Chambord affair
Original edition entitled *Soeur Angele et les Fantomes de Chambord*
3 *[Soeur Angele et les seigneurs du jour]* (1953)
No English edition
4 *[Soeur Angele et caux de la mouise]* (1953)
No English edition
5 *[Soeur Angele et les roses de Noel]* (1954)
No English edition
6 *Soeur Angele and the bellringer's niece* (1954)
Original edition entitled *Soeur Angele et l'angelus du soir*
7 *[Soeur Angele et les croix de glace]* (1955)
No English edition
8 *[Le secret de Soeur Angele]* (1956)
No English edition
9 *[Soeur Angele et l'etrangers]* (1957)
No English edition
10 *[Soeur Angele et le redresseur de torts]* (1959)
No English edition

Soft whisper trilogy
Grant, Charles Lewis
1 *Soft whisper of the dead* (1982)
2 *Dark cry of the moon* (1985)
3 *Long night of the grave* (1986)

Software series
Rucker, Rudy
1 *Software* (1982)
2 *Wetware* (1988)

Software Superslug series
Dunbar, Joyce
1 *Software Superslug* (1987)
2 *Software Superslug and the great computer stupor* (1989)
3 *Software Superslug and the nutty novelty knitting* (1990)

Soho series
Carson, Anthony
1 *Sin of summer* (1965)
Includes *The adventures of Mister Quick*
2 *Golden kiss* (1966)

Sokki series
Frison-Roche, Roger
see **Simon Sokki series**

Sola trilogy
Sandman Lilius, Irmelin
Horses of the night (1971)
Original edition entitled *Gangande Gra*
1 *Gold Crown Lane* (1969)
Original edition entitled *Gullkrona grand*
2 *Goldmaker's house* (1970)
Original edition entitled *Gripanderska garden*

Solar Pons series
This sequence has two authors; short stories
Derleth, August
1 *In re Sherlock Holmes* (1945)
Regarding Sherlock Holmes
Adventures of Solar Pons
Short stories
2 *Memoirs of Solar Pons* (1951)
Short stories
3 *Three problems for Solar Pons* (1952)
Short stories
4 *Return of Solar Pons* (1958)
Short stories
5 *Reminiscences of Solar Pons* (1961)
Short stories
6 *Adventure of the Orient Express* (1965)
Short stories
7 *Casebook of Solar Pons* (1965)
Short stories
8 *Praed Street papers* (1965)
Short stories
9 *Mister Fairlie's final journey* (1968)
10 *Adventure of the unique Dickensians* (1968)
11 *Praed Street dossier* (1968)
Short stories
12 *Chronicles of Solar Pons* (1973)
Copper, Basil
13 *Dossier of Solar Pons* (1979)
14 *Further adventures of Solar Pons* (1979)
15 *Secret files of Solar Pons* (1979)
16 *Uncollected cases of Solar Pons* (1980)

Solar Queen series
Norton, Andre
see **Dane Thorson series**

Soldano series
Webster, Ernest
see **Benni Soldano series**

Soldato series
Conroy, Al
see **Johnny Morini series**

Solden series
Turner, Bill
see **Detective Inspector Manson series**

Soldier and gentleman series
Hislop, John
1 *Far from a gentleman* (1960)
2 *Anything but a soldier* (1965)

Soldier for hire series
This sequence has two authors
Skimin, Robert
1 *Zulu blood* (1981)
2 *Trojan in Iran* (1981)
3 *U.N. sabotage* (1981)
4 *Bloodletting!* (1982)
5 *Libyan warlord* (1982)
Roberts, Mark Kelly
6 *Commando squad* (1982)
7 *Pathet vengeance* (1983)
8 *Jakarta coup* (1983)

Soldier of fortune series
McCurtin, Peter
see **Jim Rainey series**

Soldier of fortune series
This sequence has ten authors
Williams, Michael
1 *Doorgunner* (1987)
Victor, Roger
2 *Missing by choice* (1987)
Yaeger, Carl H
3 *Cult crushers* (1987)
Number four not identified
McCall, Alex
5 *Counterfeit* (1987)
Philburn, Dennis K
6 *Freedom bird* (1987)
King, Melvin
7 *Nature of the beast* (1987)
Pruitt, James H
8 *Striker one down* (1987)
Humphrey, Vernon
9 *MacGonigal's way* (1987)
Neebel, Richard
10 *Wargamer* (1987)

Soldiering series
Mays, Spike
Autobiography
1 *Reuben's corner* (1969)
2 *Fall out the officers* (1969)
3 *No more soldiering for me* (1971)
4 *Last post* (1974)
5 *Band rats* (1975)
6 *Return to Anglia* (1986)

Soldiers and officers series
Harris, Marion
1 *Soldiers' wives* (1986)
2 *Officers' ladies* (1987)

Soldiers of fortune series
Stratemeyer, Edward L
1 *On to Pekin* (1900)
Alternative title: Old Glory in China
2 *Under the Mikado's flag* (1904)
Alternative title: Young soldiers of fortune
3 *At the fall of Port Arthur* (1905)
Alternative title: A young American in the Japanese Navy
4 *Under Togo for Japan* (1906)
Alternative title: Three young Americans on land and sea

Soldiers trilogy
Moore, William
see **Mallandine family trilogy**

Soledad brother series
Jackson, George
Autobiography of an American socialist revolutionary
1 *Soledad brother* (1970)
Prison letters
2 *Blood in my eye* (1972)

Solitude trilogy
Kaye, Marvin
1 *Masters of solitude* (1978)
2 *Wintermind* (1982)
Third volume not published

Solo Malcolm series
Graham, Neill
1 *Murder makes a date* (1955)
2 *Play it Solo* (1955)
3 *Say it with murder* (1956)
4 *You can't call it murder* (1957)
5 *Hit me hard* (1958)
6 *Salute to murder* (1958)
7 *Murder rings the bell* (1959)
8 *Killers are on velvet* (1960)
9 *Murder is my weakness* (1961)
10 *Murder on the Duchess* (1961)
11 *Make mine murder* (1962)
12 *Murder makes it certain* (1963)
13 *Graft town* (1963)
14 *Label it murder* (1963)
15 *Murder made easy* (1964)
16 *Murder of a black cat* (1964)
17 *Murder on my hands* (1965)
18 *Murder's always final* (1965)
19 *Money for murder* (1966)
20 *Murder on demand* (1966)
21 *Murder makes the news* (1967)
22 *Murder has been done* (1967)
23 *Pay off* (1968)
24 *Candidate for a coffin* (1968)
25 *Death of a canary* (1969)
26 *Murder lies in waiting* (1969)
27 *Blood on the pavement* (1970)
28 *One for the book* (1970)
29 *Matter of murder* (1971)
30 *Murder double murder* (1971)
31 *Frame-up* (1972)
32 *Cop in a tight frame* (1973)
33 *Murder in a dark room* (1973)
34 *Assignment, murder* (1974)
35 *Murder on the list* (1975)
36 *Search for a missing lady* (1976)
37 *Motive for murder* (1977)

Solo series
Avallone, Michael
see **Man from U.N.C.L.E. series**

Solo series
Dahl, Roald
1 *Boy* (1984)
Tales of childhood
2 *Going solo* (1986)

Solo the dragon series
Robinson, Mike
1 *Solo the dragon learns to fly* (1986)
2 *Milky mountains* (1986)
3 *Hunter's trap* (1986)

Solomon Kane series
Howard, Robert Ervin
1 *Red shadows* (1968)
1.1 *Moon of skulls* (1969)
1.2 *Hand of Kane* (1970)
1.3 *Solomon Kane* (1971)
2 *Skulls in the stars* (1978)
3 *Hills of the dead* (1979)

Solomon trilogy
Bedford-Jones, Henry
see **John Solomon trilogy**

Solstice series
Payack, Paul J J
1 *Solstice* (1975)
Alternative title: Star-tales
2 *Solstice II* (1976)
3 *Solstice III* (1977)

Solstice series
Smith, Lisa J
1 *Night of the solstice* (1987)
2 *Heart of valor* (1990)

Solve it with Oliver series
Dicks, Terrance
see **Ask Oliver series**

Solve it yourself series
Waddell, Martin
see **Mystery Squad series**

Some women trilogy
Dawson-Scott, Catherine Amy
1 *Story of Anne Beames* (1907)
Maiden
2 *Burden* (1908)
Mother
3 *Treasure trove* (1909)
Matron

Somebody series
Rogers, Paul
Illustrated by Robin Bell Corfield
1 *Somebody's sleepy* (1988)
2 *Somebody's awake* (1988)

Someone series
Winberg, Greta
see **Maddie series**

Somers series
Somers, Jane
see **Jane Somers series**

Somerville series
Yonge, Charlotte Mary
see **Lady Herbert Somerville series**

Something queer series
Levy, Elizabeth
1 *Something queer is going on* (1973)
2 *Something queer at the ball park* (1975)
3 *Something queer at the library* (1977)
4 *Something queer on vacation* (1980)
5 *Something queer at the haunted school* (1982)
6 *Something queer at the lemonade stand* (1982)
7 *Something queer in rock 'n roll* (1987)
8 *Something queer at the birthday party* (1990)
9 *Something queer in outer space* (1993)

Something special series
Williams, Vera Baker
1 *Chair for my mother* (1982)
2 *Something special for me* (1983)
3 *Music, music for everyone* (1984)

Something to sell series
Birt, David
1 *Propaganda* (1978)
2 *Advertising* (1978)

Sometime farmer series
Perrin, Noel
Essays
1 *First person rural* (1978)
2 *Second person rural* (1980)
3 *Third person rural* (1983)

Sommers and Hanscombe series
Whalley, Peter
see **Harry Sommers and Jill Hanscombe series**

Son of Blackshirt series
Graeme, Bruce
see **Lord Blackshirt series**

Son of Erin series
Swan, Annie Shepherd
1 *Son of Erin* (1899)
2 *American woman* (1900)

Son of the Plains series
Johnston, Terry Conrad
see **General Armstrong Custer series**

Song called youth trilogy
Shirley, John
1 *Eclipse* (1985)
2 *Eclipse penumbra* (1988)
3 *Eclipse corona* (1990)

Song of Albion trilogy
Lawhead, Stephen
1 *Paradise war* (1991)
2 *Silver hand* (1993)
3 *Endless knot* (1993)

Song of earth series
Coney, Michael Greatrex
see **Greataway series**

Song of Naga Teot series
Gladney, Heather
1 *Teot's war* (1987)
2 *Blood storm* (1989)

Song of Phaid the Gambler series
Farren, Mick
1 *Phaid the gambler* (1986)
2 *Citizen Phaid* (1986)
Revised from the original one volume edition entitled *The song of Phaid the Gambler*, 1981

Song of the lioness series
Pierce, Tamora
1 *Alanna* (1983)
2 *In the hand of the goddess* (1984)
3 *Woman who rides like a man* (1986)
4 *Lioness rampant* (1988)

Song of the world trilogy
Giono, Jean
1 *Song of the world* (1933)
Original edition entitled *Le chant du monde*
2 *[Batailles dans le montagne]* (1937)
No English edition
3 *Joy of man's desiring* (1935)
Original edition entitled *Que ma joie demeure*

Song of Wirrun trilogy
Wrightson, Patricia
1 *Ice is coming* (1977)
2 *Dark bright water* (1978)
3 *Behind the wind* (1981)
Journey behind the wind
One volume edition entitled *The song of Wirrun*, 1987

Song series
Gunnarsson, Thorarinn
1 *Song of the dwarves* (1988)
2 *Revenge of the Valkyrie* (1989)

Songkiller series
Scarborough, Elizabeth Ann
1 *Phantom banjo* (1991)
2 *Picking the ballad's bones* (1991)

Songs to read series
Raffi
see **Raffi songs to read series**

Songweaver series
De Lint, Charles
see **Cerin Songweaver series**

Sonia series
McKenna, Stephen
1 *Sonia* (1917)
2 *Sonia married* (1919)
3 *Midas and Son* (1919)
4 *To-morrow and to-morrow* (1924)

Sonja series
Smith, David Claude
see **Red Sonja series**

Sonny series
Stuart, Ruth Macenery
1 *Sonny* (1896)
A Christmas guest
2 *Sonny's father* (1910)

Sons of Barrabas series
Hild, Jack
see **SOBS series**

Sons of Texas series
Early, Tom
1 *Danger, the daring* (1989)
2 *Raiders* (1989)
3 *Rebels* (1990)
4 *Proud* (1992)
5 *Bold* (1992)

Sontag series
Tuttle, Wilbur Coleman
see **Sad Sontag series**

Sookan series
Choi, Sook Nyul
1 *Year of impossible goodbyes* (1991)
2 *Echoes of the white giraffe* (1993)
3 *Gathering of pearls* (1994)

Sooper series
Wallace, Edgar
see **Superintendent Minter series**

Sooty series
Blyton, Enid
1 *Away goes Sooty* (1955)
2 *Sooty* (1955)

Sophie and Gussie series
Sharmat, Marjorie Weinman
1 *Sophie and Gussie* (1973)
2 *Trip, and other Sophie and Gussie stories* (1976)

Sophie and Jack series
Taylor, Judy
Illustrated by Susan Gantner
1 *Sophie and Jack* (1983)
2 *Sophie and Jack help out* (1983)
3 *Sophie and Jack in the snow* (1984)
4 *Sophie and Jack in the rain* (1989)

Sophie and Nicky series
Ichikawa, Satomi
see **Suzanne and Nicholas series**

Sophie, Helen, Jean and Robbie series
Dallas, Ruth
see **Jean, Robbie, Sophie and Helen series**

Sophie, Sarah and Ben series
Barrett, Peter
1 *Line Sophie drew* (1970)
2 *Circle Sarah drew* (1970)
3 *Square Ben drew* (1970)

Sophie series
Baker, Harriette Newell Woods
1 *Sophie and the gipsies* (1870)
2 *Sophie's letter-book* (1871)

Sophie series
King-Smith, Dick
1 *Sophie's snail* (1988)
2 *Sophie's tom* (1991)
3 *Sophie hits six* (1991)
4 *Sophie in the saddle* (1993)

Sophie series
Stock, Catherine
1 *Sophie's bucket* (1985)
2 *Sophie's knapsack* (1988)

Soprano series
Barnard, Charles
1 *Soprano* (1869)
2 *Money and music* (1874)

Sorak series
Richards, Harvey D
1 *Sorak of the Malay jungle* (1934)
Alternative title: How two young Americans face death and win a friend
2 *Sorak and the clouded tiger* (1934)
Alternative title: How the terrible ruler of the north is hunted and destroyed
3 *Sorak and the sultan's ankus* (1934)
Alternative title: How a perilous journey leads to a kingdom of giants
4 *Sorak and the tree-men* (1936)
Alternative title: How Sorak and his friend escape from their captives

Sorcerer trilogy
Volsky, Paula
1 *Sorcerer's lady* (1986)
2 *Sorcerer's heir* (1988)
3 *Sorcerer's curse* (1989)

Sorcerer's son series
Eisenstein, Phyllis
1 *Sorcerer's son* (1979)
2 *Crystal palace* (1988)

Sorceress trilogy
Gallizier, Nathan
1 *Castel del Monte* (1905)
A romance of the fall of the Hohenstaufen Dynasty in Italy
2 *Sorceress of Rome* (1907)
3 *Court of Lucifer* (1910)
A tale of the Renaissance

Sorcery Hall trilogy
Charnas, Suzy McKee
1 *Bronze king* (1985)
2 *Silver glove* (1988)
3 *Golden thread* (1989)

Sorcery series
Jackson, Steve
1 *Shamutanti Hills* (1984)
2 *Khare, cityport of traps* (1984)
3 *Seven serpents* (1984)
4 *Crown of kings* (1985)
Companion volume: *The sorcery spell book*, 1983

Sorcery trilogy
Simon, Morris
see **Kingdom of sorcery trilogy**

Sorme trilogy
Wilson, Colin
see **Gerard Sorme trilogy**

Sorority girls series
Lowell, Anne Hunter
1 *Getting in* (1986)
2 *Nowhere to run* (1986)
3 *Starting over* (1986)
4 *Dangerous secrets* (1986)
5 *Settling the score* (1986)
6 *Winner take all* (1986)
7 *Change of heart* (1987)
8 *Mistaken identity* (1987)
9 *Risking it all* (1987)
10 *Rumors* (1987)
11 *Breaker* (1987)
12 *Holding on* (1987)

Sorority sisters series
Sharmat, Marjorie Weinman
1 *For members only* (1986)
2 *Snobs, beware* (1986)
3 *I think I'm falling in love* (1986)
4 *Fighting over me* (1986)
5 *Nobody knows how scared I am* (1987)
6 *Here comes Mister Right* (1987)
7 *Getting closer* (1987)
8 *I'm going to get your boyfriend* (1987)

Sorrel series
Clare, Marguerite
see **Merlin Sorrel series**

Sorrows of Priapus series
Dahlberg, Edward
1 *Sorrows of Priapus* (1957)
2 *Carnal myth* (1968)
A look into Classical sensuality
One volume edition entitled *The sorrows of Priapus*, 1973

Sos trilogy
Anthony, Piers
see **Battle circle trilogy**

Sossi series
Hurwitz, Johanna
see **Aldo Sossi series**

Soul drinker trilogy
Clayton, Jo
see **Drinker of souls trilogy**

Soul enchanted series
Rolland, Romain
1 *Annette and Sylvie* (1922)
Original edition entitled *Annette et Sylvie*
2 *Summer* (1924)
Original edition entitled *L'ete*
3 *Mother and son* (1927)
Original edition entitled *Mere et fils*
4 *Combat* (1933)
Death of a world
Original edition entitled *L'annonciatrix, Anna Nuncia, la mort d'un monde*
5 *Via Sacra* (1933)
World in birth
Original edition entitled *L'annonciatrix, Anna Nuncia, l'enfantement*

Soul rider series
Chalker, Jack Laurence
1 *Spirits of Flux and Anchor* (1984)
2 *Empires of Flux and Anchor* (1984)
3 *Masters of Flux and Anchor* (1985)
4 *Birth of Flux and Anchor* (1985)
5 *Children of Flux and Anchor* (1986)

Soul's development trilogy
Strindberg, Johan August
1 *Son of a servant* (1886)
Original edition entitled *Tjenstokvinnans son*
2 *Confessions of a fool* (1893)
Original edition entitled *Die beichte eines thoren*
3 *Fair haven and foul strand* (1902)
Original edition entitled *Fagervik, och, Skamsund*
Companion volumes: *Red room, scenes of artistic and literary life*, 1879, originally published as *Roda rummet*, *The confessions of a fool*, 1888, revised edition 1893, originally published as *Le plaidoyer d'un fou*

Soup series
Peck, Robert Newton
1 *Soup* (1974)
2 *Soup and me* (1975)
3 *Soup for president* (1978)
4 *Soup's drum* (1980)
5 *Soup on wheels* (1981)
6 *Soup in the saddle* (1983)
7 *Soup's goat* (1984)
8 *Soup on ice* (1985)
9 *Soup on fire* (1987)
10 *Soup's uncle* (1988)
11 *Soup's hoop* (1989)
12 *Soup in love* (1992)
13 *Soup ahoy* (1994)

South Africa series
Butler, Guy
Autobiography
1 *Karoo morning* (1978)
1918-1935
2 *Bursting world* (1983)
1936-1945
3 *Local habitation* (1991)
1945-1990

South African history series
Gibbs, Henry
1 *Splendour and the dust* (1955)
2 *Winds of time* (1956)
3 *Thunder at dawn* (1957)
4 *Tumult and the shouting* (1958)

South African series
Scholefield, Alan
1 *View of vultures* (1966)
2 *Great elephant* (1967)
3 *Eagles of malice* (1968)
4 *Wild dog running* (1970)

South African series
Stern, Rhona
1 *Cactus land* (1964)
2 *Bird flies blind* (1965)
3 *Stop half way and look at the view* (1969)

South African trilogy
Bancroft, Francis
1 *Veldt dwellers* (1912)
2 *Thane Brandon* (1913)
3 *Dalliance and strife* (1914)

South City cops series
Eisenberg, Lisa
1 *Hit man* (1984)
2 *Kidnap* (1984)
3 *Payoff game* (1984)

South Coast series
Slaven, Roy
1 *Pants off* (1989)
2 *This is the South Coast news and I'm Paul Murphy* (1990)
3 *Five South Coast seasons* (1992)

South London series
Staples, Mary Jane
1 *Down Lambeth way* (1988)
2 *Our Emily* (1989)
3 *King of Camberwell* (1990)
4 *Two for three farthings* (1990)
5 *Lodger* (1991)
6 *Rising summer* (1991)
7 *Pearly Queen* (1992)
8 *Sergeant Joe* (1992)
9 *On Mother Brown's doorstep* (1993)
10 *Trap* (1993)
11 *Family affair* (1994)
12 *Missing person* (1994)
13 *Pride of Walworth* (1995)

South Orange River Middle School series
Avi
1 *S.O.R. losers* (1984)
2 *Romeo and Juliet, together, and alive, at last* (1988)

South Pacific series
Michener, James Albert
1 *Tales of the South Pacific* (1947)
2 *Return to paradise* (1951)
3 *Rascals in paradise* (1957)
Co-author: Arthur Grove Day

South Seas series
Melville, Herman
Fictionalized autobiography
1 *Typee* (1846)
Revised edition 1846; a peep at Polynesian life
2 *Omoo* (1847)

Southern Army campaign trilogy
Cooke, John Esten
1 *Surry of Eagle's Nest* (1866)
2 *Hilt to hilt* (1869)
Days and nights on the banks of the Shenandoah
3 *Mohun* (1869)
Alternative title: The last days of Lee and his paladins

Southwood series
Bedford, Jean
see **Anna Southwood series**

Souvenir de France series
Fleming, Arnold
1 *Four Maries* (1951)
Story of the the maids of honour to Mary, Queen of Scots
2 *Medieval Scots scholar in France* (1952)
3 *Troubadours of Provence* (1953)
Poetry
4 *Huguenot influence in Scotland* (1954)

Soviet conquest series
Drury, Allen
1 *Hill of summer* (1981)
2 *Roads of earth* (1984)

Soviet literature series
Shneidman, Noah Norman
1 *Soviet literature in the nineteen seventies* (1979)
Artistic diversity and ideological conformity
2 *Soviet literature in the nineteen eighties* (1989)
Decade of transition

Sovra and Ian series
Lyon, Elinor
see **Ian and Sovra series**

Sowing and growing series
Woolf, Leonard
Autobiography
1 *Sowing* (1960)
1880-1904
2 *Growing* (1961)
1904-1911
3 *Beginning again* (1964)
1911-1918
4 *Downhill all the way* (1967)
1919-1939
5 *Journey not the arrival matters* (1969)
1939-1969

Space age series
Corson, Hazel Wyman
see **Peter series**

Space Agent series
Macvicar, Angus
see **Jeremy Grant series**

Space Angel series
Roberts, John Maddox
1 *Space Angel* (1979)
2 *Spacer, window of the mind* (1988)

Space brat series
Coville, Bruce
1 *Space brat* (1992)
2 *Blork's evil twin* (1993)

Space cadets series
Stine, Robert Lawrence
1 *Jerks-in-training* (1991)
2 *Losers in space* (1991)
3 *Bozos on patrol* (1992)

Space Cat series
Todd, Ruthven
1 *Space Cat* (1952)
2 *Space Cat visits Venus* (1955)
3 *Space Cat meets Mars* (1957)
4 *Space Cat and the kittens* (1958)

Space cops series
Duane, Diane
1 *Mindblast* (1991)
2 *Kill station* (1992)
3 *High moon* (1992)

Space corporation series
Rankine, John
1 *Never the same door* (1967)
2 *Moons of triopus* (1968)
3 *Fingalman conspiracy* (1973)

Space demons trilogy
Rubinstein, Gillian
1 *Space demons* (1986)
2 *Skymaze* (1989)
Third volume not yet published

Space detective series
Nixon, Joan Lowery
see **Kleep, space detective series**

Space Eagle series
Pearl, Jack
1 *Operation Doomsday* (1967)
2 *Operation Star Voyage* (1970)

Space Express Company series
This sequence has two authors
Del Martia, Astron
1 *Space pirates* (1951)
Harkon, Franz
2 *Spawn of space* (1951)
Del Martia, Astron
3 *Interstellar espionage* (1952)

Space gladiators trilogy
Drake, David
1 *Space gladiators* (1989)
2 *Space infantry* (1989)
3 *Space dreadnoughts* (1990)

Space hawks series
Packard, Edward
1 *Faster than light* (1991)
2 *Alien invaders* (1991)
3 *Space fortress* (1991)
4 *Comet masters* (1991)

Space knight series
Gunson, Jonathan
1 *Space knight and the space dragon* (1987)
2 *Space knight and the galactic ice-cream* (1987)

Space mavericks series
Kring, Michael K
1 *Space mavericks* (1980)
2 *Children on the night* (1981)

Space merchants series
Pohl, Frederik
1 *Space merchants* (1953)
Co-author: Cyril M Kornbluth; revised edition 1985
2 *Merchants' war* (1984)
One volume edition entitled *Venus, Inc.*, 1985

Space nineteen ninety nine series
This sequence has five authors
Tubb, Edwin Charles
1 *Breakaway* (1975)
Rankine, John
2 *Moon odyssey* (1975)
Ball, Brian Neville
3 *Space guardians* (1975)
Tubb, Edwin Charles
4 *Collision course* (1975)
Rankine, John
5 *Lunar attack* (1975)
6 *Astral quest* (1975)
Tubb, Edwin Charles
7 *Alien seed* (1976)
Rankine, John
8 *Android planet* (1976)
Tubb, Edwin Charles
9 *Rogue planet* (1976)
Rankine, John
10 *Phoenix of Megaron* (1975)
Tubb, Edwin Charles
11 *Earthfall* (1977)
Butterworth, Michael
12 *Planets of peril* (1977)
13 *Mind-breakers of space* (1977)
Co-author: J Jeff Jones
14 *Space-jackers* (1977)
15 *Psychomorph* (1977)
16 *Time fighters* (1977)
17 *On the edge of the infinite* (1978)

Space odyssey series
Clarke, Arthur Charles
1 *Two thousand and one, a space odyssey* (1968)
Based on a screenplay
2 *Two thousand and ten* (1982)
3 *Two thousand and sixty one* (1988)
Companion volume: *The lost worlds of 2001*, 1972

Space photos series
Simon, Seymour
1 *Jupiter* (1985)
2 *Saturn* (1985)
3 *Sun* (1986)
4 *Stars* (1986)
5 *Mars* (1987)
6 *Uranus* (1987)
7 *Galaxies* (1988)
8 *Neptune* (1991)
9 *Mercury* (1992)
10 *Venus* (1992)
11 *Our solar system* (1993)

Space police series
Kelley, Leo Patrick
1 *Prison satellite* (1979)
2 *Worlds apart* (1979)
3 *Earth Two* (1979)
4 *Backward in time* (1979)
5 *Sunworld* (1979)
6 *Death sentence* (1979)
Companion volume: *Space police teacher's guide*, 1979

Space probe six series
Huntington, Charles
1 *Soul stealers* (1973)
2 *Nightmare on Vega Three* (1973)

Space puppet series
Rackham, John
1 *Space Puppet* (1954)
2 *Master weed* (1954)
3 *Jupiter equilateral* (1954)
4 *Alien virus* (1954)

Space series
Nolan, William Francis
see **Sam Space series**

Space ship series
Slobodkin, Louis
1 *Space ship under the apple tree* (1952)
2 *Space ship returns to the apple tree* (1958)
3 *Three-seated space ship* (1962)
4 *Round trip space ship* (1968)
5 *Space ship in the park* (1972)

Space travel series
Corson, Hazel Wyman
see **Peter series**

Space trilogy
Lewis, Clive Staples
1 *Out of the silent planet* (1938)
2 *Perelandra* (1943)
Voyage to Venus
3 *That hideous strength* (1945)
Tortured planet
The second title is an abridged edition; a modern fairy tale for grown-ups

Space tyrant series
Anthony, Piers
see **Bio of a space tyrant series**

Spaceache series
Wilson, Snoo
1 *Spaceache* (1984)
2 *Inside Babel* (1985)

Spacebread series
Senn, Steve
1 *Spacebread* (1981)
2 *Born of flame* (1982)

Spaceman Kowalski and Blue Maguire series
White, Teri
see **Blue Maguire and Spaceman Kowalski series**

Spacers series
Bentley, Roy
1 *Lift off to danger* (1982)
2 *Moonquake* (1983)
3 *Shuttle burn* (1984)
4 *Space crash* (1985)
5 *Far from earth* (1986)

Spaceship series
Lord, Beman
1 *Day the spaceship landed* (1967)
2 *Spaceship returns* (1970)

Spaceways series
Cleve, John
This pseudonym is used by Garry Cotton Edmondson, Roland Green, Jack Carroll Haldeman, Vol Haldeman, Robin Kincaid, Victor Koman, Andrew Jefferson Offutt, George Watt Proctor, Dwight Vreeland Swain as indicated against each title
1 *Of alien bondage* (1982)
[Offutt]
2 *Corundum's woman* (1982)
[Offutt]
3 *Escape from Macho* (1982)
[Offutt]
4 *Satana enslaved* (1982)
[Offutt]
5 *Master of misfit* (1982)
[Offutt, Proctor]
6 *Purrfect plunder* (1982)
[Offutt]
7 *Manhuntress* (1982)
[Offutt, Proctor]
8 *Under twin suns* (1982)
[Offutt]
9 *In quest of Qalara* (1983)
[Offutt]
10 *Yoke of Shen* (1983)
[Offutt, Proctor]
11 *Iceworld connection* (1983)
[Offutt, Jack Haldeman, Vol Haldeman]
12 *Star slaver* (1983)
[Offutt, Edmondson]
13 *Jonuta rising!* (1983)
[Offutt, Koman]
14 *Assignment hellhole* (1983)
[Offutt, Kincaid]
15 *Starship Sapphire* (1984)
[Offutt, Green]
16 *Planet murderer* (1984)
[Offutt, Swain]
17 *Carnadyne hoard* (1984)
[Offutt, Koman]
18 *Race across the stars* (1984)
[Offutt, Kincaid]
19 *King of the slavers* (1985)
[Offutt]

Spaceworld series
Eliott, E C
see **Kemlo series**

Spade series
Hammett, Dashiell
see **Sam Spade series**
Johnson, B B
see **Superspade series**
Spade, Danny
see **Danny Spade series**

Spaghetti series
Frascino, Edward
see **Eddie Spaghetti series**

Spaniards and Elizabethans series
Whittle, Tyler
1 *Spades and feathers* (1955)
2 *Runners of Orford* (1956)
3 *Castle Pizard* (1957)

Spanish-American empire series
Madariaga, Salvador de
1 *Rise of the Spanish-American Empire* (1945)
Original edition entitled *El auge del Imperio Espanol en America*
2 *Fall of the Spanish-American Empire* (1945)
Original edition entitled *El ocaso del Imperio Espanol en America*

Spanish bit series
Coldsmith, Don
1 *Trail of the Spanish bit* (1980)
2 *Buffalo medicine* (1981)
3 *Elk-dog heritage* (1982)
4 *Follow the wind* (1983)
5 *Man of the shadows* (1983)
6 *Daughter of the eagle* (1983)
7 *Moon of thunder* (1985)
8 *Sacred hills* (1985)
9 *Pale star* (1986)
10 *River of swans* (1986)
11 *Return to the river* (1987)
12 *Medicine knife* (1988)
13 *Flower in the mountains* (1988)
14 *Trail from Taos* (1988)
15 *Song of the rock* (1989)
16 *Fort de Chastaigne* (1990)
17 *Quest for the white bull* (1990)
18 *Return of the Spanish* (1991)
19 *Bride of the morning star* (1991)
20 *Walks in the sun* (1991)
21 *Thunderstick* (1993)
22 *Track of the bear* (1994)

Spanish bit super series
Coldsmith, Don
1 *Changing wind* (1990)
2 *Traveler* (1991)
3 *World of silence* (1992)

Spanish duet series
Clifford, Francis
1 *Trembling earth* (1955)
2 *Time is an ambush* (1962)
One volume edition entitled Spanish duet, 1966

Spanish Farm series
Mottram, Ralph Hale
1 *Spanish Farm* (1924)
2 *Sixty-four, ninety-four!* (1925)
3 *Crime at Vanderlynden's* (1926)
Numbers 1-3, with connecting pieces entitled *D'Archeville, The winner, The stranger*, published in one volume entitled *Spanish Farm trilogy*, 1927
4 *Ten years ago* (1929)
Armistice and other nenories
5 *Through the Menin Gate* (1935)
Short stories
6 *Europa's beast* (1930)
Rich man's daughter
7 *Come to the bower* (1949)
8 *Over the wall* (1955)

Spanish history series
Blasco Ibanez, Vicente
1 *Pope of the sea* (1925)
Original edition entitled *El papa del mar*; an historical medley
2 *Borgias* (1926)
Original edition entitled *A los pies de Venus*; alternative English title, At the feet of Venus
3 *Unknown lands* (1929)
Original edition entitled *En basca del Gran Kan*; based on the life of Christopher Columbus
4 *Knight of the Virgin* (1929)
Original edition entitled *El caballero de la Virgen*; based on the life of Alonso de Aleda

Spanish Inquisition trilogy
Plaidy, Jean
1 *Rise of the Spanish Inquisition* (1959)
2 *Growth of the Spanish Inquisition* (1960)
3 *End of the Spanish Inquisition* (1961)
One volume edition entitled *The Spanish Inquisition, its rise, growth and end*, 1967

Spanish trilogy
Steen, Marguerite
1 *Matador* (1934)
2 *One-eyed moon* (1935)
3 *Tavern* (1935)

Spanner series
Chastain, Thomas
see **J T Spanner series**

Spargo series
Scott, Jack Denton
1 *Spargo* (1972)
2 *Sea file* (1981)

Sparrow and Zapp series
Lodge, David
see **Rummidge University series**

Sparrow series
Ardies, Tom
see **Charlie Sparrow series**

Sparrow series
Fisker, Robert
1 *Sparrow falls out of the sky* (1978)
Original edition entitled *Peter Pjusk falder ud af reden*
2 *Sparrow flies away* (1979)
Original edition entitled *Peter Pjusk flyver bort*

Sparrow series
Hadath, John Edward Gunby
1 *Sparrow in search of expulsion* (1924)

2 *Sparrow gets going* (1928)
3 *Sparrow in search of fame* (1935)

Sparrow series
Murphy, Christopher
1 *Scream at the sea* (1981)
2 *I, said the Sparrow* (1984)

Sparrowhawk series
Easton, Thomas Atwood
1 *Sparrowhawk* (1990)
2 *Greenhouse* (1991)

Sparrows series
Brown, Roy
1 *Flight of sparrows* (1972)
2 *White sparrow* (1974)

Spartan series
Pournelle, Jerry
1 *Go tell the Spartans* (1991)
2 *Prince of Sparta* (1993)

Sparton series
Johnson, Ruth Ingrid
see **Joy Sparton series**

Spayed series
Singer, Marilyn
see **Samantha Spayed series**

Speak for me series
Graeber, Charlotte Towner
1 *Jonah, speak for God* (1986)
2 *Moses, speak for me* (1986)
3 *Paul, speak for me* (1986)
4 *Peter, speak for me* (1986)

Spear series
Cunningham, Chet
see **Agent Brad Spear series**

Speare and Cole series
Davis, Frederick Clyde
see **Schyler Cole and Luke Speare series**

Spearlake children series
Green, Roger Lancelyn
1 *Wonderful stranger* (1950)
A holiday romance
2 *Luck of the Lynns* (1952)
3 *Theft of the golden cat* (1955)

Spearman series
Jevons, Marshall
see **Henry Spearman series**

Spearpoint series
Arthur, Frank
see **Inspector Spearpoint series**

Spears series
Gielgud, Val
see **Inspector Simon Spears series**

Special Air Service series
Farran, Roy
1 *Winged dagger* (1948)
2 *Operation Tombola* (1960)

Special Air Service series
Strong, Terence
1 *Whisper who dares* (1982)
2 *Fifth hostage* (1983)

Special Boat Service trilogy
Fullerton, Alexander
1 *Special deliverance* (1986)
2 *Special dynamic* (1987)
3 *Special deception* (1988)

Special Branch series
Lilley, Tom
see **Police Special Branch series**

Special Operations Executive series
Crisp, Jack H
1 *Dragon spoor* (1978)
2 *Final act* (1978)

Special relationships series
Wheeler-Bennett, John
1 *Knaves, fools and heroes* (1974)
In Europe between the wars
2 *Special relationships* (1975)
America in peace and war

Special Squad series
Franklin, Donald
1 *Velvet hammer* (1974)
2 *Two-way witness* (1974)
3 *Lethal playground* (1975)

Specialist series
Cutter, John
1 *Talent for revenge* (1984)
2 *Manhattan revenge* (1984)
3 *Sullivan's revenge* (1984)
4 *Psycho soldiers* (1984)
5 *Maltese vengeance* (1984)
6 *Big one* (1984)
7 *Vendetta* (1985)
8 *One-man army* (1985)
9 *Vengeance mountain* (1985)
10 *Beirut retaliation* (1985)
11 *American vengeance* (1985)

Specialist series
Lecale, Errol
1 *Tigerman of Terrahpur* (1973)
2 *Castledoom* (1974)
3 *Severed hand* (1974)
4 *Death box* (1974)
5 *Zombie* (1975)
6 *Blood of my blood* (1975)

Speckled panic series
Townson, Hazel
1 *Speckled panic* (1982)
2 *Choking peril* (1985)
One volume edition entitled *The school book fair*, 1993

Specs McCann series
McNeill, Janet
1 *My friend Specs McCann* (1955)
2 *Specs fortissimo* (1958)
3 *Various Specs* (1961)
Omnibus volume: *Best Specs, his most remarkable adventures*, 1970

Spector trilogy
Strasser, Todd
see **Coming attractions trilogy**

Spectros series
Winters, Logan
1 *Silverado* (1981)
2 *Hunt the beast down* (1981)
3 *Natchez* (1981)
4 *Silver canyon* (1981)

Speed Johnson series
Savage, Buck
1 *Lariats of death* (1950)
2 *Riders of the Renegade* (1951)
3 *Destiny trail* (1951)
4 *Herds of Lampasa* (1952)
5 *Pecos plainsmen* (1953)
6 *Call of the canyon* (1953)

Speed series
Donovan, Jean Beradine
see **Bill Speed series**
Elliott, George
see **Martin Speed series**
Starnes, Richard
see **Maxwell Speed series**

Speedwell boys series
Rockwood, Roy
House pseudonym
1 *Speedwell boys on motorcycles* (1913)
Alternative title: The mystery of a great conflagration
2 *Speedwell boys and their racing auto* (1913)
Alternative title: A run for the golden cup
3 *Speedwell boys and their power launch* (1913)
Alternative title: To the rescue of the castaways
4 *Speedwell boys in a submarine* (1913)
Alternative title: The treasure of Rocky Cove
5 *Speedwell boys and their ice racer* (1915)
Alternative title: Lost in the great blizzard

Speedy series
Hamilton, Esme
1 *Speedy* (1940)
2 *Rainbow and Speedy* (1952)
3 *Starlight* (1956)
4 *Children at Moyinish* (1957)

Speer series
Tracy, Don
see **Giff Speer series**

Spelljammer series
This sequence has two authors
Cook, David
1 *Beyond the moons* (1991)
Findley, Nigel
2 *Into the void* (1991)

Spellsinger series
Foster, Alan Dean
1 *Spellsinger* (1983)
2 *Hour of the gate* (1984)
Numbers 1 and 2 also published in one volume entitled *Spellsinger at the gate*, 1983
3 *Day of the dissonance* (1984)
Numbers 1-3 also published in one volume entitled *Season of the Spellsing*, 1985
4 *Moment of the magician* (1984)
5 *Paths of the perambulator* (1985)
6 *Time of the transference* (1986)
Numbers 4-6 also published in one volume entitled *Spellsinger's scherzo*, 1987
7 *Son of Spellsinger* (1993)

Spence and Franklin series
Jenkins, Jerry Bruce
see **Margo Franklin and Philip Spence series**

Spence series
Allen, Michael
see **Superintendent Ben Spence series**

Spencer family series
Hamner, Earl
1 *Spencer's Mountain* (1961)
2 *Homecoming* (1970)

Spencer family series
Mason, Henrietta
1 *Fool's gold* (1960)
2 *Our hills cry woe* (1963)

Spencer Monroe Savage series
Theroux, Paul
Short stories
1 *Consul's file* (1977)
2 *London Embassy* (1982)

Spencer series
Beeby, Otto
see **Tony Spencer series**
Cresswell, Helen
see **Jumbo Spencer series**
Smith, Lou
see **John Spencer series**
Winski, Norman
see **Dirk Spencer series**

Spenlove series
McFee, William
1 *Harbourmaster* (1932)
2 *Beachcomber* (1935)
3 *Derelicts* (1939)
4 *Spenlove in Arcady* (1942)
5 *Family trouble* (1949)
6 *Adopted* (1952)

Spenser series
Parker, Robert Brown
1 *Godwulf manuscript* (1973)
2 *God save the child* (1974)
3 *Mortal stakes* (1975)
4 *Promised land* (1976)
5 *Judas goat* (1978)
6 *Looking for Rachel Wallace* (1980)
7 *Early autumn* (1981)
8 *Savage place* (1981)
9 *Ceremony* (1982)
10 *Widening gyre* (1983)
11 *Valediction* (1984)
12 *Catskill eagle* (1985)
13 *Taming a sea-horse* (1986)
14 *Pale kings and princes* (1987)
15 *Crimson joy* (1988)
16 *Playmates* (1989)
17 *Stardust* (1990)
18 *Pastime* (1991)
19 *Double deuce* (1992)
20 *Paper doll* (1993)
21 *Walking shadow* (1994)

Spice Islands series
Lofts, Norah
1 *Silver nutmeg* (1947)
2 *Scent of cloves* (1957)

Spicer series
Danvers, Milton
see **Robert Spicer series**

Spider and moonlight trilogy
Tabori, Paul
1 *Two forests* (1944)
2 *Uneasy giant* (1949)
3 *Heritage of mercy* (1949)

Spider Scott series
Royce, Kenneth
1 *XYY man* (1970)
2 *Concrete boot* (1971)
3 *Miniature frame* (1972)
4 *Spider underground* (1973)
Masterpiece affair
5 *Trap Spider* (1974)
6 *Woodcutter operation* (1975)
7 *Crypto man* (1984)
8 *Mosley receipt* (1985)

Spider series
Edwards, Pat
see **Sadie Spider series**

Spider series
Gear, William Michael
1 *Artifact* (1990)
2 *Warriors of Spider* (1988)
3 *Way of Spider* (1989)
4 *Web of Spider* (1989)

Spider series
Kraus, Robert
1 *Trouble with Spider* (1962)
2 *How Spider saved Christmas* (1970)
3 *How Spider saved Turkey* (1981)
4 *How Spider saved Valentine's Day* (1986)
5 *Spider's first day at school* (1987)
6 *Spider's home town* (1988)
7 *How Spider saved the baseball game* (1989)
8 *Spider's baby-sitting job* (1990)
9 *Spider's draw-a-long book* (1990)

Spider series
McCulley, Johnston
1 *Spider's den* (1925)
2 *Spider's debt* (1930)
3 *Spider's fury* (1930)

Spider series
Scott, Reginald Thomas Maitland
see **Richard Wentworth series**

Spider Stockwell series
Holden, J Railton
1 *Death flies high* (1935)
2 *Spider flies again* (1937)

Spider world series
Wilson, Colin
1 *Tower* (1987)
1.1 *Desert* (1987)
1.2 *Tower* (1987)
1.3 *Fortress* (1987)
2 *Delta* (1987)

Spiderman series
Wein, Len
see **Amazing Spiderman series**

Spike Jones series
Nickson, Arthur
see **Rusty Himes series**

Spike Russell series
Tunis, John Roberts
1 *Keystone Kids* (1943)
2 *Rookie of the year* (1944)

Spike Tracy series
Ashbrook, Harriette
see **Philip Tracy series**

Spindle Bottom series
Allan, Mabel Esther
1 *Secret of Spindle Bottom* (1984)
2 *Mystery in Spindle Bottom* (1986)

Spinnet series
Soutar, Andrew
see **Phineas Spinnet series**

Spiral ascent trilogy
Upward, Edward
see **Alan Sebrill trilogy**

Spirit and faith series
Urquhart, Colin
Autobiography
1 *When the Spirit comes* (1974)
2 *Faith for the future* (1982)

Spirit and the flesh series
Buck, Pearl Sydenstricker
1 *Exile* (1936)
Biography of the author's mother
2 *Fighting angel* (1937)
Biography of the author's father
One volume edition entitled *The spirit and the flesh*, 1944

Spirit of America series
Whited, Charles
1 *Challenge* (1982)
2 *Destiny* (1982)

Spiritual history of Great Britain trilogy
Bowen, Marjorie
1 *God and the wedding dress* (1938)
2 *Mister Tyler's saints* (1939)
3 *Circle in the water* (1939)

Spiritual life series
Bernanos, Georges
1 *Star of Satan* (1926)
Under the sun of Satan
Original edition entitled Sous le soleil de Satan
2 *[Imposture]* (1927)
No English edition
3 *Joy* (1929)
Original edition entitled *La joie*
4 *Diary of a country priest* (1936)
Original edition entitled *Journal d'un cure de campagne*

Spiritualism series
Davis, Andrew Jackson
Autobiography of a spiritualist
1 *Magic staff* (1857)
2 *Beyond the valley* (1885)

Spitznagle series
Wahl, Jan
see **Melvin Spitznagle series**

Spiv series
Worby, John
Autobiography
1 *Other half* (1938)
2 *Spiv's progress* (1939)

Spoils of war series
This sequence has two authors; based on a television series
Finch, John
1 *Flesh and blood* (1980)
Miles, Keith
2 *Spoils of war* (1980)

Spook series
Sandberg, Inger
see **Little Spook series**

Spooky series
Carlson, Natalie Savage
1 *Spooky night* (1982)
2 *Spooky and the ghost cat* (1985)
3 *Spooky and the wizard's bats* (1986)
4 *Spooky and the bad luck raven* (1988)
5 *Spooky and the witch's goat* (1989)

Spoon River series
Masters, Edgar Lee
Poetry
1 *Spoon River anthology* (1915)
Enlarged edition 1916; originally published in *Reedy's mirror*, under the pseudonym Webster Ford
2 *New Spoon River* (1924)
Companion volume: *Across Spoon River*, autobiography, 1936

Sport series
Resnicow, Herbert
1 *Murder at the Superbowl* (1986)
Co-author: Fran Tarkenton
2 *Bean ball* (1989)
Co-author: Tom Seaver
3 *World Cup murder* (1989)
Co-author: Pele

Sporting stories series
G, G
1 *Sporting stories and sketches* (1895)
2 *New sporting stories* (1896)

Sports acheivers series
Aaseng, Nathan
1 *Bruce Jenner, decathlon winner* (1979)
2 *Eric Heiden, winner in gold* (1980)
3 *Pete Rose, baseball's Charlie Hustle* (1981)
4 *Steve Carlton, baseball's silent strongman* (1984)
5 *Carl Lewis, legend chaser* (1985)
6 *Dwight Gooden, strikout king* (1988)
7 *Florence Griffith Joyner, dazzling Olympian* (1989)
8 *Jose Canseco, baseball's forty-four man* (1989)

Sports fields series
Kostlanetz, Richard
Poems
1 *Turfs-arenas-fields-pitches* (1980)
2 *Arenas-fields-pitches-turfs* (1982)
3 *Fields-pitches-turfs-arenas* (1990)

Sports for me series
Moran, Tom
1 *Roller skating is for me* (1981)
2 *BMX is for me* (1982)
3 *Frisbee disc flying is for me* (1982)
4 *Kite flying is for me* (1984)
5 *Canoeing is for me* (1984)

Sports heroes series
Aaseng, Nathan
1 *Football's fierce defenses* (1980)
2 *Basketball's high flyers* (1980)
3 *Little giants of pro sports* (1980)
4 *Winners never quit* (1980)
Athletes who beat the odds
5 *Baseball's finest pitchers* (1980)
6 *Football's winning quarterbacks* (1980)
7 *Football's breakaway backs* (1980)
8 *Football's sure-handed receivers* (1980)
9 *Winnin men of tennis* (1981)
10 *Winnin women of tennis* (1981)
11 *Track's magnificent milers* (1981)
12 *Football's cunning coaches* (1981)
13 *Football's steadiest kickers* (1981)
14 *Football's toughest tight ends* (1981)
15 *Football's super bowl champions, I-VIII* (1982)
16 *Football's super bowl champions, IX-XVI* (1982)
17 *Football's crushing blockers* (1982)
18 *World-class marathoners* (1982)
19 *Memorable World Series moments* (1982)
20 *Baseball's brilliant managers* (1982)
21 *Superstars stopped short* (1982)
22 *Baseball's hottest hitters* (1983)
23 *Basketball's sharpshooters* (1983)
24 *Supersubs of pro sports* (1983)
25 *Football's hardhitting linebackers* (1983)
26 *Baseball's power hitters* (1983)
27 *Basketball's playmakers* (1983)
28 *Comeback stars of pro sports* (1983)
29 *Baseball's ace relief pitchers* (1984)
30 *Football's daring defensive backs* (1984)
31 *Football's punishing pass rushers* (1984)
32 *Hockey's fearless goalies* (1984)
33 *Hockey super scorers* (1984)
34 *Basketball's power players* (1985)
35 *Decade of champions* (1991)
Alternative title: Super bowls, XVI-XXIV

Sports on the light side series
Paulsen, Gary
1 *Dribbling, shooting and scoring, sometimes* (1976)
2 *Hitting, pitching and running, maybe* (1976)
3 *Tackling, running and kicking, now and again* (1977)
4 *Riding, roping and bulldogging, almost* (1977)
5 *Running, jumping and throwing, if you can* (1978)
Athletics
The second title is a revised edition with Roger Barrett
6 *Forehanding and backhanding, if you're lucky* (1978)
Tennis
The second title is a revised edition with Roger Barrett
7 *Downhill, hotdogging and cross-country, if the snow isn't sticky* (1979)
Skiing
The second title is a revised edition with Roger Barrett
8 *Facing off, checking and goaltending, perhaps* (1979)
Revised edition with Roger Barrett, 1980
9 *Going very fast in a circle, if you don't run out of gas* (1979)
10 *Launching, floating high and landing, if your pilot light doesn't go out* (1979)
11 *Pummeling, falling and getting up, sometimes* (1979)
12 *Track, enduro and motorcross, unless you fall over* (1979)

Sports series
Hopgood, Alan
Three act plays
1 *And the big men fly* (1969)
2 *And here comes, Bucknuckle* (1980)
The story of a racehorse

Sports talk series
Aaseng, Nathan
1 *Baseball's greatest teams* (1986)
2 *Baseball's worst teams* (1986)
3 *Football's most controversial calls* (1986)
4 *Football's most shocking upsets* (1986)
5 *Pro sports' greatest rivalries* (1986)
6 *Record breakers of pro sports* (1987)
7 *Ultramarthons* (1987)
The world's most punishing races
8 *College football's hottest rivalries* (1987)
9 *Football's incredible hulks* (1987)
10 *Great summer Olympic moments* (1990)
11 *Great winter Olympic moments* (1990)

Spot series
Hill, Eric
1 *Where's Spot* (1980)
2 *Spot's first walk* (1981)
3 *Spot's birthday party* (1982)
4 *Puppy love* (1982)
5 *Spot's busy year* (1983)
6 *Spot's first Christmas* (1983)
7 *Spot learns to count* (1983)
8 *Spot tells the time* (1983)
9 *Spot's alphabet* (1983)
10 *Sweet dreams, Spot* (1984)
11 *Spot's friends* (1984)
12 *Spot's toys* (1984)
13 *Here's Spot* (1984)
14 *Spot goes splash!* (1984)
15 *Spot goes to school* (1984)
16 *Spot on the farm* (1985)
17 *Spot goes to the beach* (1985)
18 *Spot at play* (1985)
19 *Spot at the fair* (1985)
20 *Spot goes to the circus* (1986)
21 *Spot's first words* (1986)
22 *Spot's doghouse* (1986)
23 *Spot looks at colors* (1986)
24 *Spot looks at shapes* (1986)
25 *Spot goes to the farm* (1987)
26 *Spot's first picnic* (1987)
27 *Spot visits the hospital* (1987)
28 *Spot's big book of words* (1988)
29 *Spot's first Easter* (1988)
30 *Spot counts from one to ten* (1989)
31 *Spot looks at opposites* (1989)
32 *Spot looks at the weather* (1989)
33 *Spot's baby sister* (1989)
34 *Spot sleeps over* (1990)
35 *Spot goes to the park* (1991)
36 *Spot in the garden* (1991)
37 *Spot's toy box* (1991)
38 *Spot at home* (1991)
39 *Spot counts from one to ten* (1989)
40 *Spot goes to a party* (1993)
Companion volume: *My very own Spot book, a special book to fill in and keep*, 1993

Spotlight Detective Club series
This sequence has three authors
Heide, Florence Parry
1 *Mystery of the missing suitcase* (1972)
2 *Mystery of the silver tag* (1972)
3 *Hidden box mystery* (1973)
4 *Mystery at MacAdoo Zoo* (1973)
5 *Mystery of the whispering voice* (1974)
6 *Mystery of the melting snowman* (1974)
7 *Mystery of the vanishing visitor* (1975)
8 *Mystery of the bewitched bookmobile* (1975)

9 *Mystery of the lonely lantern* (1976)
10 *Mystery at Keyhole carnival* (1977)
11 *Mystery of the midnight message* (1977)
12 *Brillstone mystery* (1977)
13 *Mystery at Southport Cinema* (1978)
14 *Mystery of the mummy's mask* (1979)
15 *Mystery of the Forgotten Island* (1979)
16 *Mystery on Danger Road* (1983)

Spot's dogs series
Wild, Robin
1 *Spot's dogs and the alley cats* (1979)
2 *Spot's dogs and the kidnappers* (1981)

Spots of time series
Willey, Basil
Autobiography
1 *Spots of time, 1897-1920* (1965)
2 *Cambridge and other memories, 1920-1953* (1968)

Spotswood family series
Dos Passos, John
1 *Adventures of a young man* (1939)
2 *Number One* (1943)
3 *Grand design* (1949)
One volume edition entitled *District of Columbia*, 1952

Spotted Moon series
Yarbro, Chelsea Quinn
see **Charlie Spotted Moon series**

Spraggue series
Barnes, Linda
see **Michael Spraggue series**

Spratt and Hallam series
Douglas, George
see **Inspector Hallam and Sergeant Spratt series**

Spring and Glendower series
Arnold, Margot
see **Penelope Spring and Sir Tobias Glendower series**

Spring Haven series
Hatcher, Robin Lee
1 *Stormy surrender* (1984)
2 *Heart's landing* (1984)
3 *Heart storm* (1986)

Spring series
Kains, Josephine
see **Terry Spring series**

Springdale series
Bruce, Dorita Fairlie
1 *New house-captain* (1928)
2 *Best house in the school* (1930)
3 *Captain of Springdale* (1932)
4 *New house at Springdale* (1934)
5 *Prefects at Springdale* (1938)
6 *Captain Anne* (1939)

Springfield series
Sandys, James
see **Mister Springfield series**

Sprockets trilogy
Key, Alexander
1 *Sprockets, a little robot* (1963)
2 *Rivets and Sprockets* (1964)
3 *Bolts, a robot dog* (1966)

Sprout series
Wayne, Jenifer
1 *Sprout* (1970)
2 *Sprout's window-cleaner* (1971)
3 *Sprout and the dogsitter* (1972)
4 *Sprout and the helicopter* (1974)
5 *Sprout and the conjuror* (1976)
Sprout and the magician

Spud Tamson series
Campbell, R W
1 *Private Spud Tamson* (1915)
2 *Sergeant Spuds Tamson, V.C.* (1918)
3 *Spud Tamson out west* (1924)
4 *Spud Tamson's pit* (1926)

Spur McCoy giant series
Fletcher, Dirk
1 *Mint perfect madam* (1990)
2 *Denver darlin'* (1991)
3 *High Plains princess* (1992)
4 *Klondike cutie* (1993)
5 *Wilderness wanton* (1994)

Spur McCoy series
Fletcher, Dirk
1 *High Plains temptress* (1982)
2 *Arizona fancy lady* (1982)
3 *Saint Louis Jezebel* (1983)
4 *Rocky Mountain vamp* (1982)
5 *Wyoming wench* (1984)
6 *Texas tart* (1984)
7 *San Francisco strumpet* (1984)
8 *Montana minx* (1984)
9 *Cathouse kitten* (1984)
10 *Indian maid* (1984)
11 *Nebraska nymph* (1985)
12 *Gold train tramp* (1985)
13 *Red Rock redhead* (1985)
14 *Savage sisters* (1986)
15 *Hang Spur McCoy* (1986)
16 *Rawhider's woman* (1986)
17 *Saloon girl* (1986)
18 *Missouri madam* (1986)
19 *Helena Hellion* (1986)
20 *Colorado cutie* (1987)
21 *Texas tease* (1987)
22 *Dakota doxy* (1987)
23 *San Diego sirens* (1987)
24 *Dodge City doll* (1988)
25 *Laramie lovers* (1988)
26 *Bodie beauties* (1988)
27 *Frisco foxes* (1988)
28 *Kansas City chorine* (1988)
29 *Plains paramour* (1989)
30 *Boise belle* (1989)
31 *Portland pussycat* (1989)
32 *Miner's moll* (1990)
33 *Louisiana lass* (1990)
34 *Deadridge doll* (1991)
35 *Wyoming wildcat* (1992)
36 *Mountain madam* (1992)
37 *Missouri mama* (1992)
38 *Free press filly* (1993)
39 *Minetown mistress* (1993)
40 *Texas tramp* (1993)
41 *Gold ledge gold* (1994)

Spur McCoy special series
Fletcher, Dirk
1 *Phoenix filly* (1987)
2 *Tall timber trollop* (1989)
3 *Mint perfect madam* (1990)
4 *Denver darlin'* (1991)
5 *High Plains princess* (1992)

Spur series
James, Cy
see **Sam Spur series**

Spurs series
Holland, Julian
see **Tottenham Hotspur Football Club series**

Spy series
Emery, Anne
1 *Spy in old Philadelphia* (1958)
2 *Spy in old New Orleans* (1960)
3 *Spy in old New Detroit* (1963)
4 *Spy in old New West Point* (1965)

Spymaster series
Whiting, Charles
1 *Wolf hunt* (1976)
2 *Double cross* (1977)

Squadron series
Holden, Matthew
1 *Sons of the morning* (1978)
2 *Sun climbs slowly* (1978)
3 *Scramble Dieppe* (1980)
4 *Desert Spitfire* (1980)
5 *Whirlwind at Arromanches* (1981)

Squanderbug series
Fisher, Aileen
Plays
1 *Squanderbug's Christmas carol* (1943)
Based on *Christmas carol*, by Charles Dickens
2 *Squanderbug's Mother Goose* (1944)

Squanto series
Bulla, Clyde Robert
1 *Squanto, friend of the white men* (1954)
Squanto, friend of the Pilgrims
2 *John Billington, friend of Squanto* (1956)

Square of sky trilogy
David, Janina
1 *Square of sky* (1964)
2 *Touch of earth* (1966)
3 *Part of the main* (1969)

Squaw Man series
This sequence has two authors
Faversham, Julie Opp
1 *Squaw Man* (1906)
Royle, Edwin Milton
2 *Silent call* (1910)

Squeaky series
Silly, E S
1 *Squeaky* (1982)
2 *Squeaky' one man band* (1982)

Squed series
Miller, Richard
1 *Squed* (1989)
2 *Sowboy* (1991)

Squire quartet
Aldiss, Brian Wilson
1 *Life in the West* (1980)
2 *Forgotten life* (1988)
3 *Remembrance day* (1993)
4 *Somewhere east of life* (1994)

Squire's daughter series
Lillie, Lucy Cecil
1 *Squire's daughter* (1891)
2 *For honour's sake* (1891)

Squirrel series
Judson, Clara Ingram
see **Foxy Squirrel series**
Wyatt, Woodrow Lyle
see **Mister Saucy Squirrel series**

Squirrel's Island series
Trevor, Elleston
1 *Island in the pines* (1948)
2 *Squirrel's Island* (1963)

SS Stuka Squadron series
Kessler, Leo
1 *Black knights* (1983)
2 *Hawks of death* (1983)
3 *Tank-busters!* (1984)
4 *Blood mission* (1984)

Stable series
Collier, James Lincoln
see **George Stable series**

Stacey Gordon series
Shiplett, June Lund
1 *Journey to yesterday* (1979)
2 *Return to yesterday* (1983)

Staceys of Feathergrant series
Kenyon, Theda
1 *Golden feather* (1944)
2 *Dark root* (1946)

Stachel series
Hunter, Jack Dayton
see **Blue Max series**

Stack series
Fields, Frank
see **Ellis Stack series**

Stacy and Katie Rose Belford series
Weber, Lenora Mattingly
1 *Don't call me Katie Rose* (1964)
2 *Winds of March* (1965)
3 *New and different summer* (1966)
4 *I met a boy I used to know* (1967)
5 *Angel in heavy shoes* (1968)
6 *How long is always?* (1970)
7 *Hello, my love, goodbye* (1971)
8 *Sometimes a stranger* (1972)

Stacy series
Diamond, Graham
1 *Lady of the Haven* (1978)
2 *Dungeons of Kuba* (1979)
3 *Falcon of Eden* (1980)
4 *Beasts of Hades* (1981)

Stafford family trilogy
Mather, Berkely
1 *Pagoda tree* (1979)
2 *Midnight gun* (1981)
3 *Hour of the Dog* (1982)

Stafford series
Bagley, Desmond
see **Max Stafford series**

Staffordshire characters series
Godwin, John
1 *Staffordshire characters* (1982)
2 *More Staffordshire characters* (1983)

Stage coach station series
Mitchum, Hank
House pseudonym
1 *Dodge City* (1982)
2 *Laredo* (1982)
3 *Cheyenne* (1982)
4 *Tombstone* (1982)
5 *Virginia City* (1983)
6 *Santa Fe* (1983)
7 *Seattle* (1983)
8 *Fort Yuma* (1983)
9 *Sonora* (1983)
10 *Abilene* (1984)
11 *Deadwood* (1984)
12 *Tucson* (1984)
13 *Carson City* (1984)
14 *Cimarron* (1984)
15 *Wichita* (1984)
16 *Mojave* (1985)
17 *Durango* (1985)
18 *Casa Grande* (1985)
19 *Last chance* (1985)
20 *Leadville* (1985)
21 *Fargo* (1985)
22 *Devil's Canyon* (1986)
23 *El Paso* (1986)
24 *Mesa Verde* (1986)
25 *San Antonio* (1986)
26 *Tulsa* (1986)
27 *Pecos* (1986)
28 *Medicine Bow* (1987)
29 *Panhandle* (1987)
30 *Rawhide* (1987)
31 *Royal Coach* (1987)
32 *Taos* (1987)
33 *Death Valley* (1988)
34 *Deadman Butte* (1988)
35 *Bonanza City* (1988)
36 *Casper* (1988)
37 *Shawnee* (1988)
38 *Grand Teton* (1988)
39 *Fort Verde* (1989)

Stage coach station series

40 *Silverado* (1989)
41 *Red Buffalo* (1989)
42 *Fort Davis* (1989)
43 *Apache junction* (1989)
44 *Socorro* (1989)
45 *Presidio* (1990)
46 *North Platte* (1990)
47 *Huarez* (1990)
48 *Buffalo Station* (1990)
49 *Gila Bend* (1990)
50 *Buckskin Pass* (1990)
51 *Wild West* (1991)
52 *Last frontier* (1991)

Stahl series
Beresford, John Davys
see **Jacob Stahl series**
Kessler, Leo
see **Otto Stahl series**

Stainless steel rat series
Harrison, Harry
see **Jim Di Griz series**

Staircase in Surrey pentalogy
Stewart, John Innes Mackintosh
see **Duncan Pattullo series**

Stairey series
Dick, Kay
see **Robert Stairey series**

Stairway to forever series
Adams, Robert
1 *Stairway to forever* (1988)
2 *Monsters and magicians* (1989)

Stalingrad series
Konsalik, Heinz Gunther
1 *Naked earth* (1956)
Doctor of Stalingrad
Original edition entitled *Der Arzt von Stalingrad*
2 *Battalion 999* (1959)
Straf Batalion 999
Original edition entitled *Strafbattalion 999*

Stalker family trilogy
Stirling, Jessica
1 *Spoiled earth* (1974)
Strathmore
2 *Hiring fair* (1976)
Call home the heart
3 *Dark pasture* (1977)

Stalker series
Hunter, Neil
see **Bodie the Stalker series**

Stallard and Godwin series
Beare, George
see **Vincent Stallard and Cynthia Godwin series**

Stamford series
Sancha, Sheila
1 *Walter Dragun's town* (1987)
Trade in Stamford in the thirteenth century
2 *Luttrell Village* (1982)
Country life in the early fourteenth century

Standish series
Amis, Kingsley
see **Patrick Standish series**
Horler, Sydney
see **Tiger Standish series**
Sapper
see **Ronald Standish series**

Standish series
Westerman, Percy Francis
1 *Standish of the Air Police* (1935)
2 *Standish gets his man* (1938)
3 *Standish loses his man* (1939)
4 *Standish pulls it off* (1940)
5 *Standish holds on* (1941)

Stanfield series
Jones, Adrienne
see **Margery Stanfield series**

Stanislaus family series
Ferra-Mikura, Vera
1 *Voyagers* (1966)
2 *Painters* (1967)
Original edition entitled Unsere drei Stanislause

Stanislaus Priest trilogy
O'Riordan, Conal
1 *Age of miracles* (1923)
2 *Rowena Barnes* (1923)
3 *Young Lady Dazencourt* (1926)
A discovery

Stanley Bagshaw series
Wilson, Bob
1 *Stanley Bagshaw and the fourteen foot wheel* (1981)
2 *Stanley Bagshaw and the twenty-two ton whale* (1983)
3 *Stanley Bagshaw and the Mafeking Square cheese robbery* (1985)
4 *Stanley Bagshaw and the short-sighted football trainer* (1986)
5 *Stanley Bagshaw and the rather dangerous miracle cure* (1987)

Stanley Bass series
Anthony, David
1 *Organization* (1970)
2 *Stud game* (1977)

Stanley Delphond series
Halliday, Fred
1 *Chocolate mousse murders* (1974)
2 *Raspberry tart affair* (1976)
3 *Case of indelicate champagne* (1976)
Slight case of champagne
Murder in the kitchen

Stanley family series
Snyder, Zilpha Keatley
1 *Headless Cupid* (1971)
2 *Famous Stanley kidnapping case* (1979)
3 *Blair's nightmare* (1984)
4 *Janie's private eyes* (1989)

Stanley Fyles series
Cullum, Ridgwell
see **Inspector Stanley Fyles series**

Stanley Hastings series
Hall, Parnell
1 *Detective* (1987)
2 *Murder* (1988)
3 *Favor* (1988)
4 *Strangler* (1989)
5 *Client* (1990)
6 *Juror* (1990)
7 *Shot* (1991)
8 *Actor* (1993)
9 *Blackmail* (1994)
10 *Movie* (1995)

Stanley Lambchops series
Brown, Jeff
1 *Flat Stanley* (1964)
Revised edition 1974
2 *Lamb for the Lambchops* (1985)

Stanley Moodrow series
Solomita, Stephen
1 *Twist of the knife* (1988)
2 *Force of nature* (1989)
3 *Forced entry* (1990)
4 *Bad to the bone* (1991)
5 *Piece of the action* (1992)

Stanley series
Edwards, Pat
1 *Have you seen Stanley?* (1987)
2 *Go away Stanley* (1987)
3 *Stanley goes to school* (1987)
4 *Lonely Stanley* (1987)
5 *Mind the house, Stanley* (1987)

Stanley Windrush series
Hackney, Alan
1 *Private's progress* (1954)
2 *Private life* (1958)
I'm all right Jack
3 *Let's keep religion out of this!* (1963)
4 *Whatever turns you on, Jack* (1972)

Stannard series
Hershatter, Richard Lawrence
see **Rand Stannard series**

Stanton and Curwen series
Vickers, Roy
see **Inspector Peter Curwen and Hugh Stanton series**

Stanton Empire series
Blackburn, Thomas Wakefield
1 *Yanqui* (1973)
2 *Ranchero* (1974)
3 *El Segundo* (1974)
4 *Patron* (1976)
5 *Companeros* (1978)

Stanton series
Clews, Roy
see **Jethro Stanton series**

Stanton's series
Little, Sylvia
1 *Stanton's comes of age* (1947)
2 *Stanton's pulls it off* (1948)
3 *Masquerade at Stanton's* (1951)

Star challenge series
Black, Christopher
1 *Planets in peril* (1984)
2 *Android invasion* (1984)
3 *Cosmic funhouse* (1984)
4 *Exploding suns* (1984)
5 *Galactic raiders* (1984)
6 *Weird zone* (1984)
7 *Dimension of doom* (1985)
8 *Lost planet* (1985)
9 *Moons of mystery* (1985)
10 *Haunted planet* (1985)

Star colony series
This sequence has two authors
Laumer, Keith
1 *Star colony* (1981)
Denning, Troy
2 *Omega rebellion* (1987)
Combat Command in the world of Keith Laumer's *Star colony*, 1981

Star commandos series
Griffin, Pauline Margaret
1 *Star commandos* (1986)
2 *Colony in peril* (1987)
3 *Mission underground* (1988)
4 *Death planet* (1989)
5 *Mind slaver* (1990)
6 *Return to war* (1990)
7 *Fire planet* (1990)
8 *Jungle assault* (1991)
9 *Call to arms* (1991)

Star fall series
Bischoff, David
1 *Star fall* (1980)
2 *Star spring* (1982)

Star Hawks series
Dalton, Sean
see **Operation Star Hawks series**

Star Hawks series
Goulart, Ron
1 *Empire 99* (1980)
2 *Cyborg king* (1981)

Star hounds series
Bischoff, David
1 *Infinite battle* (1985)
2 *Galactic warriors* (1985)
3 *Macrocosmic conflict* (1986)

Star Island trilogy
Hall, Margery
1 *Star Island* (1953)
2 *Star Island again* (1955)
3 *Three stars for Star Island* (1958)

Star Jam Pack trilogy
Earnshaw, Brian
1 *Starclipper and the song wars* (1985)
2 *Starclipper and the snowstone* (1986)
3 *Starclipper and the galactic final* (1987)

Star Ka'at series
Norton, Andre
1 *Star Ka'at* (1976)
2 *Star Ka'at world* (1978)
3 *Star Ka'ats and the plant world* (1979)
4 *Star Ka'ats and the winged warriors* (1981)

Star Kings series
Hamilton, Edmond
see **John Gordon series**

Star lords series
Buffery, Judith
1 *Sheeg* (1979)
2 *Saffron* (1979)
3 *Iron clog* (1979)
4 *Gringol weed* (1980)

Star Man series
Byrne, Stuart James
1 *Star Man 1* (1979)
Contains *Superman of Alpha, Time window, Interstellar mutineers, Cosmium raiders, World changer*
2 *Star Man 2* (1979)
Contains *The slaves of Venus, Lost in the Milky Way, Time trap, The centurians, The emperor, The return of Star Man*
One volume edition entitled *Star Man*, 1969

Star of the guardians series
Weis, Margaret
1 *Lost king* (1990)
2 *King's test* (1990)
3 *King's sacrifice* (1991)

Star Pilot Grainger series
Stableford, Brian Michael
1 *Halcyon drift* (1972)
2 *Rhapsody in black* (1973)
3 *Promised land* (1974)
4 *Paradise game* (1974)
5 *Fenris device* (1974)
6 *Swan song* (1975)

Star pirates trilogy
Elliott, Nathan
1 *Kidnap in space* (1987)
2 *Plague moon* (1987)
3 *Treasure planet* (1987)

Star quest series
Dicks, Terrance
1 *Spacejack!* (1978)
2 *Roboworld* (1979)
3 *Terrorsaur!* (1981)

Star requiem series
Cole, Adrian
1 *Mother of storms* (1989)
2 *Thief of dreams* (1989)
3 *Warlord of Heaven* (1990)
4 *Labyrinth of worlds* (1990)

Star trek fan series
This sequence has thirty one authors
Downs, Gerry
1 *Alternative* (1976)
The epilog to Orion

Lorrah, Jean
2 *Full moon rising* (1976)
3 *Night of the twin moons* (1976)
Clark, Sheila
4 *Enterprise incidents 2* (1977)
Stories
Wright, Meg
5 *As new wine* (1979)
Lorrah, Jean
6 *Epilogue* (1979)
Two volumes
Frisbie, Carol
7 *Night visions* (1979)
Glazer, Mindy
8 *Perfect object* (1979)
Clark, Sheila
9 *Something hidden* (1979)
Coles, Lesley
10 *Tomorrow is another day* (1979)
Mason, Simone
11 *Web of Selagor* (1979)
Piacentini, Valerie
12 *Wheel turns* (1979)
13 *Wine of Calvoro* (1979)
Dexter, Carmen
14 *Beyond shattered illusions* (1980)
Lorrah, Jean
15 *Sarek collection* (1980)
Rose, Pamela
16 *Companion* (1980)
The rest of the story
Clark, Sheila
17 *Wheel of fate* (1980)
Vance, J Emily
18 *Rack* (1981)
Also includes *All the king's horses, all the king's men*
Wright, Meg
19 *Tribe of Jen-Wae* (1981)
Baddeley, Pam
20 *Weaver of dreams* (1981)
Richards, Vicki
21 *Acceptance* (1982)
Welling, Lois
22 *Displaced* (1982)
Wright, Meg
23 *Female of the species is more deadly than the male* (1982)
Richards, Vicki
24 *Home is where the heart is* (1982)
Zuk, Beverly C
25 *Third verdict* (1982)
Stewart, Janet
26 *Time is, time was, time yet to be* (1982)
Inscription on an old sun-dial
Welling, Lois
27 *Transition* (1982)
Dubois, D
28 *T'Zad'U, part 2* (1982)
Wright, Meg
29 *Closer than a brother* (1983)
Welling, Loi
30 *Continuum* (1983)
Jadis, Donna
31 *Reality barrier* (1983)
Clark, Sheila
32 *Something lost* (1983)
Tullock, Joyce
33 *When heroes die* (1983)
A starchild's quest
Hayden, Karen
34 *When the sun shines* (1983)
Pitkethley, Janice
35 *When two worlds collide* (1983)
Coles, Lesley
36 *World of difference* (1983)
Anonymous
37 *Enterprise, log entries 60* (1984)
Baddeley, Pam
38 *Fall of night* (1984)
Viviers, Lyn
39 *Know thine enemy* (1984)
Baddeley, Pam
40 *Mark of Cain* (1984)
Regan, Jackie
41 *Nineteen forty two* (1984)
From starship to Lancaster
Rousch, Catherine E
42 *Stars or dust* (1984)
Schulze, Doris
43 *Friendship and duty* (1985)
Hayden, Karen
44 *Human kind of learning* (1985)
Montgomery, Wendy
45 *Tender expressions* (1985)
Baddeley, Pam
46 *Spinner of nightmares* (1986)
Viviers, Lyn
47 *Blood of others* (1988)
Schulze, Doris
48 *Crystal clear* (1988)
Viviers, Lyn
49 *Fallen angel* (1990)

Star trek moving picture series

This sequence has three authors
Roddenberry, Gene
1 *Star trek* (1979)
2 *Wrath of Khan* (1982)
3 *Search for Spock* (1984)
McIntyre, Vondra Neil
4 *Voyage home* (1986)
Another version of the film entitled *The voyage home*, by Peter Lerangis, 1986
Dillard, Jeanne M
5 *Final frontier* (1989)
Companion volumes: *Star trek log*, 1-10, 1974-1978

Star trek original series

Blish, James
Based on a television series
1 *Star trek* (1967)
Star trek 1
2 *Star trek 2* (1968)
3 *Star trek 3* (1969)
4 *Star trek 4* (1971)
5 *Star trek 5* (1972)
6 *Star trek 6* (1972)
7 *Star trek 7* (1972)
Numbers 5-7 also published in one volume entitled *The star trek reader III*, 1977
8 *Star trek 8* (1972)
Numbers 2, 3, 8 also published in one volume entitled *The Star trek reader*, 1976
9 *Star trek 9* (1973)
Numbers 1, 4, 9 also published in one volume entitled *The star trek reader II*, 1977
10 *Star trek 10* (1974)
11 *Star trek 11* (1975)
Day of the dove
Numbers 10 and 11 and *Spock must die*, 1970, also published in one volume entitled *The star trek reader IV*, 1978
12 *Star trek 12* (1977)
Co-author: Judith Ann Lawrence; selections from Numbers 1-12 published as *Star trek, the classic episodes, 1-3*, 1991
13 *Mudd's angels* (1978)

Star trek originals sequels series

This sequence has thirteen authors; it is a list of works which relate to the original Star trek adventures and, for convenience, are numbered in order of publication
Reynolds, Mack
1 *Mission to Horatius* (1968)
Blish, James
2 *Spock must die!* (1970)
Cogswell, Theodore Rose
3 *Spock, messiah!* (1976)
Culbreath, Myrna
4 *Star trek, the new voyages* (1976)
Haldeman, Joe
5 *Planet of judgment* (1977)
Culbreath, Myrna
6 *Price of the phoenix* (1977)
7 *Star trek, the new voyages 2* (1978)
Eklund, Gordon
8 *Starless world* (1978)
Sky, Kathleen
9 *Vulcan!* (1978)
Eklund, Gordon
10 *Devil world* (1979)
Haldeman, Joe
11 *World without end* (1979)
Culbreath, Myrna
12 *Fate of the phoenix* (1979)
Goldin, Stephen
13 *Trek to madworld* (1979)
Gerrold, David
14 *Galactic whirlpool* (1980)
Haldeman, Jack Carroll
15 *Perry's planet* (1980)
Sky, Kathleen
16 *Death's angel* (1981)

Star trek sequels series

This sequence has eight authors; it is a list of works which relate to the Star trek adventures and, for convenience, are numbered in order of publication
Dillard, Jeanne M
1 *Demons* (1986)
McIntyre, Vondra Neil
2 *Enterprise, the first adventure* (1986)
Morwood, Peter
3 *Romulan way* (1987)
Bonanno, Margaret Wander
4 *Strangers from the sky* (1987)
Carey, Diane
5 *Final frontier* (1988)
Duane, Diane
6 *Spock's world* (1988)
Dillard, Jeanne M
7 *Lost years* (1989)
Reeves-Stevens, Garfield
8 *Prime directive* (1990)

Star trek series

This sequence has forty authors
Roddenberry, Gene
1 *Star trek* (1979)
Based on a moving picture
McIntyre, Vondra Neil
2 *Entropy effect* (1981)
Vardeman, Robert Edward
3 *Klingon gambit* (1981)
Weinstein, Howard
4 *Covenant of the crown* (1981)
Culbreath, Myrna
5 *Prometheus design* (1982)
Correy, Lee
6 *Abode of life* (1982)
McIntyre, Vondra Neil
7 *Wrath of Khan* (1982)
Based on a moving picture
Cooper, Sonni
8 *Black fire* (1983)
Culbreath, Myrna
9 *Triangle* (1983)
Murdock, Melinda Seabrooke
10 *Web of the Romulans* (1983)
Crispin, Ann Carol
11 *Yesterday's son* (1983)
Vardeman, Robert Edward
12 *Mutiny on the Enterprise* (1983)
Duane, Diane
13 *Wounded sky* (1983)
Dvorkin, Daniel
14 *Trellisane confrontation* (1984)
Bear, Greg
15 *Corona* (1984)
Ford, John M
16 *Final reflection* (1984)
McIntyre, Vondra Neil
17 *Search for Spock* (1984)
Based on a moving picture
Duane, Diane
18 *My enemy, my ally* (1984)
Snodgrass, Melinda Marilyn
19 *Tears of the singers* (1984)
Lorrah, Jean
20 *Vulcan academy murders* (1984)
Kagan, Janet
21 *Uhura's song* (1985)
Yep, Laurence Michael
22 *Shadow lord* (1985)
Hambly, Barbara
23 *Ishmael* (1985)
Van Hise, Della
24 *Killing time* (1985)
Bonanno, Margaret Wander
25 *Dwellers in the crucible* (1985)
Larson, Majliss
26 *Pawns and symbols* (1985)
Dillard, Jeanne M
27 *Mindshadow* (1986)
Ferguson, Brad
28 *Crisis on Centaurus* (1986)
Carey, Diane
29 *Dreadnought!* (1986)
Dillard, Jeanne M
30 *Demons* (1986)
Carey, Diane
31 *Battlestations!* (1986)
DeWeese, Gene
32 *Chain of attack* (1987)
Weinstein, Howard
33 *Deep domain* (1987)
Carter, Carmen
34 *Dreams of the raven* (1987)
Duane, Diane
35 *Romulan way* (1987)
Ford, John M
36 *How much for just the planet?* (1987)
Dillard, Jeanne M
37 *Bloodthirst* (1987)
Lorrah, Jean
38 *IDIC epidemic* (1988)
Crispin, Ann Carol
39 *Time for yesterday* (1988)
Dvorkin, David
40 *Timetrap* (1988)
Paul, Barbara
41 *Three-minute universe* (1988)
Reeves-Stevens, Garfield
42 *Memory prime* (1988)
DeWeese, Gene
43 *Final nexus* (1988)
Fontana, Dorothy Catherine
44 *Vulcan's glory* (1989)
Friedman, Michael Jan
45 *Double, double* (1989)
Klass, Judy
46 *Cry of the Onlies* (1989)
Ecklar, Julia
47 *Kobayashi Maru* (1989)
Morwood, Peter
48 *Rules of engagement* (1990)
Clowes, Carolyn
49 *Pandora principle* (1990)
Duane, Diane
50 *Doctor's orders* (1990)
Mitchell, Victoria Estelle
51 *Enemy unseen* (1990)
Kramer, Dana
52 *Home is the hunter* (1990)
Hambly, Barbara
53 *Ghost walker* (1991)
Ferguson, Brad
54 *Flag full of stars* (1991)
DeWeese, Gene
55 *Renegade* (1991)
Friedman, Michael Jan
56 *Legacy* (1991)
David, Peter
57 *Rift* (1991)
Companion volumes: *Star trek, the motion picture peel-off graphics book*, by Lee Cole, 1979, *Star trek speaks*, by Fred Goldstein and others, 1979, *Star trek spaceflight chronology*, by Stan Goldstein, 1980, *The Klingon dictionary*, by Marc Okrand, 1985, *Star trek encyclopaedia, a reference guide to the future*, by Michael Okuda and Denise and Debbie Mirek, 1994; parodies: *Up your asteroid*, by C Everett Cooper, 1977, *The Doctor and the Enterprise*, by Jean Airey, 1986, *Star wreck, the generation gap, the spacy spoof that dares to boldly go where nobody wanted to go before*, by Leah Rewolinski, 1989

Star trek, the next generation sequels series
This sequence has six authors
Gerrold, David
1 *Encounter at Farpoint* (1987)
Johnson, Shane
2 *Mister Scott's guide to Enterprise* (1987)
3 *Worlds of the Federation* (1989)
Lorrah, Jean
4 *Metemorphosis* (1990)
Friedman, Michael Jan
5 *Reunion* (1991)
David, Peter
6 *Vendetta* (1991)
Taylor, Jeri
7 *Unification* (1991)
Companion volumes: *The encyclopedia of Star trek*, by Michael Okuda, 1988, *Star trek, the next generation officer's manual*, by John Terra and Rick Stuart, 1988, *Star trek, the next generation technical manual*, by Michael Okuda, 1991

Star trek, the next generation series
This sequence has fourteen authors
Carey, Diane
1 *Ghost ship* (1988)
DeWeese, Gene
2 *Peacekeepers* (1988)
Carter, Carmen
3 *Children of Hamlin* (1988)
Lorrah, Jean
4 *Survivors* (1989)
David, Peter
5 *Strike zone* (1989)
Weinstein, Howard
6 *Power hungry* (1989)
Vornholt, John
7 *Masks* (1989)
Dvorkin, David
8 *Captain's honor* (1989)
Friedman, Michael Jan
9 *Call to darkness* (1989)
David, Peter
10 *Rock and a hard place* (1990)
Sharee, Keith
11 *Gulliver's fugitive* (1990)
Carter, Carmen
12 *Doomsday world* (1990)
Co-authors: Michael Jan Friedman, Peter David, Robert Greenberger
Crispin, Ann Carol
13 *Eyes of the beholder* (1990)
Weinstein, Howard
14 *Exiles* (1990)
Friedman, Michael Jan
15 *Fortune's light* (1991)
Vornholt, John
16 *Contamination* (1991)
Gilden, Mel
17 *Boogeymen* (1991)
David, Peter
18 *Q-in-law* (1991)
Weinstein, Howard
19 *Perchance to dream* (1991)
Duane, Diane
20 *Dark mirror* (1993)
Crispin, Ann Carol
21 *Sarek* (1994)

Star trek tie-ins series
This sequence has six authors
Schnurnberger, Lynn Edelman
1 *Star trek, the motion picture make-your-own costume book* (1979)
Rotsler, William
2 *Star trek II biographies* (1982)
3 *Distress call* (1982)
4 *Star trek II short stories* (1982)
5 *Star trek III short stories* (1984)
Weinberg, Larry
6 *Search for Spock storybook* (1984)
Rotsler, William
7 *Vulcan treasure* (1984)
Dodge, Michael J
8 *Voyage to adventure* (1984)
Siegel, Barbara
9 *Phaser fight* (1986)

Star trilogy
Conant, Constance
1 *Southern star* (1987)
2 *Falling star* (1988)
3 *Star of the West* (1988)

Star trilogy
Coulter, Catherine
1 *Midnight star* (1986)
2 *Wild star* (1986)
3 *Jade star* (1987)

Star wars series
This sequence has three authors; it follows the **Luke Skywalker series**
Zahn, Timothy
1 *Heir to the Empire* (1991)
2 *Dark Force rising* (1992)
3 *Last command* (1993)
Wolverton, Dave
4 *Courtship of Princess Leia* (1994)
McIntyre, Vondra Neil
5 *Crystal star* (1994)

Star wars storybook series
Based on moving pictures
Richelson, Geraldine
1 *Star wars storybook* (1976)
Companion volume: *Star wars, adaptation*, by Larry Weinberg, 1985
Steneman, Shep
2 *Empire strikes back storybook* (1980)
Companion volume: *The Empire strikes back*, by Larry Weinberg, 1985
Vinge, Joan Dennison
3 *Return of the Jedi* (1983)
One volume edition entitled *Star wars, the first ten years*, 1987
Companion volumes: *Esper*, by Cary A Bucar, 1981, *Knight of the shadows*, by Karen Osman, 1982

StarBridge series
Crispin, Ann Carol
1 *StarBridge* (1989)
2 *Silent dances* (1990)
Co-author: Kathleen O'Malley
3 *Shadow world* (1991)
Co-author: Jannean Elliott

Starbridge series
Park, Paul
1 *Soldiers of paradise* (1987)
2 *Sugar rain* (1989)
Numbers 1 and 2 also published in one volume entitled *The sugar festival*, 1989
3 *Cult of loving kindness* (1991)

Starbuck family series
Lasky, Kathryn
1 *Double trouble squared* (1991)
2 *Shadows in the water* (1992)
3 *Voice in the wind* (1993)

Starbuck series
Braun, Matt
see **Luke Starbuck series**
Hogan, Ray
see **Shawn Starbuck series**

Starcats trilogy
Gotlieb, Phyllis
see **Qsaprinel trilogy**

Starchild trilogy
Pohl, Frederik
see **Plan of man trilogy**

Starclipper trilogy
Earnshaw, Brian
see **Star Jam Pack trilogy**

Starcruiser Shenandoah series
Green, Roland James
1 *Squadron alert* (1989)
2 *Division of the spoils* (1990)
3 *Sum of things* (1991)

Stardance series
Robinson, Jeanne
1 *Stardance* (1979)
2 *Starseed* (1991)

Stardust series
Tall, Stephen
1 *Stardust voyages* (1975)
2 *Ramsgate paradox* (1976)

Starfarers series
McIntyre, Vondra Neil
1 *Starfarers* (1989)
2 *Transition* (1990)

Starfire series
Mumford, Edwin Embree
1 *Flight of the Starfire* (1972)
2 *Second flight of the Starfire* (1972)
3 *Third flight of the Starfire* (1972)
4 *Fourth flight of the Starfire* (1972)
5 *Voyage of the Starfire to Atlantis* (1973)
One volume edition entitled *The five flights of the Starfire*, 1974

Starfishers trilogy
Cook, Glen
1 *Shadowline* (1982)
2 *Starfishers* (1982)
3 *Stars' End* (1982)

Stargard series
Frankowski, Leo
see **Adventures of Conrad Stargard series**

Starhounds series
Bischoff, David
see **Star hounds series**

Starhunters series
Drake, David
1 *Men hunting things* (1988)
2 *Things hunting men* (1988)
3 *Bluebloods* (1990)

Stark series
Brackett, Leigh
see **Eric John Stark series**
Fisher, Clay
see **Nathan Mason Stark series**
Hedges, Joseph
see **John Stark series**
Randolph, Forrest A
see **Confederate series**

Starkadder trilogy
King, Bernard
1 *Starkadder* (1985)
2 *Vargr-moon* (1986)
3 *Death-blinder* (1988)

Starke sisters series
Mackenzie, Kathleen
1 *Starke sisters* (1963)
2 *Charlotte* (1964)
3 *Kelford dig* (1966)

Starlight series
Lister, Gladys
1 *Starlight belongs to me* (1951)
2 *Star for Starlight* (1953)
3 *Quest for Starlight* (1956)

Starlight trilogy
Wells, Marian
1 *Wishing star* (1985)
2 *Star light, star bright* (1986)
3 *Morning star* (1986)

Starling series
Hildick, Edmund Wallace
see **Jim Starling series**

StarQuest series
Smith, Gregory Jon
1 *Captive planet* (1986)
2 *Operation master planet* (1986)

Starr and Cyber series
Heath, Peter
see **Jason Starr and Adam Cyber series**

Starr family series
Jordan, Godfrey P
1 *Milky Way run* (1985)
2 *Extraterrestrial cover up* (1986)

Starr series
French, Paul
see **David Starr series**
Johnston, William
see **Doctor Starr series**
Martin, Eugene
see **Randy Starr series**

Starr trilogy
Montgomery, Lucy Maud
see **Emily Starr trilogy**

Starry flag series
Optic, Oliver
1 *Starry flag* (1867)
Alternative title: The young fisherman of Cape Ann
2 *Freaks of fortune* (1868)
Alternative title: Half round the world
3 *Breaking away* (1868)
Alternative title: The fortunes of a student
4 *Seek and find* (1868)
Alternative title: The adventures of a smart boy
5 *Make or break* (1869)
Alternative title: The rich man's daughter
6 *Down the river* (1869)
Alternative title: Buck Bradford and his tyrants

Stars and Stripes series
Cobb, Frank
1 *Winning in the air* (1915)
2 *Potter boys under Old Glory* (1918)
3 *Winning the War Cross* (1916)
4 *Hunting down the spy* (1916)
5 *Potter boys with the tanks* (1919)

Stars series
Smith, Frederick Escreet
1 *Meeting of stars* (1987)
2 *Clash of stars* (1987)

Starship Orpheus trilogy
Jade, Symon
1 *Starship Orpheus* (1982)
Return from the dead
2 *Cosmic courage* (1983)
3 *Alter evil* (1983)

Starship troopers series
This sequence has two authors
Heinlein, Robert Anson
1 *Starship troopers* (1959)
Acres, Mark
2 *Shines the name* (1987)
Combat Command in the world of Robert A Heinlein's *Starship troopers*, 1959

Sta rsky and Hutch series
Franklin, Max
Based on a television series
1 *Starsky and Hutch* (1975)
2 *Kill Huggy Bear* (1976)
3 *Death ride* (1976)
4 *Bounty hunter* (1977)
5 *Terror on the docks* (1977)
6 *Psychic* (1977)
7 *Setup* (1978)
8 *Murder on Playboy Island* (1978)

Starstormers series
Fisk, Nicholas
1 *Starstormers* (1980)

2 *Sunburst* (1980)
3 *Catfang* (1981)
4 *Evil eye* (1982)
5 *Volcano* (1983)

Start in life series
Trowbridge, John Townsend
1 *Start in life* (1889)
A story of the Genesee country
2 *Biding his time* (1889)
Alternative title: Andrew Hapnell's fortune
3 *Adventures of David Vane and David Crane* (1889)
4 *Kelp-gatherers* (1890)
A story of the Maine coast
5 *Scarlet tanager, and other bipeds* (1891)
6 *Lottery ticket* (1896)

Start right and play well series
Gutman, Bill
1 *Football* (1989)
2 *Volleyball* (1989)
Volleyball for boys and girls
3 *Basketball for boys and girls* (1990)
4 *Field hockey* (1990)
5 *Soccer for boys and girls* (1990)
6 *Softball for boys and girls* (1990)
7 *Tennis for boys and girls* (1990)

Start to finish series
Mitgutsch, Ali
Translated from the German
1 *From beet to sugar* (1981)
2 *From blossom to honey* (1981)
3 *From cacao bean to chocolate* (1981)
4 *From cement to bridge* (1981)
5 *From clay to bricks* (1981)
6 *From cotton to pants* (1981)
7 *From cow to shoe* (1981)
8 *From fruit to jam* (1981)
9 *From grain to bread* (1981)
10 *From grass to butter* (1981)
11 *From milk to ice cream* (1981)
12 *From oil to gasoline* (1981)
13 *From ore to spoon* (1981)
14 *From sand to glass* (1981)
15 *From seed to pear* (1981)
16 *From sheep to scarf* (1981)
17 *From tree to table* (1981)
18 *From gold to money* (1985)
19 *From graphite to pencil* (1985)
20 *From sea to salt* (1985)
21 *From swamp to coal* (1985)
22 *From lemon to lemonade* (1986)
23 *From rubber tree to tire* (1986)
24 *From wood to paper* (1986)
25 *From idea to toy* (1988)
26 *From picture to picture book* (1988)

Starte series
Williams, Eric Ernest
see **Roger and Kate Starte series**

Starwolf trilogy
Hamilton, Edmond
1 *Weapon from beyond* (1967)
2 *Closed Worlds* (1968)
3 *World of the Starwolves* (1968)
One volume edition entitled *Starwolf*, 1982

Starwolves series
Gunnarsson, Thorarinn
1 *Starwolves* (1988)
2 *Battle of the ring* (1989)
3 *Tactical error* (1991)

Stash Koval series
Peters, Ron
1 *Big stash* (1972)
2 *Stash spots a murder* (1973)

State Ballet School series
Curcija-Prodanovic, Nada
see **Belgrade Ballet School series**

State Fair series
Stong, Philip
1 *State Fair* (1932)
2 *Return in August* (1954)

Statistical history series
Clodfelter, Micheal D
1 *Statistical history of the Korean War* (1990)
2 *Statistical history of the Vietnam War* (1990)

Staunch series
Garvice, Charles
1 *Staunch as a woman* (1903)
Alternative title: Love's woe
2 *Led by love* (1903)

Staunton series
Hill, Peter
see **Inspector Robert Staunton series**

Staveley series
Robbins, Clifton
1 *Six sign-post murder* (1939)
2 *Death forms threes* (1940)

Staveney series
Allan, Mea
1 *Rose Cottage* (1961)
2 *Base rumour* (1962)

Stavros the Anatolian trilogy
Kazan, Elia
1 *America, America* (1962)
2 *Anatolian* (1982)
3 *Beyond the Aegean* (1994)

Steadford Abbey series
Allen, Sheila Rosalynd
see **Lovers of Steadford Abbey series**

Steady as a Rock Posse series
Alington, Adrian
see **Inspector Posse series**

Steam house series
Verne, Jules
1 *Demon of Cawnpore* (1880)
Original edition entitled *La maison a vapeur*, part 1
2 *Tigers and traitors* (1880)
Original edition entitled *La maison a vapeur*, part 2
One volume edition entitled *The steam house*, 1881

Stecher trilogy
Williams, William Carlos
1 *White mule* (1937)
2 *In the money* (1940)
3 *Build-up* (1952)

Steel Callaghan series
Chesney, Michael
see **Colonel Steel Callaghan series**

Steel series
Brooks, Collin
see **Raeburn Steel series**
Cunningham, Chet
see **Jim Steel series**
Newton, Mike
see **Jon Steel series**
Robertson, Colin
see **Alan Steel series**

Steeldust series
Brown, Joseph Paul Summers
1 *Steeldust* (1986)
2 *Flight* (1987)

Steele meets Edge series
Gilman, George G
see **Edge meets Steele series**

Steele series
Bancroft, John
see **James Steele series**
Barlow, Roger
see **Sandy Steele series**
Chambers, Dana
see **Jim Steele series**
Fitzgerald, Hugh
see **Sam Steele series**
Gilman, George G
see **Adam Steele series**
Goulart, Ron
see **Skyrocket Steele series**
Grayson, Donald
see **Bob Steele series**
Gunn, Tom
see **Sheriff Blue Steele series**
Lee, Babs
see **Argus Steele series**

Steele series
This sequence has two authors
Masters, J D
1 *Steele* (1989)
2 *Cold Steele* (1989)
3 *Killer Steele* (1990)
4 *Jagged Steele* (1990)
5 *Renegade Steele* (1990)
6 *Target Steele* (1990)
Hunter, S L
7 *Fugitive Steele* (1991)
8 *Molten Steele* (1991)

Steele series
Sanders, Brett
see **Web Steele series**
Scott, Mansfield
see **Inspector Malcome Steele series**
West, John B
see **Rocky Steele series**

Steele's war series
Gilman, George G
1 *Woman* (1980)
2 *Preacher* (1981)
3 *Storekeeper* (1981)
4 *Stranger* (1981)
5 *Big prize* (1981)

Steeley Delaroy series
Johns, William Earl
1 *Sky high* (1936)
Revised edition 1951
2 *Steeley flies again* (1936)
Revised edition 1951
3 *Murder by air* (1937)
Revised edition 1951
4 *Murder at Castle Deeping* (1938)
Revised edition 1951
5 *Wings of romance* (1939)
Revised edition 1951
Story entitled *Det forsuunne dagboksblad*, i.e. *The missing page* in *Thriller*, 16 October 1937 features Steeley Delaroy

Steeleye series
Dunn, Saul
1 *Coming of Steeleye* (1976)
2 *Wideways* (1976)
3 *Waterspace* (1976)

Steep Farm series
Sandler, Mona
1 *Young horse dealers* (1957)
2 *Steep Farm stables* (1958)

Steep Street series
Berg, Leila
1 *Having friends* (1987)
2 *Call that a hat* (1987)
3 *Loving Jonathan Jones* (1987)
4 *Rosie and Mister Brown* (1987)

Steevens series
Kiddy, Maurice George
see **Stonewall Steevens series**

Stefan and Evonn series
Cooper, Margaret Chilvers
1 *Solution, escape* (1981)
2 *Code name, Clone* (1982)

Stellar rangers series
Perry, Steve
1 *Peacemaker* (1993)
2 *Guns of honor* (1993)

Stemson family series
Barren, Charles
1 *Eighty north* (1960)
2 *Jamestown* (1961)

Sten series
Cole, Allan
1 *Sten* (1982)
2 *Wolf worlds* (1984)
3 *Court of a thousand suns* (1986)
4 *Fleet of the damned* (1988)
5 *Revenge of the damned* (1989)
6 *Return of the emperor* (1990)

Stenton series
Dexter, Ted
see **Jack Stenton series**

Step by step series
Wilmer, Diane
1 *Daytime* (1987)
2 *Night time* (1987)
3 *My house* (1987)
4 *Shopping* (1987)

Stephanie series
Gobineau, Marceline
1 *Passions of spring* (1970)
Original edition entitled *L'amour a quatre saisons*, part 1
2 *Snows of Sebastopol* (1970)
Original edition entitled *L'amour a quatre saisons*, part 2
3 *Emperor's agent* (1971)
Original edition entitled *Puisque je t'aime*, part 1
4 *All for my love* (1971)
Original edition entitled *Puisque je t'aime*, part 2
5 *Savage land* (1973)
Original edition entitled *Le prix de la liberte*, part 1
6 *Price of freedom* (1973)
Original edition entitled *Le prix de la liberte*, part 2

Stephen Armitage series
McLeave, Hugh
see **Doctor Stephen Armitage series**

Stephen Bellecroix and Sheila Roath series
Craig, David
1 *Young men may die* (1970)
2 *Walk at night* (1971)

Stephen Braby series
Dehan, Richard
see **Market place series**

Stephen Carey series
Overton, Jenny
see **Creed series**

Stephen Clay series
Porcelain, Sidney E
1 *Purple pony murders* (1944)
2 *Crimson cat murders* (1946)

Stephen Dain series
Sheckley, Robert
1 *Calibre point fifty* (1961)
2 *Dead run* (1961)
3 *Live gold* (1962)
4 *White death* (1963)
5 *Time limit* (1967)

Stephen Dedalus series
This sequence has two authors
Joyce, James
1 *Portrait of the artist as a young man* (1916)

Stephen Dedalus series

2 *Ulysses* (1922)
Costello, Peter
3 *Leopold Bloom* (1981)

Stephen Drake series
Wilcox, Collin
1 *Black door* (1967)
2 *Third figure* (1968)

Stephen Duane series
Benton, John L
1 *Duane of the FBI* (1937)
Duane of the G-men
2 *Art treasure murders* (1939)
Duane and the art murders

Stephen Fletcher series
Davison, Geoffrey
1 *Spy who swopped shoes* (1967)
2 *Nest of spies* (1968)
3 *Chessboard spies* (1969)

Stephen Harper series
Brown, Walter C
see **Inspector Stephen Harper series**

Stephen Kale series
Jon, Montague
1 *Wallington case* (1981)
2 *Question of law* (1981)

Stephen Macfarlane series
Cross, John Keir
see **Albatross series**

Stephen Marryat series
Leek, Margaret
1 *Healthy grave* (1980)
2 *We must have a trial* (1980)
3 *Voice of the past* (1981)

Stephen Maturin and Jack Aubrey series
O'Brian, Patrick
see **Jack Aubrey and Stephen Maturin series**

Stephen Mayhew series
Olsen, D B
see **Lieutenant Stephen Mayhew series**

Stephen Parkin series
Burton, Hester
1 *Rebel* (1971)
2 *Riders of the storm* (1972)

Stephen Power series
Gray, Juliet
1 *Sweet promise* (1961)
2 *Sweet rebel* (1965)

Stephen Ramsay series
Cleeves, Ann
see **Inspector Stephen Ramsay series**

Stephen Rant series
Wheeler, H E
1 *Death takes a ride* (1942)
2 *Third attempt* (1946)

Stephen Ringway series
Lott, Stanley Makepeace
1 *Twopence for a rat's tail* (1947)
2 *Judge will call it murder* (1951)

Stephen, Sandy and Jane series
Macgibbon, Jean
see **Sandy, Jane and Stephen series**

Stephen series
Farmer, Penelope
1 *Seagull* (1965)
2 *Dragonfly summer* (1971)

Stephen Wayne series
Harknett, Terry
1 *Benevolent blackmailer* (1962)
2 *Scratch on the surface* (1962)
3 *Invitation to a funeral* (1963)
4 *Dead little rich girl* (1963)
5 *Evil money* (1964)
6 *Man who did not die* (1964)
7 *Death of an aunt* (1967)
8 *Two-way frame* (1967)
9 *Softcover kill* (1971)
10 *Upmarket affair* (1973)

Stephenson series
Bernard, Elizabeth
see **Satin slippers series**
Stevenson, William Henri
see **William Stephenson series**

Stepping stones 1 2 3 series
Berridge, Celia
1 *Down the road* (1987)
2 *In the playground* (1987)
3 *At home* (1987)
4 *Going swimming* (1987)
5 *Birthday party* (1988)
6 *Going shopping* (1988)
7 *My family* (1988)
8 *Me and my friends* (1988)

Steps series
Lind, Jakov
Autobiography
1 *Counting my steps* (1969)
2 *Numbers* (1972)

Stepsisters series
Oaks, Tina
1 *War between the sisters* (1987)
2 *Sister trap* (1987)
3 *Bad sisters* (1987)
4 *Sisters in charge* (1987)
5 *That cheating sister* (1988)
6 *Guilty sister* (1988)
7 *Reckless sister* (1988)

Sterling family series
Johnston, Norma
1 *Keeping days* (1973)
2 *Glory in the flower* (1974)
3 *Mustard seed of magic* (1977)
4 *Sanctuary tree* (1977)
5 *Nice girl like you* (1980)
6 *Myself and I* (1981)

Sterling O'Blivion series
Scott, Jody
1 *Passing for human* (1977)
2 *I, vampire* (1984)

Sterling series
Grove, Harriet Pyne
see **Ann Sterling series**

Stern series
Turow, Scott
see **Sandy Stern series**

Steur series
Morrison, Margaret
see **Annette de Steur series**

Steve and Anna series
Hardcastle, Michael
1 *Crash car* (1977)
2 *Strong arm* (1977)
3 *Fire on the sea* (1977)
4 *Holiday house* (1977)

Steve Arrow and Chief Inspector Peacock series
Mantell, Laurie
see **Sergeant Steve Arrow and Chief Inspector Peacock series**

Steve Ashe series
Howard, James Arch
1 *I'll get you yet* (1954)
2 *I like it tough* (1955)
3 *Blow out my torch* (1956)
4 *Die on Easy Street* (1957)

Steve Austin series
Caidin, Martin
see **Six Million Dollar Man series**

Steve Bentley series
Dietrich, Robert
1 *Murder on the rocks* (1957)
2 *House on Q Street* (1959)
3 *End of a stripper* (1959)
4 *Mistress to murder* (1960)
5 *Murder on her mind* (1960)
6 *Angel Eyes* (1961)
7 *Steve Bentley's calypso caper* (1961)
8 *Curtains for a lover* (1961)
9 *My body* (1962)
Also published under the author's real name Everette Howard Hunt

Steve Borden series
Dougall, Bernard
1 *I don't scare easy* (1941)
2 *Singing corpse* (1943)

Steve Canyon series
Caniff, Milton
1 *Steve Canyon* (1959)
2 *Operation Snowflower* (1959)
3 *Operation Convoy* (1959)
4 *Operation Foo Ling* (1959)
5 *Operation Eel Island* (1959)

Steve Carradine series
Robertson, Manning K
1 *Seek and destroy* (1965)
2 *Blueprint for destruction* (1966)
3 *Night passage to Kano* (1967)
4 *Twelve hours to destiny* (1971)

Steve Carter series
Long, Amelia Reynolds
1 *Murder to type* (1943)
2 *Death wears a scarab* (1943)
3 *Death has a will* (1944)
4 *Murder by treason* (1944)
5 *Once acquitted* (1945)
6 *Murder by magic* (1947)
7 *House with green shutters* (1950)

Steve Conacher series
Knight, Adam
1 *Stone cold blonde* (1951)
2 *Murder for madame* (1951)
3 *Knife at my back* (1952)
4 *Sunburned corpse* (1952)
5 *Kiss and kill* (1953)
6 *I'll kill you next!* (1954)
7 *Girl running* (1956)
8 *Triple slay* (1959)

Steve Considine series
Wilmot, Robert Patrick
1 *Blood in your eye* (1952)
2 *Murder on Monday* (1953)
3 *Death rides a painted horse* (1954)

Steve Craig series
Winter, Bevis
1 *Redheads are poison* (1948)
2 *Redheads cool fast* (1952)
3 *Dead sleep for keeps* (1953)
4 *Darker grows the street* (1955)
5 *Next stop, the morgue* (1955)
6 *Noose of emeralds* (1956)
Let the lady die
7 *Night was made for murder* (1957)
8 *Sleep long, my lovely* (1958)
9 *Blondes end up dead* (1960)
10 *Dark and the deadly* (1961)

Steve Cranmer series
Knickmeyer, Steve
1 *Straight* (1976)
2 *Cranmer* (1978)

Steve Crown series
Streib, Dan
1 *Counter Force* (1983)
2 *Trident hijacking* (1983)
3 *Death shuttle* (1983)
4 *Karate killers* (1983)
5 *Terror for sale* (1984)
6 *Titan's duel* (1984)
7 *Mind breakers* (1984)
8 *Body hunters* (1984)
9 *Bloody rose* (1984)

Steve Drake series
Ellington, Richard
1 *Shoot the works* (1948)
2 *It's a crime* (1948)
3 *Stone cold dead* (1950)
4 *Exit for a dame* (1951)
5 *Just killing time* (1953)
Shakedown

Steve Essex series
Waldron, Simon
1 *Leap before you look* (1968)
2 *Hot ice* (1969)

Steve Harmas series
Chase, James Hadley
1 *Double shuffle* (1952)
2 *There's always a price tag* (1956)
3 *Shock treatment* (1959)
4 *Tell it to the birds* (1963)
5 *Ear to the ground* (1968)

Steve Harragan series
Harragan, Steve
1 *Bigamy kiss* (1952)
2 *Dope doll* (1952)
3 *Kiss of the damned* (1952)
4 *Side-show girl* (1952)
5 *Sin is a redhead* (1952)
6 *Smuggled sin* (1952)
7 *Carney's burlesque* (1953)
8 *Cuban heel* (1953)
9 *Queer sisters* (1953)
10 *Shayne dame* (1953)

Steve Harvester series
Fox, James M
1 *Dark crusade* (1954)
Also published under the pseudonym Grant Holmes
2 *Operation Dancing Dog* (1974)

Steve Johnson series
Nelson, Hugh Lawrence
1 *Title is murder* (1947)
2 *Copper lady* (1947)
3 *Fountain of death* (1948)
4 *Dark echo* (1949)
5 *Dead giveaway* (1950)

Steve McCade series
Kester, Ken
1 *Marshal of Blazing Gulch* (1958)
2 *Outlaws of Shy Valley* (1958)
3 *Crooked desert* (1959)

Steve McLaren series
Scott, Bruce
see **Superintendent Steve McLaren series**

Steve Morgan and Ginny Brandon series
Rogers, Rosemary
see **Ginny Brandon and Steve Morgan series**

Steve Morton series
Smith, Ford
see **Dark Knight series**

Steve Ramsay series
Wallace, C H
1 *Crashlanding in the Congo* (1965)
2 *Highflight to hell* (1966)
3 *Tailwind to danger* (1966)
4 *E.T.A. for death* (1967)

Steve Ransome series
Ransome, Stephen
1 *Hear no evil* (1953)
2 *Shroud off her back* (1953)

Steve Rhoden series
Walker, Ira
1 *Someone's stolen Nellie Grey* (1963)
2 *Man in the driver's seat* (1964)
Sequence continued under the author's real name Irma Walker
Walker, Irma
3 *Murder in twenty five words or less* (1980)

Steve Savage series
Lewis, David
1 *Andromeda assignment* (1976)
2 *Omega assignment* (1976)

Steve series
Bannister, S F
see **Rolling Stone series**

Steve Silk series
O'Sullivan, James Brendan
1 *Death came late* (1945)
2 *Death card* (1945)
3 *Death on ice* (1946)
4 *Death stalks the stadium* (1946)
5 *I die possessed* (1953)
6 *Nerve beat* (1953)
7 *Don't hang me too high* (1954)
8 *Someone walked ovr my grave* (1954)
9 *Stuffed man* (1955)
10 *Long spoon* (1956)
11 *Raid* (1958)
12 *Choke chain* (1958)
13 *Gate fever* (1959)
14 *Backlash* (1960)
15 *Make my coffin big* (1964)

Steve Sinclair series
Decker, Jake
1 *Deadly snow* (1984)
2 *Death's little sister* (1984)
3 *Death gambit* (1984)
4 *Death comes home* (1985)

Steve Summers series
Manor, Jason
1 *Too dead to run* (1953)
2 *Red Jaguar* (1954)
Girl in the red Jaguar
3 *Pawns of fear* (1955)
No halo for me
4 *Tramplers* (1956)

Steve Victor series
Mark, Ted
see **Man from O.R.G.Y. series**

Steve Walker series
Greaves, Jimmy
see **Soccer series**

Steve Wayne series
Harknett, Terry
see **Stephen Wayne series**

Steven Borg series
Posey, Carl Alfred
1 *Kiev footprint* (1983)
2 *Prospero drill* (1984)

Steven Bright trilogy
Caute, David
see **Confrontation trilogy**

Steven Flagg series
Day, Will B
1 *Bravo nine* (1967)
2 *Man from M.O.D.* (1968)

Steven Gale series
Leyland, Eric
1 *Calling Steven Gale* (1961)
2 *Gale hits the headlines* (1961)
3 *Scoop for Steven Gale* (1962)
4 *Gale and the sword of Mars* (1962)

Steven Kirk series
Hornig, Doug
1 *Waterman* (1987)
2 *Stinger* (1990)

Steven Malone series
Morland, Nigel
1 *Strangely she died* (1946)
2 *Death takes an editor* (1949)

Steven Mitchell series
Bell, Josephine
see **Inspector Steven Mitchell series**

Steven Rushton series
Russell, Robert
see **Doctor Steven Rushton series**

Stevens and Allain series
Graeme, Bruce
see **Superintendent William Stevens and Inspector Pierre Allain series**

Stevens and Hartley series
Tuttle, Wilbur Coleman
see **Hashknife Hartley and Sleepy Stevens series**

Stevens series
Davidson, Linda
see **Endless summer series**
Saddler, Allen
see **Dave Stevens series**

Stevens trilogy
Faulkner, William
see **Gavin Stevens trilogy**

Stevenson family series
Macdonald, Malcolm
1 *World from rough stones* (1974)
2 *Rich are with you always* (1976)
3 *Sons of fortune* (1978)
4 *Abigail* (1979)

Stevenson series
Elder, Michael
see **Mindslip series**

Stevie O'Dowda series
Finch, Matthew
1 *Eye with mascara* (1968)
2 *Eye spy* (1975)

Stewardesses series
Sutton, Penny
1 *Stewardesses* (1973)
2 *Stewardesses down under* (1973)
3 *Jumbo jet girls* (1974)
4 *I'm Penny, fly me* (1975)

Stewart daughters trilogy
Johnston, Joan
see **Sisters of the Lone Star trilogy**

Stewart empire series
Whited, Charles
see **Spirit of America series**

Stewart family series
Bourne, Peter
1 *Black saga* (1947)
Drums of destiny
2 *Ten thousand shall die* (1951)
Golden road

Stewart family series
Grey, Zane
see **Western stars series**

Stewart family series
Lowe, Eric
1 *Beyond the nineteen counties* (1948)
2 *O willing hearts* (1951)
3 *Salute to freedom* (1938)

Stewart family series
Stewart, Averil
1 *Alicella* (1955)
A memoir of Alice King Stewart and Ella Christie
2 *Family tapestry* (1961)

Stewart Hoag series
Handler, David
1 *Man who died laughing* (1988)
2 *Man who lived by night* (1989)
3 *Man who would be F Scott Fitzgerald* (1990)
4 *Woman who fell from grace* (1991)
5 *Boy who never grew up* (1992)

Stewart Noble and Laurie Grant series
Mackintosh, May
see **Laurie Grant and Stewart Noble series**

Stewart series
Fitz Roy, Olivia
see **Jamie and Jean Stewart series**
Jackson, Gabrielle Emilie
see **Peggy Stewart series**
Lamb, J Dayne
see **Teal Stewart series**
Treece, Henry
see **Gordon Stewart series**
Van Siller, Hilda
see **Allan Stewart series**

Stewarts of Badenoch series
Mackie, Charles
1 *Wolf* (1977)
2 *Blood of the Wolf* (1978)
3 *Mariota* (1981)

Stewarts series
Fitz Roy, Olivia
1 *Orders to poach* (1942)
2 *Steer by the stars* (1944)
3 *House in the hills* (1946)
4 *Hill war* (1950)
5 *Wandering star* (1953)

Steytler series
Milne, Shirley
see **Detective Sergeant Steytler series**

Stick-in-the-Mud Turtle series
Hoban, Lillian
1 *Stick-in-the-Mud Turtle* (1977)
2 *Turtle spring* (1978)

Stickit minister series
Crockett, Samuel Rutherford
1 *Stickit minister, and some common men* (1893)
2 *Stickit minister's wooing, and other Galloway stories* (1900)

Stiggins family series
Heward, Constance
see **Ameliaranne series**

Still life series
Cobb, Richard
Autobiography
1 *Still life* (1983)
Sketches from a Tunbridge Wells childhood
2 *Classical education* (1985)
3 *Something to hold on to* (1988)
Autobiographical sketches

Stillworthy series
Marshall, May
see **Sister Madge Stillworthy series**

Stingray series
Theydon, John
Based on a television series
1 *Stingray* (1965)
2 *Stingray and the monster* (1966)
Companion volume: *The Gerry Anderson's Stingray files*, by John Peel, 1986

Stinky Stanley series
Hodgman, Ann
1 *Stinky Stanley* (1993)
2 *Stinky Stanley stinks again* (1993)
3 *Superhero* (1994)

Stock series
Tourney, Leonard
see **Matthew Stock series**

Stockton series
Joyce, Cyril
see **Chief Superintendent Pat Stockton series**

Stockwell series
Holden, J Railton
see **Spider Stockwell series**

Stoddart series
Haynes, Annie
see **Inspector Stoddart series**

Stole series
Wogan, Charles
see **Sebastian Stole series**

Stolen story series
Williams, Jesse Lynch
1 *Stolen story, and other newspaper stories* (1899)
2 *Day dreamer* (1906)
3 *Girl and the game, and other college stories* (1908)

Stone age family from Viking-land series
Almqvist, Bertil
see **Stones series**

Stone book quartet
Garner, Alan
1 *Stone book* (1976)
2 *Tom Fobble's day* (1977)
3 *Granny Reardun* (1977)
4 *Aimer Gate* (1978)
One volume edition entitled *The stone book quartet*, 1983

Stone maiden series
Townley, Pamela
1 *Stone maiden* (1986)
2 *Next of kin* (1988)

Stone Park Prison series
Douglas, Felicity
see **Faye Boswell series**

Stone series
Armstrong, Raymond
see **J Rockingham Stone series**
Buchanan, Jack
see **M.I.A. Hunter series**
Edwards, Josh
see **John Stone series**
Jacks, Jeff
see **Shep Stone series**
Seward, Jack
see **Curt Stone series**
Wells, Carolyn
see **Fleming Stone series**

Stone trilogy
Bryant, Marguerite
1 *Christopher Hibbault, roadmaker* (1909)
2 *Anne Kempburn, truthseeker* (1910)
3 *Shadow on the stone* (1917)

Stonecroft series
Savory, Teo
1 *Stonecroft* (1977)
The country I remember
2 *Childhood* (1978)
3 *To raise a rainbow* (1980)

Stoner McTavish series
Dreher, Sarah
1 *Stoner McTavish* (1985)
2 *Something shady* (1986)
3 *Gray magic* (1987)
4 *Captive in time* (1990)

Stoner series
Hayes, Ralph Eugene
see **Mark Stoner series**
Valin, Jonathan
see **Harry Stoner series**

Stones series
Almqvist, Bertil
Translated from the Swedish
1 *Stone Age Kids discover America* (1950)
Stones discover America
2 *Stones explore Britain* (1971)
Original edition entitled *Barna Hedenhos besoker England*

Stonewall Inn series
Zubro, Mark Richard
1 *Simple suburban murder* (1989)
2 *Only good priest* (1991)
3 *Sorry now?* (1991)

Stonewall series
Roberts, Mark Kelly
see **Soldier for hire series**

Stonewall Steevens series
Kiddy, Maurice George
1 *Killing no murder* (1931)
2 *Stonewall Steevens investigates* (1933)
3 *Jade hatpin* (1933)

Stony Man series
Pendleton, Don
1 *Stony Man doctrine* (1983)
2 *Stony Man II* (1991)
3 *Stony Man III* (1991)
4 *Stony Man IV* (1992)
5 *Stony Man V* (1992)
6 *Stony Man VI* (1993)
7 *Stony Man VII* (1993)
8 *Stony Man VIII* (1993)

Storey series
Footner, Hulbert
see **Madame Rosika Storey series**

Stories for happiness series
Kibby, Leigh
1 *Myranda and Chester* (1993)
2 *Mignon and Peter* (1993)

Stories for telling series
Wood, William Hollingsworth
1 *Stories for telling* (1958)
2 *More stories for telling* (1962)

Stories from Cockleshell Bay series
Trueman, Brian
1 *Pirate king* (1982)
2 *Ostriches and obstacles* (1982)
3 *Bucket and spade* (1985)
4 *Dressing up* (1985)
5 *Pirate seagull* (1985)
6 *Lost and found* (1985)
7 *Name for baby Cockle* (1986)
8 *Robin and Rosie's new room* (1986)

Stories from the Bible series
De la Mare, Walter
1 *Story of Joseph* (1958)
2 *Story of Moses* (1959)
3 *Story of Samuel and Saul* (1960)
Originally published in one volume entitled *Stories from the Bible*, 1929

Stories from the past series
Vansittart, Peter
1 *Dark tower* (1965)
2 *Shadow land* (1967)

Stories from world history series
Blyton, Enid
1 *Story of the siege of Troy* (1934)
2 *Adventures of Odysseus* (1934)
3 *Tales of the ancient Greeks and Persians* (1934)
4 *Tales of the Romans* (1934)

Stories of Edinburgh life series
Kemp, Robert
1 *Malacca cane* (1954)
2 *Maestro* (1956)
3 *Highlander* (1957)

Stories of six worlds series
Baldry, Cherith
1 *Book and the phoenix* (1989)
Rush of golden wings
2 *Hostage of the sea* (1990)
3 *Carpenter's apprentice* (1992)

Stories of the Great War series
Strang, Herbert
1 *Hero of Liege* (1914)
2 *Fighting with French* (1915)
3 *Burton of the Flying Corps* (1916)
4 *With Haig on the Somme* (1918)
5 *Tom Willoughby's scouts* (1919)
A story of the War in German East Africa
6 *Blue raider* (1920)
A tale of adventure in the southern seas

Stories of the realm series
Allcock, Phil
1 *Will of Dargan* (1989)
2 *In search of the golden sceptre* (1991)

Stories of the seen and the unseen series
Oliphant, Margaret Oliphant Wilson
1 *Beleaguered city* (1878)
2 *Little pilgrim in the unseen* (1882)
3 *Land of darkness* (1888)

Stories series
Tulloch, Richard
1 *Stories from our house* (1987)
2 *Stories from our street* (1989)

Stories to tell series
Bruna, Dick
1 *Story to tell* (1968)
Original edition entitled *Boek zonder woorden*
2 *Another story to tell* (1974)
Original edition entitled *Boek zonder woorden 2*
3 *Sophie's toys* (1988)
Original edition entitled *Boek zonder woorden 3*

Storm country series
White, Grace Miller
1 *Tess of the Storm Country* (1909)
Tess of Ithaca
2 *Secret of the Storm Country* (1917)

Storm family series
Chisholm, Matt
1 *Stampede* (1970)
2 *Hard Texas trail* (1971)
3 *Riders west* (1971)
4 *One notch to death* (1972)
5 *One man, one gun* (1972)
6 *Breed of men* (1973)
7 *Thunder in the west* (1973)
8 *Battle fury* (1973)
9 *Blood on the hills* (1973)

Storm Jackson series
Buckman, Sam
1 *Guns at Fortune Ranch* (1953)
2 *Ranch of death* (1953)
3 *Texan killer* (1954)
4 *Rancher's gold* (1954)
5 *Killers of Prairie Flats* (1955)
6 *Storm on the sawdust trail* (1955)
7 *Hellfire sheriff* (1956)

Storm quartet
Nelson, Lee
see **Dan Storm quartet**

Storm series
Barber, Willetta Ann
see **Christopher Storm series**

Storm series
Maisky, Ivan Mikhailovich
1 *Before the storm* (1944)
2 *Journey into the past* (1960)
3 *Who helped Hitler?* (1962)
4 *Spanish notebooks* (1962)

Storm series
Norton, Andre
see **Arzor series**
Stevens, Steve
see **Jack Storm series**
Walsh, James Morgan
see **Inspector Storm series**

Storm troop series
Kessler, Leo
see **Stormtroop series**

Stormtroop series
Kessler, Leo
1 *Stormtroop* (1977)
2 *Blood mountain* (1978)
3 *Valley of the assassins* (1979)
4 *Red assault* (1979)
5 *Himmler's gold* (1980)
6 *Fire over Kabul* (1982)
7 *Wave of terror* (1983)
8 *Eagles in the snow* (1983)
9 *Fire over Africa* (1984)

Stormy Petrel series
Needham, Violet
1 *Black Riders* (1939)
2 *Stormy Petrel* (1942)
3 *House of the Paladin* (1945)
4 *Betrayer* (1950)

Story book series
Blyton, Enid
1 *Happy story book* (1942)
2 *Merry story book* (1943)
3 *Jolly story book* (1944)
4 *Sunny story book* (1945)
5 *Gay story book* (1946)
6 *Lucky story book* (1947)
7 *Bright story book* (1952)
8 *Friendly story book* (1954)

Story Girl series
Montgomery, Lucy Maud
1 *Story Girl* (1911)
2 *Golden road* (1913)

Story hat series
Aardema, Verna
1 *Tales from the story hat* (1960)
2 *More tales from the story hat* (1966)

Story in a picture series
Richmond, Robin
1 *Children in art* (1992)
2 *Animals in art* (1993)

Story of a life series
Paustovsky, Konstantin Georgievich
Translated from the Russian; autobiography
1 *Childhood and schooldays* (1946)
2 *Slow approach of thunder* (1954)
3 *In that dawn* (1958)
4 *Years of hope* (1960)
5 *Southern adventure* (1961)
6 *Restless years* (1946)

Story of a peasant series
Erckmann, Emile
Translated from Histoire d'un paysan
1 *States General* (1869)
2 *Country in danger* (1869)
3 *Year one of the Republic* (1869)
4 *Citizen Bonaparte* (1869)

Story of California trilogy
White, Stewart Edward
see **California trilogy**

Story of England series
Bryant, Arthur
1 *Makers of the realm* (1953)
2 *Age of chivalry* (1963)

Story of the gardener series
Mann, Phillip
1 *Master of Paxwax* (1986)
2 *Fall of the families* (1987)

Story of the stone series
Ts'ao, Hsueh-ch'in
see **Dream of the red chamber series**

Story series
Gree, Alain
1 *Story of a car* (1968)
Original edition entitled *Une voiture m'a raconte*
2 *Story of a ship* (1968)
Original edition entitled *Un navire m'a raconte*
3 *Story of a train* (1968)
Original edition entitled *Un wagon m'a raconte*
4 *Story of a truck* (1968)
Original edition entitled *Un camion m'a raconte*
5 *Story of a space rocket* (1968)
Original edition entitled *Un fusee m'a raconte*
6 *Story of an aeroplane* (1968)
Original edition entitled *Un avion m'a raconte*
7 *Story of a sailing boat* (1968)
Original edition entitled *Un voilier m'a raconte*

Story-teller series
Anderson, Sherwood
Autobiography
1 *Tar* (1926)
A mid-West childhood
2 *Story-teller's story* (1922)
The tale of an American writer's journey

Storyteller series
Ruck, Berta
Autobiography
1 *Storyteller tells the truth* (1935)
2 *Smile for the past* (1959)
3 *Trickle of Welsh blood* (1967)
4 *Asset to Wales* (1970)
5 *Ancestral voices* (1972)

Storytime series
Daly, Niki
1 *Teddy's ear* (1985)
2 *Monsters are like that* (1985)
3 *Ben's gingerbread man* (1985)
4 *Look at me!* (1986)
5 *Just like Archie* (1986)

Storytrails series
Sharp, Allen
1 *King's mission* (1982)
Can you rescue a victim from the Great Terror?
2 *Haunters of Marsh Hall* (1982)
Can you find the secret of the ghostly guardian?
3 *Evil of Mister Happiness* (1982)
Can you defeat the schemes of a criminal mastermind?
4 *Terror in the fourth dimension* (1982)

Can you return from a 2000 year journey through time?
5 *Invitation to murder* (1982)
Can you find the murderer before the murderer finds you?
6 *Stone of Badda* (1982)
Can you face the deadly guardians of Otherworld?
7 *Dirty dollars* (1983)
8 *Tomb of Amenosis* (1983)
Can you stop a war, solve a riddle as old as Genesis?
9 *Night of the comet* (1983)
Can you destroy the giants from the sea?
10 *Deadly trap* (1983)
Caught up in the web of a strange prophecy, can you avoid the trap?
11 *Sicilain contract* (1984)
Can you find the killer with a contract on your life?
12 *Conspiracy of blood* (1984)
Can you prevent the crime of the century?
13 *Unsolved case of Sherlock Holmes* (1984)
Can you solve it?
14 *Return of the undead* (1984)
Can you destroy the vampire of Valdah?
15 *Shadow over the marsh* (1985)
Can you discover the dark secret which threatens your very life?
16 *Second conquest* (1985)
Can you discover the world's future; Numbers 4, 6, 9, 16 also published in one volume entitled *The Storytrails book of science fiction,* 1987
17 *Hands of Pablo Santos* (1985)
18 *Eye of heaven* (1985)
Can you save the victim of a web of mystery; Numbers 3, 5, 8, 18 also published in one volume entitled *The Storytrails book of thrillers*, 1987
19 *Sherlock Holmes, the Meyringen papers* (1986)
Can you solve the mystery of the Reichenbach Falls?
20 *Dark awakening* (1986)
Can you destroy an ancient sorcery?
21 *Island of the walking dead* (1986)
Can you save the victim of a terrifying revenge?
22 *Busting of Frankie da Mora* (1986)
Can you outwit the Chicago mobsters?
23 *Wolf with no tail* (1987)
Can you discover Kutzka's ancient secret?
24 *Sherlock Holmes, the case of the dancing bees* (1987)
Can you solve the mystery of Perrot's Cove?
25 *Death's drum* (1988)
26 *To catch a bunyip* (1988)

Stover series
Bartlett, Philip A
see **Roy Stover series**
Huie, William Bradford
see **Mamie Stover series**

Strachey series
Holroyd, Michael
see **Lytton Strachey series**
Stevenson, Richard
see **Donald Strachey series**

Straight series
Morgan, Geoffrey
see **Ricky Straight series**

Straight talk about drugs series
Berger, Gilda
1 *Meg's story* (1992)
2 *Patty's story* (1992)
3 *Joey's story* (1992)

Strang series
Brinton, Henry
see **John and Sally Strang series**
Cagney, Peter
see **Mike Strang series**
Carnac, Carol
see **Inspector Strang series**
Dilnot, George
see **Jim Strang series**

Strange adventure series
Ellis, Edward Sylvester
1 *Teddy and Towser* (1904)
A story of early days in California
2 *Up the forked river* (1904)
Alternative title: Adventures in South America

Strange and the good trilogy
Fuller, Roy
Memoirs
1 *Souvenirs* (1980)
2 *Vamp till ready* (1982)
3 *Home and dry* (1984)
One volume edition entitled *The strange and the good*, 1989

Strange conflict series
Batchelor, John M
1 *Strange conflict* (1888)
2 *Strange people* (1888)

Strange family trilogy
Watson, Edmund Henry Lacon
1 *Strange family* (1926)
2 *Rudolph Strange* (1927)
3 *Last of the Stranges* (1928)

Strange Occurrence Squad series
Laymon, Richard Carl
1 *Beast* (1986)
2 *Night creature* (1986)
3 *Return* (1986)
4 *Thin air* (1986)

Strange paradise trilogy
Daniels, Dorothy
1 *Strange paradise* (1969)
2 *Island of evil* (1970)
3 *Raxl, voodoo princess* (1970)

Strange series
Gaines, Audrey
see **Jeff Strange series**
Quinn, Eleanor Baker
see **James Strange series**
Rotsler, William
see **Doctor Strange series**

Strange stories from nature series
Verrill, Alpheus Hyatt
1 *Strange sea shells and their stories* (1936)
2 *Strange insects and their stories* (1937)
3 *Strange reptiles and their stories* (1937)
4 *Strange birds and their stories* (1938)
5 *Strange fish and their stories* (1938)
6 *Strange animals and their stories* (1939)
7 *Strange prehistoric animals and their stories* (1948)
8 *Strange creatures of the sea* (1955)

Strange valley trilogy
Cockett, Mary
1 *Strange valley* (1967)
2 *Strange hill* (1984)
3 *Drowning valley* (1978)

Strangely series
Black, Elizabeth Best
see **Peter Strangely series**

Stranger series
Keevil, John Joyce
see **Baldwin Hamey series**

Strangers and brothers series
Snow, Charles Percy
1 *Time of hope* (1949)
2 *Strangers and brothers* (1940)
George Passant
3 *Conscience of the rich* (1958)
4 *Light and the dark* (1947)
5 *Masters* (1951)
6 *New men* (1954)
7 *Homecomings* (1956)
8 *Affair* (1960)
9 *Corridors of power* (1964)
10 *Sleep of reason* (1968)
11 *Last things* (1970)
12 *In their wisdom* (1974)

Strangeways series
Blake, Nicholas
see **Nigel Strangeways series**

Stranglers series
Belot, Adolphe
1 *Stranglers of Paris* (1879)
Original edition entitled *Les etranglers*
2 *Grande Florine* (1879)
Original edition entitled *La Grande Florine*

Stranleigh series
Barr, Robert
see **Lord Stranleigh series**

Strategic Commandoes series
White, Steve
see **S-Com series**

Stratton series
Bickers, Richard Townshend
see **Mark Stratton series**

Straussman series
Davison, Gilderoy
see **Twisted Face series**

Straw series
Crump, James Irving
see **Jack Straw series**

Strawberry Shortcake series
This sequence has thirteen authors
Smollin, Michael J
1 *Strawberry Shortcake's cooking fun* (1980)
Razzi, Jim
2 *Strawberry Shortcake toy book* (1980)
3 *Strawberry Shortcake playhouse* (1980)
Fahrion, Muriel
4 *Strawberry Shortcake's make-and-do book* (1980)
Saphore, Athena
5 *Strawberry Shortcake sunny day poems* (1981)
Sustendal, Pat
6 *Strawberry Shortcake one-two-three* (1981)
Daly, Kathleen
7 *Strawberry Shortcake pets on parade* (1983)
Rosenblatt, Arthur
8 *Strawberry Shortcake and the deep dark woods* (1983)
Winthrop, Elizabeth
9 *Strawberry Shortcake and the big balloon race* (1983)
Miller, Nell
10 *Strawberry Shortcake and the crazy baking contest* (1983)
Lexau, Joan M
11 *Strawberry Shortcake and sad Mister Sun* (1983)
Doyle, Elizabeth
12 *Strawberry Shortcake and the birthday surprise* (1983)
Smollin, Michael J
13 *Strawberry Shortcake's party fun* (1983)
Llimona, Mercedes
14 *Strawberry Shortcake's favorite Mother Goose rhymes* (1983)
Elliott, Brian
15 *Strawberry Shortcake and baby needs a name* (1984)
Companion volumes: *Strawberry Shortcake and the fake cake surprise*, 1982, *Strawberry Shortcake and the catnabbing*, 1982, *Strawberry Shortcake and the picnic plot*, 1982, *Strawberry Shortcake's bathtime book*, 1984, *Strawberry Shortcake's year-round coloring book*, by Susan Shore, 1983

Street cars trilogy
Lorimer, Graeme
1 *Men are like street cars* (1932)
2 *Stag line* (1934)
3 *Heart specialist* (1935)

Street Hawk series
Roberts, Jack
Based on a television series
1 *Street Hawk* (1985)
2 *Cons at large* (1985)

Street series
Wakefield, Hannah
see **Dee Street series**

Street vigilante series
Rawls, Philip
see **Richard Bronson series**

Streeter series
Burke, Jackson Frederick
see **Joe Streeter series**

Strega Nona series
De Paola, Tomie
1 *Strega Nona* (1975)
Magic pasta pot
An old tale
2 *Strega Nona's magic lessons* (1982)
3 *Merry Christmas, Strega Nona* (1986)

Stretch and Larry series
Grover, Marshall
see **Larry and Stretch series**

Strickland series
Dilnot, George
see **Inspector Strickland series**

Strictly personal series
Horler, Sydney
1 *Strictly personal* (1934)
An indiscreet diary
2 *More strictly personal* (1935)
Six months of my life

Strike fighters series
Willard, Tom
1 *Strike fighters* (1990)
2 *Bold forager* (1990)
3 *War chariot* (1990)
4 *Sudden fury* (1991)
5 *Red dancer* (1991)
6 *Desert star* (1991)
7 *Blood river* (1991)
8 *Golden triangle* (1992)
9 *Death squad* (1992)

Strike Force Falklands series
Hardy, Adam
1 *Operation Exocet* (1984)
2 *Raider's dawn* (1984)
3 *Red alert* (1984)
4 *Reece patrol* (1985)
5 *Covert op* (1985)
6 *'Ware mines* (1985)

Striker series
Anthony, Piers
see **Jason Striker series**

Striker series
Cope, Kenneth
1 *Striker* (1976)
2 *Striker, second leg* (1977)

String family trilogy
Cleveland-Peck, Patricia
1 *String family* (1979)
2 *String family in summer* (1983)
3 *String family moves house* (1985)
Numbers 2 and 3 also published in one volume entitled *The String family at home*, 1986

Stringer series
Cameron, Lou
1 *Stringer* (1987)
2 *Stringer on Dead Man's Range* (1987)
3 *Stringer on the assassin's trail* (1987)
4 *Stringer and the hangman's rodeo* (1988)
5 *Stringer and the wild bunch* (1988)
6 *Stringer and the hanging judge* (1988)
7 *Stringer in Tombstone* (1988)
8 *Stringer and the deadly flood* (1988)
9 *Stringer and the lost tribe* (1988)
10 *Stringer and the oil well Indians* (1989)
11 *Stringer and the border war* (1989)
12 *Stringer and the Mojave* (1989)
13 *Stringer on Pike's Peak* (1989)
14 *Stringer and the hell-bound herd* (1989)
15 *Stringer in a Texas shoot-out* (1989)

Striplings trilogy
Hooke, Nina Warner
1 *Striplings* (1933)
2 *Close of play* (1936)
3 *Own wilderness* (1938)

Stroganoff Troupe series
Brahms, Caryl
1 *Bullet in the ballet* (1937)
2 *Casino for sale* (1938)
Murder a la Stroganoff
3 *Six curtains for Stroganova* (1945)
Six curtains for Natasha

Stroheim and Moss trilogy
Bantock, Nick
see **Griffin Moss and Sabine Stroheim trilogy**

Stromlands series
Roberts, John Maddox
1 *Islander* (1990)
2 *black shields* (1991)

Strong and Matthews series
Oursler, William
see **Philip Strong and James Matthews series**

Strong series
Acres, Mark
see **Sniper series**
Barnum, Vance
see **Joe Strong series**
Nolan, Frederick
see **Davy Strong series**

Strosa light series
Pope, Ray
1 *Strosa light* (1965)
2 *Salvage from Strosa* (1967)

Stroud series
Caine, Geoffrey
see **Abraham Stroud series**

Struan family series
Clavell, James
1 *Tai-pan* (1966)
A novel of Hong Kong
2 *Noble house* (1981)
3 *Whirlwind* (1986)

Struggle for life trilogy
Baroja y Nessi, Pio
1 *Quest* (1904)
Original edition entitled *La busca*
2 *Red dawn* (1904)
Original edition entitled *Aurora roja*
3 *Weeds* (1904)
Original edition entitled *Mala hierba*

Strummar series
Fackler, Elizabeth
see **Seth Strummar series**

Struthers series
Sims, L V
see **Dixie T Struthers series**

Strydom series
Nortje, Peter Henry
see **Henk Strydom series**

Stryker series
Barnes, Dallas
see **Sergeant John Stryker series**
Cain, Jonathan
see **Saigon commandos series**
Crawford, William
see **Colin Stryker series**
Gosling, Paula
see **Lieutenant Jack Stryker series**
Nighbert, David Franklin
see **Anton Stryker series**

Stuart Bailey series
Huggins, Roy
1 *Double take* (1946)
2 *Seventy seven Sunset Strip* (1959)
Three novelettes; based on a television series

Stuart Brannon series
Bly, Stephen Arthur
1 *Hard winter at Broken Arrow Crossing* (1991)
2 *False claims at the Little Stephen Mine* (1992)
3 *Last hanging at Paradise Meadow* (1992)
4 *Standof at Sunrise Creek* (1993)

Stuart Haydon series
Lindsey, David L
1 *Cold mind* (1983)
2 *Heat from another sun* (1984)
3 *Spiral* (1986)
4 *In the lake of the moon* (1988)

Stuart kings series
Trease, Geoffrey
1 *Cue for treason* (1940)
2 *Silver guard* (1948)
Set during the English Civil War
3 *Grey adventurer* (1942)
Set during the Restoration and the early years of the American colonies
4 *Trumpets in the West* (1947)
Set during the Monmouth Rebellion

Stuart series
Coffin, Geoffrey
see **Inspector Scott Stuart series**

Stuart series
Irwin, Margaret
1 *Royal flush* (1932)
The story of Minette
2 *Proud servant* (1934)
The story of Montrose
3 *Stranger prince* (1937)
The story of Rupert of the Rhine
4 *Bride* (1939)
The story of Louise and Montrose

Stuart series
Kerr, Robert
see **Jamie Stuart series**

Stuart series
Lane, Jane
1 *Escape of the King* (1950)
2 *Escape of the Prince* (1951)
3 *Escape of the Queen* (1957)
4 *Escape of the Duke* (1960)
5 *Escape of the Princess* (1962)
6 *Trial of the King* (1963)
7 *Return of the King* (1964)
8 *March of the Prince* (1965)
9 *Champion of the King* (1966)

Stuart series
Macdougall, James K
see **David Stuart series**

Stuart series
Plaidy, Jean
1 *Murder in the Tower* (1964)
2 *Wandering prince* (1956)
3 *Health unto His Majesty* (1956)
4 *Here lies our Sovereign Lord* (1957)
Numbers 2-4 also published in one volume entitled *Charles II*, 1972
5 *Three crowns* (1965)
6 *Haunted sisters* (1966)
7 *Queen's favourites* (1966)
Numbers 5-7 also published in one volume entitled *The last of the Stuarts*, 1977

Stuart series
Remick, Grace May
see **Jane Stuart series**

Stuart series
Tranter, Nigel Godwin
1 *Lords of misrule* (1976)
2 *Folly of princes* (1977)
3 *Captive crown* (1977)
4 *Unicorn rampant* (1984)

Stuarts series
Birt, David
1 *Guy Fawkes file* (1976)
2 *Stuart navy* (1976)
3 *Eleven years' tyranny* (1976)
4 *Civil War* (1976)
5 *Cromwell* (1976)
6 *Restoration England* (1976)
7 *Science and superstition* (1976)
8 *Plague and fire* (1976)
9 *Invasion of 1688* (1976)
10 *Marlborough's wars* (1976)
11 *Stuart fashion* (1976)
12 *Buckingham's expeditions* (1976)
13 *Pilgrim Fathers* (1976)
14 *Battle of Naseby* (1976)
15 *Execution of Charles I* (1976)
16 *Popish plot* (1976)
17 *Witch finder* (1976)
18 *Rebuilding of Saint Paul's* (1976)
19 *Monmouth's Rebellion* (1976)
20 *March to Blenheim* (1976)

Stubborn soil series
Owen, William A
Autobiography
1 *This stubborn soil* (1966)
A frontier boyhood
2 *Season of weathering* (1973)

Stubbs series
Aldiss, Brian Wilson
see **Horace Stubbs series**
Campbell, R T
see **Professor John Stubbs series**

Studs Lonigan trilogy
Farrell, James Thomas
1 *Young Lonigan* (1932)
A boyhood in Chicago streete
2 *Young manhood of Studs Lonigan* (1934)
3 *Judgment day* (1935)

Study Thirteen series
Havilton, Jeffrey
1 *Luck of Study Thirteen* (1934)
2 *Study Thirteen to the rescue* (1936)
3 *Sleuth of Study Thirteen* (1938)
4 *Study Thirteen in a tangle* (1939)

Stuff Central series
Farren, Mick
see **Jeb Stuart Ho series**

Stuff Driscoll series
King, Rufus
Short stories
1 *Malice in Wonderland* (1958)
2 *Steps to murder* (1960)
3 *Faces of danger* (1964)

Stuka Squadron series
Kessler, Leo
see **SS Stuka Squadron series**

Stumpfs series
Onslow, John
1 *Stumpfs* (1966)
2 *Stumpfs and the Cornish witches* (1969)

Stumps series
Bleackley, Horace William
1 *Tales of the stumps* (1901)
2 *More tales of the stumps* (1902)

Stupids series
Allard, Harry
1 *Stupids step out* (1974)
2 *Stupids have a ball* (1978)
3 *Stupids die* (1981)
4 *Stupids take off* (1989)

Stupids series
Marshall, James
1 *Stupids step out* (1974)
2 *Stupids have a ball* (1978)
3 *Stupids die* (1981)
4 *Stupids take off* (1989)

Sturdy series
Appleton, Victor
see **Don Sturdy series**

Sturrock series
Sturrock, Jeremy
see **Bow Street Runner series**

Styles series
Philips, Judson Pentecost
see **Peter Styles series**

Sub wars series
Henrick, Richard P
1 *Silent warriors* (1985)
2 *Counterforce* (1987)
3 *Phoenix odyssey* (1988)

Subaltern series
This sequence has two authors
Edmonds, Charles
1 *Subaltern's war* (1929)
A memoir of the Great War from the point of view of a romantic young man, and an essay on militarism
Carrington, Charles
2 *Soldier from the wars returning* (1965)

Submarine boys series
Durham, Victor
1 *Submarine boys on duty* (1909)
Alternative title: Life on a diving torpedo boat
2 *Submarine boys' trail trip* (1909)
Alternative title: Making good as young experts
3 *Submarine boys and the middies* (1909)
Alternative title: The prize detail at Annapolis
4 *Submarine boys and the spies* (1910)
Alternative title: Dodging the sharks of the deep
5 *Submarine boys' lightning cruise* (1910)

Alternative title: The young kings of the deep
6 *Submarine boys for the flag* (1910)
Alternative title: Deeding their lives to Uncle Sam
7 *Submarine boys and the smugglers* (1912)
Alternative title: Breaking up the New Jersey custom frauds
8 *Submarine boys' secret mission* (1912)
Alternative title: Beating an ambassador's game

Submarine series
Collenette, Eric J
see **Ben Grant series**

Submarine series
Hudson, Alec
1 *Battle stations* (1939)
2 *Enemy sighted* (1940)
3 *Rendezvous* (1941)
4 *Night action* (1942)
One volume edition entitled *Open fire*, 1942

Submarine series
Kessler, Leo
1 *Wolf pack* (1985)
2 *Operation death watch* (1985)
3 *Convoy to catastrophe* (1986)
4 *Fire in the west* (1986)
5 *Flight to the Reich* (1988)

Submarine Service series
Hackforth-Jones, Gilbert
1 *Submarine flotilla* (1940)
2 *Rough passage* (1941)
3 *Submarine alone* (1943)
4 *Price was high* (1946)
5 *Sixteen bells* (1946)
Short stories
6 *Questing hound* (1948)
7 *Worst enemy* (1950)
8 *Dangerous trade* (1952)

Submarine U93 series
Gilson, Charles
1 *Submarine U93* (1916)
A tale of the Great War
2 *In the power of the pigmies* (1918)
3 *Mystery of Ah Jim* (1919)
A story of the Chinese underworld and of piracy and adventure in Eastern seas
4 *Fire gods* (1920)
A tale of the Congo

Submarine warfare series
Melville-Ross, Antony
1 *Trigger* (1982)
2 *Talon* (1983)
3 *Shadow* (1984)
4 *Command* (1985)

Submariner Sinclair series
Wingate, John
1 *Submariner Sinclair* (1959)
2 *Jimmy-the-One* (1960)
3 *Sinclair in command* (1961)
4 *Nuclear captain* (1962)
5 *Sub-zero* (1963)
6 *Full fathom five* (1967)
7 *In the blood* (1973)

Submariners series
Blair, Clay
1 *Swordray's first three patrols* (1980)
2 *Silent victory* (1987)

Subspace explorers series
Smith, Edward Elmer
1 *Subspace explorers* (1965)
2 *Subspace encounter* (1983)
Co-author: Lloyd Arthur Eshbach

Such is life series
Collins, Tom
1 *Such is life* (1903)
2 *Rigby's romance* (1946)
3 *Buln-Buln and the brolga* (1948)

Sudden series
This sequence has two authors
Strange, Oliver
1 *Range robbers* (1930)
2 *Law o' the lariat* (1931)
3 *Marshal of Lawless* (1933)
Lawless
4 *Sudden* (1933)
5 *Sudden outlawed* (1935)
Outlawed
6 *Sudden, gold-seeker* (1937)
7 *Sudden rides again* (1938)
8 *Sudden takes the trail* (1940)
9 *Sudden takes charge* (1940)
10 *Sudden makes war* (1942)
11 *Sudden plays a hand* (1950)
Christian, Frederick H
12 *Sudden strikes back* (1966)
13 *Sudden, troubleshooter* (1967)
14 *Sudden at bay* (1968)
15 *Sudden, apache fighter* (1969)
16 *Sudden, dead or alive!* (1970)

Sudderley series
Mansbridge, Pamela
see **Caroline series**

Sue and Andy McVeigh series
Macveigh, Sue
see **Captain Andy and Sue McVeigh series**

Sue and Bunny Brown series
Hope, Laura Lee
see **Bunny Brown and his sister Sue series**

Sue and Jenny series
Macpherson, Bruce
see **Jenny and Sue series**

Sue Barton series
Boylston, Helen Dore
1 *Sue Barton, student nurse* (1936)
2 *Sue Barton, senior nurse* (1937)
3 *Sue Barton, visiting nurse* (1938)
4 *Sue Barton, rural nurse* (1939)
5 *Sue Barton, superintendent nurse* (1940)
Sue Barton, superintendent of nurses
6 *Sue Barton, neighbourhood nurse* (1949)
7 *Sue Barton, staff nurse* (1952)

Sue Trent series
Berrisford, Judith Mary
1 *Sue's circus horse* (1951)
2 *Ponies all summer* (1956)
3 *Sue's TV pony* (1964)

Suffolk trilogy
Lofts, Norah
1 *Town house* (1959)
2 *House at Old Vine* (1961)
3 *House at Sunset* (1962)

Sugar and spice series
Quin-Harkin, Janet
1 *Two girls, one boy* (1987)
2 *Trading places* (1987)
3 *Last dance* (1987)
4 *Dear cousin* (1987)
5 *Nothing in common* (1987)
6 *Flipside* (1987)
7 *Tug of war* (1987)
8 *Surf's up* (1987)
9 *Double take* (1987)
10 *Make me a star* (1988)
11 *Big sister* (1988)
12 *Out in the cold* (1988)
13 *Blind date* (1988)
14 *It's my turn* (1988)
15 *Home sweet home* (1988)
16 *Dream come true* (1988)
17 *Campus cousins* (1989)
18 *Roadtrip* (1989)
19 *One step too far* (1989)
20 *Having a ball* (1989)

Sugar Creek Gang series
Hutchens, Paul
1 *Sugar Creek Gang* (1939)
Sugar Creek Gang and the swamp robber
2 *Further adventures of the Sugar Creek Gang* (1940)
Sugar Creek Gang and the winter rescue
3 *We killed a bear* (1940)
Sugar Creek Gang and the killer bear
4 *Sugar Creek goes camping* (1941)
Lost campers
5 *Sugar Creek in Chicago* (1941)
Sugar Creek Gang and the Chicago adventure
6 *Sugar Creek Gang in school* (1942)
Secret hideout
7 *Mystery at Sugar Creek* (1943)
Sugar Creek Gang and the mystery cave
8 *Sugar Creek Gang flies to Cuba* (1944)
Sugar Creek Gang and the palm tree mystery
9 *New Sugar Creek Gang mystery* (1946)
Sugar Creek Gang and the mystery thief
10 *One stormy day at Sugar Creek* (1946)
11 *Shenanigans at Sugar Creek* (1947)
Sugar Creek Gang and the teacher trouble
12 *Sugar Creek Gang goes north* (1947)
Sugar Creek Gang and screams in the night
13 *Adventure in an Indian cemetery* (1947)
Indian cemetery
14 *Sugar Creek Gang digs for treasure* (1948)
Sugar Creek Gang and the treasure hunt
15 *North woods manhunt* (1948)
Sugar Creek Gang and the thousand dollar fish
16 *Haunted house at Sugar Creek* (1949)
Sugar Creek Gang and the haunted house
17 *Lost in a Sugar Creek blizzard* (1950)
Sugar Creek Gang lost in the blizzard
18 *Sugar Creek Gang on the Mexican border* (1950)
On the Mexican border
19 *Green tent mystery at Sugar Creek* (1950)
Sugar Creek Gang and the green tent mystery
20 *Ten thousand minutes at Sugar Creek* (1952)
Sugar Creek Gang and the bull fighter
21 *Blue cow at Sugar Creek* (1953)
Sugar Creek Gang and the blue cow
22 *Trapline thief at Sugar Creek* (1953)
Sugar Creek Gang and the trapline thief
23 *Watermelon mystery at Sugar Creek* (1953)
Sugar Creek Gang and the watermelon mystery
24 *Sugar Creek Gang at Snow Goose Lodge* (1957)
Sugar Creek Gang and the timber wolf
25 *Sugar Creek Gang goes Western* (1957)
Sugar Creek Gang and the Western adventure
26 *Old stranger's secret at Sugar Creek* (1957)
Sugar Creek Gang and the tree house mystery
27 *Wild Horse Canyon mystery* (1959)
Sugar Creek Gang and the Colorado kidnapping
28 *Howling dog in Sugar Creek* (1960)
Sugar Creek Gang and the ghost dog
29 *We killed a wildcat at Sugar Creek* (1966)
Sugar Creek Gang and the killer cat
30 *Brown box mystery at Sugar Creek* (1970)
Sugar Creek Gang and the brown box
31 *White boat rescue at Sugar Creek* (1970)
Sugar Creek Gang and the white boat rescue
32 *Worm turns at Sugar Creek* (1972)
Sugar Creek Gang and the cemetery vandals
33 *Sleeping Beauty at Sugar Creek* (1972)
Sugar Creek Gang and the battle of the bees
34 *Down in Sugar Creek chimney* (1973)
Sugar Creek Gang locked in the attic
35 *Runaway mystery at Sugar Creek* (1973)
Sugar Creek Gang and the runaway rescue
Companion volume: *Trails of yesteryear, ye olde Sugar Creek scrapbook*, 1951

Sugar Kane series
Marshall, Lovat
1 *Sugar for the lady* (1955)
2 *Sugar on the carpet* (1956)
3 *Sugar cuts the corners* (1957)
4 *Sugar on the target* (1958)
5 *Sugar on the cuff* (1960)
6 *Sugar on the kill* (1961)
7 *Sugar on the loose* (1962)
8 *Sugar on the prowl* (1962)
9 *Murder in triplicate* (1963)
10 *Murder is the reason* (1964)
11 *Ladies can be dangerous* (1964)
12 *Death strikes in darkness* (1965)
13 *Dead are silent* (1966)
14 *Dead are dangerous* (1966)
15 *Murder of a lady* (1966)
16 *Blood on the blotter* (1968)
17 *Money means murder* (1968)
18 *Death is for ever* (1969)
19 *Murder's out of season* (1970)
20 *Murder's just for cops* (1971)
21 *Death casts a shadow* (1972)
22 *Moment for murder* (1972)
23 *Loose lady death* (1973)
24 *Date with murder* (1973)
25 *Murder town* (1974)
26 *Strangler* (1974)
27 *Key to murder* (1975)
28 *Murder to order* (1975)
29 *Murder mission* (1976)

Sugden series
Mackenzie, Lee
see **Annie Sugden series**

Sughrue series
Crumley, James
see **C W Sughrue series**

Suite Policiere series
Aveline, Claude
1 *Cat's-eye* (1970)
Original edition entitled *L'oeil-de-chat*
2 *Passenger on the U* (1947)
Original edition entitled *L'abonne de la ligne U*
3 *Fountain at Marlieux* (1954)
Original edition entitled *Le jet d'eau*

Suite Policiere series

4 *Double death of Frederic Belot* (1932)
Original edition entitled *La double mort de Frederic Belot*
5 *Carriage seven, seat fifteen* (1947)
Original edition entitled *Voiture 7, place 15*

Sula series
Derwent, Lavinia
see **Magnus series**

Suleiman the Magnificent trilogy
Crawley, Aileen
1 *Bride of Suleiman* (1981)
2 *Shadow of God* (1982)
3 *House of war* (1984)

Sullivan series
Cutter, John
see **Specialist series**
Deitz, Tom
see **David Sullivan series**
Mullally, Frederic
see **Bob Sullivan series**

Sultan series
Austin, Hugh
see **William Sultan series**

Sultan's harem series
Austin, Hugh
see **William Sultan series**

Sumi series
Uchida, Yoshiko
1 *Sumi's prize* (1964)
2 *Sumi's special happening* (1966)
3 *Sumi and the goat and the Tokyo Express* (1969)

Summer fun, winter fun series
Dubrovin, Vivian
1 *Baseball just for fun* (1974)
2 *Magic bowling ball* (1974)
3 *Track trophy* (1974)
4 *Rescue on skis* (1974)

Summer trilogy
Lipsyte, Roger
1 *One fat summer* (1977)
2 *Summer rules* (1981)
3 *Summerboy* (1982)

Summer wine series
Clarke, Roy
1 *Gala week* (1986)
2 *Moonbather* (1987)
Companion volumes: *Last of the summer wine, cartoon book*, 1983, *Summer wine country*, 1989

Summer's lease trilogy
Rothenstein, John
Autobiography
1 *Summer's lease* (1965)
1901-1938
2 *Brave day, hideous night* (1966)
1939-1965
3 *Time's thievish progress* (1970)

Summers series
Manor, Jason
see **Steve Summers series**
Marlowe, Francis
see **Doc Summers series**

Summing up trilogy
Maugham, William Somerset
Literary memoirs
1 *Summing up* (1938)
2 *Strictly personal* (1941)
3 *Writer's notebook* (1949)
One volume edition entitled *The partial view*, 1954

Sumner series
Davey, Norman
see **Pilgrim series**

Goulart, Ron
see **Barnum series**

Sumuru series
Rohmer, Sax
1 *Nude in mink* (1950)
Sins of Sumuru
2 *Sumuru* (1951)
Slaves of Sumuru
3 *Fire goddess* (1952)
Virgin in flames
4 *Moon is red* (1954)
5 *Sand and satin* (1954)
Return of Sumuru
6 *Sinister madonna* (1956)

Sun and moon series
Ormerod, Jan
Books without words
1 *Sunshine* (1981)
2 *Moonlight* (1982)

Sun Wolf series
Hambly, Barbara
1 *Ladies of Mandrigyn* (1984)
2 *Witches of Wenshar* (1987)
Numbers 1 and 2 also published in one volume entitled *The unschooled wizard*, 1987
3 *Dark hand of magic* (1990)

Sun-cross series
Hambly, Barbara
1 *Rainbow abyss* (1991)
2 *Magicians of night* (1992)

Sundance Kid and Butch Cassidy series
Essex, Saran
see **Butch Cassidy and the Sundance Kid series**

Sundance series
This sequence has three authors
Benteen, John
1 *Overkill* (1971)
2 *Dead Man's Canyon* (1972)
3 *Dakota Territory* (1972)
4 *Death in the lava* (1972)
5 *Pistoleros* (1972)
6 *Bronco trail* (1973)
7 *Wild stallions* (1973)
8 *Bring me his scalp* (1973)
9 *Taps at Little Big Horn* (1973)
10 *Ghost dancers* (1973)
Slade, Jack
11 *Comancheros* (1974)
12 *Renegade* (1974)
13 *Honcho* (1974)
Benteen, John
14 *War party* (1974)
15 *Bounty killer* (1975)
16 *Run for cover* (1976)
17 *Manhunt* (1976)
18 *Blood on the prairie* (1976)
19 *War trail* (1976)
20 *Riding shotgun* (1977)
21 *Silent enemy* (1977)
22 *Ride the man down* (1977)
23 *Gunbelt* (1977)
Slade, Jack
24 *Canyon kill* (1977)
McCurtin, Peter
25 *Loanshark* (1979)
26 *Nightriders* (1979)
27 *Death dance* (1979)
28 *Savage* (1979)
29 *Day of the halfbreeds* (1979)
30 *Los Olvidados* (1980)
31 *Marauders* (1980)
32 *Scorpion* (1980)
33 *Hangman's knot* (1980)
34 *Apache war* (1980)
35 *Gold strike* (1980)
36 *Trail drive* (1981)
37 *Iron men* (1981)
38 *Drumfire* (1981)
39 *Buffalo war* (1981)
40 *Hunters* (1981)
41 *Cage* (1982)
42 *Choctaw County war* (1982)
43 *Texas empire* (1982)
44 *Rockwell* (1984)
Companion volume: *Sundance*, by Richard Telfair, 1960

Sunday the thirteenth series
Gard, Stephen
1 *Sunday the thirteenth* (1993)
2 *Return* (1993)

Sundered series
Sagara, Michele M
1 *Into the dark lands* (1991)
2 *Children of the blood* (1992)
3 *Lady of mercy* (1993)

Sundmans trilogy
Duke, Madelaine
1 *City built to music* (1960)
2 *Ride the brooding wind* (1961)
3 *Sovereign lords* (1963)

Sunfire series
This sequence has six authors
Ransom, Candice Farris
1 *Amanda* (1984)
2 *Susannah* (1984)
Roberts, Willo Davis
3 *Elizabeth* (1984)
Schurfranz, Vivian
4 *Danielle* (1984)
Miner, Jane Claypool
5 *Joanna* (1984)
Shura, Mary Francis
6 *Jessica* (1984)
Roberts, Willo Davis
7 *Caroline* (1984)
Ransom, Candice Farris
8 *Kathleen* (1985)
Shura, Mary Francis
9 *Marilee* (1985)
Schurfranz, Vivian
10 *Laura* (1985)
Ransom, Candice Farris
11 *Emily* (1985)
Gordon, Jeffie Ross
12 *Jacquelyn* (1985)
Roberts, Willo Davis
13 *Victoria* (1985)
Schurfranz, Vivian
14 *Cassie* (1985)
Miner, Jane Claypool
15 *Roxanne* (1985)
Schurfranz, Vivian
16 *Megan* (1986)
Ransom, Candice Farris
17 *Sabrina* (1986)
Miner, Jane Claypool
18 *Veronica* (1986)
Ransom, Candice Farris
19 *Nicole* (1986)
Schurfranz, Vivian
20 *Julie* (1986)
21 *Rachel* (1986)
Miner, Jane Claypool
22 *Corey* (1986)
Schurfranz, Vivian
23 *Heather* (1987)
Shura, Mary Francis
24 *Gabrielle* (1987)
Schurfranz, Vivian
25 *Merrie* (1987)
Gordon, Jeffie Ross
26 *Nora* (1987)
Miner, Jane Claypool
27 *Margaret* (1988)
Schurfranz, Vivian
28 *Josie* (1988)
Shura, Mary Francis
29 *Diana* (1988)
Schurfranz, Vivian
30 *Renee* (1989)
Miner, Jane Claypool
31 *Jennie* (1989)
Shura, Mary Francis
32 *Darcy* (1989)

Sunglasses series
Collins, Nancy Averill
1 *Sunglasses after dark* (1989)
2 *Tempter* (1990)

Sunken danger series
Jeffries, Roderic Graeme
1 *Sunken danger* (1985)
2 *Meeting trouble* (1986)
3 *Man who couldn't be* (1987)

Sunken treasure series
Ellsberg, Edward
1 *Thirty fathoms deep* (1930)
2 *Ocean gold* (1935)
3 *Spanish ingots* (1936)
4 *Treasure below* (1940)

Sunny Boy series
White, Ramy Allison
1 *Sunny Boy in the country* (1920)
2 *Sunny Boy at the seashore* (1920)
3 *Sunny Boy in the big city* (1920)
4 *Sunny Boy in school and out* (1921)
5 *Sunny Boy and his playmates* (1922)
6 *Sunny Boy and his games* (1923)
7 *Sunny Boy in the far West* (1924)
8 *Sunny Boy on the ocean* (1925)
9 *Sunny Boy with the circus* (1926)
10 *Sunny Boy and his big dog* (1927)
11 *Sunny Boy in the snow* (1929)
12 *Sunny Boy at Willow Farm* (1929)
13 *Sunny Boy and his cave* (1930)
14 *Sunny Boy at Rainbow Lake* (1931)

Sunnybank collies series
Terhune, Albert Payson
1 *Lad, a dog* (1919)
2 *Bruce* (1920)
3 *Buff, a collie, and other stories* (1921)
4 *His dog* (1922)
5 *Further adventures of Lad* (1922)
Dog stories every child should know
6 *Lochinvar Luck* (1923)
7 *Treve* (1924)
8 *Heart of a dog* (1924)
9 *Wolf* (1925)
10 *My friend the dog* (1926)
11 *Treasure* (1927)
Faith of a collie
12 *Gray Dawn* (1927)
13 *Luck of the Laird* (1927)
Highland collie
14 *Lad of Sunnybank* (1929)
15 *Dog named Chips* (1931)
16 *Way of a dog* (1932)
Further adventures of Gray Dawn and some others
17 *Loot!* (1940)
Collie to the rescue
Companion volume: *The book of Sunnybank*, 1934, also published as *Sunnybank, home of Lad*

Sunnybrook Farm series
Wiggin, Kate Douglas
see **Rebecca series**

Sun's end series
Lupoff, Richard Allen
1 *Sun's end* (1984)
2 *Galaxy's end* (1988)
3 *Time's end* (1989)

Sunset House series
Lea, Alec
see **Varden family series**

Sunset Warrior series
Lustbader, Eric
1 *Sunset Warrior* (1977)
2 *Shallows of night* (1978)
3 *Dai-San* (1978)
4 *Beneath an opal moon* (1980)

Sunshine and shadow series
Roberts, Cecil
Autobiography
1 *Growing boy* (1967)

Covers 1892-1908
2 *Years of promise* (1968)
Covers 1908-1919
3 *Bright twenties* (1970)
Covers 1920-1929
4 *Sunshine and shadow* (1972)
Covers 1930-1946
5 *Pleasant years* (1974)
Covers 1947-1972

Sunshine Ranch series
Dickson, Helen
1 *Family at Sunshine Ranch* (1939)
2 *Dorothy of Sunshine Ranch* (1948)

Sunshine series
Klein, Norma
Based on a television series and a moving picture
1 *Sunshine* (1971)
2 *Sunshine years* (1975)
3 *Sunshine Christmas* (1978)

Sunstone scrolls trilogy
Van Scyoc, Sydney Joyce
1 *Darkchild* (1982)
2 *Bluesong* (1983)
3 *Starsilk* (1984)
One volume edition entitled *Daughters of the sunshine*, 1985

Super Adam and Rosie Wonder series
Thwaites, Lyndsay
1 *Super Adam and Rosie Wonder* (1983)
2 *Rosie's wonderful dances* (1984)
3 *Adam and Rosie run away* (1985)
4 *Adam and Rosie and the strange planet* (1987)

Super Barrabas series
Hild, Jack
1 *Barrabas strike* (1988)
2 *Barrabas sting* (1988)
3 *Barrabas blitz* (1989)
Number 4 not identified
5 *Barrabas sweep* (1990)

Super Bowl series
Resciniti, Angelo G
Based on *Countdown to thirteen Super Bowls*, 1979
1 *Victory at the Super Bowl* (1982)
2 *Super Bowl victories* (1985)
3 *Hot Super Bowl battles* (1988)
4 *Incredible Super Bowl action* (1993)

Super Cops series
This sequence has two authors; based on a television series
Whittemore, Louis Henry
1 *Super Cops* (1973)
Greenberg, Dave
2 *Play it to a bust* (1975)

Super endless quest adventure gamebook series
This sequence has three authors
Simon, Morris
1 *Prisoners of Pax Tharkas* (1985)
Blashfield, Jean
2 *Ghost tower* (1985)
Niles, Douglas
3 *Escape from Castle Quarras* (1985)

Super Gran series
Wilson, Forrest
1 *Super Gran* (1978)
2 *Super Gran rules O.K.!* (1981)
3 *Super Gran superstar* (1982)
4 *Super Gran is magic* (1983)
5 *Super Gran on holiday* (1985)
6 *Super Gran at the circus* (1987)
7 *Super Gran abroad* (1988)
8 *Super Gran to the rescue* (1990)

Super men and women series
Cooper, Jilly
1 *Men and super men* (1972)
2 *Women and super women* (1974)
One volume edition entitled *Super men and super women*, 1976

Super nova series
Macvicar, Angus
1 *Super Nova and the rogue satellite* (1969)
2 *Super Nova and the frozen man* (1970)

Super powers which way series
This sequence has three authors
Helfer, Andrew
1 *Superman, the man of steel* (1983)
2 *Supergirl, the girl of steel* (1984)
Fleming, Robert Loren
3 *Justice League of America* (1984)
Wenk, Richard
4 *Batman, the doomsday prophecy* (1986)

Super Sam Snout series
Lemieux, Anne
1 *Super Sam Snout and the case of the stolen snowman* (1994)
2 *Super Sam Snout and the case of the missing marble* (1994)
3 *Super Sam Snout and the case of the yogurt-poker* (1994)

Super Sleuth series
Christian, Mary Blount
see **Sebastian Super Sleuth series**

Super Sleuth series
Vivelo, Jacqueline Jones
1 *Super Sleuth* (1985)
Twelve solve-it-yourself mysteries
2 *Beagle in trouble* (1986)
3 *Super Sleuth and the bare bones* (1988)

Super sleuth series
Ecke, Wolfgang
Translated from the German
1 *Be a supersleuth with the case of the face at the window* (1978)
Case of the face at the window
Face at the window
2 *Be a super sleuth with the case of the stolen paintings* (1979)
Case of the stolen paintings
Stolen paintings
3 *Be a super sleuth with the case of the invisible witness* (1980)
Case of the invisible witness
Invisible witness
4 *Be a super sleuth with the case of the bank holdup* (1982)
Case of the bank holdup
Bank holdup
5 *Be a super sleuth with the case of the high-rise robbery* (1983)
Case of the high-rise robbery
6 *Case of the midnight chess game* (1985)
Midnight chess game

Super Vietnam series
Helm, Eric
1 *Raid* (1989)
2 *Shifting fires* (1989)
3 *Strike* (1989)
4 *Empire* (1990)
5 *Sniper* (1990)

SuperBolan series
Pendleton, Don
All titles in this sequence are published under the name Don Pendleton either as a real name or as a house pseudonym used by Alan Bomack, Chet Cunningham, Peter Leslie, Charlie McDade, Mike McQuay, Stephen Mertz, Mike Newton, Dick Stivers where authorship is indicated against the titles
1 *Stony Man doctrine* (1983) [Stivers]
2 *Terminal velocity* (1984) [Bomack]
3 *Resurrection day* (1985) [Cunningham]
4 *Dirty war* (1985) [Mertz]
5 *Flight seven four one* (1986) [Newton]
6 *Dead easy* (1986) [Leslie]
7 *Sudden death* (1987) [Leslie]
8 *Rogue force* (1987) [Newton]
9 *Tropic heat* (1987) [McDade]
10 *Fire in the sky* (1988) [McQuay]
11 *Anvil of hell* (1988)
12 *Flash point* (1988)
13 *Flesh and blood* (1988)

Supercops series
Greenberg, Dave
see **Super Cops series**

Superdog series
McInerney, Judith Whitelock
see **Judge Benjamin series**

Superdog series
Wilson, David Henry
1 *Superdog* (1984)
2 *Superdog the hero* (1986)
3 *Superdog in trouble* (1988)

Superintendent Adams series
Hollingsworth, Leonard
1 *Body on the bus* (1930)
2 *Death leaves us naked* (1931)
3 *Dead man's alibi* (1933)

Superintendent Anders series
Jobson, Hamilton
see **Inspector Anders series**

Superintendent Andrew Ash series
Grierson, Francis Durham
1 *Out of the ashes* (1946)
2 *He had it coming to him* (1948)
3 *No wreaths for the duchess* (1948)
4 *Buddha of Fleet Street* (1949)
5 *Strange case of Edgar Herriot* (1950)
6 *Boomerang murder* (1951)
7 *Traitor's cross* (1852)
8 *Madame Shadow* (1852)
9 *Blackmail in red* (1954)
10 *Judas, C.I.D.* (1955)
11 *Blind frog* (1955)
12 *Sign of the nine* (1956)
13 *Green evil* (1958)
14 *Red cobra* (1960)

Superintendent Andrew Dalziel and Sergeant Pascoe series
Hill, Reginald
1 *Clubbable woman* (1970)
2 *Fell of dark* (1971)
3 *Advancement of learning* (1971)
4 *Fairly dangerous thing* (1972)
5 *Ruling passion* (1973)
6 *Very good hater* (1974)
7 *April shroud* (1975)
8 *Another death in Venice* (1976)
9 *Pinch of snuff* (1978)
10 *Pascoe's ghost* (1979)
Short stories
11 *Spy's wife* (1980)
12 *Killing kindness* (1980)
13 *Deadheads* (1983)
14 *Exit lines* (1984)
15 *Child's play* (1987)
16 *Under world* (1988)
17 *Bones and silence* (1990)
18 *One small step* (1990)
19 *Recalled to life* (1992)
20 *Pictures of perfection* (1994)

Superintendent Andrew Pearson series
Shepherd, Eric
1 *Murder in a nunnery* (1940)
2 *More murder in a nunnery* (1954)

Superintendent Anthony Slade series
Gribble, Leonard Reginald
1 *Gillespie suicide mystery* (1929)
Terrace suicide mystery
2 *Case of the Marsden rubies* (1929)
3 *Grand Modena murder* (1930)
4 *Is this revenge?* (1931)
Serpentine murder
5 *Stolen home secretary* (1932)
Stolen statesman
6 *Yellow bungalow mystery* (1933)
7 *Secret of Tangles* (1933)
8 *Riddle of the ravens* (1934)
9 *Death chime* (1934)
10 *Mystery at Tudor Arches* (1935)
11 *Riley of the Special Branch* (1936)
12 *Case of the Malverne diamonds* (1936)
13 *Who killed Oliver Cromwell?* (1937)
14 *Case-book of Anthony Slade* (1937)
15 *Tragedy in E flat* (1938)
16 *Arsenal Stadium mystery* (1939)
Revised edition 1950
17 *Atomic murder* (1947)
18 *Hangman's moon* (1950)
19 *They kidnapped Stanley Matthews* (1950)
20 *Frightened chameleon* (1951)
21 *Glass alibi* (1952)
22 *Murder out of season* (1952)
23 *She died laughing* (1953)
24 *Inverted crime* (1954)
25 *Death pays the piper* (1956)
26 *Superintendent Slade investigates* (1956)
27 *Stand-in for murder* (1957)
28 *Don't argue with death* (1959)
29 *Wantons die hard* (1961)
30 *Heads you die* (1964)
31 *Violent dark* (1965)
32 *Strip-tease macabre* (1967)
33 *Diplomat dies* (1969)
34 *Alias the victim* (1971)
35 *Programmed for death* (1973)
36 *You can't die tomorrow* (1975)
37 *Midsummer slay ride* (1976)
38 *Cardinal's diamonds* (1976)
39 *Crime on her hands* (1977)
40 *Death needs no alibi* (1979)
41 *Dead end in Mayfair* (1981)
42 *Dead don't scream* (1983)
43 *Violent midnight* (1986)

Superintendent Badger Brock series
Bingham, John
1 *Brock* (1981)
2 *Brock and the defector* (1982)

Superintendent Bamsan Kiet series
Alexander, Gary
1 *Pigeon blood* (1988)
2 *Unfunny money* (1989)
3 *Kiet and the golden peacock* (1989)
4 *Kiet and the Opium War* (1990)
5 *Deadly drought* (1991)
6 *Kiet goes west* (1992)

Superintendent Battle series
Christie, Agatha
1 *Secret of Chimneys* (1925)
2 *Seven Dials mystery* (1929)
3 *Cards on the table* (1936)
4 *Murder is easy* (1939)
Easy to kill
5 *Towards zero* (1944)
Come and be hanged

Superintendent Ben Spence series
Allen, Michael
1 *Spence in Petal Park* (1977)
Spence and the holiday makers
2 *Spence at the Blue Bazaar* (1979)
3 *Spence at Marlby Manor* (1982)

Superintendent Bill Rowlands series
Lucas, Norman
1 *Corner in crime* (1952)
2 *Red dice* (1952)
3 *Testament of death* (1953)
4 *Situations vacant* (1956)

Superintendent Black series
Chance, John Newton
1 *Wheels in the forest* (1935)
2 *Death of an innocent* (1938)
3 *Ghost of truth* (1939)
4 *Red knight* (1945)

Superintendent Blayde series
Wainwright, John
1 *Urge for justice* (1981)
2 *Blayde R.I.P.* (1982)

Superintendent Bone series
Staynes, Jill
American editions published under the pseudonym Susannah Stacey
1 *Goodbye, Nanny Gray* (1987)
2 *Body of opinion* (1988)
3 *Knife at the opera* (1988)
4 *Grave responsibility* (1990)
5 *Late lady* (1992)
6 *Bone idle* (1993)

Superintendent Bowman and Sergeant Peart series
Burrows, Julie
1 *No need for violence* (1970)
2 *Like an evening gone* (1973)

Superintendent Bradley and Sergeant Raymond series
Longmate, Norman
see **Inspector Bradley and Sergeant Raymond series**

Superintendent Bradley series
Robertson, Colin
1 *Murder in the morning* (1957)
2 *Time to kill* (1961)
3 *Conflict fo shadows* (1963)
4 *Frightened widow* (1963)
5 *Dead on time* (1964)
6 *Sinister moonlight* (1965)
7 *Killer's mask* (1966)
8 *Double take* (1967)
9 *Twice dead* (1968)
10 *Devil's cloak* (1969)
11 *Green diamonds* (1970)

Superintendent Brannigan series
Mackenzie, Andrew
1 *House at the estuary* (1948)
2 *Search in the dark* (1948)
3 *Shadows on the river* (1949)
4 *Splash of red* (1949)
5 *Whisper if you dare!* (1950)
6 *Point of a gun* (1951)
7 *Man who wanted to die* (1951)

Superintendent Carmichael series
Radford, Edwin
1 *Look in at murder* (1956)
2 *Married to murder* (1959)

Superintendent Cawthorne series
Silverwood, Roger
1 *Deadly daffodils* (1970)
2 *Dying for a drink* (1971)
3 *Illegitimate spy* (1972)

Superintendent Charles Ripley series
Wainwright, John
1 *Evil intent* (1966)
2 *Worms must wait* (1967)
3 *Freeze thy blood less coldly* (1970)
4 *Touch of malice* (1973)
5 *Hard hit* (1974)
6 *Death of a big man* (1975)

Superintendent Charles Wycliffe series
Burley, William John
1 *Three-toed pussy* (1968)
2 *To kill a cat* (1970)
Wycliffe and how to kill a cat
3 *Guilt edged* (1971)
4 *Death in a salubrious place* (1973)
5 *Death in Stanley Street* (1974)
Wycliffe and death in Stanley Street
6 *Wycliffe and the pea-green boat* (1975)
7 *Wycliffe and the schoolgirls* (1976)
8 *Wycliffe and the scapegoat* (1978)
9 *Wycliffe in Paul's Court* (1980)
10 *Wycliffe's wild goose chase* (1982)
11 *Wycliffe and the Beales* (1983)
12 *Wycliffe and the four Jacks* (1985)
13 *Wycliffe and the quiet virgin* (1986)
14 *Wycliffe and the Windsor blue* (1987)
15 *Wycliffe and the tangled web* (1988)
16 *Wycliffe and the cycle of death* (1990)
17 *Wycliffe and the dead flautist* (1991)
18 *Wycliffe and the last rites* (1992)
19 *Wycliffe and the dunes mystery* (1994)

Superintendent Cissie Marlow series
Dickson, Grierson
1 *Traitor's market* (1936)
2 *Devil's torch* (1936)
3 *Design for treason* (1937)
4 *Knight's gambit* (1950)
5 *Seven screens* (1950)

Superintendent Colin Harpur series
James, Bill
1 *You'd better believe it* (1985)
2 *Lolita man* (1986)
3 *Halo parade* (1987)
4 *Protection* (1988)
5 *Come clean* (1989)
6 *Take* (1990)

Superintendent Curtis Burke series
Trevor, Ralph
1 *Death burns the candle* (1938)
2 *Murder for two pins* (1939)
3 *Sky-high terror* (1940)
4 *Front page murder* (1942)

Superintendent Daniels series
Baxter, Gregory
1 *Narrowing lust* (1928)
2 *Ainceworth mystery* (1929)
3 *Death strikes at six bells* (1930)
4 *Calamity comes of age* (1935)

Superintendent Donald Martin series
Bardsley, Michael
1 *Murder on fire* (1969)
2 *Murder for sale* (1970)
3 *Murder on ice* (1972)
4 *Hit it rich* (1972)

Superintendent Donald Reamer series
Duncan, William Murdoch
1 *Meet the Dreamer* (1963)
2 *Again the Dreamer* (1965)
3 *Presenting the Dreamer* (1966)
4 *Case for the Dreamer* (1966)
5 *Problem for the Dreamer* (1967)
6 *Dreamer intervenes* (1968)
7 *Salute the Dreamer* (1968)
8 *Challenge for the Dreamer* (1969)
9 *Dreamer deals with murder* (1970)
10 *Detail for the Dreamer* (1971)
11 *Dreamer at large* (1972)
12 *Prey for the Dreamer* (1974)
13 *Laurels for the Dreamer* (1975)

Superintendent Duffy series
Fitzgerald, Nigel
1 *Midsummer malice* (1953)
2 *Rosy pastor* (1954)
3 *House is falling* (1955)
4 *Imagine a man* (1956)
5 *Student body* (1958)
6 *Suffer a witch* (1958)
7 *This won't hurt you* (1959)
8 *Black welcome* (1961)
9 *Day of the adder* (1963)
Echo answers murder
10 *Affairs of death* (1967)

Superintendent Duncan Kincaid and Sergeant Gemma James series
Crombie, Deborah
1 *Share in death* (1993)
2 *All shall be well* (1994)

Superintendent Edmund Bendilow series
Wallace, Carlton
1 *Mister Death walks aborad* (1933)
Mister Death
2 *Sinister alibi* (1934)
3 *Death of a libertine* (1936)
4 *Devil breathes but once* (1937)
5 *Death in the kettle* (1938)

Superintendent Fergus McQueen series
Litchfield, Michael
1 *See how they run* (1984)
2 *Murder circus* (1985)

Superintendent Fillinger series
McGuire, Paul
1 *Tower mystery* (1932)
Death tolls the bell
2 *Three dead men* (1931)
3 *Murder by the law* (1932)
4 *Death fugue* (1933)
5 *There sits death* (1933)
6 *Daylight murder* (1934)
Murder at high noon
7 *Murder in haste* (1934)

Superintendent Flagg series
Duncan, William Murdoch
1 *Death beckons quietly* (1946)
Sequence continued under the pseudonym John Cassells
Cassells, John
2 *Murder comes to Rothesay* (1946)
3 *League of nameless men* (1948)
4 *Master of the dark* (1948)
5 *Castle of sin* (1949)
6 *Clue of the purple asters* (1949)
7 *Waters of sadness* (1950)
8 *Circle of dust* (1950)
9 *Exit Mister Shane* (1951)
10 *Grey ghost* (1951)
11 *Second Mrs Locke* (1952)
12 *Rattler* (1952)
13 *Salute Inspector Flagg* (1953)
14 *Case for Inspector Flagg* (1954)
15 *Inspector Flagg and the scarlet skeleton* (1955)
16 *Again Inspector Flagg* (1956)
17 *Presenting Superintendent Flagg* (1957)
18 *Case twenty nine* (1958)
19 *Enter Superintendent Flagg* (1959)
20 *Score for Superintendent Flagg* (1960)
21 *Problem for Superintendent Flagg* (1961)
22 *Brothers of benevolence* (1962)
23 *Council of the Rat* (1963)
24 *Blue Mask* (1964)
25 *Grey Face* (1965)
26 *Blackfingers* (1966)
27 *Room in Quiver Court* (1967)
28 *Call for Superintendent Flagg* (1968)
29 *Double-crosser* (1969)
30 *Grafter* (1970)
31 *Hatchet man* (1971)
32 *Enforcer* (1973)
33 *Killer's rope* (1974)
34 *Quest for Superintendent Flagg* (1975)

Superintendent Folly series
York, Jeremy
These titles include Superintendent Folly in the revised editions which are listed here; the original editions were published under the pseudonym Michael Halliday between 1945 and 1949 and did not contain Superintendent Folly
1 *Find the body* (1967)
2 *Murder came late* (1969)
3 *Run away to murder* (1970)
4 *Let's kill Uncle Lionel* (1973)
5 *Close the door on murder* (1973)
6 *Gallows are waiting* (1973)

Superintendent Francis Foy series
Black, Lionel
1 *Breakaway* (1970)
Flood
2 *Ransom for a nude* (1972)
3 *Life and death of Peter Wade* (1973)

Superintendent Gaden series
Powell, Percival Henry
1 *Why kill a butler?* (1952)
2 *Now lying dead* (1953)
3 *Death of an expert witness* (1957)

Superintendent Gaylord series
Duncan, William Murdoch
1 *Hooded man* (1960)
2 *Nighthawk* (1962)

Superintendent George Gently series
Hunter, Alan
see **Inspector George Gently series**

Superintendent George Masters series
Clark, Douglas
see **Inspector George Masters series**

Superintendent George Rogers series
Ross, Jonathan
1 *Blood running cold* (1968)
2 *Diminished by death* (1968)
3 *Dead at first hand* (1969)
4 *Deadest thing you ever saw* (1969)
5 *Here lies Nancy Frail* (1972)
6 *Burning of Billy Toober* (1974)
7 *I know what it's like to die* (1976)
8 *Rattling of old bones* (1979)
9 *Dark blue and dangerous* (1981)
10 *Death's head* (1982)
11 *Dead Eye* (1983)
12 *Dropped dead* (1984)
13 *Burial deferred* (1985)
14 *Fate accomplished* (1987)
15 *Sudden departures* (1988)
16 *Time for dying* (1989)
17 *Daphne dead and done for* (1990)
18 *Murder be hanged* (1993)

Superintendent Gilles series
Decrest, Jacques
1 *Meet a body* (1933)
Original edition entitled *Hasard*
2 *Missing formula* (1934)
Original edition entitled *Les trois jeunes filles de Vienne*
3 *Body on the beach* (1935)
Original edition entitled *Le rendez-vous du dimanche soir*

Superintendent Gilliant series
Wainwright, John
1 *Crystallised carbon pig* (1966)
2 *Requiem for a loser* (1972)
3 *Ripple of murders* (1978)

Superintendent Gloom series
King, Frank
1 *Case of the painted girl* (1931)
2 *Green gold* (1933)
3 *Case of the vanishing artist* (1956)

Superintendent Gordon Knollis series
Vivian, Francis
see **Inspector Gordon Knollis series**

Superintendent Hannasyde series
Heyer, Georgette
1 *Death in the stocks* (1935)
Merely murder
2 *Behold, here's poison!* (1936)
3 *They found him dead* (1937)
4 *Blunt instrument* (1938)

Superintendent Henry Wilson series
Cole, George Douglas Howard
1 *Brooklyn murders* (1923)
2 *Death of a millionaire* (1925)
3 *Blatchington tangle* (1926)
4 *Man from the river* (1928)
5 *Superintendent Wilson's holiday* (1928)
Short stories; *In a telephone booth*, 1944, *The missing baronet*, 1943, *The Oxford mystery*, 1943 also published separately
6 *Poison in the garden suburb* (1929)
Poison in a garden suburb
7 *Burglars in Bucks.* (1930)
Berkshire mystery
8 *Corpse in canonicals* (1930)
Corpse in the constable's garden
9 *Great Southern mystery* (1931)
Walking corpse
10 *Dead man's watch* (1931)
11 *Lesson in crime, and other stories* (1933)
Eight of the eleven stories feature Wilson; *Superintendent Wakely's mistake*, 1944, *Wilson calling*, 1944 also published separately
12 *End of an ancient mariner* (1933)
13 *Death in the quarry* (1934)
14 *Big business murder* (1935)
15 *Doctor Tancred begins* (1935)
16 *Last will and testament* (1936)
17 *Brothers Sackville* (1937)
18 *Missing aunt* (1937)
19 *Off with her head* (1938)
20 *Double blackmail* (1939)
21 *Greek tragedy* (1939)
22 *Wilson and some others* (1940)
Short stories; *Murder in broad daylight*, and, *Crime at Eslington Hall*, 1943 published separately
23 *Murder at the munition works* (1940)
24 *Counterpoint murder* (1940)
25 *Knife in the dark* (1941)
26 *Toper's end* (1942)
27 *Birthday gifts, and other stories* (1946)

Superintendent James Pibble series
Dickinson, Peter
1 *Skin deep* (1968)
Glass-sided ants' nest
2 *Pride of heroes* (1969)
Old English peep show
3 *Seals* (1970)
Sinful stones
4 *Sleep and his brother* (1971)
5 *Lizard in the cup* (1972)
6 *One foot in the grave* (1979)

Superintendent John Coffin series
Butler, Gwendoline
see **Inspector John Coffin series**

Superintendent John Crown series
Harknett, Terry
1 *Sweet and sour kill* (1974)
2 *Macao mayhem* (1974)
3 *Bamboo shoot-out* (1975)

Superintendent John Gaffney series
Ison, Graham
1 *Cold light of dawn* (1988)
2 *Confirm or deny* (1989)
3 *Home Secretary will see you now, sir* (1989)

Superintendent John Snow series
Sawkins, Raymond
1 *Snow on high ground* (1966)
2 *Snow in paradise* (1967)
3 *Snow along the border* (1968)

Superintendent Konstantin Keller trilogy
Kirst, Hans Hellmut
see **Munich trilogy**

Superintendent Lawrence Gilmartin series
Barry, Charles
1 *Smaller penny* (1925)
2 *Detective's holiday* (1926)
3 *Mouls House mystery* (1926)
4 *Witness at the window* (1927)
5 *Corpse on the bridge* (1927)
6 *Clue of the clot* (1928)
7 *Avenging ikon* (1930)
8 *Ghost of a clue* (1931)
9 *Murder on Monday?* (1932)
10 *Wrong murder mystery* (1933)
11 *Shot from the door* (1934)
12 *Death overseas* (1937)
13 *Case dead and buried* (1938)
14 *Boat train mystery* (1938)
15 *Nicholas Lattermole's case* (1939)

Superintendent Lennox series
Wainwright, John
see **Chief Inspector Lennox series**

Superintendent Leslie series
Duncan, William Murdoch
1 *Council of Comforters* (1967)
2 *Green triangle* (1969)

Superintendent Luis Bernal series
Serafin, David
1 *Saturday of glory* (1979)
2 *Madrid underground* (1982)
3 *Christmas rising* (1982)
4 *Body in Cadiz Bay* (1985)
5 *Port of light* (1987)
6 *Angel of Torremolinos* (1988)

Superintendent McCaig series
Rae, Hugh Crauford
1 *Few small bones* (1968)
House at Balnesmoor
2 *Shooting gallery* (1972)

Superintendent Macdonald series
Lorac, E C R
see **Inspector Macdonald series**

Superintendent Macneill series
Duncan, William Murdoch
1 *Death stands round the corner* (1955)
2 *Knife in the night* (1955)
3 *Pennies for his eyes* (1956)

Superintendent Mallett series
Fitt, Mary
1 *Expected death* (1938)
2 *Sky rocket* (1938)
3 *Death at dancing stones* (1939)
4 *Death starts a rumour* (1940)
5 *Death and Mary Dazill* (1941)
Aftermath of murder
6 *Death on Heron's Mere* (1941)
Death finds a target
7 *Requiem for Robert* (1942)
8 *Clue to Christabel* (1944)
9 *Death and the pleasant voices* (1946)
10 *Fine and private place* (1947)
11 *Death and the bright day* (1948)
12 *Banquet ceases* (1949)
13 *Ill wind* (1951)
14 *Death and the shortest day* (1952)
15 *Man who shot birds, and other tales* (1954)
16 *Love from Elizabeth* (1954)
17 *Sweet poison* (1956)
18 *Mizmaze* (1959)

Superintendent Manning series
Cobb, Belton
1 *Early morning poison* (1947)
2 *Secret of Superintendent Manning* (1948)
3 *Framing of Carol Woan* (1948)
4 *No last words* (1949)
5 *Stolen strychnine* (1949)
6 *No charge for the poison* (1950)

Superintendent Margetson series
Keate, Edith Murray
1 *Wild-cat scheme* (1930)
2 *Jackanapes jacket* (1931)
3 *Demon of the air* (1936)
4 *Demon again* (1937)

Superintendent Mark Nicolson series
Charles, Robert
see **Counter-terror series**

Superintendent Maxwell Quayne series
Symonds, Francis Addington
1 *Stone dead* (1961)
2 *Death goes window shopping* (1961)
3 *Spotlight on murder* (1962)

Superintendent Merlin Capricorn series
Winslow, Pauline Glen
1 *Death of an angel* (1975)
2 *Brandenburg Hotel* (1976)
3 *Witch Hill murder* (1976)
4 *Coppergold* (1978)
Copper gold
5 *Counsellor heart* (1980)
Sister Death
6 *Rockefeller gift* (1982)

Superintendent Mersey series
Clement, Frank A
1 *Picture him dead* (1935)
2 *No end of a rogue* (1936)
3 *Scandal at the Home Office* (1937)

Superintendent Michael Drexel series
Usher, Gray
1 *Death in the straw* (1955)
2 *Death sped the plough* (1956)
3 *Death takes a teacher* (1957)
4 *Death in the bag* (1958)
5 *Death goes caving* (1959)

Superintendent Mike Yeadings and Sergeant Angus Mott series
Curzon, Clare
1 *Leaven of malice* (1979)
2 *Special occasions* (1981)
3 *I give you five days* (1983)
4 *Masks and faces* (1984)
5 *Trojan hearse* (1985)
6 *Blue eyed boy* (1990)
7 *Cat's cradle* (1992)
8 *First wife, twice removed* (1993)
9 *Death prone* (1994)

Superintendent Minter series
Wallace, Edgar
1 *Big Foot* (1927)
2 *Lone house mystery* (1929)

Superintendent Mooney series
Magarshack, David
1 *Big Ben strikes eleven* (1934)
2 *Death cuts a caper* (1935)
3 *Three dead* (1937)

Superintendent O'Malley series
Kenyon, Michael
1 *May you die in Ireland* (1965)
2 *Hundred thousand welcomes* (1970)
3 *Shooting of Dan McGraw* (1972)
4 *Sorry state* (1974)
5 *Rapist* (1977)
Also published under the pseudonym Daniel Forbes
6 *Zigzag* (1981)
Elgar variations

Superintendent Owen Smith series
Barnett, James
1 *Backfire is hostile* (1979)
2 *Palmprint* (1980)
3 *Firing squad* (1981)
4 *Marked for destruction* (1982)
5 *Diminished responsibility* (1984)

Superintendent Pepper series
Smith, Frank Allan
1 *Corpse in handcuffs* (1969)
2 *Defectors are dead men* (1971)

Superintendent Perry Trethowan series
Barnard, Robert
1 *Sheer torture* (1981)
Death by sheer torture
2 *Death and the princess* (1982)
3 *Missing Bronte* (1983)
Case of the missing Bronte
4 *Bodies* (1986)
5 *Death in purple prose* (1987)
Cherry blossom corpse

Superintendent Philip Hunter series
Procter, Maurice
1 *Chief Inspector's statement* (1951)
Pennycross murders
2 *I will speak daggers* (1956)
Ripper
Ripper murders

Superintendent Quill and Inspector Glover series
Lamb, Lynton
1 *Death of a dissenter* (1969)
2 *Worse than death* (1971)
3 *Picture frame* (1972)
4 *Man in a mist* (1974)

Superintendent Richard Falcon series
Yates, Dornford
1 *Period stuff* (1942)
Short stories
2 *House that Berry built* (1945)
3 *Ne'er-do-well* (1954)

Superintendent Richard Jury series
Grimes, Martha
see **Inspector Richard Jury series**

Superintendent Richard York series
Williamson, Audrey
1 *Funeral march for Siegfried* (1979)
2 *Death of a theatre filly* (1980)

Superintendent Richardson series
Thomson, Basil
1 *P.C.Richardson's first case* (1933)
2 *Richardson scores again* (1934)
Richardson's second case
3 *Inspector Richardson, C.I.D.* (1934)
Case of Naomi Clymes
4 *Richardson goes abroad* (1935)
Case of the dead diplomat
5 *Richardson solves a Dartmoor mystery* (1935)
Dartmoor enigma
6 *Death in the bathroom* (1936)
Who killed Stella Pomeroy?
7 *Milliner's hat mystery* (1937)

Mystery of the French milliner
8 *Murder arranged* (1937)
When thieves fall out

Superintendent Robert Budd series
Verner, Gerald
1 *Sinister house* (1934)
Short stories
2 *Green mask* (1934)
3 *Crooked circle* (1935)
4 *Cleverness of Mr Budd* (1935)
Case of Mr Budd
5 *Grim joker* (1936)
6 *Jockey* (1937)
7 *Silver horseshoe* (1938)
8 *Return of Mr Budd* (1938)
9 *Witches' moon* (1938)
10 *Mister Budd again* (1939)
11 *Football pool murders* (1939)
Coupon crimes
12 *Mister Budd investigates* (1940)
13 *Huntsman* (1940)
14 *Twelve apostles* (1946)
15 *Seven lamps* (1947)
16 *Royal flush murders* (1948)
17 *Tipster* (1949)
18 *Whispering woman* (1949)
19 *Mister Midnight* (1953)
20 *Nursery rhyme murders* (1960)
21 *Red tape murders* (1962)
22 *Last warning* (1962)
23 *Murder in manuscript* (1963)
24 *Six men died* (1964)
25 *Mister Big* (1966)

Superintendent Robert Townley and Sergeant Roger Newman series
Bearshaw, Brian
1 *Day of murder* (1978)
2 *Practice makes murder* (1979)

Superintendent Roderick Alleyn series
Marsh, Ngaio
see **Inspector Roderick Alleyn series**

Superintendent Roger Ellerdine and Sergeant Cherry Blossom series
Wills, Cecil Melville
1 *Case of the R.E. pipe* (1940)
2 *Clue of the lost hour* (1949)
3 *Clue of the golden earring* (1950)
4 *Who killed Brother Treasurer?* (1951)
5 *What say the jury?* (1951)
6 *Dead voice* (1952)
7 *It pays to die* (1953)
8 *Death in the dark* (1955)
9 *Tiger strikes again* (1957)
10 *Mere murder* (1958)
11 *Justice in jeopardy* (1961)

Superintendent Roger West series
Creasey, John
see **Inspector Roger West series**

Superintendent Ross series
Connington, John Jervis
1 *Eye in the museum* (1929)
2 *Two tickets puzzle* (1930)
Two ticket puzzle

Superintendent Samuel Quan series
Begbie, Garstin
1 *Sudden death at Scotland Yard* (1933)
2 *Murder mask* (1934)

Superintendent Scarfe series
Goodwin, John
1 *Shadow man* (1932)
2 *In full cry* (1941)

Superintendent Shannon series
Ryland, Clive
1 *Notting Hill murder* (1932)
2 *Murders at the manor* (1933)
3 *Murder on the cliff* (1934)
4 *Murder on the common* (1939)

Superintendent Simmonds series
East, Roger
1 *Murder rehearsal* (1933)
2 *Twenty-five sanitary inspectors* (1935)
3 *Detectives in gum boots* (1936)

Superintendent Simon Bullion series
Dix, Maurice Buxton
1 *This is my murder* (1938)
2 *Murder strikes twice* (1939)

Superintendent Simon Kenworthy series
Hilton, John Buxton
1 *Death of an alderman* (1968)
2 *Death in midwinter* (1969)
3 *Hangman's tide* (1975)
4 *No birds sang* (1975)
5 *Some run crooked* (1978)
6 *Anathema stone* (1980)
7 *Playground of death* (1981)
8 *Surrender value* (1981)
9 *Green frontier* (1981)
10 *Sunset law* (1982)
11 *Asking price* (1983)
12 *Corridors of guilt* (1984)
13 *Hobbema prospect* (1984)
14 *Passion in the park* (1986)
15 *Moondrop to murder* (1986)
16 *Innocents at home* (1986)
17 *Displaced persons* (1987)

Superintendent Simon Manton series
Underwood, Michael
1 *Murder on trial* (1954)
2 *Murder made absolute* (1955)
3 *Death on remand* (1956)
4 *False witness* (1957)
5 *Lawful pursuit* (1958)
6 *Arm of the law* (1959)
7 *Cause of death* (1960)
8 *Death by misadventure* (1960)
9 *Adam's case* (1965)
10 *Case against Phillip Quest* (1962)
11 *Girl found dead* (1963)
12 *Crime of Colin Wise* (1964)
13 *Anxious conspirator* (1965)

Superintendent Simon Shard series
McCutchan, Philip
1 *Call for Simon Shard* (1974)
2 *Very big bang* (1975)
3 *Blood run east* (1976)
4 *Eros affair* (1977)
5 *Blackmail north* (1978)
6 *Shard calls the tune* (1981)
7 *Hoof* (1983)
8 *Shard at bay* (1984)
9 *Executioners* (1986)
10 *Overnight express* (1988)

Superintendent Steve McLaren series
Scott, Bruce
1 *Prayer mat* (1967)
2 *Secret of the elephant* (1968)
3 *Hell of a spot* (1971)

Superintendent Tetsuo Otani series
Melville, James
1 *Wages of Zen* (1979)
2 *Chrysanthemum chain* (1980)
3 *Sort of Samurai* (1981)
4 *Ninth netsuke* (1982)
5 *Sayonara, sweet Amaryllis* (1983)
6 *Death of a daimyo* (1984)
7 *Death ceremony* (1985)
8 *Go gently, Gaijin* (1986)
9 *Kimono for a corpse* (1987)
10 *Reluctant Ronin* (1988)
11 *Haiku for Hanae* (1989)
12 *Bogus Buddha* (1990)
13 *Body wore brocade* (1992)

Superintendent Thomas Littlejohn series
Bellairs, George
see **Detective Inspector Thomas Littlejohn series**

Superintendent Tom Pollard series
Lemarchand, Elizabeth
1 *Death of an old girl* (1967)
2 *Affacombe affair* (1968)
3 *Alibi for a corpse* (1969)
4 *Death on doomsday* (1971)
5 *Cyanide with compliments* (1972)
6 *Let or hindrance* (1973)
No vacation from murder
7 *Buried in the past* (1974)
8 *Step in the dark* (1976)
9 *Unhappy returns* (1977)
10 *Suddenly while gardening* (1978)
11 *Change for the worse* (1980)
12 *Nothing to do with the case* (1981)
13 *Troubled waters* (1982)
14 *Wheel turns* (1983)
15 *Light through glass* (1984)
16 *Who goes home?* (1986)
17 *Glade Manor murder* (1988)

Superintendent Tubby Green series
Goyne, Richard
see **Ex-Superintendent Tubby Green series**

Superintendent Vachell series
Huxley, Elspeth
1 *Murder at Government House* (1937)
2 *Murder on safari* (1938)
3 *Death of an aryan* (1939)
African poison murders

Superintendent William Austen series
Hocking, Anne
see **Inspector William Austen series**

Superintendent William Baker series
Mills, Osmington
1 *Unlucky break* (1955)
2 *Case of the Flying Fifteen* (1956)
3 *No match for the law* (1957)
4 *Misguided missile* (1958)
5 *Stairway to murder* (1959)
6 *Trial by ordeal* (1961)
7 *Headlines make murder* (1962)
8 *At one fell swoop* (1963)
9 *Traitor betrayed* (1964)

Superintendent William Stevens and Inspector Pierre Allain series
Graeme, Bruce
1 *Murder of some importance* (1931)
2 *Imperfect crime* (1932)
3 *Epilogue* (1933)
4 *International affair* (1934)
5 *Satan's mistress* (1935)
6 *Not proven* (1935)
7 *Mystery on the Queen Mary* (1937)
8 *Man from Michigan* (1938)
Mystery of the stolen hats
9 *Body unknown* (1939)
10 *Poisoned sleep* (1939)
11 *Corporal died in bed* (1940)
12 *Encore Allain!* (1941)
13 *News travels by night* (1943)
Companion volume: *Lord Blackshirt*, 1942

Superintendent William Winter series
Butler, Gwendoline
see **Inspector William Winter series**

Superlearning series
Ostrander, Sheila
1 *Superlearning* (1979)
2 *Superlearning 2000* (1994)
Companion volume: *Supermemory*, 1991

Superman series
This sequence has six authors
Maggin, Elliot S
1 *Superman, last son of Krypton* (1978)
2 *Miracle Monday* (1981)
Skinner, Stephanie
3 *Daily Planet, a world of news every day!* (1981)
Helfer, Andrew
4 *Superman, the man of steel* (1983)
Based on a screenplay
Kotzwinkle, William
5 *Superman III* (1983)
Based on a screenplay
Hiller, Barbara B
6 *Superman IV* (1987)
Based on a screenplay; companion volume: *Superman IV*, by Nancy E Krulik, 1987
Stern, Roger
7 *Death and life of Superman* (1994)
Companion volumes: *Superman, serial to cereal*, by Gary Howard Grossman, 1976, *The making of Superman, the movie*, by David Michael Petrou, 1978, *Superman's maze challenge*, by Vladimir Koziakin, 1978, *Superman II, the movie magazine*, by Michael Fleisher and Joe Orlando, 1981, *Superman, the movie*, by Gary Libman, 1983, *Superman and Spider-Man*, by Edward Gross, 1986, *The Superman files*, by James Van Hise, 1986, *Superman IV, the quest for peace, the official poster magazine*, by David McDonnell, 1987, *Superman at fifty, the persistence of a legend*, by Dennis Dooley and Gary Eagle, 1987, *It's a bird, it's a plane, no, it's the television adventures of Superman*, by James Van Hise, 1989

Supernatural series
Benson, Robert Hugh
1 *Sentimentalists* (1906)
2 *Conventionalists* (1908)

Supernatural series
Martin, Russell White
1 *Desecration of Susan Browning* (1981)
2 *Devil and Lisa Black* (1982)
3 *Possession of Jessica Young* (1982)
4 *Resurrection of Candy Sterling* (1982)
5 *Obsession of Sally Wing* (1983)
6 *Education of Jennifer Parrish* (1984)

Supernatural series
Smith, Keith
1 *Australian encounters* (1991)
2 *More Australian encounters* (1993)

Super-seniors series
Goudge, Eileen
1 *Old enough* (1986)
2 *Hawaiian Christmas* (1986)
3 *Something borrowed, something blue* (1988)
4 *Deep-sea summer* (1988)

Superslug series
Dunbar, Joyce
see **Software Superslug series**

Superspade series
Johnson, B B
1 *Death of a blue-eyed soul brother* (1970)
2 *Black is beautiful* (1970)
3 *That's where the cat's at, baby* (1970)
4 *Mother of the year* (1970)
5 *Bad day for a black brother* (1970)
6 *Blues for a black sister* (1971)

SuperTed series
Young, Mike
1 *SuperTed in space* (1980)
2 *SuperTed in Creepy Castle* (1980)
3 *SuperTed and the helicopter pirates* (1980)
4 *SuperTed and the lost ponies* (1980)
5 *SuperTed meets Zappy and Zoppy* (1981)
Revised edition 1985
6 *SuperTed and the green planet* (1981)
Revised edition 1985
7 *SuperTed at the bottom of the sea* (1981)
Revised edition 1985
8 *SuperTed and the hungry monkeys* (1981)
Revised edition 1985
9 *SuperTed and the stolen rocket ship* (1982)
Revised edition 1985
10 *SuperTed and the pearl fishers* (1982)
11 *SuperTed and the giant kites* (1982)
12 *SuperTed and the Inca treasure* (1982)
13 *SuperTed returns to Creepy Castle* (1983)
14 *SuperTed and the train robbers* (1983)
15 *SuperTed on planet Spot* (1983)
16 *SuperTed and the elephant graveyard* (1983)
17 *SuperTed and the crystal ball* (1984)
18 *SuperTed in the Arctic* (1984)
19 *SuperTed in Spotty and the Indians* (1984)
20 *SuperTed and the gun smugglers* (1984)
21 *SuperTed and the pothole rescue* (1985)
22 *SuperTed and the blue whales* (1985)
23 *SuperTed kicks up the dust* (1985)
24 *SuperTed and Tex's magic spell* (1985)
25 *SuperTed and Bulk's story* (1985)
26 *SuperTed in SuperTed's dream* (1985)
27 *SuperTed and the lumberjacks* (1985)
28 *SuperTed and Mother Nature* (1985)

Super-tramp series
Davies, William Henry
1 *Autobiography of a super-tramp* (1908)
2 *Later days* (1925)

Surf city series
Daniels, Lee
1 *Wipeout* (1988)
2 *Storm warnings* (1988)
3 *Riptide* (1988)
4 *Hidden reef* (1988)
5 *Capsized!* (1989)

Surgeon in series
Sava, George
1 *Surgeon in Rome* (1961)
Alternative title: Passegiata romana
2 *Surgeon in California* (1962)
Sequence continued under the pseudonym George Alexis Bankoff
Bankoff, George Alexis
3 *Surgeon in New Zealand* (1964)
4 *Surgeon in Cyprus* (1965)
5 *Surgeon in Australia* (1966)

Surgeon series
Mair, George Brown
1 *Confessions of a surgeon* (1974)
2 *Escape from surgery* (1975)

Surgeon series
Thorwald, Jurgen
see **Century of the surgeon series**

Surgeon's destiny series
Sava, George
1 *Healing knife* (1938)
2 *Surgeon's destiny* (1939)
3 *Lure of surgery* (1955)

Surgeon's stories series
Topelius, Zacharias
1 *Gustave Adolf and the Thirty Years' War* (1872)
Times of Gustaf Adolf
King's ring
1594-1632
2 *Times of battle and of rest* (1883)
Set during the 17th century
3 *Times of Charles XII* (1884)
1682-1718
4 *Times of Frederick I* (1884)
1720-1751
5 *Times of Linnaeus* (1884)
1751-1771
6 *Times of alchemy* (1884)
1771-1792
Originally published in five volumes entitled *Feltlagens historier*, 1853-67

Surgical strike series
Ahern, Jerry
1 *Surgical strike* (1988)
2 *Assault on the Empress* (1989)
3 *Infiltrator* (1990)

Surprise party series
Hutchins, Pat
1 *Surprise party* (1969)
2 *Silver Christmas tree* (1974)

Survival in Auschwitz series
Levi, Primo
1 *If this is a man* (1947)
Survival in Auschwitz
Original edition entitled *Se questo e un uomo*; the Nazi assault on humanity
2 *Reawakening* (1958)
Truce
Original edition entitled *La tregua*; a survivor's journey home from Auschwitz

Survival series
Berry, Joy
1 *What to do when your mom or dad says clean your room!* (1981)
2 *What to do when your mom or dad says get good grades!* (1981)
3 *What to do when your mom or dad says be prepared!* (1981)
4 *What to do when your mom or dad says earn your allowance!* (1981)
5 *What to do when your mom or dad says clean yourself up!* (1982)
6 *What to do when your mom or dad says be kind to your guest!* (1982)
7 *What to do when your mom or dad says take care of your clothes!* (1982)
8 *What to do when your mom or dad says be good while you're there!* (1982)
9 *What to do when your mom or dad says don't hang around with the wrong crowd* (1982)
10 *What to do when your mom or dad says help!* (1982)
11 *What to do when your mom or dad says do something besides watch TV!* (1982)
12 *What to do when your mom or dad says do your homework and schoolwork!* (1982)
13 *What to do when your mom or dad says don't overdo with video games!* (1982)
14 *What to do when your mom or dad says be careful!* (1983)
15 *What to do when your mom or dad says we can't afford it!* (1983)
16 *What to do when your mom or dad says get the phone!* (1983)
17 *What to do when your mom or dad says be good!* (1983)
18 *What to do when your mom or dad says go to bed!* (1983)
19 *What to do when your mom or dad says what should you say dear?* (1983)
20 *What to do when your mom or dad says stand up straight!* (1983)
21 *What to do when your mom or dad says don't slurp your soup!* (1984)
22 *What to do when your mom or dad says write to grandma!* (1984)
23 *What to do when your mom or dad says make your breakfast and lunch!* (1984)
24 *What to do when your mom or dad says turn off the water and lights!* (1984)
25 *What to do when your mom or dad says get dressed!* (1986)
26 *What to do when your mom or dad says baby-sit!* (1986)
27 *What to do when your mom or dad says do the yardwork!* (1986)
28 *What to do when your mom or dad says you want a pet?* (1986)
29 *What to do when your mom or dad says behave in public!* (1986)

Survival series
Skynner, Robin
1 *Families and how to survive them* (1983)
2 *Life and how to survive it* (1993)
Also published in one volume entitled *The complete works of Shakespeare and Monty Python*, volume 1, 1981

Survival series
Southall, Ivan
1 *To the wild sky* (1967)
2 *City out of sight* (1984)

Survival two thousand trilogy
McPhee, James
1 *Blood quest* (1991)
2 *Renegade war* (1991)
3 *Frozen fire* (1991)

Survivalist series
Ahern, Jerry
1 *Total war* (1981)
2 *Nightmare begins* (1981)
3 *Quest* (1981)
4 *Doomsayer* (1981)
5 *Web* (1983)
6 *Savage horde* (1983)
7 *Prophet* (1984)
8 *End is coming* (1984)
9 *Earth fire* (1984)
10 *Awakening* (1984)
11 *Reprisal* (1985)
12 *Rebellion* (1985)
13 *Pursuit* (1986)
14 *Terror* (1987)
15 *Overlord* (1987)
16 *Arsenal* (1988)
17 *Ordeal* (1988)
18 *Struggle* (1989)
19 *Final rain* (1989)
20 *Firestorm* (1990)
21 *To end all war* (1990)
22 *Brutal conquest* (1991)
23 *Call to battle* (1992)
24 *Blood assassins* (1992)
25 *War mountain* (1993)
26 *Countdown* (1993)
27 *Death watch* (1993)
Companion volumes: *Mid-wake*, 1988, *The legend*, 1991

Survivors of Nam series
Zlotnik, Donald E
1 *Baptism* (1988)
2 *P.O.W.* (1988)
3 *Black market* (1988)
4 *Court-martial* (1988)

Survivors of the Jonathan series
Verne, Jules
1 *Masterless man* (1909)
2 *Unwilling dictator* (1909)
Original one volume edition entitled *Les naufrages du Jonathan*

Survivors series
This sequence has two authors
Nation, Terry
1 *Survivors* (1976)
Eyers, John
2 *Genesis of a hero* (1977)

Survivors series
Sibson, Francis H
1 *Survivors* (1932)
2 *Stolen continent* (1934)

Survivor's tale series
Spiegelman, Art
Comic strips
1 *My father bleeds history* (1986)
2 *And here my troubles began* (1991)
Companion volume: *Breakdowns, from Maus to now, an anthology of strips*, 1977

Surya series
Gavin, Jamila
1 *Wheel of Surya* (1992)
2 *Eye of the horse* (1994)

Susan and Ann series
Wahlstedt, Viola
see **Ann and Susan series**

Susan and Bill series
Saville, Malcolm
1 *Susan, Bill and the wolf-dog* (1954)
2 *Susan, Bill and the ivy-clad oak* (1954)
3 *Susan, Bill and the vanishing boy* (1955)
4 *Susan, Bill and the golden clock* (1955)
5 *Susan, Bill and the dark stranger* (1956)
6 *Susan, Bill and the Saucy Kate* (1956)
7 *Susan, Bill and the Bright Star Circus* (1960)
8 *Susan, Bill and the pirates bold* (1961)

Susan and Christine Pratt series
Blair, Cynthia
1 *Hot fudge sundae affair* (1985)
2 *Banana split affair* (1985)
3 *Strawberry summer* (1986)
4 *Marshmallow masquerade* (1987)
5 *Candy cane caper* (1987)
6 *Double dip disguise* (1987)
7 *Pink lemonade charade* (1988)
8 *Apple pie adventure* (1989)
9 *Popcorn project* (1989)
10 *Jelly bean scheme* (1990)
11 *Lollipop plot* (1990)

Susan and Colin series
Garner, Alan
see **Alderley series**

Susan and Fenwick series
Barth, John
see **Fenwick and Susan series**

Susan and James series
Jones, Joan Clement
see **James and Susan series**

Susan and R. Dragon series
Manning, Rosemary
1 *Green smoke* (1957)
2 *Dragon in danger* (1959)
3 *Dragon's quest* (1961)
4 *Dragon in the harbour* (1980)

Susan and William series
Kirk, Thomas Hobson
see **William and Susan series**

Susan Campbell and Paul Ross series
Henneker, Philip
1 *And one must die* (1965)
2 *Don't be afraid of the dark* (1965)
3 *Too late for tears* (1966)

Susan Clegg series
Warner, Anne
1 *Susan Clegg and her friend Mrs Lathrop* (1904)
2 *Susan Clegg and her neighbors' affairs* (1906)
One volume abridged edition of Numbers 1 and 2 published as *Susan Clegg, her friend and her neighbors*, 1910
3 *Susan Clegg and a man in the house* (1907)
4 *Susan Clegg and her love affairs* (1916)

Susan Dare series
Eberhart, Mignon Good
Short stories
1 *Cases of Susan Dare* (1934)
2 *Five of my best* (1949)

Susan Denver trilogy
Black, Hermina
1 *Gold moon of Africa* (1938)
2 *Marriage of Susan* (1938)
3 *Gift of the desert* (1945)

Susan Lancaster series
Bond, Freda Constance
see **Lancasters series**

Susan Marsh series
Adam, Ruth
1 *Stepmother for Susan of Saint Bride's* (1958)
2 *Susan and the wrong baby* (1961)

Susan Melville series
Smith, Evelyn E
see **Miss Susan Melville series**

Susan Sand series
Ezell, Marilyn
1 *Mystery at Hollowhearth* (1982)
2 *Secret of Clovercrest Castle* (1982)
3 *Clue in Witchwhistle* (1982)
4 *Riddle of Raggedrock* (1982)
5 *Phantom of Featherford Falls* (1983)
6 *Password to Diamonddwarf* (1983)

Susan series
Brady, Cyrus Townsend
see **Lady Susan series**
Cleeve, Lucas
see **Lady Susan series**

Susan series
Finlay, Winifred
1 *Canal holiday* (1957)
2 *Cruise of the Susan* (1958)

Susan series
Russell, Ivy
see **Princess Susan series**

Susan series
Shaw, Jane
1 *Susan pulls the strings* (1952)
2 *Susan's helping hand* (1955)
3 *Susan rushes in* (1956)
4 *Susan interferes* (1957)
5 *Susan at school* (1958)
6 *Susan muddles through* (1960)
7 *Susan's trying term* (1961)
8 *No trouble for Susan* (1962)
9 *Susan's kind heart* (1965)
10 *Where is Susan?* (1968)
11 *Job for Susan* (1969)

Susan Shaw series
Ormondroyd, Edward
1 *Time at the top* (1963)
2 *All in good time* (1975)

Susan trilogy
Leonard, Mary Finley
1 *Everyday Susan* (1912)
2 *Christmas Tree House* (1913)
3 *Susan grows up* (1914)

Susan Turnbull series
Gunter, Archibald Clavering
1 *Susan Turnbull* (1897)
Alternative title: The power of women
2 *Ballyho Bey* (1897)

Susan Yates and Lyle Curtis series
Fetta, Emma Lou
see **Lyle Curtis and Susan Yates series**

Susannah and Henry Kable series
Whittaker, June Lovina
see **Henry and Susannah Kable series**

Susannah series
Denison, Muriel
1 *Susannah of the Mounties* (1936)
Susannah, a little girl with the Mounties
2 *Susannah of the Yukon* (1937)
3 *Susannah at boarding school* (1938)
4 *Susannah rides again* (1940)

Susannah series
Elmore, Patricia
1 *Susannah and the blue house mystery* (1980)
2 *Susannah and the posion green Halloween* (1982)
3 *Susannah and the purple mongoose mystery* (1992)

Susie and Alfred series
Craig, Helen
1 *Knight, the princess and the dragons* (1985)
2 *Susie and Alfred in the night of the paper bag monster* (1985)
3 *Susie and Alfred in a welcome for Annie* (1986)
4 *Susie and Alfred in a busy day in town* (1986)

Susie and Ann series
Wahlstedt, Viola
see **Ann and Susan series**

Susie Slagle series
Tucker, Augusta
see **Miss Susie Slagle series**

Sussex quartet
Glover, Judith
1 *Stallion man* (1982)
2 *Sisters and brothers* (1984)
3 *To everything a season* (1986)
4 *Birds in a gilded cage* (1988)

Sussex series
Leyland, Eric
1 *Gentlemen of Sussex* (1944)
2 *Hazard royal* (1945)

Sussex series
Lindsay, Philip
1 *Devil comes to Winchelsea* (1958)
2 *Sisters of Rye* (1960)

Sussex trilogy
Hastings, Phyllis
1 *All earth to love* (1968)
2 *Day of the dancing sun* (1971)
3 *Gates of morning* (1973)

Sutherland series
Eberhard, Frederick George
see **Chief of Police Sutherland series**

Sutton and Logan series
White, James G
see **Gunslick series**

Sutton Place trilogy
Lampitt, Dinah
1 *Sutton Place* (1983)
2 *Silver swan* (1984)
3 *Fortune's soldier* (1985)

Sutton series
Kelley, Leo Patrick
see **Luke Sutton series**

Suzanne and Nicholas series
Ichikawa, Satomi
1 *Suzanne and Nicholas in the garden* (1976)
Original edition entitled *Suzette et Nicolas dans leur jardin*
2 *Suzanne and Nicholas at the market* (1977)
Original edition entitled *Suzette et Nicolas au marche*; later edition with text by Robina Beckles Willson entitled *Sophie and Nicky go to market*, 1984
3 *Suzette and Nicholas and the four seasons* (1978)
Original edition entitled *L'horloge des quatre saisons*; later edition with text by Robina Beckles Willson entitled *Sophie and Nicky and the four seasons*, 1984

Suzanne series
Matchett, Grace
1 *Suzanne goes to Brittany* (1954)
2 *Suzanne goes to market* (1954)

Suzette and Nicholas series
This sequence has two authors
Mangin, Marie France
1 *Suzanne and Nicholas and the four seasons* (1978)
Sophie and Nicky and the four seasons
Suzettte and Nicholas and the seasons clock
Original edition entitled *Suzette et Nicholas et l'horloge des 4 saisons*
Lochak, Michelle
2 *Suzette and Nicholas and the Sunijudi Circus* (1979)
Original edition entitled *Suzette et Nicholas et le cirque des enfants*

Suzy and John Marshall series
Fox, James M
see **John and Suzy Marshall series**

Svenska series
Ghose, Sudhindra Nath
see **Sister Svenska series**

Sventon series
Holmberg, Ake
see **Tam Sventon series**

Swain series
Da Cruz, Daniel
see **Ape Swain series**
McQuay, Mike
see **Mathew Swain series**
Nathan, Paul
see **Bert Swain series**
Thomas, Donald
see **Inspector Swain series**

Swallow series
De Vries, Peter
see **Chick Swallow series**

Swallowdale series
This sequence has two authors
Ransome, Arthur
1 *Swallowdale* (1931)
Mace, Elisabeth
2 *Ransome revisited* (1975)
Out there
3 *Travelling man* (1976)

Swallows and Amazons series
Ransome, Arthur
1 *Swallows and Amazons* (1930)
2 *Swallowdale* (1931)
3 *Peter Duck* (1932)
4 *Winter holiday* (1933)
5 *Coot Club* (1934)
6 *Pigeon post* (1936)
7 *We didn't mean to go to sea* (1937)
8 *Secret water* (1939)
9 *Big six* (1940)
10 *Missee Lee* (1941)
11 *Picts and the Martyrs* (1943)
12 *Great Northern?* (1947)
13 *Coots in the north, and other stories* (1988)

Swallows eaves series
Ward, Ruth Cameron
1 *Swallows eaves* (1939)
2 *Snow on the high ground* (1942)

Swamp Master series
Spencer, Jake
see **John Firecloud series**

Swamp monsters series
Christian, Mary Blount
1 *Swamp monsters* (1983)
2 *Go west, swamp monsters* (1985)

Swamp Thing second series
This sequence has two authors
Cannon, Martin
1 *Swamp Thing* (1987)
2 *Green mansions* (1987)
Van Hise, James
3 *Swamp Thing finale* (1987)

Swamp Thing series
This sequence has three authors; based on screenplays
Wein, Len
1 *Swamp Thing* (1982)
David, Peter
2 *Return of Swamp Thing* (1989)

Swan series
Philmore, R
1 *Journey downstairs* (1934)
2 *Riot act* (1935)
3 *Good books* (1936)
4 *No mourning in the family* (1937)
5 *Short list* (1938)

Swan trilogy
De Blasis, Celeste
see **Wild Swan trilogy**

Swann series
Delderfield, Ronald Frederick
see **Adam Swann series**
Moody, Susan
see **Cassie Swann series**

Swan's milk series
Marlow, Louis
Autobiography
1 *Swan's milk* (1934)
2 *Forth, beast!* (1946)

Swansea Place series
Preston, Fayrene
1 *Legacy* (1990)
2 *Deceit* (1990)
3 *Promise* (1990)
4 *Jeopardy* (1990)
5 *Destiny* (1991)

Swansea series
Courtney, Edith
Reminescences
1 *Mouse ran up my nightie* (1974)
Childhood in Swansea

2 *Fares please* (1957)
Life as a bus conductress
3 *My feet are killing me* (1977)
Life in Wales during the Second World War and after

Swanson series
Park, Barbara
see **Rosie Swanson series**

Swede and Neil trilogy
Robertson, Keith
see **Neil and Swede trilogy**

Sweden series
Sagan, Francoise
1 *Castle in Sweden* (1963)
Original edition entitled *Chateau en Suede*; a play
2 *Scars on the soul* (1972)
Original edition entitled *Des bleus a l'ame*; a novel

Swedish youth series
Bjorkman, Edwin August
1 *Soul of a child* (1922)
2 *Gates of life* (1923)

Sweeney series
This sequence has two authors
Martin, Ian Kennedy
1 *Regan* (1975)
Sweeney
2 *Regan and the Manhattan file* (1975)
Manhattan file
3 *Regan and the deal of the century* (1977)
Deal of the century
Balham, Joe
4 *Regan and the Lebanese shipment* (1977)
5 *Regan and the human pipeline* (1977)
6 *Regan and the snout who cried wolf* (1977)
7 *Regan and the bent stripper* (1977)
8 *Regan and the Venetian virgin* (1978)
9 *Regan and the high rollers* (1978)
10 *Regan and the blag* (1978)

Sweepers series
Waine, Charlton
1 *Breed of the inshore* (1940)
2 *Sweepers* (1941)

Sweet Medicine's prophecy series
Bale, Karen A
1 *Sun Dancer's passion* (1981)
2 *Little Flower's desire* (1982)
3 *Winter's love song* (1983)
4 *Sun Dancer's legacy* (1986)
5 *Savage fury* (1983)

Sweet savage sophomore year series
Grimes, Frances Harley
1 *Kiss and tell* (1989)
2 *Spring break* (1989)

Sweet Thames series
Gibbings, Robert
1 *Sweet Thames run softly* (1940)
2 *Till I end my song* (1957)

Sweet trilogy
Tetel, Julie
1 *Sweet suspicions* (1992)
2 *Sweet seduction* (1993)
3 *Sweet sensations* (1993)

Sweet Valley High series
Pascal, Francine
Although other authors are credited with many of the volumes in this sequence it is listed under Francine Pascal who "maintains artistic control over every aspect of these novels" including all plot outlines, descriptions of characters, time, setting, etc.
1 *Double love* (1983)
2 *Secrets* (1983)
3 *Playing with fire* (1983)
4 *Power play* (1983)
5 *All night long* (1984)
6 *Dangerous love* (1984)
7 *Dear sister* (1984)
8 *Heartbreaker* (1984)
9 *Racing hearts* (1984)
10 *Wrong kind of girl* (1984)
11 *Too good to be true* (1984)
12 *When love dies* (1984)
13 *Kidnapped!* (1984)
14 *Deceptions* (1984)
15 *Promises* (1984)
16 *Rags to riches* (1985)
17 *Love letters* (1985)
18 *Head over heels* (1985)
19 *Shwodown* (1985)
20 *Crash landing!* (1985)
21 *Runaway* (1985)
22 *Too much in love* (1985)
23 *Say goodbye* (1985)
24 *Memories* (1985)
25 *Nowhere to run* (1986)
26 *Hostage!* (1986)
27 *Lovestruck* (1986)
28 *Alone in the crowd* (1986)
29 *Bitter rivals* (1986)
30 *Jealous lies* (1986)
31 *Taking sides* (1986)
32 *New Jessica* (1986)
33 *Starting over* (1987)
34 *Forbidden love* (1987)
35 *Out of control* (1987)
36 *Last chance* (1987)
37 *Rumors* (1987)
38 *Leaving home* (1987)
39 *Secret admirer* (1987)
40 *On the edge* (1987)
41 *Outcast* (1987)
42 *Caught in the middle* (1988)
43 *Hard choices* (1988)
44 *Pretenses* (1988)
45 *Family secrets* (1988)
46 *Decisions* (1988)
47 *Troublemaker* (1988)
48 *Slam book fever* (1988)
49 *Playing for keeps* (1988)
50 *Out of reach* (1988)
51 *Against the odds* (1988)
52 *White lies* (1989)
53 *Second chance* (1989)
54 *Two-boy weekend* (1989)
55 *Perfect shot* (1989)
56 *Lost at sea* (1989)
57 *Teacher crush* (1989)
58 *Broken-hearted* (1989)
59 *In love again* (1989)
60 *That fatal night* (1989)
61 *Boy trouble* (1990)
62 *Who's who* (1990)
63 *New Elizabeth* (1990)
64 *Ghost of Tricia Martin* (1990)
65 *Trouble at home* (1990)
66 *Who's to blame?* (1990)
67 *Parent plot* (1990)
68 *Love bet* (1990)
69 *Friend against friend* (1990)
70 *Ms Quarterback* (1990)
71 *Starring Jessica* (1991)
72 *Rock star's girl* (1991)
73 *Regina's legacy* (1991)
74 *Perfect girl* (1991)
75 *Amy's true love* (1991)
76 *Miss Teen Sweet Valley* (1991)
77 *Cheating to win* (1991)
78 *Dating game* (1991)
79 *Long-lost brother* (1991)
80 *Girl they both loved* (1991)
81 *Rosa's lie* (1992)
82 *Kidnapped by a cult* (1992)
83 *Steven's bride* (1992)
84 *Stolen diary* (1992)
85 *Soap star* (1992)
86 *Jessica against Bruce* (1992)
87 *My best friend's boyfriend* (1993)
88 *Love letters for sale* (1993)
89 *Elizabeth betrayed* (1993)
90 *Don't go home with John* (1993)
91 *In love with a prince* (1993)
92 *She's not what she seems* (1993)
93 *Stepsisters* (1993)
94 *Are we in love?* (1993)
95 *Morning after* (1993)
96 *Arrest* (1993)
97 *Verdict* (1993)
98 *Wedding* (1993)
99 *Beware the babysitter* (1993)
100 *Evil truth* (1993)
101 *Boyfriend war* (1994)
102 *Almost married* (1994)
103 *Operation love* (1994)
104 *Love and death in London* (1994)
105 *Date with a werewolf* (1994)
106 *Beware the wolfman* (1994)
107 *Jessica's secret love* (1994)
108 *Left at the altar* (1994)
109 *Double-crossed* (1994)
110 *Death threat* (1994)
111 *Deadly Christmas* (1994)

Sweet Valley High super series
Pascal, Francine
Although other authors are credited with many of the volumes in this sequence it is listed under Francine Pascal who "maintains artistic control over every aspect of these novels" including all plot outlines, descriptions of characters, time, setting, etc.
1 *Perfect summer* (1985)
2 *Special Christmas* (1985)
3 *Malibu summer* (1986)
4 *Winter carnival* (1986)
5 *Spring fever* (1987)
6 *Spring break* (1987)

Sweet Valley High super star series
Pascal, Francine
Although other authors are credited with many of the volumes in this sequence it is listed under Francine Pascal who "maintains artistic control over every aspect of these novels" including all plot outlines, descriptions of characters, time, setting, etc.
1 *Lila's story* (1989)
2 *Bruce's story* (1990)
3 *Enid's story* (1990)
4 *Todd's story* (1992)
5 *Olivia's story* (1992)

Sweet Valley High super thriller series
Pascal, Francine
Although other authors are credited with many of the volumes in this sequence it is listed under Francine Pascal who "maintains artistic control over every aspect of these novels" including all plot outlines, descriptions of characters, time, setting, etc.
1 *Double jeopardy* (1987)
2 *On the run* (1988)
3 *No place to hide* (1988)
4 *Deadly summer* (1989)
5 *Murder on the line* (1992)

Sweet Valley kids magna series
Pascal, Francine
1 *Magic Christmas* (1992)
2 *Christmas without Elizabeth* (1993)

Sweet Valley kids series
Pascal, Francine
Although other authors are credited with many of the volumes in this sequence it is listed under Francine Pascal who "maintains artistic control over every aspect of these novels" including all plot outlines, descriptions of characters, time, setting, etc.
1 *Surprise, surprise!* (1989)
2 *Runaway hamster* (1989)
3 *Substitute teacher* (1990)
4 *Elizabeth's valentine* (1990)
5 *Jessica's cat trick* (1990)
6 *Lila's secret* (1990)
7 *Jessica's big mistake* (1990)
8 *Jessica's zoo adventure* (1990)
9 *Elizabeth's super-selling lemonade* (1990)
10 *Twins and the Wild West* (1990)
11 *Crybaby Lois* (1990)
12 *Sweet Valley trick or treat* (1990)
13 *Starring Winston* (1990)
14 *Jessica the babysitter* (1991)
15 *Fearless Elizabeth* (1991)
16 *Jessica the TV star* (1991)
17 *Carolyn's mystery dolls* (1991)
18 *Bossy Steven* (1991)
19 *Jessica and Jumbo* (1991)
20 *Twins go to the hospital* (1991)
21 *Jessica and the spelling bee surprise* (1991)
22 *Sweet Valley slumber party* (1991)
23 *Lila's haunted house party* (1991)
24 *Copusin Kelly's family secret* (1991)
25 *Left-out Elizabeth* (1992)
26 *Jessica's snobby* (1992)
27 *Sweet Valley clean-up* (1992)
28 *Elizabeth meets her hero* (1992)
29 *Andy and the alien* (1992)
30 *Jessica's unburied treasure* (1992)
31 *Elizabeth and Jessica run away* (1992)
32 *Left back* (1992)
33 *Caroline's Halloween spell* (1992)
34 *Best Thanksgiving ever* (1992)
35 *Elizabeth's broken arm* (1993)
36 *Elizabeth's video fever* (1993)
37 *Big race* (1993)
38 *Good-bye Eva?* (1993)
39 *Ellen is home alone* (1993)
40 *Robin in the middle* (1993)
41 *Missing tea set* (1993)
42 *Jessica's monster nightmare* (1993)
43 *Jessica gets spooked* (1993)
44 *Twins big pow-wow* (1993)
45 *Elizabeth's piano lessons* (1994)
46 *Get the teacher* (1994)
47 *Elizabeth and the tattletale* (1994)
48 *Lila's April fool* (1994)
49 *Jessica's mermaid* (1994)
50 *Steven's twin* (1994)
51 *Lois and the sleepover* (1994)
52 *Julie and the karate kid* (1994)
53 *Magic puppets* (1994)
54 *Star of the parade* (1994)

Sweet Valley kids super snooper series
Pascal, Francine
Although other authors are credited with many of the volumes in this sequence it is listed under Francine Pascal who "maintains artistic control over every aspect of these novels" including all plot outlines, descriptions of characters, time, setting, etc.
1 *Case of the secret Santa* (1990)
2 *Case of the magic Christmas bell* (1991)
3 *Case of the haunted camp* (1992)
4 *Case of the Christmas thief* (1992)
5 *Case of the hidden treasure* (1993)
6 *Case of the million-dollar diamonds* (1993)
7 *Case of the alien princess* (1994)

Sweet Valley magna series
Pascal, Francine
1 *Wakefields of Sweet Valley* (1991)
2 *Wakefield legacy* (1992)

Sweet Valley twins magna series
Pascal, Francine
1 *Magic Christmas* (1992)
2 *Christmas without Elizabeth* (1993)

Sweet Valley twins series
Pascal, Francine
Although other authors are credited with many of the volumes in this sequence it is listed under Francine Pascal who "maintains artistic control over every

aspect of these novels" including all plot outlines, descriptions of characters, time, setting, etc.
1 *Best friends* (1986)
2 *Teacher's pet* (1986)
3 *Haunted house* (1986)
4 *Choosing sides* (1986)
5 *Sneaking out* (1987)
6 *New girl* (1987)
7 *Three's a crowd* (1987)
8 *First place* (1987)
9 *Against the rules* (1987)
10 *One of the gang* (1987)
11 *Buried treasure* (1987)
12 *Keeping secrets* (1987)
13 *Stretching the truth* (1987)
14 *Tug of war* (1987)
15 *Older boy* (1988)
16 *Second best* (1988)
17 *Boys against girls* (1988)
18 *Center of attention* (1988)
19 *Bully* (1988)
20 *Playing hooky* (1988)
21 *Left behind* (1988)
22 *Out of place* (1988)
23 *Claim to fame* (1988)
24 *Jumping to conclusions* (1988)
25 *Standing out* (1989)
26 *Taking charge* (1989)
27 *Teamwork* (1989)
28 *April fool!* (1989)
29 *Jessica and the brat attack* (1989)
30 *Princess Elizabeth* (1989)
31 *Jessica's bad idea* (1989)
32 *Jessica on stage* (1989)
33 *Elizabeth's new hero* (1989)
34 *Jessica's the rock star* (1989)
35 *Amy's pen pal* (1990)
36 *Mary is missing* (1990)
37 *War between the twins* (1990)
38 *Lois strikes back* (1990)
39 *Jessica and the money mix-up* (1990)
40 *Danny means trouble* (1990)
41 *Twins get caught* (1990)
42 *Jessica's secret* (1990)
43 *Elizabeth's first kiss* (1990)
44 *Amy moves in* (1991)
45 *Lucy takes the reins* (1991)
46 *Mademoiselle Jessica* (1991)
47 *Jessica's new look* (1991)
48 *Mansy Miller fights back* (1991)
49 *Twins' little sister* (1991)
50 *Jessica and the secret star* (1991)
51 *Elizabeth the impossible* (1991)
52 *Booster boycott* (1991)
53 *Slime that at Sweet Valley* (1991)
54 *Big party weekend* (1991)
55 *Brooke and her rock star mom* (1991)
56 *Unicorns go Hawaiian* (1991)
57 *Steven's in love* (1992)
Titles of numbers 58 and 59 not identified
60 *Ciao, Sweet Valley!* (1992)
61 *Jessica the ned* (1992)
62 *Sarah's dad and Sophia's mom* (1992)
63 *Poor Lila* (1992)
64 *Charm school mystery* (1992)
65 *Patty's last dance* (1993)
66 *Great boyfriend switch* (1993)
67 *Jessica the thief* (1993)
68 *Middle School gets married* (1993)
69 *Won't someone help Anna* (1993)
70 *Psychic sisters* (1993)
71 *Jessica saves the trees* (1993)
72 *Love potion* (1993)
73 *Lila's music video* (1993)
74 *Elizabeth the hero* (1993)
75 *Jessica and the earthquake* (1994)
76 *Yours for a day* (1994)
77 *Todd runs away* (1994)
78 *Steven and the zombie* (1994)
79 *Jessica's blind* (1994)
80 *Gossip war* (1994)
81 *Robbery at the mall* (1994)
82 *Steven's enemy* (1994)
83 *Amy's secret sister* (1994)

Sweet Valley twins super chiller series
Pascal, Francine
Although other authors are credited with many of the volumes in this sequence it is listed under Francine Pascal who "maintains artistic control over every aspect of these novels" including all plot outlines, descriptions of characters, time, setting, etc.
1 *Jessica's Christmas carol* (1989)
2 *Ghosts in the graveyard* (1990)
3 *Carnival graveyard* (1990)
4 *Ghost in the bell tower* (1992)
5 *Curse of the ruby necklace* (1993)
6 *Curse of the golden heart* (1994)
7 *Haunted burial ground* (1994)

Sweet Valley twins super series
Pascal, Francine
1 *Class trip* (1988)
2 *Holiday mischief* (1988)

Sweet Valley twins super special series
Pascal, Francine
1 *Perfect summer* (1985)
2 *Winter carnival* (1986)
3 *Spring break* (1986)

Sweet Valley University series
Pascal, Francine
1 *College girls* (1993)
2 *Love, lies and Jessica Wakefield* (1993)
3 *What your parents don't know* (1994)
4 *Anything for love* (1994)
5 *Married woman* (1994)
6 *Love of her life* (1994)
7 *Good-bye to love* (1994)
8 *Home for Christmas* (1994)

Sweethearts series
Crockett, Samuel Rutherford
1 *Sweetheart travellers* (1895)
2 *Sweethearts at home* (1912)

Swept away series
This sequence has six authors
Goudge, Eileen
1 *Gone with the wish* (1986)
Lantz, Francess Lin
2 *Woodstock magic* (1986)
Powers, Louise E
3 *Love on the range* (1986)
Lantz, Francess Lin
4 *Star struck* (1987)
Rabin, Jennifer
5 *Spellbound* (1987)
Garrido, Mar
6 *Once upon a kiss* (1987)
Steiner, Merrilee
7 *Pirate moon* (1987)
Lantz, Francess Lin
8 *All shook up* (1987)

Sweyn's Eye series
Gower, Iris
see **Copper kingdom series**

Swift Junior series
Appleton, Victor II
see **Tom Swift Junior series**

Swift series
Appleton, Victor
see **Tom Swift series**
Hornig, Doug
see **Loren Swift series**
Jones, Charles Reed
see **Leighton Swift series**

Swinbrooke series
Grace, C L
see **Kathryn Swinbrooke series**

Swinton series
Flower, Pat
see **Inspector Swinton series**
Greig, Ian
see **Inspector Swinton series**

Swiss family Robinson series
This sequence has four authors
Wyss, Johann Rudolf
1 *Swiss family Robinson* (1820)
Original edition entitled *Der Schweizerische Robinson*
Paul, Adrien
2 *Willis the pilot* (1855)
Adventures of Willis the pilot
Original edition entitled *Le pilot Willis*
Wister, Owen
3 *New Swiss family Robinson* (1882)
Verne, Jules
4 *Their island home* (1900)
Original edition entitled *Seconde patrie*
5 *Castaways of the flag* (1900)

Swithinford series
Marshall, Sybil
see **Old Swithinford series**

Swoptops series
Black, Cindy
see **Mojo Swoptops series**

Sword and circlet trilogy
Douglas, Carole Nelson
1 *Keepers of Edanvani* (1987)
2 *Heir of Reingarth* (1988)
3 *Seven of swords* (1989)

Sword and the dream series
Elliott, Janice
1 *King awakes* (1987)
2 *Empty throne* (1988)

Sword of honour trilogy
Waugh, Evelyn
see **World War II trilogy**

Sword of knowledge series
Cherryh, Carolyn Janice
1 *Dirge for Sabis* (1989)
Co-author: Leslie Fish
2 *Wizard spawn* (1989)
Co-author: Nancy Asire
3 *Reap the whirlwind* (1989)
Co-author: Mercedes Lackey

Sword of knowledge trilogy
Cherryh, Carolyn Janice
1 *Dirge for Sabis* (1989)
Co-author: Leslie Fish
2 *Wizard spawn* (1989)
Co-author: Nancy Asire
3 *Reap the whirlwind* (1989)
Co-author: Mercedes Lackey

Sword of the Raven series
Boucher, Alan Estcourt
see **Halli Thordason series**

Sword trilogy
Christopher, John
see **Prince trilogy**

Sword-dancer series
Roberson, Jennifer
see **Tiger and Del series**

SwordQuest series
Fawcett, Bill
1 *Quest for the unicorn's horn* (1985)
2 *Quest for the dragon's eye* (1985)
3 *Quest for the Demon's Gate* (1986)
4 *Quest for the elf king* (1987)

Swords of Raemllyn series
Vardeman, Robert Edward
1 *To demons bound* (1985)
2 *Yoke of magic* (1985)
3 *Blood fountain* (1985)
4 *Death's acolyte* (1986)
5 *Beasts of the mist* (1986)
6 *For crown and kingdom* (1987)

Swords series
Bulmer, Kenneth
1 *Swords of the barbarians* (1970)
2 *Electric sword swallowers* (1971)

Swords series
Leiber, Fritz
see **Fafhrd and Gray Mouser series**
Moorcock, Michael
see **Corum series**

Swords trilogy
Norton, Andre
1 *Sword is drawn* (1944)
2 *Sword in sheath* (1949)
3 *At sword's point* (1954)

Sybylla Penelope Melvyn series
Franklin, Miles
Autobiographical novels
1 *My brilliant career* (1901)
2 *My career goes bung* (1946)
End of my career

Syd Fish series
Geason, Susan
1 *Shaved fish* (1990)
Short stories
2 *Dogfish* (1991)
3 *Sharkbait* (1993)

Sydenham series
Seaman, Donald
1 *Defector* (1975)
Chameleon course
2 *Terror syndicate* (1976)
3 *Committee* (1977)

Sydney Treherne series
Saint Dennis, Madelon
1 *Death kiss* (1932)
2 *Perfumed lure* (1932)

Sydney underworld trilogy
Peters, Lance
see **Detective Sergeant Joe Church trilogy**

Sydney Vane series
Islay, Nicholas
1 *Selicombe murder* (1920)
2 *Brace of rogues* (1920)

Sylvaine and Vinca trilogy
Meyers, Roy
see **Dolphins trilogy**

Sylvania series
Allen, Hervey
see **Disinherited series**

Sylvester Horatio Pinkney series
Wills, Cecil Melville
1 *Case of the empty beehive* (1959)
2 *Death of a best seller* (1959)
3 *Colonel's foxhound* (1960)

Sylvia Arden series
Chalmers, Margaret Piper
1 *Sylvia's experiment* (1914)
Alternative title: The story of an unrelated family
2 *Sylvia of the hill top* (1916)
3 *Sylvia Arden decides* (1917)
4 *Wild wings* (1921)
5 *Peter's best seller* (1923)
6 *Babbie* (1925)

Sylvia Plotkin and Max Van Larsen series
Baxt, George
1 *Parade of cockeyed creatures* (1967)

2 *I, said the demon* (1969)
3 *Satan is a woman* (1987)

Sylvia Scarlett series
Mackenzie, Compton
1 *Early adventures of Sylvia Scarlett* (1918)
Early life and adventures of Sylvia Scarlett
Sylvia Scarlett
1.1 *Sylvia Scarlett* (1918)
1.2 *Sylvia and Arthur* (1918)
2 *Sylvia and Michael* (1919)
One volume edition entitled *The adventures of Sylvia Scarlett*, 1950

Sylvia series
Sinclair, Upton
1 *Sylvia* (1913)
2 *Sylvia's marriage* (1914)

Sylvia Smith-Smith series
Nelson, Peter N
1 *Sylvia Smith-Smith* (1987)
2 *Night of fire* (1991)
3 *Fast lane west* (1991)
4 *Scarface* (1991)
5 *Deadly games* (1992)
6 *Dangerous waters* (1992)

Sylvie and Bruno series
Carroll, Lewis
1 *Sylvie and Bruno* (1889)
2 *Sylvie and Bruno, concluded* (1893)

Symphony trilogy
Miller, Calvin
1 *Requiem of love* (1989)
2 *Symphony in sand* (1990)
3 *Overture of light* (1991)

Syn series
Thorndike, Russell
see **Doctor Syn series**

T

T.A.C.K. series
Miller, Marvin
1 *T.A.C.K. to the rescue* (1982)
2 *T.A.C.K. secret service* (1982)
3 *T.A.C.K. against time* (1983)
4 *T.A.C.K. into danger* (1983)

T and me series
Graeber, Charlotte Towner
see **Mister T and me series**

T B Smith series
Wallace, Edgar
see **Mister T B Smith series**

T-city trilogy
Adlard, Mark
see **Jan Caspol trilogy**

T.E.R.R.A. series
Maddock, Larry
see **Hannibal Fortune and Webley series**

T F Benson series
Adler, David A
1 *T F Benson and the funny money mystery* (1992)
2 *T F Benson and the dinosaur madness mystery* (1992)
3 *T F Benson and the Jewelry spy mystery* (1992)

T-Force series
Whiting, Charles
1 *Big breakout!* (1976)
2 *Massacre at Metz* (1976)
3 *Highway through hell* (1976)
4 *Last mission* (1977)

T.G. and Moonie series
Maschler, Fay
Illustrated by Sylvie Selig
1 *T.G. and Moonie move out of town* (1977)
2 *T.G. and Moonie go shopping* (1978)

T G Horne series
Mackenzie, Pierce
1 *Stolen white eagle* (1987)
2 *Fleecing of Fodder City* (1987)
3 *Winner takes nothing* (1987)
4 *Spanish Monte Fiasco* (1987)
5 *Double trouble in Skagway* (1987)
6 *Cockeyed coyote* (1987)

T-Man series
Sanders, Buck
see **Ben Slayton series**

T.O.M.C.A.T. series
Knight, Mallory T
see **Man from T.O.M. C.A.T. series**

T.R.Bear series
Dicks, Terrance
1 *Enter T.R.* (1985)
2 *T.R. goes to school* (1985)
3 *T.R.'s day out* (1985)
4 *T.R. afloat* (1986)
5 *T.R.'s Hallowe'en* (1986)
6 *T.R.'s big game* (1987)
7 *T.R.'s festival* (1987)
8 *T.R. goes to Hollywood* (1988)
9 *T.R. goes skiing* (1988)
10 *T.R. down under* (1989)
11 *T.R. in New York* (1989)
12 *T.R. Bear at the zoo* (1990)

T.S.Eliot series
Gordon, Lyndall
1 *Eliot's early years* (1977)
2 *Eliot's new life* (1988)

T S W Sheridan series
Wilcox, Stephen F
1 *Dry white tear* (1989)
2 *Saint Lawrence run* (1990)
3 *All the dead heroes* (1992)

T T Baldwin series
Ocork, Shannon
1 *Sports freak* (1980)
2 *Hell bent for heaven* (1983)
3 *End of the line* (1984)

Taash series
McKenzie, Ellen Kindt
1 *Taash and the jesters* (1968)
2 *Kashka* (1987)

Tabard series
Allison-Williams, Jean
1 *Mistress of the Tabard* (1984)
2 *Simon on the Tabard* (1984)

Tabby series
De Banke, Cecile
1 *Tabby magic* (1959)
2 *More tabby magic* (1961)

Tabitha trilogy
Brown, Ruth Alberta
see **Ivy Hall trilogy**

Tabor family series
Goolden, Barbara
1 *Minty* (1959)
2 *Five pairs of hands* (1961)
3 *Minty and the missing picture* (1963)
4 *Minty and the secret room* (1963)
5 *Trouble for the Tabors* (1966)
6 *Top secret* (1969)

Tabor series
Cruz, Mark
see **Death Squad series**

Tac One series
This sequence has two authors
Decker, Joseph
1 *Assignment North Africa* (1975)
Barker, Patrick
2 *Assignment Devil's Playground* (1975)

Tac series
Radin, Ruth Yaffe
1 *Tac's island* (1986)
2 *Tac's turn* (1987)

Tackett trilogy
Nofziger, Lyn
1 *Tackett* (1992)
2 *Tackett and the teacher* (1994)
3 *Tackett and the saloon keeper* (1994)

Tacy Kelly series
Lovelace, Maud Hart
see **Betsy Ray series**

Tad Anders series
Allbeury, Ted
1 *Snowball* (1974)
2 *Judas factor* (1984)

Tad Sheldon series
Wilson, John Fleming
1 *Tad Sheldon, Boy Scout* (1913)
Stories of his patrol
2 *Tad Sheldon's Fourth of July* (1913)

Tadgy series
Davis, Nelson
1 *Tadgy the mystery boy* (1947)
2 *Detective Tadgy* (1949)
3 *Tadgy on the trail* (1950)

Taff Roberts series
Parker, Roger
see **Inspector Taff Roberts series**

Taff series
Berrisford, Judith Mary
1 *Taff the sheepdog* (1949)
2 *Son of Taff* (1959)
3 *S.O.S.for sheepdog Taff* (1963)
4 *Taff and the stolen ponies* (1965)

Taffin series
Mallet, Lyndon
1 *Taffin* (1980)
2 *Taffin's first law* (1980)

Taffy Sinclair series
Haynes, Betsy
1 *Against Taffy Sinclair Club* (1981)
2 *Taffy Sinclair strikes again* (1984)
3 *Taffy Sinclair, queen of the soaps* (1987)
4 *Taffy Sinclair and the romance machine* (1987)
5 *Blackmailed by Taffy Sinclair* (1987)
6 *Taffy Sinclair, Baby Ashley and me* (1988)
7 *Taffy Sinclair and the secret admirer epidemic* (1988)
8 *Taffy Sinclair and the Melanie makeover* (1988)
9 *Truth about Taffy Sinclair* (1988)
10 *Taffy Sinclair goes to Hollywood* (1990)
11 *Nobody likes Taffy Sinclair* (1991)

Taggart series
Hayes, Ralph Eugene
see **Agent for Cominsec series**

Tahara series
Sherman, Harold Morrow
1 *Tahara, boy king of the desert* (1933)
2 *Tahara among African tribes* (1933)
3 *Tahara, boy mystic of India* (1933)
4 *Tahara in the land of Yucatan* (1933)

Tai-Lu series
Fraser, Shelagh
1 *Tai-Lu talking* (1952)
2 *Tai-Lu's birthday party* (1954)
3 *Tai-Lu flies abroad* (1955)

Tail End Ranch series
Culp, John Hewett
see **Martin Cameron series**

Tain series
Frost, Gregory
1 *Tain* (1986)
2 *Remscela* (1988)

Taine series
Household, Geoffrey
see **Roger Taine series**

Taiwan series
Wood, Christopher
1 *Taiwan* (1981)
2 *Dove against death* (1983)

Take one for murder series
Fulton, Eileen
see **Nina McFall series**

Takeo series
Tasaki, Hanama
see **Private Takeo series**

Takeoff series
Garrett, Randall
1 *Takeoff!* (1980)
2 *Takeoff too* (1987)

Takers series
Ahern, Jerry
1 *Takers* (1984)
2 *River of gold* (1985)

Taking a walk series
Tarsky, Sue
1 *Taking a walk in the town* (1979)
2 *Taking a walk in the park* (1979)
3 *Taking a walk on the seashore* (1979)
4 *Taking a walk in the countryside* (1979)

Taking my pet to the vet series
Kuklin, Susan
1 *Taking my cat to the vet* (1988)
2 *Taking my dog to the vet* (1988)

Tala series
Wynne, May
1 *Little Brown Tala* (1944)
2 *Brown Tala finds little Tulsi* (1945)
One volume edition entitled *Little Brown Tala stories*, 1947

Talbot Lion series
Victor, Sam
1 *Cuban inferno* (1981)
2 *White House massacre* (1981)

Talbot series
Aiken, Albert W
see **Dick Talbot series**
Mulkeen, Thomas Patrick
see **Clem Talbot series**

Talbot trilogy
Golding, William
see **Sea trilogy**

Tale of Krispos series
Turtledove, Harry
1 *Krispos rising* (1991)
2 *Krispos of Videssos* (1991)

Tale of Trotter Street series
Hughes, Shirley
1 *Angel Mae* (1989)

Tale of Trotter Street series

2 *Snow lady* (1990)
3 *Big concrete lorry* (1990)
4 *Wheels* (1991)

Talents series
Hill, Douglas
1 *Blade of the poisoner* (1987)
2 *Master of fiends* (1987)

Tales at the Mousehole trilogy
Stolz, Mary
1 *Great rebellion* (1961)
2 *Siri, the Conquistador* (1963)
3 *Maximilian's world* (1966)
One volume revised edition entitled *Tales at the Mousehole*, 1990

Tales from Camp Crystal Lake series
Morse, Eric
see **Friday the thirteenth series**

Tales from Mister Toffy's circus series
Ross, Tony
1 *Samuel* (1973)
2 *Bop* (1973)
3 *Tiger Harry* (1973)
4 *Blodwen* (1973)
5 *Big Ethel* (1973)
6 *Mister Toffy* (1973)

Tales from the Atchafalaya series
Edler, Timothy J
1 *Maurice the snake and Gaston the near-sighted turtle* (1977)
2 *T-boy and the trial for life* (1978)
3 *T-boy in Mossland* (1978)
4 *T-boy, the little Cajun* (1978)

Tales from the flat earth series
Lee, Tanith
1 *Night's master* (1978)
2 *Death's master* (1979)
3 *Delusion's master* (1981)
Numbers 1-3 also published in one volume entitled *The lords of darkness*, 1987
4 *Delirium's mistress* (1986)
5 *Night's sorceries* (1987)
Numbers 4 and 5 also published in one volume entitled *Night's daughter*, 1987

Tales from the igloo series
Nanogak, Agnes
1 *Tales from the igloo* (1972)
2 *More tales from the igloo* (1985)

Tales from the Land of Erin trilogy
Scott, Michael
1 *Bright enchantment* (1985)
2 *Golden dream* (1985)
3 *Silver wish* (1985)

Tales from the Misty Wood series
Joyner, Simon
1 *Merry Mischief* (1984)
2 *Bubbles and troubles* (1984)
3 *Riverbank rumpus* (1984)
4 *Frosty frolics* (1984)

Tales from the past series
Vansittart, Peter
see **Stories from the past series**

Tales of a fisherman series
Grey, Zane
1 *Tales of fishes* (1919)
2 *Tales of lonely trails* (1922)
3 *Tales of Southern rivers* (1924)
4 *Tales of fishing virgin seas* (1925)
5 *Tales of the angler's Eldorado, New Zealand* (1926)
Angler's El Dorado
The second title is a revised edition
6 *Tales of swordship and tuna* (1927)
7 *Tales of fresh water fishing* (1928)
8 *Tales of Tahitian waters* (1931)
Companion volumes: *An American angler in Australia*, 1937, *Adventures in fishing*, edited by Ed Zern, 1952, *Zane Grey's tales from the fisherman's log*, 1979, *The undiscovered Zane Grey fishing stories*, edited by George Reiger, 1983

Tales of a Minnesota girl series
Sterrett, Frances Roberta
see **Rusty series**

Tales of a naturalist series
Chambers, Robert William
1 *In search of the unknown* (1904)
2 *Police!* (1915)

Tales of Arthur series
Kennealy, Patricia
1 *Hawk's gray feather* (1990)
Hawk's grey feather
2 *Oak above the kings* (1994)

Tales of Clavering Grange series
Chetwynd-Hayes, Ronald
1 *Tales of darkness* (1981)
2 *King's ghost* (1985)
Grange
3 *Ghosts from the mist of time* (1985)
4 *Tales from the hidden world* (1988)
5 *Haunted grange* (1988)

Tales of George and Matilda Mouse series
Buchanan, Heather S
1 *Matilda Mouse's first adventure* (1985)
2 *George Mouse goes flying* (1985)
3 *Matilda Mouse's patchwork life-jackets* (1985)
4 *George Mouse's first summer* (1985)
5 *Matilda Mouse's garden* (1986)
6 *Matilda Mouse's shell house* (1986)
7 *George Mouse's water music* (1986)
8 *George mouse's caravan* (1986)
9 *George and Matilda Mouse and the doll's house* (1988)
10 *George and Matilda Mouse and the floating school* (1990)
11 *George and Matilda Mouse and the moon rocket* (1991)
12 *George and Matilda Mouse's Christmas journey* (1993)

Tales of Gom in the Legends of Ulm series
Chetwin, Grace
1 *Gom on Windy Mountain* (1986)
2 *Riddle and the rune* (1987)
3 *Crystal stair* (1988)
4 *Starstone* (1989)

Tales of my landlord series
Scott, Walter
1 *Count Robert of Paris* (1831)
Set in 1098
2 *Castle Dangerous* (1831)
Set in 1306-07
3 *Legend of Montrose* (1819)
Set in 1645-46
4 *Old Mortality* (1816)
Set in 1685
5 *Bride of Lammermoor* (1819)
Set in 1695
6 *Black dwarf* (1816)
Set in 1706
7 *Heart of Midlothian* (1818)
Set in 1736

Tales of South Carolina series
Rhyne, Nancy
1 *Tales of the South Carolina low country* (1982)
2 *More tales of the South Carolina low country* (1984)

Tales of stirring times series
Rutley, Cecil Bernard
1 *For Queen and freedom* (1928)
A tale of the time of Queen Boadicea and Emperor Nero
2 *Banner of the dragon* (1927)
A tale of the Norman Conquest
3 *Knight of the Cross* (1928)
A tale of the Third Crusade
4 *Crecy and Poitiers* (1929)
A tale of the Hundred Years War
5 *Frontier scout* (1928)
A tale of the conquest of Canada

Tales of Terry Trotter series
Jones, Peter
see **Terry Trotter series**

Tales of Texas series
Kelton, Elmer
1 *Horsehead Crossing* (1963)
2 *Massacre at Goliad* (1965)
3 *Llano River* (1966)
4 *After the bugles* (1967)
5 *Hanging judge* (1969)
6 *Captain's rangers* (1969)
7 *Bowie's mine* (1971)
8 *Wagontongue* (1972)
Originally published under the pseudonym Lee McElroy
9 *Manhunt* (1974)
10 *Joe Pepper* (1975)
11 *Long way to Texas* (1976)
Originally published under the pseudonym Lee McElroy
12 *Wolf and the buffalo* (1980)
13 *Eyes of the hawk* (1981)
14 *Stand proud* (1984)
15 *Dark thicket* (1985)
16 *Big brand* (1986)

Tales of the bard trilogy
Scott, Michael
1 *Magician's law* (1987)
2 *Demon's law* (1988)
3 *Death's law* (1989)

Tales of the Broad acres series
Jacob, Naomi
see **Broad acres series**

Tales of the city series
Maupin, Armistead
1 *Tales of the city* (1978)
2 *More tales of the city* (1980)
3 *Further tales of the city* (1982)
4 *Baby Cakes* (1984)
5 *Significant others* (1987)
6 *Sure of you* (1989)
Numbers 1-6 also published in one volume entitled *Twenty-eight Barbary Lane*, 1990
7 *Back to Barbary Lane* (1991)

Tales of the Concordat trilogy
Swycaffer, Jefferson Putnam
1 *Empire's legacy* (1988)
2 *Voyage of the planetslayer* (1988)
3 *Revolt and rebirth* (1988)

Tales of the continuing time series
Moran, Daniel Keys
1 *Emerald eyes* (1988)
2 *Long run* (1989)

Tales of the Crusaders series
Scott, Walter
1 *Betrothed* (1825)
2 *Talisman* (1825)

Tales of the five series
Duane, Diane
see **Epic tales of the five series**

Tales of the Five Towns series
Bennett, Arnold
1 *Tales of the Five Towns* (1905)
2 *Grim smile of the Five Towns* (1907)
3 *Matador of the Five Towns, and other stories* (1912)

Tales of the Galactic Midway series
Resnick, Mike
1 *Sideshow* (1982)
2 *Three-legged hootch dancer* (1983)
3 *Wild alien tamer* (1983)
4 *Best rootin' tootin' shootin' gunslinger in the shole damned galaxy* (1983)

Tales of the jewelled men series
Veryan, Patricia
1 *Time's fool* (1991)
2 *Had we never loved* (1992)
3 *Ask me no questions* (1993)
4 *Shadow's bliss* (1994)

Tales of the Picts series
Howard, Robert Ervin
1 *King Kull* (1967)
Kull
Co-author: Lin Carter
2 *Bran Mak Morn* (1969)
Abridged edition entitled *Worms of the earth*, 1974
Also the title story in *The dark man, and others*, 1963

Tales of the prairies series
Hunkins, Ralph Valentine
1 *Tepee days* (1941)
2 *Trapper days* (1942)
3 *Sod-house days* (1945)

Tales of the primal land series
Lumley, Brian
1 *House of Cthulhu, and other tales of the primal land* (1984)
2 *Tarra Khash, Hrossak!* (1991)
3 *Sorcery in Shad* (1991)

Tales of the Ridings series
Moorman, Frederic William
1 *Tales of the Ridings* (1920)
2 *More tales of the Ridings* (1920)

Tales of the south series
Park, Ruth
1 *Ship's cat* (1961)
2 *Uncle Matt's mountain* (1962)
3 *Road to Christmas* (1962)

Tales of the third grade series
Ransom, Candice Farris
1 *Who needs third grade?* (1992)
2 *Third grade stars* (1993)

Tales of the velvet comet series
Resnick, Mike
1 *Eros ascending* (1984)
2 *Eros at zenith* (1984)
3 *Eros descending* (1985)
4 *Eros at nadir* (1986)

Tales of the Werewolf Clan trilogy
Munn, Harold Warner
1 *Werewolf of Ponkert* (1958)
2 *In the tomb of the bishop* (1979)
3 *Master goes home* (1980)

Tales of the wild folk series
Rutley, Cecily Marianne
1 *Kingfisher blue* (1949)
2 *Tale of Tom Thrush* (1949)
3 *Sweet-Song the skylark* (1949)
4 *Greykin a squirrel* (1949)
5 *Minky the mole* (1949)
6 *Teeny the harvest mouse* (1949)
7 *Grasshopper green* (1950)
8 *White Wings, a butterfly* (1950)
9 *Wunda the wood ant* (1950)
10 *David, a dragonfly* (1950)
11 *Hum Hum, a honey bee* (1950)
12 *Queen Wasp* (1950)
13 *Little Billy Blue Tit* (1951)
14 *Hal the hedgehog* (1951)
15 *Tale of William Woodpecker* (1951)
16 *Brock the badger* (1951)
17 *Oscar the otter* (1951)
18 *Wee One, the wren* (1951)

Tales of tomorrow series
Houston, David
1 *Invaders of Ground Zero* (1981)
2 *Red dust* (1981)
3 *Substance X* (1981)
4 *Ice from space* (1982)

Tales of Uncle Remus series
Lester, Julius
Based on the stories by Joel Chandler Harris
1 *Adventures of Brer Rabbit* (1987)
2 *Further adventures of Brer Rabbit* (1988)
3 *Misadventures of Brer Rabbit, Brer Fox, Brer Wolf, Doodang & other* (1990)
creatures
4 *Last tales of Uncle Remus* (1994)

Talisend series
Kitchen, Paddy
see **Vanessa Talisend series**

Taliswoman trilogy
Douglas, Carole Nelson
1 *Cup of clay* (1991)
2 *Seed upon the wind* (1992)
3 *Lady rogue* (1993)

Talking cat series
Kubinyi, Laszlo
see **Shukru series**

Tall Bird and John Crane trilogy
Gulick, Bill
see **Northwest destiny trilogy**

Tall Man series
Fisher, Clay
see **Ben Allison series**

Tallant series
York, Andrew
see **Colonel Munroe Tallant series**

Tallboys series
Lofts, Norah
see **Sir Godfrey Tallboys series**

Tallentire family series
Bragg, Melvyn
1 *Hired man* (1969)
2 *Place in England* (1970)
3 *Kingdom come* (1980)

Talleyman series
James, John
1 *Talleyman* (1986)
2 *Talleyman in the ice* (1989)

Tallis series
L'Engle, Madeleine
see **Poly and Charles O'Keefe series**
Rossiter, John
see **Roger Tallis series**

Tallman series
Braun, Matt
see **Ash Tallman series**

Tallman series
Lord, Tom
1 *Highbinders* (1983)
2 *Crossfire* (1984)
3 *Wages of sin* (1984)

Tallon series
Ball, John
see **Jack Tallon series**

Talon family series
L'Amour, Louis
1 *Man from the broken hills* (1975)
2 *Rivers west* (1975)
3 *Milo Talon* (1981)

Talon trilogy
Eulo, Ken
see **Chandal Talon trilogy**

Talos Cord series
Macleod, Robert
1 *Drum of power* (1963)
Also published as *Drum of Ungara*, by Bill Knox
2 *Cave of bats* (1964)
3 *Lake of fear* (1966)
Iron sanctuary
4 *Isle of dragons* (1967)
5 *Place of mists* (1969)
6 *Path of ghosts* (1971)
7 *Nest of vultures* (1973)

Talvarin series
Morwood, Peter
see **Book of years series**

Tam Sventon series
Holmberg, Ake
1 *Tam Sventon and the silver-plate gang* (1954)
Original edition entitled *Ture Sventon i Stockholm*
2 *Tam Sventon, private detective* (1963)
Original edition entitled *Ture Sventon, privatdetektiv*
3 *Tam Sventon, desert detective* (1963)
Original edition entitled *Ture Sventon i oknen*
4 *Tam Sventon and discovery* (1968)
Original edition entitled *Ture Sventon i varnhuset*

Tama series
Cummings, Ray
1 *Tama of the light country* (1965)
2 *Tama, princess of Mercury* (1966)

Tamar series
Caudwell, Sarah
see **Professor Hilary Tamar series**

Tamara and Andreas Valeshoff series
Ambler, Eric
see **Andreas and Tamara Valeshoff series**

Tamara Hoyland series
Mann, Jessica
1 *Funeral sites* (1981)
2 *No man's island* (1983)
3 *Grave goods* (1984)
4 *Kind of healthy grave* (1986)
5 *Death beyond the Nile* (1988)

Tamara series
Harrison, Claire
1 *Arctic rose* (1985)
2 *Wild flower* (1986)

Tamarisk tree series
Russell, Dora
Autobiography
1 *My quest for liberty and love* (1975)
2 *My school and the years of war* (1980)

Tambai series
Porteous, Richard Sydney
1 *Tambai Island* (1955)
2 *Tambai treasure* (1958)
3 *Silent isles* (1963)

Tambari series
Saro-Wiwa, Ken
1 *Tambari* (1973)
2 *Tambari in Dukana* (1973)

Tamberly series
Byers, Irene
see **Tim Digby series**

Tami Shimoni series
Hesky, Olga
see **Inspector Tami Shimoni series**

Tamily and Dick series
Robins, Patricia
see **Dick and Tamily series**

Tammy series
Baker, Elizabeth
1 *Tammy camps out* (1958)
2 *Tammy climbs Pyramid Mountain* (1962)
3 *Tammy goes canoeing* (1966)
4 *Tammy camps in the Rocky Mountains* (1970)

Tammy Troot series
Derwent, Lavinia
1 *Tammy Troot* (1945)
2 *Tammy Troot's capers* (1947)
3 *Adventures of Tammy Troot* (1975)
Contains *Tammy Troot's telegram*, and, *Tammy Troot's refugee*
4 *Further adventures of Tammy Troot* (1975)
Contains *Tammy Troot's hide-and-seek*, and, *Tammy Troot's balloon*

Tamson series
Campbell, R W
see **Spud Tamson series**

Tamuli trilogy
Eddings, David
1 *Domes of fire* (1993)
2 *Shining ones* (1993)
3 *Hidden city* (1994)

Tamworth Pig series
Kemp, Gene
1 *Prime of Tamworth Pig* (1972)
2 *Tamworth Pig saves the trees* (1973)
3 *Tamworth Pig and the litter* (1975)
4 *Christmas with Tamworth Pig* (1977)
Numbers 1-4 also published in one volume entitled *Tamworth Pig stories*, 1987
5 *Tamworth Pig rides again* (1992)

Tanaka series
La Plante, Richard
see **Josef Tanaka series**

Tanaka Tom Fletcher series
Lee, Patrick
see **Six-Gun Samurai series**

Tancred series
Cole, George Douglas Howard
see **Doctor Benjamin Tancred series**

Tandy series
Shepherd, Neal
see **Chief Inspector Michael Tandy series**

Tanganyika series
Bates, Darrell
1 *Fly-switch from the Sultan* (1961)
2 *Mango and the palm* (1962)

Tangent series
Sanders, Lawrence
see **Peter Tangent series**

Tangier trilogy
Burroughs, William Seward
1 *Soft machine* (1961)
2 *Ticket that exploded* (1962)
Revised edition 1967
3 *Nova express* (1964)

Tangled webs series
Mudd, Steve
1 *Tangled webs* (1989)
2 *Planet beyond* (1990)

Tango Key series
Drake, Alison
1 *Tango Key* (1988)
2 *Fevered* (1988)
3 *Black moon* (1989)
4 *Lagoon* (1990)
5 *High strangeness* (1992)

Tank series
Williams, David
1 *Tank* (1977)
2 *Fortress Eagle* (1977)
3 *Sugar sugar* (1978)

Tanker and Tinker series
Scarry, Richard
see **Tinker and Tanker series**

Tankwar series
Steelbaugh, Larry
1 *Tankwar* (1990)
2 *Fireball* (1990)
3 *Firestorm* (1991)
4 *Firebrand* (1991)

Tanner series
Block, Lawrence
see **Evan Tanner series**
Donald, Anabel
see **Alex Tanner series**
Greenleaf, Stephen
see **John Marshall Tanner series**
White, Ted
see **Abdroid Tanner series**

Tanquillan series
Brindley, Louise
1 *Tanquillan* (1986)
2 *Tender leaves of hope* (1986)
3 *Our summer faces* (1987)

Tansy series
Oxenham, Elsie J
1 *Rosamund's castle* (1938)
2 *Patch and pawn* (1940)
3 *Julie Mac comes back* (1941)

Tante Martine and Pascalet series
Bosco, Henri
see **Pascalet and Aunt Martine series**

Taoist Winnie-the-Pooh series
Hoff, Benjamin
1 *Tao of Pooh* (1992)
2 *Te of Piglet* (1992)

Taormin series
Franklin, Cheryl Jean
see **Magical tales of Taormin series**

Tapioca for tea series
Shears, Sarah
Autobiography
1 *Tapioca for tea* (1971)
Memories of a Kentish childhood
2 *Gather no moss* (1972)
Reminiscences of travel
3 *Seventh Commandment* (1973)
Experience of an adulterous relationship
4 *Other people's children* (1978)
Reminiscences of childminding

Tapiola series
Nathan, Robert
1 *Journey of Tapiola* (1938)
2 *Tapiola's brave regiment* (1941)
One volume edition entitled *The adventures of Tapiola*, 1950

Tar-Aiym Krang trilogy
Foster, Alan Dean
1 *Tar-Aiym Krang* (1972)
2 *Orphan Star* (1977)
3 *End of the matter* (1977)

Tara Chadwick series
Jenkins, Jerry Bruce
1 *Springtime discovery* (1992)

Tara Chadwick series

2 *Time to tell* (1992)
3 *Operation cemetery* (1992)
4 *Scattered flowers* (1992)

Target series

This sequence has two authors; based on a television series
Masters, Simon
1 *Men they once were* (1977)
Callan, Michael Feeney
2 *Bronze heist* (1978)

Tarl Cabot series

Norman, John
1 *Tarnsman of Gor* (1966)
2 *Outlaw of Gor* (1967)
3 *Priest-kings of Gor* (1968)
Numbers 1-3 also published in one volume entitled *Gor omnibus*, 1972
4 *Nomads of Gor* (1969)
5 *Assassin of Gor* (1970)
6 *Raiders of Gor* (1971)
7 *Captive of Gor* (1972)
8 *Hunters of Gor* (1974)
9 *Marauders of Gor* (1975)
10 *Tribesmen of Gor* (1976)
11 *Slave girl of Gor* (1977)
12 *Beasts of Gor* (1978)
13 *Explorers of Gor* (1979)
14 *Fighting slave of Gor* (1980)
15 *Rogue of Gor* (1981)
16 *Guardsman of Gor* (1981)
17 *Savages of Gor* (1982)
18 *Blood brothers of Gor* (1982)
19 *Kajira of Gor* (1983)
20 *Players of Gor* (1984)
21 *Mercenaries of Gor* (1985)
22 *Dancer of Gor* (1985)
23 *Renegades of Gor* (1986)
24 *Vagabonds of Gor* (1987)
25 *Magicians of Gor* (1988)

Tarleton series

Upward, Allen
see **Doctor Frank Tarleton series**
Van de Water, Frederic Franklin
see **John Tarleton series**

Tarnham series

Tute, Warren
see **George Mado series**

Taronga Road Riders series

Martin, Toy
1 *Bird in the hand* (1991)
2 *Behind the barricade* (1991)
3 *Fakes and fast horses* (1992)
4 *Secret stock* (1992)
5 *Price of a prize* (1993)
6 *Odd bods* (1993)

Tarot trilogy

Anthony, Piers
1 *God of Tarot* (1979)
2 *Vision of Tarot* (1980)
3 *Faith of Tarot* (1980)
One volume edition entitled *Tarot*, 1987

Tarradiddle series

Atkin, Flora Blumenthal
One act plays
1 *Tarradiddle tales* (1970)
2 *Tarradiddle travels* (1971)

Tartarin series

Daudet, Alphonse
1 *Tartarin of Tarascon, traveller, Turk and lion-hunter* (1872)
Original edition entitled *Aventures prodigieuses de Tartarin*, and also published as *Tartarin de Tarascon*
2 *Tartarin on the Alps* (1885)
Original edition entitled *Tartarin sur les Alpes*
3 *Port Tarascon* (1862)
Original edition entitled Port Tarascon

Tartarus series

Greenleaf, William
1 *Tartarus incident* (1983)
2 *Pandora stone* (1984)
3 *Starjacked!* (1987)

Tarzan series

Burroughs, Edgar Rice
1 *Tarzan of the apes* (1914)
Adapted as *Tarzan, king of the apes*, by Joan Dennison Vinge, 1983
2 *Return of Tarzan* (1915)
3 *Beasts of Tarzan* (1916)
4 *Son of Tarzan* (1917)
5 *Tarzan and the jewels of Opar* (1918)
Companion volume: *Hadon of ancient Opar*, by Philip Jose Farmer, 1974
6 *Jungle tales of Tarzan* (1919)
Short stories
7 *Tarzan the untamed* (1920)
8 *Tarzan the terrible* (1921)
9 *Tarzan and the golden lion* (1923)
10 *Tarzan and the ant men* (1924)
11 *Tarzan, lord of the jungle* (1928)
12 *Tarzan and the lost empire* (1929)
13 *Tarzan at the earth's core* (1930)
14 *Tarzan the invincible* (1931)
15 *Tarzan triumphant* (1931)
Numbers 1, 4, 13, 15 also published in one volume entitled *Tarzan of the apes*, 1988
16 *Tarzan and the City of Gold* (1933)
17 *Tarzan and the lion man* (1934)
18 *Tarzan and the leopard men* (1935)
19 *Tarzan's quest* (1936)
20 *Tarzan and the forbidden city* (1938)
21 *Tarzan the magnificent* (1939)
Short stories
22 *Tarzan and the Foreign Legion* (1947)
23 *Tarzan and the madman* (1964)
24 *Tarzan and the castaways* (1964)
Short stories
Companion volumes: *Tarzan and the lightning man*, by William Gilmour, 1963, *Tarzan and the lost safari*, anonymous, 1966, *Tarzan and the valley of* gold, by Fritz Leiber, 1966, *Tarzan alive, a definitive biography of Lord Greystoke*, by Philip Jose Farmer, 1972, *Tarzan at Mars' core*, by Edward Hirschman, 1977, *Tarzan and the tower of diamonds*, by Richard Reinsmith, 1985, *Tarzan and the well of slaves*, by Douglas Niles, 1985, *Jungle scenes of Tarzan*, by Zdenek Burian, 1973, *The adventure of the peerless peer by John H Watson*, by Philip Jose Farmer, 1974, *Tarzan encyclopedia*, by John Harwood and Allan Howard, 1975, *Tarzan and the classics*, by Erling Bent Holtsmark, 1979, *Tarzan and tradition*, by Erling Bent Holtsmark, 1981, *Burroughs dictionary*, by George T McWhorter, 1987; **Bunduki series** by John Thomas Edson features the adopted son and great granddaughter of Tarzan; other series inspired by the Tarzan series: **Anjani series, Azan series, Bomba series, Kaspa series, Lord Grandith series, New Tarzan series, Shuna series, Sorak series**

Tarzan twins series

Burroughs, Edgar Rice
1 *Tarzan twins* (1927)
2 *Tarzan and the Tarzan twins with Jad-Bal-Ja, the golden lion* (1936)
One volume edition entitled *Tarzan and the Tarzan twins*, 1963; companion volume: *The eternal lover*, 1925, also published as *The eternal savage*

Tas series

Eliott, E C
1 *Tas and the space machine* (1955)
2 *Tas and the postal rocket* (1955)

Taskers series

Onions, Oliver
1 *Two kisses* (1913)
2 *Crooked mile* (1914)

Tasmania series

Chauncy, Nan
1 *They found a cave* (1949)
2 *World's End was home* (1952)
3 *Fortune for the brave* (1954)

Tasmanian prints series

Craig, Clifford
1 *Engravers of Van Diemen's Land* (1961)
2 *Old Tasmanian prints* (1964)
3 *More old Tasmanian prints* (1984)
Companion volume: *Notes on Tasmania*, 1987

Tasmanian tales series

Lyne, Nairda
see **Powranna series**

Taste series

Kruk, Zofia
Autobiography of a Polish refugee in England
1 *Taste of fear* (1973)
A Polish childhood in Germany, 1939-1946
2 *Taste of hope* (1977)

Tate and Perkins series

Babson, Marian
see **Douglas Perkins and Gerry Tate series**

Tate series

Lowry, Lois
see **Caroline Tate series**

Tattered Tom series

Alger, Horatio
1 *Tattered Tom* (1871)
Alternative title: The story of a street Arab
2 *Paul, the peddler* (1871)
Alternative title: The fortunes of a young street peddler
3 *Phil, the fiddler* (1872)
Alternative title: The story of a young street musician
4 *Slow and sure* (1872)
Alternative title: From the street to the shop
5 *Julius* (1874)
Alternative title: The street boy out West
6 *Young outlaw* (1875)
Alternative title: Adrift in the streets
7 *Sam's chance and how he improved it* (1876)
8 *Telegraph boy* (1879)

Taunt series

Murray, William Hutchinson
see **John Taunt series**

Tavern talk series

Brooks, Collin
Essays
1 *Tavern talk* (1950)
2 *More tavern talk* (1952)

Tavy Martin series

Winsor, Diana
1 *Red on Wight* (1972)
2 *Death Convention* (1974)

Taylor House trilogy

Williams, Leigh Anne
1 *Katherine's dream* (1988)
2 *Lydia's hope* (1988)
3 *Clarisse's wish* (1988)

Taylor series

Abrahams, Robert
see **Pete Taylor series**
Gifford, Griselda
see **Ben Taylor series**
Hart, Catherine
see **Kathleen Hartly Taylor and Reed Taylor series**
Ridley, Sheila
see **Nurse Jane Taylor series**
Spencer, Sally
see **Becky Taylor series**
Treat, Lawrence
see **Mitch Taylor series**

Teabury series

Asher, Sandra Fenichel
see **Teddy Teabury series**

Teacake series

Davies, Hunter
see **Flossie Teacake series**

Teach me about series

Berry, Joy
1 *Teach me about mealtime* (1984)
2 *Teach me about getting dressed* (1984)
3 *Teach me about potty training* (1984)
4 *Teach me about bathtime* (1984)
5 *Teach me about bedtime* (1984)
6 *Teach me about boredom* (1984)
7 *Teach me about crying* (1984)
8 *Teach me about danger* (1984)
9 *Teach me about illness* (1984)
10 *Teach me about security objects* (1984)
11 *Teach me about separation* (1984)
12 *Teach me about travel* (1984)
13 *Teach me about pets* (1986)
14 *Teach me about brothers and sisters* (1986)
15 *Teach me about pretending* (1986)
16 *Teach me about relatives* (1986)
17 *Teach me about friends* (1986)
18 *Teach me about the dentist* (1986)
19 *Teach me about listening* (1986)
20 *Teach me about looking* (1986)
21 *Teach me about the baby-sitter* (1986)
22 *Teach me about mommies and daddies* (1986)
23 *Teach me about the doctor* (1986)
24 *Teach me about my body* (1986)
25 *Teach me about school* (1986)
26 *Teach me about smelling* (1986)
27 *Teach me about tasting* (1986)
28 *Teach me about touching* (1986)

Teaching series

Hope, Jane
Humorous reminiscences
1 *Don't do it!* (1947)
2 *All this and Burnham too* (1948)
3 *One term at Utopia* (1950)
4 *Inspector suggests* (1951)

Teaching series

Wigg, T I G
1 *Job with the boys* (1958)
2 *For the sons of gentlemen* (1960)

Teagarden series

Harris, Charlaine
see **Aurora Teagarden series**

Teal Stewart series

Lamb, J Dayne
1 *Questionable behavior* (1993)
2 *Question of preference* (1994)

Team names series

Lessiter, Mike
1 *Name that team!* (1986)
2 *College names of the games* (1989)
Stories behind the nicknames of 293 college sports teams

Team three series

Cunningham, Chet
1 *Deadly connection* (1980)
2 *Silent murder* (1980)

Tearle series
Corbett, Scott
see **Inspector Roger Tearle series**

Tears series
Skelton, Barbara
Memoirs
1 *Tears before bedtime* (1987)
2 *Weep no more* (1989)
One volume edition 1993

Tecumseh Fox series
Stout, Rex
1 *Double for death* (1939)
2 *Bad for business* (1940)
Originally published in *The second mystery book*; first published separately 1945
3 *Broken vase* (1941)

Ted and Dolly series
Fowler, Richard
1 *Ted and Dolly's magic carpet ride* (1982)
2 *Ted and Dolly's fairytale flight* (1984)

Ted and Nap series
Tilsley, Frank
see **Nap and Ted series**

Ted and Nina series
De Angeli, Marguerite
1 *Ted and Nina go to the grocery store* (1935)
2 *Ted and Nina have a happy rainy day* (1936)

Ted and Terri series
Palmer, Bernard
1 *Ted and Terri and the broken arrow* (1971)
2 *Ted and Terri and the crooked trapper* (1971)
3 *Ted and Terri and the troubled trumpeter* (1971)
4 *Ted and Terri and the stubborn bully* (1971)
5 *Ted and Terri and the secret captive* (1971)

Ted Jones series
Patchin, Frank Gee
1 *Ted Jones, fortune hunter* (1928)
Alternative title: Perilous adventures with a Chinese pearl trader
2 *Ted Jones at Desperation Island* (1928)
Alternative title: The affair with the yellow coral prince
3 *Ted Jones' weeks of terror* (1928)
Alternative title: The Luckless Three's revolt against the Sandalwood Sharpers
4 *Ted Jones under sealed orders* (1928)
Alternative title: The mysterious treasure trail to the Red Lagoon

Ted Quantrill trilogy
Ing, Dean
1 *Systemic shock* (1981)
2 *Single combat* (1983)
3 *Wild country* (1985)

Ted Rockson series
Stacy, Ryder
see **Doomsday warrior series**

Ted S Weaver series
Keith, David
1 *Matter of iodine* (1940)
2 *Matter of accent* (1943)

Ted Scott flying series
Dixon, Franklin W
House pseudonym
1 *Over the ocean to Paris* (1927)
Alternative title: Ted Scott's daring long distance flight
2 *Rescued in the clouds* (1927)
Alternative title: Ted Scott, hero of the air
3 *Over the Rockies with the air mail* (1927)
Alternative title: Ted Scott lost in the wilderness
4 *First stop Honolulu* (1927)
Alternative title: Ted Scott over the Pacific
5 *Search for the lost flyers* (1928)
Alternative title: Ted Scott over the West Indies
6 *South of the Rio Grande* (1928)
Alternative title: Ted Scott on a secret mission
7 *Across the Pacific* (1928)
Alternative title: Ted Scott's hop to Australia
8 *Lone eagle of the border* (1929)
Alternative title: Ted Scott and the diamond smugglers
9 *Flying against time* (1929)
Alternative title: Ted Scott breaking the ocean to ocean record
10 *Over the jungle trails* (1929)
Alternative title: Ted Scott and the missing explorers
11 *Lost at the South Pole* (1930)
Alternative title: Ted Scott in blizzard land
12 *Through the air to Alaska* (1930)
Alternative title: Ted Scott's search in Nugget Valley
13 *Flying to the rescue* (1930)
Alternative title: Ted Scott and the big dirigible
14 *Danger trails of the sky* (1931)
Alternative title: Ted Scott's great mountain climb
15 *Following the sun shadow* (1932)
Alternative title: Ted Scott and the great eclipse
16 *Battling the wind* (1933)
Alternative title: Ted Scott flying around Cape Horn
17 *Brushing the mountain top* (1934)
Alternative title: Aiding the lost traveler
18 *Castaways of the stratosphere* (1935)
Alternative title: Hunting the vanquished balloonists
19 *Hunting the sky spies* (1941)
Alternative title: Testing the invisible plane
20 *Pursuit patrol* (1943)
Alternative title: Chasing the platinum pirates

Ted series
Mogenson, Jan
Translated from the Danish
1 *Just before dawn* (1982)
Original edition entitled *Har du sovet godt, Bamse?*
2 *Ted and the Chinese princess* (1983)
3 *Mary's Christmas present* (1983)
4 *Lost and found* (1985)
Original edition entitled *Bamses ven*
5 *Ted's seaside adventure* (1985)
6 *Ted runs away from home* (1986)

Ted Wallace series
Fry, Stephen
1 *Liar* (1993)
2 *Hippopotamus* (1994)

Teddies series
This sequence has two authors
Ward, Dorothy Darrell
Illustrated by Chrissie Wells
1 *Picture rhymes* (1984)
2 *Counting rhymes* (1984)
3 *Colour rhymes* (1985)
4 *Shape rhymes* (1985)
McCaughrean, Geraldine
5 *Tell the time* (1986)
6 *Seaside adventure* (1986)

Teddy and Nora series
Hurwitz, Johanna
see **Nora and Teddy series**

Teddy Bear series
Cradock, Henry Cowper, *Mrs*
1 *Adventures of a Teddy Bear* (1934)
2 *More adventures of a Teddy Bear* (1935)
3 *In Teddy Bear's house* (1936)
4 *Teddy Bear's shop* (1939)
5 *Teddy Bear's farm* (1941)

Teddy Bear series
Slier, Debby
1 *Teddy Bear's bedtime book* (1985)
2 *Teddy Bear's bedtime adventure* (1985)

Teddy bear series
Worthington, Phoebe
1 *Teddy bear coalman* (1977)
2 *Teddy bear baker* (1979)
3 *Teddy bear postman* (1981)
4 *Teddy bear gardener* (1983)
5 *Teddy bear farmer* (1985)

Teddy boy series
Stucley, Elizabeth
Autobiography
1 *Teddy boy's picnic* (1958)
2 *Life is for living* (1959)

Teddy Edward series
Matthews, Patrick
Based on a television series
1 *Teddy Edward and the contraption* (1975)
2 *Teddy Edward becomes a Red Indian* (1975)
3 *Teddy Edward in Timbuctoo* (1975)
4 *Teddy Edward goes to Mount Everest* (1975)

Teddy Edward's books for bears series
Matthews, Patrick
Based on the Watch with Mother television series
1 *Teddy Edward's magic journey* (1976)
2 *Snowy Toes and the magic music box* (1976)
3 *Teddy Edward's magic music box* (1976)

Teddy Jo series
Stahl, Hilda
1 *Teddy Jo and the terrible secret* (1982)
2 *Teddy Jo and the yellow room mystery* (1983)
3 *Teddy Jo and the stolen ring* (1983)
4 *Teddy Jo and the strangers in the pink house* (1983)
5 *Teddy Jo and the strange medallion* (1983)
6 *Teddy Jo and the wild dog* (1984)
7 *Teddy Jo and the abandoned house* (1984)
8 *Teddy Jo and the ragged beggars* (1984)
9 *Teddy Jo and the kidnapped heir* (1984)
10 *Teddy Jo and the great dive* (1985)
11 *Teddy Jo and the magic quill* (1985)
12 *Teddy Jo and the missing portrait* (1985)
13 *Teddy Jo and the broken locket mystery* (1986)
14 *Teddy Jo and the missing family* (1986)

Teddy Lester series
Finnemore, John
1 *Three school chums* (1939)
2 *His first term* (1939)
3 *Teddy Lester's chums* (1939)
4 *Teddy Lester's schooldays* (1939)
5 *Teddy Lester in the Fifth* (1939)
6 *Teddy Lester, captain of cricket* (1939)

Teddy Robinson series
Robinson, Joan Gale
1 *Teddy Robinson* (1953)
About Teddy Robinson
2 *More about Teddy Robinson* (1954)
3 *Teddy Robinson's book* (1955)
4 *Dear Teddy Robinson* (1956)
5 *Teddy Robinson himself* (1957)
6 *Another Teddy Robinson* (1960)
7 *Keeping up with Teddy Robinson* (1964)

Teddy series
Davidson, Amanda
1 *Teddy's first Christmas* (1982)
2 *Teddy at the seaside* (1984)
3 *Teddy out-of-doors* (1985)
4 *Teddy's pocket money* (1985)
5 *Teddy's wash day* (1985)
6 *Teddy's favourite food* (1985)
7 *Teddy's birthday* (1985)
8 *Teddy in the garden* (1986)

Teddy series
Hickson, Mabel
1 *Concerning Teddy* (1897)
2 *Chronicles of Teddy's village* (1899)

Teddy series
Ray, Anna Chapin
1 *Teddy, her book* (1898)
2 *Phoebe, her profession* (1900)
3 *Teddy, her daughter* (1901)
4 *Nathalie's chum* (1902)
5 *Ursula's freshman* (1903)
6 *Nathalie's sister* (1904)

Teddy tales series
Cecil, Hugh
1 *Surprise bear* (1982)
2 *Blue bears' race* (1982)
3 *Speedy bears* (1982)
4 *Bears' Christmas* (1982)

Teddy Teabury series
Asher, Sandra Fenichel
1 *Teddy Teabury's fabulous fact* (1985)
2 *Teddy Teabury's peanutty problems* (1987)

Teddy the windbag series
Windsor, Patricia
see **Weirdo and ghost series**

Teddy trucks series
Cartlidge, Michelle
1 *Teddy trucks* (1981)
2 *Gerry's seaside journey* (1988)

Teddybear board book series
Gretz, Susanna
1 *Hide and seek* (1985)
2 *Ready for bed* (1985)
3 *I'm not sleepy* (1985)
4 *Too dark!* (1985)

Teddybears series
Gretz, Susanna
1 *Teddybears one to ten* (1969)
2 *Bears who stayed indoors* (1970)
3 *Bears who went to the seaside* (1972)
4 *Teddybears ABC* (1974)
5 *Teddybears cookbook* (1978)
6 *Teddybears moving day* (1981)
7 *Teddybears go shopping* (1982)
8 *Teddybears and the cold cure* (1984)

Teddy's days series
Jungman, Ann
1 *Day Teddy didn't tidy up* (1989)
2 *Day Teddy made new friends* (1989)
3 *Day Teddy got very worried* (1989)

4 *Day Teddy wanted Grandad to notice him* (1989)

Tee-Bo series
Whitcomb, Mary Burg
1 *Tee-Bo the talking dog on the trail of the persnickety prowler* (1975)
2 *Tee-Bo the incredible talking dog leads the way in the great hort hunt* (1975)

Teed series
Montrose, David
see **Russell Teed series**

Teen-age series
Brown, Wenzell
1 *Teen-age terror* (1958)
2 *Teen-age Mafia* (1959)

Teen age stories series
Coombs, Charles Ira
1 *Teen age adventure stories* (1948)
2 *Teen age treasure chest of sports* (1948)
3 *Teen age champion sports stories* (1950)

TEEN agent series
Lancer, Jack
see **Christopher Cool series**

Teen Eastenders series
Miller, Hugh
Based on a television series
1 *Solid ground* (1986)
2 *Growing pains* (1986)
3 *Heroes* (1988)
4 *Eye for business* (1988)

Teen Power Inc. series
Rodda, Emily
1 *Cry of the cat* (1994)
2 *Ghost of Raven Hill* (1994)
3 *Sorcerer's apprentice* (1994)
4 *Disappearing TV star* (1994)
5 *Beware the gingerbread house* (1994)

Teen witch series
Barnes, Megan
1 *Lucky thirteen* (1988)
2 *Be careful what you wish for* (1988)
3 *Gone with the witch* (1989)
4 *Witch switch* (1989)

Teenage mutant ninja turtles series
This sequence has two authors
Hiller, Barbara B
1 *Teenage mutant ninja turtles* (1990)
Morris, Dave
2 *Sky-high* (1990)
3 *Red herrings* (1990)
4 *Buried treasure* (1990)
5 *Six-guns and shurikens* (1990)
Companion volumes: *Teenage mutant ninja turtles knitting book*, by Joy Gammon, 1990, *The unauthorized teenage mutant ninja turtles quiz book, an unofficial trivia guide to America's hottest phenomenon*, by Jeff Rovin, 1990, *The official teenage mutant ninja turtles treasury*, by Stanley Wiater, 1991

Teetoncey and Ben O'Neal trilogy
Taylor, Theodore
1 *Teetoncey* (1974)
2 *Teetoncey and Ben O'Neal* (1975)
3 *Odyssey of Ben O'Neal* (1977)

Tegne series
La Plante, Richard
1 *Warlord of Zendow* (1988)
2 *Killing blow* (1990)

Tekumel series
Barker, Muhammad Abd al-Rahman
1 *Man of gold* (1984)
Based on the game, Empire of the Petal Throne
2 *Flamesong* (1985)

TekWar series
Shatner, William
1 *TekWar* (1989)
2 *TekLords* (1991)
3 *TekLab* (1991)

Telepathy series
Berger, John
1 *Foot of Clive* (1962)
2 *Corker's freedom* (1964)

Telfair series
Stevenson, Florence
see **Kitty Telfair series**

Telford series
Pope, Ray
1 *Model railway men* (1970)
2 *Telford and the American visitor* (1970)
3 *Model railway men take over* (1971)
4 *Telford's holiday* (1972)
5 *Telford and the Festiniog railway* (1973)
6 *Telford saves the line* (1974)
7 *Telford goes Dutch* (1976)
8 *Telford tells the truth* (1977)
9 *Model railway men in America* (1978)
10 *Telford and the prairie battle* (1979)

Tell and draw series
Oldfield, Margaret Jean
1 *Tell and draw stories* (1961)
2 *Tell and draw animal cut-outs* (1963)
3 *More tell and draw stories* (1969)
4 *Lots more tell and draw stories* (1973)
5 *Tell and draw paper bag puppet book* (1976)
6 *Tell and draw cut-outs* (1988)

Tellford series
Fisher, Douglas George
see **Jeff Tellford series**

Telling the truth series
Backus, William
1 *Telling yourself the truth* (1980)
2 *Telling the truth to troubled people* (1985)
3 *Telling each other the truth* (1985)

Telnarian histories series
Norman, John
1 *Chieftain* (1991)
2 *Captain* (1992)
3 *King* (1993)

Telzey Amberdon and Trigger Argee series
Schmitz, James Henry
1 *Tale of two clocks* (1962)
Legacy
2 *Universe against her* (1964)
3 *Lion game* (1973)
4 *Telzey toy* (1973)
Also published in *The Telzey toy, and other stories*, 1982

Tempest family series
This sequence has two authors
Weir, Rosemary
1 *Honeysuckle Line* (1959)
Beresford, Elisabeth
2 *Danger on the Old Pull'n Push* (1962)

Tempest series
Fox-Davies, Arthur Charles
see **Ashley Tempest series**
Shand, William
see **Bill Tempest series**

Tempest series
This sequence has two authors
Williams, Tad
1 *Caliban's hour* (1994)
Shakespeare, William
2 *Tempest* (1623)

Templar series
Charteris, Leslie
see **Saint series**

Temple Drake series
Faulkner, William
1 *Sanctuary* (1931)
2 *Requiem for a nun* (1951)

Temple Fortune series
Jacobs, Thomas Curtis Hicks
1 *Dangerous Fortune* (1949)
2 *Red eyes of Kali* (1950)
3 *Lock the door, mademoiselle* (1951)
4 *Blood and Sun-Tan* (1952)
5 *Lady, what's your game?* (1952)
6 *No sleep for Elsa* (1953)
7 *Good knight, sailor* (1954)
8 *Death in the mews* (1955)
9 *Deadly race* (1958)
10 *Women are like that* (1960)
11 *Target for terror* (1961)
12 *Murder market* (1962)
13 *Danger money* (1963)
14 *Final payment* (1965)
15 *Ashes in the cellar* (1966)
16 *Sweet poison* (1966)
17 *Death of a scoundrel* (1967)
18 *Wild week-end* (1967)
19 *House of horror* (1969)
20 *Black devil* (1969)

Temple girl series
Bruce, Henry
1 *Temple girl* (1919)
2 *Bride of Shiva* (1920)

Temple Kent series
Devon, D G
1 *Temple Kent* (1982)
2 *Shattered mask* (1983)
3 *Precious objects* (1984)

Temple series
Durbridge, Francis
see **Paul Temple series**
Gorell, Ronald Gorell Barnes
see **Evelyn Temple series**

Temple Street series
Spearing, Judith
1 *Ghosts who went to school* (1966)
2 *Museum house ghosts* (1969)

Templeton series
Goyne, Richard
see **Paul Templeton series**
Luigi, Belli
see **Vernon Templeton series**
Treadgold, Mary
see **Mick and Caroline Templeton series**

Temptress series
Allcard, Edward Cecil
1 *Single-handed passage* (1950)
2 *Temptress returns* (1952)

Temptress series
Blasco Ibanez, Vicente
1 *Temptress* (1922)
Original edition entitled *La tierra de todos*
2 *Queen Calafia* (1923)
Original edition entitled *La reina Calafia*

Tempus series
Morris, Janet Ellen
1 *Beyond sanctuary* (1985)
2 *Beyond the veil* (1985)
3 *Beyond Wizardwall* (1986)
4 *Tempus* (1987)
5 *City at the edge of time* (1988)
Co-author: Chris Morris
6 *Tempus unbound* (1989)
Co-author: Chris Morris
7 *Storm seed* (1990)
Co-author: Chris Morris

Ten commandments series
Sanders, Lawrence
1 *Sixth commandment* (1979)
2 *Seventh commandment* (1991)
3 *Eighth commandment* (1986)
4 *Tenth commandment* (1980)

Ten things I know series
Wax, Wendy
1 *Ten things I know about kangaroos* (1989)
2 *Ten things I know about penguins* (1989)
3 *Ten things I know about elephants* (1990)
4 *Ten things I know about whales* (1990)

Tenko series
This sequence has three authors; based on a television series
Masters, Anthony
1 *Tenko* (1981)
Hardwick, Michael
2 *Last Tenko* (1984)
Valery, Anne
3 *Tenko reunion* (1986)

Tennessee frontier series
Steele, William Owen
1 *Buffalo knife* (1952)
2 *Winter danger* (1954)
3 *Flaming arrows* (1957)
4 *Perilous road* (1958)

Tenopia series
Packard, Edward
see **Escape from Tenopia series**

Teot series
Gladney, Heather
see **Song of Naga Teot series**

Terence Duke series
Meyerstein, Edward Henry William
1 *Pleasure-lover* (1925)
2 *Terence in love* (1928)
One volume edition entitled *Terence Duke*, 1935

Terence O'Hara series
Costello, Paul
1 *Long silence* (1957)
2 *Red beard* (1958)
3 *Mortgage for murder* (1960)
4 *Blue diamond* (1962)

Terence O'Rourke series
Vance, Louis Joseph
1 *Terence O'Rourke, gentleman adventurer* (1905)
2 *Pool of flame* (1909)

Terence series
Brandon, Gordon
see **Michael and Terry Terence series**

Terhune series
Graeme, Bruce
see **Theodore I Terhune series**

Terminator series
Frakes, Randall
1 *Terminator* (1985)
Co-author: William H Wisher; also novelized as *The terminator*, by Shaun Hutson, 1984
2 *Terminator two* (1991)
Judgment day

Companion volumes: *The making of T2, Terminator two, Judgment day*, by Don Shay and Jody Duncan, 1991, *Terminator two, Judgment day, the book of the film, an illustrated screenplay*, by James Cameron and William H Wisher, 1991

Terminator series
Quinn, John
see **Rod Gavin series**

Tern series
Wallace, Bryan Edgar
see **Bill Tern series**

Terra Magica series
Carter, Lin
1 *Kesrick* (1982)
2 *Dragonrouge* (1984)
3 *Mandricardo* (1987)
4 *Callipygia* (1988)

Terran empire series
This sequence has two authors
Cameron, Berl
1 *Cosmic echelon* (1952)
Le Page, Rand
2 *Time and space* (1952)

Terraplane trilogy
Womack, Jack
1 *Ambient* (1987)
2 *Terraplane* (1988)
3 *Heathern* (1990)

Terrel series
Maddock, Stephen
see **Timothy Terrel series**

Terrell series
Chase, James Hadley
see **Frank Terrell series**
Cook, Canfield
see **Lucky Terrell series**

Terri and Ted series
Palmer, Bernard
see **Ted and Terri series**

Terrilian series
Green, Sharon
1 *Warrior within* (1982)
2 *Warrior enchanted* (1983)
3 *Warrior rearmed* (1984)
4 *Warrior challenged* (1986)
5 *Warrior victorious* (1988)

Terry Bunker series
Ross, Paul
see **Chopper Cop series**

Terry Clane series
Gardner, Erle Stanley
1 *Murder up my sleeve* (1937)
2 *Case of the backward mule* (1946)

Terry Flynn series
This sequence has two authors
Granger, Bill
1 *Public murders* (1980)
Gash, Joe
2 *Priestly murders* (1984)
3 *Newspaper murders* (1985)

Terry Nation's Blake's Seven series
Hoyle, Trevor
see **Blake's Seven series**

Terry Rooke and Tommy Twotoes series
Alexander, David
see **Tommy Twotoes and Terry Rooke series**

Terry series
Danielsson, Bengt
1 *Terry in the South Seas* (1957)
Original edition entitled *Villervalle i Soederhavet*
2 *Terry in Australia* (1958)
Original edition entitled *Villervalles okenaventyr*
3 *Terry's Kon-Tiki adventure* (1963)
Original edition entitled *Kapten Villervalle*

Terry series
Munn, Charles Clark
see **Uncle Terry series**
Sabin, Edward Legrand
see **Great West series**

Terry Sneed series
Newman, Gordon F
see **Inspector Terry Sneed series**

Terry Spring series
Kains, Josephine
1 *Devil mask mystery* (1978)
2 *Curse of the golden skull* (1978)
3 *Green lama mystery* (1979)
4 *Whispering cat mystery* (1979)
5 *Witch's Tower mystery* (1979)
6 *Laughing dragon mystery* (1980)
7 *Lament for a lady* (1982)
8 *Affairs of state* (1983)

Terry Terence series
Brandon, Gordon
see **Michael and Terry Terence series**

Terry Trotter series
Jones, Peter
1 *Wheldon the weed* (1961)
2 *Crump the crock* (1961)
3 *Wheldon the wizard* (1962)
4 *Mathematics or blood?* (1964)

Tertius trilogy
Newman, Robert
1 *Merlin's mistake* (1970)
2 *Testing of Tertius* (1973)
3 *Shattered stone* (1975)

Tess series
Tranter, Nigel Godwin
see **Tinker Tess series**

Tessa Crichton Price series
Morice, Anne
1 *Death in the grand manor* (1970)
2 *Murder in married life* (1971)
3 *Death of a gay dog* (1971)
4 *Murder on French leave* (1972)
5 *Death and the dutiful daughter* (1973)
6 *Death of a heavenly twin* (1974)
7 *Killing with kindness* (1974)
8 *Nursery tea and poison* (1975)
9 *Death of a wedding guest* (1976)
10 *Murder in mimicry* (1977)
11 *Scared to death* (1977)
12 *Murder by proxy* (1978)
13 *Murder in outline* (1979)
14 *Death in the round* (1980)
15 *Men in her death* (1981)
16 *Hollow vengeance* (1982)
17 *Sleep of death* (1982)
18 *Getting away with murder?* (1984)
Murder post-dated
19 *Dead on cue* (1985)
20 *Publish and be killed* (1986)
21 *Treble exposure* (1987)
22 *Design for dying* (1988)
23 *Fatal charm* (1988)
24 *Planning for murder* (1990)

Tessa Crichton series
Morice, Anne
see **Tessa Crichton Price series**

Tessa series
Ritson, Kitty
1 *Tessa and some ponies* (1953)
2 *Tessa in South Africa* (1955)
3 *Tessa to the rescue* (1957)
4 *Tessa and the Rannoch Dude Ranch* (1961)

Tessie and Biddy series
Warner, Priscilla Mary
see **Biddy and Tessie series**

Tessie series
Jackson, Jesse
1 *Tessie* (1968)
2 *Tessie keeps her secret* (1970)

Tessie Venable series
Holley, Helen
1 *Blood on the beach* (1946)
2 *Dead run* (1947)

Test cricket series
Godfrey, William
1 *Malleson at Melbourne* (1956)
2 *Friendly game* (1957)

Testament of man series
Fisher, Vardis
1 *Darkness and the deep* (1943)
2 *Golden rooms* (1944)
3 *Intimations of Eve* (1946)
4 *Adam and the serpent* (1947)
5 *Divine passion* (1948)
6 *Valley of vision* (1951)
A novel of king Solomon and his time
7 *Island of the innocent* (1952)
A novel of Greek and Jew in the time of the Maccabees
8 *Jesus came again* (1956)
A parable
9 *Goat for Azazel* (1956)
A novel of Christian beginnings
10 *Peace like a river* (1957)
Passion within
A novel of Christian asceticism
11 *My holy Satan* (1958)
A novel of Christian twilight
12 *Orphans in Gethsemane* (1960)
12.1 *For passion, for heaven* (1960)
12.2 *Great confession* (1960)

Testament series
Brittain, Vera
Autobiography
1 *Testament of youth* (1933)
1900-1925
2 *Testament of friendship* (1940)
The author's friendship with Winifred Holtby
3 *Testament of experience* (1957)
1925-1950

Tetsuo Otani series
Melville, James
see **Superintendent Tetsuo Otani series**

Teverton Hall series
This sequence has two authors
Austen, Jane
1 *Pride and prejudice* (1813)
Gillespie, Jane
2 *Teverton Hall* (1983)

Tevye the milkman series
Aleichem, Sholom
1 *Old country* (1946)
2 *Tevye's daughters* (1949)
Translated from the Yiddish; dramatized by Joseph Stein as *Fiddler on the roof*, 1966

Tewkesbury series
Cecil, Henry
see **Mister Tewkesbury series**

Tex series
Garland, Sarah
1 *Tex the cowboy* (1983)
2 *Tex and Gloria* (1983)
3 *Tex and bad Hank* (1983)

Texan series
Arthur, Burt
see **Johnny Canavan series**

Texans series
Fletcher, Farris
1 *Rawhide country* (1982)
2 *Remember the Alamo* (1982)
3 *Yellow rose* (1982)
4 *Lone Star legacy* (1982)

Texar's vengeance series
Verne, Jules
see **North against South series**

Texas Anthem series
Reno, James
1 *Texas Anthem* (1986)
2 *Texas born* (1986)
3 *Shadow walker* (1987)
4 *Rogue river* (1988)
5 *Creed's law* (1988)

Texas Brazos series
Wisler, Gary Clifton
1 *Texas Brazos* (1987)
2 *Fortune Bend* (1987)
3 *Palo pinto* (1987)
4 *Caddo Creek* (1988)
5 *Baron of the Brazos* (1991)

Texas Joe and Roaming Reynolds series
Martin, Charles Morris
see **Roaming Reynolds and Texas Joe series**

Texas Lawman series
Randall, Clay
see **Amos Flagg series**

Texas legends series
Shelton, Gene
1 *Last gun* (1991)
The legend of John Selman
2 *Captain Jack* (1991)
The story of John Coffee Hayes
3 *Rawhider* (1992)
The story of Print Olive
4 *Tascosa gun* (1993)
The story of Jim East
5 *Brazos dreamer* (1993)
The story of Major Robert S Neighbors

Texas promises trilogy
Lindquiest, Marie
1 *Dream at dawn* (1987)
2 *Untamed heart* (1987)
3 *Hidden longings* (1987)

Texas Ranger series
Cole, Jackson
see **Jim Hatfield series**

Texas Rangers series
Arthur, Burt
1 *Stirrups in the dust* (1950)
2 *Trouble town* (1950)
3 *Three guns north* (1961)
Co-author: Budd Arthur

Texas series
Hoff, Carol
see **Johnny Texas series**

Texas series
Michaels, Fern
1 *Texas rich* (1985)
2 *Texas heat* (1986)
3 *Texas fury* (1989)
Numbers 1-3 also published in one volume entitled *Texas trilogy*, 1989
4 *Texas sunrise* (1993)

Texas trilogy
Altsheler, Joseph Alexander
1 *Texan star* (1912)
2 *Texan scouts* (1913)
3 *Texan triumph* (1913)

Texas trilogy
Brown, Sandra
1 *Texas lucky!* (1990)
2 *Texas sage!* (1991)
3 *Texas chase!* (1991)
One volume edition entitled *Texas trilogy*, 1992

Texas trilogy
Shefelman, Janice Jordan
1 *Paradise called Texas* (1983)
2 *Willow Creek home* (1985)
3 *Spirit of iron* (1987)

Texians series
Wyatt, Zach
1 *Texians* (1984)
2 *Horse marines* (1984)
3 *War devils* (1984)
4 *Blood moon* (1985)
5 *Death's shadow* (1985)

Texts that made history series
Boreham, Frank William
Essays on Christian life
1 *Bunch of everlastings* (1920)
2 *Handful of stars* (1922)
3 *Casket of cameos* (1924)
4 *Faggot of torches* (1926)
5 *Temple of topaz* (1928)

Thackeray and Cribb series
Lovesey, Peter
see **Sergeant Cribb and Constable Thackeray series**

Thackeray Phin series
Sladek, John Thomas
1 *Black aura* (1974)
2 *Invisible green* (1977)

Thady Corey series
Borg, Jack
1 *Badman's shadow* (1972)
2 *Badman headed north* (1974)

Thaine and Falconer trilogy
De Blasis, Celeste
see **Wild Swan trilogy**

Thake trilogy
Morton, John Bingham
see **Mister Thake trilogy**

Thalia series
McMurtry, Larry
1 *Last picture show* (1966)
2 *Texasville* (1987)
Companion volumes: *Horseman, pass by*, 1961, *Leaving Cheyenne*, 1963

Thames River Police series
Wood, Andrew
see **Bunch and Alexander series**

Thane and Moss series
Knox, Bill
see **Inspector Colin Thane and Phil Moss series**

Thanet series
Simpson, Dorothy
see **Inspector Luke Thanet series**

Thank you series
Spain, Nancy
Autobiography
1 *Thank you, Nelson* (1945)
2 *Why I'm not a millionaire* (1956)
3 *Funny thing happened on the way* (1964)

Tharn series
Browne, Howard
1 *Warrior of the dawn* (1943)
2 *Return of Tharn* (1956)

Tharrus trilogy
Maclean, Catherine Macdonald
1 *Seven for Cordelia* (1941)
2 *Three for Cordelia* (1943)
Tharrus three
3 *Farewell to Tharrus* (1944)

That boy Trog series
Butterworth, Ben
1 *Trog and his axe* (1973)
2 *Trog and the fire* (1973)
Numbers 1 and 2 also published in one volume entitled *Trog*
3 *Trog makes a trap* (1973)
4 *Grandpa has a swim* (1973)
Numbers 3 and 4 also published in one volume entitled *Trog in trouble*
5 *Trog and the horse* (1973)
6 *Trog and his boat* (1973)
Numbers 5 and 6 also published in one volume entitled *Trog tries again*
7 *Grandpa plays hide and seek* (1973)
8 *Trog and the dog* (1973)
Numbers 7 and 8 also published in one volume entitled *Trog's grandpa*
9 *Grandpa's horse race* (1973)
10 *Grandpa and the mammoth* (1973)
11 *Grandpa and the birdman* (1973)
12 *Grandpa goes hunting* (1973)

That reminds me trilogy
Graham, Winifred
Reminiscences
1 *That reminds me* (1945)
2 *Observations, casual and intimate* (1947)
3 *I introduce* (1948)

Thatcher Colt series
Abbot, Anthony
1 *About the murder of Geraldine Foster* (1930)
Murder of Geraldine Foster
2 *About the murder of the clergyman's mistress* (1931)
Murder of the clergyman's mistress
Crime of the century
3 *About the murder of the night club lady* (1931)
Murder of the night club lady
Night club lady
4 *About the murder of the circus queen* (1932)
Murder of the circus queen
5 *About the murder of a startled lady* (1935)
Murder of a startled lady
6 *About the murder of a man afraid of women* (1937)
Murder of a man afraid of women
7 *Creeps* (1939)
Murder at Buzzard's Bay
8 *Shudders* (1943)
Deadly secret

Thatcher family series
Yates, Peter
1 *Curtain call for murder* (1945)
2 *Death comes to dinner* (1945)

Thatcher series
Lathen, Emma
see **John Putnam Thatcher series**

Thea Crawford series
Mann, Jessica
1 *Only security* (1973)
Troublecross
2 *Captive audience* (1975)

Theatre series
Gibbs, Henry
1 *Theatre tapestry* (1949)
2 *Ten-thirty sharp* (1949)

Thebes series
Makepeace, Joanna
1 *Divine son of Ra* (1969)
2 *Daughter of Isis* (1969)
3 *Chosen of the Gods* (1970)

Their lives and hearts series
Hunt, Violet
1 *Their lives* (1916)
2 *Their hearts* (1921)

Thelma Mueller series
Lovelace, Maud Hart
see **Betsy Ray series**

Theo Bloomer series
Hadley, Joan
1 *Night-blooming circus* (1986)
2 *Deadly ackee* (1988)

Theobald series
Black, Lionel
see **Kate Theobald series**

Theocritus Lucius Westborough series
Clason, Clyde B
1 *Fifth tumbler* (1936)
2 *Death angel* (1936)
3 *Blind drifts* (1937)
4 *Purple parrot* (1937)
5 *Man from Tibet* (1938)
6 *Whispering ear* (1938)
7 *Murder gone Minoan* (1939)
Clue to the labyrinth
8 *Dragon's cave* (1939)
9 *Poison jasmine* (1940)
10 *Green shiver* (1941)

Theodore Bryan series
Thurston, Ida Treadwell
1 *Bishop's shadow* (1899)
2 *Big brothers of Sabin Street* (1909)

Theodore I Terhune series
Graeme, Bruce
1 *Seven clues in search of a crime* (1941)
2 *House with crooked walls* (1942)
3 *Case for Solomon* (1943)
4 *Work for the hangman* (1944)
5 *Ten trails to Tyburn* (1944)
6 *Case of books* (1946)
7 *And a bottle of rum* (1949)
8 *Dead pigs at Hungry Farm* (1951)

Theodore J Cash series
Cleary, Denis
1 *Shameful* (1971)
2 *Rattler* (1972)

Therapist series
Kottler, Jeffrey
Reminiscences of a psychotherapist
1 *On being a therapist* (1987)
2 *Imperfect therapist* (1989)
Co-author: Diane Blau; learning from failure in therapeutic practice
3 *Compleat therapist* (1991)

There will be war series
Pournelle, Jerry
1 *There will be war* (1983)
2 *Men of war* ()
3 *Blood and iron* (1984)
4 *Day of the tyrant* (1985)
5 *Warrior* (1986)
6 *Guns of darkness* (1987)
7 *Call to battle* (1988)
8 *Armageddon!* (1989)
9 *After Armageddon* (1990)

Theresa Fortunato series
Green, Kate
1 *Shooting star* (1992)
2 *Black dreams* (1993)

Theresa Terence series
Brandon, Gordon
see **Michael and Terry Terence series**

These lawless worlds series
Comstock, Jarrod
1 *Love machine* (1984)
2 *Scales of justice* (1984)
3 *Kingdom come* (1984)
4 *Hammer home* (1985)

These were the days series
Day, Clarence
see **Life series**

Theseus series
Renault, Mary
1 *King must die* (1958)
2 *Bull from the sea* (1962)

Thew series
Browne, Douglas Gordon
see **Inspector Thew series**

They call me the Mercenary series
Kilgore, Axel
1 *Killer genesis* (1980)
2 *Slaughter run* (1981)
3 *Fourth Reich Death Squad* (1981)
4 *Opium hunter* (1981)
5 *Canadian killing ground* (1981)
6 *Vengeance army* (1981)
7 *Slave of the warmonger* (1982)
8 *Assassin's express* (1982)
9 *Terror contract* (1982)
10 *Bush warfare* (1982)
11 *Death lust* (1982)
12 *Eye for eye* (1983)
13 *Naked blade, naked gun* (1983)
14 *Siberian alternative* (1983)
15 *Afghanistan penetration* (1983)
16 *China bloodhunt* (1983)
17 *Buckingham blowout* (1984)
18 *Hard men* (1984)

They came from series
Judson, Clara Ingram
1 *They came from Sweden* (1942)
Sod-house winter
2 *They came from France* (1943)
Pierre's lucky pouch
3 *They came from Scotland* (1944)
Bruce carries the flag
4 *Petar's treasure* (1945)
Alternative title: They came from Dalmatia
5 *Michael's victory* (1946)
Alternative title: They came from Ireland
6 *Lost violin* (1947)
Alternative title: They came from Bohemia
7 *Green ginger jar* (1949)
A Chinatown mystery

They came to a river series
Mackay, Allis
1 *They came to a river* (1941)
2 *Goodbye summer* (1953)

They series
Barclay, Vera Charlesworth
1 *They went to the sea* (1946)
2 *They met a wizard* (1947)
3 *They found an elephant* (1950)

Theyn chronicles trilogy
Hunt, Angela Elwell
1 *Afton of Margate Castle* (1993)
2 *Troubadour's quest* (1994)
3 *Ingram of the Irish* (1995)

Thibault family series
Martin du Gard, Roger
1 *Thibaults* (1939)
Originally published in six volumes entitled *Le cahier gris*, 1922, *Le penitencier*, 1922, *La belle saison*, 1923, *La consultation*, 1928, *La sorellina*, 1928, *La mort du pere*, 1929
2 *Summer 1914* (1941)
Originally published in two volumes entitled *L'ete* 1914, 1936, *Epilogue*, 1940

Thibault Parew and Chips Carpenter series
Eldredge, Gilbert
1 *Death for the surgeon* (1939)
2 *Murder in the stratosphere* (1940)

Thieves' world series
Asprin, Robert Lynn
see **Sanctuary series**

Thieves' world: tempus series
Morris, Janet Ellen
see **Tempus series**

Thimblefinger series
Harris, Joel Chandler
see **Mister Thimblefinger series**

Thin King series
Farmer, Derek
Based on a BBC radio programme
1 *First big radio Thin King book* (1983)
2 *Second big radio Thin King book* (1983)
3 *Third big radio Thin King book* (1983)
4 *Fourth big radio Thin King book* (1983)

Thinker series
Aldanov, Mark Aleksandrovich
Translated from the Russian
1 *Ninth thermidor* (1921)
2 *Devil's bridge* (1925)
3 *Conspiracy* (1926)
4 *Saint Helena, little island* (1921)

Thinking about series
Pluckrose, Henry
Photographic illustrations by Chris Fairclough
1 *Touching* (1985)
2 *Tasting* (1985)
3 *Smelling* (1985)
4 *Seeing* (1985)
5 *Hearing* (1985)
6 *Big and little* (1986)
7 *Shape* (1986)
8 *Floating and sinking* (1986)
9 *Hot and cold* (1986)

Thinking Machine series
Futrelle, Jacques
see **Professor Augustus S F X Van Dusen series**

Third Bilsley Pack series
Travis, Falcon
1 *Grand howl* (1965)
2 *Tawny talent* (1966)
3 *Tawny trail* (1967)

Third Crusade series
Shelby, Graham
1 *Knights of dark renown* (1969)
2 *Kings of vain intent* (1970)

Third eye series
Lobsang Rampa, Tuesday
Autobiography
1 *Third eye* (1956)
2 *Doctor from Llasa* (1959)
3 *Rampa story* (1960)

Third grade ghost series
Stine, Harlan William
see **Jeffrey and the third grade ghost series**

Third grade series
Ransom, Candice Farris
see **Tales of the third grade series**

Third World War series
Hackett, John
see **World War Three series**

Third World War trilogy
Wingate, John
1 *Frigate* (1980)
2 *Carrier* (1981)
3 *Submarine* (1982)

Thiriet series
Berna, Paul
see **Bobby Thiriet series**

Thirst series
Smith, Guy Newman
1 *Thirst* (1980)
2 *Plague* (1987)

Thirteen colonies series
Chase, Carolyn
1 *Renegade hearts* (1990)
South Carolina
2 *Scoundrel's caress* (1990)
3 *Smuggler's embrace* (1990)
Massachusetts
4 *Frontier rogue* (1990)
New York
5 *Rebel's kiss* (1990)
6 *Seafaring stranger* (1991)
Virginia

Thirteen moons series
George, Jean Craighead
1 *Moon of the bears* (1967)
2 *Moon of the owls* (1967)
3 *Moon of the salamanders* (1967)
4 *Moon of the Chackarees* (1968)
5 *Moon of the fox pups* (1968)
6 *Moon of the monarch butterflies* (1968)
7 *Moon of the wild pigs* (1968)
8 *Moon of the mountain lions* (1968)
9 *Moon of the deer* (1969)
10 *Moon of the alligators* (1969)
11 *Moon of the gray wolves* (1969)
12 *Moon of the moles* (1969)
13 *Moon of the winter bird* (1969)

Thirty nine kids on the block series
Marzollo, Jean
1 *Green ghost of Appleville* (1989)
2 *Best present ever* (1989)
3 *Roses are pink and yellow* (1990)
4 *Best Friends Club* (1990)
5 *Chicken pox strikes again* (1990)
6 *My sister, the blabbermouth* (1990)

Thirty Years War series
Henty, George Alfred
1 *Lion of the North* (1885)
2 *Won by the sword* (1899)

This land, this time series
Cosic, Dobrica
Translated from the Serbo-Croat
1 *Into the battle* (1972)
2 *Time of death* (1972)
3 *Reach to eternity* (1977)
4 *South to destiny* (1979)
4.1 *Time of death* (1978)
4.2 *Reach to eternity* (1980)
4.3 *South to destiny* (1981)

This school series
Hentoff, Nat
1 *This school is driving me crazy* (1976)
2 *Does this school have capital punishment* (1981)

Thlassa Mey series
McCarty, Dennis
1 *Flight to Thlassa Mey* (1986)
2 *Warriors of Thlassa Mey* (1987)
3 *Lords of Thlassa Mey* (1989)
4 *Across the Thlassa Mey* (1991)

Thomas and Grandfather series
Stolz, Mary
1 *Storm in the night* (1988)
2 *Go fish* (1991)
3 *Stealing home* (1992)
4 *Coco Grimes* (1994)

Thomas and Webber series
Oliver, Anthony
see **Lizzie Thomas and Inspector John Webber series**

Thomas Becket series
This sequence has two authors; plays
Eliot, Thomas Stearns
1 *Murder in the cathedral* (1935)
Pearce, Brian Louis
2 *Shrine rites* (1990)

Thomas Black series
Emerson, Earl W
1 *Rainy city* (1985)
2 *Poverty Bay* (1985)
3 *Nervous laughter* (1986)
4 *Fat Tuesday* (1987)
5 *Deviant behavior* (1988)
6 *Yellow dog party* (1991)
7 *Portland laughter* (1994)

Thomas Brunt series
Hilton, John Buxton
see **Inspector Thomas Brunt series**

Thomas Conroy series
Asbury, Herbert
see **Inspector Thomas Conroy series**

Thomas Covenant Chronicles: first series
Donaldson, Stephen Reeder
see **First chronicles of Thomas Covenant series**

Thomas Covenant Chronicles: second series
Donaldson, Stephen Reeder
see **Second chronicles of Thomas Covenant series**

Thomas Early series
Early, Richard Elliott
1 *Apprentice* (1977)
2 *Master weaver* (1980)
Companion volume: Weavers and war, 1984

Thomas Hardy series
Gittings, Robert
1 *Young Thomas Hardy* (1975)
2 *Older Hardy* (1978)
Thomas Hardy's later years

Thomas Littlejohn series
Bellairs, George
see **Detective Inspector Thomas Littlejohn series**

Thomas Lynley and Barbara Havers series
George, Elizabeth
see **Inspector Thomas Lynley and Sergeant Barbara Havers series**

Thomas Pitt series
Perry, Anne
see **Charlotte Ellison Pitt and Inspector Thomas Pitt series**

Thomas Rodolfo Rackstraw series
Hardwick, Michael
1 *Regency royal* (1978)
2 *Regency rake* (1979)
3 *Regency revenge* (1980)
4 *Regency revels* (1982)

Thomas series
Creswell, Harry Bulkeley
1 *Thomas* (1917)
2 *Thomas settles down* (1918)

Thomas series
Fitzsimmons, Cortland
see **Ethel Thomas series**
Lewis, Catherine
see **Lisa Thomas series**
Martin, Nancy
see **Jean Thomas series**

Thomas series
Wolde, Gunilla
English text by Alison Winn
1 *Thomas builds a house* (1969)
Tommy builds a house
2 *Thomas has a bath* (1969)
Tommy has a bath
3 *Thomas cleans his room* (1969)
Tommy tidies his room
4 *Thomas goes out* (1969)
Tommy goes out
5 *Thomas and Sarah dress up* (1972)
Tommy and Sarah dress up
6 *Thomas goes to the doctor* (1972)
Tommy goes to the doctor
7 *Thomas is little* (1973)
8 *Thomas bakes a cake* (1973)
9 *Thomas and his cat* (1973)
10 *Thomas is different* (1973)

Thomas Tilling series
Watkins, Ron
1 *Paper chase* (1972)
2 *Death draws the curtain* (1973)

Thomas trilogy
Hall, Patrick
see **Harry Thomas trilogy**

Thomas Wingfold trilogy
Macdonald, George
1 *Thomas Wingfold, curate* (1876)
Curate's awakening
The second title is a revised edition
2 *Paul Faber, surgeon* (1879)
Lady's confession
The second title is a revised edition
3 *There and back* (1891)
Baron's apprenticeship
The second title is a revised edition

Thomasheen James series
Walsh, Maurice
Short stories
1 *Thomasheen James* (1941)
2 *Smart fellow* (1964)
Thomasheen James gets his hair cut

Thomassy series
Stein, Sol
see **George Thomassy series**

Thompson and Larrimore series
Paull, Jessica
see **Tracy Larrimore and Mike Thompson series**

Thompson series
Cameron, Evelyn
see **Sheriff Jack Thompson series**
Daninos, Pierre
see **Major Thompson series**
Dean, Robert George
see **Pat Thompson series**
Drax, Peter
see **Chief Inspector Thompson series**
Holliday, Joe
see **Dale of the mounted series**

Thompson Travel Agency series
Verne, Jules
1 *Package holiday* (1907)
2 *End of the journey* (1907)
Original one volume edition entitled *L'agence Thompson et Cie*

Thompson trilogy
Gallacher, Tom
see **Bill Thompson trilogy**

Thomson's Yard series
Maisner, Heather
see **Tractors of Thomson's Yard series**

Thongor of Lemuria series
Carter, Lin
1 *Wizard of Lemuria* (1965)
Thongor and the wizard of Lemuria
2 *Thongor of Lemuria* (1966)
Thongor and the Dragon City
3 *Thongor against the gods* (1967)
4 *Thongor in the City of Magicians* (1968)
5 *Thongor at the end of time* (1968)
6 *Thongor fights the pirates of Tarakus* (1970)
Thongor and the pirates of Tarakus

Thordason series
Boucher, Alan Estcourt
see **Halli Thordason series**

Thorensen Dykes series
McBratney, Sam
1 *Final correction* (1978)
2 *From the Thorensen Dykes* (1980)

Thorgrim series
Bailey, Gerald Earl
see **Saga of Thorgrin series**

Thorley family series
Lofts, Norah
see **Gad's Hall series**

Thorn series
Coburn, L J
see **Caleb Thorn series**

Thorn series
Hall, James W
1 *Under cover of daylight* (1988)
2 *Tropical freeze* (1989)
3 *Mean high tide* (1994)

Thorndyke series
Freeman, Richard Austin
see **Doctor John Evelyn Thorndyke series**

Thorne and Abbot series
Penn, John
see **Inspector George Thorne and Sergeant Bill Abbot series**

Thorne series
Pugh, Dianne G
see **Iris Thorne series**
Snow, Charles Horace
see **Tommy Thorne series**
Vardeman, Robert Edward
see **Peter Thorne series**

Thornley Colton series
Stagg, Clinton Holland
1 *Silver sandals* (1915)
Thornley Colton, blind reader of hearts
2 *Thornley Colton, blind detective* (1923)

Thornton series
Anthony, Lotta Rowe
see **Anne Thornton series**
Ashton, Elizabeth
see **Renee and Leon Thornton series**
Lodwick, John
see **Desmond Thornton series**

Thornton Zane series
Massey, Morrell
1 *Left hand left* (1932)
2 *Through the lens* (1933)

Thornyold series
Almedingen, Edith Martha
see **Andrew Thornyold series**

Thorpe series
Martin, Nancy
see **Anne Clarke series**

Thorson series
Norton, Andre
see **Dane Thorson series**

Those of the lost continent series
Tucci, Niccolo
1 *Before my time* (1962)
2 *Unfinished funeral* (1964)
3 *Sun and the moon* (1977)

Those were the days series
Milne, Alan Alexander
see **Day's play series**

Thoughts of Nanushka series
Witcomb, Nan
Poems
1 *Yesterday, today and tomorrow* (1990)
2 *Loving and living* (1990)
3 *This moment is forever* (1990)
4 *Between love and loneliness* (1990)
5 *Pocketful of dreams* (1990)
6 *Wonder of tomorrow* (1990)
Numbers 1-6 also published in one volume entitled *Thoughts of Nanushka 1-6*, 1979
7 *Love, tears and dreams* (1991)
8 *Rainbows are for everyone* (1991)
9 *After the loving* (1991)
10 *Once upon a memory* (1992)
11 *Gifts of love* (1992)
12 *Tears and tenderness* (1992)
Numbers 7-12 also published in one volume entitled *Thoughts of Nanushka 7-12*, 1986; Numbers 13 and 14 published in one volume entitled *Thoughts of Nanushka 13-14*, 1990
15 *Beyond the loving* (1992)
16 *Ride on a rainbow* (1992)
Companion volume: *Nanushka's love poems, to someone I love*, 1992

Thranx series
Foster, Alan Dean
1 *Nor crystal tears* (1982)
2 *Midworld* (1975)
3 *Icerigger* (1974)
4 *Mission to Moulokin* (1979)
5 *Deluge drivers* (1987)
6 *Voyage to the city of the dead* (1984)
7 *Sentenced to Prism* (1985)

Thread of scarlet series
Williams, Ben Ames
1 *Thread of scarlet* (1939)
2 *Come spring* (1940)
3 *Strange woman* (1941)
4 *Time of peace* (1942)

Three bears series
Baker, Margaret Joyce
1 *Shoe shop bears* (1963)
2 *Hannibal and the bears* (1965)
3 *Bears back in business* (1967)
4 *Hi-Jinks joins the bears* (1968)
5 *Teabag and the bears* (1970)
6 *Boots and the ginger bears* (1972)

Three boys series
Young, Egerton Ryerson
1 *Three boys in the wild north land* (1896)
2 *Winter adventures of thre boys in Great Lone Land* (1899)

Three brothers series
Black, Margaret Katherine
1 *Two young explorers* (1945)
2 *Three brothers and a lady* (1947)

Three cities of bells series
Goudge, Elizabeth
see **Cathedrals series**

Three cities trilogy
Zola, Emile
see **Abbe Pierre Fremont trilogy**

Three college girls series
Champney, Elizabeth Williams
see **Three Vassar girls series**

Three corvettes series
Monsarrat, Nicholas
see **Corvette series**

Three damosels trilogy
Chapman, Vera
1 *Green Knight* (1975)
2 *King's damosel* (1976)
3 *King Arthur's daughter* (1976)
One volume edition entitled *The three damosels*, 1978

Three detectives series
Brett, Simon
1 *Three detectives and the missing superstar* (1986)
2 *Three detectives and the knight in armour* (1987)

Three Ds series
Gray, P D
1 *Deceit, deception, death and the carousel horse* (1993)
2 *Deceit, deception, death and the jackal-headed god* (1994)

Three faces series
Autobiography
Bard, Mary
1 *Doctor wears three faces* (1949)
2 *Forty odd* (1952)
3 *Just be yourself* (1956)
Experiences as a Brownie leader

Three Gays series
Brown, Ethel C
1 *Three Gays* (1915)
2 *Three Gays at Merryton* (1916)
3 *Three Gays in Maine* (1917)
4 *Three Gays at the old farm* (1918)

Three generations trilogy
Beresford, John Davys
see **Hillingtons trilogy**

Three Graces series
Jackson, Gabrielle Emilie
1 *Three Graces* (1903)
2 *Three Graces at college* (1904)

Three Hundred and Eighteen series
Hughes, Rupert
see **Miss Three Hundred and Eighteen series**

Three immortals trilogy
Viereck, George Sylvester
see **Wandering Jew trilogy**

Three Investigators Crimebusters series
This sequence has two authors
Arden, William
1 *Hot wheels* (1989)
Brandel, Marc
2 *Ear for danger* (1989)

Three Investigators series
This sequence has five authors
Arthur, Robert
1 *Secret of Terror Castle* (1964)
2 *Mystery of the stuttering parrot* (1964)
3 *Mystery of the whispering mummy* (1965)
4 *Mystery of the green ghost* (1965)
5 *Mystery of the vanishing treasure* (1966)
6 *Secret of Skeleton Island* (1966)
7 *Mystery of the fiery eye* (1967)
8 *Mystery of the silver spider* (1967)
9 *Mystery of the screaming clock* (1968)
Arden, William
10 *Mystery of the moaning cave* (1968)
Arthur, Robert
11 *Mystery of the talking skull* (1969)
Arden, William
12 *Mystery of the laughing shadow* (1969)
13 *Secret of the crooked cat* (1970)
West, Nick
14 *Mystery of the coughing dragon* (1970)
Carey, Mary Virginia
15 *Mystery of the flaming footprints* (1971)
West, Nick
16 *Mystery of the nervous lion* (1972)
Carey, Mary Virginia
17 *Mystery of the singing serpent* (1972)
Arden, William
18 *Mystery of the shrinking house* (1972)
19 *Secret of Phantom Lake* (1973)
Carey, Mary Virginia
20 *Mystery of monster mountain* (1973)
21 *Secret of the haunted mirror* (1974)
Arden, William
22 *Mystery of the dead man's riddle* (1974)
Carey, Mary Virginia
23 *Mystery of the invisible dog* (1975)
24 *Mystery of Death Trap Mine* (1976)
Arden, William
25 *Mystery of the dancing devil* (1976)
26 *Mystery of the headless horse* (1977)
Carey, Mary Virginia
27 *Mystery of the magic circle* (1978)
Arden, William
28 *Mystery of the deadly double* (1978)
Carey, Mary Virginia
29 *Mystery of the sinister scarecrow* (1979)
Arden, William
30 *Secret of Shark Reef* (1979)
Carey, Mary Virginia
31 *Mystery of the scar-faced beggar* (1981)
32 *Mystery of the blazing cliffs* (1981)
Arden, William
33 *Mystery of the purple pirate* (1982)
Carey, Mary Virginia
34 *Mystery of the wandering caveman* (1982)
Brandel, Marc
35 *Mystery of the kidnapped whale* (1983)
Carey, Mary Virginia
36 *Mystery of the missing mermaid* (1983)
Brandel, Marc
37 *Mystery of the two-toed pigeon* (1984)
Arden, William
38 *Mystery of the smashing glass* (1984)
Carey, Mary Virginia
39 *Mystery of the trail of terror* (1984)
Brandel, Marc
40 *Mystery of the rogue's reunion* (1985)
Carey, Mary Virginia
41 *Mystery of the creep-show crooks* (1985)
42 *Mystery of the cranky collector* (1986)
Arden, William
43 *Mystery of the Wrecker's Rock* (1986)
Carey, Mary Virginia
44 *Case of the savage statue* (1987)

Three Jays series
Smythe, Pat
1 *Jacqueline rides for a fall* (1957)
2 *Three Jays against the clock* (1958)
3 *Three Jays on holiday* (1958)
4 *Three Jays go to town* (1959)
5 *Three Jays over the border* (1960)
6 *Three Jays go to Rome* (1960)
7 *Three Jays lend a hand* (1961)

Three little folk series
Latham, Katharine Wright
see **Christabel series**

Three little rabbits series
McCarthy, Ruth
Illustrated by Marie H Henry
1 *Day with three little rabbits* (1985)
2 *Three little rabbits go visiting* (1985)

Three little women series
Jackson, Gabrielle Emilie
1 *Three little women* (1908)
2 *Three little women at work* (1909)
3 *Three little women's success* (1910)
4 *Three little women as wives* (1914)

Three Margarets series
Richards, Laura Elizabeth
1 *Three Margarets* (1897)
2 *Margaret Montfort* (1898)
3 *Peggy* (1899)
4 *Rita* (1900)
5 *Fernley House* (1901)
6 *Merryweathers* (1904)

Three marriages series
Hoff, Harry Summerfield
1 *Trina* (1934)
It happened in PRK
2 *Rhea* (1935)
3 *Lisa* (1937)
4 *Three marriages* (1946)

Three men series
Jerome, Jerome Klapka
1 *Three men in a boat, to say nothing of the dog* (1889)
2 *Three men on the bummel* (1900)
Three men on bicycles

Three Mesquiteers series
Macdonald, William Colt
This sequence was inspired by *Riders of the night*, by Eugene Cunningham, 1932
1 *Law of the Forty-Fives* (1933)
Sunrise guns
2 *Riders of the Whistling Skull* (1934)
3 *Powdersmoke Range* (1934)
4 *Singing Scorpion* (1934)
Ambush at Scorpion Valley
5 *Roarin' lead* (1935)
6 *Ghost town gold* (1935)
Town that God forgot
7 *Bullets for buckaroos* (1936)
Bullet trail
8 *Rebel ranger* (1943)
9 *Vanishing gunslinger* (1943)
10 *Three Mesquiteers* (1944)
11 *Thunderbird trail* (1946)
12 *Bad man's return* (1947)
13 *Powdersmoke justice* (1949)
14 *Mesquiteer mavericks* (1950)
15 *Galloping ghost* (1952)

Three miles square series
Corey, Peter
1 *Three miles square* (1939)
2 *Road returns* (1940)
3 *County seat* (1941)

Three Musketeers series
This sequence has two authors
Dumas, Alexandre
1 *Three Musketeers* (1844)
Three guardsmen
Original edition entitled *Les trois mousquetaires*; set between 1626 and 1648
2 *Twenty years after* (1845)
Original edition entitled *Vingt ans apres*; set during the regency of Anne of Austria, 1648-49
3 *Vicomte de Bragelonne* (1851)
Alternative English title: Ten years later; original edition entitled *Le Vicomte de Bragelonne*; set during the reign of Louis XIV
3.1 *Vicomte de Bragelonne* (1848)
3.2 *Louise de la Valliere* (1848)
3.3 *Man in the Iron Mask* (1849)
Iron Mask
3.4 *Son of Porthos* (1850)
Lestienne, Voldemar
4 *Furioso* (1971)
Original edition entitled *Furioso*

Three of a kind series
Kaye, Marilyn
1 *With friends like these* (1990)
2 *Home's a nice place to visit, but I wouldn't want to live there* (1990)
3 *Will the real Becka Morgan stand up?* (1991)
4 *Two's company* (1991)
5 *Cat Morgan, working girl* (1991)
6 *One hundred and one ways to win a homecoming queen* (1991)

Three R detectives series
Digby, Anne
1 *Three R detectives and the milk bottles mystery* (1991)
2 *Three R detectives and the mystery of the missing footprints* (1992)

Three rivers series
Curwood, James Oliver
1 *River's end* (1919)
2 *Valley of silent men* (1920)
3 *Flaming forest* (1921)s

Three series
Brambleby, Ailsa
1 *Three for trouble* (1963)
2 *Three for pack holiday* (1964)

Three trilogy
Hellman, Lillian
see **Unfinished woman trilogy**

Three Vassar girls series
Champney, Elizabeth Williams
1 *Three Vassar girls on the Rhine* (1878)
A holiday trip of three college girls through Germany by way of this celebrated river
2 *Three Vassar girls abroad* (1882)
Rambles of three college girle on a vacation trip through France and Spain for amusement and instruction, with their haps and mishaps
3 *Three Vassar girls in England* (1884)
A holiday trip of three college girls through the mother country
4 *Three Vassar girls in South America* (1884)
A holiday trip of three college girls through the southern continent, up the Aamazon, down the Madeira, across the Andes and up the Pacific coast to Panama
5 *Three Vassar girls in Italy* (1885)
A holiday trip of three college girls through the classic lands
6 *Three Vassar girls at home* (1887)
A holiday trip of three college girls through the South and West
7 *Three Vassar girls in France* (1888)
A story of the siege of Paris
8 *Three Vassar girls in Russia and Turkey* (1889)
9 *Three Vassar girls in Switzerland* (1890)
10 *Three Vassar girls in the Tyrol* (1891)
11 *Three Vassar girls in the Holy Land* (1892)

Three wives series
Seymour, Beatrice Kean
1 *Three wives* (1927)
2 *Youth rides out* (1928)

Three women trilogy
Schnitzler, Arthur
1 *Bertha Garlan* (1901)
Original edition entitled *Frau Bertha Garlan*
2 *Beatrice* (1913)
Original edition entitled *Frau Beate und ihr Sohn*
3 *Fraulein Elsa* (1924)
Original edition entitled *Fraulein Else*

Three worlds series
Daiches, David
Autobiography
1 *Two worlds* (1957)
An Edinburgh Jewish childhood
2 *Third world* (1971)

Threshold series
Morris, Janet Ellen
1 *Threshold* (1991)
2 *Trust territory* (1992)

Thrift series
Blyth, James
1 *Thrift* (1912)
2 *Respectability* (1913)

Thriller series
Hart, Ted
Based on a television series
1 *Thriller* (1974)
2 *More stories from Thriller* (1975)

Throne trilogy
Oakgrove, Artemis
1 *Raging peace* (1984)
2 *Dreams of vengeance* (1985)
3 *Throne of council* (1986)

Through on time series
Ellis, Edward Sylvester
1 *Jack Midwood* (1895)
Alternative title: Bread cast upon the waters
2 *Young conductor* (1895)
Alternative title: Winning his way
3 *Four boys* (1896)
Alternative title: The glory of a forest fire

Thrums series
Barrie, James Matthew
1 *Auld Licht idylls* (1888)
2 *Window in Thrums* (1889)
3 *Little minister* (1891)
4 *Auld Licht manse, and other sketches* (1893)
5 *Sentimental Tommy* (1896)
The story of his boyhood
6 *Tommy and Grizel* (1898)

Thrush Green series
Read, *Miss*
1 *Thrush Green* (1959)
2 *Winter in Thrush Green* (1961)
3 *News from Thrush Green* (1970)
Numbers 1-3 also published in one volume as *Life at Thrush Green*, 1984
4 *Battles at Thrush Green* (1975)
5 *Return to Thrush Green* (1978)
6 *Gossip from Thrush Green* (1981)
Numbers 4-6 also published in one volume entitled *More stories from Thrush Green*, 1985
7 *Affairs at Thrush Green* (1983)
8 *At home in Thrush Green* (1985)
9 *School at Thrush Green* (1987)
10 *World of Thrush Green* (1988)

Thunder Moon series
Brand, Max
1 *Thunder Moon's challenge* (1983)
2 *Thunder Moon's strike* (1984)

Thunder Reef series
Seligman, Adrian
1 *Thunder Reef* (1950)
2 *Thunder in the bay* (1951)
3 *Mountain of gold* (1952)
4 *Trafalgar forty-nine* (1953)

Thunderbird series
Baker, Charlotte
1 *Venture of the Thunderbird* (1960)
2 *Return of the Thunderbird* (1960)

Thunderbirds series
This sequence has two authors
Theydon, John
1 *Thunderbirds* (1966)
2 *Calling Thunderbirds* (1966)
3 *Ring of fire* (1966)
Allan, Angus P
4 *Thunderbirds are go* (1966)
Theydon, John
5 *Lady Penelope, the Albanian affair* (1967)
Companion volumes: *Lost world*, by John William Jennison, 1966, *Operation Asteroids*, by John William Jennison, 1966

Thunderbolt series
McCulley, Johnston
1 *Thunderbolt collects* (1921)
2 *Alias the Thunderbolt* (1926)
3 *Thunderbolt's jest* (1927)

Thunderbolt series
Ohlson, Hereward
1 *Thunderbolt of the spaceways* (1954)
2 *Thunderbolt and the rebel planet* (1954)

Thundercats series
This sequence has three authors
Stine, Megan
1 *Thundercats and the ghost warrior* (1985)
2 *Thundercats and the snowmen of Hook Mountain* (1985)
3 *Spear of Azzura* (1986)
Martin, Les
4 *Invisible castle* (1986)

Thunstone trilogy
Wellman, Manly Wade
see **John Thunstone trilogy**

Thursby series
Cecil, Henry
see **Roger Thursby series**

Thursday series
Bond, Michael
1 *Here comes Thursday!* (1966)
2 *Thursday rides again* (1968)
3 *Thursday ahoy!* (1969)
4 *Thursday in Paris* (1971)

Thursday series
Miller, Wade
see **Max Thursday series**

Thursday trilogy
Ure, Jean
1 *See you Thursday* (1981)
2 *After Thursday* (1985)
3 *Tomorrow is also a day* (1989)

Thursday's child series
Streatfeild, Noel
1 *Thursday's child* (1970)
2 *Far to go* (1976)

Thyrde series
Denham, Bertie
see **Derek Thyrde series**

Thyri trilogy
Weaver, Michael D
1 *Wolf-dreams* (1987)
2 *Nightreaver* (1988)

Thyri trilogy

3 *Bloodfang* (1989)
One volume edition entitled *Wolf-dreams*, 1989

Tiadatha series
Rutter, Owen
1 *Song of Tiadatha* (1920)
2 *Travels of Tiadatha* (1922)

Tiangle trilogy
Asimov, Isaac
see **Trantorian Empire trilogy**

Tib series
Lovelace, Maud Hart
see **Betsy Ray series**

Tibbet series
Payne, Laurence
see **John Tibbet series**

Tibbett series
Moyes, Patricia
see **Henry and Emmy Tibbett series**

Tibbs series
Ball, John
see **Virgil Tibbs series**

Tibet series
This sequence has two authors
Harrer, Heinrich
1 *Seven years in Tibet* (1953)
Original edition entitled *Sieben Jahre in Tibet*
Norbu, Thubten Jigme
2 *Tibet is my country* (1960)
As told to Heinrich Harrer; original edition entitled *Tibet verlorene Helmat*

Tiburon series
Silver, Richard
see **Captain Shark series**

Tichy series
Lem, Stanislaw
see **Ijon Tichy series**

Ticktock and Jim series
Robertson, Keith
1 *Ticktock and Jim* (1948)
Watch for a pony
2 *Ticktock and Jim, deputy sheriffs* (1949)

Ti-Coyo series
Richer, Clement
1 *Ti-Coyo and his shark* (1941)
Original edition entitled *Ti-Coyo et son requin*
2 *Son of Ti-Coyo* (1954)
Original edition entitled *Nouvelles aventures de Ti-Coyo et son requin*

Tidd series
Kelland, Clarence Budington
see **Mark Tidd series**

Tiddy Jeffreys series
Chappell, Mollie
1 *Ladies of Lark* (1965)
2 *Bright promise* (1966)

Tide Mill series
Trowbridge, John Townsend
1 *Tinkham Brothers' Tide Mill* (1882)
2 *Phil and his friends* (1883)
3 *Satin-wood box* (1886)
Old Lady Hemenway's legacy
4 *Little master* (1886)
5 *His one fault* (1886)
6 *Peter Budstone, the boy who was hazed* (1887)

Tidewater series
Holly, David Chauncey
see **Chesapeke steamboats series**

Tidinbilla series
Graves, Richard Harry
1 *Spear and stockwhip* (1950)
2 *Tidinbilla adventure* (1951)

Tiernan family series
Ebert, Alan
1 *Traditions* (1981)
2 *Long way home* (1984)

Tierney series
Champlin, Tim
see **Matt Tierney series**
Moroso, John Antonio
see **James Tierney series**

Tiers series
Farmer, Philip Jose
see **World of Tiers series**

Tietjens series
Ford, Ford Madox
see **Parade's end series**

Tiffany series
Reid, Meta Mayne
1 *Carrigmore Castle* (1954)
2 *Tiffany and the swallow rhyme* (1956)
3 *Cuckoo at Coolnean* (1956)
4 *Strangers in Carrigmore* (1958)
5 *Tobermillin Oracle* (1962)

Tiger and Del series
Roberson, Jennifer
1 *Sword-dancer* (1986)
2 *Sword-singer* (1988)
3 *Sword-maker* (1989)
4 *Sword-breaker* (1991)

Tiger and the rose trilogy
Scannell, Vernon
Autobiography
1 *Tiger and the rose* (1971)
2 *Proper gentleman* (1977)
3 *Argument of kings* (1987)

Tiger Bay series
Walsh, James Morgan
1 *Once in Tiger Bay* (1947)
2 *Return to Tiger Bay* (1950)
3 *King of Tiger Bay* (1952)

Tiger Gang series
Bidwell, Dafne
1 *Tiger Gang and the hijackers* (1976)
2 *Tiger Gang and the car thieves* (1977)

Tiger Lester series
Betteridge, Don
1 *Balkan spy* (1942)
2 *Escape of General Gerard* (1943)
3 *Dictator's destiny* (1945)
4 *Potsdam murder plot* (1947)
5 *Spies left!* (1950)
6 *Not single spies* (1951)
7 *Spy, counter spy* (1953)
8 *Case of the Berlin spy* (1954)
9 *Gibraltar conspiracy* (1955)
10 *Spies of Peenemunde* (1958)
11 *Contact man* (1960)
12 *Package holiday spy case* (1962)

Tiger Lillie series
Allan, Luke
1 *Masked stranger* (1930)
2 *Murder at midnight* (1930)
3 *Jungle crime* (1931)
4 *Fourth dagger* (1932)
5 *Murder at the club* (1933)
6 *Behind the wire fence* (1935)
7 *Beyond the locked door* (1938)

Tiger Mann series
Spillane, Mickey
1 *Day of the guns* (1964)
2 *Bloody sunrise* (1965)
3 *Death dealers* (1965)
4 *By-pass control* (1966)

Tiger of Tibet series
Burrard, Gerald
1 *Tiger of Tibet* (1925)
2 *Mystery of Mekong* (1928)

Tiger Patrol series
Styles, Showell
1 *Tiger Patrol* (1957)
2 *Tiger Patrol wins through* (1958)
3 *Tiger Patrol at sea* (1959)
4 *Tiger Patrol presses on* (1961)

Tiger Ransome series
Sea-Lion
1 *Pirate destroyer* (1951)
2 *Wrecked on the Goodwins* (1953)
3 *Detective Tiger Ransome* (1957)

Tiger series
Bisset, Donald
1 *Talks with a tiger* (1967)
2 *Tiger wants more* (1971)
3 *Oh dear, said Tiger* (1975)

Tiger series
Case, Patricia
1 *Tiger, tiger!* (1949)
2 *Sons of the tiger* (1952)

Tiger series
Janosch
see **Little Tiger series**
Oetting, Ray
see **Timmy Tiger series**
Oona, Katherine Deme
see **Timmy Tiger series**

Tiger series
Spain, Nancy
1 *Tiger who wouldn't eat meat* (1954)
2 *Tiger who went to the moon* (1956)
3 *Tiger who won his star* (1957)
4 *Tiger who saved the train* (1960)
5 *Tiger who found the trasure* (1961)

Tiger Shark series
Stanton, Ken
see **Aquanauts series**

Tiger Standish series
Horler, Sydney
1 *Tiger Standish* (1932)
2 *Tiger Standish comes back* (1934)
3 *Mystery of the seven cafes* (1935)
Based on a radio play
4 *Grim game* (1936)
5 *Tiger Standish takes the field* (1939)
6 *Tiger Standish steps on it* (1940)
7 *Tiger Standish does his stuff* (1941)
Two novelettes
8 *Tiger Standish has a party* (1943)
A short story
9 *Lady with the limp* (1944)
10 *Exit the Disguiser* (1948)
11 *They thought he was dead* (1949)
12 *House of jackals* (1951)

Tiger Wragge series
Capon, Paul
see **Arnold Wragge series**

Tiger's heart series
Orde, Lewis
1 *Tiger's heart* (1987)
2 *Tiger's claw* (1988)

Tigger series
Huddy, Delia
1 *Tea-on-Friday-Tigger* (1975)
2 *Gold Top Tigger* (1977)

Tightrope-tense series
Ludlum, Robert
1 *Scarlatti inheritance* (1971)
2 *Osterman weekend* (1972)
3 *Matlock paper* (1973)

Tilda Jane series
Saunders, Marshall
1 *Tilda Jane* (1901)
An orphan in search of a home
2 *Tilda Jane's orphans* (1909)

Tildy series
Fraser, Sara
1 *Tildy* (1985)
2 *Poorhouse woman* (1986)
3 *Nursing woman* (1987)
4 *Pointing woman* (1988)
5 *Radical woman* (1988)
6 *Gang woman* (1989)
7 *Widow woman* (1991)
8 *Invincible woman* (1991)

Tiller Galloway series
Poyer, David
1 *Hatteras blue* (1989)
2 *Bahamas blue* (1991)
3 *Louisiana blue* (1994)

Tillermans series
Voigt, Cynthia
1 *Homecoming* (1981)
2 *Dicey's song* (1982)
3 *Solitary blue* (1983)
Numbers 1-3 also published in one volume entitled *Tillerman saga*, 1990
4 *Come a stranger* (1987)
Companion volume: *Solitary blue*, 1986

Tilling series
Watkins, Ron
see **Thomas Tilling series**

Tillman and Muldoon series
Marshall, William Leonard
1 *New York detective* (1989)
2 *Faces in the crowd* (1991)

Tilly Mint series
Doherty, Berlie
1 *Tilly Mint tales* (1984)
2 *Tilly Mint and the dodo* (1989)

Tilly series
Hoban, Lillian
see **Silly Tilly series**

Tilly series
Jaques, Faith
1 *Tilly's house* (1979)
2 *Tilly's rescue* (1981)

Tilly Trotter trilogy
Cookson, Catherine
1 *Tilly Trotter* (1980)
Tilly
2 *Tilly Trotter wed* (1981)
Tilly wed
3 *Tilly Trotter widowed* (1982)
Tilly alone

Tim and Anna series
Ball, Duncan
see **Anna and Tim series**

Tim and Betsy series
Rhodes, John
1 *Badger's Bend, the animal hotel* (1963)
2 *Adventure at Badger's Bend* (1965)

Tim and Nick Diamond series
Horowitz, Anthony
see **Nick and Tim Diamond series**

Tim and Pistol series
Garfield, Leon
1 *Boy and the monkey* (1969)
2 *Captain's watch* (1972)
3 *Lucifer Wilkins* (1973)

Tim Asher series
Hultman, Helen Joan
1 *Find the woman* (1929)
2 *Death at Windward Hill* (1931)

Tim Blackgrove series
Mackintosh, Ian
1 *Slaying in September* (1967)
2 *Drug called power* (1968)
3 *Brave cannot yield* (1970)

Tim Corrigan series
Queen, Ellery
This pseudonym is used by Richard Deming and Talmage Powell as indicated against each title
1 *Where is Bianca?* (1966) [Powell]
2 *Why so dead?* (1966) [Deming]
3 *Who spies, who kills?* (1966) [Powell]
4 *How goes the murder?* (1967) [Deming]
5 *Which way to die?* (1966) [Deming]
6 *What's in the dark?* (1968) *When fell the night?* [Deming]

Tim Dalby series
Harper, Stephen
see **Healers series**

Tim Digby series
Byers, Irene
1 *Tim of Tamberly Forest* (1954)
2 *Tim returns to Tamberly* (1962)
3 *Trouble at Tamberly* (1964)

Tim Forest series
Dale, Norman
1 *Exciting journey* (1947)
2 *Mystery Christmas* (1948)
3 *Skeleton Island* (1949)

Tim Frazer series
Durbridge, Francis
1 *World of Tim Frazer* (1962)
2 *Tim Frazer again* (1964)
3 *Tim Frazer gets the message* (1978)

Tim Hooley series
Craigie, Dorothy
1 *Tim Hooley's hero* (1957)
2 *Tim Hooley's haunting* (1958)

Tim Kyle series
Moore, Robin
see **Pulsar series**

Tim McCoy series
This sequence has three authors
Packer, Eleanor
1 *Tim McCoy in the Prescott Kid* (1935)
2 *Tim McCoy in the Westerner* (1936)
3 *Tim McCoy on the Tomahawk Trail* (1937)
Wilson, Buck
4 *Tim McCoy fighting the Redskins* (1938)
Du Bois, Gaylord
5 *Tim McCoy and the Sandy Gulch stampede* (1939)

Tim Mouse series
Brook, Judy
1 *Tim Mouse* (1966)
2 *Tim Mouse and the major* (1967)
3 *Tim Mouse visits the farm* (1968)
4 *Tim Mouse goes down the stream* (1970)
5 *Tim Mouse and Helen Mouse* (1970)
6 *Tim Mouse and Father Christmas* (1971)

Tim Mulligan and Elsie Mae Hunt series
Stein, Aaron Marc
1 *Sun is a witness* (1940)
2 *Up to no good* (1941)
3 *Only the guilty* (1942)
4 *Case of the absent-minded professor* (1943)
5 *And high water* (1946)
6 *Who saw him die* (1947)
7 *Cradle and the grave* (1948)
8 *Death takes a paying guest* (1947)
9 *Second burial* (1949)
10 *Days of misfortune* (1949)
11 *Three, with blood* (1950)
12 *Frightened Amazon* (1950)
13 *Shoot me Dacent* (1951)
14 *Pistols for two* (1951)
15 *Mask for murder* (1952)
16 *Dead thing in the pool* (1952)
17 *Death meets four hundred rabbits* (1953)
18 *Moonmilk and murder* (1955)

Tim O'Shane series
Knight, Mallory T
see **Man from T.O.M.C.A.T. series**

Tim Parnell series
Smith, Don
1 *Man who played thief* (1969)
2 *Padrone* (1971)
3 *Payoff* (1973)
4 *Corsican takeover* (1974)

Tim Rabbit series
Uttley, Alison
see **Timothy Rabbit series**

Tim Ryder series
Rutherford, Douglas
see **Chequered flag series**

Tim series
Ardizzone, Edward
1 *Little Tim and the brave sea captain* (1936)
2 *Tim and Lucy go to sea* (1938)
3 *Tim to the rescue* (1949)
4 *Tim and Charlotte* (1951)
5 *Tim in danger* (1953)
6 *Tim all alone* (1956)
7 *Tim's friend Towser* (1962)
8 *Tim and Ginger* (1965)
9 *Tim to the lighthouse* (1968)
10 *Tim's last voyage* (1972)

Tim series
Monckton, Ella
1 *Tim minds the shop* (1957)
2 *Tim minds the baby* (1960)
3 *Tim thinks of something* (1964)

Tim series
Ryder, Eileen
1 *Tim's new friends* (1975)
2 *Tim's rainy day* (1977)

Tim series
Stevenson, Dorothy Emily
see **Mrs Tim series**

Tim Simpson series
Malcolm, John
1 *Back room in Somers Town* (1984)
2 *Godwin sideboard* (1984)
3 *Gwen John sculpture* (1985)
4 *Whistler in the dark* (1986)
5 *Gothic pursuit* (1987)
6 *Mortal ruin* (1988)
7 *Wrong impression* (1990)
8 *Sheep, goats and soap* (1991)
9 *Deceptive appearances* (1992)
10 *Burning ground* (1993)

Tim the scissors grinder series
Leslie, Madeline
1 *Tim the scissors grinder* (1861) Alternative title: Loving Christ and serving him
2 *Sequel to Tim the scissors grinder* (1862)

Timber Creek series
Clark, Mavis Thorpe
1 *Twins from Timber Creek* (1949)
2 *Home again at Timber Creek* (1950)

Timber Trail riders series
Murray, Michael
1 *Long trail* (1961)
2 *Texas tenderfoot* (1962)
3 *Luck of Black Diamond* (1963)
4 *Mystery of the Hollywood horse* (1964)

Timberlake series
Marquis, Max
see **Harry Timberlake series**

Timble family trilogy
Rikhoff, Jean
1 *Dear ones all* (1961)
2 *Voyage in, voyage out* (1963)
3 *Rites of passage* (1966)

Time agents series
Norton, Andre
see **Time war series**

Time between the stars
Greeley, Andrew Moran
1 *Virgin and martyr* (1985)
2 *Angels of September* (1986)
3 *Patience of a saint* (1987)

Time circle series
Shuler, Linda Lay
1 *She who remembers* (1988)
2 *Voice of the eagle* (1992)

Time for series
Briscoe, Jill
1 *Time for giving* (1979)
2 *Time for living* (1980)

Time gate series
Silverberg, Robert
1 *Time gate* (1989) Co-author: Bill Fawcett
2 *Dangerous interfaces* (1990)

Time has come series
Wheatley, Dennis
Autobiography
1 *Young man said* (1977) 1897-1914
2 *Officer and temporary gentleman* (1978) 1914-1919
3 *Drink and ink* (1979) 1919-1977
Companion volume: *The deception planners, my secret war*, 1980

Time keeper trilogy
Bartholomew, Barbara
1 *Time keeper* (1985)
2 *Child of tomorrow* (1985)
3 *When dreams cease to dream* (1985)

Time machine series
Darby, Joan
1 *Leonard discovers America* (1965)
2 *Leonard visits dinosaur land* (1965)
3 *Leonard visits space* (1965)
4 *Leonard visits the ocean floor* (1965)
5 *Leonard visits Sitting Bull* (1967)
6 *Leonard goes to the Olympics* (1967)
7 *Leonard equals Einstein* (1967)
8 *Leonard discovers Africa* (1969)

Time machine series
Faraday, Robert
see **Adventures in the time machine series**

Time machine series
This sequence has twenty authors
Gasperini, Jim
1 *Secrets of the knights* (1984)
Bischoff, David
2 *Search for dinosaurs* (1984)
Perry, Steve
3 *Sword of the samurai* (1984)
Gasperini, Jim
4 *Sail with pirates* (1984)
Perry, Steve
5 *Civil War secret agent* (1984)
Cover, Arthur Byron
6 *Rings of Saturn* (1985)
Dixon, Dougal
7 *Ice age explorer* (1985)
Gasperini, Jim
8 *Mystery of Atlantis* (1985)
Overholser, Stephen
9 *Wild West rider* (1985)
Cover, Arthur Byron
10 *American revolutionary* (1985)
Kornblatt, Marc
11 *Mission to World War II* (1986)
Walker, Robert Wayne
12 *Search for the Nile* (1986)
Gaskin, Carol
13 *Secret of the royal treasure* (1986)
Cover, Arthur Byron
14 *Blade of the guillotine* (1986)
Kornblatt, Marc
15 *Flame of the Inquisition* (1986)
Glatzer, Richard
16 *Quest for the cities of gold* (1987)
Reit, Seymour V
17 *Scotland Yard detective* (1987)
Stevenson, Bruce
18 *Sword of Caesar* (1987)
Gaskin, Carol
19 *Death mask of Pancho Villa* (1987)
Bailey, Nancy
20 *Bound for Australia* (1987)
Gaskin, Carol
21 *Caravan to China* (1987)
Lerangis, Peter
22 *Last of the dinosaurs* (1988)
Ashby, Ruth
23 *Quest for King Arthur* (1988)
Mueller, Richard
24 *World War I flying ace* (1988)
Lerangis, Peter
25 *World War II code breaker* (1989)

Time machine series
Keith, Donald
1 *Mutiny in the time machine* (1963)
2 *Time machine to the rescue* (1967)

Time machine series
Wells, Herbert George
see **Time traveller series**

Time master trilogy
Cooper, Louise Antell
1 *Initiate* (1985)
2 *Outcast* (1986)
3 *Master* (1987)

Time of death series
Cosic, Dobrica
see **This land, this time series**

Time of life series
Adam, Paul
1 *Force* (1899) Original edition entitled *La force*
2 *Child of the Austerlitz* (1902) Original edition entitled *L'enfant d'Austerlitz*
3 *Sun of July* (1903) Original edition entitled *Au soleil de juillet*
About 17 other volumes in this series not translated into English

Time of war series
Poyer, Joe
1 *Transgressors* (1983)
2 *Come evil days* (1985)

Time Patrol series
Anderson, Poul
1 *Guardians of time* (1960) Short stories; revised edition 1981

Time Patrol series

2 *Time Patrolman* (1983)
Numbers 1 and 2 also published in one volume entitled *Annals of the Time Patrol*, 1984
3 *Year of the ransom* (1988)
Numbers 1-3 also published in one volume entitled *Time Patrol*, 1991
4 *Shield of time* (1990)

Time police series
Norwood, Warren
1 *Vanished* (1988)
2 *Trapped!* (1989)
3 *Stranded* (1989)
Co-author: Mel Odom

Time remembered series
Barton, Arthur
Autobiography
1 *Two lamps in our street* (1967)
A time remembered
2 *Penny world* (1969)
A boyhood recalled
3 *School for love* (1976)

Time remembered series
Holland, Vyvyan
Autobiography
1 *Son of Oscar Wilde* (1954)
2 *Time remembered after Pere Lachaise* (1966)

Time remembered series
Read, *Miss*
Autobiography
1 *Fortunate grandchild* (1982)
2 *Time remembered* (1986)

Time rope series
Leeson, Robert
1 *Time rope* (1986)
2 *Three against the world* (1986)
3 *At war with tomorrow* (1986)
4 *Metro gangs attack* (1986)

Time series
Ball, Brian Neville
1 *Timepiece* (1968)
2 *Timepivot* (1970)
3 *Timepit* (1971)

Time series
Barrett, Neal
1 *Gates of time* (1970)
2 *Leaves of time* (1971)

Time series
Lansing, Karen E
1 *Time to fly* (1991)
2 *Time to be a friend* (1993)

Time squared quartet
McDonald, Gregory
1 *World too wide* (1987)
2 *Exits and entrances* (1988)
3 *Merely players* (1988)
Number 4 not yet published

Time to be born series
Lang-Sims, Lois
Autobiography
1 *Time to be born* (1971)
2 *Flower in a teacup* (1973)

Time to talk series
Tarsky, Sue
1 *Playtime* (1983)
2 *Shopping* (1983)

Time tours series
This sequence has seven authors
Wu, William Franking
1 *Robin Hood ambush* (1990)
Baron, Nick
2 *Glory's end* (1990)
Doyle, Debra
3 *Timecrime, Inc.* (1991)
Shadwell, Thomas
4 *Dinosaur trackers* (1991)
Baron, Nick
5 *Pirate paradox* (1991)
Kingston, Jeremy
6 *Caesar's time legions* (1991)

Time travel series
Norton, Andre
see **Blake Walker series**

Time traveler series
This sequence has five authors
Reit, Seymour V
1 *Voyage with Columbus* (1986)
Gaskin, Carol
2 *Legend of Hiawatha* (1986)
3 *First settlers* (1987)
Lerangis, Peter
4 *Amazing Ben Franklin* (1987)
Kornblatt, Marc
5 *Paul Revere and the Boston Tea Party* (1987)
Frankel, Ellen
6 *George Washington and the Constitution* (1987)

Time traveller series
This sequence has six authors
Wells, Herbert George
1 *Time machine* (1895)
Friedell, Egon
2 *Return of the time machine* (1972)
Priest, Christopher
3 *Space machine* (1976)
Jeter, Kevin W
4 *Morlock night* (1979)
Lake, David John
5 *Man who loved Morlocks* (1981)
Morhaim, Joe
6 *Time machine 2* (1981)
Companion volume: *The time machine*, by Tomas Ernesto Bethancourt, 1986

Time trilogy
Anderson, Margaret Jean
1 *In the keep of time* (1977)
2 *In the circle of time* (1979)
3 *Mists of time* (1984)

Time trilogy
Kirst, Hans Hellmut
see **Munich trilogy**
L'Engle, Madeleine
see **Wallace family series**

Time tunnel series
Leinster, Murray
Based on a television series
1 *Time tunnel* (1967)
2 *Timeslip!* (1967)

Time war series
Norton, Andre
1 *Time traders* (1958)
2 *Galactic derelict* (1959)
3 *Defiant agents* (1962)
4 *Key out of time* (1963)
5 *Firehand* (1994)
Co-author: Pauline Margaret Griffin

Time warp trio series
Scieszka, Jon
Illustrated by Lane Smith
1 *Knights of the kitchen table* (1991)
2 *Not-so-jolly Roger* (1991)
3 *Good, the bad and the goofy* (1992)
4 *Your mother was a neanderthal* (1993)

Time warrior series
Costello, Matthew John
1 *Time of the fox* (1990)
2 *Hour of the scorpion* (1991)

Time warriors series
North, David
1 *Fuse point* (1991)
2 *Forbidden region* (1991)
3 *Guardian strikes* (1991)

Time well spent series
Cheesman, Evelyn
Autobiography
1 *Things worthwhile* (1957)
2 *Time well spent* (1960)

Time windows series
Reiss, Kathryn
1 *Time windows* (1991)
2 *Pale phoenix* (1994)

Time without clocks series
Lindsay, Joan
Autobiography
1 *Time without clocks* (1962)
2 *Facts soft and hard* (1964)

Timebinders series
Nelson, Ray Faraday
1 *Prometheus man, a Nrobook* (1982)
2 *Revolt of the unemployables* (1978)

Timekeeper series
Rodda, Emily
1 *Finders keepers* (1990)
2 *Timekeeper* (1992)

Timeliner trilogy
Meredith, Richard Carlton
1 *At the narrow passage* (1973)
Revised edition 1979
2 *No brother, no friend* (1976)
Revised edition 1979
3 *Vestiges of time* (1978)
Revised edition 1979
One volume edition entitled *Timeliner trilogy*, 1987

Timequest trilogy
Tedford, William G
1 *Rashanyn dark* (1981)
2 *Hydrabyss red* (1981)
3 *Nemydia Deep* (1981)

Time's harvest trilogy
Charques, Dorothy
1 *Time's harvest* (1940)
2 *Returning heart* (1943)
3 *Between the twilights* (1947)
One volume edition entitled *Time's harvest*, 1949

Timewars series
Hawke, Simon
1 *Ivanhoe gambit* (1984)
2 *Timekeeper conspiracy* (1984)
3 *Pimpernel plot* (1984)
4 *Zenda vendetta* (1985)
5 *Nautilus sanction* (1985)
6 *Khyber connection* (1986)
7 *Argonaut affair* (1987)
8 *Dracula caper* (1988)
9 *Lilliput legion* (1989)
10 *Hellfire rebellion* (1990)
11 *Cleopatra crisis* (1990)
12 *Six-gun solution* (1991)

Timewyrm series
This sequence has nine authors
Peel, John
1 *Genesys* (1991)
Dicks, Terrance
2 *Exodus* (1991)
Robinson, Nigel
3 *Apocalypse* (1991)
Cornell, Paul
4 *Revelation* (1991)
Roberts, Gareth
5 *Highest science* (1993)
Robinson, Nigel
6 *Birthright* (1993)
Lyons, Steve
7 *Conundrum* (1994)
No future
Roberts, Gareth
8 *Tragedy day* (1994)
Russell, Gary
9 *Legacy* (1994)
Richards, Justin
10 *Theatre of war* (1994)
Lane, Andy
11 *All-consuming fire* (1994)
Dicks, Terrance
12 *Blood harvest* (1994)

Timms series
Avery, Gillian
see **Ellen Timms series**

Timmy series
Vallance, Rosalind
1 *Timmy Turnpenny* (1937)
2 *Timmy and Janet* (1941)
3 *Timmy and Roger* (1949)
4 *Timmy in the country* (1951)
5 *Timmy and Bingo* (1954)
6 *Timmy moves house* (1957)
7 *Timmy Turnpenny's secret* (1959)

Timmy Tiger series
Oetting, Ray
Illustrated by Vic Cantone
1 *Timmy Tiger and the elephants* (1970)
2 *Timmy Tiger to the rescue* (1970)
3 *Timmy Tiger's new coat* (1970)
4 *Timmy Tiger's new friend* (1970)

Timmy Tiger series
Oona, Katherine Deme
1 *Timmy Tiger and the masked bandit* (1980)
2 *Timmy Tiger and the butterfly net* (1981)

Timothy and Joe series
Edwards, Dorothy
see **Joe and Timothy series**

Timothy and Trudy series
Porter, Bertha Currier
see **Trudy and Timothy series**

Timothy Cone series
Sanders, Lawrence
1 *Timothy files* (1987)
2 *Timothy's game* (1988)

Timothy Cullinan series
Martin, Oliver
1 *Iron door* (1923)
2 *Mermaid* (1926)

Timothy Dane series
Ard, William
1 *Perfect frame* (1951)
2 *Point thirty eight* (1952)
This is murder
You can't stop me
3 *Diary* (1952)
4 *Private party* (1953)
Rogue's murder
5 *Don't come crying to me* (1954)
6 *Mister Trouble* (1954)
7 *Hell is a city* (1955)
8 *Cry scandal* (1956)
9 *Root of his evil* (1957)
Deadly beloved

Timothy Devlin series
Heatter, Basil
1 *Devlin's triangle* (1976)
2 *Golden stag* (1976)

Timothy Dexter series
Marquand, John Phillips
1 *Lord Timothy Dexter of Newburyport, Mass.* (1926)
2 *Timothy Dexter revisited* (1960)

Timothy Drewer series
Landon, Hilary
1 *Murder at morning prayers* (1947)
2 *Circles round a corpse* (1948)

Timothy, Ellen and Melinda series
Storey, Margaret
1 *Timothy and two witches* (1966)
2 *Quarrel of witches* (1970)
3 *Sleeping witch* (1971)
4 *War of wizards* (1976)

5 *Double wizard* (1979)
Companion volumes: *The stone sorcerer*, 1967, also published as *The stone wizard, The dragon's daughter*, and, *Timothy travels*, 1967

Timothy Fowler series
Harris, Colver
1 *Hide and go seek* (1933)
2 *Going to Saint Ives* (1936)
3 *Murder in amber* (1938)
Murder by proxy

Timothy Herring series
Torrie, Malcolm
1 *Heavy as lead* (1966)
2 *Late and cold* (1967)
3 *Your secret friend* (1968)
4 *Churchyard salad* (1969)
5 *Shade of darkness* (1970)
6 *Bismarck Herrings* (1971)

Timothy McCarty series
Ostrander, Isabel
1 *Clue in the air* (1917)
2 *Twenty-six clues* (1919)
3 *How many cards?* (1920)
4 *McCarty, incog.* (1922)
5 *Annihilation* (1924)

Timothy Rabbit series
Uttley, Alison
1 *Adventures of no ordinary rabbit* (1937)
2 *Adventures of Tim Rabbit* (1945)
3 *Tim Rabbit and company* (1959)
4 *Tim Rabbit's dozen* (1964)

Timothy Rogan series
Dutton, Charles Judson
see **Harley Manners series**

Timothy Rourke series
Wolf, Jack
1 *Two shadows for death* (1961)
2 *Payoff on Fever Street* (1962)

Timothy series
Gollancz, Victor
see **Letters to Timothy series**

Timothy series
Smyth, Reitta
1 *Tommy's pup, Timothy* (1946)
2 *Timothy in the land of storybooks* (1950)
3 *Timothy on tour* (1950)

Timothy Terrel series
Maddock, Stephen
1 *Woman of destiny* (1933)
2 *White siren* (1934)
3 *Gentlemen of the night* (1934)
4 *Danger after dark* (1934)
5 *Conspirators in Capri* (1935)
6 *Eye at the keyhole* (1935)
7 *Conspirators three* (1936)
8 *Forbidden frontiers* (1936)
9 *Conspirators at large* (1937)
10 *Lamp-post 592* (1938)
11 *Doorway to danger* (1938)
12 *Spies along the Severn* (1939)
13 *Spades at midnight* (1940)
14 *Date with a spy* (1941)
15 *Drums beat at dusk* (1943)
16 *Something on the stairs* (1944)
17 *I'll never like Friday again* (1945)
18 *Overture to trouble* (1946)

Timothy Trant series
Patrick, Q
see **Lieutenant Timothy Trant series**

Timothy Yorke series
Stranger, Joyce
1 *Vet on call* (1981)
2 *Double trouble* (1981)
Vet up the wall
3 *Vet riding high* (1982)
4 *No more horses* (1982)
5 *Dial V.E.T.* (1982)

Tims Creek series
Kenan, Randall
1 *Visitation of spirits* (1989)
2 *Let the dead bury their dead, and other stories* (1992)

Tin toys series
Holden, Ursula
1 *Tin toys* (1986)
2 *Unicorn sisters* (1988)

Tina May series
Kemp, Sarah
see **Doctor Tina May series**

Tina series
Oterdahl, Jeanna
Translated from the Swedish
1 *April adventure* (1962)
2 *Tina and the latchkey child* (1964)

Tina series
Stahl, Hilda
1 *Tina's first love* (1972)
2 *Tina's dangerous secret* (1980)
3 *Tina's elusive enemy* (1981)
4 *Tina's reluctant friend* (1981)
5 *Tina's unwelcome intruder* (1982)
6 *Tina's secret rival* (1982)
7 *Tina's eighteenth summer* (1983)
8 *Tina's surprise romance* (1983)

Tini and Pethi series
Macdonald, Shelagh
see **Pethi and Tini series**

Tinieblas trilogy
Koster, Richard Morton
1 *Prince* (1972)
2 *Dissertation* (1975)
3 *Mandragon* (1979)

Tink, tonk tales series
Mayer, Mercer
1 *Tinka bakes a cake* (1984)
2 *Tuk takes a trip* (1984)
3 *Tink goes fishing* (1984)
4 *Teep and Beep go to sleep* (1984)
5 *Trouble in Tinktonk Land* (1985)
6 *Tinktonks find a home* (1985)
7 *Tonk gives a magic show* (1985)
8 *Zoomer builds a racing car* (1985)

Tinka series
Downing, Brownie
1 *Tinka and his friends* (1960)
Co-author: John Mansfield
2 *Tinka and the bunyip* (1966)

Tinker and Tanker series
Scarry, Richard
1 *Tinker and Tanker* (1960)
2 *Tinker and Tanker out west* (1961)
3 *Tinker and Tanker and their space ship* (1961)
Numbers 1-3 also published in one volume entitled *The adventures of Tinker and Tanker*, 1968
4 *Tinker and Tanker and the pirates* (1961)
5 *Tinker and Tanker, Knights of the Round Table* (1963)
6 *Tinker and Tanker in Africa* (1963)
Numbers 4-6 also published in one volume entitled *More adventures of Tinker and Tanker*, 1971; selections from numbers 4-6 published as *Tinker and Tanker tales of pirates and knights*, 1979

Tinker series
Jepson, Edgar
1 *Admirable Tinker, child of the world* (1904)
2 *Triumph of Tinker* (1906)

Tinker Tess series
Tranter, Nigel Godwin
1 *Tinker Tess* (1967)
2 *To the rescue* (1968)

Tintagel series
Brandewyne, Rebecca
see **Chronicles of Tintagel series**
Draco, F
see **Lord and Lady Tintagel series**

Tintin series
Herge
1 *[Tintin au pays des Soviets]* (1930)
No English edition
2 *[Tintin au Congo]* (1931)
[Aventures de Tintin, reporter du Petit Vingtieme]
No English edition
3 *Tintin in America* (1932)
Original edition entitled *Tintin en Amerique*
4 *Cigars of the pharaoh* (1934)
Original edition entitled *Les cigars du pharaon*
5 *Blue lotus* (1936)
Original edition entitled *Le lotus bleu*
6 *Tintin and the broken ear* (1937)
Broken ear
Original edition entitled *L'oreille cassee*; numbers 3, 4, 6 also published in one volume entitled *Adventures of Tintin*, volume 1, 1989
7 *Black island* (1938)
Original edition entitled *L'ile noire*
8 *King Ottokar's sceptre* (1939)
Original edition entitled *Le sceptre d'Ottokar*
9 *Crab with the golden claws* (1941)
Original edition entitled *Le crabe aux pinces d'or*; numbers 7-9 also published in one volume entitled *Adventures of Tintin*, volume 2, 1989
10 *Shooting star* (1942)
Original edition entitled *L'etoile mysterieuse*
11 *Secret of the unicorn* (1943)
Original edition entitled *Le secret se la licorne*
12 *Red Rackham's treasure* (1945)
Original edition entitled *Le tresor de Rackham le Rouge*; numbers 11 and 12 also published in one volume entitled *The making of Tintin*, 1983
13 *Seven crystal balls* (1948)
Original edition entitled *Les sept boules de cristal*
14 *Prisoners of the sun* (1949)
Original edition entitled *Le temple du soleil*; numbers 13 and 14 also published in one volume entitled *The making of Tintin in the world of the Incas*, 1984
15 *Land of the black gold* (1951)
Original edition entitled *Tintin aux pays de l'or noir*
16 *Destination Moon* (1953)
Original edition entitled *Objectif Lune*
17 *Explorers on the Moon* (1954)
Original edition entitled *On a marche sur la Lune*
18 *Calculus affair* (1956)
Original edition entitled *L'affaire tournesol*
19 *Red Sea sharks* (1958)
Original edition entitled *Coke en Stock*
20 *Tintin in Tibet* (1960)
Original edition entitled *Tintin au Tibet*
21 *Tintin and the Golden Fleece* (1962)
Original edition entitled *Tintin et le mystere de la toison d'or*; based on a screenplay by Andre Barret and Remo Forlani
22 *Castafiore emerald* (1963)
Original edition entitled *Le bijoux de la Castafiore*
23 *Flight Seven One Four* (1968)
Original edition entitled *Vol 714 pour Sydney*
24 *Popol out West* (1969)
Original edition entitled *Popol et Virginie*
25 *Tintin and the lake of sharks* (1973)
Original edition entitled *Tintin et le lac aux requins*; based on a screenplay by Raymond Leblanc
26 *Tintin and the Picaros* (1976)
Original edition entitled *Tintin et les Picaros*
Companion volumes: *Tintin's moon adventure painting book*, 1972, *Tintin games book*, 1986, *Tintin action play book*, nos 1-3, 1988, *The Tintin poster book*, 1989

Tiny Meldrum and Inspector Dusty Muller series
Glanville, Alec
see **Inspector Dusty Muller and Tiny Meldrum series**

Tiny paw series
Szekeres, Cyndy
1 *Busy day* (1989)
2 *New baby* (1989)
3 *Moving day* (1989)
4 *Fine mouse band* (1989)
5 *Mouse mess* (1990)

Tiny Rider series
Boyles, William
see **Bounty Hunter series**

Tiny Spook series
Sandberg, Inger
see **Little Spook series**

Tiny Toon's adventures series
Korman, Justine
1 *Rock 'n' roar* (1990)
2 *Circus comes to town* (1991)
3 *Adventures of Buster Hood* (1991)

Tip Paine series
Batchelor, John Calvin
see **Gordon Liddy is my muse series**

Tipple in the deep series
Wood, James
Autobiography
1 *Tipple in the deep* (1962)
2 *Beer for Christmas* (1964)
3 *Drop of himself* (1967)

Tippy Parrish series
Lambert, Janet
1 *Miss Tippy* (1948)
2 *Little Miss Atlas* (1949)
3 *Miss America* (1951)
4 *Don't cry, little girl* (1952)
5 *Rainbow after rain* (1953)
6 *Welcome home, Mrs Jordan* (1953)
7 *Song in their hearts* (1956)

Tiptilt series
Wied, Marie Elisabeth
1 *Tiptilt* (1952)
Original edition entitled *Lilltrollet hos manniskoma*
2 *Tiptilt and the pixie* (1952)
Original edition entitled *Lilltrollet rymmer*
3 *Tiptilt and the trolls* (1954)
Original edition entitled *Lilltrollet pa nya aventyr*

Tiptoes series
Byers, Irene
1 *Timothy and Tiptoes* (1974)
2 *Tiptoes wins through* (1976)

Tiptop series
Stone, Raymond
see **Tommy Tiptop series**

Tirel series
Shipway, George
see **Walter Tirel series**

Tish series
Rinehart, Mary Roberts
1 *Amazing adventures of Letitia Carberry* (1911)
2 *Tish* (1916)
3 *More Tish* (1921)
4 *Tish plays the game* (1926)
5 *Tish marches on* (1937)
Omnibus volume: *The best of Tish*, 1955

Tisi series
Dutton, Geoffrey
1 *Tisi and the yabby* (1965)
2 *Tisi and the pageant* (1968)

Titan series
Horvat, Dilwyn
see **Operation Titan series**

Titania's Palace series
Wilkinson, Nevile
1 *Yvette in Italy and Titania's Palace* (1922)
2 *Grey Fairy and Titania's Palace* (1922)
3 *Yvette in Venice and Titania's Palace* (1923)
4 *Yvette in Switzerland and Titania's Palace* (1926)
5 *Yvette in the U.S.A. with Titania's Palace* (1928)

Titans series
Adkins, Patrick H
1 *Lord of the crooked paths* (1987)
2 *Master of the fearful depths* (1989)
3 *Sons of the titans* (1990)

Titch series
Hutchins, Pat
1 *Titch* (1972)
2 *You'll soon grow into them, Titch* (1983)

Tittlemouse series
Judson, Clara Ingram
see **Tommy Tittlemouse series**

Tittymouse and Tattymouse series
Vallance, Rosalind
1 *Tittymouse and Tattymouse* (1946)
2 *Titty and Tatty by the river* (1949)
3 *Titty and Tatty's housewarming* (1958)

Titus Bass series
Johnston, Terry Conrad
1 *Carry the wind* (1982)
2 *Borderlords* (1984)
3 *One-eyed dream* (1988)

Titus Bear series
Kosikowski, Renate
Illustrated by Brian Cosgrove and Mark Hall
1 *Titus Bear goes to school* (1984)
2 *Titus Bear goes to the beach* (1984)
3 *Titus Bear's spring* (1986)
4 *Titus Bear's summer* (1986)
5 *Titus Bear's autumn* (1986)
6 *Titus Bear's winter* (1986)

Titus Crow series
Lumley, Brian
1 *Burrowers beneath* (1974)
2 *Transition of Titus Crow* (1975)
Revised edition 1991
3 *Clock of dreams* (1978)
4 *Spawn of the winds* (1978)
5 *In the moons of Borea* (1979)
6 *Compleat Crow* (1987)

Titus Groan trilogy
Peake, Mervyn
1 *Titus Groan* (1946)
2 *Gormenghast* (1950)
3 *Titus alone* (1959)
Revised edition 1970
One volume editions entitled *The Titus books*, 1983 and *The Gormenghast trilogy*, 1988; companion volumes: *Boy in darkness*, by Mervyn Peake, edited by Kenyon Calthrop, 1976, *Titus unbound*, by Mervyn Peake and Colin Greenland, 1977

Tlen series
Lambert, William J
1 *Five roads to Tlen* (1970)
2 *Gods of Tlen* (1970)

TNT series
Masters, Doug
1 *TNT* (1985)
2 *Beast* (1985)
3 *Spiral of death* (1985)
4 *Devil's claw* (1985)
5 *Killer angel* (1986)
6 *Ritual of blood* (1986)
7 *Kingdom of death* (1986)

To heal series
Rodney, Jonathan
Memoirs of a doctor
1 *To heal the sick* (1957)
2 *Next patient, please* (1958)

To keep the ball rolling series
Powell, Anthony
Reminiscences
1 *Infants of the spring* (1977)
2 *Messengers of day* (1978)
3 *Faces in my time* (1980)
4 *Strangers all are gone* (1982)
One volume abridged edition entitled *To keep the ball rolling*, 1983

To please myself series
Starr, Leonard
1 *To please myself* (1948)
2 *To please myself again* (1952)

To serve them all my days series
Delderfield, Ronald Frederick
1 *Late spring* (1972)
2 *Headmaster* (1972)
One volume edition entitled *To serve them all my days*, 1972

To the stars trilogy
Harrison, Harry
1 *Homeworld* (1980)
2 *Wheelworld* (1981)
3 *Starworld* (1981)
One volume edition entitled *To the stars*, 1981

Toad Hall series
This sequence has two authors
Grahame, Kenneth
1 *Wind in the willows* (1908)
Companion volumes: *First whisper of the wind in the willows*, edited by Elspeth Grahame, 1945, *My dearest mouse, The wind in the willows letters*, 1988; dramatized as *Toad of Toad Hall*, by Alan Alexander Milne with music by H Fraser-Simson, 1929
Scott, Dixon
2 *Fresh wind in the willows* (1983)

Toad series
Erickson, Russell Everett
see **Warton Toad series**

Toad series
Locklin, Gerald
1 *Toad poems* (1970)
2 *Toad's Europe* (1973)
3 *Tarzan and Shane meet the Toad* (1975)
Co-authors: Ronald Koertge and Charles Stetler
4 *Last of Toad* (1980)
5 *Why turn a perfectly good toad into a prince?* (1983)
Selections published as *Toad turns fifty*, 1993

Toad series
Yolen, Jane
see **Commander Toad series**

Toady series
Crockett, Samuel Rutherford
see **Sir Toady series**

Toba series
Mark, Michael
1 *Toba* (1984)
2 *Toba at the hands of a thief* (1985)

Tobacco Jones and Judge Lemanuel Bates series
Floren, Lee
see **Judge Lemanuel Bates and Tobacco Jones series**

Tobey and Midge Heydon series
Du Jardin, Rosamond
1 *Practically seventeen* (1949)
2 *Class ring* (1951)
3 *Boy trouble* (1953)
4 *Real thing* (1956)
5 *Wedding in the family* (1958)
6 *One of the crowd* (1961)

Tobiah series
Silberrad, Una Lucy
1 *Wedding of the Lady of Lovell, and other matches of Tobiah's making* (1905)
2 *Second book of Tobiah* (1906)
3 *Green pastures* (1919)

Tobias Glendower and Penelope Spring series
Arnold, Margot
see **Penelope Spring and Sir Tobias Glendower series**

Tobias series
Eldon, Magdalen
1 *Tobias* (1954)
2 *Tobias two* (1954)

Tobias trilogy
Lagerkvist, Par
1 *Death of Ahasueras* (1960)
Original edition entitled *Ahasverus dod*
2 *Pilgrim at sea* (1962)
Original edition entitled *Pilgrim pa havet*
3 *Holy land* (1964)
Original edition entitled *Det helige landet*
Companion volume: *The sybil*, originally *Sibyllan*, 1956

Tobin series
Caillou, Alan
see **Colonel Matthew Tobin series**
Coe, Tucker
see **Mitchell Tobin series**

Tobin series
Gorman, Edward
1 *Murder on the aisle* (1987)
2 *Several deaths later* (1988)

Tobin series
Hughes, Dorothy Belle
see **Inspector Tobin series**
Morgan, Stanley
see **Russ Tobin series**

Toby and Jane series
Thwaite, Ann
see **Jane and Toby series**

Toby Belfer series
Pushker, Gloria
1 *Toby Belfer never had a Christmas tree* (1990)
2 *Toby Belfer's seder* (1994)
A Passover story retold

Toby Dyke series
Ferrars, Elizabeth
American editions are published under the pseudonym E X Ferrars
1 *Give a corpse a bad name* (1940)
2 *Remove the bodies* (1940)
American edition entitled *Rehearsals for murder*, by E X Ferrars
3 *Death in Botanist's Bay* (1941)
American edition entitled Murder of a suicide, by E X Ferrars
4 *Don't monkey with murder* (1942)
American edition entitled *Shape of a stain*, by E X Ferrars
5 *Your neck in a noose* (1942)
American edition entitled *Neck in a noose*, by E X Ferrars

Toby Peters series
Kaminsky, Stuart Melvin
1 *Bullet for a star* (1977)
2 *Murder on the Yellow Brick Road* (1978)
3 *You bet your life* (1978)
4 *Howard Hughes affair* (1979)
5 *Never cross a vampire* (1980)
6 *High midnight* (1981)
7 *Catch a falling clown* (1982)
8 *He done her wrong* (1983)
9 *Fala factor* (1984)
10 *Down for the count* (1985)
11 *Man who shot Lewis Vance* (1986)
12 *Smart moves* (1987)
13 *Think fast, Mister Peters* (1988)
14 *Buried Caesars* (1989)
15 *Poor butterfly* (1990)
16 *Melting clock* (1991)
17 *Devil met a lady* (1993)

Toby Roberts series
Johnson, Pamela Hansford
1 *Good listener* (1975)
2 *Good husband* (1978)

Toby series
Branscum, Robbie
1 *Toby, Grannie and George* (1976)
2 *Toby alone* (1978)
3 *Toby and Johnny Joe* (1978)

Toby series
Schley, Sturges Mason
see **Doctor Quentin Toby series**

Toby series
Weber, Christine
1 *Toby* (1983)
A dachshund's troubles
2 *Toby and his tail* (1983)

Toby Trafford series
Trowbridge, John Townsend
1 *Fortunes of Toby Trafford* (1893)
2 *Woodie Thorpe's pilgrimage, and other stories* (1893)

Toby Tyler series
Otis, James
1 *Toby Tyler* (1880)
2 *Old Ben* (1911)

Tod Claymore series
Claymore, Tod
1 *You remember the case* (1939)
This is what happened
2 *Nest of vipers* (1948)
3 *Appointment in New Orleans* (1950)
4 *Reunion in Florida* (1952)
5 *Dead men don't answer* (1954)
6 *Rendezvous on an island* (1957)

Tod Moran series
Pease, Howard
1 *Tattooed man* (1926)
2 *Jinx ship* (1927)
3 *Shanghai passage* (1929)
4 *Ship without a crew* (1934)
5 *Wind in the rigging* (1935)

6 *Hurricane weather* (1936)
7 *Foghorns* (1937)
8 *Highroad to adventure* (1939)
9 *Black tanker* (1941)
10 *Night boat, and other Tod Moran mysteries* (1942)
11 *Heart of danger* (1946)
12 *Captain of the Araby* (1953)
13 *Mystery on Telegraph Hill* (1961)

Toda and McGlynn families series
Toland, John
see **McGlynn and Toda families series**

Todd McKinnon series
Offord, Lenore Glen
1 *Skeleton key* (1943)
2 *Glass mask* (1944)
3 *Smiling tiger* (1949)
4 *Walking shadow* (1959)

Todd series
Conde, Phillip
see **Irving Todd series**
Freeman, Martin Joseph
see **Jerry Todd series**
Halstead, John
see **Inspector Todd series**
Jones, Henry Llewellyn
see **Fraser Todd series**
McCullough, David Willis
see **Ziza Todd series**
Tresillian, Richard
see **Bondmaster series**

Toddie and Budge series
Habberton, John
see **Budge and Toddie series**

Toddler's fun series
Roth, Harold
1 *Nursery school* (1987)
2 *Playground* (1987)
3 *Spring days* (1987)
4 *Summer days* (1987)

Toddlers' tales series
Kilroy, Sally
1 *What a week!* (1986)
2 *On the road* (1986)
3 *Grandpa's garden* (1986)
4 *Market day* (1986)

Toddy Nott series
Judd, Alfred
1 *Toddy Nott, schoolboy* (1927)
2 *Toddy scores again* (1923)

Toff series
Creasey, John
1 *Introducing the Toff* (1938)
Revised edition 1954
2 *Toff steps out* (1939)
Revised edition 1955
3 *Toff goes on* (1939)
Revised edition 1955
4 *Toff breaks in* (1940)
Revised edition 1955
5 *Here comes the Toff!* (1940)
6 *Salute the Toff* (1941)
7 *Toff proceeds* (1941)
8 *Toff is back* (1942)
9 *Toff goes to market* (1942)
10 *Accuse the Toff* (1943)
11 *Toff among the millions* (1943)
12 *Toff and the great illusion* (1944)
13 *Toff and the curate* (1944)
Toff and the deadly parson
14 *Feathers for the Toff* (1945)
Revised edition 1964
15 *Toff and the lady* (1946)
16 *Hammer the Toff* (1947)
17 *Toff on ice* (1947)
Poison for the Toff
Revised edition 1976
18 *Toff in town* (1948)
Revised edition 1977
19 *Toff takes shares* (1948)
20 *Toff and Old Harry* (1949)
Revised edition 1964
21 *Toff on board* (1949)
Revised edition 1973
22 *Kill the Toff* (1950)
23 *Fool the Toff* (1950)
Foul play suspected
24 *Toff goes gay* (1951)
Mask for the Toff
25 *Knife for the Toff* (1951)
26 *Hunt the Toff* (1952)
27 *Murder out of the past* (1953)
Also includes Under-cover man
28 *Call the Toff* (1953)
29 *Toff down under* (1953)
Break the Toff
30 *Toff at Butlin's* (1954)
31 *Toff at the fair* (1954)
32 *Six for the Toff* (1955)
Score for the Toff
33 *Toff and the deep blue sea* (1955)
34 *Make-up for the Toff* (1956)
Kiss the Toff
35 *Toff in New York* (1956)
36 *Toff on fire* (1957)
37 *Model for the Toff* (1957)
38 *Toff and the stolen tresses* (1958)
39 *Toff on the farm* (1958)
Terror for the Toff
40 *Toff and the runaway bride* (1959)
41 *Double for the Toff* (1959)
42 *Toff and the kidnapped girl* (1960)
43 *Rocket for the Toff* (1960)
44 *Follow the Toff* (1961)
45 *Toff and the teds* (1961)
Toff and the toughs
46 *Leave it to the Toff* (1963)
47 *Doll for the Toff* (1963)
48 *Toff and the spider* (1965)
49 *Toff in wax* (1966)
50 *Bundle for the Toff* (1967)
51 *Stars for the Toff* (1968)
52 *Toff and the golden boy* (1969)
53 *Toff and the fallen angels* (1970)
54 *Vote for the Toff* (1971)
55 *Toff and the trip-trip triplets* (1972)
56 *Toff and the terrified taxman* (1973)
57 *Toff and the sleepy cowboy* (1974)
58 *Toff and the crooked copper* (1977)
59 *Toff and the dead man's finger* (1978)
Written by William Vivian Butler on an outline by John Creasey
Companion volume: *The Toff, 3-act play*, 1963

Toffy's circus series
Ross, Tony
see **Tales from Mister Toffy's circus series**

Toggle series
Pulver, Robin
see **Mrs Toggle series**

Tolkien quest series
Ruemmler, John David
see **Middle Earth quest series**

Tolliver series
Harvey, James Neal
see **Ben Tolliver series**

Tollivers series
Stone, Alan
1 *Tollivers and the mystery of the lost pony* (1967)
2 *Tollivers and the mystery of Pirate Island* (1967)
3 *Tollivers and the mystery of the old jalopy* (1967)

Tom and Jerry series
Lewis, Jean
1 *Tom and Jerry scairdy cat* (1969)
2 *Tom and Jerry under the big top* (1969)

Tom and Lucy series
Hughes, Shirley
see **Lucy and Tom series**

Tom and Molly series
Costa, Nicoletta
see **Molly and Tom series**

Tom and Pippo series
Oxenbury, Helen
1 *Tom and Pippo go shopping* (1988)
2 *Tom and Pippo's day* (1988)
3 *Tom and Pippo in the garden* (1988)
4 *Tom and Pippo go for a walk* (1988)
5 *Tom and Pippo make a mess* (1988)
6 *Tom and Pippo read a story* (1988)
7 *Tom and Pippo see the moon* (1988)
8 *Tom and Pippo and the washing machine* (1988)
9 *Pippo gets lost* (1989)
10 *Tom and Pippo and the dog* (1989)
11 *Tom and Pippo in the snow* (1989)
12 *Tom and Pippo make a friend* (1989)

Tom and Sally series
Lynam, Terence
see **Sally and Tom series**

Tom and Sam series
Hutchins, Pat
1 *Tom and Sam* (1968)
2 *Happy birthday, Sam* (1978)

Tom Anderson series
Southworth, Louis
see **Inspector Tom Anderson series**

Tom Aragon series
Millar, Margaret
1 *Ask for me tomorrow* (1976)
2 *Murder of Miranda* (1979)
3 *Mermaid* (1982)

Tom Barber trilogy
Reid, Forrest
1 *Young Tom* (1944)
2 *Retreat* (1936)
3 *Uncle Stephen* (1931)

Tom Barnes series
Runyan, John
1 *Tom Barnes and the substitute second baseman* (1964)
2 *Tom Barnes and the blocking back* (1966)
3 *Tom Barnes, forward* (1968)

Tom Bloch series
Elkon, Jon
1 *Umfaan's heroes* (1988)
2 *Laszlo's millions* (1991)

Tom Brown series
Hughes, Thomas
1 *Tom Brown's schooldays* (1857)
2 *Tom Brown at Oxford* (1861)

Tom Buchanan series
Ward, Jonas
This pseudonym is used by William Ard, William Robert Cox and Brian Wynne Garfield as indicated against each title
1 *Name's Buchanan* (1956)
[Ard]
2 *Buchanan says no* (1957)
[Ard]
3 *Buchanan gets mad* (1958)
[Ard]
4 *One-man massacre* (1958)
[Ard]
5 *Buchanan's revenge* (1960)
[Ard]
6 *Buchanan on the prod* (1960)
[Ard]; completed by Robert Silverberg after Ard's death
7 *Buchanan's gun* (1968)
[Garfield]
8 *Buchanan gets tough* (1969)
[Garfield]
9 *Buchanan's war* (1970)
[Cox]
10 *Trap for Buchanan* (1971)
[Cox]
11 *Buchanan's gamble* (1972)
[Cox]
12 *Buchanan's siege* (1972)
[Cox]
13 *Buchanan on the run* (1973)
[Cox]
14 *Get Buchanan!* (1974)
[Cox]
15 *Buchanan takes over* (1974)
[Cox]
16 *Buchanan calls the shots* (1975)
[Cox]
17 *Buchanan's big showdown* (1975)
[Cox]
18 *Buchanan's Texas treasure* (1976)
[Cox]
19 *Buchanan's stolen railway* (1977)
[Cox]
20 *Buchanan's manhunt* (1978)
[Cox]
21 *Buchanan's range war* (1979)
[Cox]
22 *Buchanan's big fight* (1980)
[Cox]
23 *Buchanan's black sheep* (1985)
[Cox]
24 *Buchanan's stage line* (1986)
[Cox]

Tom Burton and Trevor Nichols series
Peters, Geoffrey
see **Inspector Trevor Nichols and Sergeant Tom Burton series**

Tom Carey trilogy
Greenfield, Irving A
1 *Carey blood* (1972)
2 *Carey's vengeance* (1972)
3 *Carey gun* (1974)

Tom Caxton series
Brissenden, Robert Francis
1 *Poor boy* (1987)
2 *Wildcat* (1991)

Tom Conroy series
Ames, Francis Herbert
see **Callahan series**

Tom Cook series
Tomlinson, Paul Greene
1 *Tom Cook and the German spy* (1917)
2 *Tom Cook and the German air fleet* (1918)
3 *Tom Cook's brother in the trenches* (1918)
4 *Tom Cook and the winged messenger* (1919)

Tom Corbett series
Rockwell, Carey
1 *Stand by for Mars!* (1952)
2 *Danger in deep space* (1953)
3 *On the trail of the space pirates* (1953)
4 *Space pioneers* (1953)
5 *Revolt on Venus* (1954)
6 *Treachery in outer space* (1954)
7 *Sabotage in space* (1955)
8 *Robot rocket* (1956)

Tom Cotter and Inspector Keats series
Long, Martin
see **Inspector Keats and Tom Cotter series**

Tom Craig series
Van Urk, Virginia
1 *Speaking of murder* (1951)
2 *Grounds for murder* (1958)

Tom English series
Broome, H B
1 *Meanest man in West Texas* (1985)
2 *Gunfighters* (1987)
3 *Man who had enemies* (1988)
4 *Violent summer* (1990)
5 *Dark winter* (1991)
6 *Gambler's luck* (1993)

Tom Fairfield series
Chapman, Allen
1 *Tom Fairfield's school days* (1913)
Alternative title: The chums at Elmwood Hall
2 *Tom Fairfield at sea* (1913)
Alternative title: The wreck of the Silver Star
3 *Tom Fairfield in camp* (1913)
Alternative title: The secret of the old mill
4 *Tom Fairfield's pluck and luck* (1913)
Alternative title: Working to clear his name
5 *Tom Fairfield's hunting trip* (1916)

Tom Furness series
Cottenham, Mark Pepys
1 *All out* (1932)
2 *Sicilain circuit* (1933)

Tom Galletin series
Parker, F M
1 *Highbinders* (1986)
2 *Shanghaiers* (1987)

Tom Goane series
Nolan, Christopher
see **Journals of Tom Goane series**

Tom Hickey trilogy
Kuhlken, Ken
1 *Loud adios* (1991)
2 *Venus deal* (1993)
3 *Angel gang* (1994)

Tom Holder trilogy
Wilson, Trevor Edward
see **Big Tom Holder trilogy**

Tom Holiday series
Mortimer, Derek
1 *Goodbye Angel, goodbye Joanne* (1976)
2 *Dankworth's Yard* (1976)

Tom Howard series
Howard, Tom
see **Sergeant Tom Howard series**

Tom Humboldt series
Huddy, Delia
1 *Time piper* (1976)
2 *Humboldt effect* (1982)

Tom Jones series
This sequence has two authors
Fielding, Henry
1 *Tom Jones* (1749)
Coleman, Bob
2 *Later adventures of Tom Jones* (1985)

Tom Kane and Condon series
Jordan, David
1 *Nile green* (1973)
2 *Black account* (1975)
3 *Double red* (1981)

Tom Kincaid series
Cox, William Robert
1 *Hell to pay* (1958)
2 *Murder in Vegas* (1960)
3 *Death on location* (1962)

Tom Kyd series
Harris, Timothy Hyde
1 *Kyd for hire* (1977)
2 *Goodnight and goodbye* (1979)

Tom Langley series
Monmouth, Jack
1 *Donovan case* (1955)
2 *Lonely, lovely lady* (1956)
3 *Sleepy-eyed blonde* (1957)
4 *Lightning over Mayfair* (1958)

Tom Lepski series
Chase, James Hadley
see **Frank Terrell series**

Tom Logan series
Chandler, Edna Walker
1 *Pony rider* (1966)
2 *Secret tunnel* (1967)
3 *Gold nugget* (1967)
4 *Stagecoach driver* (1968)
5 *Talking wire* (1968)
6 *Gold train* (1969)
7 *Cattle cars* (1970)
8 *Circus train* (1971)

Tom Maybridge series
Gill, B M
see **Inspector Tom Maybridge series**

Tom Merry series
Clifford, Martin
1 *Tom Merry and Company of Saint Jim's* (1949)
2 *Secret of the study* (1949)
3 *Rallying round Gussy* (1950)
4 *Scapegrace of Saint Jim's* (1951)
5 *Talbot's secret* (1951)
6 *Tom Merry's secret* (1952)
7 *Tom Merry's rival* (1952)
8 *Man from the past* (1952)
9 *Who ragged Railton?* (1952)
10 *Skimpole's sbapshot* (1952)
11 *Trouble for Trimble* (1952)
12 *D'Arcy in danger* (1952)
13 *D'Arcy on the warpath* (1952)
14 *D'Arcy's disappearance* (1952)
15 *D'Arcy the reformer* (1952)
16 *D'Arcy's day off* (1952)
Companion volumes: *Tom Merry's own*, 1952-1955

Tom More series
Percy, Walker
see **Doctor Tom More series**

Tom Pollard series
Lemarchand, Elizabeth
see **Superintendent Tom Pollard series**

Tom Quest series
Striker, Fran
1 *Sign of the spiral* (1947)
2 *Telltale scar* (1947)
3 *Clue of the cypress stump* (1948)
4 *Secret of the lost mesa* (1949)
5 *Hidden stone mystery* (1950)
6 *Secret of Thunder Mountain* (1952)
7 *Inca luck piece* (1955)
8 *Mystery of the timber grant* (1955)

Tom Red Clay trilogy
Ore, Rebecca
1 *Becoming alien* (1988)
2 *Being alien* (1989)
3 *Human to human* (1990)

Tom Ripley series
Highsmith, Patricia
1 *Talented Mister Ripley* (1955)
2 *Ripley under ground* (1970)
3 *Ripley's game* (1974)
4 *Boy who followed Ripley* (1980)

Tom Sawyer series
This sequence has two authors
Twain, Mark
1 *Adventures of Tom Sawyer* (1876)
Tom Sawyer
2 *Adventures of Huckleberry Finn* (1884)
Huckleberry Finn
Comic strip version entitled *The adventures of Huckleberry Finn*, by Clare Dwiggins, 1990
3 *Tom Sawyer abroad* (1894)
4 *Tom Sawyer, detective* (1896)
Short stories
5 *Huck Finn and Tom Sawyer among the Indians, and other unfinished stories* (1983)
Wood, Clement
6 *Tom Sawyer grows up* (1939)

Tom series
Alger, Horatio
see **Tattered Tom series**
Fitzgerald, John Dennis
see **Tom's Great Brain series**
Gree, Alain
see **Little Tom series**

Tom series
Leavy, Una
1 *Tom's garden* (1981)
2 *Shoes for Tom* (1981)

Tom Slade series
Fitzhugh, Percy Keese
1 *Tom Slade, Boy Scout* (1915)
2 *Tom Slade at Temple Camp* (1917)
3 *Tom Slade on the river* (1917)
4 *Tom Slade with the colors* (1918)
5 *Tom Slade on a transport* (1918)
6 *Tom Slade with the boys Over There* (1918)
7 *Tom Slade, motorcycle dispatch bearer* (1918)
8 *Tom Slade with the Flying Corps* (1919)
9 *Tom Slade back home* (1920)
10 *Tom Slade, Scout master* (1920)
11 *Tom Slade at Black Lake* (1921)
12 *Tom Slade on Mystery Trail* (1921)
13 *Tom Slade's double dare* (1922)
14 *Tom Slade on Overlook Mountain* (1923)
15 *Tom Slade picks a winner* (1924)
16 *Tom Slade at Bear Mountain* (1925)
17 *Tom Slade, Forest Ranger* (1926)
18 *Tom Slade in the north woods* (1927)
19 *Tom Slade at Shadow Isle* (1928)
20 *Tom Slade in the haunted cavern* (1929)
21 *Parachute jumper* (1930)

Tom Slattery series
Lawrence, Steven C
1 *Slattery* (1961)
Lynchers
2 *Bullet welcome for Slattery* (1961)
Numbers 1 and 2 originally published as one volume
3 *Walk a narrow trail* (1962)
4 *Noose for Slattery* (1962)
Numbers 3 and 4 originally published as one volume
5 *Longhorns north* (1962)
6 *Slattery's gun says no* (1962)
Numbers 5 and 6 originally published as one volume
7 *North to Montana* (1975)
8 *Slattery stands alone* (1976)
9 *Day of the Comancheros* (1977)

Tom Swift Junior series 1
Appleton, Victor II
This pseudonym is used by John Almquist, William Dougherty, Jim Lawrence, Richard McKenna, Thomas Mulvey, Richard Sklar as indicated against each title
1 *Tom Swift and his flying lab* (1954) [Dougherty]
2 *Tom Swift and his jetmarine* (1954) [Almquist]
3 *Tom Swift and his rocket ship* (1954) [Almquist]
4 *Tom Swift and his giant robot* (1954) [Sklar]
5 *Tom Swift and his atomic earth blaster* (1954) [Lawrence]
6 *Tom Swift and his outpost in space* (1955)
Tom Swift and his sky wheel [Lawrence]
7 *Tom Swift and his diving seacopter* (1956) [Lawrence]
8 *Tom Swift in the caves of nuclear fire* (1956) [Mulvey]
9 *Tom Swift on the phantom satellite* (1957) [Lawrence]
10 *Tom Swift and his ultrasonic cycloplane* (1957) [Lawrence]
11 *Tom Swift and his deep-sea hydrodome* (1958) [Lawrence]
12 *Tom Swift in the race to the moon* (1958) [Lawrence]
13 *Tom Swift and his space solartron* (1954) [Lawrence]
14 *Tom Swift and his electronic retroscope* (1959)
Tom Swift in the jungle of the Mayas [Lawrence]
15 *Tom Swift and his spectromarine selector* (1960)
Tom Swift and the city of gold [Lawrence]
16 *Tom Swift and the cosmic astronauts* (1960) [Lawrence]
17 *Tom Swift and the visitor from Planet X* (1961) [Lawrence]
18 *Tom Swift and the electric hydrolung* (1961) [Lawrence]
19 *Tom Swift and his triphibian atomicar* (1962) [Lawrence]
20 *Tom Swift and his megascope space prober* (1962) [Lawrence]
21 *Tom Swift and the asteroid pirates* (1963) [Lawrence]
22 *Tom Swift and his repelatron skyway* (1963) [Lawrence]
23 *Tom Swift and his aquatomic tracker* (1964) [Lawrence]
24 *Tom Swift and his 3-D telejector* (1964) [Lawrence]
25 *Tom Swift and his polar-ray dynasphere* (1965) [Lawrence]
26 *Tom Swift and his sonic boom trap* (1965) [Lawrence]
27 *Tom Swift and his subocean geotron* (1966) [Lawrence]
28 *Tom Swift and the mystery comet* (1966) [Lawrence]
29 *Tom Swift and the captive planetoid* (1967) [Lawrence]
30 *Tom Swift and his G-force inverter* (1968) [Lawrence]
31 *Tom Swift and the Dyna-4 capsule* (1969) [McKenna]
32 *Tom Swift and his Cosmotron Express* (1970) [McKenna]
33 *Tom Swift and the galaxy ghosts* (1971) [McKenna]

Tom Swift Junior series 2
Appleton, Victor II
This pseudonym is used by Neal Barrett, Sharman DiVono, Mike McQuay, William Rotsler, Robert Edward Vardeman ad indicated against each title
1 *City in the stars* (1981) [Rotsler; DiVono]
2 *Terror on the moons of Jupiter* (1981) [Rotsler; DiVono]
3 *Alien probe* (1981) [Rotsler; DiVono]
4 *War in outer space* (1981) [Rotsler; DiVono]
5 *Astral fortress* (1981) [Rotsler; DiVono]
6 *Rescue mission* (1981) [Rotsler; DiVono]
7 *Ark Two* (1982) [Neal Barrett]
8 *Crater of mystery* (1983) [McQuay]
9 *Gateway to doom* (1983) [Vardeman]

10 *Invisible force* (1983)
[Barrett]
11 *Planet of nightmares* (1984)
[McQuay]

Tom Swift Junior series 3

Appleton, Victor II
This pseudonym is used by several authors including Debra Doyle, Steven Grant, Bill McCay. James Douglas Macdonald, Feargus Gwynplaine Macintyre, whose authorship is indicated against those titles where it is known
1 *Black dragon* (1991)
[McCay]
2 *Negative zone* (1991)
[McCay]
3 *Cyborg kickboxer* (1991)
[Grant]
4 *DNA disaster* (1991)
[Macintyre]
5 *Monster machine* (1991)
[Macdonald; Doyle]
6 *Aquatech warriors* (1991)
[Macdonald; Doyle]
7 *Moonstalker* (1992)
8 *Microbots* (1992)
9 *Fire biker* (1992)
10 *Mind games* (1992)
11 *Mutant beach* (1992)
12 *Death quake* (1993)
13 *Quantum force* (1993)
Companion volumes: *Tom Swift and his airship*, 1992, *Tom Swift and his motor boat*, 1992, *Tom Swift and his motor cycle*, 1992

Tom Swift series

Appleton, Victor
1 *Tom Swift and his motor cycle* (1910)
Alternative title: Fun and adventures on the road
2 *Tom Swift and his motor boat* (1910)
Alternative title: The rivals of Lake Carlopa
3 *Tom Swift and his airship* (1910)
Alternative title: The stirring cruise of the Red Cloud
4 *Tom Swift and his submarine boat* (1910)
Alternative title: Under the ocean for sunken treasure
5 *Tom Swift and his electric runabout* (1910)
Alternative title: The speediest car on the road
6 *Tom Swift and his wireless message* (1911)
Alternative title: The castaways of Earthquake Island
7 *Tom Swift among the diamond makers* (1911)
Alternative title: The secret of Phantom Mountain
8 *Tom Swift in the caves of ice* (1911)
Alternative title: The wreck of the airship
9 *Tom Swift and his sky racer* (1911)
Alternative title: Then quickest flight on record
10 *Tom Swift and his electric rifle* (1911)
Alternative title: Daring adventures in elephant land
11 *Tom Swift in the city of gold* (1912)
Alternative title: Marvelous adventures underground
12 *Tom Swift and his air glider* (1912)
Alternative title: Seeking the platinum treasure
13 *Tom Swift in captivity* (1912)
Alternative title: A daring escape by airship
14 *Tom Swift and his wizard camera* (1912)
Alternative title: The perils of moving picture making
15 *Tom Swift and his great searchlight* (1912)
Alternative title: On the border for Uncle Sam
16 *Tom Swift and his giant cannon* (1913)
Alternative title: The longest shots on record
17 *Tom Swift and his photo telephone* (1914)
Alternative title: The picture that saved a fortune
18 *Tom Swift and his aerial warship* (1915)
Alternative title: The naval terror of the seas
19 *Tom Swift and his big tunnel* (1916)
Alternative title: The hidden city of the Andes
20 *Tom Swift in the land of wonders* (1917)
Alternative title: The underground search for the idol of gold
21 *Tom Swift and his war tank* (1918)
Alternative title: Doing his bit for Uncle Sam
22 *Tom Swift and his air scout* (1919)
Alternative title: Uncle Sam's mastery of the sky
23 *Tom Swift and his undersea search* (1920)
Alternative title: The treasure on the floor of the Atlantic
24 *Tom Swift among the fire fighters* (1921)
Alternative title: Battling with flames from the air
25 *Tom Swift and his electric locomotive* (1922)
Alternative title: Two miles a minute on the rails
26 *Tom Swift and his flying boat* (1923)
Alternative title: The castaways of the giant iceberg
27 *Tom Swift and his great oil gusher* (1924)
Alternative title: The treasure of Goby Farm
28 *Tom Swift and his chest of secrets* (1925)
Alternative title: Tracing the stolen inventions
29 *Tom Swift and his airline express* (1926)
Alternative title: From ocean to ocean by daylight
30 *Tom Swift circling the globe* (1927)
Alternative title: The daring cruise of the Air Monarch
31 *Tom Swift and his talking pictures* (1928)
Alternative title: The greatest invention on record
32 *Tom Swift and his house on wheels* (1929)
Alternative title: A trip to the mountain of mystery
33 *Tom Swift and his big dirigible* (1930)
Alternative title: Adventures over the forest of fire
34 *Tom Swift and his sky train* (1931)
Alternative title: Overland through the clouds
35 *Tom Swift and his giant magnet* (1932)
Alternative title: Bringing up the lost submarine
36 *Tom Swift and his television detector* (1933)
Alternative title: Trailing the secret plotters
37 *Tom Swift and his ocean airport* (1934)
Alternative title: Foiling the Haargolanders
38 *Tony Swift and his planet stone* (1935)
Alternative title: Discovering the secret of another world
39 *Tom Swift and his giant telescope* (1939)
40 *Tom Swift and his magnetic silencer* (1941)

Tom Truxton series

Lounsberry, Lionel
1 *Tom Truxton's school days* (1903)
Fun and mystery at Pickle Academy
2 *Tom Truxton's ocean liner* (1903)
Alternative title: The island of palms

Tom Tufton series

Everett-Green, Evelyn
1 *Tom Tufon's roll* (1898)
2 *Tom Tufton's travels* (1898)

Tom Tyson series

Dowling, Terry
1 *Rynosseros* (1990)
2 *Blue Tyson* (1992)

Tom Vaughan series

Macleod, Alison
1 *Trusted servant* (1968)
Hireling
2 *No need of the sun* (1969)
City of light

Tom Ward series

Farmer, Bernard James
1 *Vanished policeman* (1953)
2 *Policeman's holiday* (1954)
3 *Tom Ward, policeman* (1955)
4 *P.C.Ward lends a hand* (1957)
5 *Policeman's hobby* (1960)

Tomahawk Club series

Church, Richard
1 *Cave* (1950)
Five boys in a cave
The second title is a revised edition
2 *Down river* (1951)

Tomahawk series

Leigh, Roberta
1 *Tomahawk* (1960)
2 *Tomahawk and the river of gold* (1960)
3 *Tomahawk and the tomb of White Moose* (1961)
4 *Tomahawk and the animals of the wild* (1961)

Tomlins series

Anthony, Frank Sheldon
see **Gus Tomlins series**

Tommy and Griff series

Griffiths, John
see **Griff and Tommy series**

Tommy and Tuppence Beresford series

Christie, Agatha
1 *Secret adversary* (1922)
2 *Partners in crime* (1929)
Short stories; part reprinted as *The Sunningdale mystery*, 1933
3 *N or M?* (1941)
Short stories; part reprinted as *The Sunningdale mystery*, 1933
4 *By the pricking of my thumbs* (1968)
5 *Postern of fate* (1973)

Tommy-Anne series

Wright, Mabel Osgood
1 *Tommy-Anne and the three hearts* (1898)
2 *Wabeno, the magician* (1899)

Tommy Briggs series

Macdonald, Donald
1 *Briggs investigates* (1968)
2 *No judges' rules* (1969)
3 *Organizer* (1970)
4 *Ryan affair* (1970)
5 *Two kinds of murder* (1971)
6 *Two bullets for Briggs* (1971)

Tommy Hambledon series

Coles, Manning
1 *Drink to yesterday* (1940)
2 *Pray silence* (1940)
Toast for tomorrow
3 *They tell no tales* (1941)
4 *Without lawful authority* (1943)
5 *Green hazard* (1945)
6 *Fifth man* (1946)
7 *Brother for Hugh* (1947)
With intent to deceive
8 *Let the tiger die* (1947)
9 *Among those absent* (1948)
10 *Not negotiable* (1949)
11 *Diamonds to Amsterdam* (1949)
12 *Dangerous by nature* (1950)
13 *Now or never* (1951)
14 *Night train to Paris* (1952)
15 *Alias Uncle Hugo* (1952)
Operation Manhunt
16 *Knife for the juggler* (1953)
Vengeance man
17 *Not for export* (1954)
All that glitters
Mystery of the stolen plans
18 *Man in the green hat* (1955)
19 *Basle Express* (1956)
20 *Birdwatcher's quarry* (1956)
Three beans
21 *Death of an ambassador* (1957)
22 *No entry* (1958)
23 *Crime in concrete* (1959)
Concrete crime
24 *Nothing to declare* (1960)
Short stories
25 *Search for a sultan* (1961)
26 *House at Pluck's Gutter* (1963)

Tommy Hawke series

Patrick, Michael
1 *Tommy Hawke, detective* (1939)
2 *Tommy Hawke at school* (1940)
3 *Tommy Hawke's third case* (1953)

Tommy Lumb and Peter Marsham series

Cross, Laurence
1 *Dope dealers* (1928)
2 *White chalet* (1929)

Tommy Mac series

Barry, Margaret Stuart
1 *Tommy Mac* (1972)
2 *Tommy Mac battles on* (1974)
3 *Tommy Mac on safari* (1975)

Tommy Malins, Anthony Mornington and George Hawkins series

Dix, Maurice Buxton
1 *Twisted evidence* (1933)
2 *Golden fluid* (1935)
3 *Kidnapped scientist* (1937)
4 *Beacons of death* (1937)

Tommy Niner series

Bradman, Tony
1 *Tommy Niner and planet of danger* (1993)
2 *Tommy Niner and the mystery spaceship* (1994)

Tommy Rankin series

Propper, Milton
1 *Strange disappearance of Mary Young* (1929)
2 *Ticker-tape murder* (1930)
3 *Boudoir murder* (1931)
And then silence
4 *Student fraternity murder* (1932)
Murder of an initiate
5 *Divorce court murder* (1934)
6 *Family burial murders* (1934)
7 *Election booth murder* (1935)
Murder at the polls
8 *One murdered, two dead* (1936)
9 *Great insurance murders* (1937)
10 *Case of the cheating bride* (1938)

11 *Hide the body!* (1939)
12 *Station wagon murder* (1940)
13 *Handwriting on the wall* (1941)
You can't gag the dead
14 *Blood transfusion murders* (1943)
Murders in sequence

Tommy Rostetter series
Campbell, Alice
1 *Click of the gate* (1932)
2 *Desire to kill* (1934)
3 *Flying blind* (1938)
4 *Bloodstained toy* (1948)

Tommy series
Barrie, James Matthew
1 *Sentimental Tommy* (1896)
The story of his boyhood
2 *Tommy and Grizel* (1898)

Tommy series
Burgess, Thornton Waldo
see **Wishing Stone series**

Tommy series
Doyle, Brian
1 *Up to low* (1982)
2 *Angel Square* (1984)
see **Great War, Green front series**

Tommy series
Thatcher, Dora
1 *Tommy the tugboat* (1956)
2 *Tommy joins the navy* (1957)
3 *Tommy gets a medal* (1958)
4 *Ferryboat Tommy* (1959)
5 *Tommy's new engine* (1961)
6 *Tommy and the onion boat* (1962)
7 *Tommy and the lighthouse* (1965)
8 *Tommy and the oil rig* (1967)
9 *Tommy and the Spanish galleon* (1969)
10 *Tommy and the yellow submarine* (1971)
11 *Tommy in the Caribbean* (1974)
12 *Tommy and the island* (1977)

Tommy series
Wolde, Gunilla
see **Thomas series**

Tommy Tad and Polly Wog series
Trick, Edgar Harold
1 *Adventures of Tommy Tad and Polly Wog* (1919)
2 *More adventures of Tommy Tad and Polly Wog* (1919)

Tommy Thorne series
Snow, Charles Horace
1 *Lakeside murder* (1933)
2 *Bonanza murder case* (1934)
3 *Sign of the death circle* (1935)

Tommy Tip Paine series
Batchelor, John Calvin
see **Gordon Liddy is my muse series**

Tommy Tiptop series
Stone, Raymond
1 *Tommy Tiptop and his baseball nine* (1912)
Alternative title: The boys of Riverdale and their good times
2 *Tommy Tiptop and his football eleven* (1912)
Alternative title: A great victory and how it was won
3 *Tommy Tiptop and his winter sports* (1912)
Alternative title: Jolly times on the ice and in camp
4 *Tommy Tiptop and his boat club* (1914)
Alternative title: The young hunters of Hemlock Island
5 *Tommy Tiptop and his boy scouts* (1915)
Alternative title: The doings of the Silver Fox Patrol
6 *Tommy Tiptop and his great show* (1917)
Alternative title: Raising some money that was needed

Tommy Tittlemouse series
Judson, Clara Ingram
1 *Tommy Tittlemouse* (1918)
2 *Garden adventures of Tommy Tittlemouse* (1922)

Tommy Tompkins series
Branston, Frank
1 *Up and coming man* (1977)
2 *Sergeant Ritchie's conscience* (1978)

Tommy Twotoes and Terry Rooke series
Alexander, David
1 *Most men don't kill* (1951)
Corpse in my bed
2 *Murder in black and white* (1951)

Tommy Weston series
Sheridan, Wilfred
1 *Five brains* (1924)
2 *Tommy Weston, adventuress* (1925)

Tommycat, Anna and Paul series
Girard, Nicole
see **Anna, Paul and Tommycat series**

Tomoe Gozen trilogy
Salmonson, Jessica Amanda
1 *Tomoe Gozen* (1981)
2 *Golden Naginata* (1982)
3 *Thousand shrine warrior* (1984)

Tomorrow people series
This sequence has two authors; based on a television series
Gregory, Julian R
1 *Visitor* (1973)
Price, Roger
2 *Three in three* (1974)
3 *Four into three* (1975)
4 *One law* (1976)
5 *Lost gods* (1979)
Also includes *Hitler's last secret*, and *The Thargon menace*

To-morrow will come trilogy
Almedingen, Edith Martha
Autobiography
1 *To-morrow will come* (1941)
2 *Almond tree* (1947)
3 *Within the harbour* (1950)

Tompkins series
Branston, Frank
see **Tommy Tompkins series**
Gamow, George
see **Mister Tompkins series**

Tom's amazing machine trilogy
Snell, Gordon
1 *Tom's amazing machine* (1988)
2 *Tom's amazing machine zaps back* (1989)
3 *Tom's amazing machine takes a trip* (1990)

Tom's Great Brain series
Fitzgerald, John Dennis
1 *Great Brain* (1967)
2 *More adventures of the Great Brain* (1969)
3 *Me and my little brain* (1971)
4 *Great Brain at the Academy* (1972)
5 *Great Brain reform* (1973)
6 *Return of the Great Brain* (1974)
7 *Great Brain does it again* (1975)

Tomten series
Lindgren, Astrid
1 *Tomten* (1961)
Original edition entitled *Tomten*; adapted from a poem by Viktor Rydberg
2 *Fox and the Tomten* (1965)
Original edition entitled *Raaven och Tomten*; adapted from a poem by Karl Eric Forsslund

Tonelli series
Williams, Alexander
see **Detective Sergeant Pietro Tonelli series**

Tong series
Burgess, Eric
see **Harry Tong series**

Toni Redmond and Jill Gardner series
Quin-Harkin, Janet
1 *Ten boy summer* (1982)
2 *Great boy chase* (1985)
3 *Graduates* (1986)
4 *Trouble with Toni* (1986)
5 *Out of love* (1986)
6 *Old friends, new friends* (1986)
7 *Growing pains* (1986)
8 *Best friends forever* (1986)

Tonneman series
Meyers, Maan
see **Pieter Tonneman series**

Tony and Jay series
Hardcastle, Michael
1 *Dive to danger* (1969)
2 *Shilling a mile* (1969)
Walk for us
3 *Stop that car!* (1970)
4 *Reds and Blues* (1970)
5 *Strike!* (1970)
6 *Smashing!* (1970)
7 *Live in the sky* (1971)
8 *Come and get me* (1971)
9 *Shelter* (1971)
10 *Load of trouble* (1971)
11 *It wasn't me* (1971)
12 *Blood money* (1971)

Tony and Melissa series
Byers, Irene
1 *Jewel of the jungle* (1957)
2 *Flowers for Melissa* (1958)
3 *Kennel maid Sally* (1960)

Tony and Mister Collins series
Elwell, Felicia Rosemary
see **Mister Collins and Tony series**

Tony and Pat Pratt series
Lee, Bernie
1 *Murder at Musket Beach* (1990)
2 *Murder without reservation* (1991)
3 *Murder takes two* (1992)

Tony Bevan and Alex Smith series
Forster, Peter
see **Alex Smith and Tony Bevan series**

Tony Carlisle and Guy Laurence series
Dempster, Guy
see **Guy Laurence and Tony Carlisle series**

Tony Carter series
Hume, David
1 *You'll catch your death* (1940)
2 *Never say live!* (1942)
3 *Requiem for rogues* (1942)

Tony Cassella series
Beinhart, Larry
1 *No one rides for free* (1987)
2 *You get what you pay for* (1988)
3 *Foreign exchange* (1991)

Tony Costaine and Bert McCall series
Macneil, Neil
1 *Death takes an option* (1958)
2 *Two guns for hire* (1959)
3 *Third on a seesaw* (1959)
4 *Hot dam* (1960)
5 *Death ride* (1960)
6 *Mexican slay ride* (1962)
7 *Spy catchers* (1966)

Tony Edgwell series
Sidgwick, Ethel
1 *Promise* (1910)
2 *Succession* (1913)
A comedy of the generations

Tony Ellis and Avery Gregg series
Koehler, Robert Portner
see **Avery Gregg and Tony Ellis series**

Tony Fletcher series
Butterworth, William Edmund
1 *Fast green car* (1965)
2 *Return to racing* (1971)

Tony Garrity series
Nixon, Allan
1 *Get Garrity* (1969)
Garrity
2 *Good night, Garrity* (1969)
3 *Go for Garrity* (1970)

Tony Hawkin series
Harrison, Harry
1 *Montezuma's revenge* (1972)
2 *Queen Victoria's revenge* (1974)

Tony Hunter series
Dean, Robert George
1 *Murder makes a merry widow* (1938)
2 *Murder of convenience* (1938)
3 *Murder by marriage* (1940)
4 *Murder through the looking glass* (1940)
5 *Murder in mink* (1941)
6 *On ice* (1942)
7 *Layoff* (1942)
8 *Body was quite cold* (1951)
9 *Case of Joshua Locke* (1951)
10 *Affair at Lover's Leap* (1953)
Death at Lover's Leap

Tony Lantz and Eddie Wright series
Mullen, Clarence
1 *Thereby hangs a corpse* (1946)
2 *Good place for murder* (1948)

Tony Lonto series
Johnson, Emil Richard
1 *Silver Street* (1968)
Silver Street killer
2 *Inside man* (1969)

Tony Quinn series
Jones, G Wayman
see **Black Bat series**

Tony Rome series
Rome, Anthony
1 *Miami mayhem* (1960)
Also published as *Tony Rome*, by Marvin Henry Albert
2 *Lady in cement* (1961)
3 *My kind of game* (1962)

Tony series
Lind, Anton
1 *Tony hits out* (1937)
2 *Tony beats the band* (1938)

Tony series
Martin, Robert
1 *Tony and the champ* (1963)
2 *Tony and the secret money* (1964)

Tony Spencer series
Beeby, Otto
1 *Blank cheque for murder* (1968)
2 *Faceless men* (1969)
3 *No profit in dying* (1970)
4 *Too many innocents* (1972)

Tony Woolrich series
Raison, Milton Michael
1 *Phantom of Forty Second Street* (1936)
Co-author: Jack Harvey
2 *Nobody loves a dead man* (1945)
3 *Gay mortician* (1946)
4 *No weeds for the widow* (1946)
5 *Murder in a lighter vein* (1947)
6 *Tunnel Thirteen* (1948)

Too long a winter series
Hauxwell, Hannah
see **Daleswoman series**

Toodles series
Jackson, Gabrielle Emilie
see **Denise and Ned Toodles series**

Toole series
Wheeler, Richard Seabrook
see **Sheriff Santiago Toole series**

Toosie series
Whitaker, Evelyn
see **Miss Toosie series**

Toot series
Gramatky, Hardie
see **Little Toot series**

Tooting Corner series
Bligh, Eric
Reminiscences
1 *Tooting Corner* (1946)
2 *Faintly smiling mouth* (1961)

Tootleoo series
Darwin, Bernard
see **Mister Tootleoo series**

Tootoo series
Chetham-Strode, Warren
see **Siamese cats series**

Top of the world series
Ruesch, Hans
1 *Top of the world* (1950)
Revised edition 1974
2 *Back to the top of the world* (1973)

Top of the world trilogy
Mowat, Farley
1 *Ordeal by ice* (1960)
2 *Polar passion* (1967)
Revised edition 1973
3 *Tundra* (1973)
Selections from the great accounts of Arctic land voyages

Top-secret Educational Espionage Network series
Lancer, Jack
see **Christopher Cool series**

Tope series
Davis, Howard Charles
see **Edward Tope series**
Williams, Ben Ames
see **Inspector Tope series**

Toplitt series
Stockwell, Gail
see **Kingsley Toplitt series**

Topper series
Smith, Thorne
1 *Topper, an improbable adventure* (1926)
Jovial ghosts
2 *Topper takes a trip* (1932)

Toppin series
Brookins, Dana
see **Bobbie Toppin series**

Topsail series
Duncan, Norman
see **Doctor Luke series**

Topsy and Tim activity series
Adamson, Jean
1 *Topsy and Tim can garden* (1980)
2 *Topsy and Tim can print in colour* (1980)
3 *Topsy and Tim can cook* (1981)
4 *Topsy and Tim can sing and play* (1981)
5 *Topsy and Tim can look after their pets* (1981)
6 *Topsy and Tim can play party games* (1981)
7 *Topsy and Tim can make music* (1982)
8 *Topsy and Tim can help birds* (1982)
9 *Topsy and Tim's chocolate cook book* (1983)

Topsy and Tim board book series
Adamson, Jean
1 *Topsy and Tim's farm day* (1985)
2 *Topsy and Tim's toys* (1985)
3 *Topsy and Tim on the move* (1985)
4 *Topsy and Tim at home* (1985)

Topsy and Tim series
Adamson, Jean
1 *Topsy and Tim's Monday book* (1960)
2 *Topsy and Tim's Tuesday book* (1960)
3 *Topsy and Tim's Wednesday book* (1961)
4 *Topsy and Tim's Thursday book* (1961)
5 *Topsy and Tim's Friday book* (1962)
6 *Topsy and Tim's Saturday book* (1962)
7 *Topsy and Tim's Sunday book* (1962)
8 *Topsy and Tim's foggy day* (1962)
9 *Topsy and Tim's football match* (1963)
10 *Topsy and Tim go fishing* (1963)
11 *Topsy and Tim's bonfire night* (1964)
12 *Topsy and Tim's snowy day* (1964)
13 *Topsy and Tim go on holiday* (1965)
14 *Topsy and Tim at the seaside* (1965)
15 *Topsy and Tim on the farm* (1970)
16 *Topsy and Tim's paddling pool* (1970)
17 *Topsy and Tim's birthday party* (1971)
18 *Topsy and Tim go to hospital* (1971)
19 *Topsy and Tim at the zoo* (1971)
Topsy and Tim go to the zoo
20 *Topsy and Tim at school* (1971)
21 *Topsy and Tim go safely* (1972)
22 *Topsy and Tim go pony-trekkers* (1972)
23 *Topsy and Tim take no risks* (1973)
24 *Topsy and Tim's ups and downs* (1973)
25 *Topsy and Tim go hill walking* (1973)
26 *Topsy and Tim learn to swim* (1973)
27 *Topsy and Tim go sailing* (1973)
28 *Topsy and Tim cross the Channel* (1974)
29 *Topsy and Tim in Belgium* (1974)
30 *Topsy and Tim in Holland* (1974)
31 *Topsy and Tim visit the dentist* (1975)
Topsy and Tim meet the dentist
32 *Topsy and Tim visit the doctor* (1975)
33 *Topsy and Tim's new brother* (1975)
34 *Topsy and Tim at the wedding* (1976)
35 *Topsy and Tim visit the Tower of London* (1976)
36 *Topsy and Tim's pet show* (1976)
37 *Topsy and Tim's new school* (1976)
38 *Topsy and Tim at the circus* (1977)
39 *Topsy and Tim go camping* (1977)
40 *Topsy and Tim go shopping* (1977)
41 *Topsy and Tim's sports day* (1978)
42 *Topsy and Tim at the library* (1978)
43 *Topsy and Tim at the vet* (1978)
44 *Topsy and Tim choose a puppy* (1978)
45 *Topsy and Tim at the fairground* (1978)
46 *Topsy and Tim's school outing* (1978)
47 *Topsy and Tim's picnic* (1978)
48 *Topsy and Tim's train journey* (1978)
49 *Topsy and Tim meet the monsters* (1978)
50 *Topsy and Tim go in an aeroplane* (1979)
51 *Topsy and Tim move house* (1979)
52 *Topsy and Tim at the hairdressers* (1979)
53 *Topsy and Tim have a barbecue* (1979)
54 *Topsy and Tim at the jumble sale* (1979)
55 *Topsy and Tim at the fire station* (1979)
Topsy and Tim meet the firefighters
56 *Topsy and Tim at the pantomime* (1979)
57 *Topsy and Tim's caravan holiday* (1979)
58 *Topsy and Tim go to the doctor* (1982)
59 *Topsy and Tim go to the dentist* (1982)
60 *Topsy and Tim have their eyes tested* (1982)
Topsy and Tim's eye test
61 *Topsy and Tim's new playground* (1982)
62 *Topsy and Tim help the dustman* (1982)
63 *Topsy and Tim's school play* (1982)
64 *Topsy and Tim learn to dance* (1982)
65 *Topsy and Tim go riding* (1983)
66 *Topsy and Tim's new shoes* (1983)
67 *Topsy and Tim visit the supermarket* (1983)
68 *Topsy and Tim visit the police station* (1983)
Topsy and Tim meet the police
69 *Topsy and Tim at the football match* (1983)
70 *Topsy and Tim's playing rhymes* (1984)
71 *Topsy and Tim's garden* (1984)
72 *Topsy and Tim and the babysitter* (1985)
Topsy and Tim meet the babysitter
73 *Topsy and Tim's motorway games* (1985)
74 *Topsy and Tim's new friend* (1985)
75 *Topsy and Tim at the bank* (1985)
76 *Topsy and Tim in the gym* (1985)
77 *Topsy and Tim ride their bikes* (1985)
78 *Topsy and Tim at the safari park* (1986)
79 *Topsy and Tim's coach journey* (1986)
80 *Topsy and Tim learn to horse ride* (1986)
81 *Topsy and Tim at the post office* (1986)
82 *Topsy and Tim at the biscuit factory* (1987)
83 *Topsy and Tim at the TV studio* (1987)
84 *Topsy and Tim stay with a friend* (1987)
85 *Topsy and Tim in the farmyard* (1987)
86 *Topsy and Tim go swimming* (1988)
87 *Topsy and Tim go to the farm* (1988)
88 *Topsy and Tim go to school* (1988)
89 *Topsy and Tim have new shoes* (1989)
90 *Topsy and Tim have their hair cut* (1989)
91 *Topsy and Tim have a birthday party* (1989)
92 *Topsy and Tim have horse riding lessons* (1989)
93 *Topsy and Tim's small pets* (1990)
94 *Topsy and Tim's train journey* (1990)
95 *Topsy and Tim go to the park* (1990)
96 *Topsy and Tim and the new baby* (1992)
97 *Topsy and Tim at the school fair* (1993)
98 *Topsy and Tim at Granny and Grandpa's* (1993)
Omnibus volumes: *Adventures of Topsy and Tim*, 1970, *Topsy and Tim's weekend book*, 1970, *Hello Topsy and Tim*, 1971, *Surprises for Topsy and Tim*, 1971, *Topsy and Tim out and about*, 1974, *Topsy and Tim in Europe*, 1974, *Topsy and Tim's big fun book*, 1983, *The adventures of Topsy and Tim*, 1986

Topsy and Tim's life series
Adamson, Jean
see **Life with Topsy and Tim series**

Topsy series
Herbert, Alan Patrick
1 *Trials of Topsy* (1928)
2 *Topsy, M.P.* (1929)
3 *Topsy turvy* (1947)

Torch series
Allen, Roger Macbride
1 *Torch of honor* (1985)
2 *Rogue powers* (1986)

Torchy series
Ford, Sewell
1 *Torchy* (1911)
2 *Trying out Torchy* (1912)
3 *On with Torchy* (1914)
4 *Torchy, private sec.* (1915)
5 *Wilt thou Torchy* (1917)
6 *House of Torchy* (1918)
7 *Torchy and Vee* (1919)
8 *Torchy as a pa* (1920)

Torchy series
Leigh, Roberta
1 *Torchy in Topsy Turvy Land* (1960)
2 *Torchy and the magic beam* (1960)
3 *Torchy and the twinkling star* (1962)
4 *Torchy and Bossy Boots* (1962)
5 *Torchy and his two best friends* (1962)

Torg series
This sequence has four authors
Slavicsek, Bill
1 *Storm knights* (1990)
Kaufman, Douglas
2 *Dark realm* (1990)
Caspian, Jonatha Ariadne
3 *Nightmare dream* (1991)

Torin trilogy
Wilder, Cherry
1 *Luck of Brin's Five* (1977)
2 *Nearest fire* (1980)
3 *Tapestry warriors* (1983)

Torminster series
Goudge, Elizabeth
1 *City of bells* (1936)
2 *Sister of the angels* (1939)
A Christmas story

Torn series
Edwards, Hank
see **Judge Clay Torn series**

Torn Slater series
Cain, Jackson
1 *Hellbreak country* (1984)
2 *Savage blood* (1984)

Torn Slater series

3 *Hangman's whip* (1984)
4 *Hell hound* (1984)
5 *Devil's sting* (1985)

Tornor trilogy
Lynn, Elizabeth Anne
see **Chronicles of Tornor trilogy**

Torrent series
Cores, Lucy
see **Captain Andrew Torrent series**

Torres and Garrett
Moore, Arthur
see **Bluestar series**

Torrey series
Wales, Mike
see **Leatherhand series**

Torreyton series
Charles, Ernest F
see **Dick Torreyton series**

Torridons series
Muir, Marie
1 *Torridons' triumph* (1960)
2 *Torridons' surprise* (1961)
3 *Torridons in Spain* (1962)
4 *Torridons in trouble* (1963)

Torris series
Braenne, Berit
1 *Boy of the mountains* (1967)
Torris, the boy from Broad Valley
Original edition entitled *Torris, gutten fra Storlidalen*
2 *Reindeer boy* (1972)
Original edition entitled *Torris og Fjellvind*

Torry series
Gardner, John Edmund
see **Detective Inspector Derek Torry series**

Tortilla Joe and Buckshot McKee series
Floren, Lee
see **Buckshot McKee and Tortilla Joe series**

Tortoise and Turtle series
Gendel, Evelyn
1 *Tortoise and Turtle* (1960)
2 *Tortoise and Turtle abroad* (1963)

Tory Baxter series
Blair, Marcia
1 *Final ring* (1978)
2 *Final lie* (1978)
3 *Final pose* (1978)
4 *Final target* (1979)
5 *Final guest* (1979)
6 *Final appointment* (1979)
7 *Final fear* (1979)
8 *Finale* (1980)

Totally hot series
Cooney, Linda A
1 *Losing control* (1991)
2 *Breaking away* (1991)
3 *Standing alone* (1991)
Co-author: Kevin Cooney
4 *Making changes* (1991)
Co-author: Kevin Cooney
5 *Staying cool* (1992)
6 *Playing games* (1992)

Totem series
Harris, Christie
American Indian legends
1 *Once upon a totem* (1963)
2 *Once more upon a totem* (1973)

Toto series
Richards, Laura Elizabeth
1 *Joyous story of Toto* (1885)
2 *Toto's merry winter* (1887)

Toto's tales series
Rolfe, Frederick William
1 *Stories Toto told me* (1898)
2 *In his own image* (1901)

Tots series
Cunliffe, John Arthur
Based on a television series
1 *Tots and the windy day* (1993)
2 *Tots and the curly-tail piglets* (1994)
3 *Tots and the hedgehog* (1994)

Tottenham Hotspur Football Club series
Holland, Julian
1 *Spurs* (1955)
2 *Spurs, the double* (1961)

Toucan Tecs series
Laird, Elizabeth
1 *Grand ostrich ball* (1989)
2 *Arctic blues* (1989)
3 *Gopher gold* (1989)
4 *High flyers* (1989)
5 *Going cuckoo* (1989)
6 *Fine feathered friends* (1989)
7 *Kookaburra cackles* (1989)
8 *Peacock Palace scoop* (1989)
9 *Highland fling* (1991)
10 *Big drip* (1991)
11 *Desert island ducks* (1991)
12 *Snail's tale* (1991)

Touch of laughter series
Sinden, Donald
Autobiography
1 *Touch of the memoirs* (1982)
2 *Laughter in the second act* (1985)

Touch series
Gordon, Jeffie Ross
1 *Touch of genius* (1986)
2 *Touch of magic* (1987)

Touchfeather series
Sangster, Jimmy
see **Katy Touchfeather series**

Touchwood series
Mackenzie, Compton
see **John Touchwood series**

Tough issues for teens series
Sanders, Bill
1 *Stand tall* (1992)
Learning to really love yourself
2 *Stand up* (1993)
Making peer pressure work for you

Tough questions series
Baldwin, Stan
1 *Tough questions boys ask* (1972)
2 *Tough questions girls ask* (1972)

Toughboy sertiies
Hill, Kirkpatrick
1 *Toughboy and sister* (1990)
2 *Winter camp* (1993)

Toussaint Moore series
Lacy, Ed
1 *Room to swing* (1957)
2 *Moment of untruth* (1964)

Tower and Galt series
France, Victor
see **Oliver Galt and Hugo Tower series**

Tower family series
Willard, Barbara
1 *Family Tower* (1968)
2 *Toppling Towers* (1969)

Tower prisoners series
Birt, David
1 *Sir Thomas More* (1982)
2 *Sir Walter Raleigh* (1983)

Tower topics series
Birt, David
1 *Prisoner's life in the Tower* (1983)
2 *Torture in the Tower* (1983)
3 *Traitors in the Tower* (1983)

Town mouse and country mouse series
Hayes, Barbara
1 *Annabel visits the country* (1986)
2 *Up, up and away* (1986)
3 *Flora goes to town* (1986)
4 *Adventures on the water* (1986)

Town series
Graham, Lorenz
Novels of racism in the United States
1 *South town* (1958)
2 *North town* (1965)
3 *Whose town?* (1969)
4 *Return to South town* (1976)

Townley and Newman series
Bearshaw, Brian
see **Superintendent Robert Townley and Sergeant Roger Newman series**

Townsend series
Gordon, Fritz
see **Schuyler Townsend series**

Townshend series
Cobban, James Maclaren
see **Mister Townshend series**

Towser series
Ross, Tony
1 *Towser and Sadie's birthday* (1984)
2 *Towser and the terrible thing* (1984)
3 *Towser and the water rats* (1984)
4 *Towser and the haunted house* (1985)
5 *Towser and the funny face* (1987)
6 *Towser and the magic apple* (1987)

Toy box tale series
Bruna, Dick
1 *Apple* (1953)
Happy apple
Original edition entitled De appel; the second title is a revised edition
2 *King* (1955)
Original edition entitled *De kleine koning*, revised edition entitled *De Koning*, 1962
3 *Tilly and Tessa* (1959)
Original edition entitled *Fien en Pien*
4 *Little Bird* (1959)
Little Bird Tweet
Original edition entitled *Het vogeltje*
5 *Kitten Nell* (1959)
Pussy Nell
Original edition entitled *Poesje Nel*
6 *Circus* (1962)
Original edition entitled *Circus*
7 *Egg* (1962)
Original edition entitled *Het ei*
8 *Fish* (1962)
Original edition entitled *De vis*
9 *Sailor* (1964)
Original edition entitled *De matroos*
10 *School* (1964)
Original edition entitled De school

Toy series
Clapton, Patricia
1 *Toy* (1968)
2 *Truffles for Toy* (1971)

Toyland series
Blyton, Enid
see **Noddy series**

Toymakers series
Williams, Ursula Moray
1 *Three toymakers* (1945)
Revised edition 1970
2 *Malkin's mountain* (1948)
Revised edition 1970
3 *Toymaker's daughter* (1968)

Toytown series
Beaman, Sydney George Hulme
1 *Road to Toytown* (1925)
2 *Jerry and Joe* (1925)
3 *Trouble in Toyland* (1925)
4 *Wooden knight* (1925)
5 *Tale of the magician* (1928)
6 *Tales of the inventor* (1928)
7 *Tale of Captain Brass, the pirate* (1928)
8 *Tales of Toytown* (1928)
Ernest the policeman
9 *John Trusty* (1929)
10 *Wireless in Toytown* (1930)
11 *Toytown book* (1930)
12 *Toytown mystery* (1932)
13 *Mayor's sea voyage* (1938)
14 *Stories from Toytown* (1938)
15 *Arkville dragon* (1938)
16 *Dirty work at the Dog and Whistle* (1942)
17 *Tea for two* (1942)
18 *Brave deed of Ernest the policeman* (1942)
Ernest the brave
19 *Pistols for two* (1942)
20 *Mister Noah's holiday* (1942)
21 *Frightfulness in the Theatre Royal* (1943)
22 *Dreadful doings in Ark Street* (1943)
23 *Golf, Toytown rules* (1943)
24 *Mister Growser moves* (1943)
Mister Growser moves house
25 *Larry the lamb* (1946)
26 *Extraordingary affair of Ernest the policeman* (1947)
27 *Portrait of the mayor* (1947)
28 *Disgraceful business at Mrs Goose's* (1958)
Co-author: Betty Hulme Beaman
29 *Enchanted ark* (1958)
Co-author: Betty Hulme Beaman
30 *Toytown goes west* (1958)
Co-author: Betty Hulme Beaman
31 *Theatre Royal and Punch and Judy* (1958)
Co-author: Betty Hulme Beaman
32 *Toytown Christmas party* (1958)
33 *Toytown treasure* (1961)
Co-author: Betty Hulme Beaman
34 *Larry the plumber* (1961)
Co-author: Betty Hulme Beaman
35 *Conversion of Mrs Growser* (1961)
36 *Great Toytown war* (1961)
37 *How the radio came to Toytown* (1961)
38 *Showing up of Larry the lamb* (1963)
39 *Toytown pantomime* (1963)
40 *Book of Toytown and Larry the lamb* (1979)
41 *Toytown and Larry the Lamb* (1985)

Trace family trilogy
Selby, John
1 *Elegant journey* (1944)
2 *Island in the corn* (1942)
3 *Starbuck* (1943)

Trace Tracy series
Murphy, Warren Burton
see **Devlin Tracy series**

Tracey series
Judd, Frances K
see **Kay Tracey series**

Track series
Ahern, Jerry
see **Dan Track series**

Track series
Bishop, Samuel P
1 *Track* (1986)
2 *Partners in death* (1986)
3 *Apache gold* (1988)

Tracker series
Bensen, Donald R
see **Cole Brandon series**

Tracker series
Cutter, Tom
1 *Winning hand* (1983)
2 *Lincoln County* (1983)
3 *Blue Cut job* (1983)
4 *Chinatown chance* (1983)
5 *Oklahoma score* (1985)
6 *Barbary Coast Tong* (1985)
7 *Huntsville breakout* (1985)

Tracker series
Stillman, Ron
1 *Tracker* (1990)
2 *Green lightning* (1990)
3 *Blood money* (1991)
4 *Black phantom* (1991)
5 *Firekill* (1991)
6 *Death hunt* (1991)
7 *Shock treatment* (1992)
8 *Dynasty of evil* (1992)

Tractors of Thomson's Yard series
Maisner, Heather
1 *Jack and the combine* (1986)
2 *Sam for sale* (1986)
3 *Kate and the cutter* (1986)
4 *Rufus to the rescue* (1986)

Tracy cartoon series
Gould, Chester
see **Dick Tracy cartoon series**

Tracy Chipp series
Thiele, Colin
1 *Shatterbelt* (1989)
2 *Aftershock!* (1992)

Tracy film series
Collins, Max Allan
see **Dick Tracy film series**

Tracy Larrimore and Mike Thompson series
Paull, Jessica
see **Passport to danger series**

Tracy Scott series
Kirby, Jean
see **Scott sisters series**

Tracy series
Ashbrook, Harriette
see **Philip Tracy series**
Collins, Max Allan
see **Dick Tracy series**
Fraser, Alex
see **Inspector Noel Tracy series**
Wallace, Trevor
see **John Tracy series**

Tradd family series
Ripley, Alexandra
see **Charleston series**

Trafford series
Trowbridge, John Townsend
see **Toby Trafford series**

Tragg series
Adams, Clifton
1 *Oceola Kid* (1963)
Originally published under the pseudonym Clay Randall
2 *Tragg's choice* (1969)

Tragic life series
Fisher, Vardis
1 *In tragic life* (1932)
I see no sin
2 *Passions spin the plot* (1934)
3 *We are betrayed* (1935)
4 *No villain need be* (1936)

Trail blazers series
This sequence has three authors
Forbes-Lindsey, Charles Harcourt
1 *Captain John Smith* (1907)
2 *Daniel Boone, backwoodsman* (1908)
Allen, Charles Fletcher
3 *David Crockett, scout* (1911)
Sabin, Edward Legrand
4 *With Carson and Fremont* (1912)
5 *On the Plains with Custer* (1913)
6 *Buffalo Bill and the Overland Trail* (1914)
7 *Gold seeker of '49* (1915)
8 *With Sam Houston in Texas* (1916)
9 *Opening the West with Lewis and Clark* (1917)
10 *General Crook and the fighting Apaches* (1918)
11 *Lost with Lieutenant Pike* (1919)
12 *Into Mexico with General Scott* (1920)
13 *With George Washington into the West* (1924)
14 *In the ranks of Old Hickory* (1927)
15 *Mississippi river boy* (1932)

Trail drive series
Compton, Ralph
1 *Goodnight Trail* (1992)
2 *Western Trail* (1992)
3 *Chisholm Trail* (1993)
4 *Bandara Trail* (1993)

Trail series
Armstrong, Anthony
see **Jimmie Rezaire series**

Trail series
Verrill, Alpheus Hyatt
1 *Trail of the cloven foot* (1918)
2 *Trail of the white Indians* (1920)

Trail sinister series
Delmer, Sefton
Autobiography
1 *Trail sinister* (1961)
2 *Black boomerang* (1962)

Trailer series
Wirt, Mildred Augustine
1 *Runaway caravan* (1937)
2 *Crimson cruiser* (1937)
3 *Timbered treasure* (1937)
4 *Phantom trailer* (1938)

Trailers series
Altsheler, Joseph Alexander
1 *Young trailers* (1907)
2 *Forest runners* (1908)
3 *Free rangers* (1909)
4 *Riflemen of Ohio* (1910)
5 *Scouts of the valley* (1911)
6 *Border watch* (1912)
7 *Keepers of the trail* (1916)
8 *Eyes of the woods* (1916)

Trailsman series
Sharpe, Jon
1 *Seven wagons west* (1980)
2 *Hanging trail* (1980)
3 *Mountain man kill* (1980)
4 *Sundown searchers* (1980)
5 *River raiders* (1981)
6 *Dakota wild* (1981)
7 *Wolf country* (1981)
8 *Six gun drive* (1981)
9 *Dead man's saddle* (1982)
10 *Slave hunter* (1982)
11 *Montana maiden* (1982)
12 *Condor Pass* (1982)
13 *Blood chase* (1983)
14 *Arrowhead territory* (1983)
15 *Stalking horse* (1983)
16 *Savage shadow* (1983)
17 *Ride the wild shadow* (1983)
18 *Cry the Cheyenne* (1983)
19 *Spoon River stud* (1983)
20 *Judas killer* (1983)
21 *Whiskey guns* (1983)
22 *Border arrows* (1983)
23 *Comstock killers* (1983)
24 *Twisted noose* (1983)
25 *Maverick maiden* (1984)
26 *Warpaint rifles* (1984)
27 *Bloody heritage* (1984)
28 *Hostage trail* (1984)
29 *High mountain guns* (1984)
30 *White savage* (1984)
31 *Six-gun sombreros* (1984)
32 *Apache gold* (1984)
33 *Red River revenge* (1984)
34 *Sharpe's justice* (1984)
35 *Kiowa kill* (1984)
36 *Badge* (1984)
37 *Valley of death* (1985)
38 *Lost patrol* (1985)
39 *Tomahawk revenge* (1985)
40 *Grizzly man* (1985)
41 *Range killers* (1985)
42 *Renegade command* (1985)
43 *Mesquite manhunt* (1985)
44 *Scorpion trail* (1985)
45 *Killer caravan* (1985)
46 *Hell town* (1985)
47 *Six-gun salvation* (1985)
48 *White hell trail* (1985)
49 *Swamp slayers* (1986)
50 *Blood oath* (1986)
51 *Sioux captive* (1986)
52 *Posse from hell* (1986)
53 *Longhorn guns* (1986)
54 *Killer clan* (1986)
55 *Thief River showdown* (1986)
56 *Guns of Hungry Horse* (1986)
57 *Fortune riders* (1986)
58 *Slaughter express* (1986)
59 *Thunderhawk* (1986)
60 *Wayward lassie* (1986)
61 *Bullet caravan* (1987)
62 *Horsethief Crossing* (1987)
63 *Stagecoach to hell* (1987)
64 *Fargo's woman* (1987)
65 *River kill* (1987)
66 *Treachery Pass* (1987)
67 *Manitoba marauders* (1987)
68 *Trapper rampage* (1987)
69 *Confederate challenge* (1987)
70 *Hostage arrows* (1987)
71 *Renegade rebellion* (1987)
72 *Calico kill* (1987)
73 *Santa Fe slaughter* (1988)
74 *White hell* (1988)
75 *Colorado robber* (1988)
76 *Wildcat wagon* (1988)
77 *Devil's den* (1988)
78 *Minnesota massacre* (1988)
79 *Smoky hell trail* (1988)
80 *Blood Pass* (1988)
81 *Twisted trails* (1988)
82 *Mescalero mask* (1988)
83 *Dead man's forest* (1988)
84 *Utah slaughter* (1988)
85 *Call of the White Wolf* (1989)
86 *Texas hell country* (1989)
87 *Brothel bullets* (1989)
88 *Mexican massacre* (1989)
89 *Target Conestoga* (1989)
90 *Mesabi huntdown* (1989)
91 *Cave of death* (1989)
92 *Death's caravan* (1989)
93 *Texas train* (1989)
94 *Desperate dispatch* (1989)
95 *Cry revenge* (1989)
96 *Buzzard's Gap* (1989)
97 *Queen' high bid* (1990)
98 *Desert desperadoes* (1990)
99 *Camp Saint Lucifer* (1990)
100 *Riverboat gold* (1990)
101 *Shoshoni spirits* (1990)
102 *Coronado killers* (1990)
103 *Secret sixguns* (1990)
104 *Comanche crossing* (1990)
105 *Black Hills blood* (1990)
106 *Sierra shootout* (1990)
107 *Gunsmoke Gulch* (1990)
108 *Pawnee bargain* (1990)
109 *Lone Star lightning* (1991)
110 *Counterfeit cargo* (1991)
111 *Blood Canyon* (1991)
112 *Doomsday warriors* (1991)
113 *Southern belles* (1991)
114 *Tamarind trail* (1991)
115 *Gold mine madness* (1991)
116 *Kansas kill* (1991)
117 *Gun Valley* (1991)
118 *Arizona slaughter* (1991)
119 *Renegade rifles* (1991)
120 *Wyoming manhunt* (1991)
121 *Redwood revenge* (1992)
122 *Gold fever* (1992)
123 *Desert death* (1992)
124 *Colorado quarry* (1992)
125 *Blood prairie* (1992)
126 *Coins of death* (1992)
127 *Nevada warpath* (1992)
128 *River butcher* (1992)
129 *Silver Maria* (1992)
130 *Montana fire smoke* (1992)
131 *Beartown bloodshed* (1992)
132 *Kentucky colts* (1992)
133 *Sage River conspiracy* (1993)
134 *Cougar dawn* (1993)
135 *Montana mayhem* (1993)
136 *Texas triggers* (1993)
137 *Moon Lake massacre* (1993)
138 *Silver fury* (1993)
139 *Buffalo guns* (1993)
140 *Killing corridor* (1993)
141 *Tomahawk justice* (1993)
142 *Golden bullets* (1993)
143 *Deathblow trail* (1993)
144 *Abeline ambush* (1993)
145 *Cheyenne crossing* (1994)
146 *Nebraska nightmare* (1994)
147 *Death trails* (1994)
148 *California quarry* (1994)
149 *Springfield sharpshooters* (1994)
150 *Savage guns* (1994)
151 *Cowheart's revenge* (1994)
152 *Prairie fire* (1994)
153 *Saguaro showdown* (1994)
154 *Ambush at Skull Pass* (1994)
155 *Oklahoma ordeal* (1994)
156 *Sawdust trail* (1994)

Train series
Fischer, Bruno
see **Rick Train series**

Train to nowhere series
Leslie, Anita
Autobiography
1 *Train to nowhere* (1948)
2 *Story half told* (1983)
A wartime autobiography
3 *Gilt and the gingerbread* (1981)

Trainmasters series
Croft, Jesse Taylor
1 *Trainmasters* (1988)
2 *Railroad war* (1989)

Trakker series
Dunn, Roger
see **Matty Trakker series**

Tramont family series
Barclay, Tessa
1 *Wine widow* (1985)
2 *Champagne girls* (1986)
3 *Last heiress* (1987)

Tramp-Royal series
Marshall, Matt
1 *Tramp-Royal on the Toby* (1933)
The true history of his earlier adventures on the road in Wales and England and his later wanderings in Galloway
2 *Travels of Tramp-Royal* (1932)
The account of his two journeys afoot through the wild Highlands of Scotland and the isles of Skye and Mull
3 *Tramp-Royal in Spain* (1935)

Tramp series
Twain, Mark
1 *Tramp abroad* (1880)
2 *Following the Equator* (1897)
More Tramps abroad

Transformers series
Morris, Dave
1 *Dinobot war* (1985)
2 *Peril from the stars* (1985)
3 *Highway clash* (1986)
4 *Island of fear* (1986)

Transgressor series
Farson, Negley
Autobiography
1 *Way of a transgressor* (1935)
2 *Transgressor in the tropics* (1937)
3 *Mirror for Narcissus* (1956)

Transition series
Barkin, Carol
1 *Are we still best friends?* (1975)
2 *Doing things together* (1975)
3 *I'd rather stay home* (1975)
4 *Sometimes I hate school* (1975)

Transylvania series
Jokai, Mor
see **Michael Apafi series**

Trant series
Downing, John Hyatt
see **Anthony Trant series**
Kenyon, James William
see **Peter Trant series**
Patrick, Q
see **Lieutenant Timothy Trant series**

Trantorian Empire trilogy
Asimov, Isaac
1 *Pebble in the sky* (1950)
2 *Stars, like dust* (1951)
Rebellious stars
3 *Currents of space* (1952)
One volume edition entitled *Triangle*, 1961

Trapp family series
Trapp, Maria Augusta von
1 *Story of the Trapp family singers* (1949)
Trapp family singers
Film and musical adaptation entitled *The sound of music*, 1966
2 *Trapp family on wheels* (1959)
Co-author: Ruth Templeton Murdoch

Trapp series
Callison, Brian
see **Captain Edward Trapp series**

Trapper Bill and Clint Wade series
Weddle, Ferris
see **Clint Wade and Trapper Bill series**

Trask and Carver series
Wallingford, Lee
see **Frank Carver and Ginny Trask series**

Trask series
Heron, Jack
see **Jason Trask series**

Trauma 2020 series
Beere, Peter
1 *Urban prey* (1984)
2 *Crucifixion squad* (1984)
3 *Silent slaughter* (1985)

Travel and transport series
Burrell, Roy Eric Charles
1 *Travel and transport by muscle power* (1980)
2 *Travel and transport by machine before 1914* (1980)
3 *Travel and transport in modern times* (1980)

Travel diary series
Dodge, David
1 *How lost was my weekend* (1948)
A greenhorn in Guatemala
2 *How green was my father* (1950)
A sort of travel diary, Mexico to Guatemala
3 *High life in the Andes* (1951)

Travel series
Chase, Ilka
Reminiscences of travel
1 *Carthaginian rose* (1961)
2 *Elephants arrive at half-past five* (1963)
3 *Second spring and two potatoes* (1965)
4 *Fresh from the laundry* (1967)
5 *Varied airs of spring* (1969)
6 *Around the world and other places* (1970)
7 *Worlds apart* (1972)

Travel series
Greene, Carla
1 *Hotel holiday* (1954)
2 *Holiday in a trailer* (1955)
3 *Motor holiday* (1956)
4 *Trip on a train* (1956)
5 *Trip on a plane* (1957)
6 *Trip on a ship* (1958)
7 *Trip to Hawaii* (1959)
8 *Trip on a jet* (1960)
9 *Trip to the zoo* (1962)
10 *Trip on a bus* (1964)
11 *Trip to the aquarium* (1967)

Traveler series
Drumm, D B
This pseudonym is used by Ed Naha and John Shirley as indicated aginst each title
1 *First, you fight* (1984)
[Naha]
2 *Kingdom come* (1984)
[Shirley]
3 *Stalkers* (1984)
[Shirley]
4 *To kill a shadow* (1984)
[Shirley]
5 *Road war* (1985)
[Shirley]
6 *Border war* (1985)
[Shirley]
7 *Road ghost* (1985)
[Naha]
8 *Terminal road* (1986)
[Shirley]
9 *Stalking time* (1986)
[Naha]
10 *Hell on earth* (1986)
[Naha]
11 *Children's crusade* (1987)
[Naha]
12 *Prey* (1987)
[Naha]
13 *Ghost dancers* (1987)
[Naha]

Traveler series
Irvine, Robert Ralstone
see **Moroni Traveler series**

Traveller series
Stark, Freya
Memoirs of travel
1 *Traveller's prelude* (1950)
2 *Beyond Euphrates* (1951)
1928-1933
3 *Coast of innocence* (1953)
1933-1939; one volume abridged edition of numbers 1-3 entitled *The Freya Stark story*, 1953
4 *Dust in the lion's paw* (1961)
1939-1946

Traveller's letters series
Stark, Freya
1 *Furnace of the cup* (1974)
1914-1930
2 *Open door* (1975)
1930-1935
3 *Growth of danger* (1976)
1935-1939
4 *Bridge of the Levant* (1977)
1940-1943
5 *New worlds for old* (1978)
1943-1946

Travelling doctor series
Mair, George Brown
Reminiscences
1 *Doctor goes east* (1957)
2 *Doctor goes north* (1958)
Scotland revisited
3 *Doctor goes west* (1958)
Journey to Brazil
4 *Doctor in Turkey* (1961)

Travelling matchmaker series
Chesney, Marion
1 *Emily goes to Exeter* (1990)
2 *Belinda goes to Bath* (1991)
3 *Penelope goes to Portsmouth* (1991)
4 *Beatrice goes to Brighton* (1991)
5 *Deborah goes to Dover* (1992)

Travers series
Barrington, Pamela
see **Inspector George Travers series**
Bush, Christopher
see **Ludovic Travers series**
Deighton, Barbara
see **Felicity Travers series**
Samuels, Adelaide Florence
see **Dick Travers series; Dick and Daisy Travers series**

Travis McGee series
Macdonald, John Dann
1 *Deep blue goodbye* (1964)
2 *Nightmare in pink* (1964)
3 *Purple place for dying* (1964)
4 *Quick red fox* (1964)
5 *Deadly shade of gold* (1965)
6 *Bright orange for the shroud* (1965)
7 *Darker than amber* (1966)
8 *One fearful yellow eye* (1966)
9 *Pale gray for guilt* (1968)
Pale grey for guilt
10 *Girl in the plain brown wrapper* (1968)
11 *Dress her in indigo* (1969)
12 *Long lavender look* (1970)
13 *Tan and sandy silence* (1971)
14 *Scarlet ruse* (1973)
15 *Turquoise lament* (1973)
16 *Dreadful lemon sky* (1974)
17 *Empty copper sea* (1978)
18 *Green ripper* (1979)
19 *Free fall in crimson* (1981)
20 *Cinnamon skin* (1982)
21 *Lonely silver rain* (1985)
Omnibus volumes: *Three for McGee*, 1967, *McGee*, 1975

Travis series
Jons, Hal
see **Marshal Carl Travis series**

Travis trilogy
Cameron, Lou
see **Doc Travis trilogy**

Treacherous moon series
Blunt, Betty
1 *Treacherous moon* (1984)
2 *Deep ran the river* (1987)
3 *Star sapphire* (1988)

Treadgold series
Weymouth, Anthony
see **Inspector Treadgold series**
Williams, Valentine
see **Mister Treadgold series**

Treason in arms series
Fraser, David
1 *Kiss for the enemy* (1985)
Fortunes of war
2 *Killing times* (1986)
3 *Dragon's teeth* (1987)
4 *Seizure* (1988)
5 *Candle for Judas* (1989)

Treasure hound series
Mooser, Stephen
1 *Case of the slippery sharks* (1988)
2 *Mummy's secret* (1988)
3 *Secret gold mine* (1988)
4 *Secret in the old mansion* (1988)

Treasure Island series
This sequence has five authors; inspired by *Treasure Island*, by Robert Louis Stevenson, 1883
Smith, Arthur Douglas Howden
1 *Porto Bello gold* (1924)
Stevenson, Robert Louis
2 *Treasure Island* (1883)
Calahan, Harold Augustin
3 *Back to Treasure Island* (1936)
Wibberley, Leonard
4 *Flint's Island* (1972)
Llewellyn, Sam
5 *Last will and testament of Robert Louis Stevenson* (1981)

Treasure Seekers series
Nesbit, Edith
see **Bastable family series**

Treasure series
Williams, David
see **Mark Treasure series**

Trebizon series
Digby, Anne
1 *First term at Trebizon* (1978)
2 *Second term at Trebizon* (1979)
3 *Summer term at Trebizon* (1979)
Numbers 1-3 also published in one volume entitled *Rebecca's first year*, 1992
4 *Boy trouble at Trebizon* (1980)
5 *More trouble at Trebizon* (1981)
6 *Tennis term at Trebizon* (1981)
7 *Summer camp at Trebizon* (1982)
8 *Into the Fourth at Trebizon* (1982)
9 *Hockey term at Trebizon* (1984)
10 *Fourth year triumphs at Trebizon* (1985)
11 *Ghostly term at Trebizon* (1990)
12 *Fifth year friendships at Trebizon* (1990)
13 *Secret letters at Trebizon* (1993)

Tredana trilogy
Gregorian, Joyce Ballou
1 *Broken citadel* (1975)
2 *Castledown* (1977)
3 *Great wheel* (1987)

Tredennick series
Sanborn, Ruth Burr
see **Angeline Tredennick series**

Tree of the Folkungs series
Heidenstam, Verner von
1 *Folke Filbyter* (1905)
Original edition entitled *Folke Filbyter*
2 *Bilbo heritage* (1907)
Original edition entitled *Bjelboarfvet*

Tree series
Collins, Max Allan
see **Ms Tree series**
Foley, Craig
see **Hangman series**

Tree Tall series
Evans, Shirlee
1 *Tree Tall and the whiteskins* (1985)

2 *Tree Tall and the horse race* (1986)
3 *Tree Tall to the rescue* (1987)

Treegate family series
Wibberley, Leonard
1 *John Treegate's musket* (1959)
2 *Peter Treegate's war* (1960)
3 *Treegate's raiders* (1962)
4 *Leopard's prey* (1971)
5 *Red pawns* (1973)
6 *Last battle* (1976)

Treehorn series
Heide, Florence Parry
1 *Shrinking of Treehorn* (1971)
2 *Treehorn's treasure* (1981)
Numbers 1-2 also published in one volume entitled *The adventures of Treehorn*, 1983
3 *Treehorn's wish* (1984)
One volume edition entitled *Treehorn times three*, 1992

Treehouse Gang series
Resciniti, Angelo G
1 *Treehouse Gang* (1980)
2 *Treehouse Gang's racing revenge* (1981)

Treelake series
Melville-Ross, Antony
1 *Blindfold* (1978)
2 *Two faces of nemesis* (1979)
3 *Tightrope* (1981)
4 *Trigger* (1982)

Treelake series
Turner, George Reginald
1 *Stranger and afraid* (1961)
2 *Cupboard under the stairs* (1962)
3 *Waste of shame* (1965)
4 *Lame dog man* (1967)

Trees series
Niven, Larry
1 *Integral trees* (1984)
2 *Smoke ring* (1987)

Trees series
Q, John
see **Peter Trees series**

Tregarde series
Lackey, Mercedes
see **Diana Tregarde series**

Tregare series
Busby, Francis Marion
see **Bran Tregare series**

Treherne family series
Charlton, Moyra
1 *Pendellion* (1948)
2 *Wind from Spain* (1950)

Treherne series
Saint Dennis, Madelon
see **Sydney Treherne series**

Trelawney series
Goodchild, George
see **John Trelawney series**
Manuel, Esme
see **Trisha Trelawney series**

Trelawny series
Long, Amelia Reynolds
see **Edward Trelawny series**

Treloar series
Chance, Stephen
see **Septimus Treloar series**
O'Harris, Pixie
see **Poppy Treloar series**

Trelooe series
Greenwood, Walter
1 *So brief the spring* (1952)
2 *What everybody wants* (1954)
3 *Down by the sea* (1956)

Tremain family trilogy
Carmichael, Claire
see **Virtual reality trilogy**

Tremain series
Dengler, Sandy
see **Danile Tremain series**

Tremaine series
Duncan, Francis
see **Mordecai Euripides Tremaine series**

Tremayne series
Mackenzie, Nigel
see **Inspector Charles Tremayne series**

Tremayne's series
Mallory, Clare
see **Merry Arundel series**

Trenchard family series
Walpole, Hugh
1 *Green mirror* (1917)
2 *Young enchanted* (1921)
3 *Dark forest* (1916)

Trent and Lone Eagle series
Bittner, F Rosanne
see **Savage destiny series**

Trent series
Bentley, Edmund Clerihew
see **Philip Trent series**
Berrisford, Judith Mary
see **Sue Trent series**
Kane, Henry
see **Marla Trent series**
Martyn, Wyndham
see **Anthony Trent series**
Owen, Frank
see **Scobee Trent series**
Raymond, Evelyn Hunt
see **Jessica Trent series**
Seifert, Adele
see **Gregory Trent series**

Trenton series
Burton, Anne
see **Richard Trenton series**
Carstairs, John Paddy
see **Garaway Trenton series**
Lyon, Dana
see **Hilda Trenton series**

Tresillian series
Lewis, Harriet
1 *Tresillian Court* (1870)
2 *Guy Tresillian's fate* (1870)

Trethowan series
Barnard, Robert
see **Superintendent Perry Trethowan series**

Trev the truck series
Negus, George
Illustrated by Craig Smith
1 *Trev the truck saves the school bus* (1993)
2 *Trev the truck fights fire* (1993)
3 *Trev the truck hits the highway* (1993)
4 *Trev the truck falls in love* (1993)

Trevarvas family series
Harvey, Marianne
1 *Dark horseman* (1978)
2 *Proud hunter* (1980)
3 *Foxgate* (1982)

Trevellyan and Hope series
Kelly, Susan
see **Alison Hope and Inspector Nick Trevellyan series**

Trevor and Blythe series
Philips, Judson Pentecost
see **Carole Trevor and Max Blythe series**

Trevor Dene series
Williams, Valentine
see **Sergeant Trevor Dene series**

Trevor Lowe series
Verner, Gerald
1 *Phantom Hollow* (1933)
2 *Next to die* (1934)
3 *Lady of doom* (1934)
4 *Hangman* (1934)
5 *Terror tower* (1935)
6 *Watcher* (1936)
7 *Token* (1937)
8 *Three gnomes* (1937)
9 *Glass arrow* (1937)
10 *River house mystery* (1938)
11 *Clue of the green candle* (1938)
12 *Dene of the Secret Service* (1941)
13 *Shadow men* (1962)
14 *Death set in diamonds* (1965)

Trevor Nichols and Tom Burton series
Peters, Geoffrey
see **Inspector Trevor Nichols and Sergeant Tom Burton series**

Trevor series
Lewis, Harriet
see **Edith Trevor series**
Rogers, Alan
see **Clever Trevor series**
West, Marvin
see **Motor Rangers series**

Trevose family series
Gordon, Richard
1 *Facemaker* (1967)
2 *Surgeon at arms* (1968)

Trew twins series
Martin, Robert
1 *Golden elephant* (1959)
2 *Money mystery* (1960)
3 *Secret boat* (1961)

Treynor series
Livingston, Armstrong
see **Jimmy Treynor series**

Triad series
Arvay, Harry
1 *Triad 21* (1977)
2 *Society of fear* (1979)

Triad series
Rohmer, Richard
1 *Periscope red* (1980)
2 *Triad* (1982)

Triad trilogy
Marks, Laurie J
see **Children of Triad trilogy**

Trial of the Time Lord series
This sequence has three authors
Baker, Pip
1 *Terror of the Vervoids* (1987)
2 *Ultimate foe* (1988)
Martin, Philip
3 *Mindwarp* (1989)

Triangulum trilogy
Wallis, Redmond
1 *Starbloom* (1989)
2 *Mills of space* (1989)
Third volume not yet published

Trick series
Corbett, Scott
see **Kerby Maxwell series**

Trickster series
Greenhalgh, Zohra
1 *Contrarywise* (1989)
2 *Trickster's touch* (1989)

Tricotrin series
Merrick, Leonard
see **Parisian series**

Trig series
Peck, Robert Newton
1 *Trig* (1977)
2 *Trig sees red* (1978)
3 *Trig goes ape* (1980)
4 *Trig or treat* (1982)

Trigger Argee and Telzey Amberdon series
Schmitz, James Henry
see **Telzey Amberdon and Trigger Argee series**

Trigger series
Allum, Tom
see **Captain Michael Triggington series**

Triggington series
Allum, Tom
see **Captain Michael Triggington series**

Trigon disunity trilogy
Kube-McDowell, Michael Paul
1 *Emprise* (1985)
2 *Enigma* (1986)
3 *Empery* (1987)

Trilogy of desire
Dreiser, Theodore
see **Frank Cowperwood trilogy**

Trilogy of earth
Giono, Jean
1 *Hill of destiny* (1929)
Original edition entitled *Colline*
2 *Lovers are never losers* (1929)
Original edition entitled *Un de Beaumugnes*
3 *Harvest* (1930)
Original edition entitled *Regain*

Trina series
Braenne, Berit
1 *Trina finds a brother* (1958)
Original edition entitled *Historien om Tamar og Trine*
2 *Little sister Tai-Me* (1959)
Original edition entitled *Tai-Mi, tamars og Trines soster*

Trinidad series
De Boissiere, Ralph
1 *Crown jewel* (1952)
2 *Rum and Coca-Cola* (1956)

Trio series
Montgomery, Raymond A
see **Rebels in the New World series**

Trip Bodley series
McCall, Dan
1 *Bluebird Canyon* (1983)
2 *Triphammer* (1990)

Triple S agent series
Green, Hilary
1 *Woman called Omega* (1984)
2 *Fidelio affair* (1985)

Triple zero eight series
Allison, Clyde
see **Agent triple zero eight series**

Triplets series
Moore, Bertha B
1 *Baer's Christmas* (1938)
2 *Three Baers* (1938)
3 *Triplets in business* (1939)
4 *Triplets go south* (1940)
5 *Triplets over J.O.Y.* (1941)
6 *Triplets go places* (1942)
7 *Triplets sign up* (1943)
8 *Triplets become good neighbors* (1945)
9 *Triplets receive a reward* (1946)
10 *Triplets have an adventure* (1947)
11 *Triplets make a discovery* (1948)
12 *Triplets fly high* (1950)
13 *Triplets go to camp* (1952)
14 *Triplets take over* (1953)
15 *Triplets try television* (1954)

Tripods series
Christopher, John
1 *When the tripods came* (1988)
2 *White mountains* (1967)
3 *City of gold and lead* (1967)
4 *Pool of fire* (1968)
Numbers 2-4 also published in one volume entitled *Tripods trilogy*, 1980

Tripper and Sam series
Robinson, Nancy Konheim
1 *Phantom film crew* (1986)
2 *Danger on the sound track* (1986)
3 *Ghost who wanted to be a star* (1987)

Trisha Trelawney series
Manuel, Esme
1 *Green feather* (1954)
2 *Crimson petal* (1955)

Triumph of time trilogy
Jameson, Storm
1 *Lovely ship* (1927)
2 *Voyage home* (1930)
3 *Richer dust* (1931)
One volume edition entitled *The triumph of time*, 1932

Triumph series
Gann, Ernest Kellogg
1 *Triumph* (1986)
2 *Antagonists* (1970)

Trixie Belden series
This sequence has two authors
Campbell, Julie
1 *Trixie Belden and the secret of the mansion* (1948)
2 *Trixie Belden and the red trailer mystery* (1950)
3 *Trixie Belden and the gatehouse mystery* (1951)
4 *Trixie Belden and the mysterious visitor* (1954)
5 *Trixie Belden and the mystery off Glen Road* (1956)
6 *Trixie Belden and mystery in Arizona* (1958)
Kenny, Kathryn
7 *Trixie Belden and the mysterious code* (1961)
8 *Trixie Belden and the black jacket mystery* (1961)
9 *Trixie Belden and the Happy Valley mystery* (1962)
10 *Trixie Belden and the marshland mystery* (1962)
11 *Trixie Belden and the mystery at Bob-White Cave* (1963)
12 *Trixie Belden and the mystery of the blinking eye* (1963)
13 *Trixie Belden and the mystery on Cobbett's Island* (1964)
14 *Trixie Belden and the mystery of the emeralds* (1965)
15 *Trixie Belden and the mystery on the Mississippi* (1965)
16 *Trixie Belden and the mystery of the missing heiress* (1970)
17 *Trixie Belden and the mystery of the uninvited guest* (1977)
18 *Trixie Belden and the mystery of the phantom grasshopper* (1977)
19 *Trixie Belden and the secret of the unseen treasure* (1977)
20 *Trixie Belden and the mystery off Old Telegraph Road* (1978)
21 *Trixie Belden and the mystery of the castaway children* (1978)
22 *Trixie Belden and the mystery at Mead's Mountain* (1978)
23 *Trixie Belden and the mystery of the queen's necklace* (1979)
24 *Trixie Belden and the mystery at Saratoga* (1979)
25 *Trixie Belden and the Sasquatch mystery* (1979)
26 *Trixie Belden and the mystery of the headless horseman* (1979)
27 *Trixie Belden and the mystery of the ghostly galleon* (1979)
28 *Trixie Belden and the Hudson River mystery* (1979)
29 *Mystery of the velvet gown* (1980)
30 *Trixie Belden and the mystery of the midnight marauder* (1980)
31 *Trixie Belden and the mystery at Maypenny's* (1980)
32 *Trixie Belden and the mystery of the whispering witch* (1980)
33 *Trixie Belden and the mystery of the vanishing victim* (1980)
34 *Trixie Belden and the mystery of the missing millionaire* (1980)

Trixie Dolan and Evangeline Sinclair series
Babson, Marian
1 *Reel murder* (1987)
2 *Encore murder* (1989)

Trocher series
Walker, David Harry
see **Dougal Trocher series**

Troddles series
Andom, R
1 *We three and Troddles* (1894)
A tale of London life
2 *Troddles and us and others* (1901)
3 *Cruise of the Mock Turtle* (1904)
4 *Lighter days with Troddles* (1907)
5 *Four men with a van* (1907)
6 *On tour with Troddles* (1909)
7 *Runaways* (1909)
At school with Troddles
Some early adventures of Troddles and us
8 *Our flat* (1910)
9 *Adrift with Troddles* (1913)
10 *Troddles, not to mention ourselves* (1914)
11 *Troddles' farm* (1914)
12 *Three men and Troddles* (1916)
13 *Same old Troddles* (1919)
A book of laughter
14 *Troddles in the trenches* (1919)
15 *Out and about with Troddles* (1920)
Companion volume: *Neighbours of mine*, 1912

Trog series
Butterworth, Ben
see **That boy Trog series**

Trojan War series
This sequence has two authors; translated from the ancient Greek
Homer
1 *Iliad* (-700)
2 *Odyssey* (-700)
Kazantzakis, Nikos
3 *Odyssey* (1938)
A modern sequel, translated from the modern Greek

Trojan War trilogy
Baker, George
1 *Cry Hylas on the hills* (1945)
2 *Son of Hylas* (1952)
3 *Fidus achates* (1944)
Paris of Troy

Troll and Mole series
Johnston, Tony
see **Mole and Troll series**

Troll series
Ellis, Carol
1 *There's a troll in my closet* (1994)
2 *There's a troll in my popcorn* (1994)
3 *There's a troll in my sleeping bag* (1994)

Troll series
Torgersen, Don Arthur
1 *Troll tales of Tumble Town* (1978)
2 *Troll's three Christmas wishes* (1978)
3 *Troll who lived in the lake* (1979)
4 *Scariest night in Troll Forest* (1979)
5 *Troll who went to school* (1980)
6 *Angry giants of Troll Mountain* (1980)
7 *Wicked witch of the Troll Cave* (1981)
8 *Huff and puff and the troll hole* (1982)
9 *Secret of Cathedral Lake* (1982)
10 *Torrek and the elfin girl* (1982)
11 *Last days of Gorlock the dragon* (1982)

Troop Five series
Thurston, Ida Treadwell
1 *Scout master of Troop Five* (1912)
2 *Billy Burns of Troop Five* (1916)

Trooper Ralph Lindsey series
Benson, Ben
see **Ralph Lindsey series**

Troopers series
Tann, Roger
1 *Flower Power Joe* (1980)
2 *Mac and the caterpillar* (1980)
3 *Maggie in the porridge* (1980)
4 *Six pence for Sam* (1980)

Troot series
Derwent, Lavinia
see **Tammy Troot series**

Tropics series
Miller, Henry
1 *Tropic of Cancer* (1934)
2 *Black spring* (1936)
3 *Tropic of Capricorn* (1939)

Tros of Samothrace series
Mundy, Talbot
1 *Tros of Samothrace* (1934)
Tros
Abridged edition in three volumes 1967
1.1 *Lud of Lunden* (1934)
Tros
1.2 *Avenging Liafail* (1934)
Helma
1 3 *Praetor's dungeon* (1934)
Liafail
1 4 *Helene* (1934)
2 *Queen Cleopatra* (1929)
3 *Purple pirate* (1935)

Trot and Cap'n Bill series
Baum, Lyman Frank
1 *Sea fairies* (1911)
2 *Sky Island* (1912)

Trothe series
Llewellyn, Richard
see **Edmund Trothe series**

Trotsky series
Cliff, Tony
Biography
1 *Towards October, 1879-1917* (1989)
2 *Sword of the Revolution, 1917-1923* (1990)

Trotsky trilogy
Deutscher, Isaac
see **Leon Trotsky trilogy**

Trotter series
Jones, Peter
see **Terry Trotter series**
Keeler, Harry Stephen
see **Tuddleton Trotter series**

Trotter Street series
Hughes, Shirley
see **Tale of Trotter Street series**

Trotter trilogy
Cookson, Catherine
see **Tilly Trotter trilogy**

Trouble series
Harris, Christie
American Indian legends
1 *Trouble with princesses* (1980)
2 *Trouble with adventurers* (1982)

Trouble series
Summers, James Levingston
1 *Girl trouble* (1953)
2 *Prom trouble* (1954)
3 *Trouble on the run* (1956)
4 *Trouble on Hogback Hill* (1960)
5 *Trouble with being in love* (1963)

Trouble with series
Cole, Babette
1 *Trouble with mum* (1983)
Trouble with mom
2 *Trouble with dad* (1986)
3 *Trouble with gran* (1987)
4 *Trouble with grandad* (1988)

Troubles with machines series
Goulart, Ron
1 *Broke down engine and other troubles with machines* (1971)
2 *Nutzenbolts and more troubles with machines* (1975)

Troubleshooters series
Fuller, Ed
1 *Troubleshooters* (1963)
2 *Ransom trail* (1964)
3 *Savage west* (1966)
4 *Violence in the Black Hills* (1968)
5 *Big killing* (1970)

Trout fishing series
Webber, Edmund Godfrey
Humorous reminiscences of New Zealand trout fishing
1 *You should've been here Thursday* (1961)
2 *Try again Friday* (1965)

Trout series
Fraser, Ronald
1 *Visit to Venus* (1958)
2 *Jupiter in the chair* (1958)
3 *Trout's testament* (1960)
4 *City of the sun* (1961)

Trovo series
Lory, Robert
1 *Eyes of Bolsk* (1969)
2 *Master of the Etrax* (1970)

Troy series
Gardner, Alan Harold
see **Davis Troy series**
Roos, Kelley
see **Jeff and Haila Troy series**

Troy Town series
Quiller-Couch, Arthur
1 *Astonishing history of Troy Town* (1888)
2 *Noughts and crosses* (1891)
Stories, studies, sketches
3 *Delectable Duchy* (1893)
Stories, studies, sketches
4 *Wandering Heath* (1895)
Short stories
5 *White wolf, and other fireside tales* (1902)
6 *Mayor of Troy* (1905)
Set during 1804
7 *Corporal Sam, and other stories* (1910)
8 *Brother Copas* (1911)
9 *Hocken and Hunken* (1912)

Troyana series
Meek, Sterner St. Paul
1 *Drums of Tapajos* (1961)
2 *Troyana* (1961)

Trozen series
Carey, D L
see **Dorian Trozen series**

Truckers series
Smith, Guy Newman
1 *Black Knights* (1977)
2 *Hi-Jack!* (1977)

Trudy and Timothy series
Porter, Bertha Currier
1 *Trudy and Timothy* (1917)
2 *Trudy and Timothy out of doors* (1919)
3 *Trudy and Timothy and the trees* (1920)
4 *Trudy and Timothy, foresters* (1922)

Trudy series
Faid, Mary Alice
1 *Trudy takes charge* (1949)
2 *Trudy's island holiday* (1950)
3 *Trudy's uphill road* (1951)
4 *Trudy's college days* (1953)
5 *Schoolma'am Trudy* (1955)
6 *Trudy on her own* (1957)
7 *Trudy's small corner* (1959)
8 *Trudy married* (1961)
9 *Trudy in demand* (1964)

True game trilogy
Tepper, Sheri S
1 *King's blood four* (1983)
2 *Necromancer nine* (1983)
3 *Wizard's eleven* (1984)
One volume edition entitled *The true game*, 1985

True grit trilogy
Ellis, Edward Sylvester
1 *Secret of Coffin Island* (1897)
2 *Dorsey, the young inventor* (1899)
3 *Jim and Joe* (1902)
Two brave boys

True Ted Troop series
Garis, Lilian C
see **Girl Scouts series**

Truelance family series
Brinsmead, Hesba Fay
1 *Longtime passing* (1971)
2 *Longtime dreaming* (1982)

Truelove series
Rodgers, Sherlaw Johnston
see **Micah Truelove series**

Truffles series
Anholt, Catherine
1 *Truffles in trouble* (1987)
2 *Truffles' day in bed* (1987)
Truffles is sick

Trulsa series
Ringner-Lundgren, Ester
see **Little Trulsa series**

Truly series
Drummond, Violet Hilda
see **Miss Anna Truly series**

Truly thankful series
Toye, Francis
Autobiography
1 *For what we have received* (1950)
2 *Truly thankful?* (1957)

Truman Smith series
Crider, Bill
1 *Gator kill* (1992)
2 *When old men die* (1994)

Trump series
Lockwood, Ingersoll
see **Baron Trump series**

Trumpalar series
Bernard-Waite, Judy
1 *Riddle of the Trumpalar* (1981)
2 *Challenge of the Trumpalar* (1986)

Trumpets series
Dallas-Smith, Peter
Illustrated by Peter Cross
1 *Trouble for Trumpets* (1982)
2 *Trumpets in Grumpetland* (1984)

Trumpton series
This sequence has two authors
Dillon, Deidre
1 *Nick Fisher the bill-poster* (1967)
2 *Mrs Cobbit and the ice-cream man* (1967)
3 *Mayor's birthday present* (1968)
4 *Mister Platt and the painter* (1968)
Carruth, Jean
5 *Trouble in the mayor's parlour* (1968)
6 *Ringing up the fire brigade* (1968)
7 *Vanishing ladder* (1970)
8 *Cuthbert's missing auntie* (1970)
Companion volume: *Trumpton story book*, by Moira Maclean, 1968

Truth and democracy trilogy
Capek, Karel
1 *Hordubal* (1933)
Original edition entitled *Hordubal*
2 *Meteor* (1934)
Original edition entitled *Poevtron*
3 *Ordinary life* (1934)
Original edition entitled *Obycejny zivot*

Truxton series
Lounsberry, Lionel
see **Tom Truxton series**

Try series
Clune, Frank
1 *Try anything once* (1933)
Autobiography of a wanderer
2 *Try nothing twice* (1946)
Story of two dozen jobs

Tryggvason series
Sprague, Rosemary
see **King Olaf Tryggvason series**

Trygve Yamamura series
Anderson, Poul
1 *Perish by the sword* (1959)
2 *Murder in black letter* (1960)
3 *Murder bound* (1962)

Tschai series
Vance, Jack
1 *City of the Chasch* (1968)
Chasch
2 *Servants of the Wankh* (1969)
Wankh
3 *Dirdir* (1969)
4 *Pnume* (1970)
One volume edition entitled *The planet of adventure omnibus*, 1985

Tub People series
Conrad, Pam
Illustrated by Richard Egielski
1 *Tub People* (1989)
2 *Tub grandfather* (1993)

Tubbs series
Lofting, Hugh
see **Mrs Tubbs series**

Tubby Green series
Goyne, Richard
see **Ex-Superintendent Tubby Green series**

Tubby Hall series
Hambledon, Phyllis
see **Inspector Tubby Hall series**

Tubby series
Perkins, Al
1 *Tubby and the lantern* (1972)
2 *Tubby and the Poo-Bah* (1974)

Tuck series
Lewis, Lange
see **Lieutenant Richard Tuck series**

Tucker and Harry series
Selden, George
see **Chester Cricket series**

Tucker and Shock series
Buchanan, Patrick
see **Ben Shock and Charity Tucker series**

Tucker family series
Mendel, Jo
1 *Wonderful house* (1961)
2 *Special secret* (1961)
3 *Adventures of Plum Tucker* (1961)
4 *Trouble on Valley View* (1961)
5 *Cottage holiday* (1962)
6 *Tell a tale of Tuckers* (1962)
7 *Here comes a friend* (1963)
8 *Turn-about summer* (1963)
9 *Here come the Tuckers* (1965)
10 *Toby Tucker* (1965)

Tucker, Norrington and Di Ganzarello series
Drummond, Ivor
see **Lady Jennifer, Sandro and Colly series**

Tucker series
Coffey, Brian
see **Mike Tucker series**
Kennedy, Adam
see **Roy Tucker series**

Tucker series
This sequence has two authors; based on a character from the **Grange Hill series**
Leeson, Robert
1 *Forty days of Tucker J* (1983)
Needle, Jan
2 *Tucker's luck* (1984)
3 *Tucker in control* (1985)

Tucker series
Potter, Jerry Allen
see **Sam Tucker series**
Tunis, John Roberts
see **Roy Tucker series**

Tucker twins series
Sampson, Emma
1 *At boarding school with the Tucker twins* (1915)
2 *Vacation with the Tucker twins* (1916)
3 *Back at school with the Tucker twins* (1917)
4 *Tripping with the Tucker twins* (1919)
5 *House party with the Tucker twins* (1921)
6 *In New York with the Tucker twins* (1924)

Tuckonie series
Bingham, Lorna
see **Golden boomerang series**

Tuddleton Trotter series
Keeler, Harry Stephen
1 *Matilda Hunter murder* (1931)
Black satchel
The second title is the English abridged edition
2 *Case of the barking clock* (1947)
Barking clock
Co-author: Hazel Goodwin; the second title is the expanded English edition

Tudor series
Beamish, Noel de Vic
see **Owen Tudor series**

Tudor series
Hyde, Eleanor
1 *Tudor maid* (1972)
2 *Tudor masquerade* (1972)
3 *Tudor mayhem* (1973)
4 *Tudor mystery* (1974)
5 *Tudor myth* (1976)
6 *Tudort murder* (1977)
7 *Tudor mausoleum* (1977)
8 *Tudor mansion* (1978)
9 *Tudor malice* (1979)

Tudor series
King, Betty
1 *Owen Tudor* (1977)
2 *Lady Margaret* (1965)
3 *Lord Jasper* (1967)
4 *King's mother* (1969)

Tudor series
Nash, Anne
see **Mark Tudor series**

Tudor series
Plaidy, Jean
1 *Katharine, the virgin widow* (1961)
2 *Shadow of the pomegranate* (1962)
3 *King's secret matter* (1962)
Numbers 1-3 also published in one volume entitled *Katharine of Aragon*, 1968
4 *Murder most royal* (1949)
King's pleasure
5 *Sixth wife* (1953)
6 *Saint Thomas's Eve* (1954)
7 *Spanish bridegroom* (1954)
8 *Gay Lord Robert* (1955)
9 *Thistle and the Rose* (1963)
10 *Mary, Queen of France* (1964)
11 *Uneasy lies the head* (1982)

Tudor trilogy
Burgess, Mallory
1 *Passion rose* (1987)
2 *Passion fire* (1988)
3 *Passion star* (1988)

Tudor trilogy
Fecher, Constance
see **Ralegh family trilogy**

Tudor trilogy
Moody, Laurence
1 *Dark-eyed client* (1975)
2 *Golden princess* (1976)
3 *Greatest Tudor* (1977)

Tudor trilogy
Prole, Lozania
1 *Ghost that haunted a king* (1963)
2 *Ten-day queen* (1972)
3 *Consort to the Queen* (1959)

Tudors series
Birt, David
1 *Great Cardinal* (1975)
2 *King and Pope* (1975)
3 *Oxford martyrs* (1975)
4 *Drake's world voyage* (1975)
5 *Elizabeth and her court* (1975)
6 *Mary, Queen of Scots* (1975)
7 *Tudor Navy* (1975)
8 *Rogues and vagabonds* (1975)
9 *Elizabethan theatre* (1975)
10 *Tudor London* (1975)
11 *Field of Cloth of Gold* (1975)
12 *Pilgrimage of Grace* (1975)
13 *Nine Days' Queen* (1975)
14 *Raiding and trading* (1975)
15 *To entertain a queen* (1975)
16 *Babington plot* (1975)
17 *Drake and the Spanish Armada* (1975)
18 *London underworld* (1975)
19 *Globe Playhouse* (1975)
20 *Plots and plays* (1975)

Tuesday dogs series
Stoneley, Jack
1 *Tuesday dog* (1978)
2 *Return of the Tuesday dogs* (1979)

Tuffa series
Schroeder, Binette
1 *Tuffa and the picnic* (1983)
2 *Tuffa and the bone* (1983)
3 *Tuffa and her friends* (1983)
4 *Tuffa and the snow* (1983)
5 *Tuffa and the ducks* (1983)

Tufton series
Everett-Green, Evelyn
see **Tom Tufton series**

Tugboat Annie series
Raine, Norman Reilly
1 *Tugboat Annie* (1947)
2 *Glencannon meets Tugboat Annie* (1950)
Co-author: Guy Gilpatric; selections: *Tugboat Annie*, 1977

Tuke series
Browne, Douglas Gordon
see **Mister Harvey Tuke series**

Tula Springs trilogy
Wilcox, James
1 *Modern Baptists* (1984)
2 *North Gladiola* (1985)
3 *Miss Undine's living room* (1987)

Tuldon series
Agnus, Orme
see **Sarah Tuldon series**

Tully and Norris series
Davis, Dorothy Salisbury
see **Mrs Norris and Jasper Tully series**

Tumbleweeds series
Ryan, Tom K
Comic strips
1 *Let 'er rip, Tumbleweeds!* (1967)
2 *Tumbleweeds* (1968)
3 *Tumbleweeds 3* (1970)
4 *Tumbleweeds 4* (1971)
5 *Tumbleweeds 5* (1972)
6 *Hang in there, Tumbleweeds!* (1976)
7 *Tumbleweeds roundup!* (1977)
8 *Ride on, Tumbleweeds!* (1978)
9 *Tumbleweeds and Company* (1979)
10 *Sackside Tumbleweeds* (1980)
11 *Head 'em off, Tumbleweeds!* (1980)
12 *Tumbleweeds express* (1981)
13 *Saddle up, Tumbleweeds* (1982)
14 *Sound off, Tumbleweeds!* (1983)
15 *Tumbleweeds revisited* (1983)
16 *Tumbleweeds country* (1984)
17 *Tumbleweeds buckaroo* (1985)
18 *Tumbleweeds wild West* (1986)
19 *Tumbleweeds rodeo!* (1987)
20 *Tumbleweeds corral* (1987)

Tumpy series
Blyton, Enid
see **Mister Tumpy series**

Tumtwit series
Mallett, Jerry J
Co-author of numbers 1-5: Marian R Nartch
1 *First and last Gravelsburg School spelling bee* (1986)
2 *Bellyful of ballet!* (1986)
3 *Close curtains* (1986)
4 *Goodbye to Camp Crumb* (1986)
5 *On your mark, get set, HELP!* (1986)
Co-author of numbers 6 and 7: Timothy S Ervin
6 *Elevator* (1992)
7 *Good day, blue goose!* (1992)

Tumulty series
Williams, Charles Walter Stansby
see **Sir Giles Tumulty series**

Tunisian Jew series
Memmi, Albert
1 *Pillar of salt* (1933)
Original edition entitled *Statue de sel*
2 *Strangers* (1955)
Original edition entitled *Agar*

Tuppence and Tommy Beresford series
Christie, Agatha
see **Tommy and Tuppence Beresford series**

Tupper series
Bell, Josephine
see **Amy Tupper series**

Turbo cowboys series
Phillips, Tony
This pseudonym is used by Paul Bagdon, Chet Cunningham and John Read as indicated against each title
1 *Jump start* (1988) [Cunningham]
2 *Spin out* (1989) [Cunningham]
3 *Spark fire* (1989) [Cunningham]
4 *Full throttle* (1989) [Cunningham]
5 *Super charge* (1989) [Bagdon]
6 *Rat trap* (1989) [Read]
7 *Night riders* (1989) [Bagdon]
8 *Speed shift* (1989) [Bagdon]
9 *Duster trouble* (1989) [Read]
10 *City of glass* (1989) [Bagdon]

Turf-cutter's donkey series
Lynch, Patricia
1 *Turf-cutter's donkey* (1934)
2 *Turf-cutter's donkey goes visiting* (1935)
Donkey goes visiting
3 *Turf-cutter's donkey kicks up his heels* (1939)

Turing series
Dewdney, Alexander Keewatin
1 *Turing omnibus* (1988)
2 *New Turing omnibus* (1993)

Turkey series
Harris, Ray
1 *Adventures of Turkey* (1952)
2 *Turkey and partners* (1954)
3 *Turkey and Co.* (1961)

Turlock Loams series
Ruyle, John
Parodies on the Sherlock Holmes series, by Sir Arthur Conan Doyle
1 *Adventure of the logophagous client* (1971)
2 *Adventure of the retired weatherman* (1972)
3 *His last vow* (1973)
4 *Adventure of the Soledad cyclist* (1974)
5 *Adventure of the freckled hand* (1975)
6 *Adventure of the five buffalo chips* (1975)
7 *Adventure of the giant bat of Sonoma* (1976)
8 *Adventure of the missing third quarter* (1977)
9 *Adventure of the dancing hen* (1978)
10 *Silver haze* (1978)
11 *Adventure of the jogging man* (1979)

Turn of the screw series
Hastings, Michael
1 *Nightcomers* (1972)
A speculation
James, Henry
2 *Turn of the screw* (1898)

Turnbull series
Gunter, Archibald Clavering
see **Susan Turnbull series**
Tyndall, John
see **Roger Turnbull series**

Turner series
Palmer, Bernard
see **Mickey Turner series**

Turnpenny series
Vallance, Rosalind
see **Timmy series**

Turquoise dragon series
Wallace, David Rains
1 *Turquoise dragon* (1985)
2 *Vermilion parrot* (1991)

Turtle series
Hoban, Lillian
see **Stick-in-the-Mud Turtle series**

Tusk Smith series
Zachary, Hugh
1 *To guard the right* (1980)
2 *Top level death* (1981)

Tut Claw series
Paradis, Vincent A
1 *Castilian caper* (1978)
2 *Cocaine caper* (1978)

Tutt series
Train, Arthur
see **Ephraim Tutt series**

Tweed, Grey and Newman series
Forbes, Colin
1 *Double jeopardy* (1982)
2 *Terminal* (1984)
3 *Cover story* (1985)
4 *Janus man* (1988)
5 *Deadlock* (1988)
6 *Greek key* (1989)
7 *Shockwave* (1990)
8 *Whirlpool* (1991)

Tweedy family series
Burns, Olive Ann
1 *Cold Sassy Tree* (1984)
2 *Leaving Cold Sassy Tree* (1992)
Unfinished at the author's death

Twelfth and after series
Stanford, John Keith
see **Life and death of George Proteron series**

Twelve kingdoms series
Friesner, Esther Mona
see **Chronicles of the twelve kingdoms series**

Twelve tasks of Asterix series
Goscinny, Rene
Based on an animated film
1 *Race* (1976)
2 *Javelin* (1976)
3 *Judo match* (1976)
4 *Isle of Pleasure* (1976)
5 *Magician* (1976)
6 *Chef* (1976)
7 *Cave of the beast* (1976)
8 *Place that sends you mad* (1976)
9 *Crocociles* (1976)
10 *Old Man of the Mountains* (1976)
11 *Ghostly legionaries* (1976)
12 *Circus* (1976)
One volume edition entitled *The twelve tasks of Asterix*, 1976

Twentieth-century Europe series
Gavin, Catherine
1 *Devil in harbour* (1968)
Set during the Battle of Jutland in 1916
2 *Snow mountain* (1973)
A novel of the fall of the Romanov dynasty
3 *Give me the daggers* (1972)
A novel of the Finnish fight for independence in 1918
4 *House of war* (1970)
Based on the life and work of Kemal Ataturk

Twentieth century trilogy
Marshall, William Leonard
1 *Age of death* (1970)
2 *Middle kingdom* (1971)
3 *Shanghai* (1979)

Twenty-eight Barbary Lane series
Maupin, Armistead
see **Tales of the city series**

Twenty thousand streets under the sky series
Hamilton, Patrick
1 *Midnight bell* (1929)
2 *Siege of pleasure* (1932)
3 *Plains of cement* (1934)

Twiddle series
Blyton, Enid
see **Mister Twiddle series**

Twilight country series
Faldbakken, Knut
Translated from the Norwegian
1 *Twilight country* (1993)
2 *Sweetwater* (1994)

Twilight of the gods trilogy
Schmidt, Dennis
1 *First name* (1985)
2 *Groa's other eye* (1986)
3 *Three trumps sounding* (1988)

Twilight series
This sequence has twenty three authors
Cowan, Dale
1 *Deadly sleep* (1982)
Haynes, Betsy
2 *Power* (1982)
Brunn, Robert
3 *Initiation* (1982)
Howe, Imogen
4 *Fatal attraction* (1982)
Francis, Dorothy Brenner
5 *Blink of the mind* (1982)

Haynes, James
6 *Voices in the dark* (1982)
Veley, Charles
7 *Play to live* (1982)
Armstrong, Sarah
8 *Blood red roses* (1982)
Daniel, Colin
9 *Demon tree* (1983)
Stevenson, Edward
10 *Avenging spirit* (1983)
Laymon, Richard Carl
11 *Nightmare Lake* (1983)
Smith, Janet Patton
12 *Twisted room* (1983)
Howe, Imogen
13 *Vicious circle* (1983)
Callahan, Jay
14 *Footprints of the dead* (1983)
Coville, Bruce
15 *Spirits and spells* (1983)
Selden, Neil
16 *Drawing the dead* (1983)
Netter, Susan
17 *Storm child* (1983)
Trainor, Joseph
18 *Watery grave* (1983)
Kassem, Lou
19 *Dance of death* (1984)
Trainor, Joseph
20 *Family crypt* (1984)
Cusick, Richie Tankersley
21 *Evil on the bayou* (1984)
Blake, Susan
22 *Haunted dollhouse* (1984)
Byron, Amanda
23 *Warning* (1985)
Coville, Bruce
24 *Amulet of doom* (1985)
Gonzalez, Gloria
25 *Deadly rhyme* (1986)
Bicknell, Arthur
26 *Scavenger's hunt* (1987)

Twilight Zone series
This sequence has three authors
Serling, Rod
1 *Stories from the Twilight Zone* (1960)
2 *More stories from the Twilight Zone* (1961)
3 *New stories from the Twilight Zone* (1962)
Numbers 1-3 also published in one volume entitled *Stories from the Twilight Zone*, 1986; selections from 1-3 published as *From the Twilight Zone*, 1970
Gibson, Walter Brown
4 *Rod Serling's The Twilight Zone* (1963)
Chilling stories from the Twilight Zone
5 *Twilight Zone revisited* (1964)
Greenberg, Martin Harry
6 *New stories from the Twilight Zone* (1991)
Companion volumes: *Twilight Zone companion*, by Marc Scott Zicree, 1982, revised 1989, *Twilight Zone, the movie*, by Robert Bloch, 1983, *The Twilight Zone, the original stories*, by Martin Harry Greenberg and Richard Matheson and Charles Gordon Waugh, 1985, *The Twilight Zone files*, by John Peel, 1985-86

Twin animals series
Tompkins, Jane
see **Animal twins series**

Twin planets series
Lupoff, Richard Allen
see **Counterearth series**

Twin series
Masters, Doug
see **TNT series**

Twin series
This sequence has nine authors
Perkins, Lucy Fitch
1 *Dutch twins* (1911)
2 *Japanese twins* (1912)
3 *Irish twins* (1913)
4 *Eskimo twins* (1914)
5 *Mexican twins* (1915)
6 *Cave twins* (1916)
7 *Belgian twins* (1917)
8 *Spartan twins* (1918)
9 *French twins* (1918)
10 *Scotch twins* (1919)
11 *Italian twins* (1920)
12 *Puritan twins* (1921)
13 *Swiss twins* (1922)
14 *Filipino twins* (1923)
15 *Colonial twins of Virginia* (1924)
16 *American twins of 1812* (1925)
17 *American twins of the Revolution* (1926)
18 *Pioneer twins* (1927)
19 *Farm twins* (1928)
20 *Indian twins* (1930)
21 *Pickaninny twins* (1931)
22 *Norwegian twins* (1933)
23 *Spanish twins* (1934)
24 *Chinese twins* (1935)
Rooke, Daphne
26 *South African twins* (1953)
Twins in South Africa
27 *Australian twins* (1954)
Twins in Australia
Wuorio, Eva Lis
28 *Canadian twins* (1956)
Ucuk, Cahit
29 *Turkish twins* (1956)
Rooke, Daphne
30 *New Zealand twins* (1957)
Williams, Harry
31 *Twins of Ceylon* (1957)
Shaw, Denis
32 *Twins of India* (1959)
Jenkins, Alan Charles
33 *Twins of Lapland* (1960)
Shaw, Denis
34 *Pakistani twins* (1960)
Charnock, Joan
35 *Russian twins* (1963)
Tindall, Gillian
36 *Israeli twins* (1963)

Twin soul series
Anethan, Eleanora Mary d'
1 *Twin soul of O'Take San* (1914)
2 *Her mother's blood* (1918)

Twink series
Hurt, Freda Mary
see **Mister Twink series**

Twinkle series
Saroyan, William
see **Mama and papa series**

Twinkle tales series
Bancroft, Laura
1 *Bandit Jim Crow* (1906)
2 *Mister Woodchuck* (1906)
3 *Prairie-dog town* (1906)
4 *Prince Mud-Turtle* (1906)
5 *Sugar-Loaf Mountain* (1906)
6 *Twinkle's enchantment* (1906)
One volume edition entitled *Twinkle and Chubbins, their astonishing adventures in nature fairyland*, 1911

Twins in Ceylon series
Woolf, Bella Sidney
1 *Twins in Ceylon* (1909)
2 *More about the twins in Ceylon* (1911)

Twins series
Blyton, Enid
1 *Twins go to Nursery Rhyme Land* (1945)
2 *Tales of the twins* (1948)
3 *Hello twins* (1951)
4 *Come along twins* (1952)
5 *Here come the twins* (1953)
6 *Fun with the twins* (1954)
7 *Trouble for the twins* (1955)

Twins series
Bracken, Anne
see **Jon and Julie Howard series**

Twins series
Denton, Phyllis
1 *Tales of the twins* (1958)
2 *Twins again* (1959)

Twins series
Deveraux, Jude
see **Chandler twins series**

Twins series
Hogan, Inez
1 *Bear twins* (1935)
2 *Elephant twins* (1936)
3 *Twin kids* (1937)
4 *Kangaroo twins* (1938)
5 *Mule twins* (1939)
6 *Twin seals* (1940)
7 *Twin deer* (1941)
8 *Monkey twins* (1943)
9 *Twin colts* (1944)
10 *Raccoon twins* (1946)
11 *Giraffe twins* (1948)
12 *Twin lambs* (1951)
13 *Koala bear twins* (1955)
14 *Twin kittens* (1958)
15 *Twin puppies* (1959)
16 *Twin otters and the Indians* (1962)
17 *Fox twins* (1964)

Twins series
Kent, Margaret
1 *Twins at Hillside Farm* (1942)
2 *Twins at the seaside* (1943)
3 *Twins at home* (1947)
4 *Twins and Felicity* (1959)
5 *Twins and the move* (1962)

Twins series
Perkins, Lucy Fitch
see **Twin series**
Whitehill, Dorothy
see **Janet and Phyllis series**

Twistaplot series
This sequence has fifteen authors
Stine, Robert Lawrence
1 *Time raider* (1982)
Foley, Louise Munro
2 *Train of terror* (1982)
Stine, Megan
3 *Formula for trouble* (1983)
Stine, Robert Lawrence
4 *Golden sword of Dragonwalk* (1983)
Foley, Louise Munro
5 *Sinister studios KESP-TV* (1983)
Roth, Arthur
6 *Crash landing* (1983)
Colligan, Douglas
7 *Video avenger* (1983)
Stine, Megan
8 *Race into the past* (1983)
Stine, Robert Lawrence
9 *Horrors of the haunted museum* (1983)
Glick, Ruth
10 *Mission of the secret spy squad* (1984)
Hiller, Barbara B
11 *Camp-out on Danger mountain* (1984)
Stine, Megan
12 *Journey to Vernico 5* (1984)
Otfinoski, Steven
13 *Midnight at Monster Mansion* (1984)
Stine, Robert Lawrence
14 *Instant millionaire* (1984)
Brown, Katy
15 *Spellcaster* (1984)
Beach, Lynn
16 *Secrets of the lost island* (1984)
Siegel, Scott
17 *Ghost riders of Goldspur* (1985)
Nugent, Jean
18 *Calling outer space* (1985)

Twisted Face series
Davison, Gilderoy
1 *Man with the Twisted Face* (1931)
2 *Prince of spies* (1932)
3 *Traitor unmasked* (1932)
4 *Devil's apprentice* (1933)
5 *Twisted Face, the avenger* (1935)
6 *Twisted Face strikes again* (1939)
7 *Twisted Face defends his title* (1940)
8 *Dog fight with death* (1940)

Twister Malone series
Dresser, Davis
1 *Death rides the Pecos* (1940)
2 *Hangmen of Sleepy Valley* (1940)
Masked riders of Sleepy Valley
3 *Lynch-rope law* (1940)
4 *Murder on the mesa* (1953)

Twitchell series
Butterworth, Oliver
see **Nate Twitchell series**

Twite series
Aiken, Joan
see **Dido Twite series**

Twitmeyer series
Moore, Lilian
see **Mister Twitmeyer series**

Two American boys series
Crockett, Sherman
1 *Two American boys with the Allied armies* (1915)
2 *Two American boys in the French war trenches* (1916)
3 *Two American boys with the Dardanelles battle fleet* (1916)
4 *Two American boys aboard a submersible* (1917)
5 *Two American boys with Pershing in France* (1918)

Two brothers series
Lenski, Lois
1 *Two brothers and their animal friends* (1929)
2 *Two brothers and their baby sister* (1930)

Two by two series
This sequence has eleven authors
Casey, Sara
1 *Cassie and Chris* (19183)
Connell, Abby
2 *Jed and Jessie* (19183)
Aks, Patricia
3 *Change of heart* (19183)
Makris, Kathryn
4 *Only a dream away* (19183)
Harrell, Janice
5 *One special summer* (1984)
Malone, Lucy
6 *Handle with care* (1984)
Kennedy, Kim
7 *In-between love* (1984)
Filichia, Peter
8 *Falling in love again* (1984)
Makris, Kathryn
9 *Weekends for us* (1984)
Norby, Lisa
10 *Just the way you are* (1984)
Ellis, Carol
11 *Kiss for good luck* (1984)
Emerson, Mark
12 *Here to stay* (1984)

Two children series
Brown, Rose
1 *Two children of Brazil* (1940)
2 *Amazon adventures of two children* (1942)
3 *Two children and their jungle zoo* (1944)

Two Dianas series
Herbert, Agnes
1 *Two Dianas in Somaliland* (1908)
The record of a shooting trip
2 *Two Dianas in Alaska* (1909)

Two Feet series
Friskey, Margaret
see **Indian Two Feet series**

Two fiddlers series
Brown, George Mackay
1 *Two fiddlers* (1974)
Tales from Orkney
2 *Pictures in the cave* (1977)

Two friends series
Greenwell, Dora
1 *Two friends* (1867)
2 *Colloquia Crucis* (1871)

Two Galaxy series
Jakes, John
see **Dragonard series**

Two heads series
Ahlberg, Janet
1 *One and only two heads* (1979)
2 *Two wheels, two heads* (1979)

Two hearts series
Randall, Lindsey
1 *Two hearts too wild* (1988)
2 *Two hearts too reckless* (1989)

Two Hoots series
Cresswell, Helen
1 *Two Hoots* (1974)
2 *Two Hoots go to sea* (1974)
3 *Two Hoots and the big bad bird* (1975)
4 *Two Hoots in the snow* (1975)
5 *Two Hoots and the king* (1977)
6 *Two Hoots play hide and seek* (1977)

Two hungry mice trilogy
Piers, Helen
1 *Mouse looks for a house* (1966)
2 *Mouse looks for a friend* (1966)
3 *How did it look* (1966)
One volume edition entitled *The mouse book*, 1972

Two little women series
Wells, Carolyn
1 *Two little women* (1915)
2 *Two little women and treasure house* (1916)
3 *Two little women on a holiday* (1917)

Two-minute mysteries series
Sobol, Donald J
1 *Two-minute mysteries* (1967)
2 *More two-minute mysteries* (1971)
3 *Still more two-minute mysteries* (1975)

Two of a kind series
Albright, Molly
Illustrated by Dee De Rosa
1 *Meet Miss Dracula* (1988)
2 *Dream team* (1988)
3 *Big showoffs* (1988)
4 *Best friends* (1988)

Two thousand and sixty nine trilogy
Townsend, Larry
1 *Two thousand and sixty nine* (1969)
2 *Two thousand and sixty nine plus one* (1970)
3 *Two thousand and sixty nine plus two* (1970)

Two-Two series
Richler, Mordecai
see **Jacob Two-Two series**

Two Wild Cherries series
Garis, Howard Roger
1 *Two Wild Cherries in the country* (1924)
Alternative title: How Dick and Janet saved the mill
2 *Two Wild Cherries in the woods* (1924)
Alternative title: How Dick and Janet caught the bear
3 *Two Wild Cherries* (1924)
Alternative title: How Dick and Janet lost something
4 *Two Wild Cherries at the seashore* (1925)

Two worlds series
Corelli, Marie
1 *Romance of two worlds* (1886)
2 *Vendetta* (1886)
Alternative title: The story of one forgotten
3 *Ardath* (1889)
The story of a dead self
4 *Soul of Lilith* (1892)
5 *Barabbas* (1893)
A dream of the world's tragedy
6 *Master-Christian* (1900)

Two worlds series
Harris, Jean
1 *Stranger in two worlds* (1986)
2 *They always call us ladies* (1988)

Two worlds series
Ollivant, Alfred
1 *Two men* (1919)
2 *One woman* (1921)
A romance of Sussex

Two years' holiday series
Verne, Jules
1 *Adrift in the Pacific* (1888)
2 *Second year ashore* (1888)
One volume edition entitled *Two year's vacation*, 1889; original one volume edition entitled *Deux ans de vacation*

Two youths series
Knox, Thomas Wallace
see **Boy travellers series**

Twombley series
Williams, Sidney
see **Jabez Twombley series**

Twotoes and Rooke series
Alexander, David
see **Tommy Twotoes and Terry Rooke series**

Tyco Bass series
Cameron, Eleanor
1 *Wonderful flight to the mushroom planet* (1954)
2 *Stowaway to the mushroom planet* (1956)
3 *Mister Bass's planetoid* (1958)
4 *Mystery for Mister Bass* (1960)
5 *Time and Mister Bass* (1967)

Tyger Decker series
Riefe, Alan
1 *Tyger at bay* (1976)
2 *Tyger by the tail* (1976)
3 *Smile on the face of the tyger* (1976)
4 *Tyger and the lady* (1976)
5 *Hold that tyger* (1976)
6 *Tyger, tyger burning bright* (1976)

Tygrus Gerald Decker series
Riefe, Alan
see **Tyger Decker series**

Tygwyn series
Morgan, Alison
see **Llanwern series**

Tyldens series
Ford, Elizabeth
1 *Meeting the spring* (1954)
2 *One fine day* (1954)

Tyler brothers series
Jordan, Matt
1 *Brigham's way* (1976)
2 *Jacob's road* (1976)

Tyler McAllister series
Hayes, Daniel
1 *Trouble with lemons* (1991)
2 *Eye of the beholder* (1992)
3 *No effect* (1993)

Tyler series
Diplomat
see **Dennis Tyler series**
Evans, Kenneth
see **Crispin Tyler series**
Otis, James
see **Toby Tyler series**
Potter, J L
see **Jeff Tyler series**
Revell, Louisa
see **Julia Tyler series**
Stone, Richard H
see **Slim Tyler series**

Tyler twins series
Stahl, Hilda
1 *Tyler twins and the surprise at the Big Key Ranch* (1986)
2 *Tyler twins and the swamp monster* (1987)
3 *Tyler twins and the pet show adventure* (1988)
4 *Tyler twins and the latchkey kids* (1988)
5 *Tyler twins and the tree house hideaway* (1988)
6 *Tyler twins and the mystery of the missing grandfather* (1988)

Tylor trilogy
Burroughs, Edgar Rice
see **Bowen Tylor trilogy**

Tyrone series
Wilhelm, Hans
1 *Tyrone the horrible* (1988)
2 *Tyrone the double dirty rotten cheater* (1991)

Tyson series
Kummer, Frederic Arnold
see **Judge Henry Tyson series**

Tyson-Tyree and Pynchon series
Pedneau, Dave
see **Whit Pynchon and Annie Tyson-Tyree series**

Tzu Hang series
Smeeton, Miles
see **Chronicles of Tzu Hang series**

Tzu Hsi series
Lancing, George
1 *Imperial motherhood* (1945)
2 *Mating of the dragon* (1946)
3 *Dragon in chains* (1947)
4 *Phoenix triumphant* (1950)

U

U-boat series
Gray, Edwyn
1 *No survivors* (1974)
2 *Action Atlantic* (1975)
3 *Tokyo torpedo* (1976)

U-boat series
Horst, Karl
1 *Sink the Ark Royal* (1979)
2 *Caribbean pirate* (1980)
3 *Arctic mutiny* (1981)

U.N.A.C.O.series
This sequence has two authors; based on story outlines by Alistair Maclean
Denis, John
1 *Hostage tower* (1980)
2 *Air Force One is down* (1981)
Macneill, Alastair
3 *Death train* (1989)

U.N.C.L.E. files series
Peel, John
1 *Fifteen years later affair* (1985)
2 *Girl from U.N.C.L.E.* (1985)
3 *End of the affair* (1985)
4 *Man from Thrush* (1985)
5 *Mission begins* (1986)
Co-author: Glenn A Magee
6 *Show takes off* (1986)
Co-author: Glenn A Magee
7 *Pieces of fate* (1986)
8 *Take me to your leader* (1986)
9 *Deadly quest* (1986)

U.S.A.trilogy
Dos Passos, John
1 *Forty second parallel* (1930)
2 *Nineteen hundred and nineteen* (1932)
3 *Big money* (1936)
One volume edition entitled *U.S.A.*, 1937

U.S. midshipman series
Stirling, Yates
see **United States midshipman series**

U.S.S.A. series
This sequence has three authors
De Haven, Tom
1 *U.S.S.A., book 1* (1987)
Lewitt, Shariann N
2 *U.S.S.A., book 2* (1987)
Sykes, Sondra Catharine
3 *U.S.S.A., book 3* (1987)
Lewitt, Shariann N
4 *U.S.S.A., book 4* (1987)
Companion volumes: *U.S.S.A.*, by James Frey, 1987, *U.S.S.A.*, by David Madsen, 1989

UFO conspiracy series
Bischoff, David
1 *Abduction* (1990)
2 *Deception* (1991)
3 *Revelation* (1991)

UFO series
Miall, Robert
1 *UFO* (1970)
UFO 1
Flesh hunters
2 *UFO 2* (1971)
Sporting blood

Ugglians series
Fallaw, L M
1 *Ugglians* (1957)
2 *Ugglians at large* (1959)

Ukridge series
Wodehouse, Pelham Grenville
1 *Love among the chickens* (1906)
2 *Ukridge* (1924)
Also three Ukridge stories in *Lord Emsworth and others*, 1937, three in *Eggs, beans and crumpets*, 1940, one in *Nothing serious*, 1950, one in *A few quick ones*, 1959, one in *Plum pie*, 1966

Ulm series
Chetwin, Grace
see **Tales of Gom in the Legends of Ulm series**

Ulrich series
Musil, Robert
see **Man without qualities series**

Ulster life series
Irvine, Alexander
1 *My lady of the chimney corner* (1913)
2 *Souls of the poor folk* (1921)

Ulster series
Harbinson, Robert
Autobiography
1 *No surrender* (1960)
Ulster childhood
2 *Song of Erne* (1960)
Evacuation in Fermanagh during the Second World War
3 *Up spake the cabin boy* (1961)
4 *Protege* (1963)

Ultimate truths trilogy
Rankin, Robert
1 *Book of ultimate truths* (1993)
2 *Raiders of the lost car park* (1994)
Number three not yet published

Ultimatum series
Rohmer, Richard
1 *Ultimatum* (1973)
2 *Exxoneration* (1974)

Umslopogaas series
Haggard, Henry Rider
1 *Allan Quatermain* (1887)
Allan Quatermain and the lost city of gold
The second title is an edition abridged by Sarah Litvinoff, 1986
2 *Nada the lily* (1892)

Una Persson series
Moorcock, Michael
1 *Land leviathan* (1974)
2 *Adventures of Una Persson and Catherine Cornelius in the twentieth century* (1976)

UNACO series
Denis, John
see **U.N.A.C.O.series**

Unbalanced accounts series
Gallison, Kate
1 *Unbalanced accounts* (1986)
2 *Death tape* (1987)

Unbalanced earth trilogy
Wylie, Jonathan
1 *Dreams of stone* (1989)
2 *Lightless kingdom* (1989)
3 *Age of chaos* (1989)

Uncalled-for histories series
Nicol, Eric
1 *Say Uncle* (1961)
A completely uncalled-for history of the U.S.
2 *Russia, anyone?* (1963)
A completely uncalled-for history of the U.S.S.R.

Uncle Abner series
Post, Melville Davisson
1 *Uncle Abner, master of mysteries* (1918)
2 *Methods on Uncle Abner* (1974)
Omnibus volume: *The complete Uncle Abner*, 1977

Uncle Albert series
Stannard, Russell
1 *Time and space of Uncle Albert* (1989)
2 *Black holes and Uncle Albert* (1991)
3 *Uncle Albert and the quantum quest* (1994)

Uncle and Aunt series
McCardell, Roy Larcom
see **Aunt and Uncle series**

Uncle Barney series
Weir, Rosemary
1 *Uncle Barney and the sleep-destroyer* (1974)
2 *Uncle Barney and the shrink-drink* (1977)

Uncle Bill and David series
Serraillier, Ian
see **David and Uncle Bill series**

Uncle Bill series
James, Will
1 *Uncle Bill* (1932)
A tale of two kinds of cowboy
2 *In the saddle with Uncle Bill* (1935)
3 *Look-see with Uncle Bill* (1938)

Uncle Bill series
Wibberley, Leonard
1 *Encounter near Venus* (1967)
2 *Journey to Untor* (1970)

Uncle Charlie series
Lane, Elizabeth
Humorous reminiscences of Australian country life
1 *Mad as rabbits* (1962)
2 *Our Uncle Charlie* (1964)

Uncle Fred, Earl of Ickenham series
Wodehouse, Pelham Grenville
1 *Uncle Fred in the springtime* (1939)
2 *Uncle Dynamite* (1948)
3 *Cocktail time* (1958)
4 *Service with a smile* (1961)

Uncle George and Jack Meredith series
Leyland, Eric
see **Jack Meredith and Uncle George series**

Uncle George series
Pentecost, Hugh
see **George Crowder series**

Uncle Jock series
Taylor, Allan K
1 *My friends the beasts* (1949)
2 *African adventures* (1949)
3 *Dauntless Jock* (1951)

Uncle John series
Warner, Anne
1 *Seeing France with Uncle John* (1906)
2 *Seeing England with Uncle John* (1908)

Uncle Paul series
Blackwood, Algernon
1 *Education of Uncle Paul* (1909)
2 *Prisoner in Fairyland* (1913)
The book that Uncle Paul wrote

Uncle Remus series
Harris, Joel Chandler
1 *Uncle Remus, his songs and his sayings* (1880)
Revised editions 1895 and 1957; folklore of the old plantation
2 *Nights with Uncle Remus* (1883)
Revised edition 1917; myths and legends of the old plantation
3 *Daddy Jake, the runaway, and short stories told after dark by Uncle Remus* (1889)
4 *Uncle Remus and his friends* (1892)
Old plantation stories
5 *Told by Uncle Remus* (1905)
New stories of the old plantation
6 *Uncle Remus and Brer Rabbit* (1907)
7 *Uncle Remus and the little boy* (1910)
8 *Uncle Remus returns* (1918)
9 *Witch Wolf* (1921)
Companion volume: *The tar-baby, and other rhymes of Uncle Remus*, 1904; omnibus volume: *The complete tales of Uncle Remus*, 1955

Uncle Remus series
Lester, Julius
see **Tales of Uncle Remus series**

Uncle Rutherford series
Mathews, Joanna Hooe
1 *Uncle Rutherford's attic* (1887)
2 *Uncle Rutherford's nieces* (1888)

Uncle Sam's Army boys series
Burley, Andrew S
1 *Uncle Sam's Army boys on the Rhine* (1919)
Alternative title: Bob Hamilton in the Argonne Death Troop
2 *Uncle Sam's Army boys in Italy* (1919)
Alternative title: Bob Hamilton under fire in the Piave district
3 *Uncle Sam's Army boys in khaki under canvas* (1919)
Alternative title: Bob Hamilton and the munition plant plot
4 *Uncle Sam's Army boys with Old Glory in Mexico* (1919)
Alternative title: Bob Hamilton along Pershing's trail

Uncle Sam's boys series
Hancock, Harrie Irving
1 *Uncle Sam's boys in the ranks* (1910)
Alternative title: Two recruits in the U.S. Army
2 *Uncle Sam's boys on field duty* (1911)
Alternative title: Winning the corporal's chevrons
3 *Uncle Sam's boys as sergeants* (1911)
Alternative title: Handling their first real command
4 *Uncle Sam's boys in the Philippines* (1912)
Alternative title: Following the flag against the Moros
5 *Uncle Sam's boys on their mettle* (1916)
Alternative title: A chance to win officers commissions
6 *Uncle Sam's boys as lieutenants* (1919)
Alternative title: Serving Old Glory as line officers
7 *Uncle Sam's boys with Pershing* (1919)
Alternative title: Dick Prescott at grips with the Boche
8 *Uncle Sam's boys smash the Germans* (1919)
Alternative title: Winding up the Great War

Uncle Sam's Navy boys series
Jasper, Robert Lee
1 *Uncle Sam's Navy boys with the Submarine Chasers* (1919)
Alternative title: On patrol duty in the North Sea
2 *Uncle Sam's Navy boys afloat* (1919)
Alternative title: The raid along the Atlantic seaboard
3 *Uncle Sam's Navy boys in action* (1919)
Alternative title: Running down enemy commerce destroyers
4 *Uncle Sam's Navy boys with the Marines* (1919)
Alternative title: Standing like a rock at Shateau Thierry

Uncle Sam's service series
Armitage, Taylor
1 *Bob Spencer the life saver* (1914)
Alternative title: Guarding the coast for Uncle Sam
2 *Dave Spencer on secret service* (1918)
Alternative title: Uncle Sam's search for counterfeiters

Uncle series
Martin, John Percival
1 *Uncle* (1964)
2 *Uncle cleans up* (1965)
3 *Uncle and his detective* (1966)
4 *Uncle and the treacle trouble* (1967)
5 *Uncle and Claudius the camel* (1969)
6 *Uncle and the battle for Badgertown* (1973)

Uncle Silas series
Bates, Herbert Ernest
1 *My Uncle Silas* (1939)
2 *Sugar for the horse* (1957)

Uncle Terry series
Munn, Charles Clark
1 *Uncle Terry* (1900)
A story of the Maine coast
2 *Heart of Uncle Terry* (1915)

Uncle Tom series
Stowe, Harriet Beecher
1 *Uncle Tom's cabin* (1852)
Alternative title: Life among the lonely
2 *Key to Uncle Tom's cabin* (1853)

Uncle Walter series
Townsend, John Rowe
1 *Gumble's Yard* (1961)
Trouble in the Jungle
2 *Widdershins Crescent* (1965)
Goodbye to the Jungle
Goodbye to Gumble's Yard

Uncle Wiggily series
This sequence has two authors
Garis, Howard Roger
1 *Uncle Wiggily book* (1961)
2 *Uncle Wiggily stories* (1965)
3 *Uncle Wiggily and the pirates, and other stories* (1977)
4 *Uncle Wiggily and his woodland friends* (1977)
Garis, M R
5 *Uncle Wiggily and the Will-a-wong* (1977)
6 *Uncle Wiggily and the strange notes, and other stories* (1978)

Uncle William series
Lee, Jennette Barbour Perry
1 *Uncle William, the man who was shif'less* (1909)
2 *Happy island* (1910)

Undead series
Meyers, Richard S
see **Book of the undead series**

Under four flags series
Edwards, Herbert Wilson
Autobiography
1 *Under four flags* (1954)
Experiences at sea
2 *Their lawful occasions* (1956)
Covers 1913-1956

Under sail series
Hiscock, Eric Charles
Memoirs of voyages
1 *Wandering under sail* (1939)
Second edition 1948; third edition 1977
2 *Cruising under sail* (1950)
Second edition 1965
3 *Voyaging under sail* (1959)
Second edition 1970; numbers 2 and 3 also published in one volume entitled *Cruising under sail*, 3rd edition, 1981

Under storm's wing trilogy
Thomas, Helen
Autobiography
1 *As it was* (1926)
Originally published as by H T
2 *World without end* (1931)
3 *Time and again* (1978)
Memoirs and letters
One volume edition entitled *Under storm's wing*, 1988

Under the earth series
Casteret, Norbert
1 *Ten years under the earth* (1939)
Abridged translation of *Dix ans sous terre*, 1933 and *Au fond des gouffres*, 1936
2 *My caves* (1942)
Original edition entitled *Mes cavernes*
3 *Cave men, new and old* (1949)
Original edition entitled *Exploration*
4 *Darkness under the earth* (1952)
Original edition entitled *Tenebres*
5 *Descent of Pierre Saint-Martin* (1954)
Original edition entitled *Trente ans sous terre*
6 *More years under the earth* (1958)
Original edition entitled *Aux pays des eaux folles*
7 *Mission underground* (1964)
Original edition entitled *Mission centre terre*

Undercover Cat series
Gordons
1 *Undercover Cat* (1963)
That darn Cat
2 *Undercover Cat prowls again* (1966)
3 *Catnapped!* (1974)

Undercover series
Mazzaro, Ed
1 *One death in the red* (1976)
2 *Bootleg angel* (1977)
3 *Chicago deadline* (1978)
4 *Pawn to King's Cross* (1978)

Underfoot the cat series
Maguire, Jack
see **Many lives of Underfoot the cat series**

Underground series
Fraser, Conon
1 *Underground explorers* (1957)
2 *Underground river* (1959)

Underpeople series
Smith, Cordwainer
see **Instrumentality series**

Undersea series
Pohl, Frederik
see **Jim Eden series**

Understanding holidays series
Parker, Margot
1 *What is Columbus Day?* (1985)
2 *What is Veteran's Day?* (1986)
3 *What is Thanksgiving Day?* (1988)
4 *What is Martin Luther King, Jr. Day?* (1990)

Undertaker series
Gilman, George G
1 *Black as death* (1981)
2 *Destined to die* (1981)
3 *Funeral by the sea* (1982)
4 *Three graves to a showdown* (1982)
5 *Back from the dead* (1982)

Underwood and Carnelian series
Moorcock, Michael
see **Jherek Carnelian and Amelia Underwood series**

Uneasy series
Hunt, Violet
1 *Tales of the uneasy* (1911)
2 *More tales of the uneasy* (1925)

Unfair sex series
Farewell, Nina
1 *Unfair sex* (1953)
2 *Someone to love* (1959)

Unfinished business trilogy
Houseman, John
Autobiography
1 *Run-through* (1972)
2 *Front and centre* (1979)
3 *Final dress* (1983)
One volume edition entitled *Unfinished business*, 1986

Unfinished journey series
Jones, Jack
Autobiography
1 *Unfinished journey* (1937)
2 *Me and mine* (1946)
3 *Give me back my heart* (1950)

Unfinished woman trilogy
Hellman, Lillian
Memoirs
1 *Unfinished woman* (1969)
2 *Pentimento* (1974)
A book of portraits
3 *Scoundrel time* (1976)
One volume edition entitled *Three*, 1979

Unicorn and dragon series
Abbey, Lynn
1 *Unicorn and dragon* (1987)
2 *Conquest* (1988)
Green man

Unicorn Club series
Pascal, Francine
1 *Save the Unicorns!* (1994)
2 *Maria's movie comeback* (1994)
3 *Best friend game* (1994)
4 *Lila's little sister* (1994)

Unicorn Queen series
Hansen, Gwen
see **Secret of the Unicorn Queen series**

Unicorn series
Lindbergh, Anne Morrow
Diaries and letters
1 *Bring me a unicorn* (1972)
1920-1928
2 *Hour of gold, hour of lead* (1973)
1929-1932
3 *Locked rooms and open door* (1974)
1932-1935
4 *Flower and the nettle* (1976)
1936-1939
5 *War within and without* (1980)
1939-1944

Unicorn series
Luenn, Nancy
1 *Arctic unicorn* (1986)
2 *Unicorn crossing* (1987)

Unicorn trilogy
Lee, John
1 *Unicorn quest* (1986)
2 *Unicorn dilemma* (1988)
3 *Unicorn solution* (1991)

Unidentified flying riddles series
Cohen, Paul S
1 *Unidentified flying riddles* (1983)
2 *More unidentified flying riddles* (1985)

Uninvited trilogy
Harold, Clive
1 *Uninvited* (1979)
Sequence continued under the pseudonym Frank Taylor
Taylor, Frank
2 *Visitation* (1984)
3 *Abduction* (1985)

Union-Alliance series
Cherryh, Carolyn Janice
see **Alliance-Union series**

United Nations Anti-Crime Organization series
Denis, John
see **U.N.A.C.O.series**

United States Air Force in Vietnam series
Tilford, Earl H
see **USAF in Vietnam series**

United States Cavalry trilogy
Cook, Will
1 *Comanche captives* (1960)
Two rode together
2 *Peacemakers* (1961)
3 *Outcasts* (1965)

United States Marines series
Bishop, Giles
1 *Marines have landed* (1921)
2 *Marines have advanced* (1922)
3 *Lieutenant Comstock, U.S. Marines* (1922)
4 *Captain Comstock, U.S.M.C.* (1922)

United States midshipman series
Stirling, Yates
1 *United States midshipman afloat* (1908)
2 *United States midshipman in China* (1909)
3 *United States midshipman in the Philippines* (1910)
4 *United States midshipman in Japan* (1911)
5 *United States midshipman in the South Seas* (1913)

United States Navy series
Nicole, Christopher
1 *Old Glory* (1986)
2 *Sea and the sand* (1986)
3 *Iron ships, iron men* (1987)
4 *Wind of destiny* (1987)
5 *Raging seas, seering skies* (1988)
6 *Passion and the glory* (1988)

Universal Services series
Chase, James Hadley
see **Vic Malloy series**

Universe of time series
Farrell, James Thomas
1 *Silence of history* (1963)
2 *Lonely for the future* (1966)
3 *What time collects* (1964)
4 *Brand new life* (1968)
5 *Judith* (1969)
6 *Dunne family* (1976)
7 *Death of Nora Ryan* (1978)

Universe series
Abetti, Giorgio
1 *Sun* (1936)
Original edition entitled *Il sole, fonte di vita*
2 *Stars and planets* (1945)
Original edition entitled *Le stelle e i pianeti*
3 *Nebulae and galaxies* (1959)
Original edition entitled *Nebulose e gli universe-isole*

Universe series
Silverberg, Robert
1 *Universe one* (1990)
2 *Universe two* (1992)

University of Cosmopoli series
Blayre, Christopher
1 *Purple sapphire, and other posthumous papers* (1921)
Part of this novel were published under the title *The cheetah girl*, 1923
2 *Strange papers of Doctor Blayre* (1932)
Also includes *The purple sapphire*
3 *Some women of the University* (1934)

University series
Stokes, Roy Eliot
1 *Andy at Yale* (1914)
Alternative title: The great quadrangle mystery
2 *Chet at Harvard* (1914)
Alternative title: A young freshman's triumph

Unknown Indian series
Chaudhuri, Nirad Chandra
Autobiography
1 *Autobiography of an unknown Indian* (1951)
2 *Passage to England* (1959)
3 *Thy hand, great Anarch!* (1987)

Unnatural pursuit series
Gray, Simon
Autobiography
1 *Unnatural pursuit* (1985)
2 *How's that for telling 'em, fat lady?* (1988)

Unpacked series
Holt, William
Autobiography
1 *I haven't unpacked* (1939)
2 *I still haven't unpacked* (1953)

Unquenchable fire series
Pollack, Rachel
1 *Unquenchable fire* (1988)
2 *Temporary agency* (1994)

Unreliable memoirs series
James, Clive
1 *Unreliable memoirs* (1980)
2 *Falling towards England* (1985)
3 *May Week was in June* (1990)

Unsolved mysteries series
Daniken, Erich von
1 *Chariots of the gods* (1968)
Unsolved mysteries of the past; original edition entitled *Erinnerungen an die Zukunft*
2 *Return to the stars* (1968)
Evidence for the impossible; original edition entitled *Zuruck zu den Sternen*
3 *Gold of the gods* (1972)
Original edition entitled *Aussaart und Kosmos*
4 *In search of ancient gods* (1973)
My pictorial evidence for the impossible; original edition entitled *Meine Welt in Bildern*
5 *Miracles of the gods* (1974)
A hard look at the supernatural; original edition entitled *Erscheiningen*
6 *According to the evidence* (1977)
My proof of man's extraterrestrial origins; original edition entitled *Beseise*
7 *Signs of the gods?* (1979)
Original edition entitled *Prophet der Vergangenheit*
8 *Stones of Kiribati* (1982)
Pathways to the gods; original edition entitled *Reise nach Kiribati*
9 *Gods and their grand design* (1984)
The eighth wonder of the world; original edition entitled *Die Strategie der Gottar*

Comic strips based on this sequence by Bogulsaw Polch: *Atlantis, men and monsters*, 1978, *The war of the chariots*, 1979, *Revolt of the Titans*, 1979

Unspeakable series
Adams, Phillip
Essays
1 *Unspeakable Adams* (1977)
2 *More unspeakable Adams* (1979)
3 *Uncensored Adams* (1981)
4 *Inflammable Adams* (1983)

Untamed years trilogy
Johansen, Iris
see **Delaneys, the untamed years trilogy**

Untidy gardener series
Cragoe, Elizabeth
Memoirs
1 *Buttercups and Daisy* (1976)
2 *Cowslips and clover* (1977)
3 *Yorkshire relish* (1978)
4 *Sweet nothings* (1980)
5 *Untidy gardener* (1982)

Untouchables series
This sequence has three authors
Ness, Eliot
1 *Untouchables* (1957)
Fraley, Oscar
2 *Four against the mob* (1961)
3 *Last of the Untouchables* (1962)
Co-author: Paul Robsky

Untuswa trilogy
Mitford, Bertram
1 *King's assegai* (1894)
A Matabili story
2 *White shield* (1895)
3 *Word of the sorceress* (1902)

Unwin series
Hervey, Evelyn
see **Harriet Unwin series**

Unwisemen series
Bangs, John Kendrick
see **Mollie and the unwisemen series**

Up and doing series
Gordon, Frederick
1 *Young Crusoes of Pine Island* (1912)
Alternative title: The wreck of the Puff; reissued as *The Fairview boys afloat and ashore*, 1914
2 *Sammy Brown's treasure hunt* (1912)
Alternative title: Lost in the mountains; reissued as *The Fairview boys on Eagle Mountain*, 1914
3 *Bob Bouncer's schooldays* (1912)
Alternative title: The doings of a real, live everyday boy; reissued as *The Fairview boys and their rivals*, 1914

Up and down series
Trewin, John Courtenay
Autobiography
1 *Up from the lizard* (1948)
2 *Down to the lion* (1952)

Up the Ladder Club series
Rand, Edward Augustus
1 *Knights of the White Shield* (1885)
Play
2 *School in the light-house* (1885)
School
3 *Yard-stick and scissors* (1886)
Store
4 *Camp at Surf Bluff* (1886)
Vacation
5 *Out of the breakers* (1886)
Manhood

Upney Junction series
Butterworth, Nick
1 *Monster at Upney Junction* (1983)
2 *Invasion at Upney Junction* (1983)
3 *Windy day at Upney Junction* (1983)
4 *Treasure at Upney Junction* (1983)

Upstairs, downstairs series
This sequence has five authors; based on a television series
Hawkesworth, John
1 *Upstairs, downstairs* (1972)
Brady, Terence
2 *Rose's story* (1972)
Hardwick, Mollie
3 *Sarah's story* (1972)
Hardwick, Michael
4 *Mister Hudson's diaries* (1973)
Mister Hudson's diary
Hawkesworth, John
5 *In my lady's chamber* (1973)
Hardwick, Michael
6 *Mister Bellamy's story* (1974)
Hardwick, Mollie
7 *Years of change* (1974)
8 *War to end wars* (1975)
9 *Mrs Bridges' story* (1975)
Hardwick, Michael
10 *On with the dance* (1975)
11 *Endings and beginnings* (1975)
Numbers 4, 6, 10, 11 also published in one volume entitled *The upstairs, downstairs omnibus*, 1975
Pearson, John
12 *Bellamys of Eaton Place* (1976)
Hardwick, Mollie
13 *Thomas and Sarah* (1978)
Companion volume: *The world of upstairs, downstairs*, by Mollie Hardwick, 1976

Upstairs room series
Reiss, Johanna
1 *Upstairs room* (1972)
2 *Journey back* (1976)

Upward and onward series
Optic, Oliver
see **Onward and upward series**

Ur series
Fyson, Jenny Grace
see **Shamashazir series**

Urban disaster trilogy
Ballard, James Graham
1 *Crash* (1973)
2 *Concrete island* (1974)
3 *High-rise* (1975)

Urban nucleus series
Bishop, Michael
1 *Little knowledge* (1977)
2 *Catacomb years* (1979)
3 *Under heaven's bridge* (1981)
Co-author: Ian Watson

Urban series
Guenter, C H
see **Robert Urban series**

Urban the Ninth series
Marshall, Bruce
see **Vicar of Christ tetralogy**

Urban trilogy
McMurtry, Larry
1 *Moving on* (1970)
2 *All my friends are going to be strangers* (1972)
3 *Terms of endearment* (1975)

Urgent series
Forde, Nicholas
see **Mark Urgent series**

Urizar series
McCloy, Helen
see **Miguel Urizar series**

Urmal series
Kruse, Max
1 *Urmal from the Ice Age* (1969)
Original edition entitled *Urmel aus dem Eis*
2 *Urmal in space* (1970)
Original edition entitled *Urmel fliegt ins All*

Urruty family trilogy
Kelly, Eleanor Mercein
1 *Basquerie* (1927)
2 *Book of Bette* (1929)
3 *Nacio, his affairs* (1931)

Ursula Bear series
Lavelle, Sheila
1 *Ursula Bear* (1977)
2 *Ursula dancing* (1979)
3 *Ursula exploring* (1980)
4 *Ursula flying* (1981)
5 *Ursula sailing* (1984)
6 *Ursula riding* (1985)
7 *Ursula camping* (1986)
8 *Ursula at the zoo* (1986)
9 *Ursula by the sea* (1986)
10 *Ursula climbing* (1987)
11 *Ursula on the farm* (1987)
12 *Ursula skiing* (1989)
13 *Ursula in the snow* (1989)
14 *Ursula swimming* (1990)
15 *Ursula ballooning* (1992)
16 *Ursula on safari* (1992)

Ursula Dolling series
Clouston, Joseph Storer
1 *Colonel Dam* (1930)
2 *Virtuous vamp* (1931)

Ursula series
Boucher, Anthony
see **Sister Ursula series**

Us three series
Hawker, Ruth Marjorie
1 *Us three* (1930)
Verses
2 *Us three outback* (1932)
Stories and verses
3 *Yesterday* (1936)
Stories and verses; adventures of us three with the early colonists

USAF in Vietnam series
Tilford, Earl H
1 *Setup* (1991)
What the Air Force did in Vietnam and why
2 *Crosswinds* (1993)
The Air Force's setup in Vietnam
Companion volume: *Search and rescue operations in Southeast Asia, 1961-1975*, 1980

Use your series
Williams, Guy Richard
1 *Use your hands!* (1956)
2 *Use your eyes!* (1957)
3 *Use your leisure!* (1958)
4 *Use your head!* (1959)
5 *Use your spare time!* (1960)
6 *Use your legs!* (1961)
7 *Use your playtime!* (1962)
8 *Use your ears!* (1963)

Useless information series
Steiner, Paul
1 *Useless information* (1959)
How to know more and more about less and less
2 *More useless information* (1962)
3 *Useless facts of history* (1964)
4 *Useless facts about women* (1965)

Usher series
Davey, Jocelyn
see **Ambrose Usher series**

V

V I Warshawski series
Paretsky, Sara
1 *Indemnity only* (1982)
2 *Deadlock* (1984)
3 *Killing orders* (1985)
4 *Bitter medicine* (1987)
5 *Blood shot* (1988)
Toxic shock
6 *Burn marks* (1990)
7 *Guardian angel* (1992)
8 *Tunnel vision* (1994)

V series
This sequence has eight authors
Crispin, Ann Carol
1 *V* (1984)
2 *East Coast crisis* (1984)
Wold, Allen
3 *Pursuit of Diana* (1984)
Proctor, George Wyatt
4 *Chicago conversion* (1985)
Sullivan, Tim
5 *Florida project* (1985)
Weinstein, Howard
6 *Prisoners and pawns* (1985)
Sucharitkul, Somtow
7 *Alien swordmaster* (1985)
Wold, Allen
8 *Crivit experiment* (1985)
Sullivan, Tim
9 *New England resistance* (1985)
Crispin, Ann Carol
10 *Death tide* (1985)
Proctor, George Wyatt
11 *Texas run* (1985)
Sullivan, Tim
12 *To conquer the throne* (1987)
Weinstein, Howard
13 *Path to conquest* (1987)
Sucharitkul, Somtow
14 *Symphony of terror* (1988)
Tannehill, Jayne
15 *Oregon invasion* (1988)
Wold, Allen
16 *Below the threshold* (1988)
Companion volumes: *The arrival*, by James Van Hise, 1986, *They're back*, by Edward Gross, 1986, *Conclusion*, by Edward Gross, 1986, *A new beginning*, by Edward Gross, 1986

V series
Upward, Allen
see **Monsieur V series**

Vacation fever series
Andrews, Wendy
Also published under the author's real name Marjorie Weinman Sharmat
1 *Vacation fever!* (1984)
2 *Are we there yet?* (1985)

Vachell series
Huxley, Elspeth
see **Superintendent Vachell series**

Vagabond nights series
Keeler, Harry Stephen
1 *Defrauded yeggman* (1937)
Expanded version of the first part of *The defrauded yeggman* published as *When thief meets thief*, 1938
2 *Ten hours* (1934)
Expanded first part of *Ten hours* published as *The skull of the waltzing clown*, 1935

Vagabonds series
Berna, Paul
see **Mael family series**

Vagabonds series
Dann, Colin
1 *King of the vagabonds* (1987)
2 *City vagabonds* (1991)

Vaiden trilogy
Stribling, Thomas Sigismund
see **Colonel Miltiades Vaiden trilogy**

Val Emery series
Dilnot, George
1 *Tiger Lily* (1939)
2 *Fighting fool* (1939)

Valcour series
King, Rufus
see **Lieutenant Valcour series**

Valdemar trilogy
Lackey, Mercedes
see **Heralds of Valdemar trilogy**

Valdoro series
Armstrong, Evelyn Stewart
1 *Daughter of Valdoro* (1974)
2 *Valdoro's mistress* (1976)

Vale family series
Prouty, Olive Higgins
1 *White fawn* (1931)
2 *Lisa Vale* (1938)
3 *Now, voyager* (1941)
4 *Home port* (1947)
5 *Fabia* (1951)

Vale of Evesham series
Archer, Fred
see **Evesham Vale series**

Vale of laughter series
Travers, Ben
Autobiography
1 *Vale of laughter* (1957)
2 *A-sitting on a gate* (1978)

Valediction of Pantaloon series
Toynbee, Philip
1 *Pantaloon* (1961)
2 *Two brothers* (1964)
3 *Learned city* (1966)
4 *Views from a lake* (1968)

Valencia series
Blasco Ibanez, Vicente
1 *Three roses* (1894)
Original edition entitled *Arroz y tortana*
2 *Mayflower* (1895)
Original edition entitled *Flor de Mayo*
3 *Cabin* (1898)
Original edition entitled *La barraca*
4 *Torrent* (1900)
Original edition entitled *Entre Naranjos*
5 *Reeds and mud* (1902)
Original edition entitled *Canas y barra*

Valentine and Lovelace series
Aldyne, Nathan
see **Dan Valentine and Clarissa Lovelace series**

Valentine Flynn series
O'Shea, Sean
1 *What a way to go!* (1966)
2 *Operation Boudoir* (1967)
3 *Win with sin* (1967)
4 *Nymph island affair* (1967)
5 *Invasion of the nymphomaniacs* (1967)

Valentine Hawkehurst series
Braddon, Mary Elizabeth
1 *Birds of prey* (1867)
2 *Charlotte's inheritance* (1868)

Valentine series
Beecham, Rose
see **Amanda Valentine series**
Day, Marele
see **Claudia Valentine series**
Giff, Patricia Reilly
see **Casey Valentine series**

Valentine series
Somtow, S P
1 *Vampire junction* (1984)
2 *Valentine* (1992)

Valerie and Richard series
Held, Jacqueline
see **Richard and Valerie series**

Valerie Lambert series
Allan, Joan
1 *Who killed me?* (1979)
2 *Who's next* (1979)
3 *Who's on first?* (1979)

Valeshoff series
Ambler, Eric
see **Andreas and Tamara Valeshoff series**

Valhalla trilogy
Chesbro, George Clark
1 *Beasts of Valhalla* (1985)
2 *Two songs this archangel sings* (1986)
3 *Cold smell of sacred stone* (1988)

VALIS trilogy
Dick, Philip Kindred
1 *VALIS* (1981)
2 *Divine invasion* (1981)
3 *Transmigration of Timothy Archer* (1982)
One volume edition entitled *The VALIS trilogy*, 1989; companion volume: *In pursuit of VALIS*, selections from the exegesis, 1991

Vallance series
Proudfoot, Walter
see **Inspector Bill Vallance series**

Valley Farm series
Pellowski, Anne
1 *First farm in the valley* (1982)
Anna's story
2 *Winding Valley Farm* (1982)
Annie's story
3 *Stairstep Farm* (1981)
Anna Rose's story
4 *Willow Wind Farm* (1981)
Betsy's story
5 *Betsy's up-and-down year* (1983)

Valley series
Bacon, Ronald Leonard
1 *In the sticks* (1963)
2 *Along the road* (1964)

Vallon series
Cheyney, Peter
see **Johnny Vallon series**

Valois series
Dumas, Alexandre
1 *Ascanio* (1843)
Francis the First
Alternative English title: The sculptor's apprentice and the provost's daughter; original edition entitled *Ascanio*
2 *Two Dianas* (1847)
Original edition entitled *Les deux Dianes*
3 *Page of the Duke of Savoy* (1855)
Duke's page
Original edition entitled *Le page du duc de Savoie*
3.1 *Leone-Leona* (1855)
3.2 *Saint Quentin* (1855)
3.3 *Tourney* (1855)
Alternative title: Rue Saint Antoine
4 *Horoscope* (1860)
Brigand
Original edition entitled *L'horoscope*
5 *Marguerite de Valois* (1845)
Original edition entitled *La reine Margot*
6 *La Dame de Monsoreau* (1846)
Chicot, the jester
Diana of Meridor
Original edition entitled *La Dame de Monsereau*
7 *Forty-Five guardsmen* (1848)
Forty-Five
Original edition entitled *Les quarante-cinq*

Vampire chronicles series
Rice, Anne
1 *Interview with the vampire* (1976)
2 *Vampire Lestat* (1985)
3 *Queen of the damned* (1988)
One volume edition entitled *Vampire chronicles*, 1989

Vampire diaries series
Smith, Lisa J
1 *Awakening* (1991)
2 *Struggle* (1991)
3 *Fury* (1991)
4 *Dark reunion* (1992)

Vampire files series
Elrod, Patricia Nead
1 *Bloodlist* (1990)
2 *Lifeblood* (1990)
3 *Bloodcircle* (1990)
4 *Art in the blood* (1991)
5 *Fire in the blood* (1991)

Vampirella series
Goulart, Ron
Based on a comic strip
1 *Bloodstalk* (1975)
2 *On alien wings* (1975)
3 *Deadwalk* (1976)
4 *Blood wedding* (1976)
5 *Deathgame* (1976)
6 *Snakegod* (1976)

Vampires series
McMahan, Jeffrey N
1 *Somewhere in the night* (1989)
Short stories
2 *Vampires anonymous* (1991)

Van Alen family series
Schreiner, Samuel Agnew
1 *Possessors and the possessed* (1980)
The saga of the Van Alen family of New York
2 *Van Alens* (1981)
First family of a nation's first city

Van Bell series
Saint James, Blakely
see **Christina Van Bell series**

Van Breda family series
Knight, Brigid
1 *I struggle and I rise* (1946)
2 *Old Amsterdam* (1955)
3 *I shall maintain* (1957)

Van Buren family series
McNally, Clare
see **Ghost house series**

Vance Garde series
La Plante, Jerry
see **Chameleon series**

Vance series
Van Dine, S S
see **Philo Vance series**

Vance Weston series
Wharton, Edith
1 *Hudson River bracketed* (1930)
2 *Gods arrive* (1932)

Van der Berg family series
Cloete, Stuart
1 *Turning wheels* (1937)
2 *Watch for the dawn* (1939)
3 *Hill of doves* (1942)
4 *Mask* (1958)

Vanderi series
Chant, Joy
1 *Grey mane of morning* (1977)
2 *Red moon and black mountain* (1970)
The end of the House of Kendreth
3 *When Voiha wakes* (1983)

Van der Valk series
Freeling, Nicolas
see **Inspector Piet Van der Valk series**

Van der Valk's widow series
Freeling, Nicolas
see **Arlette Van der Valk series**

Vandervoord trilogy
Gaye, Phoebe Fenwich
1 *French prisoner* (1943)
2 *Louisa Vandervoord* (1946)
3 *On a darkling plain* (1950)

Van Doren series
Babcock, Dwight Vincent
see **Hannah Van Doren series**

Van Dusen Ormsberry series
Strange, John Stephen
1 *Man who killed Fortescue* (1928)
2 *Clue of the second murder* (1929)
3 *Murder on the ten-yard line* (1931)
Murder game

Van Dusen series
Futrelle, Jacques
see **Professor Augustus S F X Van Dusen series**

Vandoren series
Bingham, John
see **Ducane series**

Vane series
Islay, Nicholas
see **Sydney Vane series**
Sayers, Dorothy Leigh
see **Harriet Vane series**

Vaness series
Black, Mansell
see **Richard Vaness series**

Vanessa series
Storm, Joan
see **Sarah Vanessa series**

Vanessa Talisend series
Kitchen, Paddy
1 *Lying-in* (1965)
2 *Fleshly school* (1970)
3 *Linsey-Woolsey* (1971)
4 *Paradise* (1972)

Vanessa trilogy
Ure, Jean
1 *Trouble with Vanessa* (1988)
2 *There's always Danny* (1989)
3 *Say goodbye* (1989)

Vanetti series
Lovell, Marc
see **Elsie Vanetti series**

Vang trilogy
Rowley, Christopher
1 *Starhammer* (1986)
2 *Military form* (1988)
3 *Battlemaster* (1990)

Van Heerden series
Sharpe, Tom
see **Kommandant Van Heerden series**

Vanished pomps of yesterday series
Hamilton, Frederic
Autobiography
1 *Days before yesterday* (1920)
2 *Vanished pomps* (1919)
Some random reminiscences of a British diplomat
3 *Here, there and everywhere* (1921)

Vanishing Cracksman series
Hanshew, Thomas W
see **Hamilton Cleek series**

Vanity trilogy
Stoeckl, Agnes de
Autobiography
1 *Not all vanity* (1950)
2 *My dear Marquis* (1952)
3 *When men had time to love* (1953)
Co-author: Wilfrid S Edwards

Van Kill series
Bayne, Spencer
see **Hendrik Van Kill series**

Van Larsen and Plotkin series
Baxt, George
see **Sylvia Plotkin and Max Van Larsen series**

Van Riebeck series
Moray, Helga
see **Katie and Paul Van Riebeck series**

Van Rijn and Falkeyn series
Anderson, Poul
see **Polesotechnic League series**

Vansittart series
Tracy, Louis
1 *American emperor* (1897)
The story of the 4th Empire of France
2 *Lost provinces* (1898)

Van Treece and Conroy series
Tuttle, Wilbur Coleman
see **Henry Harrison Conroy and Judge Van Treece series**

Van Vernet series
Lynch, Lawrence L
1 *Dangerous ground* (1885)
Rival detectives
2 *Mountain mystery* (1886)
Alternative title: The outlaws of the Rockies

Van Vliet series
Briskin, Jacqueline
1 *Paloverde* (1978)
2 *Rich friends* (1976)

Van Zale family series
Howatch, Susan
1 *Rich are different* (1977)
2 *Sins of the fathers* (1980)
3 *Wheel of fortune* (1984)

Vanzant family trilogy
Hohl, Joan
1 *Lady Ice* (1987)
2 *One tough hombre* (1987)
3 *Forever spring* (1988)
Companion volume: *Texas gold*, 1986

Varallo series
Egan, Lesley
see **Vic Varallo series**

Varayan memoir series
Shelley, Rick
1 *Son of the hero* (1990)
2 *Hero of Varay* (1991)

Varden family series
Lea, Alec
1 *To Sunset and beyond* (1970)
2 *Beth Varden at Sunset* (1977)

Variations on a life series
Ward, Richard Heron
see **Neil Falder series**

Varney series
Barry, Jerome
see **Chick Varney series**

Varsity coach series
Hallowell, Tommy
1 *Fourth and goal* (1986)
2 *Out of bounds* (1987)

Varsity coach series
Lantz, Francess Lin
1 *Take down* (1986)
2 *Double play* (1987)

'Varsity series
Allen, Inglis
1 *'Varsity man* (1901)
Passages in the career of an impressionable undergraduate
2 *Graduate in love* (1902)

Vasily Borgneff and Eddie Mancuso series
Luckless, John
see **Eddie Mancuso and Vasily Borgneff series**

Vassar girls series
Champney, Elizabeth Williams
see **Three Vassar girls series**

Vaughan series
Macleod, Alison
see **Tom Vaughan series**

Vaughans series
Jordan, Jennifer
1 *Good weekend for murder* (1987)
2 *Murder under the mistletoe* (1988)

VCR time machine series
Pfeffer, Susan Beth
1 *Rewind to yesterday* (1988)
2 *Future forward* (1989)

Vector series
Swigart, Rob
1 *Vector* (1986)
2 *Toxin* (1989)

Vedder series
Barr, Amelia Edith
see **Shetland series**

Vee Brown series
Daly, Carroll John
1 *Murder won't wait* (1933)
2 *Emperor of evil* (1936)

Veg, Aquilon and Cal trilogy
Anthony, Piers
see **Of man and mantra trilogy**

Veil Kendry series
Chesbro, George Clark
1 *Veil* (1986)
2 *Jungle of steel and stone* (1988)

Vejay Haskell series
Dunlap, Susan
1 *Equal opportunity death* (1984)
2 *Bohemian connection* (1985)
3 *Last annual slugfest* (1986)

Vellacott series
Knight, Peter
see **Roger Vellacott series**

Veltakin series
Cristabel
1 *Manalacor of Veltakin* (1970)
2 *Cruachan and the Killane* (1970)

Velvet comet series
Resnick, Mike
see **Tales of the velvet comet series**

Velvet series
Deveraux, Jude
see **Montgomery annals series**

Velvet series
This sequence has two authors
Bagnold, Enid
1 *National Velvet* (1935)
Forbes, Bryan
2 *International Velvet* (1978)

Venable series
Holley, Helen
see **Tessie Venable series**

Venables series
Sprigg, Christopher Saint John
see **Charles Venables series**

Vendetta series
Gates, Tudor
Based on a television series
1 *Scipio* (1967)
2 *Mister Scipio* (1968)
3 *Ancora Scipio* (1970)

Vendetta series
Murdock, Melinda Seabrooke
1 *Vendetta* (1987)
2 *Dynteryx* (1988)

Vendetta series
Zacharia, Irwin
1 *Vendetta* (1982)
2 *Murder Club* (1982)

Venesz series
Thwaites, Frederick Joseph
see **Doctor Joszef Venesz series**

Vengeance Seeker series
Knott, William Cecil
1 *Vengeance Seeker, number one* (1975)
2 *Vengeance Seeker, number two* (1975)
3 *Vengeance Seeker, number three* (1976)
4 *Taste of Vengeance* (1977)
5 *Caulder's badge* (1977)

Venn series
Brock, Lynn
see **Sergeant Venn series**

Venneker series
Geddes, Paul
see **Paul Venneker series**

Vent Torrey series
Wales, Mike
see **Leatherhand series**

Venturer Twelve series
This sequence has two authors
Morgan, Dan
1 *Thunder of stars* (1968)
2 *Seed of stars* (1972)
3 *Neutral stars* (1973)
Kippax, John
4 *Where no stars guide* (1975)

Venus prime series
Preuss, Paul
1 *Breaking strain* (1987)
2 *Maelstrom* (1988)
3 *Hide and seek* (1989)
4 *Medusa encounter* (1990)
5 *Diamond moon* (1990)
6 *Shining ones* (1991)

Venus series
Burroughs, Edgar Rice
1 *Pirates of Venus* (1934)
2 *Lost on Venus* (1935)
3 *Carson of Venus* (1939)
4 *Escape on Venus* (1946)
5 *Wizard of Venus* (1964)

Venus series
Fraser, Ronald
see **Trout series**

Venus series
Lach-Szyrma, Wladislaw Somerville
1 *Voice from another world* (1874)
Aleriel
Alternative title: A voyage to other worlds; the second title is an expanded edition
2 *Under other conditions* (1892)
3 *Worlds apart* (1893)

Venus trilogy
Sargent, Pamela
1 *Venus of dreams* (1986)
2 *Venus of shadows* (1988)

Veralidaine Sarrasri series
Pierce, Tamora
see **Daine series**

Verdant Green series
Bede, Cuthbert
see **Mister Verdant Green series**

Vereker series
Forsythe, Robin
see **Anthony Vereker series**

Verena Frodesley series
Lance, Leslie
see **Nurse Verena Frodesley series**

Verity Ames and Jonas Quarrel series
Krentz, Jayne Ann
1 *Gift of gold* (1988)
2 *Gift of fire* (1989)

Verity Birdwood series
Rowe, Jennifer
1 *Grim pickings* (1987)
2 *Murder by the book* (1989)
3 *Death in store* (1991)
4 *Makeover murders* (1992)
5 *Stranglehold* (1993)

Verity series
Antony, Peter
see **Mister Verity series**
Selwyn, Francis
see **Sergeant William Verity series**

Vermilion boat series
Ghose, Sudhindra Nath
Reminiscences of student days in Calcutta
1 *Vermilion boat* (1953)
2 *Flame of the forest* (1955)

Vermont farm series
Peck, Robert Newton
Autobiography
1 *Day no pigs would die* (1972)
2 *Part of the sky* (1994)

Vermont series
Hard, Walter
1 *Some Vermonters* (1928)
2 *Salt of Vermont* (1931)
3 *Mountain township* (1933)
4 *Vermont vintage* (1937)

Vermont series

Character stories in verse; numbers 2 and 4 also published in one volume entitled *Vermont salt and vintage*, 1946
5 *Vermont valley* (1939)
Companion volume: *This is Vermont*, 1936

Vermont series
Van de Water, Frederic Franklin
see **American Revolution series**

Vernal equinox series
Harrison, Michael
1 *All the trees were green* (1936)
2 *Vernal equinox* (1939)

Vernet series
Lynch, Lawrence L
see **Van Vernet series**

Verney series
Wheatley, Dennis
see **Molly Fountain series**

Vernon series
Bateson, David
see **Larry Vernon series**

Vernon Templeton series
Luigi, Belli
1 *Mummy walks* (1950)
2 *Curse of the mummy* (1950)

Veronica and Peter series
Beech, Margaret
see **Peter and Veronica series**

Veronica Ganz series
Sachs, Marilyn
1 *Veronica Ganz* (1968)
2 *Peter and Veronica* (1969)
3 *Mary* (1970)
4 *Truth about Mary Rose* (1973)

Veronica quartet
Robinson, Nancy Konheim
1 *Veronica, the show-off* (1984)
2 *Veronica knows best* (1987)
3 *Veronica meets her match* (1990)
4 *Countess Veronica* (1994)

Veronica Ramsay series
Wallace, Kathleen
1 *Grace on their doorposts* (1944)
2 *And after that, the dark* (1946)

Veronica series
Duvoisin, Roger
1 *Veronica* (1961)
2 *Our Veronica goes to Petunia's farm* (1962)
Veronica goes to Petunia's farm
3 *Lonely Veronica* (1963)
4 *Veronica's smile* (1964)
5 *Veronica and the birthday present* (1971)

Veronica Slate series
Crews, Lary
1 *Kill cue* (1988)
2 *Extreme close-ups* (1989)
3 *Option to die* (1989)
4 *Death rehearsal* (1990)

Verrell series
Graeme, Bruce
see **Blackshirt series; Lord Blackshirt series**
Graeme, Roderic
see **Blackshirt series**

Verrick series
McBain, Laurie
see **Sabrina Verrick series**

Very merry story series
Barkan, Joanne
1 *Very merry Santa Claus story* (1992)
2 *Very merry snowman story* (1992)

Very scary story series
Barkan, Joanne
1 *Very scary haunted house* (1991)
2 *Very scary Jack o'Lantern* (1991)
3 *Very scary ghost story* (1992)
4 *Very scary witch story* (1992)

Very young series
Kremenetz, Jill
Photographic picture books
1 *Very young dancer* (1976)
2 *Very young rider* (1977)
3 *Very young gymnast* (1978)
4 *Very young circus flyer* (1979)
5 *Very young skater* (1979)
6 *Very young skier* (1990)
7 *Very young actress* (1991)
8 *Very young gardener* (1991)
9 *Very young musician* (1991)

Very young series
Milne, Alan Alexander
1 *When I was very young* (1930)
2 *It's too late now* (1939)
Autobiography

Veseloffsky series
Horler, Sydney
see **Baron Veseloffsky series**

Vesper Holly series
Alexander, Lloyd
1 *Illyrian adventure* (1986)
2 *El Dorado adventure* (1987)
3 *Drackenberg adventure* (1988)
4 *Jedera adventure* (1989)
5 *Philadelphia adventure* (1990)

Vesuvio trilogy
Finch, Simon
see **Voyager trilogy**

Vet in green pastures series
Lasgarn, Hugh
Reminiscences
1 *Vet in green pastures* (1985)
2 *Vet for all seasons* (1986)
3 *Vet in a storm* (1987)
4 *Vet in the village* (1988)

Vet in the vestry series
Cameron, Alexander
1 *Vet in the vestry* (1987)
2 *Poultry in the pulpit* (1988)

Vet series
Dawson, David
Memoirs
1 *Vet in downland* (1977)
2 *Vet in the vale* (1978)
3 *Vet in the paddocks* (1978)
Numbers 2 and 3 also published in one volume 1978

Vet series
Duncan, Alex
Reminiscences
1 *It's a vet life* (1961)
2 *Vet has nine lives* (1962)
3 *Vets in the belfry* (1964)
Numbers 1-3 also published in an abridged edition entitled *The best of vets*, 1977
4 *Vets in congress* (1977)
5 *Vet among the pigeons* (1977)
6 *Vet in the manger* (1978)
7 *Vet in a state* (1979)
8 *Vet on vacation* (1979)

Vet series
Herriot, James
Reminiscences
1 *If only they could talk* (1970)
2 *It shouldn't happen to a vet* (1972)
Numbers 1 and 2 also published in one volume entitled *All creatures great and small*, 1972
3 *Let sleeping vets lie* (1973)
4 *Vet in harness* (1974)
Numbers 3 and 4 also published in one volume entitled *All things bright and beautiful*, 1974
5 *Vets might fly* (1976)
6 *Vet in a spin* (1977)
Numbers 5 and 6 also published in one volume entitled *All things wise and wonderful*, 1977
7 *Lord God made them all* (1981)
8 *Every living thing* (1992)

Vet series
Lloyd-Jones, Buster
Memoirs of life as a vet
1 *Animals came in one by one* (1966)
2 *Come into my world* (1972)
3 *Love on a lead* (1973)

Vet series
Martin, Nancy
1 *Call the vet* (1955)
2 *Vet in the making* (1957)

Vet series
Robinson, Martha
1 *Vet's family* (1963)
2 *Vet's son* (1966)
3 *Vet's nieces* (1967)
4 *Vet's problem* (1969)
5 *Vet's holiday* (1971)

Vet series
Straiton, Eddie
Reminiscences
1 *Animals are my life* (1979)
Vet in charge
2 *Vet at large!* (1981)
3 *Positively vetted!* (1983)
4 *Vet on the set!* (1985)

Veta series
Goll, Reinhold Weimar
1 *Visitors from planet Veta* (1961)
2 *Spaceship to planet Veta* (1962)

Veteran's Day series
Kane, Rod
1 *Combat bachelor, part one* (1985)
2 *Combat bachelor, part two* (1987)
One volume edition entitled Veteran's Day, 1990

Veterinary surgeon series
Stranger, Joyce
see **Timothy Yorke series**

Vet's wife series
Bishop, Mary
Humorous reminiscences
1 *It's a dog's life* (1958)
2 *Love in the doghouse* (1962)

Vi and Marissa series
Cooney, Caroline B
1 *Cam girl-meets-boy* (1988)
2 *Camp reunion* (1988)

Viagens Interplanetarias series
De Camp, Lyon Sprague
see **Krishna series**

Vibart series
Farnol, Jeffery
1 *Broad highway* (1910)
2 *Charmian, Lady Vibart* (1932)
3 *Way beyond* (1933)

Vic and Jerry series
Dines, Glen
see **Jerry and Vic series**

Vic Brown trilogy
Barstow, Stan
1 *Kind of loving* (1960)
2 *Watchers on the shore* (1966)
3 *Right true end* (1976)

Vic Malloy series
Chase, James Hadley
1 *You're lonely when you're dead* (1949)
2 *Lay her among the lilies* (1950)
Too dangeous to be free
3 *Figure it out for yourself* (1950)
Marijuana mob

Vic Merritt series
Cafferty, Jake
1 *Death on the boardwalk* (1986)
2 *Carnation killer* (1987)

Vic Varallo series
Egan, Lesley
1 *Case for appeal* (1961)
2 *Borrowed alibi* (1962)
3 *Run to evil* (1963)
4 *Detective's due* (1965)
5 *Nameless ones* (1967)
6 *Wine of violence* (1969)
7 *Malicious mischief* (1971)
8 *Scenes of crime* (1976)
9 *Dream apart* (1978)
10 *Hunter and the hunted* (1979)
11 *Choice of crimes* (1980)
12 *Random death* (1982)
13 *Crime for Christmas* (1983)
14 *Wine of life* (1985)

Vicar of Christ tetralogy
Marshall, Bruce
1 *Bishop* (1970)
2 *Urban the Ninth* (1973)
3 *Marx the First* (1975)
4 *Peter the Second* (1976)

Vicar series
Insight, James
Reminiscences
1 *I turned my collar round* (1954)
2 *I am the vicar* (1956)
3 *Country parson* (1961)
4 *I am a guinea pig* (1964)

Vicarage Children series
Hill, Lorna
1 *Vicarage Children* (1961)
2 *More about Mandy* (1963)
3 *Vicarage Children in Skye* (1966)

Vicarage series
Streatfeild, Noel
Autobiography
1 *Vicarage family* (1963)
2 *Away from the vicarage* (1965)
On tour
3 *Beyond the vicarage* (1971)

Vicarious years series
Van Druten, John
Autobiography
1 *Vicarious years* (1955)
2 *Widening circle* (1957)

Vickery series
Hobart, Robertson
see **Grant Vickery series**
Mace, Helen
see **Noel Vickery series**

Vicki Barr series
This sequence has two authors
Wells, Helen
1 *Silver wings for Vicki* (1947)
2 *Vicki finds the answer* (1948)
3 *Hidden valley mystery* (1949)
4 *Secret of Magnolia Manor* (1949)
Tatham, Julie
5 *Clue of the broken blossom* (1950)
6 *Behind the white veil* (1951)
7 *Mystery at Hartwood House* (1952)
Wells, Helen
8 *Peril over the airport* (1953)
9 *Mystery of the vanishing lady* (1954)
10 *Search for the missing twin* (1954)
11 *Ghost at the waterfall* (1956)

12 *Clue of the gold coin* (1958)
13 *Silver ring mystery* (1960)
14 *Clue of the carved ruby* (1961)
15 *Mystery of Flight 908* (1962)
16 *Brass idol mystery* (1964)
Mystery of the brass idol

Vicky Austin series
L'Engle, Madeleine
see **Austin family series**

Vicky Bliss series
Peters, Elizabeth
1 *Borrower of the night* (1973)
2 *Street of the five moons* (1978)
3 *Silhouette in scarlet* (1983)
4 *Trojan gold* (1987)
5 *Night train to Memphis* (1994)

Vicky Gaines and Ransome Dragoon series
Diamond, Frank
see **Ransome Dragoon and Vicky Gaines series**

Vicky Loring series
Kincade, Wynn
1 *Career for Vicky* (1962)
2 *Golden buttons* (1963)

Vicky McBain series
Robertson, Colin
1 *Tiger's claws* (1951)
2 *You can keep the corpse* (1955)
3 *Venetian mask* (1956)
4 *Eastlake affair* (1957)
5 *Who rides a tiger* (1958)
6 *Golden triangle* (1959)
7 *Threatening shadows* (1959)
8 *Night trip* (1960)
9 *Murder sits pretty* (1961)

Victim trilogy
Sheckley, Robert
1 *Tenth victim* (1965)
2 *Victim prime* (1987)
3 *Hunter victim* (1988)

Victor and Maria series
Vendrell, Carme Sole
Translated from the Catalan
1 *Coat* (1982)
2 *Cherry tree* (1982)
3 *Climb* (1982)
4 *Bandstand* (1982)
5 *Sun* (1983)
6 *Moon* (1983)
7 *Parcel* (1983)
8 *Hide and seek* (1983)

Victor Bondurant series
Edwards, James G
see **Inspector Victor Bondurant series**

Victor Caryll series
Fairlie, Gerard
1 *Scissors cut paper* (1927)
2 *Man who laughed* (1928)
3 *Stone blunts scissors* (1928)
4 *That man returns* (1934)

Victor Garrison series
Kirby, Dallas
1 *Victor* (1942)
2 *Victor versus Verhasst* (1943)

Victor Grant series
Ethan, John B
1 *Black gold murders* (1959)
2 *Call girls for murder* (1960)
3 *Murder on Wall Street* (1960)

Victor series
Mark, Ted
see **Man from O.R.G.Y. series**

Victoria Albemarle trilogy
Coulter, Catherine
1 *Midsummer magic* (1988)
2 *Calypso magic* (1988)
3 *Moonspun magic* (1988)

Victoria Babenberg series
Cost, March
see **Princess Victorian Babenberg series**

Victoria Bowering series
Yeager, Dorian
1 *Cancellation by death* (1992)
2 *Eviction by death* (1993)

Victoria Edgecombe series
Brady, Terence
1 *Victoria* (1972)
2 *Victoria and company* (1974)

Victoria Martin trilogy
Pascal, Francine
1 *Hanging out with Cici* (1977)
2 *My first love and other disasters* (1979)
3 *Love and betrayal and hold the mayo!* (1985)

Victoria Plum picture book series
Rippon, Angela
1 *Victoria Plum's one, two, three* (1985)
2 *Victoria Plum's toys* (1985)
3 *Victoria Plum at the seaside* (1985)
4 *Victoria Plum on the farm* (1985)
Companion volumes: *Victoria Plum's garden, pop-up book*, 1985, *Victoria Plum's seaside adventure, pop-up book*, 1985

Victoria Plum series
Rippon, Angela
1 *Victoria Plum and her animal friends* (1982)
2 *Victoria Plum goes house hunting* (1982)
3 *Victoria Plum has a party* (1982)
4 *Victoria Plum plants a garden* (1982)
5 *Victoria Plum and the little bird* (1982)
6 *Victoria Plum goes for a walk* (1982)
7 *Victoria Plum and the magic spell* (1983)
8 *Victoria Plum and the squirrels* (1983)
9 *Victoria Plum on sports day* (1983)
10 *Victoria Plum and her woodland friends* (1983)
11 *Victoria Plum and the lost moonbeam* (1983)
12 *Victoria Plum has a surprise party* (1983)
13 *Victoria Plum goes on a picnic* (1983)
14 *Victoria Plum has a visitor* (1983)
Selections: *Victoria Plum story book*, 1983

Victoria Plumb series
Szudek, Agnes Susan Philomena
Short stories
1 *Victoria Plumb* (1978)
2 *Victoria and the Parrots Gang* (1979)

Victoria series
Plaidy, Jean
see **Queen Victoria series**

Victoria series
Wilkins, Vaughan
1 *And so Victoria* (1936)
2 *Husband for Victoria* (1958)

Victoria trilogy
Whittle, Tyler
see **Queen Victoria trilogy**

Victorian and Edwardian London life series
Stafford, Ann
1 *Light me a candle* (1949)
2 *Bess* (1951)
3 *Great Mrs Pennington* (1952)
4 *Time it takes* (1954)

Victorian boyhood series
Jones, Lawrence Evelyn
Autobiography
1 *Victorian boyhood* (1955)
2 *Edwardian youth* (1956)
3 *Geogian afternoon* (1958)
4 *I forgot to tell you* (1959)

Victorian day series
This sequence has three authors
Huggett, Frank Edward
1 *Day in the life of a Victorian farm worker* (1972)
2 *Day in the life of a Victorian factory worker* (1973)
Garforth, John
3 *Day in the life of a Victorian policeman* (1974)
Davidoff, Leonore
4 *Day in the life of a Victorian domestic servant* (1976)

Victorian England series
Kellow, Kathleen
Also published under the pseudonym Jean Plaidy
1 *Lilith* (1954)
2 *It began in Vauxhall Gardens* (1955)

Victorian England series
Lindsay, Philip
1 *Through midnight streets* (1957)
2 *Under their skin* (1959)

Victorian girls series
This sequence has two authors; biography of Emily Mary and Ellen Augusta Hall
Sherrard, Owen Aubrey
1 *Two Victorian girls* (1966)
Edited by Anthony Reginald Mills, with extracts from the Hall diaries
Mills, Anthony Reginald
2 *Halls of Ravenswood* (1967)
3 *Two Victorian ladies* (1969)

Victorian India series
Stewart, Cynthia
1 *Residency* (1963)
2 *Jethro's daughters* (1964)

Victorian lady series
Fountaine, Margaret
1 *Love among the butterflies* (1980)
2 *Butterflies and late loves* (1986)

Victorian life series
Lochhead, Marion Cleland
1 *Their first ten years* (1956)
Victorian childhood
2 *Young Victorians* (1959)
3 *Victorian household* (1964)

Victorian painting series
Gaunt, William
1 *Pre-Raphaelite tragedy* (1942)
2 *Aesthetic adventure* (1945)
3 *March of the moderns* (1949)
4 *Victorian Olympus* (1952)

Victorian series
Rita
1 *Grandmothers* (1927)
2 *Wand'ring darling* (1928)
3 *Jean and Jeanette* (1929)

Victorian son series
Cloete, Stuart
Autobiography
1 *Victorian son* (1972)
1897-1922
2 *Gambler* (1973)
1920-1939

Victorian trilogy
Tweedsmuir, Susan Buchan
1 *Cousin Harriet* (1957)
2 *Dashbury Park* (1959)
3 *Stone in the pool* (1961)

Victory series
Botsford, Charles Alexander
1 *Joining the colors* (1918)
2 *Fighting with the U.S.Army* (1919)
3 *In the trenches* (1920)
4 *At the Front* (1921)

Victory trilogy
Alger, Horatio
1 *Only an Irish boy* (1894)
Alternative title: Andy Burke's fortunes
2 *Victor Vane* (1894)
Alternative title: The young secretary
3 *Adrift in the city* (1895)
Alternative title: Oliver Conrad'a plucky fight

Victory trilogy
Leslie, Richard
1 *Dawn readiness* (1985)
2 *Raging skies* (1985)
3 *Hunters* (1986)

Vidar trilogy
Friedman, Michael Jan
1 *Hammer and the horn* (1985)
2 *Seekers and the sword* (1985)
3 *Fortress and the fire* (1988)

Video High series
Kaye, Marilyn
1 *Modern love* (1994)
2 *High life* (1994)

Videssos series
Turtledove, Harry
1 *Misplaced legion* (1987)
2 *Emperor for the legion* (1987)
3 *Legion of Videssos* (1987)
4 *Swords of the legion* (1987)
5 *World of difference* (1990)
6 *Krispos rising* (1991)
7 *Krispos of Videssos* (1991)

Vienna series
Buckley, Eunice
1 *Family from Vienna* (1941)
2 *Blue Danube* (1943)

Viennese trilogy
Gainham, Sarah
1 *Night falls on the city* (1967)
2 *Place in the country* (1969)
3 *Private worlds* (1971)

Viera Kolarova series
Powers, Elizabeth
1 *All that glitters* (1981)
Alternative title: The case of the ice-cold diamond
2 *On account of murder* (1984)

Vierges fortes series
Prevost, Marcel
Translated from the French
1 *Frederique* (1900)
2 *Lea* (1900)

Vietnam series
Helm, Eric
see **Ground Zero series**

Vietnam War series
Leib, Franklin Allen
1 *Fire dream* (1989)
2 *Valley of the shadow* (1991)

Vietnam War series
Nolan, Keith William
1 *Battle for Hue, Tet, 1958* (1983)
2 *Into Laos* (1985)
3 *Death Valley* (1987)
4 *Into Cambodia* (1990)
5 *Operation Buffalo* (1991)

Vietnam War series
O'Brien, Tim
1 *If I die in a combat zone, box me up and ship me home* (1973)
Based on the author's experiences
2 *Northern lights* (1975)
3 *Going after Cacciato* (1978)
4 *Things they carried* (1990)

Vietnam War series
Thompson, Robert
1 *No exit from Vietnam* (1969)
2 *Peace is not at hand* (1974)

Vigilante series
Ludlow, Ian
1 *Point Three Five Seven Vigilante* (1985)
2 *Make them pay* (1985)
3 *White wash* (1985)

Vigilante series
Reno, Clint
1 *Sun Mountain slaughter* (1974)
2 *Sierra massacre* (1974)

Vigilante series
Santiago, V J
see **Joseph Madden series**

Viking cipher series
Spencer, Rick
see **Eric Ivorsen series**

Viking lords series
Coulter, Catherine
1 *Lord of Hawkfell Island* (1993)
2 *Lord of Raven's Peak* (1994)

Viking trilogy
Treece, Henry
1 *Viking's dawn* (1955)
2 *Road to Miklagard* (1957)
3 *Viking's sunset* (1960)

Vikings and Saxons series
Birt, David
see **Saxons and Vikings series**

Vikings series
Langholm, Neil
This pseudonym is used by Kenneth Bulmer and Laurence James as indicated against each title
1 *Blood sacrifice* (1975)
[James]
2 *Dark return* (1975)
[Bulmer]
3 *Blood on the sun* (1975)
[James]
4 *Trail of blood* (1976)
[Bulmer]

Village cricket series
Parker, John
1 *Village cricket match* (1977)
2 *Test time at Tillingfold* (1979)
3 *Tillingfold's tour* (1986)

Village dinosaur series
Arkle, Phyllis
1 *Village dinosaur* (1968)
2 *Two village dinosaurs* (1969)

Village parson trilogy
Pellow, John
1 *Pastor's green* (1980)
2 *Parson's progress* (1981)
3 *Parson's princess* (1983)

Village series
Diack, Hunter
Autobiography of an educator
1 *Boy in a village* (1962)
2 *That village on the Don* (1965)
Companion volume: *Road fortune, a cycling journey through Europe*, by Hunter Diack and Robert Frazer Mackenzie, 1935

Village trilogy
Fraser, Mary
1 *First summer* (1979)
2 *Long winter* (1979)
3 *Time of change* (1980)

Villiers series
Gibbs, Lewis
see **Kitty Villiers series**
Muller, Mary
see **Anna and Johan de Villiers series**
Panshin, Alexei
see **Anthony Villiers series**
Rodney, Bryan
see **Francis Villiers series**

Villon trilogy
McCarthy, Justin Huntly
see **Francois Villon trilogy**

Vinca and Sylvaine trilogy
Meyers, Roy
see **Dolphins trilogy**

Vincent and Penny Mercer series
Clandon, Henrietta
see **Penny and Vincent Mercer series**

Vincent Skrene series
Richardson, Frank
1 *King's counsel* (1902)
2 *Semi-society* (1903)

Vincent Stallard and Cynthia Godwin series
Beare, George
1 *Bloody sun at noon* (1970)
2 *Very breath of hell* (1971)
3 *Bee sting deal* (1972)

Vincente and Samson series
Singer, Shelley
see **Jake Samson and Rosie Vincente series**

Vine series
Sterling, Stewart
see **Gil Vine series**

Vinegar Hill series
Free, Colin
see **Pollitt family series**

Vinegar works trilogy
Gorey, Edward
1 *Gashlycrumb* (1963)
2 *Insect god* (1963)
3 *West wing* (1963)

Vinnie Harris trilogy
Oldfield, Pamela
see **Kent trilogy**

Vinson series
Norman, Mick
see **Gerry Vinson series**

Vintage years trilogy
Leigh, Helena
1 *Grapes of paradise* (1980)
2 *Wild vines* (1984)
3 *Kingdoms of the vine* (1984)

Vinti family series
Verga, Giovanni
1 *House by the medlar tree* (1888)
Original edition entitled *I malevoglia*
2 *Master Don Gesualdo* (1889)
Don Candeloro
Maestro Don Gesualdo
Original edition entitled *Maestro Don Gesualdo*

Vintner series
Campbell, Ian Maxwell
Reminiscences
1 *Wayward tendrils on the vine* (1948)
2 *Reminiscences of a vintner* (1950)

Viola Corbett series
Edgar, Josephine
1 *Duchess* (1976)
2 *Countess* (1978)

Violence series
Berger, Gilda
1 *Violence and the media* (1989)
2 *Violence and drugs* (1989)
3 *Violence and the family* (1990)
4 *Violence in sports* (1990)

Vipers series
Walker, Frank
1 *Vipers and Co.* (1976)
2 *Pop go the Vipers* (1979)

Virgil Magus series
Davidson, Avram
1 *Phoenix and the mirror* (1969)
2 *Virgil in Averno* (1987)

Virgil Nosegay series
Biegel, Paul
1 *Dwarfs of Nosegay* (1976)
Original edition entitled *De dwergjes van Tuil*
2 *Fattest dwarf of Nosegay* (1978)
Original edition entitled *Virgilius van Tuil*
3 *Virgil Nosegay and the cake hunt* (1979)
Original edition entitled *Virgilius van Tuil op zoek van een taart*
4 *Virgil Nosegay and the hupmobile* (1980)
Original edition entitled *Virgilius van Tuil en de oom uit Zweden*
5 *Virgil Nosegay and the Wellington boots* (1982)
Original edition entitled *Virgilius van Tuil overwintert bij de mensen*
No further volumes in this sequence translated into English

Virgil Tibbs series
Ball, John
1 *In the heat of the night* (1965)
2 *Cool cottontail* (1966)
3 *Johnny get your gun* (1969)
Death for a playmate
The second title is a revised edition
4 *Five pieces of jade* (1972)
5 *Eyes of Buddha* (1976)
6 *Then came violence* (1980)
7 *Singapore* (1986)

Virgin in the garden tetralogy
Byatt, Antonia Susan
1 *Virgin in the garden* (1979)
2 *Still life* (1986)
Numbers 3 and 4 not yet published

Virgin soldiers series
Thomas, Leslie
1 *Virgin soldiers* (1966)
2 *Onward virgin soldiers* (1971)
3 *Stand up virgin soldiers* (1975)

Virginia and Felix Freer series
Ferrars, Elizabeth
American editions are published under the name E X Ferrars
1 *Last will and testament* (1978)
2 *Frog in the throat* (1980)
3 *Thinner than water* (1981)
4 *Death of a minor character* (1983)
5 *I met murder* (1985)
6 *Woman slaughter* (1989)

Virginia Davis series
North, Grace May
1 *Virginia of V.M. Ranch* (1924)
2 *Virginia at Vine Haven* (1924)
3 *Virginia's adventure club* (1924)
4 *Virginia's ranch neighbors* (1924)
5 *Virginia's romance* (1924)

Virginia Hammond trilogy
Campbell, Daisy Rhodes
1 *Fiddling girl* (1914)
2 *Proving of Virginia* (1915)
3 *Violin lady* (1916)

Virginia Kelly series
Baker, Nikki
1 *In the game* (1991)
2 *Lavender House murder* (1992)
3 *Long goodbyes* (1993)

Virginia Nixon series
Murray, Lillian
1 *Ginnie and the snow gypsies* (1958)
2 *In the track of the huskies* (1960)

Virginia series
Chase, Mary Ellen
1 *Girl from Big Horn Country* (1916)
2 *Virginia of Elk Creek Valley* (1917)

Virginia series
Collonge, Simone
Illustrated by Francoise Amadieu
1 *Virginia and the prince of the sea* (1984)
2 *Virginia and the blue bird* (1984)

Virginia series
Griffith, Helen Sherman
1 *Oh, Virginia!* (1920)
2 *No, Virginia!* (1922)
3 *Now, Virginia!* (1923)
4 *Why, Virginia!* (1924)
5 *Yes, Virginia!* (1928)
6 *Hail, Virginia!* (1930)

Virginia series
Thackeray, William Makepeace
1 *History of Henry Esmond* (1852)
Henry Esmond
2 *Virginians* (1857)

Virginia trilogy
Eggleston, George Cary
1 *Dorothy South* (1902)
A love story of Virginia just before the War
2 *Master of Warlock* (1903)
A Virginia war story
3 *Evelyn Byrd* (1904)

Virginian series
Johnston, Mary
1 *To have and to hold* (1900)
By order of the company
Set in 1621
2 *Prisoners of hope* (1898)
Old dominion
Set in the years 1649-1651
3 *Audrey* (1902)
Set in 1727
4 *Great valley* (1926)
Set in Shenandoah between 1735 and 1760

Virginian series
This sequence has two authors
Wister, Owen
1 *Virginian* (1902)
A horseman of the Plains
Owen, Dean
2 *Trail for the Virginian* (1971)
Based on the television series entitled *The men from Shiloh*

Virgins series
Rivers, Caryl
1 *Virgins* (1984)
2 *Girls forever brave and true* (1986)

Viriconium series
Harrison, Michael John
1 *Pastel city* (1971)
2 *Storm of wings* (1980)
3 *In Viriconium* (1982)
Floating gods
4 *Viriconium nights* (1984)
Revised edition 1985; numbers 3 and 4 also published in one volume entitled *Viriconium*, 1988

Virtual realities trilogy
Carmichael, Claire
1 *Virtual realities* (1992)
2 *Cybersaur* (1993)
3 *Worldwarp* (1994)

Vis trilogy
Lee, Tanith
see **Wars of Vis trilogy**

Viscount Clymping and Inspector Gregory Pellew series
Gielgud, Val
see **Inspector Gregory Pellew and Viscount Clymping series**

Vision of beasts trilogy
Lovejoy, Jack
1 *Creation descending* (1984)
2 *Second kingdom* (1984)
3 *Brotherhood of Diablo* (1984)

Vision of light series
Riley, Judith Merkle
see **Margaret of Ashbury series**

Visions of London series
Macinnes, Colin
1 *City of Spades* (1957)
2 *Absolute beginners* (1959)
3 *Mister Love and Justice* (1960)
One volume editions entitled *Visions of London*, 1969 and *The London novels*, 1969

Vivanti series
Horler, Sydney
see **Paul Vivanti series**

Vivian series
Meade, Lillie Thomas
see **Betty Vivian series**

Vivian's series
Caldwell, Patricia Kathleen
1 *Prefects at Vivian's* (1956)
2 *Head girl at Vivian's* (1957)

Vivien Le Fay Morgan series
Fortune, Dion
1 *Sea priestess* (1938)
2 *Moon magic* (1956)

Vlad the Drac series
Jungman, Ann
1 *Vlad the Drac* (1982)
2 *Vlad the Drac returns* (1984)
3 *Vlad the Drac, superstar* (1985)
4 *Vlad the Drac, vampire* (1988)
5 *Vlad the Drac down under* (1989)

Vladimer Karlov and Alexander Crane series
Hayes, Ralph Eugene
see **Check Force series**

Vladimir Gull series
Stuart, Anthony
1 *Snap judgment* (1977)
That man Gull
2 *Vicious circles* (1978)
3 *Midwinter madness* (1979)
4 *Force play* (1979)
5 *London affair* (1981)
6 *Russian leave* (1982)

Vladimir Nabokov series
Boyd, Brian
1 *Russian years* (1990)
2 *American years* (1991)

Vladimir Yabolinsky series
Schechtman, Joseph Boris
1 *Rebel and statesman* (1956)
2 *Fighter and prophet* (1961)

Voices series
Stokes, Doris
Autobiography of a medium
1 *Voices in my ear* (1980)
2 *More voices in my ear* (1981)
3 *Innocent voices in my ear* (1983)
4 *Host of voices* (1984)
5 *Whispering voices* (1985)
6 *Voices of love* (1986)
7 *Joyful voices* (1987)

Volcano god trilogy
Freund, Philip
1 *Saturnalia* (1956)
Also includes *The nomads*
2 *Roof-top* (1957)
Also includes *Eurasia*
3 *How the world began* (1958)

Von Bek family trilogy
Moorcock, Michael
1 *War hound and the world's pain* (1981)
2 *Brothel in Rosenstrasse* (1982)
3 *City in the autumn stars* (1986)

Von Helsing series
Mathewson, Joseph
see **Alicia von Helsing series**

Von Heynitz series
Le Queux, William
see **Otto von Heynitz series**

Von Kaz series
Teilhet, Darwin Le Ora
see **Baron Von Kaz series**

Von Kopf series
De Halsalle, Henry
see **Olga von Kopf series**

Vonnie and Monique series
Francis, Dorothy
see **Keepsake series**

Von Ryan series
Westheimer, David
1 *Von Ryan's express* (1964)
2 *Von Ryan's return* (1980)

Vorkosigan series
Bujold, Lois McMaster
see **Miles Naismith Vorkosigan series**

Vorland series
Norton, Andre
see **Krip Vorland series**

Vorobeitchik series
Steeman, Andre
see **Wenceslas Vorobeitchik series**

Voss series
Cameron, Donald Clough
see **Abelard Voss series**

Voula and Henry series
Stewart, Maureen
see **Henry and Voula series**

Vows and honor series
Lackey, Mercedes
1 *Oathbound* (1988)
2 *Oathbreakers* (1989)

Voyage into space series
Branley, Franklyn Mansfield
1 *Saturn, the spectacular planet* (1983)
2 *Space telescope* (1985)
3 *Sputnik to space shuttle* (1986)
4 *Star guide* (1987)
5 *Uranus, the seventh planet* (1988)
6 *Superstar* (1990)
The super nova of 1987

Voyage not completed series
Grayson, Rupert
Autobiography
1 *Voyage not completed* (1969)
2 *Standfast, the Holy Ghost* (1973)

Voyage series
Francis, Clare
1 *Come hell or high water* (1977)
2 *Come wind or weather* (1978)

Voyage that never ends series
Lowry, Malcolm
1 *Under the volcano* (1947)
2 *Dark as the grave wherein my friend is laid* (1968)
3 *Hear us O Lord from heaven thy dwelling place* (1961)

Voyage to New South Wales series
Barrington, George
1 *Voyage to New South Wales* (1795)
Includes a description of the country, the manners, customs, religion, etc. of the natives in the vicinity of Botany Bay
2 *Sequel to Barrington's Voyage to New South Wales* (1800)

Voyage to the bottom of the sea series
This sequence has two authors
Sturgeon, Theodore
1 *Voyage to the bottom of the sea* (1961)
Fairman, Paul Warren
2 *City under the sea* (1965)
Companion volume: *Voyage to the bottom of the sea*, by Raymond F Jones, 1965

Voyager trilogy
Finch, Simon
1 *Golden voyager* (1978)
2 *Pagan voyager* (1979)
3 *Voyager in bondage* (1981)

Voyagers series
Bova, Ben
1 *Voyagers* (1981)
2 *Alien within* (1986)
3 *Star brothers* (1990)

Voyages series
Davison, Ann
1 *Home was an island* (1952)
Life on an island in Loch Lomond
2 *Last voyage* (1951)
An autobiographical account of all that led up to an illicit voyage and the outcome thereof
3 *My ship is so small* (1956)
Across the Atlantic in a 23-foot yacht from Plymouth via the Canary Islands and West Indies to New York
4 *By Gemini* (1962)
Alternative title: Marshmallows in the salad; a coast-wise cruise from Miami to Miami
5 *Florida junket* (1964)
The story of a shoestring cruise

Voyageurs series
Ballinger, W A
1 *Voyageurs* (1976)
2 *There and back again* (1977)

Vridar Hunter series
Fisher, Vardis
see **In tragic life series**

Vulcan reflections series
Langsam, Devra Michele
1 *Vulcan reflections* (1975)
2 *More Vulcan reflections* (1976)
Co-author: Sherna Comerford

Vulmea series
Howard, Robert Ervin
see **Black Vulmea series**

Vulture series
Ward, Harold
1 *Vulture* (1936)
2 *Vulture strikes* (1936)

Vurt series
Noon, Jeff
1 *Vurt* (1993)
2 *Pollen* (1994)

W

WW III series
Slater, Ian
1 *WW III* (1990)
2 *World in flames* (1991)

WAAC series
WAAC
1 *Woman's story of the war* (1930)
2 *WAAC demobolized* (1931)
Her private affairs, 1918-1930

Wabash trilogy
Garlock, Dorothy
1 *Lonesome River* (1987)
2 *Dream river* (1988)
3 *River of tomorrow* (1988)

Wace series
Simons, Roger
see **Inspector Fadiman Wace series**

Wacky facts lunch bunch series
Zindel, Paul
1 *Attack of the killer* (1993)
2 *Fright party* (1993)
3 *Fifth-grade safari* (1993)
4 *One hundred per-cent laugh riot* (1994)

Wacky series
Sobol, Donald J
see **Encyclopedia Brown's wacky series**

Wacky Witch series
Lewis, Jean
1 *Wacky Witch and the royal birthday* (1971)
2 *Wacky Witch and the mystery of the king's gold* (1973)

Waco series
Edson, John Thomas
1 *Waco's debt* (1962)
2 *Waco's badge* (1981)
3 *Sagebrush sleuth* (1962)
4 *Arizona Ranger* (1962)
Originally published under the pseudonym Rod Denver
5 *Waco rides in* (1964)
6 *Drifter* (1963)
7 *Doc Leroy, M.D.* (1977)
Night hawk
8 *Hound dog man* (1967)

Wacvie series
Bandler, Faith
1 *Wacvie* (1977)
2 *Welou, my brother* (1984)

Wade and Bill series
Weddle, Ferris
see **Clint Wade and Trapper Bill series**

Wade Anthony series
Heath, Eric
1 *Murder pool* (1954)
2 *Murder of a mystery writer* (1955)
Based on *Death takes a dive*, 1938

Wade, Arcot and Morey series
Campbell, John Wood
see **Arcot, Morey and Wade series**

Wade Calhoun series
Hawkins, Clint
see **Saddletramp series**

Wade Chisholm series
Cunningham, Chet
1 *Apache ambush* (1979)
2 *Arizona gunfire* (1980)
3 *Man in two camps* (1980)

Wade Paris series
Benson, Ben
see **Inspector Wade Paris series**

Wade series
Bristow, Gwen
1 *Gutenberg murders* (1931)
2 *Mardi gras murders* (1932)

Wade series
Hogan, Robert Jasper
see **Smoke Wade series**
Lorin, Amii
see **Samantha Wade series**
McConnell, Vicki P
see **Nyla Wade series**
Short, Luke
see **Big Jim Wade series**

Wady series
Mack Bride, Johnny
see **Frank Wady series**

Wager series
Burns, Rex
see **Gabriel Wager series**

Waghorn series
Rhode, John
see **Doctor Lancelot Priestley series**

Wagon train series
Johnston, Dorothy Grunbock
1 *Cathy and carl of the covered wagon* (1953)
2 *Cathy and carl captured* (1954)
3 *Cathy and Carl join the gold rush* (1955)
4 *Cathy and Carl shipwrecked* (1956)
5 *Cathy and Carl and the sea horse mystery* (1957)
6 *Cathy and Carl ride the pony express* (1958)

Wagon train series
Stanley, Chuck
1 *Wagon train colt* (1960)
2 *Wagon train hold-up* (1961)

Wagons West series
Ross, Dana Fuller
1 *Independence!* (1979)
2 *Nebraska!* (1979)
3 *Wyoming!* (1979)
4 *Oregon!* (1980)
5 *Texas!* (1980)
6 *California!* (1981)
7 *Colorado!* (1981)
8 *Nevada!* (1981)
9 *Washington!* (1982)
10 *Montana!* (1983)
11 *Dakota!* (1983)
12 *Utah!* (1984)
13 *Idaho!* (1984)
14 *Missouri!* (1985)
15 *Mississippi!* (1985)
16 *Louisiana!* (1986)
17 *Tennessee!* (1986)
18 *Illinois!* (1986)
19 *Wisconsin!* (1987)
20 *Kentucky!* (1987)
21 *Arizona!* (1988)
22 *New Mexico!* (1988)
23 *Oklahoma!* (1989)
24 *Celebration!* (1989)

Wahl and Bertin series
Zweig, Arnold
see **Werner Bertin and Lenore Wahl series**

Wainwright series
Mather, Berkely
see **James Wainwright series**

Waiting game series
Mosco, Maisie
1 *Waiting game* (1987)
2 *After the dream* (1988)

Waiting-room tetralogy
Feuchtwanger, Lion
1 *Success* (1930)
Original edition entitled *Erfolg*
2 *Oppermanns* (1933)
Original edition entitled *Die geschwister Oppenheim*
3 *Paris gazette* (1940)
Original edition entitled *Exil*
4 *Simone* (1944)
Original edition entitled *Simone*

Wake series
Kingston, Charles
see **Inspector Wake series**

Wake series
Schildt, Goran
1 *In the wake of a wish* (1949)
Original edition entitled *Onskeresan*
2 *In the wake of Odysseus* (1951)
Original edition entitled *I Odysseus Kolvatten*
3 *Sun boat* (1956)
Original edition entitled *Solbaten*; a journey up the Nile

Wakefield series
Miller, Blaine
see **Bob Wakefield series**

Wakeley witch series
Smith, Janet
1 *Wakeley witch* (1980)
2 *Witch, the carpet and the boomash* (1982)

Walden series
This sequence has three authors
Thoreau, Henry David
1 *Walden* (1854)
Alternative title: Life in the woods
Skinner, Burrhus Frederic
2 *Walden two* (1948)
Catran, Jack
3 *Walden three* (1988)

Walden West series
Derleth, August
Autobiography
1 *Walden West* (1961)
2 *Return to Walden West* (1970)
Companion volume: *Walden Pond, homage to Thoreau*, 1968

Walderhurst series
Burnett, Frances Hodgson
see **Lady Walderhurst series**

Waldo series
Handford, Martin
see **Wally series**

Waldo series
Wilhelm, Hans
1 *Waldo and the desert island adventure* (1986)
2 *Waldo and the Christmas surprise* (1988)
3 *Waldo and the giant splash* (1988)
4 *Waldo and the boattrip* (1988)
5 *Waldo and the orchestra* (1988)
6 *One, two, three with Waldo* (1988)
7 *In the zoo with Waldo* (1988)
8 *In the morning with Waldo* (1988)
9 *Green, green are all my colors* (1988)
Companion volumes: *Waldo for old and young*, 1986, 1987, *Waldo with love*, 1986, 1987, 1988, 1989, *Waldo between friends*, 1986, 1987, 1988, *Waldo datebook*, 1988, 1989, *Waldo friendship*, 1989

Waldo, tell me series
Wilhelm, Hans
1 *Waldo, tell me about guardian angels* (1988)
2 *Waldo, tell me about me* (1988)
3 *Waldo, tell me about God* (1988)
4 *Waldo, tell me about Christ* (1988)
5 *Waldo, tell me about Christmas* (1989)

Wales series
Carter, Forrest
see **Josey Wales series**
Warde, Margaret
see **Betty Wales series**

Walk in the dark trilogy
Spedding, Alison
1 *Road and the hills* (1986)
2 *Cloud over water* (1988)
3 *Streets of the city* (1988)

Walk in the woods series
Border, Rosemary
1 *Walk in the wind* (1984)
2 *Walk in the snow* (1984)
3 *Walk in the sun* (1984)
4 *Walk in the rain* (1984)

Walk series
Daniel, Roland
see **Inspector John Walk series**

Walker series
Greaves, Jimmy
see **Soccer series**
Macdonnell, James Edmond
see **Hooky Walker series**
Norton, Andre
see **Blake Walker series**

Wallace and John Mahoney series
Flannery, Sean
1 *Kremlin conspiracy* (1979)
2 *Eagles fly* (1980)
3 *False prophets* (1983)
4 *Broken idols* (1985)

Wallace family series
Plagemann, Bentz
1 *This is Goggle* (1955)
My son Goggle
2 *Father to the man* (1964)
3 *Best is yet to be* (1966)
4 *World of difference* (1969)

Wallace series
Daniel, Roland
see **Michael Wallace series**
Fry, Stephen
see **Ted Wallace series**
Wilson, Alexander
see **Sir Leonard Wallace series**

Walled orchard series
Holt, Tom
1 *Goatsong* (1989)
2 *Walled orchard* (1990)

Wallingford series
Chester, George Randolph
see **James Rufus Wallingford series**
Cooper, James Fenimore
see **Miles Wallingford series**

Wallion series
Regis, Julius
see **Maurice Wallion series**

Wally Phipps-Mangot series
Hackforth-Jones, Gilbert
see **Commander Wally Phipps-Mangot series**

Wally series
Handford, Martin
Picture game books
1 *Where's Wally?* (1987)
Where's Waldo?
2 *Where's Wally now?* (1988)
Find Waldo now
3 *Great Wally search* (1989)
Great Waldo search
4 *Where's Wally 3, the fantastic journey* (1989)
Where's Waldo, the ultimate fun book
5 *Where's Wally in Hollywood?* (1993)
Where's Waldo in Hollywood?
Companion volume: *Where's Wally, the magnificent poster book*, 1991, also published as *Where's Waldo, the magnificent poster book*

Wallypug series
Farrow, George Edward
1 *Wallypug of Why* (1895)
2 *Wallypug in London* (1897)
3 *Adventures in Wallypug-Land* (1898)
4 *In search of the Wallypug* (1902)
5 *All about the Wallypug* (1903)
6 *Wallypug in Pog-Land* (1904)
7 *Wallypug in the moon* (1905)
Alternative title: His badjesty
Companion volumes: *Wallypug tales, verse*, 1903, *Wallypug birthday book*, 1904, *The Wallypug book*, 1905

Wally's Ward series
Andrews, Lucilla
1 *One night in London* (1979)
2 *Weekend in The Garden* (1981)
3 *In an Edinburgh drawing room* (1983)
4 *Phoenix syndrome* (1987)

Walnut Grove series
Rushing, Jane Gilmore
1 *Mary Dove* (1974)
Set in the 1870s
2 *Tamzen* (1972)
Set in the 1890s
3 *Walnut Grove* (1964)
Set about 1900
4 *Winds of blame* (1983)
Set in 1916
5 *Against the moon* (1968)
Set in the 1960s
6 *Raincrow* (1977)
Set in the 1970s

Walpole series
Plumb, John Harold
see **Sir Robert Walpole series**

Walsh and Phipps series
Hunt, Richard
see **Chief Inspector Walsh and Constable Brenda Phipps series**

Walsh series
Cohen, Octavus Roy
see **Lieutenant Marty Walsh series**

Walt Disney's Annette series
This sequence has two authors
Schroeder, Doris
1 *Sierra summer* (1960)
2 *Desert inn mystery* (1961)
3 *Mystery at Moonstone Bay* (1962)
4 *Mystery at Smugglers' Cove* (1963)
Meyers, Barlow
5 *Mystery at Medicine Wheel* (1964)

Walt Slade series
Scott, Bradford
The character of Walt Slade was inspired by Eugene Cunningham's *Buckaroo*, 1933
1 *Cowpuncher* (1942)
2 *Trail herd* (1944)
3 *Range rider* (1945)
4 *Desert gold* (1946)
5 *Gold for the dead* (1947)
6 *Whip* (1950)
Silver City
7 *Stranger in boots* (1952)
8 *Rustler's range* (1953)
9 *Trigger talk* (1956)
Sixgun talk
10 *Canyon killers* (1956)
11 *Border blood* (1956)
12 *Badland's boss* (1956)
13 *Texas terror* (1956)
14 *Texas hawk* (1957)
15 *Death Canyon* (1957)
16 *Curse of the Texas gold* (1957)
17 *Powder burn* (1957)
18 *Dead Man's Trail* (1957)
19 *Shootin' man* (1958)
Slick-iron
20 *Blaze of guns* (1958)
21 *Gun law* (1959)
22 *Texas badman* (1959)
23 *Texas vengeance* (1959)
24 *Dead in Texas* (1959)
Gunslick
25 *Range terror* (1959)
26 *Holster law* (1959)
27 *Gun gamble* (1960)
28 *Guns of the Alamo* (1960)
29 *Valley of hunted men* (1960)
30 *Ambush trail* (1960)
31 *Pecos trail* (1960)
32 *Lone Star rider* (1960)
33 *Desert killers* (1961)
34 *Rangeland guns* (1961)
35 *Rangers at bay* (1961)
36 *Skeleton trail* (1961)
37 *Smuggler's brand* (1961)
38 *Gunsmoke on the Rio Grande* (1961)
39 *Masked raider* (1962)
40 *Gunsight showdown* (1962)
41 *Death rides the Rio Grande* (1962)
42 *Doom trail* (1962)
43 *Ranger rides to death* (1962)
44 *Guns of Bang Town* (1962)
45 *Texas devil* (1962)
46 *Texas rider* (1962)
47 *Trail of blood and bones* (1962)
48 *Gundown* (1963)
49 *Gun justice* (1963)
50 *Ranger's revenge* (1963)
51 *Rattlesnake bandit* (1963)
52 *Rustler's guns* (1963)
53 *Hate trail* (1963)
54 *Gunsmoke talk* (1963)
55 *Death's corral* (1963)
56 *Outlaw land* (1963)
57 *Killer's doom* (1963)
58 *Bullets for a ranger* (1963)
59 *Outlaw gold* (1963)
60 *Trails of guns and gold* (1964)
61 *Guns for hire* (1964)
62 *Horseman of the shadows* (1964)
63 *Death calls the turn* (1964)
64 *Dead at sunset* (1964)
65 *Range ghost* (1964)
66 *Raiders of the Rio Grande* (1964)
67 *Ghost trail* (1964)
68 *Showdown at Skull Canyon* (1964)
69 *Tombstone showdown* (1964)
70 *Trails of steel* (1965)
71 *Wasteland rider* (1965)
72 *West of Laredo* (1965)
73 *Border vengeance* (1965)
74 *Bullets over the border* (1965)
75 *Death in the saddle* (1965)
76 *Thundering guns* (1965)
77 *Hot lead* (1966)
78 *Death on the Rimrock* (1967)
79 *Bullet brand* (1967)
Sixgun fury
80 *Blood on the moon* (1967)
81 *Pecos law* (1967)
82 *Death's harvest* (1967)
83 *Curse of dead man's gold* (1967)
84 *Sidewinder* (1967)
85 *Maverick showdown* (1967)
86 *Hot lead and cold nerve* (1967)
87 *Texas death* (1967)
Ranger laughs at death
88 *Thunder trail* (1967)
89 *River raiders* (1968)
90 *Death tally* (1968)
91 *Red road to vengeance* (1968)
92 *Sixguns in a bloody dawn* (1968)
Death rides the river trail
93 *Sky riders* (1968)
94 *Haunted valley* (1968)
95 *Hard Rock showdown* (1968)
96 *Border terror* (1968)
Border war
97 *Outlaw roundup* (1968)
Robber's roundup
98 *Boom town* (1968)
99 *Lead and flame* (1968)
100 *Laredo on the Rio Grande* (1969)
101 *Mountain raiders* (1969)
102 *Date with death* (1969)
103 *Bullet justice* (1969)
104 *Devil from Blazing Hill* (1969)
Ranger to the rescue
105 *Hands up!* (1969)
106 *Rider of the Mesquite Trail* (1969)
107 *Sixgun doom* (1969)
108 *Texas blood* (1969)
Blood and steel
109 *Trail of empire* (1969)
110 *Death to the ranger!* (1970)
111 *Death whispers* (1970)
112 *Ranger's roundup* (1970)
113 *Reach for gold* (1970)
114 *Ranger daring* (1971)
115 *Ranger wins* (1971)
116 *Savage gunlaw* (1971)
117 *Border terror* (1972)
118 *Spargo* (1972)
119 *Border daring* (1973)
120 *Four must die* (1973)

Walt Warren series
Langley, John
1 *Six-gun trial* (1958)
2 *Six-gun feud* (1959)
3 *Six-gun law* (1960)
4 *Six-gun war* (1960)
5 *Six-gun justice* (1961)
6 *Six-gun strife* (1963)
7 *Six-gun gamble* (1963)
8 *Six-gun champion* (1964)
9 *Six-gun citadel* (1964)
10 *Six-gun cavalier* (1965)
11 *Six-gun smoke* (1965)
12 *Six-gun vengeance* (1966)
13 *Six-gun salute* (1967)
14 *Badlands gang* (1970)

Walter Ghost series
Starrett, Vincent
1 *Murder on B Deck* (1929)
2 *Dead man inside* (1931)
3 *End of Mister Garment* (1932)

Walter Greenway series
Holmes, Robert
1 *Walter Greenway, spy and others, sometime criminal* (1916)
2 *Walter Greenway, spy and hero* (1917)
His life story

Walter McDumont series
Garner, Hugh
see **Inspector Walter McDumont series**

Walter series
Cook, David
1 *Walter* (1978)
2 *Winter doves* (1979)

Walter series
Townsend, John Rowe
see **Uncle Walter series**

Walter Tirel series
Shipway, George
1 *Paladin* (1972)
2 *Wolf time* (1973)

Walters and Skye series
Hart, Bruce
see **Jessie Walters and Michael Skye series**

Walter's schooldays series
Adams, Henry Cadwallader
1 *Doctor's birthday* (1873)
Alternative title: The force of example
2 *Walter's friend* (1873)
Alternative title: Big boys and little ones

Walters series
Sapper
see **John Walters series**

Walton boys series
Burton, Hal
1 *Walton boys and gold in the snow* (1948)
2 *Walton boys in rapids ahead* (1950)
3 *Walton boys in high country* (1952)

Walton series
Clark, Susanna Rebecca Graham
see **Yensie Walton series**
Elton, Wallace
see **Jud Walton series**
Frost, Kelman Dalgety
see **Captain John Walton series**
Green, Roger James
see **Samuel Walton series**

Waltons series
Rathjen, Carl Henry
Based on a television series
1 *Treasures* (1975)
2 *Puzzle* (1975)

Waltz series
McCormick, Claire
see **John Waltz series**

Wanawake series
Moody, Susan
see **Penny Wanawake series**

Wanderer series
Hiscock, Eric Charles
1 *Around the world in Wanderer III* (1956)
Based on Voyage of the Wanderer III, 1945
2 *Beyond the west horizon* (1963)
3 *Atlantic cruise in Wanderer III* (1968)
4 *Sou'West in Wanderer IV* (1973)
5 *Come abroad* (1978)
Companion volume: *Two yachts, two voyages*, 1984

Wanderer Springs series
Flynn, Robert
1 *Seasonal rain, and other stories* (1986)
2 *Wanderer Springs* (1987)

Wandering girl series
Ward, Glenyse
1 *Wandering girl* (1988)
2 *Unna you fellas* (1991)

Wandering Jew series
This sequence has five authors
Sue, Eugene
1 *Wandering Jew* (1844)
Original edition entitled *Le Juif errant*
Mohoao
2 *Ships of Tarshish* (1867)
Heym, Stefan
3 *Wandering Jew* (1981)
Original edition entitled *Ahasver*
Stableford, Brian Michael
4 *Tales of the Wandering Jew* (1991)
Clough, Samuel Dennis Procter
5 *Wandering Jew, an account of his last adventure* (1983)

Wandering Jew trilogy
Viereck, George Sylvester
1 *My first two thousand years* (1928)
2 *Salome, the wandering Jewess* (1930)
3 *Invincible Adam* (1932)

Wandering Will trilogy
Ballantyne, Robert Michael
1 *Sunk at sea* (1869)
Alternative title: The adventures of Wandering Will in the Pacific
2 *Lost in the forest* (1869)
Alternative title: Wandering Will's adventure in South America
3 *Over the Rocky Mountains* (1869)
Alternative title: Wandering Will in the land of the Redskin

Wanderlust Brown series
Boyd, Edward
1 *Introducing Wanderlust Brown* (1948)
2 *Wanderlust goes south* (1948)
3 *Wanderlust's third innings* (1953)

Wandlemere series
Sibley, Patricia
1 *High walk to Wandlemere* (1973)
2 *Ravens in winter* (1974)

Wandor series
Green, Roland James
1 *Wandor's ride* (1973)
2 *Wandor's journey* (1975)
3 *Wandor's voyage* (1979)
4 *Wandor's flight* (1981)

Wandy series
Chaffee, Allen
1 *Wandy the wild pony* (1933)
2 *Wandy wins* (1938)

Wang family series
Buck, Pearl Sydenstricker
1 *Good earth* (1931)
2 *Sons* (1932)
3 *House divided* (1935)
One volume edition entitled *House of earth*, 1935

Wang the Ninth trilogy
Weale, Putnam
1 *Wang the Ninth* (1920)
The story of a Chinese boy
2 *Her closed hands* (1927)
3 *China's crucifixion* (1928)

Wantoknow series for boys
Goodman, Montague
1 *Questions of Jack Wantoknow* (1936)
2 *Come to tea with me* (1937)
3 *Curiosity Joe* (1938)
Numbers 1-3 also published in one volume entitled *The first Wantoknow omnibus for boys*, 1943
4 *Worldover School* (1943)
5 *Curiosity Club* (1944)
6 *Solomon goes to school* (1945)
Numbers 4-6 also published in one volume entitled *The second Wantoknow omnibus for boys*, 1947
Companion volume: *Solomon builds a temple*, 1951

Wantoknow series for girls
Dennison, Dorothy
1 *Jill wants to know* (1938)

Wantoknow series for girls

2 *Doubting Thomasina* (1939)
3 *Jennifer Knowall* (1942)
Numbers 1-3 also published in one volume entitled *The first Wantoknow omnibus for girls*, 1944
4 *Corrie and Co.* (1946)
5 *These girls I knew* (1947)
6 *We all went sailing* (1947)
Numbers 4-6 also published in one volume entitled *The second Wantoknow omnibus for girls*, 1947

Wapshot series
Cheever, John
1 *Wapshot chronicle* (1957)
2 *Wapshot scandal* (1964)

War against the Chtorr trilogy
Gerrold, David
1 *Matter for men* (1983)
Expanded edition 1989
2 *Day for damnation* (1984)
Revised edition 1989; numbers 1-2 also published in one volume entitled *Invasion*, 1984
3 *Rage for revenge* (1989)

War and peace series
This sequence has two authors
Tolstoi, Leo Nikolaevich
1 *War and peace* (1869)
Translated from the Russian
Salisbury, Carola
2 *Count Vronsky's daughter* (1981)

War birds trilogy
This sequence has two authors
McGavock, John
1 *War birds* (1927)
Diary of an unknown aviator, edited by Elliott White Springs
Springs, Elliott White
2 *Above the bright blue sky* (1928)
3 *War birds and ladybirds* (1931)

War Cabinet trilogy
Parkinson, Roger
1 *Peace for our time* (1971)
Munich to Dunkirk, the inside story
2 *Blood, toil, tears and sweat* (1973)
The War history from Dunkirk to Alamein, based on the War Cabinet papers of 1940 to 1942
3 *Day's march nearer home* (1974)
The War history from Alamein to VE Day, based on the War Cabinet papers of 1942 to 1945

War chief series
Ellis, Edward Sylvester
1 *Iron Heart, war chief of the Iroquois* (1899)
2 *Blazing Arrow* (1900)
3 *Red Eagle* (1901)
Chieftain and the scout

War chiefs series
Dugan, Bill
1 *Geronimo* (1991)
2 *Chief Joseph* (1992)
3 *Crazy Horse* (1992)
4 *Quanah Parker* (1993)

War diary series
Millin, Sarah Gertrude
Autobiography
1 *Night is long* (1941)
2 *World blackout* (1944)
3 *Reeling earth* (1945)
4 *Pit of the abyss* (1946)
5 *Sound of the trumpet* (1947)
6 *Fire out of heaven* (1947)
7 *Seven thunders* (1948)
8 *Measure of my days* (1955)

War dogs series
Nik-Uhernik
1 *War dogs* (1984)
2 *M-sixteen jury* (1985)

War Eagle series
Buntline, Ned
1 *Ice-king* (1848)
Alternative title: The fate of the lost steamer; a fanciful tale of the far North
2 *War Eagle* (1869)
Alternative title: Ossiniwa, the Indian brave

War for the Union series
Tomlinson, Everett Titsworth
1 *For the Stars and Stripes* (1909)
2 *Young blockaders* (1910)

War game series
Wheatley, Dennis
1 *Invasion* (1938)
2 *Blockade* (1939)
3 *Alibi* (1951)

War in Crete series
Moss, William Stanley
1 *Ill met by moonlight* (1950)
An account of the kidnapping of Major-General Karl Kreipe in Crete in 1944; companion volume: *Appointment in Crete, the story of a British agent*, by Alexander Meadows Rendel, 1953
2 *War of shadows* (1952)

War in South-East Asia series
This sequence has two authors; personal accounts of World War II
McCormac, Charles
1 *You'll die in Singapore* (1954)
Allbury, Albert George
2 *Bamboo and bushido* (1955)

War in the air series
Southall, Ivan
1 *Third pilot* (1958)
2 *Flight to Gibraltar* (1958)
Terror flight
3 *Mediterranean black* (1959)
4 *Sortie in Cyrenaica* (1959)
5 *Mission in Greece* (1959)
6 *Atlantic pursuit* (1960)

War in Vietnam series
Wright, David K
1 *Eve of battle* (1989)
2 *Wider war* (1989)
3 *Vietnamization* (1989)
4 *Fall of Vietnam* (1989)

War memoirs series
Caputo, Philip
War correspondent's memoirs of the Vietnam and other wars
1 *Rumor of war* (1977)
2 *Means of escape* (1991)

War memoirs series
Gaulle, Charles de
1 *Call to honour, 1940-1942* (1955)
Original edition entitled L'appel, 1940-1942
2 *Unity, 1942-1944* (1959)
Original edition entitled L'unite
3 *Salvation, 1944-1946* (1960)
Original edition entitled Le salut
4 *Memoirs of hope* (1971)
Original edition entitled *Memoires d'espoir;* contains *Renewal, 1958-62*, and *Endeavour, 1962-*

War memoirs series
Milligan, Spike
1 *Adolf Hitler, my part in his downfall* (1971)
2 *Rommel, Gunner who?* (1974)
3 *Monty, his part in my victory* (1976)
4 *Mussolini, his part in my downfall* (1978)
5 *Where have all the bullets gone?* (1985)
6 *Goodbye soldier* (1986)
Selections entitled *Milligan's war*, 1988

War of Independence series
Mason, Francis Van Wyck
see **American War of Independence series**

War of Independence series
Mitchell, Silas Weir
1 *Hugh Wynne, Free Quaker* (1896)
Sometime brevet lieutenant-colonel in the staff of His Excellency General **War of** Washington
2 *Red City* (1908)
A novel of the second administration of President Washington

War of Independence trilogy
Taylor, David
1 *Lights across the Delaware* (1954)
2 *Farewell to Valley Forge* (1955)
3 *Storm the last rampart* (1960)

War of 1938 trilogy
Wright, Sydney Fowler
1 *Prelude in Prague* (1935)
2 *Four days' war* (1936)
3 *Megiddo's Ridge* (1937)

War of powers series
Vardeman, Robert Edward
1 *Sundered realm* (1980)
2 *City in the glacier* (1980)
3 *Destiny stone* (1980)
Numbers 1-3 also published in one volume entitled *The war of powers*, 1984
4 *Fallen ones* (1982)
5 *In the shadow of Omizantrim* (1982)
6 *Demon of the dark ones* (1982)
Numbers 4-6 also published in one volume entitled *Istu awakened*, 1985

War of the dragons series
Smeds, Dave
1 *Sorcery within* (1985)
2 *Schemes of dragons* (1989)

War of the gods on earth trilogy
Offutt, Andrew Jefferson
1 *Iron lords* (1979)
2 *Shadows out of hell* (1980)
3 *Lady of the snowmist* (1983)

War of the Ninja Master series
Barker, Wade
1 *Kohga ritual* (1988)
2 *Shibo discipline* (1988)
3 *Himitsu attack* (1988)
4 *Zakka slaughter* (1988)

War of the wizards trilogy
Offutt, Andrew Jefferson
1 *Demon in the mirror* (1978)
2 *Eyes of Sarsis* (1980)
3 *Web of the spider* (1981)

War of the worlds series
This sequence has three authors
Wells, Herbert George
1 *War of the worlds* (1898)
Parody: *The war of the Wenuses*, by Charles Larcom Graves and Edward Verrall Lucas, 1898
Serviss, Garrett Putnam
2 *Edison's conquest of Mars* (1947)
Abridged for radio as *Forrest J Ackerman presents Invasion of Mars*, 1969
Wellman, Manly Wade
3 *Sherlock Holmes's War of the worlds* (1975)

War plays series
Bond, Edward
1 *Red, black and ignorant* (1985)
2 *Tin can people* (1985)
3 *Great peace* (1985)
One volume edition entitled *The war plays*, 1991

War reminiscences series
Mant, Gilbert
1 *Grim glory* (1942)
2 *You'll be sotty* (1944)

War surplus series
Watt-Evans, Lawrence
1 *Cyborg and the sorcerers* (1982)
2 *Wizard and the war machine* (1987)

War trilogy
Doolittle, Hilda
Poetry
1 *Walls do not fall* (1944)
2 *Tribute to the angels* (1945)
3 *Flowering of the rod* (1946)
One volume edition entitled *Trilogy*, 1973

War whoop series
Jayne, R H
1 *Lost in the wilderness* (1892)
2 *Through Apache land* (1893)
3 *In the Pecos country* (1894)
4 *Cave in the mountains* (1894)

War world series
Pournelle, Jerry
1 *Burning eye* (1988)
Co-authors: John Francis Carr and Roland Green
2 *Death's head rebellion* (1990)
3 *Sauron dominion* (1991)
Co-author: John Francis Carr

War years series
Fawcett, Bill
1 *Far stars war* (1990)
2 *Siege of Arista* (1991)
3 *Jupiter war* (1991)

Warbots series
Stine, George Harry
1 *Warbots* (1988)
2 *Operation steel band* (1988)
3 *Bastaard rebellion* (1988)
4 *Sierra Madre* (1988)
5 *Operation high dragon* (1989)
6 *Lost battalion* (1989)
7 *Operation iron fist* (1989)
8 *Force of arms* (1990)
9 *Blood siege* (1990)
10 *Guts and glory* (1991)
11 *Warrior shield* (1992)
12 *Judgment day* (1992)

Warchild series
Bowes, Richard
1 *Warchild* (1986)
2 *Goblin market* (1988)

Ward series
Delannoy, Burford
see **Watson Ward series**
Farmer, Bernard James
see **Tom Ward series**
Grey, Zane
see **Ken Ward series**
Lewis, Royston
see **Eric Ward series**
Saint John, David
see **Peter Ward series**

Ware series
Andrews, Charlton
see **Drexel Ware series**
Wells, Susan
see **Anthony Ware series**

Wareham series
Brennan, Carol
see **Liz Wareham series**

Warhammer forty thousand series
Jones, Neal
see **Inquisition war series**

Warhammer series
This sequence has two authors
Yeovil, Jack
1 *Drachenfels* (1989)
2 *Ignorant armies* (1989)
Pringle, David
3 *Wolf riders* (1989)
4 *Red thirst* (1990)
Yeovil, Jack
5 *Beasts in velvet* (1991)
6 *Ignorant armies* (1992)

Warhunter series
Siegel, Scott
1 *Killer's council* (1981)
2 *Gunmen's grave* (1981)
3 *Great Salt Lake massacre* (1981)
4 *Bitter blood* (1981)

Waring series
Ebel, Suzanne
see **Sir Robert Waring series**
King, T Stanleyan
see **Scarsdale Waring series**

Warlock series
Haggard, Paul
see **Mike Warlock series**
Norton, Andre
see **Planet Warlock series**
Stasheff, Christopher
see **Gramarye series**

Warlord series
Frost, Jason
This pseudonym is used by Raymond Obstfeld and Rich Rainey as indicated against each title
1 *Warlord* (1983)
[Obstfeld]
2 *Cutthroat* (1984)
[Obstfeld]
3 *Badlands* (1984)
[Obstfeld]
4 *Prisonland* (1985)
[Obstfeld]
5 *Terminal island* (1985)
[Obstfeld]
6 *Killer's keep* (1987)
[Rainey]

Warmstry series
Pakington, Humphrey
1 *Four in family* (1931)
2 *Roving eye* (1932)
3 *In company with Crispin* (1934)
Eligible bachelor

Warne and Hilton families series
Nicole, Christopher
see **West Indies series**

Warne series
Sylvester, Martin
see **William Warne series**

Warner series
Morris, Wright
see **Floyd Warner series**

Warner series
Severn, David
1 *Ponies and poachers* (1947)
2 *Cruise of the Maiden Castle* (1948)
3 *Treasure for three* (1949)
4 *Crazy castle* (1951)
5 *Burglars and bandicoots* (1952)

Warp series
Oram, Neil
Based on the Warp cycle of ten unpublished plays
1 *Storm's howling through Tiflis* (1980)
2 *Lemmings on the edge* (1981)
3 *Balustrade paradox* (1982)

Warren and Ed Baer series
Resnicow, Herbert
see **Ed and Warren Baer series**

Warren Peace series
Shaw, Bob
1 *Warren Peace* (1993)
2 *Toga war* (1994)

Warren Remfrey series
Thompson, Edward
1 *In Araby Orion* (1930)
2 *Lament for Adonis* (1932)

Warren series
Bialk, Elisa
see **Marty Warren series**
Kitchin, Clifford Henry Benn
see **Malcolm Warren series**
Langley, John
see **Walt Warren series**
Shaw, George Bernard
see **Mrs Warren series**

Warren series
Sindall, Marjorie Aylwynn
1 *Children of The Warren* (1953)
2 *Strangers at The Warren* (1954)
3 *Holidays at The Warren* (1955)
4 *Caravan at The Warren* (1957)
5 *Surprises at The Warren* (1960)

Warren series
Warren, James
see **James Warren series**

Warrender series
Cole, George Douglas Howard
see **Mrs Elizabeth Warrender series**

Warrenders series
Wallace, Ivy Lilian
1 *Young Warrenders* (1961)
2 *Thanks to Peculiar* (1962)
3 *Strangers at Warrenders' Halt* (1963)
4 *Snake ring mystery* (1966)

Warrington-Reeve series
Bell, Josephine
see **Claude Warrington-Reeve series**

Warrior of Mars trilogy
Bradbury, Edward P
1 *Warriors of Mars* (1965)
Also published as *City of the beast*, by Michael Moorcock
2 *Blades of Mars* (1965)
Also published as *Lord of the Spiders*, by Michael Moorcock
3 *Barbarians of Mars* (1965)
Also published as *Masters of the pit*, by Michael Moorcock
One volume edition entitled *Warrior of Mars*, 1981

Warrior of vengeance series
Coe, Ross Anton
1 *Sorcerer's blood* (1982)
2 *Trails of peril* (1982)

Warrior series
Green, Sharon
see **Terrilian series**

Warrior trilogy
Stackpole, Michael
1 *Riposte* (1988)
2 *En garde* (1988)
3 *Coupe* (1989)

Warriors of America trilogy
Waite, Jon
1 *Soldiers of the sea* (1943)
2 *Wings over Europe* (1943)
3 *Tanks are coming* (1944)

Warriors series
Armstrong, Anthony
1 *Warriors at ease* (1926)
2 *Warriors still at ease* (1928)
3 *Livestock in barracks* (1929)
4 *Easy warriors* (1932)
5 *Captain Bayonet and others* (1937)
6 *Warriors at war* (1941)

Wars of independence trilogy
Marten, Jacqueline
1 *To pluck a rose* (1987)
2 *Glory in the flower* (1988)
3 *In the long green grass* (1988)

Wars of the Roses series
Fairburn, Eleanor
1 *Rose in spring* (1971)
2 *White Rose, dark summer* (1972)
3 *Rose at harvest end* (1974)
Based on the life of Cecily Neville
4 *Winter's Rose* (1976)

Wars of Vis trilogy
Lee, Tanith
1 *Storm Lord* (1976)
2 *Anackire* (1983)
Numbers 1 and 2 also published in one volume entitled *The wars of Vis*, 1984
3 *White serpent* (1988)

Warshawski series
Paretsky, Sara
see **V I Warshawski series**

Warship series
Mackintosh, Ian
Based on a television series
1 *Warship* (1973)
2 *H.M.S.Hero* (1976)
3 *Holt, R.N.* (1977)

Warton Toad series
Erickson, Russell Everett
1 *Toad for Tuesday* (1974)
2 *Warton and Morton* (1976)
3 *Warton's Christmas Eve adventure* (1977)
4 *Warton and the king of the skies* (1978)
5 *Warton and the traders* (1979)
6 *Warton and the castaways* (1982)
7 *Warton and the contest* (1986)

Warwick series
McCulley, Johnston
see **Spider series**

Warwyck family trilogy
Laker, Rosalind
see **Easthampton trilogy**

Washbourne series
Pakington, Humphrey
1 *Washbournes of Otterley* (1948)
2 *Young William Washbourne* (1949)
3 *Farewell to Otterley* (1951)

Washington crime series
Truman, Margaret
see **Capital crime series**

Washington Parke series
Curtis, Alice Turner
see **Little Washingtons series**

Washington series
Drury, Allen
1 *Advise and consent* (1959)
2 *Shade of difference* (1962)
3 *Capable of honor* (1966)
4 *Preserve and protect* (1968)
5 *Come Nineveh, come Tyre* (1973)
The presidency of Edward M Jason
6 *Promise of joy* (1975)
The presidency of Orin Knox
7 *Anna Hastings* (1977)
Story of a Washington newspaper person
8 *Mark Coffin, Senator* (1979)
A novel of Capitol Hill

Washington series
Flexner, James Thomas
see **George Washington series**

Washington series
Vidal, Gore
1 *Burr* (1973)
2 *Lincoln* (1984)
3 *Eighteen seventy six* (1976)
4 *Empire* (1987)
5 *Washington D.C.* (1967)

Wasserman series
Conford, Ellen
see **Carrie Wasserman series**

Waste triptych
Sherwin, Judith Johnson
Poetry
1 *Town scold* (1977)
2 *Transparencies* (1978)
3 *Dead's good company* (1979)

Wasteworld series
Barton, James
1 *Aftermath* (1983)
2 *Resurrection* (1983)
3 *Angels* (1985)
4 *My way* (1985)

Watch and landfall series
Sampson, Fay
1 *Watch of Patterick Fell* (1978)
2 *Landfall on Innis Michael* (1980)

Watch for series
Haigh, Sheila
1 *Watch for the ghost* (1975)
2 *Watch for smoke* (1978)
3 *Watch for the champion* (1980)
4 *Watch for danger* (1983)
5 *Watch for the tide* (1987)

Watcher series
Porter, Hal
1 *Watcher on the cast-iron balcony* (1963)
2 *Paper chase* (1965)

Watchers series
Etchemendy, Nancy
1 *Watchers of space* (1980)
2 *Crystal city* (1985)

Watchers trilogy
Gordon, Stuart
1 *Achon!* (1987)
2 *Hidden world* (1988)
3 *Mask* (1990)

Watching series
Morris, Desmond
1 *Manwatching* (1977)
A field guide to human behaviour
2 *Bodywatching* (1985)
A field guide to human species
3 *Dogwatching* (1986)
4 *Catwatching* (1987)
5 *Horsewatching* (1988)
6 *Animalwatching* (1990)
A field guide to animal behaviour

Watchman chronicles series
Finlay, D G
1 *Watchman* (1984)
2 *Grey regard* (1985)
3 *Deadly relations* (1986)
4 *Graven image* (1987)
One volume abridged edition entitled *The killing glance*, 1989

Watchman series
Garfield, Brian Wynne
see **Sam Watchman series**

Water house series
Olinto, Antonio
1 *Water house* (1969)
Original edition entitled *A Casa da Agua*
2 *King of Ketu* (1980)
Original edition entitled *O Tei de Keto*

Water series
Ling, Peter
1 *High water* (1991)
2 *Flood water* (1992)
3 *Storm water* (1993)

Water Wagon series
Gibson, William Curtis
1 *Log of the Water Wagon* (1905)
Alternative title: The cruise of the good ship Lithia
2 *Extra dry* (1906)

Watergate series
Woodward, Bob
1 *All the President's men* (1974)
2 *Final days* (1976)

Waterloo series
Herring, Christine
1 *Waterloo legacy* (1979)
2 *Waterloo's ward* (1980)

Waterlow series
Mackenzie, Compton
see **Commander Roger Waterlow series**

Waters series
Armstrong, William
see **Moses Waters series**

Watson series
Gardiner, Dorothy
see **Mister Watson series**
Mills, Robert E
see **Davy Watson series**
Resciniti, Angelo G
see **C J Watson series**
Zachary, Hugh
see **Sheriff Jug Watson series**

Watson Ward series
Delannoy, Burford
1 *Dead man's rooms* (1905)
2 *Flat beneath* (1931)

Watsons series
This sequence has two authors
Austen, Jane
1 *Watsons* (1928)
Completed in accordance with her intentions by Edith, her great grand-niece and Francis Brown; originally published in *A memoir of Jane Austen*, by J E Austen-Leigh, 1870; another edition continued and completed by John Coates, 1958
Hubback, Edith C
2 *Younger sister* (1850)

Waugh series
Stannard, Martin
see **Evelyn Waugh series**

Wave series
Ehrenburg, Ilya
Translated from the Russian
1 *Storm* (1948)
2 *Ninth wave* (1953)

Waveneys series
Wentworth, Patricia
1 *Little more than kin* (1911)
More than kin
2 *Anne Belinda* (1927)

Waxahachie Smith series
Edson, John Thomas
1 *No finger on the trigger* (1987)
2 *Slip gun* (1971)

Way ahead trilogy
Briggs, Victor
1 *Sacred ground* (1975)
2 *Reap the harvest* (1976)
3 *Yours is the earth* (1977)

Way of the Tiger series
Smith, Mark
Adventure game stories
1 *Avenger!* (1985)
2 *Assassin!* (1985)
3 *Usurper!* (1985)
4 *Overlord!* (1986)
5 *Warbringer!* (1986)
6 *Inferno!* (1987)

Way series
John, Stephen
see **Albert Divine series**

Way trilogy
McMillan, James
1 *Way we were, 1900-1914* (1978)
Social history of Britain based on the Daily Express
2 *Way it was, 1914-1934* (1979)
3 *Way it happened, 1935-1950* (1980)

Wayne and Ratcliffe series
Sutcliffe, Halliwell
1 *Shameless Wayne* (1900)
2 *Red o' the feud* (1905)

Wayne series
Blood, Matthew
see **Morgan Wayne series**
Cromwell, A G E
see **Rodney Wayne series**
Harknett, Terry
see **Stephen Wayne series**

Wayne Wilson series
McRobbie, David
1 *Wayne dynasty* (1991)
2 *Waxing with Wayne* (1991)
3 *Wages of Wayne* (1993)
4 *Little drop of Wayne* (1994)

Waynes of Wood Mount trilogy
Cadell, Elizabeth
1 *Lark shall sing* (1955)
Singing heart
2 *Blue sky of spring* (1956)
3 *Six impossible things* (1961)

Ways of animals series
Fisher, Aileen
Poetry
1 *Animal houses* (1972)
2 *Animal disguises* (1973)
3 *Animal jackets* (1973)
4 *Now that days are colder* (1973)
5 *Tail twisters* (1973)
6 *Filling the bill* (1973)
7 *Going places* (1973)
8 *Sleepy heads* (1973)
9 *You don't look like your mother, said the robin to the fawn* (1973)
10 *No accounting for tastes* (1973)

Ways of plants series
Fisher, Aileen
Poetry
1 *Now that spring is here* (1977)
2 *And a sunflower grew* (1977)
3 *Mysteries in the garden* (1977)
4 *Seeds on the go* (1977)
5 *Plant magic* (1977)
6 *Petals yellow and petals red* (1977)
7 *Swords and daggers* (1977)
8 *Prize performance* (1977)
9 *Tree with a thousadn uses* (1977)
10 *As the leaves fall down* (1977)

Wayside School series
Sachar, Louis
1 *Sideways stories from Wayside School* (1978)
2 *Wayside School is falling down* (1989)
3 *Sideways arithmetic from Wayside School* (1989)

Wayward man series
Case, Frank
Reminiscences of the owner of the Algonquin Hotel in New York
1 *Tales of a wayward man* (1938)
2 *Do not disturb* (1940)

Wayward sailor series
Jones, Tristan
Reminiscences
1 *Steady trade* (1982)
A boyhood at sea
2 *Heart of oak* (1984)
3 *Incredible voyage* (1977)
4 *Ice!* (1978)
5 *Saga of a wayward sailor* (1979)
6 *Adrift* (1980)
7 *Star to steer her by* (1985)
Outward log
8 *Improbable voyage* (1986)

Wayward series
Treat, Lawrence
see **Carl Wayward series**

We Donkeys series
Gibbons, M S
1 *We Donkeys on Dartmoor* (1886)
2 *We Donkeys on the coast of Devon* (1887)

We four series
Barr, Nora
1 *We four on Mouse Island* (1950)
2 *We four and the king's treasure* (1950)

We have series
Campbell, Rod
1 *We have a cat* (1990)
2 *We have a dog* (1990)
3 *We have a rabbit* (1990)
4 *We have a guinea pig* (1990)

We were there series
Steele, William Owen
1 *We were there on the Oregon Trail* (1955)
2 *We were there with the Pony Express* (1956)

Weapon series
Mason, Robert Caverly
1 *Weapon* (1991)
2 *Solo* (1992)

Weapons of chaos trilogy
Vardeman, Robert Edward
1 *Echoes of chaos* (1986)
2 *Equations of chaos* (1987)
3 *Colors of chaos* (1988)
One volume edition entitled *Weapons of chaos*, 1989

Weary road series
Douie, Charles
Autobiography
1 *Weary road* (1929)
Recollections of a subaltern of infantry
2 *Beyond the sunset* (1935)
3 *So long to learn* (1951)
Autobiography in terms of ideas

Weatherford series
Grand, Gordon
see **Colonel John Weatherford series**

Weatherley series
Birmingham, Maisie
see **Kate Weatherley series**

Weaver series
Keith, David
see **Ted S Weaver series**
Weaver, Nicky
see **Nicky Weaver series**

Web Steele series
Sanders, Brett
1 *Hawk* (1973)
2 *Vengeance gun* (1974)
3 *Blood bait* (1974)
4 *Shootout at Las Cruces* (1976)

Webb and Jackson series
Fraser, Anthea
see **Inspector David Webb and Sergeant Ken Jackson series**

Webb Calder series
Dailey, Janet
1 *This Calder sky* (1981)
2 *This Calder range* (1982)
3 *Stands a Calder man* (1982)
4 *Calder born, Calder bred* (1983)

Webb Carrick series
Knox, Bill
1 *Scavengers* (1964)
2 *Devilweed* (1966)
3 *Blacklight* (1967)
4 *Klondyker* (1968)
Figurehead
5 *Blueback* (1969)
6 *Seafire* (1970)
7 *Stormtide* (1972)
8 *Whitewater* (1974)
9 *Hellspout* (1976)
10 *Witchrock* (1977)
11 *Bombship* (1980)
12 *Bloodtide* (1982)
13 *Wavecrest* (1985)
14 *Dead man's mooring* (1987)

Webb series
Foster, Walter Bertram
see **Clint Webb series**
Palmer, Bernard
see **Mel Webb series**
Presnell, Frank G
see **John and Anne Webb series**

Webber and Thomas series
Oliver, Anthony
see **Lizzie Thomas and Inspector John Webber series**

Webber series
Wolfe, Thomas Clayton
see **George Webber series**

Webley and Fortune series
Maddock, Larry
see **Hannibal Fortune and Webley series**

Webster and Arnold series
Roche, Patricia K
1 *Good-bye, Arnold!* (1979)
2 *Webster and Arnold and the giant box* (1980)
3 *Webster and Arnold go camping* (1988)

Webster Daniels series
Smith, Terence Lore
1 *Thief who came to dinner* (1971)
2 *Devil and Webster Daniels* (1975)

Webster Flagg series
Johns, Veronica Parker
1 *Murder by the day* (1953)
2 *Servant's problem* (1958)

Webster series
Sale, Richard
see **Daniel Webster series**
Stanford, Don
see **Dallas Webster series**
Wright, Sydney Fowler
see **Martin Webster series**

Wedding dress series
Wells, Marian
1 *Wedding dress* (1982)
2 *With this ring* (1984)

Wee little books series
Burgess, Thornton Waldo
1 *Little Joe Otter's slide* (1929)
2 *Betty Bear's lesson* (1929)
3 *Unc' Billy gets even* (1930)
4 *Whitefoot's secret* (1931)
5 *Jimmy Skunk's justice* (1932)
6 *Peter Rabbit's carrots* (1933)

Wee Macgregor series
Bell, John Joy
1 *Wee Macgregor* (1902)
Revised edition 1909
2 *Wee Macgregor again* (1904)
Later adventures of Macgregor
3 *Wee Macgregor enlists* (1915)

Wee Winkles series
Jackson, Gabrielle Emilie
1 *Wee Winkles and Wideawake* (1905)
2 *Wee Winkles and Snowball* (1906)
3 *Wee Winkles and her friends* (1907)
4 *Wee Winkles at the mountains* (1908)

Weekday stories series
Blyton, Enid
1 *Stories for Monday* (1962)
2 *Stories for Tuesday* (1962)

Weems series
Matthews, Greg
see **Burris Weems series**

Weetzie Bat series
Block, Francesca Lia
1 *Weetzie Bat* (1989)
2 *Witch baby* (1991)
3 *Cherokee Bat and the goat guys* (1992)
4 *Missing Angel Juan* (1993)

Weir series
Durrant, Valentine
see **Saul Weir series**

Weird and wacky inventions series
Murphy, Jim
1 *Weird and wacky inventions* (1978)
2 *Guess again* (1985)

Weird heroes series
This sequence has seven authors
Preiss, Byron
1 *Weird heroes* (1975)
2 *Weird heroes, volume 2* (1975)
Goulart, Ron
3 *Quest of the gypsy* (1976)
King, Tappan
4 *Nightshade* (1976)
White, Ted
5 *Phoenix* (1977)
Preiss, Byron
6 *Weird heroes, volume 6* (1977)
Goulart, Ron
7 *Eye of the vulture* (1977)
Preiss, Byron
8 *Weird heroes, volume 8* (1977)

Weird mob series
Culotta, Nino
1 *They're a weird mob* (1957)
2 *Cop this lot* (1960)
3 *Gone fishin'* (1962)
4 *Gone gougin'* (1975)

Weirdo and ghost series
Windsor, Patricia
1 *How a weirdo and a ghost can change your entire life* (1986)
2 *Two weirdos and a ghost* (1991)

Welch series
Johns, Veronica Parker
see **Agatha Welch series**

Welch trilogy
Walden, Amelia
see **Miranda Welch trilogy**

Welcome back, Kotter series
Johnston, William
Based on a television series
1 *Sweathog trail* (1976)
2 *Sweathog newshawks* (1976)
3 *Super Sweathogs* (1976)
4 *Ten to four Sweathogs* (1976)
5 *Sweathog sit-in* (1977)
6 *Barbarino drops out* (1977)

Welgevonden trilogy
Leroux, Etienne
1 *Seven days at the Silbersteins* (1962)
Original edition entitled *Sewe dae by die Silbersteins*
2 *One for the devil* (1964)
Original edition entitled *Een vir azazel*
3 *Third eye* (1966)
Original edition entitled *Die derde oog*
One volume edition entitled *To a dubious salvation*, 1972

We'll meet again series
This sequence has two authors; based on a television series
Miles, Keith
1 *We'll meet again* (1982)
Butler, David
2 *End of an era* (1983)

Well of Souls series
Chalker, Jack Laurence
see **Well world series**

Well series
Beeler, Cecil Freeman
1 *Girl in the well* (1991)
2 *No room in the well* (1993)

Well world series
Chalker, Jack Laurence
1 *Midnight at the Well of Souls* (1977)
2 *Exiles of the Well of Souls* (1978)
3 *Quest for the Well of Souls* (1978)
4 *Return of Nathan Brazil* (1980)
5 *Twilight at the Well of Souls* (1980)
The legacy of Nathan Brazil

Welles family trilogy
Ward, Lynda
1 *Race the sun* (1988)
2 *Leap the moon* (1988)
3 *Touch the stars* (1988)

Wellies series
Reilly, David
Illustrated by Angelo Cinque
1 *Wellies drop in* (1986)
2 *Little lost cloud* (1986)
3 *Cuckoo that couldn't* (1986)
4 *Welly happy Christmas* (1986)

Wells and Sims series
Grierson, Francis Durham
see **Inspector Sims and Professor Wells series**

Wells brothers series
Adams, Andy
1 *Young cattle kings* (1911)
2 *Ranch on the beaver* (1927)

Wells family series
Pullein-Thompson, Christine
1 *Ponies in the park* (1982)
2 *Ponies in the forest* (1983)
3 *Ponies in the blizzard* (1985)

Wells Fargo series
This sequence has three authors; based on a television series
Gruber, Frank
1 *Tales of Wells Fargo* (1958)
Loomis, Noel
2 *Wells Fargo, danger station* (1958)
Stanley, Chuck
3 *Freight for Wells Fargo* (1958)
4 *Wells Fargo gunguard* (1959)
Companion volumes: *Danger at Dry Creek*, by Irving Werstein, 1959, *Tales of Wells Fargo annual*, 1961-1962, *Tales of Wells Fargo bumper book*, 1963, *Tales of Wells Fargo story book*, 1965

Wells of Ythan series
Alexander, Marc
1 *Ancient dreams* (1988)
2 *Magic casements* (1989)
3 *Shadow realm* (1991)

Wells series
Bortner, Norman Stanley
see **Professor Clifford Wells series**
Hill, Lorna
see **Sadler's Wells series**
Whitelaw, David
see **Peter Wells series**

Welpton series
Saxon, John A
see **Sam Welpton series**

Welsh island series
Skidmore, Ian
1 *Island fling* (1981)
2 *Magnificent Evan* (1983)

Welsh Mabinogion series
Walton, Evangeline
see **Mabinogion series**

Welsh migrants series
Cordell, Alexander
see **Mortymers series**

Welsh series
Fitzhugh, Louise
see **Harriet M Welsh series**

Welsh series
Young, Francis Brett
1 *Undergrowth* (1913)
Co-author: Eric Brett Young; set in the Welsh mountains
2 *Black diamond* (1921)
Set in the mining area of south Wales

Wenceslas Vorobeitchik series
Steeman, Andre
1 *Six dead men* (1931)
Original edition entitled *Six hommes morts*
2 *Night of the twelfth to thirteenth* (1931)
Original edition entitled *La nuir du 12 au 13*

Wendall trilogy
Oates, Joyce Carol
see **Jules and Maureen Wendall trilogy**

Wendy and Jinx series
Hastings, Valerie
1 *Wendy and Jinx and the Dutch stamp mystery* (1956)
2 *Wendy and Jinx and the missing scientist* (1957)

Wendy and Mark series
Egan, Ted
see **Mark and Wendy series**

Wendy and William series
Braga, Meg
see **William and Wendy series**

Wendy Brent series
Deming, Dorothy
1 *Curious calamity in Ward 8* (1954)
2 *Strange disappearance from Ward 2* (1956)
3 *Mysterious discovery in Ward K* (1959)
4 *Baffling affair in the county hospital* (1962)

Wendy series
Robinson, Nancy Konheim
1 *Wendy and the bullies* (1987)
2 *Wendy on the warpath* (1994)

Wendy series
Williams, Dorian
1 *Wendy wins a pony* (1961)
2 *Wendy wins her spurs* (1962)
3 *Wendy at Wembley* (1963)

Wentley series
Westerman, John Francis Cyril
see **John Wentley series**

Wentworth series
Ellis, Humphry Francis
see **A.J.Wentworth series**
Forrest, Richard
see **Lyon and Bea Wentworth series**
Scott, Reginald Thomas Maitland
see **Richard Wentworth series**
Stevenson, Dorothy Emily
see **Katherine Wentworth series**

Werewolf Clan trilogy
Munn, Harold Warner
see **Tales of the Werewolf Clan trilogy**

Werewolf series
Jaccoma, Richard
1 *Werewolf's tale* (1988)
2 *Werewolf's revenge* (1991)

Werewolf trilogy
Smith, Guy Newman
1 *Werewolf by moonlight* (1974)
2 *Return of the werewolf* (1977)
3 *Son of the werewolf* (1978)

Werewolves series
Stableford, Brian Michael
1 *Werewolves of London* (1989)
2 *Angel of pain* (1991)

Werner Bertin and Lenore Wahl series
Zweig, Arnold
1 *Time is ripe* (1957)
Original edition entitled *Die Zeit ist reif*
2 *Young woman of 1914* (1931)
Original edition entitled *Junge Frau von 1914*
3 *Education before Verdun* (1935)
Original edition entitled *Erziehung vor Verdun*
4 *Case of Sergeant Grischa* (1927)
Original edition entitled *Der Streit um den Sergeanten Grischa*
5 *[Die Feuerpause]* (1954)
No English edition
6 *Crowning of a king* (1937)
Winfried
Original edition entitled *Einsetzung eines Konigs*

Werner series
Weinberg, Robert
see **Alex Werner series**

Wes Hart series
Harvey, John Barton
1 *Cherokee outlet* (1980)
2 *Blood trail* (1980)
3 *Tago* (1980)
4 *Silver lie* (1980)
5 *Blood on the border* (1981)
6 *Ride the wide country* (1981)
7 *Arkansas breakout* (1982)
8 *John Wesley Hardin* (1982)
9 *California bloodlines* (1982)
10 *Skinning place* (1982)

Wesley series
Waugh, Hillary
see **Sheridan Wesley series**

West and Macadam series
Campbell, Alice
see **Geoffrey Macadam and Catherine West series**

West family series
Barrett, Helen Elizabeth-Anne
1 *Waminda* (1982)
2 *Gold through the haze* (1986)
3 *To jump a log* (1989)
4 *Return to Waminda* (1992)

West Indians series
Lamming, George
see **Caribbean series**

West Indies series
Nicole, Christopher
1 *Caribee* (1974)
2 *Devil's own* (1975)
3 *Mistress of darkness* (1976)
4 *Black dawn* (1977)
5 *Sunset* (1978)

West Indies series
Salkey, Andrew
1 *Hurricane* (1964)
2 *Earthquake* (1965)
3 *Drought* (1966)
4 *Riot* (1967)

West Meadow series
Reeder, Colin
1 *Great flood* (1989)
2 *Moving day* (1989)
3 *Billy's mistake* (1989)
4 *Ronnie's finest hour* (1989)
5 *Gerald's Saturday* (1989)
6 *Plastered for Christmas* (1989)

West Mercia series
Tunstall, Beatrice
1 *Shiny night* (1931)
2 *Long day closes* (1934)

West Mount High trilogy
Harrell, Janice
1 *Wild times at West Mount High* (1989)
2 *Easy answers* (1990)
3 *Senior year at last* (1990)

West Point series
Garrison, Frederick
1 *Off for West Point* (1903)
Alternative title: Mark Mallory's struggle
2 *Cadet's honor* (1903)
Alternative title: Mark Mallory's heroism
3 *On guard* (1903)
Alternative title: Mark Mallory's celebration
4 *West Point treasure* (1903)
Alternative title: Mark Mallory's strange find
5 *West Point rivals* (1903)
Alternative title: Mark Mallory's stratagem

West Riding series
Bentley, Phyllis
1 *Panorama* (1952)
Tales of the West Riding
2 *Take courage* (1940)
Power and the glory
3 *Manhold* (1941)
4 *House of Moreys* (1953)
5 *Inheritance* (1932)
6 *Carr* (1929)
7 *Life story* (1948)
8 *Spinner of the years* (1928)
9 *Modern tragedy* (1934)
10 *Sleep in peace* (1938)
11 *Rise of Henry Morcar* (1946)
12 *Quorum* (1950)
13 *Noble in reason* (1955)
14 *Love and money* (1957)
Seven tales of the West Riding
15 *Crescendo* (1958)
16 *Kith and kin* (1960)
Nine tales of family life
17 *Tales of the West Riding* (1965)
18 *Man of his times* (1966)
19 *Ring in the new* (1969)
20 *More tales of the West Riding* (1974)
Companion volumes: *The partnership*, 1928, *Trio*, 1930

West series
Creasey, John
see **Inspector Roger West series**
Fickling, G G
see **Honey West series**
Hogan, Ray
see **Fortuna West series**
Levene, Philip
see **Ambrose West series**
Nazel, Joseph
see **Iceman series**
O'Callaghan, Maxine
see **Delilah West series**
Welles, Elizabeth
see **Janine West series**

Westborough series
Clason, Clyde B
see **Theocritus Lucius Westborough series**

Westcott series
Walpole, Hugh
see **Peter Westcott series**

Westcotts and Lesters series
Mantle, Winifred
see **Lesters and Westcotts series**

Westerbury series
Chesney, Marion
1 *Westerbury inheritance* (1982)
2 *Westerbury sisters* (1983)

Western Australian Goldfields series
Prichard, Katharine Susannah
1 *Roaring nineties* (1946)
2 *Golden miles* (1948)
3 *Winged seeds* (1950)

Western Australian series
Vines, Freda
1 *Lonely shore* (1958)
2 *So wild the sea* (1961)

Western Highlands series
Pardoe, Margot
1 *Charles arriving* (1954)
2 *May madrigal* (1955)

Western Indian series
Gregor, Elmer Russell
1 *White Otter* (1917)
2 *War trail* (1921)
3 *Three Sioux scouts* (1922)
4 *Medicine buffalo* (1925)
5 *War chief* (1927)
6 *Spotted pony* (1930)

Western Isles trilogy
Macgregor, Alasdair Alpin
1 *Behold the Hebrides* (1925)
Alternative title: Wayfaring in the Western Isles; revised edition 1948
2 *Summer days among the Western Isles* (1929)
3 *Haunted isles* (1933)
Alternative title: Life in the Hebrides
Companion volume: *Searching the Hebrides with a camera*, 1933

Western mining series
Peterson, Richard Hermann
1 *Bonanza kings* (1977)
The social origins and business behavior of Western mining entrepreneurs, 1870-1900
2 *Bonanza rich* (1991)
Lifestyles of the Western mining entrepreneurs

Western philosophy series
This sequence has two authors
Russell, Bertrand
1 *History of western philosophy* (1945)
Ayer, Alfred Jules
2 *Philosophy in the twentieth century* (1982)

Western stars series
Grey, Zane
1 *Light of western stars* (1914)
Light of the western stars
2 *Majesty's rancho* (1938)

Western tales series
Wister, Owen
1 *Lin McLean* (1898)
2 *Jimmyjohn boss, and other stories* (1900)
3 *Virginian* (1902)
A horseman of the plains
4 *Members of the family* (1911)
Short stories

Westerners in Japan series
Barr, Pat
1 *Coming of the barbarians* (1967)
A story of Western settlement in Japan, 1853-1870
2 *Deer Cry Pavilion* (1968)
A story of Westerners in Japan, 1868-1905

Westfall series
Crisp, William
1 *Spytrap* (1982)
2 *Vengeance is thine* (1986)

Westlake series
Stagge, Jonathan
see **Doctor Hugh Westlake series**

Westmark trilogy
Alexander, Lloyd
1 *Westmark* (1981)
2 *Kestrel* (1982)
3 *Beggar queen* (1984)

Westminster series
Rae, John
1 *Golden crucifix* (1974)
2 *Treasure of Westminster* (1975)

Westmoreland family series
McNaught, Judith
1 *Kingdom of dreams* (1989)
Set in 15th century Scotland
2 *Whitney, my love* (1985)
Set in 19th century England

Weston family trilogy
Frankau, Pamela
see **Clothes of a king's son trilogy**

Weston series
Conway, Peter
see **Inspector Cathy Weston series**
Haughey, Thomas Brace
see **Geoffrey Weston series**
Lund, Trygve
see **Dick Weston series**
Meynell, Laurence Walter
see **Robin Weston series**
Sheridan, Wilfred
see **Tommy Weston series**
Thomas, Eugene
see **Mrs Caywood Weston series**
Warren, James
see **James Weston series**
Wharton, Edith
see **Vance Weston series**

Westria series
Paxson, Diana Lucile
1 *Lady of light* (1982)
2 *Lady of darkness* (1983)
Numbers 1 and 2 also published in one volume editions entitled *Lady of light, lady of darkness*, 1990 and *The mistress of the jewels*, 1991
3 *Silverhair the wanderer* (1986)
4 *Earthstone* (1987)
5 *Sea star* (1988)
6 *Wind crystal* (1990)

Westward rails trilogy
Rothweiler, Paul Roger
1 *Railroad king* (1981)
2 *Fortune's mistress* (1982)
3 *Empire builder* (1982)

Westward series
Havard, Aline
1 *Fighting westward* (1923)
2 *Where the trail divides* (1924)

Westways series
White, Constance Mary
1 *Ponies at Westways* (1956)
2 *Nutmeg comes to Westways* (1961)

Westy Martin series
Fitzhugh, Percy Keese
1 *Westy Martin* (1924)
2 *Westy Martin in the Yellowstone* (1924)
3 *Westy Martin in the Rockies* (1925)
4 *Westy Martin on the Santa Fe Trail* (1926)
5 *Westy Martin on the Old Indian Trail* (1928)
6 *Westy Martin in the land of the purple sage* (1929)
7 *Westy Martin on the Mississippi* (1930)
8 *Westy Martin in the Sierras* (1931)
9 *Out West with Westy Martin* (1933)

Wetherall series
Sutton, Stack
see **Marshal Creed Wetherall series**

Wetzon series
Meyers, Annette
see **Leslie Wetzon series**

Wexford series
Rendell, Ruth
see **Chief Inspector Reginald Wexford series**

Wharton series
Buckingham, David
see **Sam Wharton series**

What-a-Mess series
Muir, Frank
1 *What-a-Mess* (1977)
2 *What-a-Mess the good* (1978)
3 *Prince What-a-Mess* (1979)
4 *Super What-a-Mess* (1980)
5 *What-a-Mess and the cat next door* (1981)
6 *What-a-Mess in autumn* (1982)
7 *What-a-Mess in winter* (1982)
8 *What-a-Mess in spring* (1982)
9 *What-a-Mess in summer* (1982)
10 *What-a-Mess at the seaside* (1983)
11 *What-a-Mess goes to school* (1984)
12 *What-a-Mess goes camping* (1990)
13 *What-a-Mess and Little Poppet* (1990)
14 *What-a-Mess and a trip to the vet* (1990)
15 *What-a-Mess the beautiful* (1990)
16 *What-a-Mess and the hairy monster* (1990)

17 *What-a-Mess goes to town* (1991)
18 *What-a-Mess has a brainwave* (1991)

What do series
Slier, Debby
1 *What do babies do* (1985)
2 *What do toddlers do* (1985)

What do they do series
Greene, Carla
1 *Policemen and firemen* (1962)
2 *Doctors and nurses* (1963)
3 *Soldiers and sailors* (1963)
4 *Railroad engineers and airplane pilots* (1964)
5 *Animal doctors* (1967)
6 *Truck drivers* (1967)
7 *Cowboys* (1972)

What-do-you-know series
Berg, Leila
1 *How John caught the sea-horse, and other stories* (1966)
2 *Penguin who couldn't paddle, and other stories* (1967)
Originally published in one volume entitled *Fourteen what-do-you-know stories*, 1948

What might have been series
Greenberg, Martin Harry
1 *Alternate empires* (1989)
2 *Alternate heroes* (1990)
Numbers 1 and 2 also published in one volume entitled *What might have been*, 1990
3 *Alternate wars* (1991)

What to expect series
Eisenberg, Arlene
1 *What to expect when you're expecting* (1984)
2 *What to expect the first year* (1989)

What we can do about series
Bailey, Donna
1 *What we can do about litter* (1991)
2 *What we can do about recycling garbage* (1991)
3 *What we can do about noise and fumes* (1992)
4 *What we can do about wasting water* (1992)
5 *What we can do about conserving energy* (1992)
6 *What we can do about protecting nature* (1992)

What's good series
Cole, William
1 *What's good for a three-year-old?* (1974)
2 *What's good for a four-year-old?* (1967)
3 *What's good for a five-year-old?* (1969)
4 *What's good for a six-year-old?* (1965)

What's that series
Petty, Kate
1 *What's that noise?* (1986)
2 *What's that taste?* (1986)
3 *What's that shape?* (1986)
4 *What's that colour?* (1986)
5 *What's that smell?* (1986)
6 *What's that number?* (1986)
7 *What's that feel?* (1986)
8 *What's that size?* (1986)

Wheat series
Boyd, Thomas Alexander
1 *Through the wheat* (1923)
2 *In time of peace* (1935)

Wheat series
ane, Jeremy
see **Whitney Wheat series**

Wheel of time series
Jordan, Robert
1 *Eye of the world* (1990)
2 *Great hunt* (1990)
3 *Dragon reborn* (1991)
4 *Shadow rising* (1992)
5 *Fires of heaven* (1993)
6 *Lord of chaos* (1994)

Wheeler series
Brown, Carter
see **Lieutenant Al Wheeler series**

Whelan series
Raleigh, Michael
see **Paul Whelan series**
Smith, Laurence Dwight
see **Dick Whelan series**

Wheldon series
Jones, Peter
see **Terry Trotter series**

When I see series
Kuklin, Susan
1 *When I see my doctor* (1988)
2 *When I see my dentist* (1988)

When the boat comes in series
Mitchell, James
Based on a television series
1 *When the boat comes in* (1976)
2 *Hungry years* (1976)
3 *Upwards and onwards* (1977)

When the world was young trilogy
Dewes, Simon
Autobiography
1 *Suffolk childhood* (1959)
2 *Essex schooldays* (1960)
3 *When all the world was young* (1961)

Where animals live series
Hirschi, Ron
1 *Who lives in the forest* (1987)
2 *Who lives in alligator swamp* (1987)
3 *Who lives in the mountains* (1988)
4 *Who lives on the prairie* (1988)

Where do I put series
Barkan, Joanne
1 *Where do I put my books?* (1991)
2 *Where do I put my clothes?* (1991)
3 *Where do I put my food?* (1991)
4 *Where do I put my toys?* (1991)

Where does it come from series
Henderson, Kathy
1 *Water* (1986)
2 *Banana* (1986)
3 *Sweater* (1986)
4 *Lego brick* (1986)
5 *Bread* (1987)
6 *Letter* (1987)

Where is it series
Ziefert, Harriet
Illustrated by Richard Brown
1 *Birthday card, where are you?* (1985)
2 *Where's my Easter egg?* (1985)
3 *Where's the Halloween treat* (1985)
4 *Where is Nicky's Valentine?* (1987)

Where love rules series
Dubus, Elizabeth Nell
1 *Where love rules* (1985)
2 *To love and to dream* (1986)

Where series
Mayer, Mercer
1 *Where's my sneaker* (1991)
2 *Where's my frog* (1991)
3 *Where's my kitty* (1991)

Whetstone series
Warren, Lella
1 *Foundation stone* (1940)
2 *Whetstone walls* (1952)

Which way interactive series
Mooser, Stephen
1 *Space raiders and the planet of doom* (1983)
2 *Starship warrior* (1984)
3 *Nightmare planet* (1985)
4 *Invasion of the mutants* (1985)
5 *Mind bandits* (1985)
6 *Monster express* (1986)

Which way super powers series
Helfer, Andrew
see **Super powers which way series**

Which would you choose series
Kunhardt, Edith
1 *Which one would you choose?* (1989)
2 *Which pig would you choose?* (1990)

While the earth endures trilogy
Troyat, Henri
see **Danov family trilogy**

Whimsy storybooks series
Cosgrove, Stephen Edward
1 *Gimme* (1985)
2 *Tattletale* (1985)
3 *Gobble and gulp* (1985)
4 *Cranky* (1985)
5 *Chatterbox* (1985)
6 *Giggle* (1985)

Whippletree series
Hinkemeyer, Michael Thomas
see **Sheriff Emil Whippletree series**

Whiskerville series
Barkan, Joanne
1 *Whiskerville School* (1990)
2 *Whiskerville Post Office* (1990)
3 *Whiskerville Bake Shop* (1990)
4 *Whiskerville Firehouse* (1990)
5 *Whiskerville Theater* (1991)
6 *Whiskerville Train Station* (1991)
7 *Whiskerville Toy Shop* (1991)
8 *Whiskerville Grocery* (1991)

Whiskey Smith series
Allen, Eric
1 *Killer in Whiskey Smith* (1967)
2 *Hanging at Whiskey Smith* (1968)
3 *Marshal from Whiskey Smith* (1969)
4 *Raiders from Whiskey Smith* (1972)
5 *Rampage in Whiskey Smith* (1979)

Whisper series
Macrow, Brenda Grace
see **Mister Whisper series**

Whispering Hills series
Cameron, Kate
1 *Evil at Whispering Hills* (1973)
2 *Curse of Whispering Hills* (1974)
3 *Shadows of the moon* (1974)
4 *Legacy of terror* (1974)
5 *Awakening dream* (1974)
6 *Echoes of evil* (1974)

Whispering Pine series
Kellogg, Elijah
1 *Spark of genius* (1871)
Alternative title: The college life of James Trafton
2 *Sophomores of Radcliffe* (1871)
Alternative title: James Trafton and his bosom friends
3 *Whispering Pine* (1872)
Alternative title: Graduates of Radcliffe Hall
4 *Winning his spurs* (1872)
Alternative title: Henry Morton's first trial
5 *Stout heart* (1873)
Alternative title: The student from over the sea
6 *Turning of the tide* (1873)
Alternative title: Radcliffe Rich and his friends

Whispering Sands series
Gardner, Erle Stanley
Edited by Charles Gordon Waugh and Martin Harry Greenberg
1 *Whispering Sands* (1981)
Stories of gold fever and the Western Desert
2 *Pay dirt, and other Whispering Sands stories* (1983)

Whistler series
Campbell, Robert Wright
1 *In La-La Land we trust* (1986)
2 *Alice in La-La Land* (1987)
3 *Sweet La-La Land* (1990)

Whistler series
Mann, Edward Beverly
1 *Rustlers' round-up* (1935)
2 *El Sombra* (1936)
3 *Whistler* (1953)
Three Western novelettes

Whit Pynchon and Annie Tyson-Tyree series
Pedneau, Dave
1 *A.P.B.* (1987)
2 *D.O.A.* (1988)

Whit Whitney series
Dodge, David
1 *Death and taxes* (1941)
2 *Shear the black sheep* (1942)
3 *Bullets for the bridegroom* (1944)
4 *It ain't hay* (1949)
Drug on the market

Whitby trilogy
Morressy, John
see **Del Whitby trilogy**

Whitcomb series
Mitchell, James
see **Jane Whitcomb series**

White and Clark series
Andrews, Stephen
see **Nobby Clark and Snowy White series**

White Bull trilogy
Faulknor, Cliff
see **Eagle Child trilogy**

White conqueror series
Munroe, Kirk
1 *White conquerors* (1893)
A tale of Toltec and Aztec
2 *At war with Pontiac* (1895)
Alternative title: The totem of the bear; a tale of Redcoat and Redskin
3 *Through swamp and glade* (1896)
A tale of the Seminole war
4 *With Crockett and Bowie* (1897)
Alternative title: Fighting for the Lone Star flag

White crow series
Gentle, Mary
1 *Rats and gargoyles* (1990)
2 *Architecture of desire* (1991)

White Devil series
Palen, Lewis Stanton
1 *White Devil of the Black Sea* (1924)
2 *White Devil's mate* (1926)

White dog trilogy
Sharam, Norman
1 *White earth* (1986)
2 *White arrow* (1987)
3 *White rage* (1988)

White Eagle trilogy
McDonald, Kay L
see **Ross Chesnut trilogy**

White family series
White, Myrtle Rose
Account of life on cattle stations in South Australia and New South Wales
1 *No roads go by* (1932)
2 *Beyond the western waters* (1955)

White House years series
Kissinger, Henry
Memoirs
1 *White House years* (1979)
2 *Years of upheaval* (1982)

White Indian series
Porter, Donald Clayton
1 *White Indian* (1979)
2 *Renegade* (1980)
3 *War chief* (1980)
4 *Sachem* (1981)
5 *Renno* (1981)
6 *Tomahawk* (1982)
7 *War cry* (1983)
8 *Ambush* (1983)
9 *Seneca* (1983)
10 *Cherokee* (1984)
11 *Choctaw* (1985)
12 *Seminole* (1986)
13 *War drums* (1986)
14 *Apache* (1987)
15 *Spirit knife* (1988)
16 *Manitou* (1988)
17 *Seneca warriors* (1989)
18 *Father of waters* (1989)
19 *Fallen timbers* (1990)
20 *Sachem's son* (1990)
21 *Sachem's daughter* (1991)
22 *Seneca patriots* (1992)
23 *Hawk's journey* (1992)
24 *Father and son* (1993)
25 *War clouds* (1994)

White mule trilogy
Williams, William Carlos
see **Stecher trilogy**

White Pine chronicles series
Stahl, Hilda
1 *Covenant* (1991)
2 *Inheritance* (1992)
3 *Dream* (1992)

White poppy series
Osborne, Helena
1 *White poppy* (1977)
2 *Joker* (1979)

White ribbon boys series
Sperry, Raymond, junior
1 *White ribbon boys of Chester* (1915)
Alternative title: The old tavern keeper's secret
2 *White ribbon boys at Long Shore* (1916)
Alternative title: To the rescue of Dan Bates

White Russian series
Danischewsky, Monja
Autobiography
1 *White Russian, red face* (1966)
2 *Out of my mind* (1972)

White Savage series
Truman, Timothy
see **Simon Girty series**

White series
Holden, Genevieve
see **Lieutenant Al White series**
Mannon, M M
see **Sheriff George White series**
Nolan, Jeannette Covert
see **Lace White series**
Spicer, Bart
see **Colonel Peregrine White series**

White Squaw series
Hunter, E J
1 *Sioux wildfire* (1983)
2 *Boomtown bust* (1983)
3 *Virgin territory* (1984)
4 *Hot Texas tall* (1984)
5 *Buckskin bombshell* (1984)
6 *Dakota squeeze* (1984)
7 *Abilene tight spot* (1984)
8 *Horn of plenty* (1985)
9 *Twin Peaks, or bust* (1986)
10 *Solid as a rock* (1986)
11 *Hot-handed heathen* (1986)
12 *Ball and chain* (1986)
13 *Track tramp* (1987)
14 *Red top tramp* (1987)
15 *Here comes the bride* (1987)
16 *Redskin rosebud* (1988)
17 *Bullwhipped beauty* (1988)
18 *Hot pursuit* (1989)
19 *Badman's climax* (1989)
20 *Bareback beauty* (1990)
21 *Arizona laydown* (1990)
22 *Desert climax* (1991)
23 *Comanche come down* (1991)
24 *Rough and ready* (1992)

White warlord series
Dever, Joe
1 *White warlord* (1986)
2 *Black baron* (1986)

White Wolf series
Dunning, Hal
1 *Outlaw sheriff* (1928)
2 *White Wolf's law* (1928)
3 *White Wolf's pack* (1929)
4 *White Wolf's feud* (1930)
5 *Wolf deputy* (1930)
6 *White Wolf's outlaw legion* (1933)

White Wolf series
Reinius, Trish
1 *Planet of Tears* (1979)
2 *Power of the White Wolf* (1985)

Whitelands series
Browne, Reginald
1 *Fortescue of the Fourth* (1945)
2 *School in space* (1947)
3 *Rotter of Whitelands* (1947)

Whiteoak series
De la Roche, Mazo
1 *Building of Jalna* (1944)
2 *Morning at Jalna* (1960)
3 *Mary Wakefield* (1949)
4 *Young Renny* (1935)
5 *Whiteoak heritage* (1940)
6 *Whiteoak brothers* (1953)
7 *Jalna* (1927)
8 *Whiteoaks* (1929)
Whiteoaks of Jalna
9 *Finch's fortune* (1931)
10 *Master of Jalna* (1933)
11 *Whiteoak harvest* (1936)
12 *Wakefield's course* (1941)
13 *Return to Jalna* (1946)
14 *Renny's daughter* (1951)
15 *Variable winds at Jalna* (1954)
16 *Centenary at Jalna* (1958)

Whitewater dynasty series
Poole, Helen Lee
1 *Hudson!* (1980)
2 *Ohio!* (1981)
3 *Cumberland!* (1982)
4 *Wabash!* (1983)
5 *Mississippi!* (1984)
6 *Missouri!* (1985)

Whitey and Injun series
Hart, William Surrey
see **Injun and Whitey series**

Whitey series
Rounds, Glen
1 *Pay dirt* (1938)
2 *Whitey's first roundup* (1942)
3 *Whitey's Sunday horse* (1943)
Includes extracts from The blind colt
4 *Whitey looks for a job* (1944)
5 *Whitey and Jinglebob* (1946)
6 *Whitey and the rustlers* (1951)
7 *Whitey and the blizzard* (1952)
Numbers 6 and 7 also published in one volume entitled *Whitey's new saddle*, 1963
8 *Whitey takes a trip* (1954)
9 *Whitey ropes and rides* (1956)
10 *Whitey and the wild horses* (1958)
11 *Whitey and the colt killer* (1962)
12 *Wild horses of the Red Desert* (1969)
13 *Once we had a horse* (1971)

Whitfield series
Johnstone, William Wallace
see **Beasts series**
Moore, Richard A
see **Bob Whitfield series**

Whitford series
Roderus, Frank
see **J Aubrey Whitford series**

Whitgift series
Kirsten, Angela
see **Ralph Whitgift series**

Whitman series
Pearson, Diane
1 *Marigold field* (1969)
2 *Sarah Whitman* (1971)

Whitmarsh chronicles series
Richards, J T
1 *Generation apart* (1981)
2 *Generation untamed* (1981)

Whitney cousins series
Thesman, Jean
1 *Heather* (1990)
2 *Amelia* (1990)
3 *Erin* (1990)
4 *Triple trouble* (1992)

Whitney series
Dodge, David
see **Whit Whitney series**

Whitney Wheat series
Lane, Jeremy
1 *Death to drumbeat* (1944)
2 *Kill him tonight* (1946)
3 *Murder menagerie* (1946)
4 *Murder spoils everything* (1949)

Whittaker series
Popkin, Zelda
see **Mary Carner Whittaker series**

Who did it series
Salmon, Michael
1 *At the zoo* (1991)
2 *In the old castle* (1991)
3 *At the circus* (1991)
4 *At the beach* (1991)

Who framed Roger Rabbit series
Korman, Justine
see **Roger Rabbit series**

Who lives in series
Hirschi, Ron
see **Where animals live series**

Who me series
Macdonald, Betty
Humorous reminiscences
1 *Egg and I* (1946)
2 *Plague and I* (1948)
3 *Anybody can do anything* (1950)
4 *Onions in the stew* (1955)
One volume abridged edition entitled *Who me*, 1959

Whom God hath sundered trilogy
Onions, Oliver
1 *In accordance with the evidence* (1912)
2 *Debit account* (1912)
3 *Story of Louie* (1913)
One volume edition entitled *Whom God hath sundered*, 1925

Who's behind the door series
Salmon, Michael
1 *At my house* (1989)
2 *At the zoo* (1989)
3 *At my school* (1989)
4 *In the city* (1989)
5 *At the farm* (1989)
6 *In my dream* (1989)
7 *In dinosaur land* (1991)
8 *In monster land* (1991)
9 *In the jungle* (1991)
10 *Under the sea* (1991)

Why not series
Beaumont, Laura
1 *Tale of Christine Pristine* (1991)
Why you must never put your elbows on the table
2 *Tale of Doug Smug* (1992)
3 *Tale of Mitch Snitch* (1994)
Why you must never put your hands in your pockets

Wick series
Lang, Maria
see **Christer Wick series**

Wicked Willie series
Mayle, Peter
1 *Man's best friend* (1984)
2 *Wicked Willie's guide to women* (1987)
A worm's-eye view of the fair sex
3 *Wicked Willie's guide to women II* (1988)
Further adventures of man's best friend

Wicker series
Dawson, Carley
see **Mister Wicker series**

Wickford series
Sidgwick, Ethel
1 *Hatchways* (1916)
2 *Jamesie* (1918)

Wickham series
Barber, Anne Viccars
1 *Days at Wickham* (1966)
2 *Childhood in Egypt* (1968)

Wide Awake Girls series
Ellis, Katherine Ruth
1 *Wide Awake Girls* (1908)
2 *Wide Awake Girls at Winsted* (1909)
3 *Wide Awake Girls at college* (1910)

Widgeon series
Thomas, Alan
see **Inspector Widgeon series**

Widgery Winks series
Bennett, Rodney
1 *Story of Widgery Winks* (1942)
2 *Widgery Winks in the wide world* (1943)
3 *Widgery Winks and his new friends* (1945)

Widgets series
Marino, Tony
1 *Ratchet hood* (1992)
2 *Scraboolee jubilee* (1992)
3 *Intergalactic grudge match* (1992)

Widow Barnaby trilogy
Trollope, Frances
1 *Widow Barnaby* (1839)

2 *Widow married* (1840)
Widow wedded
3 *Adventures of the Barnabys in America* (1843)
Barnabys in America
Alternative title: Adventures of the widow wedded

Widows series
La Plante, Lynda
Based on a television series
1 *Widows* (1983)
2 *Widows II* (1985)

Wiegand series
Lockridge, Frances
see **Bill Wiegand series**

Wield series
Glint Green
see **Inspector Wield series**

Wife series
Burnley, Judith
1 *Wife* (1977)
2 *Unrepentant women* (1982)
3 *Woman herself* (1986)

Wife swap series
Law, Simone
1 *Swapping partners* (1972)
2 *Wife Swap Incorporated* (1972)

Wig series
Draper, Hastings
1 *Wiggery pokery* (1956)
2 *Wigged and gowned* (1958)
3 *Brief help* (1961)

Wigan series
Farmer, Bernard James
see **Sergeant Jack Wigan series**

Wiggen series
Harris, Mark
see **Henry W Wiggen series**

Wiggily series
Garis, Howard Roger
see **Uncle Wiggily series**

Wiggins series
Card, Orson Scott
see **Ender Wiggins series**
Gardner, Erle Stanley
see **Gramps Wiggins series**

Wiggly Price series
Chichester, John Jay
see **Jimmy Price series**

Wiggs series
Rice, Alice Hegan
see **Mrs Wiggs series**

Wilberforce series
Coleman, Leslie
1 *Wilberforce the whale* (1973)
2 *Wilberforce and the blue cave* (1974)
3 *Wilberforce, detective* (1975)
4 *Fort Wilberforce* (1977)
5 *Wilberforce and the McMonster* (1978)

Wilberforce series
Gordon, Margaret
1 *Wilberforce goes on a picnic* (1982)
2 *Wilberforce goes shopping* (1983)
3 *Wilberforce goes to a party* (1985)
4 *Wilberforce goes to playgroup* (1987)

Wilbur series
Rogerson, James
see **King Wilbur series**

Wilchester chronicles series
Ashton, Helen
1 *Tadpole Hall* (1941)
2 *Joanna at Littlefold* (1942)
3 *Yeoman's hospital* (1944)
4 *Captain comes home* (1947)
5 *Half-crown house* (1956)
Companion volume: *Hornet's nest*, 1934

Wild adventure series
Ellis, Edward Sylvester
1 *On the trail of Geronimo* (1889)
Alternative title: In the Apache country
2 *White mustang* (1889)
A tale of the Lone Star state

Wild and Black series
Carter, Bruce
see **Danny Black and Johnny Wild series**

Wild animals series
Drabble, Phil
1 *Weasel in my meatsafe* (1957)
2 *Badgers at my window* (1969)
3 *Country seasons* (1976)
4 *Country scene* (1978)
5 *No badgers in my wood* (1979)
6 *Country wise* (1980)
7 *Country matters* (1982)

Wild baby series
Lindgren, Barbro
Illustrated by Eva Eriksson
1 *Wild baby* (1981)
Original edition entitled *Mamman och den vilda Bebin*
2 *Wild baby's boat trip* (1983)
Wild baby goes to sea
Original edition entitled *Den vilde Bebiresan*
3 *Wild baby's dog* (1986)
Original edition entitled *Vilde Bebin far en hund*

Wild card trilogy
Stamey, Sara
1 *Wild card run* (1987)
2 *Win, lose, draw* (1988)
3 *Double blind* (1990)

Wild cards series
Martin, George Raymond Richard
1 *Wild cards* (1986)
2 *Aces high* (1987)
3 *Jokers wild* (1987)
4 *Aces abroad* (1988)
5 *Down and dirty* (1988)
6 *Ace in the hole* (1990)
Co-author: Melinda Marilyn Snodgrass
7 *Dead man's hand* (1990)
Co-authors: John Joseph Miller and Melinda Marilyn Snodgrass
8 *One-eyed jacks* (1991)
Co-author: Melinda Marilyn Snodgrass
9 *Jokertown shuffle* (1991)
Co-author: Melinda Marilyn Snodgrass

Wild flowers series
Burgess, Thornton Waldo
1 *Wild flowers we know* (1929)
2 *Wild flowers we should know* (1929)
Companion volume: *Birds you should know*, 1933

Wild flowers series
Young, Andrew
1 *Prospect of flowers* (1945)
2 *Retrospect of flowers* (1950)

Wild Geese series
Carney, Daniel
1 *Wild Geese* (1977)
2 *Square circle* (1982)
Wild Geese II

Wild geese series
Dillon, Eilis
1 *Wild geese* (1980)
2 *Citizen Burke* (1984)

Wild hearts series
Bennett, Cherie
1 *Wild hearts* (1994)
2 *Wild hearts on fire* (1994)
3 *Wild hearts forever* (1994)

Wild Horse Shorty series
Nye, Nelson Coral
1 *Wild Horse Shorty* (1944)
2 *Blood of kings* (1946)

Wild life story series
Rutley, Cecil Bernard
1 *Bru the grizzly* (1939)
2 *Kra the baboon* (1939)
3 *Peeko the beaver* (1939)
4 *Shag the caribou* (1940)
Numbers 1, 3, 4 also published in one volume entitled *Wild life in Canada*, 1943
5 *Timur the tiger* (1940)
6 *Miska the seal* (1940)
7 *Loki the wolf* (1940)
8 *Raja the elephant* (1940)
Numbers 2, 5, 8 also published in one volume entitled *Wild life in the jungle*, 1943
9 *Pogo the penguin* (1943)
Numbers 6, 7, 9 also published in one volume entitled *Wild life in the ice and snow*, 1943
10 *Inkosi the lion* (1948)
11 *Frisk the otter* (1951)
12 *Tuska the boar* (1952)
13 *Rey the fox* (1952)
14 *Thunda the buffalo* (1953)
Numbers 10, 12, 14 also published in one volume entitled *Wild life in the bush and jungle*, 1954
15 *Fleet the stag* (1956)
16 *Fulgor the golden eagle* (1959)

Wild Lorings series
Courtney, Gwendoline
1 *Wild Lorings at school* (1954)
2 *Wild Lorings, detectives!* (1956)

Wild magic trilogy
Clayton, Jo
This sequence follows the **Soul magic trilogy**
1 *Wild magic* (1991)
2 *Wildfire* (1992)
3 *Magic wars* (1993)

Wild One series
Grey, Peter
see **Kit Hunter series**

Wild sheep chase series
Murakami, Haruki
Translated from the Japanese
1 *Wild sheep chase* (1981)
2 *Dance, dance, dance* (1988)

Wild Swan trilogy
De Blasis, Celeste
1 *Wild Swan* (1984)
2 *Swan's chance* (1987)
3 *Season of Swans* (1989)

Wild talents series
Goulart, Ron
1 *Talent for the invisible* (1973)
2 *Hello, Lemuria, hello* (1979)

Wild West series
Freedman, Russell
1 *Children of the Wild West* (1983)
2 *Cowboys of the Wild West* (1985)

Wild Wood series
Clewes, Dorothy
1 *Cottage in the Wild Wood* (1945)
2 *Stream in the Wild Wood* (1946)
Numbers 1 and 2 also published in one volume entitled *The Wild Wood*, 1948
3 *Treasure in the Wild Wood* (1947)
4 *Fair in the Wild Wood* (1949)

Wild woods series
Ellis, Edward Sylvester
1 *On the trail of the moose* (1890)
2 *Through forest and fire* (1891)
3 *Across Texas* (1893)

Wildcat O'Shea series
Clinton, Jeff
1 *Fighting buckaroo* (1961)
2 *Wildcat's rampage* (1962)
3 *Wildcat against the house* (1963)
4 *Wildcat's revenge* (1964)
5 *Wildcat takes his medicine* (1966)
6 *Wanted, Wildcat O'Shea* (1967)
7 *Wildcat on the loose* (1967)
8 *Wildcat's witch hunt* (1967)
9 *Watch out for Wildcat* (1968)
10 *Wildcat meets Miss Melody* (1968)
11 *Build a box for Wildcat* (1969)
12 *Stranger named O'Shea* (1970)
13 *Wildcat's claim to fame* (1971)
14 *Bounty on Wildcat* (1971)
15 *Hang high, O'Shea* (1972)

Wildcat series
Wiley, Hugh
1 *Wildcat* (1920)
2 *Prowler* (1924)

Wildcat trilogy
Nyoongah, Mudrooroo
1 *Wildcat falling* (1965)
Originally published under the author's original name Colin Johnson
2 *Doin Wildcat* (1977)
3 *Wildcat screaming* (1992)

Wilde boys series
Bridges, Ben
1 *Wilde boys* (1988)
2 *Wilde fire* (1988)
3 *Wilde's law* (1990)
4 *Aces Wilde* (1991)

Wilde series
Spicer, Bart
see **Carney Wilde series**
York, Andrew
see **Jonas Wilde series**

Wilderness giants series
Thompson, David
1 *Season of the warrior* (1993)
2 *Hawken fury* (1993)
3 *Prairie blood* (1994)

Wilderness mystery series
Nesbit, Troy
1 *Sand dune pony* (1952)
2 *Jinx of Payrock Canyon* (1954)
3 *Indian mummy mystery* (1954)
4 *Mystery at Rustlers' Fort* (1960)
5 *Diamond Cave mystery* (1962)
6 *Forest fire mystery* (1963)

Wilderness of four series
Hancock, Niel
1 *Across the far mountain* (1982)
2 *Plains of the sea* (1963)
3 *On the boundaries of bleakness* (1982)
4 *Road to the Middle Islands* (1983)
This sequence is followed by the **Windameir Circle series**

Wilderness series
Lowry, Malcolm
see **Voyage that never ends series**

Wilderness series
Pound, Arthur
1 *Once a wilderness* (1934)
2 *Second growth* (1935)

Wilderness series
Roberts, Charles George Douglas
1 *Wisdom of the wilderness* (1922)
2 *They that walk in the wild* (1924)

Wilderness series
Thompson, David
see **Nathaniel King series**
Truman, Timothy
see **Simon Girty series**

Wilderness trilogy
Thompson, Mary Wolfe
see **Aiken family trilogy**

Wildest dreams series
Thomas, Leslie
Autobiography
1 *This time next week* (1964)
2 *In my wildest dreams* (1984)

Wildfowling series
B B
Memoirs
1 *Tide's ending* (1950)
2 *Dark estuary* (1953)

Wilding family series
Crompton, Richmal
1 *Wildings* (1925)
2 *David Wilding* (1926)
3 *Thorn bush* (1928)

Wildkeepers series
Grimshaw, Nigel
1 *Bluntstone and the Wildkeepers* (1974)
2 *Wildkeeper's guest* (1976)

Wildlife series
Williams, Elma Mary
1 *Valley of animals* (1963)
2 *Pig in paradise* (1964)
3 *Pant Glas story* (1970)
Companion volume: *Heaven on my doorstep*, 1970

Wilfred Dover series
Porter, Joyce
see **Chief Inspector Wilfred Dover series**

Wilhelm Meister series
Goethe, Johann Wolfgang von
1 *Wilhelm Meister's apprenticeship* (1795)
Original edition entitled *Wilhelm Meisters Lehrjahre*
2 *Wilhelm Meister's travels* (1796)
Original edition entitled *Wilhelm Meisters Wanderjahre*

Wilkcox Street Precinct series
Linington, Elizabeth
see **Sergeant Ivor Maddox series**

Wilkes the wizard series
Webb, Jackie
1 *Wilkes the wizard* (1985)
2 *Wilkes the wizard and the S.P.A.M.* (1986)

Wilkins series
Anderson, James
see **Inspector Wilkins series**
Beeding, Francis
see **Inspector Wilkins series**

Wilkins series
Newman, Marjorie
1 *Wilkins the armchair cat* (1978)
2 *Wilkins gets a job* (1980)
3 *Wilkins gets a blanket* (1984)

Wilkins series
Thomas, Murray
see **Inspector Wilkins series**

Will and Liz series
Resciniti, Angelo G
see **Liz and Will series**

Will Barrett series
Percy, Walker
1 *Last gentleman* (1966)
2 *Second coming* (1980)

Will Cody series
Buntline, Ned
see **Buffalo Bill series**

Will Fitzgerald trilogy
Fitzgerald, John Dennis
1 *Papa married a Mormon* (1955)
Family reminiscences
2 *Mamma's boarding house* (1958)
3 *Uncle Will and the Fitzgerald curse* (1961)

Will Foreman series
Rey, Bret
1 *Runaway* (1990)
2 *Arizona break-out* (1990)

Will Powers series
Zacharia, Irwin
see **Vendetta series**

Will trilogy
Ballantyne, Robert Michael
see **Wandering Will trilogy**

Will Woodfield series
Foote-Smith, Elizabeth
1 *Gentle albatross* (1976)
2 *Never say die* (1977)

Willa Jansson series
Matera, Lia
1 *Where lawyers fear to tread* (1987)
2 *Radical departure* (1988)
3 *Hidden agenda* (1988)

Willard and Ben series
Gilbert, Stephen
see **Ben and Willard series**

Willard series
Lynch, Miriam
see **Nell Willard series**

Willeford series
DeWeese, Gene
see **Calvin Willeford series**

Willerbys series
Oldfield, Pamela
1 *Willerbys and the burglar* (1981)
2 *Willerbys and the haunted mill* (1981)
3 *Willerbys and the sad clown* (1982)
4 *Willerbys and the old castle* (1982)
5 *Willerbys and the bank robbers* (1983)
6 *Willerbys and the mystery man* (1983)

William Ames series
Freeman, Lucy
see **Doctor William Ames series**

William and Mary trilogy
Plaidy, Jean
1 *Three crowns* (1965)
2 *Haunted sisters* (1966)
3 *Queen's favourites* (1966)
One volume edition entitled *The last of the Stuarts*, 1977

William and Ponder series
Softly, Barbara
see **Ponder and William series**

William and Susan series
Kirk, Thomas Hobson
1 *Back to the wall* (1967)
2 *River gang* (1968)
3 *Ardrey ambush* (1969)

William and Wendy series
Braga, Meg
1 *Secrets in the attic* (1970)
2 *Lollipops and apples* (1970)
3 *Pepperpots and presents* (1971)
4 *Pictures in the spring* (1971)

William Austen series
Hocking, Anne
see **Inspector William Austen series**

William Baker series
Mills, Osmington
see **Superintendent William Baker series**

William Bastion series
Harrison, Richard
see **Chief Inspector William Bastion series**

William Beef series
Bruce, Leo
see **Sergeant William Beef series**

William Beeke series
Brooks, Edwy Searles
see **Inspector William Beeke series**

William Blow and Gideon Manciple series
Hopkins, Kenneth
see **Doctor William Blow and Professor Gideon Manciple series**

William Brewer series
McElroy, Hugh
see **Inspector William Brewer series**

William Burrill series
Macleod, Adam Gordon
see **Sir William Burrill series**

William Cargoe series
Peacey, Seton
1 *Achievement of William Cargoe* (1935)
2 *They are transformed* (1937)

William Cecil series
Read, Conyers
1 *Mister Secretary Cecil* (1955)
2 *Lord Burghley and Queen Elizabeth* (1960)

William Clarke Quantrell series
Gruber, Frank
Based on the life of a Confederate guerilla
1 *Fighting man* (1948)
2 *Quantrell's raiders* (1954)

William Deacon series
Brean, Herbert
1 *Traces of Brillhart* (1960)
2 *Traces of Merrilee* (1966)

William Dougal series
Taylor, Andrew
1 *Caroline minuscule* (1982)
2 *Waiting for the end of the world* (1984)
3 *Our father's lies* (1985)
4 *Old school tie* (1986)
5 *Freelance death* (1987)
6 *Blood relation* (1990)
7 *Sleeping policeman* (1992)
8 *Odd man out* (1993)

William Harkness series
Warwick, Milligan
1 *Yawning lion* (1932)
2 *Bandit trust* (1934)

William Hart and Charlie Pearce series
Gardner, Jerome
see **Dripspring series**

William Holmes series
Bark, Conrad Voss
see **Mister William Holmes series**

William Horton series
Kilbourne, Fannie
1 *Corner in William* (1922)
2 *Mrs William Horton speaking* (1925)
3 *Horton twins* (1926)
4 *Dot and Will* (1929)
5 *Dot and Will at Home* (1931)

William III trilogy
Bowen, Marjorie
1 *I will maintain* (1910)
Revised edition 1943
2 *Defender of the Faith* (1911)
3 *God and the king* (1911)

William Jackson and Edward Razoni series
Murphy, Warren Burton
see **Edward Razoni and William Jackson series**

William Kane and Abel Rosnovski series
Archer, Jeffrey
1 *Kane and Abel* (1979)
2 *Prodigal daughter* (1982)

William Kendall and Aaron Eisenberg series
Chase, Philip
see **Aaron Eisenberg and William Kendall series**

William Mallett series
Macdonnell, James Edmond
see **Commander William Mallett series**

William Mallett series
Orgill, Douglas
1 *Death bringers* (1962)
Journey into violence
2 *Ride a tiger* (1963)
Cautious assassin

William Marshal series
Shelby, Graham
1 *Devil is loose* (1973)
2 *Wolf at the door* (1975)

William Martin series
Stanton, Ken
see **Aquanauts series**

William, Mary and Ben series
Furminger, Jo
see **Mary, Ben and William series**

William McAlpin series
Smithies, Richard Hugo Ripman
see **Inspector William McAlpin series**

William McGonagall series
Milligan, Spike
1 *Great McGonagall scrap book* (1975)
2 *William McGonagall, the truth at last* (1976)
3 *William McGonagall meets George Gershwin* (1988)
Companion volume: *The great McGonagall, a screenplay*, by Spike Milligan and Joseph McGrath, 1975

William Mitchell series
Wrenn, Harold Albert
1 *Tangle* (1953)
2 *Lady prefers murder* (1954)
3 *Toby jug murders* (1955)

4 *Due to expire* (1958)
5 *Unguarded moment* (1959)

William Monk series
Perry, Anne
see **Inspector William Monk series**

William Murgatroyd series
Osborne, William Hamilton
1 *Red mouse* (1909)
2 *Running fight* (1910)

William Power series
Clandon, Henrietta
1 *Rope by arrangement* (1935)
2 *Good by stealth* (1936)
3 *This delicate murder* (1936)
4 *Power on the scent* (1937)

William Ryder series
Boyles, William
see **Bounty Hunter series**

William Schaefer series
Estow, Daniel
1 *Moment of fiction* (1979)
2 *Moment of silence* (1980)

William series
Crompton, Richmal
1 *Just William* (1922)
2 *More William* (1922)
3 *William again* (1923)
4 *William the fourth* (1924)
5 *Still, William* (1925)
6 *William the conqueror* (1926)
7 *William in trouble* (1927)
8 *William, the outlaw* (1927)
9 *William the good* (1928)
10 *William* (1929)
11 *William the bad* (1930)
12 *William's happy days* (1930)
13 *William's crowded hours* (1931)
14 *William, the pirate* (1932)
15 *William, the rebel* (1933)
16 *William the gangster* (1934)
17 *William the detective* (1935)
18 *Sweet William* (1936)
19 *William, the showman* (1937)
20 *William, the dictator* (1938)
21 *William and A.R.P.* (1939)
William's bad resolution
22 *William and the evacuees* (1940)
William the film star
23 *William does his bit* (1941)
24 *William carries on* (1942)
25 *William and the Brains Trust* (1945)
William the hero
The second title is an abridged edition
26 *Just William's luck* (1948)
27 *William the bold* (1950)
28 *William and the tramp* (1952)
29 *William and the moon rocket* (1954)
30 *William and the space animal* (1956)
31 *William's television show* (1958)
32 *William, the explorer* (1960)
33 *William's treasure trove* (1962)
34 *William and the witch* (1964)
35 *William and the monster* (1965)
36 *William the ancient Briton* (1965)
37 *William the cannibal* (1965)
38 *William the globetrotter* (1965)
39 *William and the pop singers* (1965)
40 *William and the masked ranger* (1966)
41 *William the superman* (1968)
42 *William the lawless* (1970)
Companion volumes: *Just William, the story of the film*, 1939, *William and the artist's model, a play*, 1956

William series
Flack, Marjorie
1 *Wait for William* (1935)
2 *William and his kitten* (1938)

William series
Lee, Jennette Barbour Perry
see **Uncle William series**

William series
Winthrop, Elizabeth
1 *Castle in the attic* (1985)
2 *Battle for the castle* (1993)

William Shakespeare trilogy
Malpass, Eric Lawson
1 *Sweet Will* (1973)
2 *Cleopatra boy* (1974)
3 *House of women* (1975)

William Stephenson series
Stevenson, William Henri
Account of the career of the British Security Coordinator under Churchill
1 *Man called Intrepid* (1976)
The secret war
2 *Intrepid's last case* (1983)

William Stevens and Pierre Allain series
Graeme, Bruce
see **Superintendent William Stevens and Inspector Pierre Allain series**

William Sultan series
Austin, Hugh
1 *Drink the green water* (1948)
2 *Milkmaid's millions* (1948)

William T Bucko trilogy
Westcott, C T
see **Eagleheart trilogy**

William the Silent series
Bowen, Marjorie
1 *Prince and heretic* (1914)
2 *William, by the grace of God* (1916)
Abridged edition 1928

William the wizard series
Cleveland-Peck, Patricia
1 *William the wizard* (1980)
2 *Community magic* (1984)

William Verity series
Selwyn, Francis
see **Sergeant William Verity series**

William Walker series
Macdonnell, James Edmond
see **Hooky Walker series**

William Warne series
Sylvester, Martin
1 *Dangerous age* (1986)
2 *Lethal vintage* (1988)
3 *Rough red* (1990)

William Wilberforce Smith series
Haggard, William
1 *Martello Tower* (1986)
2 *Diplomatist* (1987)

William Winter series
Butler, Gwendoline
see **Inspector William Winter series**

Williams series
Barrington, John
see **Ken Williams series**
Clevely, Hugh
see **Inspector Williams series**
Daly, Carroll John
see **Race Williams series**
Di Mona, Joseph
see **George Williams series**
Macdonald, Hugh Chisholm
see **Paul Williams series**
Murphy, Warren Burton
see **Destroyer series**
Tippette, Giles
see **Justa Williams series**

Williams trilogy
Young, Gordon Ray
see **Hurricane Williams trilogy**

Williamsburg series
Thane, Elswyth
1 *Dawn's early light* (1943)
2 *Yankee stranger* (1944)
3 *Ever after* (1945)
4 *Light heart* (1947)
5 *Kissing kin* (1948)
6 *This was tomorrow* (1951)
7 *Homing* (1957)

Williamsburg trilogy
Fuchs, Daniel
1 *Summer in Williamsburg* (1934)
2 *Homage to Blenholt* (1936)
3 *Low company* (1937)
Neptune Beach
One volume editions entitled *Three novels*, 1961 and *The Williamsburg trilogy*, 1972

Willie Delamer series
Wisler, Gary Clifton
1 *Trident brand* (1982)
2 *Starr's showdown* (1986)
3 *Antelope Springs* (1986)
4 *Purgatory* (1987)
5 *Abrego Canyon* (1987)
6 *Wayward trail* (1988)
7 *South Pass ambush* (1988)
8 *Sweetwater Flats* (1989)
9 *Sam Delamer* (1989)
10 *Among the eagles* (1989)
11 *Clear Fork* (1990)
12 *North of Esperanza* (1991)
13 *Blood mesa* (1991)
14 *Baron of the Brazos* (1992)
15 *Wetherbys* (1992)
16 *Shawnee trail* (1993)

Willie Halliday series
Fredman, Mike
1 *You can always blame the rain* (1978)
2 *Kisses leave no fingerprints* (1979)

Willie Maddison series
Williamson, Henry
see **Flax of dream series**

Willie series
Clewes, Dorothy
1 *Upsidedown Willie* (1968)
2 *Special Branch Willie* (1969)
3 *Fire-Brigade Willie* (1970)

Willie series
Mayle, Peter
see **Wicked Willie series**
Oakden, David
see **Buttercup Willie series**

Willing series
McCloy, Helen
see **Basil Willing series**

Willis series
Hughes, William
see **George Willis series**

Williver family series
Hadfield, Alice Mary
1 *Williver's luck* (1964)
2 *Williver's quest* (1965)
3 *Williver's return* (1967)

Willoughby Chase series
Aiken, Joan
see **Dido Twite series**

Willow and Albert series
Miller, Margaret Jessy
1 *Mouse tales* (1967)
2 *Willow and Albert* (1968)
3 *Willow and Albert are stowaways* (1970)
4 *Big Brown Teapot* (1979)
5 *Mad muddle* (1982)
6 *Pocketful of mice* (1984)
7 *Two mice on holiday* (1986)
8 *Mouse outings* (1987)

Willow Farm series
Blyton, Enid
1 *Children of Willow Farm* (1942)
Adventures on Willow Farm
2 *More adventures on Willow Farm* (1943)

Willow Hill series
Hader, Berta
1 *Cock-a-doodle-doo* (1939)
The story of a little red rooster
2 *Big snow* (1948)
3 *Squirrely at Willow Hill* (1950)
4 *Little White Foot* (1952)
5 *Friendly phoebe* (1953)
6 *Wish on the moon* (1954)
7 *Little Chip of Willow Hill* (1958)

Willow King series
Cooper, Natasha
1 *Festering lilies* (1990)
2 *Poison flowers* (1991)
3 *Bloody roses* (1992)
4 *Bitter herbs* (1993)

Willow series
Bawden, Nina
see **Carrie Willow series**

Willow series
This sequence has three authors
Drew, Wayland
1 *Willow* (1988)
Vinge, Joan Dennison
2 *Willow* (1988)
Based on a screenplay
Dubowski, Cathy East
3 *Willow* (1988)
Based on a screenplay
Companion volumes: *The Willow sourcebook*, by Greg Costikyan and Allen Varney, 1988; *Willow, official movie magazine*, by David McDonnell, 1988

Willow Wood Springs trilogy
Ellis, Terry
1 *Legend of Willow Wood Springs* (1989)
2 *Explorers of Willow Wood Springs* (1989)
3 *Invasion of Willow Wood Springs* (1989)

Willows and Parker series
Gough, Laurence
1 *Goldfish bowl* (1987)
2 *Death on a number eight hook* (1988)
3 *Hot shots* (1989)
4 *Sandstorm* (1990)
5 *Serious crimes* (1990)
6 *Accidental deaths* (1991)
7 *Fall down easy* (1992)

Wills series
Brown, Sam
see **Casey Wills series**

Willum series
Watson, Clarissa
see **Persis Willum series**

Willy Freeman trilogy
Collier, James Lincoln
1 *Jump ship to freedom* (1981)
2 *War comes to Willy* (1983)
3 *Who is Carrie?* (1984)

Willy Hand series
Priestley, Brian
1 *Makariri gold* (1977)
2 *Island emperor* (1978)

Willy series
Browne, Anthony
1 *Willy the wimp* (1984)
2 *Willy the champ* (1985)

Wilmington series
Wiat, Philippa
1 *Four-poster* (1979)
2 *Shadow of Samain* (1980)

Wilshaw series
Pollard, Alfred Oliver
see **David Wilshaw series**

Wilson and Coe series
Cameron, Caddo
see **Private Badger Coe and Sergeant Blizzard Wilson series**

Wilson family trilogy
Elliott, Janice
1 *State of peace* (1971)
2 *Private life* (1972)
3 *Heaven on earth* (1975)

Wilson series
Alden, William Livingston
see **Moral Pirates series**
Cole, George Douglas Howard
see **Superintendent Henry Wilson series**
Garnet, A H
see **Cyrus Wilson series**
Haywood, Carolyn
see **Eddie Wilson series**
McRobbie, David
see **Wayne Wilson series**
Palfrey, Heather Mary
see **Ricky Wilson series**
Powell, Jonathan
see **Sam Wilson series**
Sproul, Kathleen
see **Dick Wilson series**

Wilson trilogy
Wilkinson, Brenda
see **Ludell Wilson trilogy**

Wilson Young series
Tippette, Giles
1 *Bank robber* (1970)
Spikes Gang
2 *Wilson's gold* (1980)
3 *Wilson's luck* (1980)
4 *Wilson's choice* (1981)
5 *Wilson's revenge* (1981)
6 *Wilson's woman* (1982)
7 *Hard luck money* (1982)
8 *Texas Bank Robbing Company* (1983)
9 *Wilson Young on the run* (1983)

Wilt series
Sharpe, Tom
see **Henry Wilt series**

Wilton Jacks series
Wallis, James Harold
see **Inspector Wilton Jacks series**

Wim series
Rhinehart, Luke
1 *Dice Man* (1971)
2 *Adventures of Wim* (1986)
3 *Search for the Dice Man* (1993)

Wimble series
Burnham, Helen
see **One Week Wimble series**

Wimpy series
Drake, Joan
1 *Story of Wimpy, a wump* (1940)
2 *More about Wimpy and his friends* (1942)
3 *Wimpy on holiday* (1946)
4 *Wimpy goes abroad* (1954)

Wimsey series
Sayers, Dorothy Leigh
see **Lord Peter Wimsey series**

Win Bear trilogy
Smith, Lester Neil
1 *Probability broach* (1980)
2 *Venus belt* (1981)
3 *Nagasaki vector* (1983)

Win Hadley series
Porter, Mark
1 *Winning pitcher* (1960)
2 *Keeper play* (1960)
3 *Overtime upset* (1960)
4 *Set point* (1960)
5 *Slashing blades* (1960)
6 *Duel on the cinders* (1960)

Winchester family series
Wayne, Jenifer
1 *Day the ceiling fell down* (1961)
2 *Night the rain came in* (1963)
3 *Merry by name* (1964)
4 *Ghost next door* (1965)
5 *Someone in the attic* (1967)
6 *Something in the barn* (1971)

Wincourt and Raine series
Hodge, Charles
see **Jim Raine and Bob Wincourt series**

Wind chill series
Gifford, Thomas
1 *Wind chill factor* (1992)
2 *First sacrifice* (1994)

Wind dancers series
Meluch, Rebecca M
1 *Wind dancers* (1981)
2 *Wind child* (1982)

Wind in the banner series
Lanham, Edwin
1 *Wind blew west* (1935)
2 *Banner at daybreak* (1937)

Wind in the willows series
This sequence has three authors
Grahame, Kenneth
1 *Wind in the willows* (1908)
Companion volumes: *First whisper of the wind in the willows*, edited by Elspeth Grahame, 1945
Jones, Nicholas
2 *Grand annual show* (1984)
3 *Mole's cousin* (1984)
4 *Weasel's trap* (1984)
5 *Alfred and the caravan* (1984)
6 *Buried treasure* (1985)
7 *Burglary at Toad Hall* (1985)
8 *Harvest* (1985)
9 *Labyrinth* (1985)
10 *Winter sports* (1986)
11 *Rescue* (1986)
12 *Bankruptcy* (1986)
13 *Toad, photographer* (1986)
Horwood, William
14 *Willows in winter* (1993)

Wind river series
McCarthy, Gary
1 *Wind river* (1984)
2 *Powder river* (1985)

Wind trilogy
Garlock, Dorothy
see **Colorado trilogy**

Windameir circle series
Hancock, Niel
1 *Dragon winter* (1978)
2 *Fires of Windameir* (1985)
3 *Sea of silence* (1987)
4 *Wanderer's return* (1988)
5 *Bridge of dawn* (1991)

Windhaven series
De Jourlet, Marie
1 *Windhaven Plantation* (1977)
2 *Storm over Windhaven* (1977)
3 *Legacy of Windhaven* (1978)
4 *Return to Windhaven* (1978)
5 *Windhaven's peril* (1979)
6 *Trials of Windhaven* (1980)
7 *Defenders of Windhaven* (1980)
8 *Windhaven's crisis* (1981)
9 *Windhaven's bounty* (1981)
10 *Windhaven's triumph* (1982)
11 *Windhaven's fury* (1982)
12 *Windhaven's destiny* (1983)
13 *Windhaven's hope* (1983)

Windhawk and Joanne series
O'Banyon, Constance
see **Joanne and Windhawk series**

Windhover tapes series
Norwood, Warren
1 *Image of voices* (1982)
2 *Flexing the warp* (1983)
3 *Fize of the Gabriel Ratchets* (1982)
4 *Planet of flowers* (1984)

Windmill Hill series
Evans, Stuart
1 *Centres of ritual* (1978)
2 *Occupational debris* (1979)
3 *Temporary hearths* (1982)
4 *Houses on the site* (1984)
5 *Seasonal tribal feasts* (1986)

Windmill Land series
Clarke, Allen
1 *Windmill Land* (1916)
2 *More Windmill Land* (1918)
3 *Windmill Land stories* (1924)

Window trilogy
Hohl, Joan
1 *Window on yesterday* (1988)
2 *Window on today* (1989)
3 *Window on tomorrow* (1989)

Windri series
Needham, Violet
1 *Woods of Windri* (1944)
2 *Changeling of Monte Lucio* (1946)

Windrider series
Stahl, Hilda
see **Elizabeth Gail series**

Windrose series
Hambly, Barbara
1 *Silent tower* (1986)
2 *Silicon mage* (1988)
Numbers 1 and 2 also published in one volume entitled *Darkmage*, 1988
3 *Dog wizard* (1992)

Windrush series
Hackney, Alan
see **Stanley Windrush series**

Winds of change series
Macmillan, Harold
Reminiscences
1 *Winds of change, 1914-1939* (1966)
2 *Blast of war, 1939-1945* (1967)
3 *Tides of fortune, 1945-1955* (1969)
4 *Riding the storm, 1956-1959* (1971)
5 *Pointing the way, 1959-1961* (1972)
6 *At the end of the day, 1961-1963* (1973)

Winds series
Shiplett, June Lund
1 *Raging winds of heaven* (1978)
2 *Reap the bitter winds* (1979)
3 *Wild storms of heaven* (1980)
4 *Defy the savage winds* (1980)
5 *Thunder in the wind* (1982)
6 *Wild wind's calling* (1984)
7 *Winds of betrayal* (1987)
8 *Gathering of the winds* (1988)

Windsingers series
Lindholm, Megan
1 *Harpy's flight* (1983)
2 *Windsingers* (1984)
3 *Limbreth Gate* (1984)
Numbers 1-3 also published in one volume entitled *The Windsingers*, 1986
4 *Luck of the wheels* (1989)

Windwalker series
Mayhar, Ardath
1 *Trail of the seahawks* (1987)
2 *Monkey station* (1989)

Windy Foot series
Frost, Frances Mary
1 *Windy Foot at the county fair* (1947)
2 *Sleigh bells for Windy Foot* (1948)
3 *Maple sugar for Windy Foot* (1950)

Windylaw Farm series
Hardman, Diana
1 *Children at Windylaw Farm* (1957)
2 *More about the children at Windylaw Farm* (1957)

Windyridge series
Riley, William
1 *Windyridge* (1912)
2 *Thro' a Yorkshire window* (1919)
3 *Yorkshire suburb* (1920)
4 *Windyridge revisited* (1928)

Wine series
Simon, Roger Lichtenberg
see **Moses Wine series**

Winfield and Quentin series
Peterson, Audrey
see **Jane Winfield and Andrew Quentin series**

Winfield series
Blake, Vanessa
see **Jenny Winfield series**

Winfield series
Lucas, Edward Verrall
1 *Listener's lure* (1906)
An oblique narration
2 *Over Bemerton's* (1908)
An easy-going chronicle
3 *Mister Ingleside* (1910)
4 *London lavender* (1912)
5 *Landmarks* (1914)

Wing series
Jong, Erica
see **Isadora Wing series**

Wing series
Reach, James
1 *One mad night* (1935)
2 *Lunatics at large* (1936)
3 *Case of the laughing dwarf* (1938)

Wingate series
Swift, Bryan
see **Mac Wingate series**

Winged assassin trilogy
Cooke, Catherine
1 *Winged assassin* (1987)
2 *Realm of the gods* (1988)
3 *Crimson goddess* (1989)

Wingfold trilogy
Macdonald, George
see **Thomas Wingfold trilogy**

Wingman series
Maloney, Mack
1 *Wingman* (1987)
2 *Circle war* (1987)
3 *Lucifer crusade* (1987)
4 *Thunder in the East* (1988)
5 *Twisted cross* (1989)
6 *Final storm* (1989)
7 *Freedom express* (1990)
8 *Skyfire* (1990)
9 *Return from the inferno* (1991)

Wingo series
Street, James
1 *Gauntlet* (1946)
2 *High calling* (1951)

Wings series
Thomas, Barry
1 *Wings* (1977)
2 *Wings over enemy lines* (1978)

Winifred series
Rhoades, Nina
1 *Winifred's neighbors* (1903)
2 *Children on the top floor* (1904)

Winkie series
Schermele, Willy
1 *Winkie and Woolly Wopsie* (1958)
Original edition entitled *Winkie en Wolletje Wopsie*
2 *Winkie and Ruby Robin* (1958)
Original edition entitled *Winkie en Robijntje Roodborst*
3 *Winkie and Blinkie Bear* (1958)
Original edition entitled *Winkie en Binki Beer*
4 *Winkie and his woodland friends* (1958)
Original edition entitled *Winkie en zijn woudvriendjes*
5 *Winkie and Twinkie Twiddle* (1958)
Original edition entitled *Winkie en Twinkie Toef*
6 *Winkie and his magic flute* (1958)
Original edition entitled *Winkie en zijn toverfluit*
7 *Winkie and the wily fox* (1958)
Original edition entitled *Winkie en de sluive vos*
8 *Winkie lost in the deep, deep woods* (1958)
Original edition entitled *Winkie verdwaalt in het grote bos*
9 *Winkie in Toadstool Town* (1960)
Original edition entitled *Winkie in Paddestoelenstad*
10 *Winkie and Wobbleena* (1960)
Original edition entitled *Winkie en Wiebelientje*
11 *Winkie and the secret passage* (1960)
Original edition entitled *Winkie en de geheime gang*
12 *Winkie and Brownie Bright-Eyes* (1960)
Original edition entitled *Winkie en Kabouter Kraaloog*

Winkle series
Holland, Muriel
see **Wizard Winkle series**

Winklepicker series
Moon, Heather
1 *Winklepicker* (1981)
2 *Winklepicker goes south* (1982)
3 *Winklepicker and Paper Dart* (1984)

Winkles series
Jackson, Gabrielle Emilie
see **Wee Winkles series**

Winklesea series
Cresswell, Helen
1 *Gift from Winklesea* (1969)
2 *Whatever happened to Winklesea?* (1989)

Winkley series
Rutland, Harriet
see **Mister Winkley series**

Winkman series
Von Elsner, Don
see **Jake Winkman series**

Winks series
Bennett, Rodney
see **Widgery Winks series**

Winnebagos series
Frey, Hildegarde Gertrude
1 *Camp Fire Girls in the Maine woods* (1916)
Alternative title: The Winnebagos go camping
2 *Camp Fire Girls at school* (1916)
Alternative title: The Wokelo Weavers
3 *Camp Fire Girls at Onoway House* (1916)
Alternative title: The magic garden
4 *Camp Fire Girls go motoring* (1916)
Alternative title: Along the road that leads the way
5 *Camp Fire Girls larks and pranks* (1918)
Alternative title: The house of the open door
6 *Camp Fire Girls on Ellen's Isle* (1918)
Alternative title: The trail of the seven cedars
7 *Camp Fire Girls on the open road* (1918)
Alternative title: Glorify work
8 *Camp Fire Girls do their bit* (1919)
Alternative title: Over the top with the Winnebagos
9 *Camp Fire Girls solve a mystery* (1919)
Alternative title: The Christmas adventure at Carver House
10 *Camp Fire Girls at Camp Keewaydin* (1920)
Alternative title: Down paddles

Winners and losers series
Pearson, Michael A
1 *Winners and losers* (1984)
2 *Bubble gum champion* (1986)
3 *Splashers* (1987)

Winners series
Rand, Suzanne
1 *Girl most likely* (1985)
2 *All-American girl* (1985)
3 *Good luck girl* (1986)

Winnetou trilogy
May, Karl Friedrich
1 *Winnetou, the Apache knight* (1898)
Based on Winnetou, by Karl Friedrich May, 1893
2 *Treasure of Nugget Mountain* (1898)
3 *Jack Hildreth on the Nile* (1899)

Winnie O'Wynn series
Atkey, Bertram
1 *Winnie O'Wynn and the wolves* (1921)
2 *Winnie O'Wynn and the dark horses* (1925)

Winnie-the-Pooh series
Milne, Alan Alexander
see **Piglet series**

Winning of America series
Eckert, Allan Wesley
1 *Frontiersmen* (1967)
2 *Wilderness empire, 1745* (1969)
3 *Conquerors* (1970)
4 *Wilderness war* (1978)
5 *Gateway to empire* (1983)
6 *Twilight of empire* (1988)

Winning series
Groten, Dallas
1 *Winning isn't always first place* (1983)
Short stories based on factual incidents
2 *Will the real winner please stand?* (1985)
3 *Ordinary champions* (1989)

Winning the West series
Porter, Donald Clayton
1 *Rio Grande* (1986)
2 *Fort Laramie* (1987)
3 *Union Pacific* (1987)

Winona series
Widdemer, Margaret
1 *Winona of the camp fire* (1915)
2 *Winona of Camp Karonya* (1917)
3 *Winona's war farm* (1918)
4 *Winona's way* (1919)
A story of reconstruction
5 *Winona on her own* (1922)
6 *Winona's dreams come true* (1923)

Winslow family trilogy
Keyes, Frances Parkinson
1 *Honor Bright* (1936)
2 *Blue camellia* (1957)
3 *Victorine* (1958)
Gold slippers

Winslow series
Martinek, Frank V
see **Don Wilnslow series**

Winsome series
Murphy, David John
1 *Winsome for winners* (1952)
2 *More winners for Winsome* (1954)

Winstanley trilogy
Penn, Margaret
see **Hilda Winstanley trilogy**

Winston Barrows series
Eades, Maud L
1 *Crown swindle* (1925)
2 *Torrington Square mystery* (1932)

Winston Creevy series
Lord, Jeremy
see **Colonel Winston Creevy series**

Winston S Churchill series
This sequence has two authors; authorised biography
Churchill, Randolph Spencer
1 *Youth, 1874-1900* (1966)
2 *Young politician, 1901-1914* (1967)
Gilbert, Martin
3 *Challenge of the war, 1914-1916* (1971)
Co-author: Randolph Spencer Churchill
4 *Stricken world, 1917-1922* (1974)
5 *Prophet of truth, 1923-1939* (1976)
6 *Finest hour, 1939-1941* (1983)
7 *Road to victory, 1941-1945* (1986)
8 *Never despair, 1945-1965* (1988)
Companion volume: *Winston Churchill, a collection of contemporary documents*, edited by Martin Gilbert, 1969

Winston series
Glyn, Caroline
1 *Don't knock the corners off* (1963)
2 *Love and joy in the Mabillon* (1965)

Winston series
Winston, Peter
see **Adjusters series**

Winter count series
Manfred, Frederick
1 *Winter count* (1966)
Poems, 1934-1965
2 *Winter count II* (1985)
Poems, 1966-1985

Winter fire series
Porter, Rose
1 *Summer driftwood for the winter fire* (1870)
2 *Winter fire* (1873)

Winter in the morning series
Bauman, Janina
1 *Winter in the morning* (1986)
A young girl's life in the Warsaw Ghetto and beyond, 1939-1945
2 *Dream of belonging* (1988)
My years in postwar Poland

Winter King's war trilogy
Dexter, Susan
1 *Ring of Allaire* (1981)
2 *Sword of Calandra* (1985)
3 *Mountains of Channadran* (1986)

Winter of the world trilogy
Rohan, Michael Scott
1 *Anvil of ice* (1986)
2 *Forge in the forest* (1987)
3 *Hammer of the sun* (1988)

Winter series
Bensusan, Samuel Levy
see **Joan Winter series**
Butler, Gwendoline
see **Inspector William Winter series**
Egleton, Clive
see **Charles Winter series**
Gaston, Bill
see **Lieutenant Jason Winter series**
Mackenzie, Joan
see **Mimosa Winter series**
Mackenzie, Kathleen
see **Miss Winter series**

Winter series
Service, Pamela F
1 *Winter of magic's return* (1985)
2 *Tomorrow's magic* (1987)

Winter series
Telushkin, Joseph
see **Rabbi Daniel Winter series**

Winter sisters series
Goodwin, Suzanne
1 *Winter spring* (1978)
Set in 1837
2 *Winter sisters* (1980)
Set in 1851

Winter world series
Mills, Carla Johnson
1 *Winter world* (1988)
2 *Egil's book* (1991)
3 *Kit's book* (1991)
4 *Brander's book* (1992)
5 *Zihanne's book* (1992)

Winterbottom series
Cutter, Leela
see **Lettie Winterbottom series**

Wintercombe series
Belle, Pamela
1 *Wintercombe* (1988)
2 *Herald of joy* (1989)
3 *Falling star* (1990)

Winters series
Oellrichs, Inez
see **Matt Winters series**

Wintersol series
Earnshaw, Anthony
1 *Musrum* (1968)
2 *Wintersol* (1971)

Winterstone series
Lombard, Nap
see **Lord Winterstone series**

Winterton School series
Potter, Dora Joan
1 *With Wendy at Winterton School* (1945)
2 *Wendy moves up* (1947)
3 *Wendy in charge* (1947)
4 *Althea's term at Winterton* (1948)

5 *Winterton holiday cruise* (1949)
6 *New girl for Winterton* (1950)

Winthrop series
Broughall, Helen Katherine
see **Barbara Winthrop series**
Chambers, Kate
see **Diana Winthrop series**

Wintino series
Lacy, Ed
see **Lieutenant Dave Wintino series**

Winton series
Atwater, Montgomery Meigs
see **Hank Winton series**

Wintringham series
Bell, Josephine
see **Doctor David Wintringham series**

Wirrun trilogy
Wrightson, Patricia
see **Song of Wirrun trilogy**

Wiscock series
Rice, William
see **Doctor James Wiscock series**

Wisconsin series
Derleth, August
1 *Bright journey* (1940)
2 *House on the mound* (1958)
3 *Hills stand watch* (1960)
4 *Shadow in the glass* (1963)
5 *Wisconsin harvest* (1966)
6 *Wind leans west* (1969)

Wise child series
Furlong, Monica
1 *Year and a day* (1990)
Juniper
2 *Wise child* (1987)

Wise series
Barrett, Alfred Wilson
see **Justus Wise series**
Wells, Carolyn
see **Pennington Wise series**

Wishet series
Porteous, Crichton
see **Jonas Wishet series**

Wishing Stone series
Burgess, Thornton Waldo
1 *Tommy and the Wishing Stone* (1915)
2 *Tommy's wishes come true* (1921)
3 *Tommy's change of heart* (1921)
One volume edition entitled *Wishing Stone stories*, 1935

Wishing-chair series
Blyton, Enid
1 *Adventures of the wishing-chair* (1937)
1.1 *Adventures of the wishing-chair, part 1* (1937)
1.2 *More adventures of the wishing-chair* (1937)
2 *Wishing-chair again* (1950)

Wistaria Street series
Anthony, Jane
1 *Wistaria Street will soon be gone* (1970)
2 *Young stranger* (1971)

Witch and Simon series
Barry, Margaret Stuart
see **Simon and the witch series**

Witch family series
Estes, Eleanor
1 *Witch family* (1960)
2 *Curious adventures of Jimmy McGee* (1987)

Witch finder series
Ball, Brian Neville
see **Witchfinder series**

Witch Mountain series
Key, Alexander
1 *Escape to Witch Mountain* (1968)
2 *Return from Witch Mountain* (1978)

Witch series
Bridwell, Norman
1 *Witch next door* (1965)
2 *Witch's Christmas* (1970)
3 *Witch's vacation* (1973)
4 *Witch's catalog* (1976)
5 *Witch grows up* (1979)
6 *Witch goes to school* (1992)

Witch series
Cass, Joan Evelyn
see **Molly Millikens series**

Witch series
Willson, Robina Beckles
1 *Secret witch* (1983)
2 *Holiday witch* (1983)
3 *Hungry witch* (1984)
4 *Sporty witch* (1986)

Witch series
Wright, Ralph
1 *Witch's big toe* (1983)
2 *Witch's funny bone* (1986)
3 *Witch goes for gold* (1988)

Witch war series
Prescot, Dray
1 *Werewolves of Kregen* (1985)
2 *Witches of Kregen* (1985)
3 *Omens of Kregen* (1985)
4 *Warlord of Antares* (1988)

Witch Winnie series
Champney, Elizabeth Williams
1 *Witch Winnie* (1887)
The story of a King's daughter
2 *Witch Winnie's mystery* (1891)
Alternative title: The old oak cabinet
3 *Witch Winnie's studio* (1892)
Alternative title: The King's daughter's art life
4 *Witch Winnie in Paris* (1893)
Alternative title: The King's daughters abroad
5 *Witch Winnie at Shinnecock* (1894)
Alternative title: The King's daughters in a summer art school
6 *Witch Winnie at Versailles* (1895)
7 *Witch Winnie in Holland* (1896)
8 *Witch Winnie in Venice* (1897)
Also includes The alchemist's story
9 *Witch Winnie in Spain* (1898)

Witch woman trilogy
Cabell, James Branch
1 *Music from behind the moon* (1926)
Short stories
2 *White robe* (1928)
3 *Way of Ecben* (1929)
One volume edition entitled *The witch-woman*, 1948

Witch World series
Norton, Andre
1 *Witch World* (1963)
2 *Web of the Witch World* (1964)
3 *Three against the Witch World* (1965)
4 *Year of the unicorn* (1965)
5 *Warlock of the Witch World* (1967)
6 *Sorceress of the Witch World* (1968)
7 *Crystal gryphon* (1972)
8 *Spell of the Witch World* (1972)
9 *Jargoon pard* (1974)
10 *Trey of swords* (1977)
Short stories
11 *Zarsthor's Bane* (1978)
12 *Lore of the wild witch* (1980)
13 *Gryphon in glory* (1981)
14 *Horn crown* (1981)
15 *'Ware Hawk* (1983)
16 *Were-wrath* (1984)
17 *Gryphon's eyrie* (1984)
Co-author: Ann Carol Crispin
18 *Serpent's tooth* (1987)
19 *Gate of the cat* (1987)
20 *Four from the Witch World* (1989)
21 *Turning* (1991)
Co-author: Pauline Margaret Griffin; alternative title: Storms of victory
Companion volumes: *Tales of the Witch World*, numbers 1-3, 1987-1990

Witchend series
Saville, Malcolm
see **Lone Pine Five Club series**

Witches' Sabbath series
Sachs, Maurice
1 *Witches' Sabbath* (1965)
2 *Hunt* (1967)

Witches series
Darke, James
1 *Prisoner* (1983)
2 *Trial* (1983)
3 *Torture* (1983)
4 *Escape* (1984)
5 *Meeting* (1985)
6 *Killing* (1985)
7 *Feud* (1986)
8 *Plague* (1986)

Witchfinder series
Ball, Brian Neville
1 *Mark of the beast* (1976)
2 *Evil at Monteine* (1977)

Witch's gold trilogy
Elliot, Margaret
1 *When the night crow flies* (1977)
2 *Witch's gold* (1979)
3 *To trick a witch* (1981)

Witch's sister series
Naylor, Phyllis Reynolds
1 *Witch's sister* (1975)
2 *Witch water* (1977)
3 *Witch herself* (1978)
4 *Witch's eye* (1990)
5 *Witch weed* (1991)
6 *Witch returns* (1993)

With Him, through Him, to Him series
McGloin, Joseph Thaddeus
1 *Living in God* (1965)
2 *Christ lives on* (1966)
3 *Life of man in Christ* (1967)
4 *Living in the Kingdom* (1967)

With love series
Fitzgibbon, Theodora
Autobiography of a cook
1 *With love* (1982)
2 *Love lies a loss* (1985)

Witherall series
Tilton, Alice
see **Leonard Witherall series**

Withered Man series
Deane, Norman
see **Bruce Murdoch series**

Withers series
Palmer, Stuart
see **Hildegarde Withers series**

Witherspoon and Albert series
Smith, Doris Buchanan
see **Lloyd Albert and Ancil Witherspoon series**

Within these walls series
Douglas, Felicity
see **Faye Boswell series**

Witting family series
Maclachlan, Patricia
1 *Sarah, plain and tall* (1985)
2 *Skylark* (1994)

Wittler series
McGuire, Paul
see **Inspector Wittler series**

Wives and husbands series
Atherton, Gertrude Franklin
1 *American wives and English husbands* (1898)
Transplanted
The second title is a revised edition
2 *Californians* (1898)

Wizard crystal series
Huff, Tanya
1 *Child of the grove* (1988)
2 *Last wizard* (1989)

Wizard of Oz series
Baum, Lyman Frank
see **Oz series**

Wizard series
Duane, Diane
1 *So you want to be a wizard?* (1983)
2 *Deep wizardry* (1984)
3 *High wizardry* (1990)
One volume edition entitled *Support your local wizard*, 1990

Wizard series
Hawke, Simon
1 *Wizard of Fourth Street* (1987)
2 *Wizard of Whitechapel* (1988)
3 *Wizard of Sunset Strip* (1989)
4 *Wizard of Rue Morgue* (1990)
5 *Samurai wizard* (1991)
6 *Wizard of Santa Fe* (1991)
7 *Nine lives of Catseye Gomez* (1991)

Wizard war chronicles series
Cook, Hugh
see **Chronicles of an age of darkness series**

Wizard Winkle series
Holland, Muriel
1 *Wizard Winkle won't tell* (1960)
2 *Wizard Winkle goes north* (1962)
3 *Wizard Winkle's wishing ring* (1964)
4 *Wizard Winkle goes abroad* (1967)

Wizard's bane series
Cook, Rick
1 *Wizard's bane* (1989)
2 *Wizardry compiled* (1990)
3 *Wizardry cursed* (1991)

Wizards trilogy
Offutt, Andrew Jefferson
see **War of the wizards trilogy**

Wizard's war series
Boyer, Elizabeth H
1 *Troll's grindstone* (1986)
2 *Curse of Slagfid* (1989)
3 *Dragon's carbuncle* (1990)
4 *Lord of chaos* (1991)

Wizards, warlocks and you series
This sequence has ten authors
Stine, Robert Lawrence
1 *Forest of twisted dreams* (1984)
Affabee, Eric
2 *Siege of the dragonriders* (1984)
Stine, Harlan William
3 *Who kidnapped Princess Saralinda?* (1984)
Kraft, David Anthony
4 *Ghost knights of Camelot* (1984)
Beach, Lynn
5 *Haunted castle of Ravencurse* (1985)
Siegel, Scott
6 *Revenge of the falcon knight* (1985)

Stine, Robert Lawrence
7 *Challenge of the wolf knight* (1985)
Beach, Lynn
8 *Conquest of the time master* (1985)
Affabee, Eric
9 *Dragon Queen's revenge* (1986)
Stine, Harlan William
10 *Tournament for terror* (1986)
11 *Imposter king* (1986)
Siegel, Barbara
12 *Scarlet shield of Shalimar* (1986)
Stine, Robert Lawrence
13 *Cavern of the phantoms* (1986)
Sno, William
14 *Carnival of demons* (1986)
Beach, Lynn
15 *Invaders from Darkland* (1986)
Affabee, Eric
16 *Attack on the king* (1986)
Stine, Harlan William
17 *Conquest of the barbarians* (1986)
Siegel, Barbara
18 *Warrior women of Weymouth* (1986)

Wizenbeak trilogy
Gilliland, Alexis Arnaldus
1 *Wizenbeak* (1986)
2 *Shadow Shaia* (1990)
3 *Lord of the troll-bats* (1992)

Woar series
Yates, George Worthing
see **Hazlitt Woar series**

Woffle series
Chaney, Jill
1 *Taking the Woffle to Pebblecombe-on-Sea* (1974)
2 *Woffle, B.A.* (1976)

Wolcott family series
Lincoln, Jeanie Gould
1 *Unwilling maid* (1897)
A history of certain episodes during the American Revolution in the early life of Mistress Betty Yorke, born Wolcott
2 *Luck of Rathcoole* (1912)
The romantic adventures of Mistress Faith Wolcott during her sojourn in New York at an early period of the Republic

Wolf Caulder series
Knott, William Cecil
see **Vengeance Seeker series**

Wolf hunters series
Curwood, James Oliver
1 *Wolf hunters* (1908)
A tale of adventure in the wilderness
2 *Gold hunters* (1909)
Treasure hunters
A story of life and adventure in the Hudson Bay wilds

Wolf series
Bennet, Robert Ames
1 *Branded wolf* (1929)
2 *Roped wolf* (1930)
3 *Border wolf* (1930)
4 *Gold wolf* (1930)
5 *Hunted wolf* (1931)

Wolfe and Goodwin series
Stout, Rex
see **Nero Wolfe and Archie Goodwin series**

Wolfe family series
Leahy, Syrell Rogovin
1 *Family ties* (1983)
2 *Family truths* (1985)

Wolfgang Amadeus Mozart series
Weiss, David
1 *Sacred and profane* (1968)
2 *Assassination of Mozart* (1970)

Wolfmark series
Crockett, Samuel Rutherford
1 *Red axe* (1898)
2 *Joan of the sword hand* (1900)

Wolfram series
Graves, Richard Latshaw
see **Hugo Wolfram series**

Wolfshead series
Frazier, Arthur
1 *Oath of blood* (1973)
2 *King's death* (1973)
3 *Light in the west* (1973)
4 *Viking slaughter* (1974)
5 *Flame in the fens* (1974)
6 *Axe in Miklagard* (1975)

Wolfville series
Lewis, Alfred Henry
Short stories
1 *Wolfville* (1897)
Episodes of cowboy life
2 *Sandburrs* (1900)
3 *Wolfville days* (1902)
4 *Wolfville nights* (1902)
5 *Black Lion Inn* (1903)
6 *Wolfville folks* (1908)
7 *Faro Nell and her friends* (1913)
Selections: *Old Wolfville*, edited by Louis Filler, 1968, *Wolfville yarns*, edited by Rolfe Humphries, 1968

Wolfwalker series
Harper, Tara K
1 *Wolfwalker* (1990)
2 *Shadow leader* (1991)
3 *Storm runner* (1993)

Wolverine MacAlistaire series
Messner-Loebs, William
Comic strips
1 *Tall tales* (1987)
2 *Bad weather* (1990)

Woman detective series
Kerner, Annette
Autobiography
1 *Woman detective* (1954)
2 *Further adventures of a woman detective* (1955)

Woman singer series
Sand, George
see **Consuelo series**

Woman's place series
Yorke, Katherine
1 *Woman's place* (1983)
2 *Pair bond* (1984)

Wombats series
Dugan, Michael
1 *House for wombats* (1987)
Illustrated by Jane Burrell
2 *Wombats don't have Christmas* (1988)
Illustrated by Jane Burrell
3 *Bathing Buster* (1990)
Illustrated by Wendy Elks

Wombles series
Beresford, Elisabeth
1 *Wombles* (1968)
2 *Wandering Wombles* (1970)
3 *Invisible Wombles, and other stories* (1973)
4 *Wombles in danger* (1973)
5 *Wombles at work* (1973)
6 *Wombles go to the seaside* (1974)
7 *Wombles make a clean sweep* (1975)
8 *Wombles to the rescue* (1975)
Numbers 5 and 9 also published in one volume entitled *The Wombles of Wimbledon*, 1976
9 *Wombles go round the world* (1976)
10 *World of the Wombles* (1976)
11 *Wombling free* (1978)
Companion volumes: *The Wombles gift book*, 1975, *The Wombles annual*, 1975-1978

Women of the West series
This sequence has two authors
Harrington, Emma
1 *Blue fire* (1988)
Collins, Laurel
2 *Silver Eyes* (1988)

Women of war series
Drury, Rebecca
House pseudonym
1 *Morning triumph* (1982)
2 *Blue glory* (1982)
3 *Sisters of battle* (1982)
4 *Splendid victory* (1983)
5 *Darkness at dawn* (1983)
6 *Courage at sea* (1983)
7 *Valiant wings* (1983)
8 *Desert battle* (1983)
9 *Bitter victory* (1983)

Women West series
This sequence has two authors
Hatcher, Robin Lee
1 *Promised sunrise* (1990)
Mason, Connie
2 *Beyond the horizon* (1990)

Women who won the West series
Willoughby, Lee Davis
1 *Tempest of Tombstone* (1982)
2 *Dodge City* (1982)
3 *Duchess of Denver* (1982)
4 *Lost lady of Laramie* (1982)
5 *Flame of Virginia City* (1982)
6 *Angel of Hangtown* (1982)
7 *Princess of Powder River* (1982)

Wonder book series
Hawthorne, Nathaniel
1 *Wonder book for boys and girls* (1852)
2 *Tanglewood tales for girls and boys* (1853)

Wonder Club series
Dryasdust
see **Ye Headless Lady Inn series**

Wonder of war series
Rolt-Wheeler, Francis
1 *Wonder of war in the air* (1917)
2 *Wonder of war on land* (1918)
3 *Wonder of war at sea* (1919)
4 *Wonder of war in the holy Land* (1919)

Wonderful Farm series
Ayme, Marcel
1 *Wonderful Farm* (1949)
Selections translated from *Les contes du chat perche*
2 *Return to the Wonderful Farm* (1950)
Magic pictures
Selections translated from *Autres contes du chat perche*

Wonderland series
Carroll, Lewis
see **Alice in Wonderland series**

Wonderland series
Dobkin, Kaye
1 *Queen of hearts* (1982)
2 *White rabbit* (1983)

Wonders Farm series
Williams, Zillah
1 *Treasure of Wonders Farm* (1990)
2 *Wonders Farm Gang* (1992)

Wonders of nature series
Lavine, Sigmund Arnold
1 *Wonders of the aquarium* (1957)
2 *Wonders of the hive* (1958)
3 *Wonders of the ant hill* (1960)
4 *Wonders of the wasps' nest* (1961)
5 *Wonders of the animal disguises* (1962)
6 *Wonders of the beetle world* (1962)
7 *Wonders of animal architecture* (1964)
8 *Wonders of the spider world* (1966)
9 *Wonders of the world of bats* (1969)
10 *Wonders of the fly world* (1970)
11 *Wonders of the owl world* (1971)
12 *Wonders of the hawk world* (1972)
13 *Wonders of the world of horses* (1972)
Co-author: Brigid Casey
14 *Wonders of the world of eagles* (1974)
15 *Wonders of the world of cactus* (1974)
16 *Wonders of the bison world* (1975)
Co-author: Vincent Scuro
17 *Wonders of herbs* (1976)
18 *Wonders of terrariums* (1977)
19 *Marsupials* (1978)
20 *Wonders of the donkey world* (1978)
Co-author: Vincent Scuro
21 *Wonders of the camel world* (1979)
22 *Wonders of mice* (1979)
23 *Wonders of elephants* (1979)
Co-author: Vincent Scuro
24 *Wonders of ponies* (1980)
Co-author: Brigid Casey
25 *Wonders of goats* (1980)
Co-author: Vincent Scuro
26 *Wonders of pigs* (1981)
Co-author: Vincent Scuro
27 *Wonders of peacocks* (1982)
28 *Wonders of rhinos* (1982)
29 *Wonders of hippos* (1983)
30 *Wonders of draft horses* (1983)
Co-author: Brigid Casey
31 *Wonders of coyotes* (1984)
32 *Wonders of badgers* (1985)
33 *Wonders of giraffes* (1986)
34 *Wonders of tigers* (1987)

Wonderwitch series
Muir, Helen
1 *Wonderwitch* (1988)
2 *Wonderwitch and the rooftop cats* (1991)

Wong, Richard and Kitchie series
Dalton, Clive
see **Malay series**

Wonk series
Levy, Muriel
1 *Going to the sea* (1941)
2 *Strawberries and cream* (1941)
3 *Fireworks* (1941)
4 *Secret* (1945)
5 *Circus* (1948)
6 *Snowman* (1948)

Wood Jason series
Michel, Milton Scott
1 *X-ray murders* (1942)
Sinister warning
2 *Sweet murder* (1943)
House in Harlem

Wood Mount trilogy
Cadell, Elizabeth
see **Waynes of Wood Mount trilogy**

Wood Street series
Allan, Mabel Esther
1 *Wood Street secret* (1968)
2 *Wood Street group* (1970)
3 *Wood Street rivals* (1971)
4 *Wood Street helpers* (1973)
5 *Away from Wood Street* (1975)
6 *Wood Street and Mary Ellen* (1979)
7 *Growing up in Wood Street* (1982)

Wood trilogy
Michelet, Claude
Translated from the French
1 *Firelight and woodsmoke* (1993)
2 *Applewood* (1994)
Number three not yet published

Woodbine series
Leslie, Madeline
1 *Live and learn* (1868)
2 *Governor's pardon* (1868)
Alternative title: The bridge of sighs
3 *Paul Barton* (1868)
Alternative title: The drunkard's son
4 *Walter and Frank* (1869)
Alternative title: The Apthorp farm
Companion volume: *Wilful Walter*, 1868

Woodcraft Girls series
Roy, Lillian Elizabeth
1 *Woodcraft Girls at Camp Doran* (1916)
2 *Woodcraft Girls in the city* (1918)
3 *Woodcraft Girls camping in Maine* (1928)

Wooden horse series
Suhl, Yuri
1 *One foot in America* (1950)
2 *Cowboy on a wooden horse* (1953)

Woodentops series
Bird, Maria
1 *Woodentops washing day* (1956)
2 *Woodentops at the fair* (1957)

Woodfield series
Foote-Smith, Elizabeth
see **Will Woodfield series**

Woodhead series
Clements, Eileen Helen
see **Alister Woodhead series**

Woodland Pack series
Collins, Freda
1 *Pack that ran itself* (1955)
2 *Woodland Pack* (1957)
3 *Brownie year* (1957)
4 *Barney and the Big House Pack* (1960)
5 *Good turn hunters* (1963)
6 *Brownies and the farm pig* (1964)
7 *Pack mascot* (1966)
8 *Patchwork pack* (1968)

Woodlanders series
Miller, Muriel
1 *Samantha's hungry day* (1985)
2 *Search for Otis Otter* (1985)
3 *All the rabbit's relations* (1985)
4 *Hunting with the fox cubs* (1985)
5 *Benjamin Badger's night shift* (1985)
6 *Panic in the woodland* (1985)

Woodlanders series
Trevor, Elleston
1 *Badger's Beech* (1948)
2 *Wizard of the wood* (1948)
3 *Badger's moon* (1949)
4 *Ant's castle* (1949)
5 *Mole's castle* (1951)
6 *Sweethallow Valley* (1951)
7 *Badger's Wood* (1958)

Woodlawn series
Brink, Carol Ryrie
see **Caddie Woodlawn series**

Woodlawn series
Hattie, Aunt
1 *Bertie's home* (1868)
2 *Bertie and the carpenters* (1868)
3 *Bertie and the masons* (1868)
4 *Bertie and the plumbers* (1868)
5 *Bertie and the painters* (1868)
6 *Bertie and the gardeners* (1868)
7 *Bertie and his sisters* (1871)

Woodpig series
B B
see **Monty Woodpig series**

Woodranger series
Browne, George Waldo
1 *Young woodranger* (1899)
A story of the pioneers of the debatable grounds
2 *Young gunbearer* (1900)
A tale of the neutral ground, Acadia and the siege of Louisburg
3 *Hero of the hills* (1901)
A tale of the captive-ground, St Francis and life in the northern wilderness in the days of the pioneers
4 *With Roger's Rangers* (1906)

Woodruff trilogy
Goulding, Francis Robert
1 *Sapelo* (1870)
Alternative title: Child life on the tide-water
2 *Nachoochee* (1870)
Alternative title: Boy life from home
3 *Sal-o-quah* (1870)
Alternative title: Boy life among the Cherokees

Woods Palmer series
Waller, Leslie
1 *Banker* (1963)
2 *Family* (1968)
3 *American* (1970)

Woods series
Dean, Anabel
see **Racing wheels series**
Muir, Dorothy Erskine
see **Inspector Woods series**

Woods series
Rich, Louise Dickinson
1 *We took to the woods* (1944)
2 *Happy the land* (1948)
3 *My neck of the woods* (1950)
Numbers 1 and 3 also published in one volume entitled *The forest years*, 1963
4 *Only parent* (1953)
5 *Innocence under the elms* (1955)

Woodside School series
Ure, Jean
1 *Fright* (1987)
2 *Loud Mouth* (1988)
3 *Soppy birthday* (1988)
4 *King of Spuds* (1989)
5 *Who's for the zoo?* (1989)

Woodville series
Optic, Oliver
1 *Rich and humble* (1864)
Alternative title: The mission of Bertha Grant
2 *In school and out* (1864)
Alternative title: The conquest of Richard Grant
3 *Watch and wait* (1864)
Alternative title: The young fugitives
4 *Work and win* (1865)
Alternative title: Noddy Newman on a cruise
5 *Hope and have* (1866)
Alternative title: Fanny Grant among the Indians
6 *Haste and waste* (1867)
Alternative title: The young pilot of Lake Champlain

Woodward and Bracken series
Blazer, J S
see **Donald Bracken and James Rowland Woodward series**

Woodward and Cormack series
Baddock, James
see **Cormack and Woodward series**

Woodward series
Lowndes, Joan Selby
see **Francis and Anne Woodward series**

Woodworld series
Kilworth, Garry
1 *Wizard of Woodworld* (1987)
2 *Voyage of the Vigilance* (1988)

Woody Beatty trilogy
Bonner, Cindy
see **Haywood Beatty trilogy**

Woody Woods series
Dean, Anabel
see **Racing wheels series**

Woofits series
Parkinson, Michael
1 *Woofits' day out* (1980)
2 *Woofits play cricket* (1980)
3 *Woofits play football* (1980)
4 *Daily Woofit* (1980)

Woolcot family series
Turner, Ethel
1 *Seven little Australians* (1894)
2 *Family at Misrule* (1895)
3 *Little Mother Meg* (1902)
4 *Judy and Punch* (1928)

Woolfe series
Graham, Winifred
see **Miss Woolfe series**

Woolrich series
Raison, Milton Michael
see **Tony Woolrich series**

Wooster and Jeeves series
Wodehouse, Pelham Grenville
see **Jeeves and Bertie Wooster series**

Woozy series
Barry, Margaret Stuart
1 *Woozy* (1973)
2 *Woozies go to school* (1973)
3 *Woozies on television* (1973)
4 *Woozy and the Weight Watchers* (1976)
5 *Woozies go visiting* (1976)
6 *Woozies hold a frubard week* (1977)
7 *Monster in Woozy garden* (1977)

Words series
Maestro, Betsy Crippen
Illustrated by Giulio Maestro
1 *Busy day* (1978)
A book of action words
2 *On the go* (1979)
A book of adjectives
3 *Traffic* (1981)
A book of opposites
4 *On the town* (1983)
A book of clothing words
5 *Camping out* (1984)
A book of action words
6 *Taxi* (1989)
A book of city words
7 *Delivery van* (1990)
Words for town and country

Work and wedlock series
Cooper, Jilly
Humorous pieces
1 *How to stay married* (1969)
2 *How to survive from nine to five* (1970)
One volume edition entitled *Work and wedlock*, 1977; companion volume: *How to survive Christmas*, 1987

Working dogs series
Goode, Angela
1 *Great working dog stories* (1990)
2 *More great working dog stories* (1992)
A national tribute to Australian working dogs by those who work with them
3 *Working dogs* (1993)
Stories from all round Australia

Working hard series
This sequence has two authors
Korman, Justine
1 *Working hard with the mighty dump truck* (1993)
Horowitz, Jordan
2 *Working hard with the busy fire truck* (1993)
3 *Working hard with the mighty loader* (1993)
Korman, Justine
4 *Working hard with the mighty mixer* (1993)

Working upward series
Stratemeyer, Edward L
Richard Dare's venture (1903)
Alternative title: Striking out for himself
1 *Young auctioneers* (1903)
Alternative title: The polishing of a rolling stone
2 *Bound to be an electrician* (1903)
Alternative title: Franklin Bell's road to success
3 *Shorthand Tom, the reporter* (1903)
Alternative titles: The exploits of a bright boy, The exploits of a young reporter
4 *Fighting for his own* (1903)
Alternative title: The fortunes of a young artist
5 *Oliver Bright's search* (1903)
Alternative title: The mystery of a mine

World collision series
Balmer, Edwin
see **Bronson Beta series**

World Dionysus series
Priestley, Margaret
1 *Ring of fortune* (1948)
2 *Three queens* (1950)
3 *Tomay is loyal* (1951)

World Dionysus trilogy
Trevor, Meriol
1 *Forest and the kingdom* (1949)
2 *Hunt the king, hide the fox* (1950)
3 *Fires and the stars* (1951)

World history series
Blyton, Enid
see **Stories from world history series**

World I cannot see series
Russell, Robert William
Autobiography of a man blind from five years old
1 *To catch an angel* (1962)
2 *Island* (1973)

World in Amber series
Orr, Alice
1 *World in Amber* (1985)
2 *In the ice king's palace* (1986)

World of adventure series
Bamman, Henry A
1 *Lost uranium mine* (1963)
2 *Flight to the South Pole* (1963)
3 *Hunting grizzly bears* (1963)
4 *Fire on the mountain* (1963)
5 *City beneath the sea* (1964)
6 *Search for Piranha* (1964)
7 *Sacred well of sacrifice* (1964)
8 *Viking treasure* (1964)

World of Lone Wolf series
Page, Ian
Edited by Joe Dever
1 *Grey Star the wizard* (1985)
2 *Forbidden city* (1986)
3 *Beyond the nightmare gate* (1986)
4 *War of the wizards* (1986)

World of men and women series
Collins, Jackie
1 *World is full of married men* (1968)
2 *World is full of divorced women* (1975)

World of O trilogy
Gee, Maurice
1 *Halfmen of O* (1982)
2 *Priests of Ferris* (1984)
3 *Motherstone* (1985)

World of Pern series
Nye, Jody Lynn
Adventures in Anne McCaffrey's world of Pern
1 *Dragonharper* (1987)
2 *Dragonfire* (1988)

World of racing series
Wilkinson, Sylvia
1 *Formula One* (1981)
2 *Formula Atlantic* (1981)
3 *Sprint cars* (1981)
4 *Endurance racing* (1981)
5 *Stock cars* (1981)
6 *Super Vee* (1981)
7 *Can-Am* (1981)
8 *Champ cars* (1982)
9 *Trans-Am* (1983)
10 *Karts* (1985)

World of the Alfar series
Boyer, Elizabeth H
1 *Sword and the satchel* (1980)
2 *Elves and the otterskin* (1981)
3 *Thrall and the dragon's heart* (1982)
4 *Wizard and the warlord* (1983)

World of the Eleven Kingdoms, first trilogy
Kurtz, Katherine
see **Legends of Camber of Culdi trilogy**

World of the Eleven Kingdoms, fourth trilogy
Kurtz, Katherine
see **Histories of King Kelson trilogy**

World of the Eleven Kingdoms, second trilogy
Kurtz, Katherine
see **Heirs of Saint Camber trilogy**

World of the Eleven Kingdoms, third trilogy
Kurtz, Katherine
see **Chronicles of the Deryni trilogy**

World of Tiers series
Farmer, Philip Jose
1 *Maker of universes* (1965)
The enigma of the man-leveled cosmos; revised edition 1980
2 *Gates of creation* (1966)
Revised edition 1981
3 *Private cosmos* (1967)
Revised edition 1981; numbers 1-3 also published in one volume entitled *World of Tiers*, volume 1, 1981
4 *Behind the Walls of Terra* (1970)
Revised edition 1982
5 *Lavalite world* (1977)
Revised edition 1983; numbers 4 and 5 also published in one volume entitled *World of Tiers*, volume 2, 1981
Companion volumes: *Greatheart Silver*, 1982, *The purple book*, 1982

World records series
Scheier, Michael
1 *Ridiculous world records* (1976)
2 *More ridiculous world records* (1983)

World trilogy
Bates, Herbert Ernest
Autobiography
1 *Vanished world* (1969)
2 *Blossoming world* (1971)
3 *World in ripeness* (1972)

World War I series
Remarque, Erich Maria
1 *All quiet on the Western Front* (1929)
Original edition entitled *Im Westen nichts Neues*
2 *Road back* (1931)
Original edition entitled *Der Weg zuruck*
3 *Three comrades* (1938)
Original edition entitled *Drei Kameraden*

World War I series
Spears, Edward
see **Defeat and victory series**

World War II series
Waugh, Evelyn
1 *Men at arms* (1952)
2 *Officers and gentlemen* (1955)
3 *Unconditional surrender* (1961)
End of the battle
One volume revised editions entitled *The sword of honour*, 1965 and *The sword of honour trilogy*, 1994
4 *Basil Seal rides again* (1963)
Alternative title: The rake's regress
Companion volume: *Work suspended*, 1942

World War II trilogy
Hough, Richard Alexander
1 *Angels One-Five* (1978)
Wings against the sky
2 *Fight of the few* (1979)
3 *Fight to the finish* (1979)
Wings of victory

World War II trilogy
Plievier, Theodor
1 *Moscow* (1953)
Original edition entitled *Moskau*
2 *Stalingrad* (1945)
Death of an army
Original edition entitled *Stalingrad*
3 *Berlin* (1954)
Rape of a city
Original edition entitled *Berlin*

World War III series
Adair, James B
1 *Target Texas* (1990)
2 *Target nuke* (1990)
3 *Target Iran* (1991)

World War III series
Slater, Ian
see **WW III series**

World War Three series
This sequence has two authors
Hackett, John
1 *Third World War* (1978)
A future history, August 1985
2 *Third world war, the untold story* (1982)
Coyle, Harold
3 *Team Yankee* (1987)
Companion volumes: *World War III*, by John Stanley, 1976, *World War III*, by Brian Harris, 1982, *Alternative Third World War, 1985-2035, a personal history*, by William Jackson, 1987

World War trilogy
Altsheler, Joseph Alexander
1 *Guns of Europe* (1915)
2 *Hosts of the air* (1915)
3 *Forest of swords* (1915)

World War Two series
Gibbs, Philip
see **Second World War series**

World within a world series
Lewin, Ted
1 *Everglades* (1976)
2 *Baja* (1978)
3 *Pribiloffs* (1980)

World without men series
Maine, Charles Eric
1 *World without men* (1958)
2 *Alph* (1972)

World's best games series
Barry, Sheila Anne
1 *World's best travel games* (1987)
2 *World's best party games* (1987)

World's End series
Carter, Lin
see **Gondwane epic series**
Dickens, Monica
see **Fielding family series**

World's end series
Sinclair, Upton
1 *World's end* (1940)
2 *Between two worlds* (1941)
3 *Dragon's teeth* (1942)
4 *Wide is the gate* (1943)
5 *Presidential agent* (1944)
6 *Dragon harvest* (1945)
7 *World to win* (1946)
8 *Presidential mission* (1947)
9 *One clear call* (1948)
10 *O shepherd speak* (1949)
11 *Return of Lanny Budd* (1953)

Worlds in collision series
Velikovsky, Immanuel
1 *Worlds in collision* (1950)
2 *Stargazers and gravediggers* (1983)

Worlds of Chthon series
Anthony, Piers
see **Aton series**

Worlds of power series
This sequence has five authors; based on computer games by various software companies
Singer, A L
1 *Blaster master* (1990)
Based on the game by Sunsoft
Frost, Alexandra
2 *Metal gear* (1990)
Based on the game by Ultragames
Singer, A L
3 *Ninja garden* (1990)
Based on the game by Tecmo
Howell, Christopher
4 *Castlevania II* (1990)
Simon's quest
Based on the game by Konami
Miles, Ellen
5 *Wizards and warriors* (1990)
Based on the game by Acclaim
Stamper, Judith Bauer
6 *Bionic compounds* (1991)
Based on the game by CAPCOM
Singer, A L
7 *Infiltrator* (1991)
Based on the game by MINDSCAPE
Miles, Ellen
8 *Before Shadowgate* (1990)
The prequel to the game created by ICOM Simulations
9 *Mega man two* (1990)
Based on the game by CAPCOM
Singer, A L
10 *Bases loaded II, second season* (1991)
Based on the game by Jaleco

World's wanderer trilogy
Feikema, Feike
1 *Primitive* (1949)
2 *Brother* (1950)
3 *Giant* (1951)
One volume revised edition entitled *Wanderlust*, published under the author's real name Frederick Manfred, 1962

World's war series
Fiske, James
1 *Fighting in the clouds for France* (1915)
2 *Facing the German foe* (1915)
3 *On board the mine-laying cruiser* (1915)
4 *Under fire for Servia* (1915)
5 *Belgians to the Front* (1915)
6 *In Russian trenches* (1916)
7 *Fighting in the Alps* (1916)
8 *Shelled by an unseen foe* (1916)
9 *At the fall of Warsaw* (1916)
10 *With the hero of the Marne* (1919)
11 *With Pershing for France* (1919)
12 *Fighting the U-boat menace* (1919)

Worlds without end series
Barclay, Isabel
History of world exploration
1 *Early explorers* (1957)
3 *Great age of discovery* (1959)

Worrall series
Cousins, Edmund George
see **Brigadier Worrall series**

Worrals series
Johns, William Earl
1 *Worrals of the W.A.A.F.* (1941)
2 *Worrals carries on* (1942)
3 *Worrals flies again* (1942)
4 *Worrals on the war-path* (1943)
5 *Worrals goes east* (1944)
6 *Worrals of the islands* (1945)
A story of the war in the Pacific
7 *Worrals in the wilds* (1947)
8 *Worrals down under* (1948)
9 *Worrals goes afoot* (1949)
10 *Worrals in the wastelands* (1949)
11 *Worral investigates* (1950)

Worse and Garman series
Kielland, Alexander Lange
see **Garman and Worse series**

Worst day of my life series
This sequence has three authors
Dover, Harold
1 *Up the creek* (1991)
Rees, Rod
2 *On the run* (1991)
Sharp, Alastair
3 *Out of your mind* (1991)

Worst person in the world series
Stevenson, James
1 *Worst person in the world* (1978)
2 *Worst person in the world at Crab Beach* (1988)
3 *Worst person's Chrismas* (1991)

Worst Witch series
Murphy, Jill
1 *Worst Witch* (1974)
2 *Worst Witch strikes again* (1980)
3 *Bad spell for the Worst Witch* (1982)

Wortenheimer series
Learmonth, David
see **Silas Wortenheimer series**

Worth series
Heyer, Georgette
see **Judith Taverner Worth series**

Worthing chronicles series
Card, Orson Scott
1 *Capitol* (1979)
2 *Hot sleep* (1979)
One volume edition including additional stories entitled *The Worthing saga*, 1990; selections from both volumes published as *The Worthing chronicle*, 1983

Worthing series
Drummond, John Keith
see **Matilda Worthing series**

Worthington series
Morison, Betty Jane
see **Elizabeth Lamb Worthington series**

Wortlethorpe chonicles series
Oakley, Graham
 see **Church mice series**

Worzel Gummidge series
This sequence has three authors
Todd, Barbara Euphan
1 *Worzel Gummidge* (1936)
Alternative title: The scarecrow of Scatterbrook
2 *Worzel Gummidge again* (1937)
Selections from numbers 1 and 2 published as *Worzel Gummidge, the scarecrow of Scatterbrook Farm*
3 *More about Worzel Gummidge* (1938)
4 *Worzel Gummidge and Saucy Nancy* (1947)
5 *Worzel Gummidge takes a holiday* (1949)
6 *Earthy Mangold and Worzel Gummidge* (1954)
7 *Worzel Gummidge and the railway scarecrows* (1955)
8 *Worzel Gummidge at the circus* (1956)
9 *Worzel Gummidge and the treasure ship* (1958)
10 *Detective Worzel Gummidge* (1963)
Waterhouse, Keith
11 *Television adventures of Worzel Gummidge* (1979)
12 *More television adventures of Worzel Gummidge* (1979)
Numbers 11 and 12 also published as *Worzel Gummidge's television adventures*, 1981
13 *Worzel Gummidge at the fair* (1980)
14 *Trials of Worzel Gummidge* (1980)
15 *Worzel's birthday* (1981)
16 *New television adventures of Worzel Gummidge and Aunt Sally* (1981)
17 *Worzel Gummidge and Aunt Sally* (1982)
18 *Irish adventures of Worzel Gummidge* (1984)
19 *Worzel Gummidge down under* (1987)
Companion volume: *Worzel Gummidge goes to the seaside, a picture book*, 1980

Wotan series
Kessler, Leo
1 *SS Panzer Battalion* (1974)
2 *Death's head* (1974)
3 *Claws of steel* (1974)
4 *Guns at Cassino* (1974)
5 *Devil's shield* (1975)
6 *Hammer of the gods* (1975)
7 *Forced march* (1976)
8 *Blood and ice* (1977)
9 *Sand panthers* (1977)
10 *Counter-attack* (1978)
11 *Hellfire* (1978)
12 *Panzer hunt* (1979)
13 *Slaughter ground* (1980)
14 *Flashpoint* (1980)
15 *Cauldron of blood* (1981)
16 *Schirmer's headhunters* (1981)
17 *Whores of war* (1983)
18 *Schirmer's death legion* (1983)
19 *Death ride* (1985)
20 *Slaughter at Salerno* (1985)
21 *March or die* (1985)
22 *Outcasts* (1986)
23 *Hess assault* (1987)
24 *March on Warsaw* (1988)

Wraeththu series
Constantine, Storm
 see **Book of Wraeththu series**

Wragge series
Capon, Paul
 see **Arnold Wragge series**

Wraithlea series
Taylor, Philip Neville Walker
 see **Commander Wraithlea series**

Wrangler Lewis and Dusty Jones series
Evans, Max
 see **Dusty Jones and Wrangler Lewis series**

Wrayne and her Four Adjusters series
Cross, Mark
 see **Daphne Wrayne and her Four Adjusters series**

Wreck series
Ethel
1 *Wreck* (1885)
2 *Lufness* (1886)

Wren Helen series
Carter, Dorothy
1 *Wren Helen* (1943)
2 *Wren Helen sails south* (1944)
3 *Wren Helen sails north* (1946)

Wren House series
Stahl, Hilda
1 *Mystery at Wheeler Place* (1992)
2 *Disappearance of Amos Pike* (1992)
3 *Tim Avery's secret* (1992)
4 *Missing newspaper caper* (1992)
5 *Case of the missing money* (1992)

Wren series
Berger, Thomas
 see **Russel Wren series**
Temple-Ellis, N A
 see **Inspector Wren series**
Young, Emily Hilda
 see **Jenny Wren series**

Wren twins series
Govan, Christine Noble
1 *Mystery at the Indian hide-out* (1957)
2 *Mystery at the haunted house* (1959)
3 *Mystery at Fearsome Lake* (1960)
4 *Mystery at Rock City* (1960)
5 *Mystery of the dancing skeleton* (1962)
6 *Mystery at Ghost Lodge* (1963)
7 *Mystery at the weird ruins* (1964)
8 *Mystery at the echoing cave* (1965)

Wrens series
Judd, Alfred
1 *Wrens to the rescue* (1926)
2 *Wrens on the trail* (1927)

Wright and Lantz series
Mullen, Clarence
 see **Tony Lantz and Eddie Wright series**

Wright family series
Ehle, John
 see **North Carolina series**

Wright series
Marks, James Macdonald
 see **Jason Wright series**
Scott, Mary
 see **Inspector Wright series**
Straker, John Foster
 see **David Wright series**

Writer's education series
Little, Jean
Autobiography
1 *Little by Little* (1987)
2 *Stars come out within* (1990)

Wroth family series
Carter, Reginald
1 *He and his* (1940)
2 *Nest for cuckoos* (1945)

Wrykyn School series
Wodehouse, Pelham Grenville
1 *Gold bat* (1904)
1.1 *Mike at Wrykyn* (1909)
1.2 *Mike and Psmith* (1909)
Enter Psmith
2 *White feather* (1907)
3 *Mike* (1909)

Wu and Cameron series
Sheridan, Juanita
 see **Lily Wu and Janice Cameron series**

Wu and Durant series
Thomas, Ross
 see **Artie Wu and Quincy Durant series**

Wu Fang series
Daniel, Roland
1 *Society of the spiders* (1928)
2 *Wu Fang* (1929)
3 *Ruby of a thousand dreams* (1933)
4 *Wu Fang's revenge* (1934)
5 *Son of Wu Fang* (1935)
6 *Return of Wu Fang* (1937)

Wulf series
Crossley-Holland, Kevin
1 *Sea stranger* (1973)
2 *Fire-brother* (1975)
3 *Earth-father* (1976)

Wulff series
Barry, Mike
 see **Burton Wulff series**

Wumpus series
Trevor, Elleston
1 *Wumpus* (1945)
2 *More about Wumpus* (1947)
3 *Where's Wumpus?* (1948)

Wunnerful series
Welk, Laurence
Autobiography
1 *Wunnerful, wunnerful!* (1971)
2 *Ah-one, ah-two!* (1974)
Life with my musical family
3 *My America, your America* (1976)
4 *This I believe* (1979)
5 *You're never too young* (1981)
Companion volumes: *Laurence Welk's musical family album*, 1977, *Laurence Welk's bunny rabbit concert*, 1978

Wuthering Heights series
This sequence has three authors
Bronte, Emily Jane
1 *Wuthering Heights* (1847)
Caine, Jeffrey
2 *Heathcliff* (1977)
L'Estrange, Anna
3 *Return to Wuthering Heights* (1977)
Companion volume: *H, the story of Heathcliff's journey back to Wuthering Heights*, by Lin Haire-Sargeant, 1992

Wyatt Duncan series
Mulford, Clarence Edward
1 *Black buttes* (1923)
2 *Hopalong Cassidy and the eagle's brood* (1931)

Wyatt family series
Wiat, Philippa
1 *Master of Blandeston Hall* (1973)
2 *Heir of Allington* (1973)
3 *Knight of Allington* (1974)
4 *Rebel of Allington* (1974)
5 *Tree of Vertigern* (1976)
6 *Atheling* (1977)
7 *My lute be still* (1977)
8 *Sound now the passing-bell* (1977)

Wyatt series
Disher, Garry
1 *Kickback* (1991)
2 *Paydirt* (1992)
3 *Deathdeal* (1993)
4 *Crosskill* (1994)

Wyatt series
Gethin, David
1 *Wyatt* (1983)
2 *Wyatt and the Moresby legacy* (1983)
3 *Wyatt's orphan* (1985)

Wyatt series
Skinner, Mike
 see **Luke Wyatt series**
Wright, Don
 see **Luke Wyatt series**

Wych Hazel series
Warner, Susan Bagert
1 *Wych Hazel* (1876)
2 *Gold of Chikaree* (1877)
Co-author: Anna Bartlett

Wycherly series
Harker, Lizzie Allen
 see **Mister Wycherly series**

Wyck series
Sinclair, May
1 *Mister Waddington of Wyck* (1921)
2 *Rector of Wyck* (1925)

Wycliffe series
Burley, William John
 see **Superintendent Charles Wycliffe series**

Wylde series
Hughes, Glyn
 see **Anne Wylde series**

Wyler series
Leroe, Ellen Whitney
 see **Bixby Wyler series**

Wylie King and Nels Lundberg series
Saunders, Lawrence
1 *Columnist murder* (1931)
2 *Devil's den* (1933)

Wylo series
Wightman, Frank Armstrong
Yacht voyages
1 *Wind is free* (1949)
2 *My way leads me seaward* (1952)
3 *Wylo sails again* (1957)

Wyman series
Cook, Bob
 see **Michael Wyman series**
Sawyer, Ruth
 see **Lucinda Wyman series**

Wyn Lewis series
Kaufelt, David A
1 *Fat boy murders* (1993)
2 *Winter women murders* (1994)

Wynd family trilogy
Krensky, Stephen
1 *Dragon circle* (1977)
2 *Witching hour* (1981)
3 *Ghostly business* (1984)

Wyndcliffe series
Laurence, Louise
1 *Wyndcliffe* (1974)
2 *Sing and scatter daisies* (1977)

Wyndspelle series
Vandergriff, Aola
1 *Wyndspelle* (1975)
2 *Bell tower of Wyndspelle* (1975)
3 *Wyndspelle's child* (1976)

Wyndward series
Daniels, Norman A
1 *Law of the lash* (1968)
2 *Master of Wyndward* (1969)
Numbers 1 and 2 also published in one volume entitled *Wyndward passion*, 1978

3 *Wyndward fury* (1979)
4 *Wyndward glory* (1981)
5 *Wyndward forever* (1984)

Wynn and Elizabeth series
Oke, Janette
see **Elizabeth and Wynn series**

Wynn and Lonny racing series
Speed, Eric
1 *Mexicali 1000* (1975)
2 *Road race of champions* (1975)
3 *GT challenge* (1976)
4 *Gold Cup rookies* (1976)
5 *Dead heat at Le Mans* (1977)
6 *Midnight rally* (1978)

Wynnton series
Horler, Sydney
see **Robert Wynnton series**

Wyoming Jones series
Telfair, Richard
1 *Wyoming Jones* (1958)
2 *Day of the gun* (1958)
3 *Wyoming Jones for hire* (1958)
4 *Secret of Apache Canyon* (1959)
5 *Sundance* (1960)

Wyoming series
Kidd, Russ
1 *Man from Wyoming* (1982)
2 *Wyoming's debt to a dead man* (1986)

Wyoming Valley trilogy
Ellis, Edward Sylvester
1 *Wyoming* (1888)
2 *Storm Mountain* (1889)
3 *Cabin in the clearing* (1890)
A tale of the frontier

Wyrm series
Wangerin, Walter
see **Coop series**

Wyvern quartet
Forward, Toby
1 *Wyvern winter* (1992)
2 *Wyvern spring* (1993)
3 *Wyvern summer* (1994)
Number four not yet published

XYZ

X Bar X boys series
Ferris, James Cody
House pseudonym
1 *X Bar X boys on the ranch* (1926)
2 *X Bar X boys in Thunder Canyon* (1926)
3 *X Bar X boys on Whirlpool River* (1926)
4 *X Bar X boys on Big Bison Trail* (1927)
5 *X Bar X boys at the round-up* (1927)
6 *X Bar X boys at Nugget Camp* (1928)
7 *X Bar X boys at Rustlers' Gap* (1929)
8 *X Bar X boys at Grizzly Pass* (1929)
9 *X Bar X boys lost in the Rockies* (1930)
10 *X Bar X boys riding for life* (1931)
11 *X Bar X boys in Smoky Valley* (1932)
12 *X Bar X boys at Copperhead Gulch* (1933)
13 *X Bar X boys branding the wild herd* (1934)
14 *X Bar X boys at the strange rodeo* (1935)
15 *X Bar X boys with the secret rangers* (1936)
16 *X Bar X boys hunting the prize mustangs* (1937)
17 *X Bar X boys at Triangle Mine* (1938)
18 *X Bar X boys and the sagebrush mystery* (1939)
19 *X Bar X boys in the haunted gully* (1940)
20 *X Bar X boys seeking the lost troopers* (1941)
21 *X Bar X boys following the stampede* (1942)
Companion volume: *X Bar X Ranch*, 1930

Xanth series
Anthony, Piers
1 *Spell for Chameleon* (1977)
2 *Source of magic* (1979)
3 *Castle Roogna* (1979)
Numbers 1-3 also published in one volume entitled *The magic of Xanth*, 1981
4 *Centaur Aisle* (1982)
5 *Ogre, ogre* (1982)
6 *Night mare* (1983)
7 *Dragon on a pedestal* (1983)
8 *Crewel lye* (1984)
A caustic yarn
9 *Golem in the gears* (1986)
10 *Vale of the vole* (1987)
11 *Heaven cent* (1988)
12 *Man from Mundania* (1989)
13 *Isle of view* (1990)
14 *Question quest* (1991)
15 *Color of her panties* (1992)
16 *Geis of the gargoyle* (1995)
Companion volumes: *Encyclopedia of Xanth, a Crossroads adventure in the world of Pier Anthony's Xanth*, by Jody Lynn Nye, 1987, *Ghost of a chance, a Crossroads adventure in the world of Pier Anthony's Xanth*, by Jody Lynn Nye, 1988, *Piers Anthony's visual guide to Xanth*, by Piers Anthony and Jody Lynn Nye, 1989

Xargle series
Willis, Jeanne
see **Doctor Xargle series**

Xavier Flynn series
Braine, John
see **Colonel Xavier Flynn series**

Xenogenesis trilogy
Butler, Octavia Estelle
1 *Dawn* (1987)
2 *Adulthood* (1988)
3 *Imago* (1989)
One volume edition entitled *Xenogenesis*, 1989

Xman series
Brodsky, Michael Mark
1 *Xman* (1987)
2 *X in Paris* (1988)
Short stories

Xorandor series
Brooke-Rose, Christine
1 *Xorandor* (1986)
2 *Verbivor* (1990)

Xuma series
Lake, David John
1 *Gods of Xuma* (1978)
Alternative title: Barsoom revisited
2 *Warlords of Xuma* (1983)

XYY man series
Royce, Kenneth
see **Spider Scott series**

Y.M.C.A. boys series
Henderley, Brooks
1 *Y.M.C.A. boys of Cliffwood* (1916)
Alternative title: The struggle for the Holwell prize
2 *Y.M.C.A. boys on Bass Island* (1916)
Alternative title: The mystery of Russabaga Camp
3 *Y.M.C.A. boys at football* (1917)
Alternative title: Lively doings on and off the gridiron

Yabolinsky series
Schechtman, Joseph Boris
see **Vladimir Yabolinsky series**

Yacht Club series
Optic, Oliver
1 *Little Bobtail* (1872)
2 *Yacht Club* (1873)
Alternative title: The victory of the basilisk
3 *Money maker* (1874)
4 *Coming wave* (1875)
Alternative title: The hidden treasure of High Rock
5 *Dorcas Club* (1875)
Alternative title: Our girls afloat
6 *Ocean-born* (1875)
Alternative title: The cruise of clubs

Yacht Dolly series
Dunnett, Dorothy
see **Johnson and the yacht Dolly series**

Yagodah family trilogy
Elman, Richard Martin
1 *Twenty eighth day of Elul* (1967)
2 *Lilo's diary* (1968)
3 *Reckoning* (1969)

Yak series
Bisset, Donald
1 *Yak and the seashell* (1971)
2 *Yak and the painted cave* (1971)
3 *Yak and the ice cream* (1972)
4 *Yak and the buried treasure* (1972)
5 *Yak goes home* (1973)
Omnibus volume: *The adventures of Yak*, 1978

Yakari series
Derib
Comic strips
1 *Yakari* (1977)
Original edition entitled *Yakari*
2 *Yakari and the white buffalo* (1977)
Original edition entitled *Yakari et le bison blanc*

Yale University series
Knowles, John
1 *Indian summer* (1966)
2 *Paragon* (1971)
3 *Stolen past* (1983)

Yamamura series
Anderson, Poul
see **Trygve Yamamura series**

Yamboorah series
Ottley, Reginald Leslie
1 *By the sandhills of Yamboorah* (1965)
2 *Roan colt of Yamboorah* (1966)
3 *Rain comes to Yamboorah* (1967)

Yan series
Paulden, Sydney
1 *Yan and the golden moutain robbers* (1974)
2 *Yan and the firemonsters* (1976)
3 *Yan and the battle for Bergania* (1977)

Yanaba Maddock series
McCaffrey, Anne
1 *Powers that be* (1993)
2 *Power lines* (1994)

Yandilli trilogy
Hall, Rodney
1 *Second bridegroom* (1991)
2 *Grisly wife* (1993)
3 *Captivity captive* (1988)

Yangtse run series
O'Hara, Patrick
1 *Yangtse run* (1977)
2 *Wohldorf shipment* (1978)
Originally announced as a trilogy

Yankee flier series
Avery, Al
1 *Yankee flier with the R.A.F.* (1941)
2 *Yankee flier in the Far East* (1942)
3 *Yankee flier in the South Pacific* (1943)
4 *Yankee flier in North Africa* (1943)
5 *Yankee flier in Italy* (1944)
6 *Yankee flier over Berlin* (1944)
7 *Yankee flier in Normandy* (1945)
8 *Yankee flier on a rescue mission* (1945)
9 *Yankee flier under secret orders* (1946)

Yankee girl series
Curtis, Alice Turner
1 *Yankee girl at Fort Sumter* (1920)
2 *Yankee girl at Bull Horn* (1921)
3 *Yankee girl at Shiloh* (1922)
4 *Yankee girl at Antietam* (1923)
5 *Yankee girl at Gettysburg* (1924)
6 *Yankee girl at Vicksburg* (1926)
7 *Yankee Girl at Hampton Roads* (1927)
8 *Yankee girl at Lookout Mountain* (1928)
9 *Yankee girl at the Battle of the Wilderness* (1929)
10 *Yankee girl at Richmond* (1930)

Yankee series
Johnson, Irving
1 *Westward bound in the schooner Yankee* (1936)
2 *Sailing to see* (1939)
3 *Yankee's wander world* (1949)
4 *Yankee's people and places* (1955)

Yaqui series
Castaneda, Carlos
see **Don Juan series**

Yaqui series
This sequence has two authors
Grey, Zane
1 *Desert gold* (1913)
Selections: Zane Grey's *Yaqui, and other great Indian stories*, edited by Loren Grey, 1976
Grey, Romer Zane
2 *Siege at Forlorn River* (1970)

Yard series
Hayes, Ralph Eugene
see **John Yard series**

Yardie series
Headley, Victor
1 *Yardie* (1992)
2 *Excess* (1993)

Yardley family trilogy
Kalman, Yvonne
1 *Greenstone land* (1981)
Greenstone
2 *Juliette's daughter* (1982)
3 *Riversong* (1985)

Yardley Hall series
Barbour, Ralph Henry
1 *Forward pass* (1908)
2 *Double play* (1909)
3 *Winning his Y* (1910)
4 *For Yardley* (1911)
5 *Change signals* (1912)
6 *Around the end* (1913)
7 *Guarding his goal* (1919)
8 *Fourth down* (1920)

Yardley series
Garnett, Roger
see **John Yardley series**

Yarns of a shellback series
Duff, Douglas Valder
1 *Yarns of a shellback* (1959)
2 *More yarns of a shellback* (1960)

Yarrow series
Best, Rayleigh Breton Amis
1 *House called Yarrow* (1960)
2 *Honest rogue* (1961)
3 *High tide* (1964)
4 *Idle rainbow* (1965)
5 *Green wood* (1967)
6 *Selfish ones* (1968)

Yates and Curtis series
Fetta, Emma Lou
see **Lyle Curtis and Susan Yates series**

Yates series
Drake, David
1 *Kill ratio* (1987)
2 *Target* (1989)

Ye Headless Lady Inn series
Dryasdust
1 *Tales of the Wonder Club* (1899)
2 *Tales of the Wonder Club 2* (1900)

Yeadings and Mott series
Curzon, Clare
see **Superintendent Mike Yeardings and Sergeant Angus Mott series**

Year in the life of an animal series
Stidworthy, John
1 *Year in the life of a badger* (1987)
2 *Year in the life of an elephant* (1987)
3 *Year in the life of a tiger* (1987)
4 *Year in the life of a whale* (1987)
5 *Year in the life of an owl* (1987)
6 *Year in the life of a chimpanzee* (1987)

Year of the Ninja Master series
Barker, Wade
1 *Dragon rising* (1985)
Spring
2 *Lion's fire* (1985)
Summer
3 *Serpent's eye* (1985)
Autumn
4 *Phoenix sword* (1986)
Winter
This sequence is followed by the **War of the Ninja Master series**

Years at sea series
Bisset, James
1 *Sail ho!* (1958)
My early years at sea
2 *Tramps and ladies* (1959)
My early years in steamers
3 *Commodore* (1961)
War, peace and big ships

Years between series
Feval, Paul
Numbers 1-4 have co-author M Lassez
1 *Mysterious cavalier* (1925)
Original edition entitled *Le chevalier mystere*
2 *Martyr to the Queen* (1925)
Original edition entitled *Martyre de Reine*
3 *Secret of the Bastille* (1925)
Original edition entitled *Le secret de la Bastille*
4 *Heir of Buckingham* (1925)
Original edition entitled L'heritage de Buckingham
5 *Comrades at arms* (1928)
Original edition entitled *D'Artagnon et Cyrano reconcilies*
6 *Salute to Cyrano* (1928)
Original edition entitled *Les noces de Cyrano*

Years diaries series
Beaton, Cecil
Diaries
1 *Wandering years* (1961)
1922-39
2 *Years between* (1965)
1939-44
3 *Happy years* (1972)
1944-48
4 *Strenuous years* (1973)
1948-55
5 *Restless years* (1976)
1955-63
6 *Parting years* (1978)
1963-74

Years of life series
Cartland, Barbara
1 *We danced all night* (1970)
1919-1929
2 *Isthmus years* (1943)
1919-1939
3 *Years of opportunity* (1948)
1939-1945
4 *I search for rainbows* (1967)
1946-1966
Companion volumes: *Polly, my wonderful mother*, 1956, *I seek the miraculous*, 1978

Years of love series
Widdemer, Margaret
1 *Years of love* (1933)
2 *Other lovers* (1934)

Years of Lyndon Johnson series
Caro, Robert A
1 *Path to power* (1982)
2 *Means of ascent* (1990)

Years of peace series
Macleod, Le Roy
1 *Years of peace* (1932)
2 *Crowded hill* (1934)

Years series
Douglas, William Sholto
1 *Years of combat* (1963)
2 *Years of command* (1966)

Years series
Gielgud, Val
1 *Years of the locust* (1947)
2 *Years in a mirror* (1965)
Companion volumes: *One year of grace*, 1950, *My cats and myself*, 1972

Years series
Richmond, Arthur Cyril
1 *Twenty-six years* (1961)
1879-1905
2 *Another sixty years* (1965)

Yedder series
Bond, Evelyn
see **Ira Yedder series**

Yellowstone critter series
Reese, Bob
1 *Bugle Elk and Little Toot* (1986)
2 *Buffa Buffalo* (1986)
3 *Bubba Bear* (1986)
4 *Mickey Moose* (1986)
5 *Old Faithful* (1986)
6 *Camper critters* (1986)

Yellowstone Kelly series
Bowen, Peter
1 *Yellowstone Kelly* (1988)
2 *Kelly blue* (1991)
3 *Imperial Kelly* (1992)

Yellowstone series
Lomax, Bliss
1 *Guns along the Yellowstone* (1952)
2 *Appointment on the Yellowstone* (1959)
Lawless guns

Yellowthread Street series
Marshall, William Leonard
1 *Yellowthread Street* (1975)
2 *Hatchet man* (1976)
3 *Gelignite* (1976)
4 *Thin air* (1977)
5 *Skulduggery* (1979)
6 *Sci fi* (1981)
7 *Perfect end* (1981)
8 *War machine* (1982)
9 *Far away man* (1984)
10 *Roadshow* (1985)
11 *Head first* (1986)
12 *Frogmouth* (1987)
13 *Out of nowhere* (1988)
14 *Inches* (1994)

Yen-Ching trilogy
Vare, Daniele
1 *Maker of Heavenly Trousers* (1935)
2 *Gate of Happy Sparrows* (1937)
3 *Temply of Costly Experience* (1939)

Yensie Walton series
Clark, Susanna Rebecca Graham
1 *Yensie Walton* (1879)
2 *Yensie Walton's womanhood* (1882)

Yeo series
Treherne, John
see **Doctor James Yeo series**

Yeoman series
Woodhouse, Martin
see **Giles Yeoman series**

Yesno series
Tozer, Mary
see **Queen Yesno series**

Yesterday and tomorrow series
Bethancourt, Tomas Ernesto
1 *Tune in yesterday* (1978)
2 *Tomorrow connection* (1984)

Yesterday series
O'Harris, Pixie
Autobiography
1 *Our small safe world* (1986)
2 *Was it yesterday?* (1983)

Yesterday's road series
Minton, Mary
1 *Yesterday's road* (1986)
2 *Marriage bowl* (1986)
3 *Weeping doves* (1987)
4 *Don't laugh at fools* (1988)
5 *Spinner's end* (1989)
6 *Every street* (1990)
7 *Paradise corner* (1992)
8 *House of destiny* (1993)
9 *Tracing of angels* (1994)

Ygrec series
Rippon, Marion
see **Inspector Maurice Ygrec series**

Yiktor series
Norton, Andre
see **Krip Vorland series**

Yngling series
Dalmas, John
see **Nils Jarnhan series**

Yok-yok series
Van der Essen, Anne
Illustrated by Etienne Delessert
Translated from the French
1 *Caterpillar* (1979)
2 *Magician* (1979)
3 *Night* (1979)
4 *Blackbird* (1979)
5 *Frog* (1979)
6 *Rabbit* (1979)
7 *Shadow* (1981)
8 *Circus* (1981)
9 *Cricket* (1981)
10 *Snow* (1981)
11 *Violin* (1981)
12 *Cherry* (1981)

Yolanda series
Verseau, Dominique
1 *Yolanda, the girl from the erosphere* (1975)
2 *Slaves of space* (1976)

Yonderbeyonder series
Davey, Thyrza
1 *Yonderbeyonder* (1990)
2 *Wintersmoke* (1993)

York family series
Anderson, Verily
1 *Vanload to Venice* (1961)
2 *Nine times never* (1962)
3 *Yorks in London* (1964)

York series
Durham, Mary
see **Inspector York series**
Holt, Gavin
see **Sherret York series**

York trilogy
Naylor, Phyllis Reynolds
1 *Shadows on the wall* (1980)
2 *Faces in the water* (1981)
3 *Footprints at the window* (1981)

Yorke Norroy series
Bronson-Howard, George
1 *Norroy, diplomatic agent* (1907)
Short stories
2 *Slaves of the lamp* (1917)
3 *Black book* (1920)

Yorke series
Pope, Dudley
see **Ned Yorke series**
Stranger, Joyce
see **Timothy Yorke series**

Yorkshire Dales trilogy
Sunley, Margaret
1 *Quiet earth* (1990)
2 *Fields in the sun* (1991)
3 *Sons of toil* (1992)

Yorkshire farm series
Fussey, Joyce
1 *Milk my ewes and weep* (1976)
2 *Cows in the corn* (1978)
3 *Calf love* (1984)
4 *Cats in the coffee* (1986)

Yorkshire trilogy
Braithwaite, Ruth
1 *Martha* (1983)
2 *Ben* (1984)
3 *House in Kingston Square* (1985)

You and me series
This sequence has four authors; photographic picture books
Alex, Marlee
1 *Our new baby* (1981)
2 *Grandpa and me* (1981)
Kargaard, Jens
3 *We go exploring* (1984)
Alex, Benny
4 *Our best Christmas* (1987)

You and me series
Pickles, Wilfred
1 *Between you and me* (1949)
2 *Sometime never* (1951)
3 *Ne'er forget the people* (1953)
Companion volume: *Wilfred Pickles invites you to have another go*, 1978

You and yours series
Bloom, Ursula
1 *You and your child* (1946)
2 *You and your holiday* (1947)

3 *You and your home* (1949)
4 *You and your dog* (1949)
5 *You and your looks* (1949)
6 *You and your life* (1950)
7 *You and your fun* (1950)
8 *You and your needle* (1950)

You are the coach series
Aaseng, Nathan
1 *Baseball* (1983)
You are the manager
2 *Basketball* (1983)
3 *Football* (1983)
4 *Hockey* (1983)
5 *College basketball* (1984)
6 *College football* (1983)
7 *Baseball* (1985)
It's your team
8 *Football* (1985)
It's your team

You can eat series
Cobb, Vicki
1 *Science experiments you can eat* (1972)
2 *Arts and crafts you can eat* (1974)
3 *More science experiments you can eat* (1979)

You can get there series
MacLaine, Shirley
Memoirs
1 *You can get there from here* (1975)
2 *Out on a limb* (1983)
3 *Dancing in the light* (1985)
4 *It's all in the playing* (1987)
5 *Dance while you can* (1991)
Companion volume: *Don't fall off the mountain*, 1970

You'll never guess what series
Sanford, Doris
1 *Once I told a lie* (1990)
2 *Once I was a bully* (1990)
3 *Once I was a thief* (1990)
4 *Once I was obnoxious* (1990)

Young Aeroplane Scouts series
Porter, Horace
1 *Our Young Aeroplane scouts in France and Belgium* (1915)
Alternative title: Saving the fortune of the Trouviles
2 *Our Young Aeroplane scouts in Germany* (1915)
Alternative title: Winning the Iron Cross
3 *Our Young Aeroplane scouts in Russia* (1915)
Alternative title: Lost on the frozen steppes
4 *Our Young Aeroplane scouts in Turkey* (1915)
Alternative title: Bringing the light to Yusef
5 *Our Young Aeroplane scouts in England* (1916)
Alternative title: Twin stars in the London Sky Patrol
6 *Our Young Aeroplane scouts in Italy* (1916)
Alternative title: Flying with the War Eagles in the Alps
7 *Our Young Aeroplane scouts at Verdun* (1917)
Alternative title: Driving armored meteors over flaming battle fronts
8 *Our Young Aeroplane scouts in the Balkans* (1917)
Alternative title: Wearing the red badge of courage
9 *Our Young Aeroplane scouts in the war zone* (1918)
Alternative title: Serving Uncle Sam in the cause of the Allies
10 *Our Young Aeroplane scouts fighting to the finish* (1918)
Alternative title: Striking hard over the sea for the Stars and Stripes
11 *Our Young Aeroplane scouts at the Marne* (1919)
Alternative title: Harrying the Huns from Allied battle planes
12 *Our Young Aeroplane scouts in at the victory* (1919)
Alternative title: Speedy high flyers smashing the Hindenberg Line

Young America, first series
Optic, Oliver
1 *Outward bound* (1867)
Alternative title: Young America afloat
2 *Shamrock and thistle* (1868)
Alternative title: Young America in Ireland and Scotland
3 *Red cross* (1868)
Alternative title: Young America in England and Wales
4 *Dikes and ditches* (1868)
Alternative title: Young America in Holland and Belgium
5 *Palace and cottage* (1868)
Alternative title: Young America in France and Switzerland
6 *Down the Rhine* (1869)
Alternative title: Young America in Germany

Young America, second series
Optic, Oliver
1 *Up the Baltic* (1871)
Alternative title: Young America in Norway, Sweden and Denmark
2 *Northern lands* (1872)
Alternative title: Young America in Russia and Prussia
3 *Cross and crescent* (1872)
Alternative title: Young America in Turkey and Greece
4 *Sunny shores* (1875)
Alternative title: Young America in Turkey and Greece
5 *Vine and olive* (1876)
Alternative title: Young America in Spain and Portugal
6 *Isles of the sea* (1877)
Alternative title: Young America homeward bound

Young and Keene series
Wood, Eric
see **Arnold Keene and Bernard Young series**

Young Art and old Hector series
Gunn, Neil Miller
1 *Young Art and old Hector* (1942)
2 *Green isle of the great deep* (1944)

Young Astronauts series
North, Rick
This pseudonym is used by Margaret Wander Bonanno, Mayer Alan Brenner, Shariann N Lewitt and John Peel as indicated against each title
1 *Young Astronauts* (1990)
[Lewitt]
2 *Ready for blastoff!* (1990)
[Peel]
3 *Space blazers* (1990)
[Lewitt]
4 *Destination Mars* (1991)
[Bonanno]
5 *Space pioneers* (1991)
[Brenner]
6 *Citizens of Mars* (1991)
[Bonanno]

Young birdmen series
Russell, Keith
1 *Young birdmen on the wing* (1929)
Alternative title: The rescue at Greenley Island
2 *Young birdmen across the continent* (1930)
Alternative title: The coast-to-coast flight of the night mail
3 *Young birdmen up the Amazon* (1930)
Alternative title: Secrets of the tropical jungle

Young Blueberry series
Charlier, Jean Michel
Comic strips; individual volumes illustrated by Jean Giraud or Colin Wilson
1 *Blueberry's secret* (1989)
Original edition entitled La jeunesse de Blueberry
2 *Yankee named Blueberry* (1990)
Original edition entitled Un Yankee nomme Blueberry
3 *Blue Coats* (1990)
Original edition entitled Le Cavalier Bleu
4 *Missouri Demons* (1990)
Original edition entitled Les Demons du Missouri
5 *Terror over Kansas* (1990)
Original edition entitled Terreurs sur le Kansas

Young Buffalo Bill series
Sherwood, Elmer
1 *Buffalo Bill's childhood* (1919)
2 *Buffalo Bill and the Pony Express* (1919)
Reissued anonymously in 1934
Companion volumes: *The wild West adventures of Buffalo Bill*, 1935, and *Buffalo Bill plays a lone hand*, 1936, both issued anonymously

Young cavalier series
James, George Payne Rainsford
1 *Henry Masterton* (1832)
Alternative title: The adventures of a young cavalier
2 *John Marston Hall* (1834)
Alternative title: The little ball of fire

Young Christian series
Abbott, Jacob
1 *Young Christian* (1832)
2 *Corner-stone* (1834)
3 *Way to do good* (1836)
4 *Hoaryhead and M'Donner* (1838)
5 *Hoaryhead and the vallies below* (1838)

Young Continentals series
McIntyre, John Thomas
1 *Young Continentals at Lexington* (1909)
2 *Young Continentals at Bunker Hill* (1910)
3 *Young Continentals at Trenton* (1911)
4 *Young Continentals at Monmouth* (1912)

Young detective series
Butler, William Vivian
1 *Young detective's handbook* (1979)
Revised edition 1982
2 *Young detective's whodunit* (1983)

Young detective series
Coombs, Charles Ira
1 *Young circus detective series* (1954)
2 *Young ranch detective* (1956)
3 *Young atom detective* (1958)

Young detectives series
Macgregor, Reginald James
1 *Young detectives* (1934)
2 *Young detectives incorporated* (1947)

Young Dodge Club series
De Mille, James
1 *Dodge Club* (1859)
Alternative title: Italy in 1869
2 *Among the brigands* (1872)
3 *Seven hills* (1873)
4 *Winged lion* (1877)

Young engineers series
Hancock, Harrie Irving
1 *Young engineers in Colorado* (1912)
Alternative title: At railroad building in earnest
2 *Young engineers in Arizona* (1912)
Alternative title: Laying tracks on the man-killer quicksand
3 *Young engineers in Nevada* (1913)
Alternative title: Seeking fortune on the turn of a pick
4 *Young engineers in Mexico* (1913)
Alternative title: Fighting the mine swindlers
5 *Young engineers in the Gulf* (1920)
Alternative title: The mystery of the million-dollar breakwater

Young England trilogy
Disraeli, Benjamin
1 *Coningsby* (1844)
Alternative title: The new generation
2 *Sybil* (1845)
Alternative title: The two nations
3 *Tancred* (1847)
Alternative title: The new crusade

Young farmers series
Martin, Nancy
1 *Young farmers at Greythorne* (1954)
2 *Young farmers in Denmark* (1955)
3 *Young farmers in Scotland* (1956)

Young folks colonial series
Fitzhugh, Percy Keese
1 *Story of Ethan Allen, the Green mountain boy* (1906)
2 *Story of General Anthony Wayne, Mad Anthony, the hero of Stony Point* (1906)
3 *Story of General Johann De Kalb* (1906)
4 *Story of General Richard Montgomery* (1906)
Tale of the invasion of Canada
5 *Story of John Paul Jones* (1906)
6 *Story of General Francis Marion, the Bayard of the South* (1907)

Young Indiana Jones chronicles series
This sequence has six authors
Stine, Megan
1 *Mummy's curse* (1992)
Martin, Les
2 *Field of death* (1992)
McCay, William
3 *Secret peace* (1992)
Bell, Sally
4 *Safari in Africa* (1992)
Martin, Les
5 *Trek of doom* (1992)
Calmenson, Stephanie
6 *Race to danger* (1993)
Martin, Les
7 *Prisoner of war* (1993)

Young Indiana Jones series
This sequence has five authors
McCay, William
1 *Young Indiana Jones and the plantation treasure* (1990)
Martin, Les
2 *Young Indiana Jones and the tomb of terror* (1990)
McCay, William
3 *Young Indiana Jones and the circle of death* (1990)
Martin, Les
4 *Young Indiana Jones and the secret city* (1990)
5 *Young Indiana Jones and the princess of peril* (1991)
6 *Young Indiana Jones and the gypsy revenge* (1991)
McCay, William
7 *Young Indiana Jones and the ghostly riders* (1991)

8 *Young Indiana Jones and the Curse of the ruby cross* (1992)
Young Indiana Jones and the ruby cross
Martin, Les
9 *Young Indiana Jones and the Titanic adevnture* (1993)
Stine, Megan
10 *Young Indiana Jones and the lost gold of Durango* (1993)
McCay, William
11 *Young Indiana Jones and the face of the dragon* (1994)
Stine, Megan
12 *Young Indiana Jones and the journey to the underworld* (1994)
McCay, William
13 *Young Indiana Jones and the mountain of fire* (1994)
Fox, J N
14 *Young Indiana Jones and the pirates' loot* (1994)

Young Kentuckians series
Dunn, Byron Archibald
1 *General Nelson's scout* (1898)
2 *On General Thomas' staff* (1899)
3 *Battling for Atlanta* (1900)
4 *From Atlanta to the sea* (1901)
5 *Raiding with Morgan* (1903)

Young Missourians series
Dunn, Byron Archibald
1 *With Lyon in Missouri* (1910)
2 *Scout of Pea Ridge* (1911)
3 *Courier of the Ozarks* (1912)
4 *Storming Vicksburg* (1913)
5 *Last raid* (1914)

Young Nimrods series
Knox, Thomas Wallace
see **Hunting adventures on land and sea series**

Young Pitt series
Maughan, Anne Margery
1 *Young Pitt* (1974)
2 *King's malady* (1978)

Young readers series
Coombs, Charles Ira
1 *Young readers basketball stories* (1950)
2 *Young readers football stories* ()
3 *Young readers stories of the diamond* (1951)
4 *Young readers mystery stories* (1951)
5 *Young readers detective stories* (1951)
6 *Young readers indoor sports stories* (1952)
7 *Young readers sports treasury* (1952)
8 *Young readers water sports stories* (1952)
9 *Young readers railroad stories* (1953)
10 *Young readers baseball stories* (1955)

Young rebels series
Johnston, William
Based on a television series
1 *Hedgerow incident* (1970)
2 *Seagold* (1971)

Young reporter series
Garis, Howard Roger
see **Great newspaper series**

Young Roy series
Gilroy, Beryl
1 *New people at twenty four* (1973)
2 *Visitor from home* (1973)
3 *Knock at Mrs Herbs'* (1973)

Young series
Campbell, Alice
see **Alison Young series**
Tippette, Giles
see **Wilson Young series**
Trenhaile, John
see **Simon Young series**

Young Sherlock Holmes series
Frow, Gerald
1 *Mystery of the manor house* (1982)
2 *Adventures of Ferryman's Creek* (1984)

Young trailers series
Altsheler, Joseph Alexander
see **Trailers series**

Young Virginians series
Dunn, Byron Archibald
1 *Boy scouts of the Shenandoah* (1916)
2 *With the army of the Potomac* (1917)
3 *Scouting for Sheridan* (1918)

Youngdahl series
Harris, Mark
see **Lee Youngdahl series**

Your amazing adventures series
Brightfield, Richard
1 *Castle of doom* (1984)
2 *Island of fear* (1984)
3 *Terror under the earth* (1984)
4 *Dragonmaster* (1985)
5 *Revenge of the Dragonmaster* (1985)
6 *Battle of the dragons* (1986)

Your child series
Ames, Louise Bates
1 *Your one-year-old* (1982)
Co-authors: Frances Lillian Ilg, Carol Chase Haber; subtitle: the fun-loving, fussy 12-to-24 month old
2 *Your two-year-old* (1976)
Co-author: Frances Lillian Ilg; subtitle: terrible or tender
3 *Your three-year-old* (1976)
Co-author: Frances Lillian Ilg; subtitle: friend or enemy
4 *Your four-year-old* (1976)
Co-author: Frances Lillian Ilg; subtitle: wild and wonderful
5 *Your five-year-old* (1979)
Co-author: Frances Lillian Ilg; subtitle: sunny and serene
6 *Your six-year-old* (1979)
Co-author: Frances Lillian Ilg; subtitle: defiant but loving
7 *Your seven-year-old* (1985)
Co-author: Carol Chase Haber; subtitle: life in a minor key
8 *Your eight-year-old* (1989)
Co-author: Carol Chase Haber; subtitle: lively and outgoing
9 *Your nine-year-old* (1990)
Co-author: Carol Chase Haber; subtitle: thoughtful and mysterious
10 *Your ten- to fourteen-year-old* (1988)
Co-authors: Frances Lillian Ilg, Sidney M Baker

Your future in aviation series
Scribner, Kimball
The second titles are revised editions
1 *Your future in aviation in the air* (1979)
Careers in the air
2 *Your future in aviation on the ground* (1979)
Careers on the ground

Your high-tech world series
Skurzynski, Gloria
1 *Robots* (1990)
2 *Almost the real thing* (1991)
About simulation
3 *Get the message* (1993)
About telecommunications
4 *Know the score* (1994)
About video games

Your street series
Simon, Seymour
1 *Tree in your street* (1973)
2 *Building in your street* (1973)
3 *Birds in your street* (1974)

Youth and winter series
Napier, Elma
Autobiography
1 *Youth is a blunder* (1948)
2 *Winter is in July* (1949)

Youth work series
Blandy, Mary
1 *Razor edge* (1967)
The story of a youth club
2 *Harvest from rotten apples* (1971)
An account of experimental work with detached youth

Yowder series
Rounds, Glen
see **Mister Yowder series**

Ys series
Anderson, Poul
see **King of Ys series**

Ythan series
Alexander, Marc
see **Wells of Ythan series**

Yudel Gordon series
Ebersohn, Wessel
1 *Lonely place to die* (1979)
2 *Divide the night* (1981)

Yum Yum and Koko series
Braun, Lilian Jackson
see **Jim Qwilleran series**

Yuma series
Smith, Russell
1 *Yuma* (1978)
2 *Renegade gold* (1979)

Yummers series
Marshall, James
1 *Yummers!* (1973)
2 *Yummers too* (1986)
The second course

Yuri Nevsky series
Gat, Dimitri
1 *Nevsky's return* (1982)
3 *Nevsky's demon* (1983)

Yusof series
Sherry, Sylvia
1 *Street of the small night market* (1966)
Secret of the jade pavilion
2 *Frog in a coconut shell* (1968)

Z cars series
Martin, Troy Kennedy
see **Chief Inspector Barlow series**

Z series
Farjeon, Joseph Jefferson
1 *Person called Z* (1930)
2 *Z murders* (1932)

Zachariah Tree series
Foley, Craig
see **Hangman series**

Zacharias series
Williamson, Jerry Neal
see **Lamia Zacharias series**

Zachary Jones series
Steirman, Hy
1 *Strike terror* (1968)
2 *Cry of the hawk* (1970)

Zack, Emmie and Leo series
Ehrlich, Amy
see **Leo, Zack and Emmie series**

Zack Rolfe series
Lamb, J J
1 *Nickel jackpot* (1976)
2 *Chinese straight* (1976)
3 *Losers take all* (1979)

Zag and Zig series
Young, Peter
see **Zig and Zag series**

Zailm series
Phylos the Thibetan
1 *Dweller on two planets* (1905)
Alternative title: The dividing of the way
2 *Earth dweller's return* (1940)
Rewritten from *A dweller on two planets*, 1894

Zambra series
Hill, Headon
see **Sebastian Zambra series**

Zan Hagan series
Knudson, Rozanne Ruth
1 *Zanballer* (1972)
2 *Zanbanger* (1977)
3 *Zanboomer* (1978)
4 *Zan Hagan's marathon* (1984)

Zandra trilogy
Rotsler, William
1 *Zondra* (1978)
2 *Far frontier* (1980)
3 *Hidden worlds of Zandra* (1983)

Zane family series
Grey, Zane
1 *Betty Zane* (1903)
Last ranger
2 *Spirit of the border* (1906)
3 *Last trail* (1909)

Zane series
Gardner, Erle Stanley
see **Whispering Sands series**
Massey, Morrell
see **Thornton Zane series**
Trimble, Louis
see **Martin Zane series**

Zanthar series
Williams, Robert Moore
1 *Zanthar of the many worlds* (1967)
2 *Zanthar at the edge of never* (1968)
3 *Zanthar at moon's madness* (1968)
4 *Zanthar at trip's end* (1969)

Zanzibar series
Brunner, John
1 *Stand on Zanzibar* (1968)
2 *Sheep look up* (1972)

Zanzibar series
Kaye, Mary Margaret
1 *Trade wind* (1963)
2 *House of Shade* (1959)
Death in Zanzibar
The second title is a revised edition

Zapp and Sparrow series
Lodge, David
see **Rummidge University series**

Zapt series
Pearce, Michael
see **Mamur Zapt series**

Zarathustra trilogy
Brunner, John
1 *Secret agent of Terra* (1962)
Avengers of Carrig
The second title is a revised edition
2 *Castaways' world* (1963)
Polymath
The second title is a revised edition
3 *Repairmen of Cyclops* (1965)
Also includes *Enigma from Tantalus*
One volume edition entitled *Victims of the nova*, 1989

Zarkon series
Carter, Lin
see **Prince Zarkon series**

Zarnia experiment series
Leeson, Robert
1 *Landing* (1991)
2 *Fire!* (1991)
3 *Deadline* (1993)

4 *Danger trail* (1993)
5 *Hide and seek* (1993)
6 *Blast off!* (1993)

Zebby series
Schroeder, Binette
1 *Zebby swims* (1981)
2 *Zebby gone with the wind* (1981)
3 *Zebby's breakfast* (1981)
4 *Zebby shops* (1981)
5 *Run Zebby run* (1981)

Zed series
Penrose, Gordon
see **Doctor Zed series**

Zeke Henderson and Buck Lawrence series
Pritchett, Ron
see **Buck Lawrence and Zeke Henderson series**

Zelazny's Alien speedway series
Wylde, Thomas
see **Roger Zelazny's Alien speedway series**

Zelda Hammersmith series
Hall, Lynn
1 *In trouble again, Zelda Hammersmith?* (1987)
2 *Zelda strikes again!* (1988)
3 *Here comes Zelda Claus, and other holiday disasters* (1989)

Zen series
Van de Wetering, Janwillem
Autobiography
1 *Empty mirror* (1972)
Original edition entitled *De lege spiegal*; experiences in a Japanese Zen monastery
2 *Glimpse of nothingness* (1974)
Original edition entitled *Het dagende niets*; experiences in an American Zen community

Zeno series
Svevo, Italo
1 *Confessions of Zeno* (1923)
2 *Further confessions of Zeno* (1969)
Include selections translated from *La novella del buon vecchio e della bella fanciulla*, 1929, *Corto maggio sentimentale, e altri racconti*,1949, and, *La rigenerazione*, in *Comedie*, 1960 and published in English as *Regeneration*

Zenobia and Aurelian series
Ware, William
1 *Zenobia* (1838)
Letters of Lucius M Piso from Palmyra
Last days and fall of Palmyra
2 *Probus* (1838)
Last days of Aurelian
Alternative titles: Rome in the third century, and The Nazarenes of Rome

Zenobia and Fletcher series
Gorey, Edward
see **Fletcher and Zenobia series**

Zeor series
Lichtenberg, Jacqueline
see **Sime-Gen series**

Zero and Rosalind series
Buckley, Eunice
1 *Just was my lot* (1972)
2 *Face of the tempter* (1973)
3 *Wonder-worker* (1975)

Zero stone series
Norton, Andre
see **Murdoc Jern series**

Zerzura series
Home, Michael
1 *Place of Little Birds* (1941)
Attack in the desert
2 *House of shade* (1942)
3 *City of the soul* (1943)

Zest series
McBratney, Sam
see **Jimmy Zest series**

Zette, Jocko and Jo series
Herge
see **Adventures of Jo, Zette and Jocko series**

Zevich and Kirlin series
Bourgeau, Art
see **Claude Kirlin and F T Zevich series**

Zhivago series
Pasternak, Boris
see **Doctor Zhivago series**

Zia series
O'Dell, Scott
1 *Island of the blue dolphin* (1961)
2 *Zia* (1976)

Zian series
Frison-Roche, Roger
1 *Last crevasse* (1948)
2 *Return to the mountains* (1957)

Ziax II series
Morressy, John
1 *Humans of Ziax II* (1974)
2 *Drought on Ziax II* (1978)
One volume edition 1978

Zig and Zag series
Young, Peter
1 *Zig and Zag from Planet ZV7* (1966)
2 *Zag the Great and Zig the Big* (1966)

Zimiamvian trilogy
Eddison, Eric Rucker
1 *Mezentian gate* (1958)
2 *Fish dinner in Memison* (1941)
3 *Mistress of mistresses* (1935)
Companion volume: *The worm Ouroboros*, 1922

Zimmerman series
George, Theodore
see **Lieutenant Al Zimmerman series**

Zimmerman trilogy
Bellairs, John
see **Clock trilogy**

Zip series
Caveney, Sylvia
see **Little Zip series**
Steele, William Owen
see **Hound Dog Zip series**

Zip-Zip series
Schealer, John Milton
1 *Zip-Zip and his flying saucer* (1956)
2 *Zip-Zip goes to Venus* (1958)
3 *Zip-Zip and the red planet* (1961)

Ziza Todd series
McCullough, David Willis
1 *Think on death* (1991)
A Hudson Valley mystery
2 *Point no-point* (1992)

Zoe and George series
Arendt, Veronique
1 *Magic scarf* (1987)
2 *Island of colours* (1987)

Zograffi series
Istrati, Panait
see **Adrien Zograffi series**

Zondi and Kramer series
McClure, James
see **Lieutenant Kramer and Sergeant Zondi series**

Zone series
Rouch, James
1 *Hard target* (1980)
2 *Blind fire* (1980)
3 *Hunter killer* (1981)
4 *Sky strike* (1981)
5 *Overkill* (1982)
6 *Plague bomb* (1986)
7 *Killing ground* (1988)
8 *Civilian slaughter* (1989)
9 *Body count* (1990)

Zoo doings series
Prelutsky, Jack
1 *Gopher in the garden, and other animal poems* (1967)
2 *Toucans two, and other poems* (1970)
Zoo doings, and other poems
3 *Pack rat's day, and other poems* (1974)
One volume edition entitled *Zoo doings*, 1983

Zoo in series
Taylor, David Conrad
1 *Zoo in you* (1987)
Discover the animals which live in you
2 *Zoo in the house* (1987)
Discover the animals which live in your house
3 *Zoo in the garden* (1987)
Discover the animals which live in your garden
4 *Zoo in town* (1987)
Discover the animals which live in your town

Zoo Man series
Gillespie, Thomas Haining
1 *Zoo Man talks* (1959)
2 *Zoo Man stories* (1960)
3 *Zoo Man tales* (1960)
4 *Zoo Man again* (1961)

Zoo quest series
Attenborough, David
Memoirs of the travels of a naturalist
1 *Zoo quest for Guyana* (1956)
2 *Zoo quest for a dragon* (1957)
3 *Zoo quest in Paraguay* (1958)
4 *Quest in paradise* (1960)
5 *Zoo quest in Madagascar* (1961)
6 *Quest under Capricorn* (1963)

Zoo vet series
Taylor, David
see **Zoovet series**

Zoo ways series
Gillespie, Thomas Haining
1 *Zoo ways and whys* (1930)
2 *More zoo ways* (1931)
Companion volume: *Zootales* 1936, revised edition 1962

Zoo world series
Irvine, Georgeanne
1 *Protecting endangered species at the San Diego Zoo* (1990)
2 *Raising Gordy Gorilla at the San Diego Zoo* (1990)
3 *Visit of two giant pandas at the San Diego Zoo* (1991)
4 *Work of the zoo doctors at the San Diego Zoo* (1991)

Zoom series
Wynne-Jones, Tim
1 *Zoom at sea* (1982)
2 *Zoom away* (1985)

Zoomers of Motor City series
Gilden, Mel
1 *Pokey to the rescue* (1988)
2 *RV and the haunted garage* (1988)

Zoot Marlowe series
Gilden, Mel
1 *Surfing Samurai robots* (1988)
2 *Hawaiian UFO aliens* (1991)
3 *Tubular android superheroes* (1991)
4 *Hawaiian UFO robots* (1992)

Zoovet series
Taylor, David Conrad
1 *Zoovet* (1976)
2 *Doctor in the zoo* (1978)
Is there a doctor in the zoo?
3 *Going wild* (1980)
4 *Next panda, please!* (1982)
5 *Wandering whale, and other adventures from a zoo vet's casebook* (1984)
6 *Dragon doctor* (1985)
7 *Vet on the wild side* (1990)

Zorachus series
Rogers, Mark Earl
1 *Zorachus* (1986)
2 *Nightmare of God* (1988)

Zordan series
Eastwood, James
see **Anna Zordan series**

Zork series
Meretzky, S Eric
1 *Forces of Krill* (1983)
2 *Malifestro quest* (1983)
3 *Cavern of doom* (1983)
4 *Conquest of Quendor* (1984)
Companion volumes: *The Zork chronicles*, by George Alec Effinger, 1990, *The lost city of Zork*, by Robin Wayne Bailey, 1991

Zorro series
This sequence has four authors
McCulley, Johnston
1 *Mark of Zorro* (1924)
2 *Further adventures of Zorro* (1926)
Verral, Charles Spain
3 *Zorro* (1958)
4 *Zorro and the secret plan* (1959)
Dean, Les
5 *Zorro, the gay blade* (1981)
Arneson, Don Jon
6 *Zorro and the pirate raiders* (1986)
7 *Zorro rides again* (1986)
Companion volumes: *Walt Disney's Zorro*, by Steve Frazee, 1958, *Zorro in old California*, by Nedaud and Marcello, 1986, *Zorro, the classic adventures*, 2 volumes, 1988

Zouga Ballantyne series
Smith, Wilbur Addison
1 *Falcon flies* (1980)
Flight of the falcon
2 *Men of men* (1981)
3 *Angels weep* (1982)

Zozo series
This sequence has two authors; American edition with the character Curious George is listed separately
Rey, Hans Augusto
1 *Zozo* (1942)
2 *Zozo takes a job* (1954)
3 *Zozo rides a bike* (1954)
4 *Zozo gets a medal* (1958)
Rey, Margret
5 *Zozo flies a kite* (1961)
Illustrated by Hans Augusto Rey
Rey, Hans Augusto
6 *Zozo learns the alphabet* (1964)
Rey, Margret
7 *Zozo goes to the hospital* (1967)
Illustrated by Hans Augusto Rey

Zuckerman series
Roth, Philip
see **Natan Zuckrman series**

Zulu series
Haggard, Henry Rider
1 *Nada the lily* (1892)
2 *Marie* (1912)
3 *Child of storm* (1913)
4 *Finished* (1917)

Zulu series
Mirsky, Reba Paeff
1 *Thirty-one brothers and sisters* (1952)
2 *Seven grandmothers* (1955)

TITLE INDEX

A

A
Zukofsky, Louis
A series (4)
A.B.C. investigates
Ephesian
A B C Hawkes series (2)
A B C of Babar
Brunhoff, Jean de
Babar series (4)
A.B.C. solves five
Ephesian
A B C Hawkes series (3)
A.B.C.'s test case
Ephesian
A B C Hawkes series (1)
A for Andromeda
Hoyle, Fred
Andromeda series (1)
A is for alibi
Grafton, Sue
Kinsey Millhone series (1)
A.J.Wentworth, B.A., retd.
Ellis, Humphry Francis
A.J.Wentworth series (2)
A, my name is Ami
Mazer, Norma Fox
My name series (1)
A 1-12
Zukofsky, Louis
A series (1)
A.P.B.
Pedneau, Dave
Whit Pynchon and Annie Tyson-Tyree series (1)
A.R.P. murder
Scott, Sutherland
Doctor Septimus Dodds series (5)
A.R.P. mystery
Perowne, Barry
Raffles series (11)
A-Team
Heath, Charles
A-Team series (1)
A 13-21
Zukofsky, Louis
A series (2)
A 22-23
Zukofsky, Louis
A series (3)
A 24
Zukofsky, Louis
A series (4)
Aardvark affair
Brandner, Gary
Big Brain series (1)
Aaron in the wildwoods
Harris, Joel Chandler
Aaron series (2)
Abandon and destroy
Macdonnell, James Edmond
Dutchy Holland series (1)
Abandon galaxy!
Somers, Bart
Commander Craig series (2)
Abandon ship
Macdonnell, James Edmond
Captain Peter Bentley series (25)
Abandoned
Verne, Jules
Captain Grant's children series (2)
Captain Nemo series (2)
Abandoned car crime
Evans, Gwyn
Sexton Blake series (659)
Abandoning an adopted farm
Sanborn, Katherine Abbott
Abandoned farm series (2)
Abbatical crosier
Sue, Eugene
Mysteries of the people series (8)
Abbe Mouret's sin
Zola, Emile
Rougon Macquart series (5)
Abbe Mouret's transgression
Zola, Emile
Rougon Macquart series (5)
Abbe Pierre
Hudson, Jay William
Abbe Pierre series (1)
Abbe Pierre and the ragpickers
Simon, Boris
Ragpickers series (1)
Abbe Pierre's people
Hudson, Jay William
Abbe Pierre series (2)
Abbe's temptation
Zola, Emile
Rougon Macquart series (5)
Abbey champion
Oxenham, Elsie J
Abbey girls second generation series (4)
Abbey Court murder
Haynes, Annie
Inspector Furnival series (1)
Abbey girls
Oxenham, Elsie J
Abbey girls first generation series (2)
Abbey girls again
Oxenham, Elsie J
Abbey girls first generation series (6)
Abbey girls at home
Oxenham, Elsie J
Abbey girls first generation series (12)
Abbey girls go back to school
Oxenham, Elsie J
Abbey girls first generation series (4)
Abbey girls in town
Oxenham, Elsie J
Abbey girls first generation series (7)
Abbey girls on trial
Oxenham, Elsie J
Abbey girls first generation series (14)
Abbey girls play up
Oxenham, Elsie J
Abbey girls first generation series (13)
Abbey girls win through
Oxenham, Elsie J
Abbey girls first generation series (10)
Abbey makes the grade
Leyland, Eric
Abbey series (5)
Abbey of Kilkhampton
Croft, Herbert
Abbey of Kilkhampton series (1)
Abbey on the warpath
Leyland, Eric
Abbey series (3)
Abbey School
Oxenham, Elsie J
Abbey girls first generation series (11)
Abbey sees it through
Leyland, Eric
Abbey series (1)
Abbey turns the tables
Leyland, Eric
Abbey series (4)
Abbie
Chandos, Dane
Abbie series (1)
Abbie an' Slats
Capp, Al
Abbie an' Slats series (1)
Abbie an' Slats 2
Capp, Al
Abbie an' Slats series (2)
Abbie and Arthur
Chandos, Dane
Abbie series (2)
Abbie in love
Corcoran, Barbara
Abigail trilogy (2)
Abbot
Scott, Walter
Mary, Queen of Scots series (2)
Abby is missing
Woolfolk, Dorothy
Donna Rockford series (4)
ABC affair
Winston, Peter
Adjusters series (2)
ABC murders
Christie, Agatha
Hercule Poirot series (12)
ABC of ESP
Pluis, Bridget
Psychic series (1)
ABC of flower fairies
Barker, Cicely Mary
Flower fairies series (8)
ABC with Noddy
Blyton, Enid
Noddy picture books series (12)
Abdallah and the donkey
Dombrowski, Katrina
Abdallah series (1)
Abdication
Candler, Edmund
Siri Ram series (2)
Abducted
Stahl, Hilda
Amber Ainslie series (2)
Abduction
Bischoff, David
UFO conspiracy series (1)
Taylor, Frank
Uninvited trilogy (3)
Abductors
Reid, Desmond
Sexton Blake series (1606)
Abe and Mawruss
Glass, Montague
Potash series (2)
Abe Martin almanack
Hubbard, Kin
Abe Martin series (21)
Abe Martin, hoss sense and nonsense
Hubbard, Kin
Abe Martin series (17)
Abe Martin, joker on facts
Hubbard, Kin
Abe Martin series (12)
Abe Martin of Brown County
Hubbard, Kin
Abe Martin series (1)
Abe Martin on the the War and other things
Hubbard, Kin
Abe Martin series (10)
Abe Martin on things in general
Hubbard, Kin
Abe Martin series (16)
Abe Martin primer
Hubbard, Kin
Abe Martin series (5)
Abe Martin's back country sayings
Hubbard, Kin
Abe Martin series (9)
Abe Martin's barbed wire
Hubbard, Kin
Abe Martin series (19)
Abe martin's broadcast
Hubbard, Kin
Abe Martin series (21)
Abe Martin's home cured philosophy
Hubbard, Kin
Abe Martin series (11)
Abe Martin's sayings and sketches
Hubbard, Kin
Abe Martin series (7)
Abe Martin's town pump
Hubbard, Kin
Abe Martin series (20)
Abe Martin's wise cracks
Hubbard, Kin
Abe Martin series (18)
Abel coincidence
Chance, John Newton
Jonathan Blake series (13)
Abeline ambush
Sharpe, Jon
Trailsman series (144)
Abeng
Cliff, Michelle
Clare Savage series (1)
Aberdeen conundrum
Ross, Angus
Mark Farrow series (10)
Abert and Kaibab
Reese, Bob
Grand Canyon series (1)
Abigail
Corcoran, Barbara
Abigail trilogy (1)
Macdonald, Malcolm
Stevenson family series (4)
Abigail and the bushranger
Cox, David
Abigail series (1)
Abigail and the rainmaker
Cox, David
Abigail series (2)
Abilene
Mitchum, Hank
Stage coach station series (10)
Abilene or bust
Gulick, Bill
Junior Trail Blazers series (1)
Abilene tight spot
Hunter, E J
White Squaw series (7)
Abington Abbey
Marshall, Archibald
Abington series (1)
Able McLaughlins
Wilson, Margaret
McLaughlin family series (1)
Abner Daniel
Harben, William Nathaniel
Georgians series (1)
Abner in the orphanage, atrange girl in the swamp
Capp, Al
Li'l Abner dailies series (4)
Abode of life
Correy, Lee
Star trek series (6)
Abolition of death
Anderson, James
Mikael Petros series (2)
Abolitionist legacy
McPherson, James Munro
Abolitionist series (2)
Abominable goat
Lister, Stephen
Sainte Monique series (16)
Abominable history of the man with copper fingers
Sayers, Dorothy Leigh
Lord Peter Wimsey series (16)
Abominable man
Sjowall, Maj
Inspector Martin Beck series (7)
Abominable snowman
Montgomery, Raymond A
Choose your own adventure series (13)
Abomination
Janson, Hank
Hank Janson series (196)
McGill, Gordon
Omen series (5)
About a marriage
Gordon, Giles
Edward series (1)
About Barney
Casserley, Anne
Barney series (1)
About belonging
Cone, Molly
Shema series (2)
About Catherine de Medici
Balzac, Honore de
Philosophic studies series (16)
About change and moving
Berry, Joy
Good answers to tough questions series (2)
About death
Berry, Joy
Good answers to tough questions series (3)
About divorce
Berry, Joy
Good answers to tough questions series (4)
About face
Kane, Frank
Johnny Liddell series (1)
About God
Cone, Molly
Shema series (4)
About Japhet and the rest of the Noah family
Horrabin, James Francis
Noah family series (7)
About learning
Cone, Molly
Shema series (3)
About my father's business
Beckwith, Lillian
Hebrides series (1)
About Peggy Saville
Vaizey, Jessie Bell
Peggy Saville series (1)
About physical disabilities
Berry, Joy
Good answers to tough questions series (5)
About substance abuse
Berry, Joy
Good answers to tough questions series (6)
About Teddy Robinson
Robinson, Joan Gale
Teddy Robinson series (1)
About the murder of a man afraid of women
Abbot, Anthony
Thatcher Colt series (6)
About the murder of a startled lady
Abbot, Anthony
Thatcher Colt series (5)
About the murder of Geraldine Foster
Abbot, Anthony
Thatcher Colt series (1)
About the murder of the circus queen
Abbot, Anthony
Thatcher Colt series (4)
About the murder of the clergyman's mistress
Abbot, Anthony
Thatcher Colt series (2)
About the murder of the night club lady
Abbot, Anthony
Thatcher Colt series (3)
About this village
Douglas, Peter
Norfolk village series (2)
About your heart
Simon, Seymour
Let's try it out series (5)
About yourself
Montgomery, Elizabeth
Dick, Jane and Sally series (15)
Above and below
Palmer, John
Guy Plante and Freya Matthews series (1)
Above the bright blue sky
Springs, Elliott White
War birds trilogy (2)
Abra-cadaver
Monig, Christopher
Brian Brett series (2)
Abracadaver
Lovesey, Peter
Sergeant Cribb and Constable Thackeray series (3)
McInerny, Ralph
Father Roger Dowling series (12)
Abraham
Daniel, Rebecca
Our greatest heritage series (3)
Abrar's holiday
Fletcher, Audrey
Allsorts series (2)
Abrego Canyon
Wisler, Gary Clifton
Willie Delamer series (5)
Absalom, Absalom!
Faulkner, William
Listener series (2)
Sin and salvation series (6)
Absolute beginners
MacInnes, Colin
Visions of London series (2)
Absolute Elizabeth
Dessau, Joanna
Elizabeth I trilogy (2)
Absolute hero
Humphreys, Emyr
Amy Parry series (4)
Absolute truths
Howatch, Susan
Church of England series (6)
Absolute zero
Cresswell, Helen
Bagthorpes series (2)
Absurd convictions, modest hopes
Berrigan, Daniel
Conversations series (2)
Abu Ali
Van Woerkom, Dorothy
Abu Ali series (1)
Abu Wahab caper
Spencer, Ross Harrison
Chance Purdue series (4)
Abuse and neglect
Berry, Joy
Danger zones series (1)
Abuse of justice
Parker, Roger
Inspector Taff Roberts series (2)
Abyss of light
O'Neal, Kathleen M
Powers of light series (1)
Abyssinian mystery
Chester, Gilbert
Sexton Blake series (839)
Academic question
Smithies, Richard Hugo Ripman
Inspector William McAlpin series (1)
Academic year
Enright, Dennis Joseph
Packet series (1)
Academy of terror
Charles, Steven
Private school series (2)
Acadians
Wall, Robert Emmet
Nowell family series (7)
Accent on murder
Lockridge, Frances
Inspector Merton Heimrich series (13)
Richards, Francis
Inspector Merton Heimrich series (13)
Acceptable time
L'Engle, Madeleine
Meg Murry series (5)
Acceptance
Richards, Vicki
Star trek fan series (21)

Acceptance and rejection
Burke, Kenneth
Attitudes towards history series (1)
Acceptance world
Powell, Anthony
Dance to the music of time series (3)
Accessory after
Vivian, Evelyn Charles
Inspector Head series (2)
Accessory after the fact
Thayer, Lee
Peter Clancy series (35)
Accessory to murder
Barrington, Pamela
Inspector Henderson series (1)
Accident
Wiesel, Elie
Night trilogy (3)
Accident by design
Lorac, E C R
Inspector Macdonald series (34)
Accident call
Harrison, Elizabeth
Central London Hospital series (5)
Accident for Inspector West
Creasey, John
Inspector Roger West series (21)
Accident, manslaughter or murder?
Thayer, Lee
Peter Clancy series (39)
Accident or murder?
Carter, Nicholas
Nicholas Carter series (197)
Accident prone
Penn, John
Inspector George Thorne and Sergeant Bill Abbot series (8)
Accidental deaths
Gough, Laurence
Willows and Parker series (6)
Accidental murder
Gregg, Cecil Freeman
Inspector Cuthbert Higgins series (30)
Accidental password
Carter, Nicholas
Nicholas Carter series (20)
Accidentally in transit
Laurence, Murray
Compulsive traveller series (2)
Accidents do happen
Burton, Miles
Inspector Arnold and Desmond Merrion series (32)
Accolade
Sidgwick, Ethel
Ashwin trilogy (3)
According to Jake and the Kid
Mitchell, William Ormond
Jake and the Kid series (2)
According to Jennings
Buckeridge, Anthony
Jennings series (6)
According to Maria
Lane, Anna
Maria trilogy (1)
According to plan
Jackson, Lewis
Sexton Blake series (1186)
Seton, Graham
Colonel Duncan Grant series (5)
According to Saint John
Babula, William
Saint John series (2)
According to the evidence
Cecil, Henry
Ambrose Low series (2)
Colonel Brain series (3)
Daniken, Erich von
Unsolved mysteries series (6)
Account of the state of learning in the Empire of Lilliput
Arbuthnot, John
Lilliput series (4)
Account rendered
Barrington, Pamela
Inspector George Marshall series (2)
Wentworth, Patricia
Inspector Ernest Lamb series (2)
Miss Maud Silver series (4)
Accounting for murder
Lathen, Emma
John Putnam Thatcher series (3)
Accuse the Toff
Creasey, John
Toff series (10)
Accused
Janson, Hank
Hank Janson series (36)
Ace in the hole
Curry, Gene
Jim Saddler series (6)
Martin, George Raymond Richard
Wild cards series (6)
Masters, Zeke
Faro Blake series (8)
Ace of Cads, and other stories
Arlen, Michael
Charming people series (2)
Ace of danger
Grex, Leo
Paul Irving series (7)
Ace of Diamonds
Schorr, Mark
Red Diamond series (2)
Ace of Knaves
Charteris, Leslie
Saint series (17)
Ace of shadows
Lancer, Jack
Christopher Cool series (4)
Ace of Spades
Shannon, Dell
Lieutenant Luis Mendoza series (2)
Ace of Spades murder
Keeler, Harry Stephen
Angus Macwhorter series (2)
Ace of spies
Von Elsner, Don
Jake Winkman series (2)
Ace up my sleeve
Chase, James Hadley
Helga Rolfe series (1)
Aces abroad
Martin, George Raymond Richard
Wild cards series (4)
Aces, eights and murder
Heberden, Mary Violet
Desmond Shannon series (5)
Aces high
Hooper, Kay
Hagen series (11)
Martin, George Raymond Richard
Wild cards series (2)
Aces of the White Death
Hogan, Robert Jasper
G-Eight series (2)
Aces wild
Clay, E Jefferson
Duke Benedict and Hank Brazos series (4)
Aces Wilde
Bridges, Ben
Wilde boys series (4)
Achievement
Thurston, Ernest Temple
Richard Furlong series (3)
Achievement of Richard Furlong
Thurston, Ernest Temple
Richard Furlong series (3)
Achievement of William Cargoe
Peacey, Seton
William Cargoe series (1)
Achievements of John Carruthers
Cox, Edmund Charles
John Carruthers series (2)
Achilles affair
Mather, Berkely
Peter Feltham series (1)
Achilles and Diana
Bates, Herbert Ernest
Achilles series (2)
Achilles and the twins
Bates, Herbert Ernest
Achilles series (3)
Achilles the donkey
Bates, Herbert Ernest
Achilles series (1)
Achon!
Gordon, Stuart
Watchers trilogy (1)
Achtung, Normandy!
Eckhardt, Kurt
Heroes series (4)
Acid
Imbert-Terry, Henry
Detective Inspector Du Cas series (1)
Acid rain
Snodgrass, Mary Ellen
Environmental awareness series (1)
Acid rock
Murphy, Warren Burton
Destroyer series (13)
Acid test
Lewis, Colin
Howard Hayes trilogy (2)
Acolytes of darkness
Dille, Flint
Agent thirteen series (3)
Aconite murders
Williams, Sidney
Jabez Twombley series (2)
Acquaintances
Toynbee, Arnold Joseph
Acquaintances series (1)
Acquainted with murder
Hurt, Freda Mary
Inspector Herbert Broom series (4)
Acquittal
Wainwright, John
Northern Police series (30)
Across a starlit sea
Brandewyne, Rebecca
Highclyffe Hall series (2)
Across captive seas
Du Barry, Michele
Angela Carlyle series (2)
Across India
Optic, Oliver
All-over-the-world series (9)
Across realtime
Vinge, Vernor
Realtime series (2)
Across Spoon River
Masters, Edgar Lee
Spoon River series (2)
Across Texas
Ellis, Edward Sylvester
Wild woods series (3)
Across the barricades
Lingard, Joan
Sadie and Kevin series (2)
Across the bitter sea
Dillon, Eilis
Bitter sea series (1)
Across the black waters
Anand, Mulk Raj
Lal Singh trilogy (2)
Across the continent with Paul and Peggy
Scott, Florence E
Paul and Peggy series (2)
Across the dark metropolis
De Larrabeiti, Michael
Borribles series (3)
Across the divide
Murray, Andrew
Sexton Blake series (89)
Across the far mountain
Hancock, Niel
Wilderness of four series (1)
Across the High Sierras
Mills, Robert E
Davy Watson series (2)
Across the Pacific
Dixon, Franklin W
Ted Scott flying series (7)
Across the rio Grande
Logan, Jake
John Slocum series (4)
Across the sea of suns
Benford, Gregory
Ocean series (2)
Across the Thlassa Mey
McCarty, Dennis
Thlassa Mey series (4)
Across the top of the world
Adams, Eustace Lane
Andy Lane series (11)
Across the wide Missouri
De Voto, Bernard
American West trilogy (2)
Act of anger
Spicer, Bart
Benson Kellogg series (1)
Act of fear
Collins, Michael
Dan Fortune series (1)
Act of God
Healy, Jeremiah
John Francis Cuddy series (9)
Kotani, Eric
Act of God trilogy (1)
Act of outrage
Hart, Alison
Girls in trouble series (3)
Act of providence
Brennan, Joseph Payne
Lucius Leffing series (3)
Act of silence
Graham, Anthony
Eric Marsden series (1)
Act of terror
Foxall, Peter Augustus
Catford Police series (2)
Act of violence
Saxon, Peter
Sexton Blake series (1432)
Act of war
Callison, Brian
Brevet Cable series (2)
Acting up
Sarasin, Jennifer
Cheerleaders series (37)
Action and passion
Wren, Percival Christopher
Sinbad Dysart series (1)
Action at Arcanum
Macdonald, William Colt
Gregory Quist series (9)
Action at Truxton
Arthur, Burt
Johnny Canavan series (6)
Action Atlantic
Gray, Edwyn
U-boat series (2)
Action, Division Three
Mahr, Kurt
Perry Rhodan series (94)
Action for the Picaroon
Cassells, John
Ludovic Saxon series (20)
Action in the sky
Whitehouse, Arch
Air war series (5)
Action stations
Bartimeus
Naval occasions series (8)
Actor
Hall, Parnell
Stanley Hastings series (8)
Actor's life for me
Pertwee, Roland
Patrick Faraday series (3)
Actor's secret
Hill, Harry Egbert
Sexton Blake series (283)
Actress abroad
Balzac, Honore de
Scenes of provincial life series (5)
Acts of black night
Knight, Kathleen Moore
Elisha Macomber series (6)
Acts of homicide
Davis, Kenn
Carver Bascombe series (8)
Ad for murder
Penn, John
Inspector George Thorne and Sergeant Bill Abbot series (1)
Adam and Caroline
O'Riordan, Conal
Anglo-Irish relations series (8)
Adam and Eve
Daniel, Rebecca
Our greatest heritage series (1)
Adam and evil
Kane, Martin
Martin Kane series (15)
Adam and Rosie and the strange planet
Thwaites, Lyndsay
Super Adam and Rosie Wonder series (4)
Adam and Rosie run away
Thwaites, Lyndsay
Super Adam and Rosie Wonder series (3)
Adam and the F.A. Cup
Sibley, Kathleen
Adam trilogy (2)
Adam and the football
Sibley, Kathleen
Adam trilogy (1)
Adam and the football mystery
Sibley, Kathleen
Adam trilogy (3)
Adam and the serpent
Fisher, Vardis
Testament of man series (4)
Adam Avocado
Reed, Giles
Munch Bunch character series (9)
Adam in ochre
Simpson, Colin
Adam series (1)
Adam in plumes
Simpson, Colin
Adam series (3)
Adam Link in the past
Binder, Eando
Adam Link series (1)
Adam Link, robot
Binder, Eando
Adam Link series (2)
Adam Macadam, naval cadet
Duff, Douglas Valder
Adam Macadam series (12)
Adam Mouse's book of poems
Moore, Lilian
Cucumbers trilogy (3)
Adam of Dublin
O'Riordan, Conal
Anglo-Irish relations series (7)
Adam Square
Stewart, Marjorie
Adam Square series (1)
Adam was a ploughman
Warren, Clarence Henry
Happy countryman series (5)
Adam with arrows
Simpson, Colin
Adam series (2)
Adam's balm
Martin, Bill
Freedom series (1)
Adam's case
Underwood, Michael
Superintendent Simon Manton series (9)
Adam's Eden
Baldwin, Faith
Little Oxford series (7)
Adam's fall
Ridgway, Jason
Brian Guy series (1)
Adam's rest
Millin, Sarah Gertrude
Dark river series (3)
Addams chronicles
Cox, Stephen
Addams family series (3)
Addams family
Calmenson, Stephanie
Addams family series (3)
Faucher, Elizabeth
Addams family series (3)
Sharkey, Jack
Addams family series (1)
Addams family revealed
Van Hise, James
Addams family series (3)
Addams family strikes back
Miksch, William
Addams family series (2)
Adder's brood
Carter, Nicholas
Nicholas Carter series (615)
Adders on the heath
Mitchell, Gladys
Dame Beatrice Bradley series (36)
Addie across the prairie
Lawlor, Laurie
Addie series (1)
Addie and the King of Hearts
Rock, Gail
Addie series (3)
Addie's Dakota winter
Lawlor, Laurie
Addie series (2)
Addy learns a lesson
Porter, Connie
Addy series (2)
Addy's surprise
Porter, Connie
Addy series (3)
Adela Doring at boarding-school
North, Grace May
Adele Doring series (3)
Adelaide, the enchantress
Hooper, Kay
Delaneys of Killaroo trilogy (1)
Adele and Company
Yates, Dornford
Berry series (6)
Jonah Mansel series (5)
Adele Doring at Vineyard Valley
North, Grace May
Adele Doring series (5)
Adele Doring in camp
North, Grace May
Adele Doring series (4)
Adele Doring of the Sunnyside Club
North, Grace May
Adele Doring series (1)
Adele Doring on a ranch
North, Grace May
Adele Doring series (2)
Adeline
Dickinson, Margaret
Abbeyford trilogy (2)
Adept
Kurtz, Katherine
Adept trilogy (1)
Adieu
Balzac, Honore de
Philosophic studies series (9)
Adios, Bandido
Clay, E Jefferson
Duke Benedict and Hank Brazos series (3)
Adjusters
Valentine
Daphne Wrayne and her Four Adjusters series (1)

Adventures of Billy Mink
Burgess, Thornton Waldo
Smiling Pool series (1)
Adventures of Billy Topsail
Duncan, Norman
Doctor Luke series (2)
Adventures of Bindle
Jenkins, Herbert
Bindle series (3)
Adventures of Blackshirt
Graeme, Bruce
Blackshirt series (3)
Adventures of Bob White
Burgess, Thornton Waldo
Bedtime story-books series (19)
Adventures of Bobby Coon
Burgess, Thornton Waldo
Bedtime story-books series (17)
Adventures of Bobby Orde
White, Stewart Edward
Orde family series (4)
Adventures of Brer Rabbit
Lester, Julius
Tales of Uncle Remus series (1)
Adventures of Bunny Buffin
Buckels, Alex
Bunny Buffin series (2)
Adventures of Buster Bear
Burgess, Thornton Waldo
Bedtime story-books series (11)
Adventures of Buster Hood
Korman, Justine
Tiny Toon's adventures series (3)
Adventures of Captain Al Scabbard, no 1
Crabb, Lawrence James
Captain Al Scabbard series (1)
Adventures of Captain Al Scabbard, no 2
Crabb, Lawrence James
Captain Al Scabbard series (2)
Adventures of Captain Cattle
Hyne, Charles John Cutcliffe
Captain Owen Kettle series (3)
Adventures of Captain Hatteras
Verne, Jules
Adventures of Captain Hatteras series (2)
Adventures of Captain Horn
Stockton, Frank Richard
Captain Horn series (1)
Adventures of Catkin and Codlin
Gilmore, David Hunter
Christopher Cricket series (4)
Adventures of Catkin and Codlin, Christopher Cricket and Benjamin Bumble
Gilmore, David Hunter
Christopher Cricket series (6)
Adventures of Charlotte Holmes
Bailey, Hilary
Sherlock Holmes sequels series (99)
Adventures of Chatterer the red squirrel
Burgess, Thornton Waldo
Bedtime story-books series (9)
Adventures of Chicken Little Jane
Ritchie, Lily Munsel
Chicken Little Jane series (3)
Adventures of Chunky
Berg, Leila
Chunky series (1)
Adventures of Cname Sname and the Wattle Fairy
Manners, Carol
Cname Sname series (1)
Adventures of Colonel Sellers
Twain, Mark
Colonel Sellers series (1)
Adventures of Crawfish-Man
Edler, Timothy J
Crawfish-Man series (1)
Adventures of Danny Meadow Mouse
Burgess, Thornton Waldo
Bedtime story-books series (7)
Adventures of David Vane and David Crane
Trowbridge, John Townsend
Start in life series (3)
Adventures of Desmond the dinosaur
Althea
Desmond the dinosaur series (13)
Adventures of Doctor Thorndyke
Freeman, Richard Austin
Doctor John Evelyn Thorndyke series (4)
Adventures of Doctor Who
Dicks, Terrance
Doctor Who series (22)
Adventures of Don Quixote de la Mancha
Cervantes Saavedra, Miguel de
Don Quixote series (1)
Adventures of Dougal
Thompson, Eric
Dougal series (1)
Adventures of Drowsy the Drone
Gilmore, David Hunter
Christopher Cricket series (1)
Adventures of Elizabeth Ann
Lawrence, Josephine
Elizabeth Ann series (1)
Adventures of Elizabeth in Rugen
Russell, Mary Annette
Elizabeth series (5)
Adventures of Ellery Queen
Queen, Ellery
Ellery Queen series (8)
Adventures of Ephraim Tutt
Train, Arthur
Ephraim Tutt series (7)
Adventures of Ernest in Africa
Libenzi, Ermanno
Ernest series (1)
Adventures of felix Boyd
Campbell, Scott
Felix Boyd series (4)
Adventures of Ferryman's Creek
Frow, Gerald
Young Sherlock Holmes series (2)
Adventures of Fingerling
Laan, Dick
Fingerling series (4)
Adventures of Galldora
Sedgwick, Modwena
Galldora series (1)
Adventures of Gerard
Doyle, Arthur Conan
Brigadier Gerard series (2)
Adventures of Ginger Meggs
Bancks, James Charles
Ginger Meggs series (1)
Adventures of good comrade Schweik
Putz, Helmut
Schweik series (3)
Adventures of Grandfather Frog
Burgess, Thornton Waldo
Bedtime story-books series (8)
Adventures of Hadrian the hedgehog
Lycett-Green, Candida
Hadrian series (1)
Adventures of Hajji Baba of Ispahan
Morier, James
Hajji Baba series (1)
Adventures of Harrison Keith, detective
Carter, Nicholas
Harrison Keith series (50)
Nicholas Carter series (34)
Adventures of Henrietta Hen
Judah, Aaron
Henrietta Hen series (1)
Adventures of Herlock Sholmes
Hamilton, Charles
Sherlock Holmes series (10)
Adventures of Hiram Holliday
Gallico, Paul
Hiram Holliday series (1)
Adventures of Huckleberry Finn
Dwiggins, Clare
Huckleberry Finn series (1)
Tom Sawyer series (2)
Twain, Mark
Huckleberry Finn series (1)
Tom Sawyer series (2)
Adventures of Inspector Lestrade
Trow, Meirion James
Inspector Sholto Lestrade series (4)
Adventures of Jack Ninepins
Averill, Esther
Jenny Linsky series (2)
Adventures of Jane
Stone, Gene
Jane series (2)
Adventures of Jed McLane
Honig, Donald
Jed McLane series (1)
Adventures of Jerry Muskrat
Burgess, Thornton Waldo
Bedtime story-books series (6)
Adventures of Jerry Muskrat at home
Burgess, Thornton Waldo
Smiling Pool series (3)
Adventures of Jimmie Dale
Packard, Frank Lucius
Jimmie Dale series (1)
Adventures of Jimmy Brown
Alden, William Livingston
Jimmy Brown series (1)
Adventures of Jimmy Skunk
Burgess, Thornton Waldo
Bedtime story-books series (18)
Adventures of Joel Pepper
Sidney, Margaret
Five Little Peppers series (6)
Adventures of John and Mary
James, Grace
John and Mary series (12)
Adventures of Johnny Chuck
Burgess, Thornton Waldo
Bedtime story-books series (2)
Adventures of Johnny May
Branscum, Robbie
Johnny May series (2)
Adventures of Jonny Briggs
Eadington, Joan
Jonny Briggs series (3)
Adventures of Judith Lee
Marsh, Richard
Judith Lee series (2)
Adventures of Jules de Grandin
Quinn, Seabury
Jules de Grandin series (2)
Adventures of King Rollo
McKee, David
King Rollo series (5)
Adventures of Lady Susan
Brady, Cyrus Townsend
Lady Susan series (2)
Adventures of Lester
Blake, Quentin
Lester series (2)
Adventures of Lieut. Lawless, R.N.
Bennett, Rolf
Commander Lawless series (1)
Adventures of Little Black Nickum
Robertson, Jean
Little Black Nickum series (1)
Adventures of little Fuzzy
Piper, Horace Beam
Fuzzy series (1)
Adventures of Little Joe Otter
Burgess, Thornton Waldo
Smiling Pool series (2)
Adventures of Littlenose
Grant, John
Littlenose series (3)
Adventures of Long John Silver
Judd, Denis
Long John Silver series (2)
Adventures of Longlegs the heron
Burgess, Thornton Waldo
Smiling Pool series (4)
Adventures of Lucius Leffing
Brennan, Joseph Payne
Lucius Leffing series (4)
Adventures of Margery Pym
Miller, Rosalind
Pym family series (1)
Adventures of Marmaduke the possum
O'Harris, Pixie
Marmaduke series (1)
Adventures of Martin Hewitt
Morrison, Arthur
Martin Hewitt series (3)
Adventures of Maud Noakes
Neame, Alan
Maud Noakes series (1)
Adventures of miss Gregory
Gibbon, Percival
Miss Gregory series (1)
Adventures of Mister Hero
Leigh, Roberta
Mister Hero series (1)
Adventures of Mister Mocker
Burgess, Thornton Waldo
Bedtime story-books series (5)
Adventures of Mister Pink-Whistle
Blyton, Enid
Mister Pink-Whistle series (1)
Adventures of Mister Verdant Green, an Oxford freshman
Bede, Cuthbert
Mister Verdant Green series (1)
Adventures of Mole and Troll
Johnston, Tony
Mole and Troll series (1)
Adventures of Mother West Wind's animal friends
Burgess, Thornton Waldo
Old Mother West Wind series (3)
Adventures of Mother West Wind's children
Burgess, Thornton Waldo
Old Mother West Wind series (2)
Adventures of Mother West Wind's neighbours
Burgess, Thornton Waldo
Old Mother West Wind series (4)
Adventures of Mrs May
Le Breton, Thomas
Mrs May series (5)
Adventures of Nicholas and the gang
Goscinny, Rene
Nicholas series (3)
Adventures of no ordinary rabbit
Uttley, Alison
Timothy Rabbit series (1)
Adventures of Obadiah
Turkle, Brinton
Obadiah series (3)
Adventures of Odd and Elsewhere
Roose-Evans, James
Odd and Elsewhere series (1)
Adventures of Odysseus
Blyton, Enid
Stories from world history series (2)
Adventures of Ol' Mistah Buzzard
Burgess, Thornton Waldo
Bedtime story-books series (20)
Adventures of Old Man Coyote
Burgess, Thornton Waldo
Bedtime story-books series (14)
Adventures of Old Mother West Wind
Burgess, Thornton Waldo
Old Mother West Wind series (1)
Adventures of Old Mr Toad
Burgess, Thornton Waldo
Bedtime story-books series (12)
Adventures of Paddington
Bond, Michael
Paddington series (2)
Adventures of Paddy Pork
Goodall, John Strickland
Paddy Pork series (1)
Adventures of Paddy the beaver
Burgess, Thornton Waldo
Bedtime story-books series (15)
Adventures of Peregrine Pickle
Smollett, Tobias
Morgan the Welshman series (2)
Adventures of Perrine
Malot, Hector
Remi and Perrine series (2)
Adventures of Peter and Lotta
Beskow, Elsa
Peter and Lotta series (3)
Adventures of Peter and Tim
Brown, T Burton
Peter and Tim series (1)
Adventures of Peter Cottontail
Burgess, Thornton Waldo
Bedtime story-books series (3)
Adventures of Peter Possum and his friends
Hibberd, Jean
Peter Possum series (1)
Adventures of Philip on his way through the world
Thackeray, William Makepeace
Arthur Pendennis series (3)
Adventures of Picklock Holes
Lehmann, Rudolf Chambers
Picklock Holes series (1)
Adventures of Pinkie
Ruff, Agnes
Pinkie series (1)
Adventures of Pinocchio
Collodi, Carlo
Pinocchio series (1)
Pinocchio series (2)
Adventures of Pip
Blyton, Enid
Pip series (1)
Adventures of Plum Tucker
Mendel, Jo
Tucker family series (3)
Adventures of Polly and the wolf
Storr, Catherine
Polly and the wolf series (4)
Adventures of poor Mrs Quack
Burgess, Thornton Waldo
Bedtime story-books series (16)
Adventures of Prickly Porky
Burgess, Thornton Waldo
Bedtime story-books series (13)
Adventures of Race Williams
Daly, Carroll John
Race Williams series (9)
Adventures of Reddy Fox
Burgess, Thornton Waldo
Bedtime story-books series (1)
Adventures of Remi
Malot, Hector
Remi and Perrine series (1)
Adventures of Roderick Random
Smollett, Tobias
Morgan the Welshman series (1)
Adventures of Romney Pringle
Ashdown, Clifford
Romney Pringle series (1)
Adventures of Roobarb when there was a TV show
Calveley, Grange
Roobarb series (3)
Adventures of Rosa
Barratt, Isabel
Rosa series (1)
Adventures of Rupert the Little Lost Bear
Tourtel, Mary
Rupert Bear series (1)
Adventures of Sabo
Lewis, E W
Sabo series (1)
Adventures of Sam Pig
Uttley, Alison
Sam Pig series (1)
Adventures of Sam Spade, and other stories
Hammett, Dashiell
Sam Spade series (2)
Adventures of Sammy Jay
Burgess, Thornton Waldo
Bedtime story-books series (10)
Adventures of Samurai Cat
Rogers, Mark Earl
Samurai Cat series (1)
Adventures of Satan Hall
Daly, Carroll John
Satan Hall series (3)
Adventures of Scamp
Blyton, Enid
Scamp series (1)
Pollock, Mary
Dog stories series (2)
Adventures of Scout Grey
Bellamy, Robert Lowe
Scout Grey series (1)
Adventures of Sherlock Holmes
Doyle, Arthur Conan
Sherlock Holmes sequels series (97)
Sherlock Holmes series (3)
Adventures of Sherlock Holmes' smarter brother
Pearlman, Gilbert
Sherlock Holmes sequels series (23)
Adventures of Signor McGlusky
Hales, Alfred Greenwood
McGlusky series (6)
Adventures of Silly Billy
Kitt, Tamara
Billy Brown series (1)
Adventures of Solar Pons
Derleth, August
Solar Pons series (1)
Adventures of Sylvia Scarlett
Mackenzie, Compton
Sinister Street series (4)
Sylvia Scarlett series (2)
Adventures of Tammy Troot
Derwent, Lavinia
Tammy Troot series (3)
Adventures of Tapiola
Nathan, Robert
Tapiola series (2)
Adventures of the Barnabys in America
Trollope, Frances
Widow Barnaby trilogy (3)
Adventures of the ectoplasmic man
Stashower, Daniel
Sherlock Holmes sequels series (80)
Adventures of the Gingerbread Man
Walker, Elizabeth
Gingerbread Man series (1)
Adventures of the Gumby Gang
Oldfield, Pamela
Gumby Gang series (1)
Adventures of the infallible Godahl
Anderson, Frederick Irving
Oliver Armiston series (1)
Adventures of the Little Blue Engine
Hourihane, Ursula
Little Blue Engine series (2)
Adventures of the little wooden horse
Williams, Ursula Moray
Gobbolino series (1)
Adventures of the muddle-headed wombat
Park, Ruth
Muddle-headed wombat series (4)
Adventures of the mustard jar
Suter, Jon Michael
Mustard jar series (1)
Adventures of the scarlet daffodil
Clewes, Dorothy
Hadley family series (1)
Adventures of the Scarlet Pimpernel
Orczy, Emmuska
Scarlet Pimpernel series (13)
Adventures of the So Hi
Beaton-Jones, Cynon
So Hi series (1)
Adventures of the stainless steel rat
Harrison, Harry
Jim Di Griz series (3)

Adventures of the wishing-chair
Blyton, Enid
Wishing-chair series (1)
Adventures of the wishing-chair, part 1
Blyton, Enid
Wishing-chair series (1)
Adventures of Tim Rabbit
Uttley, Alison
Timothy Rabbit series (2)
Adventures of Tinker and Tanker
Scarry, Richard
Tinker and Tanker series (3)
Adventures of Tintin
Herge
Tintin series (6)
Tintin series (9)
Adventures of Tom Sawyer
Twain, Mark
Tom Sawyer series (1)
Adventures of Tommy Tad and Polly Wog
Trick, Edgar Harold
Tommy Tad and Polly Wog series (1)
Adventures of Topsy and Tim
Adamson, Jean
Topsy and Tim series (98)
Adventures of Treehorn
Heide, Florence Parry
Treehorn series (2)
Adventures of Turkey
Harris, Ray
Turkey series (1)
Adventures of two Dutch dolls and a golliwogg
Upton, Bertha
Golliwogg series (1)
Adventures of Una Persson and Catherine Cornelius in the twentieth century
Moorcock, Michael
Catherine Cornelius series (2)
Jerry Cornelius series (7)
Una Persson series (2)
Adventures of Unc' Billy Possum
Burgess, Thornton Waldo
Bedtime story-books series (4)
Adventures of Walter
Pilgrim, Jane
Blackberry Farm series (9)
Adventures of Willis the pilot
Paul, Adrien
Swiss family Robinson series (2)
Adventures of Wim
Rhinehart, Luke
Wim series (2)
Adventures of Yak
Bisset, Donald
Yak series (5)
Adventures on the water
Hayes, Barbara
Town mouse and country mouse series (4)
Adventures on Willow Farm
Blyton, Enid
Willow Farm series (1)
Adventures with Marmaduke
Chapman, Elizabeth
Marmaduke series (4)
Adventures with the Buttonwoods
Beiler, Edna
Buttonwoods series (1)
Adventuress
Chesney, Marion
House for the season series (5)
Reeve, Arthur Benjamin
Craig Kennedy series (12)
Adventuring with Nomad
Ellison, Norman
Nomad series (5)
Adventurous Allens
Grove, Harriet Pyne
Adventurous Allens series (1)
Adventurous Allens afloat
Grove, Harriet Pyne
Adventurous Allens series (2)
Adventurous Allens find mystery
Grove, Harriet Pyne
Adventurous Allens series (3)
Adventurous Allens marooned
Grove, Harriet Pyne
Adventurous Allens series (4)
Adventurous Allens' treasure
Grove, Harriet Pyne
Adventurous Allens series (5)
Adventurous Four
Blyton, Enid
Adventurous Four series (1)
Adventurous Four again
Blyton, Enid
Adventurous Four series (2)
Adventurous Nine
Prime, Heather
Adventurous Nine series (1)
Adversary
May, Julian
Pliocene exile series (5)
Rhodes, Daniel
Guilhelm de Courdeval series (2)
Adverse report
Hammond, Gerald
Keith Calder series (12)
Simon Parbitter series (1)
Advertise for Treasure
Williams, David
Mark Treasure series (7)
Advertising
Birt, David
Something to sell series (2)
Advise and consent
Drury, Allen
Washington series (1)
Advocate
Deal, Borden
Bookman trilogy (2)
Aegean memories
Mackenzie, Compton
Memories series (4)
Aero Club mystery
Millward, Edward J
Inspector Gil Flicker series (2)
Aeroplane express
Ashton, Lamar
Aeroplane boys series (3)
Aerospace heritage of Long Island
Stoff, Joshua
Long Island aerospace series (1)
Aesop's fables retold in verse
Paxton, Tom
Aesop in verse series (1)
Aesthetic adventure
Gaunt, William
Victorian painting series (2)
Affacombe affair
Lemarchand, Elizabeth
Superintendent Tom Pollard series (2)
Affair
Snow, Charles Percy
Strangers and brothers series (8)
Affair at Barworld
Meynell, Laurence Walter
Hooky Hefferman series (19)
Affair at Cralla Voe
Shelynn, Jack
Sam Clayton trilogy (1)
Affair at Dead End
Chance, John Newton
Jonathan Blake series (1)
Affair at Flower Acres
Wells, Carolyn
Pennington Wise series (6)
Affair at Helen's Court
Carnac, Carol
Inspector Julian Rivers series (15)
Affair at Little Wokeham
Crofts, Freeman Wills
Inspector Joseph French series (24)
Affair at Lover's Leap
Dean, Robert George
Tony Hunter series (10)
Affair at Palm Springs
Knight, Clifford
Huntoon Rogers series (3)
Affair at Portstead Manor
Locke, Gladys Edson
Mercedes Quero series (1)
Affair at Sidi Brahim
Stuart, Brian
Knock-Out Kavanagh series (2)
Affair at the boat landing
Cunningham, Albert Benjamin
Sheriff Jess Roden series (6)
Affair at Thor's Head
Lorac, E C R
Inspector Macdonald series (2)
Affair for the Baron
Morton, Anthony
Baron series (39)
Affair in Araby
Mundy, Talbot
Jimgrim series (9)
Affair in Death Valley
Knight, Clifford
Huntoon Rogers series (7)
Affair next door
Green, Anna Katharine
Amelia Butterworth series (1)
Affair of Chief Strongheart
O'Malley, Patrick
Harrigan and Hoeffler series (4)
Affair of Danny the Dip
Tyrer, Walter
Sexton Blake series (1267)
Affair of John Donne
O'Malley, Patrick
Harrigan and Hoeffler series (5)
Affair of Jolie Madame
O'Malley, Patrick
Harrigan and Hoeffler series (3)
Affair of sorcerers
Chesbro, George Clark
Mongo series (3)
Affair of Swan Lake
O'Malley, Patrick
Harrigan and Hoeffler series (2)
Affair of the Atlantic mail robbery
Armour, R Coutts
Sexton Blake series (551)
Affair of the black sombrero
Knight, Clifford
Huntoon Rogers series (5)
Affair of the Blackfriars financier
Brooks, Leonard Harold
Sexton Blake series (114)
Affair of the blood-stained egg cosy
Anderson, James
Inspector Wilkins series (1)
Affair of the blue pig
O'Malley, Patrick
Harrigan and Hoeffler series (7)
Affair of the bronzed basilisk
Skene, Anthony
Sexton Blake series (1104)
Affair of the bumbling Briton
O'Malley, Patrick
Harrigan and Hoeffler series (6)
Affair of the circus queen
Knight, Clifford
Huntoon Rogers series (8)
Affair of the corpse escort
Knight, Clifford
Huntoon Rogers series (16)
Affair of the country club
Gibbons, Harry Hornaby Clifford
Sexton Blake series (336)
Affair of the crimson gull
Knight, Clifford
Huntoon Rogers series (10)
Affair of the crook explorer
Armour, R Coutts
Sexton Blake series (505)
Affair of the cross-roads
Gibbons, Harry Hornaby Clifford
Sexton Blake series (427)
Affair of the dead stranger
Knight, Clifford
Huntoon Rogers series (15)
Affair of the demobilized soldier
Bayfield, William John
Sexton Blake series (67)
Affair of the diamond star
Gibbons, Harry Hornaby Clifford
Sexton Blake series (373)
Affair of the exotic dancer
Benson, Ben
Inspector Wade Paris series (8)
Affair of the fainting butler
Knight, Clifford
Huntoon Rogers series (13)
Affair of the family diamonds
Bayfield, William John
Sexton Blake series (161)
Affair of the fraternizing soldier
Meriton, Peter
Sexton Blake series (1163)
Affair of the ginger lei
Knight, Clifford
Huntoon Rogers series (4)
Affair of the golden buzzard
Knight, Clifford
Huntoon Rogers series (17)
Affair of the heart
James, Josephine
Kathy Martin series (11)
Affair of the heavenly voice
Knight, Clifford
Huntoon Rogers series (2)
Affair of the Hollywood contract
Tyrer, Walter
Sexton Blake series (1247)
Affair of the jade monkey
Knight, Clifford
Huntoon Rogers series (14)
Affair of the kidnapped crook
Gibbons, Harry Hornaby Clifford
Sexton Blake series (474)
Affair of the limping sailor
Knight, Clifford
Huntoon Rogers series (11)
Affair of the Malacca stick
Andrews, Charlton
Drexel Ware series (1)
Affair of the missing parachutist
Parsons, Anthony
Sexton Blake series (1191)
Affair of the missing witness
Graydon, William Murray
Sexton Blake series (432)
Affair of the mutilated mink
Anderson, James
Jessica Fletcher series (1)
Affair of the mutilated mink coat
Anderson, James
Inspector Wilkins series (2)
Affair of the Oriental doctor
Lewis, Jack
Sexton Blake series (128)
Affair of the phantom car
Murray, Edgar Joyce
Sexton Blake series (390)
Affair of the red mosaic
O'Malley, Patrick
Harrigan and Hoeffler series (1)
Affair of the rival cinema kings
Shute, Walter
Sexton Blake series (534)
Affair of the scarlet crab
Knight, Clifford
Huntoon Rogers series (1)
Affair of the seven mummy cases
Bayfield, William John
Sexton Blake series (273)
Affair of the seven warnings
Philips, George Norman
Sexton Blake series (448)
Affair of the sixth button
Knight, Clifford
Huntoon Rogers series (18)
Affair of the skiing clown
Knight, Clifford
Huntoon Rogers series (9)
Affair of the smuggled millions
Dix, Maurice Buxton
Sexton Blake series (1086)
Affair of the spiv's secret
Hunter, John
Sexton Blake series (1226)
Affair of the splintered heart
Knight, Clifford
Huntoon Rogers series (12)
Affair of the substitute doctor
Rhode, John
Doctor Lancelot Priestley series (52)
Affair of the Syrian dagger
Andrews, Charlton
Drexel Ware series (2)
Affair of the three gunmen
Graydon, William Murray
Sexton Blake series (342)
Affair of the trade rivals
Armour, R Coutts
Sexton Blake series (409)
Affair of the unprincipled publisher
Garland, Lawrence
Sherlock Holmes sequels series (66)
Affair of the world's champion
Lewis, Jack
Sexton Blake series (129)
Affair on the painted desert
Knight, Clifford
Huntoon Rogers series (6)
Affair Ravel
Courage, John
Bill Britain series (3)
Affaire royale
Roberts, Nora
Cordina series (1)
Affairs at Thrush Green
Read, *Miss*
Thrush Green series (7)
Affairs of death
Fitzgerald, Nigel
Superintendent Duffy series (10)
Affairs of Paula
Janson, Hank
Hank Janson series (197)
Affairs of state
Kains, Josephine
Terry Spring series (8)
Affairs royale
Roberts, Nora
Flowers series (35)
Afghan intercept
Carter, Nick
Nick Carter series (242)
Afghan onslaught
Caillou, Alan
Colonel Matthew Tobin series (4)
Afghanistan crashout
Rosenberger, Joseph
Death Merchant series (56)
Afghanistan penetration
Kilgore, Axel
They call me the Mercenary series (15)
Afloat and ashore
Cooper, James Fenimore
Miles Wallingford series (1)
Afraid to love
Goudge, Eileen
Seniors series (4)
Africa in black and white
Dutton, Geoffrey
Long way series (2)
Africa, where do elephants live underground?
Packard, Edward
Earth inspectors series (6)
African adventure
James, Josephine
Kathy Martin series (13)
Price, Willard
Hal and Roger Hunt series (6)
African adventures
Taylor, Allan K
Uncle Jock series (2)
African alibi
Edwards, Sylvia
Sally Baxter series (5)
African apprenticship
Perham, Margery
African travels series (1)
African assignment
McAdam, Preston
Shield series (1)
African burn
Wilson, Gar
Phoenix Force series (45)
African contract
Jason, Stuart
Butcher series (14)
African follies
Tomkinson, Constance
Les Girls series (2)
African gold
Graydon, William Murray
Sexton Blake series (122)
African ivory mystery
Adams, Andy
Biff Brewster series (5)
African mercenary
Sadler, Barry
Casca series (12)
African poison murders
Huxley, Elspeth
Superintendent Vachell series (3)
Africa's garden
Rutley, Cecily Marianne
Little people in far off lands series (3)
Afrikander
Reitz, Deneys
Boer War journal trilogy (2)
Afrikorps
Dolan, Bill
Afrikorps series (1)
Afrit affair
Laumer, Keith
Avengers series (7)
Afro-Bets alphabet rap song
Hudson, Wade
Afro-Bets series (2)
Afro-Bets book of black heroes from A to Z
Hudson, Wade
Afro-Bets series (1)
Afro-Bets kids
Hudson, Wade
Afro-Bets series (3)
After a famous victory
Andrews, Lucilla
Saint Martha's Hospital series (14)
After a hundred years
McKee, Ruth Eleanor
Hawaii series (2)
After a manner
Vallins, George Henry
Parodies series (2)
After a shadow
Arthur, Timothy Shay
Home stories series (6)
After Armageddon
Pournelle, Jerry
There will be war series (9)
After dark
Wellman, Manly Wade
Silver John series (3)
After Darvray died
Meriton, Peter
Bill Langley series (2)
After Emma
Hocken, Sheila
Emma series (5)

After hours
Torres, Edwin
Carlito series (2)
After I's
Zukofsky, Louis
I's series (2)
After life
Sewell, Elizabeth Missings
Home and after life series (2)
After midnight
Nielsen, Helen
Simon Drake series (2)
After-midnight gang
Grover, Marshall
Larry and Stretch series (280)
After midnight stories
Myers, Amy
After midnight stories series (1)
After such knowledge
Blish, James
After such knowledge series (4)
After summer merrily
Miller, Connie
Seasons trilogy (1)
After the bomb
Miklowitz, Gloria Dubov
After the bomb series (1)
After the bugles
Kelton, Elmer
Buckalew tetralogy (2)
Tales of Texas series (4)
After the dinosaurs
Berenstain, Stan
Berenstain bears series (64)
Greene, Carla
Science and natural history series (2)
After the dream
Mosco, Maisie
Waiting game series (2)
After the fact
Saberhagen, Fred
Pilgrim series (2)
After the flames
Mitchell, Elizabeth
Alien stars series (2)
After the funeral
Christie, Agatha
Hercule Poirot series (28)
After the loving
Witcomb, Nan
Thoughts of Nanushka series (9)
After the monsoon
Moxon, Oliver
Monsoon trilogy (3)
After the payoff
Grover, Marshall
Larry and Stretch series (177)
After the reunion
Jaffe, Rona
Reunion series (2)
After the storm
Oldfield, Pamela
Heron saga series (3)
After the verdict
Carter, Nicholas
Nicholas Carter series (509)
Gilbert, Anthony
Arthur Crook series (36)
After Thursday
Ure, Jean
Thursday trilogy (2)
After worlds collide
Balmer, Edwin
Bronson Beta series (2)
After world's end
Williamson, Jack
Legion of time series (2)
After you with the pistol
Bonfiglioli, Kyril
Charlie Mortdecai series (3)
Afterglow
England, George Allen
Darkness and dawn series (5)
Afterglow and nightfall
Pargeter, Edith
Brothers of Gwynedd tetralogy (4)
Afterlife
Attwood, Tony
Blake's Seven series (4)
Aftermath
Allen, James Lane
Kentucky series (2)
Asprin, Robert Lynn
Sanctuary series (10)
Barton, James
Wasteworld series (1)
Habe, Hans
Occupied Germany series (1)
Romains, Jules
Men of goodwill series (18)
Aftermath of murder
Fitt, Mary
Superintendent Mallett series (5)
Afternoon
Coote, Roger
My day series (2)
Metcalfe, Penny
Baby's day series (2)
Thompson, Carol
Busy baby's day series (3)
Afternoon light
Menzies, Robert Gordon
Afternoon light series (1)
Afternoon of an autocrat
Lofts, Norah
Clevely series (2)
Afternoon of violence
Barling, Charles
Inspector George Travers series (4)
Aftershock
Corris, Peter
Cliff Hardy series (15)
O'Donnell, Lillian
Mici Anhalt series (1)
Thiele, Colin
Tracy Chipp series (2)*Aftershock*
Wilcox, Collin
Lieutenant Frank Hastings series (6)
Afton of Margate Castle
Hunt, Angela Elwell
Theyn chronicles trilogy (1)
Again Atlan
Scheer, Karl Herbert
Perry Rhodan series (46)
Again Inspector Flagg
Cassells, John
Superintendent Flagg series (16)
Again McLean
Goodchild, George
Inspector McLean series (19)
Again, Mister Sandyman
Graham, Neill
Mister Sandyman series (5)
Again Peyton Place
Fuller, Roger
Peyton Place series (3)
Again Rags
Dutton, Lewis
Rags series (3)
Again Sanders
Wallace, Edgar
Commissioner Sanders series (7)
Again the Dreamer
Duncan, William Murdoch
Superintendent Donald Reamer series (2)
Again the Remover
Daniel, Roland
Bill Saville series (6)
Remover series (4)
Again the Ringer
Wallace, Edgar
Ringer series (2)
Again the Three
Wallace, Edgar
Just Men series (6)
Again the Three Just Men
Wallace, Edgar
Just Men series (6)
Against a dark shore
Kenworthy, Christopher
Matthew and Son series (4)
Against desperate odds
Carter, Nicholas
Nicholas Carter series (144)
Against odds
Lynch, Lawrence L
Carl Masters series (1)
Against Taffy Sinclair Club
Haynes, Betsy
Taffy Sinclair series (1)
Against the Assegais
Moore, William
Mallandine family trilogy (2)
Against the evidence
Egan, Lesley
Jesse Falkenstein series (2)
Against the fall of night
Clarke, Arthur Charles
Fall of night series (1)
Fall of night series (2)
Against the horde
Gemmell, David A
Drenai series (1)
Against the moon
Rushing, Jane Gilmore
Walnut Grove series (5)
Against the odds
Pascal, Francine
Sweet Valley High series (51)
Against the prince of hell
Smith, David Claude
Red Sonja series (5)
Against the rules
Goudge, Eileen
Seniors series (20)
Pascal, Francine
Sweet Valley twins series (9)
Against the seventh flag
Martin, Larry Jay
John Clinton Ryan series (2)
Against the tide
Konsalik, Heinz Gunther
Love on the Don series (2)
Lethbridge, Mabel
Fortune grass series (2)
Against the wind
Pini, Richard
Elfquest series (5)
Against time!
Jeffries, Roderic Graeme
Police series (1)
Agatha
Colegate, Isabel
King family series (3)
Agatha Raisin and the potted gardener
Beaton, M C
Agatha Raisin series (3)
Agatha Raisin and the quiche of death
Beaton, M C
Agatha Raisin series (1)
Agatha Raisin and the vicious vet
Beaton, M C
Agatha Raisin series (2)
Agatha Webb
Green, Anna Katharine
Caleb Sweetwater series (1)
Agaton Sax and Lispington's grandfather clock
Franzen, Nils Olof
Agaton Sax series (11)
Agaton Sax and the bank robbers
Franzen, Nils Olof
Agaton Sax series (7)
Agaton Sax and the big rig
Franzen, Nils Olof
Agaton Sax series (9)
Agaton Sax and the Colossus of Rhodes
Franzen, Nils Olof
Agaton Sax series (8)
Agaton Sax and the criminal doubles
Franzen, Nils Olof
Agaton Sax series (6)
Agaton Sax and the diamond thieves
Franzen, Nils Olof
Agaton Sax series (4)
Agaton Sax and the haunted house
Franzen, Nils Olof
Agaton Sax series (3)
Agaton Sax and the incredible Max brothers
Franzen, Nils Olof
Agaton Sax series (7)
Agaton Sax and the League of Silent Exploders
Franzen, Nils Olof
Agaton Sax series (2)
Agaton Sax and the London computer plot
Franzen, Nils Olof
Agaton Sax series (10)
Agaton Sax and the Max brothers
Franzen, Nils Olof
Agaton Sax series (7)
Agaton Sax and the Scotland Yard mystery
Franzen, Nils Olof
Agaton Sax series (5)
Agave blooms just once
Jernigan, Gisela
Desert trilogy (1)
Age of chaos
Wylie, Jonathan
Unbalanced earth trilogy (3)
Age of chivalry
Bryant, Arthur
Story of England series (2)
Age of death
Marshall, William Leonard
Twentieth century trilogy (1)
Age of elegance, 1812-1822
Bryant, Arthur
Napoleonic Wars trilogy (3)
Age of miracles
O'Riordan, Conal
Stanislaus Priest trilogy (1)
Age of reason
Sartre, Jean Paul
Roads to freedom trilogy (1)
Age of scandal
White, Terence Hanbury
Scandal series (1)
Age of wonder
Jones, Richard
Benson-Williams series (1)
Agency
Meltzer, David
Agency trilogy (1)
Agent
Meltzer, David
Agency trilogy (2)
Agent B-seven
White, Ared
Captain Fox Elton series (2)
Agent counter agent
Carter, Nick
Nick Carter series (78)
Agent extraordinary
Bayne, Spencer
Hendrik Van Kill series (3)
Agent intervenes
Annesley, Michael
Lawrence Fenton series (9)
Agent Nine solves his first case
Dean, Graham
Agent Nine series (1)
Agent Nine solves the jewel mystery
Dean, Grahma
Agent Nine series (2)
Agent of change
Miller, Steve
Agent series (1)
Agent of death
Demille, Nelson
Joe Ryker series (4)
Agent of the Falcon
McFarlane, Leslie
Checkmate series (1)
Agent of the Terran Empire
Anderson, Poul
Sir Dominic Flandry series (4)
Agents of destruction
Brand, Kurt
Perry Rhodan series (134)
Agents of the League
Davy, Colin
David Sheridan series (2)
Aggravations of Minnie Ashe
Kersh, Cyril
Minnie Ashe series (1)
Agile retrieval
Hild, Jack
SOBS series (11)
Agincourt War
Burne, Alfred Higgins
Hundred Years' War series (2)
Agnes
Abbott, Jacob
Franconia series (10)
Agnes day
Fenn, Lionel
Quest for the white duck trilogy (3)
Agony column murders
Scott, Reginald Thomas Maitland
Aurelius Smith series (6)
Agony of Alice
Naylor, Phyllis Reynolds
Alice series (1)
Aground
Williams, Charles
John Ingram series (1)
Ah-choo
Mayer, Mercer
Ah-choo series (1)
Ah-one, ah-two!
Welk, Laurence
Wunnerful series (2)
Ahead of the game
Carter, Nicholas
Nicholas Carter series (147)
AI war
Berry, Stephen Ames
John Harrison series (3)
Aia
Vivian, Evelyn Charles
Aia series (2)
Aimer Gate
Garner, Alan
Stone book quartet (4)
Aims and objects
Housman, Laurence
Palace plays series (3)
Ainceworth mystery
Baxter, Gregory
Superintendent Daniels series (2)
Air
Coote, Roger
Four elements series (1)
Air apparent
Gardner, John Edmund
Boysie L Oakes series (7)
Air cargo of gold
Stone, Richard H
Slim Tyler series (3)
Air-conditioned nightmare
Miller, Henry
Air-conditioned nightmare series (1)
Air dance
Foley, Craig
Hangman series (3)
Air day for the Brownies
Sykes, Pamela
Barnwell Brownie Guide Pack series (1)
Air express holdup
Wright, Philip Lee
Air pilot series (2)
Air Force One is down
Denis, John
U.N.A.C.O.series (2)
Air Force One is haunted
Serling, Robert
Jeremy Haines series (2)
Air Patrol and the hijackers
Buddee, Paul
Air Patrol series (1)
Air Patrol and the saboteurs
Buddee, Paul
Air Patrol series (2)
Air Patrol and the secret intruders
Buddee, Paul
Air Patrol series (3)
Air Patrol and the underwater spies
Buddee, Paul
Air Patrol series (4)
Air pollution
Snodgrass, Mary Ellen
Environmental awareness series (2)
Air scout
Kay, Ross
Big war series (2)
Air service boys flying for France
Beach, Charles Amory
Air service boys series (1)
Air service boys flying for victory
Beach, Charles Amory
Air service boys series (5)
Air service boys in the big battle
Beach, Charles Amory
Air service boys series (4)
Air service boys over the Atlantic
Beach, Charles Amory
Air service boys series (6)
Air service boys over the enemy's lines
Beach, Charles Amory
Air service boys series (2)
Air service boys over the Rhine
Beach, Charles Amory
Air service boys series (3)
Air voyagers of the Arctic
Langley, John Prentice
Aviation series (5)
Aircraft boys of Lakeport
Stratemeyer, Edward L
Lakeport series (6)
Airline pirates
Gardner, John Edmund
Boysie L Oakes series (7)
Airlords of Han
Nowlan, Philip Francis
Buck Rogers series (1)
Airplane Boys at Belize
Craine, Edith Janice
Airplane Boys series (8)
Airplane Boys at Cap Rock
Craine, Edith Janice
Airplane Boys series (2)
Airplane Boys at Platinum River
Craine, Edith Janice
Airplane Boys series (5)
Airplane Boys discover the secrets of Cuzco
Craine, Edith Janice
Airplane Boys series (3)
Airplane Boys flying to Amy-Ran Fastness
Craine, Edith Janice
Airplane Boys series (4)
Airplane Boys in the Black Woods
Craine, Edith Janice
Airplane Boys series (7)
Airplane Boys on the border line
Craine, Edith Janice
Airplane Boys series (1)
Airplane Boys with the revolutionists in Bolivia
Craine, Edith Janice
Airplane Boys series (6)
Airplane mystery
Stone, Richard H
Slim Tyler series (5)
Airport
Hailey, Arthur
Airport series (1)
Airport '80
Stewart, Kerry
Airport series (2)

Airship Boys
Sayler, Harry Lincoln
Airship Boys series (1)
Airship Boys adrift
Sayler, Harry Lincoln
Airship Boys series (2)
Airship Boys as detectives
Sayler, Harry Lincoln
Airship Boys series (7)
Airship Boys due north
Sayler, Harry Lincoln
Airship Boys series (3)
Airship Boys in finance
Sayler, Harry Lincoln
Airship Boys series (5)
Airship Boys in the barren lands
Sayler, Harry Lincoln
Airship Boys series (4)
Airship Boys in the Great War
Cass, Delysle F
Airship Boys series (8)
Airship Boys' ocean flyer
Sayler, Harry Lincoln
Airship Boys series (6)
Airship Ladyship adventure
Gathorne-Hardy, Jonathan
Jane Charrington series (3)
Ajax and the drovers
Patchett, Mary Elwyn
Ajax series (10)
Ajax and the haunted mountain
Patchett, Mary Elwyn
Ajax series (9)
Ajax, golden dog of the Australian bush
Patchett, Mary Elwyn
Ajax series (1)
Ajax the warrior
Patchett, Mary Elwyn
Ajax series (1)
AK-47 Firefight
Lansing, John
Black Eagles series (6)
Akbar and Jeff's guide to life
Groening, Matt
Life in hell series (5)
Akbar contract
McCray, Mike
Black Berets series (12)
Akhnaton, King of Egypt
Merejkowski, Dmitri Sergeevich
Dio series (2)
Akimbo and the crocodile man
McCall Smith, Alexander
Akimbo series (3)
Akimbo and the elephants
McCall Smith, Alexander
Akimbo series (1)
Akimbo and the lions
McCall Smith, Alexander
Akimbo series (2)
Akin to murder
Knight, Kathleen Moore
Elisha Macomber series (14)
Al Capsella and the watchdogs
Clarke, Judith
Al Capsella series (2)
Al Capsella on holidays
Clarke, Judith
Al Capsella series (3)
Al Capsella takes a vacation
Clarke, Judith
Al Capsella series (3)
Al Jaffee gags
Jaffee, Al
Al Jaffee gags series (1)
Al Jaffee gags again
Jaffee, Al
Al Jaffee gags series (2)
Alabama bloodbath
Ham, Bob
Overload series (11)
Alamein attack
Bradley, Jack
Battlesquad 1942 series (1)
Alamo design
Evans, John
Habbakuk Parton series (3)
Alamo treasure
Hardin, J D
Raider and Doc series (66)
Alamut
Tarr, Judith
Alamut series (1)
Alamut ambush
Price, Anthony
Doctor David Audley and Jack Butler series (3)
Alan Breck again
Smith, Arthur Douglas Howden
David Balfour series (3)
Alan Carr in command
Westerman, Percy Francis
Alan Carr series (5)
Alan Carr in the Arctic
Westerman, Percy Francis
Alan Carr series (4)
Alan Carr in the Near East
Westerman, Percy Francis
Alan Carr series (3)
Alanna
Pierce, Tamora
Song of the lioness series (1)
Alarm at Black Brake
Chance, John Newton
Mister DeHavilland series (10)
Alarm bells
Escott, John
Bells series (1)
Alarm, E-boats!
Macdonnell, James Edmond
Captain Peter Bentley series (3)
Alarm in the night
Sterling, Stewart
Ben Pedley series (3)
Fire Marshal Ben Pedley series (3)
Alarm of the black cat
Olsen, D B
Rachel and Jennifer Murdock series (2)
Alarming clock
Avallone, Michael
Ed Noon series (10)
Alarms and excursions
Douglas, Felicity
Nicholas series (1)
Alarums and excursions
Grahame, Kenneth
Smith family series (1)
Alaska cat
Roe, JoAnn
Cat series (3)
Alaska conspiracy
Rosenberger, Joseph
Death Merchant series (33)
Alaska deception
Hild, Jack
SOBS series (20)
Alaska Ghost Glacier mystery
Adams, Andy
Biff Brewster series (6)
Alaska man's luck
Rutzebeck, Hjalmar
Frozen north series (1)
Alaska steel
Benteen, John
Neal Fargo series (3)
Alaskan mystery
Keene, Carolyn
Nancy Drew and the Hardy boys be a detective mystery series (5)
Alaskans
Myers, Barry
Making of America series (10)
Alastor 933
Vance, Jack
Alastor trilogy (2)
Gaean series (3)
Alastor 1716
Vance, Jack
Alastor trilogy (3)
Gaean series (5)
Alastor 2262
Vance, Jack
Alastor trilogy (1)
Gaean series (1)
Alathea
Belle, Pamela
Heron family series (3)
Alba
Delacorta
Serge Gorodish series (6)
Albanian connection
Rosenberger, Joseph
Death Merchant series (6)
Albatross
Anthony, Evelyn
Davina Graham series (3)
Albert
Jezard, Alison
Albert series (1)
Albert and Digger
Jezard, Alison
Albert series (6)
Albert and Henry
Jezard, Alison
Albert series (3)
Albert and the dragonettes
Weir, Rosemary
Albert the dragon series (4)
Albert and Tum Tum
Jezard, Alison
Albert series (7)
Albert comes back
Edgar, Marriott
Albert and the lion series (2)
Albert Gate affair
Tracy, Louis
Reginald Brett series (2)
Albert Gate mystery
Tracy, Louis
Reginald Brett series (2)
Albert goes to sea
Jezard, Alison
Albert series (8)
Albert goes treasure-hunting
Jezard, Alison
Albert series (12)
Albert goes trekking
Jezard, Alison
Albert series (10)
Albert Grope
Mann, Francis Oscar
Albert Grope series (1)
Albert Henry Hawkins, the naughtiest boy in the world
Dickens, Frank
Albert Henry Hawkins series (1)
Albert Henry Hawkins, the naughtiest boy in the world and the Olympic Games
Dickens, Frank
Albert Henry Hawkins series (3)
Albert Henry Hawkins, the naughtiest boy in the world and the space rocket
Dickens, Frank
Albert Henry Hawkins series (2)
Albert in Scotland
Jezard, Alison
Albert series (2)
Albert John in disgrace
Silcock, Ruth
Albert John series (2)
Albert John out hunting
Silcock, Ruth
Albert John series (1)
Albert, my consort
Powell, Margaret
Domestic service series (7)
Albert on the farm
Jezard, Alison
Albert series (13)
Albert, police bear
Jezard, Alison
Albert series (9)
Albert Savarus
Balzac, Honore de
Scenes of private life series (7)
Albert the dragon
Weir, Rosemary
Albert the dragon series (1)
Albert the dragon and the centaur
Weir, Rosemary
Albert the dragon series (3)
Albert up the river
Jezard, Alison
Albert series (5)
Alberta alone
Sandel, Cora
Alberta series (3)
Alberta and freedom
Sandel, Cora
Alberta series (2)
Alberta and Jacob
Sandel, Cora
Alberta series (1)
Albertine gone
Proust, Marcel
Remembrance of things past series (11)
Albert's Christmas
Jezard, Alison
Albert series (4)
Albert's circus
Jezard, Alison
Albert series (11)
Albert's Victoria
Whittle, Tyler
Queen Victoria trilogy (2)
Albert's world tour
Weir, Rosemary
Albert the dragon series (5)
Albin and his friend Ali Baba
Lofgren, Ulf
Albin series (5)
Albin and the crazy bicycle
Lofgren, Ulf
Albin series (3)
Albin and the magic wand
Lofgren, Ulf
Albin series (6)
Albin and the parrot
Lofgren, Ulf
Albin series (7)
Albin and the rainbow
Lofgren, Ulf
Albin series (8)
Albin and the strange umbrella
Lofgren, Ulf
Albin series (4)
Albin is never afraid
Lofgren, Ulf
Albin series (1)
Albin lends a hand
Lofgren, Ulf
Albin series (2)
Albino knife
Perry, Steve
Khadaji series (6)
Albino's double
Philips, George Norman
Sexton Blake series (256)
Albion case
Craig, David
Peter Gale series (1)
Albion's story
Grenville, Kate
Lilian Singer series (2)
Album of the fifties
Lindop, Edmund
Modern America series (2)
Albuquerque
Orwig, Sara
Danby trilogy (2)
Alchemists
Gravel, Geary
Autumn world series (1)
Alchemist's question
Moorcock, Michael
Jerry Cornelius series (7)
Alchemist's story
Champney, Elizabeth Williams
Witch Winnie series (8)
Alchemy deception
Holzer, Hans
Randy Knowles series (2)
Alchymists's cat
Jarvis, Robin
Deptford histories series (1)
Alcibiades, beloved of gods and men
Brun, Vincenz
Alcibiades series (1)
Alcibiades, forsaken by gods and men
Brun, Vincenz
Alcibiades series (2)
Alcott Library is falling down
Haas, Dorothy
Peanut Butter and Jilly series (9)
Aldair, across the misty sea
Barrett, Neal
Aldair series (3)
Aldair in Albion
Barrett, Neal
Aldair series (1)
Aldair, master of ships
Barrett, Neal
Aldair series (2)
Aldebaran campaign
Randle, Kevin
Seeds of war trilogy (2)
Alden among the Indians
Ellis, Edward Sylvester
Overland series (2)
Alden, the pony express rider
Ellis, Edward Sylvester
Overland series (1)
Aldo Applesauce
Hurwitz, Johanna
Aldo Sossi series (2)
Aldo Ice Cream
Hurwitz, Johanna
Aldo Sossi series (3)
Aldo Peanut Butter
Hurwitz, Johanna
Aldo Sossi series (4)
Aldringham's last chance
Rees, Arthur John
Inspector Luckraft series (6)
Aleph
Constantine, Storm
Monstrous regiment series (2)
Aleriel
Lach-Szyrma, Wladislaw Somerville
Venus series (1)
Alert state black
Nolan, Frederick
Garrett dossier series (2)
Alerting kids to the danger of abuse and neglect
Berry, Joy
Alerting kids to the danger zones series (3)
Alerting kids to the danger of kidnapping
Berry, Joy
Alerting kids to the danger zones series (1)
Alerting kids to the danger of sexual abuse
Berry, Joy
Alerting kids to the danger zones series (2)
Alessandra
Duder, Tessa
Alex series (3)
Alessandra between
Kaplow, Robert
Alessandra series (2)
Alessandra in love
Kaplow, Robert
Alessandra series (1)
Aleutian pink mink
Fox, James M
John and Suzy Marshall series (9)
Alex
Duder, Tessa
Alex series (1)
Alex and Roy
Dickinson, Mary
Alex series (2)
Alex and the baby
Dickinson, Mary
Alex series (3)
Alex Haley's queen
Haley, Alex
Roots series (2)
Alex in winter
Duder, Tessa
Alex series (2)
Alex quartet
Duder, Tessa
Alex series (4)
Alexa
Melville, Anne
Lorimer family series (2)
Alexander and the terrible, horrible, no good, very bad day
Viorst, Judith
Alexander series (1)
Alexander Botts, earthworm tractors
Upson, William Hazlett
Alexander Botts series (1)
Alexander Bunyip
Salmon, Michael
Alexander Bunyip series (5)
Alexander Bunyip and the swagman
Salmon, Michael
Alexander Bunyip series (6)
Alexander in the land of Mog
Elliott, Janice
Alexander Columbus Banyana series (2)
Alexander the greatest
Upson, William Hazlett
Alexander Botts series (1)
Alexander trilogy
Renault, Mary
Alexander the Great series (3)
Alexander, who used to be rich last Sunday
Viorst, Judith
Alexander series (2)
Alexander's feast
Solmssen, Arthur Robert George
Conyers and Dean series (2)
Alexandra
Harvey, Caroline
Legacy of love trilogy (2)
Alexandra the great
Greene, Constance Clarke
Al series (4)
Alexandria, the ambivalent
Kimbrough, Katheryn
Phenwick women series (36)
Alexandrian ring
Forstchen, William R
Gamester wars series (1)
Alex's bed
Dickinson, Mary
Alex series (1)
Alex's outing
Dickinson, Mary
Alex series (4)
Alf Gorilla
Grater, Michael
Alf Gorilla series (1)
Alf Gorilla adrift
Grater, Michael
Alf Gorilla series (2)
Alfgar the Dane
Crake, Augustus David
Chronicles of Aescendune trilogy (2)
Alfie
Naughton, Bill
Alfie series (1)
Alfie and his secret friend
Bergstrom, Gunilla
Alfie Atkins series (1)

Alfie and the monster
Bergstrom, Gunilla
Alfie Atkins series (4)
Alfie darling
Naughton, Bill
Alfie series (2)
Alfie gets in first
Hughes, Shirley
Alfie Rose series (1)
Alfie gives a hand
Hughes, Shirley
Alfie Rose series (3)
Alfie's feet
Hughes, Shirley
Alfie Rose series (2)
Alfred and the caravan
Jones, Nicholas
Wind in the willows series (5)
Alfred Hagart's household
Smith, Alexander
Alfred Hagart series (1)
Alfred summer
Slepian, Jan
Alfred and Lester series (1)
Alf's button
Darlington, William Aubrey
Alf Higgins series (1)
Alf's carpet
Darlington, William Aubrey
Alf Higgins series (2)
Alf's new button
Darlington, William Aubrey
Alf Higgins series (3)
Algarve affair
Carter, Nick
Nick Carter series (185)
Algerian adventure
Saint-Laurent, Cecil
Bernadette series (1)
Ali Baba Bernstein, lost and found
Hurwitz, Johanna
Ali Baba Bernstein series (3)
Alias Basil Willing
McCloy, Helen
Basil Willing series (9)
Alias Blackshirt
Graeme, Bruce
Blackshirt series (4)
Alias Blue Mask
Morton, Anthony
Baron series (5)
Alias Doctor Ely
Thayer, Lee
Peter Clancy series (8)
Alias Ed Dacey
Grover, Marshall
Larry and Stretch series (382)
Alias his wife
Ransome, Stephen
Lieutenant Lee Barcello series (3)
Alias Jungle Doctor
White, Paul
Jungle Doctor series (22)
Alias man
Craig, David
Roy Rickman trilogy (1)
Alias Mr Orson
Spiller, Andrew
Chief Inspector Duck Mallard series (13)
Alias Norman Conquest
Gray, Berkeley
Norman Conquest series (15)
Alias Smith and jones
Fox, Brian
Alias Smith and Jones series (6)
Alias the Baron
Morton, Anthony
Baron series (5)
Alias the Lone Wolf
Vance, Louis Joseph
Michael Lanyard series (3)
Alias the night wind
Vanardy, Varick
Bingham Harvard series (1)
Alias the Saint
Charteris, Leslie
Saint series (6)
Alias the Thunderbolt
McCulley, Johnston
Thunderbolt series (2)
Alias the victim
Gribble, Leonard Reginald
Superintendent Anthony Slade series (34)
Alias Uncle Hugo
Coles, Manning
Tommy Hambledon series (15)
Alibi
Carmichael, Harry
John Piper and Quinn series (18)
Alibi?
Creasey, John
Inspector Roger West series (39)
Alibi
Wheatley, Dennis
War game series (3)
Alibi and Doctor Morelle
Dudley, Ernest
Doctor Morelle series (12)
Alibi at dusk
Benson, Ben
Inspector Wade Paris series (2)
Alibi baby
Sterling, Stewart
Gil Vine series (4)
Alibi for a corpse
Lemarchand, Elizabeth
Superintendent Tom Pollard series (3)
Alibi for Inspector West
Creasey, John
Inspector Roger West series (39)
Alibi in black
Robertson, Colin
Peter Grayleigh series (5)
Alibi in time
Thomson, June
Inspector Finch series (7)
Alibi innings
Worsley-Gough, Barbara
Aloysius Kelly series (1)
Alibi too soon
Ormerod, Roger
Richard Patton series (4)
Alibi trail
Grant, Maxwell
Shadow series (216)
Grover, Marshall
Larry and Stretch series (345)
Alice
Lytton, Edward George Earle Lytton Bulwer-Lytton
Eleusinia series (2)
Alice in April
Naylor, Phyllis Reynolds
Alice series (5)
Alice in Blunderland
Anderson, Jack
Alice in Wonderland parodies series (9)
Bangs, John Kendrick
Alice in Wonderland parodies series (3)
Alice in La-La Land
Campbell, Robert Wright
Whistler series (2)
Alice in Music Land
La Prade, Ernest
Alice in Wonderland sequels series (3)
Alice in Orchestra Land
La Prade, Ernest
Alice in Wonderland sequels series (3)
Alice in Orchestralia
La Prade, Ernest
Alice in Wonderland sequels series (3)
Alice in Rankbustland
Otterbourg, Edwin Max
Alice in Wonderland parodies series (6)
Alice in rapture
Naylor, Phyllis Reynolds
Alice series (2)
Alice in reflection
Starling, Jill
Alice and Emily series (1)
Alice in the Delighted States
Hope, Edward
Alice in Wonderland parodies series (7)
Alice in Wonderland
Carroll, Lewis
Alice in Wonderland series (1)
Alice through the looking glass
Carroll, Lewis
Alice in Wonderland series (2)
Alice through the needle's eye
Adair, Gilbert
Alice in Wonderland sequels series (6)
Alicella
Stewart, Averil
Stewart family series (1)
Alice's adventures in Cambridge
Evarts, Richard Conover
Alice in Wonderland parodies series (4)
Alice's adventures in Wonderland
Carroll, Lewis
Alice in Wonderland series (1)
Alice's adventures under-ground
Carroll, Lewis
Alice in Wonderland series (1)
Alicia in Blunderland
Miller, Peter Schuyler
Alice in Wonderland parodies series (9)
Alicia's trump
Mathewson, Joseph
Alicia von Helsing series (1)
Alien
Foster, Alan Dean
Alien series (1)
Alien affair
Hubbard, Lafayette Ronald
Mission earth series (4)
Alien archipelago
San Antonio
Berurier series (10)
San Antonio series (10)
Alien blood
Vinge, Joan Dennison
Psion series (2)
Alien blues
Hightower, Lynn S
David Silver series (1)
Alien bounty
Dietz, William Corey
Sam McCade series (3)
Alien citadel
Hill, Douglas
Huntsman trilogy (3)
Alien debt
Busby, Francis Marion
Bran Tregare series (2)
Alien eyes
Hightower, Lynn S
David Silver series (2)
Alien, go home!
Johnson, Seddon
Choose your own adventure series (101)
Alien heart
Moorcock, Michael
Jherek Carnelian and Amelia Underwood series (1)
Alien heat
Hightower, Lynn S
David Silver series (3)
Moorcock, Michael
Dancers at the end of time series (1)
Alien invaders
Packard, Edward
Space hawks series (2)
Alien Island
Sherred, Thomas L
Alien Island series (1)
Alien main
Sherred, Thomas L
Alien Island series (2)
Alien minds
Evans, Edward Everett
George Hanlon series (2)
Alien missile threat
Newman, Paul S
Invaders series (4)
Alien probe
Appleton, Victor II
Tom Swift Junior series 2 (3)
Alien realms
Smith, Edward Elmer
Lord Tedric series (4)
Alien salute
Ingrid, Charles
Sand wars series (4)
Alien seed
Tubb, Edwin Charles
Space nineteen ninety nine series (7)
Alien stars
Mitchell, Elizabeth
Alien stars series (1)
Alien swordmaster
Sucharitkul, Somtow
V series (7)
Alien tongue
Leigh, Stephen
Next wave series (2)
Alien trace
Major, H M
Alien trace series (1)
Alien virus
Rackham, John
Space puppet series (4)
Alien web
Vardeman, Robert Edward
Masters of space trilogy (2)
Alien within
Bova, Ben
Voyagers series (2)
Alien worlds
Smith, Edward Elmer
Lord Tedric series (1)
Aliens
Foster, Alan Dean
Alien series (2)
Aliens among us
White, James
Sector General series (8)
Aliens for breakfast
Etra, Jonathan
Aliens series (1)
Aliens for lunch
Etra, Jonathan
Aliens series (2)
Alington inheritance
Wentworth, Patricia
Miss Maud Silver series (32)
Alinor
Gellis, Roberta
Roselynde chronicles series (2)
Alison and the witch's cave
Stuart, Sheila
Alison series (11)
Alison's caravan adventure
Stuart, Sheila
Alison series (15)
Alison's Christmas adventure
Stuart, Sheila
Alison series (3)
Alison's cliff adventure
Stuart, Sheila
Alison series (14)
Alison's Easter adventure
Stuart, Sheila
Alison series (5)
Alison's Highland holiday
Stuart, Sheila
Alison series (1)
Alison's island adventure
Stuart, Sheila
Alison series (9)
Alison's kidnapping adventure
Stuart, Sheila
Alison series (7)
Alison's poaching adventure
Stuart, Sheila
Alison series (6)
Alison's pony adventure
Stuart, Sheila
Alison series (8)
Alison's riding adventure
Stuart, Sheila
Alison series (13)
Alison's spy adventure
Stuart, Sheila
Alison series (10)
Alison's yacht adventure
Stuart, Sheila
Alison series (12)
Alive in the Lord!
McGloin, Joseph Thaddeus
Called to love, called to serve series (1)
Alive to the burning
Baker, Howard
Dead and alive series (2)
All aboard
Koscielniak, Bruce
Hector and Prudence series (2)
Optic, Oliver
Boat Club series (2)
All aboard for Singapore
Clune, Frank
Discovery series (6)
All aboard for sunrise lands
Rand, Edward Augustus
All aboard series (1)
All aboard for the lakes and mountains
Rand, Edward Augustus
All aboard series (2)
All about a Brownie
Hann, Dorothy Owen
Brownie series (1)
All about anthrax
Fitzgerald, Ross
Grafton Everest series (2)
All about birth and growth
Bailey, Donna
Health facts series (2)
All about Brenda Bear
Coombes, Marion
Brenda Bear series (1)
All about digestion
Bailey, Donna
Health facts series (6)
All about Emily
Stewart, Maureen
Emily series (2)
All about heart and blood
Bailey, Donna
Health facts series (4)
All about me
Kalman, Bobbie
In my world series (1)
Wolff, Margaret
Books for me series (2)
All about my naughty little sister
Edwards, Dorothy
My naughty little sister series (4)
All about Sam
Lowry, Lois
Sam series (1)
All about Semolina Silkpaws
Williams, Gladys
Semolina Silkpaws series (3)
All about Simpey and his grandmother
Roberts, Elisabeth
Simpey series (2)
All about skin, hair and teeth
Bailey, Donna
Health facts series (8)
All about Stacy
Giff, Patricia Reilly
New kids at the Polk Street School series (3)
All about the Bullerby children
Lindgren, Astrid
Bullerby series (2)
All about the Giant Alexander
Herrman, Frank
Giant Alexander series (4)
All about the Wallypug
Farrow, George Edward
Wallypug series (5)
All about your brain
Bailey, Donna
Health facts series (3)
All about your lungs
Bailey, Donna
Health facts series (7)
All about your senses
Bailey, Donna
Health facts series (1)
All about your skeleton
Bailey, Donna
Health facts series (5)
All adrift
Optic, Oliver
Boat builders series (1)
All-American girl
Rand, Suzanne
Winners series (2)
All at sea
Wells, Carolyn
Fleming Stone series (22)
All authors are equal
Warburg, Fredric
Publishing series (2)
All because of Dawks
Reid, Meta Mayne
Peyton children series (1)
All blood is red
James, William M
Apache series (10)
All brides are beautiful
Corrigan, Mark
Mark Corrigan and McLean series (10)
All but Alice
Naylor, Phyllis Reynolds
Alice series (4)
All by ourselves
Robinson, Mabel Louise
Little Lucia series (4)
All change at Cuckly Place
Streatfeild, Noel
Maitlands series (2)
All change for Medenham
Dale, Norman
Medenham series (4)
All change for murder
Gunn, Victor
Chief Inspector Bill Cromwell series (37)
All change her
Mitchison, Naomi
Small talk series (2)
All-color activity book of animals
Gree, Alain
Books and games series (4)
All-consuming fire
Lane, Andy
Timewyrm series (11)
All concerned notified
Reilly, Helen
Inspector Christopher McKee series (7)
All creatures great and small
Herriot, James
Vet series (2)
All darkness met
Cook, Glen
Dread Empire series (3)

All day long
McCord, David
Rhymes of the never was an always is series (3)
All done from memory
Lancaster, Osbert
Memory series (1)
All dreams denied
Kennedy, Adam
Bradshaw trilogy (3)
All earth to love
Hastings, Phyllis
Sussex trilogy (1)
All experience
Mannin, Ethel
Confessions and impressions series (2)
All fall down
Oxenbury, Helen
Big baby series (3)
Strong, Leonard Alfred George
Police diversion series (1)
All flags flying
Keyes, Frances Parkinson
Roses series (2)
All for a scrap of paper
Hocking, Joseph
Great War, French Front series (1)
All for my love
Gobineau, Marceline
Stephanie series (4)
All for Quinn
Hooper, Kay
Men of mysteries past series (3)
All for the love of a lady
Ford, Leslie
Colonel John Primrose series (10)
Grace Latham series (10)
All for the love of that boy
Lewis, Linda
Linda series (6)
All geared up
McEvoy, Seth
Not quite human series (2)
All God's children
Lyons, Arthur
Jacob Asch series (2)
All God's children need traveling shoes
Angelou, Maya
Heart of a woman series (5)
All grass isn't green
Fair, A A
Bertha Cool and Donald Lam series (29)
All hands on deck
Leyland, Eric
Max and Scrap series (2)
All I can get
Ard, William
Lou Largo series (1)
All I could never be
Nichols, Beverley
Candid recollections series (2)
All I ever ask
Ashley, Bernard
Clipper Street series (5)
All in a summer season
Ure, Jean
Riverside Theatre series (2)
All in good time
Ormondroyd, Edward
Susan Shaw series (2)
Stern, Gladys Bronwyn
Ragbag chronicles series (6)
All in one piece
Murphy, Jill
Larges family trilogy (2)
All in the blue unclouded weather
Klein, Robin
Melling series (1)
All is but a beginning
Neihardt, John Gneisenau
All is but a beginning series (1)
All is discovered
Cannan, Joanna
Frank Frobisher series (2)
Inspector Ronald Price series (5)
All is vanity
Bell, Josephine
Doctor David Wintringham series (6)
All Jahdu storybook
Hamilton, Virginia
Jahdu series (4)
All-Jewish cartoon collection
Gerberg, Mort
All-Jewish cartoon series (1)
All leads negative
Alding, Peter
C.I.D. Room series (1)
All Mary
Rae, Gwynedd
Mary Plain series (2)

All men are islands
Duncan, Ronald
All men are islands trilogy (1)
All men are liars
Strange, John Stephen
Captain George Honegger series (2)
All men are lonely now
Clifford, Francis
Loyalty trilogy (1)
All my days
Dayus, Kathleen
Birmingham life series (3)
All my friends are going to be strangers
McMurtry, Larry
Danny Deck series (1)
Urban trilogy (2)
All my pretty chickens
Hocking, Anne
Inspector William Austen series (9)
All nature sings
DeJonge, Joanne E
My Father's world series (4)
All night long
Pascal, Francine
Sweet Valley High series (5)
All-nighter
Blake, Susan
Hawthorne College series (1)
Wharton, Joanna
Campus fever series (2)
All-of-a-kind family
Taylor, Sydney
All-of-a-kind family series (1)
All-of-a-kind family downtown
Taylor, Sydney
All-of-a-kind family series (4)
All-of-a-kind family uptown
Taylor, Sydney
All-of-a-kind family series (3)
All on a summer's day
Wainwright, John
Northern Police series (49)
All on the Irish shore
Somerville, Edith Oenone
Irish R.M. series (2)
All on the never-never
Lindsay, Jack
British way series (6)
All or nothing
Davis, Leslie
Cheerleaders series (39)
Longstreet, Stephen
Fiore family series (1)
All, or something
Brand, Hilary
Hilary Brand series (4)
All other perils
Macleod, Robert
Andrew Laird series (1)
All our aircraft are missing
Radford, John P
Illusionist series (2)
All out
Cottenham, Mark Pepys
Tom Furness series (1)
All out of grape jelly
Blake, Susan
Fifteen series (6)
All over but the shooting
Powell, Richard
Arab and Andy Blake series (2)
All points bulletin
Weiss, Mike
Ben Henry series (2)
All possible avenues
Howard, Tom
Sergeant Tom Howard series (2)
All power to the Soviets, 1914-1917
Cliff, Tony
Lenin series (2)
All-purpose bodies
McCutchan, Philip
Commander Esmonde Shaw series (11)
All quiet on the Western Front
Remarque, Erich Maria
World War I series (1)
All roads lead to Rome
Clune, Frank
Discovery series (14)
All roads to Sospel
Bellairs, George
Detective Inspector Thomas Littlejohn series (55)
All said and done
Beauvoir, Simone de
Dutiful daughter series (4)
All screwed up
Conway, Troy
Coxeman series (22)

All shall be well
Crombie, Deborah
Superintendent Duncan Kincaid and Sergeant Gemma James series (2)
All shapes and sizes
Hughes, Shirley
Nursery series (4)
All shook up
Lantz, Francess Lin
Swept away series (8)
All shot up
Himes, Chester
Grave Digger Jones and Coffin Ed Johnson series (5)
All stations to Malta
Hackforth-Jones, Gilbert
Paul Dexter series (2)
All summer through
Saville, Malcolm
Nettleford series (1)
All suspected
Bayfield, William John
Sexton Blake series (460)
All taut
Optic, Oliver
Boat builders series (5)
All that a man has
Mackenzie, Lee
Emmerdale Farm series (3)
All that glitters
Coles, Manning
Tommy Hambledon series (17)
Hayes, Ralph Eugene
Mark Stoner series (3)
Powers, Elizabeth
Viera Kolarova series (1)
Spencer, Rick
Eric Ivorsen series (2)
All that remains
Cornwell, Patricia Daniels
Doctor Kay Scarpetta series (3)
All the beasts in the field
Fenton, Sylvia
Beasts in the field series (1)
All the Buffalo returning
Johnson, Dorothy Marie
Buffalo Woman series (2)
All the colors of darkness
Biggle, Lloyd
Jan Darzek series (1)
All the colours of darkness
Biggle, Lloyd
Jan Darzek series (1)
All the days of my life
Mais, Stuart Petre Brodie
Days of my life series (1)
All the dead heroes
Wilcox, Stephen F
T S W Sheridan series (3)
All the drowning seas
Fullerton, Alexander
Nick Everard series (6)
All the fun of the fair
Clewes, Dorothy
Kay and Rory series (3)
All the gods are dead
Baker, Howard
Dead and alive series (1)
All the gods of Eiseron
Lang, Simon
Skipjack series (1)
All the grey cats
Thomas, Craig
Kenneth Aubrey series (2)
All the king's horses, all the king's men
Vance, J Emily
Star trek fan series (18)
All the king's sons
Honeyman, Brenda
Edward III series (2)
All the myriad ways
Niven, Larry
Known Space series (6)
All the nice girls
Winton, John
Navy series (5)
All the old bargains
Schutz, Benjamin Merrill
Leo Haggerty series (1)
All the possibilities
Roberts, Nora
Flowers series (15)
Macgregor series (3)
All the President's men
Woodward, Bob
Watergate series (1)
All the pretty horses
McCarthy, Cormac
Border trilogy (1)
All the pretty people
Scott, Jack S
Detective Inspector Alfred Stanley Rosher series (9)

All the rabbit's relations
Miller, Muriel
Woodlanders series (3)
All the right moves
Hollan, Linda
Annie series (1)
All the rivers ran
Cato, Nancy
Australian trilogy (1)
All the rivers run
Cato, Nancy
Australian trilogy (3)
All the sea between
Odgers, Sally Farrell
Helen and Dominic series (2)
All the small poems
Worth, Valerie
Small poems series (5)
All the sweet tomorrows
Small, Beatrice
Skye O'Malley series (2)
All the tall men
Grover, Marshall
Larry and Stretch series (64)
All the trees were green
Harrison, Michael
Vernal equinox series (1)
All the way
Cooney, Caroline B
Cheerleaders series (5)
All the way down
Chaber, M E
Milo March series (2)
All the way home
Vail, Virginia
Animal Inn series (6)
All the weyrs of Pern
McCaffrey, Anne
Pern and the Red Planet series (11)
All the world loves a lover
Browne, Dik
Hagar the horrible series (26)
All the world wondered
Merrick, Leonard
Parisian series (2)
All things are dangerous
Daniel, Roland
Michael Grant series (3)
All things bright and beautiful
Herriot, James
Vet series (4)
All things come round
Burgin, George Brown
Four Corners series (18)
All things wise and wonderful
Herriot, James
Vet series (6)
All this and Burnham too
Hope, Jane
Teaching series (2)
All this and Cornwall too
Baker, Denys Val
Cornish series (13)
All through the night
Wainwright, John
Northern Police series (57)
All together now
Hughes, Dean
Angel Park All-Stars series (14)
All tramps are trouble
Janson, Hank
Hank Janson series (93)
All upon a sidewalk
George, Jean Craighead
All upon series (2)
All upon a stone
George, Jean Craighead
All upon series (1)
All vigil ended
Howe, Doris
Kootenay series (2)
All-white elf
Robeson, Kenneth
Doc Savage series (127)
All women are fatal
Mauriac, Claude
Interior dialogue series (1)
All wrong, Mrs Bear
Runyon, Catherine
Mister and Mrs Bear series (1)
All you've ever wanted, and other stories
Aiken, Joan
Armitage family series (1)
Allah's Eye conspiracy
Parsons, Anthony
Sexton Blake series (971)
Allan and the holy flower
Haggard, Henry Rider
Allan Quatermain series (7)
Holy flower trilogy (1)

Allan and the ice gods
Haggard, Henry Rider
Allan Quatermain series (15)
She series (5)
Allan Quatermain
Haggard, Henry Rider
Allan Quatermain series (16)
King Solomon's mines series (2)
Umslopogaas series (1)
Allan Quatermain and the lost city of gold
Haggard, Henry Rider
Allan Quatermain series (16)
King Solomon's mines series (2)
Umslopogaas series (1)
Litvinoff, Sarah
Allan Quatermain series (16)
King Solomon's mines series (2)
Umslopogaas series (1)
Allan the hunter
Haggard, Henry Rider
Allan Quatermain series (6)
Allan's wife
Haggard, Henry Rider
Allan Quatermain series (2)
King Solomon's mines series (4)
Allan's wife, and other tales
Haggard, Henry Rider
Allan Quatermain series (4)
Allan Quatermain series (6)
Allegra
Harker, Lizzie Allen
Mister Wycherly series (4)
Alley Jaggers
West, Paul
Jaggers family series (1)
Alliance
Oltion, Jerry
Robots and aliens series (4)
Allied in victory
Sellers, Con
Men at arms series (4)
Allies of Antares
Prescot, Dray
Dray Prescot series (26)
Alligator and the Everglades
Taylor, Dave
Animals and their ecosystems series (4)
Alligator case
Pene du Bois, William
Alligator case series (1)
Allingham case-book
Allingham, Margery
Albert Campion series (23)
Allingham omnibus
Allingham, Margery
Albert Campion series (23)
Allotment Lane School again
Joy, Margaret
Allotment Lane School series (2)
All's well that ends as you like it
Green, Michael
Coarse plays series (1)
Allsorts
Fletcher, Audrey
Allsorts series (3)
Allyson
Jenkins, Jerry Bruce
Margo Franklin and Philip Spence series (7)
Alma at Hadley Hall
Breitenbach, Louise Marks
Alma series (1)
Alma's junior year
Breitenbach, Louise Marks
Alma series (3)
Alma's senior year
Breitenbach, Louise Marks
Alma series (4)
Alma's sophomore year
Breitenbach, Louise Marks
Alma series (2)
Almayer's folly
Conrad, Joseph
Captain Lingard series (3)
Almond blossom fairy
Marden, Fay
Flower fairy series (1)
Almond tree
Almedingen, Edith Martha
To-morrow will come trilogy (2)
Almonds and raisins
Mosco, Maisie
Almonds and raisins trilogy (1)
Almoner at Ryeminster
Ferrari, Ivy
Ryeminster Hospital series (4)
Almost a gentleman
Benney, Mark
Low company series (3)

Almost lost
Montgomery, Raymond A
Rebels in the New World series (3)
Almost married
Pascal, Francine
Sweet Valley High series (102)
Almost murder
Jeffries, Roderic Graeme
Inspector Enrique Alvarez series (10)
Almost perfect murder
Footner, Hulbert
Madame Rosika Storey series (7)
Almost summer carnival
Chase, Emily
Canby Hall series (32)
Almost ten and a half
Ransom, Candice Farris
Growing up series (1)
Almost the real thing
Skurzynski, Gloria
Your high-tech world series (2)
Alms for oblivion
Kemp, Peter Mant Macintyre
Conflict trilogy (3)
Aloha
Tempski, Armine von
Paradise series (2)
Alone
Tibble, Anne
Greenhorn trilogy (3)
Alone among men
Coryn, Marjorie
Napoleonic trilogy (3)
Alone at Pine Street
Allan, Mabel Esther
Pine Street series (5)
Alone in the ashes
Johnstone, William Wallace
Ashes series (5)
Alone in the crowd
Pascal, Francine
Sweet Valley High series (28)
Alone, 1932-1940
Manchester, William
Last lion series (2)
Alone, together
Cooney, Linda A
Couples series (3)
Along came a llama
Ruck, Ruth Janette
Hill Farm trilogy (3)
Along comes Judy Jo
Hill, Mabel Betsy
Judy Jo series (5)
Along Janet's road
Dalgliesh, Alice
Silver pencil series (2)
Along Laughing Brook
Burgess, Thornton Waldo
Nature stories series (5)
Along my line
Harding, Gilbert
Along my line series (1)
Along the Mohawk Trail
Fitzhugh, Percy Keese
Boy Scouts series (1)
Along the road
Bacon, Ronald Leonard
Valley series (2)
Along with youth
Griffin, Peter
Ernest Hemingway series (1)
Alongshore
Reynolds, Stephen
Nautical series (2)
Alonzo Mactavish again
Cheyney, Peter
Alonzo Mactavish series (2)
Alp murder
Stein, Aaron Marc
Matt Erridge series (9)
Alpaca
Billam, Rosemary
Alpaca series (1)
Alpaca in the park
Billam, Rosemary
Alpaca series (2)
Alpaca saves Christmas
Billam, Rosemary
Alpaca series (4)
Alph
Maine, Charles Eric
World without men series (2)
Alpha Death
Conway, Norman
Adam Hunter series (2)
Alpha deception
Land, Jon
Blaine McCracken series (2)
Alphabatics
Macdonald, Suse
Discovery series (1)
Alphabet book
Burningham, John
Play and learn series (1)
Alphabet murders
Christie, Agatha
Hercule Poirot series (12)
Alphie and the dream machine
Martin, Richard E
Listen-hear series (1)
Slepian, Jan
Listen-hear series (1)
Alpine coach
Coffman, Virginia
Napoleonic Europe series (3)
Alpine gambit
Cort, Ned
Boxer Unit SS series (2)
Alps assignment
Sugar, Andrew
Israeli commandos series (4)
Alraune
Ewers, Hanns Heinz
Frank Braun series (2)
Al's blind date
Greene, Constance Clarke
Al series (6)
Alscott experiment
Stanley, Bennett
Alscott experiment series (1)
Altar in the loft
Croft-Cooke, Rupert
Sensual life series (2)
Altar of evil
Stevenson, Florence
Kitty Telfair series (3)
Altar steps
Mackenzie, Compton
Faith, hope and charity trilogy (1)
Alter ego
Linington, Elizabeth
Sergeant Ivor Maddox series (14)
Alter evil
Jade, Symon
Starship Orpheus trilogy (3)
Alternate empires
Greenberg, Martin Harry
What might have been series (1)
Alternate heroes
Greenberg, Martin Harry
What might have been series (2)
Alternate orbits
Chandler, Arthur Bertram
John Grimes series (10)
Rim series (12)
Alternate wars
Greenberg, Martin Harry
What might have been series (3)
Alternative
Downs, Gerry
Star trek fan series (1)
Alternative Third World War, 1985-2035
Jackson, William
World War Three series (3)
Althea joins the Chalet School
Brent-Dyer, Elinor Mary
Chalet School series (57)
Althea's term at Winterton
Potter, Dora Joan
Winterton School series (4)
Aluminum turtle
Kendrick, Baynard
Captain Duncan Maclain series (11)
Alvarez journal
Burns, Rex
Gabriel Wager series (1)
Alvin Fernald, foreign trader
Hicks, Clifford Byron
Alvin Fernald series (3)
Alvin Fernald, master of a thousand disguises
Hicks, Clifford Byron
Alvin Fernald series (9)
Alvin Fernald, mayor for a day
Hicks, Clifford Byron
Alvin Fernald series (4)
Alvin Fernald, superweasel
Hicks, Clifford Byron
Alvin Fernald series (5)
Alvin Fernald, TV anchorman
Hicks, Clifford Byron
Alvin Fernald series (7)
Alvin Stardust story
Tremlett, George
Rock stars series (12)
Alvin's secret code
Hicks, Clifford Byron
Alvin Fernald series (2)
Alvin's swap shop
Hicks, Clifford Byron
Alvin Fernald series (6)
Always a body to trade
Constantine, K C
Mario Balzic series (6)
Always a pair
Cole, Jennifer
Cindy and Nicole series (5)
Always a spy
Footman, Robert
Harry Ryder series (2)
Always Arthur
Graham, Amanda
Arthur trilogy (3)
Always fight back
Mackenzie, Andrew
Nicholas Cornish series (1)
Always in Vogue
Chase, Ilka
Past imperfect series (3)
Always kill a stranger
Fish, Robert Lloyd
Captain Jose da Silva series (6)
Always leave 'em dying
Prather, Richard Scott
Shell Scott series (10)
Always lock your bedroom door
Winsor, Roy
Ira Cobb series (2)
Always murder a friend
Scherf, Margaret
Emily and Henry Bryce series (1)
Always on Sunday
Chase, Glen
Cherry Delight series (20)
Always take the big ones
Chambers, Peter
Mark Preston series (10)
Always tell the sleuth
O'Hara, Kevin
Chico Brett series (4)
Always the wolf
Easton, Nat
Bill Banning series (1)
Alys-all-alone
Macdonald, Una
Alys series (1)
Alys in Happyland
Macdonald, Una
Alys series (2)
Alyx
Russ, Joanna
Adventures of Alyx series (2)
Am I too loud?
Moore, Gerald
Memoirs of an accompanist series (1)
Amabel abroad
Prior, Natalie Jane
Amabel series (2)
Amabel and Mary Verena
Hicks Beach, Susan Emily
Morville family series (2)
Amanda
Ransom, Candice Farris
Sunfire series (1)
Amanda and April
Pryor, Bonnie
Amanda and April series (1)
Amanda and the Brownies
Anderson, Verily
Brownies series (1)
Amanda and the magic garden
Himmelman, John
Amanda series (2)
Amanda and the witch switch
Himmelman, John
Amanda series (1)
Amanda goes dancing
Colbert, Anthony
Amanda series (2)
Amanda going away
Blyton, Enid
Little bedtime books series (5)
Amanda has a surprise
Colbert, Anthony
Amanda series (1)
Amanda in Berlin
Revelli, George
Amanda Nightingale series (5)
Amanda in Spain
Revelli, George
Amanda Nightingale series (4)
Amanda's castle
Revelli, George
Amanda Nightingale series (3)
Amarillo Ridge
Grover, Marshall
Larry and Stretch series (100)
Amarilly in love
Maniates, Belle Kanaris
Amarilly series (2)
Amarilly of Clothes-Line Alley
Maniates, Belle Kanaris
Amarilly series (1)
Amateur city
Forrest, Katherine V
Kate Delafield series (1)
Amateur corpse
Brett, Simon
Charles Paris series (4)
Amateur Cracksman
Hornung, Ernest William
Raffles series (1)
Amateur crook
Clevely, Hugh
Inspector Williams series (4)
Amateur gentleman
Farnol, Jeffery
Mister Jasper Shrig of Bow Street series (1)
Amateur in crime
Graydon, William Murray
Sexton Blake series (343)
Amateur in vilence
Gilbert, Michael Francis
Patrick Petrella series (5)
Amateur in violence
Gilbert, Michael Francis
Inspector Hazelrigg series (7)
Amateur murderer
Daly, Carroll John
Race Williams series (6)
Amateur night
Beck, Kathrine Kristine
Jane Da Silva series (2)
Amateur prefects
Matthewman, Phyllis
Priory series (4)
Amateur sailor
Harling, Robert
Sailor series (1)
Amateur violence
Gilbert, Michael Francis
Inspector Hazelrigg series (7)
Amateurs in alchemy
Deegan, Jon J
Old Growler trilogy (1)
Amazing adventures of Amabel
Prior, Natalie Jane
Amabel series (1)
Amazing adventures of Carolus Herbert
Leroux, Gaston
Carolus Herbert series (1)
Amazing adventures of Letitia Carberry
Rinehart, Mary Roberts
Tish series (1)
Amazing affair at Highlands
Tarrant, Elizabeth
Highlands series (4)
Amazing affair of the renegade prince
Philips, George Norman
Sexton Blake series (395)
Amazing affair of the shipyard sabotage
Hope, Stanton
Sexton Blake series (1035)
Amazing Ben Franklin
Lerangis, Peter
Time traveler series (4)
Amazing bubblegum caper
O'Connor, Jane
Pick-a-path series (4)
Amazing corpse
Robertson, Colin
Peter Grayleigh series (3)
Amazing koalas
Campbell, Peter
Amazing Koalas series (3)
Amazing Mister Blackshirt
Graeme, Roderic
Blackshirt series (15)
Amazing Mister Bunn
Atkey, Bertram
Smiler Bunn series (1)
Amazing Mister Sandyman
Graham, Neill
Mister Sandyman series (6)
Amazing Mister Whisper
Macrow, Brenda Grace
Mister Whisper series (1)
Amazing Mrs Pollifax
Gilman, Dorothy
Mrs Emily Pollifax series (2)
Amazing quest of Doctor Syn
Thorndike, Russell
Doctor Syn series (5)
Amazing scoundrel
Carter, Nicholas
Nicholas Carter series (218)
Amazing Spiderman, As the world burns
David, Peter
Marvel superheroes adventure gamebooks series (7)
Amazing Spiderman, Crime campaign
Kupperberg, Paul
Marvel superheroes, new series (8)
Amazing Spiderman, Mayhem in Manhattan
Wein, Len
Marvel superheroes, new series (1)
Amazing stories
Mooser, Stephen
All-Star Meatballs series (7)
Amazing summer
Gibbs, Philip
Second World War series (2)
Amazing test match crime
Alington, Adrian
Inspector Posse series (2)
Amazing Wiley
Campbell, Peter
Amazing Koalas series (3)
Amazon
Carter, Nick
Nick Carter series (43)
Amazon adventure
Price, Willard
Hal and Roger Hunt series (1)
Amazon adventures of two children
Brown, Rose
Two children series (2)
Amazon planet
Reynolds, Mack
Planetary Agent series (2)
Amazon slaughter
Anthony, Piers
Jason Striker series (5)
Stivers, Dick
Able Team series (4)
Amazon strike
Wilson, Gar
Phoenix Force series (41)
Amazon strikes again
Fearn, John Russell
Golden Amazon series (5)
Amazon, where do fish swim through the treetops?
Compton, Sara
Earth inspectors series (2)
Amazons
Ross, Ian
Mind Masters series (4)
Salmonson, Jessica Amanda
Amazons series (1)
Amazon's diamond quest
Fearn, John Russell
Golden Amazon series (4)
Amazons II
Salmonson, Jessica Amanda
Amazons series (2)
Ambassadors from Aurigel
Mahr, Kurt
Perry Rhodan series (64)
Ambassadors of death
Dicks, Terrance
Doctor Who series (121)
Ambassador's plot
Frances, Stephen Daniel
John Gail series (3)
Ambassador's trunk
Barton, George
Bromley Barnes series (3)
Amber effect
Prather, Richard Scott
Shell Scott series (39)
Amber enchantress
Denning, Troy
Prism pentad series (3)
Amber eyes
Crane, Frances
Pat and Jean Abbott series (25)
Amber file
Home, Michael
John Benham series (2)
Amber fire
Barbieri, Elaine
Amber trilogy (1)
Amber junk
Hanshew, Mary E
Hamilton Cleek series (9)
Amber nine
Gardner, John Edmund
Boysie L Oakes series (3)
Amber passion
Barbieri, Elaine
Amber trilogy (3)
Amber princess
Treece, Henry
Greek trilogy (3)
Amber treasure
Barbieri, Elaine
Amber trilogy (2)
Ambergris!
Murray, Andrew
Sexton Blake series (186)
Ambermere treasure
Saville, Malcolm
Jillies series (6)

Amberwell
Stevenson, Dorothy Emily
Ayrton family series (1)
Amberwood
Rundle, Anne
Amberwood series (1)
Ambient
Womack, Jack
Terraplane trilogy (1)
Ambition
Aminoff, Constance Leonie Caroline
Napoleonic series (3)
Muspratt, Eric
Fire of youth series (4)
Amboy Dukes
Shulman, Irving
Juvenile delinquency trilogy (1)
Ambridge summer
Miles, Keith
Archers of Ambridge series (3)
Ambroo Keon
Lorrah, Jean
Sime-Gen series (7)
Ambrose in London
Levene, Philip
Ambrose West series (1)
Ambrose in Paris
Levene, Philip
Ambrose West series (2)
Ambrose Kangaroo
Macintyre, Elisabeth
Ambrose Kangaroo series (1)
Ambrose Kangaroo delivers the goods
Macintyre, Elisabeth
Ambrose Kangaroo series (4)
Ambrose Kangaroo goes to town
Macintyre, Elisabeth
Ambrose Kangaroo series (3)
Ambrose Kangaroo has a busy day
Macintyre, Elisabeth
Ambrose Kangaroo series (2)
Ambrose rock
Tangye, Derek
Minack chronicles series (13)
Ambulance call
Harrison, Elizabeth
Central London Hospital series (6)
Ambulance ship
White, James
Sector General series (4)
Ambush
Edwards, Walter
Sexton Blake series (650)
Mackenzie, Steve
Seals series (1)
Porter, Donald Clayton
White Indian series (8)
Ambush at Apache Rocks
Logan, Jake
John Slocum series (177)
Ambush at Big Creek
Hobart, Donald Bayne
Masked Rider and Blue Hawk series (17)
Ambush at Derati Wells
McCurtin, Peter
Jim Rainey series (6)
Ambush at Scorpion Valley
Macdonald, William Colt
Three Mesquiteers series (4)
Ambush at Skull Pass
Sharpe, Jon
Trailsman series (154)
Ambush for Anatol
Sherwood, John
Mister Charles Blessington series (3)
Ambush for Lassiter
Grey, Loren Zane
Lassiter series (2)
Ambush House
Steel, Kurt
Hank Hyer series (9)
Ambush in Purgatory
Christian, Frederick H
Frank Angel series (4)
Ambush in the Amazon
Myers, Walter Dean
Arrow series (4)
Ambush of shadows
Williams, Paul Osborne
Pelbar series (5)
Ambush on Blood River
Pendleton, Don
Mack Bolan series (58)
Ambush trail
Scott, Bradford
Walt Slade series (30)
Ambush Valley
Hardin, J D
Raider series (40)

Ambushers
Hamilton, Donald
Matt Helm series (6)
Amelia
Thesman, Jean
Whitney cousins series (2)
Amelia and the angels
Hooper, Muriel
Amelia series (1)
Amelia and the robber rats
Hooper, Muriel
Amelia series (2)
Amelia Bedelia
Parish, Peggy
Amelia Bedelia series (1)
Amelia Bedelia and the baby
Parish, Peggy
Amelia Bedelia series (9)
Amelia Bedelia and the surprise shower
Parish, Peggy
Amelia Bedelia series (3)
Amelia Bedelia goes camping
Parish, Peggy
Amelia Bedelia series (10)
Amelia Bedelia helps out
Parish, Peggy
Amelia Bedelia series (8)
Amelia Bedelia's family album
Parish, Peggy
Amelia Bedelia series (12)
Amelia Earhart, missing, declared dead
Larsen, Anita
Histories mysteries series (2)
Amelia Jane again
Blyton, Enid
Amelia Jane series (2)
Ameliaranne and the big treasure
Joan, Natalie
Ameliaranne series (6)
Ameliaranne and the green umbrella
Heward, Constance
Ameliaranne series (1)
Ameliaranne and the jumble sale
Osborne, Eileen
Ameliaranne series (16)
Ameliaranne and the magic ring
Farjeon, Eleanor
Ameliaranne series (7)
Ameliaranne and the monkey
Heward, Constance
Ameliaranne series (3)
Ameliaranne at the circus
Gilmour, Margaret
Ameliaranne series (5)
Ameliaranne at the farm
Heward, Constance
Ameliaranne series (11)
Ameliaranne at the seaside
Gilmour, Margaret
Ameliaranne series (9)
Ameliaranne at the zoo
Thompson, K L
Ameliaranne series (10)
Ameliaranne, bridesmaid
Morris, Ethelberta
Ameliaranne series (18)
Ameliaranne camps out
Heward, Constance
Ameliaranne series (13)
Ameliaranne, cinema star
Heward, Constance
Ameliaranne series (3)
Ameliaranne gives a Christmas party
Heward, Constance
Ameliaranne series (12)
Ameliaranne gives a concert
Gilmour, Margaret
Ameliaranne series (17)
Ameliaranne goes digging
Wood, Lorna
Ameliaranne series (19)
Ameliaranne goes touring
Heward, Constance
Ameliaranne series (15)
Ameliaranne in town
Joan, Natalie
Ameliaranne series (4)
Ameliaranne keeps school
Heward, Constance
Ameliaranne series (14)
Ameliaranne keeps shop
Heward, Constance
Ameliaranne series (2)
Ameliaranne's moving day
Morris, Ethelberta
Ameliaranne series (20)
Ameliaranne's prize packet
Farjeon, Eleanor
Ameliaranne series (7)
Ameliaranne's washing day
Farjeon, Eleanor
Ameliaranne series (8)

Amelie and Pierre
Troyat, Henri
Seed and the fruit series (2)
Amelie in love
Troyat, Henri
Seed and the fruit series (1)
Amende Honorable
Housman, Laurence
Palace plays series (3)
America, America
Kazan, Elia
Stavros the Anatolian trilogy (1)
America, I know you
Martin, Bill
Freedom series (2)
America is hard to find
Berrigan, Daniel
Conversations series (2)
America lost and found
Bailey, Anthony
America and England series (1)
America two thousand and forty
Innes, Evan
American two thousand and forty series (1)
America, why is there an eye on the pyramid on the one-dollar bill?
Packard, Edward
Earth inspectors series (1)
American
Waller, Leslie
Woods Palmer series (3)
American angler in Australia
Grey, Zane
Tales of a fisherman series (8)
American boys afloat
Optic, Oliver
All-over-the-world series (5)
American claimant
Twain, Mark
Colonel Sellers series (2)
American death orbit
Stacy, Ryder
Doomsday warrior series (14)
American defiance
Stacy, Ryder
Doomsday warrior series (7)
American dream machine
Stacy, Ryder
Doomsday warrior series (18)
American duchess
Fitzroy, Rosamond
Mallamshire series (3)
American Eden
Harris, Marilyn
Eden family series (6)
Stacy, Ryder
Doomsday warrior series (11)
American emperor
Tracy, Louis
Vansittart series (1)
American family
Baldwin, Faith
Condit family series (1)
American gentleman
Castronovo, David
Gentleman series (2)
American girl at the Durbar
Bradley, Shelland
American girl series (2)
American girl in India
Bradley, Shelland
American girl series (1)
American girl in London
Cotes, Sarah Jeanette
American tourist series (1)
American glory
Stacy, Ryder
Doomsday warrior series (8)
American Gun Club
Verne, Jules
Gun Club series (1)
American gun mystery
Queen, Ellery
Ellery Queen series (6)
American history atlas
Gilbert, Martin
History atlas series (3)
American hunger
Wright, Richard Nathaniel
Horror and the glory series (2)
American in Paris
Flanner, Janet
Paris trilogy (3)
American Indian habitats
Wolfson, Evelyn
American Indian series (1)
American Indian tools and ornaments
Wolfson, Evelyn
American Indian series (3)
American Indian utensils
Wolfson, Evelyn
American Indian series (2)

American king
Ellis, Edward Sylvester
Colonial trilogy (1)
American marquis
Carter, Nicholas
Nicholas Carter series (2)
American music makers
Nichols, Janet
Music makers series (1)
American nightmare
Bainbridge, Chuck
Hard corps series (6)
Pendleton, Don
Mack Bolan series (107)
Stacy, Ryder
Doomsday warrior series (10)
American overthrow
Stacy, Ryder
Doomsday warrior series (16)
American paradise
Stacy, Ryder
Doomsday warrior series (13)
American penman
Hawthorne, Julian
Inspector Byrnes series (1)
American plaid
De Banke, Cecile
Hand over hand series (3)
American quartet
Adler, Warren
Fiona Fitzgerald series (1)
American rebellion
Stacy, Ryder
Doomsday warrior series (6)
American revolutionary
Cover, Arthur Byron
Time machine series (10)
American River
McCarthy, Gary
Rivers west series (7)
American sextet
Adler, Warren
Fiona Fitzgerald series (2)
American triptych
Sedges, John
American life series (3)
American twins of 1812
Perkins, Lucy Fitch
Twin series (16)
American twins of the Revolution
Perkins, Lucy Fitch
Twin series (17)
American ultimatum
Stacy, Ryder
Doomsday warrior series (15)
American vengeance
Cutter, John
Specialist series (11)
American wives and English husbands
Atherton, Gertrude Franklin
Wives and husbands series (1)
American woman
Swan, Annie Shepherd
Son of Erin series (2)
American years
Boyd, Brian
Vladimir Nabokov series (2)
Sinclair, Harold
American years trilogy (1)
Americanization of Emily
Huie, William Bradford
Mamie Stover series (2)
Americans
Jakes, John
Kent family series (8)
Target, George William
Post-war Britain series (5)
America's daughter
Halsey, Rena Isabelle
Nathalie Page series (2)
America's final defense
Stacy, Ryder
Doomsday warrior series (19)
America's last declaration
Stacy, Ryder
Doomsday warrior series (5)
America's secret king
Dennison, Milo
Blackstone's magical adventure series (1)
America's sword
Stacy, Ryder
Doomsday warrior series (17)
America's zero hour
Stacy, Ryder
Doomsday warrior series (9)
Amethyst ring
France, Anatole
Contemporary history series (3)
O'Dell, Scott
Julian Escobar trilogy (3)

Amethyst spectacles
Crane, Frances
Pat and Jean Abbott series (6)
Amigo, amigo
Clifford, Francis
Loyalty trilogy (3)
Amish home
Bial, Raymond
Home series (1)
Amityville curse
Holzer, Hans
Amityville horror series (3)
Amityville horror
Anson, Jay
Amityville horror series (1)
Amityville horror 2
Jones, John G
Amityville horror series (4)
Amityville horror 3
Jones, John G
Amityville horror series (5)
Amityville, the untold story
Jones, John G
Amityville horror series (7)
Amityville three-D
McGill, Gordon
Amityville horror series (6)
Amnesia trap
Ormerod, Roger
David Mallin and George Coe series (13)
Amok
Janson, Hank
Hank Janson series (48)
Among the brigands
De Mille, James
Young Dodge Club series (2)
Among the cannibals
Verne, Jules
Captain Grant's children series (1)
Captain Grant's children series (1)
Among the counterfeiters
Carter, Nicholas
Nicholas Carter series (32)
Among the eagles
Wisler, Gary Clifton
Willie Delamer series (10)
Among the farmyard people
Pierson, Clara Dillingham
Among the animals series (3)
Among the forest people
Pierson, Clara Dillingham
Among the animals series (2)
Among the garden people
Pierson, Clara Dillingham
Among the animals series (6)
Among the meadow people
Pierson, Clara Dillingham
Among the animals series (1)
Among the night people
Pierson, Clara Dillingham
Among the animals series (5)
Among the nihilists
Carter, Nicholas
Nicholas Carter series (21)
Among the pond people
Pierson, Clara Dillingham
Among the animals series (4)
Among the river pirates
Lloyd, Hugh
Skippy Dare series (1)
Among the volcanoes
Castaneda, Omar S
Isabel series (1)
Among those absent
Coles, Manning
Tommy Hambledon series (9)
Among those present
Barrington, Pamela
Inspector George Travers series (2)
Among you, taking notes
Mitchison, Naomi
Small talk series (4)
Amorous captive
Janson, Hank
Hank Janson series (81)
Amorous cheat
Creighton, Basil
Amorous cheat series (1)
Amorous Leander
Hunter, Alan
Inspector George Gently series (30)
Amorous rogue
Foxall, Raymond
John Crispin series (2)
Amorous trooper
Bassett, Ronald
Margaret family series (2)
Amorous umbrella
Kaye, Marvin
Fillmore series (2)

Amos Crowle, widow-maker
Hanson, Victor Joseph
Amos Crowle series (5)

Amos Flagg, bushwacked
Randall, Clay
Amos Flagg series (4)

Amos Flagg has his day
Randall, Clay
Amos Flagg series (5)

Amos Flagg, high gun
Randall, Clay
Amos Flagg series (2)

Amos Flagg, lawman
Randall, Clay
Amos Flagg series (1)

Amos Flagg rides out
Randall, Clay
Amos Flagg series (3)

Amos Flagg, showdown
Randall, Clay
Amos Flagg series (6)

Amos lives
Hanson, Victor Joseph
Amos Crowle series (13)

Amos Petrie's puzzle
Turner, John Victor
Amos Petrie series (3)

Ampersand
Common, Jack
Newcastle-upon-Tyne series (2)

Ampersand papers
Innes, Michael
Sir John Appleby series (31)

Amphetamines and pearls
Harvey, John Barton
Scott Mitchell series (1)

Amphibians
Wright, Sydney Fowler
Amphibians series (1)

Amphitheatre plot
Carter, Nicholas
Nicholas Carter series (619)

Ample proposition
Lehmann, John
In my own time series (3)

Ampurias exchange
Ross, Angus
Mark Farrow series (9)

Amsterdam
Carter, Nick
Nick Carter series (35)

Amsterdam diversion
Ross, Angus
Mark Farrow series (6)

Amulet
Morlan, A R
Ewerton series (2)

Amulet of doom
Coville, Bruce
Twilight series (24)

Amusement park mystery
Warner, Gertrude Chandler
Boxcar children series (25)

Amy and Laura
Sachs, Marilyn
Amy and Laura series (3)

Amy in Acadia
Reed, Helen Leah
Brenda series (6)

Amy moves in
Pascal, Francine
Sweet Valley twins series (44)
Sachs, Marilyn
Amy and Laura series (1)

Amyot crime
Nicole, Christopher
Amyot family series (3)

Amyot's Cay
Nicole, Christopher
Amyot family series (1)

Amy's pen pal
Pascal, Francine
Sweet Valley twins series (35)

Amy's secret sister
Pascal, Francine
Sweet Valley twins series (83)

Amy's true love
Pascal, Francine
Sweet Valley High series (75)

Anackire
Lee, Tanith
Wars of Vis trilogy (2)

Anaheim run
Robbins, David
Endworld series (13)

Analysis of symbolic structure
Burke, Kenneth
Attitudes towards history series (2)

Anarch lords
Chandler, Arthur Bertram
John Grimes series (21)

Anarchist
Broch, Hermann
Sleepwalkers trilogy (2)

Anarchists in love
Spencer, Colin
Simpson family series (1)

Anarchists' moon
Griffin, John
Richard Raven series (5)

Anarchy in the ashes
Johnstone, William Wallace
Ashes series (3)

Anarchy of love
Spencer, Colin
Simpson family series (1)

Anastasia again!
Lowry, Lois
Anastasia Krupnik series (2)

Anastasia, ask your analyst
Lowry, Lois
Anastasia Krupnik series (4)

Anastasia at this address
Lowry, Lois
Anastasia Krupnik series (8)

Anastasia at your service
Lowry, Lois
Anastasia Krupnik series (3)

Anastasia has the answers
Lowry, Lois
Anastasia Krupnik series (6)

Anastasia Krupnik
Lowry, Lois
Anastasia Krupnik series (1)

Anastasia on her own
Lowry, Lois
Anastasia Krupnik series (5)

Anastasia's chosen career
Lowry, Lois
Anastasia Krupnik series (7)

Anathema stone
Hilton, John Buxton
Superintendent Simon Kenworthy series (6)

Anatole
Titus, Eve
Anatole series (1)

Anatole and the cat
Titus, Eve
Anatole series (2)

Anatole and the piano
Titus, Eve
Anatole series (6)

Anatole and the Pied Piper
Titus, Eve
Anatole series (10)

Anatole and the poodle
Titus, Eve
Anatole series (5)

Anatole and the robot
Titus, Eve
Anatole series (3)

Anatole and the thirty thieves
Titus, Eve
Anatole series (7)

Anatole and the toyshop
Titus, Eve
Anatole series (8)

Anatole in Italy
Titus, Eve
Anatole series (9)

Anatole over Paris
Titus, Eve
Anatole series (4)

Anatolian
Kazan, Elia
Stavros the Anatolian trilogy (2)

Anatomy lesson
Roth, Philip
Nathan Zuckerman series (3)

Anatomy of a riot
Wainwright, John
Northern Police series (52)

Ancestors of Bantan
Gardner, Maurice Benjamin
Bantan series (11)

Ancestral voices
Lees-Milne, James
Ancestral voices series (1)
Ruck, Berta
Storyteller series (5)

Anchor for her heart
Newcomb, Ellsworth
Joan and Bill series (1)

Anchor man
Jackson, Jesse
Charley Moss series (2)

Anchor trick
Wall, Anthony
Roger Moore and the Crimefighters series (6)

Ancient
Bischoff, David
SeaQuest series (3)

Ancient Allan
Haggard, Henry Rider
Allan Quatermain series (14)
Holy flower trilogy (3)

Ancient dreams
Alexander, Marc
Wells of Ythan series (1)

Ancient evil
Brennan, James Herbert
Sagas of the Demonspawn series (3)

Ancient light
Gentle, Mary
Orthe series (2)

Ancient lights and certain new reflections
Ford, Ford Madox
Memories and impressions series (1)

Ancient one
Barron, Tom A
Heartlight series (2)

Ancora Scipio
Gates, Tudor
Vendetta series (3)

And a bottle of rum
Graeme, Bruce
Theodore I Terhune series (7)

And a sunflower grew
Fisher, Aileen
Ways of plants series (2)

And after that, the dark
Wallace, Kathleen
Veronica Ramsay series (2)

And all between
Snyder, Zilpha Keatley
Green-sky trilogy (2)

And all I learned
Cannan, Joanna
Frank Frobisher series (1)

And all that beauty
Bridges, Roy
Australian trilogy (1)

And all through the house
McBain, Ed
Eighty Seventh Precinct series (48)

And another thing
Spring, Howard
Heaven lies about us series (3)

And be a villain
Cannan, Joanna
Inspector Ronald Price series (4)
Stout, Rex
Nero Wolfe and Archie Goodwin series (13)

And being dead
Erskine, Margaret
Inspector Septimus Finch series (1)

And Berry came too
Yates, Dornford
Berry series (7)

And cauldron bubble
Flynn, Brian
Anthony Bathurst series (39)

And dangerous to know
Daly, Elizabeth
Henry Gamadge series (14)

And de fun don't done
Barrett, Robert G
Les Norton series (8)

And death came too
Gilbert, Anthony
Arthur Crook series (29)
Mace, Helen
Noel Vickery series (3)

And did murder him
Turnbull, Peter
P Division series (7)

And die she did
Oellrichs, Inez
Matt Winters series (4)

And died so?
Gielgud, Val
Inspector Gregory Pellew and Viscount Clymping series (3)

And eternity
Anthony, Piers
Incarnations of immortality series (7)

And four to go
Stout, Rex
Nero Wolfe and Archie Goodwin series (31)

And gazelles leaping
Ghose, Sudhindra Nath
Sister Svenska series (1)

And here comes, Bucknuckle
Hopgood, Alan
Sports series (2)

And here is the noose
O'Hara, Kevin
Chico Brett series (11)

And here my troubles began
Spiegelman, Art
Survivor's tale series (2)

And high water
Stein, Aaron Marc
Tim Mulligan and Elsie Mae Hunt series (5)

And hope to die
Ormerod, Roger
Philipa Lowe series (8)
Powell, Richard
Arab and Andy Blake series (5)

And I heard a bird sing
Guy, Rosa
Imamu Jones series (3)

And I quote
Lambert, Derek
Quote series (2)

And in the morning
Darrell, Elizabeth
Sheridan family series (2)

And incidentally, murder!
Lovell, B E
Edge Hannegan series (1)

And left for dead
Lockridge, Frances
Assistant District Attorney Bernie Simmons series (1)

And love thee evermore
Allan, Lennox
Living sword series (1)

And loving it!
Johnston, William
Maxwell Smart series (6)

And Maggie makes three
Nixon, Joan Lowery
Maggie series (2)

And Miss Carter wore pink
Bradley, Helen
Edwardian Lancashire series (1)

And my mean old mother will be sorry, Blackboard Bear
Alexander, Martha G
Blackboard Bear series (2)

And next the king
Carter, Nick
Nick Carter series (136)

And no one wept
Hocking, Anne
Inspector William Austen series (22)

And now all this
Sellar, Walter Carruthers
All that series (2)

And now for something completely trivial
Johnson, Kim Howard
Monty Python series (7)

And now it's sables
Spanier, Ginette
Mink and sables series (2)

And now, tomorrow
Bartlett, Vernon
My life series (2)

And on the eighth day
Queen, Ellery
Ellery Queen series (36)

And one cried murder
Thayer, Lee
Peter Clancy series (59)

And one for the dead
Audemars, Pierre
Monsieur Pinaud series (19)

And one must die
Henneker, Philip
Susan Campbell and Paul Ross series (1)

And one rode west
Graham, Heather
Civil War trilogy (3)

And one wore gray
Graham, Heather
Civil War trilogy (2)

And only man
Dick, Alexandra
Alastair Macalastair series (1)

And Peter said goodbye
Farrington, Liz
Mrs Murgatroyd series (1)

And promenade home
De Mille, Agnes
Ballet memoirs series (2)

And quiet flows the Don
Sholokhov, Mikhail
Don series (2)

And shame the devil
Woods, Sara
Sir Nicholas Harding and Antony Maitland series (13)

And she had a little knife
Linklater, Joseph Lane
Silas Booth series (4)

And so divided
Burton, Thomas
Bloodbird series (1)

And so he had to die
Cameron, Donald Clough
Abelard Voss series (3)

And so my garden grows
Spier, Peter
Mother Goose library series (4)

And so to America
Roberts, Cecil
And so series (2)

And so to Bath
Roberts, Cecil
And so series (1)

And so to bed
Ard, William
Lou Largo series (4)

And so to murder
Dickson, Carter
Sir Henry Merrivale series (12)

And so to Rome
Roberts, Cecil
And so series (3)

And so Victoria
Wilkins, Vaughan
Victoria series (1)

And sombre the valleys
Closs, Hannah
Albigensian trilogy (2)

And soon I'll come to kill you
Kelly, Susan
Liz Connors and Jack Lingemann series (6)

And sudden death
Adams, Cleve Franklin
Rex McBride series (1)

And the big men fly
Hopgood, Alan
Sports series (1)

And the deep blue sea
Knotts, Raymond
Jim Hale series (1)

And the glory
Jennings, D K
Doctor Ralph Conway series (11)

And the undead sing
Brown, Carter
Mavis Seidlitz series (12)

And the wild birds sing
Irish, Lola
Colonial trilogy (1)

And the wind blows free
Short, Luke
Big Jim Wade series (1)

And then came fear
Cumberland, Marten
Saturnin Dax series (10)

And then put out the light
Lorac, E C R
Inspector Macdonald series (33)

And then silence
Propper, Milton
Tommy Rankin series (3)

And then the screaming started
Blakeston, Oswell
Screaming series (1)

And then there was nun
Quill, Monica
Sister Mary Teresa series (3)

And then there'll be fireworks
Elgin, Suzette Haden
Ozark fantasy trilogy (3)

And then what happened, Paul Revere?
Fritz, Jean
American Revolution series (2)

And then you die
Martin, James E
Gil Disbro series (3)

And thereby hangs!
Spiller, Andrew
Chief Inspector Duck Mallard series (7)

And when she was bad she was murdered
Starnes, Richard
Barney Forge and Doctor Saint George Peachy series (2)

And when she was bad she was popular
Rhodes, Susan
Bad girls series (2)

And where she stops
Dewey, Thomas Blanchard
Pete Schofield series (1)

And which, the knave?
Scott, Barbara Montagu
Grisenbaum family series (2)

And worms have eaten them
Cumberland, Marten
Saturnin Dax series (9)

And yet so new
Lunn, Arnold
Now I see series (3)

And you wonder, Herman, why I never want to go to Italian restaurants
Unger, Jim
Herman series (2)
Anderson Crow, detective
McCutcheon, George Barr
Anderson Crow series (2)
Anderson tapes
Sanders, Lawrence
Edward X Delaney series (1)
Anderson Valley shootout
Hardin, J D
Raider series (22)
Andie and the boys
Harrell, Janice
Andie and the boys series (1)
Andree de Taverney
Dumas, Alexandre
Marie Antoinette series (5)
Andrew Connington
Irwin, Grace
Andrew Connington series (2)
Androcles and the lion, and other Aesop's fables
Paxton, Tom
Aesop in verse series (3)
Android avenger
White, Ted
Android Tanner series (1)
Android invasion
Black, Christopher
Star challenge series (2)
Android planet
Rankine, John
Space nineteen ninety nine series (8)
Andromeda assignment
Lewis, David
Steve Savage series (1)
Andromeda breakthrough
Hoyle, Fred
Andromeda series (2)
Andropov file
Carter, Nick
Nick Carter series (233)
Andy
Borntrager, Mary Christner
Ellie's people series (6)
Andy and her twin
Hurt, Freda Mary
Andy series (9)
Andy and his last parade
Taylor, Reginald
Andy series (8)
Andy and the alien
Pascal, Francine
Sweet Valley kids series (29)
Andy and the display team
Taylor, Reginald
Andy series (3)
Andy and the mascots
Taylor, Reginald
Andy series (1)
Andy and the miniature war
Taylor, Reginald
Andy series (6)
Andy and the royal review
Taylor, Reginald
Andy series (7)
Andy and the secret papers
Taylor, Reginald
Andy series (5)
Andy and the sharpshooters
Taylor, Reginald
Andy series (4)
Andy and the water crossing
Taylor, Reginald
Andy series (2)
Andy at Yale
Stokes, Roy Eliot
University series (1)
Andy finds a way
Hurt, Freda Mary
Andy series (6)
Andy gets the blame
Hurt, Freda Mary
Andy series (4)
Andy goes abroad
Hurt, Freda Mary
Andy series (7)
Andy in danger
Hurt, Freda Mary
Andy series (5)
Andy in trouble
Hurt, Freda Mary
Andy series (1)
Andy joins the BMX Bunch
Lynam, Terence
BMX Gang series (4)
Andy joins the Gang
Lynam, Terence
BMX Gang series (4)
Andy keeps a secret
Hurt, Freda Mary
Andy series (2)
Andy looks for gold
Hurt, Freda Mary
Andy series (11)
Andy meets a hero
Hurt, Freda Mary
Andy series (10)
Andy Pandy and his hobby horse
Bird, Maria
Andy Pandy series (4)
Andy Pandy and Teddy at the zoo
Bird, Maria
Andy Pandy series (15)
Andy Pandy and the baby monkey
Bird, Maria
Andy Pandy series (41)
Andy Pandy and the baby pigs
Bird, Maria
Andy Pandy series (27)
Andy Pandy and the badger
Bird, Maria
Andy Pandy series (35)
Andy Pandy and the ducklings
Bird, Maria
Andy Pandy series (8)
Andy Pandy and the gingerbread man
Bird, Maria
Andy Pandy series (5)
Andy Pandy and the green puppy
Bird, Maria
Andy Pandy series (36)
Andy Pandy and the hedgehog
Bird, Maria
Andy Pandy series (22)
Andy Pandy and the patchwork cat
Bird, Maria
Andy Pandy series (29)
Andy Pandy and the scarecrow
Bird, Maria
Andy Pandy series (37)
Andy Pandy and the snowman
Bird, Maria
Andy Pandy series (30)
Andy Pandy and the spotted cow
Bird, Maria
Andy Pandy series (40)
Andy Pandy and the teddy dog
Bird, Maria
Andy Pandy series (25)
Andy Pandy and the tiny piglet
Bird, Maria
Andy Pandy series (42)
Andy Pandy and the white kitten
Bird, Maria
Andy Pandy series (16)
Andy Pandy and the willow tree
Bird, Maria
Andy Pandy series (17)
Andy Pandy and the woolly lamb
Bird, Maria
Andy Pandy series (24)
Andy Pandy and the yellow dog
Bird, Maria
Andy Pandy series (39)
Andy Pandy builds a house for Looby Loo
Bird, Maria
Andy Pandy series (18)
Andy Pandy in the country
Bird, Maria
Andy Pandy series (12)
Andy Pandy paints his house
Bird, Maria
Andy Pandy series (20)
Andy Pandy plays lions and tigers
Bird, Maria
Andy Pandy series (33)
Andy Pandy, Teddy and Looby Loo
Bird, Maria
Andy Pandy series (11)
Andy Pandy, the baby clown
Lingstrom, Freda
Andy Pandy series (42)
Andy Pandy's adventures
Bird, Maria
Andy Pandy series (42)
Andy Pandy's busy friends
Bird, Maria
Andy Pandy series (42)
Andy Pandy's dovecot
Bird, Maria
Andy Pandy series (26)
Andy Pandy's garden
Bird, Maria
Andy Pandy series (1)
Andy Pandy's jack-in-the-box
Bird, Maria
Andy Pandy series (13)
Andy Pandy's jump-up book
Bird, Maria
Andy Pandy series (10)
Andy Pandy's kite
Bird, Maria
Andy Pandy series (19)
Andy Pandy's little goat
Bird, Maria
Andy Pandy series (28)
Andy Pandy's little house
Bird, Maria
Andy Pandy series (2)
Andy Pandy's new pet
Bird, Maria
Andy Pandy series (31)
Andy Pandy's nursery rhymes
Bird, Maria
Andy Pandy series (7)
Andy Pandy's playhouse
Bird, Maria
Andy Pandy series (34)
Andy Pandy's puppy
Bird, Maria
Andy Pandy series (23)
Andy Pandy's red motor car
Bird, Maria
Andy Pandy series (38)
Andy Pandy's shop
Bird, Maria
Andy Pandy series (14)
Andy Pandy's shopping bag
Bird, Maria
Andy Pandy series (21)
Andy Pandy's tea-party
Bird, Maria
Andy Pandy series (9)
Andy Pandy's washing day
Bird, Maria
Andy Pandy series (6)
Andy Pandy's weather house
Bird, Maria
Andy Pandy series (32)
Andy takes the lead
Hurt, Freda Mary
Andy series (3)
Andy wins the prize
Hurt, Freda Mary
Andy series (8)
Angado
Tubb, Edwin Charles
Dumarest series (29)
Ange Pitou
Dumas, Alexandre
Marie Antoinette series (3)
Angel
Brown, Carter
Lieutenant Al Wheeler series (24)
Kilworth, Garry
Angel series (1)
Vassilikos, Vassilis
Modern Greece trilogy (3)
Angel abroad
Montrose, Graham
Angel Brown series (4)
Angel alone
Ryder, Thom
Avenging Angel series (2)
Angel and the Nero
Montrose, Graham
Angel Brown series (10)
Angel and the red admiral
Montrose, Graham
Angel Brown series (13)
Angel astray
Janson, Hank
Hank Janson series (116)
Angel at arms
Montrose, Graham
Angel Brown series (12)
Angel at my table
Frame, Janet
Is-land trilogy (2)
Angel challenge
Norman, Mick
Gerry Vinson series (2)
Angel death
Moyes, Patricia
Henry and Emmy Tibbett series (15)
Angel dust
Cohen, Anthea
Nurse Agnes Carmichael series (9)
Angel Eyes
Dietrich, Robert
Steve Bentley series (6)
Estleman, Loren D
Amos Walker series (2)
Angel face
Giraud, Jean
Lieutenant Mike S Blueberry series (3)
Angel for hire
Longley, W B
Angel Eyes series (9)
Angel for Paradise
Canon, Jack
Mike Paradise series (1)
Angel gang
Kuhlken, Ken
Tom Hickey trilogy (3)
Angel Heart
Thompson, Victoria
Kid Collins series (3)
Angel hold fire
McCall, K T
Johnny Buchanan series (19)
Angel in action
Cohen, Anthea
Nurse Agnes Carmichael series (11)
Angel in charge
Delton, Judy
Angel series (2)
Angel in heavy shoes
Weber, Lenora Mattingly
Stacy and Katie Rose Belford series (5)
Angel in love
Cohen, Anthea
Nurse Agnes Carmichael series (12)
Angel in marble
Coffman, Elaine
Mackinnon brothers series (4)
Angel in Paradise
Montrose, Graham
Angel Brown series (7)
Angel Mae
Hughes, Shirley
Tale of Trotter Street series (1)
Angel of death
Carter, Nicholas
Nicholas Carter series (458)
Cohen, Anthea
Nurse Agnes Carmichael series (3)
Doherty, Paul C
Hugh Corbett series (4)
Krich, Rochelle Majer
Jessie Drake series (4)
Montrose, Graham
Angel Brown series (2)
Pike, Charles R
Jubal Cade series (15)
Angel of destruction
Hedges, Joseph
John Stark series (12)
Angel of Hangtown
Willoughby, Lee Davis
Women who won the West series (6)
Angel of light
McCutcheon, Hugh
Anthony Howard series (1)
Inspector McKeller series (1)
Angel of no mercy
Montrose, Graham
Angel Brown series (1)
Angel of pain
Stableford, Brian Michael
Werewolves series (2)
Angel of the opera
Siciliano, Sam
Sherlock Holmes sequels series (100)
Angel of the revolution
Griffith, George Chetwynd
Romanoff series (1)
Angel of Torremolinos
Serafin, David
Superintendent Luis Bernal series (6)
Angel of vengeance
Cohen, Anthea
Nurse Agnes Carmichael series (2)
De Villiers, Gerard
Malko Linge series (9)
Montrose, Graham
Angel Brown series (6)
Angel on each shoulder
Willis, William
Ancient mariner trilogy (2)
Angel Range
Reese, John
Jesus on horseback trilogy (1)
Angel, shoot to kill
Janson, Hank
Hank Janson series (6)
Angel Square
Doyle, Brian
Tommy series (2)
Angel with the sword
Cherryh, Carolyn Janice
Merovingen nights series (1)
Angel without mercy
Cohen, Anthea
Nurse Agnes Carmichael series (1)
Angela and the broken heart
Robinson, Nancy Konheim
Angela trilogy (3)
Angela and the king-size crusade
Smith, Susan
Best friends series (2)
Angela, private citizen
Robinson, Nancy Konheim
Angela trilogy (2)
Angelina and Alice
Holabird, Katharine
Angelina Ballerina series (6)
Angelina and the dragon
Holabird, Katharine
Angelina Ballerina series (7)
Angelina and the princess
Holabird, Katharine
Angelina Ballerina series (2)
Angelina at the fair
Holabird, Katharine
Angelina Ballerina series (3)
Angelina Ballerina
Holabird, Katharine
Angelina Ballerina series (1)
Angelina dances
Holabird, Katharine
Angelina Ballerina series (11)
Angelina ice-skates
Holabird, Katharine
Angelina Ballerina series (12)
Angelina on stage
Holabird, Katharine
Angelina Ballerina series (5)
Angelina's baby sister
Holabird, Katharine
Angelina Ballerina series (9)
Angelina's birthday and address book
Holabird, Katharine
Angelina Ballerina series (12)
Angelina's birthday surprise
Holabird, Katharine
Angelina Ballerina series (8)
Angelina's book and doll package
Holabird, Katharine
Angelina Ballerina series (12)
Angelina's Christmas
Holabird, Katharine
Angelina Ballerina series (4)
Angelique
Golon, Sergeanne
Angelique series (1)
Angelique and the demon
Golon, Sergeanne
Angelique series (8)
Angelique and the ghosts
Golon, Sergeanne
Angelique series (9)
Angelique and the king
Golon, Sergeanne
Angelique series (2)
Angelique and the Sultan
Golon, Sergeanne
Angelique series (3)
Angelique in Barbary
Golon, Sergeanne
Angelique series (3)
Angelique in love
Golon, Sergeanne
Angelique series (5)
Angelique in revolt
Golon, Sergeanne
Angelique series (4)
Angelo
Giono, Jean
Angelo series (1)
Angels
Barton, James
Wasteworld series (3)
Milne, Paula
Angels series (1)
Angels and ministers
Housman, Laurence
Palace plays series (3)
Angels are painted fair
Whelton, Paul
Garry Dean series (3)
Angels fell
Fischer, Bruno
Ben Helm series (4)
Angels from hell
Norman, Mick
Gerry Vinson series (1)
Angels in chains
Franklin, Max
Charlie's Angels series (4)
Angels in hell
Morris, Janet Ellen
Heroes in hell series (6)
Angels in red
Cooper, Lisa
Princess Beatrice Hospital series (3)

Angels in the snow
Lambert, Derek
Angels in the snow series (1)
Angel's law
Christian, Frederick H
Frank Angel series (12)
Angel's mother's baby
Delton, Judy
Angel series (5)
Angel's mother's boyfriend
Delton, Judy
Angel series (3)
Angel's mother's wedding
Delton, Judy
Angel series (4)
Angels of doom
Charteris, Leslie
Saint series (7)
Angels of September
Greeley, Andrew Moran
Time between the stars (2)
Angels on a string
Franklin, Max
Charlie's Angels series (3)
Angels on holiday
Sorenson, Jane
Katie Hooper series (6)
Angels on ice
Franklin, Max
Charlie's Angels series (5)
Angels on my mind
Norman, Mick
Gerry Vinson series (4)
Angels One-Five
Hough, Richard Alexander
World War II trilogy (1)
Angel's share
Graham, Heather
Donna Miro and Lorna Doria series (2)
Irvine, Robert Ralstone
Moroni Traveler series (2)
Angel's way
Christian, Frederick H
Frank Angel series (13)
Angels weep
Smith, Wilbur Addison
Zouga Ballantyne series (3)
Angelwalk
Elwood, Roger
Angelwalk series (1)
Anger at World's End
Reid, Desmond
Sexton Blake series (1562)
Anger of the bells
Rath, Virginia
Rocky Allan series (5)
Anger of the north
Clayton, John
Provence trilogy (3)
Angle of attack
Burns, Rex
Gabriel Wager series (4)
Angler's El Dorado
Grey, Zane
Tales of a fisherman series (5)
Anglo-Catholic
Leslie, Shane
Oppidan trilogy (3)
Angry
Leonard, Marcia
Feelings series (1)
Angry Amazons
Brown, Carter
Danny Boyd series (22)
Randy Roberts series (2)
Angry angel
Zilahy, Lajos
Dukay family series (2)
Angry battalion
Harris, Herbert
Hawaii Five-O series (3)
Angry canary
Robeson, Kenneth
Doc Savage series (129)
Angry ghost
Robeson, Kenneth
Doc Savage series (86)
Angry giants of Troll Mountain
Torgersen, Don Arthur
Troll series (6)
Angry gymnast
Jenkins, Jerry Bruce
Dallas O'Neil and the Baker Street Sports Club series (4)
Angry night
Baker, William Howard
Sexton Blake series (1485)
Angry ocean
Johnston, Ronald
James Bruce series (2)
Angry planet
Cross, John Keir
Albatross series (1)
Angry story
Erickson, Karen
I can do it series (8)
Angry sun
King, Robin
Merchant Navy trilogy (3)
Angry tide
Graham, Winston
Poldark series (7)
Angry young man
Paul, Leslie
Angry young man series (2)
Anguish and farewell, 1793-1799
Flexner, James Thomas
George Washington series (4)
Angus and the cat
Flack, Marjorie
Angus series (2)
Angus and the ducks
Flack, Marjorie
Angus series (1)
Angus and Topsy
Flack, Marjorie
Angus series (6)
Angus and Wag-Tail Bess
Flack, Marjorie
Angus series (4)
Angus lost
Flack, Marjorie
Angus series (3)
Animal
Emberley, Ed
First words series (3)
Animal allsorts
Oxenbury, Helen
Seven hundred and twenty nine series (1)
Animal architects
Freedman, Russell
Animal behavior series (2)
Animal babies
Kalman, Bobbie
North American wildlife series (1)
Animal builders
Lilly, Kenneth
Animal series (5)
Animal car
Barkan, Joanne
Circus train come aboard series (4)
Animal climbers
Lilly, Kenneth
Animal series (2)
Animal day
Ziefert, Harriet
Mister Rose's class series (1)
Animal disguises
Fisher, Aileen
Ways of animals series (2)
Animal doctors
Greene, Carla
What do they do series (5)
Animal fathers
Freedman, Russell
Animal behavior series (3)
Animal fun
Gree, Alain
Smashers series (6)
Animal fun 123
Brown, Mik
Animal fun series (2)
Animal fun ABC
Brown, Mik
Animal fun series (1)
Animal game
Derrick, Lionel
Penetrator series (27)
Animal games
Freedman, Russell
Animal behavior series (4)
Animal haus
Browne, Dik
Hagar the horrible series (17)
Animal hotel
Cooper, Diana Davis
Animal hotel series (1)
Animal houses
Fisher, Aileen
Ways of animals series (1)
Animal instincts
Freedman, Russell
Animal behavior series (1)
Animal jackets
Fisher, Aileen
Ways of animals series (3)
Animal jumpers
Lilly, Kenneth
Animal series (1)
Animal lore and disorder
Riddell, James
Animal lore and disorder series (1)
Animal orphan
Hart, Sharon M
Animal Rescue Farm series (2)
Animal people
Coblentz, Stanton Arthur
Outlander series (2)
Animal runners
Lilly, Kenneth
Animal series (4)
Animal shelter mystery
Warner, Gertrude Chandler
Boxcar children series (22)
Animal specialists
Aaseng, Nathan
Early nature picture book series (1)
Animal superstars
Freedman, Russell
Animal behavior series (6)
Animal swimmers
Lilly, Kenneth
Animal series (3)
Animal wife
Thomas, Elizabeth Marshall
Reindeer moon series (2)
Animal words
Tyler, Jenny
First words series (4)
Animal worlds
Kalman, Bobbie
In my world series (8)
Animals
Hill, Eric
Peek-a-book series (3)
Oxenbury, Helen
Baby board books series (3)
Animals are my life
Straiton, Eddie
Vet series (1)
Animals before breakfast
Bowring, Mary
Animals series (2)
Animals came in one by one
Lloyd-Jones, Buster
Vet series (1)
Animals come first
Bowring, Mary
Animals series (1)
Animals from Mother Goose
Hopkins, Lee Bennett
Mother Goose series (1)
Animals in art
Richmond, Robin
Story in a picture series (2)
Animals naughty and nice
Rosenberg, Amye
Animals series (1)
Animals of Farthing Wood
Dann, Colin
Farthing Wood series (1)
Animals round the clock
Bowring, Mary
Animals series (3)
Animals wild and wooly
Rosenberg, Amye
Animals series (2)
Animalwatching
Morris, Desmond
Watching series (6)
Animating Maria
Chesney, Marion
School of manners series (5)
Anjani the Mighty
Titan, Earl
Anjani series (2)
Ankle grabber
Impey, Rose
Creepies series (4)
Ann and Peter in Austria
Mannin, Ethel
Kennedys abroad series (12)
Ann and peter in Belgium
Someren, Liesje van
Kennedys abroad series (11)
Ann and Peter in Brittany
Guillemin, Anne
Kennedys abroad series (5)
Ann and Peter in Denmark
Martin, Nancy
Kennedys abroad series (4)
Ann and Peter in Greece
Vaughan, Carol
Kennedys abroad series (19)
Ann and Peter in Holland
Someren, Liesje van
Kennedys abroad series (1)
Ann and Peter in Israel
Willcox, Kathleen Mary
Kennedys abroad series (13)
Ann and Peter in Japan
Mannin, Ethel
Kennedys abroad series (7)
Ann and Peter in London
Wilson, Barbara Ker
Kennedys abroad series (18)
Ann and Peter in northern Italy
Richards, Phyllis
Kennedys abroad series (8)
Ann and Peter in Norway
Hogg, Garry
Kennedys abroad series (9)
Ann and Peter in Paris
Wilson, Barbara Ker
Kennedys abroad series (14)
Ann and Peter in Rome
Richards, Phyllis
Kennedys abroad series (15)
Ann and Peter in Scotland
Greenham, Hazel
Kennedys abroad series (16)
Ann and Peter in southern Germany
Einberg, Elizabeth
Kennedys abroad series (3)
Ann and Peter in southern Spain
Callas, Theo
Kennedys abroad series (2)
Ann and Peter in Sweden
Mannin, Ethel
Kennedys abroad series (6)
Ann and Peter in Switzerland
Willcox, Kathleen Mary
Kennedys abroad series (17)
Ann and Peter in Yugoslavia
Richards, Phyllis
Kennedys abroad series (10)
Ann and Susie keep shop
Wahlstedt, Viola
Ann and Susan series (2)
Ann and Susie pick berries
Wahlstedt, Viola
Ann and Susan series (4)
Ann and the Jolly Six
Grove, Harriet Pyne
Ann Sterling series (2)
Ann Bartlett in Bataan
Johnson, Martha
Ann Bartlett series (2)
Ann Bartlett in the South Pacific
Johnson, Martha
Ann Bartlett series (3)
Ann Bartlett, navy nurse
Johnson, Martha
Ann Bartlett series (1)
Ann Bartlett on stateside duty
Johnson, Martha
Ann Bartlett series (5)
Ann Bartlett returns to the Philippines
Johnson, Martha
Ann Bartlett series (4)
Ann crosses a secret trail
Grove, Harriet Pyne
Ann Sterling series (3)
Ann goes hunting
Smyth, John George
Ann Sheldon series (3)
Ann of Cambray
Lide, Mary
Ann of Cambray trilogy (1)
Ann Rankin and the boy who painted horses
Buddee, Paul
Ann Rankin series (3)
Ann Rankin and the great flood
Buddee, Paul
Ann Rankin series (2)
Ann Rankin and the house on Coolabah Hill
Buddee, Paul
Ann Rankin series (4)
Ann Rankin and the lost valley
Buddee, Paul
Ann Rankin series (1)
Ann Sterling
Grove, Harriet Pyne
Ann Sterling series (1)
Ann, the gentle
Kimbrough, Katheryn
Phenwick women series (20)
Ann turns detective
Daniel, Roland
Inspector John Walk series (2)
Anna
Gilchrist, Ellen
Anna Hudson series (2)
Anna all alone
Sandwall-Bergstrom, Martha
Anna series (1)
Anna and the black knight
Fynn
Anna series (3)
Anna and the magic hat
Sandberg, Inger
Anna series (1)
Anna at Bloom Farm
Sandwall-Bergstrom, Martha
Anna series (1)
Anna at the manor house
Sandwall-Bergstrom, Martha
Anna series (5)
Anna Chevron
Turner, James Ernest
Nicholas de la Haye series (3)
Anna Hastings
Drury, Allen
Washington series (7)
Anna keeps her promise
Sandwall-Bergstrom, Martha
Anna series (3)
Anna of the Five Towns
Bennett, Arnold
Five towns series (2)
Anna papers
Gilchrist, Ellen
Anna Hudson series (1)
Anna Hudson series (2)
Anna, Paul and Tommycat say hello
Girard, Nicole
Anna, Paul and Tommycat series (1)
Anna solves the mystery
Sandwall-Bergstrom, Martha
Anna series (6)
Anna Svard
Lagerlof, Selma
Ring of the Lowenskolds trilogy (3)
Anna Truly and the Christmas nights
Drummond, Violet Hilda
Little Laura series (6)
Anna, where are you?
Wentworth, Patricia
Miss Maud Silver series (20)
Anna wins through
Sandwall-Bergstrom, Martha
Anna series (4)
Annabel visits the country
Hayes, Barbara
Town mouse and country mouse series (1)
Annabella and the smugglers
Fitt, Mary
Annabella series (4)
Annabella at the lighthouse
Fitt, Mary
Annabella series (1)
Annabella takes a plunge
Fitt, Mary
Annabella series (2)
Annabella to the rescue
Fitt, Mary
Annabella series (3)
Annals of a quiet neighbourhood
Macdonald, George
Quiet neighbourhood series (1)
Annals of Ann
Sharber, Kate Trimble
Ann and Eve series (1)
Annals of the Black Company
Cook, Glen
Chronicles of the Black Company series (3)
Annals of the Heechee
Pohl, Frederik
Heechee series (4)
Annals of the Time Patrol
Anderson, Poul
Time Patrol series (2)
Annapolis alphabet
Stevens, William Oliver
Annapolis alphabet series (1)
Anna's book
Fynn
Anna series (2)
Anna's mother has a birthday
Sandberg, Inger
Anna series (4)
Anne
Remick, Grace May
Sheldon Six series (1)
Anne Belinda
Wentworth, Patricia
Waveneys series (2)
Anne Kempburn, truthseeker
Bryant, Marguerite
Stone trilogy (2)
Anne of Avonlea
Montgomery, Lucy Maud
Avonlea series (2)
Anne of Green Gables
Montgomery, Lucy Maud
Avonlea series (1)
Anne of Green Gables cookbook
Macdonald, Kate
Avonlea series (11)
Anne of Ingleside
Montgomery, Lucy Maud
Avonlea series (7)

Anne of the Blossom Shop
Mullins, Iola May
Blossom Shop series (2)
Anne of the island
Montgomery, Lucy Maud
Avonlea series (4)
Anne of Windy Poplars
Montgomery, Lucy Maud
Avonlea series (5)
Anne of Windy Willows
Montgomery, Lucy Maud
Avonlea series (5)
Anne Thornton
Anthony, Lotta Rowe
Anne Thornton series (3)
Anne Thornton, junior guide
Anthony, Lotta Rowe
Anne Thornton series (2)
Anne Thornton, Wetamoo
Anthony, Lotta Rowe
Anne Thornton series (1)
Anne's house of dreams
Montgomery, Lucy Maud
Avonlea series (6)
Anne's wedding
Mullins, Iola May
Blossom Shop series (3)
Annette and Bennett
Cannan, Gilbert
Laurie series (6)
Annette and Company
Cheyne, Irene
Annette series (2)
Annette and Sylvie
Rolland, Romain
Soul enchanted series (1)
Annette of River Bend
Cheyne, Irene
Annette series (1)
Annie
Ehrlich, Amy
Annie series (1)
Annie and the desert treasure
Manushkin, Fran
Annie series (3)
Annie and the kidnappers
Ehrlich, Amy
Annie series (3)
Annie and the new baby
Louhi, Kristiina
Annie series (4)
Annie and the party thieves
Manushkin, Fran
Annie series (4)
Annie finds a home
Ehrlich, Amy
Annie series (2)
Annie finds Sandy
Manushkin, Fran
Annie series (1)
Annie goes to the jungle
Manushkin, Fran
Annie series (2)
Annie is almost three
Louhi, Kristiina
Annie series (3)
Annie Jordan
Post, Mary Brinker
Annie Jordan series (1)
Annie Kilburn
Howells, William Dean
Annie Kilburn series (1)
Annie Marble in Germany
Forester, Cecil Scott
Annie Marble series (2)
Annie Parsons
Shears, Sarah
Annie Parsons trilogy (1)
Annie Pat and Eddie
Haywood, Carolyn
Eddie Wilson series (8)
Annie Sugden's country diary
Mackenzie, Lee
Annie Sugden series (1)
Annie's boys
Shears, Sarah
Annie Parsons trilogy (2)
Annie's day
Louhi, Kristiina
Annie series (1)
Annie's kingdom
Shears, Sarah
Annie Parsons trilogy (3)
Annie's year
Louhi, Kristiina
Annie series (2)
Annihilation
Ostrander, Isabel
Timothy McCarty series (5)
Annihilators
Hamilton, Donald
Matt Helm series (20)
Annihilist
Robeson, Kenneth
Doc Savage series (31)
Anniversaries
Johnson, Uwe
Jakob Abs series (2)
Anniversaries II
Johnson, Uwe
Jakob Abs series (3)
Anniversary
Housman, Laurence
Palace plays series (4)
Anno Domini
Oxenham, John
Jesus Christ series (2)
Anno's Britain
Anno, Mitsumasa
Anno's journey series (3)
Anno's Italy
Anno, Mitsumasa
Anno's journey series (2)
Anno's journey
Anno, Mitsumasa
Anno's journey series (1)
Anno's journey III
Anno, Mitsumasa
Anno's journey series (3)
Anno's math games
Anno, Mitsumasa
Math games series (1)
Anno's math games II
Anno, Mitsumasa
Math games series (2)
Anno's USA
Anno, Mitsumasa
Anno's journey series (4)
Annotated Alice
Carroll, Lewis
Alice in Wonderland series (2)
Annotated Clerihew
Horgan, Paul
Clerihews series (2)
Annotated Dracula
Stoker, Bram
Dracula series (1)
Annotated Innocence of Father Brown
Chesterton, Gilbert Keith
Father Brown series (1)
Annotated She
Haggard, Henry Rider
She series (3)
Annotated Sherlock Holmes
Doyle, Arthur Conan
Sherlock Holmes series (10)
Ann's ambitions
Grove, Harriet Pyne
Ann Sterling series (6)
Ann's crime
Scott, Reginald Thomas Maitland
Aurelius Smith series (3)
Ann's search rewarded
Grove, Harriet Pyne
Ann Sterling series (4)
Ann's sterling heart
Grove, Harriet Pyne
Ann Sterling series (7)
Annulet of gilt
Taylor, Phoebe Atwood
Asey Mayo series (12)
Anodyne necklace
Grimes, Martha
Inspector Richard Jury series (3)
Anomalous phenomena
Verne, Jules
Hector Servadac series (2)
Anome
Vance, Jack
Durdane trilogy (1)
Anonymous Venetian
Leon, Donna
Commissario Guido Brunetti series (3)
Another Annapolis alphabet
Stevens, William Oliver
Annapolis alphabet series (2)
Another big book about Little Bear
Clarke, Molly
Little Bear series (2)
Another bloody ratbag book
Cue, Kerry
Bloody ratbags series (2)
Another bouquet
Newman, Andrea
Bouquet series (2)
Another breath of Border air
Derwent, Lavinia
Border series (2)
Another Bunchy book
Brisley, Joyce Lankester
Bunchy series (2)
Another case for Inspector Jackson
Lindsay, David T
Inspector John Jay Jackson series (2)
Another Claudia
Franken, Rose
Claudia series (3)
Another dawn
Brown, Sandra
Coleman family and Jake Langston series (2)
Another day, another death
Bagby, George
Inspector Schmidt series (36)
Another day, another dungeon
Costikyan, Greg
Dungeon series (1)
Another day, another stiff
Brett, Michael
Pete McGrath series (7)
Another day toward dying
Marlett, Melba
Sarah O'Brien series (2)
Another death in Venice
Hill, Reginald
Superintendent Andrew Dalziel and Sergeant Pascoe series (8)
Another door opens
Mackenzie, Lee
Emmerdale Farm series (21)
Another fine mess
Needle, Jan
Size spies series (2)
Another fine myth
Asprin, Robert Lynn
Skeeve series (1)
Another fish story
Browne, Dik
Hagar the horrible series (50)
Another good friend
Odgers, Sally Farrell
Helen and Dominic series (1)
Another grain of truth
Webster, Jack
Grain of truth series (2)
Another grey ghost book
Middleton, Jessie Adelaide
Grey ghost series (2)
Another helping of Chips
Hughes, Shirley
Chips series (2)
Another holiday camp mystery
Cole, Margaret Alice
Judy Lawler series (4)
Another Jennifer
Sorenson, Jane
Jennifer series (5)
Another job for Biggles
Johns, William Earl
Biggles series (37)
Another kind of magic
Allen, Charlotte Vale
Hidden meanings series (2)
Harris, Mollie
Kind of magic series (2)
Another letter of John to James
Kater, John
John to James series (2)
Another little death
Turner, Bill
Detective Inspector Manson series (4)
Another load of cocky chaff
Nelson, Brian
Cocky chaff series (2)
Another lucky dip
Ainsworth, Ruth
Lucky dip series (2)
Another man's poison
Cleeves, Ann
George Palmer-Jones series (5)
Holman, Hugh
Sheriff Macready series (4)
Another man's shadow
Bude, John
Inspector Meredith series (26)
Another moon
Turner, Mary
Blythe family series (2)
Another morgue heard from
Davis, Frederick Clyde
Schyler Cole and Luke Speare series (5)
Another mug for the bier
Starnes, Richard
Barney Forge and Doctor Saint George Peachy series (1)
Another mystery in Suva
Arthur, Frank
Inspector Spearpoint series (2)
Another naval digression
Franklin, Gordon
Naval digressions series (2)
Another part of the city
McBain, Ed
Eighty Seventh Precinct series (39)
Another part of the forest
Stern, Gladys Bronwyn
Ragbag chronicles series (2)
Another part of the wood
Clark, Kenneth Mackenzie
Self-portrait series (1)
Mackail, Denis
Noodles series (1)
Another pony for Jean
Cannan, Joanna
Jean series (2)
Another Saturday night of wild and reckless abandon
Guisewhite, Cathy
Cathy series (1)
Another scandal
Hamilton, Cosmo
Scandal series (2)
Another secret diary
Byrd, William
Secret diary series (2)
Another self
Lees-Milne, James
Ancestral voices series (4)
Another sixty years
Richmond, Arthur Cyril
Years series (2)
Another story of a little mouse trapped in a book
Felix, Monique
Little mouse trapped in a book series (2)
Another story to tell
Bruna, Dick
Stories to tell series (2)
Another stretch of Porridge
Victor, Paul
Porridge series (2)
Another study of woman
Balzac, Honore de
Scenes of private life series (28)
Another Teddy Robinson
Robinson, Joan Gale
Teddy Robinson series (6)
Another thrilling holiday
Cole, Margaret Alice
Judy Lawler series (3)
Another way to die
Crowe, John
Buena Costa County series (1)
Another weeping woman
Zochert, Donald
Nick Caine series (1)
Another window seat
Mottram, Ralph Hale
Life observed series (2)
Another woman's man
Lee, Norma
Beautiful Gunner series (3)
Another world
Myrdal, Jan
Another world series (2)
Another world, 1897-1917
Eden, Anthony
Reckoning series (1)
Another year with Denise and Ned Toodles
Jackson, Gabrielle Emilie
Denise and Ned Toodles series (2)
Another's crime
Hawthorne, Julian
Inspector Byrnes series (4)
Answer in the negative
Hamilton, Henrietta
Johnny and Sally Heldar series (4)
Answer to building your self-image
Wright, Harry Norman
Answer series (9)
Answer to depression
Wright, Harry Norman
Answer series (2)
Answer to discipline
Wright, Harry Norman
Answer series (4)
Answer to divorce
Wright, Harry Norman
Answer series (7)
Answer to family communication
Wright, Harry Norman
Answer series (5)
Answer to frustration and anger
Wright, Harry Norman
Answer series (6)
Answer to in-law relationships
Wright, Harry Norman
Answer series (8)
Answer to loneliness
Wright, Harry Norman
Answer series (11)
Answer to parent-teen relationships
Wright, Harry Norman
Answer series (10)
Answer to submission and decision making
Wright, Harry Norman
Answer series (12)
Answer to the fulfilled marriage
Wright, Harry Norman
Answer series (3)
Answer to the tide
Ogilvie, Elisabeth May
Bennett Island series (5)
Answer to worry and anxiety
Wright, Harry Norman
Answer series (1)
Ant and Bee
Banner, Angela
Ant and Bee series (1)
Ant and Bee and Kind Dog
Banner, Angela
Ant and Bee series (7)
Kind Dog series (1)
Ant and Bee and the ABC
Banner, Angela
Ant and Bee series (9)
Ant and Bee and the doctor
Banner, Angela
Ant and Bee series (12)
Ant and Bee and the rainbow
Banner, Angela
Ant and Bee series (6)
Ant and Bee and the secret
Banner, Angela
Ant and Bee series (11)
Ant and Bee big buy bag
Banner, Angela
Ant and Bee series (13)
Ant and Bee go shopping
Banner, Angela
Ant and Bee series (14)
Ant and Bee time
Banner, Angela
Ant and Bee series (10)
Antagonists
Gann, Ernest Kellogg
Triumph series (2)
Haggard, William
Colonel Charles Russell series (6)
Thurston, Ernest Temple
Richard Furlong series (1)
Antarctic convergence
Griffin, John
Richard Raven series (8)
Antarctic mystery
Verne, Jules
Arthur Gordon Pym series (2)
Antarctic raider
McLaughlin, William Raffan Davidson
Antarctic series (1)
Antares dawn
McCollum, Michael
Antares series (1)
Antares passage
McCollum, Michael
Antares series (2)
Antelope Company ashore
Hall, Willis
Antelope Company trilogy (2)
Antelope Company at large
Hall, Willis
Antelope Company trilogy (3)
Antelope Springs
Wisler, Gary Clifton
Willie Delamer series (3)
Ante-room
Dickson, Lovat
Ante-room series (1)
O'Brien, Kate
Considine family series (2)
Anthony Dare
Marshall, Archibald
Anthony Dare series (1)
Anthony Dare's progress
Marshall, Archibald
Anthony Dare series (3)
Anthony Lyveden
Yates, Dornford
Anthony Lyveden series (1)
Anthony Ravenhill, crime merchant
Foster, Reginald Francis
Anthony Ravenhill series (3)
Anthony Trant
Downing, John Hyatt
Anthony Trant series (2)
Anthony Trent, avenger
Martyn, Wyndham
Anthony Trent series (8)
Anthony Trent, master criminal
Martyn, Wyndham
Anthony Trent series (1)

Anthropol
Trimble, Louis
Anthropol Detective Agency series (1)
Antic years
Franken, Rose
Claudia series (8)
Anti-coloring book
Striker, Susan
Anti-coloring series (1)
Anti-coloring book for adults only
Striker, Susan
Anti-coloring book series (4)
Anti-coloring book of exploring space on earth
Striker, Susan
Anti-coloring book series (1)
Anti-coloring book of masterpieces
Striker, Susan
Anti-coloring book series (3)
Anti-coloring book of red letter days
Striker, Susan
Anti-coloring book series (2)
Anti-coloring calendar
Striker, Susan
Anti-coloring book series (9)
Antidote to venom
Crofts, Freeman Wills
Inspector Joseph French series (18)
Antimacassar City
McCrone, Guy
Moorhouse family trilogy (1)
Antimatter formula
Leibold, Jay
Choose your own adventure series (57)
Antipodes
Oliver, Maria Antonia
Lonia Guiu series (2)
Antipope
Rankin, Robert
Brentford series (1)
Antique dealer's tale
Bremond d'Ars, Yvonne de
Journal of an antique dealer series (2)
Anti-woo
Potter, Stephen
Lifemanship Correspondence College series (5)
Antoine of Oregon
Otis, James
Pioneer series (4)
Antoinette
Rolland, Romain
John Christopher series (3)
Antonio and Mellida
Marston, John
Antonio series (1)
Antonio's revenge
Marston, John
Antonio series (2)
Antony Ant and the earwig pirates
Gilmore, David Hunter
Christopher Cricket series (2)
Antrian messenger
Wisler, Gary Clifton
Antrian series (1)
Antro, the life-giver
Deegan, Jon J
Old Growler trilogy (2)
Antrobus complete
Durrell, Lawrence
Antrobus series (3)
Ant's castle
Trevor, Elleston
Woodlanders series (4)
Anvil
Drake, David
Generals series (3)
Anvil of hell
Pendleton, Don
SuperBolan series (11)
Anvil of ice
Rohan, Michael Scott
Winter of the world trilogy (1)
Anvil of stars
Bear, Greg
Law series (2)
Anxious conspirator
Underwood, Michael
Superintendent Simon Manton series (13)
Any day now
Derleth, August
Sac Prairie series (4)
Any kind of danger
Cousins, Edmund George
Brigadier Worrall series (2)
Any man's death
Estleman, Loren D
Peter Macklin series (3)
Any old port
Clement, Henry
Columbo series (3)
Any other complaints, Herman?
Unger, Jim
Herman series (12)
Any shape or form
Daly, Elizabeth
Henry Gamadge series (9)
Any village
Baldwin, Faith
Doctor Bing Irvington series (2)
Little Oxford series (2)
Any way you like
John, Stephen
Albert Divine series (3)
Anybody but Anne
Wells, Carolyn
Fleming Stone series (5)
Anybody can do anything
Macdonald, Betty
Who me series (3)
Anything but a soldier
Hislop, John
Soldier and gentleman series (2)
Anything but saintly
Deming, Richard
Matt Rudd series (2)
Anything but the truth
Wells, Carolyn
Fleming Stone series (18)
Anything can happen
Shaw, Jane
Ali and Dizzy series (1)
Anything for a quiet life
Gilbert, Michael Francis
Patrick Petrella series (4)
Anything for Kelly
Sheldon, Ann
Linda Craig adventures series (10)
Anything for love
Pascal, Francine
Sweet Valley University series (4)
Anything might happen
Balfour, Hearnden
Inspector Jack Strickland series (3)
Anything once
Wyndham, Joan
Love diary series (3)
Anything to declare?
Crofts, Freeman Wills
Inspector Joseph French series (32)
Anything to win
Joyce, Rosemary
Dream girls series (1)
Anytime rings
Faraday, Robert
Adventures in the time machine series (1)
Anyway, this particular Sunday
Fitzwilliam, Jennifer
Mona series (1)
Anywhere but here
Pinney, Peter
Dust on my shoes series (3)
Apache
Porter, Donald Clayton
White Indian series (14)
Apache ambush
Cunningham, Chet
Wade Chisholm series (1)
Gentry, Buck
Eli Holten series (9)
Apache arrows
Sherman, Jory
Gunn series (8)
Apache blood
Muir, James A
Breed series (22)
Thompson, David
Nathaniel King series (12)
Apache breakout
Masterson, Louis
Morgan Kane series (30)
Apache Canyon
Goscinny, Rene
Lucky Luke series (7)
Apache caress
Gentry, Georgina
Panorama of the old West series (8)
Apache dawn
Dawson, Clay
Long Rider series (4)
Apache death
Gilman, George G
Edge series (3)
Apache devil
Burroughs, Edgar Rice
Apache series (2)
Apache gold
Bishop, Samuel P
Track series (3)
Fox, Brian
Alias Smith and Jones series (4)
Hardin, J D
Raider and Doc series (24)
Roberts, J R
Gunsmith series (73)
Sharpe, Jon
Trailsman series (32)
Apache hunter
Shirreffs, Gordon Donald
Lee Kershaw series (5)
Apache junction
Mitchum, Hank
Stage coach station series (43)
Apache Junction
Slade, Jack
Lassiter series (20)
Apache messiah
Lee, Patrick
Six-Gun Samurai series (8)
Apache moon
Bodine, J D
Pecos Kid series (3)
Apache raiders
Benteen, John
Neal Fargo series (6)
Duncan, Terence
Powell's army series (2)
Apache rampage
Edson, John Thomas
Floating Outfit series (53)
Apache ransom
Fisher, Clay
Ben Allison series (5)
Franciscan prient series (1)
Apache rifles
Dalton, Kit
Buckskin series (28)
Apache squaw
McLaglen, John J
Herne the Hunter series (5)
Apache sunrise
Logan, Jake
John Slocum series (54)
Apache thunder
Mason, Dan
Lex Cranshaw series (6)
Apache trail
Hardin, J D
Raider and Doc series (48)
Ledd, Paul
Shelter Morgan series (9)
Apache trick
Gentry, Buck
Eli Holten series (27)
Apache war
McCurtin, Peter
Sundance series (34)
Apache way
Frazee, Steve
High Chaparral series (3)
Apaches
Hall, Oakley
Legends west trilogy (3)
Apart from a little dampness, Herman, how's everything?
Unger, Jim
Herman series (1)
Ape escape
Reese, Bob
Going ape series (2)
Ape in velvet
Foley, Rae
John Harland series (2)
Ape team
Reese, Bob
Going ape series (4)
Apeman's secret
Dixon, Franklin W
Hardy boys series (62)
Apes and ivory
Packer, Joy
Pack and follow series (3)
Apocalypse
Konvitz, Jeffrey
Sentinel series (2)
Robinson, Nigel
Timewyrm series (3)
Rosenberger, Joseph
Death Merchant series (70)
Apocalypse, USA
Rosenberger, Joseph
Death Merchant series (54)
Apocrypha
Jones, Valerie
Miracleman series (5)
Apollo legacy
Barker, Albert
Reefe King series (2)
Apollo's war
Larson, Glen A
Battlestar Galactica series (13)
Apostle
Asch, Sholem
Biblical series (2)
Apostles of light
Douglas, Ellen
Homochito County series (4)
Apostles of violence
Braun, Maurice-Gilles
Al Glenne series (1)
Appalachee Red
Andrews, Raymond
Appalachee Red series (1)
Appassionata
Franzero, Carlo Maria
Mrs Caroline series (2)
Appearances of death
Shannon, Dell
Lieutenant Luis Mendoza series (28)
Appeasers
Gilbert, Martin
Appeasement series (2)
Apperson's folly
Mallory, Arthur
Doctor Kirke Montgomery series (1)
Apple
Bruna, Dick
Toy box tale series (1)
Apple Acre
Bell, Adrian
Country life series (4)
Apple and Eve
Ammers-Kuller, Jo van
Leyden trilogy (3)
Apple and pear
Tarsky, Sue
Look and see series (1)
Apple and Percival
Armstrong, Anthony
Percival series (3)
Apple Bough
Streatfeild, Noel
Shoes series (11)
Apple on a pear tree
Burress, John
Singleton family series (2)
Apple pie adventure
Blair, Cynthia
Susan and Christine Pratt series (8)
Apple pie alien
Lavelle, Sheila
Jupiter Jane series (1)
Apple spy in the sky
Lovell, Marc
Appleton Porter series (4)
Apple to the core
Lovell, Marc
Appleton Porter series (5)
Apple tree lean down
Pearce, Mary Emily
Apple tree series (1)
Apple tree saga
Pearce, Mary Emily
Apple tree series (3)
Appleby and Honeybath
Innes, Michael
Charles Honeybath series (4)
Sir John Appleby series (33)
Appleby and the ospreys
Innes, Michael
Sir John Appleby series (35)
Appleby at Allington
Innes, Michael
Sir John Appleby series (22)
Appleby file
Innes, Michael
Sir John Appleby series (29)
Appleby on Ararat
Innes, Michael
Sir John Appleby series (7)
Appleby plays chicken
Innes, Michael
Sir John Appleby series (16)
Appleby talking
Innes, Michael
Sir John Appleby series (14)
Appleby talks again
Innes, Michael
Sir John Appleby series (15)
Appleby's answer
Innes, Michael
Sir John Appleby series (27)
Appleby's end
Innes, Michael
Sir John Appleby series (10)
Appleby's other story
Innes, Michael
Sir John Appleby series (28)
Applegreen cat
Crane, Frances
Pat and Jean Abbott series (5)
Applewood
Michelet, Claude
Wood trilogy (2)
Paice, Margaret
Fletcher family series (3)
Appley Dapply's nursery rhymes
Potter, Beatrix
Peter Rabbit verse series (1)
Appleyards
Edwards, David
Appleyards series (1)
Appleyards again
Edwards, David
Appleyards series (2)
Appointed to die
Charles, Kate
David Middleton-Brown series (3)
Appointed with danger
Baker, William Howard
Sexton Blake series (1441)
Appointment at Bloodstar
Smith, Edward Elmer
Family d'Alembert series (5)
Appointment at eight
Desmond, Hugh
Alan Fraser series (13)
Appointment at nine
Disney, Doris Miles
Jim O'Neill series (3)
Appointment in Andalusia
Mackintosh, May
Laurie Grant and Stewart Noble series (1)
Appointment in Cairo
Brewer, Gil
Al Mundy series (3)
Appointment in Crete
Rendel, Alexander Meadows
War in Crete series (1)
Appointment in Haiphong
Carter, Nick
Nick Carter series (167)
Appointment in Iran
Jason, Stuart
Butcher series (23)
Appointment in Kabul
Pendleton, Don
Mack Bolan series (73)
Appointment in Kiltone
York, Andrew
Jonathan Anders series (3)
Appointment in New Orleans
Claymore, Tod
Tod Claymore series (3)
Appointment in Tangier
Wilkinson, Laurence
Mike Daryl series (4)
Appointment in Tibet
Murray, William Hutchinson
John Taunt series (1)
Appointment on the Yellowstone
Lomax, Bliss
Yellowstone series (2)
Appointment with death
Barling, Charles
Inspector George Marshall series (7)
Christie, Agatha
Hercule Poirot series (18)
Appointment with F.E.A.R.
Jackson, Steve
Fighting fantasy gamebook series (17)
Apprehensive dog
Bailey, Henry Christopher
Mister Reggie Fortune series (17)
Apprentice
Early, Richard Elliott
Thomas Early series (1)
Gallacher, Tom
Bill Thompson trilogy (1)
Apprentice in terror
Warren, Paulette
Caliban series (3)
Apprentice to fear
Brinton, Henry
John and Sally Strang series (7)
Apprentices
Garfield, Leon
Apprentices series (12)
Apprenticeship
Nexo, Martin Andersen
Pelle the conqueror series (2)
Approach to farming
Donaldson, Frances Annesley
Farming series (1)
Approved to scrap
Macdonnell, James Edmond
Dutchy Holland series (12)

Apricot ape
Reese, Bob
Going ape series (1)
April adventure
Oterdahl, Jeanna
Tina series (1)
April folly
Lucas, Saint John
First round series (2)
April fool!
Pascal, Francine
Sweet Valley twins series (28)
April fool at Hob Lane School
Leeson, Robert
Hob Lane series (1)
April Fool mystery
Nixon, Joan Lowery
First read-alone mystery series (6)
April-fool twins
Timlow, Elizabeth Weston
Dorothy Dot series (2)
April fools
Mackenzie, Compton
John Touchwood series (2)
Mooser, Stephen
All-Star Meatballs series (8)
April Fool's Day magic
Baker, James Webb
Magic series (5)
April Fool's Day mystery
Markham, Marion M
Dixon twins series (5)
April girl
Bromige, Iris
Rainwood family series (3)
April harvest
Bubb, Lillian
Christiansson family trilogy (3)
Budd, Lillian
Kristiansson trilogy (3)
April Panhasard
Hine, Muriel
April Panhasard series (2)
April rainers
Fraser, Anthea
Inspector David Webb and Sergeant Ken Jackson series (7)
April Rising
Sallis, Susan
Rising family series (1)
April Robin murders
Rice, Craig
Bingo Riggs and Handsome Kusak series (3)
April shroud
Hill, Reginald
Superintendent Andrew Dalziel and Sergeant Pascoe series (7)
April snow
Bubb, Lillian
Christiansson family trilogy (1)
Budd, Lillian
Kristiansson trilogy (1)
April story
Martin, Robert
Career adventure series (2)
Aqualung twins and the Iron Crab
Falkner, Frederick
Aqualung twins series (3)
Aqualung twins and the vanishing people
Falkner, Frederick
Aqualung twins series (2)
Aqualung twins find Chinese treasure
Falkner, Frederick
Aqualung twins series (1)
Aquarian attack
Randle, Kevin
Seeds of war trilogy (3)
Aquarius
Mark, Jan
Manipulator trilogy (3)
Aquatech warriors
Appleton, Victor II
Tom Swift Junior series 3 (6)
Aquila and the iron horse
Somtow, S P
Aquiliad trilogy (2)
Aquila and the sphinx
Somtow, S P
Aquiliad trilogy (3)
Aquila in the new world
Somtow, S P
Aquiliad trilogy (1)
Aquiliad
Sucharitkul, Somtow
Aquiliad trilogy (1)
Arab interlude
Sheridan, Clare
Nuda veritas series (2)
Arab plague
Carter, Nick
Nick Carter series (53)
Arabel and Morimer
Aiken, Joan
Arabel and Mortimer series (6)
Arabel and the escaped black mamba
Aiken, Joan
Arabel and Mortimer series (2)
Arabel's raven
Aiken, Joan
Arabel and Mortimer series (1)
Arabel and Mortimer series (3)
Arabian assault
McAdam, Preston
Shield series (2)
Arabian days
Philby, Harry St John Bridger
Arabian travel series (4)
Arabian nightmare
Blackburn, Martin
Delgado series (4)
Murphy, Warren Burton
Destroyer series (86)
Murray, Will
Destroyer series (86)
Arabian Nights murder
Carr, John Dickson
Doctor Gideon Fell series (7)
Arabian pearl
Jackson, Marian J A
Miss Abigail Patience Danforth series (2)
Arafel's saga
Cherryh, Carolyn Janice
Ealdwood series (2)
Araminta Station
Vance, Jack
Cadwal chronicles series (1)
Arapaho revenge
Gilman, George G
Edge series (43)
Ararat
Thomas, Donald Michael
Russian quartet (1)
Ara's field
Marks, Laurie J
Children of Triad trilogy (3)
Araway oath
Adams, Herbert
Major Roger Bennion series (13)
Arbiter of your fate
Walter, William Wilfred
Pastor's son trilogy (3)
Arbor Day magic
Baker, James Webb
Magic series (10)
Arc of infinity
Dicks, Terrance
Doctor Who series (80)
Arc of the dream
Attanasio, A A
Radix Tetrad series (3)
Archangel
Kilworth, Garry
Angel series (2)
Archdeacons afloat
Alington, Cyril Augustine
Archdeacon series (1)
Mister Birtley series (1)
Archdeacons ashore
Alington, Cyril Augustine
Archdeacon series (2)
Archer plus twenty
Clevely, Hugh
Maxwell Archer series (2)
Archers intervene
Webb, Geoffrey
Archers of Ambridge series (2)
Archers of Ambridge
Webb, Geoffrey
Archers of Ambridge series (1)
Archer's revenge
Roberts, J R
Gunsmith series (48)
Archery contest
Saddler, Allen
King and queen series (1)
Arches of the years
Boileau, Ethel
Hippy Buchan series (2)
Sutherland, Halliday
Arches of the years series (1)
Archie abroad
Bateman, Robert
Archibald McGillicuddy series (3)
Archie and the missing stamps
Bateman, Robert
Archibald McGillicuddy series (4)
Archie on the trail
Bateman, Robert
Archibald McGillicuddy series (7)
Archie, young detective
Bateman, Robert
Archibald McGillicuddy series (1)
Archie's Italian adventure
Bateman, Robert
Archibald McGillicuddy series (5)
Archipelago
Lafferty, Raphael Aloysius
Argos mythos series (2)
Coscuin chronicles series (3)
Architects
Fisher, Leonard Everett
Colonial Americans series (16)
Architect's secret
Bayfield, William John
Sexton Blake series (162)
Architecture of desire
Gentle, Mary
White crow series (2)
Archives of Haven
Savarin, Julian Jay
Lemmus trilogy (3)
Archivist
Alderman, Gill
Guna series (1)
Archy and Mehitabel
Marquis, Don
Archy and Mehitabel series (1)
Archy's life of Mehitabel
Marquis, Don
Archy and Mehitabel series (2)
Arctic abduction
Carter, Nick
Nick Carter series (258)
Arctic adventure
Price, Willard
Hal and Roger Hunt series (14)
Arctic animals
Kalman, Bobbie
Arctic world series (1)
Arctic assignment
Charles, Robert
Simon Larren series (5)
Arctic blues
Laird, Elizabeth
Toucan Tecs series (2)
Arctic bush pilot
Helmericks, Bud
Bob Hamilton series (3)
Arctic community
Kalman, Bobbie
Arctic world series (2)
Arctic hunter
Helmericks, Bud
Bob Hamilton series (2)
Arctic land
Kalman, Bobbie
Arctic world series (3)
Arctic mutiny
Horst, Karl
U-boat series (3)
Arctic patrol mystery
Dixon, Franklin W
Hardy boys series (48)
Arctic rose
Harrison, Claire
Tamara series (1)
Arctic trail
Graydon, William Murray
Sexton Blake series (287)
Arctic treachery
Woodman, Richard
Nathaniel Drinkwater series (5)
Arctic unicorn
Luenn, Nancy
Unicorn series (1)
Arctic whales and whaling
Kalman, Bobbie
Arctic world series (4)
Ardath
Corelli, Marie
Heliobas series (2)
Two worlds series (3)
Ardneh's world
Saberhagen, Fred
Chup trilogy (3)
Ardrey ambush
Kirk, Thomas Hobson
William and Susan series (3)
Are we in love?
Pascal, Francine
Sweet Valley High series (94)
Are we still best friends?
Barkin, Carol
Transition series (1)
Are we there yet?
Andrews, Wendy
Vacation fever series (2)
Are you listening Rabbi Low
Donleavy, James Patrick
Sigmund Schultz series (2)
Arena
Haggard, William
Colonel Charles Russell series (3)
Arena of Antares
Akers, Alan Burt
Dray Prescot series (7)
Arena of death
Smith, Mark
Duelmaster series (5)
Arenas-fields-pitches-turfs
Kostlanetz, Richard
Sports fields series (2)
Aren't you the one who?
Miller, Frances Abbott
Losers and winners series (1)
Arf
Gray, Harold
Little Orphan Annie series (12)
Arfive
Guthrie, Alfred Bertram
Settlement of the American West series (5)
Argentine deadline
Pendleton, Don
Phoenix Force series (1)
Argle's causeway
Pardoe, Margot
Macalister children series (2)
Argle's mist
Pardoe, Margot
Macalister children series (1)
Argle's oracle
Pardoe, Margot
Macalister children series (3)
Argonaut affair
Hawke, Simon
Timewars series (7)
Argument of kings
Scannell, Vernon
Tiger and the rose trilogy (3)
Argus gambit
Ross, David D
Dreamers of the day series (1)
Argus pheasant
Beecham, John Charles
Koyola series (1)
Argus steps in
Sernine, Daniel
Argus series (1)
Arigato
Condon, Richard
Captain Colin Huntington series (1)
Aristocratic detective
Marsh, Richard
Augustus Champnell series (2)
Aristocrats
Saint-Pierre, Michel de
Aristocrats series (1)
Arizona!
Ross, Dana Fuller
Wagons West series (21)
Arizona ambush
Pendleton, Don
Mack Bolan series (31)
Roberts, J R
Gunsmith series (119)
Arizona Ames
Grey, Zane
Arizona Ames series (1)
Arizona blood trail
Sadler, Jeff
Marshal Andrew Anderson series (1)
Arizona bloodline
Garrett, Charles C
Gunslinger series (5)
Arizona break-out
Rey, Bret
Will Foreman series (2)
Arizona bride
Bittner, F Rosanne
Brides series (1)
Arizona bustout
Hunter, E J
Headhunter series (6)
Arizona climax
Chisholm, Matt
Joe Blade series (7)
Arizona fancy lady
Fletcher, Dirk
Spur McCoy series (2)
Arizona gun feud
Nickson, Arthur
Rusty Hines series (8)
Arizona gunfire
Cunningham, Chet
Wade Chisholm series (2)
Arizona gunmen
Ellis, Wesley
Lone Star series (91)
Arizona hardcase
Sherman, Jory
Gunn series (13)
Arizona hellcat
Hunter, E J
Headhunter series (1)
Arizona hellride
Hardin, J D
Raider series (25)
Arizona hideout
Nickson, Arthur
Rusty Hines series (11)
Arizona laydown
Hunter, E J
White Squaw series (21)
Arizona Longhorn adventure
Dengler, Sandy
Pioneer family series (3)
Arizona outlaw
Hobart, Donald Bayne
Masked Rider and Blue Hawk series (7)
Arizona Ranger
Edson, John Thomas
Waco series (4)
Arizona round-up
Leyland, Eric
Bill, Jake and Ned series (1)
Arizona slaughter
Sharpe, Jon
Trailsman series (118)
Arizona stranger
Ellis, Wesley
Lone Star series (87)
Arizona triangle
Roberts, J R
Gunsmith series (92)
Arizona ways
Tuttle, Wilbur Coleman
Hashknife Hartley and Sleepy Stevens series (3)
Arizona wildcat
Grover, Marshall
Larry and Stretch series (2)
Ark
Benary, Margot
Lechow family series (1)
Erickson, Paul
Doctor Who series (114)
Ark in space
Marter, Ian
Doctor Who series (31)
Sarah Jane Smith series (9)
Ark of doom
Woodley, Richard
Man from Atlantis series (4)
Ark of Elm Island
Kellogg, Elijah
Elm Island series (3)
Ark on the flood
Knowles, Anne
Cotswold vet series (2)
Ark Two
Appleton, Victor II
Tom Swift Junior series 2 (7)
Arkansas breakout
Harvey, John Barton
Wes Hart series (7)
Arkansas raiders
Harte, Bryce
Slate Creed series (10)
Arkansas River
Sherman, Jory
Rivers west series (6)
Arkham evil
Diaper, John
Cthulhu Mythos series (9)
Arkville dragon
Beaman, Sydney George Hulme
Toytown series (15)
Arlette
Freeling, Nicolas
Arlette Van der Valk series (3)
Arly
Peck, Robert Newton
Arly series (1)
Arly's run
Peck, Robert Newton
Arly series (2)
Arm of the law
Underwood, Michael
Superintendent Simon Manton series (6)
Arm of the leopard
Gaunt, Mary
Doctor Craven series (1)
Arm of the starfish
L'Engle, Madeleine
Poly and Charles O'Keefe series (1)
Armada of Antares
Akers, Alan Burt
Dray Prescot series (11)
Armageddon
Pournelle, Jerry
There will be war series (8)

Rankin, Robert
Armageddon trilogy (1)
Armageddon box
Weinberg, Robert
Alex Werner series (2)
Armageddon conspiracy
Ahern, Jerry
Dan Track series (3)
Armageddon game
Washburn, Mark
Sam Boggs series (1)
Armageddon in the West
Scofield, Jonathan
Freedom fighters series (12)
Armageddon of Vesta
Murdock, Melinda Seabrooke
Martian wars trilogy (3)
Armageddon run
Austin, Richard
Guardians series (5)
Robbins, David
Endworld series (7)
Armageddon 2419A.D.
Nowlan, Philip Francis
Buck Rogers series (1)
Armageddon 2000
McGill, Gordon
Omen series (4)
Armageddon, USA
Rosenberger, Joseph
Death Merchant series (19)
Schmidt, Dan
Eagle Force series (9)
Armata
Erskine, Thomas
Armata series (1)
Armata series (2)
Armchair in hell
Kane, Henry
Peter Chambers series (2)
Armed, dangerous
Halliday, Brett
Michael Shayne series (54)
Armed protest
Bancroft, Francis
Germans in South Africa series (1)
Armed with a new terror
Du Bois, Theodora
Anne and Jeffrey McNeill series (1)
Armenians in America, 1618-1976
Wertsman, Vladimir
Ethnic groups in America series (4)
Armies of daylight
Hambly, Barbara
Darwath trilogy (3)
Armistice and other nenories
Mottram, Ralph Hale
Spanish Farm series (4)
Armitage, Armitage, fly away home
Aiken, Joan
Armitage family series (3)
Armitage secret
Howard, Hartley
Glenn Bowman series (17)
Armlet of the gods
Eshbach, Lloyd Arthur
Gates of Lucifer series (2)
Arms for oblivion
Hedges, Joseph
John Stark series (2)
Arms of death
Vivian, Francis
Inspector John Burnell series (1)
Arms of Kali
Murphy, Warren Burton
Destroyer series (59)
Arms of Nemesis
Saylor, Steven
Roma sub rosa series (2)
Arms of the mantis
Charles, Robert
Counter-terror series (8)
Arms of vengeance
Carter, Nick
Nick Carter series (253)
Armstrong
White, Alan
Inspector Armstrong series (1)
Army alphabet
Baum, Lyman Frank
Alphabet series (1)
Army boy in Alaska
Kilboure, Charles Evans
Army boy series (4)
Army boy in Mexico
Kilboure, Charles Evans
Army boy series (3)
Army boy in Pekin
Kilboure, Charles Evans
Army boy series (1)
Army boy in the Philippines
Kilboure, Charles Evans
Army boy series (2)
Army boys in France
Randall, Homer
Army boys series (1)
Army boys in the big drive
Randall, Homer
Army boys series (4)
Army boys in the French trenches
Randall, Homer
Army boys series (2)
Army boys marching into Germany
Randall, Homer
Army boys series (5)
Army boys on German soil
Randall, Homer
Army boys series (6)
Army boys on the firing line
Randall, Homer
Army boys series (3)
Army defaulter's secret
Douthwaite, Louis Charles
Sexton Blake series (1087)
Army of darkness
Walker, Hugh
Magira trilogy (2)
Army of devils
Stivers, Dick
Able Team series (8)
Army of the dead
Steele, Curtis
James Christopher series (8)
Army of the undead
Bernard, Rafe
Invaders series (3)
Army society
Winter, John Strange
Blankhampton series (2)
Arnaldo my brother
Leeming, John Fishwick
Fontana d'amore series (3)
Arnholt makes his bow
Latta, Gordon
Arnholt series (1)
Arnie and the new kid
Carlson, Nancy
Arnie series (3)
Arnie and the stolen markers
Carlson, Nancy
Arnie series (1)
Arnie goes to camp
Carlson, Nancy
Arnie series (2)
Arnold Waterlow
Sinclair, May
Mary and Arnold series (2)
Around dark corners
Pentecost, Hugh
George Crowder series (2)
Around old Chester
Deland, Margaret
Old Chester series (4)
Around the clock with Harriet
Maestro, Betsy Crippen
Harriet series (3)
Around the end
Barbour, Ralph Henry
Yardley Hall series (6)
Around the moon
Verne, Jules
Gun Club series (2)
Around the world and other places
Chase, Ilka
Travel series (6)
Around the world in eighty days
Verne, Jules
Phileas Fogg series (1)
Around the world in Wanderer III
Hiscock, Eric Charles
Wanderer series (1)
Around the world is no trip
Mark, Ted
Man from O.R.G.Y. series (5)
Around the world with Ant and Bee
Banner, Angela
Ant and Bee series (4)
Around the world with Auntie Mame
Dennis, Patrick
Auntie Mame series (2)
Around the world with Josiah Allen's wife
Holley, Marietta
Samantha and Josiah Allen series (11)
Around the year at Alectown
Crowley, Carl Campbell
Nine winds series (4)
Arouse and beware
Kantor, Mackinlay
Civil War trilogy (2)
Arrangement for murder
Simons, Roger
Inspector Fadiman Wace series (4)
Arras of youth
Onions, Oliver
Gandelyn the Jester trilogy (2)
Arrest
Pascal, Francine
Sweet Valley High series (96)
Proudfoot, Walter
Inspector Bill Vallance series (2)
Arrest and trial
Daniels, Norman A
Arrest and trial series (1)
Arrest at the Soo
Barnes, Michael
Just north series (5)
Arrest of Arsene Lupin
Leblanc, Maurice
Arsene Lupin series (2)
Arrest Sitting Bull
Jones, Douglas Clyde
General George Custer trilogy (2)
Arrest the Saint
Bloxsom, Peter
Saint series (51)
Arrest these men!
Perowne, Barry
Rick Leroy series (1)
Arrested for murder
Daniel, Roland
Brian O'Malley series (1)
Arresting Delia
Fowler, Sydney
Inspector Cleveland series (4)
Arrival
Nichols, Robert
Daily lives in Nghsi-Altai series (2)
Van Hise, James
V series (16)
Arrival and departure
Koestler, Arthur
Ends and means trilogy (3)
Arrogance
Aminoff, Constance Leonie Caroline
Napoleonic series (8)
Arrogant alibi
King, Charles Daly
Doctor L Rees Pons series (5)
Michael Lord series (4)
Arrow death
Daniel, Roland
Buddy Mustard series (8)
Arrow in the blue
Koestler, Arthur
Arrow in the blue series (1)
Arrow keeper
Cole, Judd
Cheyenne series (1)
Arrow of death
Vivian, Francis
Sergeant Ronnie Drew series (1)
Arrow of gold
Achebe, Chinua
African trilogy (3)
Arrow pointing nowhere
Daly, Elizabeth
Henry Gamadge series (7)
Arrowhead territory
Sharpe, Jon
Trailsman series (14)
Arrow's fall
Lackey, Mercedes
Heralds of Valdemar trilogy (3)
Arrow's flight
Lackey, Mercedes
Heralds of Valdemar trilogy (2)
Arrows of the queen
Lackey, Mercedes
Heralds of Valdemar trilogy (1)
Arsenal
Ahern, Jerry
Survivalist series (16)
Arsenal of death
Wallace, Robert
Phantom Detective series (31)
Arsenal Stadium mystery
Gribble, Leonard Reginald
Superintendent Anthony Slade series (16)
Arsene Lupin
Jepson, Edgar
Arsene Lupin series (16)
Arsene Lupin, gentleman burglar
Leblanc, Maurice
Arsene Lupin series (1)
Arsene Lupin intervenes
Leblanc, Maurice
Arsene Lupin series (13)
Arsene Lupin, super-sleuth
Leblanc, Maurice
Arsene Lupin series (12)
Arsene Lupin versus Herlock Sholmes
Leblanc, Maurice
Arsene Lupin series (2)
Arsene Lupin versus Holmlock Shears
Leblanc, Maurice
Arsene Lupin series (2)
Arsenic
Remenham, John
Inspector Bliss series (2)
Arsenic and gold
Atkey, Bertram
Smiler Bunn series (8)
Arsenic for the teacher
Keystone, Oliver
Paul Plush series (3)
Arsenic in Richmond
Frome, David
Evan Pinkerton series (5)
Art and artlessness
Leslie, Madeline
Little Agnes series (3)
Art in the blood
Elrod, Patricia Nead
Vampire files series (4)
Art of coarse acting
Green, Michael
Coarse series (4)
Art of coarse bridge
Hughes, Spike
Coarse series (4)
Art of coarse cookery
Hughes, Spike
Coarse series (5)
Art of coarse cricket
Hughes, Spike
Coarse series (1)
Art of coarse cruising
Green, Michael
Coarse series (9)
Art of coarse drinking
Green, Michael
Coarse series (8)
Art of coarse entertaining
Hughes, Spike
Coarse series (6)
Art of coarse gardening
Hughes, Spike
Coarse series (3)
Art of coarse golf
Green, Michael
Coarse series (6)
Art of coarse moving
Green, Michael
Coarse series (7)
Art of coarse office life
Green, Michael
Coarse series (12)
Art of coarse rugby
Green, Michael
Coarse series (1)
Art of coarse sailing
Green, Michael
Coarse series (2)
Art of coarse sex
Green, Michael
Coarse series (11)
Art of coarse travel
Hughes, Spike
Coarse series (2)
Art of deception
Roberts, Nora
Flowers series (27)
Art of living
Crowley, Carl Campbell
Nine winds series (7)
Art of The Empire strikes back
Bulluck, Vic
Luke Skywalker series (7)
Art treasure murders
Benton, John L
Stephen Duane series (2)
Artful egg
McClure, James
Lieutenant Kramer and Sergeant Zondi series (7)
Artful schemer
Carter, Nicholas
Nicholas Carter series (257)
Arthur
Graham, Amanda
Arthur trilogy (1)
Lawhead, Stephen
Pendragon trilogy (3)
Arthur and the bellybutton diamond
Coren, Alan
Arthur series (8)
Arthur and the great detective
Coren, Alan
Arthur series (7)
Arthur and the purple panic
Coren, Alan
Arthur series (9)
Arthur, Arthur
Black, Arthur
Basic Black series (4)
Arthur Brown, young captain
Kellogg, Elijah
Pleasant Cove series (1)
Arthur Conan Doyle on Sherlock Holmes
Doyle, Arthur Conan
Sherlock Holmes series (10)
Arthur Corunna's story
Morgan, Sally
My place series (2)
Arthur goes to camp
Brown, Marc
Arthur series (4)
Arthur Gordon Pym
Poe, Edgar Allan
Arthur Gordon Pym series (1)
Arthur Helmuth
Ellis, Edward Sylvester
Arthur Helmuth series (1)
Arthur meets the President
Brown, Marc
Arthur series (14)
Arthur the Kid
Coren, Alan
Arthur series (2)
Arthur versus the rest
Coren, Alan
Arthur series (10)
Arthur's April fool
Brown, Marc
Arthur series (6)
Arthur's baby
Brown, Marc
Arthur series (11)
Arthur's birthday wish
Brown, Marc
Arthur series (12)
Arthur's camp-out
Hoban, Lillian
Arthur series (9)
Arthur's Christmas
Brown, Marc
Arthur series (8)
Arthur's Christmas cookies
Hoban, Lillian
Arthur series (1)
Arthur's eyes
Brown, Marc
Arthur series (2)
Arthur's father
Wright, Kit
Arthur series (3)
Arthur's funny money
Hoban, Lillian
Arthur series (5)
Arthur's granny
Wright, Kit
Arthur series (1)
Arthur's great big valentine
Hoban, Lillian
Arthur series (8)
Arthur's Halloween
Brown, Marc
Arthur series (5)
Hoban, Lillian
Arthur series (6)
Arthur's honey bear
Hoban, Lillian
Arthur series (2)
Arthur's last stand
Coren, Alan
Arthur series (6)
Arthur's loose tooth
Hoban, Lillian
Arthur series (7)
Arthur's new power
Hoban, Russell
Arthur and Emma series (2)
Arthur's nose
Brown, Marc
Arthur series (1)
Arthur's pen pal
Hoban, Lillian
Arthur series (3)
Arthur's pet business
Brown, Marc
Arthur series (13)
Arthur's prize reader
Hoban, Lillian
Arthur series (4)
Arthur's sister
Wright, Kit
Arthur series (2)
Arthur's teacher trouble
Brown, Marc
Arthur series (10)
Arthur's Thanksgiving
Brown, Marc
Arthur series (7)
Arthur's tooth
Brown, Marc
Arthur series (9)

Arthur's uncle
Wright, Kit
Arthur series (4)
Arthur's valentine
Brown, Marc
Arthur series (3)
Artichoke hearts
Wuamett, Victor
Chase Randel series (3)
Artifact
Gear, William Michael
Spider series (1)
Artifact of evil
Gygax, Gary
Greyhawk series (2)
Artifact of the system
McKinney, Jack
Black Hole Travel Agency series (2)
Artifex intervenes
Keverne, Richard
Simon Artifex series (1)
Artificial grandma
Delton, Judy
Condo Kids series (3)
Artificial road murder
Blair, Allan
Sexton Blake series (735)
Artificial satellites
Bendick, Jeanne
Early bird astronomy series (3)
Artillery of time
Smith, Chard Powers
Lathrop family series (1)
Artist dies
Rhode, John
Doctor Lancelot Priestley series (62)
Artist in crime
Ottolengui, Rodrigues
John Barnes series (1)
Robert Leroy Mitchell series (1)
Artists in crime
Marsh, Ngaio
Inspector Roderick Alleyn series (6)
Artist's life
Munnings, Alfred
Artist's life trilogy (1)
Artless commuter
Jones, Joanna
Artless series (2)
Artless flat-hunter
Jones, Joanna
Artless series (1)
Artorius Rex
Gloag, John
Roman Britain series (3)
Arts and crafts you can eat
Cobb, Vicki
You can eat series (2)
Arundel
Roberts, Kenneth Lewis
Chronicles of Arundel series (1)
Arvada Jones and the orphans of the trail
Wayne, Les
Arvada Jones series (4)
Aryan onslaught
Derrick, Lionel
Penetrator series (29)
As a crook sows
Carter, Nicholas
Nicholas Carter series (559)
As a favor
Dunlap, Susan
Jill Smith series (2)
As a thief in the night
Freeman, Richard Austin
Doctor John Evelyn Thorndyke series (17)
As bad as I am
Ard, William
Danny Fontaine series (1)
As Berry and I were saying
Yates, Dornford
Berry series (10)
As empty as hate
Halliday, Michael
Doctor Emmanuel Cellini series (8)
As good as dead
Dewey, Thomas Blanchard
Singer Batts series (2)
As good as murdered
O'Hanlon, James
Jason Cordrey series (4)
As I lay dying
Faulkner, William
Sin and salvation series (3)
As I walked out one midsummer morning
Lee, Laurie
Cotswolds series (2)
As I was going down Sackville Street
Gogarty, Oliver St John
Sackville Street series (1)
As it chanced
Watson, Henry Brereton Marriott
Dick Ryder series (4)
As it happened
Gee, Herbert Leslie
Friendly series (7)
As it was
Thomas, Helen
Under storm's wing trilogy (1)
As lonely as the damned
Halliday, Michael
Doctor Emmanuel Cellini series (7)
As long as the fields are green
Layberry, Layton George Joseph
Oakleigh Farm series (6)
As merry as hell
Halliday, Michael
Doctor Emmanuel Cellini series (9)
As new wine
Wright, Meg
Star trek fan series (5)
As October dies
Davis, Kenn
Carver Bascombe series (7)
As of the gods
Brown, Rollo Walter
Emergency series (4)
As old as Cain
Chaber, M E
Milo March series (4)
As others see us
Brooke, Carol
Marshall family series (1)
As the devil burned
Kemp, Harold
Inspector James Brent series (3)
As the earth turns
Carroll, Gladys Hasty
Shaw family series (1)
As the Green Star rises
Carter, Lin
Green Star series (4)
As the leaves fall down
Fisher, Aileen
Ways of plants series (10)
As the stream flows by
Baker, Denys Val
Cornish series (15)
As the world burns
David, Peter
Amazing Spiderman series (4)
As they shall sow
Spiller, Andrew
Chief Inspector Duck Mallard series (14)
As time goes by
Bailey, Hilary
Polly series (2)
As time went by
Smyth, Ethel Mary
Impressions series (4)
As you were Bill!
Streeter, Edward
Mable series (4)
Asbestos mask
Nicholas, Jerome
Bill Anstruther series (2)
Ascanio
Dumas, Alexandre
Valois series (1)
Ascension
Grant, Charles Lewis
Parric family trilogy (2)
Ascension factor
Herbert, Frank
Pandora series (4)
Ascent into hell
Greeley, Andrew Moran
Passover trilogy (2)
Ascent of Everest
Hunt, John
Everest series (1)
Ascent to Omai
Harris, Wilson
Agent of personality quartet (4)
Asceptic murders
Brown, Carter
Lieutenant Al Wheeler series (44)
Ascian in rose
De Lint, Charles
Moonheart series (2)
Asey Mayo trio
Taylor, Phoebe Atwood
Asey Mayo series (22)
Ash Ock
Hinz, Christopher
Paratwa trilogy (2)
Ash on a youg man's sleeve
Abse, Dannie
Poet in the family series (1)
Ash staff
Fisher, Paul R
Ash staff trilogy (1)
Ashe of the outback
Jorgensen, Norman
Captain Ashe series (1)
Langoulant, Allan
Captain Ashe series (1)
Ashe on parade
Langoulant, Allan
Captain Ashe series (2)
Ashes and blood
Pike, Charles R
Jubal Cade series (13)
Ashes and dust
Gilman, George G
Edge series (19)
Ashes and ecstasy
Hart, Catherine
Kathleen Hartly Taylor and Reed Taylor series (3)
Ashes and stars
Zebrowski, George
Omega Point trilogy (1)
Ashes for Easter
Watmough, David
Davey Bryant series (1)
Ashes in an urn
Roffman, Jan
Sergeant Ratlin series (1)
Ashes in the cellar
Jacobs, Thomas Curtis Hicks
Temple Fortune series (15)
Ashes of a god
Bain, Francis William
Indian mystic love stories series (9)
Ashes of empire
Chambers, Robert William
Franco-Prussian war trilogy (2)
Ashes of evidence
Levison, Eric
Doctor Edward Lester series (3)
Ashes of Hiroshima
Clune, Frank
Discovery series (13)
Ashes to ashes
Housman, Laurence
Palace plays series (4)
Lathen, Emma
John Putnam Thatcher series (12)
Pendleton, Don
Ashton Ford series (1)
Pulver, Mary Monica
Kori McLeod Price and Peter Brichter series (3)
Ashiel mystery
Bryce, Charles, *Mrs*
Mister Gimblet series (2)
Ashton horror
Bridges, Laurie
Dark forces series (12)
Ashton-Kirk, criminologist
McIntyre, John Thomas
Ashton-Kirk series (4)
Ashton-Kirk, investigator
McIntyre, John Thomas
Ashton-Kirk series (1)
Ashton-Kirk, secret agent
McIntyre, John Thomas
Ashton-Kirk series (2)
Ashton-Kirk, special detective
McIntyre, John Thomas
Ashton-Kirk series (3)
Asian hellbox
Wilson, Gar
Phoenix Force series (8)
Asian mantrap
Carter, Nick
Nick Carter series (124)
Asiatic breezes
Optic, Oliver
All-over-the-world series (8)
A-sitting on a gate
Travers, Ben
Vale of laughter series (2)
Ask a policeman
Lorac, E C R
Inspector Macdonald series (41)
Ask for angel
Montrose, Graham
Angel Brown series (9)
Ask for King Billy
Treece, Henry
Gordon Stewart series (1)
Ask for me tomorrow
Millar, Margaret
Tom Aragon series (1)
Ask for Ronald Standish
Sapper
Ronald Standish series (5)
Ask me no questions
Veryan, Patricia
Tales of the jewelled men series (3)
Ask the cards a question
Muller, Marcia
Sharon McCone series (2)
Ask the dust
Fante, John
Arturo Bandini series (2)
Ask the fellows who cut the hay
Evans, George Ewart
Farm life series (1)
Ask the right question
Lewin, Michael Zinn
Albert Samson series (1)
Ask the wind, ask the sea
Thompson, Neil
Rand series (4)
Asking for it
Mayo, James
Charles Hood series (6)
Asking for trouble
Rayter, Joe
Johnny Powers series (2)
Asking price
Hilton, John Buxton
Superintendent Simon Kenworthy series (11)
Asleep in the afternoon
Large, Ernest Charles
Charles Pry series (1)
Asmodeus
Lesage, Alain Rene
Devil upon two sticks series (1)
Aspen
Hirschfeld, Burt
Aspen series (1)
Aspen affair
Hirschfeld, Burt
Aspen series (2)
Asphalt jungle
Burnett, William Riley
Chicago trilogy (2)
Assassin
Anderson, James
Mikael Petros series (1)
Blake, Ken
Professionals series (12)
Griffin, W E B
Badge of honor series (5)
Sadler, Barry
Casca series (13)
Smith, Mark
Way of the Tiger series (2)
Stone, Nick
Ben Kane series (2)
Assassin, code name Vulture
Carter, Nick
Nick Carter series (86)
Assassin convention
Carter, Nick
Nick Carter series (204)
Assassin gambit
Forstchen, William R
Gamester wars series (2)
Assassin in the greenwood
Doherty, Paul C
Hugh Corbett series (7)
Assassin of Gor
Norman, John
Tarl Cabot series (5)
Assassination affair
Holly, Joan Hunter
Man from U.N.C.L.E. series (10)
Assassination brigade
Carter, Nick
Nick Carter series (74)
Assassination factor
Derrick, Lionel
Penetrator series (40)
Assassination file
Gardner, John Edmund
Boysie L Oakes series (8)
Assassination is set for July four
Parker, Lee
Donovan's Devils series (1)
Assassination of Mozart
Weiss, David
Wolfgang Amadeus Mozart series (2)
Assassins
Falk, Lee
Phantom series (14)
Teilhet, Hildegarde Tolman
Sam Hook series (3)
Willoughby, Lee Davis
Making of America series (46)
Assassin's castle
Knight, Peter
Roger Vellacott series (2)
Assassins don't die in bed
Avallone, Michael
Ed Noon series (17)
Assassin's express
Kilgore, Axel
They call me the Mercenary series (8)
Assassins for peace
Charles, Robert
Simon Larren series (7)
Assassins for tomorrow
Heath, Peter
Jason Starr and Adam Cyber series (2)
Assassin's handbook
Murray, Will
Destroyer series (94)
Assassins play-off
Murphy, Warren Burton
Destroyer series (20)
Assassins road
Harvester, Simon
Asia in turmoil series (16)
Dorian Silk series (5)
Assassin's shadow
Striker, Randy
Dusky MacMorgan series (5)
Assassin's trail
Sharpe, Jon
Canyon O'Grady series (13)
Assault!
Mackenzie, Steve
Seals series (9)
Assault and pepper
Story, Jack Trevor
Sexton Blake series (1528)
Assault force
Agry, Ed
O'Reilly series (1)
Assault into Libya
Case, Jim
Cody's army series (2)
Assault on Agathon
Caillou, Alan
Cabot Cain series (5)
Assault on Aimata
Caillou, Alan
Cabot Cain series (6)
Assault on England
Carter, Nick
Nick Carter series (67)
Assault on Fellawi
Caillou, Alan
Cabot Cain series (4)
Assault on Khe Sanh
Hammel, Eric Maxwell
Khe Sanh series (2)
Assault on Kolchak
Caillou, Alan
Cabot Cain series (1)
Assault on Loveless
Caillou, Alan
Cabot Cain series (2)
Assault on Ming
Caillou, Alan
Cabot Cain series (3)
Assault on Omega Four
Horvat, Dilwyn
Operation Titan series (2)
Assault on Rome
Pendleton, Don
Mack Bolan series (103)
Assault on Soho
Pendleton, Don
Mack Bolan series (6)
Assault on the Empress
Ahern, Jerry
Surgical strike series (2)
Assault with intent
Kienzle, William Xavier
Father Robert Koesler series (4)
Asses in clover
O'Duffy, Eimar
Aloysius Kennedy series (2)
King Goshawk series (2)
Asset to Wales
Ruck, Berta
Storyteller series (4)
Assignment Afghan dragon
Aarons, Edward Sidney
Sam Durell series (41)
Assignment Amazon queen
Aarons, Edward Sidney
Sam Durell series (37)
Assignment Andalusia
Galway, Robert Conington
James Packard series (3)
Assignment Angelina
Aarons, Edward Sidney
Sam Durell series (6)
Assignment Ankara
Aarons, Edward Sidney
Sam Durell series (13)
Assignment Argentina
Galway, Robert Conington
James Packard series (6)

Assignment assassination
Milton, Joseph
Bart Gould series (2)
Assignment Bangkok
Aarons, Edward Sidney
Sam Durell series (32)
Assignment black gold
Aarons, Edward Sidney
Sam Durell series (39)
Assignment black Viking
Aarons, Edward Sidney
Sam Durell series (25)
Assignment Budapest
Aarons, Edward Sidney
Sam Durell series (4)
Assignment Burma girl
Aarons, Edward Sidney
Sam Durell series (15)
Assignment Carlotta Cortez
Aarons, Edward Sidney
Sam Durell series (8)
Assignment Ceylon
Aarons, Edward Sidney
Sam Durell series (35)
Assignment Cong Hai kill
Aarons, Edward Sidney
Sam Durell series (23)
Assignment death ship
Aarons, Will B
Sam Durell series (48)
Assignment death squad
Galway, Robert Conington
James Packard series (10)
Assignment Devil's Playground
Barker, Patrick
Tac One series (2)
Assignment Doomsday
Thomas, Martin
Sexton Blake series (1532)
Assignment Fenland
Galway, Robert Conington
James Packard series (7)
Assignment, Find Cherry
Seward, Jack
Curt Stone series (4)
Assignment gaolbreak
Galway, Robert Conington
James Packard series (5)
Assignment golden girl
Aarons, Edward Sidney
Sam Durell series (33)
Assignment Haiti
Thorne, Ernest Pollett
Geoff Fennell series (2)
Assignment Helene
Aarons, Edward Sidney
Sam Durell series (9)
Assignment hellhole
Cleve, John
Spaceways series (14)
Assignment Hong Kong
Dark, James
Mark Kingsley Hood series (4)
Assignment in Alaska
James, Josephine
Kathy Martin series (4)
Assignment in Algeria
Lee, John Darrell
Brian Douglas series (2)
Assignment in Andorra
Mackintosh, May
Laurie Grant and Stewart Noble series (2)
Assignment in Beirut
Stagg, James
Sexton Blake series (1407)
Assignment in Iraq
Mackinnon, Allan
Mike Darroch series (2)
Assignment Intercept
Carter, Nick
Nick Carter series (102)
Assignment Israel
Carter, Nick
Nick Carter series (27)
Assignment K
Howard, Hartley
Philip Scott series (1)
Assignment Karachi
Aarons, Edward Sidney
Sam Durell series (16)
Assignment Lili Lamaris
Aarons, Edward Sidney
Sam Durell series (10)
Assignment London
Galway, Robert Conington
James Packard series (2)
Assignment Lowlands
Aarons, Edward Sidney
Sam Durell series (14)
Assignment Madeleine
Aarons, Edward Sidney
Sam Durell series (7)
Assignment Malta
Galway, Robert Conington
James Packard series (4)
Assignment Maltese maiden
Aarons, Edward Sidney
Sam Durell series (34)
Assignment Manchurian doll
Aarons, Edward Sidney
Sam Durell series (18)
Assignment Mara Tirana
Aarons, Edward Sidney
Sam Durell series (11)
Assignment mermaid
Aarons, Will B
Sam Durell series (46)
Assignment moon girl
Aarons, Edward Sidney
Sam Durell series (26)
Assignment, murder
Graham, Neill
Solo Malcolm series (34)
Assignment New York
Galway, Robert Conington
James Packard series (1)
Assignment North Africa
Decker, Joseph
Tac One series (1)
Assignment nuclear nude
Aarons, Edward Sidney
Sam Durell series (27)
Assignment Palermo
Aarons, Edward Sidney
Sam Durell series (22)
Assignment Peking
Aarons, Edward Sidney
Sam Durell series (28)
Assignment Quayle question
Aarons, Edward Sidney
Sam Durell series (40)
Assignment Rio
Carter, Nick
Nick Carter series (191)
Assignment school for spies
Aarons, Edward Sidney
Sam Durell series (24)
Assignment sea bed
Galway, Robert Conington
James Packard series (8)
Assignment Sheba
Aarons, Will B
Sam Durell series (43)
Assignment silver scorpion
Aarons, Edward Sidney
Sam Durell series (36)
Assignment Sorrento siren
Aarons, Edward Sidney
Sam Durell series (17)
Assignment star stealers
Aarons, Edward Sidney
Sam Durell series (29)
Assignment Stella Marni
Aarons, Edward Sidney
Sam Durell series (5)
Assignment suicide
Aarons, Edward Sidney
Sam Durell series (2)
Assignment Sulu Sea
Aarons, Edward Sidney
Sam Durell series (19)
Assignment Sumatra
Aarons, Edward Sidney
Sam Durell series (38)
Assignment Sydney
Galway, Robert Conington
James Packard series (9)
Assignment Tahiti
Gardner, Alan Harold
Davis Troy series (2)
Assignment, the arranger
Deming, Richard
Mod Squad junior series (1)
Assignment the Cairo dancers
Aarons, Edward Sidney
Sam Durell series (21)
Assignment the girl in the gondola
Aarons, Edward Sidney
Sam Durell series (20)
Assignment, the hideout
Deming, Richard
Mod Squad junior series (2)
Assignment thirteenth princess
Aarons, Will B
Sam Durell series (45)
Assignment tiger devil
Aarons, Will B
Sam Durell series (44)
Assignment to Bahrein
Winston, Peter
Adjusters series (1)
Assignment to death
Leonard, Charles L
Paul Kilgerrin series (3)
Assignment to disaster
Aarons, Edward Sidney
Sam Durell series (1)
Assignment to nowhere
Laumer, Keith
Mister Curlon series (3)
Assignment Tokyo
Aarons, Edward Sidney
Sam Durell series (31)
Dark, James
Mark Kingsley Hood series (5)
Assignment treason
Aarons, Edward Sidney
Sam Durell series (3)
Assignment tyrant's bride
Aarons, Will B
Sam Durell series (47)
Assignment unicorn
Aarons, Edward Sidney
Sam Durell series (42)
Assignment white rajah
Aarons, Edward Sidney
Sam Durell series (30)
Assignment Zoraya
Aarons, Edward Sidney
Sam Durell series (12)
Assisi murders
Holme, Timothy
Inspector Achille Peroni series (4)
Assisted by Lessinger
Essex, Richard
Lessinger series (7)
Asterix and Caesar's gift
Goscinny, Rene
Asterix series (21)
Asterix and Cleopatra
Goscinny, Rene
Asterix series (5)
Asterix and his village
Bell, Anthea
Asterix push-out series (2)
Asterix and Son
Uderzo, Albert
Asterix series (28)
Asterix and the banquet
Goscinny, Rene
Asterix series (6)
Asterix and the big fight
Goscinny, Rene
Asterix series (9)
Asterix and the black gold
Uderzo, Albert
Asterix series (27)
Asterix and the cauldron
Goscinny, Rene
Asterix series (13)
Asterix and the chieftain's shield
Goscinny, Rene
Asterix series (12)
Asterix and the circis of Rome
Bell, Anthea
Asterix push-out series (4)
Asterix and the golden sickle
Goscinny, Rene
Asterix series (2)
Asterix and the Goths
Goscinny, Rene
Asterix series (3)
Asterix and the great crossing
Goscinny, Rene
Asterix series (22)
Asterix and the great divide
Uderzo, Albert
Asterix series (26)
Asterix and the laurel wreath
Goscinny, Rene
Asterix series (19)
Asterix and the magic carpet
Uderzo, Albert
Asterix series (30)
Asterix and the Normans
Goscinny, Rene
Asterix series (7)
Asterix and the pirates
Bell, Anthea
Asterix push-out series (5)
Asterix and the Roman agent
Goscinny, Rene
Asterix series (16)
Asterix and the Roman camp
Bell, Anthea
Asterix push-out series (1)
Asterix and the soothsayer
Goscinny, Rene
Asterix series (18)
Asterix and the twelve tasks
Bell, Anthea
Asterix push-out series (6)
Asterix at the Olympic Games
Goscinny, Rene
Asterix series (11)
Asterix in ancient Egypt
Bell, Anthea
Asterix push-out series (3)
Asterix in Belgium
Goscinny, Rene
Asterix series (25)
Asterix in Britain
Goscinny, Rene
Asterix series (8)
Asterix in Corsica
Goscinny, Rene
Asterix series (20)
Asterix in Spain
Goscinny, Rene
Asterix series (14)
Asterix in Switzerland
Goscinny, Rene
Asterix series (15)
Asterix, the Gaul
Goscinny, Rene
Asterix series (1)
Asterix, the gladiator
Goscinny, Rene
Asterix series (4)
Asterix series (29)
Asterix, the legionary
Goscinny, Rene
Asterix series (10)
Asterix series (29)
Asterix versus Caesar
Uderzo, Albert
Asterix series (29)
Astonishing history of Troy Town
Quiller-Couch, Arthur
Troy Town series (1)
Astonishing stereoscope
Langton, Jane
Edward, Eleanor and Georgie Hall series (3)
Astounding adventures among the comets
Verne, Jules
Hector Servadac series (1)
Hector Servadac series (2)
Astral fortress
Appleton, Victor II
Tom Swift Junior series 2 (5)
Astral quest
Rankine, John
Space nineteen ninety nine series (6)
Astride two worlds
Brata, Sasthi
Astride two worlds series (2)
Astro pilots
Mixon, Laura J
Omni odysseys trilogy (1)
Astrologer's day, and other stories
Narayan, Rasipuram Krishnaswami
Malgudi series (17)
Astropilots
Mixon, Laura J
Omni odysseys trilogy (1)
Astrosmurf
Peyo
Smurf series (5)
Astrov inheritance
Heaven, Constance
Kuragin series (2)
Astrov legacy
Heaven, Constance
Kuragin series (2)
Asutra
Vance, Jack
Durdane trilogy (3)
Aswan assignment
Sugar, Andrew
Israeli commandos series (1)
Asye Mayo trio
Taylor, Phoebe Atwood
Asey Mayo series (19)
At any price
Drake, David
Hammer's Slammers series (3)
At bat
Gutman, Bill
At bat series (1)
At Bertram's Hotel
Christie, Agatha
Miss Jane Marple series (12)
At boarding school with the Tucker twins
Sampson, Emma
Tucker twins series (1)
At close grips
Duff, Douglas Valder
Adam Macadam series (7)
At dead of night
Amey, Linda
Blair Emerson series (2)
At death's door
Bruce, Leo
Carolus Deene series (1)
At face value
Carter, Nicholas
Nicholas Carter series (359)
At Greenacres
Taggart, Marion Ames
Jack-in-the-box series (1)
At home
Berridge, Celia
Stepping stones 1 2 3 series (3)
Bingham, Charlotte
Belgravia trilogy (3)
Gree, Alain
Smashers series (5)
Hautzig, Esther Rudomin
Four languages series (2)
Hill, Eric
Baby Bear series (1)
Plomer, William
Double lives series (2)
At home and away
Black, Margaret Katherine
Honey family trilogy (3)
At home in Thrush Green
Read, *Miss*
Thrush Green series (8)
At Lady Molly's
Powell, Anthony
Dance to the music of time series (4)
At Muerto Springs
Calhoun, Wes
Chulo trilogy (2)
At my house
Salmon, Michael
Who's behind the door series (1)
At my school
Salmon, Michael
Who's behind the door series (3)
At mystery's threshold
Carter, Nicholas
Nicholas Carter series (300)
At night to die
Hamilton, Henrietta
Johnny and Sally Heldar series (3)
At odds with Scotland Yard
Carter, Nicholas
Nicholas Carter series (19)
At one fell swoop
Mills, Osmington
Superintendent William Baker series (8)
Palmer, Stuart
Hildegarde Withers series (13)
At Paddy the Beaver's pond
Burgess, Thornton Waldo
Nature stories series (6)
At Paddy the beaver's pond
Burgess, Thornton Waldo
Paddy the beaver series (2)
At Platinum River
Craine, Edith Janice
Airplane Boys series (5)
At playgroup
Jessel, Camilla
Chatterbooks series (5)
At school
Gree, Alain
Smashers series (1)
At school in Skye
Allan, Mabel Esther
Harvie family series (3)
At school in the Cannibal Islands
Houston, Edwin James
Pacific shipwreck series (4)
At school with Troddles
Andom, R
Troddles series (7)
At sixty miles per hour
Drummond, J
Sexton Blake series (1136)
At sword's point
Norton, Andre
Swords trilogy (3)
At the age of Eve
Sharber, Kate Trimble
Ann and Eve series (2)
At the back of the north wind
Macdonald, George
Faery trilogy (1)
At the beach
Salmon, Michael
Who did it series (4)
At The Cedars
Hocking, Anne
Inspector William Austen series (15)
At the circus
Salmon, Michael
Who did it series (3)
At the defense of Pittsburgh
Hancock, Harrie Irving
Conquest of the United States series (3)

At the earth's core
Burroughs, Edgar Rice
Pellucidar series (1)
At the edge of the sun
Stuart, Anne
Maggie Bennett series (3)
At the end of a Texas rope
Cameron, Caddo
Private Badger Coe and Sergeant Blizzard Wilson series (3)
At the end of the day, 1961-1963
Macmillan, Harold
Winds of change series (6)
At the end of time
Smith, Mark
Falcon series (6)
At the fall of Montreal
Stratemeyer, Edward L
Colonial series (3)
At the fall of Port Arthur
Stratemeyer, Edward L
Soldiers of fortune series (3)
At the fall of Warsaw
Fiske, James
World's war series (9)
At the farm
Salmon, Michael
Who's behind the door series (5)
At the feet of Venus
Blasco Ibanez, Vicente
Spanish history series (2)
At the foot of the rainbow
Hendryx, James Beardsley
Corporal Downey series (4)
At the forge of liberty
Carter, Alden Richardson
American Revolution series (3)
At the Front
Botsford, Charles Alexander
Victory series (4)
At the front
Optic, Oliver
Blue and the Gray on land series (5)
At the Gai-Moulin
Simenon, Georges
Inspector Jules Maigret series (5)
Inspector Jules Maigret series (9)
At the going down of the sun
Darrell, Elizabeth
Sheridan family series (1)
At the hands of another
Lyons, Arthur
Jacob Asch series (7)
At the height of the moon
Malpass, Eric Lawson
Gaylord series (2)
At the house of the priest
Adye, John
Oliver Smaile series (1)
At the Jazz Band Ball
Oakes, Philip
Middle England trilogy (3)
At the knife's point
Carter, Nicholas
Nicholas Carter series (91)
At the lake of sudden death
Holme, Timothy
Inspector Achille Peroni series (5)
At the little brown house
Brown, Ruth Alberta
Peace Greenfield series (1)
At the narrow passage
Meredith, Richard Carlton
Timeliner trilogy (1)
At the North Pole
Verne, Jules
Adventures of Captain Hatteras series (1)
At the park
Bradman, Tony
Rhymes with me series (3)
At the point of a thirty eight
Halliday, Brett
Michael Shayne series (68)
At the seaside
Newsham, Wendy
Dynamite twins series (1)
At the Seventh Level
Elgin, Suzette Haden
Coyote Jones series (3)
At the shrine of the Buddha
Graydon, William Murray
Sexton Blake series (171)
At the sign of the Cat and Racket
Balzac, Honore de
Scenes of private life series (1)
At the sign of the Reine Pedauque
France, Anatole
Abbe Coignard series (1)
At the Smiling Pool
Burgess, Thornton Waldo
Nature stories series (2)
At the tenth clue
Stanners, Harold H
Professor Harding series (2)
At the Villa Rose
Mason, Alfred Edward Woodley
Inspector Hanaud series (1)
At the zoo
Salmon, Michael
Who did it series (1)
Who's behind the door series (2)
At their departing
Thompson, Nancy
Departing and return series (1)
At Thompson's ranch
Carter, Nicholas
Nicholas Carter series (22)
At war with Pontiac
Munroe, Kirk
White conqueror series (2)
At war with tomorrow
Leeson, Robert
Time rope series (3)
At Willie Tucker's place
Morgan, Alison
Llanwern series (4)
At wind's edge
Davis, Kathryn
Dakotas series (1)
At winter's end
Silverberg, Robert
New springtime series (1)
At your service
Bemelmans, Ludwig
Hotel series (1)
Atavar, the dream dancer
Reeve, Arthur Benjamin
Craig Kennedy series (17)
Athalie
Chambers, Robert William
Athalie series (2)
Atheist's mass
Balzac, Honore de
Scenes of private life series (25)
Atheling
Wiat, Philippa
Black Boar series (5)
Wyatt family series (6)
Athelsons
Kettle, Jocelyn
Athelson family series (1)
Athletics
Paulsen, Gary
Sports on the light side series (5)
Atkinson century
Hardwick, Mollie
Atkinson family series (3)
Atkinson heritage
Hardwick, Mollie
Atkinson family series (1)
Atlan
Gaskell, Jane
Atlan saga series (2)
Atlan in danger
Brand, Kurt
Perry Rhodan series (82)
Atlanta burn
Ham, Bob
Overload series (5)
Atlanta deathwatch
Dennis, Ralph
Jim Hardman series (1)
Atlanta extreme
Ramm, Carl
James Hawker series (8)
Atlanta run
Robbins, David
Endworld series (17)
Atlantean horror
Rosenberger, Joseph
Death Merchant series (63)
Atlantic assignment
Holliday, Joe
Dale of the Mounted series (8)
Atlantic cruise in Wanderer III
Hiscock, Eric Charles
Wanderer series (3)
Atlantic pursuit
Southall, Ivan
War in the air series (6)
Atlantic scramble
Pendleton, Don
Phoenix Force series (3)
Atlantis
Mohr, Ulrich
German raider series (1)
Atlantis, men and monsters
Polch, Boguslaw
Unsolved mysteries series (9)
Atlas of Middle Earth
Fonstad, Karen Wynn
Middle Earth series (5)
Atlas of Pern
Fonstad, Karen Wynn
Pern and the Red Planet series (12)
Atlas of the DragonLance world
Fonstad, Karen Wynn
DragonLance chronicles series (3)
Atlas of World War I
Gilbert, Martin
History atlas series (5)
Atom bomb angel
James, Peter
Max Flynn series (2)
Atom Chasers
Macvicar, Angus
Atom Chasers series (1)
Atom Chasers in Tibet
Macvicar, Angus
Atom Chasers series (2)
Atom fire on Mechanica
Darlton, Clark
Perry Rhodan series (121)
Atom hell of Grautier
Mahr, Kurt
Perry Rhodan series (71)
Atom 'plane mystery
Leyland, Eric
Hunter Hawk series (2)
Atomic murder
Gribble, Leonard Reginald
Superintendent Anthony Slade series (17)
Atomic plot
Holliday, Joe
Dale of the Mounted series (9)
Atoms in action
Sheldon, Roy
Shiny spear series (1)
Atoms of death
Grant, Maxwell
Shadow series (82)
Atrocity
Ahern, Jerry
Dan Track series (2)
Atropos
De Andrea, William Louis
Clifford Driscoll series (4)
Attaboy, Sam!
Lowry, Lois
Sam series (2)
Attache
Haliburton, Thomas Chandler
Sam Slick series (5)
Attache, 2nd series
Haliburton, Thomas Chandler
Sam Slick series (6)
Attack
Coleman, Clay
Lost Island series (2)
Hardcastle, Michael
Mark Fox series (7)
Macdonnell, James Edmond
Dutchy Holland series (36)
Mackenzie, Steve
Seals series (11)
Attack and be damned
Macdonnell, James Edmond
Dutchy Holland series (13)
Attack Anzio
Lutz, Gunther
Panzer Platoon series (6)
Attack from the unseen
Darlton, Clark
Perry Rhodan series (50)
Attack in the desert
Home, Michael
Zerzura series (1)
Attack of the Cybermen
Saward, Eric
Doctor Who series (138)
Attack of the deranged mutant killer monster snow goons
Watterson, Bill
Calvin and Hobbes series (10)
Attack of the Insecticons
Beach, Lynn
Junior transformers find your fate series (3)
Attack of the killer
Zindel, Paul
Wacky facts lunch bunch series (1)
Attack of the Seventh Carrier
Albano, Peter
Seventh Carrier series (5)
Attack of the video villains
Dixon, Franklin W
Hardy boys series (106)
Attack on the king
Affabee, Eric
Wizards, warlocks and you series (16)
Attack on Vienna
Nixon, Alan
Larry Maver series (2)
Attack the Baron
Morton, Anthony
Baron series (20)
Attacking the wall
Birt, David
Roman Britain series (12)
Attar's revenge
Graham, Robert
Attar the Merman series (1)
Attending physician
Dominic, R B
Congressman Ben Safford series (6)
Attending truth
Punshon, Ernest Robertson
Bobby Owen series (30)
Attention, Saturnin Dax!
Cumberland, Marten
Saturnin Dax series (30)
Attic and area
Marton, Francesca
Jordan family series (1)
Attic in Bohemia
Watson, Edmund Henry Lacon
Bohemia series (1)
Attic murder
Fowler, Sydney
Mister Jellipot series (2)
Attic room
Wolffe, Katherine
Captain Courtney Brade series (1)
Attic term
Forest, Antonia
Marlow family series (9)
Attila the pun
Pinkwater, Daniel Manus
Magic Moscow series (2)
Attitudes towards history
Burke, Kenneth
Attitudes towards history series (2)
Aubrey Aubergine
Reed, Giles
Munch Bunch character series (17)
Auction
Henry, Marguerite
Chincoteague series (1)
Auctioned
Janson, Hank
Hank Janson series (37)
Audacious Picaroon
Cassells, John
Ludovic Saxon series (13)
Audition for murder
Carlson, Patricia McEvoy
Maggie Ryan series (1)
Audrey
Johnston, Mary
Virginian series (3)
Audrey at school
Nash, Frances Olivia Hartopp
Audrey series (3)
Audrey books
Nash, Frances Olivia Hartopp
Audrey series (4)
Audrey in camp
Nash, Frances Olivia Hartopp
Audrey series (2)
Audrey Rose
De Felitta, Frank
Audrey Rose series (1)
Audrey, the sea ranger
Nash, Frances Olivia Hartopp
Audrey series (4)
August
Hamsun, Knut
Edevart and August series (2)
August adventure
Atkinson, Mary Evelyn
Lockett family series (1)
August and Elire
Abbott, Jacob
August series (1)
August folly
Thirkell, Angela
Barsetshire series (4)
August ice
Day, Deforest
Chase Defoe series (1)
August incident
Dean, Amber
Albie Harris series (7)
August 1914
Solzhenitsyn, Alexander
Russian Revolution series (1)
Augusta steps out
Hoult, Norah
Augusta Hortense Carey series (2)
Augusta, the first
Kimbrough, Katheryn
Phenwick women series (1)
Augusta, the second
Kimbrough, Katheryn
Phenwick women series (28)
Augustus
Epstein, June
Augustus series (1)
Massie, Allan
Roman emperors quartet (1)
Augustus and the desert
Henderson, Le Grand
Augustus series (12)
Augustus and the mountain
Henderson, Le Grand
Augustus series (3)
Augustus and the river
Henderson, Le Grand
Augustus series (1)
Augustus conducts the band
Epstein, June
Augustus series (2)
Augustus drives a jeep
Henderson, Le Grand
Augustus series (7)
Augustus flies
Henderson, Le Grand
Augustus series (8)
Augustus flies a plane
Epstein, June
Augustus series (4)
Augustus goes south
Henderson, Le Grand
Augustus series (2)
Augustus helps the Army
Henderson, Le Grand
Augustus series (5)
Augustus helps the Marines
Henderson, Le Grand
Augustus series (6)
Augustus helps the Navy
Henderson, Le Grand
Augustus series (4)
Augustus hits the road
Henderson, Le Grand
Augustus series (10)
Augustus plays football
Epstein, June
Augustus series (6)
Augustus rides the border
Henderson, Le Grand
Augustus series (11)
Augustus saves a ship
Henderson, Le Grand
Augustus series (9)
Augustus teaches the children
Epstein, June
Augustus series (3)
Augustus the king
Epstein, June
Augustus series (8)
Augustus the painter
Epstein, June
Augustus series (7)
Augustus works in a factory
Epstein, June
Augustus series (5)
Auld Licht idylls
Barrie, James Matthew
Thrums series (1)
Auld Licht manse, and other sketches
Barrie, James Matthew
Thrums series (4)
Auld Reekie
Macgregor, Alasdair Alpin
Auld Reekie series (3)
Aunt Bel
McCrone, Guy
Moorhouse family trilogy (2)
Aunt Brown's birthday
Beskow, Elsa
Peter and Lotta series (2)
Aunt Eleanor
Jackson, Rosemary Elizabeth
Macgillan family series (2)
Aunt Flora
Coatsworth, Elizabeth
Once-upon-a-time-in-America series (4)
Aunt Green, Aunt Brown and Aunt Lavender
Beskow, Elsa
Peter and Lotta series (1)
Aunt Jane and Uncle James
Conyers, Dorothea
Peter series (2)
Aunt Jane of Kentucky
Hall, Eliza Calvert
Aunt Jane series (1)
Aunt Jane's nieces
Van Dyne, Edith
Aunt Jane's nieces series (1)
Aunt Jane's nieces abroad
Van Dyne, Edith
Aunt Jane's nieces series (2)
Aunt Jane's nieces and Uncle John
Van Dyne, Edith
Aunt Jane's nieces series (6)

Aunt Jane's nieces at Millville
Van Dyne, Edith
Aunt Jane's nieces series (3)
Aunt Jane's nieces at work
Van Dyne, Edith
Aunt Jane's nieces series (4)
Aunt Jane's nieces in society
Van Dyne, Edith
Aunt Jane's nieces series (5)
Aunt Jane's nieces in the Red Cross
Van Dyne, Edith
Aunt Jane's nieces series (10)
Aunt Jane's nieces on the ranch
Van Dyne, Edith
Aunt Jane's nieces series (8)
Aunt Jane's nieces on vacation
Van Dyne, Edith
Aunt Jane's nieces series (7)
Aunt Jane's nieces out west
Van Dyne, Edith
Aunt Jane's nieces series (9)
Aunt Kitty's fowls
Finley, Martha Farquharson
Pewit's nest series (8)
Aunt Nina and her nephews and nieces
Brandenberg, Franz
Aunt Nina series (1)
Aunt Nina, good night!
Brandenberg, Franz
Aunt Nina series (3)
Aunt Nina's visit
Brandenberg, Franz
Aunt Nina series (2)
Auntie Mame
Dennis, Patrick
Auntie Mame series (1)
Aunts aren't gentlemen
Wodehouse, Pelham Grenville
Jeeves and Bertie Wooster series (15)
Aupres de ma blonde
Freeling, Nicolas
Arlette Van der Valk series (1)
Inspector Piet Van der Valk series (10)
Aurelien
Aragon, Louis
Real world series (4)
Aurelius Smith, detective
Scott, Reginald Thomas Maitland
Aurelius Smith series (4)
Aurora and Socrates
Vestly, Anna Catharina
Aurora series (4)
Aurora and the little blue car
Vestly, Anna Catharina
Aurora series (3)
Aurora in Holland
Vestly, Anna Catharina
Aurora series (5)
Aurora land use plan
Hester, Randolph Thompson
Aurora series (3)
Australia Felix
Richardson, Henry Handel
Fortunes of Richard Mahony trilogy (1)
Australia, find the flying foxes!
Foley, Louise Munro
Earth inspectors series (4)
Australian encounters
Smith, Keith
Supernatural series (1)
Australian houses of the forties and fifties
Cuffley, Peter
Australian houses series (2)
Australian houses of the twenties and thirties
Cuffley, Peter
Australian houses series (1)
Australian Klondyke
Carter, Nicholas
Nicholas Carter series (13)
Australian nature trails
Rees, Leslie
Australian nature tales series (7)
Australian story, 1837-1907
Casey, Maie
Australian story series (1)
Australian twins
Rooke, Daphne
Twin series (27)
Austrian adventure
Bayley, Viola
Adventure series (11)
Author bites the dust
Upfield, Arthur William
Napoleon Bonaparte series (11)
Author in distress
Wills, Cecil Melville
Geoffrey Boscobell series (1)
Author unknown
Dane, Clemence
Sir John Saumerez series (2)
Authoritative Calvin and Hobbes
Watterson, Bill
Calvin and Hobbes series (6)
Auto boys
Braden, James Andrew
Auto boys series (1)
Auto boys' camp
Braden, James Andrew
Auto boys series (4)
Auto boys' outing
Braden, James Andrew
Auto boys series (2)
Auto boys' quest
Braden, James Andrew
Auto boys series (3)
Autobiography
Cardus, Neville
Innings series (1)
Evans, Margiad
Ray of darkness series (1)
John, Augustus
Fragments of autobiography series (2)
Milne, Alan Alexander
Very young series (2)
Autobiography of a super-tramp
Davies, William Henry
Super-tramp series (1)
Autobiography of an unknown Indian
Chaudhuri, Nirad Chandra
Unknown Indian series (1)
Autobiography of Arthur Machen
Machen, Arthur
Near and far series (2)
Autobiography of Diana Cooper
Cooper, Diana Olivia Winifred Maud
Rainbow series (3)
Autobiography of Mark Rutherford
White, William Hale
Mark Rutherford series (1)
Autobot alert!
Stamper, Judith Bauer
Junior transformers find your fate series (7)
Autocrat of the breakfast table
Holmes, Oliver Wendell
Breakfast table trilogy (1)
Autocrats of Oz
Suter, Jon Michael
Mustard jar series (6)
Oz series (42)
Automobile boys of Lakeport
Stratemeyer, Edward L
Lakeport series (5)
Automobile girls along the Hudson
Crane, Laura Dent
Automobile girls series (3)
Automobile girls at Chicago
Crane, Laura Dent
Automobile girls series (4)
Automobile girls at Newport
Crane, Laura Dent
Automobile girls series (1)
Automobile girls at Palm Beach
Crane, Laura Dent
Automobile girls series (5)
Automobile girls at Washington
Crane, Laura Dent
Automobile girls series (6)
Automobile girls in the Berkshires
Crane, Laura Dent
Automobile girls series (2)
Auton invasion
Dicks, Terrance
Doctor Who series (5)
Autumn
Allington, Richard L
Beginning to learn series (18)
Best, Jacqueline
Paul and Fritzi's year series (3)
Blyton, Enid
Round the year series (3)
Gibbs, George
Old Philadelphia series (3)
Autumn accelerator
Leslie, Peter
Invaders series (6)
Autumn adventure
Pudney, John
Fred and I series (10)
Autumn and Advent
Haughton, Rosemary
Christian year series (3)
Autumn angels
Cover, Arthur Byron
Autumn angels trilogy (1)
Autumn at Cherry-Tree Farm
Kent, Margaret
Four seasons at Cherry-Tree Farm series (3)
Autumn at Karnford
Bell, Catherine Douglas
Cousin Kate series (2)
Autumn dead
Gorman, Edward
Jack Dwyer series (5)
Autumn fields
Home, Michael
East Anglia seasons series (1)
Autumn journal
Macneice, Louis
Autumn series (1)
Autumn of an age
Hardwick, Michael
Cedar tree trilogy (2)
Autumn sequel
Macneice, Louis
Autumn series (2)
Autumn story
Barklem, Jill
Brambly Hedge series (2)
Autumn term
Forest, Antonia
Marlow family series (1)
Autumn trail
Bryant, Bonnie
Saddle Club series (30)
Avalanche patrol
Atwater, Montgomery Meigs
Hank Winton series (3)
Avalanche run
Grant, William
Matthew Faraday series (7)
Avaryan Rising
Tarr, Judith
Avaryan Rising trilogy (3)
Avatar
Cooper, Louise Antell
Indigo series (6)
Ave
Moore, George
Hail and farewell trilogy (1)
Avenger
Blood, Matthew
Morgan Wayne series (1)
Cooper, Louise Antell
Chaos gate trilogy (3)
Cunningham, Chet
Matt Hawke series (1)
Smith, Mark
Way of the Tiger series (1)
Avenger at large
Salt, Jonathan
Jonathan Salt series (2)
Avenger of Antares
Akers, Alan Burt
Dray Prescot series (10)
Avenger strikes
Masterman, Walter Sidney
Sir Arthur Sinclair series (11)
Avengers
Cunningham, Chet
Outlaws series (4)
Graves, Charles
Royal Air Force series (2)
Avengers battle the earth-wrecker
Binder, Otto
Avengers superheroes series (1)
Captain America series (1)
Marvel superheroes series (1)
Avengers of Carrig
Brunner, John
Zarathustra trilogy (1)
Avenger's trail
Elton, Wallace
Jud Walton series (5)
Avenging angel
Burns, Rex
Gabriel Wager series (5)
Copeland, Lori
Passion trilogy (1)
Avenging Angel
Longley, W B
Angel Eyes series (8)
Ryder, Thom
Avenging Angel series (1)
Avenging children
Mann, Mary E
Ronald Love series (2)
Avenging ikon
Barry, Charles
Superintendent Lawrence Gilmartin series (7)
Avenging Liafail
Mundy, Talbot
Tros of Samothrace series (1)
Avenging nymph
Janson, Hank
Hank Janson series (82)
Avenging parrot
Austin, Anne
James F Dundee series (3)
Avenging Picaroon
Cassells, John
Ludovic Saxon series (2)
Avenging Saint
Charteris, Leslie
Saint series (4)
Avenging seven
Brooks, Leonard Harold
Sexton Blake series (115)
Avenging spirit
Stevenson, Edward
Twilight series (10)
Avenging Twins
McCulley, Johnston
Avenging Twins series (1)
Avenging Twins collect
McCulley, Johnston
Avenging Twins series (2)
Avenue
Delderfield, Ronald Frederick
Avenue series (2)
Avenue goes to war
Delderfield, Ronald Frederick
Avenue series (2)
Avenue of stone
Johnson, Pamela Hansford
Helena trilogy (2)
Avenue of the dead
Anthony, Evelyn
Davina Graham series (2)
Avenue story
Delderfield, Ronald Frederick
Avenue series (2)
Average man
Fox-Davies, Arthur Charles
Ashley Tempest series (2)
Aviation stories for boys
Stone, Richard H
Slim Tyler series (4)
Aviators
Griffin, W E B
Brotherhood of war series (8)
Aviator's luck
Cobb, Frank
Aviator series (2)
Avillion, and other tale
Craik, Dinah Maria
Avillion series (2)
Awakened
Oldenbourg, Zoe
Paris series (1)
Awakeners
Tepper, Sheri S
Awakeners series (2)
Awakening
Ahern, Jerry
Survivalist series (10)
Diver, Maud
Sinclair series (1)
Galsworthy, John
Forsyte saga trilogy (3)
Macnamara, Rachel Swete
Awakening series (1)
Pringle, Eric
Doctor Who series (95)
Smith, Lisa J
Vampire diaries series (1)
Tomino, Yoshiyuki
Gundam mobile suit trilogy (1)
Awakening dream
Cameron, Kate
Whispering Hills series (5)
Awakening land
Richter, Conrad
American pioneer trilogy (3)
Awakening of Helen Ritchie
Deland, Margaret
Helen Ritchie series (1)
Awakening of Mary Fenwick
Whitby, Beatrice
Mary Fenwick series (1)
Away and ago
McCord, David
Rhymes of the never was an always is series (5)
Away boarders
Macdonnell, James Edmond
Captain Peter Bentley series (19)
Away for the night
Jessel, Camilla
Chatterbooks series (1)
Away from home
Hardcastle, Michael
Bank Vale United series (3)
Away from the vicarage
Streatfeild, Noel
Vicarage series (2)
Away from Wood Street
Allan, Mabel Esther
Wood Street series (5)
Away goes Sally
Coatsworth, Elizabeth
Sally Smith series (1)
Away goes Sooty
Blyton, Enid
Sooty series (1)
Away to the west
Tomalin, Ruth
Ralph Oliver series (3)
Away went the little fish
Bennett, Margot
John Davies series (2)
Away with them to prison
Woods, Sara
Sir Nicholas Harding and Antony Maitland series (44)
Awful dynasty
Robeson, Kenneth
Doc Savage series (148)
Awful egg
Robeson, Kenneth
Doc Savage series (92)
Awfully big adventure
Bartimeus
Naval occasions series (4)
Awkward lie
Innes, Michael
Sir John Appleby series (25)
Awkward magic
Beresford, Elisabeth
Magic series (1)
Awol at large
Shurtleff, Bertrand Leslie
Awol series (3)
Awol, K9 commando
Shurtleff, Bertrand Leslie
Awol series (1)
Awol musters out
Shurtleff, Bertrand Leslie
Awol series (3)
Ax
McBain, Ed
Eighty Seventh Precinct series (18)
Undset, Sigrid
Master of Hestviken series (1)
Axa in color
Avenell, Donne
Axa series (9)
Axa, the beginning
Avenell, Donne
Axa series (1)
Axe
McBain, Ed
Eighty Seventh Precinct series (18)
Undset, Sigrid
Master of Hestviken series (1)
Axe in Miklagard
Frazier, Arthur
Wolfshead series (6)
Axe to grind
Fair, A A
Bertha Cool and Donald Lam series (9)
Wallace, Robert
Essington Holt series (2)
Axeman's jazz
Smith, Julie
Skip Langdon series (2)
Axes of hate
Preston, James
Sergeant Bob Christie series (2)
Ayes of Texas
Da Cruz, Daniel
Forte family trilogy (1)
Ayesha
Haggard, Henry Rider
She series (4)
Aylwin
Watts-Dunton, Theodore
Aylwin series (1)
Aylwin series (2)
Azanian action
Corris, Peter
Pokerface series (5)
Azon the youth
Cooper, John R
Repositors series (2)
Azor
Crowley, Maude
Azor series (1)
Henaghan, Jim
Jeff Pride series (5)
Azor and the blue-eyed cow
Crowley, Maude
Azor series (3)
Azor and the haddock
Crowley, Maude
Azor series (2)
Azrael
De Andrea, William Louis
Clifford Driscoll series (3)
Aztec avenger
Carter, Nick
Nick Carter series (94)

Aztec Gold
Cunningham, Chet
Jim Steel series (6)
Aztecs
Lucarotti, John
Doctor Who series (88)
Azure bonds
Novak, Kate
Finder's stone trilogy (1)

B

B as in banshee
Treat, Lawrence
Carl Wayward series (1)
B-Berry and I look back
Yates, Dornford
Berry series (11)
B book
Berenstain, Stan
Berenstain bears series (11)
B-E-S-T friends
Giff, Patricia Reilly
New kids at the Polk Street School series (4)
B is for Betsy
Haywood, Carolyn
Betsy series (1)
B is for burglar
Grafton, Sue
Kinsey Millhone series (2)
B, my name is Bunny
Mazer, Norma Fox
My name series (2)
B.O.W.C.
De Mille, James
Brethren of the White Cross series (1)
Baa baa Black Sheep
Boyington, Gregory
Black Sheep Squadron series (2)
Baalbak quest
Kelly, David J
Killstar series (1)
Babar and Father Christmas
Brunhoff, Jean de
Babar series (7)
Babar and his children
Brunhoff, Jean de
Babar series (6)
Babar and that rascal Arthur
Brunhoff, Laurent de
Babar series (8)
Babar and the doctor
Brunhoff, Laurent de
Babar series (21)
Babar and the professor
Brunhoff, Laurent de
Babar series (12)
Babar and the Wully-Wully
Brunhoff, Laurent de
Babar series (34)
Babar and Zephir
Brunhoff, Jean de
Babar series (5)
Babar at home
Brunhoff, Jean de
Babar series (6)
Babar at the seashore
Brunhoff, Laurent de
Babar series (20)
Babar at the seaside
Brunhoff, Laurent de
Babar series (20)
Babar bakes a cake
Brunhoff, Laurent de
Babar series (33)
Babar comes to America
Brunhoff, Laurent de
Babar series (14)
Babar goes camping
Brunhoff, Laurent de
Babar series (28)
Babar goes on a picnic
Brunhoff, Laurent de
Babar series (18)
Babar goes skiing
Brunhoff, Laurent de
Babar series (16)
Babar goes visiting
Brunhoff, Laurent de
Babar series (23)
Babar in the snow
Brunhoff, Laurent de
Babar series (16)
Babar keeps fit
Brunhoff, Laurent de
Babar series (26)
Babar learns to drive
Brunhoff, Laurent de
Babar series (22)
Babar loses his crown
Brunhoff, Laurent de
Babar series (15)
Babar on the secret planet
Brunhoff, Laurent de
Babar series (29)
Babar saves the day
Brunhoff, Laurent de
Babar series (35)
Babar the artist
Brunhoff, Laurent de
Babar series (27)
Babar the athlete
Brunhoff, Laurent de
Babar series (26)
Babar the camper
Brunhoff, Laurent de
Babar series (28)
Babar the cook
Brunhoff, Laurent de
Babar series (33)
Babar the gardener
Brunhoff, Laurent de
Babar series (17)
Babar the king
Brunhoff, Jean de
Babar series (3)
Babar the painter
Brunhoff, Laurent de
Babar series (27)
Babar the pilot
Brunhoff, Laurent de
Babar series (31)
Babar to the rescue
Brunhoff, Laurent de
Babar series (31)
Babar visits another planet
Brunhoff, Laurent de
Babar series (29)
Babar's A B C
Brunhoff, Jean de
Babar series (4)
Babar's birthday surprise
Brunhoff, Laurent de
Babar series (25)
Babar's bookmobile
Brunhoff, Laurent de
Babar series (32)
Babar's castle
Brunhoff, Laurent de
Babar series (13)
Babar's cousin, that rascal Arthur
Brunhoff, Laurent de
Babar series (8)
Babar's day out
Brunhoff, Laurent de
Babar series (18)
Babar's fair will be opened next Sunday
Brunhoff, Laurent de
Babar series (11)
Babar's friend Zephir
Brunhoff, Jean de
Babar series (5)
Babar's games
Brunhoff, Laurent de
Babar series (19)
Babar's moon trip
Brunhoff, Laurent de
Babar series (24)
Babar's picnic
Brunhoff, Laurent de
Babar series (9)
Babar's travels
Brunhoff, Jean de
Babar series (2)
Babar's trunk
Brunhoff, Laurent de
Babar series (20)
Babar's visit to Bird Island
Brunhoff, Laurent de
Babar series (10)
Babbie
Chalmers, Margaret Piper
Sylvia Arden series (6)
Babbington case
Carter, Nicholas
Nicholas Carter series (460)
Babbitt
Lewis, Sinclair
American society series (1)
Babcock boys
Reid, Desmond
Pinkerton series (1)
Babe bound to kill
Brody, Marc
Marc Brody series (76)
Babe Ruth and the home run Derby
Mooser, Stephen
All-Star Meatballs series (1)
Babe up in arms
McCall, K T
Johnny Buchanan series (18)
Babe with the twistable arm
Stone, Hampton
Jeremiah X Gibson series (12)
Babel
Cournos, John
John Gombarov trilogy (3)
Babel in London
Haycraft, John
Babel series (2)
Babel in Spain
Haycraft, John
Babel series (1)
Babes in Birdland
Bancroft, Laura
Birdland series (2)
Babies' bodies
Kilroy, Sally
Baby series (2)
Babies' homes
Kilroy, Sally
Baby series (4)
Babies' outings
Kilroy, Sally
Baby series (5)
Babies' zoo
Kilroy, Sally
Baby series (7)
Babington plot
Birt, David
Tudors series (16)
Baboon's paw
Armour, R Coutts
Sexton Blake series (266)
Babs
Baldwin, Faith
Divine corners series (2)
Colver, Alice Ross
Babs series (1)
Babs at Birchwood
Colver, Alice Ross
Babs series (2)
Babs at college
Colver, Alice Ross
Babs series (3)
Babs at home
Colver, Alice Ross
Babs series (4)
Babushka Baba Yaga
Polacco, Patricia
Babushka series (2)
Babushka's doll
Polacco, Patricia
Babushka series (1)
Baby
Burningham, John
Little book series (4)
Baby animals
Hill, Eric
Peek-a-book series (5)
Baby Bear's bedtime
Hill, Eric
Baby Bear series (5)
Baby Beluga
Raffi
Raffi songs to read series (8)
Baby blue rip-off
Collins, Max Allan
Mallory series (1)
Baby Cakes
Maupin, Armistead
Tales of the city series (4)
Baby car
Lenski, Lois
Small family series (2)
Baby colours
Kilroy, Sally
Baby series (1)
Baby doll
Williams, Tennessee
Baby doll series (1)
Baby doll games
Maron, Margaret
Lieutenant Sigrid Harald series (5)
Baby, don't dare squeal
Janson, Hank
Hank Janson series (26)
Baby don't love hoodlums
Storm, Michael
Baby don't series (1)
Baby don't say goodbye
Storm, Michael
Baby don't series (2)
Baby Elephant and the secret wishes
Joslin, Sesyle
Baby Elephant series (4)
Baby Elephant goes to China
Joslin, Sesyle
Baby Elephant series (5)
Baby Elephant's baby book
Joslin, Sesyle
Baby Elephant series (6)
Baby Elephant's bedtime
McCue, Dick
Animal shape series (9)
Baby Elephant's trunk
Joslin, Sesyle
Baby Elephant series (2)
Baby face
Corrigan, Mark
Mark Corrigan and McLean series (8)
Baby farm animals
James, Robin
Baby animal series (1)
Baby forest animals
James, Robin
Baby animal series (3)
Baby in the ash can
Shane, Susannah
Christopher Saxe series (3)
Baby in the bulrushes
Blyton, Enid
Bible stories series (3)
Baby Koala finds a home
Tripp, Valerie
Just one more stories series (2)
Baby merchants
O'Donnell, Lillian
Detective Norah Mulcahaney series (4)
Baby mice
Cartlidge, Michelle
Mouse series (3)
Baby might be crying
Davis, Margaret Thomson
Glasgow trilogy (2)
Baby pets
James, Robin
Baby animal series (4)
Baby sister for Frances
Hoban, Russell
Frances series (2)
Baby Sweet's
Andrews, Raymond
Appalachee Red series (3)
Baby talk
Miranda, Anne
Baby series (1)
Walker, Mort
Hi and Lois series (23)
Baby unicorn
Marzollo, Jean
Baby unicorn series (1)
Baby unicorn and baby dragon
Marzollo, Jean
Baby unicorn series (2)
Baby walk
Miranda, Anne
Baby series (2)
Baby, would I lie?
Westlake, Donald Edwin
Sara Joslyn series (2)
Baby, your racket's busted
Brody, Marc
Marc Brody series (47)
Baby, your type's murder
Brody, Marc
Marc Brody series (59)
Baby zoo animals
James, Robin
Baby animal series (2)
Babyland abroad
Jesse, Louie
Babyland series (1)
Babyland in history
Jesse, Louie
Babyland series (2)
Babylon South
Cleary, Jon
Scobie Malone series (6)
Babylonians
Weinreb, Nathaniel Norsen
Biblical series (1)
Baby's bedtime
Jessel, Camilla
Babydays series (3)
Baby's clothes
Jessel, Camilla
Babydays series (4)
Baby's day
Jessel, Camilla
Babydays series (1)
Baby's food
Jessel, Camilla
Babydays series (5)
Baby's toys
Jessel, Camilla
Babydays series (2)
Baby-sitter
Jessel, Camilla
Chatterbooks series (7)
Stine, Robert Lawrence
Baby-sitter series (1)
Baby-sitter II
Stine, Robert Lawrence
Baby-sitter series (2)
Baby-Sitters at Shadow Lake
Martin, Ann Matthews
Baby-Sitters Club super specials series (8)
Baby-Sitters Club guide to baby-sitting
Martin, Ann Matthews
Baby-Sitters Club series (78)
Baby-Sitters Club notebook
Black, Sonia
Baby-Sitters Club series (78)
Baby-Sitters Club postcard book
Martin, Ann Matthews
Baby-Sitters Club series (78)
Baby-Sitters Club trivia and puzzle fun book
Adamo, Kara
Baby-Sitters Club series (78)
Baby-Sitters island adventure
Martin, Ann Matthews
Baby-Sitters Club super specials series (4)
Baby-Sitters on board!
Martin, Ann Matthews
Baby-Sitters Club super specials series (1)
Baby-Sitters remember
Martin, Ann Matthews
Baby-Sitters Club super specials series (11)
Baby-Sitters summer vacation
Martin, Ann Matthews
Baby-Sitters Club super specials series (2)
Baby-Sitters winter carnival
Martin, Ann Matthews
Baby-Sitters Club super specials series (3)
Baby-snatcher
Kendall, Carol
Kendall series (2)
Bachelor flat mystery
Walling, Robert Alfred John
Philip Tolefree series (5)
Bachelor in Arcady
Sutcliffe, Halliwell
Arcady series (2)
Bachelor maid and her brother
Thurston, Ida Treadwell
Bachelor maid series (1)
Bachelor of arts
Narayan, Rasipuram Krishnaswami
Malgudi series (6)
Bachelors anonymous
Wodehouse, Pelham Grenville
Ivor Llewellyn series (2)
Bachelors' Club
Zangwill, Israel
Celibates' Club series (1)
Bachelor's establishment
Balzac, Honore de
Scenes of provincial life series (4)
Bachelors get lonely
Fair, A A
Bertha Cool and Donald Lam series (21)
Bachelors of Broken Hill
Upfield, Arthur William
Napoleon Bonaparte series (14)
Back at our selection
Rudd, Steele
Rudd family series (4)
Back at school with the Tucker twins
Sampson, Emma
Tucker twins series (3)
Back Bay murders
Scarlett, Roger
Inspector Kane series (2)
Back country
Fuller, William
Brad Dolan series (1)
Back country folks
Hubbard, Kin
Abe Martin series (6)
Back crack boy
McKeown, Joseph
Liam series (1)
Back door to death
Foley, Rae
Hiram Potter series (8)
Back from the dead
Gilman, George G
Undertaker series (5)
Back from the grave
Masterman, Walter Sidney
Sir Arthur Sinclair series (18)

Back home
Cobb, Irwin Shrewsbury
Judge Priest series (1)
Pinkney, Gloria Jean
Ernestine series (2)
Back home at the O.R.G.Y.
Mark, Ted
Man from O.R.G.Y. series (14)
Back in daylight
Clements, Eileen Helen
Alister Woodhead series (8)
Back in Keith County
Janovy, John
Keith County series (2)
Back in Texas
Grover, Marshall
Larry and Stretch series (19)
Back in the beforetime
Curry, Jane Louise
California Indian series (2)
Back in the jug
Willans, Geoffrey
Nigel Molesworth series (4)
Back in the real world
Albert, Marvin Hubert
Pierre-Ange Sawyer series (2)
Back in the world
Mason, Robert Caverly
Chickenhawk series (2)
Back in time with Megabot
Hall, Willis
Megabot series (2)
Back of beyond
Dorrance, Ethel Smith
Sergeant Alfred Rawson series (2)
White, Stewart Edward
Simba series (3)
Back of the North Wind
Freeling, Nicolas
Henri Castang series (7)
Back room in Somers Town
Malcolm, John
Tim Simpson series (1)
Back-stage
Hill, Lorna
Sadler's Wells series (12)
Back street runner
Breeze, Paul
Billy Dancey series (2)
Back to Barbary Lane
Maupin, Armistead
Tales of the city series (7)
Back to battle
Hennessy, Max
Kelly Maguire trilogy (3)
Back to Bay Thirteen
Walker, Max
Cricketer series (2)
Back to Billabong
Bruce, Mary Grant
Billabong series (7)
Back to Black
Black, Arthur
Basic Black series (2)
Back to Bool Bool
Brent of Bin Bin
Bert Poole series (5)
Back to Cape Horn
Swale, Rosie
Rosie Darling series (4)
Back to Nam
Buchanan, Jack
M.I.A. Hunter series (14)
Back to nature
Saunders, Susan
Bad News Bunny series (2)
Back to school with Betsy
Haywood, Carolyn
Betsy series (3)
Back to the bloody border
Edson, John Thomas
American Civil War series (12)
Back to the forest
Foley, Winifred
Forest series (2)
Back to the future
Fleming, Robert Loren
Back to the future trilogy (1)
Gipe, George
Back to the future trilogy (1)
Hibbin, Sally
Back to the future trilogy (3)
Back to the future, part three
Gardner, Craig Shaw
Back to the future trilogy (3)
Back to the future, part two
Gardner, Craig Shaw
Back to the future trilogy (2)
Back to the honey-pot
Barcynska, Helena Margareta
Honey-pot series (4)
Back to the Marble Mountain
Gardner, Hugh
Marble Mountain series (2)
Back to the smoky sea
Nutchuk
Smoky sea series (2)
Back to the stone age
Burroughs, Edgar Rice
Pellucidar series (5)
Back to the top of the world
Ruesch, Hans
Top of the world series (2)
Back to the wall
Kirk, Thomas Hobson
William and Susan series (1)
Back to Treasure Island
Calahan, Harold Augustin
Treasure Island series (3)
Back trail to danger
Field, Peter
Powder Valley series (35)
Back-trailers of the Middle Border
Garland, Hamlin
Middle Border series (4)
Back with Parren
Hildick, Edmund Wallace
Parren series (2)
Backblast
McKeone, Lee
Ghoster trilogy (2)
Backblocks baby doctor
Gordon, Doris
Backblocks doctor series (1)
Backboard fever
Bee, Clair
Chip Hilton series (10)
Backcloth
Bogarde, Dirk
Orderly man series (4)
Backcourt ace
Bee, Clair
Chip Hilton series (19)
Backed by the law
Masterson, Louis
Morgan Kane series (4)
Backfield challenge
Gault, William Campbell
Gridiron series (4)
Backfire
Newman, Christopher
Joe Dante series (3)
Sauter, Eric
Robert Lee Hunter series (6)
Backfire is hostile
Barnett, James
Superintendent Owen Smith series (1)
Backflash
James, Laurence
Simon Rack series (3)
Background for murder
Smith, Shelley
Jacob Chaos series (1)
Background to danger
Ambler, Eric
Andreas and Tamara Valeshoff series (1)
Background with chorus
Swinnerton, Frank
Background and foreground series (1)
Backhand
Cody, Liza
Anna Lee series (6)
Backing up Billy Bunter
Richards, Frank
Billy Bunter series (16)
Backlash
Brunner, John
Max Curfew series (1)
Durst, Paul
Michael Carmichael series (1)
Gosling, Paula
Lieutenant Jack Stryker series (2)
O'Sullivan, James Brendan
Steve Silk series (14)
Philips, Judson Pentecost
Peter Styles series (13)
Reno, Bill
Badge series (9)
Backlash mission
Zahn, Timothy
Blackcollar series (2)
Backlash of infamy
Janson, Hank
Hank Janson series (198)
Backshot
Gilman, George G
Edge series (54)
Backstage mystery
Cohen, Octavus Roy
Jim Hanvey series (3)
Backtracking Little Red
Grover, Marshall
Larry and Stretch series (387)
Backtrail
Fackler, Elizabeth
Seth Strummar series (2)
Backup goalie
Hughes, Dean
Angel Park Soccer Stars series (5)
Backup men
Thomas, Ross
McCorkle and Padillo series (3)
Backward in time
Kelley, Leo Patrick
Space police series (4)
Backward shadow
Banks, Lynne Reid
Jane Graham trilogy (2)
Backwater
Richardson, Dorothy Miller
Pilgrimage series (2)
Backyard Angel
Delton, Judy
Angel series (1)
Bad and the beautiful
Cooney, Caroline B
Chrystal Falls series (3)
Bad April
Ross, Angus
Mark Farrow series (16)
Bad Babies' book of colours
Bradman, Tony
Bad babies series (2)
Bad babies' book of months
Bradman, Tony
Bad babies series (3)
Bad Babies' counting book
Bradman, Tony
Bad babies series (1)
Bad Bear
Ahlberg, Allan
Help your child to read series (4)
Bad blonde
Webb, Jack
Father Joseph Shanley and Sammy Golden series (5)
Bad blood
Carlson, Patricia McEvoy
Maggie Ryan series (8)
Edwards, Hank
Judge Clay Torn series (7)
McLennan, Will
Ramseys series (10)
Bad Boris and the birthday
Jenkin-Pearce, Susie
Bad Boris series (2)
Bad Boris and the new kitten
Jenkin-Pearce, Susie
Bad Boris series (1)
Bad boy abroad
Gray, Walter T
Bad boy series (2)
Bad boy at home and his experiences in trying to become an editor
Gray, Walter T
Bad boy series (3)
Bad boy in the country
Golden Rod
Bad boy series (4)
Bad boy's adventures
Little Georgie
Bad boy series (4)
Bad boy's diary
Gray, Walter T
Bad boy series (1)
Bad break
Levy, Elizabeth
Gymnasts series (6)
Bad, brown bunnies
Delton, Judy
Pee wee scout series (12)
Bad bunch
Edson, John Thomas
Floating Outfit series (19)
Bad bungle!
Davis, Anne
Pumpkin Hollow series (3)
Bad child's book of beasts
Belloc, Hilaire
Beasts series (1)
Bad company
Cody, Liza
Anna Lee series (2)
Luckey, William A
Blue Mitchell series (2)
Bad day at Agua Caliente
Christian, Frederick H
Frank Angel series (1)
Bad day at Bandera
Wales, Mike
Leatherhand series (5)
Bad day for a black brother
Johnson, B B
Superspade series (5)
Bad die young
Chambers, Peter
Mark Preston series (13)
Bad dream of death
Chance, John Newton
Jonathan Blake series (27)
Bad dreams
Gair, Malcolm
Mark Raeburn series (4)
Stine, Robert Lawrence
Fear Street series (22)
Bad End Valley
Bannerman, W B
Domingo Santos series (2)
Bad for business
Stout, Rex
Tecumseh Fox series (2)
Bad for the Baron
Morton, Anthony
Baron series (34)
Bad girl
Goudge, Eileen
Seniors series (11)
Janson, Hank
Hank Janson series (32)
Bad habits
Muir, James A
Breed series (16)
Bad hombre
Edson, John Thomas
Rockabye County series (10)
Bad intent
Hornsby, Wendy
Maggie McGowan series (3)
Bad lands
Hall, Oakley
Legends west trilogy (2)
Bad love
Cooper, M E
Couples series (12)
Bad man of Cairo
Parsons, Anthony
Sexton Blake series (1287)
Bad man's return
Macdonald, William Colt
Three Mesquiteers series (12)
Bad medicine
Keene, Carolyn
Nancy Drew files series (35)
Leslie, David Stuart
Ernie Pratt series (2)
Yarbro, Chelsea Quinn
Charlie Spotted Moon series (1)
Bad neighbor murder
Russell, Charlotte Murray
Jane Amanda Edwards series (9)
Bad news
Tippette, Giles
Justa Williams series (1)
Bad night for Ali Baba
Gardner, Craig Shaw
Arabian Nights trilogy (2)
Bad night's work
Currington, Owen Josiah
Jack Lovel series (1)
Bad rap
Dixon, Franklin W
Hardy boys case files series (73)
Bad Sam!
Lindgren, Barbro
Sam series (5)
Bad Samaritan
Gault, William Campbell
Brock Callahan series (8)
Bad scene
Copper, Basil
Mike Faraday series (50)
Bad scene at Bong Son
Lansing, John
Black Eagles series (9)
Bad sisters
Oaks, Tina
Stepsisters series (3)
Bad spell for the Worst Witch
Murphy, Jill
Worst Witch series (3)
Bad to the bone
Solomita, Stephen
Stanley Moodrow series (4)
Bad weather
Messner-Loebs, William
Wolverine MacAlistaire series (2)
Baddington horror
Masterman, Walter Sidney
Sir Arthur Sinclair series (8)
Badge
Sharpe, Jon
Trailsman series (36)
Badge and Tully McGlynn
Grover, Marshall
Larry and Stretch series (348)
Badge for a badman
Wynne, Brian
Marshal Jeremy Six series (7)
Badge for Brazos
Clay, E Jefferson
Duke Benedict and Hank Brazos series (4)
Badge in the dust
Gilman, George G
Adam Steele series (9)
Badge of glory
Reeman, Douglas
Blackwood family series (1)
Badge of honour
Barnes, Dallas
Sergeant John Stryker series (2)
Badge of infamy
Durst, Paul
Michael Carmichael series (2)
Badger and the buried treasure
Trueman, Brian
Riverbend and Wildwood tales series (1)
Badger in the bag
De Lint, Charles
Cerin Songweaver series (6)
Badger in the dusk
Brent, Nigel
Barney Hyde series (8)
Badger Wood
Bradbury, Catherine
Applebury tales series (1)
Badgers at my window
Drabble, Phil
Wild animals series (2)
Badger's Beech
Trevor, Elleston
Woodlanders series (1)
Badger's Bend, the animal hotel
Rhodes, John
Tim and Betsy series (1)
Badger's daughter
Crawford, Robert
Arthur Salisbury and Frank Shearer series (3)
Badger's fate
Hamley, Dennis
Hare's choice trilogy (2)
Badger's moon
Trevor, Elleston
Woodlanders series (3)
Badger's Wood
Trevor, Elleston
Woodlanders series (7)
Badlanders
Slade, Jack
Lassiter series (13)
Badlands
Frost, Jason
Warlord series (3)
Wheeler, Richard Seabrook
Skye's West series (7)
Badlands blood
Weston, Cole
Andrew Ryder series (6)
Badland's boss
Scott, Bradford
Walt Slade series (12)
Badlands brigade
Thorne, Ramsay
Captain Gringo series (12)
Badlands fury
Borg, Jack
Hogleg Bailey series (11)
Badlands gang
Langley, John
Walt Warren series (14)
Badlands of Hark
Stine, Robert Lawrence
Hark series (1)
Badlands patrol
Hardin, J D
Raider series (23)
Badlands run
Lambard, Creede
Car wars adventure gamebook series (4)
Badlands showdown
Allen, Chester
Justice Colt series (3)
Badman headed north
Borg, Jack
Thady Corey series (2)
Badman's bordello
Martin, Cort
Jared Bolt series (9)
Badman's climax
Hunter, E J
White Squaw series (19)

Badman's revenge
Cole, Jackson
Jim Hatfield series (39)

Badman's shadow
Borg, Jack
Thady Corey series (1)

Badmen of Bordertown
Cole, Jackson
Jim Hatfield series (50)

Badmen on Halfaday Creek
Hendryx, James Beardsley
Black John series (14)
Corporal Cameron Downey series (8)

Baer's Christmas
Moore, Bertha B
Triplets series (1)

Baffled, but not beaten
Carter, Nicholas
Nicholas Carter series (196)

Baffled heart
Miller, Hugh
Eastenders series (7)

Baffled oath
Carter, Nicholas
Nicholas Carter series (171)

Baffling affair in the county hospital
Deming, Dorothy
Wendy Brent series (4)

Bag I'm taking to grandma's
Neitzel, Shirley
My clothes series (3)

Bagatelle
Denuziere, Maurice
Clarence Dandridge series (1)

Bagdad
Dennis, Ian
Prince of Stars in the Cavern of Time series (1)

Bagful of dreams
Vance, Jack
Adventures of Cugel the Clever series (2)

Bagodia episode
Dawlish, Peter
Sam Macclellan series (2)

Bagpuss in the sun
Postgate, Oliver
Bagpuss series (1)

Bagpuss on a rainy day
Postgate, Oliver
Bagpuss series (2)

Bags of swank
Walder, David
Charles Lilburne and Rupert Inglis series (1)

Bags the lamb
Kanno, Wendy
Funny Farm series (3)

Bagthorpe triangle
Cresswell, Helen
Bagthorpes series (8)

Bagthorpes abroad
Cresswell, Helen
Bagthorpes series (5)

Bagthorpes haunted
Cresswell, Helen
Bagthorpes series (6)

Bagthorpes liberated
Cresswell, Helen
Bagthorpes series (7)

Bagthorpes unlimited
Cresswell, Helen
Bagthorpes series (3)

Bagthorpes versus the world
Cresswell, Helen
Bagthorpes series (4)

Bah, Humbug!
Balian, Lorna
Humbug series (3)

Bahamas blue
Poyer, David
Tiller Galloway series (2)

Baileaus of Desert Home
Kopsen, Dorothy Blaxland
Desert Home series (2)

Bailey chronicles
Cookson, Catherine
Bill Bailey series (3)

Bailiff's secret
Teed, George Hamilton
Sexton Blake series (977)

Bainbridge murder
Fitzsimmons, Cortland
Arthur Martinson series (1)

Bait
Black, Lionel
Emma Greaves series (2)
Uhnak, Dorothy
Christie Opara series (1)

Bait for a killer
Bagby, George
Inspector Schmidt series (34)

Bait for murder
Knight, Kathleen Moore
Elisha Macomber series (10)

Bait money
Collins, Max Allan
Nolan series (1)

Bait on the hook
Parrish, Frank
Dan Mallett series (4)

Baja
Lewin, Ted
World within a world series (2)

Baja bandidos
Derrick, Lionel
Penetrator series (7)

Baja diablo
Hardin, J D
Raider series (15)

Baja people
Willoughby, Lee Davis
Making of America series (32)

Baked bean queen
Impey, Rose
Baddies series (1)

Baked bean supper murders
Rich, Virginia
Mrs Eugenia Potter series (2)

Baker City breakout
Grover, Marshall
Larry and Stretch series (208)

Balaam's error
Webb, Michael
Giants in the earth trilogy (2)

Balance of dangers
Forrest, Anthony
Captain John Valcourt Justice series (4)

Balance of fear
Matheson, Hugh
Gregory Branscombe series (2)
Osborne, Geoffrey
James Dingle and Glyn Jones series (2)

Balance of power
Cochran, Molly
Destroyer series (44)
Murphy, Warren Burton
Destroyer series (44)
Stableford, Brian Michael
Daedalus series (5)

Balancing act
Kaye, Marilyn
Camp Sunnyside Friends series (18)
Larsen, Rebecca
Going for it series (2)

Balcony
Bell, Adrian
Roland Pace series (1)

Balkan spy
Betteridge, Don
Tiger Lester series (1)

Balkan trilogy
Manning, Olivia
Guy and Harriet Pringle series (3)

Ball and chain
Hunter, E J
White Squaw series (12)

Ball game
Greaves, Jimmy
Soccer series (2)

Ballad and the plough
Cameron, David Kerr
Scottish farm life series (1)

Ballad for a coffin
Giraud, Jean
Lieutenant Mike S Blueberry series (2)

Ballad of Cactus Jack
Benedict, Rex
Pecos Gang series (4)

Ballad of favour
Dickens, Monica
Messenger series (2)

Ballad of Gato Guerrero
Ramos, Manuel
Luis Montez series (2)

Ballad of loving Jenny
Brown, Carter
Rick Holman series (7)

Ballad of Rocky Ruiz
Ramos, Manuel
Luis Montez series (1)

Ballad of the flim-flam man
Owen, Guy
Flim-flam man series (1)

Ballade in G minor
Boileau, Ethel
Mallory family series (2)

Ballerina
Curcija-Prodanovic, Nada
Belgrade Ballet School series (1)

Ballerina mystery
Pascal, Jamie
Pick-a-path series (12)

Ballet family
Allan, Mabel Esther
Garland family series (1)

Ballet family again
Allan, Mabel Esther
Garland family series (2)

Ballet for Drina
Estoril, Jean
Drina series (1)

Ballet for Laura
Blake, Linda
Laura series (1)

Ballet for Mary
Brock, Emma Lillian
Mary series (1)

Ballet in Romilly Street
Denison, Mary
Romilly Street series (2)

Ballet of death
Anthony, Elizabeth
Pauline Lyons series (1)

Ballet of fear
Anthony, Elizabeth
Pauline Lyons series (2)

Ballet on tour
Curcija-Prodanovic, Nada
Belgrade Ballet School series (2)

Ballet school mystery
White, Constance Mary
Ballet school series (1)

Ballet school rivals
White, Constance Mary
Ballet school series (4)

Ballet shoes
Streatfeild, Noel
Shoes series (1)

Ballet shoes for Anna
Streatfeild, Noel
Shoes series (13)

Balloon pipe
Blyton, Enid
Little bedtime books series (6)

Ballooning adventures of Paddy Pork
Goodall, John Strickland
Paddy Pork series (2)

Balloons in the black bag
Donaldson, William
Ladies and gentlemen series (2)

Ballot box murders
Strange, John Stephen
Barney Gantt series (3)

Ballot box mystery
Gibbons, Harry Hornaby Clifford
Sexton Blake series (567)

Ballpoint bananas, and other jokes for kids
Keller, Charles
Ballpoint bananas series (1)

Ballycubin mystery
Webster, H M
Shamus Burke series (1)

Ballygullion
Doyle, Lynn
Ballygullion series (1)

Ballyho Bey
Gunter, Archibald Clavering
Susan Turnbull series (2)

Balsamo the magician
Dumas, Alexandre
Memoirs of a physician series (1)

Balthazar
Durrell, Lawrence
Alexandria quartet (2)

Balthazer the magus
Van der Naillen, Albert
Magi trilogy (3)

Baltic business
Corris, Peter
Pokerface series (2)

Baltic convoy
Styles, Showell
Lieutenant Michael Fitton series (3)

Baltic mission
Woodman, Richard
Nathaniel Drinkwater series (7)

Baltimore Gun Club
Verne, Jules
Gun Club series (1)

Baltimore trackdown
Pendleton, Don
Mack Bolan series (88)

Balustrade paradox
Oram, Neil
Warp series (3)

Bambi
Salten, Felix
Bambi series (1)

Bambi's children
Salten, Felix
Bambi series (2)

Bamboo and bushido
Allbury, Albert George
War in South-East Asia series (2)

Bamboo bloodbath
Anthony, Piers
Jason Striker series (3)

Bamboo bomb
Dark, James
Mark Kingsley Hood series (2)

Bamboo demons
Sherman, Jory
Doctor Russell V Childers series (3)

Bamboo in the wind
Lewin, Hugh
Second chance series (1)

Bamboo rod
George, Sidney Charles
Lim Quong series (2)

Bamboo screen
Harvester, Simon
Asia in turmoil series (1)
Malcolm Kenton series (1)

Bamboo shoot-out
Harknett, Terry
Superintendent John Crown series (3)

Bamboo whistle
Frost, Frederick
Secret service series (3)

Bamm-Bamm and Pebbles Flintstone
Lewis, Jean
Flintstones series (2)

Banana
Henderson, Kathy
Where does it come from series (2)

Banana blitz
Heide, Florence Parry
Banana series (2)

Banana boy
Norman, Frank
Bang to rights series (1)

Banana split affair
Blair, Cynthia
Susan and Christine Pratt series (2)

Banana twist
Heide, Florence Parry
Banana series (1)

Bananas gorilla
Scarry, Richard
Smallest pop-up book ever series (1)

Banbury Bog
Taylor, Phoebe Atwood
Asey Mayo series (13)

Banco
Charriere, Henri
Papillon series (2)

Bancock murder case
Cunningham, Albert Benjamin
Sheriff Jess Roden series (5)

Band rats
Mays, Spike
Soldering series (5)

Bandaged nude
Finnegan, Robert
Dan Banion series (2)

Bandara Trail
Compton, Ralph
Trail drive series (4)

Bandersnatch
Hardwick, Mollie
Doran Fairweather series (4)

Bandicoot
Condon, Richard
Captain Colin Huntington series (2)

Bandido blood
Roberts, J R
Gunsmith series (19)

Bandido hunters
Grover, Marshall
Larry and Stretch series (353)

Bandit and the priest
Lindop, Audrey Erskine
Father Keogh series (1)

Bandit bait
Grover, Marshall
Larry and Stretch series (320)

Bandit fury
Gentry, Buck
Eli Holten series (6)

Bandit gold
Leyland, Eric
Hunter Hawk series (7)
Logan, Jake
John Slocum series (65)
Roberts, J R
Gunsmith series (15)

Bandit Jim Crow
Bancroft, Laura
Birdland series (1)
Twinkle tales series (1)

Bandit of Paloduro
Ballew, Charles
Rim-Fire series (1)

Bandit queen
Ledd, Paul
Shelter Morgan series (8)

Bandit trail
Winstan, Matt
Reuben Brown series (8)

Bandit trap
Grover, Marshall
Larry and Stretch series (167)

Bandit trust
Warwick, Milligan
William Harkness series (2)

Bandits
Istrati, Panait
Adrien Zograffi series (3)
Whalley, Peter
Harry Sommers and Jill Hanscombe series (2)

Bandit's blood
Hawkins, Clint
Saddletramp series (5)

Bandit's embrace
Gentry, Georgina
Panorama of the old West series (4)

Bandits in blue
Hill, Morgan
Dan Colt series (5)

Bandits of the air
Carter, Nicholas
Nicholas Carter series (409)

Bandoleer
Benedict, Dorothy
Pagan series (3)

Bandolero
Benteen, John
Neal Fargo series (14)

Bandoleros
Paine, Lauran
Sheridan Township series (5)

Bandstand
Vendrell, Carme Sole
Victor and Maria series (4)

Bane of Lord Caladon
Mills, Craig
Caladon series (1)

Bane of nightmares
Cole, Adrian
Dream Lords trilogy (3)

Bane of the black sword
Moorcock, Michael
Elric series (5)

Bang bang birds
Diment, Adam
Philip McAlpine series (3)

Bang the drug slowly
Harris, Mark
Henry W Wiggen series (2)

Bang to rights
Norman, Frank
Bang to rights series (2)

Bang-up showman
Ledd, Paul
Shelter Morgan series (29)

Bang, you're dead!
Treece, Henry
Gordon Stewart series (4)

Banggaiyerri
Shaw, Bruce
East Kimberley series (2)

Banished from Bodie
Grover, Marshall
Larry and Stretch series (412)

Banishing of Billy Bunter
Richards, Frank
Billy Bunter series (18)

Bank draft puzzle
Carter, Nicholas
Nicholas Carter series (221)

Bank holdup
Ecke, Wolfgang
Super sleuth series (4)

Bank job
Pike, Robert L
Lieutenant Jim Reardon series (3)

Bank robber
Tippette, Giles
Wilson Young series (1)

Bank robbers
Ellis, Wesley
Lone Star series (99)

Bank shot
Westlake, Donald Edwin
Dortmunder Gang series (2)

Bank vault mystery
Booth, Louis F
Maxwell Fenner series (1)
Banker
Waller, Leslie
Woods Palmer series (1)
Banker Pook confesses
Pook, Peter
Pook series (7)
Banker's bones
Scherf, Margaret
Grace Severance series (1)
Banker's trust
Bobin, John William
Sexton Blake series (6)
Banking on death
Lathen, Emma
John Putnam Thatcher series (1)
Banking on form
Pook, Peter
Pook series (1)
Banking on murder
Williams, David
Mark Treasure series (17)
Bankruptcy
Jones, Nicholas
Wind in the willows series (12)
Banks of Colne
Phillpotts, Eden
Industries of England series (4)
Bannack
Wheeler, Richard Seabrook
Skye's West series (2)
Banner at daybreak
Lanham, Edwin
Wind in the banner series (2)
Banner for Pegasus
Bonett, John
Professor Mandrake series (2)
Banner of the Bull
Sabatini, Rafael
Cesare Borgia series (3)
Banner of the dragon
Rutley, Cecil Bernard
Tales of stirring times series (2)
Banner with a strange device
McHugh, Arona
Sally Brimmer series (1)
Bannerman
Flynn, Jay
Jim Bannerman series (1)
Bannerman case
Lord, Jeremy
Colonel Winston Creevy series (1)
Bannerman effect
Maxim, John R
Bannerman series (2)
Bannerman solution
Maxim, John R
Bannerman series (1)
Bannerman's law
Maxim, John R
Bannerman series (3)
Banners of courage
Carnegie, Sacha
Destiny of eagles series (4)
Banners of gold
Kaufman, Pamela
Richard I series (2)
Banners of love
Carnegie, Sacha
Destiny of eagles series (1)
Banners of power
Carnegie, Sacha
Destiny of eagles series (3)
Banners of revolt
Carnegie, Sacha
Destiny of eagles series (5)
Banners of war
Carnegie, Sacha
Destiny of eagles series (2)
Banquet
Mottram, Ralph Hale
Captain Dormer series (5)
Banquet ceases
Fitt, Mary
Superintendent Mallett series (12)
Banquets of the Black Widowers
Asimov, Isaac
Black Widowers series (4)
Banshee murders
Grant, Maxwell
Shadow series (271)
Bantan and the island goddess
Gardner, Maurice Benjamin
Bantan series (3)
Bantan and the mermaids
Gardner, Maurice Benjamin
Bantan series (9)
Bantan defiant
Gardner, Maurice Benjamin
Bantan series (4)
Bantan fearless
Gardner, Maurice Benjamin
Bantan series (8)
Bantan, god-like islander
Gardner, Maurice Benjamin
Bantan series (1)
Bantan incredible
Gardner, Maurice Benjamin
Bantan series (6)
Bantan of the islands
Gardner, Maurice Benjamin
Bantan series (1)
Bantan primeval
Gardner, Maurice Benjamin
Bantan series (7)
Bantan valiant
Gardner, Maurice Benjamin
Bantan series (5)
Bantan's quest
Gardner, Maurice Benjamin
Bantan series (10)
Baphomet's meteor
Barbet, Pierre
Baphomet series (1)
Baptism
Zlotnik, Donald E
Survivors of Nam series (1)
Baptism for the dead
Irvine, Robert Ralstone
Moroni Traveler series (1)
Baptism of blood
Kostov, K N
Punishment battalion series (1)
Bar B boys
Sabin, Edward Legrand
Bar B boys series (1)
Bar G bunch
Grover, Marshall
Larry and Stretch series (94)
Bar-None Ranch
Asprin, Robert Lynn
Duncan and Mallory series (2)
Bar of shadow
Van der Post, Laurens
Seed and the sower trilogy (1)
Bar-20
Mulford, Clarence Edward
Hopalong Cassidy series (1)
Bar-20 days
Mulford, Clarence Edward
Hopalong Cassidy series (3)
Bar-20 rides again
Mulford, Clarence Edward
Hopalong Cassidy series (12)
Bar-20 three
Mulford, Clarence Edward
Hopalong Cassidy series (8)
Johnny Nelson series (3)
Barabbas
Corelli, Marie
Two worlds series (5)
Barba, the slaver
Forest, Dael
Roman world series (1)
Barbapapa
Tison, Annette
Barbapapa series (1)
Barbapapa's ark
Tison, Annette
Barbapapa series (4)
Barbapapa's new house
Tison, Annette
Barbapapa series (3)
Barbapapa's school
Tison, Annette
Barbapapa series (5)
Barbapapa's theatre
Tison, Annette
Barbapapa first book series (1)
Barbapapa's voyage
Tison, Annette
Barbapapa series (2)
Barbapapa's winter
Tison, Annette
Barbapapa series (6)
Barbara Dering
Rives, Amelie
Barbara Dering series (2)
Barbara Hale, a doctor's daughter
Garis, Lilian C
Barbara Hale series (1)
Barbara Hale and Cozette
Garis, Lilian C
Barbara Hale series (2)
Barbara Nichols, fifth grade teacher
Palmer, Bernard
Career series (2)
Barbara, the valiant
Kimbrough, Katheryn
Phenwick women series (16)
Barbara Winthrop abroad
Broughall, Helen Katherine
Barbara Winthrop series (4)
Barbara Winthrop at boarding school
Broughall, Helen Katherine
Barbara Winthrop series (1)
Barbara Winthrop at camp
Broughall, Helen Katherine
Barbara Winthrop series (2)
Barbara Winthrop, graduate
Broughall, Helen Katherine
Barbara Winthrop series (3)
Barbarian
Sadler, Barry
Casca series (5)
Barbarian of World's End
Carter, Lin
Gondwane epic series (4)
Barbarians
Adams, Robert
Barbarians series (1)
Pinney, Peter
Australian soldier series (1)
Waugh, Charles Gordon
Barbarians series (1)
Barbarians II
Adams, Robert
Barbarians series (2)
Greenberg, Martin Harry
Barbarians series (2)
Barbarians of Mars
Bradbury, Edward P
Warrior of Mars trilogy (3)
Barbarino drops out
Johnston, William
Welcome back, Kotter series (6)
Barbarous coast
Macdonald, Ross
Lew Archer series (7)
Barbary Coast
Edwards, Josh
John Stone series (12)
Barbary Coast Tong
Cutter, Tom
Tracker series (6)
Barbary Coasters
Willoughby, Lee Davis
Making of America series (36)
Barbed wire and bullets
Roberts, J R
Gunsmith series (78)
Barbed wire noose
Adams, Harold
Carl Wilcox series (6)
Barber of Seville
Beaumarchais, Pierre Augustin
Caron de
Figaro series (1)
Barber's clock
Lucas, Edward Verrall
Richard series (3)
Barber's shop crime
Edwards, Walter
Sexton Blake series (862)
Barberton intrigue
Truss, Seldon
Inspector Gidleigh series (11)
Barbie and Ken
Lawrence, Cynthia
Barbie series (3)
Barbie, Midge and Ken
Lawrence, Cynthia
Barbie series (5)
Barbie solves a mystery
Lawrence, Cynthia
Barbie series (4)
Barbie's New York summer
Lawrence, Cynthia
Barbie series (1)
Barboche
Bosco, Henri
Pascalet and Aunt Martine series (3)
Barbouze
Williams, Alan
Rupert Quinn series (2)
Barchester Towers
Trollope, Anthony
Chronicles of Barsetshire series (2)
Bard
Llywelyn, Morgan
Odyssey of the Irish trilogy (3)
Taylor, Keith
Bard series (1)
Bard II
Taylor, Keith
Bard series (2)
Bardelow's heir
Vickers, Roy
Inspector J Rason series (5)
Bardel's murder
McGirr, Edmund
Jim Piron series (8)
Bardik the thief
Farrell, Simon
City of shadows series (2)
Bardolph the beastly beagle
Barratt, Isabel
Rosa series (2)
Bardot M.P., and other misleading cases
Herbert, Alan Patrick
Misleading cases series (5)
Bare acquaintances
Berne, Karin
Ellie Gordon series (1)
Bare bear
Alborough, Jez
Bare bear series (1)
Bare feet in the palace
Keith, Agnes
Borneo series (4)
Bare trap
Kane, Frank
Johnny Liddell series (6)
Bareback
Steiner, Merrilee
Going for it series (5)
Bareback beauty
Hunter, E J
White Squaw series (20)
Baree, son of Kazan
Curwood, James Oliver
Kazan series (2)
Barefoot brigade
Jones, Douglas Clyde
Comanche trilogy (2)
Hasford family series (4)
Barefoot in the sky
Scott, Sheila
Air pilot series (2)
Barefoot journey
Felicity, *Sister*
Barefoot series (1)
Barefoot mailman
Pratt, Theodore
Florida trilogy (1)
Barefoot witch
Clare, Marguerite
Merlin Sorrel series (2)
Barely seen
Kane, Frank
Johnny Liddell series (25)
Barely undercover
Bogen, M Arthur
Burchardt and Decker series (2)
Bargain
Ruddy, Jon
Dracula series (25)
Sparger, Rex
Dark forces series (5)
Bargain for death
Martin, Robert Lee
Jim Bennett series (14)
Bargain for Frances
Hoban, Russell
Frances series (6)
Bargain in blood
Maclean, Arthur
Sexton Blake series (1544)
Stanford, Don
Dallas Webster series (2)
Bargain in crime
Carter, Nicholas
Nicholas Carter series (223)
Bargain with death
Pentecost, Hugh
Pierre Chambrun series (10)
Barkham Street trilogy
Stolz, Mary
Barkham Street trilogy (3)
Barking cat
Myers, David
Sebastian, the incredible drawing dog series (2)
Barking clock
Keeler, Harry Stephen
Tuddleton Trotter series (2)
Barking dog murder case
Vivian, Evelyn Charles
Inspector Head series (7)
Barley
Cosgrove, Stephen Edward
Bugg series (28)
Barley ripe, barley reap
Palmer, Juliette
Barley series (2)
Barley sow, barley grow
Palmer, Juliette
Barley series (1)
Barlow brides
Ladd, Justin
Abilene series (15)
Barlow casebook
Jones, Elwyn
Chief Inspector Barlow series (10)
Barlow comes to judgement
Jones, Elwyn
Chief Inspector Barlow series (9)
Barlow down under
Jones, Elwyn
Chief Inspector Barlow series (12)
Barlow exposed
Jones, Elwyn
Chief Inspector Barlow series (11)
Barlow in charge
Jones, Elwyn
Chief Inspector Barlow series (8)
Barly fields
Nathan, Robert
Barly fields series (5)
Barmy Jeffers and the Quasimodo walk
Brennan, James Herbert
Barmy Jeffers series (1)
Barmy Jeffers and the shrinking potion
Brennan, James Herbert
Barmy Jeffers series (3)
Barnabas Collins
Ross, Marilyn
Barnabas Collins series (6)
Barnabas Collins and Quentin's demon
Ross, Marilyn
Barnabas Collins series (14)
Barnabas Collins and the gypsy wish
Ross, Marilyn
Barnabas Collins series (15)
Barnabas Collins and the mysterious ghost
Ross, Marilyn
Barnabas Collins series (13)
Barnabas Collins versus the warlock
Ross, Marilyn
Barnabas Collins series (10)
Barnabas, Quentin and Doctor Jekyll's son
Ross, Marilyn
Barnabas Collins series (28)
Barnabas, Quentin and the avenging ghost
Ross, Marilyn
Barnabas Collins series (18)
Barnabas, Quentin and the body snatchers
Ross, Marilyn
Barnabas Collins series (27)
Barnabas, Quentin and the crystal coffin
Ross, Marilyn
Barnabas Collins series (20)
Barnabas, Quentin and the frightened bride
Ross, Marilyn
Barnabas Collins series (22)
Barnabas, Quentin and the grave robbers
Ross, Marilyn
Barnabas Collins series (29)
Barnabas, Quentin and the haunted cave
Ross, Marilyn
Barnabas Collins series (21)
Barnabas, Quentin and the hidden tomb
Ross, Marilyn
Barnabas Collins series (32)
Barnabas, Quentin and the mad magician
Ross, Marilyn
Barnabas Collins series (31)
Barnabas, Quentin and the magic potion
Ross, Marilyn
Barnabas Collins series (26)
Barnabas, Quentin and the mummy's curse
Ross, Marilyn
Barnabas Collins series (17)
Barnabas, Quentin and the nightmare assassin
Ross, Marilyn
Barnabas Collins series (19)
Barnabas, Quentin and the Scorpio curse
Ross, Marilyn
Barnabas Collins series (23)
Barnabas, Quentin and the sea ghost
Ross, Marilyn
Barnabas Collins series (30)
Barnabas, Quentin and the serpent
Ross, Marilyn
Barnabas Collins series (24)
Barnabas, Quentin and the vampire beauty
Ross, Marilyn
Barnabas Collins series (33)
Barnabas, Quentin and the witch's curse
Ross, Marilyn
Barnabas Collins series (25)
Barnabas walks
Mayne, William
Animal library series (4)

Basketball's power players
Aaseng, Nathan
Sports heroes series (34)
Basketball's sharpshooters
Aaseng, Nathan
Sports heroes series (23)
Basle Express
Coles, Manning
Tommy Hambledon series (19)
Basque hotel
Laxalt, Robert
Basque trilogy (2)
Basquerie
Kelly, Eleanor Mercein
Urruty family trilogy (1)
Bass Derby murder
Knight, Kathleen Moore
Elisha Macomber series (11)
Bass saxophone
Skvorecky, Josef
Danny Smiricky series (4)
Bastaard rebellion
Stine, George Harry
Warbots series (3)
Bastable children
Nesbit, Edith
Bastable family series (3)
Bastard
Jakes, John
Kent family series (1)
Wainwright, John
Northern Police series (32)
Bastard king
Plaidy, Jean
Norman trilogy (1)
Bastard prince
Kurtz, Katherine
Heirs of Saint Camber trilogy (3)
Bastard verdict
Duke, Winifred
Harold Fieldend series (1)
Bastard's name was Bristow
Scott, Jack S
Detective Inspector Alfred Stanley Rosher series (2)
Bat Masterson
Lee, Wayne
Bat Masterson series (2)
O'Connor, Richard
Bat Masterson series (1)
Bat Staffel
Hogan, Robert Jasper
G-Eight series (1)
Bat-Wing
Rohmer, Sax
Paul Harley series (1)
Batarde
Leduc, Violette
Batarde series (1)
Bath comedy
Castle, Agnes
Beau Nash regime romance series (1)
Bath mysteries
Punshon, Ernest Robertson
Bobby Owen series (7)
Bath of acid
Franklin, Charles
Inspector Jim Burgess series (3)
Bathchair mystery
Murray, Andrew
Sexton Blake series (96)
Bathing Buster
Dugan, Michael
Wombats series (3)
Bathing pool mystery
Blair, Allan
Sexton Blake series (822)
Bathtime for John
Graham, Bob
John and friends series (3)
Bathtub murder case
Punshon, Ernest Robertson
Bobby Owen series (7)
Bathtubs, slides, roller coaster rails
Lampton, Christopher
Simple machines series (1)
Bathwater's hot
Hughes, Shirley
Nursery series (3)
Batman
Gardner, Craig Shaw
Batman series (4)
Schuster, Hal
Batman series (10)
Batman murders
Gardner, Craig Shaw
Batman series (5)
Batman official souvenir magazine
Gerani, Gary
Batman series (10)
Batman returns
Gardner, Craig Shaw
Batman series (10)
Batman, the doomsday prophecy
Wenk, Richard
Super powers which way series (4)
Batman versus the fearsome foursome
Lyon, Winston
Batman series (1)
Batman versus the three villains of doom
Lyon, Winston
Batman series (2)
Batmania
Van Hise, James
Batman series (10)
Baton Rouge
Willoughby, Lee Davis
Americana series (2)
Bats fly at dusk
Fair, A A
Bertha Cool and Donald Lam series (6)
Bats fly up for Inspector Ghote
Keating, Henry Reymond Fitzwalter
Inspector Ganesh Ghote series (9)
Bats in the belfry
Lorac, E C R
Inspector Macdonald series (13)
Matson, Norman
Jennifer series (2)
Bats in the pavilion
Parkinson, Michael
Daft series (3)
Battalion 999
Konsalik, Heinz Gunther
Stalingrad series (2)
Batteries not included
McEvoy, Seth
Not quite human series (1)
Batting to win
Chadwick, Lester
College sports series (3)
Battle
Romains, Jules
Men of goodwill series (16)
Battle Alley
Grover, Marshall
Larry and Stretch series (393)
Battle at the McGoverns'
Berry, Joy
Human race club series (3)
Battle begins
Ahern, Jerry
Defender series (1)
Battle below Giltspur
Macraois, Cormac
Giltspur trilogy (1)
Battle circle
Anthony, Piers
Battle circle trilogy (3)
Battle cry
Cunningham, Chet
Pony soldiers series (9)
McKinney, Jack
Robotech series (2)
Battle days
Fetterless, Arthur
Officer and gentleman series (2)
Battle drive
Siegel, Barbara
Junior transformers find your fate series (2)
Battle ensign
Macdonnell, James Edmond
Captain Peter Bentley series (4)
Battle fire
Macdonnell, James Edmond
Captain Peter Bentley series (13)
Battle for Hue, Tet, 1958
Nolan, Keith William
Vietnam War series (1)
Battle for Inspector West
Creasey, John
Inspector Roger West series (7)
Battle for Lucknow
Stuart, Vivian
Captain Alexander Sheridan series (4)
Battle for McAllister
Chisholm, Matt
Rem McAllister series (26)
Battle for Terra Two
Berry, Stephen Ames
John Harrison series (2)
Battle for the castle
Winthrop, Elizabeth
William series (2)
Battle for the Planet of the Apes
Gerrold, David
Planet of the Apes series (5)
Battle for the right
Carter, Nicholas
Nicholas Carter series (629)
Battle fury
Chisholm, Matt
Storm family series (8)
Battle hymn
Macdonnell, James Edmond
Captain Peter Bentley series (42)
Battle in Botswana
White, Steve
S-Com series (3)
Battle in the ashes
Johnstone, William Wallace
Ashes series (17)
Battle in the ice
Gunn, John
Peter Kent series (2)
Battle line
Macdonnell, James Edmond
Captain Peter Bentley series (17)
Battle lost and won
Manning, Olivia
Guy and Harriet Pringle series (5)
Battle mask
Pendleton, Don
Mack Bolan series (3)
Battle mound
Porteous, Crichton
Jonas Wishet series (3)
Battle of Agincourt
Birt, David
Middle Ages series (14)
Battle of Astar
Brightfield, Richard
Escape from the Kingdom of Frome series (4)
Battle of Blunder Ridge
Grover, Marshall
Larry and Stretch series (165)
Battle of Bunkum Bay
Ryan, John
Captain Pugwash series (17)
Battle of greed
Grant, Maxwell
Shadow series (163)
Battle of Hogan's Hole
Grover, Marshall
Larry and Stretch series (375)
Battle of Horsetooth Mountain
Carrington, G A
Marcus Cavanaugh series (6)
Battle of Maldon
Birt, David
Saxons and Vikings series (16)
Battle of Naseby
Birt, David
Stuarts series (14)
Battle of nerves
Simenon, Georges
Inspector Jules Maigret series (10)
Battle of Saint George Without
McNeill, Janet
Matt McGinley series (1)
Battle of Salamanca
Perez Galdos, Benito
National episodes series, epoch 1 (10)
Battle of the bed
Patterson, John
Johnson and friends series (2)
Battle of the dragons
Brightfield, Richard
Dragons series (1)
Your amazing adventures series (6)
Battle of the queens
Plaidy, Jean
Plantagenet series (5)
Battle of the ring
Gunnarsson, Thorarinn
Starwolves series (2)
Battle of the stallions
Henry, Marguerite
King of the wind series (4)
Battle of the Wazzir
Dennis, Clarence James
Sentimental bloke series (3)
Battle of Thunderhorse Mesa
Carrington, G A
Marcus Cavanaugh series (3)
Battle pay
McCurtin, Peter
Jim Rainey series (9)
Battle road
Harvester, Simon
Asia in turmoil series (19)
Dorian Silk series (7)
Jackson, Steven Gary
Car wars adventure gamebook series (1)
Battle smoke
Hardy, Adam
George Abercrombie Fox series (8)
Battle song
Baker, William Howard
Sexton Blake series (1395)
Battle stations
Greenfield, Irving A
Depth force series (4)
Hudson, Alec
Submarine series (1)
Battle within
Gibbs, Philip
Second World War series (4)
Battleblade warrior
Gascoigne, Marc
Fighting fantasy gamebook series (32)
Battlefield
Platt, Marc
Doctor Who series (152)
Battleground
Griffin, W E B
Corps series (4)
Battlehymn
McKinney, Jack
Robotech series (4)
Battlemaster
Rowley, Christopher
Vang trilogy (3)
Battles at Thrush Green
Read, *Miss*
Thrush Green series (4)
Battles royal down North
Duncan, Norman
Down North series (2)
Battleship boys at sea
Patchin, Frank Gee
Battleship boys series (1)
Battleship boys' first step upward
Patchin, Frank Gee
Battleship boys series (2)
Battleship boys in foreign service
Patchin, Frank Gee
Battleship boys series (3)
Battleship boys in the tropics
Patchin, Frank Gee
Battleship boys series (4)
Battleship boys in the wardroom
Patchin, Frank Gee
Battleship boys series (6)
Battleship boys on sky patrol
Patchin, Frank Gee
Battleship boys series (8)
Battleship boys under fire
Patchin, Frank Gee
Battleship boys series (5)
Battleship boys with the Adriatic chasers
Patchin, Frank Gee
Battleship boys series (7)
Battlesnake Range
Field, Peter
Powder Valley series (68)
Battlestar Galactica
Larson, Glen A
Battlestar Galactica series (1)
Lely, James A
Battlestar Galactica series (14)
Battlestar Galactica storybook
Mercer, Charles Edward
Battlestar Galactica series (14)
Battlestations!
Carey, Diane
Dreadnought series (2)
Star trek series (31)
Battling for Atlanta
Dunn, Byron Archibald
Young Kentuckians series (3)
Battling on the Somme
Kay, Ross
Big war series (6)
Battling prophet
Upfield, Arthur William
Napoleon Bonaparte series (20)
Battling the bighorns
Ashton, Lamar
Aeroplane boys series (6)
Battling the clouds
Cobb, Frank
Aviator series (1)
Battling the wind
Dixon, Franklin W
Ted Scott flying series (16)
Batu-Khan
Yan, Vasiliy Grigorievich
Mongol series (2)
Bavarian connection
Smith, Don
Secret mission series (20)
Bavarian journey
Hogg, Garry
Jonty series (8)
Bawdy house
Martin, Cort
Jared Bolt series (10)
Baxter and the golden pavements
Forsyth, Anne
Baxter series (2)
Baxter by the sea
Forsyth, Anne
Baxter series (3)
Baxter the travelling cat
Forsyth, Anne
Baxter series (1)
Baxter's last laugh
Grover, Marshall
Larry and Stretch series (160)
Baxter's second death
Greig, Ian
Inspector Swinton series (4)
Bay City blast
Murphy, Warren Burton
Destroyer series (38)
Bay City burnout
Harding, Richard
Outrider series (4)
Bay of Seals
Wood, James
James Fraser series (5)
Bay of Shadows
Free, Colin
Pollitt family series (2)
Bay prowler
Barry, Mike
Burton Wulff series (2)
Bayberry Lane
Bassett, Sara Ware
Cape Cod series (7)
Bayonets in No-Man's Land
Scofield, Jonathan
Freedom fighters series (11)
Bayonets in the sun
Moore, William
Mallandine family trilogy (1)
Bayou bluff
Tanner, Clay
Chance Sharpe series (10)
Bayou Brigade
Sanders, Buck
Ben Slayton series (5)
Bayou guns
Cole, Jackson
Jim Hatfield series (84)
Bayou moon
Lowe, Myra
Louisiana series (1)
Bayou Suzette
Lenski, Lois
Regional series (1)
Bazaar of the bizarre
Leiber, Fritz
Fafhrd and Gray Mouser series (7)
Bazza pulls it off
Humphries, Barry
Barry McKenzie series (2)
BBOC
Cosgrove, Stephen Edward
Bugg series (19)
Be a super sleuth with the case of the bank holdup
Ecke, Wolfgang
Super sleuth series (4)
Be a super sleuth with the case of the high-rise robbery
Ecke, Wolfgang
Super sleuth series (5)
Be a super sleuth with the case of the invisible witness
Ecke, Wolfgang
Super sleuth series (3)
Be a super sleuth with the case of the stolen paintings
Ecke, Wolfgang
Super sleuth series (2)
Be a supersleuth with the case of the face at the window
Ecke, Wolfgang
Super sleuth series (1)
Be a winner in baseball
Coombs, Charles Ira
Be a winner series (1)
Be a winner in basketball
Coombs, Charles Ira
Be a winner series (5)
Be a winner in football
Coombs, Charles Ira
Be a winner series (3)
Be a winner in horsemanship
Coombs, Charles Ira
Be a winner series (7)
Be a winner in ice hockey
Coombs, Charles Ira
Be a winner series (2)

Be a winner in skiing
Coombs, Charles Ira
Be a winner series (9)
Be a winner in soccer
Coombs, Charles Ira
Be a winner series (8)
Be a winner in tennis
Coombs, Charles Ira
Be a winner series (4)
Be a winner in track and field
Coombs, Charles Ira
Be a winner series (6)
Be a winner in windsurfing
Coombs, Charles Ira
Be a winner series (10)
Be brave, Baby Rabbit
Manushkin, Fran
Baby Rabbit series (2)
Be brave, little Noddy!
Blyton, Enid
Noddy series (13)
Be careful what you wish for
Barnes, Megan
Teen witch series (2)
Be good, Harry
Chalmers, Mary
Harry series (3)
Be sure to close your eyes
Hood, Hugh
New age series (9)
Beach-front murders
Howard, Tom
Sergeant Tom Howard series (4)
Beach money
Pairo, Preston
Dallas Henry series (1)
Beach party
Cooper, M E
Couples series (35)
Beach patrol
Drysdale, William
Brain and brawn series (3)
Beach queen blowout
Morgan, Patrick
Operation Hang Ten series (8)
Beach ride
Bryant, Bonnie
Saddle Club series (26)
Beachcomber
McFee, William
Spenlove series (2)
Murray, Andrew
Sexton Blake series (136)
Beachy Head murder
Gask, Arthur
Gilbert Larose series (18)
Beacon Hill murders
Scarlett, Roger
Inspector Kane series (1)
Beacon of gold
Moray, Helga
Katie and Paul Van Riebeck series (7)
Beacons of death
Dix, Maurice Buxton
Tommy Malins, Anthony Mornington and George Hawkins series (4)
Beaded banana
Scherf, Margaret
Grace Severance series (4)
Beadle
Smith, Pauline
Karoo series (2)
Beads of silence
Bamburg, Lilian
Septimus March series (1)
Beagle in trouble
Vivelo, Jacqueline Jones
Super Sleuth series (2)
Beagle scented murder
Gruber, Frank
Otis Beagle series (2)
Beam of black light
John, Owen
Haggai Godin series (3)
Bean ABC
Fowler, Richard
Beans series (3)
Bean ball
Resnicow, Herbert
Sport series (2)
Bean 123
Fowler, Richard
Beans series (4)
Chute, Carolyn
Egypt, Maine series (1)
Beany and Scamp
Bassett, Lisa
Beany series (2)
Beany and the beckoning road
Weber, Lenora Mattingly
Beany Malone series (4)
Beany has a secret life
Weber, Lenora Mattingly
Beany Malone series (5)
Beany Malone
Weber, Lenora Mattingly
Beany Malone series (2)
Beany Malone cookbook
Weber, Lenora Mattingly
Beany Malone series (14)
Beany wakes up for Christmas
Bassett, Lisa
Beany series (3)
Bear all year
Ziefert, Harriet
Guessing game series (2)
Bear and Duck on the run
Delton, Judy
Bear and Duck series (2)
Bear and forbear
Optic, Oliver
Lake Shore series (6)
Bear called Paddington
Bond, Michael
Paddington series (1)
Paddington series (6)
Bear child's book of hour
Rockwell, Anne Foote
Bear child series (1)
Bear child's book of special days
Rockwell, Anne Foote
Bear child series (2)
Bear-Claw Range
Bosworth, Frank
Earl Morton series (8)
Bear claws and furry tails
Torgersen, Don Arthur
Animal safari nature series (5)
Bear detectives
Berenstain, Stan
Berenstain bears series (18)
Bear Dinkum
Curtis, Neil
Bear Dinkum series (1)
Bear Dinkum drops his guts
Curtis, Neil
Bear Dinkum series (2)
Bear for all seasons
Roy, Anne
Bear for all seasons series (1)
Bear gets dressed
Ziefert, Harriet
Guessing game series (1)
Bear goes shopping
Ziefert, Harriet
Guessing game series (3)
Bear goes to town
Browne, Anthony
Bear series (2)
Bear hunt
Browne, Anthony
Bear series (1)
Bear raid
Follett, Ken
Piers Roper series (2)
Bear rampant
Wilson, Derek
Robert Dudley series (2)
Bear scare
Burgess, Thornton Waldo
Animal stories series (2)
Bear Scouts
Berenstain, Stan
Berenstain bears series (4)
Bear shadow
Asch, Frank
Bear series (7)
Bear twins
Hogan, Inez
Twins series (1)
Bearcat
Bamman, Henry A
Checkered flag series (3)
Bearer plot
Sela, Owen
Nicholas Maasten series (1)
Bearing an hour glass
Anthony, Piers
Incarnations of immortality series (2)
Bears' ABC book
Wild, Robin
Bears series (1)
Bears' activity book
Berenstain, Stan
Berenstain bears series (79)
Bears' almanac
Berenstain, Stan
Berenstain bears series (13)
Bears back in business
Baker, Margaret Joyce
Three bears series (3)
Bear's bad mood
Prater, John
Bear series (1)
Bear's bargain
Asch, Frank
Bear series (8)
Bear's birthday
Ahlberg, Allan
Red nose readers series (6)
Bear's busy morning
Ziefert, Harriet
Guessing game series (4)
Bears' Christmas
Berenstain, Stan
Berenstain bears series (8)
Cecil, Hugh
Teddy tales series (4)
Bears' counting book
Wild, Robin
Bears series (2)
Bear's den
Prater, John
Bear series (2)
Bears go exploring
Salmon, Michael
Animal antics series (1)
Bears' holiday
Berenstain, Stan
Berenstain bears series (5)
Bears in the caviar
Thayer, Charles Wheeler
Caviar series (1)
Bears in the night
Berenstain, Stan
Berenstain bears series (10)
Bears' nature guide
Berenstain, Stan
Berenstain bears series (17)
Bears on wheels
Berenstain, Stan
Berenstain bears series (7)
Bears' picnic
Berenstain, Stan
Berenstain bears series (3)
Bear's tears
Thomas, Craig
Kenneth Aubrey series (1)
Bears' vacation
Berenstain, Stan
Berenstain bears series (5)
Bear's water picnic
Yeoman, John
Bear series (2)
Bear's whelp
Wilson, Derek
Robert Dudley series (1)
Bears who stayed indoors
Gretz, Susanna
Teddybears series (2)
Bears who went to the seaside
Gretz, Susanna
Teddybears series (3)
Bear's winter house
Yeoman, John
Bear series (1)
Beartown bloodshed
Sharpe, Jon
Trailsman series (131)
Bear-y tale
Browne, Anthony
Bear series (4)
Beast
Laymon, Richard Carl
Strange Occurrence Squad series (1)
Masters, Doug
TNT series (2)
Stallman, Robert
Beast trilogy (3)
Beast and the babysitter
Stevens, Kathleen
Beast series (2)
Beast and the Halloween horror
Giff, Patricia Reilly
Kids of the Polk Street School series (13)
New kids at the Polk Street School series (9)
Beast in man
Zola, Emile
Rougon Macquart series (17)
Beast in Ms Rooney's room
Giff, Patricia Reilly
Kids of the Polk Street School series (1)
Beast in the bathtub
Stevens, Kathleen
Beast series (1)
Beast-king murders
Wallace, Robert
Phantom Detective series (9)
Beast master
Norton, Andre
Arzor series (1)
Beast must die
Blake, Nicholas
Nigel Strangeways series (4)
Beast of the Baskervilles
Kelly, Tim J
Sherlock Holmes drama series (23)
Beastmaker
Smith, James V
Beast series (1)
Beastmark the spy
Clouston, Joseph Storer
F T Carrington series (3)
Beasts and babies
Creaton, David
Beasts series (2)
Beasts and super-beasts
Saki
Clovis series (2)
Beasts below
Mahr, Kurt
Perry Rhodan series (128)
Beasts go west
Creaton, David
Beasts series (3)
Beasts in velvet
Yeovil, Jack
Warhammer series (5)
Beasts of Antares
Prescot, Dray
Dray Prescot series (23)
Beasts of Gor
Norman, John
Tarl Cabot series (12)
Beasts of Hades
Diamond, Graham
Haven series (5)
Stacy series (4)
Beasts of my fields
Creaton, David
Beasts series (1)
Beasts of Never
McHargue, Georgess
Natural and unnatural history series (1)
Beasts of Tarzan
Burroughs, Edgar Rice
Tarzan series (3)
Beasts of the mist
Vardeman, Robert Edward
Swords of Raemllyn series (5)
Beasts of Valhalla
Chesbro, George Clark
Mongo series (4)
Valhalla trilogy (1)
Beaststalker
Smith, James V
Beast series (2)
Beat a distant drum
Emmett, Robert
American Avenger series (1)
Beat of the drum
Sefton, Catherine
Northern Ireland trilogy (3)
Beat on an orange drum
Reid, Desmond
Sexton Blake series (1583)
Beat the devil
Siegel, Scott
Dark forces series (10)
Beat the drums slowly
Waldo, Dale
Johnny Ross series (1)
Beat to quarters
Forester, Cecil Scott
Horatio Hornblower series (6)
Beatrice
Schnitzler, Arthur
Three women trilogy (2)
Beatrice and Bertha
Turpin, Allan
Geoffrey Gillard series (3)
Beatrice goes to Brighton
Chesney, Marion
Travelling matchmaker series (4)
Beatrice of Denewood
Knipe, Emilie Benson
Denewood series (2)
Beatrix
Balzac, Honore de
Scenes of private life series (20)
Beatrix Potter's nursery rhyme book
Potter, Beatrix
Peter Rabbit verse series (2)
Beats me, Claude
Nixon, Joan Lowery
Claude series (2)
Beau Blackstone
Falkirk, Richard
Edmund Blackstone series (3)
Beau Bumbo
Sinclair, Andrew
Bumbo series (2)
Beau Geste
Wren, Percival Christopher
Beau Geste series (1)
Beau Ideal
Wren, Percival Christopher
Beau Geste series (3)
Beau Pook proposes
Pook, Peter
Pook series (15)
Beau Sabreur
Wren, Percival Christopher
Beau Geste series (2)
Beaufort bastard
King, Betty
Beaufort family series (7)
Beaufort secretary
King, Betty
Beaufort family series (6)
Beautiful birthday cake
Scherf, Margaret
Grace Severance series (2)
Beautiful dead
Pentecost, Hugh
Julian Quist series (3)
Beautiful death
Haymon, Sylvia T
Inspector Ben Jurnet series (7)
Beautiful derelict
Wells, Carolyn
Fleming Stone series (40)
Beautiful devil
Dunn, *Detective*
Beautiful devil series (1)
Beautiful empire
Ghose, Zulfikar
Incredible Brazilian trilogy (2)
Beautiful golden frame
Chambers, Peter
Mark Preston series (22)
Beautiful Gunner
Lee, Norma
Beautiful Gunner series (1)
Beautiful Jim of Blankshire Regiment
Winter, John Strange
Blankhampton series (5)
Beautiful Joe
Saunders, Marshall
Beautiful Joe series (1)
Beautiful Joe's paradise
Saunders, Marshall
Beautiful Joe series (2)
Beautiful just
Beckwith, Lillian
Hebrides series (7)
Beautiful murder
Ingersol, Jared
Carl Moore series (2)
Beautiful one
Hamilton, Alexandra
Nefertiti trilogy (1)
Beautiful place to die
Craig, Philip R
Martha's Vineyard series (1)
Beautiful room is empty
White, Edmund
Beautiful room series (2)
Beautiful years
Williamson, Henry
Flax of dream series (1)
Beauty, a snare
Glint Green
Inspector Wield series (3)
Beauty and the beast
Achilleos, Chris
Fantasy illustrations series (1)
Beauty and the Beast
Hambly, Barbara
Beauty and the Beast trilogy (1)
Beauty and the beast
McBain, Ed
Matthew Hope series (3)
Beauty and the beat
Janson, Hank
Hank Janson series (117)
Beauty and the Bounty
Randall, Joshua
Bounty Hunter series (3)
Beauty and the brigands
Grover, Marshall
Larry and Stretch series (289)
Beauty and the buccaneer
Sherwood, Valerie
Lovesong series (2)
Beauty and the bug
Mark, Ted
Man from O.R.G.Y. series (21)
Beauty and the English lord
Sherwood, Valerie
Lovesong series (1)

Beauty bazaar
Finch, Matthew
Dentist series (3)
Beauty for ashes
Fortescue, Winifred
Provence series (6)
Beauty for Inspector West
Creasey, John
Inspector Roger West series (16)
Beauty is a beast
Knight, Kathleen Moore
Elisha Macomber series (16)
Beauty kill
Hawkes, Robert
NARC series (6)
Beauty marks the spot
Roos, Kelley
Jeff and Haila Troy series (8)
Beauty-mask murder
Shore, Viola Brothers
Colin Keats and Gwynn Leith series (1)
Beauty-mask mystery
Shore, Viola Brothers
Colin Keats and Gwynn Leith series (1)
Beauty of British Columbia
Russell, Paul
Beauty of Canada series (4)
Beauty of Ontario
Russell, Paul
Beauty of Canada series (1)
Beauty of Quebec
Russell, Paul
Beauty of Canada series (2)
Beauty of the Maritimes
Russell, Paul
Beauty of Canada series (3)
Beauty parlour mystery
Chester, Gilbert
Sexton Blake series (840)
Beauty queen killer
Creasey, John
Inspector Roger West series (16)
Beauty sleep
Darby, Ruth
Peter and Janet Barron series (4)
Dolson, Hildegarde
Lucy Ramsdale series (4)
Beauty's punishment
Roquelaure, A N
Sleeping Beauty series (2)
Beauty's release
Roquelaure, A N
Sleeping Beauty series (3)
Beaver to fox
Kartun, Derek
Alfred Baum series (1)
Beaver Towers
Hinton, Nigel
Beaver Towers trilogy (1)
Beaver twins
Tompkins, Jane
Animal twins series (3)
Because it is there
Unsworth, Walter
Mountaineering trilogy (3)
Because of fear in the night
Duke, Madelaine
Modern youth trilogy (3)
Because of Lissa
Meyer, Carolyn
Hotline series (1)
Because of the cats
Freeling, Nicolas
Inspector Piet Van der Valk series (2)
Because of the night
Ellroy, James
Sergeant Lloyd Hopkins trilogy (2)
Because of Vivian
Matthewman, Phyllis
Priory series (1)
Bech, a book
Updike, John
Bech series (1)
Bech is back
Updike, John
Bech series (2)
Beckoning hills
Harris, Ruth Elwin
Quantocks quartet (2)
Beckoning lady
Allingham, Margery
Albert Campion series (17)
Beckoning land
Farre, Rowena
Seal morning series (3)
Beckoning road
Snedeker, Caroline Dale
Dencey Coffyn series (2)
Beckoning shadow
Scott, Denis
Mike James series (2)
Beckoning shore
Timms, Edward Vivian
Australian saga series (3)
Beckside lights
Ackworth, John
Clogshop trilogy (2)
Becky
Janson, Hank
Hank Janson series (199)
Lister, Stephen
Sainte Monique series (15)
Becky Bryan's secret
Baxter, Betty
Becky Bryan series (1)
Becky Compton, ex-dux
Jacberns, Raymond
Becky Compton series (1)
Becky, the rabbit
Darby, Joan
Animal adventure series (4)
Becky's birthday
Tudor, Tasha
Becky series (1)
Becky's Christmas
Tudor, Tasha
Becky series (2)
Become the hunted
Swycaffer, Jefferson Putnam
Concordat series (1)
Becoming alien
Ore, Rebecca
Tom Red Clay trilogy (1)
Bed-chamber plot
Housman, Laurence
Palace plays series (4)
Bed-knob and broomstick
Norton, Mary
Bed-knob and broomstick series (2)
Bed manners
Hopton, Ralph
Bed manners series (1)
Bed-time stories
Blyton, Enid
Little books series (2)
Bedford Row
Rayner, Claire
Performers series (5)
Bedford Village
Allen, Hervey
Disinherited series (2)
Bedrock connection
Elias, Horace J
Flintstones series (11)
Bedroll bait
Gentry, Buck
Eli Holten series (23)
Bedroll beauty
Sherman, Jory
Gunn series (23)
Bedroom bolero
Avallone, Michael
Ed Noon series (13)
Bedrooms have windows
Fair, A A
Bertha Cool and Donald Lam series (12)
Beds in the East
Burgess, Anthony
Malayan trilogy (3)
Beds in the east
Burgess, Anthony
Richard Emmis series (3)
Bedside lover boy
Berenstain, Stan
Lover boy series (2)
Bedtime
Duke, Kate
Guinea pig board books series (3)
Oxenbury, Helen
Baby board books series (5)
Thompson, Carol
Busy baby's day series (4)
Bedtime beast
Impey, Rose
Baddies series (4)
Bedtime book
Korman, Justine
Crispy Critter series (3)
Bedtime for Frances
Hoban, Russell
Frances series (1)
Bedtime words
Tyler, Jenny
First words series (3)
Bee Bopp
Cosgrove, Stephen Edward
Bugg series (22)
Bee, my Valentine!
Cohen, Miriam
Best friends series (5)
Bee sting deal
Beare, George
Vincent Stallard and Cynthia Godwin series (3)
Beebo and the Fizzimen
Gree, Alain
Beebo series (2)
Beebo and the funny machine
Gree, Alain
Beebo series (3)
Beeby's big night
Grover, Marshall
Larry and Stretch series (384)
Beechcroft at Rockstone
Yonge, Charlotte Mary
Beechcroft series (6)
Beecher's quest
Grover, Marshall
Larry and Stretch series (191)
Beechnut
Abbott, Jacob
Franconia series (5)
Beef Wellington blues
Davidson, Max
Beef Wellington series (1)
Beekeeper
Andrews, Val
Sherlock Holmes sequels series (58)
Beekeepers
Redgrove, Peter
Beekeepers series (1)
Beekeeper's apprentice
King, Laurie R
Sherlock Holmes sequels series (98)
Beelzebub business
Brandner, Gary
Big Brain series (2)
Beepers from outer space
DeWeese, Gene
Calvin Willeford series (1)
Beer and skittles
Morison, Betty Jane
Elizabeth Lamb Worthington series (3)
Beer for Christmas
Wood, James
Tipple in the deep series (2)
Bees
Berg, Leila
Small world series (4)
Bees in my bonnet
Macvicar, Angus
Confessions series (5)
Bees in our bonnet
Stewart, Flora
Flora and Dickie series (3)
Beet queen
Erdrich, Louise
Argus series (2)
Beethoven Medal
Peyton, K M
Patrick Pennington series (2)
Beetle
Marsh, Richard
Augustus Champnell series (1)
Beetle in the anthill
Strugatsky, Arkady
Maxim trilogy (2)
Beezer's end
Hassett, Margaret
Miss Dinwiddie series (2)
Beezus and Ramona
Cleary, Beverly
Beezus series (2)
Henry Huggins series (4)
Ramona Quimby series (1)
Beezus and Ramona diary
Cleary, Beverly
Beezus series (2)
Ramona Quimby series (1)
Before freedom
Hurmence, Belinda
Oral histories of slaves series (2)
Before freedom, when I just can't remember
Hurmence, Belinda
Oral histories of slaves series (2)
Before he kills again
Grover, Marshall
Larry and Stretch series (173)
Before I die
Stout, Rex
Nero Wolfe and Archie Goodwin series (14)
Before I go
Stott, Mary
Forgetting series (2)
Before it's too late
Goudge, Eileen
Seniors series (5)
Before lunch
Thirkell, Angela
Barsetshire series (8)
Before midnight
Stout, Rex
Nero Wolfe and Archie Goodwin series (25)
Before my time
Tucci, Niccolo
Those of the lost continent series (1)
Before noon
Sender, Ramon Jose
Before noon trilogy (3)
Before Shadowgate
Miles, Ellen
Worlds of power series (8)
Before the cock crowed
Hayes, William Edward
Arthur Halstead series (2)
Before the crossing
Jameson, Storm
Renn series (1)
Before the darkness falls
Price, Eugenia
Savannah quartet (3)
Before the dinosaurs
Greene, Carla
Science and natural history series (3)
Before the judge
Jenkins, Jerry Bruce
Bradford family series (4)
Before the mast
Baynham, Henry
Naval life series (2)
Before the storm
Jackson, Robert
Bomber Command series (1)
Maisky, Ivan Mikhailovich
Storm series (1)
Before the wind
Charles, Ernest F
Dick Torreyton series (3)
Beggar queen
Alexander, Lloyd
Westmark trilogy (3)
Beggarman, thief
Shaw, Irwin
Jordache family series (2)
Beggarman's country
Webster, Jan
Kate Kilgour trilogy (3)
Beggar's choice
Branson, Henry Clay
John Bent series (7)
Beggar's curse
Cheetham, Ann
Black harvest series (2)
Beggars' horses
Wren, Percival Christopher
Major Hazelrigg series (1)
Beggars of the sea
Bevan, Tom
Dutch in Spain series (1)
Beggar's Penny
Coblentz, Catherine
Beggar's Penny series (1)
Beggar's virtue
Bennett, Barbara
Calladine family series (2)
Begin, murderer!
Cory, Desmond
Lindy Grey series (1)
Begin with a gun
Cronin, Michael
Richard Maidment series (5)
Beginners
Levy, Elizabeth
Gymnasts series (1)
Beginner's luck
Bodine, J D
Pecos Kid series (1)
Somers, Paul
Hugh Curtis and Mollie Bourne series (1)
Beginning
Edwards, Gene
Chronicles of the door series (2)
Robitaille, Julie
Quantum leap series (1)
Beginning again
Woolf, Leonard
Sowing and growing series (3)
Beginning with a bash
Tilton, Alice
Leonidas Witherall series (1)
Beginnings
Dickson, Gordon Rupert
Beginnings and ends series (1)
Patterson, John
Johnson and friends series (1)
Beginnings of Mister P J Davenant
Hamilton, Frederic
P J Davenant series (4)
Begonia Walk
Holt, Gavin
Inspector Joel Saber series (5)
Beguinage
Edson, John Thomas
Floating Outfit series (38)
Beguinage is dead!
Edson, John Thomas
Floating Outfit series (39)
Behemoth
Macdonnell, James Edmond
Dutchy Holland series (10)
Behind a black mask
Grover, Marshall
Nevada Jim series (47)
McCoy, Marshall
Nevada Jim series (47)
Behind a mask
Carter, Nicholas
Nicholas Carter series (92)
Behind a throne
Carter, Nicholas
Nicholas Carter series (194)
Behind closed doors
Carter, Nicholas
Nicholas Carter series (334)
Green, Anna Katharine
Ebenezer Gryce series (4)
Behind locked doors
Poate, Ernest M
Doctor Bentiron series (1)
Behind red curtains
Scott, Mansfield
Inspector Malcome Steele series (1)
Behind that curtain
Biggers, Earl Derr
Charlie Chan series (3)
Behind that mask
Keeler, Harry Stephen
Behind that mask series (2)
Behind the arras
Graham, Anthony
Eric Marsden series (2)
Behind the barricade
Martin, Toy
Taronga Road Riders series (2)
Behind the black mask
Carter, Nicholas
Nicholas Carter series (336)
Behind the blue and gray
Ray, Delia
American Civil War series (2)
Behind the crimson blind
Dickson, Carter
Sir Henry Merrivale series (22)
Behind the curtain
Gibbs, Philip
Second World War series (7)
Behind the door
Bassani, Giorgio
Ferrara series (4)
Behind the enemy
Marlowe, Greg
Greg Marlowe series (1)
Behind the German lines
Le Queux, William
Otto von Heynitz series (2)
Behind the green door
Wirt, Mildred Augustine
Penny Parker series (4)
Behind the headlines
Chapman, Robert
Rex Banner series (5)
Behind the head-lines
Sutherland, William
Inspector Haskell series (1)
Behind the light
Meyrick, Bette
Morgan family series (2)
Behind the lines
Barbour, Ralph Henry
Erskine trilogy (1)
Behind the screen
Hill, Charles
Broadcasting memoirs series (2)
Behind the steam
Morgan, Bill
Morgan family series (1)
Behind the sunset
Jennings, D K
Doctor Ralph Conway series (17)
Behind the walls
Graydon, William Murray
Sexton Blake series (433)
Behind the Walls of Terra
Farmer, Philip Jose
World of Tiers series (4)

Benjie
Lexau, Joan M
Benjie series (1)
Benjie and his friends
Walter, Francis V
Benjie series (2)
Benjie and the flood
Walter, Francis V
Benjie series (3)
Benjie on his own
Lexau, Joan M
Benjie series (2)
Benjie's portion
Ballard, Martin
Benjie and Simon series (1)
Benjy and the barking bird
Graham, Margaret Bloy
Benjy series (1)
Benjy's dog house
Graham, Margaret Bloy
Benjy series (2)
Bennett's welcome
Fletcher, Inglis
Carolina series (2)
Bennett's world
Lewis, Elliott
Fred Bennett series (6)
Bennie and the new baby
Van Stockum, Hilda
Jeremy Bear series (3)
Benno and some of the Push
Dyson, Edward
Fact'ry 'ands series (2)
Benny
Wilmer, Diane
Benny series (1)
Benny and the builders
Wilmer, Diane
Benny series (4)
Benny and the crazy contest
Zach, Cheryl
Benny series (1)
Benny and the dolphin
Hurt, Freda Mary
Benny of Crab Island series (2)
Benny and the fair
Wilmer, Diane
Benny series (3)
Benny and the football match
Wilmer, Diane
Benny series (2)
Benny and the jumble sale
Wilmer, Diane
Benny series (5)
Benny and the no-good teacher
Zach, Cheryl
Benny series (2)
Benny and the space boy
Hurt, Freda Mary
Benny of Crab Island series (3)
Benny uncovers a mystery
Warner, Gertrude Chandler
Boxcar children series (19)
Benoni
Hamsun, Knut
Benoni series (1)
Ben's baby
Foreman, Michael
Ben series (2)
Ben's birthday party
Border, Rosemary
Out and about series (4)
Ben's box
Foreman, Michael
Ben series (1)
Ben's expedition
Gifford, Griselda
Ben Taylor series (2)
Ben's gingerbread man
Daly, Niki
Storytime series (3)
Ben's nugget
Alger, Horatio
Pacific series (4)
Benson murder case
Van Dine, S S
Philo Vance series (1)
Bent grasses
Palmer, Frank
Jim Jackson series (3)
Benton of the Royal Mounted
Kendall, Ralph Selwood
L Division series (1)
Beppo back with Rupert
Tourtel, Mary
Rupert Bear series (30)
Beppo Tate and Roy Penner
Palmer, Cyril Everard
Beppo Tate series (2)
Bequest of evil
Robeson, Kenneth
Doc Savage series (173)
Bequest to a Texan
Grover, Marshall
Larry and Stretch series (419)
Berbora
Sirota, Mike
Berbora series (1)
Bereavement
Housman, Laurence
Palace plays series (3)
Berenger's toughest case
Duff, Douglas Valder
Bill Berenger series (4)
Berenstain bears' almanac
Berenstain, Stan
Berenstain bears series (13)
Berenstain bears and mama's new job
Berenstain, Stan
Berenstain bears series (45)
Berenstain bears and the bad dream
Berenstain, Stan
Berenstain bears series (68)
Berenstain bears and the bad habit
Berenstain, Stan
Berenstain bears series (62)
Berenstain bears and the big election
Berenstain, Stan
Berenstain bears series (39)
Berenstain bears and the big road race
Berenstain, Stan
Berenstain bears series (61)
Berenstain bears and the dinosaurs
Berenstain, Stan
Berenstain bears series (43)
Berenstain bears and the double dare
Berenstain, Stan
Berenstain bears series (67)
Berenstain bears and the ghost of the forest
Berenstain, Stan
Berenstain bears series (65)
Berenstain bears and the in-crowd
Berenstain, Stan
Berenstain bears series (72)
Berenstain bears and the messy room
Berenstain, Stan
Berenstain bears series (32)
Berenstain bears and the missing dinosaur bone
Berenstain, Stan
Berenstain bears series (23)
Berenstain bears and the missing honey
Berenstain, Stan
Berenstain bears series (60)
Berenstain bears and the neighborly skunk
Berenstain, Stan
Berenstain bears series (42)
Berenstain bears and the prize pumpkin
Berenstain, Stan
Berenstain bears series (74)
Berenstain bears and the sitter
Berenstain, Stan
Berenstain bears series (25)
Berenstain bears and the slumber party
Berenstain, Stan
Berenstain bears series (73)
Berenstain bears and the spooky old tree
Berenstain, Stan
Berenstain bears series (20)
Berenstain bears and the trouble at school
Berenstain, Stan
Berenstain bears series (63)
Berenstain bears and the trouble with friends
Berenstain, Stan
Berenstain bears series (59)
Berenstain bears and the truth
Berenstain, Stan
Berenstain bears series (33)
Berenstain bears and the week at grandma's
Berenstain, Stan
Berenstain bears series (53)
Berenstain bears and the wild, wild honey
Berenstain, Stan
Berenstain bears series (34)
Berenstain bears and too much birthday
Berenstain, Stan
Berenstain bears series (54)
Berenstain bears and too much junk food
Berenstain, Stan
Berenstain bears series (46)
Berenstain bears and too much TV
Berenstain, Stan
Berenstain bears series (40)
Berenstain bears and too much vacation
Berenstain, Stan
Berenstain bears series (70)
Berenstain bears are a family
Berenstain, Stan
Berenstain bears series (76)
Berenstain bears at the super-duper market
Berenstain, Stan
Berenstain bears series (77)
Berenstain bears' bath book
Berenstain, Stan
Berenstain bears series (79)
Berenstain bears blaze a trail
Berenstain, Stan
Berenstain bears series (57)
Berenstain bears' Christmas tree
Berenstain, Stan
Berenstain bears series (24)
Berenstain bears, coughing catfish
Berenstain, Stan
Berenstain bears series (56)
Berenstain bears' counting book
Berenstain, Stan
Berenstain bears series (79)
Berenstain bears forget their manners
Berenstain, Stan
Berenstain bears series (50)
Berenstain bears get in a fight
Berenstain, Stan
Berenstain bears series (29)
Berenstain bears get stage fright
Berenstain, Stan
Berenstain bears series (51)
Berenstain bears get the gimmies
Berenstain, Stan
Berenstain bears series (66)
Berenstain bears go fly a kite
Berenstain, Stan
Berenstain bears series (36)
Berenstain bears go out for the team
Berenstain, Stan
Berenstain bears series (55)
Berenstain bears go to camp
Berenstain, Stan
Berenstain bears series (30)
Berenstain bears go to school
Berenstain, Stan
Berenstain bears series (22)
Berenstain bears go to the doctor
Berenstain, Stan
Berenstain bears series (26)
Berenstain bears in the dark
Berenstain, Stan
Berenstain bears series (31)
Berenstain bears learn about strangers
Berenstain, Stan
Berenstain bears series (48)
Berenstain bears make and do book
Berenstain, Stan
Berenstain bears series (79)
Berenstain bears meet Santa Bear
Berenstain, Stan
Berenstain bears series (44)
Berenstain bears' moving day
Berenstain, Stan
Berenstain bears series (27)
Berenstain bears' nature guide
Berenstain, Stan
Berenstain bears series (17)
Berenstain bears' new baby
Berenstain, Stan
Berenstain bears series (16)
Berenstain bears, no girls allowed
Berenstain, Stan
Berenstain bears series (52)
Berenstain bears' nursery tales
Berenstain, Stan
Berenstain bears series (14)
Berenstain bears on the job
Berenstain, Stan
Berenstain bears series (58)
Berenstain bears on the moon
Berenstain, Stan
Berenstain bears series (47)
Berenstain bears, ready, set, go!
Berenstain, Stan
Berenstain bears series (69)
Berenstain bears say goodnight
Berenstain, Stan
Berenstain bears series (78)
Berenstain bears' science fair
Berenstain, Stan
Berenstain bears series (19)
Berenstain bears shoot the rapids
Berenstain, Stan
Berenstain bears series (41)
Berenstain bears' soccer star
Berenstain, Stan
Berenstain bears series (35)
Berenstain bears' take-along library
Berenstain, Stan
Berenstain bears series (40)
Berenstain bears to the rescue
Berenstain, Stan
Berenstain bears series (37)
Berenstain bears' toy time
Berenstain, Stan
Berenstain bears series (49)
Berenstain bears' trick or treat
Berenstain, Stan
Berenstain bears series (71)
Berenstain bears' trouble with money
Berenstain, Stan
Berenstain bears series (38)
Berenstain bears' trouble with pets
Berenstain, Stan
Berenstain bears series (75)
Berenstain bears visit the dentist
Berenstain, Stan
Berenstain bears series (28)
Berenstain kids, I love colors
Berenstain, Stan
Berenstain bears series (79)
Berentain bears' four seasons
Berenstain, Stan
Berenstain bears series (79)
Beresfords in Tarndale
Lethbridge, Peter
Jeremy series (5)
Berets
Griffin, W E B
Brotherhood of war series (5)
Berg case
Bentley, John
Sir Richard Herrivell series (1)
Berg family fortune
Roche, Eliane
Fortune and power series (1)
Bergerac
Hardwick, Michael
Bergerac series (1)
Bergerac and the fatal weakness
Saville, Andrew
Bergerac series (6)
Bergerac and the Jersey rose
Saville, Andrew
Bergerac series (4)
Bergerac and the moving fever
Saville, Andrew
Bergerac series (5)
Bergerac and the traitor's child
Saville, Andrew
Bergerac series (7)
Bergerac is back!
Saville, Andrew
Bergerac series (2)
Beria papers
Williams, Alan
Beria papers series (1)
Berkshire mystery
Cole, George Douglas Howard
Everard Blatchington series (2)
Superintendent Henry Wilson series (7)
Berlin
Carter, Nick
Nick Carter series (45)
Plievier, Theodor
World War II trilogy (3)
Berlin briefing
Janson, Hank
Hank Janson series (200)
Berlin fugue
Winters, Jon
Anton Drakov series (3)
Berlin game
Deighton, Len
Bernard Samson series (1)
Game, set and match trilogy (1)
Berlin memorandum
Hall, Adam
Quiller series (1)
Berlin noir
Kerr, Philip
Berlin noir trilogy (3)
Berlin of Sally Bowles
Isherwood, Christopher
Berlin series (3)
Berlin stories
Isherwood, Christopher
Berlin series (3)
Berlin target
Carter, Nick
Nick Carter series (210)
Berlin Wall affair
Conway, Troy
Coxeman series (1)
Bermuda burial
King, Charles Daly
Michael Lord series (5)
Bermuda Triangle
Berlitz, Charles
Bermuda Triangle series (1)
Bermuda Triangle action
Rosenberger, Joseph
Death Merchant series (37)
Bernard and the catnip caper
Freschet, Berniece
Bernard series (3)
Bernard Clare
Farrell, James Thomas
Bernard Clare series (1)
Bernard Clayre
Farrell, James Thomas
Bernard Clare series (1)
Bernard into battle
Sharp, Margery
Miss Bianca series (9)
Bernard of Scotland Yard
Freschet, Berniece
Bernard series (2)
Bernard sees the world
Freschet, Berniece
Bernard series (1)
Bernard the brave
Sharp, Margery
Miss Bianca series (8)
Bernese adventure
Shaw, Jane
Caroline and Sara series (2)
Bernese holiday
Shaw, Jane
Caroline and Sara series (2)
Bernhardt's Edge
Wilcox, Collin
Alan Bernhardt series (1)
Bernie and the Bessledorf ghost
Naylor, Phyllis Reynolds
Bessledorf series (3)
Berries in the scoop
Lenski, Lois
Roundabout America series (5)
Berron's tooth
Solomon, Joan
Children's life series (4)
Berry and Company
Yates, Dornford
Berry series (3)
Jonah Mansel series (1)
Berry green
Clements, Eileen Helen
Alister Woodhead series (3)
Berry scene
Yates, Dornford
Berry series (9)
Berserker
Saberhagen, Fred
Berserker series (1)
Schmidt, Dan
Eagle Force series (6)
Berserker attack
Saberhagen, Fred
Berserker series (9)
Berserker base
Saberhagen, Fred
Berserker series (6)
Berserker lies
Saberhagen, Fred
Berserker series (10)
Berserker man
Saberhagen, Fred
Berserker series (4)
Berserker throne
Saberhagen, Fred
Berserker series (7)
Berserker wars
Saberhagen, Fred
Berserker series (1)
Berserker's planet
Saberhagen, Fred
Berserker series (3)
Bertha and a mouse in the works
Charles, Eric
Bertha series (4)
Bertha and the best machine competition
Charles, Eric
Bertha series (3)
Bertha and the flying bear
Charles, Eric
Bertha series (5)
Bertha and the great painting job
Charles, Eric
Bertha series (1)
Bertha and the lost tom
Charles, Eric
Bertha series (6)
Bertha and the windmills
Charles, Eric
Bertha series (2)
Bertha Garlan
Schnitzler, Arthur
Three women trilogy (1)
Bertie
Whittle, Tyler
Edward VII series (1)
Bertie and his sisters
Hattie, Aunt
Woodlawn series (7)

Bertie and the carpenters
Hattie, Aunt
Woodlawn series (2)
Bertie and the crime of passion
Lovesey, Peter
Bertie series (3)
Bertie and the gardeners
Hattie, Aunt
Woodlawn series (6)
Bertie and the masons
Hattie, Aunt
Woodlawn series (3)
Bertie and the painters
Hattie, Aunt
Woodlawn series (5)
Bertie and the plumbers
Hattie, Aunt
Woodlawn series (4)
Bertie and the seven bodies
Lovesey, Peter
Bertie series (2)
Bertie and the Tinman
Lovesey, Peter
Sergeant Cribb and Constable Thackeray series (9)
Bertie and tinman
Lovesey, Peter
Bertie series (1)
Bertie at the dentist's
Bouma, Paddy
Bertie series (2)
Bertie comes through
Felsen, Henry Gregor
Bertie series (1)
Bertie takes care
Felsen, Henry Gregor
Bertie series (2)
Bertie visits granny
Bouma, Paddy
Bertie series (1)
Bertie Wooster sees it through
Wodehouse, Pelham Grenville
Jeeves and Bertie Wooster series (11)
Bertie's home
Hattie, Aunt
Woodlawn series (1)
Bertioni's Hotel
Nicol, Jean
Hotel series (3)
Bertram family
Charles, Elizabeth
Bertram family series (2)
Beryl's lot
Powell, Margaret
Beryl Humphries series (1)
Beryl's lot, book two
Powell, Margaret
Beryl Humphries series (2)
Beside a Norman tower
De la Roche, Mazo
Gillian and Diggory series (1)
Beside the bonnie briar bush
Maclaren, Ian
Drumtochty series (1)
Beside the sea
Ainsworth, Ruth
Look about you series (3)
Beside the sea with Jeremy James
Wilson, David Henry
Jeremy James series (3)
Besides the wench is dead
Erskine, Margaret
Inspector Septimus Finch series (19)
Bess
Leeson, Robert
Matthew Morten trilogy (2)
Stafford, Ann
Victorian and Edwardian London life series (2)
Bessie among the mountains
Mathews, Joanna Hooe
Bessie Bradford series (5)
Bessie and her friends
Mathews, Joanna Hooe
Bessie Bradford series (4)
Bessie at school
Mathews, Joanna Hooe
Bessie Bradford series (6)
Bessie at the seaside
Mathews, Joanna Hooe
Bessie Bradford series (1)
Bessie Bradford's prize
Mathews, Joanna Hooe
Bessie Bradford series (9)
Bradford family series (5)
Bessie Bradford's secret
Mathews, Joanna Hooe
Bessie Bradford series (8)
Bessie Bunter and the gold robbers
Richards, Hilda
Bessie Bunter series (3)
Bessie Bunter joins the circus
Richards, Hilda
Bessie Bunter series (2)
Bessie Bunter of Cliff House
Richards, Hilda
Bessie Bunter series (1)
Bessie in the city
Mathews, Joanna Hooe
Bessie Bradford series (2)
Bessie on her travels
Mathews, Joanna Hooe
Bessie Bradford series (7)
Best adventure
Dale, Norman
Peter and Ginger series (3)
Best and the worst
Grover, Marshall
Larry and Stretch series (329)
Best bad thing
Uchida, Yoshiko
Rinko trilogy (2)
Best bike ever
Graeber, Charlotte Towner
Mister T and me series (1)
Best Christmas pageant ever
Robinson, Barbara
Herdman family series (1)
Best defense
Wilhelm, Kate
Barbara Holloway series (2)
Best detective stories
Crispin, Edmund
Inspector George Rason series (3)
Best Doctor Poggioli detective stories
Stribling, Thomas Sigismund
Professor Henry Poggioli series (2)
Best enemies
Leverich, Kathleen
Best enemies series (1)
Best enemies again
Leverich, Kathleen
Best enemies series (2)
Best foot forward
Weir, Molly
Feet series (2)
Best friend
Stine, Robert Lawrence
Fear Street series (17)
Best friend game
Pascal, Francine
Unicorn Club series (3)
Best friends
Albright, Molly
Two of a kind series (4)
Bard, Mary
Best friends series (1)
Cohen, Miriam
Best friends series (1)
Best friends
Pascal, Francine
Sweet Valley twins series (1)
Best friends at school
Bard, Mary
Best friends series (3)
Best Friends Club
Marzollo, Jean
Thirty nine kids on the block series (4)
Winthrop, Elizabeth
Lizzie and Harold series (2)
Best friends don't come in threes
Schwartz, Joel L
Best friends series (2)
Best friends for Frances
Hoban, Russell
Frances series (5)
Best friends forever
Chase, Emily
Canby Hall series (6)
Quin-Harkin, Janet
Toni Redmond and Jill Gardner series (8)
Best friends get better
Asher, Sandra Fenichel
Ballet One series (1)
Best friends in summer
Bard, Mary
Best friends series (2)
Best house in Stratford
Fisher, Edward
Silver falcon trilogy (3)
Best house in the school
Bruce, Dorita Fairlie
Springdale series (2)
Best intentions
Bergman, Ingmar
Bergman family series (1)
Best is yet to be
Plagemann, Bentz
Wallace family series (3)
Best laid plans
Conway, Troy
Coxeman series (10)
Hocking, Anne
Inspector William Austen series (17)
Roberts, Nora
Flowers series (44)
Best laid schemes
Cross, Mark
Daphne Wrayne and her Four Adjusters series (35)
Best man
James, William M
Apache series (13)
Best man to die
Rendell, Ruth
Chief Inspector Reginald Wexford series (4)
Best Max Carrados detective stories
Bramah, Ernest
Max Carrados series (5)
Best mom in the world
Delton, Judy
My mom series (2)
Best of all possible worlds
Ledwith, Frank
Ship insurance series (1)
Best of Antrobus
Durrell, Lawrence
Antrobus series (3)
Best of Berry
Yates, Dornford
Berry series (11)
Best of Botts
Upson, William Hazlett
Alexander Botts series (7)
Best of Brer Anansi
Makhanlall, David Paschal
Anansi series (1)
Best of Crunch and Des
Wylie, Philip
Crunch and Des series (4)
Best of Dougal
Thompson, Eric
Dougal series (5)
Best of enemies
Keene, Carolyn
Nancy Drew and Hardy boys supermystery series (9)
Best of Father Brown
Chesterton, Gilbert Keith
Father Brown series (5)
Best of friends
Humphreys, Emyr
Amy Parry series (2)
Best of Glencannon
Gilpatric, Guy
Mister Colin Andrew Macthrockle Glencannon series (9)
Best of Hagar the horrible
Browne, Dik
Hagar the horrible series (52)
Best of Jake Winkman
Von Elsner, Don
Jake Winkman series (4)
Best of Jennings
Buckeridge, Anthony
Jennings series (16)
Best of Li'l Abner
Capp, Al
Li'l Abner series (2)
Best of Mister Fortune
Bailey, Henry Christopher
Mister Reggie Fortune series (23)
Best of Myles
O'Brien, Flann
Cruiskeen Lawn series (1)
Best of Tish
Rinehart, Mary Roberts
Tish series (5)
Best of vets
Duncan, Alex
Vet series (3)
Best pest
Thomson, Pat
Share-a-story series (9)
Best present ever
Marzollo, Jean
Thirty nine kids on the block series (2)
Best rootin' tootin' shootin' gunslinger in the shole damned galaxy
Resnick, Mike
Tales of the Galactic Midway series (4)
Best Specs
McNeill, Janet
Specs McCann series (3)
Best story ever
Clouston, Joseph Storer
Mister Francis Mandell-Essington series (7)
Best Thanksgiving ever
Pascal, Francine
Sweet Valley kids series (34)
Best thing of all
Thomson, Pat
Share-a-story series (10)
Best Thinking Machine detective stories
Futrelle, Jacques
Professor Augustus S F X Van Dusen series (3)
Best wishes
Rylant, Cynthia
Best wishes series (2)
Best-worse Christmas present ever
Wilson, Budge
Blue Harbour series (1)
Best ye breed
Reynolds, Mack
Homer Crawford trilogy (3)
Bestiary Mountain
Forrester, John
Bestiary trilogy (1)
Bet you can!
Cobb, Vicki
Bet you series (2)
Bet you can't!
Cobb, Vicki
Bet you series (1)
Beth and Ernestine Graper
Corbett, Elizabeth
Graper girls series (4)
Beth Anne goes to school
Ginther, Mary Pemberton
Beth Anne series (4)
Beth Anne herself
Ginther, Mary Pemberton
Beth Anne series (1)
Beth Anne, really-for-truly
Ginther, Mary Pemberton
Beth Anne series (2)
Beth Anne's new cousin
Ginther, Mary Pemberton
Beth Anne series (3)
Beth of Old Chilton
Taggart, Marion Ames
Beth series (3)
Beth Varden at Sunset
Lea, Alec
Varden family series (2)
Bethlehem Road
Perry, Anne
Charlotte Ellison Pitt and Inspector Thomas Pitt series (10)
Beth's garden party
Burnett, Alice Hale
Merryvale girls series (1)
Beth's old home
Taggart, Marion Ames
Beth series (2)
Beth's wonder-winter
Taggart, Marion Ames
Beth series (1)
Betrayal
Cherryh, Carolyn Janice
Alliance-Union series (11)
Cyteen series (1)
Hartley, Leslie Poles
Richard Mardick series (2)
Payne, Oliver
Northwest Territory series (7)
Slovo, Gillian
Kate Baeier series (4)
Stine, Robert Lawrence
Fear Street saga series (1)
Walter, Alexia E
Sir Edgar Ewart series (2)
Betrayal in Eden
Chase, Philip
Aaron Eisenberg and William Kendall series (3)
Betrayed
Harte, Bryce
Slate Creed series (7)
Hoh, Diane
Cheerleaders series (10)
Betrayed by death
Alding, Peter
C.I.D. Room series (13)
Betrayed spring
Lindsay, Jack
British way series (1)
Betrayer
Needham, Violet
Stormy Petrel series (4)
Betrayers
Avenell, Donne
Axa series (9)
Hamilton, Donald
Matt Helm series (10)
Betrothal
Maeterlinck, Maurice
Blue bird series (2)
Betrothed
Scott, Walter
Tales of the Crusaders series (1)
Betsey Bobbet
Holley, Marietta
Betsey Bobbet series (2)
Betsy and Billy
Haywood, Carolyn
Betsy series (2)
Betsy and Joe
Lovelace, Maud Hart
Betsy Ray series (8)
Betsy and Mr Kilpatrick
Haywood, Carolyn
Betsy series (10)
Betsy and Peter are different
Wolde, Gunilla
Emma series (5)
Betsy and Tacy go down town
Lovelace, Maud Hart
Betsy Ray series (4)
Betsy and Tacy go over the big hill
Lovelace, Maud Hart
Betsy Ray series (3)
Betsy and the boys
Haywood, Carolyn
Betsy series (4)
Betsy and the chicken pox
Wolde, Gunilla
Emma series (3)
Betsy and the circus
Haywood, Carolyn
Betsy series (6)
Betsy and the doctor
Wolde, Gunilla
Emma series (10)
Betsy and the great world
Lovelace, Maud Hart
Betsy Ray series (9)
Betsy and the vacuum cleaner
Wolde, Gunilla
Emma series (6)
Betsy goes to the dentist
Wolde, Gunilla
Emma series (4)
Betsy Hale
Ginther, Mary Pemberton
Betsy Hale series (1)
Betsy Hale succeeds
Ginther, Mary Pemberton
Betsy Hale series (3)
Betsy Hale tries
Ginther, Mary Pemberton
Betsy Hale series (2)
Betsy in spite of herself
Lovelace, Maud Hart
Betsy Ray series (6)
Betsy-Tacy
Lovelace, Maud Hart
Betsy Ray series (1)
Betsy-Tacy and Tib
Lovelace, Maud Hart
Betsy Ray series (2)
Betsy was a junior
Lovelace, Maud Hart
Betsy Ray series (7)
Betsybob
Morrison, Margaret
Elizabeth Conway series (3)
Betsy's baby brother
Wolde, Gunilla
Emma series (1)
Betsy's busy summer
Haywood, Carolyn
Betsy series (7)
Betsy's first day at nursery school
Wolde, Gunilla
Emma series (7)
Betsy's fixing day
Wolde, Gunilla
Emma series (9)
Betsy's little star
Haywood, Carolyn
Betsy series (5)
Betsy's play school
Haywood, Carolyn
Betsy series (12)
Betsy's up-and-down year
Pellowski, Anne
Valley Farm series (5)
Betsy's wedding
Lovelace, Maud Hart
Betsy Ray series (10)
Betsy's winterhouse
Haywood, Carolyn
Betsy series (8)
Better bed manners
Hopton, Ralph
Bed manners series (2)
Better bit and bridle
Dubrovin, Vivian
Saddle up series (1)
Better class of business
Scott, Jack S
Detective Inspector Alfred Stanley Rosher series (2)

Better corpses
Daly, Carroll John
Race Williams series (8)
Better dead
Bagby, George
Inspector Schmidt series (43)
Bonett, John
Inspector Borges series (1)
Better mousetraps
Aaseng, Nathan
Inside business series (1)
Better not get wet, Jesse Bear
Carlstrom, Nancy White
Jesse Bear series (2)
Better off dead
Bonett, John
Inspector Borges series (1)
Better than life
Naylor, Grant
Red Dwarf series (2)
Better to arrive
Gordon, Glenda
Glenda series (1)
Better wed than dead
Kane, Henry
Peter Chambers series (23)
Better world of Reginald Perrin
Nobbs, David
Reginald Perrin series (3)
Better world than this
Joseph, Marie
Daisy Penny series (1)
Betterfly
Cosgrove, Stephen Edward
Bugg series (29)
Bettesworth book
Bourne, George
Frederick Bettesworth series (1)
Betty, a schoolgirl
Meade, Lillie Thomas
Betty Vivian series (1)
Betty Alden, the first-born daughter of the Pilgrims
Austin, Jane Goodwin
Pilgrims of Plymouth series (2)
Betty Baird
Weikel, Anna Hamline
Betty Baird trilogy (1)
Betty Baird's golden year
Weikel, Anna Hamline
Betty Baird trilogy (3)
Betty Baird's ventures
Weikel, Anna Hamline
Betty Baird trilogy (2)
Betty Bear's lesson
Burgess, Thornton Waldo
Wee little books series (2)
Betty Gaston, the seventh girl
Taggart, Marion Ames
Six girls series (5)
Betty Gordon and her school chums
Emerson, Alice B
Betty Gordon series (7)
Betty Gordon and the Hale twins
Emerson, Alice B
Betty Gordon series (12)
Betty Gordon and the lost pearls
Emerson, Alice B
Betty Gordon series (10)
Betty Gordon and the mystery girl
Emerson, Alice B
Betty Gordon series (15)
Betty Gordon at boarding school
Emerson, Alice B
Betty Gordon series (4)
Betty Gordon at Bramble Farm
Emerson, Alice B
Betty Gordon series (1)
Betty Gordon at Mountain Camp
Emerson, Alice B
Betty Gordon series (5)
Betty Gordon at Mystery Farm
Emerson, Alice B
Betty Gordon series (13)
Betty Gordon at Ocean Park
Emerson, Alice B
Betty Gordon series (6)
Betty Gordon at Rainbow Ranch
Emerson, Alice B
Betty Gordon series (8)
Betty Gordon in Mexican wilds
Emerson, Alice B
Betty Gordon series (9)
Betty Gordon in the land of oil
Emerson, Alice B
Betty Gordon series (3)
Betty Gordon in Washington
Emerson, Alice B
Betty Gordon series (2)
Betty Gordon on No-Trail Island
Emerson, Alice B
Betty Gordon series (14)
Betty Gordon on the campus
Emerson, Alice B
Betty Gordon series (11)
Betty Lee, freshman
Grove, Harriet Pyne
Betty Lee series (1)
Betty Lee, junior
Grove, Harriet Pyne
Betty Lee series (3)
Betty Lee, senior
Grove, Harriet Pyne
Betty Lee series (4)
Betty Lee, sophomore
Grove, Harriet Pyne
Betty Lee series (2)
Betty Leicester
Jewett, Sarah Orne
Betty Leicester series (1)
Betty Leicester's Christmas
Jewett, Sarah Orne
Betty Leicester series (2)
Betty of the rectory
Meade, Lillie Thomas
Betty Vivian series (2)
Betty Vivian
Meade, Lillie Thomas
Betty Vivian series (3)
Betty Wales and Company
Warde, Margaret
Betty Wales series (6)
Betty Wales, B.A.
Warde, Margaret
Betty Wales series (5)
Betty Wales, business woman
Warde, Margaret
Betty Wales series (10)
Betty Wales decides
Warde, Margaret
Betty Wales series (8)
Betty Wales, freshman
Warde, Margaret
Betty Wales series (1)
Betty Wales girls and Mister Kidd
Warde, Margaret
Betty Wales series (9)
Betty Wales, junior
Warde, Margaret
Betty Wales series (3)
Betty Wales on the campus
Warde, Margaret
Betty Wales series (7)
Betty Wales, senior
Warde, Margaret
Betty Wales series (4)
Betty Wales, sophomore
Warde, Margaret
Betty Wales series (2)
Betty Zane
Grey, Zane
Zane family series (1)
Betty's first term
Wevill, Lilian F
Betty series (1)
Betty's next term
Wevill, Lilian F
Betty series (2)
Between dances
Dean, Karen Strickler
Maggie Adams series (2)
Between day and dark
Angoff, Charles
Polonsky family series (4)
Between Devlin and the deep blue sea
Barrett, Robert G
Les Norton series (5)
Between friends
Green, Kate
Fossil family tales series (2)
Between life and death
Masterson, Louis
Morgan Kane series (15)
Between love and loneliness
Witcomb, Nan
Thoughts of Nanushka series (4)
Between moon and moon, 1946-1972
Graves, Robert
Broken images series (2)
Between the galaxies
Mahr, Kurt
Perry Rhodan series (119)
Between the larch-woods and the weir
Klickmann, Flora
Flower-patch series (2)
Between the lines
Keene, Carolyn
River Heights series (5)
Between the lines in Belgium
Ames, Franklin T
Between the lines series (1)
Between the lines in France
Ames, Franklin T
Between the lines series (2)
Between the lines on the American Front
Ames, Franklin T
Between the lines series (3)
Between the stars
Kotani, Eric
Act of God trilogy (3)
Between the tides
Street, Philip
Fisheries series (1)
Between the twilights
Charques, Dorothy
Time's harvest trilogy (3)
Between the woods and the water
Fermor, Patrick Leigh
On foot series (2)
Between the worlds
Cooke, John Byrne
Snowblind moon trilogy (1)
Between two shores
Bray, Donald
Captain Davy series (1)
Between two worlds
Mosco, Maisie
Between two worlds trilogy (1)
Sinclair, Upton
World's end series (2)
Between us and evil
Russell, Charlotte Murray
Homer Fitzgerald series (3)
Between you and me
Bailey, Pearl
Raw Pearl series (3)
Pickles, Wilfred
You and me series (1)
Beulah Land
Coleman, Lonnie
Beulah Land trilogy (1)
Bev
Miles, Keith
Sin bin series (4)
Beverly Gray at the World's Fair
Blank, Clair
Beverly Gray series (6)
Beverly Gray, freshman
Blank, Clair
Beverly Gray series (1)
Beverly Gray in the Orient
Blank, Clair
Beverly Gray series (8)
Beverly Gray, junior
Blank, Clair
Beverly Gray series (3)
Beverly Gray on a treasure hunt
Blank, Clair
Beverly Gray series (9)
Beverly Gray on a world cruise
Blank, Clair
Beverly Gray series (7)
Beverly Gray, reporter
Blank, Clair
Beverly Gray series (11)
Beverly Gray, senior
Blank, Clair
Beverly Gray series (4)
Beverly Gray, sophomore
Blank, Clair
Beverly Gray series (2)
Beverly Gray's adventure
Blank, Clair
Beverly Gray series (15)
Beverly Gray's assignment
Blank, Clair
Beverly Gray series (18)
Beverly Gray's career
Blank, Clair
Beverly Gray series (5)
Beverly Gray's challenge
Blank, Clair
Beverly Gray series (16)
Beverly Gray's discovery
Blank, Clair
Beverly Gray series (24)
Beverly Gray's fortune
Blank, Clair
Beverly Gray series (21)
Beverly Gray's island mystery
Blank, Clair
Beverly Gray series (23)
Beverly Gray's journey
Blank, Clair
Beverly Gray series (17)
Beverly Gray's mystery
Blank, Clair
Beverly Gray series (19)
Beverly Gray's problem
Blank, Clair
Beverly Gray series (14)
Beverly Gray's quest
Blank, Clair
Beverly Gray series (13)
Beverly Gray's return
Blank, Clair
Beverly Gray series (10)
Beverly Gray's romance
Blank, Clair
Beverly Gray series (12)
Beverly Gray's scoop
Blank, Clair
Beverly Gray series (25)
Beverly Gray's secret
Blank, Clair
Beverly Gray series (22)
Beverly Gray's surprise
Blank, Clair
Beverly Gray series (26)
Beverly Gray's vacation
Blank, Clair
Beverly Gray series (20)
Beverly Hills 90210
Gilden, Mel
Beverly Hills 90210 series (1)
Beverly Hills Browning
Corris, Peter
Richard Browning series (2)
Beverly Malibu
Forrest, Katherine V
Kate Delafield series (3)
Beverly of Graustark
McCutcheon, George Barr
Graustark series (2)
Bevis
Jefferies, Richard
Bevis series (2)
Beware, beware the Bight of Benin
McCutchan, Philip
Lieutenant Saint Vincent Halfhyde series (1)
Beware Dawn!
Martin, Ann Matthews
Baby-Sitters Club mystery series (2)
Beware of children
Anderson, Verily
Anderson family series (3)
Beware of the Brain Sharpeners
Curtis, Philip
Mister Browser series (5)
Beware of the dog
Corris, Peter
Cliff Hardy series (16)
Varnam, John
Inspector Semlake series (3)
Beware of the mouse
Wibberley, Leonard
Grand Fenwick series (1)
Beware of the trains
Crispin, Edmund
Gervase Fen series (9)
Beware, take care
Treloar, Bruce
Baggable tales series (1)
Beware the babysitter
Pascal, Francine
Sweet Valley High series (99)
Beware the Bight of Benin
McCutchan, Philip
Lieutenant Saint Vincent Halfhyde series (1)
Beware the crimson cord!
Edmunds, Brent
Pete Marvin series (3)
Beware the curves
Fair, A A
Bertha Cool and Donald Lam series (15)
Beware the gingerbread house
Rodda, Emily
Teen Power Inc. series (5)
Beware the hunter
Jones, Howard
John Haddon series (1)
Beware the microbats
Mahr, Kurt
Perry Rhodan series (35)
Beware the pale horse
Benson, Ben
Inspector Wade Paris series (1)
Beware, the Picaroon
Cassells, John
Ludovic Saxon series (3)
Beware the smiling stranger
Dana, Mitchell
Dakota Bush series (6)
Beware the Tektrons
Erskine, George
Counter Force series (1)
Beware the wolfman
Pascal, Francine
Sweet Valley High series (106)
Beware the yellow Packard
Malloy, Lester
Martin Moon series (4)
Beware young lovers
Pentecost, Hugh
Pierre Chambrun series (15)
Beware your neighbour
Burton, Miles
Inspector Arnold and Desmond Merrion series (43)
Bewitched
Hine, Alfred Blakelee
Bewitched series (1)
Janson, Hank
Hank Janson series (85)
Bewitched by the Brain Sharpeners
Curtis, Philip
Mister Browser series (8)
Bewitched caverns
Rienow, Leona Train
Dark pool series (1)
Bewitchments of love and hate
Constantine, Storm
Book of Wraeththu series (2)
Beyond
Galsworthy, John
Love trilogy (2)
Beyond Baker Street
Jaffee, Mary
Sherlock Holmes sequels series (14)
Beyond blame
Greenleaf, Stephen
John Marshall Tanner series (5)
Beyond Blue Hills
Meredith, Gwen
Blue Hills series (3)
Beyond chance of change
Shafer, Sara Andrew
Day before yesterday series (2)
Beyond dark hills
Stuart, Jesse
Dark hills trilogy (1)
Beyond Eden
Morgan, Jill Meredith
Eden trilogy (2)
Beyond escape!
Montgomery, Raymond A
Choose your own adventure series (61)
Beyond Euphrates
Stark, Freya
Traveller series (2)
Beyond gravity
Leiber, Justin Fritz
Beyond trilogy (3)
Beyond humanity
Leiber, Justin Fritz
Beyond trilogy (2)
Beyond Land's End
Enright, Dennis Joseph
Joke shop trilogy (3)
Beyond life
Cabell, James Branch
Dom Manuel and his descendants series (1)
Beyond my worth
Roth, Lillian
I'll cry tomorrow series (2)
Beyond pursuit
Carter, Nicholas
Nicholas Carter series (146)
Beyond reasonable doubt
Hull, Richard
Inspector Fenby series (2)
Beyond rejection
Leiber, Justin Fritz
Beyond trilogy (1)
Beyond sanctuary
Morris, Janet Ellen
Sanctuary series (12)
Tempus series (1)
Beyond shattered illusions
Dexter, Carmen
Star trek fan series (14)
Beyond sing the woods
Gulbranssen, Trygve
Bjorndal family series (1)
Beyond terror
Siegel, Barbara
Ghostworld series (1)
Beyond the Aegean
Kazan, Elia
Stavros the Anatolian trilogy (3)
Beyond the ancient cities
Merino, Jose Maria
Miguel series (2)
Beyond the back gate
Parker, Richard
Pipers series (3)
Beyond the bedroom wall
Woiwode, Larry
Neumiller family series (1)
Beyond the black enigma
Somers, Bart
Commander Craig series (1)

Beyond the blue event horizon
Pohl, Frederik
Heechee series (2)
Beyond the blue hills
Seton, Hilary
Minty Humble series (1)
Beyond the Blue Ridge
Burnap, Jennifer
Cartwright family series (2)
Beyond the Borders
Derwent, Lavinia
Border series (7)
Beyond the burning lands
Christopher, John
Prince trilogy (2)
Beyond the Chindwin
Fergusson, Bernard
Burma campaign series (1)
Beyond the chocolate war
Cormier, Robert
Chocolate war series (2)
Beyond the cross and the switchblade
Wilkerson, David
Cross and the switchblade series (3)
Beyond the Danube
Meade, Richard
John Allison series (1)
Beyond the desert gate
Ray, Mary
Early Christian series (4)
Beyond the DMZ
Lansing, John
Black Eagles series (7)
Beyond the Draak's teeth
Bennett, Marcia Joanne
Ni-lach series (3)
Beyond the fall of night
Benford, Gregory
Fall of night series (2)
Beyond the far pavilions
Cooper, Leo
Far pavilions series (2)
Beyond the Far Side
Larson, Gary
Far Side series (2)
Beyond the fourth door
Deegan, Jon J
Dysart trilogy (2)
Beyond the galactic lens
Kern, Gregory
Cap Kennedy series (16)
Beyond the Galactic Rim
Chandler, Arthur Bertram
John Grimes series (2)
Beyond the galactic rim
Chandler, Arthur Bertram
Rim series (15)
Beyond the glass
White, Antonia
Frost in May series (4)
Beyond the grass bank
Bagshaw, Joyce Margaret
Hobstones series (2)
Beyond the grave
Muller, Marcia
Elena Olivirez series (3)
Pronzini, Bill
Quincannon series (2)
Beyond the great oblivion
England, George Allen
Darkness and dawn series (2)
Beyond the great silence
Maeterlinck, Maurice
Pascalian series (1)
Beyond the Great Wall
Leibold, Jay
Choose your own adventure series (73)
Beyond the Highland line
Frere, Richard
Highland line series (2)
Beyond the horizon
Mason, Connie
Women West series (2)
Beyond the Imperium
Laumer, Keith
Mister Curlon series (3)
Beyond the law
Dana, Mitchell
Dakota Bush series (1)
Dixon, Franklin W
Hardy boys case files series (55)
Murray, Andrew
Sexton Blake series (244)
Beyond the locked door
Allan, Luke
Tiger Lillie series (7)
Beyond the loving
Witcomb, Nan
Thoughts of Nanushka series (15)
Beyond the Marble Mountain
Gardner, Hugh
Marble Mountain series (1)
Beyond the Mogollon Rim
Grey, Romer Zane
Nevada Jim Lacy series (2)
Beyond the moon
Hamilton, Edmond
John Gordon series (1)
Beyond the moons
Cook, David
Spelljammer series (1)
Beyond the nightmare gate
Page, Ian
World of Lone Wolf series (3)
Beyond the nineteen counties
Lowe, Eric
Stewart family series (1)
Beyond the Outer Mirr
Savarin, Julian Jay
Lemmus trilogy (2)
Beyond the outsider
Wilson, Colin
Outsider series (2)
Beyond the pale
Mosley, Nicholas
Sir Oswald Mosley series (2)
Beyond the pawpaw trees
Brown, Palmer
Anna Lavinia series (1)
Beyond the Poseidon adventure
Gallico, Paul
Poseidon series (2)
Beyond the prize
Denning, Mark
John Marshall series (3)
Beyond the rainbow
Thwaites, Frederick Joseph
Doctor Joszef Venesz series (2)
Beyond the reef
Kent, Alexander
Captain Richard Bolitho series (20)
Beyond the sea of ice
Sarabande, William
First Americans series (1)
Beyond the starlit frost
Brandewyne, Rebecca
Chronicles of Tintagel series (2)
Beyond the stone heaps
Anderson, Ian
Scarlet riders series (3)
Beyond the sunset
Douie, Charles
Weary road series (2)
Smith, Arthur Douglas Howden
Doom trail series (2)
Beyond the tides
Street, Philip
Fisheries series (2)
Beyond the tomorrow mountains
Engdahl, Sylvia Louise
Noren series (2)
Beyond the valley
Davis, Andrew Jackson
Spiritualism series (2)
Beyond the veil
Morris, Janet Ellen
Tempus series (2)
Beyond the vicarage
Streatfeild, Noel
Vicarage series (3)
Beyond the void
Dalton, Sean
Operation Star Hawks series (3)
Beyond the west horizon
Hiscock, Eric Charles
Wanderer series (2)
Beyond the western waters
White, Myrtle Rose
White family series (2)
Beyond tolerance
Hobson, Hank
Brad Ford series (5)
Beyond vengeance
Howard, Tom
Sergeant Tom Howard series (8)
Beyond Wizardwall
Morris, Janet Ellen
Tempus series (3)
Bhowani Junction
Masters, John
Indian trilogy (3)
Savage family series (6)
Bib and Bub
Gibbs, May
Gumnut Land series (11)
Bib and Bub in Gumnut Town
Gibbs, May
Gumnut Land series (14)
Bib and Bub painting book
Gibbs, May
Gumnut Land series (16)
Bibi, a little Danish girl
Michaelis, Karin
Bibi series (1)
Bibi goes travelling
Michaelis, Karin
Bibi series (2)
Bible cameos
Powell, Ivor
Bible series (1)
Bible gems
Powell, Ivor
Bible series (6)
Bible highway
Powell, Ivor
Bible series (5)
Bible magic tricks for children's church
Westphail, Arnold Carl
Gospel magic series (4)
Bible names of Christ
Powell, Ivor
Bible series (7)
Bible nuggets
Powell, Ivor
Bible series (8)
Bible pinnacles
Powell, Ivor
Bible series (2)
Bible promises
Powell, Ivor
Bible series (9)
Bible treasures
Powell, Ivor
Bible series (3)
Bible windows
Powell, Ivor
Bible series (4)
Bibles, bullets and brides
Hardin, J D
Raider and Doc series (22)
Bicycle mystery
Warner, Gertrude Chandler
Boxcar children series (15)
Bicycle safety
Higgs, Mike
Learn with Moonbird series (2)
Bicycle to treachery
Quackenbush, Robert Mead
Miss Mallard series (9)
Bid for beauty
Janson, Hank
Hank Janson series (227)
Bid for fortune
Boothby, Guy
Doctor Nikola series (1)
Bid time return
Ure, Jean
Riverside Theatre series (4)
Biddy Christmas
Warner, Priscilla Mary
Biddy and Tessie series (1)
Biddy's secret
Oxenham, Elsie J
Abbey girls first generation series (15)
Rachel and Damaris series (1)
Biding his time
Trowbridge, John Townsend
Start in life series (2)
Bier for a chaser
Foster, Richard
Pete Draco series (1)
Biff
Gould, Charles S
Biff series (1)
Biff finds a clue
Gould, Charles S
Biff series (2)
Biff Norris and the clue of the angry fisherman
Runyan, John
Biff Norris series (8)
Biff Norris and the clue of the disappearing wolf
Runyan, John
Biff Norris series (9)
Biff Norris and the clue of the gold ring
Runyan, John
Biff Norris series (7)
Biff Norris and the clue of the golden ram
Runyan, John
Biff Norris series (4)
Biff Norris and the clue of the half-burned book
Runyan, John
Biff Norris series (11)
Biff Norris and the clue of the lavender mink
Runyan, John
Biff Norris series (6)
Biff Norris and the clue of the lonely landing strip
Runyan, John
Biff Norris series (1)
Biff Norris and the clue of the midnight stage
Runyan, John
Biff Norris series (5)
Biff Norris and the clue of the mysterious letter
Runyan, John
Biff Norris series (10)
Biff Norris and the clue of the nervous stranger
Runyan, John
Biff Norris series (3)
Biff Norris and the clue of the worn saddle
Runyan, John
Biff Norris series (2)
Biffin and his circle
Graham, Harry
Reginald Drake Biffin series (4)
Biffin papers
Graham, Harry
Reginald Drake Biffin series (6)
Big Alfie and Annie Rose storybook
Hughes, Shirley
Alfie Rose series (4)
Big Alfie out-of-doors storybook
Hughes, Shirley
Alfie Rose series (4)
Big and little
Pluckrose, Henry
Thinking about series (6)
Big and strong
Campbell, Rod
Little people series (11)
Pocket wheels series (1)
Big apple
Myles, Simon
Apples Carstairs series (2)
Big Apple money is rotten to the core
Glazner, Joseph Mark
Billy Nevers series (4)
Big bad pig
Ahlberg, Allan
Red nose readers series (2)
Big Baja bounty
Gentry, Buck
Eli Holten series (20)
Big bands are back
Browne, Dik
Hagar the horrible series (4)
Big bang
Goulart, Ron
Odd jobs series (3)
Big bankroll
Chase, Glen
Cherry Delight series (24)
Big barn
Edmonds, Walter Dumaux
Erie Canal series (3)
Big base hit
Hughes, Dean
Angel Park All-Stars series (2)
Big Bear to the rescue
Margolis, Richard Jules
Big Bear series (2)
Big Ben strikes eleven
Magarshack, David
Superintendent Mooney series (1)
Big Ben struck twelve
Wood, Andrew
Magnus Keeble series (2)
Big Bill the bastard
Macdonnell, James Edmond
Commander William Mallett series (2)
Big black
Myles, Simon
Apples Carstairs series (1)
Big black mark
Chandler, Arthur Bertram
John Grimes series (13)
Rim series (7)
Big blackmail
King, Frank
Dormouse series (16)
Big blow up
Krulick, Nancy E
Lassie series (3)
Big blue death
Milton, Joseph
Bart Gould series (4)
Big book about Little Bear
Clarke, Molly
Little Bear series (1)
Big book of Brambly Hedge
Barklem, Jill
Brambly Hedge series (4)
Big book of Digit Dick
Rees, Leslie
Digit Dick series (4)
Big book of Josephine
Cradock, Henry Cowper, Mrs
Josephine series (3)
Big book of Mister Small
Lenski, Lois
Small family series (10)
Big book of Pegmen tales
McFadyen, Ella
Pegmen series (2)
Big boys don't cry
Corrigan, Mark
Mark Corrigan and McLean series (17)
Big brain
Gray, Berkeley
Norman Conquest series (37)
Big brand
Kelton, Elmer
Tales of Texas series (16)
Big breakout!
Whiting, Charles
T-Force series (1)
Big broad jump
Conway, Troy
Coxeman series (17)
Big brokers
Shulman, Irving
Juvenile delinquency trilogy (3)
Big brother
Eggleston, George Cary
Indian War trilogy (1)
Big brother blues
Stine, Harlan William
Jeffrey and the fourth grade ghost series (6)
Big brothers of Sabin Street
Thurston, Ida Treadwell
Theodore Bryan series (2)
Big Brown Teapot
Miller, Margaret Jessy
Willow and Albert series (4)
Big bubble
Pratt, Theodore
Florida trilogy (3)
Big bug book of counting
McKissack, Patricia Carwell
Big bug series (1)
Big bug book of opposites
McKissack, Patricia Carwell
Big bug series (2)
Big bug book of places to go
McKissack, Patricia Carwell
Big bug series (3)
Big bug book of the alphabet
McKissack, Patricia Carwell
Big bug series (4)
Big bug book of things to do
McKissack, Patricia Carwell
Big bug series (5)
Big business murder
Cole, George Douglas Howard
Superintendent Henry Wilson series (14)
Big C
Cronin, Michael
James Hellier series (6)
Big call
Ashe, Gordon
Patrick Dawlish series (40)
Big Cherokee
Borg, Jack
Hogleg Bailey series (4)
Big Chief Bunter
Richards, Frank
Billy Bunter series (34)
Big chill
Copper, Basil
Mike Faraday series (10)
Big chip
Cannon, Elliott
Guy Fosse series (2)
Big circus mystery
King, Hilary
Sexton Blake series (1325)
Big city blues
Moore, John
Dick Tracy cartoon series (7)
Big concrete lorry
Hughes, Shirley
Tale of Trotter Street series (3)
Big country
Timms, Edward Vivian
Australian saga series (11)
Big country, big men
Wynne, Brian
Marshal Jeremy Six series (10)
Big crush
Chase, Emily
Canby Hall series (8)

Big date
Adorjan, Carol
Junior High series (3)
Kenyon, Kate
Cedar Groves Junior High School series (10)
Big day at Bellbird
Vernon, Barbara
Bellbird series (2)
Big day at Blue Creek
Grover, Marshall
Larry and Stretch series (97)
Big deal
Lambert, Janet
Cinda Hollister series (3)
Big deal in Veragua
Morales, Pablo
Pedro Moreno series (2)
Big Desmond story book
Althea
Desmond the dinosaur series (13)
Big dinero
Grover, Marshall
Larry and Stretch series (67)
Big dive
Crossen, Kendell Foster
Kim Locke series (2)
Big drip
Laird, Elizabeth
Toucan Tecs series (10)
Big drive
Douglas, Thorne
Rancho Bravo series (2)
Big drop, and other Cliff Hardy stories
Corris, Peter
Cliff Hardy series (8)
Big ears
Savage, Deborah
Peregrine Piecrust series (4)
Big enchilada
Morse, Larry Alan
Sam Hunter series (1)
Big enough
James, Will
Cow camps series (1)
Big enough wreath
Garner, William
Mike Jagger series (4)
Big Ethel
Ross, Tony
Tales from Mister Toffy's circus series (5)
Big Fellow
Palmer, Vance
Macy Donovan series (3)
Big fifty
Miller, Jim
Long guns series (2)
Big fish
Charles, Robert
Simon Larren series (9)
Big Fisherman
Douglas, Lloyd Cassel
Apostle Peter series (2)
Big fix
Barker, Albert
Hawk Macrae series (1)
Simon, Roger Lichtenberg
Moses Wine series (1)
Big flood in the bush
Dallas, Ruth
Jean, Robbie, Sophie and Helen series (3)
Big Foot
Wallace, Edgar
Superintendent Minter series (1)
Big Foot's Range
Slade, Jack
Lassiter series (29)
Big four
Christie, Agatha
Hercule Poirot series (5)
Big freeze
Favors, Jean M
Micro adventure series (8)
Big gamble
Coxe, George Harmon
Kent Murdock series (17)
Masters, Zeke
Faro Blake series (1)
Big game
Gilman, George G
Adam Steele series (22)
Perry, Lawrence
Football series (2)
Big game Benn
McKee, David
Mister Benn series (3)
Big gator of the Everglades
Torgersen, Don Arthur
Animal life stories series (7)
Big gold
Gilman, George G
Edge series (14)
Big gold dream
Himes, Chester
Grave Digger Jones and Coffin Ed Johnson series (4)
Big goodbye
Chambers, Peter
Mark Preston series (3)
Big greed
Giles, Kenneth
Inspector Harry James and Sergeant Honeybody series (2)
Big grouse
Clark, Douglas
Inspector George Masters series (25)
Big gun
Edson, John Thomas
American Civil War series (3)
Big gun bushwhacker
Meek, Joseph
Mountain Jack Pike series (9)
Big gunfight
Gilman, George G
Adam Steele series (42)
Big H
Janson, Hank
Hank Janson series (228)
Peters, Bryan
Brandon and Lundstrom series (2)
Big hand for the corpse
Bagby, George
Inspector Schmidt series (22)
Big herd
Winstan, Matt
Reuben Brown series (1)
Big hit
Myles, Simon
Apples Carstairs series (3)
Big honey hunt
Berenstain, Stan
Berenstain bears series (1)
Big hunt
Edson, John Thomas
Calamity Jane series (12)
Big John Turkle
Hoban, Russell
Ponders series (2)
Big kill
Spillane, Mickey
Mike Hammer series (4)
Big killing
Fuller, Ed
Troubleshooters series (5)
Meyers, Annette
Leslie Wetzon series (1)
Big kiss-off of 1944
Bergman, Andrew
Jack LeVine series (1)
Le Vine, Jack
Jack Le Vine series (1)
Big knock-over
Hammett, Dashiell
Continental Op series (3)
Big lie
Janson, Hank
Hank Janson series (67)
Big little Davy
Lenski, Lois
Davy series (3)
Big Lobo
McCoy, Marshall
Nevada Jim series (31)
Big lonely
Brown, Sam
Casey Wills series (1)
Big loser
Kennedy, Elliot
Griff Dexter series (1)
Big Mac and the oil rig
Jungman, Ann
Big Mac series (1)
Big Mac and the satellite
Jungman, Ann
Big Mac series (2)
Big Mac goes to Mars
Jungman, Ann
Big Mac series (3)
Big Mama's funeral
Garcia Marquez, Gabriel
Macondo series (2)
Big man
McIlvanney, William
Inspector Jack Laidlaw series (3)
Big match
Dicks, Terrance
David and Goliath series (15)
Big Max
Platt, Kin
Big Max series (1)
Big Max in the mystery of the missing moose
Platt, Kin
Big Max series (2)
Big midget murders
Rice, Craig
John Joseph Malone series (6)
Big money
Dos Passos, John
U.S.A.trilogy (3)
Masur, Harold Q
Scott Jordan series (5)
Turnbull, Peter
P Division series (4)
Big mouth
Savage, Deborah
Peregrine Piecrust series (6)
Big needle
Myles, Simon
Apples Carstairs series (2)
Big Nick
Buranelli, Prosper
Nick Morro series (1)
Big Noddy books
Blyton, Enid
Noddy series (24)
Big nowhere
Ellroy, James
Los Angeles quartet (2)
Big one
Cutter, John
Specialist series (6)
Big one gets away!
Wylie, Philip
Crunch and Des series (1)
Big party weekend
Pascal, Francine
Sweet Valley twins series (54)
Big pasture
Fisher, Clay
Nathan Mason Stark series (2)
Big payoff
Law, Janice
Anna Peters series (1)
Novak, Robert
Joe Blaze series (1)
Big Peter's little Peter
Cheesman, Lilian
Peter trilogy (2)
Big pig puzzle
Hope, Laura Lee
New Bobbsey twins series (27)
Big Planet
Vance, Jack
Big Planet series (1)
Big prize
Gilman, George G
Adam Steele series (29)
Steele's war series (5)
Big race
Henry, Marguerite
Chincoteague series (1)
Pascal, Francine
Sweet Valley kids series (37)
Big racket
Daniel, Roland
Buddy Mustard series (11)
Big rain
Francoise
Jeanne-Marie series (5)
Big Red
Kjelgaard, Jim
Red series (1)
Big rip-off
Copper, Basil
Mike Faraday series (28)
Big river, big man
Duncan, Thomas
Big river, big man series (2)
Big round bed
Janson, Hank
Hank Janson series (250)
Big season
Palmer, Bernard
Career series (3)
Big shot
Daniel, Roland
Buddy Mustard series (14)
Treat, Lawrence
Bill Decker series (3)
Jub Freeman series (7)
Mitch Taylor series (4)
Big shot's final edition
Brody, Marc
Marc Brody series (13)
Big showoffs
Albright, Molly
Two of a kind series (3)
Big sin
Webb, Jack
Father Joseph Shanley and Sammy Golden series (1)
Big sister
Quin-Harkin, Janet
Sugar and spice series (11)
Big sister blues
Kaye, Marilyn
Camp Sunnyside Friends series (13)
Big sister Stephanie
Saunders, Susan
Sleepover friends series (30)
Big six
Ransome, Arthur
Swallows and Amazons series (9)
Big sky
Guthrie, Alfred Bertram
Settlement of the American West series (1)
Big sleep
Chandler, Raymond
Big sleep series (1)
Philip Marlowe series (1)
Big sleepy time book
Hodgetts, Sheila
Sleepy time tales series (4)
Big smear
Baker, William Howard
Sexton Blake series (1533)
Big snake hunters
Appleton, Victor
Don Sturdy series (2)
Big snatch
Gray, Rod
Lady from L.U.S.T. series (10)
Howard, Hartley
Glenn Bowman series (16)
Big snow
Falstaff, Jack
Jacoby's Corners trilogy (2)
Hader, Berta
Willow Hill series (2)
Big Snowy
Slater, Jim
A Mazing Monster series (12)
Big splash for Belinda
Brody, Marc
Marc Brody series (48)
Big squeeze
Corrigan, Mark
Mark Corrigan and McLean series (16)
Big stash
Peters, Ron
Stash Koval series (1)
Big steal
Story, Jack Trevor
Sexton Blake series (1502)
Big stiffs
Avallone, Michael
Ed Noon series (30)
Big story
West, Morris Langlo
George Harlequin series (1)
Big sun of Mercury
Asimov, Isaac
David Starr series (4)
Big Sur
Kerouac, Jack
Jack Duluoz series (12)
Big tickle
Cronin, Michael
Sam Harris series (6)
Wainwright, John
Northern Police series (11)
Big time
Foxall, Peter Augustus
Detective Sergeant Scamp series (2)
Leiber, Fritz
Changewar series (1)
Big timer
Duncan, William Murdoch
Mister Gilly series (2)
Big tomorrow
Bateson, David
Larry Vernon series (3)
Big top Benn
McKee, David
Mister Benn series (4)
Big top mystery
Matranga, Frances Carfi
Nina Cristina series (5)
Big top squaw
Gentry, Buck
Eli Holten series (19)
Big touch
Kane, Henry
Peter Chambers series (7)
Peter Chambers series (8)
Big trouble at the beach
Jenkins, Jerry Bruce
Bradford family series (12)
Big trouble for Roxie
Stahl, Hilda
Best friends series (2)
Big twist
Hobson, Hank
Brad Ford series (3)
Big up!
Brooke, Jonathan
Backstreets series (2)
Big wedding
Duun, Ole Julius
People of Juvik series (3)
Big wind
Macdonnell, James Edmond
Captain Peter Bentley series (27)
Big wind for summer
Black, Gavin
Paul Harris series (11)
Big X
Tracy, Don
Giff Speer series (9)
Bigamist
Chichester, John Jay
Jimmy Price series (1)
Bigamy kiss
Harragan, Steve
Steve Harragan series (1)
Bigfoot
Christian, Mary Blount
Mystery of series (1)
Bigg family
Cosgrove, Stephen Edward
Bugg series (30)
Bigger light
Clarke, Austin Chesterfield
Boysie Cumberbatch trilogy (3)
Bigger they are
Ditton, James
John Boldre series (1)
Bigger they come
Fair, A A
Bertha Cool and Donald Lam series (1)
Biggest bounty
Gilman, George G
Edge series (12)
Biggest dinosaurs
Berenstain, Michael
Dinosaurs series (1)
Biggle flying omnibus
Johns, William Earl
Biggles series (18)
Biggles adventure omnibus
Johns, William Earl
Biggles series (51)
Biggles, air commodore
Johns, William Earl
Biggles series (12)
Biggles, air detective
Johns, William Earl
Biggles series (42)
Biggles air detective omnibus
Johns, William Earl
Biggles series (39)
Biggles and Company
Johns, William Earl
Biggles series (10)
Biggles and the Black Mask
Johns, William Earl
Biggles series (76)
Biggles and the black raider
Johns, William Earl
Biggles series (43)
Biggles and the blue moon
Johns, William Earl
Biggles series (80)
Biggles and the cruise of the Condor
Johns, William Earl
Biggles series (2)
Biggles and the dark intruder
Johns, William Earl
Biggles series (85)
Biggles and the deep blue sea
Johns, William Earl
Biggles series (87)
Biggles and the gun-runners
Johns, William Earl
Biggles series (83)
Biggles and the leopards of Zinn
Johns, William Earl
Biggles series (62)
Biggles and the little green god
Johns, William Earl
Biggles series (90)
Biggles and the lost sovereigns
Johns, William Earl
Biggles series (75)
Biggles and the lost treasure
Johns, William Earl
Biggles series (75)
Biggles and the missing millionaire
Johns, William Earl
Biggles series (66)

Biggles and the noble lord
Johns, William Earl
Biggles series (91)

Biggles and the penitent thief
Johns, William Earl
Biggles series (86)

Biggles and the pirate treasure
Johns, William Earl
Biggles series (47)

Biggles and the plack peril
Johns, William Earl
Biggles series (6)

Biggles and the plane that disappeared
Johns, William Earl
Biggles series (73)

Biggles and the plot that failed
Johns, William Earl
Biggles series (79)

Biggles and the poor rich boy
Johns, William Earl
Biggles series (64)

Biggles at school
Johns, William Earl
Biggles series (38)

Biggles at world's end
Johns, William Earl
Biggles series (61)

Biggles book of beroes
Johns, William Earl
Biggles series (92)

Biggles book of treasure hunting
Johns, William Earl
Biggles series (92)

Biggles breaks the silence
Johns, William Earl
Biggles series (35)

Biggles buries a hatchet
Johns, William Earl
Biggles series (58)

Biggles, charter pilot
Johns, William Earl
Biggles series (26)

Biggles' Chinese puzzle, and other Biggles adventures
Johns, William Earl
Biggles series (50)

Biggles' combined operation
Johns, William Earl
Biggles series (60)

Biggles cuts it fine
Johns, William Earl
Biggles series (46)

Biggles defies the swastika
Johns, William Earl
Biggles series (22)

Biggles delivers the goods
Johns, William Earl
Biggles series (30)

Biggles fails to return
Johns, William Earl
Biggles series (28)

Biggles flies again
Johns, William Earl
Biggles series (4)

Biggles flies east
Johns, William Earl
Biggles series (6)
Biggles series (7)

Biggles flies north
Johns, William Earl
Biggles series (18)

Biggles flies south
Johns, William Earl
Biggles series (14)

Biggles flies to work
Johns, William Earl
Biggles series (74)

Biggles flies west
Johns, William Earl
Biggles series (13)

Biggles follows on
Johns, William Earl
Biggles series (41)

Biggles, foreign legionnaire
Johns, William Earl
Biggles series (48)

Biggles forms a syndicate
Johns, William Earl
Biggles series (65)

Biggles gets his men
Johns, William Earl
Biggles series (36)

Biggles goes alone
Johns, William Earl
Biggles series (67)

Biggles goes home
Johns, William Earl
Biggles series (63)

Biggles goes to school
Johns, William Earl
Biggles series (38)

Biggles goes to war
Johns, William Earl
Biggles series (3)
Biggles series (15)

Biggles hits the trail
Johns, William Earl
Biggles series (8)

Biggles hunts big game
Johns, William Earl
Biggles series (33)

Biggles in Africa
Johns, William Earl
Biggles series (11)

Biggles in Australia
Johns, William Earl
Biggles series (49)

Biggles in Borneo
Johns, William Earl
Biggles series (27)

Biggles in France
Johns, William Earl
Biggles series (9)

Biggles in Mexico
Johns, William Earl
Biggles series (59)

Biggles in Spain
Johns, William Earl
Biggles series (17)

Biggles in the Antarctic
Johns, William Earl
Biggles series (35)

Biggles in the Baltic
Johns, William Earl
Biggles series (20)

Biggles in the blue
Johns, William Earl
Biggles series (44)

Biggles in the cruise of the Condor
Johns, William Earl
Biggles series (2)

Biggles in the Gobi
Johns, William Earl
Biggles series (45)

Biggles in the jungle
Johns, William Earl
Biggles series (24)

Biggles in the Orient
Johns, William Earl
Biggles series (29)

Biggles in the South Seas
Johns, William Earl
Biggles series (21)

Biggles in the Terai
Johns, William Earl
Biggles series (82)

Biggles in the underworld
Johns, William Earl
Biggles series (89)

Biggles investigates, and other stories of the Air Police
Johns, William Earl
Biggles series (77)

Biggles learns to fly
Johns, William Earl
Biggles series (5)

Biggles looks back
Johns, William Earl
Biggles series (78)

Biggles makes ends meet
Johns, William Earl
Biggles series (53)

Biggles of the Camel Squadron
Johns, William Earl
Biggles series (3)

Biggles of the Interpol
Johns, William Earl
Biggles series (54)

Biggles of the Royal Flying Corps
Johns, William Earl
Biggles series (92)

Biggles of the Special Air Police
Johns, William Earl
Biggles series (1)

Biggles of two six six
Johns, William Earl
Biggles series (9)

Biggles omnibus
Johns, William Earl
Biggles series (10)

Biggles on Mystery Island
Johns, William Earl
Biggles series (57)

Biggles on the home front
Johns, William Earl
Biggles series (55)

Biggles, pioneer air fighter
Johns, William Earl
Biggles series (1)

Biggles presses on
Johns, William Earl
Biggles series (56)

Biggles' rescue flight
Johns, William Earl
Biggles series (16)

Biggles scores a bull
Johns, William Earl
Biggles series (81)

Biggles' second case
Johns, William Earl
Biggles series (32)

Biggles, secret agent
Johns, William Earl
Biggles series (19)

Biggles sees it through
Johns, William Earl
Biggles series (23)

Biggles sees too much
Johns, William Earl
Biggles series (92)

Biggles sets a trap
Johns, William Earl
Biggles series (69)

Biggles sorts it out
Johns, William Earl
Biggles series (84)

Biggles' South Seas adventure
Johns, William Earl
Biggles series (21)

Biggles' special case
Johns, William Earl
Biggles series (72)

Biggles sweeps the desert
Johns, William Earl
Biggles series (25)

Biggles takes a hand
Johns, William Earl
Biggles series (71)

Biggles takes a holiday
Johns, William Earl
Biggles series (34)

Biggles takes charge
Johns, William Earl
Biggles series (52)

Biggles takes it rough
Johns, William Earl
Biggles series (70)

Biggles takes the case
Johns, William Earl
Biggles series (40)

Biggles works it out
Johns, William Earl
Biggles series (39)

Bignose
Slater, Jim
A Mazing Monster series (2)

Bike lesson
Berenstain, Stan
Berenstain bears series (2)

Bike tycoon
Johnston, William
Happy days series (6)

Bikie birds
Hall, Stuart
Bikie series (1)

Bikie hell
Hall, Stuart
Bikie series (3)

Bikie hellcats
Hall, Stuart
Bikie series (2)

Bilbao looking glass
Macleod, Charlotte
Sarah Kelling series (4)

Bilbo heritage
Heidenstam, Verner von
Tree of the Folkungs series (2)

Bilbo's last song
Tolkien, John Ronald Reuel
Middle Earth series (5)

Bili the Axe
Adams, Robert
Horseclans series (10)

Bill and Ben and the Potato Man
Bird, Maria
Flowerpot Men series (1)

Bill and Beryl in Chinatown
Burke, Thomas
Bill and Beryl series (1)

Bill and Beryl in Old London
Burke, Thomas
Bill and Beryl series (2)

Bill and Beryl in Soho
Burke, Thomas
Bill and Beryl series (3)

Bill and Nancy
Wasson, Mildred
Nancy Prentiss series (4)

Bill and Pete
De Paola, Tomie
Bill and Pete series (1)

Bill and Pete go down the Nile
De Paola, Tomie
Bill and Pete series (2)

Bill and the ghost of Grimley Grange
Stones, Anthony
Bill of Grimley Grange series (1)

Bill and the maze at Grimley Grange
Stones, Anthony
Bill of Grimley Grange series (2)

Bill Badger and the big store robbery
B B
Bill Badger series (7)

Bill Badger and the pirates
B B
Bill Badger series (3)

Bill Badger and the wandering wind
B B
Bill Badger series (1)

Bill Badger's big mistake
B B
Bill Badger series (6)

Bill Badger's finest hour
B B
Bill Badger series (4)

Bill Badger's voyage to the world's end
B B
Bill Badger series (8)

Bill Badger's whispering reeds adventure
B B
Bill Badger series (5)

Bill Badger's winter cruise
B B
Bill Badger series (2)

Bill Bailey
Cookson, Catherine
Bill Bailey series (1)

Bill Bailey's daughter
Cookson, Catherine
Bill Bailey series (3)

Bill Bailey's lot
Cookson, Catherine
Bill Bailey series (2)

Bill Berenger to the rescue
Duff, Douglas Valder
Bill Berenger series (2)

Bill Berenger wins command
Duff, Douglas Valder
Bill Berenger series (3)

Bill Berenger's first case
Duff, Douglas Valder
Bill Berenger series (1)

Bill Bergson and the white rose rescue
Lindgren, Astrid
Bill Bergson series (3)

Bill Bergson lives dangerously
Lindgren, Astrid
Bill Bergson series (2)

Bill Bergson, master detective
Lindgren, Astrid
Bill Bergson series (1)

Bill Bolton and hidden danger
Sainsbury, Noel
Bill Bolton series (3)

Bill Bolton and the flying fish
Sainsbury, Noel
Bill Bolton series (2)

Bill Bolton and the winged cartwheels
Sainsbury, Noel
Bill Bolton series (4)

Bill Bolton, flying midshipman
Sainsbury, Noel
Bill Bolton series (1)

Bill Bruce and the pioneer aviators
Arnold, Henry
Bill Bruce series (1)

Bill Bruce and the Trans-continental Race
Arnold, Henry
Bill Bruce series (5)

Bill Bruce becomes an ace
Arnold, Henry
Bill Bruce series (3)

Bill Bruce on forest patrol
Arnold, Henry
Bill Bruce series (6)

Bill Bruce on the Border Patrol
Arnold, Henry
Bill Bruce series (4)

Bill Bruce, the flying cadet
Arnold, Henry
Bill Bruce series (2)

Bill for damages
Easton, Nat
Bill Banning series (3)

Bill for the use of a body
Wheatley, Dennis
Julian Day series (3)

Bill Holmes and the fortune-teller
Hughes, Gwilym Fielden
Bill Holmes series (3)

Bill Holmes and the red panthers
Hughes, Gwilym Fielden
Bill Holmes series (2)

Bill of Billabong
Bruce, Mary Grant
Billabong series (10)

Bill Severn's amazing magic
Severn, Bill
Magic series (16)

Bill Severn's best magic
Severn, Bill
Magic series (16)

Bill Severn's big book of close-up magic
Severn, Bill
Magic series (10)

Bill Severn's` guide to magic as a hobby
Severn, Bill
Magic series (11)

Bill Severn's impromptu magic
Severn, Bill
Magic series (14)

Bill Severn's Magic in mind
Severn, Bill
Magic series (15)

Bill Severn's magic trunk
Severn, Bill
Magic series (7)

Bill Severn's magic workshop
Severn, Bill
Magic series (8)

Bill Severn's money magic
Severn, Bill
Magic series (16)

Bill Speed on hot ice
Donovan, Jean Beradine
Bill Speed series (2)

Bill Speed, Special Squad
Donovan, Jean Beradine
Bill Speed series (3)

Bill, the galactic hero
Harrison, Harry
Bill, the galactic hero series (1)

Bill, the galactic hero on the planet of bottled brains
Harrison, Harry
Bill, the galactic hero series (2)

Bill, the galactic hero on the planet of tasteless pleasure
Harrison, Harry
Bill, the galactic hero series (3)

Bill, the galactic hero on the planet of ten thousand bars
Harrison, Harry
Bill, the galactic hero series (5)

Bill, the galactic hero on the planet of the hippies from hell
Harrison, Harry
Bill, the galactic hero series (6)

Bill, the galactic hero on the planet of the zombie vampires
Harrison, Harry
Bill, the galactic hero series (4)

Bill, the galactic hero on the planet of tobot slaves
Harrison, Harry
Bill, the galactic hero series (1)

Billa, the wombat who had a bad dream
Rees, Leslie
Australian nature tales series (12)

Billabong adventurers
Bruce, Mary Grant
Billabong series (9)

Billabong gold
Bruce, Mary Grant
Billabong series (13)

Billabong riders
Bruce, Mary Grant
Billabong series (15)

Billabong's daughter
Bruce, Mary Grant
Billabong series (8)

Billabong's luck
Bruce, Mary Grant
Billabong series (11)

Billiard-room mystery
Flynn, Brian
Anthony Bathurst series (1)

Billie Bradley and her classmates
Wheeler, Janet D
Billie Bradley series (4)

Billie Bradley and her inheritance
Wheeler, Janet D
Billie Bradley series (1)

Billie Bradley and the school mystery
Wheeler, Janet D
Billie Bradley series (8)

Billie Bradley at Sun Dial Lodge
Wheeler, Janet D
Billie Bradley series (7)

Billie Bradley at Three Towers Hall
Wheeler, Janet D
Billie Bradley series (2)

Billie Bradley at Treasure Cove
Wheeler, Janet D
Billie Bradley series (6)

Billie Bradley at Twin Lakes
Wheeler, Janet D
Billie Bradley series (5)
Billie Bradley on Lighthouse Island
Wheeler, Janet D
Billie Bradley series (3)
Billie Bradley winning the trophy
Wheeler, Janet D
Billie Bradley series (9)
Billie Impett and Doris
Ainsworth, Eustace
Billie Impett series (2)
Billingsgate shoal
Boyer, Richard Lewis
Doctor Charlie Adams series (1)
Billion dollar body
Shallit, Joseph
Dan Morrison series (1)
Billion-dollar brain
Deighton, Len
Secret file series (4)
Billion dollar death
Nazel, Joseph
Iceman series (1)
Billion dollar ransom
Dixon, Franklin W
Hardy boys series (73)
Billion dollar snatch
Conway, Troy
Coxeman series (3)
Billion for Boris
Rodgers, Mary
Annabel Andrews series (2)
Billionaire mission
Rosenberger, Joseph
Death Merchant series (8)
Billy and Blaze
Anderson, Clarence William
Billy and Blaze series (1)
Billy and the major
Sampson, Emma
Miss Minerva series (1)
Billy Blackberry
Reed, Giles
Munch Bunch character series (3)
Billy Blackberry's secret tunnel
Reed, Giles
Munch Bunch story books series (7)
Billy Brown makes something grand
Kitt, Tamara
Billy Brown series (2)
Billy Brown, the baby sitter
Kitt, Tamara
Billy Brown series (3)
Billy Bunter afloat
Richards, Frank
Billy Bunter series (20)
Billy Bunter among the cannibals
Richards, Frank
Billy Bunter series (6)
Billy Bunter and the bank robber
Richards, Frank
Billy Bunter series (47)
Billy Bunter and the blue Mauritius
Richards, Frank
Billy Bunter series (10)
Billy Bunter and the crooked captain
Richards, Frank
Billy Bunter series (49)
Billy Bunter and the man from South America
Richards, Frank
Billy Bunter series (43)
Billy Bunter and the school rebellion
Richards, Frank
Billy Bunter series (44)
Billy Bunter and the secret enemy
Richards, Frank
Billy Bunter series (45)
Billy Bunter at Butlin's
Richards, Frank
Billy Bunter series (28)
Billy Bunter butts in
Richards, Frank
Billy Bunter series (8)
Billy Bunter comes for Christmas
Richards, Frank
Billy Bunter series (24)
Billy Bunter does his best
Richards, Frank
Billy Bunter series (15)
Billy Bunter in Brazil
Richards, Frank
Billy Bunter series (4)
Billy Bunter of Greyfriars School
Richards, Frank
Billy Bunter series (1)
Billy Bunter, sportsman
Richards, Frank
Billy Bunter series (48)
Billy Bunter the bold
Richards, Frank
Billy Bunter series (14)
Billy Bunter the hiker
Richards, Frank
Billy Bunter series (22)
Billy Bunter's banknote
Richards, Frank
Billy Bunter series (3)
Billy Bunter's bargain
Richards, Frank
Billy Bunter series (23)
Billy Bunter's barring-out
Richards, Frank
Billy Bunter series (2)
Billy Bunter's beanfeast
Richards, Frank
Billy Bunter series (11)
Billy Bunter's benefit
Richards, Frank
Billy Bunter series (7)
Billy Bunter's big top
Richards, Frank
Billy Bunter series (46)
Billy Bunter's bodyguard
Richards, Frank
Billy Bunter series (31)
Billy Bunter's bolt
Richards, Frank
Billy Bunter series (21)
Billy Bunter's brainwave
Richards, Frank
Billy Bunter series (12)
Billy Bunter's Christmas party
Richards, Frank
Billy Bunter series (5)
Billy Bunter's convict
Richards, Frank
Billy Bunter series (50)
Billy Bunter's double
Richards, Frank
Billy Bunter series (17)
Billy Bunter's first case
Richards, Frank
Billy Bunter series (13)
Billy Bunter's own
Richards, Frank
Billy Bunter series (50)
Billy Bunter's postal order
Richards, Frank
Billy Bunter series (9)
Billy Bunter's treasure-hunt
Richards, Frank
Billy Bunter series (29)
Billy Burns of Troop Five
Thurston, Ida Treadwell
Troop Five series (2)
Billy Cantrell case
Waugh, Hillary
Simon Kaye series (3)
Billy Goats Gruff
Cosgrove, Stephen Edward
DreamMaker series (2)
Billy Grime's favourite
Mannering, May
Climbing the rope series (2)
Billy had a system
Holland, Marion
Billy series (1)
Billy Hull, R.I.P.
Grover, Marshall
Larry and Stretch series (332)
Billy Jack
Christina, Frank
Billy Jack series (1)
Billy Jack goes to Washington
Christina, Frank
Billy Jack series (3)
Billy Liar
Waterhouse, Keith
Billy Liar series (1)
Billy Liar on the moon
Waterhouse, Keith
Billy Liar series (2)
Billy Mink
Burgess, Thornton Waldo
Smiling Pool series (1)
Billy Phelan's greatest game
Kennedy, William
Albany series (3)
Phelan family series (1)
Billy Ray and the good news
Roderus, Frank
Billy Ray series (1)
Billy Ray's forty days
Roderus, Frank
Billy Ray series (2)
Billy Smith exploring Ace
Sainsbury, Noel
Billy Smith series (1)
Billy Smith, mystery ace
Sainsbury, Noel
Billy Smith series (3)
Billy Smith, secret service ace
Sainsbury, Noel
Billy Smith series (2)
Billy Smith shangaied ace
Sainsbury, Noel
Billy Smith series (5)
Billy Smith, trail eater ace
Sainsbury, Noel
Billy Smith series (4)
Billy the Kid
McLaglen, John J
Herne the Hunter series (13)
Billy the squirrel
Evens, George Bramwell
Romany readers series (6)
Billy Topsail and company
Duncan, Norman
Doctor Luke series (3)
Billy Topsail, M.D.
Duncan, Norman
Doctor Luke series (4)
Billy's clubhouse
Holland, Marion
Billy series (2)
Billy's mistake
Reeder, Colin
West Meadow series (3)
Biltmore call
Van Siller, Hilda
Allan Stewart series (3)
Bim, the very special bear
Lindsay, Frances
Bim series (2)
Bimbo and Blackie
Blyton, Enid
Bimbo series (4)
Bimbo and Blackie go camping
Blyton, Enid
Bimbo series (5)
Bimbo and his cousin
Blyton, Enid
Bimbo series (3)
Bimbo and Topsy
Blyton, Enid
Bimbo series (1)
Bimbo heaven
Albert, Marvin Hubert
Pierre-Ange Sawyer series (7)
Bimbo, the little kitten
Blyton, Enid
Bimbo series (2)
Binding ties
Adler, Carole Schwerdtfeger
Footsteps series (2)
Bindle
Jenkins, Herbert
Bindle series (1)
Bindles on the rocks
Jenkins, Herbert
Bindle series (5)
Bindlestiff
Pronzini, Bill
Private Eye series (11)
Bingo, Boggart and the furry cubs
Roberts, K H
Bingo Bones and the Boggart series (2)
Bingo Bones and the Boggart
Roberts, K H
Bingo Bones and the Boggart series (1)
Bingo Brown and the language of love
Byars, Betsy
Bingo Brown series (2)
Bingo Brown, gypsy lover
Byars, Betsy
Bingo Brown series (3)
Bingo palace
Erdrich, Louise
Argus series (4)
Binklebys at home
Williams, Ursula Moray
Binklebys series (1)
Binklebys on the farm
Williams, Ursula Moray
Binklebys series (2)
Binks family
Winter, John Strange
Binks family series (1)
Bio blitz
Sugar, Andrew
Enforcer series (6)
Biofab war
Berry, Stephen Ames
John Harrison series (1)
Biography for beginners
Bentley, Edmund Clerihew
Clerihews series (1)
Biology and the social crisis
Brierley, John Keith
Human behaviour trilogy (1)
Bionic compounds
Stamper, Judith Bauer
Worlds of power series (6)
Bird Boys
Langworthy, John Luther
Bird Boys series (1)
Bird Boys' aeroplane wonder
Langworthy, John Luther
Bird Boys series (5)
Bird Boys among the clouds
Langworthy, John Luther
Bird Boys series (3)
Bird Boys' flight
Langworthy, John Luther
Bird Boys series (4)
Bird Boys on the wing
Langworthy, John Luther
Bird Boys series (2)
Bird flies blind
Stern, Rhona
South African series (2)
Bird in a guilt-edged cage
Brown, Carter
Andy Kane series (2)
Bird in the hand
Cleeves, Ann
George Palmer-Jones series (1)
Martin, Toy
Taronga Road Riders series (1)
Bird in the house
Laurence, Margaret
Manawaka series (4)
Bird in the net
Parrish, Frank
Dan Mallett series (7)
Bird in the tree
Goudge, Elizabeth
Eliot family trilogy (1)
Bird of time
Effinger, George Alec
Nick of time series (2)
Bird walking weather
Bagby, George
Inspector Schmidt series (5)
Birdcage
Canning, Victor
Birdcage trilogy (1)
Birdless summer
Han, Suyin
Crippled tree series (3)
Birds
Rippon, Angela
Learn with Victoria Plum series (1)
Birds at my feeder
Kalman, Bobbie
North American wildlife series (2)
Birds, beasts and relatives
Durrell, Gerald
Corfu series (2)
Birds began to sing
Tiltman, Marjorie Hessell
Country life trilogy (3)
Birds in a gilded cage
Glover, Judith
Sussex quartet (4)
Birds in your street
Simon, Seymour
Your street series (3)
Bird's nest
Savage, Deborah
Peregrine Piecrust series (2)
Birds of a bloodied feather
Tate, Richard
Marcus Obadiah series (3)
Birds of a feather
Bradley, Mary Emily Neely
Proverb trilogy (1)
Spiller, Andrew
Chief Inspector Duck Mallard series (11)
Tranter, Nigel Godwin
Ken and Fiona series (4)
Birds of a feather affair
Avallone, Michael
Girl from U.N.C.L.E.series (1)
Birds of coasts, lakes and rivers
Ardley, Neil
Birds series (3)
Birds of death
Robeson, Kenneth
Doc Savage series (161)
Birds of prey
Braddon, Mary Elizabeth
Valentine Hawkehurst series (1)
Carter, Nicholas
Nicholas Carter series (513)
Birds of the air
Salisbury, Ray
Simon series (3)
Birds of the country
Ardley, Neil
Birds series (2)
Birds of the Limberlost
Porter, Gene Stratton
Limberlost series (3)
Birds of towns
Ardley, Neil
Birds series (1)
Birds you should know
Burgess, Thornton Waldo
Wild flowers series (2)
Birdstones
Curry, Jane Louise
Abaloc series (6)
Apple Lock series (2)
Callie series (3)
Birdwatcher's quarry
Coles, Manning
Tommy Hambledon series (20)
Birdy and the group
Hildick, Edmund Wallace
Birdy Jones series (2)
Birdy in Amsterdam
Hildick, Edmund Wallace
Birdy Jones series (4)
Birdy Jones
Hildick, Edmund Wallace
Birdy Jones series (1)
Birdy Jones and the New York heads
Hildick, Edmund Wallace
Birdy Jones series (5)
Birdy swings north
Hildick, Edmund Wallace
Birdy Jones series (3)
Birth
Edwards, Gene
Chronicles of the door series (1)
Birth of a foal
Miller, Jane
Birth series (1)
Birth of a gunman
Rey, Bret
Ralph Coates series (1)
Birth of a nation
Dixon, Thomas
Clansman series (1)
Birth of a rocket
Bergaust, Erik
Rockets series (6)
Birth of Flux and Anchor
Chalker, Jack Laurence
Soul rider series (4)
Birth of our power
Serge, Victor
Revolution trilogy (2)
Birth of piglets
Miller, Jane
Birth series (4)
Birth of Rowland
Lutyens, Emily
Blessed girl series (2)
Birth of the Firebringer
Pierce, Meredith Ann
Firebringer trilogy (1)
Birth of the gods
Merejkowski, Dmitri Sergeevich
Dio series (1)
Birth of the republic
Carter, Alden Richardson
American Revolution series (4)
Birthday
Clewes, Dorothy
Penny series (4)
Birthday band
Korman, Justine
Crispy Critter series (2)
Birthday bunnies
Cartlidge, Michelle
Press and play series (1)
Birthday card, where are you?
Ziefert, Harriet
Where is it series (1)
Birthday, deathday
Pentecost, Hugh
Pierre Chambrun series (8)
Birthday for Frances
Hoban, Russell
Frances series (4)
Birthday gifts, and other stories
Cole, George Douglas Howard
Superintendent Henry Wilson series (27)
Birthday girl
Rush, Robert
Birthday series (1)
Birthday magic
Baker, James Webb
Magic series (1)
Birthday murder
Lewis, Lange
Lieutenant Richard Tuck series (4)
Sproul, Kathleen
Dick Wilson series (1)

Birthday party
Berridge, Celia
Stepping stones 1 2 3 series (5)
Costa, Nicoletta
Molly and Tom series (4)
Dowling, Patrick
Amazing adventures of Morph series (3)
Howson, John Michael
Adventure Island story books (2)
Markham, Marion M
Dixon twins series (4)
Newsham, Wendy
Dynamite twins series (2)
Optic, Oliver
Flora Lee series (6)
Riverdale series (6)
Oxenbury, Helen
First picture books series (1)
Salmon, Michael
Alexander Bunyip series (9)
Birthday picnic
Pilgrim, Jane
Blackberry Farm series (12)
Birthday races
Berg, Leila
Snaps series (3)
Birthday treat
Rush, Robert
Birthday series (2)
Birthday unicorn
Elliott, Janice
Alexander Columbus Banyana series (1)
Birthgrave
Lee, Tanith
Birthgrave trilogy (1)
Birthright
Matthews, Clayton
Moraghan family trilogy (1)
Robinson, Nigel
Timewyrm series (6)
Wall, Robert Emmet
Nowell family series (3)
Bishop
Marshall, Bruce
Vicar of Christ tetralogy (1)
Bishop as pawn
Kienzle, William Xavier
Father Robert Koesler series (16)
McInerny, Ralph
Father Roger Dowling series (3)
Bishop in check
Rattray, Simon
Hugo Bishop series (3)
Bishop in the back seat
Watson, Clarissa
Persis Willum series (2)
Bishop murder case
Van Dine, S S
Philo Vance series (4)
Bishop of Kenelminster
Hope-Simpson, Jacynth
Bishop of Kenelminster series (1)
Bishop's cap
Linklater, Joseph Lane
Silas Booth series (3)
Bishop's cap murder
Linklater, Joseph Lane
Silas Booth series (3)
Bishop's crime
Bailey, Henry Christopher
Mister Reggie Fortune series (16)
Bishop's heir
Kurtz, Katherine
Histories of King Kelson trilogy (1)
Bishop's pawn
Perry, Ritchie
Philis series (9)
Bishop's picture
Hope-Simpson, Jacynth
Bishop of Kenelminster series (2)
Bishop's shadow
Thurston, Ida Treadwell
Theodore Bryan series (1)
Bishop's sword
Berrow, Norman
Inspector Lancelot Carolus Smith series (2)
Bishop's wife
Nathan, Robert
Barly fields series (3)
Bismarck Herrings
Torrie, Malcolm
Timothy Herring series (6)
Bison and the Great Plains
Taylor, Dave
Animals and their ecosystems series (3)
Bit of a do
Pratt, Henry
Do series (1)
Bite of an apple, and other stories
Carter, Nicholas
Nicholas Carter series (33)
Bite of death
Conant, Susan
Dog trainer mystery series (3)
Bite of the leech
Mackenzie, William Andrew
Sir Nigel Lacaita series (4)
Bite the hand
Fenisong, Ruth
Captain Gridley Nelson series (10)
Biting fortune
Mills, Woosnam
John Melrose series (4)
Bits and pieces
Masterman, John Cecil
Ernst Brendel series (2)
Bits and Pieces and the smugglers
Lindsay, Frances
Mister Bits and Pieces series (3)
Bits and Pieces solves a mystery
Lindsay, Frances
Mister Bits and Pieces series (2)
Bitter blood
Siegel, Scott
Warhunter series (4)
Bitter chalice
Seymour, Arabella
Jane Beaufort series (2)
Bitter ending
Irving, Alexander
Doctor Anthony Post series (1)
Bitter finish
Barnes, Linda
Michael Spraggue series (2)
Bitter gold hearts
Cook, Glen
Garrett series (2)
Bitter harvest
Haggard, William
Colonel Charles Russell series (14)
Bitter herb
Heath-Miller, Mavis
Raines of Rayleigh series (4)
Bitter herbs
Cooper, Natasha
Willow King series (4)
Bitter homicide
Warden, Mike
Hank Bradford series (2)
Bitter legacy
Blake, M Glaiser
Ayesthorpe trilogy (3)
Fuller, Kathleen
Riverview trilogy (1)
Miles, Rosalind
Eden series (2)
Bitter Lemon mob
Urquhart, Macgregor
Chief Inspector Joshua Smarles series (7)
Bitter lemons
Durrell, Lawrence
Island series (3)
Bitter medicine
Paretsky, Sara
V I Warshawski series (4)
Bitter monsoon
James, Stefan
Monsoon trilogy (1)
Moxon, Oliver
Monsoon trilogy (1)
Bitter path of death
Audemars, Pierre
Monsieur Pinaud series (25)
Bitter recoil
Havill, Steven F
Bill Gastner series (2)
Bitter rivals
Pascal, Francine
Sweet Valley High series (29)
Bitter rubies
Storm, Joan
Sarah Vanessa series (2)
Bitter sage
Gruber, Frank
Historical Western series (9)
Bitter shield
Adair, Denis
MacLeod family series (2)
Bitter spring
Angoff, Charles
Polonsky family series (5)
Bitter summer
Brooke, Carol
Marshall family series (3)
Bitter tea
Black, Gavin
Paul Harris series (9)
Bitter victory
Drury, Rebecca
Women of war series (9)
Bitterroot
Wheeler, Richard Seabrook
Skye's West series (5)
Bittersweet ecstasy
Taylor, Janelle
Sioux series (8)
Bivouac and battle
Optic, Oliver
Onward and upward series (5)
Bizarre hockey tournament
Jenkins, Jerry Bruce
Dallas O'Neil and the Baker Street Sports Club series (5)
Bizarre murders
Queen, Ellery
Ellery Queen series (44)
Blabber mouth
Gleitzman, Morris
Rowena Batts series (1)
Black account
Jordan, David
Tom Kane and Condon series (2)
Black ace
Dilnot, George
Inspector Strickland series (2)
Sexton Blake series (946)
Black agent
Flynn, Brian
Anthony Bathurst series (37)
Black alchemists
Wilson, Gar
Phoenix Force series (12)
Black Amos
Hanson, Victor Joseph
Amos Crowle series (10)
Black Amos, lawbringer
Hanson, Victor Joseph
Amos Crowle series (11)
Black and the red
Paul, Elliot
Homer Evans series (9)
Black and white keys
Hood, Hugh
New age series (4)
Black Apache
Fisher, Clay
Franciscan prient series (2)
Black Arab
Halstead, John
Inspector Todd series (2)
Black arrows
Beeding, Francis
Colonel Alastair Granby series (12)
Black as death
Gilman, George G
Undertaker series (1)
Black as he's painted
Marsh, Ngaio
Inspector Roderick Alleyn series (28)
Black attendant
McCutcheon, Hugh
Jimmy Carroll series (2)
Black August
Wheatley, Dennis
Gregory Sallust series (2)
Black aura
Sladek, John Thomas
Thackeray Phin series (1)
Black Banner abroad
Trease, Geoffrey
Bannermere series (4)
Black Banner players
Trease, Geoffrey
Bannermere series (3)
Black Barney
Tufts, Warren
Casey Ruggles series (2)
Black baron
Dever, Joe
Combat heroes series (2)
White warlord series (2)
Black baroness
Wheatley, Dennis
Gregory Sallust series (5)
Black Bartlemy's treasure
Farnol, Jeffery
Martin Conisby series (1)
Black bat
Murray, Andrew
Sexton Blake series (42)
Black Bat and the Dragon Trail
Jones, G Wayman
Black Bat series (10)
Black Bat and the Red Menace
Jones, G Wayman
Black Bat series (12)
Black Bat and the Trojan horse
Jones, G Wayman
Black Bat series (9)
Black Bat fights for life
Jones, G Wayman
Black Bat series (33)
Black Bat strikes again
Jones, G Wayman
Black Bat series (3)
Black Bat's challenge
Jones, G Wayman
Black Bat series (4)
Black Bat's crusade
Jones, G Wayman
Black Bat series (6)
Black Bat's flame trail
Jones, G Wayman
Black Bat series (7)
Black Bat's invisible enemy
Jones, G Wayman
Black Bat series (13)
Black Bat's justice
Jones, G Wayman
Black Bat series (11)
Black Bat's spy trail
Jones, G Wayman
Black Bat series (5)
Black Bat's triumph
Jones, G Wayman
Black Bat series (8)
Black beadle
Lorac, E C R
Inspector Macdonald series (16)
Black bear twins
Tompkins, Jane
Animal twins series (7)
Black beast
Springer, Nancy
Book of Isle series (4)
Black Beauty, his grooms and companions
Sewell, Anna
Black Beauty series (1)
Black Beauty's clan
Pullein-Thompson, Christine
Black Beauty series (3)
Pullein-Thompson, Josephine
Black Beauty series (3)
Black Beauty's family, book 1
Pullein-Thompson, Christine
Black Beauty series (4)
Black Beauty's family, book 2
Pullein-Thompson, Christine
Black Beauty series (5)
Black beret
Fry, Pete
Pete Fry series (4)
Black Berets
McCray, Mike
Black Berets series (13)
Black Betty
Mosley, Walter
Ezekiel Rawlins series (4)
Black, black witch
Robeson, Kenneth
Doc Savage series (108)
Black blood
Hart, Jon
Mercenaries series (1)
Black book
Bronson-Howard, George
Yorke Norroy series (3)
Black boomerang
Delmer, Sefton
Trail sinister series (2)
Black box
Jacobs, Thomas Curtis Hicks
Chief Inspector Barnard series (12)
Black boy
Wright, Richard Nathaniel
Horror and the glory series (1)
Black Bramble Wood
Kaye, Mollie
Potter Pinner series (2)
Black brute
Tralins, Sandor Robert
Black stud trilogy (1)
Black bullets
Holt, Gavin
Professor Luther Bastion series (15)
Black bulls
Benteen, John
Neal Fargo series (10)
Black burying
Carstairs, Henry
Lydford Long series (3)
Black butterfly
Mackenzie, William Andrew
Sir Nigel Lacaita series (3)
Black buttes
Mulford, Clarence Edward
Wyatt Duncan series (1)
Black camel
Biggers, Earl Derr
Charlie Chan series (4)
Black cameo
Baker, Donna
Glassmakers series (2)
Black cap
Evans, Gwyn
Sexton Blake series (800)
Black cap for murder
Spiller, Andrew
Chief Inspector Duck Mallard series (22)
Black cap murder
Gunn, Victor
Chief Inspector Bill Cromwell series (41)
Black cargo
Graydon, William Murray
Sexton Blake series (382)
Black casket
Powell, Lester
Philip Odell series (5)
Black castle
Daniels, Les
Don Sebastien series (1)
Black cat
Ahlberg, Allan
Funnybones series (1)
Tracy, Louis
Inspector Furneaux series (9)
Black cats are lucky
Fielding, A
Inspector Pointer series (22)
Black cat's clue
Sutton, Margaret
Judy Bolton series (23)
Black cauldron
Alexander, Lloyd
Prydain series (2)
Black champagne
Mair, George Brown
David Grant series (6)
Black charade
Burke, John Frederick
Doctor Alexander Caspian series (2)
Black chariots
Robeson, Kenneth
Avenger series (30)
Black cherry blues
Burke, James Lee
Dave Robicheaux series (3)
Black chronicle
Hayes, William Edward
Arthur Halstead series (3)
Black chrysanthemum
Murray, Andrew
Sexton Blake series (18)
Black circle
Grant, Maxwell
Shadow series (279)
Scott, Mansfield
Inspector Malcome Steele series (2)
Black cloud, white cloud
Douglas, Ellen
Homochito County series (2)
Black cockade
Suthren, Victor
Paul Gallant series (1)
Black coffin
Reno, Bill
Badge series (3)
Black Company
Cook, Glen
Chronicles of the Black Company series (1)
Black cop
Gober, Don
James Rhodes series (1)
Black Cossacks
Kessler, Leo
Black Cossacks series (1)
Black cotton gloves
Fry, Pete
Pete Fry series (15)
Black cow summer
Graber, Richard
Ray Decker series (3)
Black cypress
Crane, Frances
Pat and Jean Abbott series (11)
Black dagger
Brooks, Edwy Searles
Sexton Blake series (751)
Black dahlia
Ellroy, James
Los Angeles quartet (1)
Black dawn
Nicole, Christopher
West Indies series (4)

Black death
Adams, Herbert
Major Roger Bennion series (7)
Birt, David
Middle Ages series (12)
Carter, Nick
Nick Carter series (56)
Gilbert, Anthony
Arthur Crook series (26)
Robeson, Kenneth
Avenger series (22)
Black devil
Jacobs, Thomas Curtis Hicks
Temple Fortune series (20)
Black diamond
Young, Francis Brett
Welsh series (2)
Black dice
Pendleton, Don
Mack Bolan series (98)
Black dog mystery
Queen, Ellery, Junior
Djuna and Champ series (1)
Black doll
Hayes, William Edward
Arthur Halstead series (1)
Black door
Wilcox, Collin
Stephen Drake series (1)
Black Dougal
Walker, David Harry
Dougal Trocher series (2)
Black Douglas
Crockett, Samuel Rutherford
Douglas series (1)
Black dragon
Appleton, Victor II
Tom Swift Junior series 3 (1)
Grant, Maxwell
Shadow series (239)
Silverman, Deborah
Shogun series (2)
Walsh, James Morgan
Oliver Keene series (2)
Black dreams
Green, Kate
Theresa Fortunato series (2)
Black Dudley murder
Allingham, Margery
Albert Campion series (1)
Black Duke
Dexter, Ross
Duke Lawson series (1)
Black dwarf
Scott, Walter
Tales of my landlord series (6)
Black eagle
Teed, George Hamilton
Sexton Blake series (399)
Black eagle mystery
Bonner, Geraldine
Molly Morganthau series (2)
Black Easter
Blish, James
After such knowledge series (2)
Black Ebony
Pullein-Thompson, Christine
Black Beauty series (3)
Pullein-Thompson, Josephine
Black Beauty series (3)
Black echo
Connelly, Michael
Harry Bosch series (1)
Black edged
Flynn, Brian
Anthony Bathurst series (23)
Black emperor
Gerard, Francis
Sir John Meredith series (3)
Hawton, Hector
Colonel Max Masterson series (3)
Teed, George Hamilton
Sexton Blake series (451)
Black envelope
Frome, David
Evan Pinkerton series (9)
Black falcon
Grant, Maxwell
Shadow series (47)
Black fear
Halstead, John
Inspector Todd series (4)
Black fire
Cooper, Sonni
Star trek series (8)
Black flag
Romains, Jules
Men of goodwill series (14)
Black flame
Abbey, Lynn
Rifkind series (2)
Du Bois, William Edward Burghardt
Black flame trilogy (3)
Halstead, John
Inspector Todd series (5)
Black fog
Dutton, Charles Judson
Harley Manners series (6)
Black for the Baron
Morton, Anthony
Baron series (31)
Black Gang
Sapper
Bulldog Drummond series (2)
Black gardenia
Paul, Elliot
Homer Evans series (7)
Black genesis, fortress of evil
Hubbard, Lafayette Ronald
Mission earth series (2)
Black ghost
Newton, David C
Bunst series (1)
Black girl, white girl
Moyes, Patricia
Henry and Emmy Tibbett series (18)
Black glass city
Philips, Judson Pentecost
Peter Styles series (2)
Black gold
Bourne, Peter
Henri Christophe series (2)
Cole, Jackson
Jim Hatfield series (1)
Cox, William Robert
Bonanza series (3)
Gower, Iris
Copper kingdom series (6)
Kenyon, Paul
Baroness Penelope Saint-John Orsini series (8)
Black gold briefing
Buck, Peter
Marc Dean series (7)
Black gold murders
Ethan, John B
Victor Grant series (1)
Black gold of Malverde
Graves, Richard Latshaw
Hugo Wolfram series (1)
Black grail
Broderick, Damien
Faustus hexagram series (2)
Black hand
Reeve, Arthur Benjamin
Craig Kennedy series (1)
Black harvest
Cheetham, Ann
Black harvest series (1)
Black hat riders
Cole, Jackson
Jim Hatfield series (51)
Black hate
Halstead, John
Inspector Todd series (6)
Black Hawk's warpath
Risteen, H L
Red Indian series (4)
Black Heart Crowle
Hanson, Victor Joseph
Amos Crowle series (1)
Black Heart's bunch
Hanson, Victor Joseph
Amos Crowle series (6)
Black hearts in Battersea
Aiken, Joan
Dido Twite series (2)
Black hearts murder
Queen, Ellery
Mike McCall series (2)
Black highway
Chance, John Newton
Mister DeHavilland series (6)
Black-Hill murder case
Hardinge, Rex
Sexton Blake series (759)
Black Hills blood
Sharpe, Jon
Trailsman series (105)
Black Hills duel
Rountree, Owen
Jim Cord series (3)
Black Hills showdown
Hardin, J D
Raider and Doc series (69)
Black Hills trackdown
Hardin, J D
Raider series (20)
Black Hogan strikes again
Renwick, Peter
Leatherface Lonergan series (2)
Black holes and Uncle Albert
Stannard, Russell
Uncle Albert series (2)
Black holes, white dwarfs and superstars
Branley, Franklyn Mansfield
Exploring our universe series (7)
Black honey
Saxon, Peter
Sexton Blake series (1608)
Black hornet
Sallis, James
Lew Griffin series (3)
Black house in Harley Street
Fletcher, Joseph Smith
Richard Goulburn series (2)
Black hunter
Curwood, James Oliver
Quebec series (1)
Black hunting whip
Edwards, Monica
Punchbowl Farm series (2)
Black hush
Grant, Maxwell
Shadow series (35)
Black ice
Connelly, Michael
Harry Bosch series (2)
Black ice score
Stark, Richard
Parker series (11)
Black Invaders versus the Battle Birds
Bowen, Robert Sidney
Dusty Ayres and his Battle Birds series (5)
Black is beautiful
Johnson, B B
Superspade series (2)
Black is black
Nazel, Joseph
Black series (2)
Black is the colour of my true love's heart
Peters, Ellis
Inspector George Felse series (6)
Black island
Herge
Tintin series (7)
Black Italian
Jepson, Selwyn
Eve Gill series (4)
Black ivory
Duff, Douglas Valder
Adam Macadam series (5)
Rockman, Clint
Sable ivory series (3)
Black Jack
McClung, Robert Marshall
Endangered animals series (3)
Black jade road
Grant, Kathryn
Land of ten thousand willows trilogy (2)
Black John of Halfaday Creek
Hendryx, James Beardsley
Black John series (3)
Black joss
Brandon, John Gordon
Inspector Patrick Aloysius McCarthy series (2)
Black Judas
Wilkinson, Burke
Geoffrey Mildmay series (2)
Black key
Michel, Milton Scott
Doctor Alexander Cornell series (1)
Black Knight of the Iron Sphere
Smith, Edward Elmer
Lord Tedric series (3)
Black knights
Kessler, Leo
SS Stuka Squadron series (1)
Black Knights
Smith, Guy Newman
Truckers series (1)
Black lace blackmail
McCall, K T
Johnny Buchanan series (17)
Black lace hangover
Brown, Carter
Danny Boyd series (15)
Black land, white land
Bailey, Henry Christopher
Mister Reggie Fortune series (12)
Black laurel
Jameson, Storm
Renn series (2)
Black leather case
Cronin, Michael
Sam Harris series (3)
Black legion of Callisto
Carter, Lin
Jandar the Alien series (2)
Black lightning
Bowen, Robert Sidney
Dusty Ayres and his Battle Birds series (1)
Black limousine
Sayer, Walter William
Sexton Blake series (449)
Black Lion Inn
Lewis, Alfred Henry
Wolfville series (5)
Black magic
King, T Stanleyan
Scarsdale Waring series (1)
Black magic at Brillstone
Heide, Florence Parry
Brillstone Apartments series (5)
Black magic in New York
De Villiers, Gerard
Malko Linge series (2)
Black magician
Barker, Wade
Ninja Master series (5)
Edmondson, Garry Cotton
Cunningham trilogy (2)
Scott, Reginald Thomas Maitland
Aurelius Smith series (2)
Black mail
Disney, Doris Miles
David Madden series (2)
Black man's country
Ryan, Isobel
Black man trilogy (1)
Black man's palaver
Ryan, Isobel
Black man trilogy (3)
Black man's town
Ryan, Isobel
Black man trilogy (2)
Black Maria, M.A.
Slate, John
Black Maria series (1)
Black Maria mystery
Bayfield, William John
Sexton Blake series (556)
Black market
Daniel, Roland
Buddy Mustard series (2)
Newman, Bernard
Papa Pontivy series (6)
Zlotnik, Donald E
Survivors of Nam series (3)
Black market Green
Kaye, Barbara
Gorsefield Green series (1)
Black Marsden
Harris, Wilson
Black Marsden series (1)
Civilizations quartet (1)
Black Martinmas
Leith, Mary Charlotte Julia
Lachlan series (1)
Black mask
Hornung, Ernest William
Raffles series (2)
Black Mask trick
Corbett, Scott
Kerby Maxwell series (11)
Black massacre
Derrick, Lionel
Penetrator series (35)
Black master
Grant, Maxwell
Shadow series (8)
Black Mercedes
Boshell, Gordon
Secret Guardians series (1)
Black mischief
Waugh, Evelyn
Basil Seal series (1)
Black money
Macdonald, Ross
Lew Archer series (14)
Black moon
Drake, Alison
Tango Key series (3)
Dunn, Saul
Cabal series (2)
Graham, Winston
Poldark series (5)
Black mountain
Stout, Rex
Nero Wolfe and Archie Goodwin series (24)
Black Mountain mystery
Beresford, Elisabeth
Gappy, Jim and Jane series (10)
Black mountains
Saberhagen, Fred
Chup trilogy (2)
Tanner, Janet
Hillsbridge series (1)
Black Nat
Halstead, John
Inspector Todd series (1)
Black night in Red Square
Kaminsky, Stuart Melvin
Inspector Porfiry Petrovich Rostnikov series (2)
Black night murders
Wells, Carolyn
Fleming Stone series (58)
Black opal
Linklater, Joseph Lane
Silas Booth series (2)
Black opal mine
Murray, Andrew
Sexton Blake series (187)
Black orchid
Dudley, Terence
Doctor Who series (113)
Black orchids
Stout, Rex
Nero Wolfe and Archie Goodwin series (9)
Black-out crime
Chester, Gilbert
Sexton Blake series (1029)
Black palm
McCray, Mike
Black Berets series (3)
Black pawn
Norman, Bruce
James Mallaby series (2)
Black pearl
Harrod-Eagles, Cynthia
Morland family series (5)
O'Donnell, Peter
Modesty Blaise comic strip series (1)
Black Pearl Saloon
Roberts, J R
Gunsmith series (36)
Black pearls
Gregg, Cecil Freeman
Inspector Cuthbert Higgins series (12)
Kerr, Robert
Jamie Stuart series (2)
Black peril
Johns, William Earl
Biggles series (6)
Black phantom
Stillman, Ron
Tracker series (4)
Black pigeon
Austin, Anne
James F Dundee series (1)
Pullen, Alan
Sam and Lin series (4)
Black plumes
Allingham, Margery
Albert Campion series (12)
Black pope
Ramsay, Mark
Falcon trilogy (2)
Black powder justice
Thompson, David
Nathaniel King series (6)
Black Prince
Birt, David
Middle Ages series (11)
Black Princess
Pullein-Thompson, Christine
Black Beauty series (3)
Pullein-Thompson, Josephine
Black Beauty series (3)
Black pyramid
Tant, David
Legends of Skyfall series (2)
Black queen
Rockman, Clint
Sable ivory series (1)
Black rainbow
Michaels, Barbara
Greyhaven Manor series (1)
Black rat
Plummer, Thomas Arthur
Detective Inspector Andrew Frampton series (40)
Black renegade
Faralla, Dana
Magnificent barb series (2)
Black ribbon murders
Plummer, Thomas Arthur
Detective Inspector Andrew Frampton series (13)

Black rider
Shappiro, Herbert
Mustang Marshal series (1)

Black Riders
Needham, Violet
Stormy Petrel series (1)

Black River affair
Devine, Raynard
Flesh traders series (2)

Black River breed
Devine, Raynard
Flesh traders series (3)

Black road war
Randall, Neil
Combat Command series (6)

Black Road war
Randall, Neil
Kingdom of Amber series (1)

Black rose murder
McGuire, Paul
Chief Inspector Cummings series (1)
Inspector Wittler series (1)

Black saga
Bourne, Peter
Henri Christophe series (1)
Stewart family series (1)

Black Sambo affair
Gielgud, Val
Inspector Gregory Pellew and Viscount Clymping series (9)

Black Samurai
Olden, Marc
Robert Sand series (1)

Black satchel
Keeler, Harry Stephen
Tuddleton Trotter series (1)

Black Sea bloodbath
Carter, Nick
Nick Carter series (244)

Black Sea caper
Moore, Robin
Connection series (7)

Black Sea connection
Moore, Robin
Connection series (7)

Black Sea frigate
Stuart, Vivian
Commander Philip Hazard series (2)

Black seven
Kendall, Carol
Kendall series (1)

Black sheep of Sparshott
Richards, Frank
Schoolboy series (2)

Black sheep, run
Spicer, Bart
Carney Wilde series (4)

black shields
Roberts, John Maddox
Stromlands series (2)

Black ship
Rowley, Christopher
Fenrile trilogy (2)

Black shrouds the bride
Larbalestier, Philip George
Inspector Michael Farrant series (2)

Black skull
Verner, Gerald
Sexton Blake series (585)

Black slaver
Rockman, Clint
Sable ivory series (2)

Black Smith's telling
Sampson, Fay
Daughter of Tintagel series (3)

Black sombrero mystery
Pink, Hal
Inspector Docker series (3)

Black sorcerer of the Black Castle
Offutt, Andrew Jefferson
Conan series (69)

Black spectacles
Carr, John Dickson
Doctor Gideon Fell series (10)

Black spider
Creasey, John
Department Z series (29)
Cross, Mark
Daphne Wrayne and her Four Adjusters series (30)

Black spot
Robeson, Kenneth
Doc Savage series (76)

Black spot mystery
Soutar, Andrew
Phineas Spinnet series (6)

Black spring
Miller, Henry
Tropics series (2)

Black stage
Gilbert, Anthony
Arthur Crook series (16)

Black stallion
Farley, Walter
Black stallion series (1)

Black stallion and Flame
Farley, Walter
Black stallion series (15)

Black stallion and Satan
Farley, Walter
Black stallion series (5)

Black stallion and the girl
Farley, Walter
Black stallion series (19)

Black stallion challenged
Farley, Walter
Black stallion series (17)

Black stallion legend
Farley, Walter
Black stallion series (20)

Black stallion mesa
Hobart, Donald Bayne
Masked Rider and Blue Hawk series (15)

Black stallion picture book
Farley, Walter
Black stallion series (1)

Black stallion returns
Farley, Walter
Black stallion series (2)

Black stallion revolts
Farley, Walter
Black stallion series (9)

Black stallion's challenge
Farley, Walter
Black stallion series (17)

Black stallion's courage
Farley, Walter
Black stallion series (12)

Black stallion's filly
Farley, Walter
Black stallion series (8)

Black stallion's ghost
Farley, Walter
Black stallion series (18)

Black stallion's mystery
Farley, Walter
Black stallion series (13)

Black stallion's sulky colt
Farley, Walter
Black stallion series (10)

Black stamp
Scott, Will
Disher series (1)

Black Star
McCulley, Johnston
Black Star series (1)

Black Star again
McCulley, Johnston
Black Star series (4)

Black star passes
Campbell, John Wood
Arcot, Morey and Wade series (1)

Black Star's campaign
McCulley, Johnston
Black Star series (2)

Black Star's return
McCulley, Johnston
Black Star series (3)

Black Star's revenge
McCulley, Johnston
Black Star series (4)

Black steel
Perry, Steve
Khadaji series (7)

Black streak
Graydon, William Murray
Sexton Blake series (123)

Black stud
Tralins, Sandor Robert
Black stud trilogy (1)

Black suits from outer space
DeWeese, Gene
Calvin Willeford series (1)

Black sun
Johnston, Terry Conrad
Plainsmen series (4)

Black swan
Taylor, Day
Black swan series (1)

Black swastika
Brandon, John Gordon
Sexton Blake series (1022)

Black tanker
Pease, Howard
Tod Moran series (9)

Black tarn
Wilson, Philip Whitwell
Sir Julian Morthoe series (2)

Black Templar
Halstead, John
Inspector Todd series (3)

Black thumb mystery
Campbell, Bruce
Ken Holt series (3)

Black thunder
Mountjoy, Roberta Jean
Night wind series (2)

Black tide
Lane, Carl Daniel
Altair series (2)

Black tie rising
Greene, L Patrick
Aubrey Saint John Major series (16)

Black Tiger
O'Connor, Patrick
Black Tiger series (1)

Black Tiger at Bonneville
O'Connor, Patrick
Black Tiger series (4)

Black Tiger at Indianapolis
O'Connor, Patrick
Black Tiger series (5)

Black Tiger at Le Mans
O'Connor, Patrick
Black Tiger series (3)

Black tower
James, Phyllis Dorothy
Commander Adam Dalgliesh series (6)
Lupoff, Richard Allen
Dungeon series (1)

Black trail
Marvin, James W
Crow series (4)

Black treasure
Barlow, Roger
Sandy Steele series (1)

Black trinity
Jacobs, Thomas Curtis Hicks
Detective Superintendent John Bellamy series (6)

Black turret
Wynnton, Patrick
Black turret series (1)

Black unicorn
Brooks, Terry
Magic Kingdom of Landover series (2)

Black Valley murders
Mallory, Arthur
Doctor Kirke Montgomery series (2)

Black vein prophecy
Mason, Paul
Fighting fantasy gamebook series (42)

Black Velvet
Pullein-Thompson, Christine
Black Beauty series (3)
Pullein-Thompson, Josephine
Black Beauty series (3)

Black vengeance
Gant, Norman
Chane series (2)
Gilman, George G
Edge series (10)
Sadler, Geoffrey
Justus trilogy (3)

Black Venus contract
Atlee, Philip
Joe Gall series (21)

Black Vulmea's vengeance
Howard, Robert Ervin
Black Vulmea series (1)

Black Water Canyon
Bowden, Jim
Dan McCoy series (6)

Black welcome
Fitzgerald, Nigel
Superintendent Duffy series (8)

Black widow
Harrison, Richard
Chief Inspector William Bastion series (1)
Keene, Carolyn
Nancy Drew files series (28)
McLaglen, John J
Herne the Hunter series (3)
Quentin, Patrick
Lieutenant Timothy Trant series (4)
Peter Duluth series (8)

Black widower
Moyes, Patricia
Henry and Emmy Tibbett series (12)
Riefe, Alan
Huntington Cage series (3)

Black wizards
Niles, Douglas
Moonshae trilogy (2)

Blackbeard's ghost
Stahl, Ben
Blackbeard series (1)

Blackberry Farm storybook
Pilgrim, Jane
Blackberry Farm series (22)

Blackberry jam
Mathews, Joanna Hooe
Haps and mishaps series (3)

Blackbird
Duplechan, Larry
Johnnie Ray Rousseau series (2)
Mackenzie, Steve
Seals series (2)
Stark, Richard
Alan Grofield series (5)
Van der Essen, Anne
Yok-yok series (4)

Blackbird in amber
Warrington, Freda
Quest of the serpent series (3)

Blackbird in darkness
Warrington, Freda
Quest of the serpent series (2)

Blackbird in silver
Warrington, Freda
Quest of the serpent series (1)

Blackbird in twilight
Warrington, Freda
Quest of the serpent series (4)

Blackbirds and the gift pony
Furminger, Jo
Blackbird series (4)

Blackbirds and the midnight horse
Furminger, Jo
Blackbird series (8)

Blackbirds at the gallop
Furminger, Jo
Blackbird series (7)

Blackbirds' own gymkhana
Furminger, Jo
Blackbird series (5)

Blackbirds' pony trek
Furminger, Jo
Blackbird series (3)

Blackbirds ride a mystery trail
Furminger, Jo
Blackbird series (2)

Blackboard Bear
Alexander, Martha G
Blackboard Bear series (1)

Blackcollar
Zahn, Timothy
Blackcollar series (1)

Blackdrop Hall
Carstairs, Henry
Lydford Long series (8)

Blackfingers
Cassells, John
Superintendent Flagg series (26)

Blackfoot massacre
Thompson, David
Nathaniel King series (10)

Blackheath poisonings
Symons, Julian
Sheridan Haynes series (2)

Blackie, a lost cat
Barnum, Richard
Kneetime animal stories series (7)

Blacklight
Knox, Bill
Webb Carrick series (3)

Blackmail
Hall, Parnell
Stanley Hastings series (9)
Stahl, Hilda
Amber Ainslie series (4)

Blackmail in Blankshire
Alington, Cyril Augustine
Archdeacon series (3)

Blackmail in red
Grierson, Francis Durham
Superintendent Andrew Ash series (9)

Blackmail in red headlines
Brody, Marc
Marc Brody series (18)

Blackmail, Inc.
Kyle, Robert
Ben Gates series (1)

Blackmail is murder
Cooper, Craig
Matt Savage series (1)

Blackmail king
Grant, Maxwell
Shadow series (212)

Blackmail north
McCutchan, Philip
Superintendent Simon Shard series (5)

Blackmail ring
Grant, Maxwell
Shadow series (13)

Blackmail was a brunette
Brody, Marc
Marc Brody series (43)

Blackmail whoops it up
Jason
Jason series (10)

Blackmailed baronet
Hill, Harry Egbert
Sexton Blake series (425)

Blackmailed by Taffy Sinclair
Haynes, Betsy
Taffy Sinclair series (5)

Blackmailed refugee
Parsons, Anthony
Sexton Blake series (1145)

Blackmailer
Daniel, Roland
Bill Saville series (4)
Remover series (2)
Fenisong, Ruth
Captain Gridley Nelson series (10)

Blackmailers
Gaboriau, Emile
Dossier series (1)

Blackmailer's bluff
Carter, Nicholas
Nicholas Carter series (117)

Blackman's burden
Reynolds, Mack
Homer Crawford trilogy (1)

Blackout murders
Jones, G Wayman
Black Bat series (15)

Blackrobe
Wall, Robert Emmet
Nowell family series (1)

Blacksand!
Gascoigne, Marc
Fighting fantasy gamebook series (40)

Blackshirt
Graeme, Bruce
Blackshirt series (1)

Blackshirt again
Graeme, Bruce
Blackshirt series (3)

Blackshirt at large
Graeme, Roderic
Blackshirt series (28)

Blackshirt counter-spy
Graeme, Bruce
Blackshirt series (8)

Blackshirt finds trouble
Graeme, Roderic
Blackshirt series (22)

Blackshirt helps himself
Graeme, Roderic
Blackshirt series (18)

Blackshirt in peril
Graeme, Roderic
Blackshirt series (29)

Blackshirt interferes
Graeme, Bruce
Blackshirt series (9)

Blackshirt meets the lady
Graeme, Roderic
Blackshirt series (16)

Blackshirt mystery
Graydon, William Murray
Sexton Blake series (434)

Blackshirt on the spot
Graeme, Roderic
Blackshirt series (25)

Blackshirt passes by
Graeme, Roderic
Blackshirt series (13)

Blackshirt saves the day
Graeme, Roderic
Blackshirt series (26)

Blackshirt sees it through
Graeme, Roderic
Blackshirt series (21)

Blackshirt sets the pace
Graeme, Roderic
Blackshirt series (20)

Blackshirt stirs things up
Graeme, Roderic
Blackshirt series (30)

Blackshirt strikes back
Graeme, Bruce
Blackshirt series (10)

Blackshirt takes a hand
Graeme, Bruce
Blackshirt series (7)

Blackshirt takes the trail
Graeme, Roderic
Blackshirt series (23)

Blackshirt the adventurer
Graeme, Bruce
Blackshirt series (6)

Blackshirt the audacious
Graeme, Bruce
Blackshirt series (5)

Blackshirt wins the trick
Graeme, Roderic
Blackshirt series (12)
Blacksmiths
Fisher, Leonard Everett
Colonial Americans series (19)
Blacksmith's hammer
Sue, Eugene
Mysteries of the people series (17)
Blacksnake Trail
Field, Peter
Powder Valley series (33)
Blackstock affair
Bandy, Franklin
Kevin Macinnes series (2)
Blackstone
Falkirk, Richard
Edmund Blackstone series (1)
Blackstone and the scourge of Europe
Falkirk, Richard
Edmund Blackstone series (4)
Blackstone on Broadway
Falkirk, Richard
Edmund Blackstone series (6)
Blackstone underground
Falkirk, Richard
Edmund Blackstone series (5)
Blackstone's fancy
Falkirk, Richard
Edmund Blackstone series (2)
Blackthorn House
Rhode, John
Doctor Lancelot Priestley series (48)
Blackwash
Postgate, Oliver
Saga of Noggin the Nog series (11)
Blackwater
McDowell, Michael M
Blackwater series (6)
Blackwing puzzle
Dixon, Franklin W
Hardy boys series (82)
Blacky the crow
Burgess, Thornton Waldo
Green forest series (2)
Blade is bright
Horler, Sydney
Gerald Lissendale series (3)
Blade of the guillotine
Cover, Arthur Byron
Time machine series (14)
Blade of the poisoner
Hill, Douglas
Talents series (1)
Blade of the young samurai
Simon, Morris
Endless quest series (23)
Blades of Mars
Bradbury, Edward P
Warrior of Mars trilogy (2)
Bladesman of Antares
Akers, Alan Burt
Dray Prescot series (9)
Blaine's law
Young, Carter Travis
Cullom Blaine series (1)
Blair's nightmare
Snyder, Zilpha Keatley
Stanley family series (3)
Blaize
Melville, Anne
Lorimer family series (4)
Blakes come to Melling
Biggs, Margaret
Melling School series (1)
Blame the Baron
Morton, Anthony
Baron series (15)
Blameless woman
Winter, John Strange
Bootles series (12)
Blanche
Wendorf, Patricia
Patteran trilogy (2)
Bland beginning
Symons, Julian
Inspector Bland series (3)
Blandings Castle
Wodehouse, Pelham Grenville
Blandings Castle series (3)
Mister Mulliner series (3)
Blandings way
Hodgins, Eric
Blandings series (2)
Blane document
Rich, Nicholas
Adam Hood series (1)
Blank cheque for murder
Beeby, Otto
Tony Spencer series (1)
Blank page
Constantine, K C
Mario Balzic series (3)
Blank wall
Holding, Elisabeth Sanxay
Lieutenant Levy series (1)
Blanket
Burningham, John
Little book series (5)
Blanket of the dark
Healey, Ben
Paul Hedley series (6)
Blanket word
Arundel, Honor
Janet Meredith series (2)
Blast of trumpets
Ashe, Gordon
Patrick Dawlish series (50)
Blast of war, 1939-1945
Macmillan, Harold
Winds of change series (2)
Blast off!
Leeson, Robert
Zarnia experiment series (6)
Blast off at Woomera
Walters, Hugh
Chris Godfrey series (1)
Blast off at 0300
Walters, Hugh
Chris Godfrey series (1)
Blast out in Lebanon
Acres, Mark
Sniper series (2)
Blaster master
Singer, A L
Worlds of power series (1)
Blatchington tangle
Cole, George Douglas Howard
Everard Blatchington series (1)
Superintendent Henry Wilson series (3)
Blayde R.I.P.
Wainwright, John
Northern Police series (51)
Superintendent Blayde series (2)
Blaze
Fritch, Elizabeth
Richmond series (5)
Johnson, Susan
Blaze Braddock and Jon Hazard Black series (1)
Roberts, Kenneth
Black fire series (1)
Blaze Allan
Ross, Lillian
Big Sur series (2)
Blaze and the forest fire
Anderson, Clarence William
Billy and Blaze series (3)
Blaze and the gray spotted pony
Anderson, Clarence William
Billy and Blaze series (9)
Blaze and the gypsies
Anderson, Clarence William
Billy and Blaze series (2)
Blaze and the Indian cave
Anderson, Clarence William
Billy and Blaze series (7)
Blaze and the lost quarry
Anderson, Clarence William
Billy and Blaze series (8)
Blaze and the mountain lion
Anderson, Clarence William
Billy and Blaze series (6)
Blaze and Thunderbolt
Anderson, Clarence William
Billy and Blaze series (5)
Blaze finds forgotten roads
Anderson, Clarence William
Billy and Blaze series (11)
Blaze finds the trail
Anderson, Clarence William
Billy and Blaze series (4)
Blaze of guns
Scott, Bradford
Walt Slade series (20)
Blaze of the sun
Hougron, Jean
Monsieur Lastin series (2)
Blaze of wrath
Hawkins, Ward
Harry Borg series (3)
Blaze shows the way
Anderson, Clarence William
Billy and Blaze series (10)
Blazed trail
White, Stewart Edward
Lumbering trilogy (1)
Orde family series (1)
Blazed trail stories
White, Stewart Edward
Lumbering trilogy (3)
Blazing affair
Avallone, Michael
Girl from U.N.C.L.E.series (2)
Blazing Arrow
Ellis, Edward Sylvester
War chief series (2)
Blazing Colts
Wrexe, Charles
Bill Mitchum series (2)
Blazing express
Logan, Jake
John Slocum series (91)
Blazing garage crime
Blair, Allan
Sexton Blake series (784)
Blazing guns
Logan, Jake
John Slocum series (37)
Blazing launch murder
Hardinge, Rex
Sexton Blake series (801)
Blazing mountain
Weddle, Ferris
Clint Wade and Trapper Bill series (2)
Blazing six-gun
Dalton, Kit
Buckskin series (39)
Blazing sun
Darlton, Clark
Perry Rhodan series (86)
Bleak Creek
Grover, Marshall
Bleak Creek series (1)
Bleak morning
Tolstoi, Aleksei Nikolaevich
Ordeal trilogy (3)
Bleak spring
Cleary, Jon
Scobie Malone series (10)
Bleeders come first
Douglas, Colin
David Campbell series (3)
Bleeding Dodger Blue
Evers, Crabbe
Duffy House series (3)
Bleeding hearts
White, Teri
Blue Maguire and Spaceman Kowalski series (1)
Bleeding hooks
Rutland, Harriet
Mister Winkley series (2)
Bleeding Kansas
Sharpe, Jon
Canyon O'Grady series (8)
Blenheim
Trevelyan, George Macaulay
Queen Anne's England trilogy (1)
Blenheim boy
Passmore, Richard
Blenheim boy series (1)
Bless me again, father
Boyd, Neil
Father Charles Duddleswell series (5)
Bless me, father
Boyd, Neil
Father Charles Duddleswell series (1)
Bless this house
Lofts, Norah
Clevely series (1)
Rhodes, Evan Harold
American palace series (1)
Blessed girl
Lutyens, Emily
Blessed girl series (1)
Blessing papers
Barnwell, William
Blessing trilogy (1)
Blessing unbounded
Blamires, Harry
Heaven and Hell trilogy (3)
Blessing way
Hillerman, Tony
Lieutenant Joe Leaphorn series (1)
Bleys the man
Dickson, Gordon Rupert
Bleys quartet (4)
Dorsai series (10)
Blight
Creasey, John
Doctor Palfrey series (26)
Blind alley
Singer, Bant
Denis Delaney series (1)
Blind allies
Kendrick, Baynard
Captain Duncan Maclain series (8)
Blind barber
Carr, John Dickson
Doctor Gideon Fell series (3)
Blind beggar murder
Ryland, Clive
Inspector Beck series (1)
Blind bend
Macintyre, Lorn
Chronicles of Inverness series (2)
Blind colt
Rounds, Glen
Blind colt series (1)
Whitey series (3)
Blind corner
Yates, Dornford
Jonah Mansel series (3)
Richard Chandos series (1)
Blind date
Quin-Harkin, Janet
Sugar and spice series (13)
Blind date for a private eye
Graeme, Bruce
Henry Maxwell series (1)
Blind drifts
Clason, Clyde B
Theocritus Lucius Westborough series (3)
Blind duty
Nolan, Frederick
Davy Strong series (2)
Blind eye
Macdonnell, James Edmond
Captain Peter Bentley series (12)
Raymond, John
Dempsey and Makepeace series (2)
Blind fire
Rouch, James
Zone series (2)
Blind frog
Grierson, Francis Durham
Superintendent Andrew Ash series (11)
Blind fury
Gluck, Sinclair
Ross McCoy series (2)
Blind hypnotist
Lovell, Marc
Elsie Vanetti series (1)
Blind justice
Bernhardt, William
Justice series (2)
Blind loyalty
Haverfield, Eleanor Luisa
Our vow series (2)
Blind luck
Sayer, Mandy
Rose trilogy (2)
Blind man
Duun, Ole Julius
People of Juvik series (2)
Blind man with a pistol
Himes, Chester
Grave Digger Jones and Coffin Ed Johnson series (8)
Blind man's bluff
Jones, G Wayman
Black Bat series (24)
Kendrick, Baynard
Captain Duncan Maclain series (4)
Blind man's buff
Ryerson, Florence
Jimmy Lane series (3)
Blind man's child
Charlesworth, Maria Louisa
Ministering children series (1)
Blind man's daughter
Carter, Nicholas
Nicholas Carter series (514)
Blind man's garden
Troy, Simon
Inspector Smith series (12)
Blind man's secret
Brisbane, Coutts
Sexton Blake series (873)
Blind pig
Jackson, Jon Anthony
Sergeant Fang Mulheisen series (2)
Blind rage
Rawls, Philip
Richard Bronson series (1)
Blind reckoning
Mills, Woosnam
Sir John Howden series (3)
Blind run
Blake, Ken
Professionals series (5)
Freemantle, Brian
Charlie Muffin series (7)
Blind saw murder
Huston, Howard Chauncey
Detective Charles A Baker series (2)
Blind search
Egan, Lesley
Jesse Falkenstein series (8)
Blind side
Clifford, Francis
Loyalty trilogy (2)
Gilman, George G
Edge series (44)
Klein, Dave
Butch Lewis series (1)
Wentworth, Patricia
Inspector Ernest Lamb series (1)
Blind spot
Creasey, John
Inspector Roger West series (13)
Hall, Austin
Blind spot series (1)
Harper, Stephen
Healers series (5)
Harrington, Joseph
Lieutenant Frank Kerrigan series (2)
Blind spots
Miller, Hugh
Eastenders series (5)
Blind trust kills
Wohl, James Paul
Sam Gross series (2)
Blindfold
Melville-Ross, Antony
Treelake series (1)
Blindfold mystery
Carter, Nicholas
Nicholas Carter series (301)
Blindness of Flynn
Laurie-Long, Ernest
Captain Flynn series (12)
Blindness of Sergeant Cluff
North, Gil
Sergeant Caleb Cluff series (5)
Blink of the mind
Francis, Dorothy Brenner
Twilight series (5)
Blinky Bill and his friends
Wall, Dorothy
Blinky Bill adaptations series (7)
Blinky Bill and Nutsy
Wall, Dorothy
Blinky Bill adaptations series (3)
Blinky Bill series (3)
Blinky Bill and Nutsy have fun
Wall, Dorothy
Blinky Bill adaptations series (7)
Blinky Bill and the bull ants
Wall, Dorothy
Blinky Bill adaptations series (10)
Blinky Bill and the guest house
Wall, Dorothy
Blinky Bill adaptations series (5)
Blinky Bill and the pelicans
Wall, Dorothy
Blinky Bill adaptations series (6)
Blinky Bill and the rabbit's birthday party
Wall, Dorothy
Blinky Bill adaptations series (2)
Blinky Bill and the tree-warming
Wall, Dorothy
Blinky Bill adaptations series (7)
Blinky Bill at Frog Hollow
Wall, Dorothy
Blinky Bill adaptations series (9)
Blinky Bill at Mister Smifkin's farm
Wall, Dorothy
Blinky Bill adaptations series (4)
Blinky Bill cookbook
Coleman, Mary
Blinky Bill series (4)
Blinky Bill dress-up book
Wall, Dorothy
Blinky Bill series (4)
Blinky Bill goes to school
Wall, Dorothy
Blinky Bill adaptations series (13)
Blinky Bill goes to the doctor
Wall, Dorothy
Blinky Bill adaptations series (14)
Blinky Bill grows up
Wall, Dorothy
Blinky Bill series (2)
Blinky Bill joins the army
Wall, Dorothy
Blinky Bill series (4)
Blinky Bill magic action
Wall, Dorothy
Blinky Bill series (4)
Blinky Bill meets Nutsy
Wall, Dorothy
Blinky Bill adaptations series (12)
Blinky Bill runs away
Wall, Dorothy
Blinky Bill adaptations series (11)
Blinky Bill, the quaint little Australian
Wall, Dorothy
Blinky Bill series (1)

Blood of Amber
Zelazny, Roger
Kingdom of Amber series (7)
Blood of an Englishman
Clive, William
Joseph Dando series (5)
McClure, James
Lieutenant Kramer and Sergeant Zondi series (6)
Blood of angels
Barker, Albert
Hawk Macrae series (4)
Blood of Dracula
Teed, Jack Hamilton
Dracula series (12)
Blood of kings
Nye, Nelson Coral
Wild Horse Shorty series (2)
Blood of my blood
Lecale, Errol
Specialist series (6)
Blood of Nostradamus
Laurance, Andrew
Nostradamus trilogy (2)
Blood of others
Viviers, Lyn
Star trek fan series (47)
Blood of poets
Davis, Kenn
Carver Bascombe series (9)
Blood of strawberries
Van Dyke, Henry
Oliver series (2)
Blood of ten chiefs
Asprin, Robert Lynn
Elfquest series (2)
Pini, Richard
Elfquest series (2)
Blood of the Bondmaster
Tresillian, Richard
Bondmaster series (2)
Blood of the conquerors
Fergusson, Harry
Santa Fe Trail trilogy (1)
Fergusson, Harvey
Followers of the sun trilogy (3)
Blood of the falcon
Carter, Nick
Nick Carter series (222)
Blood of the Mountain Man
Johnstone, William Wallace
Mountain Man series (13)
Blood of the North
Hendryx, James Beardsley
Corporal Downey series (8)
Blood of the scimitar
Carter, Nick
Nick Carter series (205)
Blood of the strangers
Hartman, Dane
Dirty Harry Callahan series (10)
Blood of the tiger
Estes, Rose
Saga of lost lands trilogy (1)
Blood of the Wolf
Mackie, Charles
Stewarts of Badenoch series (2)
Blood of vintage
Kyd, Thomas
Sam Phelan series (2)
Blood on a widow's cross
Fraser, James
Inspector Bill Aveyard series (5)
Blood on Baker Street
Boucher, Anthony
Fergus O'Breen series (2)
Blood on Biscayne Bay
Halliday, Brett
Michael Shayne series (14)
Blood on his hands
Afford, Max
Jeffery Blackburn series (1)
Blood on McAllister
Chisholm, Matt
Rem McAllister series (18)
Blood on my rug
Cushing, E Louise
Inspector Mackay series (2)
Blood on my sleeve
Baker, Ivon
David Meynell series (4)
Blood on pale fingers
Malloch, Peter
Inspector Dave Norton series (1)
Blood on silver
Gilman, George G
Edge series (5)
Blood on the Baltic
Kostov, K N
Punishment battalion series (3)
Blood on the beach
Holley, Helen
Tessie Venable series (1)
Blood on the black market
Halliday, Brett
Michael Shayne series (8)
Blood on the blonde
Chambers, Dana
Nile Boyd series (1)
Blood on the blotter
Marshall, Lovat
Sugar Kane series (16)
Blood on the border
Harvey, John Barton
Wes Hart series (5)
Thorne, Ramsay
Captain Gringo series (26)
Blood on the bosom devine
Kyd, Thomas
Sam Phelan series (3)
Blood on the deck
McLaren, Jack
My adventures series (3)
Blood on the divide
Johnstone, William Wallace
First Mountain Man trilogy (2)
Mountain Man Preacher series (2)
Blood on the floor
Masterman, Walter Sidney
Sir Arthur Sinclair series (3)
Blood on the handle
Montgomery, Raymond A
Choose your own adventure series (94)
Blood on the happy highway
Radley, Sheila
Chief Inspector Douglas Quantrill series (4)
Blood on the harvest moon
Anthony, David
Morgan Butler series (2)
Blood on the hills
Chisholm, Matt
Storm family series (9)
Blood on the knight
Thayer, Lee
Peter Clancy series (50)
Blood on the land
Roberts, J R
Gunsmith series (89)
Blood on the moon
Cohen, Barry
Asher Bockhorn series (2)
Copper, Basil
Mike Faraday series (47)
Ellroy, James
Sergeant Lloyd Hopkins trilogy (1)
Longtree, Warren T
Ruff Justice series (3)
Scott, Bradford
Walt Slade series (80)
Blood on the Nueces
Jeffers, Harry Paul
Morgan trilogy (2)
Blood on the pavement
Graham, Neill
Solo Malcolm series (27)
Blood on the plains
Cole, Judd
Cheyenne series (5)
Curry, Tom
Captain Mesquite series (7)
Blood on the prairie
Benteen, John
Sundance series (18)
Blood on the rails
Stone, Ned
Other Day Logan series (3)
Blood on the rocks
Venters, Archie
Gil Kennedy series (2)
Blood on the snow
Litvinoff, Samuel
Faces of terror series (2)
Blood on the staked plains
Weston, Cole
Andrew Ryder series (10)
Blood on the stars
Halliday, Brett
Michael Shayne series (17)
Morland, Nigel
Chief Inspector Andrew McMurdo series (5)
Stein, Aaron Marc
Matt Erridge series (4)
Blood on the street
Meyers, Annette
Leslie Wetzon series (4)
Blood on the strip
Derrick, Lionel
Penetrator series (2)
Blood on the sun
Langholm, Neil
Vikings series (3)
Blood on the tracks
James, William M
Apache series (8)
Blood on the wind
Moray, Helga
Katie and Paul Van Riebeck series (4)
Blood on the Yukon trail
Hendryx, James Beardsley
Corporal Cameron Downey series (2)
Blood on the Yukon Trail
Hendryx, James Beardsley
Corporal Downey series (7)
Blood orange
Llewellyn, Sam
Charlie Agutter series (2)
Blood oranges
Hawkes, John
Blood oranges trilogy (1)
Blood order
Hunter, Jack Dayton
Blue Max series (2)
Blood Pass
Sharpe, Jon
Trailsman series (80)
Blood patrol
Fennell, George
Mike Brent series (1)
Blood-pit
Carrel, Mark
Andrew McCall series (1)
Blood prairie
Sharpe, Jon
Trailsman series (125)
Blood quest
McPhee, James
Survival two thousand trilogy (1)
Blood raid
Carter, Nick
Nick Carter series (226)
Blood ransom
Austin, Jim
John Fury series (2)
Blood red
Morton, Anthony
Baron series (30)
Blood-red badge
Carter, Nicholas
Nicholas Carter series (119)
Blood red dream
Collins, Michael
Dan Fortune series (8)
Blood red island
Croft-Cooke, Rupert
Sensual life series (13)
Blood red roses
Armstrong, Sarah
Twilight series (8)
Blood reign of the dictator
Steele, Curtis
James Christopher series (10)
Blood relation
Taylor, Andrew
William Dougal series (6)
Blood relations
Dillon, Eilis
Bitter sea series (2)
Dixon, Franklin W
Hardy boys case files series (15)
Stewart, Flora
Inspector Newsom series (2)
Blood relatives
McBain, Ed
Eighty Seventh Precinct series (30)
Blood ring
Robeson, Kenneth
Avenger series (6)
Blood rising
James, William M
Apache series (15)
Blood risk
Coffey, Brian
Mike Tucker series (1)
Blood rites
Bergstrom, Elaine
Shattered glass series (3)
Blood rival
Walker, Dalton
Shiloh series (3)
Blood river
Slade, Jack
Lassiter series (18)
Tilley, Patrick
Amtrak wars series (4)
Willard, Tom
Strike fighters series (7)
Blood river down
Fenn, Lionel
Quest for the white duck trilogy (1)
Blood royal
Yates, Dornford
Richard Chandos series (3)
Blood royal at Castle School
Little, Sylvia
Castle School series (4)
Blood run
Brady, William S
Peacemaker series (5)
Conroy, Al
Johnny Morini series (5)
Gilman, George G
Edge series (15)
Kellerman, Dan
Jesse Heller series (1)
Webb, Alex
Josh Dekker series (1)
Blood run east
McCutchan, Philip
Superintendent Simon Shard series (3)
Blood runner
Thorne, Ramsay
Captain Gringo series (2)
Blood running cold
Ross, Jonathan
Superintendent George Rogers series (1)
Blood runs cold
Cunningham, Albert Benjamin
Sheriff Jess Roden series (17)
Blood runs hot
Dacre, Richard
Sam Hoskins series (1)
Blood sacrifice
Langholm, Neil
Vikings series (1)
Blood shot
Paretsky, Sara
V I Warshawski series (5)
Blood siege
Stine, George Harry
Warbots series (9)
Blood sport
Cohler, David Keith
Sam Knight series (1)
Scott, R C
Dark forces series (14)
Blood-stock
Muir, James A
Breed series (9)
Blood stone
Allegretto, Michael
Jacob Lomax series (2)
Blood stones
Moore, Wallace
Balzan of the cat people trilogy (1)
Blood storm
Buchanan, Jack
M.I.A. Hunter series (6)
Gladney, Heather
Song of Naga Teot series (2)
McLennan, Will
Ramseys series (14)
Blood, sweat and gold
Hardin, J D
Raider and Doc series (1)
Blood sword
Morris, Dave
Blood sword series (1)
Blood tapes
Starr, Leonard
Kelly Green series (2)
Blood target
Garrett, Charles C
Gunslinger series (10)
Blood tells
Robertson, Stephen
Ryne Lanark series (2)
Blood test
Kellerman, Jonathan
Alex Delaware series (2)
Blood testament
Pendleton, Don
Mack Bolan series (100)
Blood tide
Cameron, J D
Omega sub series (4)
Blood-tie
Gardner, Jerome
Hanging Judge series (2)
Blood ties
Asprin, Robert Lynn
Sanctuary series (9)
Murphy, Warren Burton
Destroyer series (69)
Murray, Will
Destroyer series (69)
Robertson, Stephen
Ryne Lanark series (3)
Blood, toil, tears and sweat
Parkinson, Roger
War Cabinet trilogy (2)
Blood trail
Baker, William Howard
Pinkerton series (4)
Harvey, John Barton
Wes Hart series (2)
Logan, Jake
John Slocum series (186)
Reno, Bill
Badge series (10)
Blood trails
Hawkins, Jack
Chopper series (1)
Blood trance
Zimmerman, R D
Maddy and Alex Phillips series (2)
Blood transfusion murders
Propper, Milton
Tommy Rankin series (14)
Blood truce
Thompson, David
Nathaniel King series (16)
Blood type
Greenleaf, Stephen
John Marshall Tanner series (8)
Blood ultimatum
Carter, Nick
Nick Carter series (212)
Blood under the bridge
Zimmerman, Bruce
Quinn Parker series (1)
Blood upon the snow
Lawrence, Hilda
Mark East series (1)
Blood Valley
Muir, James A
Breed series (19)
Smith, Mark
Duelmaster series (2)
Blood vengeance
Jason, Stuart
Butcher series (13)
Weston, Cole
Andrew Ryder series (8)
Blood wedding
Goulart, Ron
Vampirella series (4)
James, William M
Apache series (21)
Blood will have blood
Barnes, Linda
Michael Spraggue series (1)
Blood will tell
Bagby, George
Inspector Schmidt series (18)
Carter, Nicholas
Nicholas Carter series (616)
Christie, Agatha
Hercule Poirot series (27)
Mrs Ariadne Oliver series (3)
Parker, Maude
Jim Little series (2)
Stout, Rex
Nero Wolfe and Archie Goodwin series (39)
Bloodbath
McCurtin, Peter
Jim Rainey series (16)
Bloodbeach
Harding, Ian
Assault troop series (1)
Bloodbird
Burton, Thomas
Bloodbird series (2)
Bloodbrothers
Wall, Robert Emmet
Nowell family series (2)
Bloodcircle
Elrod, Patricia Nead
Vampire files series (3)
Blooded stock
Brown, Joseph Paul Summers
Arizona saga series (1)
Bloodfang
Weaver, Michael D
Thyri trilogy (3)
Bloodheart
Tresillian, Richard
Bloodheart series (1)
Bloodheart feud
Tresillian, Richard
Bloodheart series (3)
Bloodheart royal
Tresillian, Richard
Bloodheart series (2)
Bloodhound Gang in the case of the cackling ghost
Fleischman, Sid
Bloodhound Gang series (2)
Bloodhound Gang in the case of the flying clock
Fleischman, Sid
Bloodhound Gang series (1)

Bloodhound Gang in the case of the Princess Tomorrow
Fleischman, Sid
Bloodhound Gang series (3)
Bloodhound Gang in the case of the secret message
Fleischman, Sid
Bloodhound Gang series (4)
Bloodhound Gang's secret code book
Fleischman, Sid
Bloodhound Gang series (5)
Bloodhounds Bay
Masterman, Walter Sidney
Dick Seldon series (1)
Bloodhound's revenge
Graydon, William Murray
Sexton Blake series (435)
Bloodhouse Gang in the case of the two hundred and sixty four pound burglar
Fleischman, Sid
Bloodhound Gang series (6)
Bloodhype
Foster, Alan Dean
Flinx of the Commonwealth series (5)
Bloodied ivy
Goldsborough, Robert
Nero Wolfe and Archie Goodwin series (50)
Bloodied toga
Hardy, William George
Roman trilogy (3)
Blooding of the guns
Fullerton, Alexander
Nick Everard series (1)
Bloodletting!
Skimin, Robert
Soldier for hire series (4)
Bloodline
McLaglen, John J
Herne the Hunter series (19)
Bloodline to murder
McDowell, Emmett
Jonathan Knox series (2)
Bloodlines
Conant, Susan
Dog lover's mystery series (2)
Bloodlinks
Killough, Lee
Blood hunt series (2)
Bloodlist
Elrod, Patricia Nead
Vampire files series (1)
Bloodmoon
Kalish, Robert
Skipper Gould series (3)
Bloodname
Thurston, Robert
Legend of the jade phoenix trilogy (2)
Bloodright
Tremayne, Peter
Dracula series (10)
Bloodrun
Kalish, Robert
Skipper Gould series (1)
Bloodrush
Zachary, Hugh
Sheriff Jug Watson series (1)
Bloodseed
Darby, Lyndan
Eye of time trilogy (2)
Bloodshed in Bayswater
Rowland, John
Inspector Shelley series (1)
Bloodsmoor romance
Oates, Joyce Carol
Bellefleur series (2)
Bloodsongs
Bailey, Robin Wayne
Frost trilogy (3)
Bloodsport
Pendleton, Don
Mack Bolan series (46)
Bloodstain
Alexander, David
Marty Land series (2)
Bloodstained toy
Campbell, Alice
Inspector Headcorn series (5)
Tommy Rostetter series (4)
Bloodstalk
Goulart, Ron
Vampirella series (1)
Bloodstar
Topor, Tom
Kevin Fitzgerald series (1)
Bloodstar conspiracy
Smith, Edward Elmer
Family d'Alembert series (5)
Bloodstone
Eulo, Ken
Chandal Talon trilogy (2)
Wagner, Karl Edward
Kane series (3)
Bloodstone terror
Carter, Nicholas
Nicholas Carter series (167)
Bloodthirst
Dillard, Jeanne M
Star trek series (37)
Bloodtide
Kalish, Robert
Skipper Gould series (2)
Knox, Bill
Webb Carrick series (12)
Bloodtrail to Mecca
Carter, Nick
Nick Carter series (235)
Bloodwater
Crowe, John
Buena Costa County series (3)
Sadler, Geoffrey
Justus trilogy (2)
Bloodwind
Grant, Charles Lewis
Oxrun Station series (6)
Bloody affair at Riverside Drive
Rayner, William
Missouri series (1)
Bloody America
Stacy, Ryder
Doomsday warrior series (4)
Bloody Bastogne
Davis, Gordon
Sergeant series (8)
Bloody book of law
Woods, Sara
Sir Nicholas Harding and Antony Maitland series (40)
Bloody border
Edson, John Thomas
American Civil War series (11)
Gilman, George G
Adam Steele series (13)
Bloody Boston
Derrick, Lionel
Penetrator series (12)
Bloody bounty
Hunter, Neil
Bodie the Stalker series (2)
Bloody bridgehead
Bradley, Jack
Battlesquad 1942 series (4)
Bloody bush
Davis, Gordon
Sergeant series (3)
Bloody Christmas
Pike, Charles R
Jubal Cade series (17)
Bloody cross
Ramsay, Mark
Falcon trilogy (3)
Bloody earth
Masterson, Louis
Morgan Kane series (28)
Bloody Gold
Cunningham, Chet
Jim Steel series (3)
Bloody ground
Truman, Timothy
Simon Girty series (2)
Bloody heritage
Sharpe, Jon
Trailsman series (27)
Bloody instructions
Woods, Sara
Sir Nicholas Harding and Antony Maitland series (2)
Bloody justice
Sherman, Jory
Gunn series (4)
Bloody Mary
Lewis, Hilda
Mary Tudor trilogy (3)
Bloody medallion
Telfair, Richard
Monty Nash series (1)
Bloody Monday conspiracy
Hayes, Ralph Eugene
Agent for Cominsec series (1)
Bloody moonlight
Brown, Fredric
Ed and Am Hunter series (3)
Bloody rose
Streib, Dan
Steve Crown series (9)
Bloody roses
Cooper, Natasha
Willow King series (3)
Bloody sands
Hardin, J D
Raider and Doc series (8)
Bloody seas
Greenfield, Irving A
Depth force series (3)
Bloody September
Haddad, Carolyn A
David Haham series (1)
Bloody Shiloh
Coburn, L J
Caleb Thorn series (4)
Bloody special
Babbin, Jaqueline
Clovis Kelly series (2)
Bloody success
Culpan, Maurice
Inspector Bill Houghton series (5)
Bloody summer
Gilman, George G
Edge series (9)
Bloody sun
Bradley, Marion Zimmer
Darkover series (12)
Bloody sun at noon
Beare, George
Vincent Stallard and Cynthia Godwin series (1)
Bloody Sunday
Edwards, Josh
John Stone series (11)
Scarpetta, Frank
Marksman series (21)
Bloody sunrise
Gilman, George G
Edge series (42)
Spillane, Mickey
Tiger Mann series (2)
Bloody time in Blacktower
Hardin, J D
Raider and Doc series (27)
Bloody Tower
Rhode, John
Doctor Lancelot Priestley series (29)
Bloody trail to Texas
Logan, Jake
John Slocum series (7)
Bloody wig murders
Bagby, George
Inspector Schmidt series (7)
Bloody wood
Innes, Michael
Sir John Appleby series (21)
Bloom of life
France, Anatole
Pierre Noziere series (4)
Blooming of the Rose
Beamish, Noel de Vic
Owen Tudor series (2)
Bloomsbury Fair
Henrey, Madeleine
Madeleine reminiscences series (5)
Blork's evil twin
Coville, Bruce
Space brat series (2)
Blossom
Vachss, Andrew
Burke series (5)
Blossom Culp and the sleep of death
Peck, Richard
Blossom Culp series (4)
Blossom of months
Skelton, Peter
Edwin series (3)
Blossom promise
Byars, Betsy
Blossoms series (3)
Blossom Shop
Mullins, Iola May
Blossom Shop series (1)
Blossoming love
Stahl, Hilda
Prairie series (1)
Blossoming world
Bates, Herbert Ernest
World trilogy (2)
Blossoms and the green phantom
Byars, Betsy
Blossoms series (2)
Blossoms meet the vulture lady
Byars, Betsy
Blossoms series (1)
Blow a wild bugle for Catfish Bend
Burman, Ben Lucien
Catfish Bend series (4)
Blow-and-grow year
Potter, Margaret Newman
Sinclair family series (2)
Blow for vengeance
Carter, Nicholas
Nicholas Carter series (118)
Blow hot, blow cold
Neels, Betty
Adelaide Peters series (2)
Blow me down
Ahlberg, Allan
Red nose readers series (15)
Blow my mind
Gray, Rod
Lady from L.U.S.T. series (13)
Blow of a hammer, and other stories
Carter, Nicholas
Nicholas Carter series (73)
Blow out my torch
Howard, James Arch
Steve Ashe series (3)
Blow the four winds
Arvay, Harry
Israeli Security Branch series (10)
Blow up!
Huddy, Delia
Hipster series (3)
Blow your mind job
Conway, Troy
Coxeman series (19)
Blowback
Pronzini, Bill
Private Eye series (4)
Blowholers
Reese, John
Jesus on horseback trilogy (2)
Blown
Farmer, Philip Jose
Exorcism series (2)
Blown dead
Sloane, Ben
Horn series (2)
Blown figures
Thomas, Audrey
Isobel Cleary series (3)
Blowtorch
Agry, Ed
O'Reilly series (2)
Bludgeon
Ryan, Jim
Igor Kerinsky series (1)
Blue above the chimneys
Fraser, Christine Marion
Blue above the chimneys series (1)
Blue adept
Anthony, Piers
Apprentice adept series (2)
Blue Alice
Short, Jackson
Alice in Wonderland parodies series (8)
Blue aura
Walters, Hugh
Chris Godfrey series (20)
Blue Bay mystery
Warner, Gertrude Chandler
Boxcar children series (6)
Blue bears' race
Cecil, Hugh
Teddy tales series (2)
Blue belle
Vachss, Andrew
Burke series (3)
Blue bicycle
Deforges, Regine
Lea Delmas trilogy (1)
Blue bird
Maeterlinck, Maurice
Blue bird series (1)
Blue bird chooses
Maeterlinck, Maurice
Blue bird series (2)
Blue Birds at Happy Hills
Roy, Lillian Elizabeth
Blue Birds series (4)
Blue Birds of happy times
Roy, Lillian Elizabeth
Blue Birds series (1)
Blue Birds' Uncle Ben
Roy, Lillian Elizabeth
Blue Birds series (3)
Blue Birds' winter nest
Roy, Lillian Elizabeth
Blue Birds series (2)
Blue blood will out
Heald, Tim
Simon Bognor series (2)
Blue bone
Woodhouse, Martin
Giles Yeoman series (4)
Blue bonnet
Muir, Augustus
Blue bonnet series (1)
Blue Bonnet, debutante
Richards, Lela Horn
Blue Bonnet series (5)
Blue Bonnet in Boston
Jacobs, Caroline Emilia
Blue Bonnet series (3)
Blue Bonnet keeps house
Jacobs, Caroline Emilia
Blue Bonnet series (4)
Blue Bonnet of the Seven Stars
Richards, Lela Horn
Blue Bonnet series (6)
Blue Bonnet's family
Richards, Lela Horn
Blue Bonnet series (7)
Blue Bonnet's ranch party
Jacobs, Caroline Emilia
Blue Bonnet series (2)
Blue book of Hob stories
Mayne, William
Hob stories series (2)
Blue bucket mystery
Grierson, Francis Durham
Inspector Sims and Professor Wells series (7)
Blue bullet
McCarthy, Gary
Ballou family series (4)
Blue camellia
Keyes, Frances Parkinson
Winslow family trilogy (2)
Blue car mystery
Lincoln, Natalie Sumner
Inspector Mitchell series (8)
Blue Coats
Charlier, Jean Michel
Young Blueberry series (3)
Blue cow at Sugar Creek
Hutchens, Paul
Sugar Creek Gang series (21)
Blue Cut job
Cutter, Tom
Tracker series (3)
Blue Danube
Buckley, Eunice
Vienna series (2)
Blue days and fair
Gibbs, Henry
Prior Report trilogy (2)
Blue death
Collins, Michael
Dan Fortune series (7)
Saberhagen, Fred
Berserker series (8)
Blue diamond
Costello, Paul
Terence O'Hara series (4)
Blue Door venture
Brown, Pamela
Blue Door Theatre Company series (4)
Blue dwarfs
Mahr, Kurt
Perry Rhodan series (54)
Blue evening gone
Stirling, Jessica
Beckman family trilogy (2)
Blue eyed boy
Curzon, Clare
Superintendent Mike Yeadings and Sergeant Angus Mott series (6)
Blue-eyed Buddha
Hawton, Hector
Colonel Max Masterson series (2)
Blue-eyed Manchu
Abdullah, Achmed
Red stain series (2)
Blue-eyed Shan
Becker, Stephen
Far East trilogy (3)
Blue Eyes
Charyn, Jerome
Isaac Sidel series (1)
Blue field
Moore, John Cecil
Brensham trilogy (3)
Blue fire
Harrington, Emma
Women of the West series (1)
Blue for true love
Mitchell Ruth Comfort
Old San Francisco series (1)
Blue ghost mystery
Blaine, John
Rick Brant series (15)
Blue glory
Drury, Rebecca
Women of war series (2)
Blue Grass Seminary girls' Christmas holidays
Burnett, Carolyn Judson
Blue Grass Seminary girls series (2)
Blue Grass Seminary girls in the mountains
Burnett, Carolyn Judson
Blue Grass Seminary girls series (3)
Blue Grass Seminary girls on the water
Burnett, Carolyn Judson
Blue Grass Seminary girls series (4)

Blue Grass Seminary girls' vacation adventures
Burnett, Carolyn Judson
Blue Grass Seminary girls series (1)
Blue Grotto terror
Claudy, Carl Harry
Adventures in the unknown series (4)
Blue hammer
Macdonald, Ross
Lew Archer series (19)
Blue hearts
Lehrer, Jim
One-Eyed Mack series (6)
Blue herring mystery
Queen, Ellery, Junior
Djuna and Champ series (8)
Blue Hills
Meredith, Gwen
Blue Hills series (2)
Blue Hills in the sun
Meredith, Gwen
Blue Hills series (4)
Blue horizon
Stacpoole, Henry de Vere
Blue horizon series (1)
Blue house
Hannum, Alberta
Desert trading post series (1)
Blue hurricane
Mason, Francis Van Wyck
American Civil War, naval series (2)
Blue ice affair
Carter, Nick
Nick Carter series (197)
Blue Jean Billy
Tyler, Charles Waller
Blue Jean Billy Race series (1)
Blue knight
Wambaugh, Joseph
Bumper Morgan series (2)
Blue lagoon
Stacpoole, Henry de Vere
Dick and Emmeline series (1)
Blue lamp
Willis, Ted
George Dixon series (1)
Blue leader
Wager, Walter
Alison Gordon series (1)
Blue lights
Fredericks, Arnold
Richard Duvall series (3)
Blue limbo
Lauria, Frank
Doctor Owen Orient series (7)
Blue Line murder
Moffatt, James
Johnny Canuck series (1)
Blue lotus
Herge
Tintin series (5)
Blue macaw
Edwards, Charman
Percy Aloysius Huff series (2)
Blue magic
Clayton, Jo
Drinker of souls trilogy (2)
Blue Magnolia
Smyth, John George
Beloved cats series (2)
Blue Mask
Cassells, John
Superintendent Flagg series (24)
Blue Mask at bay
Morton, Anthony
Baron series (3)
Blue Mask strikes again
Morton, Anthony
Baron series (7)
Blue Mask victorious
Morton, Anthony
Baron series (8)
Blue Mauritius
Warren, Vernon
Mark Brandon series (4)
Blue Max
Hunter, Jack Dayton
Blue Max series (1)
Blue mirror
Turner, James Ernest
Rampion Savage series (10)
Blue moon
Wager, Walter
Alison Gordon series (2)
Blue mountain
Gaan, Margaret
Red barbarian trilogy (3)
Blue movie murders
Queen, Ellery
Mike McCall series (3)
Blue Muffin book
Hogarth, Ann
Muffin book series (2)
Blue Munch Bunch word book
Reed, Giles
Munch Bunch word book series (3)
Blue murder
Hale, Edgar
Montague Migglewade series (1)
Halliday, Brett
Michael Shayne series (66)
Wager, Walter
Alison Gordon series (3)
Watson, Colin
Inspector Purbright series (10)
Blue mystery
Benary, Margot
Annegret series (1)
Blue ocean's daughter
Brady, Cyrus Townsend
Lady Susan series (1)
Blue parakeet murders
Koehler, Robert Portner
Avery Gregg and Tony Ellis series (3)
Blue Pete and the kid
Allan, Luke
Blue Pete series (19)
Blue Pete and the Pinto
Allan, Luke
Blue Pete series (13)
Blue Pete at bay
Allan, Luke
Blue Pete series (17)
Blue Pete breaks the rules
Allan, Luke
Blue Pete series (8)
Blue Pete, detective
Allan, Luke
Blue Pete series (3)
Blue Pete, half-breed
Allan, Luke
Blue Pete series (1)
Blue Pete, horsethief
Allan, Luke
Blue Pete series (4)
Blue Pete in the badlands
Allan, Luke
Blue Pete series (20)
Blue Pete, Indian scout
Allan, Luke
Blue Pete series (16)
Blue Pete, outlaw
Allan, Luke
Blue Pete series (9)
Blue Pete pays a debt
Allan, Luke
Blue Pete series (7)
Blue Pete, rebel
Allan, Luke
Blue Pete series (6)
Blue Pete rides the foothills
Allan, Luke
Blue Pete series (18)
Blue Pete to the rescue
Allan, Luke
Blue Pete series (12)
Blue Pete, unofficially
Allan, Luke
Blue Pete series (15)
Blue Pete works alone
Allan, Luke
Blue Pete series (14)
Blue Peter book of limericks
Baxter, Biddy
Blue Peter series (1)
Blue Peter book of odd odes
Baxter, Biddy
Blue Peter series (2)
Blue Pete's dilemma
Allan, Luke
Blue Pete series (10)
Blue Pete's vendetta
Allan, Luke
Blue Pete series (11)
Blue pheasant
Boswell, John
Christopher Kent series (1)
Blue poodle mystery
Hope, Laura Lee
Bobbsey twins series (73)
Blue print for execution
Parker, Lee
Donovan's Devils series (2)
Blue-print murders
Brandon, John Gordon
Inspector Patrick Aloysius McCarthy series (36)
Blue raider
Strang, Herbert
Stories of the Great War series (6)
Blue remembered hills
Robertson, Denise
Belgate trilogy (3)
Blue ribbon
Housman, Laurence
Palace plays series (2)
Blue Ridge Billy
Lenski, Lois
Regional series (3)
Blue Ridge crime
Martyn, Wyndham
Anthony Trent series (20)
Blue ring
Quinnell, A J
Creasy series (2)
Blue Robin, the girl pioneer
Halsey, Rena Isabelle
Nathalie Page series (1)
Blue scarab
Freeman, Richard Austin
Doctor John Evelyn Thorndyke series (9)
Blue shark
Torgersen, Don Arthur
Animal life stories series (12)
Blue skies, French fries
Delton, Judy
Pee wee scout series (4)
Blue sky of spring
Cadell, Elizabeth
Waynes of Wood Mount trilogy (2)
Blue smoke and mirrors
Murphy, Warren Burton
Destroyer series (78)
Murray, Will
Destroyer series (78)
Blue sphinx
Grant, Maxwell
Shadow series (70)
Blue Star Range
Slaughter, Jim
Boone Helm series (6)
Blue story book
Blyton, Enid
Colour story book series (1)
Blue sword
McKinley, Robin
Chronicles of Damar series (2)
Blue system
Scheer, Karl Herbert
Perry Rhodan series (99)
Blue, the grey and the red
Gilman, George G
Edge series (6)
Blue trousers
Murasaki Shibuku
Genji series (4)
Blue trout and black truffles
Wechsberg, Joseph
Epicure trilogy (3)
Blue Two, bale-out
Hamre, Leif
Peter Hovden series (2)
Blue Tyson
Dowling, Terry
Tom Tyson series (2)
Blue Vesuvius
Wynne, Anthony
Doctor Eustace Hailey series (11)
Blue water contract
McCray, Mike
Black Berets series (13)
Blueankle
Suter, Jon Michael
Mustard jar series (5)
Blueback
Knox, Bill
Webb Carrick series (5)
Bluebeard
Kerrigan, John
SBS series (2)
Bluebeard room
Keene, Carolyn
Nancy Drew series (77)
Bluebeard's keys
Evans, Gwyn
Double O'Day series (1)
Bluebell story book
Blyton, Enid
Flower story book series (2)
Bluebell windows
Sallis, Susan
Rising family series (3)
Blueberries for Sal
McCloskey, Robert
Sal series (1)
Blueberry Mountain
Meader, Stephen Warren
Blueberry Mountain series (1)
Blueberry's secret
Charlier, Jean Michel
Young Blueberry series (1)
Bluebird Canyon
McCall, Dan
Trip Bodley series (1)
Bluebirds over
Williams, David
Fighter series (1)
Bluebirds over Pit Row
Cresswell, Helen
Mike series (1)
Bluebloods
Drake, David
Starhunters series (3)
Bluebolt one
McCutchan, Philip
Commander Esmonde Shaw series (3)
Bluebottle
Urquhart, Macgregor
Chief Inspector Joshua Smarles series (4)
Bluefeather
Meynell, Laurence Walter
Bluefeather series (1)
Bluegate Fields
Perry, Anne
Charlotte Ellison Pitt and Inspector Thomas Pitt series (6)
Bluenose pirate
Knight, Frank
Clipper ship series (4)
Blueprint for destruction
Robertson, Manning K
Steve Carradine series (2)
Blueprint for murder
Bax, Roger
Inspector James series (1)
Blueprint invisibility
Rosenberger, Joseph
Death Merchant series (40)
Blueprint to kill
Evans, Kenneth
Crispin Tyler series (2)
Blueprints for a blonde
Brody, Marc
Marc Brody series (55)
Blueprints for murder
Brody, Marc
Marc Brody series (9)
Blues for a black sister
Johnson, B B
Superspade series (6)
Blues for Charlie Darwin
Hentoff, Nat
Noah Green series (1)
Blues for the Prince
Spicer, Bart
Carney Wilde series (2)
Bluesong
Van Scyoc, Sydney Joyce
Sunstone scrolls trilogy (2)
Bluff
Adams, Herbert
Major Roger Bennion series (5)
Bluff and Bran and the birthday
Rutherford, Meg
Bluff and Bran series (5)
Bluff and Bran and the magpie
Rutherford, Meg
Bluff and Bran series (2)
Bluff and Bran and the scarecrow
Rutherford, Meg
Bluff and Bran series (1)
Bluff and Bran and the snowdrift
Rutherford, Meg
Bluff and Bran series (4)
Bluff and Bran and the tree house
Rutherford, Meg
Bluff and Bran series (3)
Blunt darts
Healy, Jeremiah
John Francis Cuddy series (1)
Blunt instrument
Heyer, Georgette
Inspector Hemingway series (4)
Superintendent Hannasyde series (4)
Blunted lance
Hennessy, Max
Cavalry trilogy (2)
Bluntstone and the Wildkeepers
Grimshaw, Nigel
Wildkeepers series (1)
Blur
Grant, Maxwell
Shadow series (207)
Blurred reality
Lewis, Royston
Eric Ward series (5)
Blushing monkey
McDougald, Roman
Philip Cabot series (3)
BMX biker
Spurgeon, Maureen
BMX bikers series (1)
BMX bikers and the Dirt Track Racers
Spurgeon, Maureen
BMX bikers series (2)
BMX Bunch on vacation
Lynam, Terence
BMX Gang series (1)
BMX Bunch turns detective
Lynam, Terence
BMX Gang series (2)
BMX Gang on holiday
Lynam, Terence
BMX Gang series (1)
BMX Gang turns detective
Lynam, Terence
BMX Gang series (2)
BMX is for me
Moran, Tom
Sports for me series (2)
BMX star rider
Graham, Caroline
BMX series (1)
BMX'ers battle it out!
Graham, Caroline
BMX series (2)
Bo Binh command
Lansing, John
Black Eagles series (20)
Board but no breakfast
Scott, Mary
New Zealand life series (11)
Boarders away!
Hardy, Adam
George Abercrombie Fox series (10)
Boarding-house mystery
Brooks, Edwy Searles
Sexton Blake series (327)
Boarding house mystery
Osborne, Mark
Sexton Blake series (666)
Boast of the Seminole
Lange, Dietrich
American Indian series (15)
Boastful Rabbit
Manning-Sanders, Ruth
Rabbit series (1)
Boat and Bax
Collinson, Roger
Bobby Bax series (1)
Boat Club
Optic, Oliver
Boat Club series (1)
Boat Club boys of Lakeport
Stratemeyer, Edward L
Lakeport series (3)
Boat-house riddle
Connington, John Jervis
Sir Clinton Driffield series (6)
Boat seekers
Pardoe, Margot
Boat series (2)
Boat train mystery
Barry, Charles
Superintendent Lawrence Gilmartin series (14)
Boats of the Glen Carrig
Hodgson, William Hope
Glen Carrig trilogy (1)
Boatswain's boy
Du Soe, Robert C
Jonathan Amory series (1)
Bob and Jilly
Schmidt, Annie Maria Geertruida
Bob and Jilly series (1)
Bob and Jilly are friends
Schmidt, Annie Maria Geertruida
Bob and Jilly series (5)
Bob Bodden and the good ship Rover
Coatsworth, Elizabeth
Bob Bodden series (1)
Bob Bodden and the seagoing farm
Coatsworth, Elizabeth
Bob Bodden series (2)
Bob Bouncer's schooldays
Gordon, Frederick
Fairview boys series (3)
Up and doing series (3)
Bob Chase after grizzly bears
Warner, Frank A
Bob Chase series (2)
Bob Chase in the tiger's lair
Warner, Frank A
Bob Chase series (3)
Bob Chase with the big moose hunters
Warner, Frank A
Bob Chase series (1)
Bob Chase with the lion hunters
Warner, Frank A
Bob Chase series (4)

Bob Dashaway in the frozen seas
Brady, Cyrus Townsend
Bob Dashaway series (2)

Bob Dashaway, treasure hunter
Brady, Cyrus Townsend
Bob Dashaway series (1)

Bob Dexter and the aeroplane mystery
Baker, Willard F
Bob Dexter series (4)

Bob Dexter and the Beacon Beach mystery
Baker, Willard F
Bob Dexter series (2)

Bob Dexter and the club house mystery
Baker, Willard F
Bob Dexter series (3)

Bob Dexter and the radio mystery
Baker, Willard F
Bob Dexter series (7)

Bob Dexter and the red auto mystery
Baker, Willard F
Bob Dexter series (6)

Bob Dexter and the seaplane mystery
Baker, Willard F
Bob Dexter series (5)

Bob Dexter and the Storm Mountain mystery
Baker, Willard F
Bob Dexter series (1)

Bob Ford, the slayer of Jesse James
Lawson, W B
Jesse James series (7)

Bob Fulton's amazing soda-pop stretcher
Beatty, Jerome
Bob Fulton series (1)

Bob Fulton's terrific time machine
Beatty, Jerome
Bob Fulton series (2)

Bob in Jilly in trouble
Schmidt, Annie Maria Geertruida
Bob and Jilly series (6)

Bob Moran and the buccaneer's board
Verne, Henry
Bob Moran series (4)

Bob Moran and the Fawcett mystery
Verne, Henry
Bob Moran series (1)

Bob Moran and the fiery claw
Verne, Henry
Bob Moran series (6)

Bob Moran and the pirates of the air
Verne, Henry
Bob Moran series (2)

Bob Moran and the sunken galley
Verne, Henry
Bob Moran series (3)

Bob Moran in the valley of hell
Verne, Henry
Bob Moran series (5)

Bob Spencer the life saver
Armitage, Taylor
Uncle Sam's service series (1)

Bob Steele afloat in the clouds
Grayson, Donald
Bob Steele series (4)

Bob Steele from auto to airship
Grayson, Donald
Bob Steele series (3)

Bob Steele in strange waters
Grayson, Donald
Bob Steele series (6)

Bob Steele on high gear
Grayson, Donald
Bob Steele series (2)

Bob Steele's last flight
Grayson, Donald
Bob Steele series (10)

Bob Steele's motorboat
Grayson, Donald
Bob Steele series (7)

Bob Steele's motorcycle
Grayson, Donald
Bob Steele series (1)

Bob Steele's new aeroplane
Grayson, Donald
Bob Steele series (9)

Bob Steele's submarine cruise
Grayson, Donald
Bob Steele series (5)

Bob Steele's winning race
Grayson, Donald
Bob Steele series (8)

Bob Wakefield, naval aviator
Miller, Blaine
Bob Wakefield series (1)

Bob Wakefield, naval inspector
Miller, Blaine
Bob Wakefield series (2)

Bob Wakefield's flight log
Miller, Blaine
Bob Wakefield series (3)

Bobbie Bear and the blizzard
Oona, Katherine Deme
Bobbie Bear series (2)

Bobbie Bear goes to the beach
Oona, Katherine Deme
Bobbie Bear series (1)

Bobbie takes the reins
Furminger, Justine
Bobbie series (1)

Bobbies, baubles and blood
Hardin, J D
Raider and Doc series (21)

Bobbie's sponsored ride
Furminger, Justine
Bobbie series (2)

Bobbi's new year
Solomon, Joan
Children's life series (6)

Bobbsey twins
Hope, Laura Lee
Bobbsey twins series (1)

Bobbsey twins' adventure in the country
Hope, Laura Lee
Bobbsey twins series (2)

Bobbsey twins' adventure in Washington
Hope, Laura Lee
Bobbsey twins series (12)

Bobbsey twins' adventures with baby May
Hope, Laura Lee
Bobbsey twins series (17)

Bobbsey twins and baby May
Hope, Laura Lee
Bobbsey twins series (17)

Bobbsey twins and double trouble
Hope, Laura Lee
Bobbsey twins series (79)

Bobbsey twins and the Big River mystery
Hope, Laura Lee
Bobbsey twins series (56)

Bobbsey twins and the camp fire mystery
Hope, Laura Lee
Bobbsey twins series (78)

Bobbsey twins and the Cedar Camp mystery
Hope, Laura Lee
Bobbsey twins series (14)

Bobbsey twins and the circus surprise
Hope, Laura Lee
Bobbsey twins series (25)

Bobbsey twins and the country fair mystery
Hope, Laura Lee
Bobbsey twins series (15)

Bobbsey twins and the doodlebug mystery
Hope, Laura Lee
Bobbsey twins series (62)

Bobbsey twins and the flying clown
Hope, Laura Lee
Bobbsey twins series (67)

Bobbsey twins and the four-leaf clover mystery
Hope, Laura Lee
Bobbsey twins series (19)

Bobbsey twins and the Freedom Bell mystery
Hope, Laura Lee
Bobbsey twins series (69)

Bobbsey twins and the ghost in the computer
Hope, Laura Lee
Bobbsey twins series (82)

Bobbsey twins and the goldfish mystery
Hope, Laura Lee
Bobbsey twins series (55)

Bobbsey twins and the Greek hat mystery
Hope, Laura Lee
Bobbsey twins series (57)

Bobbsey twins and the grinning gargoyle mystery
Hope, Laura Lee
Bobbsey twins series (86)

Bobbsey twins and the haunted house mystery
Hope, Laura Lee
Bobbsey twins series (84)

Bobbsey twins and the horsehoe riddle
Hope, Laura Lee
Bobbsey twins series (46)

Bobbsey twins and the music box mystery
Hope, Laura Lee
Bobbsey twins series (81)

Bobbsey twins and the mystery at Snow Lodge
Hope, Laura Lee
Bobbsey twins series (5)

Bobbsey twins and the mystery of the Hindu temple
Hope, Laura Lee
Bobbsey twins series (85)

Bobbsey twins and the mystery of the king's puppet
Hope, Laura Lee
Bobbsey twins series (60)

Bobbsey twins and the mystery of the laughing dinosaur
Hope, Laura Lee
Bobbsey twins series (80)

Bobbsey twins and the play house secret
Hope, Laura Lee
Bobbsey twins series (18)

Bobbsey twins and the rose parade mystery
Hope, Laura Lee
Bobbsey twins series (77)

Bobbsey twins and the scarecrow mystery
Hope, Laura Lee
Bobbsey twins series (83)

Bobbsey twins and the secret of Candy Castle
Hope, Laura Lee
Bobbsey twins series (61)

Bobbsey twins and the Smoky Mountain mystery
Hope, Laura Lee
Bobbsey twins series (70)

Bobbsey twins and the tagalong giraffe
Hope, Laura Lee
Bobbsey twins series (66)

Bobbsey twins and the talking fox mystery
Hope, Laura Lee
Bobbsey twins series (63)

Bobbsey twins and their camel adventure
Hope, Laura Lee
Bobbsey twins series (59)

Bobbsey twins and their schoolmates
Hope, Laura Lee
Bobbsey twins series (21)

Bobbsey twins at Big Bear Pond
Hope, Laura Lee
Bobbsey twins series (47)

Bobbsey twins at Cedar Camp
Hope, Laura Lee
Bobbsey twins series (14)

Bobbsey twins at Cherry Corners
Hope, Laura Lee
Bobbsey twins series (20)

Bobbsey twins at Cloverbank
Hope, Laura Lee
Bobbsey twins series (19)

Bobbsey twins at home
Hope, Laura Lee
Bobbsey twins series (8)

Bobbsey twins at Indian Hollow
Hope, Laura Lee
Bobbsey twins series (33)

Bobbsey twins at Lighthouse Point
Hope, Laura Lee
Bobbsey twins series (32)

Bobbsey twins at London Tower
Hope, Laura Lee
Bobbsey twins series (52)

Bobbsey twins at Meadow Brook
Hope, Laura Lee
Bobbsey twins series (7)

Bobbsey twins at Mystery Mansion
Hope, Laura Lee
Bobbsey twins series (38)

Bobbsey twins at Pilgrim Rock
Hope, Laura Lee
Bobbsey twins series (50)

Bobbsey twins at school
Hope, Laura Lee
Bobbsey twins series (4)

Bobbsey twins at Snow Lodge
Hope, Laura Lee
Bobbsey twins series (5)

Bobbsey twins at Spruce Lake
Hope, Laura Lee
Bobbsey twins series (23)

Bobbsey twins at Sugar Maple Hill
Hope, Laura Lee
Bobbsey twins series (39)

Bobbsey twins at the circus
Hope, Laura Lee
Bobbsey twins series (25)

Bobbsey twins at the country fair
Hope, Laura Lee
Bobbsey twins series (15)

Bobbsey twins at the ice carnival
Hope, Laura Lee
Bobbsey twins series (34)

Bobbsey twins at the seashore
Hope, Laura Lee
Bobbsey twins series (3)

Bobbsey twins at the Tower of London
Hope, Laura Lee
Bobbsey twins series (52)

Bobbsey twins at Whitesail Harbor
Hope, Laura Lee
Bobbsey twins series (45)

Bobbsey twins at Whitesail Harbour
Hope, Laura Lee
Bobbsey twins series (45)

Bobbsey twins at Windmill Cottage
Hope, Laura Lee
Bobbsey twins series (31)

Bobbsey twins big adventure at home
Hope, Laura Lee
Bobbsey twins series (8)

Bobbsey twins camping out
Hope, Laura Lee
Bobbsey twins series (16)

Bobbsey twins' forest adventure
Hope, Laura Lee
Bobbsey twins series (51)

Bobbsey twins in a great city
Hope, Laura Lee
Bobbsey twins series (9)

Bobbsey twins in a radio play
Hope, Laura Lee
Bobbsey twins series (30)

Bobbsey twins in a TV mystery show
Hope, Laura Lee
Bobbsey twins series (71)

Bobbsey twins in Echo Valley
Hope, Laura Lee
Bobbsey twins series (36)

Bobbsey twins in Eskimo Land
Hope, Laura Lee
Bobbsey twins series (29)

Bobbsey twins in Mexico
Hope, Laura Lee
Bobbsey twins series (40)

Bobbsey twins in Rainbow Valley
Hope, Laura Lee
Bobbsey twins series (43)

Bobbsey twins in the country
Hope, Laura Lee
Bobbsey twins series (2)

Bobbsey twins in the great West
Hope, Laura Lee
Bobbsey twins series (13)

Bobbsey twins in the land of cotton
Hope, Laura Lee
Bobbsey twins series (35)

Bobbsey twins in the mystery at Cherry Corners
Hope, Laura Lee
Bobbsey twins series (20)

Bobbsey twins in the mystery cave
Hope, Laura Lee
Bobbsey twins series (53)

Bobbsey twins in Tulip Land
Hope, Laura Lee
Bobbsey twins series (42)

Bobbsey twins in Volcano Land
Hope, Laura Lee
Bobbsey twins series (54)

Bobbsey twins in Washington
Hope, Laura Lee
Bobbsey twins series (12)

Bobbsey twins keeping house
Hope, Laura Lee
Bobbsey twins series (18)

Bobbsey twins' mystery at Meadow Brook
Hope, Laura Lee
Bobbsey twins series (7)

Bobbsey twins' mystery at school
Hope, Laura Lee
Bobbsey twins series (4)

Bobbsey twins' mystery on the deep blue sea
Hope, Laura Lee
Bobbsey twins series (11)

Bobbsey twins of Lakeport
Hope, Laura Lee
Bobbsey twins series (1)

Bobbsey twins on a bicycle trip
Hope, Laura Lee
Bobbsey twins series (48)

Bobbsey twins on a houseboat
Hope, Laura Lee
Bobbsey twins series (6)

Bobbsey twins on a ranch
Hope, Laura Lee
Bobbsey twins series (28)

Bobbsey twins on an airplane trip
Hope, Laura Lee
Bobbsey twins series (26)

Bobbsey twins on Blueberry Island
Hope, Laura Lee
Bobbsey twins series (10)

Bobbsey twins on the deep blue sea
Hope, Laura Lee
Bobbsey twins series (11)

Bobbsey twins on the pony trail
Hope, Laura Lee
Bobbsey twins series (37)

Bobbsey twins on the sun-moon cruise
Hope, Laura Lee
Bobbsey twins series (68)

Bobbsey twins' own little ferryboat
Hope, Laura Lee
Bobbsey twins series (49)

Bobbsey twins' own little railroad
Hope, Laura Lee
Bobbsey twins series (44)

Bobbsey twins' own little railway
Hope, Laura Lee
Bobbsey twins series (44)

Bobbsey twins' search for the green rooster
Hope, Laura Lee
Bobbsey twins series (58)

Bobbsey twins' search in the great city
Hope, Laura Lee
Bobbsey twins series (9)

Bobbsey twins' secret at the seashore
Hope, Laura Lee
Bobbsey twins series (3)

Bobbsey twins solve a mystery
Hope, Laura Lee
Bobbsey twins series (27)

Bobbsey twins' toy shop
Hope, Laura Lee
Bobbsey twins series (41)

Bobbsey twins treasure hunting
Hope, Laura Lee
Bobbsey twins series (22)

Bobbsey twins' visit to the great West
Hope, Laura Lee
Bobbsey twins series (13)

Bobbsey twins' wonderful secret
Hope, Laura Lee
Bobbsey twins series (24)

Bobbsey twins' wonderful winter secret
Hope, Laura Lee
Bobbsey twins series (24)

Bobby and Frank
Pearce, Margaret
Home and away series (3)

Bobby Blake and his school chums
Warner, Frank A
Bobby Blake series (4)

Bobby Blake at Bass Cove
Warner, Frank A
Bobby Blake series (2)

Bobby Blake at Rockledge School
Warner, Frank A
Bobby Blake series (1)

Bobby Blake at Snowtop Camp
Warner, Frank A
Bobby Blake series (5)

Bobby Blake in the frozen North
Warner, Frank A
Bobby Blake series (11)

Bobby Blake on a cruise
Warner, Frank A
Bobby Blake series (3)

Bobby Blake on a plantation
Warner, Frank A
Bobby Blake series (10)

Bobby Blake on a ranch
Warner, Frank A
Bobby Blake series (7)

Bobby Blake on an auto tour
Warner, Frank A
Bobby Blake series (8)

Bobby Blake on Mystery Mountain
Warner, Frank A
Bobby Blake series (12)

Bobby Blake on the school eleven
Warner, Frank A
Bobby Blake series (9)

Bobby Blake on the school nine
Warner, Frank A
Bobby Blake series (6)

Bobby Brewster
Todd, Herbert Eatton
Bobby Brewster series (2)

Bobby Brewster and the ghost
Todd, Herbert Eatton
Bobby Brewster series (11)

Bobby Brewster and the magic handyman
Todd, Herbert Eatton
Bobby Brewster series (26)

Bobby Brewster and the Winker's Club
Todd, Herbert Eatton
Bobby Brewster series (1)

Bobby Brewster, bus conductor
Todd, Herbert Eatton
Bobby Brewster series (3)

Bobby Brewster, detective
Todd, Herbert Eatton
Bobby Brewster series (9)

Bolsheviks and world communism
Cliff, Tony
Lenin series (4)
Bolster book
Graham, Harry
Reginald Drake Biffin series (1)
Bolt
Francis, Dick
Kit Fielding series (2)
Bolt-action
LeBeau, Roy
Buckskin series (10)
Bolts, a robot dog
Key, Alexander
Sprockets trilogy (3)
Bolts from blue skies
Carter, Nicholas
Nicholas Carter series (516)
Bom and his magic drumstick
Blyton, Enid
Bom series (2)
Bom and the clown
Blyton, Enid
Bom series (6)
Bom and the rainbow
Blyton, Enid
Bom series (5)
Bom annual
Blyton, Enid
Bom series (11)
Bom at the seaside
Blyton, Enid
Bom series (10)
Bom goes adventuring
Blyton, Enid
Bom series (3)
Bom goes to Ho Ho Village
Blyton, Enid
Bom series (4)
Bom goes to Magic Town
Blyton, Enid
Bom series (8)
Bom goes to the circus
Blyton, Enid
Bom series (11)
Bom painting book
Blyton, Enid
Bom series (11)
Bom, the little toy drummer
Blyton, Enid
Bom series (1)
Bomb job
Kane, Henry
Peter Chambers series (26)
Bomb-scare flight 147
Chambers, Peter
Mark Preston series (33)
Bomb vessel
Woodman, Richard
Nathaniel Drinkwater series (4)
Bomba the jungle boy
Rockwood, Roy
Bomba series (1)
Bomba the jungle boy among the pygmies
Rockwood, Roy
Bomba series (12)
Bomba the jungle boy among the slaves
Rockwood, Roy
Bomba series (8)
Bomba the jungle boy and the cannibals
Rockwood, Roy
Bomba series (13)
Bomba the jungle boy and the hostile chieftain
Rockwood, Roy
Bomba series (16)
Bomba the jungle boy and the lost explorers
Rockwood, Roy
Bomba series (10)
Bomba the jungle boy and the painted hunters
Rockwood, Roy
Bomba series (14)
Bomba the jungle boy and the river demons
Rockwood, Roy
Bomba series (15)
Bomba the jungle boy at the giant cataract
Rockwood, Roy
Bomba series (3)
Bomba the jungle boy at the moving mountain
Rockwood, Roy
Bomba series (2)
Bomba the jungle boy in a strange land
Rockwood, Roy
Bomba series (11)
Bomba the jungle boy in the abandoned city
Rockwood, Roy
Bomba series (5)
Bomba the jungle boy in the land of burning lava
Rockwood, Roy
Bomba series (18)
Bomba the jungle boy in the perilous kingdom
Rockwood, Roy
Bomba series (19)
Bomba the jungle boy in the steaming grotto
Rockwood, Roy
Bomba series (20)
Bomba the jungle boy in the swamp of death
Rockwood, Roy
Bomba series (7)
Bomba the jungle boy on Jaguar Island
Rockwood, Roy
Bomba series (4)
Bomba the jungle boy on Terror Trail
Rockwood, Roy
Bomba series (6)
Bomba the jungle boy on the underground river
Rockwood, Roy
Bomba series (9)
Bomba the jungle boy trapped by the cyclone
Rockwood, Roy
Bomba series (17)
Bombay boomerang
Dixon, Franklin W
Hardy boys series (49)
Bombay mail
Blochman, Lawrence Goldtree
Inspector Leonidas Prike series (1)
Bombay Marines
Hill, Porter
Captain Adam Horne series (1)
Bombers in the sky
Whitehouse, Arch
Air war series (2)
Bombers moon
Vander Els, Betty
Ruth series (1)
Bombing run
Stein, Aaron Marc
Matt Erridge series (22)
Bombs from the murder wolves
Hogan, Robert Jasper
G-Eight series (4)
Bombshell
Brown, Carter
Lieutenant Al Wheeler series (5)
Fickling, G G
Honey West series (9)
Raine, Richard
David Martini series (3)
Bombship
Knox, Bill
Webb Carrick series (11)
Bon chance
Grover, Marshall
Larry and Stretch series (281)
Bon marche
Hagan, Chet
Dewey annals series (1)
Bon voyage Baabee
Khalsa, Dayal Kaur
Baabee series III (1)
Bonanza
Campion, Sarah
Mister Moses Burdekin series (2)
Loomis, Noel
Bonanza series (1)
Bonanza at Wishbone
Floren, Lee
Judge Lemanuel Bates and Tobacco Jones series (1)
Bonanza City
Mitchum, Hank
Stage coach station series (35)
Bonanza kings
Peterson, Richard Hermann
Western mining series (1)
Bonanza murder case
Snow, Charles Horace
Tommy Thorne series (2)
Bonanza rich
Peterson, Richard Hermann
Western mining series (2)
Boncoeur affair
Wickham, Harvey
Ferris McClue series (3)
Bond
Ehrlich, Max
Peter Proud series (2)
Bond Grayson murdered!
Bortner, Norman Stanley
Professor Clifford Wells series (1)
Bond jumper
Tully, Paul
Deputy Marshal Hooky Gibbs series (3)
Bond of love
Joyce, Rosemary
Dream girls series (4)
Bond Street murder
Brandon, John Gordon
Arthur Stukeley Pennington series (8)
Inspector Patrick Aloysius McCarthy series (14)
Bond Street raiders
Brandon, John Gordon
Sexton Blake series (919)
Bonded dead
Chaber, M E
Milo March series (20)
Bonded Fleming
Fleming, Ian
James Bond series (10)
Bonded villain
Carter, Nicholas
Nicholas Carter series (121)
Bonding
Lynde, Stan
Pardners series (1)
Bondmaster
Tresillian, Richard
Bondmaster series (1)
Bondmaster breed
Tresillian, Richard
Bondmaster series (3)
Bondmaster buck
Tresillian, Richard
Bondmaster series (6)
Bondmaster fury
Tresillian, Richard
Bondmaster series (4)
Bondmaster's revenge
Tresillian, Richard
Bondmaster series (5)
Bonds of eternity
Darlton, Clark
Perry Rhodan series (69)
Bonds of shame
Lascaux, Simon
Ebony masters series (2)
Bondwoman
Collingwood, William Gershon
Norsemen series (2)
Bone and a hank of hair
Bruce, Leo
Carolus Deene series (9)
Bone game
Owens, Louis
Cole McCurtain series (2)
Bone idle
Staynes, Jill
Superintendent Bone series (6)
Bone is pointed
Upfield, Arthur William
Napoleon Bonaparte series (6)
Bone to pick
Harris, Charlaine
Aurora Teagarden series (1)
Bone yard
Pendleton, Don
Mack Bolan series (75)
Bones
Pronzini, Bill
Private Eye series (15)
Tepper, Sheri S
Blood heritage series (2)
Wallace, Edgar
Commissioner Sanders series (4)
Bones and silence
Hill, Reginald
Superintendent Andrew Dalziel and Sergeant Pascoe series (17)
Bones gather no moss
Sherwood, John
Celia Grant series (11)
Bones in London
Wallace, Edgar
Commissioner Sanders series (13)
Bones in the barrow
Bell, Josephine
Doctor David Wintringham series (11)
Inspector Steven Mitchell series (7)
Bones in the brickfield
Burton, Miles
Inspector Arnold and Desmond Merrion series (56)
Bones in the wilderness
Bellairs, George
Detective Inspector Thomas Littlejohn series (31)
Bones of contention
Candy, Edward
Inspector Burnival series (2)
Bones of Frankenstein
Glut, Donald Frank
Frankenstein sequels series (8)
Bones of haven
Green, Simon
Hawk and Fisher series (6)
Bones of the moon
Carroll, Jonathan
Bones series (1)
Bones of the river
Wallace, Edgar
Commissioner Sanders series (5)
Bones of Zora
De Camp, Lyon Sprague
Krishna series (9)
Boneshaker
Rogers, Paul
Boneshaker series (1)
Boneshaker rides again
Rogers, Paul
Boneshaker series (2)
Bonfire murder
Plummer, Thomas Arthur
Detective Inspector Andrew Frampton series (5)
Bonfires and broomsticks
Norton, Mary
Bed-knob and broomstick series (2)
Bonhomme
Brunhoff, Laurent de
Bonhomme series (1)
Bonhomme and the huge beast
Brunhoff, Laurent de
Bonhomme series (2)
Bonifacius and Little Bonnie
Anckarsvard, Karin
Bonifacius series (2)
Bonifacius the Green
Anckarsvard, Karin
Bonifacius series (1)
Bonn blitz
Wilson, Gar
Phoenix Force series (30)
Bonnie and Clyde
Hirschfeld, Burt
Bonnie and Clyde series (1)
Bonnie Edith Copplestone
Waldy, Frances Helen
Scarsborough series (1)
Bonnie Jean
Barke, James
Immortal memory series (6)
Bonnie McSmithers is at it again!
Alderson, Sue Ann
Bonnie McSmithers series (2)
Bonnie McSmithers, you're driving me dithers
Alderson, Sue Ann
Bonnie McSmithers series (1)
Bonny book of Josephine
Cradock, Henry Cowper, Mrs
Josephine series (6)
Bonny's big day
Herriot, James
Pets series (4)
Bonus for murder
Brandon, John Gordon
Inspector Patrick Aloysius McCarthy series (21)
Bony and the black virgin
Upfield, Arthur William
Napoleon Bonaparte series (24)
Bony and the Kelly Gang
Upfield, Arthur William
Napoleon Bonaparte series (25)
Bony and the mouse
Upfield, Arthur William
Napoleon Bonaparte series (23)
Bony and the white savage
Upfield, Arthur William
Napoleon Bonaparte series (26)
Bony buys a woman
Upfield, Arthur William
Napoleon Bonaparte series (22)
Booby trap
Stout, Rex
Nero Wolfe and Archie Goodwin series (10)
Boocoo death
Lansing, John
Black Eagles series (8)
Boodle
Charteris, Leslie
Saint series (13)
Boogeymen
Gilden, Mel
Star trek, the next generation series (17)
Boogie Woogie Bears go bacvk to nature
Kraus, Robert
Boogie Woogie Bears series (1)
Boogie Woogie Bears' picnic
Kraus, Robert
Boogie Woogie Bears series (2)
Book about Moomin, Mymble and little My
Jansson, Tove
Moomin series (4)
Book and the phoenix
Baldry, Cherith
Stories of six worlds series (1)
Book for Banning
Easton, Nat
Bill Banning series (5)
Book for Jane
Farnol, Jeffery
Jane series (1)
Book-full of beans
Fowler, Richard
Beans series (1)
Book her for murder
Brody, Marc
Marc Brody series (64)
Book of Abraham
Halter, Marek
Jewish family series (1)
Book of Avis
Phillpotts, Eden
Book of Avis series (3)
Book of Bebb
Buechner, Frederick
Leo Bebb tetralogy (4)
Book of Being
Watson, Ian
Black Current trilogy (3)
Book of Bette
Kelly, Eleanor Mercein
Urruty family trilogy (2)
Book of cats and creatures
Manning-Sanders, Ruth
Folk tales series (19)
Book of charms and changelings
Manning-Sanders, Ruth
Folk tales series (10)
Book of coarse sport
Green, Michael
Coarse series (5)
Book of Dan
Rudd, Steele
Rudd family series (7)
Book of death
Grant, Maxwell
Shadow series (217)
Book of devils and demons
Manning-Sanders, Ruth
Folk tales series (9)
Book of dragons
Manning-Sanders, Ruth
Folk tales series (3)
Book of dreams
Vance, Jack
Kirth Gersen series (5)
Book of dwarfs
Manning-Sanders, Ruth
Folk tales series (2)
Book of enchantments and curses
Manning-Sanders, Ruth
Folk tales series (15)
Book of flower fairies
Barker, Cicely Mary
Flower fairies series (4)
Book of ghosts and goblins
Manning-Sanders, Ruth
Folk tales series (7)
Book of giants
Manning-Sanders, Ruth
Folk tales series (1)
Book of Giuliano Sansevero
Giovene, Andrea
Giuliano Sansevero series (1)
Book of heroes and heroines
Manning-Sanders, Ruth
Folk tales series (20)
Book of Kane
Wagner, Karl Edward
Kane series (6)
Book of King Arthur
Pyle, Howard
Arthurian legends series (1)
Book of kings and queens
Manning-Sanders, Ruth
Folk tales series (16)
Book of lost tales, part 1
Tolkien, John Ronald Reuel
History of Middle Earth series (1)
Book of lost tales, part 2
Tolkien, John Ronald Reuel
History of Middle Earth series (2)

Book of magic adventures
Manning-Sanders, Ruth
Folk tales series (21)
Book of magic animals
Manning-Sanders, Ruth
Folk tales series (13)
Book of magic horses
Manning-Sanders, Ruth
Folk tales series (22)
Book of Martha
Dowdall, Mary Frances
Martha series (1)
Book of marvels and magic
Manning-Sanders, Ruth
Folk tales series (17)
Book of Merlyn
White, Terence Hanbury
Once and future king series (4)
Book of mermaids
Manning-Sanders, Ruth
Folk tales series (6)
Book of monsters
Manning-Sanders, Ruth
Folk tales series (14)
Book of Mordred
Hanratty, Peter
Arthur series (2)
Book of Morgaine
Cherryh, Carolyn Janice
Chronicles of Morgaine series (3)
Book of murder
Anderson, Frederick Irving
Deputy Parr series (2)
Oliver Armiston series (3)
Book of my Uncle Oswald
McCardell, Roy Larcom
Aunt and Uncle series (2)
Book of naughty children
Blyton, Enid
Naughty children series (1)
Book of ogres and trolls
Manning-Sanders, Ruth
Folk tales series (11)
Book of princes and princesses
Manning-Sanders, Ruth
Folk tales series (8)
Book of Rack the Healer
Hughes, Zach
Rack the Healer series (1)
Book of Reuben
King, Tabitha
Nodd's Ridge series (5)
Book of Shai
Walther, Daniel
Shai series (1)
Book of silence
Watt-Evans, Lawrence
Lords of Dus series (4)
Book of Skaith
Brackett, Leigh
Eric John Stark series (5)
Book of sorcerers and spells
Manning-Sanders, Ruth
Folk tales series (12)
Book of sorrows
Wangerin, Walter
Coop series (2)
Book of spooks and spectres
Manning-Sanders, Ruth
Folk tales series (18)
Book of Sunnybank
Terhune, Albert Payson
Sunnybank collies series (17)
Book of suns
Springer, Nancy
Book of Isle series (1)
Book of the beast
Lee, Tanith
Secret books of Paradys series (2)
Stallman, Robert
Beast trilogy (3)
Book of the crime
Daly, Elizabeth
Henry Gamadge series (16)
Book of the damned
Lee, Tanith
Secret books of Paradys series (1)
Book of the dead
Daly, Elizabeth
Henry Gamadge series (8)
Lee, Tanith
Secret books of Paradys series (3)
Book of the dun cow
Wangerin, Walter
Coop series (1)
Book of the green planet
Kotzwinkle, William
E.T. series (2)
Book of the lion
Daly, Elizabeth
Henry Gamadge series (13)
Book of the new sun
Wolfe, Gene
Book of the new sun series (2)
Book of the River
Watson, Ian
Black Current trilogy (1)
Book of the Stars
Watson, Ian
Black Current trilogy (2)
Book of three
Alexander, Lloyd
Prydain series (1)
Book of Toytown and Larry the lamb
Beaman, Sydney George Hulme
Toytown series (40)
Book of ultimate truths
Rankin, Robert
Ultimate truths trilogy (1)
Book of Vale
Springer, Nancy
Book of Isle series (5)
Book of witches
Manning-Sanders, Ruth
Folk tales series (4)
Book of wizards
Manning-Sanders, Ruth
Folk tales series (5)
Bookcase
Greenleaf, Stephen
John Marshall Tanner series (7)
Booked for a hanging
Crider, Bill
Dan Rhodes series (7)
Booked for death
Cumberland, Marten
Saturnin Dax series (16)
Bookful of Jennings
Buckeridge, Anthony
Jennings series (16)
Bookmaker's body
Stone, Simon
Sir Brian Dinsmore Conway series (3)
Bookmaker's crime
Hardy, Arthur Steffens
Sexton Blake series (843)
Books do furnish a room
Powell, Anthony
Dance to the music of time series (10)
Books for the Baron
Morton, Anthony
Baron series (16)
Books of blood V
Barker, Clive
Books of blood series (5)
Books of blood VI
Barker, Clive
Books of blood series (6)
Books of blood, volume I
Barker, Clive
Books of blood series (1)
Books of blood, volume II
Barker, Clive
Books of blood series (2)
Books of blood, volume III
Barker, Clive
Books of blood series (3)
Books of blood, volume IV
Barker, Clive
Books of blood series (4)
Books of blood, volume V
Barker, Clive
Books of blood series (5)
Books of blood, volume VI
Barker, Clive
Books of blood series (6)
Books of Great Alta
Yolen, Jane
Great Alta series (2)
Books of Rachel
Gross, Joel
Rachel series (2)
Books of the Black Current
Watson, Ian
Black Current trilogy (3)
Boom town
Edwards, Josh
John Stone series (10)
Scott, Bradford
Walt Slade series (98)
Boom town boy
Lenski, Lois
Regional series (5)
Boom town bravados
Grover, Marshall
Larry and Stretch series (90)
Boom town guns
Hopson, William L
Masked Rider and Blue Hawk series (31)
Boom town killer
Roberts, J R
Gunsmith series (62)
Boomer down
Adair, James B
Deepcore series (2)
Boomerang murder
Grierson, Francis Durham
Inspector George Muir series (13)
Superintendent Andrew Ash series (6)
Boomerang stories for the children
Edwards, George
Golden boomerang series (2)
Boomers
Willoughby, Lee Davis
Making of America series (20)
Booming of Bunkie
Neill, Alexander Sutherland
Dominie series (4)
Boomtown bust
Hunter, E J
White Squaw series (2)
Boomtown bustout
Masters, Zeke
Faro Blake series (9)
Boone's law
Slaughter, Jim
Boone Helm series (3)
Boonie-rat body burning
Cain, Jonathan
Saigon commandos series (5)
Boori
Scott, Bill
Boori series (1)
Boosted man
Zetford, Tully
Ryder Hook series (2)
Booster boycott
Pascal, Francine
Sweet Valley twins series (52)
Boot Hill brother
Hill, Morgan
Dan Colt series (3)
Boot Hill gospel
Martin, Charles Morris
Gospel Cummings series (2)
Boot River run
Kherdian, David
Armenian girl series (2)
Boothill bounty
Sherman, Jory
Gunn series (9)
Boothill Court
Smith, Lew
Judge Lemanuel Bates and Tobacco Jones series (6)
Bootlaces for Bastion
Harrison, Richard
Chief Inspector William Bastion series (2)
Bootleg angel
Mazzaro, Ed
Undercover series (2)
Bootlegger
Torrio, Vincente
Hoods series (2)
Bootlegger's daughter
Maron, Margaret
Judge Deborah Knott series (1)
Bootlegger's victim
Armour, R Coutts
Sexton Blake series (552)
Bootles' baby
Winter, John Strange
Bootles series (3)
Bootles' children
Winter, John Strange
Bootles series (8)
Boots and Josephine
Mure, Geoffrey
Josephine series (2)
Boots and saddles
Cunningham, Chet
Pony soldiers series (7)
Boots and the ginger bears
Baker, Margaret Joyce
Three bears series (6)
Boots for Charlie
Allen, Joy
Charlie series (1)
Booty for a babe
Brown, Carter
Lieutenant Al Wheeler series (3)
Booty from a badman
L'Amour, Louis
Sackett family series (18)
Bop
Ross, Tony
Tales from Mister Toffy's circus series (2)
Boracho
Rodgers, Sherlaw Johnston
Micah Truelove series (2)
Borchester echoes
Gallagher, Jock
Archers of Ambridge series (7)
Bordeaux red
Clayton, Colin Guy
Blakeney papers series (3)
Bordello backshooter
Martin, Cort
Jared Bolt series (15)
Borden Chantry
L'Amour, Louis
Chantry family series (4)
Border affair
Sandon, J D
Gringos series (4)
Border arrows
Sharpe, Jon
Trailsman series (22)
Border bairn
Derwent, Lavinia
Border series (3)
Border bandits
Mason, Dan
Lex Cranshaw series (2)
Border blood
Scott, Bradford
Walt Slade series (11)
Border Boys across the frontier
Deering, Fremont B
Border Boys series (2)
Border Boys along the St Lawrence
Deering, Fremont B
Border Boys series (6)
Border Boys in the Canadian Rockies
Deering, Fremont B
Border Boys series (5)
Border Boys on the trail
Deering, Fremont B
Border Boys series (1)
Border Boys with the Mexican Rangers
Deering, Fremont B
Border Boys series (3)
Border Boys with the Texas Rangers
Deering, Fremont B
Border Boys series (4)
Border breed
Willoughby, Lee Davis
Making of America series (18)
Border, breed, nor birth
Reynolds, Mack
Homer Crawford trilogy (2)
Border country
Williams, Raymond
Glynmawr series (1)
Border daring
Scott, Bradford
Walt Slade series (119)
Border fury
Morgan, G J
Buck Dunne series (2)
Border hell
Cole, Jackson
Jim Hatfield series (12)
Border incident
Flynn, Jay
Jim Bannerman series (2)
Border jumpers
Benteen, John
Neal Fargo series (15)
Border killing
James, William M
Apache series (22)
Border knight
Dymoke, Juliet
Plantagenets series (7)
Border law
Hardin, J D
Raider series (34)
Border Legion
Grey, Zane
Border Legion series (1)
Border line
Masterman, Walter Sidney
Dick Seldon series (2)
Border Peel
Hill, Lorna
Marjorie series (3)
Border Riding
Tranter, Nigel Godwin
Ken and Fiona series (2)
Border showdown
Hart, Matthew S
Cody's law series (3)
Border storm
Grover, Marshall
Larry and Stretch series (73)
Border terror
Scott, Bradford
Walt Slade series (96)
Walt Slade series (117)
Border trouble
Boone, James Calder
Ned Remington series (6)
Border vengeance
Scott, Bradford
Walt Slade series (73)
Border war
Brady, William S
Jared Hawk series (14)
Drumm, D B
Traveler series (6)
Hardin, J D
Raider series (26)
Scott, Bradford
Walt Slade series (96)
Slade, Jack
Gatling series (3)
Border watch
Altsheler, Joseph Alexander
Trailers series (6)
Border way
Edwards, Hank
Judge Clay Torn series (9)
Border winds
Randle, Kevin
Global war series (2)
Border wolf
Bennet, Robert Ames
Wolf series (3)
Borderland
Calderini, Priscilla
Borderland series (2)
Hunt, Greg
Hartman family trilogy (1)
Truman, Timothy
Simon Girty series (1)
Windling, Terri
Borderland series (1)
Borderland of hell
Barker, Wade
Ninja Master series (3)
Borderline case
Dixon, Franklin W
Hardy boys case files series (25)
McLeave, Hugh
Doctor Gregor Maclean series (2)
Borderlines
Mayor, Archer Huntington
Lieutenant Joe Gunther series (2)
Borderlords
Johnston, Terry Conrad
Titus Bass series (2)
Borders of barbarism
Williams, Eric Ernest
Roger and Kate Starte series (2)
Borders of infinity
Bujold, Lois McMaster
Miles Naismith Vorkosigan series (2)
Borders omnibus
Derwent, Lavinia
Border series (7)
Bordertown
Windling, Terri
Borderland series (2)
Boreas adventure
Knight, Peter
Anthony Daintrey series (2)
Bored of the rings
Beard, Henry N
Middle Earth series (5)
Bored to death
Delving, Michael
Dave Cannon and Robert Eddison series (5)
Borgia bull
Bennetts, Pamela
Cesare Borgia series (2)
Borgia cabinet
Fletcher, Joseph Smith
Sergeant Charlesworth series (1)
Borgia dagger
Dixon, Franklin W
Hardy boys case files series (13)
Borgia Head mystery
Gunn, Victor
Chief Inspector Bill Cromwell series (18)
Borgia prince
Bennetts, Pamela
Cesare Borgia series (1)
Borgian bull
Huna, Ludwig
Borgia trilogy (1)
Borgias
Blasco Ibanez, Vicente
Spanish history series (2)
Boris and Barbara
Bruna, Dick
Boris Bear series (2)
Boris Bear
Bruna, Dick
Boris Bear series (1)

Boris on the mountain
Bruna, Dick
Boris Bear series (3)
Born beautiful
Campbell, Keith
Mike Brett series (4)
Born brothers
Woiwode, Larry
Neumiller family series (2)
Born free
Adamson, Joy
Elsa series (1)
Born in paradise
Tempski, Armine von
Paradise series (1)
Born Indian
Kinsella, William Patrick
Silas Ermineskin series (3)
Born leader
Browne, Dik
Hagar the horrible series (15)
Born loser
Brown, Carter
Lieutenant Al Wheeler series (45)
Born losers
Macbeth, George
Cadbury series (3)
Born mechanic
Martin, Robert
Ginger Pennylove series (3)
Born of flame
Senn, Steve
Spacebread series (2)
Born of the sun
Culp, John Hewett
Martin Cameron series (1)
Born soldier
Winter, John Strange
Bootles series (10)
Born to be hanged
Chaber, M E
Milo March series (21)
Born to believe
Longford, Frank Pakenham
Born to believe trilogy (1)
Born to die
James, William M
Apache series (14)
Born to drift
Grover, Marshall
Larry and Stretch series (54)
Born to exile
Eisenstein, Phyllis
Alaric the Minstrel series (1)
Born to howl
Gilden, Mel
Fifth grade monsters series (2)
Born to kill
Revere, John D
Justin Perry series (3)
Born victim
Waugh, Hillary
Chief Fred Fellows series (5)
Borneo story
Albany, James
S.A.S. series (7)
Boro Council ramp
Urquhart, Paul
Sexton Blake series (942)
Boronia babies
Gibbs, May
Gumnut Land series (3)
Boroughmonger
Mottram, Ralph Hale
Captain Dormer series (3)
Borribles
De Larrabeiti, Michael
Borribles series (1)
Borribles go for broke
De Larrabeiti, Michael
Borribles series (2)
Borrobil
Dickinson, William Croft
Donald and Jean series (1)
Borrowed alibi
Egan, Lesley
Vic Varallo series (2)
Borrowed cottage
Campbell, Alice
Inspector Headcorn series (3)
Borrowed garden
Fidler, Kathleen
Brydon family series (1)
Borrower of the night
Peters, Elizabeth
Vicky Bliss series (1)
Borrowers
Norton, Mary
Borrowers series (1)
Borrowers afield
Norton, Mary
Borrowers series (2)
Borrowers afloat
Norton, Mary
Borrowers series (3)
Borrowers aloft
Norton, Mary
Borrowers series (4)
Borrowers avenged
Norton, Mary
Borrowers series (6)
Borrowers omnibus
Norton, Mary
Borrowers series (4)
Borstal boy
Behan, Brendan
Borstal boy series (1)
Bosambo of the river
Wallace, Edgar
Commissioner Sanders series (3)
Bosnian chronicle
Andric, Ivo
Bosnian trilogy (2)
Bosnian story
Andric, Ivo
Bosnian trilogy (2)
Boss
Greaves, Jimmy
Soccer series (3)
Handler, David
Danny Levine series (2)
Boss of terror
Robeson, Kenneth
Doc Savage series (85)
Boss of the Lazy 9
Field, Peter
Powder Valley series (4)
Bossy Steven
Pascal, Francine
Sweet Valley kids series (18)
Bostock and Harris
Garfield, Leon
Bostock and Harris series (2)
Boston avenger
Barry, Mike
Burton Wulff series (3)
Boston belle meets murder
Lenehan, John Christopher
Charlie Ryan series (3)
Boston bells
Coatsworth, Elizabeth
Once-upon-a-time-in-America series (3)
Boston blitz
Pendleton, Don
Mack Bolan series (12)
Boston bust
McCurtin, Peter
Assassins series (3)
Boston crab
Usher, Frank
Amanda Curzon and Oscar Sallis series (3)
Boston run
Robbins, David
Endworld series (21)
Botanist at bay
Sherwood, John
Celia Grant series (2)
Both sides of Battle Creek
Grover, Marshall
Larry and Stretch series (215)
Both sides of the blanket
Glover, Halcott
Louise trilogy (1)
Both sides of the case
Prescot, Julian
Case books series (1)
Both sides of the hill
Hill, Charles
Broadcasting memoirs series (1)
Both sides of the medal
Sinopy, Hilda
Pelham family series (2)
Both the ladies and the gentleman
Donaldson, William
Ladies and gentlemen series (1)
Both your houses
Gibbs, Philip
Second World War series (8)
Botor chaperon
Williamson, Charles Norris
Motoring series (4)
Bottersnikes and gumbles
Wakefield, Sydney Alexander
Gumbles series (1)
Bottle and the black label
Carter, Nicholas
Nicholas Carter series (74)
Bottle imp
Taggart, Marion Ames
Jack-in-the-box series (3)
Bottom deal
Masters, Zeke
Faro Blake series (7)
Bottom dogs
Dahlberg, Edward
Bottom dogs series (1)
Bottom line
Murphy, Warren Burton
Destroyer series (37)
Bottom liner blues
Constantine, K C
Mario Balzic series (10)
Bottom of Suez
Teed, George Hamilton
Grant Rushton series (4)
Botts in war, Botts in peace
Upson, William Hazlett
Alexander Botts series (4)
Boudicca's revolt
Birt, David
Roman Britain series (14)
Boudoir murder
Propper, Milton
Tommy Rankin series (3)
Bough breaks
Hardwick, Michael
Cedar tree trilogy (3)
Boulevard mutes
Carter, Nicholas
Nicholas Carter series (170)
Bouncing back
Schuller, Gary
Bouncing series (1)
Bouncing higher
Schuller, Gary
Bouncing series (2)
Bound by desire
Rogers, Rosemary
Ginny Brandon and Steve Morgan series (4)
Bound for Australia
Bailey, Nancy
Time machine series (20)
Bound for Mars
Ballou, Arthur W
Marooned in orbit series (2)
Bound in honor
Trowbridge, John Townsend
Silver medal series (2)
Bound to be an electrician
Stratemeyer, Edward L
Bound to win series (1)
Working upward series (2)
Bound to die
Turner, Bill
Detective Inspector Manson series (1)
Bound to rise
Alger, Horatio
Luck and pluck series (6)
Boundary lines
Roberts, Nora
Flowers series (47)
Bounty for Pilgrim
Potter, Jay Hill
Pilgrim series (5)
Bounty Hunter
Fletcher, Aaron
Bounty Hunter series (1)
Bounty hunter
Franklin, Max
Starsky and Hutch series (4)
Gilman, George G
Adam Steele series (2)
Hardin, J D
Raider and Doc series (31)
Muir, James A
Breed series (13)
Bounty hunters
Ellis, Wesley
Lone Star series (97)
Roberts, J R
Gunsmith series (107)
Willoughby, Lee Davis
Making of America series (47)
Bounty hunter's moon
Hogan, Ray
Shawn Starbuck series (23)
Bounty hunter's trail
Nickson, Arthur
Rusty Hines series (6)
Bounty killer
Benteen, John
Sundance series (15)
Bounty lands
Ellis, William Donohue
Ohio frontier trilogy (1)
Bounty man
Hart, Matthew S
Cody's law series (4)
Bounty on a baron
Randall, Joshua
Bounty Hunter series (4)
Bounty on a lawman
Randall, Joshua
Bounty Hunter series (2)
Bounty on Bannister
Newton, Dwight Bennett
Jim Bannister series (10)
Bounty on Wes Durand
Grover, Marshall
Nevada Jim series (51)
McCoy, Marshall
Nevada Jim series (51)
Bounty on Wildcat
Clinton, Jeff
Wildcat O'Shea series (14)
Bounty road
Pike, Charles R
Jubal Cade series (12)
Bounty trilogy
Nordhoff, Charles
Bounty trilogy (3)
Bounty women
Roberts, J R
Gunsmith series (35)
Bouquet garni
Clark, Douglas
Inspector George Masters series (21)
Bouquet of barbed wire
Newman, Andrea
Bouquet series (1)
Bouquet of brides
Meadows, Rose
Hanover succession series (2)
Bouquet of sonnets
Crowley, Carl Campbell
Nine winds series (3)
Bouquet of thorns
Sherwood, John
Celia Grant series (7)
Bourgainville breakout
Darby, John
McLeane's Rangers series (1)
Bourne identity
Ludlum, Robert
Bourne trilogy (1)
Bourne supremacy
Ludlum, Robert
Bourne trilogy (2)
Bourne ultimatum
Ludlum, Robert
Bourne trilogy (3)
Bout with the Mildew Gang
Fowler, Sydney
Inspector Cauldron series (1)
Bow or orange ribbons
Barr, Amelia Edith
New York trilogy (1)
Bow Street brangle
Sebastian, Margaret
Bow Street series (1)
Bow Street gentleman
Sebastian, Margaret
Bow Street series (2)
Bowdrie
L'Amour, Louis
Chick Bowdrie series (1)
Bowdrie's law
L'Amour, Louis
Chick Bowdrie series (2)
Bowery murder
Smith, Willard K
Inspector Dann Carr series (1)
Bowie's mine
Kelton, Elmer
Buckalew tetralogy (3)
Tales of Texas series (7)
Bowman at a venture
Howard, Hartley
Glenn Bowman series (8)
Bowman on Broadway
Howard, Hartley
Glenn Bowman series (7)
Bowman strikes again
Howard, Hartley
Glenn Bowman series (6)
Bowman touch
Howard, Hartley
Glenn Bowman series (12)
Bowman's kid
Shirreffs, Gordon Donald
Lee Kershaw series (3)
Bowser the hound
Burgess, Thornton Waldo
Green Meadow series (3)
Bowstring murders
Dickson, Carter
Sir Henry Merrivale series (1)
Box
Turpin, Allan
Geoffrey Gillard series (2)
Box, Fox, Ox and the peacock
Bunting, Eve
Magic circle series (3)
Box in the attic
Todd, Barbara Euphan
Perdita series (1)
Box of delights
Masefield, John
Kay Harker series (2)
Box of doom
Verner, Gerald
Sexton Blake series (536)
Box of tricks
Brett, Simon
Charles Paris series (15)
Box office Browning
Corris, Peter
Richard Browning series (1)
Box office murders
Crofts, Freeman Wills
Inspector Joseph French series (5)
Boxcar
Barkan, Joanne
Come aboard series (1)
Boxcar children
Warner, Gertrude Chandler
Boxcar children series (1)
Boxed in
Steed, Neville
Peter Marklin series (6)
Boy
Dahl, Roald
Solo series (1)
Manning, Paul
Merry-go-rhymes series (4)
Boy, a dog and a frog
Mayer, Mercer
Frog series (1)
Boy adventurers in the forbidden land
Verrill, Alpheus Hyatt
Boy adventurers series (1)
Boy adventurers in the land of El Dorado
Verrill, Alpheus Hyatt
Boy adventurers series (2)
Boy adventurers in the land of the monkey men
Verrill, Alpheus Hyatt
Boy adventurers series (3)
Boy adventurers in the unknown land
Verrill, Alpheus Hyatt
Boy adventurers series (4)
Boy allies at Jutland
Drake, Robert L
Boy allies of the navy series (7)
Boy allies at Liege
Hayes, Clair Wallace
Boy allies of the army series (1)
Boy allies at Verdun
Hayes, Clair Wallace
Boy allies of the army series (8)
Boy allies in great peril
Hayes, Clair Wallace
Boy allies of the army series (5)
Boy allies in the Balkan Campaign
Hayes, Clair Wallace
Boy allies of the army series (6)
Boy allies in the Baltic
Drake, Robert L
Boy allies of the navy series (6)
Boy allies in the trenches
Hayes, Clair Wallace
Boy allies of the army series (4)
Boy allies on the firing line
Hayes, Clair Wallace
Boy allies of the army series (2)
Boy allies on the Somme
Hayes, Clair Wallace
Boy allies of the army series (7)
Boy allies under the sea
Drake, Robert L
Boy allies of the navy series (5)
Boy allies under the Stars and Stripes
Hayes, Clair Wallace
Boy allies of the army series (9)
Boy allies under two flags
Drake, Robert L
Boy allies of the navy series (2)
Boy allies with Haig in Flanders
Hayes, Clair Wallace
Boy allies of the army series (10)
Boy allies with Marshall Foch
Hayes, Clair Wallace
Boy allies of the army series (13)
Boy allies with Pershing in France
Hayes, Clair Wallace
Boy allies of the army series (11)
Boy allies with the Cossacks
Hayes, Clair Wallace
Boy allies of the army series (3)
Boy allies with the Flying Squadron
Drake, Robert L
Boy allies of the navy series (3)
Boy allies with the great advance
Hayes, Clair Wallace
Boy allies of the army series (12)
Boy allies with the North Sea Patrol
Drake, Robert L
Boy allies of the navy series (1)

Boys
Montherlant, Henry de
Alban de Bricoule trilogy (2)
Boys against girls
Pascal, Francine
Sweet Valley twins series (17)
Boys' and girls' circus book
Blyton, Enid
Boys' and girls' series (1)
Boys' and girls' story book
Blyton, Enid
Boys' and girls' series (2)
Boys and I
Molesworth, Mary Louisa
Boys and girls and I series (1)
Boys are yucko!
Hines, Anna Grossnickle
Cassie Bowen series (2)
Boys' book of airmen
Crump, James Irving
Boys' book series (8)
Boys' book of Arctic exploration
Crump, James Irving
Boys' book series (6)
Boys' book of coast guards
Crump, James Irving
Boys' book series (9)
Boys' book of cowboys
Crump, James Irving
Boys' book series (12)
Boys' book of firemen
Crump, James Irving
Boys' book series (1)
Boys' book of fisheries
Crump, James Irving
Boys' book series (10)
Boys' book of forest rangers
Crump, James Irving
Boys' book series (5)
Boys' book of mounted police
Crump, James Irving
Boys' book series (3)
Boys' book of newsreel hunters
Crump, James Irving
Boys' book series (11)
Boys' book of policemen
Crump, James Irving
Boys' book series (2)
Boys' book of railroads
Crump, James Irving
Boys' book series (4)
Boys' book of the U.S. mails
Crump, James Irving
Boys' book series (7)
Boy's fortune
Alger, Horatio
Good fortune trilogy (3)
Boys from Binjiwunyawunya
Barrett, Robert G
Les Norton series (3)
Boys from Bondi
Collins, Alan
Jacob Kaiser series (1)
Boys in the gym
Levy, Elizabeth
Gymnasts series (10)
Boys of Bob's Hill
Burton, Charles Pierce
Bob's Hill series (1)
Boys of Coastal
Kingston, Guy
Royal Air Force trilogy (3)
Boys of Columbia High
Forbes, Graham B
Columbia High School series (1)
Frank Allen series (1)
Boys of Columbia High in camp
Forbes, Graham B
Columbia High School series (8)
Frank Allen series (7)
Boys of Columbia High in track athletics
Forbes, Graham B
Columbia High School series (6)
Frank Allen series (4)
Boys of Columbia High in winter sports
Forbes, Graham B
Columbia High School series (7)
Frank Allen series (3)
Boys of Columbia High on the diamond
Forbes, Graham B
Columbia High School series (2)
Frank Allen series (5)
Boys of Columbia High on the gridiron
Forbes, Graham B
Columbia High School series (4)
Frank Allen series (11)
Boys of Columbia High on the ice
Forbes, Graham B
Columbia High School series (5)
Frank Allen series (2)
Boys of Columbia High on the river
Forbes, Graham B
Columbia High School series (3)
Frank Allen series (6)
Boys of Glen Morrock
Mackinnon, Allan
Glen Morrock series (1)
Boys of Grand Pre School
De Mille, James
Brethren of the White Cross series (2)
Boys of Pigeon Camp, their luck and fun
James, Martha
Pigeon Camp series (2)
Boys of Saint Timothy's
Pier, Arthur Stanwood
Saint Timothy's School series (1)
Boys of the big top
Mitchell, Lane
Jimmy Grier series (1)
Boys of the Fort
Bonehill, Ralph
Flag and frontier series (5)
Boys of the fort
Bonehill, Ralph
Flag of freedom series (5)
Boys of the gold fields
Stratemeyer, Edward L
Frontier series (3)
Boys of the great Northwest
Stratemeyer, Edward L
Frontier series (2)
Boys of the Otter Patrol
Martin, Edward Le Breton
Otter Patrol series (1)
Boys of the wilderness
Stratemeyer, Edward L
Frontier series (1)
Boy's own story
White, Edmund
Beautiful room series (1)
Boy's way
Derleth, August
Boy's series (1)
Bozos on patrol
Stine, Robert Lawrence
Space cadets series (3)
Bra burners' brigade
Knight, Mallory T
Man from T.O.M.C.A.T. series (11)
Brace of rogues
Islay, Nicholas
Sydney Vane series (2)
Brace of skeet
Hammond, Gerald
Keith Calder series (14)
Brace yourself
Harrell, Janice
Andie and the boys series (3)
Brach of trust
Graydon, William Murray
Sexton Blake series (172)
Brackenford story
Home, Michael
Breckland series (10)
Brad Dolan's Miami manhunt
Fuller, William
Brad Dolan series (6)
Brad Dollan's blonde cargo
Fuller, William
Brad Dolan series (4)
Brad Forrest's Calgary adventure
Maitland, Hugh
Brad Forrest series (4)
Brad Forrest's Halifax adventure
Maitland, Hugh
Brad Forrest series (7)
Brad Forrest's Hong Kong adventure
Maitland, Hugh
Brad Forrest series (1)
Brad Forrest's London adventure
Maitland, Hugh
Brad Forrest series (8)
Brad Forrest's Los Angeles adventure
Maitland, Hugh
Brad Forrest series (2)
Brad Forrest's Madagascar adventure
Maitland, Hugh
Brad Forrest series (3)
Brad Forrest's New York adventure
Maitland, Hugh
Brad Forrest series (5)
Brad Forrest's Yucatan adventure
Maitland, Hugh
Brad Forrest series (6)
Brad Foster, engineer
Palmer, Bernard
Career series (6)
Bradford business
Ross, Angus
Mark Farrow series (5)
Brading collection
Wentworth, Patricia
Miss Maud Silver series (18)
Bradmoor murder
Post, Melville Davisson
Sir Henry Marquis series (2)
Bradshaws on the trail
Pugh, Nansi
Bradshaw family series (2)
Brady Bunch
Johnston, William
Brady Bunch series (1)
Brady's back in town
Grover, Marshall
Larry and Stretch series (223)
Bragg's Bunch
Lynch, Jack
Peter Bragg series (1)
Brain damage
Burkholz, Herbert
Sensitives series (3)
Brain drain
Murphy, Warren Burton
Destroyer series (22)
Wayne, Matt
Nintendo adventure series (12)
Brain of Morbius
Dicks, Terrance
Doctor Who series (32)
Sarah Jane Smith series (10)
Brain plant tetralogy
Meltzer, David
Brain plant series (4)
Brain robbers
Munro, Hugh Macfarlane
Clutha series (7)
Brain scavengers
Edwards, Paul
John Eagle series (2)
Brain Sharpeners abroad
Curtis, Philip
Mister Browser series (9)
Brain Trust for murder
Spiller, Andrew
Chief Inspector Duck Mallard series (23)
Brain Trust murder
Diplomat
Dennis Tyler series (7)
Brain twister
Phillips, Mark
Ken Malone trilogy (1)
Brainwash
Wainwright, John
Inspector Lyle series (1)
Northern Police series (40)
Brainwashed
Thomas, Martin
Sexton Blake series (1610)
Brainz, Inc.
Goulart, Ron
Odd jobs series (4)
Brak the barbarian
Jakes, John
Brak series (1)
Brak the barbarian versus the mark of the demons
Jakes, John
Brak series (3)
Brak the barbarian versus the sorceress
Jakes, John
Brak series (2)
Brake-pedal down
Bratby, John
Break series (3)
Peter Carr series (2)
Brake up
Optic, Oliver
Lake Shore series (5)
Bramble Fortress
Knight, Peter
Anthony Daintrey series (1)
Brambleberrys animal book of alphabet
Mayer, Marianna
Brambleberrys series (1)
Brambleberrys animal book of colors
Mayer, Marianna
Brambleberrys series (2)
Brambleberrys animal book of counting
Mayer, Marianna
Brambleberrys series (3)
Brambleberrys animal book of shapes
Mayer, Marianna
Brambleberrys series (4)
Brambly Hedge pattern book
Dolman, Sue
Brambly Hedge series (7)
Bran Mak Morn
Howard, Robert Ervin
Bran Mak Morn trilogy (1)
Tales of the Picts series (2)
Bran tub
Ross, Diana
Miss Pussy series (4)
Branch for the Baron
Morton, Anthony
Baron series (33)
Branch line engines
Awdry, Wilbert
Railway series (16)
Brand image
Janson, Hank
Hank Janson series (139)
Brand McAllister
Chisholm, Matt
Rem McAllister series (27)
Brand new life
Farrell, James Thomas
Universe of time series (4)
Brand new Monty Python bok
Monty Python
Monty Python series (2)
Brand new Monty Python paperbok
Monty Python
Monty Python series (2)
Brand of fear
Lang, Brad
Fred Crockett series (3)
Brand of the beast
Lewis, Michael
Sergeant Hobbs series (1)
Brand of the black bat
Jones, G Wayman
Black Bat series (1)
Brand of the gun
Wynne, Brian
Marshal Jeremy Six series (8)
Brand of the lawless
Cole, Jackson
Jim Hatfield series (31)
Brand of the metal maiden
House, Brant
Secret Agent X series (11)
Brand of the werewolf
Robeson, Kenneth
Doc Savage series (5)
Brand of vengeance
Pike, Charles R
Jubal Cade series (11)
Brand T
Brand, Hilary
Hilary Brand series (2)
Branded spy
Merland, Oliver
Sexton Blake series (90)
Branded spy murders
Mason, Francis Van Wyck
Colonel Hugh North series (5)
Branded wolf
Bennet, Robert Ames
Wolf series (1)
Brandenburg affair
White, James Dillon
Sebastian Kettle series (3)
Brandenburg Hotel
Winslow, Pauline Glen
Superintendent Merlin Capricorn series (2)
Brander's book
Mills, Carla Johnson
Winter world series (4)
Branding needle
Sue, Eugene
Mysteries of the people series (7)
Brandon case
Connington, John Jervis
Sir Clinton Driffield series (9)
Brandon Coyle's wife
Southworth, Emma Dorothy Eliza Nevitte
Brandon Coyle series (2)
Brandon in New York
Warren, Vernon
Mark Brandon series (2)
Brandon returns
Warren, Vernon
Mark Brandon series (3)
Brandon takes over
Warren, Vernon
Mark Brandon series (1)
Brandons
Thirkell, Angela
Barsetshire series (7)
Brandon's posse
Hogan, Ray
Shawn Starbuck series (7)
Brandreths
Hope, Alexander James Beresford
Brandreths series (2)
Brandstetter
Hansen, Joseph
Dave Brandstetter series (11)
Brandstetter and others
Hansen, Joseph
Dave Brandstetter series (12)
Brandy ahoy!
Graeme, Roderic
Brandy series (1)
Brandy for the parson
Foxall, Raymond
Harry Adkins series (2)
Brandy goes a cruising
Graeme, Roderic
Brandy series (3)
Brandy pole
Chance, John Newton
Mister DeHavilland series (8)
Brandyjack
Funnell, Augustine
Brandyjack series (1)
Brannigan
Newsom, Ed
Chagro Brannigan series (1)
Ryan, Tom
Brannigan series (1)
Brannocks
Braun, Matt
Brannocks series (1)
Brannon
Free, Colin
Pollitt family series (3)
Brass bell
Sue, Eugene
Mysteries of the people series (2)
Brass boy
Miller, Jim
Long guns series (3)
Brass chills
Pentecost, Hugh
Luke Bradley series (4)
Brass circle
Cole, Jackson
Jim Hatfield series (77)
Brass diamonds
Sandberg, Berent
Matt Eberhart series (1)
Brass eagle
Duffy, Margaret
Patrick Gillard series (3)
Brass for a nude
Kane, Martin
Martin Kane series (8)
Brass go-between
Bleeck, Oliver
Philip Saint Ives series (1)
Brass halo
Webb, Jack
Father Joseph Shanley and Sammy Golden series (6)
Brass idol mystery
Wells, Helen
Vicki Barr series (16)
Brass rainbow
Collins, Michael
Dan Fortune series (2)
Brasshats and beueaucrats, 1941-1950
Pritt, Denis Nowell
Right to left trilogy (2)
Bravado
Masterson, Louis
Morgan Kane series (18)
Bravados from Texas
Grover, Marshall
Larry and Stretch series (34)
Bravados of Bandera
Grover, Marshall
Larry and Stretch series (254)
Brave
Avenell, Donne
Axa series (3)
Lipsyte, Roger
Contender trilogy (2)
Brave and bold
Alger, Horatio
Brave and bold series (1)
Brave Baby Elephant
Joslin, Sesyle
Baby Elephant series (1)
Brave, bad girls
Dewey, Thomas Blanchard
Private Eye Mac series (5)
Brave Billy
Ellis, Edward Sylvester
Bound to win trilogy (1)
Brave cannot yield
Mackintosh, Ian
Tim Blackgrove series (3)
Brave Captain Kelso
White, James Dillon
Roger Kelso series (2)
Brave captains
Stuart, Vivian
Captain Alexander Sheridan series (2)

Brave cowboy
Abbey, Edward
Jack Burns series (1)
Brave day, hideous night
Rothenstein, John
Summer's lease trilogy (2)
Brave deed of Ernest the policeman
Beaman, Sydney George Hulme
Toytown series (18)
Brave explorers
Hindley, Judy
Best of friends series (2)
Brave Fireman
Bradbury, Bianca
Brave Fireman series (1)
Brave Fireman and the firehouse cat
Bradbury, Bianca
Brave Fireman series (2)
Brave Free Men
Vance, Jack
Durdane trilogy (2)
Brave little toaster
Disch, Thomas Michael
Brave little toaster series (1)
Brave little toaster goes to Mars
Disch, Thomas Michael
Brave little toaster series (2)
Brave new world
Huxley, Aldous
New world series (1)
Brave new world revisited
Huxley, Aldous
New world series (2)
Brave Old Salt
Optic, Oliver
Army and navy series (6)
Brave pursuit
Allis, Marguerite
Ashbel Field series (3)
Brave ride tall
James, Cy
Sam Spur series (5)
Brave Tom
Ellis, Edward Sylvester
Brave and honest trilogy (1)
Brave white flag
Ford, James Allan
Hong Kong series (1)
Brave white rabbit
Gissing, Vera
Pippins series (3)
Brave wild heart
Montague, Jeanne
Loves of Carola Mountjoy series (1)
Bravo Charlie
Filgate, Macartney
Charlotte Eliot series (1)
Bravo, Ernest and Celestine!
Vincent, Gabrielle
Ernest and Celestine series (2)
Bravo nine
Day, Will B
Steven Flagg series (1)
Bravo of London
Bramah, Ernest
Max Carrados series (5)
Bravos
Wynne, Brian
Marshal Jeremy Six series (5)
Brazen
Brown, Carter
Lieutenant Al Wheeler series (19)
Brazen confession
Gregg, Cecil Freeman
Inspector Cuthbert Higgins series (4)
Brazen ecstasy
Taylor, Janelle
Sioux series (4)
Brazen seductress
Janson, Hank
Hank Janson series (140)
Brazen tongue
Mitchell, Gladys
Dame Beatrice Bradley series (11)
Brazilian gold mine mystery
Adams, Andy
Biff Brewster series (1)
Brazilian sleigh ride
Fish, Robert Lloyd
Captain Jose da Silva series (5)
Brazo feud
Bowden, Jim
Dan McCoy series (8)
Brazos dreamer
Shelton, Gene
Texas legends series (5)
Breach of promise
Hart, Roy
Detective Superintendent Roper series (6)
Bread
Henderson, Kathy
Where does it come from series (5)
McBain, Ed
Eighty Seventh Precinct series (29)
Bread-and-Butter Indian
Colver, Anne
Barbara Baum series (1)
Bread-and-Butter journey
Colver, Anne
Barbara Baum series (2)
Bread and jam for Frances
Hoban, Russell
Frances series (3)
Bread and oranges
Warner, Susan Bagert
Bread and oranges series (1)
Bread and wine
Silone, Ignazio
Pietro Spina series (1)
Bread bin
Aiken, Joan
Arabel and Mortimer series (3)
Breadfruit lotteries
Elman, Richard Martin
Professor Robert Harmon series (1)
Breadmakers
Davis, Margaret Thomson
Glasgow trilogy (1)
Breadwinners
Hay, John
Breadwinners series (1)
Breahtless
Glick, Ruth
Charisma Inc. series (2)
Break
Mather, Berkely
James Wainwright series (2)
Break away
Cooper, M E
Couples series (35)
Break 50 kill
Bratby, John
Break series (4)
Break for a lovely
Janson, Hank
Hank Janson series (103)
Break in
Francis, Dick
Kit Fielding series (1)
Break in the line
Mather, Berkely
James Wainwright series (2)
Break in the sun
Thomson, David Robert Alexander
Daniel Cullen series (2)
Break in the traffic
Wright, Steve
Barry Donovan series (3)
Break of day
Colette, Sidonie Gabrielle
Claudine series (7)
Break-out
Currington, Owen Josiah
Jack Lovel series (2)
Break out
McNeilly, Wilfred
Sexton Blake series (1571)
Break the Toff
Creasey, John
Toff series (29)
Break-up
Padoan, Gianni
Facing up series (1)
Breakaway
Black, Lionel
Superintendent Francis Foy series (1)
Hardcastle, Michael
Mark Fox series (2)
McFarlane, Leslie
Checkmate series (5)
Thornton, Jane Foster
Electric High series (1)
Tubb, Edwin Charles
Space nineteen ninety nine series (1)
Breakdown
Bratby, John
Break series (1)
Pronzini, Bill
Private Eye series (19)
Breakdown in Axeblade
Dixon, Franklin W
Hardy boys series (94)
Breakdowns, from Maus to now
Spiegelman, Art
Survivor's tale series (2)
Breaker
Lowell, Anne Hunter
Sorority girls series (11)
Breakfast
Lloyd, David
Dinosaur days series (2)
Breakfast and elevenses
Bratby, John
Break series (2)
Peter Carr series (1)
Breakfast at night
Bright, Pamela
Nursing trilogy (2)
Breakfast at six
Scott, Mary
New Zealand life series (1)
Breakfast at the Hermitage
Crabb, Alfred Leland
Nashville series (3)
Breakfast at Wimbledon
Bickham, Jack Miles
Brad Smith series (4)
Breakfast in bed
Brown, Sandra
Alicia series (1)
Breakfast in the ruins
Moorcock, Michael
Karl Glogauer series (2)
Breakfast time, Ernest Celestine
Vincent, Gabrielle
Ernest and Celestine series (7)
Breakfast with a corpse
Murray, Max
Corpse series (10)
Breaking away
Cooney, Linda A
Totally hot series (2)
Optic, Oliver
Starry flag series (3)
Breaking in
Monsarrat, Nicholas
Life is a four letter word series (1)
Breaking of Bumbo
Sinclair, Andrew
Bumbo series (1)
Breaking of Northwall
Williams, Paul Osborne
Pelbar series (1)
Breaking out
De Clements, Barthe
Jerry Johnson trilogy (3)
Monsarrat, Nicholas
Life is a four letter word series (2)
Breaking point
Copper, Basil
Mike Faraday series (14)
Macdonnell, James Edmond
Dutchy Holland series (45)
Breaking strain
Preuss, Paul
Venus prime series (1)
Breaking the ice
Lowell, Melissa
Silver blades series (1)
Breaking the rules
Ransom, Candice Farris
Chrystal Falls series (2)
Breakneck bawdy house
Gentry, Buck
Eli Holten series (17)
Breakneck Pass
Field, Peter
Powder Valley series (49)
Breakout
Kessler, Leo
Rebel series (4)
Breakthrough
Drake, David
Fleet series (3)
Kessler, Leo
Black Cossacks series (4)
Breastplate for Aaron
Harvester, Simon
Roger Fleming series (4)
Breath of Border air
Derwent, Lavinia
Border series (1)
Breath of French air
Bates, Herbert Ernest
Larkin family series (2)
Breath of spring
Coke, Peter
Brigadier Rayne series (1)
Breathe no more
Franklin, Charles
Grant Garfield series (18)
Breathe no more, my lady
Bailey, Hilea
Hilea Bailey and Hilary Dunsany Bailey series (4)
Breck's choice
Palmer, Bernard
Kid Breckinridge series (1)
Bred in the bone
Phillpotts, Eden
Book of Avis series (1)
Bred to kill
Thomas, Martin
Sexton Blake series (1505)
Brede's tale
May, Julian
Pliocene exile series (5)
Breed
Stone, Ned
Other Day Logan series (1)
Breed of men
Chisholm, Matt
Storm family series (6)
Breed of Sabre
Darby, Catherine
Sabre family series (5)
Breed of the inshore
Waine, Charlton
Sweepers series (1)
Breed woman
Gilman, George G
Edge series (60)
Breeding ground
Hutson, Shaun
Slugs series (2)
Breed's rampage
Hicks, D L
Milton Hicks series (2)
Bren Hardy again
Elliott, William James
Bren Hardy series (2)
Bren Hardy, tough dame
Elliott, William James
Bren Hardy series (1)
Brenda Bear's castle
Coombes, Marion
Brenda Bear series (2)
Brenda, her school and her club
Reed, Helen Leah
Brenda series (2)
Brenda's bargain
Reed, Helen Leah
Brenda series (5)
Brenda's cousin at Radcliffe
Reed, Helen Leah
Brenda series (4)
Brenda's murder
Wells, Tobias
Detective Knute Severson series (12)
Brenda's summer at Rockley
Reed, Helen Leah
Brenda series (3)
Brenda's ward
Reed, Helen Leah
Brenda series (7)
Brensham Village
Moore, John Cecil
Brensham trilogy (2)
Brentford triangle
Rankin, Robert
Brentford series (2)
Brentford trilogy
Rankin, Robert
Brentford series (3)
Brer Anansi strikes again
Makhanlall, David Paschal
Anansi series (3)
Brer Anansi's bag of tricks
Makhanlall, David Paschal
Anansi series (4)
Brer Rabbit
Blyton, Enid
Little books series (1)
Derwent, Lavinia
Brer Rabbit series (1)
Brer Rabbit again
Blyton, Enid
Brer Rabbit adventures series (5)
Derwent, Lavinia
Brer Rabbit series (3)
Brer Rabbit and his friends
Blyton, Enid
Brer Rabbit adventures series (4)
Brer Rabbit book
Blyton, Enid
Brer Rabbit series (1)
Brer Rabbit's a rascal
Blyton, Enid
Brer Rabbit adventures series (6)
Bret Malone, Texas marshal
Dower, Penn
Marshal Bret Malone series (1)
Breton adventure
Shaw, Jane
Caroline and Sara series (1)
Breton holiday
Shaw, Jane
Caroline and Sara series (1)
Bretons of Elm Street
Ripperger, Henrietta
Elm Street series (2)
Brewer's war
Hardin, J D
Raider and Doc series (67)
Brian Mulroney, the boy from Baie Comeau
Maur, Nick auf der
Brian Mulroney series (1)
Murphy, Rae Allan
Brian Mulroney series (1)
Brian was adopted
Sanford, Doris
In our neighborhood series (1)
Briary-bush
Dell, Floyd
Felix Fay trilogy (2)
Brickbats for Bastion
Harrison, Richard
Chief Inspector William Bastion series (3)
Brickfield
Hartley, Leslie Poles
Richard Mardick series (1)
Bricklayer's arms
Rhode, John
Doctor Lancelot Priestley series (41)
Bricky and the hobo
Nesdale, Ira
Bricky series (2)
Bridal bed murders
Martin, Archibald Edward
Pel Pelham and Detective Linley series (2)
Bridal wreath
Undset, Sigrid
Kristin Lavransdatter trilogy (1)
Bride
Irwin, Margaret
Stuart series (4)
Martin, Les
Frankenstein sequels series (14)
McIntyre, Vondra Neil
Frankenstein sequels series (15)
Bride and the Bugatti
Buron, Nicole de
Penelope and Guillaume trilogy (2)
Bride for Mister B
Saro-Wiwa, Ken
Mister B series (10)
Bride in darkness
Wiat, Philippa
Charlton Mead series (2)
Bride leads the Chalet School
Brent-Dyer, Elinor Mary
Chalet School series (27)
Bride of a moment
Wells, Carolyn
Alan Ford series (1)
Bride of chance
Blake, Vanessa
Jenny Winfield series (2)
Bride of death
Marsh, Ngaio
Inspector Roderick Alleyn series (17)
Bride of doom
Gray, Harriet
Quadroon trilogy (2)
Bride of Frankenstein
Dreadstone, Carl
Frankenstein sequels series (10)
Egremont, Michael
Frankenstein sequels series (1)
Bride of Fu-Manchu
Rohmer, Sax
Fu-Manchu series (7)
Bride of Lammermoor
Scott, Walter
Tales of my landlord series (5)
Bride of misfortune
Blake, Vanessa
Jenny Winfield series (2)
Bride of Selton Hall
Benzoni, Juliette
Marianne series (1)
Bride of Shiva
Bruce, Henry
Eurasian series (6)
Temple girl series (2)
Bride of Suleiman
Crawley, Aileen
Suleiman the Magnificent trilogy (1)
Bride of the Far Side
Larson, Gary
Far Side series (4)
Bride of the mistletoe
Allen, James Lane
Christmas season series (1)
Bride of the morning star
Coldsmith, Don
Spanish bit series (19)

Bride of the slime monster
Gardner, Craig Shaw
Cineverse trilogy (2)
Bride of the spear
Herbert, Kathleen
Cumbrian series (3)
Bride of the wilderness
McCarry, Charles
Paul Christopher series (5)
Bride of violence
Gray, Harriet
Quadroon trilogy (2)
Bride to the mountain
Firbank, Thomas
Mountain series (2)
Bride wore black
Brody, Marc
Marc Brody series (33)
Bride wore weeds
Janson, Hank
Hank Janson series (23)
Bridegroom cometh
Frank, Waldo
David Markand series (2)
Bridegroom's bodyguards
Grover, Marshall
Larry and Stretch series (369)
Bride's castle
Wilson, Philip Whitwell
Sir Julian Morthoe series (1)
Brides of Dracula
Owen, Dean
Dracula series (3)
Bridesmaids in black
Pickford, Ted
Scared to death trilogy (3)
Bridge
Tully, John
Inspector Holt series (4)
Bridge for passing
Buck, Pearl Sydenstricker
Several worlds series (2)
Bridge in the jungle
Traven, B
Gerard Gales series (3)
Bridge is lost
Nicholson, Celia Anna
Duchess series (2)
Bridge of birds
Hughart, Barry
Master Li Kao and Number Ten Ox series (1)
Bridge of dawn
Hancock, Neil
Windameir circle series (5)
Bridge of dreams
Murasaki Shibuku
Genji series (6)
Bridge of lost desire
Delany, Samuel Ray
Neveryon series (4)
Bridge of rainbows
Fitzgerald, Julia
Astromance series (10)
Bridge of the Levant
Stark, Freya
Traveller's letters series (4)
Bridge on the Drina
Andric, Ivo
Bosnian trilogy (1)
Bridge over the Yarra
Luscombe, Tom
Melbourne series (3)
Bridge that went nowhere
Fish, Robert Lloyd
Captain Jose da Silva series (7)
Bridge to Brooklyn
Idell, Albert Edward
Rogers family series (3)
Bridge too far
Ryan, Cornelius
Normandy Campaign trilogy (3)
Bridge under the water
Edwin, Maribel
Baird family series (1)
Bridget's cosmic connections
Pluis, Bridget
Psychic series (2)
Bridging the seven seas
Langley, John Prentice
Aviation series (8)
Bridle path
Bryant, Bonnie
Saddle Club series (27)
Bridle the wind
Aiken, Joan
Felix Brooke series (2)
Davis, Julia
Macleods of Virginia series (2)
Brief biography of a failure
Kolyer, John
Failure series (1)
Brief candle
Spiller, Andrew
Chief Inspector Duck Mallard series (8)
Brief candles
Gaite, Francis
James and Charles Latimer series (1)
Brief case of murder
Laing, Patrick
Patrick Laing series (4)
Brief help
Draper, Hastings
Wig series (3)
Brief sketch of my parliamentary life and times
Lang, John Dunmore
Life and times series (2)
Brief voices
Mannin, Ethel
Confessions and impressions series (4)
Brig of war
Woodman, Richard
Nathaniel Drinkwater series (3)
Brig Three Lilies
Mattson, Olle
Mickel Mickelson series (1)
Brigade
Trow, Meirion James
Inspector Sholto Lestrade series (5)
Brigade Boys and the basketball mystery
Palmer, Bernard
Brigade Boys series (5)
Brigade Boys and the disappearing stranger
Palmer, Bernard
Brigade Boys series (4)
Brigade Boys and the flight to danger
Palmer, Bernard
Brigade Boys series (1)
Brigade Boys and the phantom radio
Palmer, Bernard
Brigade Boys series (2)
Brigade Boys in the Arctic wilderness
Palmer, Bernard
Brigade Boys series (3)
Brigadier down under
Tinniswood, Peter
Brigadier series (3)
Brigadier in season
Tinniswood, Peter
Brigadier series (4)
Brigadier's brief lives
Tinniswood, Peter
Brigadier series (5)
Brigadier's collection
Tinniswood, Peter
Brigadier series (6)
Brigadier's last tour
Tinniswood, Peter
Brigadier series (6)
Brigadier's tour
Tinniswood, Peter
Brigadier series (6)
Brigand
Dumas, Alexandre
Valois series (4)
Brigands of the moon
Cummings, Ray
Gregg Haljan series (1)
Brigand's secret
Graydon, William Murray
Sexton Blake series (232)
Briggs investigates
Macdonald, Donald
Tommy Briggs series (1)
Brigham's way
Jordan, Matt
Tyler brothers series (1)
Bright and morning star
Harris, Rosemary
Egyptian trilogy (3)
Bright and shining tiger
Edwards, Claudia Jane
Forest King trilogy (3)
Bright angel
Wood, Andrew
Koregorvsky series (1)
Bright blue death
Carter, Nick
Nick Carter series (30)
Bright blue sky
Hennessy, Max
Dicken Quinney trilogy (1)
Bright companion
Llewellyn, Edward
Douglas convolution trilogy (2)
Bright days
Chastain, Madye Lee
Fripsey series (1)
Bright enchantment
Scott, Michael
Tales from the Land of Erin trilogy (1)
Bright face of danger
Ormerod, Roger
David Mallin and George Coe series (12)
Bright feathers
Culp, John Hewett
Five Civilized Tribes series (2)
bright green waistcoat
Fry, Pete
Pete Fry series (12)
Bright intervals
Clements, Eileen Helen
Bright intervals series (2)
Bright journey
Derleth, August
Wisconsin series (1)
Bright messenger
Blackwood, Algernon
Reincarnation series (2)
Bright morning
Thorne, Nicola
Askham family series (3)
Bright orange for the shroud
Macdonald, John Dann
Travis McGee series (6)
Bright pavilions
Walpole, Hugh
Herries ancestors series (1)
Bright promise
Chappell, Mollie
Tiddy Jeffreys series (2)
Bright red business men
McCutchan, Philip
Commander Esmonde Shaw series (10)
Bright serpent
Fox, James M
John and Suzy Marshall series (13)
Bright shadow
Thomas, Joyce Carol
Abyssinia Jackson series (2)
Bright star falls
Weber, Lenora Mattingly
Beany Malone series (9)
Bright story book
Blyton, Enid
Story book series (7)
Bright tomorrow
Lambert, Janet
Jordons series (10)
Bright twenties
Roberts, Cecil
Sunshine and shadow series (3)
Bright weft
De Banke, Cecile
Hand over hand series (2)
Bright young things
Vail, Amanda
Emily and Amy series (2)
Brighter buccaneer
Charteris, Leslie
Saint series (11)
Brightness falls from the air
Tiptree, James
Great Central Library series (1)
Brighton beach mystery
Kingston, Charles
Inspector Wake series (1)
Brighton Boys at Chateay Thierry
Driscoll, James R
Brighton Boys series (7)
Brighton Boys at Saint Mihiel
Driscoll, James R
Brighton Boys series (8)
Brighton Boys in a submarine treasure ship
Driscoll, James R
Brighton Boys series (11)
Brighton Boys in the Argonne Forest
Driscoll, James R
Brighton Boys series (9)
Brighton Boys in the Radio Service
Driscoll, James R
Brighton Boys series (4)
Brighton Boys in the trenches
Driscoll, James R
Brighton Boys series (2)
Brighton Boys in Translantic flight
Driscoll, James R
Brighton Boys series (10)
Brighton Boys with the Battle Fleet
Driscoll, James R
Brighton Boys series (3)
Brighton Boys with the Flying Corps
Driscoll, James R
Brighton Boys series (1)
Brighton Boys with the Submarine Fleet
Driscoll, James R
Brighton Boys series (5)
Brighton Boys with the Engineers at Cantigny
Driscoll, James R
Brighton Boys series (6)
Brightsea
Gillespie, Jane
Brightsea series (2)
Brightsuit MacBear
Smith, Lester Neil
North American Confederacy trilogy (3)
Brightwood Expedition
McDonald, Kay L
Ross Chesnut trilogy (2)
Brigid and the Cub
Turner, Ethel
Cub series (3)
Brill and the Dragators
Downing, Peggy
Exitorn series (1)
Brill and the puffire volcano
Downing, Peggy
Exitorn series (6)
Brill and the Zinders
Downing, Peggy
Exitorn series (4)
Brilliant Doctor Wogan
Montgomery, Raymond A
Choose your own adventure series (72)
Brillstone break-in
Heide, Florence Parry
Brillstone Apartments series (1)
Brillstone mystery
Heide, Florence Parry
Spotlight Detective Club series (12)
Brim sails out
Gaunt, Michael
Brim series (2)
Brimhall comes to stay
Delton, Judy
Brimhall series (1)
Brimhall turns detective
Delton, Judy
Brimhall series (3)
Brimhall turns to magic
Delton, Judy
Brimhall series (2)
Brimming cup
Canfield, Dorothy
Brimming cup series (1)
Brim's boat
Gaunt, Michael
Brim series (1)
Brim's valley
Gaunt, Michael
Brim series (3)
Brimstone Basin
Rountree, Owen
Jim Cord series (9)
Bring back yesterday
Chandler, Arthur Bertram
Rim series (15)
Bring 'em back alive
Browne, Dik
Hagar the horrible series (6)
Bring 'em back dead
Hume, David
Mick Cardby series (10)
Bring forth the body
Raven, Simon
Alms for oblivion series (9)
Bring me a unicorn
Lindbergh, Anne Morrow
Unicorn series (1)
Bring me another corpse
Rabe, Peter
Daniel Port series (4)
Bring me his scalp
Benteen, John
Sundance series (8)
Bring me sorrow
Janson, Hank
Hank Janson series (35)
Bring on the empty horses
Niven, David
Moon's a ballon series (2)
Bring the bride a shroud
Olsen, D B
Professor A Pennyfeather series (1)
Bringing home the new baby
Graham, Bob
New baby series (3)
Bringing up father
McManus, George
Maggie and Jiggs series (1)
Maggie and Jiggs series (2)
Brink of murder
Nielsen, Helen
Simon Drake series (6)
Brinkley Manor
Wodehouse, Pelham Grenville
Jeeves and Bertie Wooster series (6)
Brinkmanship of Galahad
Wodehouse, Pelham Grenville
Blandings Castle series (11)
Brinkworth Bear's alphabet book
West, Annie
Brinkworth Bear series (3)
Brinkworth Bear's colours book
West, Annie
Brinkworth Bear series (2)
Brinkworth Bear's counting book
West, Annie
Brinkworth Bear series (4)
Brinkworth Bear's opposites book
West, Annie
Brinkworth Bear series (1)
Bristling wood
Kerr, Katharine
Deverry series (3)
Bristol cousins
Ponsonby, Doris Almon
Jaspard family series (2)
Britain before the Romans
Birt, David
Roman Britain series (11)
Britain's great flood disaster
Janson, Hank
Hank Janson series (49)
British Cross
Granger, Bill
November Man series (5)
British history atlas
Gilbert, Martin
History atlas series (2)
British Museum mystery
Jardine, Warwick
Sexton Blake series (804)
British spy ring mystery
Adams, Andy
Biff Brewster series (11)
Brixham Manor mystery
Brooks, Edwy Searles
Sexton Blake series (328)
Broad highway
Farnol, Jeffery
Vibart series (1)
Broad is the way
Waldman, Emerson
Land and the way series (2)
Broad jump
Chase, Glen
Cherry Delight series (11)
Broadland adventure
Day, James Wentworth
Rural rides series (5)
Broads don't scare easy
Janson, Hank
Hank Janson series (25)
Broadsides and brass
Westcott, C T
Eagleheart trilogy (2)
Broadstrop in season
Kee, Robert
Simon Broadstrop series (2)
Broadway Bounty
Randall, Joshua
Bounty Hunter series (5)
Broadway cross
Carter, Nicholas
Nicholas Carter series (193)
Broadway jungle
Lee, Norma
Beautiful Gunner series (4)
Broadway murders
Wallace, Robert
Phantom Detective series (14)
Brock
Bingham, John
Superintendent Badger Brock series (1)
Brock and the defector
Bingham, John
Superintendent Badger Brock series (2)
Brock the badger
Rutley, Cecily Marianne
Tales of the wild folk series (16)
Brodie and the deep sea
Wylie, Ida Alexa Ross
Adam Brodie series (2)
Brogan and the bull
Tetlow, L D
Brogan McNally series (6)
Brogan and the judge killer
Tetlow, L D
Brogan McNally series (10)
Brogan for sheriff
Tetlow, L D
Brogan McNally series (4)
Brogan, passing through
Tetlow, L D
Brogan McNally series (2)

Brogan takes toll
Tetlow, L D
Brogan McNally series (8)
Brogan's Mexican stand-off
Tetlow, L D
Brogan McNally series (3)
Brogeen and the black enchanter
Lynch, Patricia
Brogeen the leprechaun series (8)
Brogeen and the bronze lizard
Lynch, Patricia
Brogeen the leprechaun series (4)
Brogeen and the little wind
Lynch, Patricia
Brogeen the leprechaun series (12)
Brogeen and the lost castle
Lynch, Patricia
Brogeen the leprechaun series (6)
Brogeen and the magic shoes
Lynch, Patricia
Brogeen the leprechaun series (3)
Brogeen and the Princess of Sheen
Lynch, Patricia
Brogeen the leprechaun series (5)
Brogeen and the red fez
Lynch, Patricia
Brogeen the leprechaun series (13)
Brogeen follows the magic tune
Lynch, Patricia
Brogeen the leprechaun series (2)
Brogeen of the stepping stones
Lynch, Patricia
Brogeen the leprechaun series (1)
Broiled alive
Buckingham, Bruce
Don Pancho series (2)
Broke down engine and other troubles with machines
Goulart, Ron
Troubles with machines series (1)
Broken alibi
Jacobs, Thomas Curtis Hicks
Detective Superintendent John Bellamy series (5)
Broken anchor
Keene, Carolyn
Nancy Drew series (70)
Broken bars
Carter, Nicholas
Nicholas Carter series (587)
Broken blossoms
Burke, Thomas
London series (1)
Broken bond
Carter, Nicholas
Nicholas Carter series (625)
Broken boy
Blackburn, John
General Charles Kirk series (3)
Broken citadel
Gregorian, Joyce Ballou
Tredana trilogy (1)
Broken cup
Browne, Edith Ophelia
Broken cup series (1)
Broken cycle
Chandler, Arthur Bertram
John Grimes series (14)
Rim series (6)
Broken doll
Webb, Jack
Father Joseph Shanley and Sammy Golden series (4)
Broken ear
Herge
Tintin series (6)
Broken face murders
Teilhet, Darwin Le Ora
Baron Von Kaz series (4)
Broken fang, and other experiences of a specialist in spooks
Key, Uel
Professor Arnold Rhymer series (1)
Broken-hearted
Pascal, Francine
Sweet Valley High series (58)
Broken hearts
Cooper, M E
Couples series (9)
Keene, Carolyn
River Heights series (11)
Stine, Robert Lawrence
Fear Street super chiller series (4)
Broken house
South, Ambrose
Broken house trilogy (1)
Broken idols
Flannery, Sean
Wallace and John Mahoney series (4)

Broken knife
Jacobs, Thomas Curtis Hicks
Chief Inspector Barnard series (10)
Broken lance
Gruber, Frank
Historical Western series (5)
Broken lands
Saberhagen, Fred
Chup trilogy (1)
Broken looking-glass
Charlesworth, Maria Louisa
Mrs Dorothy Cope series (2)
Broken mallet and the pigeon's eggs
Mathews, Joanna Hooe
Haps and mishaps series (2)
Broken melody
Thwaites, Frederick Joseph
Melody series (1)
Broken napoleons
Grant, Maxwell
Shadow series (106)
Broken O
Wells, Carolyn
Fleming Stone series (34)
Broken on crime's wheel
Carter, Nicholas
Nicholas Carter series (366)
Broken pledges
Gibbs, Philip
John Barton trilogy (2)
Broken promises
Baer, Judy
Cedar River daydreams series (5)
Campbell, Drusilla
Hopewell series (1)
Broken record
Campbell, Roy
Broken record series (1)
Broken shield
Benson, Ben
Ralph Lindsey series (4)
Broken spear
Seed, Jenny
Natal series (3)
Broken spur
Newton, Dwight Bennett
Jim Bannister series (11)
Broken stone
Monaco, Richard
Leitus series (2)
Broken toy
Maclean, Arthur
Sexton Blake series (1403)
Broken trail
Carter, Nicholas
Nicholas Carter series (148)
Murray, Andrew
Sexton Blake series (102)
Broken vase
Stout, Rex
Tecumseh Fox series (3)
Broken vase mystery
Plum, Mary
John Smith series (4)
Broken voyage
Barrington, G W
Rusty and Peter series (1)
Broken wheel
Wingrove, David
Chung Kuo series (2)
Broken wheels
Cody, Al
Montana series (7)
Brokenclaw
Gardner, John Edmund
James Bond series (26)
Broker
Collins, Max Allan
Quarry series (1)
Brokered death
Boland, John C
Donald McCarry series (2)
Broker's end
Booth, Louis F
Maxwell Fenner series (2)
Brokers of doom
Aikman, Anthony
Boyet Rhodes series (3)
Broker's wife
Collins, Max Allan
Quarry series (2)
Bromius Phenomenon
Rankine, John
Dag Fletcher series (4)
Bromley and the hidden treasure
Campbell, Alan
Bromley Bear series (3)
Bromley climbs Uluru
Campbell, Alan
Bromley Bear series (1)

Bromley to the rescue
Campbell, Alan
Bromley Bear series (2)
Bronc people
Eastlake, William
Bowman family trilogy (2)
Broncho Bill
O'Neil, Harry F
Broncho Bill series (1)
Broncho Bill in Suicide Canyon
O'Neil, Harry F
Broncho Bill series (2)
Broncho Rider Boys along the border
Fowler, Frank
Broncho Rider Boys series (3)
Broncho Rider Boys at Keystone Ranch
Fowler, Frank
Broncho Rider Boys series (1)
Broncho Rider Boys down in Arizona
Fowler, Frank
Broncho Rider Boys series (2)
Broncho Rider Boys on the Wyoming Trail
Fowler, Frank
Broncho Rider Boys series (4)
Broncho Rider Boys with Funston at Vera Cruz
Fowler, Frank
Broncho Rider Boys series (6)
Broncho Rider Boys with the Texas Rangers
Fowler, Frank
Broncho Rider Boys series (5)
Bronco justice
Borg, Jack
Hogleg Bailey series (7)
Bronco trail
Benteen, John
Sundance series (6)
Brontomek!
Coney, Michael Greatrex
Arcadia series (3)
Brontosaurus birthday cake
McCrum, Robert
Brontosaurus series (1)
Brontosaurus superstar
McCrum, Robert
Brontosaurus series (2)
Bronwyn's bane
Scarborough, Elizabeth Ann
Argonia series (3)
Bronze axe
Lord, Jeffrey
Richard Blade series (1)
Bronze bell
Silliphant, Stirling
John Locke series (3)
Bronze bird
Rybakov, Anatoli
Dirk series (2)
Bronze claws
Kruger, Paul
Phil Kramer series (4)
Bronze hand
Wells, Carolyn
Fleming Stone series (20)
Bronze heist
Callan, Michael Feeney
Target series (2)
Bronze king
Charnas, Suzy McKee
Sorcery Hall trilogy (1)
Bronze mermaid
Ernst, Paul
Jim Ryan series (2)
Bronze of Eddarta
Garrett, Randall
Gandalara cycle series (3)
Bronze Perseus
Hough, Stanley Bennett
Inspector Brentford series (1)
Bronze Star
Zlotnik, Donald E
Fields of honor series (5)
Brood of folly
Erskine, Margaret
Inspector Septimus Finch series (18)
Brood of the Eagle
Macdonnell, James Edmond
Eagle series (1)
Brood of the witch-queen
Rohmer, Sax
Anthony Ferrara series (2)
Brooke and her rock star mom
Pascal, Francine
Sweet Valley twins series (55)
Brooklands mystery
Urquhart, Paul
Sexton Blake series (731)
Brooklyn book of the dead
Stephens, Michael
J Leland Coole series (2)

Brooklyn murders
Cole, George Douglas Howard
Superintendent Henry Wilson series (1)
Brooks legend
Ellis, William Donohue
Ohio frontier trilogy (3)
Broom
Lister, Stephen
Sainte Monique series (9)
Broomsticks over Flaxborough
Watson, Colin
Inspector Purbright series (7)
Broomtail Basin
Floren, Lee
Judge Lemanuel Bates and Tobacco Jones series (4)
Broomtail, brother of Lightning
Mason, Miriam Evangeline
Lightning series (2)
Brotan, the breeder
Forest, Dael
Roman world series (3)
Brothel bullets
Sharpe, Jon
Trailsman series (87)
Brothel in Rosenstrasse
Moorcock, Michael
Von Bek family trilogy (2)
Brother
Feikema, Feike
World's wanderer trilogy (2)
Brother against brother
Dixon, Franklin W
Hardy boys case files series (11)
Optic, Oliver
Blue and the Gray on land series (1)
Brother and sister
Frank, Leonhard
Carl and Anna series (2)
Lawrence, Josephine
Brother and sister series (1)
Brother and sister at Bayport
Lawrence, Josephine
Brother and sister series (5)
Brother and sister keep house
Lawrence, Josephine
Brother and sister series (6)
Brother and sister's holidays
Lawrence, Josephine
Brother and sister series (2)
Brother and sister's schooldays
Lawrence, Josephine
Brother and sister series (3)
Brother and sister's vacation
Lawrence, Josephine
Brother and sister series (4)
Brother Assassin
Saberhagen, Fred
Berserker series (2)
Brother Berserker
Saberhagen, Fred
Berserker series (2)
Brother Bert comes to stay
Salmon, Michael
Alexander Bunyip series (8)
Brother Cadfael's penance
Peters, Ellis
Brother Cadfael series (20)
Brother Copas
Quiller-Couch, Arthur
Troy Town series (8)
Brother Death
Perry, Steve
Khadaji series (8)
Brother enemy
Gaunt, Richard
English Civil War series (1)
Brother for Hugh
Coles, Manning
Tommy Hambledon series (7)
Brother for Momoko
Iwasaki, Chihiro
Momoko series (2)
Brother for the Orphelines
Carlson, Natalie Savage
Orphelines series (2)
Brother Gun
Slade, Jack
Lassiter series (31)
Brother Nap
Tilsley, Frank
Nap and Ted series (2)
Brother o' mine
Cleaver, Hylton
Harley series (1)
Brother of Daphne
Yates, Dornford
Berry series (1)
Brother of girls
Grier, Sydney Carlyon
Princess series (4)

Brother Spy
Jacobs, Thomas Curtis Hicks
Chief Inspector Barnard series (9)
Brother to the lion
Estes, Rose
Saga of lost lands trilogy (2)
Brother wind
Harrison, Sue
Mother earth trilogy (3)
Brotherhood
Wall, Robert Emmet
Nowell family series (8)
Brotherhood of blood
Derrick, Lionel
Penetrator series (50)
Brotherhood of death
Carter, Nicholas
Nicholas Carter series (219)
Brotherhood of Diablo
Lovejoy, Jack
Vision of beasts trilogy (3)
Brotherhood of evil
Hunter, Neil
Brand series (6)
Zacharia, Irwin
Irving Martin Reddy series (1)
Brotherhood of the gun
Johnstone, William Wallace
Blood bond series (2)
Brotherhood of the Red Poppy
Troyat, Henri
Light of the just series (1)
Brotherhood of the Rose
Morrell, David
Chris Kilmoonie and Saul Grisman series (1)
Brotherly death
Coburn, L J
Caleb Thorn series (3)
Brotherly love
Fielding, Gabriel
Blaydon family trilogy (2)
Brothers
Goldman, William
Marathon man series (2)
James, Janice
Brothers series (1)
Vachell, Horace Annesley
Harrow School series (1)
Brothers and enemies
Nicole, Christopher
New Americans series (1)
Brothers and sisters
Campbell, Bebe Moore
Blues series (2)
Stine, Jane
Everything you need to survive series (1)
Brothers, book 2
James, Janice
Brothers series (2)
Brothers, book 3
Mackenzie, Lee
Brothers series (3)
Brothers, book 4
Mackenzie, Lee
Brothers series (4)
Brothers, book 5
Mackenzie, Lee
Brothers series (5)
Brothers in arms
Bujold, Lois McMaster
Miles Naismith Vorkosigan series (3)
Brothers in blood
Pendleton, Don
Mack Bolan series (50)
Saint James, Daniel
Brothers in blood series (1)
Brothers in law
Cecil, Henry
Roger Thursby series (1)
Brothers Majere
Stein, Kevin
DragonLance series (4)
Brothers of benevolence
Cassells, John
Superintendent Flagg series (22)
Brothers of consolation
Balzac, Honore de
Scenes of Parisian life series (13)
Brothers of doom
Grant, Maxwell
Shadow series (124)
Brothers of earth
Cherryh, Carolyn Janice
Alliance-Union series (17)
Brothers of the gun
Roberts, J R
Gunsmith series (93)

Brothers Sackville
Cole, George Douglas Howard
Superintendent Henry Wilson series (17)
Brought in dead
Patterson, Henry
Nick Miller series (2)
Brought to bay
Carter, Nicholas
Nicholas Carter series (56)
M'Govan, James
James M'Govan series (1)
Brought to book
Heald, Tim
Simon Bognor series (9)
Brought to light
Punshon, Ernest Robertson
Bobby Owen series (32)
Brought to the front
Kellogg, Elijah
Forest Glen series (3)
Brought to the mark
Carter, Nicholas
Nicholas Carter series (467)
Brought up in Dublin
Jeffares, Alexander Norman
Brought up series (1)
Brought up to leave
Jeffares, Alexander Norman
Brought up series (2)
Brown and white
Jennens, Frank
Mouse series (2)
Brown Beggarman series
Daykin, Lilian
Brown Beggarman series (1)
Brown box mystery at Sugar Creek
Hutchens, Paul
Sugar Creek Gang series (30)
Brown bread and butter
Wayne, Jenifer
Purple dress series (1)
Brown County almanack
Hubbard, Kin
Abe Martin series (2)
Brown County folks
Hubbard, Kin
Abe Martin series (3)
Brown cow
Branfield, John
Brown cow series (1)
Brown Ears
Lawhead, Stephen
Brown Ears series (1)
Brown Ears at sea
Lawhead, Stephen
Brown Ears series (2)
Brown fox mystery
Queen, Ellery, Junior
Djuna and Champ series (5)
Brown Mouse
Jennens, Frank
Mouse series (1)
Brown murder case
Daniel, Roland
Inspector Neville Langham series (2)
Brown of Moukden
Strang, Herbert
Russo-Japanese War series (2)
Brown satchel mystery
Allen, Betsy
Connie Blair series (9)
Brown suede jacket
Fry, Pete
Pete Fry series (13)
Brown Tala finds little Tulsi
Wynne, May
Tala series (2)
Browne fights the fifth column
Poole, Michael
Freddie Browne and Jim Fanshaw series (8)
Browne follows the clue
Poole, Michael
Freddie Browne and Jim Fanshaw series (2)
Browne of the Secret Service
Poole, Michael
Freddie Browne and Jim Fanshaw series (7)
Browne's first case
Poole, Michael
Freddie Browne and Jim Fanshaw series (1)
Brownie and the wedding day
Anderson, Verily
Brownies series (7)
Brownie campaigners
Richardson, Dorothy
Brownies series (15)
Brownie cook-book
Anderson, Verily
Brownies series (8)
Brownie discoverers
Blathwayt, Jean
Brownie series (3)
Brownie elephant hunters
Richardson, Dorothy
Brownies series (14)
Brownie entertainers
Richardson, Dorothy
Brownies series (13)
Brownie explorers
Richardson, Dorothy
Brownies series (11)
Brownie foxwatchers
Richardson, Dorothy
Brownies series (16)
Brownie from the caravans
Hann, Dorothy Owen
Brownie series (3)
Brownie rescuers
Richardson, Dorothy
Brownies series (12)
Brownie Sandford
May, Carrie L
Recovered pearl series (1)
Brownie Scouts and their tree house
Wirt, Mildred Augustine
Brownie Scout series (4)
Brownie Scouts at Silver Beach
Wirt, Mildred Augustine
Brownie Scout series (5)
Brownie Scouts at Snow Valley
Wirt, Mildred Augustine
Brownie Scout series (1)
Brownie Scouts at Windmill Farm
Wirt, Mildred Augustine
Brownie Scout series (6)
Brownie Scouts in the Cherry Festival
Wirt, Mildred Augustine
Brownie Scout series (3)
Brownie Scouts in the circus
Wirt, Mildred Augustine
Brownie Scout series (2)
Brownie venturers
Richardson, Dorothy
Brownies series (10)
Brownie year
Collins, Freda
Woodland Pack series (3)
Brownies and the christening
Anderson, Verily
Brownies series (8)
Brownies and the farm pig
Collins, Freda
Woodland Pack series (6)
Brownies and the fire
Sykes, Pamela
Barnwell Brownie Guide Pack series (3)
Brownies and the flood
Sykes, Pamela
Barnwell Brownie Guide Pack series (7)
Brownies and the golden hand
Anderson, Verily
Brownies series (2)
Brownies and the ponies
Anderson, Verily
Brownies series (4)
Brownies and their animal friends
Anderson, Verily
Brownies series (6)
Brownies at the zoo
Sykes, Pamela
Barnwell Brownie Guide Pack series (2)
Brownies' day abroad
Anderson, Verily
Brownies series (3)
Brownies in hospital
Sykes, Pamela
Barnwell Brownie Guide Pack series (5)
Brownies on television
Sykes, Pamela
Barnwell Brownie Guide Pack series (4)
Brownies on wheels
Anderson, Verily
Brownies series (5)
Brownies throw a party
Sykes, Pamela
Barnwell Brownie Guide Pack series (6)
Browning battles on
Corris, Peter
Richard Browning series (6)
Browning in buckskin
Corris, Peter
Richard Browning series (4)
Browning, P.I.
Corris, Peter
Richard Browning series (5)
Browning Sahib
Corris, Peter
Richard Browning series (7)
Browning takes off
Corris, Peter
Richard Browning series (3)
Brown's fifty thousand pound mystery
Poole, Michael
Freddie Browne and Jim Fanshaw series (3)
Brownsea silver
Peyton, K M
Mick and Rob series (3)
Brownstone
Eulo, Ken
Chandal Talon trilogy (1)
Browser's dictionary & native guide to the unknown American language
Ciardi, John
Browser's dictionary series (1)
Bru the grizzly
Rutley, Cecil Bernard
Wild life story series (1)
Bruach bland
Beckwith, Lillian
Hebrides series (8)
Bruce
Terhune, Albert Payson
Sunnybank collies series (2)
Bruce Benedict, quarterback
Gault, William Campbell
Gridiron series (3)
Bruce carries the flag
Judson, Clara Ingram
They came from series (3)
Bruce Jenner, decathlon winner
Aaseng, Nathan
Sports acheivers series (1)
Bruce's story
Pascal, Francine
Sweet Valley High super star series (2)
Brumaire
Logan, Mark
Nicholas Minnett series (3)
Brumby
Patchett, Mary Elwyn
Joey Meehan series (1)
Brumby, come home
Patchett, Mary Elwyn
Joey Meehan series (2)
Brumby foal
Patchett, Mary Elwyn
Joey Meehan series (5)
Brumby racer
Mitchell, Elyne
Silver Brumby series (10)
Brummell
Hamilton, Cosmo
Beau Brummell series (1)
Brummell again
Hamilton, Cosmo
Beau Brummell series (2)
Brunel's tower
Phillpotts, Eden
Industries of England series (1)
Brunette on the beam
Brody, Marc
Marc Brody series (68)
Brunettes are dangerous
Daniel, Roland
Michael Grant series (5)
Brush Buggs
Cosgrove, Stephen Edward
Bugg series (31)
Brush country killers
Madison, Holt
Batwing Jones trilogy (1)
Brush of death
Warren, James
James Weston series (4)
Brushing the mountain top
Dixon, Franklin W
Ted Scott flying series (17)
Brutal border
Gilman, George G
Edge series (52)
Brutal conquest
Ahern, Jerry
Survivalist series (22)
Brutal kook
Avallone, Michael
Ed Noon series (14)
Brute force
Austin, Richard
Guardians series (7)
Brutish are coming
Browne, Dik
Hagar the horrible series (11)
Brydons abroad
Fidler, Kathleen
Brydon family series (15)
Brydons at Blackpool
Fidler, Kathleen
Brydon family series (18)
Brydons at Smuggler's Creek
Fidler, Kathleen
Brydon family series (3)
Brydons catch queer fish
Fidler, Kathleen
Brydon family series (13)
Brydons do battle
Fidler, Kathleen
Brydon family series (6)
Brydons get things going
Fidler, Kathleen
Brydon family series (11)
Brydons go camping
Fidler, Kathleen
Brydon family series (5)
Brydons go canoeing
Fidler, Kathleen
Brydon family series (19)
Brydons hunt for treasure
Fidler, Kathleen
Brydon family series (12)
Brydons in a pickle
Fidler, Kathleen
Brydon family series (9)
Brydons in summer
Fidler, Kathleen
Brydon family series (7)
Brydons look for trouble
Fidler, Kathleen
Brydon family series (10)
Brydons on the Broads
Fidler, Kathleen
Brydon family series (16)
Brydons stick at nothing
Fidler, Kathleen
Brydon family series (14)
Bubba Bear
Reese, Bob
Yellowstone critter series (3)
Bubba Bugg
Cosgrove, Stephen Edward
Bugg series (33)
Bubble
Anand, Mulk Raj
Seven ages of man series (4)
Bubble Bugg
Cosgrove, Stephen Edward
Bugg series (32)
Bubble gum champion
Pearson, Michael A
Winners and losers series (2)
Bubble gum kid
Elrich, George S
Bonanza series (7)
Bubble trouble
Savage, Deborah
Peregrine Piecrust series (1)
Bubbles and troubles
Joyner, Simon
Tales from the Misty Wood series (2)
Bubbles of the foam
Bain, Francis William
Indian mystic love stories series (10)
Bubbling crocodile
Mahy, Margaret
Crocodile series (2)
Buccaneer
Pope, Dudley
Ned Yorke series (2)
Buccaneers of Lan-Kern
Tremayne, Peter
Lan-Kern trilogy (3)
Buchanan calls the shots
Ward, Jonas
Tom Buchanan series (16)
Buchanan gets mad
Ward, Jonas
Tom Buchanan series (3)
Buchanan gets tough
Ward, Jonas
Tom Buchanan series (8)
Buchanan on the prod
Ward, Jonas
Tom Buchanan series (6)
Buchanan on the run
Ward, Jonas
Tom Buchanan series (13)
Buchanan says no
Ward, Jonas
Tom Buchanan series (2)
Buchanan takes over
Ward, Jonas
Tom Buchanan series (15)
Buchanan's big fight
Ward, Jonas
Tom Buchanan series (22)
Buchanan's big showdown
Ward, Jonas
Tom Buchanan series (17)
Buchanan's black sheep
Ward, Jonas
Tom Buchanan series (23)
Buchanan's gamble
Ward, Jonas
Tom Buchanan series (11)
Buchanan's gun
Ward, Jonas
Tom Buchanan series (7)
Buchanan's manhunt
Ward, Jonas
Tom Buchanan series (20)
Buchanan's range war
Ward, Jonas
Tom Buchanan series (21)
Buchanan's revenge
Ward, Jonas
Tom Buchanan series (5)
Buchanan's siege
Ward, Jonas
Tom Buchanan series (12)
Buchanan's stage line
Ward, Jonas
Tom Buchanan series (24)
Buchanan's stolen railway
Ward, Jonas
Tom Buchanan series (19)
Buchanan's Texas treasure
Ward, Jonas
Tom Buchanan series (18)
Buchanan's war
Ward, Jonas
Tom Buchanan series (9)
Bucharest ballerina murders
Mason, Francis Van Wyck
Colonel Hugh North series (14)
Buchholz family
Stinde, Julius
Buchholz family series (2)
Buchholzes in Italy
Stinde, Julius
Buchholz family series (1)
Buck passes Flynn
McDonald, Gregory
Francis Xavier Flynn series (3)
Buck Peters, ranchman
Mulford, Clarence Edward
Hopalong Cassidy series (4)
Buck Rogers and the depth men of Jupiter
Nowlan, Philip Francis
Buck Rogers series (4)
Buck Rogers in the 25th century
Nowlan, Philip Francis
Buck Rogers series (6)
Steele, Addison E
Buck Rogers teleplay series (1)
Buck Rogers in the dangerous mission
Nowlan, Philip Francis
Buck Rogers series (3)
Buck Rogers on the moons of Saturn
Nowlan, Philip Francis
Buck Rogers series (2)
Buckaroo
Cunningham, Eugene
Walt Slade series (1)
Bucket and spade
Trueman, Brian
Stories from Cockleshell Bay series (3)
Buckingham blowout
Kilgore, Axel
They call me the Mercenary series (17)
Buckinghams at Ravenswyke
Saville, Malcolm
Buckinghams series (2)
Buckingham's expeditions
Birt, David
Stuarts series (12)
Buckled bag
Rinehart, Mary Roberts
Nurse Hilda Adams series (2)
Buckled wing
Pollard, Alfred Oliver
David Wilshaw series (5)
Buck's home run drive
Dawson, Elmer A
Buck and Larry baseball series (4)
Buck's winning hit
Dawson, Elmer A
Buck and Larry baseball series (2)
Buckskin beau
Stanley, Chuck
Buckskin series (2)

Buckskin bombshell
Hunter, E J
White Squaw series (5)

Buckskin breeches
Stong, Philip
Ivanhoe Keeler series (1)

Buckskin breed
Dalton, Kit
Buckskin series (40)

Buckskin pards
Stanley, Chuck
Buckskin series (1)

Buckskin Pass
Mitchum, Hank
Stage coach station series (50)

Buckskins and sixguns
Roberts, J R
Gunsmith series (16)

Buckskin's trail
Roberts, J R
Gunsmith series (104)

Bucky Button
McCall, Edith
Button family series (1)

Budapest action
Rosenberger, Joseph
Death Merchant series (23)

Budapest Parade murders
Mason, Francis Van Wyck
Colonel Hugh North series (8)

Budapest run
Carter, Nick
Nick Carter series (183)

Buddha of Fleet Street
Grierson, Francis Durham
Inspector George Muir series (11)
Superintendent Andrew Ash series (4)

Buddha's retreat
Kalish, Robert
Skipper Gould series (4)

Buddy Rock's race
Green, Kate
Fossil family tales series (3)

Budge and Toddie
Habberton, John
Budge and Toddie series (2)

Budgie at Bendick's Point
Sarah, Duchess of York
Budgie series (2)

Budgie, the little helicopter
Sarah, Duchess of York
Budgie series (1)

Buds of May
Seymour, Beatrice Kean
Malling-Gaywood family series (1)

Buff, a collie, and other stories
Terhune, Albert Payson
Sunnybank collies series (3)

Buff runners
Sherman, Jory
Gunn series (14)

Buffa Buffalo
Reese, Bob
Yellowstone critter series (2)

Buffalo are coming
Edson, John Thomas
Floating Outfit series (42)

Buffalo Arthur
Coren, Alan
Arthur series (1)

Buffalo Bill and his adventures in the West
Buntline, Ned
Buffalo Bill series (1)

Buffalo Bill and the Overland Trail
Sabin, Edward Legrand
Trail blazers series (6)

Buffalo Bill and the Pony Express
Sherwood, Elmer
Young Buffalo Bill series (2)

Buffalo Bill, the king of the border men
Buntline, Ned
Buffalo Bill series (1)

Buffalo Bill's best shot
Buntline, Ned
Buffalo Bill series (3)

Buffalo Bill's childhood
Sherwood, Elmer
Young Buffalo Bill series (1)

Buffalo Bill's first trail
Buntline, Ned
Buffalo Bill series (2)

Buffalo Bill's last victory
Buntline, Ned
Buffalo Bill series (4)

Buffalo box
Gruber, Frank
Simon Lash series (2)

Buffalo Gal
Weston, Cole
Andrew Ryder series (1)

Buffalo grass
Gruber, Frank
Historical Western series (13)

Buffalo guns
Sharpe, Jon
Trailsman series (139)

Buffalo hiders
Cole, Judd
Cheyenne series (10)

Buffalo hunters
Curry, Tom
Captain Mesquite series (3)
Dawson, Clay
Long Rider series (10)

Buffalo knife
Steele, William Owen
Tennessee frontier series (1)

Buffalo medicine
Coldsmith, Don
Spanish bit series (2)

Buffalo people
Willoughby, Lee Davis
Making of America series (17)

Buffalo shield
Wisler, Gary Clifton
Medicine Trail series (3)

Buffalo soldier
Hardin, J D
Raider and Doc series (45)

Buffalo Station
Mitchum, Hank
Stage coach station series (48)

Buffalo war
McCurtin, Peter
Sundance series (39)

Buffalo Woman
Johnson, Dorothy Marie
Buffalo Woman series (1)

Buffer
Macdonnell, James Edmond
Hooky Walker series (4)

Buffets and rewards
Mais, Stuart Petre Brodie
Days of my life series (2)

Buffy cleans up
Dahlerup, Rina
Buffy and Company series (1)

Bug in the system
McEvoy, Seth
Not quite human series (3)

Bugaloos and the vile Vibes
Stratton, Chris
Bugaloos series (1)

Bugg off
Cosgrove, Stephen Edward
Bugg series (34)

Buggaboo!
Cosgrove, Stephen Edward
Bugg series (35)

Buggita
Cosgrove, Stephen Edward
Bugg series (36)

Bugglar boys
Cosgrove, Stephen Edward
Bugg series (1)

Buggly
Cosgrove, Stephen Edward
Bugg series (20)

Bugle Elk and Little Toot
Reese, Bob
Yellowstone critter series (1)

Bugles and a tiger
Masters, John
British India trilogy (1)

Bugles blowing
Freeling, Nicolas
Henri Castang series (2)

Bugles on the Bighorn
Cole, Jackson
Jim Hatfield series (93)

Bugles west
Gruber, Frank
Historical Western series (11)

Bugs Bunny rides again
Lewis, Jean
Bugs Bunny series (2)

Bugs Potter, live at Nickaninny
Korman, Gordon
Bugs Potter series (2)

Build a better mouse trap
Striker, Susan
Anti-coloring book series (5)

Build a box for Wildcat
Clinton, Jeff
Wildcat O'Shea series (11)

Build-up
Williams, William Carlos
Stecher trilogy (3)

Builder of the Black Empire
Stockbridge, Grant
Richard Wentworth series (9)

Builders
Sommers, Jeanne
Making of America series (6)

Building
McGee, Shelagh
Little activity series (4)

Building estate murder
Urquhart, Paul
Sexton Blake series (818)

Building in your street
Simon, Seymour
Your street series (2)

Building of Jalna
De la Roche, Mazo
Whiteoak series (1)

Building the Party, 1893-1914
Cliff, Tony
Lenin series (1)

Building the snowman
Briggs, Raymond
Snowman series (5)

Built to kill
Harding, Richard
Outrider series (5)

Bulbulla
Eyton, John
India series (2)

Bulgarian termination
Rosenberger, Joseph
Death Merchant series (61)

Bull and the spear
Moorcock, Michael
Chronicle of Prince Corum and the silver hand trilogy (1)
Corum series (4)

Bull chief
Carlsen, Chris
Berserker series (2)

Bull from the sea
Renault, Mary
Theseus series (2)

Bull-dogs and bull-dog breeding
Cooper, Henry Saint John
Bulldog series (1)

Bull Hunter
Manning, David
Bull Hunter series (1)

Bull Hunter's romance
Manning, David
Bull Hunter series (2)

Bull whip breed
Edson, John Thomas
Calamity Jane series (3)

Bulldog and Rats
Allain, Marcel
Fantomas series (13)

Bulldog Drummond
Sapper
Bulldog Drummond series (1)

Bulldog Drummond and the female of the species
Sapper
Bulldog Drummond series (5)

Bulldog Drummond at bay
Sapper
Bulldog Drummond series (9)
Ronald Standish series (4)

Bulldog Drummond attacks
Fairlie, Gerard
Bulldog Drummond series (12)

Bulldog Drummond meets a murderess
Sapper
Bulldog Drummond series (5)

Bulldog Drummond on Dartmoor
Fairlie, Gerard
Bulldog Drummond series (11)

Bulldog Drummond returns
Sapper
Bulldog Drummond series (7)

Bulldog Drummond stands fast
Fairlie, Gerard
Bulldog Drummond series (14)

Bulldog Drummond strikes back
Sapper
Ronald Standish series (2)

Bulldog Drummond strikes nack
Sapper
Bulldog Drummond series (8)

Bulldog Drummond's third round
Sapper
Bulldog Drummond series (3)

Bulldogs and all about them
Cooper, Henry Saint John
Bulldog series (3)

Bulldogs and bulldog men
Cooper, Henry Saint John
Bulldog series (2)

Bulldozer Brown
Russell, Steven
Bulldozer Brown series (1)

Bulldozer Brown in Africa
Russell, Steven
Bulldozer Brown series (2)

Buller's Dreadnought
Hough, Richard Alexander
Archy Buller series (2)

Buller's guns
Hough, Richard Alexander
Archy Buller series (1)

Buller's victory
Hough, Richard Alexander
Archy Buller series (3)

Bullet bounty
Allen, Chester
Justice Colt series (8)

Bullet brand
Scott, Bradford
Walt Slade series (79)

Bullet Bridge
Davis, Gordon
Sergeant series (7)

Bullet caravan
Sharpe, Jon
Trailsman series (61)

Bullet for a beast
Simons, Roger
Inspector Fadiman Wace series (8)

Bullet for a star
Kaminsky, Stuart Melvin
Toby Peters series (1)

Bullet for a widow
Grover, Marshall
Larry and Stretch series (200)

Bullet for Betty
Joyce, Cyril
Chief Superintendent Pat Stockton series (12)

Bullet for Fidel
Carter, Nick
Nick Carter series (7)

Bullet for Midas
Morland, Nigel
Mrs Palmyra Pym series (20)

Bullet for Mister Texas
Hogan, Ray
Shawn Starbuck series (5)

Bullet for my baby
Brown, Carter
Mavis Seidlitz series (2)

Bullet for my love
Cohen, Octavus Roy
Lieutenant Marty Walsh series (3)

Bullet for one
Stout, Rex
Nero Wolfe and Archie Goodwin series (18)

Bullet for Rhino
Witting, Clifford
Inspector Charlton series (9)

Bullet for your dreams
Von Elsner, Don
David Danning series (8)

Bullet hole
Miles, Keith
Alan Saxton series (1)

Bullet in a bedroom
Brody, Marc
Marc Brody series (71)

Bullet in Mason's back
Grover, Marshall
Larry and Stretch series (273)

Bullet in the ballet
Brahms, Caryl
Inspector Adam Quill series (1)
Stroganoff Troupe series (1)

Bullet in the cornice
Beckett, Mark
Major Dick Burton series (6)

Bullet is faster
Grover, Marshall
Nevada Jim series (21)

Bullet justice
Scott, Bradford
Walt Slade series (103)

Bullet proof
Collins, Max Allan
Eliot Ness series (3)
Kane, Frank
Johnny Liddell series (5)

Bullet-proof man
Riefe, Alan
Huntington Cage series (5)

Bullet-proof toga
Malloy, Lester
Martin Moon series (5)

Bullet trail
Macdonald, William Colt
Three Mesquiteers series (7)

Bullet welcome for Slattery
Lawrence, Steven C
Tom Slattery series (2)

Bulletin blonde
Brody, Marc
Marc Brody series (11)

Bullets and bad times
Longley, W B
Angel Eyes series (6)

Bullets and ballots
Roberts, J R
Gunsmith series (22)

Bullets and billets
Bairnsfather, Bruce
Old Bill series (4)

Bullets and brown eyes
Corrigan, Mark
Mark Corrigan and McLean series (1)

Bullets are final
Kennedy, Elliot
Griff Dexter series (2)

Bullets are my business
West, John B
Rocky Steele series (3)

Bullets are trumps
Reid, Desmond
Sexton Blake series (1520)

Bullets, bikinis and bells
Renauld, Ron
A-Team series (7)

Bullets bite deep
Hume, David
Mick Cardby series (1)

Bullets, buzzards, boxes of pine
Hardin, J D
Raider and Doc series (4)

Bullets for a ranger
Scott, Bradford
Walt Slade series (58)

Bullets for Badwater
Nelson, Al P
Badwater series (2)

Bullets for Brandon
Warren, Vernon
Mark Brandon series (6)

Bullets for breakfast
Walsh, James Morgan
Oliver Keene series (4)

Bullets for buckaroos
Macdonald, William Colt
Three Mesquiteers series (7)

Bullets for Macbeth
Kaye, Marvin
Hilary Quayle series (3)

Bullets for Mulvane
Heuman, William
Grady Mulvane series (4)

Bullets for the bridegroom
Dodge, David
Whit Whitney series (3)

Bullets high
Cole, Jackson
Jim Hatfield series (22)

Bullets in the wind
Newton, Dwight Bennett
Jim Bannister series (3)

Bullets make holes
Bentley, John
Glen Gibson series (1)

Bullets on the border
Cole, Jackson
Jim Hatfield series (42)
Scofield, Jonathan
Freedom fighters series (5)

Bullets over the border
Scott, Bradford
Walt Slade series (74)

Bullets to Baghdad
Chambers, Philip
Sexton Blake series (1488)

Bulleymung pit
Blomefield, Mathena
Nessel series (1)

Bullfrog and Gertrude go camping
Dauer, Rosamond
Bullfrog series (3)

Bullfrog builds a horse
Dauer, Rosamond
Bullfrog series (2)

Bullfrog grows up
Dauer, Rosamond
Bullfrog series (1)

Bullion
Woodman, Michael
Paul Gane series (2)

Bullion mystery
Carter, Nicholas
Nicholas Carter series (518)

Bullion route
Grover, Marshall
Larry and Stretch series (174)

Bullitt
Pike, Robert L
Lieutenant Clancy series (1)

Bull's eye
Kennedy, Milward
Sir George Bull series (1)

Bulls in the meadows
Bull, Peter
Bulls series (2)
Bulls of Rome
Huna, Ludwig
Borgia trilogy (1)
Bullseye blood
Meek, Joseph
Mountain Jack Pike series (10)
Bullwhipped beauty
Hunter, E J
White Squaw series (17)
Bully
Pascal, Francine
Sweet Valley twins series (19)
Bully for the Beast!
Stevens, Kathleen
Beast series (3)
Bully of Barkham Street
Stolz, Mary
Barkham Street trilogy (2)
Bully on the bus
Sharmat, Marjorie Weinman
Kids on the bus series (4)
Bulman
Holdstock, Robert
Bulman series (1)
Buln-Buln and the brolga
Collins, Tom
Such is life series (3)
Bum steer
Pickard, Nancy
Jenny Cain series (6)
Bumble
Eldon, Magdalen
Bumble series (1)
Bumble B Bear cleans up
Cosgrove, Stephen Edward
Bumble B Bear series (5)
Bumble B Bear in the garden
Cosgrove, Stephen Edward
Bumble B Bear series (4)
Bumble B Bear rides in a car
Cosgrove, Stephen Edward
Bumble B Bear series (3)
Bumble B Bear takes a walk
Cosgrove, Stephen Edward
Bumble B Bear series (2)
Bumble's dream
Treloar, Bruce
Bumble series (1)
Bumble's island
Treloar, Bruce
Bumble series (2)
Bumble's journey
Treloar, Bruce
Bumble series (3)
Bump and grind murders
Brown, Carter
Mavis Seidlitz series (9)
Bump in the night
Watson, Colin
Inspector Purbright series (2)
Bumper Gumdrop omnibus
Biro, Val
Gumdrop series (39)
Bumps in the night
Ahlberg, Allan
Funnybones series (6)
Bun and Mrs Tubby
Paterson, Bettina
Bun series (1)
Bun Noel
English, David
Bunburys series (10)
Bunbury tails
English, David
Bunburys series (1)
Bunburys down under
English, David
Bunburys series (3)
Bunburys play ball
English, David
Bunburys series (5)
Bunch of everlastings
Boreham, Frank William
Texts that made history series (1)
Bunchester United
English, David
Bunburys series (9)
Bunchy
Brisley, Joyce Lankester
Bunchy series (1)
Bundle for the Toff
Creasey, John
Toff series (50)
Bundle of clews
Carter, Nicholas
Nicholas Carter series (145)
Bundle of sensations
Rees, Goronwy
Sensations and accidents series (1)
Bunduki
Edson, John Thomas
Bunduki series (1)
Bunduki and Dawn
Edson, John Thomas
Bunduki series (2)
Bundy in the Greenwood
Begbie, Harold
Bundy series (1)
Bundy on the sea
Begbie, Harold
Bundy series (2)
Bungalow crime
Urquhart, Paul
Sexton Blake series (732)
Bungalow mystery
Keene, Carolyn
Nancy Drew series (3)
Bungalow tragedy
Bayfield, William John
Sexton Blake series (68)
Bungle's ghost
Strong, Jeremy
Bungle series (2)
Bungo knows best
Beresford, Elisabeth
Little Wombles series (5)
Bunkle and Belinda
Pardoe, Margot
Bunkle series (6)
Bunkle baffles them
Pardoe, Margot
Bunkle series (7)
Bunkle began it
Pardoe, Margot
Bunkle series (2)
Bunkle bought it
Pardoe, Margot
Bunkle series (4)
Bunkle breaks away
Pardoe, Margot
Bunkle series (5)
Bunkle brings it off
Pardoe, Margot
Bunkle series (12)
Bunkle butts in
Pardoe, Margot
Bunkle series (3)
Bunkle gets busy
Pardoe, Margot
Bunkle series (9)
Bunkle scents a clue
Pardoe, Margot
Bunkle series (11)
Bunkle went for six
Pardoe, Margot
Bunkle series (8)
Bunkle's brainwave
Pardoe, Margot
Bunkle series (10)
Bunko trail
Grover, Marshall
Larry and Stretch series (418)
Bunnicula
Howe, James
Bunnicula series (1)
Bunnicula fun book
Howe, James
Bunnicula series (10)
Bunnies
Q, John
Peter Trees series (1)
Bunnies all day long
Ehrlich, Amy
Bunnies series (1)
Bunnies and their grandma
Ehrlich, Amy
Bunnies series (2)
Bunnies and their hobbies
Carlson, Nancy
Bunnies series (1)
Bunnies and their sports
Carlson, Nancy
Bunnies series (2)
Bunnies at Christmas time
Ehrlich, Amy
Bunnies series (4)
Bunnies love
McCue, Lisa
Baby animal love series (3)
Bunnies on their own
Ehrlich, Amy
Bunnies series (3)
Bunny bakes a cake
Cosgrove, Stephen Edward
Baby Bunny series (5)
Bunny Binks on the war-path
Richards, Frank
Mascot schoolboy series (2)
Bunny Brown and his sister Sue
Hope, Laura Lee
Bunny Brown and his sister Sue series (1)
Bunny Brown and his sister Sue and their Shetland pony
Hope, Laura Lee
Bunny Brown and his sister Sue series (8)
Bunny Brown and his sister Sue and their trick dog
Hope, Laura Lee
Bunny Brown and his sister Sue series (13)
Bunny Brown and his sister Sue at a sugar camp
Hope, Laura Lee
Bunny Brown and his sister Sue series (14)
Bunny Brown and his sister Sue at Aunt Lou's city home
Hope, Laura Lee
Bunny Brown and his sister Sue series (5)
Bunny Brown and his sister Sue at Berry Hill
Hope, Laura Lee
Bunny Brown and his sister Sue series (18)
Bunny Brown and his sister Sue at Camp Rest-a-While
Hope, Laura Lee
Bunny Brown and his sister Sue series (4)
Bunny Brown and his sister Sue at Christmas Tree Cove
Hope, Laura Lee
Bunny Brown and his sister Sue series (10)
Bunny Brown and his sister Sue at Shore Acres
Hope, Laura Lee
Bunny Brown and his sister Sue series (17)
Bunny Brown and his sister Sue at Sky Top
Hope, Laura Lee
Bunny Brown and his sister Sue series (19)
Bunny Brown and his sister Sue at the summer carnival
Hope, Laura Lee
Bunny Brown and his sister Sue series (20)
Bunny Brown and his sister Sue giving a show
Hope, Laura Lee
Bunny Brown and his sister Sue series (9)
Bunny Brown and his sister Sue in the big woods
Hope, Laura Lee
Bunny Brown and his sister Sue series (6)
Bunny Brown and his sister Sue in the sunny South
Hope, Laura Lee
Bunny Brown and his sister Sue series (11)
Bunny Brown and his sister Sue keeping store
Hope, Laura Lee
Bunny Brown and his sister Sue series (12)
Bunny Brown and his sister Sue on an auto tour
Hope, Laura Lee
Bunny Brown and his sister Sue series (7)
Bunny Brown and his sister Sue on grandpa's farm
Hope, Laura Lee
Bunny Brown and his sister Sue series (2)
Bunny Brown and his sister Sue on Jack Frost Island
Hope, Laura Lee
Bunny Brown and his sister Sue series (16)
Bunny Brown and his sister Sue on the rolling ocean
Hope, Laura Lee
Bunny Brown and his sister Sue series (15)
Bunny Brown and his sister Sue playing circus
Hope, Laura Lee
Bunny Brown and his sister Sue series (3)
Bunny goes to market
Cosgrove, Stephen Edward
Baby Bunny series (4)
Bunny in trouble
Pilgrim, Jane
Blackberry Farm series (18)
Bunny sees
Hands, Hargrave
Look and see series (5)
Bunny stories for young people
Jewett, John Howard
Bunny stories series (1)
Bunny trouble
Wilhelm, Hans
Bunny trouble series (1)
Bunnybados
English, David
Bunburys series (2)
Bunnykins in the kitchen
Warrener
Bunnykins series (4)
Bunnykins in the snow
Warrener
Bunnykins series (3)
Bunny's busy day
Cosgrove, Stephen Edward
Baby Bunny series (3)
Bunny's numbers
McCue, Dick
Animal shape series (5)
Bunny's playtime
Cosgrove, Stephen Edward
Baby Bunny series (1)
Bun's birthday
Paterson, Bettina
Bun series (2)
Bunst and the brown voice
Chance, John Newton
Bunst series (4)
Bunst and the flying eye
Chance, John Newton
Bunst series (6)
Bunst and the secret six
Chance, John Newton
Bunst series (5)
Bunst the bold
Chance, John Newton
Bunst series (3)
Bunter and the phantom of the towers
Richards, Frank
Billy Bunter series (37)
Bunter comes for Christmas
Richards, Frank
Billy Bunter series (24)
Bunter does his best
Richards, Frank
Billy Bunter series (15)
Bunter keeps it dark
Richards, Frank
Billy Bunter series (26)
Bunter out of bounds
Richards, Frank
Billy Bunter series (25)
Bunter the bad lad
Richards, Frank
Billy Bunter series (27)
Bunter the caravanner
Richards, Frank
Billy Bunter series (32)
Bunter the racketeer
Richards, Frank
Billy Bunter series (38)
Bunter the sportsman
Richards, Frank
Billy Bunter series (39)
Bunter the stowaway
Richards, Frank
Billy Bunter series (35)
Bunter the tough guy of Greyfriars
Richards, Frank
Billy Bunter series (40)
Bunter the ventriloquist
Richards, Frank
Billy Bunter series (30)
Bunter's Christmas party
Richards, Frank
Billy Bunter series (5)
Bunter's holiday cruise
Richards, Frank
Billy Bunter series (41)
Bunter's last fling
Richards, Frank
Billy Bunter series (42)
Bunty Brown of the Flying Squad
Wilcox, Barbara
Bunty Brown series (3)
Bunty Brown, probationer
Wilcox, Barbara
Bunty Brown series (1)
Bunty Brown's bargain
Wilcox, Barbara
Bunty Brown series (2)
Bunyip and the brolga bird
Whitlock, Judith
Bunyip series (3)
Bunyip and the bushfire
Whitlock, Judith
Bunyip series (4)
Bunyip and the tiger cats
Whitlock, Judith
Bunyip series (5)
Bunyip at the seaside
Whitlock, Judith
Bunyip series (2)
Bunyip hole
Wrightson, Patricia
Society of the Crooked Snake series (2)
Burbank the northerner
Verne, Jules
North against South series (1)
Burcliff, its sunshine and its clouds
Trowbridge, John Townsend
Brighthope series (3)
Burden
Dawson-Scott, Catherine Amy
Some women trilogy (2)
Burden of guilt
Brown, Carter
Lieutenant Al Wheeler series (40)
Burden of proof
Carter, Nicholas
Nicholas Carter series (588)
Challis, Mary
Jeremy Locke series (1)
Turow, Scott
Sandy Stern series (2)
Bureau thirteen
Pollotta, Nick
Bureau thirteen series (1)
Burgess animal book for children
Burgess, Thornton Waldo
Natural history series (2)
Burgess big book of Green Meadow stories
Burgess, Thornton Waldo
Green Meadow series (4)
Burgess bird book for children
Burgess, Thornton Waldo
Natural history series (1)
Burgess flower book for children
Burgess, Thornton Waldo
Natural history series (3)
Burgess seashore book for children
Burgess, Thornton Waldo
Natural history series (4)
Burglar bells
Escott, John
Bells series (3)
Burglar in the closet
Block, Lawrence
Bernie Rhodenbarr series (2)
Burglar of White Birches
Graydon, William Murray
Sexton Blake series (481)
Burglar who liked to quote Kipling
Block, Lawrence
Bernie Rhodenbarr series (3)
Burglar who painted like Mondrian
Block, Lawrence
Bernie Rhodenbarr series (5)
Burglar who studied Spinoza
Block, Lawrence
Bernie Rhodenbarr series (4)
Burglar who traded Tad Williams
Block, Lawrence
Bernie Rhodenbarr series (6)
Burglars and bandicoots
Severn, David
Warner series (5)
Burglars can't be choosers
Block, Lawrence
Bernie Rhodenbarr series (1)
Burglars in Bucks
Cole, George Douglas Howard
Everard Blatchington series (2)
Burglars in Bucks.
Cole, George Douglas Howard
Superintendent Henry Wilson series (7)
Burglary at Toad Hall
Jones, Nicholas
Wind in the willows series (7)
Burgle the Baron
Morton, Anthony
Baron series (45)
Burgos contract
Ross, Angus
Mark Farrow series (11)
Burial
Masterton, Graham
Manitou series (3)
Burial deferred
Ross, Jonathan
Superintendent George Rogers series (13)
Burial in Portugal
Macleod, Robert
Jonathan Gaunt series (3)

Buried Caesars
Kaminsky, Stuart Melvin
Toby Peters series (14)
Buried country
Hardy, Philip
Smith Minor series (1)
Buried evidence
Grant, Maxwell
Shadow series (130)
Buried for pleasure
Crispin, Edmund
Gervase Fen series (6)
Buried in the past
Lemarchand, Elizabeth
Superintendent Tom Pollard series (7)
Buried in time
Keene, Carolyn
Nancy Drew and Hardy boys supermystery series (6)
Buried motive
Cassidy, Bruce
Cash Madigan series (2)
Buried pleasure
De Chair, Somerset
Golden carpet series (2)
Buried secret
Carter, Nicholas
Nicholas Carter series (406)
Buried secrets
Keene, Carolyn
Nancy Drew files series (10)
Buried treasure
Jones, Nicholas
Wind in the willows series (6)
Morris, Dave
Teenage mutant ninja turtles series (4)
Pascal, Francine
Sweet Valley twins series (11)
Burke, the kingpin
Preston, Fayrene
Shamrock trilogy (2)
Burma battle
Marlowe, Greg
Greg Marlowe series (3)
Burma probe
Rosenberger, Joseph
Death Merchant series (59)
Burma ruby
Fletcher, Joseph Smith
Sergeant Charlesworth series (2)
Burma surgeon
Seagrave, Gordon Stifler
Burma surgeon trilogy (1)
Burma surgeon returns
Seagrave, Gordon Stifler
Burma surgeon trilogy (2)
Burmese dagger
Stuart, Donald
Sexton Blake series (1012)
Burn a little
McGloin, Joseph Thaddeus
Love and life series (3)
Burn, and other stories
Corris, Peter
Cliff Hardy series (17)
Burn marks
Paretsky, Sara
V I Warshawski series (6)
Burn this
McCloy, Helen
Basil Willing series (13)
Burn, witch, burn!
Merritt, Abraham
Doctor Lowell series (1)
Burned bramble
Sperber, Manes
Doino Faber trilogy (1)
Burned man
Monig, Christopher
Brian Brett series (1)
Spicer, Bart
Colonel Peregrine White series (2)
Burning
Stine, Robert Lawrence
Fear Street saga series (3)
Burning blue death
Rosenberger, Joseph
Death Merchant series (38)
Burning bush
Blyton, Enid
Bible stories series (6)
Rolland, Romain
John Christopher series (4)
Undset, Sigrid
Modern scene series (2)
Burning cresset
Pease, Howard
Border trilogy (3)
Burning eye
Green, Roland
War world series (1)
Pournelle, Jerry
War world series (1)
Burning fuse
Benson, Ben
Inspector Wade Paris series (6)
Burning ground
Malcolm, John
Tim Simpson series (10)
Burning houses
Harvey, Andrew
Burning houses series (1)
Burning is a substitute for loving
Melville, Jennie
Sergeant Charmian Daniels series (2)
Burning land
Siegel, Barbara
Firebrats series (1)
Burning man
Pike, Charles R
Jubal Cade series (6)
Burning men
Jackman, Stuart
Jesus Davidson series (3)
Burning obsession
Walker, Robert Wayne
Dean Grant series (3)
Burning of Billy Toober
Ross, Jonathan
Superintendent George Rogers series (6)
Burning of Troy
Gair, Malcolm
Mark Raeburn series (3)
Burning questions of Bingo Brown
Byars, Betsy
Bingo Brown series (1)
Burning shore
Smith, Wilbur Addison
Courtney family series (1)
Burning stone
Harris, Deborah Turner
Mages of Garillon trilogy (1).
Burning tears of Sassurum
Baker, Sharon
Naphar series (3)
Burning water
Lackey, Mercedes
Diana Tregarde series (1)
Burnt lands
Elliott, Richard
John Norris series (2)
Burnt Norton
Eliot, Thomas Stearns
Four quartets series (1)
Burnt offering
Lockridge, Frances
Inspector Merton Heimrich series (10)
Richards, Francis
Inspector Merton Heimrich series (10)
Burnton widows
McConnell, Vicki P
Nyla Wade series (1)
Burr
Vidal, Gore
Washington series (1)
Burroughs dictionary
McWhorter, George T
Tarzan series (24)
Burrowers beneath
Lumley, Brian
Titus Crow series (1)
Bursting world
Butler, Guy
South Africa series (2)
Burton of the Flying Corps
Strang, Herbert
Stories of the Great War series (3)
Bury her sweetly
Amey, Linda
Blair Emerson series (1)
Bury him darkly
Ormerod, Roger
Philipa Lowe series (3)
Wade, Henry
Inspector Poole series (5)
Bury him deeper
Walling, Robert Alfred John
Philip Tolefree series (12)
Bury in haste
Eichler, Alfred
Inspector Knickman series (6)
Bury me deep
Masur, Harold Q
Scott Jordan series (1)
Bury me not
Francis, William
Anthony Martin series (2)
Bury that poker
Wilson, Gertrude Mary
Inspector Lovick series (1)
Bury the guilty
Grover, Marshall
Nevada Jim series (37)
McCoy, Marshall
Nevada Jim series (37)
Bury the guy!
Shannon, Brad
Lefty O'Connor series (3)
Bury the hatchet
Long, Manning
Liz Parrott series (4)
Bury the past
Reinsmith, Richard
Bodyguard series (4)
Bury their dead
Fraser, Alex
Inspector Noel Tracy series (4)
Burying the hatchet
Kellogg, Elijah
Forest Glen series (6)
Bus-full of beans
Fowler, Richard
Beans series (2)
Bus of my own
Lehrer, Jim
Dreamers series (2)
Bus ran late
Wilson, Gertrude Mary
Inspector Lovick series (18)
Bus station murders
Revell, Louisa
Julia Tyler series (1)
Bus station mystery
Warner, Gertrude Chandler
Boxcar children series (18)
Bush adventure
Grey, Peter
Kit Hunter series (4)
Bush baby
Woodhouse, Martin
Giles Yeoman series (2)
Bush boys
Reid, Mayne
Bush boys series (1)
Bush fire
Salmon, Michael
Alexander Bunyip series (7)
Bush time, station time
Shaw, Bruce
East Kimberley series (4)
Bush warfare
Kilgore, Axel
They call me the Mercenary series (10)
Bushido lawman
Lee, Patrick
Six-Gun Samurai series (6)
Bushido vengeance
Lee, Patrick
Six-Gun Samurai series (2)
Bushland tales
Martin, Marianne
Golden boomerang series (6)
Bushman!
Moore, William
Mallandine family trilogy (2)
Bushman who came back
Upfield, Arthur William
Napoleon Bonaparte series (22)
Bushranger of the skies
Upfield, Arthur William
Napoleon Bonaparte series (8)
Bushwack Canyon
Borg, Jack
Hogleg Bailey series (6)
Bushwacked
Randall, Clay
Amos Flagg series (4)
Bushwhacker vengeance
Benton, Will
Bushwhacker series (1)
Bushwhacker's moon
Benton, Will
Bushwhacker series (2)
Business and legal forms for authors and self-publishers
Crawford, Tad
Business and legal forms series (2)
Business and legal forms for fine artists
Crawford, Tad
Business and legal forms series (1)
Business and legal forms for graphic designers
Crawford, Tad
Business and legal forms series (4)
Business and legal forms for illustrators
Crawford, Tad
Business and legal forms series (3)
Business and legal forms for photographers
Crawford, Tad
Business and legal forms series (5)
Business boy
Chapman, Allen
Boys of business series (4)
Business boy's pluck
Chapman, Allen
Boys of business series (4)
Business unusual
Heald, Tim
Simon Bognor series (10)
Busman's holiday
Andrews, Lucilla
Saint Martha's Hospital series (9)
Busman's honeymoon
Sayers, Dorothy Leigh
Harriet Vane series (4)
Lord Peter Wimsey series (13)
Bust-up
Christian, Petra
Sally Deenes series (6)
Busted
Chase, Glen
Cherry Delight series (16)
Busted Wheeler
Brown, Carter
Lieutenant Al Wheeler series (51)
Buster Bear's twins
Burgess, Thornton Waldo
Green forest series (4)
Buster gets dressed
Campbell, Rod
Buster series (4)
Buster keeps warm
Campbell, Rod
Buster series (5)
Buster's afternoon
Campbell, Rod
Buster series (2)
Buster's bedtime
Campbell, Rod
Buster series (3)
Buster's morning
Campbell, Rod
Buster series (1)
Busting of Frankie da Mora
Sharp, Allen
Storytrails series (22)
Busy babies
Kilroy, Sally
Baby series (6)
Busy Bear firefighter counterpack
Killingback, Julia
Busy Bears series (13)
Busy Bear to the rescue
Killingback, Julia
Busy Bears series (11)
Busy Bears at the fire station
Killingback, Julia
Busy Bears series (12)
Busy Bear's closet
Margolin, Harriet
Busy Bear series (1)
Busy Bear's cupboard
Margolin, Harriet
Busy Bear series (2)
Busy Bears' picnic
Killingback, Julia
Busy Bears series (9)
Busy Bear's refrigerator
Margolin, Harriet
Busy Bear series (3)
Busy Bear's room
Margolin, Harriet
Busy Bear series (4)
Busy day
Maestro, Betsy Crippen
Words series (1)
Szekeres, Cyndy
Tiny paw series (1)
Busy in the fog
Fitzgerald, Ross
Grafton Everest series (3)
Busy O'Brien and the caterpillar punch bunch
Poploff, Michelle
Busy O'Brien series (2)
Busy O'Brien and the great bubblegum blowout
Poploff, Michelle
Busy O'Brien series (1)
Busy streets
Gee, Herbert Leslie
Friendly series (5)
Busy year at the old squire's
Ober, Frederick Albion
Old farm series (3)
Busybody Nora
Hurwitz, Johanna
Nora and Teddy series (1)
But and ben
Cameron, Isabel
Glen folk series (3)
But beauty vanishes
Blaker, Richard
Hester Billiter series (2)
But gentlemen marry brunettes
Loos, Anita
Lorelei Lee and Dorothy series (2)
But I feed the pigeons, well I watch the sun
Gibson, Patricia Jeann
Private hells trilogy (2)
But I wouldn't want to die there
Pickard, Nancy
Jenny Cain series (8)
But I'll be back again
Rylant, Cynthia
Best wishes series (1)
But in ourselves
Maurice, Michael
Not in our stars series (2)
But it still goes on
Graves, Robert
Goodbye to all that series (2)
But look, the morn
Kantor, Mackinlay
But look trilogy (1)
But not for love
Wilson, Ivor
Gregory Flamm series (1)
But not forgotten
Fenisong, Ruth
Captain Gridley Nelson series (12)
But she's so cute
Chase, Emily
Canby Hall series (23)
But still the stream
Cato, Nancy
Australian trilogy (3)
But that's another story
Grender, Iris
Did I ever tell series (2)
But the doctor died
Rice, Craig
John Joseph Malone series (14)
But the patient died
Edwards, James G
Inspector Victor Bondurant series (7)
Sinclair, Fiona
Inspector Paul Grainger series (2)
But we didn't get the fox
Llewellyn, Richard
Edmund Trothe series (2)
But yesterday
Diver, Maud
Challoners series (2)
Butch and Bax
Collinson, Roger
Bobby Bax series (2)
Butcher block
Mandell, Mark
Nazi hunter series (4)
Butcher of Belgrade
Carter, Nick
Nick Carter series (73)
Butcher's dozen
Collins, Max Allan
Eliot Ness series (2)
Butcher's moon
Stark, Richard
Alan Grofield series (7)
Parker series (16)
Butchers of Eden
Hild, Jack
SOBS series (3)
Buthcher from Guerro
Masterson, Louis
Morgan Kane series (22)
Butler died in Brooklyn
Fenisong, Ruth
Captain Gridley Nelson series (3)
Butt of Malmsey
Williamson, Hugh Ross
Passing of the Plantagenets series (1)
Butte bloodbath
Slade, Jack
Gatling series (6)
Butter Market House
Ford, Elizabeth
Maplechester series (3)
Buttercup case
Crane, Frances
Pat and Jean Abbott series (23)
Buttercup Farm family
Blyton, Enid
Mike, Belinda and Ann series (5)
Buttercup story book
Blyton, Enid
Flower story book series (4)
Buttercup Willie is a great help
Oakden, David
Buttercup Willie series (2)

Buttercup Willie rides again
Oakden, David
Buttercup Willie series (1)
Buttercups and daisies
Mackenzie, Compton
John Touchwood series (3)
Buttercups and Daisy
Cragoe, Elizabeth
Untidy gardener series (1)
Buttered side down
Addis, Faith
Devon farm series (3)
Butterflies and late loves
Fountaine, Margaret
Victorian lady series (2)
Butterfly ball and the grasshopper's feast
Aldridge, Alan
Butterfly ball series (1)
Butterfly days
Fowkes, Aubrey
Butterfly days series (1)
Butterfly flood
Wyllie, John
Doctor Quarshie series (2)
Butterfly kid
Anderson, Chester
Greenwich Village trilogy (1)
Butterfly Max
Turk, Hanne
Max the Mouse series (13)
Buttermilk
Cosgrove, Stephen Edward
Buttermilk series (1)
Buttermilk Bear
Cosgrove, Stephen Edward
Buttermilk series (2)
Butternut Bill
McCall, Edith
Butternut Bill series (1)
Butternut Bill an the train
McCall, Edith
Butternut Bill series (8)
Butternut Bill and his friends
McCall, Edith
Butternut Bill series (7)
Butternut Bill and Little River
McCall, Edith
Butternut Bill series (5)
Butternut Bill and the bear
McCall, Edith
Butternut Bill series (4)
Butternut Bill and the bee tree
McCall, Edith
Butternut Bill series (2)
Butternut Bill and the big cash
McCall, Edith
Butternut Bill series (3)
Butternut Bill and the big pumpkin
McCall, Edith
Butternut Bill series (6)
Butterscotia
Parry, Edward Abbott
Krab series (2)
Buttes Landing
Rikhoff, Jean
Butte family series (1)
Button
Cosgrove, Stephen Edward
Bugg series (37)
Button, button
Bramhall, Marion
Kit Acton series (2)
Roth, Holly
Lieutenant Kelly series (2)
Buttons and Mister Pete
McCall, Edith
Button family series (8)
Buttons and the Boy Scouts
McCall, Edith
Button family series (9)
Buttons and the Little League
McCall, Edith
Button family series (10)
Buttons and the pet parade
McCall, Edith
Button family series (3)
Buttons and the whirlybird
McCall, Edith
Button family series (11)
Buttons at the farm
McCall, Edith
Button family series (4)
Buttons at the soap box derby
McCall, Edith
Button family series (6)
Buttons at the zoo
McCall, Edith
Button family series (2)
Buttons go camping
McCall, Edith
Button family series (5)
Buttons see things that go
McCall, Edith
Button family series (12)
Buttons take a boat ride
McCall, Edith
Button family series (7)
Buy back blues
Dennis, Ralph
Jim Hardman series (12)
Buy my silence
Landon, Herman
Picaroon series (4)
Buyer beware
Lutz, John
Alo Nudger series (1)
Buyer's market
Powell, Anthony
Dance to the music of time series (2)
Buzz
Cosgrove, Stephen Edward
Bugg series (25)
Buzzard meat
Friend, Oscar
Simon Carter series (1)
Buzzard's Gap
Sharpe, Jon
Trailsman series (96)
Buzzards pick the bones
Thomas, Murray
Inspector Wilkins series (1)
Buzzy Bear and the rainbow
Marino, Dorothy
Buzzy Bear series (4)
Buzzy Bear goes camping
Marino, Dorothy
Buzzy Bear series (2)
Buzzy Bear goes south
Marino, Dorothy
Buzzy Bear series (1)
Buzzy Bear's busy day
Marino, Dorothy
Buzzy Bear series (3)
Buzzy Bear's first day at school
Marino, Dorothy
Buzzy Bear series (5)
Bwana Pook
Pook, Peter
Pook series (5)
By a silver stream
Dudley-Smith, Trevor
Happy glade series (2)
Trevor, Elleston
Green glade trilogy (2)
By advice of counsel
Train, Arthur
Ephraim Tutt series (2)
By air express to Venus
Rockwood, Roy
Great marvel series (8)
By an unseen hand
Carter, Nicholas
Nicholas Carter series (407)
By balloon to the Sahara
Terman, Douglas
Choose your own adventure series (3)
By chaos cursed
Reichert, Mickey Zucker
Bifrost guardians series (5)
By command of the Viceroy
Macneil, Duncan
James Ogilvie series (7)
By courtesy of the cardinal
Deeley, Roger
Martin Dymoke series (2)
By dawn's early light
Clement, Henry
Columbo series (4)
By daybreak the Eagle
Dorer, Nancy
Eagle series (1)
By England's aid
Henty, George Alfred
Dutch Republic series (2)
By evil means
Prowell, Sandra West
Phoebe Siegel series (1)
By force of circumstance
Holmes, Gordon
Inspector Furneaux series (1)
By frequent anguish
Dean, S F X
Professor Neil Kelly series (1)
By Gemini
Davison, Ann
Voyages series (4)
By his own hand
Cronin, Michael
Sam Harris series (1)
By hook and by crook
Archer, Fred
Evesham Vale series (9)
By hook or by Crook
Gilbert, Anthony
Arthur Crook series (17)
By hook or by crook
Lathen, Emma
John Putnam Thatcher series (16)
Walling, Robert Alfred John
Philip Tolefree series (18)
By hook or crook
Walling, Robert Alfred John
Philip Tolefree series (18)
By Jiminy
Daniell, David Scott
Jiminy series (1)
By Jiminy ahoy
Daniell, David Scott
Jiminy series (3)
By Jiminy in the Highlands
Daniell, David Scott
Jiminy series (5)
By Jiminy in the jungle
Daniell, David Scott
Jiminy series (4)
By Jumping Cat Bridge
Wells, Kenneth McNeil
Owl Pen series (4)
By land to Xanadu
Moldoff, Sheldon
Marco Polo Junior series (2)
By misadventure
Fletcher, Robert James
Gilbert Davison series (2)
By Moonstone Creek
Wells, Kenneth McNeil
Owl Pen series (2)
By night at Dinsmore
Esteven, John
Miles Le Breton series (1)
By order of the company
Johnston, Mary
Virginian series (1)
By order of the king!
Graydon, William Murray
Sexton Blake series (383)
By order of the Soviet
Symonds, Francis Addington
Sexton Blake series (393)
By order of the Tong
Brandon, John Gordon
Sexton Blake series (830)
By our beginnings
Stubbs, Jean
Brief chronicles series (1)
By-pass control
Spillane, Mickey
Tiger Mann series (4)
By-pass murder
Frome, David
Evan Pinkerton series (2)
By pike and dyke
Henty, George Alfred
Dutch Republic series (1)
By pirate's blood
Silver, Richard
Captain Shark series (1)
By pluck, not luck
Winfield, Arthur M
Bound to win series (11)
Bright and bold series (3)
By pond and stream
Ainsworth, Ruth
Look about you series (4)
By reason of insanity
Harvey, James Neal
Ben Tolliver series (1)
By registered post
Rhode, John
Doctor Lancelot Priestley series (55)
By request
Dell, Ethel May
Nick Ratcliffe series (3)
By roaring loom
Mather, James Marshall
Lancashire idylls series (2)
By royal command
Yates, Dornford
Richard Chandos series (4)
By Saturday
Fowler, Sydney
Inspector Cleveland series (1)
By sea to Xanadu
Moldoff, Sheldon
Marco Polo Junior series (1)
By some person unknown
Barrington, Pamela
Inspector George Marshall series (4)
By space ship to Saturn
Rockwood, Roy
Great marvel series (9)
By the green of the spring
Masters, John
Loss of Eden trilogy (3)
By the lake
Dick, Kay
Robert Stairey series (1)
By the light of the Green Star
Carter, Lin
Green Star series (3)
By the light of the study lamp
Keene, Carolyn
Dana girls series (1)
By the north door
Atkins, Meg Elizabeth
Inspector Henry Beaumont series (1)
By the pricking of my thumbs
Christie, Agatha
Tommy and Tuppence Beresford series (4)
By the sandhills of Yamboorah
Ottley, Reginald Leslie
Yamboorah series (1)
By the sea
Dicks, Terrance
Camden Street kids series (3)
By the shores of Silver Lake
Wilder, Laura Ingalls
Laura series (4)
By the skin of his teeth
Armour, R Coutts
Sexton Blake series (208)
By the terms of the will
Graydon, William Murray
Sexton Blake series (124)
By the waters of Liverpool
Forrester, Helen
Mersey series (3)
By valour and arms
Street, James
Dabney family series (3)
By way of confession
Gore-Browne, Robert
Lucien Clay series (2)
By whose hand?
Baskerville, Beatrice
Briconi series (1)
Hardinge, Rex
Sexton Blake series (1402)
Bye, bye, baby!
Bond, J Harvey
Mike Lanson series (1)
Bye bye blackbird
Wendorf, Patricia
Patteran trilogy (3)
Bye bye love
Cooper, M E
Couples series (23)
Byrd of the 95th
Styles, Showell
Ensign Peter Byrd series (2)
Byron in Italy
Quennell, Peter
Lord Byron series (2)
Byron, the monster who didn't want to be alone
Salmon, Michael
Scaredy monsters series (4)
Byron, the years of fame
Quennell, Peter
Lord Byron series (1)
Bystander
Gorky, Maxim
Life of Klim Samgin series (1)
Bystander's fragments from France, volume 5
Bairnsfather, Bruce
Old Bill series (5)
Bystander's fragments from France, volume 6
Bairnsfather, Bruce
Old Bill series (6)
Bystander's fragments of France
Bairnsfather, Bruce
Old Bill series (1)
Bytes Brothers compute a clue
McCoy, Lois
Bytes Brothers series (4)
Bytes Brothers enter the evidence
McCoy, Lois
Bytes Brothers series (3)
Bytes Brothers go to a getaway
McCoy, Lois
Bytes Brothers series (6)
Bytes Brothers input an investigation
McCoy, Lois
Bytes Brothers series (1)
Bytes Brothers program a problem
McCoy, Lois
Bytes Brothers series (2)
Bytes Brothers record a robbery
McCoy, Lois
Bytes Brothers series (5)
Byzantine eagle
Deeley, Roger
Martin Dymoke series (4)
Byzantium endures
Moorcock, Michael
Colonel Pyat series (1)
Byzantium's crown
Shwartz, Susan
Heirs to Byzantium trilogy (1)

C

C.A.D.S.
Sievert, John
C.A.D.S. series (1)
C.B. convoy caper
Christian, Mary Blount
Goosehill Gang series (5)
C.I.D.
Mundy, Talbot
Chullunder Ghose series (3)
C.I.D. of Dexter Drake
Barker, Elsa
Dexter Drake series (2)
C.I.D. Room
Alding, Peter
C.I.D. Room series (1)
C is for clown
Berenstain, Stan
Berenstain bears series (12)
C is for corpse
Grafton, Sue
Kinsey Millhone series (3)
C J Watson solves the dragon's blood mystery
Resciniti, Angelo G
C J Watson series (2)
C J Watson solves the spaceport mystery
Resciniti, Angelo G
C J Watson series (3)
C J's fate
Hooper, Kay
Gold class trilogy (3)
C.L.U.T.Z.
Wilkes, Marilyn Z
C.L.U.T.Z. series (1)
C.L.U.T.Z. and the fizzion formula
Wilkes, Marilyn Z
C.L.U.T.Z. series (2)
C, my name is Cal
Mazer, Norma Fox
My name series (3)
C.O.L.A.R.
Slote, Alfred
Danny One series (3)
Cab and caboose
Munroe, Kirk
Rail and water series (3)
Cab at the door
Pritchett, Victor Sawdon
Cab series (1)
Cab driver's secret
Carter, Nicholas
Nicholas Carter series (143)
Cabal
Dibdin, Michael
Aurelio Zen series (3)
Dunn, Saul
Cabal series (1)
Cabana murders
Dane, Joel Y
Sergeant Cass Harty series (2)
Cabaret crime
Grierson, Francis Durham
Inspector George Muir series (2)
Teed, George Hamilton
Sexton Blake series (592)
Cabbagetown
Garner, Hugh
Cabbagetown series (1)
Cabin
Blasco Ibanez, Vicente
Valencia series (3)
Cabin fever
Jolley, Elizabeth
My father's moon series (2)
Cabin for Crusoe
Severn, David
Crusoe series (2)
Cabin in the clearing
Braden, James Andrew
John Jerome and Return Kingdom series (3)
Ellis, Edward Sylvester
Wyoming Valley trilogy (3)

Cabin six plays Cupid
Kaye, Marilyn
Camp Sunnyside Friends series (2)
Cabin 3033
Clarke, Anna
Professor Paula Glenning series (2)
Cabinda affair
Head, Matthew
Doctor Mary Finney series (2)
Cabinet makers
Fisher, Leonard Everett
Colonial Americans series (8)
Cabinet minister resigns
Duncan, Allan
Major Charles Douglas Kerrwood series (2)
Cabinet of Antiques
Balzac, Honore de
Scenes of provincial life series (8)
Cable car murder
Taylor, Elizabeth Atwood
Maggie Elliott series (1)
Cable car to catastrophe
Quackenbush, Robert Mead
Miss Mallard series (2)
Caboose
Barkan, Joanne
Come aboard series (2)
Caboose mystery
Warner, Gertrude Chandler
Boxcar children series (11)
Cabot
Ketchum, Philip
Elijah Cabot Pickering series (4)
Cache on the rocks
Sellers, Michael
Calouste Fisher series (3)
Cack-handed war
Blishen, Edward
Schoolmaster series (3)
Cactus
Janson, Hank
Hank Janson series (68)
Mannin, Ethel
Elspeth Rodney series (1)
Cactus and the crown
Gavin, Catherine
Second Empire quartet (3)
Cactus Clancy rides
Cody, Stetson
Cactus Clancy series (1)
Cactus justice
Cody, Stetson
Cactus Clancy series (2)
Cactus land
Stern, Rhona
South African series (1)
Cadaver of Gideon Wyck
Laing, Alexander
Doctor Scarlett series (1)
Cadbury and the born losers
Macbeth, George
Cadbury series (3)
Cadbury and the Samurai
Macbeth, George
Cadbury series (1)
Cadbury and the seven witches
Macbeth, George
Cadbury series (2)
Caddie Woodlawn
Brink, Carol Ryrie
Caddie Woodlawn series (1)
Caddo Creek
Wisler, Gary Clifton
Texas Brazos series (4)
Cade curse
Roberts, Willo Davis
Black pearl series (2)
Cadenza for Caruso
Paul, Barbara
Enrico Caruso series (1)
Cadet Alan Carr
Westerman, Percy Francis
Alan Carr series (2)
Cadet days
King, Charles
Cadet series (1)
Cadet Kit Carey
Lounsberry, Lionel
Kit Carey series (1)
Cadet nurse at Saint Mark's
White, Constance Mary
Saint Mark's Hospital series (1)
Cadet of Belgium
Grant, Allan
Boys at the Front series (1)
Cadet's honor
Garrison, Frederick
West Point series (2)
Cadets of putnam Hall
Winfield, Arthur M
Putnam Hall series (1)
Cadre Lucifer
O'Riordan, Robert
Cadre trilogy (2)
Cadre Messiah
O'Riordan, Robert
Cadre trilogy (3)
Cadre One
O'Riordan, Robert
Cadre trilogy (1)
Caesar
Massie, Allan
Roman emperors quartet (3)
Caesar is dead
Lindsay, Jack
Roman Republic trilogy (2)
Caesar of the narrow seas
Gloag, John
Roman Britain series (1)
Caesar's time legions
Kingston, Jeremy
Time tours series (6)
Cage
McCurtin, Peter
Sundance series (41)
Stirling, Stephen Michael
Fifth millenium series (3)
Cage a man
Busby, Francis Marion
Demu trilogy (1)
Cage of bone
Carrier, Jean Guy
Family trilogy (3)
Cage until tame
Henderson, Laurence
Sergeant Arthur Milton series (3)
Cage without bars
Barrington, Pamela
Inspector George Marshall series (9)
Caged beasts
Duhamel, Georges
Pasquier series (2)
Cain's Chinese puzzle
Key, Sean A
Cain series (2)
Cairo communique
Mason, Robert
Captain James Donald Macgregor series (1)
Cairo countdown
Stivers, Dick
Able Team series (5)
Cairo crisis
Martyn, Wyndham
Christopher Bond series (8)
Cairo garter murders
Mason, Francis Van Wyck
Colonel Hugh North series (12)
Cairo Jim and Doris in search of Martenarten
McSkimming, Geoffrey
Cairo Jim series (1)
Cairo Jim on the trail to ChaCha Muchos
McSkimming, Geoffrey
Cairo Jim series (2)
Cairo Mafia
Carter, Nick
Nick Carter series (65)
Cairo sleeper
Tute, Warren
George Mado series (6)
Caitlin
Dunphy, Catherine
Degrassi High School series (8)
Cajun angel
Stivers, Dick
Able Team series (27)
Cajuns of Willoughby
Willoughby, Lee Davis
Making of America series (23)
Cake for Caroline
Wilson, Gertrude Mary
Inspector Lovick series (14)
Cake in the hatbox
Upfield, Arthur William
Napoleon Bonaparte series (19)
Cakes and ale
Howard, Francis Morton
Happy Rascals series (4)
Cal Henderson, M.D.
Palmer, Bernard
Career series (9)
Calaboose Canyon
Grover, Marshall
Larry and Stretch series (102)
Calaboose express
Grover, Marshall
Larry and Stretch series (199)
Calaboose gang
Grover, Marshall
Larry and Stretch series (164)
Calamity at Harwood
Bellairs, George
Detective Inspector Thomas Littlejohn series (6)
Calamity Camp
Cox, John Roberts
Skipper series (2)
Calamity comes of age
Baxter, Gregory
Superintendent Daniels series (4)
Calamity comes to Flenton
Ashton, Charles
Jack Atherley series (4)
Calamity Conquest
Gray, Berkeley
Norman Conquest series (47)
Calamity fair
Miller, Wade
Lieutenant Austin Clapp series (5)
Max Thursday series (4)
Calamity in Kent
Rowland, John
Inspector Shelley series (19)
Calamity is a woman
Grover, Marshall
Larry and Stretch series (294)
Calamity Kate
Deary, Terry
Custard Kid series (2)
Calamity, Mark and Belle
Edson, John Thomas
Calamity Jane series (1)
Calamity spells trouble
Edson, John Thomas
Calamity Jane series (8)
Calamity town
Queen, Ellery
Ellery Queen series (22)
Calamity with the fiend
Lavelle, Sheila
Charlie Ellis and Angela Mitchell series (6)
Calcroft case
Murray, Edgar Joyce
Sexton Blake series (442)
Calculated risk
Foley, Rae
Hiram Potter series (11)
Joyce, Cyril
Chief Superintendent Pat Stockton series (11)
Calculus affair
Herge
Tintin series (18)
Calcutta affair
Elrick, George S
Man from U.N.C.L.E. series (24)
Calder born, Calder bred
Dailey, Janet
Webb Calder series (4)
Caleb in the country
Abbott, Jacob
Jonas series (3)
Caleb in town
Abbott, Jacob
Jonas series (2)
Calendar of crime
Queen, Ellery
Ellery Queen series (30)
Calendar of sin
Scott, Evelyn
American history trilogy (3)
Calf is born
Miller, Jane
Birth series (3)
Calf love
Fussey, Joyce
Yorkshire farm series (3)
Calf on Shale Hill
Farrell, Anne
Mitchell family series (2)
Calhoon
Douglas, Thorne
Rancho Bravo series (1)
Calhoun
Palmer, Diana
Long tall Texan series (1)
Caliban
Asimov, Isaac
Caliban series (1)
Caliban's castle
Warren, Paulette
Caliban series (1)
Caliban's hour
Williams, Tad
Tempest series (1)
Calibre point fifty
Sheckley, Robert
Stephen Dain series (1)
Calico Jack
Newte, Horace Wykeham Can
Calico Jack series (1)
Calico Jack and the desert critters
Reese, Bob
Critterland readers series (2)
Calico kill
Sharpe, Jon
Trailsman series (72)
Calicut lends a hand
De Selincourt, Aubrey
Rutherford series (5)
Caliente gold robbery
Roberts, J R
Gunsmith series (128)
California!
Ross, Dana Fuller
Wagons West series (6)
California bloodlines
Harvey, John Barton
Wes Hart series (9)
California copper
Hohl, Joan
Sharp family trilogy (2)
California countdown
Dever, Joe
Freeway warrior series (4)
California crossfire
Dalton, Kit
Buckskin series (23)
California girls!
Martin, Ann Matthews
Baby-Sitters Club super specials series (5)
California glory
Ross, Dana Fuller
Holt family series (4)
California gold
Ellis, Wesley
Lone Star series (105)
California gold rush
Chambers, Catherine E
Adventures in frontier America series (1)
California hit
Pendleton, Don
Mack Bolan series (11)
California Kid
Hardin, J D
Raider series (33)
California kill
Gilman, George G
Edge series (7)
California killing
Gilman, George G
Edge series (7)
California quarry
Sharpe, Jon
Trailsman series (148)
California roll
Simon, Roger Lichtenberg
Moses Wine series (4)
California runaround
Grover, Marshall
Larry and Stretch series (187)
California shakedown
Streib, Dan
Michael Hawk series (5)
California Street
Busch, Niven
San Francisco series (1)
California thriller
Byrd, Max
Mike Haller series (1)
California vengeance
Sharpe, Jon
Canyon O'Grady series (20)
Californians
Atherton, Gertrude Franklin
Wives and husbands series (2)
Caligari complex
Copper, Basil
Mike Faraday series (29)
Calix Stay
Hancock, Niel
Circle of light series (3)
Call a hearse
Stagge, Jonathan
Doctor Hugh Westlake series (5)
Call back to crime
Alding, Peter
C.I.D. Room series (6)
Call back yesterday
Dalton, Hugh
Fateful years trilogy (1)
Forman, James Douglas
Doomsday series (1)
Woods, Sara
Sir Nicholas Harding and Antony Maitland series (37)
Call-box murder
Barnett, Glyn
Inspector Gramport series (1)
Call Conquest for danger
Gray, Berkeley
Norman Conquest series (42)
Call for Blackshirt
Graeme, Roderic
Blackshirt series (24)
Call for Michael Shayne
Halliday, Brett
Michael Shayne series (18)
Call for Simon Shard
McCutchan, Philip
Superintendent Simon Shard series (1)
Call for Superintendent Flagg
Cassells, John
Superintendent Flagg series (28)
Call for the Baron
Morton, Anthony
Baron series (8)
Call for the dead
Le Carre, John
George Smiley series (1)
Call for the Saint
Charteris, Leslie
Saint series (27)
Call-girl murders
Brandon, John Gordon
Arthur Stukeley Pennington series (22)
Inspector Patrick Aloysius McCarthy series (46)
Call girls for murder
Ethan, John B
Victor Grant series (2)
Call him Amos
Hanson, Victor Joseph
Amos Crowle series (8)
Call him early for the murder
Morland, Nigel
Mrs Palmyra Pym series (16)
Call home the heart
Burke, Fielding
Call home series (1)
Stirling, Jessica
Stalker family trilogy (2)
Call in Miss Hogg
Lee, Austin
Miss Flora Hogg series (2)
Call in the Feds
G-Man
F.B.I. series (1)
Call in the night
Carter, Nicholas
Nicholas Carter series (408)
Call in the Yard
Hume, David
Inspector Sanderson series (1)
Call it accident
Foley, Rae
Hiram Potter series (10)
Call McLean
Goodchild, George
Inspector McLean series (16)
Call me Charley
Jackson, Jesse
Charley Moss series (1)
Call me Florence
Hope, Jane
Florence series (1)
Call me Pandora
Dean, Amber
Albie Harris series (3)
Call me Pilgrim
Potter, Jay Hill
Pilgrim series (1)
Call Mister Fortune
Bailey, Henry Christopher
Mister Reggie Fortune series (1)
Call of death
King, T Stanleyan
Scarsdale Waring series (2)
Call of fife and drum
Fast, Howard
Call of fife and drum trilogy (3)
Call of madness
Smith, Julie Dean
Caithan Crusade series (1)
Call of the Abbey School
Oxenham, Elsie J
Abbey girls first generation series (18)
Call of the blood
Hichens, Robert
Hermione Lester series (1)
Call of the bush
Patchett, Mary Elwyn
Ajax series (6)
Brevitt series (4)
Call of the canyon
Savage, Buck
Speed Johnson series (6)
Call of the North
White, Stewart Edward
Free forest series (1)

Call of the savage
Kline, Otis Adelbert
Jan series (1)
Call of the sword
Taylor, Roger
Hawklan series (1)
Call of the White Wolf
Sharpe, Jon
Trailsman series (85)
Call of trumpets
Lane, Jane
Charles I trilogy (3)
Call off the corpse
Bentley, John
Glen Gibson series (3)
Call on the phone
Carter, Nicholas
Nicholas Carter series (365)
Call out the Flying Squad
Holt, Henry
Inspector Silver series (6)
Call that a hat
Berg, Leila
Steep Street series (2)
Call the courier
Martin, Nancy
Anne Clarke series (2)
Call the lady indiscreet
Whelton, Paul
Garry Dean series (2)
Call the nurse
Martin, Nancy
Anne Clarke series (1)
Call the Toff
Creasey, John
Toff series (28)
Call the turn
Masters, Zeke
Faro Blake series (19)
Call the vet
Martin, Nancy
Vet series (1)
Call the Yard!
Clevely, Hugh
Inspector Williams series (1)
Call to arms
Foster, Alan Dean
Damned series (1)
Griffin, Pauline Margaret
Star commandos series (9)
Griffin, W E B
Corps series (2)
Welcome, John
Bellary Bay series (2)
Call to battle
Ahern, Jerry
Survivalist series (23)
Pournelle, Jerry
There will be war series (7)
Call to danger
Coram, Christopher
Ross Macallister series (1)
Call to darkness
Friedman, Michael Jan
Star trek, the next generation series (9)
Call to die
Coram, Christopher
Ross Macallister series (2)
Call to duty
Herman, Richard
Jack Locke series (4)
Call to honour, 1940-1942
Gaulle, Charles de
War memoirs series (1)
Call waiting
Stine, Robert Lawrence
Goosebumps series (16)
Callaghan
Cheyney, Peter
Slim Callaghan series (2)
Callaghan meets his fate
Chesney, Michael
Colonel Steel Callaghan series (3)
Callaghan of Intelligence
Chesney, Michael
Colonel Steel Callaghan series (1)
Callahan and company
Robinson, Spider
Callahan's Crosstime Saloon series (3)
Callahan goes south
Ames, Francis Herbert
Callahan series (3)
Callahan touch
Robinson, Spider
Callahan's Crosstime Saloon series (5)
Callahan's crazy crosstime bar
Robinson, Spider
Callahan's Crosstime Saloon series (3)
Callahan's Crosstime Saloon
Robinson, Spider
Callahan's Crosstime Saloon series (1)
Callahans' gamble
Ames, Francis Herbert
Callahan series (2)
Callahan's lady
Robinson, Spider
Callahan's Crosstime Saloon series (4)
Callahan's secret
Robinson, Spider
Callahan's Crosstime Saloon series (3)
Callan
Mitchell, James
David Callan series (1)
Callander Square
Perry, Anne
Charlotte Ellison Pitt and Inspector Thomas Pitt series (2)
Called home
Irvine, Robert Ralstone
Moroni Traveler series (4)
Called to account
Carter, Nicholas
Nicholas Carter series (520)
Called to love, called to serve!
McGloin, Joseph Thaddeus
Called to love, called to serve series (4)
Called to the front
Allen, Willis Boyd
Siege of Boston series (2)
Caller from eternity
Brand, Kurt
Perry Rhodan series (106)
Callers for Doctor Morelle
Dudley, Ernest
Doctor Morelle series (7)
Callie's castle
Park, Ruth
Callie series (1)
Callie's family
Park, Ruth
Callie series (2)
Calling
Jenkins, Jerry Bruce
Jennifer Grey series (5)
Calling Alan Fraser
Desmond, Hugh
Alan Fraser series (6)
Calling all cars
Holt, Henry
Inspector Silver series (8)
Calling all suspects
Wells, Carolyn
Fleming Stone series (51)
Calling all Z cars
Prendergast, William
Chief Inspector Barlow series (4)
Calling bridge
Collin, Paul Ries
Henry and Jane Ellis series (3)
Calling Bulldog Drummond
Fairlie, Gerard
Bulldog Drummond series (16)
Calling Captain Future
Hamilton, Edmond
Captain Future series (2)
Calling Doctor Conway
Jennings, D K
Doctor Ralph Conway series (2)
Calling Doctor Jane
McElfresh, Adeline
Doctor Jane series (2)
Calling Doctor Kildare
Brand, Max
Doctor Kildare series (2)
Calling Doctor Kill
Sugar, Andrew
Enforcer series (2)
Calling Doctor Patchwork
Goulart, Ron
Odd jobs series (2)
Calling for Sam
Ashley, Bernard
Clipper Street series (1)
Calling Juliet Bravo
Hardwick, Mollie
Juliet Bravo series (3)
Calling Lord Blackshirt
Graeme, Bruce
Lord Blackshirt series (3)
Calling Mister Callaghan
Cheyney, Peter
Slim Callaghan series (11)
Calling Mr Spade
Spade, Danny
Danny Spade series (24)
Calling of Dan Matthews
Wright, Harold Bell
Dan Matthews series (2)
Calling of the three
Emerson, Ru
Night-threads series (1)
Calling on dragons
Wrede, Patricia Collins
Enchanted forest series (3)
Calling outer space
Nugent, Jean
Twistaplot series (18)
Calling Peter Gayleigh
Robertson, Colin
Peter Grayleigh series (11)
Calling Questers four
Hildick, Edmund Wallace
Questers series (2)
Calling Red Lawson
Leyland, Eric
Red Lawson series (4)
Calling Scotland Yard
Holt, Henry
Inspector Silver series (12)
Calling Steven Gale
Leyland, Eric
Steven Gale series (1)
Calling Thunderbirds
Theydon, John
Thunderbirds series (2)
Calling Whitehall 1212
Clevely, Hugh
Sexton Blake series (1300)
Parsons, Anthony
Sexton Blake series (1098)
Callipygia
Carter, Lin
Terra Magica series (4)
Calvin and Hobbes
Watterson, Bill
Calvin and Hobbes series (1)
Calvin and hobbes lazy Sunday book
Watterson, Bill
Calvin and Hobbes series (5)
Calvin nullifier
DeWeese, Gene
Calvin Willeford series (3)
Calvinist martyr
Balzac, Honore de
Philosophic studies series (16)
Calypso
McBain, Ed
Eighty Seventh Precinct series (33)
Calypso magic
Coulter, Catherine
Victoria Albemarle trilogy (2)
Calypsonian
Selvon, Samuel
Peter Aswell series (2)
Cam girl-meets-boy
Cooney, Caroline B
Vi and Marissa series (1)
Cam Jansen activity book
Adler, David A
Cam Jansen series (13)
Cam Jansen and the mystery at the haunted house
Adler, David A
Cam Jansen series (13)
Cam Jansen and the mystery at the monkey house
Adler, David A
Cam Jansen series (10)
Cam Jansen and the mystery of Flight Fifty-four
Adler, David A
Cam Jansen series (12)
Cam Jansen and the mystery of the Babe Ruth baseball
Adler, David A
Cam Jansen series (6)
Cam Jansen and the mystery of the carnival prize
Adler, David A
Cam Jansen series (9)
Cam Jansen and the mystery of the circus clown
Adler, David A
Cam Jansen series (7)
Cam Jansen and the mystery of the dinodaur bones
Adler, David A
Cam Jansen series (3)
Cam Jansen and the mystery of the gold coins
Adler, David A
Cam Jansen series (5)
Cam Jansen and the mystery of the monster movie
Adler, David A
Cam Jansen series (8)
Cam Jansen and the mystery of the stolen corn popper
Adler, David A
Cam Jansen series (11)
Cam Jansen and the mystery of the stolen diamonds
Adler, David A
Cam Jansen series (1)
Cam Jansen and the mystery of the television dog
Adler, David A
Cam Jansen series (4)
Cam Jansen and the mystery of the UFO
Adler, David A
Cam Jansen series (2)
Camber of Culdi
Kurtz, Katherine
Legends of Camber of Culdi trilogy (1)
Camber the heretic
Kurtz, Katherine
Legends of Camber of Culdi trilogy (3)
Cambodia
Carter, Nick
Nick Carter series (59)
Cambodia clash
Pendleton, Don
Mack Bolan series (65)
Cambodia kill-zone
Lansing, John
Black Eagles series (10)
Cambodian hell-hole
Buchanan, Jack
M.I.A. Hunter series (2)
Cambodian sanctuary
Helm, Eric
Ground Zero series (17)
Cambri plot
Moffatt, James
Silas Manners series (1)
Cambridge and other memories, 1920-1953
Willey, Basil
Spots of time series (2)
Cambridge murders
Broome, Adam
Inspector Bramley series (2)
Daniel, Glyn
Sir Richard Cherrington series (1)
Camel with wrinkled knees
Gruelle, Johnny
Raggedy Ann series (3)
Cameliers
Hogue, Oliver
Anzac series (3)
Camelot and the vision of Albion
Ashe, Geoffrey
King Arthur series (4)
Camelot conundrum
Griffin, John
Richard Raven series (10)
Camelot in orbit
Landis, Arthur Harold
Camelot series (2)
Camels are coming
Johns, William Earl
Biggles series (1)
Camera clue
Coxe, George Harmon
Jack Fenner series (2)
Kent Murdock series (3)
Camera in Colditz
Baybutt, Ron
Colditz series (9)
Cameras on Carolyn
Byers, Irene
Carolyn series (2)
Cameras on the Conways
Morgan, Geoffrey
Conways series (1)
Cameron and the Kaiserhof
McCutchan, Philip
Donald Cameron series (9)
Cameron comes through
McCutchan, Philip
Donald Cameron series (2)
Cameron in command
McCutchan, Philip
Donald Cameron series (8)
Cameron in the gap
McCutchan, Philip
Donald Cameron series (6)
Cameron of the Castle Bay
McCutchan, Philip
Donald Cameron series (3)
Cameron, ordinary seaman
McCutchan, Philip
Donald Cameron series (1)
Camerons ahoy!
Duncan, Jane
Camerons series (5)
Camerons at the castle
Duncan, Jane
Camerons series (3)
Camerons calling
Duncan, Jane
Camerons series (4)
Cameron's chase
McCutchan, Philip
Donald Cameron series (11)
Cameron's commitment
McCutchan, Philip
Donald Cameron series (13)
Cameron's convoy
McCutchan, Philip
Donald Cameron series (5)
Cameron's crossing
McCutchan, Philip
Donald Cameron series (14)
Camerons on the hills
Duncan, Jane
Camerons series (2)
Camerons on the train
Duncan, Jane
Camerons series (1)
Cameron's raid
McCutchan, Philip
Donald Cameron series (10)
Cameron's troop lift
McCutchan, Philip
Donald Cameron series (12)
Cammie's challenge
McIlvaine, Jane
Cammie series (2)
Cammie's choice
McIlvaine, Jane
Cammie series (1)
Cammie's cousin
McIlvaine, Jane
Cammie series (3)
Camp at Surf Bluff
Rand, Edward Augustus
Up the Ladder Club series (4)
Camp Bob's Hill
Burton, Charles Pierce
Bob's Hill series (5)
Camp Duck Down
Stine, Harlan William
Jeffrey and the fourth grade ghost series (5)
Camp-fire and wigwam
Ellis, Edward Sylvester
Log cabin series (2)
Camp Fire Boys at Log Cabin Bend
Clifton, Oliver Lee
Camp Fire Boys series (1)
Camp Fire Boys' canoe cruise
Clifton, Oliver Lee
Camp Fire Boys series (3)
Camp Fire Boys in Muskrat Swamp
Clifton, Oliver Lee
Camp Fire Boys series (2)
Camp Fire Boys' tracking squad
Clifton, Oliver Lee
Camp Fire Boys series (4)
Camp fire cook-book
Anderson, Verily
Brownies series (8)
Camp Fire girls across the sea
Vandercook, Margaret
Camp Fire girls series (4)
Camp Fire girls amid the snows
Vandercook, Margaret
Camp Fire girls series (2)
Camp Fire Girls at Camp Keewaydin
Frey, Hildegarde Gertrude
Winnebagos series (10)
Camp Fire girls at Half Moon Lake
Vandercook, Margaret
Camp Fire girls series (13)
Camp Fire Girls at Long Lake
Stewart, Jane L
Camp Fire Girls series (1)
Camp Fire Girls at Onoway House
Frey, Hildegarde Gertrude
Winnebagos series (3)
Camp Fire Girls at school
Frey, Hildegarde Gertrude
Winnebagos series (2)
Camp Fire girls at Sunrise Hill
Vandercook, Margaret
Camp Fire girls series (1)
Camp Fire girls at the edge of the desert
Vandercook, Margaret
Camp Fire girls series (7)
Camp Fire girls at the end of the trail
Vandercook, Margaret
Camp Fire girls series (8)
Camp Fire Girls at the seashore
Stewart, Jane L
Camp Fire Girls series (2)
Camp Fire girls behind the lines
Vandercook, Margaret
Camp Fire girls series (9)

Camp Fire girls by the blue lagoon
Vandercook, Margaret
Camp Fire girls series (14)

Camp Fire girls' careers
Vandercook, Margaret
Camp Fire girls series (5)

Camp Fire Girls do their bit
Frey, Hildegarde Gertrude
Winnebagos series (8)

Camp Fire Girls go motoring
Frey, Hildegarde Gertrude
Winnebagos series (4)

Camp Fire girls in after years
Vandercook, Margaret
Camp Fire girls series (6)

Camp Fire girls in glorious France
Vandercook, Margaret
Camp Fire girls series (11)

Camp Fire girls in Merrie England
Vandercook, Margaret
Camp Fire girls series (12)

Camp Fire Girls in the Maine woods
Frey, Hildegarde Gertrude
Winnebagos series (1)

Camp Fire Girls in the mountains
Stewart, Jane L
Camp Fire Girls series (3)

Camp Fire girls in the outside world
Vandercook, Margaret
Camp Fire girls series (3)

Camp Fire Girls in the woods
Stewart, Jane L
Camp Fire Girls series (4)

Camp Fire Girls larks and pranks
Frey, Hildegarde Gertrude
Winnebagos series (5)

Camp Fire Girls on Ellen's Isle
Frey, Hildegarde Gertrude
Winnebagos series (6)

Camp Fire Girls on the farm
Stewart, Jane L
Camp Fire Girls series (5)

Camp Fire girls on the field of honor
Vandercook, Margaret
Camp Fire girls series (10)

Camp Fire Girls on the march
Stewart, Jane L
Camp Fire Girls series (6)

Camp Fire Girls on the open road
Frey, Hildegarde Gertrude
Winnebagos series (7)

Camp Fire Girls solve a mystery
Frey, Hildegarde Gertrude
Winnebagos series (9)

Camp Ghost-Away
Delton, Judy
Pee wee scout series (2)

Camp in the mountains
Ellis, Edward Sylvester
Deerfoot the Showanoe series 4 (2)

Camp mates in Michigan
Rathborne, Saint George
Canoe and campfire series (5)

Camp Murphy
McKenna, Colleen O'Shaughnessy
Murphy family series (8)

Camp-out mystery
Warner, Gertrude Chandler
Boxcar children series (27)

Camp-out on Danger mountain
Hiller, Barbara B
Twistaplot series (11)

Camp reunion
Cooney, Caroline B
Vi and Marissa series (2)

Camp Saint Dunstan
Eldred, Warren L
Saint Dunstan series (2)

Camp Saint Lucifer
Sharpe, Jon
Trailsman series (99)

Camp Spaghetti
Kaye, Marilyn
Camp Sunnyside Friends series (17)

Campaign of the jungle
Stratemeyer, Edward L
Old Glory series (5)

Campaigners
Harrod-Eagles, Cynthia
Morland family series (14)

Campaigning
Miller, Jim
Colt Revolver series (6)

Camper critters
Reese, Bob
Yellowstone critter series (6)

Campfire Girl in summer camp
Stewart, Jane L
Camp Fire Girls series (1)

Campfire Girl's adventure
Stewart, Jane L
Camp Fire Girls series (3)

Campfire Girls and Mount Greylock
Hornibrook, Isabel
Campfire Girls series (2)

Campfire Girls as detectives
De Vries, Julianne
Campfire Girls series (1)

Campfire Girls at Driftwood Heights
Sanderson, Margaret Love
Campfire Girls series (5)

Campfire girls at Forest Lodge
Penrose, Margaret
Campfire girls series (4)

Campfire Girls at Forest Lodge
Penrose, Margaret
Radio girls series (4)

Campfire Girls at Hillside
Sanderson, Margaret Love
Campfire Girls series (1)

Campfire Girls at Holly House
De Vries, Julianne
Campfire Girls series (2)

Campfire Girls at Lookout Pass
Sanderson, Margaret Love
Campfire Girls series (4)

Campfire Girls at Pine-Tree Camp
Sanderson, Margaret Love
Campfire Girls series (2)

Campfire Girls at Top o' the World
Sanderson, Margaret Love
Campfire Girls series (3)

Campfire Girls at Twin Lakes
Benson, Irene Elliott
Campfire Girls series (6)

Campfire Girl's chum
Stewart, Jane L
Camp Fire Girls series (5)

Campfire Girl's first council fire
Stewart, Jane L
Camp Fire Girls series (4)

Campfire Girls flying around me
De Vries, Julianne
Campfire Girls series (3)

Campfire Girl's happiness
Stewart, Jane L
Camp Fire Girls series (2)

Campfire Girls in old Kentucky
Sanderson, Margaret Love
Campfire Girls series (6)

Campfire Girls in the Alleghany Mountains
Benson, Irene Elliott
Campfire Girls series (1)

Campfire Girls in the country
Benson, Irene Elliott
Campfire Girls series (2)

Campfire Girls in the forest
Benson, Irene Elliott
Campfire Girls series (7)

Campfire Girls in war and peace
Hornibrook, Isabel
Campfire Girls series (3)

Campfire Girls' lake camp
Benson, Irene Elliott
Campfire Girls series (9)

Campfire Girls mountaineering
Benson, Irene Elliott
Campfire Girls series (8)

Campfire girls of Roselawn
Penrose, Margaret
Campfire girls series (1)
Radio girls series (1)

Campfire Girls on a hike
Benson, Irene Elliott
Campfire Girls series (5)

Campfire girls on a yacht
Sanderson, Margaret Love
Campfire Girls series (7)

Campfire Girls on Hurricane Island
Sanderson, Margaret Love
Campfire Girls series (8)

Campfire girls on Station Island
Penrose, Margaret
Campfire girls series (3)
Radio girls series (3)

Campfire girls on the program
Penrose, Margaret
Campfire girls series (2)
Radio girls series (2)

Campfire Girls on Valiban Island
De Vries, Julianne
Campfire Girls series (4)

Campfire Girls outing
Benson, Irene Elliott
Campfire Girls series (4)

Campfire Girls' rural retreat
Benson, Irene Elliott
Campfire Girls series (10)

Campfire Girl's test of friendship
Stewart, Jane L
Camp Fire Girls series (6)

Campfire Girls trip up the river
Benson, Irene Elliott
Campfire Girls series (3)

Camping out
Maestro, Betsy Crippen
Words series (5)

Camping out, as recorded by Kit
Stephens, Charles Asbury
Camping out series (1)

Camping out days at Putnam Hall
Winfield, Arthur M
Putnam Hall series (5)

Camping trip
Koontz, Robin Michal
Chicago and the cat series (2)

Campmates
Munroe, Kirk
Mates series (2)

Camp's strange visitors
Fairfax, Virginia
Girl Scouts series (6)

Campus corpse
Hopkins, Kenneth
Gerry Lee series (4)

Campus cousins
Quin-Harkin, Janet
Sugar and spice series (17)

Campus murders
Queen, Ellery
Mike McCall series (1)

Camuflage
Alais, Ernest W
Sexton Blake series (108)

Can-Am
Wilkinson, Sylvia
World of racing series (7)

Can David do it!
Asher, Sandra Fenichel
Ballet One series (4)

Can ladies kill?
Cheyney, Peter
Lemmy Caution series (4)

Can this telethon be saved?
Adams, Barbara
Kid-TV series (4)

Can you forgive her?
Trollope, Anthony
Palliser novels series (1)

Can you hear me, Grandad?
Thomson, Pat
Share-a-story series (3)

Can you tell me who they is?
Gibson, Patricia Jeann
Private hells trilogy (3)

Cana diversion
Gault, William Campbell
Brock Callahan series (9)
Joe Puma series (8)

Canaan legacy
Kahn, Michael A
Rachel Gold series (1)

Canada north
Mowat, Farley
Canada north series (1)

Canada north now
Mowat, Farley
Canada north series (2)

Canadian bomber contract
Atlee, Philip
Joe Gall series (13)

Canadian crisis
Pendleton, Don
Mack Bolan series (24)

Canadian kill
Nazel, Joseph
Iceman series (6)

Canadian killing ground
Kilgore, Axel
They call me the Mercenary series (5)

Canadian payroll
Roberts, J R
Gunsmith series (12)

Canadian twins
Wuorio, Eva Lis
Twin series (28)

Canadians
Willoughby, Lee Davis
Making of America series (38)

Canal holiday
Finlay, Winifred
Susan series (1)

Canal House
Boden, Hilda
Anna and James series (2)

Canal mystery
Remenham, John
Inspector Bliss series (1)

Canal Zone conquest
Roberts, Mark Kelly
Liberty Corps series (3)

Canals are my home
Bryce, Iris
Canals series (1)

Canals are my iris
Bryce, Iris
Canals series (2)

Canaris fragments
Winward, Walter
Canaris series (1)

Canary murder case
Van Dine, S S
Philo Vance series (2)

Canavan's trail
Arthur, Burt
Johnny Canavan series (7)

Canceled Czech
Block, Lawrence
Evan Tanner series (2)

Cancellation by death
Yeager, Dorian
Victoria Bowering series (1)

Cancelled in red
Pentecost, Hugh
Luke Bradley series (1)

Cancelled out
Redmond, Anton Edward
Bill Slaker series (1)

Candidate for a coffin
Brandon, John Gordon
Inspector Patrick Aloysius McCarthy series (42)
Graham, Neill
Solo Malcolm series (24)

Candidate for truth
Beresford, John Davys
Jacob Stahl series (2)

Candidate's blood
Derrick, Lionel
Penetrator series (37)

Candidates for murder
Hocking, Anne
Inspector William Austen series (32)

Candle for a corpse
Sterling, Stewart
Ben Pedley series (6)
Fire Marshal Ben Pedley series (6)

Candle for D'Artagnan
Yarbro, Chelsea Quinn
Atta Olivia Clemens trilogy (3)

Candle for Judas
Fraser, David
Treason in arms series (5)

Candle for the proud
Macmanus, Francis
Donnacha Mac Conmara trilogy (2)

Candle-holders
Gielgud, Val
Inspector Gregory Pellew and Viscount Clymping series (8)

Candle in the sea
Rand, Edward Augustus
Fighting the sea series (2)

Candle in the wind
White, Terence Hanbury
Once and future king series (3)

Candle rekindled
Ainsworth, Patricia
Burnley series (2)

Candle shop mystery
Hill, Eileen
Robin Kane series (4)

Candleford Green
Thompson, Flora
Lark Rise to Candleford series (3)

Candles are all out
Fitzgerald, Nigel
Alan Russell series (3)

Candles for the dead
Carmichael, Harry
John Piper and Quinn series (34)

Candles in the sun
Lutyens, Emily
Blessed girl series (3)

Candles in the wind
Diver, Maud
Desmond series (3)

Candles of night
Hastings, Phyllis
London quartet (1)

Candles to the dawn
Smith, Vian Crocker
Sappers series (2)

Candlestick with seven branches
Leblanc, Maurice
Arsene Lupin series (11)

Candy and Ginger
Mamlok, Gwyneth
Candy series (3)

Candy and Peppermint
Mamlok, Gwyneth
Candy series (1)

Candy and Sharon Ole
Daly, Ita
Candy series (2)

Candy and the golden eagle
Mamlok, Gwyneth
Candy series (4)

Candy and the pony
Mamlok, Gwyneth
Candy series (6)

Candy and the rocking horse
Mamlok, Gwyneth
Candy series (2)

Candy cane caper
Blair, Cynthia
Susan and Christine Pratt series (5)

Candy corn contest
Giff, Patricia Reilly
Kids of the Polk Street School series (3)

Candy does it again
Reed, Maud Dorothy
Candy series (3)

Candy finds the clue
Reed, Maud Dorothy
Candy series (2)

Candy Floss
Godden, Rumer
Four dolls series (4)

Candy in the Alps
Reed, Maud Dorothy
Candy series (4)

Candy in the tower
Mamlok, Gwyneth
Candy series (5)

Candy Kane
Lambert, Janet
Candy Kane series (1)

Candy killings
Stockwell, Gail
Kingsley Toplitt series (3)

Candy on the D.A.R.T.
Daly, Ita
Candy series (1)

Candywine development
Morris, John
Commissioner Robin McKay series (2)

Cane-patch mystery
Cunningham, Albert Benjamin
Sheriff Jess Roden series (8)

Cang Wan
Browne, Dik
Hagar the horrible series (29)

Canis the warrior
Sinclair, James
Boadicea series (2)

Cannaway concern
Shelby, Graham
Cannaways series (2)

Cannaways
Shelby, Graham
Cannaways series (1)

Cannery Row
Steinbeck, John
Cannery Row series (1)

Cannibal
Demille, Nelson
Joe Keller series (2)
Keller series (2)

Cannibal adventure
Price, Willard
Hal and Roger Hunt series (12)

Cannibal cult
Smith, Guy Newman
Sabat series (3)

Cannibal who overate
Pentecost, Hugh
Pierre Chambrun series (1)

Cannon fodder
Kessler, Leo
Rebel series (1)

Cannon Kid
Borg, Jack
Hogleg Bailey series (3)

Cannon Mound gang
Grover, Marshall
Larry and Stretch series (330)

Cannon's grave
Reno, Bill
Badge series (16)

Cannons in the rain
Sandon, J D
Gringos series (2)

Cannons of Lucknow
Stuart, Vivian
Captain Alexander Sheridan series (4)

Cannons of the Comstock
Thoeme, Brock
Saga of the Sierras series (4)

Canny Mister Glencannon
Gilpatric, Guy
Mister Colin Andrew Macthrockle Glencannon series (8)

Canoe mates in Canada
Rathborne, Saint George
Canoe and campfire series (1)

Canoe trip mystery
Warner, Gertrude Chandler
Boxcar children series (40)

Canoeing is for me
Moran, Tom
Sports for me series (5)

Canoemates
Munroe, Kirk
Mates series (3)

Canon
Benson, Arthur Christopher
Molly Davenant series (2)

Can't get a redbird
Scarborough, Dorothy
Cotton trilogy (2)

Can't stop us now
Lantz, Francess Lin
Overnight Sensation series (1)

Can't you make them behave, King George?
Fritz, Jean
American Revolution series (6)

Cantab
Leslie, Shane
Oppidan trilogy (2)

Canterbury kilgrims
Chance, John Newton
Jonathan Blake series (33)

Canticle
Salvatore, Robert Anthony
Cleric quintet (1)

Canto for a gypsy
Smith, Martin Cruz
Roman Grey series (2)

Canvas dagger
Reilly, Helen
Inspector Christopher McKee series (26)

Canvas jungle
Maclean, Arthur
Sexton Blake series (1404)

Canvas prison
De Marco, Gordon
Riley Kovacks series (2)

Canyon bunch
Logan, Jake
John Slocum series (36)

Canyon hideout
Field, Peter
Powder Valley series (36)

Canyon kill
Slade, Jack
Lassiter series (27)
Sundance series (24)

Canyon killers
Scott, Bradford
Walt Slade series (10)

Canyon Mountain
Murray, Earl
Dan Sleyter series (3)

Canyon of death
Field, Peter
Powder Valley series (7)
Gilman, George G
Adam Steele series (37)

Canyon showdown
Cord, Barry
Dave Chance series (2)

Canyon vigil
Grover, Marshall
Nevada Jim series (17)

Cap
Bowden, Jim
Cap Millett series (1)

Cap Fog, Texas Ranger, meet Mr J.G.Reeder
Edson, John Thomas
Cap Fog series (4)

Cap for Cathy
James, Josephine
Kathy Martin series (1)

Cap for Mary Ellis
Newell, Hope
Mary Ellis series (1)

Capable of honor
Drury, Allen
Washington series (3)

Cape Cod caper
Arnold, Margot
Penelope Spring and Sir Tobias Glendower series (2)

Cape Cod conundrum
Arnold, Margot
Penelope Spring and Sir Tobias Glendower series (9)

Cape Cod mystery
Taylor, Phoebe Atwood
Asey Mayo series (1)

Cape Lost
West, Joyce
Gabrielle Allan series (2)

Capers in my kirk
Macvicar, Angus
Confessions series (8)

Capful of glory
Collenette, Eric J
Ben Grant series (6)

Capital city
Sandoz, Mari
Nebraska trilogy (2)

Capital city mystery
Wallis, James Harold
Inspector Wilton Jacks series (3)

Capital crime
Ford, Leslie
Colonel John Primrose series (7)
Grace Latham series (7)

Capital run
Robbins, David
Endworld series (9)

Capitalistic revolution
Adler, Mortimer Jerome
Revolution series (2)

Capitol
Card, Orson Scott
Worthing chronicles series (1)

Capitol hell
Derrick, Lionel
Penetrator series (3)

Capitol offence
Davey, Jocelyn
Ambrose Usher series (1)

Cap'n Eri
Lincoln, Joseph Crosby
Captain Eri series (1)

Cappy Ricks
Kyne, Peter Bernard
Cappy Ricks series (1)

Cappy Ricks comes back
Kyne, Peter Bernard
Cappy Ricks series (3)

Cappy Ricks retires
Kyne, Peter Bernard
Cappy Ricks series (2)

Cappy Ricks special
Kyne, Peter Bernard
Cappy Ricks series (4)

Capricorn run
Cleary, Denis
Breakenridge series (1)

Capsina
Benson, Edward Frederic
Greek War of Independence series (2)

Capsized!
Daniels, Lee
Surf city series (5)

Captain
De Hartog, Jan
Captain Martinus Harinxma trilogy (1)
Norman, John
Telnarian histories series (2)

Captain America, Holocaust for hire
Silva, Joseph
Marvel superheroes, new series (4)

Captain America, The great gold steal
White, Ted
Marvel superheroes series (2)

Captain Anne
Bruce, Dorita Fairlie
Springdale series (6)

Captain Apache
Whitman, Sidney Edgerton
Captain Cullah Burnett series (1)

Captain Bayonet and others
Armstrong, Anthony
Warriors series (5)

Captain Beaky
Lloyd, Jeremy
Captain Beaky and his band series (1)

Captain Beaky and the haunted wood
Lloyd, Jeremy
Captain Beaky and his band series (4)

Captain Beaky, volume 2
Lloyd, Jeremy
Captain Beaky and his band series (6)

Captain Black
Pemberton, Max
Captain Black series (2)

Captain Blake
King, Charles
Lieutenant Sandy Ray series (3)

Captain Blood
Sabatini, Rafael
Captain Blood series (1)

Captain Blood returns
Sabatini, Rafael
Captain Blood series (2)

Captain Blossom
Nelson, Michael
Captain Blossom series (1)

Captain Blossom soldiers on
Nelson, Michael
Captain Blossom series (2)

Captain Bolton's corpse
Sturrock, Jeremy
Bow Street Runner series (6)

Captain Bowker
Parkman, Sydney
Captain Bowker series (5)

Captain Bulldog Drummond
Fairlie, Gerard
Bulldog Drummond series (13)

Captain Cain
Westerman, Percy Francis
Captain Cain series (2)

Captain Carey of the Gallant Seventh
Lounsberry, Lionel
Kit Carey series (3)

Captain Caution
Roberts, Kenneth Lewis
Chronicles of Arundel series (4)

Captain Chap
Stockton, Frank Richard
Rolling stones series (1)

Captain Cobwebb
Boshell, Gordon
Captain Cobwebb series (1)

Captain Cobwebb and the amazing cloud
Boshell, Gordon
Captain Cobwebb series (11)

Captain Cobwebb and the Chinese unicorn
Boshell, Gordon
Captain Cobwebb series (7)

Captain Cobwebb and the Crustaks
Boshell, Gordon
Captain Cobwebb series (6)

Captain Cobwebb and the magic drops
Boshell, Gordon
Captain Cobwebb series (10)

Captain Cobwebb and the mischief man
Boshell, Gordon
Captain Cobwebb series (8)

Captain Cobwebb and the Quogs
Boshell, Gordon
Captain Cobwebb series (9)

Captain Cobwebb and the red transistor
Boshell, Gordon
Captain Cobwebb series (5)

Captain Cobwebb's adventurers
Boshell, Gordon
Captain Cobwebb series (4)

Captain Cobwebb's cobra
Boshell, Gordon
Captain Cobwebb series (3)

Captain Cobwebb's cowboys
Boshell, Gordon
Captain Cobwebb series (2)

Captain comes home
Ashton, Helen
Wilchester chronicles series (4)

Captain Comstock, USMC
Bishop, Gibs
Captain Comstock series (2)

Captain Comstock, U.S.M.C.
Bishop, Giles
United States Marines series (4)

Captain Coppernob
Bourne, Lawrence R
Coppernob series (3)

Captain Cub
Turner, Ethel
Cub series (2)

Captain Dack
Meriton, Peter
Captain Dack series (1)

Captain Daley's crew and peg-legged tramp
Massey, Craig
Captain Daley's crew series (4)

Captain Daley's crew and the jungle ship
Massey, Craig
Captain Daley's crew series (5)

Captain Daley's crew and the missing houseboat
Massey, Craig
Captain Daley's crew series (1)

Captain Daley's crew at Thunderhead Lake
Massey, Craig
Captain Daley's crew series (2)

Captain Daley's crew in danger
Massey, Craig
Captain Daley's crew series (3)

Captain Danny
Camp, Walter Chauncey
Danny Fists trilogy (2)

Captain Desmond, VC
Diver, Maud
Desmond series (1)

Captain Fantom
Underhill, Charles
Captain Fantom series (1)

Captain Felonius
Cowley, Joy
Captain Felonius series (1)

Captain Firebrace
Seafarer
Captain Firebrace series (1)

Captain Firebrace and Father Kelly
Seafarer
Captain Firebrace series (3)

Captain Flint, detective
Craigie, Dorothy
Captain Flint series (1)

Captain Flint kidnapped
Craigie, Dorothy
Captain Flint series (3)

Captain Flint shipwrecked
Craigie, Dorothy
Captain Flint series (4)

Captain Flint to the rescue
Craigie, Dorothy
Captain Flint series (2)

Captain Flynn
Laurie-Long, Ernest
Captain Flynn series (3)

Captain Flynn, retd.
Laurie-Long, Ernest
Captain Flynn series (10)

Captain Flynn, sheriff
Laurie-Long, Ernest
Captain Flynn series (13)

Captain Future and the Space Emperor
Hamilton, Edmond
Captain Future series (1)

Captain Future's challenge
Hamilton, Edmond
Captain Future series (3)

Captain Geoff
Thorn, Ismay
Geoff and Jim Harrington series (4)

Captain Havoc
Healey, Ben
Captain Havoc series (1)

Captain Horatio Hornblower
Forester, Cecil Scott
Horatio Hornblower series (8)

Captain intervenes
Leyland, Eric
Captain series (4)

Captain Jack
Shelton, Gene
Texas legends series (2)

Captain Jack Lorimer
Standish, Winn
Captain Jack Lorimer series (1)

Captain January
Richards, Laura Elizabeth
Captain January series (1)

Captain Jim
Bruce, Mary Grant
Billabong series (6)

Captain Jim Mason
Gregor, Elmer Russell
Jim Mason series (3)

Captain John Hunter series
Godwin, Felix
Captain John Hunter series (1)

Captain John Smith
Forbes-Lindsey, Charles Harcourt
Trail blazers series (1)

Captain Jonas feeds the rary bird
Wheeler, Anthony George
Captain Jonas series (1)

Captain Jonas shelters the Gonk family
Wheeler, Anthony George
Captain Jonas series (2)

Captain Justice
Forrest, Anthony
Captain John Valcourt Justice series (1)

Captain Kettle, ambassador
Hyne, Charles John Cutcliffe
Captain Owen Kettle series (17)

Captain Kettle, KCB
Hyne, Charles John Cutcliffe
Captain Owen Kettle series (5)

Captain Kettle on the war-path
Hyne, Charles John Cutcliffe
Captain Owen Kettle series (11)

Captain Kettle's bit
Hyne, Charles John Cutcliffe
Captain Owen Kettle series (12)

Captain Kid and the pirates
Buckholtz, Eileen
Magic micro adventure series (1)

Captain Latymer
Moore, Frank Frankfort
Cromwellian Ireland series (2)

Captain Lucy and Lieutenant Bob
Havard, Aline
Lucy Gordon series (1)

Captain Lucy in France
Havard, Aline
Lucy Gordon series (2)

Captain Lucy in the home sector
Havard, Aline
Lucy Gordon series (4)

Captain Lucy's flying ace
Havard, Aline
Lucy Gordon series (3)

Captain Mesquite
Curry, Tom
Captain Mesquite series (1)

Captain Mettle, VC
Macdonnell, James Edmond
Hooky Walker series (5)

Captain Mettle, VC
Macnell, James
Captain Mettle series (1)

Captain Miranda
Gervaise, Mary
Miranda series (3)

Captain Nash and the honour of England
Butler, Ragan
Captain George Nash series (1)

Captain Nash and the Wroth inheritance
Butler, Ragan
Captain George Nash series (2)

Captain Nicholas
Walpole, Hugh
London Group series (8)
Peter Westcott series (5)

Captain of cadets
Frith, Henry
Britannia series (1)

Captain of Dragoons
Welch, Ronald
Carey family series (4)

Captain of England
Wright, Billy
Football captain series (1)

Captain of Foot
Welch, Ronald
Carey family series (7)

Captain of marine
White, James Dillon
Roger Kelso series (4)

Captain of Springdale
Bruce, Dorita Fairlie
Springdale series (3)

Captain of the Araby
Pease, Howard
Tod Moran series (12)

Captain of the Camp
Ellis, Edward Sylvester
Catamount Camp series (2)

Captain of the crew
Barbour, Ralph Henry
Hilton School trilogy (3)

Captain of the Guidara
Verne, Jules
Kereban the Inflexible series (1)

Captain of the Phantom
Chesterton, Rupert
Phantom battleship series (2)

Captain of the team
Levy, Elizabeth
Gymnasts series (8)

Captain on guard
Leyland, Eric
Captain series (6)

Captain Peg
Hann, Dorothy Owen
Peg series (3)

Captain Peg-Leg's war
Dawlish, Peter
Captain Peg-Leg series (1)

Captain Polly, an Annapolis co-ed
Jackson, Gabrielle Emilie
Captain Polly series (2)

Captain Polly of Annapolis
Jackson, Gabrielle Emilie
Captain Polly series (1)

Captain Pugwash
Ryan, John
Captain Pugwash series (1)

Captain Pugwash and the elephant
Ryan, John
Captain Pugwash series (7)

Captain Pugwash and the mutiny
Ryan, John
Captain Pugwash series (12)

Captain Pugwash and the new ship
Ryan, John
Captain Pugwash series (8)
Captain Pugwash and the ruby
Ryan, John
Captain Pugwash series (9)
Captain Pugwash and the treasure chest
Ryan, John
Captain Pugwash series (10)
Captain Pugwash cartoon book
Ryan, John
Captain Pugwash series (17)
Captain rides again
Leyland, Eric
Captain series (3)
Captain Salt in Oz
Thompson, Ruth Plumly
Oz series (29)
Captain Sam
Eggleston, George Cary
Indian War trilogy (2)
Captain Samson, A.B.
Douglas, Gavin
Captain Samson series (3)
Captain Scarlet
Theydon, John
Captain Scarlet series (1)
Captain Scarlet and the Mysterons
Theydon, John
Captain Scarlet series (1)
Captain Scarlet and the silent saboteur
Theydon, John
Captain Scarlet series (2)
Captain Serafina
Brunhoff, Laurent de
Serafina series (3)
Captain Sparkle, private
Carter, Nicholas
Nicholas Carter series (195)
Captain strikes back
Leyland, Eric
Captain series (5)
Captain Swing
Duplechan, Larry
Johnnie Ray Rousseau series (3)
Captains
Griffin, W E B
Brotherhood of war series (2)
Captains all
Jacobs, William Wymark
Night-Watchman series (6)
Captain's honor
Dvorkin, David
Star trek, the next generation series (8)
Captain's lady
Broster, Dorothy Kathleen
Captain Carew series (2)
Captains of death
Jones, G Wayman
Black Bat series (18)
Captains of Harley
Cleaver, Hylton
Harley series (3)
Captain's paradise
Hooper, Kay
Hagen series (9)
Captain's rangers
Kelton, Elmer
Tales of Texas series (6)
Captain's Walk
Welles, Elizabeth
Janine West series (2)
Captain's watch
Garfield, Leon
Tim and Pistol series (2)
Captain's wife
Bray, Donald
Captain Davy series (2)
Jameson, Storm
Hervey Russell series (1)
Captain's woman
Logan, Mark
Nicholas Minnett series (1)
Captivator
York, Andrew
Jonas Wilde series (8)
Captive
Colette, Sidonie Gabrielle
Renee Nere series (2)
Gordons
John Ripley series (3)
Hampton, Bill
Choose your own adventure series (93)
Hawkins, Clint
Saddletramp series (2)
O'Dell, Scott
Julian Escobar trilogy (1)
Smith, Lisa J
Secret circle series (2)
Stallman, Robert
Beast trilogy (2)
Captive audience
Mann, Jessica
Thea Crawford series (2)
Captive city
Da Cruz, Daniel
Ape Swain series (3)
Captive crown
Tranter, Nigel Godwin
Stuart series (3)
Captive embraces
Michaels, Fern
Captive series (2)
Captive in the land
Aldridge, James
Rupert Royce series (1)
Captive in time
Dreher, Sarah
Stoner McTavish series (4)
Captive innocence
Michaels, Fern
Captive series (4)
Captive James
King, Betty
Beaufort family series (2)
Captive of Gor
Norman, John
Tarl Cabot series (7)
Captive of Kensington Palace
Plaidy, Jean
Queen Victoria series (1)
Captive, part one
Proust, Marcel
Remembrance of things past series (9)
Captive, part two
Proust, Marcel
Remembrance of things past series (10)
Captive passions
Michaels, Fern
Captive series (1)
Captive planet
Simon, Morris
Endless quest series (17)
Smith, Gregory Jon
StarQuest series (1)
Captive Queen of Scots
Plaidy, Jean
Mary, Queen of Scots series (2)
Captive Scorpio
Akers, Alan Burt
Dray Prescot series (17)
Captive splendors
Michaels, Fern
Captive series (3)
Captive witness
Keene, Carolyn
Nancy Drew series (64)
Captives
Walpole, Hugh
London Group series (4)
Maradick series (1)
Captives in space
Greene, Joseph
Dig Allen series (2)
Captives of Antekirtta
Verne, Jules
Giant raft series (2)
Captives of the flame
Delany, Samuel Ray
Fall of the towers trilogy (1)
Captives of the moon
Moore, Patrick
Robin North and Rex Redmayne series (1)
Captives of the Savage Empire
Lorrah, Jean
Savage Empire series (3)
Captives three
Braden, James Andrew
John Jerome and Return Kingdom series (3)
Captive's trail
Knott, William Cecil
Golden Hawk series (8)
Captivity and ransom of John II, 1356-1370
Henneman, John Bell
Royal taxation in fourteenth century France series (2)
Captivity captive
Hall, Rodney
Yandilli trilogy (3)
Capture
Henry, Marguerite
Chincoteague series (1)
Martyn, Wyndham
Christopher Bond series (6)
Capture of Paul Beck
Bodkin, Matthias McDonnell
Dora Myrl series (2)
Paul Beck series (3)
Capture of the golden stallion
Montgomery, Rutherford George
Golden stallion series (1)
Captured
King, Charles
Lieutenant Sandy Ray series (8)
Captured by the engines
Lansdale, Joe Richard
Batman series (8)
Car park mystery
Parsons, Anthony
Sexton Blake series (1357)
Car-razy life with Dexter
Fennell, Willie
Dexter Dutton series (12)
Car that Jack built
Macnaghten, Patrick
Jack Heston series (1)
Cara
Harvey, Caroline
Legacy of love trilogy (3)
Caravaggio obsession
Banks, Oliver
Amos Hatcher series (2)
Caravan
Galsworthy, John
End of the chapter series (3)
Caravan again
Bellhouse, Lucy Wilered
Caravan series (2)
Caravan at The Warren
Sindall, Marjorie Aylwynn
Warren series (4)
Caravan children
Bellhouse, Lucy Wilered
Caravan series (1)
Caravan crime
Chester, Gilbert
Sexton Blake series (796)
Caravan family
Blyton, Enid
Caravan family series (1)
Mike, Belinda and Ann series (1)
Caravan goes home
Bellhouse, Lucy Wilered
Caravan series (4)
Caravan goes west
Bellhouse, Lucy Wilered
Caravan series (3)
Caravan island
Young, Emily Hilda
Caravan series (1)
Caravan of night
Erskine, Margaret
Inspector Septimus Finch series (3)
Caravan passes
Finlay, Eileen
Caravan series (1)
Caravan to China
Gaskin, Carol
Time machine series (21)
Caravan turns
Finlay, Eileen
Caravan series (3)
Carbon copy killer
Brody, Marc
Marc Brody series (12)
Carbon monixide
Street, James
Eugene Mulcahy series (2)
Carbonel
Sleigh, Barbara
Carbonel series (1)
Carbonel and Calidor
Sleigh, Barbara
Carbonel series (3)
Carbonel, the king of the cats
Sleigh, Barbara
Carbonel series (1)
Carbuncle clue
Hume, Fergus
Octavius Fanks series (3)
Carcajou
Rowe, John Gabriel
Northwest stories series (8)
Sergeant Dick series (2)
Carcoola backstage
Handford, Nourma
Carcoola series (4)
Carcoola holiday
Handford, Nourma
Carcoola series (3)
Carcooola
Handford, Nourma
Carcoola series (1)
Carcooola adventure
Handford, Nourma
Carcoola series (2)
Card
Bennett, Arnold
Five towns series (10)
Card from Morocco
Shaw, Robert
Cure of souls trilogy (3)
Card thirteen
Luther, Mark Lee
Arthur Raneleigh series (1)
Cardboard crown
Boyd, Martin
Langton family series (1)
Cardigan
Chambers, Robert William
American Revolution trilogy (1)
Cardigan series (1)
Cardinal and Lady Susan
Cleeve, Lucas
Lady Susan series (1)
Cardinal error
Walton, Marion
Inspector James Cardinal series (1)
Cardinal in England
Williamson, Hugh Ross
Passing of the Plantagenets series (5)
Cardinal in exile
Williamson, Hugh Ross
Passing of the Plantagenets series (4)
Cardinal of the Kremlin
Clancy, Tom
Jack Ryan series (3)
Cardinal sins
Greeley, Andrew Moran
Cardinal sins and virtues series (1)
Cardinal virtues
Greeley, Andrew Moran
Cardinal sins and virtues series (2)
Cardinal's daughter
Warfield, Catherine Ann
Ferne Fleming series (2)
Cardinal's diamonds
Gribble, Leonard Reginald
Superintendent Anthony Slade series (38)
Cardinal's page
Baker, James
Cardinal Henry Beaufort series (2)
Cardington Crescent
Perry, Anne
Charlotte Ellison Pitt and Inspector Thomas Pitt series (8)
Cardles Farm
Wall, Adrian
Cardles Farm series (1)
Cardles Farm again
Wall, Adrian
Cardles Farm series (2)
Cardles Farm once again
Wall, Adrian
Cardles Farm series (3)
Cards of death
Grant, Maxwell
Shadow series (143)
Cards on the table
Christie, Agatha
Colonel Race series (2)
Hercule Poirot series (14)
Mrs Ariadne Oliver series (2)
Superintendent Battle series (3)
Cardus for all seasons
Cardus, Neville
Innings series (6)
Cardus in the covers
Cardus, Neville
Innings series (5)
Cardus on cricket
Cardus, Neville
Innings series (4)
Care of the self
Foucault, Michel
History of sexuality series (3)
Care takers
Marquis, Max
General hospital series (1)
Career for Kelly
Kirby, Jean
Scott sisters series (1)
Career for the Baron
Morton, Anthony
Baron series (12)
Career for Vicky
Kincade, Wynn
Vicky Loring series (1)
Careers in the air
Scribner, Kimball
Your future in aviation series (1)
Careers on the ground
Scribner, Kimball
Your future in aviation series (2)
Carefree
Avenell, Donne
Axa series (5)
Careless corpse
King, Charles Daly
Doctor L Rees Pons series (4)
Michael Lord series (3)
Careless hangman
Morland, Nigel
Mrs Palmyra Pym series (10)
Careless Kate
Optic, Oliver
Riverdale series (8)
Careless Mrs Christian
Russell, Charlotte Murray
Homer Fitzgerald series (2)
Jane Amanda Edwards series (11)
Carelss corpse
Halliday, Brett
Michael Shayne series (41)
Caress of conquest
Frances, Stephen Daniel
John Gail series (4)
Caretakers
Dehn, Olive
Meredith children series (1)
King, Tabitha
Nodd's Ridge series (2)
Caretakers and the gipsy
Dehn, Olive
Meredith children series (3)
Caretakers and the poacher
Dehn, Olive
Meredith children series (2)
Caretakers and the rescue
Dehn, Olive
Meredith children series (4)
Caretakers of Wilmhurst
Dehn, Olive
Meredith children series (5)
Carey blood
Greenfield, Irving A
Tom Carey trilogy (1)
Carey gun
Greenfield, Irving A
Tom Carey trilogy (3)
Carey's vengeance
Greenfield, Irving A
Tom Carey trilogy (2)
Cargo Club
Corris, Peter
Pokerface series (4)
Cargo for crooks
Sea-Lion
John Prentice series (4)
Cargo for death
Wallace, Trevor
John Tracy series (4)
Cargo for the Styx
Trimble, Louis
Martin Zane series (1)
Cargo gods
Streib, Dan
Michael Hawk series (10)
Cargo of eagles
Allingham, Margery
Albert Campion series (21)
Cargo of horses
Edwards, Monica
Romney Marsh series (5)
Cargo of Madalena
Harnett, Cynthia
Fifteenth century London series (3)
Cargo of spent evil
Brett, John Michael
Hugo Baron series (3)
Cargo risk
Macleod, Robert
Andrew Laird series (4)
Cargo to Saigon
Leader, Charles
Rick McAdden series (2)
Cargo unknown
Robeson, Kenneth
Doc Savage series (98)
Caribbean account
Furst, Alan
Roger Levin series (3)
Caribbean adventure
Bayley, Viola
Adventure series (14)
Haynes, Betsy
Fabulous Five super series (2)
Caribbean adventurers
Patchett, Mary Elwyn
Brevitt series (2)
Caribbean affair
Thorne, Ernest Pollett
Major Brains Cunningham series (14)
Caribbean caper
Janson, Hank
Hank Janson series (258)
Rosenberger, Joseph
Murder Master series (2)

Case-book of Sherlock Holmes
Doyle, Arthur Conan
Sherlock Holmes series (9)
Case closed
Thomson, June
Inspector Finch series (4)
Case continued
Prescot, Julian
Case books series (2)
Case counterfeit
Prescot, Julian
Case books series (9)
Case dead and buried
Barry, Charles
Superintendent Lawrence Gilmartin series (13)
Case deuce
Hawkes, Zachary
Fancy Hatch series (2)
Case file, FBI
Gordons
John Ripley series (2)
Case for appeal
Egan, Lesley
Jesse Falkenstein series (1)
Vic Varallo series (1)
Case for Charley
Spencer, John
Charley Case series (1)
Case for compensation
Ross, Cameron
Alistair Duncan series (1)
Case for court
Prescot, Julian
Case books series (7)
Case for Emergency Ward 10
Falla, Roger
Emergency Ward 10 series (4)
Case for equity
Hill, Katharine
Lorna Donahue series (2)
Case for hearing
Prescot, Julian
Case books series (6)
Case for Inspector Flagg
Cassells, John
Superintendent Flagg series (14)
Case for Inspector West
Creasey, John
Inspector Roger West series (12)
Case for Jenny Archer
Conford, Ellen
Jenny Archer series (2)
Case for Mason
McCleery, William
Perry Mason series (84)
Case for M.I.5
Jardine, Warwick
Sexton Blake series (1257)
Case for Mister Crook
Gilbert, Anthony
Arthur Crook series (25)
Case for Mister Fiddle
Styles, Showell
Mister Fiddle series (4)
Case for Mister Fortune
Bailey, Henry Christopher
Mister Reggie Fortune series (7)
Case for Mister Paul Savoy
Gregory, Jackson
Paul Savoy series (2)
Case for Red Lawson
Leyland, Eric
Red Lawson series (3)
Case for Sergeant Beef
Bruce, Leo
Sergeant William Beef series (6)
Case for Solomon
Graeme, Bruce
Theodore I Terhune series (3)
Case for the accused
Prescot, Julian
Case books series (4)
Case for the Baron
Morton, Anthony
Baron series (10)
Case for the Dreamer
Duncan, William Murdoch
Superintendent Donald Reamer series (4)
Case for the prosecution
Graydon, William Murray
Sexton Blake series (173)
Case for three detectives
Bruce, Leo
Sergeant William Beef series (1)
Case for treachery
White, Valerie
John Case series (2)
Case for trial
Prescot, Julian
Case books series (5)
Case in the clinic
Lorac, E C R
Inspector Macdonald series (20)
Case is altered
Jones, Henry Llewellyn
Fraser Todd series (2)
Woods, Sara
Sir Nicholas Harding and Antony Maitland series (12)
Case is closed
Wentworth, Patricia
Miss Maud Silver series (2)
Case number 561
Knight, David
Dragnet series (1)
Case of blackmail
Alais, Ernest W
Sexton Blake series (23)
Case of books
Graeme, Bruce
Inspector Auguste Jantry series (1)
Theodore I Terhune series (6)
Case of Caroline Animus
Chambers, Dana
Jim Steele series (8)
Case of Colonel Marchand
Lorac, E C R
Inspector Macdonald series (5)
Case of Comrade Tulayev
Serge, Victor
Resistance trilogy (2)
Case of Congressman Coyd
Grant, Maxwell
Shadow series (92)
Case of conscience
Blish, James
After such knowledge series (4)
Case of Elymas the sorcerer
Flynn, Brian
Anthony Bathurst series (31)
Case of indelicate champagne
Halliday, Fred
Stanley Delphond series (3)
Case of John Muir of Merchant Navy
Jackson, Lewis
Sexton Blake series (1072)
Case of Joshua Locke
Dean, Robert George
Tony Hunter series (9)
Case of L.A.C. Dickson
Drummond, J
Sexton Blake series (1250)
Case of Larachi the Lascar
Merland, Oliver
Sexton Blake series (352)
Case of Lone Star
Friedman, Kinky
Kinky Friedman series (3)
Case of Lord Greyburn's son
Long, Derek
Sexton Blake series (1162)
Case of loyalties
Wallace, Marilyn
Jay Goldstein and Carlos Cruz series (1)
Case of many clues
Carter, Nicholas
Nicholas Carter series (589)
Case of Marie Corwin
Dean, Gregory
Deputy Commissioner Benjamin Simon series (1)
Case of Mary Fielding
Erskine, Margaret
Inspector Septimus Finch series (17)
Case of Matthew Crake
Macleod, Adam Gordon
Sir William Burrill series (2)
Case of Miss Elliott
Orczy, Emmuska
Old man in the corner series (1)
Case of Mortimer Fenley
Tracy, Louis
Inspector Furneaux series (3)
Case of Mr Budd
Verner, Gerald
Superintendent Robert Budd series (4)
Case of Naomi Clymes
Thomson, Basil
Superintendent Richardson series (3)
Case of Oscar Brodski
Freeman, Richard Austin
Doctor John Evelyn Thorndyke series (4)
Case of Peter the Lett
Simenon, Georges
Inspector Jules Maigret series (1)
Case of Richard Meynell
Ward, Mary Augusta
New Brotherhood series (2)
Case of Sergeant Grischa
Zweig, Arnold
Werner Bertin and Lenore Wahl series (4)
Case of spirits
Lovesey, Peter
Sergeant Cribb and Constable Thackeray series (6)
Case of the abominable snowman
Blake, Nicholas
Nigel Strangeways series (7)
Case of the absent corpse
Hill, Katharine
Lorna Donahue series (1)
Case of the absent-minded professor
Stein, Aaron Marc
Tim Mulligan and Elsie Mae Hunt series (4)
Case of the ace accomplice
Passingham, William John
Sexton Blake series (1331)
Case of the acid throwers
Creasey, John
Inspector Roger West series (13)
Case of the adopted daughter
Graydon, William Murray
Sexton Blake series (288)
Case of the African elephant
Hardinge, Rex
Sexton Blake series (1205)
Case of the African hoodoo
Hardinge, Rex
Sexton Blake series (1327)
Case of the African trader
Hardinge, Rex
Sexton Blake series (1234)
Case of the alien princess
Pascal, Francine
Sweet Valley kids super snooper series (7)
Case of the amateur actor
Bush, Christopher
Ludovic Travers series (47)
Case of the amber crown
Murray, Andrew
Sexton Blake series (297)
Case of the American tourists
Hunter, John
Sexton Blake series (1227)
Case of the amorous aunt
Gardner, Erle Stanley
Perry Mason series (71)
Case of the angel's trumpets
Burt, Michael
Roger Poynings series (2)
Case of the angry actress
Cunningham, E V
Masao Masuto series (1)
Case of the angry mourner
Gardner, Erle Stanley
Perry Mason series (37)
Case of the April fools
Bush, Christopher
Ludovic Travers series (10)
Case of the artful crime
Keene, Carolyn
Nancy Drew series (106)
Case of the back seat girl
Ryland, Clive
Chief Inspector George Bassett series (4)
Case of the backward mule
Gardner, Erle Stanley
Terry Clane series (2)
Case of the baffling burglary
Sivers, Brenda
Sherlock Hound series (3)
Case of the baited hook
Gardner, Erle Stanley
Perry Mason series (16)
Case of the Baker Street Irregular
Newman, Robert
Sherlock Holmes sequels series (33)
Case of the Baker Street Irregulars
Boucher, Anthony
Fergus O'Breen series (2)
Case of the bank holdup
Ecke, Wolfgang
Super sleuth series (4)
Case of the banned film
Parsons, Anthony
Sexton Blake series (1308)
Case of the barking clock
Keeler, Harry Stephen
Tuddleton Trotter series (2)
Case of the bashful bank robber
Hildick, Edmund Wallace
McGurk series (12)
Case of the beautiful beggar
Gardner, Erle Stanley
Perry Mason series (76)
Case of the beautiful body
Craig, Jonathan
Pete Selby series (4)
Case of the beckoning dead
Donavan, John
Sergeant Johnny Lamb series (2)
Case of the Bendigo heirlooms
Lewis, Jack
Sexton Blake series (242)
Case of the benevolent bookie
Bush, Christopher
Ludovic Travers series (46)
Case of the Berlin spy
Betteridge, Don
Tiger Lester series (8)
Case of the bigamous spouse
Gardner, Erle Stanley
Perry Mason series (65)
Case of the billion dollar body
Shallit, Joseph
Dan Morrison series (1)
Case of the birthday bracelet
Hunt, Angela Elwell
Nicki Holland series (7)
Case of the Biscay pirate
Jackson, Lewis
Sexton Blake series (1120)
Case of the Bismarck memoirs
Quiroule, Pierre
Sexton Blake series (1595)
Case of the black-eyed blonde
Gardner, Erle Stanley
Perry Mason series (25)
Case of the black magician
Hardinge, Rex
Sexton Blake series (846)
Case of the black orchids
Stout, Rex
Nero Wolfe and Archie Goodwin series (9)
Case of the black twenty-two
Flynn, Brian
Anthony Bathurst series (2)
Case of the blackmail boys
Dicks, Terrance
Baker Street Irregulars series (3)
Case of the blackmailed banker
Blair, Allan
Sexton Blake series (902)
Case of the blackmailed prince
Parsons, Anthony
Sexton Blake series (1309)
Case of the blind barber
Carr, John Dickson
Doctor Gideon Fell series (3)
Case of the blind mouse
Freeman, Martin Joseph
Jerry Todd series (1)
Case of the blonde bonanza
Gardner, Erle Stanley
Perry Mason series (67)
Case of the blue orchid
Desmond, Hugh
Alan Fraser series (18)
Case of the bogus baron
Tyrer, Walter
Sexton Blake series (1314)
Case of the bogus bride!
Gibbons, Harry Hornaby Clifford
Sexton Blake series (374)
Case of the bogus ingots
Bayfield, William John
Sexton Blake series (109)
Case of the bogus laird
Bobin, John William
Sexton Blake series (222)
Case of the bogus monk
Teed, George Hamilton
Sexton Blake series (544)
Case of the bogus prince
Chester, Gilbert
Sexton Blake series (752)
Case of the bogus treasure hunt
Graydon, William Murray
Sexton Blake series (436)
Case of the bonfire body
Bush, Christopher
Ludovic Travers series (15)
Case of the bookmaker baronet
Bobin, John William
Sexton Blake series (421)
Case of the borrowed brunette
Gardner, Erle Stanley
Perry Mason series (28)
Case of the Bouncing Betty
Avallone, Michael
Ed Noon series (5)
Case of the brass-bound chest
Chester, Gilbert
Sexton Blake series (878)
Case of the brazen beauty
Craig, Jonathan
Pete Selby series (10)
Case of the bronze statue
Hunter, John
Sexton Blake series (1081)
Case of the burgled blessing box
Corbett, Scott
Inspector Roger Tearle series (5)
Case of the buried clock
Gardner, Erle Stanley
Perry Mason series (22)
Case of the Burmese dagger
Murray, Andrew
Sexton Blake series (104)
Case of the burning bequest
Chastain, Thomas
Perry Mason series (84)
Case of the burnt Bohemian
Bush, Christopher
Ludovic Travers series (42)
Case of the Busy Bees
Witting, Clifford
Inspector Charlton series (10)
Inspector Peter Bradfield series (5)
Case of the cabaret girl
Sayer, Walter William
Sexton Blake series (305)
Case of the cackling car
Singer, Marilyn
Sam and Dave series (4)
Case of the Calabar bean
Wills, Cecil Melville
Geoffrey Boscobell series (10)
Case of the calendar girl
Gardner, Erle Stanley
Perry Mason series (57)
Case of the car-barkaholic dog
Erickson, John R
Hank the cowdog series (17)
Case of the careless Cupid
Gardner, Erle Stanley
Perry Mason series (79)
Case of the careless kitten
Gardner, Erle Stanley
Perry Mason series (21)
Case of the careless thief
Bush, Christopher
Ludovic Travers series (53)
Case of the caretaker's cat
Gardner, Erle Stanley
Perry Mason series (7)
Case of the cashiered officer
Graydon, William Murray
Sexton Blake series (15)
Case of the cautious coquette
Gardner, Erle Stanley
Perry Mason series (34)
Case of the chased and the unchaste
Dewey, Thomas Blanchard
Private Eye Mac series (7)
Case of the cheating bride
Propper, Milton
Tommy Rankin series (10)
Case of the chief rabbi's problem
Andrews, Val
Sherlock Holmes sequels series (46)
Case of the Chinese boxes
Day, Marele
Claudia Valentine series (2)
Case of the chinese courier
Hardinge, Rex
Sexton Blake series (1181)
Case of the Chinese gong
Bush, Christopher
Ludovic Travers series (13)
Case of the Chinese puzzle
Teed, George Hamilton
Sexton Blake series (400)
Case of the chocolate chip cookies, and other mysteries
Masters, M
Hawkeye Collins and Amy Adams series (6)
Case of the chocolate snatcher, and other mysteries
Masters, M
Hawkeye Collins and Amy Adams series (2)
Case of the chocolate-covered bugs
D'Ignazio, Fred
Chip Mitchell computer mystery series (3)
Case of the Christmas thief
Pascal, Francine
Sweet Valley kids super snooper series (4)
Case of the cinema star
Murray, Andrew
Sexton Blake series (188)
Case of the cinema swindle
Dicks, Terrance
Baker Street Irregulars series (4)

Case of the clairvoyant's ruse
Teed, George Hamilton
Sexton Blake series (359)
Case of the clever computer crooks, and other mysteries
Masters, M
Hawkeye Collins and Amy Adams series (5)
Case of the clever marathon cheat, and other mysteries
Masters, M
Hawkeye Collins and Amy Adams series (14)
Case of the climbing corpse
Evans, Gwyn
Chester Brett series (4)
Case of the climbing rat
Bush, Christopher
Ludovic Travers series (22)
Case of the close encounter
Hope, Laura Lee
New Bobbsey twins series (5)
Case of the cold coquette
Craig, Jonathan
Pete Selby series (3)
Case of the coloured wind
Donavan, John
Sergeant Johnny Lamb series (4)
Case of the comic crooks
Dicks, Terrance
Baker Street Irregulars series (8)
Case of the condemned cat
Hildick, Edmund Wallace
McGurk series (4)
Case of the confirmed bachelor
Palmer, Diana
Most wanted trilogy (2)
Case of the conscript miner
Tyrer, Walter
Sexton Blake series (1128)
Case of the constant god
King, Rufus
Lieutenant Valcour series (9)
Case of the constant suicides
Carr, John Dickson
Doctor Gideon Fell series (13)
Case of the Cool-Itch Kid
Giff, Patricia Reilly
Polka Dot series (5)
Case of the cop catchers
Dicks, Terrance
Baker Street Irregulars series (6)
Case of the copy-hook killing
Howes, Royce
Captain Ben Lucias series (6)
Case of the corner cottage
Bush, Christopher
Ludovic Travers series (38)
Case of the corporal's leave
Bush, Christopher
Ludovic Travers series (29)
Case of the cosmic kidnapping
Dixon, Franklin W
Hardy boys series (120)
Case of the cottage crime
Tyrer, Walter
Sexton Blake series (1268)
Case of the cotton beetle
Murray, Andrew
Sexton Blake series (298)
Case of the council swindle
Tyrer, Walter
Sexton Blake series (1365)
Case of the counterfeit cash
Hunt, Angela Elwell
Nicki Holland series (5)
Case of the counterfeit coin
Wyatt, George
Brains Benton series (2)
Case of the counterfeit colonel
Bush, Christopher
Ludovic Travers series (41)
Case of the counterfeit criminals
Dixon, Franklin W
Hardy boys series (114)
Case of the counterfeit eye
Gardner, Erle Stanley
Perry Mason series (6)
Case of the counterfeit race horse
Levy, Elizabeth
Jody and Jake series (2)
Case of the courteous killer
Deming, Richard
Dragnet series (2)
Case of the Courtlandt jewels
Teed, George Hamilton
Sexton Blake series (261)
Case of the crawling cockroach
Reed, Harlan
Dan Jordan series (1)
Case of the crazy collections
Hope, Laura Lee
New Bobbsey twins series (25)
Case of the crazy pilot
Conde, Phillip
Dick Pemberty series (6)
Case of the crime king
Deming, Richard
Dragnet series (3)
Case of the crime reporter
Hardinge, Rex
Sexton Blake series (1235)
Case of the criminal computer
Dicks, Terrance
Baker Street Irregulars series (10)
Case of the criminal's daughter
Clevely, Hugh
Sexton Blake series (1346)
Case of the crimson conjuror
Evans, Gwyn
Sexton Blake series (514)
Case of the crimson kiss
Gardner, Erle Stanley
Perry Mason series (82)
Case of the crimson wizard
Murray, Edgar Joyce
Sexton Blake series (253)
Case of the crook councillor
Blair, Allan
Sexton Blake series (823)
Case of the crook iron master
Osborne, Mark
Sexton Blake series (806)
Case of the crook M.P.
Philips, George Norman
Sexton Blake series (588)
Case of the crook rajah
Parsons, Anthony
Sexton Blake series (1009)
Case of the crooked banker
Black, Ladbroke
Sexton Blake series (601)
Case of the crooked candle
Gardner, Erle Stanley
Perry Mason series (24)
Case of the crooked contest
Hope, Laura Lee
New Bobbsey twins series (11)
Case of the crooked skipper
Hunter, John
Sexton Blake series (1295)
Case of the crumpled knave
Boucher, Anthony
Fergus O'Breen series (1)
Case of the crying clown
Hope, Laura Lee
New Bobbsey twins series (13)
Case of the cryuing swallow
Gardner, Erle Stanley
Perry Mason series (82)
Case of the cultured pearls
Bobin, John William
Sexton Blake series (223)
Case of the curious bride
Gardner, Erle Stanley
Perry Mason series (5)
Case of the curious chair
Powell, Richard
Arab and Andy Blake series (1)
Case of the curious client
Bush, Christopher
Ludovic Travers series (32)
Case of the curious heel
Crossen, Kendell Foster
Jason Jones and Necessary Smith series (1)
Case of the Damascus dagger
Richards, Kel
Ben Bartholomew series (4)
Case of the dangerous dowager
Gardner, Erle Stanley
Perry Mason series (10)
Case of the Dangra millions
Parsons, Anthony
Sexton Blake series (1244)
Case of the daring decoy
Gardner, Erle Stanley
Perry Mason series (54)
Case of the daring divorcee
Gardner, Erle Stanley
Perry Mason series (72)
Case of the dark hero
Cheyney, Peter
Secret service series (4)
Case of the dark stranger
Dalton, Moray
Inspector Hugh Collier series (11)
Case of the dark wanton
Cheyney, Peter
Everard Peter Quayle series (4)
Secret service series (6)
Case of the dead diplomat
Thomson, Basil
Superintendent Richardson series (4)
Case of the dead man gone
Bush, Christopher
Ludovic Travers series (56)
Case of the dead man's daughters
Gardner, Erle Stanley
Perry Mason series (55)
Case of the dead producer
Macclure, Victor
Inspector Archie Burford series (1)
Case of the dead shepherd
Bush, Christopher
Ludovic Travers series (12)
Case of the dead spy
Drummond, J
Sexton Blake series (1230)
Case of the deadly diamonds
Bush, Christopher
Ludovic Travers series (62)
Case of the deadly diary
Du Bois, William
Jack Jordan series (1)
Case of the deadly toy
Gardner, Erle Stanley
Perry Mason series (58)
Case of the death computer
Chance, John Newton
John Marsh series (1)
Case of the defaulting sailor
Hunter, John
Sexton Blake series (1173)
Case of the demented spiv
Bellairs, George
Detective Inspector Thomas Littlejohn series (15)
Case of the demure defendant
Gardner, Erle Stanley
Perry Mason series (51)
Case of the deported aliens
Bayfield, William John
Sexton Blake series (363)
Case of the deportee
Chester, Gilbert
Sexton Blake series (797)
Case of the deserted war bride
Hunter, John
Sexton Blake series (1150)
Case of the deserted wife
Bayfield, William John
Sexton Blake series (163)
Case of the desperate drummer
Hildick, Edmund Wallace
McGurk series (23)
Case of the diamond eye
Walden, Amelia
Lisa Clark series (1)
Case of the dictator's double
Blair, Allan
Sexton Blake series (1017)
Case of the disappearing deejay
Keene, Carolyn
Nancy Drew series (89)
Case of the disappearing diamonds
Keene, Carolyn
Nancy Drew series (80)
Case of the disappearing diplomat
Dicks, Terrance
Baker Street Irregulars series (7)
Case of the disappearing doctor
Keith, Brandon
Green Hornet series (4)
Case of the discharged P.C.
Shute, Walter
Sexton Blake series (580)
Case of the discharged policeman
Jackson, Lewis
Sexton Blake series (1240)
Case of the disguised Apache
Teed, George Hamilton
Sexton Blake series (499)
Case of the dog lover's legacy
Chambers, Kate
Diana Winthrop series (3)
Case of the dope dealers
Frazer, Martin
Sexton Blake series (1302)
Case of the doped favourite
Hunter, John
Sexton Blake series (1318)
Case of the doped heavyweight
Jackson, Lewis
Sexton Blake series (1211)
Case of the double event
Hunter, John
Sexton Blake series (1199)
Case of the double tangle
Bayfield, William John
Sexton Blake series (164)
Case of the dragon in distress
Hildick, Edmund Wallace
McGurk series (21)
Case of the drowning duck
Gardner, Erle Stanley
Perry Mason series (20)
Case of the drowsy mosquito
Gardner, Erle Stanley
Perry Mason series (23)
Case of the dubious bridegroom
Gardner, Erle Stanley
Perry Mason series (33)
Case of the dummy with cold eyes
Levy, Elizabeth
Magic mystery series (4)
Case of the duplicate daughter
Gardner, Erle Stanley
Perry Mason series (62)
Case of the eccentric will
Armour, R Coutts
Sexton Blake series (314)
Case of the eight brothers
Heberden, Mary Violet
Desmond Shannon series (13)
Case of the eighteenth ostrich
Curzon, Colin
Mark Antony series (2)
Case of the empty beehive
Wills, Cecil Melville
Sylvester Horatio Pinkney series (1)
Case of the empty tin
Gardner, Erle Stanley
Perry Mason series (18)
Case of the Etruscan treasure
Newman, Robert
Sherlock Holmes sequels series (69)
Case of the extra grave
Bush, Christopher
Ludovic Travers series (55)
Case of the extra man
Bush, Christopher
Ludovic Travers series (48)
Case of the fabulous fake
Gardner, Erle Stanley
Perry Mason series (80)
Case of the face at the window
Ecke, Wolfgang
Super sleuth series (1)
Case of the Fagin file
Dicks, Terrance
Baker Street Irregulars series (2)
Case of the faithful heart
Flynn, Brian
Anthony Bathurst series (24)
Case of the famished parson
Bellairs, George
Detective Inspector Thomas Littlejohn series (14)
Case of the fan-dancer's horse
Gardner, Erle Stanley
Perry Mason series (29)
Case of the fantastic footprints
Hildick, Edmund Wallace
McGurk series (24)
Case of the fast young lady
Burt, Michael
Roger Poynings series (1)
Case of the fatal film
Hunter, John
Sexton Blake series (859)
Case of the fatal souvenir
Jackson, Lewis
Sexton Blake series (1157)
Case of the fatal taxi cab
Graydon, William Murray
Sexton Blake series (522)
Case of the fear makers
Chance, John Newton
John Marsh series (2)
Case of the felon's fiddle
Hildick, Edmund Wallace
McGurk series (15)
Case of the fenced-in woman
Gardner, Erle Stanley
Perry Mason series (81)
Case of the fiery fingers
Gardner, Erle Stanley
Perry Mason series (38)
Case of the fifth key
Dean, Gregory
Deputy Commissioner Benjamin Simon series (2)
Case of the fighting padre
Jackson, Lewis
Sexton Blake series (1187)
Case of the fighting soldier
Bush, Christopher
Ludovic Travers series (25)
Case of the fire raising gang
Levy, Elizabeth
Jody and Jake series (3)
Case of the fired-up gang
Levy, Elizabeth
Jody and Jake series (3)
Case of the first-class carriage
Carnac, Carol
Inspector Ryvet series (5)
Case of the five dummy books
Sayer, Walter William
Sexton Blake series (306)
Case of the five fugitives
Jackson, Lewis
Sexton Blake series (1121)
Case of the five merchants
Graydon, William Murray
Sexton Blake series (174)
Case of the five red herrings
Jackson, Lewis
Sexton Blake series (1140)
Case of the fixed location
Singer, Marilyn
Sam and Dave series (5)
Case of the flowery corpse
Bush, Christopher
Ludovic Travers series (49)
Case of the flying ass
Bush, Christopher
Ludovic Travers series (20)
Case of the Flying Fifteen
Mills, Osmington
Superintendent William Baker series (2)
Case of the foot-loose doll
Gardner, Erle Stanley
Perry Mason series (56)
Case of the forbidden island
Tyrer, Walter
Sexton Blake series (1389)
Case of the forty thieves
Rhode, John
Doctor Lancelot Priestley series (57)
Case of the foster father
Perdue, Virginia
Eleanora Burke series (2)
Case of the four barons
Graydon, William Murray
Sexton Blake series (289)
Case of the four flying fingers
Hildick, Edmund Wallace
McGurk series (13)
Case of the four friends
Masterman, John Cecil
Ernst Brendel series (2)
Case of the four pages
Norman, John
Martin Speed series (4)
Case of the fourth detective
Bush, Christopher
Ludovic Travers series (39)
Case of the French raiders
Hunter, John
Sexton Blake series (1082)
Case of the frightened brother
King, Frank
Dormouse series (21)
Case of the frightened fish
Du Bois, William
Jack Jordan series (2)
Case of the frightened friend
Newman, Robert
Sherlock Holmes sequels series (75)
Case of the frightened girl
Hardinge, Rex
Sexton Blake series (1281)
Case of the frightened innkeeper
Charteris, Leslie
Saint series (14)
Case of the frightened man
Parsons, Anthony
Sexton Blake series (1382)
Case of the frightened mannequin
Bush, Christopher
Ludovic Travers series (37)
Case of the frightened rock star
Levy, Elizabeth
Jody and Jake series (1)
Case of the frozen scream
Haughey, Thomas Brace
Geoffrey Weston series (2)
Case of the fugitive firebug
Corbett, Scott
Inspector Roger Tearle series (2)
Case of the fugitive nurse
Gardner, Erle Stanley
Perry Mason series (43)
Case of the gangster's moll
Brandon, John Gordon
Sexton Blake series (787)
Case of the ghost grabbers
Dicks, Terrance
Baker Street Irregulars series (5)
Case of the giant killer
Branson, Henry Clay
John Bent series (3)
Case of the gilded fly
Crispin, Edmund
Gervase Fen series (1)

Case of the gilded lily
Gardner, Erle Stanley
Perry Mason series (50)
Case of the girl on remand
Hunter, John
Sexton Blake series (1319)
Case of the girl reporter
Bobin, John William
Sexton Blake series (54)
Case of the glamorous ghost
Gardner, Erle Stanley
Perry Mason series (46)
Case of the gobbling squash
Levy, Elizabeth
Magic mystery series (1)
Case of the gold coins
Wynne, Anthony
Doctor Eustace Hailey series (17)
Case of the gold-digger's purse
Gardner, Erle Stanley
Perry Mason series (26)
Case of the golden stool
Symonds, Francis Addington
Sexton Blake series (394)
Case of the gone goose
Corbett, Scott
Inspector Roger Tearle series (1)
Case of the good employer
Bush, Christopher
Ludovic Travers series (61)
Case of the Goofy game show
Hope, Laura Lee
New Bobbsey twins series (24)
Case of the grand alliance
Bush, Christopher
Ludovic Travers series (59)
Case of the graveyard ghost
Ball, Duncan
Anna and Tim series (1)
Case of the greedy grandpa
Gardner, Erle Stanley
Perry Mason series (58)
Case of the green caravan
Hardinge, Rex
Sexton Blake series (1282)
Case of the green-eyed sister
Gardner, Erle Stanley
Perry Mason series (41)
Case of the green felt hat
Bush, Christopher
Ludovic Travers series (21)
Case of the green knife
Wynne, Anthony
Doctor Eustace Hailey series (14)
Case of the grieving monkey
Perdue, Virginia
Eleanora Burke series (1)
Case of the grinning gorilla
Gardner, Erle Stanley
Perry Mason series (39)
Case of the gypsy's warning
Resnick, Sylvia
Debbie Preston, teenage reporter series (1)
Case of the half-wakened wife
Gardner, Erle Stanley
Perry Mason series (27)
Case of the Halloween ghost
Erickson, John R
Hank the cowdog series (9)
Case of the hanging rope
Bush, Christopher
Ludovic Travers series (17)
Case of the happy medium
Bush, Christopher
Ludovic Travers series (40)
Case of the happy warrior
Bush, Christopher
Ludovic Travers series (37)
Case of the hardboiled dicks
Blumenthal, John
Mac Slade series (1)
Case of the haunted brides
Du Bois, William
Jack Jordan series (3)
Case of the haunted camp
Pascal, Francine
Sweet Valley kids super snooper series (3)
Case of the haunted hermit
Wyatt, George
Brains Benton series (7)
Case of the haunted holiday
Dicks, Terrance
Baker Street Irregulars series (9)
Case of the haunted house, and other mysteries
Masters, M
Hawkeye Collins and Amy Adams series (11)
Case of the haunted husband
Gardner, Erle Stanley
Perry Mason series (19)
Case of the haunting of Lowell Lanes
Hunt, Angela Elwell
Nicki Holland series (6)
Case of the Haven Hotel
Bush, Christopher
Ludovic Travers series (33)
Case of the head dispenser
Bobin, John William
Sexton Blake series (326)
Case of the headless Jesuit
Bellairs, George
Detective Inspector Thomas Littlejohn series (16)
Case of the heavenly twin
Bush, Christopher
Ludovic Travers series (58)
Case of the hesitant hostess
Gardner, Erle Stanley
Perry Mason series (42)
Case of the hidden treasure
Pascal, Francine
Sweet Valley kids super snooper series (5)
Case of the high-rise robbery
Ecke, Wolfgang
Super sleuth series (5)
Case of the hijacked moon
Haughey, Thomas Brace
Geoffrey Weston series (5)
Case of the hold-up king
Symonds, Francis Addington
Sexton Blake series (495)
Case of the hook-billed kites
Borthwick, J S
Sarah Deane and Alex Mackenzie series (1)
Case of the hooking bull
Erickson, John R
Hank the cowdog series (18)
Case of the horrible swamp monster
Stevenson, Drew
J Huntley English series (1)
Case of the horrified heirs
Gardner, Erle Stanley
Perry Mason series (74)
Case of the housekeeper's hair
Bush, Christopher
Ludovic Travers series (34)
Case of the howling dog
Gardner, Erle Stanley
Perry Mason series (4)
Case of the hula clock
Gardiner, Dorothy
Sheriff Moss Magill series (1)
Case of the human ape
Graydon, William Murray
Sexton Blake series (482)
Case of the human mole
Townley, Houghton
Sexton Blake series (496)
Case of the hypnotised virgin
Roeburt, John
Jigger Moran series (3)
Case of the ice-cold hands
Gardner, Erle Stanley
Perry Mason series (68)
Case of the income-tax frauds
Bayfield, William John
Sexton Blake series (320)
Case of the Indian curse
Newman, Robert
Sherlock Holmes sequels series (88)
Case of the Indian dancer
Parsons, Anthony
Sexton Blake series (1288)
Case of the Indian millionaire
Parsons, Anthony
Sexton Blake series (1123)
Case of the Indian watcher
Parsons, Anthony
Sexton Blake series (1383)
Case of the innocent victims
Creasey, John
Inspector Roger West series (26)
Case of the international adventurer
Bobin, John William
Sexton Blake series (26)
Case of the invisible dog
Hildick, Edmund Wallace
McGurk series (7)
Case of the invisible thief
Haughey, Thomas Brace
Geoffrey Weston series (1)
Case of the invisible witness
Ecke, Wolfgang
Super sleuth series (3)
Case of the irate witness
Gardner, Erle Stanley
Perry Mason series (82)
Case of the island princess
Armour, R Coutts
Sexton Blake series (267)
Case of the island trader
Bobin, John William
Sexton Blake series (167)
Case of the Jack of Clubs
Evans, Gwyn
Sexton Blake series (515)
Case of the jade-handled knife
Teed, George Hamilton
Sexton Blake series (360)
Case of the Japanese contract
Parsons, Anthony
Sexton Blake series (1310)
Case of the Japanese detective
Wignall, Trevor C
Sexton Blake series (150)
Case of the jeweled ragpicker
Keeler, Harry Stephen
Angus Macwhorter series (2)
Case of the Judas spoon
Stokes, Manning Lee
Christopher Fenn series (2)
Case of the jumbo sandwich
Bush, Christopher
Ludovic Travers series (60)
Case of the kidnapped angel
Cunningham, E V
Masao Masuto series (6)
Case of the kidnapped colonel
Bush, Christopher
Ludovic Travers series (24)
Case of the kidnapped legatee
Armour, R Coutts
Sexton Blake series (315)
Case of the kidnapped prisoner
Blair, Allan
Sexton Blake series (982)
Case of the kidnapped shadow
Haughey, Thomas Brace
Geoffrey Weston series (4)
Case of the kidnapped specialist
Hardinge, Rex
Sexton Blake series (964)
Case of the king's spy
Sayer, Walter William
Sexton Blake series (152)
Case of the lame canary
Gardner, Erle Stanley
Perry Mason series (11)
Case of the late pig
Allingham, Margery
Albert Campion series (8)
Case of the laughing dwarf
Reach, James
Wing series (3)
Case of the laughing Jesuit
Burt, Michael
Roger Poynings series (3)
Case of the laughing virgin
Craig, Jonathan
Pete Selby series (8)
Case of the lazy lover
Gardner, Erle Stanley
Perry Mason series (30)
Case of the leaning man
Bush, Christopher
Ludovic Travers series (19)
Case of the legion deserter
Clevely, Hugh
Sexton Blake series (1373)
Case of the limping librarian
Suter, Jon Michael
Mustard jar series (3)
Case of the lone plantation
Murray, Edgar Joyce
Sexton Blake series (443)
Case of the lonely heiress
Gardner, Erle Stanley
Perry Mason series (32)
Case of the long-firm frauds
Bobin, John William
Sexton Blake series (422)
Case of the long-legged models
Gardner, Erle Stanley
Perry Mason series (55)
Case of the lost dogs
Smith, Beatrice Schillinger
Kate and Ben King series (1)
Case of the lucky legs
Gardner, Erle Stanley
Perry Mason series (3)
Case of the lucky loser
Gardner, Erle Stanley
Perry Mason series (52)
Case of the mad inventor
Creasey, John
Sexton Blake series (1064)
Case of the magic Christmas bell
Pascal, Francine
Sweet Valley kids super snooper series (2)
Case of the magic mirror
Bush, Christopher
Ludovic Travers series (26)
Case of the Maltese treasure
Haughey, Thomas Brace
Geoffrey Weston series (3)
Case of the Malverne diamonds
Gribble, Leonard Reginald
Superintendent Anthony Slade series (12)
Case of the man in black
Merland, Oliver
Sexton Blake series (295)
Case of the man on leave
Chester, Gilbert
Sexton Blake series (1030)
Case of the man who never slept
Evans, Gwyn
Sexton Blake series (372)
Case of the man with no name
Drummond, J
Sexton Blake series (1275)
Case of the Marsden rubies
Gribble, Leonard Reginald
Superintendent Anthony Slade series (2)
Case of the master organizer
Murray, Andrew
Sexton Blake series (299)
Case of the mesmerizing boss
Palmer, Diana
Most wanted trilogy (1)
Case of the Mexican knife
Homes, Geoffrey
Jose Manuel Madero series (1)
Case of the Michaelmas goose
Witting, Clifford
Inspector Charlton series (3)
Inspector Peter Bradfield series (1)
Case of the midnight chess game
Ecke, Wolfgang
Super sleuth series (6)
Case of the midnight rustler
Erickson, John R
Hank the cowdog series (19)
Case of the mile high race
Levy, Elizabeth
Jody and Jake series (5)
Case of the mill owner's son
Graydon, William Murray
Sexton Blake series (175)
Case of the millionaire newspaper owner
Armour, R Coutts
Sexton Blake series (316)
Case of the millionaire's blackmail
Bayfield, William John
Sexton Blake series (321)
Case of the million-dollar diamonds
Pascal, Francine
Sweet Valley kids super snooper series (6)
Case of the mind-reading mommies
Levy, Elizabeth
Magic mystery series (2)
Case of the mischievous doll
Gardner, Erle Stanley
Perry Mason series (69)
Case of the missing airmen
Elliott, George
Martin Speed series (1)
Case of the missing bills
Smith, Beatrice Schillinger
Kate and Ben King series (2)
Case of the missing bridegroom
Dilnot, George
Sexton Blake series (947)
Case of the missing Bronte
Barnard, Robert
Superintendent Perry Trethowan series (3)
Case of the missing bullion
Gordon, Peter
Sexton Blake series (1614)
Case of the missing cat
Erickson, John R
Hank the cowdog series (15)
Case of the missing corpse
Lanham, Edwin
Lieutenant Gray series (1)
Case of the missing DFC
Parsons, Anthony
Sexton Blake series (1099)
Case of the missing diary
Fielding, A
Inspector Pointer series (18)
Case of the missing dinosaur
Hope, Laura Lee
New Bobbsey twins series (16)
Palmer, Bernard
Powell family series (2)
Case of the missing estate agent
Stuart, Donald
Sexton Blake series (721)
Case of the missing G.I. bride
Parsons, Anthony
Sexton Blake series (1165)
Case of the missing major
Parsons, Anthony
Sexton Blake series (1039)
Case of the missing masterpiece
Dicks, Terrance
Baker Street Irregulars series (1)
Case of the missing men
Bush, Christopher
Ludovic Travers series (30)
Case of the missing message
Verral, Charles Spain
Brains Benton series (1)
Case of the missing minutes
Bush, Christopher
Ludovic Travers series (16)
Case of the missing money
Stahl, Hilda
Wren House series (5)
Case of the missing mummy
Bradman, Tony
Sam, the girl detective series (3)
Case of the missing musician
Hardinge, Rex
Sexton Blake series (999)
case of the missing Nazi
Tyrer, Walter
Sexton Blake series (1339)
Case of the missing poison
Gardner, Erle Stanley
Perry Mason series (51)
Case of the missing sandals
Mavity, Nancy Barr
Peter Piper series (3)
Case of the missing scientist
Parsons, Anthony
Sexton Blake series (1311)
Case of the missing secretary
Palmer, Diana
Most wanted trilogy (3)
Case of the missing ships
Hope, Stanton
Sexton Blake series (845)
Case of the missing stoker
Jackson, Lewis
Sexton Blake series (1073)
Case of the missing surgeon
Parsons, Anthony
Sexton Blake series (1245)
Case of the Monday murders
Bush, Christopher
Ludovic Travers series (14)
Case of the Monta Grandee diamonds
Hope, Stanton
Sexton Blake series (1139)
Case of the moth-eaten mink
Gardner, Erle Stanley
Perry Mason series (40)
Case of the muckrakers
McNeilly, Wilfred
Sexton Blake series (1587)
Case of the mummified hand
Teed, George Hamilton
Sexton Blake series (452)
Case of the murdered caretaker
Gates, Clifford
Sexton Blake series (1034)
Case of the murdered commissionaire
Brandon, John Gordon
Sexton Blake series (831)
Case of the murdered financier
Creasey, John
Sexton Blake series (905)
Case of the murdered Mackenzie
Cunningham, E V
Masao Masuto series (7)
Case of the murdered madame
Kane, Henry
Peter Chambers series (9)
Case of the murdered mahout
Graydon, William Murray
Sexton Blake series (571)
Case of the murdered major
Bush, Christopher
Ludovic Travers series (23)
Case of the murdered model
Dewey, Thomas Blanchard
Private Eye Mac series (3)
Case of the murdered pawn broker
Edwards, Walter
Sexton Blake series (826)
Case of the murdered players
Newman, Robert
Sherlock Holmes sequels series (84)
Case of the murdered postman
Hardinge, Rex
Sexton Blake series (965)
Case of the murdered redhead
Lockridge, Frances
Nathan Shapiro series (1)

Case of the tea-cosy's aunt
Gilbert, Anthony
Arthur Crook series (11)
Case of the tearless widow
Roeburt, John
Jigger Moran series (1)
Case of the teenager terminator
Hunt, Angela Elwell
Nicki Holland series (3)
Case of the ten diamonds
Teed, George Hamilton
Sexton Blake series (401)
Case of the terrified track star
Hunt, Angela Elwell
Nicki Holland series (4)
Case of the terrified typist
Gardner, Erle Stanley
Perry Mason series (49)
Case of the theatrical profiteer
Graydon, William Murray
Sexton Blake series (437)
Case of the threatened king
Newman, Robert
Sherlock Holmes sequels series (57)
Case of the three absconding swindlers
Brisbane, Coutts
Sexton Blake series (874)
Case of the three lost letters
Bush, Christopher
Ludovic Travers series (45)
Case of the three-ring puzzle
Bush, Christopher
Ludovic Travers series (57)
Case of the three strange faces
Bush, Christopher
Ludovic Travers series (9)
Case of the three survivors
Clevely, Hugh
Sexton Blake series (1347)
Case of the ticklish tooth
Corbett, Scott
Inspector Roger Tearle series (3)
Case of the toilet paper decorator, and other mysteries
Masters, M
Hawkeye Collins and Amy Adams series (9)
Case of the trade secret
Bobin, John William
Sexton Blake series (224)
Case of the transatlantic fliers
Lewis, Jack
Sexton Blake series (93)
Case of the treble twist
Bush, Christopher
Ludovic Travers series (51)
Case of the treetop treasure
Hildick, Edmund Wallace
McGurk series (10)
Case of the tricky trickster
Hope, Laura Lee
New Bobbsey twins series (29)
Case of the triple twist
Bush, Christopher
Ludovic Travers series (51)
Case of the troubled trustee
Gardner, Erle Stanley
Perry Mason series (75)
Case of the Tudor queen
Bush, Christopher
Ludovic Travers series (18)
Case of the turning tide
Gardner, Erle Stanley
Gramps Wiggins series (1)
Case of the twin detectives
Brooks, Edwy Searles
Sexton Blake series (12)
Case of the twin teddy bears
Keene, Carolyn
Nancy Drew series (116)
Case of the twisted trail
Symonds, Francis Addington
Sexton Blake series (254)
Case of the two bankers
Bobin, John William
Sexton Blake series (51)
Case of the two brothers
Murray, Andrew
Sexton Blake series (60)
Case of the two crooked baronets
Tyrer, Walter
Sexton Blake series (1293)
Case of the two doctors
Carter, Nicholas
Nicholas Carter series (412)
Case of the two-faced swindler
Drummond, J
Sexton Blake series (1376)
Case of the two guardians
Graydon, William Murray
Sexton Blake series (344)
Case of the two pearl necklaces
Fielding, A
Inspector Pointer series (19)
Case of the two scapegraces
Graydon, William Murray
Sexton Blake series (386)
Case of the unconquered sisters
Downing, Todd
Hugh Rennert series (4)
Case of the uncut gems
Murray, Andrew
Sexton Blake series (246)
Case of the undischarged bankrupt
Murray, Andrew
Sexton Blake series (190)
Case of the unfortunate village
Bush, Christopher
Ludovic Travers series (8)
Case of the unhappy angels
Homes, Geoffrey
Humphrey Campbell series (5)
Case of the unknown heir
Parsons, Anthony
Sexton Blake series (1336)
Case of the un-named film
Murray, Andrew
Sexton Blake series (247)
Case of the vagabond virgin
Gardner, Erle Stanley
Perry Mason series (31)
Case of the vanished husband
Bayfield, William John
Sexton Blake series (215)
Case of the vanishing artist
King, Frank
Superintendent Gloom series (3)
Case of the vanishing beauty
Prather, Richard Scott
Shell Scott series (1)
Case of the vanishing corpse
Newman, Robert
Sherlock Holmes sequels series (49)
Richards, Kel
Ben Bartholomew series (1)
Case of the vanishing house
Radnor, Alan
Dick Barton series (2)
Case of the vanishing veil
Keene, Carolyn
Nancy Drew series (83)
Case of the vanishing ventriloquist
Hildick, Edmund Wallace
McGurk series (17)
Case of the vanishing video
Hope, Laura Lee
New Bobbsey twins series (28)
Case of the velvet claws
Gardner, Erle Stanley
Perry Mason series (1)
Case of the video game smugglers, and other mysteries
Masters, M
Hawkeye Collins and Amy Adams series (3)
Case of the village tramp
Craig, Jonathan
Pete Selby series (7)
Case of the violent virgin
Avallone, Michael
Ed Noon series (6)
Case of the violet smoke
Donavan, John
Sergeant Johnny Lamb series (4)
Case of the visiting vampire
Stevenson, Drew
J Huntley English series (2)
Case of the walkabout clock
Ball, Duncan
Anna and Tim series (2)
Case of the waltzing mouse
Wyatt, George
Brains Benton series (5)
Case of the wandering weathervanes
Hildick, Edmund Wallace
McGurk series (19)
Case of the wandering werewolf
Stevenson, Drew
J Huntley English series (3)
Case of the watching boy
Newman, Robert
Sherlock Holmes sequels series (90)
Case of the waylaid wolf
Gardner, Erle Stanley
Perry Mason series (61)
Case of the weeping witch
Hildick, Edmund Wallace
McGurk series (22)
Case of the weird sisters
Armstrong, Charlotte
MacDougal Duff series (2)
Case of the wicked three
Parsons, Anthony
Sexton Blake series (1361)
Case of the wild river ride
Levy, Elizabeth
Jody and Jake series (4)
Case of the withered hand
Brandon, John Gordon
Inspector Patrick Aloysius McCarthy series (9)
Case of the woman in black
Murray, Andrew
Sexton Blake series (248)
Case of the worried waitress
Gardner, Erle Stanley
Perry Mason series (77)
Case of the would-be widow
Brandon, John Gordon
Arthur Stukeley Pennington series (19)
Case of the wounded mastiff
Harman, Neal
Protection Limited series (1)
Case of too many murders
Chastain, Thomas
Perry Mason series (83)
Case of torches
Smith, Clark
Nicky Mahoun series (3)
Case of William Smith
Wentworth, Patricia
Miss Maud Silver series (14)
Case on cloud nine
Freeman, Lucy
Doctor William Ames series (3)
Case pending
Shannon, Dell
Lieutenant Luis Mendoza series (1)
Case proceeding
Prescot, Julian
Case books series (3)
Case re-opened
Prescot, Julian
Case books series (8)
Case twenty nine
Cassells, John
Superintendent Flagg series (18)
Case with four clowns
Bruce, Leo
Sergeant William Beef series (4)
Case with nine solutions
Connington, John Jervis
Sir Clinton Driffield series (4)
Case with no conclusion
Bruce, Leo
Sergeant William Beef series (3)
Case with ropes and rings
Bruce, Leo
Sergeant William Beef series (5)
Case with three husbands
Erskine, Margaret
Inspector Septimus Finch series (15)
Case without a clue
Carter, Nicholas
Nicholas Carter series (198)
Morland, Nigel
Mrs Palmyra Pym series (6)
Case without a corpse
Bruce, Leo
Sergeant William Beef series (2)
Casebook of Doctor Holton
Hunt, Charlotte
Doctor Paul Holton series (2)
Doctor Paul Holton series (4)
Casebook of Jules de Grandin
Quinn, Seabury
Jules de Grandin series (3)
Casebook of Lucius Leffing
Brennan, Joseph Payne
Lucius Leffing series (1)
Casebook of murder
Wilson, Colin
Murder series (2)
Casebook of Solar Pons
Derleth, August
Solar Pons series (7)
Casebook of the Black Widowers
Asimov, Isaac
Black Widowers series (3)
Casefile
Pronzini, Bill
Private Eye series (22)
Cases of Susan Dare
Eberhart, Mignon Good
Susan Dare series (1)
Casey Ryan
Bower, Bertha Muzzy
Casey Ryan series (1)
Casey's revenge
Berry, Joy
Human race club series (7)
Cash my chips, croupier
Marlowe, Piers
Frank Drury and Inspector Bill Hazard series (6)
Cashbox caper
Bradman, Tony
Sam, the girl detective series (2)
Cashel Byron's profession
Shaw, George Bernard
Nonage series (4)
Cashier's secret
Carter, Nicholas
Nicholas Carter series (122)
Cashing in
Masters, Zeke
Faro Blake series (28)
Casino
Corris, Peter
Cliff Hardy series (18)
Casino for sale
Brahms, Caryl
Inspector Adam Quill series (2)
Stroganoff Troupe series (2)
Casino Greystone
Bronte, Louisa
Greystone Tavern series (4)
Casino murder case
Van Dine, S S
Philo Vance series (8)
Casino mystery
Hamilton, Elaine
Inspector Reynolds series (7)
Casino Royale
Fleming, Ian
James Bond series (1)
Casino strip
Janson, Hank
Hank Janson series (230)
Casinopoly
Janson, Hank
Hank Janson series (231)
Casket of cameos
Boreham, Frank William
Texts that made history series (3)
Caspar and the lion cub
Hyman, Robin
Caspar series (1)
Sugita, Yutaka
Caspar series (1)
Caspar and the rainbow bird
Hyman, Robin
Caspar series (2)
Caspar finds a friend
Tourneur, Dina Kathelyn
Caspar series (8)
Caspar loses his dog
Tourneur, Dina Kathelyn
Caspar series (9)
Caspar plants a seed
Tourneur, Dina Kathelyn
Caspar series (7)
Caspar's ears
Tourneur, Dina Kathelyn
Caspar series (1)
Caspar's feet
Tourneur, Dina Kathelyn
Caspar series (4)
Caspar's hair
Tourneur, Dina Kathelyn
Caspar series (3)
Caspar's hands
Tourneur, Dina Kathelyn
Caspar series (5)
Caspar's mouth
Tourneur, Dina Kathelyn
Caspar series (2)
Caspar's nose
Tourneur, Dina Kathelyn
Caspar series (6)
Casper
Mitchum, Hank
Stage coach station series (36)
Casper Carrot
Reed, Giles
Munch Bunch character series (13)
Casper Carrot's new blue jumper
Reed, Giles
Munch Bunch story books series (4)
Casque's lark
Sue, Eugene
Mysteries of the people series (5)
Cassandra Bell
Van Greenaway, Peter
Inspector Cherry and Sergeant Duff series (4)
Cassandra in red
Collins, Michael
Dan Fortune series (18)
Cassandra in Westminster
Johnson, Donald McIntosh
Publisher presents himself series (5)
Cassidy the con man
Teed, George Hamilton
Sexton Blake series (635)
Cassie
Kaye, Marilyn
Sisters series (3)
Schurfranz, Vivian
Sunfire series (14)
Cassie and Chris
Casey, Sara
Two by two series (1)
Cassie Bowen takes witch lessons
Hines, Anna Grossnickle
Cassie Bowen series (1)
Cassilee
Coon, Susan
Living planet series (2)
Cassino corpse factory
Lutz, Gunther
Nazi paratrooper series (3)
Cassiodore case
Martin, A Richard
Branders Noble series (1)
Cast a wide loop
Borg, Jack
Hogleg Bailey series (18)
Cast a yellow shadow
Thomas, Ross
McCorkle and Padillo series (2)
Cast away in the land of snow
Moore, Fenworth
Jerry Ford series (3)
Cast for death
Yorke, Margaret
Doctor Patrick Grant series (5)
Cast, in order of disappearance
Brett, Simon
Charles Paris series (1)
Cast iron man
Legat, Michael
Silk maker series (2)
Cast of criminals
Dixon, Franklin W
Hardy boys series (97)
Cast of death
Orde-Powlett, Nigel
Anthony Rillington series (1)
Cast the first stone
Lee, Elsie
Sam Benedict series (1)
Castafiore emerald
Herge
Tintin series (22)
Castanets for Caroline
Hill, Lorna
Sadler's Wells series (4)
Castang's city
Freeling, Nicolas
Henri Castang series (5)
Castaway
Avenell, Donne
Axa series (8)
Irvine, Lucy
Runaway series (2)
Castaway camp
Atkinson, Mary Evelyn
Fricka Hammond series (1)
Castaway cat
Roe, JoAnn
Cat series (1)
Castaway Christmas
Baker, Margaret Joyce
Ridley family series (1)
Castaways
Berres, Frances B
Deep-sea adventure series (12)
Verne, Jules
Captain Grant's children series (1)
Castaways in Lilliput
Winterfeld, Henry
Lilliput series (8)
Castaways in time
Adams, Robert
Castaways in time series (1)
Castaways of Pete's Patch
Rankin, Carroll Watson
Dandelion Cottage series (4)
Castaways of the flag
Verne, Jules
Swiss family Robinson series (5)
Castaways of the stratosphere
Dixon, Franklin W
Ted Scott flying series (18)
Castaways' world
Brunner, John
Zarathustra trilogy (2)
Castel del Monte
Gallizier, Nathan
Sorceress trilogy (1)
Castile for Isabella
Plaidy, Jean
Ferdinand and Isabella trilogy (1)

Castilian caper
Paradis, Vincent A
Tut Claw series (1)
Casting away of Mrs Lecks and Mrs Aleshine
Stockton, Frank Richard
Mrs Lecks and Mrs Aleshine series (1)
Casting for murder
Dunham, Mikel
Rhea Buerklin series (2)
Castle
Birt, David
Middle Ages series (8)
Kafka, Franz
K series (1)
Castle builders
Yonge, Charlotte Mary
Lady Herbert Somerville series (1)
Castle Conquest
Gray, Berkeley
Norman Conquest series (45)
Castle Crespin
Andrews, Allen
Pig Plantagenet series (2)
Castle Dangerous
Gunn, Victor
Chief Inspector Bill Cromwell series (28)
Scott, Walter
Tales of my landlord series (2)
Castle Death
Dever, Joe
Lone Wolf series (7)
Castle Dinas
Walling, Robert Alfred John
Philip Tolefree series (19)
Castle dreams
De Chancie, John
Castle Perilous series (6)
Castle Fear
Dixon, Franklin W
Hardy boys case files series (44)
Castle for four
Finlay, Winifred
Judith Norton series (6)
Castle for rent
De Chancie, John
Castle Perilous series (2)
Castle Gay
Buchan, John
Dickson McCunn series (2)
Castle in Northumbria
Hill, Lorna
Patience series (3)
Castle in Sweden
Sagan, Francoise
Sweden series (1)
Castle in the air
Jones, Diana Wynne
Howl series (2)
Castle in the attic
Winthrop, Elizabeth
William series (1)
Castle in the clouds
Simon, Morris
Fantasy forest series (7)
Castle Island
Mottram, Ralph Hale
Captain Dormer series (4)
Castle Island case
Mason, Francis Van Wyck
Colonel Hugh North series (22)
Castle kidnapped
De Chancie, John
Castle Perilous series (3)
Castle murders
De Chancie, John
Castle Perilous series (5)
Castle mystery
Warner, Gertrude Chandler
Boxcar children series (36)
Castle of adventure
Blyton, Enid
Adventure series (2)
Castle of crime
Grant, Maxwell
Shadow series (172)
Castle of dark
Lee, Tanith
Castle of dark series (1)
Castle of darkness
Brennan, James Herbert
GrailQuest series (1)
Castle of doom
Brightfield, Richard
Your amazing adventures series (1)
Grant, Maxwell
Shadow series (94)
Castle of dreams
Warren, Paulette
Caliban series (6)
Castle of Frome
Packard, Edward
Escape from the Kingdom of Frome series (1)
Castle of Hape
Murphy, Shirley Rousseau
Children of Ynell series (3)
Castle of iron
De Camp, Lyon Sprague
Harold Shea series (2)
Castle of Llyr
Alexander, Lloyd
Prydain series (3)
Castle of sin
Cassells, John
Superintendent Flagg series (5)
Castle of the enchantress
Fitzgerald, Julia
Astromance series (5)
Castle of the White Flag
Everett-Green, Evelyn
Franco-Prussian War series (1)
Castle of wizardry
Eddings, David
Belgariad series (4)
Castle Omeragh
Moore, Frank Frankfort
Cromwellian Ireland series (1)
Castle on Claw Creek
Grover, Marshall
Larry and Stretch series (277)
Castle on the rock
Meyler, Eileen
Jocelyn series (2)
Castle Perilous
De Chancie, John
Castle Perilous series (1)
Castle Pizard
Whittle, Tyler
Spaniards and Elizabethans series (3)
Castle Roogna
Anthony, Piers
Xanth series (3)
Castle School at the cross-roads
Little, Sylvia
Castle School series (6)
Castle School gets going
Little, Sylvia
Castle School series (1)
Castle School in the news
Little, Sylvia
Castle School series (8)
Castle School on holiday
Little, Sylvia
Castle School series (3)
Castle School on the screen
Little, Sylvia
Castle School series (5)
Castle School on the warpath
Little, Sylvia
Castle School series (7)
Castle sinister
Johns, William Earl
Biggles series (19)
Castle Skull
Carr, John Dickson
Henri Bencolin series (2)
Castle Spellbound
De Chancie, John
Castle Perilous series (7)
Castle war!
De Chancie, John
Castle Perilous series (4)
Castledare vigilantes
Sinclair, Dee
Castledare series (2)
Castledoom
Lecale, Errol
Specialist series (2)
Castledown
Gregorian, Joyce Ballou
Tredana trilogy (2)
Castleford conundrum
Connington, John Jervis
Sir Clinton Driffield series (8)
Castles burning
Lyons, Arthur
Jacob Asch series (5)
Castles in Spain
Clune, Frank
Discovery series (17)
Castles in the air
Cammell, Charles Richard
Continent and Edinburgh series (1)
Gallagher, Patricia
Castles series (1)
Muir, Augustus
Blue bonnet series (2)
Castlevania II
Howell, Christopher
Worlds of power series (4)
Castrato
Collins, Michael
Dan Fortune series (14)
Castro file
Rosenberger, Joseph
Death Merchant series (7)
Castrovalva
Bidmead, Christopher H
Doctor Who series (76)
Casual affairs
O'Donnell, Lillian
Detective Norah Mulcahaney series (10)
Casual murderer
Footner, Hulbert
Madame Rosika Storey series (6)
Casual slaughters
Carter, Robert A
Nicholas Barlow series (1)
Hanson, Virginia
Adam Drew and Katherine Cornish series (2)
Casualty at Saint Lawrence's
Linton, Cathy
Saint Lawrence's Hospital series (1)
Cat affair
Tangye, Derek
Minack chronicles series (9)
Cat among the pigeons
Christie, Agatha
Hercule Poirot series (31)
Cat and Capricorn
Olsen, D B
Rachel and Jennifer Murdock series (11)
Cat and Dog and the ABCs
Miller, Elizabeth
Cat and Dog series (6)
Cat and Dog and the mixed-up week
Miller, Elizabeth
Cat and Dog series (4)
Cat and Dog give a party
Miller, Elizabeth
Cat and Dog series (1)
Cat and Dog have a contest
Miller, Elizabeth
Cat and Dog series (2)
Cat and Dog have a parade
Miller, Elizabeth
Cat and Dog series (7)
Cat and Dog learn the ABCs
Miller, Elizabeth
Cat and Dog series (6)
Cat and Dog raise the roof
Miller, Elizabeth
Cat and Dog series (3)
Cat and Dog take a trip
Miller, Elizabeth
Cat and Dog series (5)
Cat and Fiddle murders
Ronald, E B
Rupert Bradley series (1)
Cat and mouse
Brand, Christianna
Inspector Chucky series (2)
Gault, William Campbell
Brock Callahan series (12)
Goldthwaite, Eaton Kenneth
Lieutenant Joseph Dickerson series (3)
Grass, Gunter
Danzig trilogy (2)
Cat and mouse murder
Goldthwaite, Eaton Kenneth
Lieutenant Joseph Dickerson series (3)
Cat and the clock
Booth, Charles Gordon
Anatole Flique series (2)
Cat and the corpse
Walling, Robert Alfred John
Philip Tolefree series (7)
Cat and the flying machine
Kubinyi, Laszlo
Shukru series (2)
Cat ate my gymsuit
Danziger, Paula
Cat and bat series (1)
Cat book
Nichols, Beverley
Cat series (2)
Cat by any other name
Adamson, Lydia
Alice Nestleton series (4)
Cat called Tootoo
Chetham-Strode, Warren
Siamese cats series (3)
Cat Cay warrant
Morgan, Allan
Mark Blood series (3)
Cat Club
Averill, Esther
Jenny Linsky series (1)
Cat for a noisy day
East, Helen
Arthur's aunt series (1)
Cat got your tongue?
Pearson, Ann
Maggie Courtney series (3)
Cat in the glass house
Adamson, Lydia
Alice Nestleton series (7)
Cat in the hat
Seuss, Doctor
Cat in the hat series (1)
Cat in the hat comes back!
Seuss, Doctor
Cat in the hat series (2)
Cat in the hat dictionary
Seuss, Doctor
Cat in the hat series (2)
Cat in the hat songbook
Seuss, Doctor
Cat in the hat series (2)
Cat in the manger
Adamson, Lydia
Alice Nestleton series (1)
Cat-in-the-manger
Bentley, Phyllis
Environment series (2)
Cat in the window
Tangye, Derek
Minack chronicles series (2)
Cat in the wings
Adamson, Lydia
Alice Nestleton series (5)
Cat in wolf's clothing
Adamson, Lydia
Alice Nestleton series (2)
Cat Island
Williams, Jon
Privateers and gentlemen series (5)
Cat jumps
Burton, Miles
Inspector Arnold and Desmond Merrion series (33)
Cat killer
Dengler, Sandy
Mirage mysteries series (1)
Cat Morgan, working girl
Kaye, Marilyn
Three of a kind series (5)
Cat-nappers
Wodehouse, Pelham Grenville
Jeeves and Bertie Wooster series (15)
Cat of a different color
Adamson, Lydia
Alice Nestleton series (3)
Cat of many tails
Queen, Ellery
Ellery Queen series (26)
Cat of silvery hue
Adams, Robert
Horseclans series (4)
Cat on a blue Monday
Douglas, Carole Nelson
Midnight Louie series (3)
Cat saw murder
Olsen, D B
Lieutenant Stephen Mayhew series (2)
Rachel and Jennifer Murdock series (1)
Cat screams
Downing, Todd
Hugh Rennert series (2)
Cat show
Cass, Joan Evelyn
Cats series (2)
Cat strikes at night
Cooper, Wendy
Do and Dare Club series (1)
Cat that could spell Mississippi
Hawkins, Laura
Riverview series (2)
Cat thief
Cass, Joan Evelyn
Cats series (1)
Cat trap
Ralston, Gilbert Alexander
Dakota series (3)
Cat walk
Olsen, D B
Rachel and Jennifer Murdock series (12)
Cat watchers
Chance, John Newton
Jonathan Blake series (22)
Cat wears a mask
Olsen, D B
Rachel and Jennifer Murdock series (9)
Cat wears a noose
Olsen, D B
Lieutenant Stephen Mayhew series (6)
Rachel and Jennifer Murdock series (5)
Cat who ate Danish modern
Braun, Lilian Jackson
Jim Qwilleran series (2)
Cat who came to breakfast
Braun, Lilian Jackson
Jim Qwilleran series (17)
Cat who could read backwards
Braun, Lilian Jackson
Jim Qwilleran series (1)
Cat who had fourteen tales
Braun, Lilian Jackson
Jim Qwilleran series (9)
Cat who knew a cradinal
Braun, Lilian Jackson
Jim Qwilleran series (13)
Cat who knew Shakespeare
Braun, Lilian Jackson
Jim Qwilleran series (7)
Cat who lived high
Braun, Lilian Jackson
Jim Qwilleran series (12)
Cat who moved a mountain
Braun, Lilian Jackson
Jim Qwilleran series (14)
Cat who played Brahms
Braun, Lilian Jackson
Jim Qwilleran series (5)
Cat who played Post Office
Braun, Lilian Jackson
Jim Qwilleran series (6)
Cat who rode cows
Lockridge, Frances
Cats series (5)
Cat who saw red
Braun, Lilian Jackson
Jim Qwilleran series (4)
Cat who sniffed glue
Braun, Lilian Jackson
Jim Qwilleran series (8)
Cat who talked to ghosts
Braun, Lilian Jackson
Jim Qwilleran series (11)
Cat who turned on and off
Braun, Lilian Jackson
Jim Qwilleran series (3)
Cat who walks through walls
Heinlein, Robert Anson
Future history series (8)
Lazarus Long series (3)
Cat who wasn't there
Braun, Lilian Jackson
Jim Qwilleran series (15)
Cat who went into the closet
Braun, Lilian Jackson
Jim Qwilleran series (16)
Cat who went underground
Braun, Lilian Jackson
Jim Qwilleran series (10)
Cat who wore a pot on her head
Slepian, Jan
Junior listen-hear series (1)
Cat with a fiddle
Adamson, Lydia
Alice Nestleton series (6)
Cat with the tulip face
Morlan, A R
Ewerton series (1)
Catacomb conspiracy
Arnold, Margot
Penelope Spring and Sir Tobias Glendower series (8)
Catacomb years
Bishop, Michael
Urban nucleus series (2)
Catalyst
Cory, Desmond
John Dobie and Kate Coyle series (1)
Hall, Penny
Miners series (2)
Catalyst Club
Dyer, George
Catalyst Club series (1)
Catamount Camp
Ellis, Edward Sylvester
Catamount Camp series (1)
Catastrophe Club
King, Frank
Dormouse series (12)
Catastrophe practice
Mosley, Nicholas
Catastrophe practice series (1)
Catastrophe's spell
Brenner, Mayer Alan
Dance of the gods series (1)

Catch a falling clown
Kaminsky, Stuart Melvin
Toby Peters series (7)
Catch a falling spy
Deighton, Len
Secret file series (7)
Catch a falling star
Van de Water, Frederic Franklin
American Revolution series (4)
Catch a killer
Martin, Robert Lee
Jim Bennett series (7)
Catch a tiger
Cameron, Owen
Deputy Sheriff Jake Brown series (1)
Thomas, Martin
Sexton Blake series (1481)
Catch and kill
Blake, Nicholas
Nigel Strangeways series (11)
Catch and squeeze
Cooper, Craig
Matt Savage series (5)
Catch colt
Paine, Lauran
Sheridan Township series (3)
Catch kitten
Schongut, Emanuel
Kitten board book series (1)
Catch me a phoenix!
Brown, Carter
Danny Boyd series (13)
Catch me a renegade
Janson, Hank
Hank Janson series (201)
Catch me and kiss me and say it again
Watson, Clyde
Father Fox series (2)
Catch me, if you can
Cobb, Belton
Bryan Armitage series (19)
Inspector Cheviot Burmann series (41)
Kitty Armitage series (16)
Catch of time
Ford, Donald
Gwyneth series (2)
Catch the red bus
Killingback, Julia
Busy Bears series (3)
Catch the Saint
Lee, Fleming
Saint series (45)
Catch the star winds
Chandler, Arthur Bertram
Rim series (8)
Catch twenty two
Heller, Joseph
Catch twenty two series (1)
Catchfire
Martin, Graham
Giftwish series (2)
Catechisms
Watts, Isaac
Catechisms and prayers series (1)
Catenary exchange
Winters, Jon
Anton Drakov series (2)
Cater Street hangman
Perry, Anne
Charlotte Ellison Pitt and Inspector Thomas Pitt series (1)
Caterpillar
Van der Essen, Anne
Yok-yok series (1)
Caterpillar at breakfast
East, Helen
Arthur's aunt series (2)
Caterpillar cop
McClure, James
Lieutenant Kramer and Sergeant Zondi series (2)
Catfang
Fisk, Nicholas
Starstormers series (3)
Catfish
Hurd, Edith Thatcher
Catfish series (1)
Catfish and the kidnapped cat
Hurd, Edith Thatcher
Catfish series (2)
Cathaline at Greycliff
Grove, Harriet Pyne
Greycliff girls series (1)
Cathedral
Huysmans, Joris Karl
Durtal series (3)
Walpole, Hugh
Provincial group series (1)
Cathedral cat
Severn, June
Cathedral cat series (1)
Cathedral courtship
Wiggin, Kate Douglas
Penelope Hamilton series (1)
Cathedral Wednesday
Mayne, William
Choir school series (3)
Catherine
Benzoni, Juliette
Catherine Legoix series (2)
Seger, Maura
Calvert trilogy (3)
Catherine and a time for love
Benzoni, Juliette
Catherine Legoix series (5)
Catherine and Arnaud
Benzoni, Juliette
Catherine Legoix series (4)
Catherine de Medici
Plaidy, Jean
Catherine de Medici trilogy (3)
Catherine goes to school
Lloyd, Joanna
Catherine series (1)
Catherine, head of the house
Lloyd, Joanna
Catherine series (2)
Catherine of Calais
De la Pasture, Elizabeth
Catherine of Calais series (1)
Catherine-Wheel
Wentworth, Patricia
Miss Maud Silver series (17)
Catherine's child
De la Pasture, Elizabeth
Catherine of Calais series (2)
Catherine's proxy
Hamlin, Myra Sawyer
Nan series (4)
Cathie runs wild
Lyon, Elinor
Ian and Sovra series (5)
Catholic
Plante, David
Francoeur family series (5)
Cathouse
Ing, Dean
Man-Kzin wars series (5)
Cathouse Canyon
Gentry, Buck
Eli Holten series (14)
Cathouse kitten
Fletcher, Dirk
Spur McCoy series (9)
Cathy and Carl and the sea horse mystery
Johnston, Dorothy Grunbock
Wagon train series (5)
Cathy and carl captured
Johnston, Dorothy Grunbock
Wagon train series (2)
Cathy and Carl join the gold rush
Johnston, Dorothy Grunbock
Wagon train series (3)
Cathy and carl of the covered wagon
Johnston, Dorothy Grunbock
Wagon train series (1)
Cathy and Carl ride the pony express
Johnston, Dorothy Grunbock
Wagon train series (6)
Cathy and Carl shipwrecked
Johnston, Dorothy Grunbock
Wagon train series (4)
Cathy and company and Bumper the bully
Schertle, Alice
Cathy and Company series (2)
Cathy and Company and Hank the horse
Schertle, Alice
Cathy and Company series (5)
Cathy and Company and mean Mister Meeker
Schertle, Alice
Cathy and Company series (3)
Cathy and Company and the green ghost
Schertle, Alice
Cathy and Company series (1)
Cathy and Company and the noisy neighbor
Schertle, Alice
Cathy and Company series (4)
Cathy and the beautiful people
Woolley, Catherine
Cathy Leonard series (6)
Cathy at home
Mitchell, Yvonne
Cathy series (2)
Cathy at the crossroads
Faber, Nancy Weingarten
Cathy series (1)
Cathy away
Mitchell, Yvonne
Cathy series (1)
Cathy Leonard calling
Woolley, Catherine
Cathy Leonard series (3)
Cathy uncovers a secret
Woolley, Catherine
Cathy Leonard series (7)
Cathy's little sister
Woolley, Catherine
Cathy Leonard series (4)
Cathy's secret kingdom
Faber, Nancy Weingarten
Cathy series (2)
Catilini's riddle
Saylor, Steven
Roma sub rosa series (3)
Catnap
Douglas, Carole Nelson
Midnight Louie series (1)
Catnapped!
Gordons
Undercover Cat series (3)
Catriona
Stevenson, Robert Louis
David Balfour series (2)
Cat's ABC
Nichols, Beverley
Cat series (1)
Cats' adventures with car thieves
Cass, Joan Evelyn
Cats series (4)
Cats and people
Lockridge, Frances
Cats series (1)
Cats and their women
Cohen, Barbara
Animals and their women series (2)
Cat's cake
Fowler, Richard
Cat series (2)
Cat's car
Fowler, Richard
Cat series (1)
Cat's claw
Olsen, D B
Lieutenant Stephen Mayhew series (4)
Rachel and Jennifer Murdock series (4)
Yarbro, Chelsea Quinn
Charlie Spotted Moon series (4)
Cat's cradle
Curzon, Clare
Superintendent Mike Yeadings and Sergeant Angus Mott series (7)
Cat's cradle murder
Barry, Jerome
Chick Varney series (2)
Cats don't bark
Dalgleish, Joan
Clarence series (1)
Cats don't need coffins
Olsen, D B
Lieutenant Stephen Mayhew series (7)
Rachel and Jennifer Murdock series (7)
Cats don't smile
Olsen, D B
Rachel and Jennifer Murdock series (6)
Cat's-eye
Aveline, Claude
Suite Policiere series (1)
Cat's eye
Freeman, Richard Austin
Doctor John Evelyn Thorndyke series (10)
Jackson, Marian J A
Miss Abigail Patience Danforth series (3)
Cat's gambit
Gadallah, Leslie
Cat's pawn series (2)
Cats go to market
Cass, Joan Evelyn
Cats series (3)
Cat's got your teeth again
Unger, Jim
Herman series (17)
Cats have no lord
Shetterly, Will
Kevin Fikkan series (1)
Cats have tall shadows
Olsen, D B
Rachel and Jennifer Murdock series (8)
Cats in May
Tovey, Doreen
Cats series (2)
Cats in the belfry
Tovey, Doreen
Cats series (1)
Cats in the coffee
Fussey, Joyce
Yorkshire farm series (4)
Cat's meow
Campbell, Robert Wright
Jimmy Flannery series (5)
Cats of Castle Mountain
Buckholtz, Eileen
Magic micro adventure series (4)
Cat's paw
Janson, Hank
Hank Janson series (246)
Lincoln, Natalie Sumner
Inspector Mitchell series (5)
Pronzini, Bill
Private Eye series (10)
Scarlett, Roger
Inspector Kane series (3)
Cats paw
Vinge, Joan Dennison
Psion series (2)
Cat's pawn
Gadallah, Leslie
Cat's pawn series (1)
Cats prowl at night
Fair, A A
Bertha Cool and Donald Lam series (8)
Cat's whiskers
Bailey, Henry Christopher
Mister Reggie Fortune series (19)
Cat's XYZ
Nichols, Beverley
Cat series (2)
Catseye
Norton, Andre
Arzor series (2)
Dipple trilogy (1)
Catskill eagle
Parker, Robert Brown
Spenser series (12)
Catspaw
Carroll, John Richard
Don Bartholomew series (1)
Murray, Andrew
Sexton Blake series (43)
Stuart, Anne
Catspaw series (1)
Vinge, Joan Dennison
Psion series (2)
Catspaw for murder
Olsen, D B
Lieutenant Stephen Mayhew series (5)
Rachel and Jennifer Murdock series (3)
Catspaw II
Stuart, Anne
Catspaw series (2)
Catt out of the bag
Witting, Clifford
Inspector Charlton series (4)
Cattle baron
Ladd, Justin
Abilene series (12)
Slade, Jack
Lassiter series (22)
Cattle cars
Chandler, Edna Walker
Tom Logan series (7)
Cattletown war
Hardin, J D
Raider and Doc series (52)
Catty Atkins
Kelland, Clarence Budington
Catty Atkins series (1)
Catty Atkins, bandmaster
Kelland, Clarence Budington
Catty Atkins series (5)
Catty Atkins, financier
Kelland, Clarence Budington
Catty Atkins series (4)
Catty Atkins, riverman
Kelland, Clarence Budington
Catty Atkins series (2)
Catty Atkins, sailorman
Kelland, Clarence Budington
Catty Atkins series (3)
Catwatching
Morris, Desmond
Watching series (4)
Catweazle
Carpenter, Richard
Catweazle series (1)
Catweazle and the magic zodiac
Carpenter, Richard
Catweazle series (2)
Catwings
Le Guin, Ursula Kroeber
Catwings series (1)
Catwings return
Le Guin, Ursula Kroeber
Catwings series (2)
Caught at last!
Donovan, Dick
Dick Donovan series (2)
Caught bird
McKimmie, Christopher
Magic day series (4)
Caught by revolution
Sava, George
Peter Slavine series (2)
Caught dead
Halliday, Brett
Michael Shayne series (65)
Caught dead in Philadelphia
Roberts, Gillian
Amanda Pepper series (1)
Caught in a whirlpool
Carter, Nicholas
Nicholas Carter series (472)
Caught in crystal
Wrede, Patricia Collins
Lyra trilogy (3)
Caught in the act
Lee, John Darrell
Brian Douglas series (1)
Nixon, Joan Lowery
Orphan train quintet (2)
Saunders, Susan
Bad News Bunny series (5)
Caught in the birdlime
Parrish, Frank
Dan Mallett series (7)
Caught in the middle
Pascal, Francine
Sweet Valley High series (42)
Caught in the moving mountains
Skurzynski, Gloria
Mountain west series (3)
Caught in the net
Gaboriau, Emile
Monsieur Lecoq series (4)
Caught in the spider's web
Home-Gall, Edward Reginald
Human Bat series (1)
Caught in the toils
Carter, Nicholas
Nicholas Carter series (14)
Caulder's badge
Knott, William Cecil
Vengeance Seeker series (5)
Cauldron of blood
Kessler, Leo
Wotan series (15)
Cauldron of fear
Dever, Joe
Lone Wolf series (9)
Cauldron of Hell
Carter, Nick
Nick Carter series (153)
Cauldron of plenty
Taylor, Keith
Danans trilogy (2)
Cause and effect
McInerny, Ralph
Andrew Broom series (1)
Cause for a killing
Wainwright, John
Northern Police series (22)
Pewter series (5)
Cause for alarm
Ambler, Eric
Andreas and Tamara Valeshoff series (2)
Cause for malice
Hurt, Freda Mary
Inspector Herbert Broom series (7)
Cause of death
Underwood, Michael
Superintendent Simon Manton series (7)
Cause of the screaming
Elias, David
Nell Bartlett series (1)
Cautionary tales for children
Belloc, Hilaire
Cautionary tales series (1)
Cautious assassin
Orgill, Douglas
William Mallett series (2)
Cautious overshoes
Scherf, Margaret
Reverend Martin Buell series (4)
Cautley conundrum
Fielding, A
Inspector Pointer series (15)
Cautley mystery
Fielding, A
Inspector Pointer series (15)
Cavalier
Hunter, Joan
Rupert of the Rhine series (2)

Cavalier case
Fraser, Antonia
Jemima Shore series (7)
Cavalier Conquest
Gray, Berkeley
Norman Conquest series (14)
Cavalier in white
Muller, Marcia
Joanna Stark series (1)
Cavalier of the night
Armstrong, Raymond
J Rockingham Stone series (2)
Cavalier woman
Hunter, Joan
Rupert of the Rhine series (1)
Cavalier's corpse
Du Bois, Theodora
Anne and Jeffrey McNeill series (18)
Cavalier's cup
Dickson, Carter
Sir Henry Merrivale series (23)
Cavalry life
Winter, John Strange
Bootles series (1)
Cavalryman
Sinclair, Harold
American Civil War series (2)
Cavanaugh's island
Carrington, G A
Marcus Cavanaugh series (2)
Cave
Church, Richard
Tomahawk Club series (1)
Cave-in!
Dixon, Franklin W
Hardy boys series (78)
Cave in the mountains
Jayne, R H
War whoop series (4)
Cave men, new and old
Casteret, Norbert
Under the earth series (3)
Cave of bats
Macleod, Robert
Talos Cord series (2)
Cave of death
Sharpe, Jon
Trailsman series (91)
Cave of the beast
Goscinny, Rene
Twelve tasks of Asterix series (7)
Cave of the Chinese skeletons
Seward, Jack
Curt Stone series (1)
Cave of the master
Syvertsen, Ryder
Mystic rebel series (5)
Cave of time
Packard, Edward
Choose your own adventure series (1)
Cave twins
Perkins, Lucy Fitch
Twin series (6)
Cavender's Balkan quest
Tokson, Elliot
Alec Cavender series (2)
Cavendish chronicles
Douglas, Kathryn
Cavendish series (1)
Cavendish pride
Douglas, Kathryn
Cavendish series (1)
Cavendish Square
Douglas, Kathryn
Cavendish series (1)
Cavendish way
Douglas, Kathryn
Cavendish series (1)
Cavern of destiny
Aronin, Ben
Raphael Drale series (2)
Cavern of doom
Meretzky, S Eric
Zork series (3)
Thorne, Ramsay
Captain Gringo series (18)
Cavern of horror
Rotsler, William
Goonies series (2)
Cavern of the damned
Steele, Curtis
James Christopher series (5)
Cavern of the phantoms
Stine, Robert Lawrence
Wizards, warlocks and you series (13)
Caverns
O'Donnell, Kevin
Journeys of McGill Feighan series (1)
Caverns of Kalte
Dever, Joe
Lone Wolf series (3)
Caverns of Mornas
Brightfield, Richard
Escape from the Kingdom of Frome series (3)
Caverns of the moon
Moore, Patrick
Robin North and Rex Redmayne series (5)
Caverns of the snow witch
Livingstone, Ian
Fighting fantasy gamebook series (9)
Caves of Androzani
Dicks, Terrance
Doctor Who series (92)
Caves of death
Norwood, Victor George Charles
Jacare series (2)
Caves of Drach
Walters, Hugh
Chris Godfrey series (17)
Caves of fear
Blaine, John
Rick Brant series (8)
Caves of fire and ice
Murphy, Shirley Rousseau
Children of Ynell series (4)
Caves of Hercules
Croft-Cooke, Rupert
Sensual life series (22)
Caves of ice
Lees-Milne, James
Ancestral voices series (3)
Caves of Klydor
Hill, Douglas
ColSec trilogy (2)
Caves of madness
Moore, Wallace
Balzan of the cat people trilogy (2)
Caves of Reglathium
Sirota, Mike
Dannus series (3)
Caves of Segada
Aikman, Anthony
Boyet Rhodes series (1)
Caves of steel
Asimov, Isaac
Elijah Baley series (1)
Robot series (2)
Border, Rosemary
Elijah Baley series (4)
Caves of terror
Mundy, Talbot
Athelstan King series (3)
Caves of the Druufs
Mahr, Kurt
Perry Rhodan series (72)
Caviar to kill
McCall, K T
Johnny Buchanan series (16)
Caxtons
Lytton, Edward George Earle Lytton Bulwer-Lytton
Real and the ideal trilogy (1)
Caxton's challenge
Harnett, Cynthia
Fifteenth century London series (3)
Cay
Taylor, Theodore
Cay series (2)
Cease firing
Johnston, Mary
American Civil War trilogy (2)
Cease upon the midnight
Troy, Simon
Inspector Smith series (8)
Ceb
Nott, Loraine
Ceb Barnes series (1)
Cecil
Gore, Catherine Grace
Cecil series (1)
Cecil, a peer
Gore, Catherine Grace
Cecil series (2)
Cecil Rosse
Lewis, Harriet
Edith Trevor series (2)
Cecile
Constant, Benjamin
Adolphe series (2)
Duhamel, Georges
Pasquier series (7)
Cecile among the Pasquiers
Duhamel, Georges
Pasquier series (8)
Cecily Parsley's nursery rhymes
Potter, Beatrix
Peter Rabbit verse series (2)
Cedar tree
Hardwick, Michael
Cedar tree trilogy (1)
Cedar's boy
Meader, Stephen Warren
Cedar series (2)
Cedeno, Rose, Bonds and Fish
Gutman, Bill
At bat series (2)
Cedro County crisis
Grover, Marshall
Larry and Stretch series (266)
Celebrated cases of Dick Tracy, 1931-1951
Gould, Chester
Dick Tracy cartoon series (2)
Celebrating life
Drucker, Malka
Jewish holidays series (6)
Celebration!
Ross, Dana Fuller
Wagons West series (24)
Celebrity circus
Maxwell, Elsa
Celebrity series (2)
Celery stalks at midnight
Howe, James
Bunnicula series (3)
Celestial hit list
Ingrid, Charles
Sand wars series (3)
Celestial omnibus
Bramah, Ernest
Kai Lung series (1)
Celestial steam locomotive
Coney, Michael Greatrex
Greataway series (1)
Celestial toymaker
Davis, Gerry
Doctor Who series (111)
Celestine decorates her house
Chica, Marcel
Celestine series (1)
Celestine goes to the market
Chica, Marcel
Celestine series (2)
Celestine high in the sky
Chica, Marcel
Celestine series (4)
Celestine to the rescue
Chica, Marcel
Celestine series (3)
Celia and her friends
Brunner, Ethel
Celia series (1)
Celia once again
Brunner, Ethel
Celia series (3)
Celia's fantastic voyage
Brunner, Ethel
Celia series (4)
Celia's house
Stevenson, Dorothy Emily
Ryddelton series (1)
Celibates
Balzac, Honore de
Scenes of provincial life series (4)
Celibates' Club
Zangwill, Israel
Celibates' Club series (2)
Cell 2455, death row
Chessman, Caryl
Death row series (1)
Cell car fifty four
Fox, James M
Jerry Long and Chuck Conley series (2)
Cellini Smith, detective
Reeves, Robert
Cellini Smith series (3)
Celluloid kid
Jeier, Thomas
Matt Bishop series (2)
Celtic fairy tales
Jacobs, Joseph
Celtic fairy tales series (1)
Celtic fairy tales series (2)
Celtic knotwork
Birt, David
Saxons and Vikings series (13)
Celtic realms
Birt, David
Saxons and Vikings series (3)
Cemetary Jones and the Tombstone war
Cox, William Robert
Cemetery Jones series (5)
Cemetery first stop!
Hume, David
Mick Cardby series (12)
Cemetery Jones
Cox, William Robert
Cemetery Jones series (1)
Cemetery Jones and the dancing guns
Cox, William Robert
Cemetery Jones series (3)
Cemetery Jones and the gunslingers
Cox, William Robert
Cemetery Jones series (4)
Cemetery Jones and the Maverick Kid
Cox, William Robert
Cemetery Jones series (2)
Cenotaph Road
Vardeman, Robert Edward
Cenotaph Road series (1)
Centaur Aisle
Anthony, Piers
Xanth series (4)
Centaur conspiracy
Stevens, Carl
Christian Daguerre series (1)
Centenary at Jalna
De la Roche, Mazo
Whiteoak series (16)
Centennial summer
Idell, Albert Edward
Rogers family series (2)
Center of attention
Pascal, Francine
Sweet Valley twins series (18)
Center of the circle
Wylie, Jonathan
Servants of Ark trilogy (2)
Center stage
Bernard, Elizabeth
Satin slippers series (2)
Central Line
Binchy, Maeve
London transports series (1)
Centre cannot hold
Stableford, Brian Michael
Asgard series (3)
Centre holds
Storey, Anthony
Second Coming trilogy (2)
Centre of the circle
Wylie, Jonathan
Servants of Ark trilogy (2)
Centres of ritual
Evans, Stuart
Windmill Hill series (1)
Centrifugal rickshaw dancer
Watkins, William John
Legrange League series (1)
Centurians
Byrne, Stuart James
Star Man series (2)
Centurion
De Hartog, Jan
Captain Martinus Harinxma trilogy (3)
Rice, Peter
Renegade legion series (2)
Centurions
Larteguy, Jean
Algerian series (1)
Centurion's son
Rutley, Cecily Marianne
Children of other days series (5)
Century of scarlet
Zilahy, Lajos
Dukay family series (3)
Century of the surgeon
Thorwald, Jurgen
Century of the surgeon series (1)
Cerberus, a wolf in the fold
Chalker, Jack Laurence
Four Lords of the Diamond series (2)
Cerberus murders
Quest, Rodney
Peter Quentin series (1)
Cereals
Owen, Dilys
Mister Munch series (2)
Ceremonial time
Mitchell, John Hanson
Scratch Flat series (1)
Ceremony
Cook, Glen
Darkwar trilogy (3)
Parker, Robert Brown
Spenser series (9)
Ceremony in Lone Tree
Morris, Wright
Lone Tree series (5)
Ceremony of innocence
Dean, S F X
Professor Neil Kelly series (4)
Highwater, Jamake
Ghost horse quartet (2)
Martin, David
Sean McCart series (2)
Certain blindness
Lewis, Royston
Eric Ward series (1)
Certain blood
Ahern, Jerry
Dan Track series (6)
Certain courage
Cooper, Gordon
Kate Bassett series (3)
Certain Doctor Thorndyke
Freeman, Richard Austin
Doctor John Evelyn Thorndyke series (16)
Certain hour
Cabell, James Branch
Dom Manuel and his descendants series (14)
Certain people of importance
Norris, Kathleen
Crabtree family series (1)
Certain sleep
Reilly, Helen
Inspector Christopher McKee series (30)
Certified check
Carter, Nicholas
Nicholas Carter series (149)
Certified insane
Armour, R Coutts
Sexton Blake series (317)
Cerulean storm
Denning, Troy
Prism pentad series (5)
Chain
Wellman, Paul Iselin
Jericho series (2)
Chain five mystery
Dengler, Sandy
Daniel Tremain series (2)
Chain gang kill
Ledd, Paul
Shelter Morgan series (3)
Chain murder
Soutar, Andrew
Phineas Spinnet series (9)
Chain murders
Richmond, Philip
Duke Renny series (4)
Chain of attack
DeWeese, Gene
Star trek series (32)
Chain of clues
Carter, Nicholas
Nicholas Carter series (224)
Chain of command
Blacker, Irwin Robert
General Le Grande and GENOPS series (2)
Randle, Kevin
Jefferson's war series (6)
Chain of death
Grant, Maxwell
Shadow series (58)
Chain of evidence
Carter, Nicholas
Nicholas Carter series (94)
Wells, Carolyn
Fleming Stone series (3)
Chain of violence
Egan, Lesley
Jesse Falkenstein series (13)
Macdonnell, James Edmond
Captain Peter Bentley series (45)
Chain reaction
Ralston, Gilbert Alexander
Dakota series (5)
Chainbearer
Cooper, James Fenimore
Littlepage manuscript trilogy (2)
Chained crocodile
Whitaker, Beryl
John Abbot series (3)
Chained reaction
Murphy, Warren Burton
Destroyer series (34)
Chaining the lady
Anthony, Piers
Cluster series (2)
Chains
Lee, Howard
Kung Fu series (2)
Chains of fate
Belle, Pamela
Heron family series (2)
Chains of love
Oldenbourg, Zoe
Paris series (2)
Chains of rage
Lascaux, Simon
Ebony masters series (1)
Chair for my mother
Williams, Vera Baker
Something special series (1)
Chair-lift
Clements, Eileen Helen
Alister Woodhead series (5)

Chair of the boulevard
Merrick, Leonard
Parisian series (4)
Chalet diabolique
Coffman, Virginia
Lucifer Cove series (5)
Chalet girl from Kenya
Brent-Dyer, Elinor Mary
Chalet School series (33)
Chalet girls in camp
Brent-Dyer, Elinor Mary
Chalet School series (8)
Chalet of the devil
Coffman, Virginia
Lucifer Cove series (5)
Chalet School and Barbara
Brent-Dyer, Elinor Mary
Chalet School series (30)
Chalet School and Jo
Brent-Dyer, Elinor Mary
Chalet School series (7)
Chalet School and Richenda
Brent-Dyer, Elinor Mary
Chalet School series (40)
Chalet School and the island
Brent-Dyer, Elinor Mary
Chalet School series (21)
Chalet School and the Lintons
Brent-Dyer, Elinor Mary
Chalet School series (10)
Chalet School at war
Brent-Dyer, Elinor Mary
Chalet School series (15)
Chalet School does it again
Brent-Dyer, Elinor Mary
Chalet School series (31)
Chalet School fete
Brent-Dyer, Elinor Mary
Chalet School series (35)
Chalet School goes to it
Brent-Dyer, Elinor Mary
Chalet School series (15)
Chalet School in exile
Brent-Dyer, Elinor Mary
Chalet School series (14)
Chalet School in the Oberland
Brent-Dyer, Elinor Mary
Chalet School series (26)
Chalet School reunion
Brent-Dyer, Elinor Mary
Chalet School series (50)
Chalet School triplets
Brent-Dyer, Elinor Mary
Chalet School series (49)
Chalet School wins the trick
Brent-Dyer, Elinor Mary
Chalet School series (46)
Chalice
Baker, Donna
Glassmakers series (3)
Chalice and the sword
Raymond, Ernest
London gallery series (12)
Chalice caper
Mackenzie, Donald
Harry Chalice and Crying Eddie series (3)
Chalk gets in your eyes
Balaam
Chalk series (2)
Chalk in my hair
Balaam
Chalk series (1)
Challenge
Ahern, Jerry
Defender series (11)
Bottome, Phyllis
Search trilogy (2)
Collins, Warwick
Challenge series (1)
Counsel, George
Land in need series (1)
Leyland, Eric
Rip Randall series (1)
Sapper
Bulldog Drummond series (10)
Ronald Standish series (6)
Timms, Edward Vivian
Australian saga series (5)
Whited, Charles
Spirit of America series (1)
Challenge Blue Mask!
Morton, Anthony
Baron series (6)
Challenge for Doctor Jane
McElfresh, Adeline
Doctor Jane series (6)
Challenge for the Chalet School
Brent-Dyer, Elinor Mary
Chalet School series (55)
Challenge for the Dreamer
Duncan, William Murdoch
Superintendent Donald Reamer series (8)
Challenge for the Picaroon
Cassells, John
Ludovic Saxon series (10)
Challenge for the Poppies
Middleton, Ivy Florence Emily
Poppies series (2)
Challenge in the dark
Leeson, Robert
Demon bike rider series (2)
Challenge met
Ingrid, Charles
Sand wars series (6)
Challenge of Smoke Wade
Hogan, Robert Jasper
Smoke Wade series (1)
Challenge of the clans
Flint, Kenneth Covey
Finn McCumhal series (1)
Challenge of the Magi
Smith, Mark
Duelmaster series (1)
Challenge of the north
Hendryx, James Beardsley
Corporal Downey series (3)
Challenge of the Seventh Carrier
Albano, Peter
Seventh Carrier series (9)
Challenge of the Trumpalar
Bernard-Waite, Judy
Trumpalar series (2)
Challenge of the unknown
Darlton, Clark
Perry Rhodan series (32)
Challenge of the war, 1914-1916
Gilbert, Martin
Winston S Churchill series (3)
Challenge of the wolf knight
Stine, Robert Lawrence
Wizards, warlocks and you series (7)
Challenge of the yukon
Snell, Leroy
Northwest stories series (5)
Challenge the guilty
Grover, Marshall
Nevada Jim series (32)
Challenge the legend
Grover, Marshall
Larry and Stretch series (397)
Challenge to adventure
Atkinson, Mary Evelyn
Lockett family series (7)
Challenge to Dracula
Lory, Robert
Dracula horror series (9)
Challenge to the Brydons
Fidler, Kathleen
Brydon family series (17)
Challenge to the Four
Cross, Mark
Daphne Wrayne and her Four Adjusters series (11)
Challenging heights
Hennessy, Max
Dicken Quinney trilogy (2)
Chambered tomb
Hunt, Charlotte
Doctor Paul Holton series (6)
Chameleon
Keeler, Harry Stephen
Mysterious Mister I series (2)
Kienzle, William Xavier
Father Robert Koesler series (13)
Chameleon Corps, and other shape changers
Goulart, Ron
Ben Jolson series (2)
Chameleon course
Seaman, Donald
Sydenham series (1)
Chameleon kill
Quinn, John
Rod Gavin series (5)
Chamois murder
Wills, Cecil Melville
Geoffrey Boscobell series (5)
Champ cars
Wilkinson, Sylvia
World of racing series (8)
Champagne and a gardener
Morison, Betty Jane
Elizabeth Lamb Worthington series (1)
Champagne for one
Stout, Rex
Nero Wolfe and Archie Goodwin series (30)
Champagne girls
Barclay, Tessa
Tramont family series (2)
Champagne killer
Pentecost, Hugh
Julian Quist series (2)
Champdoce mystery
Gaboriau, Emile
Monsieur Lecoq series (4)
Champion of Garathorm
Moorcock, Michael
Chronicles of Castle Brass series (2)
Champion of Garathorn
Moorcock, Michael
Erekose series (3)
Champion of the King
Lane, Jane
Stuart series (9)
Champion of the last battle
Adams, Robert
Horseclans series (11)
Champion's calamity
Coles, P C J
Champion series (3)
Champion's chariot
Coles, P C J
Champion series (2)
Champion's folly
Coles, P C J
Champion series (1)
Champions of Putnam Hall
Winfield, Arthur M
Putnam Hall series (3)
Champions of the gods
Lord, Jeffrey
Richard Blade series (21)
Champions of the Sidhe
Flint, Kenneth Covey
Sidhe Lugh series (2)
Championship ball
Bee, Clair
Chip Hilton series (2)
Championship crime
Brandon, John Gordon
Sexton Blake series (788)
Championship game
Hughes, Dean
Angel Park All-Stars series (8)
Championship teams of the NFL
Berger, Phil
National Football League series (1)
Chance
Conrad, Joseph
Lord Jim series (3)
Tanner, Clay
Chance Sharpe series (1)
Chance acquaintance
Howells, William Dean
Mister and Mrs March series (2)
Chance acquaintances
Gee, Herbert Leslie
Friendly series (8)
Chance discovery
Carter, Nicholas
Nicholas Carter series (25)
Chance for himself
Trowbridge, John Townsend
Jack Hazard series (2)
Chance marriage
Gaboriau, Emile
Marriage of adventure series (1)
Chance of a lifetime
Hunt, Angela Elwell
Cassie Perkins series (8)
Chance of treasure
Patchett, Mary Elwyn
Brevitt series (1)
Chance the winds of fortune
McBain, Laurie
Sabrina Verrick series (2)
Chance to die
Black, Lionel
Emma Greaves series (1)
Chance to kill
Shannon, Dell
Lieutenant Luis Mendoza series (13)
Chance to love
Bernard, Elizabeth
Satin slippers series (9)
Chance to poison
Bromley, Gordon
Inspector Severn series (2)
Chance to win
Dubrovin, Vivian
Saddle up series (2)
Chancellor
Verne, Jules
J R Kazallon series (1)
Chances
Collins, Jackie
Santangelo family series (1)
Chandler heritage
Haas, Ben
Chandler family series (1)
Chandler policy
Disney, Doris Miles
Jeff Dimarco series (8)
Chane
Gant, Norman
Chane series (1)
Chaney edge
Jacks, T J
Chaney brothers series (2)
Change at Maythorn
Trease, Geoffrey
Mike and Sandra series (2)
Change-child
Curry, Jane Louise
Abaloc series (2)
Change for the worse
Lemarchand, Elizabeth
Superintendent Tom Pollard series (11)
Change from mutton
Scott, Mary
New Zealand life series (5)
Change of command
Whitman, Sidney Edgerton
Captain Cullah Burnett series (2)
Change of heart
Aks, Patricia
Two by two series (3)
Lowell, Anne Hunter
Sorority girls series (7)
Change of hearts
Cooney, Linda A
Couples series (1)
Change of jungles
Smeeton, Miles
Hills and jungles series (2)
Change signals
Barbour, Ralph Henry
Yardley Hall series (5)
Change war
Leiber, Fritz
Changewar series (2)
Changed face
Craig, Thurlow
Lieutenant Bunjy Hearne series (3)
Changeling
Carr, Philippa
Daughters of England series (15)
Leigh, Stephen
Robots and aliens series (1)
McKenney, Kenneth
Changeling trilogy (2)
Murray, Andrew
Sexton Blake series (138)
Zelazny, Roger
Changeling series (1)
Changeling earth
Saberhagen, Fred
Chup trilogy (3)
Changeling of Monte Lucio
Needham, Violet
Windri series (2)
Changeling queen
Hamilton, Julia
Habsburg series (1)
Changer's moon
Clayton, Jo
Duel of sorcery trilogy (3)
Changes
Dickinson, Peter
Changes trilogy (3)
Changes and chances
Nevinson, Henry Woodd
Changes and chances series (1)
Changes at Dowbiggins
Vipont, Elfrida
Dowbiggins series (3)
Changes for Felicity
Tripp, Valerie
Felicity series (5)
Changes for Kirsten
Shaw, Janet
Kirsten series (5)
Changes for Molly
Tripp, Valerie
Molly series (5)
Changes for Samantha
Tripp, Valerie
Samantha series (5)
Changes for the Chalet School
Brent-Dyer, Elinor Mary
Chalet School series (28)
Changes trilogy
Dickinson, Peter
Changes trilogy (3)
Changewar
Leiber, Fritz
Changewar series (2)
Changing
Armstrong, F W
Changing series (1)
Changing city
Muller, Jorg
Changing environment series (2)
Changing countryside
Muller, Jorg
Changing environment series (1)
Changing land
Zelazny, Roger
Dilvish the Damned trilogy (2)
Changing loves
Weber, Judith
Cheerleaders series (36)
Changing partners
Bernard, Elizabeth
Satin slippers series (4)
Cooper, M E
Couples series (13)
Changing places
Lodge, David
Rummidge University series (1)
Changing tide
Brooke, Carol
Marshall family series (2)
Changing wind
Coldsmith, Don
Spanish bit super series (1)
Channel million
Collins, Gilbert
Hugh Carding series (3)
Channel's destiny
Lorrah, Jean
Sime-Gen series (5)
Channing affair
Dark, Rex
Bartholomew Dane series (4)
Channings
Wood, Ellen
Channings series (1)
Chant
Cross, David
Chant series (1)
Chant of the vanishing race
Crowley, Carl Campbell
Nine winds series (5)
Chantal
Lorrimer, Claire
Mavreen trilogy (3)
Chanticleer's muffled crow
Dean, Amber
Albie Harris series (2)
Chantry guild
Dickson, Gordon Rupert
Bleys quartet (3)
Chantry Guild
Dickson, Gordon Rupert
Dorsai series (9)
Chanur's homecoming
Cherryh, Carolyn Janice
Alliance-Union series (10)
Chanur series (4)
Chanur's venture
Cherryh, Carolyn Janice
Alliance-Union series (8)
Chanur series (2)
Chaos and order
Donaldson, Stephen Reeder
Gap series (4)
Chaos comes to Chivvy Chase
Curtis, Philip
Mister Browser series (10)
Chaos in Lagrangia
Reynolds, Mack
Lagrangia series (3)
Rex Bader series (5)
Chaos kid
Peters, David
Psi-Man series (4)
Chaos makers
Bennett, Dorothy
Allardyce series (1)
Chaos mode
Anthony, Piers
Mode series (3)
Chaos obscure
Salvatore, Robert Anthony
Cleric quintet (5)
Chaos of crime
Shannon, Dell
Lieutenant Luis Mendoza series (36)
Chaos weapon
Kapp, Colin
Chaos series (2)
Chaparral marauders
Curry, Tom
Masked Rider and Blue Hawk series (26)
Chaperon
Williamson, Charles Norris
Motoring series (4)

Chaplet of pearls
Yonge, Charlotte Mary
Rebaumont series (1)
Chapter-House Dune
Herbert, Frank
Dune series (6)
Chapter of accidents
Rees, Goronwy
Sensations and accidents series (2)
Chapter of echoes
Armitage, Aileen
Chapter series (2)
Chapter of innocence
Armitage, Aileen
Chapter series (1)
Chapter of shadows
Armitage, Aileen
Chapter series (3)
Charabanc mystery
Burton, Miles
Inspector Arnold and Desmond Merrion series (8)
Characteristics
Mitchell, Silas Weir
Doctor North series (1)
Charg, monster
Grant, Maxwell
Shadow series (57)
Charge is murder
Cumberland, Marten
Saturnin Dax series (20)
Charge is treason
Baker, William Howard
Richard Quintain series (15)
Charge it
Bacheller, Irving
Socrates Potter trilogy (2)
Charge of cowardice
Macneil, Duncan
James Ogilvie series (10)
Charing Cross
Rayner, Claire
Performers series (7)
Chariots of fire
Rusoff, Garry
Chariots of fire trilogy (1)
Chariots of Ra
Bulmer, Kenneth
Keys to the dimensions series (7)
Chariots of the gods
Daniken, Erich von
Unsolved mysteries series (1)
Chariots of the Lord
Hocking, Joseph
Religious movements series (6)
Charitas
Crowley, Carl Campbell
Nine winds series (6)
Charity child
Lindsay, Paula
Mark Rendle series (1)
Charity, Colorado
Yarbro, Chelsea Quinn
Sheriff Jason Russell series (2)
Charity ends at home
Watson, Colin
Inspector Purbright series (5)
Charity fund mystery
Chester, Gilbert
Sexton Blake series (922)
Charlemagne's champion
Van Asten, Gail
Charlemagne's champion series (1)
Charles arriving
Pardoe, Margot
Western Highlands series (1)
Charles Fort never mentioned wombats
DeWeese, Gene
Joe Karns series (3)
Charles II
Plaidy, Jean
Charles II trilogy (3)
Stuart series (4)
Charles, King of England, 1600-1637
Wingfield-Stratford, Esme
Charles I trilogy (1)
Charles stories, and others from Listen with mother
Ainsworth, Ruth
Charles series (1)
Charleston
Ripley, Alexandra
Charleston series (1)
Charleston knife's back in town
Dennis, Ralph
Jim Hardman series (2)
Charley gets the picture
Spencer, John
Charley Case series (2)
Charley Malarkey and the belly-button machine
Kennedy, William
Charley Malarkey series (1)
Charley Malarkey and the singing moose
Kennedy, William
Charley Malarkey series (2)
Charley starts from scratch
Jackson, Jesse
Charley Moss series (3)
Charlie and the chocolate factory
Dahl, Roald
Charlie Bucket series (1)
Charlie and the great glass elevator
Dahl, Roald
Charlie Bucket series (2)
Charlie and the iceman
Eller, John
Charlie Hope series (1)
Charlie Bell
Kellogg, Elijah
Elm Island series (2)
Charlie Chan and the curse of the Dragon Queen
Avallone, Michael
Charlie Chan series (8)
Charlie Chan carries on
Biggers, Earl Derr
Charlie Chan series (5)
Charlie Chan returns
Lynds, Dennis
Charlie Chan series (7)
Charlie Clown
Campbell, Rod
Little people series (1)
Charlie Clown at the circus
Brook, Judy
Charlie Clown series (2)
Charlie Clown at the seaside
Brook, Judy
Charlie Clown series (1)
Charlie Codman's cruise
Alger, Horatio
Campaign trilogy (3)
Charlie don't live here any more
Sherman, David
Night fighters series (6)
Charlie, Emma and Alberic
Greaves, Margaret
Alberic the dragon series (1)
Charlie, Emma and dragons to the rescue
Greaves, Margaret
Alberic the dragon series (4)
Charlie, Emma and the dragon family
Greaves, Margaret
Alberic the dragon series (2)
Charlie, Emma and the school dragon
Greaves, Margaret
Alberic the dragon series (3)
Charlie Lewis plays for time
Kemp, Gene
Cricklepit School series (3)
Charlie M
Freemantle, Brian
Charlie Muffin series (1)
Charlie Meadows
Hoban, Russell
Ponders series (3)
Charlie moon and the big bonanza bust up
Hughes, Shirley
Charlie Moon series (2)
Charlie Muffin
Freemantle, Brian
Charlie Muffin series (1)
Charlie Muffin and Russian Rose
Freemantle, Brian
Charlie Muffin series (6)
Charlie Muffin San
Freemantle, Brian
Charlie Muffin series (8)
Charlie Muffin, U.S.A.
Freemantle, Brian
Charlie Muffin series (4)
Charlie Muffin's Uncle Sam
Freemantle, Brian
Charlie Muffin series (4)
Charlie Parr's outlaw posse
Cody, Stone
Five Mavericks series (6)
Charlie sent me
Brown, Carter
Larry Baker series (1)
Charlie's Angels
Franklin, Max
Charlie's Angels series (1)
Charlie's apprentice
Freemantle, Brian
Charlie Muffin series (11)
Charlotte
Harvey, Caroline
Legacy of love trilogy (1)
Mackenzie, Kathleen
Starke sisters series (2)
Charlotte Cheetham, master of disaster
Holmes, Barbara Ware
Charlotte Cheetham trilogy (1)
Charlotte Lowenskold
Lagerlof, Selma
Ring of the Lowenskolds trilogy (2)
Charlotte Morel
Lodi, Maria
Charlotte Morel series (1)
Charlotte Shakespeare and Annie the great
Holmes, Barbara Ware
Charlotte Cheetham trilogy (3)
Charlotte sometimes
Farmer, Penelope
Charlotte and Emma Makepeace series (3)
Charlotte the starlet
Holmes, Barbara Ware
Charlotte Cheetham trilogy (2)
Charlotte's inheritance
Braddon, Mary Elizabeth
Valentine Hawkehurst series (2)
Charm bracelet
Dickinson, Mary Anne
Charm bracelet series (1)
Charm of hours
Skelton, Peter
Edwin series (1)
Charm school mystery
Pascal, Francine
Sweet Valley twins series (64)
Charmed life
Jones, Diana Wynne
Chrestomanci series (1)
Charmian, Lady Vibart
Farnol, Jeffery
Vibart series (2)
Charming
Polcovar, Jane
Dark forces series (15)
Charming murder
Shay, Frank
Dan Doner series (1)
Charon, a dragon at the gate
Chalker, Jack Laurence
Four Lords of the Diamond series (3)
Charred witness
Coxe, George Harmon
Jack Fenner series (4)
Kent Murdock series (7)
Charteris mystery
Fielding, A
Inspector Pointer series (2)
Chasch
Vance, Jack
Tschai series (1)
Chase
Peel, John
Doctor Who series (140)
Smith, Lisa J
Forbidden game trilogy (2)
Chase for millions
Carter, Nicholas
Nicholas Carter series (363)
Chase in the dark
Carter, Nicholas
Nicholas Carter series (220)
Chase into space
Mohan, Kim
Cyborg commando trilogy (2)
Chase of the golden plate
Futrelle, Jacques
Professor Augustus S F X Van Dusen series (1)
Chase the storm
Tyler, Alison
Jennifer Heath series (2)
Chase the sun
Tyler, Alison
Jennifer Heath series (3)
Chase the wind
Taylor, Janelle
Cordell series (2)
Thompson, Ernest Victor
Retallick family series (1)
Tyler, Alison
Jennifer Heath series (1)
Chased across the Pampas
Stratemeyer, Edward L
Pan-American series (6)
Chasing away the devil
Cooper, Susan Rogers
Milton Kovak series (4)
Chasing eights
Collins, Michael
Dan Fortune series (16)
Chasing the dragon
Kelly, Susan
Liz Connors and Jack Lingemann series (3)
Chasing the setting sun
Langley, John Prentice
Aviation series (7)
Chasm of doom
Dever, Joe
Lone Wolf series (4)
Chasms of malice
Sharp, Luke
Fighting fantasy gamebook series (30)
Chateau holiday
Mantle, Winifred
Lesters and Westcotts series (3)
Chatelaine
Lorrimer, Claire
Rochford trilogy (1)
Chatterbox
Cosgrove, Stephen Edward
Whimsy storybooks series (5)
Chattering gods
Crawley, Rayburn
Ned Shackleton series (2)
Chauffeur and the chaperon
Williamson, Charles Norris
Motoring series (4)
Chauffeur driven pyre
Hedges, Joseph
John Stark series (10)
Chautauqua girls at home
Pansy
Chautauqua series (1)
Cheap day return
Cresswell, Helen
Mike series (7)
Cheap dream
Leigh, Robert
Sam Carroll series (1)
Cheaper by the dozen
Gilbreth, Frank Bunker
Gilbreth family series (1)
Cheat
Walsh, Bill
Fishing series (2)
Cheater
Stine, Robert Lawrence
Fear Street series (18)
Cheaters
Gilman, George G
Adam Steele series (31)
Wallace, Edgar
Inspector Elk series (1)
Mister T B Smith series (1)
Cheating
Sarasin, Jennifer
Cheerleaders series (11)
Cheating butcher
Stein, Aaron Marc
Matt Erridge series (18)
Cheating heart
Keene, Carolyn
Nancy Drew files series (99)
Cheating hearts
Keene, Carolyn
River Heights series (7)
Cheating to win
Pascal, Francine
Sweet Valley High series (77)
Check number 777
Carter, Nicholas
Nicholas Carter series (23)
Check two one three four
Ellis, Edward Sylvester
Arthur Helmuth series (2)
Check-up
Oxenbury, Helen
First picture books series (4)
Check your character
Staton, Knofel L
Check series (2)
Check your commitment
Staton, Knofel L
Check series (7)
Check your discipleship
Staton, Knofel L
Check series (3)
Check your homelife
Staton, Knofel L
Check series (6)
Check your life with Christ
Staton, Knofel L
Check series (4)
Check your lifestyle
Staton, Knofel L
Check series (1)
Check your morality
Staton, Knofel L
Check series (5)
Check your relationships
Staton, Knofel L
Check series (8)
Checkerboard caper
Morris, John
Commissioner Robin McKay series (3)
Checking 'em out and sizing 'em up
Berry, Joy
Ready-set-grow series (23)
Checkmate
Dunnett, Dorothy
Francis Crawford of Lymond series (6)
Moffat, Bill
Press Gang series (3)
Stokes, Arthur M
Sherlock Holmes drama series (17)
Checkmate and stalemate
Learmonth, David
Silas Wortenheimer series (2)
Checkmate by the colonel
Griswold, George
Mister Groode series (2)
Checkmate for China
Osborne, Geoffrey
James Dingle and Glyn Jones series (4)
Checkmate in Rio
Carter, Nick
Nick Carter series (3)
Checkmate kill
Quinn, John
Rod Gavin series (6)
Checkmate to murder
Lorac, E C R
Inspector Macdonald series (25)
Checkmate universe
Mahr, Kurt
Perry Rhodan series (74)
Checkmated scoundrel
Carter, Nicholas
Nicholas Carter series (123)
Checkpoint Charlie
De Villiers, Gerard
Malko Linge series (12)
Cheer for the dead
Colter, Eli
Pat Campbell series (2)
Cheer up, little Noddy!
Blyton, Enid
Noddy series (20)
Cheerful day
Fairbrother, Nan
Cheerful day series (2)
Cheerfulness breaks in
Thirkell, Angela
Barsetshire series (9)
Cheese
Elsschot, Willem
Laarmans series (3)
Cheese from a mousetrap
Fox, James M
John and Suzy Marshall series (4)
Cheesemaker mice and the giant
Williamson, Roger
Romany Rat trilogy (1)
Cheetah chase
McQuillan, Karin
Jazz Jasper series (3)
Cheetah girl
Blayre, Christopher
University of Cosmopoli series (1)
Cheetahs of the Serengeti Plain
Torgersen, Don Arthur
Animal life stories series (11)
Chef
Goscinny, Rene
Twelve tasks of Asterix series (6)
Cheim manuscript
Prather, Richard Scott
Shell Scott series (34)
Chelsea and the alien invasion
Stahl, Hilda
Best friends series (14)
Chelsea and the outrageous phone bill
Stahl, Hilda
Best friends series (1)
Chelsea ghost
Hunter, Alan
Inspector George Gently series (33)
Chelsea mystery
Hamilton, Elaine
Inspector Reynolds series (3)
Chelsea Reach
Rayner, Claire
Performers series (9)
Chelsea's special gift
Stahl, Hilda
Best friends series (10)
Cheltenham Square murder
Bude, John
Inspector Meredith series (4)

Chemical warfare
Spiers, Edward Michael
Chemical warfare series (1)
Chemical weaponry
Spiers, Edward Michael
Chemical warfare series (2)
Chenango Pass
Shappiro, Herbert
Mustang Marshal series (3)
Cherbourg mystery
Maske, John
Clarence E Hemingway series (1)
Jeremy Flack series (2)
Cherchez la femme
Graeme, Bruce
Inspector Auguste Jantry series (2)
Cheri
Colette, Sidonie Gabrielle
Cheri series (1)
Cheri-Bibi and Cecily
Leroux, Gaston
Cheri-Bibi series (2)
Cheri-Bibi, mystery man
Leroux, Gaston
Cheri-Bibi series (3)
Cherished enemy
Veryan, Patricia
Golden chronicles series (5)
Cherished wives
Anand, Valerie
Bridges over time series (5)
Chernevog
Cherryh, Carolyn Janice
Rusalka series (2)
Cherokee
Porter, Donald Clayton
White Indian series (10)
Cherokee Bat and the goat guys
Block, Francesca Lia
Weetzie Bat series (3)
Cherokee diamondback
Reese, John
Jefferson Hewitt series (7)
Cherokee Lighthorse
McCarthy, Gary
Ballou family series (2)
Cherokee outlet
Harvey, John Barton
Wes Hart series (1)
Cherry
Van der Essen, Anne
Yok-yok series (12)
Cherry Ames, army nurse
Wells, Helen
Cherry Ames series (3)
Cherry Ames at Hilton Hospital
Wells, Helen
Cherry Ames series (20)
Cherry Ames at Spencer
Tatham, Julie
Cherry Ames series (10)
Cherry Ames, boarding-school nurse
Wells, Helen
Cherry Ames series (17)
Cherry Ames, camp nurse
Wells, Helen
Cherry Ames series (19)
Cherry Ames, chief nurse
Wells, Helen
Cherry Ames series (4)
Cherry Ames, clinic nurse
Tatham, Julie
Cherry Ames series (13)
Cherry Ames, companion nurse
Wells, Helen
Cherry Ames series (24)
Cherry Ames, country doctor's nurse
Tatham, Julie
Cherry Ames series (16)
Cherry Ames, cruise nurse
Wells, Helen
Cherry Ames series (9)
Cherry Ames, department store nurse
Wells, Helen
Cherry Ames series (18)
Cherry Ames, dude ranch nurse
Tatham, Julie
Cherry Ames series (14)
Cherry Ames, flight nurse
Wells, Helen
Cherry Ames series (5)
Cherry Ames, island nurse
Wells, Helen
Cherry Ames series (21)
Cherry Ames, jungle nurse
Wells, Helen
Cherry Ames series (25)
Cherry Ames, mountaineer nurse
Tatham, Julie
Cherry Ames series (12)
Cherry Ames, night supervisor
Tatham, Julie
Cherry Ames series (11)
Cherry Ames, private duty nurse
Wells, Helen
Cherry Ames series (7)
Cherry Ames, rest home nurse
Tatham, Julie
Cherry Ames series (15)
Cherry Ames, rural nurse
Wells, Helen
Cherry Ames series (22)
Cherry Ames, senior nurse
Wells, Helen
Cherry Ames series (2)
Cherry Ames, soldiers' nurse
Wells, Helen
Cherry Ames series (6)
Cherry Ames, staff nurse
Wells, Helen
Cherry Ames series (23)
Cherry Ames, student nurse
Wells, Helen
Cherry Ames series (1)
Cherry Ames, veterans' nurse
Wells, Helen
Cherry Ames series (6)
Cherry Ames, visiting nurse
Wells, Helen
Cherry Ames series (8)
Cherry Ann and the dragon horse
Coatsworth, Elizabeth
Once-upon-a-time-in-America series (7)
Cherry blossom corpse
Barnard, Robert
Charlie Peace series (2)
Superintendent Perry Trethowan series (5)
Cherry-boy body bag
Cain, Jonathan
Saigon commandos series (4)
Cherry harvest
Clements, Eileen Helen
Alister Woodhead series (2)
Cherry sisters
Green, Michael
Coarse plays series (2)
Cherry-stones
Adams, William
Charlton School series (1)
Cherry time at Bullerby
Lindgren, Astrid
Bullerby series (2)
Cherry tree
Bell, Adrian
Country life series (3)
Tangye, Derek
Minack chronicles series (15)
Vendrell, Carme Sole
Victor and Maria series (2)
Cherrys and company
Scott, Will
Cherrys series (2)
Cherrys and the blue balloon
Scott, Will
Cherrys series (14)
Cherrys and the double arrow
Scott, Will
Cherrys series (6)
Cherrys and the galleon
Scott, Will
Cherrys series (5)
Cherrys and the Pringles
Scott, Will
Cherrys series (4)
Cherrys and the silent rooom
Scott, Will
Cherrys series (10)
Cherrys by the sea
Scott, Will
Cherrys series (3)
Cherrys famous case
Scott, Will
Cherrys series (11)
Cherrys in the snow
Scott, Will
Cherrys series (13)
Cherrys' mystery holiday
Scott, Will
Cherrys series (9)
Cherrys of River House
Scott, Will
Cherrys series (1)
Cherrys on Indoor Island
Scott, Will
Cherrys series (7)
Cherrys on Zig-Zag Trail
Scott, Will
Cherrys series (8)
Cherrys to the rescue
Scott, Will
Cherrys series (12)
Cheshire cat's eye
Muller, Marcia
Sharon McCone series (3)
Chessboard queen
Newman, Sharan
Guinevere trilogy (2)
Chessboard spies
Davison, Geoffrey
Stephen Fletcher series (3)
Chessmaster
Carter, Nick
Nick Carter series (155)
Chessmen of doom
Bellairs, John
Johnny Dixon series (7)
Chessmen of Mars
Burroughs, Edgar Rice
Martian series (5)
Chest of Chu Chan
Grant, Maxwell
Shadow series (255)
Chest with a secret
Bremond d'Ars, Yvonne de
Journal of an antique dealer series (3)
Chester Cricket's new home
Selden, George
Chester Cricket series (5)
Chester Cricket's pigeon ride
Selden, George
Chester Cricket series (4)
Chesterfield gold
Pilkington, Roger
Branxome family series (2)
Chestnut gold
Leitch, Patricia
Jinny series (9)
Chestnut spider
Nimmo, Jenny
Snow spider trilogy (3)
Chet at Harvard
Stokes, Roy Eliot
University series (2)
Chevalier
Dumas, Alexandre
Marie Antoinette series (5)
Harrod-Eagles, Cynthia
Morland family series (7)
Chevalier de Maison Rouge
Dumas, Alexandre
Marie Antoinette series (5)
Chevalier d'Harmental
Dumas, Alexandre
Regency trilogy (1)
Cheviot Chase
Tranter, Nigel Godwin
Hawick series (1)
Cheyenne
Mitchum, Hank
Stage coach station series (3)
Riefe, A R
Fortunes west series (2)
Cheyenne at Dull Knife Pass
Denver, Lee
Cheyenne Jones series (11)
Cheyenne blood storm
Cunningham, Chet
Pony soldiers series (4)
Cheyenne bloodbath
Logan, Jake
John Slocum series (90)
Cheyenne bucks the law
Denver, Lee
Cheyenne Jones series (6)
Cheyenne captive
Gentry, Georgina
Cimarron series (1)
Panorama of the old West series (1)
Cheyenne caress
Gentry, Georgina
Panorama of the old West series (6)
Cheyenne crossing
Sharpe, Jon
Trailsman series (145)
Cheyenne dreams
Lederer, Paul Joseph
Indian heritage series (4)
Cheyenne fraud
Hardin, J D
Raider series (8)
Cheyenne gold
Baxter, George Owen
Red Hawk series (3)
Cheyenne Jones, the maverick marshal
Denver, Lee
Cheyenne Jones series (7)
Cheyenne justice
Harte, Bryce
Slate Creed series (9)
Cheyenne manhunt
Wayne, Les
Arvada Jones series (2)
Cheyenne moon
Longtree, Warren T
Ruff Justice series (15)
Cheyenne payoff
Cunningham, Chet
Agent Brad Spear series (1)
Cheyenne pays in lead
Denver, Lee
Cheyenne Jones series (4)
Cheyenne princess
Gentry, Georgina
Cimarron series (2)
Panorama of the old West series (2)
Cheyenne showdown
Ellis, Wesley
Lone Star series (100)
Cheyenne splendor
Gentry, Georgina
Cimarron series (3)
Panorama of the old West series (12)
Cheyenne swings a wide loop
Denver, Lee
Cheyenne Jones series (2)
Cheyenne trap
Chisholm, Matt
Joe Blade series (10)
Cheyenne vengeance
Flynn, Jackson
Gunsmoke series (4)
Gentry, Buck
Eli Holten series (4)
Cheyenne winter
Wheeler, Richard Seabrook
Rocky Mountain Company series (3)
Cheyenne's sixgun justice
Denver, Lee
Cheyenne Jones series (8)
Cheyenne's trail to Perdition
Denver, Lee
Cheyenne Jones series (9)
Cheyenne's two-gun shoot-out
Denver, Lee
Cheyenne Jones series (10)
Cheyne mystery
Crofts, Freeman Wills
Inspector Joseph French series (2)
Cheyney's law
Cosgrave, Patrick
Colonel Allen Cheyney series (1)
Chez James
Heaton, Rose Henniker
James Montgomerie series (2)
Chi-Lo the admiral
Macgregor, Reginald James
Chi-Lo series (1)
Chi-Lo the general
Macgregor, Reginald James
Chi-Lo series (2)
Chi Ming and the jade earring
Gladstone, Josephine
Chi Ming series (3)
Chi Ming and the lion dance
Marquand, Josephine
Chi Ming series (2)
Chi Ming and the tiger kitten
Marquand, Josephine
Chi Ming series (1)
Chiaroscuro
John, Augustus
Fragments of autobiography series (1)
Chic Chic spy
Tralins, Sandor Robert
Lee Crosley series (1)
Chicago and the cat
Koontz, Robin Michal
Chicago and the cat series (1)
Chicago assault
Ramm, Carl
James Hawker series (3)
Chicago chick
Janson, Hank
Hank Janson series (119)
Chicago conversion
Proctor, George Wyatt
V series (4)
Chicago crime
Grant, Maxwell
Shadow series (155)
Chicago deadline
Mazzaro, Ed
Undercover series (3)
Chicago deathwinds
Winski, Norman
Dirk Spencer series (1)
Chicago run
Robbins, David
Endworld series (27)
Chicago showdown
Ellis, Wesley
Lone Star series (126)
Chicago six-guns
Sharpe, Jon
Canyon O'Grady series (24)
Chicago slaughter
Barry, Mike
Burton Wulff series (6)
Chicago wipeout
Pendleton, Don
Mack Bolan series (8)
Chicago woman
Saber, Robert O
Carl Good series (3)
Chicken Little Jane
Ritchie, Lily Munsel
Chicken Little Jane series (1)
Chicken Little Jane comes to town
Ritchie, Lily Munsel
Chicken Little Jane series (4)
Chicken Little Jane in the Rockies
Ritchie, Lily Munsel
Chicken Little Jane series (5)
Chicken Little Jane on the Big John
Ritchie, Lily Munsel
Chicken Little Jane series (2)
Chicken pox strikes again
Marzollo, Jean
Thirty nine kids on the block series (5)
Chicken soup with barley
Wesker, Arnold
Chicken soup trilogy (1)
Chicken trek
Manes, Stephen
Oscar Noodleman trilogy (3)
Chickenhawk
Mason, Robert Caverly
Chickenhawk series (1)
Chickens are restless
Larson, Gary
Far Side series (14)
Chicot, the jester
Dumas, Alexandre
Valois series (6)
Chief
Lipsyte, Roger
Contender trilogy (3)
Chief commanda hi-jack
Barnes, Michael
Just north series (2)
Chief constable
Gregg, Cecil Freeman
Inspector Cuthbert Higgins series (33)
Chief Inspector McLean
Goodchild, George
Inspector McLean series (5)
Chief Inspector's daughter
Radley, Sheila
Chief Inspector Douglas Quantrill series (2)
Chief Inspector's statement
Procter, Maurice
Superintendent Philip Hunter series (1)
Chief Joseph
Dugan, Bill
War chiefs series (2)
Chief of the school
Adams, Henry Cadwallader
Nethercourt series (1)
Chief Tallon and the S.O.R.
Ball, John
Jack Tallon series (3)
Chief witness
Adams, Herbert
Major Roger Bennion series (10)
Chief's daughter
Sutcliff, Rosemary
Heather, oak and olive trilogy (1)
Chieftain
Norman, John
Telnarian histories series (1)
Chieftain and the scout
Ellis, Edward Sylvester
War chief series (3)
Child accursed
Balzac, Honore de
Philosophic studies series (8)
Child across the sky
Carroll, Jonathan
Bones series (3)
Child called Freedom
Peters, Maureen
Malone family trilogy (3)
Child called Noah
Greenfeld, Josh
Noah series (1)
Child in Chile
Howe, Bea
Childhood series (2)

Child in the forest
Foley, Winifred
Forest series (1)
Child killer
Hamill, Edson T
Joe Ryker series (6)
Child of all nations
Toer, Pramoedya Ananta
All nations series (2)
Child of gentle courage
Shears, Sarah
Courage series (1)
Child of God
Sanford, Doris
Advanced theology for very tiny persons series (1)
Child of good fortune
De Haan, Tom
Brynchmachrye series (2)
Child of Norman's End
Raymond, Ernest
London gallery series (7)
Child of pleasure
Annunzio, Gabriele d'
Romances of the rose trilogy (2)
Child of Saturn
Edgerton, Teresa
Green lion trilogy (1)
Child of silence
Padgett, Abigail
Bo Bradley series (1)
Child of storm
Haggard, Henry Rider
Allan Quatermain series (3)
Zulu series (3)
Child of the Austerlitz
Adam, Paul
Time of life series (2)
Child of the grove
Huff, Tanya
Wizard crystal series (1)
Child of the island glen
Kellogg, Elijah
Pleasant Cove series (4)
Child of the northern spring
Woolley, Persia
Guinevere trilogy (1)
Child of tomorrow
Bartholomew, Barbara
Time keeper trilogy (2)
Child proof
Lewin, Michael Zinn
Albert Samson series (10)
Childermass
Lewis, Wyndham
Human age trilogy (1)
Childhood
Carossa, Hans
Childhood, boyhood and youth trilogy (1)
Gorky, Maxim
Childhood to university trilogy (1)
Myrdal, Jan
Another world series (1)
Owen, Harold
Journey from obscurity trilogy (1)
Savory, Teo
Stonecroft series (2)
Tolstoi, Leo Nikolaevich
Nicholas Irtenyev trilogy (1)
Childhood and schooldays
Paustovsky, Konstantin Georgievich
Story of a life series (1)
Childhood in Egypt
Barber, Anne Viccars
Wickham series (2)
Childhood is hell
Groening, Matt
Life in hell series (4)
Childhood of Helen
Goode, Evelyn
Polly-Dear, Rod and Small series (2)
Childhood story of Christy Brown
Brown, Christy
Cerebral palsy series (1)
Childhood's loves
Romains, Jules
Men of goodwill series (3)
Children
Fedorova, Nina
Klimova family series (2)
Children at Happy House
Blyton, Enid
Happy House series (1)
Children at Moyinish
Hamilton, Esme
Speedy series (4)
Children at Sherburne House
Douglas, Amanda Minnie
Sherburne series (6)
Children at Windylaw Farm
Hardman, Diana
Windylaw Farm series (1)
Children grow up
Seymour, Beatrice Kean
Malling-Gaywood family series (3)
Children in art
Richmond, Robin
Story in a picture series (1)
Children in the bush
Dallas, Ruth
Jean, Robbie, Sophie and Helen series (1)
Children in the house
Fairbrother, Nan
Cheerful day series (1)
Children in the little old Red House
Douglas, Amanda Minnie
Little Red House children series (1)
Children in the wood
Smith, Naomi Royde
Rockmouth and Rockhead township trilogy (1)
Children of Abraham
Halter, Marek
Jewish family series (2)
Children of ancient Persia
Rutley, Cecily Marianne
Children of other days series (18)
Children of ancient Rome
Rutley, Cecily Marianne
Children of other days series (17)
Children of Anthi
Blakeney, Jay D
Anthi series (1)
Children of Arabic
Belden, David
Galactic connectivity series (1)
Children of Ashgaroth
Ford, Richard
Faradawn trilogy (3)
Children of Bedford Court
Le Baron, Grace
Janet trilogy (3)
Children of Cape Horn
Swale, Rosie
Rosie Darling series (2)
Children of Chaucer's day
Rutley, Cecily Marianne
Children of other days series (9)
Children of despair
Creasey, John
Doctor Palfrey series (15)
Children of Dune
Herbert, Frank
Dune series (3)
Paul Atreides trilogy (3)
Children of Flux and Anchor
Chalker, Jack Laurence
Soul rider series (5)
Children of Georgian days
Rutley, Cecily Marianne
Children of other days series (13)
Children of Green Knowe
Boston, Lucy Maria
Green Knowe series (1)
Children of Hamlin
Carter, Carmen
Star trek, the next generation series (3)
Children of Hastur
Bradley, Marion Zimmer
Darkover series (14)
Children of hate
Creasey, John
Doctor Palfrey series (15)
Children of Kaywana
Mittelholzer, Edgar
Kaywana series (1)
Children of Kaywana, part 2
Mittelholzer, Edgar
Kaywana series (2)
Children of Llyr
Walton, Evangeline
Mabinogion series (2)
Children of men
James, Phyllis Dorothy
Commander Adam Dalgliesh series (10)
Phillpotts, Eden
Dartmoor series (2)
Children of Morrow
Hoover, Helen Mary
Morrow series (1)
Children of Mu
Churchward, James
Mu series (2)
Children of Noisy Village
Lindgren, Astrid
Bullerby series (2)
Children of perestroika
Adelman, Deborah
Children of Perestroika series (1)
Children of perestroika come of age
Adelman, Deborah
Children of Perestroika series (2)
Children of promise
Tedrow, Thomas L
Days of Laura Ingalls Wilder series (2)
Children of Rhanna
Fraser, Christine Marion
Rhanna series (3)
Children of Ruth
Sutton, Marvin
Children of Ruth series (1)
Children of Sanchez
Lewis, Oscar
Sanchez family series (1)
Children of Shallowford
Williamson, Henry
Shallowford to Norfolk series (2)
Children of Stuart days
Rutley, Cecily Marianne
Children of other days series (12)
Children of the age
Hamsun, Knut
Segelfoss Town series (1)
Children of the albatross
Nin, Anais
Cities of the interior series (2)
Children of the Arbat
Rybakov, Anatoli
Arbat trilogy (1)
Children of the blood
Sagara, Michele M
Sundered series (2)
Children of the castle
Rutley, Cecily Marianne
Children of other days series (7)
Children of the Crescent
Melinsky, Renate
Crescent children series (1)
Children of the dead end
Macgill, Patrick
Moleskin Joe series (1)
Children of the downs
Rutley, Cecily Marianne
Children of other days series (2)
Children of the drake
Knaak, Richard Allen
Origin of Dragonrealm series (2)
Children of the forge
McCaughren, Tom
Irish history series (4)
Children of the fox
Walsh, Jill Paton
Children of the fox trilogy (3)
Children of the ghetto
Zangwill, Israel
Ghetto series (1)
Children of the great lake
Trezise, Percy
Ngali and Mayli series (2)
Children of the lake villages
Rutley, Cecily Marianne
Children of other days series (4)
Children of the Lens
Smith, Edward Elmer
Lensman series (6)
Children of the light
De Hartog, Jan
Peaceable kingdom series (1)
Children of the Lion
Danielson, Peter
Children of the Lion series (1)
Children of the maker
Babbitt, Lucy Cullyford
Melde series (2)
Children of the mist
Knox, Bill
Inspector Colin Thane and Phil Moss series (11)
Phillpotts, Eden
Dartmoor series (1)
Children of the night
Lackey, Mercedes
Diana Tregarde series (2)
Children of the Nile
Rutley, Cecily Marianne
Children of other days series (16)
Children of the north
Power, Maurice S
Children of the north series (3)
Children of the river
Lavender, William
Hargrave journal series (1)
Children of the spring
Wiat, Philippa
Grey family series (2)
Children of the storm
Tallis, Robyn
Planet builders series (7)
Children of the sun
Kelsey, Franklyn
James Armitage trilogy (2)
Children of the void
Dexter, William
Denis Grafton series (2)
Children of The Warren
Sindall, Marjorie Aylwynn
Warren series (1)
Children of the Wild West
Freedman, Russell
Wild West series (1)
Children of the wind
Harris, Geraldine
Seven citadels series (2)
Children of their time
Glanfield, Jenny
Hotel Quadriga series (3)
Children of Tudor times
Rutley, Cecily Marianne
Children of other days series (11)
Children of violence
Lessing, Doris
Children of violence series (2)
Children of violence series (4)
Children of Willow Farm
Blyton, Enid
Willow Farm series (1)
Children on the King's Highway
Brown, Charles
John Bunyan series (2)
Children on the night
Kring, Michael K
Space mavericks series (2)
Children on the top floor
Rhoades, Nina
Winifred series (2)
Children on Troublemaker Street
Lindgren, Astrid
Marten family series (1)
Children's children
Mosco, Maisie
Almonds and raisins trilogy (3)
Children's chronicle
Stuart, Dorothy Margaret
Clavengers series (1)
Children's crusade
Drumm, D B
Traveler series (11)
Children's friend
Evans, Adelaide Bee
Bible pictures and stories series (4)
Children's hour
Pournelle, Jerry
Man-Kzin wars series (5)
Children's life of the bee
Maeterlinck, Maurice
Insect life series (1)
Children's summer
Kaye-Smith, Sheila
Selina series (1)
Children's zoo
O'Donnell, Lillian
Detective Norah Mulcahaney series (7)
Child's garden of death
Forrest, Richard
Lyon and Bea Wentworth series (1)
Child's play
Hill, Reginald
Superintendent Andrew Dalziel and Sergeant Pascoe series (15)
Murphy, Warren Burton
Destroyer series (23)
Child's play 2
Costello, Matthew John
Child's play series (1)
Child's play 3
Costello, Matthew John
Child's play series (2)
Chilgoopie the Glad
Perry, Jean
News from Korea series (1)
Chill
Macdonald, Ross
Lew Archer series (12)
Sherman, Jory
Doctor Russell V Chillders series (2)
Chill factor
Axler, James
Deathlands series (15)
Stein, Aaron Marc
Matt Erridge series (15)
Chill of a corpse
Peters, Geoffrey
Inspector Trevor Nichols and Sergeant Tom Burton series (7)
Chill rain in January
Wright, Laurali R
Sergeant Karl Alberg series (4)
Chiller
Boyll, Randall
Darkman series (2)
Chilling deception
Castle, Jayne
Guinevere Jones series (2)
Chilling stories from the Twilight Zone
Gibson, Walter Brown
Twilight Zone series (4)
Chimaera's copper
Anthony, Piers
Dragon series (3)
Chimmie Fadden and Mister Paul
Townsend, Edward Waterman
Chimmie Fadden series (3)
Chimmie Fadden explain, Major Max expounds
Townsend, Edward Waterman
Chimmie Fadden series (2)
Chimmie Fadden, Major Max, and other stories
Townsend, Edward Waterman
Chimmie Fadden series (1)
Chimney corner stories
Blyton, Enid
Chimney corner stories series (1)
Chimney cottage
Atkinson, Mary Evelyn
Lockett family series (11)
Chimney witch Christmas
Whitehead, Victoria
Chimney witch series (3)
Chimney witches
Whitehead, Victoria
Chimney witch series (1)
Chimneys of Green Knowe
Boston, Lucy Maria
Green Knowe series (2)
Chimnmey witch chase
Whitehead, Victoria
Chimney witch series (2)
China awake
Payne, Robert
Chinese diaries series (2)
China bloodhunt
Kilgore, Axel
They call me the Mercenary series (16)
China bride
Scott, Michael William
Rakehell dynasty series (2)
China command
Wilson, Gar
Phoenix Force series (42)
China doll
Carter, Nick
Nick Carter series (2)
Ledd, Paul
Shelter Morgan series (4)
China flyer
Hill, Porter
Captain Adam Horne series (3)
China governess
Allingham, Margery
Albert Campion series (19)
China roundabout
Bell, Josephine
Doctor David Wintringham series (14)
Inspector Steven Mitchell series (8)
China Sea jigsaw
Catherall, Arthur
Bulldog tugboat series (7)
China Sea murders
Mason, Francis Van Wyck
Colonel Hugh North series (6)
China strike
Buchanan, Jack
M.I.A. Hunter series (16)
China town mystery
Teed, George Hamilton
Sexton Blake series (726)
China trader
Rasmussen, Albert Henry
Sea fever trilogy (2)
China, why was an army made of clay?
Brightfield, Richard
Earth inspectors series (7)
Chinaman's chance
Thomas, Ross
Artie Wu and Quincy Durant series (1)
China's crucifixion
Weale, Putnam
Wang the Ninth trilogy (3)
Chinatown chance
Cutter, Tom
Tracker series (4)
Chinatown hell
Roberts, J R
Gunsmith series (27)
Chinatown justice
Longley, W B
Angel Eyes series (4)

Chinese agent
Moorcock, Michael
Jerry Cornell series (1)
Chinese Alice
Barr, Pat
Alice Greenwood series (1)
Chinese bandit
Becker, Stephen
Far East trilogy (1)
Chinese bed mysteries
Martin, Archibald Edward
Pel Pelham and Detective Linley series (2)
Chinese bell murders
Gulik, Robert van
Judge Dee series (3)
Chinese box
Martin, Robert
Ginger Pennylove series (4)
Chinese chop
Sheridan, Juanita
Lily Wu and Janice Cameron series (1)
Chinese coffin
Hedges, Joseph
John Stark series (3)
Chinese conspiracy
Rosenberger, Joseph
Death Merchant series (5)
Chinese conundrum
Manson, Will
Man called Black series (2)
Chinese diaries, 1941-1946
Payne, Robert
Chinese diaries series (2)
Chinese disks
Grant, Maxwell
Shadow series (65)
Chinese doll
Tucker, Wilson
Charles Horne series (1)
Chinese Donavan
Brown, Carter
Paul Donavan series (3)
Chinese dragons
Montgomery, Raymond A
Choose your own adventure series (109)
Chinese fire drill
Wolfe, Michael
Michael Keefe series (3)
Chinese gold murders
Gulik, Robert van
Judge Dee series (4)
Chinese goose
Robertson, Helen
Inspector Lathom Dynes series (3)
Chinese gunmen
Roberts, J R
Gunsmith series (2)
Chinese hammer
Harvester, Simon
Asia in turmoil series (9)
Heron Murmur series (1)
Chinese jar
Hume, Fergus
Octavius Fanks series (2)
Chinese keyhole
Himmel, Richard
Johnny Maguire series (3)
Chinese kiss
Montague, J J
Black Swan series (1)
Chinese lake murders
Gulik, Robert van
Judge Dee series (5)
Chinese mask
Ballinger, Bill Sanborn
Joaquin Hawks series (1)
Chinese maze murders
Gulik, Robert van
Judge Dee series (1)
Chinese nail murders
Gulik, Robert van
Judge Dee series (6)
Chinese obelisks
Gorey, Edward
Alphabet series (4)
Chinese orange mystery
Queen, Ellery
Ellery Queen series (9)
Chinese parrot
Biggers, Earl Derr
Charlie Chan series (2)
Chinese paymaster
Carter, Nick
Nick Carter series (24)
Chinese pleasure girl
Seward, Jack
Curt Stone series (5)
Chinese poison
Hackforth-Jones, Gilbert
Paul Dexter series (1)
Chinese poker
Thorne, Ernest Pollett
Major Brains Cunningham series (12)
Chinese primrose
Grant, Maxwell
Shadow series (199)
Chinese puzzle
Burton, Miles
Inspector Arnold and Desmond Merrion series (54)
Murphy, Warren Burton
Destroyer series (3)
Chinese red
Burke, Richard
Quinny Hite series (3)
Chinese roulette
Kirk, Philip
Butler series (4)
Chinese secret service
Deacon, Richard
Secret service series (3)
Chinese shawl
Wentworth, Patricia
Miss Maud Silver series (6)
Chinese spur
Sandberg, Berent
Matt Eberhart series (3)
Chinese straight
Lamb, J J
Zack Rolfe series (2)
Chinese tapestry
Grant, Maxwell
Shadow series (89)
Chinese twins
Perkins, Lucy Fitch
Twin series (24)
Chinese visitor
Eastwood, James
Anna Zordan series (1)
Chinese widow
Leasor, James
Far East series (3)
Chink in the armour
Lewis, Jack
Sexton Blake series (92)
Chinks in the curtain
Porter, Joyce
Edmund Brown series (2)
Chink's victim
Brandon, John Gordon
Sexton Blake series (789)
Chip of the Flying U
Bower, Bertha Muzzy
Flying U Ranch series (1)
Chip off the bloc
Wilson, Gar
Phoenix Force series (23)
Chipped
Steed, Neville
Peter Marklin series (3)
Chippeway captive
Risteen, H L
Red Indian series (1)
Chips and Jessie
Hughes, Shirley
Chips series (1)
Chips and the Black Moth
Brown, Roy Frederick
Chips Regan series (4)
Chips and the crossword gang
Brown, Roy Frederick
Chips Regan series (2)
Chips and the river rat
Brown, Roy Frederick
Chips Regan series (3)
Chipstead of the Lone Hand
Horler, Sydney
Bunny Chipstead series (2)
Chiseller
Johnson, Duff
Gutsy Morgan series (2)
Chisholm Trail
Compton, Ralph
Trail drive series (3)
Chisholm trail
Dawson, Clay
Long Rider series (19)
Chita's Christmas tree
Howard, Elizabeth Fitzgerald
Chita series (1)
Chitty-Chitty-Bang-Bang
Burke, John Frederick
Chitty-Chitty-Bang-Bang series (3)
Chitty-Chitty-Bang-Bang, the magical car, adventure number 1
Fleming, Ian
Chitty-Chitty-Bang-Bang series (1)
Chitty-Chitty-Bang-Bang, the magical car, adventure number 2
Fleming, Ian
Chitty-Chitty-Bang-Bang series (2)
Chitty-Chitty-Bang-Bang, the magical car, adventure number 3
Fleming, Ian
Chitty-Chitty-Bang-Bang series (3)
Chivalry
Cabell, James Branch
Dom Manuel and his descendants series (8)
Chiy-une
Coon, Susan
Living planet series (4)
Chloe takes control
Matthewman, Phyllis
Daneswood series (1)
Chloris and the creeps
Platt, Kin
Chloris series (1)
Chloris and the freaks
Platt, Kin
Chloris series (2)
Chloris and the weirdos
Platt, Kin
Chloris series (3)
Chocky
Wyndham, John
Chocky series (1)
Chocky's challenge
Daniel, Mark
Chocky series (2)
Chocolate cake caper
Christian, Mary Blount
Goosehill Gang series (4)
Chocolate-covered clue
Hope, Laura Lee
New Bobbsey twins series (10)
Chocolate horse
Bryant, Bonnie
Saddle Club series (32)
Chocolate Max
Turk, Hanne
Max the Mouse series (16)
Chocolate mousse murders
Halliday, Fred
Stanley Delphond series (1)
Chocolate rabbit
Claret, Maria
Melissa Mouse series (2)
Chocolate war
Cormier, Robert
Chocolate war series (1)
Choctaw
Porter, Donald Clayton
White Indian series (11)
Choctaw County war
McCurtin, Peter
Sundance series (42)
Choice
Macdonald, Philip
Colonel Anthony Ruthven Gethryn series (5)
Choice of crimes
Egan, Lesley
Vic Varallo series (11)
Choice of times
Lindsay, Jack
British way series (9)
Choice of violence
Pentecost, Hugh
George Crowder series (1)
Choke chain
O'Sullivan, James Brendan
Steve Silk series (12)
Choke hold
Dixon, Franklin W
Hardy boys case files series (51)
Choke point
Taylor, Charles Doonan
Bernie Ryng series (2)
Choking peril
Townson, Hazel
Speckled panic series (2)
Chokra
Michael, John
Chokra series (1)
Chokra and Tags
Michael, John
Chokra series (2)
Choose your enemies carefully
Charrette, Robert N
Secrets of power series (2)
Choosing sides
Cooper, Ilene
Kids from Kennedy Middle School series (2)
Keene, Carolyn
Nancy Drew files series (84)
Pascal, Francine
Sweet Valley twins series (4)
Chopper
Cave, Peter
Hell's Angels series (1)
Chopper command
Helm, Eric
Scorpion Squad series (3)
Chopper cops
Mackin, Rick
Chopper cops series (1)
Chopper from the inside
Read, Mark Brandon
Chopper series (1)
Chops and gravy
Magoffin, Richard
Bushies series (2)
Chord in crimson
Gallagher, Gale
Gale Gallagher series (2)
Chores
Cosgrove, Stephen Edward
Simple folk series (3)
Chorine makes a killing
Brown, Carter
Lieutenant Al Wheeler series (4)
Chorister's cake
Mayne, William
Choir school series (2)
Chorus ending
Raymond, Ernest
London gallery series (5)
Chorus of detectives
Paul, Barbara
Enrico Caruso series (3)
Chorus to adventurers
Pocock, Roger
Frontiersman series (2)
Chosen
Avenell, Donne
Axa series (1)
Potok, Chaim
Danny Saunders and Reuven Malter series (1)
Chosen of Mida
Green, Sharon
Jalav series (3)
Chosen of the Gods
Makepeace, Joanna
Thebes series (3)
Chouans
Balzac, Honore de
Scenes of military life series (1)
Chris in trouble
Woolley, Catherine
Cathy Leonard series (5)
Chris Temple, patrol leader
Middleton, Ivy Florence Emily
Poppies series (1)
Chrismas with Angelina
Holabird, Katharine
Angelina Ballerina series (10)
Christ in Flanders
Balzac, Honore de
Philosophic studies series (2)
Christ lives on
McGloin, Joseph Thaddeus
With Him, through Him, to Him series (2)
Christ on trial
Dixon, Roger
Jesus Christ series (2)
Christ with us!
McGloin, Joseph Thaddeus
Called to love, called to serve series (3)
Christabel
Latham, Katharine Wright
Christabel series (1)
Christabel at Cleave
Hardy, Dorothy May
Christabel series (1)
Christabel in France
Latham, Katharine Wright
Christabel series (2)
Christable's Cornish adventure
Hardy, Dorothy May
Christabel series (2)
Christening quest
Scarborough, Elizabeth Ann
Argonia series (4)
Christian Marlowe's daughter
Keyes, Frances Parkinson
Marlowe family series (1)
Christie caper
Hart, Carolyn Gimpel
Annie Laurance and Max Darling series (7)
Christie, the king's servant
Walton, Catherine Augusta
Christie series (2)
Christie's home-making
Paull, Minnie E
Christie series (2)
Christie's next things
Paull, Minnie E
Christie series (1)
Christie's old organ
Walton, Catherine Augusta
Christie series (1)
Christina enchanted
Saint James, Blakely
Christina Van Bell series (12)
Christina in love
Saint James, Blakely
Christina Van Bell series (22)
Christina's awakening
Saint James, Blakely
Christina Van Bell series (30)
Christina's bliss
Saint James, Blakely
Christina Van Bell series (21)
Christina's challenge
Saint James, Blakely
Christina Van Bell series (39)
Christina's conquest
Saint James, Blakely
Christina Van Bell series (28)
Christina's craving
Saint James, Blakely
Christina Van Bell series (46)
Christina's delight
Saint James, Blakely
Christina Van Bell series (25)
Christina's desire
Saint James, Blakely
Christina Van Bell series (7)
Christina's ecstasy
Saint James, Blakely
Christina Van Bell series (18)
Christina's escapade
Saint James, Blakely
Christina Van Bell series (44)
Christina's essence
Saint James, Blakely
Christina Van Bell series (42)
Christina's fantasy
Saint James, Blakely
Christina Van Bell series (32)
Christina's favorite
Saint James, Blakely
Christina Van Bell series (37)
Christina's hunt
Saint James, Blakely
Christina Van Bell series (45)
Christina's island
Saint James, Blakely
Christina Van Bell series (24)
Christina's mystery
Saint James, Blakely
Christina Van Bell series (43)
Christina's need
Saint James, Blakely
Christina Van Bell series (33)
Christina's nights
Saint James, Blakely
Christina Van Bell series (6)
Christina's obsession
Saint James, Blakely
Christina Van Bell series (20)
Christina's paradise
Saint James, Blakely
Christina Van Bell series (36)
Christina's passion
Saint James, Blakely
Christina Van Bell series (2)
Christina's pleasure
Saint James, Blakely
Christina Van Bell series (13)
Christina's promise
Saint James, Blakely
Christina Van Bell series (16)
Christina's quest
Saint James, Blakely
Christina Van Bell series (1)
Christina's rapture
Saint James, Blakely
Christina Van Bell series (9)
Christina's search
Saint James, Blakely
Christina Van Bell series (8)
Christina's secret
Saint James, Blakely
Christina Van Bell series (34)
Christina's sensation
Saint James, Blakely
Christina Van Bell series (47)
Christina's sins
Saint James, Blakely
Christina Van Bell series (15)
Christina's surrender
Saint James, Blakely
Christina Van Bell series (10)
Christina's technique
Saint James, Blakely
Christina Van Bell series (41)
Christina's temptation
Saint James, Blakely
Christina Van Bell series (27)

Cimarron in the Cherokee Strip
Kelley, Leo Patrick
Cimarron series (4)
Cimarron on a Texas manhunt
Baines, Lew
Cimarron series (19)
Cimarron on hell's highway
Kelley, Leo Patrick
Cimarron series (11)
Cimarron on the high plains
Baines, Lew
Cimarron series (14)
Cimarron rides the outlaw trail
Kelley, Leo Patrick
Cimarron series (2)
Cimarron Rose
Dixon, Dorothy
Leather and lace series (5)
Cimbrians
Jensen, Johannes Vilhelm
Long journey trilogy (2)
Cimmaron Kid
James, Cy
Sam Spur series (1)
Cincinnati
Willoughby, Lee Davis
Americana series (1)
Cincinnati run
Robbins, David
Endworld series (19)
Cinda
Lambert, Janet
Cinda Hollister series (1)
Cinderella
McBain, Ed
Matthew Hope series (6)
Cinderella after midnight
Zackel, Fred
Michael Brennan series (2)
Cinderella goes to the morgue
Spain, Nancy
Miriam Birdseye series (3)
Cinderella sisters
Scannell, Florence
Cinderella series (1)
Cindy on Fire
Hirschfeld, Burt
Fire Island series (2)
Cindy's baby
Johnson, Stacie
Eighteen Pine Street series (9)
Cindy's sad and happy tree
Orgel, Doris
Cindy series (2)
Cindy's snowdrops
Orgel, Doris
Cindy series (1)
Cinema crime
Goyne, Richard
Sexton Blake series (755)
Cineverse cycle
Gardner, Craig Shaw
Cineverse trilogy (3)
Cingulum
Roberts, John Maddox
Cingulum trilogy (1)
Cinnamon murder
Crane, Frances
Pat and Jean Abbott series (9)
Cinnamon skin
Macdonald, John Dann
Travis McGee series (20)
Cipher detective
Morris, Anthony Paschel
Mark Magic series (3)
Circle C carries on
Rider, Brett
Circle C series (2)
Circle C moves in
Rider, Brett
Circle C series (1)
Circle, crescent, star
Dibell, Ansen
Kantmorie trilogy (2)
Circle in the water
Bowen, Marjorie
Spiritual history of Great Britain trilogy (3)
Circle K
Sabin, Edward Legrand
Bar B boys series (3)
Circle of confusion
White, Palmer
Mystery Island series (2)
Circle of danger
Alding, Peter
C.I.D. Room series (2)
Circle of darkness
Griffin, John
Richard Raven series (3)
Circle of death
Dutton, Charles Judson
Harley Manners series (5)
Grant, Maxwell
Shadow series (49)
Rennert, Maggie
Guy Silvestri series (1)
Circle of dust
Cassells, John
Superintendent Flagg series (8)
Circle of evil
Keene, Carolyn
Nancy Drew files series (18)
Circle of fire
Macdonnell, James Edmond
Dutchy Holland series (23)
Robertson, Jenny
Circle series (2)
Sadler, Mark
Paul Shaw series (4)
Circle of footprints
Keene, Carolyn
Dana girls series (6)
Circle of freedom
Cross, Mark
Daphne Wrayne and her Four Adjusters series (31)
Circle of guilt
Kingston, Charles
Inspector Wake series (3)
Circle of light
Middleton, Martin
Chronicles of the custodians series (1)
Circle of quiet
L'Engle, Madeleine
Crosswicks journals series (1)
Circle of Rowan
Darby, Catherine
Rowan family series (4)
Circle of scorpions
Carter, Nick
Nick Carter series (196)
Circle of shadows
Robertson, Jenny
Circle series (1)
Circle of squares
Turner, Bill
Detective Inspector Manson series (3)
Circle of stones
Macdonald, Shelagh
Pethi and Tini series (1)
Circle of the gods
Canning, Victor
Crimson chalice trilogy (2)
Circle Sarah drew
Barrett, Peter
Sophie, Sarah and Ben series (2)
Circle war
Maloney, Mack
Wingman series (2)
Circles of time
Rock, Phillip
Greville family trilogy (2)
Circles round a corpse
Landon, Hilary
Timothy Drewer series (2)
Circlet of oak leaves
Sutcliff, Rosemary
Heather, oak and olive trilogy (2)
Circuit
Snodgrass, Melinda Marilyn
Circuit trilogy (1)
Circuit breaker
Snodgrass, Melinda Marilyn
Circuit trilogy (2)
Circuit rider's widow
Harris, Corra
Circuit rider series (2)
Circuit rider's wife
Harris, Corra
Circuit rider series (1)
Circular evidence
Andrews, Colin
Crop circles series (1)
Circular study
Green, Anna Katharine
Amelia Butterworth series (3)
Ebenezer Gryce series (9)
Circumpolar!
Lupoff, Richard Allen
Counterearth series (1)
Circumstantial evidence
Carter, Nicholas
Nicholas Carter series (127)
Crofts, Freeman Wills
Inspector Joseph French series (21)
Circus
Ahlberg, Allan
Foldaways series (1)
Bruna, Dick
Toy box tale series (6)
Goscinny, Rene
Twelve tasks of Asterix series (12)
Levy, Muriel
Wonk series (5)
Van der Essen, Anne
Yok-yok series (8)
Circus brumby
Patchett, Mary Elwyn
Joey Meehan series (3)
Circus comes to town
Korman, Justine
Tiny Toon's adventures series (2)
Circus crime
Skene, Anthony
Sexton Blake series (769)
Circus day at Catnip Center
Frees, Harry Whittier
Petland photo tales series (4)
Circus days again
Blyton, Enid
Mister Galliano's circus series (3)
Circus down under
Spear, Diana
Circus series (2)
Circus has no home
Croft-Cooke, Rupert
Sensual life series (27)
Circus is coming
Streatfeild, Noel
Shoes series (3)
Circus locomotive
Barkan, Joanne
Circus train come aboard series (2)
Circus of adventure
Blyton, Enid
Adventure series (7)
Circus of death
Ledd, Paul
Shelter Morgan series (6)
Circus of fear
Estes, Rose
Endless quest series (10)
Circus of hells
Anderson, Poul
Sir Dominic Flandry series (7)
Circus shoes
Streatfeild, Noel
Shoes series (3)
Circus train
Chandler, Edna Walker
Tom Logan series (8)
Circus world
Longyear, Barry Brookes
Circus trilogy (2)
Citadel of chaos
Jackson, Steve
Fighting fantasy gamebook series (2)
Citadel of death
Thorne, Ramsay
Captain Gringo series (11)
Citadel of God
De Wohl, Louis
Lives of the saints series (3)
Citadel of the Autarch
Wolfe, Gene
Book of the new sun series (4)
Citadel run
Robbins, David
Endworld series (27)
Citadels on earth
Hagberg, David
Flash Gordon series (14)
Citadels under attack
Hagberg, David
Flash Gordon series (13)
Cities in flight
Blish, James
Cities in flight series (4)
Cities in space
Pournelle, Jerry
Endless frontier series (3)
Cities of salt
Munif, Abdelrahman
Cities of salt trilogy (1)
Cities of the dead
Barnes, Linda
Michael Spraggue series (4)
Cities of the interior
Nin, Anais
Cities of the interior series (5)
Cities of the plain, part one
Proust, Marcel
Remembrance of things past series (7)
Cities of the plain, part two
Proust, Marcel
Remembrance of things past series (8)
Cities of the red night
Burroughs, William Seward
Cities of the red night trilogy (1)
Citizen Bonaparte
Erckmann, Emile
Story of a peasant series (4)
Citizen Burke
Dillon, Eilis
Wild geese series (2)
Citizen Phaid
Farren, Mick
Song of Phaid the Gambler series (2)
Citizen vampire
Daniels, Les
Don Sebastien series (3)
Citizens of Mars
North, Rick
Young Astronauts series (6)
City
Gaskell, Jane
Atlan saga series (3)
Haigh, Richard
Farm series (2)
McCrone, Guy
Moorhouse family trilogy (1)
City adventures of Marmalade Jim
Sillitoe, Alan
Marmalade Jim series (1)
City and the dream
Raymond, Ernest
London gallery series (16)
City and the stars
Clarke, Arthur Charles
Fall of night series (1)
City at the edge of time
Morris, Janet Ellen
Tempus series (5)
City below
Carroll, James
Doyle brothers series (2)
City beneath the sea
Bamman, Henry A
World of adventure series (5)
City beyond the clouds
Rockwood, Roy
Great marvel series (7)
City built to music
Duke, Madelaine
Sundmans trilogy (1)
City by the sea
Doyle, Debra
Circle of magic series (3)
City called July
Engel, Howard
Benny Cooperman series (5)
City condemned to hell
Craig, Randolph
Octopus series (1)
City destroyer
Stockbridge, Grant
Richard Wentworth series (7)
City for sale
Messmann, Jon
Revenger series (5)
City in danger
Gunn, John
Peter Kent series (6)
City in darkness
Grubb, Jeff
Marvel superheroes adventure gamebooks series (1)
City in heat
Murphy, Warren Burton
Edward Razoni and William Jackson series (3)
City in the autumn stars
Moorcock, Michael
Von Bek family trilogy (3)
City in the glacier
Vardeman, Robert Edward
War of powers series (2)
City in the mist
Innes, Evan
American two thousand and forty series (3)
City in the Sahara
Verne, Jules
Barsac mission series (2)
City in the sand
French, Jackie
Children of the valley trilogy (2)
City in the stars
Appleton, Victor II
Tom Swift Junior series 2 (1)
City in the sun
Stableford, Brian Michael
Daedalus series (4)
City jitters
Fowler, Christopher
City jitters series (1)
City limits
Marino, Nick
Mike Macauley series (2)
City of a million legends
Lichtenberg, Jacqueline
Molt brother series (2)
City of a thousand suns
Delany, Samuel Ray
Fall of the towers trilogy (3)
City of apes
Murray, Andrew
Sexton Blake series (191)
City of Baraboo
Longyear, Barry Brookes
Circus trilogy (1)
City of beautiful nonsense
Thurston, Ernest Temple
John Grey series (1)
City of bells
Goudge, Elizabeth
Cathedrals series (1)
Torminster series (1)
City of blood
Hartman, Dane
Dirty Harry Callahan series (6)
City of Boston
Abbott, Jacob
Marco Paul's adventures in pursuit of knowledge series (5)
City of brass, and other Simon Ark stories
Hoch, Edward Dentinger
Simon Ark series (2)
City of crime
Grant, Maxwell
Shadow series (111)
City of crooks
Blake, Stacey
Sexton Blake series (603)
City of crystal shadow
Schmidt, Dennis
Questioner trilogy (2)
City of doom
Grant, Maxwell
Shadow series (102)
City of fear
Cameron, J D
Omega sub series (3)
Marsh, John
Ray Felton series (3)
City of flaming shadows
Stockbridge, Grant
Richard Wentworth series (4)
City of ghosts
Grant, Maxwell
Shadow series (175)
City of glass
Auster, Paul
New York trilogy (1)
Phillips, Tony
Turbo cowboys series (10)
City of gold
Young, Francis Brett
Boer War series (2)
City of gold and lead
Christopher, John
Tripods series (3)
City of gold and shadows
Peters, Ellis
Inspector George Felse series (12)
City of hawks
Gygax, Gary
Gord the Rogue series (3)
City of horrors
Bayfield, William John
Sexton Blake series (461)
City of illusions
Le Guin, Ursula Kroeber
Hain series (6)
City of libertines
Hardy, William George
Roman trilogy (1)
City of light
Macleod, Alison
Tom Vaughan series (2)
City of madness
House, Brant
Secret Agent X series (15)
City of masks
Murray, Edgar Joyce
Sexton Blake series (444)
City of New York
Abbott, Jacob
Marco Paul's adventures in pursuit of knowledge series (1)
City of shadows
Grant, Maxwell
Shadow series (166)
City of sorcery
Bradley, Marion Zimmer
Darkover series (9)

City of Spades
Macinnes, Colin
Visions of London series (1)
City of the beast
Moorcock, Michael
Warrior of Mars trilogy (1)
City of the Chasch
Vance, Jack
Tschai series (1)
City of the dawn
Allen, Hervey
Disinherited series (3)
City of the dead
Derrick, Lionel
Penetrator series (53)
City of the living dead
House, Brant
Secret Agent X series (3)
Lord, Jeffrey
Richard Blade series (26)
City of the soul
Home, Michael
Zerzura series (3)
City of the sun
Fraser, Ronald
Trout series (4)
City of thieves
Livingstone, Ian
Fighting fantasy gamebook series (5)
City of whispering stone
Chesbro, George Clark
Mongo series (2)
City on the moon
Leinster, Murray
Joe Kenmore trilogy (3)
City out of sight
Southall, Ivan
Survival series (2)
City outside the world
Carter, Lin
Mars series (3)
City solitary
Freeling, Nicolas
Henri Castang series (9)
City under the desert sands
Kaufmann, Herbert
Captain Gevert series (3)
City under the sea
Fairman, Paul Warren
Voyage to the bottom of the sea series (2)
City vagabonds
Dann, Colin
Vagabonds series (2)
Civil prisoners
Trevor, Meriol
Brentland series (2)
Luxembourg series (6)
Civil War
Birt, David
Stuarts series (4)
Civil War secret agent
Perry, Steve
Time machine series (5)
Civilian slaughter
Rouch, James
Zone series (8)
Civilian war zone
Peters, Lance
Detective Sergeant Joe Church trilogy (3)
Clachan days
Armstrong, Sybil
Clachan series (2)
Claim on Forty Mile Creek
Verne, Jules
Golden volcano series (1)
Claim to fame
Pascal, Francine
Sweet Valley twins series (23)
Claiming of Sleeping Beauty
Roquelaure, A N
Sleeping Beauty series (1)
Claire at sixteen
Pfeffer, Susan Beth
Sebastian sisters quintet (3)
Clammer
Hopkins, William John
Clammer trilogy (1)
Clammer and the submarine
Hopkins, William John
Clammer trilogy (3)
Clampdown
Butler, William Vivian
Old Ireland Yard series (3)
Clan and crown
Pournelle, Jerry
Janisseries trilogy (2)
Clan ground
Bell, Clare
Ratha series (2)
Clan of the cats
Adams, Robert
Horseclans series (18)
Clan of the cave bear
Auel, Jean Marie
Earth's children series (1)
Clancy's secret mission
Thayer, Lee
Peter Clancy series (48)
Clandestine betrothal
Ley, Alice Chetwynd
Eversley Family series (1)
Clansman
Dixon, Thomas
American Reconstruction series (2)
Clansman series (1)
Tranter, Nigel Godwin
Rob Roy Macgregor series (3)
Clap hands
Oxenbury, Helen
Big baby series (4)
Clap hands, here comes Charlie
Freemantle, Brian
Charlie Muffin series (2)
Clara in Blunderland
Lewis, Caroline
Alice in Wonderland parodies series (1)
Clara Quince
Partridge, Jenny
Oakapple Wood series (13)
Clare
Ross, James Davidson
Ross family series (2)
Clare Carson and the gold rush
Elliott, Mary
Clare Carson series (3)
Clare Carson and the runaways
Elliott, Mary
Clare Carson series (2)
Clare Carson and the sheep duffers
Elliott, Mary
Clare Carson series (4)
Clare Carson at Wilga Junction
Elliott, Mary
Clare Carson series (1)
Clare Street
Dugon, Nora
Kelly Ryan series (2)
Clarence and the burglar
Lauber, Patricia
Clarence series (4)
Clarence and the cat
Lauber, Patricia
Clarence series (5)
Clarence goes to town
Lauber, Patricia
Clarence series (2)
Clarence settles down
Dalgleish, Joan
Clarence series (2)
Clarence takes a vacation
Lauber, Patricia
Clarence series (3)
Clarence, the TV dog
Lauber, Patricia
Clarence series (1)
Clarence series (5)
Clarence turns sea dog
Lauber, Patricia
Clarence series (3)
Clarice Dyke, the femal detective
Rockwood, Harry
Donald Dyke series (3)
Clarisse's wish
Williams, Leigh Anne
Taylor House trilogy (3)
Clarkeville's battery
Lawton, Charles
Clarkeville series (1)
Clash
Barea, Arturo
Forging of a rebel trilogy (3)
Clash of cymbals
Blish, James
Cities in flight series (4)
Clash of hawks
Charles, Robert
Counter-terror series (4)
Clash of stars
Smith, Frederick Escreet
Stars series (2)
Clash of Steel
Robertson, Colin
Alan Steel series (1)
Clash of the sorcerers
Simon, Morris
Advanced dungeons and dragons adventure gamebook series (8)
Kingdom of sorcery trilogy (3)
Clash on the Rhine
Harding, Ian
Assault troop series (3)
Class act
Blake, Susan
Hawthorne College series (8)
Hollan, Linda
Annie series (2)
Wharton, Joanna
Campus fever series (7)
Class clown
Hurwitz, Johanna
Edison-Armstrong School series (1)
Class crush
Kenyon, Kate
Cedar Groves Junior High School series (2)
Class menagerie
Churchill, Jill
Jane Jeffry series (4)
Class president
Hurwitz, Johanna
Edison-Armstrong School series (2)
Class reunion
Jaffe, Rona
Reunion series (1)
Class ring
Du Jardin, Rosamond
Tobey and Midge Heydon series (2)
Class teacher
Bentley, Diana
My school series (5)
Class trip
Pascal, Francine
Sweet Valley twins super series (1)
Classical education
Cobb, Richard
Still life series (2)
Classroom and campus
Eldred, Warren L
Saint Dunstan series (3)
Clatter vengeance
Short, Agnes
Margaret Montgomery series (2)
Claude and Pepper
Gackenbach, Dick
Claude series (2)
Claude has a picnic
Gackenbach, Dick
Claude series (5)
Claude Lantier's struggle for fame
Zola, Emile
Rougon Macquart series (14)
Claude the dog
Gackenbach, Dick
Claude series (1)
Claudia
Franken, Rose
Claudia series (1)
Lewerth, Margaret
Roundtree women series (2)
Wallace, Barbara Brooks
Claudia series (1)
Claudia and David
Franken, Rose
Claudia series (2)
Claudia and Duffy
Wallace, Barbara Brooks
Claudia series (3)
Claudia and Mean Janine!
Martin, Ann Matthews
Baby-Sitters Club series (7)
Claudia and Middle School
Martin, Ann Matthews
Baby-Sitters Club series (40)
Claudia and the bad joke
Martin, Ann Matthews
Baby-Sitters Club series (19)
Claudia and the clue in the photograph
Martin, Ann Matthews
Baby-Sitters Club mystery series (16)
Claudia and the great search
Martin, Ann Matthews
Baby-Sitters Club series (33)
Claudia and the new girl
Martin, Ann Matthews
Baby-Sitters Club series (12)
Claudia and the perfect boy
Martin, Ann Matthews
Baby-Sitters Club series (71)
Claudia and the phantom phone calls
Martin, Ann Matthews
Baby-Sitters Club series (2)
Claudia and the sad good-bye
Martin, Ann Matthews
Baby-Sitters Club series (26)
Claudia, the genius of Elm Street
Martin, Ann Matthews
Baby-Sitters Club series (49)
Claudia's freind friend
Martin, Ann Matthews
Baby-Sitters Club series (63)
Claudia's India
Coates, Irene
Claudia series (2)
Claudia's war
Coates, Irene
Claudia series (1)
Claudine and Annie
Colette, Sidonie Gabrielle
Claudine series (4)
Claudine at Saint Clare's
Blyton, Enid
Saint Clare's series (5)
Claudine at school
Colette, Sidonie Gabrielle
Claudine series (1)
Claudine in Paris
Colette, Sidonie Gabrielle
Claudine series (2)
Claudine married
Colette, Sidonie Gabrielle
Claudine series (3)
Claudine's daughter
Laker, Rosalind
Easthampton trilogy (2)
Claudius the bee
Leeming, John Fishwick
Claudius the bee series (1)
Claudius the god and his wife Messalina
Graves, Robert
Claudius series (2)
Clause in the will
Graydon, William Murray
Sexton Blake series (438)
Claverton affair
Rhode, John
Doctor Lancelot Priestley series (15)
Claverton mystery
Rhode, John
Doctor Lancelot Priestley series (15)
Claw Creek crisis
Grover, Marshall
Larry and Stretch series (292)
Claw of a cat
Peters, Geoffrey
Inspector Trevor Nichols and Sergeant Tom Burton series (1)
Claw of the conciliator
Wolfe, Gene
Book of the new sun series (2)
Claw of the dragon
Algozin, Bruce
Endless quest series (34)
Masterson, Louis
Morgan Kane series (2)
Claws of Helgedad
Dever, Joe
Legends of Lone Wolf series (5)
Claws of steel
Kessler, Leo
Wotan series (3)
Claws of the corpse
House, Brant
Secret Agent X series (18)
Claws of the scorpions
Johnston, Gunnar
Silber series (1)
Claws of the tiger
Carter, Nicholas
Nicholas Carter series (95)
Clay
Imbert-Terry, Henry
Detective Inspector Du Cas series (2)
Clay country
Summers, Rowena
Clay mining series (2)
Clayburn
Conroy, Al
Clayburn series (1)
Clayhanger
Bennett, Arnold
Clayhanger series (1)
Five towns series (9)
Clay's ark
Butler, Octavia Estelle
Patternists series (5)
Clea
Durrell, Lawrence
Alexandria quartet (4)
Clean, bright and slightly oiled
Kersh, Gerald
Brigade of Guards series (3)
Clean straw for nothing
Johnston, George Henry
David Meredith trilogy (2)
Clean up
Barry, Joe
Rush Henry series (4)
Clean-up crew
Makris, Kathryn
Eco-Kids series (2)
Clean-up day
Duke, Kate
Guinea pig board books series (2)
Clear ahead
Rowlands, Avril
God's wonderful railway series (2)
Clear and present danger
Clancy, Tom
Jack Ryan series (4)
Kendrick, Baynard
Captain Duncan Maclain series (10)
Sanders, Buck
Ben Slayton series (1)
Clear case of murder
Desmond, Hugh
Alan Fraser series (5)
Clear-cut murder
Wallingford, Lee
Frank Carver and Ginny Trask series (2)
Clear for action
White, Simon
Penhaligon trilogy (2)
Clear Fork
Wisler, Gary Clifton
Willie Delamer series (11)
Clear horizon
Richardson, Dorothy Miller
Pilgrimage series (11)
Clear shot
Stivers, Dick
Able Team series (34)
Clear to sail
Moray, Helga
Dean Brothers series (1)
Clear water stream
Williamson, Henry
Shallowford to Norfolk series (1)
Clearance
Lingard, Joan
Maggie McKinley quartet (1)
Clearly old Ernie
Mallett, Jerry J
Ernie series (4)
Cleek of Scotland Yard
Hanshew, Thomas W
Hamilton Cleek series (2)
Cleek, the man of forty faces
Hanshew, Thomas W
Hamilton Cleek series (1)
Cleek, the master detective
Hanshew, Thomas W
Hamilton Cleek series (1)
Cleek's government cases
Hanshew, Thomas W
Hamilton Cleek series (4)
Cleek's greatest riddles
Hanshew, Thomas W
Hamilton Cleek series (4)
Cleg Kelly, the Arab of the streets
Crockett, Samuel Rutherford
Galloway series (1)
Clem and the dancing bear
Phillpotts, Beatrice
Clem series (1)
Clem and the fancy dress party
Phillpotts, Beatrice
Clem series (3)
Clem and the runaway pig
Phillpotts, Beatrice
Clem series (2)
Cleopatra boy
Malpass, Eric Lawson
William Shakespeare trilogy (2)
Cleopatra crisis
Hawke, Simon
Timewars series (11)
Cleopatra Jones
Goulart, Ron
Cleopatra Jones series (1)
Cleopatra Jones and the casino of gold
Goulart, Ron
Cleopatra Jones series (2)
Cleopatra Needle mystery
Pentelow, John Nix
Sexton Blake series (492)
Cleo's conquest
Garis, Lilian C
Cleo series (1)
Cleo's misty rainbow
Garis, Lilian C
Cleo series (2)
Cleric's secret
Deeping, Warwick
James Slade series (2)
Clerihews complete
Bentley, Edmund Clerihew
Clerihews series (3)
Clerihews of Paul Horgan
Horgan, Paul
Clerihews series (2)

Cleveland connection
Roberts, Les
Milan Jacovich series (4)

Cleveland pipeline
Pendleton, Don
Mack Bolan series (30)

Clever celestial
Carter, Nicholas
Nicholas Carter series (37)

Clever little donkey
Blyton, Enid
Little donkey series (2)

Clever Mister Twink
Hurt, Freda Mary
Mister Twink series (1)

Clever Polly, and other stories
Storr, Catherine
Polly and the wolf series (1)

Clever Polly and the stupid wolf
Storr, Catherine
Polly and the wolf series (2)

Clever Trevor knows his animals
Rogers, Alan
Clever Trevor series (1)

Clever Trevor knows his colours
Rogers, Alan
Clever Trevor series (4)

Clever Trevor knows his numbers
Rogers, Alan
Clever Trevor series (2)

Clever Trevor knows his shapes
Rogers, Alan
Clever Trevor series (3)

Cleverness of Mr Budd
Verner, Gerald
Superintendent Robert Budd series (4)

Clew against clew
Carter, Nicholas
Nicholas Carter series (590)

Clew by clew
Carter, Nicholas
Nicholas Carter series (415)

Click of the gate
Campbell, Alice
Helen Roderick series (1)
Tommy Rostetter series (1)

Clicking of Cuthbert
Wodehouse, Pelham Grenville
Oldest member series (1)

Clicky and Tiptoe
Blyton, Enid
Clicky series (3)

Clicky gets into trouble
Blyton, Enid
Clicky series (2)

Clicky the clockwork clown
Blyton, Enid
Clicky series (1)

Client
Hall, Parnell
Stanley Hastings series (5)

Client called Noah
Greenfeld, Josh
Noah series (3)

Client is cancelled
Lockridge, Frances
Inspector Merton Heimrich series (6)

Client privilege
Tapply, William George
Brady Coyne series (9)

Cliff
Matterson, Neil
Cliff series (1)

Cliff climbers
Reid, Mayne
Himalayas series (2)

Cliff face
Buckingham, David
Sam Wharton series (2)

Cliff hanger
Craig, Philip R
Martha's Vineyard series (4)

Cliff House monster
Moss, Nancy
Cliff House series (4)

Cliff Island mystery
Bartlett, Philip A
Roy Stover series (3)

Cliff Richard story
Tremlett, George
Rock stars series (9)

Cliffhanger
Matterson, Neil
Cliff series (2)

Clifford affair
Fielding, A
Inspector Pointer series (4)

Clifford and the grouchy neigbors
Bridwell, Norman
Clifford series (18)

Clifford at the circus
Bridwell, Norman
Clifford series (9)

Clifford counts bubbles
Bridwell, Norman
Clifford series (31)

Clifford gets a job
Bridwell, Norman
Clifford series (2)

Clifford goes to Hollywood
Bridwell, Norman
Clifford series (10)

Clifford, I love you
Bridwell, Norman
Clifford series (34)

Clifford mystery
Fielding, A
Inspector Pointer series (4)

Clifford takes a trip
Bridwell, Norman
Clifford series (3)

Clifford, the big red dog
Bridwell, Norman
Clifford series (1)

Clifford, the small red puppy
Bridwell, Norman
Clifford series (6)

Clifford treasury
Bridwell, Norman
Clifford series (18)
Clifford series (24)

Clifford wants a cookie
Bridwell, Norman
Clifford series (23)

Clifford, we love you
Bridwell, Norman
Clifford series (25)

Clifford's ABC
Bridwell, Norman
Clifford series (11)

Clifford's animal sounds
Bridwell, Norman
Clifford series (26)

Clifford's bathtime
Bridwell, Norman
Clifford series (29)

Clifford's bedtime
Bridwell, Norman
Clifford series (28)

Clifford's big book of stories
Bridwell, Norman
Clifford series (34)

Clifford's birthday party
Bridwell, Norman
Clifford series (21)

Clifford's Christmas
Bridwell, Norman
Clifford series (15)

Clifford's family
Bridwell, Norman
Clifford series (13)

Clifford's good deeds
Bridwell, Norman
Clifford series (8)

Clifford's Halloween
Bridwell, Norman
Clifford series (4)

Clifford's happy day
Bridwell, Norman
Clifford series (34)

Clifford's kitten
Bridwell, Norman
Clifford series (14)

Clifford's manners
Bridwell, Norman
Clifford series (20)

Clifford's neighborhood
Bridwell, Norman
Clifford series (17)

Clifford's noisy day
Bridwell, Norman
Clifford series (30)

Clifford's pals
Bridwell, Norman
Clifford series (16)

Clifford's peekaboo
Bridwell, Norman
Clifford series (27)

Clifford's puppy days
Bridwell, Norman
Clifford series (24)

Clifford's riddles
Bridwell, Norman
Clifford series (7)

Clifford's sing along
Bridwell, Norman
Clifford series (22)

Clifford's springtime
Bridwell, Norman
Clifford series (33)

Clifford's sticker book
Bridwell, Norman
Clifford series (34)

Clifford's story hour
Bridwell, Norman
Clifford series (12)

Clifford's Thanksgiving visit
Bridwell, Norman
Clifford series (32)

Clifford's tricks
Bridwell, Norman
Clifford series (5)

Clifford's word book
Bridwell, Norman
Clifford series (34)

Cliffs
O'Donnell, Kevin
Journeys of McGill Feighan series (4)

Climax Mountain
Martin, Cort
Jared Bolt series (22)

Climb
Vendrell, Carme Sole
Victor and Maria series (3)

Climb the highest mountain
Bittner, F Rosanne
Savage destiny series (5)

Climb the wall
Cronin, Michael
Richard Maidment series (3)

Climbed corpse
Brede, Arnold
Bull Rogers series (1)

Climbing high
Barrie, Alexander
Jonathan Kane series (5)

Climbing the rainbow
Hulme, Joy Nelson
Disability series (2)

Climbing the rope
Mannering, May
Climbing the rope series (1)

Climbing the stairs
Powell, Margaret
Domestic service series (2)

Clinton
Aimwell, Walter
Boy series (2)

Clinton, and others
Marshall, Archibald
Clinton series (9)

Clinton twins, and other stories
Marshall, Archibald
Clinton series (9)

Clipper of the clouds
Verne, Jules
Robur series (2)

Clipper to China
Knight, Frank
Clipper ship series (3)

Clive eats alligators
Lester, Alison
Australian children series (1)

Clive's kite
Cole, Michael
Edward and friends series (3)

Cloak
Garfield, Leon
Apprentices series (3)

Cloak of darkness
Macinnes, Helen
Robert Renwick series (2)

Cloak of guilt
Carter, Nicholas
Nicholas Carter series (125)

Cloak of illusion
Roberts, John Maddox
Cingulum trilogy (2)

Cloakroom murder
Jardine, Warwick
Sexton Blake series (805)

Clochemerle
Chevallier, Gabriel
Clochemerle series (1)

Clochemerle-Babylon
Chevallier, Gabriel
Clochemerle series (2)

Clochemerle-les Bains
Chevallier, Gabriel
Clochemerle series (3)

Clock for Beany
Bassett, Lisa
Beany series (1)

Clock in the hatbox
Gilbert, Anthony
Arthur Crook series (5)

Clock of dreams
Lumley, Brian
Titus Crow series (3)

Clock strikes thirteen
Brean, Herbert
Reynold Frame series (4)
Wirt, Mildred Augustine
Penny Parker series (7)

Clock strikes twelve
Wentworth, Patricia
Miss Maud Silver series (9)

Clock that struck fifteen
Dale, Norman
Medenham series (1)

Clock ticks on
Williams, Valentine
Sergeant Trevor Dene series (3)

Clockmaker, 1st series
Haliburton, Thomas Chandler
Sam Slick series (1)

Clockmaker, 2nd series
Haliburton, Thomas Chandler
Sam Slick series (2)

Clockmaker, 3rd series
Haliburton, Thomas Chandler
Sam Slick series (3)

Clockmaker of Heidelberg
Edmonds, Harry
Hugh Brodie series (1)

Clocks
Christie, Agatha
Hercule Poirot series (33)

Clocks of Iraz
De Camp, Lyon Sprague
Jorian series (2)

Clockwork
Steed, Neville
Peter Marklin series (4)

Clockwork testament
Burgess, Anthony
Mister Enderby series (3)

Clockwork traitor
Smith, Edward Elmer
Family d'Alembert series (3)

Clockwork twin
Brooks, Walter Rollin
Freddy the pig series (5)

Clocum's bust out
Logan, Jake
John Slocum series (157)

Clogshop chronicles
Ackworth, John
Clogshop trilogy (1)

Clorinda
Zola, Emile
Rougon Macquart series (6)

Close all roads to Sospel
Bellairs, George
Detective Inspector Thomas Littlejohn series (55)

Close and investigate
Macdonnell, James Edmond
Jim Brady series (4)

Close call for Cheyenne
Denver, Lee
Cheyenne Jones series (12)

Close calls
Aaseng, Nathan
Inside business series (6)

Close cats
Severn, June
Cathedral cat series (2)

Close combat
Albany, James
S.A.S. series (4)
Griffin, W E B
Corps series (6)

Close curtains
Mallett, Jerry J
Tumtwit series (3)

Close harmony
Thornton, Jane Foster
Electric High series (2)

Close her eyes
Simpson, Dorothy
Inspector Luke Thanet series (4)

Close in for showdown
Grover, Marshall
Larry and Stretch series (41)

Close of play
Hooke, Nina Warner
Striplings trilogy (2)

Close quarters
Gilbert, Michael Francis
Inspector Hazelrigg series (1)
Golding, William
Sea trilogy (2)
Hardy, Adam
George Abercrombie Fox series (14)
Piesman, Marissa
Nina Fischman series (4)
Thirkell, Angela
Barsetshire series (27)

Close sesame
Farah, Nuruddin
African dictatorship trilogy (3)

Close the door behind you
Salisbury, Ray
Simon series (1)

Close the door on murder
York, Jeremy
Superintendent Folly series (5)

Close to critical
Clement, Hal
Mesklin series (2)

Close to death
Crowe, John
Buena Costa County series (6)

Close to the light
Perry, Paul
Near-death series (2)

Close to the vest
Masters, Zeke
Faro Blake series (25)

Closed door
Horler, Sydney
Gerald Lissendale series (2)

Closed shutters
Tinker, Frances
Old New Orleans quartet (3)

Closed Worlds
Hamilton, Edmond
Starwolf trilogy (2)

Closely confined
Burgess, Eric
Harry Tong series (2)

Closer look at plant life
Stonehouse, Bernard
Closer look at series (2)

Closer look at reptiles
Stonehouse, Bernard
Closer look at series (3)

Closer look at whales and dolphins
Stonehouse, Bernard
Closer look at series (1)

Closer than a brother
Wright, Meg
Star trek fan series (29)

Closet hanging
Fennelly, Tony
Matty Sinclair series (2)

Closing net
Rowland, Henry Cottrell
Frank Clamart series (1)

Closing time
Heller, Joseph
Catch twenty two series (2)

Clotilde
Saint-Laurent, Cecil
Clotilde series (1)

Cloud across the moon
Muller, Mary
Anna and Johan de Villiers series (2)

Cloud and cliff
Allen, Willis Boyd
Pine cone series (5)

Cloud Howe
Gibbon, Lewis Grassic
Scots Quair trilogy (2)

Cloud kitten
Blyton, Enid
Little bedtime books series (1)

Cloud on the land
Davis, Julia
Macleods of Virginia series (1)

Cloud over water
Spedding, Alison
Walk in the dark trilogy (2)

Cloud Patrol
Crump, James Irving
Cloud Patrol series (1)

Cloud the smiter
Gask, Arthur
Gilbert Larose series (1)

Cloud warrior
Tilley, Patrick
Amtrak wars series (1)

Cloudburst
Keast, Francis
Darryl Krustov series (2)

Clouded hills
Jagger, Brenda
Barforth trilogy (1)

Clouded moon
Saltmarsh, Max
Archie Lumsden series (2)

Cloudmaker
Finkel, George
Group Captain Alan Metcalfe series (3)

Clouds of guilt
Wainwright, John
Northern Police series (56)

Clouds of Magellan
Nighbert, David Franklin
Anton Stryker series (2)

Clouds of war
Hayes, Ralph Eugene
Check Force series (2)

Clouds of witness
Sayers, Dorothy Leigh
Lord Peter Wimsey series (2)
Clover
Coolidge, Susan
Katy series (4)
Clover and blue grass
Hall, Eliza Calvert
Aunt Jane series (3)
Clover Club and the adventure that fell out of the sky
Langholm, A D
Clover Club series (2)
Clover Club and the house of mystery
Langholm, A D
Clover Club series (1)
Clovis Crawfish and Batiste bete puante
Fontenot, Mary Alice
Clovis Crawfish series (12)
Clovis Crawfish and Bertile's bon voyage
Fontenot, Mary Alice
Clovis Crawfish series (11)
Clovis Crawfish and Etienne Escargot
Fontenot, Mary Alice
Clovis Crawfish series (8)
Clovis Crawfish and his friends
Fontenot, Mary Alice
Clovis Crawfish series (1)
Clovis Crawfish and Michelle Mantis
Fontenot, Mary Alice
Clovis Crawfish series (7)
Clovis Crawfish and Petit Papillon
Fontenot, Mary Alice
Clovis Crawfish series (4)
Clovis Crawfish and Simeon Suce-Fleur
Fontenot, Mary Alice
Clovis Crawfish series (10)
Clovis Crawfish and the big betail
Fontenot, Mary Alice
Clovis Crawfish series (2)
Clovis Crawfish and the curious craupaud
Fontenot, Mary Alice
Clovis Crawfish series (6)
Clovis Crawfish and the orphan Zo-Zo
Fontenot, Mary Alice
Clovis Crawfish series (9)
Clovis Crawfish and the singing cigales
Fontenot, Mary Alice
Clovis Crawfish series (3)
Clovis Crawfish and the spinning spider
Fontenot, Mary Alice
Clovis Crawfish series (5)
Clown
Brown, Carter
Lieutenant Al Wheeler series (43)
Manning, Paul
Merry-go-rhymes series (2)
Clown and the pirates
Howson, John Michael
Adventure Island story books (3)
Clown-Arounds
Cole, Joanna
Clown-Arounds series (1)
Clown-Arounds have a party
Cole, Joanna
Clown-Arounds series (2)
Clown-Arounds go on vacation
Cole, Joanna
Clown-Arounds series (4)
Clown caboose
Barkan, Joanne
Circus train come aboard series (3)
Clown of Bombay
Judah, Aaron
Clown series (1)
Clown of fire
Judah, Aaron
Clown series (2)
Clowning about
Ahlberg, Janet
Daisychain series (5)
Cloze papers
Livingston, Kenneth
Papers series (2)
Club car mystery
Colbron, Grace Isabel
Joe Muller series (5)
Club of Masks
Upward, Allen
Doctor Frank Tarleton series (1)
Club Paradis murders
McCormick, Claire
John Waltz series (2)
Club Twelve
Williams, Amanda Kyle
Madison McGuire series (1)
Clubbable woman
Hill, Reginald
Superintendent Andrew Dalziel and Sergeant Pascoe series (1)
Clubfoot the avenger
Williams, Valentine
Clubfoot series (4)
Clubhouse mystery
Jenkins, Jerry Bruce
Bradford family series (7)
Clue
Wells, Carolyn
Fleming Stone series (1)
Clue at Casper Creek
Hope, Laura Lee
New Bobbsey twins series (26)
Clue at Skeleton Rocks
Lloyd, Hugh
Hal Keen series (6)
Clue at the zoo
Giff, Patricia Reilly
Polka Dot series (8)
Clue for Clancy
Thayer, Lee
Peter Clancy series (44)
Clue for clue
Grant, Maxwell
Shadow series (231)
Clue for Clutha
Munro, Hugh Macfarlane
Clutha series (3)
Clue for Mister Fortune
Bailey, Henry Christopher
Mister Reggie Fortune series (11)
Clue from the unknown
Carter, Nicholas
Nicholas Carter series (591)
Clue in blue
Allen, Betsy
Connie Blair series (4)
Clue in code
Singer, Marilyn
Sam and Dave series (3)
Clue in the air
Ostrander, Isabel
Timothy McCarty series (1)
Clue in the ancient disguise
Keene, Carolyn
Nancy Drew series (69)
Clue in the antique trunk
Keene, Carolyn
Nancy Drew series (105)
Clue in the camera
Keene, Carolyn
Nancy Drew series (82)
Clue in the classroom
Hope, Laura Lee
New Bobbsey twins series (9)
Clue in the clay
Olsen, D B
Lieutenant Stephen Mayhew series (1)
Clue in the cobweb
Keene, Carolyn
Dana girls series (8)
Clue in the crossword cipher
Keene, Carolyn
Nancy Drew series (44)
Clue in the crumbling wall
Keene, Carolyn
Nancy Drew series (22)
Clue in the diary
Keene, Carolyn
Nancy Drew series (7)
Clue in the embers
Dixon, Franklin W
Hardy boys series (35)
Clue in the ivy
Keene, Carolyn
Dana girls series (14)
Clue in the jewel box
Keene, Carolyn
Nancy Drew series (20)
Clue in the mirror
Morland, Nigel
Mrs Palmyra Pym series (5)
Clue in the old album
Keene, Carolyn
Nancy Drew series (24)
Clue in the old stagecoach
Keene, Carolyn
Nancy Drew series (37)
Clue in the patchwork quilt
Sutton, Margaret
Judy Bolton series (14)
Clue in the ruined castle
Sutton, Margaret
Judy Bolton series (26)
Clue in Witchwhistle
Ezell, Marilyn
Susan Sand series (3)
Clue of the artificial eye
Fletcher, Joseph Smith
Paul Campenhaye series (2)
Clue of the black cat
Berna, Paul
Bobby Thiriet series (1)
Clue of the black keys
Keene, Carolyn
Nancy Drew series (28)
Clue of the bricklayer's aunt
Morland, Nigel
Mrs Palmyra Pym series (4)
Clue of the broken blade
Dixon, Franklin W
Hardy boys series (21)
Clue of the broken blossom
Tatham, Julie
Vicki Barr series (5)
Clue of the broken locket
Keene, Carolyn
Nancy Drew series (11)
Clue of the broken wing
Sutton, Margaret
Judy Bolton series (29)
Clue of the careless hangman
Morland, Nigel
Mrs Palmyra Pym series (10)
Clue of the carved ruby
Wells, Helen
Vicki Barr series (14)
Clue of the charred diary
Bayfield, William John
Sexton Blake series (70)
Clue of the cloakroom ticket
Armour, R Coutts
Sexton Blake series (362)
Clue of the clot
Barry, Charles
Superintendent Lawrence Gilmartin series (6)
Clue of the coiled cobra
Campbell, Bruce
Ken Holt series (5)
Clue of the cypress stump
Striker, Fran
Tom Quest series (3)
Clue of the dancing puppet
Keene, Carolyn
Nancy Drew series (39)
Clue of the dead goldfish
Macclure, Victor
Inspector Archie Burford series (4)
Clue of the eyelash
Wells, Carolyn
Fleming Stone series (35)
Clue of the four wigs
Teed, George Hamilton
Sexton Blake series (402)
Clue of the fourteen keys
Burton, Miles
Inspector Arnold and Desmond Merrion series (15)
Clue of the frightening coin
Ryan, Jessica
Gregory Pavlov and O'Shaughnessey series (1)
Clue of the gold coin
Wells, Helen
Vicki Barr series (12)
Clue of the golden earring
Wills, Cecil Melville
Geoffrey Boscobell series (13)
Superintendent Roger Ellerdine and Sergeant Cherry Blossom series (3)
Clue of the green candle
Verner, Gerald
Trevor Lowe series (11)
Clue of the green-eyed girl
Burnaby, Nigel
Chief Inspector Drewry series (1)
Clue of the hissing serpent
Dixon, Franklin W
Hardy boys series (53)
Clue of the Judas tree
Ford, Leslie
Lieutenant Joseph Kelly series (2)
Clue of the leaning chimney
Keene, Carolyn
Nancy Drew series (26)
Clue of the lost hour
Wills, Cecil Melville
Geoffrey Boscobell series (12)
Superintendent Roger Ellerdine and Sergeant Cherry Blossom series (2)
Clue of the marked claw
Campbell, Bruce
Ken Holt series (4)
Clue of the missing link
Evans, Gwyn
Chester Brett series (2)
Clue of the naked eye
Russell, Charlotte Murray
Jane Amanda Edwards series (5)
Clue of the new shoe
Upfield, Arthur William
Napoleon Bonaparte series (15)
Clue of the old sea chest
Palmer, Bernard
Powell family series (3)
Clue of the phantom car
Campbell, Bruce
Ken Holt series (8)
Clue of the pin-up girl
Tyrer, Walter
Sexton Blake series (1414)
Clue of the poor man's shilling
Knight, Kathleen Moore
Elisha Macomber series (2)
Clue of the primrose petal
Wickham, Harvey
Ferris McClue series (1)
Clue of the purple asters
Cassells, John
Superintendent Flagg series (6)
Clue of the rising moon
Williams, Valentine
Sergeant Trevor Dene series (5)
Clue of the rusty key
Keene, Carolyn
Dana girls series (11)
Clue of the screeching owl
Dixon, Franklin W
Hardy boys series (41)
Clue of the second murder
Strange, John Stephen
Van Dusen Ormsberry series (2)
Clue of the second tooth
Verner, Gerald
Sexton Blake series (497)
Clue of the silken ladder
Wirt, Mildred Augustine
Penny Parker series (5)
Clue of the silver brush
Burton, Miles
Inspector Arnold and Desmond Merrion series (11)
Clue of the silver cellar
Burton, Miles
Inspector Arnold and Desmond Merrion series (14)
Clue of the silver scorpion
Campbell, Bruce
Ken Holt series (16)
Clue of the stolen rupees
Parsons, Anthony
Sexton Blake series (1056)
Clue of the stone lantern
Sutton, Margaret
Judy Bolton series (21)
Clue of the tapping heels
Keene, Carolyn
Nancy Drew series (16)
Clue of the tattooed man
Brandon, John Gordon
Sexton Blake series (951)
Clue of the twisted face
Kummer, Frederic Arnold
Judge Henry Tyson series (2)
Clue of the velvet mask
Keene, Carolyn
Nancy Drew series (30)
Clue of the whistling bagpipes
Keene, Carolyn
Nancy Drew series (41)
Clue on the desert trail
Sheldon, Ann
Linda Craig series (2)
Clue sinister
Carnac, Carol
Inspector Julian Rivers series (3)
Clue that flew away
Hope, Laura Lee
New Bobbsey twins series (3)
Clue to Christabel
Fitt, Mary
Superintendent Mallett series (8)
Clue to the black flower
Keene, Carolyn
Dana girls series (18)
Clue to the labyrinth
Clason, Clyde B
Theocritus Lucius Westborough series (7)
Clues for Dr Coffee
Blochman, Lawrence Goldtree
Doctor Daniel Webster Coffee series (3)
Clues from a detective's camera
Hill, Headon
Sebastian Zambra series (1)
Clues in the woods
Parish, Peggy
Liza, Bill and Jed series (2)
Clues of the Caribbees
Stribling, Thomas Sigismund
Professor Henry Poggioli series (1)
Clues to burn
Offord, Lenore Glen
Bill and Coco Hastings series (2)
Clunk's claimant
Bailey, Henry Christopher
Mister Joshua Clunk series (4)
Cluny problem
Fielding, A
Inspector Pointer series (6)
Cluster
Anthony, Piers
Cluster series (1)
Cluster command
Drake, David
Crisis of empire trilogy (2)
Clutch hitter!
Bee, Clair
Chip Hilton series (4)
Clutch of constables
Marsh, Ngaio
Inspector Roderick Alleyn series (25)
Clutch of coppers
Ashe, Gordon
Patrick Dawlish series (43)
Clutch of dread
Carter, Nicholas
Nicholas Carter series (457)
Clutch of vipers
Scott, Jack S
Detective Inspector Alfred Stanley Rosher series (4)
Clutching hand
Dutton, Charles Judson
John Bartley series (8)
Reeve, Arthur Benjamin
Craig Kennedy series (24)
Clutha and the lady
Munro, Hugh Macfarlane
Clutha series (4)
Clutha plays a hunch
Munro, Hugh Macfarlane
Clutha series (2)
Clutterkill
Paulsen, Gary
Lieutenant Ronnie Gold series (2)
Clyde Valley
Gavin, Catherine
Clyde Valley series (1)
Clypsis
Carver, Jeffrey Allan
Roger Zelazny's Alien speedway series (1)
Cname Sname defends the America's Cup
Smith, Peter Charles
Cname Sname series (4)
Cname Sname goes riding with Emily Emu
Manners, Carol
Cname Sname series (3)
C/o American Embassy
Cooke, David Coxe
Peter Rourke series (1)
Coal camp girl
Lenski, Lois
Regional series (13)
Coal war
Sinclair, Upton
Coal series (2)
Coarse acting show
Green, Michael
Coarse plays series (1)
Coarse acting show 2
Green, Michael
Coarse plays series (2)
Coast of innocence
Stark, Freya
Traveller series (3)
Coast road murder
Turnbull, Margaret
Juliet Jackson series (4)
Coastal adventure
Day, James Wentworth
Rural rides series (3)
Coastals and hippogriff
Montherlant, Henry de
Girls series (4)
Coastlanders
Cronin, Bernard
Coastlanders series (1)
Coat
Vendrell, Carme Sole
Victor and Maria series (1)
Coat of blackmail
McIntosh, J T
Ambrose and Dominique Frayne series (2)
Cobalt
Aldyne, Nathan
Dan Valentine and Clarissa Lovelace series (2)
Cobalt sixty
Graves, Richard Latshaw
Hugo Wolfram series (3)

Cobb Creek bunch
Grover, Marshall
Larry and Stretch series (283)
Cobbler's luck
Lynch, Patricia
Brogeen the leprechaun series (7)
Cobra
Grant, Maxwell
Shadow series (51)
Zahn, Timothy
Cobra trilogy (1)
Cobra bargain
Zahn, Timothy
Cobra trilogy (3)
Cobra candlestick
Barker, Elsa
Dexter Drake series (1)
Cobra chase
Rosenberger, Joseph
Death Merchant series (66)
Cobra connection
Foley, Louise Munro
Choose your own adventure series (104)
Cobra curse
Dolan, Bill
Afrikorps series (6)
Cobra kill
Carter, Nick
Nick Carter series (47)
Teed, Jack Hamilton
Gunships series (3)
Cobra strike
Hadley, J B
Point Team series (3)
Zahn, Timothy
Cobra trilogy (2)
Cobra venom
Rowe, Anne
Inspector Barry series (1)
West, John B
Rocky Steele series (1)
Cobweb across the moon
Darby, Catherine
Moon series (5)
Cocaine and blue eyes
Zackel, Fred
Michael Brennan series (1)
Cocaine blues
Greenwood, Kerry
Phryne Fisher series (1)
Cocaine caper
Paradis, Vincent A
Tut Claw series (2)
Cocaine connection
Brent, R L
Liquidator series (3)
Cocaine kill
De Stefano, Anthony
Mondo series (2)
Cocaine run
Ahern, Jerry
Dan Track series (10)
Cochise County war
Hardin, J D
Raider and Doc series (47)
Cock-a-doodle hill
Haines, Alice Calhoun
Dudley Graham series (2)
Cock-a-doodle-doo
Hader, Berta
Willow Hill series (1)
Cock of the walk
Gentry, Buck
Eli Holten series (28)
Cock-pit of roses
Fraser, James
Inspector Bill Aveyard series (2)
Cock who couldn't crow
Slepian, Jan
Listen-hear series (2)
Cockatoos
Brent of Bin Bin
Bert Poole series (3)
Cockeyed corpse
Prather, Richard Scott
Shell Scott series (27)
Cockeyed coyote
Mackenzie, Pierce
T G Horne series (6)
Cockeyed cuties
Conway, Troy
Coxeman series (31)
Cockleburr
Crawford, Robert
Arthur Salisbury and Frank Shearer series (1)
Cockroach sings
Campbell, Alice
Inspector Headcorn series (4)
Cock's tail murder
Austin, Hugh
Peter Quint series (5)
Cocktail time
Wodehouse, Pelham Grenville
Uncle Fred, Earl of Ickenham series (3)
Cocktails and the killer
Cheyney, Peter
Michael Kells series (2)
Cocktails with a stranger
Franklin, Charles
Grant Garfield series (2)
Cocky chaff flies again
Nelson, Brian
Cocky chaff series (3)
Coco Grimes
Stolz, Mary
Thomas and Grandfather series (4)
Coco, the gift horse
Hill, Denise
Jane and Jeremy Fortune series (2)
Coconut killings
Moyes, Patricia
Henry and Emmy Tibbett series (13)
Cocoon
Saperstein, David
Cocoon series (1)
Coco's berry party
Reese, Bob
Grand Canyon series (3)
Coda
Topor, Tom
Kevin Fitzgerald series (2)
Codd's last case, and other misleading cases
Herbert, Alan Patrick
Misleading cases series (4)
Code
Carter, Nick
Nick Carter series (77)
Code blue, emergency
White, James
Sector General series (8)
Code duello
Reynolds, Mack
Planetary Agent series (5)
Code-letter mystery
Sharp, David
Professor Henry Arthur Fielding series (3)
Code name, Clone
Cooper, Margaret Chilvers
Stefan and Evonn series (2)
Code name Cobra
Carter, Nick
Nick Carter series (241)
Code name Gadget
Rabe, Peter
Manny De Witt series (3)
Code name, Judas
Walker, Max
Mission impossible series (2)
Code name, Little Ivan
Tiger, John
Mission impossible series (4)
Code name Peregrine
Dalton, Sean
Operation Star Hawks series (2)
Code name, Rapier
Walker, Max
Mission impossible series (3)
Code name Richard
Berdin, Richard
Connection series (8)
Code name Sebastian
Johnson, James Leonard
Code name Sebastian series (1)
Code name, Werewolf
Carter, Nick
Nick Carter series (69)
Code of blood
Cross, David
Chant series (3)
Code of dishonor
Pendleton, Don
Mack Bolan series (99)
Code of dishonour
Sanders, Bruce
Howard Digburn series (3)
Code of Dusty Fog
Edson, John Thomas
Cap Fog series (6)
Floating Outfit series (29)
Code of the Kid
Gregory, Lester
Kid Cyclone series (4)
Code of the Mountain Man
Johnstone, William Wallace
Mountain Man series (9)
Code of the West
Gilman, George G
Adam Steele series (44)
Code of the Woosters
Wodehouse, Pelham Grenville
Jeeves and Bertie Wooster series (7)
Code one thousand and thirteen
Trevor, Leslie
Policewoman series (2)
Code three
Fox, James M
Jerry Long and Chuck Conley series (1)
Code zero, shots fired
Cain, Jonathan
Saigon commandos series (2)
Codebreaker kids
Stanley, George Edward
Codebreaker kids series (1)
Codebreaker kids return
Stanley, George Edward
Codebreaker kids series (2)
Codeword, Bontry
Mitchell, Lane
Jimmy Grier series (2)
Codeword, Golden Fleece
Wheatley, Dennis
Duc de Richelieu series (6)
Cody's army
Case, Jim
Cody's army series (1)
Coffee for none
Caldwell, Alfred Betts
Freddy Philpotts series (1)
Coffee for one
Hale, Edgar
Montague Migglewade series (2)
Coffee, tea of me girls round-the-world diary
Baker, Trudy
Coffee, tea or me girls series (2)
Coffee, tea or me?
Baker, Trudy
Coffee, tea or me girls series (1)
Coffee, tea or me girls get away from it all
Baker, Trudy
Coffee, tea or me girls series (4)
Coffee, tea or me girls lay it on the line
Baker, Trudy
Coffee, tea or me girls series (3)
Coffin and the paper man
Butler, Gwendoline
Inspector John Coffin series (21)
Coffin bird
Brown, Carter
Danny Boyd series (20)
Coffin corner
Bagby, George
Inspector Schmidt series (17)
Coffin Corner
Shannon, Dell
Lieutenant Luis Mendoza series (11)
Coffin corner, U.S.A.
Jason, Stuart
Butcher series (30)
Coffin country
Stein, Aaron Marc
Matt Erridge series (11)
Coffin following
Butler, Gwendoline
Inspector John Coffin series (12)
Coffin for baby
Butler, Gwendoline
Inspector John Coffin series (8)
Coffin for Charley
Butler, Gwendoline
Inspector John Coffin series (24)
Coffin for Christopher
Ames, Delano
Dagobert and Jane Brown series (8)
Coffin for Dimitrios
Ambler, Eric
Charles Latimer series (1)
Coffin for one
Beeding, Francis
Colonel Alastair Granby series (9)
Coffin for Pandora
Butler, Gwendoline
Inspector John Coffin series (15)
Coffin for Pilgrim
Potter, Jay Hill
Pilgrim series (8)
Coffin for the body
Morland, Nigel
Mrs Palmyra Pym series (12)
Coffin for the canary
Butler, Gwendoline
Inspector John Coffin series (16)
Coffin for two
Martin, Robert Lee
Jim Bennett series (13)
Coffin from the past
Butler, Gwendoline
Inspector John Coffin series (14)
Coffin full of dollars
Millard, Joseph John
Dollar series (4)
Coffin in fashion
Butler, Gwendoline
Inspector John Coffin series (18)
Coffin in Malta
Butler, Gwendoline
Inspector John Coffin series (10)
Coffin in Oxford
Butler, Gwendoline
Inspector John Coffin series (7)
Coffin in the black museum
Butler, Gwendoline
Inspector John Coffin series (20)
Coffin Island
Leblanc, Maurice
Arsene Lupin series (9)
Macdonnell, James Edmond
Captain Peter Bentley series (1)
Coffin on Murder Street
Butler, Gwendoline
Inspector John Coffin series (22)
Coffin on the water
Butler, Gwendoline
Inspector John Coffin series (17)
Coffin, scarcely used
Watson, Colin
Inspector Purbright series (1)
Coffin underground
Butler, Gwendoline
Inspector John Coffin series (19)
Coffin waiting
Butler, Gwendoline
Inspector John Coffin series (9)
Coffin's dark number
Butler, Gwendoline
Inspector John Coffin series (13)
Coffins for three
Davis, Frederick Clyde
Professor Cyrus Hatch series (1)
Coffins for two
Evans, Gwyn
Double O'Day series (3)
Coggin
Oldmeadow, Ernest James
Coggin trilogy (1)
Coil of rope
Straker, John Foster
David Wright series (1)
Coils of time
Chandler, Arthur Bertram
John Grimes series (3)
Coin of the realm
Murphy, Warren Burton
Destroyer series (77)
Murray, Will
Destroyer series (77)
Coins and treasure trove
Birt, David
Roman Britain series (20)
Coins of death
Sharpe, Jon
Trailsman series (126)
Coinspinner's story
Saberhagen, Fred
Book of lost swords series (5)
Cokkie caper
Hodgman, Ann
Lunchroom series (3)
Cold and unhonoured
Hurt, Freda Mary
Inspector Herbert Broom series (6)
Cold as ice
Keene, Carolyn
Nancy Drew files series (54)
Cold asylum
Axler, James
Deathlands series (20)
Cold bed in the clay
Wallis, Ruth Sawtell
Eric Lund series (2)
Cold blood
Bruce, Leo
Sergeant William Beef series (8)
Cold-blooded murder
Crofts, Freeman Wills
Inspector Joseph French series (15)
Cold blue death
Stanton, Ken
Aquanauts series (1)
Cold blue light
Kaye, Marvin
Blue light series (1)
Cold call
Pugh, Dianne G
Iris Thorne series (1)
Cold cash war
Asprin, Robert Lynn
Cold cash war series (1)
Combat Command series (9)
Cold cash warrior
Asprin, Robert Lynn
Combat Command series (9)
Cold Comfort Farm
Gibbons, Stella
Cold Comfort Farm series (1)
Cold coming
Kelly, Mary
Inspector Brett Nightingale series (1)
Cold copper tears
Cook, Glen
Garrett series (3)
Cold dead
Wilson, Gar
Phoenix Force super series (3)
Cold dead coed
Janson, Hank
Hank Janson series (165)
Cold death
Robeson, Kenneth
Doc Savage series (21)
Saint James, Daniel
Brothers in blood series (3)
Cold deck, hot lead
Edson, John Thomas
Calamity Jane series (2)
Cold dish
Collins, Max Allan
Ms Tree series (2)
Cold evil
Flynn, Brian
Anthony Bathurst series (21)
Cold-Eye Cordell
Grover, Marshall
Larry and Stretch series (132)
Cold finger curse
Torgerson, Edwin Dial
Pierre Montigny series (2)
Cold harbour
Higgins, Jack
Brigadier Dougal Munro and Captain Jack Carter series (2)
Cold hearts and gentle people
Riggs, John Raymond
Garth Ryland series (9)
Cold in the earth
Granger, Ann
Meredith Mitchell and Chief Inspector Alan Markby series (3)
Cold iron
Freeling, Nicolas
Henri Castang series (10)
Cold is the sea
Beach, Edward Latimer, junior
Rich Richardson series (3)
Cold jungle
Black, Gavin
Paul Harris series (7)
Cold killing
Day, Deforest
Chase Defoe series (2)
Cold light
Harvey, John Barton
Inspector Charlie Resnick series (6)
Cold light of dawn
Ison, Graham
Superintendent John Gaffney series (1)
Cold light of day
Page, Emma
Inspector Kelsey series (3)
Cold, lone and still
Mitchell, Gladys
Dame Beatrice Bradley series (64)
Cold mind
Lindsey, David L
Stuart Haydon series (1)
Cold night for murder
Thomas, Martin
Sexton Blake series (1482)
Cold ones
Kruger, Paul
Phil Kramer series (5)
Cold poison
Palmer, Stuart
Hildegarde Withers series (15)
Cold red sunrise
Kaminsky, Stuart Melvin
Inspector Porfiry Petrovich Rostnikov series (5)
Cold Sassy Tree
Burns, Olive Ann
Tweedy family series (1)
Cold seas beyond
Shirreffs, Gordon Donald
Bob Dunbar and Gary Lunt series (1)

Cold smell of sacred stone
Chesbro, George Clark
Mongo series (6)
Valhalla trilogy (3)
Cold spell
Bruce, Jean
Secret Agent O.S.S.117 series (7)
Cold steel
Tilton, Alice
Leonidas Witherall series (3)
Warren, James
James Weston series (3)
Cold Steele
Masters, J D
Steele series (2)
Cold sweat
Dixon, Franklin W
Hardy boys case files series (63)
Cold tracks
Wallingford, Lee
Frank Carver and Ginny Trask series (1)
Cold trail
Shannon, Dell
Lieutenant Luis Mendoza series (29)
Cold trail from Fort Smith
Bell, Robert Vaughn
McGowan family series (6)
Cold trail to Kirby
Grover, Marshall
Larry and Stretch series (77)
Cold vengeance
McCray, Mike
Black Berets series (2)
Cold victory
Anderson, Poul
Psychotechnic League series (2)
Cold war
Brierley, David
Cody series (1)
Cold war in a country garden
Gutteridge, Lindsay
Mathew Dilke series (1)
Cold war in Hell
Blamires, Harry
Heaven and Hell trilogy (2)
Cold war swap
Thomas, Ross
McCorkle and Padillo series (1)
Cold warrior
Murphy, Warren Burton
Destroyer series (91)
Cold wind blowing
Willard, Barbara
Mantlemass series (4)
Coldhearted lady
Hardin, J D
Raider and Doc series (15)
Coldiron
Parker, F M
Luke Coldiron series (1)
Colditz
Reid, Patrick Robert
Colditz series (2)
Colditz last stop
Pringle, Jack
Colditz series (12)
Colditz recaptured
Eggers, Reinhold
Colditz series (12)
Colditz story
Reid, Patrick Robert
Colditz series (1)
Colditz, the full story
Reid, Patrick Robert
Colditz series (3)
Colditz, the German story
Eggers, Reinhold
Colditz series (6)
Coleville skeleton
Finney, R C
Inspector Bourne series (9)
Colfax
Conley, Robert Jackson
Oliver Colfax series (2)
Colin
Benson, Edward Frederic
Colin series (1)
Colin and Patricia in Canada
Rutley, Cecil Bernard
Colin and Patricia series (1)
Colin and Patricia in South Africa and Southern Rhodesia
Rutley, Cecil Bernard
Colin and Patricia series (2)
Colin II
Benson, Edward Frederic
Colin series (2)
Coll and his white pig
Alexander, Lloyd
Prydain series (6)
Collapse of stout party
Story, Jack Trevor
Sexton Blake series (1458)
Collapsing castle
Middleton, Haydn
People in the picture series (2)
Collected letters of a nobody
Waterhouse, Keith
Nobody series (3)
Collected poems of Freddy the pig
Brooks, Walter Rollin
Freddy the pig series (25)
Collected tales from a long room
Tinniswood, Peter
Brigadier series (2)
Collected works of Buck Rogers in the 25th century
Nowlan, Philip Francis
Buck Rogers series (6)
Collection of antiquities
Balzac, Honore de
Scenes of provincial life series (8)
College basketball
Aaseng, Nathan
You are the coach series (5)
College football
Aaseng, Nathan
You are the coach series (6)
College football's hottest rivalries
Aaseng, Nathan
Sports talk series (8)
College girls
Pascal, Francine
Sweet Valley University series (1)
College league mystery
Cooper, John R
Mel Martin series (5)
College names of the games
Lessiter, Mike
Team names series (2)
Collie to the rescue
Terhune, Albert Payson
Sunnybank collies series (17)
Colliers Row
Webster, Jan
Kate Kilgour trilogy (1)
Collier's Tuesday tea
Green, Michael
Coarse plays series (1)
Collision ahead
Johnston, Ronald
James Bruce series (1)
Collision course
Bayley, Barrington John
Chronos series (1)
Birch, Claire
Lucy Hill series (2)
Dixon, Franklin W
Hardy boys case files series (33)
Grant, William
Matthew Faraday series (2)
Macdonnell, James Edmond
Dutchy Holland series (2)
Tubb, Edwin Charles
Space nineteen ninety nine series (4)
Collision with Chronos
Bayley, Barrington John
Chronos series (1)
Colloghi conspiracy
Hill, Douglas
Del Curb series (2)
Colloquia Crucis
Greenwell, Dora
Two friends series (2)
Colombia crackdown
Cunningham, Chet
Matt Hawke series (3)
Colombine and the birthday party
Fert, Valerie
Colombine series (3)
Colombine in the country
Chenneviere, Sabine
Colombine series (1)
Colombine on holiday
Fert, Valerie
Colombine series (2)
Colonel Blood
Peacock, Max
Colonel Blood series (1)
Colonel Bogus
Blackburn, John
General Charles Kirk series (5)
Colonel Butler's wolf
Price, Anthony
Doctor David Audley and Jack Butler series (4)
Colonel Carter of Cartersville
Smith, Francis Hopkinson
Colonel Carter series (1)
Colonel Carter's Christmas
Smith, Francis Hopkinson
Colonel Carter series (2)
Colonel Chabert
Balzac, Honore de
Scenes of private life series (15)
Colonel Dam
Clouston, Joseph Storer
Ursula Dolling series (1)
Colonel Death
Sharpe, Jon
Canyon O'Grady series (14)
Colonel Gore's second case
Brock, Lynn
Colonel Gore series (2)
Colonel Gore's third case
Brock, Lynn
Colonel Gore series (3)
Colonel Grant's tomorrow
Seton, Graham
Colonel Duncan Grant series (2)
Colonel Grunt
Partridge, Jenny
Oakapple Wood series (2)
Colonel of the Red Hussars
Scott, John Reed
Red Hussars series (1)
Colonel Paternoster
Inchbald, Ralph
Colonel Paternoster series (1)
Colonel Sandhurst to the rescue
Chesney, Marion
Poor relation series (5)
Colonel Sellers
Twain, Mark
Colonel Sellers series (2)
Colonel Shepparton's clock
Turner, Philip
Darnley Mills series (1)
Colonel Sun
Markham, Robert
James Bond series (15)
Colonel Weatherford and his friends
Grand, Gordon
Colonel John Weatherford series (2)
Colonels
Griffin, W E B
Brotherhood of war series (4)
Colonel's children
Supervielle, Jules
Colonel's children series (1)
Colonel's daughter
King, Charles
Lieutenant Sandy Ray series (1)
Colonel's foxhound
Wills, Cecil Melville
Sylvester Horatio Pinkney series (3)
Colonial crafts
Kalman, Bobbie
Historic communities series (7)
Colonial life
Kalman, Bobbie
Historic communities series (8)
Colonial town, Williamsburg
Kalman, Bobbie
Historic communities series (6)
Colonial twins of Virginia
Perkins, Lucy Fitch
Twin series (15)
Colonies in revolt
Carter, Alden Richardson
American Revolution series (1)
Colonists
Long, William Stuart
Australians series (6)
Colonists of space
Carr, Charles
Bel series (1)
Colonizer and the colonized
Memmi, Albert
Jewish colonist series (1)
Colonizing space
Bergaust, Erik
Colonizing series (3)
Colonizing the planets
Bergaust, Erik
Colonizing series (1)
Colonizing the sea
Bergaust, Erik
Colonizing series (2)
Colony
Vigliante, Mary
Aftermath series (2)
Colony in peril
Griffin, Pauline Margaret
Star commandos series (2)
Colophon to Love respelt
Graves, Robert
Love respelt series (2)
Color of evil
Hartwell, David Geddes
Dark descent trilogy (1)
Color of her panties
Anthony, Piers
Xanth series (15)
Color out of time
Shea, Michael
Colour out of space and time series (2)
Color war!
Kaye, Marilyn
Camp Sunnyside Friends series (3)
Colorado
McCarthy, Gary
Rivers west series (3)
Ross, Dana Fuller
Wagons West series (7)
Colorado ambush
Ellis, Wesley
Lone Star series (98)
Sharpe, Jon
Canyon O'Grady series (22)
Colorado Belle
Grover, Marshall
Larry and Stretch series (163)
Colorado crossing
Curry, Gene
Jim Saddler series (3)
Colorado cutie
Fletcher, Dirk
Spur McCoy series (20)
Colorado gold
Wells, Marian
Amy Randolph trilogy (2)
Colorado Jim
Goodchild, George
Colorado Jim series (1)
Colorado kill
Trimnell, Robert L
Loner series (1)
Colorado killers
Logan, Jake
John Slocum series (134)
Colorado kill-zone
Pendleton, Don
Mack Bolan series (25)
Colorado prey
Harte, Bryce
Slate Creed series (8)
Colorado pursuit
Grover, Marshall
Larry and Stretch series (47)
Colorado quarry
Sharpe, Jon
Trailsman series (124)
Colorado robber
Sharpe, Jon
Trailsman series (75)
Colorado silver queen
Hardin, J D
Raider and Doc series (44)
Colorado special
Grant, William
Matthew Faraday series (4)
Colorado sting
Hardin, J D
Raider and Doc series (50)
Colorado virgins
Chisholm, Matt
Joe Blade series (5)
Colorado woman
Grover, Marshall
Larry and Stretch series (275)
Colors
Allington, Richard L
Beginning to learn series (4)
Colors for murder
Robeson, Kenneth
Doc Savage series (169)
Colors in the dreamweaver's loom
Hilgartner, Beth
Dreamweaver series (1)
Dreamweaver's loom series (1)
Colors of chaos
Vardeman, Robert Edward
Weapons of chaos trilogy (3)
Colors of war
Cohen, Matt
Salem quartet (2)
Colors to talk about
Lionni, Leon
Colors, letters, numbers and words to talk about series (1)
Colossal Corcoran in Central Africa
Morgan, W Ingram
Colossal Corcoran series (1)
Colossal Corcoran in Mystery Valley
Morgan, W Ingram
Colossal Corcoran series (2)
Colossal Corcoran in the Caribbean Sea
Morgan, W Ingram
Colossal Corcoran series (5)
Colossal Corcoran in the Hindu Kush mountains
Morgan, W Ingram
Colossal Corcoran series (6)
Colossal Corcoran on Skull Atoll
Morgan, W Ingram
Colossal Corcoran series (4)
Colossal Corcoran on Smoke Island
Morgan, W Ingram
Colossal Corcoran series (3)
Colossus
Jones, Dennis Feltham
Colossus trilogy (1)
Wallace, Edgar
Inspector Elk series (3)
Colossus and the crab
Jones, Dennis Feltham
Colossus trilogy (3)
Colour and Barbapapa
Tison, Annette
Barbapapa first book series (2)
Colour in the creek
Paice, Margaret
Fletcher family series (1)
Colour of Alberta
Brooks, Bill
Colour of Canada series (2)
Colour of British Columbia
Brooks, Bill
Colour of Canada series (3)
Colour of death
Muir, James A
Breed series (18)
Colour of evil
Hartwell, David Geddes
Dark descent trilogy (1)
Colour of fear
Ormerod, Roger
David Mallin and George Coe series (6)
Colour of magic
Pratchett, Terry
Discworld series (1)
Colour of money
Tevis, Walter Stone
Hustler series (2)
Colour of murder
Winn, Patrick
Inspector Lyon series (2)
Colour of Ontario
Brooks, Bill
Colour of Canada series (1)
Colour out of space, and others
Lovecraft, Howard Phillips
Colour out of space and time series (1)
Colour out of time
Shea, Michael
Colour out of space and time series (2)
Cthulhu Mythos series (17)
Colour rhymes
Ward, Dorothy Darrell
Teddies series (3)
Colour scheme
Marsh, Ngaio
Inspector Roderick Alleyn series (12)
Colours
Browne, Eileen
Funny animals series (2)
Hughes, Shirley
Nursery series (5)
Colours aloft!
Kent, Alexander
Captain Richard Bolitho series (17)
Colours of war
Cohen, Matt
Salem quartet (2)
ColSec rebellion
Hill, Douglas
ColSec trilogy (3)
Colt and the sabre
Edson, John Thomas
American Civil War series (9)
Colt courier of the Rio
Repp, Ed Earl
Jim Hayfield series (1)
Colt Creek
LeBeau, Roy
Buckskin series (4)
Colt Crossing
Dalton, Kit
Buckskin series (24)
Colt forty-five vengeance
Dalton, Kit
Buckskin series (37)
Colt from Snowy River
Mitchell, Elyne
Silver Brumby series (8)

Colt heritage
Allen, Chester
Justice Colt series (7)
Colt hostages
Grover, Marshall
Bleak Creek series (10)
Colt in the family
Berrisford, Judith Mary
Brooke family series (2)
Colt is born
Henry, Marguerite
King of the wind series (1)
Colt lightning
Champlin, Tim
Jay McGraw series (1)
Matt Tierney series (7)
Colt named Mischief
Rabinowitz, Sandy
Mischief series (1)
Columbo
Lawrence, Alfred
Columbo series (1)
Columbo and the Samurai sword
Magee, Bill
Columbo series (7)
Columbus affair
Scheer, Karl Herbert
Perry Rhodan series (80)
Columbus Day magic
Baker, James Webb
Magic series (12)
Columnist murder
Saunders, Lawrence
Wylie King and Nels Lundberg series (1)
Comanche
Brady, William S
Peacemaker series (1)
Edson, John Thomas
American Civil War series (1)
McLennan, Will
Ramseys series (9)
Comanche captives
Cook, Will
United States Cavalry trilogy (1)
Comanche carnage
Gilman, George G
Adam Steele series (8)
Comanche come down
Hunter, E J
White Squaw series (23)
Comanche come-on
Meek, Joseph
Mountain Jack Pike series (3)
Comanche cowboy
Gentry, Georgina
Panorama of the old West series (3)
Comanche crossing
Sharpe, Jon
Trailsman series (104)
Comanche heart
Anderson, Catherine
Comanche trilogy (2)
Comanche massacre
Cunningham, Chet
Pony soldiers series (2)
Comanche moon
Anderson, Catherine
Comanche trilogy (1)
Cunningham, Chet
Pony soldiers series (3)
Comanche peak
Longtree, Warren T
Ruff Justice series (11)
Comanche raid
Cole, Judd
Cheyenne series (6)
Comanche raiders
Mason, Dan
Lex Cranshaw series (3)
Comanche scalp
Macdonald, William Colt
Gregory Quist series (7)
Comanche trail
Miller, Jim
Colt Revolver series (2)
Comanche war
Carrington, G A
Marcus Cavanaugh series (4)
Comanche woman
Johnston, Joan
Sisters of the Lone Star trilogy (2)
Comanchero
Newsom, Ed
Chagro Brannigan series (2)
Comanchero blood
Ledd, Paul
Shelter Morgan series (13)
Comanchero kill
Fieldhouse, William
Shaddrock and Cougar series (2)
Comanchero lust
Gentry, Buck
Eli Holten series (29)
Comancheros
Cole, Judd
Cheyenne series (7)
Dawson, Clay
Long Rider series (14)
Slade, Jack
Sundance series (11)
Comanche's woman
Logan, Jake
John Slocum series (5)
Combat
Rolland, Romain
Soul enchanted series (4)
Combat assignment
Macdonnell, James Edmond
Captain Kenyon series (3)
Combat bachelor, part one
Kane, Rod
Veteran's Day series (1)
Combat bachelor, part two
Kane, Rod
Veteran's Day series (2)
Combat Command in the world of David Drake's Hammer's Slammers
Johnson, Todd
Hammer's Slammers series (6)
Combat Command in the world of Jack Williamson's The Legion of Space
Keith, Andrew
Legion of Space series (4)
Combat Command in the world of Jerry E Pournelle's Janisseries
Acres, Mark
Janisseries trilogy (3)
Combat Command in the world of Piers Anthony's Bio of a space tyrant
Kramer, Dana
Bio of a space tyrant series (5)
Combat Command in the world of Robert Asprin's Cold cash warrior
Asprin, Robert Lynn
Cold cash war series (2)
Combat Command in the world of Roger Zelazny's Nine princes in Amber
Randall, Neil
Kingdom of Amber series (1)
Combat in the sky
Whitehouse, Arch
Air war series (3)
Combined forces
Smithers, Jack
Berry series (12)
Bulldog Drummond series (19)
Richard Hannay series (7)
Come a stranger
Voigt, Cynthia
Tillermans series (4)
Come abroad
Hiscock, Eric Charles
Wanderer series (5)
Come again courier
Morgan, Stanley
Russ Tobin series (4)
Come again, nurse
Grant, Jane
Nurse series (2)
Come along twins
Blyton, Enid
Twins series (4)
Come and be hanged
Christie, Agatha
Superintendent Battle series (5)
Come and be killed
Bennett, Dorothy
Dennis Devore series (2)
Come and get me
Hardcastle, Michael
Tony and Jay series (8)
Come and go
Gaite, Francis
James and Charles Latimer series (3)
Come and play, Hippo
Thaler, Mike
Hippo series (3)
Come away, death
Mitchell, Gladys
Dame Beatrice Bradley series (8)
Come away from the water, Shirley
Burningham, John
Shirley series (1)
Come back
Wells, Carolyn
Pennington Wise series (3)
Come back, Amelia Bedelia
Parish, Peggy
Amelia Bedelia series (4)
Come back, Charleston Blue
Himes, Chester
Grave Digger Jones and Coffin Ed Johnson series (7)
Come back for the body
Hume, David
Mick Cardby series (26)
Come back, Geordie
Walker, David Harry
Geordie Mactaggart series (2)
Come back, Lucy
Sykes, Pamela
Lucy series (1)
Come back to murder
Courtier, Sidney Hobson
Ambrose Mahon series (3)
Come back to Wayne County
Falstaff, Jack
Jacoby's Corners trilogy (3)
Come back, wherever you are
Weber, Lenora Mattingly
Beany Malone series (14)
Come be my O.R.G.Y.
Mark, Ted
Man from O.R.G.Y. series (15)
Come clean
James, Bill
Superintendent Colin Harpur series (5)
Come, come to my corner
Mayne, William
Animal library series (1)
Come dark, come evil
McNeilly, Wilfred
Sexton Blake series (1545)
Come death and high water
Cleeves, Ann
George Palmer-Jones series (2)
Come die with me
Dark, James
Mark Kingsley Hood series (3)
Eastwood, James
Anna Zordan series (3)
Gault, William Campbell
Brock Callahan series (4)
Come dwell with death
Glidden, Minna Wesselhoft
Carey Brent series (1)
Come endless darkness
Gygax, Gary
Gord the Rogue series (4)
Come evil days
Poyer, Joe
Time of war series (2)
Come hell or high water
Francis, Clare
Voyage series (1)
Come hither, nurse
Grant, Jane
Nurse series (1)
Come home and be killed
Melville, Jennie
Sergeant Charmian Daniels series (1)
Come home to crime
Deane, Norman
Liberator series (3)
Come home to death
Ashe, Gordon
Patrick Dawlish series (34)
Come in, doctor
Downe, Patrick
Doctor series (3)
Come in doctor
Poidevin, Leslie
Country practice series (2)
Come in, number one, your time is up
Jewell, Derek
Prospero Group series (1)
Come into my parlour
Wheatley, Dennis
Gregory Sallust series (7)
Come into my world
Lloyd-Jones, Buster
Vet series (2)
Come kill with me
Kane, Henry
Peter Chambers series (30)
Come landlord
Girtin, Tom
Landlord series (1)
Come like a storm
Cousins, Edmund George
Captain Moffat series (1)
Come like shadows
Raven, Simon
Alms for oblivion series (8)
Come, lucky April
Ure, Jean
Hal series (2)
Come Nineveh, come Tyre
Drury, Allen
Washington series (5)
Come on Alpaca
Billam, Rosemary
Alpaca series (3)
Come on Ossie!
Davies, Hunter
Ossie series (1)
Come one, come all
Conway, Troy
Coxeman series (6)
Come out and play, Little Mouse
Kraus, Robert
Little Mouse series (3)
Come out fighting, A-American
Drackett, Phil
A-American series (2)
Come out killing
Reeves, Robert
Cellini Smith series (2)
Come over, come over
Barry, Lynda
Maybonne series (1)
Come, pretty puss!
Freed, Artelle
Melanie Gaye series (1)
Come quickly, honey
Janson, Hank
Hank Janson series (19)
Come see me die
Neville, Margot
Inspector Grogan and Sergeant Manning series (16)
Come seven
Cohen, Octavus Roy
Polished ebony series (2)
Come spring
Williams, Ben Ames
Thread of scarlet series (2)
Come, sweet death
Mitchell, Scott
Brock Devlin series (5)
Come to dust
Lathen, Emma
John Putnam Thatcher series (8)
Come to judgment
Strange, John Stephen
Captain George Honegger series (2)
Come to my place
Kalman, Bobbie
In my world series (2)
Come to school, Dear Dragon
Hillert, Margaret
Dear Dragon series (9)
Come to tea with me
Goodman, Montague
Wantoknow series for boys (2)
Come to the bower
Mottram, Ralph Hale
Geoffrey Skene series (4)
Spanish Farm series (7)
Come to the circus
Blyton, Enid
Mister Galliano's circus series (4)
Come to the doctor, Harry
Chalmers, Mary
Harry series (5)
Come to town
Rockwell, Anne
Our life series (3)
Come watch him die
Jason, Stuart
Butcher series (2)
Come what may
Lunn, Arnold
Now I see series (2)
Come wind or weather
Francis, Clare
Voyage series (2)
Come winter
Hunter, Evan
David, Peter and Sandy series (2)
Jones, Douglas Clyde
Hasford family series (6)
Comeback capers
Bee, Clair
Chip Hilton series (21)
Comeback stars of pro sports
Aaseng, Nathan
Sports heroes series (28)
Comeback tour
Yeovil, Jack
Dark future series (3)
Comedian dies
Brett, Simon
Charles Paris series (5)
Comedies
Wain, John
Peter and Brian Leonard series (2)
Comedy of terrors
Innes, Michael
Sir John Appleby series (5)
Comes a stranger
Punshon, Ernest Robertson
Bobby Owen series (11)
Comet in Moominland
Jansson, Tove
Moomin series (1)
Comet kings
Hamilton, Edmond
Captain Future series (8)
Comet masters
Packard, Edward
Space hawks series (4)
Comet round the world
Leyland, Eric
Hunter Hawk series (5)
Cometeers
Williamson, Jack
Legion of Space series (2)
Comets and meteors
Bendick, Jeanne
Early bird astronomy series (2)
Comets have long tails
Johnston, Madeleine
Noah Bradshaw series (1)
Comets, meteoroids and asteroids, mavericks of the solar system
Branley, Franklyn Mansfield
Exploring our universe series (6)
Comfort letter
Solmssen, Arthur Robert George
Conyers and Dean series (3)
Comfort me with apples
De Vries, Peter
Chick Swallow series (1)
Comfort of cats
Tovey, Doreen
Cats series (10)
Comic adventures of Ginger Meggs
Kemsley, James
Ginger Meggs series (34)
Comics file magazine spotlight on The Fantastic Four files
Van Hise, James
Marvel superheroes, new series (11)
Coming attractions
Stamp, Terence
Double feature series (2)
Coming back
Norby, Lisa
Cheerleaders series (34)
Perry, Paul
Near-death series (3)
Coming event
Tubb, Edwin Charles
Dumarest series (26)
Coming from the fair
Hoult, Norah
Holy Ireland series (2)
Coming fury
Catton, Bruce
Centennial history of the Civil War series (1)
Coming my way?
John, Stephen
Albert Divine series (5)
Coming-of-age of the Chalet School
Brent-Dyer, Elinor Mary
Chalet School series (39)
Coming of Cassidy and the others
Mulford, Clarence Edward
Hopalong Cassidy series (5)
Coming of Christianity
Birt, David
Saxons and Vikings series (2)
Coming of Conan
Howard, Robert Ervin
Conan series (3)
Coming of Cuculain
O'Grady, Standish James
Cuculain trilogy (1)
Coming of Hester
Baird, Jean Katherine
Hester trilogy (1)
Coming of Hopalong Cassidy
Mulford, Clarence Edward
Hopalong Cassidy series (5)
Coming of love
Watts-Dunton, Theodore
Aylwin series (2)
Coming of Lys
Matthewman, Phyllis
Priory series (3)
Coming of Morikand
Smythe, R John
Conception series (2)
Coming of Saska
Tovey, Doreen
Cats series (9)
Coming of Steeleye
Dunn, Saul
Steeleye series (1)

Coming of the barbarians
Barr, Pat
Westerners in Japan series (1)
Coming of the Horseclans
Adams, Robert
Horseclans series (1)
Coming of the king
Hocking, Joseph
Religious movements series (5)
Coming of the monster
Dudley, Owen Francis
Problems of human happiness series (5)
Coming of the New Deal
Schlesinger, Arthur Meier
Age of Roosevelt series (2)
Coming of the Terrans
Brackett, Leigh
Mars series (3)
Coming of wisdom
Duncan, Dave
Seventh sword trilogy (2)
Coming on strong
Cooper, M E
Couples series (15)
Coming to tea
Garland, Sarah
Family life series (4)
Coming up the road
Bacheller, Irving
Cheerful Yankee trilogy (1)
Coming wave
Optic, Oliver
Yacht Club series (4)
Commanche duel
Crafton, Dennis
Lobo series (2)
Command
Macdonnell, James Edmond
Captain Peter Bentley series (2)
Melville-Ross, Antony
Submarine warfare series (4)
Command a king's ship
Kent, Alexander
Captain Richard Bolitho series (7)
Command decision
Cameron, J D
Omega sub series (2)
Command performance
Roberts, Nora
Cordina series (2)
Flowers series (37)
Command strike
Pendleton, Don
Mack Bolan series (29)
Commander Amanda Nightingale
Revelli, George
Amanda Nightingale series (1)
Commander Brady
Macdonnell, James Edmond
Jim Brady series (2)
Commander Flandry
Anderson, Poul
Sir Dominic Flandry series (6)
Commander Lawless, V.C.
Bennett, Rolf
Commander Lawless series (2)
Commander Toad and the big black hole
Yolen, Jane
Commander Toad series (2)
Commander Toad and the intergalactic spy
Yolen, Jane
Commander Toad series (3)
Commander Toad and the planet of the grapes
Yolen, Jane
Commander Toad series (1)
Commander Toad and the space pirates
Yolen, Jane
Commander Toad series (4)
Commando
Reitz, Deneys
Boer War journal trilogy (1)
Commando squad
Roberts, Mark Kelly
Soldier for hire series (6)
Commandos of the clouds
Leyland, Eric
Hunter Hawk series (4)
Comments of Abe Martin and his neighbors
Hubbard, Kin
Abe Martin series (14)
Commitments
Arnold, Judith
Keeping the faith trilogy (2)
Doyle, Roddy
Barrytown trilogy (1)
Committee
Seaman, Donald
Sydenham series (3)

Commodore
Bisset, James
Years at sea series (3)
De Hartog, Jan
Captain Martinus Harinxma trilogy (2)
Forester, Cecil Scott
Horatio Hornblower series (9)
Commodore at sea
Chandler, Arthur Bertram
John Grimes series (10)
Rim series (12)
Commodore Hornblower
Forester, Cecil Scott
Horatio Hornblower series (9)
Commodore Kelso
White, James Dillon
Roger Kelso series (6)
Common defense
Ruggero, Ed
Mark Isen series (1)
Common heart
Horgan, Paul
Mountain standard time trilogy (3)
Common murder
McDermid, Val
Lindsay Gordon series (2)
Common people
Martin, Archibald Edward
Pel Pelham and Detective Linley series (1)
Common sense is all you need
Connington, John Jervis
Sir Clinton Driffield series (17)
Commune
Margueritte, Paul
Franco-Prussian War series (4)
Commune 2000A.D.
Reynolds, Mack
Bat Hardin series (1)
Communicating door
Camp, Wadsworth
Garth series (2)
Communipath worlds
Elgin, Suzette Haden
Coyote Jones series (3)
Communipaths
Elgin, Suzette Haden
Coyote Jones series (1)
Communist's corpse
Wormser, Richard
Sergeant Joe Dixon series (2)
Community in the Lord
Hinnebusch, Paul
In the Lord series (2)
Community magic
Cleveland-Peck, Patricia
William the wizard series (2)
Community of men
Kiddell, John
Hamish, David and Bottle series (2)
Comne home, brumby
Patchett, Mary Elwyn
Joey Meehan series (2)
Companeros
Blackburn, Thomas Wakefield
Stanton Empire series (5)
Companion
Rose, Pamela
Star trek fan series (16)
Siegel, Scott
Dark forces series (8)
Companion to Sirius
Goodchild, George
Inspector McLean series (32)
Companions
Nathan-Turner, John
Doctor Who series (162)
Companions of Jehu
Dumas, Alexandre
Napoleon series (2)
Companions of Pickle
Lang, Andrew
Pickle series (2)
Companions of the day and night
Harris, Wilson
Black Marsden series (2)
Civilizations quartet (2)
Company of bandits
Story, Jack Trevor
Sexton Blake series (1579)
Company of glory
Pangborn, Edgar
Davy series (3)
Company of Saints
Anthony, Evelyn
Davina Graham series (4)
Company parade
Jameson, Storm
Hervey Russell series (3)
Mirror in darkness trilogy (1)

Compare these dead!
Rea, Margaret Lucile Paine
Lieutenant Powledge series (2)
Compare with us from the big red bus
Wood, Leslie
Big red bus series (4)
Compartment K
Reilly, Helen
Inspector Christopher McKee series (25)
Compass error
Bedford, Sybille
Constanza and Flavia series (2)
Compass points north
Atkinson, Mary Evelyn
Lockett family series (3)
Compassion
Perez Galdos, Benito
Contemporary novels of Spain series (30)
Compelling case
Underwood, Michael
Rosa Epton series (13)
Competition
Lowell, Melissa
Silver blades series (3)
Compleat Bolo
Laumer, Keith
Bolo series (2)
Compleat Crow
Lumley, Brian
Titus Crow series (6)
Compleat enchanter
De Camp, Lyon Sprague
Harold Shea series (2)
Compleat therapist
Kottler, Jeffrey
Therapist series (3)
Compleat werewolf, and other tales of fantasy and science fiction
Boucher, Anthony
Fergus O'Breen series (4)
Complete adventures of Blinky Bill
Wall, Dorothy
Blinky Bill series (3)
Complete adventures of Charlie and Mr Willy Wonka
Dahl, Roald
Charlie Bucket series (2)
Complete adventures of Olga da Polga
Bond, Michael
Olga da Polga series (4)
Complete adventures of Snugglepot and Cuddlepie
Gibbs, May
Gumnut Land series (8)
Complete adventures of the Borrowers
Norton, Mary
Borrowers series (4)
Complete and utter my word
Muir, Frank
My word series (4)
Complete book of swords
Saberhagen, Fred
Book of swords trilogy (3)
Complete browser's dictionary
Ciardi, John
Browser's dictionary series (2)
Complete change
Philip, Alexander John
James Jameson series (1)
Complete Clerihews
Bentley, Edmund Clerihew
Clerihews series (3)
Complete compleat enchanter
De Camp, Lyon Sprague
Harold Shea series (3)
Complete Father Christmas
Briggs, Raymond
Father Christmas series (2)
Complete Fursey
Wall, Mervyn
Fursey series (2)
Complete golf gamesmanship
Potter, Stephen
Lifemanship Correspondence College series (6)
Complete human boy
Phillpotts, Eden
Human boy series (5)
Complete Masters of darkness
Etchison, Dennis
Masters of darkness series (3)
Complete me and Gus
Anthony, Frank Sheldon
Gus Tomlins series (3)
Complete memoirs of George Sherston
Sassoon, Siegfried
Sherston trilogy (3)
Complete Monty Python
Monty Python
Monty Python series (5)

Complete Naff guide
Bryson, Kit
Naff series (1)
Legris, Jean-Luc
Naff series (1)
Complete Night of the living dead filmbook
Russo, John
Living dead series (2)
Complete Peterkin papers
Hale, Lucretia Peabody
Peterkin series (2)
Complete Reginald Perrin
Nobbs, David
Reginald Perrin series (3)
Complete robot
Asimov, Isaac
Robot series (5)
Complete short stories of Raffles, the Amateur Cracksman
Tremayne, Peter
Raffles series (18)
Complete sportsman
Graham, Harry
Reginald Drake Biffin series (3)
Complete state of death
Gardner, John Edmund
Detective Inspector Derek Torry series (1)
Complete steel
Aird, Catherine
Inspector C D Sloan series (3)
Complete stranger
Van Siller, Hilda
Allan Stewart series (1)
Complete tales of Uncle Remus
Harris, Joel Chandler
Uncle Remus series (9)
Complete Uncle Abner
Post, Melville Davisson
Uncle Abner series (2)
Complete upmanship
Potter, Stephen
Lifemanship Correspondence College series (4)
Complete works of Shakespeare and Monty Python
Skynner, Robin
Survival series (2)
Complex man
Farca, Marie C
Andrew Ames series (2)
Compliments of a fiend
Brown, Fredric
Ed and Am Hunter series (4)
Compound for death
Disney, Doris Miles
Jim O'Neill series (1)
Computer caper
Dank, Milton
Galaxy Gang series (1)
Computer for Charlie
Allen, Joy
Charlie series (9)
Computer game murder
Dank, Milton
Galaxy Gang series (5)
Computer kill
Banks, Raymond E
Sam King series (1)
Derrick, Lionel
Penetrator series (30)
Computer that went bananas
Elias, Horace J
Flintstones series (6)
Comrade Charlie
Freemantle, Brian
Charlie Muffin series (10)
Comrade Don Camillo
Guareschi, Giovanni
Don Camillo series (5)
Comrades at arms
Feval, Paul
Years between series (5)
Comrades from Canada
Wynne, May
Comrades from Canada series (2)
Comrades of the air
Carter, Dorothy
Marise Duncan series (5)
Comrades of the right hand
Carter, Nicholas
Nicholas Carter series (362)
Comstock crazy
Sharpe, Jon
Canyon O'Grady series (6)
Comstock gold fraud
Roberts, J R
Gunsmith series (61)
Comstock killers
Sharpe, Jon
Trailsman series (23)

Comstock Lode
Curry, Tom
Captain Mesquite series (2)
Con game
Cronin, Michael
Sam Harris series (4)
Waugh, Hillary
Chief Fred Fellows series (11)
Con man
McBain, Ed
Eighty Seventh Precinct series (4)
Verner, Gerald
Paul Rivington series (1)
Conan
Carter, Lin
Conan series (8)
Howard, Robert Ervin
Conan series (8)
Conan and the gods of the mountain
Green, Roland James
Conan series (67)
Conan and the prophecy
Moore, Roger Elwood
Conan series (44)
Endless quest series (20)
Conan and the sorcerer
Offutt, Andrew Jefferson
Conan series (34)
Conan and the spider god
De Camp, Lyon Sprague
Conan series (32)
Conan and the treasure of Python
Roberts, John Maddox
Conan series (68)
Conan chronicles
Carter, Lin
Conan series (13)
Howard, Robert Ervin
Conan series (10)
Conan grimoire
De Camp, Lyon Sprague
Conan series (69)
Conan of Aquilonia
De Camp, Lyon Sprague
Conan series (17)
Howard, Robert Ervin
Conan series (17)
Conan of Cimmeria
Carter, Lin
Conan series (9)
Howard, Robert Ervin
Conan series (9)
Conan of the isles
Carter, Lin
Conan series (18)
Conan of the Red Brotherhood
Carpenter, Leonard
Conan series (66)
Conan reader
De Camp, Lyon Sprague
Conan series (69)
Conan swordbook
De Camp, Lyon Sprague
Conan series (69)
Conan the adventurer
Howard, Robert Ervin
Conan series (12)
Conan the avenger
Howard, Robert Ervin
Conan series (16)
Nyberg, Bjorn
Conan series (16)
Conan the barbarian
Carter, Lin
Conan series (36)
Howard, Robert Ervin
Conan series (5)
Conan the bold
Roberts, John Maddox
Conan series (56)
Conan the buccaneer
Carter, Lin
Conan series (13)
Conan the champion
Roberts, John Maddox
Conan series (51)
Conan the conqueror
Howard, Robert Ervin
Conan series (1)
Conan the defender
Jordan, Robert
Conan series (35)
Conan the defiant
Perry, Steve
Conan series (52)
Conan the destroyer
Jordan, Robert
Conan series (41)
Conan the fearless
Perry, Steve
Conan series (47)

Conan the formidable
Perry, Steve
Conan series (60)

Conan the free lance
Perry, Steve
Conan series (61)

Conan the freebooter
Howard, Robert Ervin
Conan series (10)

Conan the great
Carpenter, Leonard
Conan series (59)

Conan the guardian
Green, Roland James
Conan series (62)

Conan the hero
Carpenter, Leonard
Conan series (57)

Conan the indomitable
Perry, Steve
Conan series (58)

Conan the invincible
Jordan, Robert
Conan series (37)

Conan the liberator
Carter, Lin
Conan series (29)

Conan the magnificent
Jordan, Robert
Conan series (40)

Conan the marauder
Roberts, John Maddox
Conan series (53)

Conan the mercenary
Offutt, Andrew Jefferson
Conan series (34)

Conan the outcast
Carpenter, Leonard
Conan series (63)

Conan the outlaw
Moore, Roger Elwood
Conan series (45)
Endless quest series (25)

Conan the raider
Carpenter, Leonard
Conan series (48)

Conan the rebel
Anderson, Poul
Conan series (31)

Conan the relentless
Green, Roland James
Conan series (65)

Conan the renegade
Carpenter, Leonard
Conan series (49)

Conan the rogue
Roberts, John Maddox
Conan series (64)

Conan the swordman
Nyberg, Bjorn
Conan series (26)

Conan the swordsman
Carter, Lin
Conan series (26)

Conan the triumphant
Jordan, Robert
Conan series (39)

Conan the unconquered
Jordan, Robert
Conan series (38)

Conan the undaunted
Ward, James Michael
Conan series (43)
Endless quest series (19)

Conan the usurper
Howard, Robert Ervin
Conan series (15)

Conan the valiant
Green, Roland James
Conan series (54)

Conan the valorous
Roberts, John Maddox
Conan series (46)

Conan the victorious
Jordan, Robert
Conan series (42)

Conan the wanderer
Carter, Lin
Conan series (11)
Howard, Robert Ervin
Conan series (11)

Conan the warlord
Carpenter, Leonard
Conan series (55)

Conan the warrior
Howard, Robert Ervin
Conan series (14)

Conceal and disguise
Kane, Henry
Inspector McGregor series (2)

Conceived in liberty
Fast, Howard
Call of fife and drum trilogy (1)

Concept of man in contemporary China
Munro, Donald Jacques
Man in China series (2)

Concept of man in early China
Munro, Donald Jacques
Man in China series (1)

Conception
Smythe, R John
Conception series (1)

Concerning Belinda
Brainerd, Eleanor Hoyt
Belinda series (1)

Concerning Blackshirt
Graeme, Roderic
Blackshirt series (11)

Concerning Isabel Carnaby
Fowler, Ellen Thornycroft
Isabel Carnaby trilogy (1)

Concerning Paul and Fiammetta
Harker, Lizzie Allen
Fiammetta series (2)

Concerning Peter Jackson and others
Frankau, Gilbert
Peter Jackson series (4)

Concerning Teddy
Hickson, Mabel
Teddy series (1)

Concerning the Saint
Bloxsom, Peter
Saint series (51)

Concert party murders
Norman, John
Martin Speed series (3)

Conclusion
Gross, Edward
V series (16)

Concordia
Fleetwood, Frances
Concordia series (1)

Concordia errant
Fleetwood, Frances
Concordia series (2)

Concrete blonde
Connelly, Michael
Harry Bosch series (3)

Concrete boot
Royce, Kenneth
Spider Scott series (2)

Concrete cage
Novak, Robert
Joe Blaze series (3)

Concrete castle
Gerard, Francis
Sir John Meredith series (1)

Concrete castle murders
Gerard, Francis
Sir John Meredith series (1)

Concrete crime
Coles, Manning
Tommy Hambledon series (23)

Concrete evidence
Russell, Martin
Jim Larkin series (2)

Concrete island
Ballard, James Graham
Urban disaster trilogy (2)

Concrete kimono
Carstairs, John Paddy
Garaway Trenton series (5)

Concrete maze
Morland, Nigel
Mrs Palmyra Pym series (22)

Condamine case
Dalton, Moray
Inspector Hugh Collier series (10)

Condemned
Desmond, Hugh
Alan Fraser series (24)

Condemned to live
Plummer, Thomas Arthur
Detective Inspector Andrew Frampton series (44)

Condition of Muzak
Moorcock, Michael
Jerry Cornelius series (4)

Condition purple
Turnbull, Peter
P Division series (6)

Condo kill
Barth, Richard
Margaret Binton series (4)

Condom poems
Dacey, Philip
Condom poems series (1)

Condom poems II
Dacey, Philip
Condom poems series (2)

Condor
Grant, Maxwell
Shadow series (80)

Condor Crags adventure
Brent-Dyer, Elinor Mary
Chudleigh Hold series (2)

Condor Pass
Sharpe, Jon
Trailsman series (12)

Conduct of a member
Gielgud, Val
Inspector Gregory Pellew and Viscount Clymping series (6)

Conduct of Major Maxim
Lyall, Gavin
Major Harry Maxim series (2)

Conestoga people
Sommers, Jeanne
Making of America series (3)

Confederate
Randolph, Forrest A
Confederate series (1)

Confederate challenge
Sharpe, Jon
Trailsman series (69)

Conference at Cold Comfort Farm
Gibbons, Stella
Cold Comfort Farm series (3)

Confess, Fletch
McDonald, Gregory
Fletch series (5)
Francis Xavier Flynn series (1)

Confess to Doctor Morelle
Dudley, Ernest
Doctor Morelle series (10)

Confession
Pickard, Nancy
Jenny Cain series (9)

Confession at Dripspring
Gardner, Jerome
Dripspring series (5)

Confession of Brother Halmin
Peters, Ellis
Brother Cadfael series (15)

Confession of Hercule
Audemars, Pierre
Hercule Renard series (4)

Confession of murder
Barling, Charles
Inspector George Marshall series (12)
Neville, Margot
Inspector Grogan and Sergeant Manning series (13)

Confession of Ruggieri
Balzac, Honore de
Philosophic studies series (16)

Confessional
Higgins, Jack
Liam Devlin series (3)

Confessions and impressions
Mannin, Ethel
Confessions and impressions series (1)

Confessions at midnight
Duhamel, Georges
Salavin series (1)

Confessions from a haunted house
Lea, Timothy
Confessions series (38)

Confessions from a health farm
Lea, Timothy
Confessions series (14)

Confessions from a holiday camp
Lea, Timothy
Confessions series (4)

Confessions from a hotel
Lea, Timothy
Confessions series (5)

Confessions from a luxury liner
Lea, Timothy
Confessions series (25)

Confessions from a nudist colony
Lea, Timothy
Confessions series (27)

Confessions from a package tour
Dixon, Rosie
Confessions series (23)

Confessions from a sex clinic
May, Jonathan
Confessions series (32)

Confessions from a strip club
May, Jonathan
Confessions series (30)

Confessions from a stud farm
May, Jonathan
Confessions series (37)

Confessions from an escort agency
Dixon, Rosie
Confessions series (19)

Confessions from the beat
May, Jonathan
Confessions series (21)

Confessions from the clink
Lea, Timothy
Confessions series (7)

Confessions from the Olympics
May, Jonathan
Confessions series (39)

Confessions from the pop scene
Lea, Timothy
Confessions series (12)

Confessions from the shop floor
Lea, Timothy
Confessions series (15)

Confessions of a babysitter
Dixon, Rosie
Confessions series (26)

Confessions of a beachcomber
Banfield, Edmund James
Beachcomber series (1)

Confessions of a convict
Foxall, Peter Augustus
Detective Sergeant Scamp series (3)

Confessions of a driving instructor
Lea, Timothy
Confessions series (2)

Confessions of a film extra
Lea, Timothy
Confessions series (6)

Confessions of a fool
Strindberg, Johan August
Soul's development trilogy (2)
Soul's development trilogy (3)

Confessions of a games master
May, Jonathan
Confessions series (22)

Confessions of a gasman
May, Jonathan
Confessions series (35)

Confessions of a gym mistress
Dixon, Rosie
Confessions series (13)

Confessions of a hitch hiker
Lea, Timothy
Confessions series (3)

Confessions of a housewife
May, Jonathan
Confessions series (31)

Confessions of a lady courier
Dixon, Rosie
Confessions series (17)

Confessions of a long distance lorry driver
Lea, Timothy
Confessions series (16)

Confessions of a lover
Anand, Mulk Raj
Seven ages of man series (3)

Confessions of a milkman
Lea, Timothy
Confessions series (29)

Confessions of a new boy
Horne, Donald
New boy trilogy (2)

Confessions of a night nurse
Dixon, Rosie
Confessions series (11)

Confessions of a personal secretary
Dixon, Rosie
Confessions series (28)

Confessions of a plumber's mate
Lea, Timothy
Confessions series (18)

Confessions of a pop performer
Lea, Timothy
Confessions series (12)

Confessions of a private dick
Lea, Timothy
Confessions series (24)

Confessions of a private soldier
Lea, Timothy
Confessions series (8)

Confessions of a shop assistant
May, Jonathan
Confessions series (9)

Confessions of a stuntman
May, Jonathan
Confessions series (34)

Confessions of a surgeon
Mair, George Brown
Surgeon series (1)

Confessions of a teenage frog
Smith, Susan
Samantha Slade series (2)

Confessions of a travel courier
May, Jonathan
Confessions series (20)

Confessions of a travelling salesman
Lea, Timothy
Confessions series (10)

Confessions of a window cleaner
Lea, Timothy
Confessions series (1)

Confessions of an astronaut
May, Jonathan
Confessions series (36)

Confessions of an ice cream man
Lea, Timothy
Confessions series (33)

Confessions of an innkeeper
Fothergill, John
Innkeeper series (2)

Confessions of an Irish rebel
Behan, Brendan
Borstal boy series (2)

Confessions of an only child
Klein, Norma
Only child series (1)

Confessions of Arsene Lupin
Leblanc, Maurice
Arsene Lupin series (6)

Confessions of Mrs May
Le Breton, Thomas
Mrs May series (2)

Confessions of Zeno
Svevo, Italo
Zeno series (1)

Confetti can be red
Cumberland, Marten
Saturnin Dax series (14)

Confetti for a killing
Edwards, Charman
Percy Aloysius Huff series (5)

Confidence king
Carter, Nicholas
Nicholas Carter series (367)

Confirm or deny
Ison, Graham
Superintendent John Gaffney series (2)

Confirmed in command
Macdonnell, James Edmond
Commander William Mallett series (3)

Conflict
Baldwin, Faith
Condit family series (1)
Janson, Hank
Hank Janson series (38)
Macdonnell, James Edmond
Captain Peter Bentley series (21)
Payne, Oliver
Northwest Territory series (4)

Conflict center Naator
Darlton, Clark
Perry Rhodan series (77)

Conflict fo shadows
Robertson, Colin
Superintendent Bradley series (3)

Conflict of evidence
Ottolengui, Rodrigues
John Barnes series (2)
Robert Leroy Mitchell series (2)

Conflict of interest
Williams, Brad
Sam Benedict series (3)

Conflict within
Reid, Desmond
Sexton Blake series (1496)

Confounding of Sergeant Cluff
North, Gil
Sergeant Caleb Cluff series (7)

Confrontation
Caute, David
Confrontation trilogy (3)
Tomino, Yoshiyuki
Gundam mobile suit trilogy (3)

Confusion by Cupid
Lambert, Janet
Jordons series (3)

Cong kiss
Montague, J J
Black Swan series (2)

Congleton lark
Ross, Angus
Mark Farrow series (12)

Congo diamonds
Hunter, Richard Wilkes
Congo series (1)

Congo mercenary
Hunter, Richard Wilkes
Congo series (2)

Congo mercenary major
Hunter, Richard Wilkes
Congo series (3)

Congo Venus
Head, Matthew
Doctor Mary Finney series (3)

Congo war-cry
Caillou, Alan
Colonel Matthew Tobin series (3)

Coningsby
Disraeli, Benjamin
Young England trilogy (1)

Coniston
Churchill, Winston
American national development series (4)

Conjurers
Gurney, David
Conjurers series (1)

Conjuror's alibi
Lillington, Kenneth
Soapy series (1)
Conjuror's house
White, Stewart Edward
Free forest series (1)
Connecticut boys in the western reserve
Braden, James Andrew
John Jerome and Return Kingdom series (2)
Connecticut countess
Watmough, David
Davey Bryant series (4)
Connecting door
Heppenstall, Rayner
Harold Atha series (1)
Connecting link
Carter, Nicholas
Nicholas Carter series (405)
Connector
Williamson, Tony
Lee Corey series (1)
Connie
Remick, Grace May
Sheldon Six series (3)
Connie Morgan hits the trail
Hendryx, James Beardsley
Connie Morgan series (7)
Connie Morgan in Alaska
Hendryx, James Beardsley
Connie Morgan series (1)
Connie Morgan in the Arctic
Hendryx, James Beardsley
Connie Morgan series (9)
Connie Morgan in the barren lands
Hendryx, James Beardsley
Connie Morgan series (7)
Connie Morgan in the cattle country
Hendryx, James Beardsley
Connie Morgan series (5)
Connie Morgan in the fur country
Hendryx, James Beardsley
Connie Morgan series (4)
Connie Morgan in the lumber camps
Hendryx, James Beardsley
Connie Morgan series (3)
Connie Morgan, prospector
Hendryx, James Beardsley
Connie Morgan series (8)
Connie Morgan with the forest rangers
Hendryx, James Beardsley
Connie Morgan series (6)
Connie Morgan with the Mounted
Hendryx, James Beardsley
Connie Morgan series (2)
Connie Morgan with the Northwest Mounted
Hendryx, James Beardsley
Connie Morgan series (2)
Connoisseur's case
Innes, Michael
Sir John Appleby series (20)
Conquer
Masefield, John
Byzantium series (2)
Conquering family
Costain, Thomas Bertram
History of the Plantagenets tetralogy (1)
Conquering horse
Manfred, Frederick
Buckskin Man tales series (3)
Conqueror Inn
Punshon, Ernest Robertson
Bobby Owen series (18)
Conquerors
Costain, Thomas Bertram
History of the Plantagenets tetralogy (1)
Eckert, Allan Wesley
Winning of America series (3)
Conquerors of Reglathium
Sirota, Mike
Dannus series (2)
Conquest
Abbey, Lynn
Unicorn and dragon series (2)
Payne, Oliver
Northwest Territory series (2)
Conquest after midnight
Gray, Berkeley
Norman Conquest series (33)
Conquest before autumn
Eden, Matthew
Marc Savage series (6)
Conquest calls the tune
Gray, Berkeley
Norman Conquest series (50)
Conquest goes home
Gray, Berkeley
Norman Conquest series (34)
Conquest goes west
Gray, Berkeley
Norman Conquest series (29)
Conquest in California
Gray, Berkeley
Norman Conquest series (35)
Conquest in command
Gray, Berkeley
Norman Conquest series (32)
Conquest in Ireland
Gray, Berkeley
Norman Conquest series (51)
Conquest in Scotland
Gray, Berkeley
Norman Conquest series (24)
Conquest in the underworld
Gray, Berkeley
Norman Conquest series (43)
Conquest likes it hot
Gray, Berkeley
Norman Conquest series (48)
Conquest marches on
Gray, Berkeley
Norman Conquest series (4)
Conquest of brain mysteries
Bankoff, George Alexis
Conquest of series (4)
Conquest of disease
Bankoff, George Alexis
Conquest of series (1)
Conquest of Jerusalem
Harry, Myriam
Jerusalem series (1)
Conquest of life
Behaine, Rene
History of a society series (4)
Conquest of London, 1870-1883
Edel, Leon
Henry James series (2)
Conquest of pain
Bankoff, George Alexis
Conquest of series (2)
Conquest of Plassans
Zola, Emile
Rougon Macquart series (4)
Conquest of Quendor
Meretzky, S Eric
Zork series (4)
Conquest of the Amazon
Fearn, John Russell
Golden Amazon series (7)
Conquest of the barbarians
Stine, Harlan William
Wizards, warlocks and you series (17)
Conquest of the Planet of the Apes
Jakes, John
Planet of the Apes series (4)
Conquest of the river
Fatchen, Max
Murray River series (2)
Conquest of the time master
Beach, Lynn
Wizards, warlocks and you series (8)
Conquest of tuberculosis
Bankoff, George Alexis
Conquest of series (3)
Conquest on the run
Gray, Berkeley
Norman Conquest series (40)
Conquest overboard
Gray, Berkeley
Norman Conquest series (46)
Conquest takes all
Gray, Berkeley
Norman Conquest series (6)
Conquest touch
Gray, Berkeley
Norman Conquest series (18)
Conquistador
Sadler, Barry
Casca series (10)
Conrad and his world
Sherry, Norman
Conrad's world series (2)
Conrad's Eastern world
Sherry, Norman
Conrad's world series (1)
Conrad's Western world
Sherry, Norman
Conrad's world series (2)
Cons at large
Roberts, Jack
Street Hawk series (2)
Conscience of the King
Duggan, Alfred
Saxon trilogy (1)
Conscience of the rich
Snow, Charles Percy
Strangers and brothers series (3)
Consciousness machine
Saxton, Josephine
Jane Saint series (2)
Conscript
Balzac, Honore de
Philosophic studies series (11)
Erckmann, Emile
French campaign series (1)
Consequence of crime
Linington, Elizabeth
Sergeant Ivor Maddox series (10)
Consequences
Conlon, Kathleen
Forgotten season series (2)
Consider Phlebas
Banks, Iain Menzies
Culture series (1)
Consider your verdict
Hardinge, Rex
Sexton Blake series (1238)
Consort to the Queen
Prole, Lozania
Tudor trilogy (3)
Conspiracy
Aldanov, Mark Aleksandrovich
Thinker series (3)
Meriton, Peter
Captain Dack series (2)
Proudfoot, Walter
Inspector Bill Vallance series (3)
Ward, Richard Heron
Neil Falder series (1)
Conspiracy at Abbey
Leyland, Eric
Abbey series (2)
Conspiracy at Angel
Flynn, Brian
Anthony Bathurst series (32)
Conspiracy of blood
Sharp, Allen
Storytrails series (12)
Conspiracy of poisons
Sturrock, Jeremy
Bow Street Runner series (4)
Conspiracy of rumors
Carter, Nicholas
Nicholas Carter series (592)
Conspiracy of strangers
Martin, Lee
Deb Ralston series (2)
Conspirators
Dumas, Alexandre
Regency trilogy (1)
Haggard, William
Colonel Charles Russell series (10)
Riefe, Alan
Huntington Cage series (2)
Conspirators at large
Maddock, Stephen
Timothy Terrel series (9)
Conspirators in Capri
Maddock, Stephen
Timothy Terrel series (5)
Conspirators of Trieste
Verne, Jules
Giant raft series (2)
Conspirators three
Maddock, Stephen
Timothy Terrel series (7)
Constable across the moors
Rhea, Nicholas
Aidensfield series (4)
Constable along the lane
Rhea, Nicholas
Aidensfield series (7)
Constable among the heather
Rhea, Nicholas
Aidensfield series (10)
Constable and the lady
Bude, John
Inspector Meredith series (19)
Constable around the green
Rhea, Nicholas
Aidensfield series (13)
Constable around the village
Rhea, Nicholas
Aidensfield series (3)
Constable beneath the trees
Rhea, Nicholas
Aidensfield series (14)
Constable by the sea
Rhea, Nicholas
Aidensfield series (6)
Constable by the stream
Rhea, Nicholas
Aidensfield series (11)
Constable, guard thyself!
Wade, Henry
Inspector Poole series (4)
Constable in disguise
Rhea, Nicholas
Aidensfield series (9)
Constable in the dale
Rhea, Nicholas
Aidensfield series (5)
Constable on call
Rhea, Nicholas
Aidensfield series (12)
Constable on the hill
Rhea, Nicholas
Aidensfield series (1)
Constable on the prowl
Rhea, Nicholas
Aidensfield series (2)
Constable through the meadow
Rhea, Nicholas
Aidensfield series (8)
Constables don't count
Fraser, Alex
Inspector Noel Tracy series (2)
Constance
Durrell, Lawrence
Avignon quintet (3)
Constant heart
Robins, Patricia
Dick and Tamily series (2)
Constant nymph
Kennedy, Margaret
Sanger family series (1)
Constant star
Blake, George
Oliphant series (1)
Constantinople
Loti, Pierre
Aziyade series (1)
Constellations
Boylan, James Finney
Heavenly bodies series (2)
Constructs
Kostlanetz, Richard
Constructs series (1)
Constructs five
Kostlanetz, Richard
Constructs series (5)
Constructs four
Kostlanetz, Richard
Constructs series (4)
Constructs six
Kostlanetz, Richard
Constructs series (6)
Constructs three
Kostlanetz, Richard
Constructs series (3)
Constructs two
Kostlanetz, Richard
Constructs series (2)
Consuelo
Sand, George
Consuelo series (1)
Consul's file
Theroux, Paul
Spencer Monroe Savage series (1)
Consultant
Hilton, Alec
Doctor Martin Lestrange series (1)
Consulting room crime
Osborne, Mark
Sexton Blake series (713)
Consulting room mystery
Osborne, Mark
Sexton Blake series (713)
Consumer's guide for kids
Berry, Joy
Ready-set-grow series (18)
Contaband
Janson, Hank
Hank Janson series (60)
Contact and commune
Smith, Lester Neil
Contact and commune series (1)
Contact lens
Urquhart, Macgregor
Chief Inspector Joshua Smarles series (5)
Contact lost
Craig, David
Roy Rickman trilogy (3)
Contact man
Betteridge, Don
Tiger Lester series (11)
Contact Mister Delgado
Pattinson, James
Harvey Landon series (1)
Contact with a killer
Jobson, Hamilton
Inspector Anders series (8)
Container is ready
Sanders, J R
Container series (1)
Contamination
Vornholt, John
Star trek, the next generation series (16)
Contender
Lipsyte, Roger
Contender trilogy (1)
Content assignment
Roth, Holly
Lieutenant Kelly series (1)
Content with what I have
Warren, Clarence Henry
Happy countryman series (7)
Contented Jim
Finley, Martha Farquharson
Honest Jim series (2)
Contents under pressure
Buchanan, Edna
Britt Montero series (1)
Conte's run
Lassiter, Adam
Dennison's war series (2)
Contessa came too
Bryan, John
Richard Sarel series (2)
Continent in the sky
Berna, Paul
Michael Jousse series (2)
Continent makers, and other tales of the Viagens
De Camp, Lyon Sprague
Krishna series (2)
Continental contract
Pendleton, Don
Mack Bolan series (5)
Continental dollar
Knipe, Emilie Benson
Benedict Arnold series (1)
Continental holiday
Sutton, Phyllis
Merryl Hastings series (1)
Continental Op
Hammett, Dashiell
Continental Op series (4)
Continuing adventures of Captain Gregory Dangerfield
Lloyd, Jeremy
Captain Gregory Dangerfield series (2)
Continuum
Welling, Lois
Star trek fan series (30)
Contraband
Wheatley, Dennis
Gregory Sallust series (1)
Contraband from other space
Chandler, Arthur Bertram
Rim series (10)
Contraband from Otherspace
Chandler, Arthur Bertram
John Grimes series (5)
Contract
Poyer, Joe
Cole Brogan series (3)
Contract, and other stories
Glyn, Elinor
Elizabeth series (2)
Contract for a killer
Reid, Desmond
Sexton Blake series (1497)
Contract for a killing
Brent, R L
Liquidator series (2)
Contract Terror Summit
McCray, Mike
Black Berets series (10)
Contract White Lady
McCray, Mike
Black Berets series (4)
Contract with James
Heaton, Rose Henniker
James Montgomerie series (3)
Contrarywise
Greenhalgh, Zohra
Trickster series (1)
Contrband castle
Burgoyne, Peter
Peter Burgoyne series (4)
Conundrum
Lyons, Steve
Timewyrm series (7)
Convent on Styx
Mitchell, Gladys
Dame Beatrice Bradley series (49)
Conventionalists
Benson, Robert Hugh
Supernatural series (2)
Convergant series
Niven, Larry
Known Space series (11)
Converging parallels
Williams, Timothy
Commissario Trotti series (1)
Conversations with a corpse
Dennis, Robert C
Paul Reeder series (2)

Conversations with Igor Stravinsky
Stravinsky, Igor
Conversations series (1)
Conversations with Rabbi Small
Kemelman, Harry
Rabbi David Small series (9)
Converse and conflict
Smith, Lester Neil
Contact and commune series (2)
Conversion of Mrs Growser
Beaman, Sydney George Hulme
Toytown series (35)
Convert
Macdonnell, James Edmond
Captain Kenyon series (1)
Convertible hearse
Gault, William Campbell
Brock Callahan series (3)
Convict by proxy
Murray, Andrew
Sexton Blake series (106)
Convict 1066
Gray, Berkeley
Norman Conquest series (9)
Convicts
Foote, Horton
Orphans' home series (4)
Convict's hoard
Hugi, Maurice G
Martin Speed series (8)
Convivial codfish
Macleod, Charlotte
Sarah Kelling series (5)
Convoy
Pope, Dudley
Ned Yorke series (1)
Convoy commodore
McCutchan, Philip
Convoy series (1)
Convoy east
McCutchan, Philip
Convoy series (4)
Convoy homeward
McCutchan, Philip
Convoy series (6)
Convoy north
McCutchan, Philip
Convoy series (2)
Convoy of fear
McCutchan, Philip
Convoy series (5)
Convoy of steel
Hutson, Shaun
Sergeant Rolf Kessler series (3)
Convoy south
McCutchan, Philip
Convoy series (3)
Convoy strike
McGann, Michael
Marauders series (4)
Convoy to catastrophe
Kessler, Leo
Submarine series (3)
Conway, K.C.
Stone, Simon
Sir Brian Dinsmore Conway series (2)
Conways ahoy
Morgan, Geoffrey
Conways series (2)
Conways chronicle
Grover, Marshall
Larry and Stretch series (425)
Cook
Manning, Paul
Merry-go-rhymes series (1)
Cook up a crime
Russell, Charlotte Murray
Jane Amanda Edwards series (13)
Cookies and crutches
Delton, Judy
Pee wee scout series (1)
Cooking class
Sharmat, Marjorie Weinman
Kids on the bus series (2)
Cooking school murders
Rich, Virginia
Mrs Eugenia Potter series (1)
Cool breezes
Davidson, Linda
Endless summer series (4)
Cool clear death
Halleran, Tucker
Cam Maccardle series (1)
Cool cottontail
Ball, John
Virgil Tibbs series (2)
Cool day for killing
Haggard, William
Colonel Charles Russell series (11)
Cool repentance
Fraser, Antonia
Jemima Shore series (4)
Cool Sugar
Janson, Hank
Hank Janson series (26)
Coombe Hamlet
Westron, Charles
Salty series (3)
Coombe Saint Mary's
Diver, Maud
English scene series (4)
Co-op kill
Barth, Richard
Margaret Binton series (4)
Coopersmith
Griffin, Robert J
Coopersmith series (1)
Coopersmith's dolls
Griffin, Robert J
Coopersmith series (2)
Co-ordinator
York, Andrew
Jonas Wilde series (2)
Coot Club
Ransome, Arthur
Swallows and Amazons series (5)
Coots in the north, and other stories
Ransome, Arthur
Swallows and Amazons series (13)
Cooty-Doo
Cosgrove, Stephen Edward
Bugg series (14)
Cop hater
McBain, Ed
Eighty Seventh Precinct series (1)
Cop in a tight frame
Graham, Neill
Solo Malcolm series (32)
Cop-kill
Crawford, William
Colin Stryker series (2)
Cop killer
Bagby, George
Inspector Schmidt series (27)
Sjowall, Maj
Inspector Martin Beck series (9)
Cop-killer
Stout, Rex
Nero Wolfe and Archie Goodwin series (20)
Cop out
Jones, Roger William
Inspector Evans and Sergeant Beddoes series (2)
McNab, Claire
Inspector Carol Ashton and Sergeant Mark Bourke series (4)
Cop this lot
Culotta, Nino
Weird mob series (2)
Cop without a shield
O'Donnell, Lillian
Detective Norah Mulcahaney series (8)
Copenhagen affair
Oram, John
Man from U.N.C.L.E. series (3)
Coping
Skoglund, Elizabeth
Coping series (1)
Coping with overprotective parents
Webb, Margot
Coping series (2)
Coping with parents who are activists
Webb, Margot
Coping series (3)
Coping with street gangs
Webb, Margot
Coping series (1)
Copp for hire
Pendleton, Don
Joe Copp series (1)
Copp in deep
Pendleton, Don
Joe Copp series (3)
Copp in shock
Pendleton, Don
Joe Copp series (6)
Copp in the dark
Pendleton, Don
Joe Copp series (4)
Copp on fire
Pendleton, Don
Joe Copp series (2)
Copp on ice
Pendleton, Don
Joe Copp series (5)
Copper butterfly
Harvester, Simon
Asia in turmoil series (6)
Malcolm Kenton series (5)
Copper cloud
Gower, Iris
Catrin series (1)
Copper crown
Kennealy, Patricia
Keltiad series (1)
Copper fire
Preston, Fayrene
Delaneys, the untamed years trilogy (3)
Copper gold
Winslow, Pauline Glen
Superintendent Merlin Capricorn series (4)
Copper, Gold and Treasure
Williams, David
Mark Treasure series (5)
Copper house
Regis, Julius
Maurice Wallion series (1)
Copper kingdom
Gower, Iris
Copper kingdom series (1)
Copper kings
Willoughby, Lee Davis
Making of America series (41)
Copper lady
Nelson, Hugh Lawrence
Steve Johnson series (2)
Copper snare
Williams, Lawrence
Lgendary murders series (1)
Coppergold
Winslow, Pauline Glen
Superintendent Merlin Capricorn series (4)
Copperhead Trail mystery
Lloyd, Hugh
Hal Keen series (3)
Coppering lark
Meek, Victor
Coppering series (2)
Coppernob Buckland
Bourne, Lawrence R
Coppernob series (1)
Coppernob omnibus
Bourne, Lawrence R
Coppernob series (3)
Coppernob, Second Mate
Bourne, Lawrence R
Coppernob series (2)
Coppernob, shipowner
Bourne, Lawrence R
Coppernob series (4)
Coppers and gold
Brinton, Henry
John and Sally Strang series (5)
Coppers don't cry
Wainwright, John
Northern Police series (28)
Coppins Bridge saga
Daish, Elizabeth
Coppins Bridge trilogy (3)
Cops and robbers
Meek, Victor
Coppering series (1)
Copulation explosion
Gray, Rod
Lady from L.U.S.T. series (14)
Copusin Kelly's family secret
Pascal, Francine
Sweet Valley kids series (24)
Copy-cat killings
Thomas, Martin
Sexton Blake series (1439)
Copy for crime
Carnac, Carol
Inspector Julian Rivers series (6)
Copycat killers
Pentecost, Hugh
George Crowder series (3)
Coral
Mackenzie, Compton
Jenny Pearl and Maurice Avery series (2)
Coral Island
Ballantyne, Robert Michael
Coral Island series (1)
Coral princess murders
Crane, Frances
Pat and Jean Abbott series (18)
Coral reef
Reese, Bob
Ocean critterland series (6)
Coral Reef castaway
Hallard, Peter
Con and Ginty series (1)
Coral ship
Munroe, Kirk
Rail and water series (4)
Coral turtle mystery
Hope, Laura Lee
Bobbsey twins series (72)
Coral wreck
Crisp, Frank
Dirk Rogers series (10)
Corbie
Mayne, William
Animal library series (2)
Cord
Rountree, Owen
Jim Cord series (1)
Cordelia's pathway out
Foster, Edna Abigail
Hortense series (2)
Corder index
Raine, Richard
David Martini series (1)
Cordially invited to meet death
Stout, Rex
Nero Wolfe and Archie Goodwin series (9)
Cords of vanity
Cabell, James Branch
Dom Manuel and his descendants series (15)
Tripp, Miles
John Samson series (11)
Corduroy
Bell, Adrian
Country life series (1)
Corduroy goes to the doctor
McCue, Lisa
Corduroy series (4)
Corduroy on the go
McCue, Lisa
Corduroy series (5)
Corduroy's busy street
McCue, Lisa
Corduroy series (6)
Corduroy's day
McCue, Lisa
Corduroy series (1)
Corduroy's party
McCue, Lisa
Corduroy series (2)
Corduroy's toys
McCue, Lisa
Corduroy series (3)
Coreus the prince
Farrell, Simon
City of shadows series (1)
Corey
Miner, Jane Claypool
Sunfire series (22)
Corey Lane
Zollinger, Norman
Corey Lane series (1)
Corfu affair
Phillifent, John Thomas
Man from U.N.C.L.E. series (20)
Cork and the serpent
Hastings, Macdonald
Montague Cork series (3)
Cork in bottle
Hastings, Macdonald
Montague Cork series (2)
Cork in the doghouse
Hastings, Macdonald
Montague Cork series (4)
Cork on location
Hastings, Macdonald
Montague Cork series (5)
Cork on telly
Hastings, Macdonald
Montague Cork series (5)
Cork on the water
Hastings, Macdonald
Montague Cork series (1)
Cork Street crime
Brandon, John Gordon
Arthur Stukeley Pennington series (11)
Inspector Patrick Aloysius McCarthy series (22)
Cork Street, next to the hatters
Johnson, Pamela Hansford
Daniel Skipton trilogy (3)
Corker's freedom
Berger, John
Telepathy series (2)
Corkscrew
Wood, Ted
Reid Bennett series (5)
Corky Coconut
Reed, Giles
Munch Bunch character series (20)
Corleone
Crawford, Francis Marion
Roman society series (4)
Cormack came back
Grover, Marshall
Larry and Stretch series (265)
Cormorant ahoy!
Haley, George Elvey
Cormorant series (1)
Cormorant on patrol
Haley, George Elvey
Cormorant series (4)
Cormorant sails again
Haley, George Elvey
Cormorant series (3)
Cormorant venture
Trease, Geoffrey
Mandeville trilogy (3)
Cormorant's brood
Fletcher, Inglis
Carolina series (7)
Carolina series (12)
Cormorant's commandos
Haley, George Elvey
Cormorant series (2)
Corn-fed boy
Lenski, Lois
Regional series (10)
Cornelius chronicles
Moorcock, Michael
Jerry Cornelius series (4)
Jerry Cornelius series (6)
Jerry Cornelius series (7)
Cornelius in charge
Flynn, Mary
Cornelius Rabbit series (3)
Cornelius on holidays
Flynn, Mary
Cornelius Rabbit series (2)
Cornelius Rabbit of Tang
Flynn, Mary
Cornelius Rabbit series (1)
Corner House Girls
Hill, Grace Brooks
Corner House Girls series (1)
Corner House Girls among the gypsies
Hill, Grace Brooks
Corner House Girls series (10)
Corner House Girls at school
Hill, Grace Brooks
Corner House Girls series (2)
Corner House Girls facing the world
Hill, Grace Brooks
Corner House Girls series (13)
Corner House Girls growing up
Hill, Grace Brooks
Corner House Girls series (7)
Corner House Girls in a play
Hill, Grace Brooks
Corner House Girls series (4)
Corner House Girls' odd find
Hill, Grace Brooks
Corner House Girls series (5)
Corner House Girls on a houseboat
Hill, Grace Brooks
Corner House Girls series (9)
Corner House Girls on a tour
Hill, Grace Brooks
Corner House Girls series (6)
Corner House Girls on Palm Island
Hill, Grace Brooks
Corner House Girls series (11)
Corner House Girls snowbound
Hill, Grace Brooks
Corner House Girls series (8)
Corner House Girls solve a mystery
Hill, Grace Brooks
Corner House Girls series (12)
Corner House Girls under canvas
Hill, Grace Brooks
Corner House Girls series (3)
Corner in crime
Lucas, Norman
Superintendent Bill Rowlands series (1)
Corner in William
Kilbourne, Fannie
William Horton series (1)
Corner men
Gardner, John Edmund
Detective Inspector Derek Torry series (2)
Corner of paradise
Holton, Leonard
Father Joseph Bredder series (11)
Corner of the playground
Harvester, Simon
Asia in turmoil series (24)
Corner-stone
Abbott, Jacob
Young Christian series (2)
Oldenbourg, Zoe
Corner-stone series (2)
Cornered at last
Carter, Nicholas
Nicholas Carter series (461)
Cornish adventure
McCulloch, Derek
Cornish series (1)
Cornish childhood
Rowse, Alfred Leslie
Cornishman series (1)
Cornish coast conspiracy
Ames, Delano
Sexton Blake series (1063)

Cornish coast murder
Bude, John
Inspector Meredith series (1)
Cornish crime
Weymouth, Anthony
Inspector Treadgold series (5)
Cornish fox
Kitchin, Clifford Henry Benn
Malcolm Warren series (4)
Cornish heiress
Gellis, Roberta
Heiress series (2)
Cornish mystery
McCulloch, Derek
Cornish series (2)
Cornish pixie affair
Leslie, Peter
Girl from U.N.C.L.E.series (5)
Cornish prelude
Baker, Denys Val
Cornish series (25)
Cornish Riviera mystery
Rowland, John
Inspector Shelley series (9)
Cornish summer
Tangye, Derek
Minack chronicles series (7)
Cornish trilogy
Davies, Robertson
Francis Cornish trilogy (3)
Cornish years
Treneer, Anne
Schoolhouse trilogy (2)
Cornishman abroad
Rowse, Alfred Leslie
Cornishman series (3)
Cornishman at Oxford
Rowse, Alfred Leslie
Cornishman series (2)
Cornkister days
Cameron, David Kerr
Scottish farm life series (3)
Corny-on-the-Cob's not so funny day
Reed, Giles
Munch Bunch story books series (8)
Coromandel
Masters, John
Savage family series (1)
Corona
Bear, Greg
Star trek series (15)
Coronado killers
Sharpe, Jon
Trailsman series (102)
Coronation cups and jam jars
Barnes, Ron
East End series (2)
Coronation mystery
Chester, Gilbert
Sexton Blake series (923)
Coroner doubts
Walling, Robert Alfred John
Philip Tolefree series (13)
Coroner's pidgin
Allingham, Margery
Albert Campion series (14)
Coronet among the grass
Bingham, Charlotte
Coronet series (2)
Coronet among the weeds
Bingham, Charlotte
Coronet series (1)
Corporal Cameron
Connor, Ralph
North-West Mounted Police series (1)
Corporal Cavannagh
Anderson, Ian
Scarlet riders series (1)
Corporal died in bed
Graeme, Bruce
Superintendent William Stevens and Inspector Pierre Allain series (11)
Corporal Downey takes the trail
Hendryx, James Beardsley
Corporal Cameron Downey series (3)
Corporal Downey series (9)
Corporal of the guard
Raymond, Ernest
London gallery series (10)
Corporal Sam, and other stories
Quiller-Couch, Arthur
Troy Town series (7)
Corporate bodies
Brett, Simon
Charles Paris series (14)
Corporate caper
Jason, Stuart
Butcher series (26)

Corpse
Brown, Carter
Lieutenant Al Wheeler series (10)
McCutchan, Philip
Commander Esmonde Shaw series (15)
Corpse and the lady
Strange, John Stephen
Barney Gantt series (2)
Corpse and the three ex-husbands
Macveigh, Sue
Captain Andy and Sue McVeigh series (4)
Corpse at Camp Two
Carr, Glyn
Sir Abercrombie Lewker series (9)
Corpse at Casablanca
Cobb, Belton
Inspector Cheviot Burmann series (19)
Corpse at least
Courtier, Sidney Hobson
Ambrose Mahon series (8)
Corpse at the carnival
Bellairs, George
Detective Inspector Thomas Littlejohn series (29)
Corpse at the Quill Club
Long, Amelia Reynolds
Peter Piper series (1)
Corpse came calling
Halliday, Brett
Michael Shayne series (6)
Corpse came C.O.D.
Starr, Jimmy
Joe Medford series (3)
Corpse came too
Reid, Desmond
Sexton Blake series (1521)
Corpse candle
Bagby, George
Inspector Schmidt series (35)
Corpse can't walk
Long, Harman
Franklyn Keen series (3)
Corpse cargo
Stockbridge, Grant
Richard Wentworth series (13)
Corpse cavalcade
House, Brant
Secret Agent X series (8)
Corpse contraband
House, Brant
Secret Agent X series (21)
Corpse de ballet
Cores, Lucy
Captain Andrew Torrent series (2)
Corpse died twice
Frost, Barbara
Marka de Lancey series (2)
Corpse diplomatique
Ames, Delano
Dagobert and Jane Brown series (4)
Corpse for a candidate
Geller, Michael
Bud Dugan series (2)
Corpse for breakfast
Murray, Max
Corpse series (10)
Corpse for Charybdis
Gilruth, Susan
Inspector Hugh Gordon and Liane Crawford series (4)
Corpse for Christmas
Ballinger, W A
Sexton Blake series (1535)
Brown, Carter
Lieutenant Al Wheeler series (33)
Kane, Henry
Peter Chambers series (5)
Corpse from the City
Brandon, John Gordon
Arthur Stukeley Pennington series (27)
Inspector Patrick Aloysius McCarthy series (51)
Corpse guard parade
Kennedy, Milward
Inspector Cornford series (2)
Corpse in camera
Launay, Droo
Adam Flute series (3)
Corpse in canonicals
Cole, George Douglas Howard
Superintendent Henry Wilson series (8)
Corpse in cold storage
Kennedy, Milward
Sir George Bull series (2)
Corpse in Company K
Avery, Robert
Joe Kelly series (2)

Corpse in handcuffs
Smith, Frank Allan
Superintendent Pepper series (1)
Corpse in my bed
Alexander, David
Lieutenant Romano series (1)
Tommy Twotoes and Terry Rooke series (1)
Corpse in Oozak's Pond
Macleod, Charlotte
Professor Peter Shandy series (6)
Corpse in the car
Rhode, John
Doctor Lancelot Priestley series (22)
Corpse in the cargo
Cobb, Belton
Bryan Armitage series (3)
Inspector Cheviot Burmann series (27)
Corpse in the clouds
Conde, Phillip
Irving Todd series (2)
Corpse in the constable's garden
Cole, George Douglas Howard
Superintendent Henry Wilson series (8)
Corpse in the coppice
Walling, Robert Alfred John
Philip Tolefree series (8)
Corpse in the corner saloon
Stone, Hampton
Jeremiah X Gibson series (1)
Corpse in the crevasse
Carr, Glyn
Sir Abercrombie Lewker series (7)
Corpse in the crimson slippers
Walling, Robert Alfred John
Philip Tolefree series (9)
Corpse in the derby hat
Swiggett, Howard
Garrett Maynard series (1)
Corpse in the flannel nightgown
Scherf, Margaret
Reverend Martin Buell series (6)
Corpse in the green pajamas
Walling, Robert Alfred John
Philip Tolefree series (7)
Corpse in the guest room
Wood, Clement
Skelton Keyne series (1)
Corpse in the snowman
Blake, Nicholas
Nigel Strangeways series (7)
Corpse in the waxworks
Carr, John Dickson
Henri Bencolin series (4)
Corpse incognito
Cobb, Belton
Inspector Cheviot Burmann series (15)
Corpse-maker
Wilson, David
Marshal Sam McCloud series (4)
Corpse moved upstairs
Gruber, Frank
Johnny Fletcher and Sam Cragg series (7)
Corpse on ice
Hedges, Joseph
John Stark series (6)
Corpse on London Bridge
Southworth, Louis
Inspector Tom Anderson series (2)
Corpse on the bridge
Barry, Charles
Superintendent Lawrence Gilmartin series (5)
Corpse on the dike
Van de Wetering, Janwillem
De Gier and Grijpstra series (3)
Corpse on the flying trapeze
Morland, Nigel
Mrs Palmyra Pym series (11)
Corpse on the mat
Kennedy, Milward
Inspector Cornford series (1)
Corpse on the town
Roeburt, John
Jigger Moran series (3)
Corpse on the White House lawn
Diplomat
Dennis Tyler series (4)
Corpse parade
Wallace, Robert
Phantom Detective series (10)
Corpse rode on
Brandon, John Gordon
Arthur Stukeley Pennington series (20)
Inspector Patrick Aloysius McCarthy series (44)

Corpse said no
Frost, Barbara
Marka de Lancey series (1)
Corpse steps out
Rice, Craig
John Joseph Malone series (2)
Corpse that came back
Piper, Peter
Inspector Gray series (2)
Corpse that knew everybody
Worth, Cedric
Inspector Sevrel series (2)
Corpse that murdered
House, Brant
Secret Agent X series (19)
Corpse that never was
Halliday, Brett
Michael Shayne series (46)
Corpse that refused to stay dead
Stone, Hampton
Jeremiah X Gibson series (5)
Corpse that spoke
Leitfred, Robert H
Simon Crole series (1)
Corpse that talked
Telfair, Richard
Monty Nash series (2)
Corpse that traveled
Rees, Arthur John
Inspector Luckraft series (7)
Corpse that walked
Winsor, Roy
Ira Cobb series (1)
Corpse to Cairo
O'Brine, Manning
Michael O'Kelly series (2)
Corpse to Copenhagen
Burke, Jonathan
Sexton Blake series (1419)
Corpse to Cuba
Kent, Arthur
Sexton Blake series (1586)
Corpse was no bargain at all
Stone, Hampton
Jeremiah X Gibson series (16)
Corpse was no lady
Morland, Nigel
Chief Inspector Andrew McMurdo series (4)
Corpse who had too many friends
Stone, Hampton
Jeremiah X Gibson series (6)
Corpse with one shoe
Scherf, Margaret
Emily and Henry Bryce series (3)
Corpse with sticky fingers
Bagby, George
Inspector Schmidt series (21)
Corpse with the blistered hand
Walling, Robert Alfred John
Philip Tolefree series (15)
Corpse with the blue cravat
Walling, Robert Alfred John
Philip Tolefree series (13)
Corpse with the dirty face
Walling, Robert Alfred John
Philip Tolefree series (11)
Corpse with the eerie eye
Walling, Robert Alfred John
Philip Tolefree series (19)
Corpse with the floating foot
Walling, Robert Alfred John
Philip Tolefree series (10)
Corpse with the grimy glove
Walling, Robert Alfred John
Philip Tolefree series (14)
Corpse with the listening ear
Smith, Laurence Dwight
Dick Whelan series (1)
Corpse with the missing watch
Walling, Robert Alfred John
Philip Tolefree series (23)
Corpse with the purple thighs
Bagby, George
Inspector Schmidt series (6)
Corpse with the red-headed friend
Walling, Robert Alfred John
Philip Tolefree series (16)
Corpse without a clue
Walling, Robert Alfred John
Philip Tolefree series (21)
Corpse without boots
Hill, Lawrence
Inspector Macsporran series (2)
Corpse won't sing
Courtier, Sidney Hobson
Ambrose Mahon series (6)
Corpse wore a wig
Bagby, George
Inspector Schmidt series (7)
Corpse wore rubies
Lester, Frank
Geoffrey Slade series (1)

Corpses in Enderby
Bellairs, George
Detective Inspector Thomas Littlejohn series (22)
Corpses in the cellar
Latham, Brad
Hook series (5)
Corpses never argue
Hume, David
Mick Cardby series (14)
Corpus Christmas
Maron, Margaret
Lieutenant Sigrid Harald series (6)
Corpus delectable
Powell, Talmage
Ed Rivers series (5)
Corpus delicious
Kane, Martin
Martin Kane series (9)
Correct thing
Stevens, William Oliver
Etiquette series (1)
Corrector of destinies
Post, Melville Davisson
Randolph Mason series (3)
Correspondence of the three William Byrds of Westover, Virginia
Byrd, William
Secret diary series (3)
Corridor of ghosts
Butler, Bill
Dean Street detectives series (3)
Corridor of storms
Sarabande, William
First Americans series (2)
Corridors of death
Edwards, Ruth Dudley
Robert Amiss series (1)
Corridors of guilt
Hilton, John Buxton
Superintendent Simon Kenworthy series (12)
Corridors of healing
Harrison, Elizabeth
Central London Hospital series (3)
Corridors of power
Snow, Charles Percy
Strangers and brothers series (9)
Corridors of time
Deegan, Jon J
Dysart trilogy (1)
Corrie and Co.
Dennison, Dorothy
Wantoknow series for girls (4)
Corrigan and the black riders
Maddock, Reginald Bertram
Corrigan series (3)
Corrigan and the blue crater
Maddock, Reginald Bertram
Corrigan series (7)
Corrigan and the dream makers
Maddock, Reginald Bertram
Corrigan series (6)
Corrigan and the golden pagoda
Maddock, Reginald Bertram
Corrigan series (5)
Corrigan and the green tiger
Maddock, Reginald Bertram
Corrigan series (8)
Corrigan and the little people
Maddock, Reginald Bertram
Corrigan series (10)
Corrigan and the red lions
Maddock, Reginald Bertram
Corrigan series (9)
Corrigan and the tom of Opi
Maddock, Reginald Bertram
Corrigan series (4)
Corrigan and the white cobra
Maddock, Reginald Bertram
Corrigan series (1)
Corrigan and the yellow peril
Maddock, Reginald Bertram
Corrigan series (2)
Corrigan's revenge
Kincaid, J D
Jack Stone series (1)
Corrupt and ensnare
Nevins, Francis Michael
Loren Mensing series (2)
Corruption
Janson, Hank
Hank Janson series (39)
Corsair
Pope, Dudley
Ned Yorke series (6)
Corsican adventure
Bayley, Viola
Adventure series (4)
Corsican brothers
Dumas, Alexandre
Napoleon series (4)

Corsican cross
Bradley, Michael
Johnny Adrano series (1)
Corsican death
Hawkes, Robert
NARC series (7)
Corsican takeover
Smith, Don
Tim Parnell series (4)
Corson of the J C
Mulford, Clarence Edward
J C series (1)
Cortlandts of Washington Square
Fairbank, Janet Ayer
Rich man, poor man trilogy (1)
Corundum's woman
Cleve, John
Spaceways series (2)
Corvette
Woodman, Richard
Nathaniel Drinkwater series (5)
Corvette command
Monsarrat, Nicholas
Corvette series (3)
Cosa Nostra circus
Corbin, Gary
Harry Reilly series (2)
Cosette and Marius
Hugo, Victor Marie
Fate trilogy (1)
Cosmic bomber
Wu, William Franking
Doctor Bones series (2)
Cosmic courage
Jade, Symon
Starship Orpheus trilogy (2)
Cosmic crusade
Barbet, Pierre
Baphomet series (2)
Cosmic crusaders
Barbet, Pierre
Baphomet series (2)
Cosmic decoy
Scheer, Karl Herbert
Perry Rhodan series (21)
Cosmic echelon
Cameron, Berl
Terran empire series (1)
Cosmic forces as they were taught in Mu
Churchward, James
Mu series (4)
Cosmic forces of Mu
Churchward, James
Mu series (4)
Cosmic funhouse
Black, Christopher
Star challenge series (3)
Cosmic manhunt
De Camp, Lyon Sprague
Krishna series (3)
Cosmic reality kill
Rosenberger, Joseph
Death Merchant series (36)
Cosmic traitor
Darlton, Clark
Perry Rhodan series (26)
Cosmicomics
Calvino, Italo
QFWFQ series (1)
Cosmium raiders
Byrne, Stuart James
Star Man series (1)
Cossack hide-out
Webster, Ernest
Benni Soldano series (2)
Cossacks
Bartos-Hoppner, Barbara
Mitya series (1)
Cost of a best seller
Keyes, Frances Parkinson
Roses series (2)
Cost of living
Zenowich, Christopher
Bob Bodewicz series (2)
Cost price
Yates, Dornford
Jonah Mansel series (12)
Richard Chandos series (9)
Costa Rican carnage
Thorne, Ramsay
Captain Gringo series (33)
Costa Rican chaos
Roberts, Mark Kelly
Liberty Corps series (6)
Costello
Hall, Richard
Patrick Costello series (1)
Cosy little murder
Radford, Edwin
Doctor Manson series (17)
Cotfold conundrums
Browne, Douglas Gordon
Inspector Thew series (1)
Cotswold adventure
Smythe, Pat
Peter and Carol Garret series (3)
Cotswold case
Wynne, Anthony
Doctor Eustace Hailey series (15)
Cotswold holiday
Finlay, Winifred
Judith Norton series (1)
Cottage
Porteous, Crichton
Jonas Wishet series (1)
Cottage at Drimble
Ford, Elizabeth
Maplechester series (2)
Cottage by the lock
Cockett, Mary
Dan and Grum series (2)
Cottage holiday
Mendel, Jo
Tucker family series (5)
Cottage in the Wild Wood
Clewes, Dorothy
Wild Wood series (1)
Cottage into house
Armstrong, Anthony
Margaret Cottage series (1)
Cottage murder
Punshon, Ernest Robertson
Carter and Bell series (3)
Cottage of terror
Stuart, Donald
Sexton Blake series (853)
Cottage on a cliff
Tangye, Derek
Minack chronicles series (8)
Cottage on the Green
Toms, Patricia
Chronicles of Pennycress series (3)
Cottage pie
Tiltman, Marjorie Hessell
Country life trilogy (1)
Cotton comes to Harlem
Himes, Chester
Grave Digger Jones and Coffin Ed Johnson series (6)
Cotton-farm boy
Mauzey, Merritt
Farm boy series (1)
Cotton in my sack
Lenski, Lois
Regional series (6)
Cotton-pickers
Traven, B
Gerard Gales series (2)
Cottontail caper
Roos, Stephen
Pet Lovers Club series (2)
Cottonwood Gulch
Mulford, Clarence Edward
Dave Sanders series (1)
Cottonwood pards
Floren, Lee
Buckshot McKee and Tortilla Joe series (1)
Couch potatos!
Walker, Mort
Hi and Lois series (16)
Cougar
Reno, Bill
Badge series (18)
Cougar Canyon
Field, Peter
Powder Valley series (71)
Cougar City
Pritchett, Ron
Buck Lawrence and Zeke Henderson series (2)
Cougar dawn
Sharpe, Jon
Trailsman series (134)
Could be worse!
Stevenson, James
Grandpa series (1)
Could you ever build a time machine?
Darling, David J
Could you ever series (5)
Could you ever dig a hole to China?
Darling, David J
Could you ever series (4)
Could you ever fly to the stars?
Darling, David J
Could you ever series (1)
Could you ever live forever?
Darling, David J
Could you ever series (6)
Could you ever meet an alien?
Darling, David J
Could you ever series (2)
Could you ever speak chimpanzee?
Darling, David J
Could you ever series (3)
Coulson alone
Mann, Jack
Rex Coulson series (5)
Coulson goes south
Mann, Jack
Rex Coulson series (2)
Council of captains
Macdonnell, James Edmond
Captain Peter Bentley series (48)
Commander Sainsbury series (8)
Dutchy Holland series (37)
Council of Comforters
Duncan, William Murdoch
Superintendent Leslie series (1)
Council of crooks
Bayfield, William John
Sexton Blake series (415)
Council of death
Carter, Nicholas
Nicholas Carter series (126)
Council of justice
Wallace, Edgar
Just Men series (2)
Council of kings
Pendleton, Don
Mack Bolan series (79)
Council of Seven
Snaith, John Collis
Love Lane series (2)
Council of the Rat
Cassells, John
Superintendent Flagg series (23)
Counsel for the defence
Ashford, Jeffrey
Detective Inspector Don Kerry series (1)
Counsellor
Connington, John Jervis
Mark Brand series (1)
Counsellor heart
Winslow, Pauline Glen
Superintendent Merlin Capricorn series (5)
Count backwards to zero
Halliday, Brett
Michael Shayne series (63)
Count Bakwerdz on the carpet
Hunter, Norman
Kingdom of Incredibilia series (5)
Count Boris Bolescu and the black pudding
Jungman, Ann
Count Boris Bolescu series (1)
Count Boris Bolescu and the Transylvanian tango
Jungman, Ann
Count Boris Bolescu series (2)
Count Brass
Moorcock, Michael
Chronicles of Castle Brass series (1)
Count Bunker
Clouston, Joseph Storer
Mister Francis Mandell-Essington series (2)
Count Dobermann Pinscher
Sivers, Brenda
Sherlock Hound series (4)
Count-down
Howard, Hartley
Glenn Bowman series (23)
Count down for Conquest
Gray, Berkeley
Norman Conquest series (44)
Count Dracula
Savory, Gerald
Dracula series (13)
Count Dracula and the ghost
Jungman, Ann
Count Dracula series (1)
Count Dracula and the monster
Jungman, Ann
Count Dracula series (2)
Count Dracula and the victim
Jungman, Ann
Count Dracula series (3)
Count Dracula book of classic vampire stories
Youngson, Jeanne
Dracula series (26)
Count Dracula cookbook
Youngson, Jeanne
Dracula series (26)
Count Dracula Fan Club book of vampire stories
Youngson, Jeanne
Dracula series (26)
Count Dracula meets his match
Jungman, Ann
Count Dracula series (4)
Count Dracula's favorite Christmas cookie recipes
Youngson, Jeanne
Dracula series (26)
Count Luckner, the Sea Devil
Luckner, Felix von
Sea Devil series (1)
Count of Monte Cristo
Dumas, Alexandre
Count of Monte Cristo series (1)
Count of nine
Fair, A A
Bertha Cool and Donald Lam series (18)
Count of six
Powell, Lester
Philip Odell series (1)
Count on Clifford
Bridwell, Norman
Clifford series (19)
Count on the Saint
Weaver, Graham
Saint series (50)
Count Robert of Paris
Scott, Walter
Tales of my landlord series (1)
Count up
Burningham, John
Number play series (1)
Count up to blast down
Johnston, William
Brady Bunch series (3)
Count Vronsky's daughter
Salisbury, Carola
War and peace series (2)
Count with us from the big red bus
Wood, Leslie
Big red bus series (1)
Count your way through Africa
Haskins, Jim
Count your way series (7)
Count your way through Canada
Haskins, Jim
Count your way series (6)
Count your way through China
Haskins, Jim
Count your way series (1)
Count your way through Germany
Haskins, Jim
Count your way series (12)
Count your way through India
Haskins, Jim
Count your way series (10)
Count your way through Israel
Haskins, Jim
Count your way series (9)
Count your way through Italy
Haskins, Jim
Count your way series (11)
Count your way through Japan
Haskins, Jim
Count your way series (2)
Count your way through Korea
Haskins, Jim
Count your way series (8)
Count your way through Mexico
Haskins, Jim
Count your way series (5)
Count your way through Russia
Haskins, Jim
Count your way series (3)
Count your way through the Arab world
Haskins, Jim
Count your way series (4)
Count Zero
Gibson, William
Neuromancer trilogy (2)
Countdown
Ahern, Jerry
Survivalist series (26)
Countdown for a spy
Von Elsner, Don
David Danning series (7)
Countdown for murder
Sydney, George
Sexton Blake series (1548)
Countdown to Armageddon
Carter, Nick
Nick Carter series (243)
Countdown to chaos
Pendleton, Don
Mack Bolan series (105)
Countdown to China
Thompson, Steven Lynn
Max Moss series (2)
Countdown to crisis
Eden, Matthew
Marc Savage series (1)
Countdown to terror
Derrick, Lionel
Penetrator series (18)
Dixon, Franklin W
Hardy boys case files series (28)
Countdown to thirteen Super Bowls
Resciniti, Angelo G
Super Bowl series (1)
Counter attack
Garrett, Frank
Killsquad series (1)
Counter Force
Streib, Dan
Steve Crown series (1)
Counter-attack
Brogan, Mike
Action Man series (5)
Counterattack
Drake, David
Fleet series (2)
Griffin, W E B
Corps series (3)
Counter-attack
Kessler, Leo
Wotan series (10)
Leyland, Eric
Rip Randall series (3)
Counterattack
Scarpetta, Frank
Marksman series (11)
Counter-feat
Janson, Hank
Hank Janson series (202)
Counterfeit
McCall, Alex
Soldier of fortune series (5)
Thayer, Lee
Peter Clancy series (16)
Counterfeit agent
Carter, Nick
Nick Carter series (96)
Counterfeit bill
Thayer, Lee
Peter Clancy series (16)
Counterfeit cargo
Sharpe, Jon
Trailsman series (110)
Counterfeit Christmas
Keene, Carolyn
Nancy Drew files series (102)
Counterfeit for murder
Stout, Rex
Nero Wolfe and Archie Goodwin series (36)
Counterfeit killers
Wallace, Robert
Phantom Detective series (15)
Counterfeit lady
Deveraux, Jude
James River trilogy (1)
Counterfeit madam
Sharpe, Jon
Canyon O'Grady series (9)
Counterfeit murders
Macclure, Victor
Inspector Archie Burford series (2)
Counterfeit of murder
Harrison, Ray
Sergeant Joseph Bragg and Constable James Morton series (5)
Counterfeit wife
Halliday, Brett
Michael Shayne series (15)
Counterforce
Henrick, Richard P
Sub wars series (2)
Counterlife
Roth, Philip
Nathan Zuckerman series (4)
Countermeasures
Gear, William Michael
Forbidden borders series (3)
Counterpoint murder
Cole, George Douglas Howard
Superintendent Henry Wilson series (24)
Counterpol
Boland, John
Counterpol series (1)
Counterpol in Paris
Boland, John
Counterpol series (2)
Counterprobe
Douglas, Carole Nelson
Probe series (2)
Countersolar!
Lupoff, Richard Allen
Counterearth series (2)
Counterspy
Cleeve, Brian
Sean Ryan series (1)
Counter-spy
Dilnot, George
Jim Strang series (2)
Counter-spy murders
Cheyney, Peter
Secret service series (1)

Counterstrike
Taylor, Charles Doonan
Bernie Ryng series (3)
Counterstroke
Wayland, Patrick
Lloyd Nicolson series (1)
Countertrap
Tiger, John
I spy series (4)
Countess
Edgar, Josephine
Viola Corbett series (2)
Countess and the spy
De Villiers, Gerard
Malko Linge series (5)
Countess Angelique
Golon, Sergeanne
Angelique series (6)
Countess de Charny
Dumas, Alexandre
Marie Antoinette series (4)
Countess Dracula
Parry, Michel
Dracula series (5)
Countess Kate
Yonge, Charlotte Mary
Pillars of the house series (3)
Countess of Rudolstadt
Sand, George
Consuelo series (2)
Countess Pharamond
Rita
Sheba series (2)
Countess Tekla
Barr, Robert
Mediaeval Rhine series (1)
Countess Veronica
Robinson, Nancy Konheim
Veronica quartet (4)
Counting
Pluckrose, Henry
Knowabouts series (1)
Counting and Barbapapa
Tison, Annette
Barbapapa first book series (3)
Counting my steps
Lind, Jakov
Steps series (1)
Counting rhymes
Ward, Dorothy Darrell
Teddies series (2)
Counting the cost
Drake, David
Hammer's Slammers series (4)
Countisbury
Morrison, Emmeline
Lovells trilogy (2)
Country
Plante, David
Francoeur family series (4)
Country affairs
Armfelt, Roger
Affairs series (1)
Country and fatal
Bagby, George
Inspector Schmidt series (47)
Country beat
Quinain, Louis
Country beat series (1)
Country child
Uttley, Alison
Country child series (1)
Country cousin
Daringer, Helen Fern
Endicott family trilogy (3)
Country days
Gould, Elizabeth
Green Willow Farm series (6)
Country doctor
Balzac, Honore de
Scenes of country life series (2)
Country editor
Hough, Henry Beetle
Martha's Vineyard series (1)
Country girls
O'Brien, Edna
Caithleen series (1)
Country girls trilogy and epilogue
O'Brien, Edna
Caithleen series (3)
Country heart
Bates, Herbert Ernest
Country heart series (2)
Country house
Galsworthy, John
Country house trilogy (1)
Country in danger
Erckmann, Emile
Story of a peasant series (2)
Country life
Bingham, Charlotte
Belgravia trilogy (2)
Country matters
Drabble, Phil
Wild animals series (7)
Country noisy book
Brown, Margaret Wise
Noisy book series (2)
Country of memorable honour
Firbank, Thomas
Mountain series (4)
Country of old men
Hansen, Joseph
Dave Brandstetter series (12)
Country of strangers
Richter, Conrad
Pioneer children series (2)
Country of the mind
Morgan, Dan
Sixth perception series (4)
Country parson
Balzac, Honore de
Scenes of country life series (3)
Insight, James
Vicar series (3)
Country practice
Bagster, Hubert
Country doctor series (1)
Country scene
Drabble, Phil
Wild animals series (4)
Country scrap book
Haggard, Lilias Rider
Norfolk life series (3)
Country seasons
Drabble, Phil
Wild animals series (3)
Country wise
Drabble, Phil
Wild animals series (6)
Countrygoer in the Dales
Lofthouse, Jessica
Countrygoer series (2)
Countrygoers' North
Lofthouse, Jessica
Countrygoer series (3)
Countryman's journal
Derleth, August
Sac Prairie series (15)
Countryman's year
Grayson, David
Adventures series (8)
Countrymen
Shaw, Bruce
East Kimberley series (3)
Count's millions
Gaboriau, Emile
Count's secret series (1)
Count's secret
Gaboriau, Emile
Count's secret series (2)
County chronicle
Thirkell, Angela
Barsetshire series (19)
County kill
Gault, William Campbell
Brock Callahan series (6)
County rovers for Charlie
Allen, Joy
Charlie series (10)
County seat
Corey, Peter
Three miles square series (3)
Coup de Grass
Nash, Padder
Grass series (3)
Coupe
Stackpole, Michael
Warrior trilogy (3)
Couple at Demdyke Row
Mackenzie, Lee
Emmerdale Farm series (8)
Coupon crimes
Verner, Gerald
Superintendent Robert Budd series (11)
Courage and fear
Remy
Silent company trilogy (2)
Courage at sea
Drury, Rebecca
Women of war series (6)
Courage in crisis
James, Josephine
Kathy Martin series (9)
Courage in darkness
Shears, Sarah
Courage series (2)
Courage in parting
Shears, Sarah
Courage series (5)
Courage in the ashes
Johnstone, William Wallace
Ashes series (14)
Courage in war
Shears, Sarah
Courage series (4)
Courage of Ann
Grove, Harriet Pyne
Ann Sterling series (5)
Courage of Marge O'Doone
Curwood, James Oliver
Kazan series (3)
Courage of the Mountain Man
Johnstone, William Wallace
Mountain Man series (12)
Courage to serve
Shears, Sarah
Courage series (3)
Courageous exploits of Doctor Syn
Thorndike, Russell
Doctor Syn series (6)
Courier
Morgan, Stanley
Russ Tobin series (3)
Courier for crime
Story, Jack Trevor
Sexton Blake series (1478)
Courier of the Ozarks
Dunn, Byron Archibald
Young Missourians series (3)
Courier to Marrakesh
Williams, Valentine
Clubfoot series (9)
Course of empire
De Voto, Bernard
American West trilogy (3)
Glubb, John Bagot
Arab history series (3)
Course to intercept
Macdonnell, James Edmond
Captain Peter Bentley series (28)
Commander Sainsbury series (5)
Court circle
Housman, Laurence
Palace plays series (4)
Court intrigues in a collection of original letters
Manley, Mary de la Riviere
New Atalantis series (3)
Court martial
Hardy, Adam
George Abercrombie Fox series (7)
Macdonnell, James Edmond
Dutchy Holland series (39)
Court-martial
Zlotnik, Donald E
Survivors of Nam series (4)
Court-martial of George Armstrong Custer
Jones, Douglas Clyde
General George Custer trilogy (1)
Court of a thousand suns
Cole, Allan
Sten series (3)
Court of Charles IV
Perez Galdos, Benito
National episodes series, epoch 1 (2)
Court of Lucifer
Gallizier, Nathan
Sorceress trilogy (3)
Court of memory
McConkey, James
Court of memory trilogy (3)
Court of shadows
Jackson, Giles
Nile Boyd series (2)
Courtesan
Tranter, Nigel Godwin
Patrick Gray series (2)
Courtier to death
Gilbert, Anthony
Dupuy series (2)
Courtin' Christina
Bell, John Joy
Christina series (2)
Courting disaster
Keene, Carolyn
Nancy Drew and Hardy boys supermystery series (15)
Courtney
Jenkins, Jerry Bruce
Margo Franklin and Philip Spence series (11)
Courtney entry
Harris, John
Ira Penaluna trilogy (3)
Courts of chaos
Zelazny, Roger
Kingdom of Amber series (5)
Courts of idleness
Yates, Dornford
Berry series (2)
Courts of illusion
Jarman, Rosemary Hawley
Richard III series (4)
Courts of love
Plaidy, Jean
Queens of England series (5)
Courts of the morning
Buchan, John
Richard Hannay series (5)
Courtship
Foote, Horton
Orphans' home series (5)
Courtship and adventures of Jonathan Home Bred
Haliburton, Thomas Chandler
Sam Slick series (10)
Courtship in Kenya
Strange, Nora Kathleen
Kenya series (4)
Courtship of Princess Leia
Wolverton, Dave
Star wars series (4)
Courtway case
Goyne, Richard
Padre series (5)
Cousin Aleck
Goulding, Francis Robert
Boy life among the Indians series (2)
Cousin Annabelle's Christmas
O'Farrell, Kathleen
Lattimer children series (3)
Cousin Bette
Balzac, Honore de
Poor relations series (1)
Scenes of Parisian life series (15)
Cousin Betty
Balzac, Honore de
Poor relations series (1)
Scenes of Parisian life series (15)
Cousin Emma and the green jungle
Salmon, Michael
Alexander Bunyip series (10)
Cousin from Canada
Wynne, May
Comrades from Canada series (1)
Cousin from France
Masson, Sophie
Seyrac family series (2)
Cousin Harriet
Tweedsmuir, Susan Buchan
Victorian trilogy (1)
Cousin Kate
Godwin, Catherine Grace
Cousin Kate series (1)
Cousin Lucy among the mountains
Abbott, Jacob
Cousin Lucy series (4)
Cousin Lucy at play
Abbott, Jacob
Cousin Lucy series (3)
Cousin Lucy at study
Abbott, Jacob
Cousin Lucy series (2)
Cousin Lucy on the sea-shore
Abbott, Jacob
Cousin Lucy series (5)
Cousin Lucy's conversation
Abbott, Jacob
Cousin Lucy series (6)
Cousin Lucy's stories
Abbott, Jacob
Cousin Lucy series (1)
Cousin once removed
Hammond, Gerald
Keith Calder series (6)
Cousin Pons
Balzac, Honore de
Poor relations series (2)
Scenes of Parisian life series (14)
Cousin Roc comes to stay
Salmon, Michael
Dinosaur swamp series (3)
Cousin Rosamund
West, Rebecca
Aubrey family trilogy (3)
Cousins
Foote, Horton
Orphans' home series (6)
Cousins and circuses
Sypher, Lucy Johnstone
Lucy series (2)
Cove
Ireland, Kenneth
Fogou series (2)
Coven
Brown, Carter
Rick Holman series (25)
Saint John, David
Peter Ward series (10)
Coven gibbet
Chance, John Newton
Mister DeHavilland series (7)
Covenant
Stahl, Hilda
White Pine chronicles series (1)
Covenant of the crown
Weinstein, Howard
Star trek series (4)
Covenant of the Flame
Morrell, David
Chris Kilmoonie and Saul Grisman series (4)
Covenant with death
Grierson, Francis Durham
Inspector George Muir series (1)
Covent Garden
Rayner, Claire
Performers series (6)
Covent Garden murder
Makin, William James
Inspector Evans series (1)
Covent Garden mystery
Bayfield, William John
Sexton Blake series (557)
Cover girl cries murder
Brody, Marc
Marc Brody series (23)
Cover her face
James, Phyllis Dorothy
Commander Adam Dalgliesh series (1)
McCutcheon, Hugh
Anthony Howard series (2)
Inspector McKeller series (3)
Cover story
Cullen, Robert
Colin Burke series (2)
Forbes, Colin
Tweed, Grey and Newman series (3)
Cover up!
Harris, Lavinia
Computer detectives series (4)
Cover-up
Oliver, Anthony
Lizzie Thomas and Inspector John Webber series (4)
Cover-up story
Babson, Marian
Douglas Perkins and Gerry Tate series (1)
Cover zero
Hughes, William
George Willis series (3)
Covered bridge
Doyle, Brian
Hubbo O'Driscoll series (2)
Covering fire
Janson, Hank
Hank Janson series (247)
Covert action
Reeves, James R
Navy Seals series (2)
Covert op
Hardy, Adam
Strike Force Falklands series (5)
Cow-thief Trail
Floren, Lee
Judge Lemanuel Bates and Tobacco Jones series (9)
Cow thieves
Edson, John Thomas
Calamity Jane series (5)
Cowardly lion and the hungry tiger
Baum, Lyman Frank
Little Wizard series (4)
Cowardly lion of Oz
Thompson, Ruth Plumly
Oz series (16)
Cowards
Skvorecky, Josef
Danny Smiricky series (1)
Coward's Club
Grierson, Francis Durham
Commissaire Patras series (3)
Cowboy and his friend
Anglund, Joan Walsh
Cowboy series (1)
Cowboy millionaire
O'Brien, George
George O'Brien series (1)
Cowboy on a wooden horse
Suhl, Yuri
Wooden horse series (2)
Cowboy Sam
Chandler, Edna Walker
Cowboy Sam series (1)
Cowboy Sam and Big Bill
Chandler, Edna Walker
Cowboy Sam series (14)
Cowboy Sam and Dandy
Chandler, Edna Walker
Cowboy Sam series (11)
Cowboy Sam and Flop
Chandler, Edna Walker
Cowboy Sam series (10)

Cowboy Sam and Freckles
Chandler, Edna Walker
Cowboy Sam series (15)
Cowboy Sam and Freddy
Chandler, Edna Walker
Cowboy Sam series (2)
Cowboy Sam and Miss lily
Chandler, Edna Walker
Cowboy Sam series (9)
Cowboy Sam and Porky
Chandler, Edna Walker
Cowboy Sam series (5)
Cowboy Sam and Sally
Chandler, Edna Walker
Cowboy Sam series (12)
Cowboy Sam and Shorty
Chandler, Edna Walker
Cowboy Sam series (6)
Cowboy Sam and the airplane
Chandler, Edna Walker
Cowboy Sam series (13)
Cowboy Sam and the fair
Chandler, Edna Walker
Cowboy Sam series (7)
Cowboy Sam and the Indians
Chandler, Edna Walker
Cowboy Sam series (8)
Cowboy Sam and the rodeo
Chandler, Edna Walker
Cowboy Sam series (3)
Cowboy Sam and the rustlers
Chandler, Edna Walker
Cowboy Sam series (4)
Cowboy Small
Lenski, Lois
Small family series (8)
Cowboys
Greene, Carla
What do they do series (7)
Cowboys and cattle drives
McCall, Edith
Frontiers of America series (17)
Cowboys and Indians
Carruth, Jean
Fun with Sally series (3)
Cowboys of the Wild West
Freedman, Russell
Wild West series (2)
Cowboy's revenge
Stivers, Dick
Able Team series (33)
Cowboy's secret life
Anglund, Joan Walsh
Cowboy series (2)
Cowheart's revenge
Sharpe, Jon
Trailsman series (151)
Cowleaze Farm
Whitlock, Ralph
Cowleaze Farm series (1)
Cowleaze Farm in winter
Whitlock, Ralph
Cowleaze Farm series (3)
Cowls
Sudbery, Rodie
Polly Devenish series (2)
Cowmen and rustlers
Ellis, Edward Sylvester
Northwest series (2)
Cownappers
Edwards, Monica
Punchbowl Farm series (8)
Cowpuncher
Scott, Bradford
Walt Slade series (1)
Cowpunchers of Badwater
Nelson, Al P
Badwater series (1)
Cows in the corn
Fussey, Joyce
Yorkshire farm series (2)
Cows of our planet
Larson, Gary
Far Side series (13)
Cowslip Meadow
Bradbury, Catherine
Applebury tales series (3)
Cowslips and clover
Cragoe, Elizabeth
Untidy gardener series (2)
Cowtown fury
Bexar, Phil
Billy Dupree series (5)
Cowtown marshal
Bexar, Phil
Billy Dupree series (7)
Coxswain
Macdonnell, James Edmond
Captain Peter Bentley series (10)
Coyote
Barnes, Linda
Carlotta Carlyle series (4)
Coyote connection
Carter, Nick
Nick Carter series (144)
Coyote Crossing
Roderus, Frank
Carl Heller series (5)
Coyote gold
Friend, Ed
High Chaparral series (2)
Coyote Gulch
Field, Peter
Powder Valley series (5)
Coyote waits
Hillerman, Tony
Lieutenant Joe Leaphorn series (7)
Sergeant Jim Chee series (7)
Coyote winter
Kincaid, J D
Jack Stone series (5)
Coyoteros!
Masterson, Louis
Morgan Kane series (26)
Cozumel
Hunt, Everette Howard
Jack Novak series (1)
Crab cat
Bayley, Nicola
Copycats series (4)
Crab-Flower Club
Ts'ao, Hsueh-ch'in
Dream of the red chamber series (2)
Crab Island
Hurt, Freda Mary
Benny of Crab Island series (1)
Crab with the golden claws
Herge
Tintin series (9)
Crabs' moon
Smith, Guy Newman
Crabs series (5)
Crabs on the rampage
Smith, Guy Newman
Crabs series (4)
Crabtree affair
Innes, Michael
Sir John Appleby series (20)
Crack in the sidewalk
Copper, Basil
Mike Faraday series (22)
Crack of dawn
De Polnay, Peter
Death and to-morrow series (1)
Ford, Leslie
Colonel John Primrose series (10)
Grace Latham series (10)
Crack of doom
Bruce, Leo
Carolus Deene series (12)
Crack shot
Chase, Glen
Cherry Delight series (5)
Crackdown
McDermid, Val
Kate Brannigan series (3)
Stone, Nick
Ben Kane series (6)
Cracking of spines
Lewis, Roy Harley
Matthew Coll series (1)
Cracking open a Coffin
Butler, Gwendoline
Inspector John Coffin series (23)
Cracks wi' Robbie Doo
Waugh, Joseph Laing
Robbie Doo series (2)
Cracksman on velvet
Selwyn, Francis
Sergeant William Verity series (1)
Cracksman's holiday
Mackinnon, Allan
Glen Morrock series (2)
Crackswoman
Daniel, Roland
Inspector Jack Pearson series (1)
Cradle and the grave
Stein, Aaron Marc
Tim Mulligan and Elsie Mae Hunt series (7)
Cradle builder
Schoenstedt, Walter
Crade builder series (2)
Cradle of the clouds
Ghose, Sudhindra Nath
Sister Svenska series (2)
Cradle snatch
Conway, Peter
Inspector Cathy Weston series (1)
Craft and cunning
Graydon, William Murray
Sexton Blake series (35)
Craft of light
Emerson, Ru
Night-threads series (4)
Craghold creatures
Noone, Edwina
Craghold series (3)
Craghold crypt
Noone, Edwina
Craghold series (4)
Craghold curse
Noone, Edwina
Craghold series (2)
Craghold legacy
Noone, Edwina
Craghold series (1)
Craig and the Jaguar
Benton, Kenneth
Peter Craig series (4)
Craig and the Midas touch
Benton, Kenneth
Peter Craig series (6)
Craig and the Tunisian tangle
Benton, Kenneth
Peter Craig series (5)
Craig Kennedy, detective
Reeve, Arthur Benjamin
Craig Kennedy series (4)
Craig Kennedy listens in
Reeve, Arthur Benjamin
Craig Kennedy series (16)
Craig Kennedy on the farm
Reeve, Arthur Benjamin
Craig Kennedy series (19)
Craig of the Cloud Patrol
Crump, James Irving
Cloud Patrol series (5)
Craig poisoning mystery
Fielding, A
Inspector Pointer series (9)
Craighold cross
Noone, Edwina
Craghold series (5)
Craine's first case
Healy, Eugene P
Paul Craine series (1)
Cranberry birthday
Devlin, Wende
Cranberryport series (6)
Cranberry Christmas
Devlin, Wende
Cranberryport series (2)
Cranberry Easter
Devlin, Wende
Cranberryport series (7)
Cranberry Halloween
Devlin, Wende
Cranberryport series (4)
Cranberry mystery
Devlin, Wende
Cranberryport series (3)
Cranberry summer
Devlin, Wende
Cranberryport series (8)
Cranberry Thanksgiving
Devlin, Wende
Cranberryport series (1)
Cranberry Valentine
Devlin, Wende
Cranberryport series (5)
Crane's rebound
Jackson, Alison
Leslie Crane series (2)
Crank back on roller
Stuart, Donald Robert
Conjuror's years series (5)
Crank in the corner
Bush, Christopher
Ludovic Travers series (9)
Cranks and shadows
Constantine, K C
Mario Balzic series (11)
Cranky
Cosgrove, Stephen Edward
Whimsy storybooks series (4)
Cranmer
Knickmeyer, Steve
Steve Cranmer series (2)
Crash
Ballard, James Graham
Urban disaster trilogy (1)
Crash and carry
Christie, Stephen
Sexton Blake series (1598)
Crash, bang, wallop!
Ahlberg, Allan
Red nose readers series (10)
Crash car
Hardcastle, Michael
Steve and Anna series (1)
Crash course
Blake, Susan
Hawthorne College series (2)
Wharton, Joanna
Campus fever series (3)
Crash dive
Adair, James B
Deepcore series (3)
Crash landing!
Pascal, Francine
Sweet Valley High series (20)
Crash landing
Roth, Arthur
Twistaplot series (6)
Crash of '79
Erdman, Paul
Financial series (1)
Crash of empire
Pournelle, Jerry
Imperial stars series (3)
Crashing suns
Hamilton, Edmond
Interstellar Patrol series (2)
Crashlanding in the Congo
Wallace, C H
Steve Ramsay series (1)
Crater Lake
Axler, James
Deathlands series (4)
Crater of fear
Moore, Patrick
Robin North and Rex Redmayne series (3)
Crater of mystery
Appleton, Victor II
Tom Swift Junior series 2 (8)
Craven house horrors
Milton, Hilary
Plot your own horror stories series (1)
Crawfish-Man rescues Ron Guidry
Edler, Timothy J
Crawfish-Man series (2)
Crawfish-Man rescues the old beachcomber
Edler, Timothy J
Crawfish-Man series (5)
Crawfish-Man's fifty ways to keep your kids from using drugs
Edler, Timothy J
Crawfish-Man series (3)
Crawfish-Man's night befo' Christmas
Edler, Timothy J
Crawfish-Man series (4)
Crawling dark
Dunn, Pauline
Phantoms series (2)
Crawshay jewel mystery
Daniel, Roland
Buddy Mustard series (1)
Crayfish dinner
Keith, Carlton
Jeff Green series (4)
Crazy bear
McNaughton, Colin
Crazy series (2)
Crazy castle
Severn, David
Warner series (4)
Crazy cut-out tricks and puzzles
Tong, Gary
Crazy cut-outs series (4)
Crazy cut-outs
Tong, Gary
Crazy cut-outs series (1)
Crazy cut-outs from outer space
Tong, Gary
Crazy cut-outs series (3)
Crazy Horse
Dugan, Bill
War chiefs series (3)
Crazy in Berlin
Berger, Thomas
Carlo Reinhart series (1)
Crazy Indian
Bogart, William
Doc Savage series (183)
Crazy kill
Himes, Chester
Grave Digger Jones and Coffin Ed Johnson series (3)
Crazy knife
Dawson, Clay
Long Rider series (22)
Crazy love
Cooper, M E
Couples series (6)
Crazy mixed-up corpse
Avallone, Michael
Ed Noon series (7)
Crazy mixed-up nude
Fickling, G G
Erik March series (3)
Crazy mixed-up valences
Mooser, Stephen
Creepy Creature Club series (7)
Crazy murder show
Scott, Sutherland
Doctor Septimus Dodds series (3)
Crazy pop-ups
Tong, Gary
Crazy cut-outs series (4)
Crazy woman blues
Burke, Jackson Frederick
Joe Streeter series (2)
Creaking tree mystery
Knight, Leonard Alfred
Jerry Scant series (2)
Creaky knees
Huddy, Delia
Sandwich Street series (3)
Cream of the jest
Cabell, James Branch
Dom Manuel and his descendants series (20)
Created, the Destroyer
Murphy, Warren Burton
Destroyer series (1)
Creation descending
Lovejoy, Jack
Vision of beasts trilogy (1)
Creative murders
Brown, Carter
Lieutenant Al Wheeler series (41)
Creators
Boorstin, Daniel Joseph
Discoverers and creators series (2)
Creature comforts
Fenton, Sylvia
Beasts in the field series (2)
Stirling, Jessica
Elspeth and Anna Patterson trilogy (2)
Creature of Cranberry Cove
Bunting, Eve
No such things series (1)
Creature of havoc
Jackson, Steve
Fighting fantasy gamebook series (24)
Creature was stirring
Wells, Tobias
Detective Knute Severson series (15)
creatures
Lester, Julius
Tales of Uncle Remus series (3)
Creatures from the depths
Chalk, Gary
Prince of shadows series (2)
Creatures from the past
Stidworthy, John
Creatures from the past series (4)
Crecy and Poitiers
Rutley, Cecil Bernard
Tales of stirring times series (4)
Crecy War
Burne, Alfred Higgins
Hundred Years' War series (1)
Credit for a murder
Dean, Spencer
Don Cadee series (9)
Creed
Harte, Bryce
Slate Creed series (1)
Creed country
Overton, Jenny
Creed series (1)
Creed in slow motion
Knox, Ronald Arbuthnott
Slow motion series (2)
Creed's gauntlet
Newton, Mike
Lawman series (9)
Creed's gold
Newton, Mike
Lawman series (2)
Creed's hell
Newton, Mike
Lawman series (6)
Creed's kill
Newton, Mike
Lawman series (4)
Creed's law
Reno, James
Texas Anthem series (5)
Creed's ransom
Newton, Mike
Lawman series (8)
Creed's treasure
Newton, Mike
Lawman series (5)
Creed's vendetta
Newton, Mike
Lawman series (7)
Creed's vengeance
Newton, Mike
Lawman series (1)

Creed's war
Harte, Bryce
Slate Creed series (4)
Newton, Mike
Lawman series (3)
Creek called Wounded Knee
Jones, Douglas Clyde
General George Custer trilogy (3)
Creep, shadow!
Merritt, Abraham
Doctor Lowell series (2)
Creep, shadow, creep!
Merritt, Abraham
Doctor Lowell series (2)
Creeper
Grant, Maxwell
Shadow series (84)
Creepers
Creasey, John
Inspector Roger West series (9)
Creeping attack
Macdonnell, James Edmond
Captain Peter Bentley series (26)
Creeping death
Grant, Maxwell
Shadow series (22)
Knight, Leonard Alfred
Jerry Scant series (3)
Creeping hours
Pentecost, Hugh
John Jericho series (3)
Lieutenant Pascal series (5)
Creeping Jenny
Sherwood, John
Celia Grant series (10)
Creeping Jenny mystery
Flynn, Brian
Anthony Bathurst series (7)
Creeping Siamese
Hammett, Dashiell
Continental Op series (5)
Creeping unknown
Kneale, Nigel
Quatermass series (1)
Creeping vicar
Hamilton, Ian Sydney
Pete Heysen series (2)
Creeps
Abbot, Anthony
Thatcher Colt series (7)
Schoch, Tim
Creeps series (1)
Creepy Castle
Goodall, John Strickland
Paddy Pork series (8)
Creepy tale
Perry, Ritchie
Philis series (14)
Creole moon
Lowe, Myra
Louisiana series (2)
Creoles
Willoughby, Lee Davis
Making of America series (25)
Crescendo
Bentley, Phyllis
West Riding series (15)
Crescent brotherhood
Carter, Nicholas
Nicholas Carter series (38)
Crescent children on the green
Melinsky, Renate
Crescent children series (2)
Crescent in the sky
Moffitt, Donald
Mechanical sky series (1)
Cressy
Chappell, Mollie
Cressy series (2)
Crest of the broken wave
Barke, James
Immortal memory series (4)
Cretan counterfeit
Farrer, Katharine
Inspector Richard Ringwood series (2)
Crete must fall
Lutz, Gunther
Nazi paratrooper series (2)
Crewel lye
Anthony, Piers
Xanth series (8)
Crick-ette
Cosgrove, Stephen Edward
Bugg series (13)
Cricket
Timlow, Elizabeth Weston
Cricket series (1)
Van der Essen, Anne
Yok-yok series (9)
Cricket at the breakfast table
Elias, Frank
Cricket series (2)
Cricket at the seashore
Timlow, Elizabeth Weston
Cricket series (2)
Cricket in Times Square
Selden, George
Chester Cricket series (1)
Cricket mad
Parkinson, Michael
Daft series (2)
Cricket match
De Selincourt, Hugh
Gauvinier series (1)
Cricket on the brain
Elias, Frank
Cricket series (1)
Cricket team
Forest, Antonia
Marlow family series (8)
Cricketer at the crossroads
Walker, Max
Cricketer series (1)
Cries in the night
Wallis, James Harold
Inspector Wilton Jacks series (5)
Crime and again
Stout, Rex
Nero Wolfe and Archie Goodwin series (31)
Crime and Co.
Fowler, Sydney
Inspector Cleveland series (3)
Crime and punishment
Birt, David
Saxons and Vikings series (20)
Crime and puzzlement I
Treat, Lawrence
Crime and puzzlement series (1)
Crime and puzzlement II
Treat, Lawrence
Crime and puzzlement series (2)
Crime and puzzlement III
Treat, Lawrence
Crime and puzzlement series (3)
Crime and the crystal
Ferrars, Elizabeth
Andrew Basnett series (3)
Crime and the motive
Carter, Nicholas
Nicholas Carter series (256)
Crime at Black Dudley
Allingham, Margery
Albert Campion series (1)
Crime at Christmas
Kitchin, Clifford Henry Benn
Malcolm Warren series (2)
Crime at Crooked Gables
Plummer, Thomas Arthur
Detective Inspector Andrew Frampton series (14)
Crime at Crown Inn
Frazer, Martin
Sexton Blake series (884)
Crime at Eslington Hall
Cole, George Douglas Howard
Superintendent Henry Wilson series (22)
Crime at Guildford
Crofts, Freeman Wills
Inspector Joseph French series (13)
Crime at Halfpenny Bridge
Bellairs, George
Detective Inspector Thomas Littlejohn series (9)
Crime at Lock Fourteen
Simenon, Georges
Inspector Jules Maigret series (3)
Crime at Nornes
Crofts, Freeman Wills
Inspector Joseph French series (13)
Crime at Orcival
Gaboriau, Emile
Monsieur Lecoq series (2)
Crime at Seven Oaks
Grant, Maxwell
Shadow series (190)
Crime at Tattenham Corner
Haynes, Annie
Inspector Stoddart series (1)
Crime at the crossroads
Urquhart, Paul
Sexton Blake series (819)
Crime at the Crossways
Flynn, Brian
Anthony Bathurst series (7)
Crime at the fair
King, Hilary
Sexton Blake series (1326)
Crime at the Noah's Ark
Thynne, Molly
Doctor Constantine series (1)
Crime at the quay
Blair, Allan
Sexton Blake series (860)
Crime at the seaside hotel
Blair, Allan
Sexton Blake series (785)
Crime at the Villa Gloria
Norsworthy, George
Martin Crow series (2)
Crime at Three A.M.
Clevely, Hugh
Sexton Blake series (1348)
Crime at Vanderlynden's
Mottram, Ralph Hale
Captain Dormer series (1)
Spanish Farm series (3)
Crime by chance
Linington, Elizabeth
Sergeant Ivor Maddox series (7)
Crime campaign
Kupperberg, Paul
Amazing Spiderman series (2)
Crime caravan
Grant, Maxwell
Shadow series (250)
Crime circus
Grant, Maxwell
Shadow series (52)
Crime clinic
Grant, Maxwell
Shadow series (43)
Crime coast
Gill, Elizabeth
Benvenuto Brown series (1)
Crime combine
Hume, David
Inspector Sanderson series (2)
Crime conductor
Macdonald, Philip
Colonel Anthony Ruthven Gethryn series (8)
Crime counter crime
Lorac, E C R
Inspector Macdonald series (9)
Crime county
Grant, Maxwell
Shadow series (192)
Crime crypt
Grant, Maxwell
Shadow series (56)
Crime cult
Grant, Maxwell
Shadow series (12)
Crime de luxe
Gill, Elizabeth
Benvenuto Brown series (3)
Crime file
Shannon, Dell
Lieutenant Luis Mendoza series (25)
Crime for Caroline
Mansbridge, Pamela
Caroline series (1)
Crime for Christmas
Egan, Lesley
Vic Varallo series (13)
Keene, Carolyn
Nancy Drew and Hardy boys supermystery series (2)
Crime, gentlemen, please
Ames, Delano
Dagobert and Jane Brown series (8)
Crime harvest
Richmond, Philip
Duke Renny series (6)
Crime Haters
Ashe, Gordon
Patrick Dawlish series (37)
Crime in Carson's Shack
Hardinge, Rex
Sexton Blake series (847)
Crime in concrete
Coles, Manning
Tommy Hambledon series (23)
Crime in crystal
Campbell, Harriette Russell
Simon Brade series (8)
Crime in Cumberland Court
Walling, Robert Alfred John
Philip Tolefree series (11)
Crime in Holland
Simenon, Georges
Inspector Jules Maigret series (5)
Inspector Jules Maigret series (9)
Crime in Kensington
Sprigg, Christopher Saint John
Charles Venables series (1)
Inspector Bernard Bray series (1)
Crime in Leper's Hollow
Bellairs, George
Detective Inspector Thomas Littlejohn series (19)
Crime in paradise
Carter, Nicholas
Nicholas Carter series (526)
Crime in Park Lane
Jardine, Warwick
Sexton Blake series (761)
Crime in quarantine
Lambert, Rosa
Glyn Morgan series (4)
Crime in Room Twenty Seven
Tyrer, Walter
Sexton Blake series (1367)
Crime in the arcade
Proudfoot, Walter
Inspector Bill Vallance series (1)
Crime in the crypt
Wells, Carolyn
Fleming Stone series (24)
Crime in the Dutch garden
Adams, Herbert
Jimmy Haswell series (7)
Crime in the kiosk
Brandon, John Gordon
Sexton Blake series (910)
Crime in the queen's court
Keene, Carolyn
Nancy Drew series (112)
Crime in the wood
Graydon, William Murray
Sexton Blake series (483)
Crime in Threadneedle Street
Davis, George
Roag's Syndicate series (4)
Crime in time
Burton, Miles
Inspector Arnold and Desmond Merrion series (51)
Crime in Washington Mews
Crooker, Herbert
Clay Brooke series (2)
Crime in whispers
Witting, Clifford
Inspector Peter Bradfield series (9)
Crime incarnate
Wells, Carolyn
Fleming Stone series (54)
Crime insoluble
Durham, Mary
Inspector York series (4)
Crime insured
Grant, Maxwell
Shadow series (126)
Crime is my business
Baker, William Howard
Sexton Blake series (1442)
Crime lab
Stanley, George Edward
Doctor Constance Daniels series (2)
Crime Master
Duncan, William Murdoch
Mister Gilly series (1)
Crime master
Grant, Maxwell
Shadow series (59)
Crime minister
Barclay, Ian
Richard Dartley series (1)
Crime most foul
Douglas, George
Inspector Hallam and Sergeant Spratt series (9)
Crime of a century
Carter, Nicholas
Nicholas Carter series (403)
Crime of a countess
Carter, Nicholas
Nicholas Carter series (7)
Crime of Colin Wise
Underwood, Michael
Superintendent Simon Manton series (12)
Crime of Convict 13
Graydon, William Murray
Sexton Blake series (619)
Crime of Corporal Sherwood
Chester, Gilbert
Sexton Blake series (1050)
Crime of Count Dureen
Urquhart, Paul
Sexton Blake series (858)
Crime of four
Verner, Gerald
Sexton Blake series (626)
Crime of Gunga Das
Brisbane, Coutts
Sexton Blake series (875)
Crime of Inspector Maigret
Simenon, Georges
Inspector Jules Maigret series (8)
Crime of Philip Garrison
Marlowe, Francis
Doc Summers series (2)
Crime of the camera
Carter, Nicholas
Nicholas Carter series (169)
Crime of the cashiered major
Parsons, Anthony
Sexton Blake series (1101)
Crime of the catacombs
Teed, George Hamilton
Sexton Blake series (678)
Crime of the century
Abbot, Anthony
Thatcher Colt series (2)
Ottolengui, Rodrigues
John Barnes series (4)
Robert Leroy Mitchell series (3)
Crime of the chromium bowl
Black, Elizabeth Best
Peter Strangely series (2)
Crime of the French cafe, and other stories
Carter, Nicholas
Nicholas Carter series (57)
Crime of the just
Chamson, Andre
Roux series (3)
Crime of the Reckaviles
Masterman, Walter Sidney
Sir Arthur Sinclair series (2)
Crime of their life
Kane, Frank
Johnny Liddell series (19)
Crime of violence
King, Rufus
Lieutenant Valcour series (10)
Stagg, James
Sexton Blake series (1453)
Crime on Cote des Nieges
Montrose, David
Russell Teed series (1)
Crime on Gallows Hill
Teed, George Hamilton
Sexton Blake series (679)
Crime on her hands
Gribble, Leonard Reginald
Superintendent Anthony Slade series (39)
Stout, Rex
Dol Bonner series (1)
Crime on my hands
Chapman, Robert
Rex Banner series (2)
Janson, Hank
Hank Janson series (120)
Crime on the cliff
Jackson, Lewis
Sexton Blake series (1188)
Crime on the Clyde
Chester, Gilbert
Sexton Blake series (753)
Crime on the French frontier
Hunter, John
Sexton Blake series (1370)
Crime on the heath
Frost, C Vernon
Sexton Blake series (927)
Crime on the Limited
Ridley, Nat
Nat Ridley series (4)
Crime on the moor
Bridges, Thomas Charles
Sexton Blake series (825)
Crime on the moors
Tyrer, Walter
Sexton Blake series (1172)
Crime on the promenade
Hunter, John
Sexton Blake series (943)
Crime on the Solent
Crofts, Freeman Wills
Inspector Joseph French series (12)
Crime on their hands
Shannon, Dell
Lieutenant Luis Mendoza series (17)
Crime oracle
Grant, Maxwell
Shadow series (103)
Crime out of mind
Ames, Delano
Dagobert and Jane Brown series (10)
Grant, Maxwell
Shadow series (272)
Crime over Boston
Grant, Maxwell
Shadow series (151)
Crime over Casco
Grant, Maxwell
Shadow series (274)
Crime over Miami
Grant, Maxwell
Shadow series (194)

Crime partners
Clark, Al C
Kenyatta series (1)
Crime pays no dividends
Radford, Edwin
Doctor Manson series (3)
Crime philosopher
Goyne, Richard
Padre series (1)
Crime, punishment, and resurrection
Collins, Michael
Dan Fortune series (19)
Crime ray
Grant, Maxwell
Shadow series (170)
Crime reporter's secret
Dilnot, George
Sexton Blake series (906)
Crime rides the sea
Grant, Maxwell
Shadow series (158)
Crime scientist
Webster, Frederick Annesley Michael
Ebbie Entwhistle series (3)
Crime story
Nash, Jay Robert
Jack Journey series (1)
Crime tears on
Wells, Carolyn
Fleming Stone series (52)
Crime to music
Drax, Peter
Chief Inspector Thompson series (3)
Crime under cover
Grant, Maxwell
Shadow series (204)
Crime unlimited
Hume, David
Mick Cardby series (3)
Crime upon crime
Gask, Arthur
Gilbert Larose series (29)
Underwood, Michael
Rosa Epton series (3)
Crime wave
Russell, Martin
Jim Larkin series (3)
Crime wave at Blandings
Wodehouse, Pelham Grenville
Blandings Castle series (6)
Crime wave at Little Cornford
Adams, Herbert
Major Roger Bennion series (20)
Crime within crime
Drax, Peter
Chief Inspector Thompson series (2)
Crime without a clue
Cobb, Thomas
Inspector Bedison series (1)
Crime without passion
Grayson, Richard
Inspector Gautier series (5)
Crime without reason
Douglas, George
Inspector Bonny Lee series (4)
Crime zone
David, Jake
Last rangers series (2)
Crimebeat crisis
Janson, Hank
Hank Janson series (166)
Crimes at Fenton Towers
Tyrer, Walter
Sexton Blake series (1294)
Crimes of the season
Saville, Andrew
Bergerac series (3)
Crimes past
Challis, Mary
Jeremy Locke series (2)
Crime's stronghold
Grant, Maxwell
Shadow series (215)
Criminal C.O.D.
Taylor, Phoebe Atwood
Asey Mayo series (15)
Criminal computer
Dicks, Terrance
Baker Street Irregulars series (10)
Criminal conversation
Freeling, Nicolas
Inspector Piet Van der Valk series (5)
Criminal link
Carter, Nicholas
Nicholas Carter series (96)
Criminals all
Martyn, Wyndham
Anthony Trent series (17)
Criminals caught
M'Govan, James
James M'Govan series (6)
Criminals in real life
Phelan, Jim
Real life criminals series (1)
Crimson alibi
Cohen, Octavus Roy
David Carroll series (1)
Crimson belt
Teed, George Hamilton
Sexton Blake series (309)
Crimson capsule
Coblentz, Stanton Arthur
Outlander series (2)
Crimson cat
Grierson, Francis Durham
Inspector George Muir series (7)
Crimson cat murders
Porcelain, Sidney E
Stephen Clay series (2)
Crimson chalice
Canning, Victor
Crimson chalice trilogy (1)
Crimson chalice trilogy
Canning, Victor
Crimson chalice trilogy (3)
Crimson Clown
McCulley, Johnston
Crimson Clown series (1)
Crimson Clown again
McCulley, Johnston
Crimson Clown series (2)
Crimson clue
Coxe, George Harmon
Kent Murdock series (14)
Crimson crescent
Townson, Hazel
Lenny and Jake series (5)
Crimson cruiser
Wirt, Mildred Augustine
Trailer series (2)
Crimson domino
Sayer, Walter William
Sexton Blake series (257)
Crimson doom
Bowen, Robert Sidney
Dusty Ayres and his Battle Birds series (2)
Crimson feather
Mason, Sara Elizabeth
Sheriff Bill Davies series (2)
Crimson flame
Dixon, Franklin W
Hardy boys series (77)
Crimson flash
Carter, Nicholas
Nicholas Carter series (410)
Crimson frame
Martin, Aylwin Lee
Matt Hughes series (3)
Crimson goddess
Cooke, Catherine
Winged assassin trilogy (3)
Crimson green
Zimmerman, Bruce
Quinn Parker series (4)
Crimson hair murders
Teilhet, Darwin Le Ora
Baron Von Kaz series (3)
Crimson hand
Finney, R C
Inspector Bourne series (5)
Crimson jade
Mair, George Brown
David Grant series (9)
Crimson joy
Parker, Robert Brown
Spenser series (15)
Crimson killer
Wallace, Robert
Phantom Detective series (4)
Crimson kisses
Drake, Asa
Dracula series (21)
Crimson legion
Denning, Troy
Prism pentad series (2)
Crimson mask
Hardy, Arthur Steffens
Sexton Blake series (83)
Crimson moth
Turner, James Ernest
Nicholas de la Haye series (1)
Crimson pagoda
Nicole, Christopher
China trilogy (1)
Crimson patch
Taylor, Phoebe Atwood
Asey Mayo series (8)
Crimson petal
Crow, Duncan
Simon Ire series (2)
Manuel, Esme
Trisha Trelawney series (2)
Crimson ramblers
Eldred, Warren L
Saint Dunstan series (1)
Crimson rope
Asbury, Herbert
Inspector Thomas Conroy series (1)
Crimson sea
Gygax, Gary
Sagard the Barbarian series (3)
Crimson serpent
Robeson, Kenneth
Doc Savage series (78)
Crimson shadow
Daniel, Roland
Inspector Jack Pearson series (2)
Crimson sweater
Barbour, Ralph Henry
Hudson River trilogy (1)
Crimson universe
Scheer, Karl Herbert
Perry Rhodan series (67)
Crimson wind
Hennessy, Max
Dicken Quinney trilogy (4)
Cringle and cross-tree
Optic, Oliver
Onward and upward series (4)
Crinkleroot's animal tracks and wildlife signs
Arnosky, Jim
Crinkleroot series (1)
Crinkleroot's guide to knowing the birds
Arnosky, Jim
Crinkleroot series (3)
Crinkleroot's guide to walking in wild places
Arnosky, Jim
Crinkleroot series (2)
Cripple Creek
Ellis, Wesley
Lone Star series (90)
Crippled canary
Gunn, Victor
Chief Inspector Bill Cromwell series (23)
Crippled tree
Han, Suyin
Crippled tree series (1)
Crisis
Barclay, Virginia
Mid-City Hospital series (4)
Churchill, Winston
American national development series (3)
Drake, David
Fleet series (6)
Mackenzie, Steve
Seals series (13)
Crisis at Cornerstone
McCoy, Marshall
Nevada Jim series (38)
Crisis at Starlight
Vardeman, Robert Edward
Biowarriors trilogy (2)
Crisis in Babylon
Grover, Marshall
Larry and Stretch series (68)
Crisis in space
Martin, David
Doctor Who find your fate series (2)
Crisis of the old order, 1919-1933
Schlesinger, Arthur Meier
Age of Roosevelt series (1)
Crisis on Centaurus
Ferguson, Brad
Star trek series (28)
Crisis on Citadel II
Hagberg, David
Flash Gordon series (11)
Crisis on Conshelf Ten
Hughes, Monica
Conshelf Ten series (1)
Crisp report
Matthew, Christopher
Simon Crisp series (3)
Crisscross shadow
Dixon, Franklin W
Hardy boys series (33)
Cristy at Skippinhills
Hunt, Mabel Leigh
Cristy Romano series (2)
Critical condition
Sutton, Jessica
Bel Air General series (5)
Critical threshold
Stableford, Brian Michael
Daedalus series (2)
Critter race
Reese, Bob
Desert critterland series (4)
Critter sitters
Hiser, Constance
James and gang series (4)
Crivit experiment
Wold, Allen
V series (8)
Croaker
Ashe, Gordon
Patrick Dawlish series (1)
Garnett, Roger
Chief Inspector Jonathan Black series (2)
Croaking raven
Mitchell, Gladys
Dame Beatrice Bradley series (39)
Crockett on the loose
Lang, Brad
Fred Crockett series (1)
Crocociles
Goscinny, Rene
Twelve tasks of Asterix series (9)
Crocodile Christmas
Roos, Stephen
Pet Lovers Club series (3)
Crocodile club
Broome, Adam
Commissioner Denzil Grigson series (4)
Crocodile god
Edwards, Hugh
Sea Witch series (4)
Crocodile in the garden, volume 1
Mahy, Margaret
Crocodile series (5)
Crocodile in the garden, volume 2
Mahy, Margaret
Crocodile series (6)
Crocodile in the tree
Duvoisin, Roger
Crocus series (1)
Crocodile medicine
Watts, Marjorie Ann
Crocodile series (1)
Crocodile on the sandbank
Peters, Elizabeth
Amelia Peabody Emerson series (1)
Crocodile out shopping
East, Helen
Arthur's aunt series (4)
Crocodile plaster
Watts, Marjorie Ann
Crocodile series (2)
Crocodile teeth
Watts, Marjorie Ann
Crocodile series (3)
Crocodile Trapp
Callison, Brian
Captain Edward Trapp series (4)
Crocodile's Christmas jandals
Mahy, Margaret
Crocodile series (1)
Crocus
Duvoisin, Roger
Crocus series (2)
Crocus list
Lyall, Gavin
Major Harry Maxim series (3)
Croft in Clachan
Armstrong, Sybil
Clachan series (1)
Cromwell
Birt, David
Stuarts series (5)
Cromwell of Virginia
Ellis, Edward Sylvester
Colonial trilogy (2)
Cromwell's boy
Haugaard, Erik Christian
Oliver Cutter series (2)
Cromwell's cavalier
Sanders, John
Nicholas Pym series (4)
Crone
Brennan, James Herbert
Shiva series (2)
Cronus
De Andrea, William Louis
Clifford Driscoll series (1)
Crook ahoy
Hughes, Gwilym Fielden
Roger Moore and the Crimefighters series (3)
Crook cargo
Hunter, John
Sexton Blake series (900)
Crook from Chicago
Hood, Stephen
Sexton Blake series (656)
Crook o' lune
Lorac, E C R
Inspector Macdonald series (38)
Crook of Canada
Teed, George Hamilton
Sexton Blake series (636)
Crook of Chinatown
Graydon, William Murray
Sexton Blake series (484)
Crook of Costab Blanca
Teed, George Hamilton
Sexton Blake series (680)
Crook of Crauford Court
Essex, Louis
Sexton Blake series (613)
Crook of Fleet Street
Evans, Gwyn
Sexton Blake series (426)
Crook of Marsden Manor
Teed, George Hamilton
Sexton Blake series (637)
Crook of Mayfair
Gibbons, Harry Hornaby Clifford
Sexton Blake series (376)
Crook of Monte Carlo
Teed, George Hamilton
Sexton Blake series (727)
Crook of Newmarket
Hardy, Arthur Steffens
Sexton Blake series (655)
Crook of Paris
Teed, George Hamilton
Sexton Blake series (638)
Crook of Shanghai
Teed, George Hamilton
Sexton Blake series (728)
Crook straightened
Berry, Martha Eugenie
Crook series (2)
Crook stuff
Keverne, Richard
Simon Artifex series (2)
Crook town
Skene, Anthony
Sexton Blake series (717)
Crooked and straight
Berry, Martha Eugenie
Crook series (1)
Crooked bannister
Keene, Carolyn
Nancy Drew series (48)
Crooked brownie
Arthur, Ruth Mabel
Crooked brownie series (1)
Crooked brownie at the seaside
Arthur, Ruth Mabel
Crooked brownie series (3)
Crooked brownie in town
Arthur, Ruth Mabel
Crooked brownie series (2)
Crooked circle
Verner, Gerald
Superintendent Robert Budd series (3)
Crooked cross
Dutton, Charles Judson
John Bartley series (6)
Crooked desert
Kester, Ken
Steve McCade series (3)
Crooked five
Brandon, John Gordon
Inspector Patrick Aloysius McCarthy series (27)
Crooked flight
Jackson, Basil
Air detective series (1)
Crooked furrow
Farnol, Jeffery
Mister Jasper Shrig of Bow Street series (5)
Oliver Matravers series (1)
Crooked highway
Spiller, Andrew
Chief Inspector Duck Mallard series (2)
Crooked hinge
Carr, John Dickson
Doctor Gideon Fell series (9)
Crooked house
Rowland, John
Inspector Shelley series (10)
Crooked Island
McKernan, Victoria
Chicago Nordejoong series (3)
Crooked lip
Adams, Herbert
Jimmy Haswell series (2)

Crooked little path
Burgess, Thornton Waldo
Nature stories series (3)
Crooked marshal
Evans, Tabor
Longarm series (138)
Crooked mile
De Voto, Bernard
Abbey family series (1)
Onions, Oliver
Taskers series (2)
Crooked phoenix
Jones, Bradshaw
Claude Ravel series (2)
Crooked road
West, Morris Langlo
George Harlequin series (1)
Crooked shadow
Steel, Kurt
Hank Hyer series (5)
Crooked shadows
Crowe, John
Buena Costa County series (4)
Crooked Snake
Wrightson, Patricia
Society of the Crooked Snake series (1)
Crooked staircase
Gunn, Victor
Chief Inspector Bill Cromwell series (22)
Crooked wood
Underwood, Michael
Sergeant Nick Attwell series (5)
Crooked wreath
Brand, Christianna
Inspector Cockrill series (3)
Crookery Inn
Crossley, Maude
Guy Bannister series (2)
Crooking finger
Adams, Cleve Franklin
Rex McBride series (5)
Crooks
Whalley, Peter
Harry Sommers and Jill Hanscombe series (5)
Crook's accomplice
Skene, Anthony
Sexton Blake series (630)
Crook's blind
Carter, Nicholas
Nicholas Carter series (528)
Crooks' caravan
King, Frank
Dormouse series (17)
Crooks' cargo
Brandon, John Gordon
Sexton Blake series (1023)
Crook's castle
Dilnot, George
Horace Augustus Elver series (1)
Crooks, chooks and bloody ratbags
Cue, Kerry
Bloody ratbags series (1)
Crooks' convoy
Blair, Allan
Sexton Blake series (945)
Crooks' cross
King, Frank
Dormouse series (9)
Crook's decoy
Teed, George Hamilton
Sexton Blake series (776)
Crook's deputy
Parsons, Anthony
Sexton Blake series (1337)
Crook's double
Bayfield, William John
Sexton Blake series (416)
Carter, Nicholas
Nicholas Carter series (617)
Murray, Andrew
Sexton Blake series (300)
Crooks' game
Dilnot, George
Inspector Strickland series (1)
Crooks go straight
Grant, Maxwell
Shadow series (73)
Crooks' Hill
San Antonio
Berurier series (8)
San Antonio series (8)
Crooks in clover
Teed, George Hamilton
Sexton Blake series (546)
Crooks Limited
Bidston, Lester
Sexton Blake series (562)
Crook's loot
Jardine, Warwick
Sexton Blake series (710)
Crooks of Tunis
Parsons, Anthony
Sexton Blake series (1385)
Crook's shadow
Farjeon, Joseph Jefferson
Ben the tramp series (2)
Crooks' shepherd
Truss, Seldon
Inspector Gidleigh series (1)
Crooks' vendetta
Teed, George Hamilton
Grant Rushton series (3)
Crop circles
Andrews, Colin
Crop circles series (2)
Croquet for a day
Walker, Mort
Hi and Lois series (15)
Cross
Undset, Sigrid
Kristin Lavransdatter trilogy (3)
Cross and crescent
Optic, Oliver
Young America, second series (3)
Cross and the Crescent
Birt, David
Saxons and Vikings series (4)
Cross and the eagle
Berstl, Julius
Saint Paul series (2)
Cross and the switchblade
Wilkerson, David
Cross and the switchblade series (1)
Cross-Channel crime
Teed, George Hamilton
Sexton Blake series (681)
Cross-Channel quest
Hogg, Garry
Nessa and Lance series (1)
Cross-country
Kastle, Herbert David
Sergeant Edmund Roersch series (1)
Cross-currents
Asprin, Robert Lynn
Sanctuary series (6)
Cross currents
Porter, Eleanor Hodgman
Cross currents series (1)
Cross-draw
McLaglen, John J
Herne the Hunter series (8)
Cross-eyed bear
Hughes, Dorothy Belle
Inspector Tobin series (2)
Cross-eyed bear murders
Hughes, Dorothy Belle
Inspector Tobin series (2)
Cross-fire
Gilman, George G
Adam Steele series (7)
Cross fire
Tippette, Giles
Justa Williams series (2)
Cross marks the spot
Ronald, James
Julian Mendoza series (1)
Cross of Frankenstein
Myers, Robert John
Frankenstein sequels series (4)
Cross of gold affair
Davies, Fredric
Man from U.N.C.L.E. series (14)
Cross of murder
Dickson, Carter
Sir Henry Merrivale series (13)
Cross off
Corris, Peter
Luke Dunlop series (2)
Cross purposes
Dick, Alexandra
Alastair Macalastair series (5)
Cross stitch
Gabaldon, Diana
Outlander series (1)
Cross that palm when I come to it
Southcott, Audley
Frank Marker series (2)
Cross the stars
Drake, David
Hammer's Slammers series (2)
Cross-time engineer
Frankowski, Leo
Adventures of Conrad Stargard series (1)
Crossbow murder
Dickson, Carter
Sir Henry Merrivale series (8)
Crosscurrents
Keene, Carolyn
Nancy Drew files series (68)
Crossed needles
Carter, Nicholas
Nicholas Carter series (618)
Crossed skies
Carnac, Carol
Inspector Julian Rivers series (8)
Crossed wires
Carter, Nicholas
Nicholas Carter series (58)
Crossfire
Braun, Matt
Ash Tallman series (2)
Crossfire
Lord, Tom
Tallman series (2)
Crossfire Country
LeBeau, Roy
Buckskin series (9)
Crossfire kill
Buchanan, Jack
M.I.A. Hunter series (11)
Crossfire killings
Knox, Bill
Inspector Colin Thane and Phil Moss series (19)
Crossfire Mountain
Roberts, J R
Gunsmith series (57)
Crossfire red
Carter, Nick
Nick Carter series (221)
Crossing
Churchill, Winston
American national development series (2)
Fisher, Clay
Ben Allison series (2)
McCarthy, Cormac
Border trilogy (2)
Crossing enemy lines
Montgomery, Raymond A
Rebels in the New World series (2)
Crossing fee
Warner, Esther Sietmann
Liberia series (2)
Crossing the line
Cockburn, Claud
In time of trouble series (2)
Crossing to Salamis
Walsh, Jill Paton
Children of the fox trilogy (1)
Crosskill
Disher, Garry
Wyatt series (4)
Crossroad murders
Simenon, Georges
Inspector Jules Maigret series (7)
Crossroads
McConkey, James
Court of memory trilogy (1)
Crossroads of time
Norton, Andre
Blake Walker series (1)
Crosstime agent
Norton, Andre
Blake Walker series (2)
Crosswinds
Tilford, Earl H
USAF in Vietnam series (2)
Crosswinds of freedom
Burns, James Macgregor
American experiment series (3)
Crossword code
Resnicow, Herbert
Crossword series (3)
Crossword hunt
Resnicow, Herbert
Crossword series (5)
Crossword legacy
Resnicow, Herbert
Crossword series (4)
Crossword murder
Punshon, Ernest Robertson
Bobby Owen series (3)
Crossword mystery
Punshon, Ernest Robertson
Bobby Owen series (3)
Crotal and white
Macdonald, Finlay J
Hebridean boyhood series (2)
Crouching beast
Williams, Valentine
Clubfoot series (6)
Crouching spy
Macvicar, Angus
Reverend P J Macfarlane series (2)
Crow and Mrs Gaddy
Gage, Wilson
Mrs Gaddy series (2)
Crow and the castle
Robertson, Keith
Neil and Swede trilogy (3)
Crow bait
Meek, Joseph
Mountain Jack Pike series (4)
Crow goddess
Finney, Patricia
Lugh the Harper series (2)
Crowded hill
Macleod, Le Roy
Years of peace series (2)
Crowded years, 1884-1898
Kapp, Eleanor
Eleanor Marx series (2)
Crowdie and cream
Macdonald, Finlay J
Hebridean boyhood series (1)
Crowds of Lourdes
Huysmans, Joris Karl
Durtal series (5)
Crown and mitre
Neill, Robert
Sir Harry Barnaby series (1)
Crown diamond
Carter, Nicholas
Nicholas Carter series (124)
Crown for Azora
Cole, Jackson
Jim Hatfield series (94)
Crown house
Ling, Peter
Crown series (1)
Crown in candlelight
Jarman, Rosemary Hawley
Richard III series (3)
Crown in darkness
Doherty, Paul C
Hugh Corbett series (2)
Crown jewel
De Boissiere, Ralph
Trinidad series (1)
Crown jewels
Williams, Walter Jon
Crown jewels series (1)
Crown of darkness
Parry, Anne Spencer
Bara quartet (3)
Crown of fire
Benzoni, Juliette
Marianne series (6)
Crown of glory
Jarman, Rosemary Hawley
Richard III series (2)
Crown of kings
Jackson, Steve
Sorcery series (4)
Crown of light
Parry, Anne Spencer
Bara quartet (4)
Crown of night
Audemars, Pierre
Monsieur Pinaud series (4)
Crown of splendour
Farely, Alison
Plantagenet series (2)
Crown of the sword god
Norvil, Manning
Odan the half-god trilogy (3)
Crown of thorns
Heenan, John Carmel
Crown of thorns series (2)
Crown of white olive
Sutcliff, Rosemary
Heather, oak and olive trilogy (3)
Crown of willow
Muskett, Netta
Blaike family series (1)
Crown Oklahoma
Lehrer, Jim
One-Eyed Mack series (2)
Crown papers
Ling, Peter
Crown series (2)
Crown swindle
Eades, Maud L
Winston Barrows series (1)
Crowned queen
Grier, Sydney Carlyon
Balkan series (2)
Crowner's quest
Broome, Adam
Commissioner Denzil Grigson series (1)
Crowning mercy
Kells, Susannah
Lazender family series (1)
Crowning murder
Stanners, Harold H
Professor Harding series (3)
Crowning of a king
Zweig, Arnold
Werner Bertin and Lenore Wahl series (6)
Crowning terror
Dixon, Franklin W
Hardy boys case files series (6)
Crowns can kill
Janson, Hank
Hank Janson series (104)
Crows can't count
Fair, A A
Bertha Cool and Donald Lam series (10)
Crow's Inn tragedy
Haynes, Annie
Inspector Furnival series (3)
Crowthers of Bankdam
Armstrong, Thomas
Crowther chronicles series (1)
Croyd
Wallace, Ian
Croyd series (1)
Crozier Pharaohs
Mitchell, Gladys
Dame Beatrice Bradley series (66)
Cruachan and the Killane
Cristabel
Veltakin series (2)
Crucible
Chase, Robert Reynolds
Game series (2)
O'Neill, Donal
Brian series (1)
Crucifer of blood
Giovanni, Paul
Sherlock Holmes drama series (16)
Crucifixion squad
Beere, Peter
Trauma 2020 series (2)
Crude kill
Pendleton, Don
Mack Bolan series (59)
Cruel and unusual
Cornwell, Patricia Daniels
Doctor Kay Scarpetta series (4)
Cruel as a cat
Halliday, Michael
Doctor Emmanuel Cellini series (4)
Cruel as the grave
Bayne, Isabella
Benedict Breeze series (2)
Cruel dart
Carstairs, Henry
Lydford Long series (5)
Cruel in the shadow
Macintyre, Lorn
Chronicles of Inverness series (1)
Cruel lady
Corrigan, Mark
Mark Corrigan and McLean series (19)
Cruel month
Sitwell, Osbert
Left hand, right hand series (1)
Cruel mother
Lapierre, Janet
Meg Halloran series (1)
Cruel trail
James, William M
Apache series (11)
Cruel victim
Tripp, Miles
John Samson series (4)
Cruise in the sky
Ashton, Lamar
Aeroplane boys series (5)
Cruise into chaos
Derrick, Lionel
Penetrator series (39)
Cruise of terror
Hope, Stanton
Sexton Blake series (703)
Cruise of the Canoe Club
Alden, William Livingston
Moral Pirates series (3)
Cruise of the Casco
Kellogg, Elijah
Pleasant Cove series (3)
Cruise of the Condor
Johns, William Earl
Biggles series (2)
Cruise of the Cormorant
Knight, Arthur Lee
Cormorant series (2)
Verrill, Alpheus Hyatt
Cormorant series (1)
Cruise of the Dashaway
Mannering, May
Climbing the rope series (3)
Cruise of the Deerfoot
Ellis, Edward Sylvester
Launch boys series (2)
Cruise of the Firefly
Ellis, Edward Sylvester
Firefly series (2)

Cue for murder
McCloy, Helen
Basil Willing series (5)
Cue for treason
Trease, Geoffrey
Stuart kings series (1)
Cugel's saga
Vance, Jack
Dying earth series (4)
Cult crushers
Yaeger, Carl H
Soldier of fortune series (3)
Cult of crime
Dixon, Franklin W
Hardy boys case files series (3)
Cult of darkness
Reid, Desmond
Sexton Blake series (1563)
Cult of loving kindness
Park, Paul
Starbridge series (3)
Cult of the damned
Andrews, Spike
C.A.T. series (3)
Cult of the queer people
Duncan, William Murdoch
Greensleeves series (3)
Cult point forty five
Rainey, Rich
Alex Dartanian series (4)
Cumberland!
Poole, Helen Lee
Whitewater dynasty series (3)
Cumberland Gap and trails West
McCall, Edith
Frontiers of America series (10)
Cunning as a fox
Halliday, Michael
Doctor Emmanuel Cellini series (1)
Cunning linguist
Conway, Troy
Coxeman series (20)
Cunning of the dove
Duggan, Alfred
Saxon trilogy (2)
Cunningham equations
Edmondson, Garry Cotton
Cunningham trilogy (1)
Cunningham's revenge
Macneil, Duncan
James Ogilvie series (12)
Cuoto snatch
Shelynn, Jack
Ned Parker series (2)
Cup and bowl
Tarsky, Sue
Look and see series (2)
Cup Final crime
Bidston, Lester
Sexton Blake series (687)
Cup final for Charlie
Allen, Joy
Charlie series (5)
Cup Final mystery
Edgar, Alfred
Sexton Blake series (466)
Cup of clay
Douglas, Carole Nelson
Taliswoman trilogy (1)
Cup of death
Thompson, Gene
Dade Cooley series (3)
Cup of strength
Paul, Charlotte
Snoqualmie Valley series (2)
Cup of Thanatos
Hunt, Charlotte
Doctor Paul Holton series (2)
Cup that kills
Barrett, Geoffrey John
Inspector Blessingay series (3)
Cupboard
Burningham, John
Little book series (6)
Cupboard under the stairs
Turner, George Reginald
Treelake series (2)
Cupid and Chow-Chow
Alcott, Louisa May
Aunt Jo's scrap-bag series (3)
Cupid and the jacaranda
Sitwell, Sacheverell
Quick and the dead series (5)
Cupid in Mayfair
Matthewman, Phyllis
Cupid trilogy (2)
Cupid turns killer
Janson, Hank
Hank Janson series (94)
Cupid under Capricorn
Matthewman, Phyllis
Cupid trilogy (3)
Curate's awakening
Macdonald, George
Thomas Wingfold trilogy (1)
Curate's crime
Dick, Alexandra
Alastair Macalastair series (3)
Curate's wife
Young, Emily Hilda
Jenny Wren series (2)
Cure for cancer
Moorcock, Michael
Catherine Cornelius series (1)
Jerry Cornelius series (2)
Cure for dying
Melville, Jennie
Sergeant Charmian Daniels series (10)
Cure for living
Douglas, Colin
David Campbell series (5)
Curing the Daltons
Goscinny, Rene
Lucky Luke series (9)
Curio murders
Wallace, Robert
Phantom Detective series (28)
Curiosity Club
Goodman, Montague
Wantoknow series for boys (5)
Curiosity didn't kill the cat
Wren, M K
Conan Flagg series (1)
Curiosity Joe
Goodman, Montague
Wantoknow series for boys (3)
Curiosity killed the cat
Cockin, Joan
Inspector Cam and Beaver series (1)
Curiosity of Mister Treadgold
Williams, Valentine
Mister Treadgold series (2)
Curious adventures of Jimmy McGee
Estes, Eleanor
Witch family series (2)
Curious affair of the third dog
Moyes, Patricia
Henry and Emmy Tibbett series (11)
Curious calamity in Ward 8
Deming, Dorothy
Wendy Brent series (1)
Curious case of the crook's memoirs
Graydon, William Murray
Sexton Blake series (345)
Curious coronation
Keene, Carolyn
Dana girls series (31)
Curious creatures
Oxenbury, Helen
Seven hundred and twenty nine series (3)
Curious custard pie
Scherf, Margaret
Reverend Martin Buell series (2)
Curious George
Rey, Hans Augusto
Curious George series (1)
Curious George and the dinosaur
Rey, Margret
Curious George series (28)
Curious George and the dump truck
Rey, Margret
Curious George series (8)
Curious George and the pizza
Rey, Margret
Curious George series (23)
Curious George at the airport
Rey, Margret
Curious George series (22)
Curious George at the ballet
Rey, Margret
Curious George series (16)
Curious George at the beach
Rey, Margret
Curious George series (24)
Curious George at the fire station
Rey, Margret
Curious George series (21)
Curious George at the laundromat
Rey, Margret
Curious George series (19)
Curious George at the railroad station
Rey, Margret
Curious George series (25)
Curious George bakes a cake
Rey, Margret
Curious George series (32)
Curious George flies a kite
Rey, Margret
Curious George series (5)
Curious George gets a medal
Rey, Hans Augusto
Curious George series (4)
Curious George goes camping
Rey, Margret
Curious George series (33)
Curious George goes fishing
Rey, Margret
Curious George series (18)
Curious George goes hiking
Rey, Margret
Curious George series (12)
Curious George goes sledding
Rey, Margret
Curious George series (11)
Curious George goes to a costume party
Rey, Margret
Curious George series (15)
Curious George goes to a restaurant
Rey, Margret
Curious George series (26)
Curious George goes to a toy store
Rey, Margret
Curious George series (35)
Curious George goes to an air show
Rey, Margret
Curious George series (34)
Curious George goes to an icecream shop
Rey, Margret
Curious George series (29)
Curious George goes to school
Rey, Margret
Curious George series (30)
Curious George goes to the aquarium
Rey, Margret
Curious George series (10)
Curious George goes to the circus
Rey, Margret
Curious George series (9)
Curious George goes to the dentist
Rey, Margret
Curious George series (31)
Curious George goes to the hospital
Rey, Margret
Curious George series (7)
Curious George learns the alphabet
Rey, Hans Augusto
Curious George series (6)
Curious George makes a splash
Krulick, Nancy E
Curious George series (1)
Curious George plays baseball
Rey, Margret
Curious George series (14)
Curious George rides a bike
Rey, Hans Augusto
Curious George series (3)
Curious George saves the day
Krulick, Nancy E
Curious George series (2)
Curious George takes a job
Rey, Hans Augusto
Curious George series (2)
Curious George visit4s the zoo
Rey, Margret
Curious George series (20)
Curious George visits an amusement park
Rey, Margret
Curious George series (27)
Curious George visits the police station
Rey, Margret
Curious George series (17)
Curious George walks the pets
Rey, Margret
Curious George series (13)
Curious lobster
Hatch, Richard Warren
Curious lobster series (1)
Curious lobster's island
Hatch, Richard Warren
Curious lobster series (2)
Curious magic
Beresford, Elisabeth
Magic series (8)
Curious quest
Fairfax, Virginia
Girl Scouts series (5)
Curious quests of Brigadier Ffellowes
Lanier, Sterling Edmund
Brigadier Ffellowes series (2)
Curlew Coombe mystery
Lane, Gret
John Barrin series (1)
Kate Marsh series (1)
Curlew Jon
Edwin, Maribel
Curlew Jon series (1)
Curly and the Aztec gold
Ames, James Bushnell
Curly Graham trilogy (2)
Curly Graham, cowpuncher
Ames, James Bushnell
Curly Graham trilogy (3)
Curly of the Circle-bar
Ames, James Bushnell
Curly Graham trilogy (1)
Curlytops and their pets
Garis, Howard Roger
Curlytops series (6)
Curlytops and their playmates
Garis, Howard Roger
Curlytops series (7)
Curlytops at Cherry Farm
Garis, Howard Roger
Curlytops series (1)
Curlytops at Happy House
Garis, Howard Roger
Curlytops series (13)
Curlytops at Silver Lake
Garis, Howard Roger
Curlytops series (5)
Curlytops at Sunset Beach
Garis, Howard Roger
Curlytops series (9)
Curlytops at the circus
Garis, Howard Roger
Curlytops series (14)
Curlytops at Uncle Frank's ranch
Garis, Howard Roger
Curlytops series (2)
Curlytops growing up
Garis, Howard Roger
Curlytops series (12)
Curlytops in summer camp
Garis, Howard Roger
Curlytops series (11)
Curlytops in the woods
Garis, Howard Roger
Curlytops series (8)
Curlytops on Star Island
Garis, Howard Roger
Curlytops series (3)
Curlytops snowed in
Garis, Howard Roger
Curlytops series (4)
Curlytops touring around
Garis, Howard Roger
Curlytops series (10)
Currents of space
Asimov, Isaac
Trantorian Empire trilogy (3)
Curse
Weinberg, Larry
Dark forces series (13)
Curse not the king
Anthony, Evelyn
Catherine the Great trilogy (2)
Curse of Batterslea Hall
Brightfield, Richard
Choose your own adventure series (30)
Curse of Cantire
Masterman, Walter Sidney
Sir Arthur Sinclair series (16)
Curse of Collinwood
Ross, Marilyn
Barnabas Collins series (5)
Curse of dead man's gold
Scott, Bradford
Walt Slade series (83)
Curse of Frankenstein
Brennan, James Herbert
Frankenstein sequels series (16)
Curse of Khatra
Jacobs, Thomas Curtis Hicks
Detective Superintendent John Bellamy series (2)
Curse of Leo
Lory, Robert
Horrorscope series (3)
Curse of Rathlaw
Saxon, Peter
Guardians series (3)
Curse of Sagamore
Dalkey, Kara
Sagamore series (1)
Curse of Slagfid
Boyer, Elizabeth H
Wizard's war series (2)
Curse of the blue figurine
Bellairs, John
Blue figurine trilogy (1)
Johnny Dixon series (1)
Curse of the broken feather
Work, Virginia
Jodi series (3)
Curse of the bronze lamp
Dickson, Carter
Sir Henry Merrivale series (17)
Curse of the Carrington's
Tyrer, Walter
Sexton Blake series (1105)
Curse of the claw
Beach, Lynn
Phantom Valley series (9)
Curse of the cockers
Hammond, Gerald
Captain John Cunningham series (5)
Curse of the crimson horde
House, Brant
Secret Agent X series (20)
Curse of the dancing doll
Elfman, Blossom
Mike and Ally series (4)
Curse of the Fenric
Briggs, Ian
Doctor Who series (151)
Curse of the giant hogweed
Macleod, Charlotte
Professor Peter Shandy series (5)
Curse of the golden heart
Pascal, Francine
Sweet Valley twins super chiller series (6)
Curse of the golden skull
Kains, Josephine
Terry Spring series (2)
Curse of the haunted mansion
Packard, Edward
Choose your own adventure series (5)
Curse of the incredible priceless corncob
Erickson, John R
Hank the cowdog series (7)
Curse of the Kali
Gregory, Hylton
Sexton Blake series (334)
Curse of the mandarin's fan
House, Brant
Secret Agent X series (17)
Curse of the mummy
Luigi, Belli
Vernon Templeton series (2)
Curse of the mummy's tomb
Stine, Robert Lawrence
Goosebumps series (5)
Curse of the Nibelungen
D'Agneau, Marcel
Sherlock Holmes sequels series (50)
Curse of the pharaoh
Johnson, Oliver
Golden dragon fantasy gamebooks series (5)
Curse of the pharaohs
Peters, Elizabeth
Amelia Peabody Emerson series (2)
Curse of the Reckaviles
Masterman, Walter Sidney
Sir Arthur Sinclair series (2)
Curse of the ruby necklace
Pascal, Francine
Sweet Valley twins super chiller series (5)
Curse of the Santyres
Evans, Gwyn
Sexton Blake series (371)
Curse of the Texas gold
Scott, Bradford
Walt Slade series (16)
Curse of the track
Hunter, John
Sexton Blake series (1228)
Curse of the turtle
Roy, Thomas Albert
Jimmy Brent series (1)
Curse of the two-headed bull
Falk, Lee
Phantom series (15)
Curse of the vampire
Caine, Geoffrey
Abraham Stroud series (1)
Curse of the werewolf
Martindale, T Chris
Advanced dungeons and dragons adventure gamebook series (9)
Curse of Thoth
Grant, Maxwell
Shadow series (275)
Curse of Whispering Hills
Cameron, Kate
Whispering Hills series (2)
Curse the darkness
Grant-Adamson, Lesley
Rain Morgan series (5)
Cursed
Sadler, Barry
Casca series (18)
Cursed to death
Crider, Bill
Dan Rhodes series (3)

Curses!
Elkins, Aaron J
Professor Gideon Oliver series (5)

Cursing Stones murder
Bellairs, George
Detective Inspector Thomas Littlejohn series (23)

Cursory view of the history of Lilliput for these last forty three years
Anonymous
Lilliput series (3)

Curtain
Christie, Agatha
Hercule Poirot series (38)
Mitchell Ruth Comfort
Old San Francisco series (3)

Curtain at eight
Cohen, Octavus Roy
Jim Hanvey series (3)

Curtain between
Van Siller, Hilda
Richard Massey series (2)

Curtain call
Bernard, Elizabeth
Satin slippers series (6)
Foley, Rae
Hiram Potter series (6)

Curtain call for a corpse
Bell, Josephine
Doctor David Wintringham series (4)
Inspector Steven Mitchell series (4)

Curtain call for murder
Spiller, Andrew
Chief Inspector Duck Mallard series (24)
Yates, Peter
Thatcher family series (1)

Curtain fall
Dewhurst, Eileen
Inspector Neil Carter series (1)
Ure, Jean
Riverside Theatre series (5)

Curtain falls
Druon, Maurice
Curtain falls trilogy (3)

Curtain for a jester
Lockridge, Frances
Bill Wiegand series (17)
Mister and Mrs North series (19)

Curtain for crime
Rea, Margaret Lucile Paine
Lieutenant Powledge series (1)

Curtain of fire
Hocking, Joseph
Great War, French Front series (3)

Curtain of glass
Ambler, Dail
Danny Spade series (37)

Curtain of mist
Pardoe, Margot
Macalister children series (1)

Curtain of storm
Gollomb, Joseph
Galt series (3)

Curtain up
Streatfeild, Noel
Shoes series (4)

Curtain wall
Cronin, Michael
Richard Maidment series (6)

Curtains for a lover
Dietrich, Robert
Steve Bentley series (8)

Curtains for Carla
Storm, Michael
Nick Cranley series (4)

Curtains for Conquest?
Gray, Berkeley
Norman Conquest series (49)

Curtains for Komespi
Paul, Ernest
George Barclay series (3)

Curtains for the copper
Polsky, Thomas
L F Griddle series (3)

Curtains for the editor
Polsky, Thomas
L F Griddle series (1)

Curtains for the judge
Polsky, Thomas
L F Griddle series (2)

Curtains for three
Stout, Rex
Nero Wolfe and Archie Goodwin series (18)

Curtains of the dark
McElroy, Hugh
Inspector William Brewer series (2)

Curved blades
Wells, Carolyn
Fleming Stone series (7)

Curved saber
Lamb, Harold
Khlit the Cossack series (1)

Curzon case
Durbridge, Francis
Paul Temple series (11)

Custard and Company
Nash, Ogden
Custard series (2)

Custard Kid
Deary, Terry
Custard Kid series (1)

Custard the dragon
Nash, Ogden
Custard series (1)

Custard the dragon and the wicked knight
Nash, Ogden
Custard series (2)

Custer County
Standish, Buck
Custer series (1)

Custer Meadow
Standish, Buck
Custer series (2)

Custer's gold
Ulyatt, Kenneth
Portugee Philips trilogy (3)

Custodians, and other stories
Cowper, Richard
Bird of kinship series (1)

Customer's always wrong
O'Hara, Kevin
Chico Brett series (1)

Cut and thrust
Hardy, Adam
George Abercrombie Fox series (9)

Cut by emerald
Kramer, Dana
Bio of a space tyrant series (5)
Combat Command series (1)

Cut direct
Tilton, Alice
Leonidas Witherall series (2)

Cut in diamonds
Macleod, Robert
Andrew Laird series (6)

Cut off from crumpets
Baker, Margaret Joyce
Ridley family series (2)

Cut one, they all bleed
Edson, John Thomas
Calamity Jane series (7)

Cut-rate quarterback
Gault, William Campbell
Gridiron series (7)

Cut thin to win
Fair, A A
Bertha Cool and Donald Lam series (26)

Cut throat
Bush, Christopher
Ludovic Travers series (7)

Cut-Ups
Marshall, James
Cut-Ups series (1)

Cut-Ups at Camp Custer
Marshall, James
Cut-Ups series (3)

Cut-Ups carry on
Marshall, James
Cut-Ups series (4)

Cut-Ups crack up
Marshall, James
Cut-Ups series (5)

Cut-Ups cut loose
Marshall, James
Cut-Ups series (2)

Cute and deadly surf twins
Morgan, Patrick
Operation Hang Ten series (4)

Cuthberg and the good ship Thingamabob
Chesher, Kim
Cuthbert series (4)

Cuthbert and the long winter sleep
Chesher, Kim
Cuthbert series (3)

Cuthbert and the night walkers
Chesher, Kim
Cuthbert series (5)

Cuthbert and the sea monster
Chesher, Kim
Cuthbert series (2)

Cuthbert and the thingamabob
Chesher, Kim
Cuthbert series (1)

Cuthbert Coningsby
Everett-Green, Evelyn
Maud Kingslake series (2)

Cuthbert's missing auntie
Carruth, Jean
Trumpton series (8)

Cutie cashed his chips
Brown, Carter
Mike Farrel series (1)

Cutie on call
Janson, Hank
Hank Janson series (95)

Cutlass clue
Lawrence, Jim
A.I. Gang series (2)

Cutthroat
Frost, Jason
Warlord series (2)

Cutthroat cannibals
Sargent, Craig
Last ranger series (8)

Cutting edge
Duncan, Dave
Handful of men series (1)
Harvey, John Barton
Inspector Charlie Resnick series (3)
Jackson, Ken
Jud Blade series (1)
Keene, Carolyn
Nancy Drew files series (70)
Murray, Terry
Legends of Larian series (2)

Cutting up with Ramona
Cleary, Beverly
Ramona Quimby series (7)

CV
Knight, Damon
CV trilogy (1)

Cyanide!
Toye, Stanley
Anthony Read series (1)

Cyanide for the chorister
Wogan, Charles
Sebastian Stole series (3)

Cyanide with compliments
Lemarchand, Elizabeth
Superintendent Tom Pollard series (5)

Cybermen
Banks, David
Doctor Who series (162)

Cybernarc
Cain, Robert
Cybernarc series (1)

Cybernetic samurai
Milan, Victor
Cybernetic shogun series (1)

Cybernetic shogun
Milan, Victor
Cybernetic shogun series (2)

Cybersaur
Carmichael, Claire
Virtual realities trilogy (2)

Cyberstealth
Lewitt, Shariann N
Cyberstealth series (1)

Cybertech killing zone
Sievert, John
C.A.D.S. series (8)

Cyborg
Caidin, Martin
Six Million Dollar Man series (2)
Wu, William Franking
Robot city series (3)

Cyborg and the sorcerers
Watt-Evans, Lawrence
War surplus series (1)

Cyborg II
Caidin, Martin
Six Million Dollar Man series (3)

Cyborg IV
Caidin, Martin
Six Million Dollar Man series (5)

Cyborg kickboxer
Appleton, Victor II
Tom Swift Junior series 3 (3)

Cyborg king
Goulart, Ron
Barnum series (8)
Star Hawks series (2)

Cycle of the West
Neihardt, John Gneisenau
Cycle of the West series (5)

Cyclon death machine
Larson, Glen A
Battlestar Galactica series (2)

Cyclone
Asturias, Miguel Angel
Guatemala trilogy (1)

Cyclone, and other stories
Narayan, Rasipuram Krishnaswami
Malgudi series (17)

Cyclone guns
Gregory, Lester
Kid Cyclone series (3)

Cyclops
Cussler, Clive
Dirk Pitt series (8)

Cyclops conspiracy
Carter, Nick
Nick Carter series (213)

Cyclops goblet
Blackburn, John
Bill Easter series (3)

Cymric the Saxon
Rutley, Cecily Marianne
Children of other days series (6)

Cynic's word book
Bierce, Ambrose
Devil's dictionary series (1)

Cynthia
Cunningham, E V
Harvey Krim series (2)

Cypher
Mosley, Nicholas
Catastrophe practice series (1)

Cypresses believe in God
Gironella, Jose Maria
Alvear family trilogy (1)

Cyril and the dinner party
Palin, Michael
Cyril series (2)

Cyril and the House of Commons
Palin, Michael
Cyril series (1)

Cyril Bonhamy and Operation Ping
Gathorne-Hardy, Jonathan
Cyril Bonhamy series (5)

Cyril Bonhamy and the great drain robbery
Gathorne-Hardy, Jonathan
Cyril Bonhamy series (4)

Cyril Bonhamy and the great Father Christmas robbery
Gathorne-Hardy, Jonathan
Cyril Bonhamy series (3)

Cyril Bonhamy versus Madam Big
Gathorne-Hardy, Jonathan
Cyril Bonhamy series (2)

Cyril of the apes
Gathorne-Hardy, Jonathan
Cyril Bonhamy series (6)

Cyro
Grant, Maxwell
Shadow series (68)

Cyteen
Cherryh, Carolyn Janice
Alliance-Union series (11)
Cyteen series (3)

Czar of fear
Robeson, Kenneth
Doc Savage series (22)

Czar of Halfaday Creek
Hendryx, James Beardsley
Black John series (5)

Czechmate
Johns, Larry
Jacky Ryderbeit series (3)

D

D.A. breaks a seal
Gardner, Erle Stanley
District Attorney series (7)

D.A. breaks an egg
Gardner, Erle Stanley
District Attorney series (9)

D.A. calls a turn
Gardner, Erle Stanley
District Attorney series (6)

D.A. calls it murder
Gardner, Erle Stanley
District Attorney series (1)

D.A. cooks a goose
Gardner, Erle Stanley
District Attorney series (5)

D.A. draws a circle
Gardner, Erle Stanley
District Attorney series (3)

D.A. goes to trial
Gardner, Erle Stanley
District Attorney series (4)

D.A. holds a candle
Gardner, Erle Stanley
District Attorney series (2)

D.A. takes a chance
Gardner, Erle Stanley
District Attorney series (8)

D as in dead
Treat, Lawrence
Carl Wayward series (2)

D.C. death march
McCray, Mike
Black Berets series (8)

D.C. firestrike
Case, Jim
Cody's army series (5)
Danny Orlis series (42)

D.E.A.T.H. hunters
Ahern, Jerry
Dan Track series (9)

D.E.Q.
Gorell, Ronald Gorell Barnes
Evelyn Temple series (2)
Inspector Maurice Hepburn series (1)

D.I.
Ashford, Jeffrey
Detective Inspector Don Kerry series (2)

D is for deadbeat
Grafton, Sue
Kinsey Millhone series (4)

D J Dillon and Dooger, the grasshopper hound
Roddy, Lee
Davey Dillon series (3)

D J Dillon and the city bear's adventures
Roddy, Lee
Davey Dillon series (2)

D J Dillon and the escape from the raging rapids
Roddy, Lee
Davey Dillon series (10)

D J Dillon and the ghost dog of Stony Ridge
Roddy, Lee
Davey Dillon series (4)

D J Dillon and the ghost of the moaning mansion
Roddy, Lee
Davey Dillon series (8)

D J Dillon and the hermit of Mad River
Roddy, Lee
Davey Dillon series (9)

D J Dillon and the legend of the white raccoon
Roddy, Lee
Davey Dillon series (6)

D J Dillon and the mad dog of Lobo Mountain
Roddy, Lee
Davey Dillon series (5)

D J Dillon and the mystery of the Black Hole Mine
Roddy, Lee
Davey Dillon series (7)

D J Dillon and the pair-pulling bear dog
Roddy, Lee
Davey Dillon series (1)

D, my name is Danita
Mazer, Norma Fox
My name series (4)

D notice
Graeme, Bruce
Detective Sergeant Robert Mather series (3)
Henry Maxwell series (2)

D.O.A.
Pedneau, Dave
Whit Pynchon and Annie Tyson-Tyree series (2)

D.W. all wet
Brown, Marc
D.W. series (2)

D.W. flips!
Brown, Marc
D.W. series (1)

Dab Kinzer
Stoddard, William Osborn
Cowboy and college life series (1)

Dad in politics, and other stories
Rudd, Steele
Rudd family series (5)

Dada caper
Spencer, Ross Harrison
Chance Purdue series (1)

Daddies at work
Merriam, Frank
Mommies and daddies at work series (2)

Daddy, are you married?
Campbell, Ross
Marriage series (1)

Daddy builds houses
Harper, Anita
Daddy and mummy series (4)

Daddy, daddy
Kellerman, Jonathan
Alex Delaware series (8)

Daddy drives a bus
Harper, Anita
Daddy and mummy series (3)

Daddy Jake, the runaway, and short stories told after dark by Uncle Remus
Harris, Joel Chandler
Uncle Remus series (3)
Daddy Long Ears Christmas surprise
Kraus, Robert
Daddy Long Ears series (1)
Daddy Long Ears Halloween
Kraus, Robert
Daddy Long Ears series (2)
Daddy-Long-Legs
Webster, Jean
Judy Abbott series (1)
Daddyji
Mehta, Ved
Mehta family series (1)
Daddy's girl
Milne, John
James Jenner series (3)
Jimmy Jenner series (3)
Dad's book
Ormerod, Jan
Baby books series (1)
Daemons
Sloman, Robert
Doctor Who scripts series (6)
Daffodil
Butler, Maude Mary
Daffodil series (2)
Daffodil affair
Innes, Michael
Sir John Appleby series (8)
Daffodil blonde
Crane, Frances
Pat and Jean Abbott series (13)
Daffodil story book
Blyton, Enid
Flower story book series (1)
Daffodils of Newent
Sallis, Susan
Rising family series (2)
Daffy Duck in Duck Troop to the rescue
Korman, Justine
Donald Duck series (2)
Dagger
Drake, David
Sanctuary series (12)
Wynne, Anthony
Doctor Eustace Hailey series (7)
Dagger affair
McDaniel, David
Man from U.N.C.L.E. series (4)
Dagger and the cross
Tarr, Judith
Alamut series (2)
Dagger and the flame
Saville, Malcolm
Marston Baines series (6)
Dagger before me
O'Brine, Manning
Michael O'Kelly series (7)
Dagger drawn
Hill, Lawrence
Inspector Macsporran series (1)
Dagger in the sky
Robeson, Kenneth
Doc Savage series (40)
Dagger of flesh
Prather, Richard Scott
Shell Scott series (8)
Daggers of Kali
Wallace, Robert
Phantom Detective series (22)
Daggerspell
Kerr, Katharine
Deverry series (1)
Dagmar Schultz and the Angel Edna
Hall, Lynn
Dagmar Schultz series (2)
Dagmar Schultz and the green-eyed monster
Hall, Lynn
Dagmar Schultz series (4)
Dagmar Schultz and the powers of darkness
Hall, Lynn
Dagmar Schultz series (3)
Dagon
Chappell, Fred
Cthulhu Mythos series (1)
Cthulhu Mythos series (15)
Dahlia's cargo
Pilkington, Roger
Branxome family series (4)
Dahomean
Yerby, Frank
Hwesu series (1)
Dahut
Anderson, Poul
King of Ys series (3)
Dai-San
Lustbader, Eric
Sunset Warrior series (3)
Daily Planet, a world of news every day!
Skinner, Stephanie
Superman series (3)
Daily Woofit
Parkinson, Michael
Woofits series (4)
Dain curse
Hammett, Dashiell
Continental Op series (2)
Daisy
Greig, Daisy
Daisy series (1)
Warner, Susan Bagert
Daisy trilogy (2)
Daisy and the babysitter
Bradman, Tony
Daisy series (3)
Daisy and the crying baby
Bradman, Tony
Daisy series (4)
Daisy and the dog show
Kelley, Anne
Daisy series (1)
Daisy and the washing machine
Bradman, Tony
Daisy series (1)
Daisy boy
Cleugh, Sophia
Matilda series (3)
Daisy Canfield
Haas, Ben
Chandler family series (2)
Daisy chain
Yonge, Charlotte Mary
May family series (1)
Pillars of the house series (1)
Daisy dilemma
Rico, Don
Burgess Cardigan series (1)
Daisy ducks
Boyer, Richard Lewis
Doctor Charlie Adams series (3)
Daisy earns her living
Saint John, Mabel
Daisy Peach series (1)
Daisy feels ill
Bradman, Tony
Daisy series (5)
Daisy goes swimming
Bradman, Tony
Daisy series (2)
Daisy goes to playgroup
Bradman, Tony
Daisy series (6)
Daisy in the field
Warner, Susan Bagert
Daisy trilogy (3)
Daisy Peach abroad
Saint John, Mabel
Daisy Peach series (2)
Daisy Punkin
Stahl, Hilda
Daisy Punkin series (1)
Daisy Punkin and the bratty brother
Stahl, Hilda
Daisy Punkin series (2)
Daisy reminisces
Greig, Daisy
Daisy series (2)
Daisy Travers
Samuels, Adelaide Florence
Dick and Daisy Travers series (4)
Daisy's discovery
Kelley, Anne
Daisy series (2)
Daisy's work
Mathews, Joanna Hooe
Flowerets series (2)
Dakota!
Ross, Dana Fuller
Wagons West series (11)
Dakota badlands
Benteen, John
Neal Fargo series (22)
Dakota death-trap
Grover, Marshall
Larry and Stretch series (403)
Dakota doxy
Fletcher, Dirk
Spur McCoy series (22)
Dakota gold
Champlin, Tim
Matt Tierney series (2)
Dakota massacre
Gentry, Buck
Eli Holten series (2)
Dakota Red
Grover, Marshall
Larry and Stretch series (136)
Dakota run
Robbins, David
Endworld series (5)
Dakota showdown
Tanner, Clay
Chance Sharpe series (7)
Dakota squeeze
Hunter, E J
White Squaw series (6)
Dakota Territory
Benteen, John
Sundance series (3)
Dakota warpath
Ralston, Gilbert Alexander
Dakota series (1)
Dakota wild
Sharpe, Jon
Trailsman series (6)
Dale Evans and danger in Crooked Canyon
Hale, Helen
Dale Evans series (2)
Dale of the Mounted
Holliday, Joe
Dale of the Mounted series (1)
Dale of the mounted in Hong Kong
Holliday, Joe
Dale of the Mounted series (12)
Dale of the Mounted in Newfoundland
Holliday, Joe
Dale of the Mounted series (4)
Dale of the Mounted in the Arctic
Holliday, Joe
Dale of the Mounted series (2)
Dale of the mounted in the Northwest
Holliday, Joe
Dale of the Mounted series (6)
Dale of the Mounted on the west coast
Holliday, Joe
Dale of the Mounted series (3)
Dale the whale
Reese, Bob
Ocean critterland series (1)
Dalehouse murder
Everton, Francis
Detective Inspector Allport series (1)
Dalek invasion of earth
Dicks, Terrance
Doctor Who series (29)
Daleks
Nation, Terry
Doctor Who scripts series (4)
Dalek's master plan
Peel, John
Doctor Who series (141)
Doctor Who series (142)
Dales of Parkwood Hill
Antony, Jonquil
Dale family series (2)
Dalgliesh trilogy
James, Phyllis Dorothy
Commander Adam Dalgliesh series (7)
Dalla the lion cub
Stockley, Cynthia
Dalla series (1)
Dallas
Raintree, Lee
Dallas series (2)
Dallas deception
Abshire, Richard
Jack Kyle series (3)
Dallas drop
Abshire, Richard
Jack Kyle series (1)
Dallas madam
Logan, Jake
John Slocum series (67)
Dallas run
Robbins, David
Endworld series (20)
Dalliance and strife
Bancroft, Francis
South African trilogy (3)
Dalmatian holiday
Sutton, Phyllis
Merryl Hastings series (6)
Dalmatian tapes
Smith, Don
Secret mission series (19)
Dalton Boys and the MK and T robbery
Lawson, W B
Dalton Boys series (2)
Dalton Boys in California
Lawson, W B
Dalton Boys series (1)
Dalton City
Goscinny, Rene
Lucky Luke series (4)
Dam of death
Pearl, Jack
Invaders series (6)
Damagers
Hamilton, Donald
Matt Helm series (27)
Damaris
Malet, Lucas
Damaris series (1)
Damaris at Dorothy's
Oxenham, Elsie J
Rachel and Damaris series (3)
Damaris dances
Oxenham, Elsie J
Rachel and Damaris series (5)
Damaris Hard
Malet, Lucas
Damaris series (2)
Damascus countdown
Arvay, Harry
Israeli Security Branch series (6)
Damballah
Wideman, John Edgar
Homewood trilogy (1)
Dame
Brown, Carter
Lieutenant Al Wheeler series (13)
Stark, Richard
Alan Grofield series (4)
Dame called murder
Saber, Robert O
Max Keene series (1)
Dame in danger
Dewey, Thomas Blanchard
Private Eye Mac series (1)
Dame in distress
Cooper, Craig
Matt Savage series (2)
Dame in my bed
Storm, Michael
Nick Cranley series (2)
Dame on a death round
Brody, Marc
Marc Brody series (54)
Dame on the deadline
Brody, Marc
Marc Brody series (2)
Dame on the make
McCall, K T
Johnny Buchanan series (20)
Dame plays rough
Spade, Danny
Danny Spade series (1)
Dames can be deadly
Chambers, Peter
Mark Preston series (4)
Dames don't care
Cheyney, Peter
Lemmy Caution series (3)
Dames in his death
Brody, Marc
Marc Brody series (31)
Damia
McCaffrey, Anne
Damia series (1)
Damiano
Macavoy, Roberta Ann
Lute trilogy (1)
Damiano's lute
Macavoy, Roberta Ann
Lute trilogy (2)
Damia's children
McCaffrey, Anne
Damia series (2)
Damien
Howard, Joseph
Omen series (2)
Damn Desmond Drake
Sea-Lion
Desmond Drake series (2)
Damn outlaws
Grover, Marshall
Larry and Stretch series (151)
Damn the torpedoes!
Macdonnell, James Edmond
Dutchy Holland series (26)
Damned
Sadler, Barry
Casca series (7)
Damned disciples
Sargent, Craig
Last ranger series (9)
Damned if we do
Rice, Peter
Renegade legion series (5)
Damned lovely
Webb, Jack
Father Joseph Shanley and Sammy Golden series (3)
Damned spot
Adams, Herbert
Major Roger Bennion series (6)
Damocles threat
Carter, Nick
Nick Carter series (158)
Damsel
Stark, Richard
Alan Grofield series (3)
Damsel for discount
Jason
Jason series (6)
Damsel not for drowning
Kane, Martin
Martin Kane series (4)
Damyo
Morell, William
Damyo series (1)
Damyo's revenge
Morell, William
Damyo series (2)
Dan Barry's daughter
Brand, Max
Dan Barry series (4)
Dan Carter and the cub honor
Wirt, Mildred Augustine
Dan Carter series (6)
Dan Carter and the great carved face
Wirt, Mildred Augustine
Dan Carter series (5)
Dan Carter and the haunted castle
Wirt, Mildred Augustine
Dan Carter series (4)
Dan Carter and the money box
Wirt, Mildred Augustine
Dan Carter series (3)
Dan Carter and the river camp
Wirt, Mildred Augustine
Dan Carter series (2)
Dan Carter, cub scout
Wirt, Mildred Augustine
Dan Carter series (1)
Dan Monroe
Stoddard, William Osborn
Revolutionary series (1)
Dan the shepherd
Watson, Jean
Meet the Samuel family series (2)
Dance
Pike, Christopher
Final friends series (2)
Dance a step closer
Ryan, Mary Elizabeth
Katie Kusik series (1)
Dance at Four Corners
Burgin, George Brown
Four Corners series (1)
Dance at the slaughterhouse
Block, Lawrence
Matthew Scudder series (9)
Dance, dance, dance
Murakami, Haruki
Wild sheep chase series (2)
Dance for a dead uncle
Ashton, Charles
Jack Atherley series (9)
Dance hall of the dead
Hillerman, Tony
Lieutenant Joe Leaphorn series (2)
Dance me outside
Kinsella, William Patrick
Silas Ermineskin series (1)
Dance of death
Brown, Carter
Lieutenant Al Wheeler series (31)
Gaillard, Robert
Marie series (5)
Kassem, Lou
Twilight series (19)
McCloy, Helen
Basil Willing series (1)
Potter, Jeremy
Inspector Hiscock series (3)
Dance of demons
Gygax, Gary
Gord the Rogue series (5)
Dance of dreams
Roberts, Nora
Flowers series (8)
Dance of Genghis Cohn
Gary, Romain
Genghis Cohn series (1)
Dance of Sceaux
Balzac, Honore de
Scenes of private life series (2)
Dance of the hag
Leigh, Stephen
Neweden trilogy (2)
Dance of the midnight fire
Macraois, Cormac
Giltspur trilogy (2)
Dance of the quick and the dead
Sitwell, Sacheverell
Quick and the dead series (1)
Dance of the tiger
Kurten, Bjorn
Dance series (1)

Dance till you die
Keene, Carolyn
Nancy Drew files series (100)
Dance to the music of time, first movement
Powell, Anthony
Dance to the music of time series (3)
Dance to the music of time, fourth movement
Powell, Anthony
Dance to the music of time series (12)
Dance to the music of time, second movement
Powell, Anthony
Dance to the music of time series (6)
Dance to the music of time, third movement
Powell, Anthony
Dance to the music of time series (9)
Dance to the piper
De Mille, Agnes
Ballet memoirs series (1)
Roberts, Nora
O'Hurley trilogy (2)
Dance to your Daddy
Mitchell, Gladys
Dame Beatrice Bradley series (42)
Dance while you can
MacLaine, Shirley
You can get there series (5)
Dance with me
Cooper, M E
Couples series (17)
Dance with me deadly
McCall, K T
Johnny Buchanan series (8)
Dance with the dead
Prather, Richard Scott
Shell Scott series (20)
Dancer from the Abbey
Oxenham, Elsie J
Abbey girls second generation series (9)
Dancer in danger
Hill, Lorna
Annette Dancy series (5)
Dancer in the wings
Hill, Lorna
Annette Dancy series (4)
Richardson, Jean
Moth Graham series (2)
Dancer of Gor
Norman, John
Tarl Cabot series (22)
Dancer on holiday
Hill, Lorna
Annette Dancy series (6)
Dancers at the end of time
Moorcock, Michael
Dancers at the end of time series (3)
Dancer's daughter
White, Constance Mary
Ballet school series (2)
Dancer's debt
Lutz, John
Alo Nudger series (5)
Dancer's illusion
Maxwell, Ann
Dancer trilogy (3)
Dancers in mourning
Allingham, Margery
Albert Campion series (9)
Dancer's luck
Hill, Lorna
Annette Dancy series (2)
Maxwell, Ann
Dancer trilogy (2)
Dancers of Arun
Lynn, Elizabeth Anne
Chronicles of Tornor trilogy (2)
Dancer's rise
Clayton, Jo
Dancer trilogy (1)
Dancing at the Rascal Fair
Doig, Ivan
McCaskill family trilogy (2)
Dancing bear
Conway, Peter
Inspector Cathy Weston series (2)
Crumley, James
Milo Milodragovitch series (2)
Dancing class
Oxenbury, Helen
First picture books series (2)
Dancing dead
Syvertsen, Ryder
Mystic rebel series (2)
Thomas, Eugene
Mrs Caywood Weston series (2)
Dancing death
Bush, Christopher
Ludovic Travers series (5)
Dancing doll murders
Wallace, Robert
Phantom Detective series (8)
Dancing Druids
Mitchell, Gladys
Dame Beatrice Bradley series (21)
Dancing floor
Buchan, John
Sir Edward Leithen series (3)
Dancing Garlands
Allan, Mabel Esther
Garland family series (2)
Dancing girl
Leroux, Gaston
Cheri-Bibi series (4)
Dancing horse
Vaughan, Carol
Manorfield Stud series (3)
Dancing in the light
MacLaine, Shirley
You can get there series (3)
Dancing meteorite
Mason, Anne
Dancing meteorite series (1)
Dancing Peel
Hill, Lorna
Annette Dancy series (1)
Dancing shoes
Streatfeild, Noel
Shoes series (9)
Dancing silhouette
Lincoln, Natalie Sumner
Inspector Mitchell series (10)
Dancing stones
Knight, Leonard Alfred
Jerry Scant series (6)
Dancing vac.
Lewitt, Shariann N
Cyberstealth series (2)
Dancing waiters
Hone, Joseph
Collected travels series (1)
Dancing with the dead
Lutz, John
Alo Nudger series (8)
Dandee diamond mystery
O'Connor, Jane
Pick-a-path series (1)
Dandelion caper
DeWeese, Gene
Calvin Willeford series (2)
Dandelion Cottage
Rankin, Carroll Watson
Dandelion Cottage series (1)
Dandelion days
Williamson, Henry
Flax of dream series (2)
Dando and the mad emperor
Clive, William
Joseph Dando series (4)
Dando and the Summer Palace
Clive, William
Joseph Dando series (2)
Dando on Delhi Ridge
Clive, William
Joseph Dando series (1)
Dandy of Topham
Richards, Frank
Mascot schoolboy series (3)
Dane's testament
Gethin, David
Halloran series (2)
Danger
Berry, Joy
Ready-set-grow series (12)
Danger after dark
Maddock, Stephen
Timothy Terrel series (4)
Danger ahead
Saxon, Peter
Sexton Blake series (1409)
Danger at Anchor Mine
Foley, Louise Munro
Choose your own adventure series (49)
Danger at Cliff House
Gregg, Cecil Freeman
Inspector Cuthbert Higgins series (13)
Danger at Diablo
Schroeder, Doris
Annie Oakley series (1)
Danger at Dry Creek
Werstein, Irving
Wells Fargo series (4)
Danger at Mormon Crossing
Barlow, Roger
Sandy Steele series (2)
Danger at the drawbridge
Wirt, Mildred Augustine
Penny Parker series (3)
Danger at Westway's
Stuart, Donald
Sexton Blake series (973)
Danger below
Berres, Frances B
Deep-sea adventure series (6)
Blaine, John
Rick Brant series (23)
Hackforth-Jones, Gilbert
Joe Garton series (1)
Leyland, Eric
Max and Scrap series (4)
Danger calling
Wentworth, Patricia
Benbow Smith and Frank Garratt series (1)
Danger, dame at work
Muller, Paul
Paul Muller series (5)
Danger, death at work
Garnett, Roger
Chief Inspector Jonathan Black series (3)
Danger due north
Fortune, J J
Race against time series (10)
Danger for Blackshirt
Graeme, Roderic
Blackshirt series (27)
Danger for hire
Keene, Carolyn
Nancy Drew files series (52)
Danger for McAllister
Chisholm, Matt
Rem McAllister series (20)
Danger for the Baron
Morton, Anthony
Baron series (23)
Danger for two
Foster, Kingsley
Jonathan Lamb series (2)
Danger in Danny's back yard
Plain, Neil
Boris Blundle and Gang series (3)
Danger in deep space
Rockwell, Carey
Tom Corbett series (2)
Danger in disguise
Keene, Carolyn
Nancy Drew files series (33)
Danger in paradise
Cohen, Octavus Roy
Max Gold series (1)
Jennings, D K
Doctor Ralph Conway series (12)
Danger in the ashes
Johnstone, William Wallace
Ashes series (8)
Danger in the dark
Gregg, Cecil Freeman
Inspector Cuthbert Higgins series (18)
Danger in the desert
Terman, Douglas
Choose your own adventure series (3)
Danger in the fourth dimension
Dixon, Franklin W
Hardy boys series (118)
Danger in the hills
Lethbridge, Peter
Jeremy series (4)
Danger in the old fort
Chambers, Kate
Diana Winthrop series (2)
Danger in Tibet
Quackenbush, Robert Mead
Miss Mallard series (13)
Danger is my destiny
Orsborne, Dod
Adventurer in chains series (2)
Danger is my line
Marlowe, Stephen
Chester Drum series (10)
Danger key
Carter, Nick
Nick Carter series (16)
Danger kids
Padoan, Gianni
Facing up series (3)
Danger lies east
Robeson, Kenneth
Doc Savage series (155)
Danger, Marmalade at work
Davies, Andrew
Marmalade Atkins series (4)
Danger money
Jacobs, Thomas Curtis Hicks
Temple Fortune series (13)
Danger of folly
Carter, Nicholas
Nicholas Carter series (564)
Danger on ice
Keene, Carolyn
Nancy Drew and the Hardy boys be a detective mystery series (2)
Danger on parade
Keene, Carolyn
Nancy Drew files series (77)
Danger on the air
Dixon, Franklin W
Hardy boys series (95)
Danger on the diamond
Dixon, Franklin W
Hardy boys series (90)
Danger on the flip side
Story, Jack Trevor
Sexton Blake series (1503)
Danger on the Old Pull'n Push
Beresford, Elisabeth
Tempest family series (2)
Danger on the river
Janes, Joseph Robert
Danger on the river trilogy (1)
Danger on the sound track
Robinson, Nancy Konheim
Tripper and Sam series (2)
Danger on Thunder Mountain
Roddy, Lee
American adventure series (3)
Danger on Vampire Trail
Dixon, Franklin W
Hardy boys series (50)
Danger planet
Sterling, Brett
Captain Future series (11)
Danger point
Wentworth, Patricia
Miss Maud Silver series (5)
Danger rides the dollar wagon
Grey, Romer Zane
Arizona Ames series (7)
Danger rode drag
Grover, Marshall
Nevada Jim series (55)
Danger round the corner
Meynell, Laurence Walter
Hooky Hefferman series (2)
Danger, the daring
Early, Tom
Sons of Texas series (1)
Danger to Elizabeth
Plowden, Alison
Elizabeth I series (2)
Danger trail
Leeson, Robert
Zarnia experiment series (4)
Tuttle, Wilbur Coleman
Henry Harrison Conroy and Judge Van Treece series (5)
Danger trails north
Bennett, Billy L
Northwest stories series (9)
Danger trails of the sky
Dixon, Franklin W
Ted Scott flying series (14)
Danger tree
Manning, Olivia
Guy and Harriet Pringle series (4)
Danger unlimited
Dixon, Franklin W
Hardy boys case files series (79)
Danger, women at work!
O'Hara, Kevin
Chico Brett series (9)
Danger zone
Dixon, Franklin W
Hardy boys case files series (37)
Walsh, James Morgan
Oliver Keene series (10)
Danger zones
Montgomery, Raymond A
Choose your own adventure super series (2)
Dangerous age
Michaelis, Karin
Elsie Lindtner series (1)
Sylvester, Martin
William Warne series (1)
Dangerous and deadly Australian crocodiles
Vaughan, Marcia
Dangerous and deadly series (4)
Dangerous and deadly Australian insects
Vaughan, Marcia
Dangerous and deadly series (5)
Dangerous and deadly Australian plants
Vaughan, Marcia
Dangerous and deadly series (6)
Dangerous and deadly Australian sea life
Vaughan, Marcia
Dangerous and deadly series (3)
Dangerous and deadly Australian snakes
Vaughan, Marcia
Dangerous and deadly series (1)
Dangerous and deadly Australian spiders
Vaughan, Marcia
Dangerous and deadly series (2)
Dangerous assignment
Patchett, Mary Elwyn
Jeff James series (2)
Dangerous blondes
Roos, Kelley
Jeff and Haila Troy series (2)
Dangerous business
Underwood, Michael
Rosa Epton series (15)
Dangerous by nature
Coles, Manning
Tommy Hambledon series (12)
Dangerous call
Harrison, Elizabeth
Central London Hospital series (10)
Dangerous canoe race
Roddy, Lee
Ladd family series (4)
Dangerous cargo
Catherall, Arthur
Bulldog tugboat series (6)
Footner, Hulbert
Madame Rosika Storey series (8)
Dangerous cargoes
Hobart, Robertson
Grant Vickery series (2)
Dangerous company
Rowland, John
Inspector Shelley series (5)
Dangerous curves
Cheyney, Peter
Slim Callaghan series (2)
Dangerous dames
Halliday, Brett
Michael Shayne series (51)
Dangerous Davies, the last detective
Thomas, Leslie
Dangerous Davies series (1)
Dangerous deeds
Cobb, Frank
Aviator series (3)
Dangerous domicile
Lorac, E C R
Inspector Macdonald series (43)
Dangerous exchange
Eden, Matthew
Marc Savage series (2)
Dangerous Fortune
Jacobs, Thomas Curtis Hicks
Temple Fortune series (1)
Dangerous gambler
Hardinge, Rex
Sexton Blake series (966)
Dangerous game
Dank, Milton
Game series (1)
Keene, Carolyn
Nancy Drew and Hardy boys supermystery series (4)
Dangerous games
Grant-Adamson, Lesley
Jim Rush series (2)
Johnson, Stacie
Eighteen Pine Street series (8)
Murphy, Warren Burton
Destroyer series (40)
Randall, Marta
Newhome series (2)
Dangerous gold
Cody, Stone
Five Mavericks series (4)
Dangerous ground
Lynch, Lawrence L
Van Vernet series (1)
Dangerous in love
Thomas, Leslie
Dangerous Davies series (2)
Dangerous inheritance
Wheatley, Dennis
Duc de Richelieu series (10)
Dangerous interfaces
Silverberg, Robert
Time gate series (2)
Dangerous islands
Bridge, Ann
Julia Probyn series (5)
Dangerous journey
Deane, Norman
Bruce Murdoch series (2)

Dangerous liaison
Davey, Jocelyn
Ambrose Usher series (7)
Dangerous limelight
Armstrong, Raymond
Inspector Dick Mason series (1)
Dangerous love
Pascal, Francine
Sweet Valley High series (6)
Dangerous magic
Beresford, Elisabeth
Magic series (5)
Dangerous men
Steward, Paull
Donald Everhard series (1)
Dangerous Mister Dell
Hume, David
Mick Cardby series (7)
Dangerous moment
Daniel, Roland
Michael Grant series (2)
Dangerous mourning
Perry, Anne
Inspector William Monk series (2)
Dangerous one
Manson, Will
Man called Black series (3)
Dangerous ones
Franklin, Charles
Maxine Dangerfield series (1)
Dangerous party
Krulick, Nancy E
Lassie series (6)
Dangerous place to die
Wilson, David
Marshal Sam McCloud series (5)
Dangerous places
Chase, Elaine Raco
Roman Cantrell and Nikki Holden series (1)
Golding, Louis
Elsie Silver series (4)
Dangerous playmate
Chambers, Philip
Sexton Blake series (1539)
Dangerous promise
Nixon, Joan Lowery
Orphan train quintet (5)
Dangerous quest
Creasey, John
Department Z series (21)
Dangerous relations
Keene, Carolyn
Nancy Drew files series (82)
Dangerous ride
Darroll, Sally
Home and away series (1)
Dangerous road
Newton, David C
Bunst series (2)
Dangerous secrets
Lowell, Anne Hunter
Sorority girls series (4)
Dangerous sunlight
Bude, John
Inspector Meredith series (16)
Dangerous thing
Crider, Bill
Carl Burns series (4)
Dangerous thoughts
Finnegan, Robert
Dangerous thoughts series (1)
Dangerous to lean out
Fitzgerald, Kevin
Bernard Feston series (3)
Dangerous to me
Foley, Rae
Hiram Potter series (5)
Dangerous trade
Hackforth-Jones, Gilbert
Submarine Service series (8)
Dangerous treasure
Dale, Norman
Peter and Ginger series (2)
Dangerous waters
Bentley, John
Dick Marlow series (1)
Cox, John Roberts
Skipper series (1)
Foster, Kingsley
Jonathan Lamb series (1)
Nelson, Peter N
Sylvia Smith-Smith series (6)
Dangerous years
Hennessy, Max
Kelly Maguire trilogy (2)
Danger's child
Story, Jack Trevor
Sexton Blake series (1529)
Danger's green eyes
Corrigan, Mark
Mark Corrigan and McLean series (27)
Dangerville inheritance
Fox-Davies, Arthur Charles
Ashley Tempest series (1)
Dangling man
Kane, Henry
Peter Chambers series (13)
Dangola script
Johns, Larry
Jacky Ryderbeit series (4)
Daniel
Borntrager, Mary Christner
Ellie's people series (4)
Daniel, Rebecca
Our greatest heritage series (10)
Thomson, David Robert Alexander
Daniel Cullen series (1)
Daniel and the big blizzard
Jenkins, Jerry Bruce
Bradford family series (8)
Daniel and the coconut cakes
Sandberg, Inger
Daniel series (1)
Daniel Boon and the wilderness road
Chambers, Catherine E
Adventures in frontier America series (2)
Daniel Boone, backwoodsman
Forbes-Lindsey, Charles Harcourt
Trail blazers series (2)
Daniel Deronda
Eliot, George
Daniel Deronda series (1)
Daniel in the lion's den
Blyton, Enid
Bible stories series (8)
Daniel paints a picture
Sandberg, Inger
Daniel series (4)
Danielle
Schurfranz, Vivian
Sunfire series (4)
Daniel's big decision
Jenkins, Jerry Bruce
Bradford family series (3)
Daniel's big surprise
Jenkins, Jerry Bruce
Bradford family series (5)
Daniel's helping hand
Sandberg, Inger
Daniel series (3)
Daniel's mysterious monster
Sandberg, Inger
Daniel series (2)
Dankworth's Yard
Mortimer, Derek
Tom Holiday series (2)
Danny again
Barclay, Vera Charlesworth
Danny the detective series (2)
Danny and the Easter egg
Kunhardt, Edith
Danny series (4)
Danny and the rattlesnakes
Barclay, Vera Charlesworth
Danny the detective series (4)
Danny Dunn and the anti-gravity paint
Williams, Jay
Danny Dunn series (1)
Danny Dunn and the automatic house
Williams, Jay
Danny Dunn series (9)
Danny Dunn and the fossil cave
Williams, Jay
Danny Dunn series (6)
Danny Dunn and the heat ray
Williams, Jay
Danny Dunn series (7)
Danny Dunn and the homework machine
Williams, Jay
Danny Dunn series (3)
Danny Dunn and the smallifying machine
Williams, Jay
Danny Dunn series (11)
Danny Dunn and the swamp monster
Williams, Jay
Danny Dunn series (12)
Danny Dunn and the universal glue
Williams, Jay
Danny Dunn series (15)
Danny Dunn and the voice from space
Williams, Jay
Danny Dunn series (10)
Danny Dunn and the weather machine
Williams, Jay
Danny Dunn series (4)
Danny Dunn, invisible boy
Williams, Jay
Danny Dunn series (13)
Danny Dunn on a desert island
Williams, Jay
Danny Dunn series (2)
Danny Dunn on the ocean floor
Williams, Jay
Danny Dunn series (5)
Danny Dunn, scientific detective
Williams, Jay
Danny Dunn series (14)
Danny Dunn, time traveller
Williams, Jay
Danny Dunn series (8)
Danny Fists
Camp, Walter Chauncey
Danny Fists trilogy (1)
Danny Fox
Thomson, David Robert Alexander
Danny Fox series (1)
Danny Fox at the palace
Thomson, David Robert Alexander
Danny Fox series (3)
Danny Fox meets a stranger
Thomson, David Robert Alexander
Danny Fox series (2)
Danny means trouble
Pascal, Francine
Sweet Valley twins series (40)
Danny Orlis and DeeDee's best friend
Palmer, Bernard
Danny Orlis series (55)
Danny Orlis and DeeDee's defiance
Palmer, Bernard
Danny Orlis series (54)
Danny Orlis and Doug's big disappointment
Palmer, Bernard
Danny Orlis series (65)
Danny Orlis and excitement at the Circle R
Palmer, Bernard
Danny Orlis series (47)
Danny Orlis and Fritz McCloud, high school star
Palmer, Bernard
Danny Orlis series (46)
Danny Orlis and Hal's great victory
Palmer, Bernard
Danny Orlis series (27)
Danny Orlis and his big chance
Palmer, Bernard
Danny Orlis series (16)
Danny Orlis and Jim Morgan's scholarship
Palmer, Bernard
Danny Orlis series (48)
Danny Orlis and Jim's northern adventure
Palmer, Bernard
Danny Orlis series (42)
Danny Orlis and Johnny's new life
Palmer, Bernard
Danny Orlis series (53)
Danny Orlis and Kent Gilbert's tragedy
Palmer, Bernard
Danny Orlis series (43)
Danny Orlis and Kent's encounter with law
Palmer, Bernard
Danny Orlis series (39)
Danny Orlis and Linda's new mother
Palmer, Bernard
Danny Orlis series (34)
Danny Orlis and Linda's struggle
Palmer, Bernard
Danny Orlis series (32)
Danny Orlis and Marilyn's great trial
Palmer, Bernard
Danny Orlis series (21)
Danny Orlis and Robin's big battle
Palmer, Bernard
Danny Orlis series (37)
Danny Orlis and Robin's big mistake
Palmer, Bernard
Danny Orlis series (41)
Danny orlis and Robin's rebellion
Palmer, Bernard
Danny Orlis series (40)
Danny Orlis and Ron in the Mexican jungle mystery
Palmer, Bernard
Danny Orlis series (35)
Danny Orlis and Ron Orlis in the Canadian wilderness
Palmer, Bernard
Danny Orlis series (23)
Danny Orlis and Ron's call to service
Palmer, Bernard
Danny Orlis series (29)
Danny Orlis and the accident that shook Fairview
Palmer, Bernard
Danny Orlis series (50)
Danny Orlis and the Alaskan Highway adventure
Palmer, Bernard
Danny Orlis series (61)
Danny Orlis and the Angle Inlet mystery
Palmer, Bernard
Danny Orlis series (2)
Danny Orlis and the bewildered runaway
Palmer, Bernard
Danny Orlis series (58)
Danny Orlis and the big Indian
Palmer, Bernard
Danny Orlis series (11)
Danny Orlis and the boy who would not listen
Palmer, Bernard
Danny Orlis series (14)
Danny Orlis and the Canadian caper
Palmer, Bernard
Danny Orlis series (60)
Danny Orlis and the Colorado challenge
Palmer, Bernard
Danny Orlis series (64)
Danny Orlis and the contrary Mrs Forester
Palmer, Bernard
Danny Orlis series (17)
Danny Orlis and the crisis at Cedarton
Palmer, Bernard
Danny Orlis series (57)
Danny Orlis and the defiant Kent Gilbert
Palmer, Bernard
Danny Orlis series (36)
Danny Orlis and the drug story mystery
Palmer, Bernard
Danny Orlis series (28)
Danny Orlis and the dry gulch mystery
Palmer, Bernard
Danny Orlis series (52)
Danny Orlis and the football feud
Palmer, Bernard
Danny Orlis series (56)
Danny Orlis and the girl who dared
Palmer, Bernard
Danny Orlis series (68)
Danny Orlis and the Guatemala adventure
Palmer, Bernard
Danny Orlis series (45)
Danny Orlis and the headstrong Linda Penner
Palmer, Bernard
Danny Orlis series (30)
Danny Orlis and the hunters
Palmer, Bernard
Danny Orlis series (4)
Danny Orlis and the ice fishing escapade
Palmer, Bernard
Danny Orlis series (33)
Danny Orlis and the live-in tragedy
Palmer, Bernard
Danny Orlis series (63)
Danny orlis and the man from the past
Palmer, Bernard
Danny Orlis series (18)
Danny Orlis and the Mexican kidnapping
Palmer, Bernard
Danny Orlis series (59)
Danny Orlis and the model plane mystery
Palmer, Bernard
Danny Orlis series (71)
Danny Orlis and the mysterious intruder
Palmer, Bernard
Danny Orlis series (69)
Danny Orlis and the mystery at Northwest High
Palmer, Bernard
Danny Orlis series (67)
Danny Orlis and the mystery of the sunken ship
Palmer, Bernard
Danny Orlis series (22)
Danny Orlis and the old mine mystery
Palmer, Bernard
Danny Orlis series (38)
Danny Orlis and the ordeal at camp
Palmer, Bernard
Danny Orlis series (31)
Danny Orlis and the Point Barrow mystery
Palmer, Bernard
Danny Orlis series (1)
Danny Orlis and the Rock Point rebel
Palmer, Bernard
Danny Orlis series (70)
Danny Orlis and the rocks that talk
Palmer, Bernard
Danny Orlis series (6)
Danny Orlis and the sacred cave
Palmer, Bernard
Danny Orlis series (12)
Danny Orlis and the ski slope emergency
Palmer, Bernard
Danny Orlis series (66)
Danny Orlis and the strange forest fire
Palmer, Bernard
Danny Orlis series (3)
Danny Orlis and the teen-age marriage
Palmer, Bernard
Danny Orlis series (44)
Danny Orlis and the time of testing
Palmer, Bernard
Danny Orlis series (25)
Danny Orlis and the wrecked plane
Palmer, Bernard
Danny Orlis series (10)
Danny Orlis and trouble on the Circle R Ranch
Palmer, Bernard
Danny Orlis series (49)
Danny Orlis, bid for victory
Palmer, Bernard
Danny Orlis series (51)
Danny Orlis, big brother
Palmer, Bernard
Danny Orlis series (19)
Danny Orlis, bush pilot
Palmer, Bernard
Danny Orlis series (26)
Danny Orlis changes schools
Palmer, Bernard
Danny Orlis series (9)
Danny Orlis forced down
Palmer, Bernard
Danny Orlis series (62)
Danny Orlis goes to school
Palmer, Bernard
Danny Orlis series (5)
Danny Orlis in the mysterious Zanderland
Palmer, Bernard
Danny Orlis series (24)
Danny Orlis makes the team
Palmer, Bernard
Danny Orlis series (8)
Danny Orlis on Superstition Mountain
Palmer, Bernard
Danny Orlis series (7)
Danny Orlis on the Valiant
Palmer, Bernard
Danny Orlis series (20)
Danny Orlis plays hockey
Palmer, Bernard
Danny Orlis series (15)
Danny Orlis, star back
Palmer, Bernard
Danny Orlis series (13)
Danny Spade sees red
Ambler, Dail
Danny Spade series (38)
Danny Spade spells danger
Ambler, Dail
Danny Spade series (35)
Danny the detective
Barclay, Vera Charlesworth
Danny the detective series (1)
Danny the freshman
Camp, Walter Chauncey
Danny Fists trilogy (3)
Danny's birthday
Kunhardt, Edith
Danny series (1)
Danny's Christmas star
Kunhardt, Edith
Danny series (5)
Danny's mystery valentine!
Kunhardt, Edith
Danny series (2)
Danny's pack
Barclay, Vera Charlesworth
Danny the detective series (3)
Danse macabre
Mullally, Frederic
Bob Sullivan series (1)
Dante game
Langton, Jane
Homer Kelly series (8)
Danube runs red
Meade, Richard
John Allison series (1)
Danvers jewels
Cholmondeley, Mary
Danvers family series (1)
Danzig trilogy
Grass, Gunter
Danzig trilogy (3)
Daphne
Chesney, Marion
Six sisters series (4)
Kaye, Marilyn
Sisters series (2)

Daphne Bruno
Raymond, Ernest
Daphne Bruno series (1)
Daphne dead and done for
Ross, Jonathan
Superintendent George Rogers series (17)
Daphne decisions
O'Brien, Meg
Jessica James series (1)
Daphne in Paris
Topham, Anne
Daphne series (2)
Daphne in the Fatherland
Topham, Anne
Daphne series (1)
Dar boys with General Greene
Cox, Stephen Angus
Dare boys series (8)
D'Arblay mystery
Freeman, Richard Austin
Doctor John Evelyn Thorndyke series (14)
D'Archeville
Mottram, Ralph Hale
Spanish Farm series (3)
Darci and the dance contest
Tolles, Martha
Darci Daniels series (1)
Darci in Cabin Thirteen
Tolles, Martha
Darci Daniels series (2)
Darcy
Shura, Mary Francis
Sunfire series (32)
D'Arcy in danger
Clifford, Martin
Tom Merry series (12)
D'Arcy on the warpath
Clifford, Martin
Tom Merry series (13)
D'Arcy the reformer
Clifford, Martin
Tom Merry series (15)
D'Arcy's day off
Clifford, Martin
Tom Merry series (16)
D'Arcy's disappearance
Clifford, Martin
Tom Merry series (14)
Dardanelles derelict
Mason, Francis Van Wyck
Colonel Hugh North series (17)
Dare
Stine, Robert Lawrence
Fear Street series (21)
Dare boys after Benedict Arnold
Cox, Stephen Angus
Dare boys series (6)
Dare boys at Vincennes
Cox, Stephen Angus
Dare boys series (11)
Dare boys in the North West
Cox, Stephen Angus
Dare boys series (12)
Dare boys in the Red City
Cox, Stephen Angus
Dare boys series (5)
Dare boys in Trenton
Cox, Stephen Angus
Dare boys series (3)
Dare boys in Virginia
Cox, Stephen Angus
Dare boys series (7)
Dare boys of 1776
Cox, Stephen Angus
Dare boys series (1)
Dare boys on the Brandywine
Cox, Stephen Angus
Dare boys series (4)
Dare boys on the Hudson
Cox, Stephen Angus
Dare boys series (2)
Dare boys with Lafayette
Cox, Stephen Angus
Dare boys series (9)
Dare boys with the Swamp Fox
Cox, Stephen Angus
Dare boys series (10)
Dare-Devil Conquest
Gray, Berkeley
Norman Conquest series (21)
Dare to go a-hunting
Norton, Andre
Krip Vorland series (4)
Daredevil Park
Compton, Sara
Choose your own adventure series (114)
Daredevils, Ltd.
Goulart, Ron
Barnum series (9)
Daredevils, Ltd
Goulart, Ron
Exchameleon series (1)
Daredevils of the air
Burtis, Thomson
Air combat series (1)
Darewell chums
Chapman, Allen
Darewell chums series (1)
Darewell chums in a winter camp
Chapman, Allen
Darewell chums series (5)
Darewell chums in the city
Chapman, Allen
Darewell chums series (2)
Darewell chums in the woods
Chapman, Allen
Darewell chums series (3)
Darewell chums on a cruise
Chapman, Allen
Darewell chums series (4)
Darian, master magician
Farrell, Simon
Glade of dreams series (1)
Daring abduction
Ridley, Nat
Nat Ridley series (5)
Daring trip to the moon
Nizzi, Guido
Paralyzing ray trilogy (3)
Daring twins
Baum, Lyman Frank
Daring twins series (1)
Dark
Beach, Lynn
Phantom Valley series (2)
Dark abyss
Coville, Bruce
Dungeon series (2)
Dark affair
Balzac, Honore de
Scenes of political life series (2)
Dark age of violence
Carrel, Mark
Andrew McCall series (5)
Dark and deadly pool
Nixon, Joan Lowery
Mary Elizabeth series (1)
Orphan train quintet (5)
Shirley and Claude series (1)
Dark and the deadly
Winter, Bevis
Steve Craig series (10)
Dark and the light
Bell, Josephine
Jacobean trilogy (3)
Dark angel
Andrews, Virginia Cleo
Casteel-Tatterton family series (2)
Graham, Jean
Dark angel series (1)
Dark angel riding
Longtree, Warren T
Ruff Justice series (7)
Dark arbor
Shriber, Ione Sandberg
Lieutenant Bill Grady series (2)
Dark as the grave wherein my friend is laid
Lowry, Malcolm
Voyage that never ends series (2)
Dark awakening
Sharp, Allen
Storytrails series (20)
Dark Bahama
Cheyney, Peter
Johnny Vallon series (3)
Secret service series (7)
Shaun O'Mara series (3)
Dark beyond Moura
Coffman, Virginia
Moura series (3)
Dark blood, dark terror
Cleeve, Brian
Sean Ryan series (2)
Dark blue and dangerous
Ross, Jonathan
Superintendent George Rogers series (9)
Dark bright water
Wrightson, Patricia
Song of Wirrun trilogy (2)
Dark canyon
Reno, Bill
Badge series (11)
Dark carnival
Axler, James
Deathlands series (14)
Dark castle, white horse
Lee, Tanith
Castle of dark series (2)
Dark cavalier
Rath, Virginia
Michael Dundas series (1)
Dark circle
Ashe, Gordon
Patrick Dawlish series (22)
Dark city
Collins, Max Allan
Eliot Ness series (1)
Dark corners
Chase, Elaine Raco
Roman Cantrell and Nikki Holden series (2)
Dark crusade
Fox, James M
Steve Harvester series (1)
Wagner, Karl Edward
Kane series (4)
Dark cry of the moon
Grant, Charles Lewis
Oxrun Station series (8)
Soft whisper trilogy (2)
Dark danger
Saville, Malcolm
Marston Baines series (3)
Simon series (3)
Dark death
Gilbert, Anthony
Arthur Crook series (26)
Grant, Maxwell
Shadow series (72)
Dark deeds
Donovan, Dick
Dick Donovan series (13)
Dark descent
Hartwell, David Geddes
Dark descent trilogy (3)
Dark design
Farmer, Philip Jose
Riverworld series (3)
Dark desire
Coffman, Virginia
Napoleonic Europe series (5)
Dark dimensions
Chandler, Arthur Bertram
John Grimes series (9)
Rim series (15)
Dark divide
Acres, Mark
Runesword series (5)
Dark door
Wilhelm, Kate
Charlie Miklejohn and Constance Leidl series (2)
Dark door opens
Dever, Joe
Legends of Lone Wolf series (2)
Dark dowry
Roberts, Willo Davis
Black pearl series (1)
Dark dream
Martin, Robert Lee
Jim Bennett series (1)
Dark druid
Flint, Kenneth Covey
Finn McCumhal series (3)
Dark duet
Cheyney, Peter
Secret service series (1)
Dark echo
Nelson, Hugh Lawrence
Steve Johnson series (4)
Dark emerald
Storm, Joan
Sarah Vanessa series (1)
Dark encounter
Mills, Woosnam
John Melrose series (3)
Dark entry
Copper, Basil
Mike Faraday series (33)
Dark estuary
B B
Wildfowling series (2)
Dark-eyed client
Moody, Laurence
Tudor trilogy (1)
Dark fantastic
Ellin, Stanley
John Milano series (2)
Dark fields
Macgregor, T J
Quin Saint James and Mike McClary series (2)
Dark fires
Rogers, Rosemary
Ginny Brandon and Steve Morgan series (2)
Dark flower
Galsworthy, John
Love trilogy (1)
Dark Force rising
Zahn, Timothy
Star wars series (2)
Dark forest
Foxall, Raymond
Harry Adkins series (3)
Laird, Elizabeth
Olaf the Viking series (2)
Walpole, Hugh
Mister Durward series (1)
Trenchard family series (3)
Dark frontier
Maclean, Arthur
Sexton Blake series (1405)
Dark garden
Eberhart, Mignon Good
Sarah Keate and Lance O'Leary series (6)
Punshon, Ernest Robertson
Bobby Owen series (16)
Dark gateway
Long, Martin
Inspector Keats and Tom Cotter series (2)
Dark Geraldine
Ferguson, John
Francis Macnab series (5)
Dark gods
Sherman, Josepha
Secret of the Unicorn Queen series (5)
Dark gondola
Coffman, Virginia
Moura series (3)
Dark green tunnel
Eckert, Allan Wesley
Mesmerian annals series (1)
Dark gunman
Elton, Wallace
Jud Walton series (3)
Dark hand of magic
Hambly, Barbara
Sun Wolf series (3)
Dark Harbor hunting
Ross, Clarissa
Dark Harbor series (3)
Dark harvest
Creasey, John
Doctor Palfrey series (9)
Dark hero
Cheyney, Peter
Secret service series (4)
Dark highway
Gask, Arthur
Gilbert Larose series (2)
Dark hill
Duke, Winifred
Harold Fieldend series (2)
Dark horse
Bower, Bertha Muzzy
Flying U Ranch series (8)
Herbert, Mary H
Dark horse series (1)
Murphy, Warren Burton
Destroyer series (89)
Dark horseman
Harvey, Marianne
Trevarvas family series (1)
Dark index
Turner, James Ernest
Rampion Savage series (6)
Dark interlude
Cheyney, Peter
Everard Peter Quayle series (3)
Secret service series (5)
Shaun O'Mara series (2)
Dark is a color
Lapka, Fay S
Caro series (1)
Dark is rising
Cooper, Susan Mary
Dark is rising series (2)
Dark is rising sequence
Cooper, Susan Mary
Dark is rising series (5)
Dark is the clue
Punshon, Ernest Robertson
Bobby Owen series (33)
Dark is the tunnel
Burton, Miles
Inspector Arnold and Desmond Merrion series (12)
Dark island
Barr, Robert
Nick Nicholson series (1)
Treece, Henry
Early Britain series (2)
Dark journey
Crofts, Freeman Wills
Inspector Joseph French series (29)
Morlan, A R
Ewerton series (3)
Dark kiss
Enefer, Douglas
Dale Shand series (3)
Dark knight
Robertson, Colin
Peter Grayleigh series (8)
Dark lady
Holt, Gavin
Professor Luther Bastion series (12)
Kerr, Robert
Jamie Stuart series (3)
Dark lantern
Williamson, Henry
Chronicles of ancient sunlight series (1)
Dark light
Spicer, Bart
Carney Wilde series (1)
Dark lord
Graham, Jean
Dark angel series (2)
Dark mambo
Baker, William Howard
Sexton Blake series (1396)
Dark man, and others
Howard, Robert Ervin
Tales of the Picts series (2)
Dark maze
Adcock, Thomas
Neil Hockaday series (1)
Dark messiah
Alexander, David
Phoenix series (1)
Caidin, Martin
Messiah series (2)
Dark mile
Broster, Dorothy Kathleen
Jacobite trilogy (3)
Dark mill stream
Gask, Arthur
Gilbert Larose series (22)
Dark mind
Goyne, Richard
Padre series (4)
Dark mirror
Copper, Basil
Mike Faraday series (1)
Duane, Diane
Star trek, the next generation series (20)
Dark monarch
Berlin, Sven
Lazarus series (2)
Dark moon
Pierce, Meredith Ann
Firebringer trilogy (2)
Vivian, Francis
Inspector John Burnell series (2)
Sergeant Ronnie Drew series (2)
Dark mystery
Ashe, Gordon
Patrick Dawlish series (19)
Dark Nantucket noon
Langton, Jane
Homer Kelly series (2)
Dark nemesis
Wales, Mike
Leatherhand series (8)
Dark night
Horler, Sydney
Ace series (3)
Dark night offshore
Gagnon, Maurice
Deirdre O'Hara trilogy (2)
Dark nights
Burke, Thomas
London series (5)
Dark of the moon
Carr, John Dickson
Doctor Gideon Fell series (23)
Crockett, Samuel Rutherford
Raiders series (2)
Hodgell, Patricia Christine
Kencyrath series (2)
Thayer, Lee
Peter Clancy series (21)
Dark of the night
Macdonnell, James Edmond
Dutchy Holland series (40)
Dark on Monday
Avallone, Michael
Ed Noon series (31)
Dark paradise
Mackintosh, May
Laurie Grant and Stewart Noble series (3)
Schmidt, Dennis
Questioner trilogy (3)
Dark pasture
Stirling, Jessica
Stalker family trilogy (3)

Dark peril
Creasey, John
Department Z series (22)
Dark place
Elkins, Aaron J
Professor Gideon Oliver series (2)
Dark places
Fraser, Alex
Inspector Noel Tracy series (6)
Grenville, Kate
Lilian Singer series (2)
Dark pool
Rienow, Leona Train
Dark pool series (2)
Dark portal
Furnell, John
Doctor Furnell series (1)
Jarvis, Robin
Deptford mice trilogy (1)
Dark power
Arden, William
Kane Jackson series (1)
Dark powers
McKinney, Jack
Sentinels series (2)
Dark prince
Gemmell, David A
Lion of Macedon series (2)
Dark quartet
Banks, Lynne Reid
Bronte series (1)
Dark realm
Kaufman, Douglas
Torg series (2)
Dark return
Langholm, Neil
Vikings series (2)
Dark reunion
Smith, Lisa J
Vampire diaries series (4)
Dark river
Millin, Sarah Gertrude
Dark river series (1)
Dark road
Disney, Doris Miles
Jeff Dimarco series (1)
Leroux, Gaston
Cheri-Bibi series (3)
Dark room
Narayan, Rasipuram Krishnaswami
Malgudi series (5)
Dark root
Kenyon, Theda
Staceys of Feathergrant series (2)
Dark rose
Harrod-Eagles, Cynthia
Morland family series (2)
Dark Satanic
Bradley, Marion Zimmer
Leslie Barnes series (1)
Dark secret of Josephine
Wheatley, Dennis
Roger Brook series (5)
Dark secret of Weatherend
Bellairs, John
Anthony Monday series (2)
Dark secrets
Graydon, William Murray
Sexton Blake series (86)
Dark shadow
Desmond, Hugh
Alan Fraser series (27)
Dark shadows
Ross, Marilyn
Barnabas Collins series (1)
Dark side
Davis, Kenn
Carver Bascombe series (1)
Hornig, Doug
Loren Swift series (3)
Dark side of the street
Fallon, Martin
Paul Chavasse series (5)
Dark sonata
Bond, Evelyn
Ira Yedder series (4)
Dark splendour
Almedingen, Edith Martha
Andrew Thornyold series (2)
Dark star
Muller, Marcia
Joanna Stark series (3)
Dark straits of Reglathium
Sirota, Mike
Dannus series (4)
Dark stream
Thomson, June
Inspector Finch series (12)
Dark street
Cheyney, Peter
Everard Peter Quayle series (2)
Secret service series (3)
Shaun O'Mara series (1)
Dark street murders
Cheyney, Peter
Everard Peter Quayle series (2)
Secret service series (3)
Shaun O'Mara series (1)
Dark summer
Cleary, Jon
Scobie Malone series (9)
Jennings, D K
Doctor Ralph Conway series (28)
Dark sun
Nicole, Christopher
Kenya trilogy (3)
Dark sword's lover
Van Asten, Gail
Charlemagne's champion series (2)
Dark thicket
Kelton, Elmer
Tales of Texas series (15)
Dark threat
Wentworth, Patricia
Miss Maud Silver series (11)
Dark tide
McKiernan, Dennis L
Iron tower trilogy (1)
Dark tower
Vansittart, Peter
Stories from the past series (1)
Dark towers of Fog Island
Ross, Marilyn
Fog Island series (2)
Dark trade
Lejeune, Anthony
Adam Gifford series (3)
Dark trail
Gorman, Edward
Leo Guild series (4)
Hobart, Donald Bayne
Masked Rider and Blue Hawk series (5)
Dark treasure
Chastain, Madye Lee
Lisa and Emmy and Dodie series (1)
Dark triangle
Walters, Hugh
Chris Godfrey series (22)
Dark tunnel
Millar, Kenneth
Chet Gordon series (1)
Dark vendetta
Charles, Robert
Simon Larren series (3)
Dark visions
Tilley, Patrick
Amtrak wars series (6)
Dark wanton
Cheyney, Peter
Everard Peter Quayle series (4)
Secret service series (6)
Dark way
Conley, Robert Jackson
Real people series (2)
Dark ways to death
Saxon, Peter
Guardians series (2)
Guardians series (5)
Dark wind
Hillerman, Tony
Sergeant Jim Chee series (2)
Dark winds
Coffman, Virginia
Napoleonic Europe series (4)
Dark winter
Broome, H B
Tom English series (5)
Dark woman
Wren, Percival Christopher
Major Hazelrigg series (1)
Darkangel
Pierce, Meredith Ann
Aeriel trilogy (1)
Darkangel trilogy
Pierce, Meredith Ann
Aeriel trilogy (3)
Darkchild
Van Scyoc, Sydney Joyce
Sunstone scrolls trilogy (1)
Darken ship
Monsarrat, Nicholas
Master mariner series (2)
Darkening glass
Wainwright, John
Northern Police series (9)
Darkening sea
Kent, Alexander
Captain Richard Bolitho series (21)
Darker grows the street
Winter, Bevis
Steve Craig series (4)
Darker magic
Bedard, Michael
Emily series (1)
Darker than amber
Macdonald, John Dann
Travis McGee series (7)
Darker the night
Brean, Herbert
Reynold Frame series (2)
Darker traffic
Brett, Martin
Mike Garfin series (2)
Darkest day
McKiernan, Dennis L
Iron tower trilogy (3)
Darkest hour
Andrews, Virginia Cleo
Cutler family series (5)
Nielsen, Helen
Simon Drake series (4)
Darkest hours
Carter, Alden Richardson
American Revolution series (2)
Darkest road
Kay, Guy Gavriel
Fionavar tapestry trilogy (3)
Darkest spot
Thayer, Lee
Peter Clancy series (9)
Darkest under the lamp
Sandys, James
Mister Springfield series (3)
Darkling death
Vivian, Francis
Inspector Gordon Knollis series (11)
Darkling wind
Sucharitkul, Somtow
Chronicles of the high inquest series (4)
Darkmage
Hambly, Barbara
Windrose series (2)
Darkman
Boyll, Randall
Darkman series (1)
Darkness and dawn
England, George Allen
Darkness and dawn series (1)
Darkness and dawn series (5)
Farrar, Frederic William
Early Church series (1)
Tolstoi, Aleksei Nikolaevich
Ordeal trilogy (2)
Darkness and light
Carter, Tonya R
DragonLance preludes series (1)
Darkness and the deep
Fisher, Vardis
Testament of man series (1)
Darkness at dawn
Drury, Rebecca
Women of war series (5)
Darkness at Ingraham's Crest
Yerby, Frank
Hwesu series (2)
Darkness at noon
Koestler, Arthur
Ends and means trilogy (2)
Darkness at Sethanon
Feist, Raymond Elias
Riftwar series (3)
Darkness before the dawn
Stuart, Anne
Maggie Bennett series (1)
Darkness descends
Syvertsen, Ryder
Mystic rebel series (3)
Darkness falls
Dixon, Franklin W
Hardy boys case files series (89)
Darkness in the eye
Power, Maurice S
Children of the north series (3)
Darkness missiles
Teitelbaum, Michael
Photon series (1)
Darkness of slumber
Kutak, Rosemary
Doctor Marc Castleman series (1)
Darkness under the earth
Casteret, Norbert
Under the earth series (4)
Darkness under the hills
Scott, Bill
Boori series (2)
Darkness upon the ice
Forstchen, William R
Ice prophet trilogy (3)
Darkness weaves
Wagner, Karl Edward
Kane series (1)
Darkness weaves with many shades
Wagner, Karl Edward
Kane series (1)
Darkover landfall
Bradley, Marion Zimmer
Darkover series (4)
Darkspell
Kerr, Katharine
Deverry series (2)
Darksword trilogy
Weis, Margaret
Darksword trilogy (3)
Darkthunder's way
Deitz, Tom
David Sullivan series (3)
Darkwalker on Moonshae
Niles, Douglas
Moonshae trilogy (1)
Darkwell
Niles, Douglas
Moonshae trilogy (3)
Darkworld detective
Reaves, Michael
Darkworld detective series (1)
Darling buds of May
Bates, Herbert Ernest
Larkin family series (1)
Darling delinquent
Janson, Hank
Hank Janson series (217)
Darling, don't
Campbell, Keith
Mike Brett series (3)
Darling, don't be dumb
Larbalestier, Philip George
Inspector Michael Farrant series (1)
Darling, it's death
Prather, Richard Scott
Shell Scott series (6)
Darling this is death
Chambers, Dana
Jim Steele series (7)
Darlington jaunt
Ross, Angus
Mark Farrow series (15)
Darneley Place
Bagot, Richard
Passport series (2)
Darrow enigma
Severy, Martin
George Maitland series (1)
Dartmoor burial
Peterson, Audrey
Jane Winfield and Andrew Quentin series (7)
Dartmoor enigma
Thomson, Basil
Superintendent Richardson series (5)
Darya of the bronze age
Carter, Lin
Eric Carstairs series (4)
Dashbury Park
Tweedsmuir, Susan Buchan
Victorian trilogy (2)
Dashing white cowboy
Goscinny, Rene
Lucky Luke series (10)
Dashwoods
Rudd, Steele
Dashwood family series (2)
Da Silva Da Silva's cultivated wilderness
Harris, Wilson
Civilizations quartet (3)
Da Silva series (1)
Dastardly murder of Dirty Pete
Clifford, Eth
Mary Rose Onetree series (2)
Date
Moffat, Bill
Press Gang series (4)
Date can be deadly
Pearce, Colin
Fax Pack series (1)
Date for Diane
Cavanna, Betty
Diane series (1)
Date with a dead man
Halliday, Brett
Michael Shayne series (16)
Michael Shayne series (33)
Date with a noose
Gardner, Jerome
Hanging Judge series (9)
Date with a spy
Maddock, Stephen
Timothy Terrel series (14)
Date with a werewolf
Pascal, Francine
Sweet Valley High series (105)
Date with danger
Chester, Gilbert
Sexton Blake series (1178)
Thomas, Martin
Sexton Blake series (1506)
Date with death
Goldthwaite, Eaton Kenneth
Lieutenant Joseph Dickerson series (3)
Hunsburger, Ed
Destroyer series (57)
Linington, Elizabeth
Sergeant Ivor Maddox series (3)
Murphy, Warren Burton
Destroyer series (57)
Scott, Bradford
Walt Slade series (102)
Date with deception
Keene, Carolyn
Nancy Drew files series (48)
Date with destiny
Walker, Jerry
Lawrence Marley series (2)
Date with murder
Marshall, Lovat
Sugar Kane series (24)
Date with the departed
Thorne, Ernest Pollett
Major Brains Cunningham series (8)
Dateline Darlene
Janson, Hank
Hank Janson series (141)
Dateline Debbie
Janson, Hank
Hank Janson series (142)
Dateline Diane
Janson, Hank
Hank Janson series (143)
Dating game
Pascal, Francine
Sweet Valley High series (78)
Daughter fair
Graaf, Peter
Joe Dust series (2)
Daughter of Anderson Crow
McCutcheon, George Barr
Anderson Crow series (1)
Daughter of Bonnie and Clyde
Brent, Lynton Wright
Bonnie and Clyde series (2)
Daughter of Bugle Ann
Kantor, Mackinlay
Bugle Ann series (2)
Daughter of Cathay
Keyte, John Charles
Minsan series (1)
Daughter of Delilah
Foote, John Taintor
Fatal gesture series (2)
Daughter of destiny
Salsitz, R A V
Alorie series (2)
Daughter of Eve
Balzac, Honore de
Scenes of private life series (14)
Daughter of France
Maud, Constance Elisabeth
English girl series (2)
Daughter of freedom
Blanchard, Amy Ella
Revolutionary War series (3)
Daughter of Fu-Manchu
Rohmer, Sax
Fu-Manchu series (5)
Daughter of gold
Roberts, J R
Gunsmith series (72)
Daughter of Henry VIII
Churchill, Rosemary
Mary Tudor series (2)
Daughter of Isis
Makepeace, Joanna
Thebes series (2)
Daughter of shame
Janson, Hank
Hank Janson series (144)
Daughter of the bright moon
Abbey, Lynn
Rifkind series (1)
Daughter of the coast guard
Baxter, Betty
Becky Bryan series (3)
Daughter of the Dales
Hauxwell, Hannah
Daleswoman series (2)
Daughter of the eagle
Coldsmith, Don
Spanish bit series (6)
Daughter of the Empire
Feist, Raymond Elias
Empire series (1)
Daughter of the gods
Fitzgerald, Julia
Astromance series (2)

Daughter of the house
Wells, Carolyn
Fleming Stone series (19)
Daughter of the lion
Roberson, Jennifer
Chronicles of the Cheysuli series (6)
Daughter of the Middle Border
Garland, Hamlin
Middle Border series (2)
Daughter of the morning
De Selincourt, Hugh
Constance Howard series (1)
Daughter of the Revolution
Clayton, Colin Guy
Blakeney papers series (1)
Daughter of the storm
Williams, Jeanne
Clanna series (2)
Daughter of time
Tey, Josephine
Inspector Alan Grant series (5)
Daughter of Tintagel omnibus
Sampson, Fay
Daughter of Tintagel series (5)
Daughter of Valdoro
Armstrong, Evelyn Stewart
Valdoro series (1)
Daughter of witches
Wrede, Patricia Collins
Lyra trilogy (2)
Daughter of Wolf House
Bell, Margaret Elizabeth
Florence Monroe series (4)
Daughters and mothers
Davis, Margaret Thomson
Rag woman, rich woman series (2)
Daughters of Aradale
Lyon, Elinor
Ian and Sovra series (4)
Daughters of Artemis
Douglas, Lauren Wright
Caitlin Reece series (3)
Daughters of Cameron
Malcolm, Aleen
Daughters of Cameron series (3)
Daughters of divinity
Anderson, Verily
Anderson family series (4)
Daughters of Mrs Peacock
Bullett, Gerald
Peacock family series (1)
Daughters of Spain
Plaidy, Jean
Ferdinand and Isabella trilogy (3)
Daughters of the dolphin
Meyers, Roy
Dolphins trilogy (2)
Daughters of the far islands
Vandergriff, Aola
Daughters series (3)
Daughters of the misty isles
Vandergriff, Aola
Daughters series (5)
Daughters of the opal skies
Vandergriff, Aola
Daughters series (4)
Daughters of the shining city
Vandergriff, Aola
Daughters series (6)
Daughters of the silver screen
Vandergriff, Aola
Daughters series (8)
Daughters of the Southwind
Vandergriff, Aola
Daughters series (1)
Daughters of the storm
Vandergriff, Aola
Daughters series (7)
Daughters of the sunshine
Van Scyoc, Sydney Joyce
Sunstone scrolls trilogy (3)
Daughters of the wild country
Vandergriff, Aola
Daughters series (2)
Dauntless
Evans, Alan
David Cochrane series (3)
Dauntless and the Mary Baines
Dawlish, Peter
Dauntless series (3)
Dauntless and the Poplar pirates
Dawlish, Peter
Dauntless series (4)
Dauntless and the smugglers
Dawlish, Peter
Dauntless series (2)
Dauntless and the wreck of the Mary Baines
Dawlish, Peter
Dauntless series (3)
Dauntless finds her crew
Dawlish, Peter
Dauntless series (1)
Dauntless goes home
Dawlish, Peter
Dauntless series (7)
Dauntless in danger
Dawlish, Peter
Dauntless series (6)
Dauntless Jock
Taylor, Allan K
Uncle Jock series (3)
Dauntless sails again
Dawlish, Peter
Dauntless series (2)
Dauntless sails in
Dawlish, Peter
Dauntless series (5)
Dauntless takes recruits
Dawlish, Peter
Dauntless series (4)
Dave Darrin after the mine layers
Hancock, Harrie Irving
Dave Darrin series (6)
Dave Darrin and the German submarines
Hancock, Harrie Irving
Dave Darrin series (5)
Dave Darrin at Vera Cruz
Hancock, Harrie Irving
Dave Darrin series (1)
Dave Darrin on Mediterranean service
Hancock, Harrie Irving
Dave Darrin series (2)
Dave Darrin on the Asiatic station
Hancock, Harrie Irving
Dave Darrin series (4)
Dave Darrin's South American cruise
Hancock, Harrie Irving
Dave Darrin series (3)
Dave Dashaway, air champion
Rockwood, Roy
Dave Dashaway series (5)
Dave Dashaway and his giant airship
Rockwood, Roy
Dave Dashaway series (3)
Dave Dashaway and his hydroplane
Rockwood, Roy
Dave Dashaway series (2)
Dave Dashaway around the world
Rockwood, Roy
Dave Dashaway series (4)
Dave Dashaway, the young aviator
Rockwood, Roy
Dave Dashaway series (1)
Dave Dawson at Casablanca
Bowen, Robert Sidney
Dave Dawson series (13)
Dave Dawson at Dunkirk
Bowen, Robert Sidney
Dave Dawson series (1)
Dave Dawson at Singapore
Bowen, Robert Sidney
Dave Dawson series (6)
Dave Dawson at Tobruk
Bowen, Robert Sidney
Dave Dawson series (15)
Dave Dawson, flight lieutenant
Bowen, Robert Sidney
Dave Dawson series (5)
Dave Dawson in Libya
Bowen, Robert Sidney
Dave Dawson series (3)
Dave Dawson on convoy patrol
Bowen, Robert Sidney
Dave Dawson series (4)
Dave Dawson on Guadalcanal
Bowen, Robert Sidney
Dave Dawson series (12)
Dave Dawson on the Russian front
Bowen, Robert Sidney
Dave Dawson series (10)
Dave Dawson over Berlin
Bowen, Robert Sidney
Dave Dawson series (16)
Dave Dawson with the Air Corps
Bowen, Robert Sidney
Dave Dawson series (8)
Dave Dawson with the commandos
Bowen, Robert Sidney
Dave Dawson series (9)
Dave Dawson with the Eighth Air Force
Bowen, Robert Sidney
Dave Dawson series (14)
Dave Dawson with the Flying Tigers
Bowen, Robert Sidney
Dave Dawson series (11)
Dave Dawson with the Pacific Fleet
Bowen, Robert Sidney
Dave Dawson series (7)
Dave Dawson with the RAF
Bowen, Robert Sidney
Dave Dawson series (2)
Dave Fearless after a sunken treasure
Rockwood, Roy
Dave Fearless series (1)
Dave Fearless among the cannibals
Rockwood, Roy
Dave Fearless series (17)
Dave Fearless among the icebergs
Rockwood, Roy
Dave Fearless series (4)
Dave Fearless and his big raft
Rockwood, Roy
Dave Fearless series (6)
Dave Fearless and the cave of mystery
Rockwood, Roy
Dave Fearless series (3)
Deep sea series (3)
Dave Fearless and the mutineers
Rockwood, Roy
Dave Fearless series (9)
Dave Fearless at Whirlpool Point
Rockwood, Roy
Dave Fearless series (16)
Dave Fearless captured by apes
Rockwood, Roy
Dave Fearless series (8)
Dave Fearless caught by Malay pirates
Rockwood, Roy
Dave Fearless series (13)
Dave Fearless in the black jungle
Rockwood, Roy
Dave Fearless series (11)
Dave Fearless near the South Pole
Rockwood, Roy
Dave Fearless series (12)
Dave Fearless on a floating island
Rockwood, Roy
Dave Fearless series (2)
Dave Fearless on the lost brig
Rockwood, Roy
Dave Fearless series (15)
Dave Fearless on the ship of mystery
Rockwood, Roy
Dave Fearless series (14)
Dave Fearless on Volcano Island
Rockwood, Roy
Dave Fearless series (7)
Dave Fearless under the ocean
Rockwood, Roy
Dave Fearless series (10)
Dave Fearless wrecked among savages
Rockwood, Roy
Dave Fearless series (5)
Dave Porter and his classmates
Stratemeyer, Edward L
Dave Porter series (5)
Dave Porter and his double
Stratemeyer, Edward L
Dave Porter series (12)
Dave Porter and his rivals
Stratemeyer, Edward L
Dave Porter series (7)
Dave Porter and the runaways
Stratemeyer, Edward L
Dave Porter series (9)
Dave Porter at Bear Camp
Stratemeyer, Edward L
Dave Porter series (11)
Dave Porter at Oak Hall
Stratemeyer, Edward L
Dave Porter series (1)
Dave Porter at Star Ranch
Stratemeyer, Edward L
Dave Porter series (6)
Dave Porter in the far North
Stratemeyer, Edward L
Dave Porter series (4)
Dave Porter in the gold fields
Stratemeyer, Edward L
Dave Porter series (10)
Dave Porter in the South Seas
Stratemeyer, Edward L
Dave Porter series (2)
Dave Porter on Oak Island
Stratemeyer, Edward L
Dave Porter series (8)
Dave Porter under fire
Stratemeyer, Edward L
Dave Porter series (14)
Dave Porter's great search
Stratemeyer, Edward L
Dave Porter series (13)
Dave Porter's return to school
Stratemeyer, Edward L
Dave Porter series (3)
Dave Porter's war honors
Stratemeyer, Edward L
Dave Porter series (15)
Dave Spencer on secret service
Armitage, Taylor
Uncle Sam's service series (2)
Davenports and cherry pie
Dalgliesh, Alice
Davenports series (2)
Davenports are at dinner
Dalgliesh, Alice
Davenports series (1)
David
Daniel, Rebecca
Our greatest heritage series (8)
Wensell, Ulises
Jackson family series (3)
David, a dragonfly
Rutley, Cecily Marianne
Tales of the wild folk series (10)
David Alden's daughters, and other stories of colonial times
Austin, Jane Goodwin
Pilgrims of Plymouth series (3)
David and Goliath
Blyton, Enid
Bible stories series (4)
David and Goliath on their own
Dicks, Terrance
David and Goliath series (17)
David Balfour
Stevenson, Robert Louis
David Balfour series (2)
David Betterton
Ruegg, Alfred Henry
Rosie Bright series (2)
David Blaize
Benson, Edward Frederic
David Blaize series (2)
David Blaize and the blue door
Benson, Edward Frederic
David Blaize series (1)
David Blaize of King's
Benson, Edward Frederic
David Blaize series (3)
David Bowie story
Tremlett, George
Rock stars series (10)
David Crockett, scout
Allen, Charles Fletcher
Trail blazers series (3)
David Cronenberg's Scanners
Whiteson, Leon
Scanners series (1)
David Essex story
Tremlett, George
Rock stars series (2)
David has AIDS
Sanford, Doris
In our neighborhood series (2)
David Ives
Pier, Arthur Stanwood
Saint Timothy's School series (7)
David John
Fraser, Edith
David John series (1)
David John again
Fraser, Edith
David John series (3)
David John finds out
Fraser, Edith
David John series (4)
David John hears about Jesus
Fraser, Edith
David John series (2)
David Lindsay
Southworth, Emma Dorothy Eliza Nevitte
Gloria series (2)
David of King's
Benson, Edward Frederic
David Blaize series (3)
David Starr, space ranger
French, Paul
David Starr series (1)
David the prince
Tranter, Nigel Godwin
Scottish history series (3)
David Wilding
Crompton, Richmal
Wilding family series (2)
David Wilshaw investigates
Pollard, Alfred Oliver
David Wilshaw series (1)
David's landing
Richardson, Judith Benet
Maushope's Landing series (1)
Davidson affair
Jackman, Stuart
Jesus Davidson series (1)
Davidson case
Rhode, John
Doctor Lancelot Priestley series (7)
Da Vinci rose
O'Neill, Archie
Jeff Pride series (1)
Davis Cup conspiracy
Bickham, Jack Miles
Brad Smith series (6)
Davis doesn't live here anymore
Ripley, Jack
John George Davis series (1)
Davo's little something
Barrett, Robert G
Les Norton series (7)
Davy
Pangborn, Edgar
Davy series (1)
Davy and his dog
Lenski, Lois
Davy series (4)
Davy and the goblin
Carryl, Charles Edward
Alice in Wonderland sequels series (1)
Davy Crockett and the Creek Indians
Korman, Justine
Davy Crockett series (3)
Davy Crockett and the king of the river
Korman, Justine
Davy Crockett series (1)
Singer, A L
Davy Crockett series (4)
Davy Crockett and the pirates at Cave-In Rock
Singer, A L
Davy Crockett series (3)
Davy Crockett and the pirates at Cave-in-the-Rock
Korman, Justine
Davy Crockett series (4)
Davy Crockett at the Alamo
Korman, Justine
Davy Crockett series (2)
Davy goes places
Lenski, Lois
Davy series (5)
Davy's day
Lenski, Lois
Davy series (1)
Dawg day afternoon
Walker, Mort
Hi and Lois series (10)
Dawks and the duchess
Reid, Meta Mayne
Peyton children series (4)
Dawks does it again
Reid, Meta Mayne
Peyton children series (2)
Dawks on Robbers' Mountain
Reid, Meta Mayne
Peyton children series (3)
Dawn
Andrews, Virginia Cleo
Cutler family series (1)
Butler, Octavia Estelle
Xenogenesis trilogy (1)
Rolland, Romain
John Christopher series (1)
Wiesel, Elie
Night trilogy (2)
Wright, Sydney Fowler
Martin Webster series (2)
Dawn and morning
Rolland, Romain
John Christopher series (1)
Dawn and the big sleepover
Martin, Ann Matthews
Baby-Sitters Club series (44)
Dawn and the disappearing dogs
Martin, Ann Matthews
Baby-Sitters Club mystery series (7)
Dawn and the impossible three
Martin, Ann Matthews
Baby-Sitters Club series (5)
Dawn and the older boy
Martin, Ann Matthews
Baby-Sitters Club series (37)
Dawn and the surfer ghost
Martin, Ann Matthews
Baby-Sitters Club mystery series (12)
Dawn and the We Kids Club
Martin, Ann Matthews
Baby-Sitters Club series (72)
Dawn and Whitney, friends forever
Martin, Ann Matthews
Baby-Sitters Club series (77)
Dawn for a distant earth
Modesitt, Leland Exton
Forever hero trilogy (1)
Dawn in the trees
Wibberley, Leonard
Man of liberty series (2)
Dawn of conflict
Randle, Kevin
Global war series (1)
Dawn of darkness
Creasey, John
Doctor Palfrey series (11)
Dawn of magic
Pauwels, Louis
Dawn of magic series (1)

Dawn of revenge
Sherman, Jory
Gunn series (1)
Dawn of the dead
Romero, George Andrew
Living dead series (3)
Dawn of time
Mountford, Charles Pearcy
Dreamtime series (2)
Dawn on the Coast
Martin, Ann Matthews
Baby-Sitters Club series (23)
Dawn readiness
Leslie, Richard
Victory trilogy (1)
Dawn ride
Petersen-Schaefer, Karin
Melody series (1)
Dawn riders
Gruber, Frank
Historical Western series (17)
Dawn saves the planet
Martin, Ann Matthews
Baby-Sitters Club series (57)
Dawning light
Randall, Robert
Nidor series (2)
Dawn's big date
Martin, Ann Matthews
Baby-Sitters Club series (50)
Dawn's big move
Martin, Ann Matthews
Baby-Sitters Club series (67)
Dawn's early light
Thane, Elswyth
Williamsburg series (1)
Dawn's family feud
Martin, Ann Matthews
Baby-Sitters Club series (64)
Dawn's left hand
Richardson, Dorothy Miller
Pilgrimage series (10)
Dawn's uncertain light
Barrett, Neal
Darkest America series (2)
Dawn's wicked stepsister
Martin, Ann Matthews
Baby-Sitters Club series (31)
Dawnsman planet
Reynolds, Mack
Planetary Agent series (3)
Dawnspell
Kerr, Katharine
Deverry series (3)
Dawson died twice
Grover, Marshall
Larry and Stretch series (156)
Dawson pedigree
Sayers, Dorothy Leigh
Lord Peter Wimsey series (3)
Day after judgment
Blish, James
After such knowledge series (3)
Day among many
Pegram, Lorna
Blood and fire series (2)
Day and night stories
Blackwood, Algernon
John Silence series (2)
Day and the way we met
Stolz, Mary
Connor family series (2)
Day at Bullerby
Lindgren, Astrid
Bullerby series (9)
Day at school
Reed, Giles
Munch Bunch stretch series (5)
Day at school with Noddy
Blyton, Enid
Noddy picture books series (6)
Day at the country fair
Burnett, Alice Hale
Merryvale girls series (2)
Day at the fair
Reed, Giles
Munch Bunch stretch series (6)
Day at the seaside
Coote, Roger
Outings series (4)
Reed, Giles
Munch Bunch stretch series (4)
Day at the zoo
Reed, Giles
Munch Bunch stretch series (2)
Day before yesterday
Heath-Miller, Mavis
Hardwick family series (4)
Shafer, Sara Andrew
Day before yesterday series (1)
Day breaks
VerDorn, Bethea
Moon glows series (2)
Day by day
Cramer, Helen Catherine
Grief series (2)
Day by the sea
Solomon, Joan
Children's life series (3)
Day democracy died
Gilman, George G
Edge series (24)
Day dreamer
Williams, Jesse Lynch
Stolen story series (2)
Day for damnation
Gerrold, David
War against the Chtorr trilogy (2)
Day God blew up my father's car
Krause, Jonathan
Christian situations series (1)
Day, her year in New York
Ray, Anna Chapin
Sidney and Janet series (3)
Day in the city
Coote, Roger
Outings series (1)
Day in the country
Coote, Roger
Outings series (2)
Day in the death of Dorothy Cassidy
Cleeves, Ann
Inspector Stephen Ramsay series (3)
Day in the hay
McArthur, John
Jack McBumby series (1)
Day in the life
Stine, Hank
Prisoner series (3)
Day in the life of a Victorian domestic servant
Davidoff, Leonore
Victorian day series (4)
Day in the life of a Victorian factory worker
Huggett, Frank Edward
Victorian day series (2)
Day in the life of a Victorian farm worker
Huggett, Frank Edward
Victorian day series (1)
Day in the life of a Victorian policeman
Garforth, John
Victorian day series (3)
Day in the life of Petronella Pig
Hauptmann, Tatjana
Petronella and Peregrine Pig series (1)
Day in the mountains
Coote, Roger
Outings series (3)
Day in the park
Reed, Giles
Munch Bunch stretch series (3)
Day it rained diamonds
Chaber, M E
Milo March series (15)
Day it rained forever
Lee, Robert Corwin
Michael Glenn series (2)
Day it snowed
Peterson, Hans
Day when series (1)
Day Jean-Pierre joined the circus
Gallico, Paul
Jean-Pierre series (4)
Day Jean-Pierre was pignapped
Gallico, Paul
Jean-Pierre series (2)
Day Jean-Pierre went round the world
Gallico, Paul
Jean-Pierre series (3)
Day Jimmy's boa at the washing
Noble, Trinka Hakes
Jimmy's boa series (1)
Day New York trembled
Lewis, Irwin
Horace Clarke series (2)
Day no pigs would die
Peck, Robert Newton
Vermont farm series (1)
Day of Atonement
Golding, Louis
Philip Massel series (2)
Day of atonement
Kellerman, Faye
Sergeant Peter Decker and Rina Lazarus series (4)
Day of autumn
Miles, Betty
Day of the seasons series (3)
Day of battle
Van de Water, Frederic Franklin
American Revolution series (3)
Day of death
Evans, Tabor
Longarm series (128)
Masterson, Louis
Morgan Kane series (27)
Day of disaster
Creasey, John
Department Z series (18)
Day of fear
Ashe, Gordon
Patrick Dawlish series (32)
Day of fury
Kirk, Matthew
Claw series (1)
Day of glory
Behaine, Rene
History of a society series (12)
Day of judgment
Mackenzie, Nigel
Professor Christopher Fenton series (1)
Day of mourning
Pendleton, Don
Mack Bolan series (62)
Day of murder
Bearshaw, Brian
Superintendent Robert Townley and Sergeant Roger Newman series (1)
Day of pleasure
Singer, Isaac Bashevis
Love and exile trilogy (3)
Day of plunderers
Grover, Marshall
Larry and Stretch series (312)
Day of reckoning
Carter, Nicholas
Nicholas Carter series (468)
Day of small things
Douglas, O
Priorsford series (3)
Day of spring
Miles, Betty
Day of the seasons series (4)
Day of summer
Miles, Betty
Day of the seasons series (1)
Day of the adder
Fitzgerald, Nigel
Superintendent Duffy series (9)
Day of the assassin
Carter, Nick
Nick Carter series (247)
Day of the big dollar
Chambers, Peter
Mark Preston series (21)
Day of the cheetah
Brown, Dale
Patrick McLanahan series (2)
Day of the Comancheros
Lawrence, Steven C
Tom Slattery series (9)
Day of the Daleks
Dicks, Terrance
Doctor Who series (6)
Day of the dancing sun
Hastings, Phyllis
Sussex trilogy (2)
Day of the dead
Spicer, Bart
Colonel Peregrine White series (1)
Day of the dingo
Carter, Nick
Nick Carter series (135)
Day of the dinosaur
Dixon, Franklin W
Hardy boys series (128)
Day of the dinosaurs
Bunting, Eve
Dinosaur machines series (1)
Stidworthy, John
Creatures from the past series (2)
Day of the dissonance
Foster, Alan Dean
Spellsinger series (3)
Day of the dove
Blish, James
Star trek original series (11)
Day of the Dragonstar
Bischoff, David
Dragonstar trilogy (1)
Day of the gun
Hunter, Neil
Brand series (5)
Muir, James A
Breed series (17)
Telfair, Richard
Wyoming Jones series (2)
Day of the guns
Spillane, Mickey
Tiger Mann series (1)
Day of the halfbreeds
McCurtin, Peter
Sundance series (29)
Day of the hangman
Hogan, Ray
Shawn Starbuck series (19)
Day of the hunter
Ahlswede, Ann
Doctor Cicero Smith series (1)
Day of the killers
Grover, Marshall
Larry and Stretch series (229)
Day of the Klesh
Foster, Michael Anthony
Ler series (3)
Day of the Mahdi
Carter, Nick
Nick Carter series (190)
Day of the minotaur
Swann, Thomas Burnett
Ancient history series (4)
Minotaur trilogy (3)
Day of the monster planet
Hodgman, Ann
Lunchroom series (9)
Day of the peppercorn kill
Wainwright, John
Chief Inspector Lennox series (5)
Northern Police series (35)
Day of the posse
Grover, Marshall
Larry and Stretch series (16)
Day of the Ram
Gault, William Campbell
Brock Callahan series (2)
Day of the redeemer
Redwood, Alec
Michael Grant series (3)
Day of the savage
Hunter, Neil
Bodie the Stalker series (6)
Day of the scorpion
Scott, Paul
British India quartet (2)
Day of the Starwind
Hill, Douglas
Last legionary series (4)
Day of the stranger
Ellis, Novalyne Price
Robert Ervin Howard series (2)
Day of the tornado
Grover, Marshall
Larry and Stretch series (158)
Day of the tyrant
Pournelle, Jerry
There will be war series (4)
Day of their return
Anderson, Poul
Future history series (2)
Day of vengeance
Grover, Marshall
Nevada Jim series (56)
Day of winter
Miles, Betty
Day of the seasons series (2)
Day of wrath
Stableford, Brian Michael
Dies irae trilogy (3)
Valin, Jonathan
Harry Stoner series (4)
Day on the farm
Reed, Giles
Munch Bunch stretch series (1)
Day Patch stood guard
Laird, Elizabeth
Little red tractor series (1)
Day she died
Reilly, Helen
Inspector Christopher McKee series (31)
Day Sidney ran off
Laird, Elizabeth
Little red tractor series (2)
Day Sidney was lost
Laird, Elizabeth
Little red tractor series (2)
Day Teddy didn't tidy up
Jungman, Ann
Teddy's days series (1)
Day Teddy got very worried
Jungman, Ann
Teddy's days series (3)
Day Teddy made new friends
Jungman, Ann
Teddy's days series (2)
Day Teddy wanted Grandad to notice him
Jungman, Ann
Teddy's days series (4)
Day that got lost
Lyon, Elinor
Jean and Anna series (1)
Day the ceiling fell down
Wayne, Jenifer
Winchester family series (1)
Day the chickens blew away
Peterson, Hans
Day when series (2)
Day the ducks went skating
Laird, Elizabeth
Little red tractor series (3)
Day the eighth grade ran the school
Kenyon, Kate
Cedar Groves Junior High School series (3)
Day the guinea-pig talked
Gallico, Paul
Jean-Pierre series (1)
Day the spaceship landed
Lord, Beman
Spaceship series (1)
Day the world ended
Rohmer, Sax
Gaston Max series (3)
Day they invaded New York
Lewis, Irwin
Horace Clarke series (1)
Day Veronica was nosy
Laird, Elizabeth
Little red tractor series (4)
Day we were mostly butterflies
King, Louise Wooster
Miss Moppet series (1)
Day will come
Feuchtwanger, Lion
Josephus trilogy (3)
Day with Mary Mouse
Blyton, Enid
Mary Mouse series (16)
Day with Noddy
Blyton, Enid
Noddy picture books series (2)
Day with three little rabbits
McCarthy, Ruth
Three little rabbits series (1)
Day without wind
Mayne, William
Islands series (2)
Daybook
Truitt, Anne
Journal of an artist series (1)
Daybreak
Gibbs, Anthony
John Archer series (2)
Nexo, Martin Andersen
Pelle the conqueror series (4)
Daybreak on a different mountain
Greenland, Colin
Daybreak series (1)
Daybreak 2250AD
Norton, Andre
Central Control series (1)
Daybreakers
Curry, Jane Louise
Abaloc series (3)
Apple Lock series (1)
Callie series (2)
Prince Lincoas series (1)
L'Amour, Louis
Sackett family series (6)
Daylight murder
McGuire, Paul
Chief Inspector Cummings series (3)
Superintendent Fillinger series (6)
Daylight robbery
Bobin, John William
Sexton Blake series (80)
Daymaker
Halam, Ann
Inland trilogy (1)
Days are just packed
Watterson, Bill
Calvin and Hobbes series (12)
Days at the morn
Chotzinoff, Samuel
Lost paradise series (2)
Days at Wickham
Barber, Anne Viccars
Wickham series (1)
Days before yesterday
Hamilton, Frederic
Vanished pomps of yesterday series (1)
Day's end
Bright, Pamela
Nursing trilogy (3)
Day's march nearer home
Parkinson, Roger
War Cabinet trilogy (3)
Days of Auld Lang Syne
Maclaren, Ian
Drumtochty series (2)

Days of blood
Pike, Charles R
Jubal Cade series (9)
Days of danger
Creasey, John
Department Z series (9)
Days of glory
Stableford, Brian Michael
Dies irae trilogy (1)
Days of his grace
Johnson, Eyvind
Olof tetralogy (4)
Days of misfortune
Stein, Aaron Marc
Tim Mulligan and Elsie Mae Hunt series (10)
Days of our years
Van Paassen, Pierre
Days series (1)
Days of '76
Pennington, Link
Frank Slade series (1)
Days of the phoenix
Brooks, Van Wyck
Scenes and portraits series (2)
Days of thunder
Hartmann, Michael
Ben Dryden series (2)
Days of vengeance
Guenter, C H
Robert Urban series (7)
Day's play
Milne, Alan Alexander
Day's play series (1)
Days that speak
Goode, Evelyn
Polly-Dear, Rod and Small series (1)
Days were too short
Pagnol, Marcel
Remembrances of childhood series (1)
Days with Frog and Toad
Lobel, Arnold
Frog and Toad series (4)
Daytime
Wilmer, Diane
Step by step series (1)
Daytime and Baby Jay
VerDorn, Bethea
Baby Jay series (1)
Dayworld
Farmer, Philip Jose
Dayworld series (1)
Dayworld breakup
Farmer, Philip Jose
Dayworld series (3)
Dayworld rebel
Farmer, Philip Jose
Dayworld series (2)
Dazzle
O'Brien, Edna
Dazzle series (1)
Dazzling twenties
Lindop, Edmund
Modern America series (1)
Deacon's dagger
Albany, James
S.A.S. series (3)
Dead
Perry, Mark Christopher
Morigu series (2)
Dead against my principles
Hopkins, Kenneth
Doctor William Blow and Professor Gideon Manciple series (2)
Dead aim
Dawson, Clay
Long Rider series (24)
Wilcox, Collin
Lieutenant Frank Hastings series (3)
Dead air
Lupica, Mike
Peter Finley series (1)
Dead alive
Darlton, Clark
Perry Rhodan series (48)
Dead and buried
Engel, Howard
Benny Cooperman series (7)
Dead and doggone
Conant, Susan
Dog trainer mystery series (2)
Dead and done for
Reeves, Robert
Cellini Smith series (1)
Dead and dumb
Crispin, Edmund
Gervase Fen series (4)
Dead and gone
Bird, Brandon
Hampton Hume series (3)
Dead and paid for
Olden, Marc
Hawthorne Albert Harker series (2)
Dead and the damned
Baker, William Howard
Richard Quintain series (12)
Dead and the deadly
Trimble, Louis
Martin Zane series (2)
Dead angel
Dolph, Jack
Doc Connor series (5)
Dead are blind
Afford, Max
Jeffery Blackburn series (3)
Dead are dangerous
Marshall, Lovat
Sugar Kane series (14)
Dead are discreet
Lyons, Arthur
Jacob Asch series (1)
Dead are silent
Marshall, Lovat
Sugar Kane series (13)
Dead as a dinosaur
Lockridge, Frances
Bill Wiegand series (16)
Mister and Mrs North series (17)
Dead as a dodo
Edwards, Lynne
Dodo series (1)
O'Brine, Manning
Michael O'Kelly series (3)
Dead as a dummy
Homes, Geoffrey
Jose Manuel Madero series (2)
Dead at first hand
Ross, Jonathan
Superintendent George Rogers series (3)
Dead at sunset
Scott, Bradford
Walt Slade series (64)
Dead at the take-off
Dent, Lester
Chance Malloy series (1)
Dead babes in the wood
Olsen, D B
Professor A Pennyfeather series (6)
Dead-bang
Prather, Richard Scott
Shell Scott series (36)
Dead beat
McDermid, Val
Kate Brannigan series (1)
Dead birds
Milne, John
James Jenner series (1)
Jimmy Jenner series (1)
Dead bolt
Obstfeld, Raymond
Harry Gould series (4)
Dead butler caper
Norman, Frank
Ed Nelson series (1)
Dead by morning
Simpson, Dorothy
Inspector Luke Thanet series (9)
Dead by now
Erskine, Margaret
Inspector Septimus Finch series (7)
Dead by the light of the moon
Wells, Tobias
Detective Knute Severson series (3)
Dead calm
Williams, Charles
John Ingram series (2)
Dead can tell
Reilly, Helen
Inspector Christopher McKee series (9)
Dead canary
Fox, James M
Jerry Long and Chuck Conley series (3)
Dead center
Langley, Lee
Lieutenant Christopher Jensen series (2)
Dead centre
Langley, Lee
Lieutenant Christopher Jensen series (2)
Wood, Ted
Reid Bennett series (3)
Dead certain
McNab, Claire
Inspector Carol Ashton and Sergeant Mark Bourke series (5)
Sterling, Stewart
Gil Vine series (8)
Dead certainty
Janson, Hank
Hank Janson series (225)
Dead circuit
Rattray, Simon
Hugo Bishop series (5)
Dead clever
Jeffries, Roderic Graeme
Inspector Enrique Alvarez series (13)
Dead commando
Landsborough, Gordon
Desert commandos series (4)
Dead crazy
Pickard, Nancy
Jenny Cain series (5)
Dead darling
Craig, Jonathan
Pete Selby series (1)
Dead do talk
Bentley, John
Dick Marlow series (6)
Dead dogs bite
Curtiss, Elizabeth Mangam
Nathaniel Bunce series (2)
Dead don't care
Latimer, Jonathan
Bill Crane series (4)
Dead don't scare
Marlowe, Piers
Frank Drury and Inspector Bill Hazard series (1)
Dead don't scream
Gribble, Leonard Reginald
Superintendent Anthony Slade series (42)
Dead don't speak
Erskine, Margaret
Inspector Septimus Finch series (8)
Dead drop in Havana
Guenter, C H
Robert Urban series (4)
Dead drunk
Bagby, George
Inspector Schmidt series (23)
Conway, Peter
Inspector Newton series (5)
Howard, Hartley
Glenn Bowman series (34)
Dead duck
Macnee, Patrick
Avengers series (2)
Dead easy
Pendleton, Don
SuperBolan series (6)
Russell, Enid Sherry
Ben Louis series (3)
Dead easy for Dover
Porter, Joyce
Chief Inspector Wilfred Dover series (9)
Dead end
Cruz, Mark
Kill Squad series (4)
Perry, Ritchie
Philis series (7)
Dead end delivery
Santiago, V J
Joseph Madden series (5)
Dead end game
Newman, Christopher
Joe Dante series (7)
Dead end in Mayfair
Gribble, Leonard Reginald
Superintendent Anthony Slade series (41)
Dead-end option
Obstfeld, Raymond
Harry Gould series (2)
Dead end street
Murphy, Warren Burton
Edward Razoni and William Jackson series (2)
Dead end street, no outlet
Thayer, Lee
Peter Clancy series (22)
Dead Ernest
Mitchell, James
Ron Hogget series (2)
Tilton, Alice
Leonidas Witherall series (7)
Dead Eye
Reese, John
Jefferson Hewitt series (10)
Ross, Jonathan
Superintendent George Rogers series (11)
Dead fall
Kirk, Philip
Butler series (8)
Dead file
Copper, Basil
Mike Faraday series (8)
Dead for a ducat
Bruce, Leo
Carolus Deene series (3)
Payne, Laurence
Chief Inspector Sam Birkett series (5)
Mark Savage series (4)
Reilly, Helen
Inspector Christopher McKee series (8)
Dead for a penny
Goodrum, Charles Alvin
Edwin George series (2)
Dead forger
Pollard, Alfred Oliver
David Wilshaw series (4)
Dead game
Avallone, Michael
Ed Noon series (3)
Hammond, Gerald
Keith Calder series (1)
Dead girls
Ibarguengoitia, Jorge
Dead girls series (1)
Dead girl's shoes
Cobb, Belton
Bryan Armitage series (7)
Inspector Cheviot Burmann series (31)
Kitty Armitage series (4)
Dead giveaway
Brett, Simon
Charles Paris series (11)
Nelson, Hugh Lawrence
Steve Johnson series (5)
Dead heart
Roderus, Frank
Carl Heller series (6)
Dead heat
Ayres, Paul
Flash Casey series (6)
Barnes, Linda
Michael Spraggue series (3)
Obstfeld, Raymond
Harry Gould series (3)
Prather, Richard Scott
Shell Scott series (25)
Dead heat at Le Mans
Speed, Eric
Wynn and Lonny racing series (5)
Dead heat at Long Beach
Bethancourt, Tomas Ernesto
Doris Fein series (8)
Dead hero
Gault, William Campbell
Brock Callahan series (7)
Dead in a ditch
Gunn, Victor
Chief Inspector Bill Cromwell series (31)
Dead in a row
Butler, Gwendoline
Inspector John Coffin series (1)
Inspector William Winter series (2)
Dead in Aqaba
Guenter, C H
Robert Urban series (5)
Dead in bed
Kane, Henry
Peter Chambers series (16)
Keene, Day
Johnny Aloha series (1)
Dead in no time
Temple-Ellis, N A
Inspector Wren series (2)
Montrose Arbuthnot series (4)
Dead in Texas
Scott, Bradford
Walt Slade series (24)
Dead in the morning
Yorke, Margaret
Doctor Patrick Grant series (1)
Dead in the scrub
Oliphant, B J
Shirley McClintock series (1)
Dead in the water
Smith, Julie
Rebecca Schwartz series (4)
Wood, Ted
Reid Bennett series (1)
Dead innocent
Winn, Patrick
Inspector Lyon series (4)
Dead is forever
Redmond, Anton Edward
Bill Slaker series (3)
Dead is the door-nail
Haggard, Paul
Mike Warlock series (1)
Dead kingdom
Harris, Geraldine
Seven citadels series (3)
Dead knock
Turnbull, Peter
P Division series (2)
Dead lagoon
Dibdin, Michael
Aurelio Zen series (4)
Dead letter
Clark, Douglas
Inspector George Masters series (20)
Murphy, Warren Burton
Digger Burroughs series (3)
Riggs, John Raymond
Garth Ryland series (7)
Valin, Jonathan
Harry Stoner series (3)
Dead letter drop
James, Peter
Max Flynn series (1)
Dead liberty
Aird, Catherine
Inspector C D Sloan series (12)
Dead lifeguard
Stine, Robert Lawrence
Fear Street super chiller series (6)
Dead line
McCutchan, Philip
Commander Esmonde Shaw series (7)
Dead-line
Tuttle, Wilbur Coleman
Hashknife Hartley and Sleepy Stevens series (4)
Dead lion
Bonett, John
Professor Mandrake series (1)
Dead little rich girl
Harknett, Terry
Stephen Wayne series (4)
Dead loss
Cronin, Michael
James Hellier series (2)
Petrie, Rhona
Inspector Marcus Maclurg series (4)
Dead lucky
Howard, Tom
Jack Reid series (1)
Dead man alive
Cory, Desmond
Johnny Fedora series (5)
Dead man are dangerous
Weston, Garnett
Highway series (2)
Dead man at the window
Toussant-Samat, Jean
Monsieur Levert series (2)
Dead man calling
Black, Gavin
Paul Harris series (2)
Dead man control
Reilly, Helen
Inspector Christopher McKee series (6)
Dead, man, dead
Alexander, David
Bart Hardin series (8)
Lieutenant Romano series (9)
Dead man drifting
Sewart, Alan
Detective Sergeant Chamberlayne series (5)
Dead man falling
Cory, Desmond
Johnny Fedora series (3)
Dead man in Catfish Bay
Christian, Mary Blount
High-low mysteries series (2)
Dead man in Deadwood
Dixon, Franklin W
Hardy boys case files series (87)
Dead man inside
Starrett, Vincent
Walter Ghost series (2)
Dead man laughs
Gunn, Victor
Chief Inspector Bill Cromwell series (8)
Dead man live
Grant, Maxwell
Shadow series (18)
Dead Man Manor
Williams, Valentine
Mister Treadgold series (1)
Dead man murder
Newman, Bernard
Papa Pontivy series (9)
Dead man out of mind
Charles, Kate
David Middleton-Brown series (4)

Rattray, Simon
Hugo Bishop series (4)
Dead skip
Gores, Joe
DKA file series (1)
Dead sleep for keeps
Winter, Bevis
Steve Craig series (3)
Dead sleep late
Kennedy, Elliot
Griff Dexter series (5)
Dead snake's venom
Kemp, Harold
Inspector James Brent series (2)
Dead so soon
Grayson, Richard
John Bryant series (4)
Dead-stick
Washburn, Livia Jane
Lucas Hallam series (2)
Dead stop
Burton, Miles
Inspector Arnold and Desmond Merrion series (27)
Disney, Doris Miles
Jeff Dimarco series (1)
Dead storage
Bagby, George
Inspector Schmidt series (26)
Thayer, Lee
Peter Clancy series (19)
Dead stranger
Carter, Nicholas
Nicholas Carter series (227)
Dead sure
Sterling, Stewart
Gil Vine series (2)
Dead take no bows
Burke, Richard
Quinny Hite series (1)
Dead tale-tellers
Chance, John Newton
Jonathan Blake series (26)
Dead thing in the pool
Stein, Aaron Marc
Tim Mulligan and Elsie Mae Hunt series (16)
Dead time
Bland, Eleanor Taylor
Marti MacAlister series (1)
Dead to rights
Davis, Kenn
Carver Bascombe series (3)
Dead to the world
Durbridge, Francis
Philip Holt series (2)
Sterling, Stewart
Gil Vine series (6)
Dead travel fast
Tate, Richard
Marcus Obadiah series (1)
Dead upstairs in the tub
Brett, Michael
Pete McGrath series (2)
Dead voice
Wills, Cecil Melville
Superintendent Roger Ellerdine and Sergeant Cherry Blossom series (6)
Dead walk
Collins, Gilbert
Hugh Carding series (4)
Dead water
Marsh, Ngaio
Inspector Roderick Alleyn series (23)
Radford, Edwin
Doctor Manson series (34)
Dead weight
Fenisong, Ruth
Captain Gridley Nelson series (13)
Kane, Frank
Johnny Liddell series (4)
Dead who lived
Grant, Maxwell
Shadow series (152)
Dead winter
Tapply, William George
Brady Coyne series (8)
Dead with sorrow
Audemars, Pierre
Monsieur Pinaud series (8)
Dead woman of the year
Pentecost, Hugh
John Jericho series (4)
Lieutenant Pascal series (6)
Dead woman's ditch
Nash, Simon
Inspector Montero and Adam Ludlow series (4)
Dead won't bite
Browne, Douglas Gordon
Major Maurice Hemyock series (2)
Dead wrong
Bagby, George
Inspector Schmidt series (28)
Cruz, Mark
Kill Squad series (3)
Kienzle, William Xavier
Father Robert Koesler series (15)
Sterling, Stewart
Gil Vine series (1)
Wales, Mike
Leatherhand series (4)
Dead yellow women
Hammett, Dashiell
Continental Op series (5)
Dead yesterday
Fenisong, Ruth
Captain Gridley Nelson series (6)
Dead zone strike
Robbins, David
Blade series (10)
Deader they fall
Chambers, Peter
Mark Preston series (19)
Deadest thing you ever saw
Ross, Jonathan
Superintendent George Rogers series (4)
Deadfall
Dixon, Franklin W
Hardy boys case files series (60)
Pronzini, Bill
Private Eye series (16)
Deadhead
Carpenter, Carleton
Chester Long series (2)
Deadheads
Hill, Reginald
Superintendent Andrew Dalziel and Sergeant Pascoe series (13)
Deadlier of the species
Reid, Desmond
Sexton Blake series (1589)
Deadlier sex
Striker, Randy
Dusky MacMorgan series (4)
Deadlier than the male
Conaway, Jim C
Jana Blake series (1)
Reymond, Henry
Bulldog Drummond series (18)
Deadliest dare
Dixon, Franklin W
Hardy boys case files series (30)
Deadliest game
McCurtin, Peter
Jim Rainey series (2)
Deadliest option
Meyers, Annette
Leslie Wetzon series (3)
Deadliest profession
Boyles, William
Bounty Hunter series (1)
Deadliest show in town
McQuay, Mike
Mathew Swain series (3)
Deadline
Dewey, Thomas Blanchard
Private Eye Mac series (13)
Heald, Tim
Simon Bognor series (3)
Howard, Hartley
Glenn Bowman series (18)
Leeson, Robert
Zarnia experiment series (3)
Macnee, Patrick
Avengers series (1)
Russell, Martin
Jim Larkin series (1)
Stahl, Hilda
Amber Ainslie series (1)
Deadline dolly
Enefer, Douglas
Dale Shand series (9)
Deadline for a critic
Kienzle, William Xavier
Father Robert Koesler series (9)
Deadline for a dame
Brody, Marc
Marc Brody series (35)
Deadline for a diplomat
Truss, Seldon
Inspector Bass series (1)
Deadline for a dream
Knox, Bill
Inspector Colin Thane and Phil Moss series (1)
Deadline for danger
Christian, Mary Blount
High-low mysteries series (1)
Maclean, Arthur
Sexton Blake series (1421)
Deadline for destruction
Leonard, Charles L
Paul Kilgerrin series (1)
Deadline for Macall
Fairlie, Gerard
Johnny Macall series (3)
Deadline for McGurk
Hildick, Edmund Wallace
McGurk series (2)
Deadline for murder
Halliday, Brett
Mike Shayne stories series (9)
Deadline two A.M.
Pike, Robert L
Lieutenant Jim Reardon series (4)
Deadlines
Travis, Elizabeth
Ben and Carrie Porter series (1)
Deadlock
Busby, Roger
Detective Inspector Leric series (3)
Fenisong, Ruth
Captain Gridley Nelson series (7)
Forbes, Colin
Tweed, Grey and Newman series (5)
Page, Emma
Inspector Kelsey series (7)
Paretsky, Sara
V I Warshawski series (2)
Reno, Bill
Badge series (21)
Richardson, Dorothy Miller
Pilgrimage series (6)
Deadly ackee
Hadley, Joan
Theo Bloomer series (2)
Deadly admirer
Green, Christine
Kate Kinsella series (2)
Deadly affair
Le Carre, John
George Smiley series (1)
Deadly alliance
Crawford, William
Colin Stryker series (4)
Deadly Aphrodite
Bethancourt, Tomas Ernesto
Doris Fein series (6)
Deadly aria
Myers, Paul
Mark Holland series (3)
Deadly attraction
Hoh, Diane
Nightmare Hall series (3)
Deadly avengers
Hardin, J D
Raider series (28)
Deadly bedfellows
Davis, Frederick Clyde
Schyler Cole and Luke Speare series (5)
Deadly beloved
Ard, William
Timothy Dane series (9)
Knight, Alanna
Inspector Faro series (3)
Strange, John Stephen
Barney Gantt series (7)
Deadly birdman
Buck, Peter
Marc Dean series (3)
Deadly but delectable
McCall, K T
Johnny Buchanan series (6)
Deadly cadenza
Myers, Paul
Mark Holland series (2)
Deadly caution
Page, Jake
Mo Bowdre series (2)
Deadly chase
Dixon, Franklin W
Hardy boys series (68)
Eshleman, John Morton
Lieutenant Larry Koharik series (2)
Deadly Christmas
Pascal, Francine
Sweet Valley High series (111)
Deadly climate
Barth, Richard
Margaret Binton series (5)
Deadly connection
Cunningham, Chet
Team three series (1)
Deadly cotton heart
Dennis, Ralph
Jim Hardman series (8)
Deadly crescendo
Myers, Paul
Mark Holland series (6)
Deadly crusade
Chase, Philip
Aaron Eisenberg and William Kendall series (1)
Deadly crusader
Streib, Dan
Michael Hawk series (1)
Deadly cyborgs
Edwards, Paul
John Eagle series (9)
Deadly daffodils
Silverwood, Roger
Superintendent Cawthorne series (1)
Deadly deal
Jason, Stuart
Butcher series (5)
Tanner, Clay
Chance Sharpe series (9)
Deadly deceit
Burgess, Eric
Harry Tong series (3)
Deadly delight
Stein, Aaron Marc
Matt Erridge series (6)
Deadly derringer
Roberts, J R
Gunsmith series (121)
Deadly diamond
Storm, Joan
Sarah Vanessa series (3)
Deadly discretion
Ramsay, Diana
Lieutenant Meredith series (2)
Deadly ditto
Hale, Christopher
Lieutenant Bill French series (11)
Deadly diva
Carter, Nick
Nick Carter series (245)
Deadly doctor
Jason, Stuart
Butcher series (10)
Deadly doctors
Marquis, Max
Harry Timberlake series (2)
Deadly doll
Barbette, Jay
Harry Butten series (3)
Kane, Henry
Peter Chambers series (5)
Deadly dollars
Bridges, Ben
Carter O'Brien series (5)
Grover, Marshall
Larry and Stretch series (244)
Deadly doubles
Carter, Nick
Nick Carter series (119)
Keene, Carolyn
Nancy Drew files series (7)
Deadly downbeat
Burke, Jonathan
Mike Merriman series (2)
Deadly drought
Alexander, Gary
Superintendent Bamsan Kiet series (5)
Deadly Dutchman
Blaine, John
Rick Brant series (22)
Deadly dwarf
Robeson, Kenneth
Doc Savage series (28)
Deadly earnest
Cockin, Joan
Inspector Cam and Beaver series (3)
Deadly edge
Stark, Richard
Parker series (13)
Deadly encounter
Montgomery, Raymond A
Rebels in the New World series (6)
Deadly engagement
Dixon, Franklin W
Hardy boys case files series (90)
Deadly errand
Green, Christine
Kate Kinsella series (1)
Deadly eyes
Herbert, James
Rats trilogy (1)
Deadly force
Dixon, Mark
Deadly Force series (1)
Deadly games
Nelson, Peter N
Sylvia Smith-Smith series (5)
Topol, Edward
Shamrayev series (2)
Deadly gold
Roberts, J R
Gunsmith series (138)
Rossiter, John
Roger Tallis series (4)
Deadly green
Rossiter, John
Roger Tallis series (2)
Deadly group down under
Morgan, Patrick
Operation Hang Ten series (3)
Deadly healer
Roberts, J R
Gunsmith series (58)
Deadly homecoming
George, Theodore
Lieutenant Al Zimmerman series (2)
Deadly horse-race
Janson, Hank
Hank Janson series (232)
Deadly image
Coxe, George Harmon
Flash Casey series (6)
Deadly in New York
Ramm, Carl
James Hawker series (4)
Deadly innocents
Sadler, Mark
Paul Shaw series (6)
Deadly intent
Keene, Carolyn
Nancy Drew files series (2)
Rowe, Anne
Inspector Barry series (3)
Deadly interlude
O'Brine, Manning
Michael O'Kelly series (4)
Deadly is the evil tongue
Hocking, Anne
Inspector William Austen series (4)
Deadly jailbreak
Evans, Tabor
Longarm series (133)
Deadly jest
Markham, Virgil
Myles Rusby series (2)
Deadly joke
Pentecost, Hugh
Pierre Chambrun series (7)
Deadly justice
Bernhardt, William
Justice series (3)
Colter, Dale
Regulator series (3)
Deadly kitten
Brown, Carter
Rick Holman series (17)
Deadly legacy
Arden, William
Kane Jackson series (5)
Blake, Christina
Inspector Donald Dobbs series (2)
Deadly liars
Preston, John
Mission of Alex Kane series (3)
Deadly lover
Saber, Robert O
Carl Good series (2)
Deadly lovers
Graham, Anthony
Frank Richmond series (1)
Deadly manhunt
Rosenberger, Joseph
Death Merchant series (32)
Deadly meeting
Bernard, Robert
Millicent Hetherege series (1)
Deadly memories
Roberts, J R
Gunsmith series (75)
Deadly Miss Ashley
Davis, Frederick Clyde
Schyler Cole and Luke Speare series (1)
Deadly mission
Daniel, Roland
Brian O'Malley series (2)
Janson, Hank
Hank Janson series (66)
Deadly nightcap
Carmichael, Harry
John Piper and Quinn series (3)
Hawton, Hector
Asmun Hill series (4)
Stewart, Flora
Inspector Newsom series (1)
Deadly nightshade
Cameron, Kate
Holderly Hall series (4)
Daly, Elizabeth
Henry Gamadge series (2)

Fraser, James
Inspector Bill Aveyard series (3)
Deadly noose
Foley, Rae
Hiram Potter series (7)
Deadly objectives
Taylor, Laurie Aylma
J J Jamison series (3)
Deadly orbit mission
Mason, Francis Van Wyck
Colonel Hugh North series (26)
Deadly pattern
Clark, Douglas
Inspector George Masters series (3)
Deadly perfume
Thomas, Gordon
David Morton series (1)
Deadly peril
Olden, Marc
Robert Sand series (4)
Deadly persuasion
Mitchell, Scott
Brock Devlin series (3)
Reid, Desmond
Sexton Blake series (1522)
Deadly petard
Jeffries, Roderic Graeme
Inspector Enrique Alvarez series (7)
Deadly piece
Hamill, Pete
Sam Briscoe series (2)
Deadly practice
Green, Christine
Kate Kinsella series (3)
Deadly prey
Hayes, Ralph Eugene
John Yard series (5)
Deadly promise
Nixon, Joan Lowery
Deadly promise series (2)
Deadly putter
Dexter, Ted
Jack Stenton series (2)
Deadly quest
Peel, John
U.N.C.L.E. files series (9)
Deadly quiet
Enefer, Douglas
Dale Shand series (1)
Deadly race
Jacobs, Thomas Curtis Hicks
Temple Fortune series (9)
Deadly reaper
Smith, Clark
Nicky Mahoun series (2)
Deadly reflections
Friedman, Mickey
Georgia Lee Maxwell series (1)
Deadly rehearsal
Peterson, Audrey
Jane Winfield and Andrew Quentin series (4)
Deadly relations
Finlay, D G
Watchman chronicles series (3)
Thomson, June
Inspector Finch series (6)
Deadly reunion
McCray, Mike
Black Berets series (1)
Deadly rhyme
Gonzalez, Gloria
Twilight series (25)
Deadly safari
McQuillan, Karin
Jazz Jasper series (1)
Deadly scarab
Carter, Nicholas
Nicholas Carter series (413)
Deadly score
Myers, Paul
Mark Holland series (5)
Deadly secret
Abbot, Anthony
Thatcher Colt series (8)
Adams, Nicholas
Horror High series (4)
Deadly seeds
Murphy, Warren Burton
Destroyer series (21)
Deadly sex
Webb, Jack
Father Joseph Shanley and Sammy Golden series (7)
Deadly shade of gold
Macdonald, John Dann
Travis McGee series (5)
Deadly shadow
Brightfield, Richard
Choose your own adventure series (46)
Deadly sickness
Penn, John
Inspector George Thorne and Sergeant Bill Abbot series (5)
Deadly silence
Derrick, Lionel
Penetrator series (36)
Deadly sleep
Cowan, Dale
Twilight series (1)
Deadly snow
Decker, Jake
Steve Sinclair series (1)
Deadly sonata
Myers, Paul
Mark Holland series (4)
Deadly state of mind
Hays, Lee
Columbo series (6)
Deadly stranger
McLennan, Will
Ramseys series (8)
Deadly streak
Enefer, Douglas
Sam Bawtrey series (11)
Deadly summer
Pascal, Francine
Sweet Valley High super thriller series (4)
Deadly sunshade
Taylor, Phoebe Atwood
Asey Mayo series (16)
Deadly to bed
Tracy, Don
Giff Speer series (1)
Deadly trade
Jones, Bradshaw
Claude Ravel series (9)
Deadly trap
Pentecost, Hugh
Julian Quist series (8)
Sharp, Allen
Storytrails series (10)
Deadly truth
McCloy, Helen
Basil Willing series (3)
Deadly valentine
Hart, Carolyn Gimpel
Annie Laurance and Max Darling series (6)
Deadly variations
Myers, Paul
Mark Holland series (1)
Deadly vigilantes
Ellis, Wesley
Lone Star series (111)
Deadly weapon
Miller, Wade
Lieutenant Austin Clapp series (1)
Deadly withdrawal
Martin, Cort
Jared Bolt series (21)
Deadman
Jackson, Jon Anthony
Sergeant Fang Mulheisen series (5)
Deadman Butte
Mitchum, Hank
Stage coach station series (34)
Deadman's Bay
Knight, Leonard Alfred
Jerry Scant series (1)
Deadmen shouldn't die
Darlton, Clark
Perry Rhodan series (132)
Deadpan
Schock, T A
Daniel Keel series (2)
Deadridge doll
Fletcher, Dirk
Spur McCoy series (34)
Dead's good company
Sherwin, Judith Johnson
Waste triptych (3)
Deadspawn
Lumley, Brian
Necroscope series (5)
Deadspeak
Lumley, Brian
Necroscope series (4)
Deadstick
Faherty, Terence
Owen Keane series (2)
Deadwalk
Goulart, Ron
Vampirella series (3)
Deadwood
Braun, Matt
Luke Starbuck series (6)
Mitchum, Hank
Stage coach station series (11)
Deadwood City
Packard, Edward
Choose your own adventure series (8)
Deaf, dumb and blonde
Morton, Anthony
Baron series (26)
Deal
Lefcourt, Peter
Hollywood series (1)
Deal in diamonds
Carter, Nicholas
Nicholas Carter series (93)
Deal in violence
Arden, William
Kane Jackson series (2)
Deal me out
Blazer, J S
Donald Bracken and James Rowland Woodward series (1)
Corris, Peter
Cliff Hardy series (9)
Deal of the century
Martin, Ian Kennedy
Sweeney series (3)
Deal Woods
Griswold, Latta
Deering series (3)
Dealer
Collins, Max Allan
Quarry series (3)
Torrio, Vincente
Hoods series (4)
Dealer of death
Hartman, Dane
Dirty Harry Callahan series (12)
Dealer takes three
Grover, Marshall
Larry and Stretch series (176)
Dealer's move
Wilson, Steve
Dealer series (1)
Dealer's war
Wilson, Steve
Dealer series (2)
Dealer's wheels
Wilson, Steve
Dealer series (3)
Dealing out death
Ballard, Willis Todhunter
Bill Lennox series (3)
Dealing with dragons
Wrede, Patricia Collins
Enchanted forest series (1)
Deans and Mr Popple
Fidler, Kathleen
Deans series (8)
Dean's daughters
Adams, Herbert
Major Roger Bennion series (22)
Dean's death
Lawrence, Alfred
Columbo series (2)
Deans defy danger
Fidler, Kathleen
Deans series (4)
Deans dive for treasure
Fidler, Kathleen
Deans series (5)
Deans' Dutch adventure
Fidler, Kathleen
Deans series (9)
Deans follow a clue
Fidler, Kathleen
Deans series (2)
Deans' lighthouse adventure
Fidler, Kathleen
Deans series (7)
Deans move in
Fidler, Kathleen
Deans series (1)
Deans solve a mystery
Fidler, Kathleen
Deans series (3)
Deans to the rescue
Fidler, Kathleen
Deans series (6)
Dean's watch
Goudge, Elizabeth
Cathedrals series (3)
Dear Celeste, my life is a mess
Lantz, Francess Lin
Making out series (2)
Dear cousin
Quin-Harkin, Janet
Sugar and spice series (4)
Dear daughter dead
Hough, Stanley Bennett
Inspector Brentford series (2)
Dear, dead days
Barbette, Jay
Harry Butten series (2)
Dear, dead girls
Morland, Nigel
Mrs Palmyra Pym series (23)
Dear, dead Harry
Scott, Milton
Doctor Alexander Cornell series (2)
Dear dead mother-in-law
Hill, Katharine
Lorna Donahue series (1)
Dear dead woman
Chambers, Dana
Jim Steele series (8)
Gilbert, Anthony
Arthur Crook series (7)
Dear, deadly beloved
Flagg, John
Hart Muldoon series (2)
Dear departed
Burton, Anne
Richard Trenton series (1)
Dear diary, the following is top secret
Evans, Greg
Luann series (9)
Dear doctor
Downe, Patrick
Doctor series (1)
Dear Doctor Dale
Antony, Jonquil
Dale family series (3)
Dear Doctor Heartbreak
Harrell, Janice
In crowd series (2)
Dear Ducks, and other Ballygullion stories
Doyle, Lynn
Ballygullion series (2)
Dear Emily
Stewart, Maureen
Emily series (1)
Dear Enemy
Webster, Jean
Judy Abbott series (2)
Dear Fonzie
Johnston, William
Happy days series (7)
Dear Grandad, I hate Roland Roberts
Selway, Martina
Dear Grandad series (2)
Dear Judy, did you ever like a boy who didn't like you?
Baer, Judy
Dear Judy series (2)
Dear Judy, what's it like at your house
Baer, Judy
Dear Judy series (1)
Dear Laura
Stubbs, Jean
Inspector John Joseph Lintott series (1)
Dear little girl
Blanchard, Amy Ella
Dear little girl series (1)
Dear little girl at school
Blanchard, Amy Ella
Dear little girl series (2)
Dear little girl's summer holidays
Blanchard, Amy Ella
Dear little girl series (3)
Dear little girl's Thanksgiving holidays
Blanchard, Amy Ella
Dear little girl series (4)
Dear lovely Hart, I am desperate
Conford, Ellen
Carrie Wasserman series (1)
Dear Miss Demeanor
Hess, Joan
Claire Malloy series (3)
Dear old briar-patch
Burgess, Thornton Waldo
Nature stories series (4)
Dear ones all
Rikhoff, Jean
Timble family trilogy (1)
Dear papa
Bjorn, Thyra Ferre
Pastor Pontus Franzon series (4)
Dear Santa, make me a star
Roos, Stephen
Maple Street kids series (1)
Dear sister
Pascal, Francine
Sweet Valley High series (7)
Dear Teddy Robinson
Robinson, Joan Gale
Teddy Robinson series (4)
Dearer than all
Morrow, Honore Willsie
Abraham Lincoln series (1)
Dearer than life
Hocking, Joseph
Great War, French Front series (2)
Dearest enemy
Woods, Sara
Sir Nicholas Harding and Antony Maitland series (33)
Dearest girl
Taggart, Marion Ames
Pamela series (1)
Death about face
Kane, Frank
Johnny Liddell series (1)
Death about town
Grant, Maxwell
Shadow series (227)
Death after breakfast
Pentecost, Hugh
Pierre Chambrun series (13)
Death after evensong
Clark, Douglas
Inspector George Masters series (2)
Death after lunch
Abrahams, Robert
Pete Taylor series (1)
Death against the clock
Gilbert, Anthony
Arthur Crook series (32)
Death against Venus
Chambers, Dana
Jim Steele series (9)
Death ain't commercial
Bagby, George
Inspector Schmidt series (19)
Death, American style
Stacy, Ryder
Doomsday warrior series (12)
Death among doctors
Edwards, James G
Inspector Victor Bondurant series (6)
Death among friends
Lewis, Lange
Lieutenant Richard Tuck series (1)
Death among the dunes
Infante, Anne
Micky Douglas and Inspector Reeves series (2)
Death among the orchids
Morris, Thomas Baden
Inspector Headley series (2)
Death among the professors
Sproul, Kathleen
Dick Wilson series (2)
Death among the stars
Giles, Kenneth
Inspector Harry James and Sergeant Honeybody series (6)
Death among the sunbathers
Punshon, Ernest Robertson
Bobby Owen series (2)
Death among the tulips
Hocking, Anne
Inspector William Austen series (21)
Death and Benedict
Bayne, Isabella
Benedict Breeze series (1)
Death and birth of Savid Markand
Frank, Waldo
David Markand series (1)
Death and bright water
Mitchell, James
David Callan series (3)
Death and circumstance
Waugh, Hillary
Chief Fred Fellows series (6)
Death and his brother
Bidwell, Margaret
Mister Hodson series (2)
Death and Jack Slade
Brady, William S
Jared Hawk series (12)
Death and letters
Daly, Elizabeth
Henry Gamadge series (15)
Death and life of Superman
Stern, Roger
Superman series (7)
Death and Little Girl Blue
Hanson, Victor Joseph
Sexton Blake series (1541)
Death and Mary Dazill
Fitt, Mary
Superintendent Mallett series (5)
Death and Mister Gilly
Duncan, William Murdoch
Mister Gilly series (3)
Death and Mister Potter
Foley, Rae
Hiram Potter series (1)
Death and Mister Prettyman
Giles, Kenneth
Inspector Harry James and Sergeant Honeybody series (5)

Death and still life
Launay, Droo
Adam Flute series (4)
Death and taxes
Dewey, Thomas Blanchard
Private Eye Mac series (14)
Dodge, David
Whit Whitney series (1)
Death and the archdeacon
Harman, Neal
Protection Limited series (2)
Death and the bridegroom
Hurt, Freda Mary
Inspector Herbert Broom series (5)
Death and the bright day
Fitt, Mary
Superintendent Mallett series (11)
Death and the Chapman
Sedley, Kate
Roger Chapman series (1)
Death and the chaste apprentice
Barnard, Robert
Charlie Peace series (3)
Death and the dancing footman
Marsh, Ngaio
Inspector Roderick Alleyn series (11)
Death and the dear girls
Stagge, Jonathan
Doctor Hugh Westlake series (7)
Death and the devil
Whelton, Paul
Garry Dean series (1)
Death and the diplomat
Scherf, Margaret
Emily and Henry Bryce series (5)
Death and the doctors
Housman, Laurence
Palace plays series (3)
Death and the dogwalker
Orde, A J
Jason Lynx series (2)
Death and the Dutch uncle
Moyes, Patricia
Henry and Emmy Tibbett series (8)
Death and the dutiful daughter
Morice, Anne
Tessa Crichton Price series (5)
Death and the epicure
Laurence, Janet
Darina Lisle series (5)
Death and the gentle bull
Lockridge, Frances
Inspector Merton Heimrich series (9)
Death and the gilded man
Dickson, Carter
Sir Henry Merrivale series (14)
Death and the golden boy
Morland, Nigel
Mrs Palmyra Pym series (19)
Death and the joyful woman
Peters, Ellis
Inspector George Felse series (2)
Death and the leaping ladies
Drummond, Charles
Sergeant Reed series (2)
Death and the mad heroine
Dean, S F X
Professor Neil Kelly series (5)
Death and the maiden
Macdougall, James K
David Stuart series (2)
Mitchell, Gladys
Dame Beatrice Bradley series (20)
Patrick, Q
Lieutenant Timothy Trant series (3)
Radley, Sheila
Chief Inspector Douglas Quantrill series (1)
Death and the night watches
Bell, Vicars
Doctor Douglas Baynes series (5)
Death and the pleasant voices
Fitt, Mary
Superintendent Mallett series (9)
Death and the pregnant virgin
Haymon, Sylvia T
Inspector Ben Jurnet series (1)
Death and the princess
Barnard, Robert
Superintendent Perry Trethowan series (2)
Death and the professors
Sproul, Kathleen
Dick Wilson series (2)
Death and the shortest day
Fitt, Mary
Superintendent Mallett series (14)
Death and the single girl
Lewis, Elliott
Fred Bennett series (7)
Death and the south wind
Lester, Frank
Geoffrey Slade series (2)
Death and the Spider
Stockbridge, Grant
Richard Wentworth series (8)
Death and to-morrow
De Polnay, Peter
Death and to-morrow series (2)
Death and variations
Baker, Ivon
David Meynell series (3)
Death angel
Clason, Clyde B
Theocritus Lucius Westborough series (2)
Death-angel
Williamson, Jerry Neal
Lamia Zacharias series (2)
Death Angel's shadow
Wagner, Karl Edward
Kane series (2)
Death answers the bell
Williams, Valentine
Inspector Manderton series (4)
Sergeant Trevor Dene series (2)
Death arms
Jeter, Kevin W
Doctor Adder trilogy (3)
Death as a career move
Cook, Bruce
Antonio Cervantes series (3)
Death as an extra
Gielgud, Val
Inspector Simon Spears series (2)
Death at a masquerade
Corne, Molly E
Mac McIntyre series (1)
Death at Ash House
Burton, Miles
Inspector Arnold and Desmond Merrion series (26)
Death at breakfast
Rhode, John
Doctor Lancelot Priestley series (23)
Death at Broadcasting House
Gielgud, Val
Inspector Simon Spears series (1)
Death at Charity's Point
Tapply, William George
Brady Coyne series (1)
Death at Chestnut Hill
Nicolai, Charles
John Nolan series (2)
Death at court lady
Horler, Sydney
Sir Charles Knightley series (2)
Death at Crane's Court
Dillon, Eilis
Inspector Mike Kenny series (1)
Death at dancing stones
Fitt, Mary
Superintendent Mallett series (3)
Death at Dayton's Folly
Rath, Virginia
Rocky Allan series (1)
Death at Deepwood Grange
Underwood, Michael
Rosa Epton series (9)
Death at Devil-Fish Point
Boyle, Denis
Commander Moreton Shade series (2)
Death at Dyke's Corner
Lorac, E C R
Inspector Macdonald series (19)
Death at flight
Willock, Colin Dennistoun
Nathaniel Ironsides Goss series (1)
Death at Four Corners
Gilbert, Anthony
Scott Egerton series (3)
Death at half-term
Bell, Josephine
Doctor David Wintringham series (4)
Inspector Steven Mitchell series (4)
Death at Hallows End
Bruce, Leo
Carolus Deene series (14)
Death at his elbow
Walsh, James Morgan
Oliver Keene series (8)
Death at his private zoo
Howard, Tom
Jack Reid series (2)
Death at La Fenice
Leon, Donna
Commissario Guido Brunetti series (1)
Death at Lover's Leap
Dean, Robert George
Tony Hunter series (10)
Death at low tide
Burton, Miles
Inspector Arnold and Desmond Merrion series (17)
Death at noon
Chisholm, Matt
Rem McAllister series (3)
Death at one blow
Hamilton, Henrietta
Johnny and Sally Heldar series (2)
Death at Pyford Hall
Fisher, Douglas George
Jeff Tellford series (3)
Death at Saint Anselm's
Holland, Isabelle
Claire Aldington series (2)
Death at Saint Asprey's School
Bruce, Leo
Carolus Deene series (16)
Death at sea
Robinson, Vance
Justice trilogy (1)
Death at the bank
Francis, Basil
Sergeant Paul Dean series (1)
Death at the bar
Drummond, Charles
Sergeant Reed series (5)
Marsh, Ngaio
Inspector Roderick Alleyn series (10)
Death at the BBC
Sherwood, John
Celia Grant series (5)
Death at The Bottoms
Cunningham, Albert Benjamin
Sheriff Jess Roden series (4)
Death at the cascades
Farmer, Bernard James
Sergeant Jack Wigan series (1)
Death at the chase
Innes, Michael
Sir John Appleby series (24)
Death at the Chateau Noir
Radford, Edwin
Doctor Manson series (12)
Death at the club
Burton, Miles
Inspector Arnold and Desmond Merrion series (15)
Death at the crossroads
Burton, Miles
Inspector Arnold and Desmond Merrion series (7)
Death at the dam
Adams, Cleve Franklin
Rex McBride series (2)
Death at the dance
Rhode, John
Doctor Lancelot Priestley series (56)
Death at the deep end
Wentworth, Patricia
Miss Maud Silver series (20)
Death at The Dog
Cannan, Joanna
Inspector Guy Northeast series (2)
Death at the Dolphin
Marsh, Ngaio
Inspector Roderick Alleyn series (24)
Death at the door
Gilbert, Anthony
Arthur Crook series (13)
Death at the feast
Carter, Nicholas
Nicholas Carter series (302)
Death at the furlong post
Drummond, Charles
Sergeant Reed series (1)
Death at the helm
Rhode, John
Doctor Lancelot Priestley series (34)
Death at the horse show
Loder, Vernon
Inspector Chace series (2)
Death at the inn
Freeman, Richard Austin
Doctor John Evelyn Thorndyke series (24)
Rhode, John
Doctor Lancelot Priestley series (57)
Death at the manor
Corne, Molly E
Mac McIntyre series (2)
Death at the medical board
Bell, Josephine
Doctor David Wintringham series (8)
Death at the mike
Eichler, Alfred
Inspector Knickman series (2)
Martin Ames series (2)
Death at the opera
Mitchell, Gladys
Dame Beatrice Bradley series (5)
Death at the Pelican
Wills, Cecil Melville
Geoffrey Boscobell series (2)
Death at the president's lodging
Innes, Michael
Sir John Appleby series (1)
Death at the rodeo
Queen, Ellery
Ellery Queen series (6)
Death at the strike
Willock, Colin Dennistoun
Nathaniel Ironsides Goss series (2)
Death at the wedding
Duke, Madelaine
Doctor Norah North series (2)
Hocking, Anne
Inspector William Austen series (13)
Death at three
Rice, Craig
John Joseph Malone series (1)
Death at Traitor's Gate
Gunn, Victor
Chief Inspector Bill Cromwell series (34)
Death at Victoria Dock
Greenwood, Kerry
Phryne Fisher series (4)
Death at Windward Hill
Hultman, Helen Joan
Tim Asher series (2)
Death at Yew Corner
Forrest, Richard
Lyon and Bea Wentworth series (5)
Death awaits thee
Lang, Maria
Christer Wick series (2)
Death badge
Reno, Bill
Badge series (23)
Death beckons quietly
Duncan, William Murdoch
Superintendent Flagg series (1)
Death bed
Greenleaf, Stephen
John Marshall Tanner series (2)
Death before bedtime
Box, Edgar
Peter Cutler Sergeant series (2)
Death before breakfast
Adams, Cleve Franklin
Rex McBride series (2)
Bellairs, George
Detective Inspector Thomas Littlejohn series (37)
Fearon, Diana
Arabella Frant series (1)
Death before dinner
Lorac, E C R
Inspector Macdonald series (30)
Death before dying
Wilcox, Collin
Lieutenant Frank Hastings series (16)
Death before honour
Hume, David
Mick Cardby series (16)
Death before wicket
Spain, Nancy
Johnny Duvivien series (2)
Death behind the door
Macclure, Victor
Inspector Archie Burford series (3)
Death below zero
Muir, Thomas
Roger Crammond series (4)
Death beneath the river
Rowland, John
Inspector Shelley series (14)
Death benefit
Petersen, Paul
Smugglers series (6)
Death benefits
Kahn, Michael A
Rachel Gold series (2)
Death beyond the go-thru
Kendrick, Baynard
Miles Standish Rice series (3)
Death beyond the Nile
Mann, Jessica
Tamara Hoyland series (5)
Death bird contract
Atlee, Philip
Joe Gall series (4)
Death blew out the candle
Knight, Kathleen Moore
Elisha Macomber series (1)
Death-blinder
King, Bernard
Starkadder trilogy (3)
Death boards the Lazy Lady
Darby, Ruth
Peter and Janet Barron series (1)
Death box
Lecale, Errol
Specialist series (4)
Quin, Basil Godfrey
James Clarkson-Parry series (1)
Death breaks the ring
Rath, Virginia
Michael Dundas series (4)
Death bringer
Tilley, Patrick
Amtrak wars series (5)
Death bringers
Orgill, Douglas
William Mallett series (1)
Death-bringers
Shannon, Dell
Lieutenant Luis Mendoza series (9)
Death brings in the new year
Bellairs, George
Detective Inspector Thomas Littlejohn series (16)
Death burns the candle
Trevor, Ralph
Superintendent Curtis Burke series (1)
Death business
Graham, Anthony
Frank Richmond series (2)
Death by analysis
Slovo, Gillian
Kate Baeier series (2)
Death by appointment
Bonnamy, Francis
Peter Shane series (1)
Death by arrangement
Meynell, Laurence Walter
Hooky Hefferman series (4)
Death by association
Lockridge, Frances
Inspector Merton Heimrich series (7)
Death by degrees
Wright, Eric
Inspector Charlie Salter series (10)
Death by demonstration
Carlon, Patricia
Jefferson Shields series (2)
Death by design
Keene, Carolyn
Nancy Drew files series (30)
Nash, Anne
Mark Tudor series (2)
Death by desire
Goyne, Richard
Paul Templeton series (4)
Death by dynamite
Bonney, Joseph L
Simon Rolfe series (1)
Death by fire
Pentecost, Hugh
George Crowder series (6)
Death by gaslight
Kurland, Michael
Sherlock Holmes sequels series (54)
Death by hoax
Black, Lionel
Kate Theobald series (3)
Death by inches
Shannon, Dell
Lieutenant Luis Mendoza series (10)
Death by invitation
Stockwell, Gail
Kingsley Toplitt series (1)
Death by marriage
Cousins, Edmund George
Colonel Richard Barne series (1)
Death by misadventure
Greenwood, Kerry
Phryne Fisher series (1)
Underwood, Michael
Superintendent Simon Manton series (8)
Death by night
Creasey, John
Department Z series (14)
Death by proxy
Grant, Maxwell
Shadow series (112)

Death from the air
Conde, Phillip
Dick Pemberty series (1)
Death from the ladies tee
Bartlett, James Y
Pete Hacker series (2)
Death fugue
McGuire, Paul
Superintendent Fillinger series (4)
Death gambit
Decker, Jake
Steve Sinclair series (3)
Death game
Charteris, Leslie
Saint series (38)
Death games
Pendleton, Don
Mack Bolan series (78)
Death gang
Skene, Anthony
Sexton Blake series (667)
Death gets an A
Smithies, Richard Hugo Ripman
Inspector William McAlpin series (1)
Death giver
Grant, Maxwell
Shadow series (30)
Death glow
Wallace, Robert
Phantom Detective series (16)
Death god's citadel
Coulson, Juanita
Krantin series (2)
Death goes ashore
Glanville, Alec
Inspector Dusty Muller and Tiny Meldrum series (1)
Death goes by bus
Cargill, Leslie
Morrison Sharpe series (1)
Death goes caving
Usher, Gray
Superintendent Michael Drexel series (5)
Death goes fishing
Lee, Edward
Red Blake series (2)
Death goes native
Long, Max
Komako Koa series (3)
Death goes on skis
Spain, Nancy
Johnny Duvivien series (4)
Miriam Birdseye series (1)
Death goes skiing
Schier, Norma
Kay Barth series (2)
Death goes to a reunion
Knight, Kathleen Moore
Elisha Macomber series (12)
Death goes to Brussels
Lambert, Rosa
Glyn Morgan series (1)
Death goes to the fair
Courage, John
David Cane series (2)
Death goes window shopping
Symonds, Francis Addington
Superintendent Maxwell Quayne series (2)
Death greets a guest
Ashton, Charles
Jack Atherley series (3)
Death grip
Ahern, Jerry
Defender series (9)
Conroy, Al
Johnny Morini series (2)
Death ground
Gorman, Edward
Leo Guild series (2)
Death had yellow eyes
Robeson, Kenneth
Doc Savage series (110)
Death hand play
Carter, Nick
Nick Carter series (192)
Death has a double
King, Frank
Doctor Frank King series (4)
Death has a name
Pendleton, Don
Mack Bolan series (96)
Death has a shadow
Procter, Maurice
Chief Inspector Harry Martineau series (19)
Death has a small voice
Lockridge, Frances
Bill Wiegand series (18)
Mister and Mrs North series (18)
Death has a thousand doors
Marlett, Melba
Sarah O'Brien series (1)
Death has a thousand entrances
Helm, Peter
Martin Ridgway series (2)
Death has a will
Long, Amelia Reynolds
Steve Carter series (3)
Death has deep roots
Gilbert, Michael Francis
Inspector Hazelrigg series (5)
Death has gray eyes
Grant, Maxwell
Shadow series (261)
Death has green fingers
Black, Lionel
Kate Theobald series (2)
Death has many doors
Brown, Fredric
Ed and Am Hunter series (5)
Death has no tongue
Cowdroy, Joan
Li Moh series (5)
Death has ten thousand doors
Chetwynd, Bridget
Petunia Best and Max Frend series (1)
Death has three lives
Halliday, Brett
Michael Shayne series (26)
Death has two doors
Bell, Vicars
Doctor Douglas Baynes series (3)
Death has two faces
Radford, Edwin
Doctor Manson series (35)
Death has two hands
Lawrence, David
Danny Leather series (2)
Death haunts the dark lane
Cunningham, Albert Benjamin
Sheriff Jess Roden series (15)
Death haunts the repertory
Plummer, Thomas Arthur
Detective Inspector Andrew Frampton series (31)
Death her destination
Jardine, Warwick
Sexton Blake series (1517)
Death hides a mask
Corne, Molly E
Mac McIntyre series (2)
Death house
Brisbane, Coutts
Sexton Blake series (651)
Death hunt
McCurtin, Peter
Marksman series (2)
McLennan, Will
Ramseys series (11)
Stillman, Ron
Tracker series (6)
Thompson, David
Nathaniel King series (8)
Death hunter
Thorne, Ramsay
Captain Gringo series (4)
Death hunters
Longtree, Warren T
Ruff Justice series (23)
Death importer
Chance, John Newton
Macinnes series (2)
Death in a chilly corner
Oellrichs, Inez
Matt Winters series (7)
Death in a deckchair
Beck, Kathrine Kristine
Iris Cooper and Jack Clancy series (1)
Death in a distant land
Livingston, Nancy
G D H Pringle series (4)
Death in a duffle coat
Burton, Miles
Inspector Arnold and Desmond Merrion series (53)
Death in a high latitude
Anderson, John Richard Lane
Major Peter Blair series (11)
Death in a hurry
Ashe, Gordon
Patrick Dawlish series (26)
Death in a little town
Woodthorpe, Ralph Carter
Matilda Perks series (1)
Death in a mist
Salter, Elizabeth
Inspector Michael Hornsley series (1)
Death in a pheasant's eye
Fraser, James
Inspector Bill Aveyard series (4)
Death in a quiet place
Cousins, Edmund George
Colonel Richard Barne series (6)
Death in a salubrious place
Burley, William John
Superintendent Charles Wycliffe series (4)
Death in a sleeping city
Wainwright, John
Northern Police series (1)
Death in a small world
Colburn, Laura
Carol Gates series (1)
Death in a strange country
Leon, Donna
Commissario Guido Brunetti series (2)
Death in a tenured position
Cross, Amanda
Professor Kate Fansler series (6)
Death in a white tie
Marsh, Ngaio
Inspector Roderick Alleyn series (7)
Death in aberration
Cooper, John C
Inspector James Dale series (2)
Death in Acapulco
Peterson, Jim
Mack Bolan series (26)
Death in act four
Francis, Basil
Inspector Ghent series (2)
Death in Albert Park
Bruce, Leo
Carolus Deene series (13)
Death in ambush
Bude, John
Inspector Meredith series (13)
Gilruth, Susan
Inspector Hugh Gordon and Liane Crawford series (2)
Death in Amsterdam
Freeling, Nicolas
Inspector Piet Van der Valk series (1)
Death in an armchair
Street, James
Eugene Mulcahy series (1)
Death in Ankara
Wood, Clement
Lal Reed series (1)
Death in Arcady
Phillips, Stella
Inspector Matthew Furnival series (3)
Death in arms
Philmore, R
Inspector Garnett series (1)
Death in autumn
Nabb, Magdalen
Marshal Guarnaccia series (4)
Death in B-minor
Lilly, Jean
Bruce Perkins series (2)
Death in Berlin
Kaye, Mary Margaret
Death series (2)
Death in blue folders
Maron, Margaret
Lieutenant Sigrid Harald series (3)
Death in Botanist's Bay
Ferrars, Elizabeth
Toby Dyke series (3)
Death in Budapest
Gielgud, Val
Inspector Simon Spears series (3)
Death in camera
Underwood, Michael
Rosa Epton series (7)
Death in clairvoyance
Bell, Josephine
Doctor David Wintringham series (9)
Inspector Steven Mitchell series (5)
Death in close-up
Livingston, Nancy
G D H Pringle series (5)
Death in cold print
Creasey, John
Inspector Roger West series (29)
Death in costume
McRoyd, Allan
Inspector Franklin Brady series (3)
Death in covert
Willock, Colin Dennistoun
Nathaniel Ironsides Goss series (3)
Death in Cyprus
Kaye, Mary Margaret
Death series (3)
Death in D Division
Brandon, John Gordon
Arthur Stukeley Pennington series (18)
Inspector Patrick Aloysius McCarthy series (40)
Death in dark glasses
Bellairs, George
Detective Inspector Thomas Littlejohn series (18)
Death in darkness
Douglas, George
Inspector Bonny Lee series (1)
White, Alan
Inspector Armstrong series (3)
Death in Deakins Wood
Petrie, Rhona
Inspector Marcus Maclurg series (1)
Death in denims
Gray, Dulcie
Roger Moore and the Crimefighters series (4)
Death in desolation
Bellairs, George
Detective Inspector Thomas Littlejohn series (45)
Death in despair
Bellairs, George
Detective Inspector Thomas Littlejohn series (34)
Death in diamonds
Ashe, Gordon
Patrick Dawlish series (24)
Giles, Kenneth
Inspector Harry James and Sergeant Honeybody series (4)
Death in dockland
Reid, Desmond
Sexton Blake series (1553)
Death in Don Mills
Garner, Hugh
Inspector Walter McDumont series (2)
Death in Donegal Bay
Gault, William Campbell
Brock Callahan series (10)
Death in Downing Street
Brandon, John Gordon
Arthur Stukeley Pennington series (9)
Inspector Patrick Aloysius McCarthy series (15)
Death in dream time
Courtier, Sidney Hobson
Inspector Digger Haig series (2)
Death in Dunwich
Wimble, Edward
Cthulhu Mythos series (10)
Death in duplicate
Brandon, John Gordon
Inspector Patrick Aloysius McCarthy series (41)
Douglas, George
Inspector Hallam and Sergeant Spratt series (5)
White, Alan
Inspector Armstrong series (2)
Death in Durango
Majors, E B
Slaughter and Son series (4)
Death in ecstasy
Marsh, Ngaio
Inspector Roderick Alleyn series (4)
Death in error
Usher, Frank
Daye Smith series (7)
Death in five boxes
Dickson, Carter
Sir Henry Merrivale series (9)
Death in flames
Ashe, Gordon
Patrick Dawlish series (10)
Death in four colors
Bird, Brandon
Hampton Hume series (1)
Death in gold
McLaglen, John J
Herne the Hunter series (6)
Death in grease paint
Palmer, Stuart
Howie Rook series (1)
Death in green
Infante, Anne
Micky Douglas and Inspector Reeves series (4)
Death in harbour
Goyne, Richard
Paul Templeton series (6)
Death in Harley Street
Rhode, John
Doctor Lancelot Priestley series (43)
Death in high heels
Brand, Christianna
Inspector Charlesworth series (1)
Death in high places
Ashe, Gordon
Patrick Dawlish series (9)
Thorne, Ramsay
Captain Gringo series (7)
Death in High Provence
Bellairs, George
Detective Inspector Thomas Littlejohn series (27)
Death in Hollywood
Richmond, Philip
Duke Renny series (3)
Death in Irish Town
Scott, Jack S
Detective Inspector Alfred Stanley Rosher series (10)
Death in Jermyn Street
Brandon, John Gordon
Arthur Stukeley Pennington series (17)
Inspector Patrick Aloysius McCarthy series (39)
Death in Jerusalem
Boland, John C
Donald McCarry series (4)
Death in Kashmir
Kaye, Mary Margaret
Death series (1)
Death in Kenya
Kaye, Mary Margaret
Death series (4)
Death in life
Carter, Nicholas
Nicholas Carter series (620)
Death in lilac time
Crane, Frances
Pat and Jean Abbott series (19)
Death in little houses
Robeson, Kenneth
Doc Savage series (174)
Death in melting
Grayson, Richard
John Bryant series (2)
Death in Mermaid Lane
Lane, Gret
John Barrin series (5)
Kate Marsh series (6)
Death in midwinter
Hilton, John Buxton
Superintendent Simon Kenworthy series (2)
Death in office
Longmate, Norman
Inspector Bradley and Sergeant Raymond series (5)
Potter, Jeremy
Inspector Hiscock series (1)
Death in one-two-three
Abrahams, Robert
Pete Taylor series (2)
Death in perplexity
Browne, Douglas Gordon
Mister Harvey Tuke series (5)
Death in Piccadilly
Garnett, Roger
Chief Inspector Jonathan Black series (1)
Death in Ptarmigan Forest
Coram, Christopher
Ross Macallister series (3)
Death in purple prose
Barnard, Robert
Charlie Peace series (2)
Superintendent Perry Trethowan series (5)
Death in quiet places
Bailey, Elliot
Inspector Geoffrey Fraser series (1)
Death in red
Kirk, Matthew
Claw series (6)
Death in reserve
Muir, Thomas
Roger Crammond series (1)
Death in retirement
Bell, Josephine
Doctor David Wintringham series (13)
Death in retreat
Douglas, George
Inspector Bonny Lee series (5)
Death in Room Five
Bellairs, George
Detective Inspector Thomas Littlejohn series (24)

Death in Santiago
De Villiers, Gerard
Malko Linge series (14)
Death in seven volumes
Browne, Douglas Gordon
Mister Harvey Tuke series (7)
Death in shallow water
Burton, Miles
Inspector Arnold and Desmond Merrion series (37)
Death in sheep's clothing
Phillips, Stella
Inspector Matthew Furnival series (5)
Death in silhouette
Slate, John
Black Maria series (5)
Death in silver
Robeson, Kenneth
Doc Savage series (26)
Death in slow motion
Robeson, Kenneth
Avenger series (18)
Death in small doses
Thomas, Martin
Sexton Blake series (1565)
Death in Soundings
Muir, Thomas
Roger Crammond series (8)
Death in spingtime
Nabb, Magdalen
Marshal Guarnaccia series (3)
Death in Stanley Street
Burley, William John
Superintendent Charles Wycliffe series (5)
Death in store
Rowe, Jennifer
Verity Birdwood series (3)
Death in the air
Christie, Agatha
Hercule Poirot series (11)
Hartman, Dane
Dirty Harry Callahan series (11)
Death in the Andamans
Kaye, Mary Margaret
Death series (6)
Death in the ashes
Johnstone, William Wallace
Ashes series (11)
Death in the bag
Usher, Gray
Superintendent Michael Drexel series (4)
Death in the bathroom
Thomson, Basil
Superintendent Richardson series (6)
Death in the blackout
Gilbert, Anthony
Arthur Crook series (11)
Death in the blue hour
Crane, Frances
Pat and Jean Abbott series (15)
Death in the Canongate
Piper, Peter
Inspector Gray series (2)
Death in the Caribbean
Anderson, John Richard Lane
Major Peter Blair series (9)
Death in the Channel
Anderson, John Richard Lane
Major Peter Blair series (6)
Death in the church
Giles, Kenneth
Inspector Harry James and Sergeant Honeybody series (8)
Death in the city
Anderson, John Richard Lane
Major Peter Blair series (8)
Death in the clouds
Christie, Agatha
Hercule Poirot series (11)
Death in the copse
Cromwell, A G E
Rodney Wayne series (2)
Death in the crease
Curtis, Richard
Dave Bolt series (2)
Death in the crystal
Grant, Maxwell
Shadow series (254)
Death in the dark
Dalton, Moray
Inspector Hugh Collier series (7)
Wills, Cecil Melville
Superintendent Roger Ellerdine and Sergeant Cherry Blossom series (8)
Death in the desert
Anderson, John Richard Lane
Major Peter Blair series (7)
Wellman, Paul Iselin
Death on horseback series (2)
Death in the Devil's Acre
Perry, Anne
Charlotte Ellison Pitt and Inspector Thomas Pitt series (7)
Death in the ditch
Brandon, John Gordon
Arthur Stukeley Pennington series (13)
Death in the diving-pool
Carnac, Carol
Inspector Ryvet series (6)
Death in the east
Franklin, Charles
Maxine Dangerfield series (3)
Death in the faculty
Cross, Amanda
Professor Kate Fansler series (6)
Death in the fearful night
Bellairs, George
Detective Inspector Thomas Littlejohn series (33)
Death in the fifth position
Box, Edgar
Peter Cutler Sergeant series (1)
Death in the fog
Eberhart, Mignon Good
Sarah Keate and Lance O'Leary series (6)
Death in the forest
Dalton, Moray
Inspector Hugh Collier series (8)
Harding, Ian
Assault troop series (2)
Death in the glass
Gayle, Newton
James Greer series (4)
Death in the gorge
Thayer, Lee
Peter Clancy series (21)
Death in the grand manor
Morice, Anne
Tessa Crichton Price series (1)
Death in the greenhouse
Anderson, John Richard Lane
Major Peter Blair series (10)
Death in the hands of talent
Yates, Peter
Sandy Blunt series (2)
Death in the high latitude
Anderson, John Richard Lane
Major Peter Blair series (11)
Death in the hills
Bensen, Donald R
Cole Brandon series (3)
Death in the hop fields
Rhode, John
Doctor Lancelot Priestley series (25)
Death in the Jordan
Tyndall, John
Roger Turnbull series (1)
Death in the jungle
Evans, Gwyn
Sexton Blake series (756)
Death in the kettle
Wallace, Carlton
Superintendent Edmund Bendilow series (5)
Death in the lava
Benteen, John
Sundance series (4)
Death in the Lebanon
Tyndall, John
Roger Turnbull series (2)
Death in the life
Davis, Dorothy Salisbury
Julie Hayes series (1)
Death in the lock
Muir, Thomas
Roger Crammond series (3)
Death in the mews
Jacobs, Thomas Curtis Hicks
Chief Inspector Barnard series (14)
Temple Fortune series (8)
Wood, Eric
Arnold Keene and Bernard Young series (1)
Death in the middle watch
Bruce, Leo
Carolus Deene series (22)
Death in the mist
Finney, R C
Inspector Bourne series (3)
Death in the morning
Radley, Sheila
Chief Inspector Douglas Quantrill series (1)
Death in the night watches
Bellairs, George
Detective Inspector Thomas Littlejohn series (8)
Death in the North Sea
Anderson, John Richard Lane
Major Peter Blair series (5)
Death in the old country
Wright, Eric
Inspector Charlie Salter series (3)
Death in the past
Moore, Richard A
Bob Whitfield series (1)
Death in the picture
Braddon, George
Michael Gaunt series (1)
Death in the quadrangle
Dillon, Eilis
Inspector Mike Kenny series (2)
Death in the quarry
Brandon, John Gordon
Inspector Patrick Aloysius McCarthy series (33)
Cole, George Douglas Howard
Everard Blatchington series (3)
Superintendent Henry Wilson series (13)
Death in the rain
Parrish, Frank
Dan Mallett series (5)
Death in the rising sun
Creasey, John
Doctor Palfrey series (5)
Death in the round
Morice, Anne
Tessa Crichton Price series (14)
Death in the saddle
Scott, Bradford
Walt Slade series (75)
Death in the Sanchez family
Lewis, Oscar
Sanchez family series (2)
Death in the Senate
Diplomat
Dennis Tyler series (5)
Death in the snow
Stern, Richard Martin
Johnny Ortiz series (3)
Death in the stars
Grant, Maxwell
Shadow series (185)
Death in the stocks
Heyer, Georgette
Inspector Hemingway series (1)
Superintendent Hannasyde series (1)
Death in the straw
Usher, Gray
Superintendent Michael Drexel series (1)
Death in the Thames
Anderson, John Richard Lane
Major Peter Blair series (3)
Death in the 13th dose
Cobb, Belton
Inspector Cheviot Burmann series (11)
Death in the top twenty
McNeilly, Wilfred
Sexton Blake series (1573)
Death in the trees
Ashe, Gordon
Patrick Dawlish series (29)
Death in the trooper
Muir, Thomas
Roger Crammond series (2)
Death in the tunnel
Burton, Miles
Inspector Arnold and Desmond Merrion series (12)
Death in the wasteland
Bellairs, George
Detective Inspector Thomas Littlejohn series (39)
Death in the wet
Mitchell, Gladys
Dame Beatrice Bradley series (5)
Death in the wheelbarrow
Gore, William
Inspector Penk series (1)
Death in the willows
Forrest, Richard
Lyon and Bea Wentworth series (4)
Death in the wind
Lanham, Edwin
Lieutenant Gray series (2)
Death in the wrong bed
Farrar, Stewart
Inspector Elwyn Morgan series (3)
Death in the wrong room
Gilbert, Anthony
Arthur Crook series (18)
Death in three masks
Healey, Ben
Paul Hedley series (3)
Death in time
Warner, Mignon
Mrs Edwina Charles series (3)
Death in triplicate
Lorac, E C R
Inspector Macdonald series (46)
Death in uptown
Raleigh, Michael
Paul Whelan series (1)
Death in view
Macrae, Travis
Jim and Kate Harris series (1)
Death in Wellington Road
Rhode, John
Doctor Lancelot Priestley series (54)
Death in Wessex
Peterson, Audrey
Jane Winfield and Andrew Quentin series (2)
Death in white pyjamas
Bude, John
Inspector Meredith series (12)
Death in willow pattern
Burley, William John
Doctor Henry Pym series (2)
Death in Xanadu
Halliday, Brett
Mike Shayne stories series (8)
Death in yellow
Jason, Stuart
Butcher series (31)
Death in Zanzibar
Kaye, Mary Margaret
Death series (5)
Zanzibar series (2)
Death inheritance
Swan, Phyllis
Anna J series (3)
Death invades the meeting
Rhode, John
Doctor Lancelot Priestley series (39)
Death is a circus
Jason
Jason series (2)
Death is a dirty trick
Philips, Judson Pentecost
Peter Styles series (17)
Death is a drum, beating forever
Wyllie, John
Doctor Quarshie series (4)
Death is a family affair
Sims, L V
Dixie T Struthers series (1)
Death is a friend
Mackenzie, Donald
Harry Chalice and Crying Eddie series (2)
Death is a lovely dame
Blood, Matthew
Morgan Wayne series (2)
Death is a restless sleeper
Quinn, Eleanor Baker
James Strange series (2)
Death is a round black ball
Roscoe, Mike
Johnny April series (1)
Death is a round black spot
Robeson, Kenneth
Doc Savage series (171)
Death is a ruby light
Kenyon, Paul
Baroness Penelope Saint-John Orsini series (3)
Death is a two stroke penalty
Bartlett, James Y
Pete Hacker series (1)
Death is academic
Mackay, Amanda
Hannah Land series (1)
Death is buttercups
Wilson, Gertrude Mary
Inspector Lovick series (16)
Death is for ever
Marshall, Lovat
Sugar Kane series (18)
Death is for losers
Nolan, William Francis
Bart Challis series (1)
Death is forever
Gardner, John Edmund
James Bond series (28)
O'Callaghan, Maxine
Delilah West series (1)
Death is late to lunch
Du Bois, Theodora
Anne and Jeffrey McNeill series (6)
Death is like that
Spain, John
Bill Rye series (2)
Death is merciful
Sandys, James
James Charlesworth series (4)
Death is my comrade
Marlowe, Stephen
Chester Drum series (12)
Death is my name
Wells, Susan
Anthony Ware series (3)
Death is no lady
Corne, Molly E
Mac McIntyre series (1)
Death is no sportsman
Hare, Cyril
Inspector Mallett series (2)
Death is not a passing grade
Miller, Victor Brooke
Kojak series (6)
Death is so final
Fraser, Alex
Inspector Noel Tracy series (3)
Death is the end
Cooke, Geoffrey Walter
Peter Mitchell series (3)
Death is the host
Lariar, Lawrence
Ham Macandrew and Homer Bull series (1)
Death is the last lover
Kane, Henry
Peter Chambers series (14)
Death is too good for you
Alexander, Martin
Alan Kelton series (1)
Death is waiting
Usher, Frank
Daye Smith series (5)
Death Island
Carter, Nick
Nick Carter series (188)
Death jewels
Grant, Maxwell
Shadow series (149)
Death joins the party
Boyd, Raymond
Paul Scarf series (1)
Turner, John Victor
Amos Petrie series (5)
Death kiss
Saint Dennis, Madelon
Sydney Treherne series (1)
Death knell
Kendrick, Baynard
Captain Duncan Maclain series (5)
Death knocks three times
Gilbert, Anthony
Arthur Crook series (21)
Death knows no calendar
Bude, John
Inspector Meredith series (10)
Death lady
Robeson, Kenneth
Doc Savage series (176)
Death laughs aloft
Conde, Phillip
Dick Pemberty series (9)
Death leaves a diary
Carmichael, Harry
John Piper and Quinn series (1)
Death leaves no card
Burton, Miles
Inspector Arnold and Desmond Merrion series (19)
Death leaves us naked
Hollingsworth, Leonard
Superintendent Adams series (2)
Death lifts the latch
Gilbert, Anthony
Arthur Crook series (15)
Death lights a candle
Taylor, Phoebe Atwood
Asey Mayo series (2)
Death likes it hot
Box, Edgar
Peter Cutler Sergeant series (3)
Death list
Clark, Al C
Kenyatta series (2)
Hawkes, Robert
NARC series (3)
Reno, Bill
Badge series (12)
Death list of Rico Scalisi
Deptula, Walter
Frank Arrow series (3)
Death lives next door
Butler, Gwendoline
Inspector John Coffin series (5)
Death lode
Hardin, J D
Raider and Doc series (14)

Death looks down
Long, Amelia Reynolds
Edward Trelawny series (6)
Peter Piper series (5)
Death looks in
Sale, Richard
Daniel Webster series (1)
Death loop
Conde, Phillip
Dick Pemberty series (5)
Death loves a shining mark
Hocking, Anne
Inspector William Austen series (9)
Death lust
Kilgore, Axel
They call me the Mercenary series (11)
Death machine
Robeson, Kenneth
Avenger series (32)
Death machine contract
McCray, Mike
Black Berets series (6)
Death makers
Milton, Joseph
Bart Gould series (6)
Death makers conspiracy
Hayes, Ralph Eugene
Agent for Cominsec series (6)
Death makes a claim
Hobson, Hank
Brad Ford series (2)
Death makes a prophet
Bude, John
Inspector Meredith series (15)
Death makes the scene
Phillips, Stella
Inspector Matthew Furnival series (4)
Death mask
Dentinger, Jane
Jocelyn O'Rourke and Phillip Gerard series (3)
Pentecost, Hugh
Julian Quist series (10)
Death mask of Pancho Villa
Gaskin, Carol
Time machine series (19)
Death mask of war
Marlowe, Greg
Greg Marlowe series (2)
Death masque
McLeave, Hugh
Doctor Gregor Maclean series (5)
Death master strike
Robbins, David
Blade series (12)
Death match
Kessler, Leo
Rebel series (3)
Death meets four hundred rabbits
Stein, Aaron Marc
Tim Mulligan and Elsie Mae Hunt series (17)
Death meets the coroner
Ryland, John Knox
Inspector Rodway series (3)
Death meets the king's messenger
Collins, Gilbert
Hugh Carding series (5)
Death Merchant
Rosenberger, Joseph
Death Merchant series (1)
Death message
Carter, Nick
Nick Carter series (104)
Death miser
Creasey, John
Department Z series (1)
Death mission, Havana
Carter, Nick
Nick Carter series (141)
Death must gave laughed
Turner, John Victor
Amos Petrie series (1)
Death my darling daughters
Stagge, Jonathan
Doctor Hugh Westlake series (7)
Death needs no alibi
Gribble, Leonard Reginald
Superintendent Anthony Slade series (40)
Death never forgets
Weston, Garnett
Highway series (1)
Death notes
Rendell, Ruth
Chief Inspector Reginald Wexford series (13)
Death of a banker
Wynne, Anthony
Doctor Eustace Hailey series (18)

Death of a beauty queen
Punshon, Ernest Robertson
Bobby Owen series (5)
Death of a best seller
Wills, Cecil Melville
Sylvester Horatio Pinkney series (2)
Death of a big man
Wainwright, John
Northern Police series (26)
Superintendent Charles Ripley series (6)
Death of a blue-eyed soul brother
Johnson, B B
Superspade series (1)
Death of a bookseller
Farmer, Bernard James
Sergeant Jack Wigan series (2)
Death of a borrowing mole
Mitchell, Gladys
Dame Beatrice Bradley series (62)
Death of a bovver boy
Bruce, Leo
Carolus Deene series (23)
Death of a bridegroom
Rhode, John
Doctor Lancelot Priestley series (65)
Death of a bullionaire
Cunningham, Albert Benjamin
Sheriff Jess Roden series (13)
Death of a busybody
Bellairs, George
Detective Inspector Thomas Littlejohn series (3)
Shannon, Dell
Lieutenant Luis Mendoza series (5)
Death of a butterfly
Maron, Margaret
Lieutenant Sigrid Harald series (2)
Death of a cad
Beaton, M C
Hamish Macbeth series (2)
Bude, John
Inspector Meredith series (8)
Death of a call girl
Trevor, Leslie
Policewoman series (3)
Death of a canary
Graham, Neill
Solo Malcolm series (25)
Death of a celebrity
Footner, Hulbert
Amos Lee Mappin series (2)
Death of a charming man
Beaton, M C
Hamish Macbeth series (10)
Death of a cheat
Eshleman, John Morton
Lieutenant Larry Koharik series (1)
Death of a citizen
Hamilton, Donald
Matt Helm series (1)
Death of a cloven hoof
King, Frank
Doctor Frank King series (2)
Death of a commuter
Bruce, Leo
Carolus Deene series (17)
Death of a Corinthian
Lanham, Edwin
Lieutenant Gray series (1)
Death of a courier
Hawkes, Robert
NARC series (2)
Death of a daimyo
Melville, James
Superintendent Tetsuo Otani series (6)
Death of a dancer
McGown, Jill
Chief Inspector Lloyd and Sergeant Judy Hill series (3)
Woolfolk, Dorothy
Donna Rockford series (2)
Death of a dancing lady
Harrison, Ray
Sergeant Joseph Bragg and Constable James Morton series (4)
Death of a Dandie Dinmont
Duke, Madelaine
Doctor Norah North series (3)
Death of a dastard
Kane, Henry
Peter Chambers series (19)
Death of a decent fellow
Temple-Ellis, N A
Inspector Wren series (3)
Death of a Delft blue
Mitchell, Gladys
Dame Beatrice Bradley series (37)

Death of a demon
Stout, Rex
Nero Wolfe and Archie Goodwin series (36)
Death of a destroyer
Macdonnell, James Edmond
Commander Sainsbury series (9)
Death of a difficult woman
Berry, Carole
Bonnie Indermill series (6)
Death of a dinosaur
Bunting, Eve
Dinosaur machines series (2)
Death of a dissenter
Lamb, Lynton
Superintendent Quill and Inspector Glover series (1)
Death of a dissident
Kaminsky, Stuart Melvin
Inspector Porfiry Petrovich Rostnikov series (1)
Death of a dog
Eyles, Leonora
Doctor Joan Marvin series (2)
Death of a doll
Brown, Carter
Rick Holman series (1)
Lawrence, Hilda
Mark East series (3)
Death of a don
Shaw, Howard
Inspector Barnaby series (2)
Death of a doxy
Stout, Rex
Nero Wolfe and Archie Goodwin series (42)
Death of a dude
Stout, Rex
Nero Wolfe and Archie Goodwin series (44)
Death of a Dutchman
Nabb, Magdalen
Marshal Guarnaccia series (2)
Death of a dwarf
Kemp, Harold
Inspector James Brent series (5)
Death of a fat god
Keating, Henry Reymond Fitzwalter
Mrs Craggs series (1)
Death of a fellow traveller
Ames, Delano
Dagobert and Jane Brown series (3)
Death of a fire-raiser
Davis, George
Roag's Syndicate series (6)
Death of a flack
Kane, Henry
Peter Chambers series (15)
Death of a fool
Marsh, Ngaio
Inspector Roderick Alleyn series (19)
Death of a frightened editor
Radford, Edwin
Doctor Manson series (11)
Death of a gay dog
Morice, Anne
Tessa Crichton Price series (3)
Death of a gentleman
Courage, John
Bill Britain series (4)
Hollis, Christopher
Robert Fossett trilogy (1)
Radford, Edwin
Doctor Manson series (22)
Death of a ghost
Allingham, Margery
Albert Campion series (6)
Death of a glutton
Beaton, M C
Hamish Macbeth series (8)
Death of a god
Haymon, Sylvia T
Inspector Ben Jurnet series (4)
Death of a golden girl
Fulton, Eileen
Nina McFall series (1)
Death of a golfer
Wynne, Anthony
Doctor Eustace Hailey series (22)
Death of a good woman
Straker, John Foster
Inspector Pitt series (6)
Death of a gossip
Beaton, M C
Hamish Macbeth series (1)
Death of a grandmother
Rhode, John
Doctor Lancelot Priestley series (61)

Death of a Greek
Brandon, John Gordon
Arthur Stukeley Pennington series (23)
Inspector Patrick Aloysius McCarthy series (47)
Death of a halo
King, Frank
Doctor Frank King series (1)
Death of a harbourmaster
Simenon, Georges
Inspector Jules Maigret series (17)
Death of a Harvard freshman
Silver, Victoria
Laura Adler series (1)
Death of a hawker
Van de Wetering, Janwillem
De Gier and Grijpstra series (4)
Death of a heavenly twin
Morice, Anne
Tessa Crichton Price series (6)
Death of a hippie
Brett, Michael
Pete McGrath series (8)
Death of a hitman
Davies, Frederick
Hitman series (1)
Death of a hollow man
Graham, Caroline
Inspector Tom Barnaby series (2)
Death of a holy murderer
Duke, Madelaine
Doctor Norah North series (1)
Death of a hooker
Kane, Henry
Peter Chambers series (17)
Death of a hussy
Beaton, M C
Hamish Macbeth series (5)
Death of a jester
O'Donnell, Peter
Modesty Blaise comic strip series (7)
Death of a Joyce scholar
Gill, Bartholomew
Inspector Peter McGarr series (8)
Death of a king
Wynne, Anthony
Doctor Eustace Hailey series (23)
Death of a ladies' man
Roberts, Lee
Doctor Clinton Shannon series (3)
Death of a ladykiller
Carnac, Carol
Inspector Strang series (2)
Death of a lake
Upfield, Arthur William
Napoleon Bonaparte series (18)
Death of a left-handed woman
Joyce, Cyril
Chief Superintendent Pat Stockton series (9)
Death of a legend
Adams, Robert
Horseclans series (8)
Death of a libertine
Wallace, Carlton
Superintendent Edmund Bendilow series (3)
Death of a lucky lady
Rath, Virginia
Michael Dundas series (3)
Death of a man-tamer
Tripp, Miles
John Samson series (9)
Death of a marine
Leader, Charles
Mike McCall series (2)
Death of a merchant of death
Bortner, Norman Stanley
Professor Clifford Wells series (2)
Death of a mermaid
Brandon, Gordon
Arthur Stukeley Pennington series (30)
Inspector Patrick Aloysius McCarthy series (55)
Death of a merry widow
Hunt, Richard
Chief Inspector Walsh and Constable Brenda Phipps series (3)
Death of a millionaire
Cole, George Douglas Howard
Superintendent Henry Wilson series (2)
Death of a minor character
Ferrars, Elizabeth
Virginia and Felix Freer series (4)
Death of a minor poet
Krasner, William
Sam Birge series (5)

Death of a nymph
Delman, David
Lieutenant Jacob Horowitz series (7)
Death of a peculiar rabbit
Radford, Edwin
Doctor Manson series (29)
Death of a Peeping Tom
Cobb, Belton
Bryan Armitage series (5)
Death of a peeping tom
Cobb, Belton
Inspector Cheviot Burmann series (29)
Death of a Peeping Tom
Cobb, Belton
Kitty Armitage series (2)
Death of a peer
Marsh, Ngaio
Inspector Roderick Alleyn series (9)
Death of a perfect wife
Beaton, M C
Hamish Macbeth series (4)
Death of a pornographer
Lejeune, Anthony
Adam Gifford series (3)
Death of a postman
Creasey, John
Inspector Roger West series (20)
Death of a prankster
Beaton, M C
Hamish Macbeth series (7)
Death of a prima donna
Colburn, Laura
Carol Gates series (2)
Death of a pusher
Deming, Richard
Matt Rudd series (3)
Death of a queen
Sprigg, Christopher Saint John
Charles Venables series (4)
Death of a racehorse
Creasey, John
Inspector Roger West series (25)
Death of a Radcliffe roommate
Silver, Victoria
Laura Adler series (2)
Death of a raven
Duffy, Margaret
Patrick Gillard series (2)
Death of a regiment
Randle, Kevin
Jefferson's war series (5)
Death of a Russian priest
Kaminsky, Stuart Melvin
Inspector Porfiry Petrovich Rostnikov series (8)
Death of a saboteur
Footner, Hulbert
Amos Lee Mappin series (8)
Death of a scandal sister
Brody, Marc
Marc Brody series (14)
Death of a scoundrel
Jacobs, Thomas Curtis Hicks
Temple Fortune series (17)
Death of a shadow
Bellairs, George
Detective Inspector Thomas Littlejohn series (41)
Wynne, Anthony
Doctor Eustace Hailey series (28)
Death of a shrew
Barling, Charles
Inspector Henderson series (2)
Death of a sinner
Quest, Rodney
Peter Quentin series (3)
Death of a snob
Beaton, M C
Hamish Macbeth series (6)
Death of a socialite
Brandon, John Gordon
Arthur Stukeley Pennington series (25)
Inspector Patrick Aloysius McCarthy series (49)
Death of a source
Moore, Richard A
Bob Whitfield series (2)
Death of a spinster
Dalton, Moray
Inspector Hugh Collier series (13)
Death of a swagman
Upfield, Arthur William
Napoleon Bonaparte series (9)
Death of a tall man
Lockridge, Frances
Bill Wiegand series (9)
Inspector Merton Heimrich series (1)
Mister and Mrs North series (11)

Death of a theatre filly
Williamson, Audrey
Superintendent Richard York series (2)
Death of a tin god
Bellairs, George
Detective Inspector Thomas Littlejohn series (35)
Death of a train
Crofts, Freeman Wills
Inspector Joseph French series (26)
Death of a travelling man
Beaton, M C
Hamish Macbeth series (9)
Death of a tyrant
Punshon, Ernest Robertson
Bobby Owen series (10)
Death of a viewer
Adams, Herbert
Major Roger Bennion series (29)
Death of a voodoo doll
Arnold, Margot
Penelope Spring and Sir Tobias Glendower series (4)
Death of a warrior queen
Haymon, Sylvia T
Inspector Ben Jurnet series (6)
Death of a wedding guest
Morice, Anne
Tessa Crichton Price series (9)
Death of a weirdy
Carr, Glyn
Sir Abercrombie Lewker series (16)
Death of a white witch
Oellrichs, Inez
Matt Winters series (6)
Death of a wombat
Smith, Ivan
Fire, drought and flood trilogy (1)
Death of a world
Rolland, Romain
Soul enchanted series (4)
Romains, Jules
Men of goodwill series (14)
Death of a worldly woman
Cunningham, Albert Benjamin
Sheriff Jess Roden series (14)
Death of Abbe Didier
Grayson, Richard
Inspector Gautier series (3)
Death of Ahasueras
Lagerkvist, Par
Tobias trilogy (1)
Death of an ad man
Eichler, Alfred
Inspector Knickman series (3)
Martin Ames series (4)
Death of an admiral
Hackforth-Jones, Gilbert
Commander Wally Phipps-Mangot series (2)
Death of an airman
Sprigg, Christopher Saint John
Inspector Bernard Bray series (3)
Death of an alderman
Hilton, John Buxton
Superintendent Simon Kenworthy series (1)
Death of an ambassador
Coles, Manning
Tommy Hambledon series (21)
Death of an ancient Saxon
Radford, Edwin
Doctor Manson series (28)
Death of an angel
Lockridge, Frances
Bill Wiegand series (20)
Mister and Mrs North series (21)
Rea, Margaret Lucile Paine
Lieutenant Powledge series (3)
Richards, Clay
Grant Kirby series (2)
Winslow, Pauline Glen
Superintendent Merlin Capricorn series (1)
Death of an army
Plievier, Theodor
World War II trilogy (2)
Death of an artist
Eichler, Alfred
Inspector Knickman series (4)
Martin Ames series (5)
Rhode, John
Doctor Lancelot Priestley series (62)
Death of an aryan
Huxley, Elspeth
Superintendent Vachell series (3)
Death of an assassin
Creasey, John
Inspector Roger West series (19)
Death of an aunt
Harknett, Terry
Stephen Wayne series (7)
Death of an author
Rhode, John
Doctor Lancelot Priestley series (45)
Death of an editor
Loder, Vernon
Inspector Brews series (2)
Death of an eloquent man
Russell, Charlotte Murray
Jane Amanda Edwards series (2)
Death of an Englishman
Nabb, Magdalen
Marshal Guarnaccia series (1)
Death of an expert witness
James, Phyllis Dorothy
Commander Adam Dalgliesh series (7)
Powell, Percival Henry
Superintendent Gaden series (3)
Death of an Honourable Member
Harrison, Ray
Sergeant Joseph Bragg and Constable James Morton series (2)
Death of an innocent
Chance, John Newton
Mister DeHavilland series (3)
Superintendent Black series (2)
Ormerod, Roger
Richard Patton series (7)
Death of an oddfellow
Wood, Eric
Arnold Keene and Bernard Young series (3)
Death of an oil rig
Catherall, Arthur
Bulldog tugboat series (11)
Death of an old girl
Lemarchand, Elizabeth
Superintendent Tom Pollard series (1)
Death of an old sinner
Davis, Dorothy Salisbury
Mrs Norris and Jasper Tully series (1)
Death of an outsider
Beaton, M C
Hamish Macbeth series (3)
Death of an uncle
Hambledon, Phyllis
Inspector Tubby Hall series (3)
Death of Cecilia
Howard, Hartley
Glenn Bowman series (4)
Death of cold
Bruce, Leo
Carolus Deene series (2)
Death of Cosmo Revere
Bush, Christopher
Ludovic Travers series (3)
Death of Daddy-O
Alexander, David
Marty Land series (1)
Death of Duboyne
Bayfield, William John
Sexton Blake series (558)
Death of four
Skene, Anthony
Sexton Blake series (668)
Death of his uncle
Kitchin, Clifford Henry Benn
Malcolm Warren series (3)
Death of Humpty Dumpty
Alexander, David
Bart Hardin series (6)
Death of Humpty-Dumpty
Alexander, David
Lieutenant Romano series (8)
Death of Iron Horse
Longtree, Warren T
Ruff Justice series (8)
Death of Jezebel
Brand, Christianna
Inspector Charlesworth series (4)
Inspector Chucky series (1)
Inspector Cockrill series (4)
Death of John Tait
Fielding, A
Inspector Pointer series (12)
Death of kings
Danielson, Peter
Children of the Lion series (17)
Death of Laurence Vining
Thomas, Alan
Inspector Widgeon series (1)
Death of Lorenzo Jones
Latham, Brad
Hook series (4)
Death of love
Gill, Bartholomew
Inspector Peter McGarr series (9)
Death of Mister Dodsley
Ferguson, John
Francis Macnab series (5)
Death of Monsieur Gallet
Simenon, Georges
Inspector Jules Maigret series (6)
Death of Mr Gantley
Burton, Miles
Inspector Arnold and Desmond Merrion series (4)
Death of Mr Lomas
Vivian, Francis
Inspector Gordon Knollis series (2)
Death of Mrs Preedy
Jackson, Lewis
Sexton Blake series (1241)
Death of my aunt
Kitchin, Clifford Henry Benn
Malcolm Warren series (1)
Death of Neville Norway
Rowland, John
Inspector Shelley series (13)
Death of Nora Ryan
Farrell, James Thomas
Universe of time series (7)
Death of our dear one
Erskine, Margaret
Inspector Septimus Finch series (6)
Death of papa
Foote, Horton
Orphans' home series (9)
Death of Reginald Perrin
Nobbs, David
Reginald Perrin series (1)
Death of Satan
Duncan, Ronald
Don Juan series (2)
Death of sleep
McCaffrey, Anne
Planet pirates series (2)
Death of the claimant
Martin, A Richard
Branders Noble series (2)
Death of the deputy
Didelot, Francis
Inspector Lecain series (2)
Death of the Falcon
Carter, Nick
Nick Carter series (93)
Death of the gods
Merejkowski, Dmitri Sergeevich
Christ and Antichrist trilogy (1)
Death of the Home Secretary
Thomas, Alan
Inspector Widgeon series (2)
Death of the lucky country
Horne, Donald
Lucky country series (2)
Death of the party
Cutter, Leela
Lettie Winterbottom series (3)
Fenisong, Ruth
Captain Gridley Nelson series (11)
Death of the raven
Meaney, Dee Morrison
Lady Branwen series (2)
Death of the River Kwai
De Villiers, Gerard
Malko Linge series (4)
Death of the wild bird
Chance, John Newton
Jonathan Blake series (8)
Death of Treasure Trail
Davis, Don
Rio Kid series (3)
Death of two brothers
Burton, Miles
Inspector Arnold and Desmond Merrion series (24)
Death of William Posters
Sillitoe, Alan
Frank Dawley trilogy (1)
Death off the fairway
Adams, Herbert
Major Roger Bennion series (3)
Death on a broomstick
Wilson, Gertrude Mary
Inspector Lovick series (22)
Death on a dude ranch
Bonnamy, Francis
Peter Shane series (2)
Death on a ferris wheel
Martin, Aylwin Lee
Matt Hughes series (1)
Death on a high note
Reid, Desmond
Sexton Blake series (1554)
Death on a hot summer night
Infante, Anne
Micky Douglas and Inspector Reeves series (1)
Death on a number eight hook
Gough, Laurence
Willows and Parker series (2)
Death on a pale horse
Jones, Bradshaw
Claude Ravel series (4)
Death on a quiet day
Innes, Michael
Sir John Appleby series (16)
Death on a wild, cold river
Gill, Bartholomew
Inspector Peter McGarr series (10)
Death on All Hallows
McLean, Allan Campbell
Inspector Noel Macleod series (2)
Death on Allhallowe'en
Bruce, Leo
Carolus Deene series (20)
Death on Bodmir Moor
Gunn, Victor
Chief Inspector Bill Cromwell series (33)
Death on Dartmoor
Rowland, John
Inspector Shelley series (3)
Death on deadline
Goldsborough, Robert
Nero Wolfe and Archie Goodwin series (49)
Death on delivery
Brandon, John Gordon
Inspector Patrick Aloysius McCarthy series (28)
Gore-Browne, Robert
Lucien Clay series (2)
Death on demand
Ashe, Gordon
Patrick Dawlish series (2)
Death on Demand
Hart, Carolyn Gimpel
Annie Laurance and Max Darling series (1)
Death on deposit
Grierson, Francis Durham
Inspector Sims and Professor Wells series (12)
Death on display
Simons, Roger
Inspector Fadiman Wace series (12)
Death on doomsday
Lemarchand, Elizabeth
Superintendent Tom Pollard series (4)
Death on Heron's Mere
Fitt, Mary
Superintendent Mallett series (6)
Death on horseback
Wellman, Paul Iselin
Death on horseback series (2)
Death on ice
O'Sullivan, James Brendan
Steve Silk series (3)
Death on location
Cox, William Robert
Tom Kincaid series (3)
Death on Milestone Buttress
Carr, Glyn
Sir Abercrombie Lewker series (4)
Death on my shoulder
Franklin, Charles
Grant Garfield series (16)
Death on paper
Bude, John
Inspector Meredith series (7)
Death on remand
Underwood, Michael
Superintendent Simon Manton series (3)
Death on Romney Marsh
Bruce, Leo
Carolus Deene series (18)
Death on Scurvy Street
Williams, Ben Ames
Inspector Tope series (1)
Death on Sunday
Rhode, John
Doctor Lancelot Priestley series (31)
Death on the agenda
Bidwell, Margaret
Mister Hodson series (1)
Moyes, Patricia
Henry and Emmy Tibbett series (3)
Muir, Thomas
Roger Crammond series (7)
Death on the aisle
Lockridge, Frances
Bill Wiegand series (5)
Mister and Mrs North series (5)
Death on the Barrier Reef
Antill, Elizabeth
Inspector Simon Ashton series (2)
Death on the Black Sands
Bruce, Leo
Carolus Deene series (15)
Death on the board
Rhode, John
Doctor Lancelot Priestley series (26)
Death on the boardwalk
Cafferty, Jake
Vic Merritt series (1)
Death on the boat train
Rhode, John
Doctor Lancelot Priestley series (32)
Death on the borough council
Bell, Josephine
Doctor David Wintringham series (2)
Death on the broadlands
Hunter, Alan
Inspector George Gently series (30)
Death on the Broads
Radford, Edwin
Doctor Manson series (10)
Death on the cards
Grayson, Richard
Inspector Gautier series (7)
Death on the Centre Court
Goodchild, George
Inspector McLean series (10)
Death on the Champs Elysees
Didelot, Francis
Commissaire Orestes Bignon series (4)
Death on the docks
Hartman, Dane
Dirty Harry Callahan series (2)
Death on the doormat
Heberden, Mary Violet
Desmond Shannon series (1)
Death on the doorstep
Douglas, George
Inspector Bonny Lee series (2)
Death on the double
Kane, Henry
Peter Chambers series (12)
Death on the downbeat
Brown, Carter
Lieutenant Al Wheeler series (10)
Death on the Downs
Marsden, Antony
Inspector Buck series (1)
Death on the dragon's tongue
Arnold, Margot
Penelope Spring and Sir Tobias Glendower series (5)
Death on the Eno
Mackay, Amanda
Hannah Land series (2)
Death on the first tee
Adams, Herbert
Major Roger Bennion series (28)
Death on the heath
Hunter, Alan
Inspector George Gently series (28)
Death on the highway
Robbins, Clifton
Clay Harrison series (3)
Death on the Hit Parade
Gray, Berkeley
Norman Conquest series (36)
Death on the hour
Lockridge, Richard
Assistant District Attorney Bernie Simmons series (7)
Death on the last train
Bellairs, George
Detective Inspector Thomas Littlejohn series (12)
Death on the Late Show
Michaels, Jan
Darby Castle series (2)
Death on the lawn
Rhode, John
Doctor Lancelot Priestley series (59)
Death on the Limited
Denbie, Roger
Doctor Quentin Pace series (1)
Death on the Mississippi
Forrest, Richard
Lyon and Bea Wentworth series (7)
Death on the motorway
Coram, Christopher
Ross Macallister series (4)
Death on the move
Ashe, Gordon
Patrick Dawlish series (13)
Crider, Bill
Dan Rhodes series (4)
Death on the Nile
Christie, Agatha
Colonel Race series (3)
Hercule Poirot series (16)

Death on the Oxford Road
Lorac, E C R
Inspector Macdonald series (4)

Death on the pack road
Andover, Henry
Henry Holland series (1)

Death on the pampas
Wood, Clement
Lal Reed series (2)

Death on the prairie
Wellman, Paul Iselin
Death on horseback series (1)

Death on the reserve
Bell, Josephine
Doctor Henry Frost series (2)

Death on the Rimrock
Scott, Bradford
Walt Slade series (78)

Death on the river
Mackay, Amanda
Hannah Land series (2)

Death on the Riviera
Bude, John
Inspector Meredith series (20)

Death on the rocks
Allegretto, Michael
Jacob Lomax series (1)
Anderson, John Richard Lane
Major Peter Blair series (2)
West, John B
Rocky Steele series (5)

Death on the roof
Francis, Basil
Inspector Ghent series (1)
Sergeant Paul Dean series (5)

Death on the set
Macclure, Victor
Inspector Archie Burford series (5)

Death on the Shivering Sand
Gunn, Victor
Chief Inspector Bill Cromwell series (11)

Death on the slopes
Schier, Norma
Kay Barth series (1)

Death on the spike
Reid, Desmond
Sexton Blake series (1590)

Death on the way
Crofts, Freeman Wills
Inspector Joseph French series (9)

Death on tour
Courage, John
David Cane series (3)

Death on voyage
Grayson, Richard
Inspector Gautier series (6)

Death on Widow's Walk
Grant-Adamson, Lesley
Rain Morgan series (1)

Death orbit
Carter, Nick
Nick Carter series (217)

Death out of focus
Whitman, Charles
Inspector Lindon and Sergeant Gray series (2)

Death out of season
Litvinoff, Samuel
Faces of terror series (1)

Death out of the night
Wynne, Anthony
Doctor Eustace Hailey series (16)

Death over Darien
Thorne, Ramsay
Captain Gringo series (32)

Death over deep water
Nash, Simon
Inspector Montero and Adam Ludlow series (3)

Death over Newark
Williams, Alexander
Detective Sergeant Pietro Tonelli series (2)

Death overseas
Barry, Charles
Superintendent Lawrence Gilmartin series (12)

Death packs a suitcase
Wallace, Bryan Edgar
Bill Tern series (1)

Death paints a picture
Burton, Miles
Inspector Arnold and Desmond Merrion series (61)

Death paints the picture
Lariar, Lawrence
Ham Macandrew and Homer Bull series (1)

Death parade
Desmond, Hugh
Alan Fraser series (10)

Death pays a dividend
Rhode, John
Doctor Lancelot Priestley series (30)

Death pays the piper
Gribble, Leonard Reginald
Superintendent Anthony Slade series (25)

Death pays the wages
McGirr, Edmund
Jim Piron series (6)

Death penalty
Charteris, Leslie
Saint series (10)

Death pit
Pike, Charles R
Jubal Cade series (14)

Death planet
Griffin, Pauline Margaret
Star commandos series (4)

Death plays solitaire
Goldman, Raymond Leslie
Asaph Clume series (3)

Death points a finger
Levinrew, Will
Professor Herman Brierly series (4)

Death pool
Loder, Vernon
Inspector Brews series (1)

Death prone
Curzon, Clare
Superintendent Mike Yeadings and Sergeant Angus Mott series (9)

Death prowls the cove
Lane, Gret
John Barrin series (6)
Kate Marsh series (7)

Death quake
Appleton, Victor II
Tom Swift Junior series 3 (12)

Death qualified
Wilhelm, Kate
Barbara Holloway series (1)

Death quest
Alexander, David
Phoenix series (3)
Grover, Marshall
Larry and Stretch series (235)
Hubbard, Lafayette Ronald
Mission earth series (6)

Death race
Jason, Stuart
Butcher series (6)

Death raid
Hart, Jon
Mercenaries series (5)

Death raiders
Cole, Jackson
Jim Hatfield series (13)

Death ranch
Sharpe, Jon
Canyon O'Grady series (15)

Death rattle
Caldwell, Alfred Betts
Freddy Philpotts series (4)

Death ray terror
Derrick, Lionel
Penetrator series (34)

Death rays of Ardilla
Johns, William Earl
Rex Clinton series (6)

Death rehearsal
Crews, Lary
Veronica Slate series (4)

Death rehearses
Varnam, John
Inspector Semlake series (1)

Death reign of the Vampire King
Stockbridge, Grant
Richard Wentworth series (5)

Death renders account
Spender, Jean Maud
Mary Owen series (3)

Death ride
Franklin, Max
Starsky and Hutch series (3)
Hofrichter, Paul
Roadblaster trilogy (2)
James, William M
Apache series (24)
Kessler, Leo
Wotan series (19)
Lutz, Gunther
Panzer Platoon series (5)
Macneil, Neil
Tony Costaine and Bert McCall series (5)
Stivers, Dick
Able Team series (29)

Death riders
Streib, Dan
Michael Hawk series (7)

Death riders of Hel
Drake, Asa
Hel trilogy (2)

Death rides a hobby
Howes, Royce
Captain Ben Lucias series (5)

Death rides a painted horse
Wilmot, Robert Patrick
Steve Considine series (3)

Death rides a sorrel horse
Cunningham, Albert Benjamin
Sheriff Jess Roden series (11)

Death rides in Texas
Hawkins, Clint
Saddletramp series (8)

Death rides swiftly
Shepherd, Neal
Chief Inspector Michael Tandy series (3)

Death rides the dragon
Thomas, Eugene
Mrs Caywood Weston series (1)

Death rides the forest
Grayson, Rupert
Gun Cotton series (2)

Death rides the night
Field, Peter
Powder Valley series (23)

Death rides the Pecos
Dresser, Davis
Twister Malone series (1)

Death rides the rails
Stoddard, Charles
Malloy series (7)

Death rides the Rio
Cole, Jackson
Jim Hatfield series (75)

Death rides the Rio Grande
Scott, Bradford
Walt Slade series (41)

Death rides the river trail
Scott, Bradford
Walt Slade series (92)

Death rides the skyway
Grant, Maxwell
Shadow series (95)

Death rides the Star Route
Cole, Jackson
Jim Hatfield series (85)

Death rings a bell
Fitzsimmons, Cortland
Percy Peacock series (1)

Death rings no bell
Braddon, George
Michael Gaunt series (2)

Death rites
McLaglen, John J
Herne the Hunter series (7)

Death river
Coburn, L J
Caleb Thorn series (5)

Death road
Stuart, Donald
Sexton Blake series (633)

Death round the corner
Creasey, John
Department Z series (4)

Death sails in a high wind
Du Bois, Theodora
Anne and Jeffrey McNeill series (11)

Death school
McLaglen, John J
Herne the Hunter series (14)

Death-school
Williamson, Jerry Neal
Lamia Zacharias series (3)

Death scouts
Woodley, Richard
Man from Atlantis series (2)

Death sends a cable
Yates, Margaret Tayler
Anne Davenport McLean series (2)

Death sends for the doctor
Bellairs, George
Detective Inspector Thomas Littlejohn series (28)

Death sentence
Cochran, Molly
Destroyer series (80)
Garfield, Brian Wynne
Paul Benjamin series (2)
Hunsburger, Ed
Destroyer series (80)
Kelley, Leo Patrick
Space police series (6)
Murphy, Warren Burton
Destroyer series (80)

Death set in diamonds
Verner, Gerald
Trevor Lowe series (14)

Death set to music
Hebden, Mark
Inspector Clovis Pel series (1)

Death shall overcome
Lathen, Emma
John Putnam Thatcher series (5)

Death ship
Follett, James
Earthsearch series (2)
Grant, Maxwell
Shadow series (162)
Hope, Stanton
Sexton Blake series (657)
Traven, B
Gerard Gales series (1)

Death shuttle
Streib, Dan
Steve Crown series (3)

Death sign
Evans, Gwyn
Sexton Blake series (661)

Death sits on the board
Rhode, John
Doctor Lancelot Priestley series (26)

Death sleep
Grant, Maxwell
Shadow series (64)

Death, sleep and the traveller
Hawkes, John
Blood oranges trilogy (2)

Death song
Hawkes, Robert
NARC series (9)

Death sounds grand
Hunt, Richard
Chief Inspector Walsh and Constable Brenda Phipps series (2)

Death speaks softly
Fraser, Anthea
Inspector David Webb and Sergeant Ken Jackson series (4)

Death sped the plough
Usher, Gray
Superintendent Michael Drexel series (2)

Death spins the wheel
Bellairs, George
Detective Inspector Thomas Littlejohn series (42)

Death spoke sweetly
Garnett, Roger
John Yardley series (2)

Death springs the trap
Goldthwaite, Eaton Kenneth
Lieutenant Joseph Dickerson series (1)

Death squad
Carter, Nick
Nick Carter series (223)
Copper, Basil
Mike Faraday series (25)
Demille, Nelson
Joe Keller series (4)
Kastle, Herbert David
Sergeant Edmund Roersch series (3)
Mackie, John
Rat Bastards series (2)
McCurtin, Peter
Jim Rainey series (15)
Pendleton, Don
Mack Bolan series (2)
Willard, Tom
Strike fighters series (9)

Death stage
Muir, James A
Breed series (4)

Death stalked the fells
Macleod, Adam Gordon
Sir William Burrill series (3)

Death stalks in Soho
Brandon, John Gordon
Arthur Stukeley Pennington series (28)
Inspector Patrick Aloysius McCarthy series (52)

Death stalks in Spain
Smith, Don
Secret mission series (13)

Death stalks the cobbled square
Chance, John Newton
John Newton Chance series (1)

Death stalks the Punjab
Casberg, Melvin A
Captain Prem Narayan series (1)

Death stalks the stadium
O'Sullivan, James Brendan
Steve Silk series (4)

Death stalks the Wakely family
Derleth, August
Judge Ephraim Peck series (1)

Death stands by
Creasey, John
Department Z series (10)

Death stands round the corner
Duncan, William Murdoch
Superintendent Macneill series (1)

Death star affair
Carter, Nick
Nick Carter series (170)

Death starts a rumour
Fitt, Mary
Superintendent Mallett series (4)

Death steals the show
Bude, John
Inspector Meredith series (18)

Death stops the bells
Baker, Richard Merriam
Franklin Russell series (3)

Death stops the manuscript
Baker, Richard Merriam
Franklin Russell series (1)

Death stops the rehearsal
Baker, Richard Merriam
Franklin Russell series (2)

Death stops the show
Thompson, Lloyd S
Shimoru Kyota series (1)

Death strain
Carter, Nick
Nick Carter series (60)

Death strike
Stivers, Dick
Able Team series (21)

Death strikes at Heron House
O'Neil, Kerry
Jerry Mooney series (3)

Death strikes at six bells
Baxter, Gregory
Superintendent Daniels series (3)

Death strikes from the rear
Marsden, Antony
Inspector Buck series (2)

Death strikes home
Glidden, Minna Wesselhoft
Carey Brent series (1)

Death strikes in darkness
Marshall, Lovat
Sugar Kane series (12)

Death suspended
Whitman, Charles
Inspector Lindon and Sergeant Gray series (3)

Death swap
Babson, Marian
Family holiday series (1)

Death sweet
Macgregor, T J
Quin Saint James and Mike McClary series (3)

Death symbol
Plummer, Thomas Arthur
Detective Inspector Andrew Frampton series (7)

Death syndicate
Philips, Judson Pentecost
Carole Trevor and Max Blythe series (1)

Death takes a bow
Lockridge, Frances
Bill Wiegand series (6)
Mister and Mrs North series (7)

Death takes a detour
Burton, Miles
Inspector Arnold and Desmond Merrion series (57)

Death takes a dive
Cooke, Geoffrey Walter
Peter Mitchell series (2)
Heath, Eric
Cornelius Clift series (1)
Wade Anthony series (2)
Tack, Alfred
John Harley series (4)

Death takes a flat
Burton, Miles
Inspector Arnold and Desmond Merrion series (23)

Death takes a gamble
Smithies, Richard Hugo Ripman
Inspector William McAlpin series (2)

Death takes a partner
Rhode, John
Doctor Lancelot Priestley series (67)

Death takes a paying guest
Stein, Aaron Marc
Tim Mulligan and Elsie Mae Hunt series (8)

Death takes a redhead
Gilbert, Anthony
Arthur Crook series (7)

Death takes a ride
Finney, R C
Inspector Bourne series (10)
Wheeler, H E
Stephen Rant series (1)
Death takes a teacher
Usher, Gray
Superintendent Michael Drexel series (3)
Death takes a wife
Gilbert, Anthony
Arthur Crook series (34)
Death takes an editor
Morland, Nigel
Steven Malone series (2)
Death takes an option
Macneil, Neil
Tony Costaine and Bert McCall series (1)
Death takes the joystick
Conde, Phillip
Irving Todd series (3)
Death takes the living
Burton, Miles
Inspector Arnold and Desmond Merrion series (39)
Death takes the stage
Holt, Gavin
Professor Luther Bastion series (13)
Death takes the wheel
Radford, Edwin
Doctor Manson series (15)
Death talks out of turn
Powell, Richard
Arab and Andy Blake series (2)
Death talks shop
Haggard, Paul
Mike Warlock series (2)
Death tally
Scott, Bradford
Walt Slade series (90)
Death tape
Gallison, Kate
Unbalanced accounts series (2)
Death tears a comic strip
Du Bois, Theodora
Anne and Jeffrey McNeill series (4)
Death therapy
Murphy, Warren Burton
Destroyer series (6)
Death threat
Nelson, Peter N
Mollie Fox series (5)
Pascal, Francine
Sweet Valley High series (110)
Death through the looking glass
Forrest, Richard
Lyon and Bea Wentworth series (3)
Death through the mill
Colburn, Laura
Carol Gates series (3)
Death thumbs a ride
Lilly, Jean
Bruce Perkins series (3)
Death tide
Crispin, Ann Carol
V series (10)
Death times three
Stout, Rex
Nero Wolfe and Archie Goodwin series (47)
Death to a downbeat
Brown, Carter
Danny Boyd series (30)
Death to drumbeat
Lane, Jeremy
Whitney Wheat series (1)
Death to slow music
Nichols, Beverley
Mister Horatio Green series (3)
Death to the bourgeois
Piccard, Eulalie
Episodes of the great Russian tragedy series (1)
Death to the Daleks
Dicks, Terrance
Doctor Who series (40)
Sarah Jane Smith series (14)
Death to the Deutschland
Kessler, Leo
Sea Wolves series (2)
Death to the Donnellys
Miller, Orlo
Donnellys series (2)
Death to the Fifth Column
Newman, Bernard
Papa Pontivy series (5)
Death to the ladies
Morland, Nigel
Chief Inspector Andrew McMurdo series (9)
Death to the landlords!
Peters, Ellis
Inspector George Felse series (11)
Death to the Mafia
Scarpetta, Frank
Marksman series (6)
Death to the ranger!
Scott, Bradford
Walt Slade series (110)
Death to the spy
Newman, Bernard
Papa Pontivy series (1)
Death to the windward
Brinton, Henry
John and Sally Strang series (1)
Death token
Grant, Maxwell
Shadow series (119)
Death tolls the bell
McGuire, Paul
Superintendent Fillinger series (1)
Death tolls the gong
Brandon, John Gordon
Arthur Stukeley Pennington series (7)
Inspector Patrick Aloysius McCarthy series (10)
Death too soon
Peterson, Audrey
Jane Winfield and Andrew Quentin series (8)
Death took a Greek god
Forrest, Norman
John Finnegan series (2)
Death took a publisher
Forrest, Norman
John Finnegan series (1)
Death torch terror
House, Brant
Secret Agent X series (2)
Death tower
Grant, Maxwell
Shadow series (6)
Death trail
Chisholm, Matt
Rem McAllister series (6)
Gilman, George G
Adam Steele series (12)
McLennan, Will
Ramseys series (6)
Death trails
Sharpe, Jon
Trailsman series (147)
Death train
Davis, Gordon
Sergeant series (1)
James, William M
Apache series (4)
Macneill, Alastair
U.N.A.C.O.series (3)
Death trance
Zimmerman, R D
Maddy and Alex Phillips series (1)
Death trap
Carmichael, Harry
John Piper and Quinn series (29)
Logan, Jake
John Slocum series (123)
Rosenberger, Joseph
Murder Master series (1)
Skene, Anthony
Sexton Blake series (631)
Death traps
Strahan, Kay Cleaver
Lynn Macdonald series (3)
Death treads
Wills, Cecil Melville
Geoffrey Boscobell series (3)
Death treads softly
Bellairs, George
Detective Inspector Thomas Littlejohn series (25)
Death triangle
Grant, Maxwell
Shadow series (40)
Death trick
Burke, Jackson Frederick
Samuel Moses Kelly series (2)
Jeffries, Roderic Graeme
Inspector Enrique Alvarez series (12)
Stevenson, Richard
Donald Strachey series (1)
Death turns a trick
Smith, Julie
Rebecca Schwartz series (1)
Death turns right
Dewey, Thomas Blanchard
Private Eye Mac series (15)
Mathewson, Joseph
Alicia von Helsing series (2)
Death turns the tables
Carr, John Dickson
Doctor Gideon Fell series (14)
Death turns traitor
Masterman, Walter Sidney
Sir Arthur Sinclair series (10)
Death turrets
Grant, Maxwell
Shadow series (133)
Death-twist
Tiger, John
I spy series (7)
Death under contract
Wallace, Robert
Phantom Detective series (18)
Death under par
Law, Janice
Anna Peters series (5)
Death under Snowden
Carr, Glyn
Sir Abercrombie Lewker series (8)
Death under the lilacs
Forrest, Richard
Lyon and Bea Wentworth series (6)
Death under the moonflower
Downing, Todd
Peter Bounty series (2)
Death under the stars
Bell, Vicars
Doctor Douglas Baynes series (1)
Death under Virgo
Muir, Thomas
Roger Crammond series (6)
Death unheralded
Douglas, George
Inspector Hallam and Sergeant Spratt series (4)
Death upon a spear
Brown, Hosanna
Frank Le Roux series (2)
Death Valley
Dengler, Sandy
Jack Prester series (1)
James, William M
Apache series (23)
Mitchum, Hank
Stage coach station series (33)
Nolan, Keith William
Vietnam War series (3)
Death Valley gold
Benteen, John
Neal Fargo series (21)
Death village
Netzen, Klaus
Killers series (6)
Death visits Downspring
Burton, Miles
Inspector Arnold and Desmond Merrion series (25)
Death visits the Apple Hole
Cunningham, Albert Benjamin
Sheriff Jess Roden series (9)
Death visits the summer house
Lane, Gret
Kate Marsh series (5)
Death visits the summer-house
Lane, Gret
John Barrin series (4)
Death waits in semispace
Mahr, Kurt
Perry Rhodan series (61)
Death waits in Tucson
Reid, Desmond
Pinkerton series (2)
Death walked in Berlin
Kaye, Mary Margaret
Death series (2)
Death walked in Cyprus
Kaye, Mary Margaret
Death series (3)
Death walked in Kashmir
Kaye, Mary Margaret
Death series (1)
Death walks by the river
Bell, Vicars
Doctor Douglas Baynes series (6)
Death walks in Eastrepps
Beeding, Francis
Inspector Wilkins series (1)
Death walks in scarlet
Desmond, Hugh
Alan Fraser series (4)
Death walks in shadow
Thayer, Lee
Peter Clancy series (60)
Death walks on cat feet
Haggard, Paul
Mike Warlock series (4)
Olsen, D B
Rachel and Jennifer Murdock series (13)
Death walks softly
Shepherd, Neal
Chief Inspector Michael Tandy series (2)
Death walks the post
Hanson, Virginia
Adam Drew and Katherine Cornish series (1)
Death walks the woods
Hare, Cyril
Francis Pettigrew series (4)
Death warmed over
Martin, Lee
Deb Ralston series (4)
Death warrant
Edwards, Hank
Judge Clay Torn series (10)
Death was no lady
Truss, Seldon
Inspector Gidleigh series (8)
Death watch
Ahern, Jerry
Survivalist series (27)
Death-watch
Carr, John Dickson
Doctor Gideon Fell series (5)
Death watch
Compton, David Guy
Katherine Mortenhoe series (1)
Death watch ladies
Chance, John Newton
Macinnes series (1)
Death waves
Stone, Nick
Ben Kane series (3)
Death wears a mask
Browne, Douglas Gordon
Mister Harvey Tuke series (1)
Gilbert, Anthony
Arthur Crook series (47)
Death wears a purple shirt
Woodthorpe, Ralph Carter
Nicholas Slade series (1)
Death wears a red hat
Kienzle, William Xavier
Father Robert Koesler series (2)
Death wears a scarab
Long, Amelia Reynolds
Steve Carter series (2)
Death wears a veil
Knight, Kathleen Moore
Elisha Macomber series (4)
Death wears a white gardenia
Popkin, Zelda
Mary Carner Whittaker series (1)
Death wears cat's eyes
Olsen, D B
Rachel and Jennifer Murdock series (10)
Death wears grey
Pike, Charles R
Jubal Cade series (8)
Death wears red shoes
Robertson, Colin
Peter Grayleigh series (13)
Death weed
Thayer, Lee
Peter Clancy series (19)
Death went hunting
Douglas, George
Inspector Hallam and Sergeant Spratt series (3)
Death weras a white coat
Du Bois, Theodora
Anne and Jeffrey McNeill series (2)
Death when she wakes
Morland, Nigel
Detective Inspector Rory Luccan series (1)
Death whispers
Carr, Joseph Baker
Oceola Archer series (1)
Scott, Bradford
Walt Slade series (111)
Death wish
Garfield, Brian Wynne
Paul Benjamin series (1)
Death-wish green
Crane, Frances
Pat and Jean Abbott series (24)
Death with a difference
Cobb, Belton
Bryan Armitage series (1)
Inspector Cheviot Burmann series (25)
Death with blue ribbon
Bruce, Leo
Carolus Deene series (19)
Death within the vault
Thayer, Lee
Peter Clancy series (46)
Death without question
Muir, Thomas
Roger Crammond series (5)
Death women
Chance, John Newton
Jonathan Blake series (4)
Death won a prize
Montgomery, Ione
Christopher Gibson series (2)
Death won't wait
Gilbert, Anthony
Arthur Crook series (27)
Death won't wash
Longmate, Norman
Inspector Bradley and Sergeant Raymond series (1)
Death wore a petticoat
Janson, Hank
Hank Janson series (27)
Death zone attack
Sievert, John
C.A.D.S. series (11)
Deathbed
Kienzle, William Xavier
Father Robert Koesler series (8)
Deathbell
Smith, Guy Newman
Deathbell series (1)
Deathbites
Stivers, Dick
Able Team series (12)
Deathblow Hill
Taylor, Phoebe Atwood
Asey Mayo series (7)
Deathblow trail
Sharpe, Jon
Trailsman series (143)
Deathdeal
Disher, Garry
Wyatt series (3)
Deathgame
Dixon, Franklin W
Hardy boys case files series (7)
Goulart, Ron
Vampirella series (5)
Deathics
Barth, Richard
Margaret Binton series (9)
Deathless Amazon
Fearn, John Russell
Golden Amazon series (2)
Deathlight
Carter, Nick
Nick Carter series (160)
Death's acolyte
Vardeman, Robert Edward
Swords of Raemllyn series (4)
Death's Angel
Longley, W B
Angel Eyes series (2)
Death's angel
Sky, Kathleen
Star trek originals sequels series (16)
Death's bounty
Brady, William S
Jared Hawk series (3)
Gilman, George G
Edge series (12)
Death's bright angel
Warriner, Thurman
Mister Scotter series (5)
Death's bright dart
Clinton-Baddeley, Victor Clinton
Doctor Davie series (1)
Death's busy crossroads
Mitchell, Scott
Brock Devlin series (15)
Death's caravan
Sharpe, Jon
Trailsman series (92)
Death's clenched fist
Sherburne, James
Paddy Moretti series (3)
Death's corral
Scott, Bradford
Walt Slade series (55)
Death's counterfeit
Clevely, Hugh
Inspector Williams series (5)
Death's dateless night
Warriner, Thurman
Mister Scotter series (3)
Death's deal
Hardin, J D
Raider series (6)
Death's demand
Mahr, Kurt
Perry Rhodan series (114)
Death's door
Barker, Wade
Ninja Master series (6)

Death's doorway
Gunn, Victor
Chief Inspector Bill Cromwell series (5)
Death's drum
Sharp, Allen
Storytrails series (25)
Death's duet
Carstairs, Henry
Lydford Long series (12)
Death's foot forward
Mair, George Brown
David Grant series (1)
Death's gray angel
Sherburne, James
Paddy Moretti series (2)
Death's gray land
Shupp, Mike
Destiny makers series (4)
Death's grey land
Shupp, Mike
Destiny makers series (4)
Death's harvest
Scott, Bradford
Walt Slade series (82)
Death's head
Kessler, Leo
Wotan series (2)
Logan, Jake
John Slocum series (161)
Ross, Jonathan
Superintendent George Rogers series (10)
Death's head conspiracy
Carter, Nick
Nick Carter series (83)
Death's head rebellion
Pournelle, Jerry
War world series (2)
Death's Head Trail
Sherman, Jory
Gunn series (3)
Death's inheritance
Radford, Edwin
Doctor Manson series (14)
Death's juggler
Daly, Carroll John
Satan Hall series (1)
Death's law
Scott, Michael
Tales of the bard trilogy (3)
Death's little sister
Decker, Jake
Steve Sinclair series (2)
Death's long shadow
Barbette, Jay
Harry Butten series (2)
Penn, John
Inspector George Thorne and Sergeant Bill Abbot series (12)
Wolffe, Katherine
Captain Courtney Brade series (2)
Death's lovely mask
Flagg, John
Hart Muldoon series (4)
Death's mannikins
Afford, Max
Jeffery Blackburn series (2)
Death's masquerade
Grant, Maxwell
Shadow series (237)
Death's master
Lee, Tanith
Tales from the flat earth series (2)
Death's no antidote
Osborne, Geoffrey
James Dingle and Glyn Jones series (5)
Deaths of Lora Karen
McDougald, Roman
Philip Cabot series (1)
Death's old sweet song
Stagge, Jonathan
Doctor Hugh Westlake series (8)
Death's pale horse
Sherburne, James
Paddy Moretti series (1)
Death's premium
Grant, Maxwell
Shadow series (178)
Death's running mate
Revere, John D
Justin Perry series (4)
Death's savage passion
Papazoglou, Orania
Patience Campbell McKenna series (3)
Death's shadow
Wyatt, Zach
Texians series (5)
Death's visiting card
Woodiwiss, John Cecil
Inspector Hopton series (1)
Deathscape
Peters, David
Psi-Man series (2)
Deathstar voyage
Wallace, Ian
Claudine Saint Cyr series (2)
Croyd series (3)
Pan Sagittarius series (1)
Deathstone
Eulo, Ken
Chandal Talon trilogy (3)
Deathstrike
Carter, Nick
Nick Carter series (236)
Deathtrap dungeon
Livingstone, Ian
Fighting fantasy gamebook series (6)
Deathwatch
Harrison, Ray
Sergeant Joseph Bragg and Constable James Morton series (3)
Deathwater
Infante, Anne
Micky Douglas and Inspector Reeves series (3)
Deathwind of Vedun
Rypel, Thadeus Chester
Gonji series (1)
Deathwing
Jones, Neal
Inquisition war series (1)
Deathwing over Veynaa
Hill, Douglas
Last legionary series (3)
Deathworld
Harrison, Harry
Jason Din Alt series (1)
Deathworld 1
Harrison, Harry
Jason Din Alt series (1)
Deathworld 2
Harrison, Harry
Jason Din Alt series (2)
Deathworld 3
Harrison, Harry
Jason Din Alt series (3)
Deathworld trilogy
Harrison, Harry
Jason Din Alt series (3)
Deathworms of Kratos
Avery, Richard
Expendables series (1)
Debacle
Zola, Emile
Rougon Macquart series (19)
Debbie and her dolls
Lenski, Lois
Debbie series (4)
Debbie and her family
Lenski, Lois
Debbie series (2)
Debbie and her grandma
Lenski, Lois
Debbie series (1)
Debbie and her pets
Lenski, Lois
Debbie series (6)
Debbie goes to nursery school
Lenski, Lois
Debbie series (5)
Debbie herself
Lenski, Lois
Debbie series (3)
Debbie learns to cook
Delahaye, Gilbert
Debbie learns series (1)
Debbie learns to dance
Delahaye, Gilbert
Debbie learns series (2)
Debbie of the Green Gate
Daringer, Helen Fern
Endicott family trilogy (2)
De Bercy affair
Holmes, Gordon
Inspector Furneaux series (2)
Debit account
Onions, Oliver
Whom God hath sundered trilogy (2)
Deborah
Davenat, Colette
Deborah series (1)
Deborah and the siege of Paris
Davenat, Colette
Deborah series (3)
Deborah goes to Dover
Chesney, Marion
Travelling matchmaker series (5)
Deborah's diary
Manning, Anne
Mary Powell series (2)
Debt
Hogstrand, Olle
Chief Inspector Lars Kollin series (3)
Debt collector
Morgan, Stanley
Russ Tobin series (2)
Debt of blood
James, William M
Apache series (27)
Debt of honor
Bradley, Mary Hastings
Old Chicago series (3)
Clancy, Tom
Jack Ryan series (5)
Debt of honour
Veryan, Patricia
Age of Elegance series (1)
Debt of tears
Ts'ao, Hsueh-ch'in
Dream of the red chamber series (4)
Debt to a tin star
Grover, Marshall
Larry and Stretch series (285)
Decade of champions
Aaseng, Nathan
Sports heroes series (35)
Decay of the angel
Mishima, Yukio
Sea of fertiligy quartet (4)
Deceit
Preston, Fayrene
Swansea Place series (2)
Deceit and deadly lies
Bandy, Franklin
Kevin Macinnes series (1)
Deceit, deception, death and the carousel horse
Gray, P D
Three Ds series (1)
Deceit, deception, death and the jackal-headed god
Gray, P D
Three Ds series (2)
Deceitful death
Penn, John
Inspector George Thorne and Sergeant Bill Abbot series (2)
Deceiver
Cooper, Louise Antell
Chaos gate trilogy (1)
Deceivers
Masters, John
Indian trilogy (2)
Savage family series (2)
December boys
Noonan, Michael
Choker series (2)
December passion
Logan, Mark
Nicholas Minnett series (3)
December secrets
Giff, Patricia Reilly
Kids of the Polk Street School series (4)
Decepticon poison
Stamper, Judith Bauer
Junior transformers find your fate series (6)
Deception
Bischoff, David
UFO conspiracy series (2)
Deception planners
Wheatley, Dennis
Time has come series (3)
Deception Trail
Grove, Frederick Philip
Dude McQuint series (4)
Deceptions
Michael, Judith
Deceptions series (1)
Pascal, Francine
Sweet Valley High series (14)
Deceptive appearances
Malcolm, John
Tim Simpson series (9)
Decision
Macdonnell, James Edmond
Captain Peter Bentley series (22)
Decision at Brushy Creek
Tolliver, Ruby Changes
Decision series (4)
Decision at sea
Hammel, Eric Maxwell
Guadalcanal series (3)
Tolliver, Ruby Changes
Decision series (2)
Decision at Thunder Rift
Keith, William Henry
BattleTech series (1)
Decision at Trafalgar
Woodman, Richard
Nathaniel Drinkwater series (6)
Decision for Dusty Fog
Edson, John Thomas
Floating Outfit series (27)
Decision time
Ahern, Jerry
Defender series (4)
Decisions
Pascal, Francine
Sweet Valley High series (46)
Decline and fall of Lloyd George, and great was the fall thereof
Beaverbrook, William Maxwell Aitken
Lloyd George series (4)
Decorated corpse
Stratton, Roy
Scott Gregory and Justin Bassett series (1)
Decoy
Adams, Cleve Franklin
Rex McBride series (3)
Morgan, Michael
Bill Ryan series (2)
Pope, Dudley
Ned Yorke series (4)
Robertson, Stephen
Ryne Lanark series (1)
Decoy for murder
Saxon, Peter
Sexton Blake series (1410)
Decoy hit
Carter, Nick
Nick Carter series (181)
Decoy murders
Douglas, Arthur
Mark Register series (3)
Decoys
Hoyt, Richard
John Denson series (1)
Decoys from hell
Grover, Marshall
Larry and Stretch series (17)
Decoys from Texas
Grover, Marshall
Larry and Stretch series (72)
Dectra chain
Axler, James
Deathlands series (7)
Dedicated
Jennings, D K
Doctor Ralph Conway series (7)
Dedicated man
Robinson, Peter
Chief Inspector Alan Banks series (2)
Dedicated to that boy I love
Lewis, Linda
Linda series (8)
Dedicated villain
Veryan, Patricia
Golden chronicles series (6)
Deductions of Colonel Gore
Brock, Lynn
Colonel Gore series (1)
Deed is drawn
Barber, Willetta Ann
Christopher Storm series (7)
Deed without a name
Bowers, Dorothy
Inspector Pardoe series (3)
Deedle Dumpy and castles in the air
Schermele, Willy
Deedle Dumpy series (1)
Deedle Dumpy and Mimi the mouse meet Mister Owl
Schermele, Willy
Deedle Dumpy series (3)
Deedle Dumpy and mimi's new friends
Schermele, Willy
Deedle Dumpy series (4)
Deedle Dumpy meets Mimi the Mouse
Schermele, Willy
Deedle Dumpy series (2)
Deeds ill done
Seifert, Adele
Gregory Trent series (3)
Deeds of the desperate campers
Hollands, Judith
Ketchup sisters series (2)
Deeds of the disturber
Peters, Elizabeth
Amelia Peabody Emerson series (5)
Deeds of trust
Wuamett, Victor
Chase Randel series (2)
Deep
Spillane, Mickey
Mike Hammer series (7)
Deep among the dead men
Blackburn, John
Bill Easter series (1)
Deep and crisp and even
Payne, Laurence
Chief Inspector Sam Birkett series (3)
Turnbull, Peter
P Division series (1)
Deep as the grave
Keystone, Oliver
Paul Plush series (2)
Deep blue cradle
Chambers, Peter
Mark Preston series (24)
Deep blue goodbye
Macdonald, John Dann
Travis McGee series (1)
Deep canyon kill
Meek, Joseph
Mountain Jack Pike series (11)
Deep cold green
Brown, Carter
Lieutenant Al Wheeler series (38)
Deep cover blast-off
Derrick, Lionel
Penetrator series (44)
Deep, deep freeze
Garner, William
Mike Jagger series (2)
Deep dive
Hornig, Doug
Loren Swift series (4)
Deep domain
Weinstein, Howard
Star trek series (33)
Deep empire
Axler, James
Deathlands series (19)
Deep fall
Knox, Bill
Inspector Colin Thane and Phil Moss series (8)
Deep foot
Vixen, Richard M
Deep foot series (1)
Deep freeze
Bruce, Jean
Secret Agent O.S.S.117 series (10)
Deep green death
Gaston, Bill
Roy Maclean series (1)
Deep kill
Da Cruz, Daniel
Jock Sergeant series (2)
Greenfield, Irving A
Depth force series (7)
Deep of the sky
Ronan, Tom
Deep of the sky series (1)
Deep pocket
Kenyon, Michael
Inspector Henry Peckover series (1)
Deep ran the river
Blunt, Betty
Treacherous moon series (2)
Deep reaches of space
Chandler, Arthur Bertram
Rim series (15)
Deep rescue
Greenfield, Irving A
Depth force series (14)
Deep sea death
Carter, Nick
Nick Carter series (252)
Deep sea hunters
Verrill, Alpheus Hyatt
Deep sea hunters series (1)
Deep sea hunters in the frozen seas
Verrill, Alpheus Hyatt
Deep sea hunters series (2)
Deep sea hunters in the South Seas
Verrill, Alpheus Hyatt
Deep sea hunters series (3)
Deep sea sauruses
Salmon, Michael
Dinosaur swamp series (4)
Deep-sea summer
Goudge, Eileen
Super-seniors series (4)
Deep secrets
Keene, Carolyn
Nancy Drew files series (50)
Deep shaker
Roberts, Les
Milan Jacovich series (3)
Deep shooter
Gentry, Buck
Eli Holten series (34)
Deep six
Cussler, Clive
Dirk Pitt series (7)

Demons
Dillard, Jeanne M
Star trek sequels series (1)
Star trek series (30)
Pronzini, Bill
Private Eye series (22)
Smith, Guy Newman
Deathbell series (2)
Demons at Rainbow Bridge
Chalker, Jack Laurence
Quintara Marathon series (1)
Demon's claw
Morris, Dave
Blood sword series (3)
Demon's coronation
Lambert, William J
Demon series (2)
Demon's den
Dixon, Franklin W
Hardy boys series (81)
Demon's eye
Carter, Nicholas
Nicholas Carter series (225)
Demon's law
Scott, Michael
Tales of the bard trilogy (2)
Demon's moon
Robertson, Colin
Peter Grayleigh series (15)
Demons of the Dancing Gods
Chalker, Jack Laurence
Dancing Gods series (2)
Demons of the deep
Jackson, Steven Gary
Fighting fantasy gamebook series (19)
Demons of the night
Carter, Nicholas
Nicholas Carter series (232)
Demons of Zammar
Sirota, Mike
Ro-Lan series (4)
Demon's stalk
Lambert, William J
Demon series (1)
Demonstealer
Gascoigne, Marc
Fighting fantasy gamebook series (45)
Demonstration
Brennan, James Herbert
Sagas of the Demonspawn series (4)
Caute, David
Confrontation trilogy (1)
Demu trilogy
Busby, Francis Marion
Demu trilogy (3)
Den of dragons
Brennan, James Herbert
GrailQuest series (2)
Den of savage men
Jones, Bradshaw
Claude Ravel series (8)
Dene of the Secret Service
Verner, Gerald
Michael Dene series (2)
Trevor Lowe series (12)
Denise and Ned Toodles
Jackson, Gabrielle Emilie
Denise and Ned Toodles series (1)
Denmede mystery
Martyn, Wyndham
Christopher Bond series (3)
Dennis Harper, missionary journalist
Palmer, Bernard
Career series (13)
Dennisdale tragedy
Andover, Henry
Henry Holland series (2)
Dennison documents
Jones, G Wayman
Black Bat series (30)
Dennison's war
Lassiter, Adam
Dennison's war series (1)
Dentist in the chair
Finch, Matthew
Dentist series (1)
Denver
Orwig, Sara
Danby trilogy (3)
Denver darlin'
Fletcher, Dirk
Spur McCoy giant series (2)
Spur McCoy special series (4)
Denver duchess
Longtree, Warren T
Ruff Justice series (21)
Denver duo
Roberts, J R
Gunsmith series (53)
Denver gold
Logan, Jake
John Slocum series (86)
Denver run
Robbins, David
Endworld series (8)
Denver strike
Ramm, Carl
James Hawker series (10)
Denzil's dilemma
Jordan, Sherryl
Denzil series (2)
Departed glory
Danielson, Peter
Children of the Lion series (16)
Departing friends
Glemser, Bernard
Nicholas Hart series (2)
Department K
Howard, Hartley
Philip Scott series (1)
Department of danger
Lancer, Jack
Christopher Cool series (3)
Department of Dead Ends
Vickers, Roy
Department of Dead Ends series (1)
Department of death
Creasey, John
Department Z series (25)
Departure deferred
Baker, William Howard
Dangerman series (1)
Depend on Katie John
Calhoun, Mary
Katie John series (2)
Deposit vault puzzle
Carter, Nicholas
Nicholas Carter series (24)
Depository mystery
Chester, Gilbert
Sexton Blake series (996)
Depraved indifference
Tanenbaum, Robert K
Assistant District Attorney Butch Karp series (2)
Depravity
Janson, Hank
Hank Janson series (167)
Deprived child and the community
Ford, Donald
Child and the community series (1)
Deptford trilogy
Davies, Robertson
Deptford trilogy (3)
Depth charge
Stone, Nick
Ben Kane series (5)
Depth force
Greenfield, Irving A
Depth force series (1)
Depths
Creasey, John
Doctor Palfrey series (22)
Depths and the heights
Romains, Jules
Men of goodwill series (12)
Depths of danger
Clark, Halsey
Periscope series (3)
Jones, J Farragut
Silent service series (8)
Deputies
Edson, John Thomas
Rockabye County series (6)
Deputies of death
Friend, Oscar
Simon Carter series (3)
Deputy
Ladd, Justin
Abilene series (16)
Morris, Gilbert
Jim Reno series (2)
Deputy Dan and the bank robbers
Rosenbloom, Joseph
Deputy Dan series (1)
Deputy Dan gets his man
Rosenbloom, Joseph
Deputy Dan series (2)
Deputy of Arcis
Balzac, Honore de
Scenes of political life series (3)
Deputy of violence
Hogan, Ray
Shawn Starbuck series (4)
Deputy sheriff
Mulford, Clarence Edward
J C series (3)
Deputy was king
Stern, Gladys Bronwyn
Rakonitz family series (2)
Derai
Tubb, Edwin Charles
Dumarest series (2)
Derby Downs
Cosgrove, Stephen Edward
Barely there series (4)
Derby Man
McCarthy, Gary
Derby Man series (1)
Dere Mable
Streeter, Edward
Mable series (1)
Derelict
Hyne, Charles John Cutcliffe
Captain Owen Kettle series (18)
Derelict house
Skene, Anthony
Sexton Blake series (770)
Derelict of Skull Shoal
Robeson, Kenneth
Doc Savage series (178)
Derelicts
Graydon, William Murray
Sexton Blake series (233)
McFee, William
Spenlove series (3)
Deric in Mesa Verde
Nusbaum, Deric
Deric series (1)
Deric with the Indians
Nusbaum, Deric
Deric series (2)
Dermotts rampant
McKenna, Stephen
Dermott family series (1)
Derrick devil
Robeson, Kenneth
Doc Savage series (74)
Derringer danger
Dalton, Kit
Buckskin series (38)
Derry down death
Curry, Avon
Jerome Aylwin series (1)
Dervish daughter
Tepper, Sheri S
Jinian trilogy (2)
Deryni archives
Kurtz, Katherine
Chronicles of the Deryni trilogy (3)
Deryni challenge
Billias, Stephen
Chronicles of the Deryni trilogy (3)
Deryni checkmate
Kurtz, Katherine
Chronicles of the Deryni trilogy (2)
Deryni magic
Kurtz, Katherine
Chronicles of the Deryni trilogy (3)
Deryni rising
Kurtz, Katherine
Chronicles of the Deryni trilogy (1)
Descent of Pierre Saint-Martin
Casteret, Norbert
Under the earth series (5)
Descent of the sun
Bain, Francis William
Indian mystic love stories series (2)
Desdemona affair
Allison, Clyde
Agent triple zero eight series (5)
Desdemona moves on
Keller, Beverly
Desdemona series (3)
Desdemona, twelve going on desperate
Keller, Beverly
Desdemona series (1)
Desecration
Perry, Mark Christopher
Morigu series (1)
Desecration of Susan Browning
Martin, Russell White
Supernatural series (1)
Desert
Wilson, Colin
Spider world series (1)
Desert adventure
Dale, Judith
Shirley Flight series (3)
Desert battle
Drury, Rebecca
Women of war series (8)
Desert captive
Tokson, Elliot
Alec Cavender series (1)
Desert climax
Hunter, E J
White Squaw series (22)
Desert damsels
Allison, Clyde
Agent triple zero eight series (20)
Desert danger
King, David
Rat Patrol series (2)
Desert death
Sharpe, Jon
Trailsman series (123)
Desert death raid
Buchanan, Jack
M.I.A. Hunter series (12)
Desert death trap
Hardin, J D
Raider series (37)
Desert desperadoes
Sharpe, Jon
Trailsman series (98)
Desert Eden
Morgan, Jill Meredith
Eden trilogy (1)
Desert flight
Razzi, Jim
Junior transformers find your fate series (5)
Desert fury
Janson, Hank
Hank Janson series (50)
Desert ghost
Barrington, G W
Rusty and Peter series (2)
Desert gold
Grey, Zane
Yaqui series (1)
Scott, Bradford
Walt Slade series (4)
Desert guns
Bodine, J D
Quinn's Raiders series (3)
Desert hawks on the wing
Langley, John Prentice
Aviation series (6)
Desert heat
Jance, Judith A
Joanna Brady series (1)
Desert hell
Roberts, J R
Gunsmith series (51)
Walker, Dalton
Shiloh series (2)
Desert heritage
Wren, Percival Christopher
Beau Geste series (5)
Desert Home
Kopsen, Dorothy Blaxland
Desert Home series (1)
Desert inn mystery
Schroeder, Doris
Walt Disney's Annette series (2)
Desert intrigue
Stagg, James
Sexton Blake series (1493)
Desert island ducks
Laird, Elizabeth
Toucan Tecs series (11)
Desert island wreckers
Fennell, Willie
Dexter Dutton series (9)
Desert killers
Scott, Bradford
Walt Slade series (33)
Desert lake mystery
Strahan, Kay Cleaver
Lynn Macdonald series (7)
Desert love
Conquest, Joan
Jill series (1)
Desert marauders
Landsborough, Gordon
Desert commandos series (2)
Desert masquerade
King, David
Rat Patrol series (6)
Desert mercenary
Sadler, Barry
Casca series (16)
Desert moon
Williams, Jude
McLaffertys series (2)
Desert moon mystery
Strahan, Kay Cleaver
Lynn Macdonald series (1)
Desert of death's domain
Mahr, Kurt
Perry Rhodan series (100)
Desert of doom
Graydon, William Murray
Sexton Blake series (620)
Hobart, Donald Bayne
Masked Rider and Blue Hawk series (20)
Desert of ice
Verne, Jules
Adventures of Captain Hatteras series (2)
Desert of mystery
Appleton, Victor
Don Sturdy series (1)
Desert of stolen dreams
Silverberg, Robert
Majipoor trilogy (1)
Desert pursuit
Colter, Dale
Regulator series (8)
Desert queen
Fitzgerald, Julia
Desert queen series (2)
Desert rain
Mackenzie, Steve
Seals series (6)
Desert ranch
Sanders, Charles Wesley
Mournful Martin series (1)
Desert shadow
Netton, Budleigh
Derek Carrington series (2)
Desert silver
Cody, Stone
Five Mavericks series (5)
Desert sinner
McInerny, Ralph
Father Roger Dowling series (15)
Desert Spitfire
Holden, Matthew
Squadron series (4)
Desert spread
Hunter, E J
Headhunter series (13)
Desert stalker
Barry, Mike
Burton Wulff series (4)
Desert star
Willard, Tom
Strike fighters series (6)
Desert trail
Armour, R Coutts
Sexton Blake series (269)
Deserted library mystery
Warner, Gertrude Chandler
Boxcar children series (21)
Deserted yacht
Wirt, Ann
Madge Sterling series (2)
Deserter of the Foreign Legion
Graydon, William Murray
Sexton Blake series (523)
Deservedly dead
Oliphant, B J
Shirley McClintock series (3)
Design for dupes
Janson, Hank
Hank Janson series (168)
Design for dying
Krasney, Samuel A
Abe Larson series (2)
McCloy, Helen
Basil Willing series (1)
Morice, Anne
Tessa Crichton Price series (22)
Design for murder
Hart, Carolyn Gimpel
Annie Laurance and Max Darling series (2)
Design for treason
Dickson, Grierson
Superintendent Cissie Marlow series (3)
Design for vengeance
Thomas, Martin
Sexton Blake series (1508)
Design in diamonds
Knight, Kathleen Moore
Margot Blair series (4)
Designated assassin
Nolan, Frederick
Garrett dossier series (3)
Designs in crime
Keene, Carolyn
Nancy Drew files series (89)
Desirable husband
Vernon, Frances
Edwardian trilogy (3)
Desire to kill
Campbell, Alice
Helen Roderick series (2)
Tommy Rostetter series (2)
Desired
Avenell, Donne
Axa series (2)
Brown, Carter
Lieutenant Al Wheeler series (14)
Desk and debit
Optic, Oliver
Onward and upward series (3)
Desmond and Dog Friday
Best, Herbert
Desmond series (4)

Devil at Saxon wall
Mitchell, Gladys
Dame Beatrice Bradley series (6)
Devil at the door
Seuffert, Muir
Mike Hubbard series (3)
Devil breathes but once
Wallace, Carlton
Superintendent Edmund Bendilow series (4)
Devil comes to Devon
Rowland, John
Inspector Shelley series (7)
Devil comes to Winchelsea
Lindsay, Philip
Sussex series (1)
Devil Creek crossfire
Johnstone, William Wallace
Blood bond series (5)
Devil, devil
Avallone, Michael
Satan Sleuth series (3)
Devil doctor
Rohmer, Sax
Fu-Manchu series (2)
Devil down home
Sandstrom, Eve K
Down home series (2)
Devil finds work
Delving, Michael
Dave Cannon and Robert Eddison series (2)
Green, Roger James
Samuel Walton series (3)
Devil from Blazing Hill
Scott, Bradford
Walt Slade series (104)
Devil Genghis
Robeson, Kenneth
Doc Savage series (79)
Devil gun
Edson, John Thomas
American Civil War series (8)
Devil has wings
Conde, Phillip
Dick Pemberty series (2)
Devil in a blue dress
Mosley, Walter
Ezekiel Rawlins series (1)
Devil in Bucks County
Schiddel, Edmund
Bucks County trilogy (1)
Devil in Clevely
Lofts, Norah
Clevely series (2)
Devil in Davos
Brewer, Gil
Al Mundy series (1)
Devil in Downing Street
Ladline, Robert
J A Remington series (2)
Devil in harbour
Gavin, Catherine
Twentieth-century Europe series (1)
Devil in iron
Howard, Robert Ervin
Conan series (24)
Devil in Kansas
Quinn, Simon
Inquisitor series (3)
Devil in moonlight
Procter, Maurice
Chief Inspector Harry Martineau series (16)
Devil in my arms
Fitzgerald, Julia
Astromance series (7)
Devil in the atlas
Gurney, David
Conjurers series (2)
Devil in the belfry
Thorndike, Russell
Mister Macauley series (2)
Devil in the bush
Head, Matthew
Doctor Mary Finney series (1)
Devil in the desert
Horgan, Paul
Humble powers trilogy (1)
Devil in the name
Gunn, Victor
Chief Inspector Bill Cromwell series (35)
Devil in the slot
Jahn, Mike
Black Sheep Squadron series (1)
Devil is dead
Lafferty, Raphael Aloysius
Argos mythos series (1)
Coscuin chronicles series (2)
Devil is Jones
Robeson, Kenneth
Doc Savage series (172)
Devil is loose
Shelby, Graham
William Marshal series (1)
Devil knows you're dead
Block, Lawrence
Matthew Scudder series (10)
Devil laughs again
Deforges, Regine
Lea Delmas trilogy (3)
Devil loves me
Millar, Margaret
Doctor Paul Prye series (3)
Inspector Sands series (1)
Devil mask mystery
Kains, Josephine
Terry Spring series (1)
Devil-master
Grant, Maxwell
Shadow series (209)
Devil met a lady
Kaminsky, Stuart Melvin
Toby Peters series (17)
Devil monsters
Grant, Maxwell
Shadow series (238)
Devil mountain
Bunting, James
British International Airways series (1)
Devil of Danehurst
Hunter, John
Sexton Blake series (1107)
Devil of Pei-Ling
Asbury, Herbert
Inspector Thomas Conroy series (1)
Devil on my back
Hughes, Monica
Arc One series (1)
Devil on the Moon
Robeson, Kenneth
Doc Savage series (50)
Devil on two sticks
Lesage, Alain Rene
Devil upon two sticks series (1)
Devil rides out
Wheatley, Dennis
Duc de Richelieu series (3)
Devil spider
Glint Green
Inspector Wield series (2)
Devil strike
Robbins, David
Blade series (8)
Devil take the hindmost
Green, Simon
Hawk and Fisher series (2)
Devil threw twice
Dean, Amber
Albie Harris series (8)
Devil to pay
Adams, Hunter
Man from Planet X trilogy (3)
Chase, Glen
Cherry Delight series (26)
Dolphin, Rex
Sexton Blake series (1513)
Douglas, George
Inspector Hallam and Sergeant Spratt series (6)
Kane, Henry
Peter Chambers series (23)
Parkinson, Cyril Northcote
Richard Delancey series (1)
Queen, Ellery
Ellery Queen series (13)
Devil to play
Holton, Leonard
Father Joseph Bredder series (10)
Devil to ride
Leitch, Patricia
Jinny series (2)
Devil-tree of El Dorado
Aubrey, Frank
Monella trilogy (1)
Devil upon crutches
Lesage, Alain Rene
Devil upon two sticks series (1)
Devil upon crutches in England
Lesage, Alain Rene
Devil upon two sticks series (1)
Devil upon two sticks
Lesage, Alain Rene
Devil upon two sticks series (1)
Devil upon two sticks in England
Combe, William
Devil upon two sticks series (2)
Devil was handsome
Procter, Maurice
Chief Inspector Harry Martineau series (14)
Devil wind
Bridges, Laurie
Dark forces series (4)
Devil woman
Daniel, Roland
Brian O'Malley series (3)
Devil world
Eklund, Gordon
Star trek originals sequels series (10)
Devil worshipers
Ellis, Wesley
Lone Star series (96)
Devil you don't
Wainwright, John
John George Davis series (5)
Devilday
Hall, Angus
Devilday series (1)
Devilgod
Jallim, Collins
Devilgod series (1)
Devilgod in the empire of the universal master
Jallim, Collins
Devilgod series (2)
Deville McKeene, the British ace
Walker, Rowland
Captain Deville McKeene series (1)
Devil's apprentice
Davison, Gilderoy
Twisted Face series (4)
Devil's auction
Weinberg, Robert
Alex Werner series (1)
Devil's backbone
Johnston, Terry Conrad
Plainsmen series (5)
Devil's black rock
Robeson, Kenneth
Doc Savage series (164)
Devil's bounty
Martin, Larry Jay
John Clinton Ryan series (3)
Devil's bowman
Lee, Patrick
Six-Gun Samurai series (5)
Devil's brand
Edwards, Josh
John Stone series (6)
Devil's breed
Smith, George
Glencannon family trilogy (1)
Devil's bride
Quinn, Seabury
Jules de Grandin series (6)
Devil's bridge
Aldanov, Mark Aleksandrovich
Thinker series (2)
Devils burn too
Henry, Clay
Matt Archer series (2)
Devil's can-can
Baker, William Howard
Sexton Blake series (1397)
Devil's Canyon
Mitchum, Hank
Stage coach station series (22)
Devil's cat
Johnstone, William Wallace
Beasts series (4)
Devil's chapel
Thorne, Ernest Pollett
Quentin Eady series (2)
Devil's children
Dickinson, Peter
Changes trilogy (1)
Devil's church
Draco, F
Lord and Lady Tintagel series (1)
Devil's churchyard
Willis, Ted
Dixon of Dock Green series (1)
Devil's claw
Masters, Doug
TNT series (4)
Devil's cloak
Robertson, Colin
Superintendent Bradley series (10)
Devil's cockpit
Carter, Nick
Nick Carter series (23)
Devil's Cub
Heyer, Georgette
Avon family series (2)
Devil's daughter
Edwards, Olwen
Devil series (2)
Devil's day
Blish, James
After such knowledge series (3)
Devil's deal
Austin, Richard
Guardians series (13)
Devil's den
Saunders, Lawrence
Wylie King and Nels Lundberg series (2)
Sharpe, Jon
Trailsman series (77)
Devil's diamonds
Benzoni, Juliette
Falcon series (2)
Devil's dictionary
Bierce, Ambrose
Devil's dictionary series (1)
Devil's dinero
Grover, Marshall
Larry and Stretch series (146)
Devil's dollar sign
Millard, Joseph John
Dollar series (6)
Devil's donkey
Brittain, Bill
Coven Tree series (1)
Devil's door-bell
Horowitz, Anthony
Old ones trilogy (1)
Devil's double
Roberts, Willo Davis
Black pearl series (4)
Devil's dozen
Carter, Nick
Nick Carter series (76)
Grover, Marshall
Larry and Stretch series (308)
Devil's drum
Gorell, Ronald Gorell Barnes
Inspector Maurice Hepburn series (2)
Macdonald, William Colt
Gregory Quist series (8)
Devils' drums
Meik, Vivian
Geoffrey Aylett series (1)
Devil's due
Burgin, George Brown
Four Corners series (6)
Procter, Maurice
Chief Inspector Harry Martineau series (12)
Devil's Dump
Pullen, Alan
Sam and Lin series (12)
Devil's Edge
Chance, John Newton
Jonathan Blake series (35)
Devil's Elbow
Cheney, Brainard
Adam series (2)
Devil's elbow
Mitchell, Gladys
Dame Beatrice Bradley series (24)
Devil's emissary
Grange, Peter
L'Eree family series (2)
Devil's feud
Grant, Maxwell
Shadow series (225)
Devil's finger
Emmett, Robert
American Avenger series (3)
Devil's footprints
Bond, Evelyn
Ira Yedder series (3)
Devil's footsteps
Burke, John Frederick
Doctor Alexander Caspian series (1)
Devil's gambit
Masters, Zeke
Faro Blake series (30)
Devil's garden
Pinney, Peter
Australian soldier series (3)
Devil's Gold
Cunningham, Chet
Jim Steel series (4)
Devil's gold
Hendryx, James Beardsley
Corporal Cameron Downey series (2)
Hunter, Neil
Brand series (8)
Devil's guard
Mundy, Talbot
Indian trilogy (3)
Jimgrim series (2)
Devil's gunhand
Hogan, Ray
Shawn Starbuck series (8)
Devil's guns
Dawson, Clay
Long Rider series (26)
Devil's hand
McKinney, Jack
Sentinels series (1)
Devil's heart
Johnstone, William Wallace
Beasts series (2)
Devil's heaven
Adcock, Thomas
Neil Hockaday series (3)
Devil's highway
Janson, Hank
Hank Janson series (69)
Devils' Hill
Chauncy, Nan
Lorenny family series (2)
Devil's home on leave
Raymond, Derek
Factory series (1)
Factory series (3)
Devil's horn
Pendleton, Don
Mack Bolan series (104)
Devil's horns
Robeson, Kenneth
Avenger series (4)
Devil's horse
Harrod-Eagles, Cynthia
Morland family series (16)
Devil's hunting-grounds
Blamires, Harry
Heaven and Hell trilogy (1)
Devils in waiting
Motley, Mary
Morning glory series (1)
Devil's jackpot
Masters, Zeke
Faro Blake series (12)
Devil's kiss
Johnstone, William Wallace
Beasts series (1)
Devil's kloof
Greene, L Patrick
Aubrey Saint John Major series (2)
Devil's knell
Warner, Mignon
Mrs Edwina Charles series (5)
Devil's lady
Robertson, Colin
Peter Grayleigh series (9)
Devil's laughter
Johnstone, William Wallace
Beasts series (5)
Devil's legend
Grover, Marshall
Nevada Jim series (7)
Devil's marshal
Masterson, Louis
Morgan Kane series (9)
Devil's mirror
Spencer, Rick
Eric Ivorsen series (5)
Devil's mistress
Coffman, Virginia
Lucifer Cove series (1)
Devil's Nob
Turner, Philip
Darnley Mills Railway series (2)
Devil's novice
Peters, Ellis
Brother Cadfael series (8)
Devils of the deep
Robeson, Kenneth
Doc Savage series (123)
Devil's old
Bowman, Gerald
Sexton Blake series (903)
Devil's own
Edwards, Olwen
Devil series (1)
Nicole, Christopher
West Indies series (2)
Saint Claire, Erin
Jennifer and Cage series (2)
Devil's own dear son
Cabell, James Branch
It happened in Florida trilogy (3)
Devil's playground
Robeson, Kenneth
Doc Savage series (25)
Devil's plunder
Bainbridge, Chuck
Hard corps series (8)
Devil's power
Rushton, Charles
Inspector Cadman series (5)
Devil's reckoning
Burton, Miles
Inspector Arnold and Desmond Merrion series (38)

Devils Royal
Farely, Alison
Plantagenet series (3)
Devil's shadow
Thiess, Frank
Centaur trilogy (1)
Devil's shield
Kessler, Leo
Wotan series (5)
Devil's Skull
Wilson, Gertrude Mary
Inspector Lovick series (12)
Devil's smile
Foxall, Raymond
Captain James Hind series (1)
Devil's son
Carter, Nicholas
Nicholas Carter series (360)
Devil's sonata
Hufford, Susan
Hilda Hughes tetralogy (2)
Devil's spawn
Foxall, Raymond
Captain James Hind series (2)
Devil's stagecoach
Evans, Tabor
Longarm series (135)
Devil's steps
Upfield, Arthur William
Napoleon Bonaparte series (10)
Devil's sting
Cain, Jackson
Torn Slater series (5)
Devil's stronghold
Ford, Leslie
Colonel John Primrose series (14)
Grace Latham series (14)
Devil's summer
Schiddel, Edmund
Bucks County trilogy (3)
Devil's tea-party
Plummer, Thomas Arthur
Detective Inspector Andrew Frampton series (16)
Devil's tears
Hale, Edgar
Inspector Michael Regan series (1)
Devil's torch
Dickson, Grierson
Superintendent Cissie Marlow series (2)
Devil's touch
Johnstone, William Wallace
Beasts series (3)
Devil's trail
Grover, Marshall
Bleak Creek series (11)
Devil's trashcan
Rosenberger, Joseph
Death Merchant series (43)
Devil's vicar
Coffman, Virginia
Moura series (2)
Devil's virgin
Coffman, Virginia
Lucifer Cove series (3)
Devil's waltz
Kellerman, Jonathan
Alex Delaware series (7)
Devil's work
Wells, Carolyn
Fleming Stone series (55)
Devilweed
Knox, Bill
Webb Carrick series (2)
Devine Court mystery
Symons, Beryl
Inspector Henry Doight series (1)
Devious being
Hamilton, Alexandra
Nefertiti trilogy (3)
Devious design
Olsen, D B
Professor A Pennyfeather series (3)
Devious murder
Bellairs, George
Detective Inspector Thomas Littlejohn series (53)
Devious ones
Lockridge, Frances
Assistant District Attorney Bernie Simmons series (2)
Devlin in the canyon heat
Kozlow, Mark J
Chris Devlin series (4)
Devlin's triangle
Heatter, Basil
Timothy Devlin series (1)
Devouring
Armstrong, F W
Changing series (2)
Devouring fire
Gorell, Ronald Gorell Barnes
Harry Farrant series (1)
Devouring void
Rogers, Mark Earl
Blood of the lamb series (2)
Dew and mildew
Wren, Percival Christopher
Karabad series (1)
Dew drop dead
Howe, James
Sebastian Barth series (4)
Dew in April
Clayton, John
Provence trilogy (2)
Dew Line duty
Holliday, Joe
Dale of the Mounted series (5)
Dewey decimated
Goodrum, Charles Alvin
Edwin George series (1)
De Witt's strike
Hunt, Greg
Ridge Parkman series (2)
Dexter and Ashleigh muddle on
Fennell, Willie
Dexter Dutton series (11)
Dexter at war
Hackforth-Jones, Gilbert
Paul Dexter series (7)
Dexter detects
Fennell, Willie
Dexter Dutton series (13)
Dexter gets the point
Fennell, Willie
Dexter Dutton series (10)
Dexter loses his head
Fennell, Willie
Dexter Dutton series (4)
Dexter sings
Fennell, Willie
Dexter Dutton series (5)
Dexter's court
Fennell, Willie
Dexter Dutton series (8)
Dexter's fit
Fennell, Willie
Dexter Dutton series (7)
Dhampire
Baker, Scott
Dracula series (26)
Dharma bums
Kerouac, Jack
Jack Duluoz series (10)
Di and I
Lefcourt, Peter
Hollywood series (2)
Di Di Mau or die
Cain, Jonathan
Saigon commandos series (6)
Diablo at daybreak
Colter, Dale
Regulator series (2)
Diablo double cross
Bodine, J D
Quinn's Raiders series (1)
Diablo's shadow
Grover, Marshall
Nevada Jim series (25)
Diabolic candelabra
Punshon, Ernest Robertson
Bobby Owen series (17)
Diabolus
Saint John, David
Peter Ward series (9)
Diadem from the stars
Clayton, Jo
Diadem series (1)
Diagnosis, homicide
Blochman, Lawrence Goldtree
Doctor Daniel Webster Coffee series (1)
Diagnosis, murder
Scott, Sutherland
Doctor Septimus Dodds series (10)
Dial D for disaster
Thomson, Pat
Share-a-story series (7)
Dial death
Spade, Danny
Danny Spade series (16)
Dial emergency for Doctor Ross
Dwyer-Joyce, Alice
Doctor Esmond Ross series (4)
Dial five seven seven R-A-P-E
O'Donnell, Lillian
Detective Norah Mulcahaney series (3)
Dial nine nine nine
Walsh, James Morgan
Oliver Keene series (3)
Dial O for O.R.G.Y.
Mark, Ted
Man from O.R.G.Y. series (10)
Dial of death caps
Wilson, Gertrude Mary
Inspector Lovick series (17)
Dial V.E.T.
Stranger, Joyce
Timothy Yorke series (5)
Dialogues and a diary
Stravinsky, Igor
Conversations series (4)
Diamond before you die
Wiltz, Chris
Neal Rafferty series (2)
Diamond bubble
Fish, Robert Lloyd
Captain Jose da Silva series (4)
Diamond Cave mystery
Nesbit, Troy
Wilderness mystery series (5)
Diamond contessa
Bulmer, Kenneth
Keys to the dimensions series (8)
Diamond coterie
Lynch, Lawrence L
Neil Bathurst series (2)
Diamond cross mystery
Steele, Chester K
Colonel Robert Lee Ashley series (1)
Diamond cut diamond
Carter, Nicholas
Nicholas Carter series (455)
Diamond deceit
Keene, Carolyn
Nancy Drew files series (83)
Diamond dragon
Teed, George Hamilton
Sexton Blake series (262)
Diamond exchange
Chastain, Thomas
Inspector Max Kauffman series (5)
Diamond eyes
Lutz, John
Alo Nudger series (7)
Diamond feather
Reilly, Helen
Inspector Christopher McKee series (1)
Diamond fix
Barker, Albert
Hawk Macrae series (5)
Diamond flood
Armour, R Coutts
Sexton Blake series (209)
Diamond flush
Masters, Zeke
Faro Blake series (4)
Diamond for Christina
Saint James, Blakely
Christina Van Bell series (31)
Diamond gun
Roberts, J R
Gunsmith series (52)
Diamond Head
Jackson, Marian J A
Miss Abigail Patience Danforth series (4)
Diamond hitch
Tuttle, Wilbur Coleman
Hashknife Hartley and Sleepy Stevens series (23)
Diamond hook
Quartermain, James
Raven series (1)
Diamond hostage
Quartermain, James
Raven series (4)
Diamond in the buff
Dunlap, Susan
Jill Smith series (6)
Diamond in the sky
Saville, Malcolm
Buckinghams series (6)
Diamond in the window
Langton, Jane
Edward, Eleanor and Georgie Hall series (1)
Diamond mask
May, Julian
Jack the bodiless series (2)
Diamond master
Futrelle, Jacques
Professor Augustus S F X Van Dusen series (3)
Diamond mine case
Carter, Nicholas
Nicholas Carter series (40)
Diamond moon
Preuss, Paul
Venus prime series (5)
Diamond of Ti Lingo
Brandon, John Gordon
Sexton Blake series (911)
Diamond Park dinosaur
Davis, Gibbs
Never sink nine series (9)
Diamond pin
Wells, Carolyn
Fleming Stone series (10)
Diamond queen
Dixon, Dorothy
Leather and lace series (7)
Reeve, Arthur Benjamin
Craig Kennedy series (7)
Diamond ransom murders
Child, Nellise
Jeremiah Irish series (2)
Diamond Rock
Schorr, Mark
Red Diamond series (3)
Diamond stud
Singer, Norman
Robbie Jardino series (2)
Diamond-studded typewriter
Keith, Carlton
Jeff Green series (1)
Diamond sunburst
Teed, George Hamilton
Sexton Blake series (46)
Diamond throne
Eddings, David
Elenium trilogy (1)
Diamond trail
Carter, Nicholas
Nicholas Carter series (174)
Diamondback
Bishop, Pike
Cord Diamondback series (1)
Diamonds and minx
Freed, Artelle
Melanie Gaye series (2)
Diamonds are deadly
Eastwood, James
Anna Zordan series (3)
Diamonds are for dying
Kenyon, Paul
Baroness Penelope Saint-John Orsini series (2)
Diamonds are forever
Fleming, Ian
James Bond series (4)
Diamonds are more trouble
Corbett, Scott
Diamonds series (2)
Diamonds are trouble
Corbett, Scott
Diamonds series (1)
Diamonds are trumps
Adams, Herbert
Major Roger Bennion series (19)
Diamonds bid
Rathbone, Julian
Colonel Nur Bey series (1)
Diamonds can be trouble
Harrison, Edwin
Sexton Blake series (1446)
Diamonds, emeralds, cards and colts
Edson, John Thomas
Floating Outfit series (28)
Diamonds in the dumplings
Shane, Susannah
Christopher Saxe series (4)
Diamonds in the family
Buckley, Eunice
Sandor Raimann series (3)
Diamonds of death
Jackson, Wallace
Inspector Clancy Martin series (2)
Diamonds of Loreta
Drummond, Ivor
Lady Jennifer, Sandro and Colly series (9)
Diamonds to Amsterdam
Coles, Manning
Tommy Hambledon series (11)
Diamonds to sit on
Ilf, Ilya Arnoldovich
Chairs series (1)
Diamonds wild
Caillou, Alan
Mike Benasque series (4)
Diana
Delderfield, Ronald Frederick
Sennacherib series (1)
Shura, Mary Francis
Sunfire series (29)
Diana of dreams
Burgin, George Brown
Slaves of Allah series (2)
Diana of Meridor
Dumas, Alexandre
Valois series (6)
Diana the huntress
Chesney, Marion
Six sisters series (5)
Diane's new love
Cavanna, Betty
Diane series (2)
Diaries of Adam and Eve
Twain, Mark
Diaries of Adam and Eve series (2)
Diaries of Jane Somers
Lessing, Doris
Jane Somers series (2)
Diary
Ard, William
Timothy Dane series (3)
Diary of a church mouse
Oakley, Graham
Church mice series (9)
Diary of a country doctor
Duncan, Alex
Country doctor series (3)
Diary of a country priest
Bernanos, Georges
Spiritual life series (4)
Diary of a desperado
Grover, Marshall
Larry and Stretch series (74)
Diary of a district officer
Bradley, Kenneth
District officer series (1)
Diary of a good neighbour
Somers, Jane
Jane Somers series (1)
Diary of a medical nobody
Lane, Kenneth
Medical nobody series (1)
Diary of a nobody
Grossmith, George
Nobody series (1)
Diary of a provincial lady
Delafield, E M
Provincial lady series (1)
Diary of a somebody
Matthew, Christopher
Simon Crisp series (1)
Diary of my honeymoon
Anonymous
Diary series (1)
Diary of Samuel Marchbanks
Davies, Robertson
Samuel Marchbanks series (1)
Diary of the Great Warr
Pepys, Samuel, junior
Great Warr trilogy (1)
Dice are dark
Flynn, Brian
Anthony Bathurst series (48)
Dice Man
Rhinehart, Luke
Wim series (1)
Dice of war
Giovene, Andrea
Giuliano Sansevero series (3)
Dice were loaded
Cumberland, Marten
Saturnin Dax series (33)
Dicey's song
Voigt, Cynthia
Tillermans series (2)
Dick
Bradby, Godfrey Fox
Dick series (1)
Dick and Dolly
Wells, Carolyn
Dick and Dolly series (1)
Dick and Dolly's adventures
Wells, Carolyn
Dick and Dolly series (2)
Dick Barton, special agent
Jones, Elwyn
Dick Barton series (1)
Dick Kent and the mine mystery
Richards, Milton
Dick Kent series (10)
Dick Kent at Half Way House
Richards, Milton
Dick Kent series (7)
Dick Kent, fur trader
Richards, Milton
Dick Kent series (4)
Dick Kent in the far north
Richards, Milton
Dick Kent series (2)
Dick Kent, Mounted Police deputy
Richards, Milton
Dick Kent series (8)
Dick Kent on special duty
Richards, Milton
Dick Kent series (6)
Dick Kent with the Eskimos
Richards, Milton
Dick Kent series (3)

Dick Kent with the Malamute Mail
Richards, Milton
Dick Kent series (5)
Dick Kent with the mounted police
Richards, Milton
Dick Kent series (1)
Dick Kent's mysterious mission
Richards, Milton
Dick Kent series (9)
Dick Talbot, the ranch king
Aiken, Albert W
Dick Talbot series (2)
Dick Talbot's clean out
Aiken, Albert W
Dick Talbot series (1)
Dick Tracy
Collins, Max Allan
Dick Tracy film series (1)
Johnston, William
Dick Tracy cartoon series (9)
Lerangis, Peter
Dick Tracy film series (1)
Moore, John
Dick Tracy cartoon series (9)
Dick Tracy, a catch-a-crook adventure
Lerangis, Peter
Dick Tracy film series (2)
Dick Tracy activity book
Greenberg, Martin Harry
Dick Tracy film series (2)
Dick Tracy, America's most famous detective
Gould, Chester
Dick Tracy cartoon series (6)
Dick Tracy and the nightmare machine
Collins, Max Allan
Dick Tracy series (6)
Dick Tracy and the Woo Woo sisters
Gould, Chester
Dick Tracy series (1)
Dick Tracy casebook
Collins, Max Allan
Dick Tracy series (8)
Dick Tracy fun book of puzzles and games
Krulik, Nancy E
Dick Tracy film series (2)
Dick Tracy goes to war
Collins, Max Allan
Dick Tracy series (7)
Dick Tracy in hot water
Razzi, Jim
Dick Tracy series (4)
Dick Tracy meets Angel Top
Collins, Max Allan
Dick Tracy series (2)
Dick Tracy meets his match
Collins, Max Allan
Dick Tracy series (8)
Dick Tracy meets the punks
Collins, Max Allan
Dick Tracy series (3)
Dick Tracy on the trail of Blank
Gurelle, Andrew
Dick Tracy series (5)
Dick Tracy, the official biography
Meader, Jay
Dick Tracy series (8)
Dick Tracy, the official book of the movie
Bonifer, Michael
Dick Tracy film series (2)
Dick Tracy, the secret files
Greenberg, Martin Harry
Dick Tracy film series (2)
Dick Tracy, the thirties, tommy guns and hard times
Gould, Chester
Dick Tracy cartoon series (5)
Dick Tracy versus the underworld
Moore, John
Dick Tracy cartoon series (8)
Dick Tracy's fiendish foes
Collins, Max Allan
Dick Tracy series (8)
Dick Turnip
Reed, Giles
Munch Bunch character series (25)
Dick Turnip and the crazy clowns
Reed, Giles
Munch Bunch story books series (5)
Dickie and Dorrie
Everett-Green, Evelyn
Hallowdene Hall series (1)
Dickie and Dorrie at school
Everett-Green, Evelyn
Hallowdene Hall series (2)
Dickie Dilver
Burgin, George Brown
Four Corners series (8)
Dictator of crime
Grant, Maxwell
Shadow series (211)
Dictator of the damned
Stockbridge, Grant
Richard Wentworth series (16)
Dictator's destiny
Betteridge, Don
Tiger Lester series (3)
Dictator's secret
Teed, George Hamilton
Sexton Blake series (899)
Dictator's way
Punshon, Ernest Robertson
Bobby Owen series (10)
Dictatorship of the dove
Gerard, Francis
Sir John Meredith series (4)
Dictionary Johnson
Clifford, James Lowry
Samuel Johnson series (2)
Did I ever tell you?
Grender, Iris
Did I ever tell series (1)
Did I ever tell you about my birthday party?
Grender, Iris
Did I ever tell series (5)
Did I ever tell you about my Irish great grandmother?
Grender, Iris
Did I ever tell series (4)
Did I ever tell you what the children told me?
Grender, Iris
Did I ever tell series (6)
Did she fall or was she pushed?
Disney, Doris Miles
Jeff Dimarco series (6)
Dido and pa
Aiken, Joan
Dido Twite series (6)
Dido and Rogue
Peel, Hazel Mary
Ann and Jim Henderson series (7)
Dido, the dancing bear
Barnum, Richard
Kneetime animal stories series (6)
Die after dark
Pentecost, Hugh
Julian Quist series (6)
Die again, Macready
Livingston, Jack
Joe Birney series (2)
Die all, die merrily
Bruce, Leo
Carolus Deene series (10)
Die anytime after Tuesday
Brown, Carter
Rick Holman series (19)
Die brave
McCoy, Marshall
Nevada Jim series (40)
Die-cast
Steed, Neville
Peter Marklin series (2)
Die, Chameleon!
Larson, Glen A
Battlestar Galactica series (12)
Die dreaming
Faherty, Terence
Owen Keane series (3)
Die fast, die happy
Denning, Mark
John Marshall series (2)
Die for love
Peters, Elizabeth
Jacqueline Kirby series (4)
Die-hards
Kessler, Leo
Rebel series (2)
Die in the country
Wells, Tobias
Detective Knute Severson series (11)
Die in the dark
Gilbert, Anthony
Arthur Crook series (19)
Die killer die
Scarpetta, Frank
Marksman series (15)
Die laughing
Lockridge, Richard
Nathan Shapiro series (7)
Die like a dog
Gruber, Frank
Johnny Fletcher and Sam Cragg series (3)
Halliday, Brett
Michael Shayne series (35)
Moffat, Gwen
Miss Melinda Pink series (6)
Stout, Rex
Nero Wolfe and Archie Goodwin series (26)
Die like a man
Delving, Michael
Dave Cannon and Robert Eddison series (3)
Die, little goose
Alexander, David
Bart Hardin series (5)
Lieutenant Romano series (5)
Die lonesome
Grover, Marshall
Nevada Jim series (22)
Hart, Matthew S
Cody's law series (2)
Die, my darling
Usher, Frank
Daye Smith series (8)
Die now, live later
Copper, Basil
Mike Faraday series (5)
Die of Gold
Cunningham, Chet
Jim Steel series (2)
Die on Easy Street
Howard, James Arch
Steve Ashe series (4)
Die quickly, dear mother
Wells, Tobias
Detective Knute Severson series (5)
Die rich, die happy
Munro, James
John Craig series (2)
Die to a distant dream
Arden, William
Kane Jackson series (4)
Die wearing a rose
Thorne, Ernest Pollett
Quentin Eady series (5)
Diecast
Brett, John Michael
Hugo Baron series (1)
Died in the red
Gray, Dulcie
Inspector Cardiff series (2)
Died in the wool
Marsh, Ngaio
Inspector Roderick Alleyn series (13)
Diehard
Jackson, Jon Anthony
Sergeant Fang Mulheisen series (1)
Diet to die for
Hess, Joan
Claire Malloy series (5)
Difference to me
Bryan, John
Richard Sarel series (1)
Different hero
Korman, Justine
Roger Rabbit series (1)
Different kind of summer
Melville, Jennie
Sergeant Charmian Daniels series (6)
Different night
Hesky, Olga
Inspector Tami Shimoni series (4)
Different Peter and Emma
Wolde, Gunilla
Emma series (5)
Different world
Ghose, Zulfikar
Incredible Brazilian trilogy (3)
Difficult country
Napier, Priscilla
Napier family trilogy (2)
Difficult problem, and other stories
Green, Anna Katharine
Ebenezer Gryce series (12)
Difficult summer
Baxter, Gillian
Roberta series (2)
Difficult women, and other stories
Brush, Katharine
Lillian Legendre series (1)
Difficult young man
Boyd, Martin
Langton family series (2)
Difficulties with girls
Amis, Kingsley
Patrick Standish series (2)
Difficulty with dwarves
Gardner, Craig Shaw
Ballad of Wuntvor trilogy (1)
Ebenezum series (4)
Dig a dead doll
Fickling, G G
Honey West series (6)
Dig me a grave
Spain, John
Bill Rye series (1)
Dig me later
Hagen, Miriam Ann
Hortense Clinton series (2)
Dig my grave deep
Rabe, Peter
Daniel Port series (1)
Dig that crazy grave
Prather, Richard Scott
Shell Scott series (23)
Dig the grave and let him lie
Wainwright, John
Northern Police series (15)
Dig the grave deep
Brent, Nigel
Barney Hyde series (4)
Dig the missing
Urquhart, Macgregor
Chief Inspector Joshua Smarles series (3)
Dig the spurs deep
Field, Peter
Powder Valley series (42)
Dig thos heels
Janson, Hank
Hank Janson series (121)
Dig to disaster
Quackenbush, Robert Mead
Miss Mallard series (3)
Digger Smith
Dennis, Clarence James
Sentimental bloke series (5)
Diggers
Bonner, Terry Nelsen
New South Wales series (7)
Pratchett, Terry
Book of the Nomes trilogy (2)
Diggers of Colditz
Champ, Jack
Colditz series (10)
Digging for gold
Alger, Horatio
New world trilogy (1)
Digging up danger
Krulick, Nancy E
Lassie series (2)
Digit Dick and the lost opals
Rees, Leslie
Digit Dick series (4)
Digit Dick and the Tasmanian devil
Rees, Leslie
Digit Dick series (2)
Digit Dick and the zoo plot
Rees, Leslie
Digit Dick series (5)
Digit Dick in Black Swan Island
Rees, Leslie
Digit Dick series (3)
Digit Dick on the Barrier Reef
Rees, Leslie
Digit Dick series (1)
Digit Dick on the Great Barrier Reef
Rees, Leslie
Digit Dick series (1)
Digit of the moon, and other love stories from the Hindoo
Bain, Francis William
Indian mystic love stories series (1)
Dignity and purity
Jefferies, Ian
Sergeant Craig series (2)
Dikes and ditches
Optic, Oliver
Young America, first series (4)
Dilbert and the dodo
Robertson, Kate
Dilbert series (4)
Dilbert down under
Robertson, Kate
Dilbert series (2)
Dilbert on safari
Robertson, Kate
Dilbert series (3)
Dilbert wins his wings
Robertson, Kate
Dilbert series (1)
Dilemma at Dripspring
Gardner, Jerome
Dripspring series (2)
Dilemma for Dax
Cumberland, Marten
Saturnin Dax series (8)
Dilemma of Doctor Hiley
Tyrer, Walter
Sexton Blake series (1315)
Dilemma of love
Giovene, Andrea
Giuliano Sansevero series (2)
Dilly and his swamp lizard
Bradman, Tony
Dilly series (13)
Dilly and the big kids
Bradman, Tony
Dilly series (14)
Dilly and the ghost
Bradman, Tony
Dilly series (7)
Dilly and the horror film
Bradman, Tony
Dilly series (4)
Dilly and the pirates
Bradman, Tony
Dilly series (16)
Dilly and the tiger
Bradman, Tony
Dilly series (6)
Dilly, Dinosaur, detective
Bradman, Tony
Dilly series (17)
Dilly Dinosaur, superstar
Bradman, Tony
Dilly series (8)
Dilly goes on holiday
Bradman, Tony
Dilly series (11)
Dilly goes swamp wallowing
Bradman, Tony
Dilly series (5)
Dilly goes to school
Bradman, Tony
Dilly series (12)
Dilly speaks up
Bradman, Tony
Dilly series (10)
Dilly tells the truth
Bradman, Tony
Dilly series (3)
Dilly the angel
Bradman, Tony
Dilly series (9)
Dilly the dinosaur
Bradman, Tony
Dilly series (1)
Dilly visits the dentist
Bradman, Tony
Dilly series (2)
Dilly's birthday party
Bradman, Tony
Dilly series (15)
Dilly's muddy day
Bradman, Tony
Dilly series (2)
Dilvish the Damned
Zelazny, Roger
Dilvish the Damned trilogy (3)
Dimension of deceit
Tripp, Miles
John Samson series (13)
Dimension of doom
Black, Christopher
Star challenge series (7)
Dimension of dreams
Lord, Jeffrey
Richard Blade series (11)
Dimension of horror
Lord, Jeffrey
Richard Blade series (30)
Dimension riders
Blythe, Daniel
Doctor Who series (160)
Dimension search
Mahr, Kurt
Perry Rhodan series (60)
Diminished by death
Ross, Jonathan
Superintendent George Rogers series (2)
Diminished responsibility
Barnett, James
Superintendent Owen Smith series (5)
Dimmo
Slater, Jim
A Mazing Monster series (4)
Dimple Hill
Richardson, Dorothy Miller
Pilgrimage series (12)
Dimsie among the prefects
Bruce, Dorita Fairlie
Dimsie series (4)
Dimsie carries on
Bruce, Dorita Fairlie
Dimsie series (9)
Dimsie goes back
Bruce, Dorita Fairlie
Dimsie series (7)
Dimsie goes to school
Bruce, Dorita Fairlie
Dimsie series (1)
Dimsie grows up
Bruce, Dorita Fairlie
Dimsie series (5)
Dimsie, head girl
Bruce, Dorita Fairlie
Dimsie series (6)

Dimsie intervenes
Bruce, Dorita Fairlie
Dimsie series (8)
Dimsie moves up
Bruce, Dorita Fairlie
Dimsie series (2)
Dimsie moves up again
Bruce, Dorita Fairlie
Dimsie series (3)
Dimsie takes charge
Bruce, Dorita Fairlie
Dimsie series (10)
Dinah Faire
Coffman, Virginia
Gaynor women series (2)
Dinarbas
Knight, Ellis Cornelia
Rasselas series (2)
Dinard mystery
Maske, John
Duncan Cainsforth series (1)
Dinbig of Khimmur
Williamson, Philip G
Firstworld chronicles series (1)
Dine and be dead
Butler, Gwendoline
Inspector John Coffin series (5)
Dinero fever
Grover, Marshall
Larry and Stretch series (198)
Dinero of doom
Cole, Jackson
Jim Hatfield series (86)
Dinero train
Grover, Marshall
Larry and Stretch series (311)
Ding, dong bell
Reilly, Helen
Inspector Christopher McKee series (27)
Ding-dong, bing-bong
Slepian, Jan
Junior listen-hear series (2)
Ding Palmer, air detective
Sherman, Harold Morrow
Cloud Patrol series (3)
Dingleflop chimes
Heap, Jean Walmsley
Dingleflop series (1)
Dingleflop moon
Heap, Jean Walmsley
Dingleflop series (2)
Dingo king
Smith, Ivan
Fire, drought and flood trilogy (2)
Dining with dinosaurs
Milton, Hilary
Plot your own horror stories series (7)
Dinkum oil
Mills, Frederick John
Dinkum oil series (1)
Dinkum Pommie
Hesling, Bernard
Little and orphan series (2)
Dinkumization and depomification of an artful English immigrant
Hesling, Bernard
Little and orphan series (2)
Dinky-dau death
Cain, Jonathan
Saigon commandos series (3)
Dinky died
Wells, Tobias
Detective Knute Severson series (7)
Dinner at Alberta's
Hoban, Russell
Arthur and Emma series (1)
Dinner at Antoine's
Keyes, Frances Parkinson
Joe and Judith Racina series (1)
Dinner at Belmont
Crabb, Alfred Leland
Nashville series (1)
Dinner at Dupre's
Halliday, Brett
Michael Shayne series (13)
Michael Shayne series (16)
Dinner doesn't matter
Scott, Mary
New Zealand life series (3)
Dinner for none
Sarsfield, Maureen
Inspector Lane Parry series (2)
Dinner in New York
Fowler, Sydney
Mister Jellipot series (8)
Dinner in town
Mauriac, Claude
Interior dialogue series (2)
Dinner ladies
Bentley, Diana
My school series (3)
Dinner of herbs
Verney, John
Going to the wars series (3)
Dinner on the lawn
Messerli, Douglas
River to rivet trilogy (1)
Dinner party
Mauriac, Claude
Interior dialogue series (2)
Dinner to die for
Dunlap, Susan
Jill Smith series (5)
Dinner with James
Heaton, Rose Henniker
James Montgomerie series (1)
Dinny Gordon, freshman
Emery, Anne
Dinny Gordon series (1)
Dinny Gordon, junior
Emery, Anne
Dinny Gordon series (3)
Dinny Gordon, senior
Emery, Anne
Dinny Gordon series (4)
Dinny Gordon, sophomore
Emery, Anne
Dinny Gordon series (2)
Dinobot war
Morris, Dave
Transformers series (1)
Dinobots strike back
Todd, Casey
Junior transformers find your fate series (1)
Dinosaur adventure
Logan, Nora
Pick-a-path series (11)
Dinosaur dilemma
Bosco, Clyde
Nintendo adventure series (7)
Dinosaur dreams
Ahlberg, Allan
Funnybones series (3)
Dinosaur for a day
Murphy, Jim
Last dinosaur series (2)
Dinosaur mystery
Warner, Gertrude Chandler
Boxcar children series (44)
Dinosaur Planet
McCaffrey, Anne
Ireta adventure series (1)
Dinosaur Planet survivors
McCaffrey, Anne
Ireta adventure series (2)
Dinosaur that followed me home
Coville, Bruce
Camp Haunted Hills series (3)
Dinosaur trackers
Shadwell, Thomas
Time tours series (4)
Dinosaur trap
Bunting, Eve
Dinosaur machines series (3)
Dinosaur who couldn't sleep
Salmon, Michael
Dinosaur series (7)
Dinosaur who forgot her birthday
Salmon, Michael
Dinosaur series (5)
Dinosaur who invented things
Salmon, Michael
Dinosaur series (3)
Dinosaur who wanted to fly
Salmon, Michael
Dinosaur series (2)
Dinosaur who wouldn't go to school
Salmon, Michael
Dinosaur series (4)
Dinosaurs
Roop, Peter
Great mysteries series (1)
Dinosaurs alive!
Ritthaler, Shelly
Dinosaurs series (3)
Dinosaurs alive and well!
Brown, Laurence Krasny
Dinosaurs series (3)
Brown, Marc
Dinosaurs guide book series (4)
Dinosaurs, beware!
Brown, Marc
Dinosaurs guide book series (1)
Dinosaurs divorce
Brown, Laurence Krasny
Dinosaurs series (1)
Brown, Marc
Dinosaurs guide book series (2)
Dinosaurs for lunch
Ritthaler, Shelly
Dinosaurs series (1)
Dinosaurs on holiday
Salmon, Michael
Animal antics series (3)
Dinosaurs travel
Brown, Laurence Krasny
Dinosaurs series (2)
Brown, Marc
Dinosaurs guide book series (3)
Dinosaurs wild!
Ritthaler, Shelly
Dinosaurs series (2)
Dip into murder
Ormerod, Roger
David Mallin and George Coe series (10)
Diplomacy Guild
Greenberg, Martin Harry
Isaac's universe series (1)
Diplomat and the gold piano
Scherf, Margaret
Emily and Henry Bryce series (5)
Diplomat dies
Gribble, Leonard Reginald
Superintendent Anthony Slade series (33)
Diplomatic conclusions
Peyrefitte, Roger
Diplomatic series (2)
Diplomatic corpse
Taylor, Phoebe Atwood
Asey Mayo series (24)
Diplomatic death
Forsyte, Charles
Inspector Richard Left series (1)
Diplomatic deceit
Dixon, Franklin W
Hardy boys case files series (38)
Diplomatic diversions
Peyrefitte, Roger
Diplomatic series (1)
Diplomatist
Haggard, William
William Wilberforce Smith series (2)
Dippers and Jo
Willard, Barbara
Dippers series (1)
Dippers and the high-flying kite
Willard, Barbara
Dippers series (2)
Dirdir
Vance, Jack
Tschai series (3)
Dirge for a dog
Jones, Jennifer
Daisy Jane Mott series (3)
Dirge for a Dorset druid
Arnold, Margot
Penelope Spring and Sir Tobias Glendower series (10)
Dirge for her
Rath, Virginia
Michael Dundas series (7)
Dirge for Sabis
Cherryh, Carolyn Janice
Sword of knowledge series (1)
Sword of knowledge trilogy (1)
Dirk
Rybakov, Anatoli
Dirk series (1)
Dirk Bogarde, the complete autobiography
Bogarde, Dirk
Orderly man series (4)
Dirk Gently's holistic detective gency
Adams, Douglas Noel
Dirk Gently series (1)
Dirk's return
Garrisen, Paul
Dirk Prine series (3)
Dirk's revenge
Garrisen, Paul
Dirk Prine series (2)
Dirk's run
Garrisen, Paul
Dirk Prine series (1)
Dirt bike racer
Christopher, Matt
Dirt bike racer series (1)
Dirt bike runaway
Christopher, Matt
Dirt bike racer series (2)
Dirty deeds
Dixon, Franklin W
Hardy boys case files series (49)
Dirty distant war
Nathanson, E M
John Reisman series (2)
Dirty dollars
Sharp, Allen
Storytrails series (7)
Dirty dozen
Nathanson, E M
John Reisman series (1)
Dirty duck
Grimes, Martha
Inspector Richard Jury series (4)
Dirty game
Baker, William Howard
Richard Quintain series (10)
Dirty half-mile
Peters, Lance
Detective Sergeant Joe Church trilogy (2)
Dirty Harry
Rock, Philip
Dirty Harry Callahan series (12)
Dirty laundry
Hamill, Pete
Sam Briscoe series (1)
Dirty linen
Lewis, Elliott
Fred Bennett series (2)
Dirty money can't wash both hands at once
Glazner, Joseph Mark
Billy Nevers series (3)
Dirty pool
Bagby, George
Inspector Schmidt series (34)
Dirty rotten depriving ray
Knight, Mallory T
Man from T.O.M.C.A.T. series (4)
Dirty story
Ambler, Eric
Arthur Abdel Simpson series (2)
Dirty tricks
Way, Peter
Crispin Bridge series (1)
Dirty war
Pendleton, Don
SuperBolan series (4)
Dirty way to die
Bagby, George
Inspector Schmidt series (25)
Curry, Gene
Jim Saddler series (1)
Rossi, Bruno
Sharpshooter series (15)
Dirty weekend
Raymond, John
Prospects series (2)
Dirty work at the Dog and Whistle
Beaman, Sydney George Hulme
Toytown series (16)
Disagreement with death
Gardner, Craig Shaw
Ballad of Wuntvor trilogy (3)
Disappearance
Cowdroy, Joan
Li Moh series (3)
Guy, Rosa
Imamu Jones series (1)
Wilcox, Collin
Lieutenant Frank Hastings series (2)
Disappearance of a niece
Field, Katherine
Inspector Ross Paterson series (1)
Disappearance of Amos Pike
Stahl, Hilda
Wren House series (2)
Disappearance of Doctor Bruderstein
Sherwood, John
Mister Charles Blessington series (1)
Disappearance of Helen
Hope, Laura Lee
Blythe girls series (8)
Disappearance of Julie Hintz
Truss, Seldon
Inspector Gidleigh series (4)
Disappearance of Madalena Grimaldi
Day, Marele
Claudia Valentine series (4)
Disappearing bridegroom
Erskine, Margaret
Inspector Septimus Finch series (5)
Disappearing corpse
Warren, James
James Warren series (2)
Disappearing diamond
Cooper, Wendy
Do and Dare Club series (2)
Disappearing diamonds
Donovan, Jean Beradine
Bill Speed series (2)
Walker, Holly Beth
Meg Duncan series (1)
Disappearing dog trick
Corbett, Scott
Kerby Maxwell series (3)
Disappearing dues
Christian, Mary Blount
Goosehill Gang series (3)
Disappearing dwarf
Blaylock, James Paul
Jonathan Bing series (2)
Disappearing floor
Dixon, Franklin W
Hardy boys series (19)
Disappearing island
Kyle, Elisabeth
Furze series (2)
Disappearing lady
Robeson, Kenneth
Doc Savage series (151)
Disappearing parson
Burton, Miles
Inspector Arnold and Desmond Merrion series (39)
Disappearing princess
Carter, Nicholas
Nicholas Carter series (335)
Disappearing through the skylight
Hardison, Osborne Bennett
Modern culture trilogy (2)
Disappearing trick, and other stories
Bond, Michael
Paddington series (11)
Disappearing TV star
Rodda, Emily
Teen Power Inc. series (4)
Disappointed friend mystery
Warner, Gertrude Chandler
Boxcar children series (30)
Disaster
Hubbard, Lafayette Ronald
Mission earth series (8)
Marguerritte, Paul
Franco-Prussian War series (1)
Disaster at Dungeness
Johnston, Ronald
James Bruce series (1)
Disaster for hire
Dixon, Franklin W
Hardy boys case files series (23)
Disaster with the fiend
Lavelle, Sheila
Charlie Ellis and Angela Mitchell series (5)
Discharged dead
Hart, Sydney
British migrant series (1)
Disciple of Satan
Carter, Nicholas
Nicholas Carter series (303)
Disciples of Cthulhu
Berglund, Edward Paul
Cthulhu Mythos series (3)
Disco downbeat
Geller, Michael
Bud Dugan series (3)
Discord in the air
Clements, Eileen Helen
Alister Woodhead series (6)
Discourses of Doctor O'Grady
Maurois, Andre
Doctor O'Grady series (1)
Discovered!
Greene, Yvonne
Kelly Blake series (1)
Discoverers
Armstrong, Richard
History of seafaring series (2)
Boorstin, Daniel Joseph
Discoverers and creators series (1)
Discovering Evelina
Moore, Frank Frankfort
Doctor Samuel Johnson series (2)
Discovering what crickets do
Simon, Seymour
Discovering series (5)
Discovering what earthworms do
Simon, Seymour
Discovering series (1)
Discovering what frogs do
Simon, Seymour
Discovering series (2)
Discovering what garter snakes do
Simon, Seymour
Discovering series (6)
Discovering what gerbils do
Simon, Seymour
Discovering series (4)
Discovering what goldfish do
Simon, Seymour
Discovering series (3)
Discovering what puppies do
Simon, Seymour
Discovering series (7)
Discovery
Baer, Judy
Cedar River daydreams series (20)

Discovery at the Dragon's Mouth
Sutton, Margaret
Judy Bolton series (31)
Discretion
Linzee, David
Sarah Saber and Chris Rockwell series (1)
Discursions on travel, art and life
Sitwell, Osbert
Discursions series (1)
Disease fighters
Aaseng, Nathan
Nobel Prize winners series (1)
Disgrace abounding
Reed, Douglas
Insanity fair trilogy (2)
Disgrace to the Fourth
Chaundler, Christine
Fourth Form series (7)
Disgraceful business at Mrs Goose's
Beaman, Sydney George Hulme
Toytown series (28)
Disguise for a dead gentleman
Compton, David Guy
Ben Anderson series (2)
Disguise for murder
Stout, Rex
Nero Wolfe and Archie Goodwin series (18)
Dish ran away
Janson, Hank
Hank Janson series (169)
Disher, detective
Scott, Will
Disher series (1)
Dishonest murderer
Lockridge, Frances
Bill Wiegand series (13)
Mister and Mrs North series (14)
Dishonest way to die
Foxall, Peter Augustus
Catford Police series (1)
Dishonor among thieves
Dean, Spencer
Don Cadee series (5)
Dishonour among thieves
Hume, David
Mick Cardby series (22)
Lorac, E C R
Inspector Macdonald series (47)
Dishonoured bones
Trench, John
Martin Cotterell series (2)
Disinformer
John, Owen
Haggai Godin series (2)
Disinherited
Cohen, Matt
Salem quartet (1)
Forster, Peter
Alex Smith and Tony Bevan series (3)
Matthews, Clayton
Moraghan family trilogy (2)
Disinherited lady
Perez Galdos, Benito
Contemporary novels of Spain series (8)
Disintegration machine
Doyle, Arthur Conan
Professor Challenger series (4)
Disintegrator
De Born, Edith
Jimmy Chester trilogy (1)
Dismal thing to do
Craig, Alisa
Inspector Madoc Rhys series (3)
Dismissed with prejudice
Jance, Judith A
J P Beaumont series (7)
Disney's Oliver and company movie storybook
Korman, Justine
Oliver and company series (11)
Disorderly elements
Cook, Bob
Michael Wyman series (1)
Disorderly knights
Dunnett, Dorothy
Francis Crawford of Lymond series (3)
Dispatch rider
Daniel, Jack
Desert series (2)
Displaced
Welling, Lois
Star trek fan series (22)
Displaced persons
Hilton, John Buxton
Superintendent Simon Kenworthy series (17)
Disposing mind
Smithies, Richard Hugo Ripman
Inspector William McAlpin series (2)
Dispossessed
Le Guin, Ursula Kroeber
Hain series (2)
Shannon, Dell
Lieutenant Luis Mendoza series (39)
Disputed crown
Anand, Valerie
Norman trilogy (3)
Disputed quarry
Sharp, David
Professor Henry Arthur Fielding series (7)
Disraeli in love
Edelman, Maurice
Benjamin Disraeli series (1)
Disraeli rising
Edelman, Maurice
Benjamin Disraeli series (2)
Dissemblers
Creasey, John
Inspector Roger West series (11)
Dissertation
Koster, Richard Morton
Tinieblas trilogy (2)
Dissertations by Mister Dooley
Dunne, Finley Peter
Mister Dooley series (6)
Distaff factor
Wainwright, John
Northern Police series (53)
Distaff side
Paige, Frances
McGrath family series (3)
Distance between us
Sayers, Valerie
Due East series (4)
Distant clue
Lockridge, Frances
Inspector Merton Heimrich series (17)
Richards, Francis
Inspector Merton Heimrich series (17)
Distant dream
Rhodes, Evan Harold
American palace series (4)
Distant drums
Carey, D L
Dorian Trozen series (1)
Distant journey
Yeh, Chun-Chan
Quiet are the mountains series (3)
Distant land
Braun, Matt
Brannocks series (4)
Distant lands
Green, Julian
Distant lands series (1)
Distant prospect
Berners, Gerald Hugh Tyrwhitt-Wilson
Distant prospect series (2)
Distant scene
Archer, Fred
Evesham Vale series (12)
Distant song
Bromige, Iris
Rainwood family series (8)
Distant trails, 1805-1836
Gulick, Bill
Northwest destiny trilogy (1)
Distant view of death
Scott, Jack S
Detective Inspector Alfred Stanley Rosher series (6)
Distant wood
Harrod-Eagles, Cynthia
Morland family series (3)
Distinguished provincial in Paris
Balzac, Honore de
Scenes of provincial life series (9)
Distinguished Service Cross
Zlotnik, Donald E
Fields of honor series (2)
Distress call
Rotsler, William
Star trek tie-ins series (3)
District nurse
Miller, Hugh
District nurse series (1)
District Nurse Carter
Meynell, Laurence Walter
Nurse Carter series (3)
District of Columbia
Dos Passos, John
Spotswood family series (3)
Disturbance fee
Blishen, Edward
Schoolmaster series (12)
Disturbing death of Jenkin Delaney
Bonner, Michael
Roby Maclane trilogy (3)
Ditte, beyond the stars
Nexo, Martin Andersen
Ditte trilogy (3)
Ditte, daughter of man
Nexo, Martin Andersen
Ditte trilogy (2)
Ditte, girl alive!
Nexo, Martin Andersen
Ditte trilogy (1)
Diva
Delacorta
Serge Gorodish series (2)
Diva's emeralds
Macclure, Victor
Inspector Archie Burford series (7)
Diva's ruby
Crawford, Francis Marion
Paris Opera trilogy (3)
Dive deep for danger
Rothwell, Henry Talbot
Michael Brooks series (2)
Dive into danger
Forsyte, Charles
Inspector Richard Left series (2)
Dive to danger
Hardcastle, Michael
Tony and Jay series (1)
Divergence
Sheffield, Charles
Heritage universe series (2)
Diversions of Dawson
Copplestone, Bennet
Chief Inspector Dawson series (2)
Diverting adventures of Maurin
Aicard, Jean
Maurin series (1)
Divide and conquer
Becker, Margot
G.I.Joe series (2)
Divide and rule
Mark, Jan
Manipulator trilogy (2)
Divide by seven
Chambers, Robert
Hank Moody series (2)
Divide the night
Ebersohn, Wessel
Yudel Gordon series (2)
Divided allegiance
Moon, Elizabeth
Deed of Paksenarrion series (3)
Divided loyalties
Ferguson, James
Emmerdale Farm series (23)
Divided Treasure
Williams, David
Mark Treasure series (11)
Dividend on death
Halliday, Brett
Michael Shayne series (1)
Dividends of doom
House, Brant
Secret Agent X series (12)
Dividing sea
Harris, Ruth Elwin
Quantocks quartet (3)
Divinations
Ramsay, Jay
Great return series (5)
Divinations of Kala Persad, and other stories
Hill, Headon
Sebastian Zambra series (3)
Divine and deadly
Scherf, Margaret
Reverend Martin Buell series (2)
Divine death
Derrick, Lionel
Penetrator series (23)
Divine invasion
Dick, Philip Kindred
VALIS trilogy (2)
Divine passion
Fisher, Vardis
Testament of man series (5)
Divine queen
Corby, Adam
Doom-quest of Ara-Karn series (2)
Divine right
Cherryh, Carolyn Janice
Merovingen nights series (5)
Divine son of Ra
Makepeace, Joanna
Thebes series (1)
Diviners
Laurence, Margaret
Manawaka series (5)
Diving adventure
Price, Willard
Hal and Roger Hunt series (11)
Diving dames affair
Leslie, Peter
Man from U.N.C.L.E. series (9)
Diving death
Forsyte, Charles
Inspector Richard Left series (2)
Diving rock on the Hudson
Roth, Henry
Mercy of a rude stream series (2)
Division of the spoils
Green, Roland James
Starcruiser Shenandoah series (2)
Scott, Paul
British India quartet (4)
Divorce court murder
Propper, Milton
Tommy Rankin series (5)
Dixie convoy
Pendleton, Don
Mack Bolan series (27)
Dixie death squad
Derrick, Lionel
Penetrator series (13)
Dixon of Dock Green
Edwards, Rex
George Dixon series (2)
Willis, Ted
George Dixon series (2)
Dizzy daughter
Charteris, Leslie
Saint series (39)
DNA disaster
Appleton, Victor II
Tom Swift Junior series 3 (4)
Do and dare
Alger, Horatio
Atlantic series (2)
Do goldfish play the violin?
Wilson, David Henry
Jeremy James series (5)
Do-gooders
Grossman, Alfred
Marie series (2)
Do I have to go home?
Erickson, Karen
I can do it series (13)
Do look out, Noddy!
Blyton, Enid
Noddy series (15)
Do not disturb
Case, Frank
Wayward man series (2)
Kingsbury, Kate
Pennyfoot Hotel series (2)
Thayer, Lee
Peter Clancy series (48)
Do not murder before Christmas
Iams, Jack
Rocky Rockwell series (1)
Do not sleep
Wilson, Gertrude Mary
Inspector Lovick series (15)
Do nothin' till you hear from me
Wainwright, John
Lucky Luckhurst series (2)
Do or die
Mackie, John
Rat Bastards series (9)
Do-Somethings
Optic, Oliver
Flora Lee series (3)
Riverdale series (12)
Do this, hands!
Bentley, Nancy
Busy body series (2)
Do you agree?
Gee, Herbert Leslie
Priory House series (1)
Do you deal in murder?
Allyson, Alan
Martin Ross series (2)
Do you know my friend?
Beers, Victor Gilbert
Learning to read from the Bible primer series (2)
Do you love me?
Beers, Victor Gilbert
Learning to read from the Bible primer series (3)
Do you take this woman, and more disasters
Reid, Colin
Disasters series (2)
Dobie paradox
Cory, Desmond
John Dobie and Kate Coyle series (3)
Doc Leroy, M.D.
Edson, John Thomas
Waco series (7)
Doc Rance of Rambeau
Grover, Marshall
Larry and Stretch series (237)
Doc Savage, his apocalyptic life
Farmer, Philip Jose
Doc Savage series (183)
Doc Savage omnibus
Robeson, Kenneth
Doc Savage series (130)
Doc Savage series (134)
Doc Savage series (138)
Doc Savage series (142)
Doc Savage series (147)
Doc Savage series (151)
Doc Savage series (155)
Doc Savage series (159)
Doc Savage series (163)
Doc Savage series (167)
Doc Savage series (172)
Doc Savage series (177)
Doc Savage series (182)
Doc Savage, the supreme adventurer
Nanovic, John Leonard
Doc Savage series (183)
Doc, the dog
Darby, Joan
Animal adventure series (9)
Doc Travis
Cameron, Lou
Doc Travis trilogy (1)
Docken dead
Trench, John
Martin Cotterell series (1)
Dockyard mystery
Hope, Stanton
Sexton Blake series (885)
Doctor
Cameron, Isabel
Doctor Lindsay series (1)
Connor, Ralph
Crow's Nest series (2)
Doctor Adder
Jeter, Kevin W
Doctor Adder trilogy (1)
Doctor Adriaan
Couperus, Louis
Book of small souls quartet (4)
Doctor affairs all told
Duncan, Alex
Country doctor series (4)
Doctor against witch doctor
Doell, E W
Mission doctor trilogy (1)
Doctor and his friends
Cameron, Isabel
Doctor Lindsay series (4)
Doctor and son
Gordon, Richard
Doctor series (5)
Doctor and the corpse
Murray, Max
Corpse series (7)
Doctor and the Enterprise
Airey, John
Star trek series (57)
Doctor Anger's island
Buchanan, William
Kelly McCoy series (2)
Doctor at Crow's Nest
Connor, Ralph
Crow's Nest series (2)
Doctor at large
Gordon, Richard
Doctor series (3)
Doctor at Ryeminster
Ferrari, Ivy
Ryeminster Hospital series (3)
Doctor at sea
Gordon, Richard
Doctor series (2)
Doctor Bentiron, detective
Poate, Ernest M
Doctor Bentiron series (2)
Doctor Boomer
Miller, Margaret Jessy
Kingdom of Caledon series (3)
Doctor Bruderstein vanishes
Sherwood, John
Mister Charles Blessington series (1)
Doctor Burton
Gunter, Archibald Clavering
Doctor Burton series (1)
Doctor Burton's success
Gunter, Archibald Clavering
Doctor Burton series (2)
Doctor Byam in Harley Street
Byam, William
Harley Street series (2)
Doctor called Caroline
Harrison, Elizabeth
Central London Hospital series (13)

Doctor calls again
Cameron, Isabel
Doctor Lindsay series (3)
Downe, Patrick
Doctor series (2)
Doctor comes to Bayard
Seifert, Elizabeth
Bayard series (5)
Doctor Copernicus
Banville, John
Astronomers series (1)
Doctor, darling!
Rice, William
Doctor James Wiscock series (1)
Doctor Death
Carter, Nick
Nick Carter series (98)
Whitman, Charles
Inspector Lindon and Sergeant Gray series (1)
Doctor Dee
Wesley, Elizabeth
Doctor Dorothy Dee series (1)
Doctor Dee's choice
Wesley, Elizabeth
Doctor Dorothy Dee series (2)
Doctor died at dusk
Homes, Geoffrey
Robin Bishop series (1)
Doctor DNA
Carter, Nick
Nick Carter series (171)
Doctor, doctor
Flanders, Peter
Mercenary doctor series (1)
Doctor Dodds' experiment
Scott, Sutherland
Doctor Septimus Dodds series (11)
Doctor Dolittle
Lofting, Hugh
Doctor Dolittle series (1)
Doctor Dolittle, a treasury
Lofting, Hugh
Doctor Dolittle series (12)
Doctor Dolittle and the green canary
Lofting, Hugh
Doctor Dolittle series (11)
Doctor Dolittle and the pirates
Lofting, Hugh
Doctor Dolittle series (2)
Doctor Dolittle and the secret lake
Lofting, Hugh
Doctor Dolittle series (10)
Doctor Dolittle in the moon
Lofting, Hugh
Doctor Dolittle series (8)
Doctor Dolittle's caravan
Lofting, Hugh
Doctor Dolittle series (6)
Doctor Dolittle's circus
Lofting, Hugh
Doctor Dolittle series (4)
Doctor Dolittle's garden
Lofting, Hugh
Doctor Dolittle series (7)
Doctor Dolittle's post office
Lofting, Hugh
Doctor Dolittle series (3)
Doctor Dolittle's Puddlebury adventures
Lofting, Hugh
Doctor Dolittle series (12)
Doctor Dolittle's return
Lofting, Hugh
Doctor Dolittle series (9)
Doctor Dolittle's zoo
Lofting, Hugh
Doctor Dolittle series (5)
Doctor, don't!
Rice, William
Doctor James Wiscock series (2)
Doctor Doon, superstar
Bethancourt, Tomas Ernesto
Doris Fein series (1)
Doctor Dorothy's choice
Wesley, Elizabeth
Doctor Dorothy Dee series (2)
Doctor down under
Gordon, Doris
Backblocks doctor series (2)
Doctor Dredd's wagon of wonders
Brittain, Bill
Coven Tree series (3)
Doctor Duvene's crime
Chester, Gilbert
Sexton Blake series (698)
Doctor Fell, detective, and other stories
Carr, John Dickson
Doctor Gideon Fell series (23)
Doctor Ferraro's frame-up
Brisbane, Coutts
Sexton Blake series (748)
Doctor Finlay of Tannochnrae
Cronin, Archibald Joseph
Doctor Finlay series (2)
Doctor Fix
Janson, Hank
Hank Janson series (170)
Doctor from Llasa
Lobsang Rampa, Tuesday
Third eye series (2)
Doctor Funnybone's secret
Hope, Laura Lee
Bobbsey twins series (65)
Doctor goes east
Mair, George Brown
Travelling doctor series (1)
Doctor goes north
Mair, George Brown
Travelling doctor series (2)
Doctor goes west
Mair, George Brown
Travelling doctor series (3)
Doctor Goodwood's locum
Rhode, John
Doctor Lancelot Priestley series (52)
Doctor Gordon in search of his children
Goulding, Francis Robert
Marooners series (2)
Doctor heals by faith
Woodard, Christopher Roy
Faith healing trilogy (1)
Doctor, his wife and the clock
Green, Anna Katharine
Ebenezer Gryce series (6)
Doctor Hudson's secret journal
Douglas, Lloyd Cassel
Doctor Hudson series (1)
Doctor in clover
Gordon, Richard
Doctor series (6)
Doctor in judgment
Seifert, Elizabeth
Bayard series (7)
Doctor in love
Gordon, Richard
Doctor series (4)
Doctor in Mexico
Jennings, D K
Doctor Ralph Conway series (18)
Doctor in Parliament
Johnson, Donald McIntosh
Publisher presents himself series (4)
Doctor in plaster
Cooper, Lisa
Princess Beatrice Hospital series (5)
Doctor in pursuit
Collins, Lynne
Hartlake Hospital series (4)
Doctor in the house
Gordon, Richard
Doctor series (1)
Doctor in the nest
Gordon, Richard
Doctor series (15)
Doctor in the nude
Gordon, Richard
Doctor series (13)
Doctor in the soup
Gordon, Richard
Doctor series (18)
Doctor in the swim
Gordon, Richard
Doctor series (8)
Doctor in the west
Gibson, Morris
One man series (2)
Doctor in the zoo
Taylor, David Conrad
Zoovet series (2)
Doctor in Turkey
Mair, George Brown
Travelling doctor series (4)
Doctor Jack
Rathborne, Saint George
Doctor Jack series (1)
Doctor Jack and Company
Rathborne, Saint George
Doctor Jack series (4)
Doctor Jack's Paradise Mine
Rathborne, Saint George
Doctor Jack series (3)
Doctor Jack's talisman
Rathborne, Saint George
Doctor Jack series (5)
Doctor Jack's widow
Rathborne, Saint George
Doctor Jack series (6)
Doctor Jack's wife
Rathborne, Saint George
Doctor Jack series (2)
Doctor Jamie
Seifert, Elizabeth
Bayard series (2)
Doctor Jane
McElfresh, Adeline
Doctor Jane series (1)
Doctor Jane comes home
McElfresh, Adeline
Doctor Jane series (4)
Doctor Jane, interne
McElfresh, Adeline
Doctor Jane series (7)
Doctor Jane's choice
McElfresh, Adeline
Doctor Jane series (5)
Doctor Jane's mission
McElfresh, Adeline
Doctor Jane series (3)
Doctor Jekyll and Mister Hollins
Hall, Willis
Doctor Jekyll sequels series (2)
Henry Hollins series (5)
Doctor Jekyll and Mister Holmes
Estleman, Loren D
Doctor Jekyll sequels series (1)
Sherlock Holmes sequels series (36)
Doctor Jekyll and Mister Hyde
Bethancourt, Tomas Ernesto
Doctor Jekyll series (1)
Border, Rosemary
Doctor Jekyll series (1)
McMullan, Kate
Doctor Jekyll series (1)
Stevenson, Robert Louis
Doctor Jekyll series (1)
Doctor Jekyll and Mister Hyde after one hundred years
Hirsch, Gordon
Doctor Jekyll series (2)
Doctor Kerkhoven
Wassermann, Jakob
Doctor Joseph Kerkhoven trilogy (2)
Doctor Kildare
Ackworth, Robert Charles
Doctor Kildare series (8)
Doctor Kildare assigned to trouble
Ackworth, Robert Charles
Doctor Kildare junior series (1)
Doctor Kildare takes charge
Brand, Max
Doctor Kildare series (4)
Doctor Kildare's crisis
Brand, Max
Doctor Kildare series (5)
Doctor Kildare's finest hour
Daniels, Norman A
Doctor Kildare series (10)
Doctor Kildare's hardest case
Brand, Max
Doctor Kildare series (7)
Doctor Kildare's search
Brand, Max
Doctor Kildare series (7)
Doctor Kildare's secret romance
Daniels, Norman A
Doctor Kildare series (9)
Doctor Kildare's trial
Brand, Max
Doctor Kildare series (6)
Doctor Lavendar's people
Deland, Margaret
Old Chester series (3)
Doctor, lawyer
Wilcox, Collin
Lieutenant Frank Hastings series (8)
Doctor Le Baron and his daughters
Austin, Jane Goodwin
Nameless nobleman series (2)
Doctor looks at murder
Quick, Dorothy
Lieutenant Peter Donnegan series (2)
Doctor Luke of the Labrador
Duncan, Norman
Doctor Luke series (1)
Doctor Merlin's magic shop
Corbett, Scott
Doctor Merlin series (1)
Doctor Mirabilis
Blish, James
After such knowledge series (1)
Doctor Morelle and destiny
Dudley, Ernest
Doctor Morelle series (9)
Doctor Morelle and the doll
Dudley, Ernest
Doctor Morelle series (14)
Doctor Morelle and the drummer girl
Dudley, Ernest
Doctor Morelle series (5)
Doctor Morelle at midnight
Dudley, Ernest
Doctor Morelle series (11)
Doctor Morelle meets murder, and other new adventures
Dudley, Ernest
Doctor Morelle series (4)
Doctor Morelle takes a bow
Dudley, Ernest
Doctor Morelle series (6)
Doctor Nikola
Boothby, Guy
Doctor Nikola series (2)
Doctor Nikola returns
Boothby, Guy
Doctor Nikola series (2)
Doctor Nikola's experiment
Boothby, Guy
Doctor Nikola series (4)
Doctor Nikola's vendetta
Boothby, Guy
Doctor Nikola series (1)
Doctor No
Fleming, Ian
James Bond series (6)
Doctor North and his friends
Mitchell, Silas Weir
Doctor North series (2)
Doctor Nyet
Mark, Ted
Girl from P.U.S.S.Y.C.A.T. series (2)
Man from O.R.G.Y. series (6)
Doctor of Stalingrad
Konsalik, Heinz Gunther
Stalingrad series (1)
Doctor of Tanganyika
White, Paul
Doctor of Tanganyika series (1)
Doctor omnibus
Cameron, Isabel
Doctor Lindsay series (3)
Doctor on the ball
Gordon, Richard
Doctor series (17)
Doctor on the boil
Gordon, Richard
Doctor series (11)
Doctor on the brain
Gordon, Richard
Doctor series (12)
Doctor on the job
Gordon, Richard
Doctor series (14)
Doctor on toast
Gordon, Richard
Doctor series (7)
Doctor on trial
Seifert, Elizabeth
Bayard series (3)
Doctor Orient
Lauria, Frank
Doctor Owen Orient series (1)
Doctor Orpheus
Wallace, Ian
Claudine Saint Cyr series (1)
Croyd series (2)
Doctor Pascal
Zola, Emile
Rougon Macquart series (20)
Doctor Phibes
Goldstein, William
Doctor Phibes series (1)
Doctor Phibes rises again
Goldstein, William
Doctor Phibes series (2)
Doctor Priestley investigates
Rhode, John
Doctor Lancelot Priestley series (9)
Doctor Priestley lays a trap
Rhode, John
Doctor Lancelot Priestley series (14)
Doctor Priestley's quest
Rhode, John
Doctor Lancelot Priestley series (2)
Doctor Quake
Murphy, Warren Burton
Destroyer series (5)
Doctor Quartz, magician
Carter, Nicholas
Doctor Quartz series (1)
Nicholas Carter series (201)
Doctor Quartz's quick move
Carter, Nicholas
Doctor Quartz series (2)
Nicholas Carter series (202)
Doctor Rabbit's foundling
Wahl, Jan
Doctor Rabbit series (1)
Doctor Rabbit's last scout
Wahl, Jan
Doctor Rabbit series (2)
Doctor reflects
Johnson, Donald McIntosh
Publisher presents himself series (6)
Doctor regrets
Johnson, Donald McIntosh
Publisher presents himself series (1)
Doctor returns
Johnson, Donald McIntosh
Publisher presents himself series (3)
Doctor Ricardo
Garrett, William
James Drew series (3)
Doctor Ross of Harton
Dwyer-Joyce, Alice
Doctor Esmond Ross series (1)
Doctor Sahib
Jennings, D K
Doctor Ralph Conway series (13)
Doctor Sam, Johnson, detector
De la Torre, Lillian
Doctor Sam, Johnson series (1)
Doctor Sax
Kerouac, Jack
Jack Duluoz series (2)
Doctor Scarlett
Laing, Alexander
Doctor Scarlett series (2)
Doctor Sean
Breinburg, Petronella
Sean series (2)
Doctor Shawn
Breinburg, Petronella
Sean series (2)
Doctor Sinister
Chester, Gilbert
Sexton Blake series (1089)
Evans, Gwyn
Sexton Blake series (757)
Doctor Starr
Johnston, William
Doctor Starr series (1)
Doctor Starr in crisis
Johnston, William
Doctor Starr series (2)
Doctor Strange, Nightmare
Rotsler, William
Marvel superheroes, new series (7)
Doctor Strange, Through six generations
Varney, Allen
Marvel superheroes adventure gamebooks series (4)
Doctor Syn
Thorndike, Russell
Doctor Syn series (1)
Doctor Syn alias The Scarecrow
Crume, Vic
Doctor Syn series (8)
Doctor Syn on the high seas
Thorndike, Russell
Doctor Syn series (4)
Doctor Syn returns
Thorndike, Russell
Doctor Syn series (2)
Doctor Tam O'Shanter
Robinson, Mabel Louise
Little Lucia series (1)
Doctor Tancred begins
Cole, George Douglas Howard
Doctor Benjamin Tancred series (1)
Superintendent Henry Wilson series (15)
Doctor Thornduke omnibus
Freeman, Richard Austin
Doctor John Evelyn Thorndyke series (27)
Doctor Thorndyke intervenes
Freeman, Richard Austin
Doctor John Evelyn Thorndyke series (21)
Doctor Thorndyke investigates
Freeman, Richard Austin
Doctor John Evelyn Thorndyke series (27)
Doctor Thorndyke's case book
Freeman, Richard Austin
Doctor John Evelyn Thorndyke series (9)
Doctor Thorndyke's cases
Freeman, Richard Austin
Doctor John Evelyn Thorndyke series (2)
Doctor Thorndyke's dilemma
Dirckx, John H
Doctor John Evelyn Thorndyke series (29)

Doctor Thorndyke's discovery
Freeman, Richard Austin
Doctor John Evelyn Thorndyke series (20)
Doctor Thorne
Trollope, Anthony
Chronicles of Barsetshire series (3)
Doctor Thornyke's crime file
Freeman, Richard Austin
Doctor John Evelyn Thorndyke series (27)
Doctor Time
Robeson, Kenneth
Avenger series (28)
Doctor to the stars
Leinster, Murray
Med Service series (3)
Doctor Toby finds murder
Schley, Sturges Mason
Doctor Quentin Toby series (2)
Doctor Two Guns
Field, Peter
Powder Valley series (10)
Doctor Watts' chatechisms and prayers
Watts, Isaac
Catechisms and prayers series (2)
Doctor wears three faces
Bard, Mary
Three faces series (1)
Doctor Who
Whitaker, David
Doctor Who series (1)
Doctor Who, a celebration
Haining, Peter
Doctor Who series (162)
Doctor Who and an unearthly child
Dicks, Terrance
Doctor Who series (65)
Doctor Who and death to the Daleks
Dicks, Terrance
Doctor Who series (40)
Sarah Jane Smith series (14)
Doctor Who and the abominable snowman
Dicks, Terrance
Doctor Who series (8)
Doctor Who and the android invasion
Dicks, Terrance
Doctor Who series (41)
Sarah Jane Smith series (15)
Doctor Who and the androids of Tara
Dicks, Terrance
Doctor Who series (56)
Doctor Who and the ark in space
Marter, Ian
Doctor Who series (31)
Sarah Jane Smith series (9)
Doctor Who and the Armageddon factor
Dicks, Terrance
Doctor Who series (54)
Doctor Who and the Auton invasion
Dicks, Terrance
Doctor Who series (5)
Doctor Who and the brain of Morbius
Dicks, Terrance
Doctor Who series (32)
Sarah Jane Smith series (10)
Doctor Who and the carnival of monsters
Dicks, Terrance
Doctor Who series (27)
Doctor Who and the cave monsters
Hulke, Malcolm
Doctor Who series (4)
Doctor Who and the claws of Axos
Dicks, Terrance
Doctor Who series (30)
Doctor Who and the creature from the pit
Fisher, David
Doctor Who series (62)
Doctor Who and the Crusaders
Whitaker, David
Doctor Who series (3)
Doctor Who and the curse of Peladon
Hayles, Brian
Doctor Who series (58)
Doctor Who and the Cybermen
Davis, Gerry
Doctor Who series (11)
Doctor Who and the daemons
Letts, Barry
Doctor Who series (10)
Doctor Who and the Dalek invasion of earth
Dicks, Terrance
Doctor Who series (29)
Doctor Who and the Daleks
Whitaker, David
Doctor Who series (1)
Doctor Who and the day of the Daleks
Dicks, Terrance
Doctor Who series (6)
Doctor Who and the deadly assassin
Dicks, Terrance
Doctor Who series (35)
Doctor Who and the destiny of the Daleks
Dicks, Terrance
Doctor Who series (50)
Doctor Who and the dinosaur invasion
Hulke, Malcolm
Doctor Who series (17)
Sarah Jane Smith series (6)
Doctor Who and the doomsday weapon
Hulke, Malcolm
Doctor Who series (7)
Doctor Who and the enemy of the world
Marter, Ian
Doctor Who series (64)
Doctor Who and the face of evil
Dicks, Terrance
Doctor Who series (37)
Doctor Who and the genesis of the Daleks
Dicks, Terrance
Doctor Who series (22)
Sarah Jane Smith series (3)
Doctor Who and the giant robot
Dicks, Terrance
Doctor Who series (12)
Sarah Jane Smith series (2)
Doctor Who and the green death
Hulke, Malcolm
Doctor Who series (13)
Doctor Who and the hand of fear
Dicks, Terrance
Doctor Who series (45)
Sarah Jane Smith series (17)
Doctor Who and the horns of Nimon
Dicks, Terrance
Doctor Who series (61)
Doctor Who and the horror of Fang Rock
Dicks, Terrance
Doctor Who series (42)
Doctor Who and the ice warriors
Hayles, Brian
Doctor Who series (20)
Doctor Who and the image of the Fendahl
Dicks, Terrance
Doctor Who series (48)
Doctor Who and the invasion of time
Dicks, Terrance
Doctor Who series (51)
Doctor Who and the invisible enemy
Dicks, Terrance
Doctor Who series (46)
Doctor Who and the keeper of Traken
Dicks, Terrance
Doctor Who series (68)
Doctor Who and the keys of Marinus
Hinchcliffe, Philip
Doctor Who series (57)
Doctor Who and the leisure hive
Fisher, David
Doctor Who series (69)
Doctor Who and the Loch Ness Monster
Dicks, Terrance
Doctor Who series (18)
Sarah Jane Smith series (5)
Doctor Who and the masque of Mandragora
Hinchcliffe, Philip
Doctor Who series (38)
Sarah Jane Smith series (12)
Doctor Who and the monster of Peladon
Dicks, Terrance
Doctor Who series (59)
Sarah Jane Smith series (18)
Doctor Who and the mutants
Dicks, Terrance
Doctor Who series (34)
Doctor Who and the nightmare of Eden
Dicks, Terrance
Doctor Who series (63)
Doctor Who and the planet of evil
Dicks, Terrance
Doctor Who series (33)
Sarah Jane Smith series (8)
Doctor Who and the planet of the Daleks
Dicks, Terrance
Doctor Who series (25)
Doctor Who and the planet of the giants
Dicks, Terrance
Doctor Who series (145)
Doctor Who and the planet of the spiders
Dicks, Terrance
Doctor Who series (15)
Sarah Jane Smith series (1)
Doctor Who and the power of Kroll
Dicks, Terrance
Doctor Who series (60)
Doctor Who and the pyramids of Mars
Dicks, Terrance
Doctor Who series (26)
Sarah Jane Smith series (7)
Doctor Who and the revenge of the Cybermen
Dicks, Terrance
Doctor Who series (21)
Sarah Jane Smith series (4)
Doctor Who and the Ribos operation
Marter, Ian
Doctor Who series (55)
Doctor Who and the robots of death
Dicks, Terrance
Doctor Who series (47)
Doctor Who and the sea-devils
Hulke, Malcolm
Doctor Who series (9)
Doctor Who and the seeds of doom
Hinchcliffe, Philip
Doctor Who series (28)
Sarah Jane Smith series (11)
Doctor Who and the Sontaron experiment
Marter, Ian
Doctor Who series (44)
Sarah Jane Smith series (13)
Doctor Who and the space war
Hulke, Malcolm
Doctor Who series (24)
Doctor Who and the state of decay
Dicks, Terrance
Doctor Who series (66)
Doctor Who and the stones of blood
Dicks, Terrance
Doctor Who series (53)
Doctor Who and the sunmakers
Dicks, Terrance
Doctor Who series (72)
Doctor Who and the talons of Weng-Chiang
Dicks, Terrance
Doctor Who series (36)
Doctor Who and the tenth planet
Davis, Gerry
Doctor Who series (16)
Doctor Who and the terror of the Autons
Dicks, Terrance
Doctor Who series (14)
Doctor Who and the three doctors
Dicks, Terrance
Doctor Who series (19)
Doctor Who and the time warrior
Dicks, Terrance
Doctor Who series (39)
Sarah Jane Smith series (16)
Doctor Who and the tomb of the Cybermen
Davis, Gerry
Doctor Who series (43)
Doctor Who and the underworld
Dicks, Terrance
Doctor Who series (52)
Doctor Who and the visitation
Saward, Eric
Doctor Who series (70)
Doctor Who and the war games
Hulke, Malcolm
Doctor Who series (49)
Doctor Who and the warriors' gate
Lydecker, John
Doctor Who series (67)
Doctor Who and the web of fear
Dicks, Terrance
Doctor Who series (23)
Doctor Who and the Zarbi
Strutton, Bill
Doctor Who series (2)
Doctor Who cookbook
Downie, Gary
Doctor Who series (162)
Doctor Who crossword book
Robinson, Nigel
Doctor Who series (162)
Doctor Who file
Haining, Peter
Doctor Who series (162)
Doctor Who fun book
Quinn, Tim
Doctor Who series (162)
Doctor who held hands
Footner, Hulbert
Madame Rosika Storey series (4)
Doctor Who illustrated A-Z
Sandring, Lesley
Doctor Who series (162)
Doctor Who in an exciting adventure with the Daleks
Whitaker, David
Doctor Who series (1)
Doctor Who monster book
Dicks, Terrance
Doctor Who series (162)
Doctor Who omnibus
Dicks, Terrance
Doctor Who series (29)
Doctor Who puzzle book
Holt, Michael
Doctor Who series (162)
Doctor Who quiz book
Robinson, Nigel
Doctor Who quiz book series (4)
Doctor Who quiz book of dinosaurs
Holt, Michael
Doctor Who quiz book series (1)
Doctor Who quiz book of magic
Holt, Michael
Doctor Who quiz book series (2)
Doctor Who quiz book of science
Holt, Michael
Doctor Who quiz book series (3)
Doctor Who quiz book of space
Holt, Michael
Doctor Who quiz book series (4)
Doctor Who special effects
Irvine, Mat
Doctor Who series (162)
Doctor Who technical manual
Harris, Mark
Doctor Who series (162)
Doctor Who, the early years
Bentham, Jeremy
Doctor Who series (162)
Doctor Who, the making of a television series
Road, Alan
Doctor Who series (162)
Doctor Who, the unfolding text
Tulloch, John
Doctor Who series (162)
Doctor Who timeview
Bellamy, Frank
Doctor Who series (162)
Doctor Who, twenty five glorious years
Haining, Peter
Doctor Who series (162)
Doctor who wouldn't tell
Graydon, William Murray
Sexton Blake series (524)
Doctor with a mission
Seifert, Elizabeth
Bayard series (6)
Doctor Xargle's book of earthhounds
Willis, Jeanne
Doctor Xargle series (1)
Doctor Xargle's book of earthriggers
Willis, Jeanne
Doctor Xargle series (2)
Doctor Z
Timperley, Rosemary
Hospital trilogy (3)
Doctor Zed's dazzling book of science activities
Penrose, Gordon
Doctor Zed series (2)
Doctor Zed's science surprises
Penrose, Gordon
Doctor Zed series (3)
Doctor Zed's zany brilliant book of science experiments
Penrose, Gordon
Doctor Zed series (1)
Doctor Zhivago
Pasternak, Boris
Doctor Zhivago series (1)
Doctors
Fisher, Leonard Everett
Colonial Americans series (13)
Soubiran, Andre
Jean Nerac series (1)
Doctors and nurses
Greene, Carla
What do they do series (2)
Doctors are doubtful
Weymouth, Anthony
Inspector Treadgold series (2)
Doctor's birthday
Adams, Henry Cadwallader
Nethercourt series (2)
Walter's schooldays series (1)
Doctor's boy
Anckarsvard, Karin
Jon Halvorsson series (1)
Doctor's Christmas eve
Allen, James Lane
Christmas season series (2)
Doctor's crime
Danvers, Milton
Robert Spicer series (1)
Doctor's daughter
Walter, William Wilfred
Pastor's son trilogy (2)
Doctor's daughters
Gordon, Richard
Doctor series (16)
Doctor's desperate hour
Seifert, Elizabeth
Bayard series (10)
Doctor's destiny
Seifert, Elizabeth
Bayard series (8)
Doctor's double
Alais, Ernest W
Sexton Blake series (206)
Doctor's faith holds fast
Woodard, Christopher Roy
Faith healing trilogy (2)
Doctor's faith is challenged
Woodard, Christopher Roy
Faith healing trilogy (3)
Doctor's family
Oliphant, Margaret Oliphant Wilson
Carlingford series (2)
Doctor's lady
Foyle, Kathleen
Augherim series (1)
Doctor's little girl
Taggart, Marion Ames
Doctor's little girl series (1)
Doctor's orders
Duane, Diane
Star trek series (50)
Doctor's secret
Bayfield, William John
Sexton Blake series (274)
Doctor's strategem
Carter, Nicholas
Nicholas Carter series (262)
Doctor's weekend
Bagster, Hubert
Country doctor series (2)
Documents relating to the sentimental agents in the Volyen Empire
Lessing, Doris
Canopus in Argus archives series (5)
Dodd papers
Livingston, Kenneth
Papers series (1)
Doddles
Adams, Agnes
Doddles series (1)
Doddles makes things hum
Adams, Agnes
Doddles series (2)
Dodge City
Mitchum, Hank
Stage coach station series (1)
Willoughby, Lee Davis
Women who won the West series (2)
Dodge City bombers
Derrick, Lionel
Penetrator series (9)
Dodge City doll
Fletcher, Dirk
Spur McCoy series (24)
Dodge City gang
Roberts, J R
Gunsmith series (20)
Dodge Club
De Mille, James
Young Dodge Club series (1)
Dodging the law
Carter, Nicholas
Nicholas Carter series (524)
Dodging the North Sea mines
Kay, Ross
Big war series (3)
Dodo
Bell, Vicars
Dodo series (1)
Benson, Edward Frederic
Dodo series (1)
Dodo is a solitary bird
Edwards, Lynne
Dodo series (2)
Dodo the second
Benson, Edward Frederic
Dodo series (2)
Dodo's daughter
Benson, Edward Frederic
Dodo series (2)
Dodo's delight
Ryan, John
Doodle series (1)
Dodos don't duck
O'Brine, Manning
Michael O'Kelly series (3)
Dodu, and other stories
Narayan, Rasipuram Krishnaswami
Malgudi series (17)
Does anybody care about Lou Emma Miller?
Constant, Alberta Wilson
Miller family series (3)

Does this school have capital punishment
Hentoff, Nat
This school series (2)
Dog
Burningham, John
Little book series (7)
Cobbett, Pelham
Dog series (1)
Dog and a half
Willard, Barbara
Jill and Limpet series (1)
Dog and the wolf
Anderson, Poul
King of Ys series (4)
Dog called Himself
Bird, Kenneth
Himself series (1)
Dog collar murders
Wilson, Barbara Ellen
Pam Nilsen series (3)
Dog days
Stranger, Joyce
Dog series (4)
Dog detective Ranjha
Sharma, Partap
Ranjha series (1)
Dog fight with death
Davison, Gilderoy
Peter Castle series (6)
Twisted Face series (8)
Dog heavies
Washburn, Livia Jane
Lucas Hallam series (3)
Dog in a million
Stranger, Joyce
Dog series (3)
Dog in the dark
Hammond, Gerald
Captain John Cunningham series (1)
Dog it was that died
Lorac, E C R
Inspector Macdonald series (36)
Dog Man
Procter, Maurice
Chief Inspector Harry Martineau series (24)
Dog named Chips
Terhune, Albert Payson
Sunnybank collies series (15)
Dog on Barkham Street
Stolz, Mary
Barkham Street trilogy (1)
Dog on third base
Hiser, Constance
James and gang series (3)
Dog Rock
Foster, David
D'Arcy Oliveres series (1)
Dog sled to Dread
Quackenbush, Robert Mead
Miss Mallard series (12)
Dog stories
Blyton, Enid
Dog stories series (2)
Dog stories every child should know
Terhune, Albert Payson
Sunnybank collies series (5)
Dog that never was
Lister, Stephen
Sainte Monique series (14)
Dog track murder
Osborne, Mark
Sexton Blake series (807)
Dog who would go digging
Blyton, Enid
John and Mary series (3)
Dog wizard
Hambly, Barbara
Windrose series (3)
Dog years
Grass, Gunter
Danzig trilogy (3)
Dogfish
Geason, Susan
Syd Fish series (2)
Doghouse
Hammond, Gerald
Captain John Cunningham series (2)
Dogmatix and the boar hunt
Goscinny, Rene
Dogmatix series (4)
Dogmatix and the magic potion
Goscinny, Rene
Dogmatix series (6)
Dogmatix and the storm
Goscinny, Rene
Dogmatix series (1)
Dogmatix and the ugly little eagle
Goscinny, Rene
Dogmatix series (5)
Dogmatix makes a friend
Goscinny, Rene
Dogmatix series (3)
Dogs
Berg, Leila
Small world series (1)
Dogs and their women
Cohen, Barbara
Animals and their women series (1)
Dogs do bark
Stagge, Jonathan
Doctor Hugh Westlake series (1)
Dogs of Pangers
Wood, Lorna
Pangers series (1)
Dogs of peace
Croft-Cooke, Rupert
Sensual life series (15)
Dogs of war
Baker, William Howard
Richard Quintain series (7)
Dogsbody
Sinderby, Donald
Dogsbody series (1)
Dogwatching
Morris, Desmond
Watching series (3)
Doin Wildcat
Nyoongah, Mudrooroo
Wildcat trilogy (2)
Doing his best
Trowbridge, John Townsend
Jack Hazard series (3)
Doing the washing
Garland, Sarah
Family life series (2)
Doing things together
Barkin, Carol
Transition series (2)
Doings of Dooki
Hughes, Jean
Dooki series (1)
Doings of Hilda
Garrard, Phillis
Hilda series (2)
Doings of the Bodley family in town and country
Scudder, Horace Elisha
Bodley family series (1)
Doll
McBain, Ed
Eighty Seventh Precinct series (20)
Sparger, Rex
Dark forces series (3)
Doll and drum
Tarsky, Sue
Look and see series (3)
Doll for the big house
Brown, Carter
Lieutenant Al Wheeler series (5)
Doll for the Toff
Creasey, John
Toff series (47)
Doll that fell out of the pram
Blyton, Enid
Little bedtime books series (2)
Dollar to die for
Fox, Brian
Dollar series (3)
Dollar trail to Ramirez
Grover, Marshall
Larry and Stretch series (154)
Dollars and cents for Harriet
Maestro, Betsy Crippen
Harriet series (10)
Dollars for the Reaper
Holmes, Bryan John
Reaper series (2)
Dollars of death
Bowden, Jim
Cap Millett series (2)
Dollmaker
Arnow, Harriette
Kentucky trilogy (3)
Dolls are deadly
Halliday, Brett
Michael Shayne series (37)
Doll's bad news
Chase, James Hadley
Carol Blandish series (2)
Doll's done dancing
Flynn, Brian
Anthony Bathurst series (45)
Doll's house
Gaiman, Neil
Sandman series (1)
Ibsen, Henrik
Nora Helmer series (1)
Dolls in danger
Hildick, Edmund Wallace
McGurk series (2)
Dolls of death
Afford, Max
Jeffery Blackburn series (2)
Dolly and I
Optic, Oliver
Riverdale series (4)
Dolly and Molly and the farmer men
Gordon, Elizabeth
Dolly and Molly series (1)
Dolly and Molly at the circus
Gordon, Elizabeth
Dolly and Molly series (2)
Dolly and Molly at the seashore
Gordon, Elizabeth
Dolly and Molly series (3)
Dolly and Molly on Christmas day
Gordon, Elizabeth
Dolly and Molly series (4)
Dolly and the bird of paradise
Dunnett, Dorothy
Johnson and the yacht Dolly series (6)
Dolly and the cookie bird
Dunnett, Dorothy
Johnson and the yacht Dolly series (2)
Dolly and the doctor bird
Dunnett, Dorothy
Johnson and the yacht Dolly series (3)
Dolly and the nanny bird
Dunnett, Dorothy
Johnson and the yacht Dolly series (5)
Dolly and the singing bird
Dunnett, Dorothy
Johnson and the yacht Dolly series (1)
Dolly and the starry bird
Dunnett, Dorothy
Johnson and the yacht Dolly series (4)
Dolly dolly spy
Diment, Adam
Philip McAlpine series (1)
Dolly's mixture
Scannell, Dorothy
Dolly trilogy (3)
Dolly's war
Scannell, Dorothy
Dolly trilogy (2)
Dolphin boy
Meyers, Roy
Dolphins trilogy (1)
Dolphin rider
Meyers, Roy
Dolphins trilogy (1)
Dolphin sailed north
Simons, Roger
Bruce and Ian series (2)
Dolphin summer
Edwards, Monica
Romney Marsh series (15)
Dolphin that spoke
Gilbert, Harry
Honey the dolphin series (1)
Dolphin that walked
Gilbert, Harry
Honey the dolphin series (2)
Dolphins of Pern
McCaffrey, Anne
Pern and the Red Planet series (12)
Domain
Herbert, James
Rats trilogy (3)
Domains of Darkover
Bradley, Marion Zimmer
Darkover anthologies series (6)
Dombey and Son
Dickens, Charles
Dombey series (1)
Dome in the forest
Williams, Paul Osborne
Pelbar series (3)
Domes of fire
Eddings, David
Tamuli trilogy (1)
Domes of Mars
Moore, Patrick
Maurice Gray series (2)
Domes of Pico
Walters, Hugh
Chris Godfrey series (2)
Domesday Book
Masters, Edgar Lee
Domesday Book series (1)
Domestic agency
Rhode, John
Doctor Lancelot Priestley series (60)
Domestic difference
Housman, Laurence
Palace plays series (4)
Domestic stories
Craik, Dinah Maria
Avillion series (2)
Dominant third
Hely, Elizabeth
Antoine Cirret series (1)
Dominator
York, Andrew
Jonas Wilde series (5)
Dominators
Marter, Ian
Doctor Who series (86)
Dominic Sly
Partridge, Jenny
Oakapple Wood series (5)
Dominican affair
Carter, Nick
Nick Carter series (159)
Dominie abroad
Neill, Alexander Sutherland
Dominie series (5)
Dominie dismissed
Neill, Alexander Sutherland
Dominie series (2)
Dominie in doubt
Neill, Alexander Sutherland
Dominie series (3)
Dominie's five
Neill, Alexander Sutherland
Dominie series (6)
Dominie's log
Neill, Alexander Sutherland
Dominie series (1)
Dominion
Saberhagen, Fred
Dracula series (22)
Wall, Robert Emmet
Nowell family series (6)
Domino Club
Upward, Allen
Doctor Frank Tarleton series (1)
Domino man
Grover, Marshall
Larry and Stretch series (328)
Domino principle
Kennedy, Adam
Roy Tucker series (1)
Domino vendetta
Kennedy, Adam
Roy Tucker series (2)
Dominoes
Wainwright, John
Chief Inspector Lennox series (7)
Inspector Lyle series (3)
Northern Police series (46)
Dominy's dollars
Neuman, Berman Paul
Paths of the blind trilogy (3)
Domnei
Cabell, James Branch
Dom Manuel and his descendants series (7)
Don, a runaway dog
Barnum, Richard
Kneetime animal stories series (5)
Don Camillo and his flock
Guareschi, Giovanni
Don Camillo series (2)
Don Camillo and the devil
Guareschi, Giovanni
Don Camillo series (4)
Don Camillo and the prodigal son
Guareschi, Giovanni
Don Camillo series (2)
Don Camillo, his little and his dilemma
Guareschi, Giovanni
Don Camillo series (3)
Don Camillo meets Hell's Angels
Guareschi, Giovanni
Don Camillo series (6)
Don Camillo meets the flower children
Guareschi, Giovanni
Don Camillo series (6)
Don Camillo takes the devil by the tail
Guareschi, Giovanni
Don Camillo series (4)
Don Camillo's dilemma
Guareschi, Giovanni
Don Camillo series (3)
Don Candeloro
Verga, Giovanni
Vinti family series (2)
Don flows home to the sea
Sholokhov, Mikhail
Don series (3)
Don John's ducats
Pilkington, Roger
Branxome family series (5)
Don Juan
Duncan, Ronald
Don Juan series (1)
Don Kirk's mine
Patten, Gilbert
Don Kirk series (3)
Don Orsino
Crawford, Francis Marion
Roman society series (3)
Don Q in the Sierra
Prichard, Katherine
Don Q series (2)
Don Q's love story
Prichard, Katherine
Don Q series (3)
Don Quixote de la Mancha
Cervantes Saavedra, Miguel de
Don Quixote series (1)
Don Sturdy across the North Pole
Appleton, Victor
Don Sturdy series (4)
Don Sturdy among the gorillas
Appleton, Victor
Don Sturdy series (7)
Don Sturdy captured by headhunters
Appleton, Victor
Don Sturdy series (8)
Don Sturdy in Glacier Bay
Appleton, Victor
Don Sturdy series (13)
Don Sturdy in lion land
Appleton, Victor
Don Sturdy series (9)
Don Sturdy in the desert of mystery
Appleton, Victor
Don Sturdy series (1)
Don Sturdy in the land of giants
Appleton, Victor
Don Sturdy series (10)
Don Sturdy in the land of volcanoes
Appleton, Victor
Don Sturdy series (5)
Don Sturdy in the port of lost ships
Appleton, Victor
Don Sturdy series (6)
Don Sturdy in the temples of fear
Appleton, Victor
Don Sturdy series (12)
Don Sturdy in the tombs of gold
Appleton, Victor
Don Sturdy series (3)
Don Sturdy on the ocean bottom
Appleton, Victor
Don Sturdy series (11)
Don Sturdy trapped in the flaming wilderness
Appleton, Victor
Don Sturdy series (14)
Don Sturdy with the big snake hunters
Appleton, Victor
Don Sturdy series (2)
Don Sturdy with the harpoon hunters
Appleton, Victor
Don Sturdy series (15)
Don Winslow breaks the spy net
Martinek, Frank V
Don Winslow series (3)
Don Winslow face to face with the Scorpion
Martinek, Frank V
Don Winslow series (2)
Don Winslow in the Navy
Martinek, Frank V
Don Winslow series (1)
Don Winslow saves the secret formula
Martinek, Frank V
Don Winslow series (4)
Dona Prefecta
Perez Galdos, Benito
Contemporary novels of Spain series (4)
Donal Grant
Macdonald, George
Sir Gibbie series (2)
Donald and the
Gorey, Edward
Donald series (1)
Donald Dyke, the down-east detective
Rockwood, Harry
Donald Dyke series (1)
Donald has a difficulty
Gorey, Edward
Donald series (2)
Donald O'Dare
Buncher, Walter
Donald O'Dare series (2)
Donald's buried treasure
Korman, Justine
Donald Duck series (6)
Donald's dream
Korman, Justine
Donald Duck series (5)
Donavan
Brown, Carter
Paul Donavan series (1)

Donavan's day
Brown, Carter
Paul Donavan series (2)
Donavan's delight
Brown, Carter
Paul Donavan series (4)
Done Deal
Standiford, Les
John Deal series (1)
Done in the dark
Carter, Nicholas
Nicholas Carter series (228)
Done to death
Woods, Sara
Sir Nicholas Harding and Antony Maitland series (22)
Donkey boy
Williamson, Henry
Chronicles of ancient sunlight series (2)
Donkey goes visiting
Lynch, Patricia
Turf-cutter's donkey series (2)
Donkey in danger
Richards, James
Donkey series (2)
Donkey in the meadow
Tangye, Derek
Minack chronicles series (4)
Donkey walk
Richards, James
Donkey series (1)
Donkey work
Blishen, Edward
Schoolmaster series (9)
Tovey, Doreen
Cats series (3)
Donna Parker at Cherrydale
Martin, Marcia
Donna Parker series (2)
Donna Parker in Hollywood
Martin, Marcia
Donna Parker series (1)
Donna Parker on her own
Martin, Marcia
Donna Parker series (4)
Donna Parker, special agent
Martin, Marcia
Donna Parker series (3)
Donna Parker takes a giant step
Martin, Marcia
Donna Parker series (7)
Donnellys must die
Miller, Orlo
Donnellys series (1)
Donner people
Willoughby, Lee Davis
Making of America series (24)
Donny Osmond mystery
Resnick, Sylvia
Debbie Preston, teenage reporter series (3)
Donovan
Palmer, Diana
Long tall Texan series (4)
Donovan, a modern Englishman
Lyall, Edna
Donovan series (1)
Donovan case
Monmouth, Jack
Tom Langley series (1)
Donovan's brain
Siodmak, Curt
Doctor Patrick Cory series (1)
Don't argue with death
Gribble, Leonard Reginald
Superintendent Anthony Slade series (28)
Don't be afraid, Amanda
Moore, Lilian
Cucumbers trilogy (2)
Don't be afraid of the dark
Henneker, Philip
Susan Campbell and Paul Ross series (2)
Don't be afraid of the darkness
Sanford, Doris
Children of courage series (1)
Don't be silly, Mister Twiddle
Blyton, Enid
Mister Twiddle series (2)
Don't bet on living, Alice!
Carr, Kirby
Hitman series (6)
Don't bite off more than you can chew
Conway, Troy
Coxeman series (1)
Don't bite the sun
Lee, Tanith
Don't bite the sun series (1)
Don't bleed on me
Copper, Basil
Mike Faraday series (6)
Don't bother to knock
Chambers, Peter
Mark Preston series (12)
Don't call me Katie Rose
Weber, Lenora Mattingly
Stacy and Katie Rose Belford series (1)
Don't call me madame
Kane, Henry
Peter Chambers series (24)
Don't call tonight
Gault, William Campbell
Joe Puma series (2)
Don't catch me
Powell, Richard
Arab and Andy Blake series (1)
Don't come crying to me
Ard, William
Timothy Dane series (5)
Don't count the corpses
Monig, Christopher
Brian Brett series (1)
Don't count the odds
Grover, Marshall
Larry and Stretch series (48)
Don't cry for long
Dewey, Thomas Blanchard
Private Eye Mac series (11)
Don't cry, little girl
Hastings, Beverly
Don't series (3)
Lambert, Janet
Tippy Parrish series (4)
Don't cry now
Janson, Hank
Hank Janson series (44)
Don't dare me, Sugar
Janson, Hank
Hank Janson series (21)
Don't die on me
Spade, Danny
Danny Spade series (10)
Don't do it!
Hope, Jane
Teaching series (1)
Don't do that!
Henderson, Kathy
Don't series (2)
Don't drop dead tomorrow
Pentecost, Hugh
Julian Quist series (1)
Don't ever love me
Cohen, Octavus Roy
Max Gold series (3)
Don't expect any mercy!
Treece, Henry
Gordon Stewart series (2)
Don't fall off the mountain
MacLaine, Shirley
You can get there series (5)
Don't forget to write
Selway, Martina
Dear Grandad series (1)
Don't get caught
Chaber, M E
Milo March series (1)
Don't get close
Cooper, M E
Couples series (34)
Don't get me wrong
Cheyney, Peter
Lemmy Caution series (5)
Don't give up, Josephine
Wilhelm, Hans
Merritales series (2)
Don't go away dead
Kane, Henry
Peter Chambers series (27)
Don't go home with John
Pascal, Francine
Sweet Valley High series (90)
Don't go near the magic shop
Denton, Derek
Harry Sellers series (1)
Don't go out after dark
Berrow, Norman
Inspector Lancelot Carolus Smith series (4)
Don't hang me too high
O'Sullivan, James Brendan
Steve Silk series (7)
Don't interrupt!
Henderson, Kathy
Don't series (1)
Don't just stand there, do someone
Von Elsner, Don
David Danning series (3)
Don't knock the corners off
Glyn, Caroline
Winston series (1)
Don't laugh at fools
Minton, Mary
Yesterday's road series (4)
Don't leave me this way
Smith, Joan Mary
Loretta Lawson series (3)
Don't let him kill
Ashe, Gordon
Patrick Dawlish series (36)
Don't lie to me
Coe, Tucker
Mitchell Tobin series (5)
Don't lie to the police
Cobb, Belton
Inspector Cheviot Burmann series (24)
Don't look at me
Sanford, Doris
Hurts of childhood series (1)
Don't look back
Hastings, Beverly
Don't series (4)
Don't look behind you
Erskine, Margaret
Inspector Septimus Finch series (6)
Rogers, Samuel
Professor Paul Hatfield series (1)
Don't look twice
Keene, Carolyn
Nancy Drew files series (55)
Don't make me go back, mommy
Sanford, Doris
Hurts of childhood series (7)
Don't mess with murder
Allyson, Alan
Martin Ross series (1)
Don't monkey with murder
Ferrars, Elizabeth
Toby Dyke series (4)
Don't mourn me, toots
Janson, Hank
Hank Janson series (28)
Don't neglect the body
O'Hara, Kevin
Chico Brett series (15)
Don't open the door
Gilbert, Anthony
Arthur Crook series (15)
Don't panic
Gaiman, Neil
Arthur Dent series (5)
Don't play with the rough boys
Troy, Simon
Inspector Smith series (7)
Don't point that thing at me
Bonfiglioli, Kyril
Charlie Mortdecai series (1)
Don't push your luck
Muller, Paul
Paul Muller series (10)
Don't quote me
Green, Jonathon
Famous last words series (2)
Don't quote me, but
Lambert, Derek
Quote series (1)
Don't say good-bye
Goudge, Eileen
Seniors series (12)
Don't scare easy
Janson, Hank
Hank Janson series (25)
Don't send a dude
Brady, Adam
Buck Halliday series (2)
Don't shoot, darling
Holt, Henry
Inspector Silver series (16)
Mike Logan series (3)
Don't slip, Delaney
Singer, Bant
Denis Delaney series (3)
Don't stop for Hooky Hefferman
Meynell, Laurence Walter
Hooky Hefferman series (9)
Don't take it to heart
Seaton, Stuart
Inspector Martin Laidman series (1)
Don't talk to strangers
Hastings, Beverly
Don't series (1)
Don't tell Alfred
Mitford, Nancy
Love trilogy (3)
Don't tell the police
O'Hara, Kevin
Chico Brett series (14)
Don't tell the press
Jobson, Hamilton
Inspector Anders series (14)
Don't try anything funny
Fox, James M
John and Suzy Marshall series (1)
Don't walk home alone
Hastings, Beverly
Don't series (2)
Don't wear your wedding ring
O'Donnell, Lillian
Detective Norah Mulcahaney series (2)
Doodle Bugg
Cosgrove, Stephen Edward
Bugg series (18)
Doodled asterisk
Walling, Robert Alfred John
Philip Tolefree series (20)
Doodle's homework
Ryan, John
Doodle series (2)
Doodles, the sunshine boy
Dowd, Emma C
Polly series (3)
Dooki and the little white dog
Hughes, Jean
Dooki series (2)
Dooley Mackenzie is totally weird
Harrell, Janice
Andie and the boys series (2)
Doom city
Grant, Charles Lewis
Chronicles of Greystone Bay series (2)
Doom commander
Sievert, John
C.A.D.S. series (7)
Doom dealer
Fox, David
Shadowers Inc. series (3)
Doom dollies
Knight, Mallory T
Man from T.O.M.C.A.T. series (10)
Doom fisherman
York, Andrew
Jonathan Anders series (1)
Doom in the midnight sun
Boyd, Eunice Mays
F Millard Smyth series (2)
Doom of Stark House
Lloyd, Hugh
Hal Keen series (8)
Doom of the Darksword
Weis, Margaret
Darksword trilogy (2)
Doom of the Green Planet
Petaja, Emil
Green Planet series (2)
Doom of the Reds
Carter, Nicholas
Nicholas Carter series (338)
Doom on the hill
Grant, Maxwell
Shadow series (66)
Doom River
Davis, Gordon
Sergeant series (5)
Doom service
Marlowe, Dan James
Johnny Killain series (3)
Doom stalker
Glick, Ruth
Micro adventure series (7)
Doom star
Meyers, Richard S
Doomstar series (1)
Doom star, number two
Meyers, Richard S
Doomstar series (2)
Doom town
Gilman, George G
Edge series (56)
Doom trail
Grover, Marshall
Larry and Stretch series (143)
Scott, Bradford
Walt Slade series (42)
Smith, Arthur Douglas Howden
Doom trail series (1)
Doomdate
Tiger, John
I spy series (5)
Doomed demons
Adams, Eustace
Air combat series (5)
Adams, Eustace Lane
Andy Lane series (13)
Doomed five
Wells, Carolyn
Fleming Stone series (28)
Doomed men
Jardine, Warwick
Sexton Blake series (711)
Doomed of Mesa Rico
Grover, Marshall
Larry and Stretch series (207)
Doomed planet
Hubbard, Lafayette Ronald
Mission earth series (10)
Doomed to die
Simpson, Dorothy
Inspector Luke Thanet series (10)
Doomed to failure
Carter, Nicholas
Nicholas Carter series (462)
Doomfarers of Coramonde
Daley, Brian
Coramonde series (1)
Doomsayer
Ahern, Jerry
Survivalist series (4)
Doomsday
McKinney, Jack
Robotech series (6)
Doomsday affair
Whittington, Harry
Man from U.N.C.L.E. series (2)
Doomsday bag
Avallone, Michael
Ed Noon series (20)
Doomsday brain
Tabori, Paul
Hunters series (1)
Doomsday bullet
Hogan, Ray
Doomsday Marshal series (4)
Doomsday canyon
Hogan, Ray
Doomsday Marshal series (5)
Doomsday conspiracy
Hayes, Ralph Eugene
Agent for Cominsec series (2)
Doomsday contract
Williamson, Tony
Lee Corey series (2)
Doomsday disciples
Pendleton, Don
Mack Bolan series (49)
Doomsday England
Cooney, Michael
Queen's investigator series (1)
Doomsday formula
Carter, Nick
Nick Carter series (50)
Doomsday gun
Grover, Marshall
Larry and Stretch series (383)
Doomsday list
Orvis, Kenneth
Adam Breck series (2)
Doomsday Marshal
Hogan, Ray
Doomsday Marshal series (1)
Doomsday Marshal and the Comancheros
Hogan, Ray
Doomsday Marshal series (7)
Doomsday Marshal and the hanging judge
Hogan, Ray
Doomsday Marshal series (6)
Doomsday Marshal and the mountain man
Hogan, Ray
Doomsday Marshal series (8)
Doomsday on Ajiat
Jones, Neil Ronald
Professor Jameson series (5)
Doomsday plus twelve
Forman, James Douglas
Doomsday series (2)
Doomsday posse
Hogan, Ray
Doomsday Marshal series (2)
Doomsday prophecy
Wenk, Richard
Batman series (3)
Doomsday spore
Carter, Nick
Nick Carter series (123)
Doomsday Squad
Gober, Don
James Rhodes series (2)
Doomsday syndrome
Wilson, Gar
Phoenix Force series (24)
Doomsday trail
Hogan, Ray
Doomsday Marshal series (3)
Doomsday vendetta
Winston, Peter
Adjusters series (4)
Doomsday warrior
Stacy, Ryder
Doomsday warrior series (1)
Doomsday warriors
Sharpe, Jon
Trailsman series (112)

Doomsday world
Carter, Carmen
Star trek, the next generation series (12)
David, Peter
Star trek, the next generation series (12)
Greenberger, Robert
Star trek, the next generation series (12)
Doomstalker
Cook, Glen
Darkwar trilogy (1)
Doomstar
Meyers, Richard S
Doomstar series (1)
Doomsters
Macdonald, Ross
Lew Archer series (8)
Doomwalk
Morris, Dave
Blood sword series (4)
Doomway
Bond, Evelyn
Ira Yedder series (1)
Doone Walk
Clark, Douglas
Inspector George Masters series (17)
Door
Rossmann, John F
Mind Masters series (3)
Door ajar
De Polnay, Peter
Death and to-morrow series (4)
Door between
Garden, Nancy
Fours Crossing trilogy (3)
Queen, Ellery
Ellery Queen series (12)
Door closed softly
Campbell, Alice
Alison Young series (1)
Colin Ladbroke series (2)
Door in the tree
Corlett, William
Magician's house trilogy (2)
Door into fire
Duane, Diane
Epic tales of the five series (1)
Door into shadow
Duane, Diane
Epic tales of the five series (2)
Door into sunset
Duane, Diane
Epic tales of the five series (3)
Door is always open
Baker, Denys Val
Cornish series (2)
Door nails never die
Wynne, Anthony
Doctor Eustace Hailey series (24)
Door of death
Esteven, John
Inspector Rae Norse series (1)
Door of doubt
Carter, Nicholas
Nicholas Carter series (523)
Door of life
Bagnold, Enid
Girl's journey series (2)
Door to death
Stout, Rex
Nero Wolfe and Archie Goodwin series (16)
Door to doom, and other detections
Carr, John Dickson
Doctor Gideon Fell series (23)
Henri Bencolin series (6)
Sherlock Holmes series (10)
Door to Door
Blei, Norbert
Door County trilogy (2)
Door to eternity
Glaskin, Gerald Marcus
Christos experience trilogy (3)
Door way
Blei, Norbert
Door County trilogy (1)
Doorbell rang
Stout, Rex
Nero Wolfe and Archie Goodwin series (41)
Doorgunner
Williams, Michael
Soldier of fortune series (1)
Doors of sleep
Warriner, Thurman
Mister Scotter series (4)
Doors of the universe
Engdahl, Sylvia Louise
Noren series (3)
Doors open
Gilbert, Michael Francis
Inspector Hazelrigg series (3)
Doors to death
Crosby, Lee
Eric Hazard series (2)
Doors to doom
McCay, Bill
Nintendo adventure series (6)
Doorstep murders
Wells, Carolyn
Kenneth Carlisle series (2)
Doorway to danger
Maddock, Stephen
Timothy Terrel series (11)
Doorway to death
Creasey, John
Inspector Roger West series (22)
Desmond, Hugh
Alan Fraser series (16)
Marlowe, Dan James
Johnny Killain series (1)
Doozer disaster
Muntean, Michaela
Fraggle Rock series (9)
Dop Doctor
Dehan, Richard
Dop Doctor series (1)
Dope
Rohmer, Sax
Red Kerry series (1)
Dope dealers
Cross, Laurence
Tommy Lumb and Peter Marsham series (1)
Dope devils
Elliott, William James
Royston Frere series (1)
Dope doll
Harragan, Steve
Steve Harragan series (2)
Doping affair
Pullein-Thompson, Christine
Seashore School of Equitation series (3)
Doppelganger
Van Greenaway, Peter
Inspector Cherry and Sergeant Duff series (2)
Doppelganger gambit
Killough, Lee
Brill and Maxwell trilogy (1)
Doppelgangers
Heard, Henry Fitzgerald
Mister Mycroft series (3)
Dora at Follyfoot
Dickens, Monica
Follyfoot Farm series (2)
Dora Darling
Austin, Jane Goodwin
Dora Darling series (1)
Dora Myrl, the lady detective
Bodkin, Matthias McDonnell
Dora Myrl series (1)
Dora's motto
Mathews, Joanna Hooe
Little sunbeams series (2)
Dorcas Club
Optic, Oliver
Yacht Club series (5)
Dorcas Dene, detective
Sims, George Robert
Dorcas Dene series (1)
Dorcas Dene, detective, second series
Sims, George Robert
Dorcas Dene series (2)
Dorchester boy
Viscott, David Steven
Portrait of a psychiatrist series (1)
Doreen
Dennis, Clarence James
Sentimental bloke series (4)
Doreen and the sentimental bloke
Dennis, Clarence James
Sentimental bloke series (1)
Doria Rafe case
Waugh, Hillary
Simon Kaye series (2)
Doris Archer's Ambridge diary
Gallagher, Jock
Archers of Ambridge series (7)
Doris Fein, superspy
Bethancourt, Tomas Ernesto
Doris Fein series (2)
Doris Force at Barry Manor
Duncan, Julia K
Doris Force series (4)
Doris Force at Cloudy Cove
Duncan, Julia K
Doris Force series (2)
Doris Force at Locked Gates
Duncan, Julia K
Doris Force series (1)
Doris Force at Raven Rock
Duncan, Julia K
Doris Force series (3)
Dormitory days
Pier, Arthur Stanwood
Saint Timothy's School series (6)
Dormouse has nine lives
King, Frank
Dormouse series (3)
Dormouse, peacemaker
King, Frank
Dormouse series (4)
Dormouse, undertaker
King, Frank
Dormouse series (2)
Dorothy
Raymond, Evelyn Hunt
Dorothy Chester series (5)
Dorothy and her friends
Kirk, Ellen Olney
Dorothy Deane series (2)
Dorothy and the lizard of Oz
Gardner, Richard A
Oz series (51)
Dorothy and the magic belt
Saunders, Susan
Oz series (48)
Dorothy and the wizard of Oz
Baum, Lyman Frank
Oz series (4)
Dorothy at Oak Knowe
Raymond, Evelyn Hunt
Dorothy Chester series (9)
Dorothy Brooke across the sea
Sparhawk, Frances Campbell
Dorothy Brooke series (5)
Dorothy Brooke at Ridgemore
Sparhawk, Frances Campbell
Dorothy Brooke series (4)
Dorothy Brooke's experiments
Sparhawk, Frances Campbell
Dorothy Brooke series (3)
Dorothy Brooke's schooldays
Sparhawk, Frances Campbell
Dorothy Brooke series (1)
Dorothy Brooke's vacation
Sparhawk, Frances Campbell
Dorothy Brooke series (2)
Dorothy Chester at Skyrie
Raymond, Evelyn Hunt
Dorothy Chester series (1)
Dorothy Dainty
Brooks, Amy
Dorothy Dainty series (1)
Dorothy Dainty at Crestville
Brooks, Amy
Dorothy Dainty series (14)
Dorothy Dainty at Foam Ridge
Brooks, Amy
Dorothy Dainty series (17)
Dorothy Dainty at Gem Island
Brooks, Amy
Dorothy Dainty series (19)
Dorothy Dainty at Glenmore
Brooks, Amy
Dorothy Dainty series (16)
Dorothy Dainty at home
Brooks, Amy
Dorothy Dainty series (6)
Dorothy Dainty at school
Brooks, Amy
Dorothy Dainty series (3)
Dorothy Dainty at the mountains
Brooks, Amy
Dorothy Dainty series (10)
Dorothy Dainty at the shore
Brooks, Amy
Dorothy Dainty series (4)
Dorothy Dainty at the stone house
Brooks, Amy
Dorothy Dainty series (18)
Dorothy Dainty in the city
Brooks, Amy
Dorothy Dainty series (5)
Dorothy Dainty in the country
Brooks, Amy
Dorothy Dainty series (8)
Dorothy Dainty's castle
Brooks, Amy
Dorothy Dainty series (22)
Dorothy Dainty's gay times
Brooks, Amy
Dorothy Dainty series (7)
Dorothy Dainty's holidays
Brooks, Amy
Dorothy Dainty series (11)
Dorothy Dainty's new friends
Brooks, Amy
Dorothy Dainty series (15)
Dorothy Dainty's red letter day
Brooks, Amy
Dorothy Dainty series (20)
Dorothy Dainty's treasure chest
Brooks, Amy
Dorothy Dainty series (21)
Dorothy Dainty's vacation
Brooks, Amy
Dorothy Dainty series (12)
Dorothy Dainty's visit
Brooks, Amy
Dorothy Dainty series (13)
Dorothy Dainty's winter
Brooks, Amy
Dorothy Dainty series (9)
Dorothy Dale, a girl of today
Penrose, Margaret
Dorothy Dale series (1)
Dorothy Dale and her chums
Penrose, Margaret
Dorothy Dale series (4)
Dorothy Dale at Glenwood School
Penrose, Margaret
Dorothy Dale series (2)
Dorothy Dale in the city
Penrose, Margaret
Dorothy Dale series (8)
Dorothy Dale in the West
Penrose, Margaret
Dorothy Dale series (10)
Dorothy Dale to the rescue
Penrose, Margaret
Dorothy Dale series (13)
Dorothy Dale's camping days
Penrose, Margaret
Dorothy Dale series (6)
Dorothy Dale's engagement
Penrose, Margaret
Dorothy Dale series (12)
Dorothy Dale's great secret
Penrose, Margaret
Dorothy Dale series (3)
Dorothy Dale's promise
Penrose, Margaret
Dorothy Dale series (9)
Dorothy Dale's queer holidays
Penrose, Margaret
Dorothy Dale series (5)
Dorothy Dale's school rivals
Penrose, Margaret
Dorothy Dale series (7)
Dorothy Dale's strange discovery
Penrose, Margaret
Dorothy Dale series (11)
Dorothy Deane
Kirk, Ellen Olney
Dorothy Deane series (1)
Dorothy Dixon and the double cousin
Wayne, Dorothy
Dorothy Dixon series (1)
Dorothy Dixon and the mystery plane
Wayne, Dorothy
Dorothy Dixon series (2)
Dorothy Dixon solves the Conway case
Wayne, Dorothy
Dorothy Dixon series (3)
Dorothy Dixon wins her wings
Wayne, Dorothy
Dorothy Dixon series (4)
Dorothy Dot
Timlow, Elizabeth Weston
Dorothy Dot series (1)
Dorothy Draycott's todays
Townsend, Virginia Frances
Dorothy Draycott series (1)
Dorothy Draycott's tomorrow
Townsend, Virginia Frances
Dorothy Draycott series (2)
Dorothy in California
Raymond, Evelyn Hunt
Dorothy Chester series (6)
Dorothy of Oz
Baum, Roger S
Oz series (49)
Dorothy of Sunshine Ranch
Dickson, Helen
Sunshine Ranch series (2)
Dorothy on a house boat
Raymond, Evelyn Hunt
Dorothy Chester series (7)
Dorothy on a ranch
Raymond, Evelyn Hunt
Dorothy Chester series (8)
Dorothy South
Eggleston, George Cary
Virginia trilogy (1)
Dorothy, the terrified
Kimbrough, Katheryn
Phenwick women series (19)
Dorothy's house party
Raymond, Evelyn Hunt
Dorothy Chester series (2)
Dorothy's playmates
Brooks, Amy
Dorothy Dainty series (2)
Dorothy's schooling
Raymond, Evelyn Hunt
Dorothy Chester series (3)
Dorothy's tour
Raymond, Evelyn Hunt
Dorothy Chester series (10)
Dorothy's travels
Raymond, Evelyn Hunt
Dorothy Chester series (4)
Dorothy's triumph
Raymond, Evelyn Hunt
Dorothy Chester series (11)
Dorothy's wedding
Sidgwick, Ethel
Sheriff family trilogy (3)
Dorrace domain
Wells, Carolyn
Dorrance series (1)
Dorrance doings
Wells, Carolyn
Dorrance series (2)
Dorrie and the amazing magic elixir
Coombs, Patricia
Dorrie series (11)
Dorrie and the birthday eggs
Coombs, Patricia
Dorrie series (8)
Dorrie and the blue witch
Coombs, Patricia
Dorrie series (2)
Dorrie and the dreamyard monsters
Coombs, Patricia
Dorrie series (14)
Dorrie and the fortune teller
Coombs, Patricia
Dorrie series (10)
Dorrie and the goblin
Coombs, Patricia
Dorrie series (9)
Dorrie and the Hallowe'en plot
Coombs, Patricia
Dorrie series (13)
Dorrie and the haunted house
Coombs, Patricia
Dorrie series (7)
Dorrie and the museum case
Coombs, Patricia
Dorrie series (18)
Dorrie and the Screebit ghost
Coombs, Patricia
Dorrie series (15)
Dorrie and the seather box
Coombs, Patricia
Dorrie series (4)
Dorrie and the witch doctor
Coombs, Patricia
Dorrie series (5)
Dorrie and the witch's camp
Coombs, Patricia
Dorrie series (17)
Dorrie and the witch's imp
Coombs, Patricia
Dorrie series (12)
Dorrie and the Witchville Fair
Coombs, Patricia
Dorrie series (16)
Dorrie and the wizard's spell
Coombs, Patricia
Dorrie series (6)
Dorrie's magic
Coombs, Patricia
Dorrie series (1)
Dorrie's play
Coombs, Patricia
Dorrie series (3)
Dorsai
Dickson, Gordon Rupert
Dorsai series (4)
Dorsai companion
Dickson, Gordon Rupert
Dorsai series (11)
Dorsai's command
Denning, Troy
Combat Command series (8)
Dorsai series (11)
Glaberson, Cory
Combat Command series (8)
Dorsey, the young inventor
Ellis, Edward Sylvester
True grit trilogy (2)
Dorymates
Munroe, Kirk
Mates series (1)
Dosadi experiment
Herbert, Frank
Jorj X McKie series (2)
Dossier closed
Eland, Charles
Mark Randall series (1)
Dossier number one hundred and thirteen
Gaboriau, Emile
Dossier series (1)

Dossier of Solar Pons
Copper, Basil
Solar Pons series (13)
Dossier on a mantis
Bennett, William Robert
Adam Kane series (2)
Dot and Dash at Happy Hollow
West, Dorothy
Dot and Dash series (2)
Dot and Dash at the Maple Sugar Camp
West, Dorothy
Dot and Dash series (1)
Dot and Dash at the seashore
West, Dorothy
Dot and Dash series (5)
Dot and Dash in the north woods
West, Dorothy
Dot and Dash series (3)
Dot and Dash in the Pumpkin Patch
West, Dorothy
Dot and Dash series (4)
Dot and Will
Kilbourne, Fannie
William Horton series (4)
Dot and Will at Home
Kilbourne, Fannie
William Horton series (5)
Dotted lines
Nickless, Will
Rotherside series (4)
Dotty
Lafferty, Raphael Aloysius
Argos mythos series (6)
Double
Muller, Marcia
Sharon McCone series (6)
Pronzini, Bill
Private Eye series (14)
Double acrostic
Goodchild, George
Inspector McLean series (40)
Double act
Denison, Muriel
Double act series (2)
Double action
Dalton, Kit
Buckskin series (27)
Gilman, George G
Edge meets Steele series (3)
Double affair
Thirkell, Angela
Barsetshire series (26)
Double agent
Bingham, John
Ducane series (1)
Teilhet, Hildegarde Tolman
Sam Hook series (2)
Double alibi
Rinehart, Mary Roberts
Nurse Hilda Adams series (1)
Double-barrel
Freeling, Nicolas
Inspector Piet Van der Valk series (4)
Double blackmail
Cole, George Douglas Howard
Superintendent Henry Wilson series (20)
Double blind
Stamey, Sara
Wild card trilogy (3)
Double bluff
Mitchell, Scott
Brock Devlin series (6)
Shannon, Dell
Lieutenant Luis Mendoza series (6)
Double cross
Pike, Charles R
Jubal Cade series (2)
Urquhart, Paul
Sexton Blake series (780)
Whiting, Charles
Spymaster series (2)
Double-Cross Canyon
Field, Peter
Powder Valley series (66)
Double cross purposes
Knox, Ronald Arbuthnott
Miles Bredon series (5)
Double Cross Ranch
Floren, Lee
Judge Lemanuel Bates and Tobacco Jones series (3)
Double-crossed
Pascal, Francine
Sweet Valley High series (109)
Double-crosser
Cassells, John
Superintendent Flagg series (29)
Double-crossers of Ghost Tree
Tuttle, Wilbur Coleman
Hashknife Hartley and Sleepy Stevens series (26)
Double crossfire
Pendleton, Don
Mack Bolan series (40)
Double crossing
Keene, Carolyn
Nancy Drew and Hardy boys supermystery series (1)
Double dagger
Ridley, Nat
Nat Ridley series (13)
Double danger
Birch, Claire
Lucy Hill series (3)
Double date
Du Jardin, Rosamond
Pam and Penny series (1)
Stine, Robert Lawrence
Fear Street series (23)
Double daughter
McConnell, Vicki P
Nyla Wade series (3)
Double dealing
Bogen, M Arthur
Burchardt and Decker series (1)
Double death
Chance, John Newton
Jonathan Blake series (2)
Crofts, Freeman Wills
Inspector Joseph French series (9)
Forsyte, Charles
Inspector Richard Left series (3)
Double death of Frederic Belot
Aveline, Claude
Suite Policiere series (4)
Double defector
Wayland, Patrick
Lloyd Nicolson series (2)
Double detection
Cobb, Belton
Inspector Cheviot Burmann series (10)
Double deuce
Parker, Robert Brown
Spenser series (19)
Double dip disguise
Blair, Cynthia
Susan and Christine Pratt series (6)
Double disappearance of Walter Fozbek
Senn, Steve
Fozbek series (1)
Double disguise
Judd, Frances K
Kay Tracey series (16)
Double dose
Nelson, Peter N
Mollie Fox series (2)
Double, double
Friedman, Michael Jan
Star trek series (45)
Queen, Ellery
Ellery Queen series (27)
Double, double, oil and trouble
Lathen, Emma
John Putnam Thatcher series (17)
Double ducks
Ahlberg, Allan
Help your child to read series (3)
Double eagle
Miles, Keith
Alan Saxton series (2)
Owen, Dean
Latigo series (4)
Double Ex
Rooke, Daphne
Herman Jozef series (1)
Double exposure
Anthony, Piers
Apprentice adept series (3)
Dixon, Franklin W
Hardy boys case files series (22)
McLeave, Hugh
Doctor Gregor Maclean series (3)
Taylor, John Robert
Snapshot series (2)
Double face
Barclay, Virginia
Mid-City Hospital series (5)
Double family
Balzac, Honore de
Scenes of private life series (9)
Double fault
Bickham, Jack Miles
Brad Smith series (5)
Double feature
Du Jardin, Rosamond
Pam and Penny series (2)
Fowles, Anthony
Richard Powell series (2)
Stamp, Terence
Double feature series (3)
Double for Blackshirt
Graeme, Roderic
Blackshirt series (19)
Double for death
Ashe, Gordon
Patrick Dawlish series (30)
Stout, Rex
Tecumseh Fox series (1)
Double for detection
Carnac, Carol
Inspector Julian Rivers series (1)
Double for the Toff
Creasey, John
Toff series (41)
Double four
Oppenheim, Edward Phillips
Peter Ruff series (1)
Double frame
Morton, Anthony
Baron series (29)
Rice, Craig
John Joseph Malone series (10)
Double garden
Maeterlinck, Maurice
Hours of gladness series (1)
Double halfpenny
Edwin, Maribel
Curlew Jon series (3)
Double-handed game
Carter, Nicholas
Nicholas Carter series (97)
Double horrow of Fenley Place
Keene, Carolyn
Nancy Drew series (79)
Double identities
Rhode, John
Doctor Lancelot Priestley series (50)
Double identity
Carter, Nicholas
Nicholas Carter series (464)
Carter, Nick
Nick Carter series (22)
Willis, Maud
Bionic woman series (1)
Double image, and other stories
Vickers, Roy
Inspector Peter Curwen and Hugh Stanton series (5)
Double in trouble
Marlowe, Stephen
Chester Drum series (9)
Prather, Richard Scott
Shell Scott series (19)
Double jeopardy
Forbes, Colin
Tweed, Grey and Newman series (1)
Pascal, Francine
Sweet Valley High super thriller series (1)
Underwood, Michael
Rosa Epton series (4)
Wood, Clement
Skelton Keyne series (2)
Double junk mystery
Keene, Carolyn
Nancy Drew series (50)
Double kill
Da Cruz, Daniel
Jock Sergeant series (1)
Double lives
Plomer, William
Double lives series (1)
Double love
Pascal, Francine
Sweet Valley High series (1)
Double M man
Leader, Charles
Mike McCall series (1)
Double man
Reilly, Helen
Inspector Christopher McKee series (22)
Double menace
Newman, Bernard
Papa Pontivy series (11)
Double mystery
Carter, Nicholas
Nicholas Carter series (411)
Double on Death Row
Gardner, Jerome
Hanging Judge series (8)
Double or nothing
Martin, Charles Morris
Roaming Reynolds and Texas Joe series (3)
Masters, Zeke
Faro Blake series (29)
Double or quits
Fair, A A
Bertha Cool and Donald Lam series (5)
Double page spread
James, Judi
Fashion features series (2)
Double play
Barbour, Ralph Henry
Yardley Hall series (2)
Lantz, Francess Lin
Varsity coach series (2)
Double plot
Carter, Nicholas
Nicholas Carter series (233)
Double red
Jordan, David
Tom Kane and Condon series (3)
Double shadow murders
McRoyd, Allan
Inspector Franklin Brady series (2)
Double shuffle
Chase, James Hadley
Steve Harmas series (1)
Grover, Marshall
Larry and Stretch series (194)
Double Shuffle Club
Carter, Nicholas
Nicholas Carter series (26)
Double sin, and other stories
Christie, Agatha
Hercule Poirot series (38)
Miss Jane Marple series (14)
Double smile
Leblanc, Maurice
Arsene Lupin series (15)
Double solution
Gregg, Cecil Freeman
Inspector Cuthbert Higgins series (6)
Double take
Bruce, Jean
Secret Agent O.S.S.117 series (11)
Huggins, Roy
Stuart Bailey series (1)
Janson, Hank
Hank Janson series (171)
Oleksiw, Susan
Joe Silva series (2)
Ormerod, Roger
David Mallin and George Coe series (16)
Quin-Harkin, Janet
Sugar and spice series (9)
Robertson, Colin
Superintendent Bradley series (8)
Double the bluff
Fairlie, Gerard
Johnny Macall series (4)
Double the Bounty
Randall, Joshua
Bounty Hunter series (1)
Double Thirteen
Marlowe, Piers
Double Thirteen Club series (1)
Double thirteen
Wynne, Anthony
Doctor Eustace Hailey series (2)
Double-thirteen mystery
Wynne, Anthony
Doctor Eustace Hailey series (2)
Double tragedy
Crofts, Freeman Wills
Inspector Joseph French series (24)
Double trouble
Bosco, Clyde
Nintendo adventure series (1)
Graeme, Bruce
Detective Sergeant Robert Mather series (6)
Greene, Yvonne
Kelly Blake series (5)
Grover, Marshall
Larry and Stretch series (31)
Lacy, Ed
Lieutenant Dave Wintino series (2)
Lewis, Elliott
Fred Bennett series (4)
Mallory, Roosevelt
Radcliff series (3)
Stine, Megan
Find your fate: Jem series (4)
Stranger, Joyce
Timothy Yorke series (2)
Tovey, Doreen
Cats series (7)
Double trouble in Skagway
Mackenzie, Pierce
T G Horne series (5)
Double trouble squared
Lasky, Kathryn
Starbuck family series (1)
Double turn
Carnac, Carol
Inspector Julian Rivers series (14)
Inspector Strang series (1)
Double wedding
Du Jardin, Rosamond
Pam and Penny series (4)
Double wizard
Storey, Margaret
Timothy, Ellen and Melinda series (5)
Double Z
Grant, Maxwell
Shadow series (11)
Doublecross
Livingston, Armstrong
Jimmy Treynor series (1)
Doubled in diamonds
Canning, Victor
Rex Carver series (2)
Doubleminded men
Craig, Philip R
Martha's Vineyard series (3)
Doubly dead
Cobb, Belton
Inspector Cheviot Burmann series (20)
Doubtful disciple
Haggard, William
Colonel Charles Russell series (12)
Doubtful motives
Gagnon, Maurice
Deirdre O'Hara trilogy (3)
Doubting Thomasina
Dennison, Dorothy
Wantoknow series for girls (2)
Dougal round the world
Thompson, Eric
Dougal series (3)
Dougal strikes again
Thompson, Eric
Dougal series (5)
Dougal's Scottish holiday
Thompson, Eric
Dougal series (2)
Dough for the Dormouse
King, Frank
Dormouse series (5)
Dougie
Moloney, James
Dougy and Gracey series (1)
Douglas convolution
Llewellyn, Edward
Douglas convolution trilogy (1)
Dove
Saber, Robert O
Carl Good series (3)
Tucker, Wilson
Charles Horne series (3)
Dove against death
Wood, Christopher
Taiwan series (2)
Dove on his shoulder
Glemser, Bernard
Robert Crane trilogy (3)
Dovebury murders
Rhode, John
Doctor Lancelot Priestley series (58)
Dover and the claret tappers
Porter, Joyce
Chief Inspector Wilfred Dover series (8)
Dover and the unkindest cut of all
Porter, Joyce
Chief Inspector Wilfred Dover series (4)
Dover beats the band
Porter, Joyce
Chief Inspector Wilfred Dover series (10)
Dover goes to Pott
Porter, Joyce
Chief Inspector Wilfred Dover series (5)
Dover one
Porter, Joyce
Chief Inspector Wilfred Dover series (1)
Dover strikes again
Porter, Joyce
Chief Inspector Wilfred Dover series (6)
Dover three
Porter, Joyce
Chief Inspector Wilfred Dover series (3)
Dover train mystery
Gilbert, Anthony
Dupuy series (2)
Dover two
Porter, Joyce
Chief Inspector Wilfred Dover series (2)
Dove's nest
Hardwick, Mollie
Atkinson family series (3)

Dower house mystery
Beckett, Mark
Major Dick Burton series (3)
Down a Cornish lane
Baker, Denys Val
Cornish series (20)
Down all the days
Brown, Christy
Cerebral palsy series (2)
Down-along Apple Market Street
Hill, Mabel Betsy
Judy Jo series (1)
Down among the ad men
Ballinger, W A
Sexton Blake series (1605)
Down among the dead men
Hartland, Michael
David Nairn series (1)
Moyes, Patricia
Henry and Emmy Tibbett series (2)
Down among the jocks
Dennis, Ralph
Jim Hardman series (5)
Down and dirty
Mackie, John
Rat Bastards series (5)
Martin, George Raymond Richard
Wild cards series (5)
Masters, Zeke
Faro Blake series (27)
Murphy, Warren Burton
Edward Razoni and William Jackson series (4)
Down-and-out
Ashley, Bernard
Clipper Street series (3)
Down and out
Bayfield, William John
Sexton Blake series (559)
Carter, Nicholas
Nicholas Carter series (172)
Down-beat kill
Chambers, Peter
Mark Preston series (5)
Down by the bay
Raffi
Raffi songs to read series (1)
Down by the sea
Greenwood, Walter
Trelooe series (3)
Down east
Graydon, William Murray
Sexton Blake series (290)
Jackson, Lewis
Sexton Blake series (1159)
Down east murders
Borthwick, J S
Sarah Deane and Alex Mackenzie series (2)
Down for the count
Kaminsky, Stuart Melvin
Toby Peters series (10)
Down from the lonely mountain
Curry, Jane Louise
California Indian series (1)
Down home heifer heist
Sandstrom, Eve K
Down home series (3)
Down in Sugar Creek chimney
Hutchens, Paul
Sugar Creek Gang series (34)
Down in the zero
Vachss, Andrew
Burke series (7)
Down Lambeth way
Staples, Mary Jane
South London series (1)
Down nature's byways
Ellison, Norman
Nomad series (6)
Down north on the Labrador
Grenfell, Wilfrid Thomason
Labrador series (1)
Down our street
Goodwin, Ben
Rosencrantz family series (1)
Down river
Church, Richard
Tomahawk Club series (2)
Down South
Optic, Oliver
Great Western series (5)
Down th hatch
Winton, John
Navy series (3)
Down the Amazon
Verne, Jules
Giant raft series (1)
Down the back
Hillier, Fred
Outhouse series (1)
Down the Bath rocks
O'Connor, Patrick
Glasgow series (1)
Down the bright stream
B B
Oak Tree House series (2)
Down the garden path
Cannell, Dorothy
Ellie Simons Haskell series (2)
Nichols, Beverley
Allways trilogy (1)
Down the lane
Ainsworth, Ruth
Look about you series (2)
Down the long stairs
Cawley, Winifred
Ralph Cole series (1)
Down the long wind
Bradshaw, Gillian
Arthur and Gawain trilogy (3)
Down the Mississippi
Ellis, Edward Sylvester
Great river series (1)
Down the Rhine
Optic, Oliver
Young America, first series (6)
Down the river
Optic, Oliver
Starry flag series (6)
Down the road
Berridge, Celia
Stepping stones 1 2 3 series (1)
Down the sky
Lucas, Edward Verrall
Richard series (2)
Down the stream of stars
Carver, Jeffrey Allan
Changeling star series (2)
Down the throat
Macdonnell, James Edmond
Captain Kenyon series (2)
Down the village street
Douglas, Peter
Norfolk village series (1)
Down the west branch
Farrar, Charles Alden John
Lake and forest series (3)
Down there
Huysmans, Joris Karl
Durtal series (1)
Down to a sunless sea
Carter, Lin
Mars series (4)
Down to death
Phillips, Stella
Inspector Matthew Furnival series (1)
Down to earth
Addis, Faith
Devon farm series (4)
Capon, Paul
Antigeos trilogy (3)
Elder, Michael
Barclay series (3)
Down to the lion
Trewin, John Courtenay
Up and down series (2)
Down to the sea in ships
Bloom, Ursula
Elegant Edwardian series (4)
Down town
Lovelace, Maud Hart
Betsy Ray series (4)
Down under and dirty
Streib, Dan
Michael Hawk series (9)
Down under thunder
Wilson, Gar
Phoenix Force series (25)
Down where the moon is small
Llewellyn, Richard
Huw Morgan series (3)
Down with skool
Willans, Geoffrey
Nigel Molesworth series (1)
Down yonder with Judge Priest
Cobb, Irwin Shrewsbury
Judge Priest series (5)
Downbeat for a dirge
Bird, Brandon
Hampton Hume series (3)
Downbelow Station
Cherryh, Carolyn Janice
Alliance-Union series (3)
Downbelow Station trilogy (1)
Downey of the Mounted
Hendryx, James Beardsley
Corporal Cameron Downey series (1)
Corporal Downey series (6)
Downfall
Zola, Emile
Rougon Macquart series (19)
Downhill all the way
Woolf, Leonard
Sowing and growing series (4)
Downhill, hotdogging and cross-country, if the snow isn't sticky
Paulsen, Gary
Sports on the light side series (7)
Downhill ride of Leeman Popple
Bellairs, George
Detective Inspector Thomas Littlejohn series (56)
Downing Street discovery
Brandon, John Gordon
Sexton Blake series (832)
Downright Dencey
Snedeker, Caroline Dale
Dencey Coffyn series (1)
Downriver
Estleman, Loren D
Amos Walker series (8)
Downriver to hell
Hardin, J D
Raider and Doc series (30)
Downtown and dead
Brody, Marc
Marc Brody series (21)
Downward path
Chapman, Robert
Rex Banner series (7)
Dowry of death
Casberg, Melvin A
Captain Prem Narayan series (3)
Dowtown doll
Janson, Hank
Hank Janson series (16)
Doxie Dent
Ackworth, John
Clogshop trilogy (3)
Dozen deadly dragons of joy
Knight, Mallory T
Man from T.O.M.C.A.T. series (1)
Dozen from Lakerim
Hughes, Rupert
Lakerim Athletic Club series (2)
Dozen good times that Georgiana and Dolly had
Archibald, George, *Mrs*
Lady Gay trilogy (3)
Drachenfels
Yeovil, Jack
Warhammer series (1)
Drackenberg adventure
Alexander, Lloyd
Vesper Holly series (3)
Dracula
Ambrus, Victor Gyozo
Dracula trilogy (1)
Barling, Tom
Dracula series (1)
Cameron, Joan
Dracula series (1)
Skinner, Stephanie
Dracula series (1)
Stoker, Bram
Dracula series (1)
Thorne, Ian
Dracula series (1)
Dracula and the virgins of the undead
Aubin, Etienne
Dracula series (7)
Dracula archives
Rudorff, Raymond
Dracula series (26)
Dracula began
Kimberly, Gail
Dracula series (9)
Dracula book
Glut, Donald Frank
Dracula series (26)
Dracula book of great horror stories
Shepard, Leslie
Dracula series (26)
Dracula book of great vampire stories
Shepard, Leslie
Dracula series (26)
Dracula caper
Hawke, Simon
Timewars series (8)
Dracula centneary book
Haining, Peter
Dracula series (26)
Dracula go home
Platt, Kin
Dracula series (26)
Dracula in love
Shirley, John
Dracula series (26)
Dracula is a pain in the neck
Levy, Elizabeth
Dracula series (26)
Dracula, my love
Tremayne, Peter
Dracula series (19)
Dracula play
Jungman, Ann
Count Dracula series (4)
Dracula, prince of many faces
Florescu, Radu
Dracula series (26)
Dracula, princess of darkness
Burke, John Frederick
Dracula series (1)
Dracula returns
Lory, Robert
Dracula horror series (1)
Dracula scrapbook
Haining, Peter
Dracula series (26)
Dracula tapes
Saberhagen, Fred
Dracula series (8)
Dracula, the novel and the legend
Leatherdale, Clive
Dracula series (26)
Dracula, the vampire and the critics
Carter, Margaret Louise
Dracula series (26)
Dracula unborn
Tremayne, Peter
Dracula series (10)
Dracula unbound
Aldiss, Brian Wilson
Dracula series (26)
Dracula's bedtime storybook
Ambrus, Victor Gyozo
Dracula trilogy (2)
Dracula's brood
Dalby, Richard
Dracula series (26)
Dracula's brother
Lory, Robert
Dracula horror series (3)
Dracula's castle
Brennan, James Herbert
Dracula series (26)
Dracula's children
Chetwynd-Hayes, Ronald
Dracula's children series (1)
Dracula's daughter
Dreadstone, Carl
Dracula series (11)
Dracula's diary
Corby, Michael
Dracula series (26)
Dracula's disciple
Lory, Robert
Dracula horror series (8)
Dracula's dog
Johnson, Kenneth Rayner
Dracula series (1)
Dracula's gold
Lory, Robert
Dracula horror series (4)
Dracula's guest, and other weird stories
Stoker, Bram
Dracula series (2)
Dracula's lost world
Lory, Robert
Dracula horror series (7)
Dracutwig
Knight, Mallory T
Dracula series (26)
Drafted in
Templeton, Faith
Breadwinners series (2)
Drag race
Dean, Anabel
Racing wheels series (2)
Drag the dark
Davis, Frederick Clyde
Schyler Cole and Luke Speare series (4)
Dragnet
Brandon, John Gordon
Inspector Patrick Aloysius McCarthy series (11)
Spade, Danny
Danny Spade series (18)
Dragnet 1968
Vowell, David
Dragnet series (5)
Dragnet '67
Tralins, Sandor Robert
Dragnet series (4)
Dragoman Pass
Williams, Eric Ernest
Roger and Kate Starte series (1)
Dragon
Cussler, Clive
Dirk Pitt series (10)
Frith, Nigel
Pangaia trilogy (2)
Gaskell, Jane
Atlan saga series (1)
Postgate, Oliver
Ivor the engine series (3)
Dragon ABC hunt
Leedy, Loreen
Dragon series (2)
Dragon air
Ruffell, Ann
Gribble the dragon series (4)
Dragon and the George
Dickson, Gordon Rupert
Dragon series (1)
Dragon apparent
Lewis, Norman
Dragon apparent series (1)
Dragon at noonday
Pargeter, Edith
Brothers of Gwynedd tetralogy (2)
Dragon at school
Gissing, Vera
Pippins series (5)
Dragon becomes a pet
Jungman, Ann
Dragon series (2)
Dragon catchers
Lloyd, David
Let's pretend series (2)
Dragon cauldron
Yep, Laurence Michael
Shimmer and Thorn series (3)
Dragon Christmas
Leedy, Loreen
Dragon series (4)
Dragon circle
Krensky, Stephen
Wynd family trilogy (1)
Dragon dance
Christopher, John
Fireball trilogy (3)
Dragon days
Hall, Willis
Henry Hollins series (4)
Dragon defiant
Hall, Lynn
Dragon series (3)
Dragon doctor
Taylor, David Conrad
Zoovet series (6)
Dragon earth
Ruffell, Ann
Gribble the dragon series (3)
Dragon fire
Ruffell, Ann
Gribble the dragon series (1)
Dragon flame
Carter, Nick
Nick Carter series (14)
Dragon fly
Cosgrove, Stephen Edward
Bugg series (39)
Dragon for Christmas
Black, Gavin
Paul Harris series (3)
Dragon for Edward
Bennetts, Pamela
Edward I series (1)
Dragon gets by
Pilkey, Dav
Dragon series (2)
Dragon Green
Thomas, Joyce Bissell
Dragon Green series (1)
Dragon Green series (2)
Dragon Halloween party
Leedy, Loreen
Dragon series (3)
Dragon harvest
Sinclair, Upton
World's end series (6)
Dragon in chains
Lancing, George
Tzu Hsi series (3)
Dragon in class four
Counsel, June
Dragon series (1)
Dragon in danger
Manning, Rosemary
Susan and R.Dragon series (2)
Dragon in harness
Gluck, Sinclair
Jack Clayton series (2)
Dragon in love
Jungman, Ann
Dragon series (4)
Dragon in spring
Barker, Albert
Hawk Macrae series (3)
Dragon in Spring term
Counsel, June
Dragon series (2)
Dragon in Summer
Counsel, June
Dragon series (3)
Dragon in the family
Koller, Jackie French
Dragonling series (2)

Dragon in the harbour
Manning, Rosemary
Susan and R.Dragon series (4)
Dragon in the sword
Moorcock, Michael
Eternal champion trilogy (3)
Dragon in top class!
Counsel, June
Dragon series (4)
Dragon joins the army
Jungman, Ann
Dragon series (3)
Dragon knight
Dickson, Gordon Rupert
Dragon series (2)
Dragon Lensman
Kyle, David Ackerman
Lensman series (9)
Dragon lives forever
Riggs, John Raymond
Garth Ryland series (8)
Dragon lord
Drake, David
Dragon lord series (1)
Morwood, Peter
Book of years series (3)
Dragon Lord of the Savage Empire
Lorrah, Jean
Savage Empire series (2)
Dragon Lords
Shillitoe, Tony
Andrakis trilogy (3)
Dragon magic
Norton, Andre
Magic series (4)
Dragon murder case
Van Dine, S S
Philo Vance series (7)
Dragon of doom
Estes, Rose
Endless quest series (13)
Dragon of Lung Wang
Harvey, Marion
Graydon McKelvie series (4)
Dragon of Mishbil
Clough, Brenda Wang
Averidan series (2)
Dragon of the hill
Gard, Joyce
Mark Danby series (2)
Dragon of the hills
Garis, Lilian C
Melody Lane series (6)
Dragon of the lost sea
Yep, Laurence Michael
Shimmer and Thorn series (1)
Dragon of Yang-Wong
Jungman, Ann
Dragon series (1)
Dragon on a pedestal
Anthony, Piers
Xanth series (7)
Dragon paths
Bloomfield, Frena
Darkworld legends series (1)
Dragon pond
Lloyd, Alan R
Kine trilogy (3)
Dragon prince
Rawn, Melanie
Dragon prince series (1)
Dragon Queen's revenge
Affabee, Eric
Wizards, warlocks and you series (9)
Dragon reborn
Jordan, Robert
Wheel of time series (3)
Dragon revenant
Kerr, Katharine
Deverry series (4)
Dragon riders of Pern
McCaffrey, Anne
Pern and the Red Planet series (6)
Dragon rising
Barker, Wade
Year of the Ninja Master series (1)
Dragon road
Harvester, Simon
Asia in turmoil series (3)
Dorian Silk series (1)
Malcolm Kenton series (2)
Dragon seas
Short, Agnes
Christie family series (3)
Dragon seed
Buck, Pearl Sydenstricker
Ling Tan series (1)
Dragon slay
Carter, Nick
Nick Carter series (259)
Dragon slaying
Rainey, Rich
Alex Dartanian series (6)
Dragon spoor
Crisp, Jack H
Special Operations Executive series (1)
Dragon steel
Yep, Laurence Michael
Shimmer and Thorn series (2)
Dragon stone
Manley, Ruth
Ancient Japan series (2)
Dragon sword
Baudino, Gael
Dragonsword series (1)
Dragon Thanksgiving feast
Leedy, Loreen
Dragon series (5)
Dragon token
Rawn, Melanie
Dragon star series (2)
Dragon wanted
Ruffell, Ann
Gribble the dragon series (4)
Dragon warriors
Morris, Dave
Dragon warriors series (1)
Dragon water
Ruffell, Ann
Gribble the dragon series (2)
Dragon wing
Weis, Margaret
Death Gate series (1)
Dragon winter
Hancock, Niel
Windameir circle series (1)
Dragonard
Gilchrist, Rupert
Dragonard series (1)
Dragonard blood
Gilchrist, Rupert
Dragonard series (3)
Dragonard rising
Gilchrist, Rupert
Dragonard series (4)
Dragonbards
Murphy, Shirley Rousseau
Dragonbards trilogy (3)
Dragonbone chair
Williams, Tad
Memory, sorrow and thorn series (1)
Dragonbound
Miller, Carl
Dragonbound trilogy (1)
Dragondance
Christopher, John
Fireball trilogy (3)
Dragondrums
McCaffrey, Anne
Pern and the Red Planet series (9)
Dragonfall 5 and the empty planet
Earnshaw, Brian
Dragonfall 5 series (3)
Dragonfall 5 and the haunted world
Earnshaw, Brian
Dragonfall 5 series (7)
Dragonfall 5 and the hijackers
Earnshaw, Brian
Dragonfall 5 series (4)
Dragonfall 5 and the master mind
Earnshaw, Brian
Dragonfall 5 series (5)
Dragonfall 5 and the royal beast
Earnshaw, Brian
Dragonfall 5 series (1)
Dragonfall 5 and the space cowboys
Earnshaw, Brian
Dragonfall 5 series (2)
Dragonfall 5 and the super horse
Earnshaw, Brian
Dragonfall 5 series (6)
Dragonfire
Briggs, Ian
Doctor Who series (137)
Carter, Nick
Nick Carter series (234)
Nye, Jody Lynn
Pern and the Red Planet series (12)
World of Pern series (2)
Pronzini, Bill
Private Eye series (9)
Scott, Peter Graham
Dragonfire series (1)
Dragonflight
McCaffrey, Anne
Pern and the Red Planet series (4)
Dragonfly in amber
Gabaldon, Diana
Outlander series (2)
Dragonfly summer
Farmer, Penelope
Stephen series (2)
Dragonfly years
Hunter, Mollie
Bridie McShane series (2)
Dragonharper
Nye, Jody Lynn
Pern and the Red Planet series (12)
World of Pern series (1)
DragonLance adventures
Weis, Margaret
DragonLance series (3)
DragonLance chronicles
Weis, Margaret
DragonLance chronicles series (3)
DragonLance legends
Weis, Margaret
DragonLance legends trilogy (3)
DragonLance tales
Weis, Margaret
DragonLance tales trilogy (3)
Dragonling
Koller, Jackie French
Dragonling series (1)
Dragonlover's guide to Pern
Nye, Jody Lynn
Pern and the Red Planet series (12)
Dragonmaster
Brightfield, Richard
Dragonmaster series (1)
Your amazing adventures series (4)
Dragonquest
McCaffrey, Anne
Pern and the Red Planet series (5)
Dragonrank master
Reichert, Mickey Zucker
Bifrost guardians series (3)
Dragonrouge
Carter, Lin
Terra Magica series (2)
Dragons at the party
Cleary, Jon
Scobie Malone series (4)
Dragon's blood
McDonough, Alex
Scorpio series (4)
Yolen, Jane
Pit dragons trilogy (1)
Dragons can be dangerous
Chambers, Peter
Mark Preston series (32)
Dragon's carbuncle
Boyer, Elizabeth H
Wizard's war series (3)
Dragon's cave
Clason, Clyde B
Theocritus Lucius Westborough series (8)
Dragon's claw
O'Donnell, Peter
Modesty Blaise series (9)
Dragon's daughter
Storey, Margaret
Timothy, Ellen and Melinda series (5)
Dragon's delight
Hall, Lynn
Dragon series (4)
Dragons' den
Brightfield, Richard
Choose your own adventure series (33)
Dragon's egg
Forward, Robert Lull
Dragon's egg series (1)
Dragon's fat cat
Pilkey, Dav
Dragon series (4)
Dragon's gold
Anthony, Piers
Dragon series (1)
Dragon's Halloween
Pilkey, Dav
Dragon series (5)
Dragons in the waters
L'Engle, Madeleine
Poly and Charles O'Keefe series (3)
Dragon's jaw
Helm, Eric
Ground Zero series (16)
Dragon's kill
Wilson, Gar
Phoenix Force series (7)
Dragon's knight
Dennis, Carol Larkey
Dragon's pawn trilogy (2)
Dragon's merry Christmas
Pilkey, Dav
Dragon series (3)
Dragon's milk
Fletcher, Susan
Kaeldra series (2)
Dragons of Blueland
Gannett, Ruth Stiles
Dragon series (3)
Dragons of Englor
Lord, Jeffrey
Richard Blade series (24)
Dragons of Heorot
Barnes, Steven
Heorot series (2)
Niven, Larry
Heorot series (2)
Dragons of Komako
Betancourt, John Gregory
Doctor Bones series (4)
Dragons of spring dawning
Weis, Margaret
DragonLance chronicles series (3)
Dragons of the autumn twilight
Weis, Margaret
DragonLance chronicles series (1)
Dragons of the winter night
Weis, Margaret
DragonLance chronicles series (2)
Dragons past
Gentile, Gary
Dragons series (2)
Dragon's pawn
Dennis, Carol Larkey
Dragon's pawn trilogy (1)
Dragon's queen
Dennis, Carol Larkey
Dragon's pawn trilogy (3)
Dragon's quest
Manning, Rosemary
Susan and R.Dragon series (3)
Dragon's ransom
French, Laura
Endless quest series (16)
Dragon's teeth
Fraser, David
Treason in arms series (3)
Killough, Lee
Brill and Maxwell trilogy (3)
Queen, Ellery
Ellery Queen series (15)
Sinclair, Upton
World's end series (3)
Dragonsbane
Hambly, Barbara
Dragonsbane series (2)
Dragonsdawn
McCaffrey, Anne
Pern and the Red Planet series (1)
Dragonship
Macleod, Robert
Andrew Laird series (2)
Dragonsinger
McCaffrey, Anne
Pern and the Red Planet series (8)
Dragonsong
McCaffrey, Anne
Pern and the Red Planet series (7)
Dragonspell
Kerr, Katharine
Deverry series (4)
Dragonstar destiny
Bischoff, David
Dragonstar trilogy (3)
Dragonsword
Baudino, Gael
Dragonsword series (1)
Dragonsword of Lankhmar
Ward, James Michael
Fafhrd and Gray Mouser series (8)
Dragonwall
Awlinson, Richard
Empires trilogy (2)
Dragooned by Fox
Fox, Brian
Alias Smith and Jones series (5)
Drake and the Spanish Armada
Birt, David
Tudors series (17)
Drake at the door
Tangye, Derek
Minack chronicles series (3)
Drake's world voyage
Birt, David
Tudors series (4)
Drakov memoranda
Winters, Jon
Anton Drakov series (1)
Dram-shop
Zola, Emile
Rougon Macquart series (7)
Draught of the blue
Bain, Francis William
Indian mystic love stories series (5)
Draw, aim and fire
Grover, Marshall
Larry and Stretch series (39)
Draw batons!
Knox, Bill
Inspector Colin Thane and Phil Moss series (13)
Draw the blinds
Truss, Seldon
Inspector Gidleigh series (1)
Draw the curtain close
Dewey, Thomas Blanchard
Private Eye Mac series (1)
Draw to an inside death
Roberts, J R
Gunsmith series (13)
Drawback to murder
Barber, Willetta Ann
Christopher Storm series (6)
Drawbridge Gate
Harnett, Cynthia
Fifteenth century London series (1)
Drawing of the three
King, Stephen
Dark tower trilogy (2)
Drawing the dead
Selden, Neil
Twilight series (16)
Drawn conclusion
Barber, Willetta Ann
Christopher Storm series (3)
Drawn from life
Shepard, Ernest Howard
Drawn from series (2)
Drawn from memory
Shepard, Ernest Howard
Drawn from series (1)
Drawn in colour
Jabavu, Noni
Bantu series (1)
Drayton legacy
Randall, Rona
Drayton series (1)
Draytons and the Davenants
Charles, Elizabeth
Drayton family series (1)
Dread and water
Clark, Douglas
Inspector George Masters series (7)
Dread brass shadows
Cook, Glen
Garrett series (5)
Dread cave
Courage, John
Bill Britain series (5)
Dreadful doings in Ark Street
Beaman, Sydney George Hulme
Toytown series (22)
Dreadful future of Blossom Culp
Peck, Richard
Blossom Culp series (3)
Dreadful hollow
Blake, Nicholas
Nigel Strangeways series (10)
Dreadful lemon sky
Macdonald, John Dann
Travis McGee series (16)
Dreadnaught boys aboard a destroyer
Lawton, Wilbur
Dreadnaught boys series (2)
Dreadnaught boys in home waters
Lawton, Wilbur
Dreadnaught boys series (6)
Dreadnaught boys on a submarine
Lawton, Wilbur
Dreadnaught boys series (3)
Dreadnaught boys on aero service
Lawton, Wilbur
Dreadnaught boys series (4)
Dreadnaught boys on battle practice
Lawton, Wilbur
Dreadnaught boys series (1)
Dreadnaught boys' world cruise
Lawton, Wilbur
Dreadnaught boys series (5)
Dreadnought!
Carey, Diane
Dreadnought series (1)
Star trek series (29)
Dream
Freeman, Lucy
Doctor William Ames series (1)
Lodi, Maria
Charlotte Morel series (2)
Montherlant, Henry de
Alban de Bricoule trilogy (3)
Stahl, Hilda
White Pine chronicles series (3)
Wright, Sydney Fowler
Marguerite Cranleigh series (1)
Zola, Emile
Rougon Macquart series (16)

Dream and the dead
Audemars, Pierre
Monsieur Pinaud series (5)
Dream and wonder
Redekopp, Elsa
Canadian village life series (2)
Dream apart
Egan, Lesley
Vic Varallo series (9)
Dream at dawn
Lindquiest, Marie
Texas promises trilogy (1)
Dream before dying
Alexander, Martin
Alan Kelton series (2)
Dream boat brontosaurus
McCrum, Robert
Brontosaurus series (3)
Dream catcher
Hughes, Monica
Arc One series (2)
Dream chariots
Norvil, Manning
Odan the half-god trilogy (1)
Dream child
Locke, Joseph
Nightmare on Elm Street series (2)
Dream come true
Quin-Harkin, Janet
Sugar and spice series (16)
Dream country
Gaiman, Neil
Sandman series (3)
Dream Dancer
Bolton, Evelyn
Horse book series (6)
Dream dancer
Morris, Janet Ellen
Kerrion Empire series (1)
Dream days
Grahame, Kenneth
Smith family series (2)
Dream doctor
Reeve, Arthur Benjamin
Craig Kennedy series (3)
Dream for Addie
Rock, Gail
Addie series (4)
Dream for Nurse Tessa
Collins, Lynne
Brook's Hospital series (2)
Dream for Susan
Lambert, Janet
Jordons series (4)
Dream games
Hansen, Karl
Hybrid universe series (2)
Dream girl
Lawrence, James D
Angela Harpe series (1)
Dream hunters
Lyon, Elinor
Ian and Sovra series (7)
Dream is deadly
Brown, Carter
Danny Boyd series (5)
Dream island
Lockley, Ronald Mathias
Island farm series (2)
Dream island days
Lockley, Ronald Mathias
Island farm series (3)
Dream master
Locke, Joseph
Nightmare on Elm Street series (2)
Dream merchant
Brown, Carter
Lieutenant Al Wheeler series (49)
Dream merchants
Robbins, Harold
Hollywood trilogy (1)
Dream murder
Broome, Adam
Commissioner Denzil Grigson series (7)
Dream of belonging
Bauman, Janina
Winter in the morning series (2)
Dream of fair women
Williamson, Henry
Flax of dream series (3)
Dream of flying
Moore, Alan
Miracleman series (1)
Dream of kinship
Cowper, Richard
Bird of kinship series (2)
Dream of love
Zola, Emile
Rougon Macquart series (16)
Dream of red mansions
Ts'ao, Hsueh-ch'in
Dream of the red chamber series (5)
Dream of Sadler's Wells
Hill, Lorna
Sadler's Wells series (1)
Dream of the red chamber
Ts'ao, Hsueh-ch'in
Dream of the red chamber series (5)
Dream Park
Niven, Larry
Dream Park series (1)
Dream prevails
Diver, Maud
Sinclair series (4)
Dream river
Garlock, Dorothy
Wabash trilogy (2)
Dream seekers
Longstreet, Stephen
Dream seekers series (1)
Dream sinister
Schley, Sturges Mason
Doctor Quentin Toby series (3)
Dream stuff, you're murder
Kane, Martin
Martin Kane series (5)
Dream team
Albright, Molly
Two of a kind series (2)
Dream to cherish
Hunt, Angela Elwell
Cassie Perkins series (4)
Dreamer at large
Duncan, William Murdoch
Superintendent Donald Reamer series (11)
Dreamer deals with murder
Duncan, William Murdoch
Superintendent Donald Reamer series (9)
Dreamer in discord
Mills, Craig
Caladon series (2)
Dreamer intervenes
Duncan, William Murdoch
Superintendent Donald Reamer series (6)
Dreamer wakes
Ts'ao, Hsueh-ch'in
Dream of the red chamber series (5)
Dreamers
Warren, Joanna
Conrad chronicles series (2)
Dreamers of the ghetto
Zangwill, Israel
Ghetto series (3)
Dreaming city
Moorcock, Michael
Elric series (1)
Dreaming damozel
Hardwick, Mollie
Doran Fairweather series (5)
Dreaming dragons
Broderick, Damien
Faustus hexagram series (3)
Dreaming jewels
Moorcock, Michael
Elric series (1)
Dreaming suburb
Delderfield, Ronald Frederick
Avenue series (1)
Dreaming Wolf
Wisler, Gary Clifton
Medicine Trail series (4)
Dreams
Arnold, Judith
Keeping the faith trilogy (3)
Dreams can come true
Miner, Jane Claypool
Ellynne Aleese series (1)
Dreams fade
Winn, Godfrey
Dreams of youth series (1)
Dreams from Bunker Hill
Fante, John
Arturo Bandini series (3)
Dreams of dawn
Steussy, Marti
Forest series (2)
Dreams of flesh and sand
Quick, W T
Dreams trilogy (1)
Dreams of forever
Pascal, Francine
Forever trilogy (1)
Dreams of glory
Lambert, Janet
Penny Parrish series (2)
Dreams of gods and men
Quick, W T
Dreams trilogy (2)
Dreams of roses and fire
Johnson, Eyvind
Olof tetralogy (3)
Dreams of steel
Cook, Glen
Chronicles of the Black Company series (5)
Dreams of stone
Wylie, Jonathan
Unbalanced earth trilogy (1)
Dreams of the raven
Carter, Carmen
Star trek series (34)
Dreams of vengeance
Oakgrove, Artemis
Throne trilogy (2)
Dreamspy
Lichtenberg, Jacqueline
Luren series (2)
Dreamstone
Cherryh, Carolyn Janice
Ealdwood series (1)
Rivkin, J F
Runesword series (3)
Dreamtime
Mountford, Charles Pearcy
Dreamtime series (1)
Dreamtime, Aboriginal heritage
Roberts, Melva Jean
Dreamtime series (4)
Dreamtime heritage
Roberts, Melva Jean
Dreamtime series (4)
Drega path
McKiernan, Dennis L
Silver call series (2)
Drenai tales
Gemmell, David A
Drenai series (8)
Dress circlce murders
Yates, Peter
Sandy Blunt series (1)
Dress her in indigo
Macdonald, John Dann
Travis McGee series (11)
Dress I'll wear to the party
Neitzel, Shirley
My clothes series (2)
Dress rehearsal
Hill, Lorna
Sadler's Wells series (11)
Ure, Jean
Riverside Theatre series (3)
Dress up and die
Elias, David
Nell Bartlett series (3)
Dressed for death
Leon, Donna
Commissario Guido Brunetti series (3)
Dressed to kill
Hyde, D Herbert
Sexton Blake series (1472)
Morland, Nigel
Mrs Palmyra Pym series (14)
Dresses of red and gold
Klein, Robin
Melling series (2)
Dressing
Oxenbury, Helen
Baby board books series (8)
Dressing of diamond
Freeling, Nicolas
Henri Castang series (1)
Dressing up
Briggs, Raymond
Snowman series (4)
Costa, Nicoletta
Molly and Tom series (1)
McGee, Shelagh
Little activity series (1)
Trueman, Brian
Stories from Cockleshell Bay series (4)
Drexel dream
Mackenzie, William Andrew
Sir Nigel Lacaita series (2)
Dribblesome teapot, and other incredible stories
Hunter, Norman
Kingdom of Incredibilia series (1)
Dribbling, shooting and scoring, sometimes
Paulsen, Gary
Sports on the light side series (1)
Drift!
Grover, Marshall
Larry and Stretch series (1)
Drift fence
Grey, Zane
Diamond Outfit series (1)
Drift of things
Robinson, Roland Edward
Drift of things series (1)
Drifter
Edson, John Thomas
Waco series (6)
Morris, Gilbert
Jim Reno series (1)
Drifting badge
Evans, Tabor
Longarm series (185)
Drifting death
Carstairs, Henry
Lydford Long series (2)
Gaston, Bill
Roy Maclean series (2)
Drill is death
Lockridge, Frances
Nathan Shapiro series (4)
Richards, Francis
Nathan Shapiro series (4)
Drilling for death
Wolfe, John
Johnny McCoy series (2)
Drina, ballerina
Estoril, Jean
Drina series (11)
Drina dances again
Estoril, Jean
Drina series (5)
Drina dances in exile
Estoril, Jean
Drina series (3)
Drina dances in Italy
Estoril, Jean
Drina series (4)
Drina dances in Madeira
Estoril, Jean
Drina series (8)
Drina dances in New York
Estoril, Jean
Drina series (6)
Drina dances in Paris
Estoril, Jean
Drina series (7)
Drina dances in Switzerland
Estoril, Jean
Drina series (9)
Drina goes on tour
Estoril, Jean
Drina series (10)
Drina's dancing year
Estoril, Jean
Drina series (2)
Drink
Zola, Emile
Rougon Macquart series (7)
Drink alone and die
Cobb, Belton
Inspector Cheviot Burmann series (18)
Drink and ink
Wheatley, Dennis
Time has come series (3)
Drink down the moon
De Lint, Charles
Jack, the giant-killer series (2)
Drink for Mister Cherry
Gardiner, Dorothy
Mister Watson series (2)
Drink, for once dead!
Sewart, Alan
Detective Sergeant Chamberlayne series (4)
Drink of deadly wine
Charles, Kate
David Middleton-Brown series (1)
Drink the fire from the flames
Baker, Scott
Ashlu cycle series (3)
Drink the green water
Austin, Hugh
William Sultan series (1)
Drink this
Dewhurst, Eileen
Inspector Neil Carter series (2)
Drink to yesterday
Coles, Manning
Tommy Hambledon series (1)
Drinker of souls
Clayton, Jo
Drinker of souls trilogy (1)
Drinker of the wind
Frost, Kelman Dalgety
Captain John Walton series (1)
Drinking sapphire wine
Lee, Tanith
Don't bite the sun series (2)
Drinks on the victim
Heberden, Mary Violet
Desmond Shannon series (12)
Driscoll
Grover, Marshall
Nevada Jim series (33)
Drive
Oxenbury, Helen
First picture books series (5)
Drive east on Sixty Six
Wormser, Richard
Lieutenant Andy Bastian series (1)
Drive for Devil's River
Field, Peter
Powder Valley series (63)
Drive-in
Lansdale, Joe Richard
Drive-in series (1)
Drive-in 2
Lansdale, Joe Richard
Drive-in series (2)
Drive to Dodge City
Winstan, Matt
Reuben Brown series (11)
Driven death
Orde-Powlett, Nigel
Anthony Rillington series (2)
Driven from cover
Carter, Nicholas
Nicholas Carter series (98)
Driven to death
Lenehan, John Christopher
Charlie Ryan series (5)
Driven to desperation
Carter, Nicholas
Nicholas Carter series (465)
Driven to kill
Disney, Doris Miles
Jim O'Neill series (5)
Dolphin, Rex
Sexton Blake series (1612)
Witting, Clifford
Inspector Peter Bradfield series (8)
Drop dead
Ashe, Gordon
Patrick Dawlish series (28)
Bagby, George
Inspector Schmidt series (16)
Neville, Margot
Inspector Grogan and Sergeant Manning series (15)
Drop dead, sucker!
Janson, Hank
Hank Janson series (87)
Drop in the ocean
Wright, Steve
Barry Donovan series (2)
Drop of himself
Wood, James
Tipple in the deep series (3)
Drop of hot gold
Chance, John Newton
Jonathan Blake series (44)
Drop of the dice
Carr, Philippa
Daughters of England series (8)
Drop out blues
Erlbach, Arlene
Henny series (2)
Dropped dead
Ross, Jonathan
Superintendent George Rogers series (12)
Dropped from the clouds
Verne, Jules
Captain Grant's children series (2)
Captain Nemo series (2)
Drops of blood
Sologub, Fedor
Created legend trilogy (1)
Dropshot
Bickham, Jack Miles
Brad Smith series (1)
Drought
Creasey, John
Doctor Palfrey series (20)
Salkey, Andrew
West Indies series (3)
Drought foal
Stuart, Donald Robert
Conjuror's years series (3)
Drought on Ziax II
Morressy, John
Ziax II series (2)
Drover
Granger, Bill
Jimmy Drover series (1)
Drover and the designated hitter
Granger, Bill
Jimmy Drover series (3)

Drover and the zebras
Granger, Bill
Jimmy Drover series (2)
Drovers road
West, Joyce
Gabrielle Allan series (1)
Drown all the dogs
Adcock, Thomas
Neil Hockaday series (2)
Drown her remembrance
Gilruth, Susan
Inspector Hugh Gordon and Liane Crawford series (6)
Drown him deep
Cooper, Barbara
Inspector Gibbon series (2)
Drown the wind
Hood, Margaret Page
Gil Donan series (5)
Drowned Ammet
Jones, Diana Wynne
Dalemark series (2)
Drowned hope
Westlake, Donald Edwin
Dortmunder Gang series (7)
Drowned queen
Laumer, Keith
Avengers series (8)
Drowning pool
Macdonald, Ross
Lew Archer series (2)
Drowning valley
Cockett, Mary
Strange valley trilogy (3)
Drowsy and the beanstalk
Clarke, Elf Lewis
Drowsy Dormouse series (5)
Drowsy and Timmy go south
Clarke, Elf Lewis
Drowsy Dormouse series (2)
Drowsy Dormouse
Clarke, Elf Lewis
Drowsy Dormouse series (1)
Drowsy goes to school
Clarke, Elf Lewis
Drowsy Dormouse series (6)
Drowsy's Christmas Eve
Clarke, Elf Lewis
Drowsy Dormouse series (4)
Drug called power
Mackintosh, Ian
Tim Blackgrove series (2)
Drug in the market
Baines, Cuthbert
Dennis Doyne series (2)
Drug on the market
Brinton, Henry
John and Sally Strang series (4)
Dodge, David
Whit Whitney series (4)
Sampson, George
Paola and George series (1)
Drug run
Crawford, William
Colin Stryker series (3)
Drug runner
Ahern, Jerry
Dan Track series (12)
Druid connection
Smith, Guy Newman
Sabat series (4)
Druid of Shannara
Brooks, Terry
Heritage of Shannara series (2)
Druids' world
Smith, George Henry
Duffus January series (1)
Drum
Onstott, Kyle
Falconhurst series (2)
Drum and trumpet sound
Ross, Sutherland
Clifton family series (3)
Drum beat, Berlin
Marlowe, Stephen
Chester Drum series (16)
Drum beat, Dominique
Marlowe, Stephen
Chester Drum series (17)
Drum beat, Erica
Marlowe, Stephen
Chester Drum series (19)
Drum beat, Madrid
Marlowe, Stephen
Chester Drum series (18)
Drum beat, Marianne
Marlowe, Stephen
Chester Drum series (20)
Drum beats at night
Holt, Gavin
Professor Luther Bastion series (9)
Drum of power
Macleod, Robert
Talos Cord series (1)
Drum of Ungara
Knox, Bill
Talos Cord series (1)
Drum roll
Longtree, Warren T
Ruff Justice series (17)
Drumbeat
Eyre, Donald Cuthbert
Captain O'Donnell series (2)
Pope, Dudley
Lord Nicholas Ramage series (2)
Drumfire
McCurtin, Peter
Sundance series (38)
Drums
Boyd, James
James Fraser series (1)
Drums along the Amazon
Norwood, Victor George Charles
Jacare series (7)
Drums along the Khyber
Macneil, Duncan
James Ogilvie series (1)
Drums beat at dusk
Maddock, Stephen
Timothy Terrel series (15)
Drums call the Major
Greene, L Patrick
Aubrey Saint John Major series (17)
Drums of destiny
Bourne, Peter
Henri Christophe series (1)
Stewart family series (1)
Drums of Dracula
Lory, Robert
Dracula horror series (5)
Drums of Fu-Manchu
Rohmer, Sax
Fu-Manchu series (10)
Drums of jeopardy
Macgrath, Harold
Cutty Clay series (1)
Drums of morning
Croft-Cooke, Rupert
Sensual life series (3)
Drums of Tapajos
Meek, Sterner St. Paul
Troyana series (1)
Drums of the dark gods
Baker, William Howard
Richard Quintain series (9)
Drums of time
Stirling, Jessica
Beckman family trilogy (1)
Drums of war
Clews, Roy
Jethro Stanton series (3)
Drums under the window
O'Casey, Sean
I knock at the door series (3)
Drunk and love
Gilchrist, Ellen
Anna Hudson series (2)
Drunkard
Zola, Emile
Rougon Macquart series (7)
Drunkard's end
Troy, Simon
Inspector Smith series (4)
Drury Lane's last case
Ross, Barnaby
Drury Lane series (4)
Druss the legend
Gemmell, David A
Drenai series (4)
Dry and thirsty ground
Weiss, Mike
Ben Henry series (3)
Dry-Gulch Adams
Field, Peter
Powder Valley series (2)
Dry Salvages
Eliot, Thomas Stearns
Four quartets series (3)
Dry spell
Creasey, John
Doctor Palfrey series (20)
Dry Valley war
Borg, Jack
Hogleg Bailey series (24)
Dry white tear
Wilcox, Stephen F
T S W Sheridan series (1)
Drygulched
Sherman, Jory
Gunn series (15)
Drygulchers
Cole, Jackson
Jim Hatfield series (40)
Dual enigma
Underwood, Michael
Rosa Epton series (12)
Duane and the art murders
Benton, John L
Stephen Duane series (2)
Duane of the FBI
Benton, John L
Stephen Duane series (1)
Duane of the G-men
Benton, John L
Stephen Duane series (1)
Dublin crossing
Dengler, Sandy
Heroes of the misty isle series (1)
Dublin diary of Stanislaus Joyce
Joyce, Stanislaus
Dublin series (2)
Dubrovnik massacre
Carter, Nick
Nick Carter series (149)
Ducats in her coffin
Warriner, Thurman
Mister Scotter series (2)
Duchess
Edgar, Josephine
Viola Corbett series (1)
Duchess intervenes
Lowndes, Marie Belloc
Duchess Laura series (1)
Duchess Laura, certain days of her life
Lowndes, Marie Belloc
Duchess Laura series (1)
Duchess Laura, further days of her life
Lowndes, Marie Belloc
Duchess Laura series (2)
Duchess of Bloomsbury Street
Hanff, Helene
American in London series (2)
Duchess of Denver
Willoughby, Lee Davis
Women who won the West series (3)
Duchess of Duke Street
Hardwick, Mollie
Duchess of Duke Street series (2)
Duchess of Langeais
Balzac, Honore de
Scenes of Parisian life series (1)
Duchess of Wrexe
Walpole, Hugh
London Group series (2)
Peter Westcott series (3)
Duck and his friends
Tyler, Jenny
Duck series (2)
Duck and the diesel engine
Awdry, Wilbert
Railway series (13)
Duck in trouble
Tyler, Jenny
Duck series (3)
Duck on holiday
Tyler, Jenny
Duck series (1)
Duck soup in the Black Sea
Hone, Joseph
Collected travels series (3)
Duck Street Gang
Marray, Denis
Duck Street Gang series (1)
Duck Street Gang returns
Marray, Denis
Duck Street Gang series (2)
Duckling sees
Hands, Hargrave
Look and see series (1)
Ducklings love
McCue, Lisa
Baby animal love series (4)
Ducks
Berg, Leila
Small world series (8)
Ducks and drakes
Sudbery, Rodie
Polly Devenish series (5)
Ducktales, down the drain
Korman, Justine
Donald Duck series (3)
Ducky's seasons
McCue, Dick
Animal shape series (4)
Ducrow folly
Chance, John Newton
Jonathan Blake series (43)
Dude must die
Grover, Marshall
Larry and Stretch series (305)
Dude ranch
Bryant, Bonnie
Saddle Club series (6)
Dudley and the birdmen
Swede, George
Dudley series (1)
Dudley and the Christmas thief
Swede, George
Dudley series (2)
Dudley and the monster
Taylor, Judy
Dudley Dormouse series (2)
Dudley and the strawberry snake
Taylor, Judy
Dudley Dormouse series (4)
Dudley bakes a cake
Taylor, Judy
Dudley Dormouse series (5)
Dudley goes flying
Taylor, Judy
Dudley Dormouse series (1)
Dudley in a jam
Taylor, Judy
Dudley Dormouse series (3)
Due East
Sayers, Valerie
Due East series (1)
Mary Faith Rapple series (1)
Due or die
Kane, Frank
Johnny Liddell series (18)
Due reckoning
McKenna, Stephen
Realists trilogy (3)
Due to a death
Kelly, Mary
Nicholson series (2)
Due to expire
Wrenn, Harold Albert
William Mitchell series (4)
Duel
Bradley, Mary Hastings
Old Chicago series (2)
Macdonnell, James Edmond
Dutchy Holland series (3)
Duel at Dodge City
Flynn, Jackson
Gunsmoke series (3)
Duel for cannons
Hartman, Dane
Dirty Harry Callahan series (1)
Duel for the Samurai sword
Fortune, J J
Race against time series (5)
Duel image
Roberts, Nora
Flowers series (29)
Duel in purgatory
Sherman, Jory
Gunn series (6)
Duel in the dark
Townsend, Peter
Duels in the air series (2)
Duel in the desert
Myers, Walter Dean
Arrow series (3)
Duel in the shadows
Lejeune, Anthony
Adam Gifford series (2)
Duel in Tombstone
Masterson, Louis
Morgan Kane series (23)
Duel murder
Gray, Berkeley
Norman Conquest series (20)
Duel of brains
Carter, Nicholas
Nicholas Carter series (466)
Duel of dragons
Baudino, Gael
Dragonsword series (2)
Duel of eagles
Townsend, Peter
Duels in the air series (1)
Duel of the masters
Martindale, T Chris
Endless quest series (21)
Duel of wits
Churchill, Peter
British spy series (2)
Duel on the cinders
Porter, Mark
Win Hadley series (6)
Duel on the diamond
Hallowell, Tommy
Alden All Stars series (1)
Duel on the Song Cai
Lansing, John
Black Eagles series (11)
Duel to the death
James, William M
Apache series (3)
Duel under the double sun
Scheer, Karl Herbert
Perry Rhodan series (108)
Duelmaster
Smith, Mark
Duelmaster series (3)
Dueltrack
Haring, Scott D
Car wars adventure gamebook series (3)
Duet for three spies
Rothwell, Henry Talbot
Michael Brooks series (3)
Duet for two guns
Ambler, Dail
Danny Spade series (23)
Duffers on the deep
Brown, Winifred
Duffers of the deep series (1)
Duffy
Kavanagh, Dan
Nick Duffy series (1)
Duffy's dollars
Grover, Marshall
Larry and Stretch series (296)
Dugout jinx
Bee, Clair
Chip Hilton series (8)
Dukays
Zilahy, Lajos
Dukay family series (1)
Duke comes back
Cary, Lucian
Duke series (2)
Duke decides
Tunis, John Roberts
Iron Duke series (2)
Duke Jones
Sidgwick, Ethel
Ashwin trilogy (2)
Duke of York Steps
Wade, Henry
Inspector Poole series (1)
Duke steps out
Cary, Lucian
Duke series (1)
Duke, the lost engine
Awdry, Wilbert
Railway series (25)
Duke's children
Trollope, Anthony
Palliser novels series (6)
Duke's daughter
Lang, Frances
Gillonne de Beauregard series (2)
Thirkell, Angela
Barsetshire series (20)
Duke's last trick
Gregg, Cecil Freeman
Inspector Cuthbert Higgins series (9)
Duke's page
Dumas, Alexandre
Valois series (3)
Duke's strategem
Burgin, George Brown
Four Corners series (19)
Duke's twins
Burgin, George Brown
Four Corners series (9)
Dulcie and Tottie
Everett-Green, Evelyn
Dulcie trilogy (2)
Dulcie Bligh
Clark, Gail
Dulcie Bligh series (1)
Dulcie's little brother
Everett-Green, Evelyn
Dulcie trilogy (1)
Dulcie's love story
Everett-Green, Evelyn
Dulcie trilogy (3)
Dull dead
Butler, Gwendoline
Inspector John Coffin series (2)
Inspector William Winter series (3)
Dull thud
Long, Manning
Liz Parrott series (6)
Dum-dum for the president
Brett, Martin
Mike Garfin series (3)
Dum dum murders
Brown, Carter
Lieutenant Al Wheeler series (27)
Dumb as they come
Corrigan, Mark
Mark Corrigan and McLean series (20)

Dumb cake
Garfield, Leon
Apprentices series (9)
Dumb witness
Christie, Agatha
Hercule Poirot series (15)
Plummer, Thomas Arthur
Detective Inspector Andrew Frampton series (4)
Dumb witness, and other stories
Carter, Nicholas
Nicholas Carter series (76)
Dumbo Dossier
Cannon, Elliott
Guy Fosse series (1)
Dummy murder case
Ozaki, Milton K
Professor Caldwell and Lieutenant Phelan series (3)
Dump
Remenham, John
Inspector Bliss series (3)
Dumper and the circus
Bartlett, Evelyn
Dumper series (2)
Dumper the kangaroo
Bartlett, Evelyn
Dumper series (1)
Duncan and Mallory
Asprin, Robert Lynn
Duncan and Mallory series (1)
Duncan McClure
Rudd, Steele
Duncan McClure series (2)
Duncton found
Horwood, William
Duncton chronicles series (3)
Duncton quest
Horwood, William
Duncton chronicles series (2)
Duncton tales
Horwood, William
Duncton chronicles series (4)
Duncton Wood
Horwood, William
Duncton chronicles series (1)
Dune
Border, Rosemary
Dune series (6)
Herbert, Frank
Dune series (1)
Paul Atreides trilogy (1)
Dune Bugg
Cosgrove, Stephen Edward
Bugg series (2)
Dune buggy mystery
Hope, Laura Lee
Bobbsey twins series (75)
Dune messiah
Herbert, Frank
Dune series (2)
Paul Atreides trilogy (2)
Dune storybook
Vinge, Joan Dennison
Dune series (6)
Dunfermline affair
Ross, Angus
Mark Farrow series (4)
Dungeon demons
Milton, Hilary
Plot your own horror stories series (8)
Dungeon of darkness
Kendall, John
Fantasy forest series (5)
Dungeon of doom
Dixon, Franklin W
Hardy boys series (99)
Dungeon of dread
Estes, Rose
Endless quest series (1)
Dungeons of Kuba
Diamond, Graham
Haven series (3)
Stacy series (2)
Dungeons of Torgar
Dever, Joe
Lone Wolf series (10)
Dunkel
Dugdale, Pamela
Dunkel series (1)
Dunkel again
Dugdale, Pamela
Dunkel series (2)
Dunkerley's
Spring, Howard
Dillworth trilogy (2)
Dunkirk summer
Turner, Philip
Darnley Mills series (5)
Dunlop and the eggs
Reeder, Colin
Adventures of Dunlop series (1)
Dunlop catches cold
Reeder, Colin
Adventures of Dunlop series (2)
Dunlop gives chase
Reeder, Colin
Adventures of Dunlop series (3)
Dunlop goes to the rescue
Reeder, Colin
Adventures of Dunlop series (4)
Dunne family
Farrell, James Thomas
Universe of time series (6)
Dunnybrook
Carroll, Gladys Hasty
Shaw family series (2)
Dunwich horror, and others
Lovecraft, Howard Phillips
Colour out of space and time series (1)
Dupe
Cody, Liza
Anna Lee series (1)
Dupe negative
Fowles, Anthony
Richard Powell series (1)
Duplicate
Taylor, H Baldwin
David Halliday series (1)
Duplicate death
Fox-Davies, Arthur Charles
Ashley Tempest series (4)
Heyer, Georgette
Inspector Hemingway series (7)
Duplicate stiff
O'Neill, Archie
Jeff Pride series (2)
Dupree in Alaska
Dimmock, Frederick Haydon
Dupree series (1)
Dupree's tenderfoot
Dimmock, Frederick Haydon
Dupree series (2)
Durango
Mitchum, Hank
Stage coach station series (17)
Sandon, J D
Gringos series (9)
Durango Bill
Slade, Jack
Lassiter series (19)
Durango Street
Bonham, Frank
Dogtown Ghetto series (1)
Durdane
Vance, Jack
Durdane trilogy (3)
During His Majesty's pleasure
Kyle, Sefton
Inspector J Rason series (15)
Durong warrior
Lansing, John
Black Eagles series (18)
Dusantes
Stockton, Frank Richard
Mrs Lecks and Mrs Aleshine series (2)
Dushau
Lichtenberg, Jacqueline
Dushau trilogy (1)
Dusky hour
Punshon, Ernest Robertson
Bobby Owen series (9)
Dusky limelight
Robertson, Colin
Edward North series (1)
Dust and glory
Green, Evan
Kalinda series (1)
Dust and the curious boy
Graaf, Peter
Joe Dust series (1)
Dust in my throat
Farrimond, John
Bob Howarth series (1)
Dust in the lion's paw
Stark, Freya
Traveller series (4)
Dust in the vault
Walling, Robert Alfred John
Philip Tolefree series (15)
Dust in the wind
Danoen, Emile
Jeannot and Lydie series (1)
Dust in your eye
Seaton, Stuart
Inspector Martin Laidman series (2)
Dust is forever
Farrimond, John
Bob Howarth series (2)
Dust of death
Robeson, Kenneth
Doc Savage series (32)
Dust on my shoes
Pinney, Peter
Dust on my shoes series (1)
Dust on the paw
Jenkins, Robin
Nuranian series (1)
Dust on the sea
Beach, Edward Latimer, junior
Rich Richardson series (2)
Dust to dust
Budd, Mavis
Dust to dust series (1)
Dust-up at the Royal Disco
Hunter, Norman
Kingdom of Incredibilia series (4)
Dust wants to borrow everything
Sandberg, Inger
Dusty series (2)
Dust was his shroud
Nickson, Arthur
Rusty Hines series (4)
Dust within the rock
Waters, Frank
Pike's Peak trilogy (3)
Duster trouble
Phillips, Tony
Turbo cowboys series (9)
Dustland
Hamilton, Virginia
Justice trilogy (2)
Dusty and Smudge and the bride
Schmidt, Annie Maria Geertruida
Dusty and Smudge series (4)
Dusty and Smudge and the cake
Schmidt, Annie Maria Geertruida
Dusty and Smudge series (6)
Dusty and Smudge and the soap suds
Schmidt, Annie Maria Geertruida
Dusty and Smudge series (2)
Dusty and Smudge keep cool
Schmidt, Annie Maria Geertruida
Dusty and Smudge series (3)
Dusty and Smudge spill the paint
Schmidt, Annie Maria Geertruida
Dusty and Smudge series (1)
Dusty and Smudge splash soup
Schmidt, Annie Maria Geertruida
Dusty and Smudge series (5)
Dusty coinage
Mills, Woosnam
Sir John Howden series (5)
Dusty death
Mills, Osmington
Midset C.I.D. series (3)
Sergeant Patrick Shirley and Inspector Rip Irving series (1)
Robbins, Clifton
Clay Harrison series (1)
Thayer, Lee
Peter Clancy series (60)
Dusty wants to help
Sandberg, Inger
Dusty series (1)
Dusty wheels
Smith, Lew
Judge Lemanuel Bates and Tobacco Jones series (7)
Dusty's windmill
Barne, Kitty
Farrar family series (3)
Dutch blue error
Tapply, William George
Brady Coyne series (2)
Dutch boat
Pardoe, Margot
Boat series (3)
Dutch courage
Perry, Ritchie
Philis series (8)
Dutch Pensey can ride
Mack Bride, Johnny
Frank Wady series (2)
Dutch shoe mystery
Queen, Ellery
Ellery Queen series (4)
Dutch twins
Perkins, Lucy Fitch
Dutch twins series (1)
Twin series (1)
Dutch twins and little brother
Perkins, Lucy Fitch
Dutch twins series (3)
Dutchman
Meyers, Maan
Pieter Tonneman series (1)
Duty calls
Georgeson, Valerie
Angels series (4)
Duty elsewhere
Wainwright, John
Inspector Lyle series (2)
Northern Police series (42)
Duty free
Harvey, John Barton
Duty free series (1)
Duveen letter
Leather, Edwin
Rupert Conway series (3)
Dwarfed
Avenell, Donne
Axa series (6)
Dwarfs of Nosegay
Biegel, Paul
Virgil Nosegay series (1)
Dwarks
Berenstain, Michael
Dwarks series (1)
Dwarks at the mall
Berenstain, Michael
Dwarks series (3)
Dwarks meet Skunk Momma
Berenstain, Michael
Dwarks series (2)
Dwell in danger
Lewis, Royston
Eric Ward series (2)
Dweller on two planets
Phylos the Thibetan
Zailm series (2)
Dwellers
Wright, Sydney Fowler
Amphibians series (2)
Dwellers all in time and space
Oakes, Philip
Middle England trilogy (2)
Dwellers in the crucible
Bonanno, Margaret Wander
Star trek series (25)
Dwellers in Vale Sunrise
Lloyd, John William
Natural man series (2)
Dwelling place
South, Ambrose
Broken house trilogy (2)
Dwight Gooden, strikout king
Aaseng, Nathan
Sports acheivers series (6)
Dying alderman
Wade, Henry
Inspector Lott series (1)
Dying and the damned
Muir, James A
Breed series (11)
Dying breath
Walker, Robert Wayne
Dean Grant series (4)
Dying day
Mitchell, James
Ron Hogget series (3)
Dying earth
Vance, Jack
Dying earth series (1)
Dying fall
Dolson, Hildegarde
Lucy Ramsdale series (2)
Thomson, June
Inspector Finch series (11)
Dying for a drink
Silverwood, Roger
Superintendent Cawthorne series (2)
Dying for stardom
Fulton, Eileen
Nina McFall series (3)
Dying high
Curry, Avon
Jerome Aylwin series (2)
Dying in the post-war world
Collins, Max Allan
Nathan Heller series (5)
Dying is forever
Gilman, George G
Edge series (57)
Dying of paradise
Couper, Stephen
Paradise series (1)
Dying room only
Sterling, Stewart
Ben Pedley series (8)
Fire Marshal Ben Pedley series (8)
Dying scientifically
Scalpel, Aesculapius
Saint Bernard's series (2)
Dying space
Murphy, Warren Burton
Destroyer series (47)
Dying sun
Smith, Mark
Falcon series (5)
Dying thunder
Johnston, Terry Conrad
Plainsmen series (7)
Dying trade
Corris, Peter
Cliff Hardy series (2)
Dying voices
Crider, Bill
Carl Burns series (2)
Dying ways
McLaglen, John J
Herne the Hunter series (18)
Dyke and Burr, the rival detectives
Rockwood, Harry
Donald Dyke series (2)
Dykes to watch out for
Bechdel, Alison
Dykes series (1)
Dykes to watch out for, the sequel
Bechdel, Alison
Dykes series (4)
Dynamite demon
Grover, Marshall
Larry and Stretch series (365)
Dynamite do-it-yourself pen pal kit
Stine, Robert Lawrence
Dynamite series (1)
Dynamite Drury
Greene, L Patrick
Dynamite Drury series (1)
Dynamite Drury again
Greene, L Patrick
Dynamite Drury series (2)
Dynamite Drury patrols
Greene, L Patrick
Dynamite Drury series (3)
Dynamite fever
Benteen, John
Neal Fargo series (19)
Dynamite Flynns
McFarlane, Leslie
Checkmate series (2)
Dynamite for hire
Fehler, Johann Heinrich
German raider series (2)
Dynamite justice
Roberts, J R
Gunsmith series (32)
Dynamite monster boogie concert
Ross, Paul
Chopper Cop series (3)
Dynamite trap
Carter, Nicholas
Nicholas Carter series (234)
Dynamite's funny book of the sad facts of life
Stine, Robert Lawrence
Dynamite series (2)
Dynasty of death
Caldwell, Taylor
Bouchard family trilogy (1)
Dynasty of evil
Stillman, Ron
Tracker series (8)
Dynevor Terrace
Yonge, Charlotte Mary
Beechcroft series (2)
Dyngeoneer
Gascoigne, Marc
Fighting fantasy gamebook series (38)
Dynteryx
Murdock, Melinda Seabrooke
Vendetta series (2)
Dzurlord
Architects Adventure
Jhereg series (5)

E

E is for Elisa
Hurwitz, Johanna
Elisa series (2)
E is for evidence
Grafton, Sue
Kinsey Millhone series (5)
E K Means
Means, Eldred Kurtz
Is this a title, it is not series (1)
E, my name is Emily
Mazer, Norma Fox
My name series (5)
E.T.A. for death
Wallace, C H
Steve Ramsay series (4)
E.T., the extraterrestrial
Gelfland, M Howard
E.T. series (2)
E.T., the extraterrestrial, in his adventure on earth
Kotzwinkle, William
E.T. series (1)

Easter parade
Stout, Rex
Nero Wolfe and Archie Goodwin series (31)
Easter surprise
Barkan, Joanne
Easter series (2)
Easter, the show jumper
Peel, Hazel Mary
Ann and Jim Henderson series (4)
Eastlake affair
Robertson, Colin
Vicky McBain series (4)
Eastmans find a boy
Pullein-Thompson, Christine
Eastmans series (3)
Eastmans in Brittany
Pullein-Thompson, Christine
Eastmans series (1)
Eastmans move house
Pullein-Thompson, Christine
Eastmans series (2)
Eastward ho!
Farrar, Charles Alden John
Lake and forest series (1)
Easy answers
Harrell, Janice
West Mount High trilogy (2)
Easy Avenue
Doyle, Brian
Hubbo O'Driscoll series (1)
Easy Company and the Bible salesman
Howard, John Wesley
Easy Company series (25)
Easy Company and the big blizzard
Howard, John Wesley
Easy Company series (15)
Easy Company and the big medicine
Howard, John Wesley
Easy Company series (6)
Easy Company and the big name hunter
Howard, John Wesley
Easy Company series (28)
Easy Company and the Bitter Trail
Howard, John Wesley
Easy Company series (8)
Easy Company and the Black Hills
Howard, John Wesley
Easy Company series (7)
Easy Company and the blood feud
Howard, John Wesley
Easy Company series (26)
Easy Company and the bloody flag
Howard, John Wesley
Easy Company series (12)
Easy Company and the bootleggers
Howard, John Wesley
Easy Company series (17)
Easy Company and the bullwhackers
Howard, John Wesley
Easy Company series (30)
Easy Company and the card sharps
Howard, John Wesley
Easy Company series (18)
Easy Company and the Cherokee beauty
Howard, John Wesley
Easy Company series (14)
Easy Company and the Cow Country Queen
Howard, John Wesley
Easy Company series (24)
Easy Company and the dog soldiers
Howard, John Wesley
Easy Company series (27)
Easy Company and the engineers
Howard, John Wesley
Easy Company series (11)
Easy Company and the green arrows
Howard, John Wesley
Easy Company series (3)
Easy Company and the gypsy riders
Howard, John Wesley
Easy Company series (29)
Easy Company and the headline hunter
Howard, John Wesley
Easy Company series (10)
Easy Company and the Indian doctor
Howard, John Wesley
Easy Company series (19)
Easy Company and the long marchers
Howard, John Wesley
Easy Company series (16)
Easy Company and the longhorns
Howard, John Wesley
Easy Company series (5)
Easy Company and the medicine gun
Howard, John Wesley
Easy Company series (2)
Easy Company and the mystery trooper
Howard, John Wesley
Easy Company series (23)
Easy Company and the Oklahoma Trail
Howard, John Wesley
Easy Company series (13)
Easy Company and the sheep ranchers
Howard, John Wesley
Easy Company series (21)
Easy Company and the Suicide Boys
Howard, John Wesley
Easy Company series (1)
Easy Company and the twilight sniper
Howard, John Wesley
Easy Company series (20)
Easy Company and the Whiskey Trail
Howard, John Wesley
Easy Company series (31)
Easy Company and the white man's path
Howard, John Wesley
Easy Company series (4)
Easy Company at Hat Creek Station
Howard, John Wesley
Easy Company series (22)
Easy Company in Colter's Hell
Howard, John Wesley
Easy Company series (9)
Easy connections
Berry, Liz
Easy series (1)
Easy freedom
Berry, Liz
Easy series (2)
Easy marks
Keene, Carolyn
Nancy Drew files series (62)
Easy money
Boland, John C
Donald McCarry series (1)
Sandon, J D
Gringos series (5)
Steffanson, Con
Laverne and Shirley series (2)
Easy prey
Bell, Josephine
Claude Warrington-Reeve series (1)
Inspector Steven Mitchell series (10)
Easy ride
Gray, Rod
Lady from L.U.S.T. series (15)
Easy steps in the Bible story, from creation to Joseph
Evans, Adelaide Bee
Bible pictures and stories series (1)
Easy to kill
Christie, Agatha
Superintendent Battle series (4)
Footner, Hulbert
Madame Rosika Storey series (5)
Easy warriors
Armstrong, Anthony
Warriors series (4)
Easy way to go
Coxe, George Harmon
Kent Murdock series (21)
Eat your poison, dear
Howe, James
Sebastian Barth series (3)
Eat your way to a better relationship
Guisewhite, Cathy
Cathy series (2)
Eater of worlds
Kern, Gregory
Cap Kennedy series (8)
Eating out
Oxenbury, Helen
First picture books series (3)
Ebb-tide at Coppins Bridge
Daish, Elizabeth
Coppins Bridge trilogy (3)
Ebbing tide
Ogilvie, Elisabeth May
Bennett Island series (3)
Ebdon's England
Ebdon, John
Broadcaster's Odyssey trilogy (3)
Ebdon's Iliad
Ebdon, John
Broadcaster's Odyssey trilogy (2)
Ebdon's Odyssey
Ebdon, John
Broadcaster's Odyssey trilogy (1)
Eben Holden
Bacheller, Irving
Eben Holden series (1)
Eben Holden's last day a-fishing
Bacheller, Irving
Eben Holden series (2)
Ebenezer investigates
Brady, Nicholas
Ebenezer Buckle series (3)
Ebony box
Fletcher, Joseph Smith
Ronald Camberwell series (9)
Ebony cross
Carter, Nick
Nick Carter series (118)
Ebony stag
Flynn, Brian
Anthony Bathurst series (22)
Ebony torso
Woodiwiss, John Cecil
Inspector Hopton series (2)
Ecce and old earth
Vance, Jack
Cadwal chronicles series (2)
Echo answers
Willard, Barbara
Proposed series (2)
Echo answers murder
Fitzgerald, Nigel
Superintendent Duffy series (9)
Echo in the wilderness
Brinsmead, Hesba Fay
Clippie Nancarrow series (2)
Echo Mountain hermit
Palmer, Bernard
Dell Norton series (3)
Echo of a bomb
Van Siller, Hilda
Richard Massey series (1)
Echo of thunder
Seger, Maura
Callahan and Gargano families trilogy (1)
Echo sounding
Aspinall, Ruth
Malinson brothers trilogy (3)
Echo Valley
Lyon, Elinor
Meredith family series (2)
Echoes
Brandner, Gary
Howling series (3)
Echoes of chaos
Vardeman, Robert Edward
Weapons of chaos trilogy (1)
Echoes of evil
Cameron, Kate
Whispering Hills series (6)
Echoes of the white giraffe
Choi, Sook Nyul
Sookan series (2)
Echoes of war
Gilman, George G
Edge series (23)
Echoing shore
Martin, Robert Lee
Jim Bennett series (5)
Echoing strangers
Mitchell, Gladys
Dame Beatrice Bradley series (25)
Echoing yesterday
Manners, Alexandra
Karran Kinrade series (1)
Eclipse
Shirley, John
Song called youth trilogy (1)
Eclipse corona
Shirley, John
Song called youth trilogy (3)
Eclipse of the Kai
Dever, Joe
Legends of Lone Wolf series (1)
Eclipse penumbra
Shirley, John
Song called youth trilogy (2)
Eclipsing binaries
Smith, Edward Elmer
Family d'Alembert series (8)
Ecolitan operation
Modesitt, Leland Exton
Ecolitan trilogy (2)
Ecologic envoy
Modesitt, Leland Exton
Ecolitan trilogy (1)
Ecologic secession
Modesitt, Leland Exton
Ecolitan trilogy (3)
Economics of the heart
Zenowich, Christopher
Bob Bodewicz series (1)
Ecotopia
Callenbach, Ernest
Ecotopia series (2)
Ecotopia emerging
Callenbach, Ernest
Ecotopia series (1)
Ecotopian sketchbook
Clancy, Judith S
Ecotopia series (2)
Ecstasy
Janson, Hank
Hank Janson series (96)
Ecstasy connection
Kenyon, Paul
Baroness Penelope Saint-John Orsini series (1)
Ed Emberley's big green drawing book
Emberley, Ed
Ed Emberley's big drawing book series (1)
Ed Emberley's big orange drawing book
Emberley, Ed
Ed Emberley's big drawing book series (2)
Ed Emberley's big purple drawing book
Emberley, Ed
Ed Emberley's big drawing book series (3)
Ed Emberley's big red drawing book
Emberley, Ed
Ed Emberley's big drawing book series (4)
Ed Emberley's drawing book of animals
Emberley, Ed
Ed Emberley's drawing book series (1)
Ed Emberley's drawing book of faces
Emberley, Ed
Ed Emberley's drawing book series (3)
Ed Emberley's little drawing book of birds
Emberley, Ed
Ed Emberley's little drawing books series (1)
Ed Emberley's little drawing book of farms
Emberley, Ed
Ed Emberley's little drawing books series (2)
Ed Emberley's little drawing book of fish
Emberley, Ed
Ed Emberley's little drawing books series (6)
Ed Emberley's little drawing book of horses
Emberley, Ed
Ed Emberley's little drawing books series (5)
Ed Emberley's little drawing book of more weirdos
Emberley, Ed
Ed Emberley's little drawing books series (8)
Ed Emberley's little drawing book of trains
Emberley, Ed
Ed Emberley's little drawing books series (3)
Ed Emberley's little drawing book of trucks
Emberley, Ed
Ed Emberley's little drawing books series (7)
Ed Emberley's little drawing book of weirdos
Emberley, Ed
Ed Emberley's little drawing books series (4)
Ed Noon in London
Avallone, Michael
Ed Noon series (24)
Eddie and Gardenia
Haywood, Carolyn
Eddie Wilson series (3)
Eddie and his big deals
Haywood, Carolyn
Eddie Wilson series (5)
Eddie and Louella
Haywood, Carolyn
Eddie Wilson series (7)
Eddie and the fire engine
Haywood, Carolyn
Eddie Wilson series (2)
Eddie Chapman story
Chapman, Eddie
Free agent series (1)
Eddie Engine-driver
Campbell, Rod
Little people series (3)
Eddie makes music
Haywood, Carolyn
Eddie Wilson series (6)
Eddie Spaghetti
Frascino, Edward
Eddie Spaghetti series (1)
Eddie Spaghetti on the home front
Frascino, Edward
Eddie Spaghetti series (2)
Eddie the dog holder
Haywood, Carolyn
Eddie Wilson series (10)
Eddie's green thumb
Haywood, Carolyn
Eddie Wilson series (9)
Eddie's happenings
Haywood, Carolyn
Eddie Wilson series (12)
Eddie's menagerie
Haywood, Carolyn
Eddie Wilson series (14)
Eddie's pay dirt
Haywood, Carolyn
Eddie Wilson series (4)
Eddie's valuable property
Haywood, Carolyn
Eddie Wilson series (13)
Eden
Richards, Penny
Calloway Corners series (4)
Eden and Honor
Harris, Marilyn
Eden family series (7)
Eden passion
Harris, Marilyn
Eden family series (3)
Eden rising
Harris, Marilyn
Eden family series (5)
Edgar Snow's China
Snow, Edgar
Red China series (2)
Edge of beyond
Hendryx, James Beardsley
Corporal Downey series (11)
Johns, William Earl
Rex Clinton series (5)
Edge of dawn
Seger, Maura
Callahan and Gargano families trilogy (3)
Edge of day
Lee, Laurie
Cotswolds series (1)
Edge of destruction
Dixon, Franklin W
Hardy boys case files series (5)
Robinson, Nigel
Doctor Who series (132)
Edge of extinction
Wainwright, John
Northern Police series (8)
Edge of nowhere
Sypher, Lucy Johnstone
Lucy series (1)
Edge of terror
Flynn, Brian
Anthony Bathurst series (12)
Edge of the blade
Schmidt, Dan
Eagle Force series (7)
Edge of the cloud
Peyton, K M
Flambards series (2)
Edge of the forest
Barr, Robert
Nick Nicholson series (2)
Edge of the sea
Carson, Rachel Louise
Sea series (2)
Edge of vengeance
Jones, Jenny
Flight over fire series (2)
Edie on the warpath
Spykman, Elizabeth Choate
Cares family series (4)
Edinburgh detective
M'Govan, James
Edinburgh detective series (2)
Edinburgh excursion
Andrews, Lucilla
Saint Martha's Hospital series (5)
Edinburgh exercise
Ross, Angus
Mark Farrow series (8)
Edison's conquest of Mars
Serviss, Garrett Putnam
War of the worlds series (2)
Edith Jackson
Guy, Rosa
Edith Jackson series (2)
Edith Trevor's secret
Lewis, Harriet
Edith Trevor series (1)
Editha's burglar
Burnett, Frances Hodgson
Sara Crewe series (2)
Editor
Martin, Kingsley
Father figures series (2)

Edmond Dantes
Flagg, Edmund
Count of Monte Cristo series (2)
Educated Evans
Wallace, Edgar
Educated Evans series (1)
Educated man
Wallace, Edgar
Educated Evans series (3)
Educating Marmalade
Davies, Andrew
Marmalade Atkins series (3)
Educating Arthur
Graham, Amanda
Arthur trilogy (2)
Educating Elizabeth
Hassett, Margaret
Miss Dinwiddie series (1)
Education before Verdun
Zweig, Arnold
Werner Bertin and Lenore Wahl series (3)
Education of Anthony Dare
Marshall, Archibald
Anthony Dare series (2)
Education of Eric Lane
McKenna, Stephen
Sensationalists trilogy (2)
Education of Hyman Kaplan
Ross, Leonard Q
Hyman Kaplan series (1)
Education of Jennifer Parrish
Martin, Russell White
Supernatural series (6)
Education of Mister P J Davenant
Hamilton, Frederic
P J Davenant series (3)
Education of Oversoul Seven
Roberts, Jane
Oversoul Seven series (1)
Education of Patrick Silver
Charyn, Jerome
Isaac Sidel series (3)
Education of Uncle Paul
Blackwood, Algernon
Uncle Paul series (1)
Education of young Donald
Horne, Donald
New boy trilogy (1)
Edward
Whittle, Tyler
Edward VII series (2)
Edward and the camera
Cole, Michael
Edward and friends series (1)
Edward Bringle
Owen, John
Edward Bringle series (2)
Edward gets a pet
Morgan, Michaela
Edward series (1)
Edward gets the hiccups
Cole, Michael
Edward and friends series (2)
Edward hurts his knee
Morgan, Michaela
Edward series (3)
Edward I
Birt, David
Middle Ages series (10)
Edward joins the band
Cole, Michael
Edward and friends series (3)
Edward Longshanks
Plaidy, Jean
Plantagenet series (7)
Edward loses his teddy bear
Morgan, Michaela
Edward series (4)
Edward, the blue engine
Awdry, Wilbert
Railway series (9)
Edward the warrior
Honeyman, Brenda
Edward III series (1)
Edward to the rescue
Cole, Michael
Edward and friends series (4)
Edward VII
Butler, David
Edward VII series (1)
Edwardian Christmas
Goodall, John Strickland
Edwardian series (2)
Edwardian entertainments
Goodall, John Strickland
Edwardian series (5)
Edwardian holiday
Goodall, John Strickland
Edwardian series (3)
Edwardian lady
Tweedsmuir, Susan Buchan
Edwardian lady series (3)
Edwardian season
Goodall, John Strickland
Edwardian series (4)
Edwardian summer
Goodall, John Strickland
Edwardian series (1)
Edwardian youth
Jones, Lawrence Evelyn
Victorian boyhood series (2)
Edwin of the iron shoes
Muller, Marcia
Sharon McCone series (1)
Edwin's adventures
Chell, Mary
Slimtails series (8)
Edwy the Fair
Crake, Augustus David
Chronicles of Aescendune trilogy (1)
Eel pie murders
Frome, David
Evan Pinkerton series (4)
Eel pie mystery
Frome, David
Evan Pinkerton series (4)
Eenie, meanie, Murphy, no
McKenna, Colleen O'Shaughnessy
Murphy family series (4)
Eeny meeny murder
Stout, Rex
Nero Wolfe and Archie Goodwin series (36)
Eevil Weevil
Cosgrove, Stephen Edward
Bugg series (3)
Eeyore has a birthday
Milne, Alan Alexander
Piglet series (4)
Effie in Venice
Lutyens, Mary
Effie Gray series (1)
Efford triangle
Goodchild, George
Inspector McLean series (33)
Egg
Bruna, Dick
Toy box tale series (7)
Egg and I
Macdonald, Betty
Who me series (1)
Egg-drop day
Ziefert, Harriet
Mister Rose's class series (4)
Egg Pandervil
Bullett, Gerald
History of Pandervil series (1)
Egg thoughts, and other Frances songs
Hoban, Russell
Frances series (6)
Eggs, Beans and Crumpets
Wodehouse, Pelham Grenville
Drones Club series (2)
Eggs, beans and crumpets
Wodehouse, Pelham Grenville
Mister Mulliner series (3)
Ukridge series (2)
Eggs of things
Kumin, Maxine W
Eggs of things series (1)
Egholm and his God
Buchholtz, Johannes
Egholm series (1)
Egil's book
Mills, Carla Johnson
Winter world series (2)
Ego
Agate, James
Ego series (1)
Ego 2
Agate, James
Ego series (2)
Ego 3
Agate, James
Ego series (3)
Ego 4
Agate, James
Ego series (4)
Ego 5
Agate, James
Ego series (5)
Ego 6
Agate, James
Ego series (6)
Ego 7
Agate, James
Ego series (7)
Ego 8
Agate, James
Ego series (8)
Ego 9
Agate, James
Ego series (9)
Egyptian cat mystery
Blaine, John
Rick Brant series (16)
Egyptian cross mystery
Queen, Ellery
Ellery Queen series (5)
Egyptian miracle
Schwaller de Lubicz, Isha
Homo sapiens series (2)
Egyptian nights
Mann, Jack
Rex Coulson series (3)
Egyptian scarab mystery
Adams, Andy
Biff Brewster series (9)
Egypt's choice
Broun, Daniel
Harry Egypt series (2)
Eich way to die
Evans, Kenneth
Crispin Tyler series (1)
Eiffel target
Vincent, John
James Bond junior series (2)
Eiger sanction
Trevanian
Jonathan Hemlock series (1)
Eight black horses
McBain, Ed
Eighty Seventh Precinct series (38)
Eight card Stud
Carter, Nick
Nick Carter series (139)
Eight children and a bulldozer
Vestly, Anna Catharina
Eight children series (5)
Eight children and a truck
Vestly, Anna Catharina
Eight children series (1)
Eight children and Rosie
Vestly, Anna Catharina
Eight children series (4)
Eight children in the house
Vestly, Anna Catharina
Eight children series (2)
Eight children in winter
Vestly, Anna Catharina
Eight children series (3)
Eight cousins
Alcott, Louisa May
Rose Campbell series (1)
Eight crooked trenches
Beeding, Francis
Colonel Alastair Granby series (9)
Eight days a week
Duplechan, Larry
Johnnie Ray Rousseau series (1)
Eight days at Guara
Farrell, Anne
Mitchell family series (3)
Eight defiant men
Grover, Marshall
Larry and Stretch series (189)
Eight faces at three
Rice, Craig
John Joseph Malone series (1)
Eight famous engines
Awdry, Wilbert
Railway series (12)
Eight hundred and thirteen
Leblanc, Maurice
Arsene Lupin series (4)
Eight hundred leagues on the Amazon
Verne, Jules
Giant raft series (1)
Eight million ways to die
Block, Lawrence
Matthew Scudder series (6)
Eight murders in the suburbs
Vickers, Roy
Inspector George Rason series (3)
Inspector Peter Curwen and Hugh Stanton series (5)
Eight-oared victors
Chadwick, Lester
College sports series (6)
Eight o'clock alibi
Bush, Christopher
Ludovic Travers series (16)
Eight o'clock tales
Blyton, Enid
Evening tales series (4)
Eight of swords
Carr, John Dickson
Doctor Gideon Fell series (4)
Eight-pointed star
Teed, George Hamilton
Sexton Blake series (310)
Eight skilled gentlemen
Hughart, Barry
Master Li Kao and Number Ten Ox series (3)
Eight stories from The rest of the robots
Asimov, Isaac
Robot series (4)
Eight strokes of the clock
Leblanc, Maurice
Arsene Lupin series (10)
Eight tales of Mister Pengachoosa
Rush, Caroline
Mister Pengachoosa series (2)
Eight ten from Verdugo
Grover, Marshall
Larry and Stretch series (180)
Eight three five
Soutar, Andrew
Phineas Spinnet series (3)
Eight to nine
Montgomery, Elizabeth
Dick, Jane and Sally series (13)
Walling, Robert Alfred John
Philip Tolefree series (5)
Eighteen and on her own
Richardson, Arleta
Growing up series (2)
Eighteen hundred and five
Woodman, Richard
Nathaniel Drinkwater series (6)
Eighteen seventy six
Vidal, Gore
Washington series (3)
Eighteen wheel adventure
Johnstone, William Wallace
Rig warrior series (3)
Eighteenth century clothing
Kalman, Bobbie
Historic communities series (9)
Eighth big Monster book
Blance, Ellen
Monster series (27)
Eighth Brer Rabbit book
Blyton, Enid
Brer Rabbit series (8)
Eighth champion of Christendom
Pargeter, Edith
Eighth champion of Christendom trilogy (1)
Eighth commandment
Sanders, Lawrence
Ten commandments series (3)
Eighth grade hero?
Kenyon, Kate
Cedar Groves Junior High School series (6)
Eighth grade to the rescue
Adorjan, Carol
Junior High series (1)
Kenyon, Kate
Cedar Groves Junior High School series (5)
Eighth millionaire
Teed, George Hamilton
Sexton Blake series (547)
Eighth rank
Ross, David D
Dreamers of the day series (2)
Eighty four Charing Cross Road
Hanff, Helene
American in London series (1)
Eighty million eyes
McBain, Ed
Eighty Seventh Precinct series (21)
Eighty north
Barren, Charles
Stemson family series (1)
Eighty-seven
Pansy
Chautauqua series (3)
Eildon tree
Dickinson, William Croft
Donald and Jean series (2)
Eileen at Redstone Farm
Lunt, Alice
Redstone Farm series (1)
Einstein Anderson goes to bat
Simon, Seymour
Einstein Anderson series (5)
Einstein Anderson lights up the sky
Simon, Seymour
Einstein Anderson series (6)
Einstein Anderson makes up for lost time
Simon, Seymour
Einstein Anderson series (3)
Einstein Anderson, science sleuth
Simon, Seymour
Einstein Anderson series (1)
Einstein Anderson sees through the invisible man
Simon, Seymour
Einstein Anderson series (7)
Einstein Anderson shocks his friends
Simon, Seymour
Einstein Anderson series (2)
Einstein Anderson tells a comet's tale
Simon, Seymour
Einstein Anderson series (4)
Eisenbart mystery
Pilkington, Roger
Branxome family series (7)
Eisenhower deception
Egleton, Clive
Charles Winter series (1)
Eisenhower, soldier and President
Ambrose, Stephen Edward
Eisenhower series (2)
Eisenhower, soldier, general of the army, president-elect, 1890-1952
Ambrose, Stephen Edward
Eisenhower series (1)
Eisenhower, the President
Ambrose, Stephen Edward
Eisenhower series (2)
El Capitan's enemies
Grover, Marshall
Larry and Stretch series (226)
El Dorado adventure
Alexander, Lloyd
Vesper Holly series (2)
El Gringo
Masterson, Louis
Morgan Kane series (38)
El Gringo's revenge
Masterson, Louis
Morgan Kane series (39)
El Lazo
Martin, Larry Jay
John Clinton Ryan series (1)
El Paso
Mitchum, Hank
Stage coach station series (23)
El Paso Del Norte
Richmond, Roe
Lashtrow series (8)
El Paso salt war
Roberts, J R
Gunsmith series (39)
El Segundo
Blackburn, Thomas Wakefield
Stanton Empire series (3)
El Sombra
Mann, Edward Beverly
Whistler series (2)
Elbow room
Miller, Hugh
Eastenders series (12)
Elburg collection
Oliver, Anthony
Lizzie Thomas and Inspector John Webber series (3)
Eldest son
Marshall, Archibald
Clinton series (6)
Willard, Barbara
Mantlemass series (7)
Eldorado
Orczy, Emmuska
Scarlet Pimpernel series (9)
Eleanor and Franklin
Lash, Joseph P
Eleanor Roosevelt series (1)
Eleanor, the years alone
Lash, Joseph P
Eleanor Roosevelt series (2)
Eleanora Mousie catches cold
Morris, Ann
Eleanora Mousie series (1)
Eleanora Mousie in the dark
Morris, Ann
Eleanora Mousie series (4)
Eleanora Mousie makes a mess
Morris, Ann
Eleanora Mousie series (3)
Eleanora Mousie's gray day
Morris, Ann
Eleanora Mousie series (2)
Eleanor's visit
Mathews, Joanna Hooe
Miss Ashton's girls series (4)
Elected silence
Merton, Thomas
Elected silence series (1)
Election booth murder
Propper, Milton
Tommy Rankin series (7)
Election by murder
Eichler, Alfred
Martin Ames series (3)
Electra
Treece, Henry
Greek trilogy (3)

Electric city
Beck, Kathrine Kristine
Jane Da Silva series (3)

Electric sword swallowers
Bulmer, Kenneth
Swords series (2)

Electrics come to Clachan
Armstrong, Sybil
Clachan series (4)

Electromagnetic spectrum, key to the universe
Branley, Franklyn Mansfield
Exploring our universe series (8)

Electronic hurricane
McEvoy, Seth
Arcade explorers series (3)

Electronic mind reader
Blaine, John
Rick Brant series (12)

Elegant Edwardian
Bloom, Ursula
Elegant Edwardian series (2)

Elegant journey
Selby, John
Trace family trilogy (1)

Elegant Patty
Treadgold, Mary
Patty series (1)

Elegy in a country graveyard
Peterson, Audrey
Jane Winfield and Andrew Quentin series (5)

Element of doubt
Simpson, Dorothy
Inspector Luke Thanet series (7)

Elephant
Postgate, Oliver
Ivor the engine series (4)

Elephant adventure
Price, Willard
Hal and Roger Hunt series (7)

Elephant and Mouse celebrate Halloween
Grambling, Lois Goodwin
Elephant and mouse series (3)

Elephant and Mouse get ready for Christmas
Grambling, Lois Goodwin
Elephant and mouse series (1)

Elephant and Mouse get ready for Easter
Grambling, Lois Goodwin
Elephant and mouse series (2)

Elephant and the scrub forest
Taylor, Dave
Animals and their ecosystems series (2)

Elephant came to breakfast
Wood, Amanda Jane
Look twice series (2)

Elephant cat
Bayley, Nicola
Copycats series (2)

Elephant god
Casserly, Gordon
Jungle series (1)

Elephant herds and rhino horns
Torgersen, Don Arthur
Animal safari nature series (1)

Elephant song
Longyear, Barry Brookes
Circus trilogy (3)

Elephant twins
Hogan, Inez
Twins series (2)

Elephant War
Avery, Gillian
Smith family series (4)

Elephants arrive at half-past five
Chase, Ilka
Travel series (2)

Elephants at work
Salmon, Michael
Animal antics series (4)

Elephants can remember
Christie, Agatha
Hercule Poirot series (36)
Mrs Ariadne Oliver series (8)

Elephant's cold
Thurman, Mark
Elephant series (1)

Elephants' graveyard
McQuillan, Karin
Jazz Jasper series (2)

Elephant's new bicycle
Thurman, Mark
Elephant series (2)

Elephants son't sit on cars
Wilson, David Henry
Jeremy James series (1)

Eleusinia
Lytton, Edward George Earle Lytton Bulwer-Lytton
Eleusinia series (2)

Elevated railroad mystery, and other stories
Carter, Nicholas
Nicholas Carter series (59)

Elevator
Mallett, Jerry J
Tumtwit series (6)

Eleven bullets for Mohammed
Arvay, Harry
Israeli Security Branch series (1)

Eleven crystals
Johnson, Oliver
Dragon warriors series (3)

Eleven Edward Street
Boylan, Clare
Nan and Mary Cantwell series (2)

Eleven kids, one summer
Martin, Ann Matthews
Kids series (2)

Eleven of diamonds
Kendrick, Baynard
Miles Standish Rice series (1)

Eleven were brave
Beeding, Francis
Colonel Alastair Granby series (15)

Eleven years' tyranny
Birt, David
Stuarts series (3)

Eleventh hour
Cochran, Molly
Destroyer series (70)
Fletcher, Joseph Smith
Ronald Camberwell series (10)
Murphy, Warren Burton
Destroyer series (70)
Murray, William
Destroyer series (70)

Elf defense
Friesner, Esther Mona
New York trilogy (2)

Elf Queen of Shannara
Brooks, Terry
Heritage of Shannara series (3)

Elfin ship
Blaylock, James Paul
Jonathan Bing series (1)

Elfquest
Pini, Wendy
Elfquest series (1)

Elfreda
Leslie, Emma
Leofwine series (2)

Elfshadow
Cunningham, Elaine
Harpers series (2)

Elfstones of Shannara
Brooks, Terry
Shannara series (2)

Elgar on the journey to Hanley
Alldritt, Keith
Black country series (3)

Elgar variations
Kenyon, Michael
Inspector Henry Peckover series (2)
Superintendent O'Malley series (6)

Eligible bachelor
Pakington, Humphrey
Warmstry series (3)

Elimination
Marquis, Max
Harry Timberlake series (3)

Elimination process
Joyce, Cyril
Chief Superintendent Pat Stockton series (2)

Eliminator
York, Andrew
Jonas Wilde series (1)

Elinore Colhouse
Hudson, Stephen
Kurt series (2)

Eliot's early years
Gordon, Lyndall
T.S.Eliot series (1)

Eliot's new life
Gordon, Lyndall
T.S.Eliot series (2)

Elisabeth and the marsh mystery
Holman, Felice
Elisabeth series (3)

Elisabeth, the bird watcher
Holman, Felice
Elisabeth series (1)

Elisabeth, the treasure hunter
Holman, Felice
Elisabeth series (2)

Elixir of life
Dumas, Alexandre
Memoirs of a physician series (2)

Elixir of long life
Balzac, Honore de
Philosophic studies series (17)

Eliza
Pain, Barry
Eliza series (1)

Eliza getting on
Pain, Barry
Eliza series (3)

Elizabeth
Roberts, Willo Davis
Sunfire series (3)
Seger, Maura
Calvert trilogy (2)
Troyat, Henri
Seed and the fruit series (3)

Elizabeth and her court
Birt, David
Tudors series (5)

Elizabeth and her German garden
Russell, Mary Annette
Elizabeth series (1)

Elizabeth and Jessica run away
Pascal, Francine
Sweet Valley kids series (31)

Elizabeth and the Prince of Spain
Irwin, Margaret
Elizabeth I series (3)

Elizabeth and the tattletale
Pascal, Francine
Sweet Valley kids series (47)

Elizabeth Ann
Bradburne, Elizabeth Sutton
Elizabeth Ann series (1)

Elizabeth Ann again
Bradburne, Elizabeth Sutton
Elizabeth Ann series (3)

Elizabeth Ann and Doris
Lawrence, Josephine
Elizabeth Ann series (4)

Elizabeth Ann and her friends
Bradburne, Elizabeth Sutton
Elizabeth Ann series (4)

Elizabeth Ann and Uncle Doctor
Lawrence, Josephine
Elizabeth Ann series (7)

Elizabeth Ann at Maple Spring
Lawrence, Josephine
Elizabeth Ann series (2)

Elizabeth Ann's borrowed grandma
Lawrence, Josephine
Elizabeth Ann series (5)

Elizabeth Ann's houseboat
Lawrence, Josephine
Elizabeth Ann series (8)

Elizabeth Ann's six cousins
Lawrence, Josephine
Elizabeth Ann series (3)

Elizabeth Ann's spring vacation
Lawrence, Josephine
Elizabeth Ann series (6)

Elizabeth betrayed
Pascal, Francine
Sweet Valley High series (89)

Elizabeth, captive princess
Irwin, Margaret
Elizabeth I series (2)

Elizabeth finds the body
Kilpatrick, Florence Antoinette
Elizabeth series (9)

Elizabeth Fytton of Gawsworth
Howard, Liz
Elizabeth Fytton series (1)

Elizabeth Gail and double trouble
Stahl, Hilda
Elizabeth Gail series (11)

Elizabeth Gail and the dangerous double
Stahl, Hilda
Elizabeth Gail series (4)

Elizabeth Gail and the frightened runaways
Stahl, Hilda
Elizabeth Gail series (8)

Elizabeth Gail and the great canoe conspiracy
Stahl, Hilda
Elizabeth Gail series (19)

Elizabeth Gail and the handsome stranger
Stahl, Hilda
Elizabeth Gail series (15)

Elizabeth Gail and the hidden key mystery
Stahl, Hilda
Elizabeth Gail series (20)

Elizabeth Gail and the holiday mystery
Stahl, Hilda
Elizabeth Gail series (12)

Elizabeth Gail and the missing love letters
Stahl, Hilda
Elizabeth Gail series (13)

Elizabeth Gail and the music camp romance
Stahl, Hilda
Elizabeth Gail series (14)

Elizabeth Gail and the secret box
Stahl, Hilda
Elizabeth Gail series (2)

Elizabeth Gail and the secret love
Stahl, Hilda
Elizabeth Gail series (16)

Elizabeth Gail and the secret of the gold charm
Stahl, Hilda
Elizabeth Gail series (21)

Elizabeth Gail and the silent piano
Stahl, Hilda
Elizabeth Gail series (10)

Elizabeth Gail and the strange birthday party
Stahl, Hilda
Elizabeth Gail series (6)

Elizabeth Gail and the summer for weddings
Stahl, Hilda
Elizabeth Gail series (17)

Elizabeth Gail and the Teddy Bear mystery
Stahl, Hilda
Elizabeth Gail series (3)

Elizabeth Gail and the terrifying news
Stahl, Hilda
Elizabeth Gail series (7)

Elizabeth Gail and the time for love
Stahl, Hilda
Elizabeth Gail series (18)

Elizabeth Gail and the trouble at Sandhill Ranch
Stahl, Hilda
Elizabeth Gail series (5)

Elizabeth Gail and the trouble from the past
Stahl, Hilda
Elizabeth Gail series (9)

Elizabeth Gail at the Johnson Farm
Stahl, Hilda
Elizabeth Gail series (1)

Elizabeth Glen, M.B.
Swan, Annie Shepherd
Elizabeth Glen series (1)

Elizabeth, her folks
Kay, Barbara
Elizabeth, her books series (1)

Elizabeth, her friends
Kay, Barbara
Elizabeth, her books series (2)

Elizabeth I and her parliaments, 1558-1581
Neale, John Ernest
Elizabethan England trilogy (2)

Elizabeth I and her parliaments, 1584-1601
Neale, John Ernest
Elizabethan England trilogy (3)

Elizabeth in Africa
Kilpatrick, Florence Antoinette
Elizabeth series (5)

Elizabeth in retreat
Westrup, Margaret
Elizabeth series (2)

Elizabeth in wartime
Kilpatrick, Florence Antoinette
Elizabeth series (6)

Elizabeth meets her hero
Pascal, Francine
Sweet Valley kids series (28)

Elizabeth R.I.P.
Lees, Dan
Jeff Plummer series (4)

Elizabeth Regina
Plowden, Alison
Elizabeth I series (4)

Elizabeth the hero
Pascal, Francine
Sweet Valley twins series (74)

Elizabeth the impossible
Pascal, Francine
Sweet Valley twins series (51)

Elizabeth the sleuth
Kilpatrick, Florence Antoinette
Elizabeth series (8)

Elizabeth to the rescue
Kilpatrick, Florence Antoinette
Elizabeth series (7)

Elizabeth visits America
Glyn, Elinor
Elizabeth series (2)

Elizabethan House of Commons
Neale, John Ernest
Elizabethan England trilogy (1)

Elizabethan theatre
Birt, David
Tudors series (9)

Elizabeth's broken arm
Pascal, Francine
Sweet Valley kids series (35)

Elizabeth's children
Westrup, Margaret
Elizabeth series (1)

Elizabeth's daughter
Glyn, Elinor
Elizabeth series (2)

Elizabeth's first kiss
Pascal, Francine
Sweet Valley twins series (43)

Elizabeth's new hero
Pascal, Francine
Sweet Valley twins series (33)

Elizabeth's piano lessons
Pascal, Francine
Sweet Valley kids series (45)

Elizabeth's story
Graham, Winston
Poldark series (2)

Elizabeth's super-selling lemonade
Pascal, Francine
Sweet Valley kids series (9)

Elizabeth's valentine
Pascal, Francine
Sweet Valley kids series (4)

Elizabeth's video fever
Pascal, Francine
Sweet Valley kids series (36)

Eliza's daughter
Aiken, Joan
Eliza Brandon series (2)

Eliza's galiardo
Gollin, James
Antigua Players series (2)

Eliza's husband
Pain, Barry
Eliza series (2)

Eliza's son
Pain, Barry
Eliza series (5)

Elk and the evidence
Scherf, Margaret
Reverend Martin Buell series (3)

Elk-dog heritage
Coldsmith, Don
Spanish bit series (3)

Elkhorn Tavern
Jones, Douglas Clyde
Hasford family series (1)

Ella
Aimwell, Walter
Boy series (3)

Ella at the Wells
Hill, Lorna
Sadler's Wells series (6)

Ella of all-of-a-kind family
Taylor, Sydney
All-of-a-kind family series (5)

Ella of Berry Farm
Adams, Agnes
Shepton children trilogy (3)

Ellen and the Queen
Avery, Gillian
Ellen Timms series (2)

Ellen Grae
Cleaver, Vera
Ellen Grae series (1)

Ellen is home alone
Pascal, Francine
Sweet Valley kids series (39)

Ellen Linn
Abbott, Jacob
Franconia series (7)

Ellen Montgomery's bookshelf
Wetherell, Elizabeth
Ellen Montgomery series (2)

Ellen's birthday
Avery, Gillian
Ellen Timms series (1)

Ellerby case
Rhode, John
Doctor Lancelot Priestley series (3)

Ellery Queen, master detective
Queen, Ellery
Ellery Queen series (18)

Ellery Queen's big book
Queen, Ellery
Ellery Queen series (44)

Ellery Queen's mystery parade
Queen, Ellery
Ellery Queen series (44)

Elli of the Northland
Ruthin, Margaret
Elli Sari series (1)

Ellie
Borntrager, Mary Christner
Ellie's people series (1)

Elluvon gift
Lang, Simon
Skipjack series (2)

Elm tree murder
Rhode, John
Doctor Lancelot Priestley series (31)

Elm-tree on the wall
France, Anatole
Contemporary history series (2)

Elmer
McKee, David
Elmer series (1)

Elmer again and again
McKee, David
Elmer series (2)

Elmer and the dragon
Gannett, Ruth Stiles
Dragon series (2)

Elmer makes a break
Cook, Patrick
Elmer the rat series (2)

Elmer rides the rails
Cook, Patrick
Elmer the rat series (4)

Elmer runs wild
Cook, Patrick
Elmer the rat series (3)

Elmer the rat
Cook, Patrick
Elmer the rat series (1)

Elminster
Greenwood, Ed
Avatar trilogy (3)

Elmo the pig
Kanno, Wendy
Funny Farm series (4)

Eloise
Thompson, Kay
Eloise series (1)
Tubb, Edwin Charles
Dumarest series (13)

Eloise at Christmastime
Thompson, Kay
Eloise series (3)

Eloise in Moscow
Thompson, Kay
Eloise series (4)

Eloise in Paris
Thompson, Kay
Eloise series (2)

Elope to death
Ashe, Gordon
Patrick Dawlish series (35)

Elopement
Brunner, Ethel
Celia series (2)

Elric at the end of time
Moorcock, Michael
Elric series (6)

Elric of Melnibone
Moorcock, Michael
Elric series (1)

Elric saga
Moorcock, Michael
Elric series (3)
Elric series (6)

Elsa and her cubs
Adamson, Joy
Elsa series (4)

Elsa in the night
Virin, Anna
Elsa series (3)

Elsa tidies her house
Virin, Anna
Elsa series (1)

Elsa's bears
Virin, Anna
Elsa series (2)

Elsa's bears in the playground
Virin, Anna
Elsa series (5)

Elsa's bears learn to paint
Virin, Anna
Elsa series (6)

Elsa's bears need the doctor
Virin, Anna
Elsa series (4)

Elsewhere
Windling, Terri
Elsewhere trilogy (1)

Elsewhere and the gathering of the clowns
Roose-Evans, James
Odd and Elsewhere series (4)

Elsewhere II
Windling, Terri
Elsewhere trilogy (2)

Elsewhere III
Windling, Terri
Elsewhere trilogy (3)

Elsie and her loved ones
Finley, Martha Farquharson
Elsie Dinsmore series (27)

Elsie and her namesakes
Finley, Martha Farquharson
Elsie Dinsmore series (28)

Elsie and the child
Bennett, Arnold
Elsie series (2)

Elsie and the Raymonds
Finley, Martha Farquharson
Elsie Dinsmore series (15)

Elsie at home
Finley, Martha Farquharson
Elsie Dinsmore series (22)

Elsie at Ion
Finley, Martha Farquharson
Elsie Dinsmore series (19)

Elsie at Nantucket
Finley, Martha Farquharson
Elsie Dinsmore series (10)

Elsie at the World's Fair
Finley, Martha Farquharson
Elsie Dinsmore series (20)

Elsie at Viamede
Finley, Martha Farquharson
Elsie Dinsmore series (18)

Elsie Dinsmore
Finley, Martha Farquharson
Elsie Dinsmore series (1)

Elsie in the South
Finley, Martha Farquharson
Elsie Dinsmore series (24)

Elsie Lindtner
Michaelis, Karin
Elsie Lindtner series (2)

Elsie on the Hudson and elsewhere
Finley, Martha Farquharson
Elsie Dinsmore series (23)

Elsie Tanner fights back
Kershaw, H V
Coronation Street series (3)

Elsie Venner
Holmes, Oliver Wendell
Heredity series (1)

Elsie yachting with the Raymonds
Finley, Martha Farquharson
Elsie Dinsmore series (16)

Elsie's children
Finley, Martha Farquharson
Elsie Dinsmore series (6)

Elsie's friends at Woodburn
Finley, Martha Farquharson
Elsie Dinsmore series (13)

Elsie's girlhood
Finley, Martha Farquharson
Elsie Dinsmore series (3)

Elsie's holiday and Roselands
Finley, Martha Farquharson
Roselands series (1)

Elsie's holidays at Roselands
Finley, Martha Farquharson
Elsie Dinsmore series (2)

Elsie's journey on inland waters
Finley, Martha Farquharson
Elsie Dinsmore series (21)

Elsie's kith and kin
Finley, Martha Farquharson
Elsie Dinsmore series (12)

Elsie's motherhood
Finley, Martha Farquharson
Elsie Dinsmore series (5)

Elsie's new relations
Finley, Martha Farquharson
Elsie Dinsmore series (9)

Elsie's Santa Claus
Mathews, Joanna Hooe
Miss Ashton's girls series (6)

Elsie's vacation and after events
Finley, Martha Farquharson
Elsie Dinsmore series (17)

Elsie's widowhood
Finley, Martha Farquharson
Elsie Dinsmore series (7)

Elsie's winter trip
Finley, Martha Farquharson
Elsie Dinsmore series (26)

Elsie's womanhood
Finley, Martha Farquharson
Elsie Dinsmore series (4)

Elsie's young folks in peace and war
Finley, Martha Farquharson
Elsie Dinsmore series (25)

Elusive bowman
Vivian, Francis
Inspector Gordon Knollis series (9)

Elusive Ellshaw
Charteris, Leslie
Saint series (14)

Elusive epicure
Keith, Carlton
Jeff Green series (4)

Elusive Grasshopper
Saville, Malcolm
Lone Pine Five Club series (6)

Elusive heiress
Keene, Carolyn
Nancy Drew series (68)

Elusive killer
Plummer, Thomas Arthur
Detective Inspector Andrew Frampton series (46)

Elusive knave
Carter, Nicholas
Nicholas Carter series (358)

Elusive Monsieur Drago
Jacobs, Thomas Curtis Hicks
Mike Seton series (2)

Elusive Mrs Pollifax
Gilman, Dorothy
Mrs Emily Pollifax series (3)

Elusive Picaroon
Cassells, John
Ludovic Saxon series (14)
Landon, Herman
Picaroon series (1)

Elusive Pimpernel
Orczy, Emmuska
Scarlet Pimpernel series (7)

Elusive Vicky Van
Wells, Carolyn
Fleming Stone series (9)

Elven star
Weis, Margaret
Death Gate series (2)

Elves and the otterskin
Boyer, Elizabeth H
World of the Alfar series (2)

Elvis and his friends
Gripe, Maria
Elvis Karlsson series (3)

Elvis and his secret
Gripe, Maria
Elvis Karlsson series (2)

Elvis, Jesus and Coca Cola
Friedman, Kinky
Kinky Friedman series (6)

Elvis murders
Bourgeau, Art
Claude Kirlin and F T Zevich series (3)

Elysia
Lumley, Brian
Cthulhu Mythos series (16)

Em
Southworth, Emma Dorothy Eliza Nevitte
Em series (1)

Emanuel and his parrot
Craig, Christine
Emanuel series (1)

Emanuel goes to market
Craig, Christine
Emanuel series (2)

Embankment crime
Stuart, Donald
Sexton Blake series (723)

Embarrassed ladies affair
Catalan, Henri
Soeur Angele series (1)

Embarrassed murderer
Stockwell, Gail
Kingsley Toplitt series (2)

Embassy detective
Graydon, William Murray
Sexton Blake series (37)

Embassy murders
Grant, Maxwell
Shadow series (45)

Embers
Fritch, Elizabeth
Richmond series (3)

Embers of hate
Jones, Bradshaw
Claude Ravel series (6)

Embers of the heart
Bittner, F Rosanne
Montana woman series (2)

Embrace the wild land
Bittner, F Rosanne
Savage destiny series (4)

Embrace the wolf
Schutz, Benjamin Merrill
Leo Haggerty series (2)

Embryo
Laurance, Andrew
Nostradamus trilogy (3)

Emerald Canyon
Clinton, Jeff
Emerald Canyon series (1)

Emerald chicks caper
Roper, Lester V
Jerry Roe series (2)

Emerald City of Oz
Baum, Lyman Frank
Oz series (6)

Emerald elephant gambit
Maddock, Larry
Hannibal Fortune and Webley series (3)

Emerald embassy
Gerard, Francis
Sir John Meredith series (11)

Emerald enchanter
Dever, Joe
Combat heroes series (3)
Emerald enchanter series (1)

Emerald-eyed cat mystery
Keene, Carolyn
Nancy Drew series (75)

Emerald eyes
Moran, Daniel Keys
Tales of the continuing time series (1)

Emerald murder trap
Gregory, Jackson
Paul Savoy series (3)

Emerald oil caper
Lawrence, James D
Angela Harpe series (2)

Emerald Peacock
Gordon, Katharine
Peacock series (1)

Emerald sea
Dengler, Sandy
Heroes of the misty isle series (3)

Emerald spider
Holt, Gavin
Professor Luther Bastion series (16)

Emerald valley
Tanner, Janet
Hillsbridge series (2)

Emergency
Barclay, Virginia
Mid-City Hospital series (1)
Sutton, Jessica
Bel Air General series (11)

Emergency call
Harrison, Elizabeth
Central London Hospital series (4)
Jennings, D K
Doctor Ralph Conway series (4)

Emergency entrance
Hirschfeld, Burt
General Hospital series (2)

Emergency exit
Carmichael, Harry
John Piper and Quinn series (11)
Cronin, Michael
James Hellier series (3)
Wynne, Anthony
Doctor Eustace Hailey series (26)

Emergency in the Pyrenees
Bridge, Ann
Julia Probyn series (6)

Emerson challenge
Grover, Marshall
Larry and Stretch series (61)

Emerson's hex
Grover, Marshall
Larry and Stretch series (272)

Emerson's hideout
Grover, Marshall
Larry and Stretch series (309)

Emigrants
Lamming, George
Caribbean series (2)
Moberg, Vilhelm
Emigrants series (1)

Emil and his clever pig
Lindgren, Astrid
Emil series (3)

Emil and Lina's bad tooth
Lindgren, Astrid
Emil series (5)

Emil and piggy beast
Lindgren, Astrid
Emil series (3)

Emil and the detectives
Kastner, Erich
Emil series (1)

Emil and the three twins
Kastner, Erich
Emil series (2)

Emil in the soup tureen
Lindgren, Astrid
Emil series (1)

Emile and the Dutchman
Rosenberg, Joel
Metzada series (2)

Emilia in England
Meredith, George
Sandra Belloni series (1)

Emilia's inheritance
Worboise, Emma Jane
Mister Montmorency series (2)

Emil's pranks
Lindgren, Astrid
Emil series (2)

Emily
Ransom, Candice Farris
Sunfire series (11)
Smith, Emma
Emily series (1)

Emily climbs
Montgomery, Lucy Maud
Emily Starr trilogy (2)

Emily Davis
Read, *Miss*
Fairacre series (8)

Emily Dickinson is dead
Langton, Jane
Homer Kelly series (5)

Emily Eyefinger
Ball, Duncan
Emily Eyefinger series (1)

Emily Eyefinger, secret agent
Ball, Duncan
Emily Eyefinger series (2)

Emily goes to Exeter
Chesney, Marion
Travelling matchmaker series (1)

Emily in Arlington Street
Leslie, Henrietta
Arlington Street trilogy (1)

Emily in waiting
Starling, Jill
Alice and Emily series (2)

Emily of Deep Valley
Lovelace, Maud Hart
Betsy Ray series (10)

Emily of New Moon
Montgomery, Lucy Maud
Emily Starr trilogy (1)

Emily the goat
Pilgrim, Jane
Blackberry Farm series (1)

Emily, the travelling guinea pig
Smith, Emma
Emily series (1)

Emily's quest
Montgomery, Lucy Maud
Emily Starr trilogy (3)

Emily's voyage
Smith, Emma
Emily series (2)

Eminence
Kienzle, William Xavier
Father Robert Koesler series (11)

Emlyn
Williams, Emlyn
George Emlyn series (2)

Emlyn's moon
Nimmo, Jenny
Snow spider trilogy (2)

Emma
Austen, Jane
Miss Jane Fairfax series (1)
Stevenson, James
Emma series (2)

Emma and Co.
Hocken, Sheila
Emma series (4)

Emma and I
Hocken, Sheila
Emma series (1)

Emma and the doctor
Wolde, Gunilla
Emma series (10)

Emma and the measles
Wolde, Gunilla
Emma series (3)

Emma and the vacuum cleaner
Wolde, Gunilla
Emma series (6)

Emma Apple
Reed, Giles
Munch Bunch character series (11)

Emma Apple's late birthday party
Reed, Giles
Munch Bunch story books series (12)

Emma at the beach
Stevenson, James
Emma series (4)

Emma Chizzit and the mother lode marauder
Hall, Mary Bowen
Emma Chizzit series (4)

Emma Chizzit and the NAPA nemesis
Hall, Mary Bowen
Emma Chizzit series (3)

Emma Chizzit and the Queen Anne killer
Hall, Mary Bowen
Emma Chizzit series (1)

Emma Chizzit and the Sacramento stalker
Hall, Mary Bowen
Emma Chizzit series (2)
Emma enjoys nursery school
Wolde, Gunilla
Emma series (8)
Emma expects
Foxell, Nigel
Emma Hamilton series (2)
Emma goes to the dentist
Wolde, Gunilla
Emma series (4)
Emma in love
Arundel, Honor
Emma series (3)
Emma in winter
Farmer, Penelope
Charlotte and Emma Makepeace series (2)
Emma McChesney and Co
Ferber, Edna
Emma McChesney series (3)
Emma quite contrary
Wolde, Gunilla
Emma series (2)
Emma, V.I.P.
Hocken, Sheila
Emma series (2)
Emmanuel
Pontoppidan, Henrik
Emmanuel trilogy (1)
Emmanuelle
Arsan, Emmanuelle
Emmanuelle series (1)
Emmanuelle II
Arsan, Emmanuelle
Emmanuelle series (3)
Emma's baby brother
Wolde, Gunilla
Emma series (1)
Emma's first day at nursery school
Wolde, Gunilla
Emma series (7)
Emma's glory
Hocken, Sheila
Emma series (3)
Emma's holiday
McPhail, David Michael
Emma series (3)
Emma's island
Arundel, Honor
Emma series (2)
Emma's pet
McPhail, David Michael
Emma series (2)
Emma's vacation
McPhail, David Michael
Emma series (3)
Emma's workshop
Wolde, Gunilla
Emma series (9)
Emmerdale Farm
Ferguson, James
Emmerdale Farm series (23)
Emmerdale Farm book of country love
Ferguson, James
Emmerdale Farm series (23)
Emmett's pig
Stolz, Mary
Emmett series (1)
Emmy keeps a promise
Chastain, Madye Lee
Lisa and Emmy and Dodie series (2)
Emmy Lou, her book and heart
Martin, George Madden
Emmy Lou series (1)
Emmy Lou's road to grace
Martin, George Madden
Emmy Lou series (2)
Emoke
Skvorecky, Josef
Danny Smiricky series (4)
Emotional journey
Maxwell, William Babington
Men and women trilogy (2)
Emperor
Byrne, Stuart James
Star Man series (2)
Harrod-Eagles, Cynthia
Morland family series (11)
Payne, Robert
Emperor Shah Jahan series (2)
Emperor and clown
Duncan, Dave
Man of his word series (4)
Emperor and the monster
Voltz, William
Perry Rhodan series (107)
Emperor for the legion
Turtledove, Harry
Videssos series (2)
Emperor Fu-Manchu
Rohmer, Sax
Fu-Manchu series (14)
Emperor of Eridanus
Barbet, Pierre
Eridanus series (2)
Emperor of everything
Aldridge, Ray
Emancipator series (2)
Emperor of evil
Daly, Carroll John
Vee Brown series (2)
Emperor of Mars
Fearn, John Russell
Clayton Drew series (1)
Emperor on ice
Tate, Richard
Marcus Obadiah series (2)
Emperor, swords, pentacles
Gotlieb, Phyllis
Qsaprinel trilogy (2)
Emperor's agent
Gobineau, Marceline
Stephanie series (3)
Emperor's daughter
Hamilton, Julia
Habsburg series (2)
Emperor's pearl
Gulik, Robert van
Judge Dee series (11)
Emperor's pony
Sheldon, Ann
Linda Craig series (9)
Emperor's tomb
Roth, Joseph
Radetzky series (2)
Empery
Kube-McDowell, Michael Paul
Trigon disunity trilogy (3)
Emphyrion
Lawhead, Stephen
Emphyrion series (2)
Empire
Helm, Eric
Super Vietnam series (4)
Vidal, Gore
Washington series (4)
Empire 99
Goulart, Ron
Barnum series (7)
Star Hawks series (1)
Empire builder
Rothweiler, Paul Roger
Westward rails trilogy (3)
Empire builders
Long, William Stuart
Australians series (9)
Empire City
Goodman, Paul
Empire City quartet (4)
Empire city
Goodman, Paul
Empire city series (3)
Empire of blood
Lord, Jeffrey
Richard Blade series (23)
Empire of the Arabs
Glubb, John Bagot
Arab history series (2)
Empire of the atom
Van Vogt, Alfred Elton
Clane series (1)
Empire of the East
Saberhagen, Fred
Chup trilogy (3)
Empire of time
Kilian, Crawford
Chronoplane wars trilogy (1)
Empire strikes back
Glut, Donald Frank
Luke Skywalker series (5)
Weinberg, Larry
Star wars storybook series (2)
Empire strikes back storybook
Steneman, Shep
Star wars storybook series (2)
Empire trail
Cole, Jackson
Jim Hatfield series (15)
Empire's legacy
Swycaffer, Jefferson Putnam
Tales of the Concordat trilogy (1)
Empires of Flux and Anchor
Chalker, Jack Laurence
Soul rider series (2)
Empires of foliage and flower
Wolfe, Gene
Book of the new sun series (5)
Employees
Balzac, Honore de
Scenes of Parisian life series (2)
Empress file
Camp, John
Kidd series (2)
Empress of earth
Scott, Melissa
Silence Leigh trilogy (3)
Empress of outer space
Chandler, Arthur Bertram
Empress of outer space series (1)
Empress unborn
Lorrah, Jean
Savage Empire series (7)
Emprise
Kube-McDowell, Michael Paul
Trigon disunity trilogy (1)
Empty beach
Corris, Peter
Cliff Hardy series (5)
Empty bed
Adams, Herbert
Jimmy Haswell series (4)
Empty copper sea
Macdonald, John Dann
Travis McGee series (17)
Empty field
Pullein-Thompson, Christine
Seashore School of Equitation series (1)
Empty flat
King, Frank
Dormouse series (18)
Empty heart
Ford, Elizabeth
Maplechester series (1)
Empty hours
McBain, Ed
Eighty Seventh Precinct series (15)
Empty house
Gutman, Claude
Empty house trilogy (1)
Empty house murder
Stuart, Donald
Sexton Blake series (773)
Empty mirror
Van de Wetering, Janwillem
Zen series (1)
Empty silence
Copper, Basil
Mike Faraday series (32)
Empty throne
Elliott, Janice
Sword and the dream series (2)
Empty tiger
Catto, Max
Limpie series (2)
Empty tigers
Wilson, Ivor
Gregory Flamm series (4)
Empty valley
Lister, Stephen
Sainte Monique series (10)
Em's husband
Southworth, Emma Dorothy Eliza Nevitte
Em series (2)
En garde
Stackpole, Michael
Warrior trilogy (2)
En route
Huysmans, Joris Karl
Durtal series (2)
Enamored
Palmer, Diana
Mercenary series (3)
Enchanted ark
Beaman, Sydney George Hulme
Toytown series (29)
Enchanted cup
Ainsworth, Patricia
Burnley series (4)
Enchanted island of Oz
Thompson, Ruth Plumly
Oz series (41)
Enchanted islands
Conway, Ainslie
Galapagos series (1)
Enchanted isles
Flynn, Casey
Gods of Ireland series (2)
Macgregor, Alasdair Alpin
Golden lamp trilogy (3)
Enchanted kingdom
Kushner, Ellen
Choose your own adventure series (56)
Enchanted land
Chisholm, Louey
Fairyland tales series (2)
Enchanted places
Milne, Christopher
Enchanted places series (1)
Enchanted typewriter
Bangs, John Kendrick
Associated shades series (3)
Enchanted wood
Blyton, Enid
Faraway tree series (1)
Enchanter compleated
De Camp, Lyon Sprague
Harold Shea series (3)
Enchanters' end game
Eddings, David
Belgariad series (5)
Enchanter's nightshade
Morton, John Bingham
Enchanter's nightshade series (1)
Enchantments of flesh and spirit
Constantine, Storm
Book of Wraeththu series (1)
Enchantress
Yorke, Katherine
Enchantress trilogy (1)
Enchantress from the stars
Engdahl, Sylvia Louise
Elana series (1)
Enchantress of the Nile
Lindsay, Kathleen
Cleopatra series (1)
Enchantress of World's End
Carter, Lin
Gondwane epic series (2)
Enchantress saga
Thorne, Nicola
Enchantress trilogy (3)
Encore
High, Monique Raphel
Gunzberg family series (2)
Nixon, Joan Lowery
Hollywood daughters trilogy (3)
Encore Allain!
Graeme, Bruce
Superintendent William Stevens and Inspector Pierre Allain series (12)
Encore at Dien Bien Phu
Lansing, John
Black Eagles series (13)
Encore, Clotilde
Saint-Laurent, Cecil
Clotilde series (2)
Encore murder
Babson, Marian
Trixie Dolan and Evangeline Sinclair series (2)
Encore the Lone Wolf
Vance, Louis Joseph
Michael Lanyard series (7)
Encounter
Troyat, Henri
Seed and the fruit series (5)
Encounter at Farpoint
Gerrold, David
Star trek, the next generation sequels series (1)
Encounter group
Murphy, Warren Burton
Destroyer series (56)
Encounter near Venus
Wibberley, Leonard
Uncle Bill series (1)
Encounter three
Caidin, Martin
Six Million Dollar Man series (1)
Encyclopaedia of modern murder, 1962-82
Wilson, Colin
Murder series (4)
Encyclopaedia of murder
Wilson, Colin
Murder series (1)
Encyclopaedia of the worlds of Doctor Who
Saunders, David
Doctor Who series (162)
Encyclopedia Brown and the case of the dead eagles
Sobol, Donald J
Encyclopedia Brown series (12)
Encyclopedia Brown and the case of the disgusting sneakers
Sobol, Donald J
Encyclopedia Brown series (18)
Encyclopedia Brown and the case of the exploding plumbing
Sobol, Donald J
Encyclopedia Brown series (19)
Encyclopedia Brown and the case of the midnight visitor
Sobol, Donald J
Encyclopedia Brown series (13)
Encyclopedia Brown and the case of the mysterious handprints
Sobol, Donald J
Encyclopedia Brown series (16)
Encyclopedia Brown and the case of the secret pitch
Sobol, Donald J
Encyclopedia Brown series (2)
Encyclopedia Brown and the case of the treasure hunt
Sobol, Donald J
Encyclopedia Brown series (17)
Encyclopedia Brown and the case of the two spies
Sobol, Donald J
Encyclopedia Brown series (19)
Encyclopedia Brown, boy detective
Sobol, Donald J
Encyclopedia Brown series (1)
Encyclopedia Brown carries on
Sobol, Donald J
Encyclopedia Brown series (14)
Encyclopedia Brown finds the clues
Sobol, Donald J
Encyclopedia Brown series (3)
Encyclopedia Brown gets his man
Sobol, Donald J
Encyclopedia Brown series (4)
Encyclopedia Brown keeps peace
Sobol, Donald J
Encyclopedia Brown series (6)
Encyclopedia Brown lends a hand
Sobol, Donald J
Encyclopedia Brown series (11)
Encyclopedia Brown saves the day
Sobol, Donald J
Encyclopedia Brown series (7)
Encyclopedia Brown sets the pace
Sobol, Donald J
Encyclopedia Brown series (15)
Encyclopedia Brown shows the way
Sobol, Donald J
Encyclopedia Brown series (9)
Encyclopedia Brown solves them all
Sobol, Donald J
Encyclopedia Brown series (5)
Encyclopedia Brown takes the cake
Sobol, Donald J
Encyclopedia Brown series (19)
Encyclopedia Brown takes the case
Sobol, Donald J
Encyclopedia Brown series (10)
Encyclopedia Brown tracks them down
Sobol, Donald J
Encyclopedia Brown series (8)
Encyclopedia Brown's book of strange but true crimes
Sobol, Donald J
Encyclopedia Brown series (19)
Encyclopedia Brown's book of wacky animals
Sobol, Donald J
Encyclopedia Brown's wacky series (4)
Encyclopedia Brown's book of wacky cars
Sobol, Donald J
Encyclopedia Brown's wacky series (6)
Encyclopedia Brown's book of wacky crimes
Sobol, Donald J
Encyclopedia Brown's wacky series (1)
Encyclopedia Brown's book of wacky outdoors
Sobol, Donald J
Encyclopedia Brown's wacky series (5)
Encyclopedia Brown's book of wacky spies
Sobol, Donald J
Encyclopedia Brown's wacky series (2)
Encyclopedia Brown's book of wacky sports
Sobol, Donald J
Encyclopedia Brown's wacky series (3)
Encyclopedia Brown's record book of weird and wonderful facts
Sobol, Donald J
Encyclopedia Brown series (19)
Encyclopedia Brown's second record book of weird and wonderful facts
Sobol, Donald J
Encyclopedia Brown series (19)
Encyclopedia Brown's third record book of weird and wonderful facts
Sobol, Donald J
Encyclopedia Brown series (19)
Encyclopedia Galactica
Kraus, Bruce R
Battlestar Galactica series (14)

Encyclopedia of Star trek
Okuda, Michael
Star trek, the next generation sequels series (7)
Encyclopedia of Xanth
Nye, Jody Lynn
Xanth series (16)
End and a beginning
Duncan, Thomas
Big river, big man series (1)
Hanley, James
Furys chronicle series (5)
End House
Bond, Freda Constance
Lancasters series (1)
End is coming
Ahern, Jerry
Survivalist series (8)
End of a call girl
Gault, William Campbell
Joe Puma series (2)
End of a chapter
Blake, Nicholas
Nigel Strangeways series (12)
End of a childhood, and other stories
Richardson, Henry Handel
Fortunes of Richard Mahony trilogy (3)
End of a good woman
Hinxman, Margaret
Detective Inspector Ralph Brand series (1)
End of a hate
Braddon, Russell
Hate series (2)
End of a JD
Gonzales, John
Harry Horne series (1)
End of a party
Waugh, Hillary
Chief Fred Fellows series (9)
End of a road
Allegro, John Marco
Christian origins series (2)
End of a stripper
Dietrich, Robert
Steve Bentley series (3)
End of all songs
Moorcock, Michael
Dancers at the end of time series (3)
Jherek Carnelian and Amelia Underwood series (3)
End of an ancient mariner
Cole, George Douglas Howard
Superintendent Henry Wilson series (12)
End of an era
Butler, David
We'll meet again series (2)
End of Andrew Harrison
Crofts, Freeman Wills
Inspector Joseph French series (17)
End of bad roads
Balzac, Honore de
Scenes of Parisian life series (8)
End-of-everything man
De Haven, Tom
Chronicles of the king's tramp series (2)
End of evil ways
Balzac, Honore de
Scenes of Parisian life series (8)
End of exile
Bova, Ben
Exiles trilogy (3)
End of illusion
Duhamel, Georges
Salavin series (5)
End of Mister Garment
Starrett, Vincent
Walter Ghost series (3)
End of my career
Franklin, Miles
Sybylla Penelope Melvyn series (2)
End of term
Forest, Antonia
Marlow family series (4)
End of the affair
Peel, John
U.N.C.L.E. files series (3)
End of the battle
Waugh, Evelyn
World War II series (3)
End of the chapter
Galsworthy, John
End of the chapter series (3)
End of the chase
Waye, Cecil
Christopher Perrin series (3)
End of the circle
McKinney, Jack
Robotech series (13)
End of the game
Durrenmatt, Friedrich
Kommissar Hans Barlach series (1)
Murphy, Warren Burton
Destroyer series (60)
Tepper, Sheri S
Jinian trilogy (3)
End of the hours
Thompson, Edward
Indian trilogy (3)
End of the House of Alard
Kaye-Smith, Sheila
Alard family trilogy (3)
End of the imp
Krymov, Vladimir
Imp trilogy (3)
End of the journey
Verne, Jules
Thompson Travel Agency series (2)
End of the line
Brason, John
Secret army series (3)
Busby, Francis Marion
Demu trilogy (3)
Douglas, George
Inspector Bonny Lee series (6)
Fisher, Graham
Mike King series (2)
Hart, Matthew S
Cody's law series (7)
Hitchens, Dolores
John Farrel series (1)
Mason, Dan
Lex Cranshaw series (8)
Ocork, Shannon
T T Baldwin series (3)
End of the matter
Foster, Alan Dean
Flinx of the Commonwealth series (4)
Tar-Aiym Krang trilogy (3)
End of the Mildew Gang
Fowler, Sydney
Inspector Cauldron series (3)
End of the outlaws
Patchett, Mary Elwyn
Ajax series (7)
End of the pier
Grimes, Martha
Inspector Richard Jury series (13)
End of the revolution
Piccard, Eulalie
Episodes of the great Russian tragedy series (5)
End of the rug
Llewellyn, Richard
Edmund Trothe series (1)
End of the running
Evans, Alan
Cragg and Frayne series (1)
End of the Spanish Inquisition
Plaidy, Jean
Spanish Inquisition trilogy (3)
End of the street
Procter, Maurice
Chief Inspector Harry Martineau series (3)
End of the struggle
De Born, Edith
Jimmy Chester trilogy (3)
End of the tracks
Sutton, Stack
Marshal Creed Wetherall series (4)
End of the trail
Field, Peter
Powder Valley series (24)
Giraud, Jean
Lieutenant Mike S Blueberry series (5)
Hardin, J D
Raider series (42)
End of violence
Benson, Ben
Ralph Lindsey series (6)
End on the rocks
Stuart, Ian
David Grierson series (2)
End run
Harding, Ian
Assault troop series (4)
End stage
Hawkey, Raymond
Presidential trilogy (3)
End to perfect
Newton, Suzanne
Arden Gifford series (1)
End zone
James, Laurence
American football series (2)
Endangered desert animals
Taylor, Dave
Endangered animals series (7)
Endangered forest animals
Taylor, Dave
Endangered animals series (2)
Endangered grassland animals
Taylor, Dave
Endangered animals series (1)
Endangered island animals
Taylor, Dave
Endangered animals series (5)
Endangered mountain animals
Taylor, Dave
Endangered animals series (4)
Endangered ocean animals
Taylor, Dave
Endangered animals series (6)
Endangered savannah animals
Taylor, Dave
Endangered animals series (8)
Endangered species
Burns, Rex
Devlin Kirk series (4)
Dixon, Franklin W
Hardy boys case files series (64)
Endangered wetland animals
Taylor, Dave
Endangered animals series (3)
Endeavour, 1962-
Gaulle, Charles de
War memoirs series (4)
Enderby
Burgess, Anthony
Mister Enderby series (2)
Mister Enderby series (3)
Enderby outside
Burgess, Anthony
Mister Enderby series (2)
Enderby's dark lady
Burgess, Anthony
Mister Enderby series (4)
Ender's game
Card, Orson Scott
Ender Wiggins series (1)
Ender's war
Card, Orson Scott
Ender Wiggins series (2)
Endgame
Cherryh, Carolyn Janice
Merovingen nights series (7)
Endings and beginnings
Hardwick, Michael
Upstairs, downstairs series (11)
Endithor's daughter
Smith, David Claude
Red Sonja series (4)
Endless and Company
Ridge, Antonia
Endless and Company series (3)
Endless catacombs
Weis, Margaret
Endless quest series (22)
Endless frontier
Pournelle, Jerry
Endless frontier series (1)
Endless frontier, volume 2
Pournelle, Jerry
Endless frontier series (2)
Endless knot
Lawhead, Stephen
Song of Albion trilogy (3)
Endless orgy
Geis, Richard Erwin
Roi Kunzer series (2)
Endless sky
Davis, Kathryn
Dakotas series (2)
Ends
Dickson, Gordon Rupert
Beginnings and ends series (2)
Ends of the circle
Williams, Paul Osborne
Pelbar series (2)
Endurance racing
Wilkinson, Sylvia
World of racing series (4)
Enduring hills
Giles, Janice Holt
Piney Ridge trilogy (1)
Enemies from beyond
Laumer, Keith
Invaders series (2)
Enemies of the bride
Mills, Osmington
Midset C.I.D. series (4)
Sergeant Patrick Shirley and Inspector Rip Irving series (2)
Enemies within
Lewin, Michael Zinn
Albert Samson series (3)
Enemy
Garfield, Leon
Apprentices series (12)
Enemy agents
Berres, Frances B
Deep-sea adventure series (11)
Enemy at Green Knowe
Boston, Lucy Maria
Green Knowe series (5)
Enemy at home
Trevor, Meriol
Luxembourg series (3)
Enemy from space
Kneale, Nigel
Quatermass series (2)
Enemy in sight!
Kent, Alexander
Captain Richard Bolitho series (11)
Enemy in sight
Macdonnell, James Edmond
Captain Peter Bentley series (5)
Enemy in the blanket
Burgess, Anthony
Malayan trilogy (2)
Richard Emmis series (2)
Enemy in the dark
Mahr, Kurt
Perry Rhodan series (85)
Enemy match
Keene, Carolyn
Nancy Drew series (73)
Enemy mine
Longyear, Barry Brookes
Dracon series (1)
Enemy of man
Janson, Hank
Hank Janson series (76)
Enemy of the state
Wilson, Francis Paul
LaNague Federation trilogy (3)
Enemy seas
Shirreffs, Gordon Donald
Bob Dunbar and Gary Lunt series (3)
Enemy sighted
Hudson, Alec
Submarine series (2)
Enemy unseen
Crofts, Freeman Wills
Inspector Joseph French series (25)
Mitchell, Victoria Estelle
Star trek series (51)
Enemy within
Charles, Steven
Private school series (5)
Creasey, John
Department Z series (26)
Hubbard, Lafayette Ronald
Mission earth series (3)
Streib, Dan
Michael Hawk series (8)
Enemy within the gates
Horler, Sydney
Bunny Chipstead series (4)
Enemy within the skull
Kern, Gregory
Cap Kennedy series (4)
Energy zero
Brandner, Gary
Big Brain series (3)
Enforcer
Cassells, John
Superintendent Flagg series (32)
Sugar, Andrew
Enforcer series (1)
Valley, Mel
Dirty Harry Callahan series (12)
Engagement with death
Ashe, Gordon
Patrick Dawlish series (18)
Engaging Picaroon
Cassells, John
Ludovic Saxon series (5)
Engaging the powers
Wink, Walter Philip
Powers trilogy (3)
Engine and the gun series
Barbary, James
Adventure in history series (2)
Engineer of human souls
Skvorecky, Josef
Danny Smiricky series (5)
England and the English
Ford, Ford Madox
England and the English series (3)
England before the storm, 1896-1914
Amery, Leopold Stennett
My political life trilogy (1)
England first and last
Bailey, Anthony
America and England series (2)
England for sale
Lane, Jane
Montague family series (2)
England hath need of thee
Grier, Sydney Carlyon
Century series (6)
England is a village
Warren, Clarence Henry
Happy countryman series (2)
England of Elizabeth
Rowse, Alfred Leslie
Elizabethan age series (1)
England reclaimed
Sitwell, Osbert
England reclaimed series (1)
England, what is the secret of the stones?
Stuart, Charles
Earth inspectors series (11)
English assassin
Moorcock, Michael
Jerry Cornelius series (3)
English at the North Pole
Verne, Jules
Adventures of Captain Hatteras series (1)
English Bodley family
Scudder, Horace Elisha
Bodley family series (7)
English Captain
White, Simon
Penhaligon trilogy (1)
English Channel
Abbott, Jacob
Florence series (4)
English Creek
Doig, Ivan
McCaskill family trilogy (1)
English fairy tales
Jacobs, Joseph
English fairy tales series (1)
English gentleman
Castronovo, David
Gentleman series (1)
Sutherland, Douglas
English gentleman series (1)
English gentleman's child
Sutherland, Douglas
English gentleman series (3)
English gentleman's good shooting guide
Sutherland, Douglas
English gentleman series (6)
English gentleman's mistress
Sutherland, Douglas
English gentleman series (4)
English gentleman's wife
Sutherland, Douglas
English gentleman series (2)
English girl in Paris
Maud, Constance Elisabeth
English girl series (1)
English heiress
Gellis, Roberta
Heiress series (1)
English journey
Priestley, John Boynton
English journey series (1)
English library, sources and history
Irwin, Raymond
English library series (2)
English march
D'Oyley, Elizabeth
Prince Rupert series (1)
English ribbon
Hilton, Jack
English ways series (2)
English teacher
Narayan, Rasipuram Krishnaswami
Malgudi series (4)
English way of doing things
Donaldson, William
Ladies and gentlemen series (3)
English ways
Hilton, Jack
English ways series (1)
Engravers of Van Diemen's Land
Craig, Clifford
Tasmanian prints series (1)
Enid's story
Pascal, Francine
Sweet Valley High super star series (3)
Enigma
Kube-McDowell, Michael Paul
Trigon disunity trilogy (2)
Enigma from Tantalus
Brunner, John
Zarathustra trilogy (3)

Enigma project
Rosenberger, Joseph
Death Merchant series (25)
Enlarged devil's dictionary
Bierce, Ambrose
Devil's dictionary series (1)
Enlightening Delilah
Chesney, Marion
School of manners series (3)
Enlightenment
Clegg, Barbara
Doctor Who series (85)
Ennal's Point
Richards, Alun
Ennal's Point series (1)
Ennead
Mark, Jan
Manipulator trilogy (1)
Enormous apple pie, and other Miss Pussy tales
Ross, Diana
Miss Pussy series (3)
Enormous changes at the last minute
Paley, Grace
Little disturbances series (2)
Enormous egg
Butterworth, Oliver
Nate Twitchell series (1)
Enquiries are continuing
Ashford, Jeffrey
Detective Inspector Don Kerry series (4)
Enrollment cancelled
Olsen, D B
Professor A Pennyfeather series (6)
Ensign Carey
Welch, Ronald
Carey family series (8)
Ensign Flandry
Anderson, Poul
Sir Dominic Flandry series (5)
Ensign Merrill
Lounsberry, Lionel
Merrill series (2)
Ensign O'Toole and me
Lederer, William Julius
Mister Roberts series (2)
Ensign Ralph Osborn
Beach, Edward Latimer, senior
Ralph Osborn series (3)
Enslaved
Burns, Ron
Harrison Hull series (2)
Enter a gentlewoman
Woods, Sara
Sir Nicholas Harding and Antony Maitland series (34)
Enter a murderer
Marsh, Ngaio
Inspector Roderick Alleyn series (2)
Enter certain murderers
Woods, Sara
Sir Nicholas Harding and Antony Maitland series (10)
Enter Craig Kennedy
Reeve, Arthur Benjamin
Craig Kennedy series (25)
Enter Doctor Nikola!
Boothby, Guy
Doctor Nikola series (1)
Enter, Jane
Price, Evadne
Jane series (3)
Enter Prince
Housman, Laurence
Palace plays series (3)
Enter Psmith
Wodehouse, Pelham Grenville
Psmith series (1)
Wrykyn School series (1)
Enter second murderer
Knight, Alanna
Inspector Faro series (1)
Enter Sir John
Dane, Clemence
Sir John Saumerez series (1)
Enter Sir Robert
Thirkell, Angela
Barsetshire series (24)
Enter Superintendent Flagg
Cassells, John
Superintendent Flagg series (19)
Enter T.R.
Dicks, Terrance
T.R.Bear series (1)
Enter the Ace
Horler, Sydney
Ace series (1)
Enter the corpse
Woods, Sara
Sir Nicholas Harding and Antony Maitland series (21)
Enter the Dormouse
King, Frank
Dormouse series (1)
Enter the lion
Hodel, Michael P
Sherlock Holmes sequels series (37)
Enter the Picaroon
Cassells, John
Ludovic Saxon series (1)
Enter the Saint
Charteris, Leslie
Saint series (2)
Entering the maze
Hardison, Osborne Bennett
Modern culture trilogy (1)
Enterprise incidents 2
Clark, Sheila
Star trek fan series (4)
Enterprise, log entries 60
Anonymous
Star trek fan series (37)
Enterprise Stardust
Scheer, Karl Herbert
Perry Rhodan series (1)
Enterprise, the first adventure
McIntyre, Vondra Neil
Star trek sequels series (2)
Enterprising burglar
Balfour, Hearnden
Inspector Jack Strickland series (2)
Enterprising engines
Awdry, Wilbert
Railway series (23)
Enterprising Picaroon
Cassells, John
Ludovic Saxon series (6)
Entertaining murder
Grierson, Francis Durham
Inspector George Muir series (8)
Entertaining to please him
Bradford, Barbara Taylor
How to be the perfect wife series (2)
Enthusiast
Hill, Peter
Inspector Robert Staunton series (3)
Entoverse
Hogan, James Patrick
Minervan experiment series (4)
Entrapment
Ahern, Jerry
Defender series (5)
Entropy effect
McIntyre, Vondra Neil
Star trek series (2)
Entropy tango
Moorcock, Michael
Jerry Cornelius series (6)
Entry from San Sebastian
Adkins, Bill
Dave Hill series (1)
Entry of death
McGirr, Edmund
Jim Piron series (5)
Envious Casca
Heyer, Georgette
Inspector Hemingway series (6)
Environment
Bentley, Phyllis
Environment series (1)
Envoy from mirror city
Frame, Janet
Is-land trilogy (3)
Envoy of the Emperor
Gerard, Francis
Marquess de Brussac series (2)
Envoy on excursion
Brahms, Caryl
Inspector Adam Quill series (3)
Envoy to new worlds
Laumer, Keith
Retief series (1)
Eon
Bear, Greg
Eon series (1)
Epidemic Center, Aralon
Darlton, Clark
Perry Rhodan series (37)
Epilogue
Graeme, Bruce
Superintendent William Stevens and Inspector Pierre Allain series (3)
Lorrah, Jean
Star trek fan series (6)
Epilogue for Selena
Shelynn, Jack
Sam Clayton trilogy (3)
Epiphany
Yermakov, Nicholas
Last communion trilogy (2)
Episode at Toledo
Bridge, Ann
Hetta Atherley series (2)
Julia Probyn series (7)
Episode in Arcady
Sutcliffe, Halliwell
Arcady series (1)
Episode of Flatland
Hinton, Charles Howard
Flatland series (2)
Episode of the stolen voice
Armour, R Coutts
Sexton Blake series (207)
Episode of the Terror
Balzac, Honore de
Scenes of political life series (1)
Episode under the Terror
Balzac, Honore de
Scenes of political life series (1)
Episodes of the Argo
Lafferty, Raphael Aloysius
Argos mythos series (7)
Epitaph for a dead actor
Gray, Dulcie
Inspector Cardiff series (1)
Epitaph for a dead heat
Markson, David
Harry Fannin series (3)
Epitaph for a lady
Cronin, Michael
Sam Harris series (12)
Epitaph for a lobbyist
Dominic, R B
Congressman Ben Safford series (4)
Epitaph for a nurse
Hocking, Anne
Inspector William Austen series (28)
Epitaph for a tramp
Markson, David
Harry Fannin series (2)
Epitaph for Joanna
Howard, Hartley
Glenn Bowman series (31)
Epitaph for Lemmings
Harvester, Simon
Roger Fleming series (2)
Epitaph for Lydia
Rath, Virginia
Michael Dundas series (6)
Epitaph for three women
Plaidy, Jean
Plantagenet series (12)
Epitaph of a small winner
Machado de Assis, Joachim Maria
Quincas Borba series (1)
Epitaph to a bad cop
Fredman, John
Charles Dexter series (3)
Epitaph to treason
Ballinger, W A
Sexton Blake series (1486)
Epitaphs
Pronzini, Bill
Private Eye series (21)
Eppworth case
Patterson, Innis
Sebald Craft series (1)
Equal opportunity death
Dunlap, Susan
Vejay Haskell series (1)
Equal rites
Pratchett, Terry
Discworld series (3)
Equality
Bellamy, Edward
Julian West series (2)
Equality, in the year 2000
Reynolds, Mack
Julian West series (4)
Equations of chaos
Vardeman, Robert Edward
Weapons of chaos trilogy (2)
Erewhon
Butler, Samuel
Erewhon series (1)
Erewhon revisited
Butler, Samuel
Erewhon series (2)
Ergent delivery
Forde, Nicholas
Mark Urgent series (3)
Eric
Pratchett, Terry
Discworld series (9)
Eric and Frankie in Las Vegas
Henri, Adrian
Eric series (2)
Eric and Karlsson-on-the-Roof
Lindgren, Astrid
Karlsson-on-the-Roof series (1)
Eric and the Christmas horse
Peterson, Hans
Magnus series (6)
Eric and the lost planes
Sheridan, John
Eric series (3)
Eric and the mad inventor
Sheridan, John
Eric series (2)
Eric Brighteyes
Haggard, Henry Rider
Eric Brighteyes series (1)
Eric Heiden, winner in gold
Aaseng, Nathan
Sports acheivers series (2)
Eric John Stark, outlaw of Mars
Brackett, Leigh
Eric John Stark series (6)
Eric of Zanthodon
Carter, Lin
Eric Carstairs series (5)
Eric the punk cat
Henri, Adrian
Eric series (1)
Eric, the wild car
Sheridan, John
Eric series (1)
Erica
De la Pasture, Elizabeth
Master Christopher series (2)
Erie water
Edmonds, Walter Dumaux
Erie Canal series (1)
Erin
Jenkins, Jerry Bruce
Margo Franklin and Philip Spence series (5)
Thesman, Jean
Whitney cousins series (3)
Erin and the movie star
Kaye, Marilyn
Camp Sunnyside Friends series (10)
Erin's child
Kelly, Sheelagh
Feeney family series (3)
Ermine tales
Carnarvon, Henry
No regrets series (2)
Ernest and Celestine
Vincent, Gabrielle
Ernest and Celestine series (1)
Ernest and Celestine at the circus
Vincent, Gabrielle
Ernest and Celestine series (10)
Ernest and Celestine's patchwork quilt
Vincent, Gabrielle
Ernest and Celestine series (6)
Ernest and Celestine's picnic
Vincent, Gabrielle
Ernest and Celestine series (3)
Ernest in the wild west
Libenzi, Ermanno
Ernest series (2)
Ernest Maltravers
Lytton, Edward George Earle Lytton Bulwer-Lytton
Eleusinia series (1)
Ernest Owl starts a school
Pilgrim, Jane
Blackberry Farm series (10)
Ernest the brave
Beaman, Sydney George Hulme
Toytown series (18)
Ernest the policeman
Beaman, Sydney George Hulme
Toytown series (8)
Ernestine Sophie
Cleugh, Sophia
Matilda series (2)
Ernie at school and what came of his going there
Eiloart, Elizabeth
Ernie Elton series (2)
Ernie discovers excellence
Lazare, Lewis
Ernie Astorbilt series (1)
Ernie discovers Wall Street
Lazare, Lewis
Ernie Astorbilt series (3)
Ernie discovers Washington
Lazare, Lewis
Ernie Astorbilt series (2)
Ernie Elton at school
Eiloart, Elizabeth
Ernie Elton series (2)
Ernie Elton, the lazy boy
Eiloart, Elizabeth
Ernie Elton series (1)
Ernie goes abroad
Lazare, Lewis
Ernie Astorbilt series (4)
Ernie's chemistry set
Waddell, Martin
Ernie series (1)
Ernie's flying trousers
Waddell, Martin
Ernie series (2)
Ernst Ellert returns!
Darlton, Clark
Perry Rhodan series (83)
Eros affair
McCutchan, Philip
Superintendent Simon Shard series (4)
Eros ascending
Resnick, Mike
Tales of the velvet comet series (1)
Eros at nadir
Resnick, Mike
Tales of the velvet comet series (4)
Eros at zenith
Resnick, Mike
Tales of the velvet comet series (2)
Eros descending
Resnick, Mike
Tales of the velvet comet series (3)
Eros in Paris
Romains, Jules
Men of goodwill series (4)
Eros is no hangman
Wood, Andrew
Magnus Keeble series (3)
Errant sleuth
Joyce, Cyril
Chief Superintendent Pat Stockton series (16)
Greg Allard trilogy (3)
Errant target
Joyce, Cyril
Chief Superintendent Pat Stockton series (14)
Greg Allard trilogy (2)
Errant witness
Joyce, Cyril
Chief Superintendent Pat Stockton series (10)
Greg Allard trilogy (1)
Error of judgment
Coxe, George Harmon
Flash Casey series (4)
Lewis, Royston
Inspector John Crow series (3)
Error of the moon
Woods, Sara
Sir Nicholas Harding and Antony Maitland series (5)
Erthring cycle
Drew, Wayland
Erthring cycle series (3)
Escalation
Janson, Hank
Hank Janson series (218)
Tomino, Yoshiyuki
Gundam mobile suit trilogy (2)
Escalator
Gardner, Alan Harold
Davis Troy series (1)
Escapade
Goodall, John Strickland
Paddy Pork series (12)
Escape
Ahern, Jerry
Defender series (6)
Coleman, Clay
Lost Island series (6)
Darke, James
Witches series (4)
Edwards, Gene
Chronicles of the door series (3)
Franklin, Charles
Maxine Dangerfield series (4)
Janson, Hank
Hank Janson series (70)
Montgomery, Raymond A
Choose your own adventure series (20)
Murray, Mary
Freedom series (1)
Escape a killer
Philips, Judson Pentecost
Peter Styles series (8)
Escape agents
Hyne, Charles John Cutcliffe
Captain Owen Kettle series (8)
Escape and be secret
Gibbs-Smith, Charles Harvard
Paul Harvard series (2)
Escape at sunrise
Cronin, Michael
James Hellier series (5)

Escape from Castle Quarras
Niles, Douglas
Super endless quest adventure gamebook series (3)
Escape from China
Montgomery, Raymond A
Rebels in the New World series (5)
Escape from Colditz
Eggers, Reinhold
Colditz series (12)
Escape from Dartmoor
Beckett, Mark
Major Dick Burton series (5)
Escape from France
Welch, Ronald
Carey family series (6)
Escape from Gulag Taria
Rosenberger, Joseph
Death Merchant series (67)
Escape from hell
Stuart, Vivian
Captain Alexander Sheridan series (6)
Escape from high doom
Milton, Hilary
Plot your own horror stories series (5)
Escape from Jupiter
McEvoy, Seth
Explorer series (4)
Escape from liberty
Greene, L Patrick
Aubrey Saint John Major series (18)
Escape from Loki
Farmer, Philip Jose
Doc Savage series (183)
Escape from Lost Island
Coleman, Clay
Lost Island series (1)
Escape from Macho
Cleve, John
Spaceways series (3)
Escape from Montana
Pennington, Link
Frank Slade series (2)
Escape from murder
Stand, Marguerite
Bill Rice series (1)
Escape from Nicaragua
Buchanan, Jack
M.I.A. Hunter series (8)
Escape from Raven Castle
Fortune, J J
Race against time series (2)
Escape from surgery
Mair, George Brown
Surgeon series (2)
Escape from Terror
Arrow, William
Return to the Planet of the Apes series (2)
Escape from the Amazon
Atkinson, Alex
Rocking-chair series (2)
Escape from the Cossacks
Teitelbaum, Michael
Fievel series (2)
Escape from the crater
Biemiller, Carl Ludwig
Hydronauts series (3)
Escape from the Planet of the Apes
Pournelle, Jerry
Planet of the Apes series (3)
Escape from tyrannosaurus
Bunting, Eve
Dinosaur machines series (4)
Escape in passion
Romains, Jules
Men of goodwill series (26)
Escape me never
Kennedy, Margaret
Sanger family series (2)
Escape not my love
Coffman, Elaine
Mackinnon brothers series (3)
Escape of General Gerard
Betteridge, Don
Tiger Lester series (2)
Escape of Mister Trimm
Cobb, Irwin Shrewsbury
Judge Priest series (2)
Escape of the Duke
Lane, Jane
Stuart series (4)
Escape of the King
Lane, Jane
Stuart series (1)
Escape of the Prince
Lane, Jane
Stuart series (2)
Escape of the Princess
Lane, Jane
Stuart series (5)
Escape of the Queen
Lane, Jane
Stuart series (3)
Escape on Venus
Burroughs, Edgar Rice
Venus series (4)
Escape out of darkness
Stuart, Anne
Maggie Bennett series (2)
Escape to danger
Conway, Peter
Lucy Beck series (3)
Escape to death
Franklin, Charles
Grant Garfield series (9)
Escape to destiny
Ferguson, William Blair Morton
Dan Cluer series (1)
Escape to murder
Scott, Sutherland
Doctor Septimus Dodds series (7)
Escape to Persia
Hull, Katharine
Oxus series (2)
Escape to the Andes
Croft-Cooke, Rupert
Sensual life series (25)
Escape to tomorrow
Effinger, George Alec
Planet of the Apes series (7)
Escape to Venus
Darlton, Clark
Perry Rhodan series (15)
Escape to Witch Mountain
Key, Alexander
Witch Mountain series (1)
Escape velocity
Stasheff, Christopher
Gramarye series (1)
Escape with Gun Cotton
Grayson, Rupert
Gun Cotton series (5)
Escaped black mamba
Aiken, Joan
Arabel and Mortimer series (2)
Escapemanship
Ditton, James
John Boldre series (3)
Escaping the Monawks
Robbins, Orison
French and Indian war series (3)
Escapist
Avenell, Donne
Axa series (9)
Escort job
Kane, Henry
Peter Chambers series (31)
Escort ship
Macdonnell, James Edmond
Captain Peter Bentley series (11)
Eskimo twins
Perkins, Lucy Fitch
Twin series (4)
Eskimos, Chicanos, Indians
Coles, Robert
Children of crisis series (4)
Eskimo's secret
Keene, Carolyn
Nancy Drew series (76)
ESP McGee
Packard, Edward
ESP McGee series (1)
ESP McGee and the dolphin's message
Rodgers, Jesse
ESP McGee series (6)
ESP McGee and the ghost ship
McMahan, Ian
ESP McGee series (4)
ESP McGee and the haunted mansion
Lawrence, Jim
ESP McGee series (2)
ESP McGee and the mysterious magician
Ernst, Kathryn Fitzgerald
ESP McGee series (3)
ESP McGee to the rescue
Shea, George
ESP McGee series (5)
Especially Jennings
Buckeridge, Anthony
Jennings series (15)
Esper
Bucar, Cary A
Star wars storybook series (3)
Espionage!
Marlowe, Greg
Greg Marlowe series (4)
Espionage killings
Brandon, John Gordon
Inspector Patrick Aloysius McCarthy series (53)
Esprit de corps
Durrell, Lawrence
Antrobus series (1)
Esprit de corpse
Kane, Frank
Johnny Liddell series (29)
Essence of evil
Faust, Joe Clifford
Angel's luck series (3)
Essence of murder
Klinger, Henry
Lieutenant Shomri Shomar series (3)
Essence of the dusk
Bain, Francis William
Indian mystic love stories series (6)
Essential Calvin and Hughes
Watterson, Bill
Calvin and Hobbes series (2)
Essential Dracula
Stoker, Bram
Dracula series (1)
Essex murders
Loder, Vernon
Inspector Brews series (1)
Essex Road crime
Drummond, J
Sexton Blake series (1115)
Essex schooldays
Dewes, Simon
When the world was young trilogy (2)
Essex triangle
Thurlow, David
East country crimes series (1)
Establishment
Fast, Howard
Lavette family series (3)
Estate
Singer, Isaac Bashevis
Calman Jacoby family series (2)
Estate of the beckoning lady
Allingham, Margery
Albert Campion series (17)
Estella
Knight, Alanna
Miss Havisham series (2)
Estella, her expectations
Roe, Sue
Miss Havisham series (2)
Ester Ried
Pansy
Ester Ried series (1)
Ester Ried, asleep and awake
Pansy
Ester Ried series (2)
Ester Ried yet speaking
Pansy
Ester Ried series (4)
Ester Ried's namesake
Pansy
Ester Ried series (6)
Esther
Weinreb, Nathaniel Norsen
Biblical series (3)
Esther Reid
Pansy
Ester Ried series (1)
Et nunc manet in te
Gide, Andre
Journal series (5)
Etched in violence
Cumberland, Marten
Saturnin Dax series (19)
Eternal boy
Johnson, Owen McMahon
Lawrenceville series (1)
Eternal champion
Moorcock, Michael
Erekose series (1)
Eternal champion trilogy (1)
Eternal deeps
Bassett, Sara Ware
Cape Cod series (12)
Eternal echo
Cradock, Phyllis
Atlantis series (2)
Eternal light
McAuley, Paul J
Four hundred billion stars series (3)
Eternal lover
Burroughs, Edgar Rice
Barney Custer series (1)
Tarzan twins series (2)
Eternal man
Pauwels, Louis
Dawn of magic series (2)
Eternal mercenary
Sadler, Barry
Casca series (1)
Eternal passage
Schulte, Elaine
California pioneer series (3)
Eternal savage
Burroughs, Edgar Rice
Tarzan twins series (2)
Eternal triangle
Pendleton, Don
Mack Bolan series (101)
Eternity
Bear, Greg
Eon series (2)
Eternity, here I come!
Hume, David
Mick Cardby series (18)
Eternity ring
Wentworth, Patricia
Miss Maud Silver series (15)
Ethan of Athos
Bujold, Lois McMaster
Miles Naismith Vorkosigan series (7)
Ethel Hollister's summer as a Campfire Girl
Benson, Irene Elliott
Campfire Girls series (4)
Ethel Morton and the Christmas ship
Smith, Mabell Shipple Clarke
Ethel Morton series (1)
Ethel Morton at Chautauqua
Smith, Mabell Shipple Clarke
Ethel Morton series (2)
Ethel Morton at Rose House
Smith, Mabell Shipple Clarke
Ethel Morton series (3)
Ethel Morton at Sweetbriar Lodge
Smith, Mabell Shipple Clarke
Ethel Morton series (4)
Ethel Morton's holidays
Smith, Mabell Shipple Clarke
Ethel Morton series (6)
Ethel Morton's surprise
Smith, Mabell Shipple Clarke
Ethel Morton series (5)
Ethel opens the door
Fox, David
Shadowers Inc. series (2)
Ethelbert
Hoyland, Rosemary
Ethelbert series (1)
Ethelbert and the witch doctor
Hoyland, Rosemary
Ethelbert series (4)
Ethelbert goes to the moon
Hoyland, Rosemary
Ethelbert series (2)
Ethelbert under the sea
Hoyland, Rosemary
Ethelbert series (3)
Ethical engineer
Harrison, Harry
Jason Din Alt series (2)
Ethics made easy
Douglas, Colin
David Campbell series (7)
Ethiopian's secret
Sayer, Walter William
Sexton Blake series (450)
Etiquette to please him
Bradford, Barbara Taylor
How to be the perfect wife series (1)
Eucalyptus pie
Campbell, Peter
Amazing Koalas series (3)
Eugene
Marshall, James
Four little troubles series (1)
Eugenie Grandet
Balzac, Honore de
Scenes of provincial life series (3)
Eulowirree walkabout
Kiddell, John
Hamish, David and Bottle series (1)
Eunice and Cricket
Timlow, Elizabeth Weston
Cricket series (3)
Eunice Gottlieb and the unwhitewashed truth about life
Springstubb, Tricia
Eunice Gottlieb series (2)
Eunice, the egg salad, Gottlieb
Springstubb, Tricia
Eunice Gottlieb series (3)
Eurasia
Freund, Philip
Volcano god trilogy (2)
Eurasian
Bruce, Henry
Eurasian series (1)
Eurasian virgins
Seward, Jack
Curt Stone series (3)
Euro-killers
Rathbone, Julian
Jan Argand series (1)
Europa
Briffault, Robert
Europa series (1)
Europa in limbo
Briffault, Robert
Europa series (2)
Europa's beast
Mottram, Ralph Hale
Geoffrey Skene series (3)
Spanish Farm series (6)
Europe in the melting pot
Wallace, Edgar
Black Avons series (4)
Europe, why was a city built to capture a castle?
Compton, Sara
Earth inspectors series (9)
Eustace and Hilda
Hartley, Leslie Poles
Eustace and Hilda Cherrington trilogy (3)
Eustace diamonds
Trollope, Anthony
Palliser novels series (3)
Eustacia goes to the Chalet School
Brent-Dyer, Elinor Mary
Chalet School series (6)
Euston Road mystery
Parsons, Anthony
Sexton Blake series (1192)
Eutaw
Simms, William Gilmore
American Revolution series (7)
Evangelist
Dunn, Saul
Cabal series (3)
Evangelists
Target, George William
Post-war Britain series (1)
Eva's apples
Gerhardi, William Alexander
Jazz and Jasper series (2)
Eve, it's extortion
Brown, Carter
Lieutenant Al Wheeler series (6)
Eve of battle
Wright, David K
War in Vietnam series (1)
Eve of evil
Gilman, George G
Edge series (28)
Eve of the wedding
Black, Lionel
Kate Theobald series (6)
Eve of war, 1933-1941
Ehrenburg, Ilya
Men, years and life series (4)
Eveli and Beni
Spyri, Johanna
Eveli series (2)
Eveli, the little singer
Spyri, Johanna
Eveli series (1)
Evelyn Byrd
Eggleston, George Cary
Virginia trilogy (3)
Evelyn Innes
Moore, George
Evelyn Innes series (1)
Evelyn, the ambitious
Kimbrough, Katheryn
Phenwick women series (23)
Evelyn Waugh, the early years, 1903-1939
Stannard, Martin
Evelyn Waugh series (1)
Evelyn Waugh, the later years, 1939-1966
Stannard, Martin
Evelyn Waugh series (2)
Even coarser rugby
Green, Michael
Coarse series (3)
Even coarser sport
Green, Michael
Coarse series (10)
Even doctors die
Anson, Lindsay
Peter Allen series (1)
Even if
Morgan de Groot, J
Lotus flower series (2)

Even in the best families
Stout, Rex
Nero Wolfe and Archie Goodwin series (15)
Nero Wolfe and Archie Goodwin series (17)
Even more like Annabel
Davidson, Alan
Annabel Fidelity Bunce series (3)
Even more naughty stories for good boys and girls
Milne, Christopher
Naughty stories series (3)
Even my foot's asleep
Payne, Laurence
John Tibbet series (2)
Even oddlier
Jennings, Paul Francis
Oddly series (2)
Evening
Coote, Roger
My day series (3)
Metcalfe, Penny
Baby's day series (3)
Evening at Alfie's
Hughes, Shirley
Alfie Rose series (4)
Evening in spring
Derleth, August
Sac Prairie series (6)
Evening light
De Selincourt, Hugh
Constance Howard series (3)
Evening star
McMurtry, Larry
Aurora Greenway series (2)
Evenings in Albany
Bax, Clifford
Evenings in Albany series (1)
Event called murder
Thomas, Martin
Sexton Blake series (1604)
Event horizon
McKinney, Jack
Black Hole Travel Agency series (1)
Eventer's dream
Akrill, Caroline
Eventing trilogy (1)
Eventing trilogy
Akrill, Caroline
Eventing trilogy (3)
Ever after
Thane, Elswyth
Williamsburg series (3)
Ever-loving blues
Brown, Carter
Rick Holman series (1)
Ever-Ready Eddie
Haywood, Carolyn
Eddie Wilson series (11)
Everett Anderson's Christmas coming
Clifton, Lucille
Everett Anderson series (2)
Everett Anderson's friend
Clifton, Lucille
Everett Anderson series (5)
Everett Anderson's goodbye
Clifton, Lucille
Everett Anderson series (8)
Everett Anderson's nine month long
Clifton, Lucille
Everett Anderson series (7)
Everett Anderson's one-two-three
Clifton, Lucille
Everett Anderson series (6)
Everett Anderson's year
Clifton, Lucille
Everett Anderson series (4)
Everglades
Lewin, Ted
World within a world series (1)
Everglades assault
Striker, Randy
Dusky MacMorgan series (6)
Everglades swamp terror
Affabee, Eric
Find your fate: G.I. Joe series (5)
Evergreen
Plain, Belva
Anna Friedman series (1)
Evergreen death
Fraser, James
Inspector Bill Aveyard series (1)
Evermore
Steward, Barbara
Edgar Allan Poe series (1)
Everslade
Maxwell, William Babington
Men and women trilogy (3)
Everville
Barker, Clive
Books of the art series (2)
Every bet's a sure thing
Dewey, Thomas Blanchard
Private Eye Mac series (2)
Every brilliant eye
Estleman, Loren D
Amos Walker series (6)
Every crooked nanny
Trocheck, Kathy Hogan
Callahan Garrity series (1)
Every dog has his day
Erickson, John R
Hank the cowdog series (10)
Every kid's guide to being a communicator
Berry, Joy
Living skills series (10)
Every kid's guide to being special
Berry, Joy
Living skills series (18)
Every kid's guide to coping with childhood traumas
Berry, Joy
Living skills series (25)
Every kid's guide to decision making and problem solving
Berry, Joy
Living skills series (1)
Every kid's guide to family rules and responsibilities
Berry, Joy
Living skills series (11)
Every kid's guide to good manners
Berry, Joy
Living skills series (12)
Every kid's guide to handling disagreements
Berry, Joy
Living skills series (13)
Every kid's guide to handling family arguments
Berry, Joy
Living skills series (19)
Every kid's guide to handling feelings
Berry, Joy
Living skills series (20)
Every kid's guide to handling fights with brothers or sisters
Berry, Joy
Living skills series (2)
Every kid's guide to handling illness
Berry, Joy
Living skills series (26)
Every kid's guide to intelligent spending
Berry, Joy
Living skills series (27)
Every kid's guide to laws that relate to kids in the community
Berry, Joy
Living skills series (14)
Every kid's guide to laws that relate to parents and children
Berry, Joy
Living skills series (3)
Every kid's guide to laws that relate to schools and work
Berry, Joy
Living skills series (4)
Every kid's guide to making and managing money
Berry, Joy
Living skills series (21)
Every kid's guide to making friends
Berry, Joy
Living skills series (22)
Every kid's guide to nutrition and health care
Berry, Joy
Living skills series (6)
Every kid's guide to overcoming prejudice and discrimination
Berry, Joy
Living skills series (5)
Every kid's guide to responding to danger
Berry, Joy
Living skills series (23)
Every kid's guide to the juvenile justice system
Berry, Joy
Living skills series (15)
Every kid's guide to thinking and learning
Berry, Joy
Living skills series (16)
Every kid's guide to understanding human rights
Berry, Joy
Living skills series (7)
Every kid's guide to understanding nightmares
Berry, Joy
Living skills series (24)
Every kid's guide to understanding parents
Berry, Joy
Living skills series (8)
Every kid's guide to using time wisely
Berry, Joy
Living skills series (17)
Every kid's guide to watching TV intelligently
Berry, Joy
Living skills series (9)
Every living thing
Herriot, James
Vet series (8)
Every man
Llewellyn-Jones, Derek
Everyperson series (3)
Every man an enemy
Baker, William Howard
Sexton Blake series (1418)
Every month was May
Eaton, Evelyn
North star series (1)
Every mother's son
Lindsay, Norman
Redheap trilogy (1)
Every second Thursday
Page, Emma
Inspector Kelsey series (1)
Every street
Minton, Mary
Yesterday's road series (6)
Every time I climb a tree
McCord, David
Rhymes of the never was an always is series (3)
Everybody
Llewellyn-Jones, Derek
Everyperson series (2)
Everybody always tells
Punshon, Ernest Robertson
Bobby Owen series (27)
Everybody had a gun
Prather, Richard Scott
Shell Scott series (3)
Everybody suspect
Sharp, David
Professor Henry Arthur Fielding series (9)
Everybody's come to Cosmo's
Goulart, Ron
Exchameleon series (3)
Everybody's favorite
Sheldon, Ann
Linda Craig adventures series (11)
Everyday children
Rylant, Cynthia
Everyday series (1)
Everyday garden
Rylant, Cynthia
Everyday series (2)
Everyday house
Rylant, Cynthia
Everyday series (3)
Everyday life
Wensell, Ulises
Jackson family series (9)
Everyday life in Roman Britain
Birt, David
Roman Britain series (9)
Everyday parenting
Goldstein, Robin
Everyday parenting series (1)
Everyday prayers
L'Engle, Madeleine
Prayers series (1)
Everyday school
Rylant, Cynthia
Everyday series (4)
Everyday Susan
Leonard, Mary Finley
Susan trilogy (1)
Everyday town
Rylant, Cynthia
Everyday series (5)
Everygirl
Llewellyn-Jones, Derek
Everyperson series (4)
Everything a dinosaur could want
Green, Kate
Fossil family tales series (1)
Everything but a husband
Kamins, Jeanette
Husband series (1)
Everything grows
Raffi
Raffi songs to read series (7)
Everything happens to Holley
Grover, Marshall
Larry and Stretch series (182)
Everything smelt of kippers
Lister, Stephen
Kilakura series (1)
Everything to live for
Horgan, Paul
Richard trilogy (2)
Everything to lose
Partridge, Frances
Pacifist series (2)
Everything you have is mine
Scoppettone, Sandra
Lauren Laurano series (1)
Everything's Jake with me
Von Elsner, Don
Jake Winkman series (4)
Everywoman
Llewellyn-Jones, Derek
Everyperson series (1)
Everywoman's middle years
Llewellyn-Jones, Derek
Everyperson series (5)
Eve's diary
Twain, Mark
Diaries of Adam and Eve series (2)
Eve's new career
Drake, Stan
Juliet Jones series (3)
Eviction by death
Yeager, Dorian
Victoria Bowering series (2)
Evidence by telephone
Carter, Nicholas
Nicholas Carter series (27)
Evidence I shall give
Wainwright, John
Chief Inspector Lennox series (1)
Northern Police series (21)
Evidence in blue
Vivian, Evelyn Charles
Inspector Head series (9)
Evidence of things seen
Daly, Elizabeth
Henry Gamadge series (5)
Evidence unseen
Davis, Lavinia Riker
Nora Hughes and Larry Blaine series (1)
Evidence you will hear
Jobson, Hamilton
Inspector Anders series (9)
Evil ascending
Stackpole, Michael
Dark conspiracy series (2)
Evil at Monteine
Ball, Brian Neville
Witchfinder series (2)
Evil at the root
Crider, Bill
Dan Rhodes series (5)
Evil at Whispering Hills
Cameron, Kate
Whispering Hills series (1)
Evil breed
Dancer, J B
Lawmen series (1)
Evil cargo
Stanton, Ken
Aquanauts series (9)
Evil day
Brathwaite, Errol
Maori Wars trilogy (3)
Evil escapes
Jones, John G
Amityville horror series (9)
Evil eye
Fisk, Nicholas
Starstormers series (4)
Thomas, Martin
Sexton Blake series (1463)
Evil formula
Carter, Nicholas
Nicholas Carter series (596)
Evil genius
Bagby, George
Inspector Schmidt series (31)
Evil gnome
Robeson, Kenneth
Doc Savage series (82)
Evil in a mask
Wheatley, Dennis
Roger Brook series (9)
Evil in Amsterdam
Keene, Carolyn
Nancy Drew and Hardy boys supermystery series (16)
Evil in East Anglia
Thurlow, David
East country crimes series (3)
Evil in paradise
Fortune, J J
Race against time series (6)
Evil in the cup
Thorne, Ernest Pollett
Quentin Eady series (3)
Evil, Inc.
Dixon, Franklin W
Hardy boys case files series (2)
Evil innocence
Munro, Hugh Macfarlane
Clutha series (6)
Evil intent
Wainwright, John
Northern Police series (3)
Superintendent Charles Ripley series (1)
Evil men do
Fitzsimmons, Cortland
Ethel Thomas series (4)
Hocking, Anne
Inspector William Austen series (20)
Evil messenger
Horler, Sydney
Martin Huish series (2)
Sebastian Quin series (1)
Evil money
Harknett, Terry
Stephen Wayne series (5)
Evil of Dark Harbor
Ross, Clarissa
Dark Harbor series (4)
Evil of Mister Happiness
Sharp, Allen
Storytrails series (3)
Evil of the Daleks
Peel, John
Doctor Who series (158)
Evil of the day
Sterling, Thomas
Captain Rizzi series (1)
Evil of the king cockroach
Ebejer, Francis
Lucija and Rosie series (2)
Evil on the bayou
Cusick, Richie Tankersley
Twilight series (21)
Evil one
Beach, Lynn
Phantom Valley series (1)
Evil root
Thayer, Lee
Peter Clancy series (45)
Evil shadows
Daniel, Roland
Buddy Mustard series (3)
Evil spell
Tyrer, Walter
Sexton Blake series (1270)
Evil that men do
Pentecost, Hugh
Pierre Chambrun series (3)
Spiller, Andrew
Chief Inspector Duck Mallard series (16)
Evil truth
Pascal, Francine
Sweet Valley High series (100)
Evil under the sea
Quackenbush, Robert Mead
Miss Mallard series (15)
Evil under the sun
Christie, Agatha
Hercule Poirot series (22)
Evils of Peyton Place
Fuller, Roger
Peyton Place series (7)
Evvie at sixteen
Pfeffer, Susan Beth
Sebastian sisters quintet (1)
Evy-Ivy-Over
Rudowsky, Colby
Slug series (1)
Ewe lamb
Erskine, Margaret
Inspector Septimus Finch series (16)
Ewings
O'Hara, John
Dallas series (1)
Ewings of Dallas
Hirschfeld, Burt
Dallas series (3)
Excavator's secret
Gibbons, Harry Hornaby Clifford
Sexton Blake series (430)
Excellent intentions
Hull, Richard
Inspector Fenby series (2)
Excellent mystery
Peters, Ellis
Brother Cadfael series (11)
Excellent night for a murder
Rath, Virginia
Rocky Allan series (4)
Except for me and thee
West, Jessamyn
Jess and Eliza Birdwell series (2)

Except for one thing
Blayn, Hugo
Inspector Garth series (1)
Except for the bones
Wilcox, Collin
Alan Bernhardt series (3)
Except the Lord
Cary, Joyce
Chester Nimmo trilogy (1)
Except you're a bird
Tinniswood, Peter
Brandon family series (4)
Excess
Headley, Victor
Yardie series (2)
Excess of enchantments
Gardner, Craig Shaw
Ballad of Wuntvor trilogy (2)
Exchange
Brent, R L
Liquidator series (5)
Exchange royal
Bowen, Marjorie
Exchange royal series (1)
Excitement at the Chalet School
Brent-Dyer, Elinor Mary
Chalet School series (38)
Exciting journey
Dale, Norman
Tim Forest series (1)
Exciting summer
Hurt, Freda Mary
Pinetops series (4)
Exclusive
Janson, Hank
Hank Janson series (122)
Excuse me!
Browne, Dik
Hagar the horrible series (23)
Excuse me, Mrs Meigs
Corbett, Elizabeth
Mrs Meigs series (6)
Execute!
Macdonnell, James Edmond
Captain Peter Bentley series (41)
Commander Sainsbury series (7)
Execution exchange
Carter, Nick
Nick Carter series (206)
Execution of Charles I
Birt, David
Stuarts series (15)
Execution of Deutsch
Gregg, Cecil Freeman
Inspector Cuthbert Higgins series (11)
Execution of Diamond Deutsch
Gregg, Cecil Freeman
Inspector Cuthbert Higgins series (11)
Execution of Newcome Bowles
Mickle, Alan Durward
Sherlock Holmes series (10)
Executioner
Balzac, Honore de
Philosophic studies series (12)
Torrio, Vincente
Hoods series (1)
Executioner waits
Herbst, Josephine
Decay of capitalism trilogy (2)
Executioners
Carter, Nick
Nick Carter series (55)
Creasey, John
Inspector Roger West series (35)
McCutchan, Philip
Superintendent Simon Shard series (9)
Executioner's knife
Sue, Eugene
Mysteries of the people series (15)
Executioner's rest
Stein, Aaron Marc
Matt Erridge series (5)
Executive
Anthony, Piers
Bio of a space tyrant series (4)
Executor
Hammond, Gerald
Keith Calder series (10)
Exercise Hoodwink
Procter, Maurice
Chief Inspector Harry Martineau series (22)
Exerciser
Albrecht, Howard
Lieutenant Bill Kinderman series (1)
Exhaustive enquiries
Rowlands, Betty
Melissa Craig series (4)
Exile
Buck, Pearl Sydenstricker
Spirit and the flesh series (1)
Nichols, Robert
Daily lives in Nghsi-Altai series (5)
Peters, David
Photon series (5)
Salvatore, Robert Anthony
Dark elf trilogy (2)
Weiss, Peter
Exile series (2)
Exile in Soho
Henrey, Madeleine
Madeleine series (2)
Exile kiss
Effinger, George Alec
Marid Audran series (3)
Exile of time
Cummings, Ray
Matter, space and time series (5)
Exiled from earth
Bova, Ben
Exiles trilogy (1)
Exiled to earth
Montgomery, Raymond A
Choose your own adventure series (87)
Exiles
Balzac, Honore de
Philosophic studies series (18)
Bova, Ben
Exiles trilogy (3)
Hunt, Greg
Hartman family trilogy (2)
Long, William Stuart
Australians series (1)
Weinstein, Howard
Star trek, the next generation series (14)
Exiles from home
Nolan, Winefride
Catholic Stuarts series (2)
Exile's gate
Cherryh, Carolyn Janice
Chronicles of Morgaine series (4)
Exiles in time
Deegan, Jon J
Dysart trilogy (3)
Exiles of ColSec
Hill, Douglas
ColSec trilogy (1)
Exiles of the Rynth
Douglas, Carole Nelson
Irissa and Kendric trilogy (2)
Exiles of the stars
Norton, Andre
Krip Vorland series (2)
Exiles of the Well of Souls
Chalker, Jack Laurence
Well world series (2)
Exile's quest
Meade, Richard
Gray lands series (2)
Exiles to glory
Pournelle, Jerry
Laurie Jo Hansen series (2)
Exiles trilogy
Bova, Ben
Exiles trilogy (3)
Exit
Macdonald, Peter G
Open road quartet (4)
Exit a spy
Rothwell, Henry Talbot
Michael Brooks series (1)
Exit a star
Knight, Kathleen Moore
Margot Blair series (2)
Exit actors, dying
Arnold, Margot
Penelope Spring and Sir Tobias Glendower series (1)
Exit and curtains
O'Hara, Kevin
Chico Brett series (2)
Exit Arnholt
Latta, Gordon
Arnholt series (3)
Exit Eliza
Pain, Barry
Eliza series (4)
Exit for a dame
Ellington, Richard
Steve Drake series (4)
Exit Harlequin
Gregg, Cecil Freeman
Inspector Cuthbert Higgins series (24)
Ryan, Jessica
Gregory Pavlov and O'Shaughnessey series (2)
Exit laughing
Palmer, Stuart
Hildegarde Withers series (15)
Exit lines
Hill, Reginald
Superintendent Andrew Dalziel and Sergeant Pascoe series (14)
Exit Miss Emily
Murdoch, Nina
Miss Emily trilogy (3)
Exit Mister Brent
Davison, Gilderoy
Mister Brent series (2)
Peter Castle series (4)
Exit Mister Shane
Cassells, John
Superintendent Flagg series (9)
Exit murderer
Woods, Sara
Sir Nicholas Harding and Antony Maitland series (27)
Exit only
Maddock, Stephen
Inspector Slane series (1)
Exit Pretty Poll
Burgess, Eric
Harry Tong series (4)
Exit, running
Spicer, Bart
Carney Wilde series (7)
Exit screaming
Hale, Christopher
Lieutenant Bill French series (6)
Exit Sherlock Holmes
Hall, Robert Lee
Sherlock Holmes sequels series (27)
Exit Simon Hex
Walsh, James Morgan
Bromley Kay series (4)
Exit Sir John
Flynn, Brian
Anthony Bathurst series (34)
Exit the body
Carmichael, Fred
Crane Hammond series (1)
Exit the Disguiser
Horler, Sydney
Tiger Standish series (10)
Exit the skeleton
Adams, Herbert
Major Roger Bennion series (24)
Exit this way
Heberden, Mary Violet
Desmond Shannon series (15)
Exit to music
Shepherd, Neal
Chief Inspector Michael Tandy series (4)
Exit to violence
Jobson, Hamilton
Inspector Anders series (13)
Exit who?
Carmichael, Fred
Crane Hammond series (2)
Exit without permit
Franklin, Charles
Grant Garfield series (1)
Exit wounds
Westermann, John
Orin Boyd series (1)
Exits and entrances
McDonald, Gregory
Time squared quartet (2)
Exodus
Danielson, Peter
Children of the Lion series (10)
Dicks, Terrance
Timewyrm series (2)
Exodus from hell
Buchanan, Jack
M.I.A. Hunter series (5)
Exodus, UK
Rohmer, Richard
Separation trilogy (1)
Exorcist
Blatty, William Peter
Lieutenant Bill Kinderman series (1)
Exorcist III
Blatty, William Peter
Lieutenant Bill Kinderman series (3)
Exotic
Brown, Carter
Lieutenant Al Wheeler series (23)
Exotic seductress
Janson, Hank
Hank Janson series (172)
Expansion of Elizabethan England
Rowse, Alfred Leslie
Elizabethan age series (2)
Expatriates
Haggard, William
Colonel Charles Russell series (25)
Wells, Mary
Expatriates trilogy (1)
Expect no mercy
Thorne, Ernest Pollett
Quentin Eady series (6)
Expectant nymph
Janson, Hank
Hank Janson series (173)
Expected death
Fitt, Mary
Superintendent Mallett series (1)
Expected one
Rogers, Mark Earl
Blood of the lamb series (1)
Expedition to Faollen
Beardmore, George
Lesley Allan series (3)
Expedition Venus
Walters, Hugh
Chris Godfrey series (5)
Expensive place to die
Deighton, Len
Secret file series (5)
Experiences
Toynbee, Arnold Joseph
Acquaintances series (2)
Experiences of a lady detective
Hayward, William Stephens
Lady detective series (1)
Experiment
Catling, Patrick Skene
Sex research series (1)
Experiment in crime
Rhode, John
Doctor Lancelot Priestley series (44)
Experiment in Terra
Larson, Glen A
Battlestar Galactica series (9)
Experiment in terror
Gordons
John Ripley series (4)
Expert in murder
Leonard, Charles L
Paul Kilgerrin series (5)
Expert testimony
Stockley, Grif
Gideon Page series (1)
Exploding lake
Robeson, Kenneth
Doc Savage series (177)
Exploding suns
Black, Christopher
Star challenge series (4)
Exploits of a private detective
Campbell, Scott
Felix Boyd series (3)
Exploits of Arsene Lupin
Leblanc, Maurice
Arsene Lupin series (1)
Exploits of Brigadier Gerard
Doyle, Arthur Conan
Brigadier Gerard series (1)
Exploits of Captain McKeene
Walker, Rowland
Captain Deville McKeene series (2)
Exploits of death
Shannon, Dell
Lieutenant Luis Mendoza series (34)
Exploits of Dick Tracy, detective
Gould, Chester
Dick Tracy cartoon series (1)
Exploits of Doctor Sam, Johnson
De la Torre, Lillian
Doctor Sam, Johnson series (4)
Exploits of Ebenezum
Gardner, Craig Shaw
Ebenezum series (3)
Exploits of Elaine
Reeve, Arthur Benjamin
Craig Kennedy series (6)
Elaine trilogy (1)
Exploits of Fidelity Dove
Vickers, Roy
Inspector George Rason series (2)
Exploits of Jo Salis, a British spy
Greener, William Oliver
Jo Salis series (1)
Exploits of Juve
Souvestre, Pierre
Fantomas series (2)
Exploits of Mister Saucy Squirrel
Wyatt, Woodrow Lyle
Mister Saucy Squirrel series (1)
Exploits of Moominpappa
Jansson, Tove
Moomin series (3)
Exploits of Sherlock Holmes
Doyle, Adrian Conan
Sherlock Holmes sequels series (6)
Exploits of the Chalet girls
Brent-Dyer, Elinor Mary
Chalet School series (9)
Exploits of the Chevalier Dupin
Harrison, Michael
Monsieur C Auguste Dupin series (2)
Exploration infinity
Packard, Edward
Choose your own adventure series (7)
Explorations
Knights, Lionel Charles
Explorations series (1)
Explorations III
Knights, Lionel Charles
Explorations series (3)
Explorer of Barkham Street
Stolz, Mary
Barkham Street trilogy (3)
Explorers
Lloyd, David
Let's pretend series (1)
Long, William Stuart
Australians series (4)
Explorers afloat
Hogg, Garry
Explorers trilogy (3)
Explorers awheel
Hogg, Garry
Explorers trilogy (1)
Explorers in a new world
McCall, Edith
Frontiers of America series (4)
Explorers in hell
Morris, Janet Ellen
Heroes in hell series (11)
Explorers of Gor
Norman, John
Tarl Cabot series (13)
Explorers of Willow Wood Springs
Ellis, Terry
Willow Wood Springs trilogy (2)
Explorers on the Moon
Herge
Tintin series (17)
Explorers on the wall
Hogg, Garry
Explorers trilogy (2)
Exploring chemistry
Gallant, Roy Arthur
Exploring series (6)
Exploring Mars
Gallant, Roy Arthur
Exploring series (3)
Exploring summer
Markle, Sandra
Exploring the seasons series (2)
Exploring the moon
Gallant, Roy Arthur
Exploring series (1)
Exploring the planets
Gallant, Roy Arthur
Exploring series (5)
Exploring the sun
Gallant, Roy Arthur
Exploring series (7)
Exploring the universe
Gallant, Roy Arthur
Exploring series (2)
Exploring the weather
Gallant, Roy Arthur
Exploring series (4)
Exploring under the earth
Gallant, Roy Arthur
Exploring series (8)
Exploring winter
Markle, Sandra
Exploring the seasons series (1)
Explosion!
Robertson, Colin
Peter Grayleigh series (6)
Explosion at Donner Pass
McCarthy, Gary
Derby Man series (6)
Explosive situation
Hackforth-Jones, Gilbert
Paul Dexter series (3)
Explots of Asaf Khan
Afghan
Asaf Khan series (1)
Exposition to the North Pole
Milne, Alan Alexander
Piglet series (6)
Expositions and developments
Stravinsky, Igor
Conversations series (3)
Express delivery
Walsh, James Morgan
Mike Harman series (1)

Express riders
Willoughby, Lee Davis
Making of America series (28)
Express train murder
Norman, John
Martin Speed series (5)
Express train to trouble
Quackenbush, Robert Mead
Miss Mallard series (1)
Expresso jungle
Baker, William Howard
Sexton Blake series (1465)
Expurgator
York, Andrew
Jonas Wilde series (7)
Ex-serviceman's secret
Hardinge, Rex
Sexton Blake series (887)
Ex-soldier employment swindle
Murray, Andrew
Sexton Blake series (105)
Extenuating circumstances
Valin, Jonathan
Harry Stoner series (8)
Exterminator
Ballinger, W A
Dangerman series (4)
Exton Manor
Marshall, Archibald
Clinton series (3)
Extortion
Howard, Hartley
Glenn Bowman series (19)
Extortioners
Creasey, John
Inspector Roger West series (42)
Extra body
Reinsmith, Richard
Bodyguard series (3)
Extra credit
Blake, Susan
Hawthorne College series (4)
Extra credits
Lupica, Mike
Peter Finley series (2)
Extra dry
Gibson, William Curtis
Water Wagon series (2)
Extra kill
Shannon, Dell
Lieutenant Luis Mendoza series (3)
Extra special
Lambert, Janet
Patty and Ginger series (5)
Extracts from Adam's diary
Twain, Mark
Diaries of Adam and Eve series (1)
Extracurricular activities
Lottman, Eileen
Bionic woman series (2)
Extraordinary adventures of Arsene Lupin
Leblanc, Maurice
Arsene Lupin series (1)
Extraordinary case of Mister Bell
Jackson, Wallace
Archibald Penny series (2)
Extraordinary exploits and experiences of Munchausen, M.D.
Brandeis, Julian Walter
Baron Munchausen series (10)
Extraordinary women
Mackenzie, Compton
Capri series (2)
Extraordingary affair of Ernest the policeman
Beaman, Sydney George Hulme
Toytown series (26)
Extraterrestrial cover up
Jordan, Godfrey P
Starr family series (2)
Extreme close-ups
Crews, Lary
Veronica Slate series (2)
Extreme prejudice
Wilson, Gar
Phoenix Force series (50)
Extremes meet
Housman, Laurence
Palace plays series (4)
Mackenzie, Compton
Commander Roger Waterlow series (1)
Exoneration
Rohmer, Richard
Ultimatum series (2)
Eye at the keyhole
Maddock, Stephen
Timothy Terrel series (6)
Eye for a tooth
Yates, Dornford
Jonah Mansel series (9)
Richard Chandos series (7)
Eye for an eye
Santiago, V J
Joseph Madden series (1)
West, John B
Rocky Steele series (2)
Eye for business
Miller, Hugh
Teen Eastenders series (4)
Eye for eye
Kilgore, Axel
They call me the Mercenary series (12)
Eye in attendance
Williams, Valentine
Inspector Manderton series (3)
Sergeant Trevor Dene series (1)
Eye in darkness
Chance, John Newton
John Newton Chance series (3)
Eye in the city
Nunn, Judy
Eye series (2)
Eye in the door
Barker, Pat
Billy Prior series (2)
Eye in the museum
Connington, John Jervis
Superintendent Ross series (1)
Eye in the pyramid
Shea, Robert
Illuminatus series (1)
Eye in the ring
Randisi, Robert Joseph
Miles Jacoby series (1)
Eye in the storm
Nunn, Judy
Eye series (1)
Eye of a serpent
Peters, Geoffrey
Inspector Trevor Nichols and Sergeant Tom Burton series (2)
Eye of God
Grace, C L
Kathryn Swinbrooke series (2)
Eye of heaven
Sharp, Allen
Storytrails series (18)
Eye of Itza
Aikman, Anthony
Boyet Rhodes series (2)
Eye of love
Sharp, Margery
Martha Diver series (1)
Eye of Osiris
Freeman, Richard Austin
Doctor John Evelyn Thorndyke series (3)
Eye of the beholder
Hayes, Daniel
Tyler McAllister series (2)
Wainwright, John
Northern Police series (44)
Eye of the comet
Sargent, Pamela
Earthminds trilogy (2)
Eye of the dragon
Morris, Dave
Golden dragon fantasy gamebooks series (4)
Eye of the eagle
Basile, Gloria Vitanza
Global 2000 series (1)
Eye of the fire
Hild, Jack
SOBS series (8)
Eye of the fleet
Woodman, Richard
Nathaniel Drinkwater series (1)
Eye of the gods
Owen, Richard
David Morgan series (1)
Eye of the horse
Gavin, Jamila
Surya series (2)
Eye of the hurricane
Howard, Hartley
Philip Scott series (2)
Eye of the pelican
Robinson, George Bush
James Clifton series (3)
Eye of the scarecrow
Harris, Wilson
Agent of personality quartet (1)
Eye of the storm
Higgins, Jack
Dillon series (2)
Muller, Marcia
Sharon McCone series (8)
Seger, Maura
Callahan and Gargano families trilogy (2)
Eye of the vulture
Goulart, Ron
Gypsy series (2)
Weird heroes series (7)
Eye of the world
Jordan, Robert
Wheel of time series (1)
Eye of the Zodiac
Tubb, Edwin Charles
Dumarest series (12)
Eye of Zeitoon
Mundy, Talbot
Ivory trail series (2)
Eye spy
Finch, Matthew
Stevie O'Dowda series (2)
Eye to eye
Pendleton, Don
Ashton Ford series (2)
Eye with mascara
Finch, Matthew
Stevie O'Dowda series (1)
Eye witness
Coxe, George Harmon
Kent Murdock series (12)
Levison, Eric
Doctor Edward Lester series (2)
Strange, John Stephen
Captain George Honegger series (3)
Eyes
Bailey, Jill
Animals of course series (4)
Eyes around me
Black, Gavin
Paul Harris series (4)
Eyes have it
Estes, Rose
Greyhawk series (7)
Eyes in the mist
Kendrick, Baynard
Captain Duncan Maclain series (3)
Eyes in the wall
Wells, Carolyn
Fleming Stone series (37)
Eyes of a child
Pugh, Edwin
Eyes of a child series (1)
Eyes of a killer
Grover, Marshall
Larry and Stretch series (427)
Eyes of Bolsk
Lory, Robert
Trovo series (1)
Eyes of Buddha
Ball, John
Virgil Tibbs series (5)
Eyes of death
Bentley, John
Sir Richard Herrivell series (1)
Eyes of Horus
Grant, Joan
Ra-ab Hotep series (1)
Eyes of Jungle Doctor
White, Paul
Jungle Doctor series (10)
Eyes of Max Carrados
Bramah, Ernest
Max Carrados series (2)
Eyes of night
Smith, David Claude
Fair rules series (2)
Eyes of prey
Sandford, John
Lucas Davenport series (3)
Eyes of Sarsis
Offutt, Andrew Jefferson
War of the wizards trilogy (2)
Eyes of Texas
Grover, Marshall
Larry and Stretch series (55)
Eyes of the beholder
Crispin, Ann Carol
Star trek, the next generation series (13)
Eyes of the cat
Knott, William Cecil
Golden Hawk series (7)
Eyes of the hawk
Kelton, Elmer
Tales of Texas series (13)
Eyes of the interred
Asturias, Miguel Angel
Guatemala trilogy (3)
Eyes of the killer robot
Bellairs, John
Johnny Dixon series (5)
Eyes of the Overworld
Vance, Jack
Dying earth series (2)
Eyes of the Shadow
Grant, Maxwell
Shadow series (2)
Eyes of the tarot
Coville, Bruce
Dark forces series (9)
Eyes of the tiger
Carter, Nick
Nick Carter series (9)
Eyes of the woods
Altsheler, Joseph Alexander
Trailers series (8)
Eyes on Utopia murders
D'Amato, Barbara
Doctor Garrett DeGraaf series (2)
Eyes trilogy
Gordon, Stuart
Eyes trilogy (3)
Eyre's acquittal
Mathers, Helen
Sin and acquittal series (2)
Ezekiel
Pratt, Lucy
Ezekiel series (1)
Ezekiel expands
Pratt, Lucy
Ezekiel series (2)

F

F as in flight
Treat, Lawrence
Bill Decker series (1)
Jub Freeman series (5)
F.B.I. showdown
G-Man
F.B.I. series (4)
F.B.I. special agent
G-Man
F.B.I. series (3)
F Corridor
Edwards, James G
Inspector Victor Bondurant series (3)
F.E.U.D.
Janson, Hank
Hank Janson series (233)
F is for fugitive
Grafton, Sue
Kinsey Millhone series (6)
F.O.B. murder
Hitchens, Bert
Collins and McKechnie series (1)
Fabia
Prouty, Olive Higgins
Vale family series (5)
Fables in slang
Ade, George
Fables in slang series (1)
Fabulous
Benedict, Dorothy
Pagan series (2)
Brown, Carter
Mavis Seidlitz series (5)
Fabulous clipjoint
Brown, Fredric
Ed and Am Hunter series (1)
Fabulous Famous Five
Blyton, Enid
Famous Five series (10)
Fabulous flying bicycle
Dines, Glen
Jerry and Vic series (2)
Fabulous, formless darkness
Hartwell, David Geddes
Dark descent trilogy (3)
Fabulous riverboat
Farmer, Philip Jose
Riverworld series (2)
Facade
Goldring, Douglas
Love among the artists trilogy (3)
Face
Vance, Jack
Kirth Gersen series (4)
Face at Brillstone window
Heide, Florence Parry
Brillstone Apartments series (2)
Face at the window
Ecke, Wolfgang
Super sleuth series (1)
Parrish, Frank
Dan Mallett series (5)
Face down in a coffin
Hardin, J D
Raider and Doc series (5)
Face for a clue
Simenon, Georges
Inspector Jules Maigret series (4)
Face in the Bessledorf Funeral Parlor
Naylor, Phyllis Reynolds
Bessledorf series (4)
Face in the film
Merland, Oliver
Sexton Blake series (296)
Face in the shadow
Carter, Nicholas
Nicholas Carter series (364)
Face of a stranger
Perry, Anne
Charlotte Ellison Pitt and Inspector Thomas Pitt series (11)
Face of chaos
Asprin, Robert Lynn
Sanctuary series (5)
Face of danger
Fisher, Graham
Mike King series (1)
Face of death
Grant-Adamson, Lesley
Rain Morgan series (2)
Face of doom
Grant, Maxwell
Shadow series (141)
Face of hate
Du Bois, Theodora
Anne and Jeffrey McNeill series (14)
Face of Inspector Britt
Thorne, Ernest Pollett
Major Brains Cunningham series (2)
Face of justice
Chessman, Caryl
Death row series (3)
Face of the night
Ford, Ford Madox
Poems for pictures series (2)
Face of the tempter
Buckley, Eunice
Zero and Rosalind series (2)
Face of time
Farrell, James Thomas
Danny O'Neill series (1)
Face stuffer's anonymous
Browne, Dik
Hagar the horrible series (28)
Face the gun
Grover, Marshall
Larry and Stretch series (49)
Face to face
Mehta, Ved
Face to face series (1)
Queen, Ellery
Ellery Queen series (40)
Face to face with Napoleon
Caine, Oliver Vernon
Napoleon series (1)
Face value
Greene, L Patrick
Aubrey Saint John Major series (19)
Mackenzie, Lee
Emmerdale Farm series (12)
Ormerod, Roger
David Mallin and George Coe series (18)
Richard Patton series (1)
Walsh, James Morgan
Oliver Keene series (9)
Faceless adversary
Lockridge, Frances
Nathan Shapiro series (1)
Faceless fury
House, Brant
Secret Agent X series (14)
Faceless man
Reno, Bill
Badge series (2)
Vance, Jack
Durdane trilogy (1)
Faceless men
Beeby, Otto
Tony Spencer series (2)
Faceless ones
Dicks, Terrance
Doctor Who series (116)
Hardy, Lindsay
Gregory Keen series (3)
Faceless stranger
Usher, Frank
Daye Smith series (10)
Facemaker
Gordon, Richard
Trevose family series (1)
Faces in my time
Powell, Anthony
To keep the ball rolling series (3)
Faces in the crowd
Marshall, William Leonard
Tillman and Muldoon series (2)

Faces in the flames
Tate, Peter
Simeon series (3)

Faces in the water
Naylor, Phyllis Reynolds
York trilogy (2)

Faces of a bad girl
Chance, John Newton
Jonathan Blake series (23)

Faces of Britain
Laird, Elizabeth
Faces series (1)

Faces of danger
King, Rufus
Stuff Driscoll series (3)

Faces of death
Stein, Aaron Marc
Matt Erridge series (7)

Faces of love
Johnston, William
Doctor Kildare series (12)

Faces of murder
Maccargo, J T
Mannix series (2)

Faces of U.S.A.
Laird, Elizabeth
Faces series (2)

Facilitators
Redgrove, Peter
Beekeepers series (2)

Facing east
Soutar, Andrew
Phineas Spinnet series (4)

Facing off, checking and goaltending, perhaps
Paulsen, Gary
Sports on the light side series (8)

Facing the dictators
Eden, Anthony
Reckoning series (2)

Facing the German foe
Fiske, James
World's war series (2)

Facing the world
Alger, Horatio
New world trilogy (2)

Facino Cane
Balzac, Honore de
Scenes of Parisian life series (6)

Fact X
Winn, Patrick
Inspector Lyon series (3)

Factories
Fisher, Leonard Everett
Nineteenth century America series (1)

Factory nurse
Deal, Paula
Nurse series (5)

Fact'ry 'ands
Dyson, Edward
Fact'ry 'ands series (1)
Fact'ry 'ands series (3)

Facts about Floyd
Parkman, Sydney
Captain Bowker series (3)

Facts soft and hard
Lindsay, Joan
Time without clocks series (2)

Faculty of murder
Wright, June
Inspector Savage series (1)
Mother Paul series (2)

Fade out
Jacob, Naomi
Marsden family series (2)
Upton, Robert
Amos McGuffin series (2)

Fade out the stars
Cumberland, Marten
Saturnin Dax series (17)

Fade to black
Goldsborough, Robert
Nero Wolfe and Archie Goodwin series (52)

Fadeaway
Rosen, Richard
Harvey Blissberg series (2)

Faded love
Erickson, John R
Hank the cowdog series (5)

Faded sun trilogy
Cherryh, Carolyn Janice
Alliance-Union series (16)
Faded sun trilogy (3)

Fadeout
Hansen, Joseph
Dave Brandstetter series (1)

Faerie mound of dragonkind
Blashfield, Jean
Catacombs series (1)

Faery lands forlorn
Duncan, Dave
Man of his word series (2)

Fafhrd and me
Leiber, Fritz
Fafhrd and Gray Mouser series (8)

Faggot of torches
Boreham, Frank William
Texts that made history series (4)

Fagin file
Dicks, Terrance
Baker Street Irregulars series (2)

Fahnworth Manor
Welles, Elizabeth
Janine West series (1)

Failing blonde
Denver, Paul
Cannon series (4)

Failure to appear
Jance, Judith A
J P Beaumont series (11)

Faint heart never kissed a pig
Drysdale, Ann
Pig farming trilogy (1)

Faintley speaking
Mitchell, Gladys
Dame Beatrice Bradley series (27)

Faintly smiling mouth
Bligh, Eric
Tooting Corner series (2)

Fair
Andrews, Val
Sherlock Holmes sequels series (60)

Fair American
Coatsworth, Elizabeth
Sally Smith series (3)

Fair blows the wind
L'Amour, Louis
Chantry family series (5)

Fair criminal
Carter, Nicholas
Nicholas Carter series (29)

Fair day's work
Monsarrat, Nicholas
Signs of the times series (3)

Fair do's
Pratt, Henry
Do series (2)

Fair enchantress
Schumacher, Heinrich
Lady Hamilton series (1)

Fair exchange
Bouras, Gillian
Australian wife series (2)

Fair Friday
Turnbull, Peter
P Division series (3)

Fair game
Hammond, Gerald
Keith Calder series (4)
Krich, Rochelle Majer
Jessie Drake series (2)
Wilson, Gar
Phoenix Force series (32)

Fair-haired lady
Leblanc, Maurice
Arsene Lupin series (2)

Fair haven
Almedingen, Edith Martha
Andrew Thornyold series (1)

Fair haven and foul strand
Strindberg, Johan August
Soul's development trilogy (3)

Fair in the Wild Wood
Clewes, Dorothy
Wild Wood series (4)

Fair land, fair land
Guthrie, Alfred Bertram
Settlement of the American West series (3)

Fair maids missing
Audemars, Pierre
Monsieur Pinaud series (7)

Fair Margaret
Crawford, Francis Marion
Paris Opera trilogy (3)

Fair murder
Brady, Nicholas
Ebenezer Buckle series (2)

Fair rules of evil
Smith, David Claude
Fair rules series (1)

Fair weather friend
Berry, Joy
Human race club series (4)

Fair wilderness
Eames, Marion
Secret room series (2)

Fairacre festival
Read, *Miss*
Fairacre series (7)

Fairbairn case
Bentley, John
Sir Richard Herrivell series (5)

Fairground family
Daykin, Lilian
Fairground family series (1)

Fairies afield
Molesworth, Mary Louisa
Fairies series (2)

Fairies, of sorts
Molesworth, Mary Louisa
Fairies series (1)

Fairies of the trees
Barker, Cicely Mary
Flower fairies series (5)

Fairly dangerous thing
Hill, Reginald
Superintendent Andrew Dalziel and Sergeant Pascoe series (4)

Fairly innocent little man
Meynell, Laurence Walter
Hooky Hefferman series (8)

Fairmount girls in school and camp
Baker, Etta Anthony
Fairmount girls series (3)

Fairmount quartette
Baker, Etta Anthony
Fairmount girls series (4)

Fairview boys afloat and ashore
Gordon, Frederick
Fairview boys series (1)
Up and doing series (1)

Fairview boys and their rivals
Gordon, Frederick
Fairview boys series (3)
Up and doing series (3)

Fairview boys at Camp Mystery
Gordon, Frederick
Fairview boys series (4)

Fairview boys at Lighthouse Cove
Gordon, Frederick
Fairview boys series (5)

Fairview boys on a ranch
Gordon, Frederick
Fairview boys series (6)

Fairview boys on Eagle Mountain
Gordon, Frederick
Fairview boys series (2)
Up and doing series (2)

Fairy doll
Godden, Rumer
Four dolls series (2)

Fairy tales
Hill, Eric
Peek-a-book series (7)

Faith
Deighton, Len
Bernard Samson series (7)

Faith for the future
Urquhart, Colin
Spirit and faith series (2)

Faith, hope and charity
Cobb, Irwin Shrewsbury
Judge Priest series (6)

Faith, hope and death
Craig, David
Peter Gale series (2)

Faith of a collie
Terhune, Albert Payson
Sunnybank collies series (11)

Faith of Tarot
Anthony, Piers
Tarot trilogy (3)

Faith Palmer at Fordyce Hall
Woolley, Lazelle Thayer
Faith Palmer series (2)

Faith Palmer at the Oaks
Woolley, Lazelle Thayer
Faith Palmer series (1)

Faith Palmer in New York
Woolley, Lazelle Thayer
Faith Palmer series (3)

Faith Palmer in Washington
Woolley, Lazelle Thayer
Faith Palmer series (4)

Faith to share!
McGloin, Joseph Thaddeus
Called to love, called to serve series (2)

Faithful lovers
Anand, Valerie
Bridges over time series (4)

Fake
Robertson, Colin
Inspector John Martin series (2)

Faked passports
Wheatley, Dennis
Gregory Sallust series (4)

Fakes and fast horses
Martin, Toy
Taronga Road Riders series (3)

Faking it
Haynes, Betsy
Fifteen series (2)

Fala factor
Kaminsky, Stuart Melvin
Toby Peters series (9)

Falcon
Hendry, Frances Mary
Kelpies series (3)
Quest for a queen series (1)

Falcon and the diamond reef
Somers, Derek
Major John Falconbridge series (2)

Falcon and the moon
Darby, Catherine
Falcon family series (7)

Falcon and the snowman
Lindsey, Robert
Falcon series (1)

Falcon cuts in
Drake, Drexel
Falcon series (2)

Falcon family
Adams, Henry Cadwallader
Birthday tales series (2)

Falcon flies
Smith, Wilbur Addison
Zouga Ballantyne series (1)

Falcon for a witch
Darby, Catherine
Falcon family series (1)

Falcon gold
Yorke, Katherine
Enchantress trilogy (2)

Falcon guard
Thurston, Robert
Legend of the jade phoenix trilogy (3)

Falcon meets a lady
Drake, Drexel
Falcon series (3)

Falcon of Eden
Diamond, Graham
Haven series (4)
Stacy series (3)

Falcon Queen
Manning, Val
Queens series (1)

Falcon, queen's messenger
Somers, Derek
Major John Falconbridge series (1)

Falcon rising
Darby, Catherine
Falcon family series (8)

Falcon royal
Darby, Catherine
Falcon family series (5)

Falcon strikes
Ramsay, Mark
Falcon trilogy (1)

Falcon sunset
Darby, Catherine
Falcon family series (9)

Falcon to the lure
Darby, Catherine
Falcon family series (12)

Falcon tree
Darby, Catherine
Falcon family series (6)

Falconer's lure
Forest, Antonia
Marlow family series (3)

Falconhurst fancy
Horner, Lance
Falconhurst series (4)

Falconhurst fugitive
Carter, Ashley
Falconhurst series (15)

Falcons
Rosenbaum, Ray
Army Air Corps series (1)

Falcon's claw
Darby, Catherine
Falcon family series (11)

Falcon's flight
Hohl, Joan
Flint Falcon series (2)

Falcon's Malteser
Horowitz, Anthony
Nick and Tim Diamond series (1)

Falcon's prey
Drake, Drexel
Falcon series (1)

Falconshurst
Adams, Henry Cadwallader
Birthday tales series (1)

Falkenberg's Legion
Pournelle, Jerry
Falkenberg's Legion series (2)

Falkland and Zicci
Lytton, Edward George Earle Lytton Bulwer-Lytton
Glyndon series (1)

Fall and rise of Reginald Perrin
Nobbs, David
Reginald Perrin series (1)

Fall back and kill
Stivers, Dick
Able Team series (23)

Fall down easy
Gough, Laurence
Willows and Parker series (7)

Fall from aloft
Burland, Brian
James Berkeley series (1)

Fall from grace
Wright, Laurali R
Sergeant Karl Alberg series (5)

Fall from power
Housman, Laurence
Palace plays series (3)

Fall girl
Blake, Ken
Professionals series (6)

Fall guy
Barry, Joe
Rush Henry series (2)
Howard, Hartley
Glenn Bowman series (20)
Perry, Ritchie
Philis series (1)

Fall guy for murder
Goldman, Lawrence Louis
Johnny Saturday series (1)

Fall in the shell
Williams, Paul Osborne
Pelbar series (4)

Fall into my grave
Usher, Frank
Daye Smith series (11)

Fall of a nation
Dixon, Thomas
Clansman series (2)

Fall of a sparrow
Gielgud, Val
Antony Havilland series (3)

Fall of Atlantis
Bradley, Marion Zimmer
Atlantean saga series (2)

Fall of Camp A-555
Helm, Eric
Ground Zero series (4)

Fall of Chronopolis
Bayley, Barrington John
Chronos series (2)

Fall of Colossus
Jones, Dennis Feltham
Colossus trilogy (2)

Fall of France, June 1940
Spears, Edward
Assignment to catastrophe series (2)

Fall of Fyorland
Taylor, Roger
Hawklan series (2)

Fall of Hyperion
Simmons, Dan
Hyperion series (2)

Fall of Lucas Kendrick
Hooper, Kay
Hagen series (5)

Fall of Marty Moon
Frazer, Andrew
Duncan Pride series (2)

Fall of night
Baddeley, Pam
Star trek fan series (38)

Fall of princes
Tarr, Judith
Avaryan Rising trilogy (3)

Fall of Raymond
Moore, Frank Frankfort
Raymond Monk series (2)

Fall of snow
Shelynn, Jack
Sam Clayton trilogy (2)

Fall of the families
Mann, Phillip
Story of the gardener series (2)

Fall of the House of Nire
Kita, Morio
Kiichiro Nire series (2)

Fall of the republic
Kilian, Crawford
Chronoplane wars trilogy (2)

Fall of the Shogun
Silverman, Deborah
Shogun series (1)

Fall of the sky lords
Brosnan, John
Sky lords series (3)

Fall of the Spanish-American Empire
Madariaga, Salvador de
Spanish-American empire series (2)

Fall of the towers
Delany, Samuel Ray
Fall of the towers trilogy (3)
Fall of the white ship Avatar
Daley, Brian
Alacrity FitzHugh trilogy (3)
Fall of Vietnam
Wright, David K
War in Vietnam series (4)
Fall of worlds
Mezo, Francine
Areia Darenga trilogy (1)
Fall-out of thieves
Chance, John Newton
Jonathan Blake series (39)
Fall out the officers
Mays, Spike
Soldering series (2)
Fall over cliff
Bell, Josephine
Doctor David Wintringham series (3)
Inspector Steven Mitchell series (2)
Fallen angel
Avallone, Michael
Satan Sleuth series (1)
Fallen Angel
Cohen, Anthea
Nurse Agnes Carmichael series (4)
Fallen angel
Elwood, Roger
Angelwalk series (2)
Peyton, K M
Patrick Pennington series (4)
Viviers, Lyn
Star trek fan series (49)
Fallen angels
Kells, Susannah
Lazender family series (2)
Fallen fortress
Salvatore, Robert Anthony
Cleric quintet (4)
Fallen hearts
Andrews, Virginia Cleo
Casteel-Tatterton family series (3)
Fallen into the pit
Peters, Ellis
Inspector George Felse series (1)
Fallen ones
Vardeman, Robert Edward
War of powers series (4)
Fallen sparrow
Hughes, Dorothy Belle
Inspector Tobin series (3)
Fallen star
Lewis, Jack
Sexton Blake series (243)
Fallen timbers
Porter, Donald Clayton
White Indian series (19)
Fallible fiend
De Camp, Lyon Sprague
Jorian series (3)
Falling for you
Cooper, M E
Couples series (30)
Falling in love
Sarasin, Jennifer
Cheerleaders series (29)
Falling in love again
Filichia, Peter
Two by two series (8)
Falling in with fortune
Alger, Horatio
Rise in life series (2)
Falling man
Sadler, Mark
Paul Shaw series (1)
Falling star
Belle, Pamela
Wintercombe series (3)
Conant, Constance
Star trilogy (2)
Eisenberg, Lisa
Laura Brewster series (2)
McCarthy, Maureen
Mission top secret series (1)
Moyes, Patricia
Henry and Emmy Tibbett series (5)
O'Donnell, Lillian
Mici Anhalt series (2)
Falling towards England
James, Clive
Unreliable memoirs series (2)
Falling wind
Mackenzie, Agnes Mure
Kinnellan series (2)
Fallon blood
O'Neal, Reagan
Fallon trilogy (1)
Fallon legacy
O'Neal, Reagan
Fallon trilogy (3)
Fallon pride
O'Neal, Reagan
Fallon trilogy (2)
Fallout for a spy
Hershatter, Richard Lawrence
Rand Stannard series (2)
Falls the shadow
Penman, Sharon Kay
Princes of Gwynedd trilogy (2)
False alarm
Dixon, Franklin W
Hardy boys case files series (84)
Long, Manning
Liz Parrott series (3)
False alibi
Brandon, John Gordon
Sexton Blake series (952)
Lewis, Jack
Sexton Blake series (130)
False beards
Williams, Alan
Rupert Quinn series (2)
False claimant
Carter, Nicholas
Nicholas Carter series (259)
False claims at the Little Stephen Mine
Bly, Stephen Arthur
Stuart Brannon series (2)
False colours
Macdonnell, James Edmond
Dutchy Holland series (31)
False combination
Carter, Nicholas
Nicholas Carter series (99)
False conception
Greenleaf, Stephen
John Marshall Tanner series (10)
False dawn
Levine, Paul
Jake Lassiter series (3)
Wharton, Edith
Old New York quartet (1)
False entry
Calisher, Hortense
Ruth series (1)
False evidence
Carmichael, Harry
John Piper and Quinn series (36)
False-face
Horler, Sydney
Baron Veseloffsky series (1)
Sir Brian Fordinghame series (1)
False face
Lilly, Jean
Bruce Perkins series (1)
Truss, Seldon
Inspector Gidleigh series (10)
False faces
Vance, Louis Joseph
Michael Lanyard series (2)
False fatherhood
Chandler, Arthur Bertram
John Grimes series (6)
False fatherland
Chandler, Arthur Bertram
Rim series (4)
False front
Darlton, Clark
Perry Rhodan series (103)
False impressions
Berne, Karin
Ellie Gordon series (3)
Keene, Carolyn
Nancy Drew files series (43)
False Joanna
Fredman, John
Charles Dexter series (2)
False lead
Birch, Claire
Lucy Hill series (4)
False mirror
Foster, Alan Dean
Damned series (2)
False moves
Keene, Carolyn
Nancy Drew files series (9)
False notes
Yarbro, Chelsea Quinn
Charlie Spotted Moon series (2)
False pretenses
Keene, Carolyn
Nancy Drew files series (88)
Lyons, Arthur
Jacob Asch series (11)
False prophet
Kellerman, Faye
Sergeant Peter Decker and Rina Lazarus series (5)
False prophets
Flannery, Sean
Wallace and John Mahoney series (3)
False rider
Brand, Max
Silvertip series (2)
False scent
Greig, Ian
Inspector Swinton series (5)
Marsh, Ngaio
Inspector Roderick Alleyn series (21)
False scents
Bayfield, William John
Sexton Blake series (165)
False to any man
Ford, Leslie
Colonel John Primrose series (5)
Grace Latham series (5)
False witness
Mackenzie, Lee
Emmerdale Farm series (15)
Milne, Shirley
Detective Sergeant Steytler series (3)
Nisot, Elizabeth
Commissaire Payran series (3)
Underwood, Michael
Superintendent Simon Manton series (4)
Falseface
Sharp, Marilyn
Richard Owen series (3)
Fame and fortune
Alger, Horatio
Ragged Dick series (2)
Familiar faces
Garnett, David
Golden echo trilogy (3)
Familiar spirits
Tourney, Leonard
Matthew Stock series (3)
Families
Ahlberg, Allan
Foldaways series (2)
Watmough, David
Davey Bryant series (8)
Families and how to survive them
Skynner, Robin
Survival series (1)
Families are fun
Scott, Mary
Freddie series (1)
Family
Carrier, Jean Guy
Family trilogy (2)
Everett-Green, Evelyn
Family series (1)
Fedorova, Nina
Klimova family series (1)
Gold, Herbert
Jewish emigrants series (2)
Mauriac, Francois
Leper series (2)
Oxenbury, Helen
Baby board books series (10)
Plante, David
Francoeur family series (1)
Waller, Leslie
Woods Palmer series (2)
Family affair
Innes, Michael
Sir John Appleby series (23)
Miles, Keith
Crossroads series (5)
Shriber, Ione Sandberg
Lieutenant Bill Grady series (4)
Staples, Mary Jane
South London series (11)
Stout, Rex
Nero Wolfe and Archie Goodwin series (46)
Family affairs
Rhode, John
Doctor Lancelot Priestley series (51)
Family afloat
De Selincourt, Aubrey
Rutherford series (1)
Family album
Dawes, Frank Victor
Cole family series (1)
Family apart
Nixon, Joan Lowery
Orphan train quintet (1)
Family at Dowbiggins
Vipont, Elfrida
Dowbiggins series (1)
Family at Misrule
Turner, Ethel
Woolcot family series (2)
Family at sea
Baker, Denys Val
Cornish series (17)
Caldwell, John
Family voyage series (2)
Family at Sunshine Ranch
Dickson, Helen
Sunshine Ranch series (1)
Family at Tammerton
Erskine, Margaret
Inspector Septimus Finch series (14)
Family at war
Baker, Kathleen
Ashton family series (1)
Family burial murders
Propper, Milton
Tommy Rankin series (6)
Family circles
Baker, Denys Val
Cornish series (21)
Family conspiracy
Phipson, Joan
Barker family series (1)
Family crypt
Trainor, Joseph
Twilight series (20)
Family feuds
Mackenzie, Lee
Emmerdale Farm series (19)
Family flight around home
Hale, Edward Everett
Family flight series (4)
Family flight over Egypt and Syria
Hale, Edward Everett
Family flight series (2)
Family flight through France
Hale, Edward Everett
Family flight series (1)
Family flight through Mexico
Hale, Edward Everett
Family flight series (5)
Family footlights
Barne, Kitty
Farrar family series (1)
Family for all seasons
Baker, Denys Val
Cornish series (14)
Family fortunes
Melville, Anne
Lorimer family series (6)
Shears, Sarah
Franklin family series (2)
Family from One End Street
Garnett, Eve
Ruggles family series (1)
Family from Vienna
Buckley, Eunice
Vienna series (1)
Family gold rush
Sinopy, Hilda
Pelham family series (1)
Family jewels
Dumitru, Petru
Boyars trilogy (1)
Family life, 1855-1883
Kapp, Eleanor
Eleanor Marx series (1)
Family life through Spain
Hale, Edward Everett
Family flight series (3)
Family matter
Gaite, Francis
James and Charles Latimer series (2)
Family matters
Butler, Mark
Home and away series (4)
Matthew, Christopher
Simon Crisp series (4)
Family of Jaspard
Ponsonby, Doris Almon
Jaspard family series (1)
Family on Coppins Bridge
Daish, Elizabeth
Coppins Bridge trilogy (2)
Family on the tide
Knight, Frank
Chichester Harbour series (2)
Family portrait
Housman, Laurence
Palace plays series (4)
Family secrets
Leitch, David
Family secrets series (2)
Pascal, Francine
Sweet Valley High series (45)
Family shoes
Streatfeild, Noel
Bell family series (1)
Shoes series (8)
Family skeleton
Disney, Doris Miles
Jeff Dimarco series (2)
Family skeletons
Hartman, Dane
Dirty Harry Callahan series (5)
Quentin, Patrick
Lieutenant Timothy Trant series (8)
Family stalker
Katz, Jon
Kit Deleeuw series (2)
Family tapestry
Stewart, Averil
Stewart family series (2)
Family that was
Raymond, Ernest
Once in England trilogy (1)
Family ties
Leahy, Syrell Rogovin
Wolfe family series (1)
Summers, Rowena
Clay mining series (3)
Family Tower
Willard, Barbara
Tower family series (1)
Family trouble
McFee, William
Spenlove series (5)
Family truths
Leahy, Syrell Rogovin
Wolfe family series (2)
Family vault
Macleod, Charlotte
Sarah Kelling series (1)
Family's affairs
Douglas, Ellen
Homochito County series (1)
Famine
Creasey, John
Doctor Palfrey series (25)
Famished road
Okri, Ben
Azaro series (1)
Famous adventures of Richard Halliburton
Halliburton, Richard
Famous adventures series (3)
Famous cases of Doctor Thorndyke
Freeman, Richard Austin
Doctor John Evelyn Thorndyke series (27)
Famous Five and the blue bear mystery
Voilier, Charles
Famous Five television series (8)
Famous Five and the cavalier's treasure
Voilier, Charles
Famous Five television series (9)
Famous Five and the golden galleon
Voilier, Charles
Famous Five television series (5)
Famous Five and the hijackers
Voilier, Charles
Famous Five television series (14)
Famous Five and the Inca god
Voilier, Charles
Famous Five television series (10)
Famous Five and the knights' treasure
Voilier, Charles
Famous Five television series (15)
Famous Five and the missing cheetah
Voilier, Charles
Famous Five television series (4)
Famous Five and the mystery of the emeralds
Voilier, Charles
Famous Five television series (2)
Famous Five and the pink pearls
Voilier, Charles
Famous Five television series (17)
Famous Five and the secret of the caves
Voilier, Charles
Famous Five television series (11)
Famous Five and the Stately Homes Gang
Voilier, Charles
Famous Five television series (1)
Famous Five and the strange legacy
Voilier, Charles
Famous Five television series (12)
Famous Five and the strange scientist
Voilier, Charles
Famous Five television series (13)
Famous Five and the Z-rays
Voilier, Charles
Famous Five television series (18)
Famous Five bumper double
Blyton, Enid
Famous Five series (2)
Famous Five go on television
Voilier, Charles
Famous Five television series (3)

Famous Five in deadly danger
Voilier, Charles
Famous Five television series (16)
Famous Five in fancy dress
Voilier, Charles
Famous Five television series (7)
Famous Five versus the Black Mask
Voilier, Charles
Famous Five television series (6)
Famous last words
Green, Jonathon
Famous last words series (1)
Stuart, Becky
Kellogg Brown and Carey Ashton series (4)
Famous Stanley kidnapping case
Snyder, Zilpha Keatley
Stanley family series (2)
Fan fare
Janson, Hank
Hank Janson series (174)
Fanatic of Fez
Leonard, Charles L
Paul Kilgerrin series (3)
Fanatics
Hill, Peter
Commander Allan Dice series (1)
Fanatics of Al Asad
Carter, Nick
Nick Carter series (106)
Fancy dance in Feather Town
Martin, Ann Matthews
Feather Town series (1)
Fancy Hatch
Hawkes, Zachary
Fancy Hatch series (1)
Fanfare for a tin hat
Linklater, Eric
Man on my back series (3)
Fanfare for Angel
Montrose, Graham
Angel Brown series (11)
Fanfare for murder
Desmond, Hugh
Alan Fraser series (19)
Fang, the gnome
Coney, Michael Greatrex
Greataway series (3)
Fanglith
Dalmas, John
Fanglith series (1)
Fangs of fury
Sharp, Luke
Fighting fantasy gamebook series (39)
Fangs of murder
Wallace, Robert
Phantom Detective series (11)
Fangs of the hooded demon
Marsh, Geoffrey
Lincoln Blackthorne series (4)
Fangs of the Sky Leopard
Hogan, Robert Jasper
G-Eight series (5)
Fanina
Sabbagh, Pierre
Fanina series (1)
Fanina, child of Rome
Sabbagh, Pierre
Fanina series (2)
Fannin
Markson, David
Harry Fannin series (2)
Fanny
Janson, Hank
Hank Janson series (175)
Fanny and the battle of Potter's Place
Lively, Penelope
Fanny series (3)
Fanny and the monsters
Lively, Penelope
Fanny series (2)
Fanny herself
Ferber, Edna
Emma McChesney series (4)
Fanny McBride
Cookson, Catherine
Mary Ann Shaughnessy series (8)
Fanny Witch and the Bosnatch
Strong, Jeremy
Fanny Witch series (1)
Fanny Witch and the thunder lizard
Strong, Jeremy
Fanny Witch series (2)
Fanny's birthday gift
Mathews, Joanna Hooe
Miss Ashton's girls series (1)
Fanny's first novel
Moore, Frank Frankfort
Doctor Samuel Johnson series (2)
Fanny's sister
Lively, Penelope
Fanny series (1)
Fan's notes
Exley, Frederick
Frederick Exley trilogy (1)
Fantastic Four, Doomsday
Wolfman, Marv
Marvel superheroes, new series (5)
Fantastic island
Robeson, Kenneth
Doc Savage series (14)
Fantastic journey of the space shuttle
Hiller, Barbara B
Pick-a-path series (7)
Fantastic Saint
Bloxsom, Peter
Saint series (51)
Fantastic voyage
Asimov, Isaac
Fantastic voyage series (1)
Fantastical marvellous Queen
Dessau, Joanna
Elizabeth I trilogy (3)
Fantasy summer
Pfeffer, Susan Beth
Make me a star series (1)
Fantazius Mallare
Hecht, Ben
Fantazius Mallare series (1)
Fantine
Hugo, Victor Marie
Fate trilogy (1)
Fantomas
Souvestre, Pierre
Fantomas series (1)
Fantomas recaptured
Allain, Marcel
Fantomas series (11)
Far and away
Boucher, Anthony
Fergus O'Breen series (4)
Far and few
McCord, David
Rhymes of the never was an always is series (1)
Far Away Farm
Fitzgerald, Hilary
Alastair, Elizabeth and Peter Robin series (2)
Far away man
Marshall, William Leonard
Yellowthread Street series (9)
Far better dead
Cumberland, Marten
Saturnin Dax series (24)
Far beyond desire
Riefe, Barbara
Dandridge trilogy (2)
Far canyon
Kelton, Elmer
Crow Feather series (2)
Far country
Churchill, Winston
American national development series (6)
Far cry
Kane, Henry
Peter Chambers series (8)
Far-distant Oxus
Hull, Katharine
Oxus series (1)
Far down
Corbett, Elizabeth
Mount Royal trilogy (3)
Far dreamer
Lederer, Paul Joseph
Indian heritage series (7)
Far Eastern agent
Moore, Donald
Eastern nobody series (1)
Far, far the mountain peak
Masters, John
Savage family series (5)
Far fly the eagles
Anthony, Evelyn
Catherine the Great trilogy (3)
Far from a gentleman
Hislop, John
Soldier and gentleman series (1)
Far from Cibola
Horgan, Paul
Mountain standard time trilogy (2)
Far from earth
Bentley, Roy
Spacers series (5)
Far from the madding crowd
Hardy, Thomas
Novels of character and environment series (2)
Far frontier
Rotsler, William
Zandra trilogy (2)
Far horizon
Copper, Basil
Mike Faraday series (36)
Killdeer, John
Mountain majesty series (6)
Far islanders
Willoughby, Lee Davis
Making of America series (19)
Far journey of Oudin
Harris, Wilson
Guiana series (2)
Far kingdom
Cole, Allan
Rali series (1)
Far-off place
Van der Post, Laurens
Francois Joubert series (2)
Far off the leash
Park, William Bryan
Off the leash series (2)
Far off things
Machen, Arthur
Near and far series (1)
Far past the frontier
Braden, James Andrew
John Jerome and Return Kingdom series (1)
John Jerome and Return Kingdom series (1)
Far shores of danger
Scofield, Jonathan
Freedom fighters series (14)
Far Side
Larson, Gary
Far Side series (1)
Far Side gallery
Larson, Gary
Far Side series (14)
Far Side observer
Larson, Gary
Far Side series (7)
Far side of evil
Engdahl, Sylvia Louise
Elana series (2)
Far side of fear
Copper, Basil
Mike Faraday series (44)
Far side of forever
Green, Sharon
Farside of forever series (1)
Far side of the dollar
Macdonald, Ross
Lew Archer series (13)
Far side of the hill
Livingston, Nancy
Mackie family series (1)
Far side of the world
O'Brian, Patrick
Jack Aubrey and Stephen Maturin series (10)
Far stars war
Fawcett, Bill
War years series (1)
Far to go
Streatfeild, Noel
Thursday's child series (2)
Far to seek
Diver, Maud
Sinclair series (2)
Far traveler
Chandler, Arthur Bertram
John Grimes series (17)
Far traveller
Chandler, Arthur Bertram
John Grimes series (17)
Far tribes
Wheeler, Richard Seabrook
Skye's West series (3)
Faragon Fairingay
Hancock, Niel
Circle of light series (2)
Fardingales
Brent-Dyer, Elinor Mary
Fardingdales series (1)
Fare you well, my shining city
Metcalfe, Thomas Washington
Santa Anna trilogy (3)
Fares please
Courtney, Edith
Swansea series (2)
Farewell
Balzac, Honore de
Philosophic studies series (9)
Farewell, happy fields
Raine, Kathleen
Happy fields trilogy (1)
Farewell High Fell
Brown, Alfred John
High Fell series (2)
Farewell innocence
Glynne-Jones, William
Farewell innocence series (1)
Farewell, little sister
Enefer, Douglas
Cannon series (5)
Farewell, my lovely
Chandler, Raymond
Philip Marlowe series (2)
Farewell night, welcome day
Jameson, Storm
Hervey Russell series (1)
Farewell, Nikola!
Boothby, Guy
Doctor Nikola series (5)
Farewell recital
Moore, Gerald
Memoirs of an accompanist series (2)
Farewell the trumpets
Morris, James Humphrey
British Empire trilogy (3)
Farewell to Blackoaks
Carter, Ashley
Blackoaks series (4)
Farewell to Europe
Laqueur, Walter
Doctor Richard Lasson series (2)
Farewell to India
Thompson, Edward
Indian trilogy (2)
Farewell to Otterley
Pakington, Humphrey
Washbourne series (3)
Farewell to paradise
Thiess, Frank
Centaur trilogy (3)
Farewell to Priorsford
Douglas, O
Priorsford series (6)
Farewell to Tharrus
Maclean, Catherine Macdonald
Tharrus trilogy (3)
Farewell to the admiral
Cheyney, Peter
Slim Callaghan series (7)
Farewell to the Western Isles
Finlay, Campbell Kirkman
John Macinnes series (3)
Farewell to Valley Forge
Taylor, David
War of Independence trilogy (2)
Farewell to yarns
Churchill, Jill
Jane Jeffry series (2)
Farfetch
Lichtenberg, Jacqueline
Dushau trilogy (2)
Fargo
Benteen, John
Neal Fargo series (1)
Mitchum, Hank
Stage coach station series (21)
Fargo and the Texas rangers
Benteen, John
Neal Fargo series (23)
Fargo's woman
Sharpe, Jon
Trailsman series (64)
Farm
Gree, Alain
Books and games series (1)
Keith and Sally series (8)
Haigh, Richard
Farm series (1)
Kherdian, David
Farm poems series (1)
Farm and the village
Evans, George Ewart
Farm life series (4)
Farm at King's Standing
Turner, Sheila
Mary Carrick series (3)
Farm, book two
Kherdian, David
Farm poems series (2)
Farm by the lake
Porteous, Crichton
Mossdyche series (1)
Farm holidays
Gould, Elizabeth
Green Willow Farm series (7)
Farm-house
Reilly, Helen
Inspector Christopher McKee series (18)
Farm in Normandy
Henrey, Robert
Normandy Farm series (1)
Farm on the hill
Uttley, Alison
Country child series (2)
Farm servant
Anstruther, Eileen Harriet
Farm servant trilogy (1)
Farm stories
Gould, Elizabeth
Green Willow Farm series (3)
Farm twins
Perkins, Lucy Fitch
Twin series (19)
Farm villains
Chance, John Newton
Jonathan Blake series (28)
Farmer Barnes and bluebell
Cunliffe, John Arthur
Farmer Barnes series (2)
Farmer Barnes and the goats
Cunliffe, John Arthur
Farmer Barnes series (4)
Farmer Barnes and the harvest doll
Cunliffe, John Arthur
Farmer Barnes series (8)
Farmer Barnes and the snow picnic
Cunliffe, John Arthur
Farmer Barnes series (6)
Farmer Barnes at the country fair
Cunliffe, John Arthur
Farmer Barnes series (3)
Farmer Barnes at the country show
Cunliffe, John Arthur
Farmer Barnes series (3)
Farmer Barnes buys a pig
Cunliffe, John Arthur
Farmer Barnes series (1)
Farmer Barnes fells a tree
Cunliffe, John Arthur
Farmer Barnes series (7)
Farmer Barnes goes fishing
Cunliffe, John Arthur
Farmer Barnes series (5)
Farmer Barnes' Guy Fawkes Day
Cunliffe, John Arthur
Farmer Barnes series (9)
Farmer Beans and the baby wallaby
Moffatt, Frank
Farmer Beans series (2)
Farmer Beans and the pantry frog
Moffatt, Frank
Farmer Beans series (1)
Farmer boy
Wilder, Laura Ingalls
Laura series (8)
Farmer Brown's boy becomes curious
Burgess, Thornton Waldo
Cubby Bear series (2)
Farmer Drowsy
Clarke, Elf Lewis
Drowsy Dormouse series (3)
Farmer's creed
Porteous, Crichton
Farmer's creed trilogy (1)
Farmer's wife
Turner, Sheila
Mary Carrick series (2)
Farming adventure
Day, James Wentworth
Rural rides series (1)
Farmyard Cat
Anello, Christine
Farmyard Cat series (1)
Farmyard Cat in trouble
Anello, Christine
Farmyard Cat series (2)
Farnsworth score
Burns, Rex
Gabriel Wager series (2)
Faro Nell and her friends
Lewis, Alfred Henry
Wolfville series (7)
Farrago of foxes
Leslie, Colin
House of Godwin series (1)
Farrell's war
Reno, Bill
Badge series (15)
Farrers of Howton
Haworth, Elizabeth
Howton trilogy (2)
Farrowshot Park affair
Bayfield, William John
Sexton Blake series (322)
Farseekers
Carmody, Isobelle
Obernewtyn chronicles series (2)
Farslayer's story
Saberhagen, Fred
Book of lost swords series (4)
Farther afield
Read, Miss
Fairacre series (10)
Farther north
Pinkerton, Kathrene
Ann Jackman series (3)
Farther off from heaven
Humphrey, William
Red River County trilogy (3)
Farthest shore
Le Guin, Ursula Kroeber
Earthsea series (3)

Fatherland, farewell!
Larsson, Gosta
Daily bread series (2)
Fathers
Gold, Herbert
Jewish emigrants series (1)
Fathers and children
Turgenev, Ivan Sergeevich
Nihilist series (1)
Fathers and crows
Vollman, William T
Seven dreams series (2)
Fathers and sons
Turgenev, Ivan Sergeevich
Nihilist series (1)
Father's curse
Balzac, Honore de
Philosophic studies series (8)
Father's law
Smith, Daniel Wybert
Chief Inspector Harry Fathers series (1)
Fathers of their people
Freeman, Harold Webber
Pond Hall series (1)
Fathom five
Westall, Robert
Machine gunners trilogy (2)
Fattest dwarf of Nosegay
Biegel, Paul
Virgil Nosegay series (2)
Faulkner's folly
Wells, Carolyn
Alan Ford series (2)
Fault in the structure
Mitchell, Gladys
Dame Beatrice Bradley series (51)
Fauna
Robins, Denise
Quadroon trilogy (3)
Faustus
Faustus, Johann
Doctor Johann Faustus series (1)
Favor
Guild, Nicholas
Ray Guinness series (3)
Hall, Parnell
Stanley Hastings series (3)
Favorite heart throbs of famous people
Chapple, Joseph Mitchell
Heart throbs series (2)
Favorite of the gods
Bedford, Sybille
Constanza and Flavia series (1)
Favourite of the gods
Bedford, Sybille
Constanza and Flavia series (1)
Fawn
Holden, Philip
Deer trilogy (1)
Fay Cow and the honey machine
Hunt, Peter
Honey machine series (2)
Fay Cow and the missing milk
Hunt, Peter
Honey machine series (2)
Faye's folly
Corbett, Elizabeth
Faye's folly series (1)
Fay's third book
Fay, Gerard
Passenger to London series (2)
FBI story
Gordons
John Ripley series (1)
Fear
Rybakov, Anatoli
Arbat trilogy (2)
Fear and Miss Betony
Bowers, Dorothy
Inspector Pardoe series (4)
Fear and the dead man
Smith, Lou
John Spencer series (1)
Fear and trembling
Flynn, Brian
Anthony Bathurst series (19)
Fear at Brillstone
Heide, Florence Parry
Brillstone Apartments series (3)
Fear business
Hossent, Harry
Max Heald series (6)
Fear by instalments
Burke, Jonathan
Mike Merriman series (1)
Fear Cay
Robeson, Kenneth
Doc Savage series (11)
Fear comes calling
Martin, Aylwin Lee
Matt Hughes series (4)
Fear comes to Chalfont
Crofts, Freeman Wills
Inspector Joseph French series (23)
Fear followed on
Kingston, Charles
Inspector Wake series (7)
Fear for Miss Betony
Bowers, Dorothy
Inspector Pardoe series (4)
Fear for the hero!
Welsh, Ken
Hero series (2)
Fear fortune, father
Hough, Stanley Bennett
Inspector Brentford series (4)
Fear haunts the fells
Goyne, Richard
Paul Templeton series (12)
Fear haunts the roses
Edwards, Charman
Percy Aloysius Huff series (4)
Fear in Fenway
Evers, Crabbe
Duffy House series (4)
Fear in Firland
Power, Norman
Firlanders series (2)
Fear in the deep
Plain, Neil
Boris Blundle and Gang series (2)
Fear in the wind
Jepson, Selwyn
Eve Gill series (6)
Fear in yesterday's rings
Chesbro, George Clark
Mongo series (10)
Fear is my shadow
Thomas, Martin
Sexton Blake series (1483)
Fear itself
Meyers, Richard S
Book of the undead series (1)
Fear merchant
Thorne, Ramsay
Captain Gringo series (3)
Fear merchants
House, Brant
Secret Agent X series (13)
Fear of falling
Levy, Elizabeth
Gymnasts series (16)
Fear of fear
Ryerson, Florence
Jimmy Lane series (2)
Fear of flying
Jong, Erica
Isadora Wing series (1)
Fear of Mr Taltry
Cousins, Edmund George
Colonel Richard Barne series (3)
Fear of Samuel Walton
Green, Roger James
Samuel Walton series (1)
Fear on wheels
Dixon, Franklin W
Hardy boys series (108)
Fear round about
Bellairs, George
Detective Inspector Thomas Littlejohn series (54)
Fear runs softly
Franklin, Charles
Grant Garfield series (20)
Fear sign
Allingham, Margery
Albert Campion series (5)
Fear to tread
Gilbert, Michael Francis
Inspector Hazelrigg series (6)
Fear treks the moor
Pullein-Thompson, Josephine
Moor pony series (2)
Fear walked behind
Horler, Sydney
Sebastian Quin series (2)
Fearful passage
Branson, Henry Clay
John Bent series (4)
Fearful symmetry
Waltch, Lilla M
Lisa Davis series (2)
Fearful thing
Gielgud, Val
Inspector Gregory Pellew and Viscount Clymping series (11)
Fearful way to die
Nolan, Jeannette Covert
Lace White series (4)
Fearless Elizabeth
Pascal, Francine
Sweet Valley kids series (15)
Fearless Freddy's magic wish
Gascoigne, Bamber
Fearless Freddy series (2)
Fearless Freddy's sunken treasure
Gascoigne, Bamber
Fearless Freddy series (1)
Fearless master of the jungle
Edson, John Thomas
Bunduki series (4)
Fearsome island
Miller, Margaret Jessy
Fearsome series (2)
Fearsome road
Miller, Margaret Jessy
Fearsome series (1)
Fearsome tide
Miller, Margaret Jessy
Fearsome series (3)
Feast of death
Penn, John
Inspector George Thorne and Sergeant Bill Abbot series (10)
Feast of the animals
Nickerson, Sheila Bunker
Feast of the animals series (1)
Feast of the animals II
Nickerson, Sheila Bunker
Feast of the animals series (2)
Feast of the peacock
Hastings, Phyllis
London quartet (2)
Feast of the serpent
Cawley, Winifred
Ralph Cole series (2)
Feast of the trickster
Hilgartner, Beth
Dreamweaver series (2)
Dreamweaver's loom series (2)
Feast of vultures
Scott, Peter Graham
Dragonfire series (2)
Feast unknown
Farmer, Philip Jose
Doc Caliban series (1)
Lord Grandith series (1)
Feather castles
Veryan, Patricia
Age of Elegance series (4)
Sanguinet series (2)
Feather cloak murders
Teilhet, Darwin Le Ora
Baron Von Kaz series (2)
Feathered dragon
Niles, Douglas
Maztica trilogy (3)
Feathered Octopus
Robeson, Kenneth
Doc Savage series (48)
Feathered serpent
Keene, Carolyn
Nancy Drew and the Hardy boys be a detective mystery series (3)
O'Dell, Scott
Julian Escobar trilogy (2)
Feathers for the Toff
Creasey, John
Toff series (14)
Feathers left around
Wells, Carolyn
Fleming Stone series (14)
Features editor
James, Judi
Fashion features series (3)
Featuring the Saint
Charteris, Leslie
Saint series (5)
February doll murders
Avallone, Michael
Ed Noon series (16)
February mourning
Wakefield, Hannah
Dee Street series (2)
February's road
Verney, John
Callendar family series (2)
Fed up to the top attic
Vickers, Bette
Bridlington series (1)
Federal agent
G-Man
F.B.I. series (2)
Federal bullets
Eliot, George Fielding
G-men series (1)
Fee fi fo fum
Ahlberg, Allan
Red nose readers series (8)
Feedback
Copper, Basil
Mike Faraday series (16)
Feeding frenzy
Murphy, Warren Burton
Destroyer series (94)
Feel better, Ernest!
Vincent, Gabrielle
Ernest and Celestine series (9)
Feeling run doqwn again, Herman!
Unger, Jim
Herman series (16)
Feelings
Allington, Richard L
Beginning to learn series (10)
Feet
Bailey, Jill
Animals of course series (3)
Feet first
Matthews, Stanley
Feet first series (1)
Feet first again
Matthews, Stanley
Feet first series (2)
Feet of clay
Druon, Maurice
Curtain falls trilogy (2)
Feet of death
Flynn, Brian
Anthony Bathurst series (44)
Feldisham mystery
Holmes, Gordon
Inspector Furneaux series (2)
Felicia
Gould, Elizabeth Lincoln
Felicia series (1)
Felicia Cartwright and the case of the antique bookmark
Palmer, Bernard
Felicia Cartwright series (12)
Felicia Cartwright and the case of the bad-eyed girl
Palmer, Bernard
Felicia Cartwright series (18)
Felicia Cartwright and the case of the black phantom
Palmer, Bernard
Felicia Cartwright series (16)
Felicia Cartwright and the case of the dancing fire
Palmer, Bernard
Felicia Cartwright series (8)
Felicia Cartwright and the case of the frightened student
Palmer, Bernard
Felicia Cartwright series (6)
Felicia Cartwright and the case of the honorable traitor
Palmer, Bernard
Felicia Cartwright series (15)
Felicia Cartwright and the case of the hungry fiddler
Palmer, Bernard
Felicia Cartwright series (11)
Felicia Cartwright and the case of the knotted wire
Palmer, Bernard
Felicia Cartwright series (14)
Felicia Cartwright and the case of the lonely ski boot
Palmer, Bernard
Felicia Cartwright series (17)
Felicia Cartwright and the case of the lonely teacher
Palmer, Bernard
Felicia Cartwright series (7)
Felicia Cartwright and the case of the lost puppy
Palmer, Bernard
Felicia Cartwright series (13)
Felicia Cartwright and the case of the pink poodle
Palmer, Bernard
Felicia Cartwright series (19)
Felicia Cartwright and the case of the storm scarred mountain
Palmer, Bernard
Felicia Cartwright series (10)
Felicia Cartwright and the case of the troubled rancher
Palmer, Bernard
Felicia Cartwright series (9)
Felicia Cartwright and the case of the twisted key
Palmer, Bernard
Felicia Cartwright series (5)
Felicia Cartwright and the frantic search
Palmer, Bernard
Felicia Cartwright series (1)
Felicia Cartwright and the green medallion
Palmer, Bernard
Felicia Cartwright series (3)
Felicia Cartwright and the missing sideboard
Palmer, Bernard
Felicia Cartwright series (2)
Felicia Cartwright and the uncut diamond
Palmer, Bernard
Felicia Cartwright series (4)
Feliciana
Young, Stark
Feliciana series (2)
Felicia's folks
Gould, Elizabeth Lincoln
Felicia series (4)
Felicia's friends
Gould, Elizabeth Lincoln
Felicia series (2)
Felicia's visits
Gould, Elizabeth Lincoln
Felicia series (3)
Felicity learns a lesson
Tripp, Valerie
Felicity series (2)
Felicity saves the day
Tripp, Valerie
Felicity series (6)
Felicity's surprise
Tripp, Valerie
Felicity series (3)
Felidae
Pirincci, Akif
Felidae series (1)
Felidae on the road
Pirincci, Akif
Felidae series (2)
Felimid's homecoming
Taylor, Keith
Bard series (5)
Felita
Mohr, Nicholasa
Felita series (1)
Felix Boyd's final problems
Campbell, Scott
Felix Boyd series (6)
Felix Boyd's revelations
Campbell, Scott
Felix Boyd series (5)
Felix running
Ford, Hilary
Felix series (2)
Felix walking
Ford, Hilary
Felix series (1)
Fell
Kerr, M E
John Fell series (1)
Fell back
Kerr, M E
John Fell series (2)
Fell days
Sutton, Graham
Fleming family series (4)
Fell down
Kerr, M E
John Fell series (3)
Fell Farm campers
Lloyd, Marjorie
Fell Farm series (3)
Fell Farm for Christmas
Lloyd, Marjorie
Fell Farm series (2)
Fell Farm holiday
Lloyd, Marjorie
Fell Farm series (1)
Fell murder
Lorac, E C R
Inspector Macdonald series (24)
Fell of dark
Hill, Reginald
Superintendent Andrew Dalziel and Sergeant Pascoe series (2)
Fell purpose
Derleth, August
Judge Ephraim Peck series (10)
Fellow-traveler
Montross, David
Remsen series (3)
Fellow travellers
Worsley, Thomas Cuthbert
Flannelled fool series (2)
Fellowship of fear
Elkins, Aaron J
Professor Gideon Oliver series (1)
Fellowship of the Frog
Wallace, Edgar
Inspector Elk series (2)
Fellowship of the hand
Hoch, Edward Dentinger
Carl Crader and Earl Jazine series (2)
Fellowship of the Ring
Tolkien, John Ronald Reuel
Lord of the Rings trilogy (1)
Middle Earth series (3)

Felo de se?
Freeman, Richard Austin
Doctor John Evelyn Thorndyke series (24)
Felon in disguise
Southworth, Louis
Inspector Tom Anderson series (1)
Felony at random
Shannon, Dell
Lieutenant Luis Mendoza series (30)
Felony file
Shannon, Dell
Lieutenant Luis Mendoza series (31)
Felony report
Linington, Elizabeth
Sergeant Ivor Maddox series (12)
Felthams
Tute, Warren
Felthams series (1)
Female, handle with care
Chambers, Peter
Mark Preston series (27)
Female of the species
Sapper
Bulldog Drummond series (5)
Female of the species is more deadly than the male
Wright, Meg
Star trek fan series (23)
Female spy
Daniel, Roland
Brian O'Malley series (4)
Female war
Perry, Steve
Aliens series (3)
Feminine for spy
Sanders, Bruce
Howard Digburn series (4)
Femmes fatal
Cannell, Dorothy
Ellie Simons Haskell series (5)
Femmes fatales
Mauriac, Claude
Interior dialogue series (1)
Fen country
Crispin, Edmund
Gervase Fen series (11)
Fence
Nelson, Hugh Lawrence
Jim Dunn series (7)
Fence around the cuckoo
Park, Ruth
Cuckoo series (1)
Fence busters
Bee, Clair
Chip Hilton series (11)
Fencepost chronicles
Kinsella, William Patrick
Silas Ermineskin series (5)
Fence's victim
Stuart, Donald
Sexton Blake series (634)
Fenella Fang
Perry, Ritchie
Fenella Fang series (1)
Fenella Fang and the time machine
Perry, Ritchie
Fenella Fang series (3)
Fenella Fang and the wicked witch
Perry, Ritchie
Fenella Fang series (2)
Fenella in Greece
Gentleman, David
Fenella series (2)
Fenella in Ireland
Gentleman, David
Fenella series (3)
Fenella in Spain
Gentleman, David
Fenella series (4)
Fenella in the south of France
Gentleman, David
Fenella series (1)
Fenfallow
Hill, Pamela
Fenfallow series (1)
Fenland chronicle
Edwards, William Henry
Fen family series (2)
Fenner
Coxe, George Harmon
Jack Fenner series (5)
Kent Murdock series (22)
Fenris device
Stableford, Brian Michael
Star Pilot Grainger series (5)
Fenton of the Foreign Office
Annesley, Michael
Lawrence Fenton series (1)
Fepow
Kelly, Terence
Genki boys series (1)
Fer-de-lance
Stout, Rex
Nero Wolfe and Archie Goodwin series (1)
Fer-de-lance contract
Atlee, Philip
Joe Gall series (12)
Feramontov
Cory, Desmond
Feramontov quintet (3)
Johnny Fedora series (14)
Ferguson rifle
L'Amour, Louis
Chantry family series (2)
Ferne Fleming
Warfield, Catherine Ann
Ferne Fleming series (1)
Fernley House
Richards, Laura Elizabeth
Three Margarets series (5)
Ferragus
Balzac, Honore de
Scenes of Parisian life series (1)
Ferrers Court
Winter, John Strange
Bootles series (9)
Ferret was Abraham's daughter
Urquhart, Fred
Bessie Hipkiss series (1)
Ferris wheel
Stolz, Mary
Polly Lewis series (1)
Ferry the Fearless
Oman, Carola
Johel series (1)
Ferryboat Tommy
Thatcher, Dora
Tommy series (4)
Ferryman, take him across!
Rath, Virginia
Rocky Allan series (3)
Fertility Queen
Manning, Val
Queens series (2)
Festering lilies
Cooper, Natasha
Willow King series (1)
Festival
Anderson, John Richard Lane
Inspector Piet Deventer series (2)
Bonnici, Peter
Arjuna's family series (2)
Festival for Christina
Saint James, Blakely
Christina Van Bell series (29)
Festival for spies
Saint John, David
Peter Ward series (4)
Festival holiday
Edwards, Sylvia
Sally Baxter series (9)
Festival moon
Cherryh, Carolyn Janice
Merovingen nights series (1)
Festival week
Shetterly, Will
Liavek series (5)
Fetch me a rope
Boyd, Raymond
Paul Scarf series (2)
Fete worse than death
Christmas, Joyce
Lady Margaret Priam series (3)
Fetters for twenty
Phelan, Jim
Real life criminals series (2)
Feud
Darke, James
Witches series (7)
Feud at Devil's River
Bell, Robert Vaughn
McGowan family series (2)
Feud at Mendoza
Grover, Marshall
Larry and Stretch series (53)
Feud at Silvermine
Field, Peter
Powder Valley series (78)
Feud-breakers
Grover, Marshall
Larry and Stretch series (376)
Feud fury
Bickham, Jack Miles
John Campbell and Clayton Hartung series (2)
Feud in the Chalet School
Brent-Dyer, Elinor Mary
Chalet School series (48)
Feud of fear
Graydon, William Murray
Sexton Blake series (621)
Feud royal
Leslie, Colin
House of Godwin series (2)
Feuders
Grover, Marshall
Larry and Stretch series (114)
Feuding
Norby, Lisa
Cheerleaders series (4)
Fever
Blake, Susan
Hawthorne College series (14)
Fever grass
Morris, John
Commissioner Robin McKay series (1)
Fever season
Cherryh, Carolyn Janice
Merovingen nights series (2)
Fevered
Drake, Alison
Tango Key series (2)
Fevers and chills
White, Jon Manchip
Colonel Rickman trilogy (3)
Few days in Endel
Marcus, Joanna
Romney Marsh series (1)
Few dying words
Gosling, Paula
Sheriff Matt Gabriel series (2)
Few flowers for Saint George
Burland, Brian
James Berkeley series (2)
Few quick ones
Wodehouse, Pelham Grenville
Drones Club series (3)
Mister Mulliner series (3)
Ukridge series (2)
Few small bones
Rae, Hugh Crauford
Glasgow series (3)
Superintendent McCaig series (1)
Fiasco in Fulham
Bell, Josephine
Claude Warrington-Reeve series (3)
Inspector Steven Mitchell series (12)
Fibber Bugg
Cosgrove, Stephen Edward
Bugg series (40)
Fiddle City
Kavanagh, Dan
Nick Duffy series (2)
Fiddle-playing fox
Erickson, John R
Hank the cowdog series (12)
Fiddler
Cosgrove, Stephen Edward
Barely there series (1)
Fiddler for the Abbey
Oxenham, Elsie J
Abbey girls second generation series (6)
Fiddler in barly
Nathan, Robert
Barly fields series (1)
Fiddler on the roof
Stein, Joseph
Tevye the milkman series (2)
Fiddler's Ferry
Gower, Iris
Copper kingdom series (5)
Fiddling girl
Campbell, Daisy Rhodes
Virginia Hammond trilogy (1)
Fidelio affair
Green, Hilary
Triple S agent series (2)
Fidelio score
Sinstadt, Gerald
Geoffrey Landon series (1)
Fidelity's flight
Du Bay, Sandra
Fidelity series (3)
Fido frame-up
Singer, Marilyn
Samantha Spayed series (1)
Fidus achates
Baker, George
Trojan War trilogy (3)
Field and forest
Optic, Oliver
Onward and upward series (1)
Field day mix-up
Sharmat, Marjorie Weinman
Kids on the bus series (6)
Field hockey
Gutman, Bill
Go for it series (4)
Start right and play well series (4)
Field Marshal, 1944-1976
Hamilton, Nigel
Montgomery of Alamein trilogy (3)
Field of Cloth of Gold
Birt, David
Tudors series (11)
Field of death
Martin, Les
Young Indiana Jones chronicles series (2)
Field of fire
Alding, Peter
C.I.D. Room series (7)
Field of ice
Verne, Jules
Adventures of Captain Hatteras series (2)
Field of sighing
Cameron, Donald
Eldorado series (1)
Field of vision
Morris, Wright
Lone Tree series (4)
Fielding Castle
De Born, Edith
De Kailern family series (1)
Fielding Gray
Raven, Simon
Alms for oblivion series (4)
Fields
Richter, Conrad
American pioneer trilogy (2)
Fields above the sea
Lavender, William
Hargrave journal series (3)
Fields in the sun
Sunley, Margaret
Yorkshire Dales trilogy (2)
Fields of Eden
Hinkemeyer, Michael Thomas
Sheriff Emil Whippletree series (1)
Fields of glory
Rouaud, Jean
Fields of glory series (1)
Fields of heather
Hunter, Alan
Inspector George Gently series (28)
Fields of home
Moody, Ralph
Ralph series (3)
Fields of sleep
Vivian, Evelyn Charles
Aia series (1)
Fields-pitches-turfs-arenas
Kostlanetz, Richard
Sports fields series (3)
Fiend in need
Ozaki, Milton K
Professor Caldwell and Lieutenant Phelan series (2)
Fiend next door
Lavelle, Sheila
Charlie Ellis and Angela Mitchell series (2)
Fiercely the tempest
Hunter, Claire
Island of stone series (2)
Fiery menace
Robeson, Kenneth
Doc Savage series (122)
Fiesta for Wild One
Grey, Peter
Kit Hunter series (7)
Fievel and Tiger
Teitelbaum, Michael
Fievel series (7)
Fievel's boat trip
Teitelbaum, Michael
Fievel series (6)
Fievel's friends
Teitelbaum, Michael
Fievel series (8)
Fievel's New York adventure
Teitelbaum, Michael
Fievel series (3)
Fifteen at last
Ransom, Candice Farris
Growing up series (5)
Fifteen days in the air
Adams, Eustace Lane
Andy Lane series (1)
Fifteen keys
Dawe, Carlton
Leathermouth series (3)
Fifteen minute tales
Blyton, Enid
Minute tales series (3)
Fifteen years later affair
Peel, John
U.N.C.L.E. files series (1)
Fifteenth pelican
Rios, Tere
Flying nun series (1)
Fifth anti-coloring book
Striker, Susan
Anti-coloring series (5)
Fifth big Monster book
Blance, Ellen
Monster series (18)
Fifth book of after midnight stories
Myers, Amy
After midnight stories series (5)
Fifth Brer Rabbit book
Blyton, Enid
Brer Rabbit series (5)
Fifth business
Davies, Robertson
Deptford trilogy (1)
Fifth dagger
Quick, Dorothy
Lieutenant Peter Donnegan series (1)
Fifth estate
Moore, Robin
Connection series (1)
Pat Kenney series (2)
Fifth face
Grant, Maxwell
Shadow series (191)
Fifth Form detective
Walker, Rowland
Fifth Form series (2)
Fifth form of Saint Clare's
Blyton, Enid
Saint Clare's series (6)
Fifth formers at Saint Clare's
Blyton, Enid
Saint Clare's series (6)
Fifth grade, here comes trouble
McKenna, Colleen O'Shaughnessy
Murphy family series (3)
Fifth grade magic
Gormley, Beatrice
Fifth grade magic series (1)
Fifth-grade safari
Zindel, Paul
Wacky facts lunch bunch series (3)
Fifth hostage
Strong, Terence
Special Air Service series (2)
Fifth key
Coxe, George Harmon
Kent Murdock series (9)
Fifth man
Coles, Manning
Tommy Hambledon series (6)
Fifth quarter
Chesher, Kim
Inheritance trilogy (1)
Fifth queen
Ford, Ford Madox
Fifth queen trilogy (3)
Fifth queen and how she came to court
Ford, Ford Madox
Fifth queen trilogy (1)
Fifth queen crowned
Ford, Ford Madox
Fifth queen trilogy (3)
Fifth tumbler
Clason, Clyde B
Theocritus Lucius Westborough series (1)
Fifth year friendships at Trebizon
Digby, Anne
Trebizon series (12)
Fifty calibre kill
Garrett, Charles C
Gunslinger series (4)
Fifty feet under the sea
Grant, Allan
Boys at the Front series (3)
Fifty forensic fables
O
Forensic fables series (4)
Fifty pound marriage case
Brandon, John Gordon
Inspector Patrick Aloysius McCarthy series (23)
Fifty-two caliber shoot-out
Dalton, Kit
Buckskin series (33)
Fifty two weeks of Abe Martin
Hubbard, Kin
Abe Martin series (15)
Fight against the shadows
Duhamel, Georges
Pasquier series (8)

Fight for a throne
Carter, Nicholas
Nicholas Carter series (226)
Fight for freedom
Leibold, Jay
Choose your own adventure series (107)
Fight for Pelignac
De Born, Edith
Jimmy Chester trilogy (2)
Fight for Powder Valley
Field, Peter
Powder Valley series (17)
Fight for right
Carter, Nicholas
Nicholas Carter series (522)
Fight for the drylands
Benton, Peggie
Drylands series (2)
Fight night at Sweet Saturday
Settle, Mary Lee
Beulah series (5)
Fight of the few
Hough, Richard Alexander
World War II trilogy (2)
Fight to the finish
Hough, Richard Alexander
World War II trilogy (3)
Fight with a fiend
Carter, Nicholas
Nicholas Carter series (263)
Fighter aces
Toliver, Raymond F
Fighter aces series (1)
Fighter aces of the Luftwaffe
Toliver, Raymond F
Fighter aces series (2)
Fighter aces of the U.S.A.
Toliver, Raymond F
Fighter aces series (3)
Fighter and prophet
Schechtman, Joseph Boris
Vladimir Yabolinsky series (2)
Fighters in the sky
Whitehouse, Arch
Air war series (1)
Fighting against millions
Carter, Nicholas
Nicholas Carter series (9)
Fighting agents
Baldwin, Alex
Men at war series (4)
Fighting angel
Buck, Pearl Sydenstricker
Spirit and the flesh series (2)
Fighting back
Alverson, Charles
Joe Goodey series (1)
Ellis, Carol
Cheerleaders series (42)
Gutman, Claude
Empty house trilogy (2)
Fighting blood
Young, Gordon Ray
Red Clark series (13)
Fighting buckaroo
Clinton, Jeff
Wildcat O'Shea series (1)
Fighting days, A-American
Drackett, Phil
A-American series (1)
Fighting fantasy
Jackson, Steve
Fighting fantasy gamebook series (46)
Fighting fantasy poster book
Jackson, Steve
Fighting fantasy gamebook series (46)
Fighting fool
Dilnot, George
Val Emery series (2)
Fighting for his own
Stratemeyer, Edward L
Bound to win series (10)
Working upward series (4)
Fighting for the right
Optic, Oliver
Blue and the Gray afloat series (5)
Fighting formula
Burgoyne, Peter
Peter Burgoyne series (2)
Fighting four
Brand, Max
Silvertip series (8)
Fighting Four
Channel, A R
Fighting Four series (1)
Fighting in Cuban waters
Stratemeyer, Edward L
Old Glory series (3)
Fighting in France
Kay, Ross
Big war series (5)
Fighting in the Alps
Fiske, James
World's war series (7)
Fighting in the clouds for France
Fiske, James
World's war series (1)
Fighting Irish
White, Steve
S-Com series (4)
Fighting Joe
Optic, Oliver
Army and navy series (5)
Fighting man
Gruber, Frank
Historical Western series (4)
William Clarke Quantrell series (1)
Fighting man of Mars
Burroughs, Edgar Rice
Martian series (7)
Fighting men
Cartwright, Justin
New Avengers series (4)
Fighting over me
Sharmat, Marjorie Weinman
Sorority sisters series (4)
Fighting shortstop
Cooper, John R
Mel Martin series (6)
Fighting slave of Gor
Norman, John
Tarl Cabot series (14)
Fighting the battle
Samuels, Adelaide Florence
Dick and Daisy Travers series (2)
Fighting the sea
Rand, Edward Augustus
Fighting the sea series (1)
Fighting the U-boat menace
Fiske, James
World's war series (12)
Fighting the zeppelin
Grant, Allan
Boys at the Front series (4)
Fighting vengeance
Logan, Jake
John Slocum series (23)
Fighting westward
Havard, Aline
Westward series (1)
Fighting with French
Strang, Herbert
Stories of the Great War series (2)
Fighting with the U.S.Army
Botsford, Charles Alexander
Victory series (2)
Figment, your dog, speaking
Hawkins, Laura
Riverview series (1)
Figure away
Taylor, Phoebe Atwood
Asey Mayo series (10)
Figure in hiding
Dixon, Franklin W
Hardy boys series (16)
Figure in the dust
Creasey, John
Inspector Roger West series (12)
Figure in the shadows
Bellairs, John
Clock trilogy (2)
Figure it out for yourself
Chase, James Hadley
Vic Malloy series (3)
Figure of eight
Waye, Cecil
Christopher Perrin series (1)
Figure of speech
Mazer, Norma Fox
Jenny series (1)
Figurehead
Knox, Bill
Webb Carrick series (4)
Figures in the foreground
Swinnerton, Frank
Background and foreground series (2)
Figures of earth
Cabell, James Branch
Dom Manuel and his descendants series (2)
Poictesme trilogy (1)
File for record
Tilton, Alice
Leonidas Witherall series (6)
File number one hundred and fifteen
Harper, Harry
Dossier series (3)
File number one hundred and fourteen
Young, Ernest A
Dossier series (2)
File number one hundred and thirteen
Gaboriau, Emile
Dossier series (1)
File on Bolitho Blane
Wheatley, Dennis
Lieutenant John Milton Schwab series (1)
File on Claudia Cragge
Patrick, Q
Lieutenant Timothy Trant series (2)
File on death
Giles, Kenneth
Inspector Harry James and Sergeant Honeybody series (10)
File on Robert Prentice
Wheatley, Dennis
Lieutenant John Milton Schwab series (2)
File on Saint Peter's
Andrews, Jane
Saint Peter's Hospital series (1)
File one hundred and thirteen
Gaboriau, Emile
Dossier series (1)
Files of Ms Tree
Collins, Max Allan
Ms Tree series (1)
Filipino twins
Perkins, Lucy Fitch
Twin series (14)
Fill my empty heart
Baer, Judy
Cedar River daydreams series (8)
Fillets of plaice
Durrell, Gerald
Corfu series (3)
Filling the bill
Fisher, Aileen
Ways of animals series (6)
Filly wore a rod
Janson, Hank
Hank Janson series (40)
Film mystery
Reeve, Arthur Benjamin
Craig Kennedy series (15)
Film of fear
Fredericks, Arnold
Richard Duvall series (5)
Filmi, filmi, Inspector Ghote
Keating, Henry Reymond Fitzwalter
Inspector Ganesh Ghote series (10)
Filthy beast
Garfield, Leon
Apprentices series (11)
Filthy five
Carter, Nick
Nick Carter series (29)
Final
Greaves, Jimmy
Soccer series (1)
Final act
Crisp, Jack H
Special Operations Executive series (2)
Final adventures of Sherlock Holmes
Doyle, Arthur Conan
Sherlock Holmes series (10)
Final adventures of the Robber Hotzenplotz
Preussler, Otfried
Robber Hotzenplotz series (3)
Final analysis of Doctor Stark
Telushkin, Joseph
Rabbi Daniel Winter series (2)
Final appearance
Nolan, Jeannette Covert
Lace White series (1)
Final appointment
Blair, Marcia
Tory Baxter series (6)
Final assault
Berry, Stephen Ames
John Harrison series (4)
Final battle
Lupoff, Richard Allen
Dungeon series (6)
Final burning of boats
Smyth, Ethel Mary
Impressions series (3)
Final chapter
Jones, John G
Amityville horror series (5)
Final circuit
Snodgrass, Melinda Marilyn
Circuit trilogy (3)
Final command
Norwood, Warren
Double-spiral war series (3)
Final conflict
McGill, Gordon
Omen series (3)
Final copy
Barbette, Jay
Harry Butten series (1)
Final correction
McBratney, Sam
Thorensen Dykes series (1)
Final count
Sapper
Bulldog Drummond series (4)
Final crossroads
Parker, Maude
Jim Little series (3)
Final crusade
Murphy, Warren Burton
Destroyer series (76)
Murray, Will
Destroyer series (76)
Final curtain
Adams, Nicholas
Horror High series (8)
Kane, Frank
Johnny Liddell series (24)
Marsh, Ngaio
Inspector Roderick Alleyn series (14)
Final cut
Dixon, Franklin W
Hardy boys case files series (34)
Wright, Eric
Inspector Charlie Salter series (8)
Final days
Woodward, Bob
Watergate series (2)
Final death
Meyers, Richard S
Destroyer series (29)
Murphy, Warren Burton
Destroyer series (29)
Final deduction
Stout, Rex
Nero Wolfe and Archie Goodwin series (35)
Final diary, 1961-1972
Rorem, Ned
Musical diaries series (3)
Final draw
Logan, Jake
John Slocum series (172)
Final dress
Houseman, John
Unfinished business trilogy (3)
Final edit
Carter, Robert A
Nicholas Barlow series (2)
Final edition
McDermid, Val
Lindsay Gordon series (3)
Final encyclopedia
Dickson, Gordon Rupert
Bleys quartet (2)
Dorsai series (8)
Final exam
Blake, Susan
Hawthorne College series (7)
Final fear
Blair, Marcia
Tory Baxter series (7)
Final flight
Coonts, Stephen
Jake Grafton series (2)
Final forensic fables
O
Forensic fables series (3)
Final forensic fables, second series
O
Forensic fables series (4)
Final frontier
Carey, Diane
Star trek sequels series (5)
Dillard, Jeanne M
Star trek moving picture series (5)
Final gambit
Dixon, Franklin W
Hardy boys case files series (62)
Final guest
Blair, Marcia
Tory Baxter series (5)
Final hour
Caldwell, Taylor
Bouchard family trilogy (3)
Final incoherent adventure
Harrison, Harry
Bill, the galactic hero series (7)
Final instalments
Cronin, Michael
Sam Harris series (9)
Final judgement
Barrington, Pamela
Inspector George Marshall series (6)
Final lie
Blair, Marcia
Tory Baxter series (2)
Final moments
Page, Emma
Inspector Kelsey series (5)
Final nexus
DeWeese, Gene
Star trek series (43)
Final nightmare
McKinney, Jack
Robotech series (9)
Final notes
Keene, Carolyn
Nancy Drew files series (65)
Final notice
Gores, Joe
DKA file series (2)
Valin, Jonathan
Harry Stoner series (2)
Final payment
Jacobs, Thomas Curtis Hicks
Temple Fortune series (14)
Final pose
Blair, Marcia
Tory Baxter series (3)
Final programme
Moorcock, Michael
Jerry Cornelius series (1)
Final proof
Ottolengui, Rodrigues
John Barnes series (5)
Robert Leroy Mitchell series (4)
Final quest
Monaco, Richard
Parsival series (3)
Final rain
Ahern, Jerry
Survivalist series (19)
Final reckoning
Jarvis, Robin
Deptford mice trilogy (3)
Final reflection
Ford, John M
Star trek series (16)
Final ring
Blair, Marcia
Tory Baxter series (1)
Final scene
Keene, Carolyn
Nancy Drew files series (38)
Final shot
Barth, Richard
Margaret Binton series (8)
Gilman, George G
Edge series (16)
Final storm
Maloney, Mack
Wingman series (6)
Final tally
Wheeler, Richard Seabrook
Sheriff Santiago Toole series (2)
Final target
Blair, Marcia
Tory Baxter series (4)
Final test
Perlman, Dory
Secret of the Unicorn Queen series (3)
Final witness
Straker, John Foster
David Wright series (2)
Finale
Blair, Marcia
Tory Baxter series (8)
Duke, Winifred
Harold Fieldend series (4)
Financial expert
Narayan, Rasipuram Krishnaswami
Malgudi series (2)
Financier
Dreiser, Theodore
Frank Cowperwood trilogy (1)
Finch's fortune
De la Roche, Mazo
Whiteoak series (9)
Find a victim
Macdonald, Ross
Lew Archer series (5)
Find adventure!
Danby, Mary
Famous Five and you series (2)
Find Angel
Christian, Frederick H
Frank Angel series (3)
Find Demi's baby animals
Hitz, Demi
Demi series (5)
Find Demi's dinosaurs and animal gamebook
Hitz, Demi
Demi series (5)

Fire out of heaven
Millin, Sarah Gertrude
War diary series (6)
Fire over Africa
Kessler, Leo
Stormtroop series (9)
Fire over India
Baker, William Howard
Sexton Blake series (1485)
Fire over Kabul
Kessler, Leo
Stormtroop series (6)
Fire people
Cordell, Alexander
Merthyr trilogy (1)
Mortymers series (5)
Fire planet
Griffin, Pauline Margaret
Star commandos series (7)
Fire-proof hero
Jacobs, Barbara
Fire-proof hero series (1)
Fire Rock
Wood, James
James Fraser series (6)
Fire sanctuary
Kimbriel, Katharine Eliska
Nuala series (1)
Fire sea
Weis, Margaret
Death Gate series (3)
Fire sermon
Morris, Wright
Floyd Warner series (1)
Fire song
Gellis, Roberta
Royal dynasty series (3)
Fire storm
Macdonnell, James Edmond
Dutchy Holland series (35)
Wilson, Gar
Phoenix Force super series (1)
Fire sword
Martine-Barnes, Adrienne
Chronique d'Avebury series (1)
Fire-Tongue
Rohmer, Sax
Paul Harley series (2)
Fire trap
Cameron, Owen
Deputy Sheriff Jake Brown series (2)
Fire Wolf
Brennan, James Herbert
Sagas of the Demonspawn series (1)
Fireball
Christopher, John
Fireball trilogy (1)
Janson, Hank
Hank Janson series (48)
Kerrigan, John
SBS series (1)
Steelbaugh, Larry
Tankwar series (2)
Fireball assignment
Sugar, Andrew
Israeli commandos series (2)
Firebase Seattle
Pendleton, Don
Mack Bolan series (21)
Firebird
Tyers, Kathy
Firebird series (1)
Firebird rocket
Dixon, Franklin W
Hardy boys series (57)
Firebolt
Clay, Patrick
Sergeant Hawk series (5)
Firebrace and the Java Queen
Seafarer
Captain Firebrace series (2)
Firebrand
Steelbaugh, Larry
Tankwar series (4)
Firebrands
Hardin, J D
Raider and Doc series (29)
Firebreak
Herman, Richard
Jack Locke series (3)
Firecake
Postgate, Oliver
Saga of Noggin the Nog series (6)
Fireclown
Moorcock, Michael
Dancers at the end of time series (5)
Firedance
Baker, Scott
Ashlu cycle series (2)
Firedrake
Knaak, Richard Allen
Dragonrealm series (1)
Firefly
Cosgrove, Stephen Edward
Bugg series (41)
Firefly gadroon
Gash, Jonathan
Lovejoy series (6)
Firefox
Thomas, Craig
Firefox series (1)
Firefox down!
Thomas, Craig
Firefox series (2)
Firehand
Norton, Andre
Time war series (5)
Firekill
Stillman, Ron
Tracker series (5)
Firelight and woodsmoke
Michelet, Claude
Wood trilogy (1)
Firelord
Godwin, Parke
Arthurian cycle trilogy (1)
Firemakers
Brown, Rollo Walter
Emergency series (1)
Firemen hot
Hyne, Charles John Cutcliffe
Captain Owen Kettle series (10)
Fires and the stars
Trevor, Meriol
World Dionysus trilogy (3)
Fires at Fairlawn
Bell, Josephine
Doctor David Wintringham series (12)
Fires of Azeroth
Cherryh, Carolyn Janice
Chronicles of Morgaine series (3)
Fires of Fu Manchu
Van Ash, Cay
Fu-Manchu series (16)
Fires of heaven
Jordan, Robert
Wheel of time series (5)
Fires of hell
Hayes, Ralph Eugene
Check Force series (7)
Fires of Lan-Kern
Tremayne, Peter
Lan-Kern trilogy (1)
Fires of Nuala
Kimbriel, Katharine Eliska
Nuala series (2)
Fires of Oakhurst
Johnson, Walter Reed
Oakhurst series (4)
Fires of Paris
Hughes, Zach
Hotel Destiny series (3)
Fires of Scorpio
Prescot, Dray
Dray Prescot series (29)
Fires of Sinhala
De Silva, Colin
Sinhala series (3)
Fires of summer
Kennedy, Adam
Bradshaw trilogy (2)
Fires of Windameir
Hancock, Niel
Windameir circle series (2)
Fires of winter
Lindsey, Johanna
Kristen series (1)
Fireseed
Simon, Morris
Endless quest series (30)
Fireshaper's doom
Deitz, Tom
David Sullivan series (2)
Fireship
Hardy, Adam
George Abercrombie Fox series (11)
Parkinson, Cyril Northcote
Richard Delancey series (2)
Firestorm
Ahern, Jerry
Survivalist series (20)
Steelbaugh, Larry
Tankwar series (3)
Firestorm at Dong Nam
Lansing, John
Black Eagles series (14)
Firestorm USA
Hild, Jack
SOBS series (16)
Firework for Oliver
Sanders, John
Nicholas Pym series (1)
Fireworks
Levy, Muriel
Wonk series (3)
Fireworks at Farthingale
Gervaise, Mary
Farthingale series (1)
Fireworks for Semolina Silkpaws
Williams, Gladys
Semolina Silkpaws series (2)
Fireworks galore
Townson, Hazel
Lenny and Jake series (7)
Fireworks mystery
Dicks, Terrance
Ask Oliver series (5)
Firing line
Murphy, Warren Burton
Destroyer series (41)
Firing squad
Barnett, James
Superintendent Owen Smith series (3)
Firm ambitions
Kahn, Michael A
Rachel Gold series (3)
Firm of Nucingen
Balzac, Honore de
Scenes of Parisian life series (5)
First ace
Zeybel, Henry
Gunship series (1)
First act
Christie, Anne
First act series (1)
Robinson, Martha
Matty series (2)
First adventure
Coatsworth, Elizabeth
Once-upon-a-time-in-America series (1)
Leyland, Eric
Captain series (1)
First American gentleman
Cabell, James Branch
Conquest series (3)
First and last Gravelsburg School spelling bee
Mallett, Jerry J
Tumtwit series (1)
First and ten
James, Laurence
Gridiron series (1)
First and Third Crusades
Birt, David
Middle Ages series (6)
First assignment
James, Judi
Fashion features series (1)
First Athenian memories
Mackenzie, Compton
Memories series (2)
First base jinx
Cooper, John R
Mel Martin series (4)
First battle
Michaels, Melisa C
Skyrider series (2)
First big Monster book
Blance, Ellen
Monster series (6)
First big Olga da polga book
Bond, Michael
Olga da Polga series (1)
First big radio Thin King book
Farmer, Derek
Thin King series (1)
First Biggles omnibus
Johns, William Earl
Biggles series (30)
First blood
Konrad, Klaus
Russian series (1)
Martin, Cort
Jared Bolt series (1)
McCurtin, Peter
Jim Rainey series (5)
Morrell, David
John Rambo series (1)
First blood 2
Morrell, David
John Rambo series (3)
First body
Payne, Laurence
Chief Inspector Sam Birkett series (1)
First book of Blackberry Farm
Pilgrim, Jane
Blackberry Farm series (26)
First book of Eve
Fowl
Eve series (1)
First book of Krab
Parry, Edward Abbott
Krab series (2)
First book of swords
Saberhagen, Fred
Book of swords trilogy (1)
First book of the McFlannels
Pryde, Helen W
McFlannel family series (1)
First-born
Housman, Laurence
Palace plays series (4)
First-born son
Murray, Andrew
Sexton Blake series (103)
First came a murder
Creasey, John
Department Z series (3)
First case of Mister Paul Savoy
Gregory, Jackson
Paul Savoy series (1)
First challenge book of Brownie stories
Moss, Robert Alfred
Brownie stories series (1)
First channel
Lorrah, Jean
Sime-Gen series (3)
First childhood
Berners, Gerald Hugh Tyrwhitt-Wilson
Distant prospect series (1)
First children
Rutley, Cecily Marianne
Children of other days series (1)
First chronicles of Greystone Bay
Grant, Charles Lewis
Chronicles of Greystone Bay series (1)
First chronicles of Prydain
Alexander, Lloyd
Prydain series (3)
First chronicles of Thomas Covenant, the Unbeliever
Donaldson, Stephen Reeder
First Chronicles of Thomas Covenant series (3)
First class murder
Roosevelt, Elliott
Eleanor Roosevelt series (9)
First class ticket
Chula Chakrabongse
Eastern prince series (2)
First come, first kill
Lockridge, Frances
Inspector Merton Heimrich series (16)
Richards, Francis
Inspector Merton Heimrich series (16)
First comes spring
Rockwell, Anne
Our life series (1)
First command
Macdonnell, James Edmond
Dutchy Holland series (29)
First contact?
Walters, Hugh
Chris Godfrey series (13)
First date
Levy, Elizabeth
Gymnasts series (13)
Stine, Robert Lawrence
Fear Street series (16)
First dates
Stine, Jane
Everything you need to survive series (2)
First day at preschool
Oxenbury, Helen
First picture books series (6)
First deadly sin
Sanders, Lawrence
Edward X Delaney series (1)
First death
James, William M
Apache series (1)
First directive
McNamara, Joseph D
First directive series (1)
First edition
Moffat, Bill
Press Gang series (1)
First evil
Stine, Robert Lawrence
Fear Street cheerleaders series (1)
First fair wind
Short, Agnes
Christie family series (1)
First families
Bonner, Terry Nelsen
New South Wales series (2)
First family
Tilley, Patrick
Amtrak wars series (2)
First family on the moon
Walters, Hugh
Chris Godfrey series (21)
Peter Hill series (2)
First farm in the valley
Pellowski, Anne
Valley Farm series (1)
First fast draw
L'Amour, Louis
Cullen Baker series (1)
First five lives of Annie Besant
Nethercot, Arthur Hobart
Annie Besant series (1)
First flowers of our wilderness
Flexner, James Thomas
History of American painting series (1)
First four years
Wilder, Laura Ingalls
Laura series (9)
First gentleman of America
Cabell, James Branch
Conquest series (3)
First Glencannon omnibus
Gilpatric, Guy
Mister Colin Andrew Macthrockle Glencannon series (3)
First goal
Hardcastle, Michael
Mark Fox series (1)
First good joy
Nicholson, Celia Anna
Levine family series (2)
First hard times
Smith, Doris Buchanan
Lloyd Albert and Ancil Witherspoon series (2)
First hit of the season
Dentinger, Jane
Jocelyn O'Roarke and Phillip Gerard series (2)
First horror
Stine, Robert Lawrence
Ninety-nine Fear Street series (1)
First hundred thousand
Hay, Ian
First hundred thousand series (1)
First I say the Shema
Cone, Molly
Shema series (1)
First impressions
Roberts, Nora
Flowers series (5)
First job
Sorenson, Jane
Katie Hooper series (5)
First kill
Grover, Marshall
Larry and Stretch series (148)
First kill all the lawyers
Storey, Alice
Samantha Adams series (1)
First Lensman
Smith, Edward Elmer
Lensman series (2)
First lieutenant
Macdonnell, James Edmond
Commander William Mallett series (1)
First Lieutenant
Maynard, Kenneth
Lieutenant Lamb series (2)
First longship
Taylor, Keith
Bard series (2)
First man in
Richards, Frank
Schoolboy series (3)
First man in Rome
McCullough, Colleen
Rome series (1)
First meet
Levy, Elizabeth
Gymnasts series (2)
First Mountain Man
Johnstone, William Wallace
First Mountain Man trilogy (1)
First mountain man
Johnstone, William Wallace
Mountain Man Preacher series (1)
First Mountain Man
Johnstone, William Wallace
Mountain Man series (11)
First name
Schmidt, Dennis
Twilight of the gods trilogy (1)

First named
Wylie, Jonathan
Servants of Ark trilogy (1)
First of all
Lambert, Janet
Campbells series (5)
First of June
Adams, Henry Cadwallader
Charlton School series (2)
First Olympics
Baglio, Ben M
Choose your own adventure series (77)
First on the moon
Walters, Hugh
Chris Godfrey series (3)
First person rural
Perrin, Noel
Sometime farmer series (1)
First place
Pascal, Francine
Sweet Valley twins series (8)
First power play
Miller, John Joseph
Inner planets trilogy (1)
First rains
Bonnici, Peter
Arjuna's family series (1)
First rebel
Swanson, Neil Harman
American colonial series (2)
First Republic
Dumas, Alexandre
Napoleon series (1)
First rosette
Pullein-Thompson, Christine
David and Pat series (1)
First round
Lucas, Saint John
First round series (1)
First round murder
Turner, John Victor
Amos Petrie series (1)
First Rumpole omnibus
Mortimer, John
Horace Rumpole series (3)
First sacrifice
Gifford, Thomas
Wind chill series (2)
First Saint omnibus
Bloxsom, Peter
Saint series (51)
First salvo
Taylor, Charles Doonan
Bernie Ryng series (1)
First set of catechisms and prayers
Watts, Isaac
Catechisms and prayers series (1)
First settlers
Gaskin, Carol
Time traveler series (3)
First shot
Coburn, L J
Caleb Thorn series (1)
First Sir Percy
Orczy, Emmuska
Dutch War of Independence series (4)
Scarlet Pimpernel series (1)
First step
Richardson, Jean
Moth Graham series (1)
First stop Honolulu
Dixon, Franklin W
Ted Scott flying series (4)
First strike
Robbins, David
Blade series (1)
First summer
Crow, Duncan
Simon Ire series (1)
Fraser, Mary
Village trilogy (1)
First sunrise
Mountford, Charles Pearcy
Dreamtime series (3)
First term at Malory Towers
Blyton, Enid
Malory Towers series (1)
First term at Trebizon
Digby, Anne
Trebizon series (1)
First to die
Nelson, Peter N
Mollie Fox series (1)
First to kill
Usher, Frank
Daye Smith series (6)
First to land
Reeman, Douglas
Blackwood family series (2)
First treasury of Herman
Unger, Jim
Herman treasury series (1)
First two hundred years of Monty Python
Johnson, Kim Howard
Monty Python series (6)
First Wantoknow omnibus for boys
Goodman, Montague
Wantoknow series for boys (3)
First Wantoknow omnibus for girls
Dennison, Dorothy
Wantoknow series for girls (3)
First whisper of the wind in the willows
Grahame, Kenneth
Toad Hall series (1)
Wind in the willows series (1)
First wife, twice removed
Curzon, Clare
Superintendent Mike Yeadings and Sergeant Angus Mott series (8)
First World War atlas
Gilbert, Martin
History atlas series (5)
First World War history atlas
Gilbert, Martin
History atlas series (5)
First-year's fancy
Collins, Lynne
Hartlake Hospital series (5)
First years of Revolution, 1918-21
Ehrenburg, Ilya
Men, years and life series (2)
First, you fight
Drumm, D B
Traveler series (1)
Firstborn
Carter, Tonya R
Elven nations trilogy (1)
FirstFlight
Claremont, Chris
FirstFlight series (1)
Fish
Bruna, Dick
Toy box tale series (8)
Morgan, Alison
Llanwern series (1)
Owen, Dilys
Mister Munch series (4)
Fish and chips
Rogers, Pamela
Michael series (1)
Fish and kill
Hastings, Macdonald
Montague Cork series (1)
Fish and tin fish
Wylie, Philip
Crunch and Des series (3)
Fish Creek mystery
Smith, Beatrice Schillinger
Kate and Ben King series (3)
Fish dinner in Memison
Eddison, Eric Rucker
Zimiamvian trilogy (2)
Fish Face
Giff, Patricia Reilly
Kids of the Polk Street School series (2)
Fish fly!
Browne, Dik
Hagar the horrible series (47)
Fish for murder
Lee, Edward
Red Blake series (2)
Fish in her kettle
Green, Michael
Coarse plays series (3)
Fish or cut bait
Fair, A A
Bertha Cool and Donald Lam series (24)
Fish out of water
Hackforth-Jones, Gilbert
Commander Wally Phipps-Mangot series (1)
Fish preferred
Wodehouse, Pelham Grenville
Blandings Castle series (4)
Fish story
Hoyt, Richard
John Denson series (4)
Fisher boys of Pleasant Cove
Kellogg, Elijah
Pleasant Cove series (6)
Fisherman
Manning, Paul
Merry-go-rhymes series (3)
Fisherman cat
Roe, JoAnn
Cat series (2)
Fisherman's curse
Easton, Malcolm Coleman
Kyala series (2)
Fisherman's gold
Finlay, Campbell Kirkman
John Macinnes series (1)
Fisherman's hunt
Pace, Tom
Ben Garden series (2)
Fisherman's lady
Macdonald, George
Malcolm series (1)
Fishey wishes
Delton, Judy
Pee wee scout series (20)
Fisheye
Townend, Peter
Philip Quest series (3)
Fishing competition
Saddler, Allen
King and queen series (3)
Fishing for a job
Plain, Neil
Boris Blundle and Gang series (6)
Fishing for trouble
Niall, Ian
Billy Boyo and Albert Finn series (1)
Fishing in the Styx
Park, Ruth
Cuckoo series (2)
Fishing is dangerous
Millar, Florence N
Chief Inspector Douglas Grant series (2)
Fishmans
Katz, H W
Fishmans series (1)
Fishpingle
Vachell, Horace Annesley
Fishpingle series (1)
Fishy business
Lee, Robert
Fishy business series (1)
Fist of Fatima
Edwards, Paul
John Eagle series (4)
Fistful of death
Kane, Henry
Peter Chambers series (13)
Fistful of empty
Schutz, Benjamin Merrill
Leo Haggerty series (5)
Fistful of hate
Lee, Steve
Kung Fu western series (2)
Fistfull of dollars
Chandler, Frank
Dollar series (5)
Fit for a duchess
Budd, Mavis
Dust to dust series (3)
Fit to kill
Halliday, Brett
Michael Shayne series (32)
Fitzempress' law
Norman, Diana
Henry II trilogy (2)
Fitzhug
Wheeler, Richard Seabrook
Rocky Mountain Company series (1)
Five against death
Roberts, J R
Gunsmith series (123)
Five against the law
Cody, Stone
Five Mavericks series (7)
Five alarm funeral
Sterling, Stewart
Ben Pedley series (1)
Fire Marshal Ben Pedley series (1)
Five and dime murders
Reinsmith, Richard
Bodyguard series (5)
Five are the symbols
Finch, Matthew
Dick Lingham series (1)
Five are together again
Blyton, Enid
Famous Five series (21)
Five assassins
Jerome, Owen Fox
Philip Maccray series (4)
Five at Ashefield
Govan, Christine Noble
Plummer children series (2)
Five beds to Mecca
Gray, Rod
Lady from L.U.S.T. series (4)
Five Bills and Bladebone
Grimes, Martha
Inspector Richard Jury series (9)
Five boys in a cave
Church, Richard
Tomahawk Club series (1)
Five brains
Sheridan, Wilfred
Tommy Weston series (1)
Five bullets
Thayer, Lee
Peter Clancy series (38)
Five bullets for Judge Blake
Grover, Marshall
Larry and Stretch series (247)
Five Bushel Farm
Coatsworth, Elizabeth
Sally Smith series (2)
Five card death
Roberts, J R
Gunsmith series (68)
Five Cat Club
Makris, Kathryn
Eco-Kids series (1)
Five caught in a treacherous plot
Blyton, Enid
Famous Five series (8)
Five chameleons
Grant, Maxwell
Shadow series (17)
Five children
Nesbit, Edith
Five children series (3)
Five children and it
Nesbit, Edith
Five children series (1)
Five days to oblivion
Woodbury, David Oakes
George Riam series (1)
Five diamonds
Graydon, William Murray
Sexton Blake series (85)
Five doctors
Dicks, Terrance
Doctor Who series (81)
Five dolls and the Duke
Clare, Helen
Five dolls series (5)
Five dolls and the monkey
Clare, Helen
Five dolls series (2)
Five dolls and their friends
Clare, Helen
Five dolls series (4)
Five dolls in a house
Clare, Helen
Five dolls series (1)
Five dolls in the snow
Clare, Helen
Five dolls series (3)
Five down!
Burningham, John
Number play series (2)
Five easy lessons
Odgers, Sally Farrell
Bandinangi series (1)
Five faces of murder
Flynn, Jay
McHugh series (5)
Five fall into adventure
Blyton, Enid
Famous Five series (9)
Five fathoms dead
Robeson, Kenneth
Doc Savage series (153)
Five find a secret way
Blyton, Enid
Famous Five series (2)
Five-finger discount
De Clements, Barthe
Jerry Johnson trilogy (1)
Five flamboys
Beeding, Francis
Colonel Alastair Granby series (2)
Five flights of the Starfire
Mumford, Edwin Embree
Starfire series (5)
Five for the shootout
Grover, Marshall
Larry and Stretch series (326)
Five from me, five from you
Macdonald, Shelagh
Pethi and Tini series (2)
Five frontiers
Murray, William Hutchinson
John Taunt series (1)
Five gates to Armageddon
Christian, John
Richard Deutsch series (1)
Five get into a fix
Blyton, Enid
Famous Five adventure games series (7)
Famous Five series (17)
Five get into trouble
Blyton, Enid
Famous Five series (8)
Five go adventuring
Blyton, Enid
Famous Five and you series (2)
Five go adventuring again
Blyton, Enid
Famous Five series (2)
Five go down to the sea
Blyton, Enid
Famous Five series (12)
Five go fown to the sea
Blyton, Enid
Famous Five adventure games series (2)
Five go off in a caravan
Blyton, Enid
Famous Five and you series (5)
Famous Five series (5)
Five go off to camp
Blyton, Enid
Famous Five adventure games series (1)
Famous Five series (7)
Five go to Billycock Hill
Blyton, Enid
Famous Five adventure games series (6)
Famous Five series (16)
Five go to Demon Rocks
Blyton, Enid
Famous Five adventure games series (5)
Famous Five series (19)
Five go to Mystery Moor
Blyton, Enid
Famous Five series (13)
Five go to Smuggler's Top
Blyton, Enid
Famous Five and you series (4)
Five go to Smugglers' Top
Blyton, Enid
Famous Five series (4)
Five gold rings
Wiat, Philippa
Grey family series (1)
Five graves for Lassiter
Slade, Jack
Lassiter series (26)
Five have a mystery to solve
Blyton, Enid
Famous Five adventure games series (3)
Famous Five series (20)
Five have a wonderful time
Blyton, Enid
Famous Five adventure games series (8)
Famous Five series (11)
Five have plenty of fun
Blyton, Enid
Famous Five series (14)
Five Hundred
Bamman, Henry A
Checkered flag series (8)
Five in family
Anstruther, Eileen Harriet
Farm servant trilogy (3)
Five in fear
Teed, George Hamilton
Grant Rushton series (2)
Five in the family
Montgomery, Elizabeth
Dick, Jane and Sally series (6)
Five inns
Inchbald, Ralph
Colonel Paternoster series (2)
Five ivory boxes
Grant, Maxwell
Shadow series (226)
Five keys to crime
Grant, Maxwell
Shadow series (260)
Five-leafed clover
Fraser, James
Inspector Bill Aveyard series (6)
Five Listen with mother tales about Charles
Ainsworth, Ruth
Charles series (3)
Five little ducks
Raffi
Raffi songs to read series (6)
Five Little Peppers
Sidney, Margaret
Five Little Peppers series (1)
Five Little Peppers abroad
Sidney, Margaret
Five Little Peppers series (7)
Five Little Peppers and how they grew
Sidney, Margaret
Five Little Peppers series (1)
Five Little Peppers and their friends
Sidney, Margaret
Five Little Peppers series (9)

Five Little Peppers at school
Sidney, Margaret
Five Little Peppers series (8)
Five Little Peppers grown up
Sidney, Margaret
Five Little Peppers series (3)
Five Little Peppers in the little brown house
Sidney, Margaret
Five Little Peppers series (11)
Five Little Peppers midway
Sidney, Margaret
Five Little Peppers series (2)
Five little pigs
Christie, Agatha
Hercule Poirot series (23)
Five little rich girls
Block, Lawrence
Leo Haig series (1)
Five lives
Longford, Frank Pakenham
Born to believe trilogy (2)
Five matchboxes
Blayn, Hugo
Inspector Garth series (2)
Five million years to earth
Kneale, Nigel
Quatermass series (3)
Five minute mysteries
Weber, Ken
Five minute mysteries series (1)
Five minute stories
Richards, Laura Elizabeth
Five minute stories series (1)
Five minute tales
Blyton, Enid
Minute tales series (1)
Five minutes' peace
Murphy, Jill
Larges family trilogy (1)
Five months on a derelict
Houston, Edwin James
Pacific shipwreck series (1)
Five o'clock tales
Blyton, Enid
Evening tales series (1)
Five of my best
Eberhart, Mignon Good
Susan Dare series (2)
Five on a hike together
Blyton, Enid
Famous Five adventure games series (4)
Famous Five series (10)
Five on a secret trail
Blyton, Enid
Famous Five series (15)
Five on a treasure island
Blyton, Enid
Famous Five and you series (1)
Famous Five series (1)
Five on Finniston Farm
Blyton, Enid
Famous Five series (18)
Five on Kirrin Island again
Blyton, Enid
Famous Five and you series (6)
Famous Five series (6)
Five on the track of a spook train
Blyton, Enid
Famous Five series (7)
Five pairs of hands
Goolden, Barbara
Tabor family series (2)
Five pieces of jade
Ball, John
Virgil Tibbs series (4)
Five red fingers
Flynn, Brian
Anthony Bathurst series (6)
Five red herrings
Sayers, Dorothy Leigh
Lord Peter Wimsey series (7)
Five red stars
Bolt, Ben
Bob Ponting series (2)
Five rings of fire
Stivers, Dick
Able Team series (11)
Five rivers to death
Casberg, Melvin A
Captain Prem Narayan series (2)
Five Roads Inn
Goyne, Richard
Paul Templeton series (10)
Five roads to death
Philips, Judson Pentecost
Peter Styles series (14)
Five roads to Tlen
Lambert, William J
Tlen series (1)
Five run away to danger
Blyton, Enid
Famous Five series (3)
Five run away together
Blyton, Enid
Famous Five and you series (3)
Famous Five series (3)
Five shilling holiday
Hill, Lorna
Patience series (5)
Five signs from Ruby
Macdonald, Hugh Chisholm
Paul Williams series (2)
Five Silver daughters
Golding, Louis
Elsie Silver series (1)
Five South Coast seasons
Roland, Betty
Improbable life trilogy (3)
Slaven, Roy
South Coast series (3)
Five stories of Ferrara
Bassani, Giorgio
Ferrara series (1)
Five suspects
Walling, Robert Alfred John
Philip Tolefree series (6)
Five thousand miles underground
Rockwood, Roy
Great marvel series (3)
Five times Maigret
Simenon, Georges
Inspector Jules Maigret series (45)
Inspector Jules Maigret series (46)
Inspector Jules Maigret series (54)
Inspector Jules Maigret series (56)
Five to five
Muir, Dorothy Erskine
Inspector Woods series (2)
Five-twelfths of heaven
Scott, Melissa
Silence Leigh trilogy (1)
Five way secret agent
Reynolds, Mack
Rex Bader series (1)
Five were murdered
Plummer, Thomas Arthur
Detective Inspector Andrew Frampton series (9)
Five windows
Stevenson, Dorothy Emily
Barbie France series (1)
Five years after
Graydon, William Murray
Sexton Blake series (87)
Fivepenny mystery
Shaw, Jane
Penny series (5)
Five's a crowd
Lambert, Janet
Campbells series (4)
Fix it!
McPhail, David Michael
Emma series (1)
Fix like this
Constantine, K C
Mario Balzic series (4)
Fixed alibi
Carter, Nicholas
Nicholas Carter series (521)
Fize of the Gabriel Ratchets
Norwood, Warren
Windhover tapes series (3)
Fjord adventure
Dale, Judith
Shirley Flight series (9)
Flag
Shaw, Robert
Cure of souls trilogy (1)
Flag captain
Kent, Alexander
Captain Richard Bolitho series (12)
Flag from the isles
Dickinson, William Croft
Donald and Jean series (3)
Flag full of stars
Ferguson, Brad
Star trek series (54)
Flag lieutenant
Drury, William Price
Flag lieutenant series (1)
Flag lieutenant in China
Drury, William Price
Flag lieutenant series (2)
Flag of truce
Warner, Susan Bagert
Sceptres and crowns series (2)
Flag-raising
Wiggin, Kate Douglas
Rebecca series (2)
Flagellator
Brown, Carter
Rick Holman series (20)
Flags in the dust
Faulkner, William
Narcissa series (1)
Flagstaff showdown
Cunningham, Chet
Outlaws series (6)
Flagstick
Miles, Keith
Alan Saxton series (4)
Flail and the fish
Gerard, Francis
Marquess de Brussac series (1)
Flair for affairs
Brand, Hilary
Hilary Brand series (5)
Flambards
Peyton, K M
Flambards series (1)
Flambards series (3)
Flambards divided
Peyton, K M
Flambards series (4)
Flambards in summer
Peyton, K M
Flambards series (3)
Flame
Fritch, Elizabeth
Richmond series (1)
Lutz, John
Fred Carver series (4)
Roberts, Kenneth
Black fire series (2)
Flame and the dagger
Moore, Arthur
California trilogy (2)
Flame and the frost
Gray, Harriet
Quadroon trilogy (3)
Flame and the king's ransom
Leyland, Eric
Flame series (10)
Flame and the League of Five
Leyland, Eric
Flame series (16)
Flame and the treasure trail
Leyland, Eric
Flame series (12)
Flame breathers
Robeson, Kenneth
Avenger series (12)
Flame hits back
Leyland, Eric
Flame series (8)
Flame hits the trail
Leyland, Eric
Flame series (7)
Flame in Byzantium
Yarbro, Chelsea Quinn
Atta Olivia Clemens trilogy (1)
Flame in the fens
Frazier, Arthur
Wolfshead series (5)
Flame in the mist
Audemars, Pierre
Monsieur Pinaud series (13)
Flame in the morning
Whittaker, June Lovina
Henry and Susannah Kable series (2)
Flame is green
Lafferty, Raphael Aloysius
Coscuin chronicles series (1)
Flame key
Moran, Daniel Keys
Keys to paradise trilogy (1)
Flame knife
Howard, Robert Ervin
Conan series (6)
Flame makes the grade
Leyland, Eric
Flame series (14)
Flame of Fidelity
Du Bay, Sandra
Fidelity series (2)
Flame of fire
Hocking, Joseph
Religious movements series (3)
Flame of Islam
Lamb, Harold
Crusades series (2)
Flame of life
Sillitoe, Alan
Frank Dawley trilogy (3)
Flame of murder
Neville, Margot
Inspector Grogan and Sergeant Manning series (11)
Flame of Persepolis
Griffin, John
Richard Raven series (11)
Flame of the Amazon
Leyland, Eric
Flame series (4)
Flame of the East
Fitzgerald, Julia
Astromance series (1)
Flame of the forest
Broome, Adam
Commissioner Denzil Grigson series (6)
Ghose, Sudhindra Nath
Vermilion boat series (2)
Flame of the Inquisition
Kornblatt, Marc
Time machine series (15)
Flame of the Sahara
Leyland, Eric
Flame series (9)
Flame of the Sierras
Leyland, Eric
Flame series (1)
Flame of the South
Gluyas, Constance
Deep South trilogy (3)
Flame of the West
Dixon, Dorothy
Leather and lace series (4)
Flame of Virginia City
Willoughby, Lee Davis
Women who won the West series (5)
Flame over Africa
Leyland, Eric
Flame series (3)
Flame river
Longtree, Warren T
Ruff Justice series (24)
Flame, secret agent
Leyland, Eric
Flame series (15)
Flame sets the pace
Leyland, Eric
Flame series (11)
Flame takes a chance
Leyland, Eric
Flame series (6)
Flame takes command
Leyland, Eric
Flame series (13)
Flame takes over
Leyland, Eric
Flame series (2)
Flame tree
Pratt, Theodore
Florida trilogy (2)
Flame trees of Thika
Huxley, Elspeth
Kenya childhood series (1)
Flame upon the ice
Forstchen, William R
Ice prophet trilogy (2)
Flame was fatal
Brody, Marc
Marc Brody series (30)
Flame winds
Page, Norvell W
Prester John series (1)
Flame wins through
Leyland, Eric
Flame series (5)
Flames from the ashes
Johnstone, William Wallace
Ashes series (18)
Flames of war
Sellers, Con
Men at arms series (2)
Flamesong
Barker, Muhammad Abd al-Rahman
Tekumel series (2)
Flaming arrows
Steele, William Owen
Tennessee frontier series (3)
Weston, Cole
Andrew Ryder series (5)
Flaming belt
Gibbons, Harry Hornaby Clifford
Sexton Blake series (568)
Flaming falcons
Robeson, Kenneth
Doc Savage series (30)
Flaming forest
Curwood, James Oliver
Three rivers series (3)
Flaming guns
Arthur, Burt
Mustang Marshal series (9)
Flaming man
Chaber, M E
Milo March series (18)
Flaming mountain
Blaine, John
Rick Brant series (17)
Flaming sword
Buckley, Eunice
Sandor Raimann series (4)
Flaming trap
Roddy, Lee
American adventure series (5)
Flaming youth
Fabian, Warner
Flaming youth series (1)
Flanders
Rayner, Claire
Poppy series (2)
Flanders Road
Simon, Claude
Grass quartet (2)
Flandry of Terra
Anderson, Poul
Sir Dominic Flandry series (3)
Flannel flowers and other bush babies
Gibbs, May
Gumnut Land series (4)
Flannelled fool
Worsley, Thomas Cuthbert
Flannelled fool series (1)
Flash Casey, detective
Coxe, George Harmon
Flash Casey series (3)
Flash for freedom!
Fraser, George Macdonald
Flashman series (3)
Flash Gordon
Cover, Arthur Byron
Flash Gordon series (8)
Flash Gordon book
Cover, Arthur Byron
Flash Gordon series (14)
Flash Gordon in the caverns of Mongo
Raymond, Alex
Flash Gordon series (1)
Flash, hold for murder
Whelton, Paul
Garry Dean series (1)
Flash of lightning
Adye, John
Oliver Smaile series (3)
Flash point
Bruce, Jean
Secret Agent O.S.S.117 series (8)
Pendleton, Don
SuperBolan series (12)
Flash the fox
Evens, George Bramwell
Romany readers series (3)
Flash the young deer
Burgess, Thornton Waldo
Animal stories series (7)
Flashback
Carmichael, Harry
John Piper and Quinn series (22)
Wood, Ted
Reid Bennett series (8)
Flashman
Fraser, George Macdonald
Flashman series (1)
Flashman and the dragon
Fraser, George Macdonald
Flashman series (8)
Flashman and the mountain of light
Fraser, George Macdonald
Flashman series (9)
Flashman and the Redskins
Fraser, George Macdonald
Flashman series (7)
Flashman at the Charge
Fraser, George Macdonald
Flashman series (4)
Flashman in the great game
Fraser, George Macdonald
Flashman series (5)
Flashman's lady
Fraser, George Macdonald
Flashman series (6)
Flashpoint
Blayn, Hugo
Inspector Garth series (3)
Janson, Hank
Hank Janson series (204)
Kessler, Leo
Wotan series (14)
Macdonnell, James Edmond
Captain Peter Bentley series (33)
Commander Sainsbury series (6)
Marlowe, Dan James
Earl Drake series (4)
Randall, Anthony Asheton
Roger Patten series (2)
Flashpoint for treason
Reid, Desmond
Sexton Blake series (1427)
Flat beneath
Delannoy, Burford
Watson Ward series (2)

Flat in Paris
De Born, Edith
De Kailern family series (3)
Flat man
Impey, Rose
Creepies series (1)
Flat Number 4
Bayfield, William John
Sexton Blake series (323)
Flat on my back
Baxter, Alida
Flat on my back series (1)
Flat Stanley
Brown, Jeff
Stanley Lambchops series (1)
Flat tyre in Fulham
Bell, Josephine
Claude Warrington-Reeve series (3)
Inspector Steven Mitchell series (12)
Flatboats on the Ohio, westward bound
Chambers, Catherine E
Adventures in frontier America series (3)
Flatland
Abbott, Edwin Abbott
Flatland series (1)
Flats fixed, among other things
Tracy, Don
Giff Speer series (6)
Flaunting extravagant queen
Plaidy, Jean
Louis XV trilogy (1)
Flaunting moon
Darby, Catherine
Moon series (3)
Flaw in the system
Dominic, R B
Congressman Ben Safford series (7)
Flax of dreams
Williamson, Henry
Flax of dream series (4)
Flaxborough Crab
Watson, Colin
Inspector Purbright series (6)
Flea
Bamman, Henry A
Checkered flag series (6)
Flea flicker
Cosgrove, Stephen Edward
Bugg series (42)
Fledgling
Langton, Jane
Edward, Eleanor and Georgie Hall series (4)
Fledglings
Harris, John
Martin Falconer series (1)
Fleecing of Fodder City
Mackenzie, Pierce
T G Horne series (2)
Fleet
Drake, David
Fleet series (1)
Fleet of the damned
Cole, Allan
Sten series (4)
Fleet of the springers
Mahr, Kurt
Perry Rhodan series (22)
Fleet Street eclogues
Davidson, John
Fleet Street eclogues series (1)
Fleet the stag
Rutley, Cecil Bernard
Wild life story series (15)
Fleet wings
Dempster, Guy
Guy Laurence and Tony Carlisle series (1)
Fleetwood Mansions mystery
Dix, Maurice Buxton
Inspector James Miller series (2)
Fleming of Honister
Sutton, Graham
Fleming family series (6)
Flemish shop
Simenon, Georges
Inspector Jules Maigret series (12)
Inspector Jules Maigret series (14)
Flesh and blood
Cook, Thomas H
Frank Clemons series (2)
Dixon, Franklin W
Hardy boys case files series (39)
Finch, John
Spoils of war series (1)
Harvey, James Neal
Ben Tolliver series (3)
Humphreys, Emyr
Amy Parry series (1)
Pendleton, Don
SuperBolan series (13)
Flesh and the orchid
Chase, James Hadley
Carol Blandish series (3)
Flesh hunters
Miall, Robert
UFO series (1)
Flesh of the morning
Callow, Philip
Colin Patten trilogy (3)
Flesh was cold
Fischer, Bruno
Ben Helm series (4)
Flesh wounds
Holbrook, David
Flesh wounds trilogy (1)
Pendleton, Don
Mack Bolan series (57)
Fleshly school
Kitchen, Paddy
Vanessa Talisend series (2)
Fletch
McDonald, Gregory
Fletch series (3)
Fletch and the man who
McDonald, Gregory
Fletch series (9)
Fletch and the widow Bradley
McDonald, Gregory
Fletch series (7)
Fletch chronicles
McDonald, Gregory
Fletch series (2)
Fletch series (4)
Fletch series (9)
Fletch reflected
McDonald, Gregory
Fletch series (11)
Fletch, too
McDonald, Gregory
Fletch series (2)
Fletch won
McDonald, Gregory
Fletch series (1)
Fletcher and Zenobia
Gorey, Edward
Fletcher and Zenobia series (1)
Fletcher and Zenobia save the circus
Gorey, Edward
Fletcher and Zenobia series (2)
Fletch's fortune
McDonald, Gregory
Fletch series (6)
Fletch's moxie
McDonald, Gregory
Fletch series (8)
Fleurette of Four Corners
Burgin, George Brown
Four Corners series (16)
Flexing the warp
Norwood, Warren
Windhover tapes series (2)
Flick of a fin
Peters, Geoffrey
Inspector Trevor Nichols and Sergeant Tom Burton series (5)
Flicka
O'Hara, Mary
Flicka series (1)
Flicka's friend
O'Hara, Mary
Flicka series (3)
Flicker of doom
Kenyon, Paul
Baroness Penelope Saint-John Orsini series (7)
Flickering candle
Ainsworth, Patricia
Burnley series (1)
Flickering death
Macleod, Robert
Jonathan Gaunt series (1)
Flickering torch mystery
Dixon, Franklin W
Hardy boys series (22)
Fliers of Antares
Akers, Alan Burt
Dray Prescot series (8)
Flight
Brown, Joseph Paul Summers
Steeldust series (2)
Hine, Muriel
Clodagh Laidlaw series (1)
Flight five, Africa
Daniell, David Scott
Alison and John series (5)
Flight four, India
Daniell, David Scott
Alison and John series (4)
Flight from Berbora
Sirota, Mike
Berbora series (2)
Flight from Enchantry
Williamson, Philip G
Firstworld chronicles series (3)
Flight from fear
Janson, Hank
Hank Janson series (54)
Flight from Montego Bay
Haig, Alec
Alec Haig series (3)
Flight from Neveryon
Delany, Samuel Ray
Neveryon series (3)
Flight from Paris
Macleod, Robert
Jonathan Gaunt series (9)
Flight from Tarkihl
Darlton, Clark
Atlan series (2)
Flight from the dark
Dever, Joe
Lone Wolf series (1)
Flight from the grave
Hogan, Robert Jasper
G-Eight series (6)
Flight from the palace
Sava, George
Peter Slavine series (3)
Flight in darkness
Harvester, Simon
Asia in turmoil series (15)
Flight in Yiktor
Norton, Andre
Krip Vorland series (3)
Flight into danger
Dixon, Franklin W
Hardy boys case files series (47)
Flight into fear
Saxon, Peter
Sexton Blake series (1411)
Flight into infinity
Darlton, Clark
Perry Rhodan series (24)
Flight of a witch
Peters, Ellis
Inspector George Felse series (3)
Flight of Angels
Milne, Paula
Angels series (2)
Flight of exiles
Bova, Ben
Exiles trilogy (2)
Flight of fear
Rathjen, Carl Henry
Land of the giants series (5)
Flight of hawks
Eden, Matthew
Marc Savage series (3)
Flight of honour
McEnroe, Richard S
Far stars and future times series (2)
Flight of Mavin Manyshaped
Tepper, Sheri S
Mavin Manyshaped trilogy (2)
Flight of sparrows
Brown, Roy
Sparrows series (1)
Flight of steps
Nicolson, Robert
Mrs Ross series (2)
Flight of the archangel
Holland, Isabelle
Claire Aldington series (1)
Flight of the bamboo saucer
Gordon, Fritz
Schuyler Townsend series (1)
Flight of the Dragon-kyn
Fletcher, Susan
Kaeldra series (1)
Flight of the Falcon
Lindsey, Robert
Falcon series (2)
Flight of the falcon
Smith, Wilbur Addison
Zouga Ballantyne series (1)
Flight of the Golden Goose
McCarthy, Maureen
Mission top secret series (6)
Flight of the grey goose
Canning, Victor
Smiler Miles trilogy (2)
Flight of the Hawk
James, Leigh Franklin
John Cooper Baines series (4)
Flight of the heron
Broster, Dorothy Kathleen
Jacobite trilogy (1)
Flight of the intruder
Coonts, Stephen
Jake Grafton series (1)
Flight of the lobster
Bunting, James
British International Airways series (2)
Flight of the moth-kin
Tapp, Kathy Kennedy
Moth-kin series (2)
Flight of the Old Dog
Brown, Dale
Patrick McLanahan series (1)
Flight of the phoenix
Rosenberger, Joseph
Death Merchant series (52)
Flight of the Raven
Charles, Robert
Counter-terror series (2)
Flight of the raven
Roberson, Jennifer
Chronicles of the Cheysuli series (7)
York, Rebecca
Peregrine connection trilogy (2)
Flight of the Starfire
Mumford, Edwin Embree
Starfire series (1)
Flight of the stiff
Brett, Michael
Pete McGrath series (4)
Flight of the swans
Willard, Barbara
Mantlemass series (5)
Flight of youth, 1851-1885
Pope-Hennessy, James
Monckton Milnes series (2)
Flight one, Australia
Daniell, David Scott
Alison and John series (1)
Flight seven four one
Pendleton, Don
SuperBolan series (5)
Flight Seven One Four
Herge
Tintin series (23)
Flight signals
Tralins, Sandor Robert
Jack Lund series (1)
Flight six six six
Schmidt, Dan
Eagle Force series (3)
Flight six, the Holy Land
Daniell, David Scott
Alison and John series (6)
Flight three, United States of America
Daniell, David Scott
Alison and John series (3)
Flight to adventure
Serraillier, Ian
David and Uncle Bill series (2)
Flight to an island
Sykes, Pamela
Barton family series (2)
Flight to Arras
Saint-Exupery, Antoine de
Airman's odyssey trilogy (3)
Flight to Falconhurst
Horner, Lance
Falconhurst series (7)
Flight to Gibraltar
Southall, Ivan
War in the air series (2)
Flight to Opar
Farmer, Philip Jose
Opar series (3)
Flight to terror
Elder, Michael
Barclay series (2)
Flight to the Reich
Kessler, Leo
Submarine series (5)
Flight to the Savage Empire
Lorrah, Jean
Savage Empire series (4)
Flight to the South Pole
Bamman, Henry A
World of adventure series (2)
Flight to Thlassa Mey
McCarty, Dennis
Thlassa Mey series (1)
Flight two, Canada
Daniell, David Scott
Alison and John series (2)
Flight with fear
Gerard, Francis
Sir John Meredith series (15)
Flim-flam man, and other stories
Owen, Guy
Flim-flam man series (2)
Flim-flam man and the apprentice grifter
Owen, Guy
Flim-flam man series (2)
Flint and roses
Jagger, Brenda
Barforth trilogy (2)
Flint lord
Herley, Richard
Pagans trilogy (2)
Flint the king
Kirchoff, Mary Lynn
DragonLance preludes II series (2)
Flint's Island
Wibberley, Leonard
Treasure Island series (4)
Flintstones at the circus
Lewis, Jean
Flintstones series (3)
Flintstones meet the Gruesomes
Lewis, Jean
Flintstones series (5)
Flintstone's picnic panic
Lewis, Jean
Flintstones series (4)
Flinx in flux
Foster, Alan Dean
Flinx of the Commonwealth series (6)
Flip
Dennis, Wesley
Flip series (1)
Flip and the cows
Dennis, Wesley
Flip series (2)
Flip and the morning
Dennis, Wesley
Flip series (3)
Flip-side
Copper, Basil
Mike Faraday series (30)
Flip side of life
Martin, James E
Gil Disbro series (2)
Flipside
Quin-Harkin, Janet
Sugar and spice series (6)
Flirting
Hoh, Diane
Cheerleaders series (7)
Flirting with danger
Keene, Carolyn
Nancy Drew files series (47)
Flitterfly
Cosgrove, Stephen Edward
Bugg series (43)
Flittermouse
Kartun, Derek
Alfred Baum series (2)
Flo affair
Anderson, Verily
Anderson family series (5)
Floater factor
Michaels, Melisa C
Skyrider series (5)
Floating and sinking
Pluckrose, Henry
Thinking about series (8)
Floating city
Lustbader, Eric
Ninja series (5)
Verne, Jules
Floating city series (1)
Floating continent
De Camp, Lyon Sprague
Krishna series (4)
Floating crime
Keene, Carolyn
Nancy Drew series (120)
Floating death
Derrick, Lionel
Penetrator series (25)
Floating game
Garforth, John
Avengers series (3)
Floating gods
Harrison, Michael John
Viriconium series (3)
Floating Outfit
Edson, John Thomas
Floating Outfit series (52)
Floating prison
Leroux, Gaston
Cheri-Bibi series (1)
Flock
Austin, Mary
Californian Indian series (2)
Flock of four
Thorn, Ismay
Geoff and Jim Harrington series (2)
Flood
Black, Lionel
Superintendent Francis Foy series (1)
Cole, Michael
Pigeon Street series (1)

Creasey, John
Doctor Palfrey series (18)
McDowell, Michael M
Blackwater series (1)
Vachss, Andrew
Burke series (1)
Flood and flame
Verne, Jules
Golden volcano series (2)
Flood at Dry Creek
Gorelick, Molly Chernow
Rescue series (2)
Flood tide
Bassett, Sara Ware
Cape Cod series (4)
Cherryh, Carolyn Janice
Merovingen nights series (6)
Flood-tide
Harrod-Eagles, Cynthia
Morland family series (9)
Flood warning
Romains, Jules
Men of goodwill series (9)
Flood water
Ling, Peter
Water series (2)
Floodmakers
Lyon, Elinor
Ian and Sovra series (10)
James, Alan and Roslin series (2)
Floodtide for Rafferty
Woodberry, Joan
Rafferty series (2)
Floosie goes astray
Standish, Walter
Floosie series (1)
Floosie on the spot
Standish, Walter
Floosie series (2)
Floosie passes by
Standish, Walter
Floosie series (3)
Floosie takes a fall
Standish, Walter
Floosie series (4)
Flop Ear, the funny rabbit
Barnum, Richard
Kneetime animal stories series (8)
Flora goes to town
Hayes, Barbara
Town mouse and country mouse series (3)
Florence and John
Abbott, Jacob
Florence series (1)
Florence Griffith Joyner, dazzling Olympian
Aaseng, Nathan
Sports acheivers series (7)
Florence's return
Abbott, Jacob
Florence series (6)
Florentine
Kruss, James
Florentine series (1)
Shulman, Sandra
Francesca series (1)
Florentine Madonna
Griffin, John
Richard Raven series (9)
Florentine on holiday
Kruss, James
Florentine series (2)
Florentine woman
Williamson, Hugh Ross
Catherine de Valois trilogy (1)
Florian Slappey
Cohen, Octavus Roy
Florian Slappey series (2)
Florian Slappey goes abroad
Cohen, Octavus Roy
Florian Slappey series (1)
Florians
Stableford, Brian Michael
Daedalus series (1)
Florida firefight
Ramm, Carl
James Hawker series (1)
Florida junket
Davison, Ann
Voyages series (5)
Florida project
Sullivan, Tim
V series (5)
Florida run
Grave, Stephen
Miami Vice series (1)
Flossie Teacake, again!
Davies, Hunter
Flossie Teacake series (2)
Flossie Teacake strikes back!
Davies, Hunter
Flossie Teacake series (3)
Flossie Teacake's fur coat
Davies, Hunter
Flossie Teacake series (1)
Flotilla leader
Macdonnell, James Edmond
Captain Peter Bentley series (18)
Flounder
Grass, Gunter
Danzig trilogy (3)
Flower and market girls of Paris
Zola, Emile
Rougon Macquart series (3)
Flower and the nettle
Lindbergh, Anne Morrow
Unicorn series (4)
Flower-covered corpse
Avallone, Michael
Ed Noon series (19)
Flower fairies
Dickinson, Mary Anne
Charm bracelet series (2)
Flower fairies of the autumn
Barker, Cicely Mary
Flower fairies series (3)
Flower fairies of the garden
Barker, Cicely Mary
Flower fairies series (6)
Flower fairies of the spring
Barker, Cicely Mary
Flower fairies series (1)
Flower fairies of the summer
Barker, Cicely Mary
Flower fairies series (2)
Flower fairies of the trees
Barker, Cicely Mary
Flower fairies series (5)
Flower fairies of the wayside
Barker, Cicely Mary
Flower fairies series (7)
Flower fairies of the winter
Barker, Cicely Mary
Flower fairies series (8)
Flower fairy alphabet
Barker, Cicely Mary
Flower fairies series (8)
Flower fairy picture book
Barker, Cicely Mary
Flower fairies series (8)
Flower garden donkeys
Towers, Joyce
Donkey series (2)
Flower in a teacup
Lang-Sims, Lois
Time to be born series (2)
Flower in the forest
Lewin, Hugh
Second chance series (2)
Flower in the mountains
Coldsmith, Don
Spanish bit series (13)
Flower o' the lily
Orczy, Emmuska
Dutch War of Independence series (2)
Flower of Albert Square
Miller, Hugh
Eastenders series (4)
Flower of desire
Janson, Hank
Hank Janson series (176)
Flower-patch among the hills
Klickmann, Flora
Flower-patch series (1)
Flower-patch garden book
Klickmann, Flora
Flower-patch series (6)
Flower-patch neighbours
Klickmann, Flora
Flower-patch series (4)
Flower Potts and the giant
Howson, John Michael
Adventure Island story books (1)
Flower Power Joe
Tann, Roger
Troopers series (1)
Flower show
Uttley, Alison
Little Brown Mouse series (9)
Flower that's free
Harrison, Sarah
Flowers series (2)
Flowering in the sun
Stewart, Flora
Flora and Dickie series (1)
Flowering of the Cumberland
Arnow, Harriette
Cumberland series (2)
Flowering of the rod
Doolittle, Hilda
War trilogy (3)
Flowering spring
Vipont, Elfrida
Haverard family series (4)
Flowering wilderness
Galsworthy, John
End of the chapter series (2)
Flowerpot Men and the bush baby
Bird, Maria
Flowerpot Men series (3)
Flowerpot Men and the weathercock
Bird, Maria
Flowerpot Men series (4)
Flowers
Postgate, Oliver
Saga of Noggin the Nog series (7)
Rippon, Angela
Learn with Victoria Plum series (3)
Flowers by request
Holton, Leonard
Father Joseph Bredder series (5)
Flowers for Melissa
Byers, Irene
Tony and Melissa series (2)
Flowers for Mrs Harris
Gallico, Paul
Mrs Harris series (1)
Flowers for the judge
Allingham, Margery
Albert Campion series (7)
Flowers from Caroline
Mansbridge, Pamela
Caroline series (2)
Flowers in the attic
Andrews, Virginia Cleo
Dollanganger family series (2)
Flowers of darkness
Cohen, Matt
Salem quartet (4)
Flowers of evil
Sherwood, John
Celia Grant series (4)
Flowers of Hiroshima
Morris, Edita
Hiroshima series (1)
Flowers of the field
Harrison, Sarah
Flowers series (1)
Flowers of the forest
Garnett, David
Golden echo trilogy (2)
Hone, Joseph
Peter Marlow series (3)
Flown the Koopa
Wayne, Matt
Nintendo adventure series (8)
Flunking of Joshua T Bates
Shreve, Susan Richards
Joshua T Bates series (1)
Flux
Goulart, Ron
Ben Jolson series (3)
Fly away Cinda
Lambert, Janet
Cinda Hollister series (2)
Fly away, Jill
Byrd, Max
Mike Haller series (2)
Fly away Paul
Hofmeyer, Hans
Garibaldi series (2)
Fly away, youth
Winn, Godfrey
Dreams of youth series (2)
Fly baby fly
Cosgrove, Stephen Edward
Bugg series (44)
Fly boys
Morgan, Stanley
Fly boys series (1)
Fly boys in London
Morgan, Stanley
Fly boys series (2)
Fly boys sky-jacked
Morgan, Stanley
Fly boys series (3)
Fly by night
Afford, Max
Jeffery Blackburn series (4)
Jones, Jenny
Flight over fire series (1)
Fly-by-Night
Peyton, K M
Ruth Hollis series (1)
Fly for three lives
Barrie, Alexander
Jonathan Kane series (1)
Fly home, Columbina
Fry, Rosalie Kingsmill
Lucinda series (3)
Fly in the cobweb
Parrish, Frank
Dan Mallett series (6)
Fly Jamskoni
Barry, Clive
Jamskoni Airline series (2)
Fly of the Fells
Waterhouse, Arthur
Fellside Farm series (2)
Fly paper
Collins, Max Allan
Nolan series (3)
Fly-switch from the Sultan
Bates, Darrell
Tanganyika series (1)
Flyaway
Bagley, Desmond
Max Stafford series (1)
Flyaway sister
Cooper, Lisa
Princess Beatrice Hospital series (10)
Flyaways and Cinderella
Hardy, Alice Dale
Flyaways series (1)
Flyaways and Goldilocks
Hardy, Alice Dale
Flyaways series (3)
Flyaways and Little Red Riding Hood
Hardy, Alice Dale
Flyaways series (2)
Flying against time
Dixon, Franklin W
Ted Scott flying series (9)
Flying beast
Masterman, Walter Sidney
Sir Arthur Sinclair series (6)
Flying bird
Postgate, Oliver
Pingwings series (2)
Flying blackbirds
Burtis, Thomson
Air combat series (4)
Flying blind
Bowles, Colin
Mike Hazzard series (1)
Campbell, Alice
Tommy Rostetter series (3)
Flying boys in the sky
Ellis, Edward Sylvester
Flying boys series (1)
Flying boys to the rescue
Ellis, Edward Sylvester
Flying boys series (2)
Flying carpet
Halliburton, Richard
Famous adventures series (1)
Flying clues
Dutton, Charles Judson
John Bartley series (7)
Flying colors
Mooser, Stephen
Gigglemajig series (3)
Flying colours
Forester, Cecil Scott
Horatio Hornblower series (8)
Flying dagger murder
Cowdroy, Joan
Li Moh series (1)
Flying dinosaurs
Berenstain, Michael
Dinosaurs series (5)
Flying Doctor
Noonan, Michael
Flying Doctor series (1)
Flying Doctor and the secret of the pearls
Noonan, Michael
Flying Doctor series (3)
Flying Doctor hits the headlines
Noonan, Michael
Flying Doctor series (5)
Flying Doctor mystery
Beresford, Elisabeth
Gappy, Jim and Jane series (2)
Flying Doctor on the Great Barrier Reef
Noonan, Michael
Flying Doctor series (2)
Flying Doctor shadows the mob
Noonan, Michael
Flying Doctor series (4)
Flying Doctor to the rescue
Beresford, Elisabeth
Gappy, Jim and Jane series (8)
Flying Doctor under the desert
Noonan, Michael
Flying Doctor series (6)
Flying Dutchmen
Clune, Frank
Discovery series (18)
Flying eagle
Champlin, Tim
Matt Tierney series (9)
Flying eggs and things
Livings, Henry
Ravensgill series (2)
Flying ensign
Styles, Showell
Ensign Peter Byrd series (1)
Flying feathers
Grahame, Iain
Daw's Hall series (1)
Flying fish
Brathwaite, Errol
Maori Wars trilogy (1)
Flying fish adventure
Saville, Malcolm
Michael and Mary series (3)
Flying free
Cate, Dick
Flying free series (1)
Flying girl
Van Dyne, Edith
Flying girl series (1)
Flying girl and her chum
Van Dyne, Edith
Flying girl series (2)
Flying goblin
Robeson, Kenneth
Doc Savage series (90)
Flying Hazzard
Bowles, Colin
Mike Hazzard series (2)
Flying high
Morrison, Margaret
Annetze de Steur series (1)
Flying horse
Harvester, Simon
Asia in turmoil series (13)
Heron Murmur series (2)
Flying jet
Cook, Canfield
Lucky Terrell series (7)
Dale, Judith
Shirley Flight series (14)
Flying lion
Kruse, Max
Lion series (2)
Flying machine
Postgate, Oliver
Saga of Noggin the Nog series (3)
Flying machines
Firmin, Peter
Make it work series (4)
Flying nun
Rios, Tere
Flying nun series (1)
Flying patrol
Anderson, Ian
Scarlet riders series (6)
Flying popcorn experiment
Hodgman, Ann
Lunchroom series (6)
Flying red horse
Crane, Frances
Pat and Jean Abbott series (12)
Flying reporter
Theiss, Lewis Edwin
Air mail series (4)
Flying saucer gambit
Maddock, Larry
Hannibal Fortune and Webley series (1)
Flying saucer mystery
Keene, Carolyn
Nancy Drew series (58)
Flying Smurf
Peyo
Smurf series (3)
Flying Squad tragedy
Bayfield, William John
Sexton Blake series (509)
Flying squadron
Woodman, Richard
Nathaniel Drinkwater series (12)
Flying stingaree
Blaine, John
Rick Brant series (18)
Flying summer
Sykes, Pamela
Barton family series (1)
Flying to Amy-Ran Fastness
Craine, Edith Janice
Airplane Boys series (4)
Flying to the rescue
Dixon, Franklin W
Ted Scott flying series (13)
Flying too high
Greenwood, Kerry
Phryne Fisher series (2)
Flying U Ranch
Bower, Bertha Muzzy
Flying U Ranch series (4)
Flying U strikes
Bower, Bertha Muzzy
Flying U Ranch series (10)
Flying U's last stand
Bower, Bertha Muzzy
Flying U Ranch series (5)

For a few dollars more
Millard, Joseph John
Dollar series (2)
For a girl called Isaiah
Shelynn, Jack
Ned Parker series (4)
For a madman's millions
Carter, Nicholas
Nicholas Carter series (369)
For a pawned crown
Carter, Nicholas
Nicholas Carter series (611)
For all the right reasons
Coffman, Elaine
Mackinnon brothers series (5)
For benefits received
Buckley, Eunice
Fiorina series (1)
For Brownies
Williams, Ursula Moray
Brownies series (1)
For crown and kingdom
Vardeman, Robert Edward
Swords of Raemllyn series (6)
For crying out shroud
Blakeston, Oswell
Screaming series (2)
For each other
Lambert, Janet
Campbells series (2)
For Esme, with love and squalor
Salinger, Jerome David
Glass family series (1)
For fear of little men
Blackburn, John
General Charles Kirk series (9)
For Ginger's sake
Hueston, Ethel
Ginger Ella trilogy (3)
For Godmother and country
Larkin, Rochelle T
Donna series (3)
For goodness' sake
Wells, Carolyn
Fleming Stone series (41)
For honour's sake
Lillie, Lucy Cecil
Squire's daughter series (2)
For I have lived today
Dwyer-Joyce, Alice
Doctor Catriona Chisholm series (1)
For king and company
Meacham, Ellis Kirby
Captain Percival Merewether series (3)
For life, and other stories
Rudd, Steele
Rudd family series (5)
For love of Audrey Rose
De Felitta, Frank
Audrey Rose series (2)
For love of evil
Anthony, Piers
Incarnations of immortality series (6)
For love of Imabelle
Himes, Chester
Grave Digger Jones and Coffin Ed Johnson series (1)
For love of Mother-not
Foster, Alan Dean
Flinx of the Commonwealth series (1)
For me to say
McCord, David
Rhymes of the never was an always is series (4)
For members only
Sharmat, Marjorie Weinman
Sorority sisters series (1)
For murder I charge more
McAuliffe, Frank
Augustus Mandrell series (3)
For murder will speak
Connington, John Jervis
Sir Clinton Driffield series (13)
For my brother's sins
Kelly, Sheelagh
Feeney family series (2)
For my own amusement
Delderfield, Ronald Frederick
Amusement trilogy (2)
For now, forever
Roberts, Nora
Flowers series (19)
Macgregor series (5)
For old crime's sake
Ames, Delano
Dagobert and Jane Brown series (12)
For passion, for heaven
Fisher, Vardis
Testament of man series (12)
For Queen and freedom
Rutley, Cecil Bernard
Tales of stirring times series (1)
For services to medicine
Douglas, Colin
David Campbell series (6)
For special services
Gardner, John Edmund
James Bond series (19)
For the defence, Doctor Thorndyke
Freeman, Richard Austin
Doctor John Evelyn Thorndyke series (22)
For the glory
Peters, David
Photon series (1)
For the good of the state
Price, Anthony
Doctor David Audley and Jack Butler series (16)
For the hell of it
Grover, Marshall
Larry and Stretch series (256)
For the honor of Randall
Chadwick, Lester
College sports series (5)
For the honour of the school
Barbour, Ralph Henry
Hilton School trilogy (2)
For the King
Welch, Ronald
Carey family series (3)
For the liberty of Texas
Bonehill, Ralph
Mexican war series (1)
For the love of a child
Mahmoody, Betty
Daughter series (2)
For the love of a horse
Leitch, Patricia
Jinny series (1)
For the love of murder
Scherf, Margaret
Reverend Martin Buell series (1)
For the love of Sami
Preston, Fayrene
Gold class trilogy (2)
For the religion
Drummond, Hamilton
Religious wars trilogy (1)
For the sake of Elena
George, Elizabeth
Inspector Thomas Lynley and Sergeant Barbara Havers series (5)
For the sake of revenge
Carter, Nicholas
Nicholas Carter series (470)
For the silvership
Thurston, Robert
Rugger series (1)
For the sons of gentlemen
Wigg, T I G
Teaching series (2)
For the Stars and Stripes
Tomlinson, Everett Titsworth
War for the Union series (1)
For the White Rose
Carey, Wymond
Monsieur Martin series (2)
For the witch of the mists
Smith, David Claude
Bran Mak Morn trilogy (3)
For them that trespass
Raymond, Ernest
London gallery series (8)
For this I had borne him
Bradby, Godfrey Fox
Dick series (2)
For Uncle Sam, boss
Fitzhugh, Percy Keese
Boy Scouts series (2)
For what we have received
Toye, Francis
Truly thankful series (1)
For Yardley
Barbour, Ralph Henry
Yardley Hall series (4)
For your eyes only
Fleming, Ian
James Bond series (8)
For your sighs only
Allison, Clyde
Agent triple zero eight series (9)
Forayers
Simms, William Gilmore
American Revolution series (6)
Forbidden adventure
Wuorio, Eva Lis
Jersey series (2)
Forbidden beast
Forrester, John
Bestiary trilogy (3)
Forbidden bridge
Roland, Betty
Jamie series (1)
Forbidden castle
Packard, Edward
Choose your own adventure series (14)
Forbidden chest
Sutton, Margaret
Judy Bolton series (24)
Forbidden city
Page, Ian
World of Lone Wolf series (2)
Forbidden ecstasy
Taylor, Janelle
Sioux series (3)
Forbidden fountain of Oz
McGraw, Eloise Jervis
Oz series (44)
Forbidden frontiers
Maddock, Stephen
Timothy Terrel series (8)
Forbidden ground
Swanson, Neil Harman
American colonial series (3)
Forbidden hour
Crossley, Maude
Guy Bannister series (1)
Forbidden kisses
Goudge, Eileen
Seniors series (8)
Forbidden land
Sarabande, William
First Americans series (3)
Forbidden love
Hill, Meredith
Chrystal Falls series (6)
Pascal, Francine
Sweet Valley High series (34)
Forbidden region
North, David
Time warriors series (2)
Forbidden territory
Wheatley, Dennis
Duc de Richelieu series (2)
Forbidden tower
Bradley, Marion Zimmer
Darkover series (6)
Judd, Frances K
Kay Tracey series (13)
Forbidden towers
Gaskin, Carol
Forgotten forest series (4)
Forbidden trail
Garis, Lilian C
Melody Lane series (1)
Forbidden valley
Greene, L Patrick
Aubrey Saint John Major series (11)
Forbidden Valley
Schroeder, Doris
Lassie series (5)
Force
Adam, Paul
Time of life series (1)
Force carries on
Longstreth, Thomas Morris
Royal Canadian Mounted Police series (2)
Force of arms
McKinney, Jack
Robotech series (5)
Stine, George Harry
Warbots series (8)
Force of circumstance
Beauvoir, Simone de
Dutiful daughter series (3)
Force of eagles
Herman, Richard
Jack Locke series (2)
Force of innocence
Weatherhead, John
Professor David Connell series (1)
Force of nature
Solomita, Stephen
Stanley Moodrow series (2)
Force of terror
Litvinoff, Samuel
Faces of terror series (3)
Force play
Stuart, Anthony
Vladimir Gull series (4)
Force ten from Navarone
Maclean, Alistair
Navarone series (2)
Forced entries
Carroll, Jim
New York diaries series (2)
Forced entry
Solomita, Stephen
Stanley Moodrow series (3)
Forced march
Kessler, Leo
Wotan series (7)
Forces from the Federation
Hagberg, David
Flash Gordon series (12)
Forces of Krill
Meretzky, S Eric
Zork series (1)
Forecast
Hall, Malcolm
Headlines series (2)
Forehanding and backhanding, if you're lucky
Paulsen, Gary
Sports on the light side series (6)
Foreign bodies
Petrie, Rhona
Doctor Nassim Pride series (1)
Truss, Seldon
Inspector Bass series (2)
Foreign exchange
Beinhart, Larry
Tony Cassella series (3)
Sangster, Jimmy
John Smith series (2)
Foreign wife
Bouras, Gillian
Australian wife series (1)
Foreigner
Plante, David
Francoeur family series (3)
Foreigners
Walmsley, Leo
Phantom Lobster series (1)
Forensic fables
O
Forensic fables series (1)
Forerunner
Merejkowski, Dmitri Sergeevich
Christ and Antichrist trilogy (2)
Norton, Andre
Planet Warlock series (4)
Forerunner foray
Norton, Andre
Planet Warlock series (3)
Forerunner, the second venture
Norton, Andre
Planet Warlock series (5)
Forespoken
Levin, Betty
Claudia and Evan trilogy (3)
Forest affair
Chance, John Newton
Mister DeHavilland series (11)
Forest and the fort
Allen, Hervey
Disinherited series (1)
Forest and the kingdom
Trevor, Meriol
World Dionysus trilogy (1)
Forest by night
Speakman, Frederick James
Gamekeeper trilogy (2)
Forest feud
Leyland, Eric
Max and Scrap series (7)
Forest fire alert!
Lampton, Christopher
Alert series (3)
Forest fire mystery
Nesbit, Troy
Wilderness mystery series (6)
Forest Glen
Kellogg, Elijah
Forest Glen series (5)
Forest holiday
Severn, David
Crusoe series (5)
Forest is a long time growing
Brown, Robin
Rhodesian series (2)
Forest-land
Chambers, Robert William
Land series (4)
Forest lord
Williams, Michael Leon
From thief to king series (2)
Forest mammals
Kalman, Bobbie
North American wildlife series (3)
Forest messengers
Ellis, Edward Sylvester
Paddle your own canoe trilogy (1)
Forest of Boland Light Railway
B B
Boland series (1)
Forest of doom
Livingstone, Ian
Fighting fantasy gamebook series (3)
Forest of fear
Foley, Louise Munro
Choose your own adventure series (54)
Forest of forever
Swann, Thomas Burnett
Ancient history series (3)
Minotaur trilogy (2)
Forest of fortune
Sayer, Walter William
Sexton Blake series (355)
Forest of swords
Altsheler, Joseph Alexander
World War trilogy (3)
Forest of the king
Brightfield, Richard
Escape from the Kingdom of Frome series (2)
Forest of the night
Steussy, Marti
Forest series (1)
Forest of the Railway
B B
Boland series (1)
Forest of twisted dreams
Stine, Robert Lawrence
Wizards, warlocks and you series (1)
Forest runners
Altsheler, Joseph Alexander
Trailers series (2)
Forest years
Rich, Louise Dickinson
Woods series (3)
Foresters afield
Byers, Irene
Foresters series (2)
Foresters of Fourways
Byers, Irene
Foresters series (1)
Forests of Gleor
Lord, Jeffrey
Richard Blade series (22)
Forests of Maine
Abbott, Jacob
Marco Paul's adventures in pursuit of knowledge series (3)
Forever and always
Pascal, Francine
Forever trilogy (2)
Forever and ever
Lambert, Janet
Campbells series (3)
Forever begins tomorrow
Coville, Bruce
A.I. Gang series (4)
Forever China
Payne, Robert
Chinese diaries series (1)
Forever ecstasy
Taylor, Janelle
Sioux series (9)
Forever free
Adamson, Joy
Elsa series (3)
Morrow, Honore Willsie
Great Captain trilogy (1)
Forever friend
Hunt, Angela Elwell
Cassie Perkins series (2)
Forever McLean
Goodchild, George
Inspector McLean series (46)
Forever spring
Hohl, Joan
Vanzant family trilogy (3)
Forever to remain
Timms, Edward Vivian
Australian saga series (1)
Forever wilt thou die
Byfield, Barbara
Simon Bede and Helen Bullock series (2)
Forge
Barea, Arturo
Forging of a rebel trilogy (1)
Drake, David
Generals series (1)
Stribling, Thomas Sigismund
Colonel Miltiades Vaiden trilogy (1)
Forge in the forest
Roberts, Charles George Douglas
Acadia series (1)
Rohan, Michael Scott
Winter of the world trilogy (2)

Forge of experience, 1732-1775
Flexner, James Thomas
George Washington series (1)
Forge of God
Bear, Greg
Law series (1)
Forged in fury
Rhodes, Evan Harold
American palace series (2)
Forget my fate
Wallis, Ruth Sawtell
Eric Lund series (3)
Forget what you saw
Ashford, Jeffrey
Detective Inspector Don Kerry series (5)
Forgetting
Norby, Lisa
Cheerleaders series (8)
Forgetting's no excuse
Stott, Mary
Forgetting series (1)
Forging of Fantom
Underhill, Charles
Captain Fantom series (2)
Forging the Darksword
Weis, Margaret
Darksword trilogy (1)
Forgive me, lovely lady
Easton, Nat
Bill Banning series (9)
Forgotten country
Trevor, Meriol
Luxembourg series (4)
Forgotten enemy
Grover, Marshall
Larry and Stretch series (269)
Forgotten fleet mystery
Coffin, Geoffrey
Inspector Scott Stuart series (2)
Forgotten gold
Grant, Maxwell
Shadow series (197)
Forgotten kingdom
Power, Norman
Firlanders series (1)
Forgotten life
Aldiss, Brian Wilson
Squire quartet (2)
Forgotten murders
Wainwright, John
Northern Police series (58)
Forgotten place
Fores, John
London Airport series (1)
Forgotten Realms atlas
Fonstad, Karen Wynn
Avatar trilogy (3)
Forgotten road
Harvester, Simon
Asia in turmoil series (25)
Dorian Silk series (12)
Forgotten sea of Mars
Resnick, Mike
Martian series (12)
Forgotten season
Conlon, Kathleen
Forgotten season series (1)
Forgotten star
Greene, Joseph
Dig Allen series (1)
Forgotten submarine
Catherall, Arthur
Bulldog tugboat series (3)
Forgotten treasure
Matranga, Frances Carfi
Nina Cristina series (3)
Forign body
Field, Moira
Inspector Flower series (1)
Forlorn River
Grey, Zane
Forlorn River Ranch series (1)
Form line of battle
Kent, Alexander
Captain Richard Bolitho series (10)
Former days
Maclean, Norman
Former days trilogy (1)
Former king
Corby, Adam
Doom-quest of Ara-Karn series (1)
Formula Atlantic
Wilkinson, Sylvia
World of racing series (2)
Formula for crime
Grant, Maxwell
Shadow series (220)
Formula for murder
Reynolds, Adrian
Professor Dennis Barrie series (1)
Formula for trouble
Stine, Megan
Twistaplot series (3)
Formula One
Wilkinson, Sylvia
World of racing series (1)
Fornicazione
Green, Michael
Coarse plays series (1)
Forrest J Ackerman presents Invasion of Mars
Serviss, Garrett Putnam
War of the worlds series (2)
Forsaken lady
Balzac, Honore de
Scenes of private life series (18)
Forsaken woman
Balzac, Honore de
Scenes of private life series (18)
Forsyte reprise
Dawson, Suleika
Modern comedy series (4)
Forsyte saga
Galsworthy, John
Forsyte saga trilogy (3)
Forsytes, the saga continues
Dawson, Suleika
Modern comedy series (4)
Forsythia finds murder
Payes, Rachel
Forsythia Brown series (1)
Fort
Bradley, Mary Hastings
Old Chicago series (1)
Fort Blood
Cunningham, Chet
Pony soldiers series (10)
Fort Dance
Wheeler, Richard Seabrook
Rocky Mountain Company series (2)
Fort Davis
Mitchum, Hank
Stage coach station series (42)
Fort de Chastaigne
Coldsmith, Don
Spanish bit series (16)
Fort Despair
Gilman, George G
Adam Steele series (23)
Fort Dillon
Grover, Marshall
Larry and Stretch series (217)
Fort Hayes bustout
Edwards, Josh
John Stone series (9)
Fort in the forest
Barbary, James
Adventure in history series (1)
Tomlinson, Everett Titsworth
Colonial series (2)
Fort in the jungle
Wren, Percival Christopher
Sinbad Dysart series (3)
Fort in the wilderness
Barbary, James
Adventure in history series (1)
McCall, Edith
Frontiers of America series (18)
Stratemeyer, Edward L
Colonial series (5)
Fort Laramie
Porter, Donald Clayton
Winning the West series (2)
Fort Ricks
Grover, Marshall
Nevada Jim series (61)
Fort Starvation
Gruber, Frank
Historical Western series (7)
Fort Sumter to Perryville
Foote, Shelby
Civil War trilogy (1)
Fort Terror
Anderson, Ian
Scarlet riders series (5)
Fort Terror murders
Mason, Francis Van Wyck
Colonel Hugh North series (3)
Fort Treachery
James, William M
Apache series (5)
Fort Verde
Mitchum, Hank
Stage coach station series (39)
Fort Wilberforce
Coleman, Leslie
Wilberforce series (4)
Fort Yuma
Mitchum, Hank
Stage coach station series (8)
Fortescue candle
Flynn, Brian
Anthony Bathurst series (18)
Fortescue of the Fourth
Browne, Reginald
Whitelands series (1)
Forth, beast!
Marlow, Louis
Swan's milk series (2)
Fortinbras has escaped
Malpass, Eric Lawson
Gaylord series (3)
Fortitude
Walpole, Hugh
London Group series (1)
Maradick series (3)
Peter Westcott series (1)
Fortnight
Drew, Sidney
Sexton Blake series (648)
Fortress
Drake, David
Kelly series (2)
Gavin, Catherine
Second Empire quartet (1)
Walpole, Hugh
Herries saga series (3)
Wilson, Colin
Spider world series (1)
Fortress and the fire
Friedman, Michael Jan
Vidar trilogy (3)
Fortress Atlantis
Scheer, Karl Herbert
Perry Rhodan series (52)
Fortress Eagle
Williams, David
Tank series (2)
Fortress in time
Mahr, Kurt
Perry Rhodan series (123)
Fortress London
Hughes, Zach
Hotel Destiny series (2)
Fortress of death
McGann, Michael
Marauders series (7)
Fortress of forbidden destiny
Syvertsen, Ryder
Mystic rebel series (6)
Fortress of lost worlds
Rypel, Thadeus Chester
Gonji series (4)
Fortress of solitude
Robeson, Kenneth
Doc Savage series (23)
Fortress of the pearl
Moorcock, Michael
Elric series (6)
Fortress of the six moons
Scheer, Karl Herbert
Perry Rhodan series (7)
Fortuna West, lawman
Hogan, Ray
Fortuna West series (1)
Fortunata and Jacinta
Perez Galdos, Benito
Contemporary novels of Spain series (14)
Fortunate adventure
Ponsonby, Doris Almon
Jaspard family series (1)
Fortunate belle
Gladstone, Maggie
Lacebridge ladies series (1)
Fortunate fortunes
Aaseng, Nathan
Inside business series (2)
Fortunate grandchild
Read, *Miss*
Time remembered series (1)
Fortunate marriage
Trevor, Meriol
Brentland series (1)
Fortunate name
Mahy, Margaret
Cousins quartet (2)
Fortune
McDowell, Michael M
Blackwater series (5)
Fortune and fury
Arlen, Leslie
Borodin family series (6)
Fortune Bend
Wisler, Gary Clifton
Texas Brazos series (2)
Fortune branches out
Mahy, Margaret
Cousins quartet (3)
Fortune fever
Grover, Marshall
Larry and Stretch series (407)
Fortune for a Falcon
Darby, Catherine
Falcon family series (3)
Fortune for Kregen
Prescot, Dray
Dray Prescot series (21)
Fortune for the brave
Chauncy, Nan
Tasmania series (3)
Fortune grass
Lethbridge, Mabel
Fortune grass series (1)
Fortune hunter
Morris, Ira J
Lavrin family series (1)
Fortune hunters
Edson, John Thomas
Floating Outfit series (43)
Fortune made his sword
Rofheart, Martha
Henry V series (1)
Fortune of fear
Hubbard, Lafayette Ronald
Mission earth series (5)
Fortune of the Rougons
Zola, Emile
Rougon Macquart series (1)
Fortune of war
O'Brian, Patrick
Jack Aubrey and Stephen Maturin series (6)
Fortune riders
Sharpe, Jon
Trailsman series (57)
Fortune seekers
Terry, Carolyn
King of diamonds series (2)
Fortune-teller's secret
Keene, Carolyn
Nancy Drew series (121)
Fortune's bride
Gellis, Roberta
Heiress series (4)
Fortune's favourites
McCullough, Colleen
Rome series (3)
Fortune's light
Friedman, Michael Jan
Star trek, the next generation series (15)
Fortune's mistress
Rothweiler, Paul Roger
Westward rails trilogy (2)
Fortunes of Billy
Grant, Pamela
Fortunes series (2)
Fortunes of Brak
Jakes, John
Brak series (5)
Fortunes of Captain Blood
Sabatini, Rafael
Captain Blood series (3)
Fortunes of Doria
Grant, Pamela
Fortunes series (1)
Fortunes of Faust
Butler, Eliza Marian
Faust series (3)
Fortunes of Flynn
Laurie-Long, Ernest
Captain Flynn series (2)
Fortunes of Oliver Horn
Smith, Francis Hopkinson
Civil War society series (1)
Fortunes of peace
Trevor, Meriol
Luxembourg series (7)
Fortunes of Poppy Treloar
O'Harris, Pixie
Poppy Treloar series (1)
Fortunes of Richard Mahony
Richardson, Henry Handel
Fortunes of Richard Mahony trilogy (3)
Fortunes of Toby Trafford
Trowbridge, John Townsend
Toby Trafford series (1)
Fortunes of war
Fraser, David
Treason in arms series (1)
Fortune's soldier
Lampitt, Dinah
Sutton Place trilogy (3)
Fortune's whirlwind
Jakes, John
Kent family series (1)
Forty centuries look down
Austin, Frederick Britten
Napoleon Bonaparte series (2)
Forty days of Tucker J
Leeson, Robert
Tucker series (1)
Forty eight hours
Janson, Hank
Hank Janson series (61)
Forty fathoms down
Jones, J Farragut
Silent service series (3)
Forty-first passenger
Hopkins, Kenneth
Gerry Lee series (2)
Forty-Five
Dumas, Alexandre
Valois series (7)
Forty-Five guardsmen
Dumas, Alexandre
Valois series (7)
Forty four calibre man
Edson, John Thomas
Floating Outfit series (2)
Forty four vintage
Price, Anthony
Doctor David Audley and Jack Butler series (1)
Forty guns West
Johnstone, William Wallace
First Mountain Man trilogy (3)
Forty-niners
Norman, David
Frontier rakers series (2)
Toombs, Jane
Making of America series (4)
Forty odd
Bard, Mary
Three faces series (2)
Forty second parallel
Dos Passos, John
U.S.A.trilogy (1)
Forty thieves
Wallace, Robert
Phantom Detective series (17)
Forty thousand in Gehenna
Cherryh, Carolyn Janice
Alliance-Union series (4)
Downbelow Station trilogy (3)
Forty whacks
Homes, Geoffrey
Humphrey Campbell series (4)
Forty years in the wilderness
Philby, Harry St John Bridger
Arabian travel series (5)
Forward but not too fast
Housman, Laurence
Palace plays series (4)
Forward from Babylon
Golding, Louis
Philip Massel series (1)
Forward Gunner Asch!
Kirst, Hans Hellmut
Gunner Asch series (2)
Forward pass
Barbour, Ralph Henry
Yardley Hall series (1)
Forward, staff nurse
Deal, Paula
Nurse series (2)
Forward the Foundation
Asimov, Isaac
Foundation series (7)
Forza trap
Davis, Kenn
Carver Bascombe series (2)
Fossett's memory
Hollis, Christopher
Robert Fossett trilogy (2)
Foul deeds will rise
Cross, Mark
Daphne Wrayne and her Four Adjusters series (40)
Foul ground
Macdonnell, James Edmond
Dutchy Holland series (7)
Foul play
Dixon, Franklin W
Hardy boys case files series (46)
Potter, Jeremy
Inspector Hiscock series (2)
Foul play suspected
Creasey, John
Toff series (23)
Foul shot
Hornig, Doug
Loren Swift series (1)
Foul up
Perry, Ritchie
Philis series (12)
Found and fettered
Donovan, Dick
Dick Donovan series (12)
Found dead
Brooks, Collin
O Swete McTavish series (1)

Found drowned
Burton, Miles
Inspector Arnold and Desmond Merrion series (52)
Found floating
Crofts, Freeman Wills
Inspector Joseph French series (16)
Found in the jungle
Carter, Nicholas
Nicholas Carter series (612)
Found on the beach
Carter, Nicholas
Nicholas Carter series (28)
Foundation
Asimov, Isaac
Foundation series (2)
Foundation and earth
Asimov, Isaac
Foundation series (6)
Foundation and Empire
Asimov, Isaac
Foundation series (3)
Foundation stone
Warren, Lella
Whetstone series (1)
Foundation trilogy
Asimov, Isaac
Foundation series (4)
Foundation's edge
Asimov, Isaac
Foundation series (5)
Founder
Rowley, Christopher
Fenrile trilogy (3)
Founder member
Gardner, John Edmund
Boysie L Oakes series (5)
Founder of the house
Jacob, Naomi
Gollantz series (1)
Founders
Woodruff, Philip
Men who ruled India series (1)
Founding
Harrod-Eagles, Cynthia
Morland family series (1)
Founding of fortunes
Barlow, Jane
Fortunes series (2)
Foundling, and other tales of Prydain
Alexander, Lloyd
Prydain series (6)
Fountain at Marlieux
Aveline, Claude
Suite Policiere series (3)
Fountain of death
Grant, Maxwell
Shadow series (256)
Nelson, Hugh Lawrence
Steve Johnson series (3)
Fountain overflows
West, Rebecca
Aubrey family trilogy (1)
Founts of Sinhala
De Silva, Colin
Sinhala series (2)
Four aces
Burtis, Thomson
Air combat series (2)
Four aces and the knave
Grover, Marshall
Larry and Stretch series (227)
Four afloat
Barbour, Ralph Henry
Big Four trilogy (3)
Four afoot
Barbour, Ralph Henry
Big Four trilogy (2)
Four against the mob
Fraley, Oscar
Untouchables series (2)
Four armourers
Beeding, Francis
Colonel Alastair Granby series (4)
Four at bay
Cross, Mark
Daphne Wrayne and her Four Adjusters series (12)
Four boy hunters
Bonehill, Ralph
Boy hunters series (1)
Four boys
Ellis, Edward Sylvester
Through on time series (3)
Four callers in Razor Street
Fowler, Sydney
Mister Jellipot series (4)
Four-chambered heart
Nin, Anais
Cities of the interior series (3)
Four continents
Sitwell, Osbert
Discursions series (3)
Four Corners
Blanchard, Amy Ella
Four Corners series (1)
Four Corners abroad
Blanchard, Amy Ella
Four Corners series (4)
Four Corners at college
Blanchard, Amy Ella
Four Corners series (6)
Four Corners at school
Blanchard, Amy Ella
Four Corners series (3)
Four Corners in California
Blanchard, Amy Ella
Four Corners series (2)
Four corners in camp
Blanchard, Amy Ella
Four Corners series (5)
Four Corners in Egypt
Blanchard, Amy Ella
Four Corners series (87)
Four Corners in Japan
Blanchard, Amy Ella
Four Corners series (7)
Four-D funhouse
Emery, Clayton
Amazing stories series (1)
Four days' war
Wright, Sydney Fowler
War of 1938 trilogy (2)
Four dead mice
Black, Thomas B
Al Delaney series (4)
Four defences
Connington, John Jervis
Mark Brand series (2)
Four doctors, four wives
Seifert, Elizabeth
Bayard series (9)
Four dolls
Godden, Rumer
Four dolls series (4)
Four doors to death
Courage, John
David Cane series (1)
Four false weapons
Carr, John Dickson
Henri Bencolin series (6)
Four feet in the grave
Long, Amelia Reynolds
Peter Piper series (2)
Four fifty from Paddington
Christie, Agatha
Miss Jane Marple series (9)
Four-fingered glove
Carter, Nicholas
Nicholas Carter series (173)
Four friends in Oakapple Wood
Partridge, Jenny
Oakapple Wood series (8)
Four frightened women
Coxe, George Harmon
Jack Fenner series (3)
Kent Murdock series (4)
Four from the Witch World
Norton, Andre
Witch World series (20)
Four-gated city
Lessing, Doris
Children of violence series (5)
Four generations
Jacob, Naomi
Gollantz series (4)
Four get going
Cross, Mark
Daphne Wrayne and her Four Adjusters series (10)
Four girls at Chautauqua
Pansy
Chautauqua series (2)
Four green fish
Jepson, Edgar
Lord Barradine series (2)
Four handsome negresses
Baptist, R Hernekin
African negro series (1)
Four-headed dragon
Dixon, Franklin W
Hardy boys series (69)
Four hoodoo charms
Carter, Nicholas
Nicholas Carter series (372)
Four hours to fear
Richards, Francis
Assistant District Attorney Bernie Simmons series (2)
Four hundred billion stars
McAuley, Paul J
Four hundred billion stars series (1)
Four in a family
Blyton, Enid
Caravan family series (3)
Four in camp
Barbour, Ralph Henry
Big Four trilogy (1)
Four in family
Pakington, Humphrey
Warmstry series (1)
Four into three
Price, Roger
Tomorrow people series (3)
Four is a crowd
Chase, Emily
Canby Hall series (7)
Four Jessicas
Fleischer, Leonore
Holly Hills series (2)
Four Just Men
Wallace, Edgar
Just Men series (1)
Four Little Blossoms and their winter fun
Hawley, Mabel C
Four Little Blossoms series (3)
Four Little Blossoms at Brookside Farm
Hawley, Mabel C
Four Little Blossoms series (1)
Four Little Blossoms at Oak Hill School
Hawley, Mabel C
Four Little Blossoms series (2)
Four Little Blossoms at Sunrise Beach
Hawley, Mabel C
Four Little Blossoms series (6)
Four Little Blossoms indoors and out
Hawley, Mabel C
Four Little Blossoms series (7)
Four Little Blossoms on Appletree Island
Hawley, Mabel C
Four Little Blossoms series (4)
Four Little Blossoms through the holidays
Hawley, Mabel C
Four Little Blossoms series (5)
Four little bunnies
Frees, Harry Whittier
Four little pets series (2)
Four little engines
Awdry, Wilbert
Railway series (10)
Four little kittens
Frees, Harry Whittier
Four little pets series (1)
Four little kittens' Christmas
Frees, Harry Whittier
Four little pets series (5)
Four little puppies
Frees, Harry Whittier
Four little pets series (3)
Four lords of the diamond
Chalker, Jack Laurence
Four Lords of the Diamond series (4)
Four lost ladies
Palmer, Stuart
Hildegarde Withers series (11)
Four make holiday
Cross, Mark
Daphne Wrayne and her Four Adjusters series (9)
Four Maries
Fleming, Arnold
Souvenir de France series (1)
Four men with a van
Andom, R
Troddles series (5)
Four million
Henry, O
Four million series (1)
Four monsters
Truman, Timothy
Emanuel Santana series (1)
Four moons of Darkover
Bradley, Marion Zimmer
Darkover anthologies series (5)
Four more Sherlock Holmes plays
Hardwick, Michael
Sherlock Holmes drama series (8)
Four mothers at Chautauqua
Pansy
Chautauqua series (4)
Four must die
Scott, Bradford
Walt Slade series (120)
Four mysteries solved by Norman and Henry Bones
Wilson, Anthony Clifford
Norman and Henry Bones series (4)
Four o'clock fracas
Grover, Marshall
Larry and Stretch series (115)
Four of a kind
Masters, Zeke
Faro Blake series (6)
Four of hearts
Queen, Ellery
Ellery Queen series (14)
Four on the floor
McInerny, Ralph
Father Roger Dowling series (13)
Four on the shore
Marshall, Edward
Fox series (7)
Four past four
Vickers, Roy
James Segrove series (4)
Four Pentires and Jimmy
Mackenzie, Kathleen
Pentire family series (1)
Four plays for coarse actors
Green, Michael
Coarse plays series (1)
Four plus Bunkle
Pardoe, Margot
Bunkle series (1)
Four-ply yarn
Burton, Miles
Inspector Arnold and Desmond Merrion series (29)
Four ponies
Campbell, Judith
Ponies series (1)
Four-poster
Wiat, Philippa
Wilmington series (1)
Four quarters
Peters, Daniel
Pre-Columbian trilogy (3)
Four quartets
Eliot, Thomas Stearns
Four quartets series (4)
Four rhyming puzzle books
Korman, Justine
Crispy Critter series (3)
Four seasons of Brambly Hedge
Barklem, Jill
Brambly Hedge series (4)
Four Sherlock Holmes plays
Hardwick, Michael
Sherlock Holmes drama series (4)
Four signets
Grant, Maxwell
Shadow series (69)
Four-Storey Mistake
Enright, Elizabeth
Melendy family series (2)
Four stowaways and Anna
Frow, Marion
Intelligence Corps series (3)
Four strange women
Punshon, Ernest Robertson
Bobby Owen series (14)
Four strike home
Cross, Mark
Daphne Wrayne and her Four Adjusters series (7)
Four swans
Graham, Winston
Poldark series (6)
Four times a widower
Bliss, Adam
Alice Penny series (2)
Four to doomsday
Dicks, Terrance
Doctor Who series (77)
Four trails
Graydon, William Murray
Sexton Blake series (176)
Four ugly guns
Hayes, Ralph Eugene
O'Brien, Buffalo Hunter series (2)
Four unfaithful servants
Bellairs, George
Detective Inspector Thomas Littlejohn series (2)
Four wheel drift
Carter, Bruce
Nick Bailey series (1)
Four-wheeled target
Grover, Marshall
Larry and Stretch series (372)
Four winds
Adams, Herbert
Major Roger Bennion series (16)
Four winds of heaven
High, Monique Raphel
Gunzberg family series (1)
Four year's harvest
Donaldson, Frances Annesley
Farming series (2)
Four young explorers
Optic, Oliver
All-over-the-world series (11)
Fourfingers
Brock, Lynn
Sergeant Venn series (2)
Fourpenny fair
Shaw, Jane
Penny series (4)
Fours Crossing
Garden, Nancy
Fours Crossing trilogy (1)
Foursome
Healy, Jeremiah
John Francis Cuddy series (8)
Foursquare murder
Hume, David
Mick Cardby series (2)
Fourteen and holding
Ransom, Candice Farris
Growing up series (4)
Fourteen dilemma
Pentecost, Hugh
Pierre Chambrun series (12)
Fourteen points
Reeve, Arthur Benjamin
Craig Kennedy series (18)
Fourteen seconds to hell
Carter, Nick
Nick Carter series (37)
Fourteen stories about Jonathan
Cockett, Mary
Jonathan and Felicity series (3)
Fourteen what-do-you-know stories
Berg, Leila
What-do-you-know series (2)
Fourteen years after!
Hunter, John
Sexton Blake series (1174)
Fourteenth agent
Cooke, David Coxe
Peter Rourke series (2)
Fourteenth key
Wells, Carolyn
Lorimer Lane series (2)
Fourteenth trump
Philips, Judson Pentecost
Coyle and Donovan series (2)
Fourth agency
Fredman, John
Charles Dexter series (1)
Fourth and goal
Hallowell, Tommy
Varsity coach series (1)
Fourth angel
Hunter, Robin
Simon Quarry series (1)
Fourth anti-coloring book
Striker, Susan
Anti-coloring series (4)
Fourth big Monster book
Blance, Ellen
Monster series (15)
Fourth big radio Thin King book
Farmer, Derek
Thin King series (4)
Fourth bomb
Rhode, John
Doctor Lancelot Priestley series (36)
Fourth book of after midnight stories
Myers, Amy
After midnight stories series (4)
Fourth book of Jorkens
Dunsany, Edward John Moreton Drax Plunkett
Jorkens series (4)
Fourth Brer Rabbit book
Blyton, Enid
Brer Rabbit series (4)
Fourth dagger
Allan, Luke
Tiger Lillie series (4)
Fourth deadly sin
Sanders, Lawrence
Edward X Delaney series (4)
Fourth degree
Daiger, Katherine S
Inspector Everett Anderson series (1)
Fourth down
Barbour, Ralph Henry
Yardley Hall series (8)
Fourth down, death
Hinkemeyer, Michael Thomas
Sheriff Emil Whippletree series (3)
Fourth down showdown
Bee, Clair
Chip Hilton series (13)
Fourth down to death
Halliday, Brett
Michael Shayne series (61)
Fourth finger
Wynne, Anthony
Doctor Eustace Hailey series (8)

Fourth flight of the Starfire
Mumford, Edwin Embree
Starfire series (4)
Fourth Floor twins and the fish snitch mystery
Adler, David A
Fourth Floor twins series (1)
Fourth Floor twins and the fortune cookie chase
Adler, David A
Fourth Floor twins series (2)
Fourth Floor twins and the sand castle contest
Adler, David A
Fourth Floor twins series (6)
Fourth Floor twins and the Silver Ghost Express
Adler, David A
Fourth Floor twins series (4)
Fourth Floor twins and the skyscraper parade
Adler, David A
Fourth Floor twins series (5)
Fourth Floor twins and the talking bird trick
Adler, David A
Fourth Floor twins series (3)
Fourth Form detectives
Chaundler, Christine
Fourth Form series (2)
Fourth Form rebel
Chaundler, Christine
Fourth Form series (3)
Fourth Frank Muir goes into
Muir, Frank
Frank Muir goes into series (4)
Fourth funeral
Leonard, Charles L
Paul Kilgerrin series (8)
Fourth-grade celebrity
Giff, Patricia Reilly
Casey Valentine series (1)
Fourth grade is a jinx
McKenna, Colleen O'Shaughnessy
Murphy family series (2)
Fourth hemisphere
Lake, David John
Breakout series (6)
Fourth key
Saville, Malcolm
Michael and Mary series (6)
Fourth man
Smith, Lou
John Spencer series (4)
Fourth Mary
Cleeve, Brian
Crucifixion trilogy (3)
Fourth of July
Kincaid, J D
Jack Stone series (2)
Fourth of July picnic
Stout, Rex
Nero Wolfe and Archie Goodwin series (31)
Fourth postman
Rice, Craig
John Joseph Malone series (9)
Fourth quarter fix
Nelson, Peter N
Mollie Fox series (4)
Fourth Reich
Rosenberger, Joseph
Death Merchant series (39)
Fourth Reich Death Squad
Kilgore, Axel
They call me the Mercenary series (3)
Fourth seal
Groom, Pelham
Peter Mohune series (4)
Fourth shadow
Charles, Robert
Simon Larren series (6)
Fourth side of the triangle
Queen, Ellery
Ellery Queen series (37)
Fourth stage of Gainsborough Brown
Watson, Clarissa
Persis Willum series (1)
Fourth star
Burke, Richard
Quinny Hite series (4)
Fourth Street East
Weidman, Jerome
Benny Kramer series (1)
Fourth theory
Bayfield, William John
Sexton Blake series (69)
Fourth widow
Adams, Harold
Carl Wilcox series (5)
Fourth year triumphs at Trebizon
Digby, Anne
Trebizon series (10)
Fowl play
Du Bois, Theodora
Anne and Jeffrey McNeill series (17)
Fowl play, Desdemona
Keller, Beverly
Desdemona series (2)
Fowlhaven werewolf
Andrews, Val
Sherlock Holmes sequels series (61)
Fox all week
Marshall, Edward
Fox series (6)
Fox and his friends
Marshall, Edward
Fox series (2)
Fox and the faith
Parkinson, Dan
Fox trilogy (1)
Fox and the flag
Parkinson, Dan
Fox trilogy (3)
Fox and the fury
Parkinson, Dan
Fox trilogy (2)
Fox and the Tomten
Lindgren, Astrid
Tomten series (2)
Fox at school
Marshall, Edward
Fox series (5)
Fox be nimble
Marshall, James
Fox series (9)
Fox cub bold
Dann, Colin
Farthing Wood series (4)
Fox Fair
Pullen, Alan
Sam and Lin series (10)
Fox hunt
Bryant, Bonnie
Saddle Club series (22)
Fox-hunting, as recorded by Raed
Stephens, Charles Asbury
Camping out series (5)
Fox in love
Marshall, Edward
Fox series (3)
Fox in the attic
Hughes, Richard Arthur Warren
Human predicament series (1)
Fox in the island
Bosco, Henri
Pascalet and Aunt Martine series (2)
Fox in the night
Hart, Roy
Detective Superintendent Roper series (3)
Fox in the sea
Magowan, Ronald
Shane Mackenzie series (4)
Fox Island
Pinkerton, Kathrene
Ann Jackman series (2)
Fox-magic murders
Gulik, Robert van
Judge Dee series (17)
Fox on stage
Marshall, James
Fox series (11)
Fox on the job
Marshall, James
Fox series (8)
Fox on wheels
Marshall, Edward
Fox series (4)
Fox outfoxed
Marshall, James
Fox series (10)
Fox, part 1
Shakespeare, Brian
Fox series (1)
Fox, part 2
Shakespeare, Brian
Fox series (2)
Fox run
Robbins, David
Endworld series (1)
Fox twins
Hogan, Inez
Twins series (17)
Fox under my cloak
Williamson, Henry
Chronicles of ancient sunlight series (5)
Fox Valley murders
Vance, John Holbrook
Sheriff Joe Bain series (1)
Foxcatcher
Hallahan, William Henry
Charley Brewer series (1)
Foxendale Farm
Kitchen, Fred
Foxendale series (1)
Foxer gets smart
Palfrey, Heather Mary
Norah the snorer series (1)
Foxes
Postgate, Oliver
Ivor the engine series (5)
Foxes have holes
Eyre, Donald Cuthbert
Captain O'Donnell series (1)
Foxes, owls and all
Burkett, Molly
Home for animals series (1)
Foxgate
Harvey, Marianne
Trevarvas family series (3)
Foxglove story book
Blyton, Enid
Flower story book series (7)
Foxhole
Blake, Ken
Professionals series (13)
Fox's feud
Dann, Colin
Farthing Wood series (3)
Fox's lair
McMahan, Ian
Mikrokid mystery series (2)
Foxwood kidnap
Paterson, Cynthia
Foxwood series (3)
Foxwood regatta
Paterson, Cynthia
Foxwood series (4)
Foxwood smugglers
Paterson, Cynthia
Foxwood series (5)
Foxwood treasure
Paterson, Cynthia
Foxwood series (2)
Foxx!
Tyler, Zack
Foxx series (1)
Foxx hunting
Tyler, Zack
Foxx series (3)
Foxx's foe
Tyler, Zack
Foxx series (6)
Foxx's gold
Tyler, Zack
Foxx series (2)
Foxx's herd
Tyler, Zack
Foxx series (4)
Foxx's vixen
Tyler, Zack
Foxx series (5)
Foxy
Montgomery, John
Foxy series (1)
Foxy and the badgers
Montgomery, John
Foxy series (3)
Foxy Squirrel
Judson, Clara Ingram
Foxy Squirrel series (1)
Foxy Squirrel in the garden
Judson, Clara Ingram
Foxy Squirrel series (2)
Fracas factor
Reynolds, Mack
Joe Mauser series (4)
Fracas in the foothills
Paul, Elliot
Homer Evans series (3)
Fractal mode
Anthony, Piers
Mode series (2)
Fraggle Rock
Stevenson, Jocelyn
Fraggle Rock series (4)
Fragile flag
Langton, Jane
Edward, Eleanor and Georgie Hall series (5)
Fragile years
Franken, Rose
Claudia series (7)
Fragments away from France
Bairnsfather, Bruce
Old Bill series (8)
Fragrant death
Blake, Christina
Inspector Donald Dobbs series (1)
Fragrant the fertile earth
Seymour, Aubrey
Fertile earth series (2)
Frail on North Circular
Urquhart, Macgregor
Chief Inspector Joshua Smarles series (1)
Frame and fortune
Janson, Hank
Hank Janson series (251)
Frame Angel
Christian, Frederick H
Frank Angel series (5)
Frame for murder
Simons, Roger
Inspector Fadiman Wace series (2)
Frame for the front page
Brody, Marc
Marc Brody series (50)
Frame the Baron
Morton, Anthony
Baron series (29)
Frame-up
Brandon, John Gordon
Inspector Patrick Aloysius McCarthy series (24)
Graham, Neill
Solo Malcolm series (31)
Framed
Janson, Hank
Hank Janson series (62)
Framed evidence
Cowdroy, Joan
Chief Inspector Gorham series (1)
Framed in blood
Halliday, Brett
Michael Shayne series (21)
Framework of fate
Carter, Nicholas
Nicholas Carter series (61)
Framing of Carol Woan
Cobb, Belton
Superintendent Manning series (3)
Framley Parsonage
Trollope, Anthony
Chronicles of Barsetshire series (4)
Frampton of the Yard
Plummer, Thomas Arthur
Detective Inspector Andrew Frampton series (3)
Frampton sees red
Plummer, Thomas Arthur
Detective Inspector Andrew Frampton series (36)
Franca
Moss, Merrilee
Hot pursuit series (2)
France
Maddocks, Peter
Jimbo's journeys series (1)
France reborn
Aron, Robert
Liberation of France series (3)
Frances and friends
Cooper, Ilene
Frances in the fourth grade series (4)
Frances dances
Cooper, Ilene
Frances in the fourth grade series (2)
Frances Four-Eyes
Cooper, Ilene
Frances in the fourth grade series (3)
Frances takes a chance
Cooper, Ilene
Frances in the fourth grade series (1)
Francesca
Marlowe, Stephen
Chester Drum series (15)
Francesca, madonna of the shadows
Shulman, Sandra
Francesca series (2)
Francesca, the Florentine
Shulman, Sandra
Francesca series (1)
Franchise affair
Tey, Josephine
Inspector Alan Grant series (3)
Francie
Hahn, Emily
Francie series (1)
Francie again
Hahn, Emily
Francie series (2)
Francie comes home
Hahn, Emily
Francie series (3)
Francis
Stern, David
Francis trilogy (2)
Francis goes to Washington
Stern, David
Francis trilogy (3)
Francis Quarles investigates
Symons, Julian
Francis Quarles series (2)
Francis, the army mule
Stern, David
Francis trilogy (1)
Francis the First
Dumas, Alexandre
Valois series (1)
Franciscan
Blake, Forrester
Johnny Christmas trilogy (3)
Francoeur novels
Plante, David
Francoeur family series (4)
Francoise
Romains, Jules
Men of goodwill series (26)
Francoise, in love with love
Delisle, Francoise
In love series (1)
Franfolico and after
Lindsay, Jack
Life rarely tells trilogy (3)
Frank Allen after big game
Forbes, Graham B
Frank Allen series (15)
Frank Allen and his motor boat
Forbes, Graham B
Frank Allen series (10)
Frank Allen and his rivals
Forbes, Graham B
Columbia High School series (6)
Frank Allen series (4)
Frank Allen at Gold Fork
Forbes, Graham B
Frank Allen series (9)
Frank Allen at Old Moose Lake
Forbes, Graham B
Frank Allen series (12)
Frank Allen at Rockspur Ranch
Forbes, Graham B
Frank Allen series (8)
Frank Allen at Zero Camp
Forbes, Graham B
Frank Allen series (13)
Frank Allen, captain of the team
Forbes, Graham B
Columbia High School series (4)
Frank Allen series (11)
Frank Allen, head of the crew
Forbes, Graham B
Columbia High School series (3)
Frank Allen series (6)
Frank Allen in camp
Forbes, Graham B
Columbia High School series (8)
Frank Allen series (7)
Frank Allen in winter sports
Forbes, Graham B
Columbia High School series (7)
Frank Allen series (3)
Frank Allen, pitcher
Forbes, Graham B
Columbia High School series (2)
Frank Allen series (5)
Frank Allen pitching his best
Forbes, Graham B
Frank Allen series (17)
Frank Allen playing to win
Forbes, Graham B
Columbia High School series (5)
Frank Allen series (2)
Frank Allen, snowbound
Forbes, Graham B
Frank Allen series (14)
Frank Allen with the circus
Forbes, Graham B
Frank Allen series (16)
Frank Allen's schooldays
Forbes, Graham B
Columbia High School series (1)
Frank Allen series (1)
Frank and Andy afloat
Barnum, Vance
Racer boys series (1)
Frank and Andy at boarding school
Barnum, Vance
Racer boys series (2)
Frank and Andy in a winter camp
Barnum, Vance
Racer boys series (3)
Frank and Ernest
Day, Alexandra
Frank and Ernest series (1)
Frank and Ernest on the road
Day, Alexandra
Frank and Ernest series (3)

Frank and Ernest play ball
Day, Alexandra
Frank and Ernest series (2)
Frank and fearless
Alger, Horatio
Frank and fearless trilogy (2)
Frank Beresford
Curling, Henry
Frank Beresford series (1)
Frank Gordon
Goulding, Francis Robert
Marooners series (2)
Frank Hunter's peril
Alger, Horatio
Frank and fearless trilogy (1)
Frank James in St Louis
Lawson, W B
Jesse James series (6)
Frank Merriwell, freshman pitcher
Frederic, Mike
Frank Merriwell series (2)
Frank Merriwell, freshman quarterback
Frederic, Mike
Frank Merriwell series (1)
Frank Merriwell, sports car racer
Frederic, Mike
Frank Merriwell series (3)
Frank Muir goes into
Muir, Frank
Frank Muir goes into series (1)
Frankenstein
Barling, Tom
Frankenstein series (1)
Bethancort, Tomas Ernesto
Frankenstein series (1)
Campton, David
Frankenstein series (1)
Carlson, Dale
Frankenstein series (1)
Shelley, Mary
Frankenstein series (1)
Stewart, Diana
Frankenstein series (1)
Frankenstein and the whiz kid
Crume, Vic
Frankenstein series (1)
Frankenstein catalog
Glut, Donald Frank
Frankenstein series (1)
Frankenstein diaries
Venables, Hubert
Frankenstein sequels series (13)
Frankenstein factory
Hoch, Edward Dentinger
Carl Crader and Earl Jazine series (3)
Frankenstein is alive and well and living with Mrs Frankenstein
Baxter, Alida
Frankenstein sequels series (12)
Frankenstein legend
Glut, Donald Frank
Frankenstein series (1)
Frankenstein lives again
Glut, Donald Frank
Frankenstein sequels series (6)
Frankenstein meets Dracula
Glut, Donald Frank
Frankenstein sequels series (9)
Frankenstein papers
Saberhagen, Fred
Frankenstein sequels series (17)
Frankenstein sixty nine
Martin, Ed
Frankenstein series (1)
Frankenstein unbound
Aldiss, Brian Wilson
Frankenstein series (2)
Frankenstein wheel
Fairman, Paul Warren
Frankenstein sequels series (3)
Frankenstein's aunt
Pettersson, Allan Rune
Frankenstein's aunt series (1)
Frankenstein's aunt returns
Pettersson, Allan Rune
Frankenstein's aunt series (2)
Frankie Bradford's bear
Mathews, Joanna Hooe
Bradford family series (7)
Frankie's story
Sefton, Catherine
Northern Ireland trilogy (2)
Frankincense and murder
Kendrick, Baynard
Captain Duncan Maclain series (12)
Franklin fibs
Bourgeois, Paulette
Franklin series (3)
Franklin in the dark
Bourgeois, Paulette
Franklin series (1)
Franklin is bossy
Bourgeois, Paulette
Franklin series (5)
Franklin is lost
Bourgeois, Paulette
Franklin series (4)
Frank's campaign
Alger, Horatio
Campaign trilogy (1)
Franky Doyle story
Clement, Henry
Caged women series (2)
Franny and Zooey
Salinger, Jerome David
Glass family series (2)
Frantic phantom, and other incredible stories
Hunter, Norman
Kingdom of Incredibilia series (3)
Frass
Chancellor, John
Captain Frass series (1)
Fraternity
Galsworthy, John
Country house trilogy (2)
Fraternity of the Stone
Morrell, David
Chris Kilmoonie and Saul Grisman series (2)
Fratricide is a gas
Gutteridge, Lindsay
Mathew Dilke series (3)
Fraulein Elsa
Schnitzler, Arthur
Three women trilogy (3)
Fraulein Spy
Carter, Nick
Nick Carter series (5)
Fraxilly fracas
Hill, Douglas
Del Curb series (1)
Frazer butts in
Clevely, Hugh
Inspector Williams series (2)
Freak
Collins, Michael
Dan Fortune series (11)
Freak racket
Elliott, William James
Ed Gunning series (1)
Freak show murders
Grant, Maxwell
Shadow series (251)
Freaked out stranger
Morgan, Patrick
Operation Hang Ten series (10)
Freaks of fortune
Optic, Oliver
Starry flag series (2)
Freaky Friday
Rodgers, Mary
Annabel Andrews series (1)
Freckled shark
Robeson, Kenneth
Doc Savage series (67)
Freckles
Porter, Gene Stratton
Limberlost series (1)
Freckles comes home
Porter, Jeannette Stratton
Limberlost series (3)
Fred and Barney lay an egg
Elias, Horace J
Flintstones series (8)
Fred and Olive's blessed lino
Lunn, Hugh
Lunns of Annerley Junction series (2)
Fred and the skateboard
Edwards, Pat
Fred series (5)
Fred and the wasp
Edwards, Pat
Fred series (4)
Fred Archer, farmer's son
Archer, Fred
Evesham Vale series (11)
Fred at the beach
Edwards, Pat
Fred series (7)
Fred Bradford's debt
Mathews, Joanna Hooe
Bradford family series (1)
Fred Chappell reader
Chappell, Fred
Cthulhu Mythos series (15)
Fred Fear-Alot
Watson, Jean
Alot series (1)
Fred Fenton in the line
Chapman, Allen
Fred Fenton series (2)
Fred Fenton, marathon runner
Chapman, Allen
Fred Fenton series (5)
Fred Fenton on the crew
Chapman, Allen
Fred Fenton series (3)
Fred Fenton on the track
Chapman, Allen
Fred Fenton series (4)
Fred Fenton the pitcher
Chapman, Allen
Fred Fenton series (1)
Fred in situ
Hammond, Gerald
Beau Pepys series (2)
Fred in space
Edwards, Pat
Fred series (8)
Fred makes a shelf
Edwards, Pat
Fred series (2)
Fred makes a table
Edwards, Pat
Fred series (13)
Freddie
Scott, Mary
Freddie series (3)
Freddie and the Bank of England mystery
Wainwright, Sheila
Freddie series (2)
Freddie and the Star of Africa
Wainwright, Sheila
Freddie series (1)
Freddie Fireman
Campbell, Rod
Little people series (4)
Freddie Freightliner goes to Kennedy Space Center
George, David Lester
Freddie Freightliner series (1)
Freddie Freightliner learns to talk!
George, David Lester
Freddie Freightliner series (2)
Freddie Freightliner to the rescue
George, David Lester
Freddie Freightliner series (3)
Freddy and Freginald
Brooks, Walter Rollin
Freddy the pig series (4)
Freddy and Mister Camphor
Brooks, Walter Rollin
Freddy the pig series (11)
Freddy and Simon the dictator
Brooks, Walter Rollin
Freddy the pig series (23)
Freddy and the baseball team from Mars
Brooks, Walter Rollin
Freddy the pig series (22)
Freddy and the Bean Home news
Brooks, Walter Rollin
Freddy the pig series (10)
Freddy and the dragon
Brooks, Walter Rollin
Freddy the pig series (25)
Freddy and the flying saucer plans
Brooks, Walter Rollin
Freddy the pig series (24)
Freddy and the ignoramus
Brooks, Walter Rollin
Freddy the pig series (8)
Freddy and the men from Mars
Brooks, Walter Rollin
Freddy the pig series (21)
Freddy and the perilous adventure
Brooks, Walter Rollin
Freddy the pig series (9)
Freddy and the popinjay
Brooks, Walter Rollin
Freddy the pig series (12)
Freddy and the space ship
Brooks, Walter Rollin
Freddy the pig series (20)
Freddy goes camping
Brooks, Walter Rollin
Freddy the pig series (15)
Freddy goes to Florida
Brooks, Walter Rollin
Freddy the pig series (1)
Freddy goes to the North Pole
Brooks, Walter Rollin
Freddy the pig series (2)
Freddy Kreuger's seven sweetest dreams
Greenberg, Martin Harry
Nightmare on Elm Street series (2)
Freddy plays football
Brooks, Walter Rollin
Freddy the pig series (16)
Freddy rides again
Brooks, Walter Rollin
Freddy the pig series (18)
Freddy the cowboy
Brooks, Walter Rollin
Freddy the pig series (17)
Freddy the detective
Brooks, Walter Rollin
Freddy the pig series (3)
Freddy the explorer
Brooks, Walter Rollin
Freddy the pig series (2)
Freddy the magician
Brooks, Walter Rollin
Freddy the pig series (14)
Freddy the Pied Piper
Brooks, Walter Rollin
Freddy the pig series (13)
Freddy the pilot
Brooks, Walter Rollin
Freddy the pig series (19)
Freddy the politician
Brooks, Walter Rollin
Freddy the pig series (6)
Freddy's cousin Weedly
Brooks, Walter Rollin
Freddy the pig series (7)
Freddy's first adventure
Brooks, Walter Rollin
Freddy the pig series (1)
Frederica in fashion
Chesney, Marion
Six sisters series (6)
Frederick
Lionni, Leon
Frederick series (1)
Frederick and his friends
Lionni, Leon
Frederick series (2)
Frederick's fables
Lionni, Leon
Frederick series (2)
Frederick's tales
Lionni, Leon
Frederick series (2)
Fredericksburg to Meridian
Foote, Shelby
Civil War trilogy (2)
Frederique
Prevost, Marcel
Vierges fortes series (1)
Fred's birthday
Edwards, Pat
Fred series (1)
Fred's dream
Ahlberg, Allan
Brick Street Boys series (4)
Fred's Father Christmas story
Edwards, Pat
Fred series (10)
Fred's letters
Edwards, Pat
Fred series (6)
Fred's photo album
Edwards, Pat
Fred series (11)
Free admission
Chase, Ilka
Past imperfect series (2)
Free agent
Chapman, Eddie
Free agent series (2)
Free and easy land
Clune, Frank
Discovery series (3)
Free as the breeze
Priest, Charles Ashley Vincent
Nothing to lose series (2)
Free draw
Singer, Shelley
Jake Samson and Rosie Vincente series (2)
Free enterprise
Cliff, Michelle
Clare Savage series (2)
Free fall in crimson
Macdonald, John Dann
Travis McGee series (19)
Free kick
Hardcastle, Michael
Bank Vale United series (4)
Free lancers
Mitchell, Elizabeth
Alien stars series (4)
Free lands
Arthur, Burt
Dan Lovett series (2)
Free press filly
Fletcher, Dirk
Spur McCoy series (38)
Free range
Cole, Jackson
Jim Hatfield series (53)
Free-range wife
Kenyon, Michael
Inspector Henry Peckover series (4)
Free rangers
Altsheler, Joseph Alexander
Trailers series (3)
Free rein
Peyton, K M
Hero series (2)
Free ride
Fox, James M
Jerry Long and Chuck Conley series (2)
Free soil
Allis, Marguerite
Ashbel Field series (5)
Free woman
Bonner, Terry Nelsen
New South Wales series (3)
Freebooters
Grover, Marshall
Larry and Stretch series (66)
Freedom bird
Philburn, Dennis K
Soldier of fortune series (6)
Freedom express
Maloney, Mack
Wingman series (7)
Freedom fight
Austin, Richard
Guardians series (10)
Freedom fighters
Larteguy, Jean
Central America series (2)
Freedom in December
Vercors
On the shore trilogy (3)
Freedom trail to Greystone
Bronte, Louisa
Greystone Tavern series (3)
Freedom trap
Bagley, Desmond
Slade series (2)
Freedom's apple tree
Martin, Bill
Freedom series (3)
Freedom's own island
Bryant, Arthur
History of Britain and the British people series (2)
Freedom's Rangers
Andrews, Keith William
Freedom's Rangers series (1)
Freelance death
Taylor, Andrew
William Dougal series (5)
Freemantle
Ingraham, Joseph Holt
Freemantle series (1)
Freemartin
Cohler, David Keith
Sam Knight series (2)
FreeMaster
Jensen, Kris
Ardel series (1)
Freeway fighter
Livingstone, Ian
Fighting fantasy gamebook series (13)
Freewheeling of Joshua Cobb
Hodges, Margaret
Joshua Cobb series (3)
Freeze frame
Irvine, Robert Ralstone
Robert Christopher series (2)
Freeze thy blood less coldly
Wainwright, John
Northern Police series (13)
Superintendent Charles Ripley series (3)
Freezing peril strikes
Luigi, Belli
Inspector Saint Clair series (4)
Freight for Wells Fargo
Stanley, Chuck
Wells Fargo series (3)
French admiral
Lambdin, Dewey
Alan Lewrie series (2)
French affair
Kenyon, Michael
Inspector Henry Peckover series (7)
French assignment
Hunter, Joe
Attack force series (1)
French connection
Moore, Robin
Connection series (8)
Pat Kenney series (1)

French connection II
Moore, Robin
Connection series (4)
French deal
Hughes, William
George Willis series (4)
French entrapment
Cort, Ned
Boxer Unit SS series (1)
French fried aliens
Hodgman, Ann
Lunchroom series (4)
French hazard
Mills, Woosnam
Sir John Howden series (2)
French key
Gruber, Frank
Johnny Fletcher and Sam Cragg series (1)
French key mystery
Gruber, Frank
Johnny Fletcher and Sam Cragg series (1)
French killing
Cody, James P
Brian Peterson series (3)
French kiss
Israel, Peter
B F Cage series (2)
Logan, Mark
Nicholas Minnett series (2)
Montague, J J
Black Swan series (3)
French Nan
Castle, Agnes
Beau Nash regime romance series (3)
French ordinary murder
Harrison, Ray
Sergeant Joseph Bragg and Constable James Morton series (1)
French powder mystery
Queen, Ellery
Ellery Queen series (3)
French prisoner
Gaye, Phoebe Fenwich
Vandervoord trilogy (1)
French Revolution
Thompson, James Matthew
French history trilogy (1)
French strikes oil
Crofts, Freeman Wills
Inspector Joseph French series (29)
French twins
Perkins, Lucy Fitch
Twin series (9)
Frenchman's Pass
Longtree, Warren T
Ruff Justice series (19)
Frenchman's secret
Edwards, Monica
Punchbowl Farm series (7)
Frenzy
Miller, Rex
Jack Eichord series (2)
Frenzy in the flesh
Reid, Desmond
Sexton Blake series (1591)
Frenzy of merchantmen
Callison, Brian
Brevet Cable series (2)
Frequent flyer
Friedman, Kinky
Kinky Friedman series (4)
Frequent hearses
Crispin, Edmund
Gervase Fen series (7)
Fresh at Santa Fe
Aiken, Albert W
Fresh series (2)
Fresh from the laundry
Chase, Ilka
Travel series (4)
Fresh in Montana
Aiken, Albert W
Fresh series (3)
Fresh look at creation
Gourley, Frank Alan
Even gods err trilogy (1)
Fresh news from Sherwood
Suddaby, Donald
Robin Hood series (2)
Fresh of Frisco
Aiken, Albert W
Fresh series (1)
Fresh, the race-track sport
Aiken, Albert W
Fresh series (4)
Fresh wind in the willows
Scott, Dixon
Toad Hall series (2)
Freshman
Cooney, Linda A
Class of eighty eight series (1)
Class of eighty nine series (1)
Freshman affair
Cooney, Linda A
Freshman dorm series (20)
Freshman breakup
Cooney, Linda A
Freshman dorm series (29)
Freshman celebrity
Cooney, Linda A
Freshman dorm series (28)
Freshman changes
Cooney, Linda A
Freshman dorm series (10)
Freshman choices
Cooney, Linda A
Freshman dorm series (14)
Freshman co-ed
Lee, Alice Lester
Co-ed series (1)
Freshman dorm
Cooney, Linda A
Freshman dorm series (1)
Freshman dreams
Cooney, Linda A
Freshman dorm series (5)
Freshman feud
Cooney, Linda A
Freshman dorm series (16)
Freshman flames
Cooney, Linda A
Freshman dorm series (13)
Freshman fling
Cooney, Linda A
Freshman dorm series (11)
Freshman follies
Cooney, Linda A
Freshman dorm series (17)
Freshman games
Cooney, Linda A
Freshman dorm series (6)
Freshman guys
Cooney, Linda A
Freshman dorm series (3)
Freshman heartbreak
Cooney, Linda A
Freshman dorm series (15)
Freshman heat
Cooney, Linda A
Freshman dorm series (25)
Freshman lies
Cooney, Linda A
Freshman dorm series (2)
Freshman loves
Cooney, Linda A
Freshman dorm series (7)
Freshman nights
Cooney, Linda A
Freshman dorm series (4)
Freshman obsession
Cooney, Linda A
Freshman dorm series (24)
Freshman passion
Cooney, Linda A
Freshman dorm series (27)
Freshman promises
Cooney, Linda A
Freshman dorm series (19)
Freshman quarterback
Bee, Clair
Chip Hilton series (9)
Freshman rivals
Cooney, Linda A
Freshman dorm series (12)
Freshman roommate
Cooney, Linda A
Freshman dorm series (23)
Freshman scandal
Cooney, Linda A
Freshman dorm series (22)
Freshman schemes
Cooney, Linda A
Freshman dorm series (9)
Freshman secrets
Cooney, Linda A
Freshman dorm series (8)
Freshman taboo
Cooney, Linda A
Freshman dorm series (26)
Freshman temptation
Cooney, Linda A
Freshman dorm series (30)
Freshman truths
Cooney, Linda A
Freshman dorm series (21)
Freshman wedding
Cooney, Linda A
Freshman dorm series (18)
Freshwater, 1922-1928
Todd, Laura
Lavarni family series (2)
Frey and his wife
Hewlett, Maurice
Sagas retold series (2)
Freya Stark story
Stark, Freya
Traveller series (3)
Friar Felix at large
Prescott, Hilda Frances Margaret
Friar Felix Fabri series (1)
Friday adventure
Pudney, John
Fred and I series (7)
Friday before Bank Holiday
Davis, George
Roag's Syndicate series (3)
Friday run
Wood, James
James Fraser series (7)
Friday the Rabbi slept late
Kemelman, Harry
Rabbi David Small series (1)
Friday the thirteenth, part I
Hawke, Simon
Friday the thirteenth series (1)
Friday the thirteenth, part II
Hawke, Simon
Friday the thirteenth series (2)
Friday the thirteenth, part III
Avallone, Michael
Friday the thirteenth series (3)
Hawke, Simon
Friday the thirteenth series (3)
Friday to Monday
Garrett, William
James Drew series (2)
Friday's child
Lambert, Janet
Jordons series (2)
Friday's feast
Pendleton, Don
Mack Bolan series (37)
Friday's tunnel
Verney, John
Callendar family series (1)
Friedrich
Richter, Hans Peter
Friedrich trilogy (1)
Friend
Burningham, John
Little book series (8)
Friend against friend
Pascal, Francine
Sweet Valley High series (69)
Friend comes to play
Costa, Nicoletta
Molly and Tom series (3)
Friend for Dear Dragon
Hillert, Margaret
Dear Dragon series (12)
Friend for Dragon
Pilkey, Dav
Dragon series (1)
Friend for Frances
Warner, Priscilla Mary
Frances series (1)
Friend for Mitzi Mouse
Bullock, Kathleen
Mitzi Mouse series (2)
Friend in need
Ferguson, James
Emmerdale Farm series (22)
Friend like Annabel
Davidson, Alan
Annabel Fidelity Bunce series (1)
Friend like Phoebe
Kaye, Marilyn
Sisters series (5)
Friend of the rich
Benson, Edward Frederic
Old London series (3)
Friend or foe
Christmas, Joyce
Lady Margaret Priam series (5)
Friend to mankind
Voltz, William
Perry Rhodan series (91)
Friend with the countersign
Benson, Blackwood Ketcham
American Civil War series (2)
Friendly Farm
How, Ruth W
Friendly Farm series (1)
Friendly fiends
Muller, Paul
Paul Muller series (14)
Friendly folk
Gee, Herbert Leslie
Friendly series (4)
Friendly game
Godfrey, William
Test cricket series (2)
Friendly house
Gee, Herbert Leslie
Friendly series (2)
Friendly persuasion
West, Jessamyn
Jess and Eliza Birdwell series (1)
Friendly phoebe
Hader, Berta
Willow Hill series (5)
Friendly rivals
Norby, Lisa
Heart to heart series (9)
Friendly road
Grayson, David
Adventures series (3)
Friendly story book
Blyton, Enid
Story book series (8)
Friendly Terrace quartet
Smith, Harriet Lummis
Friendly Terrace series (4)
Friendly year
Gee, Herbert Leslie
Friendly series (3)
Friends
Guy, Rosa
Edith Jackson series (1)
Oxenbury, Helen
Baby board books series (6)
Friends again
Dahlerup, Rina
Buffy and Company series (2)
Friends and heroes
Manning, Olivia
Guy and Harriet Pringle series (3)
Friends and rivals
Pier, Arthur Stanwood
Saint Timothy's School series (8)
Friends are forever
Wilhelm, Hans
Merritales series (10)
Friends at court
Cecil, Henry
Roger Thursby series (2)
Friends at Pine Street
Allan, Mabel Esther
Pine Street series (6)
Friends at the Farm
Gould, Elizabeth
Green Willow Farm series (1)
Friends in low places
Raven, Simon
Alms for oblivion series (2)
Friends in the Fourth
Chaundler, Christine
Fourth Form series (6)
Friends of Abu Ali
Van Woerkom, Dorothy
Abu Ali series (2)
Friends of Barney Gregg
Grover, Marshall
Larry and Stretch series (391)
Friends of God
Sanford, Doris
Advanced theology for very tiny persons series (2)
Friends of Lucifer
Sinclair, Dennis
Greg Ballard series (3)
Friends of my life as an Indian
Schultz, James Willard
Blackfoot series (2)
Friends of the family
Flower, Pat
Inspector Swinton series (7)
Friends of the Horseclans
Adams, Robert
Horseclans series (18)
Friends of the people
Neumann, Alfred
Napoleon III trilogy (3)
Friends times three
Chase, Emily
Canby Hall series (20)
Friendship and duty
Schulze, Doris
Star trek fan series (43)
Friendship in the Lord
Hinnebusch, Paul
In the Lord series (1)
Friendship Max
Turk, Hanne
Max the Mouse series (15)
Friendship test
Haas, Dorothy
Peanut Butter and Jilly series (7)
Friendship village
Gale, Zora
Friendship village series (1)
Friendship village love stories
Gale, Zora
Friendship village series (2)
Friendship's odyssey
Delisle, Francoise
In love series (2)
Frigate
Wingate, John
Third World War trilogy (1)
Fright
Ure, Jean
Woodside School series (1)
Fright face context
Mooser, Stephen
Creepy Creature Club series (4)
Fright party
Zindel, Paul
Wacky facts lunch bunch series (2)
Fright wave
Dixon, Franklin W
Hardy boys case files series (40)
Frightened Amazon
Stein, Aaron Marc
Tim Mulligan and Elsie Mae Hunt series (12)
Frightened baby
Burgess, Thornton Waldo
Cubby Bear series (1)
Frightened brides
Cumberland, Marten
Saturnin Dax series (21)
Frightened chameleon
Gribble, Leonard Reginald
Superintendent Anthony Slade series (20)
Frightened eyes
Daniel, Roland
Michael Grant series (1)
Frightened fiancee
Coxe, George Harmon
Sam Crombie series (1)
Frightened fingers
Dean, Spencer
Don Cadee series (1)
Frightened fisherman
Chance, John Newton
Jonathan Blake series (40)
Frightened gun
Gilman, George G
Edge series (32)
Frightened lady
Baker, William Howard
Sexton Blake series (1398)
Frightened man
Chambers, Dana
Jim Steele series (5)
Meynell, Laurence Walter
Hooky Hefferman series (1)
Frightened people
Story, Jack Trevor
Sexton Blake series (1459)
Frightened sailor
Sharp, David
Professor Henry Arthur Fielding series (8)
Frightened stiff
Roos, Kelley
Jeff and Haila Troy series (3)
Frightened widow
Robertson, Colin
Superintendent Bradley series (4)
Frightened wife
Tripp, Miles
John Samson series (10)
Frightened women
Coxe, George Harmon
Jack Fenner series (3)
Kent Murdock series (4)
Frighteners
Busby, Roger
Detective Inspector Leric series (2)
Hamilton, Donald
Matt Helm series (25)
Frightfulness in the Theatre Royal
Beaman, Sydney George Hulme
Toytown series (21)
Frigor mortis
McInerny, Ralph
Andrew Broom series (3)
Fripsey fun
Chastain, Madye Lee
Fripsey series (3)
Fripsey summer
Chastain, Madye Lee
Fripsey series (2)
Frisbee disc flying is for me
Moran, Tom
Sports for me series (3)
Frisco and Fred
Ryan, John
Flying sorcerer series (1)
Frisco and Fred and the space monster
Ryan, John
Flying sorcerer series (2)

Frisco foxes
Fletcher, Dirk
Spur McCoy series (27)
Frisco lady
Cunningham, Chet
Agent Brad Spear series (4)
'Frisco Rock
Spade, Danny
Danny Spade series (3)
Frisk the otter
Rutley, Cecil Bernard
Wild life story series (11)
Frobisher's savage
Tourney, Leonard
Matthew Stock series (8)
Frog
Van der Essen, Anne
Yok-yok series (5)
Frog and Dog at the sea
Astrop, John
Frog and Dog series (1)
Frog and Dog find a treasure
Astrop, John
Frog and Dog series (3)
Frog and Dog go to the moon
Astrop, John
Frog and Dog series (4)
Frog and Dog have a party
Astrop, John
Frog and Dog series (2)
Frog and Toad all year
Lobel, Arnold
Frog and Toad series (3)
Frog and Toad are friends
Lobel, Arnold
Frog and Toad series (1)
Frog and Toad coloring book
Lobel, Arnold
Frog and Toad series (4)
Frog and Toad pop-up book
Lobel, Arnold
Frog and Toad series (4)
Frog and Toad tales
Lobel, Arnold
Frog and Toad series (4)
Frog and Toad together
Lobel, Arnold
Frog and Toad series (2)
Frog band and the Durrington dormouse
Smith, Jim
Frog band series (2)
Frog band and the mystery of Lion Castle
Smith, Jim
Frog band series (3)
Frog band and the onion seller
Smith, Jim
Frog band series (1)
Frog band and the owlnapper
Smith, Jim
Frog band series (4)
Frog goes to dinner
Mayer, Mercer
Frog series (4)
Frog in a coconut shell
Sherry, Sylvia
Yusof series (2)
Frog in the moonflower
Drummond, Ivor
Lady Jennifer, Sandro and Colly series (3)
Frog in the throat
Ferrars, Elizabeth
Virginia and Felix Freer series (2)
Frog is born
White, William
Animal is born series (1)
Frog medicine
Teague, Mark
Johnsons trilogy (3)
Frog on his own
Mayer, Mercer
Frog series (3)
Frog punch
Hodgman, Ann
Lunchroom series (2)
Frog was yellow
Vivian, Francis
Sergeant Ronnie Drew series (3)
Frog, where are you?
Mayer, Mercer
Frog series (2)
Froggie's treasure
McCue, Dick
Animal shape series (1)
Froggy gets dressed
London, Jonathan
Froggy series (1)
Froggy's little brother
Brenda
Froggy series (1)
Frogman
Macdonnell, James Edmond
Hooky Walker series (1)
Frogman assassination
Seward, Jack
Curt Stone series (2)
Frogmen in action
Berres, Frances B
Deep-sea adventure series (5)
Frogmouth
Marshall, William Leonard
Yellowthread Street series (12)
Frolic
Waldy, Frances Helen
Scarsborough series (2)
Frolics at Fairmount
Baker, Etta Anthony
Fairmount girls series (2)
Frolicsome four
Gilbert, Edith Laura
Meenie series (1)
From a changeling star
Carver, Jeffrey Allan
Changeling star series (1)
From a limestone ledge
Graves, John
Brazos trilogy (3)
From a London notebook
Charters, Samuel
Notebook series (2)
From a prison cell
Carter, Nicholas
Nicholas Carter series (200)
From a Swedish notebook
Charters, Samuel
Notebook series (1)
From A to Z
San Antonio
Berurier series (6)
San Antonio series (7)
From airship to spaceship
Stoff, Joshua
Long Island aerospace series (2)
From Anna
Little, Jean
Anna series (1)
From Atlanta to the sea
Dunn, Byron Archibald
Young Kentuckians series (4)
From baseball to Boches
Witwer, Harry Charles
Baseball series (1)
From beet to sugar
Mitgutsch, Ali
Start to finish series (1)
From Billabong to London
Bruce, Mary Grant
Billabong series (4)
From blossom to honey
Mitgutsch, Ali
Start to finish series (2)
From cacao bean to chocolate
Mitgutsch, Ali
Start to finish series (3)
From Caesar to Arthur
Ashe, Geoffrey
King Arthur series (2)
From cement to bridge
Mitgutsch, Ali
Start to finish series (4)
From Claudia to David
Franken, Rose
Claudia series (6)
From clay to bricks
Mitgutsch, Ali
Start to finish series (5)
From clue to capture
Donovan, Dick
Dick Donovan series (10)
From clue to clue
Carter, Nicholas
Nicholas Carter series (599)
From Colditz in code
Green, Julius Morris
Colditz series (7)
From cotton to pants
Mitgutsch, Ali
Start to finish series (6)
From cow to shoe
Mitgutsch, Ali
Start to finish series (7)
From Dogpatch to Slobovia
Capp, Al
Li'l Abner series (2)
From Doon with death
Rendell, Ruth
Chief Inspector Reginald Wexford series (1)
From eternity to here
Sellers, Michael
Calouste Fisher series (2)
From farm to fortune
Alger, Horatio
Rise in life series (7)
From fear set free
Sahgal, Nayantara
Prison series (2)
From Flushing to Calvary
Dahlberg, Edward
Bottom dogs series (2)
From fruit to jam
Mitgutsch, Ali
Start to finish series (8)
From gold to money
Mitgutsch, Ali
Start to finish series (18)
From grain to bread
Mitgutsch, Ali
Start to finish series (9)
From graphite to pencil
Mitgutsch, Ali
Start to finish series (19)
From grass to butter
Mitgutsch, Ali
Start to finish series (10)
From hide and horn
Edson, John Thomas
Floating Outfit series (5)
From idea to toy
Mitgutsch, Ali
Start to finish series (25)
From information received
Donovan, Dick
Dick Donovan series (8)
Gregg, Cecil Freeman
Inspector Cuthbert Higgins series (28)
Radford, Edwin
Doctor Manson series (16)
From inside Scotland Yard
Scott, Harold
Obedient servant series (2)
From lemon to lemonade
Mitgutsch, Ali
Start to finish series (22)
From low to high gear
Ellis, Edward Sylvester
Automobile series (1)
From middle England
Oakes, Philip
Middle England trilogy (1)
From milk to ice cream
Mitgutsch, Ali
Start to finish series (11)
From mud to mufti
Bairnsfather, Bruce
Old Bill series (7)
From my experience
Bromfield, Louis
Malabar series (4)
From natural causes
Bell, Josephine
Doctor David Wintringham series (5)
From office boy to reporter
Garis, Howard Roger
Great newspaper series (1)
Larry Dexter series (1)
From oil to gasoline
Mitgutsch, Ali
Start to finish series (12)
From ore to spoon
Mitgutsch, Ali
Start to finish series (13)
From outer space
Clement, Hal
Needle series (1)
From peril to peril
Carter, Nicholas
Nicholas Carter series (261)
From picture to picture book
Mitgutsch, Ali
Start to finish series (26)
From pillar to post
Mehdevi, Anne Sinclair
Pillar to post series (1)
From rags to riches
Aaseng, Nathan
Inside business series (7)
From rapture with love
Allison, Clyde
Agent triple zero eight series (16)
From right to left, 1887-1941
Pritt, Denis Nowell
Right to left trilogy (1)
From rubber tree to tire
Mitgutsch, Ali
Start to finish series (23)
From Russia, with love
Fleming, Ian
James Bond series (5)
From sand to glass
Mitgutsch, Ali
Start to finish series (14)
From Satan, with love
Coffman, Virginia
Lucifer Cove series (6)
From sea to salt
Mitgutsch, Ali
Start to finish series (20)
From sea to sea
Foster, Walter Bertram
Clint Webb series (3)
From sea to shining sea
Thom, James Alexander
George Rogers Clark series (2)
From seed to pear
Mitgutsch, Ali
Start to finish series (15)
From selection to city
Rudd, Steele
Rudd family series (6)
From sheep to scarf
Mitgutsch, Ali
Start to finish series (16)
From stores of memory
Bacheller, Irving
Cheerful Yankee trilogy (3)
From swamp to coal
Mitgutsch, Ali
Start to finish series (21)
From the angle of seventeen
Phillpotts, Eden
Human boy series (3)
From the ashes
Hagan, Chet
Dewey annals series (2)
From the earth to the moon
Verne, Jules
Gun Club series (1)
From the east unto the west
Barlow, Jane
Lisconnel series (3)
From the Exodus to King Akhnaton
Velikovsky, Immanuel
Ages in chaos series (1)
From the grave to the cradle
Joyce, Cyril
Chief Superintendent Pat Stockton series (13)
From the heat of the day
Heath, Roy Aubrey Kelvin
Georgetown trilogy (1)
From the hidden way
Cabell, James Branch
Dom Manuel and his descendants series (16)
From the Joke Shop
Fuller, Roy
Joke Shop series (1)
From the lower deck
Baynham, Henry
Naval life series (1)
From the shadow of the mountain
Brooks, Van Wyck
Scenes and portraits series (3)
From the Thorensen Dykes
McBratney, Sam
Thorensen Dykes series (2)
From the Twilight Zone
Serling, Rod
Twilight Zone series (3)
From this dark stairway
Eberhart, Mignon Good
Sarah Keate and Lance O'Leary series (4)
From this day
Roberts, Nora
Flowers series (14)
From tree to table
Mitgutsch, Ali
Start to finish series (17)
From Waterloo to the Mutiny
Wallace, Edgar
Black Avons series (3)
From wood to paper
Mitgutsch, Ali
Start to finish series (24)
Front and centre
Houseman, John
Unfinished business trilogy (2)
Front page murder
Bentley, John
Dick Marlow series (3)
Trevor, Ralph
Superintendent Curtis Burke series (4)
Front page woman
Saxon, Peter
Sexton Blake series (1412)
Front porch stories of the one-room school
Tate, Eleanora Elaine
Margie Carson and Ethel Hardisen series (2)
Front swine
Konrad, Klaus
Russian series (3)
Frontier Boys in Colorado
Roosevelt, Wyn
Frontier Boys series (2)
Frontier Boys in Frisco
Roosevelt, Wyn
Frontier Boys series (10)
Frontier Boys in Hawaii
Roosevelt, Wyn
Frontier Boys series (7)
Frontier Boys in Mexico
Roosevelt, Wyn
Frontier Boys series (4)
Frontier Boys in the Grand Canyon
Roosevelt, Wyn
Frontier Boys series (3)
Frontier Boys in the Rockies
Roosevelt, Wyn
Frontier Boys series (5)
Frontier Boys in the saddle
Roosevelt, Wyn
Frontier Boys series (9)
Frontier Boys in the Sierras
Roosevelt, Wyn
Frontier Boys series (8)
Frontier Boys in the South Seas
Roosevelt, Wyn
Frontier Boys series (11)
Frontier Boys on Overland Trail
Roosevelt, Wyn
Frontier Boys series (1)
Frontier Boys on the coast
Roosevelt, Wyn
Frontier Boys series (6)
Frontier detectives
Willoughby, Lee Davis
Making of America series (51)
Frontier dream
Chambers, Catherine E
Adventures in frontier America series (4)
Frontier Fanny
Sherman, Jory
Gunn series (24)
Frontier farmer
Chambers, Catherine E
Adventures in frontier America series (5)
Frontier feud
Baxter, George Owen
Red Hawk series (2)
Frontier fires
Bittner, F Rosanne
Caleb Sax series (2)
Frontier girl of Chesapeke Bay
Curtis, Alice Turner
Frontier girl series (4)
Frontier girl of Massachusetts
Curtis, Alice Turner
Frontier girl series (2)
Frontier girl of New York
Curtis, Alice Turner
Frontier girl series (3)
Frontier girl of Pennsylvania
Curtis, Alice Turner
Frontier girl series (5)
Frontier girl of Virginia
Curtis, Alice Turner
Frontier girl series (1)
Frontier healers
Willoughby, Lee Davis
Making of America series (16)
Frontier home
Bial, Raymond
Home series (2)
Frontier justice
Roberts, J R
Gunsmith series (114)
Frontier legion
Cole, Jackson
Jim Hatfield series (32)
Frontier medico
Stanley, Chuck
Frontier series (2)
Frontier of violence
Leader, Charles
Paul Mason series (1)
Frontier rakers
Norman, David
Frontier rakers series (1)
Frontier renegade
Stanley, Chuck
Frontier series (1)
Frontier rogue
Chase, Carolyn
Thirteen colonies series (4)
Frontier scout
Rutley, Cecil Bernard
Tales of stirring times series (5)

Frontier village
Chambers, Catherine E
Adventures in frontier America series (6)
Frontier war
Scofield, Jonathan
Freedom fighters series (8)
Frontier woman
Johnston, Joan
Sisters of the Lone Star trilogy (1)
Frontiers of death
Turner, James Ernest
Rampion Savage series (4)
Frontiersman
Pocock, Roger
Frontiersman series (1)
Frontiersmen
Eckert, Allan Wesley
Winning of America series (1)
Frontios
Bidmead, Christopher H
Doctor Who series (91)
Frontispiece
Spring, Marion Howard
Memories and gardens series (1)
Frost
Bailey, Robin Wayne
Frost trilogy (1)
Frost death
Rice, Peter
Renegade legion series (6)
Frost in May
White, Antonia
Frost in May series (1)
Frost on the moon
Darby, Catherine
Moon series (2)
Frosted death
Robeson, Kenneth
Avenger series (5)
Frostflower and Thorn
Karr, Phyllis Ann
Frostflower series (1)
Frostflower and Windbourne
Karr, Phyllis Ann
Frostflower series (2)
Frosty frolics
Joyner, Simon
Tales from the Misty Wood series (4)
Frosty the snowman
Howson, John Michael
Adventure Island story books (4)
Frozen assets
Leasor, James
Doctor Jason Love series (9)
Frozen death
Weymouth, Anthony
Inspector Treadgold series (1)
Frozen fire
McPhee, James
Survival two thousand trilogy (3)
Frozen flame
Hanshew, Mary E
Hamilton Cleek series (6)
Frozen god
Kirk, Richard
Raven series (3)
Frozen ship
Foster, Walter Bertram
Clint Webb series (2)
Frozen stiff
Chapman, Robert
Rex Banner series (6)
Frozen treasure
Bechdolt, Jack
Barrow brothers series (2)
Frozen waves
Vardeman, Robert Edward
Jade demons quartet (2)
Fruit-gathering
Tagore, Rabindranath
Gitanjali series (2)
Fruit in the seed
Leigh, Margaret Mary
Highland series (5)
Fruit of the Sabre
Darby, Catherine
Sabre family series (7)
Fruit of the vine
Blasco Ibanez, Vicente
Roman Catholic Church in Spain series (3)
Fruit stoners
Blackwood, Algernon
Maria series (2)
Fruitfulness
Zola, Emile
Four Gospels series (1)
Fruits of the earth
Gide, Andre
Fruits of the earth series (1)
Fruits of the earth series (2)
Fruits of the poisonous tree
Mayor, Archer Huntington
Lieutenant Joe Gunther series (5)
Frustrations of Vera
Kerr, Michael
Caged women series (4)
FTL
Williams, Michael Lindsay
Martian series (2)
Fu-Manchu's bride
Rohmer, Sax
Fu-Manchu series (7)
Fudge-a-mania
Blume, Judy
Peter Hatcher series (4)
Fuel's gold
Jackson, Steven Gary
Car wars adventure gamebook series (2)
Lambard, Sharleen
Car wars adventure gamebook series (2)
Fugitive
Baker, William Howard
Sexton Blake series (1398)
Fish, Robert Lloyd
Captain Jose da Silva series (1)
Proust, Marcel
Remembrance of things past series (11)
Fugitive from murder
Heberden, Mary Violet
Desmond Shannon series (3)
Fugitive Steele
Hunter, S L
Steele series (7)
Fugitive worlds
Shaw, Bob
Land and overland trilogy (3)
Fugitives
Mackenzie, Donald
Fugitives series (1)
Trevor, Meriol
Luxembourg series (1)
Willoughby, Lee Davis
Making of America series (50)
Fulfilling
Kerin, Dorothy
Faith healing series (2)
Fulfilment of Daphne Bruno
Raymond, Ernest
Daphne Bruno series (2)
Fulfilments of fate and desire
Constantine, Storm
Book of Wraeththu series (3)
Fulgor the golden eagle
Rutley, Cecil Bernard
Wild life story series (16)
Full-bodied red
Zimmerman, Bruce
Quinn Parker series (3)
Full circle
Saxton, Judith
Neyler family series (4)
Smith, Andrew
Doctor Who series (71)
Full circle, 1951-1957
Eden, Anthony
Reckoning series (4)
Full Cleveland
Roberts, Les
Milan Jacovich series (2)
Full commission
Brennan, Carol
Liz Wareham series (2)
Full contact
Randisi, Robert Joseph
Miles Jacoby series (3)
Full cry
Tone, Teona
Kyra Keaton series (2)
Full days and pressed pants
Colwell, Max
Mike series (2)
Full fare for a corpse
Davis, Tech
Aubrey Nash series (2)
Full fathom five
Galwey, Geoffrey Valentine
Inspector Daddy Bourne series (3)
Macdonnell, James Edmond
Dutchy Holland series (14)
Dutchy Holland series (15)
Wingate, John
Submariner Sinclair series (6)
Full fathom forty
Burr, Sybil
Holly Gordon series (4)
Full flower
Piper, Warrene
Bennet family series (4)
Full fury
Ormerod, Roger
David Mallin and George Coe series (3)
Full house
Masters, Zeke
Faro Blake series (14)
Singer, Shelley
Jake Samson and Rosie Vincente series (3)
Full moon
Wodehouse, Pelham Grenville
Blandings Castle series (8)
Full moon at Sweatenham
Stanford, John Keith
Life and death of George Proteron series (2)
Full moon rising
Lorrah, Jean
Star trek fan series (2)
Full moonstar
Pollotta, Nick
Bureau thirteen series (2)
Full score
Cardus, Neville
Innings series (3)
Full stop
Mitcham, Gilroy
Nick Marshall series (1)
Full term
Stewart, John Innes Mackintosh
Duncan Pattullo series (5)
Full throttle
Phillips, Tony
Turbo cowboys series (4)
Full tilt
Murphy, Dervla
Full tilt series (1)
Full turn
Finlay, Eileen
Caravan series (2)
Fullback
Perry, Lawrence
Football series (1)
Fuller's earth
Wells, Carolyn
Fleming Stone series (32)
Fun and deadly games
Tracy, Don
Giff Speer series (3)
Fun and games with Paddington
Bond, Michael
Paddington learning and activity series (3)
Fun and games with Postman Pat
Cunliffe, John Arthur
Postman Pat series (35)
Fun at the queer trail
Burgess, Thornton Waldo
Animal stories series (6)
Fun at the seaside
Carruth, Jean
Fun with Sally series (2)
Fun for the Secret Seven
Blyton, Enid
Secret Seven series (15)
Fun house terrors!
Milton, Hilary
Plot your own horror stories series (6)
Fun next door
Hurt, Freda Mary
Pinetops series (2)
Fun with addition
Daniel, Rebecca
Fun with arithmetic series (1)
Fun with Blinky Bill
Wall, Dorothy
Blinky Bill series (4)
Fun with Clifford activity book
Bridwell, Norman
Clifford series (34)
Fun with division
Daniel, Rebecca
Fun with arithmetic series (4)
Fun with Little Lulu
Henderson, Marge
Little Lulu series (2)
Fun with Mary Mouse
Blyton, Enid
Mary Mouse series (22)
Fun with multiplication
Daniel, Rebecca
Fun with arithmetic series (3)
Fun with my friends
Kalman, Bobbie
In my world series (3)
Fun with subtraction
Daniel, Rebecca
Fun with arithmetic series (2)
Fun with the twins
Blyton, Enid
Twins series (6)
Funeral Bend
Slade, Jack
Lassiter series (6)
Funeral by the sea
Gilman, George G
Undertaker series (3)
Funeral for a commissar
Magowan, Ronald
Shane Mackenzie series (2)
Funeral for five
Stagge, Jonathan
Doctor Hugh Westlake series (4)
Funeral games
Renault, Mary
Alexander the Great series (3)
Funeral in Berlin
Deighton, Len
Secret file series (3)
Funeral march for Siegfried
Williamson, Audrey
Superintendent Richard York series (1)
Funeral of gondolas
Holme, Timothy
Inspector Achille Peroni series (2)
Funeral rites
Hedges, Joseph
John Stark series (1)
Funeral sites
Mann, Jessica
Tamara Hoyland series (1)
Funeral was in Spain
McGirr, Edmund
Jim Piron series (1)
Funerals are fatal
Christie, Agatha
Hercule Poirot series (28)
Fungus the bogeyman
Briggs, Raymond
Fungus the bogeyman series (1)
Fungus the bogeyman plop-up book
Briggs, Raymond
Fungus the bogeyman series (2)
Funneyman and the penny dodo
Mooser, Stephen
Funnyman series (2)
Funniest killer in town
Stone, Hampton
Jeremiah X Gibson series (15)
Funny bananas
McHargue, Georgess
Ben and Frito series (1)
Funny bugger, and other tales
Garvey, Keith
Outback tales series (2)
Funny bunnies
Quackenbush, Robert Mead
Funny bunnies series (1)
Funny bunnies on the run
Quackenbush, Robert Mead
Funny bunnies series (2)
Funny face
Savage, Deborah
Peregrine Piecrust series (5)
Funny Farm house
Kanno, Wendy
Funny Farm series (6)
Funny guy
Hogarth, Grace Allen
Helen Hamilton series (1)
Funny money
Murphy, Warren Burton
Destroyer series (18)
Funny sort of Christmas
Cate, Dick
Flying free series (2)
Funny thing happened on the way
Spain, Nancy
Thank you series (3)
Funnybones
Ahlberg, Allan
Funnybones series (8)
Funnyman meets the monster from outer space
Mooser, Stephen
Funnyman series (3)
Funnyman's first case
Mooser, Stephen
Funnyman series (1)
Fur magic
Norton, Andre
Magic series (3)
Fur raiders
Gibbons, Harry Hornaby Clifford
Sexton Blake series (518)
Fur-seal's tooth
Munroe, Kirk
Pacific coast series (1)
Furies
Charnas, Suzy McKee
Alldera series (3)
Jakes, John
Kent family series (4)
Furioso
Lestienne, Voldemar
Three Musketeers series (4)
Furious flycycle
Wahl, Jan
Melvin Spitznagle series (1)
Furious gulf
Benford, Gregory
Galactic Center series (5)
Furious old woman
Bruce, Leo
Carolus Deene series (8)
Furnace for a foe
Rushton, Charles
Inspector Cadman series (4)
Furnace of the cup
Stark, Freya
Traveller's letters series (1)
Furnished for murder
Barth, Richard
Margaret Binton series (7)
Furry Forest bears
Graham, Rosemary
Furry Forest series (1)
Furry tales
Lee, Leslie
Furry tales series (1)
Further adventures of a woman detective
Kerner, Annette
Woman detective series (2)
Further adventures of Albert the dragon
Weir, Rosemary
Albert the dragon series (2)
Further adventures of Barry Lyndon by himself
Wood, Christopher
Barry Lyndon series (2)
Further adventures of Batman
Greenberg, Martin Harry
Batman series (6)
Further adventures of Bib and Bub
Gibbs, May
Gumnut Land series (12)
Further adventures of Brer Anansi
Makhanlall, David Paschal
Anansi series (6)
Further adventures of Brer Rabbit
Blyton, Enid
Brer Rabbit adventures series (3)
Lester, Julius
Tales of Uncle Remus series (2)
Further adventures of Captain Gregory Dangerfield
Lloyd, Jeremy
Captain Gregory Dangerfield series (1)
Further adventures of Captain Kettle
Hyne, Charles John Cutcliffe
Captain Owen Kettle series (4)
Further adventures of Doctor A.A.A.McGurk, M.D.
White, Osmar
Doctor McGurk series (2)
Further adventures of Doctor Syn
Thorndike, Russell
Doctor Syn series (3)
Further adventures of Doctor Who
Dicks, Terrance
Doctor Who series (47)
Further adventures of Ginger Meggs, series 11
Bancks, James Charles
Ginger Meggs series (11)
Further adventures of Ginger Meggs, series 2
Bancks, James Charles
Ginger Meggs series (2)
Further adventures of Ginger Meggs, series 4
Bancks, James Charles
Ginger Meggs series (4)
Further adventures of Gobbolino and the little wooden horse
Williams, Ursula Moray
Gobbolino series (3)
Further adventures of Hank the cowdog
Erickson, John R
Hank the cowdog series (2)
Further adventures of Huckleberry Finn
Matthews, Greg
Huckleberry Finn series (3)
Further adventures of Jimmie Dale
Packard, Frank Lucius
Jimmie Dale series (2)
Further adventures of Josie, Click and Bun
Blyton, Enid
Josie, Click and Bun series (2)
Further adventures of King Rollo
McKee, David
King Rollo series (9)

Further adventures of Lad
Terhune, Albert Payson
Sunnybank collies series (5)
Further adventures of Mister Verdant Green, an Oxford freshman
Bede, Cuthbert
Mister Verdant Green series (2)
Further adventures of Monty Trio
Mackinnon, Andrew
Monty Trio series (2)
Further adventures of Nils
Lagerlof, Selma
Nils series (2)
Further adventures of Peter Possum and his friends
Hibberd, Jean
Peter Possum series (2)
Further adventures of Puss in Boots
Gray, Nicholas Stuart
Puss in Boots series (2)
Further adventures of Quincy Adams Sawyer
Pidgin, Charles Felton
Quincy Adams Sawyer series (2)
Further adventures of Rab Hewison
Douglas, G A H
Rab Hewison series (2)
Further adventures of Riverboat Bill
Green, Cliff
Riverboat Bill series (2)
Further adventures of Robinson Crusoe
Defoe, Daniel
Robinson Crusoe series (1)
Treece, Henry
Robinson Crusoe series (2)
Further adventures of Romney Pringle
Ashdown, Clifford
Romney Pringle series (2)
Further adventures of Rupert and his pet monkey
Tourtel, Mary
Rupert Bear series (13)
Further adventures of Solar Pons
Copper, Basil
Solar Pons series (14)
Further adventures of Tammy Troot
Derwent, Lavinia
Tammy Troot series (4)
Further adventures of the Amateur Cracksman
Hornung, Ernest William
Raffles series (2)
Further adventures of the Black Pilgrim
Stanley, George
Black Pilgrim series (2)
Further adventures of the family from One End Street
Garnett, Eve
Ruggles family series (2)
Further adventures of the Joker
Greenberg, Martin Harry
Batman series (7)
Further adventures of the Robber Hotzenplotz
Preussler, Otfried
Robber Hotzenplotz series (2)
Further adventures of the Sugar Creek Gang
Hutchens, Paul
Sugar Creek Gang series (2)
Further adventures of Tuckonie
Martin, Marianne
Golden boomerang series (3)
Further adventures of Zorro
McCulley, Johnston
Zorro series (2)
Further chronicles of Avonlea
Montgomery, Lucy Maud
Avonlea series (10)
Further confessions of Zeno
Svevo, Italo
Zeno series (2)
Further cuttings from Cruiskeen Lawn
O'Brien, Flann
Cruiskeen Lawn series (2)
Further doings of Milly-Molly-Mandy
Brisley, Joyce Lankester
Milly-Molly-Mandy series (3)
Further down the back
Hillier, Fred
Outhouse series (2)
Further E K Means
Means, Eldred Kurtz
Is this a title, it is not series (3)
Further education of Oversoul Seven
Roberts, Jane
Oversoul Seven series (2)
Further experiences of an Irish R.M.
Somerville, Edith Oenone
Irish R.M. series (4)
Further experiences of Emmanuelle
Arsan, Emmanuelle
Emmanuelle series (3)
Further exploits of Mister Saucy Squirrel
Wyatt, Woodrow Lyle
Mister Saucy Squirrel series (2)
Further explorations
Knights, Lionel Charles
Explorations series (2)
Further forensic fables
O
Forensic fables series (2)
Further inventions of Mister Cogg
Sloan, Carolyn
Mister Cogg series (2)
Further Northern Territory recollections
Priest, Charles Ashley Vincent
Northern Territory recollections series (3)
Further outlook unsettled
Clevely, Hugh
Inspector Williams series (3)
Further particulars
Rolph, C H
Particulars series (2)
Further perils of Dracula
Youngson, Jeanne
Dracula series (18)
Further recollections of my early days in Australia
Boswell, Annabella
Early day series (2)
Further stir of Porridge
Victor, Paul
Porridge series (3)
Further story of Lieutenant Sandy Ray
King, Charles
Lieutenant Sandy Ray series (9)
Further tales from a country practice
Jackson, Arthur
Country practice series (3)
Further tales of Mister Pengachoosa
Rush, Caroline
Mister Pengachoosa series (2)
Further tales of the city
Maupin, Armistead
Tales of the city series (3)
Further than life
Williams, Michael Lindsay
Martian series (2)
Further transports of delight
Milligan, Spike
Delight series (2)
Furthermoore
Moore, Gerald
Memoirs of an accompanist series (3)
Furthest
Elgin, Suzette Haden
Coyote Jones series (2)
Furthest fury
Wells, Carolyn
Fleming Stone series (16)
Furtive plame
Janson, Hank
Hank Janson series (205)
Fury
Austin, Jim
John Fury series (1)
Smith, Lisa J
Vampire diaries series (3)
Timms, Edward Vivian
Australian saga series (7)
Watmough, David
Davey Bryant series (5)
Fury and the mustangs
Miller, Albert Griffith
Fury series (2)
Fury and the white mare
Miller, Albert Griffith
Fury series (3)
Fury at Broken Wheel
Grover, Marshall
Nevada Jim series (30)
Fury bombs
Wilson, Gar
Phoenix Force series (5)
Fury from the deep
Pemberton, Victor
Doctor Who series (110)
Fury in the ashes
Johnstone, William Wallace
Ashes series (13)
Fury of the Mountain Man
Johnstone, William Wallace
Mountain Man series (14)
Fury, son of the wilds
Peel, Hazel Mary
Ann and Jim Henderson series (1)
Fury, stallion of Broken Wheel Ranch
Miller, Albert Griffith
Fury series (1)
Furys
Hanley, James
Furys chronicle series (1)
Fury's pilgrims
Axler, James
Deathlands series (17)
Furze the cruel
Trevena, John
Dartmoor trilogy (1)
Fuse point
North, David
Time warriors series (1)
Fusion fire
Tyers, Kathy
Firebird series (2)
Fuss E Bugg
Cosgrove, Stephen Edward
Bugg series (45)
Futile alibi
Crofts, Freeman Wills
Inspector Joseph French series (17)
Future arrived
Rock, Phillip
Greville family trilogy (3)
Future Chalet School girl
Brent-Dyer, Elinor Mary
Chalet School series (47)
Future commonwealth
Chavannes, Albert
Socioland series (1)
Future deferred
Harper, Stephen
Healers series (1)
Future Eden
Morgan, Jill Meredith
Eden trilogy (3)
Future forward
Pfeffer, Susan Beth
VCR time machine series (2)
Future history
Pournelle, Jerry
Future history series (3)
Future indefinite
Coward, Noel
Present and future series (3)
Future life
Wood, George
Peter Schlemihl series (3)
Futures past
White, James
Sector General series (5)
Futurevisions
Burgess, Mary Alice
Science fiction film series (2)
Reginald, Robert
Science fiction film series (2)
Futurological congress
Lem, Stanislaw
Ijon Tichy series (1)
Fuzz
McBain, Ed
Eighty Seventh Precinct series (22)
Fuzzer basket
Bee, Clair
Chip Hilton series (20)
Fuzzies and other people
Piper, Horace Beam
Fuzzy series (3)
Fuzzy bones
Tuning, William
Fuzzy series (4)
Fuzzy friendly tale
Ross, Katharine
Fuzzy tales series (4)
Fuzzy fussy tale
Ross, Katharine
Fuzzy tales series (1)
Fuzzy Rabbit
Billam, Rosemary
Alpaca series (1)
Fuzzy Rabbit and the little brother problem
Billam, Rosemary
Alpaca series (3)
Fuzzy Rabbit in the park
Billam, Rosemary
Alpaca series (2)
Fuzzy Rabbit saves Christmas
Billam, Rosemary
Alpaca series (4)
Fuzzy sapiens
Piper, Horace Beam
Fuzzy series (2)
Fuzzy sleepy tale
Ross, Katharine
Fuzzy tales series (2)
Fuzzy wake up tale
Ross, Katharine
Fuzzy tales series (3)
Fuzzypeg goes to school
Uttley, Alison
Fuzzypeg series (2)
Little Grey Rabbit series (9)
Fuzzypeg's brother
Uttley, Alison
Fuzzypeg series (3)
Little Grey Rabbit series (31)
Fuzzytail friends' great egg hunt
Ross, Katharine
Fuzzy tales series (4)

G

G-Eight and his battle aces
Hogan, Robert Jasper
G-Eight series (10)
G.I. Joe and the Everglades swamp terror
Affabee, Eric
Find your fate: G.I. Joe series (5)
G is for gumshoe
Grafton, Sue
Kinsey Millhone series (7)
G Man at the yard
Cheyney, Peter
Lemmy Caution series (12)
Slim Callaghan series (11)
G-man's son
Robinson, Warren F
G-man's son series (1)
G-man's son ar Porpoise Island
Robinson, Warren F
G-man's son series (2)
G-men in jeopardy
Smith, Lawrence Dwight
G-men series (2)
G-Men in the professor's ring
Eagle, William
G-men series (1)
G-men on Murder Island
Jamieson, Leland
Dan Gregory series (2)
G-men tarp the spy ring
Smith, Lawrence Dwight
G-men series (3)
G-string murders
Lee, Gypsy Rose
Gypsy Rose Lee series (1)
Gaal the conqueror
White, John
Archives of Anthropos series (4)
Gabo Djara
Wongar, B
Nuclear trilogy (3)
Gaboreau
Steward, Paull
Donald Everhard series (2)
Gaboreau the terrible
Steward, Paull
Donald Everhard series (3)
Gabriel Churchkitten
Austin, Margot
Church animals series (2)
Gabriel Churchkitten and the molts
Austin, Margot
Church animals series (3)
Gabriel set-up
O'Donnell, Peter
Modesty Blaise comic strip series (3)
Gabrielle
Shura, Mary Francis
Sunfire series (24)
Gabrielle's way
Hunter, Alan
Inspector George Gently series (27)
Gabriel's angel
Roberts, Nora
Flowers series (32)
Gaby and the new money fraud
Berna, Paul
Gaby series (3)
Gadfly
Voynich, Ethel Lillian
Gadfly series (2)
Gadget lovers
Charteris, Leslie
Saint series (39)
Gad's Hall
Lofts, Norah
Gad's Hall series (1)
Gaff Lee, detective
Stewart, William Thomas
Gaff Lee series (1)
Gahr City
Nichols, Robert
Daily lives in Nghsi-Altai series (3)
Gaian expedient
Drew, Wayland
Erthring cycle series (2)
Gail Gardner, junior cadet nurse
Sutton, Margaret
Gail Gardner series (1)
Gail Gardner wins her cap
Sutton, Margaret
Gail Gardner series (2)
Gala week
Clarke, Roy
Summer wine series (1)
Galactiad
Kern, Gregory
Cap Kennedy series (17)
Galactic alarm
Mahr, Kurt
Perry Rhodan series (3)
Galactic arena
Dane, Christopher
Myra Morgana series (2)
Galactic convoy
Baldwin, Bill
Helmsman series (2)
Galactic derelict
Norton, Andre
Time war series (2)
Galactic diplomat
Laumer, Keith
Retief series (2)
Galactic Effectuator
Vance, Jack
Gaean series (6)
Galactic patrol
Smith, Edward Elmer
Lensman series (3)
Galactic raiders
Black, Christopher
Star challenge series (5)
Galactic riddle
Darlton, Clark
Perry Rhodan series (8)
Galactic Sibyl Sue Blue
Brown, Rosel George
Sibyl Sue Blue series (1)
Galactic silver star
Randle, Kevin
Jefferson's war series (1)
Galactic warlord
Hill, Douglas
Last legionary series (2)
Galactic warriors
Bischoff, David
Star hounds series (2)
Galactic whirlpool
Gerrold, David
Star trek originals sequels series (14)
Galactica discovers earth
Larson, Glen A
Battlestar Galactica series (5)
Galahad at Blandings
Wodehouse, Pelham Grenville
Blandings Castle series (11)
Galahad of the air
Wallace, Trevor
John Tracy series (2)
Galatea McGee
Grover, Marshall
Larry and Stretch series (363)
Galaxies
Simon, Seymour
Space photos series (7)
Galaxy builder
Laumer, Keith
Lafayette O'Leary series (4)
Galaxy four
Emms, William
Doctor Who series (104)
Galaxy mission
Hamilton, Edmond
Captain Future series (4)
Galaxy of governesses
Howe, Bea
Childhood series (1)
Galaxy of the lost
Kern, Gregory
Cap Kennedy series (1)
Galaxy's end
Lupoff, Richard Allen
Sun's end series (2)
Gale and the sword of Mars
Leyland, Eric
Steven Gale series (4)
Gale force
Black, Gavin
Paul Harris series (11)

Gale hits the headlines
Leyland, Eric
Steven Gale series (2)
Gale of the world
Williamson, Henry
Chronicles of ancient sunlight series (15)
Gale warning
Yates, Dornford
Jonah Mansel series (7)
Richard Chandos series (6)
Galen beknighted
Williams, Michael Leon
DragonLance heroes series (6)
Gales of spring
Wibberley, Leonard
Man of liberty series (3)
Galileans
Slaughter, Frank Gill
Biblical series (2)
Gallagher plot
Carter, Nick
Nick Carter series (114)
Gallant
Long, William Stuart
Australians series (8)
Gallant affair
Hobson, Hank
Brad Ford series (1)
Gallant folk
Gee, Herbert Leslie
Friendly series (12)
Gallant old engine
Awdry, Wilbert
Railway series (17)
Gallantry
Cabell, James Branch
Dom Manuel and his descendants series (12)
Gallatin divergence
Smith, Lester Neil
North American Confederacy trilogy (2)
Galldora omnibus
Sedgwick, Modwena
Galldora series (3)
Galleon
Pope, Dudley
Ned Yorke series (5)
Galleon's Bay
Scott, Philip
Algy, Peter and Jeremy series (1)
Gallery of Clerihews
Horgan, Paul
Clerihews series (1)
Gallery of women
Dreiser, Theodore
Men and women series (2)
Galley slave's ring
Sue, Eugene
Mysteries of the people series (19)
Gallicenae
Anderson, Poul
King of Ys series (2)
Gallifrey chronicles
Peel, John
Doctor Who series (162)
Gallipoli memories
Mackenzie, Compton
Memories series (1)
Gallop to the hills
Leitch, Patricia
Jinny series (5)
Galloping Dick
Watson, Henry Brereton Marriott
Dick Ryder series (1)
Galloping Fred
Ridge, Antonia
Endless and Company series (4)
Galloping ghost
Macdonald, William Colt
Three Mesquiteers series (15)
Galloping gold
Tuttle, Wilbur Coleman
Henry Harrison Conroy and Judge Van Treece series (7)
Sad Sontag series (5)
Galloway
L'Amour, Louis
Sackett family series (14)
Galloway childhood
Niall, Ian
Galloway series (1)
Galloway shepherd
Niall, Ian
Galloway series (2)
Gallows
Reno, Bill
Badge series (14)
Gallows are waiting
York, Jeremy
Superintendent Folly series (6)
Gallows bait
Pike, Charles R
Jubal Cade series (22)
Gallows-bird
Duffy, Margaret
Patrick Gillard series (6)
Gallows express
Masterson, Louis
Morgan Kane series (19)
Gallows' foot
Gielgud, Val
Inspector Gregory Pellew and Viscount Clymping series (1)
Gallows for a fool
Franklin, Charles
Grant Garfield series (11)
Gallows for the groom
Olsen, D B
Professor A Pennyfeather series (2)
Gallows gal
Foley, Craig
Hangman series (5)
Gallows garden
Chaber, M E
Milo March series (7)
Gallows gold
Hobart, Donald Bayne
Masked Rider and Blue Hawk series (12)
Gallows Grange
Holt, Henry
Inspector Silver series (6)
Gallows in my garden
Deming, Richard
Manville Moon series (1)
Gallows Inn
Thorne, Ernest Pollett
Quentin Eady series (4)
Gallows tree
Muir, James A
Breed series (5)
Gallows view
Robinson, Peter
Chief Inspector Alan Banks series (1)
Gallows waiting
Hart, Matthew S
Cody's law series (10)
Gallows wedding
Martin, Rhona
Black John and Hazel series (1)
Gallows west
Allen, Chester
Justice Colt series (5)
Gallybird
Kaye-Smith, Sheila
Alard family trilogy (2)
Gal's gossip
Binstead, Arthur Morris
Gal's gossip series (1)
Galton case
Macdonald, Ross
Lew Archer series (9)
Gambara
Balzac, Honore de
Philosophic studies series (6)
Gambit
Stout, Rex
Nero Wolfe and Archie Goodwin series (37)
Gambit for Mister Goode
Griswold, George
Mister Groode series (1)
Gamble of death
Ellis, Wesley
Lone Star series (89)
Gamble with death
Simons, Roger
Inspector Fadiman Wace series (5)
Gambler
Avenell, Donne
Axa series (3)
Cloete, Stuart
Victorian son series (2)
Hogstrand, Olle
Chief Inspector Lars Kollin series (2)
Krasner, William
Sam Birge series (2)
Gambler, the minstrel and the dance hall queen
Downing, Warwick
Joe Reddman series (3)
Gamblers
Willoughby, Lee Davis
Making of America series (44)
Gambler's blood
Roberts, J R
Gunsmith series (141)
Gambler's chance
Hendryx, James Beardsley
Corporal Cameron Downey series (5)
Corporal Downey series (12)
Gambler's gold
Field, Peter
Powder Valley series (26)
Gambler's luck
Broome, H B
Tom English series (6)
Gambler's revenge
Tanner, Clay
Chance Sharpe series (4)
Gambler's syndicate
Carter, Nicholas
Nicholas Carter series (8)
Gambler's woman
Calhoun, Chad
Agent Brad Spear series (12)
Gamble's hundred
Dowdey, Clifford
Richmond, Virginia series (1)
Gambling ghost, an other tales
Stivens, Dal
Ironbark Bill series (1)
Game
Hammond, Gerald
Keith Calder series (5)
Logan, Les
Dark forces series (1)
Postgate, Oliver
Saga of Noggin the Nog series (9)
Game for empires
Frye, Pearl
Lord Horatio Nelson series (1)
Game for hawks
Severn, Richard
Jeff Cass series (2)
Game goes on
McGilvray, Alan
Cricket series (2)
Game is not the same
McGilvray, Alan
Cricket series (1)
Game keeper's secret
Graydon, William Murray
Sexton Blake series (346)
Game of craft
Carter, Nicholas
Nicholas Carter series (60)
Game of death
Roberts, J R
Gunsmith series (115)
Game of empire
Anderson, Poul
Sir Dominic Flandry series (10)
Game of Falcons
Darby, Catherine
Falcon family series (2)
Game of fox and lion
Chase, Robert Reynolds
Game series (1)
Game of hearts
Burgin, George Brown
Four Corners series (11)
Game of kings
Dunnett, Dorothy
Francis Crawford of Lymond series (1)
Game of murder
Barrington, Pamela
Inspector George Marshall series (11)
Game of plots
Carter, Nicholas
Nicholas Carter series (231)
Game of terror
Messmann, Jon
Jefferson Boone series (2)
Game of the season
De Selincourt, Hugh
Gauvinier series (2)
Game of Troy
White, Jon Manchip
Colonel Rickman trilogy (2)
Game of you
Gaiman, Neil
Sandman series (5)
Game plan for disaster
Dixon, Franklin W
Hardy boys series (76)
Game, set and match
Beresford, Elisabeth
Gappy, Jim and Jane series (9)
Deighton, Len
Game, set and match trilogy (3)
Game show girls
Radford, John P
Illusionist series (4)
Game things
Berry, Joy
Can make and do series (11)
Game well played
Carter, Nicholas
Nicholas Carter series (258)
Gamearth
Anderson, Kevin James
Gamearth trilogy (1)
Gamecock murders
Gruber, Frank
Johnny Fletcher and Sam Cragg series (11)
Gamefinger
Allison, Clyde
Agent triple zero eight series (6)
Gamekeeper's gallows
Hilton, John Buxton
Inspector Thomas Brunt series (1)
Gamemaker
Cohler, David Keith
Sam Knight series (1)
Gameplay
Anderson, Kevin James
Gamearth trilogy (2)
Gameplayers of Zan
Foster, Michael Anthony
Ler series (1)
Game's afoot
Hardwick, Michael
Sherlock Holmes drama series (5)
Game's end
Anderson, Kevin James
Gamearth trilogy (3)
Dank, Milton
Game series (2)
Games to keep the dark away
Muller, Marcia
Sharon McCone series (5)
Gaming house
Manners, Alexandra
Karran Kinrade series (4)
Gamma option
Land, Jon
Blaine McCracken series (3)
Gammage cup
Kendall, Carol
Minnipins series (1)
Gamov factor
Bannerman, David
Magic Man series (2)
Gandalara cycle
Garrett, Randall
Gandalara cycle series (3)
Gandalara cycle series (6)
Gandhi and civil disobedience
Brown, Judith Margaret
Gandhi series (2)
Gandhi, prisoner of hope
Brown, Judith Margaret
Gandhi series (2)
Gandhi's rise to power
Brown, Judith Margaret
Gandhi series (1)
Gang
Kastle, Herbert David
Sergeant Edmund Roersch series (2)
Gang in the Western Isles
Catling, Gordon
Gang series (2)
Gang on the Broads
Catling, Gordon
Gang series (1)
Gang Smasher
Clevely, Hugh
John Martinson series (1)
Gang Smasher again
Clevely, Hugh
John Martinson series (2)
Gang war
Colter, Frank
Gang war series (1)
Teed, George Hamilton
Sexton Blake series (682)
Gang woman
Fraser, Sara
Tildy series (6)
Gangdom's doom
Grant, Maxwell
Shadow series (5)
Gangs all here
Harrell, Janice
In crowd series (1)
Gang's deserter
Brisbane, Coutts
Sexton Blake series (609)
Gangs, ghosts and gypsies
Sloan, Carolyn
Mall series (3)
Gang's orders
Poole, Michael
Sexton Blake series (624)
Gang's prisoners
Bidston, Lester
Sexton Blake series (646)
Gangster
Daniel, Roland
Gangster series (1)
Gangster girl
Lait, Jack
Polack Annie series (2)
Gangster pie
Martin, Robert
Ginger Pennylove series (1)
Gangsters
Martin, Philip
John Kline series (1)
Gangster's daughter
Daniel, Roland
Buddy Mustard series (16)
Gangster series (3)
Gangster's deputy
Drew, Sidney
Sexton Blake series (605)
Gangster's girl
Hunter, John
Sexton Blake series (1416)
Gangster's last shot
Daniel, Roland
Gangster series (2)
Inspector Jack Pearson series (3)
Gangsters, number two
Martin, Philip
John Kline series (2)
Gangsters of the air
Noy, John
Rufus Deville series (3)
Gangster's revenge
Philips, George Norman
Sexton Blake series (628)
Gangway
Browne, Dik
Hagar the horrible series (31)
Gants
Abshire, Richard
Gants series (1)
Gaol gates are open
Hume, David
Mick Cardby series (8)
Gap in the curtain
Buchan, John
Sir Edward Leithen series (4)
Gap into conflict
Donaldson, Stephen Reeder
Gap series (1)
Gap into power
Donaldson, Stephen Reeder
Gap series (3)
Gap into vision
Donaldson, Stephen Reeder
Gap series (2)
Gappy goes west
Beresford, Elisabeth
Gappy, Jim and Jane series (4)
Garaucan swindle
Grant, Maxwell
Shadow series (62)
Garb of truth
Stuart, Ian
David Grierson series (3)
Garbage chronicles
Herbert, Brian
Sidney series (2)
Garbage collector
Stein, Aaron Marc
Matt Erridge series (23)
Garbage juice for breakfast
Giff, Patricia Reilly
Polka Dot series (6)
Garde save the world
La Plante, Jerry
Chameleon series (3)
Garden
Strong, Leonard Alfred George
Garden series (1)
Garden adventures of Tommy Tittlemouse
Judson, Clara Ingram
Tommy Tittlemouse series (2)
Garden by the river
Ross, Jean
Belvie family series (2)
Garden city crime
Stuart, Donald
Sexton Blake series (674)
Garden game
White, Jon Manchip
Colonel Rickman trilogy (3)
Garden house
Long, Martin
Inspector Keats and Tom Cotter series (3)
Tomalin, Ruth
Ralph Oliver series (1)
Garden in Asia
Post, Melville Davisson
Sir Henry Marquis series (2)
Garden in the hills
West, Elizabeth
Hafod Garden series (2)

Garden-land
Chambers, Robert William
Land series (6)
Garden murder case
Van Dine, S S
Philo Vance series (9)
Garden of a commuter's wife
Wright, Mabel Osgood
Commuter's wife series (1)
Garden of death
Grant, Maxwell
Shadow series (210)
Garden of earthly delights
Oates, Joyce Carol
Jules and Maureen Wendall trilogy (1)
Garden of evil
Martin, David
Doctor Who find your fate series (3)
Plante, Edward
Seed series (2)
Garden of God
Stacpoole, Henry de Vere
Dick and Emmeline series (2)
Garden of malice
Kenney, Susan
Roz Howard series (1)
Garden of Rama
Clarke, Arthur Charles
Rama series (3)
Garden of resurrection
Thurston, Ernest Temple
Bellwattle and Cruikshank series (2)
Garden of shadows
Andrews, Virginia Cleo
Dollanganger family series (1)
Garden of silent beasts
Holt, Gavin
Professor Luther Bastion series (5)
Garden of the Finzi-Continis
Bassani, Giorgio
Ferrara series (3)
Garden of the gods
Durrell, Gerald
Corfu series (4)
Garden of the incubus
Tigges, John
Incubus trilogy (1)
Garden of the shaped
Finch, Sheila
Shaper exile series (1)
Garden of weapons
Gardner, John Edmund
Herbie Kruger series (2)
Garden open today
Nichols, Beverley
Open garden series (1)
Garden open tomorrow
Nichols, Beverley
Open garden series (2)
Garden rubbish, and other country bumps
Sellar, Walter Carruthers
All that series (4)
Gardenias bruise easily
Carstairs, John Paddy
Garaway Trenton series (1)
Gardens of Camelot
Croft-Cooke, Rupert
Sensual life series (1)
Gargoni girdle
Carter, Nicholas
Nicholas Carter series (561)
Gargoyle of Polgelly
Hardinge, Rex
Sexton Blake series (1207)
Garibaldi and the making of Italy
Trevelyan, George Macaulay
Giuseppe Garibaldi trilogy (3)
Garibaldi and the Thousand, Naples and Sicily, 1858-60
Trevelyan, George Macaulay
Giuseppe Garibaldi trilogy (2)
Garibaldi's ski-boat
Hofmeyer, Hans
Garibaldi series (1)
Garland
Undset, Sigrid
Kristin Lavransdatter trilogy (1)
Garland of valour
Clevely, Hugh
Justin Kelly series (2)
Garman and Worse
Kielland, Alexander Lange
Garman and Worse series (1)
Garnet
Leigh, Petra
Garnet series (1)
Garnett Bell, detective
Bullivant, Cecil Henry
Garnett Bell series (1)
Garonsky missile
Caillou, Alan
Colonel Matthew Tobin series (7)
Garrard heritage
Grover, Marshall
Larry and Stretch series (103)
Garrett files
Cook, Glen
Garrett series (3)
Garrison
Rovin, Jeff
Roger Garrison series (1)
Garrison gossip gathered in Blankhampton
Winter, John Strange
Blankhampton series (4)
Garrison triangle
King, Charles
Lieutenant Sandy Ray series (4)
Garrison's Gorillas
Pearl, Jack
Garrison's Gorillas series (1)
Garrison's Gorillas and the fear formula
Pearl, Jack
Garrison's Gorillas series (2)
Garrity
Nixon, Allan
Tony Garrity series (1)
Garry Grayson at Lenox High
Dawson, Elmer A
Garry Grayson football series (2)
Garry Grayson at Stanley Prep
Dawson, Elmer A
Garry Grayson football series (5)
Garry Grayson hitting the line
Dawson, Elmer A
Garry Grayson football series (7)
Garry Grayson showing his speed
Dawson, Elmer A
Garry Grayson football series (4)
Garry Grayson's double signals
Dawson, Elmer A
Garry Grayson football series (9)
Garry Grayson's football rivals
Dawson, Elmer A
Garry Grayson football series (3)
Garry Grayson's forward pass
Dawson, Elmer A
Garry Grayson football series (10)
Garry Grayson's High Street Eleven
Dawson, Elmer A
Garry Grayson football series (1)
Garry Grayson's winning kick
Dawson, Elmer A
Garry Grayson football series (6)
Garry Grayson's winning touchdown
Dawson, Elmer A
Garry Grayson football series (8)
Garry Halliday and the disappearing diamonds
Blake, Justin
Garry Halliday series (1)
Garry Halliday and the Flying Foxes
Blake, Justin
Garry Halliday series (5)
Garry Halliday and the kidnapped five
Blake, Justin
Garry Halliday series (3)
Garry Halliday and the ray of death
Blake, Justin
Garry Halliday series (2)
Garry Halliday and the sands of time
Blake, Justin
Garry Halliday series (4)
Garston murder case
Bailey, Henry Christopher
Mister Joshua Clunk series (1)
Garstons
Bailey, Henry Christopher
Mister Joshua Clunk series (1)
Garth Pig and the Ice Cream Lady
Rayner, Mary
Mister and Mrs Pig series (2)
Garukan blood
Wylde, Thomas
Doctor Bones series (3)
Gary Glitter story
Tremlett, George
Rock stars series (3)
Gas-mask murder
Warren, John Russell
Inspector M'Guire series (2)
Gashlycrumb
Gorey, Edward
Vinegar works trilogy (1)
Gasworks Alley Gang
Hatcher, Jo
Gasworks Alley Gang series (1)
Gasworks Alley Gang goes west
Hatcher, Jo
Gasworks Alley Gang series (2)
Gat heat
Prather, Richard Scott
Shell Scott series (33)
Gate-crashers
Fullerton, Alexander
Nick Everard series (9)
Gate crashers
Huddy, Delia
Hipster series (2)
Gate fever
O'Sullivan, James Brendan
Steve Silk series (13)
Gate of Eden
Corlett, William
Gate of Eden trilogy (1)
Gate of Happy Sparrows
Vare, Daniele
Yen-Ching trilogy (2)
Gate of ivory
Egan, Doris
Gate of ivory series (1)
Gate of Ivrel
Cherryh, Carolyn Janice
Chronicles of Morgaine series (1)
Gate of the cat
Norton, Andre
Witch World series (19)
Gate of the giant scissors
Johnston, Annie Fellows
Little colonel series (2)
Gates flew open
O'Donnell, Peadar
Another day series (1)
Gates of Bannerdale
Trease, Geoffrey
Bannermere series (5)
Gates of creation
Farmer, Philip Jose
World of Tiers series (2)
Gates of death
Brady, William S
Jared Hawk series (7)
Hedges, Joseph
John Stark series (11)
Phillips, Terry
Advanced dungeons and dragons adventure gamebook series (10)
Gates of Exquisite View
Trenhaile, John
Simon Young series (2)
Gates of hell
Morris, Janet Ellen
Heroes in hell series (3)
Gates of ivory
Drabble, Margaret
Radiant way trilogy (3)
Gates of Kunarja
Macneil, Duncan
James Ogilvie series (4)
Gates of life
Bjorkman, Edwin August
Swedish youth series (2)
Gates of midnight
Stirling, Jessica
Beckman family trilogy (3)
Gates of morning
Hastings, Phyllis
Sussex trilogy (3)
Stacpoole, Henry de Vere
Dick and Emmeline series (3)
Gates of paradise
Andrews, Virginia Cleo
Casteel-Tatterton family series (4)
Gates of the universe
DeWeese, Gene
Joe Karns series (1)
Gates of Thorbardin
Parkinson, Dan
DragonLance heroes series (5)
Gates of time
Barrett, Neal
Time series (1)
Gates wide open
Wood, George
Peter Schlemihl series (3)
Gateway
Jenkins, Jerry Bruce
Jennifer Grey series (4)
Pohl, Frederik
Heechee series (1)
Gateway of doom
Brennan, James Herbert
GrailQuest series (3)
Gateway to doom
Appleton, Victor II
Tom Swift Junior series 2 (9)
Gateway to empire
Eckert, Allan Wesley
Winning of America series (5)
Gateway to escape
Deane, Norman
Liberator series (2)
Gateway to hell
Wheatley, Dennis
Duc de Richelieu series (11)
Gateway to life
Thiess, Frank
Centaur trilogy (2)
Gateway to Never
Chandler, Arthur Bertram
John Grimes series (11)
Gateway to never
Chandler, Arthur Bertram
Rim series (14)
Gateway to remembrance
Cradock, Phyllis
Atlantis series (1)
Gateway to Xanadu
Green, Sharon
Diana Santee series (2)
Gateway trip
Pohl, Frederik
Heechee series (5)
Gath
Tubb, Edwin Charles
Dumarest series (1)
Gather no moss
Shears, Sarah
Tapioca for tea series (2)
Gather together in my name
Angelou, Maya
Heart of a woman series (2)
Gathering
Hamilton, Virginia
Justice trilogy (3)
Gathering at Greystone
Bronte, Louisa
Greystone Tavern series (2)
Gathering clouds
Farrar, Frederic William
Early Church series (2)
Gathering clouds at Castle Rising
Cradock, Fanny
Lorme family series (7)
Gathering evil
Stackpole, Michael
Dark conspiracy series (1)
Gathering of gargoyles
Pierce, Meredith Ann
Aeriel trilogy (2)
Gathering of ghosts
Lewis, Royston
Arnold Landon series (1)
Gathering of heroes
Zimmer, Paul Edwin
Dark border series (3)
Gathering of pearls
Choi, Sook Nyul
Sookan series (3)
Gathering of stars
Moffitt, Donald
Mechanical sky series (2)
Gathering of stones
Clayton, Jo
Drinker of souls trilogy (3)
Gathering of the winds
Shiplett, June Lund
Winds series (8)
Gathering place
Breen, Jon Linn
Jerry Brogan series (2)
Rachel Hennings series (1)
Gathering storm
Sellers, Con
Men at arms series (1)
Gathering storm, 1837-1868
Gulick, Bill
Northwest destiny trilogy (2)
Gatherings of the gangs
Romains, Jules
Men of goodwill series (23)
Gator kill
Crider, Bill
Truman Smith series (1)
Gaudi afternoon
Wilson, Barbara Ellen
Cassandra Reilly series (1)
Gaudissart the Great
Balzac, Honore de
Scenes of provincial life series (5)
Gaudy
Stewart, John Innes Mackintosh
Duncan Pattullo series (1)
Gaudy empire
Neumann, Alfred
Napoleon III trilogy (2)
Gaudy night
Sayers, Dorothy Leigh
Harriet Vane series (3)
Lord Peter Wimsey series (12)
Gaunt of Pacific Command
Downie, James Millar
Gaunt series (1)
Gaunt of the Pearl Seas patrol
Downie, James Millar
Gaunt series (3)
Gaunt stranger
Wallace, Edgar
Ringer series (1)
Gaunt woman
Blackburn, John
General Charles Kirk series (4)
Gilligan, Edmund
Gaunt woman series (1)
Gauntlet
Street, James
Wingo series (1)
Gauntlet of Alceste
Moorhouse, Hopkins
Addison Kent series (1)
Gauntlet of malice
Harris, Deborah Turner
Mages of Garillon trilogy (2)
Gauvinier takes to bowls
De Selincourt, Hugh
Gauvinier series (3)
Gavel and the gun
McElwain, Dean L
Preacher's law series (3)
Gay adventurer
Barstow, John Montagu Orczy
Scarlet Pimpernel series (14)
Blakeney, John
Scarlet Pimpernel series (14)
Gay application
Christie, Robert Stuart
Book of Sarah series (2)
Gay Darius
Peel, Hazel Mary
Ann and Jim Henderson series (8)
Gay desperado
Gray, Berkeley
Norman Conquest series (13)
Gay Dolphin adventure
Saville, Malcolm
Lone Pine Five Club series (3)
Gay-Dombeys
Johnston, Harry Hamilton
Dombey series (2)
Gay from China at the Chalet School
Brent-Dyer, Elinor Mary
Chalet School series (18)
Gay gallant
Blake, Vanessa
Jenny Winfield series (1)
Gay ghastly holiday
Blayne, Sebastian
Sebastian Blayne series (1)
Gay life
Tarsis, Valeriy
Black Sea trilogy (2)
Gay Lord Robert
Plaidy, Jean
Tudor series (8)
Gay mortician
Raison, Milton Michael
Tony Woolrich series (3)
Gay phoenix
Innes, Michael
Sir John Appleby series (30)
Gay soul
Thompson, Mark
Gay spirit and soul series (2)
Gay spirit
Thompson, Mark
Gay spirit and soul series (1)
Gay story book
Blyton, Enid
Story book series (5)
Gaynor women
Coffman, Virginia
Gaynor women series (1)
Gazebo
Wentworth, Patricia
Miss Maud Silver series (30)
Gecko, the lizard who lost his tail
Rees, Leslie
Australian nature tales series (12)
Gees' first case
Mann, Jack
Gregory George Gordon Green series (1)
Geis of the gargoyle
Anthony, Piers
Xanth series (16)
Gelignite
Marshall, William Leonard
Yellowthread Street series (3)
Gelignite gang
Creasey, John
Inspector Roger West series (17)
Gem of a murder
Keith, Carlton
Jeff Green series (1)

Gemini man
Kelly, Susan
Liz Connors and Jack Lingemann series (1)
Gemini plot
Collenette, Eric J
Ben Grant series (3)
Gemini smile, Gemini kill
Lory, Robert
Horrorscope series (4)
Gemini trip
Law, Janice
Anna Peters series (2)
Gemma
Streatfeild, Noel
Gemma series (1)
Gemma alone
Streatfeild, Noel
Gemma series (3)
Gemma and sisters
Streatfeild, Noel
Gemma series (2)
Gemma and the witch
Gilbert, Pamela
Gemma series (1)
Gemma and the witch's house
Gilbert, Pamela
Gemma series (2)
Gems and life
Oyved, Moysheh
Jewels and gems series (2)
Gems of doom
Grant, Maxwell
Shadow series (189)
Gene Autry and the badmen of Broken Arrow
Miller, Snowden
Gene Autry series (4)
Gene Autry and the Big Valley grab
Hutchinson, William Henry
Gene Autry series (5)
Gene Autry and the Champion
Hill, Monica
Gene Autry tell-a-tale series (3)
Gene Autry and the ghost riders
Cole, Fannin
Gene Autry series (6)
Gene Autry and the Golden Ladder Gang
Hutchinson, William Henry
Gene Autry series (3)
Gene Autry and the golden stallion
Cole, Fannin
Gene Autry series (7)
Gene Autry and the lost dogie
Beecher, Elizabeth
Gene Autry tell-a-tale series (3)
Gene Autry and the red shirt
Beecher, Elizabeth
Gene Autry series (7)
Gene Autry and the redwood pirates
Hamilton, Bob
Gene Autry series (2)
Gene Autry and the Thief River outlaws
Hamilton, Bob
Gene Autry series (1)
Gene Autry goes to the circus
Autry, Gene
Gene Autry tell-a-tale series (1)
Gene Autry makes a new friend
Beecher, Elizabeth
Gene Autry tell-a-tale series (2)
General
Ladd, Justin
Abilene series (10)
Ponsonby, Doris Almon
Jaspard family series (1)
General Besserley's puzzle box
Oppenheim, Edward Phillips
General Besserley series (1)
General Besserley's second puzzle box
Oppenheim, Edward Phillips
General Besserley series (2)
General Bramble
Maurois, Andre
Colonel Bramble series (2)
General Crook and the fighting Apaches
Sabin, Edward Legrand
Trail blazers series (10)
General danced at dawn
Fraser, George Macdonald
Private McAuslan series (1)
General from the jungle
Traven, B
Jungle series (6)
General Golden Mane
Giraud, Jean
Lieutenant Mike S Blueberry series (9)
General Hospital
Hirschfeld, Burt
General Hospital series (1)
General murders
Estleman, Loren D
Amos Walker series (9)
General Nelson's scout
Dunn, Byron Archibald
Young Kentuckians series (1)
General practice
Tibber, Robert
General practice series (1)
General practitioner's progress to the Black Country
Smith, Francis Maylett
General practitioner series (2)
Generals
Griffin, W E B
Brotherhood of war series (6)
General's ring
Lagerlof, Selma
Ring of the Lowenskolds trilogy (1)
Generation apart
Richards, J T
Whitmarsh chronicles series (1)
Generation untamed
Richards, J T
Whitmarsh chronicles series (2)
Generation warriors
McCaffrey, Anne
Planet pirates series (3)
Generous death
Pickard, Nancy
Jenny Cain series (1)
Generous man
Price, Reynolds
Mustian family series (2)
Genesis
Harbinson, William Allen
Projekt Saucer series (2)
McKinney, Jack
Robotech series (1)
Genesis of a hero
Eyers, John
Survivors series (2)
Genesis of the clowns
Harris, Wilson
Civilizations quartet (3)
Genesis of the Daleks
Dicks, Terrance
Doctor Who series (22)
Sarah Jane Smith series (3)
Genesis quest
Moffitt, Donald
Genesis quest series (1)
Genesys
Peel, John
Timewyrm series (1)
Genetha
Heath, Roy Aubrey Kelvin
Georgetown trilogy (3)
Genetic buccaneer
Kern, Gregory
Cap Kennedy series (12)
Genetic general
Dickson, Gordon Rupert
Dorsai series (4)
Genetic soldier
Turner, George Reginald
Nugan series (2)
Genetrix
Mauriac, Francois
Leper series (2)
Geneva mystery
Durbridge, Francis
Paul Temple series (10)
Genghis Coopersmith
Griffin, Robert J
Coopersmith series (4)
Genial dinosaur
Gridban, Volsted
Clifford Brooks series (2)
Genie on the loose
Leeson, Robert
Alec Bowden series (2)
Genie trilogy
Fine, Anne
Genie trilogy (3)
Genius at the Chalet School
Brent-Dyer, Elinor Mary
Chalet School series (35)
Genius in murder
Punshon, Ernest Robertson
Carter and Bell series (4)
Genius thieves
Dixon, Franklin W
Hardy boys case files series (9)
Genki boys
Kelly, Terence
Genki boys series (2)
Genocide express
Arnett, Jack
Book of justice series (1)
Gent from Bear Creek
Howard, Robert Ervin
Breckinridge Elkins series (1)
Gentle albatross
Foote-Smith, Elizabeth
Will Woodfield series (1)
Gentle assassin
Richards, Clay
Kim Locke series (3)
Gentle bigamist
Newte, Horace Wykeham Can
Calico Jack series (2)
Gentle, gentle Thursday
Martin, Bill
Freedom series (4)
Gentle giant
Edson, John Thomas
Floating Outfit series (26)
Gentle giants of Ganymede
Hogan, James Patrick
Minervan experiment series (2)
Gentle Greaves
Raymond, Ernest
London gallery series (3)
Gentle hangman
Fox, James M
John and Suzy Marshall series (8)
Gentle house
Rose, Anna Perrott
Gentle house series (2)
Gentle killer
Barrington, Pamela
Inspector George Travers series (3)
Gentle pioneer
Blanchard, Amy Ella
Revolutionary War series (6)
Gentle Sabre
Darby, Catherine
Sabre family series (8)
Gentleman brawler
Hardin, J D
Raider and Doc series (62)
Gentleman called
Davis, Dorothy Salisbury
Mrs Norris and Jasper Tully series (2)
Gentleman from Texas
Balfour, Hearnden
Inspector Jack Strickland series (1)
Gentleman in crime
Mackenzie, Donald
Fugitives series (2)
Gentleman Jack
Daly, Jim
Gentleman Jack series (1)
Gentleman Jack's big hit
Daly, Jim
Gentleman Jack series (6)
Gentleman Jack's debut
Daly, Jim
Gentleman Jack series (2)
Gentleman Jack's mix-up
Daly, Jim
Gentleman Jack series (4)
Gentleman Jack's soft mark
Daly, Jim
Gentleman Jack series (5)
Gentleman Jack's tour
Daly, Jim
Gentleman Jack series (3)
Gentleman Jim
Briggs, Raymond
Gentleman Jim series (1)
Gentleman Solomon
Bedford-Jones, Henry
John Solomon trilogy (3)
Gentleman traitor
Williams, Alan
Beria papers series (2)
Gentleman usher
Chapman, George
Monsieur d'Olive series (1)
Gentleman with the walrus moustache
Gilpatric, Guy
Mister Colin Andrew Macthrockle Glencannon series (5)
Gentlemen and players
Vernon, Frances
Edwardian trilogy (1)
Gentlemen at large
Boland, John
John George Norman Hyde series (3)
Gentlemen farmers
Elias, Horace J
Flintstones series (7)
Gentlemen in Hades
Kummer, Frederic Arnold
Hades series (2)
Gentlemen of crime
Gask, Arthur
Gilbert Larose series (6)
Gentlemen of Gyang Gyang
Brent of Bin Bin
Bert Poole series (4)
Gentlemen of Sussex
Leyland, Eric
Sussex series (1)
Gentlemen of the night
Maddock, Stephen
Timothy Terrel series (3)
Gentlemen of the west
Owens, Agnes
Gentlemen of the west series (1)
Gentlemen prefer blondes
Loos, Anita
Lorelei Lee and Dorothy series (1)
Gentlemen reform
Boland, John
John George Norman Hyde series (2)
Gentlemen's gentlemen
Harrison, Rosina
Rose series (2)
Gently at a gallop
Hunter, Alan
Inspector George Gently series (18)
Gently between tides
Hunter, Alan
Inspector George Gently series (29)
Gently by the shore
Hunter, Alan
Inspector George Gently series (2)
Gently coloured
Hunter, Alan
Inspector George Gently series (16)
Gently continental
Hunter, Alan
Inspector George Gently series (15)
Gently does it
Hunter, Alan
Inspector George Gently series (1)
Gently down the stream
Hunter, Alan
Inspector George Gently series (3)
Gently floating
Hunter, Alan
Inspector George Gently series (11)
Gently French
Hunter, Alan
Inspector George Gently series (20)
Gently go man
Hunter, Alan
Inspector George Gently series (9)
Gently in an omnibus
Hunter, Alan
Inspector George Gently series (6)
Gently in another omnibus
Hunter, Alan
Inspector George Gently series (11)
Gently in the glens
Hunter, Alan
Inspector George Gently series (41)
Gently in the Highlands
Hunter, Alan
Inspector George Gently series (14)
Gently in the sun
Hunter, Alan
Inspector George Gently series (6)
Gently in trees
Hunter, Alan
Inspector George Gently series (21)
Gently instrumental
Hunter, Alan
Inspector George Gently series (24)
Gently north-west
Hunter, Alan
Inspector George Gently series (14)
Gently Sahib
Hunter, Alan
Inspector George Gently series (12)
Gently scandalous
Hunter, Alan
Inspector George Gently series (38)
Gently through the mill
Hunter, Alan
Inspector George Gently series (5)
Gently through the woods
Hunter, Alan
Inspector George Gently series (21)
Gently to a kill
Hunter, Alan
Inspector George Gently series (39)
Gently to a sleep
Hunter, Alan
Inspector George Gently series (25)
Gently to the summit
Hunter, Alan
Inspector George Gently series (8)
Gently tragic
Hunter, Alan
Inspector George Gently series (40)
Gently where the birds are
Hunter, Alan
Inspector George Gently series (23)
Gently where the roads go
Hunter, Alan
Inspector George Gently series (10)
Gently with love
Hunter, Alan
Inspector George Gently series (22)
Gently with the innocents
Hunter, Alan
Inspector George Gently series (17)
Gently with the ladies
Hunter, Alan
Inspector George Gently series (13)
Gently with the millions
Hunter, Alan
Inspector George Gently series (37)
Gently with the painters
Hunter, Alan
Inspector George Gently series (7)
Genuine article
Guthrie, Alfred Bertram
Sheriff Chick Charleston and Jason Beard series (2)
Genuine girl
Lincoln, Jeanie Gould
Marjorie series (2)
Geoff and Jim
Thorn, Ismay
Geoff and Jim Harrington series (3)
Geoffrey Austin, student
Sheehan, Patrick Augustine
Geoffrey Austin series (1)
Geogian afternoon
Jones, Lawrence Evelyn
Victorian boyhood series (3)
Geography of faith
Berrigan, Daniel
Conversations series (1)
Geordie
Walker, David Harry
Geordie Mactaggart series (1)
George
Williams, Emlyn
George Emlyn series (1)
George and Martha
Marshall, James
George and Martha series (1)
George and Martha back in town
Marshall, James
George and Martha series (6)
George and Martha encore
Marshall, James
George and Martha series (2)
George and Martha one fine day
Marshall, James
George and Martha series (4)
George and Martha rise and shine
Marshall, James
George and Martha series (3)
George and Martha 'round and 'round
Marshall, James
George and Martha series (7)
George and Martha, tons of fun
Marshall, James
George and Martha series (5)
George and Matilda Mouse and the doll's house
Buchanan, Heather S
Tales of George and Matilda Mouse series (9)
George and Matilda Mouse and the floating school
Buchanan, Heather S
Tales of George and Matilda Mouse series (10)

George and Matilda Mouse and the moon rocket
Buchanan, Heather S
Tales of George and Matilda Mouse series (11)

George and Matilda Mouse's Christmas journey
Buchanan, Heather S
Tales of George and Matilda Mouse series (12)

George and the dragon
Dicks, Terrance
Bears series (2)

George goes one better
Havilton, Jeffrey
George series (2)

George H Ghastly
Perry, Ritchie
George H Ghastly series (1)

George H Ghastly and the little horror
Perry, Ritchie
George H Ghastly series (3)

George H Ghastly to the rescue
Perry, Ritchie
George H Ghastly series (2)

George Mouse goes flying
Buchanan, Heather S
Tales of George and Matilda Mouse series (2)

George mouse's caravan
Buchanan, Heather S
Tales of George and Matilda Mouse series (8)

George Mouse's first summer
Buchanan, Heather S
Tales of George and Matilda Mouse series (4)

George Mouse's water music
Buchanan, Heather S
Tales of George and Matilda Mouse series (7)

George O'Brien and the Arizona bad man
Packer, Eleanor
George O'Brien series (3)

George O'Brien and the hooded riders
Du Bois, Gaylord
George O'Brien series (4)

George O'Brien in Gun law
Packer, Eleanor
George O'Brien series (2)

George Passant
Snow, Charles Percy
Strangers and brothers series (2)

George pulls it off
Havilton, Jeffrey
George series (1)

George, the fire engine
Todd, Herbert Eatton
Bobby Brewster picture book series (2)

George told Kate
Chorao, Kay
Kate series (5)

George Washington and the Constitution
Frankel, Ellen
Time traveler series (6)

George Washington and the new nation, 1783-1793
Flexner, James Thomas
George Washington series (3)

George Washington in the American Revolution, 1775-1783
Flexner, James Thomas
George Washington series (2)

George Washington's breakfast
Fritz, Jean
American Revolution series (1)

Georgians
Harben, William Nathaniel
Georgians series (2)

Georgians and Victorians
Coote, Roger
Journey through history series (5)

Georgie
Bright, Robert
Georgie series (1)

Georgie and the baby birds
Bright, Robert
Georgie series (11)

Georgie and the ball of yarn
Bright, Robert
Georgie series (10)

Georgie and the buried treasure
Bright, Robert
Georgie series (9)

Georgie and the little dog
Bright, Robert
Georgie series (12)

Georgie and the magician
Bright, Robert
Georgie series (5)

Georgie and the noisy ghost
Bright, Robert
Georgie series (6)

Georgie and the robbers
Bright, Robert
Georgie series (4)

Georgie and the runaway balloon
Bright, Robert
Georgie series (13)

Georgie goes west
Bright, Robert
Georgie series (7)

Georgie to the rescue
Bright, Robert
Georgie series (2)

Georgie's Christmas carol
Bright, Robert
Georgie series (8)

Georgie's Halloween
Bright, Robert
Georgie series (3)

Georgina and the dragon
Jellinek, Joanna
Georgina series (1)

Gerald and Elizabeth
Stevenson, Dorothy Emily
Gerald Burleigh Brown series (1)

Gerald kicks off
Cole, Michael
Pigeon Street series (2)

Geraldine
Agnew, Emily C
Geraldine series (1)

Geraldine's birthday surprise
Burnett, Alice Hale
Merryvale girls series (3)

Gerald's Saturday
Reeder, Colin
West Meadow series (5)

Geranium kiss
Harvey, John Barton
Scott Mitchell series (2)

Gerfalcon
Barringer, Leslie
Neustrian trilogy (1)

German requiem
Kerr, Philip
Berlin noir trilogy (3)

German spy
Newman, Bernard
Inspector Marshall series (3)

German terror in Belgium
Toynbee, Arnold Joseph
German terror series (1)

German terror in France
Toynbee, Arnold Joseph
German terror series (2)

Germinal
Zola, Emile
Rougon Macquart series (13)

Geronimo
Dugan, Bill
War chiefs series (1)
McLaglen, John J
Herne the Hunter series (16)

Geronimo Rex
Hannah, Barry
Harry Monroe series (1)

Geronimo's trail
Roberts, J R
Gunsmith series (60)

Gerry Anderson's Stingray files
Peel, John
Stingray series (2)

Gerry goes to school
Brent-Dyer, Elinor Mary
La Rochelle series (1)

Gerry North collects
North, Gerry
Gerry North series (2)

Gerry's seaside journey
Cartlidge, Michelle
Teddy trucks series (2)

Gertie Gardener
Campbell, Rod
Little people series (6)

Gertrude and the mermaid
Hughes, Richard Arthur Warren
Gertrude series (2)

Gertrude Haddon
Southworth, Emma Dorothy Eliza Nevitte
Gertrude Haddon trilogy (3)

Gertrude's child
Hughes, Richard Arthur Warren
Gertrude series (1)

Gervaise
Zola, Emile
Rougon Macquart series (7)

Gestapo Dormouse
King, Frank
Dormouse series (10)

Gestapo file
Cory, Desmond
Johnny Fedora series (2)

Get Buchanan!
Ward, Jonas
Tom Buchanan series (14)

Get Carter
Lewis, Ted
Jack Carter series (1)

Get Clutha
Munro, Hugh Macfarlane
Clutha series (5)

Get Garrity
Nixon, Allan
Tony Garrity series (1)

Get goin', Greeley!
Grover, Marshall
Larry and Stretch series (130)

Get in the Q annual
Milligan, Spike
Q annual series (2)

Get Maledon!
Gardner, Jerome
Hanging Judge series (5)

Get off at Babylon
Albert, Marvin Hubert
Pierre-Ange Sawyer series (3)

Get on out of here, Philip Hall
Greene, Bette
Beth Lambert series (2)

Get out the cuffs
Hume, David
Mick Cardby series (21)

Get ready to die
Gray, Berkeley
Norman Conquest series (41)

Get rich Mitch!
Sharmat, Marjorie Weinman
Rich Mitch series (2)

Get-Rich-Quick Wallingford
Chester, George Randolph
James Rufus Wallingford series (1)

Get Smart!
Johnston, William
Maxwell Smart series (1)

Get Smart once again!
Johnston, William
Maxwell Smart series (3)

Get some bread, Fred
Edwards, Pat
Fred series (3)

Get the message
Skurzynski, Gloria
Your high-tech world series (3)

Get the teacher
Pascal, Francine
Sweet Valley kids series (46)

Get thee behind me
Spence, Hartzell
Parsonage series (2)

Get Urrea
Edson, John Thomas
Ole Devil Hardin series (5)

Get Wallace!
Wilson, Alexander
Sir Leonard Wallace series (4)

Get well, Clown-Arounds!
Cole, Joanna
Clown-Arounds series (3)

Get well soon, Mallory
Martin, Ann Matthews
Baby-Sitters Club series (69)

Get your man
Dorrance, Ethel Smith
Sergeant Alfred Rawson series (1)

Getaway
Charteris, Leslie
Saint series (9)
John, Owen
Haggai Godin series (7)

Getaway for Inspector West
Creasey, John
Inspector Roger West series (2)

Getaway ring
Grant, Maxwell
Shadow series (180)

Getaway world
Smith, Edward Elmer
Family d'Alembert series (4)

Getting a way with murder
McInerny, Ralph
Father Roger Dowling series (9)

Getting away with murder?
Morice, Anne
Tessa Crichton Price series (18)

Getting closer
Sharmat, Marjorie Weinman
Sorority sisters series (7)

Getting-dressed story
Erickson, Karen
I can do it series (5)

Getting even
Chaikin, Miriam
Molly series (3)
Jukes, Mavis
Maggie and Iris series (1)
Pike, Christopher
Cheerleaders series (2)

Getting in
Lowell, Anne Hunter
Sorority girls series (1)

Getting into practice
Vernon, Edward
Practice trilogy (3)

Getting Oliver's ghost
McBrier, Michael
Oliver and company series (6)

Getting rich with Jeremy James
Wilson, David Henry
Jeremy James series (2)

Getting serious
Sarasin, Jennifer
Cheerleaders series (40)

Getting something on Maggie Marmelstein
Sharmat, Marjorie Weinman
Maggie Marmelstein series (1)

Getting to know the new baby
Graham, Bob
New baby series (4)

Getting up with fleas
Murphy, Warren Burton
Devlin Tracy series (7)

Ghetto comedies
Zangwill, Israel
Ghetto series (5)

Ghetto tragedies
Zangwill, Israel
Ghetto series (2)

Gholan Gate
Kern, Gregory
Cap Kennedy series (7)

Ghost
Bunting, Eve
No such things series (3)

Ghost and Katie Donigan
Edwards, Pat
Ghost series (1)

Ghost and the goggle box
Ball, Duncan
Ghost series (1)

Ghost and the gory story
Ball, Duncan
Ghost series (2)

Ghost and the gumshoe
Robitaille, Julie
Quantum leap series (2)

Ghost and the shutterbug
Ball, Duncan
Ghost series (3)

Ghost army
Smith, David Claude
Oron series (3)

Ghost at Dawn's house
Martin, Ann Matthews
Baby-Sitters Club series (9)

Ghost at Skeleton Rock
Dixon, Franklin W
Hardy boys series (37)

Ghost at the waterfall
Wells, Helen
Vicki Barr series (11)

Ghost Beach
Stine, Robert Lawrence
Goosebumps series (22)

Ghost belonged to me
Peck, Richard
Blossom Culp series (1)

Ghost beyond the gate
Wirt, Mildred Augustine
Penny Parker series (9)

Ghost boat
Pardoe, Margot
Boat series (1)

Ghost car
Knox, Bill
Inspector Colin Thane and Phil Moss series (8)

Ghost city killers
Martyn, Wyndham
Anthony Trent series (23)

Ghost dance
Faulcon, Robert
Nighthunter series (3)

Ghost dancers
Ahern, Jerry
Dan Track series (11)
Benteen, John
Sundance series (10)
Craig, Brian
Dark future series (5)
Dawson, Clay
Long Rider series (7)
Drumm, D B
Traveler series (13)

Ghost division
Kessler, Leo
Rommel series (1)

Ghost does a Richard III
Saxe, R B
John Dobbs series (2)

Ghost dog
Cate, Dick
Ghost dog series (1)

Ghost ferry
Cates, Emily
Haunting with Louisa series (3)

Ghost for Miss Grimscuttle
Furminger, Jo
Mary, Ben and William series (4)

Ghost, ghost are you scared?
Edwards, Pat
Ghost series (3)

Ghost girl
Webster, Henry Kitchell
Arthur Jeffrey series (2)

Ghost guns
Tuttle, Wilbur Coleman
Henry Harrison Conroy and Judge Van Treece series (3)

Ghost horse on the moor
Pullein-Thompson, Josephine
Moor pony series (4)

Ghost house
McNally, Clare
Ghost house series (1)

Ghost house revenge
McNally, Clare
Ghost house series (2)

Ghost hunter
Packard, Edward
Choose your own adventure series (52)

Ghost hunters
Brooks, Collin
Raeburn Steel series (3)

Ghost in the attic
Cates, Emily
Haunting with Louisa series (1)

Ghost in the bell tower
Pascal, Francine
Sweet Valley twins super chiller series (4)

Ghost in the big brass bed
Coville, Bruce
Ghost trilogy (3)

Ghost in the gallery
Keene, Carolyn
Dana girls series (17)

Ghost in the garage
Christian, Mary Blount
Goosehill Gang series (10)

Ghost in the gondola
Keene, Carolyn
Nancy Drew series (78)

Ghost in the machine
Murphy, Warren Burton
Destroyer series (90)

Ghost in the making
Fitzgerald, Nigel
Alan Russell series (4)

Ghost in the noonday sun
Fleischman, Sid
Ghost series (1)

Ghost in the park
Smith, Beatrice Schillinger
Kate and Ben King series (4)

Ghost in the sunlight
Herbert, Kathleen
Cumbrian series (2)

Ghost in the third row
Coville, Bruce
Ghost trilogy (1)

Ghost in the window
Wright, Betty Ren
Secret window series (2)

Ghost king
Gemmell, David A
Sipstrassi tales series (2)

Ghost knights of Camelot
Kraft, David Anthony
Wizards, warlocks and you series (4)

Ghost knows his greengages
Saxe, R B
John Dobbs series (1)

Ghost light
Platt, Marc
Doctor Who scripts series (8)
Doctor Who series (149)

Ghost makers
Grant, Maxwell
Shadow series (16)

Ghost mansion
Williamson, Jerry Neal
Minnifield series (1)

Ghost mine
Hardin, J D
Raider and Doc series (53)

Ghost Mine gold
Tompkins, Walker Allison
Masked Rider and Blue Hawk series (30)

Ghost murders
Grant, Maxwell
Shadow series (93)

Ghost next door
Stine, Robert Lawrence
Goosebumps series (10)
Wayne, Jenifer
Winchester family series (4)

Ghost of a cardinal
Maske, John
Clarence E Hemingway series (2)
Jeremy Flack series (3)

Ghost of a chance
Grover, Marshall
Larry and Stretch series (188)
Nye, Jody Lynn
Xanth series (16)
Roos, Kelley
Jeff and Haila Troy series (6)
Usher, Frank
Daye Smith series (1)

Ghost of a clue
Barry, Charles
Superintendent Lawrence Gilmartin series (8)
Mills, Osmington
Midset C.I.D. series (8)
Sergeant Patrick Shirley and Inspector Rip Irving series (6)

Ghost of an idea
Challis, Mary
Jeremy Locke series (3)

Ghost of Blackwood Hall
Keene, Carolyn
Nancy Drew series (25)

Ghost of Canby Hall
Hoh, Diane
Canby Hall series (2)

Ghost of Craven Cove
Keene, Carolyn
Nancy Drew series (92)

Ghost of Dagger Bay
Buchanan, William
Kelly McCoy series (1)

Ghost of Dark Harbor
Ross, Clarissa
Dark Harbor series (1)

Ghost of Fisher's Creek
Edwards, Pat
Ghost series (2)

Ghost of Hellsfire Street
Platt, Kin
Sinbad trilogy (3)

Ghost of June
Croft-Cooke, Rupert
Sensual life series (21)

Ghost of Melody Lane
Garis, Lilian C
Melody Lane series (2)

Ghost of Raven Hill
Rodda, Emily
Teen Power Inc. series (2)

Ghost of Sherlock Holmes
Halliwell, Leslie
Sherlock Holmes sequels series (74)

Ghost of Soapy Smith
Strong, Charles Stanley
Soapy Smith series (3)

Ghost of the lost mine
Mackenzie, Jake
Secret files of Dakota King series (4)

Ghost of the manor
Grant, Maxwell
Shadow series (32)

Ghost of Tricia Martin
Pascal, Francine
Sweet Valley High series (64)

Ghost of truth
Chance, John Newton
Superintendent Black series (3)

Ghost on Saturday night
Fleischman, Sid
Ghost series (2)

Ghost on the balcony
Marfield, Dwight
Major Krim series (2)

Ghost parade
Sutton, Margaret
Judy Bolton series (5)

Ghost pirates
Hodgson, William Hope
Glen Carrig trilogy (3)

Ghost pulls the jackpot
Saxe, R B
John Dobbs series (3)

Ghost raider
Hogan, Ray
John Mosby series (1)

Ghost rider
Bryant, Bonnie
Saddle Club series (24)

Ghost riders
Tetlow, L D
Brogan McNally series (1)

Ghost riders of Goldspur
Siegel, Scott
Twistaplot series (17)

Ghost ship
Carey, Diane
Star trek, the next generation series (1)
Stuart, Becky
Kellogg Brown and Carey Ashton series (3)

Ghost ship mystery
Warner, Gertrude Chandler
Boxcar children series (39)

Ghost ship of Fog Island
Ross, Marilyn
Fog Island series (4)

Ghost-sitter
Elfman, Blossom
Mike and Ally series (3)

Ghost Squad and the ghoul of Grunberg
Hildick, Edmund Wallace
Ghost Squad series (4)

Ghost Squad and the Halloween conspiracy
Hildick, Edmund Wallace
Ghost Squad series (2)

Ghost Squad and the menace of the Malevs
Hildick, Edmund Wallace
Ghost Squad series (6)

Ghost Squad and the prowling hermits
Hildick, Edmund Wallace
Ghost Squad series (5)

Ghost Squad breaks through
Hildick, Edmund Wallace
Ghost Squad series (1)

Ghost Squad flies Concorde
Hildick, Edmund Wallace
Ghost Squad series (3)

Ghost stories of an antiquary
James, Montague Rhodes
Ghost stories series (1)

Ghost that haunted a king
Prole, Lozania
Tudor trilogy (1)

Ghost tower
Blashfield, Jean
Super endless quest adventure gamebook series (2)

Ghost town
Roberts, J R
Gunsmith series (127)

Ghost town gold
Macdonald, William Colt
Three Mesquiteers series (6)

Ghost town guns
Sadler, Jeff
Marshal Andrew Anderson series (14)

Ghost town on the Yellowstone
Paul, Elliot
Narrow street series (3)

Ghost town secret
Schroeder, Doris
Annie Oakley series (2)

Ghost town treasure
Sheldon, Ann
Linda Craig series (5)

Ghost trail
Douthwaite, Louis Charles
Sexton Blake series (690)
Scott, Bradford
Walt Slade series (67)

Ghost trails
Tuttle, Wilbur Coleman
Hashknife Hartley and Sleepy Stevens series (16)

Ghost train
Ahlberg, Allan
Funnybones series (8)
Foley, Louise Munro
Choose your own adventure series (120)
Logan, Jake
John Slocum series (181)
Stivers, Dick
Able Team series (31)

Ghost tribe
Giraud, Jean
Lieutenant Mike S Blueberry series (4)

Ghost walker
Hambly, Barbara
Star trek series (53)

Ghost walks
Brogan, Colm
Patrick Heron series (1)

Ghost warriors
McGann, Michael
Marauders series (5)

Ghost way
Hillerman, Tony
Sergeant Jim Chee series (3)

Ghost who wanted to be a star
Robinson, Nancy Konheim
Tripper and Sam series (3)

Ghost with the golden bullets
Giraud, Jean
Lieutenant Mike S Blueberry series (11)

Ghost-woman of Castillo
Grover, Marshall
Larry and Stretch series (313)

Ghost wore grey
Coville, Bruce
Ghost trilogy (2)

Ghost wore white
Allen, Betsy
Connie Blair series (6)

Ghost writer
Roth, Philip
Nathan Zuckerman series (1)

Ghostbusters
Digby, Anne
Ghostbusters series (1)
Muller, Richard
Ghostbusters series (2)

Ghostbusters 2
Hiller, Barbara B
Ghostbusters series (2)
Naha, Ed
Ghostbusters series (2)
Stine, Robert Lawrence
Ghostbusters series (2)

Ghoster
McKeone, Lee
Ghoster trilogy (1)

Ghosthunt
Clayton, Jo
Diadem series (7)

Ghostland
Hager, Jean
Mitch Bushyhead series (3)

Ghostly business
Krensky, Stephen
Wynd family trilogy (3)

Ghostly legionaries
Goscinny, Rene
Twelve tasks of Asterix series (11)

Ghostly term at Trebizon
Digby, Anne
Trebizon series (11)

Ghostmobile
Tapp, Kathy Kennedy
Moth-kin series (3)

Ghosts
Auster, Paul
New York trilogy (2)
Crabb, Arthur
Samuel Lyle series (2)
McBain, Ed
Eighty Seventh Precinct series (34)

Ghosts at Hob Lane
Leeson, Robert
Hob Lane series (3)

Ghosts can't kill
Heberden, Mary Violet
Desmond Shannon series (14)

Ghosts from the mist of time
Chetwynd-Hayes, Ronald
Tales of Clavering Grange series (3)

Ghosts' high noon
Wells, Carolyn
Fleming Stone series (29)

Ghosts I have been
Peck, Richard
Blossom Culp series (2)

Ghosts in fourth grade
Hiser, Constance
James and gang series (2)

Ghosts in the graveyard
Pascal, Francine
Sweet Valley twins super chiller series (2)

Ghosts of Canby Hall
Chase, Emily
Canby Hall series (25)

Ghosts of Chambord affair
Catalan, Henri
Soeur Angele series (2)

Ghosts of Epidoris
Kern, Gregory
Cap Kennedy series (14)

Ghosts of Gol
Mahr, Kurt
Perry Rhodan series (10)

Ghosts of night and morning
Kaye, Marvin
Blue light series (2)

Ghosts of venery
Lundin, John Philip
Erotic autobiography series (2)

Ghosts on the range to-night
Cameron, Caddo
Private Badger Coe and Sergeant Blizzard Wilson series (4)

Ghosts who went to school
Spearing, Judith
Temple Street series (1)

Ghostwood
De Lint, Charles
Moonheart series (4)

Ghostworld
Green, Simon
Mistworld series (2)

Ghoul
King, Frank
Clarence Knight series (1)

Giant
Feikema, Feike
World's wanderer trilogy (3)

Giant Alexander
Herrman, Frank
Giant Alexander series (1)

Giant Alexander and Hannibel the elephant
Herrman, Frank
Giant Alexander series (4)

Giant Alexander and the circus
Herrman, Frank
Giant Alexander series (2)

Giant Alexander in America
Herrman, Frank
Giant Alexander series (3)

Giant Brog and the motorway
Cunliffe, John Arthur
Giant series (4)

Giant city swindle
Philips, George Norman
Sexton Blake series (498)

Giant horse of Oz
Thompson, Ruth Plumly
Oz series (21)

Giant hunchback
Wurr, H J
Inspector Grierson series (1)

Giant in chains
Bowen, Marjorie
French Revolution series (1)

Giant kill
Platt, Kin
Max Roper series (4)

Giant Kippernose, and other stories
Cunliffe, John Arthur
Giant series (3)

Giant novels
Hogan, James Patrick
Minervan experiment series (3)

Giant of Jembu Gulf
Crisp, Frank
Dirk Rogers series (8)

Giant of World's End
Carter, Lin
Gondwane epic series (6)

Giant Otto
Pene du Bois, William
Otto series (1)

Giant panda
Morris, Desmond
Men and animals series (3)

Giant raft, part 1
Verne, Jules
Giant raft series (1)

Giant raft, part 2
Verne, Jules
Giant raft series (2)

Giant rat of Sumatra
Boyer, Richard Lewis
Sherlock Holmes sequels series (19)

Giant robot
Dicks, Terrance
Doctor Who series (12)
Sarah Jane Smith series (2)

Giant under the snow
Gordon, John
Giant under the snow series (1)

Giant who stole the world
Cunliffe, John Arthur
Giant series (1)

Giant who swallowed the wind
Cunliffe, John Arthur
Giant series (2)

Giants in the earth
Rolvaag, Ole Edvart
Per Hansa trilogy (1)

Giants of Elenna
Tallis, Robyn
Planet builders series (9)

Giant's partner
Darlton, Clark
Perry Rhodan series (33)

Giants' star
Hogan, James Patrick
Minervan experiment series (3)

Giant's stride
Penton, Brian
Derek Cabell series (2)

Gibraltar conspiracy
Betteridge, Don
Tiger Lester series (9)

Gibraltar Road
McCutchan, Philip
Commander Esmonde Shaw series (1)

Gibraltar sabotage
Gunn, John
Peter Kent series (3)

Gideon
Ratye, Helene
Gideon series (3)

Gideon and his friends
Ratye, Helene
Gideon series (6)

Gideon Drexel's millions, and other stories
Carter, Nicholas
Nicholas Carter series (39)

Gideon in Africa
Rabier, Benjamin
Gideon series (1)

Gideon in the forest
Rabier, Benjamin
Gideon series (2)

Gideon of Scotland Yard
Marric, J J
Commander George Gideon series (1)

Gideon on the riverbank
Ratye, Helene
Gideon series (5)

Gideon's art
Marric, J J
Commander George Gideon series (17)

Gideon's badge
Marric, J J
Commander George Gideon series (12)

Gideon's day
Marric, J J
Commander George Gideon series (1)

Gideon's drive
Marric, J J
Commander George Gideon series (21)

Gideon's fear
Marric, J J
Commander George Gideon series (2)

Gideon's fire
Marric, J J
Commander George Gideon series (7)

Gideon's fog
Marric, J J
Commander George Gideon series (20)

Gideon's force
Butler, William Vivian
Commander George Gideon series (22)

Gideon's house
Ratye, Helene
Gideon series (4)

Gideon's law
Butler, William Vivian
Commander George Gideon series (23)

Gideon's lot
Marric, J J
Commander George Gideon series (11)

Gideon's march
Marric, J J
Commander George Gideon series (8)

Gideon's men
Marric, J J
Commander George Gideon series (18)

Gideon's month
Marric, J J
Commander George Gideon series (4)
Gideon's night
Marric, J J
Commander George Gideon series (3)
Gideon's power
Marric, J J
Commander George Gideon series (15)
Gideon's press
Marric, J J
Commander George Gideon series (19)
Gideon's raid
Butler, William Vivian
Commander George Gideon series (25)
Gideon's ride
Marric, J J
Commander George Gideon series (9)
Gideon's risk
Marric, J J
Commander George Gideon series (6)
Gideon's river
Marric, J J
Commander George Gideon series (14)
Gideon's sport
Marric, J J
Commander George Gideon series (16)
Gideon's staff
Marric, J J
Commander George Gideon series (5)
Gideon's vote
Marric, J J
Commander George Gideon series (10)
Gideon's way
Butler, William Vivian
Commander George Gideon series (24)
Gideon's week
Marric, J J
Commander George Gideon series (2)
Gideon's wrath
Marric, J J
Commander George Gideon series (13)
Gift for Lonny
Bunting, Eve
Magic circle series (2)
Gift for the giving
Cosgrove, Stephen Edward
Bumble B Bear series (6)
Gift from Berlin
Barker, Albert
Reefe King series (1)
Gift from earth
Niven, Larry
Known Space series (2)
Gift from Winklesea
Cresswell, Helen
Winklesea series (1)
Gift-giver
Hansen, Joyce
Doris series (1)
Gift horse
Gruber, Frank
Johnny Fletcher and Sam Cragg series (6)
Knef, Hildegard
Gift horse series (1)
Vail, Virginia
Animal Inn series (12)
Gift horse's mouth
Campbell, Robert Wright
Jimmy Flannery series (7)
Gift of Asher Lev
Potok, Chaim
Asher Lev series (2)
Gift of death
Ronns, Edward
Jerry Benedict series (2)
Gift of echoes
Harlow, Robert
Royal Murdoch series (2)
Gift of fire
Krentz, Jayne Ann
Verity Ames and Jonas Quarrel series (2)
Gift of gold
Krentz, Jayne Ann
Verity Ames and Jonas Quarrel series (1)
Gift of onyx
Kettle, Jocelyn
Athelson family series (2)
Gift of the deer
Hoover, Helen
Forest trilogy (1)
Gift of the desert
Black, Hermina
Susan Denver trilogy (3)
Gift of the gods
Carter, Nicholas
Nicholas Carter series (375)
Gift-wrapped pony
Farrell, Anne
Mitchell family series (1)
Gifted kids survival guide, for ages eleven to eighteen
Galbraith, Judy
Gifted kids survival guide series (2)
Gifted kids survival guide, for ages ten and under
Galbraith, Judy
Gifted kids survival guide series (1)
Gifted kids survival guide II
Delisle, James
Gifted kids survival guide series (3)
Gifts and almonds
Solomon, Joan
Children's life series (7)
Gifts of Jove
Bickers, Richard Townshend
Daedalus quartet (1)
Gifts of love
Witcomb, Nan
Thoughts of Nanushka series (11)
Gifts of the queen
Lide, Mary
Ann of Cambray trilogy (2)
Giftwish
Martin, Graham
Giftwish series (1)
Giggle
Cosgrove, Stephen Edward
Whimsy storybooks series (6)
Giggling ghosts
Robeson, Kenneth
Doc Savage series (56)
Gigolo Pook
Pook, Peter
Pook series (18)
Gila Bend
Mitchum, Hank
Stage coach station series (49)
Gila monster
Dengler, Sandy
Mirage mysteries series (4)
Gila River
McCarthy, Gary
Rivers west series (8)
Gilbert Gurney
Hook, Theodore Edward
Gilbert Gurney series (1)
Gilbert Neal
Harben, William Nathaniel
Georgians series (3)
Gilbert the page
Rutley, Cecily Marianne
Children of other days series (8)
Gilbert's last toothache
Scherf, Margaret
Reverend Martin Buell series (1)
Gilded cage
Twain, Mark
Colonel Sellers series (1)
Gilded canary
Latham, Brad
Hook series (1)
Gilded kiss
Enefer, Douglas
Dale Shand series (8)
Gilded man
Dickson, Carter
Sir Henry Merrivale series (14)
Gilded nightmare
Pentecost, Hugh
Pierre Chambrun series (5)
Gilded sarcaphogus
Leigh, Stephen
Doctor Bones series (1)
Gilded sarcophagus
Hunt, Charlotte
Doctor Paul Holton series (1)
Gilded snatch caper
Lawrence, James D
Angela Harpe series (3)
Gilded witch
Webb, Jack
Father Joseph Shanley and Sammy Golden series (9)
Gilden fire
Donaldson, Stephen Reeder
Second chronicles of Thomas Covenant series (3)
Gildenford
Anand, Valerie
Norman trilogy (1)
Gildersley's tenderfoot
Leighton, Robert
Red Patrol series (1)
Giles and the canal
Pullein-Thompson, Christine
Giles series (3)
Giles and the elephant
Pullein-Thompson, Christine
Giles series (1)
Giles and the greyhound
Pullein-Thompson, Christine
Giles series (2)
Gilgamesh the king
Silverberg, Robert
Gilgamesh series (1)
Gillespie suicide mystery
Gribble, Leonard Reginald
Superintendent Anthony Slade series (1)
Gilliane
Gellis, Roberta
Roselynde chronicles series (4)
Gillian's choice
Meyer, Carolyn
Hotline series (3)
Gilt and the gingerbread
Leslie, Anita
Train to nowhere series (3)
Gilt edge
Saddler, Allen
Dave Stevens series (2)
Gilt-edged Bonds
Fleming, Ian
James Bond series (6)
Gilt-edged guilt
Wells, Carolyn
Fleming Stone series (48)
Gilt-edged traitor
Eden, Matthew
Marc Savage series (5)
Gimlet bores in
Johns, William Earl
Gimlet series (7)
Gimlet comes home
Johns, William Earl
Gimlet series (3)
Gimlet gets the answer
Johns, William Earl
Gimlet series (9)
Gimlet goes again
Johns, William Earl
Gimlet series (2)
Gimlet lends a hand
Johns, William Earl
Gimlet series (6)
Gimlet mops up
Johns, William Earl
Gimlet series (4)
Gimlet off the map
Johns, William Earl
Gimlet series (8)
Gimlet takes a job
Johns, William Earl
Gimlet series (10)
Gimlet's Oriental quest
Johns, William Earl
Gimlet series (5)
Gimme
Cosgrove, Stephen Edward
Whimsy storybooks series (1)
Gimmel flask
Clark, Douglas
Inspector George Masters series (9)
Gin and bitters
Lane, Jane
Montague family series (3)
Gin and murder
Pullein-Thompson, Josephine
Inspector James Flecker series (1)
Gin palace
Zola, Emile
Rougon Macquart series (7)
Gina
Stratton, Alan
Gina series (2)
Ginger among the pigeons
Andrew, Prudence
Ginger Jenkins series (4)
Ginger and Batty Billy
Andrew, Prudence
Ginger Jenkins series (2)
Ginger and McGlusky
Hales, Alfred Greenwood
McGlusky series (4)
Ginger and No 10
Andrew, Prudence
Ginger Jenkins series (3)
Ginger and Pickles
Potter, Beatrix
Peter Rabbit series (15)
Ginger and Speed
Hueston, Ethel
Ginger Ella trilogy (2)
Ginger and the glacier express
Johnston, Dorothy Grunbock
Ginger series (4)
Ginger and the turkey raids
Johnston, Dorothy Grunbock
Ginger series (3)
Ginger and the witch doctor
Johnston, Dorothy Grunbock
Ginger series (6)
Ginger at Dogfish Bay
Johnston, Dorothy Grunbock
Ginger series (1)
Ginger-bread man
Baum, Lyman Frank
Snuggle tales series (5)
Ginger cat mystery
Forsythe, Robin
Anthony Vereker series (5)
Ginger Ella
Hueston, Ethel
Ginger Ella trilogy (1)
Ginger horse
Straker, John Foster
Inspector Pitt series (3)
Ginger in Alaska
Johnston, Dorothy Grunbock
Ginger series (2)
Ginger in the jungles
Johnston, Dorothy Grunbock
Ginger series (5)
Ginger Lee, war nurse
Deming, Dorothy
Penny Marsh series (4)
Ginger Meggs and Herbert the billy goat
Bancks, James Charles
Ginger Meggs series (28)
Ginger Meggs and the country cousin
Bancks, James Charles
Ginger Meggs series (30)
Ginger Meggs annual
Vivian, Ron
Ginger Meggs series (37)
Ginger Meggs at large
Kemsley, James
Ginger Meggs series (33)
Ginger Meggs in a 7th series of adventures
Bancks, James Charles
Ginger Meggs series (7)
Ginger Meggs in a 9th series of adventures
Bancks, James Charles
Ginger Meggs series (9)
Ginger Meggs' lucky break
Bancks, James Charles
Ginger Meggs series (29)
Ginger Meggs meets the test
Peach, Bill
Ginger Meggs series (32)
Ginger over the wall
Andrew, Prudence
Ginger Jenkins series (1)
Ginger Pye
Estes, Eleanor
Pye family series (1)
Ginger star
Brackett, Leigh
Eric John Stark series (3)
Gingerbread band
Althea
Gingerbread series (1)
Gingerbread Man in winter
Walker, Elizabeth
Gingerbread Man series (2)
Gingerbread men
Althea
Gingerbread series (2)
Ginnie and Geneva
Woolley, Catherine
Ginnie Fellows series (1)
Ginnie and Geneva cookbook
Woolley, Catherine
Ginnie Fellows series (11)
Ginnie and her juniors
Woolley, Catherine
Ginnie Fellows series (6)
Ginnie and the cooking contest
Woolley, Catherine
Ginnie Fellows series (7)
Ginnie and the mystery cat
Woolley, Catherine
Ginnie Fellows series (9)
Ginnie and the mystery doll
Woolley, Catherine
Ginnie Fellows series (5)
Ginnie and the mystery house
Woolley, Catherine
Ginnie Fellows series (4)
Ginnie and the mystery light
Woolley, Catherine
Ginnie Fellows series (10)
Ginnie and the new girl
Woolley, Catherine
Ginnie Fellows series (3)
Ginnie and the snow gypsies
Murray, Lillian
Virginia Nixon series (1)
Ginnie and the wedding bells
Woolley, Catherine
Ginnie Fellows series (8)
Ginnie joins in
Woolley, Catherine
Ginnie Fellows series (2)
Ginny Gordon and the broadcast mystery
Campbell, Julie
Ginny Gordon series (5)
Ginny Gordon and the lending library
Campbell, Julie
Ginny Gordon series (4)
Ginny Gordon and the missing heirloom
Campbell, Julie
Ginny Gordon series (2)
Ginny Gordon and the mystery of the disappearing candlesticks
Campbell, Julie
Ginny Gordon series (1)
Ginny Gordon and the mystery of the old barn
Campbell, Julie
Ginny Gordon series (3)
Ginzberg circle
O'Neill, Archie
Jeff Pride series (4)
Gipsy, actress
Saint John, Mabel
Gipsy trilogy (3)
Gipsy born!
Saint John, Mabel
Gipsy trilogy (2)
Gipsy in evening dress
Makin, William James
Inspector Graves series (1)
Gipsy or gentleman?
Graydon, William Murray
Sexton Blake series (177)
Gipsy, schoolgirl
Saint John, Mabel
Gipsy trilogy (1)
Giraffe hooves and antelope horns
Torgersen, Don Arthur
Animal safari nature series (3)
Giraffe hunters
Reid, Mayne
Bush boys series (3)
Giraffe twins
Hogan, Inez
Twins series (11)
Girl and her dad
Garis, Lilian C
Gloria series (1)
Girl and the deal
Harriman, Karl Edwin
Girl series (1)
Girl and the game, and other college stories
Williams, Jesse Lynch
Stolen story series (3)
Girl at Central
Bonner, Geraldine
Molly Morganthau series (1)
Girl at twenty
Henrey, Madeleine
Madeleine series (4)
Girl aviators and the phantom airship
Burnham, Margaret
Girl aviators series (1)
Girl aviators' motor butterfly
Burnham, Margaret
Girl aviators series (4)
Girl aviators on golden wings
Burnham, Margaret
Girl aviators series (2)
Girl cage
Ehrlich, Jack
Robert Flick series (4)
Girl called Al
Greene, Constance Clarke
Al series (1)
Girl called Friday Night
Gilchrist, Rupert
Slaves without masters trilogy (2)
Girl chase
Enefer, Douglas
Dale Shand series (6)

Girl died singing
Morland, Nigel
Detective Inspector Rory Luccan series (2)
Girl factory
Murphy, Robert Franklin
Girl factory series (1)
Girl found dead
Underwood, Michael
Superintendent Simon Manton series (11)
Girl from B.U.S.T.
Carnelle, Inge
Jane Blonde series (1)
Girl from Big Horn Country
Chase, Mary Ellen
Virginia series (1)
Girl from Glengarry
Connor, Ralph
Glengarry series (3)
Girl from H.A.R.D.
Moffatt, James
Girl from H.A.R.D. series (1)
Girl from Harrison High
Farris, John
Harrison High series (2)
Girl from Moscow
Corrigan, Mark
Mark Corrigan and McLean series (23)
Girl from nowhere
Bond, Evelyn
Ira Yedder series (2)
Girl from outer space
Brown, Carter
Rick Holman series (13)
Girl from P.U.S.S.Y.C.A.T.
Mark, Ted
Girl from P.U.S.S.Y.C.A.T. series (1)
Girl from Peking
Mair, George Brown
David Grant series (5)
Girl from Toronto
Clevely, Hugh
Sexton Blake series (1323)
Girl from U.N.C.L.E.
Peel, John
U.N.C.L.E. files series (2)
Girl grew up in Russia
Fen, Elisaveta
Russia series (2)
Girl hunters
Spillane, Mickey
Mike Hammer series (8)
Girl in a big brass bed
Rabe, Peter
Manny De Witt series (1)
Girl in a million
Enefer, Douglas
Sam Bawtrey series (4)
Girl in a net
Marsh, John
Simon Luck series (2)
Girl in a shroud
Brown, Carter
Lieutenant Al Wheeler series (28)
Girl in arms
Enefer, Douglas
Dale Shand series (7)
Girl in asses' milk
Baker, William Howard
Richard Quintain series (11)
Girl in hand
Janson, Hank
Hank Janson series (177)
Girl in Ocean View
Symons, Maurice
George Roberts series (1)
Girl in shadow
Franklin, Charles
Grant Garfield series (14)
Girl in the cage
Benson, Ben
Ralph Lindsey series (2)
Girl in the case
Carter, Nicholas
Nicholas Carter series (260)
Girl in the cellar
Wentworth, Patricia
Miss Maud Silver series (33)
Girl in the cockpit
Avallone, Michael
Ed Noon series (25)
Girl in the crime belt
Chance, John Newton
Jonathan Blake series (31)
Girl in the dark
Vivian, Evelyn Charles
Inspector Byrne series (1)
Girl in the frame
Fuller, William
Brad Dolan series (5)
Girl in the golden atom
Cummings, Ray
Matter, space and time series (1)
Girl in the hairy paw
Geduld, Harry Maurice
King Kong series (3)
Girl in the news
Vickers, Roy
Inspector J Rason series (14)
Girl in the plain brown wrapper
Macdonald, John Dann
Travis McGee series (10)
Girl in the punchbowl
Dewey, Thomas Blanchard
Pete Schofield series (8)
Girl in the red Jaguar
Manor, Jason
Steve Summers series (2)
Girl in the river
Miller, Victor Brooke
Kojak series (4)
Girl in the telltale bikini
Morgan, Patrick
Operation Hang Ten series (6)
Girl in the well
Beeler, Cecil Freeman
Well series (1)
Girl in the wet-look bikini
Mitchell, Scott
Brock Devlin series (11)
Girl like Wigan
Leeming, John Fishwick
Fontana d'amore series (2)
Girl most likely
Rand, Suzanne
Winners series (1)
Girl next door
Montgomery, Elizabeth
Dick, Jane and Sally series (7)
Girl nobody knows
McShane, Mark
Sergeant Norman Pink series (1)
Girl of '76
Blanchard, Amy Ella
Revolutionary War series (1)
Girl of the Limberlost
Porter, Gene Stratton
Limberlost series (2)
Girl on the Left Bank
Shepherd, Joan
Inspector Jolivet series (1)
Girl on the loose
Fickling, G G
Honey West series (2)
Girl on the M6
Enefer, Douglas
Sam Bawtrey series (6)
Girl on the prowl
Fickling, G G
Honey West series (4)
Girl on the waterfront
Urquhart, Macgregor
Chief Inspector Joshua Smarles series (2)
Girl out there
Harriman, Karl Edwin
Girl series (2)
Girl prisoner
Carter, Nicholas
Nicholas Carter series (560)
Girl running
Knight, Adam
Steve Conacher series (7)
Girl Scout pioneers
Garis, Lilian C
Girl Scouts series (1)
Girl Scouts and the open road
Vandercook, Margaret
Girl Scouts series (4)
Girl Scouts at Bellaire
Garis, Lilian C
Girl Scouts series (2)
Girl Scouts at camp
Lavell, Edith
Girl Scouts series (1)
Girl Scouts at Camp Comealong
Garis, Lilian C
Girl Scouts series (4)
Girl Scouts at Dandelion Camp
Roy, Lillian Elizabeth
Girl Scouts series (1)
Girl Scouts at home
Galt, Katherine Keene
Rosanna series (1)
Girl Scouts at Miss Allen's school
Lavell, Edith
Girl Scouts series (2)
Girl Scouts at Mystery Mansion
Wirt, Mildred Augustine
Girl Scout series (3)
Girl Scouts at Penguin Pass
Wirt, Mildred Augustine
Girl Scout series (1)
Girl Scouts at Rocky Ledge
Garis, Lilian C
Girl Scouts series (5)
Girl Scouts at Sea Crest
Garis, Lilian C
Girl Scouts series (3)
Girl Scouts at Singing Sands
Wirt, Mildred Augustine
Girl Scout series (2)
Girl Scouts' canoe trip
Lavell, Edith
Girl Scouts series (3)
Girl Scouts' captain
Lavell, Edith
Girl Scouts series (9)
Girl Scouts' director
Lavell, Edith
Girl Scouts series (10)
Girl Scouts' good turn
Lavell, Edith
Girl Scouts series (4)
Girl Scouts in Arizona and New Mexico
Roy, Lillian Elizabeth
Girl Scouts series (4)
Girl Scouts in Beechwood Forest
Vandercook, Margaret
Girl Scouts series (3)
Girl Scouts in Glacier Park
Roy, Lillian Elizabeth
Girl Scouts series (7)
Girl Scouts in Mystery Valley
Vandercook, Margaret
Girl Scouts series (5)
Girl Scouts in the Adirondacks
Roy, Lillian Elizabeth
Girl Scouts series (2)
Girl Scouts in the magic city
Roy, Lillian Elizabeth
Girl Scouts series (6)
Girl Scouts in the Redwoods
Roy, Lillian Elizabeth
Girl Scouts series (5)
Girl Scouts in the Rockies
Roy, Lillian Elizabeth
Girl Scouts series (3)
Girl Scouts' motor trip
Lavell, Edith
Girl Scouts series (7)
Girl Scouts of the Eagles Wing
Vandercook, Margaret
Girl Scouts series (1)
Girl Scouts of the Round Table
Vandercook, Margaret
Girl Scouts series (2)
Girl Scouts on the ranch
Lavell, Edith
Girl Scouts series (6)
Girl Scouts rally
Galt, Katherine Keene
Rosanna series (2)
Girl Scouts' rivals
Lavell, Edith
Girl Scouts series (5)
Girl Scouts triumph
Galt, Katherine Keene
Rosanna series (3)
Girl Scouts' vacation
Lavell, Edith
Girl Scouts series (8)
Girl, the city and the soldier
Baker, William Howard
Richard Quintain series (5)
Girl they both loved
Pascal, Francine
Sweet Valley High series (80)
Girl trouble
Summers, James Levingston
Trouble series (1)
Girl watcher's funeral
Pentecost, Hugh
Pierre Chambrun series (6)
Girl who couldn't remember
Keene, Carolyn
Nancy Drew series (91)
Girl who cried monster
Stine, Robert Lawrence
Goosebumps series (8)
Girl who died
Hopkins, Kenneth
Gerry Lee series (1)
Girl who heard dragons
McCaffrey, Anne
Pern and the Red Planet series (12)
Girl who kept knocking them dead
Stone, Hampton
Jeremiah X Gibson series (9)
Girl who knew it all
Giff, Patricia Reilly
Casey Valentine series (2)
Girl who knew too much
Brandon, John Gordon
Sexton Blake series (868)
Girl who never was
Dewey, Thomas Blanchard
Private Eye Mac series (8)
Girl who saw too much
Reid, Desmond
Sexton Blake series (1564)
Girl who was clairvoyant
Warner, Mignon
Mrs Edwina Charles series (4)
Girl who was possessed
Brown, Carter
Lieutenant Al Wheeler series (29)
Girl who wasn't there
Dewey, Thomas Blanchard
Private Eye Mac series (8)
Girl who wouldn't make friends
Oxenham, Elsie J
Robin Brent series (1)
Girl who wouldn't talk
Vickers, Roy
Inspector Peter Curwen and Hugh Stanton series (5)
Girl with green eyes
O'Brien, Edna
Caithleen series (2)
Girl with no place to hide
Quarry, Nick
Jake Barrow series (3)
Girl with six fingers
Pentecost, Hugh
John Jericho series (5)
Girl with the bright head
Leigh, Robert
Sam Carroll series (2)
Girl with the frightened eyes
Lariar, Lawrence
Ham Macandrew and Homer Bull series (4)
Girl with the golden eyes
Balzac, Honore de
Scenes of Parisian life series (1)
Girl with the Green eyes
Leblanc, Maurice
Arsene Lupin series (12)
Girl with the hole in her head
Stone, Hampton
Jeremiah X Gibson series (2)
Girl with the polka dot box
Paul, F W
Man from S.T.U.D. series (8)
Girl with the sweet plump knees
Dewey, Thomas Blanchard
Pete Schofield series (6)
Girls
Montherlant, Henry de
Girls series (4)
Girls and I
Molesworth, Mary Louisa
Boys and girls and I series (2)
Girls aviators sky cruise
Burnham, Margaret
Girl aviators series (3)
Girls forever brave and true
Rivers, Caryl
Virgins series (2)
Girls from O.R.G.Y.
Mark, Ted
Man from O.R.G.Y. series (16)
Girls in their married bliss
O'Brien, Edna
Caithleen series (3)
Girl's journey
Bagnold, Enid
Girl's journey series (2)
Girl's number doesn't answer
Powell, Talmage
Ed Rivers series (2)
Girls of Canby Hall
Hoh, Diane
Canby Hall series (1)
Girls of Central High
Morrison, Gertrude W
Girls of Central High series (1)
Girls of Central High aiding the Red Cross
Morrison, Gertrude W
Girls of Central High series (7)
Girls of Central High at basketball
Morrison, Gertrude W
Girls of Central High series (3)
Girls of Central High in camp
Morrison, Gertrude W
Girls of Central High series (6)
Girls of Central High on Lake Luna
Morrison, Gertrude W
Girls of Central High series (2)
Girls of Central High on the stage
Morrison, Gertrude W
Girls of Central High series (4)
Girls of Central High on track and field
Morrison, Gertrude W
Girls of Central High series (5)
Girls of Fairmount
Baker, Etta Anthony
Fairmount girls series (1)
Girls of Friendly Terrace
Smith, Harriet Lummis
Friendly Terrace series (1)
Girls of Gardenville
Rankin, Carroll Watson
Dandelion Cottage series (2)
Girls of Greycliff
Grove, Harriet Pyne
Greycliff girls series (2)
Girls of Greycourt
Eastways, W W
Greycourt series (2)
Girls of Highland Hall
Rankin, Carroll Watson
Dandelion Cottage series (5)
Girls of Rivercliff School
Marlowe, Amy Bell
Oriole series (3)
Girls of Rocklands School
Oxenham, Elsie J
Rocklands School trilogy (1)
Girls of Saint Bride's
Bruce, Dorita Fairlie
Nancy series (1)
Girls of the Abbey School
Oxenham, Elsie J
Abbey girls first generation series (3)
Girls of the Hamlet Club
Oxenham, Elsie J
Abbey girls first generation series (1)
Girls of the Morning-Glory Camp fire
Hornibrook, Isabel
Campfire Girls series (1)
Girls of the night
Christian, Petra
Sally Deenes series (4)
Girls together
Mack, Louise
Lennie Leighton series (2)
Girls who came to murder
Carr, Kirby
Hitman series (3)
Gitanjali
Tagore, Rabindranath
Gitanjali series (1)
Give a corpse a bad name
Ferrars, Elizabeth
Toby Dyke series (1)
Give a dog a bad name
Tranter, Nigel Godwin
Donald Macdonald series (2)
Give a dog a name
Hammond, Gerald
Captain John Cunningham series (4)
Give a man a gun
Creasey, John
Inspector Roger West series (15)
Turner, Clay
Ben Gold series (1)
Give a man rope
Holt, Gavin
Inspector Joel Saber series (4)
Give all to love
Veryan, Patricia
Age of Elegance series (8)
Sanguinet series (6)
Give death a name
Gilbert, Anthony
Arthur Crook series (31)
Give 'em an ax
Fair, A A
Bertha Cool and Donald Lam series (9)
Give fire!
Challoner, Robert
Commander Lord Charles Oakshott series (2)
Give it with love, Christopher
McKissack, Patricia Carwell
Christopher series (1)
Give me back my heart
Jones, Jack
Unfinished journey series (3)
Give me death
Myers, Isabel Briggs
Peter Jerningham series (2)
Give me murder
Ashe, Gordon
Patrick Dawlish series (16)
Give me the daggers
Gavin, Catherine
Second Empire quartet (4)
Twentieth-century Europe series (3)

Give me this woman
Ard, William
Lou Largo series (5)
Give me tomorrow
Heath-Miller, Mavis
Raines of Rayleigh series (3)
Give thanks to death
Bailey, Hilea
Hilea Bailey and Hilary Dunsany Bailey series (2)
Give the boys a great big hand
McBain, Ed
Eighty Seventh Precinct series (11)
Give the devil his due
Graaf, Peter
Joe Dust series (1)
Give the dog a bone
Ahlberg, Allan
Funnybones series (7)
Give the girl a gun
Deming, Richard
Manville Moon series (3)
Give the little corpse a great big hand
Bagby, George
Inspector Schmidt series (22)
Give up the ghost
Erskine, Margaret
Inspector Septimus Finch series (4)
Give up your lovers
Golding, Louis
Philip Massel series (2)
Give us a great big smile, Rosy Cole
Greenwald, Sheila
Rosy Cole series (1)
Give us this day
Delderfield, Ronald Frederick
Adam Swann series (3)
Glad to be here
Herzog, Arthur
America series (2)
Glade Manor murder
Lemarchand, Elizabeth
Superintendent Tom Pollard series (17)
Glade of jewels
Fitzgerald, Julia
Astromance series (9)
Gladiators
Birt, David
Roman Britain series (17)
Koestler, Arthur
Ends and means trilogy (1)
Gladiators of Hapana
Lord, Jeffrey
Richard Blade series (31)
Gladly Oddly
Jennings, Paul Francis
Oddly series (6)
Gladstone bag
Macleod, Charlotte
Sarah Kelling series (9)
Glamorous powers
Howatch, Susan
Church of England series (2)
Glance
Cosgrove, Stephen Edward
Bugg series (4)
Glass alibi
Gribble, Leonard Reginald
Superintendent Anthony Slade series (21)
Glass arrow
Verner, Gerald
Trevor Lowe series (9)
Glass ball
Mayne, William
Islands series (1)
Glass cannon
Pinney, Peter
Australian soldier series (2)
Glass cipher
Winston, Peter
Adjusters series (3)
Glass cottage
Redgrove, Peter
Geoffrey Glass series (1)
Glass dagger
Brandon, John Gordon
Sexton Blake series (790)
Glass eyes of cotton strings
De Lint, Charles
Cerin Songweaver series (3)
Glass hammer
Jeter, Kevin W
Doctor Adder trilogy (2)
Glass highway
Estleman, Loren D
Amos Walker series (4)
Glass inferno
Fremd, Angelika
Inge Heinrich series (2)
Glass interval
Turner, James Ernest
Rampion Savage series (7)
Glass knife
Thayer, Lee
Peter Clancy series (14)
Glass knight
Helwig, David
Kingston tetralogy (1)
Glass man
Robeson, Kenneth
Avenger series (34)
Glass mask
Offord, Lenore Glen
Todd McKinnon series (2)
Glass mountain
Robeson, Kenneth
Avenger series (8)
Glass of Dyskornis
Garrett, Randall
Gandalara cycle series (2)
Glass on the stairs
Scherf, Margaret
Emily and Henry Bryce series (4)
Glass salamander
Downer, Ann
Caitlin series (2)
Glass shoe
Hooper, Kay
Once upon a time series (2)
Glass-sided ants' nest
Dickinson, Peter
Superintendent James Pibble series (1)
Glass spear
Courtier, Sidney Hobson
Ambrose Mahon series (1)
Glass too many
Mann, Jack
Gregory George Gordon Green series (7)
Glass triangle
Coxe, George Harmon
Kent Murdock series (5)
Glass warrior
Vardeman, Robert Edward
Demon crown trilogy (1)
Glass window
Furman, Lucy
Quare women trilogy (2)
Glass years
Brookes, Ewart
Proud waters series (2)
Glasshouse gang
Landsborough, Gordon
Desert commandos series (1)
Glassmakers
Fisher, Leonard Everett
Colonial Americans series (1)
Gleam in the north
Broster, Dorothy Kathleen
Jacobite trilogy (2)
Gleaming dawn
Baker, James
Cardinal Henry Beaufort series (1)
Gleanings
Layberry, Layton George Joseph
Oakleigh Farm series (2)
Gleave mystery
Tracy, Louis
Inspector Furneaux series (10)
Glen Hazard
Chapman, Maristan
Happy mountain series (4)
Glencannon
Gilpatric, Guy
Mister Colin Andrew Macthrockle Glencannon series (9)
Glencannon afloat
Gilpatric, Guy
Mister Colin Andrew Macthrockle Glencannon series (6)
Glencannon meets Tugboat Annie
Gilpatric, Guy
Mister Colin Andrew Macthrockle Glencannon series (9)
Raine, Norman Reilly
Tugboat Annie series (2)
Glencannon omnibus
Gilpatric, Guy
Mister Colin Andrew Macthrockle Glencannon series (3)
Glencannon Tugboat Annie affair
Gilpatric, Guy
Mister Colin Andrew Macthrockle Glencannon series (9)
Glendower conspiracy
Biggle, Lloyd
Sherlock Holmes sequels series (95)
Glendower country
Rofheart, Martha
Henry V series (2)
Glengarry days
Connor, Ralph
Glengarry series (2)
Glengarry girl
Connor, Ralph
Glengarry series (3)
Glengarry school days
Connor, Ralph
Glengarry series (2)
Glenloch girls
Remick, Grace May
Glenloch girls series (1)
Glenloch girls abroad
Remick, Grace May
Glenloch girls series (2)
Glenloch girls at Camp West
Remick, Grace May
Glenloch girls series (4)
Glenloch girls' club
Remick, Grace May
Glenloch girls series (3)
Glenna Powers case
Waugh, Hillary
Simon Kaye series (1)
Glimmering ghost
Sheldon, Ann
Linda Craig adventures series (5)
Glimpse of death
Ormerod, Roger
David Mallin and George Coe series (7)
Glimpse of nothingness
Van de Wetering, Janwillem
Zen series (2)
Glimpses of bygone days
Priest, Charles Ashley Vincent
Northern Territory recollections series (6)
Glimpses of the moon
Crispin, Edmund
Gervase Fen series (10)
Glinda of Oz
Baum, Lyman Frank
Oz series (14)
Glipton Romeos
Waddell, Sid
Jossy's Giants series (2)
Glitterburn
Gould, Heywood
Josh Krales series (2)
Glittering hour
Hodges, Arthur
Blake family series (2)
Glittering images
Howatch, Susan
Church of England series (1)
Glittering pastures
Croft-Cooke, Rupert
Sensual life series (4)
Glittering prizes
Flynn, Brian
Anthony Bathurst series (28)
Glitterspike Hall
Jefferies, Mike
Heirs to Gnarlsmyre series (1)
Global globules affair
Latter, Simon
Girl from U.N.C.L.E.series (3)
Globe Playhouse
Birt, David
Tudors series (19)
Globe probe
Janson, Hank
Hank Janson series (248)
Gloop the bunyip
Thiele, Colin
Gloop series (2)
Gloop the gloomy bunyip
Thiele, Colin
Gloop series (1)
Gloop, the gloomy bunyip
Thiele, Colin
Gloop series (2)
Gloria
Perez Galdos, Benito
Contemporary novels of Spain series (5)
Southworth, Emma Dorothy Eliza Nevitte
Gloria series (1)
Gloria at boardinf school
Garis, Lilian C
Gloria series (2)
Gloriet Tower
Meyler, Eileen
Jocelyn series (1)
Glorious adventure
Halliburton, Richard
Royal adventures series (2)
Glorious angel
Lindsey, Johanna
Hank Chavez series (1)
Glorious folly
De Wohl, Louis
Lives of the saints series (1)
Glorious nosebleed
Gorey, Edward
Alphabet series (5)
Glory
Aminoff, Constance Leonie Caroline
Napoleonic series (7)
Joseph, Ronald S
Cameron family trilogy (3)
Saxton, Judith
Neyler family series (2)
Wouk, Herman
Hope series (2)
Glory and sorrow of Norwich
Blake, M M
Norwich series (2)
Glory and the dream
Hilliard, Noel
Netta and Paul tetralogy (4)
Kenyon, Frank Wilson
John Churchill, Duke of Marlborough series (2)
Glory be!
Lambert, Janet
Penny Parrish series (3)
Glory box mystery
Wicking, George Walter
Inspector Greenwood series (1)
Glory dust
Jacks, T J
Chaney brothers series (1)
Glory hole murders
Fennelly, Tony
Matty Sinclair series (1)
Glory hound
Riggs, John Raymond
Garth Ryland series (3)
Glory in the flower
Johnston, Norma
Sterling family series (2)
Marten, Jacqueline
Wars of independence trilogy (2)
Glory of Elsie Silver
Golding, Louis
Elsie Silver series (3)
Glory of love
Hunt, Angela Elwell
Cassie Perkins series (9)
Glory Road
Catton, Bruce
Potomac Army trilogy (2)
Glory road
Gavin, Catherine
Light woman series (2)
Glory Road
Heinlein, Robert Anson
Glory Road series (1)
Glory wagon
Grover, Marshall
Larry and Stretch series (101)
Glory's end
Baron, Nick
Time tours series (2)
Gloved hand
Carter, Nicholas
Nicholas Carter series (530)
Stevenson, Burton Egbert
Jim Godfrey series (5)
Glow job
Kane, Henry
Peter Chambers series (28)
Glub, the baby dinosaur
Salmon, Michael
Dinosaur swamp series (2)
Glue factory
Meltzer, David
Brain plant series (4)
Glut of red herrings
Bude, John
Inspector Meredith series (17)
Glyphs of gold
Edwards, Paul
John Eagle series (6)
Gnat
Brooks, Leonard Harold
Sexton Blake series (166)
Gnome king of Oz
Thompson, Ruth Plumly
Oz series (20)
Gnome man's land
Friesner, Esther Mona
Gnome series (1)
Gnomemobile
Carey, Mary Virginia
Gnomobile series (2)
Gnomes
Huygen, Willibrord
Gnomes series (1)
Gnome's engine
Edgerton, Teresa
Goblin series (2)
Gnomes-one hundred, Dragons-zero
Blashfield, Jean
Catacombs series (2)
Gnomobile
Sinclair, Upton
Gnomobile series (1)
Go ahead Secret Seven
Blyton, Enid
Secret Seven series (5)
Go away death
Creasey, John
Department Z series (17)
Go away dinosaurs
Salmon, Michael
Dinosaur swamp series (1)
Go away Stanley
Edwards, Pat
Stanley series (2)
Go away to murder
Creasey, John
Inspector Roger West series (2)
Go back to hell
Edson, John Thomas
Floating Outfit series (35)
Go-between
Housman, Laurence
Palace plays series (3)
Starr, Leonard
Kelly Green series (1)
Go die in Afghanistan
Jason, Stuart
Butcher series (33)
Go down fighting
Mackie, John
Rat Bastards series (16)
Go eat worms!
Stine, Robert Lawrence
Goosebumps series (21)
Go fish
Stolz, Mary
Thomas and Grandfather series (2)
Go for broke
Gray, Rod
New lady from L.U.S.T. series (1)
Mackie, John
Rat Bastards series (12)
Welcome, John
Richard Graham series (6)
Go for Garrity
Nixon, Allan
Tony Garrity series (3)
Go from here
Berrigan, Daniel
Prison diary series (1)
Go gently, Gaijin
Melville, James
Superintendent Tetsuo Otani series (8)
Go-go SADISTO
Allison, Clyde
Agent triple zero eight series (4)
Go hog wild!
Roop, Peter
Make me laugh series (2)
Go home, unicorn
Macpherson, Donald
Reggie Brooks series (1)
Go, Honeylou
Dewey, Thomas Blanchard
Pete Schofield series (5)
Go in beauty
Eastlake, William
Bowman family trilogy (1)
Go on, I'm listening
Russell, Robert
Doctor Steven Rushton series (1)
Go saddle the sea
Aiken, Joan
Felix Brooke series (1)
Go tell the Spartans
Pournelle, Jerry
Falkenberg's Legion series (4)
Future history series (5)
Spartan series (1)
Go to sleep, Dear Dragon
Hillert, Margaret
Dear Dragon series (11)
Go to sleep, Jeannie
Dewey, Thomas Blanchard
Pete Schofield series (2)
Go to the hoop!
Hughes, Dean
Angel Park Hoop Stars series (3)
Go west, Ben Gold
Turner, Clay
Ben Gold series (2)
Go west, Inspector Ghote
Keating, Henry Reymond Fitzwalter
Inspector Ganesh Ghote series (12)
Go west, Joe Best
Grover, Marshall
Larry and Stretch series (374)

Go west, swamp monsters
Christian, Mary Blount
Swamp monsters series (2)
Go with a jerk
Janson, Hank
Hank Janson series (146)
Goal
Bottome, Phyllis
Search trilogy (3)
Goal for Charlie
Allen, Joy
Charlie series (6)
Goal in Europe
Hardcastle, Michael
Mark Fox series (5)
Goal in the sky
Hill, Margaret
Beth Dean series (1)
Goalposts, devotions for girls
Sanders, Bill
Goalposts series (2)
Goalposts, devotions for guys
Sanders, Bill
Goalposts series (1)
Goals for Aurora
Hester, Randolph Thompson
Aurora series (1)
Goals for glory
McCann, Sean
Dove's End Football Club series (1)
Goals in the air
Hardcastle, Michael
Kenny Rider series (1)
Goat
Straker, John Foster
Johnny Inch series (4)
Goat for Azazel
Fisher, Vardis
Testament of man series (9)
Goat Island
Fuller, William
Brad Dolan series (2)
Goat-wife
Macgregor, Alasdair Alpin
Auld Reekie series (1)
Goat without horns
Swann, Thomas Burnett
Ancient history series (14)
Goatsong
Holt, Tom
Walled orchard series (1)
Gobble and gulp
Cosgrove, Stephen Edward
Whimsy storybooks series (3)
Gobblin' Halloween
Thaler, Mike
Bully brothers series (2)
Gobbolino the witch's cat
Williams, Ursula Moray
Gobbolino series (2)
Goblin market
Bowes, Richard
Warchild series (2)
Douglas, Lauren Wright
Caitlin Reece series (5)
McCloy, Helen
Basil Willing series (6)
Miguel Urizar series (1)
Goblin moon
Edgerton, Teresa
Goblin series (1)
Goblin plain war
Miller, Carl
Dragonbound trilogy (3)
Goblin tower
De Camp, Lyon Sprague
Jorian series (1)
Goblins
Robeson, Kenneth
Doc Savage series (125)
Gobseck
Balzac, Honore de
Scenes of private life series (21)
God against the gods
Drury, Allen
Akhenaten series (1)
God and my father
Day, Clarence
Life series (2)
God and Sarah Pedlock
Longstreet, Stephen
Pedlock family series (2)
God and the doctor
Duncan, Alex
Country doctor series (2)
God and the groceryman
Wright, Harold Bell
Dan Matthews series (3)
God and the king
Bowen, Marjorie
William III trilogy (3)
God and the rabbit
Home, Michael
Breckland series (1)
God and the wedding dress
Bowen, Marjorie
Spiritual history of Great Britain trilogy (1)
God beneath the sea
Garfield, Leon
Greek mythology series (1)
God bless the Borders
Derwent, Lavinia
Border series (4)
God-emperor of Dune
Herbert, Frank
Dune series (4)
God holds the key
Bull, Geoffrey Taylor
Imprisoned missionary series (2)
God in Concord
Langton, Jane
Homer Kelly series (9)
God is an Englishman
Delderfield, Ronald Frederick
Adam Swann series (1)
God is my friend
Beers, Victor Gilbert
Learning to read from the Bible series (4)
God is my helper
Beers, Victor Gilbert
Learning to read from the Bible series (1)
God killer
Green, Simon
Hawk and Fisher series (3)
God of death
Sadler, Barry
Casca series (2)
God of Glass
Redgrove, Peter
Geoffrey Glass series (2)
God of Tarot
Anthony, Piers
Tarot trilogy (1)
God of the labyrinth
Wilson, Colin
Gerard Sorme trilogy (3)
God on the mountain
Furnell, John
Doctor Furnell series (2)
God save the child
Parker, Robert Brown
Spenser series (2)
God Squad bod
Kenyon, Michael
Inspector Henry Peckover series (3)
God stalk
Hodgell, Patricia Christine
Kencyrath series (1)
God stand up for bastards
Leitch, David
Family secrets series (1)
God-whale
Bass, T J
Hive series (2)
Godbond
Springer, Nancy
Sea king trilogy (3)
Goddess of death
Underwood, Michael
Rosa Epton series (5)
Goddess of Ganymede
Resnick, Mike
Ganymede series (1)
Goddess of Mars
Fearn, John Russell
Clayton Drew series (4)
Goddess of the Green Room
Plaidy, Jean
Georgian series (10)
Goddesses never die
Mair, George Brown
David Grant series (7)
Godfather
Puzo, Mario
Godfather series (1)
Roberts, J R
Gunsmith series (125)
Godfather papers, and other confessions
Puzo, Mario
Godfather series (2)
Godforsaken
Gilman, George G
Edge series (46)
Godfrey Marten, schoolboy
Turley, Charles
Godfrey Marten series (1)
Godfrey Marten, undergraduate
Turley, Charles
Godfrey Marten series (2)
Godless icon
Thomas, Gordon
David Morton series (2)
Godmother
Larkin, Rochelle T
Donna series (1)
Godmother caper
Lawrence, James D
Angela Harpe series (4)
Gods abide
Swann, Thomas Burnett
Ancient history series (10)
Gods and their grand design
Daniken, Erich von
Unsolved mysteries series (9)
Gods arrive
Wharton, Edith
Vance Weston series (2)
God's candle
Oxenham, John
Jesus Christ series (3)
God's defector
Bingham, John
Ducane series (3)
God's fig tree
Kile, Joan
Musty the mustard seed series (4)
God's fool
Patterson, George Neilson
Asian missionary trilogy (2)
God's fruit tree
Kile, Joan
Musty the mustard seed series (3)
Gods in a vortex
Houston, David
Gods in a vortex series (1)
Gods in anger
Cole, Adrian
Omaran series (4)
God's in his heaven
Hodson, James Lansdale
Harvest in the north series (2)
Gods look down
Hoyle, Trevor
Christian Queghan series (3)
God's mustard seed
Kile, Joan
Musty the mustard seed series (1)
Gods, myths and legends
Birt, David
Roman Britain series (20)
Gods of Mars
Burroughs, Edgar Rice
Martian series (2)
Gods of Pegana
Dunsany, Edward John Moreton Drax Plunkett
Gods of Pegana series (1)
Gods of Riverworld
Farmer, Philip Jose
Riverworld series (5)
Gods of the Greataway
Coney, Michael Greatrex
Greataway series (2)
Gods of Tlen
Lambert, William J
Tlen series (2)
Gods of war
Toland, John
McGlynn and Toda families series (1)
Gods of Xuma
Lake, David John
Breakout series (4)
Xuma series (1)
God's own country
Bannister, S F
Rolling Stone series (2)
Gods reborn
Merejkowski, Dmitri Sergeevich
Christ and Antichrist trilogy (2)
God's rugged cross
Kile, Joan
Musty the mustard seed series (2)
God's warrior
Williams, Patry
Canute series (2)
Gods were kind
Willis, William
Ancient mariner trilogy (1)
God's wonderful word
DeJonge, Joanne E
God's wonderful word series (1)
Godslayer
Reichert, Mickey Zucker
Bifrost guardians series (1)
Godson
Barrett, Robert G
Les Norton series (4)
Godspeed
Lee, Laurel
Godspeed series (1)
Godwin sideboard
Malcolm, John
Tim Simpson series (2)
Godwulf manuscript
Parker, Robert Brown
Spenser series (1)
Gog
Fetterless, Arthur
Officer and gentleman series (1)
Sinclair, Andrew
Albion trilogy (1)
Goggle-box affair
Gielgud, Val
Inspector Gregory Pellew and Viscount Clymping series (4)
Goggle-eyed pirates
Falk, Lee
Phantom series (10)
Goggles!
Keats, Ezra Jack
Peter series (5)
Gogo's car breaks down
Rockwell, Anne Foote
Gogo series (2)
Gogo's pay day
Rockwell, Anne Foote
Gogo series (1)
Going after Cacciato
O'Brien, Tim
Vietnam War series (3)
Going back
Gilman, George G
Adam Steele series (48)
Going bananas
Keller, Charles
Going bananas series (1)
Reese, Bob
Going ape series (5)
Going buggy!
Roop, Peter
Make me laugh series (5)
Going concern
Aird, Catherine
Inspector C D Sloan series (14)
Going cuckoo
Laird, Elizabeth
Toucan Tecs series (5)
Going for the gold
Lathen, Emma
John Putnam Thatcher series (18)
Lowell, Melissa
Silver blades series (4)
Going gangster
Atkinson, Mary Evelyn
Lockett family series (5)
Going, going, gone
Hale, Christopher
Lieutenant Bill French series (5)
Taylor, Phoebe Atwood
Asey Mayo series (20)
Going home
Collins, Alan
Jacob Kaiser series (2)
Harthern, Ernest
Palestine home series (1)
Henry, Marguerite
Chincoteague series (1)
Mohr, Nicholasa
Felita series (2)
Going native
Gogarty, Oliver St John
Sackville Street series (3)
Going on ten
Montgomery, Elizabeth
Dick, Jane and Sally series (14)
Going on twelve
Ransom, Candice Farris
Growing up series (2)
Going places
Fisher, Aileen
Ways of animals series (7)
Going places in the air
Scarry, Richard
Going places series (2)
Going places in the car
Scarry, Richard
Going places series (3)
Going places on the water
Scarry, Richard
Going places series (1)
Going places with Goldbug
Scarry, Richard
Going places series (4)
Going shopping
Berridge, Celia
Stepping stones 1 2 3 series (6)
Garland, Sarah
Family life series (1)
Going solo
Dahl, Roald
Solo series (2)
Tripp, Miles
John Samson series (6)
Going South
Optic, Oliver
Great Western series (4)
Going straight
Victor, Paul
Porridge series (4)
Going straight in Frisbee
Grover, Marshall
Larry and Stretch series (230)
Going strong
Ellis, Carol
Cheerleaders series (24)
Going swimming
Berridge, Celia
Stepping stones 1 2 3 series (4)
Going to hospital
Jessel, Camilla
Chatterbooks series (4)
Going to Jerusalem
Dixon, Roger
Jesus Christ series (3)
Going to my ballet class
Kuklin, Susan
Going to my class series (1)
Going to my gymnastics class
Kuklin, Susan
Going to my class series (3)
Going to my nursery school
Kuklin, Susan
Going to my class series (2)
Going to Patchogue
McGonigle, Thomas
Patchogue series (2)
Going to Saint Ives
Harris, Colver
Timothy Fowler series (2)
Going to see the end of the sky
Watkins, William John
Legrange League series (2)
Going to the dentist
Petty, Kate
First timers series (5)
Going to the doctor
Jessel, Camilla
Chatterbooks series (3)
Petty, Kate
First timers series (4)
Going to the dogs
Kavanagh, Dan
Nick Duffy series (4)
Going to the fair
Uttley, Alison
Little Brown Mouse series (3)
Going to the moon
Callow, Philip
Colin Patten trilogy (1)
Going to the sea
Levy, Muriel
Wonk series (1)
Going to the wars
Verney, John
Going to the wars series (2)
Going too far
Keene, Carolyn
River Heights series (3)
Going very fast in a circle, if you don't run out of gas
Paulsen, Gary
Sports on the light side series (9)
Going West
Optic, Oliver
Great Western series (1)
Going wild
Taylor, David Conrad
Zoovet series (3)
Golconda
Palmer, Vance
Macy Donovan series (1)
Gold
Allen, Gina
History of gold series (1)
Kelland, Clarence Budington
Hard money trilogy (2)
White, Stewart Edward
California trilogy (1)
Orde family series (5)
Gold and gaiters
Alington, Cyril Augustine
Archdeacon series (4)
Mister Birtley series (3)
Gold and guns on Halfaday Creek
Hendryx, James Beardsley
Black John series (8)
Gold and lead
Hawkins, Clint
Saddletramp series (4)
Gold and wine
Vickers, Roy
Inspector Peter Curwen and Hugh Stanton series (2)
Gold at K-bar-T
Tuttle, Wilbur Coleman
Sad Sontag series (4)

Gold bag
Wells, Carolyn
Fleming Stone series (2)
Gold bat
Wodehouse, Pelham Grenville
Wrykyn School series (1)
Gold Beard's downfall
Golon, Sergeanne
Angelique series (7)
Gold bomb
Laumer, Keith
Avengers series (9)
Gold bullion swindle
Pryce, Larry
Dick Barton series (4)
Gold by Gemini
Gash, Jonathan
Lovejoy series (2)
Gold chains of empire
Padfield, Peter
Guy Grenville series (3)
Gold coast
Robinson, Kim Stanley
Orange County trilogy (2)
Gold Coast nocturne
Nielsen, Helen
Simon Drake series (1)
Gold comes in bricks
Fair, A A
Bertha Cool and Donald Lam series (3)
Gold comfit box
Williams, Valentine
Clubfoot series (7)
Gold connection
Moore, Robin
Connection series (8)
Gold Crown Lane
Sandman Lilius, Irmelin
Sola trilogy (1)
Gold Cup rookies
Speed, Eric
Wynn and Lonny racing series (4)
Gold curse
Resnicow, Herbert
Alexander Magnus and Norma Gold series (4)
Gold deadline
Resnicow, Herbert
Alexander Magnus and Norma Gold series (2)
Gold dragon
Cain, Robert
Cybernarc series (2)
Gold fever
Logan, Jake
John Slocum series (122)
Norman, David
Frontier rakers series (3)
Sharpe, Jon
Trailsman series (122)
Tanner, Clay
Chance Sharpe series (11)
Gold flake hydrant
Matthews, Greg
Burris Weems series (2)
Gold flyers
Johns, William Earl
Biggles series (10)
Gold for the dead
Scott, Bradford
Walt Slade series (5)
Gold for the gay masters
Gray, Harriet
Quadroon trilogy (1)
Gold frame
Resnicow, Herbert
Alexander Magnus and Norma Gold series (3)
Gold from Gemini
Gash, Jonathan
Lovejoy series (2)
Gold gamble
Resnicow, Herbert
Alexander Magnus and Norma Gold series (5)
Gold Gorse Common
Tempest, Margaret
Potter Pinner series (4)
Gold, guns and the girl
Grover, Marshall
Larry and Stretch series (195)
Gold hijack
Eland, Charles
Mark Randall series (3)
Gold Horse Canyon
Bancroft, Tex
Angeltown Keeps and Doc Hennessy series (1)
Gold hunters
Curwood, James Oliver
Wolf hunters series (2)
Gold in every grave
Nelson, Hugh Lawrence
Jim Dunn series (3)
Gold is
Allen, Gina
History of gold series (2)
Gold ledge gold
Fletcher, Dirk
Spur McCoy series (41)
Gold-lust city
Winstan, Matt
Reuben Brown series (13)
Gold mine madness
Sharpe, Jon
Trailsman series (115)
Gold moon of Africa
Black, Hermina
Susan Denver trilogy (1)
Gold Mountain
Paul, Charlotte
Snoqualmie Valley series (1)
Gold movers
Grover, Marshall
Larry and Stretch series (408)
Gold nugget
Chandler, Edna Walker
Tom Logan series (3)
Gold of Akada
Titan, Earl
Anjani series (1)
Gold of Chikaree
Warner, Susan Bagert
Wych Hazel series (2)
Gold of dreams
Merino, Jose Maria
Miguel series (1)
Gold of Fast Castle
Fidler, Kathleen
Archaeology series (2)
Gold of Saint Matthew
Hart-Davis, Duff
Sam Sholto series (1)
Gold of the gods
Daniken, Erich von
Unsolved mysteries series (3)
Reeve, Arthur Benjamin
Craig Kennedy series (5)
Gold of the snow goose
Knight, Peter
Roger Vellacott series (1)
Gold of Toulouse
Clayton, John
Provence trilogy (1)
Gold ogre
Robeson, Kenneth
Doc Savage series (42)
Gold on the wind
Thompson, Valerie
Howell family series (2)
Gold-plated hearse
Hedges, Joseph
John Stark series (4)
Gold-rimmed spectacles
Bassani, Giorgio
Ferrara series (2)
Gold rock of the Chippewa
Lange, Dietrich
American Indian series (14)
Gold rush
Steffanson, Con
Laverne and Shirley series (3)
Gold rush adventures
McCall, Edith
Frontiers of America series (12)
Gold rush prodigal
Thoeme, Brock
Saga of the Sierras series (1)
Gold seeker of '49
Sabin, Edward Legrand
Trail blazers series (7)
Gold seekers
Boussenard, Louis
Robinsons of Guiana series (2)
Gold shaft, gold shaft
Sherman, Jory
Gunn series (26)
Gold sickle
Sue, Eugene
Mysteries of the people series (1)
Gold slippers
Keyes, Frances Parkinson
Winslow family trilogy (3)
Gold solution
Resnicow, Herbert
Alexander Magnus and Norma Gold series (1)
Gold standard
Charteris, Leslie
Saint series (10)
Gold strike
McCurtin, Peter
Sundance series (35)
Gold thimble
Optic, Oliver
Flora Lee series (2)
Riverdale series (11)
Gold through the haze
Barrett, Helen Elizabeth-Anne
West family series (2)
Gold tipped pfitzer
Handl, Irene
Benoir family series (2)
Gold Top Tigger
Huddy, Delia
Tigger series (2)
Gold town
Dawson, Clay
Long Rider series (3)
Gold trackers
Hart-Davis, Duff
Sam Sholto series (1)
Gold train
Chandler, Edna Walker
Tom Logan series (6)
Cunningham, Chet
Jim Steel series (5)
Grant, William
Matthew Faraday series (3)
Gold train bandits
Roddy, Lee
American adventure series (8)
Gold train tramp
Fletcher, Dirk
Spur McCoy series (12)
Gold wagon
Cunningham, Chet
Jim Steel series (1)
Gold was our grave
Wade, Henry
Inspector Poole series (8)
Gold wolf
Bennet, Robert Ames
Wolf series (4)
Goldd goes to the mountain
Turner, Clay
Ben Gold series (3)
Golden age
Gaiman, Neil
Miracleman series (4)
Grahame, Kenneth
Smith family series (1)
Seymour, Harold
Baseball history series (2)
Golden Amazon
Fearn, John Russell
Golden Amazon series (1)
Golden Amazon returns
Fearn, John Russell
Golden Amazon series (2)
Golden Amazon's triumph
Fearn, John Russell
Golden Amazon series (3)
Golden angel
Brent, Nigel
Barney Hyde series (7)
Corrigan, Mark
Mark Corrigan and McLean series (5)
Golden ape
Adams, Herbert
Jimmy Haswell series (6)
Golden apple
Shea, Robert
Illuminatus series (2)
Golden Arrow
Stoddard, Charles
Malloy series (8)
Golden ashes
Crofts, Freeman Wills
Inspector Joseph French series (20)
Golden ax
Neilson, Eric
Haakon series (1)
Golden bees of Tulami
Bonham, Frank
Dogtown Ghetto series (3)
Golden belt
Eadington, Joan
Jonny Briggs series (1)
Golden belts
Murray, Andrew
Sexton Blake series (21)
Golden boats of Taradata affair
Latter, Simon
Girl from U.N.C.L.E.series (4)
Golden box
Crane, Frances
Pat and Jean Abbott series (2)
Golden Boy
Palmer, Bernard
Golden Boy series (1)
Golden Boy and the counterfeiters
Palmer, Bernard
Golden Boy series (3)
Golden Boy, outlaw
Palmer, Bernard
Golden Boy series (2)
Golden Buddha
Pollard, Alfred Oliver
David Wilshaw series (3)
Golden bull
Carter, Nick
Nick Carter series (148)
Golden bullet
Denver, Paul
Cannon series (3)
Golden bullets
Sharpe, Jon
Trailsman series (142)
Golden buttons
Kincade, Wynn
Vicky Loring series (2)
Golden calf
Ilf, Ilya Arnoldovich
Chairs series (2)
Golden carpet
De Chair, Somerset
Golden carpet series (1)
Golden casket
Symonds, Francis Addington
Sexton Blake series (198)
Golden cat
Long, Harman
Franklyn Keen series (2)
Golden circle
Falk, Lee
Phantom series (5)
Golden cloak
Capon, Paul
Artor series (4)
Golden cockatrice
Black, Gavin
Paul Harris series (10)
Golden country
West, Joyce
Gabrielle Allan series (3)
Golden creep
Bagby, George
Inspector Schmidt series (50)
Golden crucible
Stubbs, Jean
Inspector John Joseph Lintott series (3)
Golden crucifix
Rae, John
Westminster series (1)
Golden cup
Plain, Belva
Anna Friedman series (2)
Golden dagger
Punshon, Ernest Robertson
Bobby Owen series (29)
Golden dart
Jepson, Selwyn
Eve Gill series (2)
Golden days
Neill, Robert
Sir Harry Barnaby series (2)
Stevenson, Dorothy Emily
Mrs Tim series (2)
Ts'ao, Hsueh-ch'in
Dream of the red chamber series (1)
Golden dead
Pike, Charles R
Jubal Cade series (7)
Golden death
Evans, Tabor
Longarm series (178)
Golden door
Spicer, Bart
Carney Wilde series (3)
Golden dream
Mayhar, Ardath
Fuzzy series (5)
Scott, Michael
Tales from the Land of Erin trilogy (2)
Golden dreams
Schulte, Elaine
California pioneer series (2)
Golden dress
Montgomery, Ione
Christopher Gibson series (1)
Golden eagle
Clewes, Dorothy
Hadley family series (7)
Golden eagle mystery
Queen, Ellery, Junior
Djuna and Champ series (2)
Golden eagles
Torgersen, Don Arthur
Animal life stories series (4)
Golden echo
Garnett, David
Golden echo trilogy (1)
Golden elephant
Martin, Robert
Trew twins series (1)
Golden express
Thorne, Ramsay
Captain Gringo series (34)
Golden fear
Harvester, Simon
Asia in turmoil series (5)
Malcolm Kenton series (4)
Golden feather
Kenyon, Theda
Staceys of Feathergrant series (1)
Golden fires
Fritch, Elizabeth
California trilogy (2)
Golden flames
Hooper, Kay
Delaneys, the untamed years trilogy (2)
Golden fleece
Paul, Ernest
George Barclay series (4)
Golden flower
Rhodes, Kathlyn
Martin Ryott series (2)
Golden fluid
Dix, Maurice Buxton
Tommy Malins, Anthony Mornington and George Hawkins series (2)
Golden Gate killers
Roberts, J R
Gunsmith series (129)
Golden girl
Hendryx, James Beardsley
Corporal Downey series (1)
Golden girl and all
Dennis, Ralph
Jim Hardman series (3)
Golden Girl and the crystal of doom
Sherman, Josepha
Golden Girl and the Guardians of the Gemstones trilogy (3)
Golden Girl and the vanishing unicorn
Stine, Robert Lawrence
Golden Girl and the Guardians of the Gemstones trilogy (1)
Golden Girl in the land of dreams
Storey, Alice
Golden Girl and the Guardians of the Gemstones trilogy (2)
Golden goal
McCann, Sean
Dove's End Football Club series (3)
Golden god
Hayes, Ralph Eugene
Mark Stoner series (1)
Golden goddess
Grange, Peter
L'Eree family series (4)
Hill, Harry Egbert
Sexton Blake series (229)
Golden goddess gammbit
Maddock, Larry
Hannibal Fortune and Webley series (2)
Golden goose
Southall, Ivan
King of the sticks trilogy (2)
Golden goose murders
McRoyd, Allan
Inspector Franklin Brady series (1)
Golden grin
Lewis, Colin
Howard Hayes trilogy (1)
Golden grotto
Grant, Maxwell
Shadow series (29)
Golden guilt
Gerard, Francis
Sir John Meredith series (9)
Golden gun
Garrett, Charles C
Gunslinger series (2)
Golden hawk
Glick, Ruth
Charisma Inc. series (5)
Golden Hawk
Knott, William Cecil
Golden Hawk series (1)
Golden hen, and other stories
Ross, Diana
Miss Pussy series (1)
Golden hooligan
Dewey, Thomas Blanchard
Pete Schofield series (4)
Golden horn
Anderson, Poul
Last Viking trilogy (1)

Golden Horn
Tarr, Judith
Hound and the Falcon trilogy (2)
Golden horseman
Roberts, J R
Gunsmith series (43)
Golden house
Warner, Charles Dudley
Finance trilogy (2)
Golden idol
Eisenberg, Lisa
Laura Brewster series (5)
Golden key
Sheldon, Georgie
Golden key series (1)
Golden kill
Olden, Marc
Robert Sand series (2)
Golden kiss
Carson, Anthony
Soho series (2)
Golden lady
Sherman, Jory
Gunn series (18)
Golden lamp
Macgregor, Alasdair Alpin
Golden lamp trilogy (1)
Golden lure
Denning, Mark
John Marshall series (4)
Leader, Charles
Rick McAdden series (1)
Golden man
Robeson, Kenneth
Doc Savage series (117)
Golden masks
Grant, Maxwell
Shadow series (109)
Golden master
Grant, Maxwell
Shadow series (171)
Golden mean
Bantock, Nick
Griffin Moss and Sabine Stroheim trilogy (3)
Golden miles
Prichard, Katharine Susannah
Western Australian Goldfields series (2)
Golden monkey
Gunn, Victor
Chief Inspector Bill Cromwell series (27)
Golden Monkey
Knight, Frank
Clipper ship series (1)
Golden murder
Lester, Frank
Geoffrey Slade series (3)
Golden Naginata
Salmonson, Jessica Amanda
Tomoe Gozen trilogy (2)
Golden name day
Lindquist, Jennie Dorothea
Nancy Bruce series (1)
Golden pagoda
Grant, Maxwell
Shadow series (140)
Golden panther
Gluck, Sinclair
Jack Clayton series (1)
Golden Paraoh
Danielson, Peter
Children of the Lion series (5)
Golden Path adventure
Gervaise, Mary
Marstons series (1)
Golden Path pets
Gervaise, Mary
Marstons series (3)
Golden pavements
Brown, Pamela
Blue Door Theatre Company series (3)
Golden peril
Robeson, Kenneth
Doc Savage series (55)
Golden pheasant mystery
Worth, Maurice
Derek Harding series (1)
Golden princess
Moody, Laurence
Tudor trilogy (2)
Golden quest
Grant, Maxwell
Shadow series (77)
Golden rain
Clark, Douglas
Inspector George Masters series (13)
Golden road
Bourne, Peter
Stewart family series (2)
Montgomery, Lucy Maud
Story Girl series (2)
Golden roof
Bowen, Marjorie
Renaissance trilogy (1)
Golden rooms
Fisher, Vardis
Testament of man series (2)
Golden scarab
Adye, John
Oliver Smaile series (2)
Moorhouse, Hopkins
Addison Kent series (2)
Golden Scorpio
Akers, Alan Burt
Dray Prescot series (18)
Golden scorpion
Rohmer, Sax
Fu-Manchu series (4)
Gaston Max series (2)
Golden secret
Sheldon, Ann
Linda Craig adventures series (1)
Golden serpent
Carter, Nick
Nick Carter series (20)
Golden shadow
Garfield, Leon
Greek mythology series (2)
Golden shaft
Ledd, Paul
Shelter Morgan series (14)
Nazel, Joseph
Iceman series (2)
Golden sheaves, black horses
Archer, Fred
Evesham Vale series (6)
Golden skull
Blaine, John
Rick Brant series (10)
Golden sovereign
Church, Richard
Over the bridge series (2)
Housman, Laurence
Palace plays series (4)
Golden Spaniard
Wheatley, Dennis
Duc de Richelieu series (4)
Golden spiders
Stout, Rex
Nero Wolfe and Archie Goodwin series (22)
Golden Square High School
Baldwin, Mary
Fifi series (2)
Golden stag
Heatter, Basil
Timothy Devlin series (2)
Golden stallion and the mysterious feud
Montgomery, Rutherford George
Golden stallion series (7)
Golden stallion and the wolf dog
Montgomery, Rutherford George
Golden stallion series (5)
Golden stallion picture book
Montgomery, Rutherford George
Golden stallion series (7)
Golden stallion to the rescue
Montgomery, Rutherford George
Golden stallion series (3)
Golden stallion's adventure at Redstone
Montgomery, Rutherford George
Golden stallion series (6)
Golden stallion's revenge
Montgomery, Rutherford George
Golden stallion series (2)
Golden stallion's victory
Montgomery, Rutherford George
Golden stallion series (4)
Golden Staters
Willoughby, Lee Davis
Making of America series (11)
Golden steed
Lord, Jeffrey
Richard Blade series (13)
Golden strangers
Treece, Henry
Early Britain series (1)
Golden stud
Horner, Lance
Falconhurst series (9)
Golden stud series (1)
Golden swan
Springer, Nancy
Book of Isle series (5)
Golden sword
Morris, Janet Ellen
Silistra series (2)
Golden sword of Dragonwalk
Stine, Robert Lawrence
Twistaplot series (4)
Golden tally
Oldfield, Pamela
Kent trilogy (3)
Golden thread
Charnas, Suzy McKee
Sorcery Hall trilogy (3)
De Wohl, Louis
Lives of the saints series (7)
Golden threads
Hooper, Kay
Once upon a time series (1)
Golden tooth
Cobban, James Maclaren
Mister Townshend series (2)
Golden torc
May, Julian
Pliocene exile series (3)
Golden trap
Pentecost, Hugh
Pierre Chambrun series (4)
Golden triangle
Leblanc, Maurice
Arsene Lupin series (8)
McCurtin, Peter
Jim Rainey series (14)
Proud, Franklin M
Joe Sanford series (1)
Robertson, Colin
Vicky McBain series (6)
Willard, Tom
Strike fighters series (8)
Golden Venus affair
Macvicar, Angus
Bruce McLintock series (1)
Golden virgin
Rossiter, John
Roger Tallis series (4)
Williamson, Henry
Chronicles of ancient sunlight series (6)
Golden voyager
Finch, Simon
Voyager trilogy (1)
Golden vulture
Grant, Maxwell
Shadow series (148)
Golden waterwheel
Walmsley, Leo
Phantom Lobster series (6)
Golden windows
Richards, Laura Elizabeth
Fables for young and old series (1)
Golden witch
Holt, Gavin
Professor Luther Bastion series (11)
Golden witchbread
Gentle, Mary
Orthe series (1)
Golden wolf
Patchett, Mary Elwyn
Ajax series (8)
Golden world
Innes, Evan
American two thousand and forty series (2)
Golden year
Lockley, Ronald Mathias
Island farm series (6)
Golden years
Hardwick, Mollie
Duchess of Duke Street series (2)
Preston, John
Mission of Alex Kane series (2)
Golden years of Ginger Meggs, 1921-1952
Bancks, James Charles
Ginger Meggs series (30)
Golden yesterdays
Deland, Margaret
If this be I series (2)
Goldengrove
Walsh, Jill Paton
Goldengrove series (1)
Goldenrod
Slater, Jim
Goldenrod series (1)
Goldenrod and the kidnappers
Slater, Jim
Goldenrod series (2)
Goldfinger
Fleming, Ian
James Bond series (7)
Goldfish bowl
Gough, Laurence
Willows and Parker series (1)
Goldilocks
Coburn, Andrew
Rita Gardella O'Dea series (3)
Cosgrove, Stephen Edward
DreamMaker series (1)
McBain, Ed
Matthew Hope series (1)
Goldmaker's house
Sandman Lilius, Irmelin
Sola trilogy (2)
Goldseekers
Long, William Stuart
Australians series (7)
Golem in the gears
Anthony, Piers
Xanth series (9)
Golf course mystery
Steele, Chester K
Colonel Robert Lee Ashley series (2)
Golf in my gallowses
Macvicar, Angus
Confessions series (6)
Golf, Toytown rules
Beaman, Sydney George Hulme
Toytown series (23)
Golfmanship
Potter, Stephen
Lifemanship Correspondence College series (6)
Goliath
Geddes, Paul
Ludovic Fender series (4)
Goliath and the burglar
Dicks, Terrance
David and Goliath series (2)
Goliath and the buried treasure
Dicks, Terrance
David and Goliath series (1)
Goliath and the Cub Scouts
Dicks, Terrance
David and Goliath series (12)
Goliath and the dognappers
Dicks, Terrance
David and Goliath series (3)
Goliath and the school bully
Dicks, Terrance
David and Goliath series (18)
Goliath at sports day
Dicks, Terrance
David and Goliath series (11)
Goliath at the dog show
Dicks, Terrance
David and Goliath series (5)
Goliath at the seaside
Dicks, Terrance
David and Goliath series (10)
Goliath gets a job
Dicks, Terrance
David and Goliath series (16)
Goliath goes to summer school
Dicks, Terrance
David and Goliath series (9)
Goliath in the snow
Dicks, Terrance
David and Goliath series (6)
Goliath on holiday
Dicks, Terrance
David and Goliath series (4)
Goliath scheme
Arden, William
Kane Jackson series (3)
Goliath's birthday
Dicks, Terrance
David and Goliath series (13)
Goliath's Christmas
Dicks, Terrance
David and Goliath series (7)
Goliath's Easter parade
Dicks, Terrance
David and Goliath series (8)
Golightly adrift
Pike, Geoffrey
Henry Golightly series (2)
Golightly outback
Pike, Geoffrey
(3)
Gollan County gallows
Grover, Marshall
Larry and Stretch series (336)
Gollantz and Partners
Jacob, Naomi
Gollantz series (7)
Gollantz, London, Paris, Milan
Jacob, Naomi
Gollantz series (6)
Golliwog and the wireless
Blyton, Enid
Little bedtime books series (7)
Golliwogg at the seaside
Upton, Bertha
Golliwogg series (3)
Golliwogg in Holland
Upton, Bertha
Golliwogg series (9)
Golliwogg in the African jungle
Upton, Bertha
Golliwogg series (13)
Golliwogg in war
Upton, Bertha
Golliwogg series (4)
Golliwogg's air-ship
Upton, Bertha
Golliwogg series (7)
Golliwogg's auto go-cart
Upton, Bertha
Golliwogg series (6)
Golliwogg's bicycle club
Upton, Bertha
Golliwogg series (2)
Golliwogg's Christmas
Upton, Bertha
Golliwogg series (12)
Golliwogg's circus
Upton, Bertha
Golliwogg series (8)
Golliwogg's desert island
Upton, Bertha
Golliwogg series (11)
Golliwogg's fox-hunt
Upton, Bertha
Golliwogg series (10)
Golliwogg's polar adventure
Upton, Bertha
Golliwogg series (5)
Gom on Windy Mountain
Chetwin, Grace
Tales of Gom in the Legends of Ulm series (1)
Gomar, the gosling
Darby, Joan
Animal adventure series (7)
Gondola scam
Gash, Jonathan
Lovejoy series (8)
Gondola to danger
Quackenbush, Robert Mead
Miss Mallard series (4)
Gondolier of Venice
Kraus, Robert
Pinchpenny Mouse series (2)
Gondreville mystery
Balzac, Honore de
Scenes of political life series (2)
Gone afield
Roberts, Cecil
Rustic series (3)
Gone-Away Lake
Enright, Elizabeth
Portia and Julian series (1)
Gone fishin'
Culotta, Nino
Weird mob series (3)
Gone gougin'
Culotta, Nino
Weird mob series (4)
Gone, no forwarding
Gores, Joe
DKA file series (3)
Gone quiet
Bland, Eleanor Taylor
Marti MacAlister series (3)
Gone rambling
Roberts, Cecil
Rustic series (2)
Gone rustic
Roberts, Cecil
Rustic series (1)
Gone sunwards
Roberts, Cecil
Rustic series (4)
Gone the dreams and dancing
Jones, Douglas Clyde
Comanche trilogy (3)
Gone to earth
Boyer, Richard Lewis
Doctor Charlie Adams series (6)
Gone to glory
Irvine, Robert Ralstone
Moroni Traveler series (3)
Gone to ground
White, Terence Hanbury
Mister Marx series (2)
Gone to her death
Audemars, Pierre
Monsieur Pinaud series (24)
McGown, Jill
Chief Inspector Lloyd and Sergeant Judy Hill series (3)
Gone to Texas
Carter, Forrest
Josey Wales series (1)
Miller, Jim
Colt Revolver series (1)
Gone to the dogs
Conant, Susan
Dog lover's mystery series (1)

Gone tomorrow
Davis, Frederick Clyde
Professor Cyrus Hatch series (8)
Hone, Joseph
Collected travels series (2)
Gone with the wind
Mitchell, Margaret
Scarlett O'Hara series (1)
Gone with the wish
Goudge, Eileen
Swept away series (1)
Gone with the witch
Barnes, Megan
Teen witch series (3)
Gonji
Rypel, Thadeus Chester
Gonji series (5)
Good and bad weather
Schiddel, Edmund
Bucks County trilogy (3)
Good and dead
Langton, Jane
Homer Kelly series (6)
Good angel slept
Greenwood, Robert
Rosie Dawes series (1)
Good beauties
Gibbs, Lewis
Kitty Villiers series (2)
Good behavior
Westlake, Donald Edwin
Dortmunder Gang series (6)
Good books
Philmore, R
Swan series (3)
Good boy's diary
Golden Rod
Bad boy series (4)
Good by stealth
Clandon, Henrietta
William Power series (2)
Good-bye, Arnold!
Roche, Patricia K
Webster and Arnold series (1)
Good-bye, Aunt Charlotte!
Straker, John Foster
Inspector Pitt series (5)
Good-bye Eva?
Pascal, Francine
Sweet Valley kids series (38)
Good-bye, Pink Pig
Adler, Carole Schwerdtfeger
Pink Pig series (1)
Good-bye, Shirley
Muller, Paul
Paul Muller series (8)
Good-bye Stacey, good-bye
Martin, Ann Matthews
Baby-Sitters Club series (13)
Good-bye summer
Lea, Fanny Heaslip
Half-angel series (1)
Good-bye to earth
Kelley, Leo Patrick
Galaxy Five series (1)
Good-bye to life
Hume, David
Mick Cardby series (13)
Good-bye to love
Baker, Carin Greenberg
Last summer, first love series (2)
Pascal, Francine
Sweet Valley University series (7)
Good Charlotte
York, Carol Beach
Miss Know It All series (4)
Good Christmas for riding
Whitbread, Elizabeth
Georgie Pony Club series (2)
Good daughters
Hocking, Mary
Fairley family trilogy (1)
Good day
Marvin, James W
Crow series (8)
Good day, blue goose!
Mallett, Jerry J
Tumtwit series (7)
Good day for a hangin'
Boone, James Calder
Ned Remington series (2)
Good day mice
York, Carol Beach
Miss Know It All series (3)
Good dog, Carl
Day, Alexandra
Carl series (1)
Good earth
Buck, Pearl Sydenstricker
Wang family series (1)
Good enough for Nelson
Winton, John
Navy series (6)
Good Evans!
Wallace, Edgar
Educated Evans series (3)
Good fight
Ahern, Jerry
Defender series (10)
Good for the soul
Deland, Margaret
Old Chester series (2)
Good Fortunes Gang
Mahy, Margaret
Cousins quartet (1)
Good Gestes
Wren, Percival Christopher
Beau Geste series (4)
Good girl granny
Thomson, Pat
Share-a-story series (6)
Good ground
Barclay, Tessa
Craigallan family series (4)
Good hearts
Price, Reynolds
Mustian family series (3)
Good horse for riding
Whitbread, Elizabeth
Georgie Pony Club series (3)
Good housekeeping
Walker, Mort
Hi and Lois series (9)
Good hunting, Blue Sky
Lewin, Hugh
Little Indian series (1)
Good hunting, Little Indian
Lewin, Hugh
Little Indian series (1)
Good husband
Johnson, Pamela Hansford
Toby Roberts series (2)
Good intentions
Deighton, Barbara
Felicity Travers series (2)
Miller, Hugh
Eastenders series (3)
Good keen girl
Crump, Barry
Good keen series (2)
Good keen man
Crump, Barry
Good keen series (1)
Good knight, sailor
Jacobs, Thomas Curtis Hicks
Temple Fortune series (7)
Good land
Erdman, Loula Grace
Pierce family series (3)
Good lesson
Housman, Laurence
Palace plays series (3)
Good life
Esmonde, John
Good life series (1)
Good light
Bjarnhof, Karl
Blind series (2)
Good listener
Johnson, Pamela Hansford
Toby Roberts series (1)
Good Lord, not another book of snappy answers to stupid questions!
Jaffee, Al
Snappy answers to stupid questions series (4)
Good Luck Arizona Man
Benedict, Rex
Pecos Gang series (1)
Good luck girl
Rand, Suzanne
Winners series (3)
Good luck, Mick and Mandy
Schmidt, Annie Maria Geertruida
Bob and Jilly series (2)
Good luck, Mister Cain
Freeborn, Brian
Mister Cain series (1)
Good luck, Nurse Ross
Meynell, Laurence Walter
Nurse Ross series (5)
Good luck, sucker
Telfair, Richard
Monty Nash series (4)
Good luck to the corpse
Murray, Max
Corpse series (6)
Good master
Seredy, Kate
Good master series (1)
Good men do nothing
Brunner, John
Max Curfew series (2)
Good moring, Miss Gator
Kraus, Robert
Miss Gator series (1)
Good morning, Baby Bear
Hill, Eric
Baby Bear series (6)
Good morning, good people
Raymond, Ernest
My days series (3)
Good morning, Irene
Douglas, Carole Nelson
Irene Adler series (2)
Good morning, Mavis
Brown, Carter
Mavis Seidlitz series (3)
Good neighbors
Tedrow, Thomas L
Days of Laura Ingalls Wilder series (3)
Good neighbours
Mackenzie, Lee
Emmerdale Farm series (13)
Good news
Abbey, Edward
Jack Burns series (2)
Good night, Garrity
Nixon, Allan
Tony Garrity series (2)
Good night, Jessie!
Ziefert, Harriet
Jessie series (2)
Good night, ladies
Van Siller, Hilda
Pete Rector series (1)
Good night, Lewis
Ziefert, Harriet
Lewis series (2)
Good night, little ABC
Kraus, Robert
Night light series (2)
Good night, Little One
Kraus, Robert
Night light series (1)
Good night, little Richard Rabbit
Kraus, Robert
Night light series (3)
Good night, Mister Holmes
Douglas, Carole Nelson
Irene Adler series (1)
Good night, Sammy
Szekeres, Cyndy
Sammy day and night series (1)
Good night, sweet prince
Berry, Carole
Bonnie Indermill series (3)
Good night to kill
O'Donnell, Lillian
Detective Norah Mulcahaney series (13)
Good old dolls
Ahlberg, Janet
Daisychain series (6)
Good old Ernie
Mallett, Jerry J
Ernie series (1)
Good old Secret Seven
Blyton, Enid
Secret Seven series (12)
Good old times
Kellogg, Elijah
Good old times series (1)
Good peace
Conway, Troy
Coxeman series (14)
Good pit man
Alldritt, Keith
Black country series (1)
Good place for murder
Mullen, Clarence
Tony Lantz and Eddie Wright series (2)
Good place to die
Copper, Basil
Mike Faraday series (20)
Good policeman
Charyn, Jerome
Isaac Sidel series (5)
Good Samaritans
Gee, Herbert Leslie
Friendly series (11)
Good, says Jerome
Clifton, Lucille
Everett Anderson series (3)
Good soldier Schweik
Hasek, Jaroslav
Schweik series (1)
Good spies don't grow on trees
Lovell, Marc
Appleton Porter series (10)
Good sport, bad sport
Jenkins, Jerry Bruce
Bradford family series (10)
Good sport Max
Turk, Hanne
Max the Mouse series (14)
Good sports
Vail, Virginia
Horse crazy series (3)
Good Teddy
Bawden, Juliet
My Teddy series (3)
Good, the bad and the deadly
Hardin, J D
Raider and Doc series (2)
Good, the bad and the goofy
Scieszka, Jon
Time warp trio series (3)
Good, the bad and the ugly
Millard, Joseph John
Dollar series (1)
Good times
Baker, Russell
Good times series (2)
Good times with our friends
Montgomery, Elizabeth
Dick, Jane and Sally series (4)
Good timing
Trent, Trisha
Kylie series (1)
Good turn hunters
Collins, Freda
Woodland Pack series (5)
Good weekend for murder
Jordan, Jennifer
Vaughans series (1)
Good wives
Alcott, Louisa May
Jo March series (2)
Good wolf
Burnett, Frances Hodgson
Good wolf series (1)
Good woman
Bromfield, Louis
Escape series (4)
Good work, Amelia Bedelia
Parish, Peggy
Amelia Bedelia series (6)
Good work Secret Seven
Blyton, Enid
Secret Seven series (6)
Good year for dwarfs
Brown, Carter
Rick Holman series (22)
Good year for riding
Whitbread, Elizabeth
Georgie Pony Club series (1)
Goodbye Angel, goodbye Joanne
Mortimer, Derek
Tom Holiday series (1)
Goodbye, Ann and Susie
Wahlstedt, Viola
Ann and Susan series (5)
Goodbye blond
Enefer, Douglas
Dale Shand series (14)
Goodbye Charlie
Bolton, Evelyn
Horse book series (3)
Goodbye, Chicago
Burnett, William Riley
Chicago trilogy (3)
Goodbye doctor
Poidevin, Leslie
Country practice series (1)
Goodbye, Doctor Roch
Soubiran, Andre
Jean Nerac series (3)
Goodbye, Donald Thorndyke
Donaldson, Norman
Doctor John Evelyn Thorndyke series (28)
Goodbye, Dove Square
McNeill, Janet
Matt McGinley series (2)
Goodbye Gemma
Streatfeild, Noel
Gemma series (4)
Goodbye gorgeous
Campbell, Keith
Mike Brett series (1)
Goodbye Hamilton
Cookson, Catherine
Maisie Leviston series (2)
Goodbye house
Asch, Frank
Bear series (9)
Goodbye is not worthwhile
Mole, William
Casson Duker series (2)
Goodbye Island
Gunn, John
Andrew Blake series (2)
Goodbye look
Macdonald, Ross
Lew Archer series (16)
Goodbye, Melbourne town
McInnes, Graham
Road to Gundagai series (4)
Goodbye Mister Chips
Hilton, James
Mister Chips series (1)
Goodbye, Mister Shaft
Tidyman, Ernest
John Shaft series (5)
Goodbye my son
Coryn, Marjorie
Napoleonic trilogy (2)
Goodbye, Nanny Gray
Stacey, Susannah
Superintendent Bone series (1)
Staynes, Jill
Superintendent Bone series (1)
Goodbye old year, hello new year
Modell, Frank B
Milton and Marvin series (4)
Goodbye soldier
Milligan, Spike
War memoirs series (6)
Goodbye summer
Mackay, Allis
They came to a river series (2)
Prince, Alison
Nick series (1)
Goodbye, sweet William
Flower, Pat
Inspector Swinton series (2)
Goodbye to a river
Graves, John
Brazos trilogy (1)
Goodbye to all that
Graves, Robert
Goodbye to all that series (1)
Goodbye to Berlin
Isherwood, Christopher
Berlin series (3)
Goodbye to Camp Crumb
Mallett, Jerry J
Tumtwit series (4)
Goodbye to Gumble's Yard
Townsend, John Rowe
Uncle Walter series (2)
Goodbye to Pine Street
Allan, Mabel Esther
Pine Street series (4)
Goodbye to the hounds
Pullein-Thompson, Christine
Sandy and Lawrence trilogy (3)
Goodbye to the Jungle
Townsend, John Rowe
Uncle Walter series (2)
Goodbye to the purple sage
Benedict, Rex
Pecos Gang series (2)
Goodbye to yesterday
Goolden, Barbara
Consett trilogy (1)
Goodey's last stand
Alverson, Charles
Joe Goodey series (2)
Goodnight and goodbye
Harris, Timothy Hyde
Tom Kyd series (2)
Goodnight, Irene
Burke, Jan
Irene series (1)
Goodnight kiss
Stine, Robert Lawrence
Fear Street super chiller series (3)
Goodnight, Little Rabbit
Wabbes, Marie
Little Rabbit series (4)
Goodnight, Max
Turk, Hanne
Max the Mouse series (5)
Goodnight sweet prince
Hunter, Alan
Inspector George Gently series (34)
Goodnight Trail
Compton, Ralph
Trail drive series (1)
Goodnight's dream
Edson, John Thomas
Floating Outfit series (4)
Goods
Douglas, Arthur
Jonathan Craythorne series (1)
Goon cartoons
Milligan, Spike
Goon cartoons series (1)
Goonies
Kahn, James
Goonies series (1)
Goose and I
Colson, John Henry Charles
Goose series (1)
Goose at sea
Colson, John Henry Charles
Goose series (3)

Goose cathedral
Brooke, Jocelyn
Orchid trilogy (3)
Goose eggs
Taylor, E J
Biscuits, buttons and pickles series (2)
Goose up the creek
Colson, John Henry Charles
Goose series (2)
Gooseberry fool
McClure, James
Lieutenant Kramer and Sergeant Zondi series (3)
Goosehill Gang cookbook
Christian, Mary Blount
Goosehill Gang series (12)
Goosehill Gang craft book
Christian, Mary Blount
Goosehill Gang series (12)
Gopher gold
Laird, Elizabeth
Toucan Tecs series (3)
Gopher in the garden, and other animal poems
Prelutsky, Jack
Zoo doings series (1)
Gor omnibus
Norman, John
Tarl Cabot series (3)
Gorbals boy at Oxford
Glasser, Ralph
Gorbals trilogy (2)
Gorbals voices, siren songs
Glasser, Ralph
Gorbals trilogy (3)
Gordon Liddy is my muse by Tommy Tip Paine
Batchelor, John Calvin
Gordon Liddy is my muse series (1)
Gordon, the big engine
Awdry, Wilbert
Railway series (8)
Gordon, the high-speed engine
Awdry, Christopher
Railway series (31)
Gorgeous East
Croft-Cooke, Rupert
Sensual life series (14)
Gorgeous ghoul
Babcock, Dwight Vincent
Hannah Van Doren series (2)
Gorgeous ghoul murder case
Babcock, Dwight Vincent
Hannah Van Doren series (2)
Gorilla adventure
Price, Willard
Hal and Roger Hunt series (10)
Gorilla hunters
Ballantyne, Robert Michael
Coral Island series (2)
Gorky Park
Smith, Martin Cruz
Arkady Renko series (1)
Gormenghast
Peake, Mervyn
Titus Groan trilogy (2)
Gormenghast trilogy
Peake, Mervyn
Titus Groan trilogy (3)
Gory details
Elias, David
Nell Bartlett series (2)
Gory dew
Mitchell, Gladys
Dame Beatrice Bradley series (43)
Gospel in slow motion
Knox, Ronald Arbuthnott
Slow motion series (3)
Gospel lamb
Scott, Jack S
Detective Inspector Alfred Stanley Rosher series (5)
Gospel magic made easy
Westphail, Arnold Carl
Gospel magic series (2)
Gospel magic with home made stuff and things
Westphail, Arnold Carl
Gospel magic series (1)
Gospel magic you can do
Westphail, Arnold Carl
Gospel magic series (3)
Gospel makers
Fraser, Anthea
Inspector David Webb and Sergeant Ken Jackson series (10)
Gospel paper tears with surprise climax
Westphail, Arnold Carl
Paper tearing series (11)
Gospel surprise paper tears
Westphail, Arnold Carl
Paper tearing series (13)
Gossamer
Birmingham, George A
Gorman MP series (1)
Cosgrove, Stephen Edward
Barely there series (3)
Gossip from Thrush Green
Read, *Miss*
Thrush Green series (6)
Gossip war
Pascal, Francine
Sweet Valley twins series (80)
Gotham Gore
Jason, Stuart
Butcher series (35)
Gothic pursuit
Malcolm, John
Tim Simpson series (5)
Gotland deal
Crisp, Norman James
Inspector Sidney Kenyon series (1)
Gotobed dawn
Quantrill, Malcolm
Gotobed trilogy (1)
Gotobedlam
Quantrill, Malcolm
Gotobed trilogy (2)
Gotty and the guv'nor
Copping, John Edward
Gotty series (1)
Gotty in furrin parts
Copping, John Edward
Gotty series (2)
Goulden fleece
Obstfeld, Raymond
Harry Gould series (1)
Governess
Hervey, Evelyn
Harriet Unwin series (1)
Government
Traven, B
Jungle series (2)
Governor
Douglas, Felicity
Faye Boswell series (2)
Governor Ramage, R.N.
Pope, Dudley
Lord Nicholas Ramage series (4)
Governor's mansion
Laxalt, Robert
Basque trilogy (3)
Governor's pardon
Leslie, Madeline
Woodbine series (2)
Gower Street
Rayner, Claire
Performers series (1)
Gowi Corby plays chicken
Kemp, Gene
Cricklepit School series (2)
Gownsman's gallows
Farrer, Katharine
Inspector Richard Ringwood series (3)
Grab operators
Chance, John Newton
Jonathan Blake series (29)
Grace before ploughing
Masefield, John
In the mill series (3)
Grace divorce
Swinnerton, Frank
Prothero quartet (3)
Grace Hamilton's schooldays
Worboise, Emma Jane
Grace Hamilton series (1)
Grace Hardie
Melville, Anne
Hardie family series (2)
Grace Harlowe overseas
Flower, Jessie Graham
Grace Harlowe overseas series (1)
Grace Harlowe with the American Army on the Rhine
Flower, Jessie Graham
Grace Harlowe overseas series (2)
Grace Harlowe with the Marines at Chateau Thierry
Flower, Jessie Graham
Grace Harlowe overseas series (3)
Grace Harlowe with the Red Cross in France
Flower, Jessie Graham
Grace Harlowe overseas series (4)
Grace Harlowe with the US troops in the Argonne
Flower, Jessie Graham
Grace Harlowe overseas series (5)
Grace Harlowe with the Yankee Shock Boys at Saint Quentin
Flower, Jessie Graham
Grace Harlowe overseas series (6)
Grace Harlowe's first year at Overton College
Flower, Jessie Graham
Grace Harlowe at college series (1)
Grace Harlowe's fourth year at Overton College
Flower, Jessie Graham
Grace Harlowe at college series (4)
Grace Harlowe's golden summer
Flower, Jessie Graham
Grace Harlowe at college series (7)
Grace Harlowe's junior year at high school
Flower, Jessie Graham
Grace Harlowe at high school series (3)
Grace Harlowe's Overland Riders among the border guerillas
Flower, Jessie Graham
Grace Harlowe's Overland Riders series (9)
Grace Harlowe's Overland Riders among the Kentucky Mountains
Flower, Jessie Graham
Grace Harlowe's Overland Riders series (1)
Grace Harlowe's Overland Riders at Circle O Ranch
Flower, Jessie Graham
Grace Harlowe's Overland Riders series (5)
Grace Harlowe's Overland Riders in the Black Hills
Flower, Jessie Graham
Grace Harlowe's Overland Riders series (6)
Grace Harlowe's Overland Riders in the Great North Woods
Flower, Jessie Graham
Grace Harlowe's Overland Riders series (2)
Grace Harlowe's Overland Riders in the High Sierras
Flower, Jessie Graham
Grace Harlowe's Overland Riders series (7)
Grace Harlowe's Overland Riders in the Yellowstone National Park
Flower, Jessie Graham
Grace Harlowe's Overland Riders series (8)
Grace Harlowe's Overland Riders on the Great American Desert
Flower, Jessie Graham
Grace Harlowe's Overland Riders series (3)
Grace Harlowe's Overland Riders on the lost river
Flower, Jessie Graham
Grace Harlowe's Overland Riders series (10)
Grace Harlowe's Overland Riders on the Old Apache Trail
Flower, Jessie Graham
Grace Harlowe's Overland Riders series (4)
Grace Harlowe's plebe year at high school
Flower, Jessie Graham
Grace Harlowe at high school series (1)
Grace Harlowe's problem
Flower, Jessie Graham
Grace Harlowe at college series (6)
Grace Harlowe's return to Overton Campus
Flower, Jessie Graham
Grace Harlowe at college series (5)
Grace Harlowe's second year at Overton College
Flower, Jessie Graham
Grace Harlowe at college series (2)
Grace Harlowe's senior year at high school
Flower, Jessie Graham
Grace Harlowe at high school series (4)
Grace Harlowe's sophomore year at high school
Flower, Jessie Graham
Grace Harlowe at high school series (2)
Grace Harlowe's third year at Overton College
Flower, Jessie Graham
Grace Harlowe at college series (3)
Grace on their doorposts
Wallace, Kathleen
Veronica Ramsay series (1)
Gracey
Moloney, James
Dougy and Gracey series (2)
Gracie Allen murder case
Van Dine, S S
Philo Vance series (11)
Gracious lily affair
Mason, Francis Van Wyck
Colonel Hugh North series (20)
Gracus, the centurion
Forest, Dael
Roman world series (4)
Graduate in love
Allen, Inglis
'Varsity series (2)
Graduates
Quin-Harkin, Janet
Toni Redmond and Jill Gardner series (3)
Graduation
Pike, Christopher
Final friends series (3)
Graduation day
Chase, Emily
Canby Hall series (17)
Graft town
Graham, Neill
Solo Malcolm series (13)
Grafter
Cassells, John
Superintendent Flagg series (30)
Grafters
Carter, Nicholas
Nicholas Carter series (532)
Grafting of the Rose
Beamish, Noel de Vic
Owen Tudor series (1)
Graftons
Marshall, Archibald
Abington series (2)
Graham's Gang
Challen, John
Graham's Gang series (1)
Grail Tree
Gash, Jonathan
Lovejoy series (3)
Grail war
Monaco, Richard
Parsival series (2)
Grain of the wood
Home, Michael
Breckland series (8)
Grain of truth
Webster, Jack
Grain of truth series (1)
Grain of wheat
Longford, Frank Pakenham
Born to believe trilogy (3)
Grammar of motives
Burke, Kenneth
Motives series (1)
Motives series (2)
Grampa in Oz
Thompson, Ruth Plumly
Oz series (17)
Grampa-Lop
Cosgrove, Stephen Edward
Leo the Lop series (3)
Gran and grandpa
Oxenbury, Helen
First picture books series (7)
Gran at Coalgate
Cawley, Winifred
Jinnie Friend series (2)
Gran builds a house
Storr, Catherine
Grandparents series (3)
Gran camping
Cole, Michael
Gran series (7)
Gran gliding
Cole, Michael
Gran series (1)
Gran knits
Cole, Michael
Gran series (5)
Grand annual show
Jones, Nicholas
Wind in the willows series (2)
Grand Canyon
Roberts, J R
Gunsmith series (111)
Grand Canyon odyssey
Leibold, Jay
Choose your own adventure series (43)
Grand catch
Buhet, Gil
Boys' Republic series (2)
Grand Cayman slam
Striker, Randy
Dusky MacMorgan series (7)
Grand Central murder
Macveigh, Sue
Captain Andy and Sue McVeigh series (1)
Grand design
Dos Passos, John
Spotswood family series (3)
Pilgrim, David
James De la Cloche series (2)
Grand finale
Clark, Halsey
Periscope series (4)
Grand hotel of horror
Milton, Hilary
Plot your own horror stories series (4)
Grand howl
Travis, Falcon
Third Bilsley Pack series (1)
Grand jubilee
Elgin, Suzette Haden
Ozark fantasy trilogy (2)
Grand man
Cookson, Catherine
Mary Ann Shaughnessy series (1)
Grand Modena murder
Gribble, Leonard Reginald
Superintendent Anthony Slade series (3)
Grand Ole Opry murders
Kaye, Marvin
Hilary Quayle series (2)
Grand ostrich ball
Laird, Elizabeth
Toucan Tecs series (1)
Grand piano
Goodman, Paul
Empire City quartet (4)
Empire city series (4)
Grand Prix
Bamman, Henry A
Checkered flag series (7)
Grand Prix Britain
Ashford, Jeffrey
Grand Prix series (3)
Grand Prix Monaco
Ashford, Jeffrey
Grand Prix series (1)
Grand Prix United States
Ashford, Jeffrey
Grand Prix series (2)
Grand slam
James, Laurence
Baseball series (1)
Moody, Susan
Cassie Swann series (2)
Perry, Ritchie
Philis series (10)
Grand Teton
Mitchum, Hank
Stage coach station series (38)
Grand trunk knight
Williamson, Geoffrey
Silva d'Croy series (2)
Grand Trunk Road
Wiles, John
Grand Trunk Road series (1)
Grandad's gifts
Jennings, Paul Arthur
Round the twist series (4)
Granddad with snails
Baldwin, Michael
Granddad with snails series (1)
Grande Florine
Belot, Adolphe
Stranglers series (2)
Grandeur and downfall of Cesar Birotteau
Balzac, Honore de
Scenes of Parisian life series (4)
Grandfather
Baker, Jeannie
Grandparents series (1)
Grandfather and I
Buckley, Helen Elizabeth
Grandparents series (1)
Grandfather medicine
Hager, Jean
Mitch Bushyhead series (1)
Grandfather Milly's luck
Samuels, Adelaide Florence
Dick and Daisy Travers series (4)
Grandfathers
Christian, Mary Blount
God's gift to children series (2)
Grandma and Grandpa Jackson
Wensell, Ulises
Jackson family series (6)
Grandma at bat
Arnold, Emily
Grandma series (3)

Grandma Bagley leads the way
Pochocki, Ethel
Grandma Bagley series (1)

Grandma Bagley to the rescue
Pochocki, Ethel
Grandma Bagley series (2)

Grandma Cadbury's bikie gang
Bates, Dianne
Grandma Cadbury series (3)

Grandma Cadbury's safari tours
Bates, Dianne
Grandma Cadbury series (2)

Grandma Cadbury's trucking tales
Bates, Dianne
Grandma Cadbury series (1)

Grandma mixup
Arnold, Emily
Grandma series (1)

Grandma Snuffles
Partridge, Jenny
Oakapple Wood series (6)

Grandmas at the lake
Arnold, Emily
Grandma series (2)

Grandmaster
Murphy, Warren Burton
Grandmaster series (1)

Grandmother
Baker, Jeannie
Grandparents series (2)

Grandmother and I
Buckley, Helen Elizabeth
Grandparents series (2)

Grandmother dear
Molesworth, Mary Louisa
Grandmother series (1)

Grandmother Elsie
Finley, Martha Farquharson
Elsie Dinsmore series (8)

Grandmother for the Orphelines
Carlson, Natalie Savage
Orphelines series (5)

Grandmother Lucy and her hats
Wood, Joyce
Grandmother Lucy series (1)

Grandmother Lucy goes for a picnic
Wood, Joyce
Grandmother Lucy series (2)

Grandmother Lucy in her garden
Wood, Joyce
Grandmother Lucy series (3)

Grandmother Lucy's birthday
Wood, Joyce
Grandmother Lucy series (4)

Grandmother Oma
Kleberger, Ilse
Grandmother Oma series (1)

Grandmother Oma and the green caravan
Kleberger, Ilse
Grandmother Oma series (2)

Grandmothers
Christian, Mary Blount
God's gift to children series (1)
Rita
Victorian series (1)

Grandmother's house
Lapierre, Janet
Meg Halloran series (2)

Grandmother's journey
Unnerstad, Edith
Anders series (2)

Grandpa and me
Alex, Marlee
You and me series (2)

Grandpa and the birdman
Butterworth, Ben
That boy Trog series (11)

Grandpa and the mammoth
Butterworth, Ben
That boy Trog series (10)

Grandpa Bear
Pryor, Bonnie
Grandpa Bear series (1)

Grandpa Bear's Christmas
Pryor, Bonnie
Grandpa Bear series (2)

Grandpa goes hunting
Butterworth, Ben
That boy Trog series (12)

Grandpa has a swim
Butterworth, Ben
That boy Trog series (4)

Grandpa plays hide and seek
Butterworth, Ben
That boy Trog series (7)

Grandpa's birthday
Storr, Catherine
Grandparents series (4)

Grandpa's garden
Kilroy, Sally
Toddlers' tales series (3)

Grandpa's great city tour
Stevenson, James
Grandpa series (4)

Grandpa's horse race
Butterworth, Ben
That boy Trog series (9)

Grandpa's little girls
Curtis, Alice Turner
Grandpa's little girls series (1)

Grandpa's little girls and Miss Abitha
Curtis, Alice Turner
Grandpa's little girls series (5)

Grandpa's little girls and their freidns
Curtis, Alice Turner
Grandpa's little girls series (3)

Grandpa's little girls at school
Curtis, Alice Turner
Grandpa's little girls series (2)

Grandpa's little girls grown up
Curtis, Alice Turner
Grandpa's little girls series (6)

Grandpa's little girls' house-boat party
Curtis, Alice Turner
Grandpa's little girls series (4)

Grandpa's selection, and other stories
Rudd, Steele
Rudd family series (8)

Grandpa's surprise
Carruth, Jean
Fun with Sally series (1)

Grandpa's too-good garden
Stevenson, James
Grandpa series (7)

Grandpuff and Leafy
Lister, Gladys
Leafy series (1)

Grandson
Dixelius, Hildur
Sara Alelia trilogy (3)
Gillespie, Susan
Longdon-Lorristone family series (2)

Grandville Bank heist
Logan, Jake
John Slocum series (153)

Grange
Chetwynd-Hayes, Ronald
Tales of Clavering Grange series (2)

Grange at High Force
Turner, Philip
Darnley Mills series (2)

Grange Hill
Redmond, Phil
Grange Hill series (14)

Grange Hill after hours
Redmond, Phil
Grange Hill series (9)

Grange Hill for sale
Leeson, Robert
Grange Hill series (4)

Grange Hill goes wild
Leeson, Robert
Grange Hill series (2)

Grange Hill graffiti
Redmond, Phil
Grange Hill series (10)

Grange Hill heroes
Redmond, Phil
Grange Hill series (12)

Grange Hill home and away
Leeson, Robert
Grange Hill series (5)

Grange Hill on the run
Redmond, Phil
Grange Hill series (8)

Grange Hill partners
Redmond, Phil
Grange Hill series (13)

Grange Hill rebels
Redmond, Phil
Grange Hill series (11)

Grange Hill rules, OK?
Leeson, Robert
Grange Hill series (3)

Grange Hill stories
Redmond, Phil
Grange Hill series (1)

Granite
Trevena, John
Dartmoor trilogy (3)

Granite and clay
Bassett, Sara Ware
Cape Cod series (5)

Granite Men
Hogg, Garry
Jonty series (6)

Grannis of the Fifth
Pier, Arthur Stanwood
Saint Timothy's School series (5)

Granny and Grandad Parker
Wensell, Ulises
Jackson family series (5)

Granny and the desperadoes
Parish, Peggy
Granny series (2)

Granny and the Indians
Parish, Peggy
Granny series (1)

Granny Reardun
Garner, Alan
Stone book quartet (3)

Granny, the baby and the big gray thing
Parish, Peggy
Granny series (3)

Granny's lovely necklace
Blyton, Enid
John and Mary series (9)

Granny's secret attic
Wahlstedt, Viola
Ann and Susan series (3)

Gran's game
Cole, Michael
Gran series (6)

Gran's goats
Cole, Michael
Gran series (8)

Gran's good news
Cole, Michael
Gran series (4)

Gran's old bones
Cole, Michael
Gran series (2)

Gran's pets
Cole, Michael
Gran series (3)

Grant Grab-Alot
Watson, Jean
Alot series (5)

Grantham mystery
Danvers, Milton
Robert Spicer series (3)

Grant's overture
Millar, Florence N
Chief Inspector Douglas Grant series (1)

Granville Valley
Abbott, Jacob
August series (4)

Grape vine
Janson, Hank
Hank Janson series (123)

Graper girls
Corbett, Elizabeth
Graper girls series (1)

Graper girls go to college
Corbett, Elizabeth
Graper girls series (2)

Grapes of paradise
Leigh, Helena
Vintage years trilogy (1)

Grasp at straws
Dane, Joel Y
Sergeant Cass Harty series (4)

Grass
Nash, Padder
Grass series (1)
Simon, Claude
Grass quartet (1)

Grass and Supergrass
Nash, Padder
Grass series (6)

Grass beyond the mountains
Hobson, Richmond Pearson
Rancher series (1)

Grass crown
McCullough, Colleen
Rome series (2)

Grass in idleness
Nash, Padder
Grass series (4)

Grass makes hay
Nash, Padder
Grass series (7)

Grass widow
Janson, Hank
Hank Janson series (259)
McInerny, Ralph
Father Roger Dowling series (8)

Grass-widow's tale
Peters, Ellis
Inspector George Felse series (7)

Grasshopper and butterfly
Piers, Helen
Little creature series (2)

Grasshopper and the pickle factory
Slater, Jim
Grasshopper series (2)

Grasshopper and the poisoned river
Slater, Jim
Grasshopper series (3)

Grasshopper and the unwise owl
Slater, Jim
Grasshopper series (1)

Grasshopper green
Rutley, Cecily Marianne
Tales of the wild folk series (7)

Grass's fancy
Nash, Padder
Grass series (2)

Grassy knoll
Harrington, William
Columbo series (8)

Grateful to life and death
Narayan, Rasipuram Krishnaswami
Malgudi series (4)

Graustark
McCutcheon, George Barr
Graustark series (1)

Grave
Grant, Charles Lewis
Oxrun Station series (4)

Grave case of murder
Bax, Roger
Inspector James series (2)

Grave consequences
Cumberland, Marten
Saturnin Dax series (16)

Grave danger
Dixon, Franklin W
Hardy boys case files series (61)
Kane, Frank
Johnny Liddell series (8)

Grave designs
Kahn, Michael A
Rachel Gold series (1)

Grave digger of Monk's Arden
Gask, Arthur
Gilbert Larose series (13)

Grave-digger's apprentice
Grayland, Valerie Merle
Hoani Mata series (3)

Grave doubt
Baker, Ivon
David Meynell series (1)

Grave error
Greenleaf, Stephen
John Marshall Tanner series (1)

Grave fairytale
Meynell, Esther
Jakob and Melchior series (1)

Grave for Lassiter
Grey, Loren Zane
Lassiter series (6)

Grave for madam
Cagney, Peter
Mike Strang series (3)

Grave for Miss Carling
Hardie, David William Ferguson
Inspector Elwyn Hughes series (4)

Grave for two
Carmichael, Harry
John Piper and Quinn series (37)

Grave goods
Mann, Jessica
Tamara Hoyland series (3)

Grave is waiting
Mackenzie, Andrew
Nicholas Cornish series (3)

Grave matters
Rhode, John
Doctor Lancelot Priestley series (60)
Yorke, Margaret
Doctor Patrick Grant series (3)

Grave mistake
Marsh, Ngaio
Inspector Roderick Alleyn series (30)

Grave responsibility
Staynes, Jill
Superintendent Bone series (4)

Grave robbers
Montgomery, Ramsey
Choose your own adventure series (103)

Grave secrets
Hendricksen, Louise
Doctor Amy Prescott series (2)

Grave without grass
Cameron, Donald Clough
Abelard Voss series (2)

Grave witness
Levi, Peter
Ben Jonson series (1)

Gravedancer
Colter, Dale
Regulator series (5)

Gravedigger
Hansen, Joseph
Dave Brandstetter series (6)

Gravelhanger
Gielgud, Val
Antony Havilland series (1)

Graven image
Finlay, D G
Watchman chronicles series (4)

Graves in Academe
Kenney, Susan
Roz Howard series (2)

Gravestone
Carlson, Patricia McEvoy
Maggie Ryan series (9)

Graveyard never closes
Davis, Frederick Clyde
Professor Cyrus Hatch series (4)

Graveyard plot
Erskine, Margaret
Inspector Septimus Finch series (11)

Graveyard plots
Pronzini, Bill
Private Eye series (22)

Graveyard rolls
Procter, Maurice
Chief Inspector Harry Martineau series (17)

Graveyard shift
Patterson, Henry
Nick Miller series (1)

Graveyard to let
Dickson, Carter
Sir Henry Merrivale series (20)

Graveyard vultures
Smith, Guy Newman
Sabat series (1)

Gray Bunny children still learning
Crabb, Minnie Rowe
Gray Bunny series (2)

Gray creatures
Zorro
Doctor Death series (2)

Gray Dawn
Terhune, Albert Payson
Sunnybank collies series (12)

Gray dawn
White, Stewart Edward
California trilogy (2)
Orde family series (6)

Gray dusk
Cohen, Octavus Roy
David Carroll series (2)

Gray Fist
Grant, Maxwell
Shadow series (48)

Gray ghost
Grant, Maxwell
Shadow series (101)

Gray Lensman
Smith, Edward Elmer
Lensman series (4)

Gray magic
Dreher, Sarah
Stoner McTavish series (3)
Landon, Herman
Gray Phantom series (5)
Norton, Andre
Magic series (1)

Gray mask
Camp, Wadsworth
Garth series (1)

Gray menace
Allen, Betsy
Connie Blair series (8)

Gray Phantom
Landon, Herman
Gray Phantom series (1)

Gray Phantom's return
Landon, Herman
Gray Phantom series (2)

Gray Prince
Vance, Jack
Gaean series (2)

Gray terror
Landon, Herman
Gray Phantom series (3)

Graymantle
Morressy, John
Iron angel series (2)

Grease
De Christoforo, Ron
Grease series (1)

Grease 2
Rotsler, William
Grease series (2)

Great abduction mystery
Graydon, William Murray
Sexton Blake series (56)

Great adventure
Giles, Janice Holt
Fowler family series (7)

Great adventure of Hare
Uttley, Alison
Little Grey Rabbit series (3)

Great advice of Lila Fenwick
McMullan, Kate
Lila Fenwick series (2)

Great age of discovery
Barclay, Isabel
Worlds without end series (3)

Great air race
Dickens, Frank
Boffo series (2)

Great air swindle
Creasey, John
Sexton Blake series (984)

Great airport mystery
Dixon, Franklin W
Hardy boys series (9)

Great airport racket
Hunter, John
Sexton Blake series (1151)

Great airways plot
Noy, John
Rufus Deville series (2)

Great amulet
Diver, Maud
Desmond series (2)

Great and secret show
Barker, Clive
Books of the art series (1)

Great apes and monkey tails
Torgersen, Don Arthur
Animal safari nature series (8)

Great Arab conquests
Glubb, John Bagot
Arab history series (1)

Great art gallery crime
Osborne, Mark
Sexton Blake series (808)

Great auk
Eckert, Allan Wesley
Extinct birds series (1)

Great Australian legends
Hardy, Frank
Great Australian legends series (1)

Great avenging day
Draper, Alfred
Crispin Paton series (5)

Great bank robbery
Hawthorne, Julian
Inspector Byrnes series (2)

Great Barrier Reef
Patchett, Mary Elwyn
Ajax series (3)

Great baseball championship
Wenk, Richard
Pick-a-path series (3)

Great betrayal
Mowat, Farley
Canada north series (2)

Great beyond
Maeterlinck, Maurice
Pascalian series (6)

Great big especially beautiful Easter egg
Stevenson, James
Grandfather's problems series (1)

Great big fish
Blyton, Enid
John and Mary series (1)

Great big Paddington Bear picture book
Bond, Michael
Paddington picture book series (6)

Great big Paddington book
Bond, Michael
Paddington picture book series (6)

Great blizzard
Idell, Albert Edward
Rogers family series (4)

Great book raid
Leach, Christopher
Long John Silver series (7)

Great boy chase
Quin-Harkin, Janet
Toni Redmond and Jill Gardner series (2)

Great boyfriend switch
Pascal, Francine
Sweet Valley twins series (66)

Great Brain
Fitzgerald, John Dennis
Tom's Great Brain series (1)

Great Brain at the Academy
Fitzgerald, John Dennis
Tom's Great Brain series (4)

Great Brain does it again
Fitzgerald, John Dennis
Tom's Great Brain series (7)

Great Brain reform
Fitzgerald, John Dennis
Tom's Great Brain series (5)

Great brain robbery
Saddler, Allen
Dave Stevens series (1)

Great British ghosts
Chambers, Aidan
Great ghosts series (1)

Great bullion mystery
Dale, Judith
Shirley Flight series (8)

Great California game
Gash, Jonathan
Lovejoy series (14)

Great Canal plot
Teed, George Hamilton
Sexton Blake series (403)

Great captain
Morrow, Honore Willsie
Great Captain trilogy (3)

Great captains
Treece, Henry
Early Britain series (4)

Great Cardinal
Birt, David
Tudors series (1)

Great cases of the Thinking Machine
Futrelle, Jacques
Professor Augustus S F X Van Dusen series (3)

Great cattle trail
Ellis, Edward Sylvester
Forest and prairie trilogy (1)

Great circle mystery
Ridley, Nat
Nat Ridley series (8)

Great circus mystery
Murray, Edgar Joyce
Sexton Blake series (354)

Great code
Frye, Northrop
Bible and literature series (1)

Great confession
Fisher, Vardis
Testament of man series (12)

Great conspiracy
Carter, Nicholas
Nicholas Carter series (131)
Soutar, Andrew
Kharduni series (2)

Great currency racket
Chester, Gilbert
Sexton Blake series (1179)

Great custard pie panic
Corbett, Scott
Doctor Merlin series (2)

Great cycle
Vesaas, Tarjei
Per Eilevson Bufast series (1)

Great days at Grange Hill
Needle, Jan
Grange Hill series (7)

Great days in Green Street
Weir, Rosemary
Green Street series (2)

Great debate
Tedrow, Thomas L
Days of Laura Ingalls Wilder series (7)

Great deception
Elliot, Douglass
American patriot series (2)

Great deliverance
George, Elizabeth
Inspector Thomas Lynley and Sergeant Barbara Havers series (1)

Great diamond bluff
Bobin, John William
Sexton Blake series (116)

Great diamond robbery
Minahan, John
Little John Rawlings series (2)

Great diamond syndicate
Carter, Nicholas
Nicholas Carter series (331)

Great dollar fraud
Parsons, Anthony
Sexton Blake series (1262)

Great dumping mystery
Jardine, Warwick
Sexton Blake series (712)

Great Dune trilogy
Herbert, Frank
Dune series (3)

Great egg flap
Palfrey, Heather Mary
Ricky Wilson series (1)

Great eighth grade switch
Kenyon, Kate
Cedar Groves Junior High School series (11)

Great elephant
Scholefield, Alan
South African series (2)

Great enigma
Carter, Nicholas
Nicholas Carter series (10)

Great expectations
Dickens, Charles
Magwitch series (1)
Miss Havisham series (1)

Great explosion
Murray, Andrew
Sexton Blake series (249)

Great flood
Reeder, Colin
West Meadow series (1)

Great fortune
Manning, Olivia
Guy and Harriet Pringle series (1)

Great game
Bailey, Henry Christopher
Mister Joshua Clunk series (5)
Mister Reggie Fortune series (14)
Thorne, Ramsay
Captain Gringo series (10)

Great ghosts of the world
Chambers, Aidan
Great ghosts series (2)

Great gold steal
White, Ted
Captain America series (2)

Great grab
Burton, Thomas
Bloodbird series (1)

Great gradepoint mystery
Bartholomew, Barbara
Mikrokid mystery series (1)

Great Gran Gorilla and the robbers
Waddell, Martin
Great Gran Gorilla series (1)

Great Gran Gorilla to the rescue
Waddell, Martin
Great Gran Gorilla series (2)

Great-grandmother's girls in New France
Champney, Elizabeth Williams
Great-grandmother's girls series (1)

Great-grandmother's girls in New Mexico
Champney, Elizabeth Williams
Great-grandmother's girls series (2)

Great grave robbery
Minahan, John
Little John Rawlings series (5)

Great great rescuer's
Macgibbon, Jean
Sandy, Jane and Stephen series (1)

Great gulper
Slater, Jim
A Mazing Monster series (1)

Great Harvard robbery
Minahan, John
Little John Rawlings series (4)

Great horse race
Grove, Frederick Philip
Dude McQuint series (1)

Great hotel murder
Starrett, Vincent
Riley Blackwood series (1)

Great hotel robbery
Minahan, John
Little John Rawlings series (1)

Great House
Thompson, Kate
Derain family series (1)

Great housewives of art
Swain, Sally
Great housewives series (1)

Great housewives of art revisited
Swain, Sally
Great housewives series (2)

Great hunger
Bojer, Johan
Peer Holm series (1)

Great hunt
Jordan, Robert
Wheel of time series (2)

Great hush-hush mystery
Dix, Maurice Buxton
Sexton Blake series (985)

Great ice-cream crime
Townson, Hazel
Lenny and Jake series (1)

Great ideas of Lila Fenwick
McMullan, Kate
Lila Fenwick series (1)

Great insurance murders
Propper, Milton
Tommy Rankin series (9)

Great ivory swindle
Teed, George Hamilton
Sexton Blake series (361)

Great jewel robbery
Hardin, J D
Raider and Doc series (46)

Great Kate
Saunders, Susan
Sleepover friends series (19)

Great Kings' war
Green, Roland James
Lord Kalvan series (2)

Great King's war
Green, Roland James
Paratime police series (3)

Great land swindle
Sharpe, Jon
Canyon O'Grady series (10)

Great Ling plot
Martyn, Wyndham
Anthony Trent series (14)

Great little engines
Awdry, Christopher
Railway series (29)

Great man
Bennett, Arnold
Five towns series (4)

Great marathon football match
Ahlberg, Allan
Brick Street Boys series (5)

Great march west
Dicks, Terrance
Mounties series (1)

Great McGonagall
Milligan, Spike
William McGonagall series (3)

Great McGonagall scrap book
Milligan, Spike
William McGonagall series (1)

Great McGonnigle rides shotgun
Corbett, Scott
Great McGonnigle series (3)

Great McGonnigle switches pitches
Corbett, Scott
Great McGonnigle series (4)

Great McGonnigle's gray ghost
Corbett, Scott
Great McGonnigle series (1)

Great McGonnigle's key play
Corbett, Scott
Great McGonnigle series (2)

Great Merlini
Rawson, Clayton
Great Merlini series (5)

Great mogul
Payne, Robert
Emperor Shah Jahan series (1)

Great money order swindle
Carter, Nicholas
Nicholas Carter series (41)

Great morning
Sitwell, Osbert
Left hand, right hand series (3)

Great motor-cycle race
Dickens, Frank
Boffo series (1)

Great Mrs Pennington
Stafford, Ann
Victorian and Edwardian London life series (3)

Great museum mystery
Hill, Harry Egbert
Sexton Blake series (332)

Great Northern?
Ransome, Arthur
Swallows and Amazons series (12)

Great ones
Deegan, Jon J
Old Growler trilogy (3)

Great opium case
Carter, Nicholas
Nicholas Carter series (600)

Great peace
Bond, Edward
War plays series (3)

Great picture robbery
Harris, Leon
Maurice the moose series (1)

Great Pike's Peak Rush
Sabin, Edward Legrand
Great West series (2)

Great pilgrim heist
Ellis, Wesley
Lone Star series (134)

Great portrait mystery
Freeman, Richard Austin
Doctor John Evelyn Thorndyke series (7)

Great possessions
Bancroft, Francis
Germans in South Africa series (2)
Grayson, David
Adventures series (5)

Great pretender
Deane, Jim
Nick Merlotti series (1)

Great pretenders
Berry, Joy
Can make and do series (1)

Great proconsul
Grier, Sydney Carlyon
Indian history trilogy (3)

Great pumpkin switch
McDonald, Megan
Potato man series (2)

Great pyramid robbery
Minahan, John
Little John Rawlings series (3)

Great rabbit rip-off
Hildick, Edmund Wallace
McGurk series (6)

Great rabbit robbery
Hildick, Edmund Wallace
McGurk series (6)

Great rail racket
Dilnot, George
Horace Augustus Elver series (3)

Great rebellion
Stolz, Mary
Tales at the Mousehole trilogy (1)

Great refusals
Preston, Florence
Kathrine Grey series (2)

Great relief
Housman, Laurence
Palace plays series (2)

Great reminder
Irvine, Robert Ralstone
Moroni Traveler series (6)

Great revue mystery
Gibbons, Harry Hornaby Clifford
Sexton Blake series (285)

Great rip-off
Harris, Lavinia
Computer detectives series (1)

Great river
Wood, James
Ian Ross series (2)

Great riverboat race
Roberts, J R
Gunsmith series (132)

Great rock 'n roll swindle
Moorcock, Michael
Elric series (6)

Great Salt Lake massacre
Siegel, Scott
Warhunter series (3)

Great salvage swindle
Gibbons, Harry Hornaby Clifford
Sexton Blake series (475)

Great secret
Daniel, Roland
John Quicksilver series (2)

Great Shalom
Dyck, Peter J
Shalom series (1)

Great shipyard mystery
Ascott, John
Sexton Blake series (644)

Great Sioux trail
Altsheler, Joseph Alexander
Great West series (1)

Great skate mystery
Hope, Laura Lee
New Bobbsey twins series (21)

Great Skinner enterprise
Tolan, Stephanie Stein
Great Skinner series (2)

Great Skinner getaway
Tolan, Stephanie Stein
Great Skinner series (3)

Great Skinner homestead
Tolan, Stephanie Stein
Great Skinner series (4)

Great Skinner strike
Tolan, Stephanie Stein
Great Skinner series (1)

Great Sky River
Benford, Gregory
Galactic Center series (3)

Great Southern mystery
Cole, George Douglas Howard
Superintendent Henry Wilson series (9)

Great spy race
Diment, Adam
Philip McAlpine series (2)

Great stores crime
Edwards, Walter
Sexton Blake series (739)

Great stores mystery
Edwards, Walter
Sexton Blake series (1021)

Great struggle
Nexo, Martin Andersen
Pelle the conqueror series (3)

Great summer Olympic moments
Aaseng, Nathan
Sports talk series (10)

Great taxi-cab ramp
Brandon, John Gordon
Sexton Blake series (988)

Great tigers of India
Torgersen, Don Arthur
Animal life stories series (5)

Great timber race
Champlin, Tim
Matt Tierney series (5)

Great Tote fraud
Bobin, John William
Sexton Blake series (564)

Great Toytown war
Beaman, Sydney George Hulme
Toytown series (36)
Great tradition
Keyes, Frances Parkinson
Marlowe family series (2)
Great trunk mystery
Poole, Reginald Heber
Sexton Blake series (494)
Great Uncle Prickles and the moon balloon
Adams, Georgie
Great Uncle Prickles series (1)
Great Uncle Prickles and the river boat
Adams, Georgie
Great Uncle Prickles series (2)
Great valley
Johnston, Mary
Virginian series (4)
Great Waldo search
Handford, Martin
Wally series (3)
Great Wally search
Handford, Martin
Wally series (3)
Great waxworks crime
Evans, Gwyn
Sexton Blake series (704)
Great wedding
Evans, Max
Dusty Jones and Wrangler Lewis series (2)
Great wheel
Gregorian, Joyce Ballou
Tredana trilogy (3)
Great winter Olympic moments
Aaseng, Nathan
Sports talk series (11)
Great working dog stories
Goode, Angela
Working dogs series (1)
Great Yant mystery
Cunningham, Albert Benjamin
Sheriff Jess Roden series (7)
Great year for dying
Copper, Basil
Mike Faraday series (12)
Great year of our lives at the old squire's
Ober, Frederick Albion
Old farm series (2)
Greatest book ever written
Oursler, Fulton
Bible stories series (1)
Greatest breakthrough since lunchtime
Douglas, Colin
David Campbell series (2)
Greatest faith ever known
Oursler, Fulton
Bible stories series (3)
Greatest Gresham
Avery, Gillian
Julia and Henry Gresham trilogy (2)
Greatest heiress in England
Oliphant, Margaret Oliphant Wilson
Greatest heiress series (1)
Greatest show in the galaxy
Wyatt, Stephen
Doctor Who series (144)
Greatest story ever told
Oursler, Fulton
Bible stories series (2)
Greatest thing since sliced bread
Robertson, Don
Morris Bird III series (1)
Greatest thing that almost happened
Robertson, Don
Morris Bird III series (3)
Greatest Tudor
Moody, Laurence
Tudor trilogy (3)
Greatheart Silver
Farmer, Philip Jose
World of Tiers series (5)
Greatness of Josiah Porlick
Neuman, Berman Paul
Paths of the blind trilogy (1)
Grecian bloodbath
Jason, Stuart
Butcher series (18)
Gredos reckoning
Rougvie, Cameron
Robert Belcourt series (3)
Greedy killers
Radford, Edwin
Doctor Manson series (33)
Greek adventure
Bayley, Viola
Adventure series (15)
Greek and Roman times
Coote, Roger
Journey through history series (2)
Greek boat mystery
Pardoe, Margot
Boat series (5)
Greek coffin mystery
Queen, Ellery
Ellery Queen series (1)
Greek fire
Chase, Glen
Cherry Delight series (25)
Greek god affair
Deming, Richard
Mod Squad series (1)
Greek goddess
Edwards, Sylvia
Sally Baxter series (10)
Greek islands
Durrell, Lawrence
Island series (5)
Greek key
Forbes, Colin
Tweed, Grey and Newman series (6)
Greek memories
Mackenzie, Compton
Memories series (3)
Greek odyssey
Keene, Carolyn
Nancy Drew files series (74)
Passport to romance trilogy (3)
Greek summit
Carter, Nick
Nick Carter series (173)
Greek symbol mystery
Keene, Carolyn
Nancy Drew series (60)
Greek tragedy
Cole, George Douglas Howard
Superintendent Henry Wilson series (21)
Greel County outcasts
Grover, Marshall
Larry and Stretch series (250)
Green ace
Palmer, Stuart
Hildegarde Withers series (13)
Green alleys
Phillpotts, Eden
Industries of England series (3)
Green ally
Nortje, Peter Henry
Henk Strydom series (2)
Green and gold
Hamilton, Mary
Robert Erskine series (1)
Green are my mountains
Fraser, Christine Marion
Blue above the chimneys series (3)
Green arrow
Bolt, Ben
Captain Grandison series (2)
Green at Greyhouse
Bell, Robert Stanly Warren
Greyhouse series (2)
Green Bay run
Robbins, David
Endworld series (22)
Green bay tree
Bromfield, Louis
Escape series (1)
Green behind the ears
Addis, Faith
Devon farm series (2)
Green book of Hob stories
Mayne, William
Hob stories series (3)
Green box
Grant, Maxwell
Shadow series (50)
Green branch
Pargeter, Edith
Mediaeval Wales trilogy (2)
Green bunyip
Whitlock, Judith
Bunyip series (1)
Green cameo mystery
Judd, Frances K
Kay Tracey series (6)
Green circle
Cross, Mark
Daphne Wrayne and her Four Adjusters series (18)
Green circle blues
Haring, Scott D
Car wars adventure gamebook series (5)
Green crow
O'Casey, Sean
I knock at the door series (7)
Green death
Hamilton, Elaine
Inspector Reynolds series (4)
Robeson, Kenneth
Doc Savage series (65)
Green December fills the graveyard
Sarsfield, Maureen
Inspector Lane Parry series (1)
Green diamonds
Robertson, Colin
Superintendent Bradley series (11)
Green dolphin
Bassett, Sara Ware
Cape Cod series (6)
Green eagle
Robeson, Kenneth
Doc Savage series (24)
Green eagle score
Stark, Richard
Parker series (10)
Green evil
Grierson, Francis Durham
Superintendent Andrew Ash series (13)
Green eye of death
Sandys, James
Inspector Millwall series (3)
James Charlesworth series (3)
Green eyes
Brooks, Edwy Searles
Sexton Blake series (281)
Green Eyes
Grant, Maxwell
Shadow series (15)
Green feather
Manuel, Esme
Trisha Trelawney series (1)
Green fingers
Arkell, Reginald
Green fingers series (1)
Green fingers again
Arkell, Reginald
Green fingers series (3)
Green flames of Aries
Lory, Robert
Horrorscope series (1)
Green for a grave
Stokes, Manning Lee
Barnabas Jones series (2)
Green for danger
Brand, Christianna
Inspector Cockrill series (2)
Holt, Gavin
Inspector Joel Saber series (2)
Green fox
Mackenzie, Kathleen
Pentire family series (3)
Green frontier
Hilton, John Buxton
Superintendent Simon Kenworthy series (9)
Green gauntlet
Delderfield, Ronald Frederick
Craddocks of Shallowford series (2)
Green ghost of Appleville
Marzollo, Jean
Thirty nine kids on the block series (1)
Green ginger jar
Judson, Clara Ingram
They came from series (7)
Green girl
Wilmott, Phyllis
Green girl series (2)
Green glade
Trevor, Elleston
Green glade trilogy (3)
Green glare murders
Wallace, Robert
Phantom Detective series (26)
Green glory
Brophy, John
Green series (1)
Green goddess
Edwards, Paul
John Eagle series (12)
Green gold
King, Frank
Superintendent Gloom series (2)
Green grape
Ratel, Simonne
Isabelle Comtat series (2)
Green grass of Wyoming
O'Hara, Mary
Flicka series (3)
Green, green are all my colors
Wilhelm, Hans
Waldo series (9)
Green, green grass
Croft-Cooke, Rupert
Sensual life series (24)
Green, green my valley now
Llewellyn, Richard
Huw Morgan series (4)
Green grow the dollars
Lathen, Emma
John Putnam Thatcher series (19)
Green grow the graves
Chaber, M E
Milo March series (19)
Green grow the rushes
Lyon, Elinor
Meredith family series (1)
Green grow the tresses-O
Hyland, Stanley
Parliament series (2)
Green harvest
Oldfield, Pamela
Kent trilogy (1)
Green hazard
Coles, Manning
Tommy Hambledon series (5)
Green heart of heaven
Owen, Roderic
Manahoa series (1)
Green hell
Mackie, John
Rat Bastards series (6)
McCurtin, Peter
Jim Rainey series (11)
Green hell treasure
Fish, Robert Lloyd
Captain Jose da Silva series (9)
Green hills of earth
Heinlein, Robert Anson
Future history series (1)
Green hoods
Grant, Maxwell
Shadow series (150)
Green Hornet cracks down
Striker, Fran
Green Hornet series (2)
Green Hornet in the infernal light
Friend, Ed
Green Hornet series (3)
Green Hornet returns
Striker, Fran
Green Hornet series (1)
Green huntsman
Stendhal
Lucien Leeuwen series (1)
Green hydra
Gygax, Gary
Sagard the Barbarian series (2)
Green Island mystery
Allen, Betsy
Connie Blair series (5)
Green isle of the great deep
Gunn, Neil Miller
Young Art and old Hector series (2)
Green jacket
Lee, Jennette Barbour Perry
Millicent Newberry series (1)
Green killer
Dawe, Carlton
Leathermouth series (11)
Robeson, Kenneth
Avenger series (20)
Green knife
Wynne, Anthony
Doctor Eustace Hailey series (14)
Green Knight
Chapman, Vera
Three damosels trilogy (1)
Green ladies
Brophy, John
Green series (2)
Green lama mystery
Kains, Josephine
Terry Spring series (3)
Green lantern
Bolt, Ben
Inspector Godbold series (2)
Green leaves
Henrey, Madeleine
Madeleine series (7)
Green leaves of summer
Willis, Ted
Rosie Carr series (2)
Green light
Douglas, Lloyd Cassel
Newell Paige series (1)
Green light for death
Kane, Frank
Johnny Liddell series (2)
Green lightning
Stillman, Ron
Tracker series (2)
Green man
Abbey, Lynn
Unicorn and dragon series (2)
Green mansions
Cannon, Martin
Swamp Thing second series (2)
Green Mars
Robinson, Kim Stanley
Mars series (2)
Green mask
Skene, Anthony
Sexton Blake series (719)
Verner, Gerald
Superintendent Robert Budd series (2)
Green master
Robeson, Kenneth
Doc Savage series (180)
Green Mill murder
Greenwood, Kerry
Phryne Fisher series (5)
Green mirror
Walpole, Hugh
London Group series (3)
Trenchard family series (1)
Green moth
Mitton, Geraldine Edith
Diana Forbes series (2)
Green Muffin book
Hogarth, Ann
Muffin book series (3)
Green Munch Bunch word book
Reed, Giles
Munch Bunch word book series (1)
Green murders
Miles, Keith
Alan Saxton series (3)
Green musketeers and the fabulous frogs
Saint Antoine, Sara
Green musketeers series (1)
Green musketeers and the incredible energy escapade
Saint Antoine, Sara
Green musketeers series (2)
Green pastures
Silberrad, Una Lucy
Tobiah series (3)
Green peaches ripen
Muller, Mary
Anna and Johan de Villiers series (1)
Green pearl
Vance, Jack
Lyonesse series (2)
Green phoenix
Swann, Thomas Burnett
Ancient history series (6)
Mellonia trilogy (2)
Green plaid pants
Scherf, Margaret
Emily and Henry Bryce series (3)
Green Pope
Asturias, Miguel Angel
Guatemala trilogy (2)
Green reapers
Jones, Roger William
Inspector Evans and Sergeant Beddoes series (3)
Green ripper
Macdonald, John Dann
Travis McGee series (18)
Green River hunt
Meek, Joseph
Mountain Jack Pike series (5)
Green room crime
Chester, Gilbert
Sexton Blake series (611)
Green sailors
Hackforth-Jones, Gilbert
Green sailors series (1)
Green sailors ahoy
Hackforth-Jones, Gilbert
Green sailors series (3)
Green sailors and blue water
Hackforth-Jones, Gilbert
Green sailors series (5)
Green sailors and fair winds
Hackforth-Jones, Gilbert
Green sailors series (6)
Green sailors, beware
Hackforth-Jones, Gilbert
Green sailors series (4)
Green sailors in the Caribbean
Hackforth-Jones, Gilbert
Green sailors series (8)
Green sailors in the Galapagos
Hackforth-Jones, Gilbert
Green sailors series (9)
Green sailors in the South Seas
Hackforth-Jones, Gilbert
Green sailors series (10)
Green sailors on holiday
Hackforth-Jones, Gilbert
Green sailors series (2)
Green sailors to Gibraltar
Hackforth-Jones, Gilbert
Green sailors series (7)
Green scarf
Fry, Pete
Pete Fry series (6)

Green shadow
Landon, Herman
Picaroon series (2)
Green shiver
Clason, Clyde B
Theocritus Lucius Westborough series (10)
Green smoke
Manning, Rosemary
Susan and R.Dragon series (1)
Green stick
Muggeridge, Malcolm
Chronicles of wasted time series (1)
Green stone
Blanc, Suzanne
Inspector Miguel Menendes series (1)
Green story book
Blyton, Enid
Colour story book series (3)
Green talons
Holt, Gavin
Professor Luther Bastion series (3)
Green team
Makris, Kathryn
Eco-Kids series (3)
Green tent mystery at Sugar Creek
Hutchens, Paul
Sugar Creek Gang series (19)
Green Toenails Gang
Sharmat, Marjorie Weinman
Olivia Sharp series (4)
Green tree in Gedde
Sharp, Alan
John Moseby series (1)
Green triangle
Duncan, William Murdoch
Superintendent Leslie series (2)
Green triangle mystery
Pink, Hal
Inspector Docker series (1)
Green trigger fingers
Sherwood, John
Celia Grant series (1)
Green turban
Graydon, William Murray
Sexton Blake series (178)
Green turtle mystery
Queen, Ellery, Junior
Djuna and Champ series (3)
Green Willow Farm
Gould, Elizabeth
Green Willow Farm series (5)
Green wind
Fowler, Thurley
Robinson family series (1)
Green with envy
Kennealy, Jerry
Nick Polo series (6)
Green wolf connection
Carter, Nick
Nick Carter series (103)
Green wood
Best, Rayleigh Breton Amis
Yarrow series (5)
Green wound
Atlee, Philip
Joe Gall series (2)
Green wound contract
Atlee, Philip
Joe Gall series (2)
Green years
Cronin, Archibald Joseph
Robert Shannon series (1)
Lyons, Genevieve
Slievelea series (2)
Winn, Godfrey
Infirm glory series (1)
Greenacre girls
Forrester, Izola Louise
Greenacres series (1)
Greenback fever
Grover, Marshall
Larry and Stretch series (341)
Greenback trail
Grover, Marshall
Larry and Stretch series (279)
Greenbriar Queen
Gilluly, Sheila
Greenbriar Queen trilogy (1)
Greencoats against Napoleon
Styles, Showell
Ensign Peter Byrd series (1)
Greene murder case
Van Dine, S S
Philo Vance series (3)
Greenery Street
Mackail, Denis
Greenery Street trilogy (1)
Greeneye
Slater, Jim
A Mazing Monster series (6)
Greenface
King, Frank
Clarence Knight series (2)
Greenfly
McCutchan, Philip
Commander Esmonde Shaw series (18)
Greenhorn
Tibble, Anne
Greenhorn trilogy (1)
Greenhorn days
Hanson, Victor Joseph
Amos Crowle series (9)
Greenhouse
Easton, Thomas Atwood
Sparrowhawk series (2)
James, Dakota
Greenhouse series (1)
Greenland farers
Boucher, Alan Estcourt
Halli Thordason series (2)
Greenland mystery
Rosenberger, Joseph
Death Merchant series (70)
Greenmantle
Buchan, John
Richard Hannay series (2)
Greenmask!
Linington, Elizabeth
Sergeant Ivor Maddox series (1)
Greenstone
Kalman, Yvonne
Yardley family trilogy (1)
Greenstone griffins
Mitchell, Gladys
Dame Beatrice Bradley series (63)
Greenstone land
Kalman, Yvonne
Yardley family trilogy (1)
Greenwell mystery
Lorac, E C R
Inspector Macdonald series (3)
Greenwich Apartments
Corris, Peter
Cliff Hardy series (10)
Greenwich killing time
Friedman, Kinky
Kinky Friedman series (2)
Greenwitch
Cooper, Susan Mary
Dark is rising series (3)
Greenwooders
Palmer, Geoffrey
Sherwood Forest series (2)
Greenwooders' triumph
Palmer, Geoffrey
Sherwood Forest series (3)
Greetings from earth
Larson, Glen A
Battlestar Galactica series (8)
Greetings from hell
Groening, Matt
Life in hell series (6)
Gregory's dog
Stobbs, William
Gregory series (2)
Gregory's garden
Stobbs, William
Gregory series (1)
Greg's first race
Lynam, Terence
BMX Gang series (3)
Gremlin in the garden
Macvicar, Angus
Confessions series (7)
Gremlins
Gipe, George
Gremlins series (1)
Gremlin's Grampa
Pike, Robert L
Lieutenant Jim Reardon series (2)
Gremlins story book
Carey, Mary Virginia
Gremlins series (2)
Grenadiere
Balzac, Honore de
Scenes of private life series (17)
Grenadine Etching, her life and loves
Ruark, Robert
Grenadine Etching series (1)
Grenadine's spawn
Ruark, Robert
Grenadine Etching series (2)
Grenson murder case
Jacobs, Thomas Curtis Hicks
Detective Superintendent John Bellamy series (1)
Gresham ghost
Roberts, Willo Davis
Black pearl series (8)
Greta's decision
Haynes, Ambrose
Greta series (2)
Greta's dream
Haynes, Ambrose
Greta series (1)
Greta's victory
Haynes, Ambrose
Greta series (3)
Grey adventurer
Trease, Geoffrey
Stuart kings series (3)
Grey dawn
White, Stewart Edward
California trilogy (2)
Orde family series (6)
Grey dusk
Cohen, Octavus Roy
David Carroll series (2)
Grey Face
Cassells, John
Superintendent Flagg series (25)
Grey Fairy and Titania's Palace
Wilkinson, Nevile
Titania's Palace series (2)
Grey Fox of Holland
Bevan, Tom
Dutch in Spain series (2)
Grey ghost
Cassells, John
Superintendent Flagg series (10)
Grey ghost book
Middleton, Jessie Adelaide
Grey ghost series (1)
Grey goose wing
Wiat, Philippa
Edward III series (2)
Grey granite
Gibbon, Lewis Grassic
Scots Quair trilogy (3)
Grey king
Cooper, Susan Mary
Dark is rising series (4)
Grey Lensman
Smith, Edward Elmer
Lensman series (4)
Grey man
Urquhart, Macgregor
Chief Inspector Joshua Smarles series (6)
Grey mane of morning
Chant, Joy
Vanderi series (1)
Grey mask
Wentworth, Patricia
Miss Maud Silver series (1)
Grey mistress
Packer, Joy
Pack and follow series (2)
Grey Phantom
Landon, Herman
Gray Phantom series (1)
Grey Phantom's return
Landon, Herman
Gray Phantom series (2)
Grey Phantom's triumph
Landon, Herman
Gray Phantom series (5)
Grey Rabbit and the circus
Uttley, Alison
Little Grey Rabbit series (26)
Grey Rabbit and the wandering hedgehog
Uttley, Alison
Little Grey Rabbit series (18)
Grey Rabbit finds a shoe
Uttley, Alison
Little Grey Rabbit series (25)
Grey Rabbit's May Day
Uttley, Alison
Little Grey Rabbit series (27)
Grey regard
Finlay, D G
Watchman chronicles series (2)
Grey Seal
Draper, Alfred
Crispin Paton series (1)
Grey sentinels
Knox, Bill
Inspector Colin Thane and Phil Moss series (5)
Grey Shadow
Rochester, George Ernest
Grey Shadow series (1)
Grey shapes
Mann, Jack
Gregory George Gordon Green series (2)
Grey sombrero
Fry, Pete
Pete Fry series (3)
Grey Star the wizard
Page, Ian
World of Lone Wolf series (1)
Grey stranger
Crane, Frances
Pat and Jean Abbott series (22)
Grey terror
Landon, Herman
Gray Phantom series (3)
Greycliff girld' great adventure
Grove, Harriet Pyne
Greycliff girls series (7)
Greycliff girls in camp
Grove, Harriet Pyne
Greycliff girls series (4)
Greycliff girls in Georgia
Grove, Harriet Pyne
Greycliff girls series (8)
Greycliff girls ranching
Grove, Harriet Pyne
Greycliff girls series (6)
Greycliff heroines
Grove, Harriet Pyne
Greycliff girls series (5)
Greycliff wings
Grove, Harriet Pyne
Greycliff girls series (3)
Greycourt
Eastways, W W
Greycourt series (1)
Greyfax Grimwald
Hancock, Niel
Circle of light series (1)
Greyhawk adventures
Ward, James Michael
Advanced dungeons and dragons adventure gamebook series (15)
Greyhawk series (7)
Greyhouse days
Bell, Robert Stanly Warren
Greyhouse series (4)
Greykin a squirrel
Rutley, Cecily Marianne
Tales of the wild folk series (4)
Greylady
Morwood, Peter
Clan wars series (1)
Greymarsh
Rees, Arthur John
Colwin Grey series (3)
Greystone heritage
Bronte, Louisa
Greystone Tavern series (6)
Greystone Tavern
Bronte, Louisa
Greystone Tavern series (1)
Grichka and Brother Bear
Guillot, Rene
Grichka series (2)
Grichka and the wolves
Guillot, Rene
Grichka series (2)
Gridiron superstars
Gutman, Bill
Modern superstars series (9)
Grief ago
Maynard, Nan
Katheryn and Gaynor Scarlett series (2)
Grief forgotten
Finn, Ralph Leslie
Aldgate series (2)
Grievous sin
Kellerman, Faye
Sergeant Peter Decker and Rina Lazarus series (6)
Griff and Tommy
Griffiths, John
Griff and Tommy series (1)
Griff and Tommy and the golden image
Griffiths, John
Griff and Tommy series (2)
Griffin and Sabine
Bantock, Nick
Griffin Moss and Sabine Stroheim trilogy (1)
Griffith case
Bentley, John
Sir Richard Herrivell series (2)
Griffon's nest
Levin, Betty
Claudia and Evan trilogy (2)
Grig
Creswell, Harry Bulkeley
Honeywood series (3)
Grig in retirement
Creswell, Harry Bulkeley
Honeywood series (4)
Grim caretaker
Ascher, Eugene
Lucian Carolus series (3)
Grim Chancery
Mills, Woosnam
John Melrose series (1)
Grim game
Horler, Sydney
Sir Harker Bellamy series (5)
Tiger Standish series (4)
Grim glory
Mant, Gilbert
War reminiscences series (1)
Grim joker
Verner, Gerald
Superintendent Robert Budd series (5)
Grim maiden
Flynn, Brian
Anthony Bathurst series (30)
Grim pickings
Rowe, Jennifer
Verity Birdwood series (1)
Grim rehearsal
Fenisong, Ruth
Captain Gridley Nelson series (5)
Grim smile of the Five Towns
Bennett, Arnold
Tales of the Five Towns series (2)
Grim souvenir
Rowland, John
Inspector Shelley series (15)
Grim vengeance
Connington, John Jervis
Sir Clinton Driffield series (5)
Grime and punishment
Churchill, Jill
Jane Jeffry series (1)
Grimkie
Abbott, Jacob
Florence series (2)
Gringo guns
Benteen, John
Neal Fargo series (20)
Field, Peter
Powder Valley series (3)
Gringol weed
Buffery, Judith
Star lords series (4)
Gringolo
Koenig, Lilli
Kiki series (1)
Grinning pig
Lombard, Nap
Lord Winterstone series (2)
Grip of honor
Brady, Cyrus Townsend
John Paul Jones series (1)
Grip of the Four
Cross, Mark
Daphne Wrayne and her Four Adjusters series (3)
Grip of the law
Bobin, John William
Sexton Blake series (7)
Grishka and the bear
Guillot, Rene
Grichka series (1)
Grisly wife
Hall, Rodney
Yandilli trilogy (2)
Gristmill
Kalman, Bobbie
Historic communities series (1)
Grizzly man
Sharpe, Jon
Trailsman series (40)
Grizzly pass
Knott, William Cecil
Golden Hawk series (3)
Grizzly trail
Moffat, Gwen
Miss Melinda Pink series (8)
Groaning spinney
Mitchell, Gladys
Dame Beatrice Bradley series (23)
Groa's other eye
Schmidt, Dennis
Twilight of the gods trilogy (2)
Groceryman and Peck's bad boy
Peck, George Wilbur
Peck's bad boy series (2)
Grococo
Marokvia, Mireille
Ann and Paul series (3)
Groggs' day out
Bentley, Anne
Groggs series (2)
Groggs have a wonderful summer
Bentley, Anne
Groggs series (1)
Groosham Grange
Horowitz, Anthony
Groosham Grange series (1)
Grootka
Jackson, Jon Anthony
Sergeant Fang Mulheisen series (3)

Groovy way to die
Deming, Richard
Mod Squad series (2)
Grope carries on
Mann, Francis Oscar
Albert Grope series (2)
Gross carriage of justice
Fish, Robert Lloyd
Murder League series (3)
Gross purposes
Ripley, Karen
Indiana Jones series (9)
Ground for suspicion
Burton, Miles
Inspector Arnold and Desmond Merrion series (41)
Ground money
Burns, Rex
Gabriel Wager series (7)
Ground zero
Alexander, David
Phoenix series (2)
Ground Zero
Helm, Eric
Ground Zero series (1)
Ground zero
Murphy, Warren Burton
Destroyer series (84)
Murray, Will
Destroyer series (84)
Grounded!
Claremont, Chris
FirstFlight series (2)
Grounds for murder
Van Urk, Virginia
Tom Craig series (2)
Groundwater
Hoff, Mary
Our endangered planet series (1)
Group of noble dames
Hardy, Thomas
Romances and fantasies series (5)
Grouse Moor murder
Ferguson, John
Francis Macnab series (4)
Grouse Moor mystery
Ferguson, John
Francis Macnab series (4)
Grouser investigates
Brooks, Edwy Searles
Inspector William Beeke series (2)
Grove of doom
Grant, Maxwell
Shadow series (37)
Grover
Cleaver, Vera
Ellen Grae series (3)
Grow old along with me
Stuart-Wortley, Violet
Life without theory series (2)
Growing
Woolf, Leonard
Sowing and growing series (2)
Growing boy
Roberts, Cecil
Sunshine and shadow series (1)
Growing concern
Stuart, Ian
David Grierson series (5)
Growing pains
Miller, Hugh
Teen Eastenders series (2)
Quin-Harkin, Janet
Toni Redmond and Jill Gardner series (7)
Zach, Cheryl
Smyth versus Smith series (6)
Growing pains of Adrian Mole
Townsend, Sue
Adrian Mole series (2)
Growing season
Olsen, Violet
Marie Carlsen series (1)
Growing up
Baker, Russell
Good times series (1)
Thirkell, Angela
Barsetshire series (12)
Growing up in a London village
Wilmott, Phyllis
Green girl series (1)
Growing up in the Gorbals
Glasser, Ralph
Gorbals trilogy (1)
Growing up in Wood Street
Allan, Mabel Esther
Wood Street series (7)
Growing up to praise God
Beers, Victor Gilbert
Growing up series (3)
Growing up wild
Freedman, Russell
How animals series (2)
Growing up with God's friends
Beers, Victor Gilbert
Growing up series (4)
Growing up with Jesus
Beers, Victor Gilbert
Growing up series (1)
Growing up with my family
Beers, Victor Gilbert
Growing up series (2)
Growing up with the Grapers
Corbett, Elizabeth
Graper girls series (3)
Growing wild
Miller, Hugh
Eastenders series (8)
Growing years
Winn, Godfrey
Infirm glory series (1)
Growth of danger
Stark, Freya
Traveller's letters series (3)
Growth of the Spanish Inquisition
Plaidy, Jean
Spanish Inquisition trilogy (2)
Grub-and-Stakers house a haunt
Craig, Alisa
Osbert Monk series (5)
Grub-and-Stakers move a mountain
Craig, Alisa
Osbert Monk series (1)
Grub-and-Stakers pinch a poke
Craig, Alisa
Osbert Monk series (3)
Grub-and-Stakers quilt a bee
Craig, Alisa
Osbert Monk series (2)
Grub-and-Stakers spin a yarn
Craig, Alisa
Osbert Monk series (4)
Grudge
Hitchens, Dolores
John Farrel series (2)
Gruesome tide
Collenette, Eric J
Ben Grant series (1)
Gruffins
Cosgrove, Stephen Edward
Snuffin chronicles series (4)
Grug
Prior, Ted
Grug series (1)
Grug and his bicycle
Prior, Ted
Grug series (13)
Grug and his garden
Prior, Ted
Grug series (4)
Grug and his kite
Prior, Ted
Grug series (23)
Grug and his music
Prior, Ted
Grug series (20)
Grug and the big red apple
Prior, Ted
Grug series (2)
Grug and the green paint
Prior, Ted
Grug series (3)
Grug and the rainbow
Prior, Ted
Grug series (6)
Grug at the beach
Prior, Ted
Grug series (12)
Grug at the snow
Prior, Ted
Grug series (15)
Grug at the zoo
Prior, Ted
Grug series (16)
Grug builds a boat
Prior, Ted
Grug series (22)
Grug builds a car
Prior, Ted
Grug series (17)
Grug goes fishing
Prior, Ted
Grug series (10)
Grug goes shopping
Prior, Ted
Grug series (24)
Grug goes to school
Prior, Ted
Grug series (11)
Grug has a birthday
Prior, Ted
Grug series (9)
Grug in the playground
Prior, Ted
Grug series (8)
Grug learns to cook
Prior, Ted
Grug series (19)
Grug learns to dance
Prior, Ted
Grug series (21)
Grug learns to swim
Prior, Ted
Grug series (5)
Grug meets Snoot
Prior, Ted
Grug series (7)
Grug plays cricket
Prior, Ted
Grug series (18)
Grug plays soccer
Prior, Ted
Grug series (14)
Grumble day
Green, Kate
Fossil family tales series (5)
Grump and the hairy mammoth
Sampson, Derek
Grump series (1)
Grump strikes back
Sampson, Derek
Grump series (2)
Grumpy pumpkins
Delton, Judy
Pee wee scout series (5)
Grunt goes to school
Salmon, Michael
Scaredy monsters series (5)
Grunt, the monster who wouldn't eat his vegetables
Salmon, Michael
Scaredy monsters series (2)
Grunts go on a picnic
Selway, Martina
Grunts series (2)
Grunts, what a day!
Selway, Martina
Grunts series (1)
Grunty the pig
Beaman, Sydney George Hulme
Out of the ark series (3)
Gryphon in glory
Norton, Andre
High Hallack series (5)
Witch World series (13)
Gryphon's eyrie
Norton, Andre
High Hallack series (6)
Witch World series (17)
GT challenge
Speed, Eric
Wynn and Lonny racing series (3)
Guadalajara
Hunt, Everette Howard
Jack Novak series (2)
Guadaloupe caper
Halliday, Brett
Mike Shayne stories series (3)
Guaranteed to fade
Bagby, George
Inspector Schmidt series (44)
Guard against dishonor
Green, Simon
Hawk and Fisher series (5)
Guard within
Ferguson, Sarah
Guard within series (2)
Guardian
Konvitz, Jeffrey
Sentinel series (2)
Guardian Angel
Cohen, Anthea
Nurse Agnes Carmichael series (5)
Guardian angel
Holmes, Oliver Wendell
Heredity series (2)
Paretsky, Sara
V I Warshawski series (7)
Guardian Angels
Norman, Mick
Gerry Vinson series (3)
Guardian honour
Bancroft, John
James Steele series (1)
Guardian in black
Jones, G Wayman
Black Bat series (20)
Guardian of death
Grant, Maxwell
Shadow series (258)
Guardian of Isis
Hughes, Monica
Isis trilogy (2)
Guardian of Rannoch
Vanner, Lyn
Rannoch series (2)
Guardian of the Reef
Hallard, Peter
Con and Ginty series (3)
Guardian strikes
North, David
Time warriors series (3)
Guardians
Austin, Richard
Guardians series (1)
Baker, William Howard
Guardians series (1)
Richard Quintain series (10)
Mahr, Kurt
Perry Rhodan series (58)
Shillitoe, Tony
Andrakis trilogy (1)
Woodruff, Philip
Men who ruled India series (2)
Guardians of the Abbey
Oxenham, Elsie J
Abbey girls second generation series (7)
Guardians of the coral throne
Lord, Jeffrey
Richard Blade series (20)
Guardians of the gate
Mooney, Brian
Cthulhu Mythos series (4)
Guardians of the house
Boston, Lucy Maria
Green Knowe series (6)
Guardians of the Singreale
Miller, Calvin
Singreale trilogy (1)
Guardians of the tall stones
Caldecott, Moyra
Sacred stones series (3)
Guardians of the treasure
Sapper
Jim Maitland series (2)
Guardians of the West
Eddings, David
Malloreon series (1)
Guardians of time
Anderson, Poul
Time Patrol series (1)
Guarding his goal
Barbour, Ralph Henry
Yardley Hall series (7)
Guarding the skies
Barker, Dennis
People of the forces trilogy (3)
Guards, guards!
Pratchett, Terry
Discworld series (8)
Guardsman of Gor
Norman, John
Tarl Cabot series (16)
Guatemala gunman
Thorne, Ramsay
Captain Gringo series (24)
Gub-Gub's book
Lofting, Hugh
Doctor Dolittle series (12)
Gudrid the Fair
Hewlett, Maurice
Sagas retold series (4)
Guerilla
Slade, Jack
Lassiter series (8)
Guerilla games
Pendleton, Don
Phoenix Force series (2)
Guerilla tactics
Idriess, Ion Llewellyn
Australian guerilla series (3)
Guermantes way, part one
Proust, Marcel
Remembrance of things past series (5)
Guermantes way, part two
Proust, Marcel
Remembrance of things past series (6)
Guernsey man
Parkinson, Cyril Northcote
Richard Delancey series (6)
Guerra
Neumann, Alfred
Carbonari revolt series (2)
Guerrilla attack
Hart, Jon
Mercenaries series (4)
Guess again
Murphy, Jim
Weird and wacky inventions series (2)
Guest and his going
Newby, Percy Howard
Eric Blainey series (3)
Guest with the scythe
Lane, Gret
John Barrin series (7)
Kate Marsh series (8)
Guests arrive
Roberts, Cecil
Pilgrim Cottage series (2)
Guests at the beech tree
Lynch, Patricia
Brogeen the leprechaun series (14)
Guide
Narayan, Rasipuram Krishnaswami
Malgudi series (8)
Guide to the Commonwealth
Goodwin, Michael
Flinx of the Commonwealth series (6)
Guidelines
Helm, Eric
Ground Zero series (8)
Guild
Gorman, Edward
Leo Guild series (1)
Guillotine
Logan, Mark
Nicholas Minnett series (2)
Guilt edged
Burley, William John
Superintendent Charles Wycliffe series (3)
Guilt-edged
Thayer, Lee
Peter Clancy series (49)
Guilt-edged cage
Brown, Carter
Andy Kane series (2)
Guilt edged frame
Kane, Frank
Johnny Liddell series (27)
Guilt-edged ivory
Egan, Doris
Gate of ivory series (3)
Guilt-edged murder
Thayer, Lee
Peter Clancy series (49)
Guilt for innocence
Franklin, Charles
Inspector Jim Burgess series (1)
Guilt is plain
Frome, David
Evan Pinkerton series (9)
Guilt is where you find it
Thayer, Lee
Peter Clancy series (55)
Guilt of the brass thieves
Wirt, Mildred Augustine
Penny Parker series (13)
Guilt on the lily
Ormerod, Roger
Richard Patton series (6)
Guilt without proof
Alding, Peter
C.I.D. Room series (4)
Guilty
Hoh, Diane
Nightmare Hall series (6)
Thayer, Lee
Peter Clancy series (29)
Guilty accuser
Livingston, Armstrong
Peter Creighton series (4)
Guilty as hell
Halliday, Brett
Michael Shayne series (57)
Guilty, be damned!
Barrett, Geoffrey John
Inspector Blessingay series (2)
Guilty, but insane
Stuart, Donald
Sexton Blake series (774)
Guilty but not insane
Lenehan, John Christopher
Charlie Ryan series (4)
Guilty bystander
Brett, Mike
Sam Dakkers series (1)
Miller, Wade
Lieutenant Austin Clapp series (2)
Max Thursday series (1)
Guilty conscience
Underwood, Michael
Rosa Epton series (17)
Guilty governor
Carter, Nicholas
Nicholas Carter series (129)
Guilty head
Gary, Romain
Genghis Cohn series (2)
Guilty knowledge
Grant-Adamson, Lesley
Rain Morgan series (3)

Gunfighter Jory
Bass, Milton R
Jory series (4)
Gunfighters
Broome, H B
Tom English series (2)
Cotton, Donald
Doctor Who series (101)
Willoughby, Lee Davis
Making of America series (22)
Gunfighters' Hollow
Elton, Wallace
Jud Walton series (4)
Gunfighter's showdown
Hardin, J D
Raider series (21)
Gunfighter's trail
Kozlow, Mark J
Chris Devlin series (1)
Gunfire at Spanish Rock
Hardin, J D
Raider and Doc series (16)
Gunfire land
Cole, Jackson
Jim Hatfield series (60)
Gunga Sahib
Mundy, Talbot
Chullunder Ghose series (4)
Gunhawk
Reno, Bill
Badge series (19)
Gunloose
Hunter, Neil
Brand series (9)
Gunman from Tulluco
Young, Gordon Ray
Red Clark series (11)
Gunman winter
Rountree, Owen
Jim Cord series (4)
Gunman's choice
Slaughter, Jim
Boone Helm series (4)
Gunman's gamble
Bickham, Jack Miles
John Campbell and Clayton Hartung series (1)
Gunman's holiday
Elton, Wallace
Jud Walton series (2)
Gardner, Jerome
Dripspring series (1)
Gunman's inheritance
Masterson, Louis
Morgan Kane series (10)
Gunmen can't hide
Bickham, Jack Miles
John Campbell and Clayton Hartung series (5)
Gunmen's grave
Siegel, Scott
Warhunter series (2)
Gunmetal justice
Hart, Matthew S
Cody's law series (1)
Gunner Asch goes to war
Kirst, Hans Hellmut
Gunner Asch series (2)
Gunner Kelly
Price, Anthony
Doctor David Audley and Jack Butler series (13)
Gunners
Teed, George Hamilton
Sexton Blake series (593)
Gunning in England
Elliott, William James
Ed Gunning series (4)
Gunnison Butte
Slaughter, Jim
Boone Helm series (1)
Gunplay at Hobb's Hole
Logan, Jake
John Slocum series (77)
Gunpoint
Dalton, Kit
Buckskin series (13)
Gunpowder Alley
Rowland, John
Inspector Shelley series (12)
Gunpowder god
Piper, Horace Beam
Lord Kalvan series (1)
Paratime police series (1)
Gunpowder trail
Hawkins, Clint
Saddletramp series (3)
Gunpowder, treason and plot
Field, Moira
Inspector Flower series (2)
Guns across the Pecos
Cole, Jackson
Jim Hatfield series (76)
Guns across the river
Sandon, J D
Gringos series (1)
Guns across the Rockies
Grover, Marshall
Larry and Stretch series (109)
Guns along the Arrowhead
Floren, Lee
Judge Lemanuel Bates and Tobacco Jones series (8)
Guns along the Brazo
Bowden, Jim
Dan McCoy series (9)
Guns along the river
Hobart, Donald Bayne
Masked Rider and Blue Hawk series (21)
Guns along the Ruthless
Cody, Stetson
Cactus Clancy series (7)
Guns along the Yellowstone
Lomax, Bliss
Yellowstone series (1)
Guns and gold
Dawson, Clay
Long Rider series (25)
Guns and snowshoes
Bonehill, Ralph
Boy hunters series (2)
Guns at Buzzard Bend
Hardin, J D
Raider and Doc series (57)
Guns at Cassino
Kessler, Leo
Wotan series (4)
Guns at Chinooga Peak
Jons, Hal
Marshal Carl Travis series (3)
Guns at Fortune Ranch
Buckman, Sam
Storm Jackson series (1)
Guns at Goliad
Richmond, Roe
Lashtrow series (4)
Guns at Lone Star
Henderson, Colt
Lone Rider series (1)
Guns at Salt Flats
Winstan, Matt
Reuben Brown series (12)
Guns at twilight
Scofield, Jonathan
Freedom fighters series (4)
Guns blaze at noon
Nickson, Arthur
Rusty Hines series (5)
Guns don't argue
Roberts, J R
Gunsmith series (112)
Guns for Congo
Macarthur, David Wilson
Larry Pearson series (3)
Guns for Garcia
Thorne, Ramsay
Captain Gringo series (36)
Guns for Grizzly Flat
Field, Peter
Powder Valley series (56)
Guns for hire
Scott, Bradford
Walt Slade series (61)
Guns for Silver Rose
Hogan, Ray
Shawn Starbuck series (24)
Guns for the ladies
Grover, Marshall
Larry and Stretch series (131)
Guns from Powder Valley
Field, Peter
Powder Valley series (13)
Guns in the desert
Netton, Budleigh
Derek Carrington series (1)
Guns in the night
Edson, John Thomas
Floating Outfit series (61)
Guns in the saddle
Field, Peter
Powder Valley series (38)
Guns of Abilene
Roberts, J R
Gunsmith series (4)
Guns of arrest
McCutchan, Philip
Lieutenant Saint Vincent Halfhyde series (3)
Guns of Avalon
Zelazny, Roger
Kingdom of Amber series (2)
Guns of Bang Town
Scott, Bradford
Walt Slade series (44)
Guns of Black Heart
Hanson, Victor Joseph
Amos Crowle series (3)
Guns of Bull Run
Altsheler, Joseph Alexander
Civil War series (1)
Guns of darkness
Pournelle, Jerry
There will be war series (6)
Guns of Dragonard
Gilchrist, Rupert
Dragonard series (6)
Guns of Durango
Cameron, Lou
Doc Travis trilogy (3)
Guns of El Dorado
Hardin, J D
Raider series (4)
Guns of El Gato
Cole, Jackson
Jim Hatfield series (34)
Guns of Europe
Altsheler, Joseph Alexander
World War trilogy (1)
Guns of Everblack
Scheer, Karl Herbert
Perry Rhodan series (126)
Guns of Fort Griffin
Cole, Jackson
Jim Hatfield series (87)
Guns of greed
McCoy, Marshall
Nevada Jim series (42)
Guns of honor
Perry, Steve
Stellar rangers series (2)
Guns of Hungry Horse
Sharpe, Jon
Trailsman series (56)
Guns of justice
Jons, Hal
Marshal Carl Travis series (1)
Guns of liberty
Newcomb, Kerry
McQueen family series (1)
Guns of Mazatlan
Parker, Lee
Donovan's Devils series (3)
Guns of Mist River
Cole, Jackson
Jim Hatfield series (9)
Guns of Montana
Floren, Lee
Judge Lemanuel Bates and Tobacco Jones series (5)
Guns of Morgette
Boyer, Glenn G
Dolf Morgette series (1)
Guns of Navarone
Maclean, Alistair
Navarone series (1)
Guns of Palembang
McCurtin, Peter
Jim Rainey series (4)
Guns of Shiloh
Altsheler, Joseph Alexander
Civil War series (2)
Guns of South Pass
Logan, Jake
John Slocum series (63)
Guns of Stingaree
Hogan, Ray
Shawn Starbuck series (12)
Guns of summer
Paine, Lauran
Sheridan Township series (1)
Slaughter, Jim
Boone Helm series (7)
Guns of Sunset Mesa
Shane, Steve
Lone Star Kid series (3)
Guns of Taos
Martin, Cort
Jared Bolt series (4)
Guns of the Alamo
Scott, Bradford
Walt Slade series (28)
Guns of the Arrowhead
Young, Gordon Ray
Red Clark series (3)
Guns of the big hills
Hobart, Donald Bayne
Masked Rider and Blue Hawk series (11)
Guns of the clan
Hopson, William L
Masked Rider and Blue Hawk series (19)
Guns of the gods
Mundy, Talbot
Indian trilogy (1)
Guns of the lawless
Borg, Jack
Hogleg Bailey series (17)
Guns of the Reaper
Holmes, Bryan John
Reaper series (1)
Guns of the Sioux
Curry, Tom
Captain Mesquite series (5)
Guns of the valiant
Grover, Marshall
Larry and Stretch series (171)
Guns of vengeance
Cole, Jackson
Jim Hatfield series (44)
Guns on Eagle Creek
Henderson, Colt
Lone Rider series (2)
Guns roaring west
Field, Peter
Powder Valley series (43)
Guns to the Far East
Stuart, Vivian
Commander Philip Hazard series (8)
Guns wanted
Stanford, John Keith
Lieutenant-Colonel James Gore-Bunbury series (1)
Gunshot Crossing
Johnstone, William Wallace
Blood bond series (3)
Gunshot Grand Prix
Rutherford, Douglas
Chequered flag series (1)
Gunsight
Gruber, Frank
Historical Western series (3)
Gunsight Gap
LeBeau, Roy
Buckskin series (5)
Gunsight Range
Macdonald, William Colt
Gregory Quist series (2)
Gunsight showdown
Scott, Bradford
Walt Slade series (40)
Gunslammer
Hayes, Ralph Eugene
O'Brien, Buffalo Hunter series (1)
Gunslick
Scott, Bradford
Walt Slade series (24)
Gunslick code
Cody, Stetson
Cactus Clancy series (5)
Gunslick gambler
Winstan, Matt
Reuben Brown series (2)
Gunslinger
King, Stephen
Dark tower trilogy (1)
Gunslinger's range
Cole, Jackson
Jim Hatfield series (43)
Gunsmoke
Stratton, Chris
Gunsmoke series (4)
Gunsmoke and gold
Johnstone, William Wallace
Blood bond series (4)
Gunsmoke country
Hobart, Donald Bayne
Masked Rider and Blue Hawk series (16)
Gunsmoke empire
Cole, Jackson
Jim Hatfield series (78)
Gunsmoke feud
Borg, Jack
Hogleg Bailey series (8)
Gunsmoke for McAllister
Chisholm, Matt
Rem McAllister series (16)
Gunsmoke Gorge
Dalton, Kit
Buckskin series (17)
Gunsmoke Gulch
Sharpe, Jon
Trailsman series (107)
Gunsmoke in her eyes
Janson, Hank
Hank Janson series (11)
Gunsmoke in Nevada
Arthur, Burt
Johnny Canavan series (4)
Gunsmoke in Utopia
Grover, Marshall
Larry and Stretch series (124)
Gunsmoke lawyer
Floren, Lee
Buckshot McKee and Tortilla Joe series (4)
Gunsmoke on the iron trail
Winstan, Matt
Reuben Brown series (6)
Gunsmoke on the Rio Grande
Scott, Bradford
Walt Slade series (38)
Gunsmoke over Alba
Dower, Penn
Marshal Bret Malone series (2)
Gunsmoke over Tumbling T
Tyler, Clarke
Clint Lacey series (3)
Gunsmoke over Utah
Shappiro, Herbert
Mustang Marshal series (7)
Gunsmoke River
Rountree, Owen
Jim Cord series (7)
Gunsmoke talk
Scott, Bradford
Walt Slade series (54)
Gunsmoke thunder
Edson, John Thomas
Floating Outfit series (56)
Gunsmoke trail
Cole, Jackson
Jim Hatfield series (24)
Gunstock
LeBeau, Roy
Buckskin series (2)
Gunston Cotton, Secret Service agent
Grayson, Rupert
Gun Cotton series (1)
Gunther heritage heritage
Bronte, Louisa
American dynasty series (3)
Guntown
Cole, Jackson
Jim Hatfield series (21)
Guntrap Trail
Smith, Ford
Dark Knight series (4)
Guntz
Norman, Frank
Bang to rights series (4)
Gupta's Christmas
Dicks, Terrance
Ask Oliver series (6)
Gurney married
Hook, Theodore Edward
Gilbert Gurney series (2)
Gurney's release
Llewellyn, Sam
George Le Fanu Gurney trilogy (3)
Gurney's revenge
Llewellyn, Sam
George Le Fanu Gurney trilogy (1)
Gurney's reward
Llewellyn, Sam
George Le Fanu Gurney trilogy (2)
Gus and Gilly
Anson, Brian
Gus and Gilly series (1)
Gus and the baby ghost
Thayer, Jane
Gus series (4)
Gus loved his happy home
Thayer, Jane
Gus series (8)
Gus Tomlins
Anthony, Frank Sheldon
Gus Tomlins series (4)
Gus was a Christmas ghost
Thayer, Jane
Gus series (3)
Gus was a friendly ghost
Thayer, Jane
Gus series (1)
Gus was a gorgeous ghost
Thayer, Jane
Gus series (6)
Gus was a Mexican ghost
Thayer, Jane
Gus series (5)
Gus was a real dumb ghost
Thayer, Jane
Gus series (7)
Gustave Adolf and the Thirty Years' War
Topelius, Zacharias
Surgeon's stories series (1)
Gut shot
McCoy, Duff
Jeb Cutter series (2)
Gutenberg murders
Bristow, Gwen
Wade series (1)
Guts and glory
Stine, George Harry
Warbots series (10)

Gutshot
Slade, Jack
Lassiter series (11)
Guv'nor
Wallace, Edgar
Mister J G Reeder series (5)
Guv'nor, and other stories
Wallace, Edgar
Mister J G Reeder series (5)
Guy and Pauline
Mackenzie, Compton
Sinister Street series (2)
Guy Fawkes file
Birt, David
Stuarts series (1)
Guy Fawkes murder
Lester, Edward Castellain
Nathaniel Moody series (1)
Guy Tresillian's fate
Lewis, Harriet
Tresillian series (2)
Guys, dating and other disasters
Erlbach, Arlene
Henny series (1)
Gwen John sculpture
Malcolm, John
Tim Simpson series (3)
Gwenda's friend from home
Batchelor, Margaret
Gwenda series (2)
Gwendolen
Anonymous
Daniel Deronda series (2)
Gwynett of Thornhaugh
Hayes, Frederick William
Gwynett trilogy (2)
Gwythyn clay mystery
Poole, Michael
Freddie Browne and Jim Fanshaw series (6)
Gymkhana trek
Packer, Jo
Pepper series (2)
Gymnast commandoes
Levy, Elizabeth
Gymnasts series (17)
Gymnast Gilly the champ
Aykroyd, Peter
Gymnast Gilly series (3)
Gymnast Gilly the dancer
Aykroyd, Peter
Gymnast Gilly series (2)
Gymnast Gilly the expert
Aykroyd, Peter
Gymnast Gilly series (4)
Gymnast Gilly the novice
Aykroyd, Peter
Gymnast Gilly series (1)
Gymnasts's gift
Levy, Elizabeth
Gymnasts series (20)
Gypsies don't have them
Wilson, Gertrude Mary
Inspector Lovick series (20)
Gypsy and Nimblefoot
Wagner, Sharon
Gypsy series (2)
Gypsy Breynton
Phelps, Elizabeth Stuart Ward
Gypsy Breynton series (1)
Gypsy from nowhere
Wagner, Sharon
Gypsy series (1)
Gypsy goes to the country
Leyland, Mal
Kerry series (2)
Gypsy hedgehogs
Uttley, Alison
Little Brown Mouse series (7)
Gypsy in amber
Smith, Martin Cruz
Roman Grey series (1)
Gypsy vengeance
Grant, Maxwell
Shadow series (60)
Gypsy's animal alphabet
Leyland, Mal
Kerry series (2)
Gypsy's cousin Joy
Phelps, Elizabeth Stuart Ward
Gypsy Breynton series (3)
Gypsy's sowing and reaping
Phelps, Elizabeth Stuart Ward
Gypsy Breynton series (2)
Gypsy's year at golden Crescent
Phelps, Elizabeth Stuart Ward
Gypsy Breynton series (4)
Gyrth chalice mystery
Allingham, Margery
Albert Campion series (3)

H

H
Haire-Sargeant, Lin
Wuthering Heights series (3)
H as in hangman
Treat, Lawrence
Carl Wayward series (3)
H as in hunted
Treat, Lawrence
Jub Freeman series (2)
H is for homicide
Grafton, Sue
Kinsey Millhone series (8)
H M Corvette
Monsarrat, Nicholas
Corvette series (1)
H.M.S. Thule intercepts
Mars, Alastair
Royal Navy series (2)
H.M.S.Hero
Mackintosh, Ian
Warship series (2)
H, my name is Henley
Rudowsky, Colby
Slug series (2)
H.O.W.L. High
Leroe, Ellen Whitney
H.O.W.L. High series (1)
H.O.W.L. High goes bats!
Leroe, Ellen Whitney
H.O.W.L. High series (3)
Ha-ha case
Connington, John Jervis
Sir Clinton Driffield series (9)
Haakon's iron hand
Neilson, Eric
Haakon series (3)
Habit of fear
Davis, Dorothy Salisbury
Julie Hayes series (4)
Habit of loving
Thomson, June
Inspector Finch series (6)
Habsburg inheritance
Hamilton, Julia
Habsburg series (5)
Hacker
Martin, Lee
Deb Ralston series (7)
Hackett's bluff
Grover, Marshall
Larry and Stretch series (386)
Hackett's gold
Grover, Marshall
Larry and Stretch series (233)
Had any lately?
Conway, Troy
Coxeman series (12)
Had I but groaned
Brown, Carter
Larry Baker series (4)
Had we never loved
Veryan, Patricia
Tales of the jewelled men series (2)
Hades hello
Wright, Wade
Paul Cameron series (4)
Hadon of ancient Opar
Farmer, Philip Jose
Opar series (1)
Tarzan series (1)
Tarzan series (5)
Hadrian in the Orient
Lycett-Green, Candida
Hadrian series (2)
Hadrian's Wall
Birt, David
Roman Britain series (3)
Haesel, the slave
Forest, Dael
Roman world series (2)
Haffertee finds a place of his own
Perkins, Janet
Haffertee Hamster series (2)
Haffertee goes exploring
Perkins, Janet
Haffertee Hamster series (3)
Haffertee goes on holiday
Perkins, Janet
Haffertee Hamster series (7)
Haffertee goes to hospital
Perkins, Janet
Haffertee Hamster series (8)
Haffertee goes to school
Perkins, Janet
Haffertee Hamster series (5)
Haffertee Hamster
Perkins, Janet
Haffertee Hamster series (1)
Haffertee Hamster Diamond
Perkins, Janet
Haffertee Hamster series (1)
Haffertee Hamster's new house
Perkins, Janet
Haffertee Hamster series (2)
Haffertee starts school
Perkins, Janet
Haffertee Hamster series (5)
Haffertee's first Christmas
Perkins, Janet
Haffertee Hamster series (4)
Haffertee's first Easter
Perkins, Janet
Haffertee Hamster series (6)
Haffertee's new house
Perkins, Janet
Haffertee Hamster series (2)
Hag calls for help
Wood, Lorna
Hag Dowsabel series (3)
Hag in the castle
Wood, Lorna
Hag Dowsabel series (6)
Hag Wood
Shrog, J M
Bernard McFoy series (1)
Hagar again and again
Browne, Dik
Hagar the horrible series (45)
Hagar and the golden maiden
Browne, Dik
Hagar the horrible series (13)
Hagar at work
Browne, Dik
Hagar the horrible series (14)
Hagar hits the mark
Browne, Dik
Hagar the horrible series (24)
Hagar the horrible
Browne, Dik
Hagar the horrible series (1)
Hagar the horrible and the basilisk
Browne, Dik
Hagar the horrible series (5)
Hagar the horrible handyman special
Browne, Dik
Hagar the horrible series (52)
Hagar the horrible, number two
Browne, Dik
Hagar the horrible series (2)
Hagar the horrible tall tales
Browne, Dik
Hagar the horrible series (52)
Hagar the horrible's activity book
Browne, Dik
Hagar the horrible series (52)
Hagar the horrible's puzzlers
Browne, Dik
Hagar the horrible series (52)
Hagar the horrible's very nearly complete Viking handbook
Browne, Dik
Hagar the horrible series (52)
Hagar's knight out
Browne, Dik
Hagar the horrible series (25)
Haggard
Nicole, Christopher
Haggard trilogy (1)
Haggard's inheritance
Nicole, Christopher
Haggard trilogy (2)
Hags by starlight
Wood, Lorna
Hag Dowsabel series (7)
Hag's Nook
Carr, John Dickson
Doctor Gideon Fell series (1)
Hags on holiday
Wood, Lorna
Hag Dowsabel series (5)
Haiku for Hanae
Melville, James
Superintendent Tetsuo Otani series (11)
Hail for the hero!
Welsh, Ken
Hero series (1)
Hail, hail, the gangs all here!
McBain, Ed
Eighty Seventh Precinct series (25)
Hail McLean
Goodchild, George
Inspector McLean series (30)
Hail the conquering hero
Yerby, Frank
Costa Verde series (2)
Hail to the Chief
McBain, Ed
Eighty Seventh Precinct series (28)
Hail, Virginia!
Griffith, Helen Sherman
Virginia series (6)
Hailey Street murder
Jardine, Warwick
Sexton Blake series (762)
Hair of the dogma
O'Brien, Flann
Cruiskeen Lawn series (3)
Hair trigger kill
Majors, E B
Slaughter and Son series (3)
Hair's breadth
Thayer, Lee
Peter Clancy series (40)
Hairy book
Cole, Babette
Hairy book series (1)
Hairy horror trick
Corbett, Scott
Kerby Maxwell series (7)
Hairy Maclary from Donaldson's Dairy
Dodd, Lynley
Hairy Maclary series (1)
Hairy Maclary's bone
Dodd, Lynley
Hairy Maclary series (2)
Hairy Maclary's catterwaul caper
Dodd, Lynley
Hairy Maclary series (4)
Hairy Maclary's rumpus at the vet
Dodd, Lynley
Hairy Maclary series (5)
Hairy Maclary's scattercat
Dodd, Lynley
Hairy Maclary series (3)
Hairy Maclary's showbusiness
Dodd, Lynley
Hairy Maclary series (6)
Haitian vendetta
Smith, Don
Secret mission series (16)
Hajji Baba in England
Morier, James
Hajji Baba series (2)
Hakon of Rogen's Saga
Haugaard, Erik Christian
Hakon and Helga series (1)
Hal the hedgehog
Rutley, Cecily Marianne
Tales of the wild folk series (14)
Halberd, dream warrior
Saint Alcorn, Lloyd
Dream quest trilogy (1)
Halcyon drift
Stableford, Brian Michael
Star Pilot Grainger series (1)
Half a life
Barnes, James Strachey
Half a life series (1)
Half a life left
Barnes, James Strachey
Half a life series (2)
Half a sky
Lafferty, Raphael Aloysius
Coscuin chronicles series (4)
Half acre
Walsh, James Morgan
Colonel Ormiston series (9)
Half-angel
Lea, Fanny Heaslip
Half-angel series (2)
Half-back
Barbour, Ralph Henry
Hilton School trilogy (1)
Half breed
Edson, John Thomas
Floating Outfit series (16)
Half-breed
Hawk, Alex
Elfego O'Reilly series (2)
Half breed
Ladd, Justin
Abilene series (5)
Half breed's bride
Gentry, Georgina
Panorama of the old West series (10)
Half-caste
Murray, Andrew
Sexton Blake series (40)
Half-cold trail
Grover, Marshall
Larry and Stretch series (9)
Half-crown house
Ashton, Helen
Wilchester chronicles series (5)
Half days and patched pants
Colwell, Max
Mike series (1)
Half devil, half tiger
Fletcher, Robert James
Gilbert Davison series (1)
Half in earnest
Hine, Muriel
April Panhasard series (1)
Half magic
Eager, Edward
Magic series (1)
Half-mast for the Deemster
Bellairs, George
Detective Inspector Thomas Littlejohn series (21)
Half of my kingdom
Buckley, Eunice
Rex Anderson series (2)
Half-open door
Gray, Berkeley
Norman Conquest series (26)
Half-past human
Bass, T J
Hive series (1)
Half-past mortem
Saxon, John A
Sam Welpton series (2)
Half-price bear
Lindsay, Frances
Bim series (1)
Half round the world
Optic, Oliver
All-over-the-world series (10)
Half-seas over
Gilpatric, Guy
Mister Colin Andrew Macthrockle Glencannon series (2)
Half sisters
Carlson, Natalie Savage
Luvvy Savage series (1)
Half way
Roberts, Cecil
Half way series (1)
Half-term holiday
Pye, Virginia
Price family series (4)
Half way to murder
Troy, Simon
Inspector Smith series (2)
Halfhyde and the admiral
McCutchan, Philip
Lieutenant Saint Vincent Halfhyde series (15)
Halfhyde and the chain gangs
McCutchan, Philip
Lieutenant Saint Vincent Halfhyde series (12)
Halfhyde and the flag captain
McCutchan, Philip
Lieutenant Saint Vincent Halfhyde series (7)
Halfhyde and the fleet review
McCutchan, Philip
Lieutenant Saint Vincent Halfhyde series (16)
Halfhyde for the Queen
McCutchan, Philip
Lieutenant Saint Vincent Halfhyde series (5)
Halfhyde goes to war
McCutchan, Philip
Lieutenant Saint Vincent Halfhyde series (13)
Halfhyde line
McCutchan, Philip
Lieutenant Saint Vincent Halfhyde series (11)
Halfhyde on the Amazon
McCutchan, Philip
Lieutenant Saint Vincent Halfhyde series (14)
Halfhyde on the Yangtse
McCutchan, Philip
Lieutenant Saint Vincent Halfhyde series (8)
Halfhyde on Zanatu
McCutchan, Philip
Lieutenant Saint Vincent Halfhyde series (9)
Halfhyde ordered south
McCutchan, Philip
Lieutenant Saint Vincent Halfhyde series (6)
Halfhyde outward bound
McCutchan, Philip
Lieutenant Saint Vincent Halfhyde series (10)
Halfhyde to the narrows
McCutchan, Philip
Lieutenant Saint Vincent Halfhyde series (4)
Halfhyde's island
McCutchan, Philip
Lieutenant Saint Vincent Halfhyde series (2)

Halfling, and other stories
Brackett, Leigh
Eric John Stark series (6)
Halfling's gem
Salvatore, Robert Anthony
Icewind Dale trilogy (3)
Halfmen of O
Gee, Maurice
World of O trilogy (1)
Halfway around the world
Young, Gavin
Slow boats series (1)
Halfway house
Hewlett, Maurice
Sanchia and John Maxwell Senhouse series (1)
Queen, Ellery
Ellery Queen series (11)
Halfway to anywhere
Lindsay, Norman
Redheap trilogy (3)
Halfway to horror
Hume, David
Mick Cardby series (11)
Hall of the Mountain King
Tarr, Judith
Avaryan Rising trilogy (1)
Hall of whispers
Jefferies, Mike
Heirs to Gnarlsmyre series (2)
Hallersage sound
Townsend, John Rowe
Hallersage series (2)
Halliwell boys and the disappearing staircase
Palmer, Bernard
Halliwell boys series (2)
Halliwell boys and the missing film mystery
Palmer, Bernard
Halliwell boys series (6)
Halliwell boys and the mysterious treasure map
Palmer, Bernard
Halliwell boys series (5)
Halliwell boys on a dangerous voyage
Palmer, Bernard
Halliwell boys series (4)
Halliwell boys on a secret African safari
Palmer, Bernard
Halliwell boys series (8)
Halliwell boys on crusade
Palmer, Bernard
Halliwell boys series (1)
Halliwell boys on Forbidden Mountain
Palmer, Bernard
Halliwell boys series (7)
Halliwell boys on the secret expedition
Palmer, Bernard
Halliwell boys series (3)
Hallo, Aurora!
Vestly, Anna Catharina
Aurora series (1)
Hallo, how are you?
Watanabe, Shigeo
I can do it series (3)
Hallo, Little Mary Mouse
Blyton, Enid
Mary Mouse series (4)
Hallowed murder
Hart, Ellen
Jane Lawless series (1)
Halloween
Richards, Curtis
Halloween series (1)
Halloween candy mystery
Markham, Marion M
Dixon twins series (1)
Hallowe'en homicide
Thayer, Lee
Peter Clancy series (31)
Halloween howls
Maestro, Giulio
Halloween howls series (1)
Halloween II
Martin, Jack
Halloween series (2)
Halloween III
Martin, Jack
Halloween series (3)
Halloween IV
Grabowsky, Nicholas
Halloween series (4)
Halloween magic
Baker, James Webb
Magic series (3)
Halloween murder
Disney, Doris Miles
Jeff Dimarco series (4)
Halloween murders
Chance, John Newton
Jonathan Blake series (11)
Halloween mystery
Nixon, Joan Lowery
First read-alone mystery series (2)
Hallowe'en party
Christie, Agatha
Hercule Poirot series (35)
Mrs Ariadne Oliver series (7)
Halloween party
Stine, Robert Lawrence
Fear Street series (4)
Halloween treats
Haywood, Carolyn
Holiday series (3)
Halls of Ravenswood
Hall, Emily
Hall sisters series (2)
Mills, Anthony Reginald
Victorian girls series (2)
Halo
Hutten zum Stolzenberg, Bettina Riddle
Pam series (3)
Halo for nobody
Kane, Henry
Peter Chambers series (1)
Halo for Satan
Evans, John
Paul Pine series (2)
Halo highway
Bernard, Rafe
Invaders series (3)
Halo in blood
Evans, John
Paul Pine series (1)
Halo in brass
Evans, John
Paul Pine series (3)
Halo parade
James, Bill
Superintendent Colin Harpur series (3)
Halo solution
Neebel, Richard
Erik Chatham series (1)
Ham and the egg
Beaman, Sydney George Hulme
Out of the ark series (5)
Ham on rye
Bukowski, Charles
Henry Chinaski series (1)
Hamburg switch
Ross, Angus
Mark Farrow series (13)
Hamey the stranger
Keevil, John Joyce
Baldwin Hamey series (1)
Hamilton
Cookson, Catherine
Maisie Leviston series (1)
Hamilton, the hamster
Darby, Joan
Animal adventure series (10)
Hamlet
Faulkner, William
Sin and salvation series (7)
Snopes family trilogy (1)
Helm, Eric
Ground Zero series (14)
Hamlet had an uncle
Cabell, James Branch
Conquest series (2)
Hamlet problem
Jones, Bradshaw
Claude Ravel series (1)
Hamlet, revenge!
Innes, Michael
Sir John Appleby series (2)
Hamlet trap
Wilhelm, Kate
Charlie Miklejohn and Constance Leidl series (1)
Hamlet ultimatum
Sanders, Leonard
Clay Loomis series (2)
Hamlet warning
Sanders, Leonard
Clay Loomis series (1)
Hammer
Drake, David
Generals series (2)
Hammer and the horn
Friedman, Michael Jan
Vidar trilogy (1)
Hammer home
Comstock, Jarrod
These lawless worlds series (4)
Hammer Island
Styles, Showell
Sir Abercrombie Lewker series (3)
Hammer of doom
Everton, Francis
Detective Inspector Allport series (2)
Hammer of God
Demille, Nelson
Joe Ryker series (2)
Hammer of justice
Milne, Shirley
Detective Sergeant Steytler series (2)
Hammer of Mars
Murdock, Melinda Seabrooke
Martian wars trilogy (2)
Hammer of the gods
Kessler, Leo
Wotan series (6)
Hammer of the Scots
Plaidy, Jean
Plantagenet series (7)
Hammer of the sun
Rohan, Michael Scott
Winter of the world trilogy (3)
Hammer of Thor
Brown, Carter
Lieutenant Al Wheeler series (34)
Hammer the Toff
Creasey, John
Toff series (16)
Hammerhead
Cory, Desmond
Feramontov quintet (2)
Johnny Fedora series (13)
Davis, Gordon
Sergeant series (9)
Mayo, James
Charles Hood series (1)
Hammerhead Reef
Pendleton, Don
Mack Bolan series (82)
Hammerlocke
Barnao, Jack
John Locke series (1)
Hammer's horde
Grover, Marshall
Larry and Stretch series (196)
Hammer's Slammers
Drake, David
Hammer's Slammers series (1)
Hammersmith maggot
Mole, William
Casson Duker series (1)
Hammersmith murders
Frome, David
Evan Pinkerton series (1)
Hammett
Johnston, Terry Conrad
Plainsmen series (2)
Hammett homicides
Hammett, Dashiell
Continental Op series (5)
Hampstead mystery
Watson, John Reay
Crewe series (1)
Hampton heritage
Ellis, Julie
Caroline Hampton series (1)
Ellis, Odette
Hampton series (1)
Hampton women
Ellis, Julie
Caroline Hampton series (2)
Ellis, Odette
Hampton series (2)
Han Solo and the lost legacy
Daley, Brian
Luke Skywalker series (6)
Han Solo at Stars' End
Daley, Brian
Luke Skywalker series (3)
Han Solo's revenge
Daley, Brian
Luke Skywalker series (4)
Hand
Grant, Maxwell
Shadow series (144)
Hand and ring
Green, Anna Katharine
Ebenezer Gryce series (3)
Hand full of diamonds
Norwood, Victor George Charles
Man alone series (2)
Hand in glove
Marsh, Ngaio
Inspector Roderick Alleyn series (22)
Hand in the dark
Rees, Arthur John
David Colwyn series (2)
Hand in the glove
Stout, Rex
Dol Bonner series (1)
Hand me a crime
Russell, Charlotte Murray
Jane Amanda Edwards series (12)
Hand-me-down cup
Graeber, Charlotte Towner
Mister T and me series (2)
Hand of a killer
Seuffert, Muir
Mike Hubbard series (1)
Hand of chaos
Weis, Margaret
Death Gate series (5)
Hand of doom
Walsh, James Morgan
Inspector Quaile series (1)
Hand of Dracula
Lory, Robert
Dracula horror series (2)
Hand of Ethelberta
Hardy, Thomas
Novels of ingenuity series (2)
Hand of Fu-Manchu
Rohmer, Sax
Fu-Manchu series (3)
Hand of Ganz
Haiblum, Isidore
Siscoe and Block series (2)
Hand of horror
Jerome, Owen Fox
Philip Maccray series (1)
Hand of Justice
Duncan, Francis
Peter Justice series (5)
Hand of Kane
Howard, Robert Ervin
Solomon Kane series (1)
Hand of Mary Constable
Gallico, Paul
Alexander Hero series (2)
Hand of Michelangelo
Alexander, Sidney
Michelangelo Buonarotti trilogy (2)
Hand of Oberon
Zelazny, Roger
Kingdom of Amber series (4)
Hand of Seeta
Brandon, John Gordon
Inspector Patrick Aloysius McCarthy series (16)
Hand of Solange
Rippon, Marion
Inspector Maurice Ygrec series (1)
Hand of the Four
Cross, Mark
Daphne Wrayne and her Four Adjusters series (4)
Hand of the lion
Coker, Carolyn
Andrea Perkins series (3)
Hand of the Mafia
Baynes, Jack
Morocco Jones series (3)
Hand of vengeance
Desmond, Hugh
Alan Fraser series (2)
Hand of Zei
De Camp, Lyon Sprague
Krishna series (4)
Hand on the alibi
Bude, John
Inspector Meredith series (6)
Hand out
Rathbone, Julian
Colonel Nur Bey series (2)
Hand over hand
De Banke, Cecile
Hand over hand series (1)
Hand-picked for murder
Martin, Robert Lee
Jim Bennett series (8)
Hand-picked to die
Deming, Richard
Manville Moon series (2)
Hand-print mystery
Fowler, Sydney
Inspector Cleveland series (3)
Hand-reared boy
Aldiss, Brian Wilson
Horace Stubbs series (1)
Hand that hid in darkness
Graydon, William Murray
Sexton Blake series (125)
Hand that won
Carter, Nicholas
Nicholas Carter series (264)
Hand to hand
Carter, Nicholas
Nicholas Carter series (265)
Hand to hold, an opinion to reject
Guisewhite, Cathy
Cathy series (11)
Hand without mercy
Sandys, James
James Charlesworth series (2)
Handcuff wizard
Carter, Nicholas
Nicholas Carter series (380)
Handful of dominoes
Johnson, James Leonard
Code name Sebastian series (3)
Handful of sinners
Franklin, Charles
Grant Garfield series (19)
Handful of stars
Boreham, Frank William
Texts that made history series (2)
Stabenow, Dana
Second star series (2)
Handie
Abbott, Jacob
Rainbow and Lucky series (1)
Handle
Stark, Richard
Alan Grofield series (2)
Parker series (8)
Handle with care
Malone, Lucy
Two by two series (6)
Handle with fear
Dewey, Thomas Blanchard
Singer Batts series (4)
Handley Cross
Surtees, Robert Smith
Mister John Jorrocks series (2)
Handling your disagreements
Berry, Joy
Ready-set-grow series (21)
Handling your ups and downs
Berry, Joy
Ready-set-grow series (9)
Hands across the caviar
Thayer, Charles Wheeler
Caviar series (2)
Hands across the Pacific
Clune, Frank
Discovery series (15)
Hands in the dark
Grant, Maxwell
Shadow series (10)
Hands of Amos Crowle
Hanson, Victor Joseph
Amos Crowle series (4)
Hands of death
Colin, Aubrey
Inspector Bill Murray series (1)
Wood, Eric
Arnold Keene and Bernard Young series (2)
Hands of glory
Kangilaski, Jaan
Seeking sword series (2)
Hands of healing murder
D'Amato, Barbara
Doctor Garrett DeGraaf series (1)
Hands of, he's mine
Goudge, Eileen
Seniors series (7)
Hands of justice
Flynn, Brian
Anthony Bathurst series (51)
Hands of Pablo Santos
Sharp, Allen
Storytrails series (17)
Hands of the strangler
Roberts, J R
Gunsmith series (97)
Hands off Bulldog Drummond
Fairlie, Gerard
Bulldog Drummond series (15)
Hands off the lovely
Kane, Martin
Martin Kane series (3)
Hands unseen
Landon, Herman
Gray Phantom series (4)
Hands up!
Niven, Frederick
Lost Cabin Mine series (2)
Scott, Bradford
Walt Slade series (105)
Hands up at Jug Valley Juniors
Digby, Anne
Jug Valley Juniors series (3)
Hands up, Miss Seeton
Crane, Hamilton
Miss Emily Seeton series (12)
Handsome is that handsome does
Bradley, Mary Emily Neely
Proverb trilogy (2)
Handsome road
Bristow, Gwen
Louisiana trilogy (2)
Handsomest drowned man in the world
Garcia Marquez, Gabriel
Macondo series (1)

Handtalk
Charlip, Remy
Handtalk series (1)
Handtalk birthday
Charlip, Remy
Handtalk series (2)
Handwriting on the wall
Fox, David
Shadowers Inc. series (4)
Propper, Milton
Tommy Rankin series (13)
Handy Mandy in Oz
Thompson, Ruth Plumly
Oz series (30)
Handyman
Robertson, Stephen
Ryne Lanark series (4)
Hang Angel
Christian, Frederick H
Frank Angel series (6)
Hang by your neck
Kane, Henry
Peter Chambers series (3)
Hang dead Hawaiian style
Morgan, Patrick
Operation Hang Ten series (1)
Hang 'em all
Whitehead, David
Judge and Dury series (1)
Hang high, O'Shea
Clinton, Jeff
Wildcat O'Shea series (15)
Hang in there, Tumbleweeds!
Ryan, Tom K
Tumbleweeds series (6)
Hang loose
Chase, Glen
Cherry Delight series (18)
Copper, Basil
Mike Faraday series (34)
Hang McAllister
Chisholm, Matt
Rem McAllister series (22)
Hang Spur McCoy
Fletcher, Dirk
Spur McCoy series (15)
Hang the consequences
Meek, Margaret Reid Duncan
Lennox Kemp series (2)
Hang the little man
Creasey, John
Inspector Roger West series (31)
Hang-up kid
Brown, Carter
Rick Holman series (23)
Hanged for a sheep
Lockridge, Frances
Bill Wiegand series (4)
Mister and Mrs North series (6)
Hanged I'll be
Goyne, Richard
Paul Templeton series (5)
Hanged man
Dancer, J B
Lawmen series (5)
Hangfire Hill
LeBeau, Roy
Buckskin series (8)
Hanging
James, William M
Apache series (26)
McLaglen, John J
Herne the Hunter series (17)
Hanging at Whiskey Smith
Allen, Eric
Whiskey Smith series (2)
Hanging captain
Wade, Henry
Inspector Lott series (2)
Hanging doll murder
Ormerod, Roger
David Mallin and George Coe series (18)
Richard Patton series (1)
Hanging garden
Sherwood, John
Celia Grant series (9)
Hanging judge
Kelton, Elmer
Tales of Texas series (5)
Roberts, J R
Gunsmith series (106)
Hanging justice
Logan, Jake
John Slocum series (2)
Hanging moon
Ledd, Paul
Shelter Morgan series (2)
Hanging of Constance Hillier
Fowler, Sydney
Inspector Cleveland series (2)
Hanging on
Freedman, Russell
How animals series (3)
Hanging out with Cici
Pascal, Francine
Victoria Martin trilogy (1)
Hanging stones
Wellman, Manly Wade
Silver John series (5)
Hanging sword!
Soutar, Andrew
Phineas Spinnet series (1)
Hanging trail
Sharpe, Jon
Trailsman series (2)
Hanging tree
Knox, Bill
Inspector Colin Thane and Phil Moss series (18)
Hanging valley
Robinson, Peter
Chief Inspector Alan Banks series (4)
Hanging week
Gardner, Jerome
Hanging Judge series (7)
Hanging woman
Rhode, John
Doctor Lancelot Priestley series (11)
Roffman, Jan
Sergeant Ratlin series (1)
Hanging's too good
Thayer, Lee
Peter Clancy series (36)
Hangman
Ladd, Justin
Abilene series (6)
Slade, Jack
Lassiter series (23)
Verner, Gerald
Trevor Lowe series (4)
Hangman and the Ladies' League
Gardner, Jerome
Hanging Judge series (1)
Hangman for Paradise
Canon, Jack
Mike Paradise series (3)
Hangman rides tall
Chisholm, Matt
Rem McAllister series (4)
Hangman waits
Daniel, Roland
Buddy Mustard series (15)
Hangman's apprentice
Gardner, Jerome
Hanging Judge series (3)
Hangman's Creek
Braun, Matt
Luke Starbuck series (1)
Hangman's curfew
Mitchell, Gladys
Dame Beatrice Bradley series (12)
Hangman's ghost trick
Corbett, Scott
Kerby Maxwell series (12)
Hangman's hands
Wogan, Charles
Sebastian Stole series (1)
Hangman's handyman
Talbot, Hake
Rogan Kincaid series (1)
Hangman's harvest
Chaber, M E
Milo March series (1)
Hangman's hat
Ernst, Paul
Jim Ryan series (1)
Shirley Leighton and Bill Harper series (1)
Hangman's holiday
Sayers, Dorothy Leigh
Lord Peter Wimsey series (10)
Hangman's knot
Gask, Arthur
Gilbert Larose series (10)
McCurtin, Peter
Sundance series (33)
Hangman's law
Hardin, J D
Raider series (35)
Hangman's legacy
Wales, Mike
Leatherhand series (2)
Hangman's moon
Gribble, Leonard Reginald
Superintendent Anthony Slade series (18)
Hangman's noose
Bridges, Ben
Carter O'Brien series (4)
Hardin, J D
Raider and Doc series (26)
Mitchell, Gladys
Dame Beatrice Bradley series (29)
Hangman's root
Albert, Susan Wittig
China Bayles series (3)
Hangman's row
Stein, Aaron Marc
Matt Erridge series (21)
Hangman's Springs
Reese, John
Jefferson Hewitt series (6)
Hangman's territory
Bickham, Jack Miles
John Campbell and Clayton Hartung series (6)
Hangman's tide
Hilton, John Buxton
Superintendent Simon Kenworthy series (3)
Hangman's tie
Hale, Christopher
Lieutenant Bill French series (8)
Hangman's trail
Field, Peter
Powder Valley series (60)
Hangman's whip
Cain, Jackson
Torn Slater series (3)
Hangmen of Sleepy Valley
Dresser, Davis
Twister Malone series (2)
Hangmen's trail
Bowden, Jim
Cap Millett series (5)
Hangover Square
Hamilton, Patrick
Ernest Ralph Gorse series (1)
Hangrope fever
Grover, Marshall
Nevada Jim series (45)
Mason, Chuck
Lee Caton series (2)
Hangrope for Beaumont
Grover, Marshall
Larry and Stretch series (122)
Hangtown
Hunter, Neil
Bodie the Stalker series (5)
McCurtin, Peter
Carmody series (1)
Hangtown harlots
Martin, Cort
Jared Bolt series (12)
Hangtown hustle
Gentry, Buck
Eli Holten series (26)
Hangtown mistake
Kozlow, Mark J
Chris Devlin series (2)
Hangtree
Slaughter, Jim
Boone Helm series (8)
Hank Prank and hot Henrietta
Older, Jules
Hank Prank series (1)
Hank Prank in love
Older, Jules
Hank Prank series (2)
Hank the cowdog
Erickson, John R
Hank the cowdog series (1)
Hank Winton, smoke chaser
Atwater, Montgomery Meigs
Hank Winton series (1)
Hannah and the snowy highway
Stahl, Hilda
Best friends series (13)
Hannah and the special fourth of July
Stahl, Hilda
Best friends series (4)
Hannah Ann
Douglas, Amanda Minnie
Little girl series (2)
Hannah Fowler
Giles, Janice Holt
Fowler family series (2)
Hannah in North America
Hauxwell, Hannah
Daleswoman series (5)
Hannah of Kentucky
Otis, James
Pioneer series (1)
Hannah says foul play
Babcock, Dwight Vincent
Hannah Van Doren series (3)
Hannah, the complete story
Hauxwell, Hannah
Daleswoman series (5)
Hannah's dangerous mystery
Stahl, Hilda
Best friends series (12)
Hannah's North Country
Hauxwell, Hannah
Daleswoman series (5)
Hannibal and the bears
Baker, Margaret Joyce
Three bears series (2)
Hanoi
Carter, Nick
Nick Carter series (15)
Hanoi deathgrip
Buchanan, Jack
M.I.A. Hunter series (3)
Hanoi hellground
Lansing, John
Black Eagles series (1)
Hans Frost
Walpole, Hugh
London Group series (7)
Peter Westcott series (4)
Hanukkah
Drucker, Malka
Jewish holidays series (1)
Hapi and the forbidden island
Bermingham, Iris
Hapi series (2)
Hapi and the Morepork
Bermingham, Iris
Hapi series (1)
Hapless child
Gorey, Edward
Alphabet series (2)
Haply I may remember
Asquith, Cynthia
Remember series (1)
Happiest day
Clewes, Dorothy
Penny series (2)
Happiest ending
Uchida, Yoshiko
Rinko trilogy (3)
Happiest ghost in town
Malloy, Lester
Martin Moon series (2)
Happily ever after
Kaye, Marilyn
Camp Sunnyside Friends series (16)
Happiness patrol
Curry, Graeme
Doctor Who series (146)
Happy
Leonard, Marcia
Feelings series (2)
Happy anchorage
Lawson, Robert Neale
Shipmates series (2)
Happy and glorious
Housman, Laurence
Palace plays series (2)
Palace plays series (4)
Happy apple
Bruna, Dick
Toy box tale series (1)
Happy are the clean of heart
Greeley, Andrew Moran
Monsignor John Blackwood Ryan series (3)
Happy are the meek
Greeley, Andrew Moran
Monsignor John Blackwood Ryan series (2)
Happy are the merciful
Greeley, Andrew Moran
Monsignor John Blackwood Ryan series (7)
Happy are the peacemakers
Greeley, Andrew Moran
Monsignor John Blackwood Ryan series (8)
Happy are those who thirst for justice
Greeley, Andrew Moran
Monsignor John Blackwood Ryan series (5)
Happy birth day
Sorenson, Jane
Katie Hooper series (3)
Happy birthday Baabee
Khalsa, Dayal Kaur
Baabee series III (2)
Happy birthday, dear Beany
Weber, Lenora Mattingly
Beany Malone series (7)
Happy birthday, Dear Dragon
Hillert, Margaret
Dear Dragon series (1)
Happy birthday, Felicity!
Tripp, Valerie
Felicity series (4)
Happy birthday, Henrietta!
Hoff, Syd
Henrietta series (7)
Happy birthday, Jane
Chase, Emily
Canby Hall series (28)
Happy birthday, Kirsten!
Shaw, Janet
Kirsten series (4)
Happy birthday, Max!
Turk, Hanne
Max the Mouse series (10)
Happy birthday, Molly!
Tripp, Valerie
Molly series (4)
Happy birthday, Moon
Asch, Frank
Bear series (3)
Happy birthday, Mrs Felonius
Cowley, Joy
Captain Felonius series (2)
Happy birthday mystery
Nixon, Joan Lowery
First read-alone mystery series (4)
Happy birthday, Ronald Morgan
Giff, Patricia Reilly
Ronald Morgan series (2)
Happy birthday, Rotten Ralph
Gantos, Jack
Rotten Ralph series (6)
Happy birthday, Sam
Hutchins, Pat
Tom and Sam series (2)
Happy birthday, Samantha!
Tripp, Valerie
Samantha series (4)
Happy birthday, Topsy and Tim
Adamson, Jean
Life with Topsy and Tim series (10)
Happy birthday with Ant and Bee
Banner, Angela
Ant and Bee series (8)
Happy campers
Walker, Mort
Hi and Lois series (18)
Happy Christmas, Clem
Phillpotts, Beatrice
Clem series (4)
Happy countryman
Bates, Herbert Ernest
Country heart series (2)
Warren, Clarence Henry
Happy countryman series (1)
Happy days
Milne, Alan Alexander
Day's play series (4)
Happy days and our friends
Montgomery, Elizabeth
Dick, Jane and Sally series (9)
Happy days at Bullerby
Lindgren, Astrid
Bullerby series (3)
Happy days on the Farm
Gould, Elizabeth
Green Willow Farm series (8)
Happy deathday
Westbrook, Perry Dickie
Doctor Samuel Cutting series (1)
Happy Easter, Dear Dragon
Hillert, Margaret
Dear Dragon series (2)
Happy ending
Walmsley, Leo
Phantom Lobster series (7)
Happy family
Bower, Bertha Muzzy
Flying U Ranch series (3)
Happy foreigner
Bagnold, Enid
Girl's journey series (1)
Happy fortress
Bromige, Iris
Rainwood family series (9)
Happy Hannukah, Rebus
Adler, David A
Happy Rebus series (1)
Happy, happy Mother's Day
Tripp, Valerie
Just one more stories series (6)
Happy harvest
Farnol, Jeffery
Mister Jasper Shrig of Bow Street series (6)
Oliver Matravers series (2)
Happy highwayman
Charteris, Leslie
Saint series (21)
Happy highways
Croft-Cooke, Rupert
Sensual life series (9)
Happy holiday, Clicky
Blyton, Enid
Clicky series (4)

Happy holiday with the little sea urchin
Macpherson, Bruce
Jenny and Sue series (2)
Happy Hollisteres and the Swiss echo mystery
West, Jerry
Happy Hollisters series (25)
Happy Hollisters
West, Jerry
Happy Hollisters series (1)
Happy Hollisters and the Castle Rock mystery
West, Jerry
Happy Hollisters series (23)
Happy Hollisters and the cowboy mystery
West, Jerry
Happy Hollisters series (20)
Happy Hollisters and the cuckoo clock mystery
West, Jerry
Happy Hollisters series (24)
Happy Hollisters and the ghost horse mystery
West, Jerry
Happy Hollisters series (29)
Happy Hollisters and the haunted house mystery
West, Jerry
Happy Hollisters series (21)
Happy Hollisters and the ice carnival mystery
West, Jerry
Happy Hollisters series (16)
Happy Hollisters and the Indian treasure
West, Jerry
Happy Hollisters series (2)
Happy Hollisteres and the merry-go-round mystery
West, Jerry
Happy Hollisters series (8)
Happy hollisters and the monster mystery
West, Jerry
Happy Hollisters series (32)
Happy Hollisters and the mystery at Missile Town
West, Jerry
Happy Hollisters series (19)
Happy Hollisters and the mystery in Skyscraper City
West, Jerry
Happy Hollisters series (17)
Happy Hollisters and the mystery of the golden witch
West, Jerry
Happy Hollisters series (30)
Happy Hollisters and the mystery of the little mermaid
West, Jerry
Happy Hollisters series (18)
Happy Hollisters and the mystery of the Mexican idol
West, Jerry
Happy Hollisters series (31)
Happy Hollisters and the mystery of the midnight trolls
West, Jerry
Happy Hollisters series (33)
Happy Hollisters and the mystery of the totem faces
West, Jerry
Happy Hollisters series (15)
Happy Hollisters and the old clipper ship
West, Jerry
Happy Hollisters series (11)
Happy Hollisters and the Punch and Judy mystery
West, Jerry
Happy Hollisters series (28)
Happy Hollisters and the scarecrow mystery
West, Jerry
Happy Hollisters series (14)
Happy Hollisters and the sea turtle mystery
West, Jerry
Happy Hollisters series (26)
Happy Hollisters and the secret fort
West, Jerry
Happy Hollisters series (9)
Happy Hollisters and the secret of the lucky coins
West, Jerry
Happy Hollisters series (22)
Happy Hollisters and the trading post mystery
West, Jerry
Happy Hollisters series (5)
Happy Hollisters and the whistle-pig mystery
West, Jerry
Happy Hollisters series (27)
Happy Hollisters at Circus Island
West, Jerry
Happy Hollisters series (10)
Happy Hollisters at Lizard Cove
West, Jerry
Happy Hollisters series (13)
Happy Hollisters at Mystery Mountain
West, Jerry
Happy Hollisters series (6)
Happy Hollisters at Pony Hill Farm
West, Jerry
Happy Hollisters series (12)
Happy Hollisters at Sea Gull Beach
West, Jerry
Happy Hollisters series (3)
Happy Hollisters at Snowflake Camp
West, Jerry
Happy Hollisters series (7)
Happy Hollisters on a river trip
West, Jerry
Happy Hollisters series (4)
Happy hour
Browne, Dik
Hagar the horrible series (21)
Happy House children
Blyton, Enid
Happy House series (3)
Happy House children again
Blyton, Enid
Happy House series (2)
Happy island
Lee, Jennette Barbour Perry
Uncle William series (2)
Happy Islands behind the winds
Kruss, James
Captain Madirankowitch series (1)
Happy Jack
Burgess, Thornton Waldo
Green Meadow series (1)
Happy killers
Robeson, Kenneth
Avenger series (21)
Happy lion
Fatio, Louise
Happy lion series (1)
Happy lion and the bear
Fatio, Louise
Happy lion series (6)
Happy lion in Africa
Fatio, Louise
Happy lion series (2)
Happy lion roars
Fatio, Louise
Happy lion series (3)
Happy lioness
Fatio, Louise
Happy lion series (10)
Happy lion's holiday
Fatio, Louise
Happy lion series (7)
Happy lion's quest
Fatio, Louise
Happy lion series (5)
Happy lion's rabbits
Fatio, Louise
Happy lion series (9)
Happy lion's treasure
Fatio, Louise
Happy lion series (8)
Happy lion's vacation
Fatio, Louise
Happy lion series (7)
Happy little family
Caudill, Rebecca
Bonnie series (1)
Happy Moomins
Jansson, Tove
Moomin series (2)
Happy mountain
Chapman, Maristan
Happy mountain series (1)
Happy Orpheline
Carlson, Natalie Savage
Orphelines series (1)
Happy pilgrimage
Brittain, Harry Ernest
Pilgrim series (2)
Happy playtime
Grannan, Mary
Just Mary series (4)
Happy Purim night
Simon, Norma
Purim series (1)
Happy Rascals
Howard, Francis Morton
Happy Rascals series (1)
Happy return
Forester, Cecil Scott
Horatio Hornblower series (6)
Happy returns
Gaite, Francis
James and Charles Latimer series (2)
Thirkell, Angela
Barsetshire series (21)
Happy stories
Blyton, Enid
Little books series (6)
Happy story book
Blyton, Enid
Story book series (1)
Happy story of Wallace the engine
Donald, Henry
Linwoodmuir series (1)
Happy Thanksgiving, Rebus
Adler, David A
Happy Rebus series (2)
Happy the land
Rich, Louise Dickinson
Woods series (2)
Happy-Thought Hall
Burnand, Francis Cowley
Happy thoughts series (2)
Happy thoughts
Burnand, Francis Cowley
Happy thoughts series (1)
Happy times in Noisy Village
Lindgren, Astrid
Bullerby series (3)
Happy to be me
Kalman, Bobbie
In my world series (4)
Happy trails
Vail, Virginia
Horse crazy series (2)
Happy valley
Nicole, Christopher
Kenya trilogy (2)
Happy worm
Ahlberg, Allan
Red nose readers series (7)
Happy years
Beaton, Cecil
Years diaries series (3)
Haps and mishaps at the old farm
Ober, Frederick Albion
Old farm series (4)
Haps and mishaps of the Brown family
Boardman, M M
Brown family series (1)
Harald and the giant knight
Carrick, Donald
Harald series (1)
Harald and the great stag
Carrick, Donald
Harald series (2)
Harbor of doom
Greenfield, Irving A
Depth force series (12)
Harbor Road
Bassett, Sara Ware
Cape Cod series (3)
Harbor tales down North
Duncan, Norman
Down North series (1)
Harbourmaster
McFee, William
Spenlove series (1)
Hard act to follow
Conway, Troy
Coxeman series (2)
Hard as nails
Bridges, Ben
Carter O'Brien series (2)
Hard bargains
Grady, James
James Rankin series (2)
Hard bullets
Sherman, Jory
Gunn series (10)
Hard candy
Vachss, Andrew
Burke series (4)
Hard case
D'Amato, Barbara
Cat Marsala series (5)
Hard cash
Collins, Max Allan
Nolan series (5)
Reade, Charles
David Dodd and Lucy Fountain series (2)
Hard chains, soft women
Hardin, J D
Raider and Doc series (11)
Hard choices
Pascal, Francine
Sweet Valley High series (43)
Hard contract
Copper, Basil
Mike Faraday series (39)
Hard-core murder
Kenyon, Paul
Baroness Penelope Saint-John Orsini series (4)
Hard corps
Bainbridge, Chuck
Hard corps series (1)
Hard currency
Kaminsky, Stuart Melvin
Inspector Porfiry Petrovich Rostnikov series (9)
Hard day's knight
Mark, Ted
Man from O.R.G.Y. series (7)
Hard facts
Spring, Howard
Dillworth trilogy (1)
Hard for justice
Meek, Joseph
Mountain Jack Pike series (8)
Hard hit
Wainwright, John
Northern Police series (24)
Superintendent Charles Ripley series (5)
Hard in the saddle
Martin, Cort
Jared Bolt series (8)
Hard kill
Grex, Leo
Phil Sanderson series (2)
Stivers, Dick
Able Team series (25)
Hard knocker's luck
Murray, William Buckley
Lou Anderson series (2)
Hard line
Lewin, Michael Zinn
Albert Samson series (7)
Lieutenant Leroy Powder series (2)
Hard liver
Weymouth, Anthony
Inspector Treadgold series (4)
Hard luck
D'Amato, Barbara
Cat Marsala series (3)
Hard luck money
Tippette, Giles
Wilson Young series (7)
Hard luck mutt
Graeber, Charlotte Towner
Mister T and me series (3)
Hard man is good to find
Conway, Troy
Coxeman series (34)
Hard man to kill
Perry, Ritchie
Philis series (2)
Hard men
Chisholm, Matt
Rem McAllister series (2)
Kilgore, Axel
They call me the Mercenary series (18)
Ledd, Paul
Shelter Morgan series (19)
Hard money
Kelland, Clarence Budington
Hard money trilogy (1)
Hard rain
Van de Wetering, Janwillem
De Gier and Grijpstra series (11)
Hard rider
Gentry, Buck
Eli Holten series (31)
Hard riders
Edson, John Thomas
Floating Outfit series (51)
Hard-riding
Hunter, E J
Headhunter series (3)
Hard rock
Adams, Nicholas
Horror High series (5)
Hard Rock Man
Hendryx, James Beardsley
Black John series (4)
Hard Rock showdown
Scott, Bradford
Walt Slade series (95)
Hard scrabble
Graves, John
Brazos trilogy (2)
Hard sell
Haggard, William
Colonel Charles Russell series (8)
Hard tack
D'Amato, Barbara
Cat Marsala series (2)
Hard target
Rouch, James
Zone series (1)
Hard Texas trail
Chisholm, Matt
Storm family series (2)
Hard to get
Greene, Yvonne
Kelly Blake series (3)
Hard to handle
Keene, Carolyn
River Heights series (12)
Welcome, John
Richard Graham series (2)
Hard trade
Lyons, Arthur
Jacob Asch series (6)
Hard way
Ahern, Jerry
Dan Track series (4)
Gilman, George G
Adam Steele series (18)
Hard way home
Peyton, K M
Mick and Rob series (2)
Hard way up
Chandler, Arthur Bertram
John Grimes series (12)
Rim series (3)
Hard winter at Broken Arrow Crossing
Bly, Stephen Arthur
Stuart Brannon series (1)
Hard women
D'Amato, Barbara
Cat Marsala series (4)
Hardacre
Skelton, Clement Lister
Hardacre series (1)
Hardacre's luck
Skelton, Clement Lister
Hardacre series (2)
Hardball
D'Amato, Barbara
Cat Marsala series (1)
Hornig, Doug
Loren Swift series (2)
Hardcase
Hunter, Neil
Brand series (2)
Hardcase guns
Hobart, Donald Bayne
Masked Rider and Blue Hawk series (6)
Hardcase hussy
Martin, Cort
Jared Bolt series (16)
Hardcase squeeze
Hunter, E J
Headhunter series (11)
Hardcourt upset
Bee, Clair
Chip Hilton series (15)
Harden than steel
Masterson, Louis
Morgan Kane series (40)
Harder thing than triumph
Byfield, Barbara
Simon Bede and Helen Bullock series (3)
Harder you try, the harder it gets
Conway, Troy
Coxeman series (29)
Harding and the Palestine police
Duff, Douglas Valder
Jack Harding series (2)
Harding and the screaming mantle
Duff, Douglas Valder
Jack Harding series (3)
Harding of Saint Timothy's
Pier, Arthur Stanwood
Saint Timothy's School series (2)
Harding's luck
Nesbit, Edith
Arden series (2)
Harding's mountain treasure
Duff, Douglas Valder
Jack Harding series (1)
Harditts in Sawna
Nichols, Robert
Daily lives in Nghsi-Altai series (4)
Hardliners
Haggard, William
Colonel Charles Russell series (13)
Hardly a man is now alive
Brean, Herbert
Reynold Frame series (3)
Ridgway, Jason
Brian Guy series (3)
Hardneck and Amos
Hanson, Victor Joseph
Amos Crowle series (7)
Hardscrabble of Elm Island
Kellogg, Elijah
Elm Island series (6)

Hardwired
Williams, Walter Jon
Hardwired trilogy (1)

Hardy boys and Nancy Drew meet Dracula
Larsen, Glen A
Hardy boys series (129)
Nancy Drew series (122)

Hardy boys' detective handbook
Dixon, Franklin W
Hardy boys series (129)

Hardy boys' handbook
Dixon, Franklin W
Hardy boys series (129)

Hardy boys' who-dunnit mystery book
Dixon, Franklin W
Hardy boys series (129)

Hare
Oldmeadow, Ernest James
Coggin trilogy (2)

Hare and Guy Fawkes
Uttley, Alison
Little Grey Rabbit series (23)

Hare and the Easter eggs
Uttley, Alison
Little Grey Rabbit series (20)

Hare and the rainbow
Uttley, Alison
Little Grey Rabbit series (34)

Hare goes shopping
Uttley, Alison
Little Grey Rabbit series (28)

Hare joins the Home Guard
Uttley, Alison
Little Grey Rabbit series (13)

Hare sitting up
Innes, Michael
Sir John Appleby series (18)

Harem mystery
Parsons, Anthony
Sexton Blake series (1010)

Hare's choice
Hamley, Dennis
Hare's choice trilogy (1)

Hargreaves story
Stewart-Hargreaves, Eustace
Hamilton Ian
Cotswold Cider Company series (1)

Harilek
Ganpat
Harry Lake series (1)

Hark, hark, the lark!
Bates, Herbert Ernest
Larkin family series (3)

Hark, hark the watchdogs bark
Wells, Tobias
Detective Knute Severson series (14)

Harker file
Olden, Marc
Hawthorne Albert Harker series (1)

Harlem hit
Mallory, Roosevelt
Radcliff series (1)

Harlem showdown
Barry, Mike
Burton Wulff series (10)

Harlem underground
Lacy, Ed
Lee Hayes series (1)

Harlequin
West, Morris Langlo
George Harlequin series (2)

Harley First XI
Cleaver, Hylton
Harley series (2)

Harley Street hypnotist
Mitchell, Alan Williams
Harley Street series (1)

Harley Street psychiatrist
Mitchell, Alan Williams
Harley Street series (2)

Harlot's progress
Balzac, Honore de
Scenes of Parisian life series (8)

Harmer John
Walpole, Hugh
Provincial group series (2)

Harmers
Piccard, Eulalie
Episodes of the great Russian tragedy series (4)

Harm's Way
Aird, Catherine
Inspector C D Sloan series (11)

Harness bull
White, Leslie Turner
Captain Barnaby series (1)

Harness of death
Sykes, William Stanley
Inspector Dennis Drury series (2)

Harold
Cookson, Catherine
Maisie Leviston series (3)

Harold and Chester in Creepy-crawly birthday
Howe, James
Bunnicula series (8)

Harold and Chester in Hot fudge
Howe, James
Bunnicula series (7)

Harold and Chester in Scared silly
Howe, James
Bunnicula series (6)

Harold and Chester in The fright before Christmas
Howe, James
Bunnicula series (5)

Harold in London
Christie, Kate
Harold Crane series (2)

Harp in the south
Park, Ruth
Darcy family trilogy (2)

Harper
Macdonald, Ross
Lew Archer series (1)

Harper Hall of Pern
McCaffrey, Anne
Pern and the Red Planet series (6)

Harper of Heaven
Service, Robert William
Adventures in memory series (2)

Harper of heaven
Service, Robert William
Ploughman of heaven series (2)

Harper's folly
Aylward, Marcus
Harper series (1)

Harper's luck
Aylward, Marcus
Harper series (2)

Harpinger's hunch
Carstairs, Henry
Lydford Long series (1)

Harpist in the wind
McKillip, Patricia Anne
Morgon trilogy (3)

Harpy high
Friesner, Esther Mona
Gnome series (2)

Harpy's flight
Lindholm, Megan
Windsingers series (1)

Harrad experiment
Rimmer, Robert Henry
Harrad College series (1)

Harrad letters to Robert H Rimmer
Rimmer, Robert Henry
Harrad College series (2)

Harriet and the crocodiles
Waddell, Martin
Harriet the Troublemaker series (1)

Harriet and the flying teachers
Waddell, Martin
Harriet the Troublemaker series (4)

Harriet and the garden
Carlson, Nancy
Harriet series (4)

Harriet and the haunted school
Waddell, Martin
Harriet the Troublemaker series (2)

Harriet and the robot
Waddell, Martin
Harriet the Troublemaker series (3)

Harriet and the roller coaster
Carlson, Nancy
Harriet series (3)

Harriet and Walt
Carlson, Nancy
Harriet series (5)

Harriet at home
Maestro, Betsy Crippen
Harriet series (7)

Harriet at play
Maestro, Betsy Crippen
Harriet series (5)

Harriet at school
Maestro, Betsy Crippen
Harriet series (6)

Harriet at work
Maestro, Betsy Crippen
Harriet series (8)

Harriet farewell
Erskine, Margaret
Inspector Septimus Finch series (20)

Harriet goes to the circus
Maestro, Betsy Crippen
Harriet series (1)

Harriet Help-Alot
Watson, Jean
Alot series (7)

Harriet Plume
Partridge, Jenny
Oakapple Wood series (8)

Harriet reads signs and more signs
Maestro, Betsy Crippen
Harriet series (2)

Harriet the elephant
Maestro, Betsy Crippen
Harriet series (4)

Harriet, the haunted
Kimbrough, Katheryn
Phenwick women series (10)

Harriet, the spy
Fitzhugh, Louise
Harriet M Welsh series (1)

Harriet's Halloween candy
Carlson, Nancy
Harriet series (2)

Harriet's recital
Carlson, Nancy
Harriet series (1)

Harrigan's star
Grover, Marshall
Larry and Stretch series (361)

Harringtons at home
Thorn, Ismay
Geoff and Jim Harrington series (6)

Harrison High
Farris, John
Harrison High series (1)

Harrison Keith and the phantom heiress
Carter, Nicholas
Harrison Keith series (24)
Nicholas Carter series (310)

Harrison Keith at bay
Carter, Nicholas
Harrison Keith series (26)
Nicholas Carter series (308)

Harrison Keith, magician
Carter, Nicholas
Harrison Keith series (38)

Harrison, Keith, magician
Carter, Nicholas
Nicholas Carter series (307)

Harrison Keith, sleuth
Carter, Nicholas
Harrison Keith series (1)
Nicholas Carter series (243)

Harrison Keith, star reporter
Carter, Nicholas
Harrison Keith series (48)
Nicholas Carter series (348)

Harrison Keith's abduction tangle
Carter, Nicholas
Harrison Keith series (31)
Nicholas Carter series (305)

Harrison Keith's battle of nerve
Carter, Nicholas
Harrison Keith series (32)
Nicholas Carter series (304)

Harrison Keith's big stakes
Carter, Nicholas
Harrison Keith series (7)
Nicholas Carter series (242)

Harrison Keith's cameo case
Carter, Nicholas
Harrison Keith series (28)
Nicholas Carter series (317)

Harrison Keith's chance clue
Carter, Nicholas
Harrison Keith series (3)
Nicholas Carter series (235)

Harrison Keith's chance shot
Carter, Nicholas
Harrison Keith series (17)
Nicholas Carter series (275)

Harrison Keith's close quarters
Carter, Nicholas
Harrison Keith series (25)
Nicholas Carter series (316)

Harrison Keith's crooked trail
Carter, Nicholas
Harrison Keith series (12)
Nicholas Carter series (273)

Harrison Keith's cyclone clue
Carter, Nicholas
Harrison Keith series (49)
Nicholas Carter series (349)

Harrison Keith's danger
Carter, Nicholas
Harrison Keith series (9)
Nicholas Carter series (244)

Harrison Keith's death compact
Carter, Nicholas
Harrison Keith series (39)
Nicholas Carter series (313)

Harrison Keith's death watch
Carter, Nicholas
Harrison Keith series (46)
Nicholas Carter series (339)

Harrison Keith's diamond case
Carter, Nicholas
Harrison Keith series (19)
Nicholas Carter series (278)

Harrison Keith's dilemma
Carter, Nicholas
Harrison Keith series (8)
Nicholas Carter series (238)

Harrison Keith's double cross
Carter, Nicholas
Harrison Keith series (30)
Nicholas Carter series (321)

Harrison Keith's double mystery
Carter, Nicholas
Harrison Keith series (13)
Nicholas Carter series (269)

Harrison Keith's drag net
Carter, Nicholas
Harrison Keith series (16)
Nicholas Carter series (267)

Harrison Keith's dual role
Carter, Nicholas
Harrison Keith series (33)
Nicholas Carter series (306)

Harrison Keith's fight for life
Carter, Nicholas
Harrison Keith series (14)
Nicholas Carter series (266)

Harrison Keith's greatest task
Carter, Nicholas
Harrison Keith series (4)
Nicholas Carter series (240)

Harrison Keith's green diamond
Carter, Nicholas
Harrison Keith series (37)
Nicholas Carter series (309)

Harrison Keith's haunted client
Carter, Nicholas
Harrison Keith series (34)
Nicholas Carter series (311)

Harrison Keith's labyrinth
Carter, Nicholas
Harrison Keith series (44)
Nicholas Carter series (341)

Harrison Keith's lucky strike
Carter, Nicholas
Harrison Keith series (36)
Nicholas Carter series (314)

Harrison Keith's mummy mystery
Carter, Nicholas
Harrison Keith series (35)
Nicholas Carter series (315)

Harrison Keith's mystic letter
Carter, Nicholas
Harrison Keith series (15)
Nicholas Carter series (277)

Harrison Keith's oath
Carter, Nicholas
Harrison Keith series (10)
Nicholas Carter series (241)

Harrison Keith's padlock mystery
Carter, Nicholas
Harrison Keith series (27)
Nicholas Carter series (318)

Harrison Keith's perilous contract
Carter, Nicholas
Harrison Keith series (50)
Nicholas Carter series (344)

Harrison Keith's poison problem
Carter, Nicholas
Harrison Keith series (47)
Nicholas Carter series (346)

Harrison Keith's queer clue
Carter, Nicholas
Harrison Keith series (23)
Nicholas Carter series (272)

Harrison Keith's river front ruse
Carter, Nicholas
Harrison Keith series (41)
Nicholas Carter series (320)

Harrison Keith's river mystery
Carter, Nicholas
Harrison Keith series (45)
Nicholas Carter series (347)

Harrison Keith's sparkling trail
Carter, Nicholas
Harrison Keith series (40)
Nicholas Carter series (319)

Harrison Keith's strange summons
Carter, Nicholas
Harrison Keith series (22)
Nicholas Carter series (276)

Harrison Keith's struggle
Carter, Nicholas
Harrison Keith series (5)
Nicholas Carter series (237)

Harrison Keith's studio crime
Carter, Nicholas
Harrison Keith series (43)
Nicholas Carter series (342)

Harrison Keith's tact
Carter, Nicholas
Harrison Keith series (20)
Nicholas Carter series (274)

Harrison Keith's time lock case
Carter, Nicholas
Harrison Keith series (21)
Nicholas Carter series (268)

Harrison Keith's triple tragedy
Carter, Nicholas
Harrison Keith series (29)
Nicholas Carter series (312)

Harrison Keith's triumph
Carter, Nicholas
Harrison Keith series (6)
Nicholas Carter series (239)

Harrison Keith's wager
Carter, Nicholas
Harrison Keith series (42)
Nicholas Carter series (343)

Harrison Keith's warning
Carter, Nicholas
Harrison Keith series (2)
Nicholas Carter series (236)

Harrison Keith's weird partner
Carter, Nicholas
Harrison Keith series (18)
Nicholas Carter series (270)

Harrison Keith's wireless message
Carter, Nicholas
Harrison Keith series (11)
Nicholas Carter series (271)

Harrow and harvest
Willard, Barbara
Mantlemass series (8)

Harrowing of Gwynedd
Kurtz, Katherine
Heirs of Saint Camber trilogy (1)

Harrowing of Hubertus
Mittelholzer, Edgar
Kaywana series (3)

Harry and his chickens
Finley, Martha Farquharson
Pewit's nest series (7)

Harry and his cousins
Finley, Martha Farquharson
Pewit's nest series (12)

Harry and the lady next door
Zion, Gene
Harry the dirty dog series (3)

Harry at Aunt Jane's
Finley, Martha Farquharson
Pewit's nest series (11)

Harry Bradford's crusade
Mathews, Joanna Hooe
Bradford family series (2)

Harry by the sea
Zion, Gene
Harry the dirty dog series (4)

Harry Cat's pet puppy
Selden, George
Chester Cricket series (3)

Harry goes to a fancy-dress party
Keith, Shona
Harry series (2)

Harry Harding's last year
Pier, Arthur Stanwood
Saint Timothy's School series (2)

Harry in trouble
Porte, Barbara Ann
Harry series (3)

Harry Kitten and Tucker Mouse
Selden, George
Chester Cricket series (6)

Harry-O
Hays, Lee
Harry Orwell series (1)

Harry-O 2
Hays, Lee
Harry Orwell series (2)

Harry Sullivan's war
Marter, Ian
Companions of Doctor Who series (2)

Harry the dirty dog
Zion, Gene
Harry the dirty dog series (1)

Harry's alphabet
Waterman, Jill
Harry series (7)

Harry's aunt
Lavelle, Sheila
Harry series (1)

Harry's baggy jumper
Keith, Shona
Harry series (3)

Harry's cat
Lavelle, Sheila
Harry series (5)

Harry's Christmas
Finley, Martha Farquharson
Pewit's nest series (6)
Harry's colours
Waterman, Jill
Harry series (1)
Harry's dog
Lavelle, Sheila
Harry series (3)
Porte, Barbara Ann
Harry series (1)
Harry's fourth of July
Finley, Martha Farquharson
Pewit's nest series (2)
Harry's grandma
Finley, Martha Farquharson
Pewit's nest series (9)
Harry's hamster
Lavelle, Sheila
Harry series (4)
Harry's horse
Lavelle, Sheila
Harry series (2)
Harry's island
Barbour, Ralph Henry
Hudson River trilogy (3)
Harry's little sister
Finley, Martha Farquharson
Pewit's nest series (5)
Harry's mom
Porte, Barbara Ann
Harry series (2)
Harry's new hobby
Keith, Shona
Harry series (1)
Harry's numbers
Waterman, Jill
Harry series (5)
Harry's ride
Finley, Martha Farquharson
Pewit's nest series (3)
Harry's shapes
Waterman, Jill
Harry series (4)
Harry's sizes
Waterman, Jill
Harry series (6)
Harry's spots
Waterman, Jill
Harry series (2)
Harry's stripes
Waterman, Jill
Harry series (3)
Harry's walks
Finley, Martha Farquharson
Pewit's nest series (4)
Hartigan
Grover, Marshall
Nevada Jim series (65)
Hartinger's mouse
McCutchan, Philip
Commander Esmonde Shaw series (12)
Hartland case
Bentley, John
Sir Richard Herrivell series (9)
Hartwarp bakehouse
Pudney, John
Hartwarp series (5)
Hartwarp balloon
Pudney, John
Hartwarp series (4)
Hartwarp circus
Pudney, John
Hartwarp series (3)
Hartwarp dump
Pudney, John
Hartwarp series (2)
Hartwarp explosion
Pudney, John
Hartwarp series (6)
Hartwarp jets
Pudney, John
Hartwarp series (7)
Hartwarp light railway
Pudney, John
Hartwarp series (1)
Harum Scarum
Stuart, Esme
Harum Scarum series (1)
Harum Scarum married
Stuart, Esme
Harum Scarum series (3)
Harum Scarum's fortune
Stuart, Esme
Harum Scarum series (2)
Harvard has a homicide
Fuller, Timothy
Jupiter Jones series (1)
Harvest
Giono, Jean
Trilogy of earth (3)
Jones, Nicholas
Wind in the willows series (8)
Harvest adventure
Day, James Wentworth
Rural rides series (2)
Harvest at Cowleaze
Whitlock, Ralph
Cowleaze Farm series (2)
Harvest burns
Moray, Helga
Katie and Paul Van Riebeck series (3)
Harvest festival
Bentley, Diana
My school series (10)
Harvest from rotten apples
Blandy, Mary
Youth work series (2)
Harvest hell
Wilson, Gar
Phoenix Force series (13)
Harvest in the north
Hodson, James Lansdale
Harvest in the north series (1)
Harvest is past
Home, Michael
Breckland series (5)
Harvest murder
Rhode, John
Doctor Lancelot Priestley series (25)
Harvest of daring
Preston, Florence
Kathrine Grey series (1)
Harvest of death
Harrison, Ray
Sergeant Joseph Bragg and Constable James Morton series (7)
Thorne, Ramsay
Captain Gringo series (14)
Harvest of desire
Larkin, Rochelle T
Desire trilogy (2)
Harvest of fury
Williams, Jeanne
Arizona trilogy (2)
Harvest of gold
Wilson, Trevor Edward
Big Tom Holder trilogy (3)
Harvest of journeys
Innes, Hammond
Sea journeys series (1)
Harvest of tares
Dalton, Moray
Inspector Hugh Collier series (3)
Harvest of the Don
Sholokhov, Mikhail
Don series (5)
Harvest of the moor
Leigh, Margaret Mary
Highland series (2)
Harvest of the sun
Thompson, Ernest Victor
Retallick family series (2)
Harvest of thorns
Barclay, Tessa
Craigallan family series (3)
Has anyone see Emily
Dunnett, Margaret
Cobb family series (1)
Hash-Knife Outfit
Grey, Zane
Diamond Outfit series (2)
Hashknife lends a hand
Tuttle, Wilbur Coleman
Hashknife Hartley and Sleepy Stevens series (5)
Hashknife of Stormy River
Tuttle, Wilbur Coleman
Hashknife Hartley and Sleepy Stevens series (12)
Hashknife of the Canyon Trail
Tuttle, Wilbur Coleman
Hashknife Hartley and Sleepy Stevens series (8)
Hashknife of the Double Bar S
Tuttle, Wilbur Coleman
Hashknife Hartley and Sleepy Stevens series (3)
Haste and waste
Optic, Oliver
Woodville series (6)
Hastings, the pirate
Creswick, Paul
Saga the Dane trilogy (3)
Hasty heiress
Muller, Paul
Paul Muller series (6)
Hat
Rock, Nova
Bobo series (1)
Hat of authority
Sanders, John
Nicholas Pym series (2)
Hatchet man
Cassells, John
Superintendent Flagg series (31)
Marshall, William Leonard
Yellowthread Street series (2)
San Antonio
Berurier series (5)
San Antonio series (5)
Hatchet men
Hartman, Dane
Dirty Harry Callahan series (8)
Hatchetman
Dodge, David
John Abraham Lincoln series (1)
Hatching of Joshua Cobb
Hodges, Margaret
Joshua Cobb series (1)
Hatch's conspiracy
Merritt, Don
Captain Franklin Hatcher series (2)
Hatch's island
Merritt, Don
Captain Franklin Hatcher series (1)
Hatch's mission
Merritt, Don
Captain Franklin Hatcher series (3)
Hatchways
Sidgwick, Ethel
Wickford series (1)
Hate
Janson, Hank
Hank Janson series (34)
Hate finds a way
Cumberland, Marten
Saturnin Dax series (32)
Hate for sale
Cumberland, Marten
Saturnin Dax series (25)
Hate genius
Robeson, Kenneth
Doc Savage series (94)
Hate is for the hunted
Frances, Stephen Daniel
John Gail series (5)
Hate is my livery
Durham, Mary
Inspector York series (1)
Hate is thicker than blood
Latham, Brad
Hook series (3)
Hate master
Robeson, Kenneth
Avenger series (16)
Hate that kills
Carter, Nicholas
Nicholas Carter series (566)
Hate trail
Scott, Bradford
Walt Slade series (53)
Hate will find a way
Cumberland, Marten
Saturnin Dax series (9)
Hated
Gilman, George G
Edge series (13)
Edge series (33)
Hated by all!
Drummond, J
Sexton Blake series (1276)
Hated eight
Quiroule, Pierre
Sexton Blake series (968)
Hateful plateful trick
Corbett, Scott
Kerby Maxwell series (8)
Hatrack River
Card, Orson Scott
Alvin Maker series (3)
Hatshepsut
Roberts, Irene
Ancient Egypt series (2)
Hatteras blue
Poyer, David
Tiller Galloway series (1)
Hatters
Fisher, Leonard Everett
Colonial Americans series (6)
Hattie be quiet, Hattie be good
Gackenbach, Dick
Hattie Rabbit series (2)
Hattie Rabbit
Gackenbach, Dick
Hattie Rabbit series (1)
Hattie, Tom and the Chicken Witch
Gackenbach, Dick
Hattie Rabbit series (4)
Hattie's adventures
Frost, Marie Hibma
Hattie series (4)
Hattie's faraway family
Frost, Marie Hibma
Hattie series (2)
Hattie's holiday fun
Frost, Marie Hibma
Hattie series (3)
Hatton Garden mystery
Marlowe, Francis
Doc Summers series (1)
Haunt of the nightingale
Riggs, John Raymond
Garth Ryland series (4)
Haunted
Stine, Robert Lawrence
Fear Street series (11)
Haunted attic
Sutton, Margaret
Judy Bolton series (2)
Haunted bell
Futrelle, Jacques
Professor Augustus S F X Van Dusen series (3)
Haunted bookshop
Morley, Christopher
Roger and Helen Mifflin series (2)
Haunted bridge
Keene, Carolyn
Nancy Drew series (15)
Haunted burial ground
Pascal, Francine
Sweet Valley twins super chiller series (7)
Haunted bus
Sharmat, Marjorie Weinman
Kids on the bus series (3)
Haunted cabin mystery
Warner, Gertrude Chandler
Boxcar children series (20)
Haunted carousel
Keene, Carolyn
Nancy Drew series (72)
Haunted castle of Ravencurse
Beach, Lynn
Wizards, warlocks and you series (5)
Haunted castles
Alexander, Marc
Haunted Britain series (2)
Haunted churches and abbeys of Britain
Alexander, Marc
Haunted Britain series (3)
Haunted circus
McKean, Thomas
Doors into time series (2)
Haunted city of gold
Mackenzie, Jake
Secret files of Dakota King series (2)
Haunted dollhouse
Blake, Susan
Twilight series (22)
Haunted fifties, 1953-1963
Stone, Isidor Feinstein
Nonconformist history of our times series (4)
Haunted fort
Dixon, Franklin W
Hardy boys series (44)
Haunted fountain
Sutton, Margaret
Judy Bolton series (28)
Haunted grange
Chetwynd-Hayes, Ronald
Tales of Clavering Grange series (5)
Haunted hall
Avallone, Michael
Partridge family series (2)
Haunted Halloween
Stine, Harlan William
Jeffrey and the third grade ghost series (2)
Haunted hangar
Powell, Van
Air mystery series (2)
Haunted holiday
Dicks, Terrance
Baker Street Irregulars series (9)
Haunted hotel mystery
Skene, Anthony
Sexton Blake series (1059)
Haunted house
Bernede, Arthur
Chantecoq series (2)
Haas, Dorothy
Peanut Butter and Jilly series (3)
Lofts, Norah
Gad's Hall series (2)
Parish, Peggy
Liza, Bill and Jed series (3)
Pascal, Francine
Sweet Valley twins series (3)
Haunted house at Sugar Creek
Hutchens, Paul
Sugar Creek Gang series (16)
Haunted house on Honeycutt Street
Nixon, Joan Lowery
Honeycutt Street series (2)
Haunted houses
Chambers, Aidan
Haunted houses series (1)
Haunted inns
Alexander, Marc
Haunted Britain series (1)
Haunted isles
Macgregor, Alasdair Alpin
Western Isles trilogy (3)
Haunted ivy
Townson, Hazel
Lenny and Jake series (4)
Haunted lady
Rinehart, Mary Roberts
Nurse Hilda Adams series (3)
Haunted lagoon
Keene, Carolyn
Dana girls series (21)
Haunted mask
Stine, Robert Lawrence
Goosebumps series (11)
Haunted mesa
Hobart, Donald Bayne
Masked Rider and Blue Hawk series (18)
Haunted monastery
Gulik, Robert van
Judge Dee series (9)
Haunted ocean
Robeson, Kenneth
Doc Savage series (51)
Haunted planet
Black, Christopher
Star challenge series (10)
Haunted pubs in Britain and Ireland
Alexander, Marc
Haunted Britain series (4)
Haunted railway game
Blyton, Enid
Famous Five adventure games series (1)
Haunted reef
Crisp, Frank
Dirk Rogers series (2)
Haunted road
Sutton, Margaret
Judy Bolton series (25)
Haunted seventh
Ross, Charles
Haunted seventh series (1)
Haunted showboat
Keene, Carolyn
Nancy Drew series (35)
Haunted sisters
Plaidy, Jean
Stuart series (6)
William and Mary trilogy (2)
Haunted valley
Scott, Bradford
Walt Slade series (94)
Haunted Valley
Sheldon, Ann
Linda Craig series (7)
Haunters of Marsh Hall
Sharp, Allen
Storytrails series (2)
Haunting of Alan Mais
Saxon, Peter
Guardians series (6)
Haunting of Bellamy four
Dickens, Monica
Messenger series (3)
Haunting of Chas McGill, and other stories
Westall, Robert
Machine gunners trilogy (3)
Haunting of Gad's Hall
Lofts, Norah
Gad's Hall series (2)
Haunting of Hillcrest
Anderson, Mary
Mostly ghosts series (1)
Haunting of Horse Island
Keene, Carolyn
Nancy Drew series (98)
Hauser's memory
Siodmak, Curt
Doctor Patrick Cory series (2)
Hausfrau rampant
Stinde, Julius
Buchholz family series (5)

Headliners
Greene, Yvonne
Kelly Blake series (4)
Headlines
Hall, Malcolm
Headlines series (1)
Headlines for a hussy
Brody, Marc
Marc Brody series (36)
Headlines make murder
Mills, Osmington
Midset C.I.D. series (1)
Superintendent William Baker series (7)
Headlong for murder
Mace, Merlda
Christine Andersen series (1)
Headmaster
Delderfield, Ronald Frederick
To serve them all my days series (2)
Headmaster's ghost at Jug Valley Juniors
Digby, Anne
Jug Valley Juniors series (2)
Headmaster's secret
Hardinge, Rex
Sexton Blake series (1283)
Headmistress
Thirkell, Angela
Barsetshire series (13)
Heads I win
Downes, Quentin
Detective Inspector Abraham Kozminski series (2)
Heads, I win
Hermes, Patricia
Kevin Corbett series (2)
Heads you die
Gribble, Leonard Reginald
Superintendent Anthony Slade series (30)
Heads you lose
Brand, Christianna
Inspector Cockrill series (1)
Cargill, Leslie
Morrison Sharpe series (2)
Gillespie, Robert Byrne
Ralph Simmons series (2)
Halliday, Brett
Michael Shayne series (8)
Hume, David
Mick Cardby series (15)
Lancer, Jack
Christopher Cool series (5)
Starr, Jimmy
Joe Medford series (2)
Healer
Meltzer, David
Brain plant series (2)
Wilson, Francis Paul
LaNague Federation trilogy (1)
Healing blade
Cordell, Alexander
John Regan trilogy (3)
Healing breed
Jennings, D K
Doctor Ralph Conway series (6)
Healing hands of death
Audemars, Pierre
Monsieur Pinaud series (20)
Healing knife
Sava, George
Surgeon's destiny series (1)
Healing oath
Soubiran, Andre
Jean Nerac series (2)
Healing through faith
Woodard, Christopher Roy
Faith healing trilogy (3)
Healing time
Andrews, Lucilla
Saint Martha's Hospital series (4)
Health-farm murders
Howard, Tom
Sergeant Tom Howard series (3)
Health unto His Majesty
Plaidy, Jean
Charles II trilogy (2)
Stuart series (3)
Healthy body
Linscott, Gillian
Birdie Linnett and Nimue Hawthorne series (1)
Healthy grave
Leek, Margaret
Stephen Marryat series (1)
Healthy way to die
Black, Lionel
Kate Theobald series (4)
Hear no evil
Browne, Dik
Hagar the horrible series (19)
Ransome, Stephen
Steve Ransome series (1)
Hear not my steps
Thompson, Lloyd S
Shimoru Kyota series (2)
Hear the stripper scream
Cagney, Peter
Mike Strang series (2)
Hear us O Lord from heaven thy dwelling place
Lowry, Malcolm
Voyage that never ends series (3)
Heard in the dark
Carter, Nicholas
Nicholas Carter series (130)
Heard it in the playground
Ahlberg, Allan
Mrs Butler series (2)
Hearing
Allington, Richard L
Beginning to learn series (6)
Pluckrose, Henry
Thinking about series (5)
Hearing secret harmonies
Powell, Anthony
Dance to the music of time series (12)
Hearse class male
Kane, Frank
Johnny Liddell series (23)
Hearse for Cinderella
Howard, Hartley
Glenn Bowman series (11)
Hearse for Dark Harbor
Ross, Clarissa
Dark Harbor series (2)
Hearse for the boss
Eichler, Alfred
Inspector Knickman series (3)
Martin Ames series (4)
Hearse in death
Cumberland, Marten
Saturnin Dax series (8)
Hearse of another colour
Chaber, M E
Milo March series (8)
Hearse on May-Day
Mitchell, Gladys
Dame Beatrice Bradley series (45)
Hearse waiting
Wright, Wade
Bart Condor series (3)
Hearse with horses
McGirr, Edmund
Jim Piron series (3)
Heart and sword
Winter, John Strange
Bootles series (13)
Heart divided
Fritch, Elizabeth
California trilogy (3)
Heart for obedience
Gage, Joy Pennock
Obedience series (1)
Heart for sale
Goudge, Eileen
Seniors series (16)
Heart has an answer
Johnston, William
Doctor Kildare series (11)
Heart in the box
Grierson, Francis Durham
Commissaire Patras series (2)
Heart listens
Van Slyke, Helen
Elizabeth Quigly series (1)
Heart of a dog
Terhune, Albert Payson
Sunnybank collies series (8)
Heart of a goof
Wodehouse, Pelham Grenville
Oldest member series (2)
Heart of a rose
Lewis, Hilda
Mary of England series (2)
Heart of a woman
Angelou, Maya
Heart of a woman series (4)
Heart of Alsace
Schickele, Rene
Rhineland heritage series (2)
Heart of Arabia
Philby, Harry St John Bridger
Arabian travel series (1)
Heart of danger
Keene, Carolyn
Nancy Drew files series (11)
Pease, Howard
Tod Moran series (11)
Heart of gold
Brown, Ruth Alberta
Peace Greenfield series (3)
Hoag, Tami
Rainbow chasers series (1)
Heart of Isabel Carleton
Ashmun, Margaret Eliza
Isabel Carleton series (2)
Heart of jade
Madariaga, Salvador de
Conquest of Mexico series (1)
Heart of Juliet Jones
Drake, Stan
Juliet Jones series (1)
Heart of Midlothian
Scott, Walter
Tales of my landlord series (7)
Heart of oak
Jones, Tristan
Wayward sailor series (2)
Heart of Philura
Kingsley, Florence Morse
Miss Philura trilogy (3)
Heart of Rachel
Norris, Kathleen
Rachel Fairfax series (1)
Heart of red iron
Gotlieb, Phyllis
Dahlgren series (2)
Heart of R'Lyeh
Kitsch, Hieronymous
Cthulhu Mythos series (17)
Heart of Scotland
Cammell, Charles Richard
Continent and Edinburgh series (2)
Heart of the country
Ford, Ford Madox
England and the English series (2)
Heart of the dreaming
Morrissey, Di
Heart of the dreaming series (1)
Heart of the family
Goudge, Elizabeth
Eliot family trilogy (3)
Heart of the hunter
Van der Post, Laurens
Kalahari series (2)
Heart of the Lion
Plaidy, Jean
Plantagenet series (3)
Heart of the range
White, William Patterson
Lazy River series (4)
Heart of the underworld
Carter, Nicholas
Nicholas Carter series (469)
Heart of the West
Ellison, Suzanne
Living West trilogy (1)
Heart of thunder
Lindsey, Johanna
Hank Chavez series (2)
Heart of Uncle Terry
Munn, Charles Clark
Uncle Terry series (2)
Heart of valor
Smith, Lisa J
Solstice series (2)
Heart of war
Masters, John
Loss of Eden trilogy (2)
Heart specialist
Lorimer, Graeme
Street cars trilogy (3)
Heart storm
Hatcher, Robin Lee
Spring Haven series (3)
Heart throbs in prose and verse dear to the American people, part 1
Chapple, Joseph Mitchell
Heart throbs series (1)
Heart throbs in prose and verse dear to the American people, part 2
Chapple, Joseph Mitchell
Heart throbs series (2)
Heart to heart
Pendleton, Don
Ashton Ford series (5)
Heartache
Janson, Hank
Hank Janson series (147)
Heartache Hospital
Collins, Lynne
Hartlake Hospital series (1)
Heartbeat
Jenkins, Jerry Bruce
Jennifer Grey series (1)
Heartbreaker
Adams, Nicholas
Horror High series (3)
Pascal, Francine
Sweet Valley High series (8)
Thornton, Jane Foster
Electric High series (3)
Heartland
Fremd, Angelika
Inge Heinrich series (1)
Heartlight
Barron, Tom A
Heartlight series (1)
Hearts
Wolitzer, Hilma
Linda and Robin Reismann series (1)
Hearts aflame
Lindsey, Johanna
Kristen series (2)
Hearts and armor
Miller, Ron
Bronwyn trilogy (3)
Hearts and diamonds
Fleischer, Leonore
Holly Hills series (1)
Hearts and faces
Trowbridge, John Townsend
Brighthope series (2)
Hearts and masks
McGrath, Harold
Hearts and masks series (1)
Heart's blood
Yolen, Jane
Pit dragons trilogy (2)
Hearts divide
Moore, Paula
Making of America series (5)
Hearts ease in death
Fraser, James
Inspector Bill Aveyard series (9)
Heart's landing
Hatcher, Robin Lee
Spring Haven series (2)
Hearts of fire
Mills, Anita
Lady of fire series (3)
Hearts of gold
McLaglen, John J
Herne the Hunter series (20)
Stirling, Jessica
Elspeth and Anna Patterson trilogy (3)
Hearts of stone
Larson, Glen A
Knight Rider series (3)
Heart's victory
Roberts, Nora
Flowers series (16)
Heartsease
Dickinson, Peter
Changes trilogy (2)
Heartshot
Havill, Steven F
Bill Gastner series (1)
Heat
McBain, Ed
Eighty Seventh Precinct series (35)
Heat from another sun
Lindsey, David L
Stuart Haydon series (2)
Heat not a furnace
Kemp, Harold
Inspector James Brent series (4)
Heat of the sun
Birmingham, Maisie
Kate Weatherley series (2)
Heathcliff
Caine, Jeffrey
Heathcliff series (2)
Wuthering Heights series (2)
Heather
Schurfranz, Vivian
Sunfire series (23)
Thesman, Jean
Whitney cousins series (1)
Trevena, John
Dartmoor trilogy (2)
Heather blazing
Toibin, Colm
Enniscorthy series (2)
Heather in my ears
Macvicar, Angus
Confessions series (2)
Heather leaves school
Brent-Dyer, Elinor Mary
La Rochelle series (4)
Heather mixture
Cameron, Isabel
Glen folk series (5)
Heather, oak and olive
Sutcliff, Rosemary
Heather, oak and olive trilogy (3)
Heather the Second
Wynne, May
Heather series (2)
Heathern
Womack, Jack
Terraplane trilogy (3)
Heat's on
Himes, Chester
Grave Digger Jones and Coffin Ed Johnson series (7)
Heave short
Durell, Charles Pendexter
Blue water trilogy (2)
Heaven
Andrews, Virginia Cleo
Casteel-Tatterton family series (1)
Heaven and earth
Coccioli, Carlo
Ardito Piccardi series (1)
Heaven and hell
Jakes, John
North and South trilogy (3)
Heaven came so near
Skidmore, Hubert
My salvation series (2)
Heaven cent
Anthony, Piers
Xanth series (11)
Heaven chronicles
Vinge, Joan Dennison
Heaven chronicles series (2)
Heaven folk
Bonsels, Waldemar
Maya series (2)
Heaven in the house
Edwards, Charlotte
Heaven series (2)
Heaven knows
Coffman, Elaine
Mackinnon brothers series (8)
Heaven knows where
Enright, Dennis Joseph
Packet series (2)
Heaven lies about us
Spring, Howard
Heaven lies about us series (1)
Heaven on earth
Elliott, Janice
Wilson family trilogy (3)
Heaven on my doorstep
Williams, Elma Mary
Wildlife series (3)
Heaven on the doorstep
Edwards, Charlotte
Heaven series (1)
Heaven to Betsy
Lovelace, Maud Hart
Betsy Ray series (5)
Heaven tree
Pargeter, Edith
Mediaeval Wales trilogy (1)
Heavenly bodies
Warriner, Thurman
Mister Scotter series (7)
Heavenly body
Morgan, Geoffrey
Ricky Straight series (2)
Heavenly hands
Ledd, Paul
Shelter Morgan series (27)
Heavenly horse from the outermost west
Stanton, Mary
Horse series (1)
Heavenly ladder
Mackenzie, Compton
Faith, hope and charity trilogy (3)
Heavenly twins
Grand, Sarah
Heavenly twins series (2)
Heaven's command
Morris, James Humphrey
British Empire trilogy (1)
Heaven's prisoners
Burke, James Lee
Dave Robicheaux series (2)
Heavy and light
Laird, Elizabeth
Contrasts series (4)
Heavy as lead
Torrie, Malcolm
Timothy Herring series (1)
Heavy change
Housman, Laurence
Palace plays series (4)
Heavy fire
Buchanan, Jack
M.I.A. Hunter series (15)
Heavy iron
Copper, Basil
Mike Faraday series (48)
Heavy knife
McQueen, James
Clocks of death trilogy (2)
Heavy time
Cherryh, Carolyn Janice
Alliance-Union series (1)
Merchanter series (2)

Heavy weather
Wodehouse, Pelham Grenville
Blandings Castle series (5)
Heavyweight gun
Roberts, J R
Gunsmith series (9)
Heberden's seat
Clark, Douglas
Inspector George Masters series (11)
Hebridean journey
Sutherland, Halliday
Journey series (2)
Hec Ramsey
Owen, Dean
Hec Ramsey series (1)
Hecate's charms
Hanscombe, Gillian
Lesbian series (1)
Heckler
McBain, Ed
Eighty Seventh Precinct series (12)
Hector and Christina
Fatio, Louise
Hector Penguin series (2)
Hector and Prudence
Koscielniak, Bruce
Hector and Prudence series (1)
Hector of Hellas
Rutley, Cecily Marianne
Children of other days series (15)
Hector Penguin
Fatio, Louise
Hector Penguin series (1)
Hector Servadac
Verne, Jules
Hector Servadac series (2)
Hector's inheritance
Alger, Horatio
Atlantic series (3)
He'd rather be dead
Bellairs, George
Detective Inspector Thomas Littlejohn series (7)
Hedgehogs in the cellar
Jones, Olive
Barfield series (8)
Hedgerow incident
Johnston, William
Young rebels series (1)
Hedonists
Wilson, Colin
Gerard Sorme trilogy (3)
Heebie jeebies at H.O.W.L. High
Leroe, Ellen Whitney
H.O.W.L. High series (2)
Heechee rendezvous
Pohl, Frederik
Heechee series (3)
Heel of Achilles
Radford, Edwin
Doctor Manson series (8)
Verner, Gerald
Michael Dene series (3)
Heffalump?
Nilsson, Eleanor Ann
Heffalump series (1)
Heffalump and the toy hospital
Nilsson, Eleanor Ann
Heffalump series (2)
Heggerty Haggerty and the amazing loaf of bread
Lindsay, Elizabeth
Heggerty Haggerty series (7)
Heggerty Haggerty and the day at the fair
Lindsay, Elizabeth
Heggerty Haggerty series (4)
Heggerty Haggerty and the day at the farm
Lindsay, Elizabeth
Heggerty Haggerty series (8)
Heggerty Haggerty and the dreadful drought
Lindsay, Elizabeth
Heggerty Haggerty series (1)
Heggerty Haggerty and the flying saucer
Lindsay, Elizabeth
Heggerty Haggerty series (9)
Heggerty Haggerty and the great running race
Lindsay, Elizabeth
Heggerty Haggerty series (6)
Heggerty Haggerty and the Hallowe'en ghosts
Lindsay, Elizabeth
Heggerty Haggerty series (2)
Heggerty Haggerty and the magic medicine
Lindsay, Elizabeth
Heggerty Haggerty series (3)
Heggerty Haggerty and the treasure hunt
Lindsay, Elizabeth
Heggerty Haggerty series (5)
Heggerty Haggerty red storybook
Lindsay, Elizabeth
Heggerty Haggerty series (7)
Heggerty Haggerty yellow storybook
Lindsay, Elizabeth
Heggerty Haggerty series (9)
Heidi
Spyri, Johanna
Heidi series (1)
Heidi grows up
Tritten, Charles
Heidi series (2)
Heidi's children
Tritten, Charles
Heidi series (3)
Heifer of the dawn
Bain, Francis William
Indian mystic love stories series (3)
Height of danger
Dixon, Franklin W
Hardy boys case files series (56)
Height of day
Cory, Desmond
Johnny Fedora series (5)
Heights and depths
Glyn, Caroline
Fullie series (2)
Heil Britannia
Long, Patrick
Martyn Cale series (1)
Heil Harris!
Garforth, John
Avengers series (6)
Heir
Grier, Sydney Carlyon
Balkan trilogy (1)
Heir apparent
Rosenberg, Joel
Guardians of the flame series (4)
Heir for the Earl
Drysdale, Margaret
Robert Dudley series (2)
Heir of Allington
Wiat, Philippa
Allington trilogy (1)
Wyatt family series (2)
Heir of Buckingham
Feval, Paul
Years between series (4)
Heir of Redclyffe
Yonge, Charlotte Mary
Morville family series (1)
Heir of Reingarth
Douglas, Carole Nelson
Sword and circlet trilogy (2)
Heir of sea and fire
McKillip, Patricia Anne
Morgon trilogy (2)
Heir of Sherburne
Douglas, Amanda Minnie
Sherburne series (8)
Heir of Tower House
Clevely, Hugh
Sexton Blake series (1349)
Heir to Falconhurst
Horner, Lance
Falconhurst series (6)
Heir to Kuragin
Heaven, Constance
Kuragin series (3)
Heir to Lucifer
Burton, Miles
Inspector Arnold and Desmond Merrion series (35)
Heir to murder
Burton, Miles
Inspector Arnold and Desmond Merrion series (47)
Heir to the dragon
Charrette, Robert N
BattleTech series (5)
Heir to the Empire
Zahn, Timothy
Star wars series (1)
Heiress bride
Coulter, Catherine
Bride trilogy (3)
Heirs of Hammerfell
Bradley, Marion Zimmer
Darkover series (18)
Held for orders
Spearman, Frank Hamilton
Railroad stories series (2)
Held for ransom
Lloyd, Hugh
Skippy Dare series (2)
Held for trial
Carter, Nicholas
Nicholas Carter series (62)
Held in suspense
Carter, Nicholas
Nicholas Carter series (565)
Held in trust!
Graydon, William Murray
Sexton Blake series (387)
Helen and the fifth cousins
Gilchrist, Beth Bradford
Helen series (4)
Helen and the Find-Out Club
Gilchrist, Beth Bradford
Helen series (3)
Helen and the uninvited guests
Gilchrist, Beth Bradford
Helen series (2)
Helen, ballet student
Graeme, Linda
Helen series (1)
Helen Grant at Aldred House
Douglas, Amanda Minnie
Helen Grant series (3)
Helen Grant, graduate
Douglas, Amanda Minnie
Helen Grant series (6)
Helen Grant in college
Douglas, Amanda Minnie
Helen Grant series (4)
Helen Grant, senior
Douglas, Amanda Minnie
Helen Grant series (5)
Helen Grant, teacher
Douglas, Amanda Minnie
Helen Grant series (7)
Helen Grant's decision
Douglas, Amanda Minnie
Helen Grant series (8)
Helen Grant's friends
Douglas, Amanda Minnie
Helen Grant series (2)
Helen Grant's harvest year
Douglas, Amanda Minnie
Helen Grant series (9)
Helen Grant's schooldays
Douglas, Amanda Minnie
Helen Grant series (1)
Helen in musical comedy
Graeme, Linda
Helen series (2)
Helen, Margy and Rose
Hope, Laura Lee
Blythe girls series (1)
Helen Over-the-Wall
Gilchrist, Beth Bradford
Helen series (1)
Helen passes by
Punshon, Ernest Robertson
Bobby Owen series (23)
Helen, television dancer
Graeme, Linda
Helen series (3)
Helen Vardon's confession
Freeman, Richard Austin
Doctor John Evelyn Thorndyke series (8)
Helen with the high hand
Bennett, Arnold
Five towns series (8)
Helena Hellion
Fletcher, Dirk
Spur McCoy series (19)
Helene
Mundy, Talbot
Tros of Samothrace series (1)
Zola, Emile
Rougon Macquart series (8)
Helen's babies
Habberton, John
Budge and Toddie series (1)
Helen's strange boarder
Hope, Laura Lee
Blythe girls series (4)
Helen's wonderful mistake
Hope, Laura Lee
Blythe girls series (12)
Helga's revenge
Browne, Dik
Hagar the horrible series (18)
Helga's web
Cleary, Jon
Scobie Malone series (2)
Helicopter children
Bellhouse, Lucy Wilered
Helicopter series (1)
Helicopter flies again
Bellhouse, Lucy Wilered
Helicopter series (2)
Hell and high water
Sotona, Wayne
High Chaparral series (1)
Hell and the duchess
Nicholson, Celia Anna
Duchess series (1)
Hell at Yuma
Slade, Jack
Lassiter series (14)
Hell below
Robeson, Kenneth
Doc Savage series (99)
Hell below zero
Masterson, Louis
Morgan Kane series (25)
Hell-benders
Cole, Jackson
Jim Hatfield series (35)
Hell bent for heaven
Ocork, Shannon
T T Baldwin series (2)
Hell-bound express
Carter, Nick
Nick Carter series (254)
Hell brood
Janson, Hank
Hank Janson series (234)
Hell for Heather
Flower, Pat
Inspector Swinton series (5)
Hell for leather
Bridges, Ben
Carter O'Brien series (10)
Hell for McAllister
Chisholm, Matt
Rem McAllister series (17)
Hell for tomorrow
Leslie, Peter
Dangerman series (3)
Hell-gate tides
Thayer, Lee
Peter Clancy series (17)
Hell Harbor
Davis, Gordon
Sergeant series (2)
Hell hound
Cain, Jackson
Torn Slater series (4)
Hell in High County
Grover, Marshall
Nevada Jim series (67)
Hell in Hindu land
Rosenberger, Joseph
Death Merchant series (20)
Hell in paradise
Cole, Jackson
Jim Hatfield series (62)
Hell in the Palo Duro
Edson, John Thomas
Floating Outfit series (34)
Hardin, J D
Raider and Doc series (65)
Hell is a city
Ard, William
Timothy Dane series (7)
Procter, Maurice
Chief Inspector Harry Martineau series (6)
Hell is always today
Patterson, Henry
Nick Miller series (3)
Hell is where you find it
Welcome, John
Richard Graham series (4)
Hell let loose
Beeding, Francis
Colonel Alastair Granby series (11)
Hell-makers
O'Donnell, Peter
Modesty Blaise comic strip series (5)
Hell merchant
Hogan, Ray
Shawn Starbuck series (10)
Hell nest
Mandell, Mark
Nazi hunter series (5)
Hell of a dame
Janson, Hank
Hank Janson series (97)
Hell of a spot
Scott, Bruce
Superintendent Steve McLaren series (3)
Hell of a way to die
Slade, Jack
Lassiter series (7)
Hell on a holiday
Richmond, Roe
Lashtrow series (3)
Hell on earth
Drumm, D B
Traveler series (10)
Spencer, Jake
John Firecloud series (2)
Hell on Friday
Bogart, William
Johnny Saxon series (1)
Hell on Hill 457
Darby, John
McLeane's Rangers series (3)
Hell on Legg's Hill
Trimnell, Robert L
Loner series (4)
Hell on the Powder River
Hardin, J D
Raider and Doc series (73)
Hell on the way
Fox, James M
John and Suzy Marshall series (3)
Hell on wheels
Benteen, John
Neal Fargo series (16)
Lassiter, Adam
Dennison's war series (3)
Morgan, G J
Buck Dunne series (3)
Roberts, J R
Gunsmith series (54)
Hell raider
Thorne, Ramsay
Captain Gringo series (9)
Hell raisers
Grover, Marshall
Larry and Stretch series (10)
Hell ride
Hofrichter, Paul
Roadblaster trilogy (1)
Hell ship
Macdonnell, James Edmond
Dutchy Holland series (8)
Hell shot
Poyer, Joe
Cole Brogan series (1)
Hell to Hallelujah
Hogan, Ray
John Mosby series (5)
Hell to midnight
Logan, Jake
John Slocum series (178)
Hell to pay
Clevely, Hugh
Inspector Williams series (1)
Cox, William Robert
Tom Kincaid series (1)
Hell town
Sharpe, Jon
Trailsman series (46)
Walker, Dalton
Shiloh series (5)
Hell week
Reynolds, Kay
Fortune's Friends series (1)
Hell west and crooked
Cole, Tom
Hunting series (1)
Hell with a pistol
Roberts, J R
Gunsmith series (41)
Hell with the hide off
Miller, Jim
Ex-Rangers series (3)
Hellbent trail
Borg, Jack
Hogleg Bailey series (1)
Hellbinder
Pendleton, Don
Mack Bolan series (72)
Hellbirds
Mitchelson, Austin
Sherlock Holmes sequels series (21)
Hellbomb flight
Derrick, Lionel
Penetrator series (10)
Hellbomb theft
Rosenberger, Joseph
Death Merchant series (50)
Hellbottom
Corder, Eric
Shame and glory series (4)
Hellbound magic
Green, Sharon
Farside of forever series (2)
Hellbound train
Sundown, Will
Pockets series (2)
Hellbreak country
Cain, Jackson
Torn Slater series (1)
Hellburner
Cherryh, Carolyn Janice
Alliance-Union series (2)
Merchanter series (3)
Hellcat
Brown, Carter
Lieutenant Al Wheeler series (25)
Janson, Hank
Hank Janson series (77)

Hellcat of Sabrehill
Giles, Raymond
Sabrehill series (5)
Helldorado
Janson, Hank
Hank Janson series (219)
Roberts, J R
Gunsmith series (105)
Heller
Whitehead, David
Heller series (1)
Heller in the Rockies
Whitehead, David
Heller series (2)
Heller's leap
Wallace, Ian
Claudine Saint Cyr series (5)
Croyd series (6)
Hellfire
Edwards, Josh
John Stone series (5)
Kessler, Leo
Wotan series (11)
Logan, Jake
John Slocum series (27)
Hellfire conspiracy
Hayes, Ralph Eugene
Agent for Cominsec series (4)
Hellfire crusade
Pendleton, Don
Mack Bolan series (87)
Hellfire files of Jules de Grandin
Quinn, Seabury
Jules de Grandin series (4)
Hellfire heritage
Roberts, Willo Davis
Black pearl series (6)
Hellfire hideaway
Hardin, J D
Raider and Doc series (23)
Hellfire in Haiti
Case, Jim
Cody's army series (6)
Hellfire in Honduras
Thorne, Ramsay
Captain Gringo series (19)
Hellfire mound
Gentry, Buck
Eli Holten series (30)
Hellfire rebellion
Hawke, Simon
Timewars series (10)
Hellfire sheriff
Buckman, Sam
Storm Jackson series (7)
Hellgate
Macdonald, William Colt
Gregory Quist series (8)
Hellhole
Dawson, Clay
Long Rider series (8)
Hayes, Ralph Eugene
O'Brien, Buffalo Hunter series (4)
Helliconia spring
Aldiss, Brian Wilson
Helliconia trilogy (1)
Helliconia summer
Aldiss, Brian Wilson
Helliconia trilogy (2)
Helliconia trilogy
Aldiss, Brian Wilson
Helliconia trilogy (3)
Helliconia winter
Aldiss, Brian Wilson
Helliconia trilogy (3)
Hellion
Ladd, Justin
Abilene series (11)
Hellion breed
Grover, Marshall
Larry and Stretch series (121)
Hellion bride
Coulter, Catherine
Bride trilogy (2)
Hellions
Bickers, Richard Townshend
Mark Stratton series (1)
McNeill, George
Deavors family series (3)
Hello, Aurora!
Vestly, Anna Catharina
Aurora series (1)
Hello, Claudia!
Wallace, Barbara Brooks
Claudia series (2)
Hello Clifford
Bridwell, Norman
Clifford series (34)
Hello, goodbye!
McMullen, Nigel
Naughty baby series (4)
Hello Henry
Peppe, Rodney
Henry series (7)
Hello Huckleberry Heights
Delton, Judy
Condo Kids series (1)
Hello I'm Bear
Gordon, Mike
Hello series (2)
Hello I'm Frog
Gordon, Mike
Hello series (3)
Hello I'm Mouse
Gordon, Mike
Hello series (1)
Hello I'm Rabbit
Gordon, Mike
Hello series (4)
Hello Kitty can count
Sullivan, Scott
Hello Kitty series (6)
Hello Kitty on the go
Sullivan, Scott
Hello Kitty series (6)
Hello Kitty sleeps over
Harris, Robin
Hello Kitty series (1)
Hello Kitty's bedtime search
Harris, Robin
Hello Kitty series (2)
Hello Kitty's button book
Gray, J M
Hello Kitty series (6)
Hello Kitty's early day
Bright, Sarah
Hello Kitty series (5)
Hello Kitty's happy Christmas
Bright, Sarah
Hello Kitty series (4)
Hello Kitty's paper kiss
Bright, Sarah
Hello Kitty series (3)
Hello Kitty's special present
Bright, Sarah
Hello Kitty series (6)
Hello, Lemuria, hello
Goulart, Ron
Wild talents series (2)
Hello, Mallory
Martin, Ann Matthews
Baby-Sitters Club series (14)
Hello, Mister Henderson
Upson, William Hazlett
Alexander Botts series (6)
Hello Mister Twiddle
Blyton, Enid
Mister Twiddle series (1)
Hello, Mrs Piggle-Wiggle
Macdonald, Betty
Mrs Piggle-Wiggle series (4)
Hello, my love, goodbye
Weber, Lenora Mattingly
Stacy and Katie Rose Belford series (7)
Hello sailor!
Christian, Petra
Sally Deenes series (7)
Hello to ponies
Allen, Jane
Hello series (1)
Hello to riding
Allen, Jane
Hello series (2)
Hello Topsy and Tim
Adamson, Jean
Topsy and Tim series (98)
Hello twins
Blyton, Enid
Twins series (3)
Hellraisers
Gilman, George G
Adam Steele series (36)
Hellrider
Kellerman, Dan
Jesse Heller series (2)
Hell's Angel
Christian, Frederick H
Frank Angel series (10)
Cohen, Anthea
Nurse Agnes Carmichael series (6)
Hell's angel
Janson, Hank
Hank Janson series (71)
Hell's Angel kidnapping
Foxall, Peter Augustus
Inspector Frank Derben series (4)
Hell's belle
Hardin, J D
Raider and Doc series (51)
Hell's belles
Janson, Hank
Hank Janson series (106)
Hell's brew
Horler, Sydney
Ace series (2)
Hell's children
Knott, William Cecil
Golden Hawk series (4)
Hell's Edge
Townsend, John Rowe
Hallersage series (1)
Hell's forty acres
Shirreffs, Gordon Donald
Dave Hunter series (1)
Hell's fury
Logan, Jake
John Slocum series (101)
Hell's gate
Pendleton, Don
Mack Bolan series (86)
Hell's hostages
Derrick, Lionel
Penetrator series (41)
Hell's Junction
Gilman, George G
Adam Steele series (3)
Hell's march
Schmidt, Dan
Eagle Force series (8)
Hell's seven
Gilman, George G
Edge series (8)
Hellspout
Knox, Bill
Webb Carrick series (9)
Helltown trail
Logan, Jake
John Slocum series (167)
Hellworld
Green, Simon
Mistworld series (3)
Helma
Mundy, Talbot
Tros of Samothrace series (1)
Helmquist
Fickling, David
Fantasy quest book series (3)
Helmsman
Baldwin, Bill
Helmsman series (1)
Help!
Ahlberg, Allan
Red nose readers series (1)
Help for Dear Dragon
Hillert, Margaret
Dear Dragon series (7)
Help from the Baron
Morton, Anthony
Baron series (27)
Help, I'm a prisoner in the library!
Clifford, Eth
Mary Rose Onetree series (1)
Help, I'm drowning, and other emergencies
Downing, Peggy
Help series (2)
Help, I'm shrinking!
Downing, Peggy
Help series (1)
Help, Pink Pig!
Adler, Carole Schwerdtfeger
Pink Pig series (2)
Help the poor struggler
Grimes, Martha
Inspector Richard Jury series (6)
Help wanted!
Chase, Emily
Canby Hall series (26)
Help wanted, male
Stout, Rex
Nero Wolfe and Archie Goodwin series (14)
Helpful ghost
Allen, Sheila Rosalynd
Lovers of Steadford Abbey series (3)
Helpful Penny
Haynes, Ambrose
Penny series (2)
Helping
Oxenbury, Helen
Baby board books series (4)
Helping himself
Alger, Horatio
Atlantic series (4)
Helpless Annie
Tuite, Hugh
Helpless Annie series (1)
Helpless Annie's idears
Tuite, Hugh
Helpless Annie series (2)
Helter skelter murders
Harrington, William
Columbo series (9)
Hemingway's notebook
Granger, Bill
November Man series (7)
Hempfield
Grayson, David
Adventures series (4)
Hendon's first case
Rhode, John
Doctor Lancelot Priestley series (20)
Hendra's book
Benoit, Hendra
Psi Patrol trilogy (2)
Henri Quatre, King of France
Mann, Heinrich
Henry, King of France series (2)
Henrietta and the day of the iguana
Rosen, Winifred
Henrietta series (2)
Henrietta and the gong from Hong Kong
Rosen, Winifred
Henrietta series (3)
Henrietta Chuffertrain
Kruss, James
Henrietta Chuffertrain series (1)
Henrietta, circus star
Hoff, Syd
Henrietta series (2)
Henrietta goes to the fair
Hoff, Syd
Henrietta series (4)
Henrietta Goose
Pizer, Abigail
Henrietta and Nosey series (1)
Henrietta in love
Judah, Aaron
Henrietta Hen series (3)
Henrietta in the snow
Judah, Aaron
Henrietta Hen series (2)
Henrietta lays some eggs
Hoff, Syd
Henrietta series (1)
Henrietta sees it through
Dennys, Joyce
Henrietta series (2)
Henrietta, the early bird
Hoff, Syd
Henrietta series (3)
Henrietta the faithful hen
Hale, Kathleen
Henrietta series (1)
Henrietta, the wild woman of Borneo
Rosen, Winifred
Henrietta series (1)
Henrietta who?
Aird, Catherine
Inspector C D Sloan series (2)
Henrietta's Fourth of July
Hoff, Syd
Henrietta series (6)
Henrietta's Halloween
Hoff, Syd
Henrietta series (5)
Henrietta's magic egg
Hale, Kathleen
Henrietta series (2)
Henrietta's war
Dennys, Joyce
Henrietta series (1)
Henry Adams
Samuels, Ernest
Henry Adams trilogy (3)
Henry Adams, the major phase
Samuels, Ernest
Henry Adams trilogy (3)
Henry Adams, the middle years
Samuels, Ernest
Henry Adams trilogy (2)
Henry and Beezus
Cleary, Beverly
Beezus series (1)
Henry Huggins series (2)
Henry and his friends
Tippett, James Sterling
Henry series (3)
Henry and Mudge
Rylant, Cynthia
Henry and Mudge series (1)
Henry and Mudge and the bedtime thumps
Rylant, Cynthia
Henry and Mudge series (9)
Henry and Mudge and the careful cousin
Rylant, Cynthia
Henry and Mudge series (13)
Henry and mudge and the forever sea
Rylant, Cynthia
Henry and Mudge series (6)
Henry and Mudge and the happy cat
Rylant, Cynthia
Henry and Mudge series (8)
Henry and Mudge and the long weekend
Rylant, Cynthia
Henry and Mudge series (11)
Henry and Mudge and the wild wind
Rylant, Cynthia
Henry and Mudge series (12)
Henry and Mudge get the cold shivers
Rylant, Cynthia
Henry and Mudge series (7)
Henry and Mudge in puddle trouble
Rylant, Cynthia
Henry and Mudge series (2)
Henry and Mudge in the green time
Rylant, Cynthia
Henry and Mudge series (3)
Henry and Mudge in the sparkle days
Rylant, Cynthia
Henry and Mudge series (5)
Henry and Mudge take the big test
Rylant, Cynthia
Henry and Mudge series (10)
Henry and Mudge under the yellow moon
Rylant, Cynthia
Henry and Mudge series (4)
Henry and Ribsy
Cleary, Beverly
Henry Huggins series (3)
Ribsy series (1)
Henry and the astronaut
Thatcher, Dora
Henry series (8)
Henry and the clubhouse
Cleary, Beverly
Henry Huggins series (6)
Henry and the express
Awdry, Christopher
Railway series (37)
Henry and the garden
Tippett, James Sterling
Henry series (1)
Henry and the paper route
Cleary, Beverly
Henry Huggins series (5)
Henry and the traction engine
Thatcher, Dora
Henry series (9)
Henry and Voula
Stewart, Maureen
Henry and Voula series (1)
Henry babysits
Quackenbush, Robert Mead
Henry series (4)
Henry Bear's park
McPhail, David Michael
Henry Bear series (1)
Henry eats out
Peppe, Rodney
Henry series (5)
Henry Esmond
Thackeray, William Makepeace
Virginia series (1)
Henry explores the jungle
Taylor, Mark
Henry series (2)
Henry explores the mountains
Taylor, Mark
Henry series (4)
Henry goes green
Stewart, Maureen
Henry and Voula series (2)
Henry goes to town
Thatcher, Dora
Henry series (12)
Henry goes visiting
Pilgrim, Jane
Blackberry Farm series (3)
Henry goes west
Quackenbush, Robert Mead
Henry series (3)
Henry Golightly
Pike, Geoffrey
Henry Golightly series (1)
Henry Hare and the kidnapping of Selina Squirrel
Clewes, Dorothy
Henry Hare series (4)
Henry Hare, painter and decorator
Clewes, Dorothy
Henry Hare series (3)
Henry Hare's boxing match
Clewes, Dorothy
Henry Hare series (1)
Henry Hare's earthquake
Clewes, Dorothy
Henry Hare series (2)
Henry Hollins and the dinosaur
Hall, Willis
Henry Hollins series (1)

Henry Huggins
Cleary, Beverly
Henry Huggins series (1)
Henry in Iceland
Thatcher, Dora
Henry series (11)
Henry in the mountains
Thatcher, Dora
Henry series (10)
Henry in the news
Thatcher, Dora
Henry series (5)
Henry Irving
Irving, Laurence
Irving family trilogy (1)
Henry is twenty
Merwin, Samuel
Henry Calverly series (2)
Henry joins the police
Thatcher, Dora
Henry series (7)
Henry Masterton
James, George Payne Rainsford
Young cavalier series (1)
Henry McGee is not dead
Granger, Bill
November Man series (10)
Henry of the high rock
Dymoke, Juliet
Henry I trilogy (2)
Henry on safari
Thatcher, Dora
Henry series (12)
Henry Prince in action
Gregg, Cecil Freeman
Henry Prince series (2)
Henry Reed, Inc.
Robertson, Keith
Henry Reed series (1)
Henry Reed's baby-sitting service
Robertson, Keith
Henry Reed series (3)
Henry Reed's big show
Robertson, Keith
Henry Reed series (4)
Henry Reed's journey
Robertson, Keith
Henry Reed series (2)
Henry Reed's think tank
Robertson, Keith
Henry Reed series (5)
Henry Saint John, gentleman
Cooke, John Esten
Effingham series (2)
Henry the castaway
Taylor, Mark
Henry series (3)
Henry the explorer
Taylor, Mark
Henry series (1)
Henry, the green engine
Awdry, Wilbert
Railway series (6)
Henry the helicopter
Thatcher, Dora
Henry series (1)
Henry the hero
Thatcher, Dora
Henry series (3)
Henry the sheriff
Tuttle, Wilbur Coleman
Henry Harrison Conroy and Judge Van Treece series (1)
Henry the Tenth, part seven
Green, Michael
Coarse plays series (2)
Henry to the rescue
Thatcher, Dora
Henry series (2)
Henry's aeroplane
Peppe, Rodney
Henry series (4)
Henry's awful mistake
Quackenbush, Robert Mead
Henry series (1)
Henry's busy winter
Thatcher, Dora
Henry series (6)
Henry's exciting flight
Thatcher, Dora
Henry series (12)
Henry's exercises
Peppe, Rodney
Henry series (1)
Henry's garden
Peppe, Rodney
Henry series (2)
Henry's important date
Quackenbush, Robert Mead
Henry series (2)
Henry's mountain adventure
Thatcher, Dora
Henry series (12)
Henry's picnic
Keller, Holly
Henry series (2)
Henry's sunbathe
Peppe, Rodney
Henry series (3)
Henry's toy cupboard
Peppe, Rodney
Henry series (6)
Henry's world tour
Quackenbush, Robert Mead
Henry series (5)
Heor of Sparshott
Richards, Frank
Schoolboy series (5)
Her
Anonymous
Pronoun series (1)
Williams, J X
She series (3)
Her April days
Henrey, Madeleine
Madeleine series (9)
Her-Bak, Chick-Pea
Schwaller de Lubicz, Isha
Homo sapiens series (1)
Her-Bak, Egyptian initiate
Schwaller de Lubicz, Isha
Homo sapiens series (2)
Her Christmas and her Easter
Rand, Edward Augustus
Margie series (1)
Her closed hands
Weale, Putnam
Wang the Ninth trilogy (2)
Her column's a killer
Brody, Marc
Marc Brody series (6)
Her daughter Jean
Taggart, Marion Ames
Six girls series (8)
Her death of cold
McInerny, Ralph
Father Roger Dowling series (1)
Her father's sins
Cox, Josephine
Her father's sins series (1)
Her first auto tour
Thorndyke, Helen Louise
Honey Bunch series (7)
Her first big adventure
Thorndyke, Helen Louise
Honey Bunch series (14)
Her first big parade
Thorndyke, Helen Louise
Honey Bunch series (15)
Her first costume party
Thorndyke, Helen Louise
Honey Bunch series (23)
Her first days in camp
Thorndyke, Helen Louise
Honey Bunch series (6)
Her first days on the farm
Thorndyke, Helen Louise
Honey Bunch series (3)
Her first little circus
Thorndyke, Helen Louise
Honey Bunch series (17)
Her first little club
Thorndyke, Helen Louise
Honey Bunch series (19)
Her first little garden
Thorndyke, Helen Louise
Honey Bunch series (5)
Her first little mystery
Thorndyke, Helen Louise
Honey Bunch series (16)
Her first little pet show
Thorndyke, Helen Louise
Honey Bunch series (27)
Her first little treasure hunt
Thorndyke, Helen Louise
Honey Bunch series (18)
Her first summer on an island
Thorndyke, Helen Louise
Honey Bunch series (10)
Her first tour of Toy Town
Thorndyke, Helen Louise
Honey Bunch series (30)
Her first trip in a trailer
Thorndyke, Helen Louise
Honey Bunch series (20)
Her first trip in an airplane
Thorndyke, Helen Louise
Honey Bunch series (12)
Her first trip on a houseboat
Thorndyke, Helen Louise
Honey Bunch series (24)
Her first trip on the Great Lakes
Thorndyke, Helen Louise
Honey Bunch series (11)
Her first trip on the ocean
Thorndyke, Helen Louise
Honey Bunch series (8)
Her first trip to a big fair
Thorndyke, Helen Louise
Honey Bunch series (21)
Her first trip to a lighthouse
Thorndyke, Helen Louise
Honey Bunch series (28)
Her first trip to Reindeer Farm
Thorndyke, Helen Louise
Honey Bunch series (32)
Her first trip to the big woods
Thorndyke, Helen Louise
Honey Bunch series (26)
Her first trip west
Thorndyke, Helen Louise
Honey Bunch series (9)
Her first twin playmates
Thorndyke, Helen Louise
Honey Bunch series (22)
Her first visit to a pony ranch
Thorndyke, Helen Louise
Honey Bunch series (29)
Her first visit to Puppyland
Thorndyke, Helen Louise
Honey Bunch series (31)
Her first visit to the city
Thorndyke, Helen Louise
Honey Bunch series (2)
Her first visit to the seashore
Thorndyke, Helen Louise
Honey Bunch series (4)
Her first visit to the zoo
Thorndyke, Helen Louise
Honey Bunch series (13)
Her first winter at Snowtop
Thorndyke, Helen Louise
Honey Bunch series (25)
Her halo in headlines
Brody, Marc
Marc Brody series (44)
Her Honor, Katie Shannon
Haynes, Betsy
Fabulous Five series (4)
Her ladyship's elephant
Wells, David Dwight
Ladyship and lordship series (1)
Her Majesty, Grace Jones
Langton, Jane
Grace Jones series (2)
Her mother's blood
Anethan, Eleanora Mary d'
Twin soul series (2)
Her mother's keeper
Roberts, Nora
Flowers series (20)
Her people
Dayus, Kathleen
Birmingham life series (1)
Her shining splendor
Sherwood, Valerie
Geoffrey and Lenore series (2)
Her sixteenth year
Brown, Helen Dawes
Anna Lavinia series (2)
Her ways are death
Mann, Jack
Gregory George Gordon Green series (8)
Her weapon is passion
Janson, Hank
Hank Janson series (178)
Herald of doom
Ashe, Gordon
Patrick Dawlish series (49)
Herald of joy
Belle, Pamela
Wintercombe series (2)
Herald personal, and other stories
Carter, Nicholas
Nicholas Carter series (42)
Herb of grace
Goudge, Elizabeth
Eliot family trilogy (2)
Herb of healing
Burgin, George Brown
Four Corners series (10)
Herbert
Wilson, Hazel
Herbert series (1)
Herbert Carter's legacy
Alger, Horatio
Luck and pluck series (8)
Herbert the chicken
Cutler, Ivor
Herbert series (1)
Herbert the elephant
Cutler, Ivor
Herbert series (2)
Herbert's space trip
Wilson, Hazel
Herbert series (2)
Herbie goes bananas
Claro, Joe
Herbie series (4)
Herbie goes to Monte Carlo
Crume, Vic
Herbie series (3)
Herbie Jones
Kline, Suzy
Herbie Jones series (1)
Herbie Jones and Hamburger Head
Kline, Suzy
Herbie Jones series (5)
Herbie Jones and the birthday showdown
Kline, Suzy
Herbie Jones series (9)
Herbie Jones and the class gift
Kline, Suzy
Herbie Jones series (3)
Herbie Jones and the dark attic
Kline, Suzy
Herbie Jones series (8)
Herbie Jones and the monster ball
Kline, Suzy
Herbie Jones series (4)
Herbie Jones reader's theater
Kline, Suzy
Herbie Jones series (7)
Herbie rides again
Cebulash, Mel
Herbie series (2)
Herbie the matchmaker
Claro, Joe
Herbie series (5)
Hercule and the gods
Audemars, Pierre
Hercule Renard series (1)
Hercule Poirot's casebook
Christie, Agatha
Hercule Poirot series (38)
Hercule Poirot's Christmas
Christie, Agatha
Hercule Poirot series (19)
Hercule poirot's early cases
Christie, Agatha
Hercule Poirot series (37)
Hercules, Esq.
Evans, Gwyn
Bill Kellaway series (1)
Herds of Lampasa
Savage, Buck
Speed Johnson series (4)
Here am I, but please send my sister!
Rosser, Glenda Dawn
Missionary mum series (2)
Here and there with Henry
Tippett, James Sterling
Henry series (4)
Here and there with Paul and Peggy
Scott, Florence E
Paul and Peggy series (1)
Here are the Brick Street Boys
Ahlberg, Allan
Brick Street Boys series (1)
Here are the people
Watkins, Peter
Here's the church series (3)
Here at the New Yorker
Gill, Brendan
New York series (1)
Here be demons
Friesner, Esther Mona
Demons trilogy (1)
Here be dragons
Penman, Sharon Kay
Princes of Gwynedd trilogy (1)
Here be monsters
Price, Anthony
Doctor David Audley and Jack Butler series (15)
Here come Bom
Blyton, Enid
Bom series (9)
Here come the bears!
Goudey, Alice Edwards
Here come series (1)
Here come the beavers!
Goudey, Alice Edwards
Here come series (7)
Here come the bees!
Goudey, Alice Edwards
Here come series (10)
Here come the Blinkins
Teitelbaum, Michael
Blinkins series (2)
Here come the boys
Chase, Emily
Canby Hall series (13)
Here come the cottontails!
Goudey, Alice Edwards
Here come series (13)
Here come the dead
Koehler, Robert Portner
Pecos Appleby series (3)
Here come the deer!
Goudey, Alice Edwards
Here come series (2)
Here come the dolphins!
Goudey, Alice Edwards
Here come series (11)
Here come the elephants!
Goudey, Alice Edwards
Here come series (3)
Here come the Huggetts
Constanduros, Mabel
Huggetts series (1)
Here come the lions!
Goudey, Alice Edwards
Here come series (4)
Here come the raccoons!
Goudey, Alice Edwards
Here come series (9)
Here come the seals!
Goudey, Alice Edwards
Here come series (6)
Here come the squirrels!
Goudey, Alice Edwards
Here come series (12)
Here come the Tuckers
Mendel, Jo
Tucker family series (9)
Here come the twins
Blyton, Enid
Twins series (5)
Here come the whales!
Goudey, Alice Edwards
Here come series (5)
Here come the wild dogs!
Goudey, Alice Edwards
Here come series (8)
Here comes a chopper
Mitchell, Gladys
Dame Beatrice Bradley series (19)
Here comes a friend
Mendel, Jo
Tucker family series (7)
Here comes a hero
Block, Lawrence
Evan Tanner series (6)
Here comes Charlie M
Freemantle, Brian
Charlie Muffin series (2)
Here comes Charlie Moon
Hughes, Shirley
Charlie Moon series (1)
Here comes Huxley Pig
Peppe, Rodney
Huxley Pig series (1)
Here comes Jan
Roggeveen, Leonard
Jan series (1)
Here comes John
Graham, Bob
John and friends series (2)
Here comes Mary Mouse again
Blyton, Enid
Mary Mouse series (6)
Here comes McBroom
Fleischman, Sid
McBroom series (7)
Here comes Mister Right
Sharmat, Marjorie Weinman
Sorority sisters series (6)
Here comes Muffin
Mills, Annette
Muffin series (4)
Here comes Mumfie
Tozer, Katharine
Mumfie series (2)
Here comes Noddy again
Blyton, Enid
Noddy series (4)
Here comes Parren
Hildick, Edmund Wallace
Parren series (1)
Here comes Peter
Peterson, Hans
Peter Johnson series (2)
Here comes the bride
Hunter, E J
White Squaw series (15)
Here comes the bridesmaid
Chase, Emily
Canby Hall series (31)
Here comes the copper
Wade, Henry
John Bragg series (1)
Here comes the corpse
Bagby, George
Inspector Schmidt series (8)
Brandon, Gordon
Michael and Terry Terence series (2)

Here comes the Horribilly
Osborne, Maureen
Horribilly series (1)
Here comes the Toff!
Creasey, John
Toff series (5)
Here comes Theo
Graham, Bob
John and friends series (1)
Here comes Thursday!
Bond, Michael
Thursday series (1)
Here comes Tobin
Morgan, Stanley
Russ Tobin series (13)
Here comes trouble
Wilhelm, Hans
Merritales series (7)
Here comes Zelda Claus, and other holiday disasters
Hall, Lynn
Zelda Hammersmith series (3)
Here goes Kitten
Gover, Robert
Kitten series (2)
Here is an S.O.S.
Horler, Sydney
Constable Meatyard series (1)
Here is danger!
Ashe, Gordon
Patrick Dawlish series (15)
Here lies a most beautiful lady
Blaker, Richard
Hester Billiter series (1)
Here lies Andy McGraw
Grover, Marshall
Larry and Stretch series (117)
Here lies blood
Mannon, M M
Sheriff George White series (1)
Here lies Gloria Mundy
Mitchell, Gladys
Dame Beatrice Bradley series (61)
Here lies my wife
McGirr, Edmund
Jim Piron series (2)
Here lies Nancy Frail
Ross, Jonathan
Superintendent George Rogers series (5)
Here lies our Sovereign Lord
Plaidy, Jean
Charles II trilogy (3)
Stuart series (4)
Here lies the body
Burke, Richard
Quinny Hite series (2)
Here lies tomorrow
Gibbs, Anthony
John Archer series (1)
Here, there and everywhere
Hamilton, Frederic
Vanished pomps of yesterday series (3)
Here to die
Sadler, Mark
Paul Shaw series (2)
Here to stay
Emerson, Mark
Two by two series (12)
Sarasin, Jennifer
Cheerleaders series (45)
Here today, dead tomorrow
Lewis, Elliott
Fred Bennett series (5)
Here we go round the buttercups
Ainsworth, Ruth
Little Mushrooms series (1)
Here's Barbie
Lawrence, Cynthia
Barbie series (2)
Here's Benjie
Walter, Francis V
Benjie series (1)
Here's blood in your eye
Long, Manning
Liz Parrott series (1)
Here's Hermione
Greenwald, Sheila
Rosy Cole series (6)
Here's Marny
Lambert, Janet
Jordons series (11)
Here's murder done
Ashton, Charles
Jack Atherley series (7)
Here's Penny
Haywood, Carolyn
Penny series (1)
Here's Pippa again
Boegehold, Betty
Pippa Mouse series (2)
Here's Spot
Hill, Eric
Spot series (13)
Here's the church
Watkins, Peter
Here's the church series (1)
Here's the year
Watkins, Peter
Here's the church series (2)
Here's your O.R.G.Y.
Mark, Ted
Man from O.R.G.Y. series (3)
Heretic's apprentice
Peters, Ellis
Brother Cadfael series (16)
Heretics of Dune
Herbert, Frank
Dune series (5)
Herewith the clues!
Wheatley, Dennis
Lieutenant John Milton Schwab series (4)
Herines of a schoolroom
Tannenforst, Ursula
Mount Cedar series (2)
Heritage
Grier, Sydney Carlyon
Balkan trilogy (2)
Hummel, George Frederick
Heritage series (1)
Heritage in Powdersmoke
Westland, Lynn
Powdersmoke series (3)
Heritage of Blackoaks
Carter, Ashley
Blackoaks series (3)
Heritage of Hastur
Bradley, Marion Zimmer
Darkover series (13)
Heritage of love
Sheldon, Georgie
Golden key series (2)
Heritage of mercy
Tabori, Paul
Spider and moonlight trilogy (3)
Heritage of Quincas Borba
Machado de Assis, Joachim Maria
Quincas Borba series (2)
Heritage of the English library
Irwin, Raymond
English library series (2)
Heritage of the Legion
Grey, Romer Zane
Border Legion series (2)
Heritage of the lizard people
Darlton, Clark
Perry Rhodan series (113)
Heritage of the Sioux
Bower, Bertha Muzzy
Flying U Ranch series (6)
Heritage of the star
Engdahl, Sylvia Louise
Noren series (1)
Heritage of trouble
Carter, Nicholas
Nicholas Carter series (515)
Heritage perilous
Farnol, Jeffery
Mister Jasper Shrig of Bow Street series (8)
Heritors
Short, Agnes
Margaret Montgomery series (1)
Herman and the extraterrestrials
Unger, Jim
Herman series (6)
Herman, dinner's served, as soon as the smoke clears!
Unger, Jim
Herman series (11)
Herman eight
Unger, Jim
Herman treasury series (8)
Herman, M.D.
Unger, Jim
Herman series (8)
Herman out to lunch
Unger, Jim
Herman series (7)
Herman over the wall
Unger, Jim
Herman series (20)
Herman treasury series (7)
Herman Sundays
Unger, Jim
Herman series (4)
Herman, the fourth treasury
Unger, Jim
Herman treasury series (4)
Herman the helper cleans up
Kraus, Robert
Herman the helper series (2)
Herman the helper lends a hand
Kraus, Robert
Herman the helper series (1)
Herman, the sixth treasury
Unger, Jim
Herman treasury series (6)
Herman, the third treasury
Unger, Jim
Herman treasury series (3)
Herman treasury five
Unger, Jim
Herman treasury series (5)
Herman, you can get in the bathroom now
Unger, Jim
Herman series (18)
Herman, you were a much stronger man on our first honeymoon
Unger, Jim
Herman series (5)
Hermit Dan
Parish, Peggy
Liza, Bill and Jed series (5)
Hermit in the hills
Severn, David
Crusoe series (4)
Hermit of Eyton Forest
Peters, Ellis
Brother Cadfael series (14)
Hermit of Gordon's Creek
Lloyd, Hugh
Hal Keen series (1)
Hermit of Proud Hill
Garis, Lilian C
Melody Lane series (9)
Hermit of Turkey Hollow
Train, Arthur
Ephraim Tutt series (3)
Hernan Cortes
Madariaga, Salvador de
New world trilogy (2)
Hero
Rosenberg, Joel
Metzada series (4)
Hero and the crown
McKinley, Robin
Chronicles of Damar series (1)
Hero by proxy
Teilhet, Hildegarde Tolman
Sam Hook series (1)
Hero in Peyton Place
Fuller, Roger
Peyton Place series (8)
Hero of dreams
Lumley, Brian
Cthulhu Mythos series (13)
Dreamlands series (1)
Hero of Herat
Diver, Maud
Eldred Pottinger series (1)
Hero of Liege
Strang, Herbert
Stories of the Great War series (1)
Hero of Pigeon Camp
James, Martha
Pigeon Camp series (3)
Hero of the hills
Browne, George Waldo
Woodranger series (3)
Hero of Varay
Shelley, Rick
Varayan memoir series (2)
Hero of Washington Square
Estes, Rose
Endless quest series (7)
Herod's peal
Thorndike, Russell
Mister Macauley series (2)
Heroes
Miller, Hugh
Teen Eastenders series (3)
Rosenberg, Joel
Guardians of the flame series (5)
Heroes and hellers
Grover, Marshall
Larry and Stretch series (310)
Heroes in hell
Morris, Janet Ellen
Heroes in hell series (1)
Heroes, Inc.
Crocco, Kyle
Heroes, Inc. series (1)
Heroes of Bear Creek
Howard, Robert Ervin
Breckinridge Elkins series (4)
Heroes of Cassino
Eckhardt, Kurt
Heroes series (3)
Heroes of Smokeover
Jacks, Lawrence Pearsall
Smokeover series (2)
Heroes of the Western outposts
McCall, Edith
Frontiers of America series (7)
Heroes of the white shield
Sprague, Rosemary
King Olaf Tryggvason series (2)
Heroes wanted
Crocco, Kyle
Heroes, Inc. series (2)
Heroes without honour
Eckhardt, Kurt
Heroes series (1)
Heroic garrison
Stuart, Vivian
Captain Alexander Sheridan series (5)
Heroic life of Al Capsella
Clarke, Judith
Al Capsella series (1)
Heroin Annie, and other Cliff Hardy stories
Corris, Peter
Cliff Hardy series (6)
Heroin connection
Rosenberger, Joseph
C.O.B.R.A. series (1)
Heroin triple-cross
Weisman, John
Headhunters series (1)
Heroine of 1812
Blanchard, Amy Ella
Revolutionary War series (4)
Heron
Bassani, Giorgio
Ferrara series (5)
Heron ride
Treadgold, Mary
Heron series (1)
Heronbrook
Rundle, Anne
Amberwood series (2)
Heron's Island
Roberts, Gruffydd Dewi
Pikey's Steep series (2)
Heron's Nest
Ford, Elizabeth
Maplechester series (4)
Herons of Pikey's Steep
Roberts, Constance Evelyn
Pikey's Steep series (3)
Hero's return
Cook, Hugh
Chronicles of an age of darkness series (2)
Hers is a hearse
Brody, Marc
Marc Brody series (56)
Herself
Sampson, Fay
Daughter of Tintagel series (5)
Herself and Janet Reachfar
Duncan, Jane
Janet Reachfar series (1)
Herself surprised
Cary, Joyce
Art trilogy (1)
Hervey Willetts
Fitzhugh, Percy Keese
Buddy series (1)
He's got a million
Krymov, Vladimir
Imp trilogy (2)
He's late this morning
Hale, Christopher
Lieutenant Bill French series (12)
He's Valentine, I'm Emerson
Grover, Marshall
Larry and Stretch series (238)
Hess assault
Kessler, Leo
Wotan series (23)
Hester
Bigsby, Christopher
Hester Prynne series (1)
Lewerth, Margaret
Roundtree women series (3)
Hester's counterpart
Baird, Jean Katherine
Hester trilogy (2)
Hester's wage-earning
Baird, Jean Katherine
Hester trilogy (3)
Hetty married
Kilpatrick, Florence Antoinette
Hetty trilogy (2)
Hetty's son
Kilpatrick, Florence Antoinette
Hetty trilogy (3)
Heu-Heu
Haggard, Henry Rider
Allan Quatermain series (8)
Hex
Robeson, Kenneth
Doc Savage series (37)
Hexing
Faulcon, Robert
Nighthunter series (5)
Hey Hippopotamus, do babies eat cake too?
Edwards, Hazel
Hippopotamus series (3)
Hey, remember Fat Glenda?
Perle, Lila
Fat Glenda series (2)
Heyo, Brer Rabbit!
Blyton, Enid
Brer Rabbit adventures series (2)
Hi, Cat!
Keats, Ezra Jack
Peter series (6)
Hi dear, your hair looks great
Browne, Dik
Hagar the horrible series (37)
Hi honey, I'm home
Walker, Mort
Hi and Lois series (3)
Hi, I'm Eddy and here's why I read the Bible
Duffin, Andrew
Eddy series (3)
Hi, I'm Eddy and I believe in Jesus
Duffin, Andrew
Eddy series (2)
Hi, I'm Eddy and this is how I pray
Duffin, Andrew
Eddy series (1)
Hi, I'm Katie Hooper
Sorenson, Jane
Katie Hooper series (1)
Hi-Jack!
Smith, Guy Newman
Truckers series (2)
Hi-jack
Spade, Danny
Danny Spade series (21)
Hi Jinks!
Severy, Richard
Jinks Gang series (4)
Hi-Jinks joins the bears
Baker, Margaret Joyce
Three bears series (4)
Hi-spy-kick-the-can
Macclure, Victor
Inspector Archie Burford series (6)
Hi there, supermouse
Ure, Jean
Nicola Bruce series (1)
Hiccup
Mayer, Mercer
Ah-choo series (2)
Hickety pickety
Butler, Peter
Rounds series (1)
Hickory, dickory, death
Christie, Agatha
Hercule Poirot series (29)
Hickory, dickory, dock
Christie, Agatha
Hercule Poirot series (29)
Hidden agenda
Matera, Lia
Willa Jansson series (3)
Hidden blood
Tuttle, Wilbur Coleman
Hashknife Hartley and Sleepy Stevens series (9)
Hidden box mystery
Heide, Florence Parry
Spotlight Detective Club series (3)
Hidden children
Chambers, Robert William
Cardigan series (3)
Hidden city
De Lint, Charles
Dungeon series (5)
Eddings, David
Tamuli trilogy (3)
Hidden clue
Sutton, Margaret
Judy Bolton series (35)
Hidden death
Grant, Maxwell
Shadow series (14)
Hidden door
Gask, Arthur
Gilbert Larose series (8)
Hidden evil
Montgomery, Raymond A
Rebels in the New World series (4)
Hidden eyes
Levison, Eric
Doctor Edward Lester series (1)

High tide at noon
Ogilvie, Elisabeth May
Bennett Island series (1)
High tide temptress
Brody, Marc
Marc Brody series (73)
High time
Hillary, Louise
Himalayan series (2)
Lasswell, Mary
Mrs Feeley series (2)
High times in the middle of nowhere
Laurence, Murray
Compulsive traveller series (1)
High Toby
Watson, Henry Brereton Marriott
Dick Ryder series (2)
High trail to danger
Nixon, Joan Lowery
Deadly promise series (1)
High treason
Bruce, Jean
Secret Agent O.S.S.117 series (14)
Upward, Allen
High treason series (1)
High treason at Catfish Bend
Burman, Ben Lucien
Catfish Bend series (5)
High Valley River
Grey, Romer Zane
Buck Duane series (4)
High vengeance
Longtree, Warren T
Ruff Justice series (16)
High voltage
Chastain, Thomas
Inspector Max Kauffman series (4)
High walk to Wandlemere
Sibley, Patricia
Wandlemere series (1)
High wall
Copper, Basil
Mike Faraday series (18)
Truss, Seldon
Inspector Gidleigh series (9)
High water
Ling, Peter
Water series (1)
High water at Catfish Bend
Burman, Ben Lucien
Catfish Bend series (1)
High, wide and deadly
Logan, Jake
John Slocum series (102)
High, wide and ransom
Tracy, Don
Giff Speer series (7)
High window
Chandler, Raymond
Philip Marlowe series (3)
High wire
Haggard, William
Colonel Charles Russell series (5)
High wizardry
Duane, Diane
Wizard series (3)
High yield in death
Carter, Nick
Nick Carter series (111)
Highbinders
Bleeck, Oliver
Philip Saint Ives series (4)
Braun, Matt
Ash Tallman series (1)
Lord, Tom
Tallman series (1)
Parker, F M
Tom Galletin series (1)
Highcliff on tour
Little, Sylvia
Highcliff series (4)
Highcliff, top of the form
Little, Sylvia
Highcliff series (2)
Higher education
Blake, Susan
Hawthorne College series (9)
Higher Jones
Gibb, Lee
Jones series (2)
Higher on the door
Stevenson, James
Growing up series (2)
Highest science
Roberts, Gareth
Timewyrm series (5)
Highflight to hell
Wallace, C H
Steve Ramsay series (2)
Highgate Rise
Perry, Anne
Charlotte Ellison Pitt and Inspector Thomas Pitt series (12)
Highland Bumble
Eldon, Magdalen
Bumble series (3)
Highland collie
Terhune, Albert Payson
Sunnybank collies series (13)
Highland fling
Laird, Elizabeth
Toucan Tecs series (9)
Highland homespun
Leigh, Margaret Mary
Highland series (1)
Highland homicide
Austwick, John
Inspector Parker series (1)
Highland interlude
Andrews, Lucilla
Saint Martha's Hospital series (3)
Highland laddie gone
McCrumb, Sharon
Elizabeth Macpherson series (3)
Highland quest
Milroy, Clarita
Highland quest series (1)
Highland twins and the Chalet School
Brent-Dyer, Elinor Mary
Chalet School series (16)
Highland velvet
Deveraux, Jude
Montgomery annals series (2)
Highland vet
Stevenson, Robert
Highland vet series (1)
Highlander
Kemp, Robert
Stories of Edinburgh life series (3)
Highlanders
Davis, Gerry
Doctor Who series (90)
Highly explosive case
Chambers, Peter
Mark Preston series (29)
Highly inflammable
Saltmarsh, Max
Archie Lumsden series (1)
Highroad to adventure
Pease, Howard
Tod Moran series (8)
Highroller's man
Hogan, Ray
Shawn Starbuck series (13)
Highway clash
Morris, Dave
Transformers series (3)
Highway holocaust
Dever, Joe
Freeway warrior series (1)
Highway of death
Hardin, J D
Raider series (29)
Highway robbery
Dixon, Franklin W
Hardy boys case files series (41)
Highway through hell
Whiting, Charles
T-Force series (3)
Highway to heaven
Blamires, Harry
Heaven and Hell trilogy (3)
Highway to murder
Howard, Hartley
Glenn Bowman series (33)
Highway warriors
Ham, Bob
Overload series (3)
Highwayman
Gruber, Frank
Historical Western series (12)
Hijacked
Brightfield, Richard
Choose your own adventure series (106)
Marks, James Macdonald
Jason Wright series (1)
Hijacker's moon
Grover, Marshall
Larry and Stretch series (138)
Hijacking Manhattan
Derrick, Lionel
Penetrator series (4)
Hiker's secret
Edwards, Walter
Sexton Blake series (740)
Hilarious adventures of Paddington
Bond, Michael
Paddington series (7)
Hilary
Jenkins, Jerry Bruce
Margo Franklin and Philip Spence series (3)
Hilary's holidays
Ellis, Vivian
Hilary series (2)
Hilary's terms
Janson, Hank
Hank Janson series (148)
Hilary's tune
Ellis, Vivian
Hilary series (1)
Hild at Allotment Lane School
Joy, Margaret
Allotment Lane School series (3)
Hilda at school
Garrard, Phillis
Hilda series (1)
Hilda, fifteen
Garrard, Phillis
Hilda series (4)
Hilda Lessways
Bennett, Arnold
Clayhanger series (2)
Five towns series (11)
Hilda of Grey Cottage
Ginther, Mary Pemberton
Hilda series (1)
Hilda of Landis and Co.
Ginther, Mary Pemberton
Hilda series (2)
Hilda of the green smock
Ginther, Mary Pemberton
Hilda series (3)
Hilda of the Three Star Ranch
Ginther, Mary Pemberton
Hilda series (4)
Hilda's adventures
Garrard, Phillis
Hilda series (3)
Hildegarde
Norris, Kathleen
Crabtree family series (2)
Hildegarde Withers makes the scene
Palmer, Stuart
Hildegarde Withers series (17)
Hildegarde's harvest
Richards, Laura Elizabeth
Hildegarde series (5)
Hildegarde's holiday
Richards, Laura Elizabeth
Hildegarde series (2)
Hildegarde's home
Richards, Laura Elizabeth
Hildegarde series (3)
Hildegarde's neighbors
Richards, Laura Elizabeth
Hildegarde series (4)
Hill
Rigby, Ray
Hill series (1)
Vachell, Horace Annesley
Harrow School series (1)
Hill Farm story
Ruck, Ruth Janette
Hill Farm trilogy (2)
Hill fog
Chance, John Newton
Jonathan Blake series (34)
Hill of destiny
Giono, Jean
Trilogy of earth (1)
Hill of doves
Cloete, Stuart
Van der Berg family series (3)
Hill of sand
Rigby, Ray
Hill series (2)
Hill of summer
Drury, Allen
Soviet conquest series (1)
Hill of the Ring
Lupton, Joyce
Leigh family series (1)
Hill of the terrified monk
Homes, Geoffrey
Jose Manuel Madero series (2)
Hill station
Farrell, James Gordon
British Empire trilogy (3)
Hill war
Fitz Roy, Olivia
Stewarts series (4)
Hillary to the rescue
Armstrong, Jennifer
Pets, Inc. series (3)
Hilliken
Brown, Rollo Walter
Emergency series (3)
Hillingdon Hall
Surtees, Robert Smith
Mister John Jorrocks series (3)
Hills
Bernen, Robert
Blue Stacks series (2)
Hills and the valley
Tanner, Janet
Hillsbridge series (3)
Hills is lonely
Beckwith, Lillian
Hebrides series (2)
Hills of death
Grant, Maxwell
Shadow series (138)
Hills of heaven
Farrimond, John
Graham's Gang series (2)
Hills of home
Finlay, Eileen
Boyd family series (1)
Fraser, Amy Stewart
Hills of home trilogy (1)
Hills of the dead
Howard, Robert Ervin
Solomon Kane series (3)
Potter, Jay Hill
Pilgrim series (11)
Hills stand watch
Derleth, August
Wisconsin series (3)
Hilt to hilt
Cooke, John Esten
Southern Army campaign trilogy (2)
Him
Anonymous
Pronoun series (2)
Himalayan assignment
Mason, Francis Van Wyck
Colonel Hugh North series (18)
Himalayan concerto
Masters, John
Bateman family series (2)
Himitsu attack
Barker, Wade
War of the Ninja Master series (3)
Himmler's gold
Kessler, Leo
Stormtroop series (5)
Himself again
Pickering, Robert Easton
Dick Philip series (2)
Himself and a missing uncle
Bird, Kenneth
Himself series (5)
Himself and Macafferty's queen
Bird, Kenneth
Himself series (2)
Himself and the fake Santas
Bird, Kenneth
Himself series (11)
Himself and the golden ghost
Bird, Kenneth
Himself series (13)
Himself and the Kerry crucher
Bird, Kenneth
Himself series (9)
Himself and the Rooney rebellion
Bird, Kenneth
Himself series (8)
Himself and tomorrow's ogre
Bird, Kenneth
Himself series (12)
Himself and Whistler's niece
Bird, Kenneth
Himself series (7)
Himself beats the Bill
Bird, Kenneth
Himself series (10)
Himself in a yellow balloon
Bird, Kenneth
Himself series (4)
Hindu trinity
Rosenberger, Joseph
Death Merchant series (68)
Hinges of hell
Sterling, Stewart
Ben Pedley series (5)
Fire Marshal Ben Pedley series (5)
Hip-deep in alligators
Campbell, Robert Wright
Jimmy Flannery series (3)
Hip-Hippo-Ray
Ahlberg, Allan
Help your child to read series (7)
Hippo leaves home
Hargreaves, Roger
Hippo, Potto and Mouse series (4)
Hippo lemonade
Thaler, Mike
Hippo series (2)
Hippo, Potto and Mouse
Hargreaves, Roger
Hippo, Potto and Mouse series (3)
Hippopotamus
Fry, Stephen
Ted Wallace series (2)
Hippy Buchan
Boileau, Ethel
Hippy Buchan series (1)
Hira Singh's tale
Mundy, Talbot
Sikh series (3)
Hiram Golf's religion
Hepworth, George Hughes
Hiram Golf series (1)
Hiram in the Middle West
Todd, Burbank L
Back to the soil series (2)
Hiram, the young farmer
Todd, Burbank L
Back to the soil series (1)
Hire a hangman
Wilcox, Collin
Lieutenant Frank Hastings series (17)
Hire me a hearse
Marlowe, Piers
Frank Drury and Inspector Bill Hazard series (5)
Hire purchase crime
Chester, Gilbert
Sexton Blake series (960)
Hire-purchase fraud
Tyrer, Walter
Sexton Blake series (1316)
Hired help for Rabbit
Delton, Judy
Rabbit series (4)
Hired man
Bragg, Melvyn
Tallentire family series (1)
Hireling
Macleod, Alison
Tom Vaughan series (1)
Hiring fair
Stirling, Jessica
Stalker family trilogy (2)
His burial too
Aird, Catherine
Inspector C D Sloan series (5)
His butler's story
Limonov, Edward
Eddie Limonov series (3)
His dog
Terhune, Albert Payson
Sunnybank collies series (4)
His Eminence, Death
Quinn, Simon
Inquisitor series (1)
His Excellency
Zola, Emile
Rougon Macquart series (6)
His Excellency and Peter
Harper, Theodore Acland
Siberian series (3)
His Excellency Eugene Rougon
Zola, Emile
Rougon Macquart series (6)
His Excellency, Governor Wallace
Wilson, Alexander
Sir Leonard Wallace series (5)
His Excellency's English governess
Grier, Sydney Carlyon
Modern East series (2)
His Excellency's secret
Murray, Andrew
Sexton Blake series (20)
His father's crime
Graydon, William Murray
Sexton Blake series (388)
His father's son
Pier, Arthur Stanwood
Saint Timothy's School series (5)
His favourite flower
Housman, Laurence
Palace plays series (3)
His first leave
Harker, Lizzie Allen
Mister Wycherly series (3)
His first term
Finnemore, John
Teddy Lester series (2)
His Grace of Osmond
Burnett, Frances Hodgson
Lady of quality series (2)
His Highness commands Pendragon
Trevelyan, Robert
Pendragon series (2)
His last bow
Doyle, Arthur Conan
Sherlock Holmes series (8)
His last vow
Ruyle, John
Turlock Loams series (3)
His lordship's leopard
Wells, David Dwight
Ladyship and lordship series (2)
His majesty, the crook
Evans, Gwyn
Quentin Drex series (1)
His Majesty's frigate
White, Simon
Penhaligon trilogy (3)

His Majesty's peacock
Mackenzie, William Andrew
Sir Nigel Lacaita series (1)
His masterpiece?
Zola, Emile
Rougon Macquart series (14)
His one fault
Trowbridge, John Townsend
Tide Mill series (5)
His own funeral
Barrett, Geoffrey John
Inspector Blessingay series (4)
His own master
Trowbridge, John Townsend
Silver medal series (1)
His prey was man
Gask, Arthur
Gilbert Larose series (19)
His rise to power
Miller, Henry Russell
Life and love series (2)
His Royal Highness, J Aubrey Whitford
Roderus, Frank
J Aubrey Whitford series (2)
His son's honour
Bobin, John William
Sexton Blake series (117)
His unfinished voyage
Westerman, Percy Francis
Alan Carr series (1)
His weight in gold
Procter, Maurice
Chief Inspector Harry Martineau series (20)
Hissing Sid and the swimming lesson
Lloyd, Jeremy
Captain Beaky and his band series (3)
Histoire
Simon, Claude
Grass quartet (4)
Historian's holiday
Bryant, Arthur
Historian series (1)
History and adventures of Peregrine Pickle
Smollett, Tobias
Morgan the Welshman series (2)
History and environment
Braudel, Fernand
Identity of France series (1)
History of a conscript of 1813
Erckmann, Emile
French campaign series (1)
History of Henry Esmond
Thackeray, William Makepeace
Virginia series (1)
History of Middle Earth
Tolkien, John Ronald Reuel
Middle Earth series (5)
History of Northern Rhodesia
Gann, Lewis Henry
History of Rhodesia series (1)
History of Pendennis
Thackeray, William Makepeace
Arthur Pendennis series (1)
History of sexuality
Foucault, Michel
History of sexuality series (1)
History of Southern Rhodesia
Gann, Lewis Henry
History of Rhodesia series (2)
History of the British secret service
Deacon, Richard
Secret service series (1)
History of the Chinese secret service
Deacon, Richard
Secret service series (3)
History of the Japanese secret service
Deacon, Richard
Secret service series (5)
History of the Runestaff
Moorcock, Michael
History of Runestaff series (4)
History of the Russian secret service
Deacon, Richard
Secret service series (2)
History of the thirteen
Balzac, Honore de
Scenes of Parisian life series (1)
History of western philosophy
Russell, Bertrand
Western philosophy series (1)
Hit
Deming, Richard
Mod Squad series (5)
Hit and run
Ashford, Jeffrey
Detective Inspector Don Kerry series (3)
Creasey, John
Inspector Roger West series (21)
Klein, Dave
Butch Lewis series (2)
O'Callaghan, Maxine
Delilah West series (3)
Stivers, Dick
Able Team series (30)
Hit and run holiday
Keene, Carolyn
Nancy Drew files series (5)
Hit it rich
Bardsley, Michael
Superintendent Donald Martin series (4)
Hit man
Eisenberg, Lisa
South City cops series (1)
Rossi, Bruno
Sharpshooter series (10)
Hit me hard
Graham, Neill
Solo Malcolm series (5)
Hit number twenty nine
Joey
Joey series (1)
Hit on the house
Jackson, Jon Anthony
Sergeant Fang Mulheisen series (4)
Hit or myth
Asprin, Robert Lynn
Skeeve series (4)
Riddell, James
Animal lore and disorder series (2)
Hit parade
Rainey, Rich
Alex Dartanian series (3)
Hit squad
Kastle, Herbert David
Sergeant Edmund Roersch series (3)
Hit the beach!
Mackie, John
Rat Bastards series (1)
Hit the leather
Grover, Marshall
Bleak Creek series (3)
Hit the road and strike it rich
Maguire, Jack
Many lives of Underfoot the cat series (2)
Hitch-hiker
Christian, Petra
Sally Deenes series (1)
Hitch-hiker's companion
Adams, Douglas Noel
Arthur Dent series (5)
Hitch-hiker's guide to the galaxy
Adams, Douglas Noel
Arthur Dent series (1)
Hitch-hiker's quartet
Adams, Douglas Noel
Arthur Dent series (4)
Hitch-hiker's trilogy
Adams, Douglas Noel
Arthur Dent series (3)
Hitch in time
Joyce, Cyril
Chief Superintendent Pat Stockton series (8)
Hitchhike killer
Ross, Paul
Chopper Cop series (1)
Hite report
Hite, Shere
Hite report series (1)
Hite report of the family
Hite, Shere
Hite report series (3)
Hite report on male sexuality
Hite, Shere
Hite report series (2)
Hitler diamonds
Cory, Desmond
Johnny Fedora series (3)
Hitler needs you
Story, Jack Trevor
Horace Spurgeon Fenton series (1)
Hitler's high seas fleet
Humble, Richard
High seas fleet series (1)
Hitler's last secret
Price, Roger
Tomorrow people series (5)
Hits and memories
Read, Mark Brandon
Chopper series (2)
Hits and misses
Keene, Carolyn
Nancy Drew and Hardy boys supermystery series (14)
Hitting paydirt
Gilman, George G
Edge series (53)
Hitting, pitching and running, maybe
Paulsen, Gary
Sports on the light side series (2)
Hitting the line
Barbour, Ralph Henry
Grafton School trilogy (3)
HMS Cracker
Styles, Showell
Lieutenant Michael Fitton series (5)
HMS Surprise
O'Brian, Patrick
Jack Aubrey and Stephen Maturin series (3)
Ho-Ho and Too Smart
Blyton, Enid
Little books series (4)
Hoa-Tien kill
Lansing, John
Black Eagles series (19)
Hoaryhead
Abbott, Jacob
Hoaryhead series (1)
Hoaryhead and M'Donner
Abbott, Jacob
Hoaryhead series (2)
Young Christian series (4)
Hoaryhead and the vallies below
Abbott, Jacob
Young Christian series (5)
Hoax
Lawrence, Lars
Seed series (4)
Hoax on you
Singer, Marilyn
Sam and Dave series (6)
Hob and the horse-bat
Read, *Miss*
Hobby Horse Cottage series (2)
Hobbema prospect
Hilton, John Buxton
Superintendent Simon Kenworthy series (13)
Hobbit
Tolkien, John Ronald Reuel
Middle Earth series (2)
Hobbit's travels
Green, Michael
Middle Earth series (2)
Hobby for Mrs Arbuckle
Smyth, Gwenda
Mrs Arbuckle series (2)
Hobby Horse Cottage
Read, *Miss*
Hobby Horse Cottage series (1)
Hobeycomb bid
Sandberg, Berent
Matt Eberhart series (2)
Hobgoblin murder
Strahan, Kay Cleaver
Lynn Macdonald series (6)
Hobo Dog
Hurd, Thacher
Hobo Dog series (1)
Hobo Dog in the ghost town
Hurd, Thacher
Hobo Dog series (3)
Hobo Dog's Christmas tree
Hurd, Thacher
Hobo Dog series (2)
Hobo woods
Helm, Eric
Ground Zero series (7)
Hobstones
Bagshaw, Joyce Margaret
Hobstones series (1)
Hochmann miniatures
Fish, Robert Lloyd
Kek Huuygens series (1)
Hocken and Hunken
Quiller-Couch, Arthur
Troy Town series (9)
Hockey
Aaseng, Nathan
You are the coach series (4)
Hockey super scorers
Aaseng, Nathan
Sports heroes series (33)
Hockey term at Trebizon
Digby, Anne
Trebizon series (9)
Hockey trick
Corbett, Scott
Kerby Maxwell series (10)
Hockey's fearless goalies
Aaseng, Nathan
Sports heroes series (32)
Hocus Locust
Cosgrove, Stephen Edward
Bugg series (46)
Hocus-pocus dilemma
Kibbe, Pat
Pinkerton family series (1)
Hogan's last case
Charles, Wyndham
Chief Superintendent Sebastian Griffin series (1)
Hoggie
Watson, Julian
Hoggie series (1)
Hoggie and bear
Watson, Julian
Hoggie series (2)
Hogglespike
Drew, Patricia
Hogglespike series (1)
Hogglespike and Thistle
Drew, Patricia
Hogglespike series (2)
Hogglespike in danger
Drew, Patricia
Hogglespike series (3)
Hogleg Hill
Dalton, Kit
Buckskin series (36)
Hog's Back mystery
Crofts, Freeman Wills
Inspector Joseph French series (10)
Hoka!
Anderson, Poul
Hoka series (3)
Holbein mystery
Wynne, Anthony
Doctor Eustace Hailey series (20)
Hold 'em back!
Grover, Marshall
Larry and Stretch series (413)
Hold my hand, I'm dying
Davis, John Gordon
Hold my hand series (1)
Hold my hand, or else
Clark, Margaret Dianne
Sam and Leanne series (1)
Hold on to love
Hunter, Mollie
Bridie McShane series (2)
Hold out
Bruton, Eric
City of London Police series (1)
Hold that tiger
Ambler, Dail
Danny Spade series (25)
Hold that tyger
Riefe, Alan
Tyger Decker series (5)
Hold the bridge
Brogan, Mike
Action Man series (1)
Hold the dream
Bradford, Barbara Taylor
Emma Harte series (2)
Holden earth
Lewis, Norman
Dragon apparent series (2)
Holding on
Lowell, Anne Hunter
Sorority girls series (12)
Mann, Sunnie
Hostage crisis series (1)
Hold-up
Rey, Bret
Ned Butler series (1)
Hole
Ramsay, Jay
Great return series (3)
Hole in the vault
Carter, Nicholas
Nicholas Carter series (132)
Holey Moley Cow
Kanno, Wendy
Funny Farm series (1)
Holiday
Clewes, Dorothy
Penny series (5)
Grahame, Kenneth
Smith family series (1)
Holiday adventurers
Lethbridge, Peter
Jeremy series (1)
Holiday adventures of Mister P J Davenant
Hamilton, Frederic
P J Davenant series (1)
Holiday annual stories
Blyton, Enid
Holiday stories series (1)
Holiday at Dew-Drop Inn
Garnett, Eve
Ruggles family series (3)
Holiday at Roselands
Finley, Martha Farquharson
Roselands series (1)
Holiday camp donkeys
Towers, Joyce
Donkey series (4)
Holiday camp murder
Francis, Basil
Sergeant Paul Dean series (3)
Holiday camp mystery
Cole, Margaret Alice
Judy Lawler series (1)
Tyrer, Walter
Sexton Blake series (1198)
Holiday campers
Christian, Petra
Sally Deenes series (3)
Holiday engagement
Ford, Elizabeth
Maplechester series (6)
Holiday exchange
Pye, Virginia
Price family series (8)
Holiday family
Edwards, Sylvia
Sally Baxter series (6)
Holiday for Havoc
Jakes, John
Johnny Havoc series (3)
Holiday for Inspector West
Creasey, John
Inspector Roger West series (5)
Holiday for Mister Muster
Lobel, Arnold
Mister Muster series (2)
Holiday for murder
Christie, Agatha
Hercule Poirot series (19)
Holiday for Noah
Topek, Susan Remick
Noah series (1)
Holiday house
Hardcastle, Michael
Steve and Anna series (4)
Holiday in a trailer
Greene, Carla
Travel series (2)
Holiday magic stories
Blyton, Enid
Holiday stories series (2)
Holiday mischief
Pascal, Francine
Sweet Valley twins super series (2)
Holiday pixie stories
Blyton, Enid
Holiday stories series (3)
Holiday round
Milne, Alan Alexander
Day's play series (2)
Holiday toy stories
Blyton, Enid
Holiday stories series (4)
Holiday trench
Ballantyne, Jean
Maitland series (1)
Holiday witch
Willson, Robina Beckles
Witch series (2)
Holiday with a vengeance
Perry, Ritchie
Philis series (4)
Holiday with Henrietta
Kruss, James
Henrietta Chuffertrain series (2)
Holiday with murder
Carr, Glyn
Sir Abercrombie Lewker series (13)
Holiday with the fiend
Lavelle, Sheila
Charlie Ellis and Angela Mitchell series (4)
Holidays
Oxenbury, Helen
Baby board books series (1)
Holidays at Roselands
Finley, Martha Farquharson
Elsie Dinsmore series (2)
Holidays at The Warren
Sindall, Marjorie Aylwynn
Warren series (3)
Holladay case
Stevenson, Burton Egbert
Jim Godfrey series (1)
Hollow
Christie, Agatha
Hercule Poirot series (24)
Hollow chest
Tilton, Alice
Leonidas Witherall series (5)
Hollow crown affair
McDaniel, David
Man from U.N.C.L.E. series (17)
Hollow hills
Stewart, Mary
Merlin and Arthur series (2)

Hollow lands
Moorcock, Michael
Dancers at the end of time series (2)
Jherek Carnelian and Amelia Underwood series (2)
Hollow man
Carr, John Dickson
Doctor Gideon Fell series (6)
Roeburt, John
Johnny Devereaux series (2)
Hollow needle
Coxe, George Harmon
Kent Murdock series (10)
Leblanc, Maurice
Arsene Lupin series (3)
Hollow on the hill
Milne, Christopher
Enchanted places series (3)
Hollow vengeance
Morice, Anne
Tessa Crichton Price series (16)
Hollowing
Holdstock, Robert
Mythago series (3)
Hollowpoint hell
Cain, Jonathan
Saigon commandos series (11)
Holly Hotel
Kyle, Elisabeth
Furze series (4)
Holly Lane
Bradbury, Catherine
Applebury tales series (4)
Hollys of Tooting Steps
Prime, Heather
Hollys series (1)
Hollys on wheels
Prime, Heather
Hollys series (2)
Hollywood
Bukowski, Charles
Henry Chinaski series (3)
Hollywood and LeVine
Bergman, Andrew
Jack LeVine series (2)
Hollywood and Vine
Le Vine, Jack
Jack Le Vine series (2)
Hollywood assassin
Jason, Stuart
Butcher series (20)
Hollywood girl
McEvoy, Joseph Patrick
Show girl series (2)
Hollywood hell
Pendleton, Don
Mack Bolan series (77)
Hollywood hoax
Frazer, Robert Caine
Mark Kilby series (4)
Hollywood husbands
Collins, Jackie
Hollywood series (2)
Hollywood kids
Collins, Jackie
Hollywood series (3)
Hollywood murder mystery
Crooker, Herbert
Clay Brooke series (1)
Hollywood murders
Queen, Ellery
Ellery Queen series (44)
Hollywood mystery
Resnick, Sylvia
Debbie Preston, teenage reporter series (2)
Hollywood wives
Collins, Jackie
Hollywood series (1)
Holmes-Dracula file
Saberhagen, Fred
Dracula series (14)
Sherlock Holmes sequels series (32)
Holocaust auction
Edwards, Paul
John Eagle series (10)
Holocaust for hire
Silva, Joseph
Captain America series (3)
Holocaust horror
Grant, Mark
Mutants amok series (4)
Holster law
Scott, Bradford
Walt Slade series (26)
Young, Gordon Ray
Red Clark series (10)
Holt, R.N.
Mackintosh, Ian
Warship series (3)
Holy Blood and the Holy Grail
Baigent, Michael
Order of Sion series (1)
Lincoln, Henry
Order of Sion series (1)
Holy City
Lagerlof, Selma
Jerusalem series (2)
Holy day book
Weiser, Francis Xavier
Christian festivals trilogy (3)
Holy disorders
Crispin, Edmund
Gervase Fen series (2)
Holy experiment
De Hartog, Jan
Peaceable kingdom series (2)
Holy Father's navy
Purser, Philip
Colin Panton series (3)
Holy flower
Haggard, Henry Rider
Allan Quatermain series (7)
Holy flower trilogy (1)
Holy Ireland
Hoult, Norah
Holy Ireland series (1)
Holy land
Lagerkvist, Par
Tobias trilogy (3)
Holy pictures
Boylan, Clare
Nan and Mary Cantwell series (1)
Holy spirit
Leslie, Peter
Father Hayes trilogy (3)
Holy terror
Charteris, Leslie
Saint series (8)
Goodman, Paul
Empire City quartet (3)
Empire city series (3)
Murphy, Warren Burton
Destroyer series (19)
Holy thief
Peters, Ellis
Brother Cadfael series (19)
Holy Treasure!
Williams, David
Mark Treasure series (13)
Holy war
Bunyan, John
John Bunyan series (3)
Carter, Nick
Nick Carter series (225)
Holy wedlock
James, Charles Thomas Clement
Mrs Grundy series (1)
Homage to Blenholt
Fuchs, Daniel
Williamsburg trilogy (2)
Home
Emberley, Ed
First words series (1)
Gree, Alain
Books and games series (2)
Hearne, Betsy Gould
Megan series (2)
Home again at Timber Creek
Clark, Mavis Thorpe
Timber Creek series (2)
Home and dry
Fuller, Roy
Strange and the good trilogy (3)
Home and murder
Stein, Aaron Marc
Matt Erridge series (3)
Home are the hunted
Wylie, Ida Alexa Ross
Provencal Hills series (2)
Home as found
Cooper, James Fenimore
Home series (2)
Home at last
Harthern, Ernest
Palestine home series (2)
Home brewed
Davis, Oswald Harcourt
Ardencester series (3)
Home crafts
Kalman, Bobbie
Historic communities series (3)
Home farm
Fitzgerald, Hilary
Alastair, Elizabeth and Peter Robin series (1)
Home fires burning
Miller, Hugh
Eastenders series (1)
Home for animals
Burkett, Molly
Home for animals series (2)
Home for Christmas
Pascal, Francine
Sweet Valley University series (8)
Home for Jessie
Pullein-Thompson, Christine
Jessie series (1)
Home for the holidays
Peck, Winifred
Childhood series (2)
Home from sea
Packer, Joy
Pack and follow series (4)
Home from the hill
Humphrey, William
Red River County trilogy (1)
Home from the shore
Dickson, Gordon Rupert
Sea people series (1)
Home in the bear's domain
Martin, Martha
Alaska series (2)
Home in the Holy Land
Finn, Elizabeth Anne MacCaul
Jerusalem series (1)
Home influence
Aguilar, Grace
Home influence series (1)
Home is the hotel
Nicol, Jean
Hotel series (2)
Home is the hunter
Kramer, Dana
Star trek series (52)
Home is where the heart is
Richards, Vicki
Star trek fan series (24)
Home is where the quick is
Johnston, William
Mod Squad series (6)
Home-made dragon, and other incredible stories
Hunter, Norman
Kingdom of Incredibilia series (2)
Home of his children
Bayfield, William John
Sexton Blake series (110)
Home place
Morris, Wright
Lone Tree series (2)
Home port
Prouty, Olive Higgins
Vale family series (4)
Home ranch
Moody, Ralph
Ralph series (4)
Home rule
Boylan, Clare
Nan and Mary Cantwell series (2)
Home run
James, Laurence
Baseball series (2)
Home run feud
Bee, Clair
Chip Hilton series (22)
Home run Hennessey
Lawton, Charles
Clarkeville series (4)
Home run trick
Corbett, Scott
Kerby Maxwell series (9)
Home Secretary will see you now, sir
Ison, Graham
Superintendent John Gaffney series (3)
Home, sweat home
Walker, Mort
Hi and Lois series (1)
Home sweet haunted house
Sorenson, Jane
Katie Hooper series (2)
Home sweet home
Quin-Harkin, Janet
Sugar and spice series (15)
Home sweet homicide
Story, Jack Trevor
Sexton Blake series (1479)
Home, to Avalon
Landis, Arthur Harold
Camelot series (4)
Home to Numidia
Motley, Mary
Morning glory series (3)
Home to roost
Stout, Rex
Nero Wolfe and Archie Goodwin series (20)
Home to the Hermitage
Crabb, Alfred Leland
Nashville series (5)
Home to the prairie
Tedrow, Thomas L
Days of Laura Ingalls Wilder series (4)
Home to Witchend
Saville, Malcolm
Lone Pine Five Club series (20)
Home was an island
Davison, Ann
Voyages series (1)
Homecoming
Dalmas, John
Nils Jarnhan series (2)
Hamner, Earl
Spencer family series (2)
Lewin, Hugh
Jafta series (7)
Lofts, Norah
Sir Godfrey Tallboys series (2)
Mackenzie, Lee
Emmerdale Farm series (16)
McKinney, Jack
Robotech series (3)
Smith, David Alexander
Marathon trilogy (3)
Voigt, Cynthia
Tillermans series (1)
Homecomings
Snow, Charles Percy
Strangers and brothers series (7)
Homeland
Salvatore, Robert Anthony
Dark elf trilogy (1)
Homemade sin
Trocheck, Kathy Hogan
Callahan Garrity series (3)
Homemakers
Fisher, Leonard Everett
Colonial Americans series (18)
Homeplace
Chapman, Maristan
Happy mountain series (2)
Homer goes to Stratford
Baker, Margaret Joyce
Homer series (3)
Homer goes west
Baker, Margaret Joyce
Homer series (5)
Homer in orbit
Baker, Margaret Joyce
Homer series (4)
Homer sees the Queen
Baker, Margaret Joyce
Homer series (2)
Homer the tortoise
Baker, Margaret Joyce
Homer series (1)
Home's a nice place to visit, but I wouldn't want to live there
Kaye, Marilyn
Three of a kind series (2)
Homesmind
Sargent, Pamela
Earthminds trilogy (3)
Homesteader guns
Roberts, J R
Gunsmith series (67)
Homesteaders
Willoughby, Lee Davis
Making of America series (15)
Homesteader's revenge
Hardin, J D
Raider and Doc series (41)
Homesteading in Standing Bear's territory
Palmer, Bernard
Bradley series (5)
Homeward bound
Axler, James
Deathlands series (5)
Cooper, James Fenimore
Home series (1)
Lethbridge, Mabel
Fortune grass series (3)
Verne, Jules
Hector Servadac series (2)
Homeward tide
White, Alan
Aysgill family trilogy (1)
Ravenswyke series (2)
Homeward winds the river
Johnson, Barbara Ferry
Plantation series (2)
Homewood trilogy
Wideman, John Edgar
Homewood trilogy (3)
Homework
Stine, Jane
Everything you need to survive series (3)
Homework is ruining my life
Evans, Greg
Luann series (6)
Homework machine
Williams, Jay
Danny Dunn series (3)
Homeworld
Harrison, Harry
To the stars trilogy (1)
Homicidal holiday
Brandon, Gordon
Michael and Terry Terence series (5)
Homicidal horse
Pentecost, Hugh
Julian Quist series (9)
Homicidal virgin
Halliday, Brett
Michael Shayne series (38)
Homicide
White, Leslie Turner
Captain Barnaby series (2)
Homicide at Yuletide
Kane, Henry
Peter Chambers series (5)
Homicide blonde
Procter, Maurice
Chief Inspector Harry Martineau series (19)
Homicide blues
Reid, Desmond
Sexton Blake series (1428)
Homicide call
Krasney, Samuel A
Abe Larson series (4)
Homicide Club
Evans, Gwyn
Bill Kellaway series (2)
Homicide for Hannah
Babcock, Dwight Vincent
Hannah Van Doren series (1)
Homicide haven
Turner, John Victor
Amos Petrie series (6)
Homicide House
Frome, David
Evan Pinkerton series (12)
Homicide is my game
Marlowe, Stephen
Chester Drum series (8)
Homicide trinity
Stout, Rex
Nero Wolfe and Archie Goodwin series (36)
Homicide west
Krasney, Samuel A
Abe Larson series (3)
Homing
Thane, Elswyth
Williamsburg series (7)
Homing pigeons
Wilson, Robert Anton
Schrodinger's cat trilogy (3)
Homing trail
Grey, Peter
Kit Hunter series (12)
Homosexuality
West, Donald James
Homosexuality series (1)
Homosexuality re-examined
West, Donald James
Homosexuality series (2)
Honcho
Slade, Jack
Sundance series (13)
Honest ape
Reese, Bob
Going ape series (3)
Honest dealer
Gruber, Frank
Johnny Fletcher and Sam Cragg series (9)
Honest dollar
Simpson, Dorothy
Janie Marshal series (2)
Honest Jim
Finley, Martha Farquharson
Honest Jim series (1)
Honest Ned
Ellis, Edward Sylvester
Brave and honest trilogy (2)
Honest reliable corpse
Bagby, George
Inspector Schmidt series (37)
Honest rogue
Best, Rayleigh Breton Amis
Yarrow series (2)
Honestly, Katie John
Calhoun, Mary
Katie John series (3)
Honey Bunch and Norman
Thorndyke, Helen Louise
Honey Bunch series (35)
Honey Bunch and Norman and the painted pony
Thorndyke, Helen Louise
Honey Bunch series (40)

Honey Bunch and Norman and the paper lantern mystery
Thorndyke, Helen Louise
Honey Bunch series (39)
Honey Bunch and Norman and the walnut tree mystery
Thorndyke, Helen Louise
Honey Bunch series (41)
Honey Bunch and Norman in the Castle of Magic
Thorndyke, Helen Louise
Honey Bunch series (37)
Honey Bunch and Norman on Lighthouse Island
Thorndyke, Helen Louise
Honey Bunch series (28)
Honey Bunch and Norman play detective at Niagara Falls
Thorndyke, Helen Louise
Honey Bunch series (36)
Honey Bunch and Norman ride with the sky mailman
Thorndyke, Helen Louise
Honey Bunch series (33)
Honey Bunch and Norman solve the pine cone mystery
Thorndyke, Helen Louise
Honey Bunch series (38)
Honey Bunch and Norman tour Toy Town
Thorndyke, Helen Louise
Honey Bunch series (30)
Honey Bunch and Norman visit Beaver Lodge
Thorndyke, Helen Louise
Honey Bunch series (34)
Honey Bunch and Norman visit Reindeer Farm
Thorndyke, Helen Louise
Honey Bunch series (32)
Honey for me
Janson, Hank
Hank Janson series (124)
Honey for the marshal
Clements, Eileen Helen
Alister Woodhead series (11)
Honey, here's your hearse!
Brown, Carter
Mavis Seidlitz series (1)
Honey in the flesh
Fickling, G G
Honey West series (5)
Honey on her tail
Fickling, G G
Honey West series (10)
Honey-pot
Barcynska, Helena Margareta
Honey-pot series (1)
Honey siege
Buhet, Gil
Boys' Republic series (1)
Honey, take ny gun
Janson, Hank
Hank Janson series (12)
Honeybath's haven
Innes, Michael
Charles Honeybath series (2)
Honeycomb
Richardson, Dorothy Miller
Pilgrimage series (3)
Honeycutt Street celebrities
Nixon, Joan Lowery
Honeycutt Street series (1)
Honeymoon for seven
Toombs, Alfred
Raising a riot series (2)
Honeymoon in Honolulu
Mark, Ted
Man from O.R.G.Y. series (19)
Honeymoon murder
Finney, R C
Inspector Bourne series (2)
Honeymoon with death
Pentecost, Hugh
Julian Quist series (5)
Honeymoon with murder
Hart, Carolyn Gimpel
Annie Laurance and Max Darling series (4)
Honeysuckle Line
Weir, Rosemary
Tempest family series (1)
Honeysuckle love
Armstrong, Carolyn T
Leather and lace series (6)
Honeywood file
Creswell, Harry Bulkeley
Honeywood series (1)
Honeywood settlement
Creswell, Harry Bulkeley
Honeywood series (2)

Honfleur decision
Hunter, Alan
Inspector George Gently series (26)
Hong Kong air base murders
Mason, Francis Van Wyck
Colonel Hugh North series (11)
Hong Kong caper
Brown, Carter
Andy Kane series (1)
Hong Kong deadline
Edwards, Sylvia
Sally Baxter series (11)
Hong Kong hit
Carter, Nick
Nick Carter series (251)
Hong Kong hit list
Pendleton, Don
Mack Bolan series (109)
Hong Kong kill
Peters, Bryan
Brandon and Lundstrom series (1)
Hong Kong mystery
Cooper, Charles
Russell Cavendish series (2)
Hongkong escape
Goodwin, Ralph
Prisoner of war series (1)
Honky in the woodpile
Brunner, John
Max Curfew series (3)
Honolulu murder story
Ford, Leslie
Colonel John Primrose series (12)
Grace Latham series (12)
Honolulu murders
Ford, Leslie
Colonel John Primrose series (12)
Grace Latham series (12)
Honolulu slay ride
Jason
Jason series (5)
Honolulu snatch
Corrigan, Mark
Mark Corrigan and McLean series (22)
Honolulu story
Ford, Leslie
Colonel John Primrose series (12)
Grace Latham series (12)
Honor
Payne, Oliver
Northwest Territory series (8)
Honor Bright
Keyes, Frances Parkinson
Winslow family trilogy (1)
Richards, Laura Elizabeth
Honor Bright series (1)
Whitaker, Evelyn
Honor Bright series (1)
Honor Bright's new adventure
Richards, Laura Elizabeth
Honor Bright series (2)
Honor Farm
Westermann, John
Orin Boyd series (2)
Honor of Doctor Shelton
Seifert, Elizabeth
Bayard series (4)
Honor of the name
Gaboriau, Emile
Monsieur Lecoq series (3)
Honor roll
Sorenson, Jane
Katie Hooper series (4)
Honor Sherburne
Douglas, Amanda Minnie
Sherburne series (11)
Honor thy godfather
Mulkeen, Thomas Patrick
Clem Talbot series (1)
Honor thy Godmother
Larkin, Rochelle T
Donna series (2)
Honorable defense
Drake, David
Crisis of empire trilogy (1)
Honorable schoolboy
Le Carre, John
George Smiley series (6)
Honorine
Balzac, Honore de
Scenes of private life series (19)
Honour among thieves
Bailey, Henry Christopher
Mister Reggie Fortune series (22)
Honour of Doctor Shelton
Seifert, Elizabeth
Bayard series (4)
Honour of Four Corners
Burgin, George Brown
Four Corners series (20)

Honour of the Clintons
Marshall, Archibald
Clinton series (7)
Honour of thieves
Hyne, Charles John Cutcliffe
Captain Owen Kettle series (1)
Honour this day
Kent, Alexander
Captain Richard Bolitho series (18)
Honourable Bashville
Shaw, George Bernard
Nonage series (4)
Honourable Mrs Garry
De la Pasture, Elizabeth
Master Christopher series (2)
Honourable schoolboy
Le Carre, John
George Smiley series (6)
Honour's mistress
Jacob, Naomi
Crowther series (2)
Hood for a honey
Brody, Marc
Marc Brody series (77)
Hood of death
Carter, Nick
Nick Carter series (34)
Hoodd riders
Bobin, John William
Sexton Blake series (225)
Hooded circle
Grant, Maxwell
Shadow series (179)
Hooded hawk mystery
Dixon, Franklin W
Hardy boys series (34)
Hooded hordes
House, Brant
Secret Agent X series (5)
Hooded man
Duncan, William Murdoch
Superintendent Gaylord series (1)
Horowitz, Anthony
Robin of Sherwood series (2)
Hooded monster
Masterman, Walter Sidney
Sir Arthur Sinclair series (15)
Hooded raider
Stuart, Donald
Sexton Blake series (675)
Hooded riders
Edson, John Thomas
Floating Outfit series (8)
Hooded vulture murders
Koehler, Robert Portner
Avery Gregg and Tony Ellis series (2)
Hoodoo horror
Jason, Stuart
Butcher series (32)
Hoods come calling
Quarry, Nick
Jake Barrow series (2)
Hoodwink
Pronzini, Bill
Private Eye series (7)
Hoodwinkers
Edwards, Monica
Romney Marsh series (14)
Hoof
McCutchan, Philip
Superintendent Simon Shard series (7)
Hoof in the door
Akrill, Caroline
Eventing trilogy (2)
Hoofbeat
Bryant, Bonnie
Saddle Club series (9)
Hoofbeats on the turnpike
Wirt, Mildred Augustine
Penny Parker series (11)
Hook
Cleary, Denis
Breakenridge series (1)
Copper, Basil
Mike Faraday series (41)
Hook, line and sinker
Deighton, Len
Hook, line and sinker trilogy (3)
Hook or crook
Martin, Cort
Jared Bolt series (23)
Hooker-smash operation
Rosenberger, Joseph
Murder Master series (3)
Hooky and the crock of gold
Meynell, Laurence Walter
Hooky Hefferman series (10)
Hooky and the prancing horse
Meynell, Laurence Walter
Hooky Hefferman series (15)

Hooky and the villainous chauffeur
Meynell, Laurence Walter
Hooky Hefferman series (14)
Hooky catches a Tartar
Meynell, Laurence Walter
Hooky Hefferman series (20)
Hooky gets the wooden spoon
Meynell, Laurence Walter
Hooky Hefferman series (12)
Hooky goes to blazes
Meynell, Laurence Walter
Hooky Hefferman series (16)
Hooky hooked
Meynell, Laurence Walter
Hooky Hefferman series (22)
Hooky on loan
Meynell, Laurence Walter
Hooky Hefferman series (21)
Hooligan
Dodge, David
John Abraham Lincoln series (1)
Dunne, Colin
Joe Hussey series (3)
Hoop crazy
Bee, Clair
Chip Hilton series (5)
Hoop of the nation
Cooke, John Byrne
Snowblind moon trilogy (3)
Hooper Haller
Hughes, Dean
Haller series (1)
Hooray for addition facts!
Daniel, Rebecca
Hooray for arithmetic facts series (1)
Hooray for division facts!
Daniel, Rebecca
Hooray for arithmetic facts series (4)
Hooray for Father's Day
Sharmat, Marjorie Weinman
Mother's and Father's Day series (2)
Hooray for Hellywood
Friesner, Esther Mona
Demons trilogy (3)
Hooray for homicide
Anderson, James
Jessica Fletcher series (3)
Hooray for Max
Wells, Rosemary
Max series (9)
Hooray for Mervyn Mouse
Creche, Sylvia
Mervyn Mouse series (5)
Hooray for Mother's Day
Sharmat, Marjorie Weinman
Mother's and Father's Day series (1)
Hooray for multiplication facts!
Daniel, Rebecca
Hooray for arithmetic facts series (3)
Hooray for Pippa!
Boegehold, Betty
Pippa Mouse series (4)
Hooray for subtraction facts!
Daniel, Rebecca
Hooray for arithmetic facts series (2)
Hopalong Cassidy
Mulford, Clarence Edward
Hopalong Cassidy series (2)
Hopalong Cassidy and the eagle's brood
Mulford, Clarence Edward
Dave Sanders series (2)
Hopalong Cassidy series (13)
J C series (4)
Johnny Nelson series (5)
Matt Skinner series (2)
Wyatt Duncan series (2)
Hopalong Cassidy and the five men of evil
Cole, Royal King
Hopalong Cassidy series (20)
Hopalong Cassidy and the riders of High Rock
Burns, Tex
Hopalong Cassidy series (19)
Hopalong Cassidy and the rustlers of West Fork
Burns, Tex
Hopalong Cassidy series (17)
Hopalong Cassidy and the trail herd
Mulford, Clarence Edward
Hopalong Cassidy series (14)
Hopalong Cassidy and the trail to Seven Pines
Burns, Tex
Hopalong Cassidy series (18)

Hopalong Cassidy returns
Mulford, Clarence Edward
Hopalong Cassidy series (10)
Mesquite Jenkins series (1)
Hopalong Cassidy sees red
Mulford, Clarence Edward
Hopalong Cassidy series (8)
Johnny Nelson series (3)
Hopalong Cassidy serves a writ
Mulford, Clarence Edward
Hopalong Cassidy series (16)
Hopalong Cassidy, trouble shooter
Burns, Tex
Hopalong Cassidy series (20)
Hopalong Cassidy's Bar-20 rides again
Mulford, Clarence Edward
Hopalong Cassidy series (12)
Hopalong Cassidy's private war
Mulford, Clarence Edward
Hopalong Cassidy series (3)
Hopalong Cassidy's protege
Mulford, Clarence Edward
Hopalong Cassidy series (11)
Mesquite Jenkins series (2)
Hopalong Cassidy's round-up
Mulford, Clarence Edward
Hopalong Cassidy series (1)
Hopalong Cassidy's saddle mate
Mulford, Clarence Edward
Hopalong Cassidy series (11)
Mesquite Jenkins series (2)
Hope
Wouk, Herman
Hope series (1)
Hope abandoned
Mandelstam, Nadezhda
Hope series (2)
Hope against hope
Kelly, Susan
Alison Hope and Inspector Nick Trevellyan series (1)
Mandelstam, Nadezhda
Hope series (1)
Hope and glory
Arlen, Leslie
Borodin family series (4)
Hope and have
Optic, Oliver
Woodville series (5)
Hope of glory
Macdonald, Peter G
Open road quartet (1)
Hope to die
Waugh, Hillary
Sheridan Wesley series (2)
Hope will answer
Kelly, Susan
Alison Hope and Inspector Nick Trevellyan series (3)
Hopeful heart
Gibbs, Philip
Second World War series (6)
Hopeful monsters
Mosley, Nicholas
Catastrophe practice series (5)
Hopeful traveller
Hocking, Mary
Fleet Air Arm training series (2)
Hopeless case
Beck, Kathrine Kristine
Jane Da Silva series (1)
Hopes and fears
Yonge, Charlotte Mary
Honor Charlecote series (1)
Pillars of the house series (2)
Hopes and horizons
Miller, Hugh
Eastenders series (6)
Hopfellow
Partridge, Jenny
Oakapple Wood series (3)
Hopjoy was here
Watson, Colin
Inspector Purbright series (3)
Hoplaong Cassidy takes cards
Mulford, Clarence Edward
Hopalong Cassidy series (15)
Hopper hunts for spring
Pfister, Marcus
Hopper series (1)
Hopper's Easter surprise
Pfister, Marcus
Hopper series (2)
Horace Higby and the field goal
Heuman, William
Horace Higby series (1)
Horace Higby and the gentle fullback
Heuman, William
Horace Higby series (3)
Horace Higby and the scientific pitch
Heuman, William
Horace Higby series (2)

Horace Higby, coxswain of the crew
Heuman, William
Horace Higby series (4)
horace, the horse
Darby, Joan
Animal adventure series (11)
Horatio Stubbs saga
Aldiss, Brian Wilson
Horace Stubbs series (3)
Horde
Blasco Ibanez, Vicente
Roman Catholic Church in Spain series (4)
Hordes of the Red Butcher
Stockbridge, Grant
Richard Wentworth series (6)
Hordubal
Capek, Karel
Truth and democracy trilogy (1)
Horizontal hold
Irvine, Robert Ralstone
Robert Christopher series (3)
Horn
Flynn, Brian
Anthony Bathurst series (15)
Horn crown
Norton, Andre
Witch World series (14)
Horn Green
Voltz, William
Perry Rhodan series (96)
Horn of plenty
Hunter, E J
White Squaw series (8)
Hornblower and the Atropos
Forester, Cecil Scott
Horatio Hornblower series (5)
Hornblower and the crisis
Forester, Cecil Scott
Horatio Hornblower series (4)
Hornblower and the Hotspur
Forester, Cecil Scott
Horatio Hornblower series (3)
Hornblower companion
Forester, Cecil Scott
Horatio Hornblower series (11)
Hornblower during the crisis
Forester, Cecil Scott
Horatio Hornblower series (4)
Hornblower goes to sea
Forester, Cecil Scott
Horatio Hornblower cadet series (1)
Hornblower in captivity
Forester, Cecil Scott
Horatio Hornblower cadet series (3)
Hornblower in the West Indies
Forester, Cecil Scott
Horatio Hornblower series (11)
Hornblower takes command
Forester, Cecil Scott
Horatio Hornblower cadet series (2)
Hornblower's triumph
Forester, Cecil Scott
Horatio Hornblower cadet series (4)
Horned animals
Aaseng, Nathan
Early nature picture book series (2)
Horned dinosaur
Berenstain, Michael
Dinosaurs series (2)
Horned pigeon
Millar, George
Maquis series (2)
Horned warrior
Carlsen, Chris
Berserker series (3)
Hornet's nest
Ashton, Helen
Wilchester chronicles series (5)
Fischer, Bruno
Rick Train series (1)
Horns of plenty
Browne, Dik
Hagar the horrible series (30)
Horoscope
Dumas, Alexandre
Valois series (4)
Horribilly goes to school
Osborne, Maureen
Horribilly series (2)
Horrible Harry and the ant invasion
Kline, Suzy
Horrible Harry series (3)
Horrible Harry and the Christmas surprise
Kline, Suzy
Horrible Harry series (5)
Horrible Harry and the green slime
Kline, Suzy
Horrible Harry series (2)
Horrible Harry and the kickball wedding
Kline, Suzy
Horrible Harry series (6)
Horrible Harry in Room 2B
Kline, Suzy
Horrible Harry series (1)
Horrible Harry's secret
Kline, Suzy
Horrible Harry series (4)
Horrible hat
Savage, Richard
Doctor Ferenc series (2)
Horrible humes
Billias, Stephen
Runesword series (4)
Horrible man
Avallone, Michael
Ed Noon series (18)
Horrible man in Heron's Wood
Cobb, Belton
Bryan Armitage series (18)
Inspector Cheviot Burmann series (40)
Kitty Armitage series (15)
Horror
Voltz, William
Perry Rhodan series (66)
Horror at the moated mill
Desmond, Hugh
Alan Fraser series (31)
Horror at Wardens Hall
Wogan, Charles
Sebastian Stole series (2)
Horror chambers of Jules de Grandin
Quinn, Seabury
Jules de Grandin series (7)
Horror hotel!
Milton, Hilary
Plot your own horror stories series (4)
Horror house
Douthwaite, Louis Charles
Sexton Blake series (604)
Milton, Hilary
Plot your own horror stories series (1)
Horror House
Wells, Carolyn
Fleming Stone series (30)
Horror mansion
Williamson, Jerry Neal
Minnifield series (2)
Horror of Fog Island
Ross, Marilyn
Fog Island series (5)
Horror of High Ridge
Goodman, Julius
Choose your own adventure series (27)
Horror on the beach
Foster, Alan Dean
Cthulhu Mythos series (6)
Horror on the Ruby X
Crane, Frances
Pat and Jean Abbott series (20)
Horror returns
Jones, John G
Amityville horror series (10)
Horror wears blue
Carter, Lin
Prince Zarkon series (5)
Horror's head
Horler, Sydney
Emp series (1)
Horrors of the haunted museum
Stine, Robert Lawrence
Twistaplot series (9)
Horrorvid
Tallis, Robyn
Planet builders series (8)
Horse and a hound, a goat and a gander
Provensen, Alice
Maple Hill Farm series (3)
Horse and his boy
Lewis, Clive Staples
Narnia series (3)
Horse and two goats, and other stories
Narayan, Rasipuram Krishnaswami
Malgudi series (11)
Horse called Bonnie
Johnson, Pat
Julie Jefferson series (2)
Horse called Dragon
Hall, Lynn
Dragon series (1)
Horse called Mogollon
Edson, John Thomas
Floating Outfit series (3)
Horse crazy
Bryant, Bonnie
Saddle Club series (1)
Horse for Jackie
Sheldon, Ann
Linda Craig adventures series (7)
Horse games
Bryant, Bonnie
Saddle Club series (16)
Horse goddess
Llywelyn, Morgan
Odyssey of the Irish trilogy (2)
Horse in a million
Leitch, Patricia
Jinny series (6)
Horse in the camel suit
Pene du Bois, William
Alligator case series (2)
Horse in the furrow
Evans, George Ewart
Farm life series (2)
Horse lord
Morwood, Peter
Book of years series (1)
Horse marines
Wyatt, Zach
Texians series (2)
Horse nonsense
Sellar, Walter Carruthers
All that series (3)
Horse of fire
Leitch, Patricia
Jinny series (11)
Horse of his own
Rooke, Daphne
Herman Jozef series (2)
Horse on a hilltop
Webster, Joanne
Nobody's horse trilogy (2)
Horse on the hard
Wynne, Anthony
Doctor Eustace Hailey series (25)
Horse play
Bryant, Bonnie
Saddle Club series (7)
Vail, Virginia
Horse crazy series (4)
Horse sense
Bryant, Bonnie
Saddle Club series (3)
Horse show
Bryant, Bonnie
Saddle Club series (8)
Horse shy
Bryant, Bonnie
Saddle Club series (2)
Horse soldiers
Sinclair, Harold
American Civil War series (1)
Horse tale
Bryant, Bonnie
Saddle Club series (35)
Horse-tamer
Farley, Walter
Black stallion series (14)
Horse thief war
Logan, Jake
John Slocum series (143)
Horse trade
Bryant, Bonnie
Saddle Club series (38)
Horse trouble
Bryant, Bonnie
Saddle Club series (23)
Horse under water
Deighton, Len
Secret file series (2)
Horse who had his picture in the paper
McGinley, Phyllis
Joey series (2)
Horse who lived upstairs
McGinley, Phyllis
Joey series (1)
Horse who loved picnics
Dengler, Sandy
Pioneer family series (2)
Horse wise
Bryant, Bonnie
Saddle Club series (11)
Horse without a head
Berna, Paul
Gaby series (1)
Horse you came in with
Grimes, Martha
Inspector Richard Jury series (14)
Horseback summer
Vail, Virginia
Horse crazy series (1)
Horseclans odyssey
Adams, Robert
Horseclans series (7)
Horsegirl
Ash, Constance
Horsegirl series (1)
Horsehead Crossing
Kelton, Elmer
Tales of Texas series (1)
Horselords
Cook, David
Empires trilogy (1)
Horseman
Brown, Joseph Paul Summers
Arizona saga series (2)
Horseman of death
Wynne, Anthony
Doctor Eustace Hailey series (4)
Horseman of the shadows
Scott, Bradford
Walt Slade series (62)
Horseman on the roof
Giono, Jean
Angelo series (2)
Horseman, pass by
McMurtry, Larry
Thalia series (2)
Horseman riding by
Delderfield, Ronald Frederick
Craddocks of Shallowford series (1)
Horsemen
McCarthy, Gary
Ballou family series (1)
Horsenapped!
Bryant, Bonnie
Saddle Club series (17)
Horses and their women
Cohen, Barbara
Animals and their women series (3)
Horses is like people
Webster, Joanne
Nobody's horse trilogy (3)
Horse's mouth
Cary, Joyce
Art trilogy (3)
Horses of Follyfoot
Dickens, Monica
Follyfoot Farm series (3)
Horses of the night
Sandman Lilius, Irmelin
Sola trilogy (0)
Horses of the north
Adams, Robert
Horseclans series (13)
Horseshoe trail
Hobart, Donald Bayne
Masked Rider and Blue Hawk series (3)
Horsethief Crossing
Sharpe, Jon
Trailsman series (62)
Horsethieves hang high
Borg, Jack
Hogleg Bailey series (15)
Horsewatching
Morris, Desmond
Watching series (5)
Horsewoman in Godsland
Edwards, Claudia Jane
Forest King trilogy (2)
Horsin' around
Coldsmith, Don
Horsin' around series (1)
Horsin' around again
Coldsmith, Don
Horsin' around series (2)
Horsing blacksmith
Tully, Paul
Deputy Marshal Hooky Gibbs series (1)
Horstmann inheritance
Healey, Ben
Harcourt d'Espinal series (3)
Hortense
Foster, Edna Abigail
Hortense series (1)
Horton twins
Kilbourne, Fannie
William Horton series (3)
Ho's hellhounds
Lansing, John
Black Eagles series (15)
Hosanna shout
Irvine, Robert Ralstone
Moroni Traveler series (7)
Hospital across the bridge
Cooper, Lisa
Princess Beatrice Hospital series (9)
Hospital call
Harrison, Elizabeth
Central London Hospital series (9)
Hospital homicides
De Puy, Edward Spence
Sam Houston series (2)
Hospital in the bush
Doell, E W
Mission doctor trilogy (2)
Hospital murders
Davis, Means
Matthew Higgins series (1)
Hospital station
White, James
Sector General series (1)
Hospital thief
Plummer, Thomas Arthur
Detective Inspector Andrew Frampton series (47)
Hospitals
Fisher, Leonard Everett
Nineteenth century America series (3)
Host for dying
Audemars, Pierre
Monsieur Pinaud series (14)
Host of extras
Leasor, James
Aristo Autos series (3)
Doctor Jason Love series (7)
Host of voices
Stokes, Doris
Voices series (4)
Hostage
Cave, Peter
New Avengers series (6)
Johnston, William
Matt Lincoln series (2)
Pascal, Francine
Sweet Valley High series (26)
Hostage arrows
Sharpe, Jon
Trailsman series (70)
Hostage hunters
Grover, Marshall
Larry and Stretch series (381)
Hostage in Tokyo
De Villiers, Gerard
Malko Linge series (13)
Hostage of the damned
Foxall, Peter Augustus
Detective Sergeant Scamp series (7)
Hostage of the sea
Baldry, Cherith
Stories of six worlds series (2)
Hostage of Zir
De Camp, Lyon Sprague
Krishna series (7)
Hostage to death
Desmond, Hugh
Alan Fraser series (25)
Hostage tower
Denis, John
U.N.A.C.O.series (1)
Hostage trail
Sharpe, Jon
Trailsman series (28)
Hostaged island
Stivers, Dick
Able Team series (2)
Hostaged Vatican
Wilson, Gar
Phoenix Force series (26)
Hostages of Colditz
Romilly, Giles
Colditz series (5)
Hostages of hate
Dixon, Franklin W
Hardy boys case files series (10)
Hostages to fortune
Lingard, Joan
Sadie and Kevin series (5)
Hostess in the sky
Hill, Margaret
Beth Dean series (2)
Hostile beaches
Shirreffs, Gordon Donald
Bob Dunbar and Gary Lunt series (2)
Hostile intent
Egleton, Clive
Peter Ashton series (1)
Hostile shore
Gavin, Catherine
Clyde Valley series (2)
Hostile takeover
Murphy, Warren Burton
Destroyer series (81)
Murray, Will
Destroyer series (81)
Hosts of Midian
Capon, Paul
Arnold Wragge series (1)
Hosts of Rebecca
Cordell, Alexander
Mortymers series (3)

Hosts of the air
Altsheler, Joseph Alexander
World War trilogy (2)
Hosts of the flaming death
Steele, Curtis
James Christopher series (13)
Hot
Lutz, John
Fred Carver series (6)
Hot air
Breen, Jon Linn
Jerry Brogan series (5)
Hot air clew
Carter, Nicholas
Nicholas Carter series (153)
Hot and cold
Laird, Elizabeth
Contrasts series (2)
Pluckrose, Henry
Thinking about series (9)
Simon, Seymour
Let's try it out series (4)
Hot and spicy
Ledd, Paul
Shelter Morgan series (31)
Hot as a pistol
Curry, Gene
Jim Saddler series (4)
Hot body
Avallone, Michael
Ed Noon series (27)
Hot bread and chips
Flint, Elizabeth
East End series (1)
Hot corner
Bowen, Robert Sidney
Hot corner series (1)
Hot corner blues
Bowen, Robert Sidney
Hot corner series (2)
Hot dam
Macneil, Neil
Tony Costaine and Bert McCall series (4)
Hot day, hot night
Himes, Chester
Grave Digger Jones and Coffin Ed Johnson series (8)
Hot Dog Gang caper
Hiller, Barbara B
Pick-a-path series (15)
Hot freeze
Brett, Martin
Mike Garfin series (1)
Hot fudge sundae affair
Blair, Cynthia
Susan and Christine Pratt series (1)
Hot-handed heathen
Hunter, E J
White Squaw series (11)
Hot Henrietta and Nailbiters United
Older, Jules
Hank Prank series (3)
Hot, hot day
Berg, Leila
Chatterbooks series (2)
Hot house
Janson, Hank
Hank Janson series (179)
Hot ice
Casey, Robert J
Jim Sands series (4)
Waldron, Simon
Steve Essex series (2)
Hot lead
Scott, Bradford
Walt Slade series (77)
Hot lead and cold nerve
Scott, Bradford
Walt Slade series (86)
Hot lead and cold steel
Mackie, John
Rat Bastards series (8)
Hot Lead Trail
Young, Gordon Ray
Red Clark series (12)
Hot line
Bruce, Jean
Secret Agent O.S.S.117 series (9)
Janson, Hank
Hank Janson series (149)
Hot line for a honey
Brody, Marc
Marc Brody series (65)
Hot mahatma
Gray, Rod
Lady from L.U.S.T. series (5)
Hot money can cook your goose
Glazner, Joseph Mark
Billy Nevers series (5)
Hot on the warpath
Martin, Cort
Jared Bolt series (25)
Hot place
Resnicow, Herbert
Ed and Warren Baer series (2)
Hot pursuit
Hunter, E J
White Squaw series (18)
Keene, Carolyn
Nancy Drew files series (58)
Hot rain
Lewis, Colin
Howard Hayes trilogy (3)
Hot rock
Westlake, Donald Edwin
Dortmunder Gang series (1)
Hot rocks
Chase, Glen
Cherry Delight series (8)
Hot rod
Dean, Anabel
Racing wheels series (1)
Hot rod angels
Bowen, Robert Sidney
Hot rod series (1)
Hot rod doom
Bowen, Robert Sidney
Hot rod series (6)
Hot rod outlaws
Bowen, Robert Sidney
Hot rod series (5)
Hot rod pareol
Bowen, Robert Sidney
Hot rod series (3)
Hot rod rodeo
Bowen, Robert Sidney
Hot rod series (2)
Hot rod showdown
Bowen, Robert Sidney
Hot rod series (4)
Hot shot
McCann, Sean
Dove's End Football Club series (5)
Hot shots
Gough, Laurence
Willows and Parker series (3)
Hot sky over Paraiso
Grover, Marshall
Larry and Stretch series (105)
Hot sleep
Card, Orson Scott
Worthing chronicles series (2)
Hot spot
Leinster, Murray
Land of the giants series (2)
Hot summer killing
Philips, Judson Pentecost
Peter Styles series (6)
Hot Super Bowl battles
Resciniti, Angelo G
Super Bowl series (3)
Hot Texas tall
Hunter, E J
White Squaw series (4)
Hot time in old town
McQuay, Mike
Mathew Swain series (1)
Hot tip
Dolph, Jack
Doc Connor series (4)
Hot tracks
Keene, Carolyn
Nancy Drew files series (71)
Hot water
Gunning, Sally
Peter Bartholomew series (1)
Hot-water bottle mystery
Delgado, Alan
Mike and Caroline series (1)
Hot water music
Bukowski, Charles
Henry Chinaski series (3)
Hot wheels
Arden, William
Three Investigators Crimebusters series (1)
Dixon, Franklin W
Hardy boys case files series (91)
Hot wind from hell
McCutcheon, Hugh
Jimmy Carroll series (4)
Hot zone
Sloane, Ben
Horn series (1)
Hotchi the hedgehog
Evens, George Bramwell
Romany readers series (1)
Hotel Bemelmans
Bemelmans, Ludwig
Hotel series (3)
Hotel by Clachan
Armstrong, Sybil
Clachan series (3)
Hotel cat
Averill, Esther
Jenny Linsky series (13)
Hotel Cremona mystery
Lane, Gret
John Barrin series (2)
Kate Marsh series (3)
Hotel holiday
Greene, Carla
Travel series (1)
Hotel homicide
Parsons, Anthony
Sexton Blake series (1408)
Hotel in flight
Johnstone, Nancy
Hotel series (2)
Hotel in Spain
Johnstone, Nancy
Hotel series (1)
Hotel Mamie Stover
Huie, William Bradford
Mamie Stover series (3)
Hotel Morgue
Laurence, Janet
Darina Lisle series (3)
Hotel murders
Sterling, Stewart
Gil Vine series (5)
Hotel Quadriga
Glanfield, Jenny
Hotel Quadriga series (1)
Hotel Regina
Nicol, Jean
Hotel series (1)
Hotel Richelieu murders
Blackmon, Anita
Adelaide Adams series (1)
Hotel Splendide
Bemelmans, Ludwig
Hotel series (2)
Hotel Transylvania
Yarbro, Chelsea Quinn
Count Ragoczy Saint-Germain series (1)
Hotline to danger
Keene, Carolyn
Nancy Drew files series (93)
Hotsy, you'll be chilled
Janson, Hank
Hank Janson series (33)
Hound and Bear
Gackenbach, Dick
Hound and Bear series (1)
Hound and the curse of Kali
Sivers, Brenda
Sherlock Hound series (6)
Hound and the Falcon
Tarr, Judith
Hound and the Falcon trilogy (3)
Hound and the fox and the harper
Herron, Shaun
Miro series (2)
Hound and the Perilous Pekes
Sivers, Brenda
Sherlock Hound series (5)
Hound and the witching affair
Sivers, Brenda
Sherlock Hound series (2)
Hound dog man
Edson, John Thomas
Waco series (8)
Hound Dog Zip to the rescue
Steele, William Owen
Hound Dog Zip series (1)
Hound in the Highlands
Sivers, Brenda
Sherlock Hound series (1)
Hound of Culain
Flint, Kenneth Covey
Sidhe Lugh series (3)
Hound of Frankenstein
Tremayne, Peter
Frankenstein sequels series (11)
Hound of the Baskervilles
Doyle, Arthur Conan
Sherlock Holmes series (4)
Kelly, Tim J
Sherlock Holmes drama series (11)
Leslie, Frederic Andrew
Sherlock Holmes drama series (13)
Hound of the Baskervilles, and other Sherlock Holmes plays
Hardwick, Michael
Sherlock Holmes drama series (22)
Hound of the Far Side
Larson, Gary
Far Side series (8)
Hounded down
Vickers, Roy
Inspector George Rason series (1)
Hounded to death
Carter, Nicholas
Nicholas Carter series (100)
Hounds of Dracula
Johnson, Kenneth Rayner
Dracula series (1)
Hounds of God
Tarr, Judith
Hound and the Falcon trilogy (3)
Hounds of justice
Forsythe, Robin
Anthony Vereker series (2)
Hounds of Skaith
Brackett, Leigh
Eric John Stark series (4)
Hounds of Sparta
Norman, Barry
Paul Baker series (2)
Hounds of sunset
Pargeter, Edith
Brothers of Gwynedd tetralogy (3)
Hounds of vengeance
Creasey, John
Doctor Palfrey series (4)
Houp-la!
Winter, John Strange
Bootles series (4)
Hour awaits
Cost, March
Princess Victoria Babenberg series (1)
Hour before disaster
Grover, Marshall
Nevada Jim series (12)
Hour before zero
Harvester, Simon
Asia in turmoil series (8)
Hour in the morning
Cooper, Gordon
Kate Bassett series (1)
Hour of gold, hour of lead
Lindbergh, Anne Morrow
Unicorn series (2)
Hour of jeopardy
Grover, Marshall
Larry and Stretch series (99)
Hour of love
Van der Meersch, Maxence
Poor girl series (2)
Hour of the Blue Fox
Macdonald, Hugh Chisholm
Paul Williams series (1)
Hour of the Dog
Mather, Berkely
Stafford family trilogy (3)
Hour of the donkey
Price, Anthony
Doctor David Audley and Jack Butler series (10)
Hour of the dragon
Howard, Robert Ervin
Conan series (1)
Conan series (25)
Hour of the gate
Foster, Alan Dean
Spellsinger series (2)
Hour of the Oxrun dead
Grant, Charles Lewis
Oxrun Station series (1)
Hour of the scorpion
Costello, Matthew John
Time warrior series (2)
Hour of the thin ox
Greenland, Colin
Daybreak series (2)
Hour of the tiger
Roberts, Irene
China trilogy (3)
Hour of the wolf
Carter, Nick
Nick Carter series (79)
Hour of the Wolf
Charles, Robert
Counter-terror series (1)
Hourglass
Maeterlinck, Maurice
Pascalian series (2)
Hours of destiny
Jennings, D K
Doctor Ralph Conway series (24)
Hours of gladness
Maeterlinck, Maurice
Hours of gladness series (2)
House
McDowell, Michael M
Blackwater series (3)
Rolland, Romain
John Christopher series (3)
House across the street
Carter, Nicholas
Nicholas Carter series (463)
House at Balnesmoor
Rae, Hugh Crauford
Glasgow series (3)
Superintendent McCaig series (1)
House at Old Vine
Lofts, Norah
Suffolk trilogy (2)
House at Pluck's Gutter
Coles, Manning
Tommy Hambledon series (26)
House at Pooh Corner
Milne, Alan Alexander
Pooh series (2)
House at Satan's Elbow
Carr, John Dickson
Doctor Gideon Fell series (21)
House at Spaniard's Bay
Reid, Meta Mayne
Kate and Lynn series (2)
House at Sunset
Lofts, Norah
Suffolk trilogy (3)
House at the estuary
Mackenzie, Andrew
Superintendent Brannigan series (1)
House at three o'clock
Gilchrist, Rupert
Slaves without masters trilogy (1)
House at war
Mackinnon, Charles Roy
Scottish chronicle series (1)
House at Waterloo
Brooks, Edwy Searles
Sexton Blake series (282)
House at World's End
Dickens, Monica
Fielding family series (1)
House-boat on the Styx
Bangs, John Kendrick
Associated shades series (1)
House by the medlar tree
Verga, Giovanni
Vinti family series (1)
House by the road
Dutton, Charles Judson
John Bartley series (4)
House by the sea
Holland, Elizabeth
House series (2)
House called Hadlows
Walker, Victoria
Hadlows series (2)
House called Pleasance
Elsna, Hebe
Pleasance series (1)
House called Yarrow
Best, Rayleigh Breton Amis
Yarrow series (1)
House calls
Walker, Mort
Hi and Lois series (13)
House-dick
Copper, Basil
Mike Faraday series (51)
House divided
Buck, Pearl Sydenstricker
Wang family series (3)
Williams, Ben Ames
Currain family series (1)
House far from home
Wilson, Budge
Blue Harbour series (2)
House for Sister Mary
Andrews, Lucilla
Saint Barnabas' Hospital series (3)
House for wombats
Dugan, Michael
Wombats series (1)
House in Belmont Square
Erskine, Margaret
Inspector Septimus Finch series (13)
House in Charlton Crescent
Haynes, Annie
Inspector Furnival series (2)
House in Greek Street
Horler, Sydney
Sir Harker Bellamy series (9)
House in Harlem
Michel, Milton Scott
Wood Jason series (2)
House in Haven Street
Dawson, Helen
Noreen and Aunt Joan series (2)
House in hiding
Lyon, Elinor
Ian and Sovra series (1)
House in Hook Street
Erskine, Margaret
Inspector Septimus Finch series (21)

House in Kingston Square
Braithwaite, Ruth
Yorkshire trilogy (3)
House in Lordship Lane
Mason, Alfred Edward Woodley
Inspector Hanaud series (5)
House in the desert
Duhamel, Georges
Pasquier series (5)
House in the dunes
Denton, Derek
Harry Sellers series (3)
House in the forest
Cumberland, Marten
Saturnin Dax series (14)
House in the Golden Orchard
Castelhun, Dorothea
Penelope series (3)
House in the hills
Fitz Roy, Olivia
Stewarts series (3)
Ratel, Simonne
Isabelle Comtat series (1)
House in the north
Holland, Elizabeth
House series (1)
House in the park
Ommanney, Francis Downes
House in the park series (1)
House in the sun
Chandos, Dane
Mexico series (2)
House in the wood
Chester, Gilbert
Sexton Blake series (1132)
Sudbery, Rodie
Polly Devenish series (1)
House in the woods
Drummond, J
Sexton Blake series (1251)
House in town
Mayne, William
Animal library series (6)
Warner, Susan Bagert
Opportunities series (3)
House in Vienna
De Born, Edith
De Kailern family series (2)
House is falling
Fitzgerald, Nigel
Superintendent Duffy series (3)
House like a lotus
L'Engle, Madeleine
Poly and Charles O'Keefe series (4)
House mother
Owen, Frank
Scobee Trent series (2)
House next door
Stevenson, Burton Egbert
Jim Godfrey series (6)
House of a hundred animals
French, Jackie
Children of the valley trilogy (3)
House of a stranger
Bailey, Gerald Earl
Nurlingas series (3)
House of a thousand candles
Nicholson, Meredith
Rosalind series (1)
House of Arden
Nesbit, Edith
Arden series (1)
House of brass
Queen, Ellery
Ellery Queen series (41)
House of cards
Cave, Peter
New Avengers series (1)
House of cellars
Teed, George Hamilton
Sexton Blake series (729)
House of Clystevill
Atkey, Bertram
Smiler Bunn series (9)
House of Cthulhu, and other tales of the primal land
Lumley, Brian
Tales of the primal land series (1)
House of curtains
Teed, George Hamilton
Sexton Blake series (683)
House of danger
Montgomery, Raymond A
Choose your own adventure series (15)
House of dark shadows
Ross, Marilyn
Barnabas Collins series (16)
House of darkness
Hunter, John
Sexton Blake series (1046)
Mackinnon, Allan
Inspector Duncan Maccallum series (2)
House of dawn
Scoggins, Charles Elbert
Colin O'Leary series (1)
House of death
Robeson, Kenneth
Avenger series (15)
House of destiny
Minton, Mary
Yesterday's road series (8)
House of Dies Drear
Hamilton, Virginia
Dies Drear series (1)
House of discord
Hanshew, Mary E
Hamilton Cleek series (8)
House of dolls
Ka-tzetnik 135633
Harry Preleshnik series (1)
House of doom
Carter, Nicholas
Nicholas Carter series (376)
House of Dracula
Chetwynd-Hayes, Ronald
Dracula's children series (2)
House of earth
Buck, Pearl Sydenstricker
Wang family series (3)
House of Elrig
Maxwell, Gavin
Camusfearna trilogy (3)
House of entropy
Sheldon, Roy
Shiny spear series (2)
House of evil
Clevely, Hugh
Sexton Blake series (1374)
House of fear
Lewis, Jack
Sexton Blake series (294)
House of fulfilment
Barrington, E
Ormond series (2)
House of ghosts
Brooks, Leonard Harold
Sexton Blake series (218)
Grant, Maxwell
Shadow series (243)
House of Goodwinsson
Punshon, Ernest Robertson
Bobby Owen series (25)
House of Gow
Hepple, Anne
Gow family series (1)
House of green turf
Peters, Ellis
Inspector George Felse series (8)
House of hades
Jackson, Steve
Fighting fantasy gamebook series (10)
House of Hardie
Melville, Anne
Hardie family series (1)
House of hate
Mace, Helen
Noel Vickery series (2)
House of hell
Jackson, Steve
Fighting fantasy gamebook series (10)
House of her own
Allee, Marjorie Hill
Lankester family trilogy (2)
House of horror
Jacobs, Thomas Curtis Hicks
Temple Fortune series (19)
House of hospitalities
Tennant, Emma
Hospitalities series (1)
House of jackals
Horler, Sydney
Tiger Standish series (12)
House of joy
Ammers-Kuller, Jo van
Jenny Heysten series (1)
House of Kingsley Merrick
Hill, Deborah
Merrick family series (2)
House of Kuragin
Heaven, Constance
Kuragin series (1)
House of laughs
Eisenberg, Lisa
Laura Brewster series (1)
House of love
Ka-tzetnik 135633
Harry Preleshnik series (2)
House of Malory
McElroy, Hugh
Inspector William Brewer series (4)
House of many worlds
Merwin, Samuel Kimball
Elspeth Marriner and Mack Fraser series (1)
Elspeth Marriner and Mack Fraser series (2)
House of Menerdue
Benson, Arthur Christopher
Molly Davenant series (1)
House of moonlight
Derleth, August
Sac Prairie series (13)
House of Moreys
Bentley, Phyllis
West Riding series (4)
House of Mrs Caroline
Franzero, Carlo Maria
Mrs Caroline series (1)
House of murder
Wallis, James Harold
Inspector Wilton Jacks series (6)
House of Nire
Kita, Morio
Kiichiro Nire series (1)
House of Nucingen
Balzac, Honore de
Scenes of Parisian life series (5)
House of O'Shea
Irish, Lola
Colonial trilogy (3)
House of peril
Tracy, Louis
Inspector Furneaux series (6)
House of prophecy
Cannan, Gilbert
New time trilogy (3)
Round the corner trilogy (3)
House of Sabre
Darby, Catherine
Sabre family series (4)
House of scorpions
Sherman, Jory
Doctor Russell V Chillders series (6)
House of seclusion
Harvey, Marion
Graydon McKelvie series (3)
House of secrets
Bawden, Nina
Mallory children series (1)
Martyn, Wyndham
Anthony Trent series (18)
House of shade
Home, Michael
Zerzura series (2)
House of Shade
Kaye, Mary Margaret
Death series (5)
Zanzibar series (2)
House of shadows
Grant, Maxwell
Shadow series (177)
House of shame
Hart, Alison
Girls in trouble series (1)
House of shards
Williams, Walter Jon
Crown jewels series (2)
House of silence
Grant, Maxwell
Shadow series (127)
Teed, George Hamilton
Sexton Blake series (639)
House of sin
Upward, Allen
Doctor Frank Tarleton series (2)
House of sorcery
Brown, Carter
Danny Boyd series (16)
House of strange guests
Brady, Nicholas
Ebenezer Buckle series (1)
House of Sun-Goes-Down
De Voto, Bernard
Abbey family series (2)
House of the Arrow
Mason, Alfred Edward Woodley
Inspector Hanaud series (2)
House of the bears
Creasey, John
Doctor Palfrey series (7)
House of the bird of paradise
Knight, Brigid
Christina Brand series (2)
House of the damned
Rud, Anthony Melville
J C K Masters series (2)
House of the dead ones
Chance, John Newton
Jonathan Blake series (41)
House of the deer
Stevenson, Dorothy Emily
Gerald Burleigh Brown series (2)
House of the enchantress
Erskine, Margaret
Inspector Septimus Finch series (11)
House of the four winds
Buchan, John
Dickson McCunn series (3)
House of the fragrant lotus
Thorne, Ernest Pollett
Major Brains Cunningham series (11)
House of the lost
Gray, Berkeley
Norman Conquest series (31)
House of the missing
Gluck, Sinclair
Jack Clayton series (1)
House of the moving room
Chichester, John Jay
Jimmy Price series (2)
House of the opal
Gregory, Jackson
Paul Savoy series (1)
House of the Paladin
Needham, Violet
Stormy Petrel series (3)
House of the seagull
Knight, Brigid
Christina Brand series (3)
House of the seven keys
Hanshew, Mary E
Hamilton Cleek series (10)
House of the solitary maggot
Purdy, James
Sleepers in moon-crowned valleys series (2)
House of the speckled browns
Byers, Irene
Meredith family series (2)
House of the swan
Knight, Brigid
Christina Brand series (1)
House of the vanishing goblets
Edingtons
Captain Smith series (2)
House of the whispering pines
Green, Anna Katharine
Caleb Sweetwater series (3)
House of the winds
Hodge, Charles
Jim Raine and Bob Wincourt series (2)
House of the wolf
Wren, M K
Phoenix legacy trilogy (3)
House of the yellow door
Carter, Nicholas
Nicholas Carter series (377)
House of Torchy
Ford, Sewell
Torchy series (6)
House of walking corpses
Hogan, Robert Jasper
Secret Six series (2)
House of war
Crawley, Aileen
Suleiman the Magnificent trilogy (3)
Gavin, Catherine
Twentieth-century Europe series (4)
House of whispers
Carter, Nicholas
Nicholas Carter series (422)
House of women
Malpass, Eric Lawson
William Shakespeare trilogy (3)
House of words
Dickson, Lovat
Ante-room series (2)
House of Zeor
Lichtenberg, Jacqueline
Sime-Gen series (1)
House on East Eighty Eighth Street
Waber, Bernard
Lyle series (1)
House on Greek Street
Horler, Sydney
Sebastian Quin series (2)
House on Ninth Street
Strange, John Stephen
Barney Gantt series (8)
House on Q Street
Dietrich, Robert
Steve Bentley series (2)
House on the bay
Maclean, Arthur
Sexton Blake series (1451)
House on the borderlands
Hodgson, William Hope
Glen Carrig trilogy (2)
House on the cliff
Dixon, Franklin W
Hardy boys series (1)
House on the cliffs
Chester, Gilbert
Sexton Blake series (924)
House on the Downs
Locke, Gladys Edson
Inspector Burton series (4)
House on the fens
Gask, Arthur
Gilbert Larose series (16)
House on the hill
Drummond, J
Sexton Blake series (1137)
Kyle, Elisabeth
Furze series (6)
House on the island
Gask, Arthur
Gilbert Larose series (5)
House on the ledge
Grant, Maxwell
Shadow series (202)
House on the moor
Atkinson, Mary Evelyn
Lockett family series (12)
House on the mound
Derleth, August
Wisconsin series (2)
House on the range
Gilman, George G
Edge series (45)
House on the river
Drummond, J
Sexton Blake series (1301)
House on the rock
Cleeve, Brian
Crucifixion trilogy (1)
House on Tollard Ridge
Rhode, John
Doctor Lancelot Priestley series (6)
House opposite
Farjeon, Joseph Jefferson
Ben the tramp series (3)
House party
Walder, David
Charles Lilburne and Rupert Inglis series (3)
House-party mystery
Norsworthy, George
Martin Crow series (1)
House party with the Tucker twins
Sampson, Emma
Tucker twins series (5)
House remains
Mackinnon, Charles Roy
Scottish chronicle series (4)
House that beckons
Lister, Gladys
Round series (3)
House that Beebo built
Ast, Janine
Beebo series (1)
Fix, Philippe
Beebo series (1)
House that Berry built
Yates, Dornford
Berry series (8)
Jonah Mansel series (10)
Superintendent Richard Falcon series (2)
House that grew
Boston, Lucy Maria
Green Knowe series (7)
House that is our own
Douglas, O
Priorsford series (5)
House that Jack built
McBain, Ed
Matthew Hope series (8)
House that sailed away
Hutchins, Pat
House that sailed away trilogy (1)
House that vanished
Grant, Maxwell
Shadow series (88)
House that was forgotten
Roberts, Gruffydd Dewi
Pikey's Steep series (1)
House with a clock in its walls
Bellairs, John
Clock trilogy (1)
House with blnd eyes
Jobson, Hamilton
Inspector Anders series (5)

House with crooked walls
Graeme, Bruce
Theodore I Terhune series (2)
House with four rooms
Godden, Rumer
No time to weep series (3)
House with green shutters
Long, Amelia Reynolds
Steve Carter series (7)
House with steel shutters
Parsons, Anthony
Sexton Blake series (1074)
House with the blind window
Batt, Elisabeth
Dinah Campion series (1)
House with the blue door
Footner, Hulbert
Amos Lee Mappin series (7)
House with the double moat
Brooks, Edwy Searles
Sexton Blake series (29)
House with the high wall
Gask, Arthur
Gilbert Larose series (24)
House with the red blinds
Wignall, Trevor C
Sexton Blake series (151)
House without a Christmas tree
Rock, Gail
Addie series (1)
House without a key
Biggers, Earl Derr
Charlie Chan series (1)
House without the door
Daly, Elizabeth
Henry Gamadge series (4)
Houseboat boys
Rathborne, Saint George
Canoe and campfire series (3)
Houseboat girl
Lenski, Lois
Regional series (12)
Houseboat killings
Simons, Roger
Inspector Fadiman Wace series (1)
Houseboat mystery
Warner, Gertrude Chandler
Boxcar children series (12)
Household safety
Jackson, Ellen B
Safety series (2)
Householders
Henry, Margaret
Bob and Hilary Dean series (2)
Housekeeper
Powell, Margaret
Maids and mistresses series (2)
Houseman's tale
Douglas, Colin
David Campbell series (1)
Houseman's trilogy
Douglas, Colin
David Campbell series (3)
Houseman's wager
Linton, Cathy
Saint Lawrence's Hospital series (8)
Housenappers
Curry, Jane Louise
Maccubbin family series (1)
Houses of bark
Shemie, Bonnie
Native dwellings series (2)
Houses of hide and earth
Shemie, Bonnie
Native dwellings series (3)
Houses of snow, skin and bones
Shemie, Bonnie
Native dwellings series (1)
Houses of stone and adobe
Shemie, Bonnie
Native dwellings series (6)
Houses of wood
Shemie, Bonnie
Native dwellings series (4)
Houses on the site
Evans, Stuart
Windmill Hill series (4)
Houston attack
Ramm, Carl
James Hawker series (5)
Houston hellground
Cunningham, Chet
Matt Hawke series (2)
Houston in the rearview mirror
Cooper, Susan Rogers
Milton Kovak series (2)
Houston run
Robbins, David
Endworld series (12)
Hovel in the hills
West, Elizabeth
Hafod Garden series (1)
Hovering over Baja
Gardner, Erle Stanley
Baja California series (1)
Hovering with Henry
Thatcher, Dora
Henry series (4)
Hoverlight
Lapka, Fay S
Caro series (2)
How a weirdo and a ghost can change your entire life
Windsor, Patricia
Weirdo and ghost series (1)
How about this way?
John, Stephen
Albert Divine series (2)
How airplanes help us
McCall, Edith
How series (2)
How animals defend their young
Freedman, Russell
How animals series (5)
How animals learn
Freedman, Russell
How animals series (1)
How Audrey became a guide
Nash, Frances Olivia Hartopp
Audrey series (1)
How birds fly
Freedman, Russell
How animals series (4)
How dear is life
Williamson, Henry
Chronicles of ancient sunlight series (4)
How did it look
Piers, Helen
Two hungry mice trilogy (3)
How do I eat it?
Watanabe, Shigeo
I can do it series (2)
How do I put it on?
Watanabe, Shigeo
I can do it series (1)
How do you do, Mary Mouse
Blyton, Enid
Mary Mouse series (7)
How do you eat it?
Benjamin, Floella
Flo and Aston series (3)
How do you lose those ninth grade blues
De Clements, Barthe
Elsie Edwards series (3)
How do you spell dad?
Walker, Mort
Hi and Lois series (7)
How doth the little crocodile
Antony, Peter
Mister Verity series (2)
Shaffer, Peter
Mister Verity series (2)
How dumb can you get?
Kenyon, Kate
Cedar Groves Junior High School series (4)
How Ethel Hollister became a Campfire Girl
Benson, Irene Elliott
Campfire Girls series (2)
How funny you are, Noddy
Blyton, Enid
Noddy tiny strip books series (4)
How goes the murder?
Queen, Ellery
Tim Corrigan series (4)
How green was my Apple
Lovell, Marc
Appleton Porter series (6)
How green was my father
Dodge, David
Travel diary series (2)
How green was my valley
Llewellyn, Richard
Huw Morgan series (1)
How green you are
Doherty, Berlie
Fingers Finnegan series (1)
How hard to kill
Dewey, Thomas Blanchard
Private Eye Mac series (9)
How harlots love
Balzac, Honore de
Scenes of Parisian life series (8)
How I got him back
Savers, Valerie
Due East series (2)
Mary Faith Rapple series (2)
How I spent my summer vacation
Roberts, Gillian
Amanda Pepper series (5)
How I survived my summer vacation
Coville, Bruce
Camp Haunted Hills series (1)
How I trained my colt
Rabinowitz, Sandy
Mischief series (2)
How in the world do we recycle glass?
Groves, Seli
How in the world series (1)
How in the world do we recycle paper?
Groves, Seli
How in the world series (2)
How it feels to be adopted
Kremenetz, Jill
How it feels series (2)
How it feels to fight for your life
Kremenetz, Jill
How it feels series (4)
How it feels to live with a physical disability
Kremenetz, Jill
How it feels series (5)
How it feels when a parent dies
Kremenetz, Jill
How it feels series (1)
How it feels when parents divorce
Kremenetz, Jill
How it feels series (3)
How Janice Day won
Long, Helen Beecher
Do something series (3)
How Jim did it
Finley, Martha Farquharson
Honest Jim series (3)
How John caught the sea-horse, and other stories
Berg, Leila
What-do-you-know series (1)
How John got his ducklings
Blyton, Enid
John and Mary series (2)
How jolly life is!
Zola, Emile
Rougon Macquart series (12)
How Little Grey Rabbit got back his tale
Uttley, Alison
Little Grey Rabbit series (2)
How long is always?
Weber, Lenora Mattingly
Stacy and Katie Rose Belford series (6)
How lost was my weekend
Dodge, David
Travel diary series (1)
How man began
Greene, Carla
Science and natural history series (4)
How many blocks in the pile?
Meltzer, David
Agency trilogy (3)
How many cards?
Ostrander, Isabel
Timothy McCarty series (3)
How many hats?
Campbell, Rod
Little people series (8)
How many miles to Babylon
Lafferty, Raphael Aloysius
Argos mythos series (5)
How many years was it now?
Fitzwilliam, Jennifer
Mona series (2)
How much for just the planet?
Ford, John M
Star trek series (36)
How much is a million
Schwartz, David Martin
Million series (1)
How much love costs an old man
Balzac, Honore de
Scenes of Parisian life series (8)
How now brown cow
McArthur, John
Jack McBumby series (2)
How now, McLean
Goodchild, George
Inspector McLean series (4)
How Phoebe found herself
Brown, Helen Dawes
Anna Lavinia series (3)
How Private George W Peck put down the rebellion
Peck, George Wilbur
Peck's bad boy series (9)
How right you are, Jeeves
Wodehouse, Pelham Grenville
Jeeves and Bertie Wooster series (12)
How sleep the brave
Gavin, Catherine
French Resistance series (3)
How Spider saved Christmas
Kraus, Robert
Spider series (2)
How Spider saved the baseball game
Kraus, Robert
Spider series (7)
How Spider saved Turkey
Kraus, Robert
Spider series (3)
How Spider saved Valentine's Day
Kraus, Robert
Spider series (4)
How the brothers joined the Cat Club
Averill, Esther
Jenny Linsky series (8)
How the dead live
Raymond, Derek
Factory series (2)
Factory series (4)
How the Ewoks saved the trees
Howe, James
Ewok series (1)
How the gods wove in Kyrannon
Mayhar, Ardath
Kyrannon series (1)
How the Pennypackers kept the light
Swett, Sophia Miriam
Pennypackers series (2)
How the radio came to Toytown
Beaman, Sydney George Hulme
Toytown series (37)
How the reindeer saved Santa Claus
Haywood, Carolyn
Santa Claus series (2)
How the world began
Freund, Philip
Volcano god trilogy (3)
How they fared in the times of the Tudors
Wallace, Edgar
Black Avons series (1)
How to be a vampire in one easy lesson
Gilden, Mel
Fifth grade monsters series (10)
How to be analyzed by a neurotic psychoanalyst
Baker, Stephen
How to series (6)
How to be topp
Willans, Geoffrey
Nigel Molesworth series (2)
How to become a virgin
Crisp, Quentin
Naked civil servant series (2)
How to buy an island
McCormick, Donald
British Isles series (3)
How to care for your monster
Bridwell, Norman
Monster series (1)
How to catch a flying saucer
Deem, James Morgan
How to series (2)
How to eat fried worms
Rockwell, Thomas
Billy Forrester series (1)
How to fight a girl
Rockwell, Thomas
Billy Forrester series (2)
How to find a ghost
Deem, James Morgan
How to series (1)
How to get fabulously rich
Rockwell, Thomas
Billy Forrester series (3)
How to get rich, fall in love, lose weight and solve all your problems
Guisewhite, Cathy
Cathy series (3)
How to go to hell
Groening, Matt
Life in hell series (8)
How to hide a butterfly and other insects
Heller, Ruth M
How to hide an animal series (2)
How to hide a crocodile and other reptiles
Heller, Ruth M
How to hide an animal series (4)
How to hide a grey tree frog and other amphibians
Heller, Ruth M
How to hide an animal series (6)
How to hide a whip-poor-will and other birds
Heller, Ruth M
How to hide an animal series (5)
How to hide an octopus and other sea creatures
Heller, Ruth M
How to hide an animal series (3)
How to his a polar bear and other mammals
Heller, Ruth M
How to hide an animal series (1)
How to hunt buried treasure
Deem, James Morgan
How to series (3)
How to kill a man
Wells, Tobias
Detective Knute Severson series (10)
How to know dinosaurs
Greene, Carla
Science and natural history series (1)
How to live with a neurotic cat
Baker, Stephen
How to series (7)
How to live with a neurotic dog
Baker, Stephen
How to series (1)
How to live with a neurotic husband
Baker, Stephen
How to series (5)
How to live with a neurotic wife
Baker, Stephen
How to series (4)
How to look like somebody in business without being anybody
Baker, Stephen
How to series (3)
How to make enemies
Duncan, Ronald
All men are islands trilogy (2)
How to meet a gorgeous girl
Sharmat, Marjorie Weinman
Gorgeous guys and girls series (2)
How to meet a gorgeous guy
Sharmat, Marjorie Weinman
Gorgeous guys and girls series (1)
How to murder your mother-in-law
Cannell, Dorothy
Ellie Simons Haskell series (6)
How to play golf in the low 120s
Baker, Stephen
How to series (2)
How to read your mother's mind
Deem, James Morgan
How to series (5)
How to save your own life
Jong, Erica
Isadora Wing series (2)
How to stay married
Cooper, Jilly
Work and wedlock series (1)
How to stop a train with one finger
Wilson, David Henry
Jeremy James series (4)
How to succeed at murder without really trying
Von Elsner, Don
Jake Winkman series (1)
How to survive Christmas
Cooper, Jilly
Work and wedlock series (2)
How to survive from nine to five
Cooper, Jilly
Work and wedlock series (2)
How to talk to your animals
George, Jean Craighead
How to talk to your animals series (2)
How to talk to your cat
George, Jean Craighead
How to talk to your animals series (2)
How to talk to your dog
George, Jean Craighead
How to talk to your animals series (1)
How to travel through time
Deem, James Morgan
How to series (4)
How Tom beat Captain Najork and his hired sportsmen
Hoban, Russell
Captain Najork series (1)
How 'twas
Reynolds, Stephen
Nautical series (4)
How was it done?
Cross, Mark
Daphne Wrayne and her Four Adjusters series (16)
How we communicate
Kalman, Bobbie
In my world series (13)
How we get cloth
McCall, Edith
How series (4)
How we get our clothing
McCall, Edith
How series (3)
How we get our mail
McCall, Edith
How series (1)

Hunt the Toff
Creasey, John
Toff series (26)
Hunted
Gilman, George G
Adam Steele series (43)
Hartmann, Michael
Ben Dryden series (1)
Millard, Joe
Hec Ramsey series (2)
Murray, Mary
Freedom series (2)
Plummer, Thomas Arthur
Detective Inspector Andrew Frampton series (29)
Reno, Bill
Badge series (24)
Walker, Dalton
Shiloh series (4)
Hunted down
M'Govan, James
James M'Govan series (2)
Hunted gun
Palmer, Bernard
Kid Breckinridge series (2)
Hunted head
Fitz Roy, Olivia
Jamie and Jean Stewart series (2)
Hunted man
Masterman, Walter Sidney
Sir Arthur Sinclair series (13)
Hunted wolf
Bennet, Robert Ames
Wolf series (5)
Hunter
Carter, Nick
Nick Carter series (165)
Estes, Rose
Hunter series (1)
Sauter, Eric
Robert Lee Hunter series (1)
Smith, Lisa J
Forbidden game trilogy (1)
Stark, Richard
Parker series (1)
Hunter and Raven
Sauter, Eric
Robert Lee Hunter series (3)
Hunter and the hunted
Egan, Lesley
Vic Varallo series (10)
Hunter and the ikon
Sauter, Eric
Robert Lee Hunter series (2)
Hunter and Tom
Abbott, Jacob
August series (2)
Hunter hunted
Blake, Ken
Professionals series (4)
Hunter is the hunted
Cunningham, Albert Benjamin
Sheriff Jess Roden series (17)
Hunter-killer
Jenkins, Geoffrey
Commander Geoffrey Peace series (2)
Macdonnell, James Edmond
Captain Peter Bentley series (39)
Hunter killer
Rouch, James
Zone series (3)
Hunter of men
Carter, Nicholas
Nicholas Carter series (279)
Guenter, C H
Robert Urban series (1)
Hunter of worlds
Cherryh, Carolyn Janice
Alliance-Union series (18)
Hunter on Arena
Estes, Rose
Hunter series (2)
Hunter Quatermain's story
Haggard, Henry Rider
Allan Quatermain series (6)
Hunter Squadron
Jackson, Robert
Flying Officer George Yeoman series (12)
Hunter victim
Sheckley, Robert
Victim trilogy (3)
Hunters
Hill, Peter
Inspector Robert Staunton series (1)
Leslie, Richard
Victory trilogy (3)
McCurtin, Peter
Sundance series (40)
Moore, Arthur
Bluestar series (5)
Wetanson, Burt
Hunters series (1)
Hunters and the hunted
Sitwell, Sacheverell
Quick and the dead series (4)
Hunters blaze the trail
McCall, Edith
Frontiers of America series (3)
Hunter's horn
Arnow, Harriette
Kentucky trilogy (2)
Hunter's moon
Armitage, Aileen
Hawksmoor series (2)
Atkinson, Mary Evelyn
Fricka Hammond series (2)
Hayes, Ralph Eugene
O'Brien, Buffalo Hunter series (3)
Hunters of Gor
Norman, John
Tarl Cabot series (8)
Hunters of humans
Steele, V M
Chief Inspector Saunders series (2)
Hunters of Jundagai
Bulmer, Kenneth
Keys to the dimensions series (6)
Hunters of space
Kelleam, Joseph Everidge
Jack Odin series (2)
Hunters of the hills
Altsheler, Joseph Alexander
French and Indian war series (1)
Hunters of the northern forest
Nelson, Richard King
Eskimos series (2)
Hunters of the northern ice
Nelson, Richard King
Eskimos series (1)
Hunters of the Ozark
Ellis, Edward Sylvester
Deerfoot the Showanoe series 4 (1)
Hunters of the red moon
Bradley, Marion Zimmer
Red moon series (1)
Hunter's trap
Robinson, Mike
Solo the dragon series (3)
Hunting down the spy
Cobb, Frank
Stars and Stripes series (4)
Hunting for hidden gold
Dixon, Franklin W
Hardy boys series (5)
Hunting grizzly bears
Bamman, Henry A
World of adventure series (3)
Hunting ground
Riggs, John Raymond
Garth Ryland series (3)
Hunting of Wilberforce Pike
Lefebure, Molly
Scratch and Company series (2)
Hunting the fairies
Mackenzie, Compton
Highland series (4)
Hunting the sky spies
Dixon, Franklin W
Ted Scott flying series (19)
Hunting the Wolfe
Hooper, Kay
Men of mysteries past series (2)
Hunting with Jorrocks
Surtees, Robert Smith
Mister John Jorrocks series (2)
Hunting with the fox cubs
Miller, Muriel
Woodlanders series (4)
Hunting wolf
Ahlswede, Ann
Doctor Cicero Smith series (2)
Hunting Wolf
Dever, Joe
Legends of Lone Wolf series (4)
Huntingtower
Buchan, John
Dickson McCunn series (1)
Huntress is dead
Benson, Ben
Inspector Wade Paris series (10)
Hunts with Jorrocks
Surtees, Robert Smith
Mister John Jorrocks series (2)
Huntsman
Hill, Douglas
Huntsman trilogy (1)
Verner, Gerald
Superintendent Robert Budd series (13)
Huntsville breakout
Cutter, Tom
Tracker series (7)
Huntsville horror
Ham, Bob
Overload series (9)
Hurok of the stone age
Carter, Lin
Eric Carstairs series (3)
Hurrah for Henry!
Peppe, Rodney
Henry series (8)
Hurrah for little Noddy
Blyton, Enid
Noddy series (2)
Hurrah for Mary Mouse
Blyton, Enid
Mary Mouse series (8)
Hurrah for Muggins, and other stories
Ridge, Antonia
Endless and Company series (2)
Hurrah for the circus!
Blyton, Enid
Mister Galliano's circus series (2)
Hurrah, we're outward bound
Spier, Peter
Mother Goose library series (3)
Hurray for Ali Baba Bernstein
Hurwitz, Johanna
Ali Baba Bernstein series (2)
Hurray for Hattie Rabbit!
Gackenbach, Dick
Hattie Rabbit series (5)
Hurray for Peregrine Pig
Hauptmann, Tatjana
Petronella and Peregrine Pig series (2)
Hurricane
Brightfield, Richard
Choose your own adventure series (82)
Gudmundson, Shirley M
Ebbie series (2)
Salkey, Andrew
West Indies series (1)
Hurricane alert!
Lampton, Christopher
Alert series (4)
Hurricane drift
Chance, John Newton
Jonathan Blake series (5)
Hurricane Elaine
Hurwitz, Johanna
Aldo Sossi series (4)
Hurricane Harland blows in
Allum, Tom
Hurricane Harland series (1)
Hurricane Harland crashes the gate
Allum, Tom
Hurricane Harland series (4)
Hurricane Harland hits out
Allum, Tom
Hurricane Harland series (2)
Hurricane Harland takes the plunge
Allum, Tom
Hurricane Harland series (3)
Hurricane Squadron
Jackson, Robert
Flying Officer George Yeoman series (1)
Hurricane warning!
Williams, Richard
Sexton Blake series (1494)
Hurricane weather
Pease, Howard
Tod Moran series (6)
Hurricane Williams
Young, Gordon Ray
Hurricane Williams trilogy (2)
Hurricane Williams' vengeance
Young, Gordon Ray
Hurricane Williams trilogy (3)
Hurry home, Mrs Boffy!
Furminger, Jo
Mary, Ben and William series (5)
Hurry the darkness
Procter, Maurice
Chief Inspector Harry Martineau series (4)
Hurry up, Franklin
Bourgeois, Paulette
Franklin series (2)
Hurry up, Jessie
Ziefert, Harriet
Jessie series (1)
Hurting
Norby, Lisa
Cheerleaders series (13)
Husband
Anstruther, Eileen Harriet
Farm servant trilogy (2)
Husband and wife
Hoult, Norah
Monty Mallory series (2)
Husband for Gail
Corcoran, Barbara
Abigail trilogy (3)
Husband for Victoria
Wilkins, Vaughan
Victoria series (2)
Husband isn't everything
Kamins, Jeanette
Husband series (2)
Hush-a-bye baby
Huddy, Delia
Hipster series (1)
Hush-a-bye murder
Alexander, David
Bart Hardin series (7)
Lieutenant Romano series (7)
Hush, Gabriel!
Johns, Veronica Parker
Agatha Welch series (1)
Hush-hush murders
Yates, Margaret Tayler
Anne Davenport McLean series (1)
Hush kitten
Schongut, Emanuel
Kitten board book series (3)
Hush money
Collins, Max Allan
Nolan series (4)
Israel, Peter
B F Cage series (1)
Hushed up at German Headquarters
Le Queux, William
Otto von Heynitz series (1)
Husky be my guide
Thwaites, Frederick Joseph
Husky series (1)
Hussar on the roof
Giono, Jean
Angelo series (2)
Hustler
Tevis, Walter Stone
Hustler series (1)
Hut by the river
Burgin, George Brown
Four Corners series (12)
Huxley Pig at the beach
Peppe, Rodney
Huxley Pig series (6)
Huxley Pig at the circus
Peppe, Rodney
Huxley Pig series (2)
Huxley Pig at the restaurant
Peppe, Rodney
Huxley Pig series (7)
Huxley Pig in the haunted house
Peppe, Rodney
Huxley Pig series (3)
Huxley Pig the clown
Peppe, Rodney
Huxley Pig series (4)
Huxley Pig's aeroplane
Peppe, Rodney
Huxley Pig series (5)
Huxley Pig's dressing up book
Peppe, Rodney
Huxley Pig series (8)
Huxley Pig's model car
Peppe, Rodney
Huxley Pig series (9)
Huzzard buzzard
Reese, Bob
Desert critterland series (6)
Hyacinth and her brother
Mathews, Joanna Hooe
Flowerets series (5)
Hyak Inlet
Pearce, Agatha Hunt
Edward, Frank and Gerry series (2)
Hyborean age
Howard, Robert Ervin
Conan series (1)
Hyde and seek
Wolff, Benjamin
John Byron Hyde series (1)
Hyde in deep cover
Wolff, Benjamin
John Byron Hyde series (2)
Hyde Park murder
Roosevelt, Elliott
Eleanor Roosevelt series (2)
Hydra
Grant, Maxwell
Shadow series (234)
Hydra conspiracy
Kirk, Philip
Butler series (1)
Hydra monster
Falk, Lee
Phantom series (8)
Hydrabyss red
Tedford, William G
Timequest trilogy (2)
Hydronauts
Biemiller, Carl Ludwig
Hydronauts series (1)
Hydronauts meet the otter-people
Biemiller, Carl Ludwig
Hydronauts series (2)
Hyperion
Simmons, Dan
Hyperion series (1)
Hyperion cantos
Simmons, Dan
Hyperion series (2)
Hyperspace
Packard, Edward
Choose your own adventure series (21)
Hypnosis and the sexual life
Pendleton, Don
Sexual life series (1)

I

I
Anonymous
Pronoun series (7)
I am a camera
Van Druten, John
Berlin series (3)
I am a guinea pig
Insight, James
Vicar series (4)
I am Canute
Williams, Patry
Canute series (1)
I am curious about numbers
Krulick, Nancy E
Curious George series (3)
I am England
Wright, Patrick
Near and distant series (1)
I am fifteen and I do not want to die
Arnothy, Christine
Living series (1)
I am five
Fitzhugh, Louise
I am series (3)
I am four
Fitzhugh, Louise
I am series (2)
I am freedom's child
Martin, Bill
Freedom series (5)
I am helping
Mayer, Mercer
I am series (1)
I am hiding
Mayer, Mercer
I am series (2)
I am Lazarus
Berlin, Sven
Lazarus series (1)
I am Maria
Hellberg, Hans Eric
Maria series (3)
I am Mary Tudor
Lewis, Hilda
Mary Tudor trilogy (1)
I am my brother
Lehmann, John
In my own time series (2)
I am playing
Mayer, Mercer
I am series (3)
I am Saxon Ashe
Ashe, Saxon
Saxon Ashe series (1)
I am sharing
Mayer, Mercer
I am series (4)
I am the captain
Hackforth-Jones, Gilbert
Joe Garton series (2)
I am the Cat
Kutak, Rosemary
Doctor Marc Castleman series (2)
I am the only running footman
Grimes, Martha
Inspector Richard Jury series (8)
I am the vicar
Insight, James
Vicar series (2)
I am the Withered Man
Deane, Norman
Bruce Murdoch series (5)

I am three
Fitzhugh, Louise
I am series (1)
I bought a hotel
Brown, Alfred John
High Fell series (1)
I bought a mountain
Firbank, Thomas
Mountain series (1)
I bought a star
Firbank, Thomas
Mountain series (3)
I can
Tarsky, Sue
Chatterbox series (3)
I can blink
Asch, Frank
I can series (1)
I can build a house
Watanabe, Shigeo
I can do it series (7)
I can cope
Cronin, Michael
Richard Maidment series (2)
I can count
Bruna, Dick
I can series (3)
I can count more, 13-24
Bruna, Dick
I can series (4)
I can do it!
Watanabe, Shigeo
I can do it series (5)
I can do it, you can do it
Smaridge, Nora
Raggedy Ann series (49)
I can dress myself
Bruna, Dick
I can series (6)
I can get it for you wholesale
Weidman, Jerome
Harry Bogen series (1)
I can jump puddles
Marshall, Alan
I can jump puddles series (1)
I can read
Bruna, Dick
I can series (1)
I can read difficult words
Bruna, Dick
I can series (5)
I can read more
Bruna, Dick
I can series (2)
I can roar
Asch, Frank
I can series (2)
I can say no
Sanford, Doris
Hurts of childhood series (5)
I cannot get you close enough
Gilchrist, Ellen
Anna Hudson series (2)
I can't believe I ate the whole thing
Conway, Troy
Coxeman series (32)
I can't die here
Nolan, Jeannette Covert
Lace White series (2)
I can't stay long
Lee, Laurie
Cotswolds series (3)
I can't talk about it
Sanford, Doris
Hurts of childhood series (2)
I can't wait
Flynn, Rachel
Koala Hills Primary Hills series (3)
I carried the horn
Pullein-Thompson, Christine
Sandy and Lawrence trilogy (2)
I chose caviar
Buchwald, Art
Caviar series (1)
I chose freedom
Kravchenko, Viktor
Choice series (1)
I chose justice
Kravchenko, Viktor
Choice series (2)
I chose to climb
Bonington, Chris
Climbing series (1)
I, Claudius
Graves, Robert
Claudius series (1)
I come to kill you
Halliday, Brett
Michael Shayne series (64)
I could have died
Bagby, George
Inspector Schmidt series (45)
I could murder her
Lorac, E C R
Inspector Macdonald series (35)
I didn't know you cared
Tinniswood, Peter
Brandon family series (3)
I die possessed
O'Sullivan, James Brendan
Steve Silk series (5)
I die slowly
Millar, Kenneth
Chet Gordon series (1)
I died yesterday
Robeson, Kenneth
Doc Savage series (147)
I din do nuttin, and other poems
Agard, John
Caribbean series (1)
I don't feel well
Brandenberg, Franz
Edward and Elizabeth series (4)
I don't like cats
Anson, Lindsay
Peter Allen series (2)
I don't scare easy
Dougall, Bernard
Steve Borden series (1)
I don't want to go in a car
Jungman, Ann
I don't want to series (3)
I don't want to go to bed
Lindgren, Astrid
I want series (1)
I don't want to go to school
Jungman, Ann
I don't want to series (2)
I don't want to live in a house
Jungman, Ann
I don't want to series (1)
I don't want to play with my friends
Jungman, Ann
I don't want to series (4)
I don't want to, said Sara
Peterson, Hans
Sara series (3)
I dream a world, 1941-1967
Rampersad, Arnold
Life of Langston Hughes series (2)
I dream of genie
Browne, Dik
Hagar the horrible series (46)
I, Eugenie
Kenyon, Frank Wilson
Emperor Napoleon III series (1)
I fear the Greeks
Stein, Aaron Marc
Matt Erridge series (5)
I fell among thieves
Cobb, Belton
Bryan Armitage series (21)
Kitty Armitage series (21)
I for intrigue
Janson, Hank
Hank Janson series (150)
I forgot to tell you
Jones, Lawrence Evelyn
Victorian boyhood series (4)
I found adventure
Ingram, James Henry
Adventure series (1)
I found him dead
Gallagher, Gale
Gale Gallagher series (1)
I give you five days
Curzon, Clare
Superintendent Mike Yeadings and Sergeant Angus Mott series (3)
I go on the films
Berkley, Tom
Algernon Alexander Gunning Hendry series (2)
I go to nursery school
Pragoff, Fiona
Going to school series (1)
I guarded kings
Brust, Harold
Political police officer series (1)
I hate Fridays
Flynn, Rachel
Koala Hills Primary Hills series (1)
I hate my brother Harry
Dragonwagon, Crescent
I hate series (1)
I hate my sister Maggie
Dragonwagon, Crescent
I hate series (2)
I hate Roland Roberts
Selway, Martina
Dear Grandad series (2)
I have Gloria Kirby
Himmel, Richard
Johnny Maguire series (2)
I have killed a man
Gregg, Cecil Freeman
Inspector Cuthbert Higgins series (4)
I haven't unpacked
Holt, William
Unpacked series (1)
I hear
Isadora, Rachel
Senses series (1)
I heard the death bell
Russell, Charlotte Murray
Jane Amanda Edwards series (6)
I hold the four aces
Chase, James Hadley
Helga Rolfe series (3)
I introduce
Graham, Winifred
That reminds me trilogy (3)
I is for innocent
Grafton, Sue
Kinsey Millhone series (9)
I, Jan Cremer
Cremer, Jan
Jan Cremer series (1)
I kiss your little hand, madame, and more disasters abroad
Reid, Colin
Disasters series (3)
I knew McBean
Erskine, Margaret
Inspector Septimus Finch series (3)
I knock at the door
O'Casey, Sean
I knock at the door series (1)
I know about animals
Gree, Alain
I know series (7)
I know about cars
Gree, Alain
I know series (2)
I know about colours
Gree, Alain
I know series (3)
I know about counting
Gree, Alain
I know series (4)
I know about flowers
Gree, Alain
I know series (1)
I know about numbers
Bruna, Dick
I know series (1)
I know about our world
Gree, Alain
I know series (5)
I know about shapes
Bruna, Dick
I know series (3)
I know more about numbers
Bruna, Dick
I know series (2)
I know Mrs Long
Barnett, Glyn
Inspector Gramport series (3)
I know the face, but
Bull, Peter
Bulls series (3)
I know the world's worst secret
Sanford, Doris
Hurts of childhood series (6)
I know what I liked
Bartlett, Vernon
My life series (5)
I know what it's like to die
Ross, Jonathan
Superintendent George Rogers series (7)
I know why the caged bird sings
Angelou, Maya
Heart of a woman series (1)
I know you, Al
Greene, Constance Clarke
Al series (2)
I like danger
Corrigan, Mark
Mark Corrigan and McLean series (12)
I like driving
Curry, Peter
I like series (3)
I like eating
Curry, Peter
I like series (4)
I like 'em tough
Cannon, Curt
Curt Cannon series (2)
I like helping
Erickson, Karen
I can do it series (14)
I like it cool
Lawrence, Michael
Johnny Amsterdam series (2)
I like it that way
John, Stephen
Albert Divine series (1)
I like it tough
Howard, James Arch
Steve Ashe series (2)
I like playing
Curry, Peter
I like series (2)
I like wearing
Curry, Peter
I like series (1)
I like winter
Lenski, Lois
Seasons series (3)
I lile school
Kalman, Bobbie
In my world series (6)
I live in a city
Kalman, Bobbie
In my world series (10)
I lived these years
Baume, Eric
I lived series (1)
I love you, Dear Dragon
Hillert, Margaret
Dear Dragon series (3)
I, Lucifer
O'Donnell, Peter
Modesty Blaise series (3)
I married a redhead
Musselman, Morris McNeil
Marriage series (1)
I married the world
Maxwell, Elsa
Celebrity series (1)
I met a boy I used to know
Weber, Lenora Mattingly
Stacy and Katie Rose Belford series (4)
I met murder
Ferrars, Elizabeth
Virginia and Felix Freer series (5)
I, Momolu
Graham, Lorenz
Momolu series (2)
I must fly
Scott, Sheila
Air pilot series (1)
I must go back
Howe, Doris
Kootenay series (1)
I need you, Dear Dragon
Hillert, Margaret
Dear Dragon series (10)
I never miss twice
Cobb, Belton
Bryan Armitage series (8)
Inspector Cheviot Burmann series (32)
Kitty Armitage series (5)
I.O.U.
Pickard, Nancy
Jenny Cain series (7)
I.O.U. murder
Dewey, Thomas Blanchard
Pete Schofield series (1)
Francis, William
Anthony Martin series (1)
I, of all people
Kirkup, James
Only child series (3)
I play as I please
Lyttleton, Humphrey
As I please series (1)
I reach out to the morning
Martin, Bill
Freedom series (6)
I read signs
Hoban, Tana
I read series (1)
I read symbols
Hoban, Tana
I read series (2)
I, robot
Asimov, Isaac
Robot series (1)
I, Roxana
Moray, Helga
Roxana trilogy (1)
I said Oddly, diddle I?
Jennings, Paul Francis
Oddly series (8)
I, said the demon
Baxt, George
Sylvia Plotkin and Max Van Larsen series (2)
I, said the sparrow
Lincoln, Maurice
Reginald Massingham series (1)
I, said the Sparrow
Murphy, Christopher
Sparrow series (2)
I said to my wife
Duche, Jean
Juliette series (1)
I saw murder
Cobden, Guy
John Chadwick series (7)
I say, look here
Bull, Peter
Bulls series (4)
I search for rainbows
Cartland, Barbara
Years of life series (4)
I see
Isadora, Rachel
Senses series (2)
I see London, I see France
Browne, Dik
Hagar the horrible series (48)
I see no sin
Fisher, Vardis
Tragic life series (1)
I seek the miraculous
Cartland, Barbara
Years of life series (4)
I shall maintain
Knight, Brigid
Van Breda family series (3)
I, Sherlock Holmes
Harrison, Michael
Sherlock Holmes sequels series (26)
I should have kissed her more
King, Alexander
Mine enemy grows older series (3)
I should have stayed in bed!
Lexau, Joan M
I should have stayed in bed series (1)
I should worry, I should care
Chaikin, Miriam
Molly series (1)
I sit and I think and I wonder
Dark, Sidney
Guide, philosopher and friend trilogy (2)
I, Smocker
Lumbers, Eugene
Smocker series (1)
I spy
Lincoln, Natalie Sumner
Inspector Mitchell series (1)
Marzollo, Jean
I spy series (1)
Tiger, John
I spy series (1)
I spy Christmas
Marzollo, Jean
I spy series (2)
I spy funhouse
Marzollo, Jean
I spy series (3)
I spy mystery
Marzollo, Jean
I spy series (4)
I spy, you die
Brown, Hosanna
Frank Le Roux series (1)
I stand corrected
Safire, William
On language series (3)
I still haven't unpacked
Holt, William
Unpacked series (2)
I struggle and I rise
Knight, Brigid
Van Breda family series (1)
I sure am glad to see you, Blackboard Bear
Alexander, Martha G
Blackboard Bear series (3)
I swore I never would
French, Harold
I swore series (1)
I take this stranger
Warren, Paulette
Caliban series (5)
I, the criminal
Sharp, David
Professor Henry Arthur Fielding series (4)
I, the hangman
Ballinger, W A
Sexton Blake series (1597)
I, the jury
Spillane, Mickey
Mike Hammer series (1)
I think I'll live
Stuart, Donald Robert
Conjuror's years series (6)
I think I'm falling in love
Sharmat, Marjorie Weinman
Sorority sisters series (3)

I thought I never could
French, Harold
I swore series (1)
I threw a rose into the sea
Simpson, Alyse
Rose in the sea series (1)
I too, have lived in Arcadia
Lowndes, Marie Belloc
Arcadia series (1)
I, too sing America, 1902-1941
Rampersad, Arnold
Life of Langston Hughes series (1)
I touch
Isadora, Rachel
Senses series (3)
I turned my collar round
Insight, James
Vicar series (1)
I, vampire
Scott, Jody
Sterling O'Blivion series (2)
I visit the Soviets
Delafield, E M
Provincial lady series (4)
I walk alone
Wallace, Kathleen
I walk alone series (1)
I want a brother or sister
Lindgren, Astrid
I want series (3)
I want more
Wilhelm, Hans
Merritales series (9)
I want to be a baker
Greene, Carla
I want to be series (2)
I want to be a ballet dancer
Greene, Carla
I want to be series (21)
I want to be a baseball player
Greene, Carla
I want to be series (31)
I want to be a bus driver
Greene, Carla
I want to be series (5)
I want to be a carpenter
Greene, Carla
I want to be series (22)
I want to be a coal miner
Greene, Carla
I want to be series (6)
I want to be a cowboy
Greene, Carla
I want to be series (27)
I want to be a dairy farmer
Greene, Carla
I want to be series (7)
I want to be a dentist
Greene, Carla
I want to be series (28)
I want to be a doctor
Greene, Carla
I want to be series (13)
I want to be a farmer
Greene, Carla
I want to be series (23)
I want to be a fireman
Greene, Carla
I want to be series (24)
I want to be a fisherman
Greene, Carla
I want to be series (8)
I want to be a homemaker
Greene, Carla
I want to be series (32)
I want to be a librarian
Greene, Carla
I want to be series (29)
I want to be a mechanic
Greene, Carla
I want to be series (25)
I want to be a musician
Greene, Carla
I want to be series (35)
I want to be a news reporter
Greene, Carla
I want to be series (14)
I want to be a nurse
Greene, Carla
I want to be series (9)
I want to be a pilot
Greene, Carla
I want to be series (10)
I want to be a policeman
Greene, Carla
I want to be series (15)
I want to be a postman
Greene, Carla
I want to be series (16)
I want to be a restaurant owner
Greene, Carla
I want to be series (26)
I want to be a road builder
Greene, Carla
I want to be series (17)
I want to be a scientist
Greene, Carla
I want to be series (33)
I want to be a ship captain
Greene, Carla
I want to be series (36)
I want to be a space pilot
Greene, Carla
I want to be series (34)
I want to be a storekeeper
Greene, Carla
I want to be series (18)
I want to be a teacher
Greene, Carla
I want to be series (11)
I want to be a telephone operator
Greene, Carla
I want to be series (19)
I want to be a train engineer
Greene, Carla
I want to be series (3)
I want to be a truck driver
Greene, Carla
I want to be series (20)
I want to be a zoo keeper
Greene, Carla
I want to be series (12)
I want to be an airplane hostess
Greene, Carla
I want to be series (30)
I want to be an animal doctor
Greene, Carla
I want to be series (1)
I want to be an orange grower
Greene, Carla
I want to be series (4)
I want to go home
Lockridge, Frances
Inspector Merton Heimrich series (3)
I want to go to school
Lindgren, Astrid
I want series (2)
I was a teeny-bopper for the CIA
Mark, Ted
Man from O.R.G.Y. series (13)
I was following this girl
Skirrow, Desmond
John Brock series (2)
I was murdered
Wilson, Gertrude Mary
Inspector Lovick series (2)
I was there
Richter, Hans Peter
Friedrich trilogy (2)
I wear the morning star
Highwater, Jamake
Ghost horse quartet (3)
I will lift up mine eyes
Skidmore, Hubert
My salvation series (1)
I will maintain
Bowen, Marjorie
William III trilogy (1)
I will repay
Orczy, Emmuska
Scarlet Pimpernel series (6)
I will speak daggers
Procter, Maurice
Superintendent Philip Hunter series (2)
I wonder about farm animals
Watson, Jean
I wonder about series (3)
I wonder about me
Watson, Jean
I wonder about series (1)
I wonder about plants
Watson, Jean
I wonder about series (2)
I wonder about zoo animals
Watson, Jean
I wonder about series (4)
I wore my rabbit
Stewart, Flora
Flora and Dickie series (2)
I would never tell a lie
Wilhelm, Hans
Merritales series (11)
I wouldn't have missed it
Longhurst, Henry
Good while it lasted series (2)
Ian and Felicity
Mackail, Denis
Greenery Street trilogy (3)
Ian Hardy, fighting the Moors
Currey, Edward Hamilton
Ian Hardy series (4)
Ian Hardy, midshipman
Currey, Edward Hamilton
Ian Hardy series (2)
Ian Hardy, naval cadet
Currey, Edward Hamilton
Ian Hardy series (1)
Ian Hardy, senior midshipman
Currey, Edward Hamilton
Ian Hardy series (3)
Ian Munro's Monte Carlo Rally
Gibson, Michael
Motor rally series (1)
Ibiza surprise
Dunnett, Dorothy
Johnson and the yacht Dolly series (2)
Icarus
Way, Peter
Crispin Bridge series (2)
Ice
Charbonneau, Louis
Kathy McNeely series (1)
Jones, Tristan
Wayward sailor series (4)
McBain, Ed
Eighty Seventh Precinct series (36)
Ice age explorer
Dixon, Dougal
Time machine series (7)
Ice and fire
Axler, James
Deathlands series (8)
Ice axe murders
Carr, Glyn
Sir Abercrombie Lewker series (11)
Ice beast
Javor, Frank A
Eli Pike series (3)
Ice belt
Couper, Stephen
Paradise series (2)
Ice bomb zero
Carter, Nick
Nick Carter series (63)
Ice cave
Salmon, Michael
Dinosaur swamp series (5)
Ice cold kill
Pendleton, Don
Mack Bolan series (70)
Ice-cold nude
Brown, Carter
Danny Boyd series (8)
Ice cream soup
Modell, Frank B
Milton and Marvin series (6)
Ice desert
Verne, Jules
Adventures of Captain Hatteras series (2)
Ice divers
Crisp, Frank
Dirk Rogers series (9)
Ice dragon
Gygax, Gary
Sagard the Barbarian series (1)
Lord, Jeffrey
Richard Blade series (10)
Postgate, Oliver
Saga of Noggin the Nog series (2)
Ice from space
Houston, David
Tales of tomorrow series (4)
Ice goddess
Edwards, Paul
John Eagle series (7)
Ice hockey
Gutman, Bill
Go for it series (7)
Ice in the sun
Enefer, Douglas
Dale Shand series (13)
Ice is coming
Wrightson, Patricia
Song of Wirrun trilogy (1)
Ice island
Greenfield, Irving A
Depth force series (11)
Ice-king
Buntline, Ned
War Eagle series (1)
Ice maiden
Allison, Clyde
Agent triple zero eight series (17)
Ice maidens
Chance, John Newton
Jonathan Blake series (16)
Ice never F
Orlovitz, Gil
Emanuel family series (2)
Ice prophet
Forstchen, William R
Ice prophet trilogy (1)
Ice-shirt
Vollman, William T
Seven dreams series (1)
Ice trap terror
Carter, Nick
Nick Carter series (85)
Ice water
Gunning, Sally
Peter Bartholomew series (3)
Iceberg
Banks, David
Doctor Who series (159)
Cussler, Clive
Dirk Pitt series (3)
Icebergs
Postgate, Oliver
Saga of Noggin the Nog series (12)
Icebound
Spencer, Rick
Eric Ivorsen series (1)
Icebreaker
Gardner, John Edmund
James Bond series (20)
Iced on Aran, and other dreamquests
Lumley, Brian
Dreamlands series (4)
Icedragon
Knaak, Richard Allen
Dragonrealm series (2)
Iceland settlement
Birt, David
Saxons and Vikings series (19)
Iceman
Miller, Rex
Jack Eichord series (5)
Icepick
Fletcher, Aaron
Marksman series (19)
Icepick in the spine
Scarpetta, Frank
Marksman series (19)
Icequake
Kilian, Crawford
Icequake series (1)
Icerigger
Foster, Alan Dean
Icerigger series (1)
Thranx series (3)
Icetowers
McGeary, Duncan
Greylock of Godshome series (2)
Iceworld connection
Cleve, John
Spaceways series (11)
Iciest sin
Keating, Henry Reymond Fitzwalter
Inspector Ganesh Ghote series (18)
Icy clutches
Elkins, Aaron J
Professor Gideon Oliver series (6)
I'd rather be dancing
Ryan, Mary Elizabeth
Katie Kusik series (2)
I'd rather be in Philadelphia
Roberts, Gillian
Amanda Pepper series (3)
I'd rather stay home
Barkin, Carol
Transition series (3)
Ida and Betty and the secret eggs
Chorao, Kay
Ida series (3)
Ida Early comes over the mountain
Burch, Robert Joseph
Ida Early series (1)
Ida makes a movie
Chorao, Kay
Ida series (2)
Idaho!
Ross, Dana Fuller
Wagons West series (13)
Idea
Mason, Roger
Motto excelsior series (3)
Ideala
Grand, Sarah
Heavenly twins series (1)
Identity plunderers
Haiblum, Isidore
Siscoe and Block series (1)
Identity unknown
Jacobs, Thomas Curtis Hicks
Chief Inspector Barnard series (7)
Ides of April
Ray, Mary
Early Christian series (2)
IDIC epidemic
Lorrah, Jean
Star trek series (38)
Idle rainbow
Best, Rayleigh Breton Amis
Yarrow series (4)
Idly Oddly
Jennings, Paul Francis
Oddly series (7)
Idol from Pasha
Mahr, Kurt
Perry Rhodan series (98)
Idol's eye
Hill, Harry Egbert
Sexton Blake series (169)
Iduna's universe
Tubb, Edwin Charles
Dumarest series (21)
If a body
Yates, George Worthing
Hazlitt Woar series (3)
If anything happened to Hester
Morton, Anthony
Baron series (31)
If anything should happen
O'Hara, Kevin
Chico Brett series (13)
If anything should happen to me
Barker, Albert
Hawk Macrae series (2)
If confusion were a class I'd get an A
Evans, Greg
Luann series (12)
If death ever slept
Stout, Rex
Nero Wolfe and Archie Goodwin series (29)
If dying was all
Goulart, Ron
John Easy series (1)
If I could be a circus clown
Dolce, Janet Ellen
Daydreamers series (3)
If I die in a combat zone, box me up and ship me home
O'Brien, Tim
Vietnam War series (1)
If I don't, who will?
Scott, Mary
New Zealand life series (8)
If I had a hippo
Dolce, Janet Ellen
Daydreamers series (1)
If I knew how to fly a rocket
Dolce, Janet Ellen
Daydreamers series (2)
If I live to dine
Waugh, Hillary
Sheridan Wesley series (1)
If I should die before I wake
Potter, Jerry Allen
Sam Tucker series (2)
If I should murder
Laing, Patrick
Patrick Laing series (1)
If I went sailing out to sea
Dolce, Janet Ellen
Daydreamers series (4)
If I were king
McCarthy, Justin Huntly
Francois Villon trilogy (1)
If I were king of the universe
Abelson, Danny
Fraggle Rock series (6)
If it die
Gide, Andre
Journal series (7)
If it hadn't been for Frances
Warner, Priscilla Mary
Frances series (2)
If it moves, kiss it!
Moura, Joni
Air Force series (2)
If looks could kill
Keene, Carolyn
Nancy Drew files series (91)
If my love could hold you
Coffman, Elaine
Mackinnon brothers series (2)
If only they could talk
Herriot, James
Vet series (1)
If Sherlock Holmes were a woman
Kelly, Tim J
Sherlock Holmes drama series (6)
If the old could
Somers, Jane
Jane Somers series (2)
If the shoe fits
Giff, Patricia Reilly
New kids at the Polk Street School series (2)
Roberts, Lee
Doctor Clinton Shannon series (2)

If the shroud fits
Kruger, Paul
Phil Kramer series (3)
Roos, Kelley
Jeff and Haila Troy series (2)
If there be thorns
Andrews, Virginia Cleo
Dollanganger family series (4)
If this be I, as I suppose it be
Deland, Margaret
If this be I series (1)
If this be murder
Darby, Ruth
Peter and Janet Barron series (3)
If this is a man
Levi, Primo
Survival in Auschwitz series (1)
If wishes were hearses
Bond, J Harvey
Mike Lanson series (4)
If wishes were horses
Grossman, Nancy Livright
Dutch Mill Stable series (2)
If you grew up with Abraham Lincoln
McGovern, Ann
American history series (4)
If you lived in colonial times
McGovern, Ann
American history series (2)
If you lived with the circus
McGovern, Ann
American history series (5)
If you lived with the Sioux Indians
McGovern, Ann
American history series (3)
If you made a million
Schwartz, David Martin
Million series (2)
If you sailed on the Mayflower
McGovern, Ann
American history series (1)
If you say so, Claude
Nixon, Joan Lowery
Claude series (1)
Iggy
Miles, Keith
Sin bin series (1)
Ignorant armies
Yeovil, Jack
Warhammer series (2)
Warhammer series (6)
Iguana's tail
Sherlock, Philip
Caribbean stories series (1)
Ike and Mama and the block wedding
Snyder, Carol
Ike and Mama series (2)
Ike and Mama and the once-a-lifetime movie
Snyder, Carol
Ike and Mama series (3)
Ike and Mama and the once-a-year suit
Snyder, Carol
Ike and Mama series (1)
Ike and Mama and the trouble at school
Snyder, Carol
Ike and Mama series (4)
Iktomi and the berries
Goble, Paul
Iktomi series (2)
Iktomi and the boulder
Goble, Paul
Iktomi series (1)
Iktomi and the buffalo skull
Goble, Paul
Iktomi series (3)
Iktomi and the ducks
Goble, Paul
Iktomi series (4)
Ilbarana
Stuart, Donald
Ilbarana series (1)
Ilene, the superstitious
Kimbrough, Katheryn
Phenwick women series (14)
Iliad
Homer
Trojan War series (1)
I'll always love you
Wilhelm, Hans
Elfie series (1)
I'll be judge, I'll be jury
Hely, Elizabeth
Antoine Cirret series (1)
I'll be leaving you always
Scoppettone, Sandra
Lauren Laurano series (2)
I'll bring her back
Cheyney, Peter
Johnny Vallon series (3)
Secret service series (7)
Shaun O'Mara series (3)
I'll cry tomorrow
Roth, Lillian
I'll cry tomorrow series (1)
Ill deeds done
Hocking, Anne
Inspector William Austen series (2)
I'll do anything
Bateson, David
Larry Vernon series (7)
I'll eat you last
Branson, Henry Clay
John Bent series (1)
Ill fares the land
Fitzroy, Rosamond
Mallamshire series (4)
Ill fate marshalling
Cook, Glen
Dread Empire series (7)
I'll find you
Himmel, Richard
Johnny Maguire series (1)
I'll get you yet
Howard, James Arch
Steve Ashe series (1)
I'll go anywhere
Bateson, David
Larry Vernon series (6)
Ill gotten gains
Murray, Andrew
Sexton Blake series (3)
I'll hate myself in the morning
Paul, Elliot
Homer Evans series (5)
I'll kill you last
Branson, Henry Clay
John Bent series (1)
I'll kill you next!
Knight, Adam
Steve Conacher series (6)
Ill-made knight
White, Terence Hanbury
Once and future king series (3)
I'll meet you at the Cucumbers
Moore, Lilian
Cucumbers trilogy (1)
Ill met by moonlight
Ford, Leslie
Colonel John Primrose series (2)
Grace Latham series (1)
Moss, William Stanley
War in Crete series (1)
Ill met in Mexico
Russell, Charlotte Murray
Jane Amanda Edwards series (10)
I'll never like Friday again
Maddock, Stephen
Timothy Terrel series (17)
I'll say she does!
Cheyney, Peter
Lemmy Caution series (11)
I'll sing at your funeral
Pentecost, Hugh
Luke Bradley series (3)
I'll take Manhattan
Barlette, Danielle
Mirrors series (1)
I'll tell you a story
Blyton, Enid
I'll tell you a story series (1)
I'll tell you another story
Blyton, Enid
I'll tell you a story series (2)
I'll try
Leslie, Madeline
Little Agnes series (2)
Ill will
Brinton, Henry
John and Sally Strang series (6)
Ill wind
Fitt, Mary
Superintendent Mallett series (13)
Ill wind contract
Atlee, Philip
Joe Gall series (10)
Illearth war
Donaldson, Stephen Reeder
First Chronicles of Thomas Covenant series (2)
Illegal entry
Bernard, Robert
Millicent Hetherege series (2)
Illegal notion
Wharton, Joanna
Campus fever series (4)
Illegitimate spy
Silverwood, Roger
Superintendent Cawthorne series (3)
Illinois!
Ross, Dana Fuller
Wagons West series (18)
Illinois Prescott
Wisler, Gary Clifton
Darby Prescott series (1)
Illuminatus trilogy
Shea, Robert
Illuminatus series (3)
Illusion
Caute, David
Confrontation trilogy (3)
Warner, Mignon
Mrs Edwina Charles series (6)
Illusionist
Mallet-Joris, Francoise
Helene series (1)
Illusions of evil
Keene, Carolyn
Nancy Drew files series (94)
Illustrated Dracula
Stoker, Bram
Dracula series (1)
Illustrated Dune
Herbert, Frank
Dune series (1)
Paul Atreides trilogy (1)
Illyrian adventure
Alexander, Lloyd
Vesper Holly series (1)
I'm a little airplane
Tubby, I M
I'm a little series (1)
I'm a little fish
Tubby, I M
I'm a little series (2)
I'm a little house
Tubby, I M
I'm a little series (3)
I'm a little tugboat
Tubby, I M
I'm a little series (4)
I'm all right Jack
Hackney, Alan
Stanley Windrush series (2)
I'm brave!
Erickson, Karen
I can do it series (11)
I'm Cannon, for hire
Cannon, Curt
Curt Cannon series (1)
I'm Cherry, fly me!
Chase, Glen
Cherry Delight series (6)
I'm Emma, I'm a quint
Pevsner, Stella
Quints series (2)
I'm expecting to live quite soon
West, Paul
Jaggers family series (2)
I'm getting killed right here
Murray, William Buckley
Lou Anderson series (3)
I'm going for a walk
Watanabe, Shigeo
I can do it series (8)
I'm going to get your boyfriend
Sharmat, Marjorie Weinman
Sorority sisters series (8)
I'm having a bath with papa!
Watanabe, Shigeo
I can do it series (10)
I'm learning, Lord, but I still need help
Aaseng, Nathan
Devotions series (1)
I'm no hero
Howard, Hartley
Glenn Bowman series (22)
I'm no murderer
Perowne, Barry
Rick Leroy series (2)
I'm not always confused, I just look that way
Evans, Greg
Luann series (14)
I'm not sleepy
Gretz, Susanna
Teddybear board book series (3)
I'm not telling
Thesman, Jean
Birthday girls series (1)
I'm Penny, fly me
Sutton, Penny
Stewardesses series (4)
I'm playing with papa!
Watanabe, Shigeo
I can do it series (9)
I'm searching, Lord, but I need your light
Aaseng, Nathan
Devotions series (2)
I'm so-so, so what?
Graeber, Charlotte Towner
Mister T and me series (11)
I'm talking about Jerusalem
Wesker, Arnold
Chicken soup trilogy (3)
I'm telling!
Arnold, Eric H
Kids talk series (2)
I'm the king of the castle
Watanabe, Shigeo
I can do it series (6)
I'm trying to give it up
Skirrow, Desmond
John Brock series (3)
Image in the mirror
Sayers, Dorothy Leigh
Lord Peter Wimsey series (10)
Image killer
Maner, William
Parker Rowe series (1)
Image men
Priestley, John Boynton
Image men series (2)
Image of a murder
Capon, Paul
Arnold Wragge series (3)
Image of the beast
Farmer, Philip Jose
Exorcism series (1)
Exorcism series (2)
Image of voices
Norwood, Warren
Windhover tapes series (1)
Images of death
Williams, Lawrence
Lgendary murders series (3)
Imaginary mistress
Balzac, Honore de
Scenes of private life series (13)
Imagine a man
Fitzgerald, Nigel
Superintendent Duffy series (4)
Imagining Isabel
Castaneda, Omar S
Isabel series (2)
Imago
Butler, Octavia Estelle
Xenogenesis trilogy (3)
McClure, James
Lieutenant Kramer and Sergeant Zondi series (8)
Imago bird
Mosley, Nicholas
Catastrophe practice series (2)
Imaro
Saunders, Charles Robert
Imaro trilogy (1)
Immaculate deception
Adler, Warren
Fiona Fitzgerald series (3)
Immaterial murder
Symons, Julian
Inspector Bland series (1)
Immigrants
Fast, Howard
Lavette family series (1)
Immigrant's daughter
Fast, Howard
Lavette family series (5)
Immoral certainty
Tanenbaum, Robert K
Assistant District Attorney Butch Karp series (3)
Immortal of World's End
Carter, Lin
Gondwane epic series (3)
Immortal sleuth
Harrison, Michael
Life of Sherlock Holmes series (5)
Immortal wound
Canning, Victor
Crimson chalice trilogy (3)
Immortals
Garner, Rolf
Kennet trilogy (2)
Immune to murder
Stout, Rex
Dol Bonner series (2)
Nero Wolfe and Archie Goodwin series (28)
Imp of mischief
Burgess, Thornton Waldo
Cubby Bear series (5)
Impact
Copper, Basil
Mike Faraday series (19)
Impact of evidence
Carnac, Carol
Inspector Julian Rivers series (11)
Imperator plot
Spruill, Steven Gregory
Kane and Pendrake series (2)
Imperfect crime
Graeme, Bruce
Superintendent William Stevens and Inspector Pierre Allain series (2)
Imperfect joy
Stubbs, Jean
Brief chronicles series (2)
Imperfect spy
Cross, Amanda
Professor Kate Fansler series (11)
Imperfect therapist
Kottler, Jeffrey
Therapist series (2)
Imperial agent
Murari, Timeri
Kim series (2)
Imperial bounty
Dietz, William Corey
Sam McCade series (2)
Imperial Caesar
Warner, Rex
Caesar series (2)
Imperial courtesan
Kenyon, Frank Wilson
Emperor Napoleon III series (2)
Imperial Highness
Anthony, Evelyn
Catherine the Great trilogy (1)
Imperial Kelly
Bowen, Peter
Yellowstone Kelly series (3)
Imperial motherhood
Lancing, George
Tzu Hsi series (1)
Imperial Russian history atlas
Gilbert, Martin
History atlas series (6)
Imperial stars
Smith, Edward Elmer
Family d'Alembert series (1)
Imperial sunset
Delderfield, Ronald Frederick
Napoleon Bonaparte series (4)
Imperialists
Long, William Stuart
Australians series (12)
Impersonators
Brooks, Edwy Searles
Sexton Blake series (423)
Impetuous mistress
Coxe, George Harmon
Sam Crombie series (2)
Importance of being murdered
Wells, Carolyn
Fleming Stone series (53)
Importance of Crocus
Duvoisin, Roger
Crocus series (3)
Impossible people
McHargue, Georgess
Natural and unnatural history series (2)
Impossible virgin
O'Donnell, Peter
Modesty Blaise series (5)
Impossible woman
Mitchell, James
Jane Whitcomb series (2)
Impossibles
Phillips, Mark
Ken Malone trilogy (2)
Imposter
Baker, William Howard
Sexton Blake series (1557)
Reno, Bill
Badge series (7)
Imposter king
Stine, Harlan William
Wizards, warlocks and you series (11)
Impressions that remained
Smyth, Ethel Mary
Impressions series (1)
Improbable cause
Jance, Judith A
J P Beaumont series (5)
Improbable fiction
Woods, Sara
Sir Nicholas Harding and Antony Maitland series (17)
Improbable life
Roland, Betty
Improbable life trilogy (1)
Improbable voyage
Jones, Tristan
Wayward sailor series (8)
Improvement of the mind
Watts, Isaac
Logick series (2)
Imprudent professor
Weaver, Graham
Saint series (48)

Impudent widow
Gladstone, Maggie
Lacebridge ladies series (4)

Impunity Jane
Godden, Rumer
Four dolls series (1)

Imram
Barnwell, William
Blessing trilogy (2)

In a bind
Chase, Glen
Cherry Delight series (19)

In a dark garden
Slaughter, Frank Gill
American Civil War series (1)

In a deadly vein
Culpan, Maurice
Inspector Bill Houghton series (3)

In a house I know
Berg, Leila
Chatterbooks series (3)

In a hundred graves
Laxalt, Robert
Basque trilogy (3)

In a marmalade saloon
O'Connor, Patrick
Glasgow series (2)

In a new world
Alger, Horatio
New world trilogy (3)

In a pig's eye
Campbell, Robert Wright
Jimmy Flannery series (8)

In a pinch
Chase, Glen
Cherry Delight series (14)

In a quiet land
O'Donoghue, John
In a quiet land series (1)
Irish labourer trilogy (1)

In a strange land
O'Donoghue, John
In a quiet land series (2)
Irish labourer trilogy (2)

In a telephone booth
Cole, George Douglas Howard
Superintendent Henry Wilson series (5)

In a time of torment
Stone, Isidor Feinstein
Nonconformist history of our times series (5)

In accordance with the evidence
Onions, Oliver
Whom God hath sundered trilogy (1)

In Alfred's days
Creswick, Paul
Saga the Dane trilogy (1)

In all times of our tribulation
Holt, Emily Sarah
Edward II series (1)

In an average lifetime
Heymann, Tom
Average series (3)

In an Edinburgh drawing room
Andrews, Lucilla
Saint Martha's Hospital series (13)
Wally's Ward series (3)

In Araby Orion
Thompson, Edward
Warren Remfrey series (1)

In at the death
Duncan, Francis
Mordecai Euripides Tremaine series (5)

In at the deep end
Donald, Anabel
Alex Tanner series (2)

In at the kill
Knox, Bill
Inspector Colin Thane and Phil Moss series (1)
McDowell, Emmett
Jonathan Knox series (3)

In-between love
Kennedy, Kim
Two by two series (7)

In big business
Drake, Stan
Juliet Jones series (2)

In black and whitey
Lacy, Ed
Lee Hayes series (2)

In blue waters
Stacpoole, Henry de Vere
Blue horizon series (2)

In brighter climes
Chavannes, Albert
Socioland series (2)

In broken images, 1914-1946
Graves, Robert
Broken images series (1)

In cahoots
Grover, Marshall
Larry and Stretch series (409)

In camp on Bass Island
Tomlinson, Paul Greene
Four classmates series (2)

In captivity in the Pacific
Houston, Edwin James
Pacific shipwreck series (3)

In Chancery
Galsworthy, John
Forsyte saga trilogy (2)

In Chinatown
Burke, Thomas
London series (1)

In cold blood
Bagby, George
Inspector Schmidt series (15)
Livingston, Armstrong
Jimmy Treynor series (4)

In comes death
Whelton, Paul
Garry Dean series (6)

In company with Crispin
Pakington, Humphrey
Warmstry series (3)

In convent walls
Holt, Emily Sarah
Edward II series (2)

In darkest Madras
Hill, Harry Egbert
Sexton Blake series (284)

In death's grip
Carter, Nicholas
Nicholas Carter series (280)

In deep
Baines, Frank
Sea series (2)

In deep water
Jenkins, Jerry Bruce
Bradford family series (1)

In defense of Paris
Grant, Allan
Boys at the Front series (2)

In dinosaur land
Salmon, Michael
Who's behind the door series (7)

In distant waters
Woodman, Richard
Nathaniel Drinkwater series (8)

In double disguise
Graydon, William Murray
Sexton Blake series (347)

In endless twilight
Modesitt, Leland Exton
Forever hero trilogy (3)

In enemy hands
Murphy, Warren Burton
Destroyer series (26)

In face of the verdict
Rhode, John
Doctor Lancelot Priestley series (24)

In Fairyland
Chisholm, Louey
Fairyland tales series (1)

In fear of the night
Desmond, Hugh
Alan Fraser series (17)

In full cry
Goodwin, John
Superintendent Scarfe series (2)

In furthest Ind
Grier, Sydney Carlyon
Indian history trilogy (1)

In gallant company
Kent, Alexander
Captain Richard Bolitho series (4)

In Garde we trust
La Plante, Jerry
Chameleon series (2)

In grandma's attic
Richardson, Arleta
Grandma's attic series (1)

In his little black waistcoat
Kiddell-Monroe, Joan
In his little black waistcoat series (1)

In his little black waistcoat to China
Kiddell-Monroe, Joan
In his little black waistcoat series (2)

In his little black waistcoat to India
Kiddell-Monroe, Joan
In his little black waistcoat series (3)

In his little black waistcoat to Tibet
Kiddell-Monroe, Joan
In his little black waistcoat series (4)

In his own image
Rolfe, Frederick William
Toto's tales series (2)

In His steps
Sheldon, Charles Monroe
Henry Maxwell series (1)

In His steps to-day
Sheldon, Charles Monroe
Henry Maxwell series (3)

In justice's prison
Thurston, Robert
Rugger series (2)

In Kentucky with Daniel Boone
McIntyre, John Thomas
Buckskin series (1)

In Kerry long ago
O'Donoghue, John
In a quiet land series (3)
Irish labourer trilogy (3)

In khaki for the King
Lynn, Escott
Great War series (1)

In Krusach's house
Williamson, Thames
Hunky series (2)

In La-La Land we trust
Campbell, Robert Wright
Whistler series (1)

In letters of fire
Carter, Nicholas
Nicholas Carter series (78)

In like Flint
Street, Bradford
Derek Flint series (2)

In Lincoln Green
Gilliat, Edward
Robin Hood series (1)

In London
O'Riordan, Conal
Anglo-Irish relations series (9)

In love
Hayes, Alfred
Love trilogy (1)
Stanley, Carol
Cheerleaders series (16)

In love again
Pascal, Francine
Sweet Valley High series (59)

In love with a prince
Pascal, Francine
Sweet Valley High series (91)

In mask and motley
De Lint, Charles
Cerin Songweaver series (4)

In masquerade
Behrens, Margaret
Percival Soames series (1)

In memory long
Fraser, Amy Stewart
Hills of home trilogy (2)

In memory of Marty Malone
Grover, Marshall
Larry and Stretch series (192)

In mine own heart
Marshall, Alan
I can jump puddles series (3)

In Mister Knox's country
Somerville, Edith Oenone
Irish R.M. series (5)

In monster land
Salmon, Michael
Who's behind the door series (8)

In Morgan's wake
Verrill, Alpheus Hyatt
Cormorant series (2)

In muffled night
Muir, Dorothy Erskine
Inspector Woods series (1)

In my dream
Salmon, Michael
Who's behind the door series (6)

In my father's court
Singer, Isaac Bashevis
Love and exile trilogy (3)

In my father's house
Fletcher, Grace Nies
Nies family series (1)

In my lady's chamber
Hawkesworth, John
Upstairs, downstairs series (5)

In my path
Sutherland, Halliday
Arches of the years series (3)

In my wildest dreams
Thomas, Leslie
Wildest dreams series (2)

In New York with the Tucker twins
Sampson, Emma
Tucker twins series (6)

In other worlds
Attanasio, A A
Radix Tetrad series (2)

In our house
Rockwell, Anne
Our life series (2)

In Patchogue
McGonigle, Thomas
Patchogue series (1)

In perilous seas
Suthren, Victor
Paul Gallant series (3)

In plain clothes
Brust, Harold
Political police officer series (2)

In pleasant places
Grenfell, Joyce
Pleasant places series (2)

In praise of life
Schoenstedt, Walter
Crade builder series (1)

In presence of my foes
Smith, Frederick Escreet
Innocent series (2)

In pursuit of a million
Marlowe, Francis
Doc Summers series (3)

In pursuit of Quincey Budd
Grover, Marshall
Larry and Stretch series (221)

In pursuit of the green lion
Riley, Judith Merkle
Margaret of Ashbury series (2)

In pursuit of VALIS
Dick, Philip Kindred
VALIS trilogy (3)

In quarters
Winter, John Strange
Blankhampton series (1)

In quarters with the 25th
Winter, John Strange
Blankhampton series (1)

In queer quarters
Carter, Nicholas
Nicholas Carter series (423)

In quest of Qalara
Cleve, John
Spaceways series (9)

In re Sherlock Holmes
Derleth, August
Solar Pons series (1)

In record time
Carter, Nicholas
Nicholas Carter series (563)

In remembrance of Rose
Meek, Margaret Reid Duncan
Lennox Kemp series (4)

In Russian trenches
Fiske, James
World's war series (6)

In savage Hayti
Armour, R Coutts
Sexton Blake series (270)

In school
Hautzig, Esther Rudomin
Four languages series (3)

In school and out
Optic, Oliver
Woodville series (2)

In search of a shark
McEvoy, Seth
Explorer series (3)

In search of ancient gods
Daniken, Erich von
Unsolved mysteries series (4)

In search of Henry
Joynson, Cecile
Henry series (2)

In search of himself
Carter, Nicholas
Nicholas Carter series (322)

In search of MOM
Peters, David
Photon series (3)

In search of Simon
Batt, Elisabeth
Dinah Campion series (2)

In search of the dove
York, Rebecca
Peregrine connection trilogy (3)

In search of the Far Side
Larson, Gary
Far Side series (3)

In search of the golden sceptre
Allcock, Phil
Stories of the realm series (2)

In search of the perfect woman
Capp, Al
Li'l Abner dailies series (16)

In search of the unknown
Chambers, Robert William
Tales of a naturalist series (1)

In search of the Wallypug
Farrow, George Edward
Wallypug series (4)

In search of Thunder
Lethbridge, Katharine Greville
Ollafubs series (2)

In secret places
Truss, Seldon
Inspector Gidleigh series (13)

In self-defense
Dixon, Franklin W
Hardy boys case files series (45)

In Serena's web
Hooper, Kay
Hagen series (1)

In sight of the promised land
Duhamel, Georges
Pasquier series (3)

In silks she goes
Croy, Catherine
Julia Arbuthnot series (1)

In sober livery
Vachell, Horace Annesley
Methuselah series (3)

In soft garments
Knox, Ronald Arbuthnott
Oxford conferences series (1)

In spite of Henry
Joynson, Cecile
Henry series (1)

In spite of thunder
Carr, John Dickson
Doctor Gideon Fell series (20)

In step with a goat
Baldwin, Michael
Granddad with snails series (2)

In storm and calm
Andrews, Lucilla
Saint Martha's Hospital series (8)

In subjection
Fowler, Ellen Thornycroft
Isabel Carnaby trilogy (2)

In such a night
Gielgud, Val
Inspector Gregory Pellew and Viscount Clymping series (10)

In suspicion's shadow
Carter, Nicholas
Nicholas Carter series (459)

In sylvan shadows
Salvatore, Robert Anthony
Cleric quintet (2)

In Teddy Bear's house
Cradock, Henry Cowper, *Mrs*
Teddy Bear series (3)

In Texas with Davy Crockett
McIntyre, John Thomas
Buckskin series (3)
McNeil, Everett
Davy Crockett series (2)

In that dawn
Paustovsky, Konstantin Georgievich
Story of a life series (3)

In that rich earth
Sewart, Alan
Detective Sergeant Chamberlayne series (1)

In the absence of horses
Hearne, Vicki
Horses series (2)

In the ansence of the body
Bromley, Gordon
Inspector Severn series (1)

In the balance
Wentworth, Patricia
Miss Maud Silver series (5)

In the battle for New York
Hancock, Harrie Irving
Conquest of the United States series (2)

In the beginning
Blyton, Enid
Bible stories series (1)
O'Donnell, Peter
Modesty Blaise comic strip series (2)

In the beginning, said Great-Aunt Jane
Bradley, Helen
Edwardian Lancashire series (3)

In the best families
Stout, Rex
Nero Wolfe and Archie Goodwin series (17)

In the blood
Douglas, Lauren Wright
Caitlin Reece series (1)
Wingate, John
Submariner Sinclair series (7)

In the camp of the Delawares
Braden, James Andrew
John Jerome and Return Kingdom series (4)

In the castle of my skin
Lamming, George
Caribbean series (1)

In the caves of exile
Emerson, Ru
Nedao trilogy (2)

In the center of the galaxy
Darlton, Clark
Perry Rhodan series (137)
In the circle of time
Anderson, Margaret Jean
Time trilogy (2)
In the city
Salmon, Michael
Who's behind the door series (4)
In the clouds for Uncle Sam
Ashton, Lamar
Aeroplane boys series (1)
In the club
Christian, Petra
Sally Deenes series (8)
In the country
Gree, Alain
Smashers series (4)
In the dark
Brennan, Carol
Liz Wareham series (3)
Horler, Sydney
Bunny Chipstead series (1)
In the dark night
Hood, Margaret Page
Gil Donan series (3)
In the dark of the moon
Kenworthy, Christopher
Matthew and Son series (1)
In the days of gold
Hendryx, James Beardsley
Corporal Cameron Downey series (2)
In the days of the pioneers
Ellis, Edward Sylvester
Daniel Boone and Simon Kenton series (3)
In the dead of night
Cross, Mark
Daphne Wrayne and her Four Adjusters series (34)
In the death of a man
Egan, Lesley
Jesse Falkenstein series (6)
In the dinosaur's paw
Giff, Patricia Reilly
Kids of the Polk Street School series (5)
In the ditch
Emecheta, Buchi
In the ditch series (1)
In the electric mist with Confederate dead
Burke, James Lee
Dave Robicheaux series (6)
In the face of danger
Nixon, Joan Lowery
Orphan train quintet (3)
In the face of the evidence
Carter, Nicholas
Nicholas Carter series (426)
In the face of the verdict
Rhode, John
Doctor Lancelot Priestley series (24)
In the Fifth at Malory Towers
Blyton, Enid
Malory Towers series (5)
In the first degree
Scarlett, Roger
Inspector Kane series (5)
In the flesh
Barker, Clive
Books of blood series (5)
In the footsteps of Sherlock Holmes
Harrison, Michael
Life of Sherlock Holmes series (1)
In the game
Baker, Nikki
Virginia Kelly series (1)
In the gates of the north
O'Grady, Standish James
Cuculain trilogy (2)
In the gloom of night
Carter, Nicholas
Nicholas Carter series (152)
In the Great God's hair
Bain, Francis William
Indian mystic love stories series (4)
In the great wild north
Lange, Dietrich
American Indian series (4)
In the Green Star's glow
Carter, Lin
Green Star series (5)
In the grip of fate
Carter, Nicholas
Nicholas Carter series (602)
In the grip of the Gestapo
Hope, Stanton
Sexton Blake series (1036)
In the grip of the kidnappers
Ridley, Nat
Nat Ridley series (12)
In the grip of the law
Donovan, Dick
Dick Donovan series (7)
In the grip of the Tong
Bobin, John William
Sexton Blake series (226)
In the grip of winter
Dann, Colin
Farthing Wood series (2)
In the hall of the Dragon King
Lawhead, Stephen
Dragon King trilogy (1)
In the hand of the goddess
Pierce, Tamora
Song of the lioness series (2)
In the hand of the Riffs
Graydon, William Murray
Sexton Blake series (348)
In the hands of spies
Brandon, John Gordon
Sexton Blake series (990)
In the heart of Paris
Bremond d'Ars, Yvonne de
Journal of an antique dealer series (1)
In the heart of Texas
Hardin, J D
Raider and Doc series (49)
In the heart of the country
Bates, Herbert Ernest
Country heart series (1)
In the heat of the night
Ball, John
Virgil Tibbs series (1)
In the high valley
Coolidge, Susan
Katy series (5)
In the house of secret enemies
Chesbro, George Clark
Mongo series (9)
In the ice king's palace
Orr, Alice
World in Amber series (2)
In the jungle
Salmon, Michael
Who's behind the door series (9)
In the keep of time
Anderson, Margaret Jean
Time trilogy (1)
In the kingdom of the beasts
Stableford, Brian Michael
Dies irae trilogy (2)
In the King's absence
Bell, Josephine
English Civil War series (2)
In the lake of the moon
Lindsey, David L
Stuart Haydon series (4)
In the land of cotton
Scarborough, Dorothy
Cotton trilogy (1)
In the land of the Redskins
Golon, Sergeanne
Angelique series (6)
In the lap of danger
Carter, Nicholas
Nicholas Carter series (204)
In the last analysis
Cross, Amanda
Professor Kate Fansler series (1)
In the long green grass
Marten, Jacqueline
Wars of independence trilogy (3)
In the meantime
Spring, Howard
Heaven lies about us series (2)
In the melting pot
Goolden, Barbara
Consett trilogy (2)
In the midnight express
Murray, Andrew
Sexton Blake series (140)
In the midst of death
Block, Lawrence
Matthew Scudder series (2)
In the mill
Masefield, John
In the mill series (1)
In the money
Dicks, Terrance
Camden Street kids series (1)
Williams, William Carlos
Stecher trilogy (2)
In the moons of Borea
Lumley, Brian
Titus Crow series (5)
In the morning light
Angoff, Charles
Polonsky family series (2)
In the morning with Waldo
Wilhelm, Hans
Waldo series (8)
In the mummy's tomb
Beach, Lynn
Phantom Valley series (7)
In the net
Hardcastle, Michael
Bank Vale United series (1)
In the Nick of time
Carter, Nicholas
Nicholas Carter series (428)
In the nick of time
Ridley, Nat
Nat Ridley series (3)
In the night
Gorell, Ronald Gorell Barnes
Evelyn Temple series (1)
In the night watch
Brooks, Edwy Searles
Sexton Blake series (368)
In the ocean of night
Benford, Gregory
Galactic Center series (2)
Ocean series (1)
In the old castle
Salmon, Michael
Who did it series (2)
In the onyx lobby
Wells, Carolyn
Pennington Wise series (2)
In the Osage strip
Evans, Tabor
Longarm series (141)
In the park
Ainsworth, Ruth
Look about you series (6)
Hautzig, Esther Rudomin
Four languages series (1)
In the path of La Salle
Fitzhugh, Percy Keese
Boy Scouts series (3)
In the path of the storm
Dann, Colin
Farthing Wood series (6)
In the Pecos country
Jayne, R H
War whoop series (3)
In the playground
Berridge, Celia
Stepping stones 1 2 3 series (2)
In the power of the pigmies
Gilson, Charles
Submarine U93 series (2)
In the ranks
Douglas, Amanda Minnie
Kathie series (5)
In the ranks of Old Hickory
Sabin, Edward Legrand
Trail blazers series (14)
In the Red Lord's reach
Eisenstein, Phyllis
Alaric the Minstrel series (2)
In the Rockies with Kit Carson
McIntyre, John Thomas
Buckskin series (2)
In the saddle
Optic, Oliver
Blue and the Gray on land series (2)
In the saddle with Uncle Bill
James, Will
Uncle Bill series (2)
In the sanctuary
Van der Naillen, Albert
Magi trilogy (2)
In the sea nymph's lair
Hale, F J
After the spell wars series (2)
In the sealed cave
Herrman, Louis
Lemuel Gulliver series (8)
In the shadow of fear
Carter, Nicholas
Nicholas Carter series (456)
In the shadow of night
Alais, Ernest W
Sexton Blake series (265)
In the shadow of Omizantrim
Vardeman, Robert Edward
War of powers series (5)
In the shadow of the crown
Plaidy, Jean
Queens of England series (6)
In the shadow of the guillotine
Bobin, John William
Sexton Blake series (53)
In the shadow of the Oak King
Jones, Courtway
King Arthur series (1)
In the shadow of the Peacock
Gordon, Katharine
Peacock series (3)
In the shadow of the tower
Keene, Carolyn
Dana girls series (2)
In the Sherburne line
Douglas, Amanda Minnie
Sherburne series (12)
In the shop
Black, Margaret Katherine
Honey family trilogy (1)
In the smoke
Kelsall, Ernest Michael
Riverman series (2)
In the spotlight
Lowell, Melissa
Silver blades series (2)
In the steps of Moses the conqueror
Golding, Louis
Moses series (2)
In the steps of Moses the lawgiver
Golding, Louis
Moses series (1)
In the sticks
Bacon, Ronald Leonard
Valley series (1)
In the sunken garden
Judd, Frances K
Kay Tracey series (12)
In the swim
Zola, Emile
Rougon Macquart series (2)
In the teeth of adversity
Babson, Marian
Douglas Perkins and Gerry Tate series (4)
In the teeth of the evidence, and other stories
Sayers, Dorothy Leigh
Lord Peter Wimsey series (14)
In the Tennessee country
Taylor, Peter
Memphis series (2)
In the thirties
Upward, Edward
Alan Sebrill trilogy (1)
In the tiger's cage
Wells, Carolyn
Fleming Stone series (38)
In the tiger's lair
Miller, Leo Edward
Hidden people series (2)
In the time of Greenbloom
Fielding, Gabriel
Blaydon family trilogy (1)
In the toils of fear
Carter, Nicholas
Nicholas Carter series (511)
In the tomb of the bishop
Munn, Harold Warner
Tales of the Werewolf Clan trilogy (2)
In the track of the huskies
Murray, Lillian
Virginia Nixon series (2)
In the trenches
Botsford, Charles Alexander
Victory series (3)
In the twinkling of an eye
Watson, Sydney
Second Coming series (1)
In the valley of shadow
Ramsay, Jay
Great return series (4)
In the wake of a wish
Schildt, Goran
Wake series (1)
In the wake of Odysseus
Schildt, Goran
Wake series (2)
In the wake of Shark Gotch
Wetjen, Albert Richard
Shark Gotch series (5)
In the whirlpool
Zola, Emile
Rougon Macquart series (2)
In the wilderness
Undset, Sigrid
Master of Hestviken series (3)
In the world
Gorky, Maxim
Childhood to university trilogy (2)
In the year of Waterloo
Caine, Oliver Vernon
Napoleon series (2)
In the zoo with Waldo
Wilhelm, Hans
Waldo series (7)
In their wisdom
Snow, Charles Percy
Strangers and brothers series (12)
In this valley
Home, Michael
Breckland series (2)
In those days
Fergusson, Harry
Santa Fe Trail trilogy (3)
Fergusson, Harvey
Followers of the sun trilogy (2)
In time for murder
Walling, Robert Alfred John
Philip Tolefree series (3)
In time of peace
Boyd, Thomas Alexander
Wheat series (2)
In time of trouble
Cockburn, Claud
In time of trouble series (1)
In times of change
Watson, Jean
In times of series (8)
In times of courage
Watson, Jean
In times of series (7)
In times of doubt
Watson, Jean
In times of series (6)
In times of growth
Watson, Jean
In times of series (5)
In times of joy
Watson, Jean
In times of series (4)
In times of need
Watson, Jean
In times of series (3)
In times of sorrow
Watson, Jean
In times of series (2)
In times of success
Watson, Jean
In times of series (1)
In tragic life
Fisher, Vardis
Tragic life series (1)
In triple disguise
Graydon, William Murray
Sexton Blake series (17)
In trouble
Dicks, Terrance
Adventures of Buster and Betty series (2)
Haynes, Betsy
Fabulous Five super series (1)
In trouble again, Zelda Hammersmith?
Hall, Lynn
Zelda Hammersmith series (1)
In Valombrosa
Mathew, David
Post-war trilogy (2)
In Viriconium
Harrison, Michael John
Viriconium series (3)
In walks murder
Ryland, Clive
Chief Inspector George Bassett series (3)
In whose dim shadow
Connington, John Jervis
Sir Clinton Driffield series (10)
In wild Africa
Knox, Thomas Wallace
Boy travellers series (16)
In winter's shadow
Bradshaw, Gillian
Arthur and Gawain trilogy (3)
In woods and fields
Ainsworth, Ruth
Look about you series (1)
In your garden
Ainsworth, Ruth
Look about you series (5)
Inca death squad
Carter, Nick
Nick Carter series (66)
Inca file
Rosenberger, Joseph
Death Merchant series (51)
Inca gold
Becket, Jim
Choose your own adventure series (85)
Cussler, Clive
Dirk Pitt series (12)
Inca gold hijack
Derrick, Lionel
Penetrator series (42)
Inca luck piece
Striker, Fran
Tom Quest series (7)
Incarnation of the snow
Bain, Francis William
Indian mystic love stories series (7)
Incense of death
Deane, Norman
Bruce Murdoch series (7)

Inception
Harbinson, William Allen
Projekt Saucer series (1)
Inch of time
Norman, James
Gimiendo Hernandez Quinto series (2)
Inches
Marshall, William Leonard
Yellowthread Street series (14)
Incident at Elm Creek
Bowden, Jim
Cap Millett series (4)
Incident at Fort Keogh
Wheeler, Richard Seabrook
Sheriff Santiago Toole series (1)
Incident at Horcado City
Macdonald, William Colt
Gregory Quist series (12)
Incident at Parga
Livingston, Nancy
G D H Pringle series (3)
Incident at Plei Soi
Helm, Eric
Ground Zero series (10)
Incident in a Texas town
Dana, Mitchell
Dakota Bush series (5)
Incident in Iceland
Macleod, Robert
Jonathan Gaunt series (6)
Incident on Ath
Tubb, Edwin Charles
Dumarest series (18)
Incidental murder
Joyce, Cyril
Chief Superintendent Pat Stockton series (6)
Incitement to murder
Amberley, Richard
Inspector Martin series (1)
Inclining to crime
Kent, Arthur
Sexton Blake series (1401)
Income tax conspiracy
Parsons, Anthony
Sexton Blake series (1214)
Incomer
Elphinstone, Margaret
Incomer series (1)
Incomparable Bellairs
Castle, Agnes
Beau Nash regime romance series (2)
Incompleat enchanter
De Camp, Lyon Sprague
Harold Shea series (1)
Incomplete enchanter
De Camp, Lyon Sprague
Harold Shea series (1)
Incongruous spy
Le Carre, John
George Smiley series (2)
Inconsistent villains
Temple-Ellis, N A
Montrose Arbuthnot series (1)
Inconstant moon
Niven, Larry
Known Space series (8)
Inconstant star
Anderson, Poul
Man-Kzin wars series (5)
Inconvenient bride
Fox, James M
John and Suzy Marshall series (7)
Inconvenient corpse
Sharp, David
Professor Henry Arthur Fielding series (5)
Incorporated knight
De Camp, Lyon Sprague
Incorporated knight series (1)
Incredible adventures, number 1
Waedt, Carl F
Incredible adventures series (1)
Incredible adventures, number 2
Waedt, Carl F
Incredible adventures series (2)
Incredible adventures of Professor Branetawm
Hunter, Norman
Professor Branestawm series (1)
Incredible city
Henrey, Robert
London in wartime series (2)
Madeleine series (8)
Incredible elopment of Lord Peter Wimsey
Sayers, Dorothy Leigh
Lord Peter Wimsey series (10)
Incredible Hulk and Spiderman, Murdermoon
Kupperberg, Paul
Marvel superheroes, new series (11)
Incredible Hulk, Stalker from the stars
Silva, Joseph
Marvel superheroes, new series (2)
Incredible magic plant
Macdonald, Elizabeth
Magic plant series (1)
Incredible murder of Cardinal Tosca
Nowlan, Alden
Sherlock Holmes drama series (15)
Incredible planet
Campbell, John Wood
Aarn Munro series (2)
Incredible radio exploits of Doc Savage
Dent, Lester
Doc Savage series (183)
Incredible Schlock Homes
Fish, Robert Lloyd
Schlock Homes series (1)
Incredible shrinking Mork
Wagner, Robin S
Mork and Mindy series (2)
Incredible steam-driven adventures of Riverboat Bill
Green, Cliff
Riverboat Bill series (1)
Incredible Super Bowl action
Resciniti, Angelo G
Super Bowl series (4)
Incredible true adventures
Wulffson, Don L
Incredible true adventures series (1)
Incredible umbrella
Kaye, Marvin
Fillmore series (1)
Incredible voyage
Jones, Tristan
Wayward sailor series (3)
Incredulity of Father Brown
Chesterton, Gilbert Keith
Father Brown series (3)
Indecent exposure
Sharpe, Tom
Kommandant Van Heerden series (2)
Indemnity only
Paretsky, Sara
V I Warshawski series (1)
Independence!
Ross, Dana Fuller
Wagons West series (1)
Independence Day magic
Baker, James Webb
Magic series (11)
Independent education in southern Africa
Mason, Peter
Private education series (4)
Independent witness
Cecil, Henry
Colonel Brain series (4)
Indestructible
Garner, Rolf
Kennet trilogy (3)
Indestructible Jones
Styles, Showell
David Jones, R.N.V.R. series (1)
India man
Hall, Patrick
Harry Thomas trilogy (1)
India-rubber men
Wallace, Edgar
Inspector Elk series (5)
Indian brothers
Coryell, Jubert V
Sam Hilton series (1)
Indian cemetery
Hutchens, Paul
Sugar Creek Gang series (13)
Indian country
Johnson, Dorothy Marie
Man called Horse series (1)
Indian day
Thompson, Edward
Indian trilogy (1)
Indian in the cupboard
Banks, Lynne Reid
Omri series (1)
Indian incident
Chisholm, Matt
Joe Blade series (1)
Indian maid
Fletcher, Dirk
Spur McCoy series (10)
Indian moon
Dower, Penn
Marshal Bret Malone series (4)
Indian mummy mystery
Nesbit, Troy
Wilderness mystery series (3)
Indian Range
Leyland, Eric
Bill, Jake and Ned series (4)
Indian silver
Risteen, H L
Red Indian series (2)
Indian summer
Cameron, James
Point of departure series (2)
Knowles, John
Yale University series (1)
Indian summer of a Forsyte
Galsworthy, John
Forsyte saga trilogy (3)
Indian trilogy
Masters, John
Indian trilogy (3)
Indian twins
Perkins, Lucy Fitch
Twin series (20)
Indian Two Feet and his eagle feather
Friskey, Margaret
Indian Two Feet series (2)
Indian Two Feet and his horse
Friskey, Margaret
Indian Two Feet series (1)
Indian Two Feet and the ABC moose hunt
Friskey, Margaret
Indian Two Feet series (5)
Indian Two Feet and the grizzly bear
Friskey, Margaret
Indian Two Feet series (4)
Indian Two Feet and the wolf cubs
Friskey, Margaret
Indian Two Feet series (3)
Indian Two Feet rides alone
Friskey, Margaret
Indian Two Feet series (6)
Indian Wars of the West
Wellman, Paul Iselin
Death on horseback series (2)
Indiana days
Chambers, Catherine E
Adventures in frontier America series (7)
Indiana Jones and genesis
Macgregor, Rob
Indiana Jones series (8)
Indiana Jones and the ape slaves of Howling Island
Stine, Robert Lawrence
Indiana Jones find your fate series (10)
Indiana Jones and the cult of the mummy's crypt
Stine, Robert Lawrence
Indiana Jones find your fate series (7)
Indiana Jones and the cup of the vampire
Helfer, Andrew
Indiana Jones find your fate series (4)
Indiana Jones and the curse of Horror Island
Stine, Robert Lawrence
Indiana Jones find your fate series (1)
Indiana Jones and the dance of the giants
Macgregor, Rob
Indiana Jones series (5)
Indiana Jones and the dragon of vengeance
Stine, Harlan William
Indiana Jones find your fate series (8)
Indiana Jones and the eye of the fates
Wenk, Richard
Indiana Jones find your fate series (5)
Indiana Jones and the giants of the silver tower
Stine, Robert Lawrence
Indiana Jones find your fate series (3)
Indiana Jones and the gold of Genghis Khan
Weiss, Ellen
Indiana Jones find your fate series (9)
Indiana Jones and the interior world
Macgregor, Rob
Indiana Jones series (9)
Indiana Jones and the last crusade
Digby, Anne
Indiana Jones series (3)
Macgregor, Rob
Indiana Jones series (3)
Martin, Les
Indiana Jones series (3)
Indiana Jones and the Legion of Death
Wenk, Richard
Indiana Jones find your fate series (6)
Indiana Jones and the lost treasure of Sheba
Estes, Rose
Indiana Jones find your fate series (2)
Indiana Jones and the mask of the elephant
Stine, Harlan William
Indiana Jones find your fate series (11)
Indiana Jones and the peril at Delphi
Macgregor, Rob
Indiana Jones series (4)
Indiana Jones and the raiders of the lost ark
French, Michael
Indiana Jones series (1)
Indiana Jones and the seven veils
Macgregor, Rob
Indiana Jones series (6)
Indiana Jones and the temple of doom
French, Michael
Indiana Jones series (2)
Huyck, Willard
Indiana Jones series (2)
Kahn, James
Indiana Jones series (2)
Martin, Les
Indiana Jones series (2)
Indiana Jones and the unicorns legacy
Macgregor, Rob
Indiana Jones series (7)
Indiana Jones explores Egypt
Malam, John
Indiana Jones explores series (1)
Indiana Jones explores the Incas
Malam, John
Indiana Jones explores series (2)
Indiana Jones, his life and adventure
Anonymous
Indiana Jones series (9)
Indians in winter camp
Deming, Therese
Indian life series (2)
Indians of the pueblos
Deming, Therese
Indian life series (4)
Indians of the wigwams
Deming, Therese
Indian life series (5)
Indifference of Juliet
Richmond, Grace Smith
Juliet Robeson series (1)
Indifferent heroes
Hocking, Mary
Fairley family trilogy (2)
Indigo blue
Anderson, Catherine
Comanche trilogy (3)
Indigo death
Saltmarsh, Max
Archie Lumsden series (3)
Indigo necklace
Crane, Frances
Pat and Jean Abbott series (7)
Indigo necklace murders
Crane, Frances
Pat and Jean Abbott series (7)
Indiscretion of Lady Usher
Anonymous
Diary series (2)
Indiscretions of the Queen
Plaidy, Jean
Georgian series (8)
Indispensible Calvin and Hobbes
Watterson, Bill
Calvin and Hobbes series (11)
Indomitable Hornblower
Forester, Cecil Scott
Horatio Hornblower series (11)
Indoor noisy book
Brown, Margaret Wise
Noisy book series (4)
Indulgent husband
Colette, Sidonie Gabrielle
Claudine series (3)
Indy Five Hundred
Dean, Anabel
Racing wheels series (6)
Inevitable fatality
Lewis, Royston
Inspector John Crow series (11)
Inexpendable
Baker, William Howard
Richard Quintain series (8)
Infamous adventures of Ginger Meggs
Kemsley, James
Ginger Meggs series (36)
Infamous army
Heyer, Georgette
Avon family series (3)
Judith Taverner Worth series (2)
Infant of Prague
Granger, Bill
November Man series (9)
Infanta
Cooper, Louise Antell
Indigo series (3)
Infants of the spring
Powell, Anthony
To keep the ball rolling series (1)
Infant's skull
Sue, Eugene
Mysteries of the people series (11)
Infatuation of the Countess
White, Percy
Countess series (2)
Infernal device
Kurland, Michael
Sherlock Holmes sequels series (35)
Infernal grove
Muggeridge, Malcolm
Chronicles of wasted time series (2)
Inferno
Asimov, Isaac
Caliban series (2)
Cooper, Louise Antell
Indigo series (2)
Creasey, John
Doctor Palfrey series (24)
Dicks, Terrance
Doctor Who series (89)
Duncan, Thomas
Big river, big man series (2)
Smith, Mark
Way of the Tiger series (6)
Inferno of fear
Dixon, Franklin W
Hardy boys case files series (88)
Infiltrate
Mackenzie, Steve
Seals series (8)
Infiltrator
Ahern, Jerry
Surgical strike series (3)
Singer, A L
Worlds of power series (7)
Walker, Martin
Maddox series (1)
York, Andrew
Jonas Wilde series (6)
Infiltrators
Hamilton, Donald
Matt Helm series (21)
Janson, Hank
Hank Janson series (252)
Infinite battle
Bischoff, David
Star hounds series (1)
Infinite number of monkeys
Roberts, Les
Saxon series (1)
Infinity clue
Dixon, Franklin W
Hardy boys series (70)
Infinity concerto
Bear, Greg
Michael Perrin series (1)
Infinity flight
Darlton, Clark
Perry Rhodan series (24)
Infinity plague
Vardeman, Robert Edward
Biowarriors trilogy (1)
Infirm glory
Winn, Godfrey
Infirm glory series (1)
Inflammable Adams
Adams, Phillip
Unspeakable series (4)
Inflatable shop
Hall, Willis
Henry Hollins series (3)
Influenza mystery
Scott, Sutherland
Doctor Septimus Dodds series (4)
Informant
Gordons
John Ripley series (5)
Information received
Punshon, Ernest Robertson
Bobby Owen series (1)
Informer
Black, Ladbroke
Sexton Blake series (602)

Infra blood
Westbrook, Perry Dickie
Doctor Samuel Cutting series (3)
Ingenious strategem
Carter, Nicholas
Nicholas Carter series (154)
Ingram of the Irish
Hunt, Angela Elwell
Theyn chronicles trilogy (3)
Inherit the stars
Hogan, James Patrick
Minervan experiment series (1)
Inheritance
Bentley, Phyllis
Oldroyd family series (1)
West Riding series (5)
Dawes, Frank Victor
Cole family series (2)
Stahl, Hilda
White Pine chronicles series (2)
Inheritance of strangers
Candaleria, Nash
Mexican war series (2)
Inherited murder
Martin, Lee
Deb Ralston series (8)
Inheritor
Bradley, Marion Zimmer
Leslie Barnes series (2)
Inheritors
Chandler, Arthur Bertram
John Grimes series (11)
Rim series (5)
Messmann, Jon
Jefferson Boone series (6)
Nicole, Christopher
Haggard trilogy (2)
Penton, Brian
Derek Cabell series (2)
Robbins, Harold
Hollywood trilogy (3)
Wall, Robert Emmet
Nowell family series (5)
Inhuman condition
Barker, Clive
Books of blood series (4)
Inimitable Jeeves
Wodehouse, Pelham Grenville
Jeeves and Bertie Wooster series (2)
Inishfallen fare thee well
O'Casey, Sean
I knock at the door series (4)
Initials only
Green, Anna Katharine
Amelia Butterworth series (5)
Caleb Sweetwater series (4)
Ebenezer Gryce series (11)
Initiate
Cooper, Louise Antell
Time master trilogy (1)
Initiation
Brunn, Robert
Twilight series (3)
Smith, Lisa J
Secret circle series (1)
Injudicious judge
Underwood, Michael
Rosa Epton series (11)
Injun and Whitey
Hart, William Surrey
Injun and Whitey series (1)
Injun and Whitey strike out for themselves
Hart, William Surrey
Injun and Whitey series (2)
Injun and Whitey to the rescue
Hart, William Surrey
Injun and Whitey series (3)
Injustice for all
Jance, Judith A
J P Beaumont series (2)
Ink-Bottle Club
Smith, Sarah Stafford
Ink-Bottle Club series (1)
Ink-Bottle Club abroad
Smith, Sarah Stafford
Ink-Bottle Club series (2)
Ink Street murder
Grierson, Francis Durham
Inspector George Muir series (4)
Ink truck
Kennedy, William
Albany series (1)
Inkosi the lion
Rutley, Cecil Bernard
Wild life story series (10)
Inland farm
Lockley, Ronald Mathias
Island farm series (4)
Inland voyage
Stevenson, Robert Louis
Inland voyage series (1)
Inn of the hawk and the raven
McCutcheon, George Barr
Graustark series (6)
Inn of Thirteen Swords
Graeme, David
Monsieur Blackshirt series (4)
Inner ring
Gagnon, Maurice
Deirdre O'Hara trilogy (1)
Innkeeper's diary
Fothergill, John
Innkeeper series (1)
Innkeeper's horse
Henry, Marguerite
King of the wind series (2)
Innocence of Father Brown
Chesterton, Gilbert Keith
Father Brown series (1)
Innocence that kills
Levitsky, Ronald
Nate Rosen series (4)
Innocence under the elms
Rich, Louise Dickinson
Woods series (5)
Innocent
Kim, Richard Eunkook
Korea series (2)
Innocent abroad
Hauxwell, Hannah
Daleswoman series (3)
Innocent bottle
Gilbert, Anthony
Arthur Crook series (20)
Innocent bystander
Bagby, George
Inspector Schmidt series (41)
Frost, Barbara
Marka de Lancey series (3)
Innocent bystanders
Munro, James
John Craig series (4)
Innocent employments
Turpin, Allan
Geoffrey Gillard series (4)
Innocent flower
Armstrong, Charlotte
MacDougal Duff series (3)
Innocent moon
Williamson, Henry
Chronicles of ancient sunlight series (9)
Innocent tenant
Guth, Paul
Innocent series (4)
Innocent victim
Mackenzie, Lee
Emmerdale Farm series (14)
Innocent voices in my ear
Stokes, Doris
Voices series (3)
Innocent wife
Colette, Sidonie Gabrielle
Claudine series (4)
Innocents abroad
Twain, Mark
Innocents series (1)
Innocents at home
Hilton, John Buxton
Superintendent Simon Kenworthy series (16)
Twain, Mark
Innocents series (2)
Innside Nantucket
Gilbreth, Frank Bunker
Gilbreth family series (3)
Inquest betraying
Sennocke, T J R
Sergeant Mallory series (3)
Inquest on a lady
Sennocke, T J R
Sergeant Mallory series (1)
Inquest on a mistress
Sennocke, T J R
Sergeant Mallory series (2)
Inquest on Miriam
Dalton, Moray
Inspector Hugh Collier series (12)
Inquests by jury
Sennocke, T J R
Sergeant Mallory series (4)
Inquests on the deceased
Sennocke, T J R
Sergeant Mallory series (5)
Inquisition
Olden, Marc
Robert Sand series (5)
Inquisitive Penny
Haynes, Ambrose
Penny series (1)
Inquisitor
Franklin, Cheryl Jean
Network-Consortium series (2)
Walpole, Hugh
Provincial group series (4)
Watson, Ian
Inquisition war series (2)
Insanity fair
Reed, Douglas
Insanity fair trilogy (1)
Insanity machine
Maxwell, Peter
Ralph Ledermann series (1)
Inscrutable Charlie Muffin
Freemantle, Brian
Charlie Muffin series (3)
Insect god
Gorey, Edward
Vinegar works trilogy (2)
Inshore squadron
Kent, Alexander
Captain Richard Bolitho series (14)
Inside Babel
Wilson, Snoo
Spaceache series (2)
Inside man
Johnson, Emil Richard
Tony Lonto series (2)
Inside Mister Enderby
Burgess, Anthony
Mister Enderby series (1)
Inside-outside book of London
Munro, Roxie
Inside-outside series (3)
Inside-outside book of New York City
Munro, Roxie
Inside-outside series (1)
Inside-outside book of Paris
Munro, Roxie
Inside-outside series (4)
Inside-outside book of Washington D.C.
Munro, Roxie
Inside-outside series (2)
Inside, outside, upside down
Berenstain, Stan
Berenstain bears series (6)
Inside Sinanju
Murray, Will
Destroyer series (94)
Inside straight
Masters, Zeke
Faro Blake series (20)
Inside the left
Brockway, Fenner
Left right series (1)
Inside UFO 54-40
Packard, Edward
Choose your own adventure series (12)
Insidious Doctor Fu-Manchu
Rohmer, Sax
Fu-Manchu series (1)
Inspector Bedison and the Sunderland case
Cobb, Thomas
Inspector Bedison series (2)
Inspector bedison risks it
Cobb, Thomas
Inspector Bedison series (3)
Inspector Burmann's blackout
Cobb, Belton
Inspector Cheviot Burmann series (9)
Inspector Burmann's busiest day
Cobb, Belton
Inspector Cheviot Burmann series (7)
Inspector Derben and the widow maker
Foxall, Peter Augustus
Inspector Frank Derben series (3)
Inspector Derben's war
Foxall, Peter Augustus
Inspector Frank Derben series (2)
Inspector Flagg and the scarlet skeleton
Cassells, John
Superintendent Flagg series (15)
Inspector French and the Cheyne mystery
Crofts, Freeman Wills
Inspector Joseph French series (2)
Inspector French and the Starvel tragedy
Crofts, Freeman Wills
Inspector Joseph French series (3)
Inspector French's greatest case
Crofts, Freeman Wills
Inspector Joseph French series (1)
Inspector Frost and Lady Brassingham
Smith, Herbert Maynard
Inspector Frost series (3)
Inspector Frost and the Waverdale fire
Smith, Herbert Maynard
Inspector Frost series (4)
Inspector Frost and the Whitbourne murder
Smith, Herbert Maynard
Inspector Frost series (6)
Inspector Frost in Crevenna Cove
Smith, Herbert Maynard
Inspector Frost series (5)
Inspector Frost in the background
Smith, Herbert Maynard
Inspector Frost series (7)
Inspector Frost in the city
Smith, Herbert Maynard
Inspector Frost series (2)
Inspector Frost's jigsaw
Smith, Herbert Maynard
Inspector Frost series (1)
Inspector Ghote breaks an egg
Keating, Henry Reymond Fitzwalter
Inspector Ganesh Ghote series (6)
Inspector Ghote caught in meshes
Keating, Henry Reymond Fitzwalter
Inspector Ganesh Ghote series (3)
Inspector Ghote draws a line
Keating, Henry Reymond Fitzwalter
Inspector Ganesh Ghote series (11)
Inspector Ghote goes by train
Keating, Henry Reymond Fitzwalter
Inspector Ganesh Ghote series (7)
Inspector Ghote, his life and times
Keating, Henry Reymond Fitzwalter
Inspector Ganesh Ghote series (17)
Inspector Ghote hunts the peacock
Keating, Henry Reymond Fitzwalter
Inspector Ganesh Ghote series (4)
Inspector ghote plays a joker
Keating, Henry Reymond Fitzwalter
Inspector Ganesh Ghote series (5)
Inspector ghote trusts the heart
Keating, Henry Reymond Fitzwalter
Inspector Ganesh Ghote series (8)
Inspector Ghote's good crusade
Keating, Henry Reymond Fitzwalter
Inspector Ganesh Ghote series (2)
Inspector Higgins goes fishing
Gregg, Cecil Freeman
Inspector Cuthbert Higgins series (29)
Inspector Higgins hurries
Gregg, Cecil Freeman
Inspector Cuthbert Higgins series (7)
Inspector Higgins sees it through
Gregg, Cecil Freeman
Inspector Cuthbert Higgins series (10)
Inspector Holt and the fur van
Tully, John
Inspector Holt series (1)
Inspector Holt gets his man
Tully, John
Inspector Holt series (2)
Inspector Jackson goes north
Lindsay, David T
Inspector John Jay Jackson series (4)
Inspector Jackson investigates
Lindsay, David T
Inspector John Jay Jackson series (1)
Inspector Maigret and the burglar's wife
Simenon, Georges
Inspector Jules Maigret series (39)
Inspector Maigret and the dead girl
Simenon, Georges
Inspector Jules Maigret series (48)
Inspector Maigret and the strangled stripper
Simenon, Georges
Inspector Jules Maigret series (37)
Inspector Maigret in New York's underworld
Simenon, Georges
Inspector Jules Maigret series (26)
Inspector Maigret investigates
Simenon, Georges
Inspector Jules Maigret series (1)
Inspector Jules Maigret series (7)
Inspector Jules Maigret series (8)
Inspector Manson's success
Radford, Edwin
Doctor Manson series (1)
Inspector McLean 's holiday
Goodchild, George
Inspector McLean series (28)
Inspector McLean's casebook
Goodchild, George
Inspector McLean series (31)
Inspector Queen's own case
Queen, Ellery
Ellery Queen series (33)
Inspector Richardson, C.I.D.
Thomson, Basil
Superintendent Richardson series (3)
Inspector Rusby's finale
Markham, Virgil
Myles Rusby series (1)
Inspector Smart gets the message
Fowler, Richard
Inspector Smart series (1)
Inspector Smart's international mystery tour
Fowler, Richard
Inspector Smart series (2)
Inspector suggests
Hope, Jane
Teaching series (4)
Inspector Treadgold investigates
Weymouth, Anthony
Inspector Treadgold series (7)
Inspector West alone
Creasey, John
Inspector Roger West series (10)
Inspector West at bay
Creasey, John
Inspector Roger West series (13)
Inspector West at home
Creasey, John
Inspector Roger West series (3)
Inspector West cries wolf
Creasey, John
Inspector Roger West series (9)
Inspector West kicks off
Creasey, John
Inspector Roger West series (8)
Inspector West leaves town
Creasey, John
Inspector Roger West series (2)
Inspector West makes haste
Creasey, John
Inspector Roger West series (17)
Inspector West regrets
Creasey, John
Inspector Roger West series (4)
Inspector West takes charge
Creasey, John
Inspector Roger West series (1)
Inspector Wilkins reads the proofs
Thomas, Murray
Inspector Wilkins series (3)
Inspector Wilkins sees red
Thomas, Murray
Inspector Wilkins series (2)
Inspector's holiday
Lockridge, Richard
Inspector Merton Heimrich series (22)
Instant dead
Jason, Stuart
Butcher series (21)
Instant enemy
Macdonald, Ross
Lew Archer series (15)
Instant millionaire
Stine, Robert Lawrence
Twistaplot series (14)
Instant popularity
Becker, Eve
Abracadabra series (5)
Instead of evidence
Stout, Rex
Nero Wolfe and Archie Goodwin series (14)
Instead of the trees
Priestley, John Boynton
English journey series (6)
Instinct at fault
Carter, Nicholas
Nicholas Carter series (510)
Instinct for trouble
Keene, Carolyn
Nancy Drew files series (95)
Instruction from the Centre
Andrew, Christopher
K.G.B. series (2)
Instruments of darkness
Bethancourt, Tomas Ernesto
Odin series (2)
Instumentality of mankind
Smith, Cordwainer
Instrumentality series (8)
Insulators
Creasey, John
Doctor Palfrey series (30)
Integral trees
Niven, Larry
Known Space series (15)
Trees series (1)
Intelligence Corps and Anna
Frow, Marion
Intelligence Corps series (1)

Intelligence Corps saved the island
Frow, Marion
Intelligence Corps series (2)
Intelligence of flowers
Maeterlinck, Maurice
Hours of gladness series (2)
Intensive care
Johnson, Stacie
Eighteen Pine Street series (7)
Interceptor
Rice, Peter
Renegade legion series (1)
Interceptors
Harris, John
Martin Falconer series (4)
Intercom conspiracy
Ambler, Eric
Charles Latimer series (2)
Interdiction
Balzac, Honore de
Scenes of private life series (26)
Interface
Adlard, Mark
Jan Caspol trilogy (1)
Interface man
Knox, Bill
Inspector Colin Thane and Phil Moss series (20)
Intergalactic express
Sanders, J R
Container series (2)
Intergalactic grudge match
Marino, Tony
Widgets series (3)
Intergalactic kitchen
Rodgers, Frank
Intergalactic kitchen series (1)
Intergalactic kitchen goes prehistoric
Rodgers, Frank
Intergalactic kitchen series (2)
Interim
Richardson, Dorothy Miller
Pilgrimage series (5)
Interloper
Butler, Gwendoline
Inspector John Coffin series (4)
Stern, Richard Martin
Johnny Ortiz series (7)
Interlopers
Hamilton, Donald
Matt Helm series (12)
Interlude for Sally
Seymour, Beatrice Kean
Sally Dunn trilogy (2)
Interlude Silko Five
Brand, Kurt
Perry Rhodan series (59)
International affair
Graeme, Bruce
Superintendent William Stevens and Inspector Pierre Allain series (4)
International Crook League
Carter, Nicholas
Nicholas Carter series (487)
International incidents
Jahn, Mike
Six Million Dollar Man series (11)
International spy
Upward, Allen
Monsieur V series (2)
International Velvet
Forbes, Bryan
Velvet series (2)
Interplanetary war with Venus
Nowlan, Philip Francis
Buck Rogers series (6)
Interpreter
Gibbs, Philip
John Barton trilogy (3)
Interrupted friendship
Voynich, Ethel Lillian
Gadfly series (3)
Interstellar espionage
Del Martia, Astron
Space Express Company series (3)
Interstellar mutineers
Byrne, Stuart James
Star Man series (1)
Interstellar Two-Five
Rankine, John
Dag Fletcher series (2)
Intervention
Housman, Laurence
Palace plays series (3)
May, Julian
Pliocene exile series (1)
Interview with the vampire
Rice, Anne
Vampire chronicles series (1)
Interviewing's killing
Tack, Alfred
John Harley series (2)
Interworld
Haiblum, Isidore
Gunjer series (1)
Intimate journal
Gide, Andre
Journal series (6)
Intimate secrets of a magazine writer
Flanagan
Intimate secrets series (2)
Intimate secrets of an actress
Flanagan
Intimate secrets series (3)
Intimate secrets of an escort girl
Flanagan
Intimate secrets series (1)
Intimations of Eve
Fisher, Vardis
Testament of man series (3)
Intimidation, Inc.
Grant, Maxwell
Shadow series (115)
Intimidators
Hamilton, Donald
Matt Helm series (15)
Into a happy glade
Dudley-Smith, Trevor
Happy glade series (1)
Into a strange lost world
Carter, Bruce
Danny Black and Johnny Wild series (1)
Into battle!
Challoner, Robert
Commander Lord Charles Oakshott series (3)
Into Cambodia
Nolan, Keith William
Vietnam War series (4)
Into China
Acres, Mark
Sniper series (3)
Into exile
Lingard, Joan
Sadie and Kevin series (3)
Into Laos
Nolan, Keith William
Vietnam War series (2)
Into Mexico with General Scott
Sabin, Edward Legrand
Trail blazers series (12)
Into Narsindal
Taylor, Roger
Hawklan series (4)
Into Nick Carter's web
Carter, Nicholas
Nicholas Carter series (284)
Into passion's dawn
Du Barry, Michele
Angela Carlyle series (1)
Into the abyss
Verne, Jules
Family without a name series (2)
Into the alternate universe
Chandler, Arthur Bertram
John Grimes series (3)
Rim series (9)
Into the battle
Cosic, Dobrica
This land, this time series (1)
Into the dark lands
Sagara, Michele M
Sundered series (1)
Into the dream
Weyn, Suzanne
Secret of the Unicorn Queen series (4)
Into the Fourth at Trebizon
Digby, Anne
Trebizon series (8)
Into the fourth dimension
Cummings, Ray
Incredible adventures series (3)
Into the happy glad
Trevor, Elleston
Green glade trilogy (1)
Into the labyrinth
Mallet-Joris, Francoise
Helene series (1)
Scott, Peter Graham
Labyrinth series (1)
Weis, Margaret
Death Gate series (6)
Into the maze
Stivers, Dick
Able Team series (14)
Into the millenium
Musil, Robert
Man without qualities series (3)
Into the Niger Bend
Verne, Jules
Barsac mission series (1)
Into the primitive
Bennet, Robert Ames
Primitive series (1)
Into the smother
Parkin, Ray
Out of the smoke series (2)
Into the sun
Meredith, Gwen
Blue Hills series (4)
Norton, John
Magic voyage series (4)
Into the unknown
Fletcher, Lawrence
Dick Grenville series (1)
Into the valley of death
Hervey, Evelyn
Harriet Unwin series (3)
Into the void
Findley, Nigel
Spelljammer series (2)
Into the wind
Hatch, Richard Warren
Bradfords series (1)
Into thin air
Carmichael, Harry
John Piper and Quinn series (12)
Keene, Carolyn
Nancy Drew files series (57)
Intrepid enchanter
De Camp, Lyon Sprague
Harold Shea series (3)
Intrepid's last case
Stevenson, William Henri
William Stephenson series (2)
Intrigue
Cory, Desmond
Johnny Fedora series (4)
Intrigue on Halfaday Creek
Hendryx, James Beardsley
Black John series (17)
Intriguer
Parker, Maude
Jim Little series (2)
Intriguers
Hamilton, Donald
Matt Helm series (14)
Intrigues of Caroline Cherie
Saint-Laurent, Cecil
Cherie series (5)
Introducing Amanda Valentine
Beecham, Rose
Amanda Valentine series (1)
Introducing C.B.Greenfield
Kallen, Lucille
C.B.Greenfield series (1)
Introducing Inspector Maigret
Simenon, Georges
Inspector Jules Maigret series (6)
Introducing Parri
Lambert, Janet
Parri Macdonald series (1)
Introducing the Arnisons
Thompson, Edward
Arnison series (1)
Introducing the Super
Goyne, Richard
Ex-Superintendent Tubby Green series (1)
Introducing the Toff
Creasey, John
Toff series (1)
Introducing Trigger
Allum, Tom
Captain Michael Triggington series (1)
Introducing Wanderlust Brown
Boyd, Edward
Wanderlust Brown series (1)
Introduction to Elvish
Tolkien, John Ronald Reuel
Middle Earth series (5)
Intruder
Annunzio, Gabriele d'
Romances of the rose trilogy (3)
Baer, Judy
Cedar River daydreams series (6)
Blasco Ibanez, Vicente
Roman Catholic Church in Spain series (2)
Housman, Laurence
Palace plays series (2)
Thurston, Robert
Robots and aliens series (3)
Intruder in the dark
Bellairs, George
Detective Inspector Thomas Littlejohn series (43)
Intruder in the dust
Faulkner, William
Gavin Stevens trilogy (2)
Intruders
Coonts, Stephen
Jake Grafton series (6)
Fane, Bron
La noire series (1)
Garner, Hugh
Cabbagetown series (4)
Intruders at Pinetops
Hurt, Freda Mary
Pinetops series (6)
Intrusion of Nicola
Matthewman, Phyllis
Daneswood series (7)
Invade Russia!
Lutz, Gunther
Panzer Platoon series (2)
Invader from space
Moore, Patrick
Robin North and Rex Redmayne series (4)
Invaders
Danielson, Peter
Children of the Lion series (13)
Gaunt, Michael
Belle Isle series (2)
Johnston, William
Happy days series (3)
Laumer, Keith
Invaders series (1)
Treece, Henry
Early Britain series (1)
Invaders from Darkland
Beach, Lynn
Wizards, warlocks and you series (15)
Invaders from the centre
Stableford, Brian Michael
Asgard series (2)
Invaders from the infinite
Campbell, John Wood
Arcot, Morey and Wade series (3)
Invaders from the lost galaxy
Norton, John
Magic voyage series (3)
Invaders from within
Packard, Edward
Choose your own adventure series (110)
Invaders of Ground Zero
Houston, David
Tales of tomorrow series (1)
Invaders of Hark
Stine, Robert Lawrence
Hark series (2)
Invaders of the planet earth
Brightfield, Richard
Choose your own adventure series (70)
Invaders plan
Hubbard, Lafayette Ronald
Mission earth series (1)
Invasion
Gerrold, David
War against the Chtorr trilogy (2)
Janson, Hank
Hank Janson series (88)
Marter, Ian
Doctor Who series (98)
Wheatley, Dennis
War game series (1)
Invasion at Upney Junction
Butterworth, Nick
Upney Junction series (2)
Invasion from below the earth
Curtis, Philip
Mister Browser series (2)
Invasion from space
Ernsting, Walter
Perry Rhodan series (4)
Invasion of 1688
Birt, David
Stuarts series (9)
Invasion of the Brain Sharpeners
Curtis, Philip
Mister Browser series (1)
Invasion of the clones
Rosenberger, Joseph
Death Merchant series (16)
Invasion of the comet people
Curtis, Philip
Mister Browser series (3)
Invasion of the fast food
Hodgman, Ann
Lunchroom series (7)
Invasion of the mutants
Mooser, Stephen
Which way interactive series (4)
Invasion of the nymphomaniacs
O'Shea, Sean
Valentine Flynn series (5)
Invasion of the Ormazoids
Martin, Philip
Doctor Who find your fate series (5)
Invasion of the United States
Hancock, Harrie Irving
Conquest of the United States series (1)
Invasion of the yellow warlords
Steele, Curtis
James Christopher series (11)
Invasion of Willow Wood Springs
Ellis, Terry
Willow Wood Springs trilogy (3)
Invasion U.S.S.R.
Buchanan, Jack
M.I.A. Hunter series (9)
Inventors
Aaseng, Nathan
Nobel Prize winners series (2)
Inverted crime
Gribble, Leonard Reginald
Superintendent Anthony Slade series (24)
Investigating King Arthur
Birt, David
Roman Britain series (18)
Investigating the druids
Birt, David
Roman Britain series (15)
Investigation at Holman Square
Hopkins, Nevil Monroe
Mason Brant series (1)
Investigations and experiences of M. Shawtinbach at Saar Soong, Sumatra
Smile, R Elton
Manatitlans series (2)
Investigations are proceeding
Ashford, Jeffrey
Detective Inspector Don Kerry series (2)
Investigations of Colwin Grey
Rees, Arthur John
Colwin Grey series (4)
Investor's sufferings
Balzac, Honore de
Scenes of provincial life series (9)
Investor's tribulations
Balzac, Honore de
Scenes of provincial life series (9)
Invid invasion
McKinney, Jack
Robotech series (10)
Invincible Adam
Viereck, George Sylvester
Wandering Jew trilogy (3)
Invincible Brer Anansi
Makhanlall, David Paschal
Anansi series (2)
Invincible Doc Savage
Grushkin, Edward
Doc Savage series (183)
Invincible Shiwan Khan
Grant, Maxwell
Shadow series (182)
Invincible woman
Fraser, Sara
Tildy series (8)
Invincibles
Vaughan, Carter A
Lieutenant Gordon Fuller series (1)
Invisibility affair
Stratton, Thomas
Man from U.N.C.L.E. series (11)
Invisibility factor
Sherman, Josepha
Junior transformers find your fate series (9)
Invisibility Island
Beach, Lynn
G.I.Joe series (4)
Invisible assassins
Pendleton, Don
Mack Bolan series (53)
Invisible-box murders
Robeson, Kenneth
Doc Savage series (160)
Invisible castle
Martin, Les
Thundercats series (4)
Invisible chimes
Sutton, Margaret
Judy Bolton series (3)
Invisible death
Carter, Lin
Prince Zarkon series (2)
Flynn, Brian
Anthony Bathurst series (5)
Invisible empire
Dille, Flint
Agent thirteen series (1)
Steele, Curtis
James Christopher series (2)
Tourgee, Albion Winegar
Comfort Servosse series (2)

Invisible event
Beresford, John Davys
Jacob Stahl series (3)
Invisible eye
Tabori, Paul
Hunters series (2)
Invisible Flamini
Brown, Carter
Rick Holman series (26)
Invisible force
Appleton, Victor II
Tom Swift Junior series 2 (10)
Invisible green
Sladek, John Thomas
Thackeray Phin series (2)
Invisible hand
Dark, Rex
Bartholomew Dane series (5)
Invisible intruder
Keene, Carolyn
Nancy Drew series (46)
Invisible magic
Beresford, Elisabeth
Magic series (6)
Invisible man murders
Foster, Richard
Chin Kwang Kham series (2)
Invisible pickpocket
M'Govan, James
James M'Govan series (7)
Invisible president
Rohmer, Sax
Fu-Manchu series (9)
Invisible stranger
Plain, Neil
Boris Blundle and Gang series (8)
Invisible weapons
Rhode, John
Doctor Lancelot Priestley series (28)
Invisible witness
Ecke, Wolfgang
Super sleuth series (3)
Invisible woman
Quick, Herbert
Iowa pioneer life series (3)
Invisible Wombles, and other stories
Beresford, Elisabeth
Wombles series (3)
Invisible worm
Millar, Margaret
Doctor Paul Prye series (1)
Invisible writing
Koestler, Arthur
Arrow in the blue series (2)
Invisibles
Dark, James
Mark Kingsley Hood series (13)
Hurwood, Bernhardt Jackson
Invisibles series (1)
Invitation from Minerva
Cost, March
Princess Victoria Babenberg series (2)
Invitation to a dynamite party
Lovesey, Peter
Sergeant Cribb and Constable Thackeray series (5)
Invitation to a funeral
Harknett, Terry
Stephen Wayne series (3)
Invitation to a murder
Story, Jack Trevor
Sexton Blake series (1480)
Invitation to a strangling
Brent, R L
Liquidator series (4)
Invitation to adventure
Ashe, Gordon
Patrick Dawlish series (14)
Invitation to Camelot
Godwin, Parke
Arthurian cycle trilogy (3)
Invitation to death
Carter, Nick
Nick Carter series (246)
Long, Amelia Reynolds
Edward Trelawny series (3)
Invitation to die
French, Fergus
General Ogle-Oxley series (2)
Invitation to live
Douglas, Lloyd Cassel
Newell Paige series (2)
Invitation to Mather
Graeme, Bruce
Detective Sergeant Robert Mather series (8)
Invitation to murder
Long, Manning
Liz Parrott series (3)
Sharp, Allen
Storytrails series (5)
Shriber, Ione Sandberg
Lieutenant Bill Grady series (6)
Stout, Rex
Nero Wolfe and Archie Goodwin series (23)
Invitation to the waltz
Lehmann, Rosamond
Olivia, Kate and Reggie series (1)
Involuntary comedians
Balzac, Honore de
Scenes of Parisian life series (10)
Involvement in Austria
Chance, John Newton
Jonathan Blake series (12)
Ionia
Stark, Freya
Ionia series (1)
Ionian mission
O'Brian, Patrick
Jack Aubrey and Stephen Maturin series (8)
Ipcress file
Deighton, Len
Secret file series (1)
Ira says goodbye
Waber, Bernard
Ira series (2)
Ira sleeps over
Waber, Bernard
Ira series (1)
Iranian hit
Pendleton, Don
Mack Bolan series (42)
Irene at large
Douglas, Carole Nelson
Irene Adler series (3)
Irene, good night
Bensen, Donald R
Sherlock Holmes sequels series (53)
Irene's last waltz
Douglas, Carole Nelson
Irene Adler series (4)
Ireta adventure
McCaffrey, Anne
Ireta adventure series (2)
Iris, the bewitched
Kimbrough, Katheryn
Phenwick women series (39)
Irish adventures of Worzel Gummidge
Waterhouse, Keith
Worzel Gummidge series (18)
Irish beauty contract
Atlee, Philip
Joe Gall series (5)
Irish captain
Kavanagh, Patrick Joseph
Scarf Jack series (1)
Irish childhood
Hamilton, Elizabeth
Irish childhood series (2)
Irish idylls
Barlow, Jane
Lisconnel series (1)
Irish journey
Sutherland, Halliday
Journey series (5)
Irish Monte Cristo abroad
Robertson, Alexander
Irish Monte Cristo series (2)
Irish Monte Cristo's search
Robertson, Alexander
Irish Monte Cristo series (1)
Irish Monte Cristo's trail
Robertson, Alexander
Irish Monte Cristo series (3)
Irish Red, son of Big Red
Kjelgaard, Jim
Red series (2)
Irish rose
Roberts, Nora
Flowers series (3)
Irish thoroughbred
Roberts, Nora
Flowers series (1)
Irish twins
Perkins, Lucy Fitch
Twin series (3)
Irish witch
Wheatley, Dennis
Roger Brook series (11)
Irishman's horse
Collins, Michael
Dan Fortune series (17)
Iron arm of Michael Glenn
Lee, Robert Corwin
Michael Glenn series (1)
Iron arrow head
Sue, Eugene
Mysteries of the people series (10)
Iron claw
Macdonnell, James Edmond
Captain Peter Bentley series (47)
Symonds, Francis Addington
Sexton Blake series (199)
Tilton, Alice
Leonidas Witherall series (8)
Iron Claymore
Wilson, Gar
Phoenix Force series (46)
Iron clog
Buffery, Judith
Star lords series (3)
Iron collar
Sue, Eugene
Mysteries of the people series (3)
Iron door
Martin, Oliver
Timothy Cullinan series (1)
Iron Duke
Tunis, John Roberts
Iron Duke series (1)
Iron earth, copper sky
Kemal, Yashar
Meryemdje series (2)
Iron egg
Hardie, David William Ferguson
Inspector Elwyn Hughes series (1)
Iron fist, velvet glove
Dille, Flint
Agent thirteen series (4)
Iron gates
Millar, Margaret
Inspector Sands series (3)
Iron Girdle
Gaunt, Richard
English Civil War series (2)
Iron glove
Tierney, Ronald
Deets Shanahan series (3)
Iron god
O'Donnell, Peter
Modesty Blaise comic strip series (9)
Stivers, Dick
Able Team series (26)
Iron Gustav
Fallada, Hans
Germany between the wars series (3)
Iron hand
Tilton, Alice
Leonidas Witherall series (8)
Iron hand of Mars
Davis, Lindsey
Marcus Didius Falco series (4)
Iron Heart, war chief of the Iroquois
Ellis, Edward Sylvester
War chief series (1)
Iron horse
Dolan, Bill
Afrikorps series (2)
Giraud, Jean
Lieutenant Mike S Blueberry series (6)
Grant, William
Matthew Faraday series (1)
Iron horse country
Cody, Al
Montana series (5)
Iron horse gunsmoke
Hobart, Donald Bayne
Masked Rider and Blue Hawk series (9)
Iron in the soul
Sartre, Jean Paul
Roads to freedom trilogy (3)
Iron King
Druon, Maurice
Accursed kings series (1)
Iron lily
Willard, Barbara
Mantlemass series (6)
Iron lords
Offutt, Andrew Jefferson
War of the gods on earth trilogy (1)
Iron maiden
Brown, Carter
Larry Baker series (6)
Iron Man, And call my killer, Modok!
Rotsler, William
Marvel superheroes, new series (6)
Iron Mask
Dumas, Alexandre
Three Musketeers series (3)
Iron mask
Evans, Gwyn
Double O'Day series (2)
Iron master
Tilley, Patrick
Amtrak wars series (3)
Iron men
McCurtin, Peter
Sundance series (37)
Iron men and saints
Lamb, Harold
Crusades series (1)
Iron monster raid
Edmonds, Ivy Gordon
Rat Patrol series (6)
Iron mouth
Fletcher, Beryl
Khryse trilogy (2)
Iron mustang
Logan, Jake
John Slocum series (15)
Iron noose
Bonner, Michael
Roby Maclane trilogy (1)
Iron peacock
Clarke, Mary Stetson
Ross McCrae series (1)
Iron pincers
Sue, Eugene
Mysteries of the people series (13)
Iron pirate
Pemberton, Max
Captain Black series (1)
Iron rails
Shane, Bart
Iron rails trilogy (1)
Iron roads
Bramble, Forbes
Kelleway family series (2)
Iron sanctuary
Macleod, Robert
Talos Cord series (3)
Iron sceptre
White, John
Archives of Anthropos series (2)
Iron ships
Abraham, Cyril
Onedin Line series (2)
Iron ships, iron men
Nicole, Christopher
United States Navy series (3)
Iron Skull
Robeson, Kenneth
Avenger series (35)
Iron sleep
Pearsall, Ronald
Oakwood family series (2)
Iron spiders
Kendrick, Baynard
Miles Standish Rice series (2)
Iron spiders murder
Kendrick, Baynard
Miles Standish Rice series (2)
Iron stallions
Hennessy, Max
Cavalry trilogy (3)
Iron swastika plot
Rosenberger, Joseph
Death Merchant series (15)
Iron Tongue
Vardeman, Robert Edward
Cenotaph Road series (4)
Iron trail
Champlin, Tim
Matt Tierney series (6)
Iron trail to death
Hardin, J D
Raider and Doc series (64)
Iron Triangle
Helm, Eric
Ground Zero series (12)
Iron trivet
Sue, Eugene
Mysteries of the people series (14)
Iron virgin
Fox, James M
John and Suzy Marshall series (10)
Iron warrior
Thompson, David
Nathaniel King series (19)
Iron woman
Deland, Margaret
Helen Ritchie series (2)
Ironbark Bill
Stivens, Dal
Ironbark Bill series (2)
Ironbrand
Morressy, John
Iron angel series (1)
Ironhelm
Niles, Douglas
Maztica trilogy (1)
Ironman
Stivers, Dick
Able Team series (19)
Ironmaster
Stubbs, Jean
Brief chronicles series (2)
Ironsides' lone hand
Gunn, Victor
Chief Inspector Bill Cromwell series (4)
Ironsides of the Yard
Gunn, Victor
Chief Inspector Bill Cromwell series (2)
Ironsides on the spot
Gunn, Victor
Chief Inspector Bill Cromwell series (13)
Ironsides sees red
Gunn, Victor
Chief Inspector Bill Cromwell series (7)
Ironsides smashes through
Gunn, Victor
Chief Inspector Bill Cromwell series (3)
Ironsides smells blood
Gunn, Victor
Chief Inspector Bill Cromwell series (10)
Ironthorpe, the frontier preacher
Trowbridge, John Townsend
Brighthope series (4)
Ironthorpe, the pioneer preacher
Trowbridge, John Townsend
Brighthope series (4)
Ironweed
Kennedy, William
Phelan family series (2)
Iroquois and the Civil War years
Hauptman, Laurence Marc
Iroquois series (2)
Iroquois and the New Deal
Hauptman, Laurence Marc
Iroquois series (3)
Iroquois in the American Revolution
Graymont, Barbara
Iroquois series (1)
Iroquois land claims
Vesey, Christopher
Iroquois series (5)
Iroquois scout
Lange, Dietrich
American Indian series (12)
Iroquois struggle for survival
Hauptman, Laurence Marc
Iroquois series (4)
Irrational knot
Shaw, George Bernard
Nonage series (2)
Irrational season
L'Engle, Madeleine
Crosswicks journals series (3)
Irregulars strike again
Derleth, August
Mill Creek Irregulars series (2)
Irsud
Clayton, Jo
Diadem series (3)
I's
Zukofsky, Louis
I's series (1)
Is dinner ready?
Walker, Mort
Hi and Lois series (4)
Is Glennon guilty?
Grover, Marshall
Larry and Stretch series (377)
Is he biting again?
Matterson, Neil
Baby series (3)
Is it Friday yet?
Evans, Greg
Luann series (3)
Is it larger, is it smaller?
Hoban, Tana
Is it series (3)
Is it red, is it yellow, is it blue?
Hoban, Tana
Is it series (1)
Is it rough, is it smooth, is it shiny?
Hoban, Tana
Is it series (2)
Is she a lady?
Hamnett, Nana
Laughing torso series (2)
Is she dead too?
Gilbert, Anthony
Arthur Crook series (28)
Is that a monster, Alfie Atkins?
Bergstrom, Gunilla
Alfie Atkins series (7)
Is that you Mrs Pinkerton-Trunks, and other stories
Isherwood, Shirley
Get up and go series (1)

Is there a cure for sophomore year?
Steiner, Barbara
Fifteen series (1)
Is there a doctor in the zoo?
Taylor, David Conrad
Zoovet series (2)
Is there a traitor in the house?
McGerr, Patricia
Selena Mead series (1)
Is there life after birth?
King, Alexander
Mine enemy grows older series (4)
Is there life after boys?
Lewis, Linda
Linda series (2)
Is this revenge?
Gribble, Leonard Reginald
Superintendent Anthony Slade series (4)
Is this the end?
Sargent, Craig
Last ranger series (10)
Isaac Asimov omnibus
Asimov, Isaac
Foundation series (4)
Isaac quartet
Charyn, Jerome
Isaac Sidel series (4)
Isaacs
Gee, Joseph
David Isaacs series (1)
Isaacs reappears
Gee, Joseph
David Isaacs series (2)
Isabel and the sea
Millar, George
Boat travel series (1)
Isabel Carleton at home
Ashmun, Margaret Eliza
Isabel Carleton series (5)
Isabel Carleton in the West
Ashmun, Margaret Eliza
Isabel Carleton series (4)
Isabel Carleton's friends
Ashmun, Margaret Eliza
Isabel Carleton series (3)
Isabel Carleton's year
Ashmun, Margaret Eliza
Isabel Carleton series (1)
Isabella and Ferdinand
Plaidy, Jean
Ferdinand and Isabella trilogy (3)
Isabella Bella rides again
Tozer, Mary
Queen Yesno series (2)
Isabelle and little orphan Frannie
Greene, Constance Clarke
Isabelle series (3)
Isabelle shows her stuff
Greene, Constance Clarke
Isabelle series (2)
Isabelle, the frantic
Kimbrough, Katheryn
Phenwick women series (22)
Isabelle the itch
Greene, Constance Clarke
Isabelle series (1)
Ishi in two worlds
Kroeber, Theodora
Ishi series (1)
Ishi, last of his tribe
Kroeber, Theodora
Ishi series (2)
Ishmael
Hambly, Barbara
Star trek series (23)
Ishmael's wife
Vickers, Roy
James Segrove series (3)
Isis pedlar
Hughes, Monica
Isis trilogy (3)
Island
Lockley, Ronald Mathias
Island farm series (7)
Postgate, Oliver
Saga of Noggin the Nog series (5)
Russell, Robert William
World I cannot see series (2)
Smith, Naomi Royde
Rockmouth and Rockhead township trilogy (3)
Whiteing, Richard
Rich and poor series (1)
Island adventure
Lavell, Edith
Linda Carlton series (2)
Island adventurer
Simons, Roger
Bruce and Ian series (1)
Island alert
Walsh, James Morgan
Oliver Keene series (11)
Island called Moreau
Aldiss, Brian Wilson
Doctor Moreau series (2)
Island camp
Bonehill, Ralph
Lakeport series (1)
Island days
Lockley, Ronald Mathias
Island farm series (3)
Island deathtrap
Pendleton, Don
Mack Bolan series (56)
Island emperor
Priestley, Brian
Willy Hand series (2)
Island farmers
Lockley, Ronald Mathias
Island farm series (5)
Island flame
Robards, Karen
Lady Catherine Alderly series (1)
Island fling
Skidmore, Ian
Welsh island series (1)
Island girl
Berry, Carole
Bonnie Indermill series (4)
Island gold
Williams, Valentine
Clubfoot series (3)
Island harp
Williams, Jeanne
Clanna series (1)
Island home
Rutley, Cecily Marianne
Little people in far off lands series (2)
Island in revolt
Gaillard, Robert
Marie series (4)
Island in the Bay
Simpson, Dorothy
Janie Marshal series (1)
Island in the corn
Selby, John
Trace family trilogy (2)
Island in the lake
Mathews, M E
Cloud family series (2)
Island in the mist
Kelsey, Franklyn
James Armitage trilogy (1)
Island in the pines
Trevor, Elleston
Squirrel's Island series (1)
Island in the sky
Peel, John
Lost in space files series (2)
Island in the swamp
Mayhar, Ardath
Amerindian prehistory series (2)
Island intrigue
McAdam, Preston
Shield series (3)
Island mystery
Birmingham, George A
Gorman MP series (2)
Bobin, John William
Sexton Blake series (77)
Island of adventure
Blyton, Enid
Adventure series (1)
Island of birds
Fitz Roy, Olivia
Jamie and Jean Stewart series (1)
Island of colours
Arendt, Veronique
Zoe and George series (2)
Island of creeping death
Norwood, Victor George Charles
Jacare series (5)
Island of death
Broome, Adam
Commissioner Denzil Grigson series (2)
Island of destiny
Rees, Arthur John
Inspector Luckraft series (1)
Island of disaster
Lewis, Michael
Sergeant Hobbs series (2)
Island of Doctor Moreau
Wells, Herbert George
Doctor Moreau series (1)
Island of dogs
Falk, Lee
Phantom series (13)
Island of evil
Daniels, Dorothy
Strange paradise trilogy (2)
Island of fear
Bream, Freda
Reverend Jabal Jarrett series (1)
Brightfield, Richard
Your amazing adventures series (2)
Moore, Patrick
Grenfell and Wright series (2)
Morris, Dave
Transformers series (4)
Island of flowers
Roberts, Nora
Flowers series (10)
Island of forgotten men
Catherall, Arthur
Bulldog tugboat series (12)
Island of Fu-Manchu
Rohmer, Sax
Fu-Manchu series (11)
Island of peril
Creasey, John
Department Z series (15)
Island of secrets
Keene, Carolyn
Nancy Drew files series (98)
Island of Sheep
Buchan, John
Richard Hannay series (6)
Island of Sodor, its people, history and railways
Awdry, Wilbert
Sodor series (2)
Island of spies
Walsh, James Morgan
Oliver Keene series (1)
Island of stone
Hunter, Claire
Island of stone series (1)
Island of terror
Sapper
Jim Maitland series (2)
Island of the blue dolphin
O'Dell, Scott
Zia series (1)
Island of the damned
Rosenberger, Joseph
Death Merchant series (44)
Island of the dead
Elder, Michael
Barclay series (5)
Island of the grass king
Willard, Nancy
Anatole series (2)
Island of the guilty
Teed, George Hamilton
Sexton Blake series (453)
Island of the innocent
Fisher, Vardis
Testament of man series (7)
Island of the Lizard King
Livingstone, Ian
Fighting fantasy gamebook series (7)
Island of the mighty
Walton, Evangeline
Mabinogion series (4)
Island of the walking dead
Sharp, Allen
Storytrails series (21)
Weinberg, Larry
Chuck Norris and the Karate Kommandos series (2)
Island of the weird
Gilden, Mel
Fifth grade monsters series (11)
Island of time
Montgomery, Raymond A
Choose your own adventure series (115)
Island people
Coblentz, Stanton Arthur
Outlander series (3)
Island rescue
Martin, Charles E
Monhegan Island series (3)
Island snatchers
Smith, George Henry
Annwn series (5)
Island sonata
Livingston, Marjorie
Karma series (1)
Island stallion
Farley, Walter
Black stallion series (4)
Island stallion races
Farley, Walter
Black stallion series (11)
Island stallion's fury
Farley, Walter
Black stallion series (7)
Island where time stands still
Wheatley, Dennis
Gregory Sallust series (8)
Island winter
Martin, Charles E
Monhegan Island series (1)
Island worlds
Kotani, Eric
Act of God trilogy (2)
Islander
Roberts, John Maddox
Stromlands series (1)
Islanders
Knowles, Gaye
Islanders series (1)
O'Donnell, Peadar
Islanders series (2)
Pertwee, Roland
Patrick Faraday series (1)
Islanders follow a clue
Knowles, Gaye
Islanders series (4)
Islanders in danger
Knowles, Gaye
Islanders series (5)
Islanders' secret cave
Knowles, Gaye
Islanders series (2)
Islanders' strange holiday
Knowles, Gaye
Islanders series (3)
Islandia
Wright, Austin Tappan
Islandia series (1)
Islandia revisited
Farmer, Richard Neil
Islandia series (5)
Islandian world of Austin Wright
Powell, Lawrence Clark
Islandia series (5)
Islands of England and Wales
McCormick, Donald
British Isles series (1)
Islands of Ireland
McCormick, Donald
British Isles series (3)
Islands of Scotland
McCormick, Donald
British Isles series (2)
Islands of space
Campbell, John Wood
Arcot, Morey and Wade series (2)
Islands of Strangers
Beardmore, George
Lesley Allan series (2)
Islar
Saxton, Mark
Islandia series (2)
Isle of blood
Carter, Nick
Nick Carter series (255)
Isle of doubt
Grant, Maxwell
Shadow series (36)
Isle of dragons
Macleod, Robert
Talos Cord series (4)
Isle of glass
Tarr, Judith
Hound and the Falcon trilogy (1)
Isle of gold
Grant, Maxwell
Shadow series (168)
Isle of horror
Teed, George Hamilton
Sexton Blake series (777)
Isle of illusion
Simon, Madeleine
Heartquest series (4)
Isle of Pleasure
Goscinny, Rene
Twelve tasks of Asterix series (4)
Isle of the dead
Zelazny, Roger
Isle of the dead series (1)
Isle of the snakes
Fish, Robert Lloyd
Captain Jose da Silva series (2)
Isle of view
Anthony, Piers
Xanth series (13)
Isle of Wight
Abbott, Jacob
Florence series (5)
Isle of woman
Anthony, Piers
Geodyssey series (1)
Isles of the sea
Optic, Oliver
Young America, second series (6)
Ismo
Verney, John
Callendar family series (3)
Isobel Quirk in orbit
Wakefield, Tom
Margaret Davis and Isobel Quirk trilogy (2)
Isotope man
Maine, Charles Eric
Mike Delaney series (1)
Israeli connection
Carter, Nick
Nick Carter series (161)
Israeli secret service
Deacon, Richard
Secret service series (4)
Israeli twins
Tindall, Gillian
Twin series (36)
Issel, warrior king
Farrell, Simon
Glade of dreams series (2)
Issi Noho
Chatfield, Keith
Issi Noho series (1)
Issi pandemonium
Chatfield, Keith
Issi Noho series (2)
Issi's magic tonic
Chatfield, Keith
Issi Noho series (3)
Istanbul
Carter, Nick
Nick Carter series (10)
Istanbul decision
Carter, Nick
Nick Carter series (180)
Isthmus years
Cartland, Barbara
Years of life series (2)
Istu awakened
Vardeman, Robert Edward
War of powers series (6)
It
Abarbanell, Jacob Ralph
He, she and it trilogy (3)
De Morgan, John
She series (3)
Hawkey, Raymond
Presidential trilogy (3)
It ain't hay
Dodge, David
Whit Whitney series (4)
It all started with Columbus
Armour, Richard
It all started with series (1)
It all started with Europa
Armour, Richard
It all started with series (2)
It all started with Eve
Armour, Richard
It all started with series (3)
It all started with freshman English
Armour, Richard
It all started with series (7)
It all started with Hippocrates
Armour, Richard
It all started with series (5)
It all started with Marx
Armour, Richard
It all started with series (4)
It all started with nudes
Armour, Richard
It all started with series (8)
It all started with stones and clubs
Armour, Richard
It all started with series (6)
It all would have startled Columbus
Armour, Richard
It all started with series (1)
It always happens to Leona
Havill, Juanita
Leona series (1)
It always rains in Rome
Leeming, John Fishwick
Fontana d'amore series (1)
It began in Vauxhall Gardens
Kellow, Kathleen
Victorian England series (2)
It came from the Far Side
Larson, Gary
Far Side series (6)
It can't be my grave
Dean, S F X
Professor Neil Kelly series (3)
It couldn't be murder
Austin, Hugh
Peter Quint series (1)
Cross, Mark
Daphne Wrayne and her Four Adjusters series (13)
It couldn't matter less
Cheyney, Peter
Slim Callaghan series (4)
It does not die
Devi, Maitreyi
Calcutta series (2)
It had to be Ortega
Grover, Marshall
Larry and Stretch series (360)

It happened in Hamburg
Baker, William Howard
Sexton Blake series (1399)
It happened in Melgrove Square
Hunter, John
Sexton Blake series (1296)
It happened in PRK
Hoff, Harry Summerfield
Three marriages series (1)
It happened on Halfaday Creek
Hendryx, James Beardsley
Black John series (9)
Corporal Cameron Downey series (6)
It is always summer
Helwig, David
Kingston tetralogy (4)
It is not so easy to live
Arnothy, Christine
Living series (2)
It isn't all Greek to me
Bull, Peter
Bulls series (5)
It isn't all mink
Spanier, Ginette
Mink and sables series (1)
It isn't this time of year at all!
Gogarty, Oliver St John
Sackville Street series (5)
It leaves them cold
O'Hara, Kevin
Chico Brett series (5)
It lives again
Dixon, James
It's alive series (2)
It looked like for ever
Harris, Mark
Henry W Wiggen series (4)
It makes you think
Jones, Arthur E
Felix Holliday series (3)
It might have meant murder
Cargill, Leslie
Major Mosson series (2)
It might lead anywhere
Punshon, Ernest Robertson
Bobby Owen series (22)
It must be something in the ink
Guisewhite, Cathy
Cathy series (13)
It must have hurt a lot
Sanford, Doris
Hurts of childhood series (3)
It pays to die
Wills, Cecil Melville
Superintendent Roger Ellerdine and Sergeant Cherry Blossom series (7)
It rained that Friday
Wilson, Gertrude Mary
Inspector Lovick series (5)
It seems to me
Gee, Herbert Leslie
Priory House series (2)
It shouldn't happen to a dog
Watson, Colin
Inspector Purbright series (9)
It shouldn't happen to a vet
Herriot, James
Vet series (2)
It takes a thief
Hooper, Kay
Hagen series (10)
It walks by night
Carr, John Dickson
Henri Bencolin series (1)
It was all through Patience
Hill, Lorna
Patience series (2)
It was Candy's idea
Reed, Maud Dorothy
Candy series (1)
It was good while it lasted
Longhurst, Henry
Good while it lasted series (1)
It was murder, they said
Bentley, John
Glen Gibson series (4)
It was the nightingale
Ford, Ford Madox
Memories and impressions series (4)
Williamson, Henry
Chronicles of ancient sunlight series (10)
It wasn't a nightmare
Hay, Lindsay Fitzgerald
Archibald Beldrum and Nigel Blair series (1)
It wasn't me
Hardcastle, Michael
Tony and Jay series (11)
Jefferies, Ian
Sergeant Craig series (3)
It won't get you anywhere
Skirrow, Desmond
John Brock series (1)
Italian adventure
Bayley, Viola
Adventure series (8)
Italian assets
Butler, Richard
Max Farne series (2)
Italian connection
Chase, Glen
Cherry Delight series (1)
Moore, Robin
Connection series (3)
Pulsar series (2)
Italian gold
Ellis, Wesley
Lone Star series (94)
Italian holiday
Sutton, Phyllis
Merryl Hastings series (5)
Italian spaghetti mystery
Stanley, George Edward
Doctor Constance Daniels series (4)
Italian spring
Avery, Gillian
Maria Henniker-Haddon series (2)
Italian twins
Perkins, Lucy Fitch
Twin series (11)
Italian woman
Plaidy, Jean
Catherine de Medici trilogy (2)
Item seven
Nixon, Alan
Larry Maver series (1)
It's a baby
Matterson, Neil
Baby series (1)
It's a bird, it's a plane, no, it's the television adventures of Superman
Van Hise, James
Superman series (7)
It's a boy's world
Derleth, August
Boy's series (2)
It's a crime
Ellington, Richard
Steve Drake series (2)
It's a dog's life
Bishop, Mary
Vet's wife series (1)
Erickson, John R
Hank the cowdog series (3)
It's a funny game
Johnston, Brian
Funny game series (2)
It's a knock-up
Grape, Oliver
Grape family series (2)
It's a vet life
Duncan, Alex
Vet series (1)
It's about time, Jesse Bear, and other rhymes
Carlstrom, Nancy White
Jesse Bear series (3)
It's alive!
Woodley, Richard
It's alive series (1)
It's all in the playing
MacLaine, Shirley
You can get there series (4)
It's always Eve that weeps
Janson, Hank
Hank Janson series (31)
It's America for me
Martin, Bill
Freedom series (7)
It's another baby
Matterson, Neil
Baby series (2)
It's bedtime, baby!
Janson, Hank
Hank Janson series (180)
It's been a lot of fun
Johnston, Brian
Funny game series (1)
It's called Midnight Surrender, Herman
Unger, Jim
Herman series (15)
It's Christmas
Prelutsky, Jack
It's a holiday series (2)
It's circus time, Dear Dragon
Hillert, Margaret
Dear Dragon series (8)
It's death, my darling
Long, Amelia Reynolds
Peter Piper series (6)
It's different in July
Fitzgerald, Kevin
Bernard Feston series (2)
It's Doctor Zed's zany brilliant book of science experiments
Penrose, Gordon
Doctor Zed series (1)
It's easy to have a ladybird to stay
Goldsmith, John
It's easy to have series (1)
It's easy to have a wood-lice to stay
Goldsmith, John
It's easy to have series (2)
It's easy to have ants to stay
Goldsmith, John
It's easy to have series (3)
It's fun to be five
Beccaria, Mijo
Birthday series (5)
It's fun to be four
Beccaria, Mijo
Birthday series (4)
It's fun to be one
Beccaria, Mijo
Birthday series (1)
It's fun to be three
Beccaria, Mijo
Birthday series (3)
It's fun to be two
Beccaria, Mijo
Birthday series (2)
It's getting harder all the time
Conway, Troy
Coxeman series (5)
It's Halloween
Prelutsky, Jack
It's a holiday series (1)
It's Halloween time, Dear Dragon
Hillert, Margaret
Dear Dragon series (4)
It's hell to be a ranger
Cameron, Caddo
Private Badger Coe and Sergeant Blizzard Wilson series (1)
It's her funeral
Christmas, Joyce
Lady Margaret Priam series (6)
It's her own funeral
Carnac, Carol
Inspector Julian Rivers series (7)
It's here
Wallace, John
Conrad Franks series (2)
It's in the bag
Spiller, Andrew
Chief Inspector Duck Mallard series (20)
It's later than you think
Kaye, Mary Margaret
Death series (4)
It's me again
Jack, Donald
Journals of Bartholomew Bandy series (3)
It's me, Eddie
Limonov, Edward
Eddie Limonov series (2)
It's me, Hippo!
Thaler, Mike
Hippo series (1)
It's me, Jennifer
Sorenson, Jane
Jennifer series (1)
It's murder, Maguire
Himmel, Richard
Johnny Maguire series (1)
It's murder, McHugh
Flynn, Jay
McHugh series (4)
It's murder, Mister Potter
Foley, Rae
Hiram Potter series (6)
It's murder, Senorita
Bateson, David
Larry Vernon series (1)
It's murder to live
Radford, Edwin
Doctor Manson series (5)
It's murder with Dover
Porter, Joyce
Chief Inspector Wilfred Dover series (7)
It's my funeral
Rabe, Peter
Daniel Port series (2)
It's my life
Leeson, Robert
Jan series (1)
It's my nerves, doctor
Delaney, Joyce
No starch in my coat series (4)
It's my turn
Quin-Harkin, Janet
Sugar and spice series (14)
It's not easy being George
Smith, Janice Lea
Adam Joshua series (5)
It's not fair
Flynn, Rachel
Koala Hills Primary Hills series (2)
It's not how long you make it
Conway, Troy
Coxeman series (25)
It's only the sister
Du Maurier, Angela
Sister series (1)
It's raining violence
Du Bois, Theodora
Anne and Jeffrey McNeill series (16)
It's rather fight than swish
Conway, Troy
Coxeman series (15)
It's snowing, Little Rabbit
Wabbes, Marie
Little Rabbit series (2)
It's spring, Peterkin
Boon, Emilie
Peterkin series (3)
It's Sunday, Ginger Meggs
Kemsley, James
Ginger Meggs series (36)
It's Thanksgiving
Prelutsky, Jack
It's a holiday series (3)
It's the bear!
Alborough, Jez
Bear hugs series (2)
It's too late now
Milne, Alan Alexander
Very young series (2)
It's Valentine's Day
Prelutsky, Jack
It's a holiday series (4)
It's what's up front that counts
Conway, Troy
Coxeman series (11)
It's your funeral
O'Hara, Kevin
Chico Brett series (16)
It's your move, Jennifer
Sorenson, Jane
Jennifer series (2)
It's your team
Aaseng, Nathan
You are the coach series (7)
You are the coach series (8)
It's your turn, Roger
Gretz, Susanna
Roger series (1)
Ivanhoe gambit
Hawke, Simon
Timewars series (1)
Ivanhoe Keeler
Stong, Philip
Ivanhoe Keeler series (2)
I've lived another year
Baume, Eric
I lived series (2)
I've lived like a lord
Ward, Edward
Number one boy series (2)
I've met some bloody wags!
Thorne, Sandy
Queensland series (1)
Ivor the engine
Postgate, Oliver
Ivor the engine series (1)
Ivor's birthday
Postgate, Oliver
Ivor the engine series (6)
Ivory
Aldyne, Nathan
Dan Valentine and Clarissa Lovelace series (4)
Ivory and apes
Nepean, Evelyn Maud
Charles II trilogy (2)
Ivory child
Haggard, Henry Rider
Allan Quatermain series (11)
Holy flower trilogy (2)
Ivory dagger
Wentworth, Patricia
Miss Maud Silver series (21)
Ivory grin
Macdonald, Ross
Lew Archer series (4)
Ivory ladies
Holt, Gavin
Sherret York series (2)
Ivory lyre
Murphy, Shirley Rousseau
Dragonbards trilogy (2)
Ivory screen
Teed, George Hamilton
Sexton Blake series (263)
Ivory snuff box
Fredericks, Arnold
Richard Duvall series (1)
Ivory trail
Mundy, Talbot
Ivory trail series (1)
Ivory tusk
Hardinge, Rex
Sexton Blake series (760)
Ivory valley
Hyne, Charles John Cutcliffe
Captain Owen Kettle series (18)
Ivy Cottage
Taylor, E J
Biscuits, buttons and pickles series (1)
Ivy when young
Spurling, Hilary
Ivy Compton-Burnett series (1)

J

J A Whitford and the great California gold hunt
Roderus, Frank
J Aubrey Whitford series (1)
J Alfred Prufrock murders
Sawyer, Corinne Holt
Senior citizens series (1)
J D Polson and the Dillogate affair
Bond, Michael
J D Polson series (2)
J D Polson and the Liberty Head dime
Bond, Michael
J D Polson series (1)
J D Polson of the great unveiling
Bond, Michael
J D Polson series (3)
J for Jennie murders
Plummer, Thomas Arthur
Detective Inspector Andrew Frampton series (24)
J is for judgment
Grafton, Sue
Kinsey Millhone series (10)
J.O.Jones and how he earned his living
Bell, Robert Stanly Warren
Greyhouse series (6)
J.T.'s ladies
Edson, John Thomas
J.T.'s ladies series (1)
J.T.'s ladies ride again
Edson, John Thomas
J.T.'s ladies series (3)
Jack among the Indians
Grinnell, George Bird
Jack Danvers series (2)
Jack and I in Lotus Land
Little, Frances
Lady of the decoration series (4)
Jack and Susan in 1913
McDowell, Michael
Jack Beaumont and Susan Bright series (1)
Jack and Susan in 1933
McDowell, Michael
Jack Beaumont and Susan Bright series (2)
Jack and Susan in 1953
McDowell, Michael
Jack Beaumont and Susan Bright series (3)
Jack and the bean tree
Haley, Gail Einhart
Jack series (1)
Jack and the beanstalk
McBain, Ed
Matthew Hope series (4)
Jack and the combine
Maisner, Heather
Tractors of Thomson's Yard series (1)
Jack and the fire dragon
Haley, Gail Einhart
Jack series (2)
Jack Anderson against Doctor Tek!
Rheingold, Howard
Savage report series (1)
Jack Brown in China
Strang, Herbert
Russo-Japanese War series (2)
Jack Brown, the hero
Strang, Herbert
Russo-Japanese War series (2)

Jack Carter and the law
Lewis, Ted
Jack Carter series (2)
Jack Carter and the Mafia pigeon
Lewis, Ted
Jack Carter series (3)
Jack Carter's law
Lewis, Ted
Jack Carter series (2)
Jack Flax
Partridge, Jenny
Oakapple Wood series (11)
Jack Hall
Grant, Robert
Jack Hall series (1)
Jack Harding's quest
Duff, Douglas Valder
Jack Harding series (4)
Jack Harvey's adventures
Smith, Ruel Perley
Rival campers series (4)
Jack Hazard and his fortunes
Trowbridge, John Townsend
Jack Hazard series (1)
Jack Hildreth on the Nile
May, Karl Friedrich
Winnetou trilogy (3)
Jack-in-the-box
Connington, John Jervis
Sir Clinton Driffield series (16)
Jack in the bush
Grant, Robert
Jack Hall series (2)
Jack in the jungle
Barnum, Phineas Taylor
Lion Jack series (2)
Jack in the Rockies
Grinnell, George Bird
Jack Danvers series (3)
Jack Lane's Browning
Gethin, David
Halloran series (1)
Jack Lorimer, freshman
Standish, Winn
Captain Jack Lorimer series (5)
Jack Lorimer's champions
Standish, Winn
Captain Jack Lorimer series (2)
Jack Lorimer's holidays
Standish, Winn
Captain Jack Lorimer series (3)
Jack Lorimer's substitute
Standish, Winn
Captain Jack Lorimer series (4)
Jack Mercybright
Pearce, Mary Emily
Apple tree series (2)
Jack Midwood
Ellis, Edward Sylvester
Through on time series (1)
Jack North's treasure hunt
Rockwood, Roy
Deep sea series (4)
Jack o' Lantern for Judy Jo
Hill, Mabel Betsy
Judy Jo series (4)
Jack of diamonds
Longtree, Warren T
Ruff Justice series (25)
Jack of Hearts
Von Elsner, Don
Jake Winkman series (3)
Jack of swords
Tubb, Edwin Charles
Dumarest series (14)
Jack on the gallows tree
Bruce, Leo
Carolus Deene series (7)
Jack, one of us
Frankau, Gilbert
One of us series (1)
Jack Pumpkinhead
Baum, Lyman Frank
Snuggle tales series (6)
Jack Pumpkinhead and the sawhorse
Baum, Lyman Frank
Little Wizard series (1)
Jack Pumpkinhead of Oz
Thompson, Ruth Plumly
Oz series (22)
Jack Ranger's gun club
Young, Clarence
Jack Ranger series (5)
Jack Ranger's ocean cruise
Young, Clarence
Jack Ranger series (4)
Jack Ranger's school victories
Young, Clarence
Jack Ranger series (3)
Jack Ranger's schooldays
Young, Clarence
Jack Ranger series (1)
Jack Ranger's treasure box
Young, Clarence
Jack Ranger series (6)
Jack Ranger's western trip
Young, Clarence
Jack Ranger series (2)
Jack Rann
Huet, M M
Jack Rann series (1)
Jack Rann's life and adventures
Huet, M M
Jack Rann series (1)
Jack Sharp in Florida
Travers, J M
Jack Sharp series (2)
Jack Sharp, keenest detective in Gotham
Travers, J M
Jack Sharp series (1)
Jack Spot
Janson, Hank
Hank Janson series (86)
Jack Straw in Mexico
Crump, James Irving
Jack Straw series (1)
Jack Straw, lighthouse builder
Crump, James Irving
Jack Straw series (2)
Jack Tars and commodores
Fowler, William Morgan
American Navy series (2)
Jack the bodiless
May, Julian
Jack the bodiless series (1)
Jack, the clumsy sweeper, and other stories for children
Leslie, Madeline
Play and study series (3)
Jack the dog
Lloyd, David
Great escapes series (1)
Jack, the giant-killer
De Lint, Charles
Jack, the giant-killer series (1)
Jack the outlaw
Snowden, James Keighley
King Jack series (2)
Jack, the young canoeman
Grinnell, George Bird
Jack Danvers series (4)
Jack, the young cowboy
Grinnell, George Bird
Jack Danvers series (7)
Jack, the young explorer
Grinnell, George Bird
Jack Danvers series (6)
Jack, the young ranchman
Grinnell, George Bird
Jack Danvers series (1)
Jack, the young trapper
Grinnell, George Bird
Jack Danvers series (5)
Jackal Helix
Basile, Gloria Vitanza
Global 2000 series (2)
Jackals of the sea
Catherall, Arthur
Bulldog tugboat series (2)
Jackanapes jacket
Keate, Edith Murray
Superintendent Margetson series (2)
Jackdaw
Hendry, Frances Mary
Kelpies series (6)
Quest for a queen series (3)
Jacket I wear in the snow
Neitzel, Shirley
My clothes series (1)
Jackie and the misfit pony
Berrisford, Judith Mary
Jackie and Babs series (8)
Jackie and the phantom ponies
Berrisford, Judith Mary
Jackie and Babs series (11)
Jackie and the pony boys
Berrisford, Judith Mary
Jackie and Babs series (6)
Jackie and the pony thieves
Berrisford, Judith Mary
Jackie and Babs series (10)
Jackie and the pony trekkers
Berrisford, Judith Mary
Jackie and Babs series (4)
Jackie on Pony Island
Berrisford, Judith Mary
Jackie and Babs series (9)
Jackie won a pony
Berrisford, Judith Mary
Jackie and Babs series (1)
Jackie's pony camp summer
Berrisford, Judith Mary
Jackie and Babs series (5)
Jackie's pony patrol
Berrisford, Judith Mary
Jackie and Babs series (3)
Jacko
Goodall, John Strickland
Paddy Pork series (4)
Thomson, Pat
Jets series (1)
Jackpot
Pronzini, Bill
Private Eye series (18)
Jack's return home
Lewis, Ted
Jack Carter series (1)
Jack's ward
Alger, Horatio
Brave and bold series (2)
Jackson and the magpies
Ball, Brian Neville
Jackson series (4)
Jackson Hole trouble
Logan, Jake
John Slocum series (51)
Jackson's England
Rigby, Ray
Private Johnny Jackson series (3)
Jackson's friend
Ball, Brian Neville
Jackson series (2)
Jackson's holiday
Ball, Brian Neville
Jackson series (3)
Jackson's house
Ball, Brian Neville
Jackson series (1)
Jackson's peace
Rigby, Ray
Private Johnny Jackson series (2)
Jackson's war
Rigby, Ray
Private Johnny Jackson series (1)
Jacob and Joachim
Clevin, Jorgen
Jacob and Joachim series (1)
Jacob and Joachim on holiday
Clevin, Jorgen
Jacob and Joachim series (3)
Jacob and Joachim's rescue service
Clevin, Jorgen
Jacob and Joachim series (2)
Jacob Street mystery
Freeman, Richard Austin
Doctor John Evelyn Thorndyke series (27)
Jacob Two-Two and the dinosaur
Richler, Mordecai
Jacob Two-Two series (2)
Jacob Two-Two meets the hooded fang
Richler, Mordecai
Jacob Two-Two series (1)
Jacobean adventure
Bell, Josephine
Jacobean trilogy (1)
Jacobite trilogy
Broster, Dorothy Kathleen
Jacobite trilogy (3)
Jacob's road
Jordan, Matt
Tyler brothers series (2)
Jacoby's Corners
Falstaff, Jack
Jacoby's Corners trilogy (1)
Jacoby's first case
Smith, J C S
Quentin Jacoby series (1)
Jacqueline rides for a fall
Smythe, Pat
Three Jays series (1)
Jacquelyn
Gordon, Jeffie Ross
Sunfire series (12)
Jade
Barr, Pat
Alice Greenwood series (2)
Jade Darcy and the affair of honor
Goldin, Stephen
Rehumanization of Jade Darcy series (1)
Jade Darcy and the Zen pirates
Goldin, Stephen
Rehumanization of Jade Darcy series (2)
Jade demons quartet
Vardeman, Robert Edward
Jade demons quartet (4)
Jade dragon
Grant, Maxwell
Shadow series (222)
Jade eye
Ingersol, Jared
Carl Moore series (1)
Jade-eyed jinx
Brown, Carter
Rick Holman series (6)
Jade-eyed jungle
Brown, Carter
Rick Holman series (6)
Jade figurine
Foxx, Jack
Dan Connell series (1)
Jade for a lady
Chaber, M E
Milo March series (10)
Jade gate
Leasor, James
Far East series (4)
Jade green Cadillac
Clewes, Dorothy
Hadley family series (4)
Jade green judy
Enefer, Douglas
Sam Bawtrey series (8)
Jade hatpin
Kiddy, Maurice George
Stonewall Steevens series (3)
Jade in Aries
Coe, Tucker
Mitchell Tobin series (4)
Jade man's eyes
Moorcock, Michael
Elric series (6)
Jade moon
Fitzgerald, Julia
Astromance series (6)
Jade star
Coulter, Catherine
Star trilogy (3)
Jade Venus
Coxe, George Harmon
Kent Murdock series (8)
Jade warrior
Lord, Jeffrey
Richard Blade series (2)
Jade wind
Harris, John
Ira Penaluna trilogy (2)
Jade woman
Gash, Jonathan
Lovejoy series (12)
Jaen
Burton, Betty
Nugent family series (2)
Jafta
Lewin, Hugh
Jafta series (1)
Jafta and his mother
Lewin, Hugh
Jafta series (3)
Jafta and the wedding
Lewin, Hugh
Jafta series (4)
Jafta's father
Lewin, Hugh
Jafta series (2)
Jafta's mother
Lewin, Hugh
Jafta series (3)
Jagged Steele
Masters, J D
Steele series (4)
Jago
Peel, Hazel Mary
Ann and Jim Henderson series (5)
Jago series (1)
Jagua Nana
Ekwensi, Cyprian
Jagua Nana series (1)
Jagua Nana's daughter
Ekwensi, Cyprian
Jagua Nana series (2)
Jaguar!
Simon, Morris
Amazing stories series (2)
Jahdu
Hamilton, Virginia
Jahdu series (3)
Jail bait
Chambers, Peter
Mark Preston series (31)
Jailbreak moon
Logan, Jake
John Slocum series (83)
Jakarta coup
Roberts, Mark Kelly
Soldier for hire series (8)
Jake
Smith, Naomi Royde
Richard Lingard series (1)
Jake and the Kid
Mitchell, William Ormond
Jake and the Kid series (1)
Jake of diamonds
Von Elsner, Don
Jake Winkman series (1)
Jalna
De la Roche, Mazo
Whiteoak series (7)
Jamaica and Brianna
Havill, Juanita
Jamaica series (3)
Jamaica Tag-Along
Havill, Juanita
Jamaica series (2)
Jamaican exchange
Carter, Nick
Nick Carter series (127)
Jamaica's find
Havill, Juanita
Jamaica series (1)
Jamberoo Road
Spence, Eleanor
Arabella Braithwaite series (2)
James
Kathryn
James series (1)
James and Lucy
Kathryn
James series (3)
James and Susan at the seaside
Jones, Joan Clement
James and Susan series (2)
James and Susan in the country
Jones, Joan Clement
James and Susan series (1)
James and the black van
Clarke, Pauline
James series (4)
James and the diesel engines
Awdry, Christopher
Railway series (28)
James and the hat
Kathryn
James series (2)
James and the policeman
Clarke, Pauline
James series (1)
James and the robbers
Clarke, Pauline
James series (2)
James and the smugglers
Clarke, Pauline
James series (3)
James Bear and the goose gathering
Latimer, Jim
James Bear series (2)
James Bear's pie
Latimer, Jim
James Bear series (1)
James Bond
Pearson, John
James Bond series (30)
James Bond and the Moonraker
Wood, Christopher
James Bond series (17)
James Bond in Barracuda run
Otfinoski, Steven
James Bond find your fate series (4)
James Bond in Programmed for danger
Favors, Jean M
James Bond find your fate series (3)
James Bond in Strike it deadly
Siegel, Barbara
James Bond find your fate series (2)
James Bond in Win, place or die
Stine, Robert Lawrence
James Bond find your fate series (1)
James Bond, the spy who loved me
Wood, Christopher
James Bond series (16)
James, by the grace of God
Tranter, Nigel Godwin
James V trilogy (2)
James Joyce murder
Cross, Amanda
Professor Kate Fansler series (2)
James Knowland, deceased
Carmichael, Harry
John Piper and Quinn series (13)
James Tarrant, adventurer
Crofts, Freeman Wills
Inspector Joseph French series (21)
James, the red engine
Awdry, Wilbert
Railway series (3)
James without Thomas
Avery, Gillian
Smith family series (3)
Jamesie
Sidgwick, Ethel
Wickford series (2)

Jamestown
Barren, Charles
Stemson family series (2)
Jamie
Denton, John
Jamie series (1)
Jamie and Jock's present
Denton, John
Jamie series (2)
Jamie in Clachan
Armstrong, Sybil
Clachan series (5)
Jamie the Red
Dickson, Gordon Rupert
Sanctuary series (12)
Jamie's discovery
Roland, Betty
Jamie series (2)
Jamie's other grandmother
Roland, Betty
Jamie series (4)
Jamie's summer visitor
Roland, Betty
Jamie series (3)
Jampot Smith
Brooks, Jeremy
Bernard Smith series (1)
Jan alone
Leeson, Robert
Jan series (2)
Jan Cremer 2
Cremer, Jan
Jan Cremer series (2)
Jan flies down under
Carter, Dorothy
Jan series (2)
Jan in India
Kline, Otis Adelbert
Jan series (2)
Jan of the Fourth
Chaundler, Christine
Fourth Form series (4)
Jan of the jungle
Kline, Otis Adelbert
Jan series (1)
Jan Perry stories
Sedgwick, Modwena
Jan Perry series (1)
Jan, son of Finn
Dawson, Alec John
Finn series (2)
Jan the market boy
Cockett, Mary
Jan series (1)
Jan Vedder's wife
Barr, Amelia Edith
Shetland series (1)
Jancy in pursuit
Bracken, Anne
Jancy series (3)
Jancy scores again
Bracken, Anne
Jancy series (2)
Jancy stands alone
Bracken, Anne
Jancy series (4)
Jancy wins through
Bracken, Anne
Jancy series (1)
Jandar of Callisto
Carter, Lin
Jandar the Alien series (1)
Jandy Mac comes back
Oxenham, Elsie J
Abbey girls second generation series (1)
Jane Allen, center
Bancroft, Edith
Jane Allen series (3)
Jane Allen, junior
Bancroft, Edith
Jane Allen series (4)
Jane Allen of the sub-team
Bancroft, Edith
Jane Allen series (1)
Jane Allen, right guard
Bancroft, Edith
Jane Allen series (2)
Jane Allen, senior
Bancroft, Edith
Jane Allen series (5)
Jane and the Chalet School
Brent-Dyer, Elinor Mary
Chalet School series (51)
Jane and the owl
Stone, Gene
Jane series (1)
Jane and the pale faces
Barclay, Vera Charlesworth
Jane series (4)
Jane and toby start school
Thwaite, Ann
Jane and Toby series (4)
Jane and Tommy Tomkins
Barclay, Vera Charlesworth
Jane series (3)
Jane at war
Price, Evadne
Jane series (10)
Jane Carberry and the laughing fountain
Symons, Beryl
Jane Carberry series (4)
Jane Carberry, detective
Symons, Beryl
Jane Carberry series (1)
Jane Carberry investigates
Symons, Beryl
Jane Carberry series (2)
Jane Carberry's week-end
Symons, Beryl
Jane Carberry series (5)
Jane Eyre
Bronte, Charlotte
Rochester series (2)
Jane Fairfax
Aiken, Joan
Miss Jane Fairfax series (3)
Jane gets busy
Price, Evadne
Jane series (9)
Jane leaves the Wells
Hill, Lorna
Sadler's Wells series (5)
Jane Martin and the case of the icecream dog
Bunting, Eve
Jane Martin series (2)
Jane Martin, dog detective
Bunting, Eve
Jane Martin series (1)
Jane of Gowlands
Hepple, Anne
Gow family series (2)
Jane Scott
Gaye, Carol
Jane Scott series (1)
Jane Scott again
Gaye, Carol
Jane Scott series (2)
Jane Scott, crime reporter
Gaye, Carol
Jane Scott series (6)
Jane Scott married
Gaye, Carol
Jane Scott series (4)
Jane Scott meets the doctor
Gaye, Carol
Jane Scott series (3)
Jane Scott meets the Pops
Gaye, Carol
Jane Scott series (5)
Jane Stuart at Rivercroft
Remick, Grace May
Jane Stuart series (3)
Jane Stuart, comrade
Remick, Grace May
Jane Stuart series (4)
Jane Stuart, twin
Remick, Grace May
Jane Stuart series (1)
Jane Stuart's chum
Remick, Grace May
Jane Stuart series (2)
Jane, the courageous
Kimbrough, Katheryn
Phenwick women series (2)
Jane the fourth
Price, Evadne
Jane series (4)
Jane the patient
Price, Evadne
Jane series (8)
Jane the popular
Price, Evadne
Jane series (6)
Jane the sleuth
Price, Evadne
Jane series (7)
Jane the unlucky
Price, Evadne
Jane series (5)
Jane versus Jonathan
Barclay, Vera Charlesworth
Jane series (2)
Jane, will you behave
Barclay, Vera Charlesworth
Jane series (1)
Jane with green eyes
Janson, Hank
Hank Janson series (22)
Janell
Jenkins, Jerry Bruce
Margo Franklin and Philip Spence series (10)
Jane's adventures in a balloon
Gathorne-Hardy, Jonathan
Jane Charrington series (3)
Jane's adventures in and out of the book
Gathorne-Hardy, Jonathan
Jane Charrington series (1)
Jane's adventures on the Island of Peeg
Gathorne-Hardy, Jonathan
Jane Charrington series (2)
Jane's amazing woolly jumper
Hindley, Judy
Best of friends series (4)
Janet
Benson, Edward Frederic
Old London series (2)
Janet, a stock-farm scout
Roy, Lillian Elizabeth
Girl Scouts trilogy (3)
Janet, a twin
Whitehill, Dorothy
Janet and Phyllis series (1)
Janet at odds
Ray, Anna Chapin
Sidney and Janet series (5)
Janet, her winter in Quebec
Ray, Anna Chapin
Sidney and Janet series (2)
Janet Lennon and the angels
Meyers, Barlow
Janet Lennon series (1)
Janet Lennon at Camp Calamity
Meyers, Barlow
Janet Lennon series (3)
Janet Reachfar and Chickabird
Duncan, Jane
Janet Reachfar series (3)
Janet Reachfar and the kelpie
Duncan, Jane
Janet Reachfar series (2)
Janey
Pearl, Irene
Janey series (1)
Janey and her friends
Pearl, Irene
Janey series (2)
Jangada, part 1
Verne, Jules
Giant raft series (1)
Jangada, part 2
Verne, Jules
Giant raft series (2)
Jangle twang
Burningham, John
First words series (6)
Janice Day at Poketown
Long, Helen Beecher
Do something series (1)
Janice Day, the young homemaker
Long, Helen Beecher
Do something series (5)
Janie B Jones and her big fat mouth
Park, Barbara
Janie B Jones series (3)
Janie B Jones and some sneaky spying
Park, Barbara
Janie B Jones series (4)
Janie B Jones and the little monkey business
Park, Barbara
Janie B Jones series (2)
Janie B Jones and the stupid smelly bus
Park, Barbara
Janie B Jones series (1)
Janie of La Rochelle
Brent-Dyer, Elinor Mary
La Rochelle series (5)
Janie steps in
Brent-Dyer, Elinor Mary
La Rochelle series (6)
Janie's private eyes
Snyder, Zilpha Keatley
Stanley family series (4)
Janine and the carnival
Thomas, Iolette
Janine series (2)
Janine and the new baby
Thomas, Iolette
Janine series (1)
Janisseries
Pournelle, Jerry
Janisseries trilogy (1)
Jannot
Marokvia, Mireille
Ann and Paul series (1)
Jan's birthday
Roggeveen, Leonard
Jan series (2)
Jan's flying start
Carter, Dorothy
Jan series (1)
Jan's treasure
Pilkington, Roger
Branxome family series (1)
Janson, go home
Janson, Hank
Hank Janson series (107)
January platoon
Randle, Kevin
Jefferson's war series (4)
January Zone
Corris, Peter
Cliff Hardy series (11)
Janus man
Forbes, Colin
Tweed, Grey and Newman series (4)
Janus murder case
Wilson, Colin
Chief Inspector Gregory Saltfleet series (2)
Japan, how do hands make peace?
Meyer, Carolyn
Earth inspectors series (10)
Japanese corpse
Van de Wetering, Janwillem
De Gier and Grijpstra series (5)
Japanese high seas fleet
Humble, Richard
High seas fleet series (2)
Japanese job
Corris, Peter
Pokerface series (6)
Japanese marriage
Sladen, Douglas
Japanese marriage series (1)
Japanese Ronin
Stewart, William Thomas
Gaff Lee series (3)
Japanese twins
Perkins, Lucy Fitch
Twin series (2)
Japhet and Company, including Happy
Horrabin, James Francis
Noah family series (8)
Japhet and Company on Arkub Island
Horrabin, James Francis
Noah family series (11)
Japhet and Fido
Horrabin, James Francis
Noah family series (3)
Japhet and Happy annual
Horrabin, James Francis
Noah family series (11)
Japhet and Happy book
Horrabin, James Francis
Noah family series (11)
Japhet and Happy painting book
Horrabin, James Francis
Noah family series (11)
Japhet and the Arkubs at sea
Horrabin, James Francis
Noah family series (10)
Japhet and the Arkubs of the The Ark, Ararat Avenue, S.W.
Horrabin, James Francis
Noah family series (9)
Japhet book
Horrabin, James Francis
Noah family series (6)
Japhet holiday book
Horrabin, James Francis
Noah family series (11)
Jar of dreams
Uchida, Yoshiko
Rinko trilogy (1)
Jargoon pard
Norton, Andre
Arvon series (2)
High Hallack series (4)
Witch World series (9)
Jarrum Creek Gang
Smith, Ford
Dark Knight series (1)
Jarryn's miracle
Davis, Elizabeth Jane
Jarryn series (1)
Jarryn's test
Davis, Elizabeth Jane
Jarryn series (2)
Jason
Marks, James Macdonald
Jason Wright series (1)
Treece, Henry
Greek trilogy (2)
Jason affair
Chance, John Newton
Jason series (1)
Jason and the aliens down the street
Greer, Gery
Jason series (1)
Jason and the escape from Bat Planet
Greer, Gery
Jason series (3)
Jason and the lizard pirates
Greer, Gery
Jason series (2)
Jason and the sleep game
Chance, John Newton
Jason series (2)
Jason Burr's first case
Kent, David
Jason Burr series (1)
Jason Cosmo
McGirt, Dan
Jason Cosmo series (1)
Jason goes west
Chance, John Newton
Jason series (4)
Jason King
Miall, Robert
Jason King series (1)
Jason lives
Hawke, Simon
Friday the thirteenth series (6)
Jason murders
Chance, John Newton
Jason series (3)
Jason, son of Jason
Giesy, John Ulrich
Jason Croft trilogy (3)
Jason's curse
Morse, Eric
Friday the thirteenth series (2)
Jason's first quest
Moore, Roger Elwood
Fantasy forest series (9)
Jasper Club
Cockett, Mary
Jasper Club series (1)
Jaunts and jollities of that renowned sporting citizen, Mr John Jorrocks
Surtees, Robert Smith
Mister John Jorrocks series (1)
Java Sea duel
Catherall, Arthur
Bulldog tugboat series (4)
Java wreckmen
Crisp, Frank
Dirk Rogers series (3)
Javelin
Goscinny, Rene
Twelve tasks of Asterix series (2)
Javelin for Jonah
Mitchell, Gladys
Dame Beatrice Bradley series (47)
Jaws
Benchley, Peter
Jaws series (1)
Jaws 2
Searls, Hank
Jaws series (2)
Jaws log
Gottlieb, Carl
Jaws series (2)
Jaws of darkness
Cross, Mark
Daphne Wrayne and her Four Adjusters series (29)
Jaws of death
Silver, Richard
Captain Shark series (2)
Thayer, Lee
Peter Clancy series (41)
Jaws of the watcdog
Drummond, Ivor
Lady Jennifer, Sandro and Colly series (4)
Jayhawk legacy
Gardner, Jerome
Dripspring series (6)
Jays
Smedley, Elisabeth
Jays series (1)
Jays write a book
Smedley, Elisabeth
Jays series (2)
Jazz and Jasper
Gerhardi, William Alexander
Jazz and Jasper series (1)
Jazz funeral
Smith, Julie
Skip Langdon series (3)
Jazz jungle
Janson, Hank
Hank Janson series (206)
Jealous house
Kelland, Clarence Budington
Hard money trilogy (3)
Jealous lies
Pascal, Francine
Sweet Valley High series (30)

Jealousy pulls the trigger
Corne, Molly E
Mac McIntyre series (3)

Jean and Jeanette
Rita
Victorian series (3)

Jean at Jo's hospital
Swinburne, Doreen
Jean Hunter series (2)

Jean at noon
Sandison, Janet
Apology for the life of Jean Robertson series (2)

Jean behind the counter
Martin, Nancy
Jean Thomas series (1)

Jean Cabot at Ashton
Scott, Gertrude Fisher
Jean Cabot series (1)

Jean Cabot in cap and gown
Scott, Gertrude Fisher
Jean Cabot series (3)

Jean Cabot in the British Isles
Scott, Gertrude Fisher
Jean Cabot series (2)

Jean Cabot in the house with the blue shutters
Scott, Gertrude Fisher
Jean Cabot series (4)

Jean Craig finds romance
Littleton, Kay
Jean Craig series (3)

Jean Craig, graduate nurse
Littleton, Kay
Jean Craig series (5)

Jean Craig grows up
Littleton, Kay
Jean Craig series (1)

Jean Craig in New York
Littleton, Kay
Jean Craig series (2)

Jean Craig, nurse
Littleton, Kay
Jean Craig series (4)

Jean in the morning
Sandison, Janet
Apology for the life of Jean Robertson series (1)

Jean in the twilight
Sandison, Janet
Apology for the life of Jean Robertson series (3)

Jean Mary in Virginia
Lee, Ella
Jean Mary series (2)

Jean Mary solves the mystery
Lee, Ella
Jean Mary series (5)

Jean Mary's adventures
Lee, Ella
Jean Mary series (1)

Jean Mary's romance
Lee, Ella
Jean Mary series (3)

Jean Mary's summer mystery
Lee, Ella
Jean Mary series (4)

Jean of Greenacres
Forrester, Izola Louise
Greenacres series (2)

Jean of the lumber camp
Wynne, May
Jean series (2)

Jean plays her part
Wynne, May
Jean series (1)

Jean, S.R.N.
Swinburne, Doreen
Jean Hunter series (3)

Jean, teenage fashion buyer
Martin, Nancy
Jean Thomas series (2)

Jean tours a hospital
Swinburne, Doreen
Jean Hunter series (1)

Jean towards another day
Sandison, Janet
Apology for the life of Jean Robertson series (4)

Jean Valjean
Hugo, Victor Marie
Fate trilogy (1)

Jeanette in the summer term
Lunt, Alice
Jeanette series (2)

Jeanette's first term
Lunt, Alice
Jeanette series (1)

Jeanne
Colver, Alice Ross
Jeanne series (1)

Jeanne at Rainbow Lodge
Colver, Alice Ross
Jeanne series (4)

Jeanne-Marie at the fair
Francoise
Jeanne-Marie series (4)

Jeanne-Marie counts her sheep
Francoise
Jeanne-Marie series (1)

Jeanne-Marie in gay Paris
Francoise
Jeanne-Marie series (2)

Jeanne's happy year
Colver, Alice Ross
Jeanne series (3)

Jeanne's house
Colver, Alice Ross
Jeanne series (2)

Jean's new junior
Swinburne, Doreen
Jean Hunter series (4)

Jed and Jessie
Connell, Abby
Two by two series (2)

Jed and the space bandits
Marzollo, Jean
Jed series (2)

Jed McLane and Storm Cloud
Honig, Donald
Jed McLane series (2)

Jed McLane and the stranger
Honig, Donald
Jed McLane series (3)

Jed, the poorhouse boy
Alger, Horatio
How to rise trilogy (1)

Jedera adventure
Alexander, Lloyd
Vesper Holly series (4)

Jed's junior space patrol
Marzollo, Jean
Jed series (1)

Jeeves
Wodehouse, Pelham Grenville
Jeeves and Bertie Wooster series (2)

Jeeves, a gentleman's personal gentleman
Parkinson, Cyril Northcote
Jeeves and Bertie Wooster series (15)

Jeeves and the feudal spirit
Wodehouse, Pelham Grenville
Jeeves and Bertie Wooster series (11)

Jeeves and the tie that binds
Wodehouse, Pelham Grenville
Jeeves and Bertie Wooster series (14)

Jeeves in the morning
Wodehouse, Pelham Grenville
Jeeves and Bertie Wooster series (8)

Jeeves in the offing
Wodehouse, Pelham Grenville
Jeeves and Bertie Wooster series (12)

Jeffrey's ghost and the fifth grade dragon
Adler, David A
Jeffrey's ghost series (2)

Jeffrey's ghost and the leftover baseball team
Adler, David A
Jeffrey's ghost series (1)

Jeffrey's ghost and the Ziffel Fair
Adler, David A
Jeffrey's ghost series (3)

Jehad
Yermakov, Nicholas
Last communion trilogy (3)

Jehovah blues
Steen, Marguerite
Flood trilogy (3)

Jehovahs' jailbreak
Tully, Paul
Deputy Marshal Hooky Gibbs series (2)

Jekyll, alias Hyde
Thomas, Donald
Inspector Swain series (3)

Jekyll legacy
Bloch, Robert
Doctor Jekyll series (2)

Jelly bean scheme
Blair, Cynthia
Susan and Christine Pratt series (10)

Jemima Puddle-Duck's painting book
Potter, Beatrix
Peter Rabbit series (21)

Jemima Shore at the sunny grave, and other stories
Fraser, Antonia
Jemima Shore series (8)

Jemima Shore's first case, and other stories
Fraser, Antonia
Jemima Shore series (8)

Jen of the Abbey School
Oxenham, Elsie J
Abbey girls first generation series (9)

Jenghiz-Khan
Yan, Vasiliy Grigorievich
Mongol series (1)

Jenner guns
Hogan, Ray
Shawn Starbuck series (16)

Jennie
Gallico, Paul
Jennie series (1)
Miner, Jane Claypool
Sunfire series (31)

Jennie about to be
Ogilvie, Elisabeth May
Jennie Hawthorne series (1)

Jennifer
Helwig, David
Kingston tetralogy (2)

Jennifer dances
Smith, Eunice Young
Jennifer Hill series (5)

Jennifer follows a clue
Buckeridge, Anthony
Jennings series (2)

Jennifer gift
Smith, Eunice Young
Jennifer Hill series (2)

Jennifer goes to school
Denes, Gee
John and Jennifer series (1)

Jennifer is eleven
Smith, Eunice Young
Jennifer Hill series (4)

Jennifer Knowall
Dennison, Dorothy
Wantoknow series for girls (3)

Jennifer Murdley's toad
Coville, Bruce
Elvie's magic shop series (2)

Jennifer prize
Smith, Eunice Young
Jennifer Hill series (3)

Jennifer says goodbye
Sorenson, Jane
Jennifer series (4)

Jennifer stands by
Lister, Gladys
Jennifer series (1)

Jennifer wish
Smith, Eunice Young
Jennifer Hill series (1)

Jennifer's new life
Sorenson, Jane
Jennifer series (3)

Jennifer's secret
Baer, Judy
Cedar River daydreams series (3)

Jennings abounding
Buckeridge, Anthony
Jennings series (17)
Jennings series (23)

Jennings and Darbishire
Buckeridge, Anthony
Jennings series (4)

Jennings, as usual
Buckeridge, Anthony
Jennings series (10)

Jennings at large
Buckeridge, Anthony
Jennings series (23)

Jennings' diary
Buckeridge, Anthony
Jennings series (5)

Jennings goes to school
Buckeridge, Anthony
Jennings series (1)

Jennings in particular
Buckeridge, Anthony
Jennings series (18)

Jennings' little hut
Buckeridge, Anthony
Jennings series (3)

Jennings, of course!
Buckeridge, Anthony
Jennings series (14)

Jennings report
Buckeridge, Anthony
Jennings series (20)

Jenny
Strange, Nora Kathleen
Kenya series (7)

Jenny and Jupie
Fujikawa, Gyo
Jenny series (2)

Jenny and Jupie to the rescue
Fujikawa, Gyo
Jenny series (3)

Jenny and Steve
Wensell, Ulises
Jackson family series (1)

Jenny and the bantam hen
Jones, Olive
Barfield series (2)

Jenny and the Cat Club
Averill, Esther
Jenny Linsky series (13)

Jenny and the new girls
Martyn, Harriet
Balcombe Hall series (4)

Jenny and the new headmistress
Martyn, Harriet
Balcombe Hall series (3)

Jenny and the sheep thieves
Gifford, Griselda
Jenny and Mirabelle series (1)

Jenny and the sphinx
Martyn, Harriet
Balcombe Hall series (2)

Jenny and the syndicate
Martyn, Harriet
Balcombe Hall series (1)

Jenny and Tito
Merriam, Lillie Fuller
Jenny series (2)

Jenny Archer, author
Conford, Ellen
Jenny Archer series (3)

Jenny Archer to the rescue
Conford, Ellen
Jenny Archer series (5)

Jenny Bell
Fitzgerald, Percy
Jenny Bell trilogy (2)

Jenny goes to sea
Averill, Esther
Jenny Linsky series (10)

Jenny Haller
Hughes, Dean
Haller series (2)

Jenny Heysten's career
Ammers-Kuller, Jo van
Jenny Heysten series (2)

Jenny learns a lesson
Fujikawa, Gyo
Jenny series (1)

Jenny lives in Barfield
Jones, Olive
Barfield series (12)

Jenny of the Fourth
Moss, Roberta
Jenny series (1)

Jenny Rorke
Hine, Muriel
Jenny Rorke series (2)

Jenny the giraffe
Beaman, Sydney George Hulme
Out of the ark series (6)

Jenny Wren
Young, Emily Hilda
Jenny Wren series (1)

Jenny's adopted brothers
Averill, Esther
Jenny Linsky series (7)

Jenny's bedside book
Averill, Esther
Jenny Linsky series (11)

Jenny's bird house
Merriam, Lillie Fuller
Jenny series (1)

Jenny's birthday book
Averill, Esther
Jenny Linsky series (9)

Jenny's exciting term
Moss, Roberta
Jenny series (2)

Jenny's first party
Averill, Esther
Jenny Linsky series (4)

Jenny's moonlight adventure
Averill, Esther
Jenny Linsky series (5)

Jenny's one and only cat
Jones, Olive
Barfield series (1)

Jeopardy
Preston, Fayrene
Swansea Place series (4)

Jeopardy is my job
Marlowe, Stephen
Chester Drum series (14)

Jeremiah and Mrs Ming
Jennings, Sharon
Jeremiah and Mrs Ming series (1)

Jeremy
Walpole, Hugh
Jeremy trilogy (1)

Jeremy and Hamlet
Walpole, Hugh
Jeremy trilogy (2)

Jeremy at Crale
Walpole, Hugh
Jeremy trilogy (3)

Jeremy at the circus
Theulet-Luzie, Bernadette
Jeremy series (2)

Jeremy Bear
Van Stockum, Hilda
Jeremy Bear series (1)

Jeremy Fisher's painting book
Potter, Beatrix
Peter Rabbit series (21)

Jeremy in town
Theulet-Luzie, Bernadette
Jeremy series (1)

Jeremy Mouse
Althea
Jeremy Mouse series (1)

Jeremy Mouse and cat
Althea
Jeremy Mouse series (2)

Jeremy Mouse was hungry
Althea
Jeremy Mouse series (3)

Jeremy Poldark
Graham, Winston
Poldark series (3)

Jeremy Smith in trouble
Smee, Donald
Jeremy Smith series (3)

Jeremy Smith investigates
Smee, Donald
Jeremy Smith series (2)

Jeremy Smith shows the way
Smee, Donald
Jeremy Smith series (4)

Jeremy Smith to the rescue
Smee, Donald
Jeremy Smith series (1)

Jeremy Thatcher, dragon hatcher
Coville, Bruce
Elvie's magic shop series (1)

Jeremy's version
Purdy, James
Sleepers in moon-crowned valleys series (1)

Jericho mosaic
Whittemore, Edward
Jerusalem quartet (4)

Jericho's daughters
Wellman, Paul Iselin
Jericho series (3)

Jericho's scam
Raymond, John
Dempsey and Makepeace series (5)

Jerks-in-training
Stine, Robert Lawrence
Space cadets series (1)

Jerry
Aimwell, Walter
Boy series (7)

Jerry and Joe
Beaman, Sydney George Hulme
Toytown series (2)

Jerry and the inventions
Saddler, Allen
Jerry series (2)

Jerry and the monsters
Saddler, Allen
Jerry series (1)

Jerry finds ants
Darby, Joan
Jerry series (1)

Jerry finds bees
Darby, Joan
Jerry series (2)

Jerry finds spiders
Darby, Joan
Jerry series (3)

Jerry Muskrat at home
Burgess, Thornton Waldo
Smiling Pool series (3)

Jerry of the islands
London, Jack
Jerry series (1)

Jerry the backwoods boy
Alger, Horatio
Rise in life series (5)

Jersey adventure
Bayley, Viola
Adventure series (12)

Jersey bounce
Chase, Glen
Cherry Delight series (9)

Jersey guns
Pendleton, Don
Mack Bolan series (17)
Jerusalem
Lagerlof, Selma
Jerusalem series (1)
Jerusalem file
Carter, Nick
Nick Carter series (95)
Jerusalem history atlas
Gilbert, Martin
History atlas series (7)
Jerusalem illustrated history atlas
Gilbert, Martin
History atlas series (7)
Jerusalem Inn
Grimes, Martha
Inspector Richard Jury series (5)
Jerusalem journey
Prescott, Hilda Frances Margaret
Friar Felix Fabri series (1)
Jerusalem man
Gemmell, David A
Sipstrassi tales series (1)
Jerusalem poker
Whittemore, Edward
Jerusalem quartet (2)
Jess and the fish
Cunliffe, John Arthur
Jess the cat series (1)
Jess goes hunting
Cunliffe, John Arthur
Jess the cat series (2)
Jessamy bride
Moore, Frank Frankfort
Doctor Samuel Johnson series (1)
Jesse Bear, what will you wear?
Carlstrom, Nancy White
Jesse Bear series (1)
Jesse James
Goscinny, Rene
Lucky Luke series (2)
Jesse James at Coney Island
Lawson, W B
Jesse James series (1)
Jesse James at Long Beach
Lawson, W B
Jesse James series (2)
Jesse James' double
Lawson, W B
Jesse James series (3)
Jesse James in New York
Lawson, W B
Jesse James series (4)
Jesse James' oath
Lawson, W B
Jesse James series (5)
Jessi and the awful secret
Martin, Ann Matthews
Baby-Sitters Club series (61)
Jessi and the bad baby-sitter
Martin, Ann Matthews
Baby-Sitters Club series (68)
Jessi and the dance school phantom
Martin, Ann Matthews
Baby-Sitters Club series (42)
Jessi and the jewel thieves
Martin, Ann Matthews
Baby-Sitters Club mystery series (8)
Jessi and the Superbrat
Martin, Ann Matthews
Baby-Sitters Club series (27)
Jessi Ramsey, pet-sitter
Martin, Ann Matthews
Baby-Sitters Club series (22)
Jessica
Moore, Melissa
Agency series (3)
Shura, Mary Francis
Sunfire series (6)
Jessica against Bruce
Pascal, Francine
Sweet Valley High series (86)
Jessica and Jumbo
Pascal, Francine
Sweet Valley kids series (19)
Jessica and the brat attack
Pascal, Francine
Sweet Valley twins series (29)
Jessica and the earthquake
Pascal, Francine
Sweet Valley twins series (75)
Jessica and the money mix-up
Pascal, Francine
Sweet Valley twins series (39)
Jessica and the secret star
Pascal, Francine
Sweet Valley twins series (50)
Jessica and the spelling bee surprise
Pascal, Francine
Sweet Valley kids series (21)
Jessica gets spooked
Pascal, Francine
Sweet Valley kids series (43)
Jessica on stage
Pascal, Francine
Sweet Valley twins series (32)
Jessica saves the trees
Pascal, Francine
Sweet Valley twins series (71)
Jessica the babysitter
Pascal, Francine
Sweet Valley kids series (14)
Jessica, the heiress
Raymond, Evelyn Hunt
Jessica Trent series (2)
Jessica the ned
Pascal, Francine
Sweet Valley twins series (61)
Jessica the thief
Pascal, Francine
Sweet Valley twins series (67)
Jessica the TV star
Pascal, Francine
Sweet Valley kids series (16)
Jessica Trent, her life on a ranch
Raymond, Evelyn Hunt
Jessica Trent series (1)
Jessica Trent's inheritance
Raymond, Evelyn Hunt
Jessica Trent series (3)
Jessica's bad idea
Pascal, Francine
Sweet Valley twins series (31)
Jessica's big mistake
Pascal, Francine
Sweet Valley kids series (7)
Jessica's blind
Pascal, Francine
Sweet Valley twins series (79)
Jessica's cat trick
Pascal, Francine
Sweet Valley kids series (5)
Jessica's Christmas carol
Pascal, Francine
Sweet Valley twins super chiller series (1)
Jessica's first prayer
Stretton, Hesba
Jessica series (1)
Jessica's mermaid
Pascal, Francine
Sweet Valley kids series (49)
Jessica's monster nightmare
Pascal, Francine
Sweet Valley kids series (42)
Jessica's mother
Stretton, Hesba
Jessica series (2)
Jessica's new look
Pascal, Francine
Sweet Valley twins series (47)
Jessica's secret
Pascal, Francine
Sweet Valley twins series (42)
Jessica's secret love
Pascal, Francine
Sweet Valley High series (107)
Jessica's snobby
Pascal, Francine
Sweet Valley kids series (26)
Jessica's the rock star
Pascal, Francine
Sweet Valley twins series (34)
Jessica's triumph
Le Baron, Grace
Janet trilogy (2)
Jessica's unburied treasure
Pascal, Francine
Sweet Valley kids series (30)
Jessica's zoo adventure
Pascal, Francine
Sweet Valley kids series (8)
Jessie
Aimwell, Walter
Boy series (6)
Jessie's parrot
Mathews, Joanna Hooe
Little sunbeams series (4)
Jessi's baby sister
Martin, Ann Matthews
Baby-Sitters Club series (36)
Jessi's gold medal
Martin, Ann Matthews
Baby-Sitters Club series (55)
Jessi's horrible prank
Martin, Ann Matthews
Baby-Sitters Club series (75)
Jessi's secret language
Martin, Ann Matthews
Baby-Sitters Club series (16)
Jessi's wish
Martin, Ann Matthews
Baby-Sitters Club series (48)
Jess's new bed
Cunliffe, John Arthur
Jess the cat series (3)
Jest of darkness
Grayland, Valerie Merle
Hoani Mata series (4)
Jest of God
Laurence, Margaret
Manawaka series (2)
Jester at Scar
Tubb, Edwin Charles
Dumarest series (5)
Jester in the back cover
Hallowell, Tommy
Alden All Stars series (2)
Jester of Saint Timothy's
Pier, Arthur Stanwood
Saint Timothy's School series (4)
Jesting army
Raymond, Ernest
Once in England trilogy (2)
Jesuit trap
Golon, Sergeanne
Angelique series (7)
Jesus came again
Fisher, Vardis
Testament of man series (8)
Jesus Christ in Flanders
Balzac, Honore de
Philosophic studies series (2)
Jesus, gathering his disciples
Daniel, Rebecca
Life of Jesus series (3)
Jesus, his birth
Daniel, Rebecca
Life of Jesus series (1)
Jesus, his boyhood
Daniel, Rebecca
Life of Jesus series (2)
Jesus, his last days
Daniel, Rebecca
Life of Jesus series (10)
Jesus, his last hours
Daniel, Rebecca
Life of Jesus series (11)
Jesus, his parables
Daniel, Rebecca
Life of Jesus series (7)
Jesus, his resurrection
Daniel, Rebecca
Life of Jesus series (12)
Jesus II
Riley, Frank
Father Anton Dymek series (2)
Jesus incident
Herbert, Frank
Pandora series (2)
Jesus is here
Sheldon, Charles Monroe
Henry Maxwell series (2)
Jesus is my guide
Beers, Victor Gilbert
Learning to read from the Bible series (2)
Jesus is my teacher
Beers, Victor Gilbert
Learning to read from the Bible series (3)
Jesus, more parables
Daniel, Rebecca
Life of Jesus series (8)
Jesus on horseback
Reese, John
Jesus on horseback trilogy (3)
Jesus, prophecies fulfilled
Daniel, Rebecca
Life of Jesus series (9)
Jesus, the healer
Daniel, Rebecca
Life of Jesus series (5)
Jesus, the miracle
Daniel, Rebecca
Life of Jesus series (6)
Jesus, the teacher
Daniel, Rebecca
Life of Jesus series (4)
Jet Bright
Scannell, Dorothy
Bright series (2)
Jet fighter trap
Blue, Zachary
Protectors series (2)
Jet-lag
Copper, Basil
Mike Faraday series (46)
Jethro Hammer
Venning, Michael
Melville Fairr series (3)
Jethro's daughters
Stewart, Cynthia
Victorian India series (2)
Jets away
Montgomery, Rutherford George
Kent Barstow series (1)
Jew of Rome
Feuchtwanger, Lion
Josephus trilogy (2)
Jewel
Burnham, Clara Louise
Jewel series (1)
Jewel in the crown
Scott, Paul
British India quartet (1)
Jewel in the skull
Moorcock, Michael
History of Runestaff series (1)
Jewel merchants
Cabell, James Branch
Dom Manuel and his descendants series (17)
Jewel of Arwen
Bradley, Marion Zimmer
Arwen series (1)
Jewel of doom
Carter, Nick
Nick Carter series (62)
Jewel of Jarhen
Kern, Gregory
Cap Kennedy series (5)
Jewel of Tharn
Lord, Jeffrey
Richard Blade series (3)
Jewel of the jungle
Byers, Irene
Tony and Melissa series (1)
Jewel of the Nile
Wilder, Joan
Romancing the stone series (2)
Jewel of the seas
Argo, Ellen
Julia Howard trilogy (1)
Jewel sowers
Allonby, Edith
Lucifram series (1)
Jewel that was ours
Dexter, Colin
Inspector Morse series (9)
Jeweled mountain
Hild, Jack
SOBS series (30)
Jeweled mummy
Carter, Nicholas
Nicholas Carter series (370)
Jewelled eye
Clark, Douglas
Inspector George Masters series (22)
Jewels in jeopardy
Paul, Ernest
George Barclay series (1)
Jewels in the dark
Hallock, Rusty
Find your fate: Jem series (1)
Jewels of doom
Wallace, Robert
Phantom Detective series (2)
Jewels of Wu Ling
Lewis, Jack
Sexton Blake series (131)
Jewel's story book
Burnham, Clara Louise
Jewel series (2)
Jewish history atlas
Gilbert, Martin
History atlas series (4)
Jews of Arab lands
Stillman, Norman Arthur
Jews in Arab lands series (1)
Jews of Arab lands in modern times
Stillman, Norman Arthur
Jews in Arab lands series (2)
Jews Pellegrini
Sarto, Ben
Miss Otis series (3)
Jezebel's dust
Urquhart, Fred
Bessie Hipkiss series (2)
Jhereg
Brust, Steven
Jhereg series (1)
Jian
Lustbader, Eric
Jake Maroc series (1)
Jibaro death
Grant, Maxwell
Shadow series (110)
Jig
Armstrong, Campbell
Detective Frank Pagan series (1)
Jig-saw
Phillpotts, Eden
John Ringrose series (2)
Jig-time murders
Givens, Charles Garland
Jimmy Hastings series (2)
Jigger Moran
Roeburt, John
Jigger Moran series (1)
Jiggle woggle bus
Drake, Joan
Mister Grimpwinkle series (1)
Jiggs is back
McManus, George
Maggie and Jiggs series (2)
Jigsaw
McBain, Ed
Eighty Seventh Precinct series (24)
Waugh, Hillary
Chief Fred Fellows series (1)
Jihad
Hild, Jack
SOBS series (12)
Jill and Joe on holiday
Cole, Margaret Alice
Jill and Joe series (1)
Jill and Joe's return
Cole, Margaret Alice
Jill and Joe series (2)
Jill and Prince the pony
Dickins, Joan
Jill and Prince series (1)
Jill and Prince triumph again
Dickins, Joan
Jill and Prince series (2)
Jill and the perfect pony
Ferguson, Ruby
Jill series (7)
Jill at Hazelmore
Hastings, Valerie
Jill series (1)
Jill enjoys her pony
Ferguson, Ruby
Jill series (1)
Jill Graham and the adventure of the man who vanished
Chase, Lesley
Jill Graham series (3)
Jill Graham and the mystery of the haunted priory
Chase, Lesley
Jill Graham series (4)
Jill Graham and the riddle of the dwarf's shadow
Chase, Lesley
Jill Graham series (2)
Jill Graham and the secret of Druids Wood
Chase, Lesley
Jill Graham series (1)
Jill Graham and the secret of the silent pool
Chase, Lesley
Jill Graham series (1)
Jill has two ponies
Ferguson, Ruby
Jill series (4)
Jill investigates
Hastings, Valerie
Jill series (2)
Jill Nolan, R.N.
McElfresh, Adeline
Jill Nolan series (2)
Jill Nolan, surgical nurse
McElfresh, Adeline
Jill Nolan series (1)
Jill Nolan's choice
McElfresh, Adeline
Jill Nolan series (3)
Jill on a ranch
Page, Gertrude
Jill series (2)
Jill wants to know
Dennison, Dorothy
Wantoknow series for girls (1)
Jillian Jiggs
Gilman, Phoebe
Jillian Jiggs series (1)
Jill's gymkhana
Ferguson, Ruby
Jill series (2)
Jill's pony trek
Ferguson, Ruby
Jill series (9)
Jill's Rhodesian philosophy
Page, Gertrude
Jill series (1)
Jill's riding club
Ferguson, Ruby
Jill series (5)
Jilly takes over
Dickinson, Mary
Jilly series (3)
Jilly, you look terrible
Dickinson, Mary
Jilly series (1)

Jilly's boat trip
Dickinson, Mary
Jilly series (2)

Jim
Thorn, Ismay
Geoff and Jim Harrington series (5)

Jim and Jam and the band
Littler, Angela
Jim and Jam series (1)

Jim and Jam and the builders
Littler, Angela
Jim and Jam series (3)

Jim and Jam at the beach
Littler, Angela
Jim and Jam series (2)

Jim and Jam have a party
Littler, Angela
Jim and Jam series (4)

Jim and Joe
Ellis, Edward Sylvester
True grit trilogy (3)

Jim and Pete
Hindley, Judy
Best of friends series (1)

Jim and Wally
Bruce, Mary Grant
Billabong series (5)

Jim Barnett intervenes
Leblanc, Maurice
Arsene Lupin series (13)

Jim Brady, leading seaman
Macdonnell, James Edmond
Jim Brady series (1)

Jim Chee mysteries
Hillerman, Tony
Sergeant Jim Chee series (3)

Jim Dunlap and the long lunar walk
Palmer, Bernard
Jim Dunlap series (5)

Jim Dunlap and the mysterious orbiting rocket
Palmer, Bernard
Jim Dunlap series (4)

Jim Dunlap and the mysterious spy
Palmer, Bernard
Jim Dunlap series (6)

Jim Dunlap and the secret rocket formula
Palmer, Bernard
Jim Dunlap series (2)

Jim Dunlap and the strange Doctor Brockton
Palmer, Bernard
Jim Dunlap series (1)

Jim Dunlap and the wingless plane
Palmer, Bernard
Jim Dunlap series (3)

Jim Frog
Hoban, Russell
Ponders series (1)

Jim goes north
Goodchild, George
Colorado Jim series (2)

Jim Hanvey, detective
Cohen, Octavus Roy
Jim Hanvey series (1)

Jim Hedgehog and the lonesome tower
Hoban, Russell
Jim Hedgehog series (1)

Jim Hedgehog's supernatural Christmas
Hoban, Russell
Jim Hedgehog series (2)

Jim Maitland
Sapper
Jim Maitland series (1)

Jim Mason, backwoodsman
Gregor, Elmer Russell
Jim Mason series (1)

Jim Mason, scout
Gregor, Elmer Russell
Jim Mason series (2)

Jim Shelton, radio engineer
Palmer, Bernard
Career series (10)

Jim Starling
Hildick, Edmund Wallace
Jim Starling series (1)

Jim Starling and the agency
Hildick, Edmund Wallace
Jim Starling series (2)

Jim Starling and the Colonel
Hildick, Edmund Wallace
Jim Starling series (4)

Jim Starling and the spotted dog
Hildick, Edmund Wallace
Jim Starling series (7)

Jim Starling goes to town
Hildick, Edmund Wallace
Jim Starling series (5)

Jim Starling takes over
Hildick, Edmund Wallace
Jim Starling series (6)

Jim Starling's holiday
Hildick, Edmund Wallace
Jim Starling series (3)

Jimbo and the UFO
Maddocks, Peter
Jimbo series (2)

Jimbo and the whale
Maddocks, Peter
Jimbo series (1)

Jimgrim
Mundy, Talbot
Chullunder Ghose series (2)
Jimgrim series (5)

Jimgrim and Allah's peace
Mundy, Talbot
Jimgrim series (11)

Jimgrim Sahib
Mundy, Talbot
Chullunder Ghose series (2)
Jimgrim series (5)

Jimmie Dale and the blue envelope murder
Packard, Frank Lucius
Jimmie Dale series (4)

Jimmie Dale and the missing hour
Packard, Frank Lucius
Jimmie Dale series (5)

Jimmie Dale and the phantom clue
Packard, Frank Lucius
Jimmie Dale series (3)

Jimmie Rezaire
Armstrong, Anthony
Jimmie Rezaire series (1)

Jimmie Suter and the boys of Pigeon Camp
James, Martha
Pigeon Camp series (1)

Jimmy
Crompton, Richmal
Jimmy series (1)

Jimmy again
Crompton, Richmal
Jimmy series (2)

Jimmy and the giant cleaner
Morton, John
Jimmy series (1)

Jimmy and the ladder
Morton, John
Jimmy series (3)

Jimmy and the plant food
Morton, John
Jimmy series (4)

Jimmy and the rubber boat
Morton, John
Jimmy series (2)

Jimmy boa's bounces back
Noble, Trinka Hakes
Jimmy's boa series (2)

Jimmy Brown in Europe
Alden, William Livingston
Jimmy Brown series (2)

Jimmy Brown trying to find Europe
Alden, William Livingston
Jimmy Brown series (2)

Jimmy Bundobust
Stanford, John Keith
Lieutenant-Colonel James Gore-Bunbury series (2)

Jimmy Skunk's justice
Burgess, Thornton Waldo
Wee little books series (5)

Jimmy the baby elephant
Beaman, Sydney George Hulme
Out of the ark series (4)

Jimmy the Kid
Westlake, Donald Edwin
Dortmunder Gang series (3)

Jimmy-the-One
Wingate, John
Submariner Sinclair series (2)

Jimmy the Third
Crompton, Richmal
Jimmy series (3)

Jimmy Zest
McBratney, Sam
Jimmy Zest series (1)

Jimmy Zest All-Stars
McBratney, Sam
Jimmy Zest series (3)

Jimmyjohn boss, and other stories
Wister, Owen
Western tales series (2)

Jimmy's cruise in the Pinafore
Alcott, Louisa May
Aunt Jo's scrap-bag series (5)

Jindi and the bunyip
Smith, Joan Watson
Jindi series (3)

Jindi, the piccaninny fairy
Smith, Joan Watson
Jindi series (1)

Jindi's Australian ABC
Smith, Joan Watson
Jindi series (3)

Jingle bells jam
Giff, Patricia Reilly
Lincoln Lions Band series (3)

Jingle with a ball
Butler, Peter
Rounds series (2)

Jinian Footseer
Tepper, Sheri S
Jinian trilogy (1)

Jinian Star Eye
Tepper, Sheri S
Jinian trilogy (3)

Jinx high
Lackey, Mercedes
Diana Tregarde series (3)

Jinx of Payrock Canyon
Nesbit, Troy
Wilderness mystery series (2)

Jinx on a Terran inheritance
Daley, Brian
Alacrity FitzHugh trilogy (2)

Jinx ship
Pease, Howard
Tod Moran series (2)

Jinx Theatre murder
Williams, Alexander
Detective Sergeant Pietro Tonelli series (1)

Jitterbugg
Cosgrove, Stephen Edward
Bugg series (12)

Jiu San
Robeson, Kenneth
Doc Savage series (107)

Jo
Hughes, Tracy
Calloway Corners series (2)

Jo and Coney's Cavern
Hastings, Valerie
Jo series (2)

Jo and the limping boy
Hastings, Valerie
Jo series (3)

Jo and the skiffle group
Hastings, Valerie
Jo series (1)

Jo Jo and the private eye
Malloy, Lester
Martin Moon series (1)

Jo of the Chalet School
Brent-Dyer, Elinor Mary
Chalet School series (2)

Jo returns to the Chalet School
Brent-Dyer, Elinor Mary
Chalet School series (12)

Jo to the rescue
Brent-Dyer, Elinor Mary
Chalet School series (19)

Joachim the dustman
Baumann, Kurt
Joachim series (1)

Joachim the policeman
Baumann, Kurt
Joachim series (2)

Joan Foster, bride
Colver, Alice Ross
Joan Foster series (6)

Joan Foster, freshman
Colver, Alice Ross
Joan Foster series (1)

Joan Foster in Europe
Colver, Alice Ross
Joan Foster series (5)

Joan Foster, junior
Colver, Alice Ross
Joan Foster series (3)

Joan Foster, senior
Colver, Alice Ross
Joan Foster series (4)

Joan Foster, sophomore
Colver, Alice Ross
Joan Foster series (2)

Joan is angry
Hellner, Katarina
Emotions series (3)

Joan is happy
Hellner, Katarina
Emotions series (4)

Joan is sad
Hellner, Katarina
Emotions series (1)

Joan is scared
Hellner, Katarina
Emotions series (2)

Joan, just girl
Garis, Lilian C
Joan series (1)

Joan of Arc
Birt, David
Middle Ages series (15)

Joan of Juniper Inn
Elliot, Emilia
Joan series (1)

Joan of the sword hand
Crockett, Samuel Rutherford
Wolfmark series (2)

Joan Winter
Bensusan, Samuel Levy
Joan Winter series (1)

Joanna
Gellis, Roberta
Roselynde chronicles series (3)
Miner, Jane Claypool
Sunfire series (5)

Joanna at Littlefold
Ashton, Helen
Wilchester chronicles series (2)

Joanna Godden
Kaye-Smith, Sheila
Joanna Godden series (1)

Joanna Godden married, and other stories
Kaye-Smith, Sheila
Joanna Godden series (2)

Joanna rides the hills
Boden, Hilda
Joanna series (2)

Joanna's special pony
Boden, Hilda
Joanna series (1)

Joanne, the unpredictable
Kimbrough, Katheryn
Phenwick women series (8)

Joan's California summer
Jacobs, Caroline Emilia
Joan series (5)

Joan's garden of adventure
Garis, Lilian C
Joan series (2)

Joan's jolly vacation
Elliot, Emilia
Joan series (2)

Job for Jenny Archer
Conford, Ellen
Jenny Archer series (1)

Job for Noel
Boden, Hilda
Noel series (6)

Job for Susan
Shaw, Jane
Susan series (11)

Job for the Jays
Smedley, Elisabeth
Jays series (3)

Job of murder
Gruber, Frank
Johnny Fletcher and Sam Cragg series (12)

Job with the boys
Wigg, T I G
Teaching series (1)

Joc and Colette at the Natural History Museum
Barclay, Vera Charlesworth
Joc and Colette series (4)

Joc and Colette on the seashore
Barclay, Vera Charlesworth
Joc and Colette series (3)

Joc, Colette and the animals
Barclay, Vera Charlesworth
Joc and Colette series (1)

Joc, Colette and the birds
Barclay, Vera Charlesworth
Joc and Colette series (2)

Jock, Jack and the corporal
Martindale, Cyril Charlie
Mister Francis Newnes series (1)

Jockey
Verner, Gerald
Superintendent Robert Budd series (6)

Joe and the gladiator
Cookson, Catherine
Matty Doolin and Joe Darling series (2)

Joe and the nursery school
Prince, Alison
Joe series (2)

Joe and Timothy together
Edwards, Dorothy
Joe and Timothy series (2)

Joe at the fair
Roberts, Doreen
Joe series (1)

Joe Bob goes back to the drive-in
Briggs, Joe Bob
Joe Bob series (2)

Joe Bob goes to the drive-in
Briggs, Joe Bob
Joe Bob series (1)

Joe Jenkins' case book
Rosenhayn, Paul
Joe Jenkins series (2)

Joe Jenkins, detective
Rosenhayn, Paul
Joe Jenkins series (1)

Joe Leaphorn mysteries
Hillerman, Tony
Lieutenant Joe Leaphorn series (6)

Joe Mauser, mercenary from tomorrow
Reynolds, Mack
Joe Mauser series (2)

Joe movs house
Prince, Alison
Joe series (1)

Joe Muller, detective
Colbron, Grace Isabel
Joe Muller series (1)

Joe Pepper
Kelton, Elmer
Tales of Texas series (10)

Joe Quinney's Jodie
Vachell, Horace Annesley
Joe Quinney series (3)

Joe Strong and his box of mystery
Barnum, Vance
Joe Strong series (6)

Joe Strong and his wings of steel
Barnum, Vance
Joe Strong series (5)

Joe Strong on the high wire
Barnum, Vance
Joe Strong series (4)

Joe Strong on the trapeze
Barnum, Vance
Joe Strong series (2)

Joe Strong, the boy fire-eater
Barnum, Vance
Joe Strong series (7)

Joe Strong, the boy fish
Barnum, Vance
Joe Strong series (3)

Joe Strong, the boy wizard
Barnum, Vance
Joe Strong series (1)

Joe, the circus boy
Allen, Alice E
Martie twins series (1)

Joe, the hotel boy
Alger, Horatio
Rise in life series (10)

Joe's day at the market
Roberts, Doreen
Joe series (2)

Joey and Co. in Tirol
Brent-Dyer, Elinor Mary
Chalet School series (43)

Joey and the Blackbird Gang
Martin, Robert
Joey series (4)

Joey and the city ghosts
Martin, Robert
Joey series (8)

Joey and the detectives
Martin, Robert
Joey series (16)

Joey and the helicopter
Martin, Robert
Joey series (5)

Joey and the magic eye
Martin, Robert
Joey series (6)

Joey and the magic pony
Martin, Robert
Joey series (13)

Joey and the magician
Martin, Robert
Joey series (17)

Joey and the mail robbers
Martin, Robert
Joey series (3)

Joey and the master plan
Martin, Robert
Joey series (15)

Joey and the pickpocket
Martin, Robert
Joey series (18)

Joey and the river pirates
Martin, Robert
Joey series (2)

Joey and the Royalist treasure
Martin, Robert
Joey series (9)

Joey and the secret engine
Martin, Robert
Joey series (14)

Joey and the smugglers' legend
Martin, Robert
Joey series (12)

Joey and the square of gold
Martin, Robert
Joey series (7)

Joey and the squib
Martin, Robert
Joey series (10)

Joey and the train robbers
Martin, Robert
Joey series (19)
Joey collects
Joey
Joey series (3)
Joey goes to the Oberland
Brent-Dyer, Elinor Mary
Chalet School series (29)
Joey Jeremiah
Ellis, Kathryn
Degrassi High School series (4)
Joey Kills
Joey
Joey series (2)
Joey of Jasmine Street
Martin, Robert
Joey series (1)
Joey, soap box driver
Martin, Robert
Joey series (11)
Joey's case
Constantine, K C
Mario Balzic series (8)
Joey's story
Berger, Gilda
Straight talk about drugs series (3)
Johan at school
Sandberg, Inger
Johan series (2)
Johanna and the Prices
Pye, Virginia
Price family series (7)
Johan's year
Sandberg, Inger
Johan series (1)
Johel
Oman, Carola
Johel series (2)
John Adam in Eden
Wood, Christopher
John Adam series (2)
John Adam, samurai
Wood, Christopher
John Adam series (1)
John and Betty's English history visit
Williamson, Margaret
John and Betty series (1)
John and Betty's Irish history visit
Williamson, Margaret
John and Betty series (3)
John and Betty's Scotch history visit
Williamson, Margaret
John and Betty series (2)
John and Jennifer and their pets
Harris, Elsie May
John and Jennifer series (6)
John and Jennifer at London Airport
Denes, Gee
John and Jennifer series (14)
John and Jennifer at the circus
Harris, Elsie May
John and Jennifer series (5)
John and Jennifer at the farm
Desmond, D J
John and Jennifer series (4)
John and Jennifer at the zoo
Higgins, Valerie
John and Jennifer series (2)
John and Jennifer go camping
Harris, Elsie May
John and Jennifer series (9)
John and Jennifer go sailing
Denes, Gee
John and Jennifer series (12)
John and Jennifer go to London
Harris, Elsie May
John and Jennifer series (11)
John and Jennifer go travelling
Harris, Elsie May
John and Jennifer series (7)
John and Jennifer's concert party
Denes, Gee
John and Jennifer series (13)
John and Jennifer's pony club
Ritson, Kitty
John and Jennifer series (10)
John and Jennifer's treasure hunt
Harris, Elsie May
John and Jennifer series (8)
John and Mary
James, Grace
John and Mary series (1)
John and Mary abroad
James, Grace
John and Mary series (3)
John and Mary and Lisetta
James, Grace
John and Mary series (18)
John and Mary and Miss Rose Brown
James, Grace
John and Mary series (8)
John and Mary at Riverton
James, Grace
John and Mary series (11)
John and Mary at school
James, Grace
John and Mary series (9)
John and Mary by land and sea
James, Grace
John and Mary series (16)
John and Mary, detectives
James, Grace
John and Mary series (4)
John and Mary in Rome
James, Grace
John and Mary series (14)
John and Mary revisit Rome
James, Grace
John and Mary series (20)
John and Mary's aunt
James, Grace
John and Mary series (13)
John and Mary's fairy-tales
James, Grace
John and Mary series (15)
John and Mary's Japanese fairy-tales
James, Grace
John and Mary series (17)
John and Mary's secret society
James, Grace
John and Mary series (5)
John and Mary's treasures
James, Grace
John and Mary series (19)
John and Mary's visitors
James, Grace
John and Mary series (6)
John and Mary's youth club
James, Grace
John and Mary series (10)
John and Nanbaroo
Chadwick, Doris
John series (3)
John and the big dog
Iseborg, Harry
John and Hugh series (1)
John and the red parrot
Iseborg, Harry
John and Hugh series (4)
John Arnison
Thompson, Edward
Arnison series (2)
John Billington, friend of Squanto
Bulla, Clyde Robert
Squanto series (2)
John Brown's body
Lorac, E C R
Inspector Macdonald series (17)
John Burningham's ABC
Burningham, John
Play and learn series (1)
John Burningham's colors
Burningham, John
Play and learn series (2)
John Burningham's colours
Burningham, John
Play and learn series (2)
John Burningham's one two three
Burningham, John
Play and learn series (3)
John Burningham's opposites
Burningham, John
Play and learn series (4)
John Carruthers, Indian policeman
Cox, Edmund Charles
John Carruthers series (1)
John Carter and the giant of Mars
Burroughs, Edgar Rice
Martian series (11)
John Carter of Mars
Burroughs, Edgar Rice
Martian series (11)
John Christopher in Paris
Rolland, Romain
John Christopher series (3)
John Clutterbuck
Ruegg, Alfred Henry
Rosie Bright series (1)
John Dene of Toronto
Jenkins, Herbert
Malcolm Sage series (1)
John Dunmore Lang, chiefly autobiographical, 1799-1878
Lang, John Dunmore
Life and times series (2)
John Godsoe's legacy
Kellogg, Elijah
Pleasant Cove series (5)
John Gotobed alone
Quantrill, Malcolm
Gotobed trilogy (3)
John Jeremy, cracksman
Montague, Jeffrey
John Jeremy series (1)
John Jolly at Christmas time
Blyton, Enid
John Jolly series (1)
John Jolly at the circus
Blyton, Enid
John Jolly series (4)
John Jolly by the sea
Blyton, Enid
John Jolly series (2)
John Jolly on the farm
Blyton, Enid
John Jolly series (3)
John Keats, the living year
Gittings, Robert
John Keats series (1)
John Kyeling died
Radford, Edwin
Doctor Manson series (7)
John Macnab
Buchan, John
Sir Edward Leithen series (2)
John Marston Hall
James, George Payne Rainsford
Young cavalier series (2)
John of Sydney Cove
Chadwick, Doris
John series (2)
John of the Sirius
Chadwick, Doris
John series (1)
John sails his boat
Iseborg, Harry
John and Hugh series (2)
John Silence, physician extraordinary
Blackwood, Algernon
John Silence series (1)
John the balladeer
Wellman, Manly Wade
Silver John series (1)
John the junior reporter
England, Edward Oliver
John Rickshaw series (1)
John Thorndyke's cases
Freeman, Richard Austin
Doctor John Evelyn Thorndyke series (2)
John Treegate's musket
Wibberley, Leonard
Treegate family trilogy (1)
John Trusty
Beaman, Sydney George Hulme
Toytown series (9)
John Verney
Vachell, Horace Annesley
Harrow School series (2)
John W Campbell anthology
Campbell, John Wood
Arcot, Morey and Wade series (3)
John Walters
Sapper
John Walters series (3)
John Wentley investigates
Westerman, John Francis Cyril
John Wentley series (2)
John Wentley takes charge
Westerman, John Francis Cyril
John Wentley series (1)
John Wentley wins through
Westerman, John Francis Cyril
John Wentley series (3)
John Wesley Hardin
Harvey, John Barton
Wes Hart series (8)
Johnny and Marytary
Creswell, Harry Bulkeley
Marytary series (2)
Johnny and the tin tortoise
Bisset, Donald
Johnny series (2)
Johnny and the Yank
Tully, John
Johnny Goodlooks series (2)
Johnny Black, footballer
Smith, Hendy
Johnny Black series (1)
Johnny Black, pilot
Smith, Hendy
Johnny Black series (4)
Johnny Black, racing driver
Smith, Hendy
Johnny Black series (5)
Johnny Black, show-jumper
Smith, Hendy
Johnny Black series (3)
Johnny Black, special agent
Smith, Hendy
Johnny Black series (2)
Johnny Black stops dreaming
Smith, Hendy
Johnny Black series (6)
Johnny Christmas
Blake, Forrester
Johnny Christmas trilogy (1)
Johnny come lately
Kane, Frank
Johnny Liddell series (22)
Johnny Crow's garden
Brooke, Leonard Leslie
Johnny Crow series (1)
Johnny Crow's new garden
Brooke, Leonard Leslie
Johnny Crow series (3)
Johnny Crow's party
Brooke, Leonard Leslie
Johnny Crow series (2)
Johnny get your gun
Ball, John
Virgil Tibbs series (3)
Johnny gets his
Ambler, Dail
Danny Spade series (29)
Johnny goes east
Cory, Desmond
Johnny Fedora series (8)
Johnny goes north
Cory, Desmond
Johnny Fedora series (7)
Johnny goes south
Cory, Desmond
Johnny Fedora series (10)
Johnny goes under
Cory, Desmond
Feramontov quintet (1)
Johnny Fedora series (12)
Johnny goes west
Cory, Desmond
Johnny Fedora series (9)
Johnny Goodlooks
Tully, John
Johnny Goodlooks series (1)
Johnny Havoc
Jakes, John
Johnny Havoc series (1)
Johnny Havoc and the doll who had It
Jakes, John
Johnny Havoc series (3)
Johnny Havoc and the siren in red
Jakes, John
Johnny Havoc series (4)
Johnny Havoc meets Zelda
Jakes, John
Johnny Havoc series (2)
Johnny here and there
Bisset, Donald
Johnny series (1)
Johnny Jones, guttersnipe
Stuart-Young, John Morag
Johnny Jones series (1)
Johnny Liddell's morgue
Kane, Frank
Johnny Liddell series (13)
Johnny Lion's bad day
Hurd, Edith Thatcher
Johnny Lion series (2)
Johnny Lion's book
Hurd, Edith Thatcher
Johnny Lion series (1)
Johnny Lion's rubber boots
Hurd, Edith Thatcher
Johnny Lion series (3)
Johnny May
Branscum, Robbie
Johnny May series (1)
Johnny May grows up
Branscum, Robbie
Johnny May series (3)
Johnny Nelson
Mulford, Clarence Edward
Hopalong Cassidy series (7)
Johnny Nelson series (2)
Johnny Osage
Giles, Janice Holt
Fowler family series (4)
Johnny Texas
Hoff, Carol
Johnny Texas series (1)
Johnny Texas on the San Antonio road
Hoff, Carol
Johnny Texas series (2)
Johnny under ground
Moyes, Patricia
Henry and Emmy Tibbett series (6)
Johnny Vengeance
Gruber, Frank
Historical Western series (10)
John's day at sea
Iseborg, Harry
John and Hugh series (3)
John's good news of Jesus
Haughton, Rosemary
Good news of Jesus series (4)
Joie d'amour
Villefranche, Anne Marie
Erotic memoirs series (2)
Joining of the stone
Murphy, Shirley Rousseau
Children of Ynell series (5)
Joining the colors
Botsford, Charles Alexander
Victory series (1)
Joke shop
Enright, Dennis Joseph
Joke shop trilogy (1)
Joke Shop annexe
Fuller, Roy
Joke Shop series (2)
Joker
Osborne, Helena
White poppy series (2)
Wallace, Edgar
Inspector Elk series (3)
Joker in a stacked deck
Shelynn, Jack
Ned Parker series (6)
Joker in the deck
Prather, Richard Scott
Shell Scott series (26)
Joker in the pack
Chase, James Hadley
Helga Rolfe series (2)
Joker's revenge
Keene, Carolyn
Nancy Drew series (84)
Jokers wild
Grover, Marshall
Larry and Stretch series (178)
Martin, George Raymond Richard
Wild cards series (3)
Jokertown shuffle
Martin, George Raymond Richard
Wild cards series (9)
Jolly Christmas postman
Ahlberg, Janet
Jolly postman series (2)
Jolly marsupial
Cooper, Jilly
Jolly super series (6)
Jolly pets
Gould, Elizabeth
Green Willow Farm series (4)
Jolly postman
Ahlberg, Janet
Jolly postman series (1)
Jolly Roger, buccaneer
Leyland, Eric
Jolly Roger series (1)
Jolly Roger sails again
Leyland, Eric
Jolly Roger series (2)
Jolly Rogerson
McInerny, Ralph
Matthew Rogerson series (1)
Jolly rover
Trowbridge, John Townsend
Silver medal series (6)
Jolly story book
Blyton, Enid
Story book series (3)
Jolly super
Cooper, Jilly
Jolly super series (1)
Jolly super too
Cooper, Jilly
Jolly super series (2)
Jolly superlative
Cooper, Jilly
Jolly super series (3)
Jolly tales
Blyton, Enid
Little books series (3)
Jon and the break-in mystery
Palmer, Bernard
Bradley series (3)
Jonah
Daniel, Rebecca
Our greatest heritage series (11)
Jonah and Company
Yates, Dornford
Berry series (4)
Jonah Mansel series (2)
Jonah Rock
Grover, Marshall
Larry and Stretch series (366)
Jonah, speak for God
Graeber, Charlotte Towner
Speak for me series (1)
Jonas a judge
Abbott, Jacob
Jonas series (1)
Jonas on a farm in the summer
Abbott, Jacob
Jonas series (5)
Jonas on a farm in the winter
Abbott, Jacob
Jonas series (6)

Jonas's stories
Abbott, Jacob
Jonas series (4)
Jonathan and Felicity
Cockett, Mary
Jonathan and Felicity series (2)
Jonathan and the superstar
Dicks, Terrance
Jonathan's ghost series (3)
Jonathan Blair, bounty lands lawyer
Ellis, William Donohue
Ohio frontier trilogy (2)
Jonathan Drew, rover
Ward, Christopher
Jonathan Drew series (2)
Jonathan Kane climbs high
Barrie, Alexander
Jonathan Kane series (5)
Jonathan Kane's jungle run
Barrie, Alexander
Jonathan Kane series (4)
Jonathan Lamb, adventurer
Foster, Kingsley
Jonathan Lamb series (3)
Jonathan Lamb, detective
Foster, Kingsley
Jonathan Lamb series (5)
Jonathan Lamb in peril
Foster, Kingsley
Jonathan Lamb series (4)
Jonathan on the farm
Cockett, Mary
Jonathan and Felicity series (1)
Jonathan's ghost
Dicks, Terrance
Jonathan's ghost series (1)
Jondelle
Tubb, Edwin Charles
Dumarest series (10)
Jones is a rainbow
Finch, Matthew
Dick Lingham series (2)
Joneses, how to keep up with them
Gibb, Lee
Jones series (1)
Jones's little murder
Radford, Edwin
Doctor Manson series (24)
Jones's private army
Styles, Showell
David Jones, R.N.V.R. series (2)
Jongor fights back
Williams, Robert Moore
Jongor trilogy (3)
Jongor of Lost Land
Williams, Robert Moore
Jongor trilogy (1)
Jonnesty
Mantle, Winifred
Jonnesty series (1)
Jonnesty in winter
Mantle, Winifred
Jonnesty series (2)
Jonny Briggs
Eadington, Joan
Jonny Briggs series (1)
Jonny Briggs and the galloping wedding
Eadington, Joan
Jonny Briggs series (6)
Jonny Briggs and the ghost
Eadington, Joan
Jonny Briggs series (2)
Jonny Briggs and the giant cave
Eadington, Joan
Jonny Briggs series (5)
Jonny Briggs and the great razzle dazzle
Eadington, Joan
Jonny Briggs series (4)
Jonny Briggs and the jubilee concert
Eadington, Joan
Jonny Briggs series (7)
Jonny Briggs and the secret sunflowers
Eadington, Joan
Jonny Briggs series (10)
Jonny Briggs and the silver surprise
Eadington, Joan
Jonny Briggs series (11)
Jonny Briggs and the Whitby weekend
Eadington, Joan
Jonny Briggs series (3)
Jonuta rising!
Cleve, John
Spaceways series (13)
Jordan County
Foote, Shelby
Lake Jordan series (4)
Jordan intercept
Mackenzie, J Alexander
Canaan trilogy (2)
Jordans
Millin, Sarah Gertrude
Dark river series (4)
Jordans murder
Fowler, Sydney
Mister Jellipot series (5)
Joris of the Rock
Barringer, Leslie
Neustrian trilogy (2)
Jorkens borrows another whisky
Dunsany, Edward John Moreton Drax Plunkett
Jorkens series (5)
Jorkens has a large whisky
Dunsany, Edward John Moreton Drax Plunkett
Jorkens series (3)
Jorkens remembers Africa
Dunsany, Edward John Moreton Drax Plunkett
Jorkens series (2)
Jormundgand
Frith, Nigel
Pangaia trilogy (1)
Jorrocks' birthday book
Surtees, Robert Smith
Mister John Jorrocks series (2)
Jorrocks' calendar
Surtees, Robert Smith
Mister John Jorrocks series (2)
Jorrocks' jaunts and jollities
Surtees, Robert Smith
Mister John Jorrocks series (1)
Jory
Bass, Milton R
Jory series (1)
Jo's boys, and how they turned out
Alcott, Louisa May
Jo March series (4)
Jo's choice
Dart, Dorothy
Jo Lacey series (2)
Jo's search
Dart, Dorothy
Jo Lacey series (1)
Jose Canseco, baseball's forty-four man
Aaseng, Nathan
Sports acheivers series (8)
Joseph
Daniel, Rebecca
Our greatest heritage series (4)
Joseph and his jointed camel
Fletcher, Audrey
Allsorts series (1)
Joseph Balsamo
Dumas, Alexandre
Marie Antoinette series (1)
Memoirs of a physician series (2)
Joseph in Egypt
Mann, Thomas
Joseph and his brothers series (3)
Joseph Kerkhoven's third existence
Wassermann, Jakob
Doctor Joseph Kerkhoven trilogy (3)
Joseph Khassan, half-caste
Dawson, Alec John
Joseph Khassan series (1)
Joseph the provider
Mann, Thomas
Joseph and his brothers series (4)
Josephina hates her name
Engel, Diana
Josephina series (2)
Josephina, the great collector
Engel, Diana
Josephina series (1)
Josephine
Gripe, Maria
Hugo and Josephine trilogy (1)
Mure, Geoffrey
Josephine series (1)
Josephine and her dolls
Cradock, Henry Cowper, *Mrs*
Josephine series (1)
Josephine goes shopping
Cradock, Henry Cowper, *Mrs*
Josephine series (7)
Josephine goes travelling
Cradock, Henry Cowper, *Mrs*
Josephine series (11)
Josephine is busy
Cradock, Henry Cowper, *Mrs*
Josephine series (3)
Josephine, John and the puppy
Cradock, Henry Cowper, *Mrs*
Josephine series (5)
Josephine keeps house
Cradock, Henry Cowper, *Mrs*
Josephine series (9)
Josephine keeps school
Cradock, Henry Cowper, *Mrs*
Josephine series (6)
Josephine's birthday
Cradock, Henry Cowper, *Mrs*
Josephine series (4)
Josephine's Christmas party
Cradock, Henry Cowper, *Mrs*
Josephine series (8)
Josephine's dolly book
Cradock, Henry Cowper, *Mrs*
Josephine series (5)
Josephine's happy family
Cradock, Henry Cowper, *Mrs*
Josephine series (2)
Josephine's pantomime
Cradock, Henry Cowper, *Mrs*
Josephine series (10)
Josephus
Feuchtwanger, Lion
Josephus trilogy (1)
Josephus and the emperor
Feuchtwanger, Lion
Josephus trilogy (3)
Josey Wales
Carter, Forrest
Josey Wales series (2)
Joshua
Daniel, Rebecca
Our greatest heritage series (6)
Girzone, Joseph Francis
Joshua series (1)
Joshua and the children
Girzone, Joseph Francis
Joshua series (2)
Joshua in the Holy Land
Girzone, Joseph Francis
Joshua series (3)
Joshua sequence
Huebner, Frederick D
Matt Riordan series (1)
Joshua T Bates in charge
Shreve, Susan Richards
Joshua T Bates series (2)
Josiah Allen on the woman question
Holley, Marietta
Samantha and Josiah Allen series (16)
Josiah Allen's wife as a P.A. and P.I.
Holley, Marietta
Samantha and Josiah Allen series (1)
Josiah's alarm and Abel Perry's funeral
Holley, Marietta
Samantha and Josiah Allen series (8)
Josiah's secret
Holley, Marietta
Samantha and Josiah Allen series (16)
Josie
Schurfranz, Vivian
Sunfire series (28)
Josie, Click and Bun again
Blyton, Enid
Josie, Click and Bun series (3)
Josie, Click and Bun and the little tree house
Blyton, Enid
Josie, Click and Bun series (1)
Josie moves up
Matthewman, Phyllis
Daneswood series (3)
Josie O'Gorman
Van Dyne, Edith
Mary Louise and Josie O'Gorman series (9)
Josie O'Gorman and the meddlesome major
Van Dyne, Edith
Mary Louise and Josie O'Gorman series (10)
Josie Smith
Nabb, Magdalen
Josie Smith series (1)
Josie Smith and Eileen
Nabb, Magdalen
Josie Smith series (4)
Josie Smith at school
Nabb, Magdalen
Josie Smith series (3)
Josie Smith at the seaside
Nabb, Magdalen
Josie Smith series (2)
Josie Smith in hospital
Nabb, Magdalen
Josie Smith series (6)
Josie Smith's Christmas
Nabb, Magdalen
Josie Smith series (5)
Jossy's Giants
Waddell, Sid
Jossy's Giants series (1)
Journal and memories
Mersey, Charles Clive
Picture of life series (2)
Journal of a cavalry officer
Nolan, Christopher
Journals of Tom Goane series (5)
Journal of a disappointed man
Barbellion, W N P
Disappointed man series (1)
Journal of a home life
Sewell, Elizabeth Missings
Home and after life series (1)
Journal of a jailbird
Nolan, Christopher
Journals of Tom Goane series (4)
Journal of a navvy
Nolan, Christopher
Journals of Tom Goane series (2)
Journal of a prize-fighter
Nolan, Christopher
Journals of Tom Goane series (3)
Journal of a slaver
Nolan, Christopher
Journals of Tom Goane series (6)
Journal of Miss Jane Fairfax
Grey, Charlotte
Miss Jane Fairfax series (2)
Journal of young rake
Nolan, Christopher
Journals of Tom Goane series (1)
Journals, 1889-1913
Gide, Andre
Journal series (1)
Journals, 1914-1927
Gide, Andre
Journal series (2)
Journals, 1928-1939
Gide, Andre
Journal series (3)
Journals, 1939-1949
Gide, Andre
Journal series (4)
Journey
Lewin, Hugh
Jafta series (5)
Randall, Marta
Newhome series (1)
Journey back
Reiss, Johanna
Upstairs room series (2)
Journey behind the wind
Wrightson, Patricia
Song of Wirrun trilogy (3)
Journey between freedoms
Matthews, Tanya
Russian wife series (1)
Journey by boat
Coote, Roger
Journeys series (3)
Journey by car
Coote, Roger
Journeys series (1)
Journey by train
Coote, Roger
Journeys series (4)
Journey continued
Paton, Alan
Mountain journey series (2)
Journey down a rainbow
Priestley, John Boynton
English journey series (4)
Journey downstairs
Philmore, R
Swan series (1)
Journey home
Muspratt, Eric
Fire of youth series (3)
Uchida, Yoshiko
Japanese-American evacuation series (2)
Journey into danger
Fox, James M
John and Suzy Marshall series (2)
Journey into night
Charlwood, Don
Airman series (2)
Journey into space
Chilton, Charles
Jet Morgan series (1)
Journey into terror
Effinger, George Alec
Planet of the Apes series (8)
Journey into the past
Maisky, Ivan Mikhailovich
Storm series (2)
Journey into violence
Orgill, Douglas
William Mallett series (1)
Journey into war
Donaldson, Margaret
Journey into war series (1)
Journey not the arrival matters
Woolf, Leonard
Sowing and growing series (5)
Journey of August King
Ehle, John
North Carolina series (2)
Journey of Cname Sname in a UFO
Manners, Carol
Cname Sname series (2)
Journey of death
Logan, Jake
John Slocum series (78)
Journey of Mary Hervey Russell
Jameson, Storm
Hervey Russell series (6)
Journey of Tapiola
Nathan, Robert
Tapiola series (1)
Journey of the eldest brother
Fyson, Jenny Grace
Shamashazir series (2)
Journey of the Mountain Man
Johnstone, William Wallace
Mountain Man series (5)
Journey to a safe place
Black, Ian Stuart
Peter Munro series (2)
Journey to Aprilioth
Kernaghan, Eileen
Aprilioth trilogy (1)
Journey to Atlantis
Fortune, J J
Race against time series (9)
Journey to enchantment
Veryan, Patricia
Golden chronicles series (2)
Journey to England
Unnerstad, Edith
Anders series (3)
Journey to Genoa
Fawcett, Frank Dubrez
Sexton Blake series (1490)
Journey to Ixtlan
Castaneda, Carlos
Don Juan series (3)
Journey to Jamestown
Burnap, Jennifer
Cartwright family series (1)
Journey to Jupiter
Greene, Joseph
Dig Allen series (3)
Walters, Hugh
Chris Godfrey series (9)
Journey to Melbury
Darbyshire, Shirley
Melbury trilogy (1)
Journey to Membliar
Baker, Sharon
Naphar series (2)
Journey to Mesharra
Sirota, Mike
Ro-Lan series (3)
Journey to Nashville
Crabb, Alfred Leland
Nashville series (5)
Journey to nature
Mowbray, Jeanie Pearl
Journey to nature series (1)
Journey to nowhere
Baer, Judy
Cedar River daydreams series (4)
Journey to quiet waters
Lavender, William
Hargrave journal series (2)
Journey to Rilla
Wylde, Thomas
Doctor Bones series (6)
Journey to Stonehenge
Graver, Fred
Choose your own adventure series (35)
Journey to the center
Stableford, Brian Michael
Asgard series (1)
Journey to the center of the atom!
Gaskin, Carol
Explorer series (1)
Journey to the centre
Stableford, Brian Michael
Asgard series (1)
Journey to the dawn
Angoff, Charles
Polonsky family series (1)
Journey to the flame
Monaco, Richard
She series (8)
Journey to the hangman
Upfield, Arthur William
Napoleon Bonaparte series (23)
Journey to the North Pole
Verne, Jules
Adventures of Captain Hatteras series (1)
Journey to the underground world
Carter, Lin
Eric Carstairs series (1)

Journey to the year 3000
Packard, Edward
Choose your own adventure super series (1)
Journey to Topaz
Uchida, Yoshiko
Japanese-American evacuation series (1)
Journey to Untor
Wibberley, Leonard
Uncle Bill series (2)
Journey to Vernico 5
Stine, Megan
Twistaplot series (12)
Journey to yesterday
Shiplett, June Lund
Stacey Gordon series (1)
Journey under the sea
Mountain, Robert
Choose your own adventure series (2)
Journey up the years
Vyvyan, Clara Coltman
Roots and stars series (2)
Journey west
Schulte, Elaine
California pioneer series (1)
Journey with a secret
Styles, Showell
Ann and John Davies series (1)
Journeyman
Gallacher, Tom
Bill Thompson trilogy (2)
Yates, Elizabeth
Journeyman series (1)
Journeyman joiner
Sand, George
Socialist trilogy (2)
Journeys by plane
Coote, Roger
Journeys series (2)
Journey's end
Rolland, Romain
John Christopher series (4)
Stuart, Becky
Kellogg Brown and Carey Ashton series (1)
Jovial ghosts
Smith, Thorne
Topper series (1)
Joy
Bernanos, Georges
Spiritual life series (3)
Joy and Gypsy Joe
Whitehill, Dorothy
Joy Payton series (1)
Joy and her chums
Whitehill, Dorothy
Joy Payton series (3)
Joy and Pam
Whitehill, Dorothy
Joy Payton series (2)
Joy and Pam as seniors
Whitehill, Dorothy
Joy Payton series (6)
Joy and Pam a-sailing
Whitehill, Dorothy
Joy Payton series (5)
Joy and Pam at Brookside
Whitehill, Dorothy
Joy Payton series (4)
Joy in the morning
Wodehouse, Pelham Grenville
Jeeves and Bertie Wooster series (8)
Joy of it
Powys, Littleton Charles
Joy series (1)
Joy of life
Zola, Emile
Rougon Macquart series (12)
Joy of man's desiring
Giono, Jean
Song of the world trilogy (3)
Joy ride
Brandon, John Gordon
Sexton Blake series (469)
Carnelle, Inge
Jane Blonde series (2)
Joy Sparton and her problem twin
Johnson, Ruth Ingrid
Joy Sparton series (4)
Joy Sparton and the money mixup
Johnson, Ruth Ingrid
Joy Sparton series (3)
Joy Sparton and the vacation mixup
Johnson, Ruth Ingrid
Joy Sparton series (2)
Joy Sparton of Parsonage Hill
Johnson, Ruth Ingrid
Joy Sparton series (1)
Joy to the world
Sawyer, Ruth
Christmas stories series (7)
Joyce Grenfell requests the pleasure
Grenfell, Joyce
Pleasant places series (1)
Joyce, the beloved
Kimbrough, Katheryn
Phenwick women series (27)
Joyful adventures of Polly
Whitehill, Dorothy
Polly series (12)
Joyful beggar
De Wohl, Louis
Lives of the saints series (4)
Joyful Delaneys
Walpole, Hugh
London Group series (9)
Joyful voices
Stokes, Doris
Voices series (7)
Joyous story of Toto
Richards, Laura Elizabeth
Toto series (1)
Joy's new adventure
Oxenham, Elsie J
Abbey girls first generation series (19)
Juan in America
Linklater, Eric
Juan series (1)
Juan in China
Linklater, Eric
Juan series (2)
Juan Soto
Tufts, Warren
Casey Ruggles series (4)
Jubal
Daniels, Norman A
Jubal trilogy (1)
Jubal Sackett
L'Amour, Louis
Sackett family series (4)
Jubilee
Rayner, Claire
Poppy series (1)
Jubilo stage
Grover, Marshall
Larry and Stretch series (351)
Judah Lion contract
Atlee, Philip
Joe Gall series (15)
Judas boy
Raven, Simon
Alms for oblivion series (5)
Judas, C.I.D.
Grierson, Francis Durham
Superintendent Andrew Ash series (10)
Judas diary
Baker, William Howard
Richard Quintain series (16)
Judas factor
Allbeury, Ted
Tad Anders series (2)
Shelynn, Jack
Ned Parker series (5)
Judas figures
Lindop, Audrey Erskine
Father Keogh series (2)
Judas flowering
Hodge, Jane Aiken
Purchis family series (1)
Judas freak
Pentecost, Hugh
Julian Quist series (4)
Judas freaks
Cave, Peter
Hell's Angels series (4)
Judas goat
Cleeve, Brian
Sean Ryan series (3)
Muir, James A
Breed series (6)
Parker, Robert Brown
Spenser series (5)
Judas horse
Newton, Dwight Bennett
Jim Bannister series (7)
Judas, Incorporated
Steel, Kurt
Hank Hyer series (6)
Judas judge
Jason, Stuart
Butcher series (27)
Judas killer
Sharpe, Jon
Trailsman series (20)
Judas kiss
Adams, Herbert
Major Roger Bennion series (27)
Judas mandala
Broderick, Damien
Faustus hexagram series (1)
Judas mandate
Egleton, Clive
David Garnett trilogy (3)
Judas pair
Gash, Jonathan
Lovejoy series (1)
Judas Priest
McInerny, Ralph
Father Roger Dowling series (14)
Judas rat
Macdonnell, James Edmond
Dutchy Holland series (16)
Judas rose
Elgin, Suzette Haden
Native tongue series (2)
Judas scrolls
Rosenberger, Joseph
Death Merchant series (53)
Judas soldiers
Garrett, Frank
Killsquad series (4)
Judas spies
Robertson, Colin
Alan Steel series (2)
Judas spy
Carter, Nick
Nick Carter series (33)
Judas tree
Braun, Matt
Luke Starbuck series (7)
Swanson, Neil Harman
American colonial series (1)
Judas window
Dickson, Carter
Sir Henry Merrivale series (8)
Judd for the defense
Goldman, Lawrence Louis
Clinton Judd series (1)
Jude
Burton, Betty
Nugent family series (1)
Jude the obscure
Hardy, Thomas
Novels of character and environment series (3)
Judge
Edwards, Hank
Judge Clay Torn series (1)
Judge and his hangman
Durrenmatt, Friedrich
Kommissar Hans Barlach series (1)
Judge Benjamin, superdog
McInerney, Judith Whitelock
Judge Benjamin series (1)
Judge Burnham's daughters
Pansy
Ruth Erskine series (2)
Judge Colt
Mills, Robert E
Davy Watson series (4)
Judge Dee at work
Gulik, Robert van
Judge Dee series (8)
Judge is reversed
Lockridge, Frances
Bill Wiegand series (25)
Mister and Mrs North series (25)
Judge is seeing double
Grossman, Nancy Livright
Dutch Mill Stable series (1)
Judge Lawless
Grant, Maxwell
Shadow series (229)
Judge me tomorrow
Jobson, Hamilton
Inspector Anders series (11)
Judge of the Four Corners
Burgin, George Brown
Four Corners series (2)
Judge Priest turns detective
Cobb, Irwin Shrewsbury
Judge Priest series (7)
Judge will call it murder
Lott, Stanley Makepeace
Stephen Ringway series (2)
Judgement at Firecreek
Roberts, J R
Gunsmith series (95)
Judgement by fire
Huebner, Frederick D
Matt Riordan series (2)
Judgement day
Dancer, J B
Lawmen series (3)
Judgement of dragons
Gotlieb, Phyllis
Qsaprinel trilogy (1)
Judgement of the sword
Diver, Maud
Eldred Pottinger series (2)
Judges of Hades, and other Simon Ark stories
Hoch, Edward Dentinger
Simon Ark series (1)
Judges of the secret court
Stacton, David
American history trilogy (2)
Judging of Jurgen
Cabell, James Branch
Dom Manuel and his descendants series (25)
Judgment at Poisoned Well
Bishop, Pike
Cord Diamondback series (2)
Judgment day
Farrell, James Thomas
Studs Lonigan trilogy (3)
Frakes, Randall
Terminator series (2)
Hayes, Ralph Eugene
Check Force series (3)
Murphy, Warren Burton
Destroyer series (14)
Stine, George Harry
Warbots series (12)
Judgment of Deke Hunter
Higgins, George Vincent
Jerry Kennedy series (1)
Judgment of Eve
Pangborn, Edgar
Davy series (2)
Judgment of Larose
Gask, Arthur
Gilbert Larose series (7)
Judgment on Janus
Norton, Andre
Dipple trilogy (2)
Janus series (1)
Judith
Farrell, James Thomas
Universe of time series (5)
Mosley, Nicholas
Catastrophe practice series (4)
Judith in Hanover
Finlay, Winifred
Judith Norton series (2)
Judith Lammeter
Rundle, Anne
Amberwood series (3)
Judith Lankester
Allee, Marjorie Hill
Lankester family trilogy (1)
Judith Lee, some pages from her life
Marsh, Richard
Judith Lee series (1)
Judith Paris
Walpole, Hugh
Herries saga series (2)
Judith Quinn
O'Riordan, Conal
Anglo-Irish relations series (5)
Judith's love
O'Riordan, Conal
Anglo-Irish relations series (6)
Judo match
Goscinny, Rene
Twelve tasks of Asterix series (3)
Judy
Baldwin, Faith
Divine corners series (1)
Judy and Chris
Govan, Christine Noble
Plummer children series (3)
Judy and Punch
Turner, Ethel
Woolcot family series (4)
Judy and the baby elephant
Haar, Jaap ter
Judy series (2)
Judy at the zoo
Haar, Jaap ter
Judy series (1)
Judy in the garden
Shoesmith, Kathleen Anne
Judy series (1)
Judy in the snow
Shoesmith, Kathleen Anne
Judy series (3)
Judy in the wind
Shoesmith, Kathleen Anne
Judy series (2)
Judy Jordan
Garis, Lilian C
Judy Jordan series (1)
Judy Jordan's discovery
Garis, Lilian C
Judy Jordan series (2)
Judy Jo's magic island
Hill, Mabel Betsy
Judy Jo series (7)
Judy on the sand
Shoesmith, Kathleen Anne
Judy series (4)
Judy's journey
Lenski, Lois
Regional series (4)
Jugger
Stark, Richard
Parker series (6)
Juke box king
Kane, Frank
Mickey Denton series (1)
Julia
Henrey, Madeleine
Madeleine series (3)
Riefe, Barbara
Shackleford legacy trilogy (2)
Julia and the hand of God
Cameron, Eleanor
Julia Redfern series (1)
Julia in Ireland
Bridge, Ann
Julia Probyn series (9)
Julia involved
Bridge, Ann
Julia Probyn series (3)
Julia Ried
Pansy
Ester Ried series (5)
Julia Ried, listening and led
Pansy
Ester Ried series (3)
Julian stories
Cameron, Ann
Julian stories series (1)
Julian the Apostate
Merejkowski, Dmitri Sergeevich
Christ and Antichrist trilogy (1)
Julia's house
Gripe, Maria
Elvis Karlsson series (1)
Julia series (2)
Julia's magic
Cameron, Eleanor
Julia Redfern series (3)
Julie
Schurfranz, Vivian
Sunfire series (20)
Taylor, Cora
Julie series (1)
Julie and the karate kid
Pascal, Francine
Sweet Valley kids series (52)
Julie Barden, district nurse
Manley-Tucker, Audrie
Julie Barden series (1)
Julie Barden, doctor's wife
Manley-Tucker, Audrie
Julie Barden series (2)
Julie Gordon and the New Guinea smugglers
Grey, Estelle
Julie Gordon series (2)
Julie Gordon and the pony club camp
Grey, Estelle
Julie Gordon series (3)
Julie Gordon and the school fashion contest
Grey, Estelle
Julie Gordon series (1)
Julie Mac comes back
Oxenham, Elsie J
Tansy series (3)
Julie's daughter
Rudowsky, Colby
Slug series (2)
Julie's secret
Taylor, Cora
Julie series (2)
Juliet Bravo, volume 1
Hardwick, Mollie
Juliet Bravo series (1)
Juliet Bravo, volume 2
Hardwick, Mollie
Juliet Bravo series (2)
Juliet dies twice
Lewis, Lange
Lieutenant Richard Tuck series (2)
Juliette's daughter
Kalman, Yvonne
Yardley family trilogy (2)
Julius
Alger, Horatio
Tattered Tom series (5)
Julius and Cleopatra
Green, Michael
Coarse plays series (3)
Julius Le Vallon
Blackwood, Algernon
Reincarnation series (1)
July at Fritham
Home, Michael
Breckland series (6)

Justice limited
Duncan, Francis
Peter Justice series (4)

Justice of Company Z
Edson, John Thomas
Cap Fog series (3)

Justice of Sanders
Gerard, Francis
Commissioner Sanders series (10)

Justice of the Duke
Sabatini, Rafael
Cesare Borgia series (2)

Justice on Halfaday Creek
Hendryx, James Beardsley
Black John series (13)

Justice on the rocks
Knox, Bill
Inspector Colin Thane and Phil Moss series (9)

Justice returns
Duncan, Francis
Peter Justice series (3)

Justin
Palmer, Diana
Long tall Texan series (2)

Justin Kelly
Clevely, Hugh
Justin Kelly series (1)

Justin Perry, the Assassin
Revere, John D
Justin Perry series (1)

Justine
Durrell, Lawrence
Alexandria quartet (1)

Justus Wise
Barrett, Alfred Wilson
Justus Wise series (1)

Jutland Cottage
Thirkell, Angela
Barsetshire series (22)

Juve in the dock
Allain, Marcel
Fantomas series (10)

Juvenile delinquent
Deming, Richard
Manville Moon series (4)

Juvenile moods
Shallit, Joseph
Dan Morrison series (4)

Juxtaposition
Anthony, Piers
Apprentice adept series (3)

K

K code plan
Seton, Graham
Colonel Duncan Grant series (4)

K.F. conspiracy
Hall, Aylmer
K.F. series (2)

K.G.B., the inside story
Andrew, Christopher
K.G.B. series (1)

K is for killer
Grafton, Sue
Kinsey Millhone series (11)

K-Nine Corps
Von Gunden, Kenneth
K-Nine series (1)

K Section
Lilley, Tom
Police Special Branch series (2)

K9 and company
Dudley, Terence
Companions of Doctor Who series (3)

Kabongo
Baker, Richard Saint Barbe
Kabongo series (1)

Kabumpo in Oz
Thompson, Ruth Plumly
Oz series (15)

Kachina doll mystery
Keene, Carolyn
Nancy Drew series (62)

Kaeti and company
Roberts, Keith
Kaeti series (1)

Kaeti's apocalypse
Roberts, Keith
Kaeti series (2)

Kahuna killer
Sheridan, Juanita
Lily Wu and Janice Cameron series (2)

Kai Ling's golden hours
Bramah, Ernest
Kai Lung series (2)

Kai Lung beneath the mulberry tree
Bramah, Ernest
Kai Lung series (6)

Kai Lung omnibus
Bramah, Ernest
Kai Lung series (4)

Kai Lung, six
Bramah, Ernest
Kai Lung series (7)

Kai Lung unrolls his mat
Bramah, Ernest
Kai Lung series (4)

Kaisho
Lustbader, Eric
Ninja series (4)

Kajira of Gor
Norman, John
Tarl Cabot series (19)

Kak-Abdullah conspiracy
Macao, Marshall
K'ing Kung-Fu series (4)

Kalahari
McCurtin, Peter
Jim Rainey series (13)

Kalasanda
Kimenye, Barbara
Kalasanda series (1)

Kalasanda revisited
Kimenye, Barbara
Kalasanda series (2)

Kaleidoscope
Janes, Joseph Robert
Jean-Louis Saint-Cyr and Hermann Kohler series (3)

Kali death cafe
Carter, Nick
Nick Carter series (176)

Kali-flowers, Sally the Sleuth!
Barreaux
Sally the Sleuth series (2)

Kalif's war
Dalmas, John
Regiment series (3)

Kalin
Tubb, Edwin Charles
Dumarest series (4)

Kalinda
Green, Evan
Kalinda series (2)

Kalispell run
Robbins, David
Endworld series (4)

Kama Sutra tango
Burke, Jackson Frederick
Joe Streeter series (1)

Kamikaze assignment
Sugar, Andrew
Israeli commandos series (3)

Kamikaze justice
Lee, Patrick
Six-Gun Samurai series (4)

Kamiti
Baker, Richard Saint Barbe
Kabongo series (2)

Kamus of Kadizhar
Shirley, John
Darkworld detective series (2)

Kanata
Adair, Denis
MacLeod family series (1)

Kane
Frank, Lee
Kane Richards series (1)

Kane and Abel
Archer, Jeffrey
William Kane and Abel Rosnovski series (1)

Kane and Miss Able
Kane, Martin
Martin Kane series (13)

Kane and the goldbar killers
Frank, Lee
Kane Richards series (2)

Kane and the outlaw's double-cross
Frank, Lee
Kane Richards series (3)

Kane's war
Stone, Nick
Ben Kane series (1)

Kanga and the Baby Roo come to the forest
Milne, Alan Alexander
Piglet series (5)

Kangaroo twins
Hogan, Inez
Twins series (4)

Kansan's lady
Mills, Robert E
Davy Watson series (10)

Kansan's woman
Mills, Robert E
Davy Watson series (9)

Kansas, bloody Kansas
Dancer, J B
Lawmen series (2)

Kansas City chorine
Fletcher, Dirk
Spur McCoy series (28)

Kansas hex
Grover, Marshall
Larry and Stretch series (184)

Kansas kill
Sharpe, Jon
Trailsman series (116)

Kansas kitten
Sherman, Jory
Gunn series (22)

Kansas trail
Borg, Jack
Hogleg Bailey series (10)

Kar-Chee reign
Davidson, Avram
Kar-Chee series (2)

Kar Kaballa
Smith, George Henry
Annwn series (2)

Karan
Wongar, B
Nuclear trilogy (2)

Karate killers
Streib, Dan
Steve Crown series (4)

Karate Princess
Strong, Jeremy
Karate Princess series (1)

Karate Princess and the cut-throat robbers
Strong, Jeremy
Karate Princess series (2)

Karate Princess to the rescue
Strong, Jeremy
Karate Princess series (3)

Karen
Killilea, Marie
Karen series (1)

Karen and Vicki
McHugh, Elisabet
Karen series (2)

Karen, Hannie and Nancy, the three musketeers
Martin, Ann Matthews
Baby-Sitters little sister super specials series (4)

Karen Simms, private secretary
Palmer, Bernard
Career series (7)

Karen Travers story
O'Shell, Maggie
Caged women series (3)

Karen's baby
Martin, Ann Matthews
Baby-Sitters little sister super specials series (5)

Karen's baby-sitter
Martin, Ann Matthews
Baby-Sitters little sister series (46)

Karen's big joke
Martin, Ann Matthews
Baby-Sitters little sister series (27)

Karen's big lie
Martin, Ann Matthews
Baby-Sitters little sister series (38)

Karen's big top
Martin, Ann Matthews
Baby-Sitters little sister series (51)

Karen's big weekend
Martin, Ann Matthews
Baby-Sitters little sister series (44)

Karen's birthday
Martin, Ann Matthews
Baby-Sitters little sister series (7)

Karen's brothers
Martin, Ann Matthews
Baby-Sitters little sister series (17)

Karen's bully
Martin, Ann Matthews
Baby-Sitters little sister series (31)

Karen's campout
Martin, Ann Matthews
Baby-Sitters little sister super specials series (6)

Karen's carnival
Martin, Ann Matthews
Baby-Sitters little sister series (20)

Karen's cartwheel
Martin, Ann Matthews
Baby-Sitters little sister series (29)

Karen's curiosity
Provensen, Alice
Karen series (1)

Karen's doll
Martin, Ann Matthews
Baby-Sitters little sister series (23)

Karen's doll house
Martin, Ann Matthews
Baby-Sitters little sister series (35)

Karen's ducklings
Martin, Ann Matthews
Baby-Sitters little sister series (26)

Karen's ghost
Martin, Ann Matthews
Baby-Sitters little sister series (12)

Karen's goldfish
Martin, Ann Matthews
Baby-Sitters little sister series (16)

Karen's good-bye
Martin, Ann Matthews
Baby-Sitters little sister series (19)

Karen's grandmother
Martin, Ann Matthews
Baby-Sitters little sister series (10)

Karen's haircut
Martin, Ann Matthews
Baby-Sitters little sister series (8)

Karen's home run
Martin, Ann Matthews
Baby-Sitters little sister series (18)

Karen's in love
Martin, Ann Matthews
Baby-Sitters little sister series (15)

Karen's kite
Martin, Ann Matthews
Baby-Sitters little sister series (47)

Karen's kittens
Martin, Ann Matthews
Baby-Sitters little sister series (30)

Karen's Kittycat Club
Martin, Ann Matthews
Baby-Sitters little sister series (4)

Karen's little sister
Martin, Ann Matthews
Baby-Sitters little sister series (6)

Karen's little witch
Martin, Ann Matthews
Baby-Sitters little sister series (22)

Karen's lucky penny
Martin, Ann Matthews
Baby-Sitters little sister series (50)

Karen's mermaid
Martin, Ann Matthews
Baby-Sitters little sister series (52)

Karen's mystery
Martin, Ann Matthews
Baby-Sitters little sister super specials series (3)

Karen's new friend
Martin, Ann Matthews
Baby-Sitters little sister series (36)

Karen's new teacher
Martin, Ann Matthews
Baby-Sitters little sister series (21)

Karen's New Year
Martin, Ann Matthews
Baby-Sitters little sister series (14)

Karen's newspaper
Martin, Ann Matthews
Baby-Sitters little sister series (40)

Karen's opposites
Provensen, Alice
Karen series (2)

Karen's pen pal
Martin, Ann Matthews
Baby-Sitters little sister series (25)

Karen's pizza party
Martin, Ann Matthews
Baby-Sitters little sister series (42)

Karen's plane trip
Martin, Ann Matthews
Baby-Sitters little sister super specials series (2)

Karen's prize
Martin, Ann Matthews
Baby-Sitters little sister series (11)

Karen's pumpkin patch
Martin, Ann Matthews
Baby-Sitters little sister series (32)

Karen's roller skates
Martin, Ann Matthews
Baby-Sitters little sister series (2)

Karen's school
Martin, Ann Matthews
Baby-Sitters little sister series (41)

Karen's school picture
Martin, Ann Matthews
Baby-Sitters little sister series (5)

Karen's school trip
Martin, Ann Matthews
Baby-Sitters little sister series (24)

Karen's secret
Martin, Ann Matthews
Baby-Sitters little sister series (33)

Karen's sister
McHugh, Elisabet
Karen series (1)

Karen's sleepover
Martin, Ann Matthews
Baby-Sitters little sister series (9)

Karen's snowy day
Martin, Ann Matthews
Baby-Sitters little sister series (34)

Karen's stepmother
Martin, Ann Matthews
Baby-Sitters little sister series (49)

Karen's surprise
Martin, Ann Matthews
Baby-Sitters little sister series (13)

Karen's tea party
Martin, Ann Matthews
Baby-Sitters little sister series (28)

Karen's toothache
Martin, Ann Matthews
Baby-Sitters little sister series (43)

Karen's tuba
Martin, Ann Matthews
Baby-Sitters little sister series (37)

Karen's twin
Martin, Ann Matthews
Baby-Sitters little sister series (45)

Karen's two families
Martin, Ann Matthews
Baby-Sitters little sister series (48)

Karen's wedding
Martin, Ann Matthews
Baby-Sitters little sister series (39)

Karen's wish
Martin, Ann Matthews
Baby-Sitters little sister super specials series (1)

Karen's witch
Martin, Ann Matthews
Baby-Sitters little sister series (1)

Karen's worst day
Martin, Ann Matthews
Baby-Sitters little sister series (3)

Karl and Rosa
Doblin, Alfred
German revolution series (2)

Karl Krinken, his Christmas stocking
Warner, Susan Bagert
Mister Rutherford series (2)

Karlsson-on-the-Roof
Lindgren, Astrid
Karlsson-on-the-Roof series (1)

Karlsson flies again
Lindgren, Astrid
Karlsson-on-the-Roof series (2)

Karlyn
Jenkins, Jerry Bruce
Margo Franklin and Philip Spence series (2)

Karma
Dunlap, Susan
Jill Smith series (1)

Karoleena
Steiner, Charlotte
Karoleena series (2)

Karoleena's red coat
Steiner, Charlotte
Karoleena series (1)

Karoo morning
Butler, Guy
South Africa series (1)

Karran Kinrade
Manners, Alexandra
Karran Kinrade series (2)

Karts
Wilkinson, Sylvia
World of racing series (10)

Kashka
McKenzie, Ellen Kindt
Taash series (2)

Kashmir adventure
Bayley, Viola
Adventure series (3)

Kasia and the empress
Carnegie, Sacha
Destiny of eagles series (3)

Kaspa, the lion man
Stoneham, Charles Thurley
Kaspa series (2)

Katana
Olden, Marc
Robert Sand series (8)

Katawampus, its treatment and cure
Parry, Edward Abbott
Krab series (1)

Kate
Little, Jean
Emily Blair and Kate Bloomfield series (2)
Moore, Melissa
Agency series (2)

Kate Alanna
Peters, Maureen
Malone family trilogy (2)
Kate and Sam go out
Cole, Michael
Kate and Sam series (4)
Kate and Sam's new home
Cole, Michael
Kate and Sam series (2)
Kate and Sam's pet
Cole, Michael
Kate and Sam series (3)
Kate and Sam's tea
Cole, Michael
Kate and Sam series (1)
Kate and the cutter
Maisner, Heather
Tractors of Thomson's Yard series (3)
Kate be late
York, Carol Beach
Miss Know It All series (7)
Kate Carnegie and those ministers
Maclaren, Ian
Drumtochty series (3)
Kate heads west
Brisson, Pat
Kate series (2)
Kate, Kate come and help
Sandberg, Inger
Kate series (4)
Kate Meredith
Hyne, Charles John Cutcliffe
Captain Owen Kettle series (7)
Kate Meredith, financier
Hyne, Charles John Cutcliffe
Captain Owen Kettle series (7)
Kate on the coast
Brisson, Pat
Kate series (3)
Kate plus ten
Wallace, Edgar
Mister T B Smith series (3)
Kate the boss
Saunders, Susan
Sleepover friends series (29)
Kate, the cat
Darby, Joan
Animal adventure series (8)
Kate, the curious
Kimbrough, Katheryn
Phenwick women series (13)
Kate the winner
Saunders, Susan
Sleepover friends series (34)
Kate's bouncy ball
Sandberg, Inger
Kate series (3)
Kate's box
Chorao, Kay
Kate series (2)
Kate's campout
Saunders, Susan
Sleepover friends series (6)
Kate's car
Chorao, Kay
Kate series (1)
Kate's Christmas present
Sandberg, Inger
Kate series (1)
Kate's crush
Saunders, Susan
Sleepover friends series (16)
Kate's party
Solomon, Joan
Children's life series (1)
Kate's quilt
Chorao, Kay
Kate series (3)
Kate's sleepover disaster
Saunders, Susan
Sleepover friends series (12)
Kate's snowman
Chorao, Kay
Kate series (4)
Kate's surprise
Saunders, Susan
Sleepover friends series (3)
Kate's surprise visitor
Saunders, Susan
Sleepover friends series (23)
Kate's upside down day
Sandberg, Inger
Kate series (2)
Katharine of Aragon
Plaidy, Jean
Katharine of Aragon trilogy (3)
Tudor series (3)
Katharine, the virgin widow
Plaidy, Jean
Katharine of Aragon trilogy (1)
Tudor series (1)
Katherine Christian
Walpole, Hugh
Herries ancestors series (2)
Katherine Lauderdale
Crawford, Francis Marion
Lauderdale family series (1)
Paul Griggs series (3)
Katherine Parr
Evans, Jean
Katherine Parr series (1)
Katherine, queen dowager
Evans, Jean
Katherine Parr series (2)
Katherine, the returned
Kimbrough, Katheryn
Phenwick women series (30)
Katherine Walton
Simms, William Gilmore
American Revolution series (4)
Katherine Wentworth
Stevenson, Dorothy Emily
Ardfalloch series (2)
Katherine Wentworth series (1)
Katherine's dream
Williams, Leigh Anne
Taylor House trilogy (1)
Katherine's marriage
Stevenson, Dorothy Emily
Ardfalloch series (3)
Katherine Wentworth series (2)
Kathie's Aunt Ruth
Douglas, Amanda Minnie
Kathie series (2)
Kathie's harvest days
Douglas, Amanda Minnie
Kathie series (6)
Kathie's soldiers
Douglas, Amanda Minnie
Kathie series (4)
Kathie's summer at Cedarwood
Douglas, Amanda Minnie
Kathie series (3)
Kathie's three wishes
Douglas, Amanda Minnie
Kathie series (1)
Kathleen
Ransom, Candice Farris
Sunfire series (8)
Kathleen and Frank
Isherwood, Christopher
Christopher series (1)
Kathy
Bacon, Josephine Dodge
Lowry series (2)
Kathy and the babysitting hassle
Stahl, Hilda
Best friends series (3)
Kathy in charge
Sheldon, Ann
Linda Craig adventures series (12)
Kathy's new brother
Stahl, Hilda
Best friends series (6)
Kati in America
Lindgren, Astrid
Kati series (1)
Kati in Italy
Lindgren, Astrid
Kati series (2)
Kati in Paris
Lindgren, Astrid
Kati series (3)
Katie and Kit at the beach
De Paola, Tomie
Katie and Kit series (1)
Katie and those boys
Tolles, Martha
Katie series (1)
Katie can
McDaniel, Becky Bring
Katie series (3)
Katie couldn't
McDaniel, Becky Bring
Katie series (2)
Katie did it
McDaniel, Becky Bring
Katie series (1)
Katie for president
Tolles, Martha
Katie series (2)
Katie gets a bed
Aston, Elizabeth
I am growing up series (2)
Katie, James and the Moonster
Johnson, Patricia Irene
Moonster series (1)
Katie, James and the Moonster go to Mars
Johnson, Patricia Irene
Moonster series (2)
Katie John
Calhoun, Mary
Katie John series (1)
Katie John and Heathcliff
Calhoun, Mary
Katie John series (4)
Katie kicks off
Davis, Gibbs
Never sink nine series (8)
Katie, Kit and Cousin Tom
De Paola, Tomie
Katie and Kit series (4)
Katie Morag and the big boy cousins
Hedderwick, Mairi
Katie Morag series (4)
Katie Morag and the new pier
Hedderwick, Mairi
Katie Morag series (5)
Katie Morag and the tiresome Ted
Hedderwick, Mairi
Katie Morag series (3)
Katie Morag and the two grandmothers
Hedderwick, Mairi
Katie Morag series (2)
Katie Morag delivers the mail
Hedderwick, Mairi
Katie Morag series (1)
Katie steals the show
Kaye, Marilyn
Camp Sunnyside Friends series (6)
Katie's babysitting job
Tolles, Martha
Katie series (3)
Katie's good idea
De Paola, Tomie
Katie and Kit series (3)
Katmandu contract
Carter, Nick
Nick Carter series (100)
Katrinka
Haskell, Helen Eggleston
Katrinka series (1)
Katrinka grows up
Haskell, Helen Eggleston
Katrinka series (2)
Katy and Dom
Oldfield, Pamela
Katy and Dom series (1)
Katy and Dom and the lost cat
Oldfield, Pamela
Katy and Dom series (2)
Katy-Didd
Cosgrove, Stephen Edward
Bugg series (17)
Katy goes to the seaside
Border, Rosemary
Out and about series (5)
Kavin's world
Mason, David
Kavin series (1)
Kay assignation
Janson, Hank
Hank Janson series (260)
Kay Thompson's Eloise
Thompson, Kay
Eloise series (1)
Kay Thompson's Eloise at Christmastime
Thompson, Kay
Eloise series (3)
Kay Thompson's Eloise in Moscow
Thompson, Kay
Eloise series (4)
Kay Thompson's Eloise in Paris
Thompson, Kay
Eloise series (2)
Kayak!
Odgers, Sally Farrell
Bandinangi series (2)
Kayla O'Brien and the dangerous journey
Stahl, Hilda
Kayla O'Brien series (1)
Kayla O'Brien and the runaway orphans
Stahl, Hilda
Kayla O'Brien series (3)
Kayla O'Brien and the trouble at Bitter Creek Ranch
Stahl, Hilda
Kayla O'Brien series (2)
Kayles of Bushy Lodge
Dwyer, Vera Gladys
Kayle family series (2)
Kaywana blood
Mittelholzer, Edgar
Kaywana series (4)
Kaywana heritage
Mittelholzer, Edgar
Kaywana series (2)
Kaywana stock
Mittelholzer, Edgar
Kaywana series (3)
Kaz, the minotaur
Knaak, Richard Allen
DragonLance heroes series (4)
Kazan, the wolf-dog
Curwood, James Oliver
Kazan series (1)
Kedrigern and the charming couple
Morressy, John
Kedrigern series (4)
Kedrigern in Wanderland
Morressy, John
Kedrigern series (3)
Keep
Becker, Jillian
Simon and Josephine Leyton series (1)
Wilson, Francis Paul
Adversary series (1)
Keep Allison alive
Grover, Marshall
Larry and Stretch series (213)
Keep calm if you can
Hillary, Louise
Himalayan series (2)
Keep cool, Mr Jones
Fuller, Timothy
Jupiter Jones series (5)
Keep 'em crawling
Upson, William Hazlett
Alexander Botts series (3)
Keep it a secret
Chambers, Philip
Sexton Blake series (1510)
Keep it clean
Knott, Tina Spencer
Fools series (2)
Keep it up, Rod!
Conway, Troy
Coxeman series (8)
Keep of the ancient king
Carr, Mike
Fantasy forest series (4)
Keep of the Lich-Lord
Jackson, Steve
Fighting fantasy gamebook series (43)
Keep off, death
Echlin, Elizabeth Gladys
Chronicles trilogy (1)
Keep out, Claudia!
Martin, Ann Matthews
Baby-Sitters Club series (56)
Keep the Home Guard turning
Mackenzie, Compton
Highland series (2)
Keep your fingers cross
O'Hara, Kevin
Chico Brett series (7)
Keep your fingers crossed
Maddock, Stephen
Inspector Slane series (3)
Keep your mouth closed, dear
Aliki
Dear series (1)
Keeper of the black hounds
Carter, Nicholas
Nicholas Carter series (527)
Keeper of the city
Morwood, Peter
Guardians of the Three series (2)
Keeper of the door
Dell, Ethel May
Nick Ratcliffe series (2)
Keeper of the Isis Light
Hughes, Monica
Isis trilogy (1)
Keeper of the keys
Biggers, Earl Derr
Charlie Chan series (6)
Wurts, Janny
Cycle of fire trilogy (2)
Keeper of the secrets
Farmer, Philip Jose
Doc Caliban series (2)
Keeper play
Porter, Mark
Win Hadley series (2)
Keeper's gold
Grant, Maxwell
Shadow series (132)
Keepers of death
Jason, Stuart
Butcher series (3)
Keepers of Edanvani
Douglas, Carole Nelson
Irissa and Kendric trilogy (3)
Sword and circlet trilogy (1)
Keepers of the gate
Grier, Sydney Carlyon
Century series (4)
Keepers of the king's peace
Wallace, Edgar
Commissioner Sanders series (11)
Keepers of the people
Jepson, Edgar
Passion for romance series (2)
Keepers of the trail
Altsheler, Joseph Alexander
Trailers series (7)
Keeper's price, and other stories
Bradley, Marion Zimmer
Darkover anthologies series (1)
Keeper's tale
Speakman, Frederick James
Gamekeeper trilogy (1)
Keeping company
Hoag, Tami
Rainbow chasers series (2)
Keeping days
Johnston, Norma
Sterling family series (1)
Keeping secrets
Chase, Emily
Canby Hall series (4)
Pascal, Francine
Sweet Valley twins series (12)
Keeping the faith
James, Dean
Melrose Place series (3)
Keeping up with Lizzie
Bacheller, Irving
Socrates Potter trilogy (1)
Keeping up with Teddy Robinson
Robinson, Joan Gale
Teddy Robinson series (7)
Keeping your body alive and well
Berry, Joy
Ready-set-grow series (3)
Keeps death his court
Durham, Mary
Inspector York series (3)
Keith and Sally at the seaside
Gree, Alain
Keith and Sally series (2)
Keith and Sally' bird book
Gree, Alain
Keith and Sally series (18)
Keith and Sally by the river
Gree, Alain
Keith and Sally series (9)
Keith and Sally go abroad
Gree, Alain
Keith and Sally series (1)
Keith and Sally in the garden
Gree, Alain
Keith and Sally series (14)
Keith and Sally look at television
Gree, Alain
Keith and Sally series (11)
Keith and Sally look for oil
Gree, Alain
Keith and Sally series (6)
Keith and Sally's plant book
Gree, Alain
Keith and Sally series (19)
Keith County journal
Janovy, John
Keith County series (1)
Keith Garvey omnibus
Garvey, Keith
Outback tales series (4)
Keith o' Kinnellan
Mackenzie, Agnes Mure
Kinnellan series (2)
Keith Partridge, master spy
Stanton, Vance
Partridge family series (4)
Keith, the hero
Avallone, Michael
Partridge family series (3)
Kek Huuygens, smuggler
Fish, Robert Lloyd
Kek Huuygens series (5)
Kelford dig
Mackenzie, Kathleen
Starke sisters series (3)
Kellogg Junction
Spicer, Bart
Benson Kellogg series (2)
Kelly among the nightingales
Burke, Jackson Frederick
Samuel Moses Kelly series (3)
Kelly blue
Bowen, Peter
Yellowstone Kelly series (2)
Kelly country
Chandler, Arthur Bertram
John Grimes series (25)
Kelly, Dot and Esmeralda
Goodall, John Strickland
Paddy Pork series (5)
Kelly Pencarrow
Scanlan, Nelle Margaret
Pencarrow family series (4)
Kelp
Allen, Willis Boyd
Pine cone series (4)

Kelp-gatherers
Trowbridge, John Townsend
Start in life series (4)
Kelso of the Paragon
White, James Dillon
Roger Kelso series (3)
Kelston of Kells
Anderson, Helen M
Kelston of Kells series (1)
Kemlo and the craters of the moon
Eliott, E C
Kemlo series (5)
Kemlo and the crazy planet
Eliott, E C
Kemlo series (2)
Kemlo and the end of time
Eliott, E C
Kemlo series (10)
Kemlo and the gravity rays
Eliott, E C
Kemlo series (8)
Kemlo and the Martian ghosts
Eliott, E C
Kemlo series (4)
Kemlo and the masters of space
Eliott, E C
Kemlo series (15)
Kemlo and the purple dawn
Eliott, E C
Kemlo series (9)
Kemlo and the satellite builders
Eliott, E C
Kemlo series (13)
Kemlo and the sky horse
Eliott, E C
Kemlo series (3)
Kemlo and the space invaders
Eliott, E C
Kemlo series (14)
Kemlo and the space lanes
Eliott, E C
Kemlo series (6)
Kemlo and the space men
Eliott, E C
Kemlo series (12)
Kemlo and the star men
Eliott, E C
Kemlo series (7)
Kemlo and the zombie men
Eliott, E C
Kemlo series (11)
Kemlo and the zones of silence
Eliott, E C
Kemlo series (1)
Kempei Tai
Deacon, Richard
Secret service series (5)
Ken and the cattle thieves
Miller, Basil
Ken series (13)
Ken and the lost Indian treasure
Miller, Basil
Ken series (17)
Ken and the Navajo treasure map
Miller, Basil
Ken series (15)
Ken bails out
Miller, Basil
Ken series (2)
Ken, Candy and Co
Thomas, Millicent Inglis
Ken, Candy and Co series (1)
Ken, Candy and the castle secret
Thomas, Millicent Inglis
Ken, Candy and Co series (3)
Ken, Candy and the hunt for spies
Thomas, Millicent Inglis
Ken, Candy and Co series (2)
Ken captures a foreign agent
Miller, Basil
Ken series (3)
Ken follows the chuck wagon
Miller, Basil
Ken series (10)
Ken hits the cowboy trail
Miller, Basil
Ken series (11)
Ken in Alaska
Miller, Basil
Ken series (5)
Ken on the Anchor D Ranch
Miller, Basil
Ken series (16)
Ken on the Argentine pampas
Miller, Basil
Ken series (7)
Ken on the Navajo trail
Miller, Basil
Ken series (9)
Ken, range detective
Miller, Basil
Ken series (12)
Ken, range hero
Miller, Basil
Ken series (14)
Ken rides the range
Miller, Basil
Ken series (1)
Ken saddles up
Miller, Basil
Ken series (6)
Ken south of the border
Miller, Basil
Ken series (8)
Ken Ward in the jungle
Grey, Zane
Ken Ward series (4)
Kender, gully dwarves and gnomes
Weis, Margaret
DragonLance tales trilogy (2)
Kendermore
Kirchoff, Mary Lynn
DragonLance preludes series (2)
Kennedy for the defense
Higgins, George Vincent
Jerry Kennedy series (2)
Kennedy Square
Smith, Francis Hopkinson
Civil War society series (2)
Kennedy's killing
Venters, Archie
Gil Kennedy series (1)
Kennel maid Sally
Byers, Irene
Tony and Melissa series (3)
Kennel murder case
Van Dine, S S
Philo Vance series (6)
Kennels crime
Osborne, Mark
Sexton Blake series (715)
Ken's mercy flight to Australia
Miller, Basil
Ken series (4)
Kensho
Schmidt, Dennis
Kensho series (2)
Kent Barstow aboard the Dyna Soar
Montgomery, Rutherford George
Kent Barstow series (8)
Kent Barstow and the commando flight
Montgomery, Rutherford George
Kent Barstow series (6)
Kent Barstow on a B-70 mission
Montgomery, Rutherford George
Kent Barstow series (7)
Kent Barstow, space man
Montgomery, Rutherford George
Kent Barstow series (5)
Kent Barstow, special agent
Montgomery, Rutherford George
Kent Barstow series (2)
Kent heiress
Gellis, Roberta
Heiress series (3)
Kent Montana and the once and future thing
Fenn, Lionel
Kent Montana trilogy (3)
Kent Montana and the really ugly thing from Mars
Fenn, Lionel
Kent Montana trilogy (1)
Kent Montana and the reasonably invisible man
Fenn, Lionel
Kent Montana trilogy (2)
Kent squire
Hayes, Frederick William
Gwynett trilogy (1)
Kentish Manor murders
Symons, Julian
Sheridan Haynes series (5)
Kentish manor murders
Symons, Julian
Sherlock Holmes sequels series (92)
Kentuckians
Giles, Janice Holt
Fowler family series (1)
Kentucky!
Ross, Dana Fuller
Wagons West series (20)
Kentucky cardinal
Allen, James Lane
Kentucky series (1)
Kentucky colts
Sharpe, Jon
Trailsman series (132)
Kentucky spitfire, Caitlyn McGregor
Brown, Kitt
Frontier women series (1)
Kenworthys
Wilson, Margaret
Kenworthys series (1)
Kenya calling
Strange, Nora Kathleen
Kenya series (2)
Kenya dawn
Strange, Nora Kathleen
Kenya series (3)
Kenya moon
Strange, Nora Kathleen
Kenya series (5)
Kenyatta's escape
Clark, Al C
Kenyatta series (3)
Kenyatta's last hit
Clark, Al C
Kenyatta series (4)
Kepler
Banville, John
Astronomers series (2)
Kept women can't quit
Fair, A A
Bertha Cool and Donald Lam series (20)
Kerrigan's quality
Barlow, Jane
Fortunes series (1)
Kerry's lost dog
Leyland, Mal
Kerry series (1)
Kesrick
Carter, Lin
Terra Magica series (1)
Kesrith
Cherryh, Carolyn Janice
Alliance-Union series (14)
Faded sun trilogy (1)
Kessler
Brason, John
Secret army series (4)
Kessler's raid
Hutson, Shaun
Sergeant Rolf Kessler series (2)
Kestrel
Alexander, Lloyd
Westmark trilogy (2)
Kestrel House mystery
Jacobs, Thomas Curtis Hicks
Chief Inspector Barnard series (2)
Kestrel Syndicate
Lewis, Jack
Sexton Blake series (91)
Kestrel's claw
Lewis, Jack
Sexton Blake series (132)
Kestrel's conspiracy
Lewis, Jack
Sexton Blake series (184)
Kestrels dare danger
Mason, Stanley Weston
Kestrels series (3)
Kestrels jetty
Mason, Stanley Weston
Kestrels series (2)
Kestrels over the beacon
Mason, Stanley Weston
Kestrels series (1)
Kestrels plot adventure
Mason, Stanley Weston
Kestrels series (4)
Kettel Mill mystery
Oellrichs, Inez
Matt Winters series (2)
Kettle's great adventure
Muir, Marie
Kettle series (2)
Kettleship pirates
Peppe, Rodney
Mice series (2)
Kevin Corbett eats flies
Hermes, Patricia
Kevin Corbett series (1)
Kewpie doll
Hanrahan, Barbara
Eucalyptus series (2)
Key
Cresswell, Helen
Mike series (5)
Grant, Maxwell
Shadow series (55)
Thayer, Lee
Peter Clancy series (6)
Wentworth, Patricia
Miss Maud Silver series (8)
Key for the nonesuch
Gravel, Geary
Fading worlds series (1)
Key of England
Divine, David
Mig and Peter Manson series (2)
Key of ice and steel
Moran, Daniel Keys
Keys to paradise trilogy (3)
Key out of time
Norton, Andre
Time war series (4)
Key ring clew
Carter, Nicholas
Nicholas Carter series (176)
Key to death
Lockridge, Frances
Bill Wiegand series (19)
Mister and Mrs North series (20)
Key to Irunium
Bulmer, Kenneth
Keys to the dimensions series (2)
Key to murder
Marshall, Lovat
Sugar Kane series (27)
Key to the case
Ormerod, Roger
Philipa Lowe series (4)
Key to the morgue
Howard, Hartley
Glenn Bowman series (13)
Martin, Robert Lee
Jim Bennett series (10)
Key to the treasure
Parish, Peggy
Liza, Bill and Jed series (1)
Key to Uncle Tom's cabin
Stowe, Harriet Beecher
Uncle Tom series (2)
Key to Venudine
Bulmer, Kenneth
Keys to the dimensions series (3)
Key West connection
Striker, Randy
Dusky MacMorgan series (1)
Key without a door
Lejeune, Anthony
Glowrey series (2)
Keys for the criminal
Hambledon, Phyllis
Inspector Tubby Hall series (1)
Keys of hell
Fallon, Martin
Paul Chavasse series (3)
Keys of Mantlemass
Willard, Barbara
Mantlemass series (9)
Keys of paradise
Moran, Daniel Keys
Keys to paradise trilogy (3)
Keystone Kids
Tunis, John Roberts
Spike Russell series (1)
Kezzy
Burns, Patricia
Kezzy series (2)
KGB doublecross
Acres, Mark
Sniper series (4)
KGB frame
Rosenberger, Joseph
Death Merchant series (12)
Khaki Boys along the Rhine
Bates, Gordon
Khaki Boys series (6)
Khaki Boys at Camp Sterling
Bates, Gordon
Khaki Boys series (1)
Khaki Boys at the Front
Bates, Gordon
Khaki Boys series (3)
Khaki Boys fighting to win
Bates, Gordon
Khaki Boys series (5)
Khaki Boys on the way
Bates, Gordon
Khaki Boys series (2)
Khaki Boys over the top
Bates, Gordon
Khaki Boys series (4)
Khaki Girls at Windsor Barracks
Brooks, Edna
Khaki Girls series (3)
Khaki Girls behind the lines
Brooks, Edna
Khaki Girls series (2)
Khaki Girls in victory
Brooks, Edna
Khaki Girls series (4)
Khaki Girls of the Motor Corps
Brooks, Edna
Khaki Girls series (1)
Khaki wings
Dank, Milton
Edward Burton series (1)
Khalindaine
Burns, Richard
Khalindaine series (1)
Kharduni
Soutar, Andrew
Kharduni series (1)
Khare, cityport of traps
Jackson, Steve
Sorcery series (2)
Khrush
Janson, Hank
Hank Janson series (224)
Khyber connection
Hawke, Simon
Timewars series (6)
Khyberie
Enriquez, Colin Metcalfe
Khyberie series (1)
Khyberie in Burma
Enriquez, Colin Metcalfe
Khyberie series (2)
Kiai!
Anthony, Piers
Jason Striker series (1)
Kick back
McDermid, Val
Kate Brannigan series (2)
Kick in the Kiomies
Capp, Al
Li'l Abner dailies series (15)
Kick off
Hardcastle, Michael
Mark Fox series (6)
Kick the can
Lehrer, Jim
One-Eyed Mack series (1)
Kickback
Disher, Garry
Wyatt series (1)
Harrell, Andrew
Sam Shank series (4)
Kickoff time
Hughes, Dean
Angel Park Soccer Stars series (1)
Kid Breckenridge
Palmer, Bernard
Kid Breckinridge series (3)
Kid comes back
Tunis, John Roberts
Roy Tucker series (4)
Kid Cyclone
Gregory, Lester
Kid Cyclone series (2)
Kid Daybreak
Grover, Marshall
Nevada Jim series (26)
Kid from Tomkinsville
Tunis, John Roberts
Roy Tucker series (1)
Kid Lightfingers
Grover, Marshall
Larry and Stretch series (239)
Kid next door, and other headaches
Smith, Janice Lea
Adam Joshua series (2)
Kid power
Pfeffer, Susan Beth
Kid power series (1)
Kid power strikes back
Pfeffer, Susan Beth
Kid power series (2)
Kid stakes
Lawler, Ray
Doll trilogy (1)
Kid was last seen hanging ten
Stone, Hampton
Jeremiah X Gibson series (14)
Kid who came home with a corpse
Stone, Hampton
Jeremiah X Gibson series (18)
Kid who only hit homers
Christopher, Matt
Home Run Kid series (1)
Kid Wichita
Grover, Marshall
Larry and Stretch series (29)
Kid with a Colt
Borg, Jack
Hogleg Bailey series (16)
Kiddar's luck
Common, Jack
Newcastle-upon-Tyne series (1)
Kiddie of the camp
Leighton, Robert
Kiddie trilogy (1)
Kiddie, the prairie rider
Leighton, Robert
Kiddie trilogy (3)
Kiddie the scout
Leighton, Robert
Kiddie trilogy (2)
Kiddo
Handler, David
Danny Levine series (1)
Kidnap
Eisenberg, Lisa
South City cops series (2)

Maguire, Michael
Mylor series (2)
Kidnap Castle
Styles, Showell
Sir Abercrombie Lewker series (2)
Kidnap club
Reeve, Arthur Benjamin
Craig Kennedy series (23)
Kidnap Hotel
Andrews, Spike
C.A.T. series (2)
Kidnap in space
Elliott, Nathan
Star pirates trilogy (1)
Kidnap Island
Vickers, Roy
Inspector J Rason series (9)
Kidnap murder case
Van Dine, S S
Philo Vance series (10)
Kidnap report
Townson, Hazel
Lenny and Jake series (10)
Kidnaped child
Ashe, Gordon
Patrick Dawlish series (31)
Kidnapped!
Packard, Edward
Choose your own adventure series (116)
Pascal, Francine
Sweet Valley High series (13)
Kidnapped
Stevenson, Robert Louis
David Balfour series (1)
Kidnapped again
Crozier, John
Falcon series (2)
Kidnapped by a cult
Pascal, Francine
Sweet Valley High series (82)
Kidnapped child
Ashe, Gordon
Patrick Dawlish series (31)
Kidnapped in the jungle
Lloyd, Hugh
Hal Keen series (2)
Kidnapped on Astarr
Nixon, Joan Lowery
Kleep, space detective series (1)
Kidnapped Santa Claus
Baum, Lyman Frank
Santa Claus series (2)
Kidnapped scientist
Dix, Maurice Buxton
Tommy Malins, Anthony Mornington and George Hawkins series (3)
Kidnapped wife
Daniel, Roland
Buddy Mustard series (17)
Kidnapper
Thomson, Basil
Peter Graham series (2)
Kidnappers
Daniel, Roland
Michael Grant series (4)
Kidnappers at Coombe
Ballantyne, Jean
Maitland series (2)
Kidnapper's victim
Goyne, Richard
Sexton Blake series (799)
Kidnapping
Berry, Joy
Danger zones series (2)
Kidnapping of Madame Storey, and other stories
Footner, Hulbert
Madame Rosika Storey series (6)
Kidnapping of Toad
Trueman, Brian
Riverbend and Wildwood tales series (4)
Kid's best friend
Vail, Virginia
Animal Inn series (2)
Kid's guide to making friends
Berry, Joy
Ready-set-grow series (7)
Kid's guide to managing money
Berry, Joy
Ready-set-grow series (17)
Kid's guide to managing time
Berry, Joy
Ready-set-grow series (16)
Kid's guide to understanding parents
Berry, Joy
Ready-set-grow series (22)
Kid's TV guide
Berry, Joy
Ready-set-grow series (15)
Kiet and the golden peacock
Alexander, Gary
Superintendent Bamsan Kiet series (3)
Kiet and the Opium War
Alexander, Gary
Superintendent Bamsan Kiet series (4)
Kiet goes west
Alexander, Gary
Superintendent Bamsan Kiet series (6)
Kiev footprint
Posey, Carl Alfred
Steven Borg series (1)
Kif strikes back
Cherryh, Carolyn Janice
Alliance-Union series (9)
Chanur series (3)
Kigsdown Lodge
Worboise, Emma Jane
Grace Hamilton series (2)
Kiki and Muffy
Steiner, Charlotte
Kiki series (1)
Kiki dances
Steiner, Charlotte
Kiki series (2)
Kiki goes to camp
Steiner, Charlotte
Kiki series (4)
Kiki is an actress
Steiner, Charlotte
Kiki series (6)
Kiki loves music
Steiner, Charlotte
Kiki series (5)
Kiki skates
Steiner, Charlotte
Kiki series (3)
Kiki's playhouse
Steiner, Charlotte
Kiki series (7)
Kilbourne connection
Larsen, Gaylord D
Henry Garrett series (1)
Kilburn
Victor, Sam
Kilburn series (1)
Kilburn tale
Raymond, Ernest
London gallery series (6)
Kilkenny
L'Amour, Louis
Lance Kilkenny series (1)
Kill
Hunter, Neil
Brand series (4)
Macdonnell, James Edmond
Dutchy Holland series (38)
Scarpetta, Frank
Marksman series (14)
Smith, Lisa J
Forbidden game trilogy (3)
Kill all the young girls
Halliday, Brett
Michael Shayne series (67)
Kill and kill again
Pentecost, Hugh
Julian Quist series (16)
Kill and tell
Kienzle, William Xavier
Father Robert Koesler series (6)
Kill Angel
Christian, Frederick H
Frank Angel series (1)
Kill city
Sugar, Andrew
Enforcer series (3)
Kill crazy
Mackie, John
Rat Bastards series (10)
Kill Crazy Horse!
Dawson, Clay
Long Rider series (5)
Kill cue
Crews, Lary
Veronica Slate series (1)
Kill cure
Rathbone, Julian
Colonel Nur Bey series (4)
Kill deadline
Sugar, Andrew
Enforcer series (4)
Kill Dusty Fog!
Edson, John Thomas
American Civil War series (7)
Kill flash
Macgregor, T J
Quin Saint James and Mike McClary series (1)
Kill for it
Hawkes, Robert
NARC series (8)
Kill for the millions
Kane, Henry
Peter Chambers series (32)
Kill gently, but sure
Jason, Stuart
Butcher series (15)
Kill Hawk
Knott, William Cecil
Golden Hawk series (5)
Kill her with love
Gray, Rod
New lady from L.U.S.T. series (6)
Kill her with passion
Janson, Hank
Hank Janson series (151)
Kill her, you'll like it!
Avallone, Michael
Ed Noon series (26)
Kill him quickly, it's raining
Brett, Michael
Pete McGrath series (1)
Kill him tonight
Lane, Jeremy
Whitney Wheat series (2)
Kill him twice
Prather, Richard Scott
Shell Scott series (29)
Kill hole
Highwater, Jamake
Ghost horse quartet (4)
Kill Huggy Bear
Franklin, Max
Starsky and Hutch series (2)
Kill is a four-letter word
Stein, Aaron Marc
Matt Erridge series (8)
Kill Jason King!
Miall, Robert
Jason King series (2)
Kill Kissinger
De Villiers, Gerard
Malko Linge series (10)
Kill McAllister
Chisholm, Matt
Rem McAllister series (9)
Kill me again
Bentley, John
Glen Gibson series (3)
Kill me and live
Franklin, Charles
Inspector Jim Burgess series (2)
Kill me in Atami
Norman, Earl
Burns Bannion series (6)
Kill me in Roppongi
Norman, Earl
Burns Bannion series (8)
Kill me in Shimbashi
Norman, Earl
Burns Bannion series (2)
Kill me in Shinjuku
Norman, Earl
Burns Bannion series (4)
Kill me in Tokyo
Norman, Earl
Burns Bannion series (1)
Kill me in Yokohama
Norman, Earl
Burns Bannion series (3)
Kill me in Yoshiwara
Norman, Earl
Burns Bannion series (5)
Kill me on the Ginza
Norman, Earl
Burns Bannion series (7)
Kill me tomorrow
Prather, Richard Scott
Shell Scott series (35)
Kill me with kindness
Bond, J Harvey
Mike Lanson series (3)
Kill now, pay later
Kyle, Robert
Ben Gates series (3)
Kill now, play later
Stout, Rex
Nero Wolfe and Archie Goodwin series (39)
Kill of consequence
Wainwright, John
Northern Police series (47)
Kill or be killed
Ashe, Gordon
Patrick Dawlish series (21)
Santiago, V J
Joseph Madden series (3)
Kill or cure
Murphy, Warren Burton
Destroyer series (11)
Sutton, Jessica
Bel Air General series (9)
Kill Petrosino!
Nolan, Frederick
Lieutenant Joe Petrosino series (2)
Kill quick or die
Jason, Stuart
Butcher series (1)
Kill ratio
Drake, David
Yates series (1)
Kill school
Stivers, Dick
Able Team series (9)
Kill Squad
Cruz, Mark
Kill Squad series (1)
Kill squad
Quinn, John
Rod Gavin series (3)
Kill station
Duane, Diane
Space cops series (2)
Kill, sweet Charity, kill
Potter, J L
Jeff Tyler series (2)
Kill the butler!
Kenyon, Michael
Inspector Henry Peckover series (6)
Kill the clown
Prather, Richard Scott
Shell Scott series (24)
Kill the dragon
Hawkes, Robert
NARC series (5)
Kill the girls and make them cry
Wainwright, John
Northern Police series (23)
Kill the hack!
Bradley, Michael
Johnny Adrano series (2)
Kill the reporter
Olden, Marc
Hawthorne Albert Harker series (4)
Kill the Stuart
Bassett, Ronald
Margaret family series (4)
Kill the Toff
Creasey, John
Toff series (22)
Kill them all
Scarpetta, Frank
Marksman series (3)
Kill them silently
Jason, Stuart
Butcher series (28)
Kill this man
Janson, Hank
Hank Janson series (83)
Kill time
Jason, Stuart
Butcher series (8)
Kill to fit
Fischer, Bruno
Rick Train series (2)
Kill with care
Nelson, Hugh Lawrence
Jim Dunn series (6)
Kill with kindness
Shannon, Dell
Lieutenant Luis Mendoza series (15)
Kill your darlings
Collins, Max Allan
Mallory series (3)
Kill your own snakes
Seifert, Adele
Gregory Trent series (3)
Kill zone
Estleman, Loren D
Peter Macklin series (1)
Hawkins, Jack
Chopper series (7)
Killashandra
McCaffrey, Anne
Killashandra series (2)
Kille her if you can
Janson, Hank
Hank Janson series (41)
Kille me for kicks
Janson, Hank
Hank Janson series (125)
Killed by scandal
Nash, Simon
Inspector Montero and Adam Ludlow series (2)
Killed in paradise
De Andrea, William Louis
Matt Cobb series (5)
Killed in the act
De Andrea, William Louis
Matt Cobb series (2)
Killed in the ratings
De Andrea, William Louis
Matt Cobb series (1)
Killed on the ice
De Andrea, William Louis
Matt Cobb series (4)
Killed on the rocks
De Andrea, William Louis
Matt Cobb series (6)
Killed with a passion
De Andrea, William Louis
Matt Cobb series (3)
Killer
Brady, William S
Jared Hawk series (15)
Grant, Maxwell
Shadow series (41)
Janson, Hank
Hank Janson series (42)
Wells, Carolyn
Fleming Stone series (49)
Killer among us
Martin, Robert Lee
Jim Bennett series (9)
Killer angel
Masters, Doug
TNT series (5)
Killer at Fort Norman
Stoddard, Charles
Malloy series (3)
Killer at large
Mackenzie, Nigel
Inspector Charles Tremayne series (1)
Procter, Maurice
Chief Inspector Harry Martineau series (11)
Killer bait
McCoy, Marshall
Nevada Jim series (44)
Killer be killed
Chase, Kip
Justine Carmichael series (3)
Killer boy was here
Bagby, George
Inspector Schmidt series (38)
Killer breath
Wyllie, John
Doctor Quarshie series (6)
Killer by proxy
Jepson, Selwyn
Eve Gill series (1)
Killer caravan
Sharpe, Jon
Trailsman series (45)
Killer chromosomes
Murphy, Warren Burton
Destroyer series (32)
Killer clan
Sharpe, Jon
Trailsman series (54)
Killer comet
Moore, Patrick
Scott Saunders series (4)
Killer Conquest
Gray, Berkeley
Norman Conquest series (17)
Killer cop
Findley, Ferguson
Johnny Malone series (1)
Gober, Don
James Rhodes series (3)
Killer country
Cole, Jackson
Jim Hatfield series (17)
Killer crabs
Smith, Guy Newman
Crabs series (2)
Killer dog
Edwards, Monica
Romney Marsh series (12)
Killer Dolphin
Marsh, Ngaio
Inspector Roderick Alleyn series (24)
Killer elite
Rostand, Robert
Mike Locken series (1)
Killer fish
Freedman, Russell
Killer series (1)
Killer for a song
Gardner, John Edmund
Boysie L Oakes series (9)
Killer genesis
Kilgore, Axel
They call me the Mercenary series (1)

Killer grew tired
Davis, George
Roag's Syndicate series (5)
Killer grizzly
Roberts, J R
Gunsmith series (24)
Killer group
Macdonnell, James Edmond
Captain Peter Bentley series (29)
Killer in dark glasses
Treece, Henry
Gordon Stewart series (3)
Killer in the chorus
McCall, K T
Johnny Buchanan series (12)
Killer in the crowd
Tey, Josephine
Inspector Alan Grant series (1)
Killer in the shade
Marlowe, Piers
Frank Drury and Inspector Bill Hazard series (7)
Killer in the straw
Lockridge, Frances
Inspector Merton Heimrich series (9)
Killer in the street
Nielsen, Helen
Simon Drake series (3)
Killer in Whiskey Smith
Allen, Eric
Whiskey Smith series (1)
Killer instinct
Boggis, David
Killer instinct series (1)
Mandell, Mark
Nazi hunter series (3)
Killer is loose
Nicolai, Charles
John Nolan series (1)
Killer is mine
Powell, Talmage
Ed Rivers series (1)
Killer Kane
Masterson, Louis
Morgan Kane series (41)
Killer lion
Frazee, Steve
Bonanza series (7)
Killer loose!
Holden, Genevieve
Lieutenant Al White series (1)
Killer moon
Black, Gavin
Paul Harris series (12)
Killer mountains
Gilman, George G
Adam Steele series (30)
Killer music
Eisenberg, Lisa
Laura Brewster series (3)
Killer mustang
Dawson, Clay
Long Rider series (12)
Killer of Sheep River
Stoddard, Charles
Malloy series (5)
Killer on the keys
Avallone, Michael
Ed Noon series (28)
Killer on the prowl
Scarpetta, Frank
Marksman series (17)
Killer on the track
Rutherford, Douglas
Chequered flag series (2)
Killer orchid
McCall, K T
Johnny Buchanan series (11)
Killer pack
McNeilly, Wilfred
Sexton Blake series (1546)
Killer patrol
Fennell, George
Mike Brent series (2)
Killer pine
Gutteridge, Lindsay
Mathew Dilke series (2)
Killer plants of Binaark
Lord, Jeffrey
Richard Blade series (33)
Killer reaction
Chance, John Newton
Jonathan Blake series (14)
Killer robot
McEvoy, Seth
Not quite human series (6)
Killer satellites
Kirk, Philip
Butler series (10)
Killer sea
Shirreffs, Gordon Donald
Bob Dunbar and Gary Lunt series (6)
Killer shales and dolphin play
Torgersen, Don Arthur
Animal safari nature series (4)
Killer ship
Macdonnell, James Edmond
Captain Peter Bentley series (6)
Killer silver
Pike, Charles R
Jubal Cade series (4)
Killer snakes
Freedman, Russell
Killer series (2)
Killer spores
Woodley, Richard
Man from Atlantis series (3)
Killer-stalk
Robinson, Vance
Justice trilogy (3)
Killer Steele
Masters, J D
Steele series (3)
Killer virus
Kirk, Philip
Butler series (7)
Killer warrior
Olden, Marc
Robert Sand series (3)
Killer watches the manhunt
Cunningham, Albert Benjamin
Sheriff Jess Roden series (18)
Killer winter
Bradley, Jack
Battlesquad 1942 series (3)
Killer with a key
Marlowe, Dan James
Johnny Killain series (2)
Killer with the golden touch
Riefe, Alan
Huntington Cage series (6)
Killers
Macdonnell, James Edmond
Dutchy Holland series (46)
McCurtin, Peter
Carmody series (5)
Killers are my meat
Marlowe, Stephen
Chester Drum series (5)
Killers are on velvet
Graham, Neill
Solo Malcolm series (8)
Killers' breed
Brady, William S
Jared Hawk series (13)
Killer's breed
Gilman, George G
Edge series (4)
Killers came at noon
McCoy, Marshall
Nevada Jim series (41)
Killer's cargo
Jason, Stuart
Butcher series (12)
Killer's choice
McBain, Ed
Eighty Seventh Precinct series (5)
Killer's club
Sharpe, Jon
Canyon O'Grady series (17)
Killer's council
Siegel, Scott
Warhunter series (1)
Killers don't cry
Brody, Marc
Marc Brody series (49)
Killer's doom
Scott, Bradford
Walt Slade series (57)
Killers for hire
Colter, Frank
Gang war series (2)
Killers from hyperspace
Voltz, William
Perry Rhodan series (120)
Killers from the Keys
Halliday, Brett
Michael Shayne series (39)
Killer's gold
Roberts, J R
Gunsmith series (126)
Killer's heritage
Elton, Wallace
Jud Walton series (1)
Killer's highway
Avallone, Michael
Ed Noon series (20)
Killer's keep
Frost, Jason
Warlord series (6)
Killer's kiss
Kane, Henry
Marla Trent series (2)
Peter Chambers series (18)
Killer's mask
Robertson, Colin
Superintendent Bradley series (7)
Killer's moon
Benteen, John
Neal Fargo series (17)
Hardin, J D
Raider series (39)
Muir, James A
Breed series (12)
Killers must eat
O'Brine, Manning
Michael O'Kelly series (1)
Killer's noon
Grover, Marshall
Nevada Jim series (5)
Killers of innocence
Creasey, John
Doctor Palfrey series (15)
Killers of Prairie Flats
Buckman, Sam
Storm Jackson series (5)
Killer's paradise
Bickham, Jack Miles
John Campbell and Clayton Hartung series (3)
Killer's payoff
McBain, Ed
Eighty Seventh Precinct series (6)
Killer's playground
Harrison, Edwin
Sexton Blake series (1470)
Killer's race
Roberts, J R
Gunsmith series (109)
Killer's rope
Cassells, John
Superintendent Flagg series (33)
Killers' round-up
Madison, Holt
Batwing Jones trilogy (3)
Killer's town
Falk, Lee
Phantom series (9)
Killer's wedge
McBain, Ed
Eighty Seventh Precinct series (8)
Killers wore black
Grover, Marshall
Nevada Jim series (64)
Killfactor five
Maxwell, Peter
Ralph Ledermann series (2)
Killigrew clay
Summers, Rowena
Clay mining series (1)
Killing
Darke, James
Witches series (6)
Wilson, David
Marshal Sam McCloud series (3)
Killing art
Gilman, George G
Adam Steele series (6)
Killing at Buffalo Crossing
Dexter, Ross
Duke Lawson series (2)
Killing blow
La Plante, Richard
Tegne series (2)
Killing bone
Saxon, Peter
Guardians series (4)
Killing chase
Simons, Roger
Inspector Fadiman Wace series (6)
Killing circle
Wiltz, Chris
Neal Rafferty series (1)
Killing claim
Gilman, George G
Edge series (41)
Killing cold
Wood, Ted
Reid Bennett series (2)
Killing comes easy
Chester, Peter
Johnny Preston series (1)
Killing connection
Hartman, Dane
Dirty Harry Callahan series (9)
Killing corridor
Sharpe, Jon
Trailsman series (140)
Killing cousins
Knight, Alanna
Inspector Faro series (4)
Killing cup
Van Greenaway, Peter
Inspector Cherry and Sergeant Duff series (6)
Killing cure
Hart, Ellen
Jane Lawless series (4)
Killing easy
Cronin, Michael
Sam Harris series (7)
Killing experiment
Chance, John Newton
Jonathan Blake series (15)
Killing floor
Lyons, Arthur
Jacob Asch series (3)
Killing for the law
Masterson, Louis
Morgan Kane series (21)
Killing frost
Burgess, Eric
Harry Tong series (1)
Killing game
Knox, Bill
Inspector Colin Thane and Phil Moss series (6)
Killing games
Carter, Nick
Nick Carter series (228)
Killing glance
Finlay, D G
Watchman chronicles series (4)
Killing ground
Carter, Nick
Nick Carter series (209)
Gober, Don
James Rhodes series (4)
Pike, Charles R
Jubal Cade series (10)
Rouch, James
Zone series (7)
Settle, Mary Lee
Beulah series (5)
Killing in antiques
Knox, Bill
Inspector Colin Thane and Phil Moss series (17)
Killing in gold
Hensley, Joe Louis
Donald Robak series (4)
Killing in hats
Davey, Jocelyn
Ambrose Usher series (4)
Killing in Malta
Macleod, Robert
Jonathan Gaunt series (2)
Killing in Moscow
Egleton, Clive
Peter Ashton series (2)
Killing in Rome
Rostand, Robert
Mike Locken series (3)
Killing in the market
Dixon, Franklin W
Hardy boys case files series (18)
Killing jazz
Booth, Christopher B
Jim Bliss series (2)
Killing kin
Hocking, Anne
Inspector William Austen series (18)
Killing kind
Franklin, Max
Charlie's Angels series (2)
Killing kindness
Hill, Reginald
Superintendent Andrew Dalziel and Sergeant Pascoe series (12)
Killing machine
Rossi, Bruno
Sharpshooter series (1)
Vance, Jack
Kirth Gersen series (2)
Killing man
Spillane, Mickey
Mike Hammer series (13)
Killing mask
Stall, Mike
Daniel Lacey series (1)
Killing match
Severn, Richard
Jeff Cass series (3)
Killing no murder
Kiddy, Maurice George
Stonewall Steevens series (1)
Shaw, Howard
Inspector Barnaby series (1)
Killing of Judge McFarlane
Plum, Mary
John Smith series (1)
Killing of Kirby
Grover, Marshall
Larry and Stretch series (201)
Killing of Monday Brown
Prowell, Sandra West
Phoebe Siegel series (2)
Killing of Paris Norton
Garnett, Roger
R I Perkins series (2)
Killing of Richard the Third
Farrington, Robert
Henry Morane series (1)
Killing of Xanadu
Pronzini, Bill
Private Eye series (22)
Killing of yesterday's children
Power, Maurice S
Children of the north series (1)
Killing orders
Paretsky, Sara
V I Warshawski series (3)
Killing run
Barry, Mike
Burton Wulff series (13)
Killing spree
Benteen, John
Neal Fargo series (12)
Killing strain
Gilman, George G
Adam Steele series (41)
Killing strike
Creasey, John
Inspector Roger West series (23)
Killing the goose
Lockridge, Frances
Bill Wiegand series (7)
Mister and Mrs North series (8)
Killing time
Brady, William S
Jared Hawk series (4)
Conley, Robert Jackson
Oliver Colfax series (1)
Murphy, Warren Burton
Destroyer series (50)
Van Hise, Della
Star trek series (24)
Killing times
Fraser, David
Treason in arms series (2)
Killing to hide
Penn, John
Inspector George Thorne and Sergeant Bill Abbot series (11)
Killing trade
Boyles, William
Bounty Hunter series (2)
Killing trail
Hunter, Neil
Bodie the Stalker series (4)
Pike, Charles R
Jubal Cade series (1)
Killing wedge
Ahern, Jerry
Defender series (2)
Killing wind
Lee, John Darrell
Brian Douglas series (2)
Killing with kindness
Morice, Anne
Tessa Crichton Price series (7)
Killing zone
Burns, Rex
Gabriel Wager series (8)
Teed, Jack Hamilton
Gunships series (1)
Killings at Badger's Drift
Graham, Caroline
Inspector Tom Barnaby series (1)
Killraine
Douglas, Thorne
Rancho Bravo series (3)
Killtown
Stark, Richard
Alan Grofield series (1)
Parker series (5)
Kilroy gambit
Blacker, Irwin Robert
General Le Grande and GENOPS series (1)
Kim
Kipling, Rudyard
Kim series (1)
Kim and the buried treasure
Holm, Jens K
Kim the detective series (2)
Kim the detective
Holm, Jens K
Kim the detective series (1)
Kimberley killing
Corris, Peter
Pokerface series (3)

Kimono for a corpse
Melville, James
Superintendent Tetsuo Otani series (9)
Kin dread
Macgregor, T J
Quin Saint James and Mike McClary series (5)
Kin to the wild wind
Grover, Marshall
Larry and Stretch series (96)
Kin Weng and the miraculous tusk
Bramah, Ernest
Kai Lung series (4)
Kincaid's last ride
Grover, Marshall
Larry and Stretch series (314)
Kind and gentle ladies
Cosgrove, Stephen Edward
Simple folk series (2)
Kind Dog on Monday
Banner, Angela
Kind Dog series (2)
Kind Dog up and down the hill
Banner, Angela
Kind Dog series (3)
Kind of healthy grave
Mann, Jessica
Tamara Hoyland series (4)
Kind of loving
Barstow, Stan
Vic Brown trilogy (1)
Kind of magic
Ferber, Edna
Peculiar treasure series (2)
Harris, Mollie
Kind of magic series (1)
Kind of prisoner
Creasey, John
Department Z series (28)
Kind relations
Liddell, Robert
Relations series (1)
Kind Uncle Buckby
Gloag, John
Lionel Buckby series (4)
Kinda
Dicks, Terrance
Doctor Who series (84)
Kindest use a knife
Revell, Louisa
Julia Tyler series (4)
Kindly light
Wilson, Andrew Norman
Norman Shotover series (2)
Kindly ones
Powell, Anthony
Dance to the music of time series (6)
Kindred spirits
Anthony, Mark
Meetings series (1)
Kinds of love, kinds of death
Coe, Tucker
Mitchell Tobin series (1)
Kine
Lloyd, Alan R
Kine trilogy (1)
King
Bruna, Dick
Toy box tale series (2)
Norman, John
Telnarian histories series (3)
King Alfred
Birt, David
Saxons and Vikings series (7)
King and joker
Dickinson, Peter
King Victor series (1)
King and Pope
Birt, David
Tudors series (2)
King and the corpse
Murray, Max
Corpse series (2)
King and the invisible dwarf
Saddler, Allen
King and queen series (4)
King and two queens
Mackintosh, May
Laurie Grant and Stewart Noble series (2)
King Arthur's Avalon
Ashe, Geoffrey
King Arthur series (1)
King Arthur's daughter
Chapman, Vera
Three damosels trilogy (3)
King at Christmas
Saddler, Allen
King and queen series (5)
King awakes
Elliott, Janice
Sword and the dream series (1)
King beyond the gate
Gemmell, David A
Drenai series (2)
King, bishop, knight
Emmett, Robert
American Avenger series (4)
King Change-a-Lot
Cole, Babette
Princess Smartypants series (3)
King Charles and King Pym, 1637-1643
Wingfield-Stratford, Esme
Charles I trilogy (2)
King Charles and the conspirators
Wingfield-Stratford, Esme
Charles I trilogy (3)
King Charles the martyr, 1643-1649
Wingfield-Stratford, Esme
Charles I trilogy (3)
King Chondos' ride
Zimmer, Paul Edwin
Dark border series (2)
King Coal
Sinclair, Upton
Coal series (1)
King Cobra
Channing, Mark
Colin Gray series (1)
King Conan
Howard, Robert Ervin
Conan series (4)
King Conger
Lee, Robert
Fishy business series (4)
King Coopersmith
Griffin, Robert J
Coopersmith series (3)
King Creole
Grange, Peter
L'Eree family series (1)
King David's spaceship
Pournelle, Jerry
Future history series (5)
King Emmett the Second
Stolz, Mary
Emmett series (2)
King gets fit
Saddler, Allen
King and queen series (2)
King Goblin and his forest friends
Grimm, Geraldine
King Goblin series (1)
King Goblin and the golden treasure
Grimm, Geraldine
King Goblin series (2)
King Goblin loses his throne
Grimm, Geraldine
King Goblin series (3)
King Goblin returns
Grimm, Geraldine
King Goblin series (5)
King Goshawk and the birds
O'Duffy, Eimar
King Goshawk series (1)
King hunters
Garron, Marco
Azan series (6)
King in check
Mundy, Talbot
Jimgrim series (9)
King is dead
Queen, Ellery
Ellery Queen series (29)
King is dead on Queen Street
Bonnamy, Francis
Peter Shane series (5)
King Jack
Snowden, James Keighley
King Jack series (1)
King Javan's year
Kurtz, Katherine
Heirs of Saint Camber trilogy (2)
King Joe Cay
Robeson, Kenneth
Doc Savage series (133)
King John
Birt, David
Middle Ages series (7)
King John of Jingalo
Housman, Laurence
Jingalo series (1)
King Kangaroo
Ahlberg, Allan
Help your child to read series (8)
King-killers
Dewey, Thomas Blanchard
Private Eye Mac series (15)
King Kobold
Stasheff, Christopher
Gramarye series (3)
King Kobold revived
Stasheff, Christopher
Gramarye series (3)
King Kong
Lovelace, Delos
King Kong series (1)
Thorne, Ian
King Kong series (3)
King Kong story
Pascall, Jeremy
King Kong series (3)
King Kull
Howard, Robert Ervin
Tales of the Picts series (1)
King Lear at Hordle
Gilbert, Bernard
Old England series (2)
King Leopold's Congo
Slade, Ruth
Congo series (1)
King Leopold's legacy
Anstey, Roger
Congo series (2)
King Ludd
Sinclair, Andrew
Albion trilogy (3)
King maker
Robeson, Kenneth
Doc Savage series (80)
King murder
Jones, Charles Reed
Leighton Swift series (1)
King must die
Renault, Mary
Theseus series (1)
King of Athelney
Duggan, Alfred
Saxon trilogy (3)
King of beasts
Todd, Herbert Eatton
Bobby Brewster picture book series (4)
King of Camberwell
Staples, Mary Jane
South London series (3)
King of Colorado
Rountree, Owen
Jim Cord series (6)
Sharpe, Jon
Canyon O'Grady series (7)
King of diamonds
Chichester, John Jay
Maxwell Sanderson series (4)
Terry, Carolyn
King of diamonds series (1)
King of Four Corners
Burgin, George Brown
Four Corners series (7)
King of Grey Corrie
Lyon, Elinor
Ian and Sovra series (9)
James, Alan and Roslin series (1)
King of Kenilwick
West, Colin
King of Kenilwick Castle series (1)
King of Ketu
Olinto, Antonio
Water house series (2)
King of Kingston
White, Steve
S-Com series (5)
King of Kor
Marshall, Sidney John
She series (6)
King of light and shadows
Cole, Adrian
Omaran series (3)
King of No Man's Land
Friel, Arthur Olney
McKay, Knowlton and Ryan series (3)
King of Satan's eyes
Marsh, Geoffrey
Lincoln Blackthorne series (1)
King of Spades
Manfred, Frederick
Buckskin Man tales series (5)
King of Spuds
Ure, Jean
Woodside School series (4)
King of terror
Robeson, Kenneth
Doc Savage series (120)
King of the black market
Grant, Maxwell
Shadow series (244)
King of the border
Roberts, J R
Gunsmith series (38)
King of the castle
Vaughan, Carol
Manorfield Stud series (5)
King of the Commandos
Johns, William Earl
Gimlet series (1)
King of the corner
Estleman, Loren D
Detroit trilogy (3)
King of the dead
Aubrey, Frank
Monella trilogy (3)
Macavoy, Roberta Ann
Lens of the world trilogy (2)
King of the dinosaurs
Berenstain, Michael
Dinosaurs series (3)
King of the highbinders
Champlin, Tim
Jay McGraw series (2)
Matt Tierney series (8)
King of the Jews
Borden, Mary
Mary of Nazareth series (2)
King of the jungle
Stoneham, Charles Thurley
Kaspa series (1)
King of the Khyber Rifles
Mundy, Talbot
Athelstan King series (1)
Sikh series (2)
King, of the Khybers
Mundy, Talbot
Athelstan King series (1)
Sikh series (2)
King of the last days
Norman, Diana
Henry II trilogy (3)
King of the mountain
Lassiter, Adam
Dennison's war series (4)
Thompson, David
Nathaniel King series (1)
King of the Murgos
Eddings, David
Malloreon series (2)
King of the Nogs
Postgate, Oliver
Saga of Noggin the Nog series (1)
King of the outlaw horde
Grey, Romer Zane
Arizona Ames series (5)
Arizona Ames series (7)
King of the rainy country
Freeling, Nicolas
Inspector Piet Van der Valk series (6)
King of the range
Grey, Romer Zane
Buck Duane series (6)
King of the Royal Mounted
Grey, Zane
King of the Royal Mounted series (1)
King of the Royal Mounted and the ghost guns of Roaring River
Grey, Zane
King of the Royal Mounted series (10)
King of the Royal Mounted and the great jewel mystery
Grey, Zane
King of the Royal Mounted series (3)
King of the Royal Mounted and the northern treasure
Grey, Zane
King of the Royal Mounted series (2)
King of the Royal Mounted gets his man
Grey, Zane
King of the Royal Mounted series (5)
King of the Royal mounted in Arctic law
Grey, Zane
King of the Royal Mounted series (4)
King of the Royal Mounted in law of the north
Grey, Zane
King of the Royal Mounted series (8)
King of the Royal Mounted in the far north
Grey, Zane
King of the Royal Mounted series (6)
King of the Royal Mounted policing the frozen north
Grey, Zane
King of the Royal Mounted series (7)
King of the Royal Mounted, the long arm of the law
Grey, Zane
King of the Royal Mounted series (9)
King of the scepter'd isle
Coney, Michael Greatrex
Greataway series (4)
King of the slavers
Cleve, John
Spaceways series (19)
King of the stars
Kelley, Leo Patrick
Galaxy Five series (6)
King of the sticks
Southall, Ivan
King of the sticks trilogy (1)
King of the Swords
Moorcock, Michael
Corum series (3)
King of the underworld
Carter, Nicholas
Nicholas Carter series (379)
Evans, Gwyn
Sexton Blake series (516)
King of the vagabonds
Dann, Colin
Vagabonds series (1)
King of the wind
Henry, Marguerite
King of the wind series (6)
King of the world's edge
Munn, Harold Warner
Gwalchmai trilogy (1)
King of Tiger Bay
Walsh, James Morgan
Tiger Bay series (3)
King of Ys
Anderson, Poul
King of Ys series (2)
King of Ys series (4)
King of Zunga
Lord, Jeffrey
Richard Blade series (12)
King Offa of Mercia
Birt, David
Saxons and Vikings series (12)
King Oleg
Brisville, Jean Claude
Oleg series (2)
King or knave, which wins?
Johnson, William Henry
Huguenot series (2)
King Ottokar's sceptre
Herge
Tintin series (8)
King Rat
Clavell, James
Asian series (3)
King Richard's friend
Viney, Jayne
Richard III series (1)
King Ricky
Lofgren, Ulf
Ricky series (3)
King Roll and the bread
McKee, David
King Rollo series (2)
King Rollo and King Frank
McKee, David
King Rollo series (9)
King Rollo and Santa's beard
McKee, David
King Rollo series (20)
King Rollo and the balloons
McKee, David
King Rollo series (4)
King Rollo and the bath
McKee, David
King Rollo series (8)
King Rollo and the birthday
McKee, David
King Rollo series (1)
King Rollo and the breakfast
McKee, David
King Rollo series (10)
King Rollo and the dishes
McKee, David
King Rollo series (6)
King Rollo and the dog
McKee, David
King Rollo series (11)
King Rollo and the letter
McKee, David
King Rollo series (14)
King Rollo and the masks
McKee, David
King Rollo series (12)
King Rollo and the new shoes
McKee, David
King Rollo series (3)

King Rollo and the playroom
McKee, David
King Rollo series (13)
King Rollo and the search
McKee, David
King Rollo series (7)
King Rollo and the tree
McKee, David
King Rollo series (5)
King Rollo's autumn
McKee, David
King Rollo series (16)
King Rollo's letter, and other stories
McKee, David
King Rollo series (19)
King Rollo's playroom, and other stories
McKee, David
King Rollo series (13)
King Rollo's spring
McKee, David
King Rollo series (15)
King Rollo's summer
McKee, David
King Rollo series (17)
King Rollo's winter
McKee, David
King Rollo series (18)
King Silky!
Rosten, Leo
Silky Pincus series (2)
King-sized murder
Herber, William
Jimmy Rehm series (1)
King Smurf
Peyo
Smurf series (1)
King Solomon's mines
Haggard, Henry Rider
Allan Quatermain series (13)
King Solomon's mines series (1)
Webb, Jean Francis
Allan Quatermain series (13)
King Solomon's treasures
De Morgan, John
Allan Quatermain series (13)
King Solomon's wives
De Morgan, John
Allan Quatermain series (13)
Ragged, Hyder
Allan Quatermain series (13)
King Vagabond
Wood, Andrew
Sasha series (2)
King was in his counting house
Cabell, James Branch
Conquest series (1)
King who never smiled
Frees, Harry Whittier
Petland photo tales series (3)
King Wilbur and the bath
Rogerson, James
King Wilbur series (2)
King Wilbur and the bicycle
Rogerson, James
King Wilbur series (4)
King Wilbur rebuilds his palace
Rogerson, James
King Wilbur series (1)
King Wilbur's birthday present
Rogerson, James
King Wilbur series (3)
King Wolf
Farely, Alison
Plantagenet series (6)
King Wren
Mann, Heinrich
Henry, King of France series (1)
Kingdom
Joseph, Ronald S
Cameron family trilogy (1)
Kingdom come
Bragg, Melvyn
Tallentire family series (3)
Comstock, Jarrod
These lawless worlds series (3)
Drumm, D B
Traveler series (2)
Kingdom for a song
Morris, Ira J
Duke of Burgundy series (1)
Kingdom of Carbonel
Sleigh, Barbara
Carbonel series (2)
Kingdom of death
Allingham, Margery
Albert Campion series (5)
Masters, Doug
TNT series (7)
Kingdom of dreams
McNaught, Judith
Westmoreland family series (1)
Kingdom of evil
Hecht, Ben
Fantazius Mallare series (2)
Kingdom of horror
Brennan, James Herbert
GrailQuest series (5)
Kingdom of Leon-Castilla under King Alfonso VI, 1065-1109
Reilly, Bernard F
Kingdom of Leon-Castilla series (1)
Kingdom of Leon-Castilla under Queen Urraca, 1109-1126
Reilly, Bernard F
Kingdom of Leon-Castilla series (2)
Kingdom of Royth
Lord, Jeffrey
Richard Blade series (9)
Kingdom of summer
Bradshaw, Gillian
Arthur and Gawain trilogy (2)
Kingdom of the bulls
Capon, Paul
Artor series (2)
Kingdom of the cats
Gotlieb, Phyllis
Qsaprinel trilogy (3)
Kingdom of the Sun
Roberts, Irene
Ancient Egypt series (3)
Kingdom of waste lands
Grier, Sydney Carlyon
Island series (2)
Kingdom of Wyrd
Morris, Dave
Blood sword series (2)
Kingdom that was
Lambourne, John
Jim Burnett series (1)
Kingdom to win
Sprague, Rosemary
King Olaf Tryggvason series (1)
kingdom under tyranny
Farely, Alison
Plantagenet series (7)
Kingdoms of Asia, the Middle East and Africa
Gurney, Gene
Kingdoms series (2)
Kingdoms of Europe
Gurney, Gene
Kingdoms series (1)
Kingdoms of terror
Dever, Joe
Lone Wolf series (6)
Kingdoms of the vine
Leigh, Helena
Vintage years trilogy (3)
Kingfisher blue
Rutley, Cecily Marianne
Tales of the wild folk series (1)
Kingmaker
Shillitoe, Tony
Andrakis trilogy (2)
Kingmaker's knight
Morgan, Denise
Ralph de Giret trilogy (2)
Kingpin
Miller, Hugh
McBain family series (2)
Kings
Logue, Christopher
Iliad adaptations series (1)
King's acre
Fraser, Christine Marion
King's series (2)
King's adversary
Beardsworth, Millicent Monica
Charles I series (4)
King's assegai
Mitford, Bertram
Untuswa trilogy (1)
King's bastard
Denis, Charlotte
Charles II series (2)
King's blood four
Tepper, Sheri S
True game trilogy (1)
King's bounty
Clews, Roy
Jethro Stanton series (2)
King's buccaneer
Feist, Raymond Elias
Riftwar series (5)
King's cannon
Scofield, Jonathan
Freedom fighters series (3)
King's close
Fraser, Christine Marion
King's series (4)
King's Club murder
Greig, Ian
Inspector Swinton series (1)
King's coat
Lambdin, Dewey
Alan Lewrie series (1)
King's commission
Lambdin, Dewey
Alan Lewrie series (3)
King's contest
Beardsworth, Millicent Monica
Charles I series (5)
King's counsel
Richardson, Frank
Vincent Skrene series (1)
King's critic
Lane, Jane
Montague family series (1)
King's croft
Fraser, Christine Marion
King's series (1)
King's curse
Murphy, Warren Burton
Destroyer series (24)
King's cutter
Woodman, Richard
Nathaniel Drinkwater series (2)
King's damosel
Chapman, Vera
Three damosels trilogy (2)
King's daughter
Churchill, Rosemary
Mary Tudor series (1)
King's death
Frazier, Arthur
Wolfshead series (2)
King's demons
Dudley, Terence
Doctor Who series (108)
King's diary
White, Percy
Countess series (1)
King's endeavour
Beardsworth, Millicent Monica
Charles I series (3)
King's enemies
Walsh, James Morgan
Oliver Keene series (5)
King's exile
Fraser, Christine Marion
King's series (3)
King's Falcon
Darby, Catherine
Falcon family series (2)
King's farewell
Fraser, Christine Marion
King's series (5)
King's friend
Beardsworth, Millicent Monica
Charles I series (2)
King's ghost
Chetwynd-Hayes, Ronald
Tales of Clavering Grange series (2)
King's grey mare
Jarman, Rosemary Hawley
Richard III series (2)
King's henchman
Johnson, William Henry
Huguenot series (1)
King's highway
Watson, Henry Brereton Marriott
Dick Ryder series (3)
Kings in grass castles
Durack, Mary
Grass castles series (1)
Kings in hell
Morris, Janet Ellen
Heroes in hell series (5)
Kings in the counting house
Mitgang, Herbert
Sam Linkum series (2)
King's justice
Kurtz, Katherine
Histories of King Kelson trilogy (2)
King's legacy
Fecher, Constance
Ralegh family trilogy (3)
King's malady
Maughan, Anne Margery
Young Pitt series (2)
King's man
Deeley, Roger
Martin Dymoke series (1)
King's mate
Murphy, Robert Franklin
Girl factory series (2)
King's messenger
Walsh, James Morgan
Colonel Ormiston series (3)
King's minister
Plumb, John Harold
Sir Robert Walpole series (2)
King's mission
Sharp, Allen
Storytrails series (1)
King's mistress
Watson, Julia
Gentian trilogy (2)
King's mother
King, Betty
Beaufort family series (4)
Tudor series (4)
Kings of crime
Grant, Maxwell
Shadow series (20)
Kings of space
Johns, William Earl
Rex Clinton series (1)
Kings of the East
Grier, Sydney Carlyon
Balkan series (3)
Kings of vain intent
Shelby, Graham
Third Crusade series (2)
King's pawn
Drummond, Hamilton
Religious wars trilogy (3)
King's pleasure
Plaidy, Jean
Tudor series (4)
King's prisoner
Carter, Nicholas
Nicholas Carter series (345)
King's privateer
Lambdin, Dewey
Alan Lewrie series (4)
King's quest
McGowen, Tom
Endless quest series (18)
King's ransom
Hayes, Ralph Eugene
Mark Stoner series (4)
McBain, Ed
Eighty Seventh Precinct series (10)
Suthren, Victor
Paul Gallant series (2)
King's rescue
Duff, Douglas Valder
Adam Macadam series (11)
King's ring
Topelius, Zacharias
Surgeon's stories series (1)
Kings Row
Bellamann, Henry
Kings Row series (1)
King's royal
Quigley, John
King family series (1)
King's sacrifice
Weis, Margaret
Star of the guardians series (3)
King's secret
Gibbons, Harry Hornaby Clifford
Sexton Blake series (337)
Poole, Reginald Heber
Sexton Blake series (147)
King's secret matter
Plaidy, Jean
Katharine of Aragon trilogy (3)
Tudor series (3)
King's servant
Beardsworth, Millicent Monica
Charles I series (1)
King's stockbroker
Gunter, Archibald Clavering
Princess of Paris series (2)
King's test
Weis, Margaret
Star of the guardians series (2)
King's toothache
West, Colin
King of Kenilwick Castle series (2)
King's victory
Beardsworth, Millicent Monica
Charles I series (6)
King's wench
Denis, Charlotte
Charles II series (1)
Kingsbane
Morressy, John
Iron angel series (3)
Kingsbridge plot
Meyers, Maan
Pieter Tonneman series (2)
Kingsmead
Hutten zum Stolzenberg, Bettina Riddle
Pam series (4)
Kingston carnage
Wilson, Gar
Phoenix Force series (35)
Kink
Brock, Lynn
Colonel Gore series (3)
Kinky Friedman crime club
Friedman, Kinky
Kinky Friedman series (3)
Kinslayer wars
Niles, Douglas
Elven nations trilogy (2)
Kinsman
Bova, Ben
Chet Kinsman series (2)
Simms, William Gilmore
American Revolution series (3)
Kinsman saga
Bova, Ben
Chet Kinsman series (2)
Kinsmen
Haggard, William
Paul Martiny series (2)
Kinsmen of the Grail
Roberts, Dorothy James
Arthurian series (2)
Kioga of the unknown land
Chester, William L
Kioga series (4)
Kioga of the wilderness
Chester, William L
Kioga series (2)
Kiowa
Chisholm, Matt
Rem McAllister series (5)
Kiowa kill
Sharpe, Jon
Trailsman series (35)
Kiowa killer
Cole, Jackson
Jim Hatfield series (29)
Kip at the coast
Odaga, Asenath
Kip series (2)
Kip goes to the city
Odaga, Asenath
Kip series (3)
Kip on the farm
Odaga, Asenath
Kip series (1)
Kipling dictionary
Young, William Arthur
Rewards and fairies series (2)
Kipper skips
Darke, Marjorie
Kipper series (2)
Kipper stew
Flint, Elizabeth
East End series (2)
Kipper's turn
Darke, Marjorie
Kipper series (1)
Kippy Koala and the bushfire
Morgan, Win
Kippy Koala series (1)
Kippy Koala's Christmas present
Morgan, Win
Kippy Koala series (2)
Kiriov tapes
Sela, Owen
Nicholas Maasten series (3)
Kirk of the Corrie
Cameron, Isabel
Glen folk series (6)
Kirkbride and Company
Blamires, Harry
Kirkbride series (2)
Kirkbride conversations
Blamires, Harry
Kirkbride series (1)
Kirlian quest
Anthony, Piers
Cluster series (3)
Kirsten learns a lesson
Shaw, Janet
Kirsten series (2)
Kirsten saves the day
Shaw, Janet
Kirsten series (6)
Kirsten's surprise
Shaw, Janet
Kirsten series (3)
Kiss
Cole, Jennifer
Cindy and Nicole series (3)
Lutz, John
Fred Carver series (3)
McBain, Ed
Eighty Seventh Precinct series (46)
Kiss a day keeps the corpses away
Yardley, James
Kiss Darling and Angus Fane series (2)
Kiss a stranger
Sinclair, Heather
Kiss series (2)

Kiss and kill
Knight, Adam
Steve Conacher series (5)
Meyers, Martin
Patrick Hardy series (1)
Kiss and make up
Goudge, Eileen
Seniors series (13)
Kiss and run
Cooper, M E
Couples series (18)
Kiss and tell
Grimes, Frances Harley
Sweet savage sophomore year series (1)
Kiss for a killer
Fickling, G G
Honey West series (7)
Kiss for Christina
Saint James, Blakely
Christina Van Bell series (19)
Kiss for good luck
Ellis, Carol
Two by two series (11)
Kiss for Little Bear
Minarik, Else Holmelund
Little Bear series (5)
Kiss for the enemy
Fraser, David
Treason in arms series (1)
Kiss for the leper
Mauriac, Francois
Leper series (2)
Kiss from Aphrodite
Fitzgerald, Julia
Astromance series (4)
Kiss, kiss, kill, kill
Kane, Henry
Peter Chambers series (32)
Kiss me as you go
Spade, Danny
Danny Spade series (30)
Kiss me, deadly
Spillane, Mickey
Mike Hammer series (6)
Kiss Michelle goodbye
Brown, Carter
Danny Boyd series (31)
Kiss my assassin
Gray, Rod
Lady from L.U.S.T. series (7)
Kiss not the child
Tigges, John
Incubus trilogy (3)
Kiss of death
Scarpetta, Frank
Marksman series (13)
Kiss of leather
Townsend, Larry
Leather bondage series (3)
Kiss of the damned
Harragan, Steve
Steve Harragan series (3)
Kiss the book
Spiller, Andrew
Chief Inspector Duck Mallard series (15)
Kiss the boss goodbye
Crawford, Robert
Arthur Salisbury and Frank Shearer series (2)
Kiss the boys and make them die
Yardley, James
Kiss Darling and Angus Fane series (1)
Kiss the killer
Shallit, Joseph
Dan Morrison series (4)
Kiss the loot goodbye
Grover, Marshall
Larry and Stretch series (159)
Kiss the tiger
Davis, Franklin Milton
Quinn Leland series (1)
Kiss the Toff
Creasey, John
Toff series (34)
Kiss time
Morris, Ann
Sleepy series (2)
Kiss to the leper
Mauriac, Francois
Leper series (1)
Kissed corpse
Baker, Asa
Jerry Burke series (2)
Kisses
McLerran, Alice
Hugs and kisses series (2)
Kisses from Satan
Mair, George Brown
David Grant series (4)
Kisses leave no fingerprints
Fredman, Mike
Willie Halliday series (2)
Kisses of death
Kane, Henry
Marla Trent series (2)
Peter Chambers series (18)
Kissing covens
Watson, Colin
Inspector Purbright series (7)
Kissing gourami
Platt, Kin
Max Roper series (2)
Kissing kin
Thane, Elswyth
Williamsburg series (5)
Kit
Gardam, Jane
Kit series (1)
Kit and Kat
Perkins, Lucy Fitch
Dutch twins series (2)
Kit Carey's protege
Lounsberry, Lionel
Kit Carey series (4)
Kit Carson scout
Helm, Eric
Ground Zero series (6)
Kit Clayton
Huet, M M
Jack Rann series (2)
Kit in boots
Gardam, Jane
Kit series (2)
Kit Kennedy
Crockett, Samuel Rutherford
Galloway series (2)
Kit of Greenacre Farm
Forrester, Izola Louise
Greenacres series (3)
Kitchen
Kalman, Bobbie
Historic communities series (2)
Kitchen cake murder
Bush, Christopher
Ludovic Travers series (11)
Kitchen in the hills
West, Elizabeth
Hafod Garden series (2)
Kite flying is for me
Moran, Tom
Sports for me series (4)
Kith and kin
Bentley, Phyllis
West Riding series (16)
Kit's book
Mills, Carla Johnson
Winter world series (3)
Kit's Hill
Stubbs, Jean
Brief chronicles series (1)
Kitten Nell
Bruna, Dick
Toy box tale series (5)
Kitten that disappeared
Blyton, Enid
John and Mary series (6)
Kitten you're a killer
Brody, Marc
Marc Brody series (75)
Kitten's Christmas
McCue, Dick
Animal shape series (8)
Kittens love
McCue, Lisa
Baby animal love series (1)
Kitty Cry-Alot
Watson, Jean
Alot series (9)
Kitty from the start
Delton, Judy
Kitty series (4)
Kitty in high school
Delton, Judy
Kitty series (3)
Kitty in the middle
Delton, Judy
Kitty series (1)
Kitty in the summer
Delton, Judy
Kitty series (2)
Kitty Villiers
Gibbs, Lewis
Kitty Villiers series (1)
Kittyboy's Christmas
Blanchard, Amy Ella
Lad and Lassie (1)
Kitty's colors
McCue, Dick
Animal shape series (2)
Kitty's first day at Catnip School
Frees, Harry Whittier
Petland photo tales series (5)
Kitty's robins
Mathews, Joanna Hooe
Kitty and Lulu series (2)
Kitty's scrapbook
Mathews, Joanna Hooe
Kitty and Lulu series (6)
Kitty's visit to grandmamma
Mathews, Joanna Hooe
Kitty and Lulu series (5)
Kiwi at large
Allison, Errol Sampson
Kiwi series (1)
Kiwi Club
Leslie, Norman
Jumbo Rutherford series (2)
Kiwi contract
Atlee, Philip
Joe Gall series (16)
Kiwi vagabond
Allison, Errol Sampson
Kiwi series (2)
Klaw
Fieldhouse, William
Klaw series (1)
Kleenum
Slater, Jim
A Mazing Monster series (10)
Kleinert case
Mann, Jack
Gregory George Gordon Green series (4)
Klingon dictionary
Okrand, Mark
Star trek series (57)
Klingon gambit
Vardeman, Robert Edward
Star trek series (3)
Klondike Arthur
Coren, Alan
Arthur series (5)
Klondike claim
Carter, Nicholas
Nicholas Carter series (15)
Klondike cutie
Fletcher, Dirk
Spur McCoy giant series (4)
Klondyker
Knox, Bill
Webb Carrick series (4)
Knave and Company
Horler, Sydney
Sebastian Quin series (2)
Knave and the game
Janifer, Laurence Mark
Gerald Knave trilogy (3)
Knave in hand
Janifer, Laurence Mark
Gerald Knave trilogy (2)
Knave of clubs
Brown, Eric
Mountaineering series (1)
Knave of Diamonds
Karney, Jack
Jim Breen series (1)
Knave of hearts
Carr, Philippa
Daughters of England series (10)
Knave of Hearts
Shannon, Dell
Lieutenant Luis Mendoza series (4)
Knave of swords
Rayner, William
Devil's picture book series (2)
Knave's castle
Robertson, Colin
Peter Grayleigh series (10)
Knaves, fools and heroes
Wheeler-Bennett, John
Special relationships series (1)
Knaves in high places
Carter, Nicholas
Nicholas Carter series (525)
Knaves rampant
Mills, Woosnam
John Melrose series (2)
Knaves Templar
Tourney, Leonard
Matthew Stock series (6)
Knavish crows
Woods, Sara
Sir Nicholas Harding and Antony Maitland series (19)
Knee-deep in thunder
Moon, Sheila
Maris series (1)
Knife
O'Donnell, Peadar
Adrigoole series (2)
Stine, Robert Lawrence
Fear Street series (14)
Knife at my back
Knight, Adam
Steve Conacher series (3)
Knife at the opera
Staynes, Jill
Superintendent Bone series (3)
Knife between the ribs
Scott, Jack S
Detective Inspector Alfred Stanley Rosher series (11)
Knife-edged thing
Mitchell, Scott
Brock Devlin series (7)
Knife for Harry Dodd
Bellairs, George
Detective Inspector Thomas Littlejohn series (20)
Knife for the juggler
Coles, Manning
Tommy Hambledon series (16)
Knife for the killer
Morland, Nigel
Mrs Palmyra Pym series (8)
Knife for the Toff
Creasey, John
Toff series (25)
Knife for your heart
Marlowe, Piers
Frank Drury and Inspector Bill Hazard series (4)
Knife in my back
Merwin, Samuel Kimball
Amy Brewster series (1)
Knife in the dark
Cole, George Douglas Howard
Mrs Elizabeth Warrender series (2)
Superintendent Henry Wilson series (25)
Knife in the light
Ramsay, Jay
Great return series (2)
Knife in the night
Duncan, William Murdoch
Superintendent Macneill series (2)
James, William M
Apache series (2)
Knife is silent
Kent, David
Jason Burr series (2)
Knife will fall
Cumberland, Marten
Saturnin Dax series (4)
Knight and his armour
Oakeshott, Ronald Ewart
Knight series (1)
Knight and his horse
Oakeshott, Ronald Ewart
Knight series (2)
Knight and his weapons
Oakeshott, Ronald Ewart
Knight series (3)
Knight and knave of swords
Leiber, Fritz
Fafhrd and Gray Mouser series (8)
Knight and the castle
Chance, John Newton
Mister DeHavilland series (5)
Knight crusader
Welch, Ronald
Carey family series (1)
Knight fall
Payne, Laurence
Mark Savage series (5)
Knight Flandry
Anderson, Poul
Sir Dominic Flandry series (8)
Knight in battle
Oakeshott, Ronald Ewart
Knight series (5)
Knight in his castle
Oakeshott, Ronald Ewart
Knight series (4)
Knight missing
Stone, Simon
Sir Brian Dinsmore Conway series (1)
Knight of Allington
Wiat, Philippa
Allington trilogy (2)
Wyatt family series (3)
Knight of ghost and shadows
Anderson, Poul
Sir Dominic Flandry series (8)
Knight of shadows
Zelazny, Roger
Kingdom of Amber series (9)
Knight of the black rose
Lowder, James
Ravenloft series (2)
Knight of the Cross
Rutley, Cecil Bernard
Tales of stirring times series (3)
Knight of the shadows
Osman, Karen
Star wars storybook series (3)
Knight of the Swords
Moorcock, Michael
Corum series (1)
Knight of the Virgin
Blasco Ibanez, Vicente
Spanish history series (4)
Knight Rider
Larson, Glen A
Knight Rider series (1)
Knight sinister
Rattray, Simon
Hugo Bishop series (1)
Knight Templar
Charteris, Leslie
Saint series (4)
Knight, the princess and the dragons
Craig, Helen
Susie and Alfred series (1)
Knightfall
Linscott, Gillian
Birdie Linnett and Nimue Hawthorne series (3)
Knightmare
Child, Tim
Knightmare series (1)
Knight's Acre
Lofts, Norah
Sir Godfrey Tallboys series (1)
Knights and tournaments
Birt, David
Middle Ages series (3)
Knight's castle
Eager, Edward
Magic series (2)
Knight's gambit
Dickson, Grierson
Superintendent Cissie Marlow series (4)
Faulkner, William
Gavin Stevens trilogy (3)
Knights of Arabia
San Antonio
Berurier series (9)
San Antonio series (9)
Knights of dark renown
Shelby, Graham
Third Crusade series (1)
Knights of illusion
Kirchoff, Mary Lynn
Endless quest series (33)
Knights of the air
Lynn, Escott
British Army trilogy (1)
Knights of the kitchen table
Scieszka, Jon
Time warp trio series (1)
Knights of the limits
Bayley, Barrington John
Chronos series (3)
Knights of the lost domain
Atterton, Julian
Knights trilogy (2)
Knights of the Round Table
Kushner, Ellen
Choose your own adventure series (86)
Knights of the sacred blade
Atterton, Julian
Knights trilogy (1)
Knights of the White Shield
Rand, Edward Augustus
Up the Ladder Club series (1)
Knit one, drop one
Levi, Peter
Ben Jonson series (2)
Knives have edges
Woods, Sara
Sir Nicholas Harding and Antony Maitland series (14)
Knives in the night
Sherman, David
Night fighters series (1)
Knock and come in
Goodchild, George
Nigel Rix series (2)
Knock and wait
Grant, Gwen
Private, keep out series (2)
Knock at Mrs Herbs'
Gilroy, Beryl
Young Roy series (3)
Knock, knock who's there?
Gilbert, Anthony
Arthur Crook series (41)
Knock, knock, you're dead
Santiago, V J
Joseph Madden series (4)
Knock knocks
Cole, William
Knock knocks series (1)
Knock knocks you've never heard before
Cole, William
Knock knocks series (2)

Knock, murderer, knock!
Rutland, Harriet
Mister Winkley series (1)
Knock on any door
Motley, Willard
Romano series (1)
Knock-out
Sapper
Bulldog Drummond series (8)
Ronald Standish series (2)
Knock-Out Kavanagh
Stuart, Brian
Knock-Out Kavanagh series (1)
Knockabout Club alongshore
Stephens, Charles Asbury
Knockabout Club series (2)
Knockabout Club in North Africa
Ober, Frederick Albion
Knockabout Club series (7)
Knockabout Club in search of treasures
Ober, Frederick Albion
Knockabout Club series (9)
Knockabout Club in Spain
Ober, Frederick Albion
Knockabout Club series (6)
Knockabout Club in the Antilles and thereabouts
Ober, Frederick Albion
Knockabout Club series (5)
Knockabout Club in the Everglades
Ober, Frederick Albion
Knockabout Club series (4)
Knockabout Club in the tropics
Stephens, Charles Asbury
Knockabout Club series (3)
Knockabout Club in the woods
Stephens, Charles Asbury
Knockabout Club series (1)
Knockabout Club on the Spanish Main
Ober, Frederick Albion
Knockabout Club series (8)
Knocked for a loop
Rice, Craig
John Joseph Malone series (10)
Knocker on death's door
Peters, Ellis
Inspector George Felse series (10)
Knot in the grain, and other stories
McKinley, Robin
Chronicles of Damar series (3)
Knot Squirrel tied
Uttley, Alison
Little Grey Rabbit series (8)
Knots in the noose
Carter, Nicholas
Nicholas Carter series (477)
Knotted silk
Barrett, Monte
Peter Cardigan series (2)
Know it all
Cranfield, Ingrid
Q challenge quiz series (1)
Know nothing
Settle, Mary Lee
Beulah series (3)
Know the score
Skurzynski, Gloria
Your high-tech world series (4)
Know thine enemy
Viviers, Lyn
Star trek fan series (39)
Koala and Emu and the unexpected box
De Fossard, Esta
Koala series (7)
Koala and the billycan
De Fossard, Esta
Koala series (2)
Koala and the bunyip
De Fossard, Esta
Koala series (1)
Koala and the dragon
De Fossard, Esta
Koala series (3)
Koala and the great comet search
De Fossard, Esta
Koala series (11)
Koala and the Tasmanian devil and the possum hunt
De Fossard, Esta
Koala series (8)
Koala bear twins
Hogan, Inez
Twins series (13)
Koala catches a thief, almost
De Fossard, Esta
Koala series (5)
Koala finds a most peculiar ver strange hole in the ground
De Fossard, Esta
Koala series (6)
Koala goes to the rainbow's end
De Fossard, Esta
Koala series (4)
Koala has a whole lot of things going on
De Fossard, Esta
Koala series (12)
Koala party
Campbell, Peter
Amazing Koalas series (1)
Koala teaches Emu a lesson
De Fossard, Esta
Koala series (10)
Koala's book of poems
De Fossard, Esta
Koala series (9)
Koalas' spring clean
Campbell, Peter
Amazing Koalas series (2)
Kobayashi Maru
Ecklar, Julia
Star trek series (47)
Koberg link
Maling, Arthur
Brock Potter series (4)
Kobo
Strang, Herbert
Russo-Japanese War series (1)
Kobra manifesto
Hall, Adam
Quiller series (7)
Kocska formula
Riley, Frank
Father Anton Dymek series (1)
Kohga ritual
Barker, Wade
War of the Ninja Master series (1)
Kojak
Mann, Abby
Kojak series (1)
Kolwezi
Perry, Ritchie
Philis series (13)
Komani mystery
Sampson, Victor
Inspector Downes and Sergeant Hopkins series (2)
Komantcia
Keith, Harold
Komantcia series (1)
Komespi affair
Paul, Ernest
George Barclay series (2)
Kondrashev chase
Rosenberger, Joseph
Death Merchant series (22)
Konrad
Ferring, David
Konrad trilogy (1)
Kookaburra cackles
Laird, Elizabeth
Toucan Tecs series (7)
Koopa capers
McCay, Bill
Nintendo adventure series (4)
Korean carnage
Roberts, Mark Kelly
Liberty Corps series (4)
Korean combat
Jackson, Robert
Flying Officer George Yeoman series (10)
Korean kill
Carter, Nick
Nick Carter series (248)
Korean killground
Wilson, Gar
Phoenix Force series (10)
Korean tiger
Carter, Nick
Nick Carter series (26)
Koren
Lukeman, Tim
Lhas'kar series (2)
Koronglea adventures
Stevens, Fae Hewston
Koronglea series (4)
Koronglea cobbers
Stevens, Fae Hewston
Koronglea series (1)
Koronglea holidays
Stevens, Fae Hewston
Koronglea series (3)
Koronglea ponies
Stevens, Fae Hewston
Koronglea series (2)
Koronglea twins
Stevens, Fae Hewston
Koronglea series (5)
Kothar and the conjuror's curse
Fox, Gardner Francis
Kothar series (5)
Kothar and the Demon Queen
Fox, Gardner Francis
Kothar series (3)
Kothar and the wizard slayer
Fox, Gardner Francis
Kothar series (4)
Kothar, barbarian swordsman
Fox, Gardner Francis
Kothar series (1)
Kothar of the magic sword
Fox, Gardner Francis
Kothar series (2)
Kowloon contract
Atlee, Philip
Joe Gall series (19)
Koyama's diamond
Berry, Adrian
Koyama series (1)
Kra the baboon
Rutley, Cecil Bernard
Wild life story series (2)
Kregoff necklace
Carter, Nicholas
Nicholas Carter series (478)
Kremlin conspiracy
Flannery, Sean
Wallace and John Mahoney series (1)
Kremlin devils
Hild, Jack
SOBS series (22)
Kremlin file
Carter, Nick
Nick Carter series (81)
Kremlin kill
Carter, Nick
Nick Carter series (193)
Krispos of Videssos
Turtledove, Harry
Tale of Krispos series (2)
Videssos series (7)
Krispos rising
Turtledove, Harry
Tale of Krispos series (1)
Videssos series (6)
Kristi
Moss, Merrilee
Hot pursuit series (6)
Kristin Lavransdatter
Undset, Sigrid
Kristin Lavransdatter trilogy (3)
Kristy and the baby parade
Martin, Ann Matthews
Baby-Sitters Club series (45)
Kristy and the copycat
Martin, Ann Matthews
Baby-Sitters Club series (74)
Kristy and the haunted mansion
Martin, Ann Matthews
Baby-Sitters Club mystery series (9)
Kristy and the missing child
Martin, Ann Matthews
Baby-Sitters Club mystery series (4)
Kristy and the Mother's Day surprise
Martin, Ann Matthews
Baby-Sitters Club series (24)
Kristy and the secret of Susan
Martin, Ann Matthews
Baby-Sitters Club series (32)
Kristy and the snobs
Martin, Ann Matthews
Baby-Sitters Club series (11)
Kristy and the vampires
Martin, Ann Matthews
Baby-Sitters Club mystery series (15)
Kristy and the walking disaster
Martin, Ann Matthews
Baby-Sitters Club series (20)
Kristy and the worst kid ever
Martin, Ann Matthews
Baby-Sitters Club series (62)
Kristy for president
Martin, Ann Matthews
Baby-Sitters Club series (53)
Kristy's big day
Martin, Ann Matthews
Baby-Sitters Club series (6)
Kristy's great idea
Martin, Ann Matthews
Baby-Sitters Club series (1)
Kristy's mystery admirer
Martin, Ann Matthews
Baby-Sitters Club series (38)
Kristy's queer Christmas
Miller, Olive Thorne
Kristy series (1)
Kristy's rainy day picnic
Miller, Olive Thorne
Kristy series (3)
Kristy's surprise party
Miller, Olive Thorne
Kristy series (2)
Krokodil tears
Yeovil, Jack
Dark future series (2)
Kronos plot
Rosenberger, Joseph
Death Merchant series (24)
Krotons
Dicks, Terrance
Doctor Who series (99)
Krozair of Kregen
Akers, Alan Burt
Dray Prescot series (14)
Kubla Khan caper
Prather, Richard Scott
Shell Scott series (32)
Kubrik the outlaw
Harper, Theodore Acland
Siberian series (2)
Kulaks
Piccard, Eulalie
Episodes of the great Russian tragedy series (3)
Kull
Howard, Robert Ervin
Tales of the Picts series (1)
Kulla of the carts
Eyton, John
India series (1)
Kutath
Cherryh, Carolyn Janice
Alliance-Union series (16)
Faded sun trilogy (3)
Kutnar, son of Pic
Langford, George
Pic series (2)
Kwahari
Hicks, D L
Milton Hicks series (1)
Kwame's girl
Johnson, Stacie
Eighteen Pine Street series (10)
Kwasi and the parrot, and other stories
Kaye, Geraldine
Kwasi series (1)
Kwasi goes to town
Kaye, Geraldine
Kwasi series (2)
Kyd for hire
Harris, Timothy Hyde
Tom Kyd series (1)
Kylie's concert
Sheehan, Patti
Kylie series (2)
Kylie's song
Sheehan, Patti
Kylie series (1)
Kyra Kyralina
Istrati, Panait
Adrien Zograffi series (1)
Kyra, my sister
Istrati, Panait
Adrien Zograffi series (1)
Kyrik and the lost queen
Fox, Gardner Francis
Kyrik series (4)
Kyrik and the wizard's sword
Fox, Gardner Francis
Kyrik series (3)
Kyrik fights the demon world
Fox, Gardner Francis
Kyrik series (2)
Kyrik, warlock warrior
Fox, Gardner Francis
Kyrik series (1)
Kyril
Trenhaile, John
General Povin series (1)

L

L.A. confidential
Ellroy, James
Los Angeles quartet (3)
L.A. gang war
Buchanan, Jack
M.I.A. Hunter series (13)
L.A. massacre
Winski, Norman
Dirk Spencer series (2)
L.A. payback
McCray, Mike
Black Berets series (13)
L.A. strike
Robbins, David
Blade series (9)
L.A. wars
Ramm, Carl
James Hawker series (2)
L-shaped room
Banks, Lynne Reid
L.U.S.T. be a lady tonight
Gray, Rod
Lady from L.U.S.T. series (1)
Jane Graham trilogy (1)
La Bodega
Blasco Ibanez, Vicente
Roman Catholic Church in Spain series (3)
La Dame de Monsoreau
Dumas, Alexandre
Valois series (6)
La vendee
Dumas, Alexandre
Napoleon series (3)
Label it murder
Graham, Neill
Solo Malcolm series (14)
Labour in vain
Garfield, Leon
Apprentices series (5)
Labours of Hercules
Christie, Agatha
Hercule Poirot series (25)
Labrador days
Grenfell, Wilfrid Thomason
Labrador series (3)
Labrador doctor
Grenfell, Wilfrid Thomason
Labrador series (3)
Labyrinth
Faulcon, Robert
Nighthunter series (6)
Jones, Nicholas
Wind in the willows series (9)
Pronzini, Bill
Private Eye series (6)
Schmidt, Dennis
Questioner trilogy (1)
Labyrinth makers
Price, Anthony
Doctor David Audley and Jack Butler series (2)
Labyrinth of dreams
Chalker, Jack Laurence
G.O.D. Inc. series (1)
Labyrinth of lies
Berry, Adrian
Koyama series (2)
Labyrinth of worlds
Cole, Adrian
Star requiem series (4)
Labyrinths of fear
Morris, Dave
Knightmare series (2)
Lace
Conran, Shirley
Lace series (1)
Lace 2
Conran, Shirley
Lace series (2)
Lachlan's widow
Leith, Mary Charlotte Julia
Lachlan series (2)
Lack of the Bodkins
Wodehouse, Pelham Grenville
Ivor Llewellyn series (1)
Lacquer screen
Gulik, Robert van
Judge Dee series (10)
Lactus cactus
Reese, Bob
Desert critterland series (1)
Lad, a dog
Terhune, Albert Payson
Sunnybank collies series (1)
Lad of Evesham Vale
Archer, Fred
Evesham Vale series (4)
Lad of Sunnybank
Terhune, Albert Payson
Sunnybank collies series (14)
Lad of the O'Friel's
Macmanus, Seumas
O'Friel trilogy (2)
Ladder of death
Flynn, Brian
Anthony Bathurst series (16)
Ladder of snow
Styles, Showell
Simon and Mag series (2)
Ladders to fire
Nin, Anais
Cities of the interior series (1)
Laddie
Whitaker, Evelyn
Miss Toosie series (2)

Ladies
Barrington, E
Bennet family series (2)
Ladies always talk
Truss, Seldon
Inspector Gidleigh series (6)
Ladies' bane
Wentworth, Patricia
Miss Maud Silver series (23)
Ladies can be dangerous
Marshall, Lovat
Sugar Kane series (11)
Ladies' day
Smith, Chard Powers
Lathrop family series (2)
Ladies' delight
Zola, Emile
Rougon Macquart series (11)
Ladies in ermine
Holt, Gavin
Inspector Joel Saber series (6)
Ladies in Hades
Kummer, Frederic Arnold
Hades series (1)
Ladies in the dark
Neville, Margot
Inspector Grogan and Sergeant Manning series (18)
Ladies Lindores
Oliphant, Margaret Oliphant Wilson
Lady Car series (1)
Ladies of Alderley
Mitford, Nancy
Alderley series (1)
Stanley, Maria Josepha
Alderley series (1)
Ladies of Lark
Chappell, Mollie
Tiddy Jeffreys series (1)
Ladies of Locksley
Vivian, Francis
Inspector Gordon Knollis series (10)
Ladies of Mandrigyn
Hambly, Barbara
Dragonsbane series (1)
Sun Wolf series (1)
Ladies of Spain
Beardmore, George
Lesley Allan series (5)
Ladies of the Rachmaninoff eyes
Van Dyke, Henry
Oliver series (1)
Ladies' paradise
Zola, Emile
Rougon Macquart series (11)
Ladies won't wait
Cheyney, Peter
Michael Kells series (2)
Ladino
Brown, Joseph Paul Summers
Arizona saga series (3)
Ladis and the ant
Sanchez-Silva, Jose Maria
Ladis series (1)
Lads of Lunda
Saxby, Jessie Margaret Edmonston
Shetland series (1)
Lads of the Lothians
Lynn, Escott
British Army trilogy (3)
Lady
Stratton, Alan
Gina series (1)
Lady Addle at home
Dunn, Mary
Lady Addle of Eigg series (2)
Lady Addle remembers
Dunn, Mary
Lady Addle of Eigg series (1)
Lady and Sada San
Little, Frances
Lady of the decoration series (3)
Lady and the lawman
Brandon, Joyce
Lady series (2)
Lady and the lion
Hooper, Kay
Once upon a time series (5)
Lady and the outlaw
Brandon, Joyce
Lady series (1)
Lady and unicorn
Johansen, Iris
Gold class trilogy (1)
Lady, be bad
Halliday, Brett
Michael Shayne series (60)
Lady, behave!
Cheyney, Peter
Johnny Vallon series (2)
Lady Betty across the water
Williamson, Charles Norris
Lord and Lady Loveland series (1)
Lady, beware!
Cheyney, Peter
Johnny Vallon series (2)
Lady Bountiful
Birmingham, George A
Gorman MP series (3)
Lady came by night
Halliday, Brett
Michael Shayne series (24)
Lady came to kill
Chaber, M E
Milo March series (7)
Lady Car
Oliphant, Margaret Oliphant Wilson
Lady Car series (2)
Lady Chatterley's daughter
Robins, Patricia
Lady Chatterley series (3)
Lady Chatterley's lover
Lawrence, David Herbert
Lady Chatterley series (1)
Lady Chatterley's second husband
D'Orliac, Jehanne
Lady Chatterley series (2)
Lady Cicely
Wilson, Sandra
Lady Cicely Plantagenet trilogy (3)
Lady, don't die on my doorstep
Shallit, Joseph
Dan Morrison series (2)
Lady, don't shroud me
Brody, Marc
Marc Brody series (72)
Lady, drop dead
Treat, Lawrence
Jub Freeman series (9)
Mitch Taylor series (6)
Lady Ellen Grae
Cleaver, Vera
Ellen Grae series (2)
Lady for Ludovic
McCulloch, Sarah
Georgian series (2)
Lady Fortescue steps out
Chesney, Marion
Poor relation series (1)
Lady from L.U.S.T.
Gray, Rod
Lady from L.U.S.T. series (20)
Lady from Tokyo
Corrigan, Mark
Mark Corrigan and McLean series (26)
Lady Gay
Archibald, George, Mrs
Lady Gay trilogy (2)
Lady Gay and her sister
Archibald, George, Mrs
Lady Gay trilogy (1)
Lady, get your gun
Ernst, Paul
Shirley Leighton and Bill Harper series (2)
Lady had a gun
Morland, Nigel
Mrs Palmyra Pym series (15)
Lady had a tiger
Brodie, Gordon
John Borham series (1)
Lady has a scar
Janson, Hank
Hank Janson series (17)
Lady has claws
Desmond, Hugh
Alan Fraser series (30)
Lady holds a gun
Spade, Danny
Danny Spade series (5)
Lady Ice
Hohl, Joan
Vanzant family trilogy (1)
Lady in a million
Shane, Susannah
Christopher Saxe series (2)
Lady in black
Graeme, Bruce
Inspector Auguste Jantry series (3)
Lady in blue
Groner, Augusta
Joe Muller series (4)
Lady in cement
Rome, Anthony
Tony Rome series (2)
Lady in danger
Shane, Susannah
Christopher Saxe series (1)
Lady in distress
Thomas, Martin
Sexton Blake series (1464)
Lady in green, and other stories
Cheyney, Peter
Alonzo Mactavish series (5)
Lady in heat
Gray, Rod
Lady from L.U.S.T. series (11)
Lady in peril
Williams, Ben Ames
Inspector Tope series (2)
Lady in scarlet
Daniel, Roland
Buddy Mustard series (5)
Lady in the lake
Chandler, Raymond
Philip Marlowe series (4)
Lady in the morgue
Latimer, Jonathan
Bill Crane series (3)
Lady in the Tower
Plaidy, Jean
Queens of England series (4)
Lady in the wood
Dellbridge, John
Rupert Hambledon series (2)
Lady Incognito
Walsh, James Morgan
Inspector Quaile series (3)
Lady is a spy
Black, Lionel
Emma Greaves series (3)
Lady is a target
Grover, Marshall
Larry and Stretch series (240)
Lady is a vamp
Dekobra, Maurice
Bradley Adams series (2)
Lady is afraid
Coxe, George Harmon
Max Hale series (2)
Lady is available
Brown, Carter
Lieutenant Al Wheeler series (30)
Lady is dead
Laing, Patrick
Patrick Laing series (5)
Lady is lethal
Muller, Paul
Paul Muller series (3)
Lady is not available
Brown, Carter
Lieutenant Al Wheeler series (30)
Lady is not fooling
Redwood, Alec
Michael Grant series (1)
Lady is poison
Gray, Berkeley
Norman Conquest series (25)
Lady is transparent
Brown, Carter
Lieutenant Al Wheeler series (26)
Lady killer
Coxe, George Harmon
Kent Murdock series (11)
Lady-killer
Gilbert, Anthony
Arthur Crook series (24)
Lady killer
Gray, Rod
Lady from L.U.S.T. series (19)
McBain, Ed
Eighty Seventh Precinct series (7)
Lady killer affair
Arliss, Joen
Kate Graham series (2)
Lady killers
Riefe, Alan
Huntington Cage series (1)
Lady, lady I did it!
McBain, Ed
Eighty Seventh Precinct series (14)
Lady, lie low
Janson, Hank
Hank Janson series (108)
Lady likes to sin
Spade, Danny
Danny Spade series (32)
Lady Lilith
McKenna, Stephen
Sensationalists trilogy (1)
Lady lost
Cory, Desmond
Lindy Grey series (3)
Lady Loudly the goose
Lloyd, David
Great escapes series (2)
Lady loved too well
Donahue, Jackson
Harlan Cole series (2)
Lady Luck and F J Beck
Grover, Marshall
Larry and Stretch series (287)
Lady Macbeth
Freeling, Nicolas
Henri Castang series (11)
Lady Margaret
King, Betty
Beaufort family series (1)
Tudor series (2)
Lady married
Little, Frances
Lady of the decoration series (3)
Lady, mind that corpse
Janson, Hank
Hank Janson series (4)
Lady Monster and the bike ride
Blance, Ellen
Monster series (15)
Lady Monster and the great search
Blance, Ellen
Monster series (28)
Lady Monster has a plan
Blance, Ellen
Monster series (24)
Lady Monster helps out
Blance, Ellen
Monster series (14)
Lady Noggs assists
Jepson, Edgar
Lady Noggs series (3)
Lady Noggs intervenes
Jepson, Edgar
Lady Noggs series (2)
Lady Noggs, peeress
Jepson, Edgar
Lady Noggs series (1)
Lady of burlesque
Lee, Gypsy Rose
Gypsy Rose Lee series (1)
Lady of China Street
Corrigan, Mark
Mark Corrigan and McLean series (9)
Lady of darkness
Paxson, Diana Lucile
Westria series (2)
Lady of despair
Grierson, Francis Durham
Commissaire Patras series (1)
Lady of doom
Verner, Gerald
Trevor Lowe series (3)
Lady of fire
Mills, Anita
Lady of fire series (1)
Lady of grace
Hamilton, Alexandra
Nefertiti trilogy (2)
Lady of Han-Gilden
Tarr, Judith
Avaryan Rising trilogy (2)
Lady of justice
Morrison, Margaret
Elizabeth Conway series (2)
Lady of leisure
Sidgwick, Ethel
Ashwin trilogy (1)
Lady of light
Paxson, Diana Lucile
Westria series (1)
Lady of light, lady of darkness
Paxson, Diana Lucile
Westria series (2)
Lady of mercy
Sagara, Michele M
Sundered series (3)
Lady of night
Barry, Jerome
Chick Varney series (3)
Lady of quality
Burnett, Frances Hodgson
Lady of quality series (1)
Lady of Ravensedge
Lewis, Jack
Sexton Blake series (185)
Lady of shadows
Carter, Nicholas
Nicholas Carter series (283)
Lady of the barge
Jacobs, William Wymark
Night-Watchman series (4)
Lady of the bees
Swann, Thomas Burnett
Ancient history series (7)
Mellonia trilogy (3)
Lady of the boat
Murasaki Shibuku
Genji series (5)
Lady of the decoration
Little, Frances
Lady of the decoration series (1)
Lady of the Garter
Dymoke, Juliet
Plantagenets series (4)
Lady of the Haven
Diamond, Graham
Haven series (2)
Stacy series (1)
Lady of the lakes
Yorke, Katherine
Enchantress trilogy (3)
Lady of the manse
Derwent, Lavinia
Border series (5)
Lady of the night wind
Vanardy, Varick
Bingham Harvard series (4)
Lady of the snowmist
Offutt, Andrew Jefferson
War of the gods on earth trilogy (3)
Lady of the winds
Novak, Kate
Heartquest series (6)
Lady on the lam
Kane, Martin
Martin Kane series (1)
Lady on the line
Tone, Teona
Kyra Keaton series (1)
Lady Penelope, the Albanian affair
Theydon, John
Thunderbirds series (5)
Lady Perfecta
Perez Galdos, Benito
Contemporary novels of Spain series (4)
Lady policeman
Lock, Joan
Lady policeman series (1)
Lady prefers murder
Wrenn, Harold Albert
William Mitchell series (2)
Lady regrets
Fox, James M
John and Suzy Marshall series (5)
Lady rogue
Douglas, Carole Nelson
Taliswoman trilogy (3)
Lady rustler
Calhoun, Chad
Agent Brad Spear series (10)
Lady said no
Allyson, Alan
Martin Ross series (3)
Lady Sativa
Lauria, Frank
Doctor Owen Orient series (3)
Lady saw red
Long, Amelia Reynolds
Peter Piper series (7)
Lady says when
Ambler, Dail
Danny Spade series (26)
Lady Sharlow's secret
Graydon, William Murray
Sexton Blake series (235)
Lady Sinister
Warren, Paulette
Caliban series (4)
Lady Susan and not the Cardinal
Cleeve, Lucas
Lady Susan series (2)
Lady, take care
Robertson, Colin
Edward North series (3)
Lady takes it all off
Gray, Rod
Lady from L.U.S.T. series (16)
Lady, the guy is dead
Ronns, Edward
Jerry Benedict series (1)
Lady, this is murder
Chambers, Peter
Mark Preston series (6)
Lady, throw me a curve
Ross, Gene
Shaun O'Malley series (2)
Lady to kill
Dent, Lester
Chance Malloy series (2)
Lady toll that bell
Janson, Hank
Hank Janson series (24)
Lady Velvet
Carter, Nicholas
Nicholas Carter series (63)
Lady was a spy
Daniel, Roland
Michael Wallace series (2)
Lady was an outlaw
Longtree, Warren T
Ruff Justice series (28)
Lady was disturbed
Warren, James
James Warren series (1)

Lady, what's your game?
Jacobs, Thomas Curtis Hicks
Temple Fortune series (5)
Lady, where are you?
Desmond, Hugh
Alan Fraser series (14)
Lady who never was
Chambers, Peter
Mark Preston series (26)
Lady with a cool eye
Moffat, Gwen
Miss Melinda Pink series (1)
Lady with a gun
Thorne, Ernest Pollett
Major Brains Cunningham series (9)
Lady with the limp
Horler, Sydney
Sir Harker Bellamy series (9)
Tiger Standish series (9)
Lady yesterday
Estleman, Loren D
Amos Walker series (7)
Lady, you're killing me
Chambers, Peter
Mark Preston series (20)
Lady you're lethal
Brody, Marc
Marc Brody series (81)
Ladybirds are in
Janson, Hank
Hank Janson series (235)
Ladygrove
Burke, John Frederick
Doctor Alexander Caspian series (3)
Ladykiller
O'Donnell, Lillian
Detective Norah Mulcahaney series (9)
Lady's a decoy
McCall, K T
Johnny Buchanan series (7)
Lady's confession
Macdonald, George
Thomas Wingfold trilogy (2)
Lady's girl
Bolton, Evelyn
Horse book series (2)
Lady's out of circulation
Brody, Marc
Marc Brody series (51)
Ladysmead
Gillespie, Jane
Mansfield Park series (3)
Lafitte, the pirate of the Gulf
Ingraham, Joseph Holt
Lafitte series (1)
Lagoon
Drake, Alison
Tango Key series (4)
Lagrange Five
Reynolds, Mack
Lagrangia series (1)
Rex Bader series (3)
Lagrangists
Reynolds, Mack
Lagrangia series (2)
Rex Bader series (4)
Laid in the future
Gray, Rod
Lady from L.U.S.T. series (12)
Laidlaw
McIlvanney, William
Inspector Jack Laidlaw series (1)
Lair
Herbert, James
Rats trilogy (2)
Lair of the Lich
Algozin, Bruce
Endless quest series (27)
Laird of evil
Thomas, Martin
Sexton Blake series (1580)
Lake breezes
Optic, Oliver
Great Western series (3)
Lake District murder
Bude, John
Inspector Meredith series (2)
Lake fear
McMahan, Ian
Mikrokid mystery series (3)
Lake Frome monster
Upfield, Arthur William
Napoleon Bonaparte series (29)
Lake House
Rhode, John
Doctor Lancelot Priestley series (42)
Lake isle
Freeling, Nicolas
Henri Castang series (3)
Lake loot
Janson, Hank
Hank Janson series (181)
Lake of fear
Macleod, Robert
Talos Cord series (3)
Lake of fire
Bailey, Robin Wayne
Dungeon series (4)
Lake of the dead
Greene, L Patrick
Aubrey Saint John Major series (15)
Lake Wobegon days
Keillor, Garrison
Lake Wobegon series (1)
Lakeland adventure
Lethbridge, Peter
Jeremy series (2)
Lakeland tragedy
Courage, John
Bill Britain series (2)
Lakeland vet
Stranger, Joyce
Dai Evans series (2)
Lakeport Bank mystery
Bartlett, Philip A
Roy Stover series (1)
Lakerim Athletic Club
Hughes, Rupert
Lakerim Athletic Club series (1)
Lakerim cruise
Hughes, Rupert
Lakerim Athletic Club series (3)
Lakeside murder
Snow, Charles Horace
Tommy Thorne series (1)
Lakeside zero
Enefer, Douglas
Sam Bawtrey series (7)
Lal
Hammond, William Alexander
Lal series (1)
Lalage in love
Evans, Cherry
Belinda and Lalage series (2)
Lallia
Tubb, Edwin Charles
Dumarest series (6)
Lam to the slaughter
Fair, A A
Bertha Cool and Donald Lam series (1)
Lama
Tangye, Derek
Minack chronicles series (5)
Lamarchos
Clayton, Jo
Diadem series (2)
Lama's secret
Graydon, William Murray
Sexton Blake series (236)
Lamb for the Lambchops
Brown, Jeff
Stanley Lambchops series (2)
Lamb in command
Maynard, Kenneth
Lieutenant Lamb series (3)
Lamb in the lounge
Warren, Rebecca
Pet lamb series (2)
Lamb Shenkin
Mayne, William
Animal library series (5)
Lambing at Sheepfold Farm
Williams, Susan
Sheepfold Farm series (1)
Lambing time
Miller, Jane
Birth series (2)
Lamb's mixed fortunes
Maynard, Kenneth
Lieutenant Lamb series (4)
Lame crusade
Pargeter, Edith
Eighth champion of Christendom trilogy (1)
Lame devil
Lesage, Alain Rene
Devil upon two sticks series (1)
Lame dog man
Turner, George Reginald
Treelake series (4)
Lame dog murder
Halliday, Michael
Martin and Richard Fane series (2)
Lament for a lady
Kains, Josephine
Terry Spring series (7)
Lament for a lost lover
Carr, Philippa
Daughters of England series (5)
Lament for a lousy lover
Brown, Carter
Lieutenant Al Wheeler series (20)
Mavis Seidlitz series (7)
Lament for a lovely
Brody, Marc
Marc Brody series (27)
Lament for a lover
Janson, Hank
Hank Janson series (253)
Lament for a maker
Innes, Michael
Sir John Appleby series (3)
Lament for Adonis
Thompson, Edward
Warren Remfrey series (2)
Lament for Christobel
Peterson, Audrey
Jane Winfield and Andrew Quentin series (6)
Lament for Leto
Mitchell, Gladys
Dame Beatrice Bradley series (44)
Lament for the bride
Reilly, Helen
Inspector Christopher McKee series (21)
Lament for William
Russell, Charlotte Murray
Homer Fitzgerald series (1)
Lamp from the warlock's tomb
Bellairs, John
Anthony Monday series (3)
Lamp of God
Queen, Ellery
Ellery Queen series (16)
Lamp-post 592
Maddock, Stephen
Timothy Terrel series (10)
Lamplighter's funeral
Garfield, Leon
Apprentices series (1)
Lancashire countrygoer
Lofthouse, Jessica
Countrygoer series (1)
Lancashire idylls
Mather, James Marshall
Lancashire idylls series (1)
Lancasters at Lynford
Bond, Freda Constance
Lancasters series (2)
Lance and his friends
Bearne, David
Ridingdale series (2)
Lancer spy
McKenna, Marthe
Clive Granville series (1)
Lances and longships
Campbell, Marion
Richard De Brun series (2)
Land
Vigliante, Mary
Aftermath series (1)
Land bandits
Dawson, Clay
Long Rider series (9)
Land baron
Reese, John
Jesus on horseback trilogy (3)
Land behind the world
Parry, Anne Spencer
Bara quartet (1)
Land below the wind
Keith, Agnes
Borneo series (1)
Land beyond
Alderman, Gill
Guna series (2)
Corlett, William
Gate of Eden trilogy (2)
Land beyond the gate
Eshbach, Lloyd Arthur
Gates of Lucifer series (1)
Land beyond the map
Bulmer, Kenneth
Keys to the dimensions series (1)
Land beyond the mountains
Giles, Janice Holt
Fowler family series (8)
Land breakers
Ehle, John
North Carolina series (1)
Land endures
Pearce, Mary Emily
Apple tree series (4)
Land fit for heroes
Mann, Phillip
Escape to the wild wood series (1)
Land grab
Cole, Jackson
Jim Hatfield series (19)
Land grabbers
Newton, Dwight Bennett
Johnny Logan series (3)
Land in flames
Marcus, David
Land of Ireland series (2)
Land is large
Waldman, Emerson
Land and the way series (1)
Land is yours
Warren, Clarence Henry
Happy countryman series (3)
Land leviathan
Moorcock, Michael
Oswald Bastable series (2)
Una Persson series (1)
Land not theirs
Marcus, David
Land of Ireland series (1)
Land of Always-Night
Robeson, Kenneth
Doc Savage series (13)
Land of Australia
Clune, Frank
Discovery series (19)
Land of darkness
Oliphant, Margaret Oliphant Wilson
Stories of the seen and the unseen series (3)
Land of dreams
Nixon, Joan Lowery
Ellis Island series (3)
Land of fear
Robeson, Kenneth
Doc Savage series (75)
Land of heart's desire
Gage, Joy Pennock
Seventh child series (1)
Land of hope
Nixon, Joan Lowery
Ellis Island series (1)
Land of hope and glory
Clune, Frank
Discovery series (12)
Land of little rain
Austin, Mary
Californian Indian series (1)
Land of long ago
Hall, Eliza Calvert
Aunt Jane series (2)
Land of long juju
Robeson, Kenneth
Doc Savage series (47)
Land of lost content
Robertson, Denise
Belgate trilogy (1)
Belgate trilogy (3)
Land of mist
Doyle, Arthur Conan
Professor Challenger series (3)
Land of mountains
Rutley, Cecily Marianne
Little people in far off lands series (1)
Land of mud castles
Ingram, James Henry
Adventure series (2)
Land of my fathers
Cordell, Alexander
Merthyr trilogy (3)
Mortymers series (7)
Land of no shadow
Claudy, Carl Harry
Adventures in the unknown series (3)
Land of our dreams
Livingston, Nancy
Mackie family series (2)
Land of Oz
Baum, Lyman Frank
Oz series (2)
Land of promise
Nixon, Joan Lowery
Ellis Island series (2)
Tedrow, Thomas L
Days of Laura Ingalls Wilder series (8)
Land of silence
Burgin, George Brown
Four Corners series (4)
Land of strangers
Bubb, Lillian
Christiansson family trilogy (2)
Budd, Lillian
Kristiansson trilogy (2)
Land of terror
Burroughs, Edgar Rice
Pellucidar series (6)
Robeson, Kenneth
Doc Savage series (8)
Land of the black gold
Herge
Tintin series (15)
Land of the children
Orenburgsky, Sergei Gussiev
Russian history series (2)
Land of the fathers
Orenburgsky, Sergei Gussiev
Russian history series (1)
Land of the giants
Leinster, Murray
Land of the giants series (1)
Land of the kangaroo
Knox, Thomas Wallace
Boy travellers series (17)
Land of the mountains and the flood
Macgregor, Alasdair Alpin
Golden lamp trilogy (2)
Land of the ten thousand smokes
Barlow, Roger
Sandy Steele series (7)
Land of the thundering herds
Denzel, Justin Francis
Prehistoric adventure series (3)
Land of tomorrow
Maile, Ben
Land of tomorrow series (1)
Land pirates
Cole, Jackson
Jim Hatfield series (92)
Land pollution
Snodgrass, Mary Ellen
Environmental awareness series (3)
Land rushers
Zachary, Elizabeth
Making of America series (7)
Land seekers
Boucher, Alan Estcourt
Halli Thordason series (5)
Land that time forgot
Burroughs, Edgar Rice
Bowen Tylor trilogy (1)
Bowen Tylor trilogy (3)
Land truant
Porteous, Crichton
Farmer's creed trilogy (3)
Land unknown
Raine, Kathleen
Happy fields trilogy (2)
Land where I belong
Seymour, Aubrey
Fertile earth series (1)
Land where serpents rule
Lee, Samantha
Owen Lightbringer trilogy (2)
Landed Gently
Hunter, Alan
Inspector George Gently series (4)
Landfall
Macarthur, David Wilson
Alec Sinclair series (2)
Landfall finesse
Da Cruz, Daniel
Ape Swain series (1)
Landfall on Innis Michael
Sampson, Fay
Watch and landfall series (2)
Landgrabbers
Willoughby, Lee Davis
Making of America series (13)
Landing
Leeson, Robert
Zarnia experiment series (1)
Landing in Cloud Valley
Leeson, Robert
Cloud Valley series (1)
Landlocked
Lessing, Doris
Children of violence series (4)
Landmarks
Lucas, Edward Verrall
Winfield series (5)
Lando
L'Amour, Louis
Cullen Baker series (2)
Sackett family series (8)
Lando Calrissian and the Flamewind of Oseon
Smith, Lester Neil
Lando Calrissian trilogy (2)
Lando Calrissian and the Mindharp of Sharu
Smith, Lester Neil
Lando Calrissian trilogy (1)
Lando Calrissian and the Starcave of ThonBoka
Smith, Lester Neil
Lando Calrissian trilogy (3)
Landor case
Bentley, John
Sir Richard Herrivell series (6)
Lands of legend
Morris, Dave
Dragon warriors series (6)

Last escape
Lorac, E C R
Inspector Macdonald series (47)
Last express
Kendrick, Baynard
Captain Duncan Maclain series (1)
Last ferry from the Lido
Healey, Ben
Harcourt d'Espinal series (4)
Paul Hedley series (8)
Last flight to Moscow
Carter, Nick
Nick Carter series (201)
Last four lives of Annie Besant
Nethercot, Arthur Hobart
Annie Besant series (2)
Last fraulein
Meade, Richard
John Allison series (2)
Last frontier
Mitchum, Hank
Stage coach station series (52)
Last full measure
Morrow, Honore Willsie
Great Captain trilogy (3)
Last gamble
Foley, Rae
Hiram Potter series (2)
Graham, Winston
Poldark series (4)
Masur, Harold Q
Scott Jordan series (7)
Last generation
Howard, Tom
Sergeant Tom Howard series (6)
Last genie
Leeson, Robert
Alec Bowden series (3)
Last gentleman
Percy, Walker
Will Barrett series (1)
Last Glencannon omnibus
Gilpatric, Guy
Mister Colin Andrew Macthrockle Glencannon series (8)
Last good kiss
Crumley, James
C W Sughrue series (1)
Last great auk
Eckert, Allan Wesley
Extinct birds series (1)
Last guardian
Gemmell, David A
Sipstrassi tales series (4)
Last gun
Shelton, Gene
Texas legends series (1)
Last gunfight
McElwain, Dean L
Preacher's law series (4)
Last hanging at Paradise Meadow
Bly, Stephen Arthur
Stuart Brannon series (3)
Last heiress
Barclay, Tessa
Tramont family series (3)
Last Herald-Mage
Lackey, Mercedes
Last Herald-Mage trilogy (3)
Last hero
Charteris, Leslie
Saint series (3)
Last heroes
Baldwin, Alex
Men at war series (1)
Last honest woman
Roberts, Nora
O'Hurley trilogy (1)
Last howl of the Wolf
Farely, Alison
Plantagenet series (8)
Last human
De Haven, Tom
Chronicles of the king's tramp series (3)
Naylor, Grant
Red Dwarf series (3)
Last hurdle
Grey, Peter
Kit Hunter series (10)
Last hurrah!
McLaglen, John J
Herne the Hunter series (24)
Last husband, and other stories
Humphrey, William
Red River County trilogy (3)
Last incarnation of Vautrin
Balzac, Honore de
Scenes of Parisian life series (8)
Last Jacobite
Foxall, Raymond
Harry Adkins series (5)

Last journal
Barbellion, W N P
Disappointed man series (2)
Last judge
Jenkins, Gwyn
Samuel and David series (1)
Last judgement
Clarke, Anna
Professor Paula Glenning series (1)
Last knight of Albion
Hanratty, Peter
Arthur series (1)
Last known address
Harrington, Joseph
Lieutenant Frank Kerrigan series (1)
Last lady
Janson, Hank
Hank Janson series (182)
Last laugh
Dixon, Franklin W
Hardy boys case files series (42)
Graham, Winifred
Miss Woolfe series (2)
Riggs, John Raymond
Garth Ryland series (1)
Last laugh for the Baron
Morton, Anthony
Baron series (42)
Last laugh, Mister Moto
Marquand, John Phillips
Mister Moto series (5)
Last leap
Enefer, Douglas
Sam Bawtrey series (12)
Last leaves from Dunk Island
Banfield, Edmund James
Beachcomber series (4)
Last legend of Smokeover
Jacks, Lawrence Pearsall
Smokeover series (3)
Last legends of earth
Attanasio, A A
Radix Tetrad series (4)
Last letter home
Moberg, Vilhelm
Emigrants series (3)
Emigrants series (3)
Last letters to a friend, 1952-1958
Macaulay, Rose
Letters to a friend series (2)
Last licks
Conway, Troy
Coxeman series (7)
Last lift from Crete
Fullerton, Alexander
Nick Everard series (5)
Last man at Arlington
Di Mona, Joseph
George Williams series (1)
Last man club
Queen, Ellery
Ellery Queen series (17)
Last mandarin
Becker, Stephen
Far East trilogy (2)
Last men in London
Stapledon, Olaf
Last men series (2)
Last migration
Frison-Roche, Roger
Simon Sokki series (2)
Last minute clue
Kelly, Vince
Detective Inspector Price series (1)
Last mission
Whiting, Charles
T-Force series (4)
Last monsoon
Moxon, Oliver
Monsoon trilogy (2)
Last mophrey
Layberry, Layton George Joseph
Oakleigh Farm series (5)
Last Mountain Man
Johnstone, William Wallace
Mountain Man series (1)
Last move in the game
Carter, Nicholas
Nicholas Carter series (340)
Last notes from home
Exley, Frederick
Frederick Exley trilogy (3)
Last of Cheri
Colette, Sidonie Gabrielle
Cheri series (2)
Last of Mister Moto
Marquand, John Phillips
Mister Moto series (6)
Last of Mister Norris
Isherwood, Christopher
Berlin series (3)

Last of Sherlock Holmes
Kelly, Tim J
Sherlock Holmes drama series (7)
Last of spring
Croft-Cooke, Rupert
Sensual life series (6)
Last of the Armageddon wars
Dennis, Ralph
Jim Hardman series (11)
Last of the Biffins
Graham, Harry
Reginald Drake Biffin series (5)
Last of the Cybernauts
Cave, Peter
New Avengers series (5)
Last of the dinosaurs
Lerangis, Peter
Time machine series (22)
Last of the Duanes
Grey, Zane
Buck Duane series (9)
Last of the Lorimers
Melville, Anne
Lorimer family series (5)
Last of the Lovells
Morrison, Emmeline
Lovells trilogy (1)
Last of the Mohicans
Cooper, James Fenimore
Leatherstocking series (2)
Last of the Peterkins
Hale, Lucretia Peabody
Peterkin series (2)
Last of the provincials
Geismar, Maxwell
American novel series (2)
Last of the Stranges
Watson, Edmund Henry Lacon
Strange family trilogy (3)
Last of the Stuarts
Plaidy, Jean
Stuart series (7)
William and Mary trilogy (3)
Last of the summer wine cartoon book
Clarke, Roy
Summer wine series (2)
Last of the Untouchables
Fraley, Oscar
Untouchables series (3)
Last of the Valois
Williamson, Hugh Ross
Catherine de Valois trilogy (2)
Last of the Vikings
Treece, Henry
Harald Hardrada series (1)
Last of the Wild Bunch
Fulman, Al
Harry Long series (1)
Last of the Zinja
Shea, Robert
Shike series (2)
Last of Toad
Locklin, Gerald
Toad series (4)
Last one home
Ehle, John
North Carolina series (5)
Last pack of dingoes
Wongar, B
Dingo series (2)
Last paradise
Cole, Tom
Hunting series (2)
Last picture show
McMurtry, Larry
Thalia series (1)
Last plane from Nice
Watson, Clarissa
Persis Willum series (4)
Last planet
Norton, Andre
Central Control series (2)
Last Plantagenets
Costain, Thomas Bertram
History of the Plantagenets tetralogy (4)
Last post
Ford, Ford Madox
Parade's end series (4)
Mays, Spike
Soldering series (4)
Last post for a partisan
Egleton, Clive
David Garnett trilogy (2)
Last quarter hour
Bruce, Jean
Secret Agent O.S.S.117 series (5)
Last raid
Dunn, Byron Archibald
Young Missourians series (5)
Last rainbow
Godwin, Parke
Arthurian cycle trilogy (3)

Last ranger
Grey, Zane
Zane family series (1)
Sargent, Craig
Last ranger series (1)
Last recall
Ingrid, Charles
Marked man series (2)
Last reckoning
Shupp, Mike
Destiny makers series (5)
Last redoubt
Goodchild, George
Inspector McLean series (38)
Last resort
Johnston, William
Munsters series (3)
Keene, Carolyn
Nancy Drew and Hardy boys supermystery series (5)
Last respects
Aird, Catherine
Inspector C D Sloan series (10)
Weidman, Jerome
Benny Kramer series (2)
Last reunion
Andrews, Val
Sherlock Holmes sequels series (62)
Last ride
Wales, Mike
Leatherhand series (7)
Last ride of Sheriff of Medicine Creek
Benedict, Rex
Pecos Gang series (2)
Last rights
Douglas, Arthur
Jonathan Craythorne series (2)
Last rites for the vulture
Quinn, Simon
Inquisitor series (6)
Last roar of the Lion
Farely, Alison
Plantagenet series (5)
Last rose of summer
Gallagher, Stephen
Paradise series (1)
Last Samurai
Carter, Nick
Nick Carter series (156)
Last scourge
Martyn, Wyndham
Anthony Trent series (26)
Last secret
Chambers, Dana
Jim Steele series (6)
Last seen alive
Simpson, Dorothy
Inspector Luke Thanet series (5)
Last seen breathing
Williams, David
Mark Treasure series (18)
Last seen hitchhiking
Halliday, Brett
Michael Shayne series (69)
Last seen in London
Clarke, Anna
Professor Paula Glenning series (4)
Last seen wearing
Dexter, Colin
Inspector Morse series (2)
Last set
Ellery, Jan
Adrienne Bishop series (1)
Last Shaft
Tidyman, Ernest
John Shaft series (7)
Last Sherlock Holmes story
Dibdin, Michael
Sherlock Holmes sequels series (29)
Last shot
Thayer, Lee
Peter Clancy series (12)
Last Sinhala lions
De Silva, Colin
Sinhala series (4)
Last smile
Albert, Marvin Hubert
Pierre-Ange Sawyer series (5)
Last stage to Delarno
Grover, Marshall
Larry and Stretch series (202)
Last stage to Eternity
Hill, Morgan
Dan Colt series (9)
Last stand
Macdonnell, James Edmond
Dutchy Holland series (24)
Last stand at Goodbye Gulch
Benedict, Rex
Pecos Gang series (3)

Last stand at Indigo Flats
Grey, Romer Zane
Laramie Nelson series (2)
Last stand of the DNA cowboys
Farren, Mick
Jeb Stuart Ho series (4)
Last straw
Disney, Doris Miles
Jim O'Neill series (5)
Pullen, Alan
Sam and Lin series (8)
Shriber, Ione Sandberg
Lieutenant Bill Grady series (8)
Last stronghold
Pattinson, James
Harvey Landon series (3)
Last summer
Hunter, Evan
David, Peter and Sandy series (1)
Last supper
McCarry, Charles
Paul Christopher series (4)
Last suspect
Rhode, John
Doctor Lancelot Priestley series (51)
Last sword of power
Gemmell, David A
Sipstrassi tales series (3)
Last tales of Uncle Remus
Lester, Julius
Tales of Uncle Remus series (4)
Last tango of Dolores Delgado
Day, Marele
Claudia Valentine series (3)
Last temple
Murphy, Warren Burton
Destroyer series (27)
Last Tenko
Hardwick, Michael
Tenko series (2)
Last term at Malory Towers
Blyton, Enid
Malory Towers series (6)
Last term for Helen
Biggs, Margaret
Melling School series (3)
Last things
Snow, Charles Percy
Strangers and brothers series (11)
Last tiger
Ballinger, W A
Sexton Blake series (1558)
Last time I saw Harris
Remkiewicz, Frank
Harris series (1)
Last time I saw hell
Quinn, Simon
Inquisitor series (4)
Last time I saw Mary
Corbin, Gary
Harry Reilly series (1)
Last time I saw Paris
Paul, Elliot
Narrow street series (1)
Last trail
Grey, Zane
Zane family series (3)
Last train north
Taulbert, Clifton Lemoure
Once upon a time series (2)
Last train to Bannock
Conroy, Al
Clayburn series (2)
Last train to Limbo
Chance, John Newton
Jonathan Blake series (25)
Last train to Rock Ferry
Enefer, Douglas
Sam Bawtrey series (9)
Last trap
Gluck, Sinclair
Paul Bernard series (1)
Last trump
Thayer, Lee
Peter Clancy series (23)
Last trumpet
Downing, Todd
Hugh Rennert series (5)
Last valley
Guthrie, Alfred Bertram
Settlement of the American West series (6)
Last vampire
Hall, Willis
Henry Hollins series (2)
Last vanity
Howard, Hartley
Glenn Bowman series (3)
Last victory
Murari, Timeri
Kim series (3)

Last Viking
Treece, Henry
Harald Hardrada series (1)
Last voyage
Davison, Ann
Voyages series (2)
Last voyage of the ghost ship
Garcia Marquez, Gabriel
Macondo series (1)
Last walk home
Page, Emma
Inspector Kelsey series (2)
Last war
Michaels, Melisa C
Skyrider series (3)
Last war dance
Murphy, Warren Burton
Destroyer series (17)
Last war trail
Ellis, Edward Sylvester
Deerfoot the Showanoe series 4 (3)
Last warning
Verner, Gerald
Superintendent Robert Budd series (22)
Last was Lloyd
Smith, Doris Buchanan
Lloyd Albert and Ancil Witherspoon series (1)
Last will and testament
Cole, George Douglas Howard
Doctor Benjamin Tancred series (2)
Superintendent Henry Wilson series (16)
Ferrars, Elizabeth
Virginia and Felix Freer series (1)
Last will and testament of Robert Louis Stevenson
Llewellyn, Sam
Treasure Island series (5)
Last will of a wanton
Brody, Marc
Marc Brody series (34)
Last witness
Grover, Marshall
Larry and Stretch series (270)
Last wizard
Huff, Tanya
Wizard crystal series (2)
Last woman in his life
Queen, Ellery
Ellery Queen series (43)
Last year's blood
Branson, Henry Clay
John Bent series (5)
Lastingham murder
Tracy, Louis
Inspector Furneaux series (13)
Laszlo's millions
Elkon, Jon
Tom Bloch series (2)
Late and cold
Torrie, Malcolm
Timothy Herring series (2)
Late delivery
Anderson, John Richard Lane
Inspector Piet Deventer series (3)
Late final blonde
Brody, Marc
Marc Brody series (67)
Late knight
Payne, Laurence
Mark Savage series (5)
Late lady
Staynes, Jill
Superintendent Bone series (5)
Late lamented
Brown, Fredric
Ed and Am Hunter series (6)
Late, lamented lady
Blizard, Marie
Eve Macwilliams series (1)
Late, late in the evening
Mitchell, Gladys
Dame Beatrice Bradley series (50)
Late Miss Trimming
Carnac, Carol
Inspector Julian Rivers series (14)
Late Mister Sherlock Homes, and other literary studies
Hall, Trevor Henry
Sherlock Holmes literary studies series (2)
Late Mrs D
Waugh, Hillary
Chief Fred Fellows series (4)
Late night revel
Janson, Hank
Hank Janson series (109)
Late payments
Lewin, Michael Zinn
Albert Samson series (9)
Lieutenant Leroy Powder series (4)
Late phoenix
Aird, Catherine
Inspector C D Sloan series (4)
Late spring
Delderfield, Ronald Frederick
To serve them all my days series (1)
Late unlamented
Carmichael, Harry
John Piper and Quinn series (17)
Walling, Robert Alfred John
Philip Tolefree series (22)
Late Yuma Smith
Grover, Marshall
Larry and Stretch series (358)
Later adventures of Macgregor
Bell, John Joy
Wee Macgregor series (2)
Later adventures of Tom Jones
Coleman, Bob
Tom Jones series (2)
Later Churchills
Rowse, Alfred Leslie
Churchill family series (2)
Later days
Davies, William Henry
Super-tramp series (2)
Later diaries
Rorem, Ned
Musical diaries series (3)
Later fruits of the earth
Gide, Andre
Fruits of the earth series (2)
Later Herods
Perowne, Stewart
Herod family series (2)
Later life
Couperus, Louis
Book of small souls quartet (2)
Later litanies
Watson, Kathleen
Litanies series (2)
Later Pratt portraits
Fuller, Anna
Pratt portraits series (2)
Later than you think
Kaye, Mary Margaret
Death series (4)
Later the same day
Paley, Grace
Little disturbances series (3)
Lateral thinking
De Bono, Edward
Lateral thinking series (2)
Lateral thinking for management
De Bono, Edward
Lateral thinking series (3)
Latest Herman
Unger, Jim
Herman series (3)
Lathe of heaven
Le Guin, Ursula Kroeber
Hain series (1)
Latigo
Lynde, Stan
Latigo series (4)
Latimer mercy
Richardson, Robert
Augustus Maltravers series (1)
Latimer's loot
Grover, Marshall
Larry and Stretch series (267)
Latin for all occasions
Beard, Henry
Lingua Latina series (1)
Latin for even more occasions
Beard, Henry
Lingua Latina series (2)
Latitude zero
Axler, James
Deathlands series (12)
Latter days
Reid, Patrick Robert
Colditz series (2)
Latter days at Colditz
Reid, Patrick Robert
Colditz series (2)
Latter end
Wentworth, Patricia
Miss Maud Silver series (12)
Latticed echoes
Mittelholzer, Edgar
Leitmotiv series (1)
Laugh of death
Robeson, Kenneth
Doc Savage series (119)
Laugh was on Lazarus
Garforth, John
Avengers series (4)
Laughing bacchante
Yates, Dornford
Jonah Mansel series (12)
Richard Chandos series (9)
Laughing Buddha murders
Foster, Richard
Chin Kwang Kham series (1)
Laughing carpenter
Martin, Robert
Ginger Pennylove series (2)
Laughing Cavalier
Orczy, Emmuska
Dutch War of Independence series (3)
Laughing cavalier
Turpin, Allan
Geoffrey Gillard series (5)
Laughing death
Brown, Walter C
Inspector Stephen Harper series (2)
Edwards, Paul
John Eagle series (3)
Laughing diplomat
Vare, Daniele
Diplomat series (1)
Laughing dog
Lochte, Dick
Leo Bloodworth and Serendipity Dahlquist series (2)
Vivian, Francis
Inspector Gordon Knollis series (6)
Laughing dragon mystery
Kains, Josephine
Terry Spring series (6)
Laughing dragon of Oz
Baum, Frank Joslyn
Oz series (51)
Laughing fish
Jepson, Selwyn
Eve Gill series (5)
Laughing fox
Gruber, Frank
Johnny Fletcher and Sam Cragg series (2)
Laughing grave
Gunn, Victor
Chief Inspector Bill Cromwell series (24)
Laughing horse
Donovan, Jean Beradine
Bill Speed series (1)
Laughing kitten
Blyton, Enid
Mischief series (1)
Laughing man
Jacobs, Thomas Curtis Hicks
Chief Inspector Barnard series (6)
Laughing policeman
Bruton, Eric
City of London Police series (2)
Sjowall, Maj
Inspector Martin Beck series (4)
Laughing through the Orient
Bairnsfather, Bruce
Old Bill series (9)
Laughing time, and other poems
Smith, William Jay
Laughing time series (1)
Laughing time collected nonsense
Smith, William Jay
Laughing time series (2)
Laughing time nonsense poems
Smith, William Jay
Laughing time series (2)
Laughing torso
Hamnett, Nana
Laughing torso series (1)
Laughs with Little Lulu
Henderson, Marge
Little Lulu series (1)
Laughter at the door
Trease, Geoffrey
Burnt boats series (2)
Laughter in Provence
Fortescue, Winifred
Provence series (7)
Laughter in the alehouse
Kane, Henry
Inspector McGregor series (3)
Laughter in the leaves
De Lint, Charles
Cerin Songweaver series (5)
Laughter in the next room
Sitwell, Osbert
Left hand, right hand series (4)
Laughter in the second act
Sinden, Donald
Touch of laughter series (2)
Laughter of Carthage
Moorcock, Michael
Colonel Pyat series (2)
Laughter on the stairs
Nichols, Beverley
Merry Hall trilogy (2)
Laughter trap
Philips, Judson Pentecost
Peter Styles series (1)
Launcelot, my brother
Roberts, Dorothy James
Arthurian series (1)
Launch boys' adventures in northern waters
Ellis, Edward Sylvester
Launch boys series (1)
Launch boys' cruise in the Deerfoot
Ellis, Edward Sylvester
Launch boys series (2)
Launching, floating high and landing, if your pilot light doesn't go out
Paulsen, Gary
Sports on the light side series (10)
Launching of Roger Brook
Wheatley, Dennis
Roger Brook series (1)
Laura
Schurfranz, Vivian
Sunfire series (10)
Sidgwick, Ethel
Sheriff family trilogy (1)
Laura, Alice's new puppy
Dumas, Philippe
Laura series (1)
Laura and Edmund
Harrison, Sarah
Laura from Lark Rise series (2)
Laura and old lumber
Harrison, Sarah
Laura from Lark Rise series (1)
Laura and the bandits
Dumas, Philippe
Laura series (2)
Laura and the lady
Harrison, Sarah
Laura from Lark Rise series (3)
Laura and the squire
Harrison, Sarah
Laura from Lark Rise series (4)
Laura in the mountains
Eliot, Henrietta Robins
Laura series (2)
Laura Lee Hope's The Bobbsey twins
Kline, Bennett
Bobbsey twins series (1)
Laura loses her head
Dumas, Philippe
Laura series (4)
Laura on the road
Dumas, Philippe
Laura series (3)
Laura, the imperiled
Kimbrough, Katheryn
Phenwick women series (38)
Laura's holiday
Eliot, Henrietta Robins
Laura series (1)
Laura's luck
Sachs, Marilyn
Amy and Laura series (2)
Laura's summer ballet
Blake, Linda
Laura series (2)
Laure
Arsan, Emmanuelle
Emmanuelle series (4)
Laurel and Hardy murders
Kaye, Marvin
Hilary Quayle series (4)
Laurell'd captains
Preedy, George Runnell
French Revolution series (2)
Laurels are poison
Mitchell, Gladys
Dame Beatrice Bradley series (14)
Laurels for McLean
Goodchild, George
Inspector McLean series (53)
Laurels for the Dreamer
Duncan, William Murdoch
Superintendent Donald Reamer series (13)
Lauren I
Saunders, Susan
Sleepover friends series (20)
Lauren saves the day
Saunders, Susan
Sleepover friends series (37)
Laurence Welk's bunny rabbit concert
Welk, Laurence
Wunnerful series (5)
Laurence Welk's musical family album
Welk, Laurence
Wunnerful series (5)
Lauren's afterschool job
Saunders, Susan
Sleepover friends series (31)
Lauren's big mixup
Saunders, Susan
Sleepover friends series (5)
Lauren's double disaster
Saunders, Susan
Sleepover friends series (33)
Lauren's new address
Saunders, Susan
Sleepover friends series (28)
Lauren's new friend
Saunders, Susan
Sleepover friends series (24)
Lauren's sleepover exchange
Saunders, Susan
Sleepover friends series (10)
Lauren's treasure
Saunders, Susan
Sleepover friends series (8)
Lava
O'Donnell, Kevin
Journeys of McGill Feighan series (3)
Lava flow murders
Long, Max
Komako Koa series (2)
Lavalite world
Farmer, Philip Jose
World of Tiers series (5)
Lavender blossom
Dixon, Dorothy
Leather and lace series (1)
Lavender-green magic
Norton, Andre
Magic series (5)
Lavender House murder
Baker, Nikki
Virginia Kelly series (2)
Lavender laughs in the Chalet School
Brent-Dyer, Elinor Mary
Chalet School series (17)
Lavengro
Borrow, George
Gypsy series (1)
Lavinia Bat
Hoban, Russell
Ponders series (4)
Lavinia's cottage
Goodall, John Strickland
Paddy Pork series (17)
Lavondyss
Holdstock, Robert
Mythago series (2)
Law always wins
Grover, Marshall
Larry and Stretch series (261)
Law and order
Newman, Gordon F
Law and order trilogy (3)
Law and order on Halfaday Creek
Hendryx, James Beardsley
Black John series (6)
Law and order, unlimited
Macdonald, William Colt
Gregory Quist series (4)
Law and the McLaughlins
Wilson, Margaret
McLaughlin family series (2)
Law badge
Field, Peter
Powder Valley series (12)
Law breakers
Cullum, Ridgwell
Inspector Stanley Fyles series (1)
Law busters
Lomax, Bliss
Rainbow Ripley series (3)
Law comes to Cold Rain
Logan, Jake
John Slocum series (39)
Law courts mystery
Blair, Allan
Sexton Blake series (597)
Law for Tombstone
Martin, Charles Morris
Alamo Bowie series (1)
Law in Charity
Yarbro, Chelsea Quinn
Sheriff Jason Russell series (1)
Law is a lady
Roberts, Nora
Flowers series (2)
Law man of Powder Valley
Field, Peter
Powder Valley series (16)
Law o' the lariat
Strange, Oliver
Sudden series (2)
Law of Amos C
Hanson, Victor Joseph
Amos Crowle series (12)

Law of the Forty-Fives
Macdonald, William Colt
Three Mesquiteers series (1)
Law of the Four Just Men
Wallace, Edgar
Just Men series (4)
Law of the gun
Cullum, Ridgwell
Inspector Stanley Fyles series (2)
Edson, John Thomas
Floating Outfit series (31)
Whitehead, David
Judge and Dury series (3)
Law of the jungle
Masterson, Louis
Morgan Kane series (13)
Law of the knife
Dawe, Carlton
Leathermouth series (6)
Law of the lash
Daniels, Norman A
Wyndward series (1)
Law of the Mountain Man
Johnstone, William Wallace
Mountain Man series (6)
Law of the river
Gerard, Francis
Commissioner Sanders series (9)
Law of the rope
Sherman, Jory
Gunn series (7)
Law of the talon
Tracy, Louis
Inspector Furneaux series (11)
Law of the Three Just Men
Wallace, Edgar
Just Men series (6)
Law unto themselves
Prior, Loveday
Feilmar family series (1)
Lawdog's bite
Cody, Stetson
Cactus Clancy series (4)
Lawful pursuit
Underwood, Michael
Superintendent Simon Manton series (5)
Lawless
Jakes, John
Kent family series (7)
Strange, Oliver
Sudden series (3)
Lawless and the lotus
Pinney, Peter
Dust on my shoes series (4)
Lawless clan
Boone, James Calder
Ned Remington series (9)
Lawless guns
Lomax, Bliss
Yellowstone series (2)
Lawless justice
Edgar, Alfred
Sexton Blake series (219)
Lawless land
Edwards, Hank
Judge Clay Torn series (6)
Grey, Romer Zane
Laramie Nelson series (4)
Lawless marshal
Madison, Holt
Batwing Jones trilogy (2)
Lawless miles
Grover, Marshall
Larry and Stretch series (33)
Lawley Road, and other stories
Narayan, Rasipuram Krishnaswami
Malgudi series (17)
Lawman
Ladd, Justin
Abilene series (14)
Lawman for Slaughter Valley
Hogan, Ray
Shawn Starbuck series (11)
Lawman for the slaughter
Hogan, Ray
Shawn Starbuck series (11)
Lawman wore black
Grover, Marshall
Larry and Stretch series (399)
Lawman's justice
Boone, James Calder
Ned Remington series (4)
Lawmen
Willoughby, Lee Davis
Making of America series (40)
Lawmen of Rockabye County
Edson, John Thomas
Rockabye County series (2)
Lawrence's adventures
Trowbridge, John Townsend
Jack Hazard series (5)

Law's delay
Woods, Sara
Sir Nicholas Harding and Antony Maitland series (25)
Lawsons
Meredith, Gwen
Blue Hills series (1)
Lawton girl
Frederic, Harold
New York series (2)
Lax of Poplar
Lax, William Henry
Poplar series (1)
Lay her among the lilies
Chase, James Hadley
Vic Malloy series (2)
Lay me odds
Gray, Rod
Lady from L.U.S.T. series (2)
Lay of the land
Ledd, Paul
Shelter Morgan series (28)
Paul, F W
Man from S.T.U.D. series (9)
Lay on, Mac Duff!
Armstrong, Charlotte
MacDougal Duff series (1)
Lay out my lady
Brody, Marc
Marc Brody series (10)
Lay siege to heaven
De Wohl, Louis
Lives of the saints series (6)
Lay that pistol down
Powell, Richard
Arab and Andy Blake series (3)
Lay the ghosts
Buckley, Eunice
Castelferrante series (2)
Layers of deceit
Jeffries, Roderic Graeme
Inspector Enrique Alvarez series (9)
{laying the odds
Roberts, Nora
Flowers series (12)
Layoff
Dean, Robert George
Tony Hunter series (7)
Layout for murder
Karney, Jack
Jim Breen series (2)
Lays of Beleriand
Tolkien, John Ronald Reuel
History of Middle Earth series (3)
Layton Court mystery
Berkeley, Anthony
Roger Sheringham series (1)
Lazarus effect
Herbert, Frank
Pandora series (3)
Lazarus guns
Ledd, Paul
Shelter Morgan series (5)
Lazarus lie
Van Greenaway, Peter
Inspector Cherry and Sergeant Duff series (5)
Lazarus murder seven
Sale, Richard
Daniel Webster series (1)
Lazarus number seven
Sale, Richard
Daniel Webster series (1)
Lazarus plot
Dixon, Franklin W
Hardy boys case files series (4)
Laziest robot in Zone One
Hoban, Lillian
Robot series (2)
Lazy Lawrence murders
Downing, Todd
Peter Bounty series (3)
Lazy lions
Giff, Patricia Reilly
Kids of the Polk Street School series (7)
Lea
Deforges, Regine
Lea Delmas trilogy (2)
Prevost, Marcel
Vierges fortes series (2)
Lead and flame
Scott, Bradford
Walt Slade series (99)
Lead disk
Snell, Leroy
Northwest stories series (1)
Lead hungry lobos
Arthur, Burt
Mustang Marshal series (8)

Lead-lined coffin
McGirr, Edmund
Jim Piron series (4)
Lead-lined coffins
Hardin, J D
Raider and Doc series (36)
Lead on, McLean
Goodchild, George
Inspector McLean series (11)
Lead with your left
Lacy, Ed
Lieutenant Dave Wintino series (1)
Leaden bubble
Branson, Henry Clay
John Bent series (6)
Leader in the Chalet School
Brent-Dyer, Elinor Mary
Chalet School series (45)
Leader of the resistance
Verne, Jules
Family without a name series (1)
Leading lady
Mitchell, James
Jane Whitcomb series (3)
Leading-strings
Housman, Laurence
Palace plays series (2)
Leadtown
Roberts, J R
Gunsmith series (6)
Leadville
Mitchum, Hank
Stage coach station series (20)
Leaf storm, and other stories
Garcia Marquez, Gabriel
Macondo series (1)
Leafy and Prince Brumby
Lister, Gladys
Leafy series (2)
Leafy's seventh wave
Lister, Gladys
Leafy series (3)
League of 89
Hebden, Mark
Colonel Mostyn series (3)
League of dark men
Creasey, John
Department Z series (24)
League of death
Grant, Maxwell
Shadow series (203)
League of discontent
Beeding, Francis
Colonel Alastair Granby series (5)
League of Faceless Men
Jones, G Wayman
Black Bat series (34)
League of Frightened Men
Stout, Rex
Nero Wolfe and Archie Goodwin series (2)
League of Gentlemen
Boland, John
John George Norman Hyde series (1)
League of hawks
Caillou, Alan
Ian Quayle series (1)
League of Justice
Duncan, Francis
Peter Justice series (2)
League of light
Creasey, John
Doctor Palfrey series (12)
League of Matthias
Flynn, Brian
Anthony Bathurst series (14)
League of missing men
Walsh, James Morgan
Bromley Kay series (3)
League of nameless men
Cassells, John
Superintendent Flagg series (3)
League of Night and fog
Morrell, David
Chris Kilmoonie and Saul Grisman series (3)
League of the lawless
Grover, Marshall
Nevada Jim series (9)
League of the Purple Dagger
Plant, Jack
Rusty Mason series (2)
League of the Scarlet Pimpernel
Orczy, Emmuska
Scarlet Pimpernel series (12)
League of the Signet Ring
Du Bois, Mary Constance
Silver sword series (2)
Leah's children
Goldreich, Gloria
Leah Goldfeder series (2)

Leah's journey
Goldreich, Gloria
Leah Goldfeder series (1)
Lean mean machine
Berry, Joy
Human race club series (1)
Leaning man
Bush, Christopher
Ludovic Travers series (19)
Leap before you look
Waldron, Simon
Steve Essex series (1)
Leap of the lion
Norris, Curtis
Narnia solo games series (3)
Leap the moon
Ward, Lynda
Welles family trilogy (2)
Leapfrog
Mayne, William
Animal library series (7)
Leaping lizards
Bosco, Clyde
Nintendo adventure series (2)
Learn a little!
McGloin, Joseph Thaddeus
Love and life series (1)
Learn animal shapes with Noddy
Blyton, Enid
Learn with Noddy series (3)
Learn opposites with the Munch Bunch
Reed, Giles
Learn with the Munch Bunch series (4)
Learn the Alphabet with the Munch Bunch
Reed, Giles
Learn with the Munch Bunch series (1)
Learn the days of the week with the Munch Bunch
Reed, Giles
Learn with the Munch Bunch series (3)
Learn to count with Noddy
Blyton, Enid
Learn with Noddy series (1)
Learn to count with the Munch Bunch
Reed, Giles
Learn with the Munch Bunch series (2)
Learn to go shopping with Noddy
Blyton, Enid
Learn with Noddy series (2)
Learn to read about animals with Noddy
Blyton, Enid
Learn with Noddy series (3)
Learn to tell the time with Noddy
Blyton, Enid
Learn with Noddy series (4)
Learn to tell time with the Munch Bunch
Reed, Giles
Learn with the Munch Bunch series (5)
Learned city
Toynbee, Philip
Valediction of Pantaloon series (3)
Learning to cruise
Calahan, Harold Augustin
Sailing series (3)
Learning to race
Calahan, Harold Augustin
Sailing series (2)
Learning to sail
Calahan, Harold Augustin
Sailing series (1)
Lear's daughters
Kellogg, Marjorie Bradley
Lear's daughters series (2)
Lease of Convict 308
Alais, Ernest W
Sexton Blake series (5)
Least of all saints
Irwin, Grace
Andrew Connington series (1)
Least one
Deal, Borden
Olden times series (1)
Leather Ad-M
Townsend, Larry
Sado-masochism series (1)
Leather Ad-S
Townsend, Larry
Sado-masochism series (2)
Leather duke
Gruber, Frank
Johnny Fletcher and Sam Cragg series (12)
Leatherface
Orczy, Emmuska
Dutch War of Independence series (1)

Leatherface Lonergan stakes a claim
Renwick, Peter
Leatherface Lonergan series (1)
Leatherhand
Wales, Mike
Leatherhand series (1)
Leathermouth
Dawe, Carlton
Leathermouth series (1)
Leathermouth's luck
Dawe, Carlton
Leathermouth series (7)
Leathers after big game
Chrystie, Edward M
Leathers Auckland series (3)
Leathers again
Chrystie, Edward M
Leathers Auckland series (2)
Leathers in Mozambique
Chrystie, Edward M
Leathers Auckland series (4)
Leathers in the wild coast
Chrystie, Edward M
Leathers Auckland series (5)
Leathers steps in
Chrystie, Edward M
Leathers Auckland series (1)
Leatherstocking saga
Cooper, James Fenimore
Leatherstocking series (5)
Leatherwood
Sutton, Stack
Marshal Creed Wetherall series (2)
Leave a message for Willie
Muller, Marcia
Sharon McCone series (4)
Leave eveything to me
Jerome, Owen Fox
Philip Maccray series (5)
Leave it Lisa
Burr, Sybil
Lisa Longland series (2)
Leave it to Augie
Roos, Stephen
Maple Street kids series (2)
Leave it to Beany
Weber, Lenora Mattingly
Beany Malone series (3)
Leave it to Conquest
Gray, Berkeley
Norman Conquest series (5)
Leave it to Florence
Hope, Jane
Florence series (2)
Leave it to Jennings
Buckeridge, Anthony
Jennings series (13)
Leave it to Madge
Saunders, Marjorie
Madge series (2)
Leave it to Psmith
Wodehouse, Pelham Grenville
Blandings Castle series (2)
Psmith series (4)
Leave it to the Fripseys
Chastain, Madye Lee
Fripsey series (4)
Leave it to the hangman
Knox, Bill
Inspector Colin Thane and Phil Moss series (3)
Leave it to the Toff
Creasey, John
Toff series (46)
Leave the salt earth
Hatch, Richard Warren
Bradfords series (2)
Leaven of malice
Curzon, Clare
Superintendent Mike Yeadings and Sergeant Angus Mott series (1)
Davies, Robertson
Salterton trilogy (2)
Leavenworth case
Green, Anna Katharine
Ebenezer Gryce series (1)
Leaves of time
Barrett, Neal
Time series (2)
Leavetaking
Weiss, Peter
Exile series (1)
Leaving Cheyenne
McMurtry, Larry
Thalia series (2)
Leaving Cold Sassy Tree
Burns, Olive Ann
Tweedy family series (2)
Leaving home
Keillor, Garrison
Lake Wobegon series (2)

Pascal, Francine
Sweet Valley High series (38)
Leaving Kansas
Roderus, Frank
Harrison Wilke series (1)
Leaving point
Vander Els, Betty
Ruth series (2)
Leaving the snow country
Noonan, Diana
Country and city series (1)
Lebanon adventure
Bayley, Viola
Adventure series (2)
Le Buns twenty four hour race
English, David
Bunburys series (8)
Led astray
Saint Claire, Erin
Jennifer and Cage series (1)
Led by love
Garvice, Charles
Staunch series (2)
Ledge between the streams
Mehta, Ved
Mehta family series (4)
Ledger
Uhnak, Dorothy
Christie Opara series (3)
Ledger is kept
Postgate, Raymond
Inspector Holly series (2)
Lee
Perdue, Tito
Leland and Judy Pefley series (2)
Lee Sloan, missionary pilot
Palmer, Bernard
Career series (12)
Lee Williams's quest
Gage, Joy Pennock
Seventh child series (2)
Leechtime
Davis, Albert Belisle
Mondebon trilogy (1)
Leeds fiasco
Ross, Angus
Mark Farrow series (7)
Leering house
Symons, Beryl
Inspector Henry Doight series (2)
Left at the altar
Pascal, Francine
Sweet Valley High series (108)
Left back
Pascal, Francine
Sweet Valley kids series (32)
Left behind
Pascal, Francine
Sweet Valley twins series (21)
Sorenson, Jane
Katie Hooper series (8)
Left foot forward
Mather, Bertrand
Robinson family series (2)
Left hand left
Massey, Morrell
Thornton Zane series (1)
Left-Hand Luke
Grover, Marshall
Larry and Stretch series (175)
Left hand of darkness
Le Guin, Ursula Kroeber
Hain series (7)
Left hand, right hand
Sitwell, Osbert
Left hand, right hand series (1)
Left-handed humming bird
Orman, Kate
Doctor Who series (161)
Left-handed shortstop
Giff, Patricia Reilly
Casey Valentine series (3)
Left leg
Tilton, Alice
Leonidas Witherall series (4)
Left on Labrador
Stephens, Charles Asbury
Camping out series (2)
Left-out Elizabeth
Pascal, Francine
Sweet Valley kids series (25)
Left till called for
Treadgold, Mary
Mick and Caroline Templeton series (1)
Lefty cuts loose
Shannon, Brad
Lefty O'Connor series (2)
Lefty hands it out
Shannon, Brad
Lefty O'Connor series (4)
Lefty Leighton
Fitzhugh, Percy Keese
Buddy series (5)
Lefty O'Connor moves in
Shannon, Brad
Lefty O'Connor series (1)
Lefty takes over
Shannon, Brad
Lefty O'Connor series (5)
Leg
Elsschot, Willem
Laarmans series (2)
Leg up for Lucinda
Grossman, Nancy Livright
Dutch Mill Stable series (3)
Legacy
Fast, Howard
Lavette family series (4)
Friedman, Michael Jan
Star trek series (56)
Lynde, Stan
Pardners series (2)
Mackenzie, Lee
Emmerdale Farm series (1)
Preston, Fayrene
Swansea Place series (1)
Russell, Gary
Timewyrm series (9)
Schmitz, James Henry
Hub series (1)
Telzey Amberdon and Trigger Argee series (1)
Vinge, Joan Dennison
Heaven chronicles series (2)
Legacy from Tenerife
Macleod, Robert
Jonathan Gaunt series (8)
Legacy in blood
Allingham, Margery
Albert Campion series (7)
Legacy lenders
Masur, Harold Q
Scott Jordan series (11)
Legacy of Beulah Land
Coleman, Lonnie
Beulah Land trilogy (3)
Legacy of danger
McGerr, Patricia
Selena Mead series (2)
Legacy of death
Burton, Miles
Inspector Arnold and Desmond Merrion series (60)
Grant, Maxwell
Shadow series (228)
Penn, John
Inspector George Thorne and Sergeant Bill Abbot series (13)
Walling, Robert Alfred John
Philip Tolefree series (6)
Legacy of doom
Murray, Edgar Joyce
Sexton Blake series (391)
Legacy of earth
Coulson, Juanita
Children of the stars series (3)
Legacy of evil
Hunter, Neil
Brand series (7)
Legacy of fear
Skene, Anthony
Sexton Blake series (669)
Legacy of hate
Carter, Nicholas
Nicholas Carter series (247)
Hardinge, Rex
Sexton Blake series (1237)
Legacy of Heorot
Barnes, Steven
Heorot series (1)
Niven, Larry
Heorot series (1)
Legacy of love
Harvey, Caroline
Legacy of love trilogy (3)
Legacy of Lucian Van Zandt
Chambers, Kate
Diana Winthrop series (5)
Legacy of magic
Kooiker, Leonie
Chris series (2)
Legacy of shame
Bobin, John William
Sexton Blake series (28)
Legacy of terror
Bethancourt, Tomas Ernesto
Doris Fein series (9)
Cameron, Kate
Whispering Hills series (4)
Legacy of the sword
Roberson, Jennifer
Chronicles of the Cheysuli series (3)
Legacy of vengeance
Bobin, John William
Sexton Blake series (279)
Legacy of Windhaven
De Jourlet, Marie
Windhaven series (3)
Legend
Ahern, Jerry
Survivalist series (27)
Gemmell, David A
Drenai series (1)
Legend days
Highwater, Jamake
Ghost horse quartet (1)
Legend in autumn
Woolley, Persia
Guinevere trilogy (3)
Legend-maker
Roberts, J R
Gunsmith series (55)
Legend of Amos
Hanson, Victor Joseph
Amos Crowle series (15)
Legend of Bell Canyon
Grover, Marshall
Larry and Stretch series (92)
Legend of Chilili
Slaughter, Jim
Boone Helm series (9)
Legend of Coyote Ford
Grover, Marshall
Larry and Stretch series (378)
Legend of fire
Roddy, Lee
Ladd family series (2)
Legend of Hiawatha
Gaskin, Carol
Time traveler series (2)
Legend of Holderly Hall
Cameron, Kate
Holderly Hall series (1)
Legend of Huma
Knaak, Richard Allen
DragonLance heroes series (1)
Legend of Joseph Nokato
Bachmann, Lawrence Paul
Ben Clancy series (1)
Legend of Miner's Creek
Keene, Carolyn
Nancy Drew series (107)
Legend of Montrose
Scott, Walter
Tales of my landlord series (3)
Legend of Shadd's torment
Williamson, Philip G
Firstworld chronicles series (2)
Legend of the Corrib king
McCaughren, Tom
Irish history series (3)
Legend of the golden key
McCaughren, Tom
Irish history series (1)
Legend of the Lone Ranger
McCarthy, Gary
Lone Ranger series (22)
Legend of the phantom highwayman
McCaughren, Tom
Irish history series (2)
Legend of the shadow warriors
Hand, Stephen
Fighting fantasy gamebook series (41)
Legend of the slain soldiers
Muller, Marcia
Elena Olivirez series (2)
Legend of Weathertop
Kubasch, Heike
Middle Earth quest series (2)
Legend of Willow Wood Springs
Ellis, Terry
Willow Wood Springs trilogy (1)
Legendary castles of the Broder
Alexander, Marc
Legendary castles of Britain series (2)
Legendary castles of the south
Alexander, Marc
Legendary castles of Britain series (1)
Legends from the end of time
Moorcock, Michael
Dancers at the end of time series (4)
Jherek Carnelian and Amelia Underwood series (4)
Legends of Angria
Bronte, Charlotte
Angria series (2)
Legends of Smokeover
Jacks, Lawrence Pearsall
Smokeover series (1)
Legion
Blatty, William Peter
Lieutenant Bill Kinderman series (2)
Grant, Charles Lewis
Parric family trilogy (3)
Legion from the shadows
Wagner, Karl Edward
Bran Mak Morn trilogy (2)
Legion of beasts
Barrett, Neal
Aldair series (4)
Legion of Space
Williamson, Jack
Legion of Space series (1)
Legion of the dead
Caine, Geoffrey
Abraham Stroud series (3)
Legion of the living dead
House, Brant
Secret Agent X series (9)
Legion of the Lost
Creasey, John
Doctor Palfrey series (3)
Legion of time
Williamson, Jack
Legion of time series (1)
Legion of time series (2)
Legion of Videssos
Turtledove, Harry
Videssos series (3)
Legion of war
Keith, Andrew
Combat Command series (5)
Legion of War
Keith, Andrew
Legion of Space series (4)
Legionnaire
Rice, Peter
Renegade legion series (4)
Sadler, Barry
Casca series (11)
Legions of Antares
Prescot, Dray
Dray Prescot series (25)
Legions of hell
Cherryh, Carolyn Janice
Heroes in hell series (8)
Legions of leave
Birt, David
Roman Britain series (8)
Legions of starvation
Steele, Curtis
James Christopher series (7)
Legions of the Death Master
Steele, Curtis
James Christopher series (12)
Legions of the eagle
Treece, Henry
Roman Britain series (1)
Legislative body
Hensley, Joe Louis
Donald Robak series (2)
Lego brick
Henderson, Kathy
Where does it come from series (4)
Legs
Kennedy, William
Albany series (2)
Leila
Donleavy, James Patrick
Darcy Dancer series (2)
Fogazzaro, Antonio
Maironi family trilogy (3)
Tytler, Ann Fraser
Leila trilogy (1)
Leila at home
Tytler, Ann Fraser
Leila trilogy (3)
Leila in England
Tytler, Ann Fraser
Leila trilogy (2)
Leipzig affair
White, James Dillon
Sebastian Kettle series (1)
Leipzig vampire
Anderson, Mary
Mostly ghosts series (2)
Leisure dying
O'Donnell, Lillian
Detective Norah Mulcahaney series (5)
Le Mans 24 hours
Gibson, Michael
Motor rally series (2)
Lemmings on the edge
Oram, Neil
Warp series (2)
Lemon and a star
Spykman, Elizabeth Choate
Cares family series (1)
Lemon Kelly
Hildick, Edmund Wallace
Lemon Kelly series (1)
Lemon Kelly and the home-made boy
Hildick, Edmund Wallace
Lemon Kelly series (3)
Lemon Kelly digs deep
Hildick, Edmund Wallace
Lemon Kelly series (2)
Lemonade trick
Corbett, Scott
Kerby Maxwell series (1)
Lemons never lie
Stark, Richard
Alan Grofield series (6)
Lena hates men
Neville, Margot
Inspector Grogan and Sergeant Manning series (1)
Lena Wingo, the Mohawk
Ellis, Edward Sylvester
River and wilderness trilogy (3)
Lend a hand
Blazer, J S
Donald Bracken and James Rowland Woodward series (2)
Lend-a-hand boys sanitary squad
Rathborne, Saint George
Lend-a-hand boys series (2)
Lend-a-hand boys team-work
Rathborne, Saint George
Lend-a-hand boys series (1)
Lend-a-hand boys wild game
Rathborne, Saint George
Lend-a-hand boys series (3)
Lend me your ears
Stein, Aaron Marc
Matt Erridge series (12)
Lengthening shadow
Green, Roger James
Samuel Walton series (2)
Lenin in Zurich
Solzhenitsyn, Alexander
Russian Revolution series (2)
Lenny and Jake adventures
Townson, Hazel
Lenny and Jake series (9)
Lens of the world
Macavoy, Roberta Ann
Lens of the world trilogy (1)
Lensman from Rigel
Kyle, David Ackerman
Lensman series (10)
Lent is for children
Kelemen, Julie
For children series (1)
Leo and Emily
Brandenberg, Franz
Leo and Emily series (1)
Leo and Emily and the dragon
Brandenberg, Franz
Leo and Emily series (3)
Leo and Emily's big ideas
Brandenberg, Franz
Leo and Emily series (2)
Leo and Emily's zoo
Brandenberg, Franz
Leo and Emily series (3)
Leo conversion
Smith, David
Jim Stevens series (1)
Leo the circus boy
Bonehill, Ralph
Bound to win series (12)
Leo the late bloomer bakes a cake
Kraus, Robert
Leo the late bloomer series (1)
Leo the late bloomer takes a bath
Kraus, Robert
Leo the late bloomer series (2)
Leo the Lop
Cosgrove, Stephen Edward
Leo the Lop series (1)
Leo the Lop, tail three
Cosgrove, Stephen Edward
Leo the Lop series (3)
Leo the Lop, tail two
Cosgrove, Stephen Edward
Leo the Lop series (2)
Leo, Zack and Emmie
Ehrlich, Amy
Leo, Zack and Emmie series (1)
Leo, Zack and Emmie together again
Ehrlich, Amy
Leo, Zack and Emmie series (2)
Leofwine the monk
Leslie, Emma
Leofwine series (3)
Leofwine the Saxon
Leslie, Emma
Leofwine series (1)

Leon Roch
Perez Galdos, Benito
Contemporary novels of Spain series (7)
Leona and Ike
Havill, Juanita
Leona series (2)
Leonard discovers Africa
Darby, Joan
Time machine series (8)
Leonard discovers America
Darby, Joan
Time machine series (1)
Leonard equals Einstein
Darby, Joan
Time machine series (7)
Leonard goes to the Olympics
Darby, Joan
Time machine series (6)
Leonard visits dinosaur land
Darby, Joan
Time machine series (2)
Leonard visits Sitting Bull
Darby, Joan
Time machine series (5)
Leonard visits space
Darby, Joan
Time machine series (3)
Leonard visits the ocean floor
Darby, Joan
Time machine series (4)
Leonardo and others
Sellers, Michael
Calouste Fisher series (1)
Leone-Leona
Dumas, Alexandre
Valois series (3)
Leonora
Bennett, Arnold
Five towns series (3)
Leopard
La Plante, Richard
Josef Tanaka series (2)
Leopard and the noisy monkeys
Maestro, Giulio
Leopard series (2)
Leopard cat's cradle
Barry, Jerome
Chick Varney series (2)
Leopard died too
Brent, Nigel
Barney Hyde series (6)
Leopard from Anjou
Farely, Alison
Plantagenet series (1)
Leopard in the bush
Stockley, Cynthia
Dalla series (2)
Leopard is sick
Maestro, Giulio
Leopard series (1)
Leopard man
Armour, R Coutts
Sexton Blake series (157)
Leopard of Poitain
Capella, Raul Garcia
Conan series (69)
Leopard Woman
White, Stewart Edward
Simba series (1)
Leopards on the Loire
Willson, Robina Beckles
Sarah and Alastair series (1)
Leopard's prey
Wibberley, Leonard
Treegate family trilogy (4)
Leopard's spots
Dixon, Thomas
American Reconstruction series (1)
Leopold Bloom
Costello, Peter
Stephen Dedalus series (3)
Leper of Saint Giles
Peters, Ellis
Brother Cadfael series (5)
Lepers
Montherlant, Henry de
Girls series (4)
Leprechaun murders
Reynolds, Adrian
Professor Dennis Barrie series (2)
Lerios Mecca
Lancour, Gene
Dirshan series (1)
Leroni of Darkover
Bradley, Marion Zimmer
Darkover anthologies series (8)
Lerouge case
Gaboriau, Emile
Monsieur Lecoq series (1)
Leroy is missing
Singer, Marilyn
Sam and Dave series (1)
Les Girls
Tomkinson, Constance
Les Girls series (1)
Les miserables
Hugo, Victor Marie
Fate trilogy (1)
Les Norton in between the Devlin and the deep blue sea
Barrett, Robert G
Les Norton series (5)
Lesley's great adventure
Beardmore, George
Lesley Allan series (1)
Less fortunate than fair
Wilson, Sandra
Lady Cicely Plantagenet trilogy (1)
Less of a stranger
Roberts, Nora
Flowers series (36)
Less than a treason
Griffin, Peter
Ernest Hemingway series (2)
Lesser Antilles case
King, Rufus
Lieutenant Valcour series (7)
Lesser evil
Chambers, Robert
Hank Moody series (2)
Lessinger comes back
Essex, Richard
John Slade series (3)
Lessinger series (3)
Lessinger laughs last
Essex, Richard
Lessinger series (6)
Lesson
Macdonnell, James Edmond
Captain Peter Bentley series (14)
Commander Sainsbury series (2)
Lesson for Janie
Simpson, Dorothy
Janie Marshal series (3)
Lesson for Max
Turk, Hanne
Max the Mouse series (6)
Lesson in crime, and other stories
Cole, George Douglas Howard
Mrs Elizabeth Warrender series (2)
Superintendent Henry Wilson series (11)
Lesson in dying
Cleeves, Ann
Inspector Stephen Ramsay series (1)
Lesson in love
Colette, Sidonie Gabrielle
Claudine series (7)
Zola, Emile
Rougon Macquart series (10)
Lessons in love
Keene, Carolyn
River Heights series (6)
Lessons in murder
McNab, Claire
Inspector Carol Ashton and Sergeant Mark Bourke series (1)
Lessons learned
Roberts, Nora
Flowers series (25)
Lessons on decorative design
Jackson, Frank George
Decorative design series (1)
Lest we forget
Hocking, Joseph
Religious movements series (2)
Lester and the sea monster
Slepian, Jan
Listen-hear series (3)
Lester at the seaside
Blake, Quentin
Lester series (1)
Lester's luck
Alger, Horatio
How to rise trilogy (3)
Lester's turn
Slepian, Jan
Alfred and Lester series (2)
Lestrade and the brother of death
Trow, Meirion James
Inspector Sholto Lestrade series (12)
Lestrade and the dead man's hand
Trow, Meirion James
Inspector Sholto Lestrade series (6)
Lestrade and the deadly game
Trow, Meirion James
Inspector Sholto Lestrade series (10)
Lestrade and the gift of the prince
Trow, Meirion James
Inspector Sholto Lestrade series (9)
Lestrade and the guardian angel
Trow, Meirion James
Inspector Sholto Lestrade series (7)
Lestrade and the hallowed house
Trow, Meirion James
Inspector Sholto Lestrade series (8)
Lestrade and the leviathan
Trow, Meirion James
Inspector Sholto Lestrade series (11)
Lestrade and the magpie
Trow, Meirion James
Inspector Sholto Lestrade series (13)
Lestrade and the Ripper
Trow, Meirion James
Inspector Sholto Lestrade series (3)
Lestrade and the sawdust ring
Trow, Meirion James
Inspector Sholto Lestrade series (1)
Lestrade and the sign of nine
Trow, Meirion James
Inspector Sholto Lestrade series (2)
L'Estrange case
Bentley, John
Sir Richard Herrivell series (3)
Let Bridget be your guide
Pluis, Bridget
Psychic series (3)
Let dead enough alone
Lockridge, Frances
Inspector Merton Heimrich series (11)
Richards, Francis
Inspector Merton Heimrich series (11)
Let 'er rip, Tumbleweeds!
Ryan, Tom K
Tumbleweeds series (1)
Let him die
Clements, Eileen Helen
Alister Woodhead series (1)
Bright intervals series (1)
Let him stay dead
Jacobs, Thomas Curtis Hicks
Jim Malone series (1)
Let loose the tigers
Cox, Josephine
Her father's sins series (2)
Let me kill you sweetheart!
Carr, Kirby
Hitman series (2)
Let my people be
Reid, Desmond
Sexton Blake series (1577)
Let no man write my epitaph
Motley, Willard
Romano series (2)
Let not thy left hand
Gorell, Ronald Gorell Barnes
Inspector Gordon Ross series (1)
Let or hindrance
Clements, Eileen Helen
Alister Woodhead series (13)
Lemarchand, Elizabeth
Superintendent Tom Pollard series (6)
Let sleepign dogs lie
Erickson, John R
Hank the cowdog series (6)
Let sleeping dogs lie
Heald, Tim
Simon Bognor series (4)
Riggs, John Raymond
Garth Ryland series (2)
Let sleeping girls lie
Mayo, James
Charles Hood series (2)
Let sleeping vets lie
Herriot, James
Vet series (3)
Let the circle be unbroken
Taylor, Mildred Davis
Logan family series (3)
Let the dead bury their dead, and other stories
Kenan, Randall
Tims Creek series (2)
Let the lady die
Winter, Bevis
Steve Craig series (6)
Let the man die
Courtier, Sidney Hobson
Ambrose Mahon series (5)
Let the skeletons rattle
Davis, Frederick Clyde
Professor Cyrus Hatch series (5)
Let the spacemen beware!
Anderson, Poul
Future history series (1)
Polesotechnic League series (1)
Let the tiger die
Coles, Manning
Tommy Hambledon series (8)
Let them all starve
Barrie, Alexander
Jonathan Kane series (3)
Let them prey
Harvester, Simon
Roger Fleming series (1)
Let us prey
Hammond, Gerald
Keith Calder series (15)
Quill, Monica
Sister Mary Teresa series (2)
Let well alone
Lorac, E C R
Inspector Macdonald series (39)
Let X be the murderer
Witting, Clifford
Inspector Charlton series (7)
Inspector Peter Bradfield series (3)
Lethal assault
Garrett, Frank
Killsquad series (3)
Lethal cargo
Dixon, Franklin W
Hardy boys case files series (67)
Lethal heritage
Stackpole, Michael
Blood of Kerensky trilogy (1)
Lethal innocents
Duke, Madelaine
Modern youth trilogy (2)
Lethal playground
Franklin, Donald
Special Squad series (3)
Lethal prey
Carter, Nick
Nick Carter series (237)
Lethal secrets
Preston, John
Mission of Alex Kane series (6)
Lethal vintage
Sylvester, Martin
William Warne series (2)
Letitia, the dreamer
Kimbrough, Katheryn
Phenwick women series (35)
Letourneau's used auto parts
Chute, Carolyn
Egypt, Maine series (2)
Let's be friends again!
Wilhelm, Hans
Elfie series (2)
Let's call him Blinky Bill
Wall, Dorothy
Blinky Bill adaptations series (1)
Let's celebrate!
Roop, Peter
Make me laugh series (6)
Let's choose executioners
Woods, Sara
Sir Nicholas Harding and Antony Maitland series (11)
Let's do it
Macdonald, Amy
Let's series (1)
Let's get invisible
Stine, Robert Lawrence
Goosebumps series (6)
Let's go
Macdonald, Amy
Let's series (6)
Let's go, Ben
Bradman, Tony
Ben series (1)
Let's go, Dear Dragon
Hillert, Margaret
Dear Dragon series (5)
Let's go, feet!
Bentley, Nancy
Busy body series (1)
Let's go for broke
Lasswell, Mary
Mrs Feeley series (6)
Let's go, Froggy!
London, Jonathan
Froggy series (2)
Let's go shopping, Ned
Zinnemann-Hope, Pam
Ned series (4)
Let's go to Poplar
Lax, William Henry
Poplar series (2)
Let's hear it for the deaf man
McBain, Ed
Eighty Seventh Precinct series (27)
Let's keep religion out of this!
Hackney, Alan
Stanley Windrush series (3)
Let's kill Ames
Robeson, Kenneth
Doc Savage series (145)
Let's kill Uncle Lionel
York, Jeremy
Superintendent Folly series (4)
Let's learn about lighthouses
Greene, Carla
Let's learn about series (5)
Let's learn about the orchestra
Greene, Carla
Let's learn about series (3)
Let's make a noise
Macdonald, Amy
Let's series (2)
Let's make it go in and out
Fowler, Richard
Let's make it series (2)
Let's make it go round and round
Fowler, Richard
Let's make it series (3)
Let's make it go up and down
Fowler, Richard
Let's make it series (1)
Let's meet the chemist
Greene, Carla
Let's learn about series (2)
Let's play
Macdonald, Amy
Let's series (3)
Let's play ball, Ned
Zinnemann-Hope, Pam
Ned series (3)
Let's pretend
Bradman, Tony
Rhymes with me series (4)
Macdonald, Amy
Let's series (5)
Let's talk about being a bad sport
Berry, Joy
Let's talk about series (28)
Let's talk about being bossy
Berry, Joy
Let's talk about series (24)
Let's talk about being bullied
Berry, Joy
Let's talk about series (23)
Let's talk about being careless
Berry, Joy
Let's talk about series (26)
Let's talk about being destructive
Berry, Joy
Let's talk about series (17)
Let's talk about being forgetful
Berry, Joy
Let's talk about series (27)
Let's talk about being greedy
Berry, Joy
Let's talk about series (20)
Let's talk about being lazy
Berry, Joy
Let's talk about series (2)
Let's talk about being mean
Berry, Joy
Let's talk about series (29)
Let's talk about being messy
Berry, Joy
Let's talk about series (19)
Let's talk about being rude
Berry, Joy
Let's talk about series (12)
Let's talk about being selfish
Berry, Joy
Let's talk about series (1)
Let's talk about being wasteful
Berry, Joy
Let's talk about series (25)
Let's talk about breaking promises
Berry, Joy
Let's talk about series (4)
Let's talk about cheating
Berry, Joy
Let's talk about series (15)
Let's talk about complaining
Berry, Joy
Let's talk about series (9)
Let's talk about disobeying
Berry, Joy
Let's talk about series (5)
Let's talk about fighting
Berry, Joy
Let's talk about series (18)
Let's talk about gossiping
Berry, Joy
Let's talk about series (22)

Life at the top
Braine, John
Joe Lampton series (2)
Life at Thrush Green
Read, *Miss*
Thrush Green series (3)
Life before, and after, Monty Python
Johnson, Kim Howard
Monty Python series (8)
Life begins
Stidworthy, John
Creatures from the past series (1)
Life begins too early
De Manio, Jack
Auntie series (2)
Life between
Vickers, Roy
Inspector J Rason series (16)
Life class
James, Elizabeth
Life series (1)
Life cycle
Carmichael, Harry
John Piper and Quinn series (38)
Life for a death
Ashe, Gordon
Patrick Dawlish series (48)
Life for Kregen
Prescot, Dray
Dray Prescot series (19)
Life for me
Croft-Cooke, Rupert
Sensual life series (16)
Life for sale
Horler, Sydney
Bunny Chipstead series (1)
Life for the stars
Blish, James
Cities in flight series (2)
Life golden time
Vickers, Bette
Bridlington series (2)
Life he stole
Kyle, Sefton
Inspector J Rason series (8)
Life hunt
Brand, Kurt
Perry Rhodan series (43)
Life in a Devon village
Williamson, Henry
Devon village series (2)
Life in Anglo-Saxon England
Birt, David
Saxons and Vikings series (10)
Life in Emergency Ward 10
Falla, Roger
Emergency Ward 10 series (1)
Life in our hands
Bright, Pamela
Nursing trilogy (1)
Life in the air
Coote, Roger
Habitats series (1)
Life in the Highlands
Housman, Laurence
Palace plays series (4)
Life in the sea
Coote, Roger
Habitats series (3)
Hoff, Mary
Our endangered planet series (7)
Life in the West
Aldiss, Brian Wilson
Squire quartet (1)
Life is a cucumber
Bull, Peter
Bulls series (6)
Life is for living
Stucley, Elizabeth
Teddy boy series (2)
Life is no fairytale
Bloom, Ursula
Elegant Edwardian series (6)
Life its ownself
Jenkins, Dan
Billy Clyde Puckett series (2)
Life lines
Ireland, Jill
Life series (2)
James, Elizabeth
Life series (2)
Life of a provincial lady
Powell, Violet
Provincial lady series (5)
Life of adventure
Grant-Adamson, Lesley
Jim Rush series (1)
Life of man in Christ
McGloin, Joseph Thaddeus
With Him, through Him, to Him series (3)
Life of one's own
Brenan, Gerald
Life of one's own series (1)
Life of the ant
Maeterlinck, Maurice
Insect life series (3)
Life of the bee
Maeterlinck, Maurice
Insect life series (1)
Life of the party
Goudge, Eileen
Seniors series (17)
Life of the white ant
Maeterlinck, Maurice
Insect life series (2)
Life on land
Hoff, Mary
Our endangered planet series (6)
Life on the border
Windling, Terri
Borderland series (2)
Life on the land
Coote, Roger
Habitats series (2)
Life PROBE
McCollum, Michael
Makers series (1)
Life rarely tells
Lindsay, Jack
Life rarely tells trilogy (1)
Life rarely tells trilogy (3)
Life sentence
Bailey, Henry Christopher
Mister Reggie Fortune series (21)
Life story
Bentley, Phyllis
West Riding series (7)
Life support
Barclay, Virginia
Mid-City Hospital series (6)
Life, the universe and everything
Adams, Douglas Noel
Arthur Dent series (3)
Life through the ages
Kalman, Bobbie
In my world series (15)
Life to life
Pendleton, Don
Ashton Ford series (4)
Life underground
Coote, Roger
Habitats series (4)
Life up the creek
Baker, Denys Val
Cornish series (5)
Life wish
Ireland, Jill
Life series (1)
Life with Daktari
Hart, Susanne
African wildlife series (2)
Life with Dexter
Fennell, Willie
Dexter Dutton series (1)
Life with father
Day, Clarence
Life series (1)
Life with grandma
Tovey, Doreen
Cats series (4)
Life with Lisa
Burr, Sybil
Lisa Longland series (1)
Life with mother
Day, Clarence
Life series (3)
Life with my wife, and other disasters
Reid, Colin
Disasters series (1)
Life without theory
Stuart-Wortley, Violet
Life without theory series (1)
Lifeblood
Elrod, Patricia Nead
Vampire files series (2)
Lifeboat Earth
Schmidt, Stanley
Kyyra series (2)
Lifeline of Texas
Richmond, Roe
Lashtrow series (6)
Life's joy
Zola, Emile
Rougon Macquart series (12)
Life's little ironies
Hardy, Thomas
Novels of character and environment series (8)
Life's work
Valin, Jonathan
Harry Stoner series (6)
Liffey runs black
Macgregor, Bill
Liffey series (1)
Lift and the drop
Galwey, Geoffrey Valentine
Inspector Daddy Bourne series (2)
Lift murder
Foster, Reginald Francis
Anthony Ravenhill series (2)
Lift off to danger
Bentley, Roy
Spacers series (1)
Lift shaft crime
Jardine, Warwick
Sexton Blake series (967)
Lift up the lid
Gilbert, Anthony
Arthur Crook series (20)
Light and dark
Laird, Elizabeth
Contrasts series (3)
Simon, Seymour
Let's try it out series (2)
Light and the dark
Snow, Charles Percy
Strangers and brothers series (4)
Light beyond
Perry, Paul
Near-death series (1)
Light beyond the forest
Sutcliff, Rosemary
Arthurian knights trilogy (1)
Light fantastic
Pratchett, Terry
Discworld series (2)
Light fingered ladies
Livingston, Armstrong
Peter Creighton series (2)
Light fingers
Morrison, Emmeline
Light fingers series (1)
Light freights
Jacobs, William Wymark
Night-Watchman series (3)
Light from a lantern
Stagge, Jonathan
Doctor Hugh Westlake series (6)
Light from tomorrow
Leighton, Edward
Muvian series (2)
Light heart
Hewlett, Maurice
Sagas retold series (6)
Thane, Elswyth
Williamsburg series (4)
Light in August
Faulkner, William
Sin and salvation series (5)
Light in exile
Franklin, Cheryl Jean
Network-Consortium series (1)
Light in the forest
Richter, Conrad
Pioneer children series (1)
Light in the sky
Cole, Michael
Pigeon Street series (3)
Light in the ward
Andrews, Lucilla
Saint Martha's Hospital series (2)
Light in the west
Frazier, Arthur
Wolfshead series (3)
Light Infantry ball
Basso, Hamilton
Pompey's Head series (1)
Light me a candle
Stafford, Ann
Victorian and Edwardian London life series (1)
Light of common day
Cooper, Diana Olivia Winifred Maud
Rainbow series (2)
Light of day
Ambler, Eric
Arthur Abdel Simpson series (1)
Light of distant skies
Flexner, James Thomas
History of American painting series (2)
Light of other days
Corbett, Elizabeth
Mount Royal trilogy (2)
Light of the western stars
Grey, Zane
Western stars series (1)
Light of western stars
Grey, Zane
Western stars series (1)
Light on a dark horse
Campbell, Roy
Broken record series (2)
Light on Dumyat
Fraser, Christine Marion
Light on Dumyat series (1)
Light on Lucrezia
Plaidy, Jean
Lucrezia Borgia series (2)
Light on Quests Mountain
Kirchoff, Mary Lynn
Endless quest series (12)
Light on the sound
Sucharitkul, Somtow
Chronicles of the high inquest series (1)
Light thickens
Marsh, Ngaio
Inspector Roderick Alleyn series (32)
Light through glass
Lemarchand, Elizabeth
Superintendent Tom Pollard series (15)
Light woman
Gavin, Catherine
Light woman series (1)
Lighten our darkness
Keable, Robert
Peter Graham series (3)
Lighter days with Troddles
Andom, R
Troddles series (4)
Lightfoot the deer
Burgess, Thornton Waldo
Green forest series (1)
Lightfoot, the leaping goat
Barnum, Richard
Kneetime animal stories series (10)
Lighthearted quest
Bridge, Ann
Julia Probyn series (1)
Lighthouse
Price, Eugenia
Saint Simons trilogy (1)
Lighthouse keeper's catastrophe
Armitage, Ronda
Lighthouse keeper series (2)
Lighthouse keeper's lunch
Armitage, Ronda
Lighthouse keeper series (1)
Lighthouse keeper's rescue
Armitage, Ronda
Lighthouse keeper series (3)
Lighthouse mystery
Armour, R Coutts
Sexton Blake series (210)
Warner, Gertrude Chandler
Boxcar children series (8)
Lightless kingdom
Wylie, Jonathan
Unbalanced earth trilogy (2)
Lightly poached
Beckwith, Lillian
Hebrides series (6)
Lightnin' Calvert
Ferguson, William Blair Morton
Lightnin' Calvert series (1)
Lightning
McBain, Ed
Eighty Seventh Precinct series (37)
Lightning conductor
Williamson, Charles Norris
Motoring series (1)
Lightning conductor comes back
Williamson, Alice Muriel
Motoring series (7)
Lightning conductress
Williamson, Charles Norris
Motoring series (6)
Lightning conductress discovers America
Williamson, Charles Norris
Motoring series (6)
Lightning crime
Luigi, Belli
Inspector Saint Clair series (1)
Lightning express
Optic, Oliver
Lake Shore series (2)
Lightning in the bottle
Beamer, Charles
Legends of Eorthe series (2)
Lightning Lucy
Strong, Jeremy
Lightning Lucy series (1)
Lightning Lucy storms ahead
Strong, Jeremy
Lightning Lucy series (3)
Lightning Lucy strikes again
Strong, Jeremy
Lightning Lucy series (2)
Lightning over Giltspur
Macraois, Cormac
Giltspur trilogy (3)
Lightning over Mayfair
Monmouth, Jack
Tom Langley series (4)
Lightning strikes twice
Thayer, Lee
Peter Clancy series (27)
Lightning time
Maguire, Gregory
Daniel Rider series (1)
Lightning tree
Aiken, Joan
Petworth series (2)
Lightning's daughter
Herbert, Mary H
Dark horse series (2)
Lights across the Delaware
Taylor, David
War of Independence trilogy (1)
Lights, action, land-ho!
Delton, Judy
Pee wee scout series (18)
Lights, action, murder!
Chase, Glen
Cherry Delight series (23)
Lights, camera, attitude
Cooper, Ilene
Hollywood wars series (2)
Lights, camera, death
Fulton, Eileen
Nina McFall series (4)
Lights, camera, murder
Shepherd, John
Bill Lennox series (4)
Lights go on again
Pearson, Kit
Evacuee trilogy (3)
Lights of London
Andrews, Lucilla
Saint Martha's Hospital series (15)
Lights of Zetar
Moore, Wallace
Balzan of the cat people trilogy (3)
Lights off shore
Durell, Charles Pendexter
Blue water trilogy (3)
Lights on in the house of the dead
Berrigan, Daniel
Prison diary series (2)
Lights on the lake
Maguire, Gregory
Daniel Rider series (2)
Lights out
Arnold, Eric H
Kids talk series (1)
Stine, Robert Lawrence
Fear Street series (9)
Lights that did not fail
Annesley, Michael
Lawrence Fenton series (14)
Like a guilty thing
Cobb, Belton
Inspector Cheviot Burmann series (5)
Like a lamb to the slaughter
Block, Lawrence
Matthew Scudder series (11)
Like an evening gone
Burrows, Julie
Superintendent Bowman and Sergeant Peart series (2)
Like another Helen
Grier, Sydney Carlyon
Indian history trilogy (2)
Like as the roaring waves
Wiat, Philippa
Howard series (1)
Like birds in the wilderness
Owens, Agnes
Gentlemen of the west series (2)
Like crazy
Janson, Hank
Hank Janson series (126)
Like ice she was
Ard, William
Lou Largo series (2)
Like lethal
Janson, Hank
Hank Janson series (127)
Like love
McBain, Ed
Eighty Seventh Precinct series (16)
Like of it now happens
Musil, Robert
Man without qualities series (1)
Like of it now happens, part 2
Musil, Robert
Man without qualities series (2)
Like poison
Janson, Hank
Hank Janson series (128)

Like victors and lords
Stuart, Vivian
Captain Alexander Sheridan series (1)
Likely lads
Clement, Dick
Likely lads series (1)
Likely story
York, Carol Beach
Heart to heart series (6)
Li'l Abner dailies, 1934-1935
Capp, Al
Li'l Abner dailies series (1)
Li'l Abner dailies, 1936
Capp, Al
Li'l Abner dailies series (2)
Li'l Abner dailies, 1937
Capp, Al
Li'l Abner dailies series (3)
Li'l Abner dailies, 1938
Capp, Al
Li'l Abner dailies series (4)
Li'l Abner dailies, 1939
Capp, Al
Li'l Abner dailies series (5)
Li'l Abner dailies, 1940
Capp, Al
Li'l Abner dailies series (6)
Li'l Abner dailies, 1941
Capp, Al
Li'l Abner dailies series (7)
Li'l Abner dailies, 1942
Capp, Al
Li'l Abner dailies series (8)
Li'l Abner dailies, 1943
Capp, Al
Li'l Abner dailies series (9)
Li'l Abner dailies, 1944
Capp, Al
Li'l Abner dailies series (10)
Li'l Abner dailies, 1945
Capp, Al
Li'l Abner dailies series (11)
Li'l Abner dailies, 1946
Capp, Al
Li'l Abner dailies series (12)
Li'l Abner dailies, 1947
Capp, Al
Li'l Abner dailies series (13)
Li'l Abner dailies, 1948
Capp, Al
Li'l Abner dailies series (14)
Li'l Abner dailies, 1949
Capp, Al
Li'l Abner dailies series (15)
Li'l Abner dailies, 1950
Capp, Al
Li'l Abner dailies series (16)
Li'l Abner dailies, 1951
Capp, Al
Li'l Abner dailies series (17)
Lilac and flag
Berger, John
Into their labours trilogy (3)
Lilac and the rose
Tweedsmuir, Susan Buchan
Edwardian lady series (1)
Lilac lady
Brown, Ruth Alberta
Peace Greenfield series (2)
Lila's April fool
Pascal, Francine
Sweet Valley kids series (48)
Lila's haunted house party
Pascal, Francine
Sweet Valley kids series (23)
Lila's little sister
Pascal, Francine
Unicorn Club series (4)
Lila's music video
Pascal, Francine
Sweet Valley twins series (73)
Lila's secret
Pascal, Francine
Sweet Valley kids series (6)
Lila's story
Pascal, Francine
Sweet Valley High super star series (1)
Lilian's story
Grenville, Kate
Lilian Singer series (1)
Lilies for my lovely
Janson, Hank
Hank Janson series (9)
Lilies in her garden grew
Davis, Frederick Clyde
Schyler Cole and Luke Speare series (2)
Lilies that fester
Wilson, Ivor
Gregory Flamm series (3)
Lilimani
Diver, Maud
Sinclair series (1)
Lilith
Kellow, Kathleen
Victorian England series (1)
Lewerth, Margaret
Roundtree women series (4)
Southworth, Emma Dorothy Eliza Nevitte
Lilith series (2)
Lilith, a snake in the grass
Chalker, Jack Laurence
Four Lords of the Diamond series (1)
Lilli Barr
Bromfield, Louis
Escape series (2)
Lillibulero
Neill, Robert
Sir Harry Barnaby series (3)
Lillie of Watts, a birthday discovery
Walter, Mildred Pitts
Lillie of Watts series (1)
Lillie of Watts takes a giant step
Walter, Mildred Pitts
Lillie of Watts series (2)
Lilliesleaf
Oliphant, Margaret Oliphant Wilson
Mrs Margaret Maitland series (2)
Lilliput
Gulliver, Lemuel, junior
Lilliput series (5)
Lilliput legion
Hawke, Simon
Timewars series (9)
Lilo's diary
Elman, Richard Martin
Yagodah family trilogy (2)
Lily
Bonner, Cindy
Haywood Beatty trilogy (1)
Lily and the lion
Druon, Maurice
Accursed kings series (6)
Lily Dale
Foote, Horton
Orphans' home series (7)
Lily in her coffin
Benson, Ben
Inspector Wade Paris series (3)
Lily loses her lollipop
Webb, Diana
Lily series (2)
Lily Norris' enemy
Mathews, Joanna Hooe
Little sunbeams series (3)
Lily of the valley
Balzac, Honore de
Scenes of provincial life series (1)
Lily the lollipop lady
Webb, Diana
Lily series (1)
Lily's lesson
Mathews, Joanna Hooe
Flowerets series (4)
Lily's lollipop wand
Webb, Diana
Lily series (3)
Limanora, the island of progress
Sweven, Godfrey
Antarctic Utopia series (2)
Limb of Satan
Souvestre, Pierre
Fantomas series (8)
Limbo lover
Janson, Hank
Hank Janson series (183)
Limbo Pass
McCoy, Marshall
Nevada Jim series (34)
Limbreth Gate
Lindholm, Megan
Windsingers series (3)
Lime pit
Valin, Jonathan
Harry Stoner series (1)
Lime Street at two
Forrester, Helen
Mersey series (4)
Limehouse nights
Burke, Thomas
London series (1)
Limerick trick
Corbett, Scott
Kerby Maxwell series (4)
Limited hold-up
Carter, Nicholas
Nicholas Carter series (203)
Limited liability
Gibbons, Harry Hornaby Clifford
Sexton Blake series (377)
Limited partner
Lupica, Mike
Peter Finley series (3)
Limited vision
Lewis, Royston
Eric Ward series (3)
Limners
Fisher, Leonard Everett
Colonial Americans series (15)
Limpid lady
Kane, Martin
Martin Kane series (11)
Limping goose
Gruber, Frank
Johnny Fletcher and Sam Cragg series (13)
Limping man
Erskine, Margaret
Inspector Septimus Finch series (1)
Grierson, Francis Durham
Inspector Sims and Professor Wells series (1)
Lin McLean
Wister, Owen
Western tales series (1)
Lincoln
Vidal, Gore
Washington series (2)
Lincoln assignment
Sharpe, Jon
Canyon O'Grady series (5)
Lincoln County
Cutter, Tom
Tracker series (2)
Lincoln diddle
Steward, Barbara
Edgar Allan Poe series (2)
Lincoln stories of Honore Morrow
Morrow, Honore Willsie
Abraham Lincoln series (3)
Lincoln's Inn tragedy
Bayfield, William John
Sexton Blake series (111)
Linda
Hentz, Caroline Lee Whiting
Belle Creole series (1)
Linda and the silver greyhounds
Donald, Winifred
Linda Carroll series (3)
Linda Cambridge
Donald, Winifred
Linda Carroll series (4)
Linda Carlton, air pilot
Lavell, Edith
Linda Carlton series (1)
Linda Carlton's Hollywood flight
Lavell, Edith
Linda Carlton series (5)
Linda Carlton's ocean flight
Lavell, Edith
Linda Carlton series (3)
Linda Carlton's perilous summer
Lavell, Edith
Linda Carlton series (4)
Linda Craig and the clue on the desert trail
Sheldon, Ann
Linda Craig series (2)
Linda Craig and the ghost town treasure
Sheldon, Ann
Linda Craig series (5)
Linda Craig and the mystery in Mexico
Sheldon, Ann
Linda Craig series (6)
Linda Craig and the mystery of Horseshoe Canyon
Sheldon, Ann
Linda Craig series (4)
Linda Craig and the Palomino mystery
Sheldon, Ann
Linda Craig series (1)
Linda Craig and the secret of Rancho del Sol
Sheldon, Ann
Linda Craig series (3)
Linda goes on a cruise
Dudley, Nancy
Linda series (5)
Linda goes to a TV studio
Dudley, Nancy
Linda series (4)
Linda goes to the hospital
Dudley, Nancy
Linda series (1)
Linda in Lucerne
Donald, Winifred
Linda Carroll series (2)
Linda in New York
Donald, Winifred
Linda Carroll series (5)
Linda Lane
Lawrence, Josephine
Linda Lane series (1)
Linda Lane helps out
Lawrence, Josephine
Linda Lane series (2)
Linda Lane's big sister
Lawrence, Josephine
Linda Lane series (6)
Linda Lane's experiments
Lawrence, Josephine
Linda Lane series (4)
Linda Lane's plan
Lawrence, Josephine
Linda Lane series (3)
Linda Lane's problem
Lawrence, Josephine
Linda Lane series (5)
Linda, the schoolgirl detective
Donald, Winifred
Linda Carroll series (1)
Linda travels alone
Dudley, Nancy
Linda series (2)
Linda's first flight
Dudley, Nancy
Linda series (3)
Linden on the Saugus branch
Paul, Elliot
Narrow street series (2)
Lindsey
Jenkins, Jerry Bruce
Margo Franklin and Philip Spence series (9)
Line drive
Hughes, Dean
Angel Park All-Stars series (7)
Line of fire
Dixon, Franklin W
Hardy boys case files series (16)
Griffin, W E B
Corps series (5)
Line of love
Cabell, James Branch
Dom Manuel and his descendants series (10)
Line of succession
Murphy, Warren Burton
Destroyer series (73)
Murray, Will
Destroyer series (73)
Line Sophie drew
Barrett, Peter
Sophie, Sarah and Ben series (1)
Line-up
Reilly, Helen
Inspector Christopher McKee series (3)
Lineage of Lichfield
Cabell, James Branch
Dom Manuel and his descendants series (21)
Liners of time
Statten, Vargo
Liners of time series (1)
Linger-Nots and the mystery house
Miller, Agnes
Linger-Nots series (1)
Linger-Nots and the secret maze
Miller, Agnes
Linger-Nots series (5)
Linger-Nots and the valley feud
Miller, Agnes
Linger-Nots series (2)
Linger-Nots and the whispering charm
Miller, Agnes
Linger-Nots series (4)
Linger-Nots and their golden quest
Miller, Agnes
Linger-Nots series (3)
Lingo
Grant, Maxwell
Shadow series (75)
Link
Carmichael, Harry
John Piper and Quinn series (19)
Laurance, Andrew
Nostradamus trilogy (2)
Macdonald, Philip
Colonel Anthony Ruthven Gethryn series (3)
Link by link
Bobin, John William
Sexton Blake series (118)
Donovan, Dick
Dick Donovan series (9)
Link in the chain
Heimler, Eugene
Mist series (2)
Links in the chain
Rhode, John
Doctor Lancelot Priestley series (46)
Linnea in Monet's garden
Bjork, Christina
Linnea series (1)
Linnea's almanac
Bjork, Christina
Linnea series (3)
Linnea's windowsill garden
Bjork, Christina
Linnea series (2)
Linsey-Woolsey
Kitchen, Paddy
Vanessa Talisend series (3)
Lion adventure
Price, Willard
Hal and Roger Hunt series (9)
Lion and Albert
Edgar, Marriott
Albert and the lion series (1)
Lion and Lamb
Hooks, William H
Lion and Lamb series (1)
Lion and Lamb step out
Brenner, Barbara
Lion and Lamb series (2)
Lion and the savannah
Taylor, Dave
Animals and their ecosystems series (1)
Lion and the unicorn
Bryant, Arthur
Historian series (2)
Lion and the Wolf
Farely, Alison
Plantagenet series (4)
Lion at sea
Hennessy, Max
Kelly Maguire trilogy (1)
Lion Ben of Elm Island
Kellogg, Elijah
Elm Island series (1)
Lion by the mane
Dane, Eva
Schroeder family series (2)
Lion country
Buechner, Frederick
Leo Bebb tetralogy (1)
Lion dormant
Wensby-Scott, Carol
Percy trilogy (2)
Lion game
Schmitz, James Henry
Telzey Amberdon and Trigger Argee series (3)
Lion in Egypt
Danielson, Peter
Children of the Lion series (4)
Lion in the garden
Seton, Hilary
Minty Humble series (2)
Lion in the valley
Peters, Elizabeth
Amelia Peabody Emerson series (4)
Lion in wait
Gardiner, Dorothy
Sheriff Moss Magill series (3)
Lion invincible
Wensby-Scott, Carol
Percy trilogy (3)
Lion Jack
Barnum, Phineas Taylor
Lion Jack series (1)
Lion Men of Mongo
Steffanson, Con
Flash Gordon series (2)
Lion mountain
Dolan, Bill
Afrikorps series (5)
Lion of Alnwick
Wensby-Scott, Carol
Percy trilogy (1)
Lion of England
Butler, Margaret
Henry II series (1)
Lion of Ireland
Llywelyn, Morgan
Odyssey of the Irish trilogy (1)
Lion of justice
Butler, Margaret
Henry II series (2)
Lion of Justice
Plaidy, Jean
Norman trilogy (2)
Lion of Macedon
Gemmell, David A
Lion of Macedon series (1)
Lion of Mortimer
Dymoke, Juliet
Plantagenets series (3)
Lion of Petra
Mundy, Talbot
Jimgrim series (8)

Lion of the North
Henty, George Alfred
Thirty Years War series (1)
Lion on Tharthee
Callin, Grant
Saturnalia series (2)
Lion on the hearth
Ehle, John
North Carolina series (6)
Lion on the loose
Kruse, Max
Lion series (1)
Lion, or murder?
Gardiner, Dorothy
Sheriff Moss Magill series (3)
Lion prides and tiger tracks
Torgersen, Don Arthur
Animal safari nature series (2)
Lion-tamer
Elsschot, Willem
Ship trilogy (2)
Lion, the witch and the wardrobe
Lewis, Clive Staples
Narnia series (2)
Lion triumphant
Carr, Philippa
Daughters of England series (2)
Lion without claws
Wiat, Philippa
Howard series (3)
Lionel and Louise
Krensky, Stephen
Lionel series (4)
Lionel and the spy
Allen, Linda
Lionel series (2)
Lionel at large
Krensky, Stephen
Lionel series (1)
Lionel in the fall
Krensky, Stephen
Lionel series (2)
Lionel in the spring
Krensky, Stephen
Lionel series (3)
Lionel in winter
Krensky, Stephen
Lionel series (5)
Lionel the lone wolf
Allen, Linda
Lionel series (3)
Lionel's car
Cole, Michael
Edward and friends series (4)
Lionel's finest hour
Allen, Linda
Lionel series (1)
Lionel's party
Cole, Michael
Edward and friends series (1)
Lioness
Bell, Frank
Shen series (2)
Lioness rampant
Pierce, Tamora
Song of the lioness series (4)
Lions and shadows
Isherwood, Christopher
Christopher series (2)
Lion's fire
Barker, Wade
Year of the Ninja Master series (2)
Lion's heart
Wehrstein, Karen
Fifth millenium series (6)
Lion's legacy
Dymoke, Juliet
Henry I trilogy (3)
Lion's mouth
Raine, Kathleen
Happy fields trilogy (3)
Lions of Oakhurst
Johnson, Walter Reed
Oakhurst series (3)
Lion's paw
Padfield, Peter
Guy Grenville series (1)
Lion's progress
Orde, Lewis
Daniel Kerr series (2)
Lion's share
Fuller, Kathleen
Riverview trilogy (2)
Lion's soul
Wehrstein, Karen
Fifth millenium series (7)
Lion's way
Orde, Lewis
Daniel Kerr series (1)
Stoneham, Charles Thurley
Kaspa series (1)
Liquidator
Brent, R L
Liquidator series (1)
Carter, Nick
Nick Carter series (75)
Gardner, John Edmund
Boysie L Oakes series (1)
Liquor is quicker
Janson, Hank
Hank Janson series (221)
Lisa
Hoff, Harry Summerfield
Three marriages series (3)
Lisa Bastian
Wood, James
James Fraser series (4)
Lisa settles in
Peterson, Hans
Lisa series (2)
Lisa Vale
Prouty, Olive Higgins
Vale family series (2)
Lisa's parents fight
Sanford, Doris
In our neighborhood series (3)
Lisdalia
Caswell, Brian
Mike and Lisdalia series (2)
Liselott and the goloff
Peterson, Hans
Lisa series (1)
List
Carter, Nick
Nick Carter series (105)
List of Adrian Messenger
Macdonald, Philip
Colonel Anthony Ruthven Gethryn series (11)
Listen!
Berry, Joy
Can make and do series (8)
Listen for the click
Breen, Jon Linn
Jerry Brogan series (1)
Listen for the singing
Little, Jean
Anna series (2)
Listen lovely
Campbell, Keith
Mike Brett series (2)
Listen to me with love
Quick, Larry
Love trilogy (2)
Listen to the wild
Hart, Susanne
African wildlife series (3)
Listen to this, ears!
Bentley, Nancy
Busy body series (3)
Listener
Caldwell, Taylor
Listener series (1)
Listeners
Emerson, Sally
Second sight series (2)
Listener's lure
Lucas, Edward Verrall
Winfield series (1)
Listening eye
Wentworth, Patricia
Miss Maud Silver series (29)
Listening man
Moroso, John Antonio
James Tierney series (2)
Listening valley
Stevenson, Dorothy Emily
Ryddelton series (2)
Listening woman
Hillerman, Tony
Lieutenant Joe Leaphorn series (3)
Lists, lists, lists!
Davis, Anne
Pumpkin Hill fact series (1)
Litanies of life
Watson, Kathleen
Litanies series (1)
Little aeroplane
Lenski, Lois
Small family series (4)
Little airplane
Lenski, Lois
Small family series (4)
Little aliens
Kelly, Myra
School life trilogy (3)
Little and orphan
Hesling, Bernard
Little and orphan series (1)
Little Anna and the magic hat
Sandberg, Inger
Anna series (1)
Little Anna and the tall uncle
Sandberg, Inger
Anna series (6)
Little Anna's mother has a birthday
Sandberg, Inger
Anna series (4)
Little auto
Lenski, Lois
Small family series (2)
Little Bear
Minarik, Else Holmelund
Little Bear series (1)
Little Bear and the fairy child
Tourtel, Mary
Rupert Bear series (2)
Little Bear and the ogres
Tourtel, Mary
Rupert Bear series (4)
Little Bear and the oompah-pah
Crespi, Francesca
Little Bear series (2)
Little Bear and the Papagini circus
Greaves, Margaret
Little Bear series (1)
Little bear book
Browne, Anthony
Bear series (3)
Little Bear stories
Minarik, Else Holmelund
Little Bear series (4)
Little Bear tales
Chapman, Gillian
Little Bear series (1)
Little Bear the brave
Davies, Evelyn
Little Bear trilogy (2)
Little Bear's Christmas
Tourtel, Mary
Rupert Bear series (3)
Little Bear's colour
Chapman, Gillian
Little Bear series (6)
Little Bear's feather
Davies, Evelyn
Little Bear trilogy (1)
Little Bear's food
Chapman, Gillian
Little Bear series (4)
Little Bear's friend
Minarik, Else Holmelund
Little Bear series (3)
Little Bear's friends
Chapman, Gillian
Little Bear series (3)
Little Bear's journey
Davies, Evelyn
Little Bear trilogy (3)
Little Bear's visit
Minarik, Else Holmelund
Little Bear series (4)
Little Bear's weather
Chapman, Gillian
Little Bear series (5)
Little Billy Blue Tit
Rutley, Cecily Marianne
Tales of the wild folk series (13)
Little Bird
Bruna, Dick
Toy box tale series (4)
Little Bird Tweet
Bruna, Dick
Toy box tale series (4)
Little black princess
Gunn, Jeannie
Never-Never series (1)
Little black princess of the Never-Never
Gunn, Jeannie
Never-Never series (1)
Little Blue Engine stories
Hourihane, Ursula
Little Blue Engine series (3)
Little Blue Engine that wanted a drink
Hourihane, Ursula
Little Blue Engine series (1)
Little Bobtail
Optic, Oliver
Yacht Club series (1)
Little boy in search of God
Singer, Isaac Bashevis
Love and exile trilogy (1)
Little boy lost
Egan, Lesley
Jesse Falkenstein series (12)
Little breathing room
Graber, Richard
Ray Decker series (1)
Little Britches
Moody, Ralph
Ralph series (1)
Little brother
Cannan, Gilbert
Laurie series (1)
Little brown bear
Blyton, Enid
John and Mary series (7)
Little Brown bear can cook!
Lebrun, Claude
Little Brown Bear series (15)
Little Brown Bear gets dressed
Lebrun, Claude
Little Brown Bear series (1)
Little Brown Bear is big!
Lebrun, Claude
Little Brown Bear series (16)
Little Brown Bear is cross
Lebrun, Claude
Little Brown Bear series (8)
Little Brown Bear is ill
Lebrun, Claude
Little Brown Bear series (2)
Little Brown Bear says no
Lebrun, Claude
Little Brown Bear series (3)
Little Brown Bear takes a bath
Lebrun, Claude
Little Brown Bear series (4)
Little Brown Bear wakes up
Lebrun, Claude
Little Brown Bear series (5)
Little Brown Bear wants a kiss
Lebrun, Claude
Little Brown Bear series (6)
Little Brown Bear won't eat!
Lebrun, Claude
Little Brown Bear series (12)
Little Brown Bear's bad days
Lebrun, Claude
Little Brown Bear series (13)
Little Brown Bear's breakfast egg
Lebrun, Claude
Little Brown Bear series (14)
Little Brown Bear's cold
Lebrun, Claude
Little Brown Bear series (7)
Little Brown Bear's playtime
Lebrun, Claude
Little Brown Bear series (17)
Little Brown Bear's snowball
Lebrun, Claude
Little Brown Bear series (18)
Little Brown Bear's story
Lebrun, Claude
Little Brown Bear series (9)
Little Brown Bear's tricycle
Lebrun, Claude
Little Brown Bear series (10)
Little Brown Bear's walk
Lebrun, Claude
Little Brown Bear series (11)
Little Brown Tala
Wynne, May
Tala series (1)
Little Brown Tala stories
Wynne, May
Tala series (2)
Little Brute family
Hoban, Russell
Brute family series (1)
Little Buggaroo
Cosgrove, Stephen Edward
Bugg series (47)
Little Bun Rabbit
Baum, Lyman Frank
Snuggle tales series (1)
Little bush maid
Bruce, Mary Grant
Billabong series (1)
Little by Little
Little, Jean
Writer's education series (1)
Little by little
Optic, Oliver
Boat Club series (6)
Little Caesar
Burnett, William Riley
Chicago trilogy (1)
Little camp on Eagle Hill
Warner, Susan Bagert
Eagle Hill series (1)
Little Canary
Osgood, Mary A
Little Canary series (2)
Little Canary's black Cato
Osgood, Mary A
Little Canary series (4)
Little Canary's cousin Eugene
Osgood, Mary A
Little Canary series (3)
Little Canary's Daisy
Osgood, Mary A
Little Canary series (1)
Little captain
Bailey, Henry Christopher
Mister Joshua Clunk series (7)
Biegel, Paul
Little captain series (1)
Little captain and the pirate treasure
Biegel, Paul
Little captain series (3)
Little captain and the seven towers
Biegel, Paul
Little captain series (2)
Little car
Berg, Leila
Little car series (1)
Gay, Michael
Little vehicle series (2)
Little car has a day out
Berg, Leila
Little car series (2)
Little chick's big day
Kwitz, Mary DeBall
Little Chick series (2)
Little Chick's breakfast
Kwitz, Mary DeBall
Little Chick series (3)
Little Chick's friend Duckling
Kwitz, Mary DeBall
Little Chick series (4)
Little Chick's story
Kwitz, Mary DeBall
Little Chick series (1)
Little China
Brodrick, Alan Hough
Indo-China series (1)
Little Chip of Willow Hill
Hader, Berta
Willow Hill series (7)
Little Chuck's adventure
Burgess, Thornton Waldo
Little color classics series (2)
Little circus
Peppe, Rodney
Little toy board books series (1)
Little circus dog
Barr, Jene
Little dog series (2)
Little citizens
Kelly, Myra
School life trilogy (1)
Little class on murder
Hart, Carolyn Gimpel
Annie Laurance and Max Darling series (5)
Little cliff-dweller
Bayliss, Clara Kern
Lolami series (3)
Little cockalorum
Simkins, Wallis
Little cockalorum series (1)
Little cockalorum crows again
Simkins, Wallis
Little cockalorum series (2)
Little cockalorum finds romance
Simkins, Wallis
Little cockalorum series (4)
Little cockalorum on her own
Simkins, Wallis
Little cockalorum series (3)
Little colonel
Johnston, Annie Fellows
Little colonel series (1)
Little colonel at boarding school
Johnston, Annie Fellows
Little colonel series (7)
Little colonel in Arizona
Johnston, Annie Fellows
Little colonel series (8)
Little colonel, maid of honor
Johnston, Annie Fellows
Little colonel series (10)
Little colonel's Christmas vacation
Johnston, Annie Fellows
Little colonel series (9)
Little colonel's doll book
Johnston, Annie Fellows
Little colonel series (15)
Little colonel's good times book
Johnston, Annie Fellows
Little colonel series (14)
Little colonel's hero
Johnston, Annie Fellows
Little colonel series (6)
Little colonel's holidays
Johnston, Annie Fellows
Little colonel series (5)
Little colonel's house party
Johnston, Annie Fellows
Little colonel series (3)
Little colonel's knight comes riding
Johnston, Annie Fellows
Little colonel series (11)
Little coquette
McCormick, Renee
Coquette series (1)

Kelleam, Joseph Everidge
Jack Odin series (1)
Little men, big world
Burnett, William Riley
Chicago trilogy (3)
Little merchant
Optic, Oliver
Riverdale series (1)
Little Millers
Merriman, Effie Woodward
Millers series (1)
Little minister
Barrie, James Matthew
Thrums series (3)
Little Miss Atlas
Lambert, Janet
Tippy Parrish series (2)
Little Miss Cricket
Jackson, Gabrielle Emilie
Little Miss Cricket trilogy (1)
Little Miss Cricket at school
Jackson, Gabrielle Emilie
Little Miss Cricket trilogy (2)
Little Miss Cricket's new home
Jackson, Gabrielle Emilie
Little Miss Cricket trilogy (3)
Little Miss Faith
Le Baron, Grace
Falcons-Height trilogy (1)
Little Miss Fales
Knipe, Emilie Benson
Little Miss Fales series (1)
Little Miss Murder
Avallone, Michael
Ed Noon series (22)
Little Miss Phoebe Gay
Brown, Helen Dawes
Anna Lavinia series (1)
Little Miss Pink
Bennett, Rodney
Little Miss Pink series (1)
Little Miss Pink at Greytoes
Bennett, Rodney
Little Miss Pink series (2)
Little Miss Pink at the Great House
Bennett, Rodney
Little Miss Pink series (4)
Little Miss Pink's school
Bennett, Rodney
Little Miss Pink series (3)
Little Miss Pink's splendid summer
Bennett, Rodney
Little Miss Pink series (5)
Little Miss Pink's wedding
Bennett, Rodney
Little Miss Pink series (6)
Little Miss Rosamund
Rhoades, Nina
Miss Rosamund series (2)
Little Miss Stoneybrook, and Dawn
Martin, Ann Matthews
Baby-Sitters Club series (15)
Little Mister Bouncer and his friend, Mister Verdant Green
Bede, Cuthbert
Mister Verdant Green series (4)
Little Mister Thimblefinger and his queer country
Harris, Joel Chandler
Mister Thimblefinger series (1)
Little monkeys
Airault, Dominique
Little animal series (4)
Little Monster at home
Mayer, Mercer
Little monster series (2)
Little Monster at school
Mayer, Mercer
Little monster series (3)
Little Monster at work
Mayer, Mercer
Little monster series (4)
Little monster cook book
Salmon, Jan
Alexander Bunyip series (12)
Little Monster's alphabet book
Mayer, Mercer
Little monster series (5)
Little Monster's bedtime book
Mayer, Mercer
Little monster series (7)
Little Monster's counting book
Mayer, Mercer
Little monster series (8)
Little Monster's Mother Goose
Mayer, Mercer
Little monster series (10)
Little Monster's neighborhood
Mayer, Mercer
Little monster series (9)
Little Monster's scratch and sniff mystery
Mayer, Mercer
Little monster series (11)
Little Monster's word book
Mayer, Mercer
Little monster series (1)
Little Monster's you-can-make-it book
Mayer, Mercer
Little monster series (6)
Little moorland princess
Marlitt, E
Moorland princess series (2)
Little more than kin
Wentworth, Patricia
Waveneys series (1)
Little Mother Meg
Turner, Ethel
Woolcot family series (3)
Little mouse ABC
Holabird, Katharine
Little mouse series (1)
Little Mouse makes
Cartlidge, Michelle
Little Mouse series (4)
Little Mouse makes a garden
Cartlidge, Michelle
Little Mouse series (4)
Little Mouse makes a mobile
Cartlidge, Michelle
Little Mouse series (1)
Little Mouse makes cards
Cartlidge, Michelle
Little Mouse series (3)
Little Mouse makes sweets
Cartlidge, Michelle
Little Mouse series (2)
Little mouse one two three
Holabird, Katharine
Little mouse series (2)
Little mule
Burress, John
Singleton family series (1)
Little murder music
Ramsay, Diana
Lieutenant Meredith series (1)
Little myth maker
Asprin, Robert Lynn
Skeeve series (6)
Little neighborhood murder
Orde, A J
Jason Lynx series (1)
Little Noddy goes to Toyland
Blyton, Enid
Noddy series (1)
Little numbers
Peppe, Rodney
Little toy board books series (4)
Little O
Unnerstad, Edith
Larsson family series (4)
Little Obelia, and further adventures of Ragged Blossom, Snugglepot and
Gibbs, May
Gumnut Land series (8)
Little of what you fancy
Bates, Herbert Ernest
Larkin family series (5)
Little old bear
Van Stockum, Hilda
Jeremy Bear series (2)
Little old engine
Awdry, Wilbert
Railway series (14)
Little old Mrs Pepperpot, and other stories
Proysen, Alf
Mrs Pepperpot series (1)
Little Orphan Annie
Gray, Harold
Little Orphan Annie series (1)
Little Orphan Annie and the Gila Monster Gang
Gray, Harold
Little Orphan Annie series (10)
Little Orphan Annie and the Gooneyville mystery
Gray, Harold
Little Orphan Annie series (11)
Little Orphan Annie and the haunted house
Gray, Harold
Little Orphan Annie series (3)
Little Orphan Annie and Uncle Dan
Gray, Harold
Little Orphan Annie series (9)
Little Orphan Annie bucking the world
Gray, Harold
Little Orphan Annie series (4)
Little Orphan Annie in Cosmic City
Gray, Harold
Little Orphan Annie series (8)
Little Orphan Annie in the circus
Gray, Harold
Little Orphan Annie series (2)
Little Orphan Annie in the Great Depression
Gray, Harold
Little Orphan Annie series (12)
Little Orphan Annie, never say die
Gray, Harold
Little Orphan Annie series (5)
Little Orphan Annie shipwrecked
Gray, Harold
Little Orphan Annie series (6)
Little Orphan Annie, willing helper
Gray, Harold
Little Orphan Annie series (7)
Little Outlaw
Grey, Peter
Kit Hunter series (9)
Little Owl and the tree house
Boyle, Constance
Little Owl series (4)
Little Owl and the weed
Boyle, Constance
Little Owl series (2)
Little Owl's favourite uncle
Boyle, Constance
Little Owl series (3)
Little pandas
Airault, Dominique
Little animal series (2)
Little Panjandrum's dodo
Farrow, George Edward
Panjandrum series (1)
Little Pear
Lattimore, Eleanor Frances
Little Pear series (1)
Little Pear and his friends
Lattimore, Eleanor Frances
Little Pear series (2)
Little Pear and the rabbits
Lattimore, Eleanor Frances
Little Pear series (3)
Little Peter Cottontail
Burgess, Thornton Waldo
Peter Rabbit series (4)
Little Pete's adventure
Burgess, Thornton Waldo
Little color classics series (1)
Little Pierre
France, Anatole
Pierre Noziere series (3)
Little pilgrim in the unseen
Oliphant, Margaret Oliphant Wilson
Stories of the seen and the unseen series (2)
Little place called King's Standing
Turner, Sheila
Mary Carrick series (3)
Little place in the country
Tiltman, Marjorie Hessell
Country life trilogy (2)
Little plane
Gay, Michael
Little vehicle series (3)
Little Plum
Godden, Rumer
Nona Fell series (2)
Little Polly Prentiss
Gould, Elizabeth Lincoln
Polly Prentiss series (1)
Little prairie dog
Barr, Jene
Little dog series (1)
Little princess
Burnett, Frances Hodgson
Sara Crewe series (3)
Little princess of Tenopah
Higgins, Aileen Cleveland
Little princess series (1)
Little princess of the patio
Higgins, Aileen Cleveland
Little princess series (3)
Little princess of the Pines
Higgins, Aileen Cleveland
Little princess series (2)
Little princess of the ranch
Higgins, Aileen Cleveland
Little princess series (4)
Little princess of the Stars and Stripes
Higgins, Aileen Cleveland
Little princess series (5)
Little puppies
Airault, Dominique
Little animal series (1)
Little Puritan bound-girl
Robinson, Edith
Little Puritan series (7)
Little Puritan cavalier
Robinson, Edith
Little Puritan series (8)
Little Puritan pioneer
Robinson, Edith
Little Puritan series (5)
Little Puritan rebel
Robinson, Edith
Little Puritan series (2)
Little Puritan stories
Robinson, Edith
Little Puritan series (7)
Little Puritan's first Christmas
Robinson, Edith
Little Puritan series (4)
Little Rabbit's baby brother
Manushkin, Fran
Baby Rabbit series (1)
Little Rabbit's birthday
Wabbes, Marie
Little Rabbit series (3)
Little Rabbit's garden
Wabbes, Marie
Little Rabbit series (1)
Little raccoon and no trouble at all
Moore, Lilian
Little raccoon series (3)
Little raccoon and poems from the woods
Moore, Lilian
Little raccoon series (4)
Little raccoon and the outside world
Moore, Lilian
Little raccoon series (2)
Little raccoon and the thing in the pool
Moore, Lilian
Little raccoon series (1)
Little raccoon takes charge
Moore, Lilian
Little raccoon series (5)
Little raccoon's nighttime adventure
Moore, Lilian
Little raccoon series (6)
Little Ragged Blossom
Gibbs, May
Gumnut Land series (7)
Little red captain
Hyne, Charles John Cutcliffe
Captain Owen Kettle series (1)
Little red engine and the rocket
Ross, Diana
Little red engine series (6)
Little red engine and the Taddlecombe outing
Ross, Diana
Little red engine series (9)
Little red engine gets a name
Ross, Diana
Little red engine series (1)
Little red engine goes carolling
Ross, Diana
Little red engine series (10)
Little red engine goes home
Ross, Diana
Little red engine series (7)
Little red engine goes to be mended
Ross, Diana
Little red engine series (8)
Little red engine goes to market
Ross, Diana
Little red engine series (3)
Little red engine goes to town
Ross, Diana
Little red engine series (4)
Little red engine goes travelling
Ross, Diana
Little red engine series (5)
Little Red Fox and Cinderella
Uttley, Alison
Little Red Fox series (2)
Little Red Fox and the great big tree
Uttley, Alison
Little Red Fox series (5)
Little Red Fox and the magic moon
Uttley, Alison
Little Red Fox series (3)
Little Red Fox and the unicorn
Uttley, Alison
Little Red Fox series (4)
Little Red Fox and the wicked uncle
Uttley, Alison
Little Red Fox series (1)
Little red metro finds a home
Rowlands, Avril
Little red metro series (2)
Little red metro for sale
Rowlands, Avril
Little red metro series (1)
Little red metro gets cold feet
Rowlands, Avril
Little red metro series (4)
Little red metro gets started
Rowlands, Avril
Little red metro series (3)
Little red rooster
Matthews, Greg
Burris Weems series (1)
Little Red's adventure
Burgess, Thornton Waldo
Little color classics series (3)
Little regiment, and other episodes of the American Civil War
Crane, Stephen
American Civil War episodes series (2)
Little Rhodesian
Batchelor, Margaret
Gwenda series (1)
Little Ripper
West, Charles
Paul Crook series (2)
Little robins' friends
Leslie, Madeline
Little robins series (5)
Little robins in the nest
Leslie, Madeline
Little robins series (1)
Little robins in trouble
Leslie, Madeline
Little robins series (3)
Little robins learning to fly
Leslie, Madeline
Little robins series (2)
Little robins love one another
Leslie, Madeline
Little robins series (4)
Little round garden
Lister, Gladys
Round series (1)
Little round house
Lister, Gladys
Round series (2)
Little round stairway
Lister, Gladys
Round series (4)
Little round world
Lister, Gladys
Round series (5)
Little runaways
Curtis, Alice Turner
Little runaways series (1)
Little runaways and mother
Curtis, Alice Turner
Little runaways series (3)
Little runaways at home
Curtis, Alice Turner
Little runaways series (2)
Little runaways at Orchard House
Curtis, Alice Turner
Little runaways series (4)
Little sail boat
Lenski, Lois
Small family series (3)
Little sailing boat
Lenski, Lois
Small family series (3)
Little Sally Shrimp
Gissing, Vera
Pippins series (2)
Little shop in Fore Street
Howard, Francis Morton
Happy Rascals series (2)
Little silver house
Lindquist, Jennie Dorothea
Nancy Bruce series (2)
Little sister
Chandler, Raymond
Philip Marlowe series (5)
Little sister Prue
Brooks, Amy
Prue series (1)
Little Sister Snow
Little, Frances
Lady of the decoration series (2)
Little sister Tai-Me
Braenne, Berit
Trina series (2)
Little smasher
Impey, Rose
Baddies series (5)
Little Soup's birthday
Peck, Robert Newton
Little Soup series (2)
Little Soup's bunny
Peck, Robert Newton
Little Soup series (4)
Little Soup's hayride
Peck, Robert Newton
Little Soup series (1)
Little Soup's turkey
Peck, Robert Newton
Little Soup series (3)
Little Spaniard
Mannering, May
Climbing the rope series (4)

Little sparrow
Eagar, Frances
Laura and Harry series (1)
Little Spook
Sandberg, Inger
Little Spook series (1)
Little Spook and the lost doll
Sandberg, Inger
Little Spook series (8)
Little Spook haunts again
Sandberg, Inger
Little Spook series (7)
Little Spook's baby sister
Sandberg, Inger
Little Spook series (5)
Little Spook's grubby day
Sandberg, Inger
Little Spook series (2)
Little stories of courtship
Cutting, Mary Stewart
Little stories of life series (1)
Little stories of married life
Cutting, Mary Stewart
Little stories of life series (2)
Little talks about God and you
Beers, Victor Gilbert
Little talks series (1)
Little tea, a little chat
Stead, Christina
New York trilogy (2)
Little Tiger, get well soon
Janosch
Little Tiger series (4)
Little Tim and the brave sea captain
Ardizzone, Edward
Tim series (1)
Little Tom and some animal friends
Gree, Alain
Little Tom series (2)
Little Tom learns about the environment
Gree, Alain
Little Tom series (1)
Gree, Gerard
Little Tom series (1)
Little Tom learns about the time
Gree, Alain
Little Tom series (4)
Little Tom makes ten discoveries
Gree, Alain
Little Tom series (3)
Little Toot
Gramatky, Hardie
Little Toot series (1)
Little Toot on the Grand Canal
Gramatky, Hardie
Little Toot series (3)
Little Toot on the Mississippi
Gramatky, Hardie
Little Toot series (4)
Little Toot on the Thames
Gramatky, Hardie
Little Toot series (2)
Little Toot through the Golden Gate
Gramatky, Hardie
Little Toot series (5)
Little town, big trouble
Grover, Marshall
Larry and Stretch series (252)
Little town on the prairie
Wilder, Laura Ingalls
Laura series (6)
Little train
Lenski, Lois
Small family series (5)
Little tree house
Blyton, Enid
Josie, Click and Bun series (1)
Little truck
Gay, Michael
Little vehicle series (1)
Little Trulsa
Ringner-Lundgren, Ester
Little Trulsa series (1)
Little Trulsa's birthday
Ringner-Lundgren, Ester
Little Trulsa series (4)
Little Trulsa's secret
Ringner-Lundgren, Ester
Little Trulsa series (3)
Little Trulsa's tea-party
Ringner-Lundgren, Ester
Little Trulsa series (2)
Little vampire
Sommer-Bodenburg, Angela
Little vampire series (1)
Little vampire and the mystery patient
Sommer-Bodenburg, Angela
Little vampire series (9)
Little vampire and the wicked plot
Sommer-Bodenburg, Angela
Little vampire series (13)
Little vampire gets a surprise
Sommer-Bodenburg, Angela
Little vampire series (12)
Little vampire goes on holiday
Sommer-Bodenburg, Angela
Little vampire series (4)
Little vampire in danger
Sommer-Bodenburg, Angela
Little vampire series (6)
Little vampire in despair
Sommer-Bodenburg, Angela
Little vampire series (8)
Little vampire in love
Sommer-Bodenburg, Angela
Little vampire series (5)
Little vampire in the lion's den
Sommer-Bodenburg, Angela
Little vampire series (10)
Little vampire in the vale of doom
Sommer-Bodenburg, Angela
Little vampire series (7)
Little vampire learns to be brave
Sommer-Bodenburg, Angela
Little vampire series (11)
Little vampire moves in
Sommer-Bodenburg, Angela
Little vampire series (2)
Little vampire on the farm
Sommer-Bodenburg, Angela
Little vampire series (4)
Little vampire takes a trip
Sommer-Bodenburg, Angela
Little vampire series (3)
Little vehicle
Brodrick, Alan Hough
Indo-China series (2)
Little victims play
Hocking, Anne
Inspector William Austen series (1)
Little Washingtons
Nourse, S Waukley Roy
Little Washingtons series (1)
Little Washingtons at school
Roy, Lillian Elizabeth
Little Washingtons series (4)
Little Washingtons, farmers
Roy, Lillian Elizabeth
Little Washingtons series (6)
Little Washingtons' holidays
Roy, Lillian Elizabeth
Little Washingtons series (5)
Little Washingtons' relative
Roy, Lillian Elizabeth
Little Washingtons series (2)
Little Washingtons' travels
Roy, Lillian Elizabeth
Little Washingtons series (3)
Little weather house
Macdonald, Elizabeth
Magic plant series (2)
Little wheels
Peppe, Rodney
Little toy board books series (5)
Little white bird
Barrie, James Matthew
Peter Pan series (2)
Little White Foot
Hader, Berta
Willow Hill series (4)
Little witch presents a monster joke book
Glovach, Linda
Little witch series (15)
Little witch's birthday book
Glovach, Linda
Little witch series (8)
Little witch's black magic book of disguises
Glovach, Linda
Little witch series (2)
Little witch's black magic book of games
Glovach, Linda
Little witch series (3)
Little witch's black magic cookbook
Glovach, Linda
Little witch series (1)
Little witch's book of toys
Glovach, Linda
Little witch series (15)
Little witch's book of yoga
Glovach, Linda
Little witch series (7)
Little witch's carnival book
Glovach, Linda
Little witch series (9)
Little witch's cat book
Glovach, Linda
Little witch series (13)
Little witch's Christmas book
Glovach, Linda
Little witch series (4)
Little witch's dinosaur book
Glovach, Linda
Little witch series (12)
Little witch's Halloween book
Glovach, Linda
Little witch series (5)
Little witch's spring holiday book
Glovach, Linda
Little witch series (10)
Little witch's summertime book
Glovach, Linda
Little witch series (14)
Little witch's Thanksgiving book
Glovach, Linda
Little witch series (6)
Little witch's Valentine book
Glovach, Linda
Little witch series (11)
Little wizard stories of Oz
Baum, Lyman Frank
Little Wizard series (6)
Oz series (51)
Little women
Alcott, Louisa May
Jo March series (1)
Jo March series (2)
Little women married
Alcott, Louisa May
Jo March series (2)
Little world of D H Gilmore
Gilmore, David Hunter
Christopher Cricket series (7)
Little world of Don Camillo
Guareschi, Giovanni
Don Camillo series (1)
Little world of the past
Fogazzaro, Antonio
Maironi family trilogy (1)
Little yearnings of Annabel
Davidson, Alan
Annabel Fidelity Bunce series (5)
Little Zip's dressing-up book
Caveney, Sylvia
Little Zip series (1)
Little Zip's night-time book
Caveney, Sylvia
Little Zip series (4)
Little Zip's water book
Caveney, Sylvia
Little Zip series (3)
Little Zip's zoo counting book
Caveney, Sylvia
Little Zip series (2)
Littlejohn on leave
Bellairs, George
Detective Inspector Thomas Littlejohn series (1)
Littlenose
Grant, John
Littlenose series (1)
Littlenose and Two-eyes
Grant, John
Littlenose series (11)
Littlenose moves house
Grant, John
Littlenose series (2)
Littlenose the fisherman
Grant, John
Littlenose series (5)
Littlenose the hero
Grant, John
Littlenose series (3)
Littlenose the hunter
Grant, John
Littlenose series (4)
Littlenose the joker
Grant, John
Littlenose series (10)
Littlenose the leader
Grant, John
Littlenose series (7)
Littlenose the marksman
Grant, John
Littlenose series (9)
Littlenose to the rescue
Grant, John
Littlenose series (6)
Littlenose's birthday
Grant, John
Littlenose series (8)
Littlest angel
Tazewell, Charles
Littlest series (1)
Littlest angel earns his halo
Kidd, Ronald
Littlest angel series (1)
Littlest angel meets the newest angel
Kidd, Ronald
Littlest angel series (2)
Littlest house
Coatsworth, Elizabeth
Plum Daffy series (1)
Littlest rebels
Johnston, William
Flying nun series (3)
Littlest snowman
Tazewell, Charles
Littlest series (3)
Littlest stork
Tazewell, Charles
Littlest series (2)
Live Albom
Albom, Mitch
Live Albom series (1)
Live Albom II
Albom, Mitch
Live Albom series (2)
Live Albom III
Albom, Mitch
Live Albom series (3)
Live and kicking Ned
Masefield, John
Autobiography of a corpse series (2)
Live and learn
Leslie, Madeline
Woodbine series (1)
Live and let die
Fleming, Ian
James Bond series (2)
Live and let's dance
Vincent, John
James Bond junior series (3)
Live bait
Knox, Bill
Inspector Colin Thane and Phil Moss series (16)
Walsh, Bill
Fishing series (1)
Wood, Ted
Reid Bennett series (3)
Live bait for murder
Herber, William
Jimmy Rehm series (2)
Live boys
Morecamp, Arthur
Live boys series (1)
Live boys in the Black Hills
Morecamp, Arthur
Live boys series (2)
Live for love
Carroll, Shana
Paxton women series (4)
Live gold
Sheckley, Robert
Stephen Dain series (3)
Live in the sky
Hardcastle, Michael
Tony and Jay series (7)
Live, love and cry
Mair, George Brown
David Grant series (3)
Live now, pay later
Story, Jack Trevor
Albert Argyle series (1)
Live Oak boys
Kellogg, Elijah
Good old times series (4)
Live unafraid
Echlin, Elizabeth Gladys
Chronicles trilogy (2)
Live wire
Bruce, Jean
Secret Agent O.S.S.117 series (5)
Live wire clue
Carter, Nicholas
Nicholas Carter series (381)
Live wires
Allen, Austen
Inspector Ord series (3)
Lively game of death
Kaye, Marvin
Hilary Quayle series (1)
Lively Lady
Roberts, Kenneth Lewis
Chronicles of Arundel series (3)
Liverpool cats
Sherry, Sylvia
Rocky O'Rourke series (1)
Liverpool characters and eccentrics
Whittington-Egan, Richard
Liverpool series (4)
Liverpool colonnade
Whittington-Egan, Richard
Liverpool series (1)
Liverpool Daisy
Forrester, Helen
Mersey series (2)
Liverpool miss
Forrester, Helen
Mersey series (1)
Liverpool roundabout
Whittington-Egan, Richard
Liverpool series (2)
Liverpool soundings
Whittington-Egan, Richard
Liverpool series (5)
Liverpool, this is my city
Whittington-Egan, Richard
Liverpool series (6)
Livery of Eve
Bain, Francis William
Indian mystic love stories series (12)
Lives and times of Jerry Cornelius
Moorcock, Michael
Jerry Cornelius series (5)
Lives of Christopher Chant
Jones, Diana Wynne
Chrestomanci series (4)
Lives of Rachel
Gross, Joel
Rachel series (1)
Livestock in barracks
Armstrong, Anthony
Warriors series (3)
Livia
Durrell, Lawrence
Avignon quintet (1)
Living at the end of time
Mitchell, John Hanson
Scratch Flat series (2)
Living bomb
Avallone, Michael
Ed Noon series (11)
Living daylights
Fleming, Ian
James Bond series (14)
Living death
Carter, Nick
Nick Carter series (48)
Living end
Kane, Frank
Johnny Liddell series (11)
Living-fire menace
Robeson, Kenneth
Doc Savage series (61)
Living free
Adamson, Joy
Elsa series (2)
Living god
Duncan, Dave
Handful of men series (4)
Living hedge
Paul, Leslie
Angry young man series (3)
Living hell
Meyers, Richard S
Book of the undead series (2)
Living in Croesor
O'Connor, Philip
Lower view series (3)
Living in fear
Parsons, Anthony
Sexton Blake series (1263)
Living in God
McGloin, Joseph Thaddeus
With Him, through Him, to Him series (1)
Living in the Kingdom
McGloin, Joseph Thaddeus
With Him, through Him, to Him series (4)
Living it up
Sarasin, Jennifer
Cheerleaders series (14)
Living joss
Grant, Maxwell
Shadow series (33)
Living legend
Larson, Glen A
Battlestar Galactica series (6)
Living mask
Carter, Nicholas
Nicholas Carter series (175)
Living portrait
Sutton, Margaret
Judy Bolton series (18)
Living Shadow
Grant, Maxwell
Shadow series (1)
Living shadow
Sayer, Walter William
Sexton Blake series (154)
Living sword
Allan, Lennox
Living sword series (2)
Living, the dying and the dead
Gilman, George G
Edge series (29)
Living toilets
Disrobeson, Kin I
Doc Savage series (183)
Living touch
Kerin, Dorothy
Faith healing series (1)

Living with Leanne
Clark, Margaret Dianne
Sam and Leanne series (2)
Living with Minka and Curdy
White, Antonia
Minka and Curdy series (2)
Liz
Macgibbon, Jean
Molly and Liz series (2)
Liz and Will solve mini-mysteries
Resciniti, Angelo G
Liz and Will series (1)
Liz assignation
Janson, Hank
Hank Janson series (261)
Lizard in the cup
Dickinson, Peter
Superintendent James Pibble series (5)
Lizzie and Harold
Winthrop, Elizabeth
Lizzie and Harold series (1)
Lizzie Dripping
Cresswell, Helen
Lizzie Dripping series (1)
Lizzie Dripping again
Cresswell, Helen
Lizzie Dripping series (2)
Lizzie Dripping and the little angel
Cresswell, Helen
Lizzie Dripping series (3)
Lizzie Dripping and the witch
Cresswell, Helen
Lizzie Dripping series (6)
Lizzie Dripping by the sea
Cresswell, Helen
Lizzie Dripping series (4)
Lizzie Leek
Reed, Giles
Munch Bunch character series (6)
Lizzie Pye
Blishen, Edward
Schoolmaster series (8)
Lizzie Silver of Sherwood Forest
Singer, Marilyn
Lizzie Silver series (2)
Llana of Gathol
Burroughs, Edgar Rice
Martian series (10)
Llano River
Kelton, Elmer
Tales of Texas series (3)
Load every rifle
Grover, Marshall
Larry and Stretch series (246)
Load of trouble
Hardcastle, Michael
Tony and Jay series (10)
Load of unicorn
Harnett, Cynthia
Fifteenth century London series (3)
Loaded dice
Marlowe, Piers
Double Thirteen Club series (2)
Masters, Zeke
Faro Blake series (22)
Loaded stick
Jacob, Naomi
Broad acres series (2)
Loanshark
McCurtin, Peter
Sundance series (25)
Lobo
Hunter, Neil
Brand series (3)
Kantor, Mackinlay
But look trilogy (2)
Lobo brand
Friend, Oscar
Simon Carter series (2)
Lobo breed
Martin, Charles Morris
Gospel Cummings series (1)
Lobo colonel
Cole, Jackson
Jim Hatfield series (88)
Lobo legion
Cole, Jackson
Jim Hatfield series (83)
Lobo moon
Sadler, Jeff
Marshal Andrew Anderson series (5)
Lobo Trail
Harris, Larry
Masked Rider and Blue Hawk series (25)
Lobo wolf
Murray, Earl
Dan Sleyter series (2)
Lob's silver spoon
Ainsworth, Ruth
Little Mushrooms series (1)
Lobster books
Hatch, Richard Warren
Curious lobster series (2)
Lobster pink murder
Heberden, Mary Violet
Desmond Shannon series (4)
Local habitation
Butler, Guy
South Africa series (3)
Lindsay, Jack
British way series (4)
Local hero
Roberts, Nora
Flowers series (48)
Local lads
Scott, Jack S
Detective Inspector Alfred Stanley Rosher series (8)
Local talent
Fuller, William
Brad Dolan series (2)
Location shots
Burke, Jackson Frederick
Samuel Moses Kelly series (1)
Lochinvar
Crockett, Samuel Rutherford
English Revolution series (2)
Lochinvar Luck
Terhune, Albert Payson
Sunnybank collies series (6)
Lock at Charenton
Simenon, Georges
Inspector Jules Maigret series (18)
Inspector Jules Maigret series (19)
Lock the door, mademoiselle
Jacobs, Thomas Curtis Hicks
Temple Fortune series (3)
Locked doors
Rinehart, Mary Roberts
Nurse Hilda Adams series (2)
Locked room
Auster, Paul
New York trilogy (3)
Sjowall, Maj
Inspector Martin Beck series (8)
Locked rooms and open door
Lindbergh, Anne Morrow
Unicorn series (3)
Lockestep
Barnao, Jack
John Locke series (2)
Lockie Leonard, human torpedo
Winton, Tim
Lockie Leonard series (1)
Lockie Leonard, scumbuster
Winton, Tim
Lockie Leonard series (2)
Lockout
O'Donnell, Lillian
Detective Norah Mulcahaney series (15)
Locomotive
Barkan, Joanne
Come aboard series (3)
Lodestar
Belle, Pamela
Heron family series (4)
Lodestar of death
Sandys, James
Mister Springfield series (2)
Lodge of the lynx
Kurtz, Katherine
Adept trilogy (2)
Lodger
Staples, Mary Jane
South London series (5)
Lodgers at Highlands
Tarrant, Elizabeth
Highlands series (3)
Lodges of the Blackfeet
Schultz, James Willard
Blackfoot series (1)
Lodging at the Saint Cloud
Crabb, Alfred Leland
Nashville series (4)
Lodging-house mystery
Hardinge, Rex
Sexton Blake series (1352)
Log book I
Seferis, George
Log book series (1)
Log book II
Seferis, George
Log book series (2)
Log book III
Seferis, George
Log book series (3)
Log-cabin home
Chambers, Catherine E
Adventures in frontier America series (8)
Log fort adventures
McCall, Edith
Frontiers of America series (1)
Log hut
Firbank, Thomas
Mountain series (5)
Log of no lady
Bloom, Ursula
No lady series (1)
Log of the Bombastes
Frith, Henry
Britannia series (2)
Log of the Flying Fish
Collingwood, Harry
Flying Fish trilogy (1)
Log of the Water Wagon
Gibson, William Curtis
Water Wagon series (1)
Logan
Nolan, William Francis
Logan series (3)
Logan Bruno, boy baby-sitter
Martin, Ann Matthews
Baby-Sitters Club readers special request series (2)
Logan likes Mary Ann!
Martin, Ann Matthews
Baby-Sitters Club series (10)
Logan's army
Longley, W B
Angel Eyes series (5)
Logan's run
Nolan, William Francis
Logan series (1)
Logan's search
Nolan, William Francis
Logan series (3)
Logan's story
Martin, Ann Matthews
Baby-Sitters Club readers special request series (1)
Logan's world
Nolan, William Francis
Logan series (2)
Logantown looters
Grover, Marshall
Larry and Stretch series (343)
Logick
Watts, Isaac
Logick series (1)
Logopolis
Bidmead, Christopher H
Doctor Who series (73)
Lois and the sleepover
Pascal, Francine
Sweet Valley kids series (51)
Lois strikes back
Pascal, Francine
Sweet Valley twins series (38)
Loki the wolf
Rutley, Cecil Bernard
Wild life story series (7)
Lola
Delacorta
Serge Gorodish series (4)
Lola brought her wreath
Janson, Hank
Hank Janson series (16)
Lolami in Tusayan
Bayliss, Clara Kern
Lolami series (2)
Lolami, the little cliff-dweller
Bayliss, Clara Kern
Lolami series (1)
Lolita man
James, Bill
Superintendent Colin Harpur series (2)
Lollipop lady
Bentley, Diana
My school series (4)
Lollipop man
Bentley, Diana
My school series (13)
Lollipop plot
Blair, Cynthia
Susan and Christine Pratt series (11)
Lollipops and apples
Braga, Meg
William and Wendy series (2)
Lombard cavalcade
Coffman, Virginia
Cavalcade series (2)
Lombard heiress
Coffman, Virginia
Cavalcade series (3)
Lombard Street mystery
Blair, Allan
Sexton Blake series (606)
Lona of Hollybush Creek
Fox, Genevieve May
Mountain girl series (3)
London
Henrey, Madeleine
Madeleine reminiscences series (7)
London adventure
Bayley, Viola
Adventure series (7)
London adventures of Mister Collin
Heller, Frank
Mister Collin series (1)
London affair
Stuart, Anthony
Vladimir Gull series (5)
London assignment
Ross, Angus
Mark Farrow series (3)
London at home
Hughes, Mary Vivian
London family series (3)
London beneath the pavement
Harrison, Michael
London archaeology series (1)
London, bloody London
Avallone, Michael
Ed Noon series (24)
London Bridge is falling down
Spier, Peter
Mother Goose library series (1)
London calling
Gielgud, Val
Inspector Simon Spears series (1)
London child of the seventies
Hughes, Mary Vivian
London family series (1)
London connection
Moore, Robin
Connection series (2)
Pulsar series (1)
London crimes
Grant, Maxwell
Shadow series (86)
London deal
Crisp, Norman James
Inspector Sidney Kenyon series (3)
London diary
Byrd, William
Secret diary series (3)
London Embassy
Theroux, Paul
Spencer Monroe Savage series (2)
London end
Priestley, John Boynton
Image men series (2)
London family between the wars
Hughes, Mary Vivian
London family series (3)
London family chronicle
Hughes, Mary Vivian
London family series (3)
London general
Willis, Frederick
Edwardian London trilogy (3)
London girl of the eighties
Hughes, Mary Vivian
London family series (2)
London home in the nineties
Hughes, Mary Vivian
London family series (3)
London lavender
Lucas, Edward Verrall
Winfield series (4)
London match
Deighton, Len
Bernard Samson series (3)
Game, set and match trilogy (3)
London morning
Avery, Valerie
London trilogy (1)
London novels
Macinnes, Colin
Visions of London series (3)
London of Sherlock Holmes
Harrison, Michael
Life of Sherlock Holmes series (2)
London particular
Brand, Christianna
Inspector Charlesworth series (2)
Inspector Cockrill series (5)
London particulars
Rolph, C H
Particulars series (1)
London season
Powell, Margaret
Domestic service series (4)
London shadows
Avery, Valerie
London trilogy (2)
London spring
Avery, Valerie
London trilogy (3)
London spy murders
Cheyney, Peter
Everard Peter Quayle series (1)
Secret service series (2)
London switch
Moore, Robin
Connection series (2)
Pulsar series (1)
London that was Rome
Harrison, Michael
London archaeology series (2)
London to Philadelphia
Graveson, Caroline Cassandra
Farthing family series (2)
London transports
Binchy, Maeve
London transports series (2)
London under fire, 1940-45
Henrey, Madeleine
Madeleine series (8)
London underworld
Birt, David
Tudors series (18)
London's revenge
Reno, Bill
Badge series (5)
Lone Arthur
Coren, Alan
Arthur series (3)
Lone Bull's horse raid
Goble, Paul
Red Indian trilogy (3)
Lone eagle of the border
Dixon, Franklin W
Ted Scott flying series (8)
Lone fighter
Sanders, Charles Wesley
Mournful Martin series (2)
Lone footprint
Judd, Frances K
Kay Tracey series (15)
Lone gun war
Saddler, Jeff
Apache Anderson series (12)
Lone gunhawk
Gruber, Frank
Historical Western series (6)
Lone Hand Emerson
Grover, Marshall
Larry and Stretch series (249)
Lone Hand in Texas
Aiken, Albert W
Lone Hand series (1)
Lone Hand on the Caddo
Aiken, Albert W
Lone Hand series (2)
Lone Hand, the shadow
Aiken, Albert W
Lone Hand series (3)
Lone house mystery
Wallace, Edgar
Superintendent Minter series (2)
Lone Hunter and the Cheyennes
Worcester, Donald Emmet
Lone Hunter series (2)
Lone Hunter and the wild horses
Worcester, Donald Emmet
Lone Hunter series (4)
Lone Hunter's first buffalo hunt
Worcester, Donald Emmet
Lone Hunter series (3)
Lone Hunter's gray pony
Worcester, Donald Emmet
Lone Hunter series (1)
Lone Indian
Braden, James Andrew
John Jerome and Return Kingdom series (2)
Lone killer
Nickson, Arthur
Rusty Hines series (7)
Lone Lodge mystery
Hawk, John
Mortimer Sark series (1)
Lone Pine Five
Saville, Malcolm
Lone Pine Five Club series (5)
Lone Pine London
Saville, Malcolm
Lone Pine Five Club series (10)
Lone prairie
Bexar, Phil
Billy Dupree series (4)
Lone Ranger
Du Dois, Gaylord
Lone Ranger series (22)
Fletcher, Steffi
Lone Ranger series (22)
Striker, Fran
Lone Ranger series (1)

Lone Ranger adventure stories
Lewis, Richard
Lone Ranger series (22)

Lone Ranger and the Bitter Spring feud
Striker, Fran
Lone Ranger series (19)

Lone Ranger and the code of the West
Striker, Fran
Lone Ranger series (20)

Lone Ranger and the gold robbery
Striker, Fran
Lone Ranger series (3)

Lone Ranger and the mystery ranch
Striker, Fran
Lone Ranger series (2)

Lone Ranger and the outlaw stronghold
Striker, Fran
Lone Ranger series (5)

Lone Ranger and the secret of Thunder Mountain
Striker, Fran
Lone Ranger series (7)

Lone Ranger and the silver bullet
Striker, Fran
Lone Ranger series (13)

Lone Ranger and the Texas renegades
Striker, Fran
Lone Ranger series (4)

Lone Ranger and Tonto
Striker, Fran
Lone Ranger series (6)

Lone Ranger at the Haunted Gulch
Striker, Fran
Lone Ranger series (9)

Lone Ranger in Wild Horse Canyon
Striker, Fran
Lone Ranger series (15)

Lone Ranger on Gunsight Mesa
Striker, Fran
Lone Ranger series (18)

Lone Ranger on Powderhorn Trail
Striker, Fran
Lone Ranger series (14)

Lone Ranger on the Red Butte Trail
Striker, Fran
Lone Ranger series (22)

Lone Ranger rides
Striker, Fran
Lone Ranger series (8)

Lone Ranger rides again
Striker, Fran
Lone Ranger series (11)

Lone Ranger rides north
Striker, Fran
Lone Ranger series (12)

Lone Ranger traps the smugglers
Striker, Fran
Lone Ranger series (10)

Lone Ranger, trouble on the Santa Fe
Striker, Fran
Lone Ranger series (21)

Lone Ranger west of Maverick Pass
Striker, Fran
Lone Ranger series (16)

Lone Ranger's new deputy
Striker, Fran
Lone Ranger series (17)

Lone Rider
Henderson, Colt
Lone Rider series (3)

Lone Rider's day
Henderson, Colt
Lone Rider series (10)

Lone Rider's guns
Henderson, Colt
Lone Rider series (4)

Lone Rider's justice
Henderson, Colt
Lone Rider series (5)

Lone Rider's law
Henderson, Colt
Lone Rider series (11)

Lone Rider's quest
Henderson, Colt
Lone Rider series (8)

Lone Rider's ranch
Henderson, Colt
Lone Rider series (7)

Lone Rider's return
Henderson, Colt
Lone Rider series (12)

Lone Rider's trail
Henderson, Colt
Lone Rider series (6)

Lone Rider's war
Henderson, Colt
Lone Rider series (9)

Lone Star and a saloon called Hell
Ellis, Wesley
Lone Star series (143)

Lone Star and Hickok's ghost
Ellis, Wesley
Lone Star series (70)

Lone Star and the Alaskan guns
Ellis, Wesley
Lone Star series (40)

Lone Star and the Alaskan renegades
Ellis, Wesley
Lone Star series (104)

Lone Star and the Amarillo rifles
Ellis, Wesley
Lone Star series (29)

Lone Star and the Apache revenge
Ellis, Wesley
Lone Star series (21)

Lone Star and the Apache warrior
Ellis, Wesley
Lone Star series (37)

Lone Star and the Aztec treasure
Ellis, Wesley
Lone Star series (123)

Lone Star and the badlands war
Ellis, Wesley
Lone Star series (16)

Lone Star and the Barbary killers
Ellis, Wesley
Lone Star series (80)

Lone Star and the bellwether kid
Ellis, Wesley
Lone Star series (133)

Lone Star and the biggest gun in the West
Ellis, Wesley
Lone Star series (36)

Lone Star and the Black Bandana Gang
Ellis, Wesley
Lone Star series (117)

Lone Star and the border bandits
Ellis, Wesley
Lone Star series (3)

Lone Star and the Brutus Gang
Ellis, Wesley
Lone Star series (127)

Lone Star and the buccaneers
Ellis, Wesley
Lone Star series (122)

Lone Star and the buffalo hunters
Ellis, Wesley
Lone Star series (35)

Lone Star and the California oil war
Ellis, Wesley
Lone Star series (39)

Lone Star and the Cheyenne trackdown
Ellis, Wesley
Lone Star series (67)

Lone Star and the Comancheros
Ellis, Wesley
Lone Star series (69)

Lone Star and the Comstock crossfire
Ellis, Wesley
Lone Star series (78)

Lone Star and the con man's ransom
Ellis, Wesley
Lone Star series (52)

Lone Star and the deadly stranger
Ellis, Wesley
Lone Star series (71)

Lone Star and the deadly vixens
Ellis, Wesley
Lone Star series (142)

Lone Star and the death chase
Ellis, Wesley
Lone Star series (138)

Lone Star and the death merchants
Ellis, Wesley
Lone Star series (77)

Lone Star and the death mine
Ellis, Wesley
Lone Star series (136)

Lone Star and the death train
Ellis, Wesley
Lone Star series (57)

Lone Star and the deep water pirates
Ellis, Wesley
Lone Star series (116)

Lone Star and the Denver madam
Ellis, Wesley
Lone Star series (13)

Lone Star and the diamond swindlers
Ellis, Wesley
Lone Star series (85)

Lone Star and the gemstone robbers
Ellis, Wesley
Lone Star series (102)

Lone Star and the ghost dancers
Ellis, Wesley
Lone Star series (112)

Lone Star and the ghost pirates
Ellis, Wesley
Lone Star series (18)

Lone Star and the ghost ship pirates
Ellis, Wesley
Lone Star series (130)

Lone Star and the gold mine
Ellis, Wesley
Lone Star series (128)

Lone Star and the gold mine war
Ellis, Wesley
Lone Star series (38)

Lone Star and the gold raiders
Ellis, Wesley
Lone Star series (12)

Lone Star and the golden mesa
Ellis, Wesley
Lone Star series (33)

Lone Star and the gulf pirates
Ellis, Wesley
Lone Star series (49)

Lone Star and the gunpowder cure
Ellis, Wesley
Lone Star series (47)

Lone Star and the gunrunners
Ellis, Wesley
Lone Star series (121)

Lone Star and the hangrope heritage
Ellis, Wesley
Lone Star series (23)

Lone Star and the hardrock payoff
Ellis, Wesley
Lone Star series (9)

Lone Star and the hellbound pilgrims
Ellis, Wesley
Lone Star series (113)

Lone Star and the horse thieves
Ellis, Wesley
Lone Star series (115)

Lone Star and the Indian rebellion
Ellis, Wesley
Lone Star series (50)

Lone Star and the James Gang's loot
Ellis, Wesley
Lone Star series (65)

Lone Star and the Kansas wolves
Ellis, Wesley
Lone Star series (4)

Lone Star and the land barons
Ellis, Wesley
Lone Star series (48)

Lone Star and the land grabbers
Ellis, Wesley
Lone Star series (6)

Lone Star and the lost gold mine
Ellis, Wesley
Lone Star series (68)

Lone Star and the master of death
Ellis, Wesley
Lone Star series (66)

Lone Star and the medicine lodge shoot out
Ellis, Wesley
Lone Star series (79)

Lone Star and the Mescalero outlaws
Ellis, Wesley
Lone Star series (28)

Lone Star and the Mexican standoff
Ellis, Wesley
Lone Star series (15)

Lone Star and the mission war
Ellis, Wesley
Lone Star series (46)

Lone Star and the Montana land grab
Ellis, Wesley
Lone Star series (64)

Lone Star and the Montana marauders
Ellis, Wesley
Lone Star series (140)

Lone Star and the Montana troubles
Ellis, Wesley
Lone Star series (24)

Lone Star and the Moon Trail feud
Ellis, Wesley
Lone Star series (32)

Lone Star and the mountain man
Ellis, Wesley
Lone Star series (25)

Lone Star and the Nevada bloodbath
Ellis, Wesley
Lone Star series (73)

Lone Star and the Nevada mustangs
Ellis, Wesley
Lone Star series (51)

Lone Star and the Oklahoma rustlers
Ellis, Wesley
Lone Star series (110)

Lone Star and the opium rustlers
Ellis, Wesley
Lone Star series (2)

Lone Star and the Oregon rail sabotage
Ellis, Wesley
Lone Star series (45)

Lone Star and the outlaw posse
Ellis, Wesley
Lone Star series (60)

Lone Star and the phantom gunmen
Ellis, Wesley
Lone Star series (63)

Lone Star and the railroad war
Ellis, Wesley
Lone Star series (14)

Lone Star and the Redemption massacre
Ellis, Wesley
Lone Star series (137)

Lone Star and the renegade Comanches
Ellis, Wesley
Lone Star series (10)

Lone Star and the Rio Grande bandits
Ellis, Wesley
Lone Star series (34)

Lone Star and the riverboat
Ellis, Wesley
Lone Star series (27)

Lone Star and the rogue grizzlies
Ellis, Wesley
Lone Star series (81)

Lone Star and the rustler's ambush
Ellis, Wesley
Lone Star series (58)

Lone Star and the San Antonio Rais
Ellis, Wesley
Lone Star series (17)

Lone Star and the San Diego bonanza
Ellis, Wesley
Lone Star series (129)

Lone Star and the Santa Fe showdown
Ellis, Wesley
Lone Star series (120)

Lone Star and the school for outlaws
Ellis, Wesley
Lone Star series (30)

Lone Star and the showdowners
Ellis, Wesley
Lone Star series (8)

Lone Star and the Sierra swindlers
Ellis, Wesley
Lone Star series (55)

Lone Star and the silver bandits
Ellis, Wesley
Lone Star series (72)

Lone Star and the sky warriors
Ellis, Wesley
Lone Star series (61)

Lone Star and the slaughter showdown
Ellis, Wesley
Lone Star series (139)

Lone Star and the stagecoach war
Ellis, Wesley
Lone Star series (53)

Lone Star and the steel rail
Ellis, Wesley
Lone Star series (132)

Lone Star and the stockyard showdown
Ellis, Wesley
Lone Star series (26)

Lone Star and the suicide spread
Ellis, Wesley
Lone Star series (75)

Lone Star and the tall timbers
Ellis, Wesley
Lone Star series (7)

Lone Star and the Texas gambler
Ellis, Wesley
Lone Star series (22)

Lone Star and the Texas killers
Ellis, Wesley
Lone Star series (86)

Lone Star and the Texas Rangers
Ellis, Wesley
Lone Star series (76)

Lone Star and the timber pirates
Ellis, Wesley
Lone Star series (7)

Lone Star and the timberland terror
Ellis, Wesley
Lone Star series (43)

Lone Star and the tombstone gamble
Ellis, Wesley
Lone Star series (42)

Lone Star and the Tong's revenge
Ellis, Wesley
Lone Star series (59)

Lone Star and the trail of blood
Ellis, Wesley
Lone Star series (141)

Lone Star and the trail of murder
Ellis, Wesley
Lone Star series (124)

Lone Star and the trail to Abilene
Ellis, Wesley
Lone Star series (114)

Lone Star and the two gun kid
Ellis, Wesley
Lone Star series (54)

Lone Star and the Utah Kid
Ellis, Wesley
Lone Star series (5)

Lone Star and the White River curse
Ellis, Wesley
Lone Star series (41)

Lone Star and the Yuma Prison break
Ellis, Wesley
Lone Star series (109)

Lone Star bodyguards
Grover, Marshall
Larry and Stretch series (25)

Lone Star brand
Cole, Jackson
Jim Hatfield series (4)

Lone Star firebrands
Grover, Marshall
Larry and Stretch series (75)

Lone Star fury
Grover, Marshall
Larry and Stretch series (46)

Lone Star godfathers
Grover, Marshall
Larry and Stretch series (179)

Lone Star hellions
Grover, Marshall
Larry and Stretch series (21)

Lone Star in a range war
Ellis, Wesley
Lone Star series (62)

Lone Star in Hell's Canyon
Ellis, Wesley
Lone Star series (82)

Lone Star in the Big Horn Mountains
Ellis, Wesley
Lone Star series (56)

Lone Star in the big thicket
Ellis, Wesley
Lone Star series (74)

Lone Star in the Cherokee Strip
Ellis, Wesley
Lone Star series (44)

Lone Star in the Choctaw nation
Ellis, Wesley
Lone Star series (108)

Lone Star in the Devil's Playground
Ellis, Wesley
Lone Star series (106)

Lone Star in the Sierra Diablos
Ellis, Wesley
Lone Star series (144)

Lone Star in Timberlands
Ellis, Wesley
Lone Star series (118)

Lone Star Kid
Shane, Steve
Lone Star Kid series (1)

Lone Star killers
Edson, John Thomas
Floating Outfit series (63)

Lone Star law
Cole, Jackson
Jim Hatfield series (4)

Lone Star legacy
Fletcher, Farris
Texans series (4)

Lone Star legion
Cole, Jackson
Jim Hatfield series (5)

Lone Star lightning
Sharpe, Jon
Trailsman series (109)

Lone Star Lucky
Grover, Marshall
Larry and Stretch series (28)

Lone Star massacre
Hardin, J D
Raider and Doc series (20)

Lone Star on Devil's Trail
Ellis, Wesley
Lone Star series (20)

Lone Star on Outlaw Mountain
Ellis, Wesley
Lone Star series (11)

Lone Star on Owlhoot Trail
Ellis, Wesley
Lone Star series (19)

Lone Star on the hangman's trail
Ellis, Wesley
Lone Star series (131)

Lone Star on the treachery trail
Ellis, Wesley
Lone Star series (1)

Lone Star on the Treasure River
Ellis, Wesley
Lone Star series (31)

Lone Star peril
Cole, Jackson
Jim Hatfield series (74)

Lone Star Ranger
Grey, Zane
Buck Duane series (1)

Lone Star reckless
Grover, Marshall
Larry and Stretch series (70)

Lone Star reckoning
Grover, Marshall
Larry and Stretch series (82)

Lone Star rider
Scott, Bradford
Walt Slade series (32)

Lone Star rowdy
Grover, Marshall
Larry and Stretch series (87)

Lone Star silver
Cole, Jackson
Jim Hatfield series (2)

Lone-Star stud
Martin, Cort
Jared Bolt series (17)

Lone Star survivors
Grover, Marshall
Larry and Stretch series (243)

Lone Star terror
Cole, Jackson
Jim Hatfield series (6)

Lone Star treasure
Cole, Jackson
Jim Hatfield series (8)

Lone Star valiant
Grover, Marshall
Larry and Stretch series (43)

Lone Star vengeance
Grover, Marshall
Larry and Stretch series (59)

Lone tiger
Grant, Maxwell
Shadow series (160)

Lone trail for Cheyenne
Denver, Lee
Cheyenne Jones series (5)

Lone Trail omnibus
Lund, Trygve
Dick Weston series (2)

Lone Wolf
Tuttle, Wilbur Coleman
Hashknife Hartley and Sleepy Stevens series (29)
Vance, Louis Joseph
Michael Lanyard series (1)

Lone Wolf adventures
Dever, Joe
Lone Wolf series (2)

Lone Wolf returns
Vance, Louis Joseph
Michael Lanyard series (5)

Lone Wolf's last prowl
Vance, Louis Joseph
Michael Lanyard series (8)

Lone Wolf's son
Vance, Louis Joseph
Michael Lanyard series (6)

Loneliness of Castle Rising
Cradock, Fanny
Lorme family series (10)

Loneliness of Mia
Beckman, Gunnel
Mia series (2)

Lonely
Romains, Jules
Men of goodwill series (7)

Lonely astronomer
Gridban, Volsted
Adam Quirke series (2)

Lonely beat
Keenan, William
Chief Superintendent Charles Miller series (1)

Lonely bungalow
Taffrail
Pirates series (2)

Lonely cage
Usher, Frank
Daye Smith series (2)

Lonely for the future
Farrell, James Thomas
Universe of time series (2)

Lonely furrow
Diver, Maud
Challoners series (1)
Lofts, Norah
Sir Godfrey Tallboys series (3)

Lonely girl
Baer, Judy
Cedar River daydreams series (17)
O'Brien, Edna
Caithleen series (2)

Lonely graves
Monig, Christopher
Brian Brett series (4)

Lonely hearts
Harvey, John Barton
Inspector Charlie Resnick series (1)

Lonely house
Gask, Arthur
Gilbert Larose series (3)

Lonely hunt
Muir, James A
Breed series (1)

Lonely hunter
Wilcox, Collin
Lieutenant Frank Hastings series (1)

Lonely Inn mystery
Grex, Leo
Paul Irving series (2)

Lonely Londoners
Selvon, Samuel
Lonely Londoners trilogy (1)

Lonely, lovely lady
Monmouth, Jack
Tom Langley series (2)

Lonely Magdalen
Wade, Henry
Inspector Poole series (6)

Lonely men
L'Amour, Louis
Sackett family series (11)

Lonely now
Cruz, Nicky
New York gang series (2)

Lonely on the mountain
L'Amour, Louis
Sackett family series (18)

Lonely only mouse
Smith, Wendy
Only mouse series (1)

Lonely place
Copper, Basil
Mike Faraday series (21)

Lonely place to die
Ebersohn, Wessel
Yudel Gordon series (1)
Robertson, Colin
Peter Grayleigh series (17)

Lonely shore
Vines, Freda
Western Australian series (1)

Lonely shroud
Mitchell, Scott
Brock Devlin series (4)

Lonely silver rain
Macdonald, John Dann
Travis McGee series (21)

Lonely Stanley
Edwards, Pat
Stanley series (4)

Lonely summers
Dugon, Nora
Kelly Ryan series (1)

Lonely target
Pentecost, Hugh
Grant Simon series (2)
Lieutenant Pascal series (3)

Lonely the man without heroes
Power, Maurice S
Children of the north series (2)

Lonely Veronica
Duvoisin, Roger
Veronica series (3)

Lonely vigils
Wellman, Manly Wade
John Thunstone trilogy (1)

Lonely vombatus
Plain, Neil
Boris Blundle and Gang series (7)

Lonely walk
Chaber, M E
Milo March series (6)

Lonely way to die
Bourgeau, Art
Claude Kirlin and F T Zevich series (1)

Lonelyheart 4122
Watson, Colin
Inspector Purbright series (4)

Loner
Gilman, George G
Edge series (1)

Lonesome badger
Gruber, Frank
Otis Beagle series (3)

Lonesome cowboys
Reese, John
Jesus on horseback trilogy (2)

Lonesome dove
McMurtry, Larry
Lonesome dove series (1)

Lonesome River
Garlock, Dorothy
Wabash trilogy (1)

Lonesome river
Gruber, Frank
Historical Western series (14)

Lonesome River range
Hankins, Robert Maxwell
Lonesome River series (1)

Lonesome road
Furman, Lucy
Quare women trilogy (3)
Wentworth, Patricia
Miss Maud Silver series (3)

Lonesome Swamp mystery
Lloyd, Hugh
Hal Keen series (7)

Lonesome trail
Bower, Bertha Muzzy
Flying U Ranch series (2)

Long Acre
Rayner, Claire
Performers series (6)

Long-ago murders
Jones, G Wayman
Black Bat series (28)

Long alert
Gibbs, Philip
Second World War series (3)

Long and happy life
Price, Reynolds
Mustian family series (1)

Long arm
Cecil, Henry
Mister Tewkesbury series (3)
Janson, Hank
Hank Janson series (254)

Long arm of Fantomas
Souvestre, Pierre
Fantomas series (8)

Long ARM of Gil Hamilton
Niven, Larry
Gil Hamilton series (1)
Known Space series (10)

Long arm of murder
Gruber, Frank
Simon Lash series (3)

Long avenue
Turner, James Ernest
Nicholas de la Haye series (2)

Long body
McCloy, Helen
Basil Willing series (10)

Long chance
Enefer, Douglas
Dale Shand series (2)

Long chase
Eshleman, John Morton
Lieutenant Larry Koharik series (2)

Long Christmas
Sawyer, Ruth
Christmas stories series (2)

Long dark night of Baron Samedi
Wyllie, John
Doctor Quarshie series (8)

Long dark tea-time of the soul
Adams, Douglas Noel
Dirk Gently series (2)

Long day
Cresswell, Helen
Mike series (4)

Long day closes
Tunstall, Beatrice
West Mercia series (2)

Long day Monday
Turnbull, Peter
P Division series (8)

Long day wanes
Burgess, Anthony
Malayan trilogy (3)

Long days
Jennings, D K
Doctor Ralph Conway series (27)

Long day's dying
White, Alan
Commando series (1)

Long death
Dyer, George
Catalyst Club series (2)
Hartman, Dane
Dirty Harry Callahan series (3)

Long divorce
Crispin, Edmund
Gervase Fen series (8)

Long drift
Brown, Sam
Casey Wills series (2)

Long drop
White, Alan
Commando series (3)

Long dusk
Serge, Victor
Resistance trilogy (3)

Long escape
Dodge, David
Al Colby series (1)

Long farewell
Innes, Michael
Sir John Appleby series (17)

Long fighter
Sanders, Charles Wesley
Mournful Martin series (2)

Long fuse
White, Alan
Commando series (6)

Long goodbye
Chandler, Raymond
Philip Marlowe series (7)

Long goodbyes
Baker, Nikki
Virginia Kelly series (3)

Long green
Spicer, Bart
Carney Wilde series (5)

Long gun war
Sadler, Jeff
Marshal Andrew Anderson series (12)

Long hand of death
White, Alan
Commando series (9)

Long hard cure
Anthony, David
Morgan Butler series (3)

Long hard look
Gair, Malcolm
Mark Raeburn series (2)

Long, hard ride
Mills, Robert E
Davy Watson series (6)

Long haul
Macdonnell, James Edmond
Captain Peter Bentley series (20)

Long hot night
Enefer, Douglas
Dale Shand series (5)

Long house in danger
Laird, Elizabeth
Olaf the Viking series (1)

Long Island murders
Glidden, Minna Wesselhoft
Carey Brent series (2)

Long journey
Jensen, Johannes Vilhelm
Long journey trilogy (3)

Long knife
De Puy, Edward Spence
Sam Houston series (1)
Thom, James Alexander
George Rogers Clark series (1)

Long lane to happiness
Ayres, Ruby Mildred
Richard Chatterton series (2)

Long lavender look
Macdonald, John Dann
Travis McGee series (12)

Long leah
Shurtleff, Bertrand Leslie
Awol series (4)

Long leather cord
Townsend, Larry
Leather bondage series (4)

Long-legged fly
Sallis, James
Lew Griffin series (1)

Long line of dead men
Block, Lawrence
Matthew Scudder series (11)

Long live Brer Anansi
Makhanlall, David Paschal
Anansi series (5)

Long long dances
Malpass, Eric Lawson
Gaylord series (4)

Long Look House
Abbott, Edward
Long Look trilogy (1)

Long-lost brother
Pascal, Francine
Sweet Valley High series (79)

Long love
Sedges, John
American life series (1)

Long memory
Cronin, Michael
James Hellier series (4)

Long midnight
White, Alan
Commando series (5)

Long night
Anderson, Poul
Polesotechnic League series (8)
Howard, Hartley
Glenn Bowman series (14)
Truss, Seldon
Inspector Gidleigh series (10)

Long night of the grave
Grant, Charles Lewis
Oxrun Station series (9)
Soft whisper trilogy (3)

Long night's walk
White, Alan
Commando series (2)

Long odds
Haggard, Henry Rider
Allan Quatermain series (4)
Masters, Zeke
Faro Blake series (23)

Long overcoat
Fry, Pete
Pete Fry series (1)

Long passage
Saville, Malcolm
Buckinghams series (3)

Long patrol
Larson, Glen A
Battlestar Galactica series (10)

Long pig
Foreman, Russell
Oliver Slater Fijiian series (1)

Long Pony race
Lengstrand, Rof
Pony Club series (1)

Long rest
Copper, Basil
Mike Faraday series (31)

Long revenge
Thomson, June
Inspector Finch series (3)

Long ride
Dawson, Clay
Long Rider series (1)
Patchett, Mary Elwyn
Joey Meehan series (6)

Long ride to hell
Christian, Frederick H
Frank Angel series (14)

Long ride to nowhere
Luckey, William A
Blue Mitchell series (1)

Long ride to vengeance
White, James G
Gunslick series (3)

Long-riders
Bosworth, Frank
Earl Morton series (4)

Long rifle
White, Stewart Edward
Andy Burnett series (1)

Long road to freedom
Spanier, Ginette
Mink and sables series (2)

Long road to paradise
Settle, Mary Lee
Beulah series (1)

Long roll
Johnston, Mary
American Civil War trilogy (1)

Long rope
Miller, Jim
Ex-Rangers series (2)

Long run
Moran, Daniel Keys
Tales of the continuing time series (2)

Long run south
Williams, Alan
Rupert Quinn series (1)

Long search
Ashe, Gordon
Patrick Dawlish series (28)

Long secret
Fitzhugh, Louise
Harriet M Welsh series (2)

Long shadow
Gilbert, Anthony
Scott Egerton series (7)
Gilman, George G
Adam Steele series (49)
Harrod-Eagles, Cynthia
Morland family series (6)

Long shadows
Cannan, Joanna
Inspector Ronald Price series (3)
Carnac, Carol
Inspector Julian Rivers series (15)

Long shot
Blake, Ken
Professionals series (2)
McDonnell, Jinny
Kim Aldrich series (4)

Long shot for Rosinante
Gilliland, Alexis Arnaldus
Rosinante trilogy (2)

Long silence
Costello, Paul
Terence O'Hara series (1)
Freeling, Nicolas
Arlette Van der Valk series (1)
Inspector Piet Van der Valk series (10)
White, Alan
Commando series (8)

Long skeleton
Lockridge, Frances
Bill Wiegand series (23)
Mister and Mrs North series (23)

Long spoon
O'Sullivan, James Brendan
Steve Silk series (10)

Long summer
Jennings, D K
Doctor Ralph Conway series (9)

White, Alan
Commando series (7)
Long summer day
Delderfield, Ronald Frederick
Craddocks of Shallowford series (1)
Long tall Texan
Palmer, Diana
Long tall Texan series (1)
Long tattoo
Corder, Eric
Shame and glory series (2)
Long teeth
Albert, Marvin Hubert
Pierre-Ange Sawyer series (4)
Long the imperial way
Tasaki, Hanama
Private Takeo series (1)
Long time dead
Chambers, Peter
Mark Preston series (25)
Long time no Leela
Brown, Carter
Rick Holman series (18)
Long time no see
McBain, Ed
Eighty Seventh Precinct series (32)
Long trail
Murray, Michael
Timber Trail riders series (1)
Long Trail Boys and the gray cloaks
Wilkins, Dale
Long Trail Boys series (2)
Long Trail Boys and the mystery of the fingerprints
Wilkins, Dale
Long Trail Boys series (5)
Long Trail Boys and the mystery of the unknown messenger
Wilkins, Dale
Long Trail Boys series (6)
Long Trail Boys and the scarlet sign
Wilkins, Dale
Long Trail Boys series (3)
Long Trail Boys and the vanishing rider
Wilkins, Dale
Long Trail Boys series (4)
Long Trail Boys at Sweet Water Ranch
Wilkins, Dale
Long Trail Boys series (1)
Long trail to nowhere
Grey, Romer Zane
Buck Duane series (5)
Long trek
Bartimeus
Naval occasions series (3)
Long vacation
Yonge, Charlotte Mary
Beechcroft series (7)
Long vacation series (2)
Long view
Busby, Francis Marion
Rissa Kerguelen series (2)
Rissa Kerguelen series (2)
Long wait
Robins, Patricia
Dick and Tamily series (1)
Long watch
White, Alan
Commando series (4)
Long way down
Wilcox, Collin
Lieutenant Frank Hastings series (5)
Long way from heaven
Kelly, Sheelagh
Feeney family series (1)
Long way from home
Pegram, Lorna
Blood and fire series (3)
Long way home
Conley, Robert Jackson
Real people series (5)
Croft-Cooke, Rupert
Sensual life series (23)
Ebert, Alan
Tiernan family series (2)
Long way south
Dutton, Geoffrey
Long way series (1)
Long way to Land's End
Baker, Denys Val
Cornish series (11)
Long way to Pitt Street
Enefer, Douglas
Sam Bawtrey series (5)
Long way to Texas
Kelton, Elmer
Buckalew tetralogy (4)
Tales of Texas series (11)
Long weekend
Chapman, Jennifer
Long weekend series (1)
Long window
Eshleman, John Morton
Lieutenant Larry Koharik series (1)
Long winter
Fraser, Mary
Village trilogy (2)
Wilder, Laura Ingalls
Laura series (5)
Long winter gone
Johnston, Terry Conrad
General Armstrong Custer series (1)
Longarm
Evans, Tabor
Longarm series (1)
Longarm and the Arizona showdown
Evans, Tabor
Longarm series (157)
Longarm and the Arkansas ambush
Evans, Tabor
Longarm series (156)
Longarm and the avenging angels
Evans, Tabor
Longarm series (3)
Longarm and the big outfit
Evans, Tabor
Longarm series (59)
Longarm and the big posse
Evans, Tabor
Longarm series (105)
Longarm and the big shoot-out
Evans, Tabor
Longarm series (85)
Longarm and the Blackfoot guns
Evans, Tabor
Longarm series (77)
Longarm and the blindman's vengeance
Evans, Tabor
Longarm series (72)
Longarm and the blood bounty
Evans, Tabor
Longarm series (116)
Longarm and the blood harvest
Evans, Tabor
Longarm series (108)
Longarm and the bloody trackdown
Evans, Tabor
Longarm series (109)
Longarm and the blue norther
Evans, Tabor
Longarm series (35)
Longarm and the bone skinners
Evans, Tabor
Longarm series (96)
Longarm and the Boot Hillers
Evans, Tabor
Longarm series (34)
Longarm and the border showdown
Evans, Tabor
Longarm series (174)
Longarm and the bounty hunters
Evans, Tabor
Longarm series (57)
Longarm series (187)
Longarm and the bounty huntress
Evans, Tabor
Longarm series (148)
Longarm and the bounty of blood
Evans, Tabor
Longarm series (181)
Longarm and the buckskin rogue
Evans, Tabor
Longarm series (53)
Longarm and the Calico Kid
Evans, Tabor
Longarm series (54)
Longarm and the captive woman
Evans, Tabor
Longarm series (176)
Longarm and the carnival killer
Evans, Tabor
Longarm series (175)
Longarm and the cattle baron
Evans, Tabor
Longarm series (64)
Longarm and the Cheyenne Kid
Evans, Tabor
Longarm series (164)
Longarm and the Chinese puzzle
Evans, Tabor
Longarm series (145)
Longarm and the Colorado gundown
Evans, Tabor
Longarm series (154)
Longarm and the Comancheros
Evans, Tabor
Longarm series (17)
Longarm series (38)
Longarm and the cottonwood curse
Evans, Tabor
Longarm series (101)
Longarm and the cowboy revenge
Evans, Tabor
Longarm series (79)
Longarm and the crooked railman
Ellis, Wesley
Longarm series (92)
Evans, Tabor
Longarm series (92)
Longarm and the cross fire
Evans, Tabor
Longarm series (177)
Longarm and the Custer County war
Evans, Tabor
Longarm series (61)
Longarm and the dead ringers
Evans, Tabor
Longarm series (180)
Longarm and the Denver bustout
Evans, Tabor
Longarm series (149)
Longarm and the desert duchess
Evans, Tabor
Longarm series (68)
Longarm and the desert spirits
Evans, Tabor
Longarm series (99)
Longarm and the desperate manhunt
Evans, Tabor
Longarm series (102)
Longarm and the devil's railroad
Evans, Tabor
Longarm series (39)
Longarm and the diamond snatchers
Evans, Tabor
Longarm series (173)
Longarm and the doomed witness
Evans, Tabor
Longarm series (126)
Longarm and the double eagles
Evans, Tabor
Longarm series (166)
Longarm and the dragon hunters
Evans, Tabor
Longarm series (26)
Longarm and the Durango payroll
Evans, Tabor
Longarm series (74)
Longarm and the eastern dudes
Evans, Tabor
Longarm series (49)
Longarm and the escape artist
Ellis, Wesley
Longarm series (95)
Evans, Tabor
Longarm series (95)
Longarm and the fool killer
Evans, Tabor
Longarm series (167)
Longarm and the Fort Reno
Evans, Tabor
Longarm series (73)
Longarm and the French actress
Evans, Tabor
Longarm series (55)
Longarm and the frontier duchess
Evans, Tabor
Longarm series (81)
Longarm and the Gallagher Gang
Evans, Tabor
Longarm series (188)
Longarm and the ghost dancers
Evans, Tabor
Longarm series (22)
Longarm and the gold hunters
Evans, Tabor
Longarm series (153)
Longarm and the golden lady
Evans, Tabor
Longarm series (32)
Longarm and the grave robbers
Evans, Tabor
Longarm series (155)
Longarm and the great cattle kill
Evans, Tabor
Longarm series (91)
Longarm and the Great Train Robbery
Evans, Tabor
Longarm series (46)
Longarm and the hangman's list
Evans, Tabor
Longarm series (130)
Longarm and the hangman's noose
Evans, Tabor
Longarm series (66)
Longarm series (125)
Longarm and the hangman's vengeance
Evans, Tabor
Longarm series (110)
Longarm and the hatchet men
Evans, Tabor
Longarm series (9)
Longarm and the high rollers
Evans, Tabor
Longarm series (186)
Longarm and the highgraders
Evans, Tabor
Longarm series (7)
Longarm and the Indian raiders
Evans, Tabor
Longarm series (122)
Longarm and the island passage
Evans, Tabor
Longarm series (89)
Longarm and the James County war
Evans, Tabor
Longarm series (63)
Longarm and the lady sheriff
Evans, Tabor
Longarm series (161)
Longarm and the Laredo Loop
Evans, Tabor
Longarm series (33)
Longarm and the last man
Evans, Tabor
Longarm series (184)
Longarm and the loggers
Evans, Tabor
Longarm series (6)
Longarm and the Lone Star bounty
Evans, Tabor
Longarm and Lone Star series (3)
Longarm and the Lone Star captive
Evans, Tabor
Longarm and Lone Star series (10)
Longarm and Lone Star series (11)
Longarm and the Lone Star deliverance
Evans, Tabor
Longarm and Lone Star series (5)
Longarm and the Lone Star frame
Evans, Tabor
Longarm and Lone Star series (8)
Longarm and the Lone Star legend
Evans, Tabor
Longarm and Lone Star series (1)
Longarm and the Lone Star mission
Evans, Tabor
Longarm and Lone Star series (7)
Longarm and the Lone Star rescue
Evans, Tabor
Longarm and Lone Star series (4)
Longarm and the Lone Star rustlers
Evans, Tabor
Longarm and Lone Star series (9)
Longarm and the Lone Star showdown
Evans, Tabor
Longarm and Lone Star series (6)
Longarm and the Lone Star vengeance
Evans, Tabor
Longarm and Lone Star series (2)
Longarm and the mad dog killer
Evans, Tabor
Longarm series (124)
Longarm and the medicine wolf
Evans, Tabor
Longarm series (121)
Longarm and the Mexican line-up
Evans, Tabor
Longarm series (97)
Longarm and the Molly Maguires
Evans, Tabor
Longarm series (10)
Longarm and the Montana massacre
Evans, Tabor
Longarm series (146)
Longarm and the moonshiners
Evans, Tabor
Longarm series (42)
Longarm and the Mounties
Evans, Tabor
Longarm series (16)
Longarm and the Navaho drums
Evans, Tabor
Longarm and Lone Star series (13)
Longarm and the nesters
Evans, Tabor
Longarm series (8)
Longarm and the Nevada swindle
Evans, Tabor
Longarm series (171)
Longarm and the New Mexico shoot out
Evans, Tabor
Longarm series (118)
Longarm and the Omaha Tinhorns
Evans, Tabor
Longarm series (67)
Longarm and the outlaw lawman
Evans, Tabor
Longarm series (56)
Longarm and the outlaw sheriff
Evans, Tabor
Longarm series (127)
Longarm and the quiet guns
Evans, Tabor
Longarm series (114)
Longarm and the railroad to Hell
Evans, Tabor
Longarm series (151)
Longarm and the railroaders
Evans, Tabor
Longarm series (24)
Longarm and the rancher's showdown
Evans, Tabor
Longarm series (88)
Longarm and the rebel brand
Evans, Tabor
Longarm series (165)
Longarm and the rebel killers
Evans, Tabor
Longarm series (129)
Longarm and the renegade sergeant
Evans, Tabor
Longarm series (119)
Longarm and the river of death
Evans, Tabor
Longarm series (152)
Longarm and the Rocky Mountains chase
Evans, Tabor
Longarm series (103)
Longarm and the runaway thieves
Evans, Tabor
Longarm series (94)
Longarm and the Rurales
Evans, Tabor
Longarm series (27)
Longarm and the San Joaquin war
Evans, Tabor
Longarm and Lone Star series (12)
Longarm and the Santa Anna's gold
Evans, Tabor
Longarm series (60)
Longarm and the Santee killing grounds
Evans, Tabor
Longarm and Lone Star series (14)
Longarm and the shepherders
Evans, Tabor
Longarm series (21)
Longarm and the Shoshoni River
Evans, Tabor
Longarm series (168)
Longarm and the Sierra Madres
Evans, Tabor
Longarm series (120)
Longarm and the Skull Canyon Gang
Evans, Tabor
Longarm series (150)
Longarm and the snake dancers
Evans, Tabor
Longarm series (51)
Longarm and the stagecoach bandits
Evans, Tabor
Longarm series (84)
Longarm and the stalking corpse
Evans, Tabor
Longarm series (37)
Longarm and the steer swindlers
Evans, Tabor
Longarm series (65)
Longarm and the tenderfoot
Evans, Tabor
Longarm series (83)
Longarm and the Texas Rangers
Evans, Tabor
Longarm series (11)
Longarm and the town tamer
Evans, Tabor
Longarm series (23)
Longarm and the trail drive sham
Evans, Tabor
Longarm series (98)
Longarm and the train robbers
Evans, Tabor
Longarm series (182)
Longarm and the treacherous trail
Evans, Tabor
Longarm series (117)
Longarm and the Ute nation
Evans, Tabor
Longarm series (158)
Longarm and the Wendigo
Evans, Tabor
Longarm series (4)
Longarm at Robber's Roost
Evans, Tabor
Longarm series (20)
Longarm in a desert showdown
Evans, Tabor
Longarm series (123)
Longarm in Boulder Canyon
Evans, Tabor
Longarm series (44)
Longarm in Deadwood
Evans, Tabor
Longarm series (45)

Longarm in Leadville
Evans, Tabor
Longarm series (14)
Longarm in Lincoln county
Evans, Tabor
Longarm series (12)
Longarm in no man's land
Evans, Tabor
Longarm series (58)
Longarm in Northfield
Evans, Tabor
Longarm series (31)
Longarm in Silver City
Evans, Tabor
Longarm series (40)
Longarm in the badlands
Evans, Tabor
Longarm series (47)
Longarm in the Big Bend
Evans, Tabor
Longarm series (50)
Longarm in the big burnout
Evans, Tabor
Longarm series (113)
Longarm in the big thicket
Evans, Tabor
Longarm series (48)
Longarm in the Bighorn Basin
Evans, Tabor
Longarm series (107)
Longarm in the Bitterroots
Evans, Tabor
Longarm series (82)
Longarm in the Clearwaters
Evans, Tabor
Longarm series (131)
Longarm in the four corners
Evans, Tabor
Longarm series (19)
Longarm in the Hard Rock country
Evans, Tabor
Longarm series (86)
Longarm in the Indian nation
Evans, Tabor
Longarm series (5)
Longarm in the Ruby Range
Evans, Tabor
Longarm series (90)
Longarm in the sand hills
Evans, Tabor
Longarm series (13)
Longarm in the Sierra Oriental
Evans, Tabor
Longarm series (159)
Longarm in the Texas Panhandle
Evans, Tabor
Longarm series (87)
Longarm in the Valley of Death
Evans, Tabor
Longarm series (115)
Longarm in Virginia City
Evans, Tabor
Longarm series (62)
Longarm in Yuma
Evans, Tabor
Longarm series (43)
Longarm of the painted desert
Evans, Tabor
Longarm series (69)
Longarm on Deadman's Trail
Evans, Tabor
Longarm series (106)
Longarm on Death mountain
Evans, Tabor
Longarm series (100)
Longarm on the Arkansas
Evans, Tabor
Longarm series (71)
Longarm on the Barbary Coast
Evans, Tabor
Longarm series (41)
Longarm on the Big Muddy
Evans, Tabor
Longarm series (29)
Longarm on the border
Evans, Tabor
Longarm series (2)
Longarm on the devil's highway
Evans, Tabor
Longarm series (162)
Longarm on the Devil's Trail
Evans, Tabor
Longarm series (15)
Longarm on the Fever Coast
Evans, Tabor
Longarm series (183)
Longarm on the Goodnight Trail
Evans, Tabor
Longarm series (80)
Longarm on the Great Divide
Evans, Tabor
Longarm series (52)
Longarm on the Humbolt
Evans, Tabor
Longarm series (28)
Longarm on the Nevada line
Evans, Tabor
Longarm series (76)
Longarm on the Ogallala Trail
Evans, Tabor
Longarm series (70)
Longarm on the Old Mission Trail
Evans, Tabor
Longarm series (25)
Longarm on the overland trail
Evans, Tabor
Longarm series (104)
Longarm on the Santa Cruz
Evans, Tabor
Longarm series (78)
Longarm on the Santa Fe
Evans, Tabor
Longarm series (36)
Longarm on the Siwash Trail
Evans, Tabor
Longarm series (93)
Longarm on the Thunderbird Run
Evans, Tabor
Longarm series (111)
Longarm on the Yellowstone
Evans, Tabor
Longarm series (18)
Longarm, south of the Gila
Evans, Tabor
Longarm series (30)
Longarm, west of the Pecos
Evans, Tabor
Longarm series (75)
Longbridge murders
Dalton, Moray
Inspector Hugh Collier series (9)
Longer bodies
Mitchell, Gladys
Dame Beatrice Bradley series (3)
Longer the thread
Lathen, Emma
John Putnam Thatcher series (13)
Longest day
Ryan, Cornelius
Normandy Campaign trilogy (1)
Longest manhunt
Hardin, J D
Raider and Doc series (59)
Longest pleasure
Clark, Douglas
Inspector George Masters series (15)
Longest way round
Lynch, Patricia
Brogeen the leprechaun series (11)
Longhorn
James, Cy
Sam Spur series (2)
Longhorn guns
Sharpe, Jon
Trailsman series (53)
Longhorn sisters
Weston, Cole
Andrew Ryder series (2)
Longhorn territory
Newman, Marc
Choose your own adventure series (74)
Longhorn trail
Hobart, Donald Bayne
Masked Rider and Blue Hawk series (13)
Ulyatt, Kenneth
Portugee Philips trilogy (2)
Longhorn war
Roberts, J R
Gunsmith series (7)
Longhorns north
Lawrence, Steven C
Tom Slattery series (5)
Longing ring
Kubasik, Christopher
Earthdawn series (1)
Longlegs the heron
Burgess, Thornton Waldo
Smiling Pool series (4)
Longley legend
Evans, Tabor
Longarm series (143)
Longship
Birt, David
Saxons and Vikings series (15)
Longtime dreaming
Brinsmead, Hesba Fay
Truelance family series (2)
Longtime passing
Brinsmead, Hesba Fay
Truelance family series (1)
Loo sanction
Trevanian
Jonathan Hemlock series (2)
Look!
Berry, Joy
Can make and do series (9)
Look-about Club and the curious live things they found
Bamford, Mary Ellen
Look-about Club series (1)
Look again with Fingermouse
Cole, Michael
Fingermouse series (2)
Look alive
Burton, Miles
Inspector Arnold and Desmond Merrion series (40)
Look alive, Libby!
Woolley, Catherine
Libby series (1)
Look at me!
Daly, Niki
Storytime series (4)
Look away, Beulah Land
Coleman, Lonnie
Beulah Land trilogy (2)
Look back on death
Egan, Lesley
Jesse Falkenstein series (9)
Look back on murder
Gray, Malcolm
Alan Craig series (1)
Look back with astonishment
Smith, Dodie
Look back series (3)
Look back with gratitude
Smith, Dodie
Look back series (4)
Look back with love
Smith, Dodie
Look back series (1)
Look back with mixed feelings
Smith, Dodie
Look back series (2)
Look behind you
Barbette, Jay
Harry Butten series (4)
Look behind you, lady
Erskine, Margaret
Inspector Septimus Finch series (6)
Look down on her dying
Tracy, Don
Giff Speer series (4)
Look goes round
Gree, Alain
Look series (1)
Look homeward, angel
Wolfe, Thomas Clayton
Eugene Gant series (1)
Look in any doorway
Morland, Nigel
Mrs Palmyra Pym series (18)
Look in at murder
Radford, Edwin
Doctor Manson series (9)
Superintendent Carmichael series (1)
Look inside Ginger Meggs
Kemsley, James
Ginger Meggs series (35)
Look into my eyes
Sapir, Richard
Destroyer series (67)
Look into the sun
Kelly, James Patrick
Messenger chronicles series (2)
Look kitten
Schongut, Emanuel
Kitten board book series (5)
Look out, Charlie
Allen, Joy
Charlie series (12)
Look out, Doctor
Clifford, Robert
Doctor series (5)
Look out for space
Nolan, William Francis
Sam Space series (2)
Look out for the seals!
Ahlberg, Allan
Red nose readers series (14)
Look out, it's April Fool's Day
Modell, Frank B
Milton and Marvin series (5)
Look out, it's Little Ed!
Tully, Tom
Little Ed series (3)
Look out Secret Seven
Blyton, Enid
Secret Seven series (14)
Look out with Fingermouse
Cole, Michael
Fingermouse series (1)
Look-see with Uncle Bill
James, Will
Uncle Bill series (3)
Look sharp
Browne, Dik
Hagar the horrible series (40)
Look three ways at murder
Creasey, John
Inspector Roger West series (32)
Look through my window
Little, Jean
Emily Blair and Kate Bloomfield series (1)
Look to the lady
Allingham, Margery
Albert Campion series (3)
Look to the West
Fidler, Kathleen
Heritage series (5)
Look towards the sea
Baines, Frank
Sea series (1)
Look up at the sky
Campbell, Rod
Little people series (9)
Look what flies
Gree, Alain
Look series (3)
Look what smokes
Gree, Alain
Look series (2)
Look your last
Strange, John Stephen
Barney Gantt series (5)
Looking
Allington, Richard L
Beginning to learn series (5)
Looking after Lamb
Richards, Frank
Schoolboy series (4)
Looking after Lily
Bonner, Cindy
Haywood Beatty trilogy (2)
Looking ahead
Morris, Alfred
Looking backward responses series (1)
Looking at the moon
Pearson, Kit
Evacuee trilogy (2)
Looking backward, from the year 2000
Reynolds, Mack
Julian West series (3)
Looking backward, 2000-1887
Bellamy, Edward
Julian West series (1)
Looking backward responses series (1)
Looking backward sequels series (1)
Looking beyond
Geissler, Ludwig A
Looking backward sequels series (4)
Looking for a bluebird
Wechsberg, Joseph
Epicure trilogy (1)
Looking for elephants
Berg, Leila
Snaps series (2)
Looking for love
Goudge, Eileen
Seniors series (14)
Looking for Rachel Wallace
Parker, Robert Brown
Spenser series (6)
Looking for Tommycat
Girard, Nicole
Anna, Paul and Tommycat series (2)
Looking for trouble
Kaye, Marilyn
Camp Sunnyside Friends series (5)
Looking forward
Bird, Arthur
Looking backward responses series (3)
Looking further backward
Vinton, Arthur Dudley
Looking backward sequels series (3)
Looking further forward
Michaelis, Richard
Looking backward sequels series (1)
Looking glass
Steen, Marguerite
Glass series (1)
Looking glass murder
Gilbert, Anthony
Arthur Crook series (43)
Looking glass murders
Browne, Douglas Gordon
Major Maurice Hemyock series (3)
Lore, Phillips
Leo Roi series (3)
Looking-glass war
Le Carre, John
George Smiley series (4)
Looking good
Ellis, Carol
Cheerleaders series (18)
Looking within
Roberts, J W
Looking backward responses series (2)
Lookout Mountain
Ledd, Paul
Shelter Morgan series (7)
Loom of ice
Macdonnell, James Edmond
Captain Peter Bentley series (34)
Loop current
Sewart, Alan
Detective Chief Superintendent Evans series (3)
Loose connection
Meek, Margaret Reid Duncan
Lennox Kemp series (7)
Loose end
Kane, Henry
Peter Chambers series (7)
Peter Chambers series (8)
Loose lady death
Marshall, Lovat
Sugar Kane series (23)
Loose lips
Breen, Jon Linn
Jerry Brogan series (4)
Loose rib
Allen, Austen
Inspector Ord series (4)
Loose screw
Hammond, Gerald
Beau Pepys series (1)
Loosely engaged
Matthew, Christopher
Simon Crisp series (2)
Loot!
Murray, Andrew
Sexton Blake series (65)
Terhune, Albert Payson
Sunnybank collies series (17)
Loot of death
Grant, Maxwell
Shadow series (117)
Loot of France
Parsons, Anthony
Sexton Blake series (1147)
Loot of Nana Sahib
Hill, Harry Egbert
Sexton Blake series (333)
Loot of Pakistan
Parsons, Anthony
Sexton Blake series (1215)
Looters of Tharn
Lord, Jeffrey
Richard Blade series (19)
Lop-ear
Partridge, Jenny
Oakapple Wood series (7)
Loraine and the little people
Gordon, Elizabeth
Loraine series (1)
Loraine and the little people of spring
Gordon, Elizabeth
Loraine series (2)
Loraine and the little people of summer
Gordon, Elizabeth
Loraine series (3)
Loraine and the little people of the ocean
Gordon, Elizabeth
Loraine series (4)
Lord
Antonius, Soraya
Lord series (1)
Lord and Lady Bugg
Cosgrove, Stephen Edward
Bugg series (6)
Lord and Mary Ann
Cookson, Catherine
Mary Ann Shaughnessy series (2)
Lord and master
Tranter, Nigel Godwin
Patrick Gray series (1)
Lord and the gypsy
Veryan, Patricia
Age of Elegance series (1)
Lord Billy Bunter
Richards, Frank
Billy Bunter series (19)

Lord Blackshirt
Graeme, Bruce
Lord Blackshirt series (2)
Superintendent William Stevens and Inspector Pierre Allain series (13)
Lord Burghley and Queen Elizabeth
Read, Conyers
William Cecil series (2)
Lord Chatham and America
Sherrard, Owen Aubrey
Lord Chatham trilogy (3)
Lord Conrad's lady
Frankowski, Leo
Adventures of Conrad Stargard series (5)
Lord Count Drakulya
Doherty, Paul C
Drakulya series (2)
Lord Darcy
Garrett, Randall
Lord Darcy series (3)
Lord Darcy investigates
Garrett, Randall
Lord Darcy series (3)
Lord Edgware dies
Christie, Agatha
Hercule Poirot series (8)
Lord Edward Fitzgerald
Bodkin, Matthias McDonnell
Lord Edward Fitzgerald series (1)
Lord Emsworth and others
Wodehouse, Pelham Grenville
Blandings Castle series (6)
Mister Mulliner series (3)
Ukridge series (2)
Lord falcon
Cooper, John R
Repositors series (1)
Lord Foul's bane
Donaldson, Stephen Reeder
First Chronicles of Thomas Covenant series (1)
Lord God made them all
Herriot, James
Vet series (7)
Lord Grizzly
Manfred, Frederick
Buckskin Man tales series (1)
Lord Hornblower
Forester, Cecil Scott
Horatio Hornblower series (10)
Lord Jasper
King, Betty
Beaufort family series (3)
Tudor series (3)
Lord Jim
Conrad, Joseph
Lord Jim series (1)
Lord Kalvan of Otherwhen
Piper, Horace Beam
Lord Kalvan series (1)
Paratime police series (1)
Lord Loveland discovers America
Williamson, Charles Norris
Lord and Lady Loveland series (2)
Lord M
Cecil, David
Lord Melbourne series (2)
Lord Mayor's Show mystery
Blair, Allan
Sexton Blake series (741)
Lord Mullion's secret
Innes, Michael
Charles Honeybath series (3)
Lord of blood
Van Arnam, Dave
Jamnar series (2)
Lord of chaos
Boyer, Elizabeth H
Wizard's war series (4)
Jordan, Robert
Wheel of time series (6)
Lord of Cragsclaw
Fawcett, Bill
Guardians of the Three series (1)
Lord of Greenwich
Dymoke, Juliet
Plantagenets series (5)
Lord of Hawkfell Island
Coulter, Catherine
Viking lords series (1)
Lord of lances
Acres, Mark
Combat Command series (7)
Lord of misrule
Jones, Gareth
Misrule series (1)
Lord of nightmares
Cole, Adrian
Dream Lords trilogy (2)
Lord of Raven's Peak
Coulter, Catherine
Viking lords series (2)
Lord of Ravensley
Heaven, Constance
Oliver Aylsham series (1)
Lord of Shadow Keep
Johnson, Oliver
Golden dragon fantasy gamebooks series (3)
Lord of terror
Horler, Sydney
Paul Vivanti series (5)
Lord of the apes
Effinger, George Alec
Planet of the Apes series (9)
Lord of the Black Boar
Wiat, Philippa
Black Boar series (2)
Lord of the chariots
Capon, Paul
Artor series (3)
Lord of the crooked paths
Adkins, Patrick H
Titans series (1)
Lord of the dance
Greeley, Andrew Moran
Passover trilogy (3)
Lord of the Green Planet
Petaja, Emil
Green Planet series (1)
Lord of the horizon
Grant, Joan
Ra-ab Hotep series (2)
Lord of the Lances
Acres, Mark
Janisseries trilogy (3)
Lord of the lightning
Leighton, Edward
Muvian series (3)
Lord of the Nile
Danielson, Peter
Children of the Lion series (6)
Lord of the plains
Silver, Alfred
Red River trilogy (2)
Lord of the Rings
Tolkien, John Ronald Reuel
Lord of the Rings trilogy (3)
Middle Earth series (5)
Lord of the shadows
Kirk, Richard
Raven series (4)
Lord of the sorcerors
Dickson, Carter
Sir Henry Merrivale series (17)
Lord of the Spiders
Moorcock, Michael
Warrior of Mars trilogy (2)
Lord of the trees
Farmer, Philip Jose
Lord Grandith series (2)
Lord of the troll-bats
Gilliland, Alexis Arnaldus
Wizenbeak trilogy (3)
Lord of the Wolf
Wiat, Philippa
Black Boar series (7)
Lord of thunder
Norton, Andre
Arzor series (3)
Lord of Wensley
Raymond, Ernest
London gallery series (14)
Lord or Terror
Allain, Marcel
Fantomas series (9)
Lord Peter
Sayers, Dorothy Leigh
Lord Peter Wimsey series (16)
Lord Peter views the body
Sayers, Dorothy Leigh
Lord Peter Wimsey series (5)
Lord Samarkand
Vachell, Horace Annesley
Harrow School series (3)
Lord Stranleigh abroad
Barr, Robert
Lord Stranleigh series (4)
Lord Stranleigh, philanthropist
Barr, Robert
Lord Stranleigh series (3)
Lord Tedric
Smith, Edward Elmer
Lord Tedric series (1)
Lord Timothy Dexter of Newburyport, Mass.
Marquand, John Phillips
Timothy Dexter series (1)
Lord Tony's wife
Orczy, Emmuska
Scarlet Pimpernel series (8)
Lord Valentine's castle
Silverberg, Robert
Majipoor trilogy (1)
Lordly isle
Duncan, Kathleen Mary
Saxonhill series (2)
Lords and ladies
Pratchett, Terry
Discworld series (14)
Lord's anointed
McKee, Ruth Eleanor
Hawaii series (1)
Lords of darkness
Lee, Tanith
Tales from the flat earth series (3)
Lords of destruction
Silke, James R
Death dealer series (2)
Lords of doom
Niles, Douglas
Advanced dungeons and dragons adventure gamebook series (7)
DragonLance series (2)
Lords of misrule
Tranter, Nigel Godwin
Stuart series (1)
Lords of Serpent Land
Connell, Alan
Serpent Land trilogy (1)
Lords of the Crimson River
Lord, Jeffrey
Richard Blade series (35)
Lords of the earth
Murphy, Warren Burton
Destroyer series (61)
Lords of the middle dark
Chalker, Jack Laurence
Rings of the master series (1)
Lords of the Red Lattice
Dodd, Catherine Isabel
Red Lattice series (1)
Lords of the starship
Geston, Mark Symington
Havengore series (1)
Lords of the Stoney Mountains
Swithin, Antony
Perilous quest for Lyonesse series (2)
Lords of the sword
Cook, Hugh
Chronicles of an age of darkness series (4)
Lords of the triple moons
Mayhar, Ardath
House of Enthala trilogy (1)
Lords of the wild
Altsheler, Joseph Alexander
French and Indian war series (5)
Lords of Thlassa Mey
McCarty, Dennis
Thlassa Mey series (3)
Lord's prayer
Davidson, Alice Joyce
Alice in Bibleland series (24)
Lore of the wild witch
Norton, Andre
Witch World series (12)
Loretta P Sweeny, where are you?
Giff, Patricia Reilly
Abby Jones series (3)
Lori Adams and the adopted rebel
Palmer, Bernard
Lori Adams series (2)
Lori Adams and the jungle search
Palmer, Bernard
Lori Adams series (4)
Lori Adams and the Old Carter House mystery
Palmer, Bernard
Lori Adams series (1)
Lori Adams and the river boat mystery
Palmer, Bernard
Lori Adams series (3)
Lorimer legacy
Melville, Anne
Lorimer family series (2)
Lorimer line
Melville, Anne
Lorimer family series (1)
Lorimer loyalties
Melville, Anne
Lorimer family series (6)
Lorimers at war
Melville, Anne
Lorimer family series (3)
Lorimers in love
Melville, Anne
Lorimer family series (4)
Loring mystery
Farnol, Jeffery
Mister Jasper Shrig of Bow Street series (3)
Lormes of Castle Rising
Cradock, Fanny
Lorme family series (1)
Lorna at Wynyards
Brent-Dyer, Elinor Mary
Lorna series (1)
Lorna Doone
Blackmore, Richard Doddridge
Lorna Doone series (1)
Lorraine
Chambers, Robert William
Franco-Prussian war trilogy (1)
Los Angeles holocaust
Barry, Mike
Burton Wulff series (8)
Los Olvidados
McCurtin, Peter
Sundance series (30)
Lose this gun
Janson, Hank
Hank Janson series (40)
Loser
Deal, Borden
Bookman trilogy (1)
Losers
Gilman, George G
Adam Steele series (10)
Losers and winners
Miller, Frances Abbott
Losers and winners series (2)
Losers in space
Stine, Robert Lawrence
Space cadets series (2)
Losers take all
Lamb, J J
Zack Rolfe series (3)
Losing control
Cooney, Linda A
Totally hot series (1)
Losing fight
Chambers, Rosamund Mary
Napoleon and Josephine series (2)
Chambers, Rosemary Mary
Little Creole series (2)
Losing game
Crofts, Freeman Wills
Inspector Joseph French series (22)
Loss of a head
Bude, John
Inspector Meredith series (5)
Loss of innocence
Hill, Meredith
Chrystal Falls series (5)
Loss of patients
McInerny, Ralph
Father Roger Dowling series (7)
Loss of the Jane Vosper
Crofts, Freeman Wills
Inspector Joseph French series (14)
Lost
Brady, William S
Peacemaker series (8)
Lost and found
Baer, Judy
Cedar River daydreams series (15)
Jessel, Camilla
Chatterbooks series (6)
Lehrer, Jim
One-Eyed Mack series (4)
Mogenson, Jan
Ted series (4)
Trueman, Brian
Stories from Cockleshell Bay series (6)
Lost, and never found
Larsen, Anita
Lost series (1)
Lost, and never found II
Larsen, Anita
Lost series (2)
Lost and the lurking
Wellman, Manly Wade
Silver John series (4)
Lost at sea
Alger, Horatio
Rise in life series (6)
Pascal, Francine
Sweet Valley High series (56)
Lost at the South Pole
Dixon, Franklin W
Ted Scott flying series (11)
Lost ballerina
Edwards, Sylvia
Sally Baxter series (12)
Lost battalion
Stine, George Harry
Warbots series (6)
Lost bay
Sperber, Manes
Doino Faber trilogy (3)
Lost bomb
Allison, Clyde
Agent triple zero eight series (10)
Lost borders
Austin, Mary
Californian Indian series (3)
Lost buckaroo
Lomax, Bliss
Rainbow Ripley series (2)
Lost Cabin Mine
Niven, Frederick
Lost Cabin Mine series (1)
Lost campers
Hutchens, Paul
Sugar Creek Gang series (4)
Lost Chittendens
Carter, Nicholas
Nicholas Carter series (281)
Lost city
Blaine, John
Rick Brant series (2)
Garron, Marco
Azan series (2)
Lost city of Uranus
Greene, Joseph
Dig Allen series (6)
Lost city of Zork
Bailey, Robin Wayne
Zork series (4)
Lost colony
Randle, Kevin
Jefferson's war series (3)
Lost continent of Mu
Churchward, James
Mu series (1)
Lost crowns of Cair Paravel
Lientz, Gerald
Narnia solo games series (4)
Lost daughter
Cormany, Michael
Dan Kruger series (1)
Lost Dorsai
Dickson, Gordon Rupert
Dorsai series (6)
Lost Dragon
Ellis, Edward Sylvester
Automobile series (2)
Lost Dutchman's Mine
Giraud, Jean
Lieutenant Mike S Blueberry series (10)
Lost emeralds of Black Howe
Finlay, Winifred
Judith Norton series (5)
Lost expedition
Sayer, Walter William
Sexton Blake series (307)
Lost farm
Curry, Jane Louise
Maccubbin family series (2)
Lost fight
Prescott, Hilda Frances Margaret
Mediaeval France trilogy (2)
Lost fisherman of Carrigmor
Lynch, Patricia
Brogeen the leprechaun series (10)
Lost forest
McMahan, Ian
Mikrokid mystery series (4)
Lost gallows
Carr, John Dickson
Henri Bencolin series (3)
Lost giant
Robeson, Kenneth
Doc Savage series (100)
Lost girl
Boswell, John
Christopher Kent series (2)
Lost gods
Price, Roger
Tomorrow people series (5)
Lost half hour
Meynell, Laurence Walter
Hooky Hefferman series (11)
Lost hunters
Altsheler, Joseph Alexander
Great West series (2)
Lost illusions
Balzac, Honore de
Scenes of provincial life series (9)
Lost in a Sugar Creek blizzard
Hutchens, Paul
Sugar Creek Gang series (17)
Lost in America
Singer, Isaac Bashevis
Love and exile trilogy (3)
Lost in Blunderland
Lewis, Caroline
Alice in Wonderland parodies series (2)
Lost in Cambodia
Graydon, William Murray
Sexton Blake series (237)

Lost in space files
Peel, John
Lost in space files series (4)
Lost in space technical manual
Messmann, Richard R
Lost in space files series (4)
Lost in space tribute book
Van Hise, James
Lost in space files series (4)
Lost in space twenty fifth annivesary tribute book
Van Hise, James
Lost in space files series (4)
Lost in the Amazon
Quackenbush, Robert Mead
Miss Mallard series (14)
Lost in the blinded blizzard
Erickson, John R
Hank the cowdog series (16)
Lost in the caves of gold
Moore, Fenworth
Jerry Ford series (2)
Lost in the dark enchanted forest
Erickson, John R
Hank the cowdog series (11)
Lost in the Devil's Desert
Skurzynski, Gloria
Mountain west series (1)
Lost in the fog
De Mille, James
Brethren of the White Cross series (3)
Lost in the forbidden land
Ellis, Edward Sylvester
Foreign adventure trilogy (1)
Lost in the forest
Ballantyne, Robert Michael
Wandering Will trilogy (2)
Lost in the fur country
Lange, Dietrich
American Indian series (3)
Lost in the Milky Way
Byrne, Stuart James
Star Man series (2)
Lost in the outback
Power, Phyllis Mary
Hannah Maine series (1)
Lost in the storm
Carrick, Carol
Sleep out series (2)
Lost in the wilderness
Jayne, R H
War whoop series (1)
Lost in the wilds
Ellis, Edward Sylvester
Great river series (3)
Lost in time
Smith, Mark
Falcon series (4)
Lost in Umbagog
Allen, Willis Boyd
Camp and tramp series (1)
Lost jewels of Nabooti
Montgomery, Raymond A
Choose your own adventure series (10)
Lost Keats
Faherty, Terence
Owen Keane series (1)
Lost king
Weis, Margaret
Star of the guardians series (1)
Lost king of Oz
Thompson, Ruth Plumly
Oz series (18)
Lost Kinnellan
Mackenzie, Agnes Mure
Kinnellan series (1)
Lost koala
Macpherson, Bruce
Jenny and Sue series (1)
Lost lady
Deveraux, Jude
James River trilogy (2)
Lost lady of Laramie
Willoughby, Lee Davis
Women who won the West series (4)
Lost ladybirds
Gilmore, David Hunter
Christopher Cricket series (1)
Lost legacy
Stackpole, Michael
Blood of Kerensky trilogy (3)
Lost legend of Finn
Tannen, Mary
Finn series (2)
Lost locket
Keene, Carolyn
Nancy Drew notebooks series (2)
Lost love found
Small, Beatrice
Skye O'Malley series (5)
Lost love, last love
Rogers, Rosemary
Ginny Brandon and Steve Morgan series (3)
Lost man's lane
Green, Anna Katharine
Amelia Butterworth series (2)
Ebenezer Gryce series (8)
Lost mine
Evans, Tabor
Longarm series (142)
Lost mine of the Amazon
Lloyd, Hugh
Hal Keen series (9)
Lost naval papers
Copplestone, Bennet
Chief Inspector Dawson series (1)
Lost ninja
Leibold, Jay
Choose your own adventure series (113)
Lost oasis
Robeson, Kenneth
Doc Savage series (6)
Lost on Jupiter
Gilmour, William
Martian series (12)
Lost on the Amazon
Montgomery, Raymond A
Choose your own adventure series (24)
Lost on the moon
Rockwood, Roy
Great marvel series (5)
Lost on the Orinoco
Stratemeyer, Edward L
Pan-American series (1)
Lost on Venus
Burroughs, Edgar Rice
Venus series (2)
Lost over Greenland
Stone, Richard H
Slim Tyler series (2)
Lost paradise
Chotzinoff, Samuel
Lost paradise series (1)
Lost patrol
Sharpe, Jon
Trailsman series (38)
Lost pearl
Grierson, Francis Durham
Inspector Sims and Professor Wells series (3)
Lost planet
Black, Christopher
Star challenge series (8)
Macvicar, Angus
Jeremy Grant series (1)
Lost pony
Pullein-Thompson, Christine
David and Pat series (4)
Lost prince
Zimmer, Paul Edwin
Dark border series (1)
Lost princess of Oz
Baum, Lyman Frank
Oz series (11)
Lost property
Dicks, Terrance
Bears series (1)
Lost provinces
Tracy, Louis
Vansittart series (2)
Lost railway
Avery, Gillian
Onlookers series (1)
Lost rifle
Adams, Henry Cadwallader
Nethercourt series (4)
Lost River loot
Cole, Jackson
Jim Hatfield series (89)
Lost road
Scoggins, Charles Elbert
Colin O'Leary series (2)
Lost road, and other writings
Tolkien, John Ronald Reuel
History of Middle Earth series (5)
Lost Sahara trail
Kaufmann, Herbert
Captain Gevert series (1)
Lost silver of Langdon
Finlay, Winifred
Judith Norton series (4)
Lost souls of the twilight
Parry, Anne Spencer
Bara quartet (2)
Lost speech of Abraham Lincoln
Morrow, Honore Willsie
Abraham Lincoln series (3)
Lost squadron
Cook, Canfield
Lucky Terrell series (4)
Lost swords, the first triad
Saberhagen, Fred
Book of lost swords series (3)
Lost swords, the second triad
Saberhagen, Fred
Book of lost swords series (6)
Lost tar
Samuels, Adelaide Florence
Dick Travers series (2)
Lost tower treasure
Clewes, Dorothy
Hadley family series (5)
Lost trail!
Ellis, Edward Sylvester
Log cabin series (1)
Lost traveller
White, Antonia
Frost in May series (2)
Lost treasure cave
McNeil, Everett
Davy Crockett series (1)
Lost treasure of Wales
Roose-Evans, James
Odd and Elsewhere series (7)
Lost tribe
Aronin, Ben
Raphael Drale series (1)
Edwards, George
Golden boomerang series (4)
Foley, Louise Munro
Choose your own adventure series (23)
Lost trooper
Mundy, Talbot
Jimgrim series (7)
Lost uranium mine
Bamman, Henry A
World of adventure series (1)
Lost valley
Hawton, Hector
Colonel Max Masterson series (4)
Lost valley of Iskander
Howard, Robert Ervin
El Borak trilogy (1)
Lost Vikings
Bechdolt, Jack
Barrow brothers series (5)
Lost violin
Judson, Clara Ingram
They came from series (6)
Lost Wallowa, 1869-1879
Gulick, Bill
Northwest destiny trilogy (3)
Lost weekend
Jackson, Charles Reginald
Don Birman series (2)
Lost wild America
McClung, Robert Marshall
Endangered animals series (7)
Lost wild worlds
McClung, Robert Marshall
Endangered animals series (7)
Lost with Lieutenant Pike
Sabin, Edward Legrand
Trail blazers series (11)
Lost without trace
Cobb, Belton
Bryan Armitage series (12)
Inspector Cheviot Burmann series (36)
Kitty Armitage series (9)
Lost wizard
Gray, Michael
Fantasy forest series (10)
Lost world
Doyle, Arthur Conan
Professor Challenger series (1)
Jennison, John William
Thunderbirds series (5)
Lost world of the Kalahari
Van der Post, Laurens
Kalahari series (1)
Lost worlds of Cronus
Kapp, Colin
Cageworld series (2)
Lost worlds of 2001
Clarke, Arthur Charles
Space odyssey series (3)
Lost years
Dillard, Jeanne M
Star trek sequels series (7)
Lost yesterday
Sapir, Richard
Destroyer series (65)
Lot forty one, dead auctioneer
Symons, Maurice
George Roberts series (3)
Lot of Bod
Cole, Michael
Bod series (12)
Lots more tell and draw stories
Oldfield, Margaret Jean
Tell and draw series (4)
Lots of animals
Campbell, Rod
Little people series (7)
Lotta
Lindgren, Astrid
Marten family series (2)
Lotta leaves home
Lindgren, Astrid
Marten family series (2)
Lotta on Troublemaker Street
Lindgren, Astrid
Marten family series (2)
Lotta's bike
Lindgren, Astrid
Marten family series (1)
Lotta's Christmas surprise
Lindgren, Astrid
Marten family series (3)
Lotta's Easter surprise
Lindgren, Astrid
Marten family series (4)
Lottery of death
Wales, Mike
Leatherhand series (3)
Lottery ticket
Trowbridge, John Townsend
Start in life series (6)
Lottie Lie-Alot
Watson, Jean
Alot series (10)
Lottie Trago
Thompson, Ernest Victor
Retallick family series (6)
Lotus affair
Wells, Tobias
Detective Knute Severson series (9)
Lotus and the wind
Masters, John
Savage family series (4)
Lotus flower
Morgan de Groot, J
Lotus flower series (1)
Lotus leaves and larceny
Chambers, Philip
Sexton Blake series (1511)
Lotus vellum
Hunt, Charlotte
Doctor Paul Holton series (3)
Lou in the limelight
Hunter, Kristin
Lourette Hawkins series (2)
Louanne Pig in making the team
Carlson, Nancy
Louanne Pig series (2)
Louanne Pig in the mysterious valentine
Carlson, Nancy
Louanne Pig series (5)
Louanne Pig in the perfect family
Carlson, Nancy
Louanne Pig series (1)
Louanne Pig in the talent show
Carlson, Nancy
Louanne Pig series (4)
Louanne Pig in Witch Lady
Carlson, Nancy
Louanne Pig series (3)
Loud adios
Kuhlken, Ken
Tom Hickey trilogy (1)
Loud halo
Beckwith, Lillian
Hebrides series (4)
Loud Mouth
Ure, Jean
Woodside School series (2)
Loudmouth George and the big race
Carlson, Nancy
Loudmouth George series (3)
Loudmouth George and the cornet
Carlson, Nancy
Loudmouth George series (2)
Loudmouth George and the fishing trip
Carlson, Nancy
Loudmouth George series (1)
Loudmouth George and the new neighbors
Carlson, Nancy
Loudmouth George series (4)
Loudmouth George and the sixth-grade bully
Carlson, Nancy
Loudmouth George series (5)
Louie
Keats, Ezra Jack
Louie series (1)
Louie Maude
Sherman, Helen
Louie Maude series (1)
Louie Maude and the caravan
Sherman, Helen
Louie Maude series (3)
Louie Maude and the Mary Ann
Sherman, Helen
Louie Maude series (4)
Louie's lot
Hildick, Edmund Wallace
Louie series (1)
Louie's ransom
Hildick, Edmund Wallace
Louie series (4)
Louie's S.O.S.
Hildick, Edmund Wallace
Louie series (2)
Louie's search
Keats, Ezra Jack
Louie series (3)
Louie's snowstorm
Hildick, Edmund Wallace
Louie series (3)
Louis Bromfield at Malabar
Bromfield, Louis
Malabar series (4)
Louis Lambert
Balzac, Honore de
Philosophic studies series (19)
Louis Napoleon and the Second Empire
Thompson, James Matthew
French history trilogy (3)
Louis the Well-Beloved
Plaidy, Jean
Louis XV trilogy (2)
Louisa Elliot
Roberts, Ann Victoria
Louisa Elliot series (1)
Louisa Vandervoord
Gaye, Phoebe Fenwich
Vandervoord trilogy (2)
Louise
Moss, Merrilee
Hot pursuit series (3)
Shears, Sarah
Louise trilogy (1)
Louise and Barnavaux
Mille, Pierre
Barnavaux series (2)
Louise and Mister Tudor
Glover, Halcott
Louise trilogy (2)
Louise builds a boat
Pfanner, Louise
Louise series (2)
Louise builds a house
Pfanner, Louise
Louise series (1)
Louise de la Valliere
Dumas, Alexandre
Three Musketeers series (3)
Louise in London
Glover, Halcott
Louise trilogy (3)
Louise, the restless
Kimbrough, Katheryn
Phenwick women series (24)
Louise's daughters
Shears, Sarah
Louise trilogy (2)
Louise's inheritance
Shears, Sarah
Louise trilogy (3)
Louisiana
Denuziere, Maurice
Clarence Dandridge series (1)
Ross, Dana Fuller
Wagons West series (16)
Louisiana blue
Poyer, David
Tiller Galloway series (3)
Louisiana firestorm
McCray, Mike
Black Berets series (5)
Louisiana gold race
Sharpe, Jon
Canyon O'Grady series (23)
Louisiana lass
Fletcher, Dirk
Spur McCoy series (33)
Lourdes
Zola, Emile
Abbe Pierre Fremont trilogy (1)
Louse for the hangman
Bruce, Leo
Carolus Deene series (5)
Lovable Lyle
Waber, Bernard
Lyle series (4)
Lovable outlaw
Williamson, Geoffrey
Silva d'Croy series (1)
Love
Aminoff, Constance Leonie Caroline
Napoleonic series (2)
Love affair
Zola, Emile
Rougon Macquart series (8)

Love affairs of Pixie
Vaizey, Jessie Bell
Pixie O'Shaughnessy series (3)
Love-all
Leasor, James
Doctor Jason Love series (6)
Love alters not
Veryan, Patricia
Golden chronicles series (4)
Love among the artists
Shaw, George Bernard
Nonage series (3)
Love among the butterflies
Fountaine, Margaret
Victorian lady series (1)
Love among the chickens
Wodehouse, Pelham Grenville
Ukridge series (1)
Love among the daughters
Huxley, Elspeth
Kenya childhood series (3)
Love among the ruins
Thirkell, Angela
Barsetshire series (17)
Love and betrayal and hold the mayo!
Pascal, Francine
Love series (2)
Victoria Martin trilogy (3)
Love and death in London
Pascal, Francine
Sweet Valley High series (104)
Love and dreams
Hagan, Patricia
Coltrane series (6)
Love and exile
Singer, Isaac Bashevis
Love and exile trilogy (3)
Love and friendship
Rolland, Romain
John Christopher series (4)
Love and fury
Hagan, Patricia
Coltrane series (4)
Love and games
Keene, Carolyn
River Heights series (14)
Love and glory
Hagan, Patricia
Coltrane series (2)
Love and honor
Arlen, Leslie
Borodin family series (1)
Hagan, Patricia
Coltrane series (7)
Love and honour
Arlen, Leslie
Borodin family series (1)
Love and joy in the Mabillon
Glyn, Caroline
Winston series (2)
Love and lamentation
Janson, Hank
Hank Janson series (152)
Love and liberty
Dumas, Alexandre
Nelson in Naples series (2)
Love and Mary Ann
Cookson, Catherine
Mary Ann Shaughnessy series (4)
Love and money
Bentley, Phyllis
West Riding series (14)
Love and peace
Payne, Robert
Lifeng, Shaofeng and Rose series (1)
Love and Sir Launcelot
Gordon, Richard
Doctor series (10)
Love and splendor
Hagan, Patricia
Coltrane series (5)
Love and the land beyond
Leasor, James
Doctor Jason Love series (8)
Love and the loveless
Williamson, Henry
Chronicles of ancient sunlight series (7)
Love and the waiting game
Watmough, David
Davey Bryant series (2)
Love and triumph
Hagan, Patricia
Coltrane series (8)
Love and war
Hagan, Patricia
Coltrane series (1)
Jakes, John
North and South trilogy (2)
Weis, Margaret
DragonLance tales trilogy (3)

Love at all ages
Thirkell, Angela
Barsetshire series (28)
Love at second sight
Leverson, Ada
Edith Ottley trilogy (3)
Love, Avalon
Wright, Steve
Barry Donovan series (1)
Love besieged
Pearce, Charles Edward
Indian mutiny trilogy (1)
Love bet
Pascal, Francine
Sweet Valley High series (68)
Love, blood and tears
Weaver, Nicky
Nicky Weaver series (1)
Love Bug
Cebulash, Mel
Herbie series (1)
Love Bugg
Cosgrove, Stephen Edward
Bugg series (8)
Love burning bright
Hunt, Angela Elwell
Cassie Perkins series (6)
Love-child
Carr, Philippa
Daughters of England series (6)
Love comes by ambulance
Cooper, Lisa
Princess Beatrice Hospital series (7)
Love comes softly
Oke, Janette
Davis family series (1)
Love comes to Keith Partridge
Stanton, Vance
Partridge family series (8)
Love-death thing
Dewey, Thomas Blanchard
Private Eye Mac series (16)
Love down under
Leasor, James
Doctor Jason Love series (10)
Love duel
Gladstone, Maggie
Lacebridge ladies series (2)
Love episode
Zola, Emile
Rougon Macquart series (8)
Love exchange
Cooper, M E
Couples series (25)
Love feast
Buechner, Frederick
Leo Bebb tetralogy (3)
Love finds Doctor Starr
Johnston, William
Doctor Starr series (3)
Love for all time
Small, Beatrice
Skye O'Malley series (4)
Love for sale
Corrigan, Mark
Mark Corrigan and McLean series (14)
Love for the Baron
Morton, Anthony
Baron series (47)
Love from Belinda
Evans, Cherry
Belinda and Lalage series (1)
Love from Elizabeth
Fitt, Mary
Superintendent Mallett series (16)
Love from Mick and Mandy
Schmidt, Annie Maria Geertruida
Bob and Jilly series (3)
Love from the fifth grade celebrity
Giff, Patricia Reilly
Casey Valentine series (6)
Love gilds the scene and women guide the plot
Castle, Agnes
Beau Nash regime romance series (4)
Love has no alibi
Cohen, Octavus Roy
Max Gold series (2)
Love in a cold climate
Mitford, Nancy
Love trilogy (2)
Love in a dry season
Foote, Shelby
Lake Jordan series (3)
Love in Amsterdam
Freeling, Nicolas
Inspector Piet Van der Valk series (1)

Love in Easingden
Sinclair, John George
Easingden series (2)
Love in Emergency Ward 10
Falla, Roger
Emergency Ward 10 series (2)
Love in the doghouse
Bishop, Mary
Vet's wife series (2)
Love in the ruins
Percy, Walker
Doctor Tom More series (1)
Love in the sun
Walmsley, Leo
Phantom Lobster series (5)
Love in the temperate zone
Wright, Laurali R
Sergeant Karl Alberg series (3)
Love in winter
Jameson, Storm
Hervey Russell series (4)
Mirror in darkness trilogy (2)
Love is a blanket word
Arundel, Honor
Janet Meredith series (2)
Love is a deadly weapon
Quentin, Patrick
Peter Duluth series (5)
Love is a three-letter word
Johnston, William
Room 222 series (3)
Love is blue
Wyndham, Joan
Love diary series (2)
Love is forever
Bell, Margaret Elizabeth
Florence Monroe series (3)
Love is hell
Groening, Matt
Life in hell series (1)
Love Lane
Snaith, John Collis
Love Lane series (1)
Love lessons
Wyndham, Joan
Love diary series (1)
Love letters
Pascal, Francine
Sweet Valley High series (17)
Love letters for sale
Pascal, Francine
Sweet Valley High series (88)
Love letters of an Anzac
Hogue, Oliver
Anzac series (1)
Love lies a loss
Fitzgibbon, Theodora
With love series (2)
Love, lies and Jessica Wakefield
Pascal, Francine
Sweet Valley University series (2)
Love lies bleeding
Crispin, Edmund
Gervase Fen series (5)
Love lost
Campbell, Joanna
Caitlin trilogy (2)
Pascal, Francine
Love trilogy (2)
Love machine
Comstock, Jarrod
These lawless worlds series (1)
Love Maggy
Barcynska, Helena Margareta
Honey-pot series (2)
Love makers
Janson, Hank
Hank Janson series (153)
Love me a little
Vail, Amanda
Emily and Amy series (1)
Love me deadly
Elfman, Blossom
Mike and Ally series (1)
Love me in death
Olsen, D B
Professor A Pennyfeather series (5)
Love me little, love me long
Reade, Charles
David Dodd and Lucy Fountain series (1)
Love me, love my werewolf
Roos, Stephen
Pet Lovers Club series (1)
Love me, Marietta
Wilde, Jennifer
Marietta Danvers series (2)
Love me to death
Kirk, Philip
Butler series (5)

Love medicine
Erdrich, Louise
Argus series (1)
Love nest
Coburn, Andrew
Rita Gardella O'Dea series (2)
Love of her life
Pascal, Francine
Sweet Valley University series (6)
Love of Philip Hampden
Winter, John Strange
Blankhampton series (10)
Love on a lead
Lloyd-Jones, Buster
Vet series (3)
Love on my list
Tibber, Robert
General practitioner series (2)
Love on the Don
Konsalik, Heinz Gunther
Love on the Don series (2)
Love on the range
Powers, Louise E
Swept away series (3)
Love only once
Lindsey, Johanna
Anthony Mallory series (1)
Love or glory
Joyce, Rosemary
Dream girls series (2)
Love or kill them all
Weaver, Nicky
Nicky Weaver series (2)
Love potion
Becker, Eve
Abracadabra series (2)
Pascal, Francine
Sweet Valley twins series (72)
Love respelt
Graves, Robert
Love respelt series (1)
Love respelt again
Graves, Robert
Love respelt series (3)
Love riddle
Kenneth, Claire
Cynthia Doanides series (1)
Love scenes
Pfeffer, Susan Beth
Make me a star series (5)
Love secretaries
Janson, Hank
Hank Janson series (184)
Love siege
Wakefield, Tom
Margaret Davis and Isobel Quirk trilogy (3)
Love so bold
Kamada, Annelise
Love so bold series (1)
Love song for Joyce
Kerry, Lois
Joyce series (1)
Love storm
Johnson, Susan
Kuzan family trilogy (2)
Love story
Segal, Erich
Oliver and Jenny series (1)
Love struck
Cooper, M E
Couples series (28)
Love talker
Peters, Elizabeth
Jacqueline Kirby series (3)
Love taps gently
Lambert, Janet
Jordons series (5)
Love, tears and dreams
Witcomb, Nan
Thoughts of Nanushka series (7)
Love that kills
Levitsky, Ronald
Nate Rosen series (1)
Love times three
Keene, Carolyn
River Heights series (1)
Love to spare
Lambert, Janet
Cinda Hollister series (5)
Love you to death
Savage, Jack
Dempsey and Makepeace series (6)
Loveleaves returns to the bush
O'Harris, Pixie
Loveleaves series (2)
Loveleaves the koala
O'Harris, Pixie
Loveleaves series (1)
Lovely
Meltzer, David
Brain plant series (1)

Lovely but dangerous
Daniel, Roland
Michael Wallace series (1)
Lovely, but lethal!
Saxon, Peter
Sexton Blake series (1527)
Lovely corpse
Cumberland, Marten
Saturnin Dax series (7)
Lovely in her bones
McCrumb, Sharon
Elizabeth Macpherson series (2)
Lovely ladies
Freeling, Nicolas
Inspector Piet Van der Valk series (9)
Lovely lady
Corrigan, Mark
Mark Corrigan and McLean series (3)
Lovely ship
Jameson, Storm
Triumph of time trilogy (1)
Lovely wanton
Fecher, Constance
Ralegh family trilogy (3)
Lover
Brown, Carter
Lieutenant Al Wheeler series (11)
Janson, Hank
Hank Janson series (154)
Lover boy
Berenstain, Stan
Lover boy series (1)
Lover, don't come back!
Brown, Carter
Danny Boyd series (9)
Lover next door
Alldritt, Keith
Black country series (2)
Lover, say it with mink!
Lee, Norma
Beautiful Gunner series (2)
Lover scorned
Holland, Isabelle
Claire Aldington series (3)
Lover too many
Lewis, Royston
Inspector John Crow series (1)
Lovers
Payne, Robert
Lifeng, Shaofeng and Rose series (2)
Lovers and other killers
Anderson, James
Jessica Fletcher series (4)
Lovers and outlaws
Nicole, Christopher
New Americans series (2)
Lovers are never losers
Giono, Jean
Trilogy of earth (2)
Lover's feud
Finney, R C
Inspector Bourne series (7)
Lovers in Acadia
Roberts, Charles George Douglas
Acadia series (2)
Lovers in war
Spencer, Colin
Simpson family series (3)
Lovers, make moan
Mitchell, Gladys
Dame Beatrice Bradley series (60)
Lovers' meeting
Mackenzie, Lee
Emmerdale Farm series (4)
Lovers of the market place
Dehan, Richard
Market place series (2)
Lover's tale
Hewlett, Maurice
Sagas retold series (1)
Love's abiding joy
Oke, Janette
Davis family series (4)
Loves and ambitions
Naglerowa, Herminia
Krauzes and others trilogy (1)
Love's detective
Landis, James David
Sisters impossible series (2)
Love's duet
Veryan, Patricia
Age of Elegance series (2)
Love's enduring promise
Oke, Janette
Davis family series (2)
Love's fragile flame
Caggiano, Phyllis
Rose series (1)

Love's labour's won
Fisher, Edward
Silver falcon trilogy (2)
Love's long journey
Oke, Janette
Davis family series (3)
Loves of Caroline Cherie
Saint-Laurent, Cecil
Cherie series (2)
Loves of Catrin
Gower, Iris
Catrin series (2)
Love's pilgrimage
Caggiano, Phyllis
Rose series (2)
Love's prisoner
Finney, R C
Inspector Bourne series (11)
Love's shadow
Leverson, Ada
Edith Ottley trilogy (1)
Love's tender fury
Wilde, Jennifer
Marietta Danvers series (1)
Love's unending legacy
Oke, Janette
Davis family series (5)
Love's wine
Hagan, Patricia
Coltrane series (3)
Lovesong
Sherwood, Valerie
Carolina Lightfoot trilogy (1)
Lovestruck
Pascal, Francine
Sweet Valley High series (27)
Lovey Mary
Rice, Alice Hegan
Mrs Wiggs series (2)
Loving
Campbell, Joanna
Caitlin trilogy (1)
Pascal, Francine
Love trilogy (1)
Loving and living
Witcomb, Nan
Thoughts of Nanushka series (2)
Loving and the dead
Brown, Carter
Mavis Seidlitz series (4)
Loving cup
Graham, Winston
Poldark series (10)
Wynne, Anthony
Doctor Eustace Hailey series (16)
Loving Emma
Foxell, Nigel
Emma Hamilton series (1)
Loving imprint
Breese, Andrea
Setting out series (2)
Loving Jack
Roberts, Nora
Flowers series (42)
Loving Jonathan Jones
Berg, Leila
Steep Street series (3)
Loving maid
Jahoda, Gloria
Bickley family series (1)
Loving mistress
Friedman, Rosemary
Mistress and wife series (1)
Loving two is hard to do
Lewis, Linda
Linda series (9)
Low company
Benney, Mark
Low company series (1)
Fuchs, Daniel
Williamsburg trilogy (3)
Low dive for Lola
Brody, Marc
Marc Brody series (79)
Low treason
Tourney, Leonard
Matthew Stock series (2)
Lower, higher, you're a liar!
Chaikin, Miriam
Molly series (4)
Lower view
O'Connor, Philip
Lower view series (2)
Lowlife
Baron, Alexander
Harryboy Boas series (1)
Lowly Worm cars and trucks book
Scarry, Richard
Lowly Worm series (5)
Lowly Worm coloring book
Scarry, Richard
Lowly Worm series (4)
Lowspeak
Morton, James
Lowspeak series (1)
Lowspeak 2
Morton, James
Lowspeak series (2)
Loxfinger
Weinstein, Sol
Israel Bond series (1)
Loyal lass
Blanchard, Amy Ella
Revolutionary War series (5)
Loyal little maid
Robinson, Edith
Little Puritan series (1)
Loyal rebel
Gibbs, George
Old Philadelphia series (1)
Lucia in London
Benson, Edward Frederic
Lucia Billson series (2)
Lucia in wartime
Holt, Tom
Lucia Billson series (8)
Lucia triumphant
Holt, Tom
Lucia Billson series (9)
Lucia's progress
Benson, Edward Frederic
Lucia Billson series (6)
Lucien's tombs
Rippon, Marion
Inspector Maurice Ygrec series (4)
Lucifer before sunrise
Williamson, Henry
Chronicles of ancient sunlight series (14)
Lucifer comet
Wallace, Ian
Croyd series (7)
Lucifer crusade
Maloney, Mack
Wingman series (3)
Lucifer Wilkins
Garfield, Leon
Tim and Pistol series (3)
Lucifer's weekend
Murphy, Warren Burton
Digger Burroughs series (4)
Lucille, bringer of joy
Duffield, Elizabeth M
Lucille series (3)
Lucille on the heights
Duffield, Elizabeth M
Lucille series (4)
Lucille, the torch bearer
Duffield, Elizabeth M
Lucille series (1)
Lucille triumphant
Duffield, Elizabeth M
Lucille series (2)
Lucinda and the painted bell
Fry, Rosalie Kingsmill
Lucinda series (1)
Lucinda and the sailor kitten
Fry, Rosalie Kingsmill
Lucinda series (2)
Lucinda's year of Jubilo
Sawyer, Ruth
Lucinda Wyman series (2)
Luck and pluck
Alger, Horatio
Luck and pluck series (1)
Luck of Barry Lyndon
Thackeray, William Makepeace
Barry Lyndon series (1)
Luck of Black Diamond
Murray, Michael
Timber Trail riders series (3)
Luck of Brin's Five
Wilder, Cherry
Torin trilogy (1)
Luck of Denewood
Knipe, Emilie Benson
Denewood series (4)
Luck of Huemac
Peters, Daniel
Pre-Columbian trilogy (1)
Luck of Lowry
Bacon, Josephine Dodge
Lowry series (1)
Luck of Rathcoole
Lincoln, Jeanie Gould
Wolcott family series (2)
Luck of Sallowby
Saville, Malcolm
Jillies series (5)
Luck of Study Thirteen
Havilton, Jeffrey
Study Thirteen series (1)
Luck of the Bodkins
Wodehouse, Pelham Grenville
Monty Bodkin series (1)
Luck of the Darrells
Murray, Andrew
Sexton Blake series (58)
Luck of the draw
Masters, Zeke
Faro Blake series (2)
Luck of the Dudley Grahams
Haines, Alice Calhoun
Dudley Graham series (1)
Luck of the Laird
Terhune, Albert Payson
Sunnybank collies series (13)
Luck of the Legion
Bond, Geoffrey
Sergeant Luck series (1)
Luck of the Legion's desert adventure
Bond, Geoffrey
Sergeant Luck series (5)
Luck of the Legion's secret mission
Bond, Geoffrey
Sergeant Luck series (4)
Luck of the Lynns
Green, Roger Lancelyn
Spearlake children series (2)
Luck of the Mounted
Kendall, Ralph Selwood
L Division series (2)
Luck of the wheels
Lindholm, Megan
Windsingers series (4)
Luck runs out
Macleod, Charlotte
Professor Peter Shandy series (2)
Luckiest day of your life
Packard, Edward
Choose your own adventure series (132)
Lucky
Collins, Jackie
Santangelo family series (2)
Lucky breaks loose
Hughes, Dean
Lucky Ladd series (2)
Lucky Bucky in Oz
Neill, John Rea
Oz series (35)
Lucky cat
Lockridge, Frances
Cats series (3)
Lucky country
Horne, Donald
Lucky country series (1)
Lucky country revisited
Horne, Donald
Lucky country series (3)
Lucky devil
Maling, Arthur
Brock Potter series (3)
Lucky dip
Ainsworth, Ruth
Lucky dip series (1)
Lucky dog days
Delton, Judy
Pee wee scout series (3)
Lucky fall
Paice, Margaret
Kathy Brown series (1)
Lucky fights back
Hughes, Dean
Lucky Ladd series (4)
Lucky for some
Mackenzie, Lee
Emmerdale Farm series (11)
Lucky Harry
Ridgway, Bill
Lucky Harry series (1)
Lucky Harry takes his time, and other stories
Ridgway, Bill
Lucky Harry series (2)
Lucky in love
Hughes, Dean
Lucky Ladd series (9)
Lucky Jake
Grover, Marshall
Larry and Stretch series (264)
Lucky Jane
Ames, Delano
Dagobert and Jane Brown series (12)
Lucky Lacey
Reynolds, Kay
Fortune's Friends series (2)
Lucky numbers
Glass, Montague
Potash series (5)
Lucky penny
Barnes, Linda
Carlotta Carlyle series (1)
Lucky Pierre
Endfield, Mercedes
Ms. Squad series (1)
Lucky policeman
Penny, Rupert
Chief Inspector Edward Beale series (4)
Lucky seventh
Barbour, Ralph Henry
Purple Pennant trilogy (1)
Lucky sixpence
Knipe, Emilie Benson
Denewood series (1)
Lucky socks
Davis, Gibbs
Never sink nine series (1)
Lucky Starr and the big sun of Mercury
French, Paul
David Starr series (4)
Lucky Starr and the moons of Jupiter
French, Paul
David Starr series (5)
Lucky Starr and the oceans of Venus
French, Paul
David Starr series (3)
Lucky Starr and the pirates of the asteroids
French, Paul
David Starr series (2)
Lucky Starr and the rings of Saturn
French, Paul
David Starr series (6)
Lucky stiff
Rice, Craig
John Joseph Malone series (8)
Lucky story book
Blyton, Enid
Story book series (6)
Lucky streak
Raymond, John
Dempsey and Makepeace series (3)
Lucky the detective
Hughes, Dean
Lucky Ladd series (7)
Lucky thirteen
Barnes, Megan
Teen witch series (1)
Lucky's cool club
Hughes, Dean
Lucky Ladd series (8)
Lucky's crash landing
Hughes, Dean
Lucky Ladd series (1)
Lucky's gold mine
Hughes, Dean
Lucky Ladd series (3)
Lucky's mud festival
Hughes, Dean
Lucky Ladd series (5)
Lucky's tricks
Hughes, Dean
Angel Park Hoop Stars series (2)
Lucky Ladd series (6)
Lucretia
Riefe, Barbara
Shackleford legacy trilogy (3)
Lucrezia Borgia
Plaidy, Jean
Lucrezia Borgia series (2)
Lucrezia Borgia's lover
Gaunt, Richard
Borgia series (5)
Lucy
Sadiq, Nazneen
Degrassi High School series (7)
Storr, Catherine
Lucy series (1)
Lucy and the babysitter
Jungman, Ann
Lucy series (3)
Lucy and the big bad wolf
Jungman, Ann
Lucy series (1)
Lucy and the wolf in sheep's clothing
Jungman, Ann
Lucy series (2)
Lucy and Tom at the seaside
Hughes, Shirley
Lucy and Tom series (3)
Lucy and Tom go to school
Hughes, Shirley
Lucy and Tom series (2)
Lucy and Tom's ABC
Hughes, Shirley
Lucy and Tom series (4)
Lucy and Tom's Christmas
Hughes, Shirley
Lucy and Tom series (4)
Lucy and Tom's day
Hughes, Shirley
Lucy and Tom series (1)
Lucy and Tom's 1-2-3
Hughes, Shirley
Lucy and Tom series (4)
Lucy Bettesworth
Bourne, George
Frederick Bettesworth series (3)
Lucy, beware
Sykes, Pamela
Lucy series (2)
Lucy, Edward's daughter
Dumas, Philippe
Edward series (2)
Lucy goes to playgroup
Border, Rosemary
Out and about series (6)
Lucy Hardinge
Cooper, James Fenimore
Miles Wallingford series (2)
Lucy helps in the garden
Border, Rosemary
Out and about series (1)
Lucy keeps the wolf from the door
Jungman, Ann
Lucy series (3)
Lucy Laugh-Alot
Watson, Jean
Alot series (8)
Lucy Lemon
Reed, Giles
Munch Bunch character series (12)
Lucy Mouse keeps a secret
Pilgrim, Jane
Blackberry Farm series (11)
Lucy runs away
Storr, Catherine
Lucy series (2)
Lucy takes the reins
Pascal, Francine
Sweet Valley twins series (45)
Lucy's Brownie road
Blathwayt, Jean
Brownie series (1)
Lucy's last Brownie challenge
Blathwayt, Jean
Brownie series (2)
Lud of Lunden
Mundy, Talbot
Tros of Samothrace series (1)
Ludell
Wilkinson, Brenda
Ludell Wilson trilogy (1)
Ludell and Willie
Wilkinson, Brenda
Ludell Wilson trilogy (2)
Ludell's New York time
Wilkinson, Brenda
Ludell Wilson trilogy (3)
Lufness
Ethel
Wreck series (2)
Luke Sutton, avenger
Kelley, Leo Patrick
Luke Sutton series (4)
Luke Sutton, bounty hunter
Kelley, Leo Patrick
Luke Sutton series (6)
Luke Sutton, gunfighter
Kelley, Leo Patrick
Luke Sutton series (2)
Luke Sutton, hired gun
Kelley, Leo Patrick
Luke Sutton series (7)
Luke Sutton, Indian fighter
Kelley, Leo Patrick
Luke Sutton series (3)
Luke Sutton, lawman
Kelley, Leo Patrick
Luke Sutton series (8)
Luke Sutton, mustanger
Kelley, Leo Patrick
Luke Sutton series (9)
Luke Sutton, outlaw
Kelley, Leo Patrick
Luke Sutton series (1)
Luke Sutton, outrider
Kelley, Leo Patrick
Luke Sutton series (5)
Luke's good news of Jesus
Haughton, Rosemary
Good news of Jesus series (3)
Lullaby of murder
Davis, Dorothy Salisbury
Julie Hayes series (3)
Lullafly
Cosgrove, Stephen Edward
Bugg series (48)
Lulu and the witch baby
O'Connor, Jane
Lulu series (1)
Lulu goes to witch school
O'Connor, Jane
Lulu series (2)
Lulu versus love
Springstubb, Tricia
Lulu series (2)

Luminous face
Wells, Carolyn
Pennington Wise series (4)
Luna
Delacorta
Serge Gorodish series (3)
Lunar attack
Rankine, John
Space nineteen ninety nine series (5)
Lunar descent
Steele, Allen
Orbital decay series (2)
Lunatic at large
Clouston, Joseph Storer
Mister Francis Mandell-Essington series (1)
Lunatic at large again
Clouston, Joseph Storer
Mister Francis Mandell-Essington series (3)
Lunatic in charge
Clouston, Joseph Storer
Mister Francis Mandell-Essington series (5)
Lunatic in love
Clouston, Joseph Storer
Mister Francis Mandell-Essington series (6)
Lunatic still at large
Clouston, Joseph Storer
Mister Francis Mandell-Essington series (4)
Lunatics at large
Reach, James
Wing series (2)
Lunch with Mussolini
Hansen, Derek
Lunch series (2)
Lunch with the generals
Hansen, Derek
Lunch series (1)
Lure of distant trails
Grey, Romer Zane
Buck Duane series (2)
Lure of fantasy, 1918-1950
Holroyd, Michael
Bernard Shaw series (3)
Lure of gold
Carter, Nicholas
Nicholas Carter series (205)
Lure of surgery
Sava, George
Surgeon's destiny series (3)
Lure of sweet death
Kemp, Sarah
Doctor Tina May series (2)
Lure of the basilisk
Watt-Evans, Lawrence
Lords of Dus series (1)
Lure of the black hills
Lange, Dietrich
American Indian series (5)
Lure of the bush
Upfield, Arthur William
Napoleon Bonaparte series (1)
Lure of the Falcon
Benzoni, Juliette
Falcon series (1)
Lure of the Mississippi
Lange, Dietrich
American Indian series (6)
Lure of the wild
Thompson, David
Nathaniel King series (2)
Lures of death
Whelton, Paul
Garry Dean series (3)
Lust for gold
Slade, Jack
Lassiter series (24)
Lust for murder
Klinger, Henry
Lieutenant Shomri Shomar series (3)
Lust for vengeance
Janson, Hank
Hank Janson series (208)
Lust is no lady
Avallone, Michael
Ed Noon series (14)
Lust of hate
Boothby, Guy
Doctor Nikola series (3)
Lust to kill
Lee, Edward
Red Blake series (2)
Lusty wind for Carolina
Fletcher, Inglis
Carolina series (6)
Luttrell Village
Sancha, Sheila
Stamford series (2)
Luvvy and the girls
Carlson, Natalie Savage
Luvvy Savage series (2)
Luxembourg run
Ross, Angus
Mark Farrow series (17)
Luxury ladies
Smith, Helen Zenna
Skinny series (2)
Lycian shore
Stark, Freya
Ionia series (2)
Lydia
Cunningham, E V
Harvey Krim series (1)
Kaye, Marilyn
Sisters series (4)
Lydia's hope
Williams, Leigh Anne
Taylor House trilogy (2)
Lying at death's door
Cumberland, Marten
Saturnin Dax series (23)
Lying down below
Carstairs, Henry
Lydford Long series (9)
Lying-in
Kitchen, Paddy
Vanessa Talisend series (1)
Lying in bed
Harris, Mark
Lee Youngdahl series (2)
Lying in wait
Jance, Judith A
J P Beaumont series (12)
Lying jade
Ford, Leslie
Colonel John Primrose series (15)
Grace Latham series (15)
Lying ladies
Finnegan, Robert
Dan Banion series (1)
Lying three
McInerny, Ralph
Father Roger Dowling series (4)
Lyle and the birthday party
Waber, Bernard
Lyle series (3)
Lyle finds his mother
Waber, Bernard
Lyle series (5)
Lyle, Lyle, crocodile
Waber, Bernard
Lyle series (2)
Lynch law
Brady, William S
Peacemaker series (4)
Edwards, Josh
John Stone series (2)
Lynch lawyers
White, William Patterson
Lazy River series (1)
Lynch-rope law
Dresser, Davis
Twister Malone series (3)
Lynch town
Gilman, George G
Adam Steele series (11)
Murphy, Warren Burton
Edward Razoni and William Jackson series (5)
Lynchers
Lawrence, Steven C
Tom Slattery series (1)
Lyndell Sherburne
Douglas, Amanda Minnie
Sherburne series (2)
Lynx, counterspy
Vigilant
Barry Link series (3)
Lynx-hunting
Stephens, Charles Asbury
Camping out series (4)
Lynx, spyflyer
Vigilant
Barry Link series (2)
Lynx, V.C.
Vigilant
Barry Link series (1)
Lynx, V.C., flies again
Vigilant
Barry Link series (4)
Lyonnais Club
Duhamel, Georges
Salavin series (4)
Lyon's pride
McCaffrey, Anne
Damia series (3)
Rowan series (2)
Lyre of Orpheus
Davies, Robertson
Francis Cornish trilogy (3)
Lyssa
Jenkins, Jerry Bruce
Margo Franklin and Philip Spence series (12)
Lythande
Bradley, Marion Zimmer
Sanctuary series (12)
Lytton Strachey
Holroyd, Michael
Lytton Strachey series (1)
Lytton Strachey and the Bloomsbury Group, his work, their influence
Holroyd, Michael
Lytton Strachey series (2)
Lytton Strachey, the unknown years, 1880-1910
Holroyd, Michael
Lytton Strachey series (1)
Lytton Strachey, the years of achievement, 1910-1932
Holroyd, Michael
Lytton Strachey series (2)

M

M.A.S.H.
Hooker, Richard
M.A.S.H. series (1)
M.A.S.H. goes to Hollywood
Hooker, Richard
M.A.S.H. series (8)
M.A.S.H. goes to Las Vegas
Hooker, Richard
M.A.S.H. series (7)
M.A.S.H. goes to London
Hooker, Richard
M.A.S.H. series (6)
M.A.S.H. goes to Maine
Hooker, Richard
M.A.S.H. series (2)
M.A.S.H. goes to Miami
Hooker, Richard
M.A.S.H. series (10)
M.A.S.H. goes to Montreal
Hooker, Richard
M.A.S.H. series (15)
M.A.S.H. goes to Morocco
Hooker, Richard
M.A.S.H. series (5)
M.A.S.H. goes to Moscow
Hooker, Richard
M.A.S.H. series (14)
M.A.S.H. goes to New Orleans
Hooker, Richard
M.A.S.H. series (4)
M.A.S.H. goes to Paris
Hooker, Richard
M.A.S.H. series (3)
M.A.S.H. goes to San Francisco
Hooker, Richard
M.A.S.H. series (11)
M.A.S.H. goes to Texas
Hooker, Richard
M.A.S.H. series (12)
M.A.S.H. goes to Vienna
Hooker, Richard
M.A.S.H. series (9)
M.A.S.H. mania
Hooker, Richard
M.A.S.H. series (13)
M and M and the bad news babies
Ross, Pat
M and M series (4)
M and M and the big bag
Ross, Pat
M and M series (3)
M and M and the haunted house
Ross, Pat
M and M series (2)
M and M and the mummy mess
Ross, Pat
M and M series (5)
M and M and the Santa secrets
Ross, Pat
M and M series (6)
M and M and the superchild afternoon
Ross, Pat
M and M series (7)
M for murder
Brandon, John Gordon
Inspector Patrick Aloysius McCarthy series (43)
M.I.A. Hunter
Buchanan, Jack
M.I.A. Hunter series (1)
M is for monster
Gilden, Mel
Fifth grade monsters series (1)
M-sixteen jury
Nik-Uhernik
War dogs series (2)
M.Y.T.H. Inc. in action
Asprin, Robert Lynn
Skeeve series (9)
M.Y.T.H. Inc. link
Asprin, Robert Lynn
Skeeve series (7)
Ma
Abarbanell, Jacob Ralph
Pa and ma series (2)
Ma and pa
Lindsay, Rose
Ma and pa series (1)
Ma Dalton
Goscinny, Rene
Lucky Luke series (8)
Ma Pettengill
Wilson, Harry Leon
Red Gap series (3)
Ma Pettengill talks
Wilson, Harry Leon
Red Gap series (4)
Mabel Walton's experiment
Mathews, Joanna Hooe
Miss Ashton's girls series (5)
Mabel's mishaps
Blanchard, Amy Ella
Lad and Lassie (2)
Mac and the caterpillar
Tann, Roger
Troopers series (2)
Macabre ones!
Fane, Bron
La noire series (7)
Macalastair looks on
Dick, Alexandra
Alastair Macalastair series (4)
Macall gets curious
Fairlie, Gerard
Johnny Macall series (5)
McAllister
Chisholm, Matt
Rem McAllister series (1)
Macallister
Perry, Ritchie
Macallister series (1)
McAllister and Cheyenne death
Chisholm, Matt
Rem McAllister series (35)
McAllister and quarry
Chisholm, Matt
Rem McAllister series (36)
McAllister and the Spanish gold
Chisholm, Matt
Rem McAllister series (34)
McAllister fights
Chisholm, Matt
Rem McAllister series (13)
McAllister gambles
Chisholm, Matt
Rem McAllister series (21)
McAllister in Die-Hard
Chisholm, Matt
Rem McAllister series (37)
McAllister in Fire-Brand
Chisholm, Matt
Rem McAllister series (39)
McAllister in Wolf-Bait
Chisholm, Matt
Rem McAllister series (38)
McAllister justice
Chisholm, Matt
Rem McAllister series (15)
McAllister legend
Chisholm, Matt
Rem McAllister series (31)
McAllister makes war
Chisholm, Matt
Rem McAllister series (10)
McAllister must die
Chisholm, Matt
Rem McAllister series (30)
McAllister never surrenders
Chisholm, Matt
Rem McAllister series (33)
McAllister on the Comanche crossing
Chisholm, Matt
Rem McAllister series (32)
McAllister rides
Chisholm, Matt
Rem McAllister series (8)
McAllister runs wild
Chisholm, Matt
Rem McAllister series (25)
McAllister says no
Chisholm, Matt
Rem McAllister series (19)
McAllister strikes
Chisholm, Matt
Rem McAllister series (11)
McAllister trapped
Chisholm, Matt
Rem McAllister series (29)
McAllister's fury
Chisholm, Matt
Rem McAllister series (12)
McAllister's victims
Grover, Marshall
Larry and Stretch series (367)
Macao
Carter, Nick
Nick Carter series (31)
Macao massacre
Carter, Nick
Nick Carter series (198)
Macao mayhem
Harknett, Terry
Superintendent John Crown series (2)
McAuslan in the rough, and other stories
Fraser, George Macdonald
Private McAuslan series (2)
McBain's ladies
McBain, Ed
Eighty Seventh Precinct series (42)
McBain's ladies, too
McBain, Ed
Eighty Seventh Precinct series (43)
Macbeth the king
Tranter, Nigel Godwin
Scottish history series (1)
McBroom and the beanstalk
Fleischman, Sid
McBroom series (8)
McBroom and the big wind
Fleischman, Sid
McBroom series (2)
McBroom and the great race
Fleischman, Sid
McBroom series (9)
McBroom tells a lie
Fleischman, Sid
McBroom series (7)
McBroom tells the truth
Fleischman, Sid
McBroom series (1)
McBroom the rainmaker
Fleischman, Sid
McBroom series (6)
McBroom's almanac
Fleischman, Sid
McBroom series (10)
McBroom's ghost
Fleischman, Sid
McBroom series (4)
McBroom's wonderful one-acre farm
Fleischman, Sid
McBroom series (4)
McBroom's zoo
Fleischman, Sid
McBroom series (5)
McCade's bounty
Dietz, William Corey
Sam McCade series (4)
McCarthy, C.I.D.
Brandon, John Gordon
Inspector Patrick Aloysius McCarthy series (12)
McCarty, incog.
Ostrander, Isabel
Timothy McCarty series (4)
Macchiavelli interface
Perry, Steve
Khadaji series (4)
Macclellan's lake
Dawlish, Peter
Sam Macclellan series (1)
McCloud
Wilcox, Collin
Marshal Sam McCloud series (1)
McCracken's marauders
Grover, Marshall
Larry and Stretch series (128)
Mace!
Grant, James
Mace series (1)
Mace of souls
Fergusson, Bruce
Six kingdoms series (2)
Macedonia
Williams, Jon
Privateers and gentlemen series (4)
Macedonian mixup
Bentley, John
Dick Marlow series (5)
Mace's luck
Grant, James
Mace series (2)

Made for each other
Cooper, M E
Couples series (4)
Made for man
Herbert, Alan Patrick
Admiral of the Fleet, Earl of Caraway series (2)
Made for murder
McGrew, Fenn
Lieutenant Charles Hillary series (2)
Made in Japan
Chase, Glen
Cherry Delight series (10)
Made-over Chelsea
Stahl, Hilda
Best friends series (7)
Made up for murder
Roos, Kelley
Jeff and Haila Troy series (1)
Made up to kill
Roos, Kelley
Jeff and Haila Troy series (1)
Madeleine
Gavin, Catherine
Second Empire quartet (4)
Madeleine grown up
Henrey, Madeleine
Madeleine series (5)
Madeleine young wife
Henrey, Madeleine
Madeleine series (6)
Madeleine's journal
Henrey, Madeleine
Madeleine reminiscences series (2)
Madeline
Bemelmans, Ludwig
Madeline series (1)
Madeline and the bad hat
Bemelmans, Ludwig
Madeline series (4)
Madeline and the gypsies
Bemelmans, Ludwig
Madeline series (5)
Madeline in London
Bemelmans, Ludwig
Madeline series (6)
Madeline Payne, the detective's daughter
Lynch, Lawrence L
Madeline Payne series (1)
Madeline's Christmas
Bemelmans, Ludwig
Madeline series (7)
Madeline's Christmas in Texas
Bemelmans, Ludwig
Madeline series (3)
Madeline's rescue
Bemelmans, Ludwig
Madeline series (2)
Mademoiselle
Symons, Geraldine
Atalanta and Pansy series (5)
Mademoiselle Jessica
Pascal, Francine
Sweet Valley twins series (46)
Madge Morton, captain of the Merry Maid
Chalmers, Amy D V
Madge Morton series (1)
Madge Morton's secret
Chalmers, Amy D V
Madge Morton series (2)
Madge Morton's trust
Chalmers, Amy D V
Madge Morton series (3)
Madge Morton's victory
Chalmers, Amy D V
Madge Morton series (4)
Madge's sister
Saunders, Marjorie
Madge series (1)
Madhouse
Hall, Angus
Devilday series (1)
Madigan's day
Grover, Marshall
Larry and Stretch series (134)
Madison murder
Grex, Leo
Paul Irving series (3)
Madman of Bergerac
Simenon, Georges
Inspector Jules Maigret series (13)
Inspector Jules Maigret series (15)
Madman of the marshes
Jardine, Warwick
Sexton Blake series (1243)
Madman run
Robbins, David
Endworld series (26)
Madman's army
Adams, Robert
Horseclans series (17)
Madman's Bend
Upfield, Arthur William
Napoleon Bonaparte series (28)
Madman's blade
Hardin, J D
Raider series (13)
Madman's buff
Steel, Kurt
Hank Hyer series (8)
Madman's mansion
Sargent, Craig
Last ranger series (3)
Madman's Peak
Leyland, Eric
Rip Randall series (4)
Madman's whisper
Grayson, Richard
John Bryant series (3)
Madness in Maggody
Hess, Joan
Arly Hanks series (4)
Madonna in Hollywood
Dekobra, Maurice
Madonna series (2)
Madonna of the Astrolabe
Stewart, John Innes Mackintosh
Duncan Pattullo series (4)
Madonna of the black market
Webster, Ernest
Benni Soldano series (1)
Madonna of the Seven Hills
Plaidy, Jean
Lucrezia Borgia series (1)
Madonna of the sleeping cars
Dekobra, Maurice
Lady Diana trilogy (2)
Madonna series (1)
Madouc
Vance, Jack
Lyonesse series (3)
Madrid underground
Serafin, David
Superintendent Luis Bernal series (2)
Madrigal
Gardner, John Edmund
Boysie L Oakes series (4)
Madrigal for Charlie Muffin
Freemantle, Brian
Charlie Muffin series (5)
Mad's Al Jaffee spews out snappy answers to stupid questions
Jaffee, Al
Snappy answers to stupid questions series (1)
Mad's Al Jaffee spews out still more snappy answers to stupid questions
Jaffee, Al
Snappy answers to stupid questions series (2)
Madwand
Zelazny, Roger
Changeling series (2)
Maelstrom
Preuss, Paul
Venus prime series (2)
Maestro
Kemp, Robert
Stories of Edinburgh life series (2)
Maestro Don Gesualdo
Verga, Giovanni
Vinti family series (2)
Maestro murders
Wees, Frances Shelley
Michael Forrester series (1)
Maeve
Clayton, Jo
Diadem series (4)
Maeve's daughter
Paige, Frances
McGrath family series (2)
Mafia death watch
Rossi, Bruno
Sharpshooter series (16)
Mafia diaries
Nash, Jay Robert
Jack Journey series (2)
Mafia dynasty
Davis, John H
Mafia series (2)
Mafia fix
Murphy, Warren Burton
Destroyer series (4)
Mafia kingfish
Davis, John H
Mafia series (1)
Mafia massacre
Scarpetta, Frank
Marksman series (12)
Mafia wipe out
Scarpetta, Frank
Marksman series (4)
Mage-born child
Wylie, Jonathan
Servants of Ark trilogy (3)
Magepa the buck
Haggard, Henry Rider
Allan Quatermain series (12)
Maggie Adams, dancer
Dean, Karen Strickler
Maggie Adams series (1)
Maggie and a horse named Devildust
Alter, Judy
Maggie and Devildust series (1)
Maggie and Bessie and their way to do good
Mathews, Joanna Hooe
Bessie Bradford series (3)
Maggie Bradford series (1)
Maggie and Devildust, ridin' high!
Alter, Judy
Maggie and Devildust series (3)
Maggie and the birthday surprise
Hollowood, Jane
Maggie series (3)
Maggie and the chickens
Hollowood, Jane
Maggie series (1)
Maggie and the roundabout
Hollowood, Jane
Maggie series (2)
Maggie and the search for Devildust
Alter, Judy
Maggie and Devildust series (2)
Maggie Bradford's club
Mathews, Joanna Hooe
Bradford family series (3)
Maggie Bradford series (2)
Maggie Bradford's fair
Mathews, Joanna Hooe
Bradford family series (6)
Maggie bradford's fair
Mathews, Joanna Hooe
Maggie Bradford series (4)
Maggie Bradford's school-mates
Mathews, Joanna Hooe
Bradford family series (4)
Maggie Bradford series (3)
Maggie Cassidy
Kerouac, Jack
Jack Duluoz series (3)
Maggie forevermore
Nixon, Joan Lowery
Maggie series (3)
Maggie Gumption
Barry, Margaret Stuart
Maggie Gumption series (1)
Maggie Gumption flies high
Barry, Margaret Stuart
Maggie Gumption series (2)
Maggie in the porridge
Tann, Roger
Troopers series (3)
Maggie in the snow
Hollowood, Jane
Maggie series (4)
Maggie Marmelstein for president
Sharmat, Marjorie Weinman
Maggie Marmelstein series (2)
Maggie Muggins
Grannan, Mary
Maggie Muggins series (1)
Maggie muggins and her animal friends
Grannan, Mary
Maggie Muggins series (7)
Maggie Muggins and the cottontail
Grannan, Mary
Maggie Muggins series (12)
Maggie Muggins and the fieldmouse
Grannan, Mary
Maggie Muggins series (11)
Maggie Muggins bedtime stories
Grannan, Mary
Maggie Muggins series (8)
Maggie Muggins by the sea
Grannan, Mary
Maggie Muggins series (9)
Maggie Muggins gives a party
Grannan, Mary
Maggie Muggins series (13)
Maggie Muggins in the meadow
Grannan, Mary
Maggie Muggins series (4)
Maggie Muggins stories
Grannan, Mary
Maggie Muggins series (2)
Maggie Rose, her birthday Christmas
Sawyer, Ruth
Christmas stories series (5)
Maggie, too
Nixon, Joan Lowery
Maggie series (1)
Maggody in Manhattan
Hess, Joan
Arly Hanks series (6)
Magic across the table
Severn, Bill
Magic series (6)
Magic and magicians
Severn, Bill
Magic series (16)
Magic Arthur and the giant
Slepian, Jan
Listen-hear series (4)
Magic ball from Mars
Biemiller, Carl Ludwig
Jonny series (1)
Magic bed-knob
Norton, Mary
Bed-knob and broomstick series (1)
Magic bowling ball
Dubrovin, Vivian
Summer fun, winter fun series (2)
Magic by the lake
Eager, Edward
Magic series (3)
Magic carpet
Romains, Jules
Men of goodwill series (25)
Magic carpet to Animal Rhyme Land
Mamlok, Gwyneth
Magic carpet series (1)
Magic carpet to Nursery Rhyme Land
Mamlok, Gwyneth
Magic carpet series (2)
Magic carpet to Pudding Pie Land
Mamlok, Gwyneth
Magic carpet series (3)
Magic carpet to Story Rhyme Land
Mamlok, Gwyneth
Magic carpet series (4)
Magic casement
Duncan, Dave
Man of his word series (1)
Magic casements
Alexander, Marc
Wells of Ythan series (2)
Magic casket
Freeman, Richard Austin
Doctor John Evelyn Thorndyke series (15)
Magic Christmas
Pascal, Francine
Sweet Valley kids magna series (1)
Sweet Valley twins magna series (1)
Magic cloak
Baum, Lyman Frank
Snuggle tales series (4)
Magic comedy
Severn, Bill
Magic series (5)
Magic day
McKimmie, Christopher
Magic day series (2)
Magic drawing pencil
Storr, Catherine
Marianne series (1)
Magic eye for Ida
Chorao, Kay
Ida series (1)
Magic faraway tree
Blyton, Enid
Faraway tree series (2)
Magic forest
Robeson, Kenneth
Doc Savage series (149)
Magic fun for everyone
Severn, Bill
Magic series (16)
Magic goes away
Niven, Larry
Magic trilogy (1)
Magic in Ithkar
Adams, Robert
Magic in Ithkar series (1)
Magic in Ithkar I
Adams, Robert
Magic in Ithkar series (1)
Magic in Ithkar II
Adams, Robert
Magic in Ithkar series (2)
Magic in Ithkar III
Adams, Robert
Magic in Ithkar series (3)
Magic in Ithkar IV
Adams, Robert
Magic in Ithkar series (4)
Magic in mind
Severn, Bill
Magic series (16)
Magic in your pockets
Severn, Bill
Magic series (4)
Magic Island
Chastain, Madye Lee
Lisa and Emmy and Dodie series (3)
Magic island
Robeson, Kenneth
Doc Savage series (89)
Magic journey
Nichols, John
New Mexico trilogy (2)
Magic key
Johnston, William
Doctor Kildare junior series (2)
Magic kingdom for sale, sold!
Brooks, Terry
Magic Kingdom of Landover series (1)
Magic labyrinth
Farmer, Philip Jose
Riverworld series (4)
Magic-lantern murders
Dickson, Carter
Sir Henry Merrivale series (6)
Magic makers and the bramble bush man
Sutton, Margaret
Magic makers series (1)
Magic makers and the golden charm
Sutton, Margaret
Magic makers series (2)
Magic makers in Backwards Land
Sutton, Margaret
Magic makers series (3)
Magic makes murder
Campbell, Harriette Russell
Simon Brade series (6)
Magic Man
Bannerman, David
Magic Man series (1)
Magic man at Jug Valley Juniors
Digby, Anne
Jug Valley Juniors series (6)
Magic master
Packard, Edward
Choose your own adventure series (122)
Magic may return
Niven, Larry
Magic trilogy (2)
Magic messages for pulpit, pew and pint sized people
Westphail, Arnold Carl
Gospel magic series (5)
Magic mirror
Friedman, Mickey
Georgia Lee Maxwell series (1)
Magic mix-up
Becker, Eve
Abracadabra series (3)
Magic monsters around the year
Tester, Sylvia Root
Magic monsters series (2)
Magic monsters' Halloween
Tester, Sylvia Root
Magic monsters series (4)
Magic monsters learn about safety
Tester, Sylvia Root
Magic monsters series (3)
Magic monsters learn about weather
Tester, Sylvia Root
Magic monsters series (5)
Magic Moscow
Pinkwater, Daniel Manus
Magic Moscow series (1)
Magic necklace
Carter, Nicholas
Nicholas Carter series (603)
Magic of Krynn
Weis, Margaret
DragonLance tales trilogy (1)
Magic of Oz
Baum, Lyman Frank
Oz series (13)
Magic of the Glits
Adler, Carole Schwerdtfeger
Glits series (1)
Magic of the unicorn
Goodman, Deborah Lerme
Choose your own adventure series (51)
Magic of Xanth
Anthony, Piers
Xanth series (3)
Magic or not?
Eager, Edward
Magic series (5)
Magic pasta pot
De Paola, Tomie
Strega Nona series (1)
Magic people
Softly, Barbara
Magic people series (1)

Magic people around the world
Softly, Barbara
Magic people series (2)
Magic pictures
Ayme, Marcel
Wonderful Farm series (2)
Magic place
Bromige, Iris
Rainwood family series (6)
Magic pony
Leitch, Patricia
Jinny series (7)
Magic puppets
Pascal, Francine
Sweet Valley kids series (53)
Magic ring
Grahame, Kenneth
Smith family series (2)
Magic scarf
Arendt, Veronique
Zoe and George series (1)
Magic school bus at the waterworks
Cole, Joanna
Magic school bus series (1)
Magic school bus inside the earth
Cole, Joanna
Magic school bus series (2)
Magic school bus inside the human body
Cole, Joanna
Magic school bus series (3)
Magic school bus lost in the solar system
Cole, Joanna
Magic school bus series (4)
Magic show
Bridges, Laurie
Dark forces series (2)
Magic shows you can give
Severn, Bill
Magic series (16)
Magic staff
Davis, Andrew Jackson
Spiritualism series (1)
Magic stone
Kooiker, Leonie
Chris series (1)
Magic tale of Harvanger and Yolande
Baker, George Philip
Greenwood series (1)
Magic talisman
Blaine, John
Rick Brant series (24)
Magic top mystery
O'Connor, Jane
Pick-a-path series (8)
Magic wars
Clayton, Jo
Wild magic trilogy (3)
Magic wherever you are
Severn, Bill
Magic series (1)
Magic with coins and bills
Severn, Bill
Magic series (9)
Magic with paper
Severn, Bill
Magic series (3)
Magic with rope
Severn, Bill
Magic series (13)
Magic world
Beresford, Elisabeth
Magic series (1)
Magic year
Maass, Joachim
Astride the times series (1)
Magical cupboard
Curry, Jane Louise
Rosemary series (2)
Magical fellowship
McGowen, Tom
Age of magic trilogy (1)
Magical melons
Brink, Carol Ryrie
Caddie Woodlawn series (2)
Magical mimics
Snow, Jack
Oz series (36)
Magician
Feist, Raymond Elias
Riftwar series (1)
Goscinny, Rene
Twelve tasks of Asterix series (5)
Stein, Sol
George Thomassy series (1)
Van der Essen, Anne
Yok-yok series (2)
Wales, Mike
Leatherhand series (6)
Magician and double trouble
McKee, David
Melric the magician series (6)
Magician and the balloon
McKee, David
Melric the magician series (4)
Magician and the crown
McKee, David
Melric the magician series (8)
Magician and the dragon
McKee, David
Melric the magician series (5)
Magician and the petnapping
McKee, David
Melric the magician series (3)
Magician and the sorcerer
McKee, David
Melric the magician series (2)
Magician apprentice
Feist, Raymond Elias
Riftwar series (1)
Magician master
Feist, Raymond Elias
Riftwar series (1)
Magician of Mars
Hamilton, Edmond
Captain Future series (5)
Magician who lost his magic
McKee, David
Melric the magician series (1)
Magician's apprentice
McGowen, Tom
Magician trilogy (1)
McKee, David
Melric the magician series (7)
Magician's bane
Beamer, Charles
Legends of Eorthe series (1)
Magician's challenge
McGowen, Tom
Magician trilogy (3)
Magician's company
McGowen, Tom
Magician trilogy (2)
Magician's gambit
Eddings, David
Belgariad series (3)
Magician's law
Scott, Michael
Tales of the bard trilogy (1)
Magician's nephew
Lewis, Clive Staples
Narnia series (1)
Magicians of Caprona
Jones, Diana Wynne
Chrestomanci series (2)
Magicians of Gor
Norman, John
Tarl Cabot series (25)
Magicians of night
Hambly, Barbara
Sun-cross series (2)
Magician's ring
Gaskin, Carol
Forgotten forest series (2)
Magick of Camelot
Landis, Arthur Harold
Camelot series (3)
Magic's pawn
Lackey, Mercedes
Last Herald-Mage trilogy (1)
Magic's price
Lackey, Mercedes
Last Herald-Mage trilogy (3)
Magic's promise
Lackey, Mercedes
Last Herald-Mage trilogy (2)
Magigals murder
Grant, Maxwell
Shadow series (278)
Maginot Line murder
Newman, Bernard
Papa Pontivy series (2)
Magnates
Druon, Maurice
Curtain falls trilogy (1)
Magnet
Gorky, Maxim
Life of Klim Samgin series (2)
Magnet for murder
Corne, Molly E
Mac McIntyre series (3)
Symons, Beryl
Jane Carberry series (3)
Magnetic ghost of Shadow Island
McEvoy, Seth
Arcade explorers series (4)
Magnetic man
Daniels, Norman A
Avengers series (10)
Magnificent Ambersons
Tarkington, Booth
Growth trilogy (1)
Magnificent barb
Faralla, Dana
Magnificent barb series (1)
Magnificent century
Costain, Thomas Bertram
History of the Plantagenets tetralogy (2)
Magnificent Evan
Skidmore, Ian
Welsh island series (2)
Magnificent Max
Dicks, Terrance
Cat called Max series (1)
Magnificent obsession
Douglas, Lloyd Cassel
Doctor Hudson series (2)
Magnificent showboats of the Lower Vissel River, Lune 23 South, Big Planet
Vance, Jack
Big Planet series (2)
Magnum for Schneider
Mitchell, James
David Callan series (1)
Magnus and the ship's mascot
Peterson, Hans
Magnus series (5)
Magnus and the squirrel
Peterson, Hans
Magnus series (1)
Magnus and the van horse
Peterson, Hans
Magnus series (2)
Magnus and the wagon horse
Peterson, Hans
Magnus series (2)
Magnus in danger
Peterson, Hans
Magnus series (4)
Magnus in the harbour
Peterson, Hans
Magnus series (3)
Magnus Sinclair
Pease, Howard
Border trilogy (1)
Magnus Think-Alot
Watson, Jean
Alot series (3)
Magog
Sinclair, Andrew
Albion trilogy (2)
Magpie and Miss Winter
Mackenzie, Kathleen
Miss Winter series (2)
Magpie boy
Roberts, Beth
Drenee series (1)
Magpie murder
Warren, John Russell
Inspector M'Guire series (4)
Magpies' hoard
Duke, Winifred
Harold Fieldend series (6)
Magwitch
Noonan, Michael
Magwitch series (2)
Magyar massacre
Saint Germain, Gregory
Resistance series (2)
Mah-Jongg spies
Trenhaile, John
Simon Young series (1)
Mahars of Pellucidar
Holmes, John Eric
Pellucidar series (8)
Mahogany pirates
Thorne, Ramsay
Captain Gringo series (13)
Mahogany trimrose
Lichtenberg, Jacqueline
Sime-Gen series (4)
Maia
Adams, Richard
Beklan Empire series (2)
Maid-at-arms
Chambers, Robert William
American Revolution trilogy (2)
Cardigan series (2)
Maid for murder
Franklin, Charles
Grant Garfield series (8)
Maid for the morgue
Brody, Marc
Marc Brody series (25)
Maid in Paris
Kane, Frank
Johnny Liddell series (30)
Maid in waiting
Galsworthy, John
End of the chapter series (1)
Maid Margaret of Galloway
Crockett, Samuel Rutherford
Douglas series (2)
Maid Mary Anne
Martin, Ann Matthews
Baby-Sitters Club series (66)
Maid of destiny
Seymour, Arabella
Jane Beaufort series (1)
Maid of gold
Wiat, Philippa
Howard series (4)
Maid of Killeena, and other stories
Black, William
Hebrides series (2)
Maid of Maiden Lane
Barr, Amelia Edith
New York trilogy (2)
Maid of the Abbey
Oxenham, Elsie J
Abbey girls second generation series (2)
Maid of the Isles
Beardmore, George
Lesley Allan series (4)
Maid of the isles
Swan, Annie Shepherd
Highland maid series (1)
Maid of the Nettuno
Huna, Ludwig
Borgia trilogy (3)
Maid-up for murder
Brody, Marc
Marc Brody series (41)
Maida's little cabins
Irwin, Inez Haynes
Maida series (9)
Maida's little camp
Irwin, Inez Haynes
Maida series (5)
Maida's little farm
Irwin, Inez Haynes
Maida series (13)
Maida's little hospital
Irwin, Inez Haynes
Maida series (12)
Maida's little house
Irwin, Inez Haynes
Maida series (2)
Maida's little house party
Irwin, Inez Haynes
Maida series (14)
Maida's little houseboat
Irwin, Inez Haynes
Maida series (7)
Maida's little island
Irwin, Inez Haynes
Maida series (4)
Maida's little lighthouse
Irwin, Inez Haynes
Maida series (11)
Maida's little school
Irwin, Inez Haynes
Maida series (3)
Maida's little shop
Irwin, Inez Haynes
Maida series (1)
Maida's little theater
Irwin, Inez Haynes
Maida series (8)
Maida's little treasure hunt
Irwin, Inez Haynes
Maida series (15)
Maida's little village
Irwin, Inez Haynes
Maida series (6)
Maida's little zoo
Irwin, Inez Haynes
Maida series (10)
Maiden
Dawson-Scott, Catherine Amy
Some women trilogy (1)
Harrod-Eagles, Cynthia
Morland family series (8)
Maiden and married life of Mary Powell
Manning, Anne
Mary Powell series (1)
Maiden possessed
Chance, John Newton
Mister DeHavilland series (2)
Maiden you slay me
Jason
Jason series (7)
Maidlin bears the torch
Oxenham, Elsie J
Abbey girls first generation series (21)
Rachel and Damaris series (4)
Maidlin to the rescue
Oxenham, Elsie J
Abbey girls first generation series (17)
Rachel and Damaris series (2)
Maids and mistresses
Powell, Margaret
Maids and mistresses series (1)
Seymour, Beatrice Kean
Sally Dunn trilogy (1)
Maids of La Rochelle
Brent-Dyer, Elinor Mary
La Rochelle series (3)
Maids of paradise
Chambers, Robert William
Franco-Prussian war trilogy (3)
Maigret abroad
Simenon, Georges
Inspector Jules Maigret series (5)
Inspector Jules Maigret series (9)
Maigret afraid
Simenon, Georges
Inspector Jules Maigret series (44)
Maigret and Monsieur Charles
Simenon, Georges
Inspector Jules Maigret series (78)
Maigret and Monsieur L'Abbe
Simenon, Georges
Inspector Jules Maigret series (17)
Maigret and the apparition
Simenon, Georges
Inspector Jules Maigret series (65)
Maigret and the black sheep
Simenon, Georges
Inspector Jules Maigret series (60)
Maigret and the bum
Simenon, Georges
Inspector Jules Maigret series (64)
Maigret and the burglar's wife
Simenon, Georges
Inspector Jules Maigret series (39)
Maigret and the Calme Report
Simenon, Georges
Inspector Jules Maigret series (47)
Maigret and the Concarneau murders
Simenon, Georges
Inspector Jules Maigret series (4)
Maigret and the coroner
Simenon, Georges
Inspector Jules Maigret series (31)
Maigret and the dead girl
Simenon, Georges
Inspector Jules Maigret series (48)
Maigret and the dosser
Simenon, Georges
Inspector Jules Maigret series (64)
Maigret and the enigmatic Lett
Simenon, Georges
Inspector Jules Maigret series (1)
Maigret and the flea
Simenon, Georges
Inspector Jules Maigret series (77)
Maigret and the fortune teller
Simenon, Georges
Inspector Jules Maigret series (25)
Maigret and the gangsters
Simenon, Georges
Inspector Jules Maigret series (41)
Maigret and the ghost
Simenon, Georges
Inspector Jules Maigret series (65)
Maigret and the headless corpse
Simenon, Georges
Inspector Jules Maigret series (50)
Maigret and the Hotel Majestic
Simenon, Georges
Inspector Jules Maigret series (22)
Maigret and the hundred gibbets
Simenon, Georges
Inspector Jules Maigret series (8)
Maigret and the informer
Simenon, Georges
Inspector Jules Maigret series (77)
Maigret and the killer
Simenon, Georges
Inspector Jules Maigret series (73)
Maigret and the killers
Simenon, Georges
Inspector Jules Maigret series (41)
Maigret and the lazy burglar
Simenon, Georges
Inspector Jules Maigret series (59)
Maigret and the loner
Simenon, Georges
Inspector Jules Maigret series (76)
Maigret and the madwoman
Simenon, Georges
Inspector Jules Maigret series (74)
Maigret and the man on the bench
Simenon, Georges
Inspector Jules Maigret series (43)
Maigret and the man on the boulevard
Simenon, Georges
Inspector Jules Maigret series (43)
Maigret and the millionaires
Simenon, Georges
Inspector Jules Maigret series (53)
Maigret and the minister
Simenon, Georges
Inspector Jules Maigret series (47)

Maigret and the Nahour case
Simenon, Georges
Inspector Jules Maigret series (68)
Inspector Jules Maigret series (69)
Maigret and the old lady
Simenon, Georges
Inspector Jules Maigret series (32)
Maigret and the reluctant witnesses
Simenon, Georges
Inspector Jules Maigret series (54)
Inspector Jules Maigret series (56)
Maigret and the Saturday caller
Simenon, Georges
Inspector Jules Maigret series (61)
Maigret and the spinster
Simenon, Georges
Inspector Jules Maigret series (20)
Maigret and the surly inspector
Simenon, Georges
Inspector Jules Maigret series (62)
Maigret and the toy village
Simenon, Georges
Inspector Jules Maigret series (23)
Maigret and the wine merchant
Simenon, Georges
Inspector Jules Maigret series (75)
Maigret at the coroner's
Simenon, Georges
Inspector Jules Maigret series (31)
Maigret at the crossroads
Simenon, Georges
Inspector Jules Maigret series (7)
Maigret bides his time
Simenon, Georges
Inspector Jules Maigret series (67)
Maigret cinq
Simenon, Georges
Inspector Jules Maigret series (32)
Inspector Jules Maigret series (34)
Inspector Jules Maigret series (48)
Maigret goes home
Simenon, Georges
Inspector Jules Maigret series (11)
Maigret goes to school
Simenon, Georges
Inspector Jules Maigret series (46)
Maigret has doubts
Simenon, Georges
Inspector Jules Maigret series (55)
Maigret has scruples
Simenon, Georges
Inspector Jules Maigret series (54)
Inspector Jules Maigret series (56)
Maigret hesitates
Simenon, Georges
Inspector Jules Maigret series (72)
Maigret in court
Simenon, Georges
Inspector Jules Maigret series (57)
Maigret in exile
Simenon, Georges
Inspector Jules Maigret series (21)
Maigret in Montmartre
Simenon, Georges
Inspector Jules Maigret series (37)
Inspector Jules Maigret series (45)
Maigret in New York
Simenon, Georges
Inspector Jules Maigret series (26)
Maigret in New York's underworld
Simenon, Georges
Inspector Jules Maigret series (26)
Maigret in retirement
Simenon, Georges
Inspector Jules Maigret series (27)
Maigret in society
Simenon, Georges
Inspector Jules Maigret series (58)
Maigret in Vichy
Simenon, Georges
Inspector Jules Maigret series (71)
Maigret keeps a rendezvous
Simenon, Georges
Inspector Jules Maigret series (2)
Inspector Jules Maigret series (11)
Maigret loses his temper
Simenon, Georges
Inspector Jules Maigret series (63)
Maigret meets a milord
Simenon, Georges
Inspector Jules Maigret series (3)
Maigret mystified
Simenon, Georges
Inspector Jules Maigret series (16)
Maigret omnibus
Simenon, Georges
Inspector Jules Maigret series (45)
Inspector Jules Maigret series (46)
Inspector Jules Maigret series (54)
Inspector Jules Maigret series (56)
Maigret on holiday
Simenon, Georges
Inspector Jules Maigret series (25)
Inspector Jules Maigret series (30)
Maigret on the defensive
Simenon, Georges
Inspector Jules Maigret series (66)
Maigret quartet
Simenon, Georges
Inspector Jules Maigret series (51)
Inspector Jules Maigret series (58)
Inspector Jules Maigret series (59)
Maigret rents a room
Simenon, Georges
Inspector Jules Maigret series (38)
Maigret returns
Simenon, Georges
Inspector Jules Maigret series (18)
Inspector Jules Maigret series (19)
Maigret right and wrong
Simenon, Georges
Inspector Jules Maigret series (37)
Inspector Jules Maigret series (45)
Maigret sets a trap
Simenon, Georges
Inspector Jules Maigret series (49)
Maigret sits it out
Simenon, Georges
Inspector Jules Maigret series (18)
Inspector Jules Maigret series (19)
Maigret stonewalled
Simenon, Georges
Inspector Jules Maigret series (6)
Maigret takes a room
Simenon, Georges
Inspector Jules Maigret series (38)
Maigret takes the waters
Simenon, Georges
Inspector Jules Maigret series (71)
Maigret to the rescue
Simenon, Georges
Inspector Jules Maigret series (12)
Inspector Jules Maigret series (14)
Maigret travels south
Simenon, Georges
Inspector Jules Maigret series (13)
Inspector Jules Maigret series (15)
Maigret's boyhood friend
Simenon, Georges
Inspector Jules Maigret series (70)
Maigret's Christmas
Simenon, Georges
Inspector Jules Maigret series (27)
Inspector Jules Maigret series (62)
Maigret's dead man
Simenon, Georges
Inspector Jules Maigret series (29)
Maigret's failure
Simenon, Georges
Inspector Jules Maigret series (51)
Maigret's first case
Simenon, Georges
Inspector Jules Maigret series (34)
Maigret's little joke
Simenon, Georges
Inspector Jules Maigret series (52)
Maigret's memoirs
Simenon, Georges
Inspector Jules Maigret series (40)
Maigret's mistake
Simenon, Georges
Inspector Jules Maigret series (45)
Maigret's pickpocket
Simenon, Georges
Inspector Jules Maigret series (68)
Inspector Jules Maigret series (69)
Maigret's pipe
Simenon, Georges
Inspector Jules Maigret series (28)
Maigret's revolver
Simenon, Georges
Inspector Jules Maigret series (42)
Maigret's rival
Simenon, Georges
Inspector Jules Maigret series (24)
Maigret's special murder
Simenon, Georges
Inspector Jules Maigret series (29)
Maigret's war of nerves
Simenon, Georges
Inspector Jules Maigret series (10)
Mail Order Frank
Chapman, Allen
Boys of business series (3)
Mail-order wings
Gormley, Beatrice
Focus pocus series (1)
Mail pilot's hunch
Wright, Philip Lee
Air pilot series (3)
Mail riders
McCall, Edith
Frontiers of America series (11)
Mail royal
Tranter, Nigel Godwin
Patrick Gray series (4)
Mail-van mystery
Brandon, John Gordon
Inspector Patrick Aloysius McCarthy series (17)
Mailbox trick
Corbett, Scott
Kerby Maxwell series (2)
Mailed fist
Albany, James
S.A.S. series (2)
Main event
Beebee, Chris
Cipola series (2)
Main force
Kingston, Guy
Royal Air Force trilogy (1)
Main force assault
Sherman, David
Night fighters series (2)
Main line engines
Awdry, Wilbert
Railway series (21)
Main line west
Horgan, Paul
Mountain standard time trilogy (1)
Main offensive
Wilson, Gar
Phoenix Force series (44)
Main Street D.O.A.
Peters, David
Psi-Man series (3)
Main Street Gallego
Grover, Marshall
Nevada Jim series (13)
Maine massacre
Van de Wetering, Janwillem
De Gier and Grijpstra series (7)
Mainline plot
Rosenberger, Joseph
Death Merchant series (10)
Maisie McFlannel
Pryde, Helen W
McFlannel family series (5)
Maitland's master mystery
Severy, Martin
George Maitland series (3)
Maiwa's revenge
Haggard, Henry Rider
Allan Quatermain series (5)
King Solomon's mines series (3)
Majestic Max
Dicks, Terrance
Cat called Max series (3)
Majesty of Grace
Langton, Jane
Grace Jones series (2)
Majesty's rancho
Grey, Zane
Western stars series (2)
Majii
Robeson, Kenneth
Doc Savage series (60)
Majipoor chronicles
Silverberg, Robert
Majipoor trilogy (2)
Major
Ross, John
Major Hutton Seary series (2)
Major adventures
Greene, L Patrick
Aubrey Saint John Major series (3)
Major changes
Blake, Susan
Hawthorne College series (3)
Major crime
Keystone, Oliver
Paul Plush series (1)
Major developments
Greene, L Patrick
Aubrey Saint John Major series (8)
Major, diamond buyer
Greene, L Patrick
Aubrey Saint John Major series (1)
Major enquiry
Henderson, Laurence
Sergeant Arthur Milton series (4)
Major exploits
Greene, L Patrick
Aubrey Saint John Major series (7)
Major hazards
Greene, L Patrick
Aubrey Saint John Major series (10)
Major, knight errant
Greene, L Patrick
Aubrey Saint John Major series (5)
Major-league Melissa
Davis, Gibbs
Never sink nine series (2)
Major Mitchell's cocky chaff
Nelson, Brian
Cocky chaff series (1)
Major occasions
Greene, L Patrick
Aubrey Saint John Major series (9)
Major operation
White, James
Sector General series (3)
Major steps out
Ross, John
Major Hutton Seary series (3)
Major Thompson and I
Daninos, Pierre
Major Thompson series (2)
Major Thompson goes French
Daninos, Pierre
Major Thompson series (3)
Major Thompson lives in France and discovers the French
Daninos, Pierre
Major Thompson series (1)
Majors
Griffin, W E B
Brotherhood of war series (3)
Major's candlesticks
Birmingham, George A
Reverend J J Meldon series (4)
Major's favourite
Winter, John Strange
Bootles series (11)
Major's niece
Birmingham, George A
Reverend J J Meldon series (3)
Makariri gold
Priestley, Brian
Willy Hand series (1)
Makassar Strait contract
Atlee, Philip
Joe Gall series (22)
Make a cow laugh
Holgate, John
Farm life series (1)
Make a face
Ahlberg, Allan
Red nose readers series (3)
Make a killing
Masur, Harold Q
Scott Jordan series (10)
Make-a-mistake story
Erickson, Karen
I can do it series (7)
Make a wish for me
Weber, Lenora Mattingly
Beany Malone series (6)
Make a world
Emberley, Ed
Ed Emberley's drawing book series (2)
Make death love me
Rendell, Ruth
Chief Inspector Reginald Wexford series (11)
Make me a murderer
Butler, Gwendoline
Inspector John Coffin series (6)
Make me a star
Chase, Emily
Canby Hall series (10)
Quin-Harkin, Janet
Sugar and spice series (10)
Make me rich
Corris, Peter
Cliff Hardy series (7)
Make mine a harlot
Storm, Michael
Nick Cranley series (1)
Make mine Maclain
Kendrick, Baynard
Captain Duncan Maclain series (12)
Make mine Mavis
Ard, William
Lou Largo series (3)
Make mine mayhem
Muller, Paul
Paul Muller series (2)
Make mine mink
Janson, Hank
Hank Janson series (229)
Make mine murder
Bowen, Robert Sidney
Gerry Barnes series (1)
Graham, Neill
Solo Malcolm series (11)
Make my bed soon
Strange, John Stephen
Barney Gantt series (6)
Make my coffin big
O'Sullivan, James Brendan
Steve Silk series (15)
Make no bones
Elkins, Aaron J
Professor Gideon Oliver series (7)
Make no mistake
Keene, Carolyn
Nancy Drew files series (56)
Make or break
Counsel, George
Land in need series (2)
Optic, Oliver
Starry flag series (5)
Make out with murder
Harrison, Chip
Leo Haig series (1)
Make peace, not war
Carr-Martindale, Jesse
Dempsey and Makepeace series (1)
Make the world laugh
Korman, Justine
Roger Rabbit series (2)
Make them pay
Ludlow, Ian
Vigilante series (2)
Make us happy
Herzog, Arthur
America series (1)
Make way for dragons!
Gunnarsson, Thorarinn
Dragons series (1)
Make way for murder
Marcus, Arthur A
Pete Hunter series (3)
Make way for the mourners
Hume, David
Mick Cardby series (17)
Makeover murders
Rowe, Jennifer
Verity Birdwood series (4)
Maker of Heavenly Trousers
Vare, Daniele
Yen-Ching trilogy (1)
Maker of shadows
Mann, Jack
Gregory George Gordon Green series (5)
Maker of universes
Farmer, Philip Jose
World of Tiers series (1)
Makers of the realm
Bryant, Arthur
Story of England series (1)
Makeshift husband
Stahl, Hilda
Prairie series (3)
Make-up for murder
Wright, June
Inspector Savage series (2)
Mother Paul series (3)
Make-up for the Toff
Creasey, John
Toff series (34)
Making a wish
York, Carol Beach
Heart to heart series (4)
Making changes
Cooney, Linda A
Totally hot series (4)
Making friends
Chase, Emily
Canby Hall series (18)
Matthews, Andrew
Human relations series (2)
Ormerod, Jan
New baby books series (3)
Making good blood
Melville, Jennie
Sergeant Charmian Daniels series (11)
Making it
Blake, Susan
Cheerleaders series (19)
Making it big
Jakes, John
Johnny Havoc series (4)
Making it on our own
Lantz, Francess Lin
Overnight Sensation series (2)
Making of a European
Whelpton, Eric
Making series (1)
Making of a general, 1887-1942
Hamilton, Nigel
Montgomery of Alamein trilogy (1)
Making of a lawman
Edson, John Thomas
Floating Outfit series (24)
Making of a marchioness
Burnett, Frances Hodgson
Lady Walderhurst series (1)
Making of a psychiatrist
Viscott, David Steven
Portrait of a psychiatrist series (2)

Making of a statesman
Plumb, John Harold
Sir Robert Walpole series (1)
Making of an admiral, 1854-1904
Fisher, John Arbuthnot
Fear God and dread nought trilogy (1)
Making of an Englishman
Whelpton, Eric
Making series (2)
Making of Fingers Finnegan
Doherty, Berlie
Fingers Finnegan series (2)
Making of Joshua Cobb
Hodges, Margaret
Joshua Cobb series (2)
Making of Meenie
Gilbert, Edith Laura
Meenie series (2)
Making of Megabot
Hall, Willis
Megabot series (1)
Making of Red Dwarf
Naylor, Grant
Red Dwarf series (3)
Making of Superman, the movie
Petrou, David Michael
Superman series (7)
Making of T2
Shay, Don
Terminator series (2)
Making of the representative for Planet Eight
Lessing, Doris
Canopus in Argus archives series (4)
Making of Tintin
Herge
Tintin series (12)
Making of Tintin in the world of the Incas
Herge
Tintin series (14)
Making over Martha
Lippmann, Julie Mathilde
Martha trilogy (2)
Making promises
Cooper, M E
Couples series (8)
Making room for Katherine
Mulford, Philippa Greene
Abbey series (2)
Making the best of it
Rand, Edward Augustus
Look ahead series (1)
Making the grade
Blake, Susan
Hawthorne College series (11)
Wharton, Joanna
Campus fever series (1)
Making the horse laugh
Tovey, Doreen
Cats series (8)
Making the stand for Old Glory
Hancock, Harrie Irving
Conquest of the United States series (4)
Making the team
Hughes, Dean
Angel Park All-Stars series (1)
Making up your own mind
Berry, Joy
Ready-set-grow series (8)
Making waves
Chandler, A C
Going for it series (1)
Cole, Jennifer
Cindy and Nicole series (8)
Keene, Carolyn
Nancy Drew files series (81)
Malabang pearl
Archer, Frank
Inspector Joseph Delaney series (1)
Malabar Farm
Bromfield, Louis
Malabar series (2)
Malacca cane
Kemp, Robert
Stories of Edinburgh life series (1)
Malady in Madeira
Bridge, Ann
Julia Probyn series (8)
Malady of magicks
Gardner, Craig Shaw
Ebenezum series (1)
Malay boy
Dalton, Clive
Malay series (2)
Malay canoe
Dalton, Clive
Malay series (1)
Malay cruise
Dalton, Clive
Malay series (4)
Malay island
Dalton, Clive
Malay series (3)
Malay pirate
Dalton, Clive
Malay series (7)
Malay schooner
Dalton, Clive
Malay series (5)
Malay treasure
Dalton, Clive
Malay series (6)
Malayan trilogy
Burgess, Anthony
Malayan trilogy (3)
Malcolm
Macdonald, George
Malcolm series (1)
Malcolm Sage, detective
Jenkins, Herbert
Malcolm Sage series (2)
Malcontent
Lang, Frances
Gillonne de Beauregard series (3)
Male impersonator
Benson, Edward Frederic
Lucia Billson series (4)
Maledon calls the shots
Gardner, Jerome
Hanging Judge series (10)
Malgudi days
Narayan, Rasipuram Krishnaswami
Malgudi series (13)
Malibu summer
Pascal, Francine
Sweet Valley High super series (3)
Malice domestic
Cameron, Evelyn
Sheriff Jack Thompson series (2)
Hardwick, Mollie
Doran Fairweather series (1)
Woods, Sara
Sir Nicholas Harding and Antony Maitland series (3)
Malice in camera
Payne, Laurence
Mark Savage series (2)
Malice in Kulturland
Wyatt, Horace
Alice in Wonderland parodies series (5)
Malice in Maggody
Hess, Joan
Arly Hanks series (1)
Malice in wonderland
Blake, Nicholas
Nigel Strangeways series (6)
Malice in Wonderland
King, Rufus
Stuff Driscoll series (1)
Malice with murder
Blake, Nicholas
Nigel Strangeways series (6)
Malicious mischief
Egan, Lesley
Vic Varallo series (7)
Malifestro quest
Meretzky, S Eric
Zork series (2)
Malign fiesta
Lewis, Wyndham
Human age trilogy (3)
Malignant metaphysical menace
Knight, Mallory T
Man from T.O.M.C.A.T. series (6)
Malignant showman
Laing, Kenneth
Rolling Stone series (1)
Malinsay massacre
Wheatley, Dennis
Lieutenant John Milton Schwab series (3)
Malkin's mountain
Williams, Ursula Moray
Toymakers series (2)
Mallen girl
Cookson, Catherine
Mallen family trilogy (2)
Mallen litter
Cookson, Catherine
Mallen family trilogy (3)
Mallen lot
Cookson, Catherine
Mallen family trilogy (3)
Mallen novels
Cookson, Catherine
Mallen family trilogy (3)
Mallen streak
Cookson, Catherine
Mallen family trilogy (1)
Malleson at Melbourne
Godfrey, William
Test cricket series (1)
Malleville
Abbott, Jacob
Franconia series (1)
Malloonkai
Stuart, Donald
Ilbarana series (2)
Mallory
Marshall, Raymond
Brick-Top Corridon series (1)
Mallory and the ghost cat
Martin, Ann Matthews
Baby-Sitters Club mystery series (3)
Mallory and the secret diary
Martin, Ann Matthews
Baby-Sitters Club series (29)
Mallory and the trouble with the twins
Martin, Ann Matthews
Baby-Sitters Club series (21)
Mallory hates boys, and gym
Martin, Ann Matthews
Baby-Sitters Club series (59)
Mallory on strike
Martin, Ann Matthews
Baby-Sitters Club series (47)
Mallory's dream horse
Martin, Ann Matthews
Baby-Sitters Club series (54)
Malloy of the Royal Mounted
Stoddard, Charles
Malloy series (2)
Malmordo
Grant, Maxwell
Shadow series (276)
Malone dies
Beckett, Samuel
Jacques Moran series (2)
Malone rides in
Dower, Penn
Marshal Bret Malone series (5)
Malta conspiracy
Mullally, Frederic
Bob Sullivan series (3)
Malta victory
Jackson, Robert
Flying Officer George Yeoman series (4)
Maltese Falcon
Hammett, Dashiell
Sam Spade series (1)
Maltese feline
Christian, Mary Blount
Determined detectives series (4)
Maltese vengeance
Cutter, John
Specialist series (5)
Mama
Cave, Peter
Hell's Angels series (2)
Hopkins, Lee Bennett
Mama series (1)
Mama and her boys
Hopkins, Lee Bennett
Mama series (2)
Mama doll
Woodhouse, Martin
Giles Yeoman series (3)
Mama Hattie's girl
Lenski, Lois
Regional series (9)
Mama, I love you
Saroyan, William
Mama and papa series (1)
Mama Liz drinks deep
Rheingold, Howard
Sisterhood trilogy (1)
Mama Liz tastes flesh
Rheingold, Howard
Sisterhood trilogy (2)
Mamaji
Mehta, Ved
Mehta family series (2)
Mama's way
Bjorn, Thyra Ferre
Pastor Pontus Franzon series (3)
Mambo
Armstrong, Campbell
Detective Frank Pagan series (3)
Mamelukes
Stewart, Desmond
Sequence of roles trilogy (3)
Mamie's watchword
Mathews, Joanna Hooe
Little sunbeams series (5)
Mamma's boarding house
Fitzgerald, John Dennis
Will Fitzgerald trilogy (2)
Mammoth hunters
Allen, Willis Boyd
Camp and tramp series (2)
Auel, Jean Marie
Earth's children series (3)
Mammoth man
Sheldon, Roy
Magdah series (1)
Mamo murders
Sheridan, Juanita
Lily Wu and Janice Cameron series (3)
Ma'mselle it's murder
McCall, K T
Johnny Buchanan series (9)
Mamur Zapt and the camel of destruction
Pearce, Michael
Mamur Zapt series (7)
Mamur Zapt and the donkey-vous
Pearce, Michael
Mamur Zapt series (3)
Mamur Zapt and the girl in the Nile
Pearce, Michael
Mamur Zapt series (5)
Mamur Zapt and the men behind
Pearce, Michael
Mamur Zapt series (4)
Mamur Zapt and the night of the dog
Pearce, Michael
Mamur Zapt series (2)
Mamur Zapt and the return of the carpet
Pearce, Michael
Mamur Zapt series (1)
Mamur Zapt and the spoils of Egypt
Pearce, Michael
Mamur Zapt series (6)
Mam'zelle Guillotine
Orczy, Emmuska
Scarlet Pimpernel series (10)
Man
Scott, Will
Disher series (3)
Man above suspicion
Mayo, James
Charles Hood series (5)
Man against man
Carter, Nicholas
Nicholas Carter series (101)
Deming, Richard
Law at work series (2)
Man against man-eaters
Corbett, Jim
Man-eaters series (2)
Man alive
Cronin, Michael
James Hellier series (1)
Stout, Rex
Nero Wolfe and Archie Goodwin series (16)
Man alone
Norwood, Victor George Charles
Man alone series (1)
Man and ancient civilizations
Greene, Carla
Science and natural history series (6)
Man and his price
Carter, Nicholas
Nicholas Carter series (102)
Man and master
Lynch, Lawrence L
Carl Masters series (3)
Man and monster
Scheer, Karl Herbert
Perry Rhodan series (36)
Man and society
Deming, Richard
Law at work series (1)
Man and the world
Deming, Richard
Law at work series (3)
Man at the wheel
Kenyon, Michael
Inspector Henry Peckover series (3)
Man at the window
Carter, Nicholas
Nicholas Carter series (80)
Man behind the curtain
Murray, Andrew
Sexton Blake series (301)
Walsh, James Morgan
Bromley Kay series (2)
Man behind the murder
Jones, G Wayman
Black Bat series (25)
Man born of woman
Ronald, James
Quentin Gourlay series (1)
Man called Alamo
Moore, Arthur
Alamo series (1)
Man called Black
Manson, Will
Man called Black series (1)
Man called Drago
McCoy, Marshall
Nevada Jim series (28)
Man called Horse
Johnson, Dorothy Marie
Man called Horse series (1)
Man called Hughes
Lillington, Kenneth
Soapy series (2)
Man called Intrepid
Stevenson, William Henri
William Stephenson series (1)
Man called Jones
Symons, Julian
Inspector Bland series (2)
Man called Kyril
Trenhaile, John
General Povin series (1)
Man called Milo Morai
Adams, Robert
Horseclans series (14)
Man called Peter
Marshall, Catherine
Peter Marshall series (1)
Man called Spade
Hammett, Dashiell
Sam Spade series (3)
Man called Storm
Stevens, Steve
Jack Storm series (1)
Man called Tempest
Shand, William
Bill Tempest series (1)
Man called Trent
L'Amour, Louis
Lance Kilkenny series (2)
Man condemned
Alding, Peter
C.I.D. Room series (12)
Man could stand up
Ford, Ford Madox
Parade's end series (3)
Man died talking
Garnett, Roger
Chief Inspector Jonathan Black series (4)
Man-eater
Conway, Troy
Coxeman series (9)
Man-eater of Malgudi
Narayan, Rasipuram Krishnaswami
Malgudi series (9)
Man-eaters and Masai spears
Ludwig, Charles Shelton
Missionary adventure series (1)
Man-eater's clauw
Ludwig, Charles Shelton
Missionary adventure series (4)
Man-eaters don't knock
Ludwig, Charles Shelton
Missionary adventure series (2)
Man-eaters don't laugh
Ludwig, Charles Shelton
Missionary adventure series (3)
Man-eaters of Cascalon
Lancour, Gene
Dirshan series (4)
Man-eaters of Kumaon
Corbett, Jim
Man-eaters series (1)
Man-eating animals
Aaseng, Nathan
Early nature picture book series (3)
Man-eating leopard of Rudraprayag
Corbett, Jim
Man-eaters series (2)
Man everybody was afraid of
Hansen, Joseph
Dave Brandstetter series (4)
Man for Marcy
Du Jardin, Rosamond
Marcy series (3)
Man for the ages
Bacheller, Irving
Abraham Lincoln trilogy (2)
Man from Algiers
Jardine, Warwick
Sexton Blake series (1213)
Man from Arnheim
Jackson, Lewis
Sexton Blake series (1141)
Man from Atlantis
Robeson, Kenneth
Avenger series (25)
Woodley, Richard
Man from Atlantis series (1)
Man from Australia
Symonds, Francis Addington
Sexton Blake series (535)

Man from Bar Harbour
Mitcham, Gilroy
Nick Marshall series (2)
Man from Bar-20
Mulford, Clarence Edward
Hopalong Cassidy series (6)
Johnny Nelson series (1)
Man from Barbarossa
Gardner, John Edmund
James Bond series (27)
Man from Broken Hills
L'Amour, Louis
Sackett family series (16)
Man from C.H.A.R.I.S.M.A.
Mark, Ted
Man from C.H.A.R.I.S.M.A. series (1)
Man from Checkmate
Bennett, William Robert
Adam Kane series (1)
Man from Cheyenne
Slade, Jack
Lassiter series (3)
Man from China
Parsons, Anthony
Sexton Blake series (1040)
Man from Chun King
Hardinge, Rex
Sexton Blake series (1156)
Man from Dahomey
Yerby, Frank
Hwesu series (1)
Man from Dartmoor
Evans, Gwyn
Sexton Blake series (705)
Man from Del Rio
Slade, Jack
Lassiter series (5)
Man from Dieppe
King, Hilary
Sexton Blake series (1303)
Man from Dublin
Blair, Allan
Sexton Blake series (742)
Man from everywhere
Simenon, Georges
Inspector Jules Maigret series (17)
Man from Fleet Street
Creasey, John
Sexton Blake series (1019)
Man from Furnace Creek
Ryan, Tom
Brannigan series (2)
Man from Glengarry
Connor, Ralph
Glengarry series (1)
Man from Holland
Hardinge, Rex
Sexton Blake series (802)
Man from India
Carter, Nicholas
Nicholas Carter series (30)
Man from Internal Affairs
Hentoff, Nat
Noah Green series (2)
Man from Italy
Brandon, John Gordon
Sexton Blake series (912)
Man from Kabul
De Villiers, Gerard
Malko Linge series (8)
Man from Kenya
Parsons, Anthony
Sexton Blake series (1193)
Man from Kura-Kura
Murray, Andrew
Sexton Blake series (141)
Man from London
Carter, Nicholas
Nicholas Carter series (79)
Man from Lordsburg
Slade, Jack
Lassiter series (9)
Man from M.O.D.
Day, Will B
Steven Flagg series (2)
Man from Madagascar
Grierson, Francis Durham
Commissaire Patras series (4)
Man from Madrid
Meriton, Peter
Sexton Blake series (1094)
Man from Maybrick Road
Parsons, Anthony
Sexton Blake series (1362)
Man from Michigan
Graeme, Bruce
Superintendent William Stevens and Inspector Pierre Allain series (8)
Man from Mongolia
Hardinge, Rex
Sexton Blake series (1182)
Man from Moscow
Chester, Gilbert
Sexton Blake series (925)
McCutchan, Philip
Commander Esmonde Shaw series (4)
Usher, Frank
Amanda Curzon and Oscar Sallis series (1)
Man from Mundania
Anthony, Piers
Xanth series (12)
Man from Mustang
Brand, Max
Silvertip series (4)
Man from Norway
Chester, Gilbert
Sexton Blake series (1051)
Man from O.R.G.Y.
Mark, Ted
Man from O.R.G.Y. series (1)
Man from occupied France
Parsons, Anthony
Sexton Blake series (1057)
Man from P.A.N.S.Y.
Rico, Don
Burgess Cardigan series (2)
Man from Papago Wells
Slade, Jack
Lassiter series (21)
Man from Paris
Daniel, Roland
Buddy Mustard series (12)
Man from Pecos
Reid, Desmond
Pinkerton series (3)
Man from Persia
Jackson, Lewis
Sexton Blake series (1285)
Man from Robber's Roost
Field, Peter
Powder Valley series (57)
Man from S.T.U.D. versus the Mafia
Paul, F W
Man from S.T.U.D. series (9)
Man from Saint Louis
Charteris, Leslie
Saint series (10)
Man from Scotland Yard
Frome, David
Evan Pinkerton series (3)
Grant, Maxwell
Shadow series (83)
Man from Shanghai
Grant, Maxwell
Shadow series (100)
Man from Singapore
Brandon, John Gordon
Sexton Blake series (991)
Man from Snowy River
Mitchell, Elyne
Man from Snowy River series (1)
Silver Brumby series (10)
Man from Snowy River, and other verses
Paterson, Andrew Barton
Man from Snowy River series (2)
Man from space
Hardinge, Rex
Sexton Blake series (1304)
Man from Texas
Edson, John Thomas
Floating Outfit series (55)
Man from the broken hills
L'Amour, Louis
Talon family series (1)
Man from the Far East
Hunter, John
Sexton Blake series (1130)
Man from the jungle
Hardinge, Rex
Sexton Blake series (1037)
Man from the Norlands
Buchan, John
Richard Hannay series (6)
Man from the north
Bennett, Arnold
Five towns series (1)
Man from the past
Clifford, Martin
Tom Merry series (8)
Mackenzie, Andrew
Nicholas Cornish series (6)
Man from the river
Cole, George Douglas Howard
Superintendent Henry Wilson series (4)
Man from the rock
Bateson, David
Larry Vernon series (2)
Man from Thief River
Field, Peter
Powder Valley series (11)
Man from Thrush
Peel, John
U.N.C.L.E. files series (4)
Man from Tibet
Clason, Clyde B
Theocritus Lucius Westborough series (5)
Man from Tokyo
Jardine, Warwick
Sexton Blake series (763)
Man from Tombstone
Slade, Jack
Lassiter series (15)
Man from U.N.C.L.E.
Avallone, Michael
Man from U.N.C.L.E. series (1)
Man from U.N.C.L.E. and the affair of the gentle saboteur
Keith, Brandon
Man from U.N.C.L.E. series (24)
Man from U.N.C.L.E. and the affair of the gun-runner's gold
Keith, Brandon
Man from U.N.C.L.E. series (24)
Man from U.N.C.L.E.'s ABCs of espionage
Hill, John
Man from U.N.C.L.E. series (24)
Man from White Hat
Jason, Stuart
Butcher series (34)
Man from Whitehall
Walsh, James Morgan
Colonel Ormiston series (5)
Man from Wyoming
Kidd, Russ
Wyoming series (1)
Man from Yuma
Slade, Jack
Lassiter series (2)
Man higher up
Miller, Henry Russell
Life and love series (1)
Man hunt
Household, Geoffrey
Raymond Ingelram series (1)
Man-hunter
Donovan, Dick
Dick Donovan series (1)
Man in a mist
Lamb, Lynton
Superintendent Quill and Inspector Glover series (4)
Man in ambush
Procter, Maurice
Chief Inspector Harry Martineau series (10)
Man in black
Conroy, Al
Clayburn series (4)
Man in brown
Edwards, Walter
Sexton Blake series (827)
Man in button boots
Gilbert, Anthony
Dupuy series (1)
Man in Europe Street
Croft-Cooke, Rupert
Sensual life series (26)
Man in fifteen
Lee, Benjamin
Mike and Bill Hendry series (2)
Man in gray
Crane, Frances
Pat and Jean Abbott series (22)
Vivian, Evelyn Charles
Inspector Head series (9)
Man in grey
Perry, Jean
News from Korea series (2)
Man in his times
Bentley, Phyllis
Oldroyd family series (3)
Man in my shoes
Chance, John Newton
John Newton Chance series (4)
Man in the auto
Carter, Nicholas
Nicholas Carter series (374)
Man in the blue mask
Morton, Anthony
Baron series (1)
Man in the bottle
Knox, Bill
Inspector Colin Thane and Phil Moss series (6)
Man in the brown suit
Christie, Agatha
Colonel Race series (1)
Man in the cloak
Horler, Sydney
Robert Wynnton series (1)
Man in the corner
Orczy, Emmuska
Old man in the corner series (2)
Man in the dark
Ferguson, John
Francis Macnab series (1)
Man in the driver's seat
Walker, Ira
Steve Rhoden series (2)
Man in the glass booth
Shaw, Robert
Cure of souls trilogy (2)
Man in the gray flannel shroud
Orenstein, Frank
Ev Franklin series (2)
Man in the gray flannel suit
Wilson, Sloan
Man in the gray flannel suit series (1)
Man in the gray flannel suit II
Wilson, Sloan
Man in the gray flannel suit series (2)
Man in the green Chevy
Cooper, Susan Rogers
Milton Kovak series (1)
Man in the green hat
Coles, Manning
Tommy Hambledon series (18)
Man in the grey cowl
Murray, Andrew
Sexton Blake series (193)
Man in the grey flannel suit
Wilson, Sloan
Man in the gray flannel suit series (1)
Man in the Iron Mask
Dumas, Alexandre
Three Musketeers series (3)
Man in the jury box
Chipperfield, Robert Orr
Barry O'Dell series (2)
Man in the making
Bryant, Arthur
Samuel Pepys series (1)
Man in the middle
Chaber, M E
Milo March series (16)
Man in the mist
Bonnamy, Francis
Peter Shane series (8)
Man in the moonlight
McCloy, Helen
Basil Willing series (2)
Man in the queue
Tey, Josephine
Inspector Alan Grant series (1)
Man in the red mask
Vickers, Roy
Inspector J Rason series (11)
Man in the sandhills
Marsden, Antony
Jim Beverley series (1)
Man in the shadow
Kyle, Sefton
Inspector J Rason series (2)
Man in the shadows
Corris, Peter
Cliff Hardy series (12)
Man in the train
Pullen, Alan
Sam and Lin series (3)
Man in the tricorn hat
Ames, Delano
Juan Llorca series (1)
Man in two camps
Cunningham, Chet
Wade Chisholm series (3)
Man inside
Chaber, M E
Milo March series (3)
Man-Kzin wars
Anderson, Poul
Man-Kzin wars series (1)
Ing, Dean
Known Space series (17)
Niven, Larry
Known Space series (17)
Man-Kzin wars series (1)
Man-Kzin wars II
Ing, Dean
Known Space series (18)
Niven, Larry
Known Space series (18)
Man-Kzin wars series (2)
Pournelle, Jerry
Man-Kzin wars series (2)
Stirling, Stephen Michael
Known Space series (18)
Man-Kzin wars series (2)
Man-Kzin wars III
Anderson, Poul
Known Space series (19)
Niven, Larry
Known Space series (19)
Man-Kzin wars series (3)
Pournelle, Jerry
Man-Kzin wars series (3)
Stirling, Stephen Michael
Known Space series (19)
Man-Kzin wars series (3)
Man-Kzin wars IV
Niven, Larry
Known Space series (22)
Man-Kzin wars series (4)
Man-Kzin wars V
Niven, Larry
Man-Kzin wars series (5)
Man lay dead
Marsh, Ngaio
Inspector Roderick Alleyn series (1)
Man made of tin
Martin, Shane
Professor Ronald Challis series (3)
Man made woman
Murphy, Robert Franklin
Girl factory series (1)
Man Miss Susie loved
Tucker, Augusta
Miss Susie Slagle series (2)
Man missing
Eberhart, Mignon Good
Sarah Keate and Lance O'Leary series (8)
Man named Thin
Hammett, Dashiell
Continental Op series (5)
Man nobody knew
Lindsay, David T
Inspector John Jay Jackson series (3)
Man nobody saw
Cheyney, Peter
Johnny Vallon series (1)
Man o' War
Farley, Walter
Black stallion series (16)
Man of a ghost
Wren, Percival Christopher
Khairastan series (1)
Man of bronze
Robeson, Kenneth
Doc Savage series (1)
Man of death
Gask, Arthur
Gilbert Larose series (21)
Man of December
Neumann, Alfred
Napoleon III trilogy (2)
Man of glass
Zochert, Donald
Nick Caine series (2)
Man of gold
Barker, Muhammad Abd al-Rahman
Tekumel series (1)
Hervey, Evelyn
Harriet Unwin series (2)
Man of his age
Drummond, Hamilton
Religious wars trilogy (2)
Man of his times
Bentley, Phyllis
West Riding series (18)
Man of iron
Carter, Nicholas
Nicholas Carter series (246)
Man of last resort
Post, Melville Davisson
Randolph Mason series (2)
Man of many faces
Carter, Nicholas
Nicholas Carter series (604)
Man of many minds
Evans, Edward Everett
George Hanlon series (1)
Man of mystery
Carter, Nicholas
Nicholas Carter series (77)
Man of property
Galsworthy, John
Forsyte saga trilogy (1)
Man of riddles
Carter, Nicholas
Nicholas Carter series (529)
Man of straw
Giono, Jean
Angelo series (3)
Man of substance
Hodges, Arthur
Blake family series (1)

Man of the family
Moody, Ralph
Ralph series (2)
Man of the forty faces
Hanshew, Thomas W
Hamilton Cleek series (1)
Man of the moors
Sutcliffe, Halliwell
Griff Lomax series (1)
Man of the shadows
Coldsmith, Don
Spanish bit series (5)
Man of the world
Fogazzaro, Antonio
Maironi family trilogy (2)
Man of two tribes
Upfield, Arthur William
Napoleon Bonaparte series (21)
Man on a leash
Williams, Charles
John Ingram series (2)
Man on a string
Wolfe, Michael
Michael Keefe series (1)
Man on all fours
Derleth, August
Judge Ephraim Peck series (2)
Man on my back
Linklater, Eric
Man on my back series (1)
Man on Pulpit Rock
Grover, Marshall
Larry and Stretch series (141)
Man on the balcony
Sjowall, Maj
Inspector Martin Beck series (3)
Man on the bridge
Black, Ian Stuart
Peter Munro series (1)
Man on the dole
Urquhart, Paul
Sexton Blake series (978)
Man on the end of a rope
Townend, Peter
McGill series (1)
Man on the rope
Buckley, Eunice
Sandor Raimann series (2)
Man on the run
Halliday, Michael
Martin and Richard Fane series (4)
Kirby, Arthur
Sexton Blake series (1491)
Man on the run
Stewart-Hargreaves, Eustace
Hamilton Ian
Cotswold Cider Company series (2)
Man on the spot
Mason, S C
Derek Glover series (2)
Man overboard
Crofts, Freeman Wills
Inspector Joseph French series (15)
Leyland, Eric
Max and Scrap series (5)
Mackinnon, Allan
Donald Kendrick series (2)
Man pursued
White, James G
Gunslick series (1)
Man rides through
Donaldson, Stephen Reeder
Mordant's need series (2)
Man running
Jepson, Selwyn
Eve Gill series (1)
Man-Shy
Davison, Frank Dalby
Man-Shy series (1)
Man, the fugitive
Effinger, George Alec
Planet of the Apes series (6)
Man, the hunted animal
Arrow, William
Return to the Planet of the Apes series (3)
Man they could not convict
Hardinge, Rex
Sexton Blake series (930)
Man they couldn't buy
Chester, Gilbert
Sexton Blake series (1109)
Man they feared
Plummer, Thomas Arthur
Detective Inspector Andrew Frampton series (6)
Man they held back
Carter, Nicholas
Nicholas Carter series (614)
Man they put away
Plummer, Thomas Arthur
Detective Inspector Andrew Frampton series (8)
Man to be feared
Carter, Nicholas
Nicholas Carter series (282)
Man to match the hour
Truss, Seldon
Inspector Gidleigh series (14)
Man who asked why
Ryan, Jessica
Gregory Pavlov and O'Shaughnessey series (1)
Man who ate a car
Mooser, Stephen
Creepy Creature Club series (10)
Man who backed out!
Parsons, Anthony
Sexton Blake series (1216)
Man who bailed out
Chester, Gilbert
Sexton Blake series (1065)
Man who bit snakes
Hardin, J D
Raider and Doc series (6)
Man who bombed the world
Milton, Joseph
Bart Gould series (7)
Man who came back
Bryan, John
Richard Sarel series (3)
Graydon, William Murray
Sexton Blake series (572)
Man who captivated New York
Lieberman, Rosalie
Brother Angelo series (2)
Man who caught the 4.15
Spiller, Andrew
Chief Inspector Duck Mallard series (10)
Man who changed faces
Carter, Nicholas
Nicholas Carter series (519)
Man who changed his face
Plummer, Thomas Arthur
Detective Inspector Andrew Frampton series (17)
Man who changed his name
Wright, Eric
Inspector Charlie Salter series (4)
Man who convicted himself
Fox, David
Shadowers Inc. series (1)
Man who could not shudder
Carr, John Dickson
Doctor Gideon Fell series (12)
Man who couldn't be
Jeffries, Roderic Graeme
Sunken danger series (3)
Man who counts
Anderson, Poul
Polesotechnic League series (5)
Man who covered mirrors
Cumberland, Marten
Saturnin Dax series (12)
Man who crawled away
Butler, Leslie
Horton and Jordan series (3)
Man who did not die
Harknett, Terry
Stephen Wayne series (6)
Man who didn't answer
Oellrichs, Inez
Matt Winters series (1)
Man who didn't exist
Homes, Geoffrey
Robin Bishop series (3)
Man who didn't mind hanging
Mavity, Nancy Barr
Peter Piper series (5)
Man who died laughing
Handler, David
Stewart Hoag series (1)
Man who died on Friday
Underwood, Michael
Richard Monk series (1)
Man who died too soon
Coxe, George Harmon
Flash Casey series (5)
Man who dressed to kill
Spiller, Andrew
Chief Inspector Duck Mallard series (27)
Man who drove on
Graydon, William Murray
Sexton Blake series (485)
Man who fainted
Carter, Nicholas
Nicholas Carter series (485)
Man who fell
Eden, Matthew
Marc Savage series (4)
Man who fell through the earth
Wells, Carolyn
Pennington Wise series (1)
Man who fell up
Robeson, Kenneth
Doc Savage series (112)
Man who followed women
Hitchens, Bert
Collins and McKechnie series (2)
Man who forgot
Armour, R Coutts
Sexton Blake series (158)
Man who grew tomatoes
Mitchell, Gladys
Dame Beatrice Bradley series (32)
Man who had enemies
Broome, H B
Tom English series (3)
man who had to quit
Parsons, Anthony
Sexton Blake series (1168)
Man who had too much to lose
Stone, Hampton
Jeremiah X Gibson series (7)
Man who heard too much
Granger, Bill
November Man series (11)
Man who hunts Jenner
Grover, Marshall
Nevada Jim series (16)
Man who killed Fortescue
Strange, John Stephen
Van Dusen Ormsberry series (1)
Man who killed his brother
Stephens, Reed
Mick Axbrewder series (1)
Man who killed me
Maclean, Arthur
Sexton Blake series (1452)
Man who killed the king
Wheatley, Dennis
Roger Brook series (4)
Man who killed too soon
Underwood, Michael
Richard Monk series (2)
Man who knew Coolidge
Lewis, Sinclair
American society series (2)
Man who knew too much
Baker, William Howard
Sexton Blake series (1371)
Man who laughed
Fairlie, Gerard
Victor Caryll series (2)
Man who laughed at murder
Ashe, Gordon
Patrick Dawlish series (36)
Man who left home
Jackson, Lewis
Sexton Blake series (1242)
Man who liked slow tomatoes
Constantine, K C
Mario Balzic series (5)
Man who liked to look at himself
Constantine, K C
Mario Balzic series (2)
Man who listens
Caldwell, Taylor
Listener series (1)
Man who lived by night
Handler, David
Stewart Hoag series (2)
Man who looked death in the eye
Stone, Hampton
Jeremiah X Gibson series (11)
Man who lost his memory
Skene, Anthony
Sexton Blake series (1197)
Man who lost his shadow
Denham, Bertie
Derek Thyrde series (1)
Man who loved chocolates
Batchelor, Denzil
Inspector Johnson series (1)
Man who loved Mars
Carter, Lin
Mars series (1)
Man who loved Morlocks
Lake, David John
Time traveller series (5)
Man who loved spiders
Horler, Sydney
Constable Meatyard series (2)
Man who made custard
Myers, David
Sebastian, the incredible drawing dog series (1)
Man who mastered time
Cummings, Ray
Matter, space and time series (3)
Man who met the train
Adams, Harold
Carl Wilcox series (7)
Man who missed the party
Adams, Harold
Carl Wilcox series (8)
Man who murdered Goliath
Homes, Geoffrey
Robin Bishop series (4)
Man who murdered himself
Homes, Geoffrey
Robin Bishop series (2)
Man who never blundered
Gluck, Sinclair
Ross McCoy series (1)
Man who never missed
Perry, Steve
Khadaji series (2)
Man who never slept!
Evans, Gwyn
Sexton Blake series (372)
Man who never was
Picard, Sam
John Scott series (2)
Man who paid
Carter, Nicholas
Nicholas Carter series (517)
Man who played patience
Truss, Seldon
Inspector Gidleigh series (2)
Man who played thief
Smith, Don
Tim Parnell series (1)
Man who plundered the city
Elvestad, Sven
Osborne Crag series (1)
Man who rang the bell
Kennedy, Milward
Inspector Cornford series (1)
Man who risked his partner
Stephens, Reed
Mick Axbrewder series (2)
Man who rocked the earth
Train, Arthur
Benjamin Hooker series (1)
Man who shook earth
Horler, Sydney
Sir Charles Knightley series (2)
Man who shook the earth
Horler, Sydney
Sir Charles Knightley series (1)
Robeson, Kenneth
Doc Savage series (43)
Man who shook the world
Creasey, John
Doctor Palfrey series (13)
Man who shot birds, and other tales
Fitt, Mary
Superintendent Mallett series (15)
Man who shot Lewis Vance
Kaminsky, Stuart Melvin
Toby Peters series (11)
Man who slept all day
Venning, Michael
Melville Fairr series (1)
Man who sold Christmas
Lieberman, Rosalie
Brother Angelo series (1)
Man who sold death
Carter, Nick
Nick Carter series (90)
Munro, James
John Craig series (1)
Man who sold Leadville
Ketchum, Philip
Elijah Cabot Pickering series (3)
Man who sold secrets
Daniel, Roland
Jim Maitland series (2)
Man who sold the moon
Heinlein, Robert Anson
Future history series (2)
Man who squealed
Philips, George Norman
Sexton Blake series (589)
Man who stole heaven
Ingersol, Jared
Carl Moore series (4)
Man who stole millions, and other stories
Carter, Nicholas
Nicholas Carter series (65)
Man who stole tomorrow
Michelinie, David
Avengers superheroes series (2)
Marvel superheroes, new series (10)
Man who tamed Dodge
Ketchum, Philip
Elijah Cabot Pickering series (1)
Man who turned king's evidence
Hunter, John
Sexton Blake series (980)
Man who turned outlaw
Ketchum, Philip
Elijah Cabot Pickering series (2)
Man who understood women, and other stories
Merrick, Leonard
Parisian series (1)
Man who upset the universe
Asimov, Isaac
Foundation series (3)
Man who used perfume
Horler, Sydney
Robert Wynnton series (2)
Man who vanished
Carter, Nicholas
Nicholas Carter series (43)
Man who vanished into space
Johns, William Earl
Rex Clinton series (10)
Man who walked like a bear
Kaminsky, Stuart Melvin
Inspector Porfiry Petrovich Rostnikov series (6)
Man who walked on diamonds
Quartermain, James
Raven series (2)
Man who walked with death
Horler, Sydney
Brett Carstairs series (1)
Man who wanted to die
Mackenzie, Andrew
Superintendent Brannigan series (7)
Man who was cursed
Carter, Nicholas
Nicholas Carter series (206)
Man who was dead
Sykes, William Stanley
Inspector Dennis Drury series (1)
Man who was God
Chase, Glen
Cherry Delight series (29)
Man who was murdered twice
Leitfred, Robert H
Simon Crole series (2)
Man who was not himself
Halliday, Michael
Doctor Emmanuel Cellini series (11)
Man who was scared
Robeson, Kenneth
Doc Savage series (104)
Man who was taller than God
Adams, Harold
Carl Wilcox series (9)
Man who was there
Morris, Wright
Lone Tree series (1)
Temple-Ellis, N A
Montrose Arbuthnot series (2)
Man who was three jumps ahead
Stone, Hampton
Jeremiah X Gibson series (10)
Man who was too clever
Gilbert, Anthony
Scott Egerton series (10)
Man who was too much
Gardner, Alan Harold
Davis Troy series (4)
Man who wasn't there
Gilbert, Anthony
Arthur Crook series (2)
Sandys, James
Mister Springfield series (4)
Wainwright, John
Inspector Lyle series (4)
Northern Police series (60)
Whitaker, Beryl
John Abbot series (4)
Man who went up in smoke
Sjowall, Maj
Inspector Martin Beck series (2)
Man who went wrong
Jackson, Lewis
Sexton Blake series (1212)
Man who would be F Scott Fitzgerald
Handler, David
Stewart Hoag series (3)
Man who would do anything
Ross, Ivan T
Ben Gordon series (4)
Man who wouldn't out
Chester, Gilbert
Sexton Blake series (1110)
Man with a crutch
Carter, Nicholas
Nicholas Carter series (416)
Man with a double
Carter, Nicholas
Nicholas Carter series (418)
Man with a grievance
Jardine, Warwick
Sexton Blake series (1307)

Man with a load of mischief
Grimes, Martha
Inspector Richard Jury series (1)

Man with a monocle
Gregg, Cecil Freeman
Inspector Cuthbert Higgins series (26)

Man with a number
Blakesley, Stephen
Sexton Blake series (1298)

Man with a paper skull
Marfield, Dwight
Dudley Brent series (2)
Gail McGurk series (2)
Inspector Skane series (2)

Man with a scar
Vivian, Evelyn Charles
Inspector Byrne series (2)

Man with bated breath
Carr, Joseph Baker
Oceola Archer series (2)

Man with Bogart's face
Fenady, Andrew J
Sam Marlow series (1)

Man with five enemies
Hardinge, Rex
Sexton Blake series (1378)

Man with half a face
Davison, Gilderoy
Peter Castle series (5)

Man with jitters
Brandon, John Gordon
Sexton Blake series (992)

Man with no bones
Helm, Peter
Martin Ridgway series (3)

Man with no face
Hardin, J D
Raider and Doc series (28)
Sayers, Dorothy Leigh
Lord Peter Wimsey series (5)

Man with tattooed face
Burton, Miles
Inspector Arnold and Desmond Merrion series (16)

Man with the big ideas
Myers, David
Sebastian, the incredible drawing dog series (4)

Man with the black cord
Groner, Augusta
Joe Muller series (2)

Man with the black wallet
Sayer, Walter William
Sexton Blake series (357)

Man with the broken nose, and other stories
Arlen, Michael
Charming people series (1)

Man with the brown paper face
Hamilton, Ian Sydney
Pete Heysen series (2)

Man with the clubfoot
Williams, Valentine
Clubfoot series (1)

Man with the crooked arm
Plummer, Thomas Arthur
Detective Inspector Andrew Frampton series (23)

Man with the getaway face
Stark, Richard
Parker series (2)

Man with the glaring eyes
Blair, Allan
Sexton Blake series (864)

Man with the golden gun
Fleming, Ian
James Bond series (13)

Man with the green eyes
Goddard, Norman
Sexton Blake series (32)

Man with the iron chest
Williams, Richard
Sexton Blake series (1575)

Man with the iron fists
Lee, Steve
Kung Fu western series (1)

Man with the lumpy nose
Lariar, Lawrence
Ham Macandrew and Homer Bull series (3)

Man with the tiny head
Drummond, Ivor
Lady Jennifer, Sandro and Colly series (1)

Man with the Twisted Face
Davison, Gilderoy
Peter Castle series (1)
Twisted Face series (1)

Man with the wax face
Wormser, Richard
Sergeant Joe Dixon series (1)

Man with the yellow eyes
Atkey, Bertram
Smiler Bunn series (5)

Man with three chins
Ames, Delano
Juan Llorca series (3)

Man with three fingers
Saville, Malcolm
Lone Pine Five Club series (16)

Man with three Jaguars
Ames, Delano
Juan Llorca series (2)

Man with three passports
Ames, Delano
Juan Llorca series (4)

Man with two faces
Brand, Kurt
Perry Rhodan series (104)

Man with two heads
Chance, John Newton
Jonathan Blake series (24)

Man with two left feet
Wodehouse, Pelham Grenville
Jeeves and Bertie Wooster series (15)

Man with two wives
Quentin, Patrick
Lieutenant Timothy Trant series (6)

Man without a conscience
Carter, Nicholas
Nicholas Carter series (248)

Man without a face
Robbins, Clifton
Clay Harrison series (2)

Man without a passport
Parsons, Anthony
Sexton Blake series (1312)

Man without a planet
Carter, Lin
History of the Great Imperium trilogy (1)

Man without a shadow
Wilson, Colin
Gerard Sorme trilogy (2)

Man without a soul
Burroughs, Edgar Rice
Mucker series (2)

Man without a will
Carter, Nicholas
Nicholas Carter series (584)

Managing your money
James, Elizabeth
Money series (1)

Manalacor of Veltakin
Cristabel
Veltakin series (1)

Manatitlans
Smile, R Elton
Manatitlans series (1)

Manchester connection
Ross, Angus
Mark Farrow series (1)

Manchester fourteen miles
Penn, Margaret
Hilda Winstanley trilogy (1)

Manchester thing
Ross, Angus
Mark Farrow series (1)

Manchu Jade
Jepson, Selwyn
Ian Macarthur series (1)

Mandarin cypher
Hall, Adam
Quiller series (6)

Mandarin-gold
Leasor, James
Far East series (2)

Mandarin's pearl
Montague, Jeffrey
John Jeremy series (2)

Mandarin's sapphire
Marfield, Dwight
Inspector Skane series (5)

Mandarin's seal
Murray, Andrew
Sexton Blake series (99)

Mandevilla
Thompson, Kate
Derain family series (2)

Mandeville
Trease, Geoffrey
Mandeville trilogy (1)

Mandie and the abandoned mine
Leppard, Lois Gladys
Mandie series (8)

Mandie and the angel's secret
Leppard, Lois Gladys
Mandie series (22)

Mandie and the Charleston phantom
Leppard, Lois Gladys
Mandie series (7)

Mandie and the Cherokee legend
Leppard, Lois Gladys
Mandie series (2)

Mandie and the dangerous imposter
Leppard, Lois Gladys
Mandie series (23)

Mandie and the fiery rescue
Leppard, Lois Gladys
Mandie series (21)

Mandie and the forbidden attic
Leppard, Lois Gladys
Mandie series (4)

Mandie and the foreign spies
Leppard, Lois Gladys
Mandie series (15)

Mandie and the ghost bandits
Leppard, Lois Gladys
Mandie series (3)

Mandie and the hidden treasure
Leppard, Lois Gladys
Mandie series (9)

Mandie and the holiday surprise
Leppard, Lois Gladys
Mandie series (11)

Mandie and the jumping juniper
Leppard, Lois Gladys
Mandie series (18)

Mandie and the medicine man
Leppard, Lois Gladys
Mandie series (6)

Mandie and the midnight journey
Leppard, Lois Gladys
Mandie series (13)

Mandie and the mysterious bells
Leppard, Lois Gladys
Mandie series (10)

Mandie and the mysterious fisherman
Leppard, Lois Gladys
Mandie series (19)

Mandie and the secret tunnel
Leppard, Lois Gladys
Mandie series (1)

Mandie and the shipboard mystery
Leppard, Lois Gladys
Mandie series (14)

Mandie and the silent catacombs
Leppard, Lois Gladys
Mandie series (16)

Mandie and the singing chalet
Leppard, Lois Gladys
Mandie series (17)

Mandie and the trunk's secret
Leppard, Lois Gladys
Mandie series (5)

Mandie and the Washington nightmare
Leppard, Lois Gladys
Mandie series (12)

Mandie and the windmill's message
Leppard, Lois Gladys
Mandie series (20)

Mandie's cookbook
Leppard, Lois Gladys
Mandie series (23)

Mandingo
Onstott, Kyle
Falconhurst series (1)

Mandingo Mansa
Carter, Ashley
Falconhurst series (16)

Mandragon
Koster, Richard Morton
Tinieblas trilogy (3)

Mandrake in Granada
Haythorne, John
Oliver Mandrake series (3)

Mandrake in the monastery
Haythorne, John
Oliver Mandrake series (4)

Mandrakes in the cupboard
Morris, Thomas Baden
Inspector Headley series (3)

Mandricardo
Carter, Lin
Terra Magica series (3)

Mandy and the dentist
Coles, Alison
Michael and Mandy series (6)

Mandy and the hospital
Coles, Alison
Michael and Mandy series (3)

Mandy and the train journey
Coles, Alison
Michael and Mandy series (4)

Mandy, Mops and Cubby again
Blyton, Enid
Mandy, Mops and Cubby series (2)

Mandy, Mops and Cubby and the whitewash
Blyton, Enid
Mandy, Mops and Cubby series (3)

Mandy, Mops and Cubby find a house
Blyton, Enid
Mandy, Mops and Cubby series (1)

Manetta's marriage
Burgin, George Brown
Four Corners series (14)

Maneuvers
Neuman, Fredric
Captain Redder series (2)

Manganinnie
Roberts, Beth
Drenee series (2)

Mango and the palm
Bates, Darrell
Tanganyika series (2)

Mango on the mango tree
Mathew, David
Post-war trilogy (1)

Mango season
Osbourne, Ivor
Mango season series (1)

Mangrove chronicles
Treherne, John
Doctor James Yeo series (2)

Mangrove murder
Scott, Mary
Inspector Wright series (2)

Manhattan cowboy
Brown, Carter
Danny Boyd series (23)

Manhattan file
Martin, Ian Kennedy
Sweeney series (2)

Manhattan ghost story
Wright, Terrance Michael
Manhattan series (1)

Manhattan massacre
Cunningham, Chet
Matt Hawke series (4)
McCurtin, Peter
Assassins series (1)

Manhattan night
Wolff, William Almon
Lieutenant Charley Mitchell series (1)

Manhattan revenge
Cutter, John
Specialist series (2)

Manhattan underworld
Roeburt, John
Jigger Moran series (2)

Manhattan wipeout
Rosenberger, Joseph
Death Merchant series (11)

Manhold
Bentley, Phyllis
West Riding series (3)

Manhounds of Antares
Akers, Alan Burt
Dray Prescot series (6)

Manhunt
Benteen, John
Sundance series (17)
Gilman, George G
Adam Steele series (24)
Kelton, Elmer
Tales of Texas series (9)

Manhunt at the UN
Holliday, Joe
Dale of the Mounted series (11)

Manhunt for a general
York, Andrew
Jonathan Anders series (2)

Manhunt in Chihuahua
Sadler, Jeff
Marshal Andrew Anderson series (8)

Manhunt in murder
Martyn, Wyndham
Anthony Trent series (28)

Manhunt is my mission
Marlowe, Stephen
Chester Drum series (13)

Manhunter
Braun, Matt
Luke Starbuck series (5)

Manhunter
Shirreffs, Gordon Donald
Lee Kershaw series (2)

Manhunters
Newton, Dwight Bennett
Jim Bannister series (4)

Manhuntress
Cleve, John
Spaceways series (7)

Mani
Fermor, Patrick Leigh
Greek travels series (1)

Mania for blondes
Krasney, Samuel A
Lieutenant Ben Krahmer series (2)

Manifesto
Messerli, Douglas
River to rivet trilogy (3)

Manifesto of the third millenium
Wenger, Peter
Logic and order in society series (2)

Manila Bay
Marshall, William Leonard
Battling Mendez series (1)

Manila menfish
Crisp, Frank
Dirk Rogers series (4)

Manila stranger
Crisp, Frank
Dirk Rogers series (5)

Manipulator
Brookins, Dana
Bobbie Toppin series (2)

Manipulators
Rossiter, John
Criminal Court series (1)

Manitoba marauders
Sharpe, Jon
Trailsman series (67)

Manitou
Masterton, Graham
Manitou series (1)
Porter, Donald Clayton
White Indian series (16)

Manitou's daughter
Lederer, Paul Joseph
Indian heritage series (1)

Mankill sport
Derrick, Lionel
Penetrator series (14)

Mankiller
Cole, Judd
Cheyenne series (12)
Wilcox, Collin
Lieutenant Frank Hastings series (11)

Manners
Higgs, Mike
Learn with Moonbird series (1)

Manning-Burke murder
Tracy, Louis
Inspector Furneaux series (14)

Mannix
Avallone, Michael
Mannix series (1)

Mano a mano
Hart, Matthew S
Cody's law series (5)

Manoeuvres
Neuman, Fredric
Captain Redder series (2)

Manor
Singer, Isaac Bashevis
Calman Jacoby family series (1)

Manor house menace
Drummond, J
Sexton Blake series (1116)

Manor of Brays
Fitzroy, Rosamond
Mallamshire series (1)

Man's best friend
Mayle, Peter
Wicked Willie series (1)

Man's desiring
Gallie, Menna
Cilhendre Village series (2)

Man's enemies
Thayer, Lee
Peter Clancy series (24)

Man's illegal life
Heller, Keith
George Man series (2)

Man's loving family
Heller, Keith
George Man series (3)

Man's storm
Heller, Keith
George Man series (1)

Mansart builds a school
Du Bois, William Edward Burghardt
Black flame trilogy (2)

Manse
Cantrell, Lisa Wright
Manse series (1)

Mansfield mystery
Lenehan, John Christopher
Inspector Kilby series (3)

Mansfield Park
Austen, Jane
Mansfield Park series (1)

Mansfield revisited
Aiken, Joan
Mansfield Park series (2)

Mansion
Faulkner, William
Sin and salvation series (10)
Snopes family trilogy (3)

Mansion House mystery
Drew, Sidney
Sexton Blake series (649)

Mansion of crime
Grant, Maxwell
Shadow series (200)
Mansion of secrets
Judd, Frances K
Kay Tracey series (17)
Mansion of shadows
Murray, Edgar Joyce
Sexton Blake series (304)
Mansion on the moor
Purley, John
Sexton Blake series (1095)
Mansions of the gods
Goscinny, Rene
Asterix series (17)
Mansy Miller fights back
Pascal, Francine
Sweet Valley twins series (48)
Manticore
Davies, Robertson
Deptford trilogy (2)
Mantis
La Plante, Richard
Josef Tanaka series (1)
Mantle of Ishmael
Fletcher, Joseph Smith
Richard Goulburn series (1)
Mantrap
Chance, John Newton
Jonathan Blake series (7)
Evans, Alan
Cragg and Frayne series (2)
Mantrap garden
Sherwood, John
Celia Grant series (3)
Manuscript murders
Lewis, Roy Harley
Matthew Coll series (2)
Manville murders
Fitzsimmons, Cortland
Arthur Martinson series (2)
Manwatching
Morris, Desmond
Watching series (1)
Manx murders
De Andrea, William Louis
Niccolo Benedetti series (2)
Many a monster
Finnegan, Robert
Dan Banion series (3)
Many a slip
Crofts, Freeman Wills
Inspector Joseph French series (30)
Mills, Osmington
Midset C.I.D. series (7)
Sergeant Patrick Shirley and Inspector Rip Irving series (5)
Many a wide mile
Grover, Marshall
Larry and Stretch series (85)
Many brave hearts
Douglass, Donald McNutt
Bolivar Manchenil series (2)
Many cargoes
Jacobs, William Wymark
Night-Watchman series (1)
Many-colored land
May, Julian
Pliocene exile series (2)
Many-headed monster
Lett, Gordon
Italian Resistance series (2)
Many deadly returns
Moyes, Patricia
Henry and Emmy Tibbett series (9)
Many dimensions
Williams, Charles Walter Stansby
Sir Giles Tumulty series (2)
Many faces of love
Davenat, Colette
Deborah series (2)
Many Junes
Marshall, Archibald
Clinton series (4)
Many memories
Burgin, George Brown
Clubman series (3)
Many murders
Irwin, Inez Haynes
Patrick O'Brien series (4)
Many things begin for change
Ulasi, Adaora Lily
Nigerian series (2)
Many things you no understand
Ulasi, Adaora Lily
Nigerian series (1)
Many waters
L'Engle, Madeleine
Meg Murry series (4)
Street, Pamela
Lodge family series (3)

Many ways of death
Didelot, Francis
Commissaire Orestes Bignon series (1)
Maori girl
Hilliard, Noel
Netta and Paul tetralogy (1)
Maori murder case
Albert, Andrew I
Paul Decker series (1)
Maori woman
Hilliard, Noel
Netta and Paul tetralogy (3)
Maple sugar for Windy Foot
Frost, Frances Mary
Windy Foot series (3)
Mapp and Lucia
Benson, Edward Frederic
Lucia Billson series (5)
Mappo, the merry monkey
Barnum, Richard
Kneetime animal stories series (3)
Maquis
Millar, George
Maquis series (1)
Maracaibo
Silliphant, Stirling
John Locke series (2)
Maracaibo affair
Gray, Rod
New lady from L.U.S.T. series (4)
Maracaibo massacre
Roberts, Mark Kelly
Liberty Corps series (2)
Maracaibo mission
Mason, Francis Van Wyck
Colonel Hugh North series (25)
Maracot Deep, and other stories
Doyle, Arthur Conan
Professor Challenger series (4)
Maradick at forty
Walpole, Hugh
Maradick series (2)
Maranas
Balzac, Honore de
Philosophic studies series (10)
Marathon
Smith, David Alexander
Marathon trilogy (1)
Marathon man
Goldman, William
Marathon man series (1)
Marathon Miranda
Winthrop, Elizabeth
Miranda series (1)
Marathon mystery
Stevenson, Burton Egbert
Jim Godfrey series (2)
Marauders
McCurtin, Peter
Sundance series (31)
McGann, Michael
Marauders series (1)
Shirreffs, Gordon Donald
Lee Kershaw series (6)
Marauders at the Lazy Mare
Field, Peter
Powder Valley series (37)
Marauders by night
Gask, Arthur
Gilbert Larose series (28)
Marauders of Gallows Valley
Grey, Romer Zane
Arizona Ames series (6)
Marauders of Gor
Norman, John
Tarl Cabot series (9)
Marble Arch mystery
Bayfield, William John
Sexton Blake series (112)
Marble city
Burgin, George Brown
Four Corners series (5)
Marble foot
Quennell, Peter
Marble foot series (1)
Marble jungle
Richards, Clay
Grant Kirby series (1)
Marble orchard
Copper, Basil
Mike Faraday series (7)
Marble tomb mystery
Robertson, Colin
Inspector Robert Strong series (2)
Marbles, roller skates, doorknobs
Lampton, Christopher
Simple machines series (2)
Marc Bolan story
Tremlett, George
Rock stars series (5)

Marceau case
Keeler, Harry Stephen
Marceau case trilogy (1)
Marcella
Ward, Mary Augusta
Marcella Boyce series (1)
March
Kuniczak, Wieslaw Stanislaw
Polish war trilogy (2)
March moonlight
Richardson, Dorothy Miller
Pilgrimage series (13)
March of Militant
Crick, Michael
Militant series (2)
March of the demons
Jennings, Gary
March series (4)
March of the flame marauders
Steele, Curtis
James Christopher series (9)
March of the gods
Jennings, Gary
March series (3)
March of the heroes
Jennings, Gary
March series (2)
March of the moderns
Gaunt, William
Victorian painting series (3)
March of the Prince
Lane, Jane
Stuart series (8)
March of the robots
Jennings, Gary
March series (1)
March of the twenty six
Delderfield, Ronald Frederick
Napoleon Bonaparte series (2)
March on Moscow
Konrad, Klaus
Russian series (2)
March on Warsaw
Kessler, Leo
Wotan series (24)
March or die
Kessler, Leo
Wotan series (21)
March to Blenheim
Birt, David
Stuarts series (20)
March to Caobaland
Traven, B
Jungle series (3)
March to Corunna
Dymoke, Juliet
French Revolution series (2)
March to the Monteria
Traven, B
Jungle series (3)
March violets
Kerr, Philip
Berlin noir trilogy (1)
Marchester Royal
Fletcher, Joseph Smith
Inspector Skarratt series (1)
Marching as to war
Charlwood, Don
Airman series (1)
Marching fire
Albany, James
S.A.S. series (5)
Marching notes
La Prade, Ernest
Alice in Wonderland sequels series (4)
Marching on
Boyd, James
James Fraser series (2)
Marching on Niagara
Stratemeyer, Edward L
Colonial series (2)
Marching through Georgia
Stirling, Stephen Michael
Draka trilogy (1)
Marchioness of Grofnek
Tufts, Warren
Casey Ruggles series (5)
Marcia, the innocent
Kimbrough, Katheryn
Phenwick women series (12)
Marco Polo
Birt, David
Middle Ages series (16)
Lucarotti, John
Doctor Who series (94)
Marco Polo, if you can
Buckley, William Frank
Blackford Oakes series (4)
Marcus
Aimwell, Walter
Boy series (5)

Marcy catches up
Du Jardin, Rosamond
Marcy series (2)
Mardi gras masks
Tinker, Frances
Old New Orleans quartet (4)
Mardi gras massacre
Derrick, Lionel
Penetrator series (5)
Mardi gras murders
Bristow, Gwen
Wade series (2)
Mardi Gras mystery
Foley, Louise Munro
Choose your own adventure series (65)
Mardi gras mystery
Grant, Maxwell
Shadow series (85)
Keene, Carolyn
Nancy Drew series (81)
Mardie
Lindgren, Astrid
Mardie series (1)
Mardie to the rescue
Lindgren, Astrid
Mardie series (2)
Margaret
Miner, Jane Claypool
Sunfire series (27)
Ross, James Davidson
Ross family series (1)
Margaret Dashwood
Brown, Edith Charlotte
Margaret Dashwood series (2)
Margaret days
Avery, Elizabeth
Babs series (1)
Margaret Montfort
Richards, Laura Elizabeth
Three Margarets series (2)
Margaret Powell down under
Powell, Margaret
Domestic service series (8)
Margaret Powell in America
Powell, Margaret
Domestic service series (6)
Margaret, the faithful
Kimbrough, Katheryn
Phenwick women series (3)
Margaret the queen
Tranter, Nigel Godwin
Scottish history series (2)
Margery's son
Holt, Emily Sarah
Mistress Margery series (2)
Marget Pow
Slater, Catherine Ponton
Marget Pow trilogy (3)
Marget Pow comes home
Slater, Catherine Ponton
Marget Pow trilogy (2)
Marget Pow in foreign parts
Slater, Catherine Ponton
Marget Pow trilogy (1)
Marget Pow looks back
Slater, Catherine Ponton
Marget Pow trilogy (3)
Margie
Cunningham, E V
John Comaday and Larry Cohen series (2)
Margie at Harbour Light
Rand, Edward Augustus
Margie series (2)
Margin
Stuart, Ian
Graham Lorimer series (2)
Margin for murder
Kane, Martin
Martin Kane series (12)
Margin for terror
Kane, Frank
Johnny Liddell series (31)
Margin released
Priestley, John Boynton
English journey series (5)
Margo
Jenkins, Jerry Bruce
Margo Franklin and Philip Spence series (1)
Margo's reunion
Jenkins, Jerry Bruce
Margo Franklin and Philip Spence series (13)
Margot the midget
Tourtel, Mary
Rupert Bear series (3)
Marguerite de Valois
Dumas, Alexandre
Valois series (5)

Margy's mysterious visitor
Hope, Laura Lee
Blythe girls series (10)
Margy's queer inheritance
Hope, Laura Lee
Blythe girls series (2)
Margy's secret mission
Hope, Laura Lee
Blythe girls series (6)
Maria
Canfield, Sandra
Calloway Corners series (1)
Hellberg, Hans Eric
Maria series (1)
Maria again
Lane, Anna
Maria trilogy (2)
Maria and Martin
Hellberg, Hans Eric
Maria series (2)
Maria Capponi
Schickele, Rene
Rhineland heritage series (1)
Maria escapes
Avery, Gillian
Maria Henniker-Haddon series (1)
Mister Copplestone series (1)
Smith family series (1)
Maria in love
Stewart, Maureen
Maria series (2)
Maria Looney and the cosmic circus
Beatty, Jerome
Maria Looney series (2)
Maria Looney and the remarkable robot
Beatty, Jerome
Maria Looney series (3)
Maria Looney on the red planet
Beatty, Jerome
Maria Looney series (1)
Maria marches on
Slate, John
Black Maria series (2)
Maria of England in the rain
Blackwood, Algernon
Maria series (1)
Mariah Delany lending library disaster
Greenwald, Sheila
Mariah Delany series (1)
Mariah Delany's author of the month club
Greenwald, Sheila
Mariah Delany series (2)
Marianela
Perez Galdos, Benito
Contemporary novels of Spain series (6)
Marianne
Benzoni, Juliette
Marianne series (1)
Mullally, Frederic
Bob Sullivan series (1)
Marianne and Mark
Storr, Catherine
Marianne series (2)
Marianne and the crown of fire
Benzoni, Juliette
Marianne series (6)
Marianne and the Lords of the East
Benzoni, Juliette
Marianne series (5)
Marianne and the masked prince
Benzoni, Juliette
Marianne series (2)
Marianne and the privateer
Benzoni, Juliette
Marianne series (3)
Marianne and the rebels
Benzoni, Juliette
Marianne series (4)
Marianne dreams
Storr, Catherine
Marianne series (1)
Marianne, the madame and the momentary gods
Tepper, Sheri S
Marianne trilogy (2)
Marianne, the magus and the manticore
Tepper, Sheri S
Marianne trilogy (1)
Marianne, the matchbox and the malachite mouse
Tepper, Sheri S
Marianne trilogy (3)
Marianne trilogy
Tepper, Sheri S
Marianne trilogy (3)
Maria's diary
Stewart, Maureen
Maria series (1)

Marlows dig for treasure
Boden, Hilda
Marlows series (3)
Marlows in town
Boden, Hilda
Marlows series (9)
Marlows into danger
Boden, Hilda
Marlows series (4)
Marlows' Irish holiday
Boden, Hilda
Marlows series (7)
Marlows' pigeon post
Boden, Hilda
Marlows series (8)
Marlows win a prize
Boden, Hilda
Marlows series (2)
Marmaduke
Monkhouse, Allan
Helen and Marmaduke series (2)
Marmaduke and his friends
Chapman, Elizabeth
Marmaduke series (6)
Marmaduke and Joe
Chapman, Elizabeth
Marmaduke series (2)
Marmaduke and Margaret
O'Harris, Pixie
Marmaduke series (2)
Marmaduke and the elephant
Chapman, Elizabeth
Marmaduke series (7)
Marmaduke and the lambs
Chapman, Elizabeth
Marmaduke series (8)
Marmaduke goes to America
Chapman, Elizabeth
Marmaduke series (11)
Marmaduke goes to France
Chapman, Elizabeth
Marmaduke series (9)
Marmaduke goes to Holland
Chapman, Elizabeth
Marmaduke series (10)
Marmaduke goes to Italy
Chapman, Elizabeth
Marmaduke series (12)
Marmaduke goes to Switzerland
Chapman, Elizabeth
Marmaduke series (13)
Marmaduke the lorry
Chapman, Elizabeth
Marmaduke series (1)
Marmaduke the possum
O'Harris, Pixie
Marmaduke series (1)
Marmaduke the possum in the cave of the gnomes
O'Harris, Pixie
Marmaduke series (3)
Marmalade and Rufus
Davies, Andrew
Marmalade Atkins series (1)
Marmalade Atkins' dreadful deeds
Davies, Andrew
Marmalade Atkins series (1)
Marmalade Atkins in space
Davies, Andrew
Marmalade Atkins series (2)
Marmalade hits the big time
Davies, Andrew
Marmalade Atkins series (5)
Marmalade Jim and the fox
Sillitoe, Alan
Marmalade Jim series (3)
Marmalade Jim at the farm
Sillitoe, Alan
Marmalade Jim series (2)
Marmalade's Christmas present
Wheeler, Cindy
Marmalade series (5)
Marmalade's nap
Wheeler, Cindy
Marmalade series (3)
Marmalade's picnic
Wheeler, Cindy
Marmalade series (4)
Marmalade's snowy day
Wheeler, Cindy
Marmalade series (1)
Marmalade's yellow leaf
Wheeler, Cindy
Marmalade series (2)
Marngit
Wongar, B
Dingo series (1)
Maroon boy
Leeson, Robert
Matthew Morten trilogy (1)
Marooned!
Murray, Andrew
Sexton Blake series (194)
Marooned
Verne, Jules
Captain Grant's children series (2)
Captain Nemo series (2)
Marooned in Fraggle Rock
Young, David
Fraggle Rock series (13)
Marooned in orbit
Ballou, Arthur W
Marooned in orbit series (1)
Marooned in realtime
Vinge, Vernor
Realtime series (2)
Marooned with murder
Walling, Robert Alfred John
Philip Tolefree series (12)
Marooner's Island
Goulding, Francis Robert
Marooners series (2)
Marquis at bay
Davis, Albert Belisle
Mondebon trilogy (2)
Marquis of Lossie
Macdonald, George
Malcolm series (2)
Marquis of Loveland
Williamson, Charles Norris
Lord and Lady Loveland series (1)
Marquis' secret
Macdonald, George
Malcolm series (2)
Marquise of the Angels
Golon, Sergeanne
Angelique series (1)
Marquise went out at five
Mauriac, Claude
Interior dialogue series (3)
Marrakesh
Diamond, Graham
Marrakesh series (1)
Marrakesh nights
Diamond, Graham
Marrakesh series (2)
Marriage and Mary Ann
Cookson, Catherine
Mary Ann Shaughnessy series (6)
Marriage and murder
Sharp, David
Professor Henry Arthur Fielding series (6)
Marriage at a venture
Gaboriau, Emile
Marriage of adventure series (1)
Marriage between Zones Three, Four and Five
Lessing, Doris
Canopus in Argus archives series (2)
Marriage bowl
Minton, Mary
Yesterday's road series (2)
Marriage contract
Balzac, Honore de
Scenes of private life series (27)
Marriage has been arranged
Macnamara, Rachel Swete
Awakening series (2)
Marriage is murder
Pickard, Nancy
Jenny Cain series (4)
Marriage made in blood
Williamson, Hugh Ross
Passing of the Plantagenets series (2)
Marriage of adventure
Gaboriau, Emile
Marriage of adventure series (2)
Marriage of Captain Kettle
Hyne, Charles John Cutcliffe
Captain Owen Kettle series (9)
Marriage of Claudia
Franken, Rose
Claudia series (5)
Marriage of Figaro
Beaumarchais, Pierre Augustin Caron de
Figaro series (2)
Marriage of Josephine
Coryn, Marjorie
Napoleonic trilogy (1)
Marriage of Katherine
Stevenson, Dorothy Emily
Ardfalloch series (3)
Katherine Wentworth series (2)
Marriage of Kettle
Hyne, Charles John Cutcliffe
Captain Owen Kettle series (9)
Marriage of Susan
Black, Hermina
Susan Denver trilogy (2)
Marriage settlement
Balzac, Honore de
Scenes of private life series (27)
Marriage with my kingdom
Plowden, Alison
Elizabeth I series (3)
Married life
O'Riordan, Conal
Anglo-Irish relations series (10)
Married life, its shadows and sunshine
Arthur, Timothy Shay
Household library series (1)
Married Miss Binks
Winter, John Strange
Binks family series (2)
Married past redemption
Veryan, Patricia
Age of Elegance series (5)
Sanguinet series (3)
Married to a single life
Blunt, Wilfrid
Single life series (1)
Married to murder
Radford, Edwin
Superintendent Carmichael series (2)
Married woman
Pascal, Francine
Sweet Valley University series (5)
Marrowby myth
Martyn, Wyndham
Christopher Bond series (4)
Marryers
Bacheller, Irving
Socrates Potter trilogy (3)
Marrying a doctor
Harrison, Elizabeth
Central London Hospital series (16)
Marrying Harriet
Chesney, Marion
School of manners series (6)
Mars
Simon, Seymour
Space photos series (5)
Marsanne
Coffman, Virginia
Napoleonic Europe series (2)
Marseilles
Caillou, Alan
Mike Benasque series (2)
Marseilles enforcer
Smith, Don
Secret mission series (14)
Marsh
Raymond, Ernest
London gallery series (2)
Marsh blood
Marcus, Joanna
Romney Marsh series (2)
Marsh king
Hodges, Cyril Walter
King Alfred series (2)
Marshal and murderer
Masterson, Louis
Morgan Kane series (6)
Marshal and the madwoman
Nabb, Magdalen
Marshal Guarnaccia series (6)
Marshal and the murderer
Nabb, Magdalen
Marshal Guarnaccia series (5)
Marshal at the Villa Torrini
Nabb, Magdalen
Marshal Guarnaccia series (9)
Marshal Blueberry
Giraud, Jean
Lieutenant Mike S Blueberry series (12)
Marshal from Whiskey Smith
Allen, Eric
Whiskey Smith series (3)
Marshal makes his report
Nabb, Magdalen
Marshal Guarnaccia series (8)
Marshal of Babylon
Hogan, Ray
Shawn Starbuck series (6)
Marshal of Blazing Gulch
Kester, Ken
Steve McCade series (1)
Marshal of Gunsmoke
Allen, Chester
Justice Colt series (2)
Marshal of Lawless
Strange, Oliver
Sudden series (3)
Marshal of Wichita
Curry, Tom
Captain Mesquite series (6)
Marshal's gun
Sutton, Stack
Marshal Creed Wetherall series (3)
Marshal's own case
Nabb, Magdalen
Marshal Guarnaccia series (7)
Marshland adventure
Day, James Wentworth
Rural rides series (4)
Marshmallow
Dixon, Rachel
Jo and Gemma series (1)
Marshmallow masquerade
Blair, Cynthia
Susan and Christine Pratt series (4)
Marshmead murders
Taylor, Selman
Inspector May series (1)
Marshworld
Lloyd, Alan R
Kine trilogy (1)
Marston, master spy
Saville, Malcolm
Marston Baines series (7)
Marsupials
Lavine, Sigmund Arnold
Wonders of nature series (19)
Martello Tower
Haggard, William
William Wilberforce Smith series (1)
Martello Tower mystery
Teed, George Hamilton
Sexton Blake series (856)
Marten mystery
Ironside, John
Detective Inspector John Freeman series (2)
Martha
Braithwaite, Ruth
Yorkshire trilogy (1)
Martha and Cupid
Lippmann, Julie Mathilde
Martha trilogy (3)
Martha and the eye of love
Sharp, Margery
Martha Diver series (1)
Martha B Rabbit address book
Barber, Shirley
Martha B Rabbit series (2)
Martha B Rabbit and how she became the fairies' cook
Barber, Shirley
Martha B Rabbit series (1)
Martha B Rabbit and the unexpected guests
Barber, Shirley
Martha B Rabbit series (2)
Martha B Rabbit birthday book
Barber, Shirley
Martha B Rabbit series (2)
Martha by-the-day
Lippmann, Julie Mathilde
Martha trilogy (1)
Martha calling
Meddaugh, Susan
Martha series (2)
Martha Do-Alot
Watson, Jean
Alot series (4)
Martha, Eric and George
Sharp, Margery
Martha Diver series (3)
Martha in Paris
Sharp, Margery
Martha Diver series (2)
Martha is afraid of the dark
Watson, Jean
Meet the Samuel family series (3)
Martha Jane at college
Specking, Inez
Martha Jane series (2)
Martha Jane, sophomore
Specking, Inez
Martha Jane series (3)
Martha of California
Otis, James
Pioneer series (5)
Martha Plover
Leslie, Henrietta
Arlington Street trilogy (2)
Martha Quest
Lessing, Doris
Children of violence series (1)
Martha speaks
Meddaugh, Susan
Martha series (1)
Martha's best friend
Steel, Danielle
Martha series (1)
Martha's busy morning
Watson, Jean
Meet the Samuel family series (1)
Martha's new daddy
Steel, Danielle
Martha series (2)
Martha's new puppy
Steel, Danielle
Martha series (4)
Martha's new school
Steel, Danielle
Martha series (3)
Martian spring
Williams, Michael Lindsay
Martian series (1)
Martians in Maggody
Hess, Joan
Arly Hanks series (8)
Martie the unconquered
Norris, Kathleen
Rachel Fairfax series (2)
Martie twins
Allen, Alice E
Martie twins series (2)
Martin Conisby's vengeance
Farnol, Jeffery
Martin Conisby series (2)
Martin Hewitt, investigator
Morrison, Arthur
Martin Hewitt series (1)
Martin Magnus on Mars
Temple, William Frederick
Martin Magnus trilogy (3)
Martin Magnus on Venus
Temple, William Frederick
Martin Magnus trilogy (2)
Martin Magnus, planet rover
Temple, William Frederick
Martin Magnus trilogy (1)
Martin Paz
Verne, Jules
J R Kazallon series (2)
Martin Pippin in the apple-orchard
Farjeon, Eleanor
Martin Pippin series (1)
Martin Pippin in the daisy-field
Farjeon, Eleanor
Martin Pippin series (2)
Martin Speed versus The Snatcher
Hugi, Maurice G
Martin Speed series (7)
Martin the warrior
Jacques, Brian
Redwall series (1)
Martinis and murder
Kane, Henry
Peter Chambers series (1)
Marty
Bialk, Elisa
Marty Warren series (1)
Marty goes to Hollywood
Bialk, Elisa
Marty Warren series (2)
Marty on the campus
Bialk, Elisa
Marty Warren series (3)
Martyr
Gillespie, Susan
Longdon-Lorristone family series (1)
Martyr to the Queen
Feval, Paul
Years between series (2)
Martyred
Kim, Richard Eunkook
Korea series (1)
Martyr's heir
Cripps, Arthur Shearly
John Kent series (2)
Martyr's servant
Cripps, Arthur Shearly
John Kent series (1)
Marune
Vance, Jack
Alastor trilogy (2)
Gaean series (3)
Marvel superheroes
Wein, Len
Marvel superheroes, new series (9)
Marvellous adventures of Percy Pig
Bennett, Rodney
Percy Pig series (1)
Marvellous boy
Corris, Peter
Cliff Hardy series (4)
Marvellous story of Puss in Boots
Gray, Nicholas Stuart
Puss in Boots series (1)
Marvelous boy
Corris, Peter
Cliff Hardy series (4)
Marvelous inventions of Alvin Fernald
Hicks, Clifford Byron
Alvin Fernald series (1)
Marvelous land of Oz
Baum, Lyman Frank
Oz series (2)

Marvin's monster
Dicks, Terrance
Horror series (2)
Marx the First
Marshall, Bruce
Vicar of Christ tetralogy (3)
Mary
Asch, Sholem
Biblical series (3)
Sachs, Marilyn
Veronica Ganz series (3)
Mary and Florence
Tytler, Ann Fraser
Mary and Florence series (1)
Mary and Florence at sixteen
Tytler, Ann Fraser
Mary and Florence series (2)
Mary and her family
Delahaye, Gilbert
Mary series (11)
Mary and her friends
Delahaye, Gilbert
Mary series (10)
Mary and her garden
Delahaye, Gilbert
Mary series (11)
Mary and Mark
Delahaye, Gilbert
Mary series (9)
Mary Ann and Bill
Cookson, Catherine
Mary Ann Shaughnessy series (8)
Mary Ann omnibus
Cookson, Catherine
Mary Ann Shaughnessy series (8)
Mary Anne and Miss priss
Martin, Ann Matthews
Baby-Sitters Club series (73)
Mary Anne and the great romance
Martin, Ann Matthews
Baby-Sitters Club series (30)
Mary Anne and the library mystery
Martin, Ann Matthews
Baby-Sitters Club mystery series (13)
Mary Anne and the search for Tigger
Martin, Ann Matthews
Baby-Sitters Club series (25)
Mary Anne and the secret in the attic
Martin, Ann Matthews
Baby-Sitters Club mystery series (5)
Mary Anne and too many babies
Martin, Ann Matthews
Baby-Sitters Club series (52)
Mary Anne and too many boys
Martin, Ann Matthews
Baby-Sitters Club series (34)
Mary Anne misses Logan
Martin, Ann Matthews
Baby-Sitters Club series (46)
Mary Anne saves the day
Martin, Ann Matthews
Baby-Sitters Club series (4)
Mary Anne versus Logan
Martin, Ann Matthews
Baby-Sitters Club series (41)
Mary Anne's makeover
Martin, Ann Matthews
Baby-Sitters Club series (60)
Mary Ann's angels
Cookson, Catherine
Mary Ann Shaughnessy series (7)
Mary Ann's bad-luck mystery
Martin, Ann Matthews
Baby-Sitters Club series (17)
Mary at the flower festival
Delahaye, Gilbert
Mary series (13)
Mary Bell
Abbott, Jacob
Franconia series (4)
Mary Cary, frequently Martha
Bosher, Kate Lee Langley
Mary Cary series (1)
Mary Dove
Rushing, Jane Gilmore
Walnut Grove series (1)
Mary Ellis, student nurse
Newell, Hope
Mary Ellis series (2)
Mary Emma and Company
Moody, Ralph
Ralph series (5)
Mary entertains the Sewing Club
Burnett, Alice Hale
Merryvale girls series (4)
Mary Erskine
Abbott, Jacob
Franconia series (3)
Mary Fenwick's daughter
Whitby, Beatrice
Mary Fenwick series (2)
Mary goes camping
Delahaye, Gilbert
Mary series (3)
Mary goes to the park
Delahaye, Gilbert
Mary series (7)
Mary goes to the sea
Delahaye, Gilbert
Mary series (6)
Mary goes travelling
Delahaye, Gilbert
Mary series (16)
Mary-in-the-Middle
Asher, Sandra Fenichel
Ballet One series (2)
Mary is missing
Pascal, Francine
Sweet Valley twins series (36)
Mary Jane and the visitors
Carson, Hilda
Mary Jane series (2)
Mary Jane at school
Judson, Clara Ingram
Mary Jane series (8)
Mary Jane down South
Judson, Clara Ingram
Mary Jane series (4)
Mary Jane, her book
Judson, Clara Ingram
Mary Jane series (1)
Mary Jane, her visit
Judson, Clara Ingram
Mary Jane series (2)
Mary Jane in Canada
Judson, Clara Ingram
Mary Jane series (9)
Mary Jane in England
Judson, Clara Ingram
Mary Jane series (13)
Mary Jane in France
Judson, Clara Ingram
Mary Jane series (15)
Mary Jane in Italy
Judson, Clara Ingram
Mary Jane series (17)
Mary Jane in New England
Judson, Clara Ingram
Mary Jane series (6)
Mary Jane in Scotland
Judson, Clara Ingram
Mary Jane series (14)
Mary Jane in Spain
Judson, Clara Ingram
Mary Jane series (18)
Mary Jane in Switzerland
Judson, Clara Ingram
Mary Jane series (16)
Mary Jane married
Sims, George Robert
Mary Jane series (2)
Mary Jane's city home
Judson, Clara Ingram
Mary Jane series (5)
Mary Jane's country home
Judson, Clara Ingram
Mary Jane series (7)
Mary Jane's friends in Holland
Judson, Clara Ingram
Mary Jane series (19)
Mary Jane's kindergarten
Judson, Clara Ingram
Mary Jane series (3)
Mary Jane's memoirs
Sims, George Robert
Mary Jane series (1)
Mary Jane's summer fun
Judson, Clara Ingram
Mary Jane series (10)
Mary Jane's vacation
Judson, Clara Ingram
Mary Jane series (12)
Mary Jane's winter sports
Judson, Clara Ingram
Mary Jane series (11)
Mary Kate
Morgan, Helen
Mary Kate series (3)
Mary Kate and the Jumble Bear, and other stories
Morgan, Helen
Mary Kate series (2)
Mary Kate and the school bus, and other stories
Morgan, Helen
Mary Kate series (3)
Mary learns to cook
Delahaye, Gilbert
Mary series (14)
Mary learns to dance
Delahaye, Gilbert
Mary series (12)
Mary learns to ride
Delahaye, Gilbert
Mary series (8)
Mary learns to ski
Delahaye, Gilbert
Mary series (16)
Mary learns to swim
Delahaye, Gilbert
Mary series (15)
Mary Leith
Raymond, Ernest
Once in England trilogy (3)
Mary Livingstone, M.D.
Allen, Julia
Mary Livingstone series (1)
Mary Lou
Baldwin, Faith
Divine corners series (3)
Mary-Lou at the Chalet School
Brent-Dyer, Elinor Mary
Chalet School series (34)
Mary-Lou of the Chalet School
Brent-Dyer, Elinor Mary
Chalet School series (34)
Mary Louise
Van Dyne, Edith
Mary Louise and Josie O'Gorman series (1)
Mary Louise adopts a soldier
Van Dyne, Edith
Mary Louise and Josie O'Gorman series (5)
Mary Louise and Josie O'Gorman
Van Dyne, Edith
Mary Louise and Josie O'Gorman series (8)
Mary Louise and the Liberty girls
Van Dyne, Edith
Mary Louise and Josie O'Gorman series (4)
Mary Louise at Dorfield
Van Dyne, Edith
Mary Louise and Josie O'Gorman series (6)
Mary Louise in the country
Van Dyne, Edith
Mary Louise and Josie O'Gorman series (2)
Mary Louise solves a mystery
Van Dyne, Edith
Mary Louise and Josie O'Gorman series (3)
Mary Louise stands the test
Van Dyne, Edith
Mary Louise and Josie O'Gorman series (7)
Mary makes a cake
Brock, Emma Lillian
Mary series (4)
Mary Marony and the snake
Kline, Suzy
Mary Marony series (1)
Mary Marony hides out
Kline, Suzy
Mary Marony series (2)
Mary, Mary
McBain, Ed
Matthew Hope series (10)
Mary-Mary
Robinson, Joan Gale
Mary-Mary series (1)
Mary-Mary stories
Robinson, Joan Gale
Mary-Mary series (3)
Mary Mouse and her bicycle
Blyton, Enid
Mary Mouse series (12)
Mary Mouse and her family
Blyton, Enid
Mary Mouse series (5)
Mary Mouse and the doll's house
Blyton, Enid
Mary Mouse series (1)
Mary Mouse and the garden party
Blyton, Enid
Mary Mouse series (17)
Mary Mouse and the little donkey
Blyton, Enid
Mary Mouse series (23)
Mary Mouse and the Noah's Ark
Blyton, Enid
Mary Mouse series (13)
Mary Mouse goes out for the day
Blyton, Enid
Mary Mouse series (21)
Mary Mouse goes to sea
Blyton, Enid
Mary Mouse series (20)
Mary Mouse goes to the fair
Blyton, Enid
Mary Mouse series (18)
Mary Mouse has a wonderful idea
Blyton, Enid
Mary Mouse series (19)
Mary Mouse in Nursery Rhyme Land
Blyton, Enid
Mary Mouse series (15)
Nursery Rhyme Land series (2)
Mary Mouse to the rescue
Blyton, Enid
Mary Mouse series (14)
Mary 'n' Mary
Foster, Edith Francis
Marigold series (1)
Mary of Nazareth
Borden, Mary
Mary of Nazareth series (1)
Mary Olivier
Sinclair, May
Mary and Arnold series (1)
Mary on roller skates
Brock, Emma Lillian
Mary series (5)
Mary Osborn
Abbott, Jacob
Juno series (2)
Mary Plain and the twins
Rae, Gwynedd
Mary Plain series (10)
Mary Plain goes bob-a-jobbing
Rae, Gwynedd
Mary Plain series (11)
Mary Plain goes to America
Rae, Gwynedd
Mary Plain series (12)
Mary Plain home again
Rae, Gwynedd
Mary Plain series (8)
Mary Plain in town
Rae, Gwynedd
Mary Plain series (3)
Mary Plain in trouble
Rae, Gwynedd
Mary Plain series (5)
Mary Plain in wartime
Rae, Gwynedd
Mary Plain series (6)
Mary Plain lends a paw
Rae, Gwynedd
Mary Plain series (6)
Mary Plain on holiday
Rae, Gwynedd
Mary Plain series (4)
Mary Plain to the rescue
Rae, Gwynedd
Mary Plain series (9)
Mary Plain, V.I.P.
Rae, Gwynedd
Mary Plain series (13)
Mary Plain's big adventure
Rae, Gwynedd
Mary Plain series (7)
Mary Plain's whodunit
Rae, Gwynedd
Mary Plain series (14)
Mary Poppins
Travers, Pamela Lyndon
Mary Poppins series (1)
Mary Poppins and the house next door
Travers, Pamela Lyndon
Mary Poppins series (7)
Mary Poppins comes back
Travers, Pamela Lyndon
Mary Poppins series (2)
Mary Poppins from A to Z
Travers, Pamela Lyndon
Mary Poppins series (5)
Mary Poppins in Cherry Tree Lane
Travers, Pamela Lyndon
Mary Poppins series (6)
Mary Poppins in the kitchen
Travers, Pamela Lyndon
Mary Poppins series (7)
Mary Poppins in the park
Travers, Pamela Lyndon
Mary Poppins series (4)
Mary Poppins opens the door
Travers, Pamela Lyndon
Mary Poppins series (3)
Mary Powell
Manning, Anne
Mary Powell series (1)
Mary, Queen of France
Plaidy, Jean
Tudor series (10)
Mary, Queen of Scotland, the triumphant years
Plaidy, Jean
Mary, Queen of Scots series (1)
Mary, Queen of Scots
Birt, David
Tudors series (6)
Mary Regan
Scott, Leroy
Bob Clifford series (2)
Mary Roberts Rinehart's crime book
Rinehart, Mary Roberts
Nurse Hilda Adams series (2)
Mary Rose at boarding school
Wirries, Mary Mabel
Mary Rose series (1)
Mary Rose at Rose Gables
Wirries, Mary Mabel
Mary Rose series (5)
Mary Rose, graduate
Wirries, Mary Mabel
Mary Rose series (4)
Mary Rose in Friendville
Wirries, Mary Mabel
Mary Rose series (6)
Mary Rose keeps house
Wirries, Mary Mabel
Mary Rose series (2)
Mary Rose, sophomore
Wirries, Mary Mabel
Mary Rose series (3)
Mary Rose's sister Bess
Wirries, Mary Mabel
Mary Rose series (7)
Mary Stewart's Merlin trilogy
Stewart, Mary
Merlin and Arthur series (3)
Mary the Queen
Lewis, Hilda
Mary Tudor trilogy (2)
Mary Wakefield
De la Roche, Mazo
Whiteoak series (3)
Mary Ware doll book
Johnston, Annie Fellows
Little colonel series (17)
Mary Ware in Texas
Johnston, Annie Fellows
Little colonel series (13)
Mary Ware, the little colonel's chum
Johnston, Annie Fellows
Little colonel series (12)
Mary Ware's promised land
Johnston, Annie Fellows
Little colonel series (16)
Marylebone miser
Phillpotts, Eden
John Ringrose series (2)
Mary's birthday party
Delahaye, Gilbert
Mary series (10)
Mary's camera
Brock, Emma Lillian
Mary series (3)
Mary's Christmas present
Mogenson, Jan
Ted series (3)
Mary's happy year
Delahaye, Gilbert
Mary series (4)
Mary's holidays
Delahaye, Gilbert
Mary series (16)
Mary's mountain holiday
Delahaye, Gilbert
Mary series (2)
Mary's seaside holiday
Delahaye, Gilbert
Mary series (5)
Mary's secret
Brock, Emma Lillian
Mary series (2)
Marytary
Creswell, Harry Bulkeley
Marytary series (1)
Mascarada Pass
Macdonald, William Colt
Gregory Quist series (5)
Mascot
Hardcastle, Michael
Mascot series (2)
Masculaine ending
Smith, Joan
Masculine ending series (1)
Masculine ending
Smith, Joan Mary
Loretta Lawson series (1)
Masha
Kay, Mara
Masha series (1)
Mask
Cloete, Stuart
Van der Berg family series (4)
Cournos, John
John Gombarov trilogy (1)
Gordon, Stuart
Watchers trilogy (3)
Scott, Will
Disher series (3)

Mask for crime
Roberts, Marion
Anne and David Layton series (2)
Mask for Dimitrios
Ambler, Eric
Charles Latimer series (1)
Mask for murder
Stein, Aaron Marc
Tim Mulligan and Elsie Mae Hunt series (15)
Mask for the Toff
Creasey, John
Toff series (24)
Mask of Cthulhu
Derleth, August
Cthulhu series (1)
Mask of Fu-Manchu
Rohmer, Sax
Fu-Manchu series (6)
Mask of fury
Maclean, Arthur
Sexton Blake series (1423)
Mask of innocence
Ormerod, Roger
Philipa Lowe series (7)
Mask of Kane
Franklin, Charles
Grant Garfield series (5)
Mask of Keats
Gittings, Robert
John Keats series (2)
Mask of Mephisto
Grant, Maxwell
Shadow series (264)
Mask of murder
Radford, Edwin
Doctor Manson series (20)
Mask of pursuit
Chance, John Newton
Jonathan Blake series (3)
Mask of terror
Desmond, Hugh
Alan Fraser series (33)
Mask of the Tracker
Bensen, Donald R
Cole Brandon series (1)
Mask of the wizard
Cooke, Catherine
Mask trilogy (1)
Mask of violence
Hebden, Mark
Colonel Mostyn series (1)
Mask of words
Roffman, Jan
Sergeant Ratlin series (2)
Mask of Zeus
Cory, Desmond
John Dobie and Kate Coyle series (2)
Maske
Vance, Jack
Gaean series (4)
Masked blackmailer
Lenehan, John Christopher
Charlie Ryan series (1)
Masked dancer
Bayfield, William John
Sexton Blake series (599)
Masked dictator
Graydon, William Murray
Sexton Blake series (486)
Masked forgers
Bayfield, William John
Sexton Blake series (560)
Masked gunman
Ashe, Gordon
Patrick Dawlish series (3)
Masked headsman
Grant, Maxwell
Shadow series (122)
Masked invasion
Steele, Curtis
James Christopher series (1)
Masked killer
Teed, George Hamilton
Sexton Blake series (640)
Masked lady
Grant, Maxwell
Shadow series (173)
Masked man
Jones, G Wayman
Black Bat series (27)
Masked man of the desert
Brisbane, Coutts
Sexton Blake series (920)
Masked marauder
Graydon, Robert Murray
Sexton Blake series (614)
Masked monkey
Dixon, Franklin W
Hardy boys series (51)
Masked raider
Scott, Bradford
Walt Slade series (39)
Masked raiders
Armour, R Coutts
Sexton Blake series (598)
Masked riders of Sleepy Valley
Dresser, Davis
Twister Malone series (2)
Masked slayer
Hardinge, Rex
Sexton Blake series (707)
Masked stranger
Allan, Luke
Tiger Lillie series (1)
Masks
Vornholt, John
Star trek, the next generation series (7)
Masks and faces
Curzon, Clare
Superintendent Mike Yeadings and Sergeant Angus Mott series (4)
Lindsay, Jack
British way series (8)
Sutton, Jessica
Bel Air General series (3)
Masks of mayhem
Waterfield, Robin
Fighting fantasy gamebook series (23)
Masks of Scorpio
Prescot, Dray
Dray Prescot series (31)
Masks of the martyrs
Chalker, Jack Laurence
Rings of the master series (4)
Masks off at midnight
Williams, Valentine
Sergeant Trevor Dene series (4)
Mason and his rangers
Gregor, Elmer Russell
Jim Mason series (4)
Masque of Mandragora
Dicks, Terrance
Doctor Who series (155)
Masque of Satan
Coffman, Virginia
Lucifer Cove series (4)
Masque world
Panshin, Alexei
Anthony Villiers series (3)
Masquerade
Kienzle, William Xavier
Father Robert Koesler series (12)
Morton, William
Biff Corrigan series (1)
Masquerade at Stanton's
Little, Sylvia
Stanton's series (3)
Masquerade at the ballet
Hill, Lorna
Sadler's Wells series (3)
Masquerade at the Wells
Hill, Lorna
Sadler's Wells series (3)
Masquerade of vengeance
Ley, Alice Chetwynd
Justin Rutherford and Anthea series (3)
Masquerader
Graydon, Robert Murray
Sexton Blake series (81)
Masques
Emerson, Ru
Beauty and the Beast trilogy (2)
Mass in slow motion
Knox, Ronald Arbuthnott
Slow motion series (1)
Mass murder
Drummond, John Keith
Matilda Worthing series (3)
Massacre
Kessler, Leo
Rommel series (2)
Lucarotti, John
Doctor Who series (122)
McLaglen, John J
Herne the Hunter series (9)
Massacre at Cawnpore
Stuart, Vivian
Commander Philip Hazard series (6)
Massacre at Goliad
Kelton, Elmer
Buckalew tetralogy (1)
Tales of Texas series (2)
Massacre at Metz
Whiting, Charles
T-Force series (2)
Massacre at Russian River
Hartman, Dane
Dirty Harry Callahan series (7)
Massacre at Umtali
McCurtin, Peter
Jim Rainey series (1)
Massacre Canyon
Cole, Jackson
Jim Hatfield series (16)
Massacre in Madison
Christian, Frederick H
Frank Angel series (7)
Massacre in Milan
Carter, Nick
Nick Carter series (87)
Massacre in Rome
Rosenberger, Joseph
Death Merchant series (35)
Massacre in the hills
Dicks, Terrance
Mounties series (2)
Massacre mission
Gilman, George G
Edge series (38)
Massacre in the 22nd century
Hagberg, David
Flash Gordon series (9)
Massacre mountain
Ledd, Paul
Shelter Morgan series (10)
Massacre river
Benteen, John
Neal Fargo series (4)
Massacre trail
Garrett, Charles C
Gunslinger series (1)
Newton, Mike
Bounty Man series (2)
Massacre Valley
Newton, Dwight Bennett
Johnny Logan series (1)
Massimilla Doni
Balzac, Honore de
Philosophic studies series (4)
Massingham butterfly, and other stories
Fletcher, Joseph Smith
Paul Campenhaye series (2)
Master
Brown, Carter
Rick Holman series (28)
Cooper, Louise Antell
Time master trilogy (3)
Master and commander
O'Brian, Patrick
Jack Aubrey and Stephen Maturin series (1)
O'Brien, Patrick
Captain Jack Aubrey series (1)
Master and man
Zola, Emile
Rougon Macquart series (13)
Master assassin
Carter, Nick
Nick Carter series (219)
Master baiter
Conway, Troy
Coxeman series (23)
Master Bun the baker's boy
Ahlberg, Allan
Happy family series (13)
Master-Christian
Corelli, Marie
Two worlds series (6)
Master Christopher
De la Pasture, Elizabeth
Master Christopher series (1)
Master Cornelius
Balzac, Honore de
Philosophic studies series (14)
Master criminal
Carter, Nicholas
Nicholas Carter series (420)
Master detective
Brebner, Percy
Christopher Quarles series (2)
Master Don Gesualdo
Verga, Giovanni
Vinti family series (2)
Master goes home
Munn, Harold Warner
Tales of the Werewolf Clan trilogy (3)
Master idol
Burton, Anthony
Navigators trilogy (1)
Master mind
Janson, Hank
Hank Janson series (110)
Moffett, Cleveland
Paul Coquenil series (2)
Master-mind menace
Luigi, Belli
Inspector Saint Clair series (3)
Master mind of Mars
Burroughs, Edgar Rice
Martian series (6)
Master Money the millionaire
Ahlberg, Allan
Happy family series (11)
Master mosaic workers
Sand, George
Socialist trilogy (1)
Master murderer
Wells, Carolyn
Fleming Stone series (36)
Master must die
Gridban, Volsted
Adam Quirke series (1)
Master, 1901-1916
Edel, Leon
Henry James series (5)
Master of Black River
Devine, Raynard
Flesh traders series (1)
Master of Blackoaks
Carter, Ashley
Blackoaks series (1)
Master of Blandeston Hall
Wiat, Philippa
Wyatt family series (1)
Master of Boranga
Sirota, Mike
Ro-Lan series (1)
Master of broken men
Steele, Curtis
James Christopher series (6)
Master of chaos
Adams, Terry A
Sentience series (2)
Master of D.E.A.T.H.
Ahern, Jerry
Dan Track series (7)
Master of death
Grant, Maxwell
Shadow series (38)
Master of deception
Mure, David
Deception series (2)
Master of deviltry
Carter, Nicholas
Nicholas Carter series (323)
Master of Dragonard Hill
Gilchrist, Rupert
Dragonard series (2)
Master of evil
Smith, David Claude
Fall of the first world trilogy (1)
Master of Falconhurst
Onstott, Kyle
Falconhurst series (3)
Master of fear
Rushton, Charles
James O'Hannay and Floyd East series (2)
Master of fiends
Hill, Douglas
Talents series (2)
Master of fortune
Hyne, Charles John Cutcliffe
Captain Owen Kettle series (4)
Master of Gray
Tranter, Nigel Godwin
Patrick Gray series (1)
Master of Hestviken
Undset, Sigrid
Master of Hestviken series (4)
Master of Jalna
De la Roche, Mazo
Whiteoak series (10)
Master of karate
Brightfield, Richard
Choose your own adventure series (108)
Master series (3)
Master of kung fu
Brightfield, Richard
Choose your own adventure series (88)
Master series (1)
Master of Littlecote Manor
Howard, Liz
Elizabeth Fytton series (2)
Master of martial arts
Brightfield, Richard
Choose your own adventure series (126)
Master of Maryknoll
Saville, Malcolm
Buckinghams series (1)
Master of mazes
Gaskin, Carol
Forgotten forest series (3)
Master of misfit
Cleve, John
Spaceways series (5)
Master of Morholm
Wilson, Timothy R
Fenland series (1)
Master of none
Harding, Gilbert
Along my line series (2)
Master of Norriya
Drew, Wayland
Erthring cycle series (3)
Master of Paxwax
Mann, Phillip
Story of the gardener series (1)
Master of Ravenloft
Blashfield, Jean
Advanced dungeons and dragons adventure gamebook series (3)
Master of shadows
Lawrence, Margery
Miles Pennoyer series (2)
Master of tae kwon do
Brightfield, Richard
Choose your own adventure series (102)
Master series (2)
Master of the battlefield, 1942-1944
Hamilton, Nigel
Montgomery of Alamein trilogy (2)
Master of the dark
Cassells, John
Superintendent Flagg series (4)
Master of the dark gate
Jakes, John
Gavin Black series (1)
Master of the death madness
Stockbridge, Grant
Richard Wentworth series (10)
Master of the Etrax
Lory, Robert
Trovo series (2)
Master of the fearful depths
Adkins, Patrick H
Titans series (2)
Master of the five magics
Hardy, Lyndon
Arcadia trilogy (1)
Master of the Hashomi
Lord, Jeffrey
Richard Blade series (27)
Master of the moon
Moore, Patrick
Grenfell and Wright series (1)
Master of the Sidhe
Flint, Kenneth Covey
Sidhe Lugh series (3)
Master of the stars
Hoskins, Robert
Master of the stars trilogy (1)
Master of the world
Verne, Jules
Robur series (1)
Master of triggernometry
Edson, John Thomas
Floating Outfit series (40)
Master of venom
Horler, Sydney
Emp series (2)
Master of Warlock
Eggleston, George Cary
Virginia trilogy (2)
Master of Wyndward
Daniels, Norman A
Wyndward series (2)
Master plan
Stuart, Ian
Graham Lorimer series (3)
Master plot
Smith, Lou
John Spencer series (5)
Master Salt the sailor's son
Ahlberg, Allan
Happy family series (4)
Master spy
Gask, Arthur
Gilbert Larose series (11)
Pendower, Jacques
Slade McGinty series (4)
Master villain
Carter, Nicholas
Nicholas Carter series (157)
Master weaver
Early, Richard Elliott
Thomas Early series (2)
Master weed
Rackham, John
Space puppet series (2)
Master Wolf
Estes, Rose
Greyhawk series (3)
Master wolf
Estes, Rose
Mika trilogy (1)
Masterdillo
Wawn, F T
Masterdillo series (1)

Masterful monk
Dudley, Owen Francis
Problems of human happiness series (3)
Masterful Wilhelmine
Stinde, Julius
Buchholz family series (2)
Masterless man
Verne, Jules
Survivors of the Jonathan series (1)
Masterly trick
Carter, Nicholas
Nicholas Carter series (373)
Mastermind wears mink
Brody, Marc
Marc Brody series (16)
Masterpiece
Zola, Emile
Rougon Macquart series (14)
Masterpiece affair
Royce, Kenneth
Spider Scott series (4)
Masterpiece merchant
Lee, Fleming
Saint series (45)
Masterpiece of crime
Carter, Nicholas
Nicholas Carter series (133)
Masters
Snow, Charles Percy
Strangers and brothers series (5)
Master's challenge
Cochran, Molly
Destroyer series (55)
Murphy, Warren Burton
Destroyer series (55)
Masters' counterpoints
Townsend, Larry
Mind master series (1)
Master's golden years
Oxenham, John
Jesus Christ series (2)
Masters in hell
Morris, Janet Ellen
Heroes in hell series (4)
Masters of darkness
Dever, Joe
Lone Wolf series (12)
Etchison, Dennis
Masters of darkness series (1)
Masters of darkness II
Etchison, Dennis
Masters of darkness series (2)
Masters of darkness III
Etchison, Dennis
Masters of darkness series (3)
Masters of death
Grant, Maxwell
Shadow series (186)
Masters of Flux and Anchor
Chalker, Jack Laurence
Soul rider series (3)
Masters of glass
Easton, Malcolm Coleman
Kyala series (1)
Masters of Luxor
Coburn, Anthony
Doctor Who scripts series (5)
Masters of solitude
Kaye, Marvin
Solitude trilogy (1)
Masters of space
Vardeman, Robert Edward
Masters of space trilogy (3)
Masters of the airlanes
Langley, John Prentice
Aviation series (3)
Masters of the lamp
Lory, Robert
Shamryke Odell series (1)
Masters of the Peaks
Altsheler, Joseph Alexander
French and Indian war series (4)
Masters of the pit
Moorcock, Michael
Warrior of Mars trilogy (3)
Masters of the vortex
Smith, Edward Elmer
Lensman series (7)
Master's quilt
Webb, Michael
Giants in the earth trilogy (1)
Masterstroke
Heald, Tim
Simon Bognor series (7)
Sharp, Marilyn
Richard Owen series (2)
Tiger, John
I spy series (2)
Masterthinker
De Bono, Edward
Masterthinker series (1)
Masterthinker II
De Bono, Edward
Masterthinker series (2)
Masterthinker's handbook
De Bono, Edward
Masterthinker series (3)
Matador
Montherlant, Henry de
Alban de Bricoule trilogy (1)
Steen, Marguerite
Spanish trilogy (1)
Matador of the Five Towns, and other stories
Bennett, Arnold
Tales of the Five Towns series (3)
Matadora
Perry, Steve
Khadaji series (3)
Matador's fortune
Bobin, John William
Sexton Blake series (75)
Match
Saint Meyer, Ned
Match series (1)
Match as a fakir
Saint Meyer, Ned
Match series (2)
Match boy
Sabatier, Robert
Olivier Chateauneuf series (1)
Match for a murderer
Dunnett, Dorothy
Johnson and the yacht Dolly series (3)
Match point for murder
Platt, Kin
Max Roper series (5)
Match race
Grove, Frederick Philip
Dude McQuint series (2)
Match wits with Sherlock Holmes
Shaw, Murray
Sherlock Holmes series (10)
Matching pair
Gilman, George G
Edge meets Steele series (2)
Mate and the midshipman
Robinson, George Bush
James Clifton series (1)
Matelot, little sailor of Brittany
Fry, Rosalie Kingsmill
Lucinda series (2)
Material witness
Tanenbaum, Robert K
Assistant District Attorney Butch Karp series (5)
Maternity nurse
Treger, Anne
Nurse series (2)
Mates at Billabong
Bruce, Mary Grant
Billabong series (2)
Mathematics or blood?
Jones, Peter
Terry Trotter series (4)
Mather again
Graeme, Bruce
Detective Sergeant Robert Mather series (7)
Mather investigates
Graeme, Bruce
Detective Sergeant Robert Mather series (9)
Maths is kids' stuff
Baker, Ann
Kids' stuff series (3)
Matilda and the chickens
Henrey, Robert
Normandy Farm series (3)
Matilda, governess of the English
Cleugh, Sophia
Matilda series (1)
Matilda Hunter murder
Keeler, Harry Stephen
Tuddleton Trotter series (1)
Matilda Mouse's first adventure
Buchanan, Heather S
Tales of George and Matilda Mouse series (1)
Matilda Mouse's garden
Buchanan, Heather S
Tales of George and Matilda Mouse series (5)
Matilda Mouse's patchwork life-jackets
Buchanan, Heather S
Tales of George and Matilda Mouse series (3)
Matilda Mouse's shell house
Buchanan, Heather S
Tales of George and Matilda Mouse series (6)
Matilda, the adventuress
Johansen, Iris
Delaneys of Killaroo trilogy (2)
Matilda's stepchildren
Chandler, Arthur Bertram
John Grimes series (19)
Mating of hawks
Williams, Jeanne
Arizona trilogy (3)
Mating of the dragon
Lancing, George
Tzu Hsi series (2)
Mating season
Wodehouse, Pelham Grenville
Jeeves and Bertie Wooster series (9)
Matlock paper
Ludlum, Robert
Tightrope-tense series (3)
Mato Grosso horror
Rosenberger, Joseph
Death Merchant series (13)
Matriarch
Stern, Gladys Bronwyn
Rakonitz family series (1)
Matrimonial causes
Corris, Peter
Cliff Hardy series (1)
Matrix cubed
Bloom, Britton
Inner planets trilogy (3)
Matrix for muscle gain
Laura, Ronald S
Matrix principle series (2)
Matrix principle
Laura, Ronald S
Matrix principle series (1)
Matron
Dawson-Scott, Catherine Amy
Some women trilogy (3)
Matt Ramsey
McLennan, Will
Ramseys series (3)
Matt Regan's woman
Post, Mary Brinker
Annie Jordan series (2)
Matter for men
Gerrold, David
War against the Chtorr trilogy (1)
Matter for the regiment
Macneil, Duncan
James Ogilvie series (14)
Matter of accent
Keith, David
Ted S Weaver series (2)
Matter of blood
Whitaker, Beryl
John Abbot series (2)
Matter of business, and other stories
Farnol, Jeffery
Mister Jasper Shrig of Bow Street series (10)
Matter of confidence
Williams, Brad
Sam Benedict series (4)
Matter of consequences
Skinner, Burrhus Frederic
Behaviorist trilogy (3)
Matter of diplomacy
Tute, Warren
George Mado series (1)
Matter of feeling
Boissard, Janine
Moreau trilogy (1)
Matter of honour
Edson, John Thomas
American Civil War series (6)
Matter of iodine
Keith, David
Ted S Weaver series (1)
Matter of life
Marquis, Max
General hospital series (2)
Matter of love and death
Wells, Tobias
Detective Knute Severson series (1)
Matter of Mandrake
Norman, Barry
Paul Baker series (1)
Matter of martyrdom
Williamson, Hugh Ross
Passing of the Plantagenets series (3)
Matter of millions
Bayfield, William John
Sexton Blake series (50)
Green, Anna Katharine
Ebenezer Gryce series (5)
Matter of motive
Montrose, Graham
Angel Brown series (5)
Matter of murder
Graham, Neill
Solo Malcolm series (29)
Matter of policy
Merwin, Samuel Kimball
Amy Brewster series (3)
Matter of pride
Simpson, Dorothy
Janie Marshal series (4)
Matter of record
Gray, Malcolm
Alan Craig series (2)
Matter of skill
Carter, Nicholas
Nicholas Carter series (371)
Matter of spunk
Jones, Adrienne
Margery Stanfield series (2)
Matter of taste
Saberhagen, Fred
Dracula series (24)
Matterhorn Man
Unsworth, Walter
Mountaineering trilogy (1)
Matthew goes to market
Watson, Jean
Meet the Samuel family series (4)
Matthew Looney and the space pirates
Beatty, Jerome
Matthew Looney series (4)
Matthew Looney in the outback
Beatty, Jerome
Matthew Looney series (3)
Matthew Looney's invasion of the earth
Beatty, Jerome
Matthew Looney series (2)
Matthew Looney's voyage to the earth
Beatty, Jerome
Matthew Looney series (1)
Matthew Ratton
Knowles, Anne
Matthew Ratton series (1)
Matthew's car
Prime, Honor
Moonface series (3)
Matthew's good news of Jesus
Haughton, Rosemary
Good news of Jesus series (1)
Matthew's hand
Larson, Charles
Nils-Frederick Blixen series (2)
Mattimeo
Jacques, Brian
Redwall series (4)
Matty Doolin
Cookson, Catherine
Matty Doolin and Joe Darling series (1)
Matty in films
Robinson, Martha
Matty series (1)
Matty in television
Robinson, Martha
Matty series (3)
Matty Trakker and the money men
Dunn, Roger
Matty Trakker series (1)
Matty Trakker and the UFO
Dunn, Roger
Matty Trakker series (2)
Matzohball
Weinstein, Sol
Israel Bond series (2)
Mau Len death zone
Lansing, John
Black Eagles series (17)
Maud Kinglake's collect
E, H F
Maud Kingslake series (1)
Maud Noakes, guerrilla
Neame, Alan
Maud Noakes series (2)
Mauleverer murders
Fox-Davies, Arthur Charles
Ashley Tempest series (3)
Maurice Dravidoff
Bensusan, Samuel Levy
Joan Winter series (2)
Maurice goes to sea
Harris, Leon
Maurice the moose series (2)
Maurice the snake and Gaston the near-sighted turtle
Edler, Timothy J
Tales from the Atchafalaya series (1)
Maurin the Illustrious
Aicard, Jean
Maurin series (2)
Mauritius command
O'Brian, Patrick
Jack Aubrey and Stephen Maturin series (4)
Maurizius case
Wassermann, Jakob
Doctor Joseph Kerkhoven trilogy (1)
Maverick
Bethke, Bruce
Robots and aliens series (5)
Maverick gunfighter
Bexar, Phil
Billy Dupree series (9)
Maverick maiden
Sharpe, Jon
Trailsman series (25)
Maverick mistress
Martin, Cort
Jared Bolt series (26)
Maverick showdown
Scott, Bradford
Walt Slade series (85)
Maverick's return
Field, Peter
Powder Valley series (21)
Mavreen
Lorrimer, Claire
Mavreen trilogy (1)
Mawdryn undead
Grimwade, Peter
Doctor Who series (82)
Mawpath millions
Reynolds, Warwick
Sexton Blake series (1164)
Max all over
Kaye, Marilyn
Out of this world series (6)
Max and Diana and the beach day
Ziefert, Harriet
Max and Diana series (3)
Max and Diana and the birthday present
Ziefert, Harriet
Max and Diana series (4)
Max and Diana and the shopping trip
Ziefert, Harriet
Max and Diana series (2)
Max and Diana and the snowy day
Ziefert, Harriet
Max and Diana series (1)
Max and me and the time machine
Greer, Gery
Max and me series (1)
Max and me and the Wild West
Greer, Gery
Max and me series (2)
Max and the baby-sitter
Steel, Danielle
Max series (1)
Max and the cat burglar
Dicks, Terrance
Cat called Max series (5)
Max and the fire crystals
Dixon, Rachel
Jo and Gemma series (2)
Max and the missing megastar
Dicks, Terrance
Cat called Max series (6)
Max and the quiz kids
Dicks, Terrance
Cat called Max series (2)
Max Carrados
Bramah, Ernest
Max Carrados series (1)
Max Carrados mysteries
Bramah, Ernest
Max Carrados series (4)
Max flips out
Kaye, Marilyn
Out of this world series (4)
Max goes bad
Kaye, Marilyn
Out of this world series (5)
Max in America
Whitmore, Adam
Max the cat series (2)
Max in Australia
Whitmore, Adam
Max the cat series (4)
Max in India
Whitmore, Adam
Max the cat series (3)
Max in love
Kaye, Marilyn
Out of this world series (2)
Max is back
Stine, Harlan William
Jeffrey and the fourth grade ghost series (1)
Max leaves home
Whitmore, Adam
Max the cat series (1)
Max Malone and the great cereal rip-off
Herman, Charlotte
Max Malone series (1)

Max Malone makes a million
Herman, Charlotte
Max Malone series (2)
Max Malone, superstar
Herman, Charlotte
Max Malone series (3)
Max on earth
Kaye, Marilyn
Out of this world series (1)
Max on fire
Kaye, Marilyn
Out of this world series (3)
Max onstage
Stine, Harlan William
Jeffrey and the third grade ghost series (5)
Max packs
Turk, Hanne
Max the Mouse series (11)
Max runs away
Steel, Danielle
Max series (4)
Max saves the day
Stine, Harlan William
Jeffrey and the third grade ghost series (6)
Max Smart and the ghastly ghost affair
Johnston, William
Maxwell Smart series (9)
Max Smart and the perilous pellets
Johnston, William
Maxwell Smart series (4)
Max Smart loses control
Johnston, William
Maxwell Smart series (8)
Max Smart, the spy who went out to the cold
Johnston, William
Maxwell Smart series (7)
Max the art lover
Turk, Hanne
Max the Mouse series (7)
Max versus the cube
Turk, Hanne
Max the Mouse series (3)
Maxie, an adorable girl
Gardner, Elsie Bell
Maxie series (1)
Maxie and her adventures in Spain
Gardner, Elsie Bell
Maxie series (5)
Maxie and the golden bird
Gardner, Elsie Bell
Maxie series (7)
Maxie at Brinksome Hall
Gardner, Elsie Bell
Maxie series (4)
Maxie in the jungle
Gardner, Elsie Bell
Maxie series (6)
Maxie in Venezuela
Gardner, Elsie Bell
Maxie series (2)
Maxie, Rosie and Earl, partners in grime
Park, Barbara
Rosie Swanson series (1)
Maxie searching for her parents
Gardner, Elsie Bell
Maxie series (3)
Maximal demotion
Nolan, Frederick
Garrett dossier series (5)
Maximilian's gold
Hardin, J D
Raider and Doc series (54)
Shirreffs, Gordon Donald
Dave Hunter series (2)
Maximilian's world
Stolz, Mary
Tales at the Mousehole trilogy (3)
Maximina
Palacio Valdes, Armando
Riverita series (2)
Maximum effort
Edmondson, Garry Cotton
Cunningham trilogy (3)
Max's amazing summer
Dicks, Terrance
Cat called Max series (4)
Max's bath
Wells, Rosemary
Max series (5)
Max's bedtime
Wells, Rosemary
Max series (6)
Max's birthday
Wells, Rosemary
Max series (8)
Max's book
Hurley, Maxwell
Psi Patrol trilogy (3)
Max's breakfast
Wells, Rosemary
Max series (7)
Max's chocolate chicken
Wells, Rosemary
Max series (11)
Max's Christmas
Wells, Rosemary
Max series (10)
Max's daddy goes to the hospital
Steel, Danielle
Max series (2)
Max's dragon shirt
Wells, Rosemary
Max series (12)
Max's first word
Wells, Rosemary
Max series (1)
Max's new baby
Steel, Danielle
Max series (3)
Max's new suit
Wells, Rosemary
Max series (2)
Max's old-fashioned Christmas
Dicks, Terrance
Cat called Max series (7)
Max's ride
Wells, Rosemary
Max series (3)
Max's secret formula
Stine, Harlan William
Jeffrey and the fourth grade ghost series (3)
Max's toys
Wells, Rosemary
Max series (4)
Maxwell mystery
Wells, Carolyn
Fleming Stone series (4)
Maxwell's ghost
Frere, Richard
Highland line series (1)
May basket mystery
Christian, Mary Blount
Goosehill Gang series (8)
May Day in Magadan
Olcott, Anthony
Ivan Kovakin series (2)
May Day mystery
Cohen, Octavus Roy
Jim Hanvey series (2)
May Fair
Arlen, Michael
Charming people series (2)
May I cross your golden river
Dixon, Paige
Skipper series (1)
May I help you?
Beers, Victor Gilbert
Learning to read from the Bible primer series (1)
May I, please, thank you!
Berry, Joy
Ready-set-grow series (11)
May in Manhattan
Kenneth, Claire
Cynthia Doanides series (2)
May Iverson, her book
Jordan, Elizabeth Garver
May Iverson trilogy (1)
May Iverson tackles life
Jordan, Elizabeth Garver
May Iverson trilogy (2)
May Iverson's career
Jordan, Elizabeth Garver
May Iverson trilogy (3)
May madrigal
Pardoe, Margot
Western Highlands series (2)
May this house be safe from tigers
King, Alexander
Mine enemy grows older series (2)
May week murders
Browne, Douglas Gordon
Major Maurice Hemyock series (4)
May Week was in June
James, Clive
Unreliable memoirs series (3)
May you die in Ireland
Kenyon, Michael
Superintendent O'Malley series (1)
Maya
Bonsels, Waldemar
Maya series (1)
Mayan connection
Carter, Nick
Nick Carter series (194)
Maybe a trumpet
Harvester, Simon
Roger Fleming series (3)
Mayday!
Cussler, Clive
Dirk Pitt series (2)
Mayday from Malaga
Macleod, Robert
Andrew Laird series (5)
Mayday orbit
Anderson, Poul
Sir Dominic Flandry series (3)
Mayday over Manhattan
Jason, Stuart
Butcher series (19)
Mayenne
Tubb, Edwin Charles
Dumarest series (9)
Mayfair mystery
Holt, Henry
Inspector Silver series (1)
Mayfair slayride
Janson, Hank
Hank Janson series (223)
Mayflower
Blasco Ibanez, Vicente
Valencia series (2)
Mayhem
James, Joseph Robert
Jean-Louis Saint-Cyr and Hermann Kohler series (1)
Mayhem at Mission Bay
Thorne, Ramsay
Captain Gringo series (30)
Mayhem in B flat
Paul, Elliot
Homer Evans series (4)
Mayhem in Manhattan
Wein, Len
Amazing Spiderman series (1)
Mayhem in Morton Episcopi
Lees, Dan
Constable Craig series (2)
Mayhem in motion
Dixon, Franklin W
Hardy boys case files series (69)
Mayhem in Parva
Livingston, Nancy
G D H Pringle series (6)
Mayhem madchen
Chance, John Newton
Jonathan Blake series (46)
Mayhem on Bear Creek
Howard, Robert Ervin
Breckinridge Elkins series (3)
Mayhem on the Coney beat
Geller, Michael
Bud Dugan series (1)
Mayor for a day
Elias, Horace J
Flintstones series (9)
Mayor of Troy
Quiller-Couch, Arthur
Troy Town series (6)
Mayor's birthday present
Dillon, Deidre
Trumpton series (3)
Mayor's sea voyage
Beaman, Sydney George Hulme
Toytown series (13)
Maythorn story
Trease, Geoffrey
Mike and Sandra series (1)
Mazatlan
Hunt, Everette Howard
Jack Novak series (3)
Sandon, J D
Gringos series (6)
Maze
Garnet, A H
Cyrus Wilson series (2)
Macdonald, Philip
Colonel Anthony Ruthven Gethryn series (6)
Maze in the mirror
Chalker, Jack Laurence
G.O.D. Inc. series (3)
Maze of motives
Carter, Nicholas
Nicholas Carter series (488)
Mazes of Antares
Prescot, Dray
Dray Prescot series (27)
Mazurka
Armstrong, Campbell
Detective Frank Pagan series (2)
Me
Anonymous
Pronoun series (5)
Jacob, Naomi
Me series (1)
Wolff, Margaret
Books for me series (1)
Me again
Jacob, Naomi
Me series (2)
Me an' th' son
Rudd, Steele
Rudd family series (9)
Me and Alice go to the gallery
Rogers, Paul
Me and Alice series (2)
Me and Alice go to the museum
Rogers, Paul
Me and Alice series (1)
Me and Fat
Perle, Lila
Fat Glenda series (1)
Me and Gus
Anthony, Frank Sheldon
Gus Tomlins series (1)
Me and Gus again
Anthony, Frank Sheldon
Gus Tomlins series (3)
Me and mine
Jones, Jack
Unfinished journey series (2)
Me and mine, you and yours
Jacob, Naomi
Me series (7)
Me and my friend
Ahlberg, Allan
Red nose readers series (11)
Me and my friends
Berridge, Celia
Stepping stones 1 2 3 series (8)
Me and my little brain
Fitzgerald, John Dennis
Tom's Great Brain series (3)
Me and the doctors
Godfrey, Jan
Me series (1)
Me and the Mediterranean
Jacob, Naomi
Me series (5)
Me and the stags
Jacob, Naomi
Me series (13)
Me and the swans
Jacob, Naomi
Me series (12)
Me at playschool
Wolff, Margaret
Books for me series (7)
Me at the playgroup
Godfrey, Jan
Me series (3)
Me at the supermarket
Godfrey, Jan
Me series (2)
Me Bandy, you Cissie
Jack, Donald
Journals of Bartholomew Bandy series (4)
Me in puddles
Wolff, Margaret
Books for me series (10)
Me in the kitchen
Jacob, Naomi
Me series (14)
Me in the park
Wolff, Margaret
Books for me series (8)
Me in wartime
Jacob, Naomi
Me series (4)
Me, Jill Robinson and the Christmas pantomime
Digby, Anne
Me and Jill Robinson series (3)
Me, Jill Robinson and the Perdou painting
Digby, Anne
Me and Jill Robinson series (5)
Me, Jill Robinson and the school camp adventure
Digby, Anne
Me and Jill Robinson series (4)
Me, Jill Robinson and the seaside mystery
Digby, Anne
Me and Jill Robinson series (2)
Me, Jill Robinson and the stepping stones mystery
Digby, Anne
Me and Jill Robinson series (6)
Me, Jill Robinson and the television quiz
Digby, Anne
Me and Jill Robinson series (1)
Me, likes and dislikes
Jacob, Naomi
Me series (10)
Me, looking back
Jacob, Naomi
Me series (8)
Me, Mop and the Moondance Kid
Myers, Walter Dean
Mop and Moondance series (1)
Me 'n' Shorty
Mulford, Clarence Edward
J C series (2)
Me on a rainy day
Godfrey, Jan
Me series (4)
Me outside
Wolff, Margaret
Books for me series (12)
Me over there
Jacob, Naomi
Me series (6)
Me shopping
Wolff, Margaret
Books for me series (14)
Me so far
Jack, Donald
Journals of Bartholomew Bandy series (7)
Me Tanner, you Jane
Block, Lawrence
Evan Tanner series (7)
Me thinking things over
Jacob, Naomi
Me series (14)
Me too
Jack, Donald
Journals of Bartholomew Bandy series (5)
Me, yesterday and today
Jacob, Naomi
Me series (11)
Meadow-Brook girls across country
Aldridge, Janet
Meadow-Brook girls series (1)
Meadow-Brook girls afloat
Aldridge, Janet
Meadow-Brook girls series (3)
Meadow-Brook girls by the sea
Aldridge, Janet
Meadow-Brook girls series (5)
Meadow-Brook girls in the hills
Aldridge, Janet
Meadow-Brook girls series (4)
Meadow-Brook girls on the tennis courts
Aldridge, Janet
Meadow-Brook girls series (6)
Meadow-Brook girls under canvas
Aldridge, Janet
Meadow-Brook girls series (2)
Meadowlark Basin
Bower, Bertha Muzzy
Meadowlark series (1)
Meagham
Jenkins, Jerry Bruce
Margo Franklin and Philip Spence series (8)
Mealtime words
Tyler, Jenny
First words series (2)
Mean city
Bradwell, James
Land of the giants series (4)
Mean high tide
Hall, James W
Thorn series (3)
Mean streak
Cooper, Ilene
Kids from Kennedy Middle School series (3)
Mean streets
Chalk, Gary
Prince of shadows series (1)
Dewey, Thomas Blanchard
Private Eye Mac series (4)
Mean to me
Cooper, M E
Couples series (33)
Meandering corpse
Prather, Richard Scott
Shell Scott series (31)
Meanest man in West Texas
Broome, H B
Tom English series (1)
Meaning of liff
Adams, Douglas Noel
Meaning of liff series (1)
Means of ascent
Caro, Robert A
Years of Lyndon Johnson series (2)
Means of escape
Caputo, Philip
War memoirs series (2)
Means of evil, and other stories
Rendell, Ruth
Chief Inspector Reginald Wexford series (12)
Meanwhile back at the morgue
Avallone, Michael
Ed Noon series (9)

Melander's millions
Gregg, Cecil Freeman
Inspector Cuthbert Higgins series (22)
Melanie
Miles, Keith
Sin bin series (2)
Nielsen, Susin
Degrassi High School series (6)
Melanie Brown and the jar of sweets
Oldfield, Pamela
Melanie Brown series (3)
Melanie Brown climbs a tree
Oldfield, Pamela
Melanie Brown series (2)
Melanie Brown goes to school
Oldfield, Pamela
Melanie Brown series (1)
Melbourne
Cecil, David
Lord Melbourne series (2)
Melbourne after the gold rush
Cannon, Michael
Old Melbourne series (2)
Melbourne House
Warner, Susan Bagert
Daisy trilogy (1)
Melbourne mystery
Brandon, John Gordon
Sexton Blake series (913)
Mele kalimaka, Mr Walker
Barrett, Robert G
Les Norton series (9)
Melendy family
Enright, Elizabeth
Melendy family series (3)
Melissa
Francis, Jaye
Hot pursuit series (1)
Melissa Mouse
Claret, Maria
Melissa Mouse series (1)
Melissa Mouse's birthday surprise
Claret, Maria
Melissa Mouse series (3)
Mellichampe
Simms, William Gilmore
American Revolution series (2)
Mellymobile, 1970-1981
Melly, George
Owning up series (4)
Melmoth reconciled
Balzac, Honore de
Philosophic studies series (3)
Melodie's year
Sabey, Ian
Melodie series (1)
Melody
Richards, Laura Elizabeth
Melody trilogy (1)
Melody lingers
Thwaites, Frederick Joseph
Melody series (2)
Melody moth
Cosgrove, Stephen Edward
Bugg series (49)
Melody murders
Wallace, Robert
Phantom Detective series (25)
Melody of death
Plummer, Thomas Arthur
Detective Inspector Andrew Frampton series (12)
Melody of Oddly
Blake, Jon
Oddly series (2)
Melome
Tubb, Edwin Charles
Dumarest series (28)
Melon hound
Dengler, Sandy
Pioneer family series (4)
Melric and the balloon
McKee, David
Melric the magician series (4)
Melric and the dragon
McKee, David
Melric the magician series (5)
Melric and the sorcerer
McKee, David
Melric the magician series (2)
Melric's apprentice
McKee, David
Melric the magician series (7)
Melrose Place
Nelson, Peter N
Melrose Place series (1)
Reisfeld, Randi
Melrose Place series (4)
Meltdown
Pendleton, Don
Mack Bolan series (97)
Melted coins
Dixon, Franklin W
Hardy boys series (23)
Melting clock
Kaminsky, Stuart Melvin
Toby Peters series (16)
Melting man
Canning, Victor
Rex Carver series (4)
Melting point
Davis, Kenn
Carver Bascombe series (5)
Melvaig's vision
Ford, Richard
Faradawn trilogy (2)
Melwood mystery
Hay, James
Jefferson Hastings series (1)
Member for Arcis
Balzac, Honore de
Scenes of political life series (3)
Members of the family
Wister, Owen
Western tales series (4)
Memed, my hawk
Kemal, Yashar
Slim Memed series (1)
Memoir of a Russian punk
Limonov, Edward
Eddie Limonov series (1)
Memoir of Jane Austen
Austen-Leigh, J E
Watsons series (1)
Memoirs of a clubman
Burgin, George Brown
Clubman series (1)
Memoirs of a dutiful daughter
Beauvoir, Simone de
Dutiful daughter series (1)
Memoirs of a fox-hunting man
Sassoon, Siegfried
Sherston trilogy (1)
Memoirs of a physician
Dumas, Alexandre
Marie Antoinette series (1)
Memoirs of a physician series (1)
Memoirs of a public baby
O'Connor, Philip
Lower view series (1)
Memoirs of a secret agent of Free France
Remy
Silent company trilogy (1)
Memoirs of a space traveler
Lem, Stanislaw
Ijon Tichy series (3)
Memoirs of a Surrey labourer
Bourne, George
Frederick Bettesworth series (2)
Memoirs of Alcheringia
Drew, Wayland
Erthring cycle series (1)
Memoirs of an aesthete
Acton, Harold
Aesthete series (1)
Memoirs of an infantry officer
Sassoon, Siegfried
Sherston trilogy (2)
Memoirs of an old bastard
Hibberd, Jack
Melbourne series (1)
Memoirs of Arsene Lupin
Leblanc, Maurice
Arsene Lupin series (11)
Memoirs of Barry Lyndon, Esq.
Thackeray, William Makepeace
Barry Lyndon series (1)
Memoirs of 1891-1917
Ehrenburg, Ilya
Men, years and life series (1)
Memoirs of Europe, towards the close of the eighth century
Manley, Mary de la Riviere
New Atalantis series (2)
Memoirs of George Sherston
Sassoon, Siegfried
Sherston trilogy (3)
Memoirs of hope
Gaulle, Charles de
War memoirs series (4)
Memoirs of Mipsie
Dunn, Mary
Lady Addle of Eigg series (3)
Memoirs of murder
Payes, Rachel
Forsythia Brown series (2)
Memoirs of Schlock Homes
Fish, Robert Lloyd
Schlock Homes series (2)
Memoirs of Sherlock Holmes
Doyle, Arthur Conan
Sherlock Holmes series (5)
Memoirs of Solar Pons
Derleth, August
Solar Pons series (2)
Memoirs of the court of Lilliput
Gulliver, Captain
Lilliput series (2)
Memorable World Series moments
Aaseng, Nathan
Sports heroes series (19)
Memorial hall murder
Langton, Jane
Homer Kelly series (3)
Memorial service
Stewart, John Innes Mackintosh
Duncan Pattullo series (3)
Memories
Emery, Ralph
Country music series (1)
Pascal, Francine
Sweet Valley High series (24)
Memories and developments
Stravinsky, Igor
Conversations series (2)
Memories and gardens
Spring, Marion Howard
Memories and gardens series (2)
Memories and impressions
Ford, Ford Madox
Memories and impressions series (1)
Memories beyond bloomers, 1924-1954
Lee, Mabel
Bloomer girl series (2)
Memories of a bloomer girl, 1894-1924
Lee, Mabel
Bloomer girl series (1)
Memories of a Victorian
Jepson, Edgar
Memories series (1)
Memories of an Edwardian
Jepson, Edgar
Memories series (2)
Memories of an Edwardian and neo-Georgian
Jepson, Edgar
Memories series (2)
Memories of evil days
Green, Julian
Days series (2)
Memories of happy days
Green, Julian
Days series (1)
Memories of Milo Morai
Adams, Robert
Horseclans series (15)
Memories of Ronald Love
Mann, Mary E
Ronald Love series (1)
Memory be green
Miller, Connie
Seasons trilogy (3)
Memory in a house
Boston, Lucy Maria
Green Knowe series (7)
Memory in a house series (2)
Memory of autumn
Angoff, Charles
Polonsky family series (7)
Memory of murder
Pentecost, Hugh
Doctor John Smith series (1)
Luke Bradley series (4)
Memory of treason
Hossent, Harry
Max Heald series (3)
Memory of youth
Moberg, Vilhelm
Earth is ours trilogy (1)
Memory prime
Reeves-Stevens, Garfield
Star trek series (42)
Memory to memory
Lunn, Arnold
Now I see series (3)
Memory trap
Price, Anthony
Doctor David Audley and Jack Butler series (19)
Memphis run
Robbins, David
Endworld series (18)
Men against the sea
Nordhoff, Charles
Bounty trilogy (2)
Men and apes
Morris, Desmond
Men and animals series (2)
Men and memories
Rothenstein, William
Men and memories series (3)
Men and memories, 1872-1900
Rothenstein, William
Men and memories series (1)
Men and memories, 1900-1922
Rothenstein, William
Men and memories series (2)
Men and pandas
Morris, Desmond
Men and animals series (3)
Men and power, 1917-18
Beaverbrook, William Maxwell Aitken
Lloyd George series (3)
Men and snakes
Morris, Desmond
Men and animals series (1)
Men and super men
Cooper, Jilly
Super men and women series (1)
Men and work
Citrine, Walter McLennan
Men and work series (1)
Men are like animals
Macpherson, Donald
Reggie Brooks series (2)
Men are like street cars
Lorimer, Graeme
Street cars trilogy (1)
Men at arms
Pratchett, Terry
Discworld series (15)
Waugh, Evelyn
World War II series (1)
Men die at Cyprus Lodge
Rhode, John
Doctor Lancelot Priestley series (38)
Men for counters
Fairlie, Gerard
Mister Malcolm series (3)
Men for pieces
Flynn, Brian
Anthony Bathurst series (36)
Men from Shadow Ridge
Thoeme, Brock
Saga of the Sierras series (2)
Men hunting things
Drake, David
Starhunters series (1)
Men in arms
Crosby, John Campbell
Horatio Cassidy series (2)
Men in blue
Griffin, W E B
Badge of honor series (1)
Men in her death
Blizard, Marie
Eve Macwilliams series (2)
Marlowe, Piers
Frank Drury and Inspector Bill Hazard series (2)
Morice, Anne
Tessa Crichton Price series (15)
Men in mid-life crisis
Conway, Jim
Mid-life crisis series (1)
Men in prison
Serge, Victor
Revolution trilogy (1)
Men, maids and mustard-pot
Frankau, Gilbert
Peter Jackson series (3)
Men of Albemarle
Fletcher, Inglis
Carolina series (5)
Men of blood
Hutson, Shaun
Sergeant Rolf Kessler series (5)
Men of Dallas
Hirschfeld, Burt
Dallas series (5)
Men of fear
Robeson, Kenneth
Doc Savage series (140)
Men of good will
Romains, Jules
Men of goodwill series (2)
Men of men
Smith, Wilbur Addison
Zouga Ballantyne series (2)
Men of might
Evans, Adelaide Bee
Bible pictures and stories series (2)
Men of subtle craft
Lewis, Royston
Arnold Landon series (4)
Men of the frontier force
Diver, Maud
Desmond series (3)
Men of the moss-hag
Crockett, Samuel Rutherford
English Revolution series (1)
Men of war
Gaillard, Robert
Marie series (6)
Pournelle, Jerry
There will be war series (2)
Men of wrath
Peacock, Max
Colonel Blood series (2)
Men on iron horses
McCall, Edith
Frontiers of America series (5)
Men should come with instruction booklets
Guisewhite, Cathy
Cathy series (4)
Men they once were
Masters, Simon
Target series (1)
Men vanished
Robeson, Kenneth
Doc Savage series (152)
Men went to Cattraeth
James, John
Photinus the Greek series (3)
Men who die twice
Heath, Peter
Jason Starr and Adam Cyber series (3)
Men who explained miracles
Carr, John Dickson
Doctor Gideon Fell series (23)
Sir Henry Merrivale series (23)
Men who march away
Paige, Frances
McGrath family series (4)
Men who smiled no more
Robeson, Kenneth
Doc Savage series (45)
Men with double faces
Loder, Vernon
Donald Cairn series (1)
Men with three eyes
Revell, Louisa
Julia Tyler series (5)
Men withering
Macmanus, Francis
Donnacha Mac Conmara trilogy (3)
Men without faces
Martyn, Wyndham
Anthony Trent series (25)
Menace
Creasey, John
Department Z series (11)
Janson, Hank
Hank Janson series (63)
Keverne, Richard
Franklin Parry and Leonard Harris series (2)
Menace for Doctor Morelle
Dudley, Ernest
Doctor Morelle series (3)
Menace from the moon
Walters, Hugh
Chris Godfrey series (2)
Menace in Siam
Corrigan, Mark
Mark Corrigan and McLean series (21)
Menace in space
Weinberg, Larry
Chuck Norris and the Karate Kommandos series (1)
Menace of atomigeddon
Mahr, Kurt
Perry Rhodan series (137)
Menace of the mutant master
Mahr, Kurt
Perry Rhodan series (18)
Menace of the saucers
Binder, Eando
Saucer series (1)
Menace of the silent death
Murray, Edgar Joyce
Sexton Blake series (445)
Menace on the Downs
Burton, Miles
Inspector Arnold and Desmond Merrion series (3)
Menace on the moor
Oliver, Marjorie Mary
Alex and Beryl series (1)
Menace to Mrs Kershaw
Allen, Austen
Inspector Ord series (1)
Menaced midget
Hildick, Edmund Wallace
McGurk series (3)
Menacers
Hamilton, Donald
Matt Helm series (11)
Menaces, menaces
Underwood, Michael
Rosa Epton series (2)
Sergeant Nick Attwell series (2)

Menacing groves
Sherwood, John
Celia Grant series (6)
Menage a trois
Villefranche, Anne Marie
Erotic memoirs series (3)
Mendelov conspiracy
Caidin, Martin
Six Million Dollar Man series (1)
Mendip holiday
Nuttall, Nesta
Meri Newman series (2)
Mendip money-makers
Boshell, Gordon
Secret Guardians series (3)
Mendip mystery
Brock, Lynn
Colonel Gore series (5)
Mendoza manuscript
Carter, Nick
Nick Carter series (169)
Mene tekel
Groner, Augusta
Joe Muller series (3)
Menehune murders
Arnold, Margot
Penelope Spring and Sir Tobias Glendower series (6)
Mensa murders
Martin, Lee
Deb Ralston series (6)
Mental monster
Robeson, Kenneth
Doc Savage series (156)
Mental wizard
Robeson, Kenneth
Doc Savage series (53)
Mentor
Jensen, Kris
Ardel series (2)
Menu cypher
Elman, Richard Martin
Professor Robert Harmon series (2)
Menwith tangle
Ross, Angus
Mark Farrow series (14)
Mercenaries
Baldwin, Bill
Helmsman series (4)
Harris, John
Ira Penaluna trilogy (2)
Mercenaries of Gor
Norman, John
Tarl Cabot series (21)
Mercenary
Anthony, Piers
Bio of a space tyrant series (2)
Pournelle, Jerry
Falkenberg's Legion series (1)
Future history series (2)
Mercenary calling
Walker, Martin
Maddox series (2)
Mercenary doctor
Flanders, Peter
Mercenary doctor series (2)
Mercenary from tomorrow
Reynolds, Mack
Joe Mauser series (1)
Mercenary justice
Bainbridge, Chuck
Hard corps series (5)
Mercenary kill
Quinn, John
Rod Gavin series (1)
Mercenary mountain
Carter, Nick
Nick Carter series (211)
Mercenary's star
Keith, William Henry
BattleTech series (2)
Merchant men
Armstrong, Richard
History of seafaring series (3)
Merchant of murder
Dean, Spencer
Don Cadee series (6)
Merchanter's luck
Cherryh, Carolyn Janice
Alliance-Union series (5)
Downbelow Station trilogy (2)
Merchanter series (1)
Merchants of death
Chase, Philip
Aaron Eisenberg and William Kendall series (2)
Merchants of disaster
Robeson, Kenneth
Doc Savage series (41)
Merchant's secret
Bobin, John William
Sexton Blake series (8)
Merchants' war
Pohl, Frederik
Space merchants series (2)
Mercies
Vanauken, Sheldon
Mercy series (3)
Merciless mermaids
Allison, Clyde
Agent triple zero eight series (11)
Mercury
Simon, Seymour
Space photos series (9)
Mercy trap
Martin, James E
Gil Disbro series (1)
Mere folly
Cooper, Diana Davis
Animal hotel series (3)
Mere murder
Wills, Cecil Melville
Superintendent Roger Ellerdine and Sergeant Cherry Blossom series (10)
Meredith mystery
Lincoln, Natalie Sumner
Inspector Mitchell series (6)
Merediths of Mappins
Byers, Irene
Meredith family series (1)
Merely a gentleman
McCulloch, Sarah
Georgian series (4)
Merely murder
Heyer, Georgette
Inspector Hemingway series (1)
Superintendent Hannasyde series (1)
Merely players
McDonald, Gregory
Time squared quartet (3)
Merger on the Orient Expressway
Christian, Mary Blount
Determined detectives series (2)
Merilyn at Camp Meenahga
Grove, Harriet Pyne
Merilyn Forrester series (1)
Merilyn enters Beechwold
Grove, Harriet Pyne
Merilyn Forrester series (2)
Merilyn Forrester, co-ed
Grove, Harriet Pyne
Merilyn Forrester series (3)
Merilyn tests loyalty
Grove, Harriet Pyne
Merilyn Forrester series (5)
Merilyn's new adventure
Grove, Harriet Pyne
Merilyn Forrester series (4)
Merilyn's rose garden
Grove, Harriet Pyne
Merilyn Forrester series (8)
Merilyn's senior dreams
Grove, Harriet Pyne
Merilyn Forrester series (7)
Meritocrats
Haggard, William
Colonel Charles Russell series (24)
Meriweather
Strahan, Kay Cleaver
Lynn Macdonald series (5)
Merlin
Lawhead, Stephen
Pendragon trilogy (2)
Merlin of the crystal cave
Stewart, Mary
Merlin and Arthur series (1)
Merlin trilogy
Stewart, Mary
Merlin and Arthur series (3)
Merlin's furlong
Mitchell, Gladys
Dame Beatrice Bradley series (26)
Merlin's godson
Munn, Harold Warner
Gwalchmai trilogy (2)
Merlin's mistake
Newman, Robert
Tertius trilogy (1)
Merlin's ring
Munn, Harold Warner
Gwalchmai trilogy (3)
Mermaid
Martin, Oliver
Timothy Cullinan series (2)
Millar, Margaret
Tom Aragon series (3)
Mermaid Madonna
Myrivilis, Stratis
Mermaid Madonna series (1)
Mermaid on the rocks
Halliday, Brett
Michael Shayne series (56)
Mermaid singing
Clift, Charmian
Greek island series (1)
Merridrew fights again
Fearn, John Russell
Jenkinson Talbot Merridrew series (4)
Merridrew follows the trail
Fearn, John Russell
Jenkinson Talbot Merridrew series (5)
Merridrew marches on
Fearn, John Russell
Jenkinson Talbot Merridrew series (3)
Merridrew rides again
Fearn, John Russell
Jenkinson Talbot Merridrew series (2)
Merrie
Schurfranz, Vivian
Sunfire series (25)
Merrie tales of Jaques Tournebroche, and, Child life in town and country
France, Anatole
Abbe Coignard series (3)
Merriweather girls and the mystery of the queen's fan
Edholm, Lizette
Merriweather girls series (1)
Merriweather girls at good old Rockhill
Edholm, Lizette
Merriweather girls series (2)
Merriweather girls in quest of treasure
Edholm, Lizette
Merriweather girls series (3)
Merriweather girls on Campers' Trail
Edholm, Lizette
Merriweather girls series (4)
Merrow ponies
Campbell, Judith
Ponies series (2)
Merry again
Mallory, Clare
Merry Arundel series (2)
Merry begins
Mallory, Clare
Merry Arundel series (1)
Merry by name
Wayne, Jenifer
Winchester family series (3)
Merry Christmas, Amanda and April
Pryor, Bonnie
Amanda and April series (2)
Merry Christmas, Amelia Bedelia
Parish, Peggy
Amelia Bedelia series (11)
Merry Christmas Baabee
Khalsa, Dayal Kaur
Baabee series III (3)
Merry Christmas, Dear Dragon
Hillert, Margaret
Dear Dragon series (6)
Merry Christmas, Ernest and Celestine
Vincent, Gabrielle
Ernest and Celestine series (5)
Merry Christmas from Betsy
Haywood, Carolyn
Betsy series (11)
Merry Christmas from Eddie
Haywood, Carolyn
Eddie Wilson series (15)
Merry Christmas, Harry
Chalmers, Mary
Harry series (4)
Merry Christmas Little Mouse
Wheeler, Cindy
Little Mouse series (1)
Merry Christmas, Max
Turk, Hanne
Max the Mouse series (8)
Merry Christmas, Strega Nona
De Paola, Tomie
Strega Nona series (3)
Merry coasting party
Burgess, Thornton Waldo
Animal stories series (6)
Merry devils
Marston, Edward
Merry-go-round
Cowdroy, Joan
Li Moh series (6)
Ross, Diana
Miss Pussy series (5)
Elizabethan whodunits series (2)
Merry go round in Oz
McGraw, Eloise Jervis
Oz series (39)
Merry Hall
Nichols, Beverley
Merry Hall trilogy (1)
Merry Lynn Mine
Grove, Harriet Pyne
Merilyn Forrester series (6)
Merry mailman
Martin, Marcia
Merry mailman series (1)
Merry mailman around the world
Martin, Marcia
Merry mailman series (2)
Merry marches on
Mallory, Clare
Merry Arundel series (3)
Merry Marmaduke
Chapman, Elizabeth
Marmaduke series (5)
Merry merry Huckleberry
Delton, Judy
Condo Kids series (6)
Merry Mischief
Joyner, Simon
Tales from the Misty Wood series (1)
Merry Mister Meddle
Blyton, Enid
Mister Meddle series (3)
Merry mix-ups
Oxenbury, Helen
Seven hundred and twenty nine series (1)
Merry Mrs Macbeth
Grant, Maxwell
Shadow series (259)
Merry Slimtails
Chell, Mary
Slimtails series (3)
Merry story book
Blyton, Enid
Story book series (2)
Merry widow
Cosgrove, Stephen Edward
Bugg series (50)
Merry wives of Westminster
Lowndes, Marie Belloc
Arcadia series (3)
Merrylees mystery
Goyne, Richard
Paul Templeton series (8)
Merrymole the intrepid
Dodd, Maurice
Merrymole series (2)
Merrymole the magnificent
Dodd, Maurice
Merrymole series (1)
Merryvale girls at the seaside
Burnett, Alice Hale
Merryvale girls series (5)
Merryvale girls in the country
Burnett, Alice Hale
Merryvale girls series (6)
Merryweathers
Richards, Laura Elizabeth
Three Margarets series (6)
Merv Marrow
Reed, Giles
Munch Bunch character series (26)
Merv Marrow's new police car
Reed, Giles
Munch Bunch story books series (10)
Mervyn Mouse at the fair
Creche, Sylvia
Mervyn Mouse series (2)
Mervyn Mouse at the zoo
Creche, Sylvia
Mervyn Mouse series (5)
Mervyn Mouse goes camping
Creche, Sylvia
Mervyn Mouse series (4)
Mervyn Mouse joins the sports club
Creche, Sylvia
Mervyn Mouse series (3)
Mervyn's Christmas
Peguero, Leone
Mervyn series (2)
Mervyn's revenge
Peguero, Leone
Mervyn series (1)
Mesa Verde
Mitchum, Hank
Stage coach station series (24)
Mesabi huntdown
Sharpe, Jon
Trailsman series (90)
Mescalero dawn
Logan, Jake
John Slocum series (85)
Mescalero mask
Sharpe, Jon
Trailsman series (82)
Mesmerist's victim
Dumas, Alexandre
Marie Antoinette series (5)
Mesquite Jenkins
Mulford, Clarence Edward
Johnny Nelson series (4)
Mesquite Jenkins series (3)
Mesquite Jenkins, Tumbleweed
Mulford, Clarence Edward
Johnny Nelson series (6)
Mesquite Jenkins series (4)
Mesquite manhunt
Sharpe, Jon
Trailsman series (43)
Mesquite marauders
Cole, Jackson
Jim Hatfield series (73)
Mesquiteer mavericks
Macdonald, William Colt
Three Mesquiteers series (14)
Message
Balzac, Honore de
Scenes of private life series (16)
Message ends
Craig, David
Roy Rickman trilogy (2)
Message for Doctor Ross
Dwyer-Joyce, Alice
Doctor Esmond Ross series (5)
Message from a corpse
Merwin, Samuel Kimball
Amy Brewster series (2)
Message from a dead man
Roberts, J R
Gunsmith series (86)
Message from Arkmae
Cutt, William Towrie
Arkmae series (1)
Message from Moscow
Keith, Brandon
I spy series (7)
Message from space
Packard, Edward
Choose your own adventure series (7)
Message in the haunted mansion
Keene, Carolyn
Nancy Drew series (122)
Message in the hollow oak
Keene, Carolyn
Nancy Drew series (12)
Message in the sand dunes
Judd, Frances K
Kay Tracey series (9)
Message of the mute dog
Russell, Charlotte Murray
Jane Amanda Edwards series (7)
Message to Moosonee
Barnes, Michael
Just north series (4)
Messages
Thomson, Pat
Jets series (3)
Messages from Michael on the nature of the evolution of the human soul
Yarbro, Chelsea Quinn
Messages from Michael series (1)
Messenger
Dickens, Monica
Messenger series (1)
Messenger dog's secret
Hunt, Francis
Mary and Jerry Denton series (1)
Messenger for Parliament
Haugaard, Erik Christian
Oliver Cutter series (1)
Messenger of death
Grant, Maxwell
Shadow series (242)
Messengers of darkness
Walker, Hugh
Magira trilogy (3)
Messengers of day
Powell, Anthony
To keep the ball rolling series (2)
Messengers of evil
Souvestre, Pierre
Fantomas series (3)
Messiah
Dixon, Roger
Jesus Christ series (1)
Messiah at the end of time
Moorcock, Michael
Dancers at the end of time series (5)
Jherek Carnelian and Amelia Underwood series (5)
Messiah stone
Caidin, Martin
Messiah series (1)
Messianic legacy
Baigent, Michael
Order of Sion series (2)
Lincoln, Henry
Order of Sion series (2)

Messmates
Stevens, William Oliver
Peewee Clinton series (2)
Messy baby
Ormerod, Jan
Baby books series (4)
ssy Bessey
McKissack, Patricia Carwell
Messy Bessey series (1)
ssy Bessey's closet
McKissack, Patricia Carwell
Messy Bessey series (2)
ssy Bessey's garden
McKissack, Patricia Carwell
Messy Bessey series (3)
ssy Malcolm
Taylor, Jenny
Messy Malcolm series (1)
essy Malcolm's birthday
Taylor, Jenny
Messy Malcolm series (2)
essy Malcolm's dream
Taylor, Jenny
Messy Malcolm series (3)
etaconcert
May, Julian
Pliocene exile series (1)
etal fire
McKinney, Jack
Robotech series (8)
etal flask
Thomson, Basil
Peter Graham series (1)
etal gear
Frost, Alexandra
Worlds of power series (2)
etal green Mercedes
Williams, Timothy
Commissario Trotti series (2)
etal Master
Robeson, Kenneth
Doc Savage series (72)
etal monster
Merritt, Abraham
Doctor Goodwin series (2)
etal storm
Alexander, David
Phoenix series (4)
etamorphosis
McKinney, Jack
Robotech series (11)
Saperstein, David
Cocoon series (2)
Metemorphosis
Lorrah, Jean
Star trek, the next generation sequels series (4)
Meteor
Capek, Karel
Truth and democracy trilogy (2)
Meteor men
Le Baron, Anthony
Invaders series (1)
Meteor menace
Robeson, Kenneth
Doc Savage series (3)
Method in his murder
Warriner, Thurman
Mister Scotter series (1)
Method in madness
Disney, Doris Miles
Jeff Dimarco series (5)
Method three for murder
Stout, Rex
Nero Wolfe and Archie Goodwin series (33)
Methodist idylls
Lindsay, Harry
Methodist idylls series (1)
Methods of Doctor Scarlett
Laing, Alexander
Doctor Scarlett series (3)
Methods of extinction
Huebner, Frederick D
Matt Riordan series (4)
Methods of Lady Walderhurst
Burnett, Frances Hodgson
Lady Walderhurst series (2)
Methods of Maigret
Simenon, Georges
Inspector Jules Maigret series (33)
Methods of Sergeant Cluff
North, Gil
Sergeant Caleb Cluff series (2)
Methods on Uncle Abner
Post, Melville Davisson
Uncle Abner series (2)
Methuselah factor
Rosenberger, Joseph
Death Merchant series (60)
Methuselah's children
Heinlein, Robert Anson
Future history series (5)
Lazarus Long series (1)
Methuselah's diary
Vachell, Horace Annesley
Methuselah series (4)
Methylated murder
Robbins, Clifton
Clay Harrison series (5)
Metro gangs attack
Leeson, Robert
Time rope series (4)
Metropolis
Bradley, Mary Hastings
Old Chicago series (4)
Sinclair, Upton
New York trilogy (1)
Mettle at Woomera
Macnell, James
Captain Mettle series (3)
Mettle dives deep
Macnell, James
Captain Mettle series (2)
Mexicali 1000
Speed, Eric
Wynn and Lonny racing series (1)
Mexican badlands
Evans, Tabor
Longarm series (147)
Mexican brown death
Derrick, Lionel
Penetrator series (26)
Mexican hit
Rosenberger, Joseph
Death Merchant series (26)
Mexican jackpot
Grover, Marshall
Larry and Stretch series (127)
Mexican marauder
Thorne, Ramsay
Captain Gringo series (16)
Mexican massacre
Sharpe, Jon
Trailsman series (88)
Mexican mourning
Hedges, Joseph
John Stark series (8)
Mexican muskets
Ellis, Wesley
Lone Star series (119)
Mexican proposition
Chisholm, Matt
Joe Blade series (6)
Mexican road race
O'Connor, Patrick
Black Tiger series (2)
Mexican showdown
Hardin, J D
Raider series (32)
Sherman, Jory
Gunn series (2)
Mexican silver
Logan, Jake
John Slocum series (131)
Mexican slay ride
Dewey, Thomas Blanchard
Pete Schofield series (4)
Macneil, Neil
Tony Costaine and Bert McCall series (6)
Mexican standoff
Chase, Glen
Cherry Delight series (21)
Cook, Bruce
Antonio Cervantes series (1)
Hawk, Alex
Elfego O'Reilly series (1)
Masters, Zeke
Faro Blake series (10)
Mexican tamale mystery
Stanley, George Edward
Doctor Constance Daniels series (5)
Mexican tree duck
Crumley, James
C W Sughrue series (2)
Mexican twins
Perkins, Lucy Fitch
Twin series (5)
Mexico breakout
Bridges, Ben
Carter O'Brien series (3)
Mexico is forever
Schutz, Benjamin Merrill
Leo Haggerty series (6)
Mexico kill
Hartman, Dane
Dirty Harry Callahan series (4)
Mexico novice
Evans, John
Habbakuk Parton series (2)
Mexico set
Deighton, Len
Bernard Samson series (2)
Game, set and match trilogy (2)
Mezentian gate
Eddison, Eric Rucker
Zimiamvian trilogy (1)
Mia
Beckman, Gunnel
Mia series (1)
Mia alone
Beckman, Gunnel
Mia series (1)
Miami blues
Willeford, Charles
Hoke Moseley series (1)
Miami crash
Stivers, Dick
Able Team series (28)
Miami, it's murder
Buchanan, Edna
Britt Montero series (2)
Miami marauder
Barry, Mike
Burton Wulff series (9)
Miami massacre
Pendleton, Don
Mack Bolan series (4)
Miami mayhem
Rome, Anthony
Tony Rome series (1)
Miami mob
Frazer, Robert Caine
Mark Kilby series (3)
Miami run
Robbins, David
Endworld series (16)
Miami war zone
Buchanan, Jack
M.I.A. Hunter series (10)
Miau
Perez Galdos, Benito
Contemporary novels of Spain series (15)
Mice and the clockwork bus
Peppe, Rodney
Mice series (4)
Mice and the flying basket
Peppe, Rodney
Mice series (3)
Mice and the travel machine
Peppe, Rodney
Mice series (6)
Mice on the moon
Peppe, Rodney
Mice series (5)
Mice who lived in a shoe
Peppe, Rodney
Mice series (1)
Michael and the sea
Coles, Alison
Michael and Mandy series (5)
Michael, brother of Jerry
London, Jack
Jerry series (2)
Michael Forth
Johnston, Mary
American Civil War trilogy (3)
Michael Green book of coarse sport
Green, Michael
Coarse series (5)
Michael in the dark
Coles, Alison
Michael and Mandy series (2)
Michael Kemp, the happy farmer's lad
Woodrooffe, Anne
Michael Kemp series (1)
Michael Shayne investigates
Halliday, Brett
Michael Shayne series (6)
Michael Shayne takes a hand
Halliday, Brett
Michael Shayne series (8)
Michael Shayne takes over
Halliday, Brett
Michael Shayne series (4)
Michael Shayne's fiftieth case
Halliday, Brett
Michael Shayne series (50)
Michael Shayne's long chance
Halliday, Brett
Michael Shayne series (9)
Michael Shayne's triple mystery
Halliday, Brett
Michael Shayne series (16)
Michael Shayne series (33)
Michael shows off Baltimore
Curtin, Patricia Romero
Show off series (1)
Michael, the Finn
Waltari, Mika
Michael Carvajel series (1)
Michael, the married man
Woodrooffe, Anne
Michael Kemp series (2)
Michael, the masterful monk
Dudley, Owen Francis
Problems of human happiness series (7)
Michael's first day at school
Coles, Alison
Michael and Mandy series (1)
Michael's people
Yarbro, Chelsea Quinn
Messages from Michael series (3)
Michael's victory
Judson, Clara Ingram
They came from series (5)
Michelangelo the Florentine
Alexander, Sidney
Michelangelo Buonarotti trilogy (1)
Michigan madness
Ham, Bob
Overload series (10)
Mick and Muff
Stiessel, Lena
Mick and Muff series (1)
Mick and Muff and the little car
Stiessel, Lena
Mick and Muff series (4)
Mick and Muff in the country
Stiessel, Lena
Mick and Muff series (2)
Mick and Muff painting
Stiessel, Lena
Mick and Muff series (3)
Mick Cardby works overtime
Hume, David
Mick Cardby series (23)
Mickel seafarer
Mattson, Olle
Mickel Mickelson series (2)
Mickey Moose
Reese, Bob
Yellowstone critter series (4)
Mickey Turner and the phantom dog
Palmer, Bernard
Mickey Turner series (3)
Mickey Turner, ranger's son
Palmer, Bernard
Mickey Turner series (4)
Micro kill
Janson, Hank
Hank Janson series (243)
Microbe murders
Eberhard, Frederick George
Chief of Police Sutherland series (2)
Microbe of crime
Carter, Nicholas
Nicholas Carter series (512)
Microbes of power
Wilson, Alexander
Sir Leonard Wallace series (6)
Microbots
Appleton, Victor II
Tom Swift Junior series 3 (8)
Microcolony
Williams, Gordon Maclean
Micronauts series (2)
Microfish
Lee, Robert
Fishy business series (2)
Micronaut world
Williams, Gordon Maclean
Micronauts series (2)
Micronauts
Williams, Gordon Maclean
Micronauts series (1)
Micro-techs
Darlton, Clark
Perry Rhodan series (55)
Midas and Son
McKenna, Stephen
Sonia series (3)
Midas coffin
Quinn, Simon
Inquisitor series (5)
Midas kill
Kirk, Philip
Butler series (12)
Midas man
Robeson, Kenneth
Doc Savage series (46)
Midas operation
Griffin, John
Richard Raven series (1)
Mid-century
Angoff, Charles
Polonsky family series (10)
Middle Ages I, 1066-1154
Birt, David
Involvement in history series (1)
Middle Ages II, 1154-1327
Birt, David
Involvement in history series (2)
Middle Ages III, 1327-1485
Birt, David
Involvement in history series (3)
Middle-class
Millin, Sarah Gertrude
Dark river series (2)
Middle classes
Balzac, Honore de
Scenes of Parisian life series (12)
Middle Earth
Carter, Lin
Middle Earth series (5)
Middle Earth quiz book
Buchholz, Suzanne
Middle Earth series (5)
Middle East massacre
Carter, Nick
Nick Carter series (249)
Middle generation
Beresford, John Davys
Hillingtons trilogy (2)
Middle kingdom
Marshall, William Leonard
Twentieth century trilogy (2)
Wingrove, David
Chung Kuo series (1)
Middle link
Carter, Nicholas
Nicholas Carter series (562)
Middle Moffat
Estes, Eleanor
Moffat family series (2)
Middle of the negro's head
Brisbane, Coutts
Sexton Blake series (995)
Middle School gets married
Pascal, Francine
Sweet Valley twins series (68)
Middle span
Santayana, George
Persons and places trilogy (2)
Middle years, 1884-1894
Edel, Leon
Henry James series (3)
Middlefold murders
Radford, Edwin
Doctor Manson series (25)
Middles and Tessa
Soderback, Marianne
Middles series (2)
Middles run away
Soderback, Marianne
Middles series (1)
Midget Mouse finds a house
Lindsay, Hilarie
Midget Mouse series (1)
Midget Mouse goes to sea
Lindsay, Hilarie
Midget Mouse series (2)
Midlander
Tarkington, Booth
Growth trilogy (3)
Midlanders
Coxhead, Elizabeth
Alney series (2)
Midnight
Cohen, Octavus Roy
David Carroll series (4)
Midnight adventures of Kelly, Dot and Esmeralda
Goodall, John Strickland
Paddy Pork series (5)
Midnight and Percy Jones
Starrett, Vincent
Riley Blackwood series (2)
Midnight at Monster Mansion
Otfinoski, Steven
Twistaplot series (13)
Midnight at the Well of Souls
Chalker, Jack Laurence
Well world series (1)
Midnight baby
Hornsby, Wendy
Maggie McGowan series (2)
Midnight bell
Hamilton, Patrick
Twenty thousand streets under the sky series (1)
Midnight cavalier
Armstrong, Raymond
J Rockingham Stone series (1)
Midnight chess game
Ecke, Wolfgang
Super sleuth series (6)
Midnight chill
Siegel, Barbara
Ghostworld series (2)

Midnight eye
Roscoe, Mike
Johnny April series (5)
Midnight ferry to Venice
Healey, Ben
Harcourt d'Espinal series (4)
Paul Hedley series (8)
Midnight folk
Masefield, John
Kay Harker series (1)
Midnight gun
Mather, Berkely
Stafford family trilogy (2)
Midnight hangman
Hill, Morgan
Dan Colt series (6)
Midnight horse
Edwards, Monica
Romney Marsh series (3)
Midnight in the century
Serge, Victor
Resistance trilogy (1)
Midnight in the doll house
Stover, Marjorie Filley
Dolls series (2)
Midnight lady and the mourning man
Anthony, David
Morgan Butler series (1)
Midnight lorry crime
Brooks, Edwy Searles
Sexton Blake series (921)
Midnight mail
Holt, Henry
Inspector Silver series (2)
Midnight man
Estleman, Loren D
Amos Walker series (3)
Kane, Henry
Inspector McGregor series (1)
Murphy, Warren Burton
Destroyer series (43)
Midnight marauders
Grover, Marshall
Larry and Stretch series (183)
Midnight message
Carter, Nicholas
Nicholas Carter series (491)
Midnight munchies
Browne, Dik
Hagar the horrible series (7)
Midnight murder
Robeson, Kenneth
Avenger series (24)
Stuart, Donald
Lionel Crane series (2)
Midnight mystery
Hardinge, Rex
Sexton Blake series (579)
Midnight never comes
Fallon, Martin
Paul Chavasse series (4)
Midnight oil
Pritchett, Victor Sawdon
Cab series (2)
Midnight on the desert
Priestley, John Boynton
English journey series (2)
Midnight patrol
Eagar, Frances
Laura and Harry series (3)
Midnight plumber
Procter, Maurice
Chief Inspector Harry Martineau series (8)
Midnight rally
Speed, Eric
Wynn and Lonny racing series (6)
Midnight rogue
Davis, Graeme
Fighting fantasy gamebook series (29)
Midnight roundup
Field, Peter
Powder Valley series (22)
Midnight sailing
Hufford, Susan
Hilda Hughes tetralogy (1)
Midnight sister
Albert, Marvin Hubert
Pierre-Ange Sawyer series (6)
Midnight star
Coulter, Catherine
Star trilogy (1)
Midnight visitor
Sutton, Margaret
Judy Bolton series (12)
Midnight walkers
Laing, Kenneth
Rolling Stone series (3)
Midnight whispers
Andrews, Virginia Cleo
Cutler family series (4)
Midnight wireless
Alington, Cyril Augustine
Mister Birtley series (2)
Mid-ocean tragedy
Hawk, John
Mortimer Sark series (3)
Midpoint
Holt, Isabella
Rampole family series (2)
Midshipman Bolitho
Kent, Alexander
Captain Richard Bolitho series (2)
Midshipman Bolitho and the Avenger
Kent, Alexander
Captain Richard Bolitho series (2)
Midshipman Lee
White, Robb
Midshipman Lee series (1)
Midshipman Lee of the Naval Academy
White, Robb
Midshipman Lee series (2)
Midshipman Merrill
Lounsberry, Lionel
Merrill series (1)
Midshipman Quinn
Styles, Showell
Midshipman Quinn series (1)
Midshipman Quinn and Denise the spy
Styles, Showell
Midshipman Quinn series (3)
Midshipman Quinn wins through
Styles, Showell
Midshipman Quinn series (3)
Midshipman Ralph Osborn at sea
Beach, Edward Latimer, senior
Ralph Osborn series (2)
Midshipmen cruise south
Pearson, Parry
Jeremy Barton and Samuel Best series (1)
Midst Balkan perils
Brooks, Edwy Searles
Sexton Blake series (10)
Midst moving waters
Rutley, Cecily Marianne
Little people in far off lands series (4)
'Midst the wild Carpathians
Jokai, Mor
Michael Apafi series (1)
Midstream
Keller, Helen
My life series (2)
Midstream changes
Aaseng, Nathan
Inside business series (8)
Midsummer ball
Marden, Fay
Flower fairy series (2)
Midsummer killing
Barnes, Trevor
Blanche Hampton series (1)
Midsummer magic
Coulter, Catherine
Victoria Albemarle trilogy (1)
Midsummer malice
Fitzgerald, Nigel
Alan Russell series (1)
Superintendent Duffy series (1)
Midsummer mink
Coke, Peter
Brigadier Rayne series (2)
Midsummer mountains
Lamplugh, Lois
Allen family series (6)
Midsummer murder
Witting, Clifford
Inspector Charlton series (2)
Midsummer nightmare
Hale, Christopher
Lieutenant Bill French series (10)
Midsummer night's crime
Bromley, Gordon
Inspector Severn series (3)
Midsummer night's killing
Barnes, Trevor
Blanche Hampton series (1)
Midsummer notebook of a country rat
Firmin, Peter
Country rat series (2)
Midsummer slay ride
Gribble, Leonard Reginald
Superintendent Anthony Slade series (37)
Midsummer tempest
Anderson, Poul
Alternate world series (2)
Midsummer's eve
Carr, Philippa
Daughters of England series (13)
Midtown North
Newman, Christopher
Joe Dante series (4)
Midtown South
Newman, Christopher
Joe Dante series (1)
Mid-wake
Ahern, Jerry
Survivalist series (27)
Midway between
Norwood, Warren
Double-spiral war series (1)
Midway on the waves
Lees-Milne, James
Ancestral voices series (4)
Midway to murder
Yates, Margaret Tayler
Anne Davenport McLean series (3)
Midwife
Courter, Gay
Midwife series (1)
Midwife of Pont Clery
Sandstrom, Flora
Pont Clery series (1)
Midwife's advice
Courter, Gay
Midwife series (2)
Midwinter madness
Stuart, Anthony
Vladimir Gull series (3)
Midwinter tale
Marden, Fay
Flower fairy series (4)
Midworld
Foster, Alan Dean
Thranx series (2)
Miernik dossier
McCarry, Charles
Paul Christopher series (1)
Miffy
Bruna, Dick
Miffy series (1)
Miffy and her friend
Bruna, Dick
Miffy series (12)
Miffy at the beach
Bruna, Dick
Miffy series (4)
Miffy at the playground
Bruna, Dick
Miffy series (7)
Miffy at the seaside
Bruna, Dick
Miffy series (4)
Miffy at the zoo
Bruna, Dick
Miffy series (2)
Miffy books
Bruna, Dick
Miffy series (8)
Miffy goes flying
Bruna, Dick
Miffy series (6)
Miffy goes to school
Bruna, Dick
Miffy series (11)
Miffy goes to stay
Bruna, Dick
Miffy series (13)
Miffy in hospital
Bruna, Dick
Miffy series (8)
Miffy in the hospital
Bruna, Dick
Miffy series (8)
Miffy in the snow
Bruna, Dick
Miffy series (3)
Miffy painting book
Bruna, Dick
Miffy series (13)
Miffy's bicycle
Bruna, Dick
Miffy series (10)
Miffy's birthday
Bruna, Dick
Miffy series (5)
Miffy's dream
Bruna, Dick
Miffy series (9)
Might as well be dead
Stout, Rex
Nero Wolfe and Archie Goodwin series (27)
Mightiest machine
Campbell, John Wood
Aarn Munro series (1)
Mighty blockhead
Gruber, Frank
Johnny Fletcher and Sam Cragg series (7)
Mighty mammals of the past
Stidworthy, John
Creatures from the past series (3)
Mighty manslayer
Lamb, Harold
Khlit the Cossack series (2)
Mighty years
Morley, Iris
Monmouth series (3)
Mignon and Peter
Kibby, Leigh
Stories for happiness series (2)
Mignon's husband
Winter, John Strange
Bootles series (7)
Mignon's secret
Winter, John Strange
Bootles series (6)
Migrants, sharecroppers, mountaineers
Coles, Robert
Children of crisis series (2)
Migrations
Scott, Evelyn
American history trilogy (1)
Mike
Caswell, Brian
Mike and Lisdalia series (1)
Wodehouse, Pelham Grenville
Psmith series (1)
Wrykyn School series (3)
Mike and Psmith
Wodehouse, Pelham Grenville
Psmith series (1)
Wrykyn School series (1)
Mike at Wrykyn
Wodehouse, Pelham Grenville
Psmith series (1)
Wrykyn School series (1)
Mike Dime
Fantoni, Barry
Mike Dime series (1)
Mike Mars and the mystery satellite
Wollheim, Donald Allen
Mike Mars series (7)
Mike Mars around the moon
Wollheim, Donald Allen
Mike Mars series (8)
Mike Mars, astronaut
Wollheim, Donald Allen
Mike Mars series (1)
Mike Mars at Cape Canaveral
Wollheim, Donald Allen
Mike Mars series (3)
Mike Mars at Cape Kennedy
Wollheim, Donald Allen
Mike Mars series (3)
Mike Mars flies the Dyna-Soar
Wollheim, Donald Allen
Mike Mars series (5)
Mike Mars flies the X-15
Wollheim, Donald Allen
Mike Mars series (2)
Mike Mars in orbit
Wollheim, Donald Allen
Mike Mars series (4)
Mike Mars, South Pole spaceman
Wollheim, Donald Allen
Mike Mars series (6)
Mike Shayne mysteries
Halliday, Brett
Mike Shayne stories series (6)
Mike's mystery
Warner, Gertrude Chandler
Boxcar children series (5)
Miko
Lustbader, Eric
Ninja series (2)
Milady in love
Chesney, Marion
House for the season series (6)
Milady took the rap
Janson, Hank
Hank Janson series (29)
Milagro Beanfield War
Nichols, John
New Mexico trilogy (1)
Milan grill room
Oppenheim, Edward Phillips
Major Charles Lyson series (2)
Mild case of murder
Brandon, Gordon
Michael and Terry Terence series (4)
Mildred and Elsie
Finley, Martha Farquharson
Elsie Dinsmore series (28)
Mildred Keith series (1)
Mildred Arkell
Wood, Ellen
Mildred Arkell series (1)
Mildred at home
Finley, Martha Farquharson
Mildred Keith series (5)
Mildred at Roselands
Finley, Martha Farquharson
Mildred Keith series (3)
Roselands series (2)
Mildred Keith
Finley, Martha Farquharson
Mildred Keith series (2)
Mildred's boys and girls
Finley, Martha Farquharson
Mildred Keith series (6)
Mildred's married life
Finley, Martha Farquharson
Mildred Keith series (4)
Mildred's married life and a winter with Elsie Dinsmore
Finley, Martha Farquharson
Elsie Dinsmore series (28)
Mildred's new daughter
Finley, Martha Farquharson
Mildred Keith series (7)
Mile deep grave
Hedges, Joseph
John Stark series (7)
Mile-high madness
Hunter, E J
Headhunter series (5)
Miles from anywhere
Warren, Clarence Henry
Happy countryman series (4)
Miles Wallingford
Cooper, James Fenimore
Miles Wallingford series (2)
Milestones of murder
Wallace, Robert
Phantom Detective series (3)
Militant
Crick, Michael
Militant series (1)
Military form
Rowley, Christopher
Vang trilogy (2)
Military orchid
Brooke, Jocelyn
Orchid trilogy (1)
Military philosophers
Powell, Anthony
Dance to the music of time series (9)
Milk
Owen, Dilys
Mister Munch series (1)
Milk and honey
Burgess, Thornton Waldo
Cubby Bear series (9)
Kellerman, Faye
Sergeant Peter Decker and Rina Lazarus series (3)
Milk-churn murders
Burton, Miles
Inspector Arnold and Desmond Merrion series (11)
Milk my ewes and weep
Fussey, Joyce
Yorkshire farm series (1)
Milk River Range
Floren, Lee
Buckshot McKee and Tortilla Joe series (2)
Milk train does'nt stop here anymore
Williams, Tennessee
Baby doll series (2)
Milkbottle H
Orlovitz, Gil
Emanuel family series (1)
Milkmaid's millions
Austin, Hugh
William Sultan series (2)
Milkshakes, men and melodies
Rosenthal, Lesley Sharon
Esmeralda Bloom series (2)
Milky mountains
Robinson, Mike
Solo the dragon series (2)
Milky Way
Maymaru, Narritjan
Mark and Wendy series (2)
Milky Way, galaxy number one
Branley, Franklyn Mansfield
Exploring our universe series (5)
Milky Way run
Jordan, Godfrey P
Starr family series (1)
Mill at Sandy Creek
Rand, Edward Augustus
Fighting the sea series (3)
Mill Creek Irregulars
Derleth, August
Mill Creek Irregulars series (1)
Mill house
Bell, Adrian
Roland Pace series (3)

Mill House murder
Fletcher, Joseph Smith
Ronald Camberwell series (11)
Mill in the valley
Baker, Denys Val
Cornish series (22)
Mill of fear
Bidston, Lester
Sexton Blake series (688)
Mill on the Po
Bacchelli, Riccardo
Mill on the Po series (1)
Mill on the shore
Cleeves, Ann
George Palmer-Jones series (6)
Mill pond mystery
Hill, Harry Egbert
Sexton Blake series (230)
Mill-race
Street, Pamela
Lodge family series (1)
Mill-race quartet
Street, Pamela
Lodge family series (4)
Mill-town massacres
Stockbridge, Grant
Richard Wentworth series (16)
Millais and the Ruskins
Lutyens, Mary
Effie Gray series (2)
Millenium
Bova, Ben
Chet Kinsman series (1)
Miller of Angibault
Sand, George
Socialist trilogy (3)
Millers and their playmates
Pierson, Clara Dillingham
Millers series (4)
Millers at Pencroft
Pierson, Clara Dillingham
Millers series (2)
Miller's boy
Willard, Barbara
Mantlemass series (2)
Miller's dance
Graham, Winston
Poldark series (9)
Millie Cooper
Herman, Charlotte
Millie Cooper series (1)
Millie Cooper takes a chance
Herman, Charlotte
Millie Cooper series (2)
Milligan's war
Milligan, Spike
War memoirs series (6)
Millijoy, the determined
Kimbrough, Katheryn
Phenwick women series (15)
Milliner's hat mystery
Thomson, Basil
Superintendent Richardson series (7)
Million dollar babe
Brown, Carter
Mike Farrel series (1)
Million-dollar bloodhunt
Millard, Joseph John
Dollar series (7)
Million-dollar diamond
Fletcher, Joseph Smith
Richard Goulburn series (2)
Million dollar gamble
West, Chassie L
Micro adventure series (3)
Million dollar handling
Halliday, Brett
Michael Shayne series (70)
Million-dollar hit
Starr, Leonard
Kelly Green series (3)
Million-dollar massacre
Barker, Wade
Ninja Master series (4)
Million dollar mayhem
McCall, K T
Johnny Buchanan series (21)
Million dollar murder
Black, Thomas B
Al Delaney series (4)
Million dollar nightmare
Dixon, Franklin W
Hardy boys series (103)
Million dollar snapshot
Howard, Hartley
Glenn Bowman series (29)
Million-dollar stand-in
Webster, Ernest
Benni Soldano series (6)
Million dollar suitcase
Macgowan, Alice
Jerry Boyne series (1)
Million dollar tramp
Gault, William Campbell
Joe Puma series (6)
Million-dollar wound
Collins, Max Allan
Nathan Heller series (3)
Million in diamonds
Carter, Nicholas
Nicholas Carter series (429)
Million missing maidens
Knight, Mallory T
Man from T.O.M.C.A.T. series (2)
Million pound ransom
Boshell, Gordon
Secret Guardians series (2)
Millionaire at sixteen
Optic, Oliver
All-over-the-world series (2)
Millionaire gangster
Wallace, John
Millionaire gangster series (1)
Millionaire gangster again
Wallace, John
Detective Sergeant Fuller series (2)
Millionaire gangster series (2)
Millionaire partner
Carter, Nicholas
Nicholas Carter series (31)
Millionaire's love story
Boothby, Guy
Jacob Burrell series (2)
Millionaire's mania
Carter, Nicholas
Nicholas Carter series (492)
Millionaire's nest egg
Parsons, Anthony
Sexton Blake series (1289)
Millions at stake, and other stories
Carter, Nicholas
Nicholas Carter series (83)
Millions for a murderer
Jones, G Wayman
Black Bat series (17)
Mills
O'Brine, Manning
Mills series (1)
Mills and the big wheels
Firmin, Peter
Make it work series (1)
Mills of space
Wallis, Redmond
Triangulum trilogy (2)
Mills of the law
Carter, Nicholas
Nicholas Carter series (473)
Millstone men
Healey, Ben
Paul Hedley series (2)
Milly-Molly-Mandy again
Brisley, Joyce Lankester
Milly-Molly-Mandy series (4)
Milly-Molly-Mandy and Billy Blunt
Brisley, Joyce Lankester
Milly-Molly-Mandy series (6)
Milly-Molly-Mandy and Company
Brisley, Joyce Lankester
Milly-Molly-Mandy series (5)
Milly-Molly-Mandy stories
Brisley, Joyce Lankester
Milly-Molly-Mandy series (1)
Milly Mouse
Cass, Joan Evelyn
Milly Mouse series (1)
Milly Mouse's measles
Cass, Joan Evelyn
Milly Mouse series (2)
Milly's whims
Mathews, Joanna Hooe
Haps and mishaps series (4)
Milo Talon
L'Amour, Louis
Talon family series (3)
Milou's daughter
Henrey, Madeleine
Madeleine reminiscences series (6)
Milton the early riser
Kraus, Robert
Milton series (1)
Milton the early riser takes a trip
Kraus, Robert
Milton series (2)
Milwaukee the beautiful
James, Dakota
Greenhouse series (2)
Mimff
Kaeser, Hildegarde Johanna
Mimff series (1)
Mimff in charge
Kaeser, Hildegarde Johanna
Mimff series (2)
Mimff-Robinson
Kaeser, Hildegarde Johanna
Mimff series (4)
Mimff takes over
Kaeser, Hildegarde Johanna
Mimff series (3)
Mimi at camp
Davis, Anne Pence
Mimi series (1)
Mimi at Sheridan
Davis, Anne Pence
Mimi series (3)
Mimic a murderer
Courtier, Sidney Hobson
Ambrose Mahon series (7)
Mimics of Dephene
Kern, Gregory
Cap Kennedy series (15)
Mimi's houseparty
Davis, Anne Pence
Mimi series (2)
Mimosa and her man
Mackenzie, Joan
Mimosa Winter series (2)
Mimosa and the mango
Saint Albans, Suzanne Marie Adele Beauclerk
Mimosa series (1)
Mimosa Winter
Mackenzie, Joan
Mimosa Winter series (1)
Mind bandits
Mooser, Stephen
Which way interactive series (5)
Mind breakers
Streib, Dan
Steve Crown series (7)
Mind-breakers of space
Butterworth, Michael
Space nineteen ninety nine series (13)
Mind brothers
Heath, Peter
Jason Starr and Adam Cyber series (1)
Mind-call
Belden, Wilanne Schneider
Mind series (1)
Mind-find
Belden, Wilanne Schneider
Mind series (3)
Mind games
Appleton, Victor II
Tom Swift Junior series 3 (10)
Bogen, M Arthur
Burchardt and Decker series (3)
Mind guest
Green, Sharon
Diana Santee series (1)
Mind-hold
Belden, Wilanne Schneider
Mind series (2)
Mind killers
Carter, Nick
Nick Carter series (57)
Thomas, Martin
Sexton Blake series (1581)
Mind master
Hurwood, Bernhardt Jackson
Invisibles series (2)
Townsend, Larry
Mind master series (3)
Mind Masters
Rossmann, John F
Mind Masters series (1)
Mind-murders
Van de Wetering, Janwillem
De Gier and Grijpstra series (8)
Mind of Doctor Morelle
Dudley, Ernest
Doctor Morelle series (8)
Mind of evil
Dicks, Terrance
Doctor Who series (96)
Mind of her own
Keene, Carolyn
River Heights series (13)
Mind of John Meredith
Gerard, Francis
Sir John Meredith series (12)
Mind of Mister J G Reeder
Wallace, Edgar
Mister J G Reeder series (2)
Mind of Mister Mosley
Greenwood, John
Inspector Mosley series (5)
Mind of my mind
Butler, Octavia Estelle
Patternists series (2)
Mind over matter
Roberts, Nora
Flowers series (45)
Mind over murder
Kienzle, William Xavier
Father Robert Koesler series (3)
Mind poisoners
Carter, Nick
Nick Carter series (18)
Mind reader
Stine, Robert Lawrence
Fear Street series (26)
Mind readers
Allingham, Margery
Albert Campion series (20)
Mind robber
Ling, Peter
Doctor Who series (115)
Mind slaver
Griffin, Pauline Margaret
Star commandos series (5)
Mind the house, Stanley
Edwards, Pat
Stanley series (5)
Mind to mind
Pendleton, Don
Ashton Ford series (3)
Mind to murder
James, Phyllis Dorothy
Commander Adam Dalgliesh series (2)
Mind trap
Morgan, Dan
Sixth perception series (3)
Wisler, Gary Clifton
Antrian series (3)
Mind twisters
Streib, Dan
Michael Hawk series (2)
Mind-twisters affair
Stratton, Thomas
Man from U.N.C.L.E. series (12)
Mind wizards of Callisto
Carter, Lin
Jandar the Alien series (5)
Mindbenders
Buckholtz, Eileen
Micro adventure series (5)
Quinn, Jake
Patrick Shannon series (3)
Mindblast
Duane, Diane
Space cops series (1)
Mindbond
Springer, Nancy
Sea king trilogy (2)
Minden curse
Roberts, Willo Davis
Minden curse series (1)
Mindkiller
Robinson, Spider
Mindkiller series (1)
Mindless monsters
Robeson, Kenneth
Doc Savage series (131)
Mindquest
Elder, Michael
Mindslip series (2)
Mind's eye
Dean, Basil
Seven ages series (2)
Mindshadow
Dillard, Jeanne M
Star trek series (27)
Mindslip
Elder, Michael
Mindslip series (1)
Mindsword's story
Saberhagen, Fred
Book of lost swords series (6)
Mindwarp
Martin, Philip
Doctor Who series (139)
Trial of the Time Lord series (3)
Mindy's mysterious miniature
Curry, Jane Louise
Maccubbin family series (1)
Mine and yours
Berry, Joy
Ready-set-grow series (1)
Mine enemy grows older
King, Alexander
Mine enemy grows older series (1)
Mine inheritance
Niven, Frederick
Flying years trilogy (2)
Mine of faults
Bain, Francis William
Indian mystic love stories series (8)
Mine of serpents
Brooke, Jocelyn
Orchid trilogy (2)
Mine shaft
Sherman, Jory
Gunn series (29)
Mine sinister hunt
Sayer, Walter William
Barnaby Grayle series (3)
Mine were of trouble
Kemp, Peter Mant Macintyre
Conflict trilogy (1)
Miner's moll
Fletcher, Dirk
Spur McCoy series (32)
Miner's showdown
Roberts, J R
Gunsmith series (47)
Minerva
Chesney, Marion
Six sisters series (1)
Minervan experiment
Hogan, James Patrick
Minervan experiment series (3)
Minerva's stepchild
Forrester, Helen
Mersey series (2)
Minetown mistress
Fletcher, Dirk
Spur McCoy series (39)
Ming
Smyth, John George
Beloved cats series (3)
Ming vase mystery
Dark, Rex
Bartholomew Dane series (1)
Mingled with venom
Mitchell, Gladys
Dame Beatrice Bradley series (54)
Mini and Maxi in Muffkinland
Beers, Victor Gilbert
Muffkin series (1)
Miniature frame
Royce, Kenneth
Spider Scott series (3)
Miniature murder mystery
Chambers, Peter
Mark Preston series (30)
Miniature mystery
Pugh, Nansi
Bradshaw family series (1)
Minikin and her friends
Hillyard, Mary Dorothea
Minikin series (3)
Minikin's new home
Hillyard, Mary Dorothea
Minikin series (2)
Minikins of Yam
Swann, Thomas Burnett
Ancient history series (1)
Minikin's visit
Hillyard, Mary Dorothea
Minikin series (1)
Minimal Farm
Carmichael, Claire
Minimal Farm series (1)
Mini-murders
Brown, Carter
Danny Boyd series (17)
Mini-mysteries
Stanley, George Edward
Doctor Constance Daniels series (1)
Mini-skirt murders
Thomas, Martin
Sexton Blake series (1613)
Minister
Edelman, Maurice
Geoffrey Melville series (1)
Minister of Injustice
Culpan, Maurice
Inspector Bill Houghton series (2)
Ministering Angel
Cohen, Anthea
Nurse Agnes Carmichael series (7)
Ministering children
Charlesworth, Maria Louisa
Ministering children series (1)
Ministering children, a sequel
Charlesworth, Maria Louisa
Ministering children series (2)
Minister's daughter
Dixelius, Hildur
Sara Alelia trilogy (1)
Minister's naughty grandchildren
Bexell, Eva
Minister series (1)
Ministry of Death
Bingham, John
Ducane series (3)
Minka and Curdy
White, Antonia
Minka and Curdy series (1)
Minky the mole
Rutley, Cecily Marianne
Tales of the wild folk series (5)
Minnesota massacre
Sharpe, Jon
Trailsman series (78)
Minnesota run
Robbins, David
Endworld series (6)

Minnesota Strip
Collins, Michael
Dan Fortune series (12)
Minnie Ashe at war
Kersh, Cyril
Minnie Ashe series (2)
Minnie Santangelo and the evil eye
Mancini, Anthony
Minnie Santangelo series (2)
Minnie Santangelo's mortal sin
Mancini, Anthony
Minnie Santangelo series (1)
Minnie's pet cat
Leslie, Madeline
Minnie's pets series (1)
Minnie's pet dog
Leslie, Madeline
Minnie's pets series (2)
Minnie's pet horse
Leslie, Madeline
Minnie's pets series (3)
Minnie's pet lamb
Leslie, Madeline
Minnie's pets series (4)
Minnie's pet monkey
Leslie, Madeline
Minnie's pets series (5)
Minnie's pet parrot
Leslie, Madeline
Minnie's pets series (6)
Minnipins
Kendall, Carol
Minnipins series (1)
Minor in possession
Jance, Judith A
J P Beaumont series (8)
Minor murders
Hensley, Joe Louis
Donald Robak series (5)
Minor operation
Connington, John Jervis
Sir Clinton Driffield series (11)
Minos of Sardanes
Stilson, Charles Billings
Polaris trilogy (2)
Minotaur
Coonts, Stephen
Jake Grafton series (3)
Minsan series
Keyte, John Charles
Minsan series (2)
Minstrel's lute
Wood, Bridget
Lute series (1)
Mint mystery
Bayfield, William John
Sexton Blake series (561)
Mint perfect madam
Fletcher, Dirk
Spur McCoy giant series (1)
Spur McCoy special series (3)
Minty
Goolden, Barbara
Tabor family series (1)
Minty and the missing picture
Goolden, Barbara
Tabor family series (3)
Minty and the secret room
Goolden, Barbara
Tabor family series (4)
Mintyglo Kid
Cross, Gillian
Clipper series (2)
Minute boys of Boston
Otis, James
Minute boys series (9)
Minute boys of Bunker Hill
Stratemeyer, Edward L
Minute boys series (2)
Minute boys of Lexington
Stratemeyer, Edward L
Minute boys series (1)
Minute boys of Long Island
Otis, James
Minute boys series (7)
Minute boys of New York
Otis, James
Minute boys series (8)
Minute boys of Philadelphia
Otis, James
Minute boys series (10)
Minute boys of South Carolina
Otis, James
Minute boys series (6)
Minute boys of the Green Mountains
Otis, James
Minute boys series (3)
Minute boys of the Mohawk Valley
Otis, James
Minute boys series (4)
Minute boys of the Wyoming Valley
Otis, James
Minute boys series (5)
Minute boys of Yorktown
Otis, James
Minute boys series (11)
Minute for murder
Blake, Nicholas
Nigel Strangeways series (8)
Minute man murder
Langton, Jane
Homer Kelly series (1)
Minute to pray, a second to die
De Stefano, Anthony
Mondo series (3)
Minutes to midnight
Spain, Nancy
Miriam Birdseye series (3)
Mirabelle's secret
Gifford, Griselda
Jenny and Mirabelle series (2)
Miracle at Carville
Martin, Betty
Miracle series (1)
Miracle at Dry Fork
Grover, Marshall
Larry and Stretch series (286)
Miracle at San Tanco
Johnston, William
Flying nun series (2)
Miracle game
Skvorecky, Josef
Danny Smiricky series (3)
Miracle man
Duff, Douglas Valder
Jeremy series (2)
Miracle mission
Rosenberger, Joseph
Death Merchant series (69)
Miracle Monday
Maggin, Elliot S
Superman series (2)
Miracle of revenge
Longley, W B
Angel Eyes series (1)
Miracle of Saint Bruno's
Carr, Philippa
Daughters of England series (1)
Miracles of Clara van Haag
Buchholtz, Johannes
Egholm series (2)
Miracles of the gods
Daniken, Erich von
Unsolved mysteries series (5)
Mirador collection
Flynn, Brian
Anthony Bathurst series (47)
Mirage
Janes, Joseph Robert
Jean-Louis Saint-Cyr and Hermann Kohler series (1)
Miranda at Merryfield
Gervaise, Mary
Miranda series (2)
Miranda in the middle
Winthrop, Elizabeth
Miranda series (2)
Mirkheim
Anderson, Poul
Polesotechnic League series (6)
Miro
Herron, Shaun
Miro series (1)
Miro papers
Herron, Shaun
Miro series (2)
Mirror crack'd
Christie, Agatha
Miss Jane Marple series (10)
Mirror crack'd from side to side
Christie, Agatha
Miss Jane Marple series (10)
Mirror dance
Bujold, Lois McMaster
Miles Naismith Vorkosigan series (7)
Mirror for Narcissus
Farson, Negley
Transgressor series (3)
Mirror for princes
De Haan, Tom
Brynchmachrye series (1)
Mirror image
Coney, Michael Greatrex
Arcadia series (1)
Larson, Glen A
Knight Rider series (5)
Prior, Ann
Felan series (2)
Sadler, Mark
Paul Shaw series (3)
Mirror, mirror
Garfield, Leon
Apprentices series (2)
Thesman, Jean
Birthday girls series (2)
Mirror of Dionysos
Comer, Ralph
Robert Lawson series (2)
Mirror of dreams
Donaldson, Stephen Reeder
Mordant's need series (1)
Mirror of hell
Holton, Leonard
Father Joseph Bredder series (9)
Mirror of minds
Zebrowski, George
Omega Point trilogy (3)
Mirror train
Chance, John Newton
Jonathan Blake series (18)
Mirrored murder
Eyles, Alfred W
Paul Chisholm series (2)
Mirrors and lonely
Richardson, Judith Benet
Maushope's Landing series (2)
Misadventures of Athelstan Digby
Harvey, William Fryer
Athelstan Digby series (1)
Misadventures of Brer Rabbit, Brer Fox, Brer Wolf, Doodang & other
Lester, Julius
Tales of Uncle Remus series (3)
Misadventures of Dougal
Thompson, Eric
Dougal series (4)
Misadventures of Esmeralda Bloom
Rosenthal, Lesley Sharon
Esmeralda Bloom series (1)
Misadventures of Sherlock Holmes
Queen, Ellery
Sherlock Holmes series (10)
Miscalculated risk
McDonnell, Jinny
Kim Aldrich series (1)
Miscarriage of justice
Carter, Nicholas
Nicholas Carter series (508)
Miscast for murder
Fenisong, Ruth
Captain Gridley Nelson series (9)
Mischief
McBain, Ed
Eighty Seventh Precinct series (47)
Mischief again
Blyton, Enid
Mischief series (2)
Mischief among the penguins
Tilman, Harold William
Mischief series (2)
Mischief in Greenland
Tilman, Harold William
Mischief series (3)
Mischief in Maggody
Hess, Joan
Arly Hanks series (2)
Mischief in Patagonia
Tilman, Harold William
Mischief series (1)
Mischief in the lane
Derleth, August
Judge Ephraim Peck series (8)
Mischief-makers
Haggard, William
Colonel Charles Russell series (22)
Mischievous Martens
Lindgren, Astrid
Marten family series (1)
Misdemeanors of Nancy
Brainerd, Eleanor Hoyt
Nancy series (1)
Misenchanted sword
Watt-Evans, Lawrence
Legend of Ethshar series (1)
Miser
Egan, Lesley
Jesse Falkenstein series (11)
Miser lord
Curling, Henry
Frank Beresford series (2)
Miser of Mayfair
Chesney, Marion
House for the season series (1)
Miseracordia
Perez Galdos, Benito
Contemporary novels of Spain series (30)
Misery guts
Gleitzman, Morris
Misery guts series (1)
Misfits
Macdonnell, James Edmond
Captain Peter Bentley series (37)
Wilson, Colin
Outsider series (4)
Misfortunes of Mister Teal
Charteris, Leslie
Saint series (12)
Misguided missile
Mills, Osmington
Superintendent William Baker series (4)
Mishmash
Cone, Molly
Mishmash series (1)
Mishmash and the big fat problem
Cone, Molly
Mishmash series (7)
Mishmash and the robot
Cone, Molly
Mishmash series (6)
Mishmash and the sauerkraut mystery
Cone, Molly
Mishmash series (3)
Mishmash and the substitute teacher
Cone, Molly
Mishmash series (2)
Mishmash and the Venus flytrap
Cone, Molly
Mishmash series (5)
Mishmash and Uncle Looey
Cone, Molly
Mishmash series (4)
Miska the seal
Rutley, Cecil Bernard
Wild life story series (6)
Misleading cases in the common law
Herbert, Alan Patrick
Misleading cases series (1)
Misplaced legion
Turtledove, Harry
Videssos series (1)
Miss America
Lambert, Janet
Tippy Parrish series (3)
Miss Anna Truly
Drummond, Violet Hilda
Miss Anna Truly series (1)
Miss Anna Truly and the Christmas lights
Drummond, Violet Hilda
Miss Anna Truly series (2)
Miss Bagshot goes to Moscow
Telscombe, Anne
Miss Bagshot series (1)
Miss Bagshot goes to Tibet
Telscombe, Anne
Miss Bagshot series (2)
Miss Bianca
Sharp, Margery
Miss Bianca series (2)
Miss Bianca and the bridesmaid
Sharp, Margery
Miss Bianca series (7)
Miss Bianca in the Antarctic
Sharp, Margery
Miss Bianca series (6)
Miss Bianca in the Orient
Sharp, Margery
Miss Bianca series (5)
Miss Bianca in the salt mines
Sharp, Margery
Miss Bianca series (4)
Miss Billy
Porter, Eleanor Hodgman
Miss Billy series (1)
Miss Billy, married
Porter, Eleanor Hodgman
Miss Billy series (3)
Miss Billy's decision
Porter, Eleanor Hodgman
Miss Billy series (2)
Miss Boo is sixteen
Runbeck, Margaret Lee
Miss Boo series (2)
Miss Brick the builder's baby
Ahlberg, Allan
Happy family series (7)
Miss Buncle
Stevenson, Dorothy Emily
Miss Buncle series (3)
Miss Buncle married
Stevenson, Dorothy Emily
Miss Buncle series (2)
Miss Buncle's book
Stevenson, Dorothy Emily
Miss Buncle series (1)
Miss Bunting
Thirkell, Angela
Barsetshire series (14)
Miss Carter came with us
Bradley, Helen
Edwardian Lancashire series (2)
Miss Cathy Leonard
Woolley, Catherine
Cathy Leonard series (2)
Miss Clare remembers
Read, *Miss*
Fairacre series (4)
Miss Doll, go home
Markson, David
Harry Fannin series (1)
Miss Dose the doctor's daughter
Ahlberg, Allan
Happy family series (15)
Miss Dynamite
Gray, Berkeley
Norman Conquest series (3)
Miss Emily in black lace
Murdoch, Nina
Miss Emily trilogy (1)
Miss Esperance and Mycherly
Harker, Lizzie Allen
Mister Wycherly series (1)
Miss Flora McFlimsey and Little Laughing Water
Mariana
Miss Flora McFlimsey series (5)
Miss Flora McFlimsey and the baby new year
Mariana
Miss Flora McFlimsey series (3)
Miss Flora McFlimsey and the little red school house
Mariana
Miss Flora McFlimsey series (6)
Miss Flora McFlimsey, Queen of the May
Mariana
Miss Flora McFlimsey series (8)
Miss Flora McFlimsey's birthday
Mariana
Miss Flora McFlimsey series (4)
Miss Flora McFlimsey's Christmas eve
Mariana
Miss Flora McFlimsey series (1)
Miss Flora McFlimsey's Easter bonnet
Mariana
Miss Flora McFlimsey series (2)
Miss Flora McFlimsey's Halloween
Mariana
Miss Flora McFlimsey series (9)
Miss Flora McFlimsey's May Day
Mariana
Miss Flora McFlimsey series (8)
Miss Flora McFlimsey's valentine
Mariana
Miss Flora McFlimsey series (7)
Miss Frances Baird, detective
Kauffman, Reginald Wright
Frances Baird series (1)
Miss from S.I.S.
Tralins, Sandor Robert
Lee Crosley series (2)
Miss Gator's school house
Kraus, Robert
Miss Gator series (2)
Miss Gibbie Gault
Bosher, Kate Lee Langley
Mary Cary series (2)
Miss Happiness and Miss Flower
Godden, Rumer
Nona Fell series (1)
Miss Hogg and the Bronte murders
Lee, Austin
Miss Flora Hogg series (3)
Miss Hogg and the Covent Garden murders
Lee, Austin
Miss Flora Hogg series (7)
Miss Hogg and the dead dean
Lee, Austin
Miss Flora Hogg series (5)
Miss Hogg and the missing sisters
Lee, Austin
Miss Flora Hogg series (8)
Miss Hogg and the squash club murder
Lee, Austin
Miss Flora Hogg series (4)
Miss Hogg flies high
Lee, Austin
Miss Flora Hogg series (6)
Miss Hogg's last case
Lee, Austin
Miss Flora Hogg series (9)
Miss Jump the jockey
Ahlberg, Allan
Happy family series (3)
Miss Know It All
York, Carol Beach
Miss Know It All series (1)
Miss Know It All and the magic house
York, Carol Beach
Miss Know It All series (10)
Miss Know It All and the three-ring circus
York, Carol Beach
Miss Know It All series (9)
Miss Know It All and the wishing lamp
York, Carol Beach
Miss Know It All series (8)

Miss Know It All returns
York, Carol Beach
Miss Know It All series (6)
Miss Lochinvar
Taggart, Marion Ames
Miss Lochinvar series (1)
Miss Lochinvar's return
Taggart, Marion Ames
Miss Lochinvar series (2)
Miss Lou and the tall men
Grover, Marshall
Larry and Stretch series (251)
Miss Mapp
Benson, Edward Frederic
Lucia Billson series (3)
Miss Marjoribanks
Oliphant, Margaret Oliphant Wilson
Carlingford series (4)
Miss Marple and the thirteen problems
Christie, Agatha
Miss Jane Marple series (2)
Miss Marple, complete short stories
Christie, Agatha
Miss Jane Marple series (14)
Miss Marple's final cases, and two other stories
Christie, Agatha
Miss Jane Marple series (14)
Miss McFlimsey
Butler, William Allen
Miss Flora McFlimsey series (1)
Miss Melville regrets
Smith, Evelyn E
Miss Susan Melville series (1)
Miss Melville returns
Smith, Evelyn E
Miss Susan Melville series (2)
Miss Melville rides a tiger
Smith, Evelyn E
Miss Susan Melville series (4)
Miss Melville runs for cover
Smith, Evelyn E
Miss Susan Melville series (5)
Miss Melville's revenge
Smith, Evelyn E
Miss Susan Melville series (3)
Miss Mephistopheles
Hume, Fergus
Madame Midas series (2)
Miss Milverton
Hocking, Anne
Inspector William Austen series (7)
Miss Minerva broadcasts Billy
Sampson, Emma
Miss Minerva series (4)
Miss Minerva goin' places
Sampson, Emma
Miss Minerva series (7)
Miss Minerva on the old plantation
Sampson, Emma
Miss Minerva series (3)
Miss Minerva's baby
Sampson, Emma
Miss Minerva series (2)
Miss Minerva's cook book
Sampson, Emma
Miss Minerva series (10)
Miss Minerva's mystery
Sampson, Emma
Miss Minerva series (8)
Miss Minerva's neighbors
Sampson, Emma
Miss Minerva series (6)
Miss Minerva's problem
Sampson, Emma
Miss Minerva series (9)
Miss Minerva's scallywags
Sampson, Emma
Miss Minerva series (5)
Miss Minerva's vacation
Sampson, Emma
Miss Minerva series (10)
Miss Mystery
Horler, Sydney
Baron Veseloffsky series (2)
Miss Nancy Prentiss
Wasson, Mildred
Nancy Prentiss series (2)
Miss nelson has a field day
Allard, Harry
Miss Nelson series (3)
Miss Nelson is back
Allard, Harry
Miss Nelson series (2)
Miss Nelson is missing!
Allard, Harry
Miss Nelson series (1)
Miss Oona McQuarrie
Smith, Alexander
Alfred Hagart series (2)
Miss Otis blows town
Sarto, Ben
Miss Otis series (6)
Miss Otis comes to Piccadilly
Sarto, Ben
Miss Otis series (2)
Miss Otis desires
Sarto, Ben
Miss Otis series (14)
Miss Otis gets fresh
Sarto, Ben
Miss Otis series (17)
Miss Otis goes French
Sarto, Ben
Miss Otis series (13)
Miss Otis goes up
Sarto, Ben
Miss Otis series (4)
Miss Otis has a daughter
Sarto, Ben
Miss Otis series (5)
Miss Otis hits back
Sarto, Ben
Miss Otis series (11)
Miss Otis makes a date
Sarto, Ben
Miss Otis series (7)
Miss Otis makes hay
Sarto, Ben
Miss Otis series (15)
Miss Otis moves in
Sarto, Ben
Miss Otis series (8)
Miss otis plays ball
Sarto, Ben
Miss Otis series (16)
Miss Otis plays Eve
Sarto, Ben
Miss Otis series (10)
Miss Otis relents
Sarto, Ben
Miss Otis series (18)
Miss Otis says yes
Sarto, Ben
Miss Otis series (12)
Miss Otis takes the rap
Sarto, Ben
Miss Otis series (9)
Miss Otis throws a come-back
Sarto, Ben
Miss Otis series (1)
Miss Pat and Company, Limited
Ginther, Mary Pemberton
Miss Pat series (4)
Miss Pat and her sisters
Ginther, Mary Pemberton
Miss Pat series (1)
Miss Pat at Artemis Lodge
Ginther, Mary Pemberton
Miss Pat series (7)
Miss Pat at school
Ginther, Mary Pemberton
Miss Pat series (2)
Miss Pat in Buenos Ayres
Ginther, Mary Pemberton
Miss Pat series (9)
Miss Pat in the Old World
Ginther, Mary Pemberton
Miss Pat series (3)
Miss Pat with the Russian Army
Ginther, Mary Pemberton
Miss Pat series (6)
Miss Pat's career
Ginther, Mary Pemberton
Miss Pat series (10)
Miss Pat's great idea
Ginther, Mary Pemberton
Miss Pat series (11)
Miss Pat's holidays at Greycroft
Ginther, Mary Pemberton
Miss Pat series (5)
Miss Pat's problem
Ginther, Mary Pemberton
Miss Pat series (8)
Miss Philura's wedding gown
Kingsley, Florence Morse
Miss Philura trilogy (2)
Miss Pickerell and the blue whales
Macgregor, Ellen
Miss Pickerell series (15)
Miss Pickerell and the geiger counter
Macgregor, Ellen
Miss Pickerell series (2)
Miss Pickerell and the lost world
Pantell, Dora
Miss Pickerell series (17)
Miss Pickerell and the supertanker
Macgregor, Ellen
Miss Pickerell series (12)
Miss Pickerell and the war of the computers
Pantell, Dora
Miss Pickerell series (16)
Miss Pickerell and the weather satellite
Macgregor, Ellen
Miss Pickerell series (8)
Miss Pickerell goes on a dig
Macgregor, Ellen
Miss Pickerell series (6)
Miss Pickerell goes to Mars
Macgregor, Ellen
Miss Pickerell series (1)
Miss Pickerell goes to the Arctic
Macgregor, Ellen
Miss Pickerell series (4)
Miss Pickerell goes undersea
Macgregor, Ellen
Miss Pickerell series (3)
Miss Pickerell harvests the sea
Macgregor, Ellen
Miss Pickerell series (7)
Miss Pickerell meets Mister H.U.M.
Macgregor, Ellen
Miss Pickerell series (9)
Miss Pickerell on the moon
Macgregor, Ellen
Miss Pickerell series (5)
Miss Pickerell on the trail
Macgregor, Ellen
Miss Pickerell series (14)
Miss Pickerell tackles the energy crisis
Macgregor, Ellen
Miss Pickerell series (13)
Miss Pickerell takes the bull by the horns
Macgregor, Ellen
Miss Pickerell series (10)
Miss Pickerell to the earthquake rescue
Macgregor, Ellen
Miss Pickerell series (11)
Miss Pink at the edge of the world
Moffat, Gwen
Miss Melinda Pink series (2)
Miss Pinkerton
Rinehart, Mary Roberts
Nurse Hilda Adams series (1)
Miss Pinnegar disappears
Gilbert, Anthony
Arthur Crook series (25)
Miss Priscilla scares 'em stiff
Zabel, Jennifer
Miss Priscilla series (1)
Miss Priscilla strikes again
Zabel, Jennifer
Miss Priscilla series (3)
Miss Priscilla's secret
Zabel, Jennifer
Miss Priscilla series (2)
Miss Rivers and Miss Bridges
Symons, Geraldine
Atalanta and Pansy series (4)
Miss Sainte Monique
Lister, Stephen
Sainte Monique series (5)
Miss Seeton at the helm
Charles, Hampton
Miss Emily Seeton series (9)
Miss Seeton bewitched
Carvic, Heron
Miss Emily Seeton series (3)
Miss Seeton by appointment
Charles, Hampton
Miss Emily Seeton series (7)
Miss Seeton by moonlight
Crane, Hamilton
Miss Emily Seeton series (13)
Miss Seeton cracks the case
Crane, Hamilton
Miss Emily Seeton series (10)
Miss Seeton draws the line
Carvic, Heron
Miss Emily Seeton series (2)
Miss Seeton goes to bat
Crane, Hamilton
Miss Emily Seeton series (15)
Miss Seeton paints the town
Crane, Hamilton
Miss Emily Seeton series (11)
Miss Seeton plants suspicion
Crane, Hamilton
Miss Emily Seeton series (16)
Miss Seeton rocks the candle
Crane, Hamilton
Miss Emily Seeton series (14)
Miss Seeton rules
Crane, Hamilton
Miss Emily Seeton series (19)
Miss Seeton sings
Carvic, Heron
Miss Emily Seeton series (4)
Miss Seeton undercover
Crane, Hamilton
Miss Emily Seeton series (18)
Miss Silver comes to stay
Wentworth, Patricia
Miss Maud Silver series (16)
Miss Silver deals with death
Wentworth, Patricia
Miss Maud Silver series (7)
Miss Silver intervenes
Wentworth, Patricia
Miss Maud Silver series (7)
Miss Slimmens' boarding house
Victor, Metta Victoria
Miss Slimmens series (2)
Miss Slimmens' window, and other papers
Victor, Metta Victoria
Miss Slimmens series (1)
Miss Susie Slagle's
Tucker, Augusta
Miss Susie Slagle series (1)
Miss Teen Sweet Valley
Pascal, Francine
Sweet Valley High series (76)
Miss Theodora
Reed, Helen Leah
Brenda series (1)
Miss Three Hundred and Eighteen
Hughes, Rupert
Miss Three Hundred and Eighteen series (1)
Miss Three Hundred and Eighteen and Mister Thirty Seven
Hughes, Rupert
Miss Three Hundred and Eighteen series (2)
Miss Tippy
Lambert, Janet
Tippy Parrish series (1)
Miss Tonks turns to crime
Chesney, Marion
Poor relation series (2)
Miss Toosie's mission
Whitaker, Evelyn
Miss Toosie series (1)
Miss Tu
Lin, Yutang
Chinese village series (1)
Miss Turquoise
Mair, George Brown
David Grant series (2)
Miss Undine's living room
Wilcox, James
Tula Springs trilogy (3)
Miss Willie
Giles, Janice Holt
Piney Ridge trilogy (2)
Miss Withers regrets
Palmer, Stuart
Hildegarde Withers series (9)
Missed by that much!
Johnston, William
Maxwell Smart series (5)
Missee Lee
Ransome, Arthur
Swallows and Amazons series (10)
Missile
Mackenzie, Andrew
Nicholas Cornish series (7)
Missile away
Montgomery, Rutherford George
Kent Barstow series (3)
Missile menace
Wilson, Gar
Phoenix Force series (38)
Missile mob
Janson, Hank
Hank Janson series (209)
Missing
Stine, Robert Lawrence
Fear Street series (3)
Valin, Jonathan
Harry Stoner series (11)
Missing ace
Crauford, William Harold Lane
Detective Kellerway series (1)
Missing agent
Annesley, Michael
Lawrence Fenton series (4)
Missing and the dead
Lynch, Jack
Peter Bragg series (2)
Missing Angel Juan
Block, Francesca Lia
Weetzie Bat series (4)
Missing at Marshlands
Garis, Cleo Fausta
Arden Blake series (1)
Missing aunt
Cole, George Douglas Howard
Superintendent Henry Wilson series (18)
Missing background
Cargill, Leslie
Major Mosson series (3)
Missing bank manager
Poole, Michael
Freddie Browne and Jim Fanshaw series (4)
Missing banker
Brandon, Charles
John Fortescue series (2)
Missing baronet
Cole, George Douglas Howard
Superintendent Henry Wilson series (5)
Missing body
Daniel, Roland
Buddy Mustard series (13)
Missing bookkeeper
Keith, Carlton
Jeff Green series (5)
Missing Bronte
Barnard, Robert
Superintendent Perry Trethowan series (3)
Missing by choice
Victor, Roger
Soldier of fortune series (2)
Missing cat
Costa, Nicoletta
Molly and Tom series (2)
Missing chums
Dixon, Franklin W
Hardy boys series (6)
Missing cotton king
Carter, Nicholas
Nicholas Carter series (82)
Missing deputy chief
Carter, Nicholas
Nicholas Carter series (433)
Missing diamond
Pollard, Alfred Oliver
David Wilshaw series (6)
Missing doctor
Fletcher, Robert James
Gilbert Davison series (3)
Missing formula
Decrest, Jacques
Superintendent Gilles series (2)
Wirt, Ann
Madge Sterling series (1)
Missing formula mystery
Beresford, Elisabeth
Gappy, Jim and Jane series (7)
Missing from her home
Gilbert, Anthony
Arthur Crook series (46)
Missing from his home
Cross, Mark
Daphne Wrayne and her Four Adjusters series (26)
Missing from home
Clewes, Dorothy
Carrie and Maxwell series (1)
Missing gates
Foster, Reginald Francis
Anthony Ravenhill series (1)
Missing hazelnuts
Marden, Fay
Flower fairy series (3)
Missing in Manhattan
Adams Round Table
Manhattan series (1)
Missing in Mexico
Pentelow, John Nix
Sexton Blake series (392)
Missing initial
Lincoln, Natalie Sumner
Inspector Mitchell series (7)
Missing Joseph
George, Elizabeth
Inspector Thomas Lynley and Sergeant Barbara Havers series (6)
Missing lady
Daniel, Roland
Inspector John Walk series (4)
Missing link
Farrer, Katharine
Inspector Richard Ringwood series (1)
Murphy, Warren Burton
Destroyer series (39)
Wells, Carolyn
Fleming Stone series (50)
Missing Madonna
O'Marie, Carol Anne
Sister Mary Helen series (3)
Missing man
Carter, Nicholas
Nicholas Carter series (156)
Stern, Richard Martin
Johnny Ortiz series (6)
Waugh, Hillary
Chief Fred Fellows series (8)
Missing masterpiece
Byers, Irene
Jeremy and Fenella series (2)
Dicks, Terrance
Baker Street Irregulars series (1)

Missing Matilda
Vaughan, Carol
Manorfield Stud series (1)
Missing mayor
King, T Stanleyan
Dixon Brett series (1)
Missing men
Leroux, Gaston
Cheri-Bibi series (2)
Skene, Anthony
Sexton Blake series (811)
Missing million
Optic, Oliver
All-over-the-world series (1)
Missing minx
Goyne, Richard
Ex-Superintendent Tubby Green series (2)
Missing Mister Mosley
Greenwood, John
Inspector Mosley series (3)
Missing money mystery
Keene, Carolyn
Nancy Drew and the Hardy boys be a detective mystery series (6)
Missing money-lender
Sykes, William Stanley
Inspector Dennis Drury series (1)
Missing moon
Adams, Harold
Carl Wilcox series (3)
Missing newspaper caper
Stahl, Hilda
Wren House series (4)
Missing of Janice Day
Long, Helen Beecher
Do something series (4)
Missing or dead?
Ashe, Gordon
Patrick Dawlish series (25)
Missing or murdered
Forsythe, Robin
Anthony Vereker series (1)
Missing page
Johns, William Earl
Steeley Delaroy series (5)
Missing panel
Pilkington, Roger
Branxome family series (3)
Missing pearls
Knipe, Emilie Benson
Little Miss Fales series (2)
Missing person
Staples, Mary Jane
South London series (12)
Missing pony mystery
Hope, Laura Lee
Bobbsey twins series (76)
Missing presumed dead
Keith, Carlton
Jeff Green series (2)
Missing rope
Carnac, Carol
Inspector Ryvet series (2)
Missing safari
Garron, Marco
Azan series (1)
Missing scapegoat
Cobb, Belton
Inspector Cheviot Burmann series (22)
Missing scientist game
Blyton, Enid
Famous Five adventure games series (8)
Missing ships
Murray, Andrew
Sexton Blake series (57)
Missing spy
Sayer, Walter William
Sexton Blake series (152)
Missing tea set
Pascal, Francine
Sweet Valley kids series (41)
Missing tin box
Winfield, Arthur M
Bound to win series (5)
Bright and bold series (4)
Missing treaty
Dawe, Carlton
Leathermouth series (5)
Missing widow
Gilbert, Anthony
Arthur Crook series (19)
Missing witness
Daniels, Norman A
Arrest and trial series (2)
Missing woman
Lewin, Michael Zinn
Albert Samson series (6)
Missing years
Laqueur, Walter
Doctor Richard Lasson series (1)
Missing you
Haynes, Betsy
Fabulous Five super series (3)
Mission accomplished
Channel, A R
Fighting Four series (4)
Walker, Jerry
Lawrence Marley series (1)
Mission begins
Peel, John
U.N.C.L.E. files series (5)
Mission code, Acropolis
Swift, Bryan
Mac Wingate series (7)
Mission code, granite island
Swift, Bryan
Mac Wingate series (4)
Mission code, king's pawn
Swift, Bryan
Mac Wingate series (2)
Mission code, minotaur
Swift, Bryan
Mac Wingate series (3)
Mission code, scorpion
Swift, Bryan
Mac Wingate series (10)
Mission code, snow queen
Swift, Bryan
Mac Wingate series (6)
Mission code, springboard
Swift, Bryan
Mac Wingate series (5)
Mission code, survival
Swift, Bryan
Mac Wingate series (11)
Mission code, symbol
Swift, Bryan
Mac Wingate series (1)
Mission code, track and destroy
Swift, Bryan
Mac Wingate series (9)
Mission code, volcano
Swift, Bryan
Mac Wingate series (8)
Mission Deadly Snow
Rosenberger, Joseph
Death Merchant series (65)
Mission doctor sees the wind of change
Doell, E W
Mission doctor trilogy (3)
Mission for Oliver
Daniell, David Scott
Drummer Oliver Crowe series (1)
Mission from Vitrium
Norton, John
Magic voyage series (1)
Mission hopeless
Macdonnell, James Edmond
Captain Peter Bentley series (40)
Dutchy Holland series (17)
Jim Brady series (6)
Mission House murder
Hobson, Hank
Brad Ford series (4)
Mission impossible
Tiger, John
Mission impossible series (1)
Mission in Greece
Southall, Ivan
War in the air series (5)
Mission into Auschwitz
Netzen, Klaus
Killers series (3)
Mission intruder
Montgomery, Rutherford George
Kent Barstow series (4)
Mission Mayhem
Dixon, Franklin W
Hardy boys case files series (93)
Mission million
Jones, G Wayman
Black Bat series (32)
Mission, Moonfire
Lancer, Jack
Christopher Cool series (2)
Mission of Black Rifle
Kellogg, Elijah
Forest Glen series (4)
Mission of doom
Evans, Gwyn
Sexton Blake series (617)
Mission of gravity
Clement, Hal
Mesklin series (1)
Mission of magic
Smith, Julie Dean
Caithan Crusade series (2)
Mission of menace
Hardinge, Rex
Sexton Blake series (623)
Mission of murder
Charles, Robert
Simon Larren series (4)
Mission of the secret spy squad
Glick, Ruth
Twistaplot series (10)
Mission of vengeance
Hardinge, Rex
Sexton Blake series (664)
Mission revenge
Garrett, Frank
Killsquad series (2)
Mission River justice
Tuttle, Wilbur Coleman
Hashknife Hartley and Sleepy Stevens series (21)
Mission to Cathay
Scott, Michael William
Rakehell dynasty series (4)
Mission to darkness
Hunt, Greg
Ridge Parkman series (5)
Mission to Horatius
Reynolds, Mack
Star trek originals sequels series (1)
Mission to Magnus
Martin, Philip
Doctor Who series (162)
Mission to Mars
Moore, Patrick
Maurice Gray series (1)
Mission to Mercury
Walters, Hugh
Chris Godfrey series (8)
Mission to Mexico
Maclean, Arthur
Sexton Blake series (1492)
Mission to Moulokin
Foster, Alan Dean
Icerigger series (2)
Thranx series (4)
Mission to Rome
Romains, Jules
Men of goodwill series (13)
Mission to Siena
Marshall, Raymond
Don Micklem series (2)
Mission to the gods
Hunter, Joe
Attack force series (2)
Mission to the moon
Del Rey, Lester
Moon trilogy (2)
Mission to the unknown
Peel, John
Doctor Who series (141)
Mission to Venice
Carter, Nick
Nick Carter series (28)
Marshall, Raymond
Don Micklem series (1)
Mission to Venus
Emms, William
Doctor Who find your fate series (4)
Mission to World War II
Kornblatt, Marc
Time machine series (11)
Mission underground
Casteret, Norbert
Under the earth series (7)
Griffin, Pauline Margaret
Star commandos series (3)
Missionaries
Target, George William
Post-war Britain series (3)
Mississippi!
Poole, Helen Lee
Whitewater dynasty series (5)
Ross, Dana Fuller
Wagons West series (15)
Mississippi bridge
Taylor, Mildred Davis
Logan family series (4)
Mississippi massacre
Roberts, J R
Gunsmith series (91)
Mississippi river boy
Sabin, Edward Legrand
Trail blazers series (15)
Mississippi rogue
Tanner, Clay
Chance Sharpe series (6)
Missouri!
Poole, Helen Lee
Whitewater dynasty series (6)
Ross, Dana Fuller
Wagons West series (14)
Missouri bittersweet
Kantor, Mackinlay
But look trilogy (3)
Missouri deathwatch
Pendleton, Don
Mack Bolan series (83)
Missouri Demons
Charlier, Jean Michel
Young Blueberry series (4)
Missouri flame, Deborah Leigh
Foster, Jeanne
Frontier women series (2)
Missouri guns
Harte, Bryce
Slate Creed series (5)
Missouri homestead
Tedrow, Thomas L
Days of Laura Ingalls Wilder series (1)
Missouri madam
Fletcher, Dirk
Spur McCoy series (18)
Missouri mama
Fletcher, Dirk
Spur McCoy series (37)
Missouri massacre
Tanner, Clay
Chance Sharpe series (8)
Missouri woodhawks
Duncan, Terence
Powell's army series (7)
Missus
Park, Ruth
Darcy family trilogy (1)
Mistake
Macdonnell, James Edmond
Captain Peter Bentley series (30)
Mistake me not
Easton, Nat
Bill Banning series (4)
Mistaken identity
Lowell, Anne Hunter
Sorority girls series (8)
Mistakenly in Mallorca
Jeffries, Roderic Graeme
Inspector Enrique Alvarez series (1)
Mister and Mrs Bear and friends
Gibbs, May
Gumnut Land series (16)
Mister and Mrs Craw
Bell, John Joy
Mister Craw series (2)
Mister and Mrs Hay the horse
Ahlberg, Allan
Happy family series (9)
Mister and Mrs May
Le Breton, Thomas
Mrs May series (3)
Mister and Mrs Meigs
Corbett, Elizabeth
Mrs Meigs series (5)
Mister and Mrs North
Lockridge, Frances
Mister and Mrs North series (1)
Mister and Mrs North and the poisoned playboy
Lockridge, Frances
Bill Wiegand series (20)
Mister and Mrs North series (21)
Mister and Mrs North meet murder
Lockridge, Frances
Bill Wiegand series (1)
Mister and Mrs North series (2)
Mister and Mrs Pig's evening out
Rayner, Mary
Mister and Mrs Pig series (1)
Mister and Mrs Sen
Miln, Louise Jordan
Sen family series (1)
Mister B
Saro-Wiwa, Ken
Mister B series (1)
Mister B again
Saro-Wiwa, Ken
Mister B series (3)
Mister B goes to Lagos
Saro-Wiwa, Ken
Mister B series (4)
Mister B goes to the moon
Saro-Wiwa, Ken
Mister B series (9)
Mister B is dead
Saro-Wiwa, Ken
Mister B series (5)
Mister Babbacombe dies
Burton, Miles
Inspector Arnold and Desmond Merrion series (20)
Mister Bailey-Martin
White, Percy
Mister Bailey-Martin series (1)
Mister Bailey-Martin, O.B.E.
White, Percy
Mister Bailey-Martin series (2)
Mister Ball of Fire
Gray, Berkeley
Norman Conquest series (16)
Mister Barnes, American
Gunter, Archibald Clavering
Mister Barnes series (2)
Mister Barnes of New York
Gunter, Archibald Clavering
Mister Barnes series (1)
Mister Bass's planetoid
Cameron, Eleanor
Tyco Bass series (3)
Mister Bear and apple jam
Kuratomi, Chizuko
Mister Bear series (7)
Mister Bear and the ghost
Kuratomi, Chizuko
Mister Bear series (17)
Mister Bear and the robbers
Kuratomi, Chizuko
Mister Bear series (5)
Mister Bear, babyminder
Kuratomi, Chizuko
Mister Bear series (10)
Mister Bear, baker
Kuratomi, Chizuko
Mister Bear series (14)
Mister Bear goes to sea
Kuratomi, Chizuko
Mister Bear series (2)
Mister Bear in the air
Kuratomi, Chizuko
Mister Bear series (3)
Mister Bear, postman
Kuratomi, Chizuko
Mister Bear series (12)
Mister Bear, shipwrecked
Kuratomi, Chizuko
Mister Bear series (19)
Mister Bear, station-master
Kuratomi, Chizuko
Mister Bear series (6)
Mister Bear's birthday
Kuratomi, Chizuko
Mister Bear series (18)
Mister Bear's Christmas
Kuratomi, Chizuko
Mister Bear series (8)
Mister Bear's drawing
Kuratomi, Chizuko
Mister Bear series (9)
Mister Bear's journey
Kuratomi, Chizuko
Mister Bear series (16)
Mister Bear's meal
Kuratomi, Chizuko
Mister Bear series (11)
Mister Bear's shadow
Kuratomi, Chizuko
Mister Bear series (13)
Mister Bear's trumpet
Kuratomi, Chizuko
Mister Bear series (4)
Mister Bear's winter sleep
Kuratomi, Chizuko
Mister Bear series (15)
Mister Bellamy's story
Hardwick, Michael
Upstairs, downstairs series (6)
Mister Benn
McKee, David
Mister Benn series (1)
Mister Benn annual
McKee, David
Mister Benn series (4)
Mister Biff the boxer
Ahlberg, Allan
Happy family series (1)
Mister Big
Verner, Gerald
Superintendent Robert Budd series (25)
Mister Big Time
Levy, Elizabeth
Fat Albert series (2)
Mister Bill and the flying fish
Adams, Georgie
Mister Bill series (2)
Mister Bill and the runaway sausages
Adams, Georgie
Mister Bill series (1)
Mister Bits and Pieces
Lindsay, Frances
Mister Bits and Pieces series (1)
Mister Blandings builds his dream house
Hodgins, Eric
Blandings series (1)
Mister Blessington's imperialist
Sherwood, John
Mister Charles Blessington series (2)
Mister Blessington's plot
Sherwood, John
Mister Charles Blessington series (2)

Mister Bodley abroad
Scudder, Horace Elisha
Bodley family series (5)
Mister Brading's collection
Wentworth, Patricia
Miss Maud Silver series (18)
Mister Bridge
Connell, Evan Shelby
Bridge series (2)
Mister Brown's bodies
Blackburn, John
Bill Easter series (2)
Mister Browser and the Brain Sharpeners
Curtis, Philip
Mister Browser series (1)
Mister Browser and the comet crisis
Curtis, Philip
Mister Browser series (3)
Mister Browser and the mini-meteorites
Curtis, Philip
Mister Browser series (6)
Mister Browser and the space maggots
Curtis, Philip
Mister Browser series (11)
Mister Browser in the space museum
Curtis, Philip
Mister Browser series (7)
Mister Browser meets the Borrowers
Curtis, Philip
Mister Browser series (2)
Mister Browser meets the mind shrinkers
Curtis, Philip
Mister Browser series (12)
Mister B's mattress
Saro-Wiwa, Ken
Mister B series (8)
Mister Bubbus and the apple-green engine
Drake, Joan
Mister Bubbus series (1)
Mister Bubbus and the railway smugglers
Drake, Joan
Mister Bubbus series (2)
Mister Buckby is not at home
Gloag, John
Lionel Buckby series (3)
Mister Budd again
Verner, Gerald
Superintendent Robert Budd series (10)
Mister Budd investigates
Verner, Gerald
Superintendent Robert Budd series (12)
Mister Budge builds a house
Adamson, Gareth
Mister Budge series (1)
Mister Budge buys a car
Adamson, Gareth
Mister Budge series (2)
Mister Bumblemoose and the flying boy
Andreus, Hans
Mister Bumblemoose series (2)
Mister Bumblemoose and the glad dog
Andreus, Hans
Mister Bumblemoose series (3)
Mister Bumblemoose and the laughing record
Andreus, Hans
Mister Bumblemoose series (5)
Mister Bumblemoose and the Mumblepuss
Andreus, Hans
Mister Bumblemoose series (6)
Mister Bumblemoose and the tiger skin rug
Andreus, Hans
Mister Bumblemoose series (7)
Mister Bumblemoose buys a motor car
Andreus, Hans
Mister Bumblemoose series (4)
Mister Bumblemoose goes to Paris
Andreus, Hans
Mister Bumblemoose series (8)
Mister Bunny and the magic pool
Frees, Harry Whittier
Petland photo tales series (1)
Mister Bunting
Greenwood, Robert
Mister Bunting series (1)
Mister Bunting at war
Greenwood, Robert
Mister Bunting series (2)
Mister Bunting in the promised land
Greenwood, Robert
Mister Bunting series (3)
Mister Burdekin
Campion, Sarah
Mister Moses Burdekin series (1)
Mister Buzz the beeman
Ahlberg, Allan
Happy family series (8)
Mister Campion and others
Allingham, Margery
Albert Campion series (11)
Mister Campion, criminologist
Allingham, Margery
Albert Campion series (8)
Albert Campion series (11)
Mister Campion's falcon
Carter, Philip Youngman
Albert Campion series (23)
Mister Campion's farthing
Carter, Philip Youngman
Albert Campion series (22)
Mister Campion's quarry
Carter, Philip Youngman
Albert Campion series (23)
Mister Caution, Mister Callaghan
Cheyney, Peter
Lemmy Caution series (7)
Slim Callaghan series (5)
Mister Chang of Scotland Yard
Apple, A E
Mister Chang series (1)
Mister Chang's crime ray
Apple, A E
Mister Chang series (2)
Mister Charlie, the fireman's friend
Hurd, Edith Thatcher
Mister Charlie series (4)
Mister Charlie's camping trip
Hurd, Edith Thatcher
Mister Charlie series (3)
Mister Charlie's chicken house
Hurd, Edith Thatcher
Mister Charlie series (1)
Mister Charlie's farm
Hurd, Edith Thatcher
Mister Charlie series (6)
Mister Charlie's gas station
Hurd, Edith Thatcher
Mister Charlie series (2)
Mister Charlie's pet shop
Hurd, Edith Thatcher
Mister Charlie series (5)
Mister Clackworthy
Booth, Christopher B
Amos Clackworthy series (1)
Mister Clackworthy, con man
Booth, Christopher B
Amos Clackworthy series (2)
Mister Clerihew, wine merchant
Allen, Herbert Warner
Mister Clerihew series (1)
Mister Clunk's text
Bailey, Henry Christopher
Mister Joshua Clunk series (6)
Mister Cogg and his computer
Sloan, Carolyn
Mister Cogg series (1)
Mister Cogg and the exploding Easter eggs
Sloan, Carolyn
Mister Cogg series (3)
Mister Collin is ruined
Heller, Frank
Mister Collin series (2)
Mister Collins and Tony and the sleeping mouse
Dudley, Christine
Mister Collins and Tony series (4)
Mister Collins and Tony by the sea
Elwell, Felicia Rosemary
Mister Collins and Tony series (5)
Mister Collins and Tony go fishing
Dudley, Christine
Mister Collins and Tony series (1)
Mister Collins and Tony go tracking
Dudley, Christine
Mister Collins and Tony series (3)
Mister Collins and Tony in London
Elwell, Felicia Rosemary
Mister Collins and Tony series (6)
Mister Collins and Tony visit Heron Wood
Dudley, Christine
Mister Collins and Tony series (2)
Mister Commissioner Sanders
Wallace, Edgar
Commissioner Sanders series (6)
Mister Cosmo the conjuror
Ahlberg, Allan
Happy family series (2)
Mister Craw
Bell, John Joy
Mister Craw series (1)
Mister Creep the crook
Ahlberg, Allan
Happy family series (14)
Mister Crewe's career
Churchill, Winston
American national development series (5)
Mister Cromwell is dead
Ford, Leslie
Colonel John Primrose series (4)
Grace Latham series (4)
Mister Crook lifts the mask
Gilbert, Anthony
Arthur Crook series (47)
Mister Death
Wallace, Carlton
Superintendent Edmund Bendilow series (1)
Mister Death walks aborad
Wallace, Carlton
Superintendent Edmund Bendilow series (1)
Mister Dooley in peace and war
Dunne, Finley Peter
Mister Dooley series (1)
Mister Dooley in the hearts of his countrymen
Dunne, Finley Peter
Mister Dooley series (2)
Mister Dooley on making a will, and other necessary evils
Dunne, Finley Peter
Mister Dooley series (8)
Mister Dooley says
Dunne, Finley Peter
Mister Dooley series (7)
Mister Dooley's opinions
Dunne, Finley Peter
Mister Dooley series (4)
Mister Dooley's philosophy
Dunne, Finley Peter
Mister Dooley series (3)
Mister Emmanuel
Golding, Louis
Elsie Silver series (2)
Mister Essington in love
Clouston, Joseph Storer
Mister Francis Mandell-Essington series (6)
Mister Fairlie's final journey
Derleth, August
Solar Pons series (9)
Mister Faraday's formula
Woodbury, David Oakes
George Riam series (2)
Mister Fiddle
Styles, Showell
Mister Fiddle series (1)
Mister Fiddle's band
Styles, Showell
Mister Fiddle series (3)
Mister Fiddle's pig
Styles, Showell
Mister Fiddle series (2)
Mister Finchley discovers his England
Canning, Victor
Mister Finchley series (1)
Mister Finchley goes to Paris
Canning, Victor
Mister Finchley series (2)
Mister Finchley takes the road
Canning, Victor
Mister Finchley series (3)
Mister Finchley's holiday
Canning, Victor
Mister Finchley series (1)
Mister Fitton's commission
Styles, Showell
Lieutenant Michael Fitton series (2)
Mister Fix-It
Scarry, Richard
Smallest pop-up book ever series (2)
Mister Fortune explains
Bailey, Henry Christopher
Mister Reggie Fortune series (6)
Mister Fortune finds a pig
Bailey, Henry Christopher
Mister Reggie Fortune series (18)
Mister Fortune here
Bailey, Henry Christopher
Mister Reggie Fortune series (15)
Mister Fortune objects
Bailey, Henry Christopher
Mister Reggie Fortune series (10)
Mister Fortune, please
Bailey, Henry Christopher
Mister Reggie Fortune series (4)
Mister Fortune speaking
Bailey, Henry Christopher
Mister Reggie Fortune series (5)
Mister Fortune wonders
Bailey, Henry Christopher
Mister Reggie Fortune series (8)
Mister Fortune's casebook
Bailey, Henry Christopher
Mister Reggie Fortune series (23)
Mister Fortune's practice
Bailey, Henry Christopher
Mister Reggie Fortune series (2)
Mister Fortune's trials
Bailey, Henry Christopher
Mister Reggie Fortune series (3)
Mister Francis Newnes
Martindale, Cyril Charlie
Mister Francis Newnes series (2)
Mister Fred
Hilton, John Buxton
Inspector Thomas Brunt series (4)
Mister Fullback
Gault, William Campbell
Gridiron series (1)
Mister Fumble
Scarry, Richard
Smallest pop-up book ever series (3)
Mister Galliano's circus
Blyton, Enid
Mister Galliano's circus series (1)
Mister Glencannon
Gilpatric, Guy
Mister Colin Andrew Macthrockle Glencannon series (3)
Mister Glencannon ignores the war
Gilpatric, Guy
Mister Colin Andrew Macthrockle Glencannon series (7)
Mister God, this is Anna
Fynn
Anna series (1)
Mister Gosling and the great art robbery
Cunliffe, John Arthur
Mister Gosling series (2)
Mister Gosling and the runaway chair
Cunliffe, John Arthur
Mister Gosling series (1)
Mister Grimpwinkle
Drake, Joan
Mister Grimpwinkle series (2)
Mister Grimpwinkle buys a bus
Drake, Joan
Mister Grimpwinkle series (5)
Mister Grimpwinkle, pirate cook
Drake, Joan
Mister Grimpwinkle series (4)
Mister Grimpwinkle's holiday
Drake, Joan
Mister Grimpwinkle series (6)
Mister Grimpwinkle's marrow
Drake, Joan
Mister Grimpwinkle series (3)
Mister Grimpwinkle's visitor
Drake, Joan
Mister Grimpwinkle series (8)
Mister Growser moves
Beaman, Sydney George Hulme
Toytown series (24)
Mister Growser moves house
Beaman, Sydney George Hulme
Toytown series (24)
Mister Guelpa
Thompson, Vance
Mister Guelpa series (2)
Mister Gumpy's motor car
Burningham, John
Mister Gumpy series (2)
Mister Gumpy's outing
Burningham, John
Mister Gumpy series (1)
Mister Gurney and Mister Slade
Deeping, Warwick
James Slade series (2)
Mister Hare and the honey bees
Holland, Muriel
Mister Hare series (2)
Mister Hare has a bright idea
Holland, Muriel
Mister Hare series (3)
Mister Hare makes stone soup
Holland, Muriel
Mister Hare series (1)
Mister Henry
Miller, Jim
Long guns series (1)
Mister Hercules
Evans, Gwyn
Bill Kellaway series (1)
Mister Hero and the Raggler children
Leigh, Roberta
Mister Hero series (2)
Mister Holmes and the fair Armenian
Bark, Conrad Voss
Mister William Holmes series (3)
Mister Holmes at sea
Bark, Conrad Voss
Mister William Holmes series (1)
Mister Holmesand the love bank
Bark, Conrad Voss
Mister William Holmes series (4)
Mister Homes goes to ground
Bark, Conrad Voss
Mister William Holmes series (2)
Mister Horrocks, purser
Hyne, Charles John Cutcliffe
Captain Owen Kettle series (18)
Mister Hoyland looks round
Williams, Philip Claxton
Mister Hoyland series (1)
Mister Hudson's diaries
Hardwick, Michael
Upstairs, downstairs series (4)
Mister Hudson's diary
Hardwick, Michael
Upstairs, downstairs series (4)
Mister Ingleside
Lucas, Edward Verrall
Winfield series (3)
Mister Isaacs
Crawford, Francis Marion
Paul Griggs series (1)
Mister J G Reeder returns
Wallace, Edgar
Mister J G Reeder series (5)
Mister Jelly's business
Upfield, Arthur William
Napoleon Bonaparte series (4)
Mister Jones tips the scales
Matthewman, Phyllis
Mister Jones series (3)
Mister Jorkens remembers Africa
Dunsany, Edward John Moreton Drax Plunkett
Jorkens series (2)
Mister Jorrocks' jaunts and jollities
Surtees, Robert Smith
Mister John Jorrocks series (1)
Mister Jorrocks' lectors
Surtees, Robert Smith
Mister John Jorrocks series (2)
Mister Jory
Bass, Milton R
Jory series (2)
Mister Justice Raffles
Hornung, Ernest William
Raffles series (4)
Mister Kettle, third mate
Hyne, Charles John Cutcliffe
Captain Owen Kettle series (16)
Mister Kilmer sees red
Urquhart, Paul
Sexton Blake series (781)
Mister Knitted and the family tree
Meyer, Renate
Knittle and Threadle series (2)
Mister Lincoln's army
Catton, Bruce
Potomac Army trilogy (1)
Mister Little's noisy ABC
Fowler, Richard
Mister Little series (4)
Mister Little's noisy boat
Fowler, Richard
Mister Little series (2)
Mister Little's noisy car
Fowler, Richard
Mister Little series (1)
Mister Little's noisy fire engine
Fowler, Richard
Mister Little series (7)
Mister Little's noisy 123
Fowler, Richard
Mister Little series (3)
Mister Little's noisy plane
Fowler, Richard
Mister Little series (5)
Mister Little's noisy truck
Fowler, Richard
Mister Little series (6)
Mister Love and Justice
Macinnes, Colin
Visions of London series (3)
Mister Majeika
Carpenter, Humphrey
Mister Majeika series (1)
Mister Majeika and the dinner lady
Carpenter, Humphrey
Mister Majeika series (4)
Mister Majeika and the haunted hotel
Carpenter, Humphrey
Mister Majeika series (3)
Mister Majeika and the music teacher
Carpenter, Humphrey
Mister Majeika series (2)
Mister Majeika and the school book week
Carpenter, Humphrey
Mister Majeika series (7)

Mister Majeika and the school inspector
Carpenter, Humphrey
Mister Majeika series (8)
Mister Majeika and the school play
Carpenter, Humphrey
Mister Majeika series (6)
Mister Malcolm presents
Fairlie, Gerard
Mister Malcolm series (2)
Mister Marlow chooses wine
Bentley, John
Dick Marlow series (2)
Mister Marlow stops for brandy
Bentley, John
Dick Marlow series (3)
Mister Marlow takes to Rye
Bentley, John
Dick Marlow series (1)
Mister McGee
Allen, Pamela
Mister McGee series (1)
Mister McGee and the blackberry jam
Allen, Pamela
Mister McGee series (3)
Mister McGee goes to sea
Allen, Pamela
Mister McGee series (2)
Mister Meddle's mischief
Blyton, Enid
Mister Meddle series (1)
Mister Meddle's muddles
Blyton, Enid
Mister Meddle series (2)
Mister Merlin, episode one
Rotsler, William
Mister Merlin series (1)
Mister Merlin, episode two
Rotsler, William
Mister Merlin series (2)
Mister Merston's hounds
Welcome, John
Mister Merston series (2)
Mister Merston's money
Welcome, John
Mister Merston series (1)
Mister Midas
Catto, Max
Limpie series (1)
Mister Midnight
Verner, Gerald
Superintendent Robert Budd series (19)
Mister Midshipman Hornblower
Forester, Cecil Scott
Horatio Hornblower series (1)
Mister Midshipman Murdock and the Barbary pirates
Icenhower, Joseph Bryan
Mister Midshipman Murdock series (1)
Mister Mole takes charge
Pilgrim, Jane
Blackberry Farm series (25)
Mister Montmorency's money
Worboise, Emma Jane
Mister Montmorency series (1)
Mister Mortimer gets the jitters
Gray, Berkeley
Norman Conquest series (1)
Mister Moto is so sorry
Marquand, John Phillips
Mister Moto series (4)
Mister Moto takes a hand
Marquand, John Phillips
Mister Moto series (1)
Mister Mulliner speaking
Wodehouse, Pelham Grenville
Mister Mulliner series (2)
Mister Munchausen
Bangs, John Kendrick
Baron Munchausen series (8)
Mister Munday and the rustlers
Pryor, Bonnie
Mister Munday series (1)
Mister Munday and the space creatures
Pryor, Bonnie
Mister Munday series (2)
Mister Murdock takes command
Icenhower, Joseph Bryan
Mister Midshipman Murdock series (2)
Mister Mysterious and Company
Fleischman, Sid
Mister Mysterious series (1)
Mister Mysterious's secrets of magic
Fleischman, Sid
Mister Mysterious series (2)
Mister Nibble calls the doctor
Pilgrim, Jane
Blackberry Farm series (22)
Mister Noah
Horrabin, James Francis
Noah family series (4)
Mister Noah's holiday
Beaman, Sydney George Hulme
Toytown series (20)
Mister Norris changes trains
Isherwood, Christopher
Berlin series (1)
Mister Parker Pyne, detective
Christie, Agatha
Mrs Ariadne Oliver series (1)
Mister Pendlebury and the Suicide Club
Webb, Anthony
Mister Pendlebury series (7)
Mister Pendlebury makes a catch
Webb, Anthony
Mister Pendlebury series (4)
Mister Pendlebury's hat trick
Webb, Anthony
Mister Pendlebury series (5)
Mister Pendlebury's second case
Webb, Anthony
Mister Pendlebury series (2)
Mister Pennington barges in
Brandon, John Gordon
Arthur Stukeley Pennington series (15)
Inspector Patrick Aloysius McCarthy series (34)
Mister Pennington comes through
Brandon, John Gordon
Arthur Stukeley Pennington series (12)
Inspector Patrick Aloysius McCarthy series (29)
Mister Pennington goes nap
Brandon, John Gordon
Arthur Stukeley Pennington series (14)
Inspector Patrick Aloysius McCarthy series (32)
Mister Pennington sees red
Brandon, John Gordon
Arthur Stukeley Pennington series (16)
Inspector Patrick Aloysius McCarthy series (38)
Mister Penny
Ets, Marie Hall
Mister Penny series (1)
Mister Penny's circus
Ets, Marie Hall
Mister Penny series (3)
Mister Penny's racehorse
Ets, Marie Hall
Mister Penny series (2)
Mister Peter
Beskow, Elsa
Peter and Lotta series (5)
Mister Pettigrew and the bell ringers
Clark, Leonard
Mister Pettigrew series (3)
Mister Pettigrew's harvest festival
Clark, Leonard
Mister Pettigrew series (1)
Mister Pettigrew's train
Clark, Leonard
Mister Pettigrew series (2)
Mister Pickwick's second time on earth
Harper, Charles George
Pickwick series (3)
Mister Pig and family
Hoban, Lillian
Mister Pig series (2)
Mister Pig and Sonny Too
Hoban, Lillian
Mister Pig series (1)
Mister Pigeon's island
Berkeley, Anthony
Roger Sheringham series (10)
Mister Pinkerton and the Old Angel
Frome, David
Evan Pinkerton series (10)
Mister Pinkerton at the Old Angel
Frome, David
Evan Pinkerton series (10)
Mister Pinkerton finds a body
Frome, David
Evan Pinkerton series (6)
Mister Pinkerton goes to Scotland Yard
Frome, David
Evan Pinkerton series (5)
Mister Pinkerton grows a beard
Frome, David
Evan Pinkerton series (7)
Mister Pinkerton has the clue
Frome, David
Evan Pinkerton series (8)
Mister Pink-Whistle interferes
Blyton, Enid
Mister Pink-Whistle series (2)
Mister Pink-Whistle's big book
Blyton, Enid
Mister Pink-Whistle series (3)
Mister Pink-Whistle's party
Blyton, Enid
Mister Pink-Whistle series (3)
Mister Platt and the painter
Dillon, Deidre
Trumpton series (4)
Mister Plod and little Noddy
Blyton, Enid
Noddy series (22)
Mister Plum's oasis
Trimby, Elisa
Mister Plum series (2)
Mister Plum's paradise
Trimby, Elisa
Mister Plum series (1)
Mister Polton explains
Freeman, Richard Austin
Doctor John Evelyn Thorndyke series (26)
Mister Pomander
Hakansson, Gunvor
Pomander series (1)
Mister Pooter's advice to his son
Waterhouse, Keith
Nobody series (3)
Mister Poppleberry and Fred the white cockatoo
Lindsay, Hilarie
Mister Poppleberry series (3)
Mister Poppleberry and the Dog's Own Daily
Lindsay, Hilarie
Mister Poppleberry series (1)
Mister Poppleberry and the milk thieves
Lindsay, Hilarie
Mister Poppleberry series (2)
Mister Poppleberry's birthday
Lindsay, Hilarie
Mister Poppleberry series (4)
Mister Popplecorn and four little hens
Musson, Margaret
Mister Popplecorn series (1)
Mister Popplecorn, Tasker and Moo
Musson, Margaret
Mister Popplecorn series (2)
Mister Popularity
Adams, Nicholas
Horror High series (1)
Mister Popularity!
Walker, Mort
Hi and Lois series (20)
Mister Poskitt
Fletcher, Joseph Smith
Mister Poskitt trilogy (2)
Mister Poskitt's nightcaps
Fletcher, Joseph Smith
Mister Poskitt trilogy (3)
Mister Potato Head's new tool set
Slier, Debby
Potato Head series (1)
Mister Potter and the parrots
Fenwick, Jill
Mister Potter's garden series (2)
Mister Pottermack's oversight
Freeman, Richard Austin
Doctor John Evelyn Thorndyke series (18)
Mister Potter's parsnip
Fenwick, Jill
Mister Potter's garden series (1)
Mister Pratt
Lincoln, Joseph Crosby
Mister Pratt series (1)
Mister Pratt's patients
Lincoln, Joseph Crosby
Mister Pratt series (2)
Mister Preed investigates
Black, Ladbroke
Mister Preed series (1)
Mister Preed's gangster
Black, Ladbroke
Mister Preed series (2)
Mister Puffett's caravan
Catling, Gordon
Mister Puffett series (2)
Mister Puffett's teamboat
Catling, Gordon
Mister Puffett series (1)
Mister Pump's legacy
Herge
Adventures of Jo, Zette and Jocko series (2)
Mister Putter and Tabby pour the tea
Rylant, Cynthia
Mister Putter and Tabby series (1)
Mister Putter and Tabby walk the dog
Rylant, Cynthia
Mister Putter and Tabby series (2)
Mister Q 33
Goodchild, George
John Trelawney series (2)
Mister Quarterback
Gault, William Campbell
Gridiron series (2)
Mister Rabbit at home
Harris, Joel Chandler
Mister Thimblefinger series (2)
Mister Reeder returns
Wallace, Edgar
Mister J G Reeder series (5)
Mister Roberts
Heggen, Thomas
Mister Roberts series (1)
Mister Rumbletum's gumboot
Postgate, Oliver
Bagpuss beginners series (1)
Mister Rutherford's children
Warner, Susan Bagert
Mister Rutherford series (1)
Mister Sampath
Narayan, Rasipuram Krishnaswami
Malgudi series (3)
Mister Sandman loses his life
Healy, Eugene P
Paul Craine series (2)
Mister Scipio
Gates, Tudor
Vendetta series (2)
Mister Scott's guide to Enterprise
Johnson, Shane
Star trek, the next generation sequels series (2)
Mister Scraggs, introduced by Red Saunders
Phillips, Henry Wallace
Red Saunders series (3)
Mister Secretary Cecil
Read, Conyers
William Cecil series (1)
Mister Secretary Peel
Gash, Norman
Sir Robert Peel series (1)
Mister Seidman and the geisha
Moll, Elick
Morris Seidman series (2)
Mister Simpson finds a body
Frome, David
Evan Pinkerton series (3)
Mister Sipple and the naughty princess
Slepian, Jan
Listen-hear series (5)
Mister Sixgun
Wynne, Brian
Marshal Jeremy Six series (3)
Mister Slim Goodbody presents the inside story
Burstein, John
Slim Goodbody series (1)
Mister Smith's hat
Reilly, Helen
Inspector Christopher McKee series (5)
Mister Smithson's bones
Conroy, Richard Timothy
Henry Scruggs series (2)
Mister Splitfoot
McCloy, Helen
Basil Willing series (12)
Mister Squint
Partridge, Jenny
Oakapple Wood series (1)
Mister Standfast
Buchan, John
Richard Hannay series (3)
Mister Stimpson and Mister Gorse
Hamilton, Patrick
Ernest Ralph Gorse series (3)
Mister Stoat walks in
Uttley, Alison
Little Brown Mouse series (11)
Mister Sun
O'Donnell, Peter
Modesty Blaise comic strip series (4)
Mister Thake again
Morton, John Bingham
Mister Thake trilogy (2)
Mister Thake and the ladies
Morton, John Bingham
Mister Thake trilogy (3)
Mister Thake, his life and letters
Morton, John Bingham
Mister Thake trilogy (1)
Mister Tick the teacher
Ahlberg, Allan
Happy family series (12)
Mister Tinker of Oz
Howe, James
Oz series (47)
Mister Toffy
Ross, Tony
Tales from Mister Toffy's circus series (6)
Mister Tolefree's reluctant witnesses
Walling, Robert Alfred John
Philip Tolefree series (8)
Mister Tompkins explores the atom
Gamow, George
Mister Tompkins series (2)
Mister Tompkins in Wonderland
Gamow, George
Mister Tompkins series (1)
Mister Tompkins inside himself
Gamow, George
Mister Tompkins series (4)
Mister Tompkins learns the facts of life
Gamow, George
Mister Tompkins series (3)
Mister Tootleoo and Company
Darwin, Bernard
Mister Tootleoo series (3)
Mister Tottleoo
Darwin, Bernard
Mister Tootleoo series (2)
Mister Treadgold cuts in
Williams, Valentine
Mister Treadgold series (2)
Mister Trouble
Ard, William
Timothy Dane series (6)
Mister Tumpy and his caravan
Blyton, Enid
Mister Tumpy series (1)
Mister Tumpy in the land of boys and girls
Blyton, Enid
Mister Tumpy series (4)
Mister Tumpy in the land of wishes
Blyton, Enid
Mister Tumpy series (3)
Mister Tumpy plays a trick on Saucepan
Blyton, Enid
Mister Tumpy series (2)
Mister Tutt at his best
Train, Arthur
Ephraim Tutt series (13)
Mister Tutt comes home
Train, Arthur
Ephraim Tutt series (11)
Mister Tutt finds a way
Train, Arthur
Ephraim Tutt series (13)
Mister Tutt takes the stand
Train, Arthur
Ephraim Tutt series (9)
Mister Tutt's case book
Train, Arthur
Ephraim Tutt series (13)
Mister Twee Deedle
Gruelle, Johnny
Mister Twee Deedle series (1)
Mister Twee Deedle's further adventures
Gruelle, Johnny
Mister Twee Deedle series (2)
Mister Twink and the cat-thief
Hurt, Freda Mary
Mister Twink series (9)
Mister Twink and the jungle garden
Hurt, Freda Mary
Mister Twink series (7)
Mister Twink and the kitten mystery
Hurt, Freda Mary
Mister Twink series (5)
Mister Twink and the pirates
Hurt, Freda Mary
Mister Twink series (6)
Mister Twink, detective
Hurt, Freda Mary
Mister Twink series (4)
Mister Twink finds a family
Hurt, Freda Mary
Mister Twink series (8)
Mister Twink finds out
Hurt, Freda Mary
Mister Twink series (3)
Mister Twink takes charge
Hurt, Freda Mary
Mister Twink series (2)
Mister Twitmeyer and the poodle
Moore, Lilian
Mister Twitmeyer series (2)
Mister Tyler's saints
Bowen, Marjorie
Spiritual history of Great Britain trilogy (2)
Mister Verdant Green
Bede, Cuthbert
Mister Verdant Green series (3)
Mister Verdant Green married and done for
Bede, Cuthbert
Mister Verdant Green series (3)
Mister Waddington of Wyck
Sinclair, May
Wyck series (1)

Mister Watson intervenes
Gardiner, Dorothy
Mister Watson series (2)
Mister Westerby missing
Burton, Miles
Inspector Arnold and Desmond Merrion series (22)
Mister Wicker's window
Dawson, Carley
Mister Wicker series (1)
Mister Wolf
Ahlberg, Allan
Help your child to read series (9)
Mister Woodchuck
Bancroft, Laura
Twinkle tales series (2)
Mister Wycherly's wards
Harker, Lizzie Allen
Mister Wycherly series (2)
Mister X
Brooks, Collin
Raeburn Steel series (1)
Mister Yesterday
Chaze, Elliot
Kiel Saint James and Orson Boles series (1)
Mister Yowder and the giant bullsnake
Rounds, Glen
Mister Yowder series (3)
Mister Yowder and the lion roar capsules
Rounds, Glen
Mister Yowder series (1)
Mister Yowder and the steamboat
Rounds, Glen
Mister Yowder series (2)
Mister Yowder and the train robbers
Rounds, Glen
Mister Yowder series (5)
Mister Yowder and the windwagon
Rounds, Glen
Mister Yowder series (6)
Mister Yowder, the peripatetic sign painter
Rounds, Glen
Mister Yowder series (4)
Misterioso
Sorrentino, Gilbert
Misterioso trilogy (3)
Mistigris
Quin, Basil Godfrey
James Clarkson-Parry series (3)
Mistletoe bough
Wiat, Philippa
Charlton Mead series (1)
Mistral Hotel
Lister, Stephen
Sainte Monique series (1)
Mistress
Brown, Carter
Lieutenant Al Wheeler series (12)
Mistress for the Valois
Watson, Julia
Gentian trilogy (1)
Mistress Margery
Holt, Emily Sarah
Mistress Margery series (1)
Mistress Masham's repose
White, Terence Hanbury
Lilliput series (7)
Mistress of ambiguities
Rivkin, J F
Silverglass series (4)
Mistress of darkness
Nicole, Christopher
West Indies series (3)
Mistress of death
Anthony, Piers
Jason Striker series (2)
Mistress of desire
Larkin, Rochelle T
Desire trilogy (1)
Mistress of Devil's Manor
Stevenson, Florence
Kitty Telfair series (4)
Mistress of Falconhurst
Horner, Lance
Falconhurst series (8)
Mistress of fear
Janson, Hank
Hank Janson series (80)
Mistress of Howton
Haworth, Elizabeth
Howton trilogy (1)
Mistress of Husaby
Undset, Sigrid
Kristin Lavransdatter trilogy (2)
Mistress of mistresses
Eddison, Eric Rucker
Zimiamvian trilogy (3)
Mistress of myself
Henrey, Madeleine
Madeleine reminiscences series (4)
Mistress of Oakhurst
Johnson, Walter Reed
Oakhurst series (2)
Mistress of Shenstone
Barclay, Florence Louisa
Shenstone series (2)
Mistress of Sherburne
Douglas, Amanda Minnie
Sherburne series (5)
Mistress of the air
Carter, Dorothy
Marise Duncan series (1)
Mistress of the boards
Sumner, Richard
Nell Gwynne trilogy (2)
Mistress of the empire
Feist, Raymond Elias
Empire series (3)
Mistress of the jewels
Paxson, Diana Lucile
Westria series (2)
Mistress of the King
Sumner, Richard
Nell Gwynne trilogy (3)
Mistress of the streets
Sumner, Richard
Nell Gwynne trilogy (1)
Mistress of the Sun King
Du Bay, Sandra
Fidelity series (1)
Mistress of the Tabard
Allison-Williams, Jean
Tabard series (1)
Mistress of Willowvale
Veryan, Patricia
Golden chronicles series (6)
Mistress Pat
Montgomery, Lucy Maud
Silver Bush series (2)
Mistress to murder
Dietrich, Robert
Steve Bentley series (4)
Mistresses
Lundin, John Philip
Erotic autobiography series (2)
Mists of doom
Offutt, Andrew Jefferson
Cormac Mac Art series (1)
Mists of fear
Creasey, John
Doctor Palfrey series (17)
Mists of time
Anderson, Margaret Jean
Time trilogy (3)
Mists of treason
Chance, John Newton
Jonathan Blake series (17)
Mists over Mosley
Greenwood, John
Inspector Mosley series (4)
Mistworld
Green, Simon
Mistworld series (1)
Misty Morgan
Cosgrove, Stephen Edward
Morgan series (5)
Misty of Chincoteague
Henry, Marguerite
Chincoteague series (1)
Misty, the wonder pony
Henry, Marguerite
Chincoteague series (3)
Misty treasury
Henry, Marguerite
Chincoteague series (4)
Misty's twilight
Henry, Marguerite
Chincoteague series (5)
Mitch Miller
Masters, Edgar Lee
Mitch Miller series (1)
Mitsy Buttonwood
Beiler, Edna
Buttonwoods series (2)
Mitzi and Frederick the Great
Williams, Barbara
Mitzi series (3)
Mitzi and the elephants
Williams, Barbara
Mitzi series (4)
Mitzi and the terrible tyrannosaurus rex
Williams, Barbara
Mitzi series (1)
Mitzi's honeymoon with Nana Potts
Williams, Barbara
Mitzi series (2)
Mixed blessing
Van Slyke, Helen
Elizabeth Quigly series (2)
Mixed emotions
Keene, Carolyn
River Heights series (10)
Mixed signals
Keene, Carolyn
Nancy Drew files series (63)
Mixed-up mess
Carter, Nicholas
Nicholas Carter series (586)
Mixed-up Mice clean house
Kraus, Robert
Mixed-up Mice series (1)
Mixed-up Mice in the big birthday mix-up
Kraus, Robert
Mixed-up Mice series (2)
Mixture of frailties
Davies, Robertson
Salterton trilogy (3)
Miz Lucretia of Falconhurst
Carter, Ashley
Falconhurst series (14)
Mizmaze
Fitt, Mary
Superintendent Mallett series (18)
Mizz Buggly
Cosgrove, Stephen Edward
Bugg series (51)
Mm-mmm-minx
McCall, K T
Johnny Buchanan series (15)
Moab is my washpot
Cousins, Edmund George
Larry Grail series (3)
Moana
Gorsky, Bernard
Moana series (1)
Moana returns
Gorsky, Bernard
Moana series (2)
Moat house mystery
Foster, Reginald Francis
Anthony Ravenhill series (5)
Mob
Blasco Ibanez, Vicente
Roman Catholic Church in Spain series (4)
Mob psychology
Murphy, Warren Burton
Destroyer series (87)
Mobile
Avenell, Donne
Axa series (7)
Mobsmen on the spot
Grant, Maxwell
Shadow series (9)
Moby Dick
Green, Michael
Coarse plays series (2)
Moccasin man
Ross, John
Major Hutton Seary series (1)
Moccasin telegraph
Kinsella, William Patrick
Silas Ermineskin series (4)
Moddle Ages
Coote, Roger
Journey through history series (3)
Model body
Reinsmith, Richard
Bodyguard series (9)
Model crime
Keene, Carolyn
Nancy Drew files series (51)
Model for murder
Brown, Carter
Lieutenant Al Wheeler series (52)
Kyle, Robert
Ben Gates series (2)
Warden, Mike
Hank Bradford series (3)
Model for the Toff
Creasey, John
Toff series (37)
Model in mayhem
Janson, Hank
Hank Janson series (210)
Model is murdered
Lee, Babs
Argus Steele series (1)
Model killer
Kane, Martin
Martin Kane series (16)
Model murder
Dengler, Sandy
Jack Prester series (2)
Model oddlies
Jennings, Paul Francis
Oddly series (5)
Model railway men
Pope, Ray
Telford series (1)
Model railway men in America
Pope, Ray
Telford series (9)
Model railway men take over
Pope, Ray
Telford series (3)
Model student
Blake, Susan
Hawthorne College series (13)
Model wife
Lindsay, Rose
Ma and pa series (2)
Modeled in murder
Long, Manning
Liz Parrott series (1)
Modern Atalantis
Manley, Mary de la Riviere
New Atalantis series (4)
Modern Baptists
Wilcox, James
Tula Springs trilogy (1)
Modern baseball superstars
Gutman, Bill
Modern superstars series (1)
Modern basketball superstars
Gutman, Bill
Modern superstars series (3)
Modern broods
Yonge, Charlotte Mary
Beechcroft series (8)
Long vacation series (3)
Modern chaos
Walker, Mort
Hi and Lois series (14)
Modern comedy
Galsworthy, John
Modern comedy series (3)
Modern football superstars
Gutman, Bill
Modern superstars series (2)
Modern girl's diary
Cooke, Kaz
Modern girl series (2)
Modern girl's guide to everything
Cooke, Kaz
Modern girl series (1)
Modern girl's guide to safe sex
Cooke, Kaz
Modern girl series (2)
Modern hockey superstars
Gutman, Bill
Modern superstars series (4)
Modern Lilliput
Wilson, David Alec
Lilliput series (6)
Modern love
Kaye, Marilyn
Video High series (1)
Modern minister
Durrant, Valentine
Saul Weir series (1)
Modern prelude
Fausset, Hugh l'Anson
Fidelity series (1)
Modern Prometheus
Shelley, Mary
Frankenstein series (1)
Modern soccer superstars
Gutman, Bill
Modern superstars series (7)
Modern times
Coote, Roger
Journey through history series (6)
Modern tragedy
Bentley, Phyllis
West Riding series (9)
Modern wizard
Ottolengui, Rodrigues
John Barnes series (3)
Modern women superstars
Gutman, Bill
Modern superstars series (5)
Modeste Mignon
Balzac, Honore de
Scenes of private life series (5)
Modesty Blaise
O'Donnell, Peter
Modesty Blaise series (1)
Modi'in Motel
McDaniel, Becky Bring
Jewish tales series (3)
Moffats
Estes, Eleanor
Moffat family series (1)
Mog
Tinniswood, Peter
Brandon family series (2)
Mog and me
Kerr, Judith
Mog series (5)
Mog and the baby
Kerr, Judith
Mog series (3)
Mog at the zoo
Nicoll, Helen
Meg and Mog series (9)
Mog in the dark
Kerr, Judith
Mog series (4)
Mog in the fog
Nicoll, Helen
Meg and Mog series (10)
Mog, the forgetful cat
Kerr, Judith
Mog series (1)
Mog's amazing birthday caper
Kerr, Judith
Mog series (7)
Mog's box
Nicoll, Helen
Meg and Mog series (12)
Mog's Christmas
Kerr, Judith
Mog series (2)
Mog's family of cats
Kerr, Judith
Mog series (6)
Mog's games
Nicoll, Helen
Meg and Mog series (13)
Mog's mumps
Nicoll, Helen
Meg and Mog series (8)
Mohawk
Russo, Richard
Mohawk series (1)
Mohawk ranger
Lange, Dietrich
American Indian series (11)
Mohawk Valley
Welch, Ronald
Carey family series (5)
Mohicans of Paris
Dumas, Alexandre
Mohicans of Paris series (1)
Mohole menace
Walters, Hugh
Chris Godfrey series (11)
Mohole mystery
Walters, Hugh
Chris Godfrey series (11)
Mohun
Cooke, John Esten
Southern Army campaign trilogy (3)
Mohune's nine lives
Groom, Pelham
Peter Mohune series (2)
Moina
Lynch, Lawrence L
Madeline Payne series (2)
Mojave
Mitchum, Hank
Stage coach station series (16)
Mojave Crossing
L'Amour, Louis
Sackett family series (9)
Mojo Swoptops cleans up
Black, Cindy
Mojo Swoptops series (3)
Mojo Swoptops fights a fire
Black, Cindy
Mojo Swoptops series (5)
Mojo Swoptops gets all mixed up
Black, Cindy
Mojo Swoptops series (1)
Mojo Swoptops goes to school
Black, Cindy
Mojo Swoptops series (6)
Mojo Swoptops goes to the races
Black, Cindy
Mojo Swoptops series (4)
Mojo Swoptops keeps his cool
Black, Cindy
Mojo Swoptops series (2)
Mokee, the white possum
Rees, Leslie
Australian nature tales series (12)
Moldy Warp, the mole
Uttley, Alison
Little Grey Rabbit series (11)
Mole and Troll trim the tree
Johnston, Tony
Mole and Troll series (2)
Molehill file
Kenyon, Michael
Inspector Henry Peckover series (1)
Molepie
Nickless, Will
Rotherside series (3)
Mole's castle
Trevor, Elleston
Woodlanders series (5)
Mole's cousin
Jones, Nicholas
Wind in the willows series (3)

Trueman, Brian
Riverbend and Wildwood tales series (3)
Moleskin Joe
Macgill, Patrick
Moleskin Joe series (3)
Molesworth rites again
Brett, Simon
Nigel Molesworth series (5)
Mollie and the unwisemen
Bangs, John Kendrick
Mollie and the unwisemen series (1)
Mollie and the unwisemen abroad
Bangs, John Kendrick
Mollie and the unwisemen series (2)
Mollie in love
Cole, Jennifer
Cindy and Nicole series (12)
Mollie Miller
Merriman, Effie Woodward
Millers series (2)
Molloy
Beckett, Samuel
Jacques Moran series (1)
Molly and the confidence man
Overholser, Stephen
Molly Owens series (1)
Molly and the gambler
Overholser, Stephen
Molly Owens series (6)
Molly and the gold baron
Overholser, Stephen
Molly Owens series (2)
Molly and the Indian agent
Overholser, Stephen
Molly Owens series (4)
Molly and the railroad tycoon
Overholser, Stephen
Molly Owens series (5)
Molly Brown of Kentucky
Speed, Nell
Molly Brown series (7)
Molly Brown's college friends
Speed, Nell
Molly Brown series (8)
Molly Brown's freshman days
Speed, Nell
Molly Brown series (1)
Molly Brown's junior days
Speed, Nell
Molly Brown series (3)
Molly Brown's orachard home
Speed, Nell
Molly Brown series (6)
Molly Brown's post-graduate days
Speed, Nell
Molly Brown series (5)
Molly Brown's senior days
Speed, Nell
Molly Brown series (4)
Molly Brown's sophomore days
Speed, Nell
Molly Brown series (2)
Molly Hilton, library assistant
Lonsdale, Bertha
Molly Hilton series (1)
Molly learns a lesson
Tripp, Valerie
Molly series (2)
Molly on the outlaw trail
Overholser, Stephen
Molly Owens series (3)
Molly qualifies as a librarian
Lonsdale, Bertha
Molly Hilton series (2)
Molly saves the day
Tripp, Valerie
Molly series (6)
Molly Weir's trilogy of Scottish childhood
Weir, Molly
Feet series (3)
Mollyday holiday
Storey, Margaret
Molly series (3)
Molly's lies
Chorao, Kay
Molly series (2)
Molly's Moe
Chorao, Kay
Molly series (1)
Molly's surprise
Tripp, Valerie
Molly series (3)
Molt brother
Lichtenberg, Jacqueline
Molt brother series (1)
Molten Steele
Hunter, S L
Steele series (8)
Mom or pop
Levy, Elizabeth
Fat Albert series (5)
Mom, where's my homework?
Walker, Mort
Hi and Lois series (5)
Moment for murder
Eichler, Alfred
Inspector Knickman series (5)
Marshall, Lovat
Sugar Kane series (22)
Moment in time
Wellard, James
Lucius Hunt series (2)
Moment of choice
Lindsay, Jack
British way series (3)
Moment of fiction
Estow, Daniel
William Schaefer series (1)
Moment of silence
Estow, Daniel
William Schaefer series (2)
Moment of the magician
Foster, Alan Dean
Spellsinger series (4)
Moment of untruth
Lacy, Ed
Toussaint Moore series (2)
Moment on ice
Easton, Nat
Bill Banning series (8)
Mommies at work
Merriam, Frank
Mommies and daddies at work series (1)
Momoko and the pretty bird
Iwasaki, Chihiro
Momoko series (3)
Momoko's birthday
Iwasaki, Chihiro
Momoko series (4)
Momoko's lovely day
Iwasaki, Chihiro
Momoko series (1)
Mona Lisa is missing!
Montgomery, Ramsey
Choose your own adventure series (76)
Mona Lisa mix-up
McCarthy, Maureen
Mission top secret series (3)
Mona Lisa mystery
Hutchins, Pat
House that sailed away trilogy (3)
Mona Lisa overdrive
Gibson, William
Neuromancer trilogy (3)
Monach light
Morrison, J Strang
Monach light series (2)
Monarch of the Glen
Mackenzie, Compton
Highland series (1)
Monastery
Birt, David
Middle Ages series (9)
Scott, Walter
Mary, Queen of Scots series (1)
Monastery mystery
Chester, Gilbert
Sexton Blake series (997)
Monday adventure
Pudney, John
Fred and I series (3)
Monday in summer
Sanders, Dorothy Lucie
Montgomery family series (6)
Monday is washing day
Killingback, Julia
Busy Bears series (1)
Monday morning father
Johnston, William
Room 222 series (2)
Monday mutiny
Collenette, Eric J
Ben Grant series (5)
Monday never came
Ryland, Clive
Chief Inspector George Bassett series (2)
Monday the Rabbi took off
Kemelman, Harry
Rabbi David Small series (4)
Monday theory
Clark, Douglas
Inspector George Masters series (18)
Monday's mob
Pendleton, Don
Mack Bolan series (33)
Mondego Bay
Bushby, John
Captain James Rollo series (2)
Mondo
De Stefano, Anthony
Mondo series (1)
Mondo SADISTO
Allison, Clyde
Agent triple zero eight series (12)
Moneta papers
Messmann, Jon
Jefferson Boone series (1)
Money
Zola, Emile
Rougon Macquart series (18)
Money and music
Barnard, Charles
Soprano series (2)
Money buys everything
Vickers, Roy
Inspector J Rason series (7)
Money by menaces
Adams, Shipley
Inspector Harrow series (2)
Money explosion
Powell, Talmage
Mission impossible series (6)
Money for murder
Carmichael, Harry
John Piper and Quinn series (7)
Graham, Neill
Solo Malcolm series (19)
Money hunt
Dixon, Franklin W
Hardy boys series (101)
Money mad murders
Wallace, Robert
Phantom Detective series (19)
Money maker
Optic, Oliver
Yacht Club series (3)
Money master
Grant, Maxwell
Shadow series (235)
Money masters
Gregoire, Jean Albert
Auguste Maller series (2)
Money matters
Sloan, Carolyn
Mall series (4)
Money means murder
Marshall, Lovat
Sugar Kane series (17)
Money men
Haggard, William
Colonel Charles Russell series (21)
Petievich, Gerald
Charles Carr and Jack Kelly series (1)
Money mountain
Macleod, Robert
Jonathan Gaunt series (9)
Money murder
Ingersol, Jared
Carl Moore series (3)
Money, murder and the McNeills
Du Bois, Theodora
Anne and Jeffrey McNeill series (16)
Money murders
Franklin, Eugene
Berkeley Barnes and Larry Howe series (2)
Money musk
Wells, Carolyn
Fleming Stone series (44)
Williams, Ben Ames
Inspector Tope series (2)
Money mystery
Martin, Robert
Trew twins series (2)
Money on the black
Mackinnon, Allan
Inspector Duncan Maccallum series (1)
Money problems
Stine, Jane
Everything you need to survive series (4)
Money soldiers
Walker, Martin
Maddox series (2)
Money spider
Waterfield, Robin
Fighting fantasy gamebook series (31)
Money that money can't die
Munro, James
John Craig series (3)
Money trouble
Reynolds, William J
Nebraska series (3)
Moneychangers
Sinclair, Upton
New York trilogy (2)
Moneymaster
Spencer, Rick
Eric Ivorsen series (3)
Mongol
Sadler, Barry
Casca series (22)
Mongol mask
Saint John, David
Peter Ward series (7)
Mongoose, R.I.P.
Buckley, William Frank
Blackford Oakes series (8)
Monica joins the W.R.A.C.
Allum, Nancy
Monica series (1)
Monica takes a commission
Allum, Nancy
Monica series (2)
Monimbo
De Borchgrave, Arnaud
Robert Hockney series (2)
Monk of Hambledon
Livingston, Armstrong
Peter Creighton series (3)
Monkey and the tiger
Gulik, Robert van
Judge Dee series (14)
Monkey business
Erickson, John R
Hank the cowdog series (14)
Vail, Virginia
Animal Inn series (3)
Monkey god
Casserly, Gordon
Jungle series (3)
Monkey murder, and other Hildegarde Withers stories
Palmer, Stuart
Hildegarde Withers series (12)
Monkey Planet
Boulle, Pierre
Planet of the Apes series (1)
Monkey puzzle
Gosling, Paula
Lieutenant Jack Stryker series (1)
Monkey see, monkey do
De Clements, Barthe
Jerry Johnson trilogy (2)
Monkey station
Mayhar, Ardath
Windwalker series (2)
Monkey suit
Robeson, Kenneth
Doc Savage series (144)
Monkey twins
Hogan, Inez
Twins series (8)
Monkey Wrench Gang
Abbey, Edward
George W Hayduke series (1)
Monkhurst murder
Grierson, Francis Durham
Richard Furling series (3)
Monk's-hood
Peters, Ellis
Brother Cadfael series (3)
Monk's hood murders
Edingtons
Captain Smith series (3)
Monmouth's Rebellion
Birt, David
Stuarts series (19)
Monogram
Stern, Gladys Bronwyn
Ragbag chronicles series (1)
Monologue of Isabel watching it rain
Garcia Marquez, Gabriel
Macondo series (1)
Monomaniac
Zola, Emile
Rougon Macquart series (17)
Monomark mystery
Carlton, Lewis
Sexton Blake series (511)
Monopoly menace
Hunter, John
Sexton Blake series (1108)
Monopoly to murder
Magowan, Ronald
Shane Mackenzie series (1)
Monsieur
Durrell, Lawrence
Avignon quintet (2)
Monsieur Bergeret in Paris
France, Anatole
Contemporary history series (4)
Monsieur Blackshirt
Graeme, David
Monsieur Blackshirt series (1)
Monsieur de Chauvelin's will
Dumas, Alexandre
Marie Antoinette series (6)
Monsieur de Rochefort
Stacpoole, Henry de Vere
Old Paris series (2)
Monsieur d'Olive
Chapman, George
Monsieur d'Olive series (2)
Monsieur Dupin
Poe, Edgar Allan
Monsieur C Auguste Dupin series (1)
Monsieur Faux-Pas
Lambert, Rosa
Glyn Morgan series (1)
Monsieur Judas
Hume, Fergus
Octavius Fanks series (1)
Monsieur Lecoq
Gaboriau, Emile
Monsieur Lecoq series (3)
Monsieur Lecoq series (3)
Monsieur Lecoq in action
Du Boisgobey, Fortune
Monsieur Lecoq series (5)
Monsieur Lecoq in retirement
Du Boisgobey, Fortune
Monsieur Lecoq series (5)
Monsieur Martin
Carey, Wymond
Monsieur Martin series (1)
Monsieur Pamplemousse
Bond, Michael
Monsieur Pamplemousse series (1)
Monsieur Pamplemousse aloft
Bond, Michael
Monsieur Pamplemousse series (6)
Monsieur Pamplemousse and the secret mission
Bond, Michael
Monsieur Pamplemousse series (3)
Monsieur Pamplemousse en fete
Bond, Michael
Monsieur Pamplemousse series (2)
Monsieur Pamplemousse on location
Bond, Michael
Monsieur Pamplemousse series (9)
Monsieur Pamplemousse on the spot
Bond, Michael
Monsieur Pamplemousse series (4)
Monsieur Pamplemousse rests his case
Bond, Michael
Monsieur Pamplemousse series (7)
Monsieur Pamplemousse stands firm
Bond, Michael
Monsieur Pamplemousse series (8)
Monsieur Pamplemousse takes the cure
Bond, Michael
Monsieur Pamplemousse series (5)
Monsieur Pamplemousse takes the train
Bond, Michael
Monsieur Pamplemousse series (10)
Monsieur Prousthe
Vercors
On the shore trilogy (2)
Monsieur Rififi
Le Breton, Auguste
Rififi series (2)
Monsoon hellhole
Lansing, John
Black Eagles series (16)
Monster
Postgate, Oliver
Saga of Noggin the Nog series (10)
Monster and the magic umbrella
Blance, Ellen
Monster series (6)
Monster and the mural
Blance, Ellen
Monster series (13)
Monster and the surprise cookie
Blance, Ellen
Monster series (20)
Monster and the toy sale
Blance, Ellen
Monster series (22)
Monster at school
Blance, Ellen
Monster series (10)
Monster at Upney Junction
Butterworth, Nick
Upney Junction series (1)
Monster at Wolf Point
Hill, Eileen
Robin Kane series (6)
Monster blood
Stine, Robert Lawrence
Goosebumps series (3)

Monster blood 2
Stine, Robert Lawrence
Goosebumps series (18)
Monster boy
Gilden, Mel
Fifth grade monsters series (13)
Monster buys a pet
Blance, Ellen
Monster series (23)
Monster cleans his house
Blance, Ellen
Monster series (3)
Monster comes to the city
Blance, Ellen
Monster series (1)
Monster express
Mooser, Stephen
Which way interactive series (6)
Monster flies a kite
Blance, Ellen
Monster series (26)
Monster flower show
Forsyth, Anne
Monster series (4)
Monster from the slimes
Barnes, Michael
Just north series (1)
Monster from Yuma
Masterson, Louis
Morgan Kane series (8)
Monster gets a job
Blance, Ellen
Monster series (19)
Monster goes around the town
Blance, Ellen
Monster series (21)
Monster goes camping
Blance, Ellen
Monster series (30)
Monster goes to school
Blance, Ellen
Monster series (9)
Monster goes to the beach
Blance, Ellen
Monster series (18)
Monster goes to the circus
Blance, Ellen
Monster series (16)
Monster goes to the hospital
Blance, Ellen
Monster series (17)
Monster goes to the museum
Blance, Ellen
Monster series (7)
Monster goes to the zoo
Blance, Ellen
Monster series (12)
Monster has a party
Blance, Ellen
Monster series (11)
Monster holiday
Mooser, Stephen
Creepy Creature Club series (3)
Monster holidays
Bridwell, Norman
Monster series (3)
Monster in Creeps Head Bay
Gilden, Mel
Fifth grade monsters series (9)
Monster in space
Salmon, Michael
Alexander Bunyip series (4)
Monster in the pool
Livingston, Armstrong
Jimmy Treynor series (2)
Monster in the third dresser drawer, and other stories about Adam Joshua
Smith, Janice Lea
Adam Joshua series (1)
Monster in Woozy garden
Barry, Margaret Stuart
Woozy series (7)
Monster jokes and riddles
Bridwell, Norman
Monster series (2)
Monster knock knocks
Cole, William
Knock knocks series (4)
Monster, Lady Monster and the garden
Blance, Ellen
Monster series (27)
Monster, Lady Monster and the pet shop
Blance, Ellen
Monster series (25)
Monster looks for a friend
Blance, Ellen
Monster series (4)
Monster looks for a house
Blance, Ellen
Monster series (2)
Monster machine
Appleton, Victor II
Tom Swift Junior series 3 (5)
Monster makes music
Blance, Ellen
Monster series (29)
Monster manners
Cole, Joanna
Monster series (1)
Monster mashers
Gilden, Mel
Fifth grade monsters series (6)
Monster meets Lady Monster
Blance, Ellen
Monster series (5)
Monster mix-up
McCay, Bill
Nintendo adventure series (3)
Monster Monday
Forsyth, Anne
Monster series (1)
Monster mouse mystery
Hope, Laura Lee
New Bobbsey twins series (23)
Monster movie
Cole, Joanna
Monster series (2)
Monster munch
Ahlberg, Janet
Daisychain series (7)
Monster of Metaleze
Kern, Gregory
Cap Kennedy series (3)
Monster of the maze
Lord, Jeffrey
Richard Blade series (6)
Monster of the outfield
Mooser, Stephen
Creepy Creature Club series (1)
Monster of the year
Mooser, Stephen
Creepy Creature Club series (5)
Monster of Widgeon Weir
Atkinson, Mary Evelyn
Lockett family series (8)
Monster on the bus
Blance, Ellen
Monster series (8)
Monster-sitter
Smith, Susan
Samantha Slade series (1)
Monster that ate Canberra
Salmon, Michael
Alexander Bunyip series (1)
Monster valentines
Cole, Joanna
Monster series (3)
Monster wheel affair
McDaniel, David
Man from U.N.C.L.E. series (8)
Monster who ate Australia
Salmon, Michael
Alexander Bunyip series (11)
Monsters
Ahlberg, Allan
Foldaways series (3)
Robeson, Kenneth
Doc Savage series (7)
Monsters and magicians
Adams, Robert
Stairway to forever series (2)
Monsters are like that
Daly, Niki
Storytime series (2)
Monsters of the marsh
Tant, David
Legends of Skyfall series (1)
Monsters on earth
May, Stephen
Planet of the monsters series (2)
Monsters on the move
Salmon, Michael
Animal antics series (2)
Monstre gai
Lewis, Wyndham
Human age trilogy (2)
Monstrous regiment
Chance, John Newton
Jonathan Blake series (36)
Constantine, Storm
Monstrous regiment series (1)
Mont Cant gold
Fisher, Paul R
Ash staff trilogy (4)
Montagu Wycherly
Harker, Lizzie Allen
Mister Wycherly series (3)
Montana!
Ross, Dana Fuller
Wagons West series (10)
Montana deadlock
Chisholm, Matt
Joe Blade series (9)
Montana fire smoke
Sharpe, Jon
Trailsman series (130)
Montana fury
Cody, Al
Montana series (1)
Montana gold
Risteen, H L
Red Indian series (6)
Montana, here I be!
Cushman, Dan
Comanche John series (1)
Montana horseman
McCord, John S
Baynes clan trilogy (1)
Montana maiden
Sharpe, Jon
Trailsman series (11)
Montana mail
Grover, Marshall
Larry and Stretch series (325)
Montana maverick
Field, Peter
Powder Valley series (44)
Montana mayhem
Sharpe, Jon
Trailsman series (135)
Montana melodrama
Gilman, George G
Edge series (40)
Montana mine
Sadler, Jeff
Marshal Andrew Anderson series (10)
Montana minx
Fletcher, Dirk
Spur McCoy series (8)
Montana mistress
Martin, Cort
Jared Bolt series (13)
Montana Pass
Norman, David
Frontier rakers series (5)
Montana rides!
Evans, Evan
Montana Kid series (1)
Montana rides again
Evans, Evan
Montana Kid series (2)
Montana runaway
Grover, Marshall
Larry and Stretch series (120)
Montana showdown
Colter, Dale
Regulator series (9)
Logan, Jake
John Slocum series (13)
Montana woman
Bittner, F Rosanne
Montana woman series (1)
Montana's golden gamble
Cody, Al
Montana series (4)
Montana's territory
Cody, Al
Montana series (3)
Montauk fault
Mitgang, Herbert
Sam Linkum series (1)
Montenegran plot
Trevelyan, Robert
Pendragon series (3)
Monterant affair
Grayson, Richard
Inspector Gautier series (2)
Monterey
Lynch, Jack
Peter Bragg series (6)
Montezuma's missing treasure
Larsen, Anita
Histories mysteries series (3)
Montezuma's revenge
Harrison, Harry
Tony Hawkin series (1)
Month in Paris
Henrey, Madeleine
Madeleine reminiscences series (3)
Month of Sundays
Lynde, Stan
Rick O'Shay series (2)
Montmartre murders
Grayson, Richard
Inspector Gautier series (4)
Montrose, the Captain-General
Tranter, Nigel Godwin
James Graham, Earl of Montrose series (2)
Monty bites back
West, Colin
Monty series (2)
Monty, his part in my victory
Milligan, Spike
War memoirs series (3)
Monty Python and the Holy Grail
Monty Python
Monty Python series (3)
Monty Python's big red book
Monty Python
Monty Python series (1)
Monty Python's life of Brian
Monty Python
Monty Python series (4)
Monty Python's meaning of life
Monty Python
Monty Python series (5)
Monty, the man behind the legend
Hamilton, Nigel
Montgomery of Alamein trilogy (3)
Monty Trio explore
Mackinnon, Andrew
Monty Trio series (5)
Monty Trio investigate
Mackinnon, Andrew
Monty Trio series (3)
Monty Trio's fourth adventure
Mackinnon, Andrew
Monty Trio series (4)
Monty Trio's great adventure
Mackinnon, Andrew
Monty Trio series (1)
Monty, up to his neck in trouble
West, Colin
Monty series (1)
Monty Woodpig and his bubblebuzz car
B B
Monty Woodpig series (2)
Monty Woodpig's caravan
B B
Monty Woodpig series (1)
Mooch the messy
Sharmat, Marjorie Weinman
Mooch series (1)
Mooch the messy meets Prudence the neat
Sharmat, Marjorie Weinman
Mooch series (2)
Moochers
Shaw, Jane
Moochers series (1)
Moochers abroad
Shaw, Jane
Moochers series (2)
Mood for murder
Gruber, Frank
Otis Beagle series (3)
Van Siller, Hilda
Allan Stewart series (2)
Mood indigo
Sayer, Mandy
Rose trilogy (1)
Moods of Ginger Mick
Dennis, Clarence James
Sentimental bloke series (2)
Moody man
Milne, John
James Jenner series (2)
Moog-Moog, space barber
Teague, Mark
Johnsons trilogy (2)
Moominland midwinter
Jansson, Tove
Moomin series (6)
Moominpappa at sea
Jansson, Tove
Moomin series (8)
Moominsummer madness
Jansson, Tove
Moomin series (5)
Moomintroll
Jansson, Tove
Moomin series (9)
Moominvalley in November
Jansson, Tove
Moomin series (9)
Moon
Higgs, Mike
Learn with Moonbird series (5)
Vendrell, Carme Sole
Victor and Maria series (6)
Moon and the face
McKillip, Patricia Anne
Kyreol series (2)
Moon Base One
Walters, Hugh
Chris Godfrey series (4)
Moon Bear
Asch, Frank
Bear series (1)
Moon by night
L'Engle, Madeleine
Austin family series (2)
Moon cake
Asch, Frank
Bear series (4)
Moon-Calf
Dell, Floyd
Felix Fay trilogy (1)
Moon cusser
Helm, Eric
Ground Zero series (15)
Moon dance
Thorne, Ernest Pollett
Major Brains Cunningham series (6)
Moon dragon summer
Lowery, Linda
Heartquest series (5)
Moon dreams
Strickland, Brad
Jeremy Moon series (1)
Moon, earth's natural satellite
Branley, Franklyn Mansfield
Exploring our universe series (2)
Moon endureth
Buchan, John
Sir Edward Leithen series (6)
Moon express
Daniels, Norman A
Avengers series (11)
Moon fate
Axler, James
Deathlands series (16)
Moon filly
Mitchell, Elyne
Silver Brumby series (5)
Moon-Flash
McKillip, Patricia Anne
Kyreol series (1)
Moon for killers
Black, Gavin
Paul Harris series (12)
Moon glows
VerDorn, Bethea
Moon glows series (1)
Moon Hill
Woodhouse, Martin
Giles Yeoman series (5)
Moon in hiding
Edgerton, Teresa
Green lion trilogy (2)
Moon in my pocket
Croft-Cooke, Rupert
Sensual life series (11)
Moon in Pisces
Darby, Catherine
Moon series (6)
Moon in the cloud
Harris, Rosemary
Egyptian trilogy (1)
Moon in the water
Belle, Pamela
Heron family series (1)
Moon into blood
Gavin, Catherine
Second Empire quartet (2)
Moon is red
Rohmer, Sax
Sumuru series (4)
Moon Lake massacre
Sharpe, Jon
Trailsman series (137)
Moon magic
Fortune, Dion
Vivien Le Fay Morgan series (2)
Moon maid
Burroughs, Edgar Rice
Moon series (1)
Moon series (2)
Moon maker
Train, Arthur
Benjamin Hooker series (2)
Moon men
Burroughs, Edgar Rice
Moon series (2)
Moon murders
Morland, Nigel
Mrs Palmyra Pym series (1)
Moon odyssey
Rankine, John
Space nineteen ninety nine series (2)
Moon of Gomrath
Garner, Alan
Alderley series (2)
Moon of much gladness
Bramah, Ernest
Kai Lung series (5)
Moon of mutiny
Del Rey, Lester
Moon trilogy (3)
Moon of skulls
Howard, Robert Ervin
Solomon Kane series (1)
Moon of the alligators
George, Jean Craighead
Thirteen moons series (10)
Moon of the bears
George, Jean Craighead
Thirteen moons series (1)

Moon of the Chackarees
George, Jean Craighead
Thirteen moons series (4)
Moon of the deer
George, Jean Craighead
Thirteen moons series (9)
Moon of the fox pups
George, Jean Craighead
Thirteen moons series (5)
Moon of the gray wolves
George, Jean Craighead
Thirteen moons series (11)
Moon of the moles
George, Jean Craighead
Thirteen moons series (12)
Moon of the monarch butterflies
George, Jean Craighead
Thirteen moons series (6)
Moon of the mountain lions
George, Jean Craighead
Thirteen moons series (8)
Moon of the owls
George, Jean Craighead
Thirteen moons series (2)
Moon of the salamanders
George, Jean Craighead
Thirteen moons series (3)
Moon of the wild pigs
George, Jean Craighead
Thirteen moons series (7)
Moon of the winter bird
George, Jean Craighead
Thirteen moons series (13)
Moon of three rings
Norton, Andre
Krip Vorland series (1)
Moon of thunder
Coldsmith, Don
Spanish bit series (7)
Moon on an iron meadow
Tate, Peter
Simeon series (2)
Moon over Miami
Deane, Jim
Nick Merlotti series (2)
Moon people
Coblentz, Stanton Arthur
Outlander series (1)
Moon pool
Merritt, Abraham
Doctor Goodwin series (1)
Moon raiders
Moore, Patrick
Scott Saunders series (3)
Moon trip
Stern, Simon
Astonishing adventures of Captain Ketchup series (2)
Moon was made for murder
Morland, Nigel
Chief Inspector Andrew McMurdo series (7)
Moon was red
Sage, Dana
Donald O'Keefe Adams series (1)
Moon-winners
Muirden, James
Eric Kendall series (2)
Moonbane mage
Marks, Laurie J
Children of Triad trilogy (2)
Moonbather
Clarke, Roy
Summer wine series (2)
Moonbird
Higgs, Mike
Moonbird series (1)
Moonbird and the fire fountain
Higgs, Mike
Moonbird series (6)
Moonbird and the fun palace
Higgs, Mike
Moonbird series (8)
Moonbird and the green dog
Higgs, Mike
Moonbird series (5)
Moonbird and the lonely ghost
Higgs, Mike
Moonbird series (7)
Moonbird and the space pirates
Higgs, Mike
Moonbird series (4)
Moonbird and the unicorn
Higgs, Mike
Moonbird series (3)
Moonbird to the rescue
Higgs, Mike
Moonbird series (2)
Moonchild
McKenney, Kenneth
Changeling trilogy (1)
Moondance
Asch, Frank
Bear series (10)
Moondrop to murder
Hilton, John Buxton
Superintendent Simon Kenworthy series (15)
Mooney moves around
O'Neil, Kerry
Jerry Mooney series (1)
Moonface
Prime, Honor
Moonface series (1)
Moonface and Matthew
Prime, Honor
Moonface series (2)
Moonflower
Nichols, Beverley
Mister Horatio Green series (2)
Moonflower murder
Nichols, Beverley
Mister Horatio Green series (2)
Moongame
Asch, Frank
Bear series (5)
Moongather
Clayton, Jo
Duel of sorcery trilogy (1)
Moonheart
De Lint, Charles
Moonheart series (1)
Moonlight
Ormerod, Jan
Sun and moon series (2)
Moonlight and gunsmoke
Grover, Marshall
Larry and Stretch series (421)
Moonlight at Greystone
Bronte, Louisa
Greystone Tavern series (5)
Moonlight flitting
Procter, Maurice
Chief Inspector Harry Martineau series (17)
Moonmilk and murder
Stein, Aaron Marc
Tim Mulligan and Elsie Mae Hunt series (18)
Moonpearl
Roberts, Irene
China trilogy (1)
Moonquake
Bentley, Roy
Spacers series (2)
Moonraker
Fleming, Ian
James Bond series (3)
Moonrock
Weverka, Robert
Search series (2)
Moon's a balloon
Niven, David
Moon's a ballon series (1)
Moons and rings
Bendick, Jeanne
Early bird astronomy series (1)
Moon's fire-eating daughter
Myers, John Myers
Silverlock series (2)
Moons of Jupiter
Asimov, Isaac
David Starr series (5)
Moons of Madeleine
Clark, Joan
Barrow family series (2)
Moons of mystery
Black, Christopher
Star challenge series (9)
Moons of triopus
Rankine, John
Space corporation series (2)
Moon's on fire
Donaldson, Margaret
Journey into war series (2)
Moonscatter
Clayton, Jo
Duel of sorcery trilogy (2)
Moonspell
Hansen, Gwen
Secret of the Unicorn Queen series (6)
Moonspender
Gash, Jonathan
Lovejoy series (11)
Moonspun magic
Coulter, Catherine
Victoria Albemarle trilogy (3)
Moonstalker
Appleton, Victor II
Tom Swift Junior series 3 (7)
Moonstone Castle mystery
Keene, Carolyn
Nancy Drew series (40)
Moonstone jungle
Harvester, Simon
Asia in turmoil series (11)
Moonstone mystery
Marsden, Antony
Jim Beverley series (2)
Moonstruck madness
McBain, Laurie
Sabrina Verrick series (1)
Moor fires mystery
Campbell, Harriette Russell
Simon Brade series (3)
Moor Grange mystery
Grey, Peter
Kit Hunter series (6)
Moorland monster
Chase, Glen
Cherry Delight series (27)
Moorland Mousie
Golden Gorse
Mousie series (1)
Mop, Moondance and the Nagasaki knights
Myers, Walter Dean
Mop and Moondance series (2)
Mopoke and the necklace
Smith, Joan Watson
Jindi series (3)
Moppy is angry
Asher, Jane
Moppy series (1)
Moppy is happy
Asher, Jane
Moppy series (2)
Moral life of children
Coles, Robert
Life of children series (1)
Moral Pirates
Alden, William Livingston
Moral Pirates series (1)
Morals Squad
Krasney, Samuel A
Lieutenant Ben Krahmer series (1)
Morbid symptoms
Slovo, Gillian
Kate Baeier series (1)
Morbid taste for bones
Peters, Ellis
Brother Cadfael series (1)
Mordred
Niven, Larry
Buck Rogers series (7)
Pournelle, Jerry
Buck Rogers series (7)
More about Amelia Jane
Blyton, Enid
Amelia Jane series (3)
More about being an author
Allan, Mabel Esther
Author series (2)
More about Brenda Bear
Coombes, Marion
Brenda Bear series (3)
More about Charles, and other stories from Listen with mother
Ainsworth, Ruth
Charles series (2)
More about Dowbiggins
Vipont, Elfrida
Dowbiggins series (2)
More about Froggy
Brenda
Froggy series (2)
More about God's wonderful word
DeJonge, Joanne E
God's wonderful word series (2)
More about John and Mary
James, Grace
John and Mary series (2)
More about Jonathan
Cockett, Mary
Jonathan and Felicity series (4)
More about Josie, Click and Bun
Blyton, Enid
Josie, Click and Bun series (4)
More about Little Pear
Lattimore, Eleanor Frances
Little Pear series (4)
More about Mandy
Hill, Lorna
Vicarage Children series (2)
More about me
Jacob, Naomi
Me series (3)
More about Muffin
Mills, Annette
Muffin series (2)
More about P J< the secret service boy
Hamilton, Frederic
P J Davenant series (6)
More about Paddington
Bond, Michael
Paddington series (2)
More about Peggy
Vaizey, Jessie Bell
Peggy Saville series (2)
More about Pixie
Vaizey, Jessie Bell
Pixie O'Shaughnessy series (2)
More about Rebecca of Sunnybrook Farm
Wiggin, Kate Douglas
Rebecca series (2)
More about Teddy Robinson
Robinson, Joan Gale
Teddy Robinson series (2)
More about the children at Windylaw Farm
Hardman, Diana
Windylaw Farm series (2)
More about the Doctor
Cameron, Isabel
Doctor Lindsay series (2)
More about the early Methodist people
Church, Leslie Frederic
Methodist people series (2)
More about the fairground family
Daykin, Lilian
Fairground family series (2)
More about the four little kittens
Frees, Harry Whittier
Four little pets series (4)
More about the Gumby Gang
Oldfield, Pamela
Gumby Gang series (3)
More about the Noahs, and Tim Tosset
Horrabin, James Francis
Noah family series (5)
More about the twins in Ceylon
Woolf, Bella Sidney
Twins in Ceylon series (2)
More about Thomas the tank engine
Awdry, Christopher
Railway series (30)
More about Wimpy and his friends
Drake, Joan
Wimpy series (2)
More about Worzel Gummidge
Todd, Barbara Euphan
Worzel Gummidge series (3)
More about Wumpus
Trevor, Elleston
Wumpus series (2)
More adventures at Foxendale Farm
Kitchen, Fred
Foxendale series (2)
More adventures of a Teddy Bear
Cradock, Henry Cowper, *Mrs*
Teddy Bear series (2)
More adventures of Alison
Stuart, Sheila
Alison series (2)
More adventures of an A.D.C.
Bradley, Shelland
A.D.C. series (2)
More adventures of Captin Kettle, KCB
Hyne, Charles John Cutcliffe
Captain Owen Kettle series (5)
More adventures of Ginger Meggs, series 10
Bancks, James Charles
Ginger Meggs series (10)
More adventures of Ginger Meggs, series 12
Bancks, James Charles
Ginger Meggs series (12)
More adventures of Ginger Meggs, series 13
Bancks, James Charles
Ginger Meggs series (13)
More adventures of Ginger Meggs, series 14
Bancks, James Charles
Ginger Meggs series (14)
More adventures of Ginger Meggs, series 15
Bancks, James Charles
Ginger Meggs series (15)
More adventures of Ginger Meggs, series 16
Bancks, James Charles
Ginger Meggs series (16)
More adventures of Ginger Meggs, series 17
Bancks, James Charles
Ginger Meggs series (17)
More adventures of Ginger Meggs, series 18
Bancks, James Charles
Ginger Meggs series (18)
More adventures of Ginger Meggs, series 19
Bancks, James Charles
Ginger Meggs series (19)
More adventures of Ginger Meggs, series 20
Bancks, James Charles
Ginger Meggs series (20)
More adventures of Ginger Meggs, series 21
Bancks, James Charles
Ginger Meggs series (21)
More adventures of Ginger Meggs, series 22
Bancks, James Charles
Ginger Meggs series (22)
More adventures of Ginger Meggs, series 23
Bancks, James Charles
Ginger Meggs series (23)
More adventures of Ginger Meggs, series 24
Bancks, James Charles
Ginger Meggs series (24)
More adventures of Ginger Meggs, series 25
Bancks, James Charles
Ginger Meggs series (25)
More adventures of Ginger Meggs, series 26
Bancks, James Charles
Ginger Meggs series (26)
More adventures of Ginger Meggs, series 27
Bancks, James Charles
Ginger Meggs series (27)
More adventures of Ginger Meggs, series 3
Bancks, James Charles
Ginger Meggs series (3)
More adventures of Ginger Meggs, series 5
Bancks, James Charles
Ginger Meggs series (5)
More adventures of Ginger Meggs, series 6
Bancks, James Charles
Ginger Meggs series (6)
More adventures of Ginger Meggs, series 8
Bancks, James Charles
Ginger Meggs series (8)
More adventures of Huckleberry Finn
Wood, Clement
Huckleberry Finn series (4)
More adventures of Little Black Nickum
Robertson, Jean
Little Black Nickum series (2)
More adventures of Littlenose
Grant, John
Littlenose series (6)
More adventures of Mary Mouse
Blyton, Enid
Mary Mouse series (2)
More adventures of Pinkie
Ruff, Agnes
Pinkie series (2)
More adventures of Pip
Blyton, Enid
Pip series (2)
More adventures of Samurai Cat
Rogers, Mark Earl
Samurai Cat series (2)
More adventures of the Brydons
Fidler, Kathleen
Brydon family series (4)
More adventures of the Great Brain
Fitzgerald, John Dennis
Tom's Great Brain series (2)
More adventures of the grey mouse family
Dubois, Ivy Millicent
Grey mouse series (2)
More adventures of the McGills
Fidler, Kathleen
McGills series (2)
More adventures of the muddle-headed wombat
Park, Ruth
Muddle-headed wombat series (8)
More adventures of the wishing-chair
Blyton, Enid
Wishing-chair series (1)
More adventures of Tinker and Tanker
Scarry, Richard
Tinker and Tanker series (6)
More adventures of Tommy Tad and Polly Wog
Trick, Edgar Harold
Tommy Tad and Polly Wog series (2)
More adventures on Willow Farm
Blyton, Enid
Willow Farm series (2)

More Alice
Wilson, Yates
Alice in Wonderland sequels series (5)
More all-Jewish cartoons, yet
Gerberg, Mort
All-Jewish cartoon series (2)
More all-of-a-kind family
Taylor, Sydney
All-of-a-kind family series (2)
More allsorts
Fletcher, Audrey
Allsorts series (6)
More and more Ant and Bee
Banner, Angela
Ant and Bee series (5)
More Ant and Bee
Banner, Angela
Ant and Bee series (2)
More Australian encounters
Smith, Keith
Supernatural series (2)
More babies
Matterson, Neil
Baby series (3)
More ballpoint bananas
Keller, Charles
Ballpoint bananas series (2)
More beasts, for worse children
Belloc, Hilaire
Beasts series (2)
More beautiful than murder
Cohen, Octavus Roy
Lieutenant Marty Walsh series (2)
More bedtime tales
Paull, Minnie E
Mother's bedtime tales series (2)
More biography
Bentley, Edmund Clerihew
Clerihews series (2)
More Brer Rabbit
Derwent, Lavinia
Brer Rabbit series (2)
More Brown Beggarman stories
Daykin, Lilian
Brown Beggarman series (2)
More bunny stories for young people
Jewett, John Howard
Bunny stories series (2)
More Bunny trouble
Wilhelm, Hans
Bunny trouble series (2)
More butterfly days
Fowkes, Aubrey
Butterfly days series (2)
More cargoes
Jacobs, William Wymark
Night-Watchman series (2)
More caviar
Buchwald, Art
Caviar series (2)
More Celtic fairy tales
Jacobs, Joseph
Celtic fairy tales series (2)
More championship teams of the NFL
Berger, Phil
National Football League series (2)
More changes, more chances
Nevinson, Henry Woodd
Changes and chances series (2)
More chimney corner stories
Blyton, Enid
Chimney corner stories series (2)
More city jitters
Fowler, Christopher
City jitters series (2)
More crazy cut-outs
Tong, Gary
Crazy cut-outs series (2)
More dangerous thoughts
Finnegan, Robert
Dangerous thoughts series (2)
More dead than alive
Ormerod, Roger
David Mallin and George Coe series (15)
More deaths for Sergeant Cluff
North, Gil
Sergeant Caleb Cluff series (4)
More deaths than one
Fischer, Bruno
Ben Helm series (2)
Stout, Rex
Nero Wolfe and Archie Goodwin series (13)
More duty free
Harvey, John Barton
Duty free series (2)
More dykes to watch out for
Bechdel, Alison
Dykes series (2)
More E K Means
Means, Eldred Kurtz
Is this a title, it is not series (2)
More educated Evans
Wallace, Edgar
Educated Evans series (2)
More eggs of things
Kumin, Maxine W
Eggs of things series (2)
More English fairy tales
Jacobs, Joseph
English fairy tales series (2)
More everyday parenting
Goldstein, Robin
Everyday parenting series (2)
More exploits of Sherlock Holmes
Doyle, Adrian Conan
Sherlock Holmes sequels series (6)
More fables
Ade, George
Fables in slang series (2)
More fifth grade magic
Gormley, Beatrice
Fifth grade magic series (2)
More five minute mysteries
Weber, Ken
Five minute mysteries series (2)
More five minute stories
Richards, Laura Elizabeth
Five minute stories series (2)
More for Brownies
Williams, Ursula Moray
Brownies series (2)
More for Timothy
Gollancz, Victor
Letters to Timothy series (2)
More fragments from France
Bairnsfather, Bruce
Old Bill series (2)
More friends of the Doctor
Cameron, Isabel
Doctor Lindsay series (5)
More from Hound and Bear
Gackenbach, Dick
Hound and Bear series (2)
More from Methuselah
Vachell, Horace Annesley
Methuselah series (5)
More from the primeval forest
Schweitzer, Albert
Primeval forest series (2)
More funny ones
Hough, Charlotte
Funny ones series (2)
More funny stories about old friends, Bib and Bub
Gibbs, May
Gumnut Land series (13)
More furry tales
Lee, Leslie
Furry tales series (2)
More gal's gossip
Binstead, Arthur Morris
Gal's gossip series (2)
More ghost stories
James, Montague Rhodes
Ghost stories series (2)
More ghost stories of an antiquary
James, Montague Rhodes
Ghost stories series (2)
More gilt-edged Bonds
Fleming, Ian
James Bond series (4)
More Goon cartoons
Milligan, Spike
Goon cartoons series (2)
More great pretenders
Berry, Joy
Can make and do series (2)
More great working dog stories
Goode, Angela
Working dogs series (2)
More green fingers
Arkell, Reginald
Green fingers series (2)
More Halloween howls
Maestro, Giulio
Halloween howls series (2)
More happy thoughts
Burnand, Francis Cowley
Happy thoughts series (3)
More haunted houses
Chambers, Aidan
Haunted houses series (2)
More heart throbs contributed by the people
Chapple, Joseph Mitchell
Heart throbs series (3)
More impertinence
Arnott, Peter
Impertinence series (2)
More incredible true adventures
Wulffson, Don L
Incredible true adventures series (2)
More instruction from the Centre
Andrew, Christopher
K.G.B. series (3)
More J.T.'s ladies
Edson, John Thomas
J.T.'s ladies series (2)
More Jan Perry stories
Sedgwick, Modwena
Jan Perry series (2)
More Janey stories
Pearl, Irene
Janey series (3)
More life with Dexter
Fennell, Willie
Dexter Dutton series (2)
More Limehouse nights
Burke, Thomas
London series (2)
More little Bear tales
Chapman, Gillian
Little Bear series (2)
More little Mushrooms
Ainsworth, Ruth
Little Mushrooms series (2)
More little talks about God and you
Beers, Victor Gilbert
Little talks series (2)
More lives than one
Wells, Carolyn
Lorimer Lane series (1)
More Lizzie Dripping
Cresswell, Helen
Lizzie Dripping series (5)
More Maggie Muggins
Grannan, Mary
Maggie Muggins series (6)
More magic
Niven, Larry
Magic trilogy (3)
More magic in your pockets
Severn, Bill
Magic series (12)
More magic people
Softly, Barbara
Magic people series (2)
More Mary-Mary
Robinson, Joan Gale
Mary-Mary series (2)
More me and Gus
Anthony, Frank Sheldon
Gus Tomlins series (2)
More memoirs, and some travels
Burgin, George Brown
Clubman series (2)
More memoirs of an aesthete
Acton, Harold
Aesthete series (2)
More memories
Emery, Ralph
Country music series (2)
More messages from Michael
Yarbro, Chelsea Quinn
Messages from Michael series (2)
More Methodist idylls
Lindsay, Harry
Methodist idylls series (2)
More Milligan letters
Milligan, Spike
Milligan letters series (2)
More Minden curses
Roberts, Willo Davis
Minden curse series (2)
More mini-mysteries for Liz and Will
Resciniti, Angelo G
Liz and Will series (2)
More misleading cases
Herbert, Alan Patrick
Misleading cases series (2)
More Mister Small
Lenski, Lois
Small family series (4)
More modern baseball superstars
Gutman, Bill
Modern superstars series (6)
More modern women superstars
Gutman, Bill
Modern superstars series (8)
More Mrs 'Arris
Poultney, Clifford Blake
Mrs 'Arris series (2)
More murder in a nunnery
Shepherd, Eric
Superintendent Andrew Pearson series (2)
More murder in the Carolinas
Rhyne, Nancy
Murder in the Carolinas series (2)
More naughty stories for good boys and girls
Milne, Christopher
Naughty stories series (2)
More news from the Middle East
Mason, Robert
Captain James Donald Macgregor series (2)
More nights of Jean Macaque
Cloete, Stuart
Jean Macaque series (2)
More of Elizabeth Ann
Bradburne, Elizabeth Sutton
Elizabeth Ann series (2)
More of Milly-Molly-Mandy
Brisley, Joyce Lankester
Milly-Molly-Mandy series (2)
More of my life
Ayer, Alfred Jules
My life series (2)
More of the good life
Esmonde, John
Good life series (2)
More of us
Frankau, Gilbert
One of us series (2)
More old Tasmanian prints
Craig, Clifford
Tasmanian prints series (3)
More opposites
Hill, Eric
Peek-a-book series (6)
More people like us
Bye, Beryl
People like us series (2)
More perfect union
Jance, Judith A
J P Beaumont series (6)
More poems for Peter
Borie, Lysbeth Boyd
Poems for Peter series (2)
More poems to solve
Swenson, May
Poems to solve series (2)
More ponies for Jean
Cannan, Joanna
Jean series (3)
More potted stories to tell Scouts and Cubs
Barclay, Vera Charlesworth
Potted stories series (2)
More prefabulous animiles
Reeves, James
Animiles series (2)
More puppets with pizazz
Berry, Joy
Can make and do series (5)
More rain unravelled tales
Heylin, Clinton
Rain unravelled tales series (2)
More Rawhides
Russell, Charles Marion
Rawhide Rawlins series (2)
More ridiculous world records
Scheier, Michael
World records series (2)
More ringside seats
Wilson, Peter
Boxing series (2)
More ripping yarns
Palin, Michael
Ripping yarns series (2)
More room for the Pipkins
Wahl, Jan
Pipkins series (2)
More Sabo stories
Lewis, E W
Sabo series (2)
More Salty
Westron, Charles
Salty series (2)
More science experiments you can eat
Cobb, Vicki
You can eat series (3)
More science surprised from Doctor Zed
Penrose, Gordon
Doctor Zed series (5)
More shapes and stories
Grigson, Geoffrey
Shapes and stories series (2)
More short sixes
Bunner, Henry Cuyler
Short sixes series (2)
More Slimtails
Chell, Mary
Slimtails series (2)
More small poems
Worth, Valerie
Small poems series (2)
More snappy answers to stupid questions
Jaffee, Al
Snappy answers to stupid questions series (3)
More Staffordshire characters
Godwin, John
Staffordshire characters series (2)
More stately mansions
O'Neill, Eugene
Possessors self-possessed series (2)
More stories for telling
Wood, William Hollingsworth
Stories for telling series (2)
More stories from grandma's attic
Richardson, Arleta
Grandma's attic series (2)
More stories from the Twilight Zone
Serling, Rod
Twilight Zone series (2)
More stories from Thriller
Hart, Ted
Thriller series (2)
More stories from Thrush Green
Read, *Miss*
Thrush Green series (6)
More stories Julian tells
Cameron, Ann
Julian stories series (2)
More stories of married life
Cutting, Mary Stewart
Little stories of life series (3)
More strictly personal
Horler, Sydney
Strictly personal series (2)
More T.V. adventures of Mister Majeika
Carpenter, Humphrey
Mister Majeika series (5)
More tabby magic
De Banke, Cecile
Tabby series (2)
More tales from a country practice
Jackson, Arthur
Country practice series (2)
More tales from a long room
Tinniswood, Peter
Brigadier series (2)
More tales from the forbidden planet
Kaveney, Roz
Forbidden planet series (2)
More tales from the igloo
Nanogak, Agnes
Tales from the igloo series (2)
More tales from the story hat
Aardema, Verna
Story hat series (2)
More tales of Oliver Pig
Van Leeuwen, Jean
Oliver Pig series (2)
More tales of Pirx the pilot
Lem, Stanislaw
Pirx series (2)
More tales of prestidigitection
Gibson, Walter Brown
Norgil series (2)
More tales of Shellover
Ainsworth, Ruth
Shellover series (2)
More tales of the Black Widowers
Asimov, Isaac
Black Widowers series (2)
More tales of the city
Maupin, Armistead
Tales of the city series (2)
More tales of the Ridings
Moorman, Frederic William
Tales of the Ridings series (2)
More tales of the South Carolina low country
Rhyne, Nancy
Tales of South Carolina series (2)
More tales of the stumps
Bleackley, Horace William
Stumps series (2)
More tales of the uneasy
Hunt, Violet
Uneasy series (2)
More tales of the West Riding
Bentley, Phyllis
West Riding series (20)
More tales told near a crocodile
Harman, Humphrey
African tales series (2)
More tavern talk
Brooks, Collin
Tavern talk series (2)
More television adventures of Worzel Gummidge
Waterhouse, Keith
Worzel Gummidge series (12)
More tell and draw stories
Oldfield, Margaret Jean
Tell and draw series (3)

Most immoral murder
Ashbrook, Harriette
Philip Tracy series (4)
Most important thing
Ure, Jean
Nicola Bruce series (2)
Most insistent lady
McCulloch, Sarah
Georgian series (3)
Most likely suspects
Bourgeau, Art
Claude Kirlin and F T Zevich series (2)
Most likely to die
Keene, Carolyn
Nancy Drew files series (27)
Most men don't kill
Alexander, David
Lieutenant Romano series (1)
Tommy Twotoes and Terry Rooke series (1)
Most powerful horse in the world
Maguire, Michael
Mylor series (1)
Most secret, most immediate
Swiggett, Howard
Garrett Maynard series (2)
Most suspicious star
Ebel, Suzanne
Sir Robert Waring series (2)
Most unnatural murder
Sinclair, Fiona
Inspector Paul Grainger series (5)
Most wanted
Bagby, George
Inspector Schmidt series (51)
Mostly canallers
Edmonds, Walter Dumaux
Erie Canal series (4)
Mostly harmless
Adams, Douglas Noel
Arthur Dent series (5)
Mostly magic
Forsyth, Anne
Monster series (3)
Mostly Mary
Rae, Gwynedd
Mary Plain series (1)
Mostly Mischief
Tilman, Harold William
Mischief series (3)
Mostly on Martha's Vineyard
Hough, Henry Beetle
Martha's Vineyard series (2)
Mosultha's magic
Smith, David Claude
Oron series (1)
Mot the mouse
Lloyd, David
Great escapes series (3)
Mote in God's eye
Pournelle, Jerry
Future history series (1)
Moth
Sallis, James
Lew Griffin series (2)
Moth in a rag shop
Chambers, Robert
Hank Moody series (1)
Moth-watch murder
Burton, Miles
Inspector Arnold and Desmond Merrion series (55)
Mother
Dawson-Scott, Catherine Amy
Some women trilogy (2)
Mother and daughter
Morgan, Sally
My place series (3)
Mother and son
Rolland, Romain
Soul enchanted series (3)
Mother beaver
Hurd, Edith Thatcher
Mother animal series (1)
Mother chimpanzee
Hurd, Edith Thatcher
Mother animal series (6)
Mother deer
Hurd, Edith Thatcher
Mother animal series (2)
Mother Earth
McQuay, Mike
Ramon and Morgan series (2)
Mother earth, father sky
Harrison, Sue
Mother earth trilogy (1)
Mother Farthing's luck
Morgan, Helen
Satchkin Patchkin series (2)
Mother finds a body
Lee, Gypsy Rose
Gypsy Rose Lee series (2)
Mother Goose in prose
Baum, Lyman Frank
Mother and Father Goose series (1)
Mother Goose murders
Grant, Maxwell
Shadow series (273)
Mother Hen and Mary
Pilgrim, Jane
Blackberry Farm series (7)
Mother hunt
Stout, Rex
Nero Wolfe and Archie Goodwin series (38)
Mother, I'm disappointed
Daniel, Rebecca
Mother series (4)
Mother, I'm embarrassed
Daniel, Rebecca
Mother series (2)
Mother, I'm mad
Daniel, Rebecca
Mother series (1)
Mother, I'm worried
Daniel, Rebecca
Mother series (3)
Mother-in-law
Boardman, M M
Nellie Gates series (2)
Mother kangaroo
Hurd, Edith Thatcher
Mother animal series (5)
Mother knew best
Scannell, Dorothy
Dolly trilogy (1)
Mother Luck
Petersen, Paul
Smugglers series (4)
Mother Murphy
McKenna, Colleen O'Shaughnessy
Murphy family series (7)
Mother of invention
Johnston, William
Flying nun series (4)
Mother of storms
Cole, Adrian
Star requiem series (1)
Mother of the year
Johnson, B B
Superspade series (4)
Mother owl
Hurd, Edith Thatcher
Mother animal series (4)
Mother Rabbit's son Tom
Gackenbach, Dick
Hattie Rabbit series (3)
Mother sea
Karlsson, Elis
Mother sea series (1)
Mother speaks
Kubasik, Christopher
Earthdawn series (2)
Mother West Wind how stories
Burgess, Thornton Waldo
Old Mother West Wind series (6)
Mother West Wind when stories
Burgess, Thornton Waldo
Old Mother West Wind series (7)
Mother West Wind where stories
Burgess, Thornton Waldo
Old Mother West Wind series (8)
Mother West Wind why stories
Burgess, Thornton Waldo
Old Mother West Wind series (5)
Mother West Wind's animal friends
Burgess, Thornton Waldo
Old Mother West Wind series (3)
Mother West Wind's children
Burgess, Thornton Waldo
Old Mother West Wind series (2)
Mother West Wind's neighbors
Burgess, Thornton Waldo
Old Mother West Wind series (4)
Mother whale
Hurd, Edith Thatcher
Mother animal series (3)
Mother, where are you?
Woolfolk, Dorothy
Donna Rockford series (1)
Motherless children
Leslie, Madeline
Play and study series (1)
Motherlines
Charnas, Suzy McKee
Alldera series (2)
Mother's bedtime tales
Paull, Minnie E
Mother's bedtime tales series (1)
Mother's blessing
Spinka, Penina Keen
Chumash series (1)
Mother's Day
Morse, Eric
Friday the thirteenth series (1)
Mother's recompense
Aguilar, Grace
Home influence series (2)
Mother's secret
Buncher, Walter
Donald O'Dare series (1)
Mothers to men
Gale, Zora
Friendship village series (3)
Motherstone
Gee, Maurice
World of O trilogy (3)
Moth-kin magic
Tapp, Kathy Kennedy
Moth-kin series (1)
Moths of the Limberlost
Porter, Gene Stratton
Limberlost series (3)
Motion menace
Robeson, Kenneth
Doc Savage series (64)
Motion picture boys' outdoor exhibition
Appleton, Victor
Moving picture boys series (14)
Motion picture chums at Seaside Park
Appleton, Victor
Motion picture chums series (2)
Movie boys series (12)
Moving picture boys series (12)
Motion picture chums at the fair
Appleton, Victor
Motion picture chums series (6)
Movie boys series (16)
Motion picture chums' first venture
Appleton, Victor
Motion picture chums series (1)
Movie boys series (11)
Moving picture boys series (11)
Motion picture chums' new idea
Appleton, Victor
Motion picture chums series (5)
Movie boys series (15)
Moving picture boys series (15)
Motion picture chums on Broadway
Appleton, Victor
Motion picture chums series (3)
Movie boys series (13)
Moving picture boys series (13)
Motion picture chums' outdoor exhibition
Appleton, Victor
Motion picture chums series (4)
Movie boys series (14)
Moving picture boys series (14)
Motion picture chums' war spectacle
Appleton, Victor
Motion picture chums series (7)
Movie boys series (17)
Motion picture comnrades' great venture
Barnes, Elmer Tracey
Motion picture comrades series (1)
Motion picture comrades aboard a submarine
Barnes, Elmer Tracey
Motion picture comrades series (4)
Motion picture comrades along the Orinoco
Barnes, Elmer Tracey
Motion picture comrades series (3)
Motion picture comrades in African jungles
Barnes, Elmer Tracey
Motion picture comrades series (2)
Motion picture comrades producing a success
Barnes, Elmer Tracey
Motion picture comrades series (5)
Motion picture comrades through African jungles
Barnes, Elmer Tracey
Motion picture comrades series (2)
Motive
Carmichael, Harry
John Piper and Quinn series (35)
Motive for a kill
Chance, John Newton
Jonathan Blake series (42)
Motive for murder
Barling, Charles
Inspector George Marshall series (5)
Brent, Nigel
Barney Hyde series (2)
Graham, Neill
Solo Malcolm series (37)
Hamill, Edson T
Joe Ryker series (5)
Motive for revenge
Conway, Peter
Lucy Beck series (1)
Motive for the crime
Soutar, Andrew
Phineas Spinnet series (13)
Motive in shadow
Egan, Lesley
Jesse Falkenstein series (10)
Motive on record
Shannon, Dell
Lieutenant Luis Mendoza series (33)
Motley and murder
Holt, Henry
Inspector Silver series (13)
Motley crew
Browne, Dik
Hagar the horrible series (51)
Motor boat boys among the Florida Keys
Arundel, Louis
Motor boat boys series (5)
Motor boat boys down the coast
Arundel, Louis
Motor boat boys series (4)
Motor boat boys down the Danube
Arundel, Louis
Motor boat boys series (7)
Motor boat boys' Mississippi cruise
Arundel, Louis
Motor boat boys series (1)
Motor boat boys on the Great Lakes
Arundel, Louis
Motor boat boys series (3)
Motor boat boys on the Saint Lawrence
Arundel, Louis
Motor boat boys series (2)
Motor boat boys' river chase
Arundel, Louis
Motor boat boys series (6)
Motor Boat Club and the wireless
Hancock, Harrie Irving
Motor Boat Club series (4)
Motor Boat Club at Nantucket
Hancock, Harrie Irving
Motor Boat Club series (2)
Motor Boat Club at the Golden Gate
Hancock, Harrie Irving
Motor Boat Club series (6)
Motor Boat Club in Florida
Hancock, Harrie Irving
Motor Boat Club series (5)
Motor Boat Club of the Kennebec
Hancock, Harrie Irving
Motor Boat Club series (1)
Motor Boat Club off Long Island
Hancock, Harrie Irving
Motor Boat Club series (3)
Motor Boat Club on the Great Lakes
Hancock, Harrie Irving
Motor Boat Club series (7)
Motor boys
Young, Clarence
Motor boys series (1)
Motor boys across the plains
Young, Clarence
Motor boys series (4)
Motor boys afloat
Young, Clarence
Motor boys series (5)
Motor boys after a fortune
Young, Clarence
Motor boys series (13)
Motor boys at Boxwood Hall
Young, Clarence
Motor boys series (17)
Motor boys bound for home
Young, Clarence
Motor boys series (21)
Motor boys in Mexico
Young, Clarence
Motor boys series (3)
Motor boys in Ottowa
Hood, Hugh
New age series (6)
Motor boys in strange waters
Young, Clarence
Motor boys series (7)
Motor boys in the army
Young, Clarence
Motor boys series (19)
Motor boys in the clouds
Young, Clarence
Motor boys series (9)
Motor boys on a ranch
Young, Clarence
Motor boys series (18)
Motor boys on road and river
Young, Clarence
Motor boys series (16)
Motor boys on the Atlantic
Young, Clarence
Motor boys series (6)
Motor boys on the border
Young, Clarence
Motor boys series (14)
Motor boys on the firing line
Young, Clarence
Motor boys series (20)
Motor boys on the Pacific
Young, Clarence
Motor boys series (8)
Motor boys on the wing
Young, Clarence
Motor boys series (12)
Motor boys on Thunder Mountain
Young, Clarence
Motor boys series (22)
Motor boys over the ocean
Young, Clarence
Motor boys series (11)
Motor boys over the Rockies
Young, Clarence
Motor boys series (10)
Motor boys overland
Young, Clarence
Motor boys series (2)
Motor boys under the sea
Young, Clarence
Motor boys series (15)
Motor bus murder
Stuart, Donald
Sexton Blake series (813)
Motor City blue
Estleman, Loren D
Amos Walker series (1)
Motor coach murder
Bidston, Lester
Sexton Blake series (736)
Motor coach mystery
Murray, Andrew
Sexton Blake series (250)
Tyrer, Walter
Sexton Blake series (1224)
Motor cycle chums around the world
Payson, Howard
Motor cycle chums series (1)
Motor cycle chums in the goldfields
Payson, Howard
Motor cycle chums series (3)
Motor cycle chums of the Northwest Patrol
Payson, Howard
Motor cycle chums series (2)
Motor cycle chums south of the Equator
Payson, Howard
Motor cycle chums series (5)
Motor cycle chums through historic America
Payson, Howard
Motor cycle chums series (6)
Motor cycle chums' whirlwind tour
Payson, Howard
Motor cycle chums series (4)
Motor girls
Penrose, Margaret
Motor girls series (1)
Motor girls at Camp Surprise
Penrose, Margaret
Motor girls series (9)
Motor girls at Lookout Beach
Penrose, Margaret
Motor girls series (3)
Motor girls in the mountains
Penrose, Margaret
Motor girls series (10)
Motor girls on a tour
Penrose, Margaret
Motor girls series (2)
Motor girls on Cedar Lake
Penrose, Margaret
Motor girls series (5)
Motor girls on Crystal Bay
Penrose, Margaret
Motor girls series (7)
Motor girls on the coast
Penrose, Margaret
Motor girls series (6)
Motor girls on waters blue
Penrose, Margaret
Motor girls series (8)
Motor girls through New England
Penrose, Margaret
Motor girls series (4)
Motor holiday
Greene, Carla
Travel series (3)
Motor maid
Williamson, Charles Norris
Motoring series (5)
Motor Maids across the continent
Stokes, Katherine
Motor Maids series (6)

Motor Maids at Sunrise Camp
Stokes, Katherine
Motor Maids series (5)
Motor Maids by palm and pine
Stokes, Katherine
Motor Maids series (2)
Motor Maids by rose, shamrock and thistle
Stokes, Katherine
Motor Maids series (3)
Motor Maids in fair Japan
Stokes, Katherine
Motor Maids series (4)
Motor Maids' school days
Stokes, Katherine
Motor Maids series (1)
Motor pirate
Paternoster, George Sidney
Randolph Mannering series (1)
Motor rally mystery
Rhode, John
Doctor Lancelot Priestley series (14)
Motor Rangers' cloud cruiser
West, Marvin
Motor Rangers series (4)
Motor Rangers' lost mine
West, Marvin
Motor Rangers series (1)
Motor Rangers on Blue Water
West, Marvin
Motor Rangers series (3)
Motor Rangers through the Sierras
West, Marvin
Motor Rangers series (2)
Motor Rangers touring for the trophy
West, Marvin
Motor Rangers series (6)
Motor Rangers' wireless station
West, Marvin
Motor Rangers series (5)
Motor show mystery
Gibbons, Harry Hornaby Clifford
Sexton Blake series (569)
Hardinge, Rex
Sexton Blake series (888)
Motorcycle chums in New England
Lincoln, Andrew Carey
Motorcycle chums series (1)
Motorcycle chums in the Adirondacks
Lincoln, Andrew Carey
Motorcycle chums series (5)
Motorcycle chums in the land of the sky
Lincoln, Andrew Carey
Motorcycle chums series (2)
Motorcycle chums in Yellowstone Park
Lincoln, Andrew Carey
Motorcycle chums series (4)
Motorcycle chums on the Santa Fe Trail
Lincoln, Andrew Carey
Motorcycle chums series (3)
Motorcycle chums stormbound
Lincoln, Andrew Carey
Motorcycle chums series (6)
Motoring Millers
Constant, Alberta Wilson
Miller family series (2)
Motown
Estleman, Loren D
Detroit trilogy (2)
Mott Street maulers
Teitelbaum, Michael
Fievel series (4)
Mottled lizard
Huxley, Elspeth
Kenya childhood series (2)
Motto excelsior, book I
De Vere, V C
Motto excelsior series (1)
Motto excelsior, book V-VIII
De Vere, V C
Motto excelsior series (3)
Motto excelsior, books II-IV
De Vere, V C
Motto excelsior series (2)
Mottram Park
Chaney, Jill
Mottram Park series (1)
Mould
Wheeler, David
Edwin Mould series (1)
Moulded in earth
Vaughan, Richard
Justin Peele series (1)
Mouls House mystery
Barry, Charles
Superintendent Lawrence Gilmartin series (3)
Mounds of earth and shell
Shemie, Bonnie
Native dwellings series (5)
Mount Blossom girls
Mullins, Iola May
Blossom Shop series (4)
Mount fire
Truman, Timothy
Emanuel Santana series (2)
Mount Subasio
Calderini, Priscilla
Borderland series (1)
Mountain bike book
Van de Plas, Rob
Mountain bike series (1)
Mountain bike magic
Van de Plas, Rob
Mountain bike series (2)
Mountain bike maintenance
Van de Plas, Rob
Mountain bike series (3)
Mountain bike technology
Van de Plas, Rob
Mountain bike series (4)
Mountain born
Yates, Elizabeth
Mountain born series (1)
Mountain breed
Fletcher, Aaron
Making of America series (2)
Mountain cat
Thompson, David
Nathaniel King series (18)
Mountain days
Romains, Jules
Men of goodwill series (21)
Mountain devil
Thompson, David
Nathaniel King series (9)
Mountain engines
Awdry, Wilbert
Railway series (19)
Mountain fury
Brady, Taylor
Kincaids series (3)
Mountain girl
Fox, Genevieve May
Mountain girl series (1)
Mountain girl comes home
Fox, Genevieve May
Mountain girl series (2)
Mountain gorilla
Torgersen, Don Arthur
Animal life stories series (3)
Mountain green
Calhoun, Chad
Agent Brad Spear series (11)
Mountain inn mystery
Ridley, Nat
Nat Ridley series (14)
Mountain Jack Pike
Meek, Joseph
Mountain Jack Pike series (1)
Mountain killer
Dawson, Clay
Long Rider series (20)
Mountain-land
Chambers, Robert William
Land series (5)
Mountain light
Yep, Laurence Michael
Cassia series (2)
Mountain madam
Fletcher, Dirk
Spur McCoy series (36)
Mountain madness
Fortescue, Winifred
Provence series (5)
Mountain man kill
Sharpe, Jon
Trailsman series (3)
Mountain manhunt
Grey, Loren Zane
Lassiter series (7)
Thompson, David
Nathaniel King series (13)
Mountain Man's vengeance
Johnstone, William Wallace
Mountain Man series (7)
Mountain massacre
Buchanan, Jack
M.I.A. Hunter series (4)
Stone, Ned
Other Day Logan series (2)
Mountain meadow
Buchan, John
Sir Edward Leithen series (6)
Mountain men
Neihardt, John Gneisenau
Cycle of the West series (5)
Mountain monster
Robeson, Kenneth
Doc Savage series (84)
Mountain mystery
Lynch, Lawrence L
Van Vernet series (2)
Mountain of adventure
Blyton, Enid
Adventure series (5)
Mountain of fear
Barker, Wade
Ninja Master series (2)
Mountain of gold
Ellis, Wesley
Lone Star series (84)
Seligman, Adrian
Thunder Reef series (3)
Mountain of light
Johns, William Earl
Biggles series (8)
Mountain of magic
Nichols, Beverley
Judy series (3)
Mountain of mirrors
Estes, Rose
Endless quest series (2)
Mountain of skulls
Kessler, Leo
Black Cossacks series (3)
Mountain of stolen dreams
Tallis, Robyn
Planet builders series (1)
Mountain path
Arnow, Harriette
Kentucky trilogy (1)
Mountain-peak mystery
Keene, Carolyn
Dana girls series (33)
Mountain pony
Larom, Henry V
Mountain pony series (1)
Mountain pony and the elkhorn mystery
Larom, Henry V
Mountain pony series (4)
Mountain pony and the pinto colt
Larom, Henry V
Mountain pony series (2)
Mountain pony and the rodeo mystery
Larom, Henry V
Mountain pony series (3)
Mountain raiders
Scott, Bradford
Walt Slade series (101)
Mountain rampage
Pendleton, Don
Mack Bolan series (54)
Mountain riders
Brand, Max
Silvertip series (12)
Mountain run
Dever, Joe
Freeway warrior series (2)
Mountain sheriff
Murray, Earl
Dan Sleyter series (1)
Mountain standard time
Horgan, Paul
Mountain standard time trilogy (3)
Mountain star
Ellis, Edward Sylvester
Paddle your own canoe trilogy (2)
Mountain survival
Packard, Edward
Choose your own adventure series (28)
Mountain top mystery
Warner, Gertrude Chandler
Boxcar children series (9)
Mountain township
Hard, Walter
Vermont series (3)
Mountain trek
Salmon, Ross
Payo series (2)
Mountain village
Yeh, Chun-Chan
Quiet are the mountains series (1)
Mountain walks
Green, Roland James
Peace Company trilogy (3)
Mountainhead
Cory, Desmond
Johnny Fedora series (8)
Mountains
Gree, Alain
Keith and Sally series (10)
Mountains have a secret
Upfield, Arthur William
Napoleon Bonaparte series (12)
Mountains of Brega
Lord, Jeffrey
Richard Blade series (17)
Mountains of Channadran
Dexter, Susan
Winter King's war trilogy (3)
Mountains of mystery
Friel, Arthur Olney
McKay, Knowlton and Ryan series (4)
Mountains remain
Tasaki, Hanama
Private Takeo series (2)
Mountains west of town
Downing, Warwick
Joe Reddman series (2)
Mountainside Acres
Welles, Elizabeth
Janine West series (6)
Mountolive
Durrell, Lawrence
Alexandria quartet (3)
Moura
Coffman, Virginia
Moura series (1)
Mourned on Sunday
Reilly, Helen
Inspector Christopher McKee series (12)
Mourner
Stark, Richard
Parker series (4)
Mourner's voyage
Martin, Shane
Professor Ronald Challis series (5)
Mournful Martin
Sanders, Charles Wesley
Mournful Martin series (6)
Mournful Martin makes his bow
Sanders, Charles Wesley
Mournful Martin series (2)
Mournful rides again
Sanders, Charles Wesley
Mournful Martin series (5)
Mourning after
Dewey, Thomas Blanchard
Singer Batts series (3)
Kane, Frank
Johnny Liddell series (16)
Masur, Harold Q
Scott Jordan series (12)
Mourning for flamingoes
Burke, James Lee
Dave Robicheaux series (4)
Mourning into dancing
Lee, Laurel
Godspeed series (4)
Mourning is red
Pike, Charles R
Jubal Cade series (16)
Mourning raga
Peters, Ellis
Inspector George Felse series (9)
Mouse and Mole
Dunbar, Joyce
Mouse and Mole series (1)
Mouse and Mole have a party
Dunbar, Joyce
Mouse and Mole series (2)
Mouse and the motorcycle
Cleary, Beverly
Ralph S Mouse series (1)
Mouse ballet
Crump, Fred H
Mouse series (2)
Mouse book
Piers, Helen
Two hungry mice trilogy (3)
Mouse gets caught
Hargreaves, Roger
Hippo, Potto and Mouse series (2)
Mouse in school
Gibson, Gloria
Rachel Payne series (2)
Mouse in the attic
Gibson, Gloria
Rachel Payne series (1)
Mouse in the manse
Derwent, Lavinia
Border series (6)
Mouse looks for a friend
Piers, Helen
Two hungry mice trilogy (2)
Mouse looks for a house
Piers, Helen
Two hungry mice trilogy (1)
Mouse mess
Szekeres, Cyndy
Tiny paw series (5)
Mouse numbers and letters
Arnosky, Jim
Mouse series (1)
Mouse on the moon
Wibberley, Leonard
Grand Fenwick series (3)
Mouse on Wall Street
Wibberley, Leonard
Grand Fenwick series (4)
Mouse opera house
Crump, Fred H
Mouse series (1)
Mouse outings
Miller, Margaret Jessy
Willow and Albert series (8)
Mouse ran up my nightie
Courtney, Edith
Swansea series (1)
Mouse soup
Lobel, Arnold
Mouse series (2)
Mouse tales
Lobel, Arnold
Mouse series (1)
Miller, Margaret Jessy
Willow and Albert series (1)
Mouse telegram
Uttley, Alison
Little Brown Mouse series (10)
Mouse that roared
Wibberley, Leonard
Grand Fenwick series (2)
Mouse that saved the West
Wibberley, Leonard
Grand Fenwick series (5)
Mouse trapped
Dengler, Sandy
Mirage mysteries series (2)
Mouse wedding
Cartlidge, Michelle
Mouse series (5)
Mouse who wouldn't play ball
Gilbert, Anthony
Arthur Crook series (12)
Mouse Woman and the mischief-makers
Harris, Christie
Mouse Woman series (2)
Mouse Woman and the muddleheads
Harris, Christie
Mouse Woman series (3)
Mouse Woman and the vanished princesses
Harris, Christie
Mouse Woman series (1)
Mouse writing
Arnosky, Jim
Mouse series (2)
Mousekin finds a friend
Miller, Edna
Mousekin series (2)
Mousekin takes a trip
Miller, Edna
Mousekin series (7)
Mousekin's ABC's
Miller, Edna
Mousekin series (4)
Mousekin's birth
Miller, Edna
Mousekin series (10)
Mousekin's Christmas Eve
Miller, Edna
Mousekin series (5)
Mousekin's close call
Miller, Edna
Mousekin series (9)
Mousekin's Easter basket
Miller, Edna
Mousekin series (14)
Mousekin's fables
Miller, Edna
Mousekin series (11)
Mousekin's family
Miller, Edna
Mousekin series (3)
Mousekin's frosty friend
Miller, Edna
Mousekin series (15)
Mousekin's golden house
Miller, Edna
Mousekin series (1)
Mousekin's lost woodland
Miller, Edna
Mousekin series (16)
Mousekin's mystery
Miller, Edna
Mousekin series (12)
Mousekin's Thanksgiving
Miller, Edna
Mousekin series (13)
Mousekin's woodland birthday
Miller, Edna
Mousekin series (6)
Mousekin's woodland sleepers
Miller, Edna
Mousekin series (8)
Mouse's Christmas house
Cartlidge, Michelle
Mouse series (4)
Mouse's diary
Cartlidge, Michelle
Mouse series (1)
Mousetrap, and other stories
Christie, Agatha
Hercule Poirot series (38)
Miss Jane Marple series (14)

Mousewing
Mayne, William
Animal library series (8)
Mousework
Cartlidge, Michelle
Mouse series (2)
Mousme
Holland, Clive
Mousme series (2)
Mouthful of sand
Meek, Margaret Reid Duncan
Lennox Kemp series (6)
Mouthpiece of Zitu
Giesy, John Ulrich
Jason Croft trilogy (2)
Mouths
Bailey, Jill
Animals of course series (2)
Move fast, brother
Spade, Danny
Danny Spade series (7)
Move for Charlie
Allen, Joy
Charlie series (3)
Move in the dark
Carter, Nicholas
Nicholas Carter series (103)
Move on Miss Mayhem
Brody, Marc
Marc Brody series (53)
Movement on the sofa
Harewood, Jocelyn
Peregrine Merritt series (2)
Movie
Hall, Parnell
Stanley Hastings series (10)
Movie boys and the flood
Appleton, Victor
Movie boys series (6)
Movie boys and the wreckers
Appleton, Victor
Movie boys series (3)
Movie boys at Seaside Park
Appleton, Victor
Movie boys series (12)
Movie boys at the big fair
Appleton, Victor
Movie boys series (16)
Movie boys' first showhouse
Appleton, Victor
Movie boys series (11)
Movie boys in earthquake land
Appleton, Victor
Movie boys series (5)
Movie boys in peril
Appleton, Victor
Movie boys series (7)
Movie boys in the jungle
Appleton, Victor
Movie boys series (4)
Movie boys in the Wild West
Appleton, Victor
Movie boys series (2)
Movie boys' new idea
Appleton, Victor
Movie boys series (15)
Movie boys on Broadway
Appleton, Victor
Movie boys series (13)
Movie boys on call
Appleton, Victor
Movie boys series (1)
Movie boys' outdoor exhibition
Appleton, Victor
Movie boys series (14)
Movie boys under fire
Appleton, Victor
Movie boys series (9)
Movie boys under the sea
Appleton, Victor
Movie boys series (8)
Movie boys under Uncle Sam
Appleton, Victor
Movie boys series (10)
Movie boys' war spectacle
Appleton, Victor
Movie boys series (17)
Movie magic
Daniel Mark
Ghostbusters series (2)
Movie mystery
Armour, R Coutts
Sexton Blake series (457)
Movie shoes
Streatfeild, Noel
Shoes series (6)
Moving cage
Gilman, George G
Edge series (47)
Moving day
Margolin, Harriet
Days series (1)
Reeder, Colin
West Meadow series (2)
Szekeres, Cyndy
Tiny paw series (3)
Moving day in Feather Town
Martin, Ann Matthews
Feather Town series (2)
Moving finger
Barrington, John
Ken Williams series (1)
Christie, Agatha
Miss Jane Marple series (4)
Fitzsimmons, Cortland
Ethel Thomas series (2)
Lincoln, Natalie Sumner
Inspector Mitchell series (4)
Moving graveyard
Avallone, Michael
Ed Noon series (23)
Moving house
Jessel, Camilla
Chatterbooks series (2)
Petty, Kate
First timers series (2)
Moving moosevan
Palmer, Jane
Planet dweller series (2)
Moving on
McMurtry, Larry
Urban trilogy (1)
Moving picture boys
Appleton, Victor
Movie boys series (1)
Moving picture boys series (1)
Moving picture boys and the flood
Appleton, Victor
Movie boys series (6)
Moving picture boys series (6)
Moving picture boys at Panama
Appleton, Victor
Movie boys series (7)
Moving picture boys series (7)
Moving picture boys at Seaside Park
Appleton, Victor
Moving picture boys series (12)
Moving picture boys' first showhouse
Appleton, Victor
Moving picture boys series (11)
Moving picture boys in earthquake land
Appleton, Victor
Movie boys series (5)
Moving picture boys series (5)
Moving picture boys in the jungle
Appleton, Victor
Movie boys series (4)
Moving picture boys series (4)
Moving picture boys in the West
Appleton, Victor
Movie boys series (2)
Moving picture boys series (2)
Moving picture boys' new idea
Appleton, Victor
Moving picture boys series (15)
Moving picture boys on Broadway
Appleton, Victor
Moving picture boys series (13)
Moving picture boys on French battlefields
Appleton, Victor
Movie boys series (10)
Moving picture boys series (10)
Moving picture boys on the coast
Appleton, Victor
Movie boys series (3)
Moving picture boys series (3)
Moving picture boys on the war front
Appleton, Victor
Movie boys series (9)
Moving picture boys series (9)
Moving picture boys under the sea
Appleton, Victor
Movie boys series (8)
Moving picture boys series (8)
Moving picture girls
Hope, Laura Lee
Moving picture girls series (1)
Moving picture girls at Oak Farm
Hope, Laura Lee
Moving picture girls series (2)
Moving picture girls at Rocky Ranch
Hope, Laura Lee
Moving picture girls series (5)
Moving picture girls at sea
Hope, Laura Lee
Moving picture girls series (6)
Moving picture girls in war plays
Hope, Laura Lee
Moving picture girls series (7)
Moving picture girls snowbound
Hope, Laura Lee
Moving picture girls series (3)
Moving picture girls under the palms
Hope, Laura Lee
Moving picture girls series (4)
Moving picture mystery
Carter, Nicholas
Nicholas Carter series (476)
Moving picture writes
Chambers, Peter
Mark Preston series (34)
Moving pictures
Pratchett, Terry
Discworld series (10)
Moving stone
Fraser, Christine Marion
Light on Dumyat series (3)
Moving target
Keene, Carolyn
Nancy Drew files series (87)
Macdonald, Ross
Lew Archer series (1)
Moving targets
Reynolds, William J
Nebraska series (2)
Moving tent
Passmore, Richard
Blenheim boy series (2)
Moving too fast
Cooper, M E
Couples series (5)
Moving toyshop
Crispin, Edmund
Gervase Fen series (3)
Moving up
Davis, Leslie
Cheerleaders series (35)
Mox
Grant, Maxwell
Shadow series (42)
Mozart score
Leather, Edwin
Rupert Conway series (2)
Mrs Appleyard and I
Kent, Louise Andrews
Appleyard family series (6)
Mrs Appleyard's family kitchen
Kent, Louise Andrews
Appleyard family series (6)
Mrs Appleyard's kitchen
Kent, Louise Andrews
Appleyard family series (2)
Mrs Appleyard's summer kitchen
Kent, Louise Andrews
Appleyard family series (4)
Mrs Appleyard's winter kitchen
Kent, Louise Andrews
Appleyard family series (5)
Mrs Appleyard's year
Kent, Louise Andrews
Appleyard family series (1)
Mrs 'Arris
Poultney, Clifford Blake
Mrs 'Arris series (1)
Mrs 'Arris again
Poultney, Clifford Blake
Mrs 'Arris series (3)
Mrs 'Arris carries on
Poultney, Clifford Blake
Mrs 'Arris series (5)
Mrs 'Arris goes to Moscow
Gallico, Paul
Mrs Harris series (4)
Mrs 'Arris goes to New York
Gallico, Paul
Mrs Harris series (2)
Mrs 'Arris goes to Paris
Gallico, Paul
Mrs Harris series (1)
Mrs 'Arris goes to Parliament
Gallico, Paul
Mrs Harris series (3)
Mrs Babcary goes to sea
Goldsmith, John
Mrs Babcary series (1)
Mrs Babcary goes to town
Goldsmith, John
Mrs Babcary series (2)
Mrs Babcary goes west
Goldsmith, John
Mrs Babcary series (3)
Mrs Babcary's driving machine
Goldsmith, John
Mrs Babcary series (6)
Mrs Babcary's steam car
Goldsmith, John
Mrs Babcary series (5)
Mrs Babcary's treat
Goldsmith, John
Mrs Babcary series (4)
Mrs Benger carries on
Lax, William Henry
Poplar series (4)
Mrs Betsey
Marton, Francesca
Jordan family series (2)
Mrs Bindle
Jenkins, Herbert
Bindle series (4)
Mrs Blood
Thomas, Audrey
Isobel Cleary series (2)
Mrs Boffy's birthday
Furminger, Jo
Mary, Ben and William series (2)
Mrs Boffy's dreadful day
Furminger, Jo
Mary, Ben and William series (6)
Mrs Bridge
Connell, Evan Shelby
Bridge series (1)
Mrs Bridges' story
Hardwick, Mollie
Upstairs, downstairs series (9)
Mrs Brown's pearls
Crabb, Arthur
Samuel Lyle series (2)
Mrs Bubble's baby
Mahy, Margaret
Crocodile series (3)
Mrs Budley falls from grace
Chesney, Marion
Poor relation series (3)
Mrs Cliff's yacht
Stockton, Frank Richard
Captain Horn series (2)
Mrs Cobbit and the ice-cream man
Dillon, Deidre
Trumpton series (2)
Mrs Coverlet's detectives
Nash, Mary
Mrs Coverlet series (3)
Mrs Coverlet's magicians
Nash, Mary
Mrs Coverlet series (2)
Mrs Craggs, crimes cleaned up
Keating, Henry Reymond Fitzwalter
Mrs Craggs series (2)
Mrs Dale
Antony, Jonquil
Dale family series (1)
Mrs Dale at home
Antony, Jonquil
Dale family series (3)
Mrs Dale's bedside book
Antony, Jonquil
Dale family series (3)
Mrs Dale's friendship book
Antony, Jonquil
Dale family series (3)
Mrs Dalloway
Woolf, Virginia
Mrs Dalloway series (2)
Mrs Dalloway's party
Woolf, Virginia
Mrs Dalloway series (3)
Mrs De Winter
Hill, Susan
Rebecca De Winter series (2)
Mrs Donald Dyke, detective
Rockwood, Harry
Donald Dyke series (4)
Mrs Dose, the doctor's wife
Dennys, Joyce
Dose series (1)
Mrs Easter and the Golden Bounder
Drummond, Violet Hilda
Mrs Easter series (3)
Mrs Easter and the storks
Drummond, Violet Hilda
Mrs Easter series (2)
Mrs Easter's Christmas flight
Drummond, Violet Hilda
Mrs Easter series (4)
Mrs Easter's parasol
Drummond, Violet Hilda
Mrs Easter series (1)
Mrs Fluster and family
Ogden, Angela
Mrs Fluster series (1)
Mrs Fluster's circus
Ogden, Angela
Mrs Fluster series (2)
Mrs Frisby and the rats of NIMH
O'Brien, Robert C
NIMH series (1)
Mrs Gaddy and the fast-growing vine
Gage, Wilson
Mrs Gaddy series (3)
Mrs Gaddy and the ghost
Gage, Wilson
Mrs Gaddy series (1)
Mrs Gray Bunny's children
Crabb, Minnie Rowe
Gray Bunny series (1)
Mrs Green
Rynd, Evelyne Elise
Mrs Green series (1)
Mrs Green again
Rynd, Evelyne Elise
Mrs Green series (2)
Mrs Grundy at home
James, Charles Thomas Clement
Mrs Grundy series (2)
Mrs Harris goes to Moscow
Gallico, Paul
Mrs Harris series (4)
Mrs Harris goes to New York
Gallico, Paul
Mrs Harris series (2)
Mrs Harris, M.P.
Gallico, Paul
Mrs Harris series (3)
Mrs Jim and Mrs Jimmie
Conrad, Stephen
Mrs Jim series (2)
Mrs Jolly's joke shop
Ahlberg, Allan
Happy family series (16)
Mrs Keats Bradford
Pool, Maria Louise
Roweny series (2)
Mrs Keith Hamilton, M.B.
Swan, Annie Shepherd
Elizabeth Glen series (2)
Mrs Lancelot
Hewlett, Maurice
Mrs Lancelot series (1)
Mrs Lather's laundry
Ahlberg, Allan
Happy family series (10)
Mrs May
Le Breton, Thomas
Mrs May series (1)
Mrs May's latest
Le Breton, Thomas
Mrs May series (6)
Mrs May's lectures
Le Breton, Thomas
Mrs May series (4)
Mrs McGinty's dead
Christie, Agatha
Hercule Poirot series (27)
Mrs Ariadne Oliver series (3)
Mrs McNab and the pirates
Lockhart, John Gilbert
Mrs McNab series (1)
Mrs McNab goes west
Lockhart, John Gilbert
Mrs McNab series (2)
Mrs Meeker's money
Disney, Doris Miles
David Madden series (3)
Mrs Meigs and Mister Cunningham
Corbett, Elizabeth
Mrs Meigs series (4)
Mrs Mouse spring-cleans
Uttley, Alison
Little Brown Mouse series (5)
Mrs Murdock takes a case
Coxe, George Harmon
Kent Murdock series (6)
Mrs Murphy's underpants
Brown, Fredric
Ed and Am Hunter series (7)
Mrs Nibble
Pilgrim, Jane
Blackberry Farm series (2)
Mrs Nibble moves house
Pilgrim, Jane
Blackberry Farm series (15)
Mrs Noah and the animals
Brook, Judy
Noah series (2)
Mrs Noah's ABC 123
Brook, Judy
Noah series (3)
Mrs Pargeter's package
Brett, Simon
Mrs Melita Pargeter series (3)
Mrs Pargeter's pound of flesh
Brett, Simon
Mrs Melita Pargeter series (4)
Mrs Pepperpot again, and other stories
Proysen, Alf
Mrs Pepperpot series (2)
Mrs Pepperpot in the Magic Wood, and other stories
Proysen, Alf
Mrs Pepperpot series (4)
Mrs Pepperpot to the rescue, and other stories
Proysen, Alf
Mrs Pepperpot series (3)
Mrs Pepperpot's busy day
Proysen, Alf
Mrs Pepperpot series (5)

Mrs Pepperpot's outing, and other stories
Proysen, Alf
Mrs Pepperpot series (6)
Mrs Pepperpot's year
Proysen, Alf
Mrs Pepperpot series (7)
Mrs Peter Rabbit
Burgess, Thornton Waldo
Green Meadow series (2)
Mrs Pig gets cross, and other stories
Rayner, Mary
Mister and Mrs Pig series (4)
Mrs Piggle-Wiggle
Macdonald, Betty
Mrs Piggle-Wiggle series (1)
Mrs Piggle-Wiggle's farm
Macdonald, Betty
Mrs Piggle-Wiggle series (3)
Mrs Piggle-Wiggle's magic
Macdonald, Betty
Mrs Piggle-Wiggle series (2)
Mrs Pig's bulk buy
Rayner, Mary
Mister and Mrs Pig series (3)
Mrs Pinny and the blowing day
Morgan, Helen
Mrs Pinny series (1)
Mrs Pinny and the salty sea day
Morgan, Helen
Mrs Pinny series (3)
Mrs Pinny and the sudden snow
Morgan, Helen
Mrs Pinny series (2)
Mrs Plug the plumber
Ahlberg, Allan
Happy family series (5)
Mrs Pollifax and the Golden Triangle
Gilman, Dorothy
Mrs Emily Pollifax series (8)
Mrs Pollifax and the Hong Kong Buddha
Gilman, Dorothy
Mrs Emily Pollifax series (7)
Mrs Pollifax and the second thief
Gilman, Dorothy
Mrs Emily Pollifax series (10)
Mrs Pollifax and the whirling dervish
Gilman, Dorothy
Mrs Emily Pollifax series (9)
Mrs Pollifax on safari
Gilman, Dorothy
Mrs Emily Pollifax series (5)
Mrs Pollifax on the China station
Gilman, Dorothy
Mrs Emily Pollifax series (6)
Mrs Pollifax pursued
Gilman, Dorothy
Mrs Emily Pollifax series (11)
Mrs Pollifax, spy
Gilman, Dorothy
Mrs Emily Pollifax series (1)
Mrs Pooter's diary
Waterhouse, Keith
Nobody series (2)
Mrs Porter's letter
McConnell, Vicki P
Nyla Wade series (2)
Mrs Potato Head's new hat
Slier, Debby
Potato Head series (2)
Mrs Pottleton's bridge parties
Tuite, Hugh
Pottleton series (1)
Mrs, presumed dead
Brett, Simon
Mrs Melita Pargeter series (2)
Mrs Pym, and other stories
Morland, Nigel
Mrs Palmyra Pym series (23)
Mrs Pym of Scotland Yard
Morland, Nigel
Mrs Palmyra Pym series (13)
Mrs Red Pepper
Richmond, Grace Smith
Red Pepper Burns series (2)
Mrs Ross
Nicolson, Robert
Mrs Ross series (1)
Mrs Rushworth
Gordon, Victor
Mansfield Park series (3)
Mrs Sherwood's summer
Toms, Patricia
Chronicles of Pennycress series (1)
Mrs Simkin and the groovy old gramophone
Allen, Linda
Mrs Simkin series (3)
Mrs Simkin and the magic wheelbarrow
Allen, Linda
Mrs Simkin series (2)
Mrs Simkin and the very big mushroom
Allen, Linda
Mrs Simkin series (1)
Mrs Simkin and the wishing well
Allen, Linda
Mrs Simkin series (4)
Mrs Slimtails goes shopping
Chell, Mary
Slimtails series (7)
Mrs Squirrel and Hazel
Pilgrim, Jane
Blackberry Farm series (13)
Mrs Tim
Stevenson, Dorothy Emily
Mrs Tim series (2)
Mrs Tim carries on
Stevenson, Dorothy Emily
Mrs Tim series (3)
Mrs Tim Christie
Stevenson, Dorothy Emily
Mrs Tim series (1)
Mrs Tim flies home
Stevenson, Dorothy Emily
Mrs Tim series (5)
Mrs Tim gets a job
Stevenson, Dorothy Emily
Mrs Tim series (4)
Mrs Tim of the Regiment
Stevenson, Dorothy Emily
Mrs Tim series (1)
Mrs Toggle and the dinosaur
Pulver, Robin
Mrs Toggle series (2)
Mrs Toggle's beautiful blue shoe
Pulver, Robin
Mrs Toggle series (3)
Mrs Toggle's zipper
Pulver, Robin
Mrs Toggle series (1)
Mrs Tree
Richards, Laura Elizabeth
Mrs Tree series (1)
Mrs Tree's will
Richards, Laura Elizabeth
Mrs Tree series (2)
Mrs Vanderstein's jewels
Bryce, Charles, *Mrs*
Mister Gimblet series (1)
Mrs Warrender's profession
Cole, George Douglas Howard
Mrs Elizabeth Warrender series (1)
Mrs Warren's daughter
Johnston, Harry Hamilton
Mrs Warren series (2)
Mrs Warren's profession
Shaw, George Bernard
Mrs Warren series (1)
Mrs Wiggs of the Cabbage Patch
Rice, Alice Hegan
Mrs Wiggs series (1)
Mrs William Horton speaking
Kilbourne, Fannie
William Horton series (2)
Mrs Wobble the waitress
Ahlberg, Allan
Happy family series (6)
Ms Quarterback
Pascal, Francine
Sweet Valley High series (70)
Much ado about Aldo
Hurwitz, Johanna
Aldo Sossi series (1)
Much ado in Maggody
Hess, Joan
Arly Hanks series (3)
Much-adored Sandy Shore
Hunt, Angela Elwell
Cassie Perkins series (5)
Much in evidence
Cecil, Henry
Mister Tewkesbury series (3)
Much obliged, Jeeves
Wodehouse, Pelham Grenville
Jeeves and Bertie Wooster series (14)
Mucker
Burroughs, Edgar Rice
Mucker series (1)
Mucker series (2)
Muckfield and the muckoid menace
Pressman, Lee
Muckfield series (2)
Muckfield's midnight monster match
Pressman, Lee
Muckfield series (1)
Mucking round five continents over fifty years
Mitchison, Naomi
Small talk series (4)
Mud in his eye
Hammond, Gerald
Beau Pepys series (3)
Mud larks
Garstin, Crosbie
Mud larks series (1)
Mud larks again
Garstin, Crosbie
Mud larks series (2)
Muddle-headed wombat
Park, Ruth
Muddle-headed wombat series (1)
Muddle-headed wombat and the bush band
Park, Ruth
Muddle-headed wombat series (9)
Muddle-headed wombat and the invention
Park, Ruth
Muddle-headed wombat series (10)
Muddle-headed wombat at school
Park, Ruth
Muddle-headed wombat series (4)
Muddle-headed wombat in the snow
Park, Ruth
Muddle-headed wombat series (5)
Muddle-headed wombat in the spring-time
Park, Ruth
Muddle-headed wombat series (7)
Muddle-headed wombat in the treetops
Park, Ruth
Muddle-headed wombat series (3)
Muddle-headed wombat is very bad
Park, Ruth
Muddle-headed wombat series (12)
Muddle-headed wombat on a rainy day
Park, Ruth
Muddle-headed wombat series (6)
Muddle-headed wombat on clean-up day
Park, Ruth
Muddle-headed wombat series (11)
Muddle-headed wombat on holiday
Park, Ruth
Muddle-headed wombat series (2)
Muddle-headed wombat on the river
Park, Ruth
Muddle-headed wombat series (8)
Muddle-headed wombat stays at home
Park, Ruth
Muddle-headed wombat series (13)
Mudd's angels
Blish, James
Star trek original series (13)
Muddy boots and Sunday suits
Archer, Fred
Evesham Vale series (5)
Mudflats of the dead
Mitchell, Gladys
Dame Beatrice Bradley series (56)
Mudhen
Allen, Merritt Parmelee
Mudhen series (1)
Mudhen acts naturally
Allen, Merritt Parmelee
Mudhen series (3)
Mudhen and the walrus
Allen, Merritt Parmelee
Mudhen series (2)
Mudlarks and mysteries
Knight, Frank
Chichester Harbour series (1)
Mudtime and more Nathaniel stories
Arnosky, Jim
Nathaniel series (2)
Muffin and Louise
Mills, Annette
Merry Muffin series (1)
Muffin and Peregrine
Mills, Annette
Merry Muffin series (2)
Muffin and the magic hat
Mills, Annette
Muffin series (3)
Muffin at the seaside
Mills, Annette
Muffin series (5)
Muffin climbs high
Hogarth, Ann
Merry Muffin series (4)
Muffin sings a song
Hogarth, Ann
Merry Muffin series (5)
Muffin the mule
Mills, Annette
Muffin series (1)
Muffin's birthday
Mills, Annette
Merry Muffin series (3)
Muffin's splendid adventure
Mills, Annette
Muffin series (6)
Muffin's thinking cap
Hogarth, Ann
Merry Muffin series (6)
Muffkins on parade
Beers, Victor Gilbert
Muffkin series (2)
Muffletump storybook
Wahl, Jan
Muffletump series (2)
Muffletumps
Wahl, Jan
Muffletump series (1)
Muffletumps' Christmas party
Wahl, Jan
Muffletump series (3)
Muffletumps' Halloween scare
Wahl, Jan
Muffletump series (4)
Mugger
McBain, Ed
Eighty Seventh Precinct series (2)
Mugger blood
Murphy, Warren Burton
Destroyer series (30)
Muggers
Grant, Maxwell
Shadow series (245)
Mugger's day
Bagby, George
Inspector Schmidt series (46)
Muir's blood
Larson, Charles
Nils-Frederick Blixen series (3)
Mulatto
Wilson, Jeanne
Island trilogy (3)
Mulberry leaf
Marshall, May
Sister Madge Stillworthy series (1)
Mule on the motorway
Berna, Paul
Bobby Thiriet series (2)
Mule twins
Hogan, Inez
Twins series (5)
Mullah from Kashmir
Macneil, Duncan
James Ogilvie series (8)
Mulliner nights
Wodehouse, Pelham Grenville
Mister Mulliner series (3)
Multiface
Adlard, Mark
Jan Caspol trilogy (3)
Multi-million dollar murders
Mason, Francis Van Wyck
Colonel Hugh North series (22)
Multiple choice
Blake, Susan
Hawthorne College series (10)
Multiple murder
Macrae, Travis
Jim and Kate Harris series (2)
Multitude of monsters
Gardner, Craig Shaw
Ebenezum series (2)
Multitude of sins
Wren, M K
Conan Flagg series (2)
Mulvane on the prod
Heuman, William
Grady Mulvane series (6)
Mulvane's war
Heuman, William
Grady Mulvane series (5)
Mum and dad
Wensell, Ulises
Jackson family series (2)
Mumbo jumbo
Reed, Ishmael
Papa LaBas series (1)
Mumfie marches on
Tozer, Katharine
Mumfie series (6)
Mumfie the admiral
Tozer, Katharine
Mumfie series (3)
Mumfie's magic box
Tozer, Katharine
Mumfie series (4)
Mumfie's picture book
Tozer, Katharine
Mumfie series (6)
Mumfie's Uncle Samuel
Tozer, Katharine
Mumfie series (5)
Mummy case
Dixon, Franklin W
Hardy boys series (63)
Peters, Elizabeth
Amelia Peabody Emerson series (3)
Mummy is a health visitor
Harper, Anita
Daddy and mummy series (2)
Mummy know best
Kraus, Robert
Mummy series (1)
Mummy monster game
Pond, Roy
Mummy series (1)
Mummy runs a cafe
Harper, Anita
Daddy and mummy series (1)
Mummy, the will and the crypt
Bellairs, John
Blue figurine trilogy (2)
Johnny Dixon series (2)
Mummy tomb hunt
Pond, Roy
Mummy series (2)
Mummy vanishes
Kraus, Robert
Mummy series (2)
Mummy walks
Luigi, Belli
Vernon Templeton series (1)
Mummy, who is your husband?
Campbell, Ross
Marriage series (2)
Mummy's curse
Stine, Megan
Young Indiana Jones chronicles series (1)
Mummy's secret
Mooser, Stephen
Treasure hound series (2)
Mum's girl was no lady
Bloom, Ursula
No lady series (7)
Mum's home
Ormerod, Jan
New baby books series (4)
Mum's the word
Cannell, Dorothy
Ellie Simons Haskell series (4)
Mum's the word for murder
Baker, Asa
Jerry Burke series (1)
Munch Bunch
Reed, Giles
Munch Bunch series (1)
Munch Bunch at the seaside
Reed, Giles
Munch Bunch series (3)
Munch Bunch goes camping
Reed, Giles
Munch Bunch series (2)
Munch Bunch have a party
Reed, Giles
Munch Bunch series (4)
Munch Bunch welcomes new friends
Reed, Giles
Munch Bunch series (5)
Munchausen at the Pole
Raspe, Rudolf Erich
Baron Munchausen series (7)
Munchausen at Walcheron
Raspe, Rudolf Erich
Baron Munchausen series (4)
Munchausen XX
Worfel, W G
Baron Munchausen series (9)
Munde and his friends
Odaga, Asenath
Munde series (1)
Munde goes to the market
Odaga, Asenath
Munde series (2)
Mungo Dabney
Street, James
Dabney family series (5)
Munich involvement
Mullally, Frederic
Bob Sullivan series (2)
Munitions master
Robeson, Kenneth
Doc Savage series (58)
Munitions ship murders
Mason, Francis Van Wyck
Colonel Hugh North series (10)
Munsters
Cooper, Morton
Munsters series (1)
Munsters and the great camera caper
Johnston, William
Munsters series (2)
Murder
Adams, Harold
Carl Wilcox series (1)
Hall, Parnell
Stanley Hastings series (2)
Janson, Hank
Hank Janson series (43)
Murder a day
Avery, Robert
Joe Kelly series (1)

Murder a la mode
Moyes, Patricia
Henry and Emmy Tibbett series (4)
Murder a la Richelieu
Blackmon, Anita
Adelaide Adams series (1)
Murder a la Stroganoff
Brahms, Caryl
Inspector Adam Quill series (2)
Stroganoff Troupe series (2)
Murder a mile high
Dean, Elizabeth
Emma Marsh and Hank Fairbanks series (3)
Murder abroad
Punshon, Ernest Robertson
Bobby Owen series (13)
Murder across and down
Resnicow, Herbert
Crossword series (1)
Murder adrift
Bellairs, George
Detective Inspector Thomas Littlejohn series (52)
Murder after a fashion
Dean, Spencer
Don Cadee series (8)
Murder after hours
Christie, Agatha
Hercule Poirot series (24)
Murder after tea-time
Cutter, Leela
Lettie Winterbottom series (1)
Murder after the blitz
Piper, Peter
Inspector Gray series (1)
Murder against the grain
Lathen, Emma
John Putnam Thatcher series (6)
Murder al fresco
Jones, Jennifer
Daisy Jane Mott series (2)
Murder all over
Adams, Cleve Franklin
Rex McBride series (4)
Murder among children
Coe, Tucker
Mitchell Tobin series (2)
Murder among friends
Lewis, Lange
Lieutenant Richard Tuck series (1)
McConnell, Frank
Harry Garnish and Bridget O'Toole series (1)
Murder among members
Carnac, Carol
Inspector Julian Rivers series (12)
Murder among the Angells
Scarlett, Roger
Inspector Kane series (4)
Murder among the dying
Jones, G Wayman
Black Bat series (23)
Murder among the nudists
Hunt, Peter
Alan Miller series (3)
Murder among thieves
Alding, Peter
C.I.D. Room series (3)
Murder among those present
Mace, Helen
Noel Vickery series (1)
Murder among us
Granger, Ann
Meredith Mitchell and Chief Inspector Alan Markby series (4)
Murder, and Ariadne
Wray, I
Inspector Digby series (2)
Murder and blueberry pie
Lockridge, Frances
Nathan Shapiro series (3)
Murder and chips
Mantell, Laurie
Sergeant Steve Arrow and Chief Inspector Peacock series (3)
Murder and Co.
Gray, Berkeley
Norman Conquest series (38)
Murder and gardenias
Neville, Margot
Inspector Grogan and Sergeant Manning series (2)
Murder and magic
Garrett, Randall
Lord Darcy series (2)
Murder and marigold
Brandon, Gordon
Michael and Terry Terence series (6)
Murder and Miss Ming
Hambledon, Phyllis
Inspector Tubby Hall series (2)
Murder and poor Jenny
Neville, Margot
Inspector Grogan and Sergeant Manning series (8)
Murder and the First Lady
Roosevelt, Elliott
Eleanor Roosevelt series (1)
Murder and the married virgin
Halliday, Brett
Michael Shayne series (10)
Murder and the red-haired girl
Balfour, Hearnden
Inspector Jack Strickland series (3)
Murder and the wanton bride
Halliday, Brett
Michael Shayne series (31)
Murder anonymous
Gilbert, Anthony
Arthur Crook series (45)
Murder arranged
Philips, Judson Pentecost
Peter Styles series (15)
Thomson, Basil
Superintendent Richardson series (8)
Murder as a fine art
Bonnamy, Francis
Peter Shane series (6)
Carnac, Carol
Inspector Julian Rivers series (9)
Murder as an ornament
Boniface, Marjorie
Sheriff Hiram Odom series (1)
Murder as arranged
Cross, Mark
Daphne Wrayne and her Four Adjusters series (19)
Murder as the curtain rises
Philips, Judson Pentecost
Peter Styles series (18)
Murder at a cottage
Daniel, Roland
Buddy Mustard series (7)
Murder at Arroways
Reilly, Helen
Inspector Christopher McKee series (20)
Murder at Avalon Arms
Jerome, Owen Fox
Philip Maccray series (3)
Murder at Bador
Mason, S C
Derek Glover series (1)
Murder at Brambles
Collins, Gilbert
Hugh Carding series (2)
Murder at Bratton Grange
Rhode, John
Doctor Lancelot Priestley series (7)
Murder at bridge
Austin, Anne
James F Dundee series (4)
Murder at Brownhill
Plummer, Thomas Arthur
Detective Inspector Andrew Frampton series (50)
Murder at Buzzard's Bay
Abbot, Anthony
Thatcher Colt series (7)
Murder at Castle Deeping
Johns, William Earl
Steeley Delaroy series (4)
Murder at Coney Island
O'Hanlon, James
Jason Cordrey series (3)
Murder at Covent Garden
Makin, William James
Inspector Evans series (1)
Murder at Deer Lick
Cunningham, Albert Benjamin
Sheriff Jess Roden series (1)
Murder at Derivale
Rhode, John
Doctor Lancelot Priestley series (66)
Murder at Endor
Wolff, William Almon
Lieutenant Charley Mitchell series (2)
Murder at Fenwold
Bush, Christopher
Ludovic Travers series (3)
Murder at full moon
Makin, William James
Inspector Graves series (2)
Murder at god's gate
Robinson, Lynda S
Lord Meren series (2)
Murder at Government House
Huxley, Elspeth
Superintendent Vachell series (1)
Murder at Grassmere Abbey
Dix, Maurice Buxton
Inspector James Miller series (1)
Murder at H.Q.
Hawton, Hector
Asmun Hill series (1)
Murder at Hermit's Cottage
Hardinge, Rex
Sexton Blake series (889)
Murder at high noon
McGuire, Paul
Chief Inspector Cummings series (3)
Superintendent Fillinger series (6)
Murder at high tide
Booth, Charles Gordon
Anatole Flique series (1)
Murder at Hobcaw Barony
Roosevelt, Elliott
Eleanor Roosevelt series (3)
Murder at Horsethief
O'Hanlon, James
Jason Cordrey series (5)
Murder at Lancaster Gate
Grierson, Francis Durham
Inspector Sims and Professor Wells series (10)
Murder at Landred Hall
Turner, James Ernest
Rampion Savage series (1)
Murder at Lantern Corner
Plummer, Thomas Arthur
Detective Inspector Andrew Frampton series (45)
Murder at Lilac Cottage
Rhode, John
Doctor Lancelot Priestley series (33)
Murder at Lintercombe
Greig, Ian
Inspector Swinton series (3)
Murder at Little Malling
Daniel, Roland
Inspector Jack Pearson series (4)
Murder at Littlegreen House
Christie, Agatha
Hercule Poirot series (15)
Murder at Malibu
O'Hanlon, James
Jason Cordrey series (1)
Murder at Maneuvers
Howes, Royce
Captain Ben Lucias series (3)
Murder at Manor House
Gorell, Ronald Gorell Barnes
Inspector Gordon Ross series (2)
Murder at Marble Arch
Holt, Gavin
Professor Luther Bastion series (4)
Murder at Markenden Court
Stanners, Harold H
Professor Harding series (1)
Murder at Marlington
Plummer, Thomas Arthur
Detective Inspector Andrew Frampton series (34)
Murder at Marston Manor
Forsythe, Robin
Anthony Vereker series (5)
Murder at Mavering
Gorell, Ronald Gorell Barnes
Inspector Maurice Hepburn series (3)
Murder at Melton Peveril
Ashton, Charles
Jack Atherley series (8)
Murder at mid-day
Hocking, Anne
Inspector William Austen series (25)
Murder at midnight
Allan, Luke
Tiger Lillie series (2)
Gregg, Cecil Freeman
Inspector Cuthbert Higgins series (25)
Walling, Robert Alfred John
Garstang series (2)
Philip Tolefree series (2)
Murder at Mocking House
Brown, Walter C
Inspector Stephen Harper series (3)
Murder at Monk's Farm
Waye, Cecil
Christopher Perrin series (2)
Murder at Monticello
Brown, Rita Mae
Mrs Murphy series (3)
Murder at Moose Jaw
Heald, Tim
Simon Bognor series (6)
Murder at morning prayers
Landon, Hilary
Timothy Drewer series (1)
Murder at Mornington
Carnac, Carol
Inspector Ryvet series (3)
Murder at Musket Beach
Lee, Bernie
Tony and Pat Pratt series (1)
Murder at out-patients
Eyles, Alfred W
Paul Chisholm series (4)
Murder at Plenders
Everton, Francis
Inspector George Annesley series (1)
Murder at Plum's
Myers, Amy
Auguste Didier series (3)
Murder at Radio City
Morland, Nigel
Mrs Palmyra Pym series (8)
Murder at Scotland Yard
Dilnot, George
Horace Augustus Elver series (4)
Murder at teatime
Matteson, Stefanie
Charlotte Graham series (2)
Murder at ten thousand feet
Conde, Phillip
Irving Todd series (5)
Murder at the Angel
McCutcheon, Hugh
Anthony Howard series (1)
Inspector McKeller series (1)
Murder at the bank
Grayson, Rupert
Gun Cotton series (14)
Murder at the Black Crook
Matschat, Cecile Hulse
Andrea Reid and David Ramsay series (2)
Murder at the Blue Owl
Martin, Lee
Deb Ralston series (3)
Murder at the bookstall
Holt, Henry
Inspector Silver series (9)
Murder at the casino
Wells, Carolyn
Fleming Stone series (59)
Murder at the cat show
Babson, Marian
Douglas Perkins and Gerry Tate series (2)
Murder at the Cheatin' Heart Motel
Bourgeau, Art
Claude Kirlin and F T Zevich series (4)
Murder at the club
Allan, Luke
Tiger Lillie series (5)
Murder at the cookout
De Fraga, Geoff
Peter Cardiman and Quong series (1)
Murder at the falls
Matteson, Stefanie
Charlotte Graham series (5)
Murder at the FBI
Truman, Margaret
Capital crime series (6)
Murder at the Flea Club
Head, Matthew
Doctor Mary Finney series (4)
Murder at the flower show
Beckett, Mark
Major Dick Burton series (1)
Murder at the gallop
Christie, Agatha
Hercule Poirot series (28)
Murder at the Gardner
Langton, Jane
Homer Kelly series (7)
Murder at the hunting club
Plum, Mary
John Smith series (3)
Murder at the inn
Goyne, Richard
Paul Templeton series (3)
Murder at the Kennedy Center
Truman, Margaret
Capital crime series (9)
Murder at the mardi gras
Stone, Elizabet M
Maggie Slone series (2)
Murder at the margin
Jevons, Marshall
Henry Spearman series (1)
Murder at the masque
Myers, Amy
Auguste Didier series (4)
Murder at the Mimosa Inn
Hess, Joan
Claire Malloy series (2)
Murder at the motel
Gunn, Victor
Chief Inspector Bill Cromwell series (40)
Murder at the motor show
Rhode, John
Doctor Lancelot Priestley series (21)
Murder at the munition works
Cole, George Douglas Howard
Superintendent Henry Wilson series (23)
Murder at the National Cathedral
Truman, Margaret
Capital crime series (10)
Murder at the Nightwood Bar
Forrest, Katherine V
Kate Delafield series (2)
Murder at the Nook
Fielding, A
Inspector Pointer series (8)
Murder at the old stone house
Russell, Charlotte Murray
Jane Amanda Edwards series (1)
Murder at the old vicarage
McGown, Jill
Chief Inspector Lloyd and Sergeant Judy Hill series (2)
Murder at the Palace
Roosevelt, Elliott
Eleanor Roosevelt series (5)
Murder at the Pentagon
Truman, Margaret
Capital crime series (11)
Murder at the piano
Bagby, George
Inspector Schmidt series (1)
Murder at the polls
Propper, Milton
Tommy Rankin series (7)
Murder at the Red October
Olcott, Anthony
Ivan Kovakin series (1)
Murder at the Savoy
Sjowall, Maj
Inspector Martin Beck series (6)
Murder at the schoolhouse
Cunningham, Albert Benjamin
Sheriff Jess Roden series (2)
Murder at the spa
Matteson, Stefanie
Charlotte Graham series (1)
Murder at the Superbowl
Resnicow, Herbert
Sport series (1)
Murder at the vicarage
Christie, Agatha
Miss Jane Marple series (1)
Murder at the war
Pulver, Mary Monica
Kori McLeod Price and Peter Brichter series (2)
Murder at the wedding
Grierson, Francis Durham
Inspector Sims and Professor Wells series (8)
Murder at the World's Fair
Plum, Mary
John Smith series (4)
Murder at the Yard
Brandon, John Gordon
Inspector Patrick Aloysius McCarthy series (13)
Murder at three hundred to one
O'Hanlon, James
Jason Cordrey series (2)
Murder at twenty eight ten
Gayle, Newton
James Greer series (3)
Murder at Vassar
Taylor, Elizabeth Atwood
Maggie Elliott series (2)
Murder at Willow Run
Collins, Michelle
Megan Marshall series (1)
Murder at Wrides Park
Fletcher, Joseph Smith
Ronald Camberwell series (1)
Murder backstairs
Austin, Anne
James F Dundee series (2)
Murder be hanged
Ross, Jonathan
Superintendent George Rogers series (18)

Murder beat
Lenton, Anthony
Graham Darren series (1)
Murder before breakfast
Offord, Lenore Glen
Bill and Coco Hastings series (1)
Murder before dinner
Franklin, Charles
Inspector Jim Burgess series (4)
Murder before marriage
Neville, Margot
Inspector Grogan and Sergeant Manning series (5)
Murder before midnight
Cunningham, Albert Benjamin
Sheriff Jess Roden series (10)
Murder before Tuesday
Hamilton, Elaine
Inspector Reynolds series (8)
Murder begets murder
Jeffries, Roderic Graeme
Inspector Enrique Alvarez series (4)
Murder begins at home
Ames, Delano
Dagobert and Jane Brown series (2)
Murder behind closed doors
Lore, Phillips
Leo Roi series (2)
Murder behind the mike
Goldman, Raymond Leslie
Asaph Clume series (5)
Murder being once done
Rendell, Ruth
Chief Inspector Reginald Wexford series (7)
Murder beneath the trees
Coram, Christopher
Ross Macallister series (6)
Murder between dark and dark
Long, Max
Komako Koa series (1)
Murder beyond the pale
Neville, Margot
Inspector Grogan and Sergeant Manning series (14)
Murder, bless it!
Spain, Nancy
Johnny Duvivien series (3)
Murder book of Mister J G Reeder
Wallace, Edgar
Mister J G Reeder series (2)
Murder bound
Anderson, Poul
Trygve Yamamura series (3)
Murder breaks trail
Boyd, Eunice Mays
F Millard Smyth series (1)
Murder brewing
Eyles, Alfred W
Paul Chisholm series (3)
Murder, but natch
Hagen, Miriam Ann
Hortense Clinton series (3)
Murder by air
Johns, William Earl
Steeley Delaroy series (3)
Murder by an aristocrat
Eberhart, Mignon Good
Sarah Keate and Lance O'Leary series (5)
Murder by an idiot
Plummer, Thomas Arthur
Detective Inspector Andrew Frampton series (19)
Murder by chance
Drax, Peter
Chief Inspector Thompson series (1)
Murder by deception
Meredith, Doris R
John Lloyd Branson series (2)
Murder by decree
Weverka, Robert
Sherlock Holmes sequels series (38)
Murder by degrees
Pearson, Ann
Maggie Courtney series (1)
Murder by design
Simons, Roger
Inspector Fadiman Wace series (16)
Murder by experiment
Knight, Leonard Alfred
Jerry Scant series (4)
Murder by experts
Gilbert, Anthony
Arthur Crook series (1)
Murder by formula
Wallis, James Harold
Inspector Wilton Jacks series (1)
Murder by Gemini
Gallagher, Richard
Cannon series (1)
Murder by impulse
Meredith, Doris R
John Lloyd Branson series (1)
Murder by inches
Hopkins, Stanley
Peter Marrell series (1)
Murder by invitation
McLean, Allan Campbell
Inspector Noel Macleod series (3)
Murder by jury
Sanborn, Ruth Burr
Angeline Tredennick series (1)
Murder by latitude
King, Rufus
Lieutenant Valcour series (3)
Murder by magic
Grant, Maxwell
Shadow series (265)
Long, Amelia Reynolds
Steve Carter series (6)
Murder by marriage
Dean, Robert George
Tony Hunter series (3)
Murder by masquerade
Meredith, Doris R
John Lloyd Branson series (3)
Murder by matchlight
Lorac, E C R
Inspector Macdonald series (26)
Murder by mistake
Urquhart, Paul
Sexton Blake series (820)
Murder by moonlight
Grant, Maxwell
Shadow series (246)
Reid, Desmond
Sexton Blake series (1524)
Murder by multiplication
Durham, Mary
Inspector York series (5)
Murder by nail
Farnol, Jeffery
Mister Jasper Shrig of Bow Street series (7)
Murder by owl light
Sawyer, Corinne Holt
Senior citizens series (3)
Murder by precedent
Petrie, Rhona
Inspector Marcus Maclurg series (2)
Murder by prescription
Stagge, Jonathan
Doctor Hugh Westlake series (2)
Murder by proxy
Carmichael, Harry
John Piper and Quinn series (26)
Halliday, Brett
Michael Shayne series (43)
Harris, Colver
Timothy Fowler series (3)
Morice, Anne
Tessa Crichton Price series (12)
Nielsen, Helen
Simon Drake series (1)
Ogan, George
Johnny Bordelon series (3)
Williams, Richard
Sexton Blake series (1559)
Murder by reference
Meredith, Doris R
John Lloyd Branson series (4)
Murder by request
Nichols, Beverley
Mister Horatio Green series (5)
Murder by sacrilege
Meredith, Doris R
John Lloyd Branson series (5)
Murder by scripture
Long, Amelia Reynolds
Peter Piper series (4)
Murder by the book
Hays, Lee
Columbo series (5)
Lockridge, Frances
Mister and Mrs North series (28)
Rowe, Jennifer
Verity Birdwood series (2)
Schier, Norma
Kay Barth series (3)
Stout, Rex
Nero Wolfe and Archie Goodwin series (19)
Murder by the clock
King, Rufus
Lieutenant Valcour series (1)
Murder by the day
Johns, Veronica Parker
Webster Flagg series (1)
Murder by the lake
Coram, Christopher
Ross Macallister series (5)
Murder by the law
McGuire, Paul
Superintendent Fillinger series (3)
Murder by the mile
Russell, Martin
Jim Larkin series (5)
Murder by the minute
Wood, Andrew
Magnus Keeble series (4)
Murder by the tale
Shannon, Dell
Lieutenant Luis Mendoza series (38)
Murder by the yard
Yates, Margaret Tayler
Anne Davenport McLean series (4)
Murder by treason
Long, Amelia Reynolds
Steve Carter series (4)
Murder by wash of light
De Fraga, Geoff
Peter Cardiman and Quong series (2)
Murder calling 50
Bagby, George
Inspector Schmidt series (10)
Murder calls Doctor Hailey
Wynne, Anthony
Doctor Eustace Hailey series (23)
Murder calls the Black Bat
Jones, G Wayman
Black Bat series (2)
Murder calls the tune
Duncan, William Murdoch
Laurie Hume series (1)
Murder came late
York, Jeremy
Superintendent Folly series (2)
Murder can't stop
Ballard, Willis Todhunter
Bill Lennox series (2)
Murder can't wait
Lockridge, Richard
Inspector Merton Heimrich series (18)
Nathan Shapiro series (5)
Murder case number thirty three
Cornell, Louis
Michael Joyce series (2)
Murder challenges Valcour
King, Rufus
Lieutenant Valcour series (7)
Murder charge
Miller, Wade
Lieutenant Austin Clapp series (6)
Max Thursday series (5)
Murder cheats the bride
Gilbert, Anthony
Arthur Crook series (16)
Murder chop chop
Norman, James
Gimiendo Hernandez Quinto series (1)
Murder circus
Litchfield, Michael
Superintendent Fergus McQueen series (2)
Murder city
Lenton, Anthony
Graham Darren series (2)
Murder Club
Zacharia, Irwin
Vendetta series (2)
Murder comes at night
Oellrichs, Inez
Matt Winters series (3)
Murder comes back
Ashbrook, Harriette
Philip Tracy series (6)
Murder comes calling
Reid, Desmond
Sexton Blake series (1498)
Murder comes first
Lockridge, Frances
Bill Wiegand series (15)
Mister and Mrs North series (16)
Murder comes high
Nelson, Hugh Lawrence
Jim Dunn series (2)
Murder comes home
Child, Nellise
Jeremiah Irish series (1)
Gilbert, Anthony
Arthur Crook series (22)
Murder comes smiling
Brandon, Gordon
Arthur Stukeley Pennington series (29)
Inspector Patrick Aloysius McCarthy series (54)
Murder comes to Rothesay
Cassells, John
Superintendent Flagg series (2)
Murder confounded
Jeffries, Roderic Graeme
Inspector Enrique Alvarez series (16)
Murder cries out
Hocking, Anne
Inspector William Austen series (34)
Murder cum laude
Dane, Joel Y
Sergeant Cass Harty series (1)
Murder cuts diamonds
Wallace, Robert
Phantom Detective series (33)
Murder doesn't always out
Ransome, Stephen
Professor Cyrus Hatch series (3)
Murder doll
Saber, Robert O
Carl Good series (4)
Murder double murder
Graham, Neill
Solo Malcolm series (30)
Murder down below
Stagg, James
Sexton Blake series (1454)
Murder down under
Upfield, Arthur William
Napoleon Bonaparte series (4)
Murder draws a line
Barber, Willetta Ann
Christopher Storm series (1)
Murder en route
Flynn, Brian
Anthony Bathurst series (8)
Murder enters the picture
Barber, Willetta Ann
Christopher Storm series (4)
Murder every hour
Grant, Maxwell
Shadow series (79)
Murder expert
Koehler, Robert Portner
Al Bronson series (2)
Murder, extra special
Brody, Marc
Marc Brody series (17)
Murder fantastical
Moyes, Patricia
Henry and Emmy Tibbett series (7)
Murder first class
Simons, Roger
Inspector Fadiman Wace series (13)
Murder flies the Atlantic
Page, Stanley Hart
Christopher Hand series (3)
Murder follows Desmond Shannon
Heberden, Mary Violet
Desmond Shannon series (6)
Murder for a hollow shell
Albert, Andrew I
Paul Decker series (2)
Murder for art's sake
Lockridge, Richard
Nathan Shapiro series (6)
Murder for breakfast
Hunt, Peter
Alan Miller series (2)
Murder for Christmas
Christie, Agatha
Hercule Poirot series (19)
Murder for fun
Savage, Richard
Doctor Ferenc series (1)
Murder for Hannah
Babcock, Dwight Vincent
Hannah Van Doren series (1)
Murder for her birthday
Cobden, Guy
John Chadwick series (5)
Murder for his money
Cobden, Guy
John Chadwick series (4)
Murder for madame
Knight, Adam
Steve Conacher series (2)
Murder for Missemily
Straker, John Foster
Inspector Pitt series (7)
Murder for sale
Bardsley, Michael
Superintendent Donald Martin series (2)
Grant, Maxwell
Shadow series (147)
Murder for the asking
Coxe, George Harmon
Max Hale series (1)
Murder for the million
Chapman, Robert
Rex Banner series (4)
Murder for the millions
Kane, Henry
Peter Chambers series (20)
Murder for the mind
Laing, Patrick
Patrick Laing series (3)
Murder for Treasure
Williams, David
Mark Treasure series (4)
Murder for two
Coxe, George Harmon
Flash Casey series (2)
Murder for two pins
Trevor, Ralph
Superintendent Curtis Burke series (2)
Murder for what?
Steel, Kurt
Hank Hyer series (2)
Murder forestalled
Chester, Peter
Johnny Preston series (2)
Murder from beyond
Foster, Reginald Francis
Anthony Ravenhill series (6)
Murder from the east
Daly, Carroll John
Race Williams series (7)
Murder from the grave
Levinrew, Will
Professor Herman Brierly series (3)
Murder from three angles
Loder, Vernon
Inspector Chace series (1)
Warren, John Russell
Inspector M'Guire series (1)
Murder game
Batchelor, Reg
Sergeant Fenwick series (1)
Strange, John Stephen
Van Dusen Ormsberry series (3)
Murder gang
Daniel, Roland
Buddy Mustard series (10)
Murder gets around
Bowen, Robert Sidney
Gerry Barnes series (2)
Murder gets Jean Holton
Knight, Kathleen Moore
Elisha Macomber series (3)
Murder gives a lovely light
Strange, John Stephen
Captain George Honegger series (1)
Murder go round
Halliday, Brett
Mike Shayne stories series (1)
Murder goes astray
Heberden, Mary Violet
Desmond Shannon series (8)
Murder goes fishing
Brace, Timothy
Anthony Adams series (1)
Murder goes in a trailer
Brace, Timothy
Anthony Adams series (2)
Murder goes mumming
Craig, Alisa
Inspector Madoc Rhys series (2)
Murder goes nap
Dolphin, Rex
Sexton Blake series (1585)
Murder goes rolling along
Moore, Harry F S
Casey Peters series (1)
Murder goes round and round
Pentecost, Hugh
Pierre Chambrun series (22)
Murder goes south
Long, Amelia Reynolds
Peter Piper series (3)
Murder goes to college
Steel, Kurt
Hank Hyer series (3)
Murder goes to the dogs
Brace, Timothy
Anthony Adams series (3)
Murder goes to the World's Fair
Brace, Timothy
Anthony Adams series (4)
Murder gone mad
Bellairs, George
Detective Inspector Thomas Littlejohn series (48)

Stone, Simon
Sir Brian Dinsmore Conway series (4)
Murder gone Minoan
Clason, Clyde B
Theocritus Lucius Westborough series (7)
Murder gone to earth
Stagge, Jonathan
Doctor Hugh Westlake series (1)
Murder grows roots
Taylor, Selman
Inspector May series (2)
Murder half-baked
Bagby, George
Inspector Schmidt series (3)
Murder has a motive
Duncan, Francis
Mordecai Euripides Tremaine series (2)
Murder has a pretty face
Melville, Jennie
Sergeant Charmian Daniels series (8)
Murder has been done
Graham, Neill
Solo Malcolm series (22)
Murder has its points
Lockridge, Frances
Bill Wiegand series (26)
Mister and Mrs North series (26)
Murder has no calories
Sawyer, Corinne Holt
Senior citizens series (5)
Murder has no tongue
Gilbert, Anthony
Arthur Crook series (3)
Murder has three dimensions
Spiller, Andrew
Chief Inspector Duck Mallard series (5)
Murder has your number
Garner, Hugh
Inspector Walter McDumont series (3)
Murder helps
Oellrichs, Inez
Matt Winters series (5)
Murder house
Grant, Maxwell
Shadow series (120)
Murder humane
Kemp, Harold
Inspector James Brent series (1)
Murder in a blue room
Neville, Margot
Inspector Grogan and Sergeant Manning series (3)
Murder in a church
Wynne, Anthony
Doctor Eustace Hailey series (27)
Murder in a dark room
Graham, Neill
Solo Malcolm series (33)
Murder in a good cause
Sale, Medora
Inspector John Sanders and Harriet Jeffries series (2)
Murder in a hurry
Lockridge, Frances
Bill Wiegand series (14)
Mister and Mrs North series (15)
Murder in a library
Dutton, Charles Judson
Harley Manners series (3)
Murder in a lighter vein
Raison, Milton Michael
Tony Woolrich series (5)
Murder in a mummy case
Beck, Kathrine Kristine
Iris Cooper and Jack Clancy series (2)
Murder in a nunnery
Shepherd, Eric
Superintendent Andrew Pearson series (1)
Murder in absence
Burton, Miles
Inspector Arnold and Desmond Merrion series (48)
Murder in Advent
Williams, David
Mark Treasure series (9)
Murder in amber
Harris, Colver
Timothy Fowler series (3)
Murder in Amityville
Holzer, Hans
Amityville horror series (2)
Murder in Amsterdam
Baantjer, Albert Cornelis
Inspector De Kok series (2)
Murder in any language
Roos, Kelley
Jeff and Haila Troy series (7)
Murder in Bethnal Square
Fowler, Sydney
Mister Jellipot series (6)
Murder in black
Cross, Mark
Daphne Wrayne and her Four Adjusters series (21)
Grierson, Francis Durham
Inspector Sims and Professor Wells series (11)
Murder in black and white
Alexander, David
Lieutenant Romano series (2)
Tommy Twotoes and Terry Rooke series (2)
Murder in black letter
Anderson, Poul
Trygve Yamamura series (2)
Murder in blue
Petersen, Paul
Smugglers series (3)
Witting, Clifford
Inspector Charlton series (1)
Murder in Blue Street
Crane, Frances
Pat and Jean Abbott series (15)
Murder in Bostall
McGuire, Paul
Chief Inspector Cummings series (1)
Inspector Wittler series (1)
Murder in bright red
Crane, Frances
Pat and Jean Abbott series (17)
Murder in broad daylight
Cole, George Douglas Howard
Superintendent Henry Wilson series (22)
Murder in Burgundy
Peterson, Audrey
Jane Winfield and Andrew Quentin series (3)
Murder in camera
Ballinger, W A
Sexton Blake series (1536)
Murder in Canton
Gulik, Robert van
Judge Dee series (12)
Murder in Chelsea
Lorac, E C R
Inspector Macdonald series (7)
Murder in college
Dane, Joel Y
Sergeant Cass Harty series (1)
Murder in cowboy bronze
McCormick, Claire
John Waltz series (3)
Murder in Crown Passage
Burton, Miles
Inspector Arnold and Desmond Merrion series (16)
Murder in disguise
Kingston, Charles
Inspector Wake series (5)
Murder in E minor
Goldsborough, Robert
Nero Wolfe and Archie Goodwin series (48)
Murder in Earl's Court
Gordon, Neil
Peter Kerrigan series (1)
Murder in false face
Childerness, George
Chet Phelps series (1)
Murder in fancy dress
Irwin, Inez Haynes
Patrick O'Brien series (1)
Mantell, Laurie
Sergeant Steve Arrow and Chief Inspector Peacock series (1)
Murder in Fiji
Vandercook, John Womack
Bertram Lynch and Robert Deane series (2)
Murder in five columns
Diamond, Frank
Ransome Dragoon and Vicky Gaines series (1)
Murder in Flat Fourteen
Cromwell, A G E
Rodney Wayne series (1)
Murder in focus
Dunnett, Dorothy
Johnson and the yacht Dolly series (4)
Sale, Medora
Inspector John Sanders and Harriet Jeffries series (1)
Murder in four degrees
Fletcher, Joseph Smith
Ronald Camberwell series (2)
Murder in Georgetown
Truman, Margaret
Capital crime series (7)
Murder in gray and white
Sawyer, Corinne Holt
Senior citizens series (2)
Murder in G-sharp
Steel, Kurt
Hank Hyer series (4)
Murder in Haiti
Vandercook, John Womack
Bertram Lynch and Robert Deane series (3)
Murder in haste
Halliday, Brett
Michael Shayne series (40)
McGuire, Paul
Chief Inspector Cummings series (4)
Superintendent Fillinger series (7)
Weston, Garnett
Highway series (1)
Murder in high place
Dominic, R B
Congressman Ben Safford series (2)
Murder in high places
Pentecost, Hugh
Pierre Chambrun series (18)
Murder in hospital
Bell, Josephine
Doctor David Wintringham series (1)
Inspector Steven Mitchell series (1)
Eyles, Alfred W
Paul Chisholm series (1)
Murder in Jackson Hole
Parker, Maude
Jim Little series (3)
Murder in luxury
Pentecost, Hugh
Pierre Chambrun series (16)
Murder in make-up
Ashton, Charles
Jack Atherley series (1)
Murder in Manchuria
Teed, George Hamilton
Sexton Blake series (816)
Murder in Manhattan
Roeburt, John
Jigger Moran series (2)
Murder in manuscript
Verner, Gerald
Superintendent Robert Budd series (23)
Murder in married life
Morice, Anne
Tessa Crichton Price series (2)
Murder in Maryland
Ford, Leslie
Lieutenant Joseph Kelly series (1)
Murder in Mayfair
Brandon, John Gordon
Arthur Stukeley Pennington series (2)
Inspector Patrick Aloysius McCarthy series (4)
Murder in Maytime
Brandon, Gordon
Michael and Terry Terence series (3)
Murder in melancholy
Keenan, William
Chief Superintendent Charles Miller series (3)
Murder in Mellingham
Oleksiw, Susan
Joe Silva series (1)
Murder in Merida
Thorne, Ramsay
Captain Gringo series (29)
Murder in Mesopotamia
Christie, Agatha
Hercule Poirot series (13)
Murder in mid-Atlantic
Antill, Elizabeth
Inspector Simon Ashton series (1)
Murder in mimicry
Morice, Anne
Tessa Crichton Price series (10)
Murder in mink
Dean, Robert George
Tony Hunter series (5)
Murder in Monaco
Flagg, John
Hart Muldoon series (3)
Murder in Mortimer Square
Grierson, Francis Durham
Richard Furling series (1)
Murder in my backyard
Cleeves, Ann
Inspector Stephen Ramsay series (2)
Murder in my fashion
Brody, Marc
Marc Brody series (8)
Murder in New Guinea
Vandercook, John Womack
Bertram Lynch and Robert Deane series (4)
Murder in Ocean Drive
Daniel, Roland
Michael Grant series (9)
Murder in Okefenokee
Matschat, Cecile Hulse
Andrea Reid and David Ramsay series (1)
Murder in orbit
Coville, Bruce
Omni odysseys trilogy (2)
Murder in ordinary time
O'Marie, Carol Anne
Sister Mary Helen series (4)
Murder in outline
Morice, Anne
Tessa Crichton Price series (13)
Murder in paradise
Cleeves, Ann
George Palmer-Jones series (3)
Davey, Jocelyn
Ambrose Usher series (6)
Murder in Piccadilly
Kingston, Charles
Inspector Wake series (2)
Murder in Pimlico
Brandon, John Gordon
Arthur Stukeley Pennington series (26)
Inspector Patrick Aloysius McCarthy series (50)
Murder in plain sight
Brown, Gerald
Duke McCale series (2)
Murder in public
Crozier, John
Falcon series (1)
Murder in Pug's Parlour
Myers, Amy
Auguste Didier series (1)
Murder in Queer Street
Ryland, Clive
Chief Inspector George Bassett series (1)
Murder in retrospect
Christie, Agatha
Hercule Poirot series (23)
Murder in reverse
Webb, Anthony
Mister Pendlebury series (8)
Murder in Rockwater
Neville, Margot
Inspector Grogan and Sergeant Manning series (1)
Murder in ruins
Hunt, Richard
Chief Inspector Walsh and Constable Brenda Phipps series (1)
Murder in Saint John's Wood
Lorac, E C R
Inspector Macdonald series (6)
Murder in Shinbone Alley
Reilly, Helen
Inspector Christopher McKee series (11)
Murder in silence
Selmark, George
Inspector Bass series (3)
Murder in Soho
Brandon, John Gordon
Inspector Patrick Aloysius McCarthy series (18)
Murder in striplicate
Kane, Martin
Martin Kane series (18)
Murder in style
Fetta, Emma Lou
Lyle Curtis and Susan Yates series (1)
Stout, Rex
Dol Bonner series (3)
Nero Wolfe and Archie Goodwin series (32)
Murder in Switzerland
Snell, Edmund
Reggie Faulkner series (3)
Murder in the act
Saint Clair, Elizabeth
Marilyn Ambers series (1)
Murder in the air
Brisbane, Coutts
Sexton Blake series (696)
Cross, Mark
Daphne Wrayne and her Four Adjusters series (20)
Hunter, John
Sexton Blake series (1393)
Teilhet, Darwin Le Ora
Jean Henri Saint Amand series (1)
Murder in the Atlantic
Dickson, Carter
Sir Henry Merrivale series (11)
Murder in the bank
Essex, Richard
John Slade series (4)
Lessinger series (4)
Murder in the basement
Berkeley, Anthony
Roger Sheringham series (8)
Murder in the bath
Didelot, Francis
Inspector Lecain series (1)
Inspector Lecain series (2)
Murder in the blackout
Warren, John Russell
Inspector M'Guire series (2)
Murder in the Blue Room
Roosevelt, Elliott
Eleanor Roosevelt series (8)
Murder in the bookshop
Wells, Carolyn
Fleming Stone series (45)
Murder in the borough library
Austwick, John
Inspector Parker series (2)
Murder in the Calais coach
Christie, Agatha
Hercule Poirot series (9)
Murder in the Carolinas
Rhyne, Nancy
Murder in the Carolinas series (1)
Murder in the cathedral
Eliot, Thomas Stearns
Thomas Becket series (1)
Murder in the CIA
Truman, Margaret
Capital crime series (8)
Murder in the coalhole
Burton, Miles
Inspector Arnold and Desmond Merrion series (21)
Murder in the cockpit
Conde, Phillip
Irving Todd series (1)
Murder in the collective
Wilson, Barbara Ellen
Pam Nilsen series (1)
Murder in the Cotswolds
Guthrie, Alfred Bertram
Sheriff Chick Charleston and Jason Beard series (5)
Murder in the dentist chair
Thynne, Molly
Doctor Constantine series (2)
Murder in the dog days
Carlson, Patricia McEvoy
Maggie Ryan series (7)
Murder in the East Room
Roosevelt, Elliott
Eleanor Roosevelt series (12)
Murder in the Embassy
Diplomat
Dennis Tyler series (2)
Murder in the family
Brown, Carter
Randy Roberts series (1)
Delman, David
Lieutenant Jacob Horowitz series (6)
Murder in the Fine Arts
Nicolai, Charles
John Nolan series (3)
Murder in the first person
Adams, Shipley
Inspector Harrow series (3)
Murder in the flagship
Taylor, Philip Neville Walker
Commander Wraithlea series (1)
Murder in the fog
Hamilton, Elaine
Inspector Reynolds series (2)
Murder in the game reserve
Taylor, Philip Neville Walker
Commander Wraithlea series (2)
Murder in the garden
Grierson, Francis Durham
Inspector Sims and Professor Wells series (4)
Murder in the green sedan
Koehler, Robert Portner
Pecos Appleby series (2)
Murder in the Harem Club
Brown, Carter
Rick Holman series (3)

Murder in the haunted sentry box
Gayle, Newton
James Greer series (2)
Murder in the hotel
Hanshew, Hazel Phillips
Hamilton Cleek series (12)
Murder in the inn
Brock, Lynn
Colonel Gore series (5)
Murder in the Key Club
Brown, Carter
Rick Holman series (3)
Murder in the kitchen
Halliday, Fred
Stanley Delphond series (3)
Murder in the limelight
Myers, Amy
Auguste Didier series (2)
Murder in the madhouse
Latimer, Jonathan
Bill Crane series (1)
Murder in the making
Petersen, Herman
Doc Miller series (1)
Murder in the market
Janes, Joseph Robert
Danger on the river trilogy (3)
Murder in the maze
Connington, John Jervis
Sir Clinton Driffield series (1)
Murder in the melody
Berrow, Norman
Michael Revel series (2)
Murder in the mews
Christie, Agatha
Hercule Poirot series (17)
Reilly, Helen
Inspector Christopher McKee series (2)
Murder in the mews, and three other Poirot cases
Christie, Agatha
Hercule Poirot series (17)
Murder in the middle pasture
Erickson, John R
Hank the cowdog series (4)
Murder in the mill-race
Lorac, E C R
Inspector Macdonald series (37)
Murder in the mirror
Thayer, Lee
Peter Clancy series (22)
Murder in the mist
Popkin, Zelda
Mary Carner Whittaker series (3)
Murder in the mobile unit
Scott, Sutherland
Doctor Septimus Dodds series (6)
Murder in the moonlight
Brown, Fredric
Ed and Am Hunter series (3)
Murder in the morning
Robertson, Colin
Superintendent Bradley series (1)
Wynne, Anthony
Doctor Eustace Hailey series (22)
Murder in the museum
Heath, Eric
Cornelius Clift series (2)
Rowland, John
Inspector Shelley series (6)
Murder in the O.P.M.
Ford, Leslie
Colonel John Primrose series (8)
Grace Latham series (8)
Murder in the outlands
Hendryx, James Beardsley
Corporal Cameron Downey series (7)
Murder in the Oval Office
Roosevelt, Elliott
Eleanor Roosevelt series (6)
Murder in the park
Gregg, Cecil Freeman
Inspector Cuthbert Higgins series (11)
Murder in the place of Anubis
Robinson, Lynda S
Lord Meren series (1)
Murder in the pool
Cross, Mark
Daphne Wrayne and her Four Adjusters series (15)
Murder in the procession
Cargill, Leslie
Major Mosson series (1)
Murder in the Queen's Armes
Elkins, Aaron J
Professor Gideon Oliver series (3)
Murder in the radio department
Eichler, Alfred
Inspector Knickman series (1)
Martin Ames series (1)
Murder in the raw
Gault, William Campbell
Brock Callahan series (1)
Murder in the Red Room
Roosevelt, Elliott
Eleanor Roosevelt series (10)
Murder in the Rose Garden
Roosevelt, Elliott
Eleanor Roosevelt series (7)
Murder in the round
Dunnett, Dorothy
Johnson and the yacht Dolly series (2)
Murder in the Rue Royale
Harrison, Michael
Monsieur C Auguste Dupin series (2)
Murder in the ruins
Temple-Ellis, N A
Inspector Wren series (2)
Murder in the sanctuary
Grex, Leo
Paul Irving series (4)
Murder in the Senate
Coffin, Geoffrey
Inspector Scott Stuart series (1)
Mason, Francis Van Wyck
Inspector Scott Stuart series (1)
Murder in the Smithsonian
Truman, Margaret
Capital crime series (4)
Murder in the smokehouse
Myers, Amy
Auguste Didier series (7)
Murder in the squire's pew
Fletcher, Joseph Smith
Ronald Camberwell series (3)
Murder in the stars
Halliday, Michael
Martin and Richard Fane series (3)
Stagge, Jonathan
Doctor Hugh Westlake series (3)
Murder in the State Department
Diplomat
Dennis Tyler series (1)
Murder in the stratosphere
Eldredge, Gilbert
Thibault Parew and Chips Carpenter series (2)
Murder in the submarine zone
Dickson, Carter
Sir Henry Merrivale series (11)
Murder in the Suez Canal
Taylor, Philip Neville Walker
Commander Wraithlea series (3)
Murder in the sun
Story, Jack Trevor
Sexton Blake series (1460)
Murder in the Supreme Court
Truman, Margaret
Capital crime series (3)
Murder in the surgery
Edwards, James G
Inspector Victor Bondurant series (1)
Plummer, Thomas Arthur
Detective Inspector Andrew Frampton series (41)
Murder in the Tajmahal
Taylor, Philip Neville Walker
Commander Wraithlea series (4)
Murder in the telephone exchange
Wright, June
Sergeant Matheson series (1)
Murder in the title
Brett, Simon
Charles Paris series (9)
Murder in the top drawer
Cousins, Edmund George
Colonel Richard Barne series (4)
Murder in the Tower
Plaidy, Jean
Stuart series (1)
Murder in the tropic night
Arthur, Frank
Inspector Spearpoint series (3)
Murder in the village
Plummer, Thomas Arthur
Detective Inspector Andrew Frampton series (21)
Murder in the walls
Stern, Richard Martin
Johnny Ortiz series (1)
Murder in the West Wing
Roosevelt, Elliott
Eleanor Roosevelt series (11)
Murder in the White House
Truman, Margaret
Capital crime series (1)
Murder in the Willett family
King, Rufus
Lieutenant Valcour series (4)
Murder in the wind
Ogan, George
Johnny Bordelon series (2)
Murder in the wings
Gorman, Edward
Jack Dwyer series (4)
Murder in the WPA
Williams, Alexander
Detective Sergeant Pietro Tonelli series (3)
Murder in thin air
Wynne, Anthony
Doctor Eustace Hailey series (21)
Murder in three acts
Christie, Agatha
Hercule Poirot series (10)
Murder in time
Day, Lillian
Frederick Hunt series (1)
Murder in tow
Hale, Christopher
Lieutenant Bill French series (7)
Murder in Trinidad
Vandercook, John Womack
Bertram Lynch and Robert Deane series (1)
Murder in triplicate
Austin, Hugh
Peter Quint series (2)
Marshall, Lovat
Sugar Kane series (9)
Murder in twenty five words or less
Walker, Irma
Steve Rhoden series (3)
Murder in two flats
Vickers, Roy
Inspector Peter Curwen and Hugh Stanton series (4)
Murder in vain
Mantell, Laurie
Sergeant Steve Arrow and Chief Inspector Peacock series (5)
Murder in Vegas
Cox, William Robert
Tom Kincaid series (2)
Murder in Venice
Sterling, Thomas
Captain Rizzi series (1)
Murder in Vienna
Lorac, E C R
Inspector Macdonald series (42)
Murder in Wardour Street
Morland, Nigel
Mrs Palmyra Pym series (9)
Murder in Washington
Woolfolk, Dorothy
Donna Rockford series (3)
Murder in white
Zachary, Hugh
Sheriff Jug Watson series (2)
Murder in White Pit
Barrington, John
Ken Williams series (2)
Murder in Windy Coppice
Plummer, Thomas Arthur
Detective Inspector Andrew Frampton series (38)
Murder in Wonderland
Bagby, George
Inspector Schmidt series (33)
Murder in Wrigley Field
Evers, Crabbe
Duffy House series (1)
Murder in writing
Clarke, Anna
Professor Paula Glenning series (5)
Murder in Y Division
Brandon, John Gordon
Sexton Blake series (833)
Murder included
Cannan, Joanna
Inspector Ronald Price series (1)
Murder inherited
Cobden, Guy
John Chadwick series (6)
Murder intended
Beeding, Francis
Inspector Wilkins series (2)
Murder is a collector's item
Dean, Elizabeth
Emma Marsh and Hank Fairbanks series (1)
Murder is a furtive thing
Boyd, Raymond
Paul Scarf series (3)
Murder is a gamble
Barns, Glenn Miller
Jonathan Marks series (1)
Murder is a habit
Halliday, Brett
Michael Shayne series (17)
Murder is a maiden's handicap
Brody, Marc
Marc Brody series (57)
Murder is a package deal
Brown, Carter
Rick Holman series (10)
Murder is a pendulum
Joyce, Cyril
Chief Superintendent Pat Stockton series (15)
Murder is a serious business
Dean, Elizabeth
Emma Marsh and Hank Fairbanks series (2)
Murder is a shady business
Spiller, Andrew
Chief Inspector Duck Mallard series (18)
Murder is academic
Carlson, Patricia McEvoy
Maggie Ryan series (2)
Murder is an art
Innes, Michael
Sir John Appleby series (13)
Murder is an evil business
Bramhall, Marion
Kit Acton series (4)
Murder is announced
Christie, Agatha
Miss Jane Marple series (6)
Murder is cheap
Gilbert, Anthony
Arthur Crook series (14)
Murder is contagious
Bramhall, Marion
Kit Acton series (5)
Murder is corny
Stout, Rex
Nero Wolfe and Archie Goodwin series (39)
Murder is easy
Christie, Agatha
Superintendent Battle series (4)
Murder is for keeps
Chambers, Peter
Mark Preston series (1)
Murder is forgetful
Bogart, William
Johnny Saxon series (2)
Murder is germane
Saum, Karen
Brigid Donovan series (2)
Murder is grim
Rogers, Samuel
Professor Paul Hatfield series (2)
Murder is infectious
Scott, Sutherland
Doctor Septimus Dodds series (2)
Murder is insane
Barns, Glenn Miller
Jonathan Marks series (3)
Murder is its own reward
Chambers, Peter
Mark Preston series (28)
Murder is mutuel
Dolph, Jack
Doc Connor series (2)
Murder is my business
Halliday, Brett
Michael Shayne series (11)
Murder is my dish
Marlowe, Stephen
Chester Drum series (4)
Murder is my mistress
Brown, Carter
Danny Boyd series (6)
Murder is my racket
Leitfred, Robert H
Simon Crole series (3)
Murder is my weakness
Graham, Neill
Solo Malcolm series (9)
Murder is no joke
Bethancourt, Tomas Ernesto
Doris Fein series (7)
Stout, Rex
Nero Wolfe and Archie Goodwin series (31)
Murder is not enough
Wells, Susan
Anthony Ware series (1)
Murder is not mute
Newell, Audrey
Patrick Michael Doyle series (2)
Murder is only skin deep
Sims, L V
Dixie T Struthers series (2)
Murder is out
Thayer, Lee
Peter Clancy series (33)
Murder is pathological
Carlson, Patricia McEvoy
Maggie Ryan series (3)
Murder is relative
Saum, Karen
Brigid Donovan series (1)
Murder is ruby red
Radford, Edwin
Doctor Manson series (31)
Murder is served
Lockridge, Frances
Bill Wiegand series (12)
Mister and Mrs North series (13)
Murder is so nostalgic
Brown, Carter
Mavis Seidlitz series (11)
Murder is suggested
Lockridge, Frances
Bill Wiegand series (24)
Mister and Mrs North series (24)
Murder is suspected
Alding, Peter
C.I.D. Room series (10)
Murder is the message
Brown, Carter
Danny Boyd series (18)
Murder is the reason
Marshall, Lovat
Sugar Kane series (10)
Murder Island
Jamieson, Leland
Dan Gregory series (1)
Murder island
Martyn, Wyndham
Anthony Trent series (9)
Murder isn't cricket
Radford, Edwin
Doctor Manson series (4)
Murder isn't enough
Flynn, Don
Ed Fitzgerald series (1)
Murder isn't funny
Bond, J Harvey
Mike Lanson series (2)
Murder jigsaw
Radford, Edwin
Doctor Manson series (2)
Murder joins the chorus
Simons, Roger
Inspector Fadiman Wace series (3)
Murder lake
Grant, Maxwell
Shadow series (241)
Murder Las Vegas style
Ballard, Willis Todhunter
Bill Lennox series (5)
Murder League
Fish, Robert Lloyd
Murder League series (1)
Murder lies in waiting
Graham, Neill
Solo Malcolm series (26)
Murder limps by
Plummer, Thomas Arthur
Detective Inspector Andrew Frampton series (18)
Murder line
Alding, Peter
C.I.D. Room series (8)
Murder listens in
Daly, Elizabeth
Henry Gamadge series (7)
Murder, London-Australia
Creasey, John
Inspector Roger West series (33)
Murder, London-Miami
Creasey, John
Inspector Roger West series (37)
Murder, London-New York
Creasey, John
Inspector Roger West series (24)
Murder, London-South Africa
Creasey, John
Inspector Roger West series (34)
Murder, M.D.
Burton, Miles
Inspector Arnold and Desmond Merrion series (28)
Murder machine
Foxall, Peter Augustus
Inspector Frank Derben series (1)
Scarpetta, Frank
Marksman series (20)
Murder made absolute
Underwood, Michael
Superintendent Simon Manton series (2)
Murder made easy
Goyne, Richard
Paul Templeton series (11)
Graham, Neill
Solo Malcolm series (15)
Reid, Desmond
Sexton Blake series (1499)

Murder, maestro, please
Ames, Delano
Dagobert and Jane Brown series (6)
Sharkey, Jack
George Herbert Henry series (1)
Murder magnified
Radford, Edwin
Doctor Manson series (21)
Murder magnifique
Janson, Hank
Hank Janson series (89)
Murder maker
Chance, John Newton
Jonathan Blake series (37)
Jones, G Wayman
Black Bat series (29)
Murder makers
Rossiter, John
Roger Tallis series (1)
Murder makes a date
Graham, Neill
Solo Malcolm series (1)
Murder makes a merry widow
Dean, Robert George
Tony Hunter series (1)
Murder makes a movie
Wallace, Robert
Phantom Detective series (32)
Murder makes a pilgrimage
O'Marie, Carol Anne
Sister Mary Helen series (5)
Murder makes a racket
Heberden, Mary Violet
Desmond Shannon series (7)
Murder makes a villain
Scott, Denis
Mike James series (1)
Murder makes an entree
Myers, Amy
Auguste Didier series (5)
Murder makes by-lines
Secrist, Kelliher
Sham Payne series (2)
Murder makes haste
Creasey, John
Inspector Roger West series (17)
Murder makes it certain
Graham, Neill
Solo Malcolm series (12)
Murder makes me nervous
Scherf, Margaret
Lieutenant Ryan series (2)
Murder makes mistakes
Bellairs, George
Detective Inspector Thomas Littlejohn series (30)
Murder makes murder
Ashbrook, Harriette
Philip Tracy series (5)
Murder makes the mare go
Dolph, Jack
Doc Connor series (3)
Murder makes the news
Graham, Neill
Solo Malcolm series (21)
Murder makes the wheels go round
Lathen, Emma
John Putnam Thatcher series (4)
Murder makes tracks
Linscott, Gillian
Birdie Linnett and Nimue Hawthorne series (2)
Murder man
Bogart, William
Johnny Saxon series (1)
Duncan, William Murdoch
Laurie Hume series (3)
Murder mansion
Grant, Maxwell
Shadow series (214)
Wallis, James Harold
Inspector Wilton Jacks series (6)
Murder Mansion
Wilson, Alexander
Sir Leonard Wallace series (2)
Murder maritime
Cranston, Claudia
Clarice Claremont series (2)
Murder market
Jacobs, Thomas Curtis Hicks
Temple Fortune series (12)
Murder marsh
Grant, Maxwell
Shadow series (63)
Murder mask
Begbie, Garstin
Superintendent Samuel Quan series (2)
Horler, Sydney
Sir Brian Fordinghame series (2)
Murder masks Miami
King, Rufus
Lieutenant Valcour series (11)
Murder masquerade
Bellairs, George
Detective Inspector Thomas Littlejohn series (36)
Dilnot, George
Horace Augustus Elver series (2)
Irwin, Inez Haynes
Patrick O'Brien series (1)
Murder master
Grant, Maxwell
Shadow series (139)
Murder may pass unpunished
Everton, Francis
Detective Inspector Allport series (4)
Inspector George Annesley series (2)
Murder melody
Robeson, Kenneth
Doc Savage series (15)
Secrist, Kelliher
Sham Payne series (1)
Murder, men only
Cobb, Belton
Bryan Armitage series (4)
Inspector Cheviot Burmann series (28)
Kitty Armitage series (1)
Murder menagerie
Lane, Jeremy
Whitney Wheat series (3)
Murder mirage
Robeson, Kenneth
Doc Savage series (71)
Murder misread
Carlson, Patricia McEvoy
Maggie Ryan series (5)
Murder mission
Conroy, Al
Johnny Morini series (4)
Marshall, Lovat
Sugar Kane series (29)
Murder, Mister Mosley
Greenwood, John
Inspector Mosley series (1)
Murder money
Wallace, Robert
Phantom Detective series (35)
Murder most artistic
Gore, William
Inspector Penk series (2)
Murder most foul
Ashe, Gordon
Patrick Dawlish series (7)
Hawton, Hector
Asmun Hill series (2)
Murder most fouled up
Wells, Tobias
Detective Knute Severson series (4)
Murder most fowl
Crider, Bill
Dan Rhodes series (8)
Murder most ingenious
Chase, Kip
Justine Carmichael series (2)
Murder most intimate
Baker, William Howard
Sexton Blake series (1443)
Murder most royal
Plaidy, Jean
Tudor series (4)
Murder most strange
Shannon, Dell
Lieutenant Luis Mendoza series (32)
Murder, murder!
Symons, Julian
Francis Quarles series (1)
Murder must advertise
Sayers, Dorothy Leigh
Lord Peter Wimsey series (9)
Murder must wait
Creasey, John
Department Z series (12)
Upfield, Arthur William
Napoleon Bonaparte series (17)
Murder, my sweet
Holt, Henry
Inspector Silver series (14)
Murder mystery
Thompson, Gene
Dade Cooley series (1)
Murder needs a face
Fenisong, Ruth
Captain Gridley Nelson series (1)
Murder needs a name
Fenisong, Ruth
Captain Gridley Nelson series (2)
Murder next year
Farmer, Bernard James
Sergeant Jack Wigan series (4)
Murder, nine and out
Turner, John Victor
Amos Petrie series (4)
Murder ninety seven
Gruber, Frank
Simon Lash series (3)
Murder now and then
Brean, Herbert
Reynold Frame series (3)
Murder observed
Boylan, Eleanor
Henry Gamadge series (18)
Murder of a banker
Fletcher, Joseph Smith
Ronald Camberwell series (7)
Murder of a black cat
Graham, Neill
Solo Malcolm series (16)
Murder of a chemist
Burton, Miles
Inspector Arnold and Desmond Merrion series (13)
Murder of a dead man
Steel, Kurt
Hank Hyer series (1)
Murder of a fifth columnist
Ford, Leslie
Colonel John Primrose series (7)
Grace Latham series (7)
Murder of a lady
Marshall, Lovat
Sugar Kane series (15)
Wynne, Anthony
Doctor Eustace Hailey series (12)
Murder of a magnate
Beckett, Mark
Major Dick Burton series (2)
Murder of a man afraid of women
Abbot, Anthony
Thatcher Colt series (6)
Murder of a martinet
Lorac, E C R
Inspector Macdonald series (35)
Murder of a matriarch
Austin, Hugh
Peter Quint series (3)
Murder of a missing man
Chase, Arthur Minturn
Lieutenant Dan Durkin series (2)
Murder of a mistress
Kuttner, Henry
Doctor Michael Gray series (3)
Sherwood, John
Mister Charles Blessington series (3)
Murder of a mystery writer
Hawk, John
Mortimer Sark series (5)
Heath, Eric
Wade Anthony series (2)
Murder of a nymph
Neville, Margot
Inspector Grogan and Sergeant Manning series (4)
Murder of a quack
Bellairs, George
Detective Inspector Thomas Littlejohn series (5)
Murder of a startled lady
Abbot, Anthony
Thatcher Colt series (5)
Murder of a stuffed man
Heberden, Mary Violet
Desmond Shannon series (9)
Murder of a suicide
Ferrars, E X
Toby Dyke series (3)
Murder of a wife
Kuttner, Henry
Doctor Michael Gray series (4)
Murder of Alonzo
Cheyney, Peter
Alonzo Mactavish series (3)
Murder of an initiate
Propper, Milton
Tommy Rankin series (4)
Murder of an MP
Gore-Browne, Robert
Lucien Clay series (1)
Murder of an old man
Frome, David
Major Gregory Lewis series (1)
Murder of an owl
Carr, Glyn
Sir Abercrombie Lewker series (10)
Murder of Ann Avery
Kuttner, Henry
Doctor Michael Gray series (1)
Murder of Becket
Birt, David
Middle Ages series (5)
Murder of busy Lizzie
Mitchell, Gladys
Dame Beatrice Bradley series (46)
Murder of Cecily Thane
Ashbrook, Harriette
Philip Tracy series (1)
Murder of Constable Cartwright
Blair, Allan
Sexton Blake series (607)
Murder of convenience
Dean, Robert George
Tony Hunter series (2)
Murder of crows
Buchanan, Patrick
Ben Shock and Charity Tucker series (1)
Duffy, Margaret
Patrick Gillard series (1)
Murder of Dave Brandon
Lund, Trygve
Dick Weston series (3)
Murder of Doctor Gray
Plummer, Thomas Arthur
Detective Inspector Andrew Frampton series (33)
Murder of Eleanor Pope
Kuttner, Henry
Doctor Michael Gray series (2)
Murder of Estelle Cantor
Gregg, Cecil Freeman
Henry Prince series (1)
Murder of Geraldine Foster
Abbot, Anthony
Thatcher Colt series (1)
Murder of Harvey Blake
Goldman, Raymond Leslie
Asaph Clume series (1)
Murder of Lalla Lee
Burnham, Helen
One Week Wimble series (1)
Murder of Lydia
Cowdroy, Joan
Li Moh series (2)
Murder of Marion Mason
Dewey, Thomas Blanchard
Singer Batts series (1)
Murder of Martin Fotherill
Lester, Edward Castellain
Nathaniel Moody series (2)
Murder of Miranda
Millar, Margaret
Tom Aragon series (2)
Murder of Miss Betty Sloan
Williams, Sidney
Jabez Twombley series (1)
Murder of Mrs Davenport
Gilbert, Anthony
Scott Egerton series (2)
Murder of my patient
Eberhart, Mignon Good
Sarah Keate and Lance O'Leary series (5)
Murder of Olympia
Neville, Margot
Inspector Grogan and Sergeant Manning series (9)
Murder of Paul Rougier
Sampson, Victor
Inspector Downes and Sergeant Hopkins series (1)
Murder of quality
Le Carre, John
George Smiley series (2)
Murder of Roger Ackroyd
Christie, Agatha
Hercule Poirot series (4)
Murder of Sherlock Holmes
Anderson, James
Jessica Fletcher series (2)
Murder of Sigurd Sharon
Ashbrook, Harriette
Philip Tracy series (3)
Murder of some importance
Graeme, Bruce
Superintendent William Stevens and Inspector Pierre Allain series (1)
Murder of Steven Kester
Ashbrook, Harriette
Philip Tracy series (2)
Murder of the admiral
Gould, Stephen
Sheridan Doome series (1)
Murder of the circus queen
Abbot, Anthony
Thatcher Colt series (4)
Murder of the clergyman's mistress
Abbot, Anthony
Thatcher Colt series (2)
Murder of the lawyer's clerk
Fletcher, Joseph Smith
Ronald Camberwell series (5)
Murder of the night club lady
Abbot, Anthony
Thatcher Colt series (3)
Murder of the Ninth Baronet
Fletcher, Joseph Smith
Ronald Camberwell series (4)
Murder of the only witness
Fletcher, Joseph Smith
Ronald Camberwell series (6)
Murder of the Park Avenue playgirl
Kane, Henry
Peter Chambers series (4)
Murder of the pigboat skipper
Fisher, Steve
Sheridan Doome series (2)
Murder of the secret agent
Fletcher, Joseph Smith
Ronald Camberwell series (8)
Murder of the well-beloved
Neville, Margot
Inspector Grogan and Sergeant Manning series (7)
Murder of three ghosts
Radford, Edwin
Doctor Manson series (18)
Murder of Whistler's brother
Alexander, David
Bart Hardin series (4)
Lieutenant Romano series (6)
Murder off Broadway
Klinger, Henry
Lieutenant Shomri Shomar series (2)
Murder off key
Sproul, Kathleen
Dick Wilson series (3)
Murder off Miami
Wheatley, Dennis
Lieutenant John Milton Schwab series (1)
Murder off stage
Barrett, Monte
Peter Cardigan series (2)
Murder on a monument
Lorac, E C R
Inspector Macdonald series (45)
Murder on a shoestring
Spiller, Andrew
Chief Inspector Duck Mallard series (25)
Murder on a tangent
Disney, Doris Miles
Jim O'Neill series (2)
Murder on Alternative
Davis, Tech
Aubrey Nash series (3)
Murder on Angler's Island
Reilly, Helen
Inspector Christopher McKee series (16)
Murder on B Deck
Starrett, Vincent
Walter Ghost series (1)
Murder on Bag Hill
Ryland, Clive
Inspector Beck series (3)
Murder on Beacon Hill
Brown, Gerald
Duke McCale series (1)
Murder on Broadway
Masur, Harold Q
Scott Jordan series (7)
Murder on Cape Cod
Shay, Frank
Dan Doner series (2)
Murder on Capitol Hill
Truman, Margaret
Capital crime series (2)
Murder on cue
Dentinger, Jane
Jocelyn O'Roarke and Phillip Gerard series (1)
Murder on delivery
Dean, Spencer
Don Cadee series (4)
Murder on demand
Graham, Neill
Solo Malcolm series (20)
Murder on display
Hale, Christopher
Lieutenant Bill French series (3)
Murder on duty
Burton, Miles
Inspector Arnold and Desmond Merrion series (45)
Murder on Embassy Row
Truman, Margaret
Capital crime series (5)

Murder on Fifth Avenue
Cranston, Claudia
Clarice Claremont series (1)
Murder on fire
Bardsley, Michael
Superintendent Donald Martin series (1)
Murder on French leave
Morice, Anne
Tessa Crichton Price series (4)
Murder on Friday
Ashbrook, Harriette
Philip Tracy series (7)
Murder on Ghost Tree Island
Daiger, Katherine S
Inspector Everett Anderson series (2)
Murder on Halfaday Creek
Hendryx, James Beardsley
Black John series (15)
Murder on her mind
Dietrich, Robert
Steve Bentley series (5)
Howard, Vechel
Johnny Church series (2)
Murder on high
Brown, Carter
Randy Roberts series (4)
Matteson, Stefanie
Charlotte Graham series (6)
Murder on high Avon
Kennedy, George
George Kennedy series (2)
Murder on holiday
Malim, Barbara
Simon Chard series (1)
Murder-on-Hudson
Jones, Jennifer
Daisy Jane Mott series (1)
Murder on ice
Bardsley, Michael
Superintendent Donald Martin series (3)
Gunn, Victor
Chief Inspector Bill Cromwell series (17)
Keene, Carolyn
Nancy Drew files series (3)
Wood, Ted
Reid Bennett series (2)
Murder on leave
Galwey, Geoffrey Valentine
Inspector Daddy Bourne series (1)
Murder on location
Engel, Howard
Benny Cooperman series (3)
Kennedy, George
George Kennedy series (1)
Thayer, Lee
Peter Clancy series (34)
Murder on Madison Avenue
Orenstein, Frank
Ev Franklin series (1)
Murder on margin
Dean, Robert George
Pat Thompson series (4)
Murder on Mars
Walters, Hugh
Chris Godfrey series (16)
Murder on mike
Jeffers, Harry Paul
Harry Macneil series (2)
Murder on Monday
Barnett, Glyn
Inspector Grampport series (2)
Murder on Monday?
Barry, Charles
Superintendent Lawrence Gilmartin series (9)
Murder on Monday
Wilmot, Robert Patrick
Steve Considine series (2)
Wilson, Gertrude Mary
Inspector Lovick series (10)
Murder on Mondays
Bush, Christopher
Ludovic Travers series (14)
Murder on my conscience
Radford, Edwin
Doctor Manson series (13)
Murder on my hands
Graham, Neill
Solo Malcolm series (17)
Murder on my street
Lanham, Edwin
Frank Luther series (1)
Murder on page three
Griffiths, Ella
Rudolph and Karsten Nilsen series (1)
Murder on parade
Wells, Carolyn
Fleming Stone series (56)
Murder on Playboy Island
Franklin, Max
Starsky and Hutch series (8)
Murder on Russian Hill
Offord, Lenore Glen
Bill and Coco Hastings series (1)
Murder on safari
Huxley, Elspeth
Superintendent Vachell series (2)
Murder-on-sea
Harrison, Richard
Chief Inspector William Bastion series (4)
Murder on show
Babson, Marian
Douglas Perkins and Gerry Tate series (2)
Murder on Silk Road
Matteson, Stefanie
Charlotte Graham series (4)
Murder on stage
Scott, Sutherland
Doctor Septimus Dodds series (3)
Murder on stilts
Dean, Gregory
Deputy Commissioner Benjamin Simon series (3)
Murder-on-Thames
Fearon, Diana
Arabella Frant series (2)
Murder on the aisle
Gorman, Edward
Tobin series (1)
Murder on the Aphrodite
Sanborn, Ruth Burr
Angeline Tredennick series (2)
Murder on the Ballarat train
Greenwood, Kerry
Phryne Fisher series (3)
Murder on the beam
Brandon, John Gordon
Arthur Stukeley Pennington series (24)
Inspector Patrick Aloysius McCarthy series (48)
Murder on the blackboard
Palmer, Stuart
Hildegarde Withers series (3)
Murder on the boat express
Hardinge, Rex
Sexton Blake series (890)
Murder on the bridge
Brock, Lynn
Colonel Gore series (6)
Murder on the Broads
Chester, Gilbert
Sexton Blake series (699)
Murder on the burrows
Lorac, E C R
Inspector Macdonald series (1)
Murder on the bus
Gregg, Cecil Freeman
Inspector Cuthbert Higgins series (3)
Murder on the Canadian
Wilson, Eric
Canadian trilogy (1)
Murder on the cliff
Matteson, Stefanie
Charlotte Graham series (3)
Ryland, Clive
Superintendent Shannon series (3)
Murder on the common
Ryland, Clive
Superintendent Shannon series (4)
Murder on the Costa Brava
Bonett, John
Inspector Borges series (3)
Murder on the day of judgment
Rath, Virginia
Rocky Allan series (2)
Murder on the Duchess
Graham, Neill
Solo Malcolm series (10)
Murder on the face of it
Fetta, Emma Lou
Lyle Curtis and Susan Yates series (2)
Murder on the fourth floor
Brandon, John Gordon
Sexton Blake series (869)
Murder on the glass floor
Shore, Viola Brothers
Colin Keats and Gwynn Leith series (2)
Murder on the high seas
Brandon, John Gordon
Sexton Blake series (953)
Murder on the Hudson
Flynn, Don
Ed Fitzgerald series (2)
Murder on the ice rink
Brandon, John Gordon
Sexton Blake series (993)
Murder on the Left Bank
Paul, Elliot
Homer Evans series (6)
Murder on the line
Creasey, John
Inspector Roger West series (27)
Pascal, Francine
Sweet Valley High super thriller series (5)
Murder on the links
Christie, Agatha
Hercule Poirot series (2)
Murder on the list
Graham, Neill
Solo Malcolm series (35)
Murder on the loose
Jones, G Wayman
Black Bat series (22)
Murder on the marsh
Ferguson, John
Francis Macnab series (2)
Murder on the marshes
Chester, Gilbert
Sexton Blake series (653)
Murder on the Matterhorn
Carr, Glyn
Sir Abercrombie Lewker series (5)
Murder on the merry-go-round
Bell, Josephine
Doctor David Wintringham series (14)
Inspector Steven Mitchell series (8)
Murder on the mesa
Dresser, Davis
Twister Malone series (4)
Murder on the Monte
Richards, Ross
Sexton Blake series (1588)
Murder on the moor
Desmond, Hugh
Alan Fraser series (32)
Edwards, Walter
Sexton Blake series (691)
Murder on the Mount
Dengler, Sandy
Jack Prester series (3)
Murder on the nose
Bagby, George
Inspector Schmidt series (4)
Murder on the Orient Express
Christie, Agatha
Hercule Poirot series (9)
Murder on the Pacific
Thayer, Lee
Peter Clancy series (52)
Murder on the Palisades
Levinrew, Will
Professor Herman Brierly series (2)
Murder on the pier
Chester, Gilbert
Sexton Blake series (841)
Murder on the Potomac
Truman, Margaret
Capital crime series (12)
Murder on the program
Mannon, M M
Sheriff George White series (2)
Murder on the prowl
Spender, Jean Maud
Mary Owen series (2)
Murder on the purple water
Crane, Frances
Pat and Jean Abbott series (10)
Murder on the rails
Hardin, J D
Raider and Doc series (63)
Murder on the rocks
Dietrich, Robert
Steve Bentley series (1)
Murder on the S-23
Fisher, Steve
Sheridan Doome series (2)
Murder on the sixth hole
Frome, David
Major Gregory Lewis series (2)
Murder on the square
Frome, David
Evan Pinkerton series (12)
Murder on the stage
Brandon, John Gordon
Sexton Blake series (791)
Murder on the ten-yard line
Strange, John Stephen
Van Dusen Ormsberry series (3)
Murder on the thirty-first floor
Wahloo, Per
Chief Inspector Peter Jensen series (1)
Murder on the tropic train
Downing, Todd
Peter Bounty series (1)
Murder on the wild side
Jacks, Jeff
Shep Stone series (1)
Murder on the yacht
King, Rufus
Lieutenant Valcour series (5)
Murder on the Yellow Brick Road
Kaminsky, Stuart Melvin
Toby Peters series (2)
Murder on their minds
Coxe, George Harmon
Kent Murdock series (16)
Murder on tour
Downing, Todd
Hugh Rennert series (1)
Murder on trial
Underwood, Michael
Superintendent Simon Manton series (1)
Murder on trust
Rushton, Charles
Inspector Cadman series (2)
Murder on Wall Street
Ethan, John B
Victor Grant series (3)
Murder on wheels
Palmer, Stuart
Hildegarde Withers series (2)
Robeson, Kenneth
Avenger series (13)
Murder on Whispering Sands
Gunn, Victor
Chief Inspector Bill Cromwell series (42)
Murder one
Copper, Basil
Mike Faraday series (26)
Gruber, Frank
Johnny Fletcher and Sam Cragg series (13)
Howard, Hartley
Glenn Bowman series (30)
Murder, one, two, three
Creasey, John
Inspector Roger West series (18)
Murder or mercy
Stagge, Jonathan
Doctor Hugh Westlake series (2)
Murder or three
Mantell, Laurie
Sergeant Steve Arrow and Chief Inspector Peacock series (2)
Murder out of commission
Dominic, R B
Congressman Ben Safford series (5)
Murder out of court
Cowdroy, Joan
Chief Inspector Gorham series (2)
Dominic, R B
Congressman Ben Safford series (3)
Murder out of school
Burton, Miles
Inspector Arnold and Desmond Merrion series (44)
Ross, Ivan T
Ben Gordon series (1)
Murder out of season
Gribble, Leonard Reginald
Superintendent Anthony Slade series (22)
Murder out of the past
Creasey, John
Toff series (27)
Murder out of tune
Rushton, Charles
Inspector Cadman series (1)
Murder out of turn
Lockridge, Frances
Bill Wiegand series (2)
Mister and Mrs North series (3)
Murder out of wedlock
Pentecost, Hugh
Julian Quist series (13)
Murder over Dorval
Montrose, David
Russell Teed series (2)
Murder plays and ugly scene
Strong, Leonard Alfred George
Police diversion series (2)
Murder pluperfect
Giles, Kenneth
Inspector Harry James and Sergeant Honeybody series (9)
Murder plus
Wells, Carolyn
Fleming Stone series (57)
Murder points a finger
Alexander, David
Lieutenant Romano series (3)
Murder pool
Heath, Eric
Wade Anthony series (1)
Murder post-dated
Morice, Anne
Tessa Crichton Price series (18)
Murder R.F.D.
Petersen, Herman
Doc Miller series (2)
Murder recalls Van Kill
Bayne, Spencer
Hendrik Van Kill series (1)
Murder rehearsal
East, Roger
Superintendent Simmonds series (1)
Quin, Basil Godfrey
James Clarkson-Parry series (2)
Murder rents a room
Mason, Sara Elizabeth
Sheriff Bill Davies series (1)
Murder rides a rocket
Diamond, Frank
Ransome Dragoon and Vicky Gaines series (2)
Murder rides the express
Reilly, Helen
Inspector Christopher McKee series (25)
Murder rides the gale
Taylor, Phoebe Atwood
Asey Mayo series (22)
Murder rings the bell
Graham, Neill
Solo Malcolm series (7)
Murder road
Moore, Arthur
Bluestar series (4)
Murder round the clock
Pentecost, Hugh
Pierre Chambrun series (20)
Murder roundabout
Lockridge, Richard
Inspector Merton Heimrich series (19)
Murder runs a fever
Fenisong, Ruth
Captain Gridley Nelson series (4)
Murder seeks an agent
Brown, Wenzell
Peter Aswell series (1)
Murder sees the light
Engel, Howard
Benny Cooperman series (4)
Murder set to music
Campbell, Harriette Russell
Simon Brade series (5)
Murder she said
Christie, Agatha
Miss Jane Marple series (9)
Murder ship
Teed, George Hamilton
Grant Rushton series (1)
Murder sits pretty
Robertson, Colin
Vicky McBain series (9)
Murder solves a problem
Bramhall, Marion
Kit Acton series (1)
Murder, somewhere in this city
Procter, Maurice
Chief Inspector Harry Martineau series (6)
Murder song
Cleary, Jon
Scobie Malone series (7)
Murder speaks
Radford, Edwin
Doctor Manson series (32)
Murder, special edition!
Brody, Marc
Marc Brody series (3)
Murder spins the wheel
Halliday, Brett
Michael Shayne series (55)
Murder spoils everything
Lane, Jeremy
Whitney Wheat series (4)
Murder stalks a billion
Wallace, Robert
Phantom Detective series (30)
Murder stalks the circle
Thayer, Lee
Peter Clancy series (42)
Murder stalks the mayor
Scott, Reginald Thomas Maitland
Aurelius Smith series (5)

Murder stalks the Wakely family
Derleth, August
Judge Ephraim Peck series (1)

Murder starts from Fishguard
Davis, Howard Charles
Hugh Rudd series (2)

Murder straight up
Gorman, Edward
Jack Dwyer series (3)

Murder strikes an atomic unit
Du Bois, Theodora
Anne and Jeffrey McNeill series (12)

Murder strikes at dawn
Desmond, Hugh
Alan Fraser series (28)

Murder strikes pink
Pullein-Thompson, Josephine
Inspector James Flecker series (3)

Murder strikes twice
Dix, Maurice Buxton
Superintendent Simon Bullion series (2)

Murder sunny side up
Dominic, R B
Congressman Ben Safford series (1)

Murder sweet and sour
Pentecost, Hugh
George Crowder series (5)

Murder swings high
Brent, Nigel
Barney Hyde series (5)

Murder takes no holiday
Halliday, Brett
Michael Shayne series (36)

Murder takes two
Lee, Bernie
Tony and Pat Pratt series (3)

Murder that had everything
Footner, Hulbert
Amos Lee Mappin series (3)

Murder that wouldn't stay solved
Stone, Hampton
Jeremiah X Gibson series (4)

Murder through Room 45
Plummer, Thomas Arthur
Detective Inspector Andrew Frampton series (35)

Murder through the looking glass
Dean, Robert George
Tony Hunter series (4)
Venning, Michael
Melville Fairr series (2)

Murder through the window
Everton, Francis
Inspector George Annesley series (1)

Murder times three
Long, Amelia Reynolds
Edward Trelawny series (2)

Murder tips the scales
Creasey, John
Inspector Roger West series (18)

Murder to burn
Mantell, Laurie
Sergeant Steve Arrow and Chief Inspector Peacock series (4)

Murder to come
Halliday, Brett
Mike Shayne stories series (7)

Murder to follow
Field, Katherine
Inspector Ross Paterson series (3)

Murder to go
Lathen, Emma
John Putnam Thatcher series (10)

Murder to music
Chester, Gilbert
Sexton Blake series (754)
Crauford, William Harold Lane
Detective Kellerway series (2)
Edingtons
Captain Smith series (2)

Murder to order
Marshall, Lovat
Sugar Kane series (28)

Murder to type
Long, Amelia Reynolds
Steve Carter series (1)

Murder to welcome her
Neville, Margot
Inspector Grogan and Sergeant Manning series (10)

Murder today, money tomorrow
Messmann, Jon
Jefferson Boone series (3)

Murder too late
Ashe, Gordon
Patrick Dawlish series (17)

Murder too many
Ferrars, Elizabeth
Andrew Basnett series (5)

Murder town
Grant, Maxwell
Shadow series (104)
Marshall, Lovat
Sugar Kane series (25)

Murder trail
Grant, Maxwell
Shadow series (26)
Wallace, Robert
Phantom Detective series (21)

Murder train
Holt, Gavin
Sherret York series (1)

Murder trap
Livingston, Armstrong
Jimmy Treynor series (3)

Murder Trapp
Franklin, Eugene
Berkeley Barnes and Larry Howe series (1)

Murder tree
McFarlane, Leslie
Michael Brent series (2)

Murder triangle
Williams, Lawrence
Lgendary murders series (2)

Murder uncensored
Jason
Jason series (1)

Murder under construction
Macveigh, Sue
Captain Andy and Sue McVeigh series (2)

Murder under the big top
Wallace, Robert
Phantom Detective series (36)

Murder under the kissing bough
Myers, Amy
Auguste Didier series (6)

Murder under the mistletoe
Jordan, Jennifer
Vaughans series (2)

Murder underground
Arden, William
Kane Jackson series (4)

Murder unleashed
Bennett, Dorothy
Dennis Devore series (1)

Murder unlimited
Heberden, Mary Violet
Desmond Shannon series (17)

Murder unmourned
Douglas, George
Inspector Hallam and Sergeant Spratt series (8)

Murder unprompted
Brett, Simon
Charles Paris series (8)

Murder unrecognized
Burton, Miles
Inspector Arnold and Desmond Merrion series (50)

Murder unrenovated
Carlson, Patricia McEvoy
Maggie Ryan series (6)

Murder unsolved
Adams, Shipley
Inspector Harrow series (1)

Murder unsuspected
Cowdroy, Joan
Li Moh series (4)

Murder up my sleeve
Gardner, Erle Stanley
Terry Clane series (1)

Murder upstairs
Bliss, Adam
Alice Penny series (1)

Murder, very dry!
Baker, Samm Sinclair
Clark Clark Clark series (2)

Murder walks on tiptoe
Graham, Neill
Mister Sandyman series (3)

Murder walks the deck
Martyn, Wyndham
Anthony Trent series (21)

Murder walks the stairs
Barns, Glenn Miller
Jonathan Marks series (2)

Murder ward
Murphy, Warren Burton
Destroyer series (15)

Murder was her welcome
Neville, Margot
Inspector Grogan and Sergeant Manning series (10)

Murder was my neighbour
Cobden, Guy
John Chadwick series (1)

Murder was their medicine
Cobden, Guy
John Chadwick series (3)

Murder wears a cowl
Doherty, Paul C
Hugh Corbett series (6)

Murder wears a mantilla
Brown, Carter
Mavis Seidlitz series (8)

Murder wears a mummer's mask
Halliday, Brett
Michael Shayne series (7)

Murder wears mukluks
Boyd, Eunice Mays
F Millard Smyth series (3)

Murder well begun
Adams, Shipley
Inspector Harrow series (4)

Murder well done
Shriber, Ione Sandberg
Lieutenant Bill Grady series (3)

Murder will in
Wells, Carolyn
Alan Ford series (4)

Murder will out
Vickers, Roy
Department of Dead Ends series (2)
Inspector George Rason series (3)
Williams, Philip Claxton
Mister Hoyland series (3)

Murder will speak
Bellairs, George
Detective Inspector Thomas Littlejohn series (4)
Connington, John Jervis
Sir Clinton Driffield series (13)
Cross, Mark
Daphne Wrayne and her Four Adjusters series (32)

Murder with a kiss
Gunn, Victor
Chief Inspector Bill Cromwell series (39)

Murder with a theme song
Rath, Virginia
Michael Dundas series (2)
Rocky Allan series (6)

Murder with a vengeance
Quest, Rodney
Peter Quentin series (2)

Murder with love
Howard, Vechel
Johnny Church series (1)
Shannon, Dell
Lieutenant Luis Mendoza series (21)

Murder, with love
Story, Jack Trevor
Sexton Blake series (1413)

Murder with malice
Underwood, Michael
Sergeant Nick Attwell series (3)

Murder with mirrors
Christie, Agatha
Miss Jane Marple series (7)

Murder with mushrooms
Ashe, Gordon
Patrick Dawlish series (23)

Murder with orange blossoms
Darby, Ruth
Peter and Janet Barron series (5)

Murder with pictures
Coxe, George Harmon
Jack Fenner series (1)
Kent Murdock series (1)

Murder with variety
Arthur, William
Sexton Blake series (1417)

Murder with your malted
Barry, Jerome
Chick Varney series (1)

Murder within murder
Lockridge, Frances
Bill Wiegand series (10)
Mister and Mrs North series (10)

Murder without clues
Bonney, Joseph L
Simon Rolfe series (2)

Murder without crime
Healey, Ben
Paul Hedley series (4)

Murder without icing
Lathen, Emma
John Putnam Thatcher series (14)

Murder without malice
Spiller, Andrew
Chief Inspector Duck Mallard series (19)

Murder without motive
Goldman, Raymond Leslie
Asaph Clume series (2)

Murder without mourners
Scott, Sutherland
Doctor Septimus Dodds series (1)

Murder without regret
Cushing, E Louise
Inspector Mackay series (1)

Murder without reservation
Lee, Bernie
Tony and Pat Pratt series (2)

Murder without weapons
Cunningham, Albert Benjamin
Sheriff Jess Roden series (16)
Davis, Means
Matthew Higgins series (2)

Murder won't out
Hobson, Polly
Inspector Basil series (1)

Murder won't wait
Daly, Carroll John
Vee Brown series (1)

Murder wore green
Koehler, Robert Portner
Pecos Appleby series (2)

Murder yet to come
Myers, Isabel Briggs
Peter Jerningham series (1)

Murdered but not dead
Austin, Anne
James F Dundee series (6)

Murdered manservant
Gregg, Cecil Freeman
Inspector Cuthbert Higgins series (1)

Murdered millionaire
Queen, Ellery
Ellery Queen series (20)

Murdered one by one
Beeding, Francis
Inspector George Martin series (2)

Murderer
Griffin, W E B
Badge of honor series (6)
Morton, William
Biff Corrigan series (3)

Murderer among us
Brown, Carter
Rick Holman series (4)

Murderer at large
Ballinger, W A
Sexton Blake series (1567)
Horler, Sydney
Emp series (3)

Murderer in this house
King, Rufus
Lieutenant Valcour series (2)

Murderer is a fox
Queen, Ellery
Ellery Queen series (24)

Murderer returns
Torgerson, Edwin Dial
Pierre Montigny series (1)

Murderer who wanted more
Kendrick, Baynard
Captain Duncan Maclain series (12)

Murderer's bluff
Duncan, Francis
Mordecai Euripides Tremaine series (3)

Murderer's challenge
Footner, Hulbert
Madame Rosika Storey series (4)

Murderer's choice
Wells, Anna Mary
Doctor Hillis Owen series (2)

Murderers' houses
Melville, Jennie
Sergeant Charmian Daniels series (3)

Murderer's luck
Holt, Henry
Inspector Silver series (5)

Murderers make mistakes
Crofts, Freeman Wills
Inspector Joseph French series (27)

Murderer's maze
Marsh, John
Ray Felton series (1)

Murderer's mistake
Lorac, E C R
Inspector Macdonald series (28)

Murderer's moon
Goyne, Richard
Paul Templeton series (13)

Murderers of Monty
Hull, Richard
Inspector Fenby series (1)

Murderer's row
Batchelor, Reg
Sergeant Fenwick series (2)
Evers, Crabbe
Duffy House series (2)
Hamilton, Donald
Matt Helm series (4)

Murderer's stand-in
Brandon, John Gordon
Arthur Stukeley Pennington series (21)
Inspector Patrick Aloysius McCarthy series (45)

Murderer's trail
Farjeon, Joseph Jefferson
Ben the tramp series (4)

Murderer's vanity
Footner, Hulbert
Amos Lee Mappin series (5)

Murdering ghost
Grant, Maxwell
Shadow series (233)

Murdering kind
Butler, Gwendoline
Inspector John Coffin series (3)
Inspector William Winter series (4)

Murdermoon
Kupperberg, Paul
Amazing Spiderman series (3)
Incredible Hulk series (3)

Murderous journey
McGirr, Edmund
Jim Piron series (9)

Murder's a swine
Lombard, Nap
Lord Winterstone series (2)

Murder's a waiting game
Gilbert, Anthony
Arthur Crook series (49)

Murder's always final
Graham, Neill
Solo Malcolm series (18)

Murders at Impass Louvain
Grayson, Richard
Inspector Gautier series (1)

Murders at Scandal House
Hunt, Peter
Alan Miller series (1)

Murders at the manor
Ryland, Clive
Superintendent Shannon series (2)

Murder's coming
Cameron, Donald Clough
Abelard Voss series (1)

Murders for fours
Hume, David
Mick Cardby series (2)

Murders in Praed Street
Rhode, John
Doctor Lancelot Priestley series (4)

Murders in sequence
Propper, Milton
Tommy Rankin series (14)

Murders in the Rue Morgue
Poe, Edgar Allan
Monsieur C Auguste Dupin series (1)

Murders in volume two
Daly, Elizabeth
Henry Gamadge series (3)

Murder's just for cops
Marshall, Lovat
Sugar Kane series (20)

Murder's little helper
Bagby, George
Inspector Schmidt series (32)

Murder's long memory
Jeffries, Roderic Graeme
Inspector Enrique Alvarez series (15)

Murder's money
Ralston, Gilbert Alexander
Dakota series (4)

Murders near Mapleton
Flynn, Brian
Anthony Bathurst series (4)

Murder's no accident
Fleischman, Sid
Max Brindle series (2)

Murder's not an odd job
Dennis, Ralph
Jim Hardman series (6)

Murders of Richard III
Peters, Elizabeth
Jacqueline Kirby series (2)

Murders on Fox Island
Hood, Margaret Page
Gil Donan series (3)

Murders on the square
George, Theodore
Lieutenant Al Zimmerman series (1)

Murder's out of season
Marshall, Lovat
Sugar Kane series (19)

Murder's out of tune
Woods, Sara
Sir Nicholas Harding and Antony Maitland series (41)

Murder's playground
Jones, G Wayman
Black Bat series (31)
Murder's Rock
Reid, Desmond
Sexton Blake series (1525)
Murder's shield
Murphy, Warren Burton
Destroyer series (9)
Murdock's acid test
Coxe, George Harmon
Kent Murdock series (2)
Murdock's law
Estleman, Loren D
Page Murdock series (3)
Murky shadows
Low, Ona
Arvo Laurila series (2)
Murmering portrait
Judd, Frances K
Kay Tracey series (10)
Murmurs in the Rue Morgue
Cumberland, Marten
Saturnin Dax series (27)
Murphy
Paulsen, Gary
Al Murphy series (1)
Murphy and Co.
Masters, Anthony
Murphy's mob series (2)
Murphy's gold
Paulsen, Gary
Al Murphy series (2)
Murphy's herd
Paulsen, Gary
Al Murphy series (3)
Murphy's island
McKenna, Colleen O'Shaughnessy
Murphy family series (5)
Murphy's mob
Saunders, Michael
Murphy's mob series (1)
Murphy's stand
Paulsen, Gary
Al Murphy series (5)
Murphy's war
Paulsen, Gary
Al Murphy series (4)
Murray Hill mystery
Carter, Nicholas
Nicholas Carter series (81)
Muscle mania
Mooser, Stephen
All-Star Meatballs series (6)
Muscle tussle
Graeber, Charlotte Towner
Mister T and me series (12)
Muse of the department
Balzac, Honore de
Scenes of provincial life series (5)
Muse Theatre murder
Plummer, Thomas Arthur
Detective Inspector Andrew Frampton series (11)
Museum murders
Grant, Maxwell
Shadow series (236)
Museum mystery
Soutar, Andrew
Phineas Spinnet series (5)
Museum of the living dead
Milton, Hilary
Plot your own horror stories series (7)
Museum house ghosts
Spearing, Judith
Temple Street series (2)
Music from behind the moon
Cabell, James Branch
Dom Manuel and his descendants series (4)
Witch woman trilogy (1)
Music from the past
Cameron, Kate
Holderly Hall series (5)
Music from the sea
French, Jackie
Children of the valley trilogy (1)
Music gallery murder
Foster, Reginald Francis
Anthony Ravenhill series (4)
Music in the hills
Stevenson, Dorothy Emily
Drumberley trilogy (2)
Music lovers
Valin, Jonathan
Harry Stoner series (10)
Music master
Gissing, Vera
Pippins series (6)
Music, music for everyone
Williams, Vera Baker
Something special series (3)
Music room
Long, Martin
Inspector Keats and Tom Cotter series (1)
Music tells all
Punshon, Ernest Robertson
Bobby Owen series (24)
Music when sweet voices die
Yarbro, Chelsea Quinn
Charlie Spotted Moon series (2)
Musical chairs
Friedman, Kinky
Kinky Friedman series (5)
Musical comedy crime
Gilbert, Anthony
Scott Egerton series (8)
Musician as outsider
Wilson, Colin
Outsider series (3)
Musket boys of old Boston
Warren, George A
Musket boys series (1)
Musket boys on the Delaware
Warren, George A
Musket boys series (3)
Musket boys under Washington
Warren, George A
Musket boys series (2)
Muskets of '76
Scofield, Jonathan
Freedom fighters series (2)
Musrum
Earnshaw, Anthony
Wintersol series (1)
Mussolini, his part in my downfall
Milligan, Spike
War memoirs series (4)
Mussolini murder plot
Newman, Bernard
Inspector Marshall series (4)
Mustang fever
McCarthy, Gary
Derby Man series (3)
Mustang hunters
Roberts, J R
Gunsmith series (82)
Mustang man
L'Amour, Louis
Sackett family series (13)
Roberts, J R
Gunsmith series (124)
Mustang Marshal
Shappiro, Herbert
Mustang Marshal series (4)
Mustang men
Douglas, Thorne
Rancho Bravo series (5)
Mustang mesa
Bosworth, Frank
Earl Morton series (1)
Mustang Mesa
Field, Peter
Powder Valley series (6)
Mustang nonstop in London
Lytton, Shel
Mustang Terry Simmons series (2)
Mustang on the Matterhorn
Lytton, Shel
Mustang Terry Simmons series (1)
Mustang Trail
Cody, Stone
Five Mavericks series (2)
Mustang trail
Foreman, Leonard London
Rogue Bishop series (2)
Mustang warriors
Duncan, Terence
Powell's army series (3)
Mustapha and his wise dog
Friesner, Esther Mona
Chronicles of the twelve kingdoms series (1)
Mustard and company
Graham, Rosemary
Furry Forest series (2)
Mustard seed of magic
Johnston, Norma
Sterling family series (3)
Mustee
Horner, Lance
Falconhurst series (5)
Mustering of the hawks
Harris, John
Ira Penaluna trilogy (1)
Mutant beach
Appleton, Victor II
Tom Swift Junior series 3 (11)
Mutant garbage
Hodgman, Ann
Lunchroom series (10)
Mutant hell
Grant, Mark
Mutants amok series (2)
Mutant legacy
Haber, Karen
Mutant series (4)
Mutant prime
Haber, Karen
Mutant series (2)
Mutant season
Haber, Karen
Mutant series (1)
Mutant star
Haber, Karen
Mutant series (3)
Mutant weapon
Leinster, Murray
Med Service series (1)
Mutants amok
Grant, Mark
Mutants amok series (1)
Mutants are coming
Haiblum, Isidore
Mutants series (1)
Mutants versus mutants
Darlton, Clark
Perry Rhodan series (19)
Mutation of time
Peel, John
Doctor Who series (142)
Mute witness
Pike, Robert L
Lieutenant Clancy series (1)
Muted strings
Livingston, Marjorie
Karma series (2)
Muted swan
Arnold, Bruce
Coppinger tetralogy (3)
Mutiny
Coleman, Clay
Lost Island series (3)
Macdonnell, James Edmond
Hooky Walker series (2)
Nordhoff, Charles
Bounty trilogy (1)
Mutiny at dawn
Stuart, Vivian
Captain Alexander Sheridan series (3)
Mutiny in Meerut
Stuart, Vivian
Captain Alexander Sheridan series (3)
Mutiny in space
Packard, Edward
Choose your own adventure series (90)
Mutiny in the time machine
Keith, Donald
Time machine series (1)
Mutiny on the Bounty
Nordhoff, Charles
Bounty trilogy (1)
Mutiny on the Enterprise
Vardeman, Robert Edward
Star trek series (12)
Muzzle blast
Rossi, Bruno
Sharpshooter series (6)
My African garden
Macdonald, Sheila
Rhodesia series (2)
My afterdream
West, Julian
Looking backward responses series (4)
My afternoon with Pierre the clown
Cooper, Elizabeth
Pierre the clown series (3)
My Alaskan idyll
Rutzebeck, Hjalmar
Frozen north series (2)
My America, your America
Welk, Laurence
Wunnerful series (3)
My American diary
Citrine, Walter McLennan
My diary series (2)
My animal friends
Nakatani, Chiyoko
My series (4)
My apprenticeship
Gorky, Maxim
Childhood to university trilogy (2)
Webb, Beatrice
Partnership series (1)
My apprenticeships
Colette, Sidonie Gabrielle
Claudine series (9)
My Aunt Angie
McCardell, Roy Larcom
Aunt and Uncle series (1)
My aunt's rhinoceros, and other reflections
Fleming, Peter
Reflections and excursions series (1)
My baby brother Ned
Sumiko
My life series (1)
My baby was blasted
Brody, Marc
Marc Brody series (29)
My babysitter
Young, Ruth
My series (2)
My bad boy
Neville, Margot
Inspector Grogan and Sergeant Manning series (17)
My bathtime
Wolff, Margaret
Books for me series (3)
My bedroom
Wolff, Margaret
Books for me series (13)
My bedroom and other environmental hazards
Evans, Greg
Luann series (15)
My bedtime with Pierre the clown
Cooper, Elizabeth
Pierre the clown series (4)
My best fiend
Lavelle, Sheila
Charlie Ellis and Angela Mitchell series (1)
My best friend's boyfriend
Pascal, Francine
Sweet Valley High series (87)
My big brother
Coote, Roger
My family series (4)
My Big-Ears picture book
Blyton, Enid
Noddy series (24)
My birthday
Wolff, Margaret
Books for me series (6)
My blanket
Young, Ruth
My series (1)
My blue tongue
Roos, Stephen
Maple Street kids series (4)
My body
Dietrich, Robert
Steve Bentley series (9)
My bones will keep
Mitchell, Gladys
Dame Beatrice Bradley series (35)
My book of the Farm
Gould, Elizabeth
Green Willow Farm series (9)
My boys
Alcott, Louisa May
Aunt Jo's scrap-bag series (1)
My brilliant career
Franklin, Miles
Sybylla Penelope Melvyn series (1)
My brother Jack
Johnston, George Henry
David Meredith trilogy (1)
My brother Sammy
Van der Meer, Ron
Sammy and Mara series (1)
My brother Sean
Breinburg, Petronella
Sean series (1)
My brother, the druggist
Kaye, Marvin
Marty Gold series (2)
My brother, the star
Jackson, Alison
Leslie Crane series (1)
My brother the vampire
Dicks, Terrance
Macmagics series (2)
My brother's keeper
Joyce, Stanislaus
Dublin series (1)
My brown bear Barney
Butler, Dorothy
Barney series (1)
My brown bear Barney in trouble
Butler, Dorothy
Barney series (2)
My business is murder
Kane, Henry
Peter Chambers series (7)
My busy body
Kalman, Bobbie
In my world series (5)
My camp memory book
Kaye, Marilyn
Camp Sunnyside Friends specials series (1)
My candle the moon
Burr, Sybil
Holly Gordon series (2)
My career goes bung
Franklin, Miles
Sybylla Penelope Melvyn series (2)
My cat
Taylor, Judy
My pet series (2)
My cats and myself
Gielgud, Val
Years series (2)
My caves
Casteret, Norbert
Under the earth series (2)
My childhood
Gorky, Maxim
Childhood to university trilogy (1)
My children and I
Powell, Margaret
Domestic service series (9)
My civilised adventure
McLaren, Jack
My adventures series (5)
My class at Christmas
Thomson, Ruth
My class series (10)
My class at Diwali
Thomson, Ruth
My class series (7)
My class at Harvest Festival
Thomson, Ruth
My class series (8)
My class enjoys cooking
Thomson, Ruth
My class series (14)
My class goes swimming
Griffiths, Vivien
My class series (2)
My class goes to the library
Griffiths, Vivien
My class series (1)
My class goes to the seaside
Flanders, Jill
My class series (5)
My class likes dancing
Thomson, Ruth
My class series (13)
My class looks after pets
Lee, Vicki
My class series (3)
My class makes music
Lee, Vicki
My class series (9)
My class on sports day
Thomson, Ruth
My class series (6)
My class visits a museum
Griffiths, Vivien
My class series (12)
My class visits a nature centre
Griffiths, Vivien
My class series (11)
My class visits a park
Lee, Vicki
My class series (4)
My cologne backfired
Guisewhite, Cathy
Cathy series (9)
My colour book
Farmer, Lynne
My book series (2)
My commonplace book
Stocks, Mary
Commonplace series (1)
My cooking pot
Barkan, Joanne
My first kitchen gadgets series (2)
My cooking spoon
Barkan, Joanne
My first kitchen gadgets series (3)
My Cornish world
Baker, Denys Val
Cornish series (24)
My co-star, my enemy
Cooper, Ilene
Hollywood wars series (1)
My counting book
Farmer, Lynne
My book series (1)
My country of the pelican dreaming
Shaw, Bruce
East Kimberley series (1)
My crowded solitude
McLaren, Jack
My adventures series (2)
My daughter Helen
Monkhouse, Allan
Helen and Marmaduke series (1)
My Davy
Lambert, Janet
Parri Macdonald series (4)

My day
Wolff, Margaret
Books for me series (4)
My day begins with Pierre the clown
Cooper, Elizabeth
Pierre the clown series (1)
My day on the farm
Nakatani, Chiyoko
My series (2)
My days and nights on the battlefield
Coffin, Charles Carleton
Civil War trilogy (1)
My days of anger
Farrell, James Thomas
Danny O'Neill series (5)
My dead body
Bagby, George
Inspector Schmidt series (40)
My deadly valentine
Keene, Carolyn
Nancy Drew files series (92)
My dear Marquis
Stoeckl, Agnes de
Vanity trilogy (2)
My dear Timothy
Gollancz, Victor
Letters to Timothy series (1)
My dearest Holmes
Piercy, Rohase
Sherlock Holmes sequels series (91)
My dearest mouse
Grahame, Kenneth
Toad Hall series (1)
My diary, my world
Yates, Elizabeth
One writer's trilogy (1)
My dinner
Wolff, Margaret
Books for me series (19)
My dog
Taylor, Judy
My pet series (1)
My dog and the birthday mystery
Adler, David A
My dog series (4)
My dog and the green sock mystery
Adler, David A
My dog series (3)
My dog and the key mystery
Adler, David A
My dog series (1)
My dog and the knock knock mystery
Adler, David A
My dog series (2)
My enemy, my ally
Duane, Diane
Star trek series (18)
My enemy, my love
Coffman, Elaine
Mackinnon brothers series (1)
My face for the world to see
Hayes, Alfred
Love trilogy (2)
My family
Berridge, Celia
Stepping stones 1 2 3 series (7)
Morris, Neil
My life series (3)
My family and other animals
Durrell, Gerald
Corfu series (1)
My father
Lewin, Hugh
Jafta series (2)
My father bleeds history
Spiegelman, Art
Survivor's tale series (1)
My father, his son
Joensson, Reidar
Ingemar Johansson series (2)
My father in his dizziebell
Hayes, Douglas
History of a selfish man series (1)
My father sleeps
Mitchell, Gladys
Dame Beatrice Bradley series (17)
My father's darkest hour
Day, Clarence
Life series (2)
My father's dragon
Gannett, Ruth Stiles
Dragon series (1)
My father's glory
Pagnol, Marcel
Remembrances of childhood series (1)
My father's house
Carrier, Jean Guy
Family trilogy (1)
Troyat, Henri
Danov family trilogy (1)
My father's moon
Jolley, Elizabeth
My father's moon series (1)
My father's son
O'Connor, Frank
Only child series (2)
My feet are killing me
Courtney, Edith
Swansea series (3)
My feet are really drunk
Browne, Dik
Hagar the horrible series (16)
My Finnish diary
Citrine, Walter McLennan
My diary series (1)
My first animal ride
Allen, Julia
My first series (4)
My first camping trip
Allen, Julia
My first series (5)
My first day at playgroup
Smith, Wendy
My first day series (1)
My first day at the swimming pool
Smith, Wendy
My first day series (3)
My first day on an aeroplane
Smith, Wendy
My first day series (4)
My first day with the babysitter
Smith, Wendy
My first day series (2)
My first dentist visit
Allen, Julia
My first series (1)
My first doctor visit
Allen, Julia
My first series (2)
My first Easter
De Paola, Tomie
My first series (1)
My first Halloween
De Paola, Tomie
My first series (3)
My first job
Allen, Julia
My first series (6)
My first love and other disasters
Pascal, Francine
Love series (1)
Victoria Martin trilogy (2)
My first Passover
De Paola, Tomie
My first series (2)
My first phone call
Allen, Julia
My first series (3)
My first pop-up book of opposites
Brown, Graham
My first pop-up series (1)
My first pop-up book of togethers
Brown, Graham
My first pop-up series (2)
My first two thousand years
Viereck, George Sylvester
Wandering Jew trilogy (1)
My first voyage
McLaren, Jack
My adventures series (3)
My flat and her apartment
Turpin, Allan
Geoffrey Gillard series (1)
My foe outstrech'd beneath the tree
Clinton-Baddeley, Victor Clinton
Doctor Davie series (2)
My folks don't want me to talk about slavery
Hurmence, Belinda
Oral histories of slaves series (1)
My folks in Maine
Ober, Frederick Albion
Old farm series (4)
My friend
Sanford, Doris
Children of courage series (3)
My friend Annie
Duncan, Jane
Reachfar series (4)
My friend Cousin Emmie
Duncan, Jane
Reachfar series (10)
My friend Flicka
O'Hara, Mary
Flicka series (1)
My friend Flora
Duncan, Jane
Reachfar series (7)
My friend Foxy
Montgomery, John
Foxy series (2)
My friend Madame Zora
Duncan, Jane
Reachfar series (8)
My friend Maigret
Simenon, Georges
Inspector Jules Maigret series (33)
My friend Martha's aunt
Duncan, Jane
Reachfar series (6)
My friend, Mister Morris
Thomson, Pat
Share-a-story series (4)
My friend Monica
Duncan, Jane
Reachfar series (3)
My friend Muriel
Duncan, Jane
Reachfar series (2)
My friend my father
Duncan, Jane
Reachfar series (13)
My friend Rose
Duncan, Jane
Reachfar series (9)
My friend Sandy
Duncan, Jane
Reachfar series (5)
My friend Sashie
Duncan, Jane
Reachfar series (17)
My friend Specs McCann
McNeill, Janet
Specs McCann series (1)
My friend the chauffeur
Williamson, Charles Norris
Motoring series (3)
My friend the dog
Terhune, Albert Payson
Sunnybank collies series (10)
My friend the professor
Andrews, Lucilla
Saint Martha's Hospital series (1)
My friend the swallow
Duncan, Jane
Reachfar series (16)
My friend, the vampire
Sommer-Bodenburg, Angela
Little vampire series (1)
My friends
Morris, Neil
My life series (4)
My friend's book
France, Anatole
Pierre Noziere series (1)
My friends from Cairnton
Duncan, Jane
Reachfar series (12)
My friends George and Tom
Duncan, Jane
Reachfar series (19)
My friends the beasts
Taylor, Allan K
Uncle Jock series (1)
My friends the hungry generation
Duncan, Jane
Reachfar series (15)
My friends the Macleans
Duncan, Jane
Reachfar series (14)
My friends the Miss Boyds
Duncan, Jane
Reachfar series (1)
My friends the Miss Millers
Duncan, Jane
Reachfar series (11)
My friends the Misses Kindness
Duncan, Jane
Reachfar series (18)
My frying pan
Barkan, Joanne
My first kitchen gadgets series (1)
My garden
Coote, Roger
My world series (1)
Wolff, Margaret
Books for me series (5)
My girls
Alcott, Louisa May
Aunt Jo's scrap-bag series (4)
My god died young
Brata, Sasthi
Astride two worlds series (1)
My god, how the money rolls in
Ripley, Jack
John George Davis series (4)
My grandparents
Coote, Roger
My family series (2)
My guess was murder
Cobden, Guy
John Chadwick series (2)
My gun is justice
James, Cy
Rem McAllister series (15)
My gun is quick
Spillane, Mickey
Mike Hammer series (3)
My Halloween boyfriend
Mooser, Stephen
Creepy Creature Club series (2)
My heart and Stephanie
Kauffman, Reginald Wright
Frances Baird series (2)
My heart belongs to that boy
Lewis, Linda
Linda series (5)
My hippopotamus is on our caravan roof getting sunburnt
Edwards, Hazel
Hippopotamus series (2)
My holidays
Sumiko
My life series (3)
My holy Satan
Fisher, Vardis
Testament of man series (11)
My home in Tasmania, during a residence of nine years
Meredith, Louisa Anne
Notes and sketches series (2)
My horrible secret
Roos, Stephen
New Eden series (1)
My hospital in the hills
Seagrave, Gordon Stifler
Burma surgeon trilogy (3)
My host, Michael
Cole, John Alfred
Just back series (2)
My host the world
Santayana, George
Persons and places trilogy (3)
My house
Coote, Roger
My world series (2)
Wilmer, Diane
Step by step series (3)
My house has two doors
Han, Suyin
Crippled tree series (4)
My Indian family
Wernher, Hilda
Indian family series (1)
My Indian son-in-law
Wernher, Hilda
Indian family series (2)
My Japanese wife
Holland, Clive
Mousme series (1)
My journey
Anno, Mitsumasa
Anno's journey series (1)
My journey II
Anno, Mitsumasa
Anno's journey series (2)
My killer doesn't understand me
Mulkeen, Thomas Patrick
Clem Talbot series (2)
My kind of game
Rome, Anthony
Tony Rome series (3)
My kingdom for a grave
Plowman, Stephanie
Alexei Hamilton series (2)
Hamilton family series (2)
My kingdom for a hearse
Rice, Craig
John Joseph Malone series (11)
My kingdom for a horse
Leigh, Margaret Mary
Highland series (3)
My lady dangerous
Horler, Sydney
Sir Harker Bellamy series (1)
My lady of the chimney corner
Irvine, Alexander
Ulster life series (1)
My lady of the moor
Oxenham, John
Beatrice Chase series (1)
My lady's slipper
Brady, Cyrus Townsend
John Paul Jones series (2)
My land and water friends
Bamford, Mary Ellen
Land and water friends series (1)
My late wives
Dickson, Carter
Sir Henry Merrivale series (18)
My left foot
Brown, Christy
Cerebral palsy series (1)
My life
Ellis, Havelock
In love series (2)
My life and soft times
Longhurst, Henry
Good while it lasted series (4)
My life as a dog
Joensson, Reidar
Ingemar Johansson series (1)
My life as a man
Roth, Philip
Nathan Zuckerman series (4)
My life as an Indian
Schultz, James Willard
Blackfoot series (1)
My life is done
Woods, Sara
Sir Nicholas Harding and Antony Maitland series (24)
My life of absurdity
Himes, Chester
Quality of hurt series (2)
My listening ears
DeJonge, Joanne E
My Father's world series (3)
My little big sister
Leonard, Marcia
Fifteen series (5)
My little sister
Coote, Roger
My family series (1)
My love wears black
Cohen, Octavus Roy
Lieutenant Marty Walsh series (1)
My lute be still
Wiat, Philippa
Wyatt family series (7)
My man Jeeves
Wodehouse, Pelham Grenville
Jeeves and Bertie Wooster series (1)
My many years
Rubinstein, Arthur
Many years series (2)
My master mariner
Turner, Judy
Sir Francis Drake series (2)
My measuring cup
Barkan, Joanne
My first kitchen gadgets series (5)
My Mister T doll
Graeber, Charlotte Towner
Mister T and me series (4)
My mom hates me in January
Delton, Judy
My mom series (1)
My mom made me go to camp
Delton, Judy
My mom series (4)
My mom made me go to school
Delton, Judy
My mom series (5)
My mom made me take piano lessons
Delton, Judy
My mom series (6)
My morning with Pierre the clown
Cooper, Elizabeth
Pierre the clown series (2)
My mother
Lewin, Hugh
Jafta series (3)
My mother and I
Powell, Margaret
Domestic service series (5)
My mother lost her job today
Delton, Judy
My mom series (3)
My mother, the mayor, maybe
Kibbe, Pat
Pinkerton family series (2)
My mother's castle
Pagnol, Marcel
Remembrances of childhood series (1)
My mother's house
Colette, Sidonie Gabrielle
Claudine series (6)
My name is Asher Lev
Potok, Chaim
Asher Lev series (1)
My name is Black
Nazel, Joseph
Black series (1)
My name is death
Egan, Lesley
Jesse Falkenstein series (3)
My naughty little sister
Edwards, Dorothy
My naughty little sister series (1)
My naughty little sister and bad Harry
Edwards, Dorothy
My naughty little sister series (6)

My naughty little sister and Bad Harry's rabbit
Edwards, Dorothy
My naughty little sister series (8)
My naughty little sister and some others
Edwards, Dorothy
My naughty little sister series (2)
My naughty little sister at the fair
Edwards, Dorothy
My naughty little sister series (9)
My naughty little sister goes fishing
Edwards, Dorothy
My naughty little sister series (7)
My naughty little sister stories
Edwards, Dorothy
My naughty little sister series (5)
My naughty little sister's birthday book
Edwards, Dorothy
My naughty little sister series (9)
My naughty little sister's friends
Edwards, Dorothy
My naughty little sister series (3)
My neck of the woods
Rich, Louise Dickinson
Woods series (3)
My new baby
Wolff, Margaret
Books for me series (9)
Young, Ruth
My series (3)
My new house
Morris, Neil
My life series (5)
My new school
Morris, Neil
My life series (6)
My Noddy picture book
Blyton, Enid
Noddy picture books series (3)
My novel
Lytton, Edward George Earle Lytton Bulwer-Lytton
Real and the ideal trilogy (2)
My odyssey
McLaren, Jack
My adventures series (1)
My old Kentucky home
Paul, Elliot
Narrow street series (4)
My old man's badge
Findley, Ferguson
Johnny Malone series (1)
My opinions and Betsey Bobbet's
Holley, Marietta
Betsey Bobbet series (1)
Betsey Bobbet series (2)
My own fairy book
Lang, Andrew
Pantouflia series (2)
My own story
Baruch, Bernard Mannes
My own story series (1)
My own way
Parry, Edward Abbott
Judge trilogy (3)
My parents
Coote, Roger
My family series (3)
My parents are driving me crazy
Vedral, Joyce Lauretta
Driving me crazy series (1)
My particular murder
Sharp, David
Professor Henry Arthur Fielding series (2)
My perfect life
Barry, Lynda
Maybonne series (2)
My pets
Hill, Eric
Baby Bear series (2)
My place
Morgan, Sally
My place series (1)
My Postman Pat storytime book
Cunliffe, John Arthur
Postman Pat beginners series (5)
My potty chair
Young, Ruth
My series (4)
My prairie Christmas
Harvey, Brett
My prairie series (2)
My prairie year
Harvey, Brett
My prairie series (1)
My pruning shears
Barkan, Joanne
My first gardening tools series (4)
My pussycat
Wolff, Margaret
Books for me series (16)
My quest for liberty and love
Russell, Dora
Tamarisk tree series (1)
My rake
Barkan, Joanne
My first gardening tools series (2)
My ratbag relations
Cue, Kerry
Bloody ratbags series (3)
My robot buddy
Slote, Alfred
Danny One series (1)
My rolling pin
Barkan, Joanne
My first kitchen gadgets series (6)
My school
Coote, Roger
My world series (3)
Sumiko
My life series (2)
My school and the years of war
Russell, Dora
Tamarisk tree series (2)
My secret admirer
Roos, Stephen
New Eden series (3)
My secret gorilla
Christie, Anne
First act series (2)
My several worlds
Buck, Pearl Sydenstricker
Several worlds series (1)
My ship is so small
Davison, Ann
Voyages series (3)
My side
Wager, Walter
King Kong series (2)
My sister, the blabbermouth
Marzollo, Jean
Thirty nine kids on the block series (6)
My sister the creep
Ransom, Candice Farris
My sister series (3)
My sister the meanie
Ransom, Candice Farris
My sister series (1)
My sister the moon
Harrison, Sue
Mother earth trilogy (2)
My sister the traitor
Ransom, Candice Farris
My sister series (2)
My small country living
McMullen, Jeanine
Country living series (1)
My son
Harris, Corra
Circuit rider series (3)
My son Goggle
Plagemann, Bentz
Wallace family series (1)
My son the double agent
Mark, Ted
Man from O.R.G.Y. series (8)
My son, the druggist
Kaye, Marvin
Marty Gold series (1)
My son, the murderer
Quentin, Patrick
Lieutenant Timothy Trant series (5)
My South Sea island
Muspratt, Eric
Fire of youth series (1)
My South Seas adventures
McLaren, Jack
My adventures series (4)
My spatula
Barkan, Joanne
My first kitchen gadgets series (4)
My street
Coote, Roger
My world series (4)
My sweet untraceable you
Scoppettone, Sandra
Lauren Laurano series (3)
My teacher flunked the planet
Coville, Bruce
My teacher series (4)
My teacher fried my brains
Coville, Bruce
My teacher series (2)
My teacher glows in the dark
Coville, Bruce
My teacher series (3)
My teacher is an alien
Coville, Bruce
My teacher series (1)
My Teddy
Bawden, Juliet
My Teddy series (4)
My teddy
Wolff, Margaret
Books for me series (17)
My teddy bear
Nakatani, Chiyoko
My series (1)
My teenager is driving me crazy
Vedral, Joyce Lauretta
Driving me crazy series (3)
My three inns
Fothergill, John
Innkeeper series (3)
My toys
Wolff, Margaret
Books for me series (15)
My treasures
Nakatani, Chiyoko
My series (3)
My trip to Alpha I
Slote, Alfred
Danny One series (2)
My tropic isle
Banfield, Edmund James
Beachcomber series (2)
My trowel
Barkan, Joanne
My first gardening tools series (3)
My truck
Wolff, Margaret
Books for me series (18)
My turn to make the tea
Dickens, Monica
One pair series (3)
My two kings, 1674-1686
Nepean, Evelyn Maud
Charles II trilogy (3)
My Uncle Harry
Garvey, Keith
Outback tales series (1)
My Uncle Silas
Bates, Herbert Ernest
Uncle Silas series (1)
My universities
Gorky, Maxim
Childhood to university trilogy (3)
My university days
Gorky, Maxim
Childhood to university trilogy (3)
My very first book of colors
Carle, Eric
My very first series (1)
My very first book of food
Carle, Eric
My very first series (11)
My very first book of growth
Carle, Eric
My very first series (5)
My very first book of heads and tales
Carle, Eric
My very first series (9)
My very first book of homes
Carle, Eric
My very first series (7)
My very first book of motion
Carle, Eric
My very first series (6)
My very first book of numbers
Carle, Eric
My very first series (2)
My very first book of shapes
Carle, Eric
My very first series (3)
My very first book of sounds
Carle, Eric
My very first series (12)
My very first book of tools
Carle, Eric
My very first series (10)
My very first book of touch
Carle, Eric
My very first series (8)
My very first book of words
Carle, Eric
My very first series (4)
My very own Spot book
Hill, Eric
Spot series (40)
My visit to a museum
Davies, Sophie
My visit series (11)
My visit to the airport
Bentley, Diana
My visit series (3)
My visit to the birthday party
Davies, Sophie
My visit series (9)
My visit to the dentist
Bentley, Diana
My visit series (5)
My visit to the doctor
Bentley, Diana
My visit series (1)
My visit to the fire station
Davies, Sophie
My visit series (10)
My visit to the hospital
Davies, Sophie
My visit series (8)
My visit to the seaside
Bentley, Diana
My visit series (2)
My visit to the supermarket
Bentley, Diana
My visit series (6)
My visit to the swimming pool
Bentley, Diana
My visit series (4)
My visit to the theme park
Davies, Sophie
My visit series (12)
My visit to the zoo
Davies, Sophie
My visit series (7)
My watering can
Barkan, Joanne
My first gardening tools series (1)
My way
Barton, James
Wasteworld series (4)
My way leads me seaward
Wightman, Frank Armstrong
Wylo series (2)
My wayward pardner
Holley, Marietta
Samantha and Josiah Allen series (2)
My week
Morris, Neil
My life series (1)
Teague, Kati
My life series (1)
My widening world
Yates, Elizabeth
One writer's trilogy (2)
My wife and I
Stowe, Harriet Beecher
Harry Henderson series (1)
My word you should have seen us
Ripley, Jack
John George Davis series (3)
My world's the stage
Walden, Amelia
Miranda Welch trilogy (3)
My year
Morris, Neil
My life series (2)
My young years
Rubinstein, Arthur
Many years series (1)
Mycroft memoranda
Walsh, Ray
Sherlock Holmes sequels series (82)
Mympho named Sylvia
Janson, Hank
Hank Janson series (211)
Myra
Baldwin, Faith
Divine corners series (4)
Myra Breckenridge
Vidal, Gore
Myra, Myron series (1)
Myranda and Chester
Kibby, Leigh
Stories for happiness series (1)
Myron
Vidal, Gore
Myra, Myron series (2)
Myrtle
Hudson, Stephen
Kurt series (5)
Myrtle Albertina's secret
Pohlmann, Lillian
Myrtle Albertina series (1)
Myrtle Albertina's song
Pohlmann, Lillian
Myrtle Albertina series (2)
Myself and I
Johnston, Norma
Sterling family series (6)
Lambert, Janet
Jordons series (7)
Myself, my enemy
Plaidy, Jean
Queens of England series (1)
Myself when young
Lockley, Ronald Mathias
Island farm series (1)
Mystere d'amour
Villefranche, Anne Marie
Erotic memoirs series (4)
Mysteries in the garden
Fisher, Aileen
Ways of plants series (3)
Mysteries of Black Valley
Mallory, Arthur
Doctor Kirke Montgomery series (3)
Mysteries of life on earth and beyond
Branley, Franklyn Mansfield
Mysteries of the universe series (4)
Mysteries of Louis Napoleon's court
Zola, Emile
Rougon Macquart series (6)
Mysteries of outer space
Branley, Franklyn Mansfield
Mysteries of the universe series (2)
Mysteries of the court of Louis Napoleon
Zola, Emile
Rougon Macquart series (6)
Mysteries of the planet earth
Branley, Franklyn Mansfield
Mysteries of the universe series (6)
Mysteries of the planets
Branley, Franklyn Mansfield
Mysteries of the universe series (5)
Mysteries of the satellites
Branley, Franklyn Mansfield
Mysteries of the universe series (3)
Mysteries of the universe
Branley, Franklyn Mansfield
Mysteries of the universe series (1)
Mysteries of the worm
Bloch, Robert
Cthulhu Mythos series (8)
Mysteries of Winterthurn
Oates, Joyce Carol
Bellefleur series (3)
Mysterious affair at Styles
Christie, Agatha
Hercule Poirot series (1)
Mysterious ambassador
Falk, Lee
Phantom series (6)
Mysterious Arab
Lloyd, Hugh
Hal Keen series (5)
Mysterious camper
Fairfax, Virginia
Girl Scouts series (1)
Mysterious caravan
Dixon, Franklin W
Hardy boys series (54)
Mysterious case case
Christian, Mary Blount
Determined detectives series (1)
Mysterious castle
Carter, Nicholas
Nicholas Carter series (386)
Mysterious cavalier
Feval, Paul
Years between series (1)
Mysterious cavern
Carter, Nicholas
Nicholas Carter series (432)
Mysterious chateau
Bremond d'Ars, Yvonne de
Journal of an antique dealer series (4)
Mysterious commission
Innes, Michael
Charles Honeybath series (1)
Mysterious death of Meriwether Lewis
Burns, Ron
Harrison Hull series (1)
Mysterious disappearance of a bride
Danvers, Milton
Robert Spicer series (5)
Mysterious discovery in Ward K
Deming, Dorothy
Wendy Brent series (3)
Mysterious document
Verne, Jules
Captain Grant's children series (1)
Mysterious fireplace
Keene, Carolyn
Dana girls series (10)
Mysterious foe
Carter, Nicholas
Nicholas Carter series (158)
Mysterious football team
Jenkins, Jerry Bruce
Dallas O'Neil and the Baker Street Sports Club series (3)
Mysterious game
Carter, Nicholas
Nicholas Carter series (134)
Mysterious graft
Carter, Nicholas
Nicholas Carter series (181)
Mysterious half cat
Sutton, Margaret
Judy Bolton series (9)
Mysterious image
Keene, Carolyn
Nancy Drew series (74)
Mysterious island
Verne, Jules
Captain Grant's children series (2)
Captain Nemo series (2)

Mysterious letter
Palmer, Bernard
Bradley series (1)
Mysterious machine
Dines, Glen
Jerry and Vic series (1)
Mysterious mademoiselle
Grierson, Francis Durham
Inspector Sims and Professor Wells series (9)
Mysterious mail robbery
Carter, Nicholas
Nicholas Carter series (16)
Mysterious mannequin
Keene, Carolyn
Nancy Drew series (47)
Mysterious Max
Stine, Harlan William
Jeffrey and the third grade ghost series (1)
Mysterious Mickey Finn
Paul, Elliot
Homer Evans series (1)
Mysterious Miss Death
Evans, Gwyn
Chester Brett series (1)
Mysterious Mister Badman
Harvey, William Fryer
Athelstan Digby series (2)
Mysterious Mister Brent
Davison, Gilderoy
Mister Brent series (1)
Mysterious Mister Frame
Merrick, Mollie
Red Hanlon series (2)
Mysterious Mister Garland
Martyn, Wyndham
Anthony Trent series (3)
Mysterious Mister I
Keeler, Harry Stephen
Mysterious Mister I series (1)
Mysterious Mister Maynard
Hunter, John
Sexton Blake series (1047)
Mysterious Mister Reece
Graydon, Robert Murray
Sexton Blake series (33)
Mysterious Mister Sabin
Oppenheim, Edward Phillips
Mister Sabin series (1)
Mysterious monoplane
Adams, Eustace Lane
Andy Lane series (7)
Mysterious neighbors
Judd, Frances K
Kay Tracey series (18)
Mysterious office
Lee, Jennette Barbour Perry
Millicent Newberry series (2)
Mysterious partner
Fielding, A
Inspector Pointer series (7)
Mysterious planet
Dicks, Terrance
Doctor Who series (128)
Mysterious prowler
Matranga, Frances Carfi
Nina Cristina series (2)
Mysterious queen of magic
Nixon, Joan Lowery
Kleep, space detective series (2)
Mysterious rifleman
Tomlinson, Everett Titsworth
American scouting series (3)
Mysterious suspect
Rhode, John
Doctor Lancelot Priestley series (55)
Mysterious valley
Wicking, George Walter
Inspector Greenwood series (2)
Mysterious way
Stewart, Marjorie
Adam Square series (2)
Mysteriouser and mysteriouser
Bagby, George
Inspector Schmidt series (33)
Mysteriously yours, Maggie Marmelstein
Sharmat, Marjorie Weinman
Maggie Marmelstein series (3)
Mystery
White, Stewart Edward
Percy Darrow series (1)
Mystery animals?
Davis, Anne
Pumpkin Hollow series (5)
Mystery anti-coloring book
Striker, Susan
Anti-coloring book series (8)
Mystery at Arawak
Martin, Marcia
Donna Parker series (6)
Mystery at ballpark
Jenkins, Jerry Bruce
Bradford family series (11)
Mystery at Bellwood Estate
Stahl, Hilda
Best friends series (11)
Mystery at Black Pony Inn
Pullein-Thompson, Christine
Black Pony Inn series (2)
Mystery at Blizzard Mesa
Scott, Dan
Bret King series (5)
Mystery at Calico Pass
Smith, Ford
Dark Knight series (2)
Mystery at Camp Triumph
Christian, Mary Blount
High-low mysteries series (3)
Mystery at Chillery
Foster, Reginald Francis
Anthony Ravenhill series (7)
Mystery at Chung's Chinese restaurant
Mallett, Jerry J
Malcolm P Muddle series (1)
Mystery at Claudia's house
Martin, Ann Matthews
Baby-Sitters Club mystery series (6)
Mystery at Dark Cedars
Lavell, Edith
Mary Lou series (1)
Mystery at Dark Star Ranch
Lloyd, Hugh
Hal Keen series (10)
Mystery at Devil's Paw
Dixon, Franklin W
Hardy boys series (38)
Mystery at Fearsome Lake
Govan, Christine Noble
Wren twins series (3)
Mystery at Ghost Lodge
Govan, Christine Noble
Wren twins series (6)
Mystery at Greycombe Farm
Rhode, John
Doctor Lancelot Priestley series (12)
Mystery at Greystone Hall
Smaridge, Norah
Robin Miller series (2)
Mystery at Hartwood House
Tatham, Julie
Vicki Barr series (7)
Mystery at Hidden Harbor
Fitzsimmons, Cortland
Ethel Thomas series (3)
Mystery at Hollowhearth
Ezell, Marilyn
Susan Sand series (1)
Mystery at Keyhole carnival
Heide, Florence Parry
Spotlight Detective Club series (10)
Mystery at Lilac Inn
Keene, Carolyn
Nancy Drew series (4)
Mystery at Littlegreen House
Christie, Agatha
Hercule Poirot series (15)
Mystery at Lovers' Cave
Berkeley, Anthony
Roger Sheringham series (3)
Mystery at Lynden Sands
Connington, John Jervis
Sir Clinton Driffield series (3)
Mystery at MacAdoo Zoo
Heide, Florence Parry
Spotlight Detective Club series (4)
Mystery at Madame Darkle's wax museum
Mallett, Jerry J
Malcolm P Muddle series (2)
Mystery at Magnolia Mansion
Keene, Carolyn
Nancy Drew series (97)
Mystery at McGeehan Ranch
Dengler, Sandy
Pioneer family series (6)
Mystery at Medicine Wheel
Meyers, Barlow
Walt Disney's Annette series (5)
Mystery at Merrilees
Poole, Michael
Freddie Browne and Jim Fanshaw series (5)
Mystery at Midget Falls
Gezi, Kal
Maple Street Five series (8)
Mystery at Miser's Mountain
Work, Virginia
Jodi series (4)
Mystery at Mockingbird Manor
Pascal, Laurie
Pick-a-path series (6)
Mystery at Moonstone Bay
Schroeder, Doris
Walt Disney's Annette series (3)
Mystery at Moor Street
Gregg, Cecil Freeman
Inspector Cuthbert Higgins series (16)
Mystery at Musket Bay
Bradman, Tony
Bluebeards series (2)
Mystery at Olympia
Rhode, John
Doctor Lancelot Priestley series (21)
Mystery at Poor Boy's Folly
Palmer, Bernard
Powell family series (4)
Mystery at Putnam Hall
Winfield, Arthur M
Putnam Hall series (6)
Mystery at Raider Stadium
Jenkins, Jerry Bruce
Bradford family series (2)
Mystery at Redstone Farm
Lunt, Alice
Redstone Farm series (2)
Mystery at Rock City
Govan, Christine Noble
Wren twins series (4)
Mystery at Rogue's Cave
Wells, Helen
Cherry Ames series (21)
Mystery at Rustlers' Fort
Nesbit, Troy
Wilderness mystery series (4)
Mystery at Sherwood
Palmer, Geoffrey
Sherwood Forest series (1)
Mystery at Smugglers' Cove
Schroeder, Doris
Walt Disney's Annette series (4)
Mystery at Snowflake Inn
Warner, Gertrude Chandler
Boxcar children special series (3)
Mystery at Southport Cinema
Heide, Florence Parry
Spotlight Detective Club series (13)
Mystery at Sugar Creek
Hutchens, Paul
Sugar Creek Gang series (7)
Mystery at the crossroads
Keene, Carolyn
Dana girls series (16)
Mystery at the dog show
Warner, Gertrude Chandler
Boxcar children series (35)
Mystery at the echoing cave
Govan, Christine Noble
Wren twins series (8)
Mystery at the haunted house
Govan, Christine Noble
Wren twins series (2)
Mystery at the Hollender Hotel
Mallett, Jerry J
Malcolm P Muddle series (3)
Mystery at the Indian hide-out
Govan, Christine Noble
Wren twins series (1)
Mystery at the Laff-a-Lott amusement park
Mallett, Jerry J
Malcolm P Muddle series (4)
Mystery at the meet
Levy, Elizabeth
Gymnasts series (11)
Mystery at the rectory
Fielding, A
Inspector Pointer series (20)
Mystery at the Seesaw Cinema Company
Mallett, Jerry J
Malcolm P Muddle series (5)
Mystery at the ski jump
Keene, Carolyn
Nancy Drew series (29)
Mystery at the tree house
Gezi, Kal
Maple Street Five series (9)
Mystery at the weird ruins
Govan, Christine Noble
Wren twins series (7)
Mystery at Tudor Arches
Gribble, Leonard Reginald
Superintendent Anthony Slade series (10)
Mystery at Wheeler Place
Stahl, Hilda
Wren House series (1)
Mystery at Witchend
Saville, Malcolm
Lone Pine Five Club series (1)
Mystery behind the wall
Warner, Gertrude Chandler
Boxcar children series (17)
Mystery box
Sayer, Walter William
Sexton Blake series (156)
Mystery boxes
Hale, Susan
Ronnie Smithers series (2)
Mystery cases of C J Watson
Resciniti, Angelo G
C J Watson series (1)
Mystery cat
Saunders, Susan
Mystery cat series (1)
Mystery cat and the chocolate trap
Saunders, Susan
Mystery cat series (2)
Mystery cat and the monkey business
Saunders, Susan
Mystery cat series (3)
Mystery Christmas
Dale, Norman
Tim Forest series (2)
Mystery crash
Powell, Van
Air mystery series (1)
Mystery cruise
Warner, Gertrude Chandler
Boxcar children series (29)
Wood, Andrew
Bunch and Alexander series (1)
Mystery day
Ziefert, Harriet
Mister Rose's class series (5)
Mystery dolls from Planet Urd
Nixon, Joan Lowery
Kleep, space detective series (3)
Mystery for Archie
Bateman, Robert
Archibald McGillicuddy series (2)
Mystery for Mary
Hanson, Virginia
Adam Drew and Katherine Cornish series (3)
Mystery for Meg
Ladd, Elizabeth
Meg of Heron's Neck series (2)
Mystery for Mister Bass
Cameron, Eleanor
Tyco Bass series (4)
Mystery gangster
Chester, Gilbert
Sexton Blake series (654)
Mystery girl
Warner, Gertrude Chandler
Boxcar children series (28)
Wells, Carolyn
Fleming Stone series (13)
Mystery hand
Bolt, Ben
Captain Grandison series (1)
Mystery horse
Warner, Gertrude Chandler
Boxcar children series (34)
Mystery house
Burrough, Reath J
Smiley Adams series (2)
Mystery in glass
Kilvington, Edwin
Crispin Quane series (1)
Mystery in Mexico
Sheldon, Ann
Linda Craig series (6)
Mystery in Newfoundland
Wees, Frances Shelley
Patterson family series (2)
Mystery in Spindle Bottom
Allan, Mabel Esther
Spindle Bottom series (2)
Mystery in Studio Thirteen
Woolfolk, Dorothy
Donna Rockford series (5)
Mystery in the Channel
Crofts, Freeman Wills
Inspector Joseph French series (7)
Mystery in the clouds
Hill, Eileen
Robin Kane series (5)
Mystery in the doctor's office
Wells, Helen
Cherry Ames series (26)
Mystery in the English Channel
Crofts, Freeman Wills
Inspector Joseph French series (7)
Mystery in the old mine
Dixon, Franklin W
Hardy boys series (121)
Mystery in the sand
Warner, Gertrude Chandler
Boxcar children series (16)
Mystery in the snow
Warner, Gertrude Chandler
Boxcar children series (32)
Mystery in the woodshed
Gilbert, Anthony
Arthur Crook series (10)
Mystery in Washington, D.C.
Warner, Gertrude Chandler
Boxcar children special series (2)
Mystery in Williamsburg
Walker, Holly Beth
Meg Duncan series (6)
Mystery island
Blyton, Enid
Adventure series (1)
Robeson, Kenneth
Doc Savage series (139)
Mystery Island
White, Palmer
Mystery Island series (1)
Mystery lady
Clarke, Anna
Professor Paula Glenning series (3)
Mystery lights on Blue Harbour
Wilson, Budge
Blue Harbour series (3)
Mystery mandarin
Bobin, John William
Sexton Blake series (280)
Mystery manor
Atkinson, Mary Evelyn
Lockett family series (2)
Mystery men of Mars
Claudy, Carl Harry
Adventures in the unknown series (1)
Mystery mile
Allingham, Margery
Albert Campion series (2)
Mystery miliataman
Black, Ladbroke
Sexton Blake series (1018)
Mystery mine
Saville, Malcolm
Lone Pine Five Club series (12)
Mystery of a butcher's shop
Mitchell, Gladys
Dame Beatrice Bradley series (2)
Mystery of a hansom cab
Hume, Fergus
Detective Kilsip and Duncan Calton series (1)
Mystery of a hidden painting
Warner, Gertrude Chandler
Boxcar children series (24)
Mystery of Ah Jim
Gilson, Charles
Submarine U93 series (3)
Mystery of Angelina Frood
Freeman, Richard Austin
Doctor John Evelyn Thorndyke series (11)
Mystery of Atlantis
Gasperini, Jim
Time machine series (8)
Mystery of Avenue Road
Parsons, Anthony
Sexton Blake series (1217)
Mystery of Bandit Gulch
Scott, Dan
Bret King series (9)
Mystery of Banshee Towers
Blyton, Enid
Fatty series (15)
Mystery of Becker's Brook
Blair, Allan
Sexton Blake series (828)
Mystery of being Jewish
Cone, Molly
Shema series (5)
Mystery of Bullen Point
Armour, R Coutts
Sexton Blake series (410)
Mystery of Burnt Hill
Robertson, Keith
Neil and Swede trilogy (1)
Mystery of Cabin Island
Dixon, Franklin W
Hardy boys series (7)
Mystery of Cell Thirteen
Teed, George Hamilton
Sexton Blake series (817)
Mystery of Chimney Rock
Packard, Edward
Choose your own adventure series (5)
Mystery of Collinwood
Ross, Marilyn
Barnabas Collins series (4)
Mystery of Comanche Caves
Scott, Dan
Bret King series (7)

Mystery of Comanche Caves
Scott, Dan
Bret King series (7)
Mystery of Crocodile Island
Keene, Carolyn
Nancy Drew series (55)
Mystery of Death Trap Mine
Carey, Mary Virginia
Three Investigators series (24)
Mystery of Doctor Fu-Manchu
Rohmer, Sax
Fu-Manchu series (1)
Mystery of Drear House
Hamilton, Virginia
Dies Drear series (2)
Mystery of D's 24
Wallace, Trevor
John Tracy series (3)
Mystery of Echo Lodge
Foley, Louise Munro
Choose your own adventure series (42)
Mystery of Fell Castle
Gask, Arthur
Gilbert Larose series (20)
Mystery of fifty-two
Masterman, Walter Sidney
Sir Arthur Sinclair series (5)
Mystery of Flight 908
Wells, Helen
Vicki Barr series (15)
Mystery of Gallows Cliff
Campbell, Bruce
Ken Holt series (15)
Mystery of Ghost Canyon
Scott, Dan
Bret King series (1)
Mystery of Glengary Castle
Hill, Eileen
Robin Kane series (3)
Mystery of Glyn Castle
Brooks, Leonard Harold
Sexton Blake series (276)
Mystery of Gruden's Gap
Cross, Mark
Daphne Wrayne and her Four Adjusters series (17)
Mystery of Hanging Sword Alley
Bayfield, William John
Sexton Blake series (418)
Mystery of High Eldersham
Burton, Miles
Inspector Arnold and Desmond Merrion series (1)
Mystery of Holly Lane
Blyton, Enid
Fatty series (11)
Mystery of Horseshoe Canyon
Sheldon, Ann
Linda Craig series (4)
Mystery of Hunting's End
Eberhart, Mignon Good
Sarah Keate and Lance O'Leary series (3)
Mystery of Hurricane Castle
Nixon, Joan Lowery
Huricane Castle series (1)
Mystery of Joan Marryat
Cross, Mark
Daphne Wrayne and her Four Adjusters series (22)
Mystery of Jockey Hollow
Garis, Cleo Fausta
Arden Blake series (2)
Mystery of June thirteen
Severy, Martin
George Maitland series (2)
Mystery of Khufri's tomb
Mundy, Talbot
Jimgrim series (10)
Mystery of King Cobra
Marfield, Dwight
Dudley Brent series (4)
Inspector Skane series (4)
Major Krim series (1)
Mystery of King's Everard
Brandon, Charles
John Fortescue series (1)
Mystery of Marie Roget
Poe, Edgar Allan
Monsieur C Auguste Dupin series (1)
Mystery of Mekong
Burrard, Gerald
Tiger of Tibet series (2)
Mystery of Merlyn Mansions
Shute, Walter
Sexton Blake series (582)
Mystery of Mister Cross
Robbins, Clifton
Clay Harrison series (2)
Mystery of Mister Jones's disappearing taxi
Aiken, Joan
Arabel and Mortimer series (7)
Mystery of Mister Mock
Walling, Robert Alfred John
Philip Tolefree series (10)
Mystery of Misty Canyon
Keene, Carolyn
Nancy Drew series (86)
Mystery of Misty Island Inn
Cates, Emily
Haunting with Louisa series (2)
Mystery of Mitcham Common
Evans, Gwyn
Sexton Blake series (517)
Mystery of Moat Farm
Hunter, John
Sexton Blake series (1175)
Mystery of Monks' Island
Rambeau, John
Morgan Bay series (6)
Mystery of monster mountain
Carey, Mary Virginia
Three Investigators series (20)
Mystery of Monte Carlo
Graydon, William Murray
Sexton Blake series (525)
Mystery of Morgan Castle
Rambeau, John
Morgan Bay series (1)
Mystery of Mr Jessop
Punshon, Ernest Robertson
Bobby Owen series (8)
Mystery of number one
Horler, Sydney
Paul Vivanti series (1)
Mystery of number seven Bitton Court
Quiroule, Pierre
Sexton Blake series (969)
Mystery of number thirteen Cavendish Square
Quiroule, Pierre
Sexton Blake series (897)
Mystery of Oldham
Bidston, Lester
Sexton Blake series (600)
Mystery of Orcival
Gaboriau, Emile
Monsieur Lecoq series (2)
Mystery of Pig's Nose
Leyland, Eric
Max and Scrap series (1)
Mystery of Rackety's way
Friskey, Margaret
Magic meadow series (2)
Mystery of Rawhide Gap
Scott, Dan
Bret King series (4)
Mystery of Rodney's Cove
Brooks, Edwy Searles
Sexton Blake series (331)
Mystery of Saint-Salgue
Berna, Paul
Gaby series (4)
Mystery of Secret Beach
Finkel, George
Group Captain Alan Metcalfe series (1)
Mystery of Sherwood Towers
Verner, Gerald
Sexton Blake series (537)
Mystery of Smuggler's Cove
Dixon, Franklin W
Hardy boys series (64)
Mystery of Spider Lake
McFarlane, Leslie
Checkmate series (3)
Mystery of Squadron X
Tyrer, Walter
Sexton Blake series (1106)
Mystery of Stingyman's Alley
Garis, Lilian C
Melody Lane series (7)
Mystery of Stockmere School
Westerman, Percy Francis
Sinclair series (1)
Mystery of Swordship Reef
Upfield, Arthur William
Napoleon Bonaparte series (7)
Mystery of Tally-Ho Cottage
Blyton, Enid
Fatty series (12)
Mystery of the abandoned cttage
Graydon, William Murray
Sexton Blake series (349)
Mystery of the Abbe Montrose
Elvestad, Sven
Osborne Crag series (2)
Mystery of the African expedition
Hardinge, Rex
Sexton Blake series (931)
Mystery of the African farm
Hardinge, Rex
Sexton Blake series (1000)
Mystery of the African mine
Hardinge, Rex
Sexton Blake series (891)
Mystery of the Agony
Bobin, John William
Sexton Blake series (74)
Mystery of the Albanian avenger
Sayer, Walter William
Sexton Blake series (397)
Mystery of the Alpine pass
Adams, Andy
Biff Brewster series (13)
Mystery of the ambush in India
Adams, Andy
Biff Brewster series (7)
Mystery of the American envoy
Hunter, John
Sexton Blake series (1176)
Mystery of the ancients
Simon, Morris
Endless quest series (28)
Mystery of the Anti
Scheer, Karl Herbert
Perry Rhodan series (88)
Mystery of the Arab agent
Jardine, Warwick
Sexton Blake series (1330)
Mystery of the Arabian stallion
Adams, Andy
Biff Brewster series (12)
Mystery of the ashes
Wynne, Anthony
Doctor Eustace Hailey series (3)
Mystery of the Aztec chain
Norman, John
Martin Speed series (6)
Mystery of the Aztec warrior
Dixon, Franklin W
Hardy boys series (43)
Mystery of the ball park
Cooper, John R
Mel Martin series (1)
Mystery of the bamboo bird
Keene, Carolyn
Dana girls series (22)
Mystery of the bankrupt estate
Parsons, Anthony
Sexton Blake series (1169)
Mystery of the bewitched bookmobile
Heide, Florence Parry
Spotlight Detective Club series (8)
Mystery of the Black-Magic Cave
Walker, Holly Beth
Meg Duncan series (5)
Mystery of the blackmailed baronet
Gregory, Hylton
Sexton Blake series (425)
Mystery of the blazing cliffs
Carey, Mary Virginia
Three Investigators series (32)
Mystery of the blind writer
Gezi, Kal
Maple Street Five series (6)
Mystery of the blitzed tower
Parsons, Anthony
Sexton Blake series (1290)
Mystery of the Blue Admiral
Clewes, Dorothy
Hadley family series (2)
Mystery of the blue geranium, and other Tuesday Club murders
Christie, Agatha
Miss Jane Marple series (2)
Mystery of the blue pelican
Hill, Eileen
Robin Kane series (1)
Mystery of the blue ring
Giff, Patricia Reilly
Polka Dot series (1)
Mystery of the Blue Train
Christie, Agatha
Hercule Poirot series (6)
Mystery of the body on the cliff
Hardinge, Rex
Sexton Blake series (1328)
Mystery of the bombed hotel
Skene, Anthony
Sexton Blake series (1080)
Mystery of the bombed monastery
Parsons, Anthony
Sexton Blake series (1125)
Mystery of the Boule cabinet
Stevenson, Burton Egbert
Jim Godfrey series (4)
Mystery of the brass bound trunk
Keene, Carolyn
Nancy Drew series (17)
Mystery of the brass idol
Wells, Helen
Vicki Barr series (16)
Mystery of the bullion robbery
Martin, Robert
Dance and Company series (5)
Mystery of the burning ocean
Lyle, Mel
Power boys series (3)
Mystery of the burnt cottage
Blyton, Enid
Fatty series (1)
Mystery of the Cairo express
Parsons, Anthony
Sexton Blake series (1126)
Mystery of the Cape Cod players
Taylor, Phoebe Atwood
Asey Mayo series (3)
Mystery of the Cape Cod tavern
Taylor, Phoebe Atwood
Asey Mayo series (4)
Mystery of the car bandits
Martin, Robert
Dance and Company series (2)
Mystery of the Caribbean pearls
Adams, Andy
Biff Brewster series (8)
Mystery of the cashiered officer
Teed, George Hamilton
Sexton Blake series (857)
Mystery of the championship belt
Hardy, Arthur Steffens
Sexton Blake series (424)
Mystery of the Chinese junk
Dixon, Franklin W
Hardy boys series (39)
Mystery of the Chinese ring
Adams, Andy
Biff Brewster series (2)
Mystery of the circle of fire
Bartlett, Philip A
Roy Stover series (4)
Mystery of the clasped hands
Boothby, Guy
Jacob Burrell series (1)
Mystery of the clock
Murray, Andrew
Sexton Blake series (251)
Mystery of the closed car
Sproul, Kathleen
Dick Wilson series (4)
Mystery of the colonel's clock
Turner, Philip
Darnley Mills series (1)
Mystery of the condemned cottage
Chester, Gilbert
Sexton Blake series (998)
Mystery of the confiscated ship
Chester, Gilbert
Sexton Blake series (1133)
Mystery of the corded box
Cross, Mark
Daphne Wrayne and her Four Adjusters series (37)
Mystery of the coughing dragon
West, Nick
Three Investigators series (14)
Mystery of the cranky collector
Carey, Mary Virginia
Three Investigators series (42)
Mystery of the crashed air liner
Chester, Gilbert
Sexton Blake series (1180)
Mystery of the creeping man
Wees, Frances Shelley
Michael Forrester series (2)
Mystery of the creep-show crooks
Carey, Mary Virginia
Three Investigators series (41)
Mystery of the Crested Falcon
Noy, John
Rufus Deville series (4)
Mystery of the crooked gift
Parsons, Anthony
Sexton Blake series (1264)
Mystery of the crooked tree
Hunt, Francis
Mary and Jerry Denton series (5)
Mystery of the cupboard
Banks, Lynne Reid
Omri series (4)
Mystery of the dancing devil
Arden, William
Three Investigators series (25)
Mystery of the dancing skeleton
Govan, Christine Noble
Wren twins series (5)
Mystery of the David M
Macarthur, David Wilson
Alec Sinclair series (1)
Mystery of the dead man's riddle
Arden, William
Three Investigators series (22)
Mystery of the dead man's wallet
Brandon, John Gordon
Sexton Blake series (954)
Mystery of the deadly diamond
Howard, Elizabeth Howard
My name is Paris series (4)
Mystery of the deadly double
Arden, William
Three Investigators series (28)
Mystery of the demobilized soldier
Chester, Gilbert
Sexton Blake series (1111)
Mystery of the desert giant
Dixon, Franklin W
Hardy boys series (40)
Mystery of the deserted camp
Drummond, J
Sexton Blake series (1202)
Mystery of the devil mask
Hardinge, Rex
Sexton Blake series (1238)
Mystery of the disappearing cat
Blyton, Enid
Fatty series (2)
Mystery of the docks
Graydon, William Murray
Sexton Blake series (574)
Mystery of the double burglary
Chester, Gilbert
Sexton Blake series (1154)
Mystery of the double kidnapping
Lyle, Mel
Power boys series (5)
Mystery of the Dover Road
Graydon, William Murray
Sexton Blake series (291)
Mystery of the Downs
Watson, John Reay
Crewe series (2)
Mystery of the east wind
Marfield, Dwight
Dudley Brent series (1)
Gail McGurk series (1)
Inspector Skane series (1)
Mystery of the engraved skull
Hope, Stanton
Sexton Blake series (1351)
Mystery of the evil eye
Wynne, Anthony
Doctor Eustace Hailey series (1)
Mystery of the fallen tree
Christian, Mary Blount
Sherlock Street detectives series (8)
Mystery of the fat cat
Bonham, Frank
Dogtown Ghetto series (2)
Mystery of the fiery eye
Arthur, Robert
Three Investigators series (7)
Mystery of the film city
Teed, George Hamilton
Sexton Blake series (500)
Mystery of the fire dragon
Keene, Carolyn
Nancy Drew series (38)
Mystery of the fires
Lavell, Edith
Mary Lou series (2)
Mystery of the five guilty men
Drummond, J
Sexton Blake series (1350)
Mystery of the flaming footprints
Carey, Mary Virginia
Three Investigators series (15)
Mystery of the flying express
Dixon, Franklin W
Hardy boys series (20)
Mystery of the flying skeleton
Lyle, Mel
Power boys series (2)
Mystery of the folded paper
Footner, Hulbert
Amos Lee Mappin series (1)
Mystery of the forbidden territory
Hardinge, Rex
Sexton Blake series (1254)
Mystery of the Forgotten Island
Heide, Florence Parry
Spotlight Detective Club series (15)
Mystery of the four rooms
Gibbons, Harry Hornaby Clifford
Sexton Blake series (476)
Mystery of the free Frenchmen
Parsons, Anthony
Sexton Blake series (1041)
Mystery of the French milliner
Thomson, Basil
Superintendent Richardson series (7)
Mystery of the friendly forger
Martin, Robert
Dance and Company series (3)
Mystery of the Fulton Gardens and the moorland tragedy
Orczy, Emmuska
Old man in the corner series (7)

Mystery of the galaxy game
Carlson, Dale
James Budd series (4)
Mystery of the galloping horse
Campbell, Bruce
Ken Holt series (9)
Mystery of the German prisoner
Frazer, Martin
Sexton Blake series (1033)
Mystery of the girl in green
Parsons, Anthony
Sexton Blake series (1291)
Mystery of the glass bullet
Atkey, Bertram
Smiler Bunn series (7)
Mystery of the glowing eye
Keene, Carolyn
Nancy Drew series (51)
Mystery of the gold box
Williams, Valentine
Clubfoot series (7)
Mystery of the golden angel
Grierson, Francis Durham
Richard Furling series (2)
Mystery of the golden chalice
Graydon, William Murray
Sexton Blake series (526)
Mystery of the golden palomino
Jenkins, Jerry Bruce
Dallas O'Neil mysteries series (6)
Mystery of the golden skulls
Martin, Robert
Dance and Company series (1)
Mystery of the golden wings
Lambert, Rosa
Glyn Morgan series (3)
Mystery of the Greek exile
Chester, Gilbert
Sexton Blake series (879)
Mystery of the green bottle
Brandon, John Gordon
Sexton Blake series (994)
Mystery of the green flame
Campbell, Bruce
Ken Holt series (10)
Mystery of the green ghost
Arthur, Robert
Three Investigators series (4)
Mystery of the green gloves
Smith, Beatrice Schillinger
Kate and Ben King series (5)
Mystery of the grey car
Bobin, John William
Sexton Blake series (73)
Mystery of the grinning tiger
Campbell, Bruce
Ken Holt series (11)
Mystery of the hasty arrow
Green, Anna Katharine
Amelia Butterworth series (6)
Caleb Sweetwater series (5)
Ebenezer Gryce series (12)
Mystery of the haunted hospital
Dicks, Terrance
Ask Oliver series (2)
Mystery of the haunted skyscraper
Lyle, Mel
Power boys series (1)
Mystery of the haunted square
Drummond, J
Sexton Blake series (1252)
Mystery of the haunted woods
Nixon, Joan Lowery
Huricane Castle series (2)
Mystery of the headless horse
Arden, William
Three Investigators series (26)
Mystery of the hidden beach
Warner, Gertrude Chandler
Boxcar children series (41)
Mystery of the hidden house
Blyton, Enid
Fatty series (6)
Mystery of the hidden room
Harvey, Marion
Graydon McKelvie series (1)
Mystery of the hidden trap
Carlson, Dale
Jenny Dean series (2)
Mystery of the Highland crest
Foley, Louise Munro
Choose your own adventure series (34)
Mystery of the Hollywood horse
Murray, Michael
Timber Trail riders series (4)
Mystery of the human bookcase
Morton, William
Biff Corrigan series (2)
Mystery of the hundred chests
Murray, Andrew
Sexton Blake series (195)
Mystery of the hush-hush factory
Chester, Gilbert
Sexton Blake series (1052)
Mystery of the ice-cream man
Brandon, John Gordon
Sexton Blake series (950)
Mystery of the Indian relic
Parsons, Anthony
Sexton Blake series (1127)
Mystery of the invisible dog
Carey, Mary Virginia
Three Investigators series (23)
Mystery of the invisible enemy
Campbell, Bruce
Ken Holt series (14)
Mystery of the invisible thief
Blyton, Enid
Fatty series (8)
Mystery of the iron box
Campbell, Bruce
Ken Holt series (7)
Mystery of the island jungle
Roddy, Lee
Ladd family series (3)
Mystery of the Isle of Fortune
Armour, R Coutts
Sexton Blake series (506)
Mystery of the Italian ruins
Long, Derek
Sexton Blake series (1260)
Mystery of the ivory charm
Keene, Carolyn
Nancy Drew series (13)
Mystery of the jade-green Cadillac
Clewes, Dorothy
Hadley family series (4)
Mystery of the jade tiger
Keene, Carolyn
Nancy Drew series (104)
Mystery of the khaki tunic
Orczy, Emmuska
Old man in the corner series (3)
Mystery of the kidnapped kid
Jenkins, Jerry Bruce
Dallas O'Neil mysteries series (1)
Mystery of the kidnapped kidnapper
Garden, Nancy
Monster hunters series (4)
Mystery of the kidnapped munition worker
Chester, Gilbert
Sexton Blake series (1090)
Mystery of the kidnapped whale
Brandel, Marc
Three Investigators series (35)
Mystery of the king cobra
Marfield, Dwight
Gail McGurk series (4)
Mystery of the kneeling woman
Dalton, Moray
Inspector Hugh Collier series (6)
Mystery of the laughing horses
Donovan, Jean Beradine
Bill Speed series (1)
Mystery of the laughing shadow
Arden, William
Three Investigators series (12)
Mystery of the live ghosts
Gezi, Kal
Maple Street Five series (2)
Mystery of the living shadow
Sayer, Walter William
Sexton Blake series (154)
Mystery of the locked room
Keene, Carolyn
Dana girls series (7)
Mystery of the London banker
Fletcher, Joseph Smith
Ronald Camberwell series (7)
Mystery of the lonely lantern
Heide, Florence Parry
Spotlight Detective Club series (9)
Mystery of the long shadow
Martin, Robert
Dance and Company series (4)
Mystery of the lorry driver
Urquhart, Paul
Sexton Blake series (1015)
Mystery of the lost battle-ship
Sayer, Walter William
Sexton Blake series (356)
Mystery of the lost dogs
Keene, Carolyn
Nancy Drew picture books series (1)
Mystery of the lost legionnaire
Osborne, Mark
Sexton Blake series (767)
Mystery of the lost loot
King, Hilary
Sexton Blake series (1278)
Mystery of the lost princess
Carlson, Dale
James Budd series (3)
Mystery of the lost tower treasure
Clewes, Dorothy
Hadley family series (5)
Mystery of the lost village
Warner, Gertrude Chandler
Boxcar children series (37)
Mystery of the Louvre
Bernede, Arthur
Chantecoq series (1)
Mystery of the mad millionaires
Tyrer, Walter
Sexton Blake series (1391)
Mystery of the madman at Cornwall Cragg
Carlson, Dale
James Budd series (1)
Mystery of the magic circle
Carey, Mary Virginia
Three Investigators series (27)
Mystery of the magic meadow
Friskey, Margaret
Magic meadow series (1)
Mystery of the magician
Howard, Elizabeth Howard
My name is Paris series (2)
Mystery of the Malay schooner
Dalton, Clive
Malay series (5)
Mystery of the man from Rio
Teed, George Hamilton
Sexton Blake series (594)
Mystery of the mandarin's idol
Graydon, Robert Murray
Sexton Blake series (512)
Mystery of the manor house
Frow, Gerald
Young Sherlock Holmes series (1)
Mystery of the mansion fire
Gibbons, Harry Hornaby Clifford
Sexton Blake series (477)
Mystery of the marauder's gold
Rambeau, John
Morgan Bay series (7)
Mystery of the marble angel
Rambeau, John
Morgan Bay series (2)
Mystery of the marchers
Edwards, Walter
Sexton Blake series (908)
Mystery of the masked rider
Keene, Carolyn
Nancy Drew series (109)
Mystery of the mason's arms
Parsons, Anthony
Sexton Blake series (1313)
Mystery of the Maya
Montgomery, Raymond A
Choose your own adventure series (11)
Mystery of the melting snowman
Heide, Florence Parry
Spotlight Detective Club series (6)
Mystery of the merry magician
Queen, Ellery, Junior
Gulliver Queen series (1)
Mystery of the message from the sky
Christian, Mary Blount
Sherlock Street detectives series (9)
Mystery of the Metro
Howard, Elizabeth Howard
My name is Paris series (1)
Mystery of the Mexican treasure
Adams, Andy
Biff Brewster series (4)
Mystery of the midget clown
Gezi, Kal
Maple Street Five series (7)
Mystery of the midnight menace
Garden, Nancy
Monster hunters series (2)
Mystery of the midnight message
Heide, Florence Parry
Spotlight Detective Club series (11)
Mystery of the midnight raider
Christian, Mary Blount
Sherlock Street detectives series (5)
Mystery of the midnight smugglers
Clewes, Dorothy
Hadley family series (8)
Mystery of the midnight visitor
Rambeau, John
Morgan Bay series (3)
Mystery of the million-dollar penny
Lyle, Mel
Power boys series (4)
Mystery of the mine
Grey, Peter
Kit Hunter series (5)
Mystery of the missing angler
Tyrer, Walter
Sexton Blake series (1248)
Mystery of the missing aviator
Sayer, Walter William
Sexton Blake series (205)
Mystery of the missing cat
Warner, Gertrude Chandler
Boxcar children series (42)
Mystery of the missing constable
Blair, Allan
Sexton Blake series (949)
Mystery of the missing corpses
Elliott, George
Martin Speed series (2)
Mystery of the missing diamond
Dicks, Terrance
Ask Oliver series (1)
Mystery of the missing doctor
Brisbane, Coutts
Sexton Blake series (959)
Mystery of the missing dogs
Gezi, Kal
Maple Street Five series (4)
Mystery of the missing envoy
Quiroule, Pierre
Sexton Blake series (1005)
Mystery of the missing footprints
Gezi, Kal
Maple Street Five series (5)
Mystery of the missing formula
Dorrell, Mike
Dick Barton series (3)
Mystery of the missing fossil
Palmer, Bernard
Bradley series (8)
Mystery of the missing journalist
Bayfield, William John
Sexton Blake series (216)
Mystery of the missing man
Blyton, Enid
Fatty series (13)
Mystery of the missing Marlin
Rambeau, John
Morgan Bay series (4)
Mystery of the missing mascot
Keene, Carolyn
Nancy Drew series (119)
Mystery of the missing mermaid
Carey, Mary Virginia
Three Investigators series (36)
Mystery of the missing message
Work, Virginia
Jodi series (1)
Mystery of the missing millionairess
Keene, Carolyn
Nancy Drew series (101)
Mystery of the missing money
McMullan, Kate
Pick-a-path series (10)
Mystery of the missing mummy
Hope, Laura Lee
New Bobbsey twins series (14)
Mystery of the missing necklace
Blyton, Enid
Fatty series (5)
Mystery of the missing passenger
Martin, Robert
Dance and Company series (10)
Mystery of the missing raccoon
Gezi, Kal
Maple Street Five series (1)
Mystery of the missing red wagon
Christian, Mary Blount
Sherlock Street detectives series (6)
Mystery of the missing refugee
Scott, Hedley
Sexton Blake series (1008)
Mystery of the missing scarf
Christian, Mary Blount
Sherlock Street detectives series (1)
Mystery of the missing sister
Jenkins, Jerry Bruce
Dallas O'Neil mysteries series (3)
Mystery of the missing suitcase
Heide, Florence Parry
Spotlight Detective Club series (1)
Mystery of the missing train
Dicks, Terrance
Ask Oliver series (4)
Mystery of the missing will
Matranga, Frances Carfi
Nina Cristina series (4)
Mystery of the mixed-up mall
Hope, Laura Lee
New Bobbsey twins series (30)
Mystery of the mixed-up teacher
Jenkins, Jerry Bruce
Dallas O'Neil mysteries series (2)
Mystery of the mixed-up zoo
Warner, Gertrude Chandler
Boxcar children series (26)
Mystery of the moaning cave
Arden, William
Three Investigators series (10)
Mystery of the monument
Blair, Allan
Sexton Blake series (608)
Mystery of the moss-covered mansion
Keene, Carolyn
Nancy Drew series (18)
Mystery of the motorway
Martin, Robert
Dance and Company series (7)
Mystery of the mummy's mask
Heide, Florence Parry
Spotlight Detective Club series (14)
Mystery of the murdered blonde
Brandon, John Gordon
Sexton Blake series (870)
Mystery of the murdered chef
Hardinge, Rex
Sexton Blake series (803)
Mystery of the murdered ice cream man
Brandon, John Gordon
Sexton Blake series (955)
Mystery of the murdered sentry
Brandon, John Gordon
Sexton Blake series (914)
Mystery of the musical ghost
Rambeau, John
Morgan Bay series (5)
Mystery of the musty ledger
Palmer, Bernard
Career series (4)
Mystery of the Myrmidon's journey
Rambeau, John
Morgan Bay series (8)
Mystery of the nervous lion
West, Nick
Three Investigators series (16)
Mystery of the new sky
Palmer, Bernard
Bradley series (2)
Mystery of the new tenant
Hunter, John
Sexton Blake series (1297)
Mystery of the night raiders
Garden, Nancy
Monster hunters series (1)
Mystery of the ninety nine steps
Keene, Carolyn
Nancy Drew series (43)
Mystery of the old age pensioner
Teed, George Hamilton
Sexton Blake series (778)
Mystery of the Old Curiosity Shop
Chester, Gilbert
Sexton Blake series (880)
Mystery of the one-day alibi
Parsons, Anthony
Sexton Blake series (1218)
Mystery of the open window
Gilbert, Anthony
Scott Egerton series (4)
Mystery of the outlawed black
Hardinge, Rex
Sexton Blake series (1379)
Mystery of the painted nude
Gore, William
Inspector Penk series (2)
Mystery of the pantomime cat
Blyton, Enid
Fatty series (7)
Mystery of the pay-snatchers
Martin, Robert
Dance and Company series (9)
Mystery of the peacock's eye
Flynn, Brian
Anthony Bathurst series (3)
Mystery of the pearl necklace and the tragedy in Bishop's Road
Orczy, Emmuska
Old man in the corner series (4)
Mystery of the phantom
Hill, Eileen
Robin Kane series (2)
Mystery of the phantom blackmailer
Verner, Gerald
Sexton Blake series (538)
Mystery of the phantom gold
Roddy, Lee
American adventure series (7)
Mystery of the phony murder
Jenkins, Jerry Bruce
Dallas O'Neil mysteries series (8)
Mystery of the platinum nugget!
Sayer, Walter William
Sexton Blake series (398)
Mystery of the plumed serpent
Campbell, Bruce
Ken Holt series (17)

Mystery of the poisoned puppet
Martin, Robert
Dance and Company series (8)
Mystery of the polluted stream
Christian, Mary Blount
Sherlock Street detectives series (10)
Mystery of the Polly Harris
Treadgold, Mary
Mick and Caroline Templeton series (2)
Mystery of the Pot-bank
Bayfield, William John
Sexton Blake series (366)
Mystery of the purple pirate
Arden, William
Three Investigators series (33)
Mystery of the purple pool
Warner, Gertrude Chandler
Boxcar children series (38)
Mystery of the rajah's jewels
Urquhart, Paul
Sexton Blake series (733)
Mystery of the rajah's son
Brisbane, Coutts
Sexton Blake series (836)
Mystery of the red chateau
Hunter, John
Sexton Blake series (1152)
Mystery of the red cockatoo
Parsons, Anthony
Sexton Blake series (1219)
Mystery of the red flame
Barton, George
Bromley Barnes series (2)
Mystery of the red-haired valet
Davison, Gilderoy
Peter Castle series (3)
Mystery of the red tower
Brisbane, Coutts
Sexton Blake series (1028)
Mystery of the red triangle
Tuttle, Wilbur Coleman
Hashknife Hartley and Sleepy Stevens series (11)
Mystery of the reunion dinner
Hardinge, Rex
Sexton Blake series (708)
Mystery of the Rio Star
Tyrer, Walter
Sexton Blake series (1271)
Mystery of the rogue's reunion
Brandel, Marc
Three Investigators series (40)
Mystery of the ruby queens
Allen, Betsy
Connie Blair series (12)
Mystery of the Russian prince and of Dog's Tooth Cliff
Orczy, Emmuska
Old man in the corner series (5)
Mystery of the sabotaged jet
Drummond, J
Sexton Blake series (1277)
Mystery of the sacred stones
Foley, Louise Munro
Choose your own adventure series (79)
Mystery of the Samurai sword
Dixon, Franklin W
Hardy boys series (60)
Mystery of the scar-faced beggar
Carey, Mary Virginia
Three Investigators series (31)
Mystery of the scarlet daffodil
Clewes, Dorothy
Hadley family series (1)
Mystery of the scented death
Vickers, Roy
Inspector J Rason series (1)
Mystery of the scorpion threat
Jenkins, Jerry Bruce
Dallas O'Neil mysteries series (4)
Mystery of the screaming clock
Arthur, Robert
Three Investigators series (9)
Mystery of the sea horse
Falk, Lee
Phantom series (7)
Mystery of the sealed room
Andrews, Val
Sherlock Holmes sequels series (42)
Mystery of the seaside hotel
Bayfield, William John
Sexton Blake series (419)
Mystery of the secret band
Lavell, Edith
Mary Lou series (3)
Mystery of the secret club house
Gezi, Kal
Maple Street Five series (3)
Mystery of the secret marks
Garden, Nancy
Monster hunters series (3)
Mystery of the secret room
Blyton, Enid
Fatty series (3)
Kushner, Ellen
Choose your own adventure series (63)
Mystery of the Seine
Teed, George Hamilton
Sexton Blake series (404)
Mystery of the seven cafes
Horler, Sydney
Sir Harker Bellamy series (4)
Tiger Standish series (3)
Mystery of the shadowed footballer
Frazer, Martin
Sexton Blake series (1204)
Mystery of the shattered glass
Campbell, Bruce
Ken Holt series (13)
Mystery of the shining children
Carlson, Dale
Jenny Dean series (1)
Mystery of the shot P.C.
Philips, George Norman
Sexton Blake series (541)
Mystery of the shrinking house
Arden, William
Three Investigators series (18)
Mystery of the silver spider
Arthur, Robert
Three Investigators series (8)
Mystery of the silver star
Dixon, Franklin W
Hardy boys series (86)
Mystery of the silver tag
Heide, Florence Parry
Spotlight Detective Club series (2)
Mystery of the singing ghost
Warner, Gertrude Chandler
Boxcar children series (31)
Mystery of the singing serpent
Carey, Mary Virginia
Three Investigators series (17)
Mystery of the singing strings
Clewes, Dorothy
Hadley family series (6)
Mystery of the sinister scarecrow
Carey, Mary Virginia
Three Investigators series (29)
Mystery of the skinny sophomore
Jenkins, Jerry Bruce
Dallas O'Neil mysteries series (7)
Mystery of the sleeping car express
Crofts, Freeman Wills
Inspector Joseph French series (31)
Mystery of the smashing glass
Arden, William
Three Investigators series (38)
Mystery of the smoking gun
Daly, Carroll John
Satan Hall series (1)
Mystery of the smugglers' treasure
Dicks, Terrance
Ask Oliver series (3)
Mystery of the snowbound express
Bartlett, Philip A
Roy Stover series (2)
Mystery of the spiral bridge
Dixon, Franklin W
Hardy boys series (45)
Mystery of the spiteful letters
Blyton, Enid
Fatty series (4)
Mystery of the stolen despatches
Parsons, Anthony
Sexton Blake series (1075)
Mystery of the stolen hats
Graeme, Bruce
Superintendent William Stevens and Inspector Pierre Allain series (8)
Mystery of the stolen plans
Coles, Manning
Tommy Hambledon series (17)
Mystery of the stone tiger
Keene, Carolyn
Dana girls series (25)
Mystery of the strange bundle
Blyton, Enid
Fatty series (10)
Mystery of the strange messages
Blyton, Enid
Fatty series (14)
Mystery of the street musician
Brandon, John Gordon
Sexton Blake series (956)
Mystery of the stuttering parrot
Arthur, Robert
Three Investigators series (2)
Mystery of the sultan's scimitar
Campbell, Bruce
Ken Holt series (18)
Mystery of the sunken road
Armour, R Coutts
Sexton Blake series (211)
Mystery of the swamp
Graydon, William Murray
Sexton Blake series (238)
Mystery of the Swanley Viaduct
Philips, George Norman
Sexton Blake series (396)
Mystery of the swaying curtains
Judd, Frances K
Kay Tracey series (3)
Mystery of the swindler's stooge
Tyrer, Walter
Sexton Blake series (1341)
Mystery of the sycamore
Wells, Carolyn
Fleming Stone series (12)
Mystery of the talking skull
Arthur, Robert
Three Investigators series (11)
Mystery of the tarn
Wells, Carolyn
Fleming Stone series (46)
Mystery of the thirteenth chest
Urquhart, Paul
Sexton Blake series (686)
Mystery of the thirteenth floor
Thayer, Lee
Peter Clancy series (1)
Mystery of the thousand peaks
Murray, Andrew
Sexton Blake series (142)
Mystery of the three acrobats
Brandon, John Gordon
Sexton Blake series (871)
Mystery of the three city's
Brandon, John Gordon
Sexton Blake series (792)
Mystery of the three demobbed men
Tyrer, Walter
Sexton Blake series (1415)
Mystery of the Tibetan canvas
Adams, Andy
Biff Brewster series (10)
Mystery of the timber grant
Striker, Fran
Tom Quest series (8)
Mystery of the tolling bell
Keene, Carolyn
Nancy Drew series (23)
Mystery of the toy bank
Hunt, Francis
Mary and Jerry Denton series (2)
Mystery of the trail of terror
Carey, Mary Virginia
Three Investigators series (39)
Mystery of the tramp steamer
Brisbane, Coutts
Sexton Blake series (749)
Mystery of the Turkish agreement
Sayer, Walter William
Sexton Blake series (155)
Mystery of the TV crooks
Martin, Robert
Dance and Company series (6)
Mystery of the two-faced man
Grierson, Francis Durham
Inspector George Muir series (3)
Mystery of the two hundred and fifty thousand rupees
Parsons, Anthony
Sexton Blake series (1170)
Mystery of the two-toed pigeon
Brandel, Marc
Three Investigators series (37)
Mystery of the underground factory
Chester, Gilbert
Sexton Blake series (1066)
Mystery of the uninvited guest
Shute, Walter
Sexton Blake series (583)
Mystery of the unknown victim
Jardine, Warwick
Sexton Blake series (764)
Mystery of the unsigned valentine
Christian, Mary Blount
Sherlock Street detectives series (7)
Mystery of the vanished prince
Blyton, Enid
Fatty series (9)
Mystery of the vanished trainer
Hunter, John
Sexton Blake series (1394)
Mystery of the vanished victim
Queen, Ellery, Junior
Gulliver Queen series (2)
Mystery of the vanishing aerodrome
Conde, Phillip
Dick Pemberty series (7)
Mystery of the vanishing lady
Lyle, Mel
Power boys series (6)
Wells, Helen
Vicki Barr series (9)
Mystery of the vanishing magician
Campbell, Bruce
Ken Holt series (12)
Mystery of the vanishing treasure
Arthur, Robert
Three Investigators series (5)
Mystery of the vanishing visitor
Heide, Florence Parry
Spotlight Detective Club series (7)
Mystery of the velvet gown
Kenny, Kathryn
Trixie Belden series (29)
Mystery of the wandering caveman
Carey, Mary Virginia
Three Investigators series (34)
Mystery of the watchful witches
Garden, Nancy
Monster hunters series (5)
Mystery of the wax queen
Keene, Carolyn
Dana girls series (28)
Mystery of the whale tattoo
Dixon, Franklin W
Hardy boys series (47)
Mystery of the whispering mummy
Arthur, Robert
Three Investigators series (3)
Mystery of the whispering voice
Heide, Florence Parry
Spotlight Detective Club series (5)
Mystery of the white carnation and the Montmartre hat
Orczy, Emmuska
Old man in the corner series (6)
Mystery of the Whitehall bomb
Parsons, Anthony
Sexton Blake series (1194)
Mystery of the wild surfer
Roddy, Lee
Ladd family series (6)
Mystery of the winged lion
Keene, Carolyn
Nancy Drew series (65)
Mystery of the witch who wouldn't
Platt, Kin
Sinbad trilogy (2)
Mystery of the woman in red
Gilbert, Anthony
Arthur Crook series (9)
Mystery of the woman overboard
Tyrer, Walter
Sexton Blake series (1225)
Mystery of the Wrecker's Rock
Arden, William
Three Investigators series (43)
Mystery of the yellow room
Leroux, Gaston
Joseph Rouletabille series (1)
Mystery of Thirty One New Inn
Freeman, Richard Austin
Doctor John Evelyn Thorndyke series (5)
Mystery of Tunnel 51
Wilson, Alexander
Sir Leonard Wallace series (1)
Mystery of Ura Senke
Gilligan, Shannon
Choose your own adventure series (44)
Mystery of Vaucluse
Wallis, James Harold
Inspector Wilton Jacks series (4)
Mystery of X04
Lewis, Jack
Sexton Blake series (133)
Mystery of X20
Brandon, John Gordon
Sexton Blake series (915)
Mystery on Danger Road
Heide, Florence Parry
Spotlight Detective Club series (16)
Mystery on Happy Bones
Robeson, Kenneth
Doc Savage series (96)
Mystery on Makatunk Island
Dixon, Franklin W
Hardy boys series (125)
Mystery on Rainbow Island
Clewes, Dorothy
Hadley family series (3)
Mystery on Southampton Water
Crofts, Freeman Wills
Inspector Joseph French series (12)
Mystery on stage
Warner, Gertrude Chandler
Boxcar children series (43)
Mystery on Stuart Street
Plain, Neil
Boris Blundle and Gang series (1)
Mystery on Telegraph Hill
Pease, Howard
Tod Moran series (13)
Mystery on the Clyde
Duncan, William Murdoch
Greensleeves series (1)
Mystery on the ice
Warner, Gertrude Chandler
Boxcar children special series (1)
Mystery on the menu
Keene, Carolyn
Nancy Drew series (117)
Mystery on the Midway
Jenkins, Jerry Bruce
Dallas O'Neil mysteries series (5)
Mystery on the Mississippi
Hope, Laura Lee
New Bobbsey twins series (6)
Mystery on the moor
Hogg, Garry
Nessa and Lance series (2)
Pullein-Thompson, Josephine
Moor pony series (6)
Mystery on the Queen Mary
Graeme, Bruce
Superintendent William Stevens and Inspector Pierre Allain series (7)
Mystery on the snow
Robeson, Kenneth
Doc Savage series (69)
Mystery pig
Severy, Richard
Jinks Gang series (1)
Mystery ranch
Warner, Gertrude Chandler
Boxcar children series (4)
Mystery Squad and Mr Midnight
Waddell, Martin
Mystery Squad series (3)
Mystery Squad and the Artful Dodger
Waddell, Martin
Mystery Squad series (2)
Mystery Squad and the candid camera
Waddell, Martin
Mystery Squad series (6)
Mystery Squad and the cannonball kid
Waddell, Martin
Mystery Squad series (8)
Mystery Squad and the creeping castle
Waddell, Martin
Mystery Squad series (5)
Mystery Squad and the dead man's message
Waddell, Martin
Mystery Squad series (1)
Mystery Squad and the robot's revenge
Waddell, Martin
Mystery Squad series (7)
Mystery Squad and the whistling teeth
Waddell, Martin
Mystery Squad series (4)
Mystery that never was
Blyton, Enid
Fatty series (16)
Mystery tour
Ahlberg, Allan
Funnybones series (4)
Mystery trail
Gregor, Elmer Russell
Eastern Indians series (5)
Leyland, Eric
Jack Meredith and Uncle George series (1)
Mystery train
Keene, Carolyn
Nancy Drew and Hardy boys supermystery series (7)
Mystery under the sea
Robeson, Kenneth
Doc Savage series (27)
Mystery villa
Punshon, Ernest Robertson
Bobby Owen series (4)
Mystery with a dangerous boat
Dixon, Franklin W
Hardy boys series (124)
Mystery woman
Macgowan, Alice
Jerry Boyne series (2)
Mystic ball
Sutton, Margaret
Judy Bolton series (7)
Mystic diagram
Carter, Nicholas
Nicholas Carter series (155)
Mystic Mullah
Robeson, Kenneth
Doc Savage series (9)

Mystic rebel
Syvertsen, Ryder
Mystic rebel series (1)
Mystical paths
Howatch, Susan
Church of England series (5)
Myth adventures
Asprin, Robert Lynn
Skeeve series (4)
Myth alliances
Asprin, Robert Lynn
Skeeve series (7)
Myth conceptions
Asprin, Robert Lynn
Skeeve series (2)
Myth directions
Asprin, Robert Lynn
Skeeve series (3)
Myth is murder
Martin, Shane
Professor Ronald Challis series (4)
Myth makers
Cotton, Donald
Doctor Who series (97)
Myth of the magus
Butler, Eliza Marian
Faust series (1)
Mythago Wood
Holdstock, Robert
Mythago series (1)
Myth-ing persons
Asprin, Robert Lynn
Skeeve series (5)
Mythistorema
Seferis, George
Log book series (3)
Myth-nomers and im-pervections
Asprin, Robert Lynn
Skeeve series (8)
Mythology abroad
Nye, Jody Lynn
Mythology series (2)
Mythology 101
Nye, Jody Lynn
Mythology series (1)

N

N or M?
Christie, Agatha
Tommy and Tuppence Beresford series (3)
N-space
Niven, Larry
Known Space series (20)
N three conspiracy
Carter, Nick
Nick Carter series (91)
Nabo
Garcia Marquez, Gabriel
Macondo series (1)
Nabob and knave
Carter, Nicholas
Nicholas Carter series (286)
Nabob of Bahour
Du Boisgobey, Fortune
Monsieur Lecoq series (6)
Nachoochee
Goulding, Francis Robert
Woodruff trilogy (2)
Nacio, his affairs
Kelly, Eleanor Mercein
Urruty family trilogy (3)
Nada the lily
Haggard, Henry Rider
Umslopogaas series (2)
Zulu series (1)
Nadeem makes samosas
Stone, Susheila
Duets series (1)
Nadya makes her bow
Haskell, Helen Eggleston
Katrinka series (5)
Naff sex guide
Bryson, Kit
Naff series (2)
Legris, Jean-Luc
Naff series (2)
Naga path
Bower, Ursula Graham
Assam series (1)
Nagasaki vector
Smith, Lester Neil
Win Bear trilogy (3)
Nail cruncher
Cohen, Albert
Gallants series (2)
Nail down the stairs
Morressy, John
Del Whitby trilogy (2)
Nairn in darkness and light
Thomson, David
Highlands youth series (1)
Naja
Savarin, Julian Jay
Gordon Gallagher series (4)
Naked and alone
Lawrence, Michael
Johnny Amsterdam series (1)
Naked and the savage
James, William M
Apache series (9)
Naked angel
Webb, Jack
Father Joseph Shanley and Sammy Golden series (2)
Naked blade
Saxon, Peter
Sexton Blake series (1456)
Naked blade, naked gun
Kilgore, Axel
They call me the Mercenary series (13)
Naked civil servant
Crisp, Quentin
Naked civil servant series (1)
Naked earth
Konsalik, Heinz Gunther
Stalingrad series (1)
Naked ebony
Cushman, Dan
Crawford series (1)
Naked eye
Reynolds, William J
Nebraska series (5)
Naked five
France, Victor
Oliver Galt and Hugo Tower series (2)
Naked island
Braddon, Russell
Hate series (1)
Naked lady
Corrigan, Mark
Mark Corrigan and McLean series (13)
Naked liar
Adams, Harold
Carl Wilcox series (4)
Naked mistress
Deptula, Walter
Frank Arrow series (1)
Naked nuns
Watson, Colin
Inspector Purbright series (8)
Naked once more
Peters, Elizabeth
Jacqueline Kirby series (5)
Naked outpost
Ledd, Paul
Shelter Morgan series (17)
Naked she died
Tracy, Don
Giff Speer series (2)
Naked sun
Asimov, Isaac
Elijah Baley series (2)
Robot series (3)
Naked to my enemy
Jobson, Hamilton
Inspector Anders series (3)
Naked to the grave
Carmichael, Harry
John Piper and Quinn series (32)
Naked villainy
Davey, Jocelyn
Ambrose Usher series (2)
Woods, Sara
Sir Nicholas Harding and Antony Maitland series (48)
Name for baby Cockle
Trueman, Brian
Stories from Cockleshell Bay series (7)
Name in lights
Ebel, Suzanne
Sir Robert Waring series (1)
Name is Archer
Macdonald, Ross
Lew Archer series (6)
Name is Chambers
Kane, Henry
Peter Chambers series (32)
Name is Jordan
Masur, Harold Q
Scott Jordan series (9)
Name is Malone
Rice, Craig
John Joseph Malone series (12)
Name is O'Brien
Hayes, Ralph Eugene
O'Brien, Buffalo Hunter series (4)
Name of the catastrophe
Moorcock, Michael
Jerry Cornelius series (7)
Name of the game
Cory, Desmond
Mister Dee series (2)
Estes, Rose
Greyhawk series (6)
Roberts, Nora
Flowers series (33)
Name of the game is death
Marlowe, Dan James
Earl Drake series (1)
Name of the rose
Eco, Umberto
Rose series (1)
Name of the sun
Clough, Brenda Wang
Averidan series (4)
Name on the bracelet
Sutton, Margaret
Judy Bolton series (13)
Name on the bullet
Grover, Marshall
Nevada Jim series (59)
Name that team!
Lessiter, Mike
Team names series (1)
Name to conjure with
Aamodt, Donald
Name to conjure with series (1)
Stern, Gladys Bronwyn
Ragbag chronicles series (5)
Name your poison
Reilly, Helen
Inspector Christopher McKee series (14)
Nameless boat
Pardoe, Margot
Boat series (4)
Nameless cat
Lockridge, Frances
Cats series (4)
Nameless Coffin
Butler, Gwendoline
Inspector John Coffin series (11)
Nameless crime
Masterman, Walter Sidney
Sir Arthur Sinclair series (7)
Nameless five
Skene, Anthony
Sexton Blake series (670)
Nameless man
Lincoln, Natalie Sumner
Inspector Mitchell series (2)
Nameless nobleman
Austin, Jane Goodwin
Nameless nobleman series (1)
Nameless ones
Egan, Lesley
Vic Varallo series (5)
Scott, Reginald Thomas Maitland
Aurelius Smith series (7)
Nameless road
Harvester, Simon
Asia in turmoil series (21)
Dorian Silk series (9)
Names and faces of the heroes
Price, Reynolds
Mustian family series (2)
Name's Buchanan
Ward, Jonas
Tom Buchanan series (1)
Name's Maguire
Himmel, Richard
Johnny Maguire series (2)
Names of God
Sanford, Doris
Advanced theology for very tiny persons series (3)
Namesake
Hodges, Cyril Walter
King Alfred series (1)
Naming the powers
Wink, Walter Philip
Powers trilogy (1)
Nan at Camp Chicopee
Hamlin, Myra Sawyer
Nan series (1)
Nan in the city
Hamlin, Myra Sawyer
Nan series (2)
Nan Sherwood at Lakeview Hall
Carr, Annie Roe
Nan Sherwood series (2)
Nan Sherwood at Palm Beach
Carr, Annie Roe
Nan Sherwood series (5)
Nan Sherwood at Pine Camp
Carr, Annie Roe
Nan Sherwood series (1)
Nan Sherwood at Rose Ranch
Carr, Annie Roe
Nan Sherwood series (4)
Nan Sherwood on the Mexican border
Carr, Annie Roe
Nan Sherwood series (7)
Nan Sherwood's summer holidays
Carr, Annie Roe
Nan Sherwood series (6)
Nan Sherwood's winter holidays
Carr, Annie Roe
Nan Sherwood series (3)
Nana
Delacorta
Serge Gorodish series (1)
Zola, Emile
Rougon Macquart series (9)
Nana's mother
Zola, Emile
Rougon Macquart series (7)
Nancy
Wasson, Mildred
Nancy Prentiss series (1)
Nancy and Nick in Helter-Skelter-Land
Barton, Olive Roberts
Nancy and Nick series (2)
Nancy and Nick in Scrub-Up-Land
Barton, Olive Roberts
Nancy and Nick series (3)
Nancy and Nick in the Land-of-Dear-Knows-Where
Barton, Olive Roberts
Nancy and Nick series (4)
Nancy and Nick in the Land-of-Near-by
Barton, Olive Roberts
Nancy and Nick series (5)
Nancy and Nick in Topsy-Turvy-Land
Barton, Olive Roberts
Nancy and Nick series (6)
Nancy and the Coggs twins
Taggart, Marion Ames
Doctor's little girl series (5)
Nancy at Saint Bride's
Bruce, Dorita Fairlie
Nancy series (5)
Nancy calls the tune
Bruce, Dorita Fairlie
Nancy series (8)
Nancy, Canadian schoolgirl
Garrard, Phillis
Nancy series (1)
Nancy Drew and the Hardy boys camp fire stories
Keene, Carolyn
Nancy Drew and the Hardy boys be a detective mystery series (8)
Nancy Drew and the Hardy boys super sleuths
Keene, Carolyn
Nancy Drew and the Hardy boys be a detective mystery series (8)
Nancy Drew book of hidden clues
Keene, Carolyn
Nancy Drew series (122)
Nancy Drew cookbook
Keene, Carolyn
Nancy Drew series (122)
Nancy Drew ghost stories
Keene, Carolyn
Nancy Drew series (122)
Nancy Drew sleuth book
Keene, Carolyn
Nancy Drew series (122)
Nancy goes camping
Large, Jean Henry
Nancy, Girl Scout series (3)
Nancy goes Girl Scouting
Large, Jean Henry
Nancy, Girl Scout series (1)
Nancy in the sixth
Bruce, Dorita Fairlie
Nancy series (6)
Nancy Kimball, nurse's aide
Laklan, Carli
Nancy Kimball series (1)
Nancy Lee
Warde, Margaret
Nancy Lee series (1)
Nancy Lee's lookout
Warde, Margaret
Nancy Lee series (3)
Nancy Lee's namesake
Warde, Margaret
Nancy Lee series (4)
Nancy Lee's spring term
Warde, Margaret
Nancy Lee series (2)
Nancy Naylor, air pilot
Lansing, Elizabeth
Nancy Naylor series (1)
Nancy Naylor, captain of flight nurses
Lansing, Elizabeth
Nancy Naylor series (4)
Nancy Naylor flies south
Lansing, Elizabeth
Nancy Naylor series (2)
Nancy Naylor, flight nurse
Lansing, Elizabeth
Nancy Naylor series (3)
Nancy Naylor, visiting nurse
Lansing, Elizabeth
Nancy Naylor series (5)
Nancy Nurse
Campbell, Rod
Little people series (2)
Nancy Pembroke, college maid
Van Epps, Margaret T
Nancy Pembroke series (1)
Nancy Pembroke in New Orleans
Van Epps, Margaret T
Nancy Pembroke series (4)
Nancy Pembroke in Nova Scotia
Van Epps, Margaret T
Nancy Pembroke series (6)
Nancy Pembroke, junior
Van Epps, Margaret T
Nancy Pembroke series (5)
Nancy Pembroke, senior
Van Epps, Margaret T
Nancy Pembroke series (7)
Nancy Pembroke, sophomore at Roxford
Van Epps, Margaret T
Nancy Pembroke series (3)
Nancy Pembroke's vacation in Canada
Van Epps, Margaret T
Nancy Pembroke series (2)
Nancy Porter's opportunity
Taggart, Marion Ames
Doctor's little girl series (4)
Nancy returns to Saint Bride's
Bruce, Dorita Fairlie
Nancy series (7)
Nancy sails
Wasson, Mildred
Nancy Prentiss series (3)
Nancy, the daring
Kimbrough, Katheryn
Phenwick women series (11)
Nancy, the doctor's little partner
Taggart, Marion Ames
Doctor's little girl series (3)
Nancy to the rescue
Bruce, Dorita Fairlie
Nancy series (4)
Nancy, young Canadian
Garrard, Phillis
Nancy series (2)
Nancy's country Christmas
Brainerd, Eleanor Hoyt
Nancy series (2)
Nancy's lone Girl Scouts
Large, Jean Henry
Nancy, Girl Scout series (2)
Nancy's mysterious letter
Keene, Carolyn
Nancy Drew series (8)
Nanette
Marokvia, Mireille
Ann and Paul series (2)
Veryan, Patricia
Age of Elegance series (3)
Sanguinet series (1)
Nannies for hire
Hest, Amy
Pajama party series (2)
Nanny and the professor
Johnston, William
Nanny and the professor series (1)
Nanny Noony and the dust queen
Frascino, Edward
Nanny Noony series (2)
Nanny Noony and the magic spell
Frascino, Edward
Nanny Noony series (1)
Nanny's miracle
Johnston, William
Nanny and the professor series (3)
Nan's Chicopee children
Hamlin, Myra Sawyer
Nan series (3)
Nantucket diary
Rorem, Ned
Musical diaries series (4)
Nantucket diet murders
Rich, Virginia
Mrs Eugenia Potter series (3)
Nantucket soap opera
Dean, S F X
Professor Neil Kelly series (6)

Nanushka's love poems, to someone I love
Witcomb, Nan
Thoughts of Nanushka series (16)

Naomi Mitchison
Mitchison, Naomi
Small talk series (4)

Nap on Nighthawk
Horler, Sydney
Nighthawk series (6)

Napoleon Bonaparte, his rise and fall
Thompson, James Matthew
French history trilogy (2)

Napoleon in love
Delderfield, Ronald Frederick
Napoleon Bonaparte series (1)

Napoleon passes
O'Riordan, Conal
Anglo-Irish relations series (2)

Napoleon wager
Forstchen, William R
Gamester wars series (3)

Napoleon's marshals
Delderfield, Ronald Frederick
Napoleon Bonaparte series (2)

Napoleons of Eridanus
Barbet, Pierre
Eridanus series (1)

Napper goes for goal
Waddell, Martin
Napper series (1)

Napper strikes again
Waddell, Martin
Napper series (2)

Napper's golden goals
Waddell, Martin
Napper series (3)

Naptime and Baby Jay
VerDorn, Bethea
Baby Jay series (3)

NARC
Hawkes, Robert
NARC series (1)

Narcissus an' de chillun
Govan, Christine Noble
Plummer children series (4)

Narnia explored
Karkainen, Paul A
Narnia series (7)

Narracong riddle
Derleth, August
Judge Ephraim Peck series (6)

Narrative of Arthur Gordon Pym of Nantucket
Poe, Edgar Allan
Arthur Gordon Pym series (1)

Narrow boat
Postgate, Oliver
Pingwings series (1)

Narrow corner
Copper, Basil
Mike Faraday series (40)

Narrow escape
Saunders, Susan
Bad News Bunny series (6)

Narrow passage
Butterworth, Oliver
Nate Twitchell series (2)

Narrow stair
Heath-Miller, Mavis
Raines of Rayleigh series (5)

Narrow street
Paul, Elliot
Narrow street series (1)

Narrowing circle
Hill, Headon
Sebastian Zambra series (4)

Narrowing lust
Baxter, Gregory
Superintendent Daniels series (1)
Kane, Henry
Peter Chambers series (10)

Nasty competition
Levy, Elizabeth
Gymnasts series (15)

Nasty name murders
Howes, Royce
Captain Ben Lucias series (4)

Nat Borden's find
Chapman, Allen
Boys of business series (5)

Natalie, a garden scout
Roy, Lillian Elizabeth
Girl Scouts trilogy (1)

Natchez
Winters, Logan
Spectros series (3)

Nate the great
Sharmat, Marjorie Weinman
Nate the great series (1)

Nate the great and the boring beach bag
Sharmat, Marjorie Weinman
Nate the great series (10)

Nate the great and the fishy prize
Sharmat, Marjorie Weinman
Nate the great series (8)

Nate the great and the Halloween hunt
Sharmat, Marjorie Weinman
Nate the great series (12)

Nate the great and the lost list
Sharmat, Marjorie Weinman
Nate the great series (3)

Nate the great and the missing key
Sharmat, Marjorie Weinman
Nate the great series (6)

Nate the great and the musical note
Sharmat, Marjorie Weinman
Nate the great series (13)

Nate the great and the phony clue
Sharmat, Marjorie Weinman
Nate the great series (4)

Nate the great and the snowy trail
Sharmat, Marjorie Weinman
Nate the great series (7)

Nate the great and the sticky case
Sharmat, Marjorie Weinman
Nate the great series (5)

Nate the great and the stolen base
Sharmat, Marjorie Weinman
Nate the great series (14)

Nate the great goes down in the dumps
Sharmat, Marjorie Weinman
Nate the great series (11)

Nate the great goes undercover
Sharmat, Marjorie Weinman
Nate the great series (2)

Nate the great stalks Stupidweed
Sharmat, Marjorie Weinman
Nate the great series (9)

Nathalie's chum
Ray, Anna Chapin
Teddy series (4)

Nathalie's sister
Ray, Anna Chapin
Teddy series (6)

Nathaniel
Arnosky, Jim
Nathaniel series (1)

Nation torn
Ray, Delia
American Civil War series (1)

National Avenue
Tarkington, Booth
Growth trilogy (3)

National Lampoon's Doon
Werner, Ellis
Dune series (6)

National Velvet
Bagnold, Enid
Velvet series (1)

Nationalists
Long, William Stuart
Australians series (11)

Nation's missing guest
Footner, Hulbert
Amos Lee Mappin series (4)

Nation's peril
Carter, Nicholas
Nicholas Carter series (353)

Native
Ghose, Zulfikar
Incredible Brazilian trilogy (1)
Plante, David
Francoeur family series (6)

Native tongue
Elgin, Suzette Haden
Native tongue series (1)

Nat's braces
Iwamura, Kazuo
Nat series (2)

Nat's hat
Iwamura, Kazuo
Nat series (1)

Natural causes
Cecil, Henry
Colonel Brain series (2)
Mister Tewkesbury series (2)
Valin, Jonathan
Harry Stoner series (5)

Natural curiosity
Drabble, Margaret
Radiant way trilogy (2)

Natural enemy
Langton, Jane
Homer Kelly series (4)

Natural history of man
Brierley, John Keith
Human behaviour trilogy (2)

Natural history of nonsense
Evans, Bergen Baldwin
Nonsense series (1)

Natural man
Lloyd, John William
Natural man series (1)

Natural resources
Kalman, Bobbie
In my world series (17)

Naturalized animals of the British Isles
Lever, Christopher
Naturalized animals series (1)

Naturalized birds of the world
Lever, Christopher
Naturalized animals series (3)

Naturalized mammals of the world
Lever, Christopher
Naturalized animals series (2)

Nature and human nature
Haliburton, Thomas Chandler
Sam Slick series (9)

Nature of Alexander
Renault, Mary
Alexander the Great series (3)

Nature of the beast
King, Melvin
Soldier of fortune series (7)

Nature of the universe
Gallant, Roy Arthur
Exploring series (2)

Nature of the weather
Gallant, Roy Arthur
Exploring series (4)

Nature's god
Wilson, Robert Anton
Historical illuminatus trilogy (3)

Naughiest girl again
Blyton, Enid
Naughtiest girl series (2)

Naughtiest girl in the school
Blyton, Enid
Naughtiest girl series (1)

Naughtiest girl is a monitor
Blyton, Enid
Naughtiest girl series (3)

Naughty Amelia Jane!
Blyton, Enid
Amelia Jane series (1)

Naughty but dead
Fickling, G G
Erik March series (1)

Naughty comet, and other fables and stories
Richards, Laura Elizabeth
Fables for young and old series (4)

Naughty George
Pilgrim, Jane
Blackberry Farm series (14)

Naughty girl's diary
Gray, Walter T
Bad boy series (4)

Naughty Nancy goes to school
Goodall, John Strickland
Paddy Pork series (17)

Naughty Nancy, the bad bridesmaid
Goodall, John Strickland
Paddy Pork series (7)

Naughty Sammy
Van der Meer, Ron
Sammy and Mara series (4)

Naughty stories for good boys and girls
Milne, Christopher
Naughty stories series (1)

Naughty stories for good boys and girls, number 4
Milne, Christopher
Naughty stories series (4)

Naughty stories for good boys and girls, number 5
Milne, Christopher
Naughty stories series (5)

Naughty Teddy
Bawden, Juliet
My Teddy series (1)

Nautilus sanction
Hawke, Simon
Timewars series (5)

Nautipuss
Allison, Clyde
Agent triple zero eight series (3)

Navaho devil
Roberts, J R
Gunsmith series (45)

Navaho trail
Chisholm, Matt
Joe Blade series (11)

Naval digression
Franklin, Gordon
Naval digressions series (1)

Naval occasions and some traits of the sailor-men
Bartimeus
Naval occasions series (1)

Navigator of Rhada
Gilman, Robert Cham
Rhada series (3)

Navigators
Burton, Anthony
Navigators trilogy (2)

Navigator's sindrome
Carr, Jayge
Navigator trilogy (1)

Navu boys in the track of the enemy
Chipman, William Pendleton
Navy boys series (3)

Navy alphabet
Baum, Lyman Frank
Alphabet series (2)

Navy boys after the submarines
Davidson, Halsey
Navy boys of World War I series (1)

Navy boys at the big surrender
Davidson, Halsey
Navy boys of World War I series (5)

Navy boys at the siege of Havana
Otis, James
Navy boys series (4)

Navy boys behind the big guns
Davidson, Halsey
Navy boys of World War I series (3)

Navy boys chasing a sea raider
Davidson, Halsey
Navy boys of World War I series (2)

Navy boys' cruise on the Pickering
Otis, James
Navy boys series (11)

Navy boys' cruise to the Bahamas
Chipman, William Pendleton
Navy boys series (7)

Navy boys' cruise with Columbus
Ober, Frederick Albion
Navy boys series (8)

Navy boys' cruise with Paul Jones
Otis, James
Navy boys series (1)

Navy boys' daring capture
Chipman, William Pendleton
Navy boys series (6)

Navy boys in defense of liberty
Chipman, William Pendleton
Navy boys series (9)

Navy boys in New York Bay
Otis, James
Navy boys series (2)

Navy boys on Lake Ontario
Otis, James
Navy boys series (10)

Navy boys on Long Island Sound
Otis, James
Navy boys series (5)

Navy boys on special service
Davidson, Halsey
Navy boys of World War I series (6)

Navy boys to the rescue
Davidson, Halsey
Navy boys of World War I series (4)

Navy boys with Grant at Vicksburg
Otis, James
Navy boys series (12)

Navy colt
Gruber, Frank
Johnny Fletcher and Sam Cragg series (4)

Navy spy murders
Eliot, George Fielding
G-men series (3)

Nazarene
Asch, Sholem
Biblical series (1)

Nazi assassins
Cory, Desmond
Johnny Fedora series (1)

Nazi hunter
Mandell, Mark
Nazi hunter series (1)

NcBroom's ear
Fleischman, Sid
McBroom series (3)

Nea
Arsan, Emmanuelle
Emmanuelle series (2)

Neapolitan lovers
Dumas, Alexandre
Nelson in Naples series (1)

Neapolitan streak
Holme, Timothy
Inspector Achille Peroni series (1)

Near and the far
Myers, Leopold Hamilton
Prince Jali series (1)

Near thing for Captain Najork
Hoban, Russell
Captain Najork series (2)

Nearest fire
Wilder, Cherry
Torin trilogy (2)

Nearly Neptune
Walters, Hugh
Chris Godfrey series (12)

Neastly birthday book
Cole, Babette
Hairy book series (5)

Neat little corpse
Murray, Max
Corpse series (4)

Nebraska!
Ross, Dana Fuller
Wagons West series (2)

Nebraska burnout
Logan, Jake
John Slocum series (56)

Nebraska nightmare
Ham, Bob
Overload series (6)
Sharpe, Jon
Trailsman series (146)

Nebraska nymph
Fletcher, Dirk
Spur McCoy series (11)

Nebraska quotient
Reynolds, William J
Nebraska series (1)

Nebraska trackdown
Grover, Marshall
Larry and Stretch series (193)

Nebula alert
Chandler, Arthur Bertram
Empress of outer space series (3)
Rim series (13)

Nebulae and galaxies
Abetti, Giorgio
Universe series (3)

Necessary corpse
Woodthorpe, Ralph Carter
Nicholas Slade series (2)

Necessary dealing
Lewis, Royston
Eric Ward series (7)

Necessary end
Fraser, Anthea
Inspector David Webb and Sergeant Ken Jackson series (2)
Gielgud, Val
Inspector Gregory Pellew and Viscount Clymping series (7)
Robinson, Peter
Chief Inspector Alan Banks series (3)

Neck and neck
Bruce, Leo
Sergeant William Beef series (7)

Neck in a noose
Ferrars, E X
Toby Dyke series (5)

Necklace and calabash
Gulik, Robert van
Judge Dee series (16)

Necklace of death
Holt, Henry
Inspector Silver series (3)

Necklace of glaciers
Styles, Showell
Simon and Mag series (3)

Necklace of skulls
Drummond, Ivor
Lady Jennifer, Sandro and Colly series (7)

Necktie party
Logan, Jake
John Slocum series (35)

Necromancer
Dickson, Gordon Rupert
Dorsai series (1)

Necromancer nine
Tepper, Sheri S
True game trilogy (2)

Necroscope
Lumley, Brian
Necroscope series (1)

Nectar of heaven
Tubb, Edwin Charles
Dumarest series (24)

Ned, Bob and Jerry at Boxwood Hall
Young, Clarence
Motor boys series (17)

Ned, Bob and Jerry bound for home
Young, Clarence
Motor boys series (21)

Ned, Bob and Jerry in the army
Young, Clarence
Motor boys series (19)

Ned, Bob and Jerry on a ranch
Young, Clarence
Motor boys series (18)

Ned, Bob and Jerry on the firing line
Young, Clarence
Motor boys series (20)
Ned Butler, bounty hunter
Rey, Bret
Ned Butler series (2)
Ned in the block-house
Ellis, Edward Sylvester
Boy pioneer series (1)
Ned in the woods
Ellis, Edward Sylvester
Boy pioneer series (2)
Ned on the river
Ellis, Edward Sylvester
Boy pioneer series (3)
Neddy the little donkey
Blyton, Enid
Little donkey series (1)
Need a body tell?
Cobb, Belton
Inspector Cheviot Burmann series (16)
Need to know
Haggard, William
Colonel Charles Russell series (23)
Needing each other
Berry, Joy
Ready-set-grow series (2)
Needle
Clement, Hal
Needle series (1)
Needle eye
Brathwaite, Errol
Maori Wars trilogy (2)
Needle that wouldn't hold still
Stone, Hampton
Jeremiah X Gibson series (3)
Needle track
Conway, Peter
Inspector Newton series (4)
Needles and pins
McCarthy, Justin Huntly
Francois Villon trilogy (2)
Needle's eye
Lee, Edward
Red Blake series (1)
Needles of death
Edwards, Paul
John Eagle series (1)
Needy Nine
Carter, Nicholas
Nicholas Carter series (613)
Ne'er-do-well
Yates, Dornford
Jonah Mansel series (13)
Richard Chandos series (10)
Superintendent Richard Falcon series (3)
Ne'er forget the people
Pickles, Wilfred
You and me series (3)
Nefarious quest
Janson, Hank
Hank Janson series (222)
Negative in blue
Brown, Carter
Rick Holman series (29)
Negative man
Galway, Robert Conington
James Packard series (11)
Negative zone
Appleton, Victor II
Tom Swift Junior series 3 (2)
Neglected mountain
Saville, Malcolm
Lone Pine Five Club series (7)
Negrohead
Bridges, Roy
Australian trilogy (2)
Negro's ring
Scott, Philip
Algy, Peter and Jeremy series (2)
Neighborhood
Blei, Norbert
Door County trilogy (3)
Neighborhood stories
Gale, Zora
Friendship village series (4)
Neighbour
Gillespie, Susan
Longdon-Lorristone family series (4)
Neighbours
Shears, Sarah
Neighbours series (1)
Neighbours' children
Shears, Sarah
Neighbours series (2)
Neighbours of mine
Andom, R
Troddles series (15)

Neil in the country
Finley, Martha Farquharson
Honest Jim series (6)
Neil, the beggar boy
Finley, Martha Farquharson
Honest Jim series (5)
Neither a candle nor a pitchfork
Porter, Joyce
Edmund Brown series (3)
Nell alone
Melville, Jennie
Sergeant Charmian Daniels series (5)
Nellie Gates and the little missionary
Boardman, M M
Nellie Gates series (1)
Nellie Milton's house keeping
May, Carrie L
Recovered pearl series (2)
Nellie, the obvious
Kimbrough, Katheryn
Phenwick women series (21)
Nellie's housekeeping
Mathews, Joanna Hooe
Little sunbeams series (6)
Nelson boys and their cobalt adventure
Barnes, Michael
Nelson boys series (1)
Nelson boys and their Wawa adventure
Barnes, Michael
Nelson boys series (2)
Nelson in love
Smith, Janice Lea
Adam Joshua series (8)
Nelson Malone meets the man from Mush-Nut
Hawes, Louise
Nelson Malone series (1)
Nelson Malone saves Flight 942
Hawes, Louise
Nelson Malone series (2)
Nelson the newsboy
Alger, Horatio
Rise in life series (4)
Nelson's last love
Schumacher, Heinrich
Lady Hamilton series (2)
Nemesis
Christie, Agatha
Miss Jane Marple series (13)
Cooper, Louise Antell
Indigo series (1)
Fane, Bron
La noire series (5)
Nemesis at Raynham Parva
Connington, John Jervis
Sir Clinton Driffield series (5)
Nemesis Club
Sayer, Walter William
Barnaby Grayle series (2)
Nemesis from Terra
Brackett, Leigh
Mars series (1)
Nemesis of evil
Carter, Lin
Prince Zarkon series (1)
Nemydia Deep
Tedford, William G
Timequest trilogy (3)
Neon madman
Harvey, John Barton
Scott Mitchell series (4)
Neon mirage
Collins, Max Allan
Nathan Heller series (4)
Neon preacher
Chambers, Robert
Hank Moody series (3)
Neon rain
Burke, James Lee
Dave Robicheaux series (1)
Nepomuk of the river
Pilkington, Roger
Branxome family series (6)
Neptune
Simon, Seymour
Space photos series (8)
Neptune Beach
Fuchs, Daniel
Williamsburg trilogy (3)
Neptune landing
Bassett, Ronald
Lobby Ludd trilogy (3)
Neptune One is missing
Walters, Hugh
Chris Godfrey series (12)
Neptune's treasure
Stern, Simon
Astonishing adventures of Captain Ketchup series (1)
Neq the sword
Anthony, Piers
Battle circle trilogy (3)

Nerilka's story
McCaffrey, Anne
Pern and the Red Planet series (3)
Nerissa Claire case
Waugh, Hillary
Simon Kaye series (4)
Nero, the circus lion
Barnum, Richard
Kneetime animal stories series (13)
Nero Wolfe cook book
Stout, Rex
Nero Wolfe and Archie Goodwin series (52)
Nerve beat
O'Sullivan, James Brendan
Steve Silk series (6)
Nerve centre
Janson, Hank
Hank Janson series (155)
Nerve end
Harper, Stephen
Healers series (4)
Nerve of Foley, and other railroad stories
Spearman, Frank Hamilton
Railroad stories series (1)
Nervous horses
Hearne, Vicki
Horses series (1)
Nervous laughter
Emerson, Earl W
Thomas Black series (3)
Nervous wreck
Lee, Robert
Fishy business series (3)
Nessa's fish
Luenn, Nancy
Nessa series (1)
Nessa's story
Luenn, Nancy
Nessa series (2)
Nessie goes to Hollywood
Mosley, Francis
Nessie series (4)
Nessie goes to Mars
Mosley, Francis
Nessie series (1)
Nessie on holiday
Mosley, Francis
Nessie series (2)
Nest egg for the Baron
Morton, Anthony
Baron series (26)
Nest for cuckoos
Carter, Reginald
Wroth family series (2)
Nest of magpies
Marshall, Sybil
Old Swithinford series (1)
Nest of rats
Wainwright, John
Northern Police series (34)
Nest of spies
Davison, Geoffrey
Stephen Fletcher series (2)
Souvestre, Pierre
Fantomas series (4)
Nest of teachers
Blishen, Edward
Schoolmaster series (6)
Nest of the scarecrow
Atkinson, Mary Evelyn
Lockett family series (9)
Nest of traitors
Ashe, Gordon
Patrick Dawlish series (46)
Nest of vipers
Claymore, Tod
Tod Claymore series (2)
Mitchell, Gladys
Dame Beatrice Bradley series (55)
Nest of vultures
Macleod, Robert
Talos Cord series (7)
Nestor the monster
Tranter, Nigel Godwin
Ken and Fiona series (3)
Net around Joan Ingleby
Fielding, A
Inspector Pointer series (5)
Nettle shade
Turner, James Ernest
Rampion Savage series (8)
Network of crime
Carter, Nicholas
Nicholas Carter series (623)
Neural atrocity
Farren, Mick
Jeb Stuart Ho series (3)
Neuromancer
Gibson, William
Neuromancer trilogy (1)

Neutral stars
Morgan, Dan
Venturer Twelve series (3)
Neutron nightmare
Derrick, Lionel
Penetrator series (51)
Neutron solstice
Axler, James
Deathlands series (3)
Neutron star
Niven, Larry
Known Space series (3)
Nevada
Arthur, Burt
Dan Lovett series (1)
Grey, Zane
Forlorn River Ranch series (2)
Nevada Jim Lacy series (1)
Ross, Dana Fuller
Wagons West series (8)
Nevada claim stripper
Hunter, E J
Headhunter series (8)
Nevada dawn
Gentry, Georgina
Panorama of the old West series (11)
Nevada death trap
Roberts, J R
Gunsmith series (98)
Nevada gunner
Logan, Jake
John Slocum series (142)
Nevada guns
Roberts, J R
Gunsmith series (137)
Nevada mustang
Chisholm, Matt
Joe Blade series (8)
Nevada nightmare
Winski, Norman
Dirk Spencer series (3)
Nevada nights
Gentry, Georgina
Panorama of the old West series (5)
Nevada Queen high
Richmond, Roe
Lashtrow series (5)
Nevada run
Robbins, David
Endworld series (15)
Nevada silver
Hohl, Joan
Flint Falcon series (1)
Sharp family trilogy (3)
Nevada swindle
Logan, Jake
John Slocum series (74)
nevada timber war
Roberts, J R
Gunsmith series (76)
Nevada war
Rountree, Owen
Jim Cord series (2)
Nevada warpath
Sharpe, Jon
Trailsman series (127)
Never a dull moment
Cheyney, Peter
Lemmy Caution series (9)
Slim Callaghan series (6)
Cole, Jennifer
Cindy and Nicole series (11)
Never call retreat
Catton, Bruce
Centennial history of the Civil War series (3)
Never cheat a Texan
Grover, Marshall
Larry and Stretch series (357)
Never contract
Gerrity, David
Frank Cardolini series (1)
Never cross a vampire
Kaminsky, Stuart Melvin
Toby Peters series (5)
Never deal with a dragon
Charrette, Robert N
Secrets of power series (1)
Never despair, 1945-1965
Gilbert, Martin
Winston S Churchill series (8)
Never die in Honolulu
Hamilton, Ian Sydney
Pete Heysen series (3)
Never enough
Sargeson, Frank
Enough series (3)
Never fight a lady
Truss, Seldon
Inspector Gidleigh series (7)

Never give a millionaire an even break
Kane, Henry
Peter Chambers series (20)
Never go back
Heath-Miller, Mavis
Raines of Rayleigh series (1)
Never go to sea
Winton, John
Navy series (4)
Never had a spanner on her
Leasor, James
Aristo Autos series (2)
Never kill a client
Halliday, Brett
Michael Shayne series (44)
Never kill a cop
West, John B
Rocky Steele series (6)
Never kiss frogs!
Leeson, Robert
Frogs series (1)
Never let up
Maine, Charles Eric
Mike Delaney series (3)
Never lonely again
Wilhelm, Hans
Merritales series (8)
Never mind
McMullen, Nigel
Naughty baby series (1)
Never need an enemy
Stein, Aaron Marc
Matt Erridge series (2)
Never no more
Laverty, Maura
Delia Scully series (1)
Never prod a Texan
Grover, Marshall
Larry and Stretch series (40)
Never put off till tomorrow what you can kill today
Godey, John
Jack Albany series (2)
Never say dead
Kennedy, Elliot
Griff Dexter series (4)
Never say die
Foote-Smith, Elizabeth
Will Woodfield series (2)
Keene, Carolyn
Nancy Drew files series (16)
Never say live!
Hume, David
Tony Carter series (2)
Never say quit
Grover, Marshall
Larry and Stretch series (406)
Never send flowers
Gardner, John Edmund
James Bond series (29)
Never shoot a lady
Hale, Edgar
Inspector Michael Regan series (3)
Never such innocence
Thorne, Nicola
Askham family series (1)
Never the same door
Rankine, John
Space corporation series (1)
Never too late
Baer, Judy
Cedar River daydreams series (19)
Thirkell, Angela
Barsetshire series (25)
Never trust a friend
Pearce, Colin
Fax Pack series (2)
Never turn your back
Scherf, Margaret
Reverend Martin Buell series (5)
Never wake a dead man
Bird, Brandon
Hampton Hume series (2)
Never-was girl
Brown, Carter
Rick Holman series (9)
Neveryona
Delany, Samuel Ray
Neveryon series (2)
Nevlo
Robeson, Kenneth
Avenger series (17)
Nevsky's demon
Gat, Dimitri
Yuri Nevsky series (3)
Nevsky's return
Gat, Dimitri
Yuri Nevsky series (1)
New Abbey girls
Oxenham, Elsie J
Abbey girls first generation series (5)

New adventures of Alice in Rainforest Land
Amadio, Nadine
Alice in Wonderland sequels series (7)
New adventures of Bantan
Gardner, Maurice Benjamin
Bantan series (12)
New adventures of Ellery Queen
Queen, Ellery
Ellery Queen series (16)
New adventures of Galldora
Sedgwick, Modwena
Galldora series (2)
New adventures of Pippi Longstocking
Lindgren, Astrid
Pippi Longstocking series (4)
New adventures of the Mad Scientists' Club
Brinley, Bertrand Russell
Mad Scientists' Club series (2)
New age
Middleton, Martin
Chronicles of the custodians series (4)
New Alice in the old Wonderland
Richards, Anna Matlock
Alice in Wonderland sequels series (2)
New and different summer
Weber, Lenora Mattingly
Stacy and Katie Rose Belford series (3)
New and improved Sarah
Kaye, Marilyn
Camp Sunnyside Friends series (9)
New Angels
Milne, Paula
Angels series (3)
New aristocrats
Saint-Pierre, Michel de
Aristocrats series (2)
New Athens
Hood, Hugh
New age series (2)
New austerities
Perdue, Tito
Leland and Judy Pefley series (1)
New baby
Petty, Kate
First timers series (1)
Szekeres, Cyndy
Tiny paw series (2)
New baby is lost
Van Stockum, Hilda
Jeremy Bear series (4)
New barbarians
Mitchell, Kirk
Procurator trilogy (2)
New batch
Bischoff, David
Gremlins series (2)
New beginning
Dicks, Terrance
Adventures of Buster and Betty series (1)
Gross, Edward
V series (16)
Hulke, Malcolm
Crossroads series (1)
New big sleepy time annual
Hodgetts, Sheila
Sleepy time tales series (4)
New big sleepy time book
Hodgetts, Sheila
Sleepy time tales series (4)
New book for Jane
Farnol, Jeffery
Jane series (2)
New boy
Pier, Arthur Stanwood
Saint Timothy's School series (3)
Stine, Robert Lawrence
Fear Street series (20)
Tovey, Doreen
Cats series (6)
New breed
Elliot, Douglass
American patriot series (1)
Griffin, W E B
Brotherhood of war series (7)
New breed heroes in pro baseball
Gutman, Bill
New breed heroes series (1)
New breed heroes in pro football
Gutman, Bill
New breed heroes series (2)
New bridge
Peterson, Hans
New series (3)
New Caesar
Neumann, Alfred
Napoleon III trilogy (1)
New camera
Carruth, Jean
Fun with Sally series (3)
New cautionary tales
Belloc, Hilaire
Cautionary tales series (2)
New centurions
Wambaugh, Joseph
Bumper Morgan series (1)
New Chalet School
Brent-Dyer, Elinor Mary
Chalet School series (13)
New chronicles of Don Q
Prichard, Katherine
Don Q series (2)
New chronicles of Rebecca of Sunnybrook Farm
Wiggin, Kate Douglas
Rebecca series (2)
New chum
Masefield, John
In the mill series (2)
New clothes for Alex
Dickinson, Mary
Alex series (5)
New coach
Levy, Elizabeth
Gymnasts series (18)
New dawn
Rolland, Romain
John Christopher series (4)
New day
Romains, Jules
Men of goodwill series (20)
New day for Dragon
Hall, Lynn
Dragon series (2)
New deal for death
Roosevelt, Elliott
Blackjack Endicott series (2)
New Decameron
Potocki, Jan
Saragossa manuscript series (2)
New devil's dictionary
Williamson, Jerry Neal
Devil's dictionary series (2)
New doctor
Seifert, Elizabeth
Bayard series (2)
New driftage
Christian, Petra
Sally Deenes series (2)
New dunkum oil
Mills, Frederick John
Dinkum oil series (3)
New earth
Layberry, Layton George Joseph
Oakleigh Farm series (7)
New Elizabeth
Pascal, Francine
Sweet Valley High series (63)
New England resistance
Sullivan, Tim
V series (9)
New Eve
Fowl
Eve series (2)
New evil
Stine, Robert Lawrence
Fear Street cheerleaders series (4)
New Forest adventure
Mogridge, Stephen
New Forest series (1)
New Forest detectives
Mogridge, Stephen
New Forest series (9)
New Forest discoveries
Mogridge, Stephen
New Forest series (5)
New Forest exploits
Mogridge, Stephen
New Forest series (4)
New Forest mystery
Mogridge, Stephen
New Forest series (2)
New Forest pirates
Mogridge, Stephen
New Forest series (7)
New Forest quest
Mogridge, Stephen
New Forest series (3)
New Forest smugglers
Mogridge, Stephen
New Forest series (6)
New Forest spies
Mogridge, Stephen
New Forest series (11)
New Forest treasure
Mogridge, Stephen
New Forest series (10)
New Forest vagabond
Mogridge, Stephen
New Forest series (8)
New found land
Christopher, John
Fireball trilogy (2)
New friends
Haas, Dorothy
Peanut Butter and Jilly series (1)
New friends for John and Mary
James, Grace
John and Mary series (7)
New friends in old Chester
Deland, Margaret
Old Chester series (6)
New girl
Pascal, Francine
Sweet Valley twins series (6)
Stine, Robert Lawrence
Fear Street series (1)
New girl and Nancy
Bruce, Dorita Fairlie
Nancy series (3)
New girl at ballet school
White, Constance Mary
Ballet school series (3)
New girl at Highlands
Tarrant, Elizabeth
Highlands series (2)
New girl at Melling
Biggs, Margaret
Melling School series (6)
New girl for Winterton
Potter, Dora Joan
Winterton School series (6)
New girl in Cabin six
Kaye, Marilyn
Camp Sunnyside Friends series (4)
New girl in town
Baer, Judy
Cedar River daydreams series (1)
Baldwin, Faith
Little Oxford series (5)
New girls at Wood End
Oxenham, Elsie J
Robin Brent series (4)
New Gulliver
Dodderidge, Esme
Lemuel Gulliver series (10)
Garrison, Wendell Phillips
Lemuel Gulliver series (6)
New guys around the block
Guy, Rosa
Imamu Jones series (2)
New Holland heritage
Weaver, Rix
New Holland series (2)
New home, a new friend
Wilhelm, Hans
Merritales series (1)
New hope for the dead
Willeford, Charles
Hoke Moseley series (2)
New horizons
Simpson, Dorothy
Janie Marshal series (5)
New house
Peterson, Hans
New series (1)
New house at Springdale
Bruce, Dorita Fairlie
Springdale series (4)
New house at the Chalet School
Brent-Dyer, Elinor Mary
Chalet School series (11)
New house-captain
Bruce, Dorita Fairlie
Springdale series (1)
New house for Little Mouse
Wheeler, Cindy
Little Mouse series (2)
New idol
Leroux, Gaston
Cheri-Bibi series (5)
New, improved, dykes to watch out for!
Bechdel, Alison
Dykes series (3)
New, improved Gretchen Hubbard
Cooper, Ilene
Kids from Kennedy Middle School series (4)
New, improved murder
Gorman, Edward
Jack Dwyer series (2)
New Jan Perry stories
Sedgwick, Modwena
Jan Perry series (3)
New Jersey showdown
Mallory, Roosevelt
Radcliff series (4)
New Jessica
Pascal, Francine
Sweet Valley High series (32)
New Just Mary stories
Grannan, Mary
Just Mary series (3)
New Kate
Saunders, Susan
Sleepover friends series (26)
New kid in town
Kroll, Steven
Hit and Run Gang series (1)
New kid on the block
Adams, Nicholas
Horror High series (4)
New kids on the block
Catalano, Grace
New kids on the block series (1)
New kids on the block scrapbook
Catalano, Grace
New kids on the block series (2)
New kind of killer
Melville, Jennie
Sergeant Charmian Daniels series (7)
New kind of killer, an old kind of death
Melville, Jennie
Sergeant Charmian Daniels series (7)
New kind of war
Price, Anthony
Doctor David Audley and Jack Butler series (17)
New knock knocks
Cole, William
Knock knocks series (3)
New lease of death
Rendell, Ruth
Chief Inspector Reginald Wexford series (2)
New leash on death
Conant, Susan
Dog trainer mystery series (1)
New Lensman
Ellern, William Bert
Lensman series (8)
New life for old
James, Laurence
Simon Rack series (5)
New lives
Piper, Warrene
Bennet family series (3)
New Maggie Muggins stories
Grannan, Mary
Maggie Muggins series (3)
New me
Sorenson, Jane
Katie Hooper series (7)
New men
Snow, Charles Percy
Strangers and brothers series (6)
New Mexico!
Ross, Dana Fuller
Wagons West series (22)
New Mexico connection
Wilcox, Collin
Marshal Sam McCloud series (2)
New Mexico massacre
Trimnell, Robert L
Loner series (2)
New Mexico showdown
Roberts, J R
Gunsmith series (77)
New minds
Morgan, Dan
Sixth perception series (1)
New mistress at the Chalet School
Brent-Dyer, Elinor Mary
Chalet School series (37)
New money
Roche, Eliane
Fortune and power series (2)
New monster that ate Canberra
Salmon, Michael
Alexander Bunyip series (12)
New moon
Snyder, Midori
Queen's quarter series (1)
New moon rising
Price, Eugenia
Saint Simons trilogy (2)
New neighbors for Nora
Hurwitz, Johanna
Nora and Teddy series (3)
New neighbours
Gissing, Vera
Pippins series (4)
New Noddy colour strip book
Blyton, Enid
Noddy tiny strip books series (10)
New order
Kimball, Janus
Scanners series (2)
Middleton, Martin
Chronicles of the custodians series (5)
New Orleans beat
Smith, Julie
Skip Langdon series (4)
New Orleans five
Roberts, J R
Gunsmith series (10)
New Orleans gamble
Masterson, Louis
Morgan Kane series (29)
New Orleans holocaust
McCurtin, Peter
Assassins series (2)
New Orleans knockout
Pendleton, Don
Mack Bolan series (20)
New Orleans mourning
Smith, Julie
Skip Langdon series (1)
New Orleans run
Robbins, David
Endworld series (24)
New Panjandrum
Farrow, George Edward
Panjandrum series (2)
New people at twenty four
Gilroy, Beryl
Young Roy series (1)
New prefect at Melling
Biggs, Margaret
Melling School series (2)
New promise
Pascal, Francine
Promise trilogy (3)
New pupil midwife
Cooper, Lisa
Princess Beatrice Hospital series (6)
New road
Peterson, Hans
New series (2)
New role for Natasha
Matthewman, Phyllis
Daneswood series (4)
New sayings
Hubbard, Kin
Abe Martin series (8)
New scholars
Mathews, Joanna Hooe
Miss Ashton's girls series (2)
New school at Highcliff
Little, Sylvia
Highcliff series (1)
New shining white murder
Launay, Droo
Adam Flute series (2)
New shoe
Upfield, Arthur William
Napoleon Bonaparte series (15)
New shoes
Streatfeild, Noel
Bell family series (2)
Shoes series (10)
New Sister Theatre
Andrews, Lucilla
Saint Barnabas' Hospital series (2)
New Spoon River
Masters, Edgar Lee
Spoon River series (2)
New sporting stories
G, G
Sporting stories series (2)
New springtime
Silverberg, Robert
New springtime series (2)
New Stephanie
Saunders, Susan
Sleepover friends series (35)
New stories from the Twilight Zone
Greenberg, Martin Harry
Twilight Zone series (6)
Serling, Rod
Twilight Zone series (3)
New Sugar Creek Gang mystery
Hutchens, Paul
Sugar Creek Gang series (9)
New Swiss family Robinson
Wister, Owen
Swiss family Robinson series (3)
New tales of Robin Hood
Suddaby, Donald
Robin Hood series (1)
New teacher
Cohen, Miriam
Best friends series (2)
New television adventures of Worzel Gummidge and Aunt Sally
Waterhouse, Keith
Worzel Gummidge series (16)
New temple
Bojer, Johan
Peer Holm series (2)

New territory
James, Colin
New Zealand revolution series (2)
New theories on the birth of the universe
Lampton, Christopher
New theories series (3)
New theories on the dinosaurs
Lampton, Christopher
New theories series (1)
New theories on the origins of the human race
Lampton, Christopher
New theories series (2)
New think
De Bono, Edward
Lateral thinking series (1)
New, thinking Annabel
Davidson, Alan
Annabel Fidelity Bunce series (4)
New Town
Streatfeild, Noel
Bell family series (2)
Shoes series (10)
New trails blaze west
Winstan, Matt
Reuben Brown series (5)
New Treasure Seekers
Nesbit, Edith
Bastable family series (3)
New Turing omnibus
Dewdney, Alexander Keewatin
Turing series (2)
New voyage to the country of the Houyhnhnms
Hodgart, Matthew
Lemuel Gulliver series (9)
New war
Pendleton, Don
Mack Bolan series (39)
New war book
Pendleton, Don
Mack Bolan series (63)
New wizard of Oz
Baum, Lyman Frank
Oz series (1)
New world
Collins, Warwick
Challenge series (2)
New worlds for old
Stark, Freya
Traveller's letters series (5)
New worlds to conquer
Halliburton, Richard
Royal adventures series (3)
New Year's Day
Wharton, Edith
Old New York quartet (4)
New Year's Day magic
Baker, James Webb
Magic series (6)
New Year's Eve in Lan-Fang
Gulik, Robert van
Judge Dee series (2)
New Year's evil
Keene, Carolyn
Nancy Drew and Hardy boys supermystery series (11)
New Year's mystery
Nixon, Joan Lowery
First read-alone mystery series (1)
New York by knight
Friesner, Esther Mona
New York trilogy (1)
New York connection
Moore, Robin
Connection series (5)
New York detective
Marshall, William Leonard
Tillman and Muldoon series (1)
New York diary
Rorem, Ned
Musical diaries series (2)
New York in flashmaps, 1974-75
George, Jean Craighead
New York in maps series (2)
New York in maps, 1972-73
George, Jean Craighead
New York in maps series (1)
New York life
Gill, Brendan
New York series (2)
New York murders
Queen, Ellery
Ellery Queen series (44)
New York necromancy
Macao, Marshall
K'ing Kung-Fu series (6)
New York, New York
Martin, Ann Matthews
Baby-Sitters Club super specials series (6)
New York run
Robbins, David
Endworld series (10)
New York trilogy
Auster, Paul
New York trilogy (3)
New Yorkers
Calisher, Hortense
Ruth series (2)
New Zealand Jack
Wilson, Phillip
Roberts family series (2)
New Zealand twins
Rooke, Daphne
Twin series (30)
Newcomers
Wilson, Trevor Edward
Big Tom Holder trilogy (1)
Newcomes
Thackeray, William Makepeace
Arthur Pendennis series (2)
News from Havre
Duhamel, Georges
Pasquier series (1)
News from Thrush Green
Read, *Miss*
Thrush Green series (3)
News girl
Brand, Hilary
Hilary Brand series (1)
News of murder
Lejeune, Anthony
Adam Gifford series (1)
News of Paul Temple
Durbridge, Francis
Paul Temple series (3)
News of spring, and other nature studies
Maeterlinck, Maurice
Hours of gladness series (2)
News reel
Casey, Robert J
Jim Sands series (3)
News reel murder
Buranelli, Prosper
Nick Morro series (2)
News travels by night
Graeme, Bruce
Superintendent William Stevens and Inspector Pierre Allain series (13)
Newsman Ned and the broken rules
Kroll, Steven
Newsman Ned series (2)
Newsman Ned meets the new family
Kroll, Steven
Newsman Ned series (1)
Newspaper anti-coloring book
Striker, Susan
Anti-coloring book series (9)
Newspaper Children
De la Mahotiere, Mary
Newspaper Children series (1)
Newspaper murders
Gash, Joe
Terry Flynn series (3)
Newspaper seller's secret
Edwards, Walter
Sexton Blake series (948)
Newspapers
Fisher, Leonard Everett
Nineteenth century America series (5)
Newton letter
Banville, John
Astronomers series (3)
Newts in the pond
Jones, Olive
Barfield series (10)
Next, after Lucifer
Rhodes, Daniel
Guilhelm de Courdeval series (1)
Next door to death
Cobb, Belton
Inspector Cheviot Burmann series (13)
Next door to murder
Cargill, Leslie
Major Mosson series (4)
Next horizon
Bonington, Chris
Climbing series (2)
Next o' kin
Graydon, William Murray
Sexton Blake series (350)
Next of kin
Goodchild, George
Inspector McLean series (45)
Murphy, Warren Burton
Destroyer series (46)
Townley, Pamela
Stone maiden series (2)
Next one to die
Gunn, Victor
Chief Inspector Bill Cromwell series (32)
Next panda, please!
Taylor, David Conrad
Zoovet series (4)
Next patient, please
Rodney, Jonathan
To heal series (2)
Next Saturday in Milan
Tute, Warren
George Mado series (5)
Next stop, the morgue
Winter, Bevis
Steve Craig series (5)
Next to die
Verner, Gerald
Trevor Lowe series (2)
Next to oddliness
Jennings, Paul Francis
Oddly series (4)
Next victim
Stuart, Donald
Sexton Blake series (676)
Next witnesses
Stout, Rex
Nero Wolfe and Archie Goodwin series (26)
Nexus
Miller, Henry
Rosy crucifixion trilogy (3)
Nghu night falls
Sherman, David
Night fighters series (5)
Nguy Hiem war zone
Lansing, John
Black Eagles series (21)
Nhu sting
Helm, Eric
Scorpion Squad series (2)
Nibbled to death by ducks
Campbell, Robert Wright
Jimmy Flannery series (6)
Nibs
Nokes, Ethel
Billy Bunker series (1)
Nibs in clover
Nokes, Ethel
Billy Bunker series (2)
Niccolo rising
Dunnett, Dorothy
House of Niccolo series (1)
Nice class of corpse
Brett, Simon
Mrs Melita Pargeter series (1)
Nice cup of tea
Gilbert, Anthony
Arthur Crook series (23)
Nice day for a funeral
Howard, Hartley
Glenn Bowman series (32)
Nice day for murder
Gunn, Victor
Chief Inspector Bill Cromwell series (9)
Nice day for screaming, and other tales of The Hub
Schmitz, James Henry
Hub series (2)
Nice day out?
Cate, Dick
Flying free series (4)
Nice derangement of epitaphs
Peters, Ellis
Inspector George Felse series (4)
Nice enough to murder
Russell, Enid Sherry
Ben Louis series (2)
Nice fillies finish last
Halliday, Brett
Michael Shayne series (52)
Nice girl like you
Johnston, Norma
Sterling family series (5)
Wormser, Richard
Lieutenant Andy Bastian series (2)
Nice guys don't win
Mitchell, Scott
Brock Devlin series (13)
Nice little business
Dewhurst, Eileen
Inspector Neil Carter series (5)
Nice little killing
Gilbert, Anthony
Arthur Crook series (50)
Nice long evening
Corbett, Elizabeth
Mrs Meigs series (3)
Nice murderers
Delman, David
Lieutenant Jacob Horowitz series (5)
Nice new neighbors
Brandenberg, Franz
Fieldmouse children series (2)
Nice place to die
Culpan, Maurice
Inspector Bill Houghton series (1)
Nice place to live
Sloane, Robert C
Marino family series (1)
Nice sound alibi
Lauben, Philip
Captain Homer Clay series (1)
Nice way to die
Janson, Hank
Hank Janson series (156)
Warner, Mignon
Mrs Edwina Charles series (1)
Nice weekend for a murder
Collins, Max Allan
Mallory series (5)
Nice work
Lodge, David
Rummidge University series (3)
Nicest day of the year
Delahaye, Gilbert
Mary series (1)
Nicholas and the gang
Goscinny, Rene
Nicholas series (2)
Nicholas and the gang again
Goscinny, Rene
Nicholas series (4)
Nicholas and the gang at school
Goscinny, Rene
Nicholas series (3)
Nicholas at large
Goscinny, Rene
Nicholas series (6)
Nicholas Carey
Welch, Ronald
Carey family series (9)
Nicholas' favorite pet
Sandberg, Inger
Nicholas series (2)
Nicholas kept on writing
Glemser, Bernard
Nicholas Hart series (1)
Nicholas Lattermole's case
Barry, Charles
Superintendent Lawrence Gilmartin series (15)
Nicholas on holiday
Goscinny, Rene
Nicholas series (5)
Nicholas' red day
Sandberg, Inger
Nicholas series (1)
Nicholas the weaver, and other Quaker stories
Robinson, Maude
Quaker tales series (2)
Nicholas'ideal pet
Sandberg, Inger
Nicholas series (2)
Nichovev plot
Carter, Nick
Nick Carter series (112)
Nick and Company clean up
Croson, Bob
Nick and Company series (4)
Nick and Company in a fix
Croson, Bob
Nick and Company series (1)
Nick and Company on holiday
Croson, Bob
Nick and Company series (2)
Nick and Company to the rescue
Croson, Bob
Nick and Company series (3)
Nick Carter and the green goods men
Carter, Nicholas
Nicholas Carter series (45)
Nick Carter and the red button
Carter, Nicholas
Nicholas Carter series (481)
Nick Carter down east
Carter, Nicholas
Nicholas Carter series (66)
Nick Carter's auto trail
Carter, Nicholas
Nicholas Carter series (288)
Nick Carter's chance clue
Carter, Nicholas
Nicholas Carter series (431)
Nick Carter's Chinese puzzle
Carter, Nicholas
Nicholas Carter series (250)
Nick Carter's cipher
Carter, Nicholas
Nicholas Carter series (285)
Nick Carter's clever protege
Carter, Nicholas
Nicholas Carter series (44)
Nick Carter's clever ruse
Carter, Nicholas
Nicholas Carter series (64)
Nick Carter's close call
Carter, Nicholas
Nicholas Carter series (249)
Nick Carter's close finish
Carter, Nicholas
Nicholas Carter series (430)
Nick Carter's convict client
Carter, Nicholas
Nicholas Carter series (350)
Nick Carter's counterplot
Carter, Nicholas
Nicholas Carter series (427)
Nick Carter's death warrant
Carter, Nicholas
Nicholas Carter series (104)
Nick Carter's double catch
Carter, Nicholas
Nicholas Carter series (179)
Nick Carter's Egyptain clew
Carter, Nicholas
Nicholas Carter series (425)
Nick Carter's fall
Carter, Nicholas
Nicholas Carter series (208)
Nick Carter's girl detective
Carter, Nicholas
Nicholas Carter series (67)
Nick Carter's intuition
Carter, Nicholas
Nicholas Carter series (387)
Nick Carter's last card
Carter, Nicholas
Nicholas Carter series (424)
Nick Carter's masterpiece
Carter, Nicholas
Nicholas Carter series (210)
Nick Carter's menace
Carter, Nicholas
Nicholas Carter series (421)
Nick Carter's new assistant
Carter, Nicholas
Nicholas Carter series (482)
Nick Carter's persistence
Carter, Nicholas
Nicholas Carter series (352)
Nick Carter's promise
Carter, Nicholas
Nicholas Carter series (287)
Nick Carter's retainer
Carter, Nicholas
Nicholas Carter series (70)
Nick Carter's roundup
Carter, Nicholas
Nicholas Carter series (389)
Nick Carter's star pupils
Carter, Nicholas
Nicholas Carter series (68)
Nick Carter's subtle foe
Carter, Nicholas
Nicholas Carter series (419)
Nick Carter's swim to victory
Carter, Nicholas
Nicholas Carter series (324)
Nick Carter's treasure chest case
Carter, Nicholas
Nicholas Carter series (483)
Nick Carter's wildest chase
Carter, Nicholas
Nicholas Carter series (351)
Nick Fisher the bill-poster
Dillon, Deidre
Trumpton series (1)
Nick of time
Effinger, George Alec
Nick of time series (1)
Nick the weasel
Evens, George Bramwell
Romany readers series (7)
Nickel jackpot
Lamb, J J
Zack Rolfe series (1)
Nicknames only
Donaldson, William
Ladies and gentlemen series (2)
Nick's October
Prince, Alison
Nick series (2)
Nicky and Nigger and the pirate
Craigie, Dorothy
Nicky and Nigger series (2)
Nicky and Nigger join the circus
Craigie, Dorothy
Nicky and Nigger series (1)
Nicky, son of Egg
Bullett, Gerald
History of Pandervil series (2)
Nicky upstairs and down
Ziefert, Harriet
Nicky series (8)

Nicky's Christmas surprise
Ziefert, Harriet
Nicky series (1)
Nicky's friends
Ziefert, Harriet
Nicky series (4)
Nicky's noisy night
Ziefert, Harriet
Nicky series (3)
Nicky's picnic
Ziefert, Harriet
Nicky series (5)
Nicodemus
Alexander, Sidney
Michelangelo Buonarotti trilogy (3)
Nicola Mimosa
Ure, Jean
Nicola Bruce series (2)
Nicole
Ransom, Candice Farris
Sunfire series (19)
Nicolette detects
Cameron, Margaret Locherbie
Nicolette series (1)
Nicolette finds her
Cameron, Margaret Locherbie
Nicolette series (2)
Nifft the Lean
Shea, Michael
Dying earth series (5)
Nigel Knight
Campbell, Rod
Little people series (5)
Night
Coote, Roger
My day series (4)
Metcalfe, Penny
Baby's day series (4)
Van der Essen, Anne
Yok-yok series (3)
Wiesel, Elie
Night trilogy (1)
Night action
Hudson, Alec
Submarine series (4)
Night after night
Goudge, Eileen
Seniors series (18)
Night after the wedding
Gordons
Frank and Gail Mitchell series (2)
Night and fog
Netzen, Klaus
Killers series (3)
Saint Germain, Gregory
Resistance series (1)
Night and silence, who is here?
Johnson, Pamela Hansford
Daniel Skipton trilogy (2)
Night and the city
Kersh, Gerald
Harry Fabian series (1)
Night and the dream
Gunnarsson, Gunar
Ships in the sky series (2)
Night and the judgment
Butler, Leslie
Horton and Jordan series (1)
Night angel
Green, Kate
Shattered series (2)
Reaves, Michael
Shattered series (2)
Night arrant
Gygax, Gary
Gord the Rogue series (2)
Night at sea
Lane, Margaret
Shipwreck series (1)
Night at the Mocking Widow
Dickson, Carter
Sir Henry Merrivale series (21)
Night at the Vulcan
Marsh, Ngaio
Inspector Roderick Alleyn series (16)
Night beat
Maclean, Arthur
Sexton Blake series (1406)
Night before the wedding
Gordons
Frank and Gail Mitchell series (1)
Night birds on Nantucket
Aiken, Joan
Dido Twite series (3)
Night-blooming circus
Hadley, Joan
Theo Bloomer series (1)
Night boat, and other Tod Moran mysteries
Pease, Howard
Tod Moran series (10)
Night branders
Evans, Tabor
Longarm series (169)
Night club
Jenkins, Herbert
Bindle series (2)
Night-club, and other stories
Brush, Katharine
Lillian Legendre series (1)
Night-club crime
Skene, Anthony
Sexton Blake series (671)
Night club lady
Abbot, Anthony
Thatcher Colt series (3)
Night club murder
Brandon, John Gordon
Inspector Patrick Aloysius McCarthy series (19)
Daniel, Roland
Michael Wallace series (3)
Night-club mystery
Teed, George Hamilton
Sexton Blake series (501)
Night counting
Morris, Ann
Sleepy series (3)
Night cover
Lewin, Michael Zinn
Albert Samson series (4)
Lieutenant Leroy Powder series (1)
Night creature
Laymon, Richard Carl
Strange Occurrence Squad series (2)
Night daddy
Gripe, Maria
Julia series (1)
Night date
Straker, Philip
Night series (1)
Night, dawn, day
Wiesel, Elie
Night trilogy (3)
Night drop
Davis, Frederick Clyde
Schyler Cole and Luke Speare series (6)
Night Eighth ran mall
Kenyon, Kate
Cedar Groves Junior High School series (15)
Night encounter
Gilbert, Anthony
Arthur Crook series (45)
Macdonnell, James Edmond
Hooky Walker series (3)
Night face
Anderson, Poul
Future history series (1)
Polesotechnic League series (1)
Night falls on the city
Gainham, Sarah
Viennese trilogy (1)
Night ferry to death
Moyes, Patricia
Henry and Emmy Tibbett series (17)
Night flight
Saint-Exupery, Antoine de
Airman's odyssey trilogy (1)
Night flight to Arras
Saint-Exupery, Antoine de
Airman's odyssey trilogy (3)
Night flight to Zurich
Gregg, Cecil Freeman
Inspector Cuthbert Higgins series (32)
Night frost
Copper, Basil
Mike Faraday series (2)
Night games
Wilcox, Collin
Lieutenant Frank Hastings series (14)
Night has eyes
Backhouse, Elizabeth
Inspector Christopher Marsden series (2)
Night hawk
Edson, John Thomas
Waco series (7)
Night horseman
Brand, Max
Dan Barry series (2)
Night in the Netherhells
Gardner, Craig Shaw
Ebenezum series (3)
Night in town
Pullen, Alan
Sam and Lin series (5)
Night is a child
Llewellyn, Richard
Edmund Trothe series (4)
Night is for violence
Bateson, David
Larry Vernon series (5)
Night is long
Millin, Sarah Gertrude
War diary series (1)
Night is the time to die
Wainwright, John
Northern Police series (16)
Night it rained bullets
Wynne, Brian
Marshal Jeremy Six series (4)
Night lady
Gault, William Campbell
Joe Puma series (3)
Night landings
Prince, Alison
Airfield series (2)
Night lords
Freeling, Nicolas
Henri Castang series (4)
Night lust
Straker, Philip
Night series (2)
Night marches
Shelynn, Jack
Ned Parker series (3)
Night mare
Anthony, Piers
Xanth series (6)
Night masks
Salvatore, Robert Anthony
Cleric quintet (3)
Night McLennan died
Grover, Marshall
Nevada Jim series (1)
Night moves
Roberts, Nora
Flowers series (7)
Night, night!
McMullen, Nigel
Naughty baby series (3)
Night, night, Ben
Bradman, Tony
Ben series (2)
Night noises and other Mole and Troll stories
Johnston, Tony
Mole and Troll series (3)
Night of a thousand pizzas
Hodgman, Ann
Lunchroom series (1)
Night of crime
Livingston, Armstrong
Jimmy Treynor series (5)
Night of dragons
Salsitz, R A V
Dragons trilogy (3)
Night of errors
Innes, Michael
Sir John Appleby series (11)
Night of fear
Dalton, Moray
Inspector Hugh Collier series (2)
Mackenzie, Nigel
Inspector Charles Tremayne series (3)
Night of fire
Nelson, Peter N
Sylvia Smith-Smith series (2)
Night of ghosts and lightning
Tallis, Robyn
Planet builders series (2)
Night of horror
Soutar, Andrew
Phineas Spinnet series (2)
Night of masks
Norton, Andre
Dipple trilogy (3)
Night of Morningstar
O'Donnell, Peter
Modesty Blaise series (11)
Night of shadows
Lockridge, Frances
Paul Lane series (1)
Richards, Francis
Paul Lane series (1)
Night of the Apache
Longtree, Warren T
Ruff Justice series (2)
Night of the assassin
Smith, Don
Secret mission series (15)
Night of the assassins
Rossi, Bruno
Sharpshooter series (5)
Night of the avenger
Carter, Nick
Nick Carter series (72)
Night of the comet
Sharp, Allen
Storytrails series (9)
Night of the Condor
Carter, Nick
Nick Carter series (231)
Night of the crabs
Smith, Guy Newman
Crabs series (1)
Night of the crash-test dummies
Larson, Gary
Far Side series (9)
Night of the crime
Desmond, Hugh
Alan Fraser series (9)
Night of the Dragonstar
Bischoff, David
Dragonstar trilogy (2)
Night of the fog
Gilbert, Anthony
Scott Egerton series (5)
Night of the fox
Higgins, Jack
Brigadier Dougal Munro and Captain Jack Carter series (1)
Night of the full moon
Chance, John Newton
Mister DeHavilland series (9)
Night of the garter murder
Howes, Royce
Captain Ben Lucias series (1)
Night of the gila
Roberts, J R
Gunsmith series (34)
Night of the guns
Grover, Marshall
Larry and Stretch series (333)
Night of the Hawk
James, Leigh Franklin
John Cooper Baines series (5)
Night of the hawk
Raine, Richard
David Martini series (2)
Night of the jackals
Hayes, Ralph Eugene
John Yard series (2)
Night of the jaguar
McCray, Mike
Black Berets series (9)
Night of the kill
James, Breni
Sergeant Gunnar Matson series (1)
Night of the living dead
Russo, John
Living dead series (1)
Night of the living dummy
Stine, Robert Lawrence
Goosebumps series (7)
Night of the mist
Heimler, Eugene
Mist series (1)
Night of the Nazgul
Ruemmler, John David
Middle Earth quest series (1)
Night of the peacock
Rosenberger, Joseph
Death Merchant series (49)
Night of the phantom
Ross, Marilyn
Phantoms series (3)
Night of the phoenix
Austin, Richard
Guardians series (4)
Demille, Nelson
Joe Keller series (3)
Keller series (3)
Night of the Picaroon
Cassells, John
Ludovic Saxon series (15)
Night of the reaper
Grayland, Valerie Merle
Hoani Mata series (2)
Night of the red horse
Leitch, Patricia
Jinny series (4)
Night of the saucers
Binder, Eando
Saucer series (2)
Night of the scorpion
Horowitz, Anthony
Old ones trilogy (2)
Night of the Shadow
Grant, Maxwell
Shadow series (288)
Night of the short knives
Wilkinson, Burke
Geoffrey Mildmay series (4)
Night of the solstice
Smith, Lisa J
Solstice series (1)
Night of the storm
Foote, Horton
Orphans' home series (1)
Gask, Arthur
Gilbert Larose series (12)
Night of the thuggie
Wilson, Gar
Phoenix Force series (18)
Night of the toads
Collins, Michael
Dan Fortune series (3)
Night of the trilobites
Leslie, Peter
Invaders series (5)
Night of the twelfth to thirteenth
Steeman, Andre
Wenceslas Vorobeitchik series (2)
Night of the twenty third
Jackson, Lewis
Sexton Blake series (1189)
Night of the twin moons
Lorrah, Jean
Star trek fan series (3)
Night of the vampire kitty
Mooser, Stephen
Creepy Creature Club series (9)
Night of the warheads
Carter, Nick
Nick Carter series (189)
Night of the watchman
Creasey, John
Inspector Roger West series (17)
Night of the werewolf
Dixon, Franklin W
Hardy boys series (59)
Night of the white hunter
Halliday, Brett
Mike Shayne stories series (10)
Night of the Wolf
Baker, William Howard
Richard Quintain series (13)
Night of the wolverine
Epperson, Jerry
Marvel superheroes adventure gamebooks series (3)
Night of two new moons
Tallis, Robyn
Planet builders series (6)
Night of violence
Barrington, Pamela
Inspector George Marshall series (3)
Night on the Devil's Pathway
Russell, Charlotte Murray
Jane Amanda Edwards series (4)
Night on the island
Kaye, Mary Margaret
Death series (6)
Night on the pathway
Russell, Charlotte Murray
Jane Amanda Edwards series (4)
Night outlasts the whippoorwill
North, Sterling
Plowing series (2)
Night over Mexico
Downing, Todd
Hugh Rennert series (6)
Night passage to Kano
Robertson, Manning K
Steve Carradine series (3)
Night pillow
Rae, Hugh Crauford
Glasgow series (2)
Night plague
Masterton, Graham
Night warriors series (3)
Night prey
Sandford, John
Lucas Davenport series (6)
Night probe!
Cussler, Clive
Dirk Pitt series (6)
Night raider
Barry, Mike
Burton Wulff series (1)
Hogan, Ray
John Mosby series (7)
Night raiders
Skene, Anthony
Sexton Blake series (632)
Night remembers
Gorman, Edward
Jack Dwyer series (7)
Night rider
Wrexe, Charles
Bill Mitchum series (4)
Night riders
Douglas, Thorne
Rancho Bravo series (4)
Ladd, Justin
Abilene series (4)
Moore, Arthur
Alamo series (2)
Phillips, Tony
Turbo cowboys series (7)

Redmayne, John
Peter Maclean series (3)
Tranter, Nigel Godwin
Hawick series (2)
Night rider's moon
Dalton, Kit
Buckskin series (40)
Night run from Java
Black, Gavin
Paul Harris series (13)
Night safe mystery
Carlton, Lewis
Sexton Blake series (689)
Night secrets
Cook, Thomas H
Frank Clemons series (3)
Night shadows
Robertson, Colin
Inspector John Martin series (1)
Night she died
Simpson, Dorothy
Inspector Luke Thanet series (1)
Night stalker
Rice, Jeff
Carl Kolchak series (1)
Night Storm, the flat racer
Peel, Hazel Mary
Ann and Jim Henderson series (6)
Night strangler
Rice, Jeff
Carl Kolchak series (2)
Night striker
Lorin, Amii
Samantha Wade series (2)
Night the fog came down
Bude, John
Inspector Sherwood series (2)
Night the ghost walked
Sinclair, Dee
Castledare series (1)
Night the gods smiled
Wright, Eric
Inspector Charlie Salter series (1)
Night the rain came in
Wayne, Jenifer
Winchester family series (2)
Night, the woman
Ransome, Stephen
Lieutenant Lee Barcello series (1)
Night they killed Joss Varran
Bellairs, George
Detective Inspector Thomas Littlejohn series (50)
Night time
Wilmer, Diane
Step by step series (2)
Night-time story
Erickson, Karen
I can do it series (6)
Night to forget
Hoh, Diane
Chrystal Falls series (7)
Night train
James, Martin
Rick Muldoon series (1)
Millar, Kenneth
Chet Gordon series (2)
Night train to Memphis
Peters, Elizabeth
Vicky Bliss series (5)
Night train to Paris
Coles, Manning
Tommy Hambledon series (14)
Night trilogy
Wiesel, Elie
Night trilogy (3)
Night trip
Robertson, Colin
Vicky McBain series (8)
Night vision
Levine, Paul
Jake Lassiter series (2)
Night visions
Frisbie, Carol
Star trek fan series (7)
Night walk
Daly, Elizabeth
Henry Gamadge series (12)
Night walker
Hager, Jean
Mitch Bushyhead series (2)
Night walkers
Norman, James
Gimiendo Hernandez Quinto series (3)
Night warriors
Masterton, Graham
Night warriors series (1)
Night was made for murder
Winter, Bevis
Steve Craig series (7)
Night watch
McCutcheon, Hugh
Jimmy Carroll series (6)
Night watches
Jacobs, William Wymark
Night-Watchman series (10)
Night Wheeler
Brown, Carter
Lieutenant Al Wheeler series (47)
Night whistlers
Trevor, Dan
Night whistlers series (1)
Night whistlers trilogy (1)
Night wind
Mountjoy, Roberta Jean
Night wind series (1)
Night winds
Wagner, Karl Edward
Kane series (5)
Night wind's promise
Vanardy, Varick
Bingham Harvard series (3)
Night without darkness
Orvis, Kenneth
Adam Breck series (1)
Nightbird
Edwards, Monica
Romney Marsh series (9)
Nightcap
Dobson, Margaret
Jane Bailey series (4)
Smith, J C S
Quentin Jacoby series (2)
Nightchild
Baker, Scott
Ashlu cycle series (1)
Nightclimber
White, Jon Manchip
Colonel Rickman trilogy (1)
Nightclub mystery
Clevely, Hugh
Sexton Blake series (1324)
Nightcomers
Hastings, Michael
Turn of the screw series (1)
Nightfeeder
Reeves-Stevens, Garfield
Chronicles of Galen Sword series (2)
Nighthawk
Duncan, William Murdoch
Superintendent Gaylord series (2)
Nighthawk mops up
Horler, Sydney
Nighthawk series (4)
Nighthawk strikes to kill
Horler, Sydney
Nighthawk series (3)
Nighthawk swears vengeance
Horler, Sydney
Nighthawk series (7)
Nighthunter
Faulcon, Robert
Nighthunter series (1)
Nightingale legacy
Coulter, Catherine
Legacy trilogy (2)
Nightingale trivet
Mead, Russell
Doctor Peter Casey series (2)
Nightlines
Lutz, John
Alo Nudger series (2)
Nightmare
Owen, Richard
David Morgan series (2)
Rotsler, William
Doctor Strange series (1)
Nightmare Alley
Mackie, John
Rat Bastards series (11)
Nightmare asylum
Perry, Steve
Aliens series (2)
Nightmare at dawn
Philips, Judson Pentecost
Peter Styles series (7)
Nightmare at noon
Gilman, George G
Adam Steele series (16)
Sterling, Stewart
Ben Pedley series (4)
Fire Marshal Ben Pedley series (4)
Nightmare begins
Ahern, Jerry
Survivalist series (2)
Nightmare Castle
Martyn, Wyndham
Anthony Trent series (16)
Nightmare clowns
Butler, Bill
Dean Street detectives series (2)
Nightmare conspiracy
Hayes, Ralph Eugene
Agent for Cominsec series (5)
Nightmare cottage
Wilson, Gertrude Mary
Inspector Lovick series (9)
Nightmare dream
Caspian, Jonatha Ariadne
Torg series (3)
Nightmare fair
Williams, Graham
Doctor Who series (162)
Nightmare Farm
Mann, Jack
Gregory George Gordon Green series (3)
Nightmare file
Livingston, Jack
Joe Birney series (3)
Nightmare for Doctor Morelle
Dudley, Ernest
Doctor Morelle series (13)
Nightmare has triplets
Cabell, James Branch
Nightmare trilogy (3)
Nightmare honeymoon
Foley, Rae
Hiram Potter series (8)
Nightmare house
Gray, Berkeley
Norman Conquest series (39)
Nightmare in Algeria
Rosenberger, Joseph
Death Merchant series (18)
Nightmare in Angel City
Dixon, Franklin W
Hardy boys case files series (19)
Nightmare in Laos
Lansing, John
Black Eagles series (3)
Nightmare in Naples
Stagg, James
Sexton Blake series (1424)
Nightmare in New York
Pendleton, Don
Mack Bolan series (7)
Nightmare in Panama
Rosenberger, Joseph
C.O.B.R.A. series (4)
Nightmare in pink
Macdonald, John Dann
Travis McGee series (2)
Nightmare in rust
Audemars, Pierre
Monsieur Pinaud series (18)
Nightmare Island
Hayes, Ralph Eugene
Check Force series (5)
Nightmare Lake
Laymon, Richard Carl
Twilight series (11)
Nightmare machine
Larson, Glen A
Battlestar Galactica series (11)
Nightmare merchants
Wilson, Gar
Phoenix Force series (29)
Nightmare network
Rainey, Rich
Alex Dartanian series (5)
Nightmare of God
Rogers, Mark Earl
Zorachus series (2)
Nightmare on Elm Street companion
Cooper, Jeffrey
Nightmare on Elm Street series (2)
Nightmare on Vega Three
Huntington, Charles
Space probe six series (2)
Nightmare planet
Mooser, Stephen
Which way interactive series (3)
Nightmare point
Berry, Carole
Bonnie Indermill series (5)
Nightmare realm of Baba Yaga
Moore, Roger Elwood
Advanced dungeons and dragons adventure gamebook series (5)
Nightmare seasons
Grant, Charles Lewis
Oxrun Station series (5)
Nightmare session
Charles, Steven
Private school series (1)
Nightmare store
Milton, Hilary
Plot your own horror stories series (2)
Nightmare time
Pentecost, Hugh
Pierre Chambrun series (21)
Nightmare town
Hammett, Dashiell
Continental Op series (5)
Nightmare trail
Majors, E B
Slaughter and Son series (2)
Nightmare world
Stern, David
Doctor Bones series (5)
Nightmares
Prelutsky, Jack
Poems to trouble your sleep series (1)
Nightmares in the mist
Farrington, Liz
Mrs Murgatroyd series (4)
Nightmares on Elm Street
Greenberg, Martin Harry
Nightmare on Elm Street series (2)
Nightmares on Elm Street, parts 1, 2, 3
Cooper, Jeffrey
Nightmare on Elm Street series (1)
Nightmares on Elm Street, parts 4, 5
Locke, Joseph
Nightmare on Elm Street series (2)
Nightpool
Murphy, Shirley Rousseau
Dragonbards trilogy (1)
Nightreaver
Weaver, Michael D
Thyri trilogy (2)
Nightriders
McCurtin, Peter
Sundance series (26)
Willoughby, Lee Davis
Making of America series (26)
Nightrunners
Collins, Michael
Dan Fortune series (9)
Nightrunners of Bengal
Masters, John
Indian trilogy (1)
Savage family series (3)
Night's candles
Hocking, Anne
Inspector William Austen series (6)
Night's cloak
Punshon, Ernest Robertson
Bobby Owen series (19)
Night's daughter
Lee, Tanith
Tales from the flat earth series (5)
Night's evil
McShane, Mark
Sergeant Norman Pink series (2)
Night's master
Lee, Tanith
Tales from the flat earth series (1)
Nights of the Round Table
Lawrence, Margery
Club of the Round Table series (1)
Night's sorceries
Lee, Tanith
Tales from the flat earth series (5)
Nights with Uncle Remus
Harris, Joel Chandler
Uncle Remus series (2)
Nightshade
King, Tappan
Weird heroes series (4)
Nightshade ring
Hardy, Lindsay
Gregory Keen series (2)
Nightshades
Pronzini, Bill
Private Eye series (13)
Nightsong
Sherwood, Valerie
Carolina Lightfoot trilogy (3)
Nightstalker
Rizzi, Timothy
Major General Duke James series (1)
Nightwatch winter
Overton, Jenny
Creed series (2)
Nightwatchmen
Hannah, Barry
Harry Monroe series (2)
Nightwitch devil
Robeson, Kenneth
Avenger series (29)
Nightwork
Hansen, Joseph
Dave Brandstetter series (7)
Nightworld
Bischoff, David
Nightworld series (1)
Wilson, Francis Paul
Adversary series (4)
Nighty-nightmare
Howe, James
Bunnicula series (4)
Nijinsky is dead
Davis, Kenn
Carver Bascombe series (6)
Nile green
Hocking, Anne
Inspector William Austen series (11)
Jordan, David
Tom Kane and Condon series (1)
Nile shadows
Whittemore, Edward
Jerusalem quartet (3)
Nim and his food
Joanny, Andre
Nim series (3)
Nim and his money
Joanny, Andre
Nim series (2)
Nim and his world
Joanny, Andre
Nim series (1)
Nim buys and sells
Joanny, Andre
Nim series (4)
Nimbus and the crown jewels
Smith, Jim
Nimbus series (1)
Nimbus and the explorer
Smith, Jim
Nimbus series (2)
Nimby factor
Wilcox, Stephen F
Elias Hackshaw series (2)
Nine afloat
Prime, Heather
Adventurous Nine series (3)
Nine and death make ten
Dickson, Carter
Sir Henry Merrivale series (11)
Nine bears
Wallace, Edgar
Inspector Elk series (1)
Mister T B Smith series (1)
Nine bright shiners
Fraser, Anthea
Inspector David Webb and Sergeant Ken Jackson series (5)
Lamplugh, Lois
Allen family series (2)
Nine cuts
Flynn, Brian
Anthony Bathurst series (52)
Nine days' murder
Mackinnon, Allan
Inspector Duncan Maccallum series (1)
Nine Days' Queen
Birt, David
Tudors series (13)
Nine doctors and a madman
Curtiss, Elizabeth Mangam
Nathaniel Bunce series (1)
Nine giants
Marston, Edward
Elizabethan whodunits series (4)
Nine had no vet
Silverman, Marguerite Ruth
Inspector Christopher Adrian series (3)
Nine holiday adventures of Mister P J Davenant in the year 1915
Hamilton, Frederic
P J Davenant series (1)
Nine hundred and eleven
Chastain, Thomas
Inspector Max Kauffman series (2)
Nine lives
Channing, Mark
Colin Gray series (4)
Nine lives of Alphonse
Johnson, James Leonard
Code name Sebastian series (2)
Nine lives of Bill Nelson
Kersh, Gerald
Brigade of Guards series (2)
Nine lives of Catseye Gomez
Hawke, Simon
Wizard series (7)
Nine-month caper
Mark, Ted
Man from O.R.G.Y. series (2)
Nine more lives
Morgan, Michael
Bill Ryan series (1)
Nine o'clock shadow
Story, Jack Trevor
Sexton Blake series (1461)
Nine on the trail
Prime, Heather
Adventurous Nine series (2)
Nine planets
Branley, Franklyn Mansfield
Exploring our universe series (1)

Nine princes in Amber
Zelazny, Roger
Kingdom of Amber series (1)

Nine singing apes
Hawton, Hector
Asmun Hill series (5)

Nine-spoked wheel
Anderson, John Richard Lane
Major Peter Blair series (4)

Nine stories
Salinger, Jerome David
Glass family series (1)

Nine tailors
Sayers, Dorothy Leigh
Lord Peter Wimsey series (11)

Nine times never
Anderson, Verily
York family series (2)

Nine times nine
Holmes, H H
Sister Ursula series (1)

Nine unknown
Mundy, Talbot
Athelstan King series (2)
Chullunder Ghose series (1)
Indian trilogy (2)
Jimgrim series (1)

Nine waxed faces
Beeding, Francis
Colonel Alastair Granby series (10)

Nine winds
Crowley, Carl Campbell
Nine winds series (1)

Nineteen and wedding bells ahead
Richardson, Arleta
Growing up series (3)

Nineteen eighteen
Foote, Horton
Orphans' home series (3)
Tolstoi, Aleksei Nikolaevich
Ordeal trilogy (2)

Nineteen eighty five
Burgess, Anthony
Big Brother series (2)
Dalos, Gyorgy
Big Brother series (2)

Nineteen eighty four
Orwell, George
Big Brother series (1)

Nineteen forty two
Regan, Jackie
Star trek fan series (41)

Nineteen fourteen
Johnson, Eyvind
Olof tetralogy (1)
Spears, Edward
Defeat and victory series (1)

Nineteen hundred and nineteen
Dos Passos, John
U.S.A.trilogy (2)

Nineteenth century clothing
Kalman, Bobbie
Historic communities series (10)

Nineteenth hole mystery
Adams, Herbert
Major Roger Bennion series (8)

Nineteenth Precinct
Newman, Christopher
Joe Dante series (5)

Ninety feet to the sun
Collenette, Eric J
Ben Grant series (2)

Ninety million dollar mouse
Nevins, Francis Michael
Loren Mensing series (4)

Ninety minutes at Entebbe
Stevenson, William Henri
Israeli armed services series (3)

Ninety-nine
Ahern, Jerry
Dan Track series (1)

Ninety seventh step
Perry, Steve
Khadaji series (1)

Ninety trillion Fausts
Chalker, Jack Laurence
Quintara Marathon series (3)

Nini at carnival
Lloyd, Errol
Nini series (1)

Nini on time
Lloyd, Errol
Nini series (2)

Ninja
Lustbader, Eric
Ninja series (1)

Ninja blood
Wilson, Gar
Phoenix Force series (33)

Ninja garden
Singer, A L
Worlds of power series (3)

Ninja's revenge
Anthony, Piers
Jason Striker series (4)

Nintendo action games
Lampton, Christopher
Nintendo series (1)

Nintendo role-playing games
Lampton, Christopher
Nintendo series (2)

Ninth big Monster book
Blance, Ellen
Monster series (30)

Ninth directive
Hall, Adam
Quiller series (2)

Ninth earl
Farnol, Jeffery
Mister Jasper Shrig of Bow Street series (9)

Ninth enemy
Vivian, Francis
Inspector Gordon Knollis series (5)

Ninth floor, Middle City Tower
O'Neil, Kerry
Jerry Mooney series (2)

Ninth hour
Benson, Ben
Inspector Wade Paris series (7)

Ninth life
Douglas, Lauren Wright
Caitlin Reece series (2)
Mann, Jack
Gregory George Gordon Green series (6)

Ninth netsuke
Melville, James
Superintendent Tetsuo Otani series (4)

Ninth tentacle
Rippon, Marion
Inspector Maurice Ygrec series (3)

Ninth thermidor
Aldanov, Mark Aleksandrovich
Thinker series (1)

Ninth vibration, and other stories
Barrington, E
Ormond series (1)

Ninth wave
Ehrenburg, Ilya
Wave series (2)

Nipped in the bud
Palmer, Stuart
Hildegarde Withers series (14)

Nipponese nightmare
Rosenberger, Joseph
Death Merchant series (28)

Nirvana blues
Nichols, John
New Mexico trilogy (3)

Nirvana can also mean death
Kane, Henry
Peter Chambers series (14)

Nirvana contracts
Wohl, James Paul
Sam Gross series (1)

Nitehood
Nickless, Will
Rotherside series (2)

Nitty-gritty of family life
Berry, Joy
Ready-set-grow series (6)

Niven's laws
Niven, Larry
Known Space series (14)

Nixon, ruin and recovery, 1973-1990
Ambrose, Stephen Edward
Richard Nixon series (3)

Nixon, the education of a politician, 1913-1962
Ambrose, Stephen Edward
Richard Nixon series (1)

Nixon, the triumph of a politician, 1962-1972
Ambrose, Stephen Edward
Richard Nixon series (2)

No abiding city
Stannard, Martin
Evelyn Waugh series (2)

No accounting for tastes
Fisher, Aileen
Ways of animals series (10)

No alibi
Cobb, Belton
Inspector Cheviot Burmann series (1)

No badgers in my wood
Drabble, Phil
Wild animals series (5)

No bail for the judge
Cecil, Henry
Ambrose Low series (1)
Colonel Brain series (1)

No barrier
Dark, Eleanor
Mannion family series (3)

No bean sprouts, please!
Hiser, Constance
James and gang series (1)

No beast so fierce
Rushton, Charles
Inspector Cadman series (3)

No bed of roses
Baldwin, Faith
Little Oxford series (3)

No better fiend
McGirr, Edmund
Jim Piron series (7)

No better place to die
Cozzens, Peter
American Civil War battles series (1)

No birds sang
Hilton, John Buxton
Superintendent Simon Kenworthy series (4)

No blonde is an island
Brown, Carter
Larry Baker series (2)

No blood spilled
Daniels, Les
Don Sebastien series (5)

No boats on Bannermere
Trease, Geoffrey
Bannermere series (1)

No body
Pickard, Nancy
Jenny Cain series (3)

No bones about it
Wallis, Ruth Sawtell
Eric Lund series (1)

No bouquets for Brandon
Warren, Vernon
Mark Brandon series (5)

No boys allowed
Kaye, Marilyn
Camp Sunnyside Friends series (1)

No brains at all
Dunstan, Keith
Brains series (1)

No brains on Tuesday
Dunstan, Keith
Brains series (2)

No branding fire
Winstan, Matt
Reuben Brown series (10)

No brother, no friend
Meredith, Richard Carlton
Timeliner trilogy (2)

No business being a cop
O'Donnell, Lillian
Detective Norah Mulcahaney series (6)

No case for the police
Clinton-Baddeley, Victor Clinton
Doctor Davie series (4)

No castanets at the Wells
Hill, Lorna
Sadler's Wells series (4)

No cause to kill
Ramsay, Diana
Lieutenant Meredith series (3)

No chance in hell
Quarry, Nick
Jake Barrow series (4)

No charge for the poison
Cobb, Belton
Superintendent Manning series (6)

No choice for Sergeant Cluff
North, Gil
Sergeant Caleb Cluff series (10)

No clue
Hay, James
Jefferson Hastings series (2)

No clues for Caroline
Mansbridge, Pamela
Caroline series (4)

No coffin for the corpse
Rawson, Clayton
Great Merlini series (4)

No colours or crest
Kemp, Peter Mant Macintyre
Conflict trilogy (2)

No common glory
Pilgrim, David
James De la Cloche series (1)

No contest
Blake, Susan
Hawthorne College series (12)
Cooper, M E
Couples series (20)

No copyright on murder
Brody, Marc
Marc Brody series (7)

No coupons for a shroud
Morland, Nigel
Chief Inspector Andrew McMurdo series (2)

No crest for the wicked
Morgan, Geoffrey
Ricky Straight series (1)

No crime for a lady
Popkin, Zelda
Mary Carner Whittaker series (5)

No crime like the present
Gaines, Audrey
Jeff Strange series (2)

No crime so great
Bailey, Elliot
Inspector Geoffrey Fraser series (2)

No crown of glory
Goldthorpe, John
Early Christian series (2)

No cure for death
Collins, Max Allan
Mallory series (2)

No darker crime
Creasey, John
Department Z series (20)

No day for murder
Halliday, Brett
Mike Shayne stories series (2)

No deals, Mister Bond
Gardner, John Edmund
James Bond series (23)

No diamonds for a doll
Cagney, Peter
Mike Strang series (1)

No dignity in death
Richards, Francis
Inspector Merton Heimrich series (15)

No distress signals
Brown, Winifred
Duffers of the deep series (2)

No dust in the attic
Gilbert, Anthony
Arthur Crook series (38)

No duty on a corpse
Murray, Max
Corpse series (3)

No earth for foxes
O'Brine, Manning
Mills series (2)

No earthly shore
Mezo, Francine
Areia Darenga trilogy (3)

No effect
Hayes, Daniel
Tyler McAllister series (3)

No end of a rogue
Clement, Frank A
Superintendent Mersey series (2)

No end to fear
Hossent, Harry
Max Heald series (2)

No entry
Coles, Manning
Tommy Hambledon series (22)
Edwards, Monica
Romney Marsh series (8)

No epitaph for Mister Zarke
Smith, C I D
Inspector Barlowe series (2)

No escape
Kemp, Sarah
Doctor Tina May series (1)

No escape trail
Grover, Marshall
Nevada Jim series (8)

No evil angel
Linington, Elizabeth
Sergeant Ivor Maddox series (2)

No exit
Heath-Miller, Mavis
Raines of Rayleigh series (2)
Redmond, Anton Edward
Bill Slaker series (2)

No exit from Vietnam
Thompson, Robert
Vietnam War series (1)

No face in the mirror
McLeave, Hugh
Doctor Gregor Maclean series (4)
Doctor Stephen Armitage series (1)

No finger on the trigger
Edson, John Thomas
Waxahachie Smith series (1)

No flowers, by request
Thomson, June
Inspector Finch series (13)

No flowers for the general
Copper, Basil
Mike Faraday series (3)

No flowers in Braslov
Usher, Frank
Amanda Curzon and Oscar Sallis series (2)

No footprints in the bush
Upfield, Arthur William
Napoleon Bonaparte series (8)

No friendly drop
Wade, Henry
Inspector Poole series (2)
Major Faide series (1)

No friends
Stevenson, James
Grandfather's problems series (5)
Grandpa series (6)

no friends for Hannah
Stahl, Hilda
Best friends series (8)

No fury
Beeding, Francis
Inspector George Martin series (2)

No future
Lyons, Steve
Timewyrm series (7)

No future for dragons
Gentile, Gary
Dragons series (3)

No future for Luana
Derleth, August
Judge Ephraim Peck series (9)

No go on Jackson Street
Weiss, Mike
Ben Henry series (1)

No going back
Edwards, Monica
Romney Marsh series (13)

No gold when you go
Chambers, Peter
Mark Preston series (11)

No good deed
Nathan, Paul
Bert Swain series (2)

No grave for a lady
Bonett, John
Professor Mandrake series (3)

No grave for March
Chaber, M E
Milo March series (2)

No greater love
Gallagher, Patricia
Castles series (2)

No gun is neutral
McCoy, Marshall
Nevada Jim series (39)

No halo for me
Manor, Jason
Steve Summers series (3)

No halo for Mimosa
Mackenzie, Joan
Mimosa Winter series (3)

No haloes in hell
Wright, Wade
Paul Cameron series (3)

No hands on the clock
Homes, Geoffrey
Humphrey Campbell series (2)

No haven for the guilty
Green, Simon
Hawk and Fisher series (1)

No head for her pillow
Taylor, Sam S
Neal Cotton series (2)

No hero
Marquand, John Phillips
Mister Moto series (1)

No hiding place
Lanham, Edwin
Frank Luther series (2)

No-hitter
Bee, Clair
Chip Hilton series (17)

No holiday for crime
Shannon, Dell
Lieutenant Luis Mendoza series (23)

No holiday for death
Thayer, Lee
Peter Clancy series (53)

No holly for Miss Quinn
Read, *Miss*
Fairacre series (11)

No home but the struggle
Upward, Edward
Alan Sebrill trilogy (3)

No honour among spies
Rothwell, Henry Talbot
Michael Brooks series (4)

No judges' rules
Macdonald, Donald
Tommy Briggs series (2)

No kisses from the Kremlin
Rothwell, Henry Talbot
Michael Brooks series (5)

No ladder for Tom Bates
Huddy, Delia
Hipster series (4)
No lady buys a cot
Bloom, Ursula
No lady series (2)
No lady has a dog's day
Bloom, Ursula
No lady series (8)
No lady in bed
Bloom, Ursula
No lady series (3)
No lady in the cart
Bloom, Ursula
No lady series (6)
No lady in the house
Kallen, Lucille
C.B.Greenfield series (3)
No lady meets no gentleman
Bloom, Ursula
No lady series (5)
No lady with a pen
Bloom, Ursula
No lady series (4)
No last words
Cobb, Belton
Superintendent Manning series (4)
No laughing matter
Keene, Carolyn
Nancy Drew files series (79)
Simpson, Dorothy
Inspector Luke Thanet series (12)
No law against angels
Brown, Carter
Lieutenant Al Wheeler series (7)
No lesser plea
Tanenbaum, Robert K
Assistant District Attorney Butch Karp series (1)
No letters from the grave
Copper, Basil
Mike Faraday series (9)
No life for a loser
Foxall, Peter Augustus
Detective Sergeant Scamp series (5)
No light came on
Campbell, Alice
Geoffrey Macadam and Catherine West series (2)
No light to die by
Robeson, Kenneth
Doc Savage series (143)
No lilies
Holt, Henry
Mike Logan series (1)
No little enemy
Bayer, Oliver Weld
Paper chase series (2)
No longer at ease
Achebe, Chinua
African trilogy (2)
No love for Miss Stent
Charles, Wyndham
Chief Superintendent Sebastian Griffin series (2)
No love for Paradise
Canon, Jack
Mike Paradise series (2)
No love in a bullet
Kennedy, Elliot
Griff Dexter series (6)
No love lost
Reeves, Robert
Cellini Smith series (2)
No man rides alone
Waldo, Dale
Johnny Ross series (2)
No man's fund
Bonney, Joseph L
Simon Rolfe series (2)
No man's island
Mann, Jessica
Tamara Hoyland series (2)
No man's land
Sapper
John Walters series (2)
No man's laughter
Laing, Kenneth
Rolling Stone series (2)
No man's street
Nichols, Beverley
Mister Horatio Green series (1)
No match for the law
Mills, Osmington
Superintendent William Baker series (3)
No mean tartar
Hay, Lindsay Fitzgerald
Archibald Beldrum and Nigel Blair series (3)
No medals for Guy
Hill, Lorna
Marjorie series (5)
No mercy
Dixon, Franklin W
Hardy boys case files series (65)
No mercy for Margaret
Cobb, Belton
Inspector Cheviot Burmann series (12)
No middle way
Marston, Jeffery
Octave trilogy (3)
No mistaking Corker
Edwards, Monica
Punchbowl Farm series (1)
No more a-roving
Troy, Simon
Inspector Smith series (9)
No more broken promises
Hunt, Angela Elwell
Cassie Perkins series (1)
No more chances
Spade, Danny
Danny Spade series (19)
No more dying then
Rendell, Ruth
Chief Inspector Reginald Wexford series (6)
No more horses
Stranger, Joyce
Timothy Yorke series (4)
No more into the garden
Watmough, David
Davey Bryant series (3)
No more murders
Lang, Maria
Christer Wick series (1)
No more parades
Ford, Ford Madox
Parade's end series (2)
No more romance
Warde, Joan
Forrester family series (1)
No more soldiering for me
Mays, Spike
Soldering series (3)
No more than human
Laverty, Maura
Delia Scully series (2)
No mourners present
Presnell, Frank G
John and Anne Webb series (2)
No mourning for the matador
Ames, Delano
Dagobert and Jane Brown series (7)
No mourning in the family
Philmore, R
Swan series (4)
No murder
Bailey, Henry Christopher
Mister Reggie Fortune series (17)
No murder of mine
Campbell, Alice
Inspector Headcorn series (3)
No mystery to the Maitlands
Ballantyne, Jean
Maitland series (3)
No name gang
Grover, Marshall
Larry and Stretch series (396)
No need for violence
Burrows, Julie
Superintendent Bowman and Sergeant Peart series (1)
No need of the sun
Macleod, Alison
Tom Vaughan series (2)
No news on Monday
Clapperton, Richard
Peter Fleck series (1)
No, no, Nicky!
Ziefert, Harriet
Nicky series (6)
No nudes is good news
Wodehouse, Pelham Grenville
Blandings Castle series (13)
No obelisk for Emily
Courtier, Sidney Hobson
Inspector Digger Haig series (6)
No one hears but him
Caldwell, Taylor
Listener series (2)
No one must ever know
Martin, Betty
Miracle series (2)
No one rides for free
Beinhart, Larry
Tony Cassella series (1)
No one writes to the colonel
Garcia Marquez, Gabriel
Macondo series (2)
No-option contract
Ball, Brian Neville
Keegan series (1)
No orchids for Miss Blandish
Chase, James Hadley
Carol Blandish series (1)
No other victim
Franklin, Charles
Grant Garfield series (10)
No outspan
Reitz, Deneys
Boer War journal trilogy (3)
No paradise
King, Robin
Merchant Navy trilogy (1)
No part in your death
Freeling, Nicolas
Henri Castang series (8)
No past is dead
Connington, John Jervis
Sir Clinton Driffield series (15)
No peace for Archer
Clevely, Hugh
Maxwell Archer series (4)
No peace for the wicked
Chambers, Peter
Mark Preston series (15)
No peace on earth
Larteguy, Jean
Central America series (1)
No place for murder
Coxe, George Harmon
Jack Fenner series (7)
No place for strangers
Baker, William Howard
Richard Quintain series (4)
No place like home
Korman, Justine
Crispy Critter series (1)
Reeve, Dominic
Gypsy life series (2)
No place to be a cop
Nolan, Frederick
Lieutenant Joe Petrosino series (1)
No place to cry
Kennedy, Adam
Bradshaw trilogy (1)
No place to hide
Pascal, Francine
Sweet Valley High super thriller series (3)
No place to live
Ronns, Edward
Jerry Benedict series (1)
No pockets in shrouds
Revell, Louisa
Julia Tyler series (2)
No pony like Pepper
Packer, Jo
Pepper series (1)
No presents for Sam
Lambert, Thelma
Sam series (3)
No prize for Sam
Lambert, Thelma
Sam series (2)
No profit in dying
Beeby, Otto
Tony Spencer series (3)
No proud chivalry
Procter, Maurice
Chief Inspector Harry Martineau series (1)
No quarter
Leyland, Eric
Red Lawson series (2)
No quarter given
Rossi, Bruno
Sharpshooter series (8)
No questions asked
Bleeck, Oliver
Philip Saint Ives series (5)
No rain in these clouds
Smith, David
Sky all over series (1)
No rainbow in the sky
Thwaites, Frederick Joseph
Doctor Joszef Venesz series (1)
No reason for murder
Radford, Edwin
Doctor Manson series (23)
No red herrings
Scott, Mary
Inspector Wright series (3)
No regrets
Carnarvon, Henry
No regrets series (1)
No regrets for Clara
Janson, Hank
Hank Janson series (8)
No relations
Malot, Hector
Remi and Perrine series (1)
No rest for Biggles
Johns, William Earl
Biggles series (51)
No rest for Botts
Upson, William Hazlett
Alexander Botts series (7)
No roads go by
White, Myrtle Rose
White family series (1)
No room for Joanna
Ford, Elizabeth
Maplechester series (7)
No room for man
Dickson, Gordon Rupert
Dorsai series (1)
No room in the well
Beeler, Cecil Freeman
Well series (2)
No roses for Harry
Zion, Gene
Harry the dirty dog series (2)
No rules, no referee
Wilson, Gar
Phoenix Force series (16)
No sad songs
Scott, Mary
Freddie series (2)
No safe place
Hild, Jack
SOBS series (21)
No safe trail
Grover, Marshall
Bleak Creek series (5)
No sanctuary
Hild, Jack
SOBS series (13)
No school today!
Brandenberg, Franz
Edward and Elizabeth series (2)
No second wind
Guthrie, Alfred Bertram
Sheriff Chick Charleston and Jason Beard series (3)
No secrets
Gilden, Mel
Beverly Hills 90210 series (2)
No sentiment in murder
Cumberland, Marten
Saturnin Dax series (34)
No shame for the devil
Cobb, Belton
Bryan Armitage series (6)
Inspector Cheviot Burmann series (30)
Kitty Armitage series (3)
No sign of life
Delving, Michael
Dave Cannon and Robert Eddison series (6)
Ormerod, Roger
Richard Patton series (8)
No sign of murder
Reed, Wallace
Sheriff Bill Lloyd series (3)
No, Sir Jeremy
Weymouth, Anthony
Inspector Treadgold series (3)
No sleep at all
Warren, James
James Weston series (1)
No sleep for Elsa
Jacobs, Thomas Curtis Hicks
Temple Fortune series (6)
No sleep for Hob Lane
Leeson, Robert
Hob Lane series (2)
No sleep for Macall
Fairlie, Gerard
Johnny Macall series (2)
No smoke, no flame
Downes, Quentin
Detective Inspector Abraham Kozminski series (1)
No snow in Latching
Home, Michael
Breckland series (7)
No soul above money
Raymond, Walter
Mendip Hills series (2)
No space for murder
Brent, Nigel
Barney Hyde series (9)
No star for the deputy
Nickson, Arthur
Rusty Hines series (1)
No star is lost
Farrell, James Thomas
Danny O'Neill series (3)
No starch in my coat
Delaney, Joyce
No starch in my coat series (1)
No stone
Blake, Ken
Professionals series (9)
No surrender
Ammers-Kuller, Jo van
Leyden trilogy (2)
Harbinson, Robert
Ulster series (1)
No survivors
Ahern, Jerry
Defender series (12)
Gray, Edwyn
U-boat series (1)
Hutson, Shaun
Sergeant Rolf Kessler series (6)
No swimming for Sam
Lambert, Thelma
Sam series (1)
No target for Bowman
Howard, Hartley
Glenn Bowman series (9)
No tears for Morgan Kane
Masterson, Louis
Morgan Kane series (14)
No tears for the dead
Audemars, Pierre
Monsieur Pinaud series (17)
No tears from the widow
Brown, Carter
Rick Holman series (16)
No tears in Aldgate
Finn, Ralph Leslie
Aldgate series (1)
No tears shed
Caldwell, Alfred Betts
Freddy Philpotts series (3)
No thanks for the shroud
Carstairs, John Paddy
Garaway Trenton series (7)
No time for crime
Russell, Charlotte Murray
Jane Amanda Edwards series (8)
No time for murder
Grant, Maxwell
Shadow series (257)
No time for sleeping
Lambert, Derek
Living and sleeping series (2)
No time to kill
Bonett, John
Inspector Borges series (5)
No time to live
Baker, William Howard
Sexton Blake series (1444)
No tomorrow for Tobin
Grover, Marshall
Nevada Jim series (63)
No traveler returns
Dean, Amber
Albie Harris series (5)
No trial, no error
Robertson, Colin
Edward North series (4)
No trouble at all
Thomson, Pat
Share-a-story series (8)
No trouble for Susan
Shaw, Jane
Susan series (8)
No turning back
Baer, Judy
Cedar River daydreams series (13)
No vacation for Maigret
Simenon, Georges
Inspector Jules Maigret series (30)
No vacation from murder
Lemarchand, Elizabeth
Superintendent Tom Pollard series (6)
No villain need be
Fisher, Vardis
Tragic life series (4)
Linington, Elizabeth
Sergeant Ivor Maddox series (9)
No, Virginia!
Griffith, Helen Sherman
Virginia series (2)
No way back
Carroll, John Richard
Dennis Gatz series (1)
No way home
Coburn, Andrew
James Morgan series (1)
No way out
Dixon, Franklin W
Hardy boys case files series (75)
McNeilly, Wilfred
Dangerman series (5)
No weeds for the widow
Raison, Milton Michael
Tony Woolrich series (4)

No white coat
Tibber, Robert
General practitioner series (1)
No wind of blame
Heyer, Georgette
Inspector Hemingway series (5)
No winding-sheet
Mitchell, Gladys
Dame Beatrice Bradley series (65)
No wings on a cop
Adams, Cleve Franklin
John J Shannon series (2)
No wooden overcoat
Carstairs, John Paddy
Garaway Trenton series (2)
No word from Winifred
Cross, Amanda
Professor Kate Fansler series (8)
No wreath for Manuela
Mackinnon, Allan
Donald Kendrick series (2)
No wreaths for the duchess
Grierson, Francis Durham
Inspector George Muir series (10)
Superintendent Andrew Ash series (3)
Noah
Daniel, Rebecca
Our greatest heritage series (2)
Noah builds his ark
Blyton, Enid
Bible stories series (2)
Noah Pandre
Schneour, Salman
Noah Pandre series (1)
Noah Pandre's village
Schneour, Salman
Noah Pandre series (2)
Noah's ark
Brook, Judy
Noah series (1)
Noah's Ark murders
Douglas, Arthur
Mark Register series (2)
Noah's Ark river
Wood, Andrew
Bunch and Alexander series (2)
Noahs on holiday, with Japhet
Horrabin, James Francis
Noah family series (2)
Nobby
Wallace, Edgar
Smithy series (3)
Noble beginnings
Fraser, Christine Marion
Blue above the chimneys series (4)
Noble essences
Sitwell, Osbert
Left hand, right hand series (5)
Noble house
Clavell, James
Asian series (4)
Struan family series (2)
Noble in reason
Bentley, Phyllis
West Riding series (13)
Noble pirate
Foxall, Raymond
John Crispin series (3)
Noble purpose
Carnegie, Sacha
Major Gair Mainwaring series (1)
Noble savage
Jones, Gareth
Misrule series (2)
Noblest experiment in the galaxy
Trimble, Louis
Anthropol Detective Agency series (2)
Noblest family
Veryan, Patricia
Age of Elegance series (6)
Sanguinet series (4)
Nobody cared for Kate
Thompson, Gene
Dade Cooley series (2)
Nobody is safe
Cumberland, Marten
Saturnin Dax series (18)
Nobody knows
Goldring, Douglas
Love among the artists trilogy (1)
Nobody knows how scared I am
Sharmat, Marjorie Weinman
Sorority sisters series (5)
Nobody knows my name
Baldwin, James Arthur
Native son series (2)
Nobody likes Taffy Sinclair
Haynes, Betsy
Taffy Sinclair series (11)
Nobody lives forever
Chambers, Peter
Mark Preston series (8)
Gardner, John Edmund
James Bond series (22)
Nobody loves a dead man
Raison, Milton Michael
Tony Woolrich series (2)
Nobody loves a loser
Kane, Henry
Peter Chambers series (21)
Nobody needs a corpse
Cronin, Michael
Sam Harris series (5)
Nobody nowhere
Williams, Donna
Nobody somebody series (1)
Nobody shouted author
Delderfield, Ronald Frederick
Amusement trilogy (1)
Nobody wants Riley
Grover, Marshall
Larry and Stretch series (56)
Nobody wore black
Ames, Delano
Dagobert and Jane Brown series (3)
Nobody's boy
Malot, Hector
Remi and Perrine series (1)
Nobody's business
Keene, Carolyn
Nancy Drew files series (67)
Nobody's girl
Malot, Hector
Remi and Perrine series (2)
Nobody's horse
Webster, Joanne
Nobody's horse trilogy (1)
Nobody's perfect
Clark, Douglas
Inspector George Masters series (1)
Levy, Elizabeth
Gymnasts series (3)
Reinsmith, Richard
Bodyguard series (10)
Westlake, Donald Edwin
Dortmunder Gang series (4)
Nobody's pony
Bye, Beryl
Cathy, Belinda and Jane series (1)
Nobody's sorry he got killed
Goldstein, Arthur David
Max Guttman series (3)
Nobody's vineyard
Bailey, Henry Christopher
Mister Joshua Clunk series (8)
Nocturne
Cooper, Louise Antell
Indigo series (4)
Nocturne for the General
Trenhaile, John
General Povin series (3)
Nocturne murder
Peterson, Audrey
Jane Winfield and Andrew Quentin series (1)
Nodding canaries
Mitchell, Gladys
Dame Beatrice Bradley series (34)
Noddy and Big Ears
Blyton, Enid
Noddy picture books series (1)
Noddy and Big Ears have a picnic
Blyton, Enid
Noddy stories series (1)
Noddy and his car
Blyton, Enid
Noddy series (3)
Noddy and his friends
Blyton, Enid
Noddy picture books series (7)
Noddy pop-up books series (2)
Noddy and his passengers
Blyton, Enid
Noddy stories series (16)
Noddy and Tessie Bear
Blyton, Enid
Noddy series (12)
Noddy and the aeroplane
Blyton, Enid
Noddy series (24)
Noddy and the bear who lost his growl
Blyton, Enid
Noddy tiny strip books series (5)
Noddy and the bumpy dog
Blyton, Enid
Noddy series (14)
Noddy and the bunkey
Blyton, Enid
Noddy series (19)
Noddy and the cuckoo's nest
Blyton, Enid
Noddy stories series (10)
Noddy and the magic rubber
Blyton, Enid
Noddy series (9)
Noddy and the Noah's Ark adventure picture book
Blyton, Enid
Noddy picture books series (8)
Noddy and the runaway wheel
Blyton, Enid
Noddy tiny strip books series (8)
Noddy and the snow house
Blyton, Enid
Noddy tiny strip books series (3)
Noddy and the Tootles
Blyton, Enid
Noddy series (23)
Noddy and the tricky teddy
Blyton, Enid
Noddy tiny strip books series (6)
Noddy and the witch's wand
Blyton, Enid
Noddy stories series (7)
Noddy at the seaside
Blyton, Enid
Noddy series (7)
Noddy be careful
Blyton, Enid
Noddy stories series (14)
Noddy colour strip book
Blyton, Enid
Noddy tiny strip books series (10)
Noddy cut-out model book
Blyton, Enid
Noddy series (24)
Noddy gets captured
Blyton, Enid
Noddy stories series (11)
Noddy gets into trouble
Blyton, Enid
Noddy series (8)
Noddy giant painting book
Blyton, Enid
Noddy series (24)
Noddy goes dancing
Blyton, Enid
Noddy tiny strip books series (1)
Noddy goes to school
Blyton, Enid
Noddy series (6)
Noddy goes to sea
Blyton, Enid
Noddy picture books series (12)
Noddy series (18)
Noddy goes to the fair
Blyton, Enid
Noddy pop-up books series (1)
Noddy series (21)
Noddy goes to the seaside
Blyton, Enid
Noddy stories series (4)
Noddy goes to Toyland
Blyton, Enid
Noddy series (1)
Noddy has a shock
Blyton, Enid
Noddy stories series (2)
Noddy has an adventure
Blyton, Enid
Noddy series (17)
Noddy has more adventures
Blyton, Enid
Noddy stories series (3)
Noddy in Toyland
Blyton, Enid
Noddy series (24)
Noddy stories series (16)
Noddy in Toyland picture book
Blyton, Enid
Noddy picture books series (9)
Noddy is very silly
Blyton, Enid
Noddy stories series (12)
Noddy meets Father Christmas
Blyton, Enid
Noddy series (11)
Noddy nursery rhymes
Blyton, Enid
Noddy series (24)
Noddy off to Rocking Horse Land
Blyton, Enid
Noddy stories series (5)
Noddy painting books
Blyton, Enid
Noddy series (24)
Noddy play day painting book
Blyton, Enid
Noddy series (24)
Noddy song book
Blyton, Enid
Noddy series (24)
Noddy tall blue book
Blyton, Enid
Noddy tall colour series (1)
Noddy tall green book
Blyton, Enid
Noddy tall colour series (2)
Noddy tall orange book
Blyton, Enid
Noddy tall colour series (3)
Noddy tall pink book
Blyton, Enid
Noddy tall colour series (4)
Noddy tall red book
Blyton, Enid
Noddy tall colour series (5)
Noddy tall yellow book
Blyton, Enid
Noddy tall colour series (6)
Noddy the cry-baby
Blyton, Enid
Noddy tiny strip books series (2)
Noddy Toyland ABC picture book
Blyton, Enid
Noddy picture books series (10)
Noddy tricks Mr Sly
Blyton, Enid
Noddy tiny strip books series (7)
Noddy's aeroplane picture book
Blyton, Enid
Noddy picture books series (11)
Noddy's bag of money
Blyton, Enid
Noddy tiny strip books series (9)
Noddy's car gets a squeak
Blyton, Enid
Noddy stories series (8)
Noddy's car gets into trouble
Blyton, Enid
Noddy tiny strip books series (10)
Noddy's car picture book
Blyton, Enid
Noddy picture books series (4)
Noddy's chimney pot
Blyton, Enid
Noddy pop-up books series (3)
Noddy's grand adventure
Blyton, Enid
Noddy stories series (15)
Noddy's one, two, three book
Blyton, Enid
Noddy picture books series (12)
Noddy's own nursery rhymes
Blyton, Enid
Noddy picture books series (12)
Noddy series (24)
Noddy's penny wheel car
Blyton, Enid
Noddy stories series (9)
Noddy's Toyland ABC
Blyton, Enid
Noddy picture books series (10)
Noddy's Toyland train picture book
Blyton, Enid
Noddy picture books series (5)
Noel and the donkeys
Boden, Hilda
Noel series (1)
Noel for Jeanne-Marie
Francoise
Jeanne-Marie series (6)
Noel the brave
Boden, Hilda
Noel series (4)
Noel the explorer
Boden, Hilda
Noel series (5)
Noel's Christmas holiday
Boden, Hilda
Noel series (3)
Noel's happy day
Boden, Hilda
Noel series (2)
Nogbad and the elephant
Postgate, Oliver
Noggin series (6)
Nogbad comes back
Postgate, Oliver
Noggin series (4)
Noggin and the dragon
Postgate, Oliver
Noggin series (3)
Noggin and the flowers
Postgate, Oliver
Saga of Noggin the Nog series (7)
Noggin and the island
Postgate, Oliver
Saga of Noggin the Nog series (5)
Noggin and the money
Postgate, Oliver
Noggin series (7)
Noggin and the moon mouse
Postgate, Oliver
Noggin series (5)
Noggin and the storks
Postgate, Oliver
Noggin series (8)
Noggin and the whale
Postgate, Oliver
Noggin series (1)
Noggin the king
Postgate, Oliver
Noggin series (2)
Nogmania
Postgate, Oliver
Saga of Noggin the Nog series (13)
Noisy
Hughes, Shirley
Nursery series (2)
Noisy bird book
Brown, Margaret Wise
Noisy book series (5)
Noisy book
Brown, Margaret Wise
Noisy book series (1)
Noisy garbage-truck problem
Plain, Neil
Boris Blundle and Gang series (4)
Noisy homes
Kilroy, Sally
Baby series (3)
Nomad of time
Moorcock, Michael
Oswald Bastable series (3)
Nomads
Freund, Philip
Volcano god trilogy (1)
Nomads from Texas
Grover, Marshall
Larry and Stretch series (35)
Nomads of Gor
Norman, John
Tarl Cabot series (4)
Nomads of the night
Leroux, Gaston
Cheri-Bibi series (4)
Nonborn king
May, Julian
Pliocene exile series (4)
None but the lethal heart
Brown, Carter
Mavis Seidlitz series (5)
None dare call it treason
Gavin, Catherine
French Resistance series (2)
None of Maigret's business
Simenon, Georges
Inspector Jules Maigret series (52)
None of my business
Sharp, David
Professor Henry Arthur Fielding series (3)
None of us cared for Kate
Haythorne, John
Oliver Mandrake series (1)
None shall sleep tonight
McCutcheon, Hugh
Inspector McKeller series (2)
None turn back
Jameson, Storm
Hervey Russell series (5)
Mirror in darkness trilogy (3)
Nonsense novels
Leacock, Stephen
Nonsense novels series (1)
Nonsense, said the tortoise
Baker, Margaret Joyce
Homer series (1)
Noon stage to Denver
Grover, Marshall
Larry and Stretch series (69)
Noon train to Breslow
Grover, Marshall
Larry and Stretch series (76)
Noonday and night
Mitchell, Gladys
Dame Beatrice Bradley series (52)
Noonday devils
Martyn, Wyndham
Christopher Bond series (5)
Noonday thread
Morrow, Charlotte
Lisa Knighton series (2)
Noose
Macdonald, Philip
Colonel Anthony Ruthven Gethryn series (4)
Noose-cheaters
Grover, Marshall
Larry and Stretch series (111)
Noose for a lady
Carmichael, Harry
John Piper and Quinn series (8)
Verner, Gerald
Simon Gale series (1)

Noose for her
Crispin, Edmund
Gervase Fen series (8)
Noose for Slattery
Lawrence, Steven C
Tom Slattery series (4)
Noose for Slocum
Logan, Jake
John Slocum series (141)
Noose for the Desperado
Adams, Clifton
Desperado series (2)
Noose is drawn
Barber, Willetta Ann
Christopher Storm series (5)
Noose of emeralds
Winter, Bevis
Steve Craig series (6)
Noose of light
Cullen, Seamus
Noose series (1)
Nop's hope
McCaig, Donald
Nop series (1)
Nop series (2)
Nor crystal tears
Foster, Alan Dean
Thranx series (1)
Nor live so long
Woods, Sara
Sir Nicholas Harding and Antony Maitland series (47)
Nora
Gordon, Jeffie Ross
Sunfire series (26)
Nora and Mrs Mind-Your-Own-Business
Hurwitz, Johanna
Nora and Teddy series (2)
Norah and the whale
Swindells, Robert
Norah series (4)
Norah at Billabong
Bruce, Mary Grant
Billabong series (3)
Norah the snorer
Palfrey, Heather Mary
Norah the snorer series (2)
Norah to the rescue
Swindells, Robert
Norah series (3)
Norah's ark
Swindells, Robert
Norah series (1)
Norah's shark
Swindells, Robert
Norah series (2)
Nora's castle
Ichikawa, Satomi
Nora series (1)
Nora's duck
Ichikawa, Satomi
Nora series (3)
Nora's friends
Leith, Mary Charlotte Julia
Nora's friends series (1)
Nora's return
Cheney, Ednah Dow
Nora Helmer series (2)
Nora's roses
Ichikawa, Satomi
Nora series (4)
Nora's stars
Ichikawa, Satomi
Nora series (2)
Nora's surprise
Ichikawa, Satomi
Nora series (5)
Norby and the court jester
Asimov, Isaac
Norby series (10)
Norby and the invaders
Asimov, Isaac
Norby series (4)
Norby and the lost princess
Asimov, Isaac
Norby series (3)
Norby and the oldest dragon
Asimov, Isaac
Norby series (9)
Norby and the queen's necklace
Asimov, Isaac
Norby series (5)
Norby and Yobo's great adventure
Asimov, Isaac
Norby series (8)
Norby chronicles
Asimov, Isaac
Norby series (2)
Norby down to earth
Asimov, Isaac
Norby series (7)
Norby finds a villain
Asimov, Isaac
Norby series (6)
Norby, robot for hire
Asimov, Isaac
Norby series (4)
Norby, the mixed-up robot
Asimov, Isaac
Norby series (1)
Norby through space and time
Asimov, Isaac
Norby series (6)
Norby's other secret
Asimov, Isaac
Norby series (2)
Noreen and the Barclay affair
Dawson, Helen
Noreen and Aunt Joan series (3)
Noreen and the Henry affair
Dawson, Helen
Noreen and Aunt Joan series (5)
Noreen and the missing schoolgirl
Dawson, Helen
Noreen and Aunt Joan series (4)
Noreen and the mystery hero
Dawson, Helen
Noreen and Aunt Joan series (6)
Noreen's first case
Dawson, Helen
Noreen and Aunt Joan series (1)
Norfolk life
Haggard, Lilias Rider
Norfolk life series (1)
Norfolk nightmare
Thurlow, David
East country crimes series (2)
Norfolk notebook
Haggard, Lilias Rider
Norfolk life series (2)
Norgil the magician
Gibson, Walter Brown
Norgil series (1)
Norma, a flower scout
Roy, Lillian Elizabeth
Girl Scouts trilogy (2)
Norman
Ingraham, Joseph Holt
Freemantle series (2)
Norman and Henry Bones
Wilson, Anthony Clifford
Norman and Henry Bones series (2)
Norman and Henry Bones investigate
Wilson, Anthony Clifford
Norman and Henry Bones series (3)
Norman and Henry follow the trail
Wilson, Anthony Clifford
Norman and Henry Bones series (6)
Norman and Henry solve the problem
Wilson, Anthony Clifford
Norman and Henry Bones series (5)
Norman Bones, detective
Wilson, Anthony Clifford
Norman and Henry Bones series (1)
Norman Conquest
Birt, David
Middle Ages series (1)
Norman pretender
Anand, Valerie
Norman trilogy (2)
Normandy code
Carter, Nick
Nick Carter series (202)
Norroy, diplomatic agent
Bronson-Howard, George
Yorke Norroy series (1)
Norse code
Browne, Dik
Hagar the horrible series (33)
Norstrilia
Smith, Cordwainer
Instrumentality series (5)
North against the sioux
Ulyatt, Kenneth
Portugee Philips trilogy (1)
North and South
Jakes, John
North and South trilogy (1)
North beat
Wood, James
Jumbo Collins series (1)
North chase
McCarthy, Gary
Derby Man series (7)
North Country maid
Craddock, Mary
Rainton series (1)
North for danger
Robertson, Colin
Edward North series (2)
North Gladiola
Wilcox, James
Tula Springs trilogy (2)
North kill
Wood, James
Jumbo Collins series (2)
North of Esperanza
Wisler, Gary Clifton
Willie Delamer series (12)
North of fifty five degrees
Murray, Andrew
Sexton Blake series (302)
North of Texas
Grover, Marshall
Larry and Stretch series (18)
North of the border
Bridges, Ben
Carter O'Brien series (7)
Roberts, J R
Gunsmith series (25)
Van Gieson, Judith
Neil Hamel series (1)
North of Welfare
Krasner, William
Sam Birge series (3)
North Platte
Mitchum, Hank
Stage coach station series (46)
North Pole mystery
Christian, Mary Blount
Sherlock Street detectives series (2)
North Star
Gibbs, George
Old Philadelphia series (4)
Lederer, Paul Joseph
Indian heritage series (6)
Sutton, Graham
Fleming family series (5)
North star is nearer
Eaton, Evelyn
North star series (2)
North to Cheyenne
Cameron, Lou
Doc Travis trilogy (2)
North to Dakota
Logan, Jake
John Slocum series (8)
North to Montana
Lawrence, Steven C
Tom Slattery series (7)
North to Powder River
Floren, Lee
Buckshot McKee and Tortilla Joe series (10)
North to the rails
L'Amour, Louis
Chantry family series (1)
North town
Graham, Lorenz
Town series (2)
North Wales for the countrygoer
Lofthouse, Jessica
Countrygoer series (4)
North wind of love
Mackenzie, Compton
Four winds of love series (4)
North woods manhunt
Hutchens, Paul
Sugar Creek Gang series (15)
North Woods mystery
Grant, Maxwell
Shadow series (96)
Northanger Abbey
Austen, Jane
Northanger Abbey series (1)
Northbridge Rectory
Thirkell, Angela
Barsetshire series (10)
Northern correspondent
Stubbs, Jean
Brief chronicles series (4)
Northern Cross
Allen, Willis Boyd
Pine cone series (3)
Northern girl
Lynn, Elizabeth Anne
Chronicles of Tornor trilogy (3)
Northern lands
Optic, Oliver
Young America, second series (2)
Northern lights
O'Brien, Tim
Vietnam War series (2)
Northern mission
Wood, James
Ian Ross series (1)
James Fraser series (1)
Northern Territory recollections
Priest, Charles Ashley Vincent
Northern Territory recollections series (2)
Northland marauders
Hardin, J D
Raider and Doc series (60)
Northlight
Hall, Adam
Quiller series (12)
Northrepp grandchildren
Anderson, Verily
Anderson family series (6)
Norths meet murder
Lockridge, Frances
Bill Wiegand series (1)
Mister and Mrs North series (2)
Northshore
Tepper, Sheri S
Awakeners series (1)
Northstar rising
Axler, James
Deathlands series (10)
Northwards with Nomad
Ellison, Norman
Nomad series (6)
Northwest by north
Macdonnell, James Edmond
Dutchy Holland series (28)
Northwest contract
Derrick, Lionel
Penetrator series (8)
Northwest murders
Taylor, Elizabeth Atwood
Maggie Elliott series (3)
Northwest Passage
Thompson, David
Nathaniel King series (11)
Northwest railroad
Hardin, J D
Raider series (12)
Northworld
Drake, David
Northworld series (1)
Norwegian holiday
Hogg, Garry
Jonty series (4)
Norwegian journey
Hogg, Garry
Jonty series (3)
Norwegian twins
Perkins, Lucy Fitch
Twin series (22)
Norwegian typhoon
Carter, Nick
Nick Carter series (164)
Norwich victims
Beeding, Francis
Inspector George Martin series (1)
Nose for it
Stein, Aaron Marc
Matt Erridge series (19)
Nose for trouble
Singer, Marilyn
Samantha Spayed series (2)
Nose knows
Hildick, Edmund Wallace
McGurk series (1)
Nose on my face
Payne, Laurence
Chief Inspector Sam Birkett series (1)
Noses
Bailey, Jill
Animals of course series (1)
Nosey birds
Cosgrove, Stephen Edward
Simple folk series (4)
Nosey Gilbert
Pizer, Abigail
Henrietta and Nosey series (2)
Nostradamus traitor
Gardner, John Edmund
Herbie Kruger series (1)
Not a bad show
Beeding, Francis
Colonel Alastair Granby series (14)
Not a blessed thing!
Quill, Monica
Sister Mary Teresa series (1)
Not a leg to stand on
Burton, Miles
Inspector Arnold and Desmond Merrion series (31)
Not a word for Himself
Bird, Kenneth
Himself series (6)
Not all vanity
Stoeckl, Agnes de
Vanity trilogy (1)
Not another day like this
Wilhelm, Hans
Merritales series (4)
Not anything for peace, and other stories
Arthur, Timothy Shay
Home stories series (5)
Not as far as Velma
Freeling, Nicolas
Henri Castang series (12)
Not at home
Duche, Jean
Juliette series (2)
Not by the sword
Candaleria, Nash
Mexican war series (1)
Not dead, only resting
Brett, Simon
Charles Paris series (10)
Not-do-great place
Graeber, Charlotte Towner
Mister T and me series (5)
Not enough horses
Roberts, Les
Saxon series (2)
Not entirely serious
Girtin, Tom
Landlord series (2)
Not exactly a Brahmin
Dunlap, Susan
Jill Smith series (3)
Not expected to live
Cumberland, Marten
Saturnin Dax series (6)
Not for all the gold in Ireland
James, John
Photinus the Greek series (2)
Not for export
Coles, Manning
Tommy Hambledon series (17)
Not for glory
Rosenberg, Joel
Metzada series (3)
Not guilty, My Lord
Desmond, Hugh
Alan Fraser series (29)
Not honour more
Cary, Joyce
Chester Nimmo trilogy (3)
Not I, said the sparrow
Lockridge, Richard
Inspector Merton Heimrich series (23)
Not in our stars
Maurice, Michael
Not in our stars series (1)
Swycaffer, Jefferson Putnam
Concordat series (2)
Not in single spies
Lewis, Catherine
Lisa Thomas series (2)
Not in the script
Bonett, John
Professor Mandrake series (2)
Not killed, just dead
Ambler, Dail
Danny Spade series (15)
Not long to live
Cross, Mark
Daphne Wrayne and her Four Adjusters series (42)
Not me, Inspector
Reilly, Helen
Inspector Christopher McKee series (28)
Not negotiable
Coles, Manning
Tommy Hambledon series (10)
Not nice people
Clevely, Hugh
Maxwell Archer series (6)
Not on the records
Carter, Nicholas
Nicholas Carter series (536)
Not one of us
Thomson, June
Inspector Finch series (1)
Not proven
Graeme, Bruce
Superintendent William Stevens and Inspector Pierre Allain series (6)
Not quite a lady
McCulloch, Sarah
Georgian series (1)
Not quite dead enough
Stout, Rex
Nero Wolfe and Archie Goodwin series (10)
Not-quite-ready-for-prime-time bandits
Adams, Barbara
Kid-TV series (2)
Not quite sisters
McKenna, Colleen O'Shaughnessy
Cousins series (1)
Not scarlet but gold
Saville, Malcolm
Lone Pine Five Club series (14)

Not single spies
Betteridge, Don
Tiger Lester series (6)
Not sleeping, just dead
Alverson, Charles
Joe Goodey series (3)
Not-so-jolly Roger
Scieszka, Jon
Time warp trio series (2)
Not so quiet
Smith, Helen Zenna
Skinny series (1)
Not so Rotten Ralph
Gantos, Jack
Rotten Ralph series (7)
Not starring Jilly!
Haas, Dorothy
Peanut Butter and Jilly series (5)
Not such a bad life
Dark, Sidney
Guide, philosopher and friend trilogy (1)
Not the final word
Inchfawn, Fay
Personal recording series (3)
Not the whole truth
Heenan, John Carmel
Crown of thorns series (1)
Not there, Doctor
Clifford, Robert
Doctor series (2)
Not to the swift
Gibbs, Henry
Prior Report trilogy (1)
Not wanted on voyage
Spain, Nancy
Miriam Birdseye series (5)
Not without my daughter
Mahmoody, Betty
Daughter series (1)
Not-world
Swann, Thomas Burnett
Ancient history series (13)
Notch on the knife
Haggard, William
Colonel Charles Russell series (15)
Notched hairpin
Heard, Henry Fitzgerald
Mister Mycroft series (4)
Note of enchantment
Clements, Eileen Helen
Alister Woodhead series (12)
Notebooks
Picard, Sam
John Scott series (1)
Notebooks for Frank Herbert's Dune
Herbert, Frank
Dune series (6)
Notebooks of Lazarus Long
Heinlein, Robert Anson
Future history series (7)
Notebooks of Lazarus long
Heinlein, Robert Anson
Lazarus Long series (2)
Lazarus Long series (4)
Notebooks of Major Thompson
Daninos, Pierre
Major Thompson series (1)
Notes and sketches of New South Wales
Meredith, Louisa Anne
Notes and sketches series (1)
Notes of a native son
Baldwin, James Arthur
Native son series (1)
Notes on Tasmania
Craig, Clifford
Tasmanian prints series (3)
Nothing but foxes
Lewis, Royston
Inspector John Crow series (9)
Nothing but money
Arthur, Timothy Shay
Nothing but money series (1)
Nothing but net
Hughes, Dean
Angel Park Hoop Stars series (1)
Nothing but the night
Blackburn, John
General Charles Kirk series (7)
Nothing but the truth
Orum, Poul
Inspector Jonas Morck series (2)
Rhode, John
Doctor Lancelot Priestley series (44)
Nothing can rescue me
Daly, Elizabeth
Henry Gamadge series (6)
Nothing doing
Campbell, Michael
Peter Perry series (2)
Nothing ever happens
Lincoln, Maurice
Reginald Massingham series (2)
Macgregor, Reginald James
Nothing and something series (1)
Nothing happened after all
Shaw, Jane
Ali and Dizzy series (2)
Nothing in common
Quin-Harkin, Janet
Sugar and spice series (5)
Nothing is the number when you die
Fleming, Joan
Nuri Iskirlak series (2)
Nothing larger than life
Holbrook, David
Flesh wounds trilogy (3)
Nothing last forever
Thorp, Roderick
Joe Leland series (2)
Nothing like blood
Bruce, Leo
Carolus Deene series (11)
Nothing new under the sun
Bacchelli, Riccardo
Mill on the Po series (2)
Nothing personal
Chambers, Peter
Mark Preston series (23)
Nothing serious
Wodehouse, Pelham Grenville
Oldest member series (3)
Ukridge series (2)
Nothing stays the same
Mackenzie, Lee
Emmerdale Farm series (7)
Nothing to declare
Coles, Manning
Tommy Hambledon series (24)
Nothing-to-do puppy
Szekeres, Cyndy
Puppy series (1)
Nothing to do with the case
Lemarchand, Elizabeth
Superintendent Tom Pollard series (12)
Nothing to hide
Spade, Danny
Danny Spade series (33)
Nothing to lose
Charles, Robert
Simon Larren series (1)
Priest, Charles Ashley Vincent
Nothing to lose series (1)
Nothing too good for a cowboy
Hobson, Richmond Pearson
Rancher series (2)
Nothing's certain but death
Wren, M K
Conan Flagg series (4)
Nothing's fair in fifth grade
De Clements, Barthe
Elsie Edwards series (1)
Notice of death
Penn, John
Inspector George Thorne and Sergeant Bill Abbot series (1)
Notorious
Keene, Day
Les Ferron series (2)
Notorious Sophie Lang
Anderson, Frederick Irving
Deputy Parr series (1)
Oliver Armiston series (2)
Notre Dame de Paris
Hugo, Victor Marie
Fate trilogy (3)
Notting Hill murder
Ryland, Clive
Superintendent Shannon series (1)
Noughts and crosses
Quiller-Couch, Arthur
Troy Town series (2)
Noumea
Hall, Richard
Patrick Costello series (2)
Nova express
Burroughs, William Seward
Tangier trilogy (3)
November Man
Granger, Bill
November Man series (1)
November wind
Geddes, Paul
Ludovic Fender series (2)
Paul Venneker series (2)
Novena for murder
O'Marie, Carol Anne
Sister Mary Helen series (1)
Now a stranger
Wolfe, Humbert
Anguish series (1)
Now and then
Buechner, Frederick
Sacred journey series (2)
Now and then, amen
Cleary, Jon
Scobie Malone series (5)
Now Barabbas was a robber
Mann, Deborah
Early Christian series (2)
Reign of Herod Antipas trilogy (1)
Now came still evening on
Vachell, Horace Annesley
Methuselah series (1)
Now dead is any man
Audemars, Pierre
Monsieur Pinaud series (21)
Now, God be thanked
Masters, John
Loss of Eden trilogy (1)
Now he is legend
Shirreffs, Gordon Donald
Quint Kershaw trilogy (1)
Now I lay me down
Laurence, Margaret
Manawaka series (2)
Now I see
Lunn, Arnold
Now I see series (1)
Now it's fall
Lenski, Lois
Seasons series (2)
Now it's my turn
Chaber, M E
Milo March series (3)
Now like to die
Brinton, Henry
John and Sally Strang series (3)
Now lying dead
Powell, Percival Henry
Superintendent Gaden series (2)
Now or never
Coles, Manning
Tommy Hambledon series (13)
Optic, Oliver
Boat Club series (4)
Now seek my bones
Courtier, Sidney Hobson
Inspector Digger Haig series (1)
Now, Texan!
Grover, Marshall
Larry and Stretch series (58)
Now that days are colder
Fisher, Aileen
Ways of animals series (4)
Now that he's asked you out
Hunt, Gary
Asked out series (2)
Now that I'm fifty
Terhune, Albert Payson
My memory series (1)
Now that spring is here
Fisher, Aileen
Ways of plants series (1)
Now that you've asked her out
Hunt, Gary
Asked out series (1)
Now to the stars
Johns, William Earl
Rex Clinton series (3)
Now, Virginia!
Griffith, Helen Sherman
Virginia series (3)
Now, voyager
Prouty, Olive Higgins
Vale family series (3)
Now we are free
Allis, Marguerite
Ashbel Field series (1)
Now we are six
Milne, Alan Alexander
Christopher Robin series (2)
Now what are you up to, Herman?
Unger, Jim
Herman series (14)
Now you don't
Greth, Roma
Hana Shaner series (1)
Now you see her, now you don't
Murray, William Buckley
Lou Anderson series (5)
Now you see it, him, them
DeWeese, Gene
Joe Karns series (2)
Now you'll think I'm awful
Rhodes, Susan
Bad girls series (1)
Nowhere
Berger, Thomas
Russel Wren series (2)
Nowhere?
Stein, Aaron Marc
Matt Erridge series (14)
Nowhere hunt
Clayton, Jo
Diadem series (6)
Nowhere man
Oster, Jerry
Jake Neuman series (2)
Perry, Ritchie
Philis series (2)
Nowhere on earth
Elder, Michael
Barclay series (1)
Nowhere to run
Dixon, Franklin W
Hardy boys case files series (27)
Krich, Rochelle Majer
Jessie Drake series (3)
Lowell, Anne Hunter
Sorority girls series (2)
Pascal, Francine
Sweet Valley High series (25)
Nowhere weapon
Carter, Nick
Nick Carter series (133)
Nuclear captain
Wingate, John
Submariner Sinclair series (4)
Nuda veritas
Sheridan, Clare
Nuda veritas series (1)
Nude in mink
Rohmer, Sax
Sumuru series (1)
Nude in Nevada
Dewey, Thomas Blanchard
Pete Schofield series (9)
Nude on the rocks
Henry, Clay
Matt Archer series (3)
Nude who did
Mark, Ted
Girl from P.U.S.S.Y.C.A.T. series (5)
Nude who never
Mark, Ted
Girl from P.U.S.S.Y.C.A.T. series (4)
Nude who wore black
Mark, Ted
Girl from P.U.S.S.Y.C.A.T. series (6)
Nude with a view
Brown, Carter
Rick Holman series (12)
Nueces strip
Mason, Dan
Lex Cranshaw series (7)
Null-A three
Van Vogt, Alfred Elton
Null-A series (3)
Nul's quest
Strickland, Brad
Jeremy Moon series (2)
Number eighteen
Wills, Cecil Melville
Geoffrey Boscobell series (1)
Number file
Dixon, Franklin W
Hardy boys case files series (17)
Number five John Street
Whiteing, Richard
Rich and poor series (2)
Number nine
Herbert, Alan Patrick
Admiral of the Fleet, Earl of Caraway series (1)
Number nine Belmont Square
Erskine, Margaret
Inspector Septimus Finch series (13)
Number nineteen
Farjeon, Joseph Jefferson
Ben the tramp series (8)
Number of dragons
Leedy, Loreen
Dragon series (1)
Number One
Dos Passos, John
Spotswood family series (2)
Number one boy
Ward, Edward
Number one boy series (1)
Number one two three
Gerard, Francis
Sir John Meredith series (2)
Number seven, Queer Street
Lawrence, Margery
Miles Pennoyer series (1)
Number seventeen
Farjeon, Joseph Jefferson
Ben the tramp series (1)
Tracy, Louis
Inspector Furneaux series (4)
Number Ten
Clark, William
Patrick Pyrton series (1)
Number ten Green Street
Weir, Rosemary
Green Street series (1)
Number thirteen Toroni
Regis, Julius
Maurice Wallion series (2)
Number three
Vincent, Kitty
Gyp Kidnadze series (1)
Number twenty one Castle Street
Katz, H W
Fishmans series (2)
Numbered account
Bridge, Ann
Julia Probyn series (3)
Numbers
Allington, Richard L
Beginning to learn series (2)
Browne, Eileen
Funny animals series (1)
Lind, Jakov
Steps series (2)
Pluckrose, Henry
Knowabouts series (2)
Numbers came
Croft-Cooke, Rupert
Sensual life series (5)
Numbers man
Gerrity, David
Frank Cardolini series (3)
Numbers to talk about
Lionni, Leon
Colors, letters, numbers and words to talk about series (3)
Numbers up!
Mooser, Stephen
Gigglemajig series (1)
Numblers
Macdonald, Suse
Discovery series (2)
Nun of the above
Quill, Monica
Sister Mary Teresa series (4)
Nungu and the crocodile
Cole, Babette
Nungu series (1)
Nungu and the elephant
Cole, Babette
Nungu series (3)
Nungu and the hippopotamus
Cole, Babette
Nungu series (2)
Nunquam
Durrell, Lawrence
Revolt of Aphrodite series (2)
Nuns go car racing
Routh, Jonathan
Nuns series (5)
Nuns go east
Routh, Jonathan
Nuns series (3)
Nuns go to Africa
Routh, Jonathan
Nuns series (2)
Nuns go to Penguin Island
Routh, Jonathan
Nuns series (1)
Nuns go west
Routh, Jonathan
Nuns series (4)
Nuplex Red
Quinn, Simon
Inquisitor series (2)
Nurse Anne
Jennings, D K
Doctor Ralph Conway series (5)
Nurse at Butlins
Deal, Paula
Nurse series (3)
Nurse at Ryeminster
Ferrari, Ivy
Ryeminster Hospital series (2)
Nurse at Saint Mark's
White, Constance Mary
Saint Mark's Hospital series (3)
Nurse Carter married
Darbyshire, Shirley
Nurse Carter series (2)
Nurse in action
Prentis, Evelyn
Nurse series (2)
Nurse in danger
Ridley, Sheila
Nurse Jane Taylor series (1)
Nurse in doubt
Ridley, Sheila
Nurse Jane Taylor series (2)
Nurse in parts
Prentis, Evelyn
Nurse series (3)

Nurse in the Mutiny
Ridley, Sheila
Nurse Jane Taylor series (5)
Nurse in the South Seas
Ridley, Sheila
Nurse Jane Taylor series (3)
Nurse in the woods
Lance, Leslie
Nurse Verena Frodesley series (1)
Nurse in time
Prentis, Evelyn
Nurse series (1)
Nurse in training
Laklan, Carli
Nancy Kimball series (2)
Nurse is a neighbour
Jones, Joanna
Nurse Jones series (1)
Nurse Matilda
Brand, Christianna
Nurse Matilda series (1)
Nurse Matilda goes to hospital
Brand, Christianna
Nurse Matilda series (3)
Nurse Matilda goes to town
Brand, Christianna
Nurse Matilda series (2)
Nurse near by
Prentis, Evelyn
Nurse series (4)
Nurse Nolan's private duty
McElfresh, Adeline
Jill Nolan series (4)
Nurse, nurse, nurse!
Deal, Paula
Nurse series (1)
Nurse on call
Jennings, D K
Doctor Ralph Conway series (23)
Nurse on the district
Jones, Joanna
Nurse Jones series (2)
Nurse on the moors
Lance, Leslie
Nurse Verena Frodesley series (3)
Nurse on Ward Nine
Cooper, Lisa
Princess Beatrice Hospital series (2)
Nurse Plum
Reed, Giles
Munch Bunch character series (22)
Nurse power
Seide, Diane
Medical power series (1)
Nurse Ross and the doctor
Meynell, Laurence Walter
Nurse Ross series (4)
Nurse Ross saves the day
Meynell, Laurence Walter
Nurse Ross series (3)
Nurse Ross shows the way
Meynell, Laurence Walter
Nurse Ross series (2)
Nurse Ross takes over
Meynell, Laurence Walter
Nurse Ross series (1)
Nurse Verena at Weirwater
Lance, Leslie
Nurse Verena Frodesley series (2)
Nursemaid who disappeared
Macdonald, Philip
Colonel Anthony Ruthven Gethryn series (10)
Nursery
Phillpotts, Eden
Industries of England series (4)
Nursery rhyme murders
Verner, Gerald
Superintendent Robert Budd series (20)
Nursery rhymes
Hill, Eric
Peek-a-book series (1)
Nursery rhymes for Bill and Ben, the Flowerpot Men
Bird, Maria
Flowerpot Men series (2)
Nursery school
Roth, Harold
Toddler's fun series (1)
Nursery tea and poison
Morice, Anne
Tessa Crichton Price series (8)
Nurses and ladies
Ridley, Sheila
Nurse Jane Taylor series (4)
Nurses three, first assignment
Kirby, Jean
Scott sisters series (2)
Nursing home crime
Brisbane, Coutts
Sexton Blake series (837)
Nursing-home murder
Marsh, Ngaio
Inspector Roderick Alleyn series (3)
Nursing in the outback
Power, Phyllis Mary
Hannah Maine series (2)
Nursing woman
Fraser, Sara
Tildy series (3)
Nut case
Conway, Peter
Inspector Newton series (3)
Nutcracker Ballet mystery
Keene, Carolyn
Nancy Drew series (110)
Nutmeg comes to Westways
White, Constance Mary
Westways series (2)
Nutmeg of Consolation
O'Brian, Patrick
Jack Aubrey and Stephen Maturin series (14)
Nuts in the rockery
Blomefield, Mathena
Nessel series (2)
Nutty and the case of the mastermind thief
Hughes, Dean
Nutty Nutsell series (2)
Nutty and the case of the ski-slope spy
Hughes, Dean
Nutty Nutsell series (3)
Nutty can't miss
Hughes, Dean
Nutty Nutsell series (4)
Nutty for president
Hughes, Dean
Nutty Nutsell series (1)
Nutty knows all
Hughes, Dean
Nutty Nutsell series (5)
Nutty the movie star
Hughes, Dean
Nutty Nutsell series (6)
Nuttybub and Nittersing
Gibbs, May
Gumnut Land series (9)
Nutty's ghost
Hughes, Dean
Nutty Nutsell series (7)
Nutzenbolts and more troubles with machines
Goulart, Ron
Troubles with machines series (2)
Nyloned avenger
Janson, Hank
Hank Janson series (51)
Nymph in the night
Janson, Hank
Hank Janson series (129)
Nymph island affair
O'Shea, Sean
Valentine Flynn series (4)
Nymph to the slaughter
Brown, Carter
Danny Boyd series (10)
NYPD
Nolan, Frederick
Lieutenant Joe Petrosino series (1)

O

O Albany
Kennedy, William
Albany series (4)
O as in omen
Treat, Lawrence
Carl Wayward series (4)
O Beulah Land
Settle, Mary Lee
Beulah series (2)
O Gang
Edwards, Hazel
O Gang series (1)
O Gang again
Edwards, Hazel
O Gang series (2)
O Kaplan, my Kaplan
Rosten, Leo
Hyman Kaplan series (2)
O little town of Maggody
Hess, Joan
Arly Hanks series (7)
O master Caliban!
Gotlieb, Phyllis
Dahlgren series (1)
O mistress mine
Greenwood, Robert
Rosie Dawes series (2)
O, more than happy countryman
Bates, Herbert Ernest
Country heart series (2)
O rugged land of gold
Martin, Martha
Alaska series (1)
O shepherd speak
Sinclair, Upton
World's end series (10)
O willing hearts
Lowe, Eric
Stewart family series (2)
Oak above the kings
Kennealy, Patricia
Tales of Arthur series (2)
Oak and iron
Hendryx, James Beardsley
Corporal Downey series (5)
Oak and the ram
Moorcock, Michael
Chronicle of Prince Corum and the silver hand trilogy (2)
Corum series (5)
Oak apple
Harrod-Eagles, Cynthia
Morland family series (4)
Oak king's daughter
De Lint, Charles
Cerin Songweaver series (1)
Oakapple Wood treasury
Partridge, Jenny
Oakapple Wood series (4)
Oaken throne
Jarvis, Robin
Deptford histories series (2)
Oakhurst
Johnson, Walter Reed
Oakhurst series (1)
Oasis
Creasey, John
Doctor Palfrey series (27)
Oath of blood
Frazier, Arthur
Wolfshead series (1)
Oath of fear
Bayfield, William John
Sexton Blake series (462)
Oath of gold
Moon, Elizabeth
Deed of Paksenarrion series (4)
Oath of the renunciates
Bradley, Marion Zimmer
Darkover series (8)
Oath to Mida
Green, Sharon
Jalav series (2)
Oathbound
Lackey, Mercedes
Vows and honor series (1)
Oathbreakers
Lackey, Mercedes
Vows and honor series (2)
Obadiah the Bold
Turkle, Brinton
Obadiah series (1)
Obedience
Hansen, Joseph
Dave Brandstetter series (10)
Obelists at sea
King, Charles Daly
Doctor L Rees Pons series (1)
Obelists en route
King, Charles Daly
Doctor L Rees Pons series (2)
Michael Lord series (1)
Obelists fly high
King, Charles Daly
Doctor L Rees Pons series (3)
Obelix and Company
Goscinny, Rene
Asterix series (23)
Oberland
Richardson, Dorothy Miller
Pilgrimage series (9)
Obernewtyn
Carmody, Isobelle
Obernewtyn chronicles series (1)
Obituary blonde
Brody, Marc
Marc Brody series (40)
Obituary Club
Pentecost, Hugh
Grant Simon series (1)
Lieutenant Pascal series (2)
Object for a walk
Liddell, Robert
Charles Harbord series (3)
Oblate
Huysmans, Joris Karl
Durtal series (4)
Obligations of Hercule
Audemars, Pierre
Hercule Renard series (3)
Obols for Charon
Harvester, Simon
Roger Fleming series (6)
Obscure grave
Woods, Sara
Sir Nicholas Harding and Antony Maitland series (43)
Obsequies at Oxford
Crispin, Edmund
Gervase Fen series (1)
Observations by Mister Dooley
Dunne, Finley Peter
Mister Dooley series (5)
Observations, casual and intimate
Graham, Winifred
That reminds me trilogy (2)
Observer Corps mystery
Hardinge, Rex
Sexton Blake series (1038)
Observers
Knight, Damon
CV trilogy (2)
Obsessed
Duncan, Ronald
All men are islands trilogy (3)
Obsession
Janson, Hank
Hank Janson series (90)
Mitchell, Scott
Brock Devlin series (16)
Tripp, Miles
John Samson series (1)
Obsession for two
Bentley, John
Glen Gibson series (5)
Obsession of Sally Wing
Martin, Russell White
Supernatural series (5)
Obsidian oracle
Denning, Troy
Prism pentad series (4)
Obslists fly high
King, Charles Daly
Michael Lord series (2)
Obstinate Captain Samson
Douglas, Gavin
Captain Samson series (2)
Obvious solution
Gregg, Cecil Freeman
Inspector Cuthbert Higgins series (35)
Occident
Halliburton, Richard
Book of marvels series (1)
Occupation
Caute, David
Confrontation trilogy (2)
Toland, John
McGlynn and Toda families series (2)
Occupation for gentlemen
Warburg, Fredric
Publishing series (1)
Occupation, thief
Mackenzie, Donald
Fugitives series (1)
Occupational debris
Evans, Stuart
Windmill Hill series (2)
Ocean-born
Optic, Oliver
Yacht Club series (6)
Ocean fish school
Reese, Bob
Ocean critterland series (3)
Ocean gold
Ellsberg, Edward
Sunken treasure series (2)
Ocean haul
Duff, Douglas Valder
Adam Macadam series (2)
Ocean heritage
Bassett, Sara Ware
Cape Cod series (14)
Ocean waifs
Reid, Mayne
Ocean waifs series (2)
Ocean Wireless Boys and the lost liner
Lawton, Wilbur
Ocean Wireless Boys series (2)
Ocean Wireless Boys and the navy code
Lawton, Wilbur
Ocean Wireless Boys series (4)
Ocean Wireless Boys of the Iceberg Patrol
Lawton, Wilbur
Ocean Wireless Boys series (3)
Ocean Wireless Boys on the Atlantic
Lawton, Wilbur
Ocean Wireless Boys series (1)
Ocean Wireless Boys on the Pacific
Lawton, Wilbur
Ocean Wireless Boys series (5)
Ocean Wireless Boys on warswept seas
Lawton, Wilbur
Ocean Wireless Boys series (6)
Oceans
Hoff, Mary
Our endangered planet series (3)
Oceans of Venus
Asimov, Isaac
David Starr series (3)
Oceola Kid
Adams, Clifton
Tragg series (1)
Ochre people
Jabavu, Noni
Bantu series (2)
Octagon House
Taylor, Phoebe Atwood
Asey Mayo series (11)
Octagon magic
Norton, Andre
Magic series (2)
Octave
Marston, Jeffery
Octave trilogy (1)
October
Isherwood, Christopher
Christopher series (4)
October heat
De Marco, Gordon
Riley Kovacks series (1)
October House
Strahan, Kay Cleaver
Lynn Macdonald series (4)
October men
Price, Anthony
Doctor David Audley and Jack Butler series (5)
October story
Martin, Robert
Career adventure series (1)
October treasure
Wuorio, Eva Lis
Jersey series (1)
October's baby
Cook, Glen
Dread Empire series (2)
Octopus
Norris, Frank
Epic of wheat series (1)
Octopus of crime
House, Brant
Secret Agent X series (4)
Octopus of Paris
Leroux, Gaston
Joseph Rouletabille series (5)
Octopussy
Fleming, Ian
James Bond series (14)
Odd
Le Feuvre, Amy
Odd series (2)
Odd and the Great Bear
Roose-Evans, James
Odd and Elsewhere series (3)
Odd bods
Martin, Toy
Taronga Road Riders series (6)
Odd craft
Jacobs, William Wymark
Night-Watchman series (5)
Odd job man
Crisp, Norman James
Inspector Sidney Kenyon series (2)
Odd jobs
Johnston, Tony
Odd jobs series (1)
Odd jobs and friends
Johnston, Tony
Odd jobs series (2)
Odd jobs number one hundred and one, and other future crimes and intrigues
Goulart, Ron
Odd jobs series (1)
Odd made even
Le Feuvre, Amy
Odd series (2)
Odd man out
Taylor, Andrew
William Dougal series (8)
Odd man out at Abbey
Leyland, Eric
Abbey series (6)
Odd numbers
Ford, Sewell
Shorty McCabe series (3)

Sorrentino, Gilbert
Misterioso trilogy (1)
Odd one
Le Feuvre, Amy
Odd series (1)
Odd to the rescue
Roose-Evans, James
Odd and Elsewhere series (5)
Odd warlock out
Stasheff, Christopher
Gramarye series (10)
Odd woman out
Douglas, George
Inspector Hallam and Sergeant Spratt series (1)
Fox, Sebastian
George Lydney series (2)
Linklater, Joseph Lane
Silas Booth series (5)
Oddly
Blake, Jon
Oddly series (1)
Oddly ad lib
Jennings, Paul Francis
Oddly series (10)
Oddly Bodlikins
Jennings, Paul Francis
Oddly series (3)
Oddly enough
Jennings, Paul Francis
Oddly series (1)
Odds against
Francis, Dick
Sid Halley series (1)
Odds against O'Shay
Grover, Marshall
Larry and Stretch series (139)
Odds against Sundown
Hawkes, Zachary
Fancy Hatch series (4)
Odds are murder
McQuay, Mike
Mathew Swain series (4)
Odds on Bluefeather
Meynell, Laurence Walter
Bluefeather series (2)
Odds on death
Drummond, Charles
Sergeant Reed series (3)
Odds on gold
Hughes, William
George Willis series (2)
Odds on its murder
Jason
Jason series (8)
Odds on Miss Seeton
Carvic, Heron
Miss Emily Seeton series (5)
Odds-on murder
Dolph, Jack
Doc Connor series (1)
Odds on the hot seat
Philips, Judson Pentecost
Coyle and Donovan series (1)
Odds run out
Waugh, Hillary
Sheridan Wesley series (3)
Odin grows up
Duun, Ole Julius
People of Juvik series (5)
Odin in fairyland
Duun, Ole Julius
People of Juvik series (4)
Odious child
Zinkin, Taya
Odious child series (1)
Odor of bitter almonds
Edwards, James G
Inspector Victor Bondurant series (4)
Odor of violets
Kendrick, Baynard
Captain Duncan Maclain series (3)
Odour of violets
Kendrick, Baynard
Captain Duncan Maclain series (3)
Odtaa
Masefield, John
Sard Harker series (2)
Odyssey
Homer
Trojan War series (2)
Kazantzakis, Nikos
Trojan War series (3)
Kube-McDowell, Michael Paul
Robot city series (1)
Odyssey of Ben O'Neal
Taylor, Theodore
Teetoncey and Ben O'Neal trilogy (3)
Oedipus
Treece, Henry
Greek trilogy (1)
Oedipus and Akhnaton
Velikovsky, Immanuel
Ages in chaos series (3)
Oedipus at Colonnus
Sophocles
Oedipus series (2)
Oedipus Rex
Sophocles
Oedipus series (1)
Oedipus Tyrannus
Sophocles
Oedipus series (1)
Of age and innocence
Lamming, George
San Cristobal series (1)
Of alien bondage
Cleve, John
Spaceways series (1)
Of all the bloody cheek
McAuliffe, Frank
Augustus Mandrell series (1)
Of beginnings and endings
Adams, Robert
Castaways in time series (6)
Of chiefs and champions
Adams, Robert
Castaways in time series (4)
Of course Lotta can do almost everything
Lindgren, Astrid
Marten family series (3)
Of course Polly can ride a bike
Lindgren, Astrid
Marten family series (1)
Of gods and men
O'Neill, Donal
Brian series (2)
Of illustrious men
Rouaud, Jean
Fields of glory series (2)
Of man and mantra
Anthony, Piers
Of man and mantra trilogy (3)
Of mice and murder
Whitaker, Beryl
John Abbot series (1)
Of Mistress Eve
Pease, Howard
Border trilogy (2)
Of myths and monsters
Adams, Robert
Castaways in time series (5)
Of quests and kings
Adams, Robert
Castaways in time series (3)
Of skies and seas
DeJonge, Joanne E
My Father's world series (2)
Of the fall
McAuley, Paul J
Four hundred billion stars series (2)
Of the Ring of Earls
Dymoke, Juliet
Henry I trilogy (1)
Of the thunder of hooves
Sabey, Ian
Melodie series (2)
Of the wall at Callahan's
Robinson, Spider
Callahan's Crosstime Saloon series (6)
Of their own choice
Churchill, Peter
British spy series (1)
Of time and of seasons
Johnston, Norma
Of time series (1)
Of time and the river
Wolfe, Thomas Clayton
Eugene Gant series (2)
Of truth as related to self and society
Gourley, Frank Alan
Even gods err trilogy (3)
Of unsound mind
Carmichael, Harry
John Piper and Quinn series (20)
O'Fear
Corris, Peter
Cliff Hardy series (13)
Off-duty nurse
James, Josephine
Kathy Martin series (10)
Off for Hawaii
Bonehill, Ralph
Flag and frontier series (7)
Flag of freedom series (3)
Off for West Point
Garrison, Frederick
West Point series (1)
Off key
McNab, Claire
Inspector Carol Ashton and Sergeant Mark Bourke series (5)
Off minor
Harvey, John Barton
Inspector Charlie Resnick series (4)
Off on a comet!
Verne, Jules
Hector Servadac series (2)
Off on a comet
Verne, Jules
Hector Servadac series (2)
Off season
Craig, Philip R
Martha's Vineyard series (5)
Ketchum, Jack
Off season series (1)
Off the beaten track in Baja
Gardner, Erle Stanley
Baja California series (3)
Off the leash
Park, William Bryan
Off the leash series (1)
Off the rails
Stonier, George Walter
Rhodesian series (1)
Off the record
Mills, Bart
Melrose Place series (2)
Off the reservation
Ellis, Edward Sylvester
Arizona trilogy (1)
Off the Skelligs
Ingelow, Jean
Skelligs series (1)
Off to Philadelphia
Allee, Marjorie Hill
Lankester family trilogy (3)
Off to the geysers
Stephens, Charles Asbury
Camping out series (3)
Off to the sea with Annabelle
O'Farrell, Kathleen
Lattimer children series (2)
Off with her head
Cole, George Douglas Howard
Superintendent Henry Wilson series (19)
Off with his head
Marsh, Ngaio
Inspector Roderick Alleyn series (19)
Offenders
Ward, Richard Heron
Neil Falder series (3)
Offered in evidence
Romains, Jules
Men of goodwill series (24)
Office lover boy
Berenstain, Stan
Lover boy series (3)
Officer and temporary gentleman
Wheatley, Dennis
Time has come series (2)
Officer from Special Branch
Lilley, Tom
Police Special Branch series (1)
Officers and gentlemen
Waugh, Evelyn
World War II series (2)
Officers' ladies
Harris, Marion
Soldiers and officers series (2)
Official Batman handbook
Eisner, Joel
Batman series (10)
Official Counter Force reference book
Erskine, George
Counter Force series (2)
Official Doctor Who and the Daleks book
Nation, Terry
Doctor Who series (162)
Official secret
Duncan, Allan
Major Charles Douglas Kerrwood series (1)
Official teenage mutant ninja turtles treasury
Wiater, Stanley
Teenage mutant ninja turtles series (5)
Offspring
Ketchum, Jack
Off season series (2)
McKenney, Kenneth
Changeling trilogy (3)
Og, boy of battle
Crump, James Irving
Og series (2)
Og of the cave people
Crump, James Irving
Og series (3)
Og, son of fire
Crump, James Irving
Og series (1)
Og, son of Og
Crump, James Irving
Og series (4)
Oggy and the holiday
Lawrence, Ann
Oggy series (3)
Oggy at home
Lawrence, Ann
Oggy series (2)
Ogilvie, Tallant and Moon
Yarbro, Chelsea Quinn
Charlie Spotted Moon series (1)
Oglala outbreak
Gentry, Buck
Eli Holten series (13)
Ogre castle
Hale, F J
After the spell wars series (1)
Ogre, ogre
Anthony, Piers
Xanth series (5)
Oh, Abigail!
Miller, Moira
Abigail series (1)
Oh, brother
Zach, Cheryl
Smyth versus Smith series (1)
Oh, bury me not
Wren, M K
Conan Flagg series (3)
Oh, Christina!
Bell, John Joy
Christina series (1)
Oh dear!
McMullen, Nigel
Naughty baby series (2)
Vail, Virginia
Animal Inn series (11)
Oh dear, Doctor
Clifford, Robert
Doctor series (4)
Oh dear, said Tiger
Bisset, Donald
Tiger series (3)
Oh honestly, Angela!
Robinson, Nancy Konheim
Angela trilogy (1)
Oh, Joshua
Taffrail
Royal Navy series (2)
Oh, murderer mine
Davis, Norbert
Doan and Carstairs series (2)
Oh, my word
Muir, Frank
My word series (4)
Oh no, Aunt Belladonna!
Furminger, Jo
Mary, Ben and William series (3)
Oh, no, you don't
Carstairs, Henry
Lydford Long series (10)
Oh promised land
Street, James
Dabney family series (1)
Oh really, Rabbit!
Manning-Sanders, Ruth
Rabbit series (2)
Oh to be in England
Bates, Herbert Ernest
Larkin family series (4)
Oh, Virginia!
Griffith, Helen Sherman
Virginia series (1)
Ohio!
Poole, Helen Lee
Whitewater dynasty series (2)
Oil for the lamps of China
Hobart, Alice Tisdale
China series (2)
Oil-planet
Elder, Michael
Oil-seeker series (2)
Oil rig
Roderus, Frank
Carl Heller series (1)
Oil seventy four two
Carter, Nick
Nick Carter series (104)
Oil-seeker
Elder, Michael
Oil-seeker series (1)
Oil slick
Murphy, Warren Burton
Destroyer series (16)
Oilfield boy
Mauzey, Merritt
Farm boy series (3)
Oink and Pearl
Chorao, Kay
Oink and Pearl series (1)
Ojo in Oz
Thompson, Ruth Plumly
Oz series (26)
Okewood of the Secret Service
Williams, Valentine
Clubfoot series (2)
Okkie and his little friends
Roggeveen, Leonard
Okkie series (2)
Okkie Gingernut
Roggeveen, Leonard
Okkie series (1)
Okkie in the cold
Roggeveen, Leonard
Okkie series (4)
Okkie knows what to do!
Roggeveen, Leonard
Okkie series (3)
Oklahoma!
Ross, Dana Fuller
Wagons West series (23)
Oklahoma ambush
Ellis, Wesley
Lone Star series (103)
Oklahoma firefight
Derrick, Lionel
Penetrator series (31)
Oklahoma gun-song
Smith, Ford
Dark Knight series (3)
Oklahoma ordeal
Sharpe, Jon
Trailsman series (155)
Oklahoma pride
Ross, Dana Fuller
Holt family series (2)
Oklahoma score
Cutter, Tom
Tracker series (5)
Ola
D'Aulaire, Ingri
Ola series (1)
Ola and Blakken and Line, Sine, Trine
D'Aulaire, Ingri
Ola series (2)
Olaf is late
Lexau, Joan M
Olaf series (2)
Olaf reads
Lexau, Joan M
Olaf series (1)
Old acquaintance
Guild, Nicholas
Ray Guinness series (2)
Old age of Lecoq, the detective
Du Boisgobey, Fortune
Monsieur Lecoq series (5)
Old age of Monsieur Lecoq
Du Boisgobey, Fortune
Monsieur Lecoq series (5)
Old Amsterdam
Knight, Brigid
Van Breda family series (2)
Old Bailey mystery
Blair, Allan
Sexton Blake series (865)
Old Bank House
Thirkell, Angela
Barsetshire series (18)
Old battle ground
Trowbridge, John Townsend
Brighthope series (5)
Old Bear
Hissey, Jane
Old Bear series (1)
Old Bear tales
Hissey, Jane
Old Bear series (2)
Old Ben
Otis, James
Toby Tyler series (2)
Old Bill and son
Bairnsfather, Bruce
Old Bill series (12)
Old Bill does it again
Bairnsfather, Bruce
Old Bill series (11)
Old Bill stands by
Bairnsfather, Bruce
Old Bill series (10)
Old Black Witch
Devlin, Wende
Old Witch series (1)
Old blood
Mittelholzer, Edgar
Kaywana series (4)

Old bone betrayed
Bishop, Pike
Cord Diamondback series (7)
Old bones
Elkins, Aaron J
Professor Gideon Oliver series (4)
Old Chester days
Deland, Margaret
Old Chester series (6)
Old Chester secret
Deland, Margaret
Old Chester series (5)
Old Chester series (6)
Old Chester tales
Deland, Margaret
Old Chester series (2)
Old contemporaries
Lucas, Edward Verrall
Ancestors series (2)
Old Contemptibles
Grimes, Martha
Inspector Richard Jury series (12)
Old country
Aleichem, Sholom
Tevye the milkman series (1)
Old country and seven more years
Sassoon, Siegfried
Siegfried series (1)
Old Delabole
Phillpotts, Eden
Industries of England series (2)
Old detective's pupil
Carter, Nicholas
Nicholas Carter series (3)
Old die young
Lockridge, Richard
Nathan Shapiro series (12)
Old dog, new tricks
Cate, Dick
Flying free series (3)
Old dominion
Johnston, Mary
Virginian series (2)
Old Ebbie, detective up-to-date
Webster, Frederick Annesley Michael
Ebbie Entwhistle series (1)
Old Ebbie returns
Webster, Frederick Annesley Michael
Ebbie Entwhistle series (2)
Old enemies
Lapierre, Janet
Meg Halloran series (3)
Old England
Gilbert, Bernard
Old England series (1)
Old English peep show
Dickinson, Peter
Superintendent James Pibble series (2)
Old enough
Goudge, Eileen
Super-seniors series (1)
Old Eve
Creighton, Basil
Amorous cheat series (2)
Old Faithful
Reese, Bob
Yellowstone critter series (5)
Old-fashioned Christmas
Dick, Alexandra
Alastair Macalastair series (2)
Old-fashioned Thanksgiving
Alcott, Louisa May
Aunt Jo's scrap-bag series (6)
Old-fashioned war
Sapir, Richard
Destroyer series (68)
Old Father Antic
Lawrence, Lars
Seed series (3)
Old flames
Mackenzie, Lee
Emmerdale Farm series (17)
Old Four-Toes
Sabin, Edward Legrand
Bar B boys series (4)
Old fox deceiv'd
Grimes, Martha
Inspector Richard Jury series (2)
Old friend of the family
Saberhagen, Fred
Dracula series (17)
Old friends, new friends
Quin-Harkin, Janet
Toni Redmond and Jill Gardner series (6)
Old Glory
Nicole, Christopher
United States Navy series (1)
Old gods laugh
Yerby, Frank
Costa Verde series (1)
Old gods waken
Wellman, Manly Wade
Silver John series (2)
Old Gorgon Graham
Lorimer, George Horace
John Graham series (2)
Old Goriot
Balzac, Honore de
Scenes of private life series (23)
Old Granny Fox
Burgess, Thornton Waldo
Green Meadow series (4)
Old hat, new hat
Berenstain, Stan
Berenstain bears series (9)
Old Home House
Lincoln, Joseph Crosby
Captain Eri series (2)
Old house
Pullen, Alan
Sam and Lin series (1)
Old Jew mystery
Adams, Herbert
Major Roger Bennion series (2)
Old judge
Haliburton, Thomas Chandler
Sam Slick series (7)
Old Judge Priest
Cobb, Irwin Shrewsbury
Judge Priest series (3)
Old June weather
Raymond, Ernest
London gallery series (15)
Old ladies
Walpole, Hugh
Provincial group series (3)
Old lady dies
Gilbert, Anthony
Scott Egerton series (9)
Old looking-glass
Charlesworth, Maria Louisa
Mrs Dorothy Cope series (1)
Old lover's ghost
Ford, Leslie
Colonel John Primrose series (6)
Grace Latham series (6)
Old maid
Balzac, Honore de
Scenes of provincial life series (7)
Wharton, Edith
Old New York quartet (2)
Old Maids' Club
Zangwill, Israel
Celibates' Club series (2)
Old maids remember
Du Maurier, Angela
Sister series (2)
Old man, and other Colonel Weatherford stories
Grand, Gordon
Colonel John Weatherford series (3)
Old man and the boy
Ruark, Robert
Old man series (1)
Old man dies
Bellairs, George
Detective Inspector Thomas Littlejohn series (57)
Old man in the corner
Orczy, Emmuska
Old man in the corner series (2)
Old man of the moors
Jardine, Warwick
Sexton Blake series (1258)
Old Man of the Mountains
Goscinny, Rene
Twelve tasks of Asterix series (10)
Old man Tutt
Train, Arthur
Ephraim Tutt series (10)
Old manor
Gregg, Cecil Freeman
Inspector Cuthbert Higgins series (23)
Old manor crime
Martyn, Wyndham
Anthony Trent series (19)
Old man's boy grows older
Ruark, Robert
Old man series (2)
Old Man's marriage
Burgin, George Brown
Four Corners series (3)
Old masters
Haggard, William
Colonel Charles Russell series (15)
Old meadow
Selden, George
Chester Cricket series (7)
Old Melbourne town before the gold rush
Cannon, Michael
Old Melbourne series (1)
Old mill
Wilson, Philip Whitwell
Sir Julian Morthoe series (3)
Old mill by the stream
Baker, Denys Val
Cornish series (7)
Old moccasins on the trail
Edson, John Thomas
Floating Outfit series (47)
Old Mortality
Scott, Walter
Tales of my landlord series (4)
Old motel mystery
Warner, Gertrude Chandler
Boxcar children series (23)
Old Mother West Wind
Burgess, Thornton Waldo
Old Mother West Wind series (1)
Old Mrs Fitzgerald
Hocking, Anne
Inspector William Austen series (4)
Old Mrs Ommanney is dead
Erskine, Margaret
Inspector Septimus Finch series (8)
Old must die
Gaines, Audrey
Chauncey O'Day series (1)
Old New York
Wharton, Edith
Old New York quartet (4)
Old order changeth
Marshall, Archibald
Clinton series (8)
Old people
Beresford, John Davys
Hillingtons trilogy (1)
Old pony
Clewes, Dorothy
Kay and Rory series (2)
Old Possum's book of practical cats
Eliot, Thomas Stearns
Old Possum series (1)
Old roses
Sandys, Oliver
Pleasure garden series (2)
Old Saxon blood
Tourney, Leonard
Matthew Stock series (5)
Old school tie
Taylor, Andrew
William Dougal series (4)
Old scores to settle
Heath, Charles
A-Team series (4)
Old silent
Grimes, Martha
Inspector Richard Jury series (10)
Old sinners never die
Davis, Dorothy Salisbury
Mrs Norris and Jasper Tully series (3)
Old stranger's secret at Sugar Creek
Hutchens, Paul
Sugar Creek Gang series (26)
Old students never die
Ross, Ivan T
Ben Gordon series (3)
Old Tasmanian prints
Craig, Clifford
Tasmanian prints series (2)
Old-timers in the Sangre de Cristos
Miller, Jim
Old-timers series (2)
Old-timers of Gun Shy
Miller, Jim
Old-timers series (1)
Old-timers on the open range
Miller, Jim
Old-timers series (3)
Old tin sorrows
Cook, Glen
Garrett series (4)
Old Tollgate mystery
Bayfield, William John
Sexton Blake series (324)
Old ugly face
Mundy, Talbot
Jimgrim series (14)
Old Vengeful
Price, Anthony
Doctor David Audley and Jack Butler series (12)
Old warriors
Gordon, Glenda
Glenda series (2)
Old ways in the new world
Conroy, Richard Timothy
Henry Scruggs series (3)
Old Whirlwind
Coatsworth, Elizabeth
Once-upon-a-time-in-America series (5)
Old Whistler Gang
Roberts, J R
Gunsmith series (71)
Old Witch and the polka dot ribbon
Devlin, Wende
Old Witch series (2)
Old Witch rescues Halloween
Devlin, Wende
Old Witch series (3)
Old wives' tale
Bennett, Arnold
Five towns series (7)
Old Wolfville
Lewis, Alfred Henry
Wolfville series (7)
Old Yeller
Gipson, Fred
Old Yeller series (1)
Old Zion
Mayne, William
Islands series (3)
Older boy
Pascal, Francine
Sweet Valley twins series (15)
Older Hardy
Gittings, Robert
Thomas Hardy series (2)
Older Mousie
Golden Gorse
Mousie series (2)
Oldest city in the world, its sieges and battles
Brown, Charles
John Bunyan series (3)
Oldtimers
Gardner, Jerome
Dripspring series (4)
Oldtown folks
Stowe, Harriet Beecher
Oldtown series (1)
Ole Devil and the Caplocks
Edson, John Thomas
Ole Devil Hardin series (2)
Ole Devil and the mule train
Edson, John Thomas
Ole Devil Hardin series (3)
Ole Devil at San Jacinto
Edson, John Thomas
Ole Devil Hardin series (4)
Ole Devil's hands and feet
Edson, John Thomas
Floating Outfit series (49)
Ole Devil Hardin series (6)
Oleg the snow leopard
Brisville, Jean Claude
Oleg series (1)
Olga carries on
Bond, Michael
Olga da Polga series (3)
Olga counts her blessings
Bond, Michael
Olga da Polga picture books series (1)
Olga makes a friend
Bond, Michael
Olga da Polga picture books series (2)
Olga makes a wish
Bond, Michael
Olga da Polga picture books series (3)
Olga makes her mark
Bond, Michael
Olga da Polga picture books series (4)
Olga meets her match
Bond, Michael
Olga da Polga series (2)
Olga Romanoff
Griffith, George Chetwynd
Romanoff series (2)
Olga takes a bite
Bond, Michael
Olga da Polga picture books series (5)
Olga takes charge
Bond, Michael
Olga da Polga series (4)
Olga, the disillusioned
Kimbrough, Katheryn
Phenwick women series (32)
Olga's new home
Bond, Michael
Olga da Polga picture books series (6)
Olga's second house
Bond, Michael
Olga da Polga picture books series (7)
Olga's special day
Bond, Michael
Olga da Polga picture books series (8)
Oliver and the amazing spy
McBrier, Michael
Oliver and company series (7)
Oliver and the lucky duck
McBrier, Page
Oliver and company series (1)
Oliver and the runaway alligator
McBrier, Michael
Oliver and company series (3)
Oliver Bright's search
Stratemeyer, Edward L
Bound to succeed series (2)
Working upward series (5)
Oliver finds a home
Korman, Justine
Oliver and company series (10)
Oliver Hastings, V.C.
Lynn, Escott
Great War series (2)
Oliver smells trouble
McBrier, Michael
Oliver and company series (8)
Oliver, the western engine
Awdry, Wilbert
Railway series (24)
Oliver's back-yard circus
McBrier, Michael
Oliver and company series (4)
Oliver's barnyard blues
McBrier, Michael
Oliver and company series (9)
Oliver's high-flying adventure
McBrier, Michael
Oliver and company series (5)
Oliver's kind women
Gibbs, Philip
Oliver series (2)
Oliver's lucky day
McBrier, Page
Oliver and company series (2)
Oliver's story
Segal, Erich
Oliver and Jenny series (2)
Olivia
Butler, Gwendoline
Inspector John Coffin series (15)
Riefe, Barbara
Shackleford legacy trilogy (1)
Olivia, the tormented
Kimbrough, Katheryn
Phenwick women series (9)
Olivia's story
Pascal, Francine
Sweet Valley High super star series (5)
Ollie's family
Solomon, Helen
Ollie series (2)
Ollie's trolley
Solomon, Helen
Ollie series (1)
Olly Onion
Reed, Giles
Munch Bunch character series (1)
Olly Onion's fancy dress party
Reed, Giles
Munch Bunch story books series (3)
Olmeg's eventful morning
Jordan, William Johnston
Olmeg series (2)
Olmeg's lucky escape
Jordan, William Johnston
Olmeg series (1)
Olmeg's tiring journey
Jordan, William Johnston
Olmeg series (3)
Olympe de Cleves
Dumas, Alexandre
Regency trilogy (3)
Olympiad
Frith, Nigel
Pangaia trilogy (3)
Olympia's inheritance
Petrocelli, Orlando Ralph
Giacomo Carlona series (2)
Olympic duty
Kirby, Jean
Scott sisters series (4)
Olympics
Gutman, Bill
Smitty series (2)
Olympics Otis
Davis, Gibbs
Never sink nine series (7)
Olympus
Moore, Alan
Miracleman series (3)

Olympus, what is the secret of the oracle?
Packard, Edward
Earth inspectors series (3)
Om
Mundy, Talbot
Cotswold Ommony series (1)
Omaha
Willoughby, Lee Davis
Americana series (4)
Omega assignment
Lewis, David
Steve Savage series (2)
Omega cage
Perry, Steve
Khadaji series (5)
Omega command
Land, Jon
Blaine McCracken series (1)
Omega document
Mackenzie, J Alexander
Canaan trilogy (1)
Omega operation
Conway, Norman
Adam Hunter series (1)
Omega Point
Zebrowski, George
Omega Point trilogy (2)
Omega Point trilogy
Zebrowski, George
Omega Point trilogy (3)
Omega rebellion
Denning, Troy
Combat Command series (3)
Star colony series (2)
Omega Station
Slote, Alfred
Danny One series (4)
Omega sub
Cameron, J D
Omega sub series (1)
Omega terror
Carter, Nick
Nick Carter series (68)
Omega threat
Washburn, Mark
Sam Boggs series (2)
Omega zone
Dever, Joe
Freeway warrior series (3)
Omen
Seltzer, David
Omen series (1)
Omens of Kregen
Prescot, Dray
Dray Prescot series (36)
Witch war series (3)
Omicron invasion
Smith, Edward Elmer
Family d'Alembert series (9)
Omicron legion
Land, Jon
Blaine McCracken series (4)
Omina uncharted
Starr, Roland
Omina series (2)
Ominous orgy
Knight, Mallory T
Man from T.O.M.C.A.T. series (7)
Omit flowers
Gaines, Audrey
Jeff Strange series (1)
Stout, Rex
Nero Wolfe and Archie Goodwin series (16)
Omnivore
Anthony, Piers
Of man and mantra trilogy (1)
Omoo
Melville, Herman
South Seas series (2)
Omruds
Postgate, Oliver
Saga of Noggin the Nog series (4)
On
Belloc, Hilaire
On series (5)
On a balcony
Stacton, David
Invincible questions trilogy (2)
Stanton, David
Invincible questions series (2)
On a crimson trail
Carter, Nicholas
Nicholas Carter series (417)
On a darkling plain
Gaye, Phoebe Fenwich
Vandervoord trilogy (3)
On a lark to the planets
Montgomery, Frances Trego
Electric elephant series (2)
On a million dollar trail
Carter, Nicholas
Nicholas Carter series (572)
On a pale horse
Anthony, Piers
Incarnations of immortality series (1)
On a pig's back
Holgate, John
Farm life series (2)
On a summer day
Lenski, Lois
Seasons series (4)
On account of murder
Powers, Elizabeth
Viera Kolarova series (2)
On alien wings
Goulart, Ron
Vampirella series (2)
On an Australian farm
Rudd, Steele
Dashwood family series (1)
On an average day
Heymann, Tom
Average series (1)
On an average day in Japan
Heymann, Tom
Average series (4)
On an average day in the Soviet Union
Heymann, Tom
Average series (2)
On anything
Belloc, Hilaire
On series (3)
On Arctic ice
Machetanz, Frederick
Andy and Panuck series (2)
On being a therapist
Kottler, Jeffrey
Therapist series (1)
On board the Mary Sands
Richards, Laura Elizabeth
Calvin Parks series (3)
On board the mine-laying cruiser
Fiske, James
World's war series (3)
On both sides of the sea
Charles, Elizabeth
Drayton family series (2)
On call
Harrison, Elizabeth
Central London Hospital series (8)
On call for trouble
Kirby, Jean
Scott sisters series (3)
On call with Doctor Finlay
Haining, Peter
Doctor Finlay series (2)
On compassionate leave
Jackson, Lewis
Sexton Blake series (1142)
On Dangerous
Winfield, Julia
Private eyes series (3)
On dangerous ground
Higgins, Jack
Sean Dillon series (2)
On eagle's wings
Howe, Doris
Kootenay series (4)
On Emu Creek
Rudd, Steele
Rudd family series (10)
On everything
Belloc, Hilaire
On series (2)
On Forsyte 'change
Galsworthy, John
End of the chapter series (3)
On General Thomas' staff
Dunn, Byron Archibald
Young Kentuckians series (2)
On guard
Garrison, Frederick
West Point series (3)
On guard, against Tory and Tarleton
True, John Preston
Revolution series (3)
On hazardous duty
Saint John, David
Peter Ward series (1)
On Her Majesty's secret service
Fleming, Ian
James Bond series (11)
On her own
Lambert, Janet
Patty and Ginger series (6)
On holiday again, Doctor?
Clifford, Robert
Doctor series (8)
On ice
Dean, Robert George
Tony Hunter series (6)
Macgregor, T J
Quin Saint James and Mike McClary series (4)
On language
Safire, William
On language series (1)
On leaving Charleston
Ripley, Alexandra
Charleston series (2)
On march
Winter, John Strange
Blankhampton series (3)
On Monday the giant
Grater, Michael
Giant series (2)
On Mother Brown's doorstep
Staples, Mary Jane
South London series (9)
On my home ground
Moffat, Gwen
Mountaineering series (2)
On my own
Roosevelt, Eleanor
On my own series (1)
On my own terms
Seymour, John
Fat of the land series (2)
On my way
Gee, Herbert Leslie
Friendly series (10)
On nothing and kindred subjects
Belloc, Hilaire
On series (1)
On our selection
Rudd, Steele
Rudd family series (1)
Rudd family series (1)
On our way to the barn
Ziefert, Harriet
On our way series (2)
On our way to the forest
Ziefert, Harriet
On our way series (3)
On our way to the water
Ziefert, Harriet
On our way series (4)
On our way to the zoo
Ziefert, Harriet
On our way series (1)
On purpose
Birch, Louis Charles
Science and religion series (1)
On something
Belloc, Hilaire
On series (4)
On Sunday the giant
Grater, Michael
Giant series (1)
On Sundays we wore white
Elias, Eileen
Lewisham series (1)
On T.V.
Dicks, Terrance
Camden Street kids series (2)
On the air and off the wall
Adams, Barbara
Kid-TV series (1)
On the Amazons
Stephens, Charles Asbury
Camping out series (6)
On the ball
Hardcastle, Michael
Mark Fox series (3)
Jeffery, Gordon
Milbury series (1)
On the banks of Plum Creek
Wilder, Laura Ingalls
Laura series (3)
On the bed of the ocean
Brooks, Edwy Searles
Sexton Blake series (227)
On the blockade
Optic, Oliver
Blue and the Gray afloat series (3)
On the borders with Andrew Jackson
McIntyre, John Thomas
Buckskin series (4)
On the boundaries of bleakness
Hancock, Niel
Wilderness of four series (3)
On the brink
Batchelor, Denzil
Inspector Johnson series (2)
Endfield, Mercedes
Ms. Squad series (2)
On the Butterfield Spur
Evans, Tabor
Longarm series (172)
On the company's service
Meacham, Ellis Kirby
Captain Percival Merewether series (2)
On the Continent
Sitwell, Osbert
England reclaimed series (3)
On the danger list
Cumberland, Marten
Saturnin Dax series (13)
On the day of the shooting
Franklin, Charles
Maxine Dangerfield series (2)
On the dead run
Murphy, Warren Burton
Edward Razoni and William Jackson series (6)
On the dodge
Newton, Dwight Bennett
Jim Bannister series (1)
On the edge
Davidson, Linda
Endless summer series (3)
Pascal, Francine
Sweet Valley High series (40)
Thornton, Jane Foster
Electric High series (4)
On the edge of the Arctic
Ashton, Lamar
Aeroplane boys series (8)
On the edge of the infinite
Butterworth, Michael
Space nineteen ninety nine series (17)
On the edge of the primeval forest
Schweitzer, Albert
Primeval forest series (1)
On the edge of the Rift
Huxley, Elspeth
Kenya childhood series (2)
On the eleven forty down
King, Hilary
Sexton Blake series (1279)
On the Erie Canal
Abbott, Jacob
Marco Paul's adventures in pursuit of knowledge series (2)
On the eve of triumph
Carter, Nicholas
Nicholas Carter series (489)
On the fur trail
Lange, Dietrich
American Indian series (16)
On the go
Maestro, Betsy Crippen
Words series (2)
On the green meadows
Burgess, Thornton Waldo
Nature stories series (1)
On the heights of Himalay
Van der Naillen, Albert
Magi trilogy (1)
On the hook
Pullen, Alan
Sam and Lin series (6)
On the inside
Wood, Ted
Reid Bennett series (7)
On the line
Hughes, Dean
Angel Park Hoop Stars series (4)
On the loose
Browne, Dik
Hagar the horrible series (8)
On the Mexican border
Hutchens, Paul
Sugar Creek Gang series (18)
On the midnight beat
Brandon, John Gordon
Sexton Blake series (793)
On the night express
Gibbons, Harry Hornaby Clifford
Sexton Blake series (378)
On the night in question
Wills, Cecil Melville
Geoffrey Boscobell series (8)
On the night of the 14th
Cross, Mark
Daphne Wrayne and her Four Adjusters series (27)
On the Oregon trail
Allen, Gina
Prairie children series (2)
On the other hand
Stevenson, Richard
Donald Strachey series (2)
On the outskirts
Dark, Sidney
Guide, philosopher and friend trilogy (3)
On the overland stage
Sabin, Edward Legrand
Great West series (3)
On the pig's back
Naughton, Bill
Saintly Billy trilogy (2)
On the Plains with Custer
Sabin, Edward Legrand
Trail blazers series (5)
On the Prime Minister's account
Hogstrand, Olle
Chief Inspector Lars Kollin series (1)
On the rack
Browne, Dik
Hagar the horrible series (9)
On the ragged edge
Carter, Nicholas
Nicholas Carter series (535)
On the red world
Kelley, Leo Patrick
Galaxy Five series (2)
On the right wrists
Livingston, Armstrong
Peter Creighton series (1)
On the road
Kerouac, Jack
Jack Duluoz series (6)
Kilroy, Sally
Toddlers' tales series (2)
On the run
Bawden, Nina
Mallory children series (2)
Pascal, Francine
Sweet Valley High super thriller series (2)
Rees, Rod
Worst day of my life series (2)
On the seas of destiny
Emerson, Ru
Nedao trilogy (3)
On the secret service of His Majesty the Queen
Weinstein, Sol
Israel Bond series (3)
On the shores of endless worlds
Tomas, Andrew
Ancient science series (2)
On the shoulders of giants
Saint Alcorn, Lloyd
Dream quest trilogy (2)
On the staff
Optic, Oliver
Blue and the Gray on land series (4)
On the stretch
Welcome, John
Richard Graham series (5)
On the stroke of nine
Parsons, Anthony
Sexton Blake series (1058)
On the torn-away world
Rockwood, Roy
Great marvel series (6)
On the town
Maestro, Betsy Crippen
Words series (4)
On the track
Verne, Jules
Captain Grant's children series (1)
On the trail of Big Finger Street
Campbell, Scott
Felix Boyd series (2)
On the trail of Geronimo
Ellis, Edward Sylvester
Wild adventure series (1)
On the trail of Pontiac
Stratemeyer, Edward L
Colonial series (4)
On the trail of the Albatross
Marsh, Jean Evelyn
Rick and Pete Clayton series (1)
On the trail of the moose
Ellis, Edward Sylvester
Wild woods series (1)
On the trail of the Sioux
Lange, Dietrich
American Indian series (1)
On the trail of the space pirates
Rockwell, Carey
Tom Corbett series (3)
On the trail of the Tumbling T
Mulford, Clarence Edward
J C series (6)
On the warpath
Schultz, James Willard
Pitamaken series (4)
On the wave
Samuels, Adelaide Florence
Dick Travers series (3)
On the way
Davis, Anne
Pumpkin Hollow series (2)
On the wings of flame
Adams, Eustace Lane
Andy Lane series (6)

On their return
Thompson, Nancy
Departing and return series (2)
On thin ice
Cole, Jennifer
Cindy and Nicole series (6)
On ticket of leave
Blake, Stacey
Sexton Blake series (737)
Brandon, John Gordon
Sexton Blake series (1024)
On time
Optic, Oliver
Lake Shore series (3)
On to Cheyenne
Cole, Jackson
Jim Hatfield series (95)
On to Pekin
Stratemeyer, Edward L
Soldiers of fortune series (1)
On top of the world
Scott, Sheila
Air pilot series (2)
On tour
Streatfeild, Noel
Vicarage series (2)
On tour with Troddles
Andom, R
Troddles series (6)
On Tuesday the giant
Grater, Michael
Giant series (3)
On Valentine's Day
Foote, Horton
Orphans' home series (2)
On with the dance
Hardwick, Michael
Upstairs, downstairs series (10)
On with Torchy
Ford, Sewell
Torchy series (3)
On your mark
Barbour, Ralph Henry
Erskine trilogy (3)
On your mark, get set, HELP!
Mallett, Jerry J
Tumtwit series (5)
Once a district officer
Bradley, Kenneth
District officer series (2)
Once a mutt
Murphy, Warren Burton
Devlin Tracy series (4)
Once a prostitute
Hunter, Alan
Inspector George Gently series (32)
Once a spy
Footman, Robert
Harry Ryder series (1)
Once a week
Milne, Alan Alexander
Day's play series (3)
Once a widow
Roberts, Lee
Doctor Clinton Shannon series (1)
Once a wilderness
Pound, Arthur
Wilderness series (1)
Once a year man
Tripp, Miles
John Samson series (2)
Once acquitted
Long, Amelia Reynolds
Steve Carter series (5)
Once again Mad's Al Jaffee spews out snappy answers to stupid questions
Jaffee, Al
Snappy answers to stupid questions series (6)
Once and always murder
Papazoglou, Orania
Patience Campbell McKenna series (5)
Once and future king
White, Terence Hanbury
Once and future king series (3)
Once, and then the funeral
Farmer, Bernard James
Sergeant Jack Wigan series (3)
Once dying, twice dead
Lewis, Royston
Eric Ward series (4)
Once I told a lie
Sanford, Doris
You'll never guess what series (1)
Once I was a bully
Sanford, Doris
You'll never guess what series (2)
Once I was a thief
Sanford, Doris
You'll never guess what series (3)
Once I was obnoxious
Sanford, Doris
You'll never guess what series (4)
Once in a lifetime
Mayo, James
Charles Hood series (4)
Once in Europa
Berger, John
Into their labours trilogy (2)
Once in the saddle
Waldo, Dale
Johnny Ross series (3)
Once in Tiger Bay
Walsh, James Morgan
Tiger Bay series (1)
Once is enough
Sargeson, Frank
Enough series (1)
Smeeton, Miles
Chronicles of Tzu Hang series (1)
Once more the hawks
Hennessy, Max
Dicken Quinney trilogy (3)
Once more the Hero
Overgard, William
Hero Haggity series (2)
Once more the Saint
Charteris, Leslie
Saint series (10)
Once more upon a totem
Harris, Christie
Totem series (2)
Once over deadly
Gruber, Frank
Johnny Fletcher and Sam Cragg series (1)
Once over lightly
Robeson, Kenneth
Doc Savage series (146)
Once there was a bagman
Ronan, Tom
Deep of the sky series (3)
Once there were bluebirds
Martin, Bill
Freedom series (8)
Once to Sinai
Prescott, Hilda Frances Margaret
Friar Felix Fabri series (2)
Once too often
Cross, Mark
Daphne Wrayne and her Four Adjusters series (45)
Once upon a crime
Monig, Christopher
Brian Brett series (3)
Once upon a gallows
Grover, Marshall
Larry and Stretch series (405)
Once upon a kiss
Garrido, Mar
Swept away series (6)
Once upon a memory
Witcomb, Nan
Thoughts of Nanushka series (10)
Once upon a private eye
Quinn, Patrick
Pete Riley series (1)
Once upon a time
Baum, Lyman Frank
Snuggle tales series (2)
Cross, Mark
Daphne Wrayne and her Four Adjusters series (46)
Once upon a time when we were colored
Taulbert, Clifton Lemoure
Once upon a time series (1)
Once upon a tombstone
Salter, Elizabeth
Inspector Michael Hornsley series (5)
Once upon a totem
Harris, Christie
Totem series (1)
Once upon another
Macdonald, Suse
Discovery series (3)
Once we had a horse
Rounds, Glen
Whitey series (13)
One against a wilderness
Chester, William L
Kioga series (3)
One against eternity
Van Vogt, Alfred Elton
Isher Empire series (2)
One against the Legion
Williamson, Jack
Legion of Space series (3)
One against time
Janson, Hank
Hank Janson series (72)
One among none
Stratton, Roy
Scott Gregory and Justin Bassett series (2)
One and last love
Braine, John
Last love series (1)
One and only two heads
Ahlberg, Janet
Two heads series (1)
One angel less
Roden, Henry Wisdom
Sid Ames series (3)
One angry man
Daniels, Norman A
Kelly Carvel series (2)
One boy too many
Chase, Emily
Canby Hall series (19)
One braver thing
Dehan, Richard
Dop Doctor series (1)
One by one they disappeared
Dalton, Moray
Inspector Hugh Collier series (1)
One clear call
Sinclair, Upton
World's end series (9)
One coffee with
Maron, Margaret
Lieutenant Sigrid Harald series (1)
One corpse missing
Ross, Zola Helen
Beau Smith and Pogy Rogers series (2)
One corpse too many
Peters, Ellis
Brother Cadfael series (2)
One cried murder
Courtier, Sidney Hobson
Ambrose Mahon series (2)
Leslie, Jean
Peter Ponsonby series (1)
One damn thing after another
Freeling, Nicolas
Arlette Van der Valk series (3)
One day event
Pullein-Thompson, Josephine
Major Holbrooke series (4)
One day in ancient Rome
Kirtland, G B
One day series (1)
One day in Aztec Mexico
Kirtland, G B
One day series (3)
One day in Elizabethan England
Kirtland, G B
One day series (2)
One day in the alpine tundra
George, Jean Craighead
One day series (2)
One day in the desert
George, Jean Craighead
One day series (1)
One day in the prairie
George, Jean Craighead
One day series (3)
One day in the tropical rain forest
George, Jean Craighead
One day series (5)
One day in the woods
George, Jean Craighead
One day series (4)
One day, my love
Bromige, Iris
Rainwood family series (10)
One dead dean
Crider, Bill
Carl Burns series (1)
One dead debutante
Gould, Heywood
Josh Krales series (1)
One dead judge
Pairo, Preston
Dallas Henry series (2)
One death in the red
Mazzaro, Ed
Undercover series (1)
One deathless hour
Ormerod, Roger
David Mallin and George Coe series (17)
One dip dead
Stein, Aaron Marc
Matt Erridge series (17)
One dog too many
Vail, Virginia
Animal Inn series (9)
One dollar death
Barth, Richard
Margaret Binton series (3)
One-dollar rip-off
Dennis, Ralph
Jim Hardman series (9)
One down and two to slay
Brinton, Henry
John and Sally Strang series (2)
One drop of blood
Austin, Anne
James F Dundee series (5)
One endless hour
Marlowe, Dan James
Earl Drake series (2)
One evil summer
Stine, Robert Lawrence
Fear Street series (25)
One-Eye
Gordon, Stuart
Eyes trilogy (1)
One-eyed death
Marvin, James W
Crow series (7)
One-eyed dream
Johnston, Terry Conrad
Titus Bass series (3)
One-eyed jacks
Martin, George Raymond Richard
Wild cards series (8)
One-eyed moon
Steen, Marguerite
Spanish trilogy (2)
One-eyed mystic
Robeson, Kenneth
Doc Savage series (111)
One false move
Roos, Kelley
Jeff and Haila Troy series (9)
One fat summer
Lipsyte, Roger
Summer trilogy (1)
One fearful yellow eye
Macdonald, John Dann
Travis McGee series (8)
One fine day
Ford, Elizabeth
Tyldens series (2)
Gee, Herbert Leslie
Friendly series (9)
One fine day the Rabbi bought a cross
Kemelman, Harry
Rabbi David Small series (9)
One flew over the cuckoo's nest
Kesey, Ken
Chief Bromden series (1)
One foot in America
Suhl, Yuri
Wooden horse series (1)
One foot in heaven
Spence, Hartzell
Parsonage series (1)
One foot in the grave
Cumberland, Marten
Saturnin Dax series (15)
Dickinson, Peter
Superintendent James Pibble series (6)
One foot on the ground
Richardson, Jean
Moth Graham series (3)
One for the book
Graham, Neill
Solo Malcolm series (28)
One for the books
Taylor, Laurie Aylma
J J Jamison series (1)
One for the devil
Leroux, Etienne
Welgevonden trilogy (2)
One for the master, tow for the fool
Townsend, Larry
Mind master series (2)
One for the money
Lambert, Janet
Candy Kane series (3)
One frog too many
Leeson, Robert
Frogs series (2)
One generation
Heath, Roy Aubrey Kelvin
Georgetown trilogy (2)
One ghost too many
Stevenson, Drew
Sarah Capshaw series (1)
One girl in a million
Tracy, Louis
Inspector Furneaux series (14)
One good death deserves another
Perry, Ritchie
Philis series (6)
One good Tern
De Selincourt, Aubrey
Rutherford series (3)
One good turn
Easton, Nat
Bill Banning series (2)
One grave too many
Goulart, Ron
John Easy series (4)
One green mesquite tree
Jernigan, Gisela
Desert trilogy (2)
One-gun justice
Winstan, Matt
Reuben Brown series (4)
One-handed gun
Roberts, J R
Gunsmith series (11)
One hell of a showdown
Grover, Marshall
Larry and Stretch series (414)
One horse race
Stone, Thomas H
Chester Fortune series (2)
One hundred and one Jubilee Road
Willis, Frederick
Edwardian London trilogy (1)
One hundred and one ways to win a homecoming queen
Kaye, Marilyn
Three of a kind series (6)
One hundred and seventeen days adrift
Bailey, Maurice
Small boat series (1)
One hundred and six thousand dollars blood money
Hammett, Dashiell
Continental Op series (3)
One hundred and twelve Elm Street
Ripperger, Henrietta
Elm Street series (1)
One hundred and twenty hour clock
Nevins, Francis Michael
Loren Mensing series (3)
One hundred and twenty-eight witnesses
Mottram, Ralph Hale
Geoffrey Skene series (5)
One hundred caps and all that
Wright, Billy
Football captain series (4)
One hundred dollar misunderstanding
Gover, Robert
Kitten series (1)
One hundred fathoms under
Blaine, John
Rick Brant series (4)
One hundred megaton kill
Hayes, Ralph Eugene
Check Force series (1)
One hundred per-cent laugh riot
Zindel, Paul
Wacky facts lunch bunch series (4)
One hundred scenes from married life
Gordon, Giles
Edward series (2)
One hundred thousand dollar kiss
Carter, Nicholas
Nicholas Carter series (582)
One hundred thousand pound insurance swindle
Sayer, Walter William
Sexton Blake series (449)
One hundred years of solitude
Garcia Marquez, Gabriel
Macondo series (3)
One hundredth thing about Caroline
Lowry, Lois
Caroline Tate series (1)
One is one
Rankine, John
Dag Fletcher series (5)
One jump ahead
Chapman, Robert
Rex Banner series (1)
Smythe, Pat
Show jumping series (2)
One lady, two cats
Lockridge, Richard
Cats series (6)
One land, one duke
Emerson, Ru
Night-threads series (3)
One law
Price, Roger
Tomorrow people series (4)
One light, one sun
Raffi
Raffi songs to read series (3)
One lonely knight
Collins, Max Allan
Mike Hammer series (13)
One lonely night
Spillane, Mickey
Mike Hammer series (5)

One love is enough
Benzoni, Juliette
Catherine Legoix series (1)
One lover too many
Tripp, Miles
John Samson series (7)
One mad last embrace
Story, Jack Trevor
Horace Spurgeon Fenton series (2)
One mad night
Reach, James
Wing series (1)
One man against the drylands
Benton, Peggie
Drylands series (1)
One-man army
Cutter, John
Specialist series (8)
One man came back
Erskine, Laurie York
Douglas Renfrew series (8)
One man in his time
Janson, Hank
Hank Janson series (2)
One-man jury
Ransome, Stephen
Lieutenant Lee Barcello series (2)
Stone, Ned
Other Day Logan series (4)
One man jury
Grover, Marshall
Nevada Jim series (6)
One-man massacre
Ward, Jonas
Tom Buchanan series (4)
One man, one gun
Chisholm, Matt
Storm family series (5)
One man saw them die
Webb, Anthony
Mister Pendlebury series (6)
One-man show
Innes, Michael
Sir John Appleby series (13)
One man with courage
Thompson, Thomas
Bonanza series (2)
One man's art
Roberts, Nora
Flowers series (17)
Macgregor series (4)
One man's death
Truss, Seldon
Inspector Gidleigh series (15)
One man's enemies
Truss, Seldon
Inspector Gidleigh series (15)
One man's justice
Alding, Peter
C.I.D. Room series (14)
One man's meat
Watson, Colin
Inspector Purbright series (9)
One man's medicine
Gibson, Morris
One man series (1)
One man's muddle
Quinn, Eleanor Baker
James Strange series (1)
One man's murder
Delman, David
Lieutenant Jacob Horowitz series (4)
One man's poison
Fox, Sebastian
George Lydney series (1)
Riggs, John Raymond
Garth Ryland series (6)
One mean town
Grover, Marshall
Larry and Stretch series (359)
One million dead
Gironella, Jose Maria
Alvear family trilogy (2)
One million francs
Fredericks, Arnold
Richard Duvall series (2)
One million pound film murder
Stuart, Donald
Sexton Blake series (775)
One million pound plot
Skene, Anthony
Sexton Blake series (672)
One-minute murder
Brandon, John Gordon
Arthur Stukeley Pennington series (3)
Inspector Patrick Aloysius McCarthy series (5)
One more showdown
Grover, Marshall
Larry and Stretch series (228)
One more summer
De Selincourt, Aubrey
Rutherford series (4)
One morning in Maine
McCloskey, Robert
Sal series (2)
One murder too many
Coxe, George Harmon
Flash Casey series (4)
Lanham, Edwin
Lieutenant Madigan series (3)
Ransome, Stephen
Professor Cyrus Hatch series (1)
One murdered, two dead
Propper, Milton
Tommy Rankin series (8)
One must die
Cunningham, Albert Benjamin
Sheriff Jess Roden series (12)
One must survive
Charles, Robert
Simon Larren series (2)
One night in London
Andrews, Lucilla
Saint Martha's Hospital series (11)
Wally's Ward series (1)
One night in Santa Anna
Metcalfe, Thomas Washington
Santa Anna trilogy (1)
One night stand
Murphy, Warren Burton
Edward Razoni and William Jackson series (1)
One night to kill
Franklin, Charles
Grant Garfield series (7)
One night with Nora
Halliday, Brett
Michael Shayne series (24)
One notch to death
Chisholm, Matt
Storm family series (4)
One object in life
Carter, Nicholas
Nicholas Carter series (557)
One of Berrian's novels
Stone, C H
Looking backward sequels series (2)
One of my sons
Green, Anna Katharine
Amelia Butterworth series (4)
Ebenezer Gryce series (10)
One of our agents is missing
Saint John, David
Peter Ward series (6)
One of our pigeons is missing
Holdstock, Robert
Bulman series (2)
One of seven
Hardinge, Rex
Sexton Blake series (1055)
One of the crowd
Du Jardin, Rosamond
Tobey and Midge Heydon series (6)
One of the eleven
Tyrer, Walter
Sexton Blake series (1249)
One of the Flying Squad
Graydon, William Murray
Sexton Blake series (179)
One of the gang
Pascal, Francine
Sweet Valley twins series (10)
One of the Raymonds
Rikhoff, Jean
Butte family series (2)
One of them
Frankau, Gilbert
One of us series (2)
One of these days
Thomson, Pat
Share-a-story series (2)
One of us
Frankau, Gilbert
One of us series (1)
One old Oxford ox
Williams, Ferelith Eccles
Oxford Ox trilogy (1)
One on one
King, Tabitha
Nodd's Ridge series (4)
One on the house
Lasswell, Mary
Mrs Feeley series (3)
One page missing
Soutar, Andrew
Phineas Spinnet series (8)
One pair of feet
Dickens, Monica
One pair series (2)
One pair of hands
Dickens, Monica
One pair series (1)
One positive hope
Winn, Godfrey
Infirm glory series (2)
One quest, hold the dragons
Costikyan, Greg
Dungeon series (2)
One rainy day
McKimmie, Christopher
Magic day series (3)
One red rose for Christmas
Horgan, Paul
Humble powers trilogy (2)
One remained seated
Slate, John
Black Maria series (3)
One rose less
Flower, Pat
Inspector Swinton series (4)
One sane man
Beeding, Francis
Colonel Alastair Granby series (8)
One shall be taken
Hocking, Anne
Inspector William Austen series (8)
One shipwreck too many
Carter, Nicholas
Nicholas Carter series (577)
One shot dead
Petievich, Gerald
Charles Carr and Jack Kelly series (2)
One shot for Sadie
Brody, Marc
Marc Brody series (74)
One sister too many
Adler, Carole Schwerdtfeger
Sisters series (2)
One small footprint
Weir, Molly
Feet series (6)
One small step
Hill, Reginald
Superintendent Andrew Dalziel and Sergeant Pascoe series (18)
One special summer
Harrell, Janice
Two by two series (5)
One step too far
Carter, Nicholas
Nicholas Carter series (289)
Quin-Harkin, Janet
Sugar and spice series (19)
One stormy day at Sugar Creek
Hutchens, Paul
Sugar Creek Gang series (10)
One summer
Roberts, Nora
Flowers series (31)
One summer on Majorca
Hoberg, Marielis
Heiner and Elsie series (1)
One tear for my grave
Roscoe, Mike
Johnny April series (4)
One term at Utopia
Hope, Jane
Teaching series (3)
One that got away
McCloy, Helen
Basil Willing series (7)
One thousand and one shoplifters
Smyth, Robin
Roger Moore and the Crimefighters series (2)
One thousand dollar death
Brady, William S
Peacemaker series (7)
One thousand dollar target
Grover, Marshall
Nevada Jim series (11)
One thrilling night
Berrow, Norman
Inspector Courtenay series (2)
One ticket to Sun Rock
Grover, Marshall
Larry and Stretch series (362)
One to jump
Douglas, George
Inspector Hallam and Sergeant Spratt series (11)
One to play
Adams, Herbert
Major Roger Bennion series (21)
One too many
Chan, Melissa
Inspector Joe Barnaby and Francesca Miles series (2)
One too many mornings
Sandon, J D
Gringos series (7)
One touch of blood
Baker, Samm Sinclair
Clark Clark Clark series (1)
One tough hombre
Hohl, Joan
Vanzant family trilogy (2)
One tree
Donaldson, Stephen Reeder
Second chronicles of Thomas Covenant series (2)
One true Santa
Ahlberg, Janet
Daisychain series (9)
One, two, buckle my shoe
Christie, Agatha
Hercule Poirot series (21)
One, two, button my shoe
McGee, Shelagh
Little nursery rhyme series (4)
One two flea!
Ahlberg, Allan
Red nose readers series (13)
One-two-three die
Starr, Leonard
Kelly Green series (4)
One two three four five six seven eight nine Benn
McKee, David
Mister Benn series (2)
One, two, three, go!
Killingback, Julia
Busy Bears series (4)
One two three murders
Gerard, Francis
Sir John Meredith series (2)
One, two, three with Ant and Bee
Banner, Angela
Ant and Bee series (3)
One, two, three with Waldo
Wilhelm, Hans
Waldo series (6)
One-upmanship
Potter, Stephen
Lifemanship Correspondence College series (3)
One-way cemetery
Hinxman, Margaret
Detective Inspector Ralph Brand series (2)
One-way deal
Ball, Brian Neville
Keegan series (2)
One way of living
Bridie, James
Mavor series (2)
One way only
Grant, Gwen
Private, keep out series (3)
One way split
Janson, Hank
Hank Janson series (236)
One way street
Macdonald, Peter G
Open road quartet (3)
Marino, Nick
Mike Macauley series (1)
One-way ticket
Howard, Hartley
Glenn Bowman series (37)
One way to die
Dancer, J B
Lawmen series (6)
One who walked alone
Ellis, Novalyne Price
Robert Ervin Howard series (1)
One woman
Ollivant, Alfred
Two worlds series (2)
One woman's story
Tibble, Anne
Greenhorn trilogy (2)
One wore blue
Graham, Heather
Civil War trilogy (1)
One writer's way
Yates, Elizabeth
One writer's trilogy (3)
One year of grace
Gielgud, Val
Years series (2)
One year of life
Roberts, Cecil
Half way series (2)
One zillion valentines
Modell, Frank B
Milton and Marvin series (3)
Onions in the stew
Macdonald, Betty
Who me series (4)
Onlookers
Avery, Gillian
Onlookers series (2)
Only a dream away
Makris, Kathryn
Two by two series (4)
Only a girl's heart
Southworth, Emma Dorothy Eliza Nevitte
Gertrude Haddon trilogy (1)
Only a matter of time
Clinton-Baddeley, Victor Clinton
Doctor Davie series (3)
Only an Irish boy
Alger, Horatio
Victory trilogy (1)
Only bank in town
Grover, Marshall
Larry and Stretch series (186)
Only boy in the ring
Grossman, Nancy Livright
Dutch Mill Stable series (4)
Only child
Kirkup, James
Only child series (1)
O'Connor, Frank
Only child series (1)
Only Fiona
Keller, Beverly
Fiona series (3)
Only good Apple in a barrel of spies
Lovell, Marc
Appleton Porter series (7)
Only good priest
Zubro, Mark Richard
Stonewall Inn series (2)
Only half a hoax
Taylor, Laurie Aylma
J J Jamison series (2)
Only her hairdresser knew
Carpenter, Carleton
Chester Long series (1)
Only in L.A.
Sinclair, Murray
Ben Crandel series (2)
Only me from over the sea
Treloar, Bruce
Baggable tales series (2)
Only nine chairs
McDaniel, Becky Bring
Jewish tales series (1)
Only on Tuesdays
Dewey, Thomas Blanchard
Pete Schofield series (7)
Only one woof
Herriot, James
Pets series (2)
Only one year
Alliluyeva, Svetlana
Letters to a friend series (2)
Only parent
Rich, Louise Dickinson
Woods series (4)
Only security
Mann, Jessica
Thea Crawford series (1)
Only son
Bobin, John William
Sexton Blake series (119)
Only the dead know Brooklyn
Boyle, Thomas
Detective Francis De Sales series (1)
Only the gallant
Newcomb, Kerry
McQueen family series (3)
Only the good die
Barker, Wade
Ninja Master series (8)
Only the guilty
Stein, Aaron Marc
Tim Mulligan and Elsie Mae Hunt series (3)
Only the rich die young
Pentecost, Hugh
Lieutenant Pascal series (4)
Only the very rich?
Brown, Carter
Danny Boyd series (19)
Only victor
Kent, Alexander
Captain Richard Bolitho series (19)
Only way is up
Grover, Marshall
Larry and Stretch series (317)
Only with a bargepole
Porter, Joyce
Edmund Brown series (4)
Onward virgin soldiers
Thomas, Leslie
Virgin soldiers series (2)
Oodles of oddlies
Jennings, Paul Francis
Oddly series (9)

Oola Oyster
Reese, Bob
Ocean critterland series (4)
Oolak's brother
Helmericks, Bud
Bob Hamilton series (1)
Oops
Mayer, Mercer
Ah-choo series (3)
Opal
Hoover, Bessie Ray
Flickinger series (2)
Opal murder case
Symons, Beryl
Inspector Henry Doight series (3)
Open city
Miller, Hugh
McBain family series (1)
Open contract
Scarpetta, Frank
Marksman series (10)
Open country
Hewlett, Maurice
Sanchia and John Maxwell Senhouse series (2)
Open door
Lutyens, Mary
Krishnamurti series (3)
Meynell, Laurence Walter
Hooky Hefferman series (18)
Stark, Freya
Traveller's letters series (2)
Open-eyed conspiracy
Howells, William Dean
Mister and Mrs March series (5)
Open fields
Yeh, Chun-Chan
Quiet are the mountains series (2)
Open fire
Hudson, Alec
Submarine series (4)
Open for business
Sloan, Carolyn
Mall series (2)
Open gate
Pullein-Thompson, Christine
Seashore School of Equitation series (2)
Open heart
Buechner, Frederick
Leo Bebb tetralogy (2)
Open house
Innes, Michael
Sir John Appleby series (26)
Open mouth
Urquhart, Macgregor
Chief Inspector Joshua Smarles series (8)
Open season
Dixon, Franklin W
Hardy boys case files series (59)
Mayor, Archer Huntington
Lieutenant Joe Gunther series (1)
Open secret
Morrison, Emmeline
Lovells trilogy (3)
Open secrets
Humphreys, Emyr
Amy Parry series (5)
Open the door
Tarsky, Sue
Chatterbox series (2)
Open the gate
Dubrovin, Vivian
Saddle up series (4)
Open verdict
Keverne, Richard
Inspector Mace series (2)
Rhode, John
Doctor Lancelot Priestley series (63)
Open window
Ormerod, Roger
Richard Patton series (5)
Opening
Ramsay, Jay
Great return series (1)
Opening bars
Hughes, Spike
Opening bars series (1)
Opening door
Reilly, Helen
Inspector Christopher McKee series (15)
Opening night
Marsh, Ngaio
Inspector Roderick Alleyn series (16)
Opening the iron trail
Sabin, Edward Legrand
Great West series (4)
Opening the West with Lewis and Clark
Sabin, Edward Legrand
Trail blazers series (9)
Opera club
Masson, Sophie
Seyrac family series (1)
Operation Afrika
Whiting, Charles
Destroyer series (1)
Operation Aladdin
Finkel, George
Sabotage series (2)
Operation Alcestis
Rennert, Maggie
Guy Silvestri series (2)
Operation Alpha Death
Conway, Norman
Adam Hunter series (2)
Operation Apocalypse
De Villiers, Gerard
Malko Linge series (6)
Operation Apricot
Haddad, Carolyn A
David Haham series (2)
Operation Asteroids
Jennison, John William
Thunderbirds series (5)
Operation Atlantis
Braun, Maurice-Gilles
Al Glenne series (3)
Operation Barbarossa
Newman, Bernard
Papa Pontivy series (12)
Operation Black Fang
Mackenzie, Jake
Secret files of Dakota King series (1)
Operation Black Sea
Davies, W X
Countdown WWIII series (2)
Operation Blindbell
Burr, Sybil
Holly Gordon series (5)
Operation Boudoir
O'Shea, Sean
Valentine Flynn series (2)
Operation Breakthrough
Marlowe, Dan James
Earl Drake series (5)
Operation Buffalo
Nolan, Keith William
Vietnam War series (5)
Operation Calpurnia
Rennert, Maggie
Guy Silvestri series (3)
Operation Carlo
Pendower, Jacques
Slade McGinty series (2)
Operation Caroline
Gibbs-Smith, Charles Harvard
Paul Harvard series (1)
Operation Caucasian Fox
Whiting, Charles
Destroyer series (3)
Operation cemetery
Jenkins, Jerry Bruce
Tara Chadwick series (3)
Operation chaos
Bennett, Dorothy
Allardyce series (2)
Operation Che Guevara
Carter, Nick
Nick Carter series (49)
Operation Checkmate
Marlowe, Dan James
Earl Drake series (6)
Operation Choke Point
Davies, W X
Countdown WWIII series (3)
Operation Cobra
Smith, Frederick Escreet
Six Three Three Squadron series (5)
Operation cocaine
Romano, Don
Mafia series (2)
Operation Columbus
Walters, Hugh
Chris Godfrey series (3)
Operation Conquest
Gray, Berkeley
Norman Conquest series (23)
Operation Convoy
Caniff, Milton
Steve Canyon series (3)
Operation Counter-Scorch
Cort, Ned
Boxer Unit SS series (3)
Operation Counterpunch
Marlowe, Dan James
Earl Drake series (12)
Operation Crucible
Smith, Frederick Escreet
Six Three Three Squadron series (3)
Operation Cuttlefish
Mounce, David R
Paul Fox series (2)
Operation Dancing Dog
Fox, James M
Steve Harvester series (2)
Operation, deadline
Dines, Michael
Johnny Manning series (1)
Operation deadly decoy
Stine, Robert Lawrence
Find your fate: G.I. Joe series (7)
Operation death-ray
Stine, Harlan William
Find your fate: G.I. Joe series (8)
Operation death stone
Siegel, Barbara
Find your fate: G.I. Joe series (6)
Operation death watch
Kessler, Leo
Submarine series (2)
Operation Deathmaker
Marlowe, Dan James
Earl Drake series (11)
Operation Deep Six
Stanton, Ken
Aquanauts series (7)
Operation Desert Son
Heath, Charles
A-Team series (6)
Operation destruct
Nicole, Christopher
Jonathan Anders series (1)
Operation Diver
Jackson, Robert
Flying Officer George Yeoman series (6)
Operation doctors
Roth, Holly
Inspector Medford series (2)
Operation Doomsday
Kenyon, Paul
Baroness Penelope Saint-John Orsini series (5)
Pearl, Jack
Space Eagle series (1)
Operation Dragnet
Thorne, Ernest Pollett
Major Brains Cunningham series (15)
Operation dragon fire
Sno, William
Find your fate: G.I. Joe series (2)
Operation Drumfire
Marlowe, Dan James
Earl Drake series (7)
Operation Eel Island
Caniff, Milton
Steve Canyon series (5)
Operation Endless Hour
Marlowe, Dan James
Earl Drake series (2)
Operation exile
Price, Edgar Hoffmann
Operation series (3)
Operation Exocet
Hardy, Adam
Strike Force Falklands series (1)
Operation Fireball
Marlowe, Dan James
Earl Drake series (3)
Operation Firedog
Jackson, Robert
Flying Officer George Yeoman series (9)
Operation Flashpoint
Marlowe, Dan James
Earl Drake series (4)
Operation Foo Ling
Caniff, Milton
Steve Canyon series (4)
Operation Fox Hunt
Whiting, Charles
Destroyer series (3)
Operation Getafix
Uderzo, Albert
Asterix series (30)
Operation Getaway
Seth, Ronald
Brian Grant series (1)
Operation Halter
King, Frank
Dormouse series (13)
Operation Hammerlock
Marlowe, Dan James
Earl Drake series (10)
Operation high dragon
Stine, George Harry
Warbots series (5)
Operation hijack
Romano, Don
Mafia series (3)
Operation hit man
Romano, Don
Mafia series (4)
Operation Honeymoon
King, Frank
Dormouse series (14)
Operation Hong Kong
McCurtin, Peter
Jim Rainey series (7)
Operation Ice Cap
Dark, James
Mark Kingsley Hood series (14)
Operation Icicle
Buck, Peter
Marc Dean series (4)
Operation Il Duce
Whiting, Charles
Destroyer series (4)
Operation iron fist
Stine, George Harry
Warbots series (7)
Operation Isis
Price, Edgar Hoffmann
Operation series (4)
Operation Jackal
Dark, James
Mark Kingsley Hood series (7)
Macdonnell, James Edmond
Dutchy Holland series (21)
Operation Jealousy
Braun, Maurice-Gilles
Al Glenne series (2)
Operation jungle doom
Beach, Lynn
Find your fate: G.I. Joe series (12)
Operation K
Daniels, Norman A
Man from A.P.E. series (4)
Operation Kill Ike
Whiting, Charles
Destroyer series (5)
Operation, kill or be killed
Dines, Michael
Johnny Manning series (3)
Operation killer comet
Ballard, S M
Find your fate: G.I. Joe series (18)
Operation Kuwait
Arvay, Harry
Israeli Security Branch series (2)
Operation Lama
Seth, Ronald
Brian Grant series (2)
Operation loan shark
Romano, Don
Mafia series (5)
Operation longlife
Price, Edgar Hoffmann
Operation series (2)
Operation love
Pascal, Francine
Sweet Valley High series (103)
Operation Manhattan
Edmonds, Harry
Hugh Brodie series (2)
Operation Manhunt
Coles, Manning
Tommy Hambledon series (15)
Operation manhunt
Nicole, Christopher
Jonathan Anders series (2)
Operation master planet
Smith, Gregory Jon
StarQuest series (2)
Operation McMurdo Sound
Carter, Nick
Nick Carter series (166)
Operation Mermaid
Stanton, Ken
Aquanauts series (11)
Operation midnight
Barrie, Alexander
Jonathan Kane series (2)
Operation Mind Murder
Rosenberger, Joseph
Death Merchant series (34)
Operation mindbender
Stine, Robert Lawrence
Find your fate: G.I. Joe series (9)
Operation misfit
Price, Edgar Hoffmann
Operation series (1)
Operation Moon Rocket
Carter, Nick
Nick Carter series (32)
Operation N
Daniels, Norman A
Man from A.P.E. series (5)
Operation Neptune
Nicole, Christopher
Jonathan Anders series (3)
Operation New York
De Villiers, Gerard
Malko Linge series (2)
Operation night flight
Sno, William
Find your fate: G.I. Joe series (10)
Operation Norfolk
Ramm, Carl
James Hawker series (11)
Operation North Africa
Davies, W X
Countdown WWIII series (1)
Operation Nuke
Caidin, Martin
Six Million Dollar Man series (3)
Operation Obliterate
Janson, Hank
Hank Janson series (237)
Operation Octopus
Dark, James
Mark Kingsley Hood series (11)
Operation Omina
Starr, Roland
Omina series (1)
Operation Ormer
Seth, Ronald
Brian Grant series (3)
Operation Overkill
Marlowe, Dan James
Earl Drake series (1)
Rosenberger, Joseph
Death Merchant series (2)
Operation Pax
Innes, Michael
Sir John Appleby series (12)
Operation Peeg
Gathorne-Hardy, Jonathan
Jane Charrington series (2)
Operation Persian Gulf
Davies, W X
Countdown WWIII series (4)
Operation Petrograd
Carter, Nick
Nick Carter series (220)
Operation piracy
Somers, Paul
Hugh Curtis and Mollie Bourne series (2)
Operation poison dart
Stine, Harlan William
Find your fate: G.I. Joe series (16)
Operation porno
Romano, Don
Mafia series (1)
Operation Retriever
Seth, Ronald
Brian Grant series (1)
Operation Rhine Maiden
Smith, Frederick Escreet
Six Three Three Squadron series (2)
Operation robot assassin
Macrae, G V
Find your fate: G.I. Joe series (4)
Operation Royal Family
Null, Gary
Secret circle series (2)
Operation S-L
Daniels, Norman A
Man from A.P.E. series (8)
Operation Scuba
Dark, James
Mark Kingsley Hood series (10)
Operation Sea Monster
Stanton, Ken
Aquanauts series (10)
Operation Seabird
Edwards, Monica
Romney Marsh series (10)
Operation Sharkbite
Carter, Nick
Nick Carter series (187)
Operation Sherlock
Coville, Bruce
A.I. Gang series (1)
Operation sink or swim
Siegel, Barbara
Find your fate: G.I. Joe series (17)
Operation sky-drop
Brogan, Mike
Action Man series (4)
Operation Skyhook
Rosenberger, Joseph
Death Merchant series (47)
Operation Smuggle
Clewes, Dorothy
Hadley family series (8)
Operation Snake
Carter, Nick
Nick Carter series (51)

Operation Snatch
Marsh, John
Ray Felton series (2)
Operation snow job
Siegel, Barbara
Find your fate: G.I. Joe series (13)
Operation Snowflower
Caniff, Milton
Steve Canyon series (2)
Operation Stalag
Whiting, Charles
Destroyer series (2)
Operation star raider
Affabee, Eric
Find your fate: G.I. Joe series (1)
Operation Star Voyage
Pearl, Jack
Space Eagle series (2)
Operation Starvation
Carter, Nick
Nick Carter series (17)
Operation steel band
Stine, George Harry
Warbots series (2)
Operation Steelfish
Stanton, Ken
Aquanauts series (8)
Operation Stranglehold
Marlowe, Dan James
Earl Drake series (8)
Operation sunpower
Duff, Douglas Valder
Jeremy series (3)
Operation Susie
Blake, Ken
Professionals series (15)
Operation T
Daniels, Norman A
Man from A.P.E. series (6)
Operation terror
Gordons
John Ripley series (4)
Operation terror trap
Stine, Harlan William
Find your fate: G.I. Joe series (3)
Operation thunderbolt
Edwards, K C
Find your fate: G.I. Joe series (14)
Operation Thunderbolt
Rosenberger, Joseph
Death Merchant series (31)
Operation tiger strike
Sno, William
Find your fate: G.I. Joe series (19)
Operation time machine
Beach, Lynn
Find your fate: G.I. Joe series (15)
Operation Titan
Horvat, Dilwyn
Operation Titan series (1)
Smith, Frederick Escreet
Six Three Three Squadron series (6)
Operation, to kill a man
Dines, Michael
Johnny Manning series (2)
Operation Tombola
Farran, Roy
Special Air Service series (2)
Operation urgent
Scott, Sutherland
Doctor Septimus Dodds series (8)
Operation V2
Channel, A R
Fighting Four series (3)
Operation Valkyrie
Smith, Frederick Escreet
Six Three Three Squadron series (4)
Operation VC
Daniels, Norman A
Man from A.P.E. series (7)
Operation Vendetta
Carter, Nick
Nick Carter series (177)
Operation Vengeance
Crane, Robert
Ben Corbin series (3)
Operation weapons disaster
Ward, James Michael
Find your fate: G.I. Joe series (11)
Operation Weatherkill
Edwards, Paul
John Eagle series (13)
Operation Werewolf
Whiting, Charles
Destroyer series (6)
Operation Whiplash
Marlowe, Dan James
Earl Drake series (9)
Operation Wild Goose
Pertwee, Roland
Patrick Faraday series (4)
Operation, World War Three
Milton, Joseph
Bart Gould series (8)
Operational immediate
Macdonnell, James Edmond
Captain Peter Bentley series (49)
Ophelia, the anxious
Kimbrough, Katheryn
Phenwick women series (18)
Opinions of a cheerful Yankee
Bacheller, Irving
Cheerful Yankee trilogy (2)
Opinions of Jerome Coignard
France, Anatole
Abbe Coignard series (2)
Opium generals, and other stories
Moorcock, Michael
Jerry Cornelius series (7)
Opium hunter
Kilgore, Axel
They call me the Mercenary series (4)
Opium queen
Longtree, Warren T
Ruff Justice series (22)
Opperman case
Bentley, John
Sir Richard Herrivell series (4)
Oppermanns
Feuchtwanger, Lion
Waiting-room tetralogy (2)
Oppidan
Leslie, Shane
Oppidan trilogy (1)
Opportunities
Warner, Susan Bagert
Opportunities series (2)
Opposite sex is driving me crazy
Vedral, Joyce Lauretta
Driving me crazy series (2)
Opposite the cross keys
Haymon, Sylvia T
East Anglian childhood series (1)
Opposite uncle
Johnston, William
Bewitched series (2)
Opposites
Allington, Richard L
Beginning to learn series (3)
Hill, Eric
Peek-a-book series (2)
Opposites attract
Roberts, Nora
Flowers series (9)
Option to die
Crews, Lary
Veronica Slate series (3)
Or be he dead
Carmichael, Harry
John Piper and Quinn series (14)
Or murder for free
Potter, J L
Jeff Tyler series (3)
Or the bambino dies
Inchbald, Peter
Inspector Franco Corti series (4)
Or was he pushed?
Lockridge, Richard
Nathan Shapiro series (10)
'Orace and Co.
Howard, Francis Morton
Happy Rascals series (3)
Oracle
Cook, Hugh
Chronicles of an age of darkness series (3)
Resnick, Mike
Oracle trilogy (2)
Orange axe
Flynn, Brian
Anthony Bathurst series (9)
Orange divan
Williams, Valentine
Inspector Manderton series (2)
Orange knight of Oz
Suter, Jon Michael
Mustard jar series (2)
Oz series (43)
Orange necktie
Fry, Pete
Pete Fry series (11)
Orange Street and Brickhole Lane
Arnold, Ralph
Orange Street series (2)
Orange-tree mystery
Rowland, John
Inspector Shelley series (17)
Oranges and UFOs
Leeson, Muriel
Promise keeper series (1)
Orbital decay
Steele, Allen
Orbital decay series (1)
Orbiting Omega
Pendleton, Don
Mack Bolan series (66)
Orbitsville
Shaw, Bob
Orbitsville trilogy (1)
Orbitsville departure
Shaw, Bob
Orbitsville trilogy (2)
Orbitsville judgement
Shaw, Bob
Orbitsville trilogy (3)
Orc wars
Dalmas, John
Nils Jarnhan series (2)
Orchard
Grant, Charles Lewis
Oxrun Station series (10)
Orchard-land
Chambers, Robert William
Land series (2)
Orchard of the crescent moon
Nimmo, Jenny
Snow spider trilogy (2)
Orchard secret
Garis, Cleo Fausta
Arden Blake series (3)
Orchid
Nathan, Robert
Barly fields series (4)
Orchid trilogy
Brooke, Jocelyn
Orchid trilogy (3)
Orchids for Biggles
Johns, William Earl
Biggles series (68)
Orchids to murder
Footner, Hulbert
Amos Lee Mappin series (10)
Orchids with murder
Morris, Thomas Baden
Inspector Headley series (4)
Orc's opal
Anthony, Piers
Dragon series (4)
Orcutt girls
Vaile, Carlotte Marion
Orcutt girls series (1)
Ordeal
Ahern, Jerry
Survivalist series (17)
Macdonnell, James Edmond
Captain Peter Bentley series (15)
Tolstoi, Aleksei Nikolaevich
Ordeal trilogy (3)
Ordeal by ice
Mowat, Farley
Top of the world trilogy (1)
Ordeal in otherwise
Norton, Andre
Planet Warlock series (2)
Ordeal of Alick Hillersdon
Graydon, William Murray
Sexton Blake series (48)
Ordeal of Elizabeth
Russell, Mary Annette
Elizabeth series (4)
Ordeal of Mansart
Du Bois, William Edward Burghardt
Black flame trilogy (1)
Ordeal of the Seventh Carrier
Albano, Peter
Seventh Carrier series (8)
Order of assassins
Wilson, Colin
Murder series (3)
Order of release
Stacpoole, Henry de Vere
Old Paris series (1)
Order of the octopus
Horler, Sydney
Paul Vivanti series (1)
Orderly man
Bogarde, Dirk
Orderly man series (3)
Orders for Cameron
McCutchan, Philip
Donald Cameron series (7)
Orders to poach
Fitz Roy, Olivia
Stewarts series (1)
Ordinary accident
Amberley, Richard
Inspector Martin series (3)
Ordinary champions
Groten, Dallas
Winning series (3)
Ordinary day
Brinton, Henry
John and Sally Strang series (7)
Ordinary Jack
Cresswell, Helen
Bagthorpes series (1)
Ordinary life
Capek, Karel
Truth and democracy trilogy (3)
Ordways
Humphrey, William
Red River County trilogy (2)
Oregon!
Ross, Dana Fuller
Wagons West series (4)
Oregon bride
Bittner, F Rosanne
Brides series (4)
Oregon invasion
Tannehill, Jayne
V series (15)
Oregon legacy
Ross, Dana Fuller
Holt family series (1)
Oregon strangler
Roberts, J R
Gunsmith series (116)
Organ hunters
Thomas, Gordon
David Morton series (3)
Organ speaks
Lorac, E C R
Inspector Macdonald series (8)
Organization
Anthony, David
Stanley Bass series (1)
Organizer
Macdonald, Donald
Tommy Briggs series (3)
Orgy at Madame Dracula's
Paul, F W
Man from S.T.U.D. series (2)
Orgy in orbit
Tea, Traves
Luke Skywalker series (7)
Orielton
Lockley, Ronald Mathias
Island farm series (8)
Orient
Halliburton, Richard
Book of marvels series (2)
Orient affair
Scott, Michael William
Rakehell dynasty series (3)
Oriental adventures
Cook, David
Advanced dungeons and dragons adventure gamebook series (15)
Origin of a vendetta
Ahern, Jerry
Dan Track series (5)
Origin of evil
Queen, Ellery
Ellery Queen series (28)
Origin of the crabs
Smith, Guy Newman
Crabs series (3)
Original carcase
Bagby, George
Inspector Schmidt series (12)
Original letters of Alexander Botts
Upson, William Hazlett
Alexander Botts series (7)
Original sin
Pulver, Mary Monica
Kori McLeod Price and Peter Brichter series (4)
Origins of the English library
Irwin, Raymond
English library series (1)
Orinoco runs away
Beresford, Elisabeth
Little Wombles series (2)
Oriole's adventures
Marlowe, Amy Bell
Oriole series (3)
Orion
Bova, Ben
Orion series (1)
Orion in the dying time
Bova, Ben
Orion series (3)
Orion's sword
Bretnor, Reginald
Future at war series (3)
Orkney Islands
Abbott, Jacob
Florence series (3)
Orlando and the three Graces
Hale, Kathleen
Orlando series (16)
Orlando at the brazen threshold
Colegate, Isabel
King family series (2)
Orlando King
Colegate, Isabel
King family series (1)
Orlando the judge
Hale, Kathleen
Orlando series (10)
Orlando, the marmalade cat, a camping holiday
Hale, Kathleen
Orlando series (1)
Orlando, the marmalade cat, a seaside holiday
Hale, Kathleen
Orlando series (11)
Orlando, the marmalade cat, a trip abroad
Hale, Kathleen
Orlando series (2)
Orlando, the marmalade cat, and the water cats
Hale, Kathleen
Orlando series (18)
Orlando, the marmalade cat, becomes a doctor
Hale, Kathleen
Orlando series (6)
Orlando, the marmalade cat, buys a cottage
Hale, Kathleen
Orlando series (15)
Orlando, the marmalade cat, buys a farm
Hale, Kathleen
Orlando series (5)
Orlando, the marmalade cat, goes to the moon
Hale, Kathleen
Orlando series (17)
Orlando, the marmalade cat, his silver wedding
Hale, Kathleen
Orlando series (7)
Orlando, the marmalade cat, keeps a dog
Hale, Kathleen
Orlando series (9)
Orlando, the marmalade cat, the frisky housewife
Hale, Kathleen
Orlando series (13)
Orlando's camping holiday
Hale, Kathleen
Orlando series (1)
Orlando's country life
Hale, Kathleen
Orlando series (18)
Orlando's evening out
Hale, Kathleen
Orlando series (3)
Orlando's home life
Hale, Kathleen
Orlando series (4)
Orlando's invisible pyjamas
Hale, Kathleen
Orlando series (8)
Orlando's magic carpet
Hale, Kathleen
Orlando series (14)
Orlando's seaside holiday
Hale, Kathleen
Orlando series (11)
Orlando's silver wedding
Hale, Kathleen
Orlando series (7)
Orlando's trip abroad
Hale, Kathleen
Orlando series (2)
Orlando's zoo
Hale, Kathleen
Orlando series (12)
Orlis twins and Jim Morgan's ordeal
Palmer, Bernard
Orlis twins series (7)
Orlis twins and Mike's last chance
Palmer, Bernard
Orlis twins series (5)
Orlis twins and Ron's big problem
Palmer, Bernard
Orlis twins series (6)
Orlis twins and Roxie's triumph
Palmer, Bernard
Orlis twins series (8)
Orlis twins and the High School Gang
Palmer, Bernard
Orlis twins series (2)
Orlis twins and the new coach
Palmer, Bernard
Orlis twins series (4)
Orlis twins and the secret of the mountain
Palmer, Bernard
Orlis twins series (1)
Orlis twins live for Christ
Palmer, Bernard
Orlis twins series (3)

Orloff diamond
Teed, George Hamilton
Sexton Blake series (311)

Orn
Anthony, Piers
Of man and mantra trilogy (2)

Oron
Smith, David Claude
Oron series (4)

Orp
Kline, Suzy
Orp series (1)

Orp and the chop suey burgers
Kline, Suzy
Orp series (2)

Orp goes to the hoop
Kline, Suzy
Orp series (3)

Orphan
Stallman, Robert
Beast trilogy (1)

Orphan Ann
Bailey, Henry Christopher
Mister Joshua Clunk series (7)

Orphan army
Derrick, Lionel
Penetrator series (47)

Orphan star
Foster, Alan Dean
Flinx of the Commonwealth series (3)

Orphan Star
Foster, Alan Dean
Tar-Aiym Krang trilogy (2)

Orphan train quartet
Nixon, Joan Lowery
Shirley and Claude series (2)

Orphans in Gethsemane
Fisher, Vardis
Testament of man series (12)

Orphans of Brandenberg
Edmonds, Harry
Hugh Brodie series (3)

Orphans of the sky
Heinlein, Robert Anson
Future history series (3)

Orphans preferred
Miller, Jim
Colt Revolver series (5)

Orphelines in the enchanted castle
Carlson, Natalie Savage
Orphelines series (4)

Orpheus machine
Aldridge, Ray
Emancipator series (3)

Orwell, the transformation
Stansky, Peter
George Orwell series (2)

Osage bow
Macdonald, William Colt
Gregory Quist series (11)

Oscar
Aimwell, Walter
Boy series (1)

Oscar J Noodleman television network
Manes, Stephen
Oscar Noodleman trilogy (2)

Oscar the otter
Rutley, Cecily Marianne
Tales of the wild folk series (17)

Osiris died in autumn
Langley, Lee
Lieutenant Christopher Jensen series (1)

Osmond story
Tremlett, George
Rock stars series (1)

Osprey Reef
McKernan, Victoria
Chicago Nordejoong series (1)

Ossie goes supersonic
Davies, Hunter
Ossie series (2)

Ossie the millionaire
Davies, Hunter
Ossie series (3)

Osterman weekend
Ludlum, Robert
Tightrope-tense series (2)

Ostriches and obstacles
Trueman, Brian
Stories from Cockleshell Bay series (2)

O'Sullivan twins
Blyton, Enid
Saint Clare's series (2)

Oswald Bastable and others
Nesbit, Edith
Bastable family series (4)

Otan plot
Newman, Bernard
Papa Pontivy series (13)

Othello's occupation
Strong, Leonard Alfred George
Police diversion series (2)

Other
Dickson, Gordon Rupert
Dorsai series (11)

Other body in Grant's Tomb
Starnes, Richard
Barney Forge and Doctor Saint George Peachy series (3)

Other bullet
Mavity, Nancy Barr
Peter Piper series (4)

Other, darker Ned
Fine, Anne
Ione Muffet series (2)

Other David
Coker, Carolyn
Andrea Perkins series (1)

Other day
Whipple, Dorothy
Other day series (1)

Other devil's name
Ferrars, Elizabeth
Andrew Basnett series (4)

Other Edens
Evans, Chris
Other Edens series (1)

Other Edens II
Evans, Chris
Other Edens series (2)

Other Edens III
Evans, Chris
Other Edens series (3)

Other fires
Gorky, Maxim
Life of Klim Samgin series (3)

Other girls
Whitney, Adeline Dutton Train
Girls series (3)

Other half
Clark, Kenneth Mackenzie
Self-portrait series (2)
Worby, John
Spiv series (1)

Other half of the planet
Capon, Paul
Antigeos trilogy (2)

Other human race
Piper, Horace Beam
Fuzzy series (2)

Other island
Clements, Eileen Helen
Alister Woodhead series (7)

Other log of Phileas Fogg
Farmer, Philip Jose
Phileas Fogg series (2)

Other lovers
Widdemer, Margaret
Years of love series (2)

Other man
Wallace, Edgar
Inspector Elk series (1)
Mister T B Smith series (1)

Other man's wife
Winter, John Strange
Blankhampton series (6)

Other paths to glory
Price, Anthony
Doctor David Audley and Jack Butler series (6)

Other people
Stein, Sol
George Thomassy series (2)

Other people's children
Habberton, John
Budge and Toddie series (2)
Shears, Sarah
Tapioca for tea series (4)

Other people's houses
Cooper, Susan Rogers
Milton Kovak series (3)

Other people's money
Lyons, Arthur
Jacob Asch series (10)

Other people's shoes
Foyle, Kathleen
Augherim series (3)

Other room
Deal, Borden
Olden times series (2)

Other side
Kahn, James
Poltergeist series (2)

Other side of death
Van Gieson, Judith
Neil Hamel series (3)

Other side of the canyon
Grey, Romer Zane
Arizona Ames series (2)

Other side of the door
Howard, Hartley
Glenn Bowman series (5)
Hulme, Joy Nelson
Disability series (1)
O'Donnell, Lillian
Detective Norah Mulcahaney series (12)

Other side of the mirror, and other Darkover stories
Bradley, Marion Zimmer
Darkover anthologies series (3)

Other side of the river
Grey, Romer Zane
Laramie Nelson series (3)
Snow, Edgar
Red China series (2)

Other side of the sun
Capon, Paul
Antigeos trilogy (1)

Other side of the wall
Truss, Seldon
Inspector Gidleigh series (9)

Other side of time
Laumer, Keith
Mister Curlon series (2)

Other Sinbad
Gardner, Craig Shaw
Arabian Nights trilogy (1)

Other sins only speak
Kane, Henry
Inspector McGregor series (1)

Other small poems again
Worth, Valerie
Small poems series (5)

Other than natural causes
Cross, Mark
Daphne Wrayne and her Four Adjusters series (25)

Other times
Lawler, Ray
Doll trilogy (2)

Other voices
Greenland, Colin
Daybreak series (3)

Other way round
Kerr, Judith
Anna series (2)

Other women
Brush, Katharine
Lillian Legendre series (3)

Other world
Robeson, Kenneth
Doc Savage series (29)

Others
Bonanno, Margaret Wander
Others trilogy (1)

OtherWhere
Bonanno, Margaret Wander
Others trilogy (2)

OtherWise
Bonanno, Margaret Wander
Others trilogy (3)

Otherwise known as Sheila the Great
Blume, Judy
Peter Hatcher series (2)

Othmar
Ouida
Princess Napraxine series (2)

Otley
Waddell, Martin
Gerald Otley quartet (1)

Otley forever
Waddell, Martin
Gerald Otley quartet (3)

Otley pursued
Waddell, Martin
Gerald Otley quartet (2)

Otley victorious
Waddell, Martin
Gerald Otley quartet (4)

Ottawa allegation
Geddes, Paul
Paul Venneker series (3)

Ottawa unbuttoned
McIntosh, Dave
Canadian life series (3)

Otter Three Two calling
Hamre, Leif
Peter Hovden series (1)

Otter twins
Tompkins, Jane
Animal twins series (9)

Otter's tale
Maxwell, Gavin
Camusfearna trilogy (1)

Otters to the rescue
Martin, Edward Le Breton
Otter Patrol series (2)

Otto and the Himmler love letters
Kessler, Leo
Otto Stahl series (6)

Otto and the magic potatoes
Pene du Bois, William
Otto series (4)

Otto and the Reds
Kessler, Leo
Otto Stahl series (3)

Otto and the SS
Kessler, Leo
Otto Stahl series (5)

Otto and the Yanks
Kessler, Leo
Otto Stahl series (4)

Otto at sea
Pene du Bois, William
Otto series (2)

Otto in Africa
Pene du Bois, William
Otto series (1)

Otto in Texas
Pene du Bois, William
Otto series (3)

Ottoline
Morrell, Ottoline
Ottoline series (1)

Ottoline at Garsington
Morrell, Ottoline
Ottoline series (2)

Otto's blitzkrieg
Kessler, Leo
Otto Stahl series (2)

Otto's phoney war
Kessler, Leo
Otto Stahl series (1)

Ould Flynn
Laurie-Long, Ernest
Captain Flynn series (11)

Our agent in Rome is missing
Carter, Nick
Nick Carter series (80)

Our airliners
Crump, James Irving
Our services series (5)

Our airmen
Crump, James Irving
Our services series (2)

Our American adventure
Doyle, Arthur Conan
American adventure series (1)

Our animal friends
Provensen, Alice
Maple Hill Farm series (1)

Our animal friends at Maple Hill Farm
Provensen, Alice
Maple Hill Farm series (1)

Our army engineers
Crump, James Irving
Our services series (11)

Our baby doesn't
Hessell, Jenny
Our baby series (2)

Our baby gets dressed
Hessell, Jenny
Our baby series (3)

Our baby helps
Hessell, Jenny
Our baby series (1)

Our best Christmas
Alex, Benny
You and me series (4)

Our boat
Phillpotts, Beatrice
Rainy day playbooks series (1)

Our brother Nick and the African drums
Hayle, Felicity
Our brother Nick series (4)

Our brother Nick and the hole in the dyke
Hayle, Felicity
Our brother Nick series (6)

Our brother Nick and the old quarry
Hayle, Felicity
Our brother Nick series (2)

Our brother Nick and the tattooed gardener
Hayle, Felicity
Our brother Nick series (3)

Our brother Nick and the tolling bell
Hayle, Felicity
Our brother Nick series (1)

Our brother Nick and the ugly idol
Hayle, Felicity
Our brother Nick series (5)

Our clerk from Barkton
Rand, Edward Augustus
Look ahead series (4)

Our crowd
Birmingham, Stephen
American Jewry series (1)

Our daily bread
Larsson, Gosta
Daily bread series (1)

Our Davie Pepper
Sidney, Margaret
Five Little Peppers series (12)

Our dog
Oxenbury, Helen
First picture books series (8)

Our earth
Kalman, Bobbie
In my world series (18)

Our Elizabeth
Kilpatrick, Florence Antoinette
Elizabeth series (1)

Our Elizabeth again
Kilpatrick, Florence Antoinette
Elizabeth series (2)

Our Elizabeth in America
Kilpatrick, Florence Antoinette
Elizabeth series (4)

Our Elizabeth returns
Kilpatrick, Florence Antoinette
Elizabeth series (3)

Our Emily
Staples, Mary Jane
South London series (2)

Our Everest adventure
Hunt, John
Everest series (2)

Our father's house
Longstreet, Stephen
Fiore family series (2)

Our father's lies
Taylor, Andrew
William Dougal series (3)

Our firemen
Crump, James Irving
Our services series (4)

Our first murder
Chanslor, Torrey
Lutie and Amanda Beagle series (1)

Our flat
Andom, R
Troddles series (8)

Our friend Jennings
Buckeridge, Anthony
Jennings series (7)

Our friend Manso
Perez Galdos, Benito
Contemporary novels of Spain series (9)

Our friend, public nuisance number one
Smith, Susan
Samantha Slade series (3)

Our friends
Wensell, Ulises
Jackson family series (7)

Our G-men
Crump, James Irving
Our services series (3)

Our girl from MEPHISTO
Allison, Clyde
Agent triple zero eight series (2)

Our Hawaii kai
Stump, Jane Barr
Hawaii kai series (1)

Our hearts were young and gay
Skinner, Cornelia Otis
Our hearts series (1)

Our hills cry woe
Mason, Henrietta
Spencer family series (2)

Our home
Wensell, Ulises
Jackson family series (10)

Our human condition
Ward, Anthony
George trilogy (3)

Our jubilee is death
Bruce, Leo
Carolus Deene series (6)

Our kind of love
Grover, Marshall
Larry and Stretch series (110)

Our late member
Raymond, Ernest
London gallery series (17)

Our Lil
Adams, Agnes
Shepton children trilogy (1)

Our living earth, its origins and ecology of our planet
Greene, Carla
Science and natural history series (5)

Our London office
Armstrong, Thomas
Crowther chronicles series (4)

Our man Flint
Pearl, Jack
Derek Flint series (1)

Our man from SADISTO
Allison, Clyde
Agent triple zero eight series (1)

Our man in Camelot

Outdoor chums at Cabin Point
Allen, Quincy
Outdoor chums series (8)
Outdoor chums in the big woods
Allen, Quincy
Outdoor chums series (7)
Outdoor chums in the forest
Allen, Quincy
Outdoor chums series (3)
Outdoor chums on a houseboat
Allen, Quincy
Outdoor chums series (6)
Outdoor chums on the gulf
Allen, Quincy
Outdoor chums series (4)
Outdoor chums on the lake
Allen, Quincy
Outdoor chums series (2)
Outdoor girls along the coast
Hope, Laura Lee
Outdoor girls series (16)
Outdoor girls around the campfire
Hope, Laura Lee
Outdoor girls series (13)
Outdoor girls at Bluff Point
Hope, Laura Lee
Outdoor girls series (10)
Outdoor girls at Cape Cod
Hope, Laura Lee
Outdoor girls series (14)
Outdoor girls at Cedar Ridge
Hope, Laura Lee
Outdoor girls series (21)
Outdoor girls at Foaming Falls
Hope, Laura Lee
Outdoor girls series (15)
Outdoor girls at New Moon Ranch
Hope, Laura Lee
Outdoor girls series (18)
Outdoor girls at Ocean View
Hope, Laura Lee
Outdoor girls series (6)
Outdoor girls at Rainbow lake
Hope, Laura Lee
Outdoor girls series (2)
Outdoor girls at Spring Hill Farm
Hope, Laura Lee
Outdoor girls series (17)
Outdoor girls at the Hostess House
Hope, Laura Lee
Outdoor girls series (9)
Outdoor girls at Wild Rose Lodge
Hope, Laura Lee
Outdoor girls series (11)
Outdoor girls in a motor car
Hope, Laura Lee
Outdoor girls series (3)
Outdoor girls in a winter camp
Hope, Laura Lee
Outdoor girls series (4)
Outdoor girls in Desert Valley
Hope, Laura Lee
Outdoor girls series (23)
Outdoor girls in Florida
Hope, Laura Lee
Outdoor girls series (5)
Outdoor girls in the air
Hope, Laura Lee
Outdoor girls series (22)
Outdoor girls in the saddle
Hope, Laura Lee
Outdoor girls series (12)
Outdoor girls of Deepdale
Hope, Laura Lee
Outdoor girls series (1)
Outdoor girls on a canoe trip
Hope, Laura Lee
Outdoor girls series (20)
Outdoor girls on a hike
Hope, Laura Lee
Outdoor girls series (19)
Outdoor girls on Pine Island
Hope, Laura Lee
Outdoor girls series (7)
Outdoor words
Tyler, Jenny
First words series (5)
Outdoorland
Chambers, Robert William
Land series (1)
Outdoot girls in army service
Hope, Laura Lee
Outdoor girls series (8)
Outerworld
Haiblum, Isidore
Gunjer series (2)
Outfit
Stark, Richard
Parker series (3)
Outing for Oliver
Chappell, Audrey
Oliver series (2)
Outing for three
Rogers, Pamela
Michael series (3)
Outland strip
Sloane, Ben
Horn series (3)
Outlander
Gabaldon, Diana
Outlander series (1)
Outlands strike
Robbins, David
Blade series (2)
Outlaw
Gruber, Frank
Historical Western series (2)
Hewlett, Maurice
Sagas retold series (5)
Outlaw blood
Logan, Jake
John Slocum series (12)
Outlaw canyon
Gentry, Buck
Eli Holten series (3)
Outlaw deputy
Field, Peter
Powder Valley series (74)
Outlaw Derek
Hooper, Kay
Hagen series (7)
Outlaw empire
Cole, Jackson
Jim Hatfield series (38)
Slade, Jack
Gatling series (2)
Outlaw express
Field, Peter
Powder Valley series (64)
Outlaw gold
Bodine, J D
Quinn's Raiders series (4)
Scott, Bradford
Walt Slade series (59)
Outlaw Gulch
Leyland, Eric
Bill, Jake and Ned series (3)
Outlaw gulch
Montgomery, Ramsey
Choose your own adventure series (125)
Outlaw hell
Bodine, J D
Pecos Kid series (4)
Cole, Jackson
Jim Hatfield series (63)
Outlaw herd
Field, Peter
Powder Valley series (72)
Outlaw Island
Hilliard, Alec Rowley
Judge Manfred series (2)
Outlaw Josey Wales
Carter, Forrest
Josey Wales series (1)
Outlaw land
Scott, Bradford
Walt Slade series (56)
Outlaw marshal
Bexar, Phil
Billy Dupree series (2)
Outlaw of Castle Canyon
Field, Peter
Powder Valley series (50)
Outlaw of Eagle Nest
Field, Peter
Powder Valley series (8)
Outlaw of Gor
Norman, John
Tarl Cabot series (2)
Outlaw posse
Cody, Stone
Five Mavericks series (6)
Outlaw Red, son of Big Red
Kjelgaard, Jim
Red series (3)
Outlaw road
Muir, James A
Breed series (10)
Outlaw rope
Foley, Craig
Hangman series (6)
Outlaw roundup
Scott, Bradford
Walt Slade series (97)
Outlaw sheriff
Dunning, Hal
White Wolf series (1)
Outlaw trail
Fox, Brian
Alias Smith and Jones series (1)
Hardin, J D
Raider and Doc series (40)
Roberts, J R
Gunsmith series (66)
Outlaw Valley
Cole, Jackson
Jim Hatfield series (54)
Field, Peter
Powder Valley series (31)
Outlaw women
Roberts, J R
Gunsmith series (134)
Outlaw world
Hamilton, Edmond
Captain Future series (13)
Outlawed
Cole, Jackson
Jim Hatfield series (3)
Hogan, Ray
Shawn Starbuck series (2)
Strange, Oliver
Sudden series (5)
Outlaws
Brady, William S
Peacemaker series (2)
Moore, Arthur
Bluestar series (6)
Willoughby, Lee Davis
Making of America series (49)
Outlaw's fortune
Lee, W W
Jefferson Birch series (5)
Outlaws of Halfaday Creek
Hendryx, James Beardsley
Black John series (2)
Outlaws of Mars
Kline, Otis Adelbert
Mars series (2)
Outlaws of Partinico
Dolci, Danilo
Sicilian inquiry series (1)
Outlaws of Sherwood Forest
Kushner, Ellen
Choose your own adventure series (47)
Outlaws of Shy Valley
Kester, Ken
Steve McCade series (2)
Outlaws of the air
Leyland, Eric
Hunter Hawk series (1)
Outlaws of the Big Bend
Cole, Jackson
Jim Hatfield series (49)
Outlaws of the blue
Carter, Nicholas
Nicholas Carter series (607)
Outlaws of the moon
Hamilton, Edmond
Captain Future series (7)
Outlaws of Yugo-Slavia
Sayer, Walter William
Sexton Blake series (308)
Outlaw's silver
Dixon, Franklin W
Hardy boys series (67)
Outlaws three
Field, Peter
Powder Valley series (1)
Outpost
Austin, Jane Goodwin
Dora Darling series (2)
Outpost of Jupiter
Del Rey, Lester
Ganymede series (1)
Outpost on the moon
Walters, Hugh
Chris Godfrey series (4)
Outrage in Manchukuo
Gielgud, Val
Antony Havilland series (2)
Outrage on Gallows Hill
Bellairs, George
Detective Inspector Thomas Littlejohn series (13)
Outrageous exposures
Penn, John
Inspector George Thorne and Sergeant Bill Abbot series (9)
Outreach
Lichtenberg, Jacqueline
Dushau trilogy (3)
Outrider
Harding, Richard
Outrider series (1)
Outrun the constable
Jepson, Selwyn
Eve Gill series (1)
Outside contributor
Blishen, Edward
Schoolmaster series (11)
Outside edge
Moffat, Gwen
Miss Melinda Pink series (14)
Outside job
Brede, Arnold
Bull Rogers series (2)
Outside the right
Brockway, Fenner
Left right series (2)
Outside the universe
Hamilton, Edmond
Interstellar Patrol series (1)
Outsider
Edwards, Monica
Punchbowl Farm series (9)
Wilson, Colin
Outsider series (1)
Outsider in Amsterdam
Van de Wetering, Janwillem
De Gier and Grijpstra series (1)
Outsiders
Martin, Archibald Edward
Pel Pelham and Detective Linley series (1)
Outtakes for girls
Sanders, Bill
Outtakes series (2)
Outtakes for guys
Sanders, Bill
Outtakes series (1)
Outward bound
Coulson, Juanita
Children of the stars series (2)
Optic, Oliver
Young America, first series (1)
Outward log
Jones, Tristan
Wayward sailor series (7)
Outworlder
Carter, Lin
History of the Great Imperium trilogy (3)
Oval amulet
Babbitt, Lucy Cullyford
Melde series (1)
Over Bemerton's
Lucas, Edward Verrall
Winfield series (2)
Over her dead body
Prather, Richard Scott
Shell Scott series (18)
Over my dead body
Mitchell, Scott
Brock Devlin series (14)
Stout, Rex
Nero Wolfe and Archie Goodwin series (7)
Over on the dry side
L'Amour, Louis
Chantry family series (3)
Over prairie trails
Grove, Frederick Philip
Canadian prairie series (1)
Over sea, under stone
Cooper, Susan Mary
Dark is rising series (1)
Over seventy
Wodehouse, Pelham Grenville
Performing flea series (2)
Over the Andes to hell
Thorne, Ramsay
Captain Gringo series (8)
Over the big hill
Lovelace, Maud Hart
Betsy Ray series (3)
Over the bridge
Church, Richard
Over the bridge series (1)
Courtney, Edith
Kit Hemsworthy series (2)
Over the counter
Turner, Sheila
Mary Carrick series (1)
Over the edge
Keene, Carolyn
Nancy Drew files series (36)
Kellerman, Jonathan
Alex Delaware series (3)
Rowlands, Betty
Melissa Craig series (3)
Treat, Lawrence
Bill Decker series (2)
Jub Freeman series (6)
Over the edge of the world
Carter, Nicholas
Nicholas Carter series (598)
Over the garden wall
Carnac, Carol
Inspector Julian Rivers series (4)
Over the gate
Read, *Miss*
Fairacre series (5)
Over the green mask
Cooper, Lisa
Princess Beatrice Hospital series (4)
Over the high side
Freeling, Nicolas
Inspector Piet Van der Valk series (9)
Over-the-hill ghost
Calif, Ruth
Over-the-hill series (1)
Over-the-hill witch
Calif, Ruth
Over-the-hill series (2)
Over the hills with Nomad
Ellison, Norman
Nomad series (3)
Over the hump
Chase, Glen
Cherry Delight series (13)
Over the jungle trails
Dixon, Franklin W
Ted Scott flying series (10)
Over the mountains
Frankau, Pamela
Clothes of a king's son trilogy (3)
Over the ocean to Paris
Dixon, Franklin W
Ted Scott flying series (1)
Over the Polar ice
Adams, Eustace Lane
Andy Lane series (2)
Over the range
Butler, Samuel
Erewhon series (1)
Over the river
Galsworthy, John
End of the chapter series (3)
Over the Rockies with the air mail
Dixon, Franklin W
Ted Scott flying series (3)
Over the Rocky Mountains
Ballantyne, Robert Michael
Wandering Will trilogy (3)
Over the sea to death
Moffat, Gwen
Miss Melinda Pink series (3)
Over the sea to school
Allan, Mabel Esther
Harvie family series (1)
Over the seas
Bell, Josephine
Jacobean trilogy (2)
Over the sea's edge
Curry, Jane Louise
Abaloc series (4)
Prince Lincoas series (2)
Over the top with Jim
Lunn, Hugh
Lunns of Annerley Junction series (1)
Over the wall
Mottram, Ralph Hale
Geoffrey Skene series (6)
Spanish Farm series (8)
Pullen, Alan
Sam and Lin series (9)
Over thin ice
Cross, Mark
Daphne Wrayne and her Four Adjusters series (39)
Over to Candleford
Thompson, Flora
Lark Rise to Candleford series (2)
Overblown collection
Jaffee, Al
Snappy answers to stupid questions series (9)
Overboard!
Schurfranz, Vivian
Cheerleaders series (46)
Overdose of death
Christie, Agatha
Hercule Poirot series (21)
Overhead
Bickham, Jack Miles
Brad Smith series (3)
Overkill
Benteen, John
Sundance series (1)
Daniels, Norman A
Man from A.P.E. series (2)
Garner, William
Mike Jagger series (1)
Rouch, James
Zone series (5)
Overland escape
Roddy, Lee
American adventure series (1)
Overload
Cory, Desmond
Johnny Fedora series (10)
Overlord
Ahern, Jerry
Survivalist series (15)

Smith, Mark
Way of the Tiger series (4)
Overlord of the damned
Stockbridge, Grant
Richard Wentworth series (11)
Overnight
Stine, Robert Lawrence
Fear Street series (10)
Overnight express
McCutchan, Philip
Superintendent Simon Shard series (10)
Overnight sensation
Nixon, Joan Lowery
Hollywood daughters trilogy (2)
Oversoul Seven and the museum of time
Roberts, Jane
Oversoul Seven series (3)
Overtime upset
Porter, Mark
Win Hadley series (3)
Overture and beginners
Denison, Muriel
Double act series (1)
Overture for beginners
Delderfield, Ronald Frederick
Amusement trilogy (3)
Overture of light
Miller, Calvin
Symphony trilogy (3)
Overture to death
Marsh, Ngaio
Inspector Roderick Alleyn series (8)
Overture to trouble
Maddock, Stephen
Timothy Terrel series (18)
Owd Poskitt
Fletcher, Joseph Smith
Mister Poskitt trilogy (1)
Owen Tudor
King, Betty
Tudor series (1)
Owl
Forward, Robert Dodson
Owl series (1)
King, Frank
Clarence Knight series (3)
Owl and Billy
Waddell, Martin
Owl and Billy series (1)
Owl and Billy and the space days
Waddell, Martin
Owl and Billy series (2)
Owl at school
Nicoll, Helen
Meg and Mog series (11)
Owl at the vet
Nicoll, Helen
Meg and Mog series (13)
Owl flies home
Rodney, Bryan
Francis Villiers series (3)
Owl hoots
Rodney, Bryan
Francis Villiers series (1)
Owl hoots twice at Catfish Bend
Burman, Ben Lucien
Catfish Bend series (3)
Owl hunters
Niall, Ian
Billy Boyo and Albert Finn series (2)
Owl in the cellar
Scherf, Margaret
Lieutenant Ryan series (1)
Owl meets the Devil
Rodney, Bryan
Francis Villiers series (2)
Owl of darkness
Afford, Max
Jeffery Blackburn series (4)
Owl Pen
Wells, Kenneth McNeil
Owl Pen series (1)
Owl sang three times
Kelsey, Vera
Lieutenant Diego series (1)
Owl too many
Macleod, Charlotte
Professor Peter Shandy series (8)
Owlglass
Nickless, Will
Rotherside series (1)
Owlhoot
Edson, John Thomas
Rockabye County series (8)
Owlhoot convention
Gardner, Jerome
Dripspring series (9)
Owlhoot Express
Grant, William
Matthew Faraday series (8)
Owlhoot justice
Clancy, Eugene A
Masked Rider and Blue Hawk series (33)
Owlhooter
Borg, Jack
Hogleg Bailey series (23)
Owliver
Kraus, Robert
Owliver series (1)
Owliver the actor takes a bow
Kraus, Robert
Owliver series (2)
Owls
Kalman, Bobbie
North American wildlife series (4)
Owls and artificers
Fuller, Roy
Oxford lectures on poetry series (1)
Owls don't blink
Fair, A A
Bertha Cool and Donald Lam series (7)
Owl's House
Garstin, Crosbie
Penhales trilogy (1)
Own wilderness
Hooke, Nina Warner
Striplings trilogy (3)
Owning up
Melly, George
Owning up series (3)
Ox
Anthony, Piers
Of man and mantra trilogy (3)
Oxford blood
Fraser, Antonia
Jemima Shore series (5)
Oxford gambit
Hone, Joseph
Peter Marlow series (3)
Oxford life
Balsdon, Dacre
Oxford life series (1)
Oxford martyrs
Birt, David
Tudors series (3)
Oxford murders
Broome, Adam
Inspector Bramley series (1)
Oxford mystery
Cole, George Douglas Howard
Superintendent Henry Wilson series (5)
Oxford now and then
Balsdon, Dacre
Oxford life series (2)
Oxford Ox's alphabet
Williams, Ferelith Eccles
Oxford Ox trilogy (2)
Oxford Ox's calendar
Williams, Ferelith Eccles
Oxford Ox trilogy (3)
Oxford tragedy
Masterman, John Cecil
Ernst Brendel series (1)
Oxus in summer
Hull, Katharine
Oxus series (3)
Oyster-bed mystery
Murray, Andrew
Sexton Blake series (303)
Ozark outlaws
Hardin, J D
Raider and Doc series (43)
Ozark payback
Ham, Bob
Overload series (8)
Ozark trilogy
Elgin, Suzette Haden
Ozark fantasy trilogy (3)
Ozma and the Little Wizard
Baum, Lyman Frank
Little Wizard series (3)
Ozma of Oz
Baum, Lyman Frank
Oz series (3)
Ozmar the mystic
Hulme-Beaman, Emeric
Ozmar series (1)
Ozoplaning with the Wizard of Oz
Thompson, Ruth Plumly
Oz series (32)

P

P as in police
Treat, Lawrence
Jub Freeman series (10)
Mitch Taylor series (7)
P.C.Richardson's first case
Thomson, Basil
Superintendent Richardson series (1)
P.C.Ward lends a hand
Farmer, Bernard James
Tom Ward series (4)
P.D.Peebles' summer or winter book
Hedderwick, Mairi
Peedie Peebles series (1)
P J, the secret service boy
Hamilton, Frederic
P J Davenant series (5)
P-K
Walters, Hugh
Chris Godfrey series (24)
P.O.W.
Helm, Eric
Ground Zero series (2)
Zlotnik, Donald E
Survivors of Nam series (2)
P.P.C. Appleton
Lincoln, Natalie Sumner
Inspector Mitchell series (9)
Pa
Abarbanell, Jacob Ralph
Pa and ma series (1)
Pa Flickinger's folks
Hoover, Bessie Ray
Flickinger series (1)
Pace that kills
Fuller, William
Brad Dolan series (3)
O'Hara, Kevin
Chico Brett series (6)
Pacific castaways
Dale, Judith
Shirley Flight series (10)
Pacific cavalcade
Coffman, Virginia
Cavalcade series (1)
Pacific edge
Robinson, Kim Stanley
Orange County trilogy (3)
Pacific hellfire
Scofield, Jonathan
Freedom fighters series (13)
Pacific Northwest
Enefer, Douglas
Dale Shand series (11)
Pacific shores
Optic, Oliver
All-over-the-world series (12)
Pacific standoff
Clark, Halsey
Periscope series (1)
Jones, J Farragut
Silent service series (6)
Pacific vortex!
Cussler, Clive
Dirk Pitt series (1)
Pacifist's war
Partridge, Frances
Pacifist series (1)
Pack and follow
Packer, Joy
Pack and follow series (1)
Pack mascot
Collins, Freda
Woodland Pack series (7)
Pack of lies
Ashe, Gordon
Patrick Dawlish series (34)
Pack rat's day, and other poems
Prelutsky, Jack
Zoo doings series (3)
Pack that ran itself
Collins, Freda
Woodland Pack series (1)
Pack trip
Bryant, Bonnie
Saddle Club series (18)
Package holiday
Verne, Jules
Thompson Travel Agency series (1)
Package holiday spy case
Betteridge, Don
Tiger Lester series (12)
Package included murder
Porter, Joyce
Honourable Constance Ethel Morrison-Burke series (3)
Packed for murder
Blackburn, John
General Charles Kirk series (5)
Packhorse and pearling boat
Ronan, Tom
Deep of the sky series (2)
Pact
Petrocelli, Orlando Ralph
Giacomo Carlona series (1)
Pact with Satan
Holton, Leonard
Father Joseph Bredder series (2)
Pact with the Devil
Desmond, Hugh
Alan Fraser series (7)
Padded cell
Conway, Peter
Lucy Beck series (2)
Padded door
Flynn, Brian
Anthony Bathurst series (11)
Paddington abroad
Bond, Michael
Paddington series (4)
Paddington activity book
Bond, Michael
Paddington learning and activity series (8)
Paddington and Auny Lucy
Bond, Michael
Paddington picture book series (17)
Paddington and the knicker-bocker rainbow
Bond, Michael
Paddington picture book series (23)
Paddington and the marmalade maze
Bond, Michael
Paddington picture book series (31)
Paddington and the snowbear
Bond, Michael
Paddington pop-up series (5)
Paddington at home
Bond, Michael
Paddington picture book series (16)
Paddington at large
Bond, Michael
Paddington series (5)
Paddington at the airport
Bond, Michael
Paddington slot book series (1)
Paddington at the circus
Bond, Michael
Paddington picture book series (3)
Paddington at the fair
Bond, Michael
Paddington picture book series (25)
Paddington at the launderette
Bond, Michael
Paddington pop-up series (2)
Paddington at the palace
Bond, Michael
Paddington picture book series (26)
Paddington at the seaside
Bond, Michael
Paddington picture book series (6)
Paddington at the station
Bond, Michael
Paddington picture book series (10)
Paddington at the Tower
Bond, Michael
Paddington picture book series (5)
Paddington at the zoo
Bond, Michael
Paddington picture book series (22)
Paddington at work
Bond, Michael
Paddington series (7)
Paddington Bear
Bond, Michael
Paddington picture book series (1)
Paddington carpenter
Bond, Michael
Paddington learning and activity series (5)
Paddington cleans up
Bond, Michael
Paddington picture book series (29)
Paddington colouring book
Bond, Michael
Paddington learning and activity series (8)
Paddington conjurer
Bond, Michael
Paddington learning and activity series (6)
Paddington cook
Bond, Michael
Paddington learning and activity series (7)
Paddington does it himself
Bond, Michael
Paddington picture book series (12)
Paddington goes out
Bond, Michael
Paddington picture book series (14)
Paddington goes shopping
Bond, Michael
Paddington picture book series (4)
Paddington goes to the sales
Bond, Michael
Paddington picture book series (8)
Paddington goes to town
Bond, Michael
Paddington series (8)
Paddington golfer
Bond, Michael
Paddington learning and activity series (8)
Paddington Green
Rayner, Claire
Performers series (3)
Paddington has fun
Bond, Michael
Paddington picture book series (19)
Paddington helps out
Bond, Michael
Paddington series (3)
Paddington hits out
Bond, Michael
Paddington picture book series (11)
Paddington in the kitchen
Bond, Michael
Paddington picture book series (13)
Paddington in touch
Bond, Michael
Paddington picture book series (18)
Paddington mails a letter
Bond, Michael
Paddington slot book series (2)
Paddington marches on
Bond, Michael
Paddington series (6)
Paddington minds the house
Bond, Michael
Paddington picture book series (27)
Paddington mystery
Rhode, John
Doctor Lancelot Priestley series (1)
Paddington on screen
Bond, Michael
Paddington's Blue Peter story series (2)
Paddington on stage
Bond, Michael
Paddington series (11)
Paddington on the river
Bond, Michael
Paddington picture book series (21)
Paddington on top
Bond, Michael
Paddington series (10)
Paddington posts a letter
Bond, Michael
Paddington slot book series (2)
Paddington spring cleans
Bond, Michael
Paddington picture book series (28)
Paddington sticker book
Bond, Michael
Paddington learning and activity series (8)
Paddington takes a bath
Bond, Michael
Paddington picture book series (7)
Paddington takes the air
Bond, Michael
Paddington series (9)
Paddington takes the test
Bond, Michael
Paddington series (11)
Paddington takes to TV
Bond, Michael
Paddington's Blue Peter story series (1)

Paddington weighs in
Bond, Michael
Paddington picture book series (15)
Paddington works hard
Bond, Michael
Paddington picture book series (20)
Paddington's art exhibition
Bond, Michael
Paddington picture book series (24)
Paddington's birthday party
Bond, Michael
Paddington learning and activity series (4)
Paddington's birthday treat
Bond, Michael
Paddington pop-up series (3)
Paddington's Blue Peter story book
Bond, Michael
Paddington's Blue Peter story series (1)
Paddington's bus ride
Bond, Michael
Paddington slot book series (5)
Paddington's busy day
Bond, Michael
Paddington picture book series (30)
Paddington's cartoon book
Bond, Michael
Paddington picture book series (32)
Paddington's clock book
Bond, Michael
Paddington slot book series (3)
Paddington's colours
Bond, Michael
Paddington play and learn series (2)
Paddington's first book
Bond, Michael
Paddington pastime series (1)
Paddington's first counting book
Bond, Michael
Paddington pastime series (2)
Paddington's first play book
Bond, Michael
Paddington pastime series (4)
Paddington's first puzzle book
Bond, Michael
Paddington play and learn series (2)
Paddington's first word book
Bond, Michael
Paddington pastime series (3)
Paddington's garden
Bond, Michael
Paddington picture book series (2)
Paddington's London, on four wheels
Bond, Michael
Paddington slot book series (4)
Paddington's loose end book
Bond, Michael
Paddington learning and activity series (1)
Paddington's lucky day
Bond, Michael
Paddington picture book series (4)
Paddington's magical Christmas
Bond, Michael
Paddington picture book series (32)
Paddington's new room
Bond, Michael
Paddington picture book series (9)
Paddington's numbers
Bond, Michael
Paddington play and learn series (1)
Paddington's painting exhibition
Bond, Michael
Paddington picture book series (24)
Paddington's party book
Bond, Michael
Paddington learning and activity series (2)
Paddington's picture book
Bond, Michael
Paddington picture book series (6)
Paddington's pop-up book
Bond, Michael
Paddington pop-up series (1)
Paddington's second puzzle book
Bond, Michael
Paddington play and learn series (2)
Paddington's shopping adventure
Bond, Michael
Paddington pop-up series (4)
Paddington's storybook
Bond, Michael
Paddington picture book series (32)
Paddy finds a job
Goodall, John Strickland
Paddy Pork series (17)
Paddy goes traveling
Goodall, John Strickland
Paddy Pork series (13)
Paddy Joe
Stranger, Joyce
Paddy Joe series (1)
Paddy Joe and Tomkin's folly
Stranger, Joyce
Paddy Joe series (4)
Paddy Joe at Deep Hollow Farm
Stranger, Joyce
Paddy Joe series (3)
Paddy Pork, odd jobs
Goodall, John Strickland
Paddy Pork series (15)
Paddy Pork to the rescue
Goodall, John Strickland
Paddy Pork series (16)
Paddy Pork's holiday
Goodall, John Strickland
Paddy Pork series (9)
Paddy the Beaver's visitor
Burgess, Thornton Waldo
Animal stories series (5)
Paddy the beaver's visitor
Burgess, Thornton Waldo
Paddy the beaver series (1)
Paddy under water
Goodall, John Strickland
Paddy Pork series (14)
Paddy's evening out
Goodall, John Strickland
Paddy Pork series (6)
Paddy's new hat
Goodall, John Strickland
Paddy Pork series (11)
Paddy's surprise visitor
Burgess, Thornton Waldo
Animal stories series (5)
Paddy the beaver series (1)
Padre in Colditz
Platt, Jock Ellison
Colditz series (8)
Padrone
Smith, Don
Tim Parnell series (2)
Paduan conspiracy
Walton, Marion
Inspector James Cardinal series (2)
Pagan blossoms
Fitzgerald, Julia
Astromance series (11)
Pagan Joe
Plummer, Thomas Arthur
Detective Inspector Andrew Frampton series (42)
Pagan pagoda
Mundy, Max
Russell Jones series (1)
Pagan queen
Treece, Henry
Early Britain series (3)
Pagan the black
Benedict, Dorothy
Pagan series (1)
Pagan voyager
Finch, Simon
Voyager trilogy (2)
Paganini strikes again
Lee, Benjamin
Mike and Bill Hendry series (1)
Pagans
Bates, Arlo
Pagans series (1)
Herley, Richard
Pagans trilogy (3)
Moore, Arthur
River of fortune trilogy (2)
Page me a pin-up
Brody, Marc
Marc Brody series (5)
Page Mister Tutt
Train, Arthur
Ephraim Tutt series (5)
Page of the Duke of Savoy
Dumas, Alexandre
Valois series (3)
Pageant of life
Dudley, Owen Francis
Problems of human happiness series (4)
Pageant of murder
Mitchell, Gladys
Dame Beatrice Bradley series (38)
Pages from a cold island
Exley, Frederick
Frederick Exley trilogy (2)
Pagett calling
Drury, William Price
Pagett series (2)
Paging Blackshirt
Graeme, Roderic
Blackshirt series (17)
Paging the Saint
Charteris, Leslie
Saint series (6)
Pagoda
Phillips, James Atlee
Joe Gall series (1)
Pagoda mystery
Worth, Maurice
Derek Harding series (3)
Pagoda tree
Mather, Berkely
Stafford family trilogy (1)
Paid and loving eyes
Gash, Jonathan
Lovejoy series (16)
Paid in full
Cronin, Michael
Richard Maidment series (1)
Paid servant
Braithwaite, Edward Ricardo
Sir series (2)
Paid with death
Carter, Nicholas
Nicholas Carter series (135)
Paige
Jenkins, Jerry Bruce
Margo Franklin and Philip Spence series (4)
Pain of confinement
Boyle, Jimmy
Prison diaries series (2)
Painful necessity
Housman, Laurence
Palace plays series (3)
Painful predicament of Sherlock Holmes
Gillette, William
Sherlock Holmes drama series (3)
Painless extractions
Anderson, Oliver
Guy Random series (1)
Painswick Line
Cecil, Henry
Mister Tewkesbury series (1)
Paint out
Wallace, Robert
Essington Holt series (3)
Paint-stained flannels
Fry, Pete
Pete Fry series (10)
Paint the town black
Alexander, David
Bart Hardin series (2)
Paint the town red
Adams, Harold
Carl Wilcox series (2)
Paint the wind
Hannum, Alberta
Desert trading post series (2)
Painted cave
Mantle, Winifred
Lesters and Westcotts series (4)
Painted caves
Thompson, Kate
Derain family series (5)
Painted dagger
Drummond, J
Sexton Blake series (1117)
Painted death
Enefer, Douglas
Dale Shand series (4)
Painted desert
Munroe, Kirk
Pacific coast series (4)
Painted devil
Bedard, Michael
Emily series (2)
Painted dog
Gunn, Victor
Chief Inspector Bill Cromwell series (25)
Painted doll affair
Macvicar, Angus
Bruce McLintock series (2)
Painted face
Stubbs, Jean
Inspector John Joseph Lintott series (2)
Painted faces
Robertson, Colin
Inspector Robert Strong series (1)
Painted for the kill
Cores, Lucy
Captain Andrew Torrent series (1)
Painted garden
Streatfeild, Noel
Shoes series (6)
Painted ladies
Harvey, James Neal
Ben Tolliver series (2)
Painted lady
Wilcox, Stephen F
Elias Hackshaw series (3)
Painted mask
Erskine, Margaret
Inspector Septimus Finch series (1)
Painted minx
Chambers, Robert William
Cardigan series (4)
Painted monster
Rowe, Anne
Inspector Pettengill series (2)
Painted ports
Smith, Cicely Fox
Barty Dale series (2)
Painted Post gunplay
Gunn, Tom
Sheriff Blue Steele series (5)
Painted Post law
Gunn, Tom
Sheriff Blue Steele series (3)
Painted post outlaws
Gunn, Tom
Sheriff Blue Steele series (1)
Painted Post range
Gunn, Tom
Sheriff Blue Steele series (4)
Painted room
Wilson, Margaret
Kenworthys series (2)
Painted tent
Canning, Victor
Smiler Miles trilogy (3)
Painted women
Cunningham, Chet
Agent Brad Spear series (5)
Painter of signs
Narayan, Rasipuram Krishnaswami
Malgudi series (12)
Painter of souls
Lisle, David
Isola Dering series (1)
Painters
Ferra-Mikura, Vera
Stanislaus family series (2)
Painter's mate
Hale, Susan
Ronnie Smithers series (1)
Painting the fire
Farrington, Liz
Mrs Murgatroyd series (2)
Pair bond
Yorke, Katherine
Woman's place series (2)
Pair of blue eyes
Hardy, Thomas
Romances and fantasies series (1)
Pair of desert wellies
Sherry, Sylvia
Rocky O'Rourke series (2)
Pair of deuces
Reese, John
Jefferson Hewitt series (9)
Pair of Jesus-boots
Sherry, Sylvia
Rocky O'Rourke series (1)
Pair of knaves
Cronin, Michael
Sam Harris series (10)
Pair of patient lovers
Howells, William Dean
Mister and Mrs March series (7)
Pajama party
Hest, Amy
Pajama party series (1)
Pajamas for Kit
De Paola, Tomie
Katie and Kit series (2)
Pakistan kill
Rosenberger, Joseph
Death Merchant series (64)
Pakistani twins
Shaw, Denis
Twin series (34)
Palace
Simon, Claude
Grass quartet (3)
Yarbro, Chelsea Quinn
Count Ragoczy Saint-Germain series (2)
Palace and cottage
Optic, Oliver
Young America, first series (5)
Palace for the Buckinghams
Saville, Malcolm
Buckinghams series (4)
Palace guard
Macleod, Charlotte
Sarah Kelling series (3)
Palace of desire
Mahfouz, Naguib
Cairo trilogy (2)
Palace of kings
Jefferies, Mike
Loremasters of Elundium trilogy (2)
Palace of love
Vance, Jack
Kirth Gersen series (3)
Palace of terror
Murray, Edgar Joyce
Sexton Blake series (490)
Palace of the peacock
Harris, Wilson
Guiana series (1)
Palace plays
Housman, Laurence
Palace plays series (1)
Palace scenes
Housman, Laurence
Palace plays series (4)
Palace walk
Mahfouz, Naguib
Cairo trilogy (1)
Palaces and prisons
Miller, Ron
Bronwyn trilogy (1)
Paladin
Shipway, George
Walter Tirel series (1)
Paladin of the night
Weis, Margaret
Rose of the prophet trilogy (2)
Palais de Danse tragedy
Chester, Gilbert
Sexton Blake series (700)
Pale blue crochet coathanger
Foster, David
D'Arcy Oliveres series (2)
Pale country pursuit
Kneifel, Hans
Atlan series (3)
Pale criminal
Kerr, Philip
Berlin noir trilogy (2)
Pale gray for guilt
Macdonald, John Dann
Travis McGee series (9)
Pale grey for guilt
Macdonald, John Dann
Travis McGee series (9)
Pale grey men
Duff, Douglas Valder
Adam Macadam series (6)
Pale horse
Christie, Agatha
Hercule Poirot series (38)
Mrs Ariadne Oliver series (5)
Pale kings and princes
Parker, Robert Brown
Spenser series (14)
Pale moon
Burnett, William Riley
San Miguel series (2)
Pale phoenix
Reiss, Kathryn
Time windows series (2)
Pale star
Coldsmith, Don
Spanish bit series (9)
Palimpsest
Atkins, Meg Elizabeth
Inspector Henry Beaumont series (3)
Pall for a painter
Lorac, E C R
Inspector Macdonald series (10)
Palm for Mrs Pollifax
Gilman, Dorothy
Mrs Emily Pollifax series (4)
Palm land
Samuels, Adelaide Florence
Dick Travers series (1)
Palmprint
Barnett, James
Superintendent Owen Smith series (2)
Palo pinto
Wisler, Gary Clifton
Texas Brazos series (3)
Paloma
Henrey, Madeleine
Madeleine reminiscences series (1)
Palomino mystery
Sheldon, Ann
Linda Craig series (1)

Palomino stud
Martin, Cort
Jared Bolt series (19)
Sadler, Jeff
Marshal Andrew Anderson series (13)
Palos of the Dog Star Pack
Giesy, John Ulrich
Jason Croft trilogy (1)
Paloverde
Briskin, Jacqueline
Van Vliet series (1)
Palzer experiment
Murray, Andrew
Sexton Blake series (143)
Pam
Hutten zum Stolzenberg, Bettina Riddle
Pam series (1)
Pam at fifty
Hutten zum Stolzenberg, Bettina Riddle
Pam series (5)
Pam decides
Hutten zum Stolzenberg, Bettina Riddle
Pam series (2)
Pam, Pot and Kettle
Muir, Marie
Kettle series (1)
Pam Wilson, registered nurse
Deming, Dorothy
Penny Marsh series (7)
Pamela
Hadath, Florence Gunby
Pamela series (1)
Pamela Calling
Hadath, Florence Gunby
Pamela series (2)
Pamela's legacy
Taggart, Marion Ames
Pamela series (2)
Pamela's spring song
Roberts, Cecil
Pamela series (1)
Pamplona affair
Carter, Nick
Nick Carter series (122)
Pam's own story
Hutten zum Stolzenberg, Bettina Riddle
Pam series (6)
Pan Michael
Sienkiewicz, Henryk
Polish history trilogy (3)
Pan Sagittarius
Wallace, Ian
Pan Sagittarius series (2)
Panama dead
Arnett, Jack
Book of justice series (4)
Panama gold
Benteen, John
Neal Fargo series (2)
Panama gunner
Thorne, Ramsay
Captain Gringo series (6)
Panama of today
Verrill, Alpheus Hyatt
Panama series (2)
Panama paradox
Wolfe, Michael
Michael Keefe series (4)
Panama, past and present
Verrill, Alpheus Hyatt
Panama series (1)
Panama plot
Reeve, Arthur Benjamin
Craig Kennedy series (13)
Panama power play
Derrick, Lionel
Penetrator series (19)
Panda and the ball
Taro, Oda
Panda series (12)
Panda and the bunyips
Foreman, Michael
Panda series (3)
Panda and the bushfire
Foreman, Michael
Panda series (4)
Panda and the circus
Taro, Oda
Panda series (9)
Panda and the odd lion
Foreman, Michael
Panda series (2)
Panda and the snow
Taro, Oda
Panda series (10)
Panda and the sparrow
Taro, Oda
Panda series (8)
Panda at the seaside
Taro, Oda
Panda series (11)
Panda One investigates
Walker, Peter Norman
Panda One series (2)
Panda One on duty
Walker, Peter Norman
Panda One series (1)
Panda the builder
Taro, Oda
Panda series (7)
Panda the doctor
Taro, Oda
Panda series (2)
Panda the explorer
Taro, Oda
Panda series (3)
Panda the racing driver
Taro, Oda
Panda series (4)
Panda the soldier
Taro, Oda
Panda series (5)
Panda the train driver
Taro, Oda
Panda series (1)
Panda the wizard
Taro, Oda
Panda series (6)
Panda's alphabet book
Taro, Oda
Panda series (12)
Panda's book of colours
Taro, Oda
Panda series (12)
Panda's book of numbers
Taro, Oda
Panda series (12)
Panda's Club tree house
Berenstain, Michael
Panda series (1)
Panda's new pet
Berenstain, Michael
Panda series (2)
Panda's playtime
McCue, Dick
Animal shape series (7)
Panda's puzzle and his voyage of discovery
Foreman, Michael
Panda series (1)
Pandemic
Ardies, Tom
Charlie Sparrow series (3)
Pandervils, Egg and Nicky
Bullett, Gerald
History of Pandervil series (2)
Pandora
Reeve, Arthur Benjamin
Craig Kennedy series (21)
Pandora plague
Matthias, Lee A
Sherlock Holmes sequels series (51)
Pandora principle
Clowes, Carolyn
Star trek series (49)
Pandora secret
Forrest, Anthony
Captain John Valcourt Justice series (2)
Pandora stone
Greenleaf, William
Tartarus series (2)
Pandora's box
Chastain, Thomas
Inspector Max Kauffman series (1)
J T Spanner series (1)
Pandora's children
Lance, Kathryn
Pandora series (2)
Pandora's genes
Lance, Kathryn
Pandora series (1)
Pangers' pup
Wood, Lorna
Pangers series (2)
Pangersbourne murders
Sturrock, Jeremy
Bow Street Runner series (7)
Pangur Ban the white cat
Sampson, Fay
Pangur Ban series (1)
Panhandle
Mitchum, Hank
Stage coach station series (29)
Panhandle bandits
Cole, Jackson
Jim Hatfield series (72)
Panhandle payback
McCoy, Duff
Jeb Cutter series (1)
Panhandle search
Roberts, J R
Gunsmith series (28)
Panic!
Creasey, John
Department Z series (13)
Panic in Box C
Carr, John Dickson
Doctor Gideon Fell series (22)
Panic in Philly
Pendleton, Don
Mack Bolan series (15)
Panic in the night
Stagg, James
Sexton Blake series (1425)
Panic in the woodland
Miller, Muriel
Woodlanders series (6)
Panic of '89
Erdman, Paul
Financial series (2)
Panic on Gull Island
Dixon, Franklin W
Hardy boys series (107)
Panic party
Berkeley, Anthony
Roger Sheringham series (10)
Panky and the saddle
Saxon, Nancy
Panky series (2)
Panky and William
Saxon, Nancy
Panky series (1)
Panorama
Bentley, Phyllis
West Riding series (1)
Pant Glas story
Williams, Elma Mary
Wildlife series (3)
Pantaloon
Toynbee, Philip
Valediction of Pantaloon series (1)
Pantomime ponies
Baxter, Gillian
Angela and Ian Kendall series (1)
Pants off
Slaven, Roy
South Coast series (1)
Panuck
Machetanz, Frederick
Andy and Panuck series (1)
Panzer hunt
Kessler, Leo
Wotan series (12)
Panzer soldier
Sadler, Barry
Casca series (4)
Papa married a Mormon
Fitzgerald, John Dennis
Will Fitzgerald trilogy (1)
Papa Pasquier
Duhamel, Georges
Pasquier series (1)
Papa Pontivy and the Maginot Line
Newman, Bernard
Papa Pontivy series (2)
Papa Small
Lenski, Lois
Small family series (9)
Papa tells Chita a story
Howard, Elizabeth Fitzgerald
Chita series (2)
Papa, you're crazy
Saroyan, William
Mama and papa series (2)
Papa's daughter
Bjorn, Thyra Ferre
Pastor Pontus Franzon series (2)
Papa's pizza
Berenstain, Stan
Berenstain bears series (21)
Papa's wife
Bjorn, Thyra Ferre
Pastor Pontus Franzon series (1)
Paper and scissors truth talks
Westphail, Arnold Carl
Paper tearing series (5)
Paper bag
Rhode, John
Doctor Lancelot Priestley series (46)
Paper chase
Balfour, Hearnden
Inspector Jack Strickland series (1)
Bayer, Oliver Weld
Paper chase series (1)
Egan, Lesley
Jesse Falkenstein series (7)
Fielding, A
Inspector Pointer series (16)
Porter, Hal
Watcher series (2)
Watkins, Ron
Thomas Tilling series (1)
Paper chase mystery
Fielding, A
Inspector Pointer series (16)
Paper circle
Fischer, Bruno
Ben Helm series (6)
Paper doll
Parker, Robert Brown
Spenser series (20)
Paper dragon
Gruelle, Johnny
Raggedy Ann series (8)
Paper gun
Browne, Howard
Paul Pine series (5)
Paper lives
Mackenzie, Compton
Oliver Huffam series (2)
Paper nights
Filion, Pierre
Pikolo series (1)
Paper pistol contract
Atlee, Philip
Joe Gall series (6)
Paper salvage crime
Chester, Gilbert
Sexton Blake series (1067)
Paper tearing Bible talks
Westphail, Arnold Carl
Paper tearing series (4)
Paper tearing evangels
Westphail, Arnold Carl
Paper tearing series (8)
Paper tearing Gospel illustrations
Westphail, Arnold Carl
Paper tearing series (3)
Paper tearing trick talks
Westphail, Arnold Carl
Paper tearing series (1)
Paper tears with a Gospel message
Westphail, Arnold Carl
Paper tearing series (14)
Paper thunderbolt
Innes, Michael
Sir John Appleby series (12)
Paperbag
Russell, Richard
Angel Graham series (3)
Paperchaser
Hall, Penny
Miners series (1)
Papermakers
Fisher, Leonard Everett
Colonial Americans series (3)
Papers of A.J.Wentworth, B.A.
Ellis, Humphry Francis
A.J.Wentworth series (1)
Papers of A.J.Wentworth, B.A., retd.
Ellis, Humphry Francis
A.J.Wentworth series (2)
Papers of Samuel Marchbanks
Davies, Robertson
Samuel Marchbanks series (3)
Papers of Tony Veitch
McIlvanney, William
Inspector Jack Laidlaw series (2)
Papersnake
Meynell, Laurence Walter
Hooky Hefferman series (13)
Papillon
Charriere, Henri
Papillon series (1)
Papyrus murder
Morris, Thomas Baden
Inspector Headley series (1)
Parables of grace
Capon, Robert
Parables series (2)
Parables of judgment
Capon, Robert
Parables series (3)
Parables of nature
Gatty, Margaret
Hedgerow tales series (1)
Parables of the Kingdom
Capon, Robert
Parables series (1)
Parachute jumper
Fitzhugh, Percy Keese
Tom Slade series (21)
Parachutes and kisses
Jong, Erica
Isadora Wing series (3)
Parade of cockeyed creatures
Baxt, George
Sylvia Plotkin and Max Van Larsen series (1)
Parade of peacocks
Ashton, Elizabeth
Renee and Leon Thornton series (2)
Parade's end
Ford, Ford Madox
Parade's end series (4)
Paradine's gauntlet
Pendleton, Don
Mack Bolan series (55)
Paradise
Kitchen, Paddy
Vanessa Talisend series (4)
Paradise and the Perrys
Turner, Lilian
Perry family series (1)
Paradise Bend
White, William Patterson
Lazy River series (3)
Paradise called Texas
Shefelman, Janice Jordan
Texas trilogy (1)
Paradise coal-boat
Hyne, Charles John Cutcliffe
Captain Owen Kettle series (2)
Paradise corner
Minton, Mary
Yesterday's road series (7)
Paradise Creek
Walmsley, Leo
Phantom Lobster series (8)
Paradise game
Stableford, Brian Michael
Star Pilot Grainger series (4)
Paradise gun
Flagg, John
Hart Muldoon series (5)
Paradise Island
Smyth, John George
Ann Sheldon series (1)
Paradise loses
Gilman, George G
Edge series (15)
Paradise men
Harvester, Simon
Asia in turmoil series (4)
Malcolm Kenton series (3)
Paradise Mountain
Colter, Dale
Regulator series (7)
Paradise of death
Letts, Barry
Doctor Who series (162)
Paradise plot
Naha, Ed
Harry Porter series (1)
Paradise spells danger
Mair, George Brown
David Grant series (10)
Paradise Towers
Wyatt, Stephen
Doctor Who series (134)
Paradise trap
Crane, Robert
Ben Corbin series (4)
Paradise Valley
Rountree, Owen
Jim Cord series (8)
Paradise war
Lawhead, Stephen
Song of Albion trilogy (1)
Paradox Alley
De Chancie, John
Skyway trilogy (3)
Paradox of the sets
Stableford, Brian Michael
Daedalus series (6)
Paradox planet
Spruill, Steven Gregory
Kane and Pendrake series (3)
Paragon
Knowles, John
Yale University series (2)
Paragon man
Garrison, Christian
Ace Chaney series (2)
Paragon Walk
Perry, Anne
Charlotte Ellison Pitt and Inspector Thomas Pitt series (3)
Paralyzing ray versus the nuclears
Nizzi, Guido
Paralyzing ray trilogy (2)
Paramilitary plot
Pendleton, Don
Mack Bolan series (45)
Paratime
Piper, Horace Beam
Paratime police series (2)
Paratwa
Hinz, Christopher
Paratwa trilogy (3)
Parcel
Vendrell, Carme Sole
Victor and Maria series (7)

Parcel for Henry
Collin, Paul Ries
Henry and Jane Ellis series (1)
Parcel of their fortunes
Byfield, Barbara
Simon Bede and Helen Bullock series (4)
Parcels for Inspector West
Creasey, John
Inspector Roger West series (20)
Parched sea
Awlinson, Richard
Harpers series (1)
Parchment key
Hopkins, Stanley
Peter Marrell series (2)
Pardon my blood
Whelton, Paul
Garry Dean series (5)
Pardon my gun
Campbell, Keith
Mike Brett series (6)
Carstairs, John Paddy
Garaway Trenton series (4)
Parent plot
Pascal, Francine
Sweet Valley High series (67)
Parent's guide to the danger zones
Berry, Joy
Alerting kids to the danger zones series (3)
Pariah
Wilcox, Collin
Lieutenant Frank Hastings series (15)
Paris
Zola, Emile
Abbe Pierre Fremont trilogy (3)
Paris adventure
Bayley, Viola
Adventure series (1)
Paris and New York diaries, 1951-1961
Rorem, Ned
Musical diaries series (2)
Paris connection
Keene, Carolyn
Nancy Drew and Hardy boys supermystery series (8)
Paris diary
Rorem, Ned
Musical diaries series (1)
Paris drop
Furst, Alan
Roger Levin series (2)
Paris gazette
Feuchtwanger, Lion
Waiting-room tetralogy (3)
Paris is with us
Stil, Andre
First clash trilogy (3)
Paris is worth a mass
Williamson, Hugh Ross
Catherine de Valois trilogy (3)
Paris journal, 1944-65
Flanner, Janet
Paris trilogy (2)
Paris journal, 1965-1971
Flanner, Janet
Paris trilogy (3)
Paris kill
Kirk, Philip
Butler series (6)
Paris kill-ground
Rosenberger, Joseph
C.O.B.R.A. series (2)
Paris market girls
Zola, Emile
Rougon Macquart series (3)
Paris nights
Greene, Yvonne
Kelly Blake series (6)
Paris of Troy
Baker, George
Trojan War trilogy (3)
Paris puzzle
McConnor, Vincent
Inspector Damiot series (3)
Paris was yesterday, 1925-39
Flanner, Janet
Paris trilogy (1)
Parisian adventure
Ashton, Elizabeth
Renee and Leon Thornton series (1)
Parisian affair
Carter, Nick
Nick Carter series (154)
Parisian pigeon drop
Radford, John P
Illusionist series (3)
Parisians in provincial France
Balzac, Honore de
Scenes of provincial life series (5)
Park
Hill, Eric
Baby Bear series (3)
Park Avenue executioner
Wilson, David
Marshal Sam McCloud series (6)
Parker ransom
Gardner, Jerome
Hanging Judge series (6)
Parliament of owls
Buchanan, Patrick
Ben Shock and Charity Tucker series (2)
Parlicoot, and how he sets out to find a playmate
Macleod, Alex W
Parlicoot series (1)
Parlicoot's house
Macleod, Alex W
Parlicoot series (2)
Parnassus on wheels
Morley, Christopher
Roger and Helen Mifflin series (1)
Parole
Ehrlich, Jack
Robert Flick series (1)
Parris Mitchell of Kings Row
Bellamann, Henry
Kings Row series (2)
Parrot cat
Bayley, Nicola
Copycats series (1)
Parrot fever
Vail, Virginia
Animal Inn series (10)
Parrot in the house
Allen, Linda
Parrot in the house series (1)
Parsival
Monaco, Richard
Parsival series (1)
Parslay's tail
Bond, Michael
Parsley series (1)
Parsley and the herbs
Bond, Michael
Parsley series (7)
Parsley, sage, rosemary and time
Curry, Jane Louise
Rosemary series (1)
Parsley the lion
Bond, Michael
Parsley series (6)
Parsley's good deed
Bond, Michael
Parsley series (2)
Parsley's last stand
Bond, Michael
Parsley series (3)
Parsley's parade
Bond, Michael
Parsley series (5)
Parsley's problem present
Bond, Michael
Parsley series (4)
Parson extraordinary
Bloom, Ursula
Father and mother series (1)
Parson's daughter
Newbery, Esylt
Parson's daughter series (1)
Parson's daughter again
Newbery, Esylt
Parson's daughter series (2)
Parson's pleasure
Hardwick, Mollie
Doran Fairweather series (2)
Parson's princess
Pellow, John
Village parson trilogy (3)
Parson's progress
Mackenzie, Compton
Faith, hope and charity trilogy (2)
Pellow, John
Village parson trilogy (2)
Part for a poisoner
Lorac, E C R
Inspector Macdonald series (31)
Part for a policeman
Creasey, John
Inspector Roger West series (38)
Part of my life
Ayer, Alfred Jules
My life series (1)
Part of the main
David, Janina
Square of sky trilogy (3)
Part of the sky
Peck, Robert Newton
Vermont farm series (2)
Part of virtue
Lewis, Royston
Inspector John Crow series (7)
Partial view
Maugham, William Somerset
Summing up trilogy (3)
Particulars of my life
Skinner, Burrhus Frederic
Behaviorist trilogy (1)
Parting breath
Aird, Catherine
Inspector C D Sloan series (7)
Parting of Arwen
Bradley, Marion Zimmer
Arwen series (2)
Parting years
Beaton, Cecil
Years diaries series (6)
Partisan
Simms, William Gilmore
American Revolution series (1)
Partisan demolition
Cort, Ned
Boxer Unit SS series (5)
Partners
Roberts, Nora
Flowers series (21)
Partners in brine
Raymond, John
Prospects series (1)
Partners in crime
Christie, Agatha
Tommy and Tuppence Beresford series (2)
King, Hilary
Sexton Blake series (1280)
Winfield, Julia
Private eyes series (1)
Partners in death
Bishop, Samuel P
Track series (2)
Partners in peril
Carter, Nicholas
Nicholas Carter series (624)
Partners of the night
Scott, Leroy
Bob Clifford series (1)
Partnership
Bentley, Phyllis
West Riding series (20)
Partridge family
Avallone, Michael
Partridge family series (1)
Parts unknown
Burns, Rex
Devlin Kirk series (2)
Party
Briggs, Raymond
Snowman series (2)
Johnson, Stacie
Eighteen Pine Street series (2)
Pike, Christopher
Final friends series (1)
Party at the penthouse
Chase, Arthur Minturn
Lieutenant Dan Durkin series (1)
Party for Lawty
Sarsfield, Maureen
Inspector Lane Parry series (2)
Party for the shooting
Revell, Louisa
Julia Tyler series (7)
Party frock
Streatfeild, Noel
Shoes series (5)
Party killer
Pentecost, Hugh
Julian Quist series (15)
Party of the year
Crosby, John Campbell
Horatio Cassidy series (1)
Party shoes
Streatfeild, Noel
Shoes series (5)
Party summer
Stine, Robert Lawrence
Fear Street super chiller series (1)
Party time!
Chase, Emily
Canby Hall series (21)
Party to murder
Underwood, Michael
Rosa Epton series (6)
Party was the pay-off
Holding, Elisabeth Sanxay
Lieutenant Levy series (2)
Pasadoble
Fitzgerald, Julia
Astromance series (3)
Pascal and the lioness
Guillot, Rene
Grichka series (2)
Pascoe's ghost
Hill, Reginald
Superintendent Andrew Dalziel and Sergeant Pascoe series (10)
Pasquier chronicles
Duhamel, Georges
Pasquier series (5)
Pass and a prayer
Bee, Clair
Chip Hilton series (7)
Pass beyond Kashmir
Mather, Berkely
Idwal Rees series (1)
Pass of morning
Styles, Showell
Simon and Mag series (4)
Pass the body
Sprigg, Christopher Saint John
Inspector Bernard Bray series (1)
Pass the gravy
Fair, A A
Bertha Cool and Donald Lam series (19)
Pass the happy pills
Delaney, Joyce
No starch in my coat series (3)
Passage for one
Frome, David
Evan Pinkerton series (11)
Passage of stars
Rasmussen, Alis A
Highroad trilogy (1)
Passage to Dodge City
Hogan, Ray
Shawn Starbuck series (9)
Passage to England
Chaudhuri, Nirad Chandra
Unknown Indian series (2)
Passage to mutiny
Kent, Alexander
Captain Richard Bolitho series (8)
Passage to Pluto
Walters, Hugh
Chris Godfrey series (14)
Passage to Pontefract
Plaidy, Jean
Plantagenet series (10)
Passage to Quivera
Zollinger, Norman
Macandrews Clan series (2)
Passage west
Killdeer, John
Mountain majesty series (5)
Passages in the life of Mrs Margaret Maitland
Oliphant, Margaret Oliphant Wilson
Mrs Margaret Maitland series (1)
Passenger car
Barkan, Joanne
Come aboard series (4)
Passenger on the U
Aveline, Claude
Suite Policiere series (2)
Passenger to London
Fay, Gerard
Passenger to London series (1)
Passenger to nowhere
Gilbert, Anthony
Arthur Crook series (42)
Passengers for Painted Rock
Tuttle, Wilbur Coleman
Hashknife Hartley and Sleepy Stevens series (24)
Passengers of destiny
Aragon, Louis
Real world series (3)
Passers by
Galsworthy, John
Modern comedy series (3)
Passing bells
Rock, Phillip
Greville family trilogy (1)
Passing for human
Scott, Jody
Sterling O'Blivion series (1)
Passing of Charles Lanson
Tracy, Louis
Inspector Furneaux series (8)
Passing of Fu Manchu
Suter, John Michael
Fu-Manchu series (16)
Suter, Jon Michael
Mustard jar series (4)
Passing of Gloria Munday
Garforth, John
Avengers series (5)
Passing of the gods
Smith, David Claude
Fall of the first world trilogy (3)
Passing of Tony Blount
Parkman, Sydney
Captain Bowker series (4)
Passing strange
Aird, Catherine
Inspector C D Sloan series (9)
Sale, Richard
Daniel Webster series (2)
Passing world
Lowndes, Marie Belloc
Arcadia series (4)
Passion and the glory
Nicole, Christopher
United States Navy series (6)
Passion fire
Burgess, Mallory
Tudor trilogy (2)
Passion Flower Hotel
Erskine, Rosalind
Passion Flowers series (1)
Passion Flowers in business
Erskine, Rosalind
Passion Flowers series (3)
Passion Flowers in Italy
Erskine, Rosalind
Passion Flowers series (2)
Passion for romance
Jepson, Edgar
Passion for romance series (1)
Passion in the desert
Balzac, Honore de
Scenes of military life series (2)
Passion in the park
Hilton, John Buxton
Superintendent Simon Kenworthy series (14)
Passion moon rising
Brandewyne, Rebecca
Chronicles of Tintagel series (1)
Passion of Joseph Pasquier
Duhamel, Georges
Pasquier series (10)
Passion pact
Janson, Hank
Hank Janson series (157)
Passion rose
Burgess, Mallory
Tudor trilogy (1)
Passion star
Burgess, Mallory
Tudor trilogy (3)
Passion within
Fisher, Vardis
Testament of man series (10)
Passionate
Brown, Carter
Lieutenant Al Wheeler series (15)
Janson, Hank
Hank Janson series (98)
Passionate enemies
Plaidy, Jean
Norman trilogy (3)
Passionate ghost
Allen, Sheila Rosalynd
Lovers of Steadford Abbey series (4)
Passionate Kensington
Ferguson, Rachel
Kensington series (1)
Passionate pagan
Brown, Carter
Danny Boyd series (11)
Passionate pilgrim
Merwin, Samuel
Henry Calverly series (3)
Passionate playmate
Janson, Hank
Hank Janson series (185)
Passionate victims
Lewis, Lange
Lieutenant Richard Tuck series (5)
Passionate witch
Smith, Thorne
Jennifer series (1)
Passions
Moore, Arthur
River of fortune trilogy (1)
Passion's captive
Copeland, Lori
Passion trilogy (2)
Passions of spring
Gobineau, Marceline
Stephanie series (1)
Passion's pilgrims
Romains, Jules
Men of goodwill series (4)
Passions spin the plot
Fisher, Vardis
Tragic life series (2)
Passion's trail
Fritch, Elizabeth
California trilogy (1)
Passover
Drucker, Malka
Jewish holidays series (2)
Passport
Bagot, Richard
Passport series (1)

Passport for a pilgrim
Leasor, James
Doctor Jason Love series (4)
Passport in suspense
Leasor, James
Doctor Jason Love series (3)
Passport into fear
Baker, William Howard
Sexton Blake series (1466)
Passport murder
Graham, Neill
Mister Sandyman series (2)
Passport to danger
Keene, Carolyn
Nancy Drew and Hardy boys supermystery series (18)
Paull, Jessica
Passport to danger series (1)
Stagg, James
Sexton Blake series (1426)
Passport to eternity
Goodwin, Ralph
Prisoner of war series (2)
Passport to oblivion
Leasor, James
Doctor Jason Love series (1)
Lee, Babs
Argus Steele series (2)
Passport to Perdition
Cole, Jackson
Jim Hatfield series (96)
Passport to peril
Buck, Peter
Marc Dean series (9)
Leasor, James
Doctor Jason Love series (2)
Passport to treason
O'Brine, Manning
Michael O'Kelly series (5)
Password to Diamonddwarf
Ezell, Marilyn
Susan Sand series (6)
Password to Larkspur Lane
Keene, Carolyn
Nancy Drew series (10)
Past conditional
Coward, Noel
Present and future series (2)
Past forgetting
Cushing, Peter
Past forgetting series (2)
Past imperfect
Chase, Ilka
Past imperfect series (1)
Past is myself
Bielenberg, Christabel
Past and future series (1)
Past Master
Tranter, Nigel Godwin
Patrick Gray series (3)
Past of forever
Coulson, Juanita
Children of the stars series (4)
Past praying for
Woods, Sara
Sir Nicholas Harding and Antony Maitland series (15)
Past, present and murder
Pentecost, Hugh
Julian Quist series (12)
Past reason hated
Robinson, Peter
Chief Inspector Alan Banks series (5)
Past recaptured
Proust, Marcel
Remembrance of things past series (12)
Past reckoning
Thomson, June
Inspector Finch series (16)
Past through tomorrow
Heinlein, Robert Anson
Future history series (5)
Lazarus Long series (1)
Pastel city
Harrison, Michael John
Viriconium series (1)
Pastime
Parker, Robert Brown
Spenser series (18)
Pastors and masters
Duhamel, Georges
Pasquier series (6)
Pastor's green
Pellow, John
Village parson trilogy (1)
Pastor's son
Walter, William Wilfred
Pastor's son trilogy (1)
Pat at the helm
Matthewman, Phyllis
Daneswood series (6)
Pat Collins and the captive scientist
Palmer, Bernard
Pat Collins series (6)
Pat Collins and the hidden treasure
Palmer, Bernard
Pat Collins series (3)
Pat Collins and the mysterious orbiting rocket
Palmer, Bernard
Jim Dunlap series (4)
Pat Collins series (5)
Pat Collins and the peculiar Doctor Brockton
Palmer, Bernard
Jim Dunlap series (1)
Pat Collins series (1)
Pat Collins and the secret engine
Palmer, Bernard
Jim Dunlap series (2)
Pat Collins series (2)
Pat Collins and the wingless plane
Palmer, Bernard
Jim Dunlap series (3)
Pat Collins series (4)
Pat of Silver Bush
Montgomery, Lucy Maud
Silver Bush series (1)
Pat, the parakeet
Darby, Joan
Animal adventure series (12)
Patch and a pawn
Oxenham, Elsie J
Patch series (1)
Rhoda series (2)
Patch and his friend Pom-Pom
Bracken, Anne
Patch series (2)
Patch and pawn
Oxenham, Elsie J
Tansy series (2)
Patch of the Odin soldier
Marsh, Geoffrey
Lincoln Blackthorne series (3)
Patchwork cat
Bayley, Nicola
Copycats series (5)
Patchwork child
Astor, Brooke
Patchwork child series (1)
Patchwork girl
Niven, Larry
Gil Hamilton series (2)
Known Space series (13)
Patchwork Girl of Oz
Baum, Lyman Frank
Oz series (7)
Patchwork hero
Noonan, Michael
Choker series (1)
Patchwork pack
Collins, Freda
Woodland Pack series (8)
Patchwork papers
Thurston, Ernest Temple
Bellwattle and Cruikshank series (1)
Path
White, Edmund Valentine
Indian romance series (1)
Path in the ravine
Ellis, Edward Sylvester
Forest and prairie trilogy (2)
Path of Exoterra
McBain, Gordon
Exoterra series (1)
Path of fear
Graydon, William Murray
Sexton Blake series (292)
Path of fire
Ingrid, Charles
Patterns of chaos series (2)
Path of ghosts
Macleod, Robert
Talos Cord series (6)
Path of peril
Fickling, David
Fantasy quest book series (1)
Path of the eclipse
Yarbro, Chelsea Quinn
Count Ragoczy Saint-Germain series (4)
Path of the hero king
Tranter, Nigel Godwin
Robert the Bruce trilogy (2)
Path of the promise keeper
Leeson, Muriel
Promise keeper series (2)
Path of the Raven
Boucher, Alan Estcourt
Halli Thordason series (1)
Path of the spendthrift
Carter, Nicholas
Nicholas Carter series (442)
Path through the circle of time
Lee, Samantha
Owen Lightbringer trilogy (3)
Path through the sea
Blyton, Enid
Bible stories series (7)
Path through the trees
Milne, Christopher
Enchanted places series (2)
Path to conquest
Weinstein, Howard
V series (13)
Path to honour
Grier, Sydney Carlyon
Century series (3)
Path to power
Caro, Robert A
Years of Lyndon Johnson series (1)
Path to the silent country
Banks, Lynne Reid
Bronte series (2)
Pathet vengeance
Roberts, Mark Kelly
Soldier for hire series (7)
Pathfinder
Cole, Judd
Cheyenne series (9)
Cooper, James Fenimore
Leatherstocking series (3)
Pathfinders
Gravel, Geary
Autumn world series (2)
Pathfinder's great flight
Langley, John Prentice
Aviation series (4)
Pathless trail
Friel, Arthur Olney
McKay, Knowlton and Ryan series (1)
Paths of love
Vercors
On the shore trilogy (3)
Paths of the perambulator
Foster, Alan Dean
Spellsinger series (5)
Pathway
Williamson, Henry
Flax of dream series (4)
Pathway to the sun
Timms, Edward Vivian
Australian saga series (2)
Patience of a saint
Greeley, Andrew Moran
Time between the stars (3)
Patience of Maigret
Simenon, Georges
Inspector Jules Maigret series (4)
Inspector Jules Maigret series (10)
Inspector Jules Maigret series (67)
Patient in Room 18
Eberhart, Mignon Good
Sarah Keate and Lance O'Leary series (1)
Patient in 202
James, Josephine
Kathy Martin series (5)
Patients of a saint
Tibber, Robert
General practitioner series (3)
Patricia
Elliot, Emilia
Joan series (3)
Patricia and the other girls
Murphy, Marguerite
Patricia trilogy (2)
Patricia from New York
Murphy, Marguerite
Patricia trilogy (1)
Patricia, the beautiful
Kimbrough, Katheryn
Phenwick women series (4)
Patrician
Galsworthy, John
Country house trilogy (3)
Patricia's problem
Murphy, Marguerite
Patricia trilogy (3)
Patrick Butler for the defence
Carr, John Dickson
Patrick Butler series (2)
Patrick engaged
Armstrong, Anthony
Patrick Kennedy series (2)
Patrick helps
Armstrong, Anthony
Patrick Kennedy series (3)
Patrick takes a trip
Daly, Maureen
Patrick series (2)
Patrick, undergraduate
Armstrong, Anthony
Patrick Kennedy series (1)
Patrick visits the farm
Daly, Maureen
Patrick series (1)
Patrick visits the library
Daly, Maureen
Patrick series (3)
Patrick visits the zoo
Daly, Maureen
Patrick series (4)
Patrick's aeroplane
Lofgren, Ulf
Patrick series (1)
Patrick's circus
Lofgren, Ulf
Patrick series (3)
Patrick's dinosaurs
Carrick, Carol
Patrick's dinosaurs series (1)
Patrick's workshop
Lofgren, Ulf
Patrick series (2)
Patrimony
Adams, Robert
Horseclans series (6)
Patriot
Fogazzaro, Antonio
Maironi family trilogy (1)
Walter, Alexia E
Sir Edgar Ewart series (1)
Patriot games
Clancy, Tom
Jack Ryan series (1)
Patriotic murders
Christie, Agatha
Hercule Poirot series (21)
Patriots
Jakes, John
Kent family series (2)
Long, William Stuart
Australians series (8)
Target, George William
Post-war Britain series (8)
Wall, Robert Emmet
Nowell family series (4)
Patrocleia
Logue, Christopher
Iliad adaptations series (2)
Patrol car
Jeffries, Roderic Graeme
Police series (3)
Patrol of the Sun Dance Trail
Connor, Ralph
North-West Mounted Police series (2)
Patrol to the Golden Horn
Fullerton, Alexander
Nick Everard series (3)
Patron
Blackburn, Thomas Wakefield
Stanton Empire series (4)
Pat's promise
Asher, Sandra Fenichel
Ballet One series (3)
Patsy Carroll at Wilderness Lodge
Gordon, Grace
Patsy Carroll series (1)
Patsy Carroll in old New England
Gordon, Grace
Patsy Carroll series (4)
Patsy Carroll in the Golden West
Gordon, Grace
Patsy Carroll series (3)
Patsy Carroll under southern skies
Gordon, Grace
Patsy Carroll series (2)
Pattern for murder
Knight, David
Shell Scott series (16)
Shriber, Ione Sandberg
Lieutenant Bill Grady series (7)
Warman, Erik
Inspector John Isidore Bloom series (2)
Pattern for panic
Prather, Richard Scott
Shell Scott series (21)
Pattern for perfidy
Bentley, John
Glen Gibson series (2)
Pattern in poison-ivy
Bowman, Gerald
Michael Shannon series (1)
Pattern of islands
Grimble, Arthur
Gilbert and Ellice Islands series (1)
Pattern of murder
Symons, Maurice
George Roberts series (2)
Pattern of silver strings
De Lint, Charles
Cerin Songweaver series (2)
Pattern of violence
Busby, Roger
Detective Inspector Leric series (5)
Pattern under the plough
Evans, George Ewart
Farm life series (3)
Patterned rape
Janson, Hank
Hank Janson series (186)
Patternmaster
Butler, Octavia Estelle
Patternists series (1)
Patterns and coincidences
Neihardt, John Gneisenau
All is but a beginning series (2)
Patterns in the dust
Grant-Adamson, Lesley
Rain Morgan series (1)
Patterns of chaos
Kapp, Colin
Chaos series (1)
Patterns on the wall
Yates, Elizabeth
Journeyman series (1)
Patterns we see from the big red bus
Wood, Leslie
Big red bus series (3)
Patti
Saunders, Susan
Sleepover friends series (17)
Patti's city adventure
Saunders, Susan
Sleepover friends series (38)
Patti's last sleepover
Saunders, Susan
Sleepover friends series (9)
Patti's luck
Saunders, Susan
Sleepover friends series (1)
Patti's new look
Saunders, Susan
Sleepover friends series (4)
Patti's secret wish
Saunders, Susan
Sleepover friends series (13)
Patty and Azalea
Wells, Carolyn
Patty Fairfield series (17)
Patty and Priscilla
Webster, Jean
Patty series (1)
Patty at home
Wells, Carolyn
Patty Fairfield series (2)
Patty Blossom
Wells, Carolyn
Patty Fairfield series (15)
Patty-bride
Wells, Carolyn
Patty Fairfield series (16)
Patty Cake
Dolce, Janet Ellen
Baby doll board books series (4)
Patty Fairfield
Wells, Carolyn
Patty Fairfield series (1)
Patty in Paris
Wells, Carolyn
Patty Fairfield series (4)
Patty in the city
Wells, Carolyn
Patty Fairfield series (3)
Patty Lou and the Seminole Indians
Miller, Basil
Patty Lou series (14)
Patty Lou and the White Gold Ranch
Miller, Basil
Patty Lou series (2)
Patty Lou at Sunset Pass
Miller, Basil
Patty Lou series (11)
Patty Lou, flying missionary
Miller, Basil
Patty Lou series (7)
Patty Lou home on the range
Miller, Basil
Patty Lou series (10)
Patty Lou in the Coast Guard
Miller, Basil
Patty Lou series (4)
Patty Lou in the wilds
Miller, Basil
Patty Lou series (8)
Patty Lou lost in the jungle
Miller, Basil
Patty Lou series (12)
Patty Lou of the Golden West
Miller, Basil
Patty Lou series (1)
Patty Lou, range nurse
Miller, Basil
Patty Lou series (13)

Patty Lou, the flying nurse
Miller, Basil
Patty Lou series (5)
Patty Lou, the girl forester
Miller, Basil
Patty Lou series (6)
Patty Lou under Western skies
Miller, Basil
Patty Lou series (9)
Patty Lou's pot of gold
Miller, Basil
Patty Lou series (3)
Patty's butterfly days
Wells, Carolyn
Patty Fairfield series (10)
Patty's fortune
Wells, Carolyn
Patty Fairfield series (14)
Patty's friends
Wells, Carolyn
Patty Fairfield series (5)
Patty's last dance
Pascal, Francine
Sweet Valley twins series (65)
Patty's motor car
Wells, Carolyn
Patty Fairfield series (9)
Patty's pleasure trip
Wells, Carolyn
Patty Fairfield series (7)
Patty's romance
Wells, Carolyn
Patty Fairfield series (13)
Patty's social season
Wells, Carolyn
Patty Fairfield series (11)
Patty's story
Berger, Gilda
Straight talk about drugs series (2)
Patty's success
Wells, Carolyn
Patty Fairfield series (8)
Patty's suitors
Wells, Carolyn
Patty Fairfield series (12)
Patty's summer days
Wells, Carolyn
Patty Fairfield series (6)
Patuffa
Harraden, Beatrice
Patuffa series (2)
Paul
Kingsley, Florence Morse
Early Christian series (3)
Paul and Arthur and the little explorer
Rockwell, Anne Foote
Paul and Arthur series (2)
Paul and Arthur search for the egg
Rockwell, Anne Foote
Paul and Arthur series (1)
Paul and Perdita
Dodd, Catherine Isabel
Red Lattice series (2)
Paul and Sally at Christmas
Iseborg, Harry
Paul and Sally series (3)
Paul Barton
Leslie, Madeline
Woodbine series (3)
Paul Beck, detective
Bodkin, Matthias McDonnell
Paul Beck series (6)
Paul Beck, the rule of thumb detective
Bodkin, Matthias McDonnell
Paul Beck series (1)
Paul Bunyan swings his axe
McCormick, Dell J
Paul Bunyan series (1)
Paul Campenhaye, specialist in criminology
Fletcher, Joseph Smith
Paul Campenhaye series (2)
Paul Faber, surgeon
Macdonald, George
Thomas Wingfold trilogy (2)
Paul Ferroll
Clive, Caroline
Paul Ferroll series (1)
Paul Jones
Dumas, Alexandre
Paul Jones series (2)
Paul McCartney story
Tremlett, George
Rock stars series (8)
Paul Patoff
Crawford, Francis Marion
Paul Griggs series (2)
Paul Prescott's charge
Alger, Horatio
Campaign trilogy (2)
Paul Revere and the Boston Tea Party
Kornblatt, Marc
Time traveler series (5)
Paul, Sally and Little Grey
Iseborg, Harry
Paul and Sally series (2)
Paul, Sally and the fox cub
Iseborg, Harry
Paul and Sally series (1)
Paul, Sally and the wash-tub
Iseborg, Harry
Paul and Sally series (4)
Paul, speak for me
Graeber, Charlotte Towner
Speak for me series (3)
Paul Temple and the front page men
Durbridge, Francis
Paul Temple series (2)
Paul Temple and the Harkdale robbery
Durbridge, Francis
Paul Temple series (8)
Paul Temple and the Kelby affair
Durbridge, Francis
Paul Temple series (9)
Paul Temple and the Madison case
Durbridge, Francis
Paul Temple series (13)
Paul Temple and the Margo mystery
Durbridge, Francis
Paul Temple series (12)
Paul Temple intervenes
Durbridge, Francis
Paul Temple series (4)
Paul, the peddler
Alger, Horatio
Tattered Tom series (2)
Pauline
Carter, Nicholas
Nicholas Carter series (388)
Chardonne, Jacques
House of Barnery series (2)
Paulton plot
Adams, Herbert
Jimmy Haswell series (8)
Paulus and mole
Dulieu, Jean
Paulus series (7)
Paulus and Solomon
Dulieu, Jean
Paulus series (11)
Paulus and the acornmen
Dulieu, Jean
Paulus series (14)
Paulus and the dragon
Dulieu, Jean
Paulus series (12)
Paulus and the three robbers
Dulieu, Jean
Paulus series (9)
Pavement artist mystery
Jardine, Warwick
Sexton Blake series (933)
Pavilion
Vipont, Elfrida
Haverard family series (5)
Pavilion by the lake
Rees, Arthur John
Inspector Luckraft series (3)
Pawn
Macdonnell, James Edmond
Captain Peter Bentley series (31)
Pawn in frankincense
Dunnett, Dorothy
Francis Crawford of Lymond series (4)
Pawn in jeopardy
Rattray, Simon
Hugo Bishop series (4)
Pawn of prophecy
Eddings, David
Belgariad series (1)
Pawn to King's Cross
Mazzaro, Ed
Undercover series (4)
Pawnee bargain
Sharpe, Jon
Trailsman series (108)
Pawnee kid
Evans, Tabor
Longarm series (134)
Pawnee rampage
Gentry, Buck
Eli Holten series (8)
Pawns and symbols
Larson, Majliss
Star trek series (26)
Pawns of fear
Manor, Jason
Steve Summers series (3)
Pawns of Null-A
Van Vogt, Alfred Elton
Null-A series (2)
Pawnshop murder
Brandon, John Gordon
Arthur Stukeley Pennington series (5)
Inspector Patrick Aloysius McCarthy series (7)
Paws before dying
Conant, Susan
Dog trainer mystery series (4)
Paws with numbers
Bisset, Donald
Paws series (2)
Paws with shapes
Bisset, Donald
Paws series (1)
Pax
Logue, Christopher
Iliad adaptations series (4)
Pax Britannica
Morris, James Humphrey
British Empire trilogy (2)
Paxton pride
Carroll, Shana
Paxton women series (1)
Pay as you die
Crawford, Robert
Arthur Salisbury and Frank Shearer series (1)
Pay dirt
Rounds, Glen
Whitey series (1)
Pay dirt, and other Whispering Sands stories
Gardner, Erle Stanley
Whispering Sands series (2)
Pay-off
Barry, Joe
Rush Henry series (5)
Pay off
Graham, Neill
Solo Malcolm series (23)
Pay-off for a penny
Kane, Martin
Martin Kane series (19)
Pay-off in blood
Halliday, Brett
Michael Shayne series (42)
Pay off in lead
Winstan, Matt
Reuben Brown series (7)
Pay-off in Switzerland
Macleod, Robert
Jonathan Gaunt series (5)
Pay-off pitch
Bee, Clair
Chip Hilton series (16)
Pay your respects
Graber, Richard
Ray Decker series (2)
Payback
Colter, Dale
Regulator series (10)
Helm, Eric
Ground Zero series (18)
Paydirt
Disher, Garry
Wyatt series (2)
Paying the piper
McCrumb, Sharon
Elizabeth Macpherson series (4)
Paying the price
Carter, Nicholas
Nicholas Carter series (609)
Payment in blood
George, Elizabeth
Inspector Thomas Lynley and Sergeant Barbara Havers series (2)
Payment in full
Bobin, John William
Sexton Blake series (9)
Payment in kind
Jance, Judith A
J P Beaumont series (9)
Payment suspended
Bobin, John William
Sexton Blake series (168)
Payoff
Howard, Hartley
Glenn Bowman series (36)
Smith, Don
Tim Parnell series (3)
Payoff for the banker
Lockridge, Frances
Bill Wiegand series (8)
Mister and Mrs North series (9)
Payoff for Wells Fargo
Denver, Lee
Deputy Marshal Dave Halloran series (4)
Payoff game
Eisenberg, Lisa
South City cops series (3)
Payoff in Panama
Thorne, Ramsay
Captain Gringo series (22)
Payoff on Fever Street
Wolf, Jack
Timothy Rourke series (2)
Payola
Keene, Day
Johnny Aloha series (2)
Payroll of fate
Tuttle, Wilbur Coleman
Hashknife Hartley and Sleepy Stevens series (28)
Pazenger problem
Plain, Josephine
Colin Anstruther series (3)
PB on ice
Rose, Gerald
PB series (2)
PB takes a holiday
Rose, Gerald
PB series (1)
Peabody's all at sea
Thomson, Ruth
Detective Peabody series (2)
Peabody's first case
Thomson, Ruth
Detective Peabody series (1)
Peacable kingdom
De Hartog, Jan
Peaceable kingdom series (2)
Kelland, Clarence Budington
Peacable kingdom series (1)
Kennelly, Ardyth
Mormon series (1)
Peace after war
Gironella, Jose Maria
Alvear family trilogy (3)
Peace and dripping toast
Willis, Frederick
Edwardian London trilogy (2)
Peace and the Protestant succession
Trevelyan, George Macaulay
Queen Anne's England trilogy (3)
Peace at last
Murphy, Jill
Peace series (1)
Peace breaks out
Knowles, John
Devon School series (2)
Thirkell, Angela
Barsetshire series (15)
Peace comes to Sainte monique
Lister, Stephen
Sainte Monique series (3)
Peace Company
Green, Roland James
Peace Company trilogy (1)
Peace Corps nurse
James, Josephine
Kathy Martin series (12)
Peace for our time
Parkinson, Roger
War Cabinet trilogy (1)
Peace in Friendship village
Gale, Zora
Friendship village series (5)
Peace in the house
Balzac, Honore de
Scenes of private life series (10)
Peace is not at hand
Thompson, Robert
Vietnam War series (2)
Peace like a river
Fisher, Vardis
Testament of man series (10)
Peace marshal
Gruber, Frank
Historical Western series (1)
Peace of the household
Balzac, Honore de
Scenes of private life series (10)
Peace on earth
Lem, Stanislaw
Ijon Tichy series (4)
Peace seekers
Aaseng, Nathan
Nobel Prize winners series (3)
Peace war
Vinge, Vernor
Realtime series (1)
Peace with honour
Grier, Sydney Carlyon
Modern East series (3)
Milne, Alan Alexander
Peace and war series (1)
Peaceable man
Grover, Marshall
Bleak Creek series (2)
Peaceful guns
Pritchett, Ron
Buck Lawrence and Zeke Henderson series (1)
Peacekeeper
Newsom, Ed
Chagro Brannigan series (4)
Peacekeepers
DeWeese, Gene
Star trek, the next generation series (2)
Peacelord of the universe
Scheer, Karl Herbert
Perry Rhodan series (13)
Peacemaker
Butler, David
Edward VII series (2)
Cook, Will
Guthrie McCabe trilogy (2)
Garrett, Charles C
Gunslinger series (8)
Ladd, Justin
Abilene series (1)
Perry, Steve
Stellar rangers series (1)
Peacemaker, and other stories
Arthur, Timothy Shay
Home stories series (4)
Peacemaker Pass
Dalton, Kit
Buckskin series (21)
Peacemakers
Cook, Will
United States Cavalry trilogy (2)
Edson, John Thomas
Floating Outfit series (32)
Peacock
Jones, Olive
Barfield series (12)
Peacock brides
Bullett, Gerald
Peacock family series (2)
Peacock duck
Gissing, Vera
Pippins series (1)
Peacock feather murders
Dickson, Carter
Sir Henry Merrivale series (7)
Peacock House
Avery, Gillian
Julia and Henry Gresham trilogy (3)
Peacock in flight
Gordon, Katharine
Peacock series (2)
Peacock in jeopardy
Gordon, Katharine
Peacock series (5)
Peacock is a bird of prey
Foley, Rae
Hiram Potter series (1)
Peacock Palace scoop
Laird, Elizabeth
Toucan Tecs series (8)
Peacock party
Aldridge, Alan
Butterfly ball series (2)
Peacock ring
Gordon, Katharine
Peacock series (4)
Peacock's feather
Woodhouse, Sarah
Season of mists series (2)
Peak of frenzy
Brand, Hilary
Hilary Brand series (3)
Peak performance
Baker, Ivon
David Meynell series (2)
Peanut and Jilly forever
Haas, Dorothy
Peanut Butter and Jilly series (2)
Peanut butter and jelly is not for kids
Kelly, Bill
Pepperoni Hero series (2)
Peanut butter murders
Sawyer, Corinne Holt
Senior citizens series (4)
Peanut-butter pilgrims
Delton, Judy
Pee wee scout series (6)
Peanut in charge
Haas, Dorothy
Peanut Butter and Jilly series (6)
Peanuts for Billy Ben
Lenski, Lois
Roundabout America series (2)
Pearl divers
Coleman, James Covington
Deep-sea adventure series (4)
Pearl galleon
Tufts, Warren
Casey Ruggles series (6)
Pearl Harbor periscopes
Jones, J Farragut
Silent service series (4)
Pearl-headed pin
Durham, David
Inspector J Rason series (3)

Pearl of blood
Netzen, Klaus
Killers series (5)
Pearl of Lima
Verne, Jules
J R Kazallon series (2)
Pearl of Patmos
Lord, Jeffrey
Richard Blade series (7)
Pearl of the Habsburgs
Hamilton, Julia
Habsburg series (3)
Pearl of the soul of the world
Pierce, Meredith Ann
Aeriel trilogy (3)
Pearl pirates
Edwards, Hugh
Sea Witch series (2)
Pearlhanger
Gash, Jonathan
Lovejoy series (9)
Pearls before swine
Allingham, Margery
Albert Campion series (14)
Drysdale, Ann
Pig farming trilogy (3)
Pearls, girls and Monty Bodkin
Wodehouse, Pelham Grenville
Monty Bodkin series (2)
Pearls of doom
Teed, George Hamilton
Sexton Blake series (595)
Pearl's pirates
Asch, Frank
Pearl series (2)
Pearl's promise
Asch, Frank
Pearl series (1)
Pearly Queen
Staples, Mary Jane
South London series (7)
Pearson County raiders
Grover, Marshall
Larry and Stretch series (214)
Peasantry
Balzac, Honore de
Scenes of country life series (1)
Peasants
Balzac, Honore de
Scenes of country life series (1)
Peasants' Revolt
Birt, David
Middle Ages series (13)
Peas-Blossom
Whitaker, Evelyn
Honor Bright series (2)
Peat Moss and ivy and the birthday present
Berenstain, Michael
Peat Moss and Ivy series (2)
Peat Moss and Ivy meet Santa Claws
Berenstain, Michael
Peat Moss and Ivy series (3)
Peat Moss and Ivy's backyard adventure
Berenstain, Michael
Peat Moss and Ivy series (1)
Pebble in the sky
Asimov, Isaac
Trantorian Empire trilogy (1)
Pebbles Flintstone
Lewis, Jean
Flintstones series (1)
Pebbles go to sea
Cooper, Michael
Pebbles series (5)
Pebbles go to town
Cooper, Michael
Pebbles series (2)
Pebbles in the country
Cooper, Michael
Pebbles series (3)
Pebbles' night adventure
Cooper, Michael
Pebbles series (4)
Peckover holds the baby
Kenyon, Michael
Inspector Henry Peckover series (5)
Peckover joins the choir
Kenyon, Michael
Inspector Henry Peckover series (8)
Peck's bad boy abroad
Peck, George Wilbur
Peck's bad boy series (6)
Peck's bad boy and his pa
George, Charles
Peck's bad boy series (1)
Peck, George Wilbur
Peck's bad boy series (1)
Peck's bad boy and the groceryman
Peck, George Wilbur
Peck's bad boy series (2)
Peck's bad boy in an airship
Peck, George Wilbur
Peck's bad boy series (9)
Peck's bad boy with the circus
Peck, George Wilbur
Peck's bad boy series (7)
Peck's bad boy with the cowboys
Peck, George Wilbur
Peck's bad boy series (8)
Peck's fun
Peck, George Wilbur
Peck's bad boy series (9)
Peck's Irish friend
Peck, George Wilbur
Peck's bad boy series (3)
Peck's red-headed boy
Peck, George Wilbur
Peck's bad boy series (5)
Peck's sunshine book
Peck, George Wilbur
Peck's bad boy series (9)
Peck's Uncle Ike and the red headed boy
Peck, George Wilbur
Peck's bad boy series (4)
Pecos
Mitchum, Hank
Stage coach station series (27)
Pecos dollars
Hardin, J D
Raider and Doc series (38)
Pecos law
Scott, Bradford
Walt Slade series (81)
Pecos manhunt
Chisholm, Matt
Joe Blade series (4)
Pecos plainsmen
Savage, Buck
Speed Johnson series (5)
Pecos poison
Cole, Jackson
Jim Hatfield series (64)
Pecos trail
Scott, Bradford
Walt Slade series (31)
Peculiar exploits of Brigadier Ffellowes
Lanier, Sterling Edmund
Brigadier Ffellowes series (1)
Peculiar treasure
Ferber, Edna
Peculiar treasure series (1)
Peculiar triumph of Professor Branestawm
Hunter, Norman
Professor Branestawm series (4)
Peddlers
Fisher, Leonard Everett
Colonial Americans series (12)
Peder victorious
Rolvaag, Ole Edvart
Per Hansa trilogy (2)
Pedlock and Sons
Longstreet, Stephen
Pedlock family series (3)
Pedlock inheritance
Longstreet, Stephen
Pedlock family series (5)
Pedlock saint, Pedlock sinner
Longstreet, Stephen
Pedlock family series (4)
Pedlocks
Longstreet, Stephen
Pedlock family series (1)
Pedlocks in love
Longstreet, Stephen
Pedlock family series (6)
Pedro Orange
Reed, Giles
Munch Bunch character series (10)
Pee wee Christmas
Delton, Judy
Pee wee scout series (7)
Pee-Wee Harris
Fitzhugh, Percy Keese
Pee-Wee Harris series (1)
Pee-Wee Harris adrift
Fitzhugh, Percy Keese
Pee-Wee Harris series (5)
Pee-Wee Harris and the sunken treasure
Fitzhugh, Percy Keese
Pee-Wee Harris series (10)
Pee-Wee Harris, as good as his word
Fitzhugh, Percy Keese
Pee-Wee Harris series (8)
Pee-Wee Harris fixer
Fitzhugh, Percy Keese
Pee-Wee Harris series (7)
Pee-Wee Harris, F.O.B. Bridgeboro
Fitzhugh, Percy Keese
Pee-Wee Harris series (6)
Pee-Wee Harris in camp
Fitzhugh, Percy Keese
Pee-Wee Harris series (3)
Pee-Wee Harris in darkest Africa
Fitzhugh, Percy Keese
Pee-Wee Harris series (12)
Pee-Wee Harris in luck
Fitzhugh, Percy Keese
Pee-Wee Harris series (4)
Pee-Wee Harris, mayor for a day
Fitzhugh, Percy Keese
Pee-Wee Harris series (9)
Pee-Wee Harris on the briny deep
Fitzhugh, Percy Keese
Pee-Wee Harris series (11)
Pee-Wee Harris on the trail
Fitzhugh, Percy Keese
Pee-Wee Harris series (2)
Pee-Wee Harris turns detective
Fitzhugh, Percy Keese
Pee-Wee Harris series (13)
Pee wee jubilee
Delton, Judy
Pee wee scout series (11)
Pee wees on parade
Delton, Judy
Pee wee scout series (17)
Pee wees on skis
Delton, Judy
Pee wee scout series (21)
Peedie Peebles colour book
Hedderwick, Mairi
Peedie Peebles series (2)
Peedie Peebles' summer or winter book
Hedderwick, Mairi
Peedie Peebles series (1)
Peeko the beaver
Rutley, Cecil Bernard
Wild life story series (3)
Peel me a lotus
Clift, Charmian
Greek island series (2)
Peep in the dark
Astrop, John
Peep series (2)
Peep-Larssons go sailing
Unnerstad, Edith
Larsson family series (2)
Peep show
Wilkinson, Walter
Puppets series (1)
Peeping Tom murders
Baynes, Jack
Morocco Jones series (4)
Peep's bath
Astrop, John
Peep series (3)
Peep's diary
Astrop, John
Peep series (1)
Peep's pals
Astrop, John
Peep series (4)
Peewee Clinton, plebe
Stevens, William Oliver
Peewee Clinton series (1)
Peg and her company
Hann, Dorothy Owen
Peg series (4)
Peg and James and the new baby
Batchelor, Mary
Peg and James series (2)
Peg and James go to market
Batchelor, Mary
Peg and James series (1)
Peg and James go to the park
Batchelor, Mary
Peg and James series (4)
Peg and james plant some bulbs
Batchelor, Mary
Peg and James series (3)
Peg, junior
Hann, Dorothy Owen
Peg series (6)
Peg-Leg and the fur pirates
Dawlish, Peter
Captain Peg-Leg series (2)
Peg-Leg and the invaders
Dawlish, Peter
Captain Peg-Leg series (3)
Peg-Leg sweeps the sea
Dawlish, Peter
Captain Peg-Leg series (4)
Peg, lieutenant
Hann, Dorothy Owen
Peg series (2)
Peg o' the Ring, a maid of Denewood
Knipe, Emilie Benson
Denewood series (3)
Pegasus in flight
McCaffrey, Anne
Pegasus series (2)
Peggy
Richards, Laura Elizabeth
Three Margarets series (3)
Peggy and the giant's aunt
Hillyard, Mary Dorothea
Peggy series (2)
Peggy and the pony
Sewell, Helen
Peggy series (1)
Peggy and the pup
Sewell, Helen
Peggy series (2)
Peggy Archer, missionary candidate
Palmer, Bernard
Career series (5)
Peggy by request
Dell, Ethel May
Nick Ratcliffe series (3)
Peggy covers London
Bugbee, Emma
Peggy series (3)
Peggy covers the clipper
Bugbee, Emma
Peggy series (4)
Peggy covers the news
Bugbee, Emma
Peggy series (1)
Peggy covers Washington
Bugbee, Emma
Peggy series (2)
Peggy finds the theater
Hughes, Virginia
Peggy Lane series (1)
Peggy goes Hollywood
Hughes, Virginia
Peggy Lane series (5)
Peggy goes overseas
Bugbee, Emma
Peggy series (5)
Peggy goes straw hat
Hughes, Virginia
Peggy Lane series (3)
Peggy keeps house
Haskell, Helen Eggleston
Katrinka series (4)
Peggy of the Chalet School
Brent-Dyer, Elinor Mary
Chalet School series (22)
Peggy on the road
Hughes, Virginia
Peggy Lane series (4)
Peggy Owen
Madison, Lucy Foster
Peggy Owen series (1)
Peggy Owen and liberty
Madison, Lucy Foster
Peggy Owen series (4)
Peggy Owen at Yorktown
Madison, Lucy Foster
Peggy Owen series (3)
Peggy Owen, patriot
Madison, Lucy Foster
Peggy Owen series (2)
Peggy Pendleton
Jameson, E M
Pendletons trilogy (2)
Peggy Pendleton's plan
Jameson, E M
Pendletons trilogy (2)
Peggy plays off-Broadway
Hughes, Virginia
Peggy Lane series (2)
Peggy plays Paris
Hughes, Virginia
Peggy Lane series (7)
Peggy Raymond's school days
Smith, Harriet Lummis
Friendly Terrace series (3)
Peggy Raymond's vacation
Smith, Harriet Lummis
Friendly Terrace series (2)
Peggy Raymond's way
Smith, Harriet Lummis
Friendly Terrace series (5)
Peggy Stewart
Jackson, Gabrielle Emilie
Peggy Stewart series (1)
Peggy Stewart at home
Jackson, Gabrielle Emilie
Peggy Stewart series (2)
Peggy Stewart at school
Jackson, Gabrielle Emilie
Peggy Stewart series (3)
Peggy Stewart, navy girl
Jackson, Gabrielle Emilie
Peggy Stewart series (4)
Peggy, the concerned
Kimbrough, Katheryn
Phenwick women series (31)
Peggy's giant
Hillyard, Mary Dorothea
Peggy series (1)
Peggy's London debut
Hughes, Virginia
Peggy Lane series (6)
Peggy's Roman holiday
Hughes, Virginia
Peggy Lane series (8)
Pegmen go walkabout
McFadyen, Ella
Pegmen series (2)
Pegmen tales
McFadyen, Ella
Pegmen series (1)
Peg's babies
Hann, Dorothy Owen
Peg series (5)
Peg's patrol
Hann, Dorothy Owen
Peg series (1)
Pekin target
Hall, Adam
Quiller series (11)
Peking
Carter, Nick
Nick Carter series (42)
Peking connection
Smith, Don
Secret mission series (18)
Peking dossier
Carter, Nick
Nick Carter series (84)
Peking duck
Simon, Roger Lichtenberg
Moses Wine series (3)
Peking plot
Hayes, Ralph Eugene
Check Force series (4)
Peking pornographer
Knight, Mallory T
Man from T.O.M.C.A.T. series (8)
Peking target
Hall, Adam
Quiller series (11)
Pel among the Pueblos
Hebden, Mark
Inspector Clovis Pel series (11)
Pel and the bombers
Hebden, Mark
Inspector Clovis Pel series (6)
Pel and the faceless corpse
Hebden, Mark
Inspector Clovis Pel series (2)
Pel and the missing person
Hebden, Mark
Inspector Clovis Pel series (15)
Pel and the Paris mob
Hebden, Mark
Inspector Clovis Pel series (10)
Pel and the party spirit
Hebden, Mark
Inspector Clovis Pel series (14)
Pel and the perfect partner
Hebden, Juliet
Inspector Clovis Pel series (19)
Pel and the picture of innocence
Hebden, Mark
Inspector Clovis Pel series (13)
Pel and the pirates
Hebden, Mark
Inspector Clovis Pel series (8)
Pel and the predators
Hebden, Mark
Inspector Clovis Pel series (7)
Pel and the promised land
Hebden, Mark
Inspector Clovis Pel series (16)
Pel and the prowler
Hebden, Mark
Inspector Clovis Pel series (9)
Pel and the sepulchre job
Hebden, Mark
Inspector Clovis Pel series (17)
Pel and the staghound
Hebden, Mark
Inspector Clovis Pel series (5)
Pel and the touch of pitch
Hebden, Mark
Inspector Clovis Pel series (12)
Pel is puzzled
Hebden, Mark
Inspector Clovis Pel series (4)
Pel picks up the pieces
Hebden, Juliet
Inspector Clovis Pel series (18)
Pel under pressure
Hebden, Mark
Inspector Clovis Pel series (3)
Pelham murder case
Barrett, Monte
Peter Cardigan series (1)

Pelican at Blandings
Wodehouse, Pelham Grenville
Blandings Castle series (13)
Peligro's last hour
Grover, Marshall
Larry and Stretch series (288)
Pelle in the big city
Peterson, Hans
Pelle Jansson series (2)
Pelle in trouble
Peterson, Hans
Pelle Jansson series (3)
Pelle Jansson
Peterson, Hans
Pelle Jansson series (1)
Pellucidar
Burroughs, Edgar Rice
Pellucidar series (2)
Pemberley
Tennant, Emma
Pride and prejudice series (2)
Pembroke Mason affair
Barton, George
Bromley Barnes series (4)
Pemex chart
Carter, Nick
Nick Carter series (129)
Pemrose Lorry, camp fire girl
Hornibrook, Isabel
Pemrose Lorry series (1)
Pemrose Lorry, radio amateur
Hornibrook, Isabel
Pemrose Lorry series (2)
Pemrose Lorry, sky sailor
Hornibrook, Isabel
Pemrose Lorry series (3)
Pemrose Lorry, torchbearer
Hornibrook, Isabel
Pemrose Lorry series (4)
Penance for Jerry Kennedy
Higgins, George Vincent
Jerry Kennedy series (4)
Pencarrow
Scanlan, Nelle Margaret
Pencarrow family series (1)
Pencil points to murder
Barber, Willetta Ann
Christopher Storm series (2)
Pendellion
Charlton, Moyra
Treherne family series (1)
Pendennis
Thackeray, William Makepeace
Arthur Pendennis series (1)
Pendleton fortune
Harding, Dolores Charlotte Frederica
Pendleton series (1)
Pendleton harvest
Harding, Dolores Charlotte Frederica
Pendleton series (2)
Pendleton twins
Jameson, E M
Pendletons trilogy (3)
Pendletons
Jameson, E M
Pendletons trilogy (1)
Pendragon, late of Prince Albert's Own
Trevelyan, Robert
Pendragon series (1)
Penelope
Anderson, William Charles
Penelope series (1)
Bullingham, Ann
Penelope series (1)
Cunningham, E V
John Comaday and Larry Cohen series (1)
Penelope and Curlew
Bullingham, Ann
Penelope series (2)
Penelope and the Golden Orchard
Castelhun, Dorothea
Penelope series (2)
Penelope goes to Portsmouth
Chesney, Marion
Travelling matchmaker series (3)
Penelope in California
Castelhun, Dorothea
Penelope series (4)
Penelope, the damp detective
Anderson, William Charles
Penelope series (2)
Penelope's English experience
Wiggin, Kate Douglas
Penelope Hamilton series (1)
Penelope's English experiences
Wiggin, Kate Douglas
Penelope Hamilton series (1)
Penelope's experiences in Scotland
Wiggin, Kate Douglas
Penelope Hamilton series (2)
Penelope's Irish experiences
Wiggin, Kate Douglas
Penelope Hamilton series (3)
Penelope's postscripts
Wiggin, Kate Douglas
Penelope Hamilton series (4)
Penelope's problems
Castelhun, Dorothea
Penelope series (1)
Penelope's progress
Wiggin, Kate Douglas
Penelope Hamilton series (2)
Penetrate
Trevor, Dan
Night whistlers series (2)
Night whistlers trilogy (2)
Penetrator
Conway, Troy
Coxeman series (27)
Penguin Pete
Pfister, Marcus
Penguin Pete series (1)
Penguin Pete ahoy!
Pfister, Marcus
Penguin Pete series (4)
Penguin Pete and Pat
Pfister, Marcus
Penguin Pete series (3)
Penguin Pete's new friends
Pfister, Marcus
Penguin Pete series (2)
Penguin pool murder
Palmer, Stuart
Hildegarde Withers series (1)
Penguin twins
Tompkins, Jane
Animal twins series (2)
Penguin who couldn't paddle, and other stories
Berg, Leila
What-do-you-know series (2)
Penguins paint
Tripp, Valerie
Just one more stories series (3)
Peninsula Place
Mackail, Denis
Greenery Street trilogy (3)
Pennies for his eyes
Duncan, William Murdoch
Superintendent Macneill series (3)
Pennies on a dead woman's eyes
Muller, Marcia
Sharon McCone series (13)
Pennine tales
Livings, Henry
Ravensgill series (1)
Pennington's heir
Peyton, K M
Patrick Pennington series (3)
Pennington's last term
Peyton, K M
Patrick Pennington series (1)
Pennington's seventeenth summer
Peyton, K M
Patrick Pennington series (1)
Penny and Dorabella at the beach
Bracken, Anne
Penny and Dorabella series (1)
Penny and Dorabella at the circus
Bracken, Anne
Penny and Dorabella series (2)
Penny and pam, nurse and cadet
Deming, Dorothy
Penny Marsh series (6)
Penny and Peter
Haywood, Carolyn
Penny series (2)
Penny and Sue
Ramstedt, Viveka
Penny series (2)
Penny and the pageant
Tring, A Stephen
Penny series (7)
Penny black
Moody, Susan
Penny Wanawake series (1)
Penny boss
Bowie, Janetta
Clydeside series (2)
Penny buff
Bowie, Janetta
Clydeside series (1)
Penny change
Bowie, Janetta
Clydeside series (3)
Penny dramatic
Tring, A Stephen
Penny series (5)
Penny dreadful
Moody, Susan
Penny Wanawake series (2)
Tring, A Stephen
Penny series (1)
Penny ferry
Boyer, Richard Lewis
Doctor Charlie Adams series (2)
Penny foolish
Shaw, Jane
Penny series (1)
Penny for the guy
Roffman, Jan
Sergeant Ratlin series (2)
Penny for the harp
Onions, Oliver
Gandelyn the Jester trilogy (3)
Penny goes a-camping
Milligan, Elsie
Penny Dawson series (5)
Penny goes a-flying
Milligan, Elsie
Penny Dawson series (4)
Penny goes a-sailing
Milligan, Elsie
Penny Dawson series (1)
Penny goes exploring
Milligan, Elsie
Penny Dawson series (2)
Penny goes home again
Milligan, Elsie
Penny Dawson series (6)
Penny goes to camp
Haywood, Carolyn
Penny series (3)
Penny goes to Rhodesia
Milligan, Elsie
Penny Dawson series (3)
Penny in Italy
Tring, A Stephen
Penny series (6)
Penny in the clouds
Clarke, Austin
Memories of Ireland and England series (2)
Penny Marsh and Ginger Lee, wartime nurses
Deming, Dorothy
Penny Marsh series (5)
Penny Marsh finds adventure in public health nursing
Deming, Dorothy
Penny Marsh series (3)
Penny Marsh, public health nurse
Deming, Dorothy
Penny Marsh series (1)
Penny Marsh, R.N., director of nurses
Deming, Dorothy
Penny Marsh series (8)
Penny Marsh, supervisor of public health nurses
Deming, Dorothy
Penny Marsh series (2)
Penny murders
Black, Lionel
Kate Theobald series (5)
Penny Nichols and the black imp
Clark, Joan
Penny Nichols series (3)
Penny Nichols and the Knob Hill mystery
Clark, Joan
Penny Nichols series (4)
Penny Nichols and the mystery of the lost key
Clark, Joan
Penny Nichols series (2)
Penny Nichols finds a clue
Clark, Joan
Penny Nichols series (1)
Penny Parsnip
Reed, Giles
Munch Bunch character series (18)
Penny penitent
Tring, A Stephen
Penny series (3)
Penny pinching
Moody, Susan
Penny Wanawake series (6)
Penny plain
Douglas, O
Priorsford series (1)
Penny Pollard in print
Klein, Robin
Penny Pollard series (3)
Penny Pollard's diary
Klein, Robin
Penny Pollard series (1)
Penny Pollard's guide to modern manners
Klein, Robin
Penny Pollard series (5)
Penny Pollard's letters
Klein, Robin
Penny Pollard series (2)
Penny Pollard's passport
Klein, Robin
Penny Pollard series (4)
Penny post
Moody, Susan
Penny Wanawake series (3)
Penny puzzled
Tring, A Stephen
Penny series (4)
Penny royal
Moody, Susan
Penny Wanawake series (4)
Morton, John Bingham
Enchanter's nightshade series (2)
Penny saving
Moody, Susan
Penny Wanawake series (7)
Penny says goodbye
Tring, A Stephen
Penny series (8)
Penny to spend
Brown, Edward
Major Adrian Titterton series (1)
Penny triumphant
Tring, A Stephen
Penny series (2)
Penny wise
Moody, Susan
Penny Wanawake series (5)
Penny world
Barton, Arthur
Time remembered series (2)
Pennybridge
Lushington, Franklin
Pigeon Hoo series (2)
Pennycross murders
Procter, Maurice
Superintendent Philip Hunter series (1)
Penrod
Tarkington, Booth
Penrod trilogy (1)
Penrod again
Christian, Mary Blount
Penrod series (2)
Penrod and Sam
Tarkington, Booth
Penrod trilogy (2)
Penrod, his complete story
Tarkington, Booth
Penrod trilogy (3)
Penrod Jashber
Tarkington, Booth
Penrod trilogy (3)
Penrod's pants
Christian, Mary Blount
Penrod series (1)
Penrod's party
Christian, Mary Blount
Penrod series (3)
Penrod's picture
Christian, Mary Blount
Penrod series (4)
Penrose mystery
Freeman, Richard Austin
Doctor John Evelyn Thorndyke series (23)
Pension for death
Lewis, Roy Harley
Matthew Coll series (3)
Pentagon spy
Dixon, Franklin W
Hardy boys series (61)
Pentecost and the chosen one
Corbett, William Jesse
Pentecost trilogy (2)
Pentecost of Lickey Top
Corbett, William Jesse
Pentecost trilogy (3)
Penthouse mystery
Queen, Ellery
Ellery Queen series (19)
Penthouse preview
Brody, Marc
Marc Brody series (70)
Pentimento
Hellman, Lillian
Unfinished woman trilogy (2)
Penultimate adventure
Davey, Norman
Pilgrim series (2)
Penultimate problem of Sherlock Holmes
Nassivera, John
Sherlock Holmes drama series (19)
Peony lantern
Manley, Ruth
Ancient Japan series (3)
People
Henderson, Zenna
People series (2)
People against Nancy Preston
Moroso, John Antonio
James Tierney series (1)
People and places
Kalman, Bobbie
In my world series (19)
People and production
Braudel, Fernand
Identity of France series (2)
People are starting to complain about too much violence on cave walls
Unger, Jim
Herman series (10)
People ask death
Dyer, George
Catalyst Club series (3)
People at play
Kalman, Bobbie
In my world series (16)
People at work
Kalman, Bobbie
In my world series (11)
People betrayed
Doblin, Alfred
German revolution series (1)
People can be animals
Pearce, Colin
Fax Pack series (3)
People collection
Henderson, Zenna
People series (2)
People from Mother Goose
Hopkins, Lee Bennett
Mother Goose series (2)
People in a diary
Behrman, Samuel Nathaniel
People in a diary series (2)
People in glass houses
Lewis, Elliott
Fred Bennett series (3)
Ridgway, Jason
Brian Guy series (2)
People in my family
Kalman, Bobbie
In my world series (7)
Moss, Jeffrey
Sesame Street people series (2)
People in Pineapple Place
Lindbergh, Anne Morrow
Pineapple Place series (1)
People in the garden
Wood, Lorna
Hag Dowsabel series (1)
People in the picture
Middleton, Haydn
People in the picture series (1)
People in your neighborhood
Moss, Jeffrey
Sesame Street people series (1)
People like us
Bye, Beryl
People like us series (1)
People of darkness
Hillerman, Tony
Sergeant Jim Chee series (1)
People of the abyss
England, George Allen
Darkness and dawn series (3)
People of the black circle
Howard, Robert Ervin
Conan series (19)
People of the darkness
Vivian, Evelyn Charles
Aia series (2)
People of the deer
Mowat, Farley
Canadian North series (1)
People of the earth
Gear, William Michael
People series (3)
People of the fire
Gear, William Michael
People series (2)
People of the mesa
Mayhar, Ardath
Amerindian prehistory series (1)
People of the river
Gear, William Michael
People series (4)
Wallace, Edgar
Commissioner Sanders series (2)
People of the sea
Gear, William Michael
People series (5)
Velikovsky, Immanuel
Ages in chaos series (4)
People of the Talisman
Brackett, Leigh
Eric John Stark series (1)
People of the whirlpool
Wright, Mabel Osgood
Commuter's wife series (2)

People of the wind
Anderson, Poul
Future history series (3)
Polesotechnic League series (2)
People of the wolf
Gear, William Michael
People series (1)
People that time forgot
Burroughs, Edgar Rice
Bowen Tylor trilogy (2)
People versus Withers and Malone
Palmer, Stuart
Hildegarde Withers series (16)
Rice, Craig
John Joseph Malone series (13)
People who come to our house
Judson, Clara Ingram
People series (1)
People who work near our house
Judson, Clara Ingram
People series (2)
People will talk
Lorac, E C R
Inspector Macdonald series (46)
People with the dogs
Stead, Christina
New York trilogy (3)
People's game
Seymour, Harold
Baseball history series (3)
Pep rally
Adams, Nicholas
Horror High series (7)
Pepe Moreno
Allen, Eric
Pepe Moreno series (1)
Pepe Moreno and the dilapidated donkey
Allen, Eric
Pepe Moreno series (4)
Pepe Moreno and the roller skates
Allen, Eric
Pepe Moreno series (2)
Pepe Moreno's Quixotic adventure
Allen, Eric
Pepe Moreno series (5)
Pepe on the run
Allen, Eric
Pepe Moreno series (3)
Pepper and all the legs
Gackenbach, Dick
Claude series (3)
Pepper leads the string
Packer, Jo
Pepper series (3)
Pepper Pike
Roberts, Les
Milan Jacovich series (1)
Pepper Street hero
Smith, Joan Mary
Pepper Street series (3)
Pepper Street papers
Smith, Joan Mary
Pepper Street series (2)
Pepper Tree Bay
Sanders, Dorothy Lucie
Montgomery family series (5)
Pepperpots and presents
Braga, Meg
William and Wendy series (3)
Pepper's good and bad day
McGill, Marci
Six little possums series (3)
Pepys and the Revolution
Bryant, Arthur
Samuel Pepys series (3)
Peradventures or Private Pagett
Drury, William Price
Pagett series (1)
Perchance of death
Linington, Elizabeth
Sergeant Ivor Maddox series (8)
Perchance to dream
Parker, Robert Brown
Big sleep series (2)
Weinstein, Howard
Star trek, the next generation series (19)
Percival and I
Armstrong, Anthony
Percival series (1)
Percival at play
Armstrong, Anthony
Percival series (2)
Percy
Hitchcock, Raymond
Percy series (1)
Percy and the kite
Awdry, Christopher
Railway series (35)
Percy goes on holiday
Allen, Joy
Percy series (1)
Percy goes to Spain
Allen, Joy
Percy series (2)
Percy Pig ahoy!
Bennett, Rodney
Percy Pig series (2)
Percy Pig goes to town
Bennett, Rodney
Percy Pig series (3)
Percy Prune
Reed, Giles
Munch Bunch character series (16)
Percy, the small engine
Awdry, Wilbert
Railway series (11)
Percy's progress
Hitchcock, Raymond
Percy series (2)
Perdita
Hibberd, Jack
Melbourne series (2)
Perdita's prince
Plaidy, Jean
Georgian series (6)
Perdition Express
Lang, Brad
Fred Crockett series (2)
Perdition Range
Carter, Nevada
Perdition series (2)
Perdition Wells
Carter, Nevada
Perdition series (1)
Peregrination twenty two
Purser, Philip
Colin Panton series (1)
Peregrine Pickle
Smollett, Tobias
Morgan the Welshman series (2)
Peregrine primus
Davidson, Avram
Peregrine series (1)
Peregrine secundus
Davidson, Avram
Peregrine series (2)
Peregrine's progress
Farnol, Jeffery
Mister Jasper Shrig of Bow Street series (2)
Perelandra
Lewis, Clive Staples
Space trilogy (2)
Perennial boarder
Taylor, Phoebe Atwood
Asey Mayo series (17)
Perfect address book
Heaton, Rose Henniker
Perfect series (5)
Perfect alibi
Sprigg, Christopher Saint John
Charles Venables series (3)
Inspector Bernard Bray series (2)
Perfect assignment
Moffatt, James
Girl from H.A.R.D. series (3)
Perfect Christmas
Heaton, Rose Henniker
Perfect series (3)
Perfect crime
Queen, Ellery
Ellery Queen series (21)
Perfect cruise and other holidays
Heaton, Rose Henniker
Perfect series (4)
Perfect day for dying
Christmas, Joyce
Lady Margaret Priam series (7)
Perfect end
Marshall, William Leonard
Yellowthread Street series (7)
Perfect fools
Green, Edith
Dearborn V Pinch series (3)
Perfect frame
Ard, William
Timothy Dane series (1)
Perfect gentleman
Graham, Harry
Reginald Drake Biffin series (2)
McCulloch, Sarah
Georgian series (5)
Perfect getaway
Dixon, Franklin W
Hardy boys case files series (12)
Perfect girl
Pascal, Francine
Sweet Valley High series (74)
Perfect horse
Baxter, Gillian
Roberta series (3)
Perfect hostess
Heaton, Rose Henniker
Perfect series (1)
Perfect justice
Bernhardt, William
Justice series (4)
Perfect kill
Quinnell, A J
Creasy series (1)
Perfect match
McGown, Jill
Chief Inspector Lloyd and Sergeant Judy Hill series (1)
Veryan, Patricia
Age of Elegance series (2)
Perfect murder
Keating, Henry Reymond Fitzwalter
Inspector Ganesh Ghote series (1)
Perfect murder case
Bush, Christopher
Ludovic Travers series (2)
Perfect object
Glazer, Mindy
Star trek fan series (8)
Perfect pair
Lowell, Melissa
Silver blades series (5)
Perfect planet
Packard, Edward
Choose your own adventure series (80)
Perfect plot
Keene, Carolyn
Nancy Drew files series (76)
Perfect schoolgirl
Heaton, Rose Henniker
Perfect series (2)
Perfect shot
Pascal, Francine
Sweet Valley High series (55)
Perfect summer
Pascal, Francine
Sweet Valley High super series (1)
Sweet Valley twins super special series (1)
Perfect wife
Pendower, Jacques
Slade McGinty series (1)
Perfecting Fiona
Chesney, Marion
School of manners series (2)
Perfectly proper murder
Adams, Harold
Carl Wilcox series (10)
Perfectly pure and good
Fyfield, Frances
Sarah Fortune series (4)
Performance
Clark, Douglas
Inspector George Masters series (23)
Performers' car
Barkan, Joanne
Circus train come aboard series (1)
Performing flea
Wodehouse, Pelham Grenville
Performing flea series (1)
Perfume from Provence
Fortescue, Winifred
Provence series (1)
Perfume of the lady in black
Leroux, Gaston
Joseph Rouletabille series (2)
Perfumed lure
Saint Dennis, Madelon
Sydney Treherne series (2)
Perfumed nemesis
Janson, Hank
Hank Janson series (52)
Perfumed planet
Elder, Michael
Barclay series (2)
Perhaps it's love
Warde, Joan
Forrester family series (2)
Perihelion
Wu, William Franking
Robot city series (6)
Peril ahead
Creasey, John
Department Z series (23)
Peril all the way
Kennett, John
Black Circle Gang series (3)
Peril at Cranbury Hall
Rhode, John
Doctor Lancelot Priestley series (8)
Peril at End House
Christie, Agatha
Hercule Poirot series (7)
Peril at midnight
Hamilton, Elaine
Inspector Reynolds series (5)
Peril at the pirate school
Bradman, Tony
Bluebeards series (3)
Peril for the guy
Kennett, John
Black Circle Gang series (1)
Peril from the stars
Morris, Dave
Transformers series (2)
Peril in Lakeland
Finlay, Winifred
Gillian Lindsay series (2)
Peril in pink
Allen, Betsy
Connie Blair series (10)
Peril in the north
Robeson, Kenneth
Doc Savage series (118)
Peril in the Pennines
Finlay, Winifred
Gillian Lindsay series (3)
Peril is my pay
Marlowe, Stephen
Chester Drum series (11)
Peril of Barnabas Collins
Ross, Marilyn
Barnabas Collins series (12)
Peril of the prince!
Brooks, Edwy Searles
Sexton Blake series (13)
Peril on Ice Planet
Mahr, Kurt
Perry Rhodan series (23)
Peril on Mars
Moore, Patrick
Maurice Gray series (4)
Peril on the lost planet
Macvicar, Angus
Jeremy Grant series (5)
Peril over the airport
Wells, Helen
Vicki Barr series (8)
Peril rides the Pecos
Cole, Jackson
Jim Hatfield series (81)
Peril under the palms
Beck, Kathrine Kristine
Iris Cooper and Jack Clancy series (3)
Peril unlimited
Brand, Kurt
Perry Rhodan series (130)
Perilous country
Creasey, John
Doctor Palfrey series (2)
Perilous descent into a strange lost world
Carter, Bruce
Danny Black and Johnny Wild series (1)
Perilous hazard
Cross, Mark
Daphne Wrayne and her Four Adjusters series (47)
Perilous parole
Carter, Nicholas
Nicholas Carter series (538)
Perilous road
Steele, William Owen
Tennessee frontier series (4)
Perilous seas
Duncan, Dave
Man of his word series (3)
Perilous spring of Morris Seidman
Moll, Elick
Morris Seidman series (3)
Perilous transactions of Mister Collin
Heller, Frank
Mister Collin series (1)
Perils of Petrograd
Graydon, William Murray
Sexton Blake series (31)
Period of evil
Halliday, Michael
Doctor Emmanuel Cellini series (6)
Period of violence
Wood, Kenneth
Gulls series (2)
Period stuff
Yates, Dornford
Superintendent Richard Falcon series (1)
Periscope red
Rohmer, Richard
Triad series (1)
Perish by the sword
Anderson, Poul
Trygve Yamamura series (1)
Perish the thought
Bonett, John
Inspector Borges series (6)
Perishable goods
Yates, Dornford
Berry series (5)
Jonah Mansel series (4)
Richard Chandos series (2)
Permanent Californians
Culbertson, Judi
Guides to the cemeteries of the world's great cities series (3)
Permanent Londoners
Culbertson, Judi
Guides to the cemeteries of the world's great cities series (4)
Permanent New Yorkers
Culbertson, Judi
Guides to the cemeteries of the world's great cities series (2)
Permanent Parisians
Culbertson, Judi
Guides to the cemeteries of the world's great cities series (1)
Permanent way
Rowlands, Avril
God's wonderful railway series (1)
Perpetual curate
Oliphant, Margaret Oliphant Wilson
Carlingford series (3)
Perrin murder case
Morton, Guy
Konrad Roque series (1)
Perry girls
Turner, Lilian
Perry family series (2)
Perry's planet
Haldeman, Jack Carroll
Star trek originals sequels series (15)
Persecutor
Hamilton, Ian Sydney
Pete Heysen series (1)
Persia is my heart
Najafi, Najmeli
Persia trilogy (1)
Persia revisited
Mehdevi, Anne Sinclair
Pillar to post series (3)
Persian
Sadler, Barry
Casca series (6)
Persian adventure
Mehdevi, Anne Sinclair
Pillar to post series (2)
Persian boy
Renault, Mary
Alexander the Great series (2)
Persian death-trap
Christian, John
Richard Deutsch series (2)
Persian gold
Walsh, Jill Paton
Children of the fox trilogy (3)
Persian pride
Janson, Hank
Hank Janson series (53)
Persimmon sequence
Fretland, Donald John
Oleandre series (1)
Persis Putnam's treasure
Hamlin, Myra Sawyer
Nan series (5)
Person called Z
Farjeon, Joseph Jefferson
Z series (1)
Person shouldn't die like that
Goldstein, Arthur David
Max Guttman series (1)
Persona non grata
Williams, Timothy
Commissario Trotti series (3)
Personal conduct of Belinda
Brainerd, Eleanor Hoyt
Belinda series (2)
Personal effects
Piesman, Marissa
Nina Fischman series (2)
Personal record, 1920-1972
Brenan, Gerald
Life of one's own series (2)
Personal war
Ham, Bob
Overload series (1)
Personality plus
Ferber, Edna
Emma McChesney series (2)
Persons and places
Santayana, George
Persons and places trilogy (1)
Persons unknown
Macdonald, Philip
Colonel Anthony Ruthven Gethryn series (6)
Moffat, Gwen
Miss Melinda Pink series (5)
Thayer, Lee
Peter Clancy series (32)

Perspectives of the world
Braudel, Fernand
Civilization and capitalism trilogy (3)
Persuaders
Smith, Frederick Escreet
Persuaders series (1)
Persuaders again
Smith, Frederick Escreet
Persuaders series (2)
Persuaders at large
Smith, Frederick Escreet
Persuaders series (3)
Persuaders, book three
Smith, Frederick Escreet
Persuaders series (3)
Persuaders, book two
Smith, Frederick Escreet
Persuaders series (2)
Peruvian nightmare
Barry, Mike
Burton Wulff series (7)
Peruvian printout
Haig, Alec
Alec Haig series (2)
Perverse and foolish
Boston, Lucy Maria
Memory in a house series (1)
Perversity of Pipers
Parker, Richard
Pipers series (2)
Pescatons
Pemberton, Victor
Doctor Who series (153)
Pet day
Smith, Janice Lea
Adam Joshua series (4)
Ziefert, Harriet
Mister Rose's class series (1)
Pet day mystery
Christian, Mary Blount
Sherlock Street detectives series (4)
Pet day surprise
Stine, Harlan William
Jeffrey and the third grade ghost series (4)
Pet for Bear and Duck
Delton, Judy
Bear and Duck series (1)
Pet for Mrs Arbuckle
Smyth, Gwenda
Mrs Arbuckle series (1)
Pet for the Orphelines
Carlson, Natalie Savage
Orphelines series (3)
Pet makeover
Vail, Virginia
Animal Inn series (7)
Pet of Frankenstein
Gilden, Mel
Fifth grade monsters series (4)
Pet shop
Ahlberg, Allan
Funnybones series (2)
Pet show!
Keats, Ezra Jack
Peter series (7)
Petals on the wind
Andrews, Virginia Cleo
Dollanganger family series (3)
Petals yellow and petals red
Fisher, Aileen
Ways of plants series (6)
Petar's treasure
Judson, Clara Ingram
They came from series (4)
Pete
Morgan, Alison
Llanwern series (2)
Pete and Penny know and grow
Johnston, Dorothy Grunbock
Pete and Penny series (2)
Pete and Penny live and learn
Johnston, Dorothy Grunbock
Pete and Penny series (3)
Pete and Penny play and pray
Johnston, Dorothy Grunbock
Pete and Penny series (1)
Pete and Penny think and thank
Johnston, Dorothy Grunbock
Pete and Penny series (4)
Pete and Prue the partridges
Evens, George Bramwell
Romany readers series (5)
Pete and the prairie people
Dixon, Rex
Pete series (1)
Pete and the Wild Grass Country
Dixon, Rex
Pete series (2)
Pete Pack Rat
Quackenbush, Robert Mead
Pete Pack Rat series (1)
Pete Pack Rat and the Christmas Eve surprise
Quackenbush, Robert Mead
Pete Pack Rat series (3)
Pete Pack Rat and the Gila Monster Gang
Quackenbush, Robert Mead
Pete Pack Rat series (2)
Pete Pepper
Reed, Giles
Munch Bunch character series (4)
Pete Rose, baseball's Charlie Hustle
Aaseng, Nathan
Sports acheivers series (3)
Pete the Magnificent
Davis, Gibbs
Never sink nine series (4)
Peter
Cheesman, Lilian
Peter trilogy (1)
Peter and Alexis
Merejkowski, Dmitri Sergeevich
Christ and Antichrist trilogy (3)
Peter and Company
Bruce, Mary Grant
Peter series (2)
Peter and Cub
Beech, Margaret
Peter and Veronica series (2)
Peter and his magic pebble
Schermele, Willy
Peter series (1)
Peter and his pets
Schermele, Willy
Peter series (2)
Peter and his playmates
Schermele, Willy
Peter series (3)
Peter and his pony
Schermele, Willy
Peter series (4)
Peter and his puppy
Schermele, Willy
Peter series (5)
Peter and Polly in autumn
Lucia, Rose
Peter and Polly series (4)
Peter and Polly in spring
Lucia, Rose
Peter and Polly series (3)
Peter and Polly in summer
Lucia, Rose
Peter and Polly series (1)
Peter and Polly in winter
Lucia, Rose
Peter and Polly series (2)
Peter and the atomic valley
Mogridge, Stephen
Peter series (2)
Peter and the big balloon
Corson, Hazel Wyman
Peter series (5)
Peter and the flying saucers
Mogridge, Stephen
Peter series (1)
Peter and the flying submarine
Mogridge, Stephen
Peter series (4)
Peter and the moon bomb
Mogridge, Stephen
Peter series (3)
Peter and the moon trip
Corson, Hazel Wyman
Peter series (3)
Peter and the rocket fishing trip
Corson, Hazel Wyman
Peter series (7)
Peter and the rocket ship
Corson, Hazel Wyman
Peter series (1)
Peter and the two-hour moon
Corson, Hazel Wyman
Peter series (2)
Peter and the unlucky rocket
Corson, Hazel Wyman
Peter series (4)
Peter and Tim on the trail
Brown, T Burton
Peter and Tim series (2)
Peter and Tim's schooldays
Brown, T Burton
Peter and Tim series (3)
Peter and Veronica
Beech, Margaret
Peter and Veronica series (1)
Sachs, Marilyn
Veronica Ganz series (2)
Peter and Veronica growing up
Beech, Margaret
Peter and Veronica series (3)
Peter and Wendy
Barrie, James Matthew
Peter Pan series (1)
Peter at the stampede
Hall, Gordon Langley
Peter Jumping Horse series (2)
Peter Binney, undergraduate
Marshall, Archibald
Clinton series (1)
Peter Budstone, the boy who was hazed
Trowbridge, John Townsend
Tide Mill series (6)
Peter Churchmouse
Austin, Margot
Church animals series (1)
Peter comes back
Peterson, Hans
Peter Johnson series (3)
Peter Cottontail and Reddy Fox
Burgess, Thornton Waldo
Peter Rabbit series (3)
Reddy Fox series (2)
Peter Cottontail's own paint book
Burgess, Thornton Waldo
Peter Rabbit series (4)
Peter Cushing
Cushing, Peter
Past forgetting series (1)
Peter Devlin and the road bandits
Buddee, Paul
Peter Devlin series (4)
Peter Devlin, buffalo hunter
Buddee, Paul
Peter Devlin series (3)
Peter Devlin fights for survival
Buddee, Paul
Peter Devlin series (1)
Peter Devlin, range rider
Buddee, Paul
Peter Devlin series (2)
Peter Duck
Ransome, Arthur
Swallows and Amazons series (3)
Peter Gayleigh flies high
Robertson, Colin
Peter Grayleigh series (14)
Peter Jackson, cigar merchant
Frankau, Gilbert
Peter Jackson series (2)
Peter Jameson
Frankau, Gilbert
Peter Jackson series (2)
Peter Johnson and his guitar
Peterson, Hans
Peter Johnson series (1)
Peter Jumping Horse
Hall, Gordon Langley
Peter Jumping Horse series (1)
Peter, Katrinka's brother
Haskell, Helen Eggleston
Katrinka series (3)
Peter Kent's command
Gunn, John
Peter Kent series (5)
Peter Lawson, camper
Davidson, Helen Beatrice
Peter Lawson series (2)
Peter Lawson, wolf-cub
Davidson, Helen Beatrice
Peter Lawson series (1)
Peter makes his way
Peterson, Hans
Peter Johnson series (4)
Peter, new girl
Matthewman, Phyllis
Mister Jones series (2)
Peter Pan
Barrie, James Matthew
Peter Pan series (1)
Peter Pan, an afterthought
Barrie, James Matthew
Peter Pan series (3)
Peter Pan and the only children
Adair, Gilbert
Peter Pan series (4)
Peter Pan and Wendy
Barrie, James Matthew
Peter Pan series (1)
Peter Pan in Kensington Gardens
Barrie, James Matthew
Peter Pan series (2)
Peter Pan saves the day
Korman, Justine
Peter Pan series (5)
Peter Perry
Campbell, Michael
Peter Perry series (1)
Peter Pig's number play book
Wada, Yoshiomi
Peter Pig series (2)
Peter Pig's telephone book
Wada, Yoshiomi
Peter Pig series (1)
Peter Pipers at the wildlife park
Moss, Elaine
Peter Pipers series (3)
Peter Pipers' birthday party
Moss, Elaine
Peter Pipers series (4)
Peter Pipers go to the fair
Moss, Elaine
Peter Pipers series (1)
Peter Pipers in the garden
Moss, Elaine
Peter Pipers series (2)
Peter plan
Peter, Laurence Johnston
Peter series (3)
Peter plays sleuth
Matthewman, Phyllis
Mister Jones series (4)
Peter prescription
Peter, Laurence Johnston
Peter series (2)
Peter principle
Peter, Laurence Johnston
Peter series (1)
Peter pyramid
Peter, Laurence Johnston
Peter series (8)
Peter Rabbit and Reddy Fox
Burgess, Thornton Waldo
Peter Rabbit series (3)
Reddy Fox series (2)
Peter Rabbit goes scouting
Burgess, Thornton Waldo
Animal stories series (3)
Peter Rabbit series (2)
Peter Rabbit proves a friend
Burgess, Thornton Waldo
Animal stories series (3)
Peter Rabbit series (2)
Peter Rabbit's almanac for 1929
Potter, Beatrix
Peter Rabbit series (21)
Peter Rabbit's carrots
Burgess, Thornton Waldo
Peter Rabbit series (1)
Wee little books series (6)
Peter Rabbit's gardening book
Garland, Sarah
Peter Rabbit series (4)
Peter Rabbit's painting book
Potter, Beatrix
Peter Rabbit series (21)
Peter Ruff
Oppenheim, Edward Phillips
Peter Ruff series (2)
Peter Ruff and the double four
Oppenheim, Edward Phillips
Peter Ruff series (1)
Peter Schlemihl
Chamisso, Adalbert von
Peter Schlemihl series (1)
Peter Schlemihl in America
Wood, George
Peter Schlemihl series (2)
Peter, speak for me
Graeber, Charlotte Towner
Speak for me series (4)
Peter the Great
Merejkowski, Dmitri Sergeevich
Christ and Antichrist trilogy (3)
Peter the prentice
Rutley, Cecily Marianne
Children of other days series (10)
Peter, the rocket sitter
Corson, Hazel Wyman
Peter series (6)
Peter the Second
Marshall, Bruce
Vicar of Christ tetralogy (4)
Peter Trant, cricketer-detective
Kenyon, James William
Peter Trant series (1)
Peter Trant, heavyweight champion
Kenyon, James William
Peter Trant series (2)
Peter Trant, speed king
Kenyon, James William
Peter Trant series (3)
Peter Treegate's war
Wibberley, Leonard
Treegate family trilogy (2)
Peterkin meets a star
Boon, Emilie
Peterkin series (1)
Peterkin papers
Hale, Lucretia Peabody
Peterkin series (1)
Peterkin Pollensnuff
Partridge, Jenny
Oakapple Wood series (4)
Peterkin's wet walk
Boon, Emilie
Peterkin series (2)
Peterloo inheritance
Blake, M Glaiser
Ayesthorpe trilogy (2)
Peterloo weaver
Blake, M Glaiser
Ayesthorpe trilogy (1)
Peter's adventurous holiday
Haynes, Ambrose
Peter series (1)
Peter's almanac
Peter, Laurence Johnston
Peter series (6)
Peter's best seller
Chalmers, Margaret Piper
Sylvia Arden series (5)
Peter's chair
Keats, Ezra Jack
Peter series (3)
Peter's Denmark adventure
Mogridge, Stephen
Peter series (5)
Peter's long walk
Kingman, Lee
Peter series (1)
Peter's pedigree
Conyers, Dorothea
Peter series (1)
Peter's people and their marvelous ideas
Peter, Laurence Johnston
Peter series (5)
Peter's pony
Kingman, Lee
Peter series (2)
Peter's predicament
Scannell, Florence
Cinderella series (2)
Peter's quotations
Peter, Laurence Johnston
Peter series (4)
Peter's return
Haynes, Ambrose
Peter series (2)
Peter's room
Forest, Antonia
Marlow family series (5)
Peter's voyage
Beskow, Elsa
Peter and Lotta series (5)
Petnapped!
Vail, Virginia
Animal Inn series (8)
Petrella at Q
Gilbert, Michael Francis
Patrick Petrella series (2)
Petrified mariner
Baker, Denys Val
Cornish series (6)
Petrova twist
Blue, Zachary
Protectors series (1)
Pets are for keeps
Vail, Virginia
Animal Inn series (1)
Pets in Barfield
Jones, Olive
Barfield series (5)
Pets in the barn
Warwick, Audrey
Carroll family series (1)
Petticoat express
Longtree, Warren T
Ruff Justice series (12)
Petticoat Lane murders
Gunn, Victor
Chief Inspector Bill Cromwell series (43)
Petty bourgeois
Balzac, Honore de
Scenes of Parisian life series (12)
Petty Officer Brady
Macdonnell, James Edmond
Jim Brady series (5)
Petunia
Duvoisin, Roger
Petunia series (1)
Petunia and the song
Duvoisin, Roger
Petunia series (2)
Petunia, beware!
Duvoisin, Roger
Petunia series (5)
Petunia, I love you
Duvoisin, Roger
Petunia series (6)
Petunia takes a trip
Duvoisin, Roger
Petunia series (4)
Petunia's Christmas
Duvoisin, Roger
Petunia series (3)
Petunia's treasure
Duvoisin, Roger
Petunia series (7)

Peverills
Leslie, Doris
Folliets and Peverills series (2)

Pew group
Oliver, Anthony
Lizzie Thomas and Inspector John Webber series (1)

Pewit's nest
Finley, Martha Farquharson
Pewit's nest series (1)

Peyton Place
Metalious, Grace
Peyton Place series (1)

Phaid the gambler
Farren, Mick
Song of Phaid the Gambler series (1)

Phalanx dragon
Rizzi, Timothy
Major General Duke James series (3)

Phantom and the curio murders
Wallace, Robert
Phantom Detective series (28)

Phantom and the daggers of Kali
Wallace, Robert
Phantom Detective series (22)

Phantom and the green glare murders
Wallace, Robert
Phantom Detective series (26)

Phantom and the melody murders
Wallace, Robert
Phantom Detective series (25)

Phantom and the Scorpia menace
Falk, Lee
Phantom series (3)

Phantom and the slave market of Macar
Falk, Lee
Phantom series (2)

Phantom and the uniformed killers
Wallace, Robert
Phantom Detective series (23)

Phantom and the vampire murders
Wallace, Robert
Phantom Detective series (24)

Phantom banjo
Scarborough, Elizabeth Ann
Songkiller series (1)

Phantom bat
Elliott, Robert Cowell
Sexton Blake series (612)

Phantom battleship
Chesterton, Rupert
Phantom battleship series (1)

Phantom called glory
Turnbull, Patrick
Bonaparte series (1)

Phantom carousel, and other ghostly tales
Ainsworth, Ruth
Ghostly tales series (3)

Phantom circus
Spiller, Andrew
Chief Inspector Duck Mallard series (9)

Phantom City
Robeson, Kenneth
Doc Savage series (10)

Phantom clue
Leroux, Gaston
Joseph Rouletabille series (4)

Phantom cyclist, and other ghost stories
Ainsworth, Ruth
Ghostly tales series (1)

Phantom cyclist, and other stories
Ainsworth, Ruth
Ghostly tales series (1)

Phantom-fighter
Quinn, Seabury
Jules de Grandin series (1)

Phantom film crew
Robinson, Nancy Konheim
Tripper and Sam series (1)

Phantom fingers
Farjeon, Joseph Jefferson
Ben the tramp series (4)

Phantom fisherboy
Ainsworth, Ruth
Ghostly tales series (2)

Phantom fleet
Darlton, Clark
Perry Rhodan series (97)
Sea-Lion
John Prentice series (1)

Phantom freighter
Dixon, Franklin W
Hardy boys series (26)

Phantom friend
Sutton, Margaret
Judy Bolton series (30)

Phantom from the east
Loti, Pierre
Aziyade series (2)

Phantom gondola
Dekobra, Maurice
Lady Diana trilogy (3)

Phantom gunman
Benteen, John
Neal Fargo series (11)
Morland, Nigel
Mrs Palmyra Pym series (2)

Phantom herd
Bower, Bertha Muzzy
Flying U Ranch series (7)

Phantom holiday
Russell, Martin
Jim Larkin series (4)

Phantom Hollow
Verner, Gerald
Trevor Lowe series (1)

Phantom homer
Cooper, John R
Mel Martin series (3)

Phantom horde
Darlton, Clark
Perry Rhodan series (137)

Phantom horse
Grey, Peter
Kit Hunter series (8)
Pullein-Thompson, Christine
Phantom horse series (1)

Phantom horse comes home
Pullein-Thompson, Christine
Phantom horse series (2)

Phantom horse goes to Ireland
Pullein-Thompson, Christine
Phantom horse series (3)

Phantom horse goes to Scotland
Pullein-Thompson, Christine
Phantom horse series (5)

Phantom horse in danger
Pullein-Thompson, Christine
Phantom horse series (4)

Phantom lady
Brown, Carter
Rick Holman series (35)

Phantom Lobster
Walmsley, Leo
Phantom Lobster series (4)

Phantom murderer
Quin, Basil Godfrey
James Clarkson-Parry series (4)

Phantom musketeer
Brandon, Charles
John Fortescue series (3)

Phantom of Barnabas Collins
Ross, Marilyn
Barnabas Collins series (9)

Phantom of Burlap Hall
Ironside, Virginia
Burlap Hall series (3)

Phantom of Dark Oaks
Sheldon, Ann
Linda Craig series (10)

Phantom of Featherford Falls
Ezell, Marilyn
Susan Sand series (5)

Phantom of Fog Island
Ross, Marilyn
Fog Island series (1)
Phantoms series (1)

Phantom of Fortuna
Grover, Marshall
Larry and Stretch series (206)

Phantom of Forty Second Street
Raison, Milton Michael
Tony Woolrich series (1)

Phantom of Pine Hill
Keene, Carolyn
Nancy Drew series (42)

Phantom of the casino
Bethancourt, Tomas Ernesto
Doris Fein series (4)

Phantom of the creek
Teed, George Hamilton
Sexton Blake series (730)

Phantom of the mill
Bidston, Lester
Sexton Blake series (465)

Phantom of the operetta
Christian, Mary Blount
Determined detectives series (3)

Phantom of the Pacific
Sayer, Walter William
Sexton Blake series (258)

Phantom of the river
Ellis, Edward Sylvester
Daniel Boone and Simon Kenton series (2)

Phantom of the rivers
Snell, Leroy
Northwest stories series (6)

Phantom of the snow
Ross, Marilyn
Phantoms series (6)

Phantom of the swamp
Ross, Marilyn
Phantoms series (2)

Phantom of the temple
Gulik, Robert van
Judge Dee series (15)

Phantom of the thirteenth floor
Ross, Marilyn
Phantoms series (4)

Phantom of Venice
Keene, Carolyn
Nancy Drew series (78)

Phantom of Wolf Creek
Scott, Dan
Bret King series (8)

Phantom roundabout, and other ghostly tales
Ainsworth, Ruth
Ghostly tales series (3)

Phantom shark
Blaine, John
Rick Brant series (6)

Phantom submarine
Brightfield, Richard
Choose your own adventure series (26)

Phantom surfer
Keene, Carolyn
Dana girls series (30)

Phantom torpedo-boats
Upward, Allen
Monsieur V series (2)

Phantom tourer
Collins, Gilbert
Hugh Carding series (2)

Phantom trailer
Wirt, Mildred Augustine
Trailer series (4)

Phantom wedding
Ross, Marilyn
Phantoms series (5)

Phantom whale
Robinson, Warren F
G-man's son series (3)

Phantom wires
Stringer, Arthur
James Durkin series (2)

Phantom yacht
Norton, Carol
Mystery and adventure series (1)

Phantoms
Koontz, Dean Ray
Phantoms series (1)

Phantom's gamble with death
Wallace, Robert
Phantom Detective series (20)

Phantom's murder trail
Wallace, Robert
Phantom Detective series (21)

Phantoms of fear
Waterfield, Robin
Fighting fantasy gamebook series (28)

Phantoms on the wind
Vardeman, Robert Edward
Demon crown trilogy (2)

Pharaoh contract
Aldridge, Ray
Emancipator series (1)

Pharaoh's ghost
Robeson, Kenneth
Doc Savage series (101)

Phaser fight
Siegel, Barbara
Star trek tie-ins series (9)

Phases in chaos
Greenberg, Martin Harry
Isaac's universe series (2)

Phaze doubt
Anthony, Piers
Apprentice adept series (7)

Phil and his friends
Trowbridge, John Townsend
Tide Mill series (2)

Phil Bradley at the wheel
Boone, Silas K
Phil Bradley series (2)

Phil Bradley's big exploit
Boone, Silas K
Phil Bradley series (6)

Phil Bradley's Mountain Boys
Boone, Silas K
Phil Bradley series (1)

Phil Bradley's shooting box
Boone, Silas K
Phil Bradley series (3)

Phil Bradley's snowshoe trail
Boone, Silas K
Phil Bradley series (4)

Phil Bradley's winning
Boone, Silas K
Phil Bradley series (5)

Phil, the fiddler
Alger, Horatio
Tattered Tom series (3)

Phil, the showman
Norris, Stanley
Phil, the showman series (1)

Philadelphia adventure
Alexander, Lloyd
Vesper Holly series (5)

Philadelphia blowup
Barry, Mike
Burton Wulff series (14)

Philadelphia murder story
Ford, Leslie
Colonel John Primrose series (11)
Grace Latham series (11)

Philip
Thackeray, William Makepeace
Arthur Pendennis series (3)

Philip and his wife
Deland, Margaret
Old Chester series (1)

Philip Berkeley
Stockton, Frank Richard
Rolling stones series (2)

Philip Hall likes me, I reckon maybe
Greene, Bette
Beth Lambert series (1)

Philip of Texas
Otis, James
Pioneer series (6)

Philippa at the chateau
Gerry, Margarita Spalding
Philippa trilogy (2)

Philippa's experiments
Gerry, Margarita Spalding
Philippa trilogy (3)

Philippa's fortune
Gerry, Margarita Spalding
Philippa trilogy (1)

Philippine hardpunch
Case, Jim
Cody's army series (3)

Philistines
Bates, Arlo
Pagans series (2)
McCrone, Guy
Moorhouse family trilogy (1)

Philly stakes
Roberts, Gillian
Amanda Pepper series (2)

Philomel Foundation
Gollin, James
Antigua Players series (1)

Philosopher's hemlock
Cranston, Maurice
Inspector Mortimer Blunt series (2)

Philosophy in the twentieth century
Ayer, Alfred Jules
Western philosophy series (2)

Phineas Finn
Trollope, Anthony
Palliser novels series (2)

Phineas redux
Trollope, Anthony
Palliser novels series (4)

Phoebe
Kaye, Marilyn
Sisters series (1)

Phoebe and Ernest
Gillmore, Inez Haynes
Phoebe and Ernest series (1)

Phoebe Daring
Baum, Lyman Frank
Daring twins series (2)

Phoebe, Ernest and Cupid
Gillmore, Inez Haynes
Phoebe and Ernest series (2)

Phoebe, her profession
Ray, Anna Chapin
Teddy series (2)

Phoebe, junior
Oliphant, Margaret Oliphant Wilson
Carlingford series (5)

Phoenix
Brust, Steven
Jhereg series (5)
Sadler, Barry
Casca series (14)
White, Ted
Weird heroes series (5)

Phoenix and the carpet
Nesbit, Edith
Five children series (2)

Phoenix and the mirror
Davidson, Avram
Virgil Magus series (1)

Phoenix bells
Grant, Kathryn
Land of ten thousand willows trilogy (1)

Phoenix cup
Morris, James Humphrey
Japan series (2)

Phoenix equation
Dixon, Franklin W
Hardy boys case files series (66)

Phoenix filly
Fletcher, Dirk
Spur McCoy special series (1)

Phoenix fire
Darby, Lyndan
Eye of time trilogy (3)

Phoenix generation
Williamson, Henry
Chronicles of ancient sunlight series (12)

Phoenix in flames
Wilson, Gar
Phoenix Force series (14)

Phoenix in obsidian
Moorcock, Michael
Erekose series (2)
Eternal champion trilogy (2)

Phoenix inferno
Barry, Mike
Burton Wulff series (12)

Phoenix man
Sherman, Jory
Doctor Russell V Childers series (5)

Phoenix odyssey
Henrick, Richard P
Sub wars series (3)

Phoenix of Megaron
Rankine, John
Space nineteen ninety nine series (10)

Phoenix prime
White, Ted
Qanar series (1)

Phoenix reaction
Phillips, Leon
Hugh Melling series (2)

Phoenix rising
Steen, Marguerite
Flood trilogy (3)

Phoenix sword
Barker, Wade
Year of the Ninja Master series (4)

Phoenix syndrome
Andrews, Lucilla
Wally's Ward series (4)

Phoenix triumphant
Lancing, George
Tzu Hsi series (4)

Phone calls
O'Donnell, Lillian
Detective Norah Mulcahaney series (1)

Phony-Baloney, the counterfeit kid
Graeber, Charlotte Towner
Mister T and me series (6)

Photo finish
Bruce, Jean
Secret Agent O.S.S.117 series (12)

Photo-finish
Marsh, Ngaio
Inspector Roderick Alleyn series (31)

Photo history of armoured cars in two world wars
Forty, George
Photo history of two world wars series (2)

Photo history of tanks in two world wars
Forty, George
Photo history of two world wars series (1)

Photofit mystery at Jug Valley Juniors
Digby, Anne
Jug Valley Juniors series (4)

Photogenic soprano
Dunnett, Dorothy
Johnson and the yacht Dolly series (1)

Photographer's evidence
Carter, Nicholas
Nicholas Carter series (136)

Phreak-out!
Brown, Carter
Rick Holman series (31)

Phronsie Pepper
Sidney, Margaret
Five Little Peppers series (4)

Phrynette and London
Troly-Curtin, Marthe
Phrynette series (1)

Phrynette married
Troly-Curtin, Marthe
Phrynette series (2)

Phthor
Anthony, Piers
Aton series (2)

Phule's company
Asprin, Robert Lynn
Phule series (1)
Phule's paradise
Asprin, Robert Lynn
Phule series (2)
Phyllis, a twin
Whitehill, Dorothy
Janet and Phyllis series (2)
Phyllis, the cautious
Kimbrough, Katheryn
Phenwick women series (33)
Physical attraction
Janson, Hank
Hank Janson series (220)
Physician power
Seide, Diane
Medical power series (2)
Physicians
Harrison, Elizabeth
Central London Hospital series (1)
Physiology of marriage
Balzac, Honore de
Marriage series (1)
Piano bird
Kallen, Lucille
C.B.Greenfield series (4)
Piano box mystery
Carter, Nicholas
Nicholas Carter series (11)
Piano lessons can be murder
Stine, Robert Lawrence
Goosebumps series (13)
Pic, the weapon-maker
Langford, George
Pic series (1)
Picaroon and the burglar tools
Landon, Herman
Picaroon series (9)
Picaroon collects
Cassells, John
Ludovic Saxon series (17)
Picaroon does justice
Landon, Herman
Picaroon series (3)
Picaroon gets the run-around
Cassells, John
Ludovic Saxon series (21)
Picaroon goes west
Cassells, John
Ludovic Saxon series (8)
Picaroon in pursuit
Landon, Herman
Picaroon series (7)
Picaroon, knight errant
Landon, Herman
Picaroon series (8)
Picaroon laughs last
Cassells, John
Ludovic Saxon series (19)
Picaroon resumes practice
Landon, Herman
Picaroon series (6)
Piccadilly
Rayner, Claire
Performers series (11)
Piccadilly murder
Berkeley, Anthony
Ambrose Chitterwick series (2)
Piccolo
Hewett, Anita
Piccolo series (1)
Piccolo and Maria
Hewett, Anita
Piccolo series (2)
Pick a new dream
Weber, Lenora Mattingly
Beany Malone series (11)
Pick-up nine
Dawson, Elmer A
Buck and Larry baseball series (1)
Pick-up on Noon Street
Chandler, Raymond
Philip Marlowe series (6)
Pick up sticks
Lathen, Emma
John Putnam Thatcher series (11)
Pick up the pieces
Straker, John Foster
Inspector Pitt series (2)
Pickaninny twins
Perkins, Lucy Fitch
Twin series (21)
Picked up adrift
De Mille, James
Brethren of the White Cross series (5)
Picking the ballad's bones
Scarborough, Elizabeth Ann
Songkiller series (2)
Pickle and Penny
Ramstedt, Viveka
Penny series (1)
Pickle puss
Giff, Patricia Reilly
Kids of the Polk Street School series (12)
Pickle the spy
Lang, Andrew
Pickle series (1)
Pickled poodles
Harris, Larry Mark
John Joseph Malone series (14)
Pickles of the Lower Fifth
Walker, Rowland
Fifth Form series (1)
Pickwick abroad
Reynolds, George Macarthur
Pickwick series (2)
Pickwick papers
Dickens, Charles
Pickwick series (1)
Picnic
Cosgrove, Stephen Edward
Simple folk series (1)
Picnic at Hanging Rock
Lindsay, Joan
Hanging Rock series (1)
Picnic at Sakkara
Newby, Percy Howard
Eric Blainey series (1)
Picnic for Bunnykins
Warrener
Bunnykins series (1)
Picnic, hurrah!
Brandenberg, Franz
Edward and Elizabeth series (5)
Picnic on paradise
Russ, Joanna
Adventures of Alyx series (1)
Picnic party
Optic, Oliver
Flora Lee series (1)
Riverdale series (10)
Picnic with Piggins
Yolen, Jane
Piggins series (2)
Pictorial life story of Misty
Henry, Marguerite
Chincoteague series (4)
Picts and the Martyrs
Ransome, Arthur
Swallows and Amazons series (11)
Picture a country vicarage
Brode, Anthony
Country vicarage series (1)
Picture book of Hannukah
Adler, David A
Picture book of Jewish holidays series (3)
Picture book of Jewish holidays
Adler, David A
Picture book of Jewish holidays series (1)
Picture book of Passover
Adler, David A
Picture book of Jewish holidays series (2)
Picture frame
Lamb, Lynton
Superintendent Quill and Inspector Glover series (3)
Picture him dead
Clement, Frank A
Superintendent Mersey series (1)
Picture Miss Seeton
Carvic, Heron
Miss Emily Seeton series (1)
Picture of David
Singer, Shelley
Barrett Lake series (2)
Picture of death
Giles, Kenneth
Inspector Harry James and Sergeant Honeybody series (3)
Lorac, E C R
Inspector Macdonald series (44)
Simons, Roger
Inspector Fadiman Wace series (15)
Picture of guilt
Innes, Michael
Sir John Appleby series (23)
Keene, Carolyn
Nancy Drew files series (101)
Picture of life, 1872-1940
Mersey, Charles Clive
Picture of life series (1)
Picture of the victim
Strange, John Stephen
Barney Gantt series (4)
Picture perfect
Cooper, M E
Couples series (14)
Picture-perfect murders
Chastain, Thomas
Robins family series (3)
Picture perfect mystery
Keene, Carolyn
Nancy Drew series (94)
Picture postcard
Huebner, Frederick D
Matt Riordan series (3)
Picture rhymes
Ward, Dorothy Darrell
Teddies series (1)
Pictures and conversations
Bowen, Elizabeth
Seven winters series (2)
Pictures in the cave
Brown, George Mackay
Two fiddlers series (2)
Pictures in the hallway
O'Casey, Sean
I knock at the door series (2)
Pictures in the spring
Braga, Meg
William and Wendy series (4)
Pictures of death
Robeson, Kenneth
Avenger series (19)
Pictures of perfection
Hill, Reginald
Superintendent Andrew Dalziel and Sergeant Pascoe series (20)
Pictures of war
Crane, Stephen
American Civil War episodes series (2)
Pidgin cargo
Hobart, Alice Tisdale
China series (1)
Pie
Postgate, Oliver
Saga of Noggin the Nog series (8)
Pie and the patty-pan
Potter, Beatrix
Peter Rabbit series (7)
Piece of cake
Murphy, Jill
Larges family trilogy (3)
Taylor, Geoff
Bomber Command series (1)
Piece of resistance
Egleton, Clive
David Garnett trilogy (1)
Piece of the action
Solomita, Stephen
Stanley Moodrow series (5)
Piece of the moon is missing
Johnson, James Leonard
Code name Sebastian series (4)
Piece of the pie
Browne, Dik
Hagar the horrible series (43)
Piece of the silence
Livingston, Jack
Joe Birney series (1)
Pieces of a Hero
Overgard, William
Hero Haggity series (1)
Pieces of cream
Hilary, Richard
Ezell Barnes series (2)
Pieces of death
Lynch, Jack
Peter Bragg series (3)
Pieces of fate
Peel, John
U.N.C.L.E. files series (7)
Pieces of Modesty
O'Donnell, Peter
Modesty Blaise series (6)
Pied Piper of Medenham
Dale, Norman
Medenham series (3)
Pier glass
Steen, Marguerite
Glass series (2)
Pierce with a skin
Hopkins, Kenneth
Gerry Lee series (3)
Pierced ear murders
Plummer, Thomas Arthur
Detective Inspector Andrew Frampton series (26)
Piercing the darkness
Peretti, Frank E
Darkness series (2)
Pierhead jump
Bassett, Ronald
Lobby Ludd trilogy (2)
Pierhead 627
Enefer, Douglas
Sam Bawtrey series (1)
Pierre and his people
Parker, Gilbert
Pretty Pierre series (1)
Pierre Grassou
Balzac, Honore de
Scenes of private life series (24)
Pierre Noziere
France, Anatole
Pierre Noziere series (2)
Pierre's lucky pouch
Judson, Clara Ingram
They came from series (2)
Pierrette
Balzac, Honore de
Scenes of provincial life series (4)
Piers Anthony's visual guide to Xanth
Anthony, Piers
Xanth series (16)
Piet Potter on the run
Quackenbush, Robert Mead
Piet Potter series (5)
Piet Potter returns
Quackenbush, Robert Mead
Piet Potter series (2)
Piet Potter strikes again
Quackenbush, Robert Mead
Piet Potter series (3)
Piet Potter to the rescue
Quackenbush, Robert Mead
Piet Potter series (4)
Piet Potter's first case
Quackenbush, Robert Mead
Piet Potter series (1)
Piet Potter's hot clue
Quackenbush, Robert Mead
Piet Potter series (6)
Pietro Ghisleri
Crawford, Francis Marion
Saracinesca family series (2)
Pig brother, and other fables and stories
Richards, Laura Elizabeth
Fables for young and old series (3)
Pig earth
Berger, John
Into their labours trilogy (1)
Pig got up and slowly walked away
Ripley, Jack
John George Davis series (2)
Pig in a muddle
Lobe, Mira
Pig series (1)
Pig in a poke
Thayer, Lee
Peter Clancy series (44)
Pig in paradise
Williams, Elma Mary
Wildlife series (2)
Pig on the run
Lobe, Mira
Pig series (2)
Pig Pig and the magic photo album
McPhail, David Michael
Pig Pig series (4)
Pig Pig gets a job
McPhail, David Michael
Pig Pig series (5)
Pig Pig goes to camp
McPhail, David Michael
Pig Pig series (3)
Pig Pig grows up
McPhail, David Michael
Pig Pig series (1)
Pig Pig rides
McPhail, David Michael
Pig Pig series (2)
Pig Plantagenet
Andrews, Allen
Pig Plantagenet series (1)
Pig, the prince and the unicorn
Brush, Karen Alexandra
Pig series (1)
Pig William
Dubanevich, Arlene
Pigs series (2)
Pigeon at sea
Cole, Michael
Pigeon Street series (4)
Pigeon blood
Alexander, Gary
Superintendent Bamsan Kiet series (1)
Pigeon blood rubies
Bodkin, Matthias McDonnell
Paul Beck series (5)
Pigeon Hoo
Lushington, Franklin
Pigeon Hoo series (1)
Pigeon loft crime
Brandon, John Gordon
Sexton Blake series (957)
Pigeon post
Ransome, Arthur
Swallows and Amazons series (6)
Pigeongram family
Lamplugh, Lois
Allen family series (1)
Pigeons
Jones, Olive
Barfield series (6)
Piggest show on earth
Dubanevich, Arlene
Pigs series (4)
Piggins
Yolen, Jane
Piggins series (1)
Piggins and the royal wedding
Yolen, Jane
Piggins series (3)
Piggy Grunter and the town hall fire
Shelley, Noreen
Piggy Grunter series (2)
Piggy Grunter at the circus
Shelley, Noreen
Piggy Grunter series (1)
Piggy Grunter's red umbrella
Shelley, Noreen
Piggy Grunter series (3)
Piglet meets a heffalump
Milne, Alan Alexander
Piglet series (3)
Pigman
Zindel, Paul
Pigman series (1)
Pigman's legacy
Zindel, Paul
Pigman series (2)
Pigs at Christmas
Dubanevich, Arlene
Pigs series (3)
Pigs get fat
Murphy, Warren Burton
Devlin Tracy series (5)
Pigs have wings
Wodehouse, Pelham Grenville
Blandings Castle series (9)
Pigs in hiding
Dubanevich, Arlene
Pigs series (1)
Pigs in the kitchen
Jones, Olive
Barfield series (7)
Pigs plus
Burningham, John
Number play series (4)
Pigwig
Dyke, John
Pigwig series (1)
Pigwig and the pirates
Dyke, John
Pigwig series (2)
Pike and the sword
Barbary, James
Adventure in history series (4)
Pike's Peak
Waters, Frank
Pike's Peak trilogy (3)
Pikes Peak shoot-out
Logan, Jake
John Slocum series (185)
Piketown flood
Grover, Marshall
Larry and Stretch series (293)
Pikolo's night voyage
Filion, Pierre
Pikolo series (2)
Pilate's wife
Mann, Deborah
Early Christian series (3)
Reign of Herod Antipas trilogy (2)
Piles on pets
Delton, Judy
Pee wee scout series (19)
Pilgrim at sea
Lagerkvist, Par
Tobias trilogy (2)
Pilgrim at the gate
Cory, Desmond
Mister Pilgrim series (1)
Pilgrim Cottage
Roberts, Cecil
Pilgrim Cottage series (1)
Pilgrim Fathers
Birt, David
Stuarts series (13)
Pilgrim in Arabia
Philby, Harry St John Bridger
Arabian travel series (3)
Pilgrim Kate
Daringer, Helen Fern
Endicott family trilogy (1)
Pilgrim kill
Potter, Jay Hill
Pilgrim series (9)

Pilgrim of a smile
Davey, Norman
Pilgrim series (1)
Pilgrim series (2)
Pilgrim of adversity
McFee, William
Pilgrims and sailors series (1)
Pilgrim of hate
Peters, Ellis
Brother Cadfael series (10)
Pilgrim on the island
Cory, Desmond
Mister Pilgrim series (2)
Pilgrim partners
Brittain, Harry Ernest
Pilgrim series (2)
Pilgrim raid
Potter, Jay Hill
Pilgrim series (7)
Pilgrim son
Masters, John
British India trilogy (3)
Pilgrimage
Henderson, Zenna
People series (1)
Lingard, Joan
Maggie McKinley quartet (3)
Richardson, Dorothy Miller
Pilgrimage series (3)
Pilgrimage series (5)
Pilgrimage series (8)
Pilgrimage series (12)
Pilgrimage series (13)
Pilgrimage of Grace
Birt, David
Tudors series (12)
Pilgrimage of Premnath
White, Edmund Valentine
Indian romance series (2)
Pilgrimage to hell
Adrian, Jack
Deathlands series (1)
Pilgrims and partners
Brittain, Harry Ernest
Pilgrim series (1)
Pilgrim's blood
Potter, Jay Hill
Pilgrim series (4)
Pilgrim's Inn
Goudge, Elizabeth
Eliot family trilogy (2)
Pilgrim's progress from this world to that which is to come
Bunyan, John
John Bunyan series (1)
John Bunyan series (2)
Pilgrim's rest
Wentworth, Patricia
Miss Maud Silver series (11)
Young, Francis Brett
N'dala series (1)
Pilgrim's revenge
Potter, Jay Hill
Pilgrim series (10)
Pilgrim's shell
Sue, Eugene
Mysteries of the people series (12)
Pilgrim's trail
Potter, Jay Hill
Pilgrim series (2)
Pillage idiot
Browne, Dik
Hagar the horrible series (32)
Pillar of night
Vardeman, Robert Edward
Cenotaph Road series (6)
Pillar of salt
Memmi, Albert
Tunisian Jew series (1)
Pillars of Pentegarn
Estes, Rose
Endless quest series (3)
Pillars of the house
Yonge, Charlotte Mary
Beechcroft series (4)
Honor Charlecote series (2)
Lady Herbert Somerville series (2)
Pillars of the house series (5)
Pilling always pays
Armstrong, Thomas
Crowther chronicles series (2)
Pillow of the community
Hilary, Richard
Ezell Barnes series (3)
Pilot
Cooper, James Fenimore
Paul Jones series (1)
Pilot at Swan Creek
Connor, Ralph
Sky Pilot series (2)
Pilot error
Barbree, Jay
Six Million Dollar Man series (8)
Knox, Bill
Inspector Colin Thane and Phil Moss series (15)
Pilot of the Cloud Patrol
Crump, James Irving
Cloud Patrol series (2)
Pilot, the chaser
Peel, Hazel Mary
Ann and Jim Henderson series (3)
Pilot the chaser
Peel, Hazel Mary
Pilot series (2)
Pilot, the hunter
Peel, Hazel Mary
Ann and Jim Henderson series (2)
Pilot the hunter
Peel, Hazel Mary
Pilot series (1)
Piloting the U.S. mail
Theiss, Lewis Edwin
Air mail series (1)
Pilot's graveyard
Conde, Phillip
Dick Pemberty series (3)
Piltditch puzzle
Ferguson, William Blair Morton
Biff Corrigan series (3)
Pimp for the dead
Dennis, Ralph
Jim Hardman series (4)
Pimpernel and Rosemary
Orczy, Emmuska
Scarlet Pimpernel series (14)
Pimpernel and the poodle
Walker, David Esdaile
Pimpernel series (2)
Pimpernel plot
Hawke, Simon
Timewars series (3)
Pin a rose on me
Blumenfeld, Josephine
Pin a rose on me series (1)
Pinball murders
Black, Thomas B
Al Delaney series (3)
Pinch of poison
Lockridge, Frances
Bill Wiegand series (3)
Mister and Mrs North series (4)
Pinch of snuff
Hill, Reginald
Superintendent Andrew Dalziel and Sergeant Pascoe series (9)
Underwood, Michael
Rosa Epton series (1)
Pinchbeck masterpiece
Cleife, Philip
Martyn Finch series (1)
Pincher Martin
Taffrail
Royal Navy series (1)
Pinchpenny Mouse
Kraus, Robert
Pinchpenny Mouse series (1)
Pine cones
Allen, Willis Boyd
Pine cone series (1)
Pine Street goes camping
Allan, Mabel Esther
Pine Street series (2)
Pine Street pageant
Allan, Mabel Esther
Pine Street series (1)
Pine Street problem
Allan, Mabel Esther
Pine Street series (3)
Pineapple child, and other tales from Ashanti
Appiah, Peggy
Ashanti series (2)
Pineapple Palace
Willson, Robina Beckles
Sarah and Alastair series (3)
Pinehurst
Rhode, John
Doctor Lancelot Priestley series (9)
Pink lady
Robeson, Kenneth
Doc Savage series (157)
Pink lemonade charade
Blair, Cynthia
Susan and Christine Pratt series (7)
Pink Panther
Albert, Marvin Hubert
Inspector Clouseau series (1)
Pink Panther strikes again
Waldman, Frank
Inspector Clouseau series (2)
Pink sugar
Douglas, O
Priorsford series (2)
Pink umbrella
Crane, Frances
Pat and Jean Abbott series (4)
Pink umbrella murder
Crane, Frances
Pat and Jean Abbott series (4)
Pink 'un and a pelican
Binstead, Arthur Morris
Random reminiscences series (1)
Pinkerton, behave!
Kellogg, Steven
Pinkerton series (1)
Pinkerton killers
Hardin, J D
Raider series (30)
Pinkie and the rabbits
Mathews, Joanna Hooe
Flowerets series (6)
Pinky and Rex
Howe, James
Pinky and Rex series (1)
Pinky and Rex and the mean old witch
Howe, James
Pinky and Rex series (4)
Pinky and Rex and the new baby
Howe, James
Pinky and Rex series (6)
Pinky and rex and the spelling bee
Howe, James
Pinky and Rex series (3)
Pinky and Rex get married
Howe, James
Pinky and Rex series (2)
Pinky and Rex go to camp
Howe, James
Pinky and Rex series (5)
Pinky Pye
Estes, Eleanor
Pye family series (2)
Pinned man
Griswold, George
Mister Groode series (4)
Pinny and the bird
Firmin, Peter
Pinny series (1)
Pinny and the floppy dog
Firmin, Peter
Pinny series (5)
Pinny finds a house
Firmin, Peter
Pinny series (2)
Pinny in the snow
Firmin, Peter
Pinny series (3)
Pinny's party
Firmin, Peter
Pinny series (4)
Pinocchio
Collodi, Carlo
Pinocchio series (1)
Pinocchio and Geppetto
Parsons, Virginia
Pinocchio series (3)
Pinocchio and the money tree
Parsons, Virginia
Pinocchio series (4)
Pinocchio goes on the stage
Parsons, Virginia
Pinocchio series (2)
Pinocchio in Venice
Coover, Robert
Pinocchio series (6)
Pinocchio plays truant
Parsons, Virginia
Pinocchio series (5)
Pinpricks of married life
Balzac, Honore de
Marriage series (2)
Pint of murder
Craig, Alisa
Inspector Madoc Rhys series (1)
Pioneer boys of Kansas
Adams, Harrison
Pioneer boys series (8)
Pioneer boys of the Colorado
Adams, Harrison
Pioneer boys series (7)
Pioneer boys of the Columbia
Adams, Harrison
Pioneer boys series (6)
Pioneer boys of the gold fields
Bonehill, Ralph
Flag and frontier series (3)
Frontier series (3)
Pioneer boys of the great Northwest
Bonehill, Ralph
Flag and frontier series (2)
Frontier series (2)
Pioneer boys of the Mississippi
Adams, Harrison
Pioneer boys series (3)
Pioneer boys of the Missouri
Adams, Harrison
Pioneer boys series (4)
Pioneer boys of the Ohio
Adams, Harrison
Pioneer boys series (1)
Pioneer boys of the Yellowstone
Adams, Harrison
Pioneer boys series (5)
Pioneer boys on the Great Lakes
Adams, Harrison
Pioneer boys series (2)
Pioneer girls and the Dutch mill mystery
Palmer, Bernard
Pioneer girls series (7)
Pioneer girls and the mysterious bedouin cave
Palmer, Bernard
Pioneer girls series (6)
Pioneer girls and the mystery of missing cocker
Palmer, Bernard
Pioneer girls series (2)
Pioneer girls and the mystery of Oak Ridge Manor
Palmer, Bernard
Pioneer girls series (1)
Pioneer girls and the secret of the jungle
Palmer, Bernard
Pioneer girls series (5)
Pioneer girls and the strange adventures on Tomahawk Hill
Palmer, Bernard
Pioneer girls series (3)
Pioneer girls at Caribou Flats
Palmer, Bernard
Pioneer girls series (4)
Pioneer scouts of the Ohio
Tomlinson, Everett Titsworth
American scouting series (7)
Pioneer show folk
McCall, Edith
Frontiers of America series (15)
Pioneer spirit
Calder, Stephen
Bonanza series (6)
Pioneer traders
McCall, Edith
Frontiers of America series (16)
Pioneer twins
Perkins, Lucy Fitch
Twin series (18)
Pioneering on the Plains
McCall, Edith
Frontiers of America series (13)
Pioneers
Bonner, Terry Nelsen
New South Wales series (4)
Cooper, James Fenimore
Leatherstocking series (4)
Jakes, John
Kent family series (4)
Pioneers of the early waterways
McCall, Edith
Frontiers of America series (8)
Pious agent
Braine, John
Colonel Xavier Flynn series (1)
Pious deception
Dunlap, Susan
Kiernan O'Shaughnessy series (1)
Pip and Andrew in danger
Wilson, Keane
Pip and Andrew series (3)
Pip and Andrew, schoolmates
Wilson, Keane
Pip and Andrew series (2)
Pip and seagull
Jones, Olive
Barfield series (9)
Pip-Larssons go sailing
Unnerstad, Edith
Larsson family series (2)
Pip of Pynalong
Wilson, Keane
Pip and Andrew series (1)
Pipa Pear
Reed, Giles
Munch Bunch character series (7)
Pipe carriers
Cooke, John Byrne
Snowblind moon trilogy (2)
Pipe down!
Bosco, Clyde
Nintendo adventure series (5)
Pipe dream finesse
Da Cruz, Daniel
Ape Swain series (2)
Pipeline from hell
Bannerman, David
Magic Man series (3)
Pipeline strike
Robbins, David
Blade series (4)
Pipeline to death
Eichler, Alfred
Martin Ames series (6)
Piper and the gates of dawn
Cowper, Richard
Bird of kinship series (1)
Piper at the gate
Stanton, Mary
Horse series (2)
Piper at the gates of dawn
Stanton, Mary
Horse series (2)
Piper on the mountain
Peters, Ellis
Inspector George Felse series (5)
Piper to the clan
Clarke, Mary Stetson
Ross McCrae series (2)
Piper's fee
Adams, Samuel Hopkins
Ruyland family series (2)
Pipers of the market place
Dehan, Richard
Market place series (1)
Pipes are calling
Brown, Carter
Danny Boyd series (27)
Piping hot
Zola, Emile
Rougon Macquart series (10)
Piping on the wind
Knight, Brigid
Ashenden series (2)
Pipkins go camping
Wahl, Jan
Pipkins series (1)
Pippa and James
Ohlson, Edith Emilie
Pippa series (4)
Pippa at Brighton
Ohlson, Edith Emilie
Pippa series (3)
Pippa at home
Ohlson, Edith Emilie
Pippa series (1)
Pippa in Switzerland
Ohlson, Edith Emilie
Pippa series (2)
Pippa Mouse
Boegehold, Betty
Pippa Mouse series (1)
Pippa pops out!
Boegehold, Betty
Pippa Mouse series (3)
Pippa's mystery horse
Berrisford, Judith Mary
Pippa series (3)
Pippi goes aboard
Lindgren, Astrid
Pippi Longstocking series (2)
Pippi goes on board
Lindgren, Astrid
Pippi Longstocking series (2)
Pippi in the South Seas
Lindgren, Astrid
Pippi Longstocking series (3)
Pippi Longstocking
Lindgren, Astrid
Pippi Longstocking series (1)
Pippi on the run
Lindgren, Astrid
Pippi Longstocking series (4)
Pippo gets lost
Oxenbury, Helen
Tom and Pippo series (9)
Piracy wears pink
Kane, Martin
Martin Kane series (6)
Piraeus plot
Arvay, Harry
Israeli Security Branch series (5)
Piranha, piranha
Zacharia, Irwin
Landshark series (2)
Pirate
Sadler, Barry
Casca series (15)
Pirate destroyer
Sea-Lion
Tiger Ransome series (1)
Pirate Island adventure
Parish, Peggy
Liza, Bill and Jed series (4)
Pirate isle
Robeson, Kenneth
Doc Savage series (115)

Pirate king
Trueman, Brian
Stories from Cockleshell Bay series (1)
Pirate moon
Steiner, Merrilee
Swept away series (7)
Pirate of the Pacific
Robeson, Kenneth
Doc Savage series (19)
Pirate of World's End
Carter, Lin
Gondwane epic series (5)
Pirate paradox
Baron, Nick
Time tours series (5)
Pirate prince
Michaels, Melisa C
Skyrider series (4)
Pirate Saint
Charteris, Leslie
Saint series (16)
Pirate seagull
Trueman, Brian
Stories from Cockleshell Bay series (5)
Pirate strike
Robbins, David
Blade series (5)
Pirate submarine
Westerman, Percy Francis
Captain Cain series (1)
Pirates
Lloyd, David
Let's pretend series (3)
Taffrail
Pirates series (1)
Pirates aboard!
Duff, Douglas Valder
Adam Macadam series (13)
Pirates and privateers
McCall, Edith
Frontiers of America series (14)
Pirate's ghost
Robeson, Kenneth
Doc Savage series (62)
Pirates in Oz
Thompson, Ruth Plumly
Oz series (24)
Pirates of Gohar
Lord, Jeffrey
Richard Blade series (32)
Pirates of Rosinante
Gilliland, Alexis Arnaldus
Rosinante trilogy (3)
Pirates of Shan
Blaine, John
Rick Brant series (14)
Pirates of the air
Adams, Eustace Lane
Andy Lane series (5)
Pirates of the air way
Armour, R Coutts
Sexton Blake series (458)
Pirates of the asteroids
Asimov, Isaac
David Starr series (2)
Pirates of the thunder
Chalker, Jack Laurence
Rings of the master series (2)
Pirates of Venus
Burroughs, Edgar Rice
Venus series (1)
Piro and the digger
Baumann, Kurt
Piro series (4)
Piro and the fire brigade
Baumann, Kurt
Piro series (1)
Piro and the runaway train
Baumann, Kurt
Piro series (3)
Piro and the treasure hunt
Baumann, Kurt
Piro series (2)
Piro the pilot
Baumann, Kurt
Piro series (5)
Pistol grip
Dalton, Kit
Buckskin series (20)
Pistol whipped
Dalton, Kit
Buckskin series (35)
Pistoleer
Ladd, Justin
Abilene series (13)
Pistolero
Masterson, Louis
Morgan Kane series (7)
Pistoleros
Benteen, John
Sundance series (5)
Pistols for two
Beaman, Sydney George Hulme
Toytown series (19)
Stein, Aaron Marc
Tim Mulligan and Elsie Mae Hunt series (14)
Pistoltown
LeBeau, Roy
Buckskin series (3)
Pit
Cheetham, Ann
Black harvest series (4)
Norris, Frank
Epic of wheat series (2)
Pit of the abyss
Millin, Sarah Gertrude
War diary series (4)
Pitcairn's Island
Nordhoff, Charles
Bounty trilogy (3)
Pitcher in paradise
Binstead, Arthur Morris
Random reminiscences series (2)
Pitcher to center field
Bunting, Eve
High point series (1)
Pitchers' duel
Bee, Clair
Chip Hilton series (6)
Pitching trouble
Kroll, Steven
Hit and Run Gang series (5)
Pitchman healer
Gardner, Jerome
Dripspring series (7)
Pitfall
Wylde, Thomas
Roger Zelazny's Alien speedway series (2)
Pitt and the Seven Years' War
Sherrard, Owen Aubrey
Lord Chatham trilogy (2)
Pity for women
Montherlant, Henry de
Girls series (2)
Pity is not enough
Herbst, Josephine
Decay of capitalism trilogy (1)
Pixie O'Shaughnessy
Vaizey, Jessie Bell
Pixie O'Shaughnessy series (1)
Pixilated peeress
De Camp, Lyon Sprague
Incorporated knight series (2)
Pizza isn't everything but is comes close
Evans, Greg
Luann series (8)
Pizza monster
Sharmat, Marjorie Weinman
Olivia Sharp series (1)
Pizza mystery
Warner, Gertrude Chandler
Boxcar children series (33)
Place among the fallen
Cole, Adrian
Omaran series (1)
Place between
Newton, Suzanne
Arden Gifford series (2)
Place called Purgatory
Shelynn, Jack
Ned Parker series (1)
Place for a poisoner
Lorac, E C R
Inspector Macdonald series (31)
Place for Jeremy
Hermes, Patricia
Jeremy series (2)
Place for murder
Lathen, Emma
John Putnam Thatcher series (2)
Place for Noah
Greenfeld, Josh
Noah series (2)
Place for Peter
Yates, Elizabeth
Mountain born series (2)
Place in England
Bragg, Melvyn
Tallentire family series (2)
Place in life
Miller, Hugh
Eastenders series (9)
Place in the country
Gainham, Sarah
Viennese trilogy (2)
Place in the sun
Thorne, Nicola
Askham family series (4)
Place in the woods
Hoover, Helen
Forest trilogy (2)
Place like home
Todd, Laura
Lavarni family series (1)
Place Mill
Softly, Barbara
English Civil War series (2)
Place of dead roads
Burroughs, William Seward
Cities of the red night trilogy (2)
Place of demons
Graat, Heinrich
Ben Camden series (3)
Place of execution
Vinter, Michael
Barry Kegan series (1)
Place of hawks
Derleth, August
Sac Prairie series (1)
Place of Little Birds
Home, Michael
Zerzura series (1)
Place of mists
Macleod, Robert
Talos Cord series (5)
Place of stones
Ruck, Ruth Janette
Hill Farm trilogy (1)
Place of the swan
Irish, Lola
Colonial trilogy (2)
Place that sends you mad
Goscinny, Rene
Twelve tasks of Asterix series (8)
Place to belong
Nixon, Joan Lowery
Orphan train quintet (4)
Place to play
Ahlberg, Allan
Brick Street Boys series (2)
Place to stand
Burton, Anthony
Navigators trilogy (3)
Place your bets
Masters, Zeke
Faro Blake series (15)
Places where they sing
Raven, Simon
Alms for oblivion series (6)
Plague
Darke, James
Witches series (8)
Smith, Guy Newman
Thirst series (2)
Plague and fire
Birt, David
Stuarts series (8)
Plague and I
Macdonald, Betty
Who me series (2)
Plague bomb
Rouch, James
Zone series (6)
Plague Court murders
Dickson, Carter
Sir Henry Merrivale series (2)
Plague demon
Craig, Brian
Minstrel Orfeo series (2)
Plague in paradise
Vardeman, Robert Edward
Masters of space trilogy (3)
Plague moon
Elliott, Nathan
Star pirates trilogy (2)
Plague nineteen ninety
Ure, Jean
Hal series (1)
Plague of demons
Ashe, Gordon
Patrick Dawlish series (51)
Plague of dragons
Brett, John Michael
Hugo Baron series (2)
Plague of knives
Silke, James R
Death dealer series (4)
Plague of nightmares
Cole, Adrian
Dream Lords trilogy (1)
Plague of oblivion
Darlton, Clark
Perry Rhodan series (28)
Plague of sailors
Callison, Brian
Brevet Cable series (1)
Plague of silence
Creasey, John
Doctor Palfrey series (19)
Plague of sound
Steffanson, Con
Flash Gordon series (3)
Plague of spies
Kurland, Michael
Mission series (4)
Plague of violence
Pentecost, Hugh
John Jericho series (6)
Plague on both your causes
Brunner, John
Max Curfew series (1)
Plague over London
Craig, Thurlow
Lieutenant Bunjy Hearne series (2)
Plague ship
Norton, Andre
Dane Thorson series (2)
Plague years
Austin, Richard
Guardians series (12)
Plain case of murder
Thayer, Lee
Peter Clancy series (37)
Plain Jane
Chesney, Marion
House for the season series (2)
Softly, Barbara
English Civil War series (1)
Plain Mary Jane
Carson, Hilda
Mary Jane series (1)
Plain Mary Smith
Phillips, Henry Wallace
Red Saunders series (2)
Plain murder
Greth, Roma
Hana Shaner series (2)
Plain old man
Macleod, Charlotte
Sarah Kelling series (6)
Plain sailing
Clark, Douglas
Inspector George Masters series (26)
Plains murder
Roberts, J R
Gunsmith series (74)
Plains of Abraham
Curwood, James Oliver
Quebec series (2)
Plains of cement
Hamilton, Patrick
Twenty thousand streets under the sky series (3)
Plains of fire
Hild, Jack
SOBS series (2)
Plains of passage
Auel, Jean Marie
Earth's children series (4)
Plains of the sea
Hancock, Niel
Wilderness of four series (2)
Plains paramour
Fletcher, Dirk
Spur McCoy series (29)
Plains war
McLennan, Will
Ramseys series (18)
Plaintext
Mairs, Nancy
Plaintext series (1)
Plaisir d'amour
Villefranche, Anne Marie
Erotic memoirs series (1)
Plan B
Himes, Chester
Grave Digger Jones and Coffin Ed Johnson series (9)
Plan XVI
Browne, Douglas Gordon
Inspector Thew series (2)
Plando and the nightingale
Bryce, Charles
Plando series (2)
Plando the mouse deer
Bryce, Charles
Plando series (1)
Plane and plank
Optic, Oliver
Onward and upward series (2)
Plane without a pilot
Adams, Eustace Lane
Andy Lane series (9)
Planet beyond
Mudd, Steve
Tangled webs series (2)
Planet buyer
Smith, Cordwainer
Instrumentality series (2)
Planet called Krishna
De Camp, Lyon Sprague
Krishna series (3)
Planet dweller
Palmer, Jane
Planet dweller series (1)
Planet in peril
Mohan, Kim
Cyborg commando trilogy (1)
Planet Mechanica
Scheer, Karl Herbert
Perry Rhodan series (112)
Planet murderer
Cleve, John
Spaceways series (16)
Planet of adventure
Main, Carol
Fraser family trilogy (3)
Planet of adventure omnibus
Vance, Jack
Tschai series (4)
Planet of dread
Kern, Gregory
Cap Kennedy series (10)
Planet of evil
Main, Carol
Fraser family trilogy (2)
Planet of exile
Le Guin, Ursula Kroeber
Hain series (5)
Planet of fear
Moore, Patrick
Scott Saunders series (2)
Planet of fire
Grimwade, Peter
Doctor Who series (93)
Planet of flowers
Norwood, Warren
Windhover tapes series (4)
Planet of judgment
Haldeman, Joe
Star trek originals sequels series (5)
Planet of night
Jones, Raymond F
Ron Barron series (2)
Planet of nightmares
Appleton, Victor II
Tom Swift Junior series 2 (11)
Planet of no return
Harrison, Harry
Brion Brandd series (2)
Planet of peril
Kline, Otis Adelbert
Grandon trilogy (1)
Planet of robot slaves
Harrison, Harry
Bill, the galactic hero series (1)
Planet of Tears
Reinius, Trish
White Wolf series (1)
Planet of the Apes
Boulle, Pierre
Planet of the Apes series (1)
Planet of the blind
James, Laurence
Simon Rack series (4)
Planet of the damned
Harrison, Harry
Brion Brandd series (1)
Planet of the double sun
Jones, Neil Ronald
Professor Jameson series (1)
Planet of the dragons
Brightfield, Richard
Choose your own adventure series (75)
Dragons series (2)
Planet of the dying man
Mahr, Kurt
Perry Rhodan series (11)
Planet of the giants
Dicks, Terrance
Doctor Who series (145)
Planet of the gods
Mahr, Kurt
Perry Rhodan series (27)
Planet of the monsters
May, Stephen
Planet of the monsters series (1)
Planet of the spiders
Dicks, Terrance
Doctor Who series (15)
Sarah Jane Smith series (1)
Planet of the Warlord
Hill, Douglas
Last legionary series (5)
Planet of treachery
Smith, Edward Elmer
Family d'Alembert series (7)
Planet of whispers
Kelly, James Patrick
Messenger chronicles series (1)
Planet poachers
Lightner, Alice Martha
Rock trilogy (2)

Planet Probability
Ball, Brian Neville
Probability series (2)
Planet savers
Bradley, Marion Zimmer
Darkover series (16)
Planet Toride, please reply!
Brand, Kurt
Perry Rhodan series (75)
Planet wizard
Jakes, John
Dragonard series (2)
Planetary Agent X
Reynolds, Mack
Planetary Agent series (1)
Planetfall
Cover, Arthur Byron
Planetfall series (1)
Planets
Bendick, Jeanne
Early bird astronomy series (7)
Boylan, James Finney
Heavenly bodies series (1)
Planets in peril
Black, Christopher
Star challenge series (1)
Hamilton, Edmond
Captain Future series (9)
Planets of peril
Butterworth, Michael
Space nineteen ninety nine series (12)
Planned parenthood caper
Paul, F W
Man from S.T.U.D. series (7)
Planning for murder
Morice, Anne
Tessa Crichton Price series (24)
Planning on murder
Williams, David
Mark Treasure series (16)
Plant
King, Stephen
Plant trilogy (1)
Vassilikos, Vassilis
Modern Greece trilogy (1)
Plant hunters
Reid, Mayne
Himalayas series (1)
Plant magic
Fisher, Aileen
Ways of plants series (5)
Plant me now
Hagen, Miriam Ann
Hortense Clinton series (1)
Plant, part 2
King, Stephen
Plant trilogy (2)
Plant, part 3
King, Stephen
Plant trilogy (3)
Plant that ate dirty socks
McArthur, Nancy
Plant that ate dirty socks series (1)
Plantagenet prelude
Plaidy, Jean
Plantagenet series (1)
Plantation
Denuziere, Maurice
Clarence Dandridge series (1)
McNeill, George
Deavors family series (1)
Plantation trilogy
Bristow, Gwen
Louisiana trilogy (3)
Plantos affair
Rankine, John
Dag Fletcher series (3)
Plasher's Mead
Mackenzie, Compton
Sinister Street series (2)
Plasm
Platt, Charles
Aton series (3)
Plasma monster
Mahr, Kurt
Perry Rhodan series (95)
Plaster sinners
Watson, Colin
Inspector Purbright series (11)
Plastered for Christmas
Reeder, Colin
West Meadow series (6)
Plastic man
Gerrity, David
Frank Cardolini series (2)
Plate of red herrings
Lockridge, Richard
Assistant District Attorney Bernie Simmons series (4)
Platinum ass
Storey, Anthony
Platinum series (2)
Platinum bullet
Graves, Richard Latshaw
Hugo Wolfram series (2)
Platinum cat
Burton, Miles
Inspector Arnold and Desmond Merrion series (18)
Platinum Jag
Storey, Anthony
Platinum series (1)
Platinum smugglers
Armour, R Coutts
Sexton Blake series (318)
Platte River crossing
Bell, Robert Vaughn
McGowan family series (4)
Platypus of doom, and other nihilists
Cover, Arthur Byron
Autumn angels trilogy (2)
Platypussy
Allison, Clyde
Agent triple zero eight series (19)
Play and study
Leslie, Madeline
Play and study series (4)
Play ball!
Walker, Mort
Hi and Lois series (21)
Play ball, Amelia Bedelia
Parish, Peggy
Amelia Bedelia series (5)
Play for millions
Carter, Nicholas
Nicholas Carter series (434)
Play it quiet
Janson, Hank
Hank Janson series (18)
Play it Solo
Graham, Neill
Solo Malcolm series (2)
Play it to a bust
Greenberg, Dave
Super Cops series (2)
Play kitten
Schongut, Emanuel
Kitten board book series (4)
Play now, kill later
Brown, Carter
Rick Holman series (15)
Play of passion
Holbrook, David
Flesh wounds trilogy (2)
Play-off
Hughes, Dean
Angel Park All-Stars series (13)
Play the ball
Forster, Peter
Alex Smith and Tony Bevan series (1)
Play the man
Forster, Peter
Alex Smith and Tony Bevan series (2)
Play time
Bradman, Tony
Rhymes with me series (2)
Play to live
Veley, Charles
Twilight series (7)
Play toward
Coxhead, Elizabeth
Alney series (1)
Playback
Chandler, Raymond
Philip Marlowe series (8)
Playboy Pook
Pook, Peter
Pook series (11)
Playboy prince
Roberts, Nora
Cordina series (3)
Flowers series (39)
Played out
Morgan, Damian
Andrea Quill series (2)
Played to a finish
Carter, Nicholas
Nicholas Carter series (105)
Player
Downing, Warwick
Joe Reddman series (1)
Player of games
Banks, Iain Menzies
Culture series (2)
Player on the other side
Queen, Ellery
Ellery Queen series (35)
Player queen
Fecher, Constance
Ralegh family trilogy (3)
Players
Cooper, Jilly
Rupert Campbell-Black series (2)
Players and the rebels
Forest, Antonia
Marlow Ancestors series (2)
Player's boy
Forest, Antonia
Marlow Ancestors series (1)
Player's boy is dead
Tourney, Leonard
Matthew Stock series (1)
Players come again
Cross, Amanda
Professor Kate Fansler series (10)
Player's hide
Hayes, Douglas
History of a selfish man series (5)
Players of Gor
Norman, John
Tarl Cabot series (20)
Players of hell
Van Arnam, Dave
Konarr series (1)
Players of luck
Shetterly, Will
Liavek series (2)
Players of Null-A
Van Vogt, Alfred Elton
Null-A series (2)
Playgirl
Janson, Hank
Hank Janson series (158)
Playgirl for keeps
McCall, K T
Johnny Buchanan series (14)
Playground
Duke, Kate
Guinea pig board books series (4)
Roth, Harold
Toddler's fun series (2)
Playground bunnies
Cartlidge, Michelle
Press and play series (3)
Playground of death
Hilton, John Buxton
Superintendent Simon Kenworthy series (7)
Playgrounds of the mind
Niven, Larry
Known Space series (21)
Playing
Oxenbury, Helen
Baby board books series (7)
Playing a bold game
Carter, Nicholas
Nicholas Carter series (17)
Playing a lone hand
Carter, Nicholas
Nicholas Carter series (159)
Playing catch-up
Guthrie, Alfred Bertram
Sheriff Chick Charleston and Jason Beard series (4)
Playing dirty
Cooper, M E
Couples series (32)
Playing favorites
Kroll, Steven
Hit and Run Gang series (2)
Playing for a fortune
Carter, Nicholas
Nicholas Carter series (180)
Playing for keeps
Morgan, Damian
Andrea Quill series (1)
Pascal, Francine
Sweet Valley High series (49)
Playing for the Ashes
George, Elizabeth
Inspector Thomas Lynley and Sergeant Barbara Havers series (7)
Playing games
Cooney, Linda A
Totally hot series (6)
Theis, Jody Sorenson
Cheerleaders series (9)
Playing hooky
Pascal, Francine
Sweet Valley twins series (20)
Playing safe
Dewhurst, Eileen
Helen Johnson series (2)
Playing story
Erickson, Karen
I can do it series (1)
Playing the game
Sladen, Douglas
Japanese marriage series (2)
Playing the odds
Roberts, Nora
Macgregor series (1)
Playing with Andy Pandy
Bird, Maria
Andy Pandy series (3)
Playing with fire
Keene, Carolyn
Nancy Drew files series (26)
Pascal, Francine
Sweet Valley High series (3)
Sampson, George
Paola and George series (2)
Playmates
Parker, Robert Brown
Spenser series (16)
Plaything of fate
Carter, Nicholas
Nicholas Carter series (325)
Playtime
Tarsky, Sue
Time to talk series (1)
Playtime and Baby Jay
VerDorn, Bethea
Baby Jay series (2)
Plaza mystery
Worth, Maurice
Derek Harding series (2)
Plea for justice
Carter, Nicholas
Nicholas Carter series (486)
Pleading guilty
Turow, Scott
Sandy Stern series (3)
Pleasant day diversions
Wells, Carolyn
Diversions series (2)
Pleasant Fieldmouse
Wahl, Jan
Pleasant Fieldmouse series (1)
Pleasant Fieldmouse storybook
Wahl, Jan
Pleasant Fieldmouse series (3)
Pleasant Fieldmouse Valentine trick
Wahl, Jan
Pleasant Fieldmouse series (4)
Pleasant Fieldmouse's Halloween party
Wahl, Jan
Pleasant Fieldmouse series (2)
Pleasant Grove murders
Vance, John Holbrook
Sheriff Joe Bain series (2)
Pleasant Valley
Bromfield, Louis
Malabar series (1)
Pleasant years
Roberts, Cecil
Sunshine and shadow series (5)
Pleasantries of Old Quong
Burke, Thomas
London series (4)
Please come home
Sanford, Doris
Hurts of childhood series (4)
Please keep off the mud
Knight, Frank
Chichester Harbour series (3)
Please kill my cousin
Fairlie, Gerard
Johnny Macall series (6)
Please look after this bear
Bond, Michael
Paddington learning and activity series (8)
Please Mrs Butler
Ahlberg, Allan
Mrs Butler series (1)
Please omit funeral
Dolson, Hildegarde
Lucy Ramsdale series (3)
Please pass the guilt
Stout, Rex
Nero Wolfe and Archie Goodwin series (45)
Please save Jessie
Pullein-Thompson, Christine
Jessie series (2)
Please to look pleasant
Housman, Laurence
Palace plays series (4)
Please write back
Stewart, Maureen
Henry and Voula series (3)
Please you, draw near
Raymond, Ernest
My days series (2)
Pleasure cruise murder
Jardine, Warwick
Sexton Blake series (765)
Pleasure cruise mystery
Forsythe, Robin
Anthony Vereker series (4)
Pleasure factory
Tarsis, Valeriy
Black Sea trilogy (1)
Pleasure garden
Sandys, Oliver
Pleasure garden series (1)
Pleasure Island
Carter, Nick
Nick Carter series (152)
Pleasure-lover
Meyerstein, Edward Henry William
Terence Duke series (1)
Pleasures of Peyton Place
Fuller, Roger
Peyton Place series (5)
Pledge of the twin knights
Sutton, Margaret
Judy Bolton series (36)
Pledge to a doomed man
Grover, Marshall
Larry and Stretch series (278)
Pleistocene mammals of Europe
Kurten, Bjorn
Pleistocene mammals series (1)
Pleistocene mammals of North America
Kurten, Bjorn
Pleistocene mammals series (2)
Plexus
Miller, Henry
Rosy crucifixion trilogy (2)
Pliocene companion
May, Julian
Pliocene exile series (5)
Plot for a warship
Carter, Nicholas
Nicholas Carter series (438)
Plot for an empire
Carter, Nicholas
Nicholas Carter series (384)
Plot for the Fourth Reich
Carter, Nick
Nick Carter series (115)
Plot it yourself
Stout, Rex
Dol Bonner series (3)
Nero Wolfe and Archie Goodwin series (32)
Plot master
Grant, Maxwell
Shadow series (71)
Plot of the Placards at Rennes, 1802
Thierry, Gilbert Augustin
Conspirators and police under Napoleon series (1)
Plot of the yellow emperor
Parsons, Anthony
Sexton Blake series (1076)
Plot that failed
Carter, Nicholas
Nicholas Carter series (178)
Plot uncovered
Carter, Nicholas
Nicholas Carter series (329)
Plot within a plot
Carter, Nicholas
Nicholas Carter series (211)
Plots and plays
Birt, David
Tudors series (20)
Plotters
Caillou, Alan
Mike Benasque series (1)
Ploughman of heaven
Service, Robert William
Ploughman of heaven series (1)
Ploughman of the moon
Service, Robert William
Adventures in memory series (1)
Plowing on Sunday
North, Sterling
Plowing series (1)
Pluck
Winter, John Strange
Bootles series (5)
Pluck will tell
Richards, Frank
Schoolboy series (6)
Pluckrose's horse
Fearon, Ethelind
Pluckrose series (2)
Plucky Dick
Ellis, Edward Sylvester
Bound to win trilogy (2)
Plugged nickle
Campbell, Robert Wright
Jake Hatch series (1)
Plum Daffy adventure
Coatsworth, Elizabeth
Plum Daffy series (2)
Plum pie
Wodehouse, Pelham Grenville
Blandings Castle series (12)
Blandings Castle series (14)
Jeeves and Bertie Wooster series (15)
Ukridge series (2)
Plum rain scroll
Manley, Ruth
Ancient Japan series (1)

Plumb
Gee, Maurice
Plumb trilogy (1)
Plumley inheritance
Bush, Christopher
Ludovic Travers series (1)
Plummer's last posse
Grover, Marshall
Larry and Stretch series (352)
Plunder
Goulart, Ron
Barnum series (3)
Meriton, Peter
Captain Dack series (3)
Van de Water, Frederic Franklin
John Tarleton series (2)
Plunder bar
Parkman, Sydney
Captain Bowker series (1)
Plunder for the Picaroon
Cassells, John
Ludovic Saxon series (12)
Plunder of the sun
Dodge, David
Al Colby series (2)
Plunder squad
Stark, Richard
Parker series (15)
Plundered paradise
Derrick, Lionel
Penetrator series (52)
Plunge
Brogan, Colm
Patrick Heron series (2)
Plunge into crime
Carter, Nicholas
Nicholas Carter series (290)
Plush-lined coffin
Brown, Carter
Lieutenant Al Wheeler series (36)
Plymouth cloak
Sedley, Kate
Roger Chapman series (2)
Pnume
Vance, Jack
Tschai series (4)
Poacher's bag
Clark, Douglas
Inspector George Masters series (12)
Poacher's pie
Archer, Fred
Evesham Vale series (8)
Pocket Bible
Sue, Eugene
Mysteries of the people series (16)
Pocket full of clues
Langham, James R
Samuel G Abbott series (2)
Pocket full of dead
Wyllie, John
Doctor Quarshie series (5)
Pocket full of rye
Christie, Agatha
Miss Jane Marple series (8)
Layberry, Layton George Joseph
Oakleigh Farm series (4)
Pocket history of American painting
Flexner, James Thomas
History of American painting series (3)
Pocket park problem
Christian, Mary Blount
Goosehill Gang series (6)
Pocket-rifle
Trowbridge, John Townsend
Silver medal series (5)
Pocketful of clues
Langham, James R
Samuel G Abbott series (2)
Pocketful of dreams
Witcomb, Nan
Thoughts of Nanushka series (5)
Pocketful of mice
Miller, Margaret Jessy
Willow and Albert series (6)
Pocketful of rye
Cronin, Archibald Joseph
Laurence Carroll series (2)
Pockets of resistance
Sundown, Will
Pockets series (1)
Pocomoto and the canyon treasure
Dixon, Rex
Pocomoto series (5)
Pocomoto and the circus folk
Dixon, Rex
Pocomoto series (16)
Pocomoto and the desert gold
Dixon, Rex
Pocomoto series (15)
Pocomoto and the golden herd
Dixon, Rex
Pocomoto series (21)
Pocomoto and the Indian trails
Dixon, Rex
Pocomoto series (12)
Pocomoto and the lazy river
Dixon, Rex
Pocomoto series (10)
Pocomoto and the lazy sheriff
Dixon, Rex
Pocomoto series (18)
Pocomoto and the l'il fella
Dixon, Rex
Pocomoto series (7)
Pocomoto and the lost hunters
Dixon, Rex
Pocomoto series (19)
Pocomoto and the Mexican bandits
Dixon, Rex
Pocomoto series (23)
Pocomoto and the night riders
Dixon, Rex
Pocomoto series (3)
Pocomoto and the robbers' trail
Dixon, Rex
Pocomoto series (13)
Pocomoto and the snow wolf
Dixon, Rex
Pocomoto series (11)
Pocomoto and the Spanish steed
Dixon, Rex
Pocomoto series (14)
Pocomoto and the Texas pioneers
Dixon, Rex
Pocomoto series (17)
Pocomoto and the Texas ranger
Dixon, Rex
Pocomoto series (20)
Pocomoto and the warrior braves
Dixon, Rex
Pocomoto series (22)
Pocomoto, bronco buster
Dixon, Rex
Pocomoto series (4)
Pocomoto, brush popper
Dixon, Rex
Pocomoto series (6)
Pocomoto, buffalo hunter
Dixon, Rex
Pocomoto series (8)
Pocomoto, cowboy cavalier
Dixon, Rex
Pocomoto series (9)
Pocomoto, pony express rider
Dixon, Rex
Pocomoto series (1)
Pocomoto, tenderfoot
Dixon, Rex
Pocomoto series (2)
Poddy the winner
Judd, Alfred
Poddy series (2)
Poddy's progress
Judd, Alfred
Poddy series (1)
Poder charge
Dalton, Kit
Buckskin series (25)
Poems
Seferis, George
Log book series (3)
Poems for Peter
Borie, Lysbeth Boyd
Poems for Peter series (1)
Poems for pictures and for notes of music
Ford, Ford Madox
Poems for pictures series (1)
Poems to solve
Swenson, May
Poems to solve series (1)
Poet at the breakfast table
Holmes, Oliver Wendell
Breakfast table trilogy (3)
Poet in the family
Abse, Dannie
Poet in the family series (2)
Poetic justice
Cross, Amanda
Professor Kate Fansler series (3)
Poets and murder
Gulik, Robert van
Judge Dee series (17)
Pogo the penguin
Rutley, Cecil Bernard
Wild life story series (9)
Point blank
Hild, Jack
SOBS series (17)
Macdonnell, James Edmond
Dutchy Holland series (33)
Stark, Richard
Parker series (1)
Point Deception
McKernan, Victoria
Chicago Nordejoong series (2)
Point no-point
McCullough, David Willis
Ziza Todd series (2)
Point of a gun
Mackenzie, Andrew
Superintendent Brannigan series (6)
Point of a thousand spears
Greene, L Patrick
Aubrey Saint John Major series (13)
Sergeant Lancey series (3)
Point of contact
Edson, John Thomas
Rockabye County series (7)
Point of departure
Cameron, James
Point of departure series (1)
Macdonnell, James Edmond
Dutchy Holland series (9)
Point of honor
Gethin, David
Halloran series (1)
Point of reference
Russell, Richard
Angel Graham series (2)
Point Team
Hadley, J B
Point Team series (1)
Point thirty eight
Ard, William
Timothy Dane series (2)
Point thirty eight automatic
Vivian, Evelyn Charles
Inspector Head series (8)
Point Three Five Seven Vigilante
Ludlow, Ian
Vigilante series (1)
Pointed roofs
Richardson, Dorothy Miller
Pilgrimage series (1)
Pointed tower
Thompson, Vance
Mister Guelpa series (1)
Pointer to a crime
Fielding, A
Inspector Pointer series (23)
Pointing the way, 1959-1961
Macmillan, Harold
Winds of change series (5)
Pointing woman
Fraser, Sara
Tildy series (4)
Points to crime
Carter, Nicholas
Nicholas Carter series (484)
Poirot and the regatta mystery
Christie, Agatha
Hercule Poirot series (38)
Poirot investigates
Christie, Agatha
Hercule Poirot series (3)
Poirot knows the murderer
Christie, Agatha
Hercule Poirot series (38)
Poirot lends a hand
Christie, Agatha
Hercule Poirot series (38)
Poirot loses a client
Christie, Agatha
Hercule Poirot series (15)
Poirot on holiday
Christie, Agatha
Hercule Poirot series (38)
Poirot's early cases
Christie, Agatha
Hercule Poirot series (37)
Poison
McBain, Ed
Eighty Seventh Precinct series (40)
Thayer, Lee
Peter Clancy series (7)
Poison a la carte
Stout, Rex
Nero Wolfe and Archie Goodwin series (33)
Poison and the root
Savage, Richard
Doctor Ferenc series (3)
Poison Bay
Bishop, Pike
Cord Diamondback series (9)
Poison belt
Doyle, Arthur Conan
Professor Challenger series (2)
Poison case number ten
Cornell, Louis
Michael Joyce series (1)
Poison cross mystery
Irwin, Inez Haynes
Patrick O'Brien series (2)
Poison death
Glint Green
Inspector Wield series (4)
Poison flowers
Cooper, Natasha
Willow King series (2)
Poison fly murder
Rutland, Harriet
Mister Winkley series (2)
Poison for one
Rhode, John
Doctor Lancelot Priestley series (18)
Poison for teacher
Spain, Nancy
Johnny Duvivien series (5)
Miriam Birdseye series (2)
Poison for the Toff
Creasey, John
Toff series (17)
Poison from a wealthy widow
Haggard, Paul
Mike Warlock series (3)
Poison fruit
Yarbro, Chelsea Quinn
Charlie Spotted Moon series (3)
Poison in a garden suburb
Cole, George Douglas Howard
Superintendent Henry Wilson series (6)
Poison in jest
Carr, John Dickson
Henri Bencolin series (5)
Poison in paradise
Hocking, Anne
Inspector William Austen series (23)
Poison in play
Spain, Nancy
Johnny Duvivien series (1)
Poison in the garden suburb
Cole, George Douglas Howard
Superintendent Henry Wilson series (6)
Poison in the pen
Wentworth, Patricia
Miss Maud Silver series (28)
Poison is a bitter brew
Hocking, Anne
Inspector William Austen series (7)
Poison Island
Robeson, Kenneth
Doc Savage series (57)
Poison ivy
Cheyney, Peter
Lemmy Caution series (2)
Poison jasmine
Clason, Clyde B
Theocritus Lucius Westborough series (9)
Poison of poppies
Brodie, Gordon
John Borham series (2)
Poison pen
Keene, Carolyn
Nancy Drew files series (60)
Poison pen at Jug Valley Juniors
Digby, Anne
Jug Valley Juniors series (5)
Poison pen at Pyford
Fisher, Douglas George
Jeff Tellford series (2)
Poison pen playgirl
Brody, Marc
Marc Brody series (80)
Poison people
Haggard, William
Colonel Charles Russell series (18)
Poison plague
Levinrew, Will
Professor Herman Brierly series (1)
Poison, poker and pistols
Stone, Elizabet M
Maggie Slone series (1)
Poison pool
Collins, Gilbert
Hugh Carding series (6)
Poison trail
Armstrong, Anthony
Jimmie Rezaire series (5)
Poison unknown
Dutton, Charles Judson
Harley Manners series (4)
Poisoned chalice
Hocking, Anne
Inspector William Austen series (30)
Poisoned chocolates case
Berkeley, Anthony
Ambrose Chitterwick series (1)
Roger Sheringham series (5)
Poisoned crown
Druon, Maurice
Accursed kings series (3)
Poisoned goblet
Gask, Arthur
Gilbert Larose series (9)
Poisoned memories
Kubasik, Christopher
Earthdawn series (3)
Poisoned mountain
Channing, Mark
Colin Gray series (3)
Poisoned paradise
Dixon, Franklin W
Hardy boys case files series (82)
Roberts, Mark Kelly
Liberty Corps series (5)
Poisoned pen
Reeve, Arthur Benjamin
Craig Kennedy series (2)
Poisoned pilot
Pollard, Alfred Oliver
David Wilshaw series (2)
Poisoned pins
Hess, Joan
Claire Malloy series (8)
Poisoned pussy
Gray, Rod
Lady from L.U.S.T. series (9)
Poisoned sleep
Graeme, Bruce
Superintendent William Stevens and Inspector Pierre Allain series (10)
Poisoned treasure
Stone, Nick
Ben Kane series (4)
Poisoners
Hamilton, Donald
Matt Helm series (13)
Poisoner's base
Cobb, Belton
Inspector Cheviot Burmann series (21)
Poisoner's mistake
Cobb, Belton
Inspector Cheviot Burmann series (2)
Poisonous relations
Cannan, Joanna
Inspector Ronald Price series (1)
Poisons of Exili
Carter, Nicholas
Nicholas Carter series (480)
Poisons unknown
Kane, Frank
Johnny Liddell series (7)
Pokerface
Corris, Peter
Pokerface series (1)
Pokey to the rescue
Gilden, Mel
Zoomers of Motor City series (1)
Polar assault
Garrett, Frank
Killsquad series (7)
Polar bear cat
Bayley, Nicola
Copycats series (3)
Polar bear twins
Tompkins, Jane
Animal twins series (1)
Polar bears and the seals
Torgersen, Don Arthur
Animal life stories series (2)
Polar fleet
Norwood, Warren
Double-spiral war series (2)
Polar passion
Mowat, Farley
Top of the world trilogy (2)
Polar Star
Smith, Martin Cruz
Arkady Renko series (2)
Polar treasure
Robeson, Kenneth
Doc Savage series (4)
Polaris and the immortals
Stilson, Charles Billings
Polaris trilogy (3)
Polaris, of the snows
Stilson, Charles Billings
Polaris trilogy (1)
Polaroid man
Cormany, Michael
Dan Kruger series (4)
Poldark's Cornwall
Graham, Winston
Poldark series (11)

Poldark's Cornwall
Graham, Winston
Poldark series (11)

Pole reaction
Bruce, Jean
Secret Agent O.S.S.117 series (1)

Pole Star family
Blyton, Enid
Mike, Belinda and Ann series (3)

Pole Star secret
Rosenberger, Joseph
Death Merchant series (21)

Polemics and prophecies, 1967-1970
Stone, Isidor Feinstein
Nonconformist history of our times series (6)

Polferry mystery
Macdonald, Philip
Colonel Anthony Ruthven Gethryn series (5)

Polferry riddle
Macdonald, Philip
Colonel Anthony Ruthven Gethryn series (5)

Police!
Chambers, Robert William
Tales of a naturalist series (2)

Police action
Kurland, Michael
Mission series (3)

Police and detection
Jeffries, Roderic Graeme
Police series (1)

Police at the funeral
Allingham, Margery
Albert Campion series (4)

Police blotter
Pike, Robert L
Lieutenant Clancy series (3)

Police car
Jeffries, Roderic Graeme
Police series (3)

Police Chief
Ball, John
Jack Tallon series (1)

Police dog
Jeffries, Roderic Graeme
Police series (2)

Police patrol, 2000A.D.
Reynolds, Mack
Bat Hardin series (4)

Police rescue 1
Green, Bill
Mickey McClintock series (1)

Police rescue 2
Green, Bill
Mickey McClintock series (2)

Police station mystery
Hardinge, Rex
Sexton Blake series (1001)

Policeboat mystery
Blair, Allan
Sexton Blake series (692)

Policeman at the door
Carnac, Carol
Inspector Julian Rivers series (10)

Policeman Bluejay
Bancroft, Laura
Birdland series (2)

Policeman in armour
Penny, Rupert
Chief Inspector Edward Beale series (3)

Policeman in the precinct
Lorac, E C R
Inspector Macdonald series (33)

Policeman on the green
Quinain, Louis
Country beat series (2)

Policeman Small
Lenski, Lois
Small family series (10)

Policeman's dread
Creasey, John
Inspector Roger West series (30)

Policeman's evidence
Penny, Rupert
Chief Inspector Edward Beale series (5)

Policeman's gazette
Cole, Harry
Policeman's life series (7)

Policeman's hobby
Farmer, Bernard James
Tom Ward series (5)

Policeman's holiday
Farmer, Bernard James
Tom Ward series (2)
Penny, Rupert
Chief Inspector Edward Beale series (2)

Policeman's lot
Cole, Harry
Policeman's life series (2)
Linington, Elizabeth
Sergeant Ivor Maddox series (5)
Wade, Henry
Inspector Poole series (3)

Policeman's nightmare
Cumberland, Marten
Saturnin Dax series (11)

Policeman's patch
Cole, Harry
Policeman's life series (3)

Policeman's patrol
Cole, Harry
Policeman's life series (4)

Policeman's prelude
Cole, Harry
Policeman's life series (5)

Policeman's progress
Cole, Harry
Policeman's life series (1)

Policeman's story
Cole, Harry
Policeman's life series (6)

Policemen and firemen
Greene, Carla
What do they do series (1)

Polish pony puzzle
McCarthy, Maureen
Mission top secret series (5)

Polished ebony
Cohen, Octavus Roy
Polished ebony series (1)

Political life of children
Coles, Robert
Life of children series (2)

Politician
Anthony, Piers
Bio of a space tyrant series (3)
Torrio, Vincente
Hoods series (3)

Politicians and the War, 1914-1916, volume 1
Beaverbrook, William Maxwell Aitken
Lloyd George series (1)

Politicians and the War, 1914-1916, volume 2
Beaverbrook, William Maxwell Aitken
Lloyd George series (2)

Politics is murder
Lanham, Edwin
Lieutenant Madigan series (2)

Politics of Africa's economic recovery
Sandbrook, Richard
African politics series (3)

Politics of Africa's economic stagnation
Sandbrook, Richard
African politics series (2)

Politics of basic needs
Sandbrook, Richard
African politics series (1)

Politics of upheaval
Schlesinger, Arthur Meier
Age of Roosevelt series (3)

Polkadot murder
Crane, Frances
Pat and Jean Abbott series (14)

Pollen
Noon, Jeff
Vurt series (2)

Pollie Green
Saint John, Mabel
Pollie Green series (1)

Pollie Green at Cambridge
Saint John, Mabel
Pollie Green series (3)

Pollie Green at Coosha
Saint John, Mabel
Pollie Green series (2)

Pollie Green at twenty-one
Saint John, Mabel
Pollie Green series (6)

Pollie Green, engaged
Saint John, Mabel
Pollie Green series (5)

Pollie Green in society
Saint John, Mabel
Pollie Green series (4)

Polly
Borntrager, Mary Christner
Ellie's people series (7)

Polly and Bob
Whitehill, Dorothy
Polly series (6)

Polly and Carola
Roy, Lillian Elizabeth
Polly Brewster series (13)

Polly and Carola at Ravenswood
Roy, Lillian Elizabeth
Polly Brewster series (14)

Polly and Eleanor
Roy, Lillian Elizabeth
Polly Brewster series (2)

Polly and her friends abroad
Roy, Lillian Elizabeth
Polly Brewster series (4)

Polly and Lois
Whitehill, Dorothy
Polly series (5)

Polly and Oliver
Daniell, David Scott
Drummer Oliver Crowe series (2)

Polly and Oliver at sea
Daniell, David Scott
Drummer Oliver Crowe series (3)

Polly and Oliver besieged
Daniell, David Scott
Drummer Oliver Crowe series (4)

Polly and Oliver pursued
Daniell, David Scott
Drummer Oliver Crowe series (5)

Polly and the princess
Dowd, Emma C
Polly series (4)

Polly and the surprising stranger
Lewis, Francine
Polly French series (4)

Polly and the wolf again
Storr, Catherine
Polly and the wolf series (4)

Polly at Pixie's Haunt
Whitehill, Dorothy
Polly series (9)

Polly Bright
Scannell, Dorothy
Bright series (1)

Polly finds out
Lewis, Francine
Polly French series (2)

Polly French of Whitford High
Lewis, Francine
Polly French series (1)

Polly Harris
Treadgold, Mary
Mick and Caroline Templeton series (2)

Polly in Alaska
Roy, Lillian Elizabeth
Polly Brewster series (9)

Polly in Egypt
Roy, Lillian Elizabeth
Polly Brewster series (11)

Polly in New York
Roy, Lillian Elizabeth
Polly Brewster series (3)

Polly in South America
Roy, Lillian Elizabeth
Polly Brewster series (7)

Polly in the Orient
Roy, Lillian Elizabeth
Polly Brewster series (10)

Polly in the Southwest
Roy, Lillian Elizabeth
Polly Brewster series (8)

Polly learns to fly
Roy, Lillian Elizabeth
Polly Brewster series (15)

Polly learns to play
Roy, Lillian Elizabeth
Polly Brewster series (16)

Polly, my wonderful mother
Cartland, Barbara
Years of life series (4)

Polly of Lady Gay Cottage
Dowd, Emma C
Polly series (2)

Polly of Pebbly Pit
Roy, Lillian Elizabeth
Polly Brewster series (1)

Polly of the hospital staff
Dowd, Emma C
Polly series (1)

Polly Oliver's problem
Wiggin, Kate Douglas
Polly Oliver series (2)

Polly Page Camping Club
Forrester, Izola Louise
Polly Page series (4)

Polly Page Motor Club
Forrester, Izola Louise
Polly Page series (3)

Polly Page Ranch Club
Forrester, Izola Louise
Polly Page series (2)

Polly Page Yacht Club
Forrester, Izola Louise
Polly Page series (1)

Polly Prentiss goes a-visiting
Gould, Elizabeth Lincoln
Polly Prentiss series (3)

Polly Prentiss goes to school
Gould, Elizabeth Lincoln
Polly Prentiss series (2)

Polly Prentiss keeps a promise
Gould, Elizabeth Lincoln
Polly Prentiss series (4)

Polly put the kettle on
Bailey, Hilary
Polly series (1)

Polly sees the world at war
Whitehill, Dorothy
Polly series (4)

Polly takes charge
Lewis, Francine
Polly French series (3)

Polly, the giant's bride
Storr, Catherine
Polly and the wolf series (3)

Polly, the worried
Kimbrough, Katheryn
Phenwick women series (25)

Pollyanna
Porter, Eleanor Hodgman
Pollyanna series (1)

Pollyanna and the secret mission
De Trevino, Elizabeth Borton
Pollyanna series (14)

Pollyanna at Six Star Ranch
Moffitt, Virginia May
Pollyanna series (12)

Pollyanna grows up
Porter, Eleanor Hodgman
Pollyanna series (2)

Pollyanna in Hollywood
De Trevino, Elizabeth Borton
Pollyanna series (7)

Pollyanna of Magic Valley
Moffitt, Virginia May
Pollyanna series (13)

Pollyanna of the orange blossoms
Smith, Harriet Lummis
Pollyanna series (3)

Pollyanna's castle in Mexico
De Trevino, Elizabeth Borton
Pollyanna series (8)

Pollyanna's debt of honor
Smith, Harriet Lummis
Pollyanna series (5)

Pollyanna's door to happiness
De Trevino, Elizabeth Borton
Pollyanna series (9)

Pollyanna's golden horseshoe
De Trevino, Elizabeth Borton
Pollyanna series (10)

Pollyanna's jewels
Smith, Harriet Lummis
Pollyanna series (4)

Pollyanna's western adventure
Smith, Harriet Lummis
Pollyanna series (6)

Pollyooly
Jepson, Edgar
Pollyooly series (1)

Pollyooly dances
Jepson, Edgar
Pollyooly series (3)

Polly's business venture
Roy, Lillian Elizabeth
Polly Brewster series (5)

Polly's dance
Hindley, Judy
Best of friends series (3)

Polly's first year at boarding school
Whitehill, Dorothy
Polly series (1)

Polly's house party
Whitehill, Dorothy
Polly series (10)

Polly's new friends
Roy, Lillian Elizabeth
Polly Brewster series (12)

Polly's Polly
Whitehill, Dorothy
Polly series (8)

Polly's Polly and Priscilla
Whitehill, Dorothy
Polly series (13)

Polly's Polly at boarding school
Whitehill, Dorothy
Polly series (11)

Polly's reunion
Whitehill, Dorothy
Polly series (7)

Polly's senior year at boarding school
Whitehill, Dorothy
Polly series (3)

Polly's southern cruise
Roy, Lillian Elizabeth
Polly Brewster series (6)

Polly's summer vacation
Whitehill, Dorothy
Polly series (2)

Polo, anyone?
Kennealy, Jerry
Nick Polo series (2)

Polo ground mystery
Forsythe, Robin
Anthony Vereker series (3)

Polo in the rough
Kennealy, Jerry
Nick Polo series (4)

Polo solo
Kennealy, Jerry
Nick Polo series (1)

Polonius Penguin and the flying doctor
Abrahams, Anthony
Polonius Penguin series (2)

Polonius Penguin comes to town
Abrahams, Anthony
Polonius Penguin series (1)

Polo's ponies
Kennealy, Jerry
Nick Polo series (3)

Polo's wild card
Kennealy, Jerry
Nick Polo series (5)

Polrudden
Thompson, Ernest Victor
Nathan Jago series (2)

Polson of Greyhouse
Bell, Robert Stanly Warren
Greyhouse series (5)

Poltergeist
Jackson, Rosemary Elizabeth
Macgillan family series (1)
Kahn, James
Poltergeist series (1)

Poltergeist of Burlap Hall
Ironside, Virginia
Burlap Hall series (4)

Poltergeists
Roop, Peter
Great mysteries series (2)

Polyanna's protege
Chalmers, Margaret Piper
Pollyanna series (11)

Polymath
Brunner, John
Zarathustra trilogy (2)

Polynesian art
Dodd, Edward Howard
Ring of fire series (1)

Polynesian seafaring
Dodd, Edward Howard
Ring of fire series (2)

Polynesia's sacred isle
Dodd, Edward Howard
Ring of fire series (3)

Pomanders of Little Chipping
Hakansson, Gunvor
Pomander series (2)

Pomeroy
Williams, Gordon Maclean
Pomeroy series (1)

Pomeroy, deceased
Bellairs, George
Detective Inspector Thomas Littlejohn series (51)

Pomeroy unleashed
Williams, Gordon Maclean
Pomeroy series (2)

Pomfret Towers
Thirkell, Angela
Barsetshire series (6)

Pommie migrant
Hart, Sydney
British migrant series (2)

Pommy cow
Campion, Sarah
Mister Moses Burdekin series (3)

Pomo uprising
Tufts, Warren
Casey Ruggles series (3)

Pomona's travels
Stockton, Frank Richard
Rudder Grange series (3)

Pompey's Head
Basso, Hamilton
Pompey's Head series (2)

Pond day
Ziefert, Harriet
Mister Rose's class series (3)

Pond Hall's progress
Freeman, Harold Webber
Pond Hall series (2)

Ponder and William
Softly, Barbara
Ponder and William series (1)

Ponder and William at home
Softly, Barbara
Ponder and William series (3)

Ponder and William at the weekend
Softly, Barbara
Ponder and William series (4)

Ponder and William on holiday
Softly, Barbara
Ponder and William series (2)

Ponderosa empire
Calder, Stephen
Bonanza series (7)
Ponderosa kill
Owen, Dean
Bonanza series (5)
Ponderosa war
Roberts, J R
Gunsmith series (30)
Poniard's hilt
Sue, Eugene
Mysteries of the people series (6)
Ponies all summer
Berrisford, Judith Mary
Sue Trent series (2)
Ponies and holidays
Gervaise, Mary
G for Georgia series (2)
Ponies and mysteries
Gervaise, Mary
G for Georgia series (4)
Ponies and poachers
Severn, David
Warner series (1)
Ponies at Westways
White, Constance Mary
Westways series (1)
Ponies by the sea
Baxter, Gillian
Angela and Ian Kendall series (3)
Ponies in clover
Gervaise, Mary
G for Georgia series (3)
Ponies in harness
Baxter, Gillian
Angela and Ian Kendall series (4)
Ponies in peril
Pullein-Thompson, Diana
Pony seekers series (3)
Ponies in the blizzard
Pullein-Thompson, Christine
Wells family series (3)
Ponies in the forest
Pullein-Thompson, Christine
Wells family series (2)
Ponies in the park
Pullein-Thompson, Christine
Wells family series (1)
Ponies in the valley
Pullein-Thompson, Diana
Pony seekers series (1)
Ponies of Cuckoo Mill Farm
Harris, Catherine
Marsham family series (2)
Ponies on the trail
Pullein-Thompson, Diana
Pony seekers series (2)
Pontifex, Son and Thorndyke
Freeman, Richard Austin
Doctor John Evelyn Thorndyke series (19)
Pony
Dicks, Terrance
Sally Ann series (6)
Pony at Blackbird Cottage
Furminger, Jo
Blackbird series (1)
Pony called Lightning
Mason, Miriam Evangeline
Lightning series (1)
Pony club camp
Pullein-Thompson, Josephine
Major Holbrooke series (5)
Pony club team
Pullein-Thompson, Josephine
Major Holbrooke series (2)
Pony Club through smoke and fire
Lengstrand, Rof
Pony Club series (2)
Pony clue
Gervaise, Mary
G for Georgia series (6)
Pony dopers
Pullein-Thompson, Christine
Seashore School of Equitation series (3)
Pony express
McLaglen, John J
Herne the Hunter series (21)
Pony express war
McCarthy, Gary
Derby Man series (4)
Pony for Belinda
Gervaise, Mary
Belinda Gordon series (1)
Pony for Jean
Cannan, Joanna
Jean series (1)
Pony for sale
Bye, Beryl
Cathy, Belinda and Jane series (2)
Pony for two
Hill, Denise
Jane and Jeremy Fortune series (1)
Pony found
Pullein-Thompson, Diana
Pony seekers series (5)
Pony from the farm
Gervaise, Mary
G for Georgia series (5)
Pony in the family
Berrisford, Judith Mary
Brooke family series (1)
Pony Island
Gervaise, Mary
G for Georgia series (7)
Pony jobs for Jilll
Ferguson, Ruby
Jill series (8)
Pony of your own
Gervaise, Mary
G for Georgia series (1)
Pony patrol
Pullein-Thompson, Christine
Pony patrol series (1)
Pony patrol and the mystery horse
Pullein-Thompson, Christine
Pony patrol series (4)
Pony patrol fights back
Pullein-Thompson, Christine
Pony patrol series (3)
Pony patrol S.O.S.
Pullein-Thompson, Christine
Pony patrol series (2)
Pony rider
Chandler, Edna Walker
Tom Logan series (1)
Pony Rider Boys in Alaska
Patchin, Frank Gee
Pony Rider Boys series (12)
Pony Rider Boys in Louisiana
Patchin, Frank Gee
Pony Rider Boys series (11)
Pony Rider Boys in Montana
Patchin, Frank Gee
Pony Rider Boys series (3)
Pony Rider Boys in New England
Patchin, Frank Gee
Pony Rider Boys series (10)
Pony Rider Boys in New Mexico
Patchin, Frank Gee
Pony Rider Boys series (6)
Pony Rider Boys in Texas
Patchin, Frank Gee
Pony Rider Boys series (2)
Pony Rider Boys in the Alkali
Patchin, Frank Gee
Pony Rider Boys series (5)
Pony Rider Boys in the Grand Canyon
Patchin, Frank Gee
Pony Rider Boys series (7)
Pony Rider Boys in the Ozarks
Patchin, Frank Gee
Pony Rider Boys series (4)
Pony Rider Boys in the Rockies
Patchin, Frank Gee
Pony Rider Boys series (1)
Pony Rider Boys on the Blue Ridge
Patchin, Frank Gee
Pony Rider Boys series (9)
Pony Rider Boys with the Texas Rangers
Patchin, Frank Gee
Pony Rider Boys series (8)
Pony soldiers
Axler, James
Deathlands series (6)
Pony, the bear and the parrot
Heuck, Sigrid
Pony and bear series (2)
Pony, the bear and the stolen apples
Heuck, Sigrid
Pony and bear series (1)
Pony-trekkers, go home!
Berrisford, Judith Mary
Pippa series (1)
Poodle Springs
Chandler, Raymond
Philip Marlowe series (9)
Pooh and Piglet nearly catch a woozle
Milne, Alan Alexander
Piglet series (2)
Pooh goes visiting
Milne, Alan Alexander
Piglet series (2)
Pook
Pook, Peter
Pook series (6)
Pook and partners
Pook, Peter
Pook series (10)
Pook at college
Pook, Peter
Pook series (8)
Pook in boots
Pook, Peter
Pook series (2)
Pook in business
Pook, Peter
Pook series (3)
Pook Sahib
Pook, Peter
Pook series (4)
Pookie
Wallace, Ivy Lilian
Pookie series (1)
Pookie and his shop
Wallace, Ivy Lilian
Pookie series (10)
Pookie and the gypsies
Wallace, Ivy Lilian
Pookie series (2)
Pookie and the swallows
Wallace, Ivy Lilian
Pookie series (7)
Pookie at the seaside
Wallace, Ivy Lilian
Pookie series (5)
Pookie believes in Santa Claus
Wallace, Ivy Lilian
Pookie series (9)
Pookie in search of a home
Wallace, Ivy Lilian
Pookie series (4)
Pookie in Wonderland
Wallace, Ivy Lilian
Pookie series (8)
Pookie puts the world right
Wallace, Ivy Lilian
Pookie series (3)
Pookie's big day
Wallace, Ivy Lilian
Pookie series (6)
Pook's china doll
Pook, Peter
Pook series (20)
Pook's class war
Pook, Peter
Pook series (12)
Pook's curiosity shop
Pook, Peter
Pook series (21)
Pook's Eastern promise
Pook, Peter
Pook series (14)
Pook's love nest
Pook, Peter
Pook series (19)
Pook's tale of woo
Pook, Peter
Pook series (13)
Pook's tender years
Pook, Peter
Pook series (9)
Pook's tours
Pook, Peter
Pook series (16)
Pook's Viking virgins
Pook, Peter
Pook series (23)
Pool of fire
Christopher, John
Tripods series (4)
Pool of flame
Vance, Louis Joseph
Terence O'Rourke series (2)
Pool of radiance
Hong, James Cooper
Avatar trilogy (3)
Pool of Saint Brunok
Carr, Philippa
Daughters of England series (14)
Pool of tears
Wainwright, John
Chief Inspector Lennox series (4)
Northern Police series (33)
Pool of the black one
Howard, Robert Ervin
Conan series (50)
Pool of Vishnu
Myers, Leopold Hamilton
Prince Jali series (4)
Poop, and other poems
Locklin, Gerald
Poop series (1)
Pooped troop
Delton, Judy
Pee wee scout series (10)
Poor and proud
Optic, Oliver
Boat Club series (3)
Poor and the land
Haggard, Henry Rider
Salvation Army series (1)
Poor boy
Brissenden, Robert Francis
Tom Caxton series (1)
Poor but plucky
Winfield, Arthur M
Bound to win series (8)
Bright and bold series (1)
Poor butterfly
Kaminsky, Stuart Melvin
Toby Peters series (15)
Poor girl
Van der Meersch, Maxence
Poor girl series (1)
Poor Lila
Pascal, Francine
Sweet Valley twins series (63)
Poor Mallory
Martin, Ann Matthews
Baby-Sitters Club series (39)
Poor mamma
Housman, Laurence
Palace plays series (2)
Poor man's house
Reynolds, Stephen
Nautical series (1)
Poor man's orange
Park, Ruth
Darcy family trilogy (3)
Poor man's shilling
Knight, Kathleen Moore
Elisha Macomber series (2)
Poor man's tapestry
Onions, Oliver
Gandelyn the Jester trilogy (1)
Poor Mister Nibble
Pilgrim, Jane
Blackberry Farm series (20)
Poor old Ernie
Mallett, Jerry J
Ernie series (2)
Poor old lady's dead
Scott, Jack S
Detective Inspector Alfred Stanley Rosher series (1)
Poor old Morph!
Dowling, Patrick
Amazing adventures of Morph series (4)
Poor old Uncle Sam
Martin, Bill
Freedom series (9)
Poor parson
Rudd, Steele
Duncan McClure series (1)
Poor Patty
Treadgold, Mary
Patty series (2)
Poor, poor, Ophelia
Weston, Carolyn
Casey Kellog and Al Krug series (1)
Poor, poor Yorick
Davis, Frederick Clyde
Professor Cyrus Hatch series (3)
Poor relations
Mackenzie, Compton
John Touchwood series (1)
Poor Stainless
Norton, Mary
Borrowers series (5)
Poor Teddy
Bawden, Juliet
My Teddy series (2)
Poorhouse woman
Fraser, Sara
Tildy series (2)
Poorly Pig
Ahlberg, Allan
Help your child to read series (5)
Pop corn contest
Giff, Patricia Reilly
Kids of the Polk Street School series (3)
Pop go the Vipers
Walker, Frank
Vipers series (2)
Popcorn project
Blair, Cynthia
Susan and Christine Pratt series (9)
Pope of the sea
Blasco Ibanez, Vicente
Spanish history series (1)
Popeye among the savages
Segar, Elzie Crisler
Popeye the Sailor series (2)
Popeye and the haunted house
Verral, Charles Spain
Popeye series (2)
Popeye and the pirates
Segar, Elzie Crisler
Popeye the Sailor series (4)
Popeye climbs a mountain
Verral, Charles Spain
Popeye series (3)
Popeye goes fishing
Verral, Charles Spain
Popeye series (1)
Popeye, the cartoon book
Segar, Elzie Crisler
Popeye the Sailor series (4)
Popeye the Sailor
Segar, Elzie Crisler
Popeye the Sailor series (1)
Popeye, the sailor man
Segar, Elzie Crisler
Popeye the Sailor series (3)
Popish plot
Birt, David
Stuarts series (16)
Pople who work in the country and the city
Judson, Clara Ingram
People series (3)
Popol out West
Herge
Tintin series (24)
Popp fly
Cosgrove, Stephen Edward
Bugg series (52)
Poppies and Mandy
Middleton, Ivy Florence Emily
Poppies series (3)
Poppies of death
Edwards, Paul
John Eagle series (11)
Poppy and the gems
O'Harris, Pixie
Poppy Treloar series (2)
Poppy faces the world
O'Harris, Pixie
Poppy Treloar series (3)
Poppy Pig
Bruna, Dick
Poppy Pig series (1)
Poppy Pig goes to market
Bruna, Dick
Poppy Pig series (3)
Poppy Pig's birthday
Bruna, Dick
Poppy Pig series (4)
Poppy Pig's garden
Bruna, Dick
Poppy Pig series (2)
Poppy seeds too
McDaniel, Becky Bring
Jewish tales series (2)
Poppy story book
Blyton, Enid
Flower story book series (3)
Poppy's pluck
Taggart, Marion Ames
Jack-in-the-box series (4)
Popular girl
Baldwin, Mary
Sibyl series (1)
Popular voice
Housman, Laurence
Palace plays series (4)
Popularity plan
Vernon, Rosemary
Frannie Bronson series (1)
Popularity summer
Vernon, Rosemary
Frannie Bronson series (2)
Popularity trap
Haynes, Betsy
Fabulous Five series (3)
Population growth
Hoff, Mary
Our endangered planet series (4)
Porcelain fish
Campbell, Harriette Russell
Simon Brade series (2)
Porcelain fish mystery
Campbell, Harriette Russell
Simon Brade series (2)
Porch
Church, Richard
John Quickshott series (1)
Porcupine twins
Tompkins, Jane
Animal twins series (8)
Porn tapes
Rainey, Rich
Alex Dartanian series (2)
Pornbroker
Brown, Carter
Rick Holman series (27)
Porpoise Bay
Pearce, Agatha Hunt
Edward, Frank and Gerry series (1)

Porpoises and the sailor
Torgersen, Don Arthur
Animal life stories series (8)
Porridge
Marshall, Jonathan
Porridge series (1)
Porridge, the inside story
Ableman, Paul
Porridge series (5)
Port and a star boarder
Morison, Betty Jane
Elizabeth Lamb Worthington series (2)
Port of destination
Laurie-Long, Ernest
Lizzie Collins series (1)
Port of intrigue
Mason, Francis Van Wyck
Colonel Hugh North series (10)
Port of light
Serafin, David
Superintendent Luis Bernal series (5)
Port of London murders
Bell, Josephine
Inspector Steven Mitchell series (3)
Port of peril
Kline, Otis Adelbert
Grandon trilogy (3)
Port Tarascon
Daudet, Alphonse
Tartarin series (3)
Portal of ancient evil
Darvill-Evans, Peter
Fighting fantasy gamebook series (37)
Portland
Willoughby, Lee Davis
Americana series (3)
Portland laughter
Emerson, Earl W
Thomas Black series (7)
Portland murders
Larson, Charles
Nils-Frederick Blixen series (4)
Portland pussycat
Fletcher, Dirk
Spur McCoy series (31)
Portly peregrine
Traill, Peter
Mister Prentice trilogy (1)
Porto Bello gold
Smith, Arthur Douglas Howden
Treasure Island series (1)
Portobello virgin
Evans, John
Habbakuk Parton series (1)
Portrait in blood
Kirchoff, Mary Lynn
Amazing stories series (3)
Portrait in crime
Keene, Carolyn
Nancy Drew files series (49)
Portrait in the sand
Keene, Carolyn
Dana girls series (12)
Portrait invisible
Gollomb, Joseph
Galt series (1)
Portrait of a beautiful harlot
Howard, Hartley
Glenn Bowman series (24)
Portrait of a dead heiress
Dewey, Thomas Blanchard
Private Eye Mac series (12)
Portrait of a Jew
Memmi, Albert
Jewish colonist series (2)
Portrait of a killer
Fulman, Al
Harry Long series (2)
Portrait of a man with red hair
Walpole, Hugh
Maradick series (4)
Portrait of a spy
Remy
Silent company trilogy (3)
Portrait of an artist and twenty-six horses
Eastlake, William
Bowman family trilogy (3)
Portrait of an English nobleman
Benson, Edward Frederic
Old London series (1)
Portrait of an optimist
Horne, Donald
New boy trilogy (3)
Portrait of Elmbury
Moore, John Cecil
Brensham trilogy (1)
Portrait of fear
Usher, Frank
Daye Smith series (3)
Portrait of Lilith
Thomson, June
Inspector Finch series (9)
Portrait of Miss Emily
Murdoch, Nina
Miss Emily trilogy (2)
Portrait of the artist as a dead man
Bonnamy, Francis
Peter Shane series (6)
Portrait of the artist as a young man
Joyce, James
Stephen Dedalus series (1)
Portrait of the mayor
Beaman, Sydney George Hulme
Toytown series (27)
Portraits of the past
Cameron, Kate
Holderly Hall series (6)
Portuguese defection
De Villiers, Gerard
Malko Linge series (15)
Portuguese escape
Bridge, Ann
Hetta Atherley series (1)
Julia Probyn series (2)
Portuguese fragment
Sela, Owen
Nicholas Maasten series (2)
Portuguese journey
Hogg, Garry
Jonty series (7)
Portulaca
Harris, Bernice
Purslane series (2)
Poseidon adventure
Gallico, Paul
Poseidon series (1)
Poseidon target
Carter, Nick
Nick Carter series (232)
Poseidon's gold
Davis, Lindsey
Marcus Didius Falco series (5)
Positively vetted!
Straiton, Eddie
Vet series (3)
Posse
Roberts, J R
Gunsmith series (33)
Posse from hell
Sharpe, Jon
Trailsman series (52)
Posse of killers
Victor, Sam
Kilburn series (6)
Posse plus two
Grover, Marshall
Larry and Stretch series (222)
Posse thunder
Denver, Lee
Deputy Marshal Dave Halloran series (3)
Possessed
Dostoevsky, Thedor Mikhailovich
Nihilist series (2)
Powe, Ronald
Possessed series (1)
Possessed II
Powe, Ronald
Possessed series (2)
Possession
Bromfield, Louis
Escape series (2)
Possession of Jessica Young
Martin, Russell White
Supernatural series (3)
Possessors and the possessed
Schreiner, Samuel Agnew
Van Alen family series (1)
Post after post-mortem
Lorac, E C R
Inspector Macdonald series (11)
Post captain
O'Brian, Patrick
Jack Aubrey and Stephen Maturin series (2)
O'Brien, Patrick
Captain Jack Aubrey series (2)
Post mortem
Carmichael, Harry
John Piper and Quinn series (24)
Post of honour
Delderfield, Ronald Frederick
Craddocks of Shallowford series (1)
Post office
Bukowski, Charles
Henry Chinaski series (2)
Post Office case
Disney, Doris Miles
David Madden series (1)
Posted for murder
Rath, Virginia
Michael Dundas series (5)
Postern of fate
Christie, Agatha
Tommy and Tuppence Beresford series (5)
Posthumous papers of the Pickwick Club
Dickens, Charles
Pickwick series (1)
Postillion struck
Bogarde, Dirk
Orderly man series (1)
Postman Joe
Pilgrim, Jane
Blackberry Farm series (8)
Postman Pat and his village
Cunliffe, John Arthur
Postman Pat series (11)
Postman Pat and the barometer
Cunliffe, John Arthur
Postman Pat series (35)
Postman Pat and the bees
Cunliffe, John Arthur
Postman Pat readers series (14)
Postman Pat and the Christmas puddings
Cunliffe, John Arthur
Postman Pat readers series (8)
Postman Pat and the cleaning day
Cunliffe, John Arthur
Postman Pat readers series (9)
Postman Pat and the dinosaur bone
Cunliffe, John Arthur
Postman Pat readers series (10)
Postman Pat and the flood
Cunliffe, John Arthur
Postman Pat series (33)
Postman Pat and the Greendale ghost
Cunliffe, John Arthur
Postman Pat readers series (7)
Postman Pat and the harvest parcel
Cunliffe, John Arthur
Postman Pat series (16)
Postman Pat and the letter puzzle
Cunliffe, John Arthur
Postman Pat series (20)
Postman Pat and the mystery thief
Cunliffe, John Arthur
Postman Pat series (2)
Postman Pat and the pet show
Cunliffe, John Arthur
Postman Pat readers series (11)
Postman Pat and the puzzle parcels
Cunliffe, John Arthur
Postman Pat series (24)
Postman Pat and the toy soldiers
Cunliffe, John Arthur
Postman Pat series (28)
Postman Pat and the tuba
Cunliffe, John Arthur
Postman Pat series (34)
Postman Pat fun book
Cunliffe, John Arthur
Postman Pat series (35)
Postman Pat gets a pet
Cunliffe, John Arthur
Postman Pat series (19)
Postman Pat gets fat
Cunliffe, John Arthur
Postman Pat beginners series (3)
Postman Pat goes sledging
Cunliffe, John Arthur
Postman Pat series (10)
Postman Pat goes to town
Cunliffe, John Arthur
Postman Pat series (17)
Postman Pat makes a present
Cunliffe, John Arthur
Postman Pat series (29)
Postman Pat makes a splash
Cunliffe, John Arthur
Postman Pat readers series (5)
Postman Pat, plant-sitter
Cunliffe, John Arthur
Postman Pat series (32)
Postman Pat plays for Greendale
Cunliffe, John Arthur
Postman Pat readers series (2)
Postman Pat takes a message
Cunliffe, John Arthur
Postman Pat series (8)
Postman Pat takes the bus
Cunliffe, John Arthur
Postman Pat series (30)
Postman Pat to the rescue
Cunliffe, John Arthur
Postman Pat series (14)
Postman Pat wins a psize
Cunliffe, John Arthur
Postman Pat series (26)
Postman Pat's ABC story
Cunliffe, John Arthur
Postman Pat beginners series (1)
Postman Pat's breezy day
Cunliffe, John Arthur
Postman Pat series (12)
Postman Pat's cat-up-a-tree party
Cunliffe, John Arthur
Postman Pat series (18)
Postman Pat's Christmas surprise
Cunliffe, John Arthur
Postman Pat series (22)
Postman Pat's Christmas tree
Cunliffe, John Arthur
Postman Pat series (23)
Postman Pat's day in bed
Cunliffe, John Arthur
Postman Pat readers series (6)
Postman Pat's difficult day
Cunliffe, John Arthur
Postman Pat series (6)
Postman Pat's discovery
Cunliffe, John Arthur
Postman Pat series (21)
Postman Pat's foggy day
Cunliffe, John Arthur
Postman Pat series (5)
Postman Pat's Greendale storybook
Cunliffe, John Arthur
Postman Pat's storybook series (4)
Postman Pat's letters on ice
Cunliffe, John Arthur
Postman Pat series (13)
Postman Pat's lost hat
Cunliffe, John Arthur
Postman Pat series (25)
Postman Pat's market day
Cunliffe, John Arthur
Postman Pat series (15)
Postman Pat's messy day
Cunliffe, John Arthur
Postman Pat readers series (3)
Postman Pat's 1, 2, 3 story
Cunliffe, John Arthur
Postman Pat beginners series (2)
Postman Pat's rainy day
Cunliffe, John Arthur
Postman Pat series (4)
Postman Pat's safari
Cunliffe, John Arthur
Postman Pat readers series (1)
Postman Pat's secret
Cunliffe, John Arthur
Postman Pat series (3)
Postman Pat's sleepy day
Cunliffe, John Arthur
Postman Pat series (27)
Postman Pat's sore tooth
Cunliffe, John Arthur
Postman Pat readers series (13)
Postman Pat's summer storybook
Cunliffe, John Arthur
Postman Pat's storybook series (2)
Postman Pat's thirsty day
Cunliffe, John Arthur
Postman Pat series (9)
Postman Pat's three wishes
Cunliffe, John Arthur
Postman Pat beginners series (4)
Postman Pat's tractor express
Cunliffe, John Arthur
Postman Pat series (7)
Postman Pat's treasure hunt
Cunliffe, John Arthur
Postman Pat series (1)
Postman Pat's washing day
Cunliffe, John Arthur
Postman Pat readers series (12)
Postman Pat's wet day
Cunliffe, John Arthur
Postman Pat readers series (4)
Postman Pat's white Christmas
Cunliffe, John Arthur
Postman Pat beginners series (5)
Postman Pat's wild cat chase
Cunliffe, John Arthur
Postman Pat series (31)
Postman Pat's winter storybook
Cunliffe, John Arthur
Postman Pat's storybook series (1)
Postman Pat's zodiac storybook
Cunliffe, John Arthur
Postman Pat's storybook series (3)
Postman's knock
Straker, John Foster
Inspector Pitt series (1)
Post-mark homicide
Marcus, Arthur A
Pete Hunter series (1)
Postmarked the stars
Norton, Andre
Dane Thorson series (4)
Postmaster's daughter
Tracy, Louis
Inspector Furneaux series (5)
Post-mortem
Collins, Gilbert
Hugh Carding series (1)
Postmortem
Cornwell, Patricia Daniels
Doctor Kay Scarpetta series (1)
Post-mortem effects
Boyle, Thomas
Detective Francis De Sales series (2)
Post-mortem evidence
Fowler, Sydney
Mister Jellipot series (3)
Postscript to a death
Cumberland, Marten
Saturnin Dax series (31)
Postscript to murder
Winn, Patrick
Inspector Lyon series (1)
Postscript to Penelope
Gilruth, Susan
Inspector Hugh Gordon and Liane Crawford series (3)
Postscript to poison
Bowers, Dorothy
Inspector Pardoe series (1)
Postscript to The name of the rose
Eco, Umberto
Rose series (2)
Post-war years, 1945-1954
Ehrenburg, Ilya
Men, years and life series (6)
Posy Bates, again!
Cresswell, Helen
Posy Bates series (2)
Posy Bates and the bag lady
Cresswell, Helen
Posy Bates series (3)
Pot of gold at rainbow's end
Frees, Harry Whittier
Petland photo tales series (2)
Pot of trouble
Tracy, Don
Giff Speer series (5)
Potash and Perlmutter in society
Glass, Montague
Potash series (3)
Potash and Perlmutter, their co-partnership, ventures and adventures
Glass, Montague
Potash series (1)
Potato eaters
Branson, Karen
Maureen O'Connor series (1)
Potato man
McDonald, Megan
Potato man series (1)
Potsdam murder plot
Betteridge, Don
Tiger Lester series (4)
Potted plant book
Tarsky, Sue
How does your garden grow series (3)
Potted stories to tell Scouts and Cubs
Barclay, Vera Charlesworth
Potted stories series (1)
Potter boys under Old Glory
Cobb, Frank
Stars and Stripes series (2)
Potter boys with the tanks
Cobb, Frank
Stars and Stripes series (5)
Potter Pinner Meadow
Kaye, Mollie
Potter Pinner series (1)
Potters
Fisher, Leonard Everett
Colonial Americans series (14)
Potter's field
Peters, Ellis
Brother Cadfael series (17)
Potter's niece
Randall, Rona
Drayton series (2)
Pottery in Roman Britain
Birt, David
Roman Britain series (19)
Pottleton bridge club
Tuite, Hugh
Pottleton series (2)
Potto finds a job
Hargreaves, Roger
Hippo, Potto and Mouse series (1)
Poultry in the pulpit
Cameron, Alexander
Vet in the vestry series (2)
Pound of flesh
Barnes, Trevor
Blanche Hampton series (2)

Pound puppies in public nuisance
Korman, Justine
Pound puppies series (2)
Pound puppies, problem puppies
Korman, Justine
Pound puppies series (1)
Pour a swindle through a loophole
Von Elsner, Don
David Danning series (6)
Poverty Bay
Emerson, Earl W
Thomas Black series (2)
Powder barrel
Haggard, William
Colonel Charles Russell series (7)
Powder burn
Scott, Bradford
Walt Slade series (17)
Powder keg
Harte, Bryce
Slate Creed series (3)
Powder monkey
Hardy, Adam
George Abercrombie Fox series (5)
Powder, patches and Patty
Knipe, Emilie Benson
Benedict Arnold series (2)
Powder puff puzzle
Giff, Patricia Reilly
Polka Dot series (4)
Powder Quay
Turner, Philip
Darnley Mills Railway series (3)
Powder River
Blevins, Winfred
Rivers west series (4)
Powder river
McCarthy, Gary
Wind river series (2)
Powder River
Reno, Bill
Badge series (4)
Powder River massacre
Logan, Jake
John Slocum series (171)
Powder train
Tute, Warren
George Mado series (2)
Powder Valley ambush
Field, Peter
Powder Valley series (34)
Powder Valley deadlock
Field, Peter
Powder Valley series (45)
Powder Valley getaway
Field, Peter
Powder Valley series (75)
Powder Valley hold-up
Field, Peter
Powder Valley series (39)
Powder Valley manhunt
Field, Peter
Powder Valley series (58)
Powder Valley pay-off
Field, Peter
Powder Valley series (14)
Powder Valley plunder
Field, Peter
Powder Valley series (67)
Powder Valley ransom
Field, Peter
Powder Valley series (73)
Powder Valley renegade
Field, Peter
Powder Valley series (53)
Powder Valley showdown
Field, Peter
Powder Valley series (27)
Powder Valley stampede
Field, Peter
Powder Valley series (46)
Powder Valley vengeance
Field, Peter
Powder Valley series (18)
Powderhorn passage
Townsend, Tom
Pirates series (2)
Powdersmoke justice
Macdonald, William Colt
Three Mesquiteers series (13)
Powdersmoke lawyer
Floren, Lee
Buckshot McKee and Tortilla Joe series (4)
Powdersmoke Pass
Westland, Lynn
Powdersmoke series (1)
Powdersmoke payoff
Westland, Lynn
Powdersmoke series (2)
Powdersmoke Range
Macdonald, William Colt
Three Mesquiteers series (3)
Power
Haynes, Betsy
Twilight series (2)
Joseph, Ronald S
Cameron family trilogy (2)
Smith, Lisa J
Secret circle series (3)
Power and glory
Easton, Robert
Saga of California series (2)
Power and the glory
Bentley, Phyllis
West Riding series (2)
Power and the prophet
Hughes, Robert Don
Pelmen trilogy (3)
Power artist
Charteris, Leslie
Saint series (38)
Power barons
Streib, Dan
Michael Hawk series (3)
Power bug
Osborne, Geoffrey
James Dingle and Glyn Jones series (1)
Power cube affair
Phillifent, John Thomas
Man from U.N.C.L.E. series (19)
Power house
Buchan, John
Sir Edward Leithen series (1)
Haggard, William
Colonel Charles Russell series (9)
Power hungry
Weinstein, Howard
Star trek, the next generation series (6)
Power instead
Coryn, Marjorie
Napoleonic trilogy (3)
Power key
Scheer, Karl Herbert
Perry Rhodan series (78)
Power killers
Philips, Judson Pentecost
Peter Styles series (11)
Power lines
McCaffrey, Anne
Yanaba Maddock series (2)
Power of Daleks
Nation, Terry
Doctor Who scripts series (7)
Power of darkness
Johnson, Oliver
Dragon warriors series (5)
Power of joy
Hilliard, Noel
Netta and Paul tetralogy (2)
Power of love
Montague, Jeanne
Loves of Carola Mountjoy series (2)
Power of one
Courtenay, Bryce
Peekay series (1)
Power of Pinjarra
Dengler, Sandy
Australian destiny series (1)
Power of silence
Castaneda, Carlos
Don Juan series (8)
Power of suggestion
Keene, Carolyn
Nancy Drew files series (80)
Power of the bug
Drummond, Ivor
Lady Jennifer, Sandro and Colly series (5)
Power of the Daleks
Peel, John
Doctor Who series (156)
Power of the dead
Williamson, Henry
Chronicles of ancient sunlight series (11)
Power of the keys
Grier, Sydney Carlyon
Century series (1)
Power of the range
Cole, Jackson
Jim Hatfield series (67)
Power of the serpent
Timlett, Peter Valentine
Atlantis trilogy (2)
Power of the sword
Smith, Wilbur Addison
Courtney family series (2)
Power of the unknown
Edgar, Alfred
Sexton Blake series (220)
Power of the White Wolf
Reinius, Trish
White Wolf series (2)
Power of three
Saville, Malcolm
Marston Baines series (5)
Power on the scent
Clandon, Henrietta
Penny and Vincent Mercer series (3)
William Power series (4)
Power play
Dixon, Franklin W
Hardy boys case files series (50)
Johns, Larry
Jacky Ryderbeit series (1)
Murphy, Warren Burton
Destroyer series (36)
Pascal, Francine
Sweet Valley High series (4)
Power plays
Wilcox, Collin
Lieutenant Frank Hastings series (10)
Power pole
Longtree, Warren T
Ruff Justice series (13)
Power that preserves
Donaldson, Stephen Reeder
First Chronicles of Thomas Covenant series (3)
Powers of the Sapphire
Miller, Margaret Jessy
Kingdom of Caledon series (2)
Power's price
Brand, Kurt
Perry Rhodan series (89)
Powers that be
McCaffrey, Anne
Yanaba Maddock series (1)
Romains, Jules
Men of goodwill series (10)
Practical Possum
Eliot, Thomas Stearns
Old Possum series (2)
Practically perfect
Lambert, Janet
Penny Parrish series (5)
Practically seventeen
Du Jardin, Rosamond
Tobey and Midge Heydon series (1)
Practice makes murder
Bearshaw, Brian
Superintendent Robert Townley and Sergeant Roger Newman series (2)
Practice makes perfect
Tibber, Robert
General practice series (2)
Vernon, Edward
Practice trilogy (1)
Practice to deceive
Linington, Elizabeth
Sergeant Ivor Maddox series (6)
Lockridge, Frances
Inspector Merton Heimrich series (12)
Veryan, Patricia
Golden chronicles series (1)
Practise to deceive
Mure, David
Deception series (1)
Richards, Francis
Inspector Merton Heimrich series (12)
Practise what you preach
Vernon, Edward
Practice trilogy (2)
Praed Street dossier
Derleth, August
Solar Pons series (11)
Praed Street papers
Derleth, August
Solar Pons series (8)
Praesidium of Archive
Swycaffer, Jefferson Putnam
Concordat series (4)
Praetorians
Larteguy, Jean
Algerian series (2)
Praetor's dungeon
Mundy, Talbot
Tros of Samothrace series (1)
Prague orgy
Roth, Philip
Nathan Zuckerman series (3)
Prairie
Cooper, James Fenimore
Leatherstocking series (5)
Prairie blood
Thompson, David
Wilderness giants series (3)
Prairie bush
Gentry, Buck
Eli Holten series (7)
Prairie Caesar
Lee, Patrick
Six-Gun Samurai series (7)
Prairie child
Stringer, Arthur
Prairie trilogy (3)
Prairie children
Allen, Gina
Prairie children series (1)
Prairie Dusters
Bancroft, Tex
Angeltown Keeps and Doc Hennessy series (2)
Prairie fire
Pendleton, Don
Mack Bolan series (68)
Sharpe, Jon
Trailsman series (152)
Prairie mother
Stringer, Arthur
Prairie trilogy (2)
Prairie school
Lenski, Lois
Regional series (8)
Prairie thunder
Brady, Taylor
Kincaids series (2)
Prairie Town dog
Torgersen, Don Arthur
Animal life stories series (9)
Prairie wife
Stringer, Arthur
Prairie trilogy (1)
Prairie-dog town
Bancroft, Laura
Twinkle tales series (3)
Pranks of Doria
Grant, Pamela
Fortunes series (3)
Pratfall
Schock, T A
Daniel Keel series (1)
Pratt of the Argus
Nobbs, David
Henry Pratt series (2)
Pratt, Henry
Second from last series (2)
Pratt portraits
Fuller, Anna
Pratt portraits series (1)
Pray silence
Coles, Manning
Tommy Hambledon series (2)
Pray to the hustlers' god
Donahue, Jackson
Harlan Cole series (1)
Prayer is for children
Kelemen, Julie
For children series (3)
Prayer mat
Scott, Bruce
Superintendent Steve McLaren series (1)
Prayers and graces
Davidson, Alice Joyce
Alice in Bibleland series (9)
Prayers for Sunday
L'Engle, Madeleine
Prayers series (2)
Praying mantis kills
Lee, Howard
Kung Fu series (4)
Praying monkey
Holt, Gavin
Professor Luther Bastion series (2)
Preach no more
Lockridge, Richard
Nathan Shapiro series (8)
Preacher
Gilman, George G
Adam Steele series (26)
Steele's war series (2)
Preacher's kids
Fletcher, Grace Nies
Nies family series (2)
Precarious crust
Irving, Laurence
Irving family trilogy (3)
Precinct command
Newman, Christopher
Joe Dante series (6)
Precious cargo
Faust, Joe Clifford
Angel's luck series (2)
Precious days
Lambert, Janet
Campbells series (1)
Precious moment through the day
Beers, Victor Gilbert
Precious moments series (2)
Precious moment through the year
Beers, Victor Gilbert
Precious moments series (1)
Precious objects
Devon, D G
Temple Kent series (3)
Predator
Monette, Paul
Predator series (1)
York, Andrew
Jonas Wilde series (3)
Predator two
Hawke, Simon
Predator series (2)
Predators
Grover, Marshall
Larry and Stretch series (137)
Sauter, Eric
Robert Lee Hunter series (4)
Streib, Dan
Michael Hawk series (4)
Preep and the Queen
Shulman, Milton
Preep series (3)
Preep in Paris
Shulman, Milton
Preep series (2)
Preep, the little pigeon of Trafalgar Square
Shulman, Milton
Preep series (1)
Prefabulous animiles
Reeves, James
Animiles series (1)
Preface to the past
Cabell, James Branch
Dom Manuel and his descendants series (24)
Prefects at Springdale
Bruce, Dorita Fairlie
Springdale series (5)
Prefects at Vivian's
Caldwell, Patricia Kathleen
Vivian's series (1)
Prefects of the Chalet School
Brent-Dyer, Elinor Mary
Chalet School series (58)
Prehistoric Pinkerton
Kellogg, Steven
Pinkerton series (4)
Prehistoric times
Coote, Roger
Journey through history series (1)
Prehistory of the Far Side
Larson, Gary
Far Side series (14)
Prelude
L'Engle, Madeleine
Katherine Forrester series (1)
McConnell, Ashley
Quantum leap series (4)
Romains, Jules
Men of goodwill series (15)
Prelude for war
Charteris, Leslie
Saint series (19)
Prelude in Prague
Wright, Sydney Fowler
War of 1938 trilogy (1)
Prelude to a showdown
Grover, Marshall
Larry and Stretch series (168)
Prelude to chaos
Llewellyn, Edward
Douglas convolution trilogy (3)
Prelude to Dunkirk, July 1939-May 1940
Spears, Edward
Assignment to catastrophe series (1)
Prelude to Foundation
Asimov, Isaac
Foundation series (1)
Prelude to healing
Macmillan, William John
Faith healing series (1)
Prelude to murder
Gilbert, Anthony
Arthur Crook series (33)
Prelude to peril
Toye, Stanley
Anthony Read series (3)
Prelude to trouble
Bentley, John
Dick Marlow series (2)
Prelude to victory
Spears, Edward
Defeat and victory series (2)
Preludes and nocturnes
Gaiman, Neil
Sandman series (2)

Premar experiments
Rimmer, Robert Henry
Harrad College series (2)
Premeditated murder
Clark, Douglas
Inspector George Masters series (6)
Premiere at Willow Run
Collins, Michelle
Megan Marshall series (2)
Premium on death
Lewis, Royston
Eric Ward series (6)
Premonition
Laurance, Andrew
Nostradamus trilogy (1)
Premonitions of an inherited mind
Laurance, Andrew
Nostradamus trilogy (1)
Prentice Alvin
Card, Orson Scott
Alvin Maker series (3)
Prepare for action
Creasey, John
Department Z series (19)
Pre-Raphaelite tragedy
Gaunt, William
Victorian painting series (1)
Prescott's challenge
Wisler, Gary Clifton
Darby Prescott series (4)
Prescott's law
Wisler, Gary Clifton
Darby Prescott series (3)
Prescott's trail
Wisler, Gary Clifton
Darby Prescott series (2)
Prescription for Melissa
Dwyer-Joyce, Alice
Doctor Catriona Chisholm series (2)
Prescription for murder
Williams, David
Mark Treasure series (14)
Present for granny
Wahlstedt, Viola
Ann and Susan series (1)
Present for mum
Solomon, Joan
Children's life series (8)
Present indicative
Coward, Noel
Present and future series (1)
Present slaughter
Green, Michael
Coarse plays series (3)
Presenting Patti
Saunders, Susan
Sleepover friends series (36)
Presenting Superhunk
Goudge, Eileen
Seniors series (10)
Presenting Superintendent Flagg
Cassells, John
Superintendent Flagg series (17)
Presenting the Dreamer
Duncan, William Murdoch
Superintendent Donald Reamer series (3)
Presents
Berg, Leila
Snaps series (1)
Preserve and protect
Drury, Allen
Washington series (4)
Preserver
Foster, Michael Anthony
Morphodite trilogy (3)
President Fu-Manchu
Rohmer, Sax
Fu-Manchu series (9)
President has been kidnapped!
Richards, Paul
Grant Fowler series (2)
President Kettle
Hyne, Charles John Cutcliffe
Captain Owen Kettle series (15)
President McGlusky
Hales, Alfred Greenwood
McGlusky series (5)
Presidential agent
Sinclair, Upton
World's end series (5)
Presidential mission
Sinclair, Upton
World's end series (8)
President's agent
Hilton, Joseph
Bart Gould series (1)
Milton, Joseph
Bart Gould series (1)
President's daughter
White, Ellen Emerson
President's daughter series (1)
President's Day magic
Baker, James Webb
Magic series (7)
President's man
Roosevelt, Elliott
Blackjack Endicott series (1)
President's plane is missing
Serling, Robert
Jeremy Haines series (1)
President's segundo
Grover, Marshall
Larry and Stretch series (338)
Presidio
Mitchum, Hank
Stage coach station series (45)
Press gang
Hardy, Adam
George Abercrombie Fox series (1)
Press on regardless
Thwaites, Frederick Joseph
Husky series (2)
Pressing peril
Carter, Nicholas
Nicholas Carter series (606)
Pressure play
Hughes, Dean
Angel Park All-Stars series (6)
Pressure point
Carter, Nick
Nick Carter series (230)
Pressure-point
Copper, Basil
Mike Faraday series (38)
Presumed dead
Perry, Ritchie
Macallister series (2)
Urquhart, Paul
Sexton Blake series (734)
Presumed innocent
Turow, Scott
Sandy Stern series (1)
Presumed sunk
Macdonnell, James Edmond
Captain Peter Bentley series (7)
Presumption
Barrett, Julia
Presumption series (2)
Pre-Teen means in between
Lewis, Linda
Linda series (11)
Pretend we've never met
Agee, Jonis
Divinity series (1)
Pretended mistress
Balzac, Honore de
Scenes of private life series (13)
Pretender
Cooper, Louise Antell
Chaos gate trilogy (2)
Pretender to the throne
Voinovich, Vladimir Nikolaevich
Private Ivan Chonkin series (2)
Pretending
McGee, Shelagh
Little activity series (2)
Pretenses
Pascal, Francine
Sweet Valley High series (44)
Pretty dear
Barcynska, Helena Margareta
Honey-pot series (3)
Pretty maids all in a row
Fraser, Anthea
Inspector David Webb and Sergeant Ken Jackson series (3)
Meadows, Rose
Hanover succession series (3)
Pretty maids all in arow
McCarthy, Justin Huntly
Francois Villon trilogy (3)
Pretty Miss Murder
Ballard, Willis Todhunter
Lieutenant Max Hunter series (1)
Pretty place for a murder
Hart, Roy
Detective Superintendent Roper series (2)
Pretty sinister
Beeding, Francis
Colonel Alastair Granby series (3)
Pretty stenographer mystery
Carter, Nicholas
Nicholas Carter series (183)
Pretzel
Rey, Margret
Pretzel series (1)
Pretzel and the puppies
Rey, Margret
Pretzel series (2)
Previously reported missing, now?
Chester, Gilbert
Sexton Blake series (1112)
Prey
Drumm, D B
Traveler series (12)
Goddard, Kenneth
Prey series (1)
Prey animals
Aaseng, Nathan
Early nature picture book series (4)
Prey for a newshawk
Janson, Hank
Hank Janson series (7)
Prey for me
Dewey, Thomas Blanchard
Private Eye Mac series (3)
Prey for the Dreamer
Duncan, William Murdoch
Superintendent Donald Reamer series (12)
Prey for the Picaroon
Cassells, John
Ludovic Saxon series (9)
Prey of the falcon
Charles, Robert
Counter-terror series (5)
Prey of the rogue riders
Grover, Marshall
Larry and Stretch series (231)
Prey to murder
Cleeves, Ann
George Palmer-Jones series (4)
Pribiloffs
Lewin, Ted
World within a world series (3)
Price
Newman, Gordon F
Inspector Terry Sneed series (3)
Price above rubies
Bloom, Ursula
Father and mother series (2)
Price of a prize
Martin, Toy
Taronga Road Riders series (5)
Price of a secret
Carter, Nicholas
Nicholas Carter series (84)
Price of a throne
Hocking, Joseph
Great War, Greek front series (3)
Price of command
Randle, Kevin
Jefferson's war series (2)
Price of death
Usher, Frank
Daye Smith series (4)
Price of fame
Lynde, Stan
Rick O'Shay series (4)
Mosco, Maisie
Between two worlds trilogy (3)
Price of freedom
Gobineau, Marceline
Stephanie series (6)
Price of glory
Keith, William Henry
BattleTech series (3)
Price of life
Sutton, Jessica
Bel Air General series (2)
Price of love
Bennett, Arnold
Five towns series (13)
Price of loving
Courtney, Edith
Kit Hemsworthy series (1)
Price of paradise
Gerard, Francis
Sir John Meredith series (8)
Price of power
Estes, Rose
Greyhawk series (4)
Mika trilogy (2)
Price of ransom
Rasmussen, Alis A
Highroad trilogy (3)
Price of silence
Pentecost, Hugh
George Crowder series (4)
Price of the King's peace
Tranter, Nigel Godwin
Robert the Bruce trilogy (3)
Price of the phoenix
Culbreath, Myrna
Star trek originals sequels series (6)
Price of treachery
Carter, Nicholas
Nicholas Carter series (182)
Price of victory
Asprin, Robert Lynn
Sanctuary series (12)
Price tag for murder
Dean, Spencer
Don Cadee series (7)
Price was high
Hackforth-Jones, Gilbert
Submarine Service series (4)
Price you pay
Wakefield, Hannah
Dee Street series (1)
Priceless particle
Powell, Talmage
Mission impossible series (5)
Prices return
Pye, Virginia
Price family series (5)
Pricking thumb
Branson, Henry Clay
John Bent series (2)
Prickle Farm
Hayes, Mike
Prickle Farm series (1)
Prickle Farm greener pastures
Hayes, Mike
Prickle Farm series (3)
Prickle Farm round two
Hayes, Mike
Prickle Farm series (2)
Prickly plant book
Tarsky, Sue
How does your garden grow series (1)
Pride
Saxton, Judith
Neyler family series (1)
Pride and penalties
Blacker, Terence
Hotshots series (1)
Pride and prejudice
Austen, Jane
Bennet family series (1)
Presumption series (1)
Pride and prejudice series (1)
Teverton Hall series (1)
Pride of Bear Creek
Howard, Robert Ervin
Breckinridge Elkins series (2)
Pride of Chanur
Cherryh, Carolyn Janice
Alliance-Union series (7)
Chanur series (1)
Pride of dolphins
Hebden, Mark
Colonel Mostyn series (2)
Pride of Falcons
Darby, Catherine
Falcon family series (5)
Pride of heroes
Dickinson, Peter
Superintendent James Pibble series (2)
Pride of kings
Dymoke, Juliet
Plantagenets series (1)
Pride of monsters
Schmitz, James Henry
Hub series (4)
Pride of Parson Carnaby
Emerson, David
Parson Carnaby series (1)
Pride of pigs
Wainwright, John
Northern Police series (18)
Pride of Pine Street
Allan, Mabel Esther
Pine Street series (7)
Pride of place
Fuller, Kathleen
Riverview trilogy (3)
Pride of princes
Roberson, Jennifer
Chronicles of the Cheysuli series (5)
Pride of the stable
Murray, Edgar Joyce
Sexton Blake series (196)
Pride of tigers
Marshall, Sybil
Fen family series (2)
Pride of Walworth
Staples, Mary Jane
South London series (13)
Pride of women
Platt, Kin
Max Roper series (3)
Pride's Court
Carroll, Joy
Court family series (2)
Pride's harvest
Cleary, Jon
Scobie Malone series (8)
Priest and the governor
Luscombe, Tom
Melbourne series (1)
Priest in the house
Zola, Emile
Rougon Macquart series (4)
Priestess
Lauria, Frank
Doctor Owen Orient series (5)
Priestess of the damned
Coffman, Virginia
Lucifer Cove series (2)
Priest-kings of Gor
Norman, John
Tarl Cabot series (3)
Priestly murders
Gash, Joe
Terry Flynn series (2)
Priests of Ferris
Gee, Maurice
World of O trilogy (2)
Priests of the abomination
Drummond, Ivor
Lady Jennifer, Sandro and Colly series (2)
Priest's secret
Graydon, William Murray
Sexton Blake series (389)
Maxwell, Allan
Sexton Blake series (896)
Prillilgirl
Wells, Carolyn
Fleming Stone series (17)
Prima donna at large
Paul, Barbara
Enrico Caruso series (2)
Prima-donna
Crawford, Francis Marion
Paris Opera trilogy (2)
Paul Griggs series (6)
Primary justice
Bernhardt, William
Justice series (1)
Primary target
Collins, Max Allan
Quarry series (5)
Wallace, Marilyn
Jay Goldstein and Carlos Cruz series (2)
Prime directive
Reeves-Stevens, Garfield
Star trek sequels series (8)
Prime Minister
Trollope, Anthony
Palliser novels series (5)
Prime minister's brain
Cross, Gillian
Demon headmaster series (2)
Prime minister's daughter
Edelman, Maurice
Geoffrey Melville series (2)
Prime Minister's pencil
Waye, Cecil
Christopher Perrin series (4)
Prime of life
Beauvoir, Simone de
Dutiful daughter series (2)
Prime of Tamworth Pig
Kemp, Gene
Tamworth Pig series (1)
Prime squared
Murdock, Melinda Seabrooke
Inner planets trilogy (2)
Prime time
Pfeffer, Susan Beth
Make me a star series (4)
Prime time corpse
Babbin, Jaqueline
Clovis Kelly series (1)
Prime-time crime
Dixon, Franklin W
Hardy boys series (109)
Primitive
Feikema, Feike
World's wanderer trilogy (1)
Primrose
Dobson, Margaret
Jane Bailey series (2)
Primrose Polly
Pye, Virginia
Price family series (3)
Primrose, the fourth man
Smith, Lou
John Spencer series (4)
Primrose way
Housman, Laurence
Palace plays series (4)
Primula
Preedy, George Runnell
French Revolution series (3)
Prince
Johnson, Stacie
Eighteen Pine Street series (3)

Koster, Richard Morton
Tinieblas trilogy (1)
Prince and heretic
Bowen, Marjorie
William the Silent series (1)
Prince and the Quakeress
Plaidy, Jean
Georgian series (4)
Prince and the tobacco lords
Davis, Margaret Thomson
Scottish historical trilogy (1)
Prince at Black Pony Inn
Pullein-Thompson, Christine
Black Pony Inn series (3)
Prince Caspian
Lewis, Clive Staples
Narnia series (4)
Prince Cinders
Cole, Babette
Princess Smartypants series (2)
Prince Dimple and his everyday doings
Paull, Minnie E
Prince Dimple trilogy (1)
Prince Dimple on his travels
Paull, Minnie E
Prince Dimple trilogy (3)
Prince Dimple's further doings
Paull, Minnie E
Prince Dimple trilogy (2)
Prince Dusty
Munroe, Kirk
Rail and water series (2)
Prince for Inspector West
Creasey, John
Inspector Roger West series (19)
Prince Hempseed
Hudson, Stephen
Kurt series (3)
Prince in waiting
Christopher, John
Prince trilogy (1)
Prince in waiting trilogy
Christopher, John
Prince trilogy (3)
Prince Jali
Myers, Leopold Hamilton
Prince Jali series (2)
Prince Mud-Turtle
Bancroft, Laura
Twinkle tales series (4)
Prince of Abyssinia
Johnson, Samuel
Rasselas series (1)
Prince of Annwn
Walton, Evangeline
Mabinogion series (1)
Prince of Bohemia
Balzac, Honore de
Scenes of Parisian life series (9)
Prince of chaos
Zelazny, Roger
Kingdom of Amber series (10)
Prince of darkness
Doherty, Paul C
Hugh Corbett series (5)
Plaidy, Jean
Plantagenet series (4)
Prince of Drakulya
Doherty, Paul C
Drakulya series (1)
Prince of Eden
Harris, Marilyn
Eden family series (2)
Prince of evil
Stockbridge, Grant
Richard Wentworth series (14)
Prince of Graustark
McCutcheon, George Barr
Graustark series (4)
Prince of Hearts
Butler, David
Edward VII series (1)
Prince of Hindustan
Voegeli, Max
Adventures of Ali series (2)
Prince of liars
Carter, Nicholas
Nicholas Carter series (294)
Prince of mercenaries
Pournelle, Jerry
Falkenberg's Legion series (3)
Future history series (4)
Prince of murder
Wallace, Robert
Phantom Detective series (5)
Prince of my country
Stuart, Donald Robert
Conjuror's years series (1)
Prince of peril
Kline, Otis Adelbert
Grandon trilogy (2)
Prince of Plunder
Horler, Sydney
Sir Brian Fordinghame series (4)
Prince of rogues
Carter, Nicholas
Nicholas Carter series (85)
Prince of Scorpio
Akers, Alan Burt
Dray Prescot series (5)
Prince of Sparta
Pournelle, Jerry
Spartan series (2)
Prince of spies
Davison, Gilderoy
Peter Castle series (2)
Twisted Face series (2)
Prince of Stars
Dennis, Ian
Prince of Stars in the Cavern of Time series (2)
Prince of Stars in the Cavern of Time
Dennis, Ian
Prince of Stars in the Cavern of Time series (2)
Prince of the bay
Seed, Jenny
Natal series (2)
Prince of the blood
Feist, Raymond Elias
Riftwar series (4)
Prince of the captivity
Grier, Sydney Carlyon
Balkan series (4)
Prince of the Dragon Green
Thomas, Joyce Bissell
Dragon Green series (2)
Prince of the Godborn
Harris, Geraldine
Seven citadels series (1)
Prince of thieves
Dumas, Alexandre
Robin Hood series (1)
Martindale, T Chris
Advanced dungeons and dragons adventure gamebook series (15)
Prince of Wales's Feathers
Mathew, David
Post-war trilogy (3)
Prince on a white horse
Lee, Tanith
Castle of dark series (2)
Prince Prigio
Lang, Andrew
Pantouflia series (1)
Prince Ricardo of Pantouflia
Lang, Andrew
Pantouflia series (2)
Prince Rupert's daughter
D'Oyley, Elizabeth
Prince Rupert series (2)
Prince What-a-Mess
Muir, Frank
What-a-Mess series (3)
Princeling
Harrod-Eagles, Cynthia
Morland family series (3)
Prince's diamond
Hulme-Beaman, Emeric
Ozmar series (2)
Princes of Sandastre
Swithin, Antony
Perilous quest for Lyonesse series (1)
Prince's players
Doyle, Debra
Circle of magic series (4)
Princess and Bungle
Strong, Jeremy
Bungle series (1)
Princess and Curdie
Macdonald, George
Faery trilogy (3)
Princess and the goblin
Macdonald, George
Faery trilogy (2)
Princess and the thorn
Fisher, Paul R
Ash staff trilogy (3)
Princess Anne
Oldmeadow, Katharine Louise
Princess series (4)
Princess Candida
Oldmeadow, Katharine Louise
Princess series (1)
Princess Casamassima
James, Henry
Princess Casamassima series (2)
Princess Charming
Oldmeadow, Katharine Louise
Princess series (2)
Princess Dehra
Scott, John Reed
Red Hussars series (2)
Princess Elizabeth
Oldmeadow, Katharine Louise
Princess series (5)
Pascal, Francine
Sweet Valley twins series (30)
Princess Flower Hat
Wright, Mabel Osgood
Commuter's wife series (4)
Princess Napraxine
Ouida
Princess Napraxine series (1)
Princess of Celle
Plaidy, Jean
Georgian series (1)
Princess of crime
Carter, Nicholas
Nicholas Carter series (69)
Princess of darkness
Zacharia, Irwin
Irving Martin Reddy series (2)
Princess of desire
Peters, Maureen
History's most fascinating women series (1)
Princess of Fairwood High
Norton, Nancy
Homeroom series (2)
Princess of Mars
Burroughs, Edgar Rice
Martian series (1)
Princess of Paris
Gunter, Archibald Clavering
Princess of Paris series (1)
Princess of Persia
White, James Dillon
Roger Kelso series (5)
Princess of Powder River
Willoughby, Lee Davis
Women who won the West series (7)
Princess of the atom
Cummings, Ray
Matter, space and time series (2)
Princess of the Chalet School
Brent-Dyer, Elinor Mary
Chalet School series (3)
Princess of the Chameln
Wilder, Cherry
Rulers of Hylor trilogy (1)
Princess of the Fillimore Street School
Sharmat, Marjorie Weinman
Olivia Sharp series (2)
Princess of the moor
Marlitt, E
Moorland princess series (1)
Princess of Thule
Black, William
Hebrides series (1)
Princess Ozma of Oz
Baum, Lyman Frank
Oz series (3)
Princess passes
Williamson, Charles Norris
Motoring series (2)
Princess Pat
Oldmeadow, Katharine Louise
Princess series (3)
Princess Pat saves the day
Palmer, Bernard
Bradley series (6)
Princess Polly
Brooks, Amy
Princess Polly series (1)
Princess Polly at Cliffmore
Brooks, Amy
Princess Polly series (7)
Princess Polly at play
Brooks, Amy
Princess Polly series (6)
Princess Polly at school
Brooks, Amy
Princess Polly series (3)
Princess Polly by the sea
Brooks, Amy
Princess Polly series (4)
Princess Polly's gay winter
Brooks, Amy
Princess Polly series (5)
Princess Polly's playmates
Brooks, Amy
Princess Polly series (2)
Princess Prunella
Oldmeadow, Katharine Louise
Princess series (6)
Princess Smartypants
Cole, Babette
Princess Smartypants series (1)
Princess stakes murder
Platt, Kin
Max Roper series (3)
Princess Susan
Russell, Ivy
Princess Susan series (1)
Princess who?
Chase, Emily
Canby Hall series (24)
Princess's secrets
Balzac, Honore de
Scenes of Parisian life series (7)
Princess's tragedy
Grier, Sydney Carlyon
Princess series (2)
Princeton boy in the Revolution
Tomlinson, Paul Greene
Princeton boy series (2)
Princeton boy under the King
Tomlinson, Paul Greene
Princeton boy series (1)
Princeton stories
Williams, Jesse Lynch
Princeton series (1)
Principal role
Hill, Lorna
Sadler's Wells series (9)
Printer of Malgudi
Narayan, Rasipuram Krishnaswami
Malgudi series (3)
Printers
Fisher, Leonard Everett
Colonial Americans series (4)
Printer's devil
Barclay, Bill
Jerry Cornell series (2)
Nick Allard series (2)
Dane, Clemence
Sir John Saumerez series (2)
Printer's error
Mitchell, Gladys
Dame Beatrice Bradley series (10)
Print-out
Copper, Basil
Mike Faraday series (52)
Gillespie, Robert Byrne
Ralph Simmons series (1)
Prinvest-London
Gielgud, Val
Inspector Gregory Pellew and Viscount Clymping series (5)
Priority murder
Ford, Leslie
Colonel John Primrose series (8)
Grace Latham series (8)
Priorsford
Douglas, O
Priorsford series (4)
Priscilla at Hunting Hill
Sampson, Emma
Priscilla Payson series (2)
Priscilla Copperwaite case
Waugh, Hillary
Simon Kaye series (6)
Priscilla Payson
Sampson, Emma
Priscilla Payson series (1)
Prison and chocolate cake
Sahgal, Nayantara
Prison series (1)
Prison at Obregon
Adkins, Bill
Dave Hill series (2)
Prison breakers
Poole, Reginald Heber
Sexton Blake series (148)
Prison of night
Tubb, Edwin Charles
Dumarest series (17)
Prison satellite
Kelley, Leo Patrick
Space police series (1)
Prisoner
Daniel, Roland
Michael Wallace series (4)
Darke, James
Witches series (1)
Disch, Thomas Michael
Prisoner series (1)
Prisoner 2
McDaniel, David
Prisoner series (2)
Prisoner 3
McDaniel, David
Prisoner series (4)
Prisoner, Cell Block H
Sinclair, Murray
Caged women series (1)
Prisoner files
McDaniel, David
Prisoner series (4)
Prisoner in Fairyland
Blackwood, Algernon
Uncle Paul series (2)
Prisoner in the hold
Parsons, Anthony
Sexton Blake series (1386)
Prisoner in the mask
Wheatley, Dennis
Count de Quesnoy and Condesa Guilia series (1)
Duc de Richelieu series (8)
Prisoner in the opal
Mason, Alfred Edward Woodley
Inspector Hanaud series (3)
Prisoner of dreams
Ripley, Karen
Prisoner of dreams series (1)
Prisoner of Elderwood
Algozin, Bruce
Endless quest series (32)
Prisoner of Ellis Island
Graydon, William Murray
Sexton Blake series (351)
Prisoner of grace
Cary, Joyce
Chester Nimmo trilogy (2)
Prisoner of Lost Island
Hunter, John
Sexton Blake series (944)
Prisoner of love
Hart, Alison
Girls in trouble series (2)
Prisoner of Pineapple Place
Lindbergh, Anne Morrow
Pineapple Place series (2)
Prisoner of Reglathium
Sirota, Mike
Dannus series (1)
Prisoner of revenge
Ledd, Paul
Shelter Morgan series (1)
Prisoner of the ant people
Montgomery, Raymond A
Choose your own adventure series (25)
Prisoner of the Buddha
Armour, R Coutts
Sexton Blake series (459)
Prisoner of the chateau
Teed, George Hamilton
Sexton Blake series (596)
Prisoner of the devil
Hardwick, Michael
Sherlock Holmes sequels series (40)
Prisoner of the horned helmet
Silke, James R
Death dealer series (1)
Prisoner of the Kremlin
Murray, Andrew
Sexton Blake series (252)
Prisoner of the manor
Hardinge, Rex
Sexton Blake series (1305)
Prisoner of the mountains
Golon, Sergeanne
Angelique series (6)
Graydon, William Murray
Sexton Blake series (439)
Prisoner of the past
Knight, Brigid
Ardleigh family series (2)
Prisoner of the pyramid
Gerard, Francis
Sir John Meredith series (14)
Prisoner of time
Darlton, Clark
Perry Rhodan series (56)
Prisoner of vampires
Garden, Nancy
Dracula series (23)
Prisoner of war
Martin, Les
Young Indiana Jones chronicles series (7)
Prisoner of Zenda
Hope, Anthony
Rudolf Rassendyl series (1)
Prisoner of Zhamanak
De Camp, Lyon Sprague
Krishna series (8)
Prisoner pleads not guilty
Thayer, Lee
Peter Clancy series (51)
Prisoners
Gilman, George G
Edge series (39)
Hart, Matthew S
Cody's law series (9)
Prisoners and pawns
Weinstein, Howard
V series (6)
Prisoner's Base
Stout, Rex
Nero Wolfe and Archie Goodwin series (21)
Prisoner's in Devil's Bog
Lloyd, Hugh
Skippy Dare series (3)

Prisoners in Serpent Land
Connell, Alan
Serpent Land trilogy (2)
Prisoner's life in the Tower
Birt, David
Tower topics series (1)
Prisoners of Bell Castle
Doyle, Debra
Circle of magic series (5)
Prisoners of evil
Teitelbaum, Michael
Photon series (2)
Prisoners of hope
Johnston, Mary
Virginian series (2)
Prisoners of Pax Tharkas
Simon, Morris
Super endless quest adventure gamebook series (1)
Prisoners of Peru
Evans, Gwyn
Sexton Blake series (473)
Prisoners of power
Strugatsky, Arkady
Maxim trilogy (1)
Prisoners of the clouds
Adams, Eustace Lane
Andy Lane series (12)
Prisoners of the desert
Blake, Stacey
Sexton Blake series (563)
Prisoners of the sun
Herge
Tintin series (14)
Prisoners of time
Dever, Joe
Lone Wolf series (11)
Prisoners on the pirate ship
Moore, Fenworth
Jerry Ford series (4)
Prisoner's plea
Waugh, Hillary
Chief Fred Fellows series (7)
Prisoner's tale
Newman, Gordon F
Law and order trilogy (2)
Prisoners under the sea
Catherall, Arthur
Bulldog tugboat series (8)
Prisonland
Frost, Jason
Warlord series (4)
Prisons
Settle, Mary Lee
Beulah series (1)
Private Carter's crime
Creasey, John
Sexton Blake series (1085)
Private cosmos
Farmer, Philip Jose
World of Tiers series (3)
Private education in Australia and New Zealand
Mason, Peter
Private education series (3)
Private education in North America
Mason, Peter
Private education series (2)
Private education in the EEC
Mason, Peter
Private education series (1)
Private enterprise
Thirkell, Angela
Barsetshire series (16)
Private eye
Adams, Cleve Franklin
John J Shannon series (1)
Private eyeful
Kane, Henry
Marla Trent series (1)
Private eyes
Kellerman, Jonathan
Alex Delaware series (6)
Private face of murder
Bonett, John
Inspector Borges series (2)
Private Gollantz
Jacob, Naomi
Gollantz series (5)
Private I
Sangster, Jimmy
John Smith series (1)
Private, keep out
Grant, Gwen
Private, keep out series (1)
Private knowledge
Nelson, Betty Palmer
Honest women series (1)
Private life
Elliott, Janice
Wilson family trilogy (2)
Hackney, Alan
Stanley Windrush series (2)
Private life of Doctor Watson
Hardwick, Michael
Sherlock Holmes sequels series (68)
Private life of Sherlock Holmes
Hardwick, Michael
Sherlock Holmes sequels series (11)
Private line
Maddock, Stephen
Inspector Slane series (4)
Private matter
Ewing, Kathryn
Marcy Benson series (1)
Private nurse
James, Josephine
Kathy Martin series (6)
Private party
Ard, William
Timothy Dane series (4)
Private pavilion
Edwards, James G
Inspector Victor Bondurant series (2)
Private pilot's handbook of navigation
Gurney, Gene
Private pilot's series (2)
Private pilot's handbook of weather
Gurney, Gene
Private pilot's series (1)
Private practice of Michael Shayne
Halliday, Brett
Michael Shayne series (2)
Private revenge
Woodman, Richard
Nathaniel Drinkwater series (9)
Private sector
Hone, Joseph
Peter Marlow series (1)
Private Spud Tamson
Campbell, R W
Spud Tamson series (1)
Private vendetta
Jones, Bradshaw
Claude Ravel series (5)
Private view
Innes, Michael
Sir John Appleby series (13)
Private worlds
Gainham, Sarah
Viennese trilogy (3)
Private worlds of Julia Redfern
Cameron, Eleanor
Julia Redfern series (5)
Privateer
Williams, Jon
Privateers and gentlemen series (1)
Private's progress
Hackney, Alan
Stanley Windrush series (1)
Privileged children
Vernon, Frances
Edwardian trilogy (2)
Privileged nightmare
Romilly, Giles
Colditz series (5)
Privileged ones
Coles, Robert
Children of crisis series (5)
Privileged spectator
Mannin, Ethel
Confessions and impressions series (3)
Privy Seal, his last venture
Ford, Ford Madox
Fifth queen trilogy (2)
Prize
Grier, Sydney Carlyon
Balkan trilogy (3)
Prize for Mary Mouse
Blyton, Enid
Mary Mouse series (11)
Prize money
Hardy, Adam
George Abercrombie Fox series (2)
Prize performance
Fisher, Aileen
Ways of plants series (8)
Prizefighter
Ladd, Justin
Abilene series (7)
Prizzi's family
Condon, Richard
Prizzi family series (1)
Prizzi's glory
Condon, Richard
Prizzi family series (3)
Prizzi's honor
Condon, Richard
Prizzi family series (2)
Prizzi's honour
Condon, Richard
Prizzi family series (2)
Prizzi's money
Condon, Richard
Prizzi family series (4)
Pro sports' greatest rivalries
Aaseng, Nathan
Sports talk series (5)
Pro-Am murders
Cake, Patrick
Dion Quince series (2)
Probability broach
Smith, Lester Neil
Win Bear trilogy (1)
Probability man
Ball, Brian Neville
Probability series (1)
Probability pad
Waters, Thomas Allen
Greenwich Village trilogy (3)
Probable cause
Stockley, Grif
Gideon Page series (2)
Probationer nurse
Treger, Anne
Nurse series (1)
Probe
Douglas, Carole Nelson
Probe series (1)
Problem at Piha
Bream, Freda
Reverend Jabal Jarrett series (6)
Problem at Saint Peter's
Andrews, Jane
Saint Peter's Hospital series (5)
Problem by rail
Vivian, Evelyn Charles
Inspector Head series (11)
Problem for Superintendent Flagg
Cassells, John
Superintendent Flagg series (21)
Problem for the Chalet School
Brent-Dyer, Elinor Mary
Chalet School series (36)
Problem for the Dreamer
Duncan, William Murdoch
Superintendent Donald Reamer series (5)
Problem in angels
Holton, Leonard
Father Joseph Bredder series (8)
Problem in Prague
Macleod, Robert
Jonathan Gaunt series (7)
Problem of Cell 13
Futrelle, Jacques
Professor Augustus S F X Van Dusen series (2)
Problem of the Derby favorite
Bobin, John William
Sexton Blake series (76)
Problem of the green capsule
Carr, John Dickson
Doctor Gideon Fell series (10)
Problem of the purple maculas
Iraldi, James C
Sherlock Holmes sequels series (9)
Problem of the wire cage
Carr, John Dickson
Doctor Gideon Fell series (11)
Problem party
Atkinson, Mary Evelyn
Lockett family series (10)
Problem solvers
Aaseng, Nathan
Inside business series (3)
Problem with parents
Kaye, Marilyn
Camp Sunnyside Friends series (11)
Problem with Sidney
Meyer, Carolyn
Hotline series (2)
Problematic characters
Spielhagen, Friedrich
Prussian series (1)
Probus
Ware, William
Zenobia and Aurelian series (2)
Procane chronicle
Bleeck, Oliver
Philip Saint Ives series (3)
Proceed at will
Wilkinson, Burke
Geoffrey Mildmay series (1)
Proceed, Sergeant Lamb
Graves, Robert
Sergeant Lamb series (2)
Proceed to judgement
Woods, Sara
Sir Nicholas Harding and Antony Maitland series (29)
Proceed with caution
Rhode, John
Doctor Lancelot Priestley series (27)
Procession of two
Philmore, R
Inspector Garnett series (2)
Procrastination of Sergeant Cluff
North, Gil
Sergeant Caleb Cluff series (9)
Procurator
Mitchell, Kirk
Procurator trilogy (1)
Procyon's promise
McCollum, Michael
Makers series (2)
Prodigal
Osbourne, Ivor
Mango season series (2)
Prodigal daughter
Archer, Jeffrey
William Kane and Abel Rosnovski series (2)
Prodigal son
Davidson, Alice Joyce
Alice in Bibleland series (13)
Prodigals
Dumitru, Petru
Boyars trilogy (2)
Prodigal's progress
Mackenzie, Lee
Emmerdale Farm series (2)
Prodigious Hickey
Johnson, Owen McMahon
Lawrenceville series (1)
Prodigy
Cover, Arthur Byron
Robot city series (4)
Produce the body
Goyne, Richard
Paul Templeton series (2)
Professional jealousy
Gregg, Cecil Freeman
Inspector Cuthbert Higgins series (36)
Professional killers
Edson, John Thomas
Rockabye County series (4)
Professionals
Harris, John
Martin Falconer series (2)
Professor
Bronte, Charlotte
Brussels series (1)
Daniel, Roland
Buddy Mustard series (4)
Professor at the breakfast table
Holmes, Oliver Wendell
Breakfast table trilogy (2)
Professor Boffin's robot
Alexander, Louis George
Professor Boffin series (1)
Professor Boffin's umbrella
Alexander, Louis George
Professor Boffin series (2)
Professor Branestawm and the wild letters
Hunter, Norman
Professor Branestawm series (9)
Professor Branestawm round the bend
Hunter, Norman
Professor Branestawm series (7)
Professor Branestawm up the pole
Hunter, Norman
Professor Branestawm series (5)
Professor Branestawm's building bust-up
Hunter, Norman
Professor Branestawm series (11)
Professor Branestawm's compendium
Hunter, Norman
Professor Branestawm series (14)
Professor Branestawm's crunchy crockery
Hunter, Norman
Professor Branestawm series (13)
Professor Branestawm's dictionary
Hunter, Norman
Professor Branestawm series (14)
Professor Branestawm's do-it-yourself handbook
Hunter, Norman
Professor Branestawm series (14)
Professor Branestawm's great revolution
Hunter, Norman
Professor Branestawm series (6)
Professor Branestawm's hair-raising idea
Hunter, Norman
Professor Branestawm series (14)
Professor Branestawm's mouse war
Hunter, Norman
Professor Branestawm series (12)
Professor Branestawm's perilous pudding
Hunter, Norman
Professor Branestawm series (8)
Professor Branestawm's pocket motor car
Hunter, Norman
Professor Branestawm series (10)
Professor Branestawm's treasure hunt, and other incredible adventures
Hunter, Norman
Professor Branestawm series (2)
Professor Challenger stories
Doyle, Arthur Conan
Professor Challenger series (4)
Professor dies
Rowland, John
Inspector Shelley series (2)
Professor in peril
Lejeune, Anthony
Glowrey series (1)
Professor on the case
Futrelle, Jacques
Professor Augustus S F X Van Dusen series (3)
Professor Pook
Pook, Peter
Pook series (6)
Professor Popkin's prodigious polish
Brittain, Bill
Coven Tree series (4)
Professor Potts meets the animals in Africa
Spence, Peter
Professor Potts series (1)
Professor Potts meets the animals in Asia
Spence, Peter
Professor Potts series (3)
Professor Potts meets the animals in North America
Spence, Peter
Professor Potts series (2)
Professor Wormbog in search of the zipperump-a-zoo
Mayer, Mercer
Professor Wormbog series (1)
Professor Wormbog's crazy cut-ups
Mayer, Mercer
Professor Wormbog series (4)
Professor Wormbog's cut it, glue it, tape it, do-it book
Mayer, Mercer
Professor Wormbog series (3)
Professor Wormbog's gloomy kerploppus
Mayer, Mercer
Professor Wormbog series (2)
Professors and gods
Fuller, Roy
Oxford lectures on poetry series (2)
Profile of a murder
King, Rufus
Lieutenant Valcour series (8)
Profit for the Picaroon
Cassells, John
Ludovic Saxon series (18)
Profit motive
Murphy, Warren Burton
Destroyer series (48)
Program for destruction
Dixon, Franklin W
Hardy boys series (87)
Programmed for death
Gribble, Leonard Reginald
Superintendent Anthony Slade series (35)
Progress of Hugh Rendal
Portman, Lionel
Hugh Rendal series (2)
Project Avalon
Hoyle, Trevor
Blake's Seven series (2)
Project Black Bear
Johnson, Lissa Halls
China Tate series (3)
Project boy
Lenski, Lois
Roundabout America series (4)
Project brain drain
Siegel, Barbara
Junior transformers find your fate series (8)
Project discovery
Greenfield, Irving A
Depth force series (9)
Project Earthsave
Brand, Kurt
Perry Rhodan series (38)

Project X
Robertson, Colin
Alan Steel series (3)
Projects Section
Lilley, Tom
Police Special Branch series (1)
Prologue to the gallows
McGuire, Paul
Inspector Wittler series (2)
Prom concert murders
Wood, Andrew
Magnus Keeble series (1)
Prom date
Cooper, M E
Couples series (31)
Prom queen
Stine, Robert Lawrence
Fear Street series (15)
Prom trouble
Summers, James Levingston
Trouble series (2)
Prometheus design
Culbreath, Myrna
Star trek series (5)
Prometheus man, a Nrobook
Nelson, Ray Faraday
Timebinders series (1)
Promise
Buck, Pearl Sydenstricker
Ling Tan series (2)
Hughes, Monica
Sandwriter series (2)
Potok, Chaim
Danny Saunders and Reuven Malter series (2)
Preston, Fayrene
Swansea Place series (3)
Sidgwick, Ethel
Tony Edgwell series (1)
Promise and the monster
Cole, Babette
Promise series (2)
Promise for death
Messmann, Jon
Revenger series (6)
Promise for Joyce
Kerry, Lois
Joyce series (2)
Promise keeper
Leeson, Muriel
Promise keeper series (1)
Promise me forever
Copeland, Lori
Promise me series (3)
Promise me today
Copeland, Lori
Promise me series (1)
Promise me tomorrow
Copeland, Lori
Promise me series (2)
Promise of dawn
Romains, Jules
Men of goodwill series (19)
Promise of days
Skelton, Peter
Edwin series (2)
Promise of diamonds
Ashe, Gordon
Patrick Dawlish series (41)
Promise of glory
Nolan, Frederick
Davy Strong series (1)
Promise of his return
Aspinall, Ruth
Malinson brothers trilogy (2)
Promise of joy
Drury, Allen
Washington series (6)
Promise of marriage
Gaboriau, Emile
Marriage of adventure series (2)
Promise of the phoenix
Gerard, Francis
Sir John Meredith series (17)
Promise solves the problem
Cole, Babette
Promise series (1)
Promise to kill
Marlowe, Piers
Frank Drury and Inspector Bill Hazard series (3)
Promised land
Danielson, Peter
Children of the Lion series (12)
Parker, Robert Brown
Spenser series (4)
Pontoppidan, Henrik
Emmanuel trilogy (2)
Stableford, Brian Michael
Star Pilot Grainger series (3)
Sutton, Marvin
Children of Ruth series (2)
Promised sunrise
Hatcher, Robin Lee
Women West series (1)
Promises
Arnold, Judith
Keeping the faith trilogy (1)
Pascal, Francine
Sweet Valley High series (15)
Promises broken
Pascal, Francine
Promise trilogy (2)
Promises of marriage
Gaboriau, Emile
Marriage of adventure series (2)
Promontory goats
Lafferty, Raphael Aloysius
Argos mythos series (4)
Promotion cometh
Housman, Laurence
Palace plays series (2)
Proof counter proof
Punshon, Ernest Robertson
Carter and Bell series (2)
Proof of poison
Thorwald, Jurgen
Century of the detective series (3)
Proof of the pudding
Taylor, Phoebe Atwood
Asey Mayo series (21)
Proofs of affection
Friedman, Rosemary
Shelton family series (1)
Propaganda
Birt, David
Something to sell series (1)
Propellor Island
Verne, Jules
Floating city series (1)
Proper carve-up
Cronin, Michael
Sam Harris series (2)
Proper gentleman
Scannell, Vernon
Tiger and the rose trilogy (2)
Proper little Nooryeff
Ure, Jean
Jamie Carr series (1)
Proper marriage
Lessing, Doris
Children of violence series (2)
Proper place
Lingard, Joan
Sadie and Kevin series (4)
Property and value
Hood, Hugh
New age series (8)
Property in Cyprus
Macleod, Robert
Jonathan Gaunt series (1)
Property of a lady
Oliver, Anthony
Lizzie Thomas and Inspector John Webber series (2)
Prophecy
Danielson, Peter
Children of the Lion series (7)
Prophesying peace
Lees-Milne, James
Ancestral voices series (2)
Prophet
Ahern, Jerry
Survivalist series (7)
Asch, Sholem
Biblical series (5)
Resnick, Mike
Oracle trilogy (3)
Prophet armed, 1879-1921
Deutscher, Isaac
Leon Trotsky trilogy (1)
Prophet at home
Reed, Douglas
Insanity fair trilogy (3)
Prophet of Akhran
Weis, Margaret
Rose of the prophet trilogy (3)
Prophet of evil
W, W
Qhe series (4)
Prophet of fire
Creasey, John
Doctor Palfrey series (14)
Prophet of Lamath
Hughes, Robert Don
Pelmen trilogy (1)
Prophet of truth, 1923-1939
Gilbert, Martin
Winston S Churchill series (5)
Prophet outcast, 1929-1940
Deutscher, Isaac
Leon Trotsky trilogy (3)
Prophet unarmed, 1921-1929
Deutscher, Isaac
Leon Trotsky trilogy (2)
Prophet without honour
Green, Russell
Prophet series (1)
Prophets and warriors
Danielson, Peter
Children of the Lion series (15)
Prophets in hell
Morris, Janet Ellen
Heroes in hell series (12)
Prophet's people
Willoughby, Lee Davis
Making of America series (39)
Proposed and seconded
Willard, Barbara
Proposed series (1)
Prospect of Ferrara
Bassani, Giorgio
Ferrara series (1)
Prospect of flowers
Young, Andrew
Wild flowers series (1)
Prospect of love
Budd, Mavis
Dust to dust series (2)
Prospect of vengeance
Price, Anthony
Doctor David Audley and Jack Butler series (18)
Prospector
Connor, Ralph
Crow's Nest series (1)
Prospect's dead
Tack, Alfred
John Harley series (3)
Prospero drill
Posey, Carl Alfred
Steven Borg series (2)
Prospero's cell
Durrell, Lawrence
Island series (1)
Prospero's island
Wham, Tom
Harold Shea series (4)
Protecting endangered species at the San Diego Zoo
Irvine, Georgeanne
Zoo world series (1)
Protection
James, Bill
Superintendent Colin Harpur series (4)
Protector
Niven, Larry
Known Space series (7)
Protectors
Haggard, William
Paul Martiny series (1)
Protege
Harbinson, Robert
Ulster series (4)
Proteus manifest
Sheffield, Charles
Proteus series (2)
Proteus unbound
Sheffield, Charles
Proteus series (2)
Protocol for a kidnapping
Bleeck, Oliver
Philip Saint Ives series (2)
Protocol for murder
Nathan, Paul
Bert Swain series (1)
Proud
Early, Tom
Sons of Texas series (4)
Moore, Arthur
River of fortune trilogy (3)
Romains, Jules
Men of goodwill series (5)
Proud and lazy
Optic, Oliver
Riverdale series (7)
Proud and the free
Fast, Howard
Call of fife and drum trilogy (3)
Proud and the meek
Romains, Jules
Men of goodwill series (6)
Proud blood
Carroll, Joy
Court family series (1)
Proud cat
Lockridge, Frances
Cats series (2)
Proud enemy
Busby, Francis Marion
Demu trilogy (2)
Proud flesh
Humphrey, William
Red River County trilogy (3)
Proud hunter
Harvey, Marianne
Trevarvas family series (2)
Proud Mary
Gower, Iris
Copper kingdom series (2)
Proud new flags
Mason, Francis Van Wyck
American Civil War, naval series (1)
Proud riders
Wynne, Brian
Marshal Jeremy Six series (6)
Proud servant
Irwin, Margaret
Stuart series (2)
Proud suitor
Dyson, Elizabeth
Revill-Gordon series (2)
Proud villeins
Anand, Valerie
Bridges over time series (1)
Proud waters
Brookes, Ewart
Proud waters series (1)
Prove it, Mr Tolliver
Walling, Robert Alfred John
Philip Tolefree series (4)
Prove yourself a hero
Peyton, K M
Hero series (1)
Provenance of death
Giles, Kenneth
Inspector Harry James and Sergeant Honeybody series (3)
Provence puzzle
McConnor, Vincent
Inspector Damiot series (1)
Proverbial murder case
Sutherland, William
Inspector Haskell series (2)
Providence file
Williams, Amanda Kyle
Madison McGuire series (2)
Provincial daughter
Dashwood, Rosamond Margaret
Provincial lady series (5)
Provincial great man in Paris
Balzac, Honore de
Scenes of provincial life series (9)
Provincial interlude
Romains, Jules
Men of goodwill series (8)
Provincial lady goes further
Delafield, E M
Provincial lady series (2)
Provincial lady in America
Delafield, E M
Provincial lady series (3)
Provincial lady in London
Delafield, E M
Provincial lady series (2)
Provincial lady in war-time
Delafield, E M
Provincial lady series (5)
Provincials in Paris
Balzac, Honore de
Scenes of provincial life series (8)
Proving it
Hoh, Diane
Cheerleaders series (23)
Proving of Virginia
Campbell, Daisy Rhodes
Virginia Hammond trilogy (2)
Prowler
Wiley, Hugh
Wildcat series (2)
Prowlers of the deep
Kelsey, Franklyn
James Armitage trilogy (3)
Prowling through Papua
Clune, Frank
Discovery series (7)
Prudence of the parsonage
Hueston, Ethel
Prudence series (1)
Prudence says so
Hueston, Ethel
Prudence series (2)
Prudence's daughter
Hueston, Ethel
Prudence series (4)
Prudence's omnibus
Hueston, Ethel
Prudence series (4)
Prudence's sisters
Hueston, Ethel
Prudence series (3)
Prue at school
Brooks, Amy
Prue series (2)
Prue flies north
Buzo, Alexander
Prue Foster series (2)
Prue's jolly winter
Brooks, Amy
Prue series (6)
Prue's little friends
Brooks, Amy
Prue series (5)
Prue's merry times
Brooks, Amy
Prue series (4)
Prue's playmates
Brooks, Amy
Prue series (3)
Pruneface
Gould, Chester
Dick Tracy cartoon series (3)
Prussian blue
Hocking, Anne
Inspector William Austen series (14)
Prydain chronicles
Alexander, Lloyd
Prydain series (6)
Prynter's devil
Wainwright, John
Northern Police series (12)
Pewter series (4)
Psalms and Proverbs for you
Davidson, Alice Joyce
Alice in Bibleland series (4)
Pseudo one
Darlton, Clark
Perry Rhodan series (44)
Psi-Man
Peters, David
Psi-Man series (1)
Psion
Vinge, Joan Dennison
Psion series (1)
Psionics war
Rosenberger, Joseph
Death Merchant series (48)
Psmith in the city
Wodehouse, Pelham Grenville
Psmith series (2)
Psmith, journalist
Wodehouse, Pelham Grenville
Psmith series (3)
Psychamok
Lumley, Brian
Psych trilogy (3)
Psyched!
Hughes, Dean
Angel Park Soccer Stars series (4)
Psychiatrist says murder
Freeman, Lucy
Doctor William Ames series (2)
Psychic
Franklin, Max
Starsky and Hutch series (6)
Psychic sisters
Pascal, Francine
Sweet Valley twins series (70)
Psycho
Bloch, Robert
Psycho series (1)
Psycho deal
Voltz, William
Perry Rhodan series (116)
Psycho II
Bloch, Robert
Psycho series (2)
Psycho in focus
Smith, Lou
John Spencer series (2)
Psycho soldiers
Cutter, John
Specialist series (4)
Psychodrome
Hawke, Simon
Psychodrome series (1)
Psycho-house
Bloch, Robert
Psycho series (3)
Psychomech
Lumley, Brian
Psych trilogy (1)
Psychomorph
Butterworth, Michael
Space nineteen ninety nine series (15)
Psychopath plague
Spruill, Steven Gregory
Kane and Pendrake series (1)
Psychosphere
Lumley, Brian
Psych trilogy (2)
Psychotechnic League
Anderson, Poul
Psychotechnic League series (1)
Psychotron plot
Rosenberger, Joseph
Death Merchant series (3)

Pub crawler
Procter, Maurice
Chief Inspector Harry Martineau series (7)
Public enemy number two
Horowitz, Anthony
Nick and Tim Diamond series (2)
Public exposure
Moffat, Bill
Press Gang series (2)
Public murders
Granger, Bill
November Man series (2)
Terry Flynn series (1)
Public years
Baruch, Bernard Mannes
My own story series (2)
Publish and be killed
Morice, Anne
Tessa Crichton Price series (20)
Publish and perish
Nevins, Francis Michael
Loren Mensing series (1)
Puck in petticoats
Behrens, Margaret
Percival Soames series (2)
Puck of Crooks' Hill
San Antonio
Berurier series (8)
San Antonio series (8)
Puck of Pook's Hill
Kipling, Rudyard
Rewards and fairies series (1)
Pucky's greatest hour
Brand, Kurt
Perry Rhodan series (81)
Pudgy I love you book
Shine, Deborah
Pudgy series (1)
Pudgy noisy book
Shine, Deborah
Pudgy series (2)
Pudgy, the beaver
Darby, Joan
Animal adventure series (1)
Puff in Canada
Shepherd, Jo
Puff trilogy (3)
Puff to the rescue
Shepherd, Jo
Puff trilogy (1)
Puffin, Twink and Waggle at home
Bennett, Rodney
Puffin, Twink and Waggle series (1)
Puffin, Twink and Waggle at the fair
Bennett, Rodney
Puffin, Twink and Waggle series (3)
Puffin, Twink and Waggle at the seaside
Bennett, Rodney
Puffin, Twink and Waggle series (4)
Puffin, Twink and Waggle at the zoo
Bennett, Rodney
Puffin, Twink and Waggle series (2)
Pugs and peacocks
Cannan, Gilbert
New time trilogy (1)
Pugwall
Clark, Margaret Dianne
Pugwall series (1)
Pugwall's summer
Clark, Margaret Dianne
Pugwall series (2)
Pugwash aloft
Ryan, John
Captain Pugwash series (2)
Pugwash and the buried treasure
Ryan, John
Captain Pugwash series (11)
Pugwash and the fancy dress party
Ryan, John
Captain Pugwash series (13)
Pugwash and the ghost ship
Ryan, John
Captain Pugwash series (3)
Pugwash and the midnight feast
Ryan, John
Captain Pugwash series (16)
Pugwash and the sea monster
Ryan, John
Captain Pugwash series (5)
Pugwash and the wreckers
Ryan, John
Captain Pugwash series (15)
Pugwash in the Pacific
Ryan, John
Captain Pugwash series (4)
Pugwash the smuggler
Ryan, John
Captain Pugwash series (6)
Puller of strings
Burgin, George Brown
Four Corners series (13)
Pulling together
Hoh, Diane
Cheerleaders series (21)
Pully-haul
Karlsson, Elis
Mother sea series (2)
Pulpit in the grill room
Oppenheim, Edward Phillips
Major Charles Lyson series (1)
Puma pistoleers
Floren, Lee
Judge Lemanuel Bates and Tobacco Jones series (2)
Pummeling, falling and getting up, sometimes
Paulsen, Gary
Sports on the light side series (11)
Pumpkin Hollow countdown
Davis, Anne
Pumpkin Hollow series (1)
Pumpkins for the pot
Davis, Anne
Pumpkin Hill fact series (3)
Punch and judy murders
Dickson, Carter
Sir Henry Merrivale series (6)
Punch with care
Taylor, Phoebe Atwood
Asey Mayo series (23)
Punchbowl harvest
Edwards, Monica
Punchbowl Farm series (6)
Punchbowl midnight
Edwards, Monica
Punchbowl Farm series (3)
Punchers of Phantom Pass
Macdonald, William Colt
Nogales Scott and Caliper Maxwell series (1)
Pungi patrol
Lansing, John
Black Eagles series (4)
Punjat's ruby
Jackson, Marian J A
Miss Abigail Patience Danforth series (1)
Punky Brewster at Camp Chipmunk
Matthews, Ann
Punky Brewster series (2)
Punography
McMillan, Bruce
Punography series (1)
Punography too
McMillan, Bruce
Punography series (2)
Puppet for a corpse
Simpson, Dorothy
Inspector Luke Thanet series (3)
Puppet master
Carter, Nick
Nick Carter series (157)
O'Donnell, Peter
Modesty Blaise comic strip series (8)
Puppet soldiers
Helm, Eric
Ground Zero series (21)
Puppet stages and props with pizazz
Berry, Joy
Can make and do series (4)
Puppeteer
Williams, Timothy
Commissario Trotti series (2)
Puppets and I
Bussell, Jan
Puppets series (1)
Puppets and pizazz
Berry, Joy
Can make and do series (3)
Puppets in Wales
Wilkinson, Walter
Puppets series (8)
Puppets in Yorkshire
Wilkinson, Walter
Puppets series (3)
Puppets into Scotland
Wilkinson, Walter
Puppets series (5)
Puppet's progress
Bussell, Jan
Puppets series (2)
Puppets through America
Wilkinson, Walter
Puppets series (7)
Puppets through Lancashire
Wilkinson, Walter
Puppets series (6)
Puppies love
McCue, Lisa
Baby animal love series (2)
Puppy fat!
Gleitzman, Morris
Misery guts series (3)
Puppy learns to share
Szekeres, Cyndy
Puppy series (3)
Puppy lost
Szekeres, Cyndy
Puppy series (2)
Puppy love
Hill, Eric
Spot series (4)
Puppy problems
Krulick, Nancy E
Lassie series (1)
Puppy ptoject
Armstrong, Jennifer
Pets, Inc. series (1)
Puppy sees
Hands, Hargrave
Look and see series (2)
Puppy's day school
McCue, Dick
Animal shape series (6)
Purchase of the North Pole
Verne, Jules
Gun Club series (3)
Pure blood
McQuay, Mike
Ramon and Morgan series (1)
Pure bred
Bryant, Bonnie
Saddle Club series (39)
Pure evil
Robeson, Kenneth
Doc Savage series (142)
Pure flame
Mannin, Ethel
Elspeth Rodney series (2)
Pure poison
Keene, Carolyn
Nancy Drew files series (29)
Waugh, Hillary
Chief Fred Fellows series (10)
Purgatory
Wisler, Gary Clifton
Willie Delamer series (4)
Purim party
Simon, Norma
Purim series (2)
Puritan knight errant
Robinson, Edith
Little Puritan series (6)
Puritan strain
Baldwin, Faith
Condit family series (2)
Puritan twins
Perkins, Lucy Fitch
Twin series (12)
Puritans
McCrone, Guy
Moorhouse family trilogy (1)
Purity plot
Smith, Edward Elmer
Family d'Alembert series (6)
Purity's ecstasy
Seymour, Janette
Purity series (2)
Purity's passion
Seymour, Janette
Purity series (1)
Purity's shame
Seymour, Janette
Purity series (3)
Purloined letter
Poe, Edgar Allan
Monsieur C Auguste Dupin series (1)
Purloined planet
Carter, Lin
Hautley Quicksilver series (2)
Purloined prince
Wallace, Ian
Claudine Saint Cyr series (3)
Purple aces
Hogan, Robert Jasper
G-Eight series (3)
Purple bird mystery
Queen, Ellery, Junior
Gulliver Queen series (3)
Purple book
Farmer, Philip Jose
World of Tiers series (5)
Purple climbing days
Giff, Patricia Reilly
Kids of the Polk Street School series (9)
Purple Dragon
Robeson, Kenneth
Doc Savage series (91)
Purple dress
Wayne, Jenifer
Purple dress series (2)
Purple dressing gown
Fry, Pete
Pete Fry series (5)
Purple legion
Eliot, George Fielding
G-men series (2)
Purple mist
Locke, Gladys Edson
Inspector Burton series (3)
Purple mountain
Clewes, Dorothy
Hadley family series (7)
Purple Muffin book
Hogarth, Ann
Muffin book series (4)
Purple onion mystery
Ashbrook, Harriette
Philip Tracy series (7)
Purple parrot
Clason, Clyde B
Theocritus Lucius Westborough series (4)
Purple Pennant
Barbour, Ralph Henry
Purple Pennant trilogy (3)
Purple pirate
Mundy, Talbot
Tros of Samothrace series (3)
Purple place for dying
Macdonald, John Dann
Travis McGee series (3)
Purple pony murders
Porcelain, Sidney E
Stephen Clay series (1)
Purple prince of Oz
Thompson, Ruth Plumly
Oz series (25)
Purple robe
Hocking, Joseph
Religious questions series (2)
Purple sapphire
Blayre, Christopher
University of Cosmopoli series (2)
Purple sapphire, and other posthumous papers
Blayre, Christopher
University of Cosmopoli series (1)
Purple sash
Nunez Alonso, Alejandro
Early Christianity series (1)
Purple sea
Owen, Frank
Chinese color series (2)
Purple shell
Goldman, Raymond Leslie
Asaph Clume series (6)
Purple sickle murders
Crofts, Freeman Wills
Inspector Joseph French series (5)
Purple-six
Brinton, Henry
John and Sally Strang series (8)
Purple spot
Carter, Nicholas
Nicholas Carter series (479)
Purple streak
Croft-Cooke, Rupert
Sensual life series (7)
Purple tornado
Bowen, Robert Sidney
Dusty Ayres and his Battle Birds series (3)
Purple twilight
Groom, Pelham
Peter Mohune series (5)
Purple valley
Saville, Malcolm
Marston Baines series (2)
Simon series (2)
Purple zombie
Robeson, Kenneth
Avenger series (27)
Purrfect plunder
Cleve, John
Spaceways series (6)
Purse
Balzac, Honore de
Scenes of private life series (4)
Purser's mate
Laurie-Long, Ernest
Lizzie Collins series (2)
Purslane
Harris, Bernice
Purslane series (1)
Pursued by shadows
Sale, Medora
Inspector John Sanders and Harriet Jeffries series (3)
Pursued by the law
Cobban, James Maclaren
Mister Townshend series (1)
Pursuers
Ladd, Justin
Abilene series (3)
Pursuit
Ahern, Jerry
Survivalist series (13)
Janson, Hank
Hank Janson series (54)
Tranter, Nigel Godwin
Donald Macdonald series (3)
Pursuit in Peru
Leonard, Charles L
Paul Kilgerrin series (6)
Pursuit in the desert
Sava, George
Peter Slavine series (4)
Pursuit of a parcel
Wentworth, Patricia
Inspector Ernest Lamb series (3)
Pursuit of arms
Hammond, Gerald
Keith Calder series (8)
Pursuit of bliss
Nelson, Betty Palmer
Honest women series (3)
Pursuit of Diana
Wold, Allen
V series (3)
Pursuit of happiness, and other sobering thoughts
Will, George Frederick
Pursuit series (1)
Pursuit of Kadath
Diaper, John
Cthulhu Mythos series (11)
Pursuit of love
Mitford, Nancy
Love trilogy (1)
Pursuit of power, 1898-1918
Holroyd, Michael
Bernard Shaw series (2)
Pursuit of the Apache chief
Tomlinson, Everett Titsworth
American scouting series (1)
Pursuit of the deadly diamonds
Fortune, J J
Race against time series (3)
Pursuit of the eagle
Carter, Nick
Nick Carter series (199)
Pursuit of the flying smugglers
Theiss, Lewis Edwin
Air mail series (5)
Pursuit of the house-boat
Bangs, John Kendrick
Associated shades series (2)
Pursuit of the Mountain Man
Johnstone, William Wallace
Mountain Man series (10)
Pursuit of the Screamer
Dibell, Ansen
Kantmorie trilogy (1)
Pursuit of virtue, and other Tory notions
Will, George Frederick
Pursuit series (2)
Pursuit on Ganymede
Resnick, Mike
Ganymede series (2)
Pursuit on the Saint Lawrence
Holliday, Joe
Dale of the Mounted series (10)
Pursuit party
Grover, Marshall
Larry and Stretch series (262)
Pursuit patrol
Dixon, Franklin W
Ted Scott flying series (20)
Pursuit to Algeria
Maclean, Arthur
Sexton Blake series (1518)
Pursuit trail
Grover, Marshall
Larry and Stretch series (126)
Push the dog
Ahlberg, Allan
Red nose readers series (9)
Pushbutton butterfly
Platt, Kin
Max Roper series (1)
Pushed from the wings
Fitzgerald, Ross
Grafton Everest series (1)
Pusher
McBain, Ed
Eighty Seventh Precinct series (3)
Pushing ahead
Rand, Edward Augustus
School and camp series (1)
Pushover
O'Donnell, Lillian
Detective Norah Mulcahaney series (14)

Puss in Boots
McBain, Ed
Matthew Hope series (7)
Pussy Nell
Bruna, Dick
Toy box tale series (5)
Pussycat, Pussycat
Mark, Ted
Girl from P.U.S.S.Y.C.A.T. series (3)
Pussycat transplant
Mark, Ted
Girl from P.U.S.S.Y.C.A.T. series (7)
Pussyfoot
Douglas, Carole Nelson
Midnight Louie series (2)
Put off thy shoes
Voynich, Ethel Lillian
Gadfly series (1)
Put on by Cunning
Rendell, Ruth
Chief Inspector Reginald Wexford series (13)
Put on the spot
Lait, Jack
Polack Annie series (1)
Put out more flags
Waugh, Evelyn
Basil Seal series (2)
Put out that star
Carmichael, Harry
John Piper and Quinn series (12)
Put out the light
Woods, Sara
Sir Nicholas Harding and Antony Maitland series (45)
Putnam Hall cadets
Winfield, Arthur M
Putnam Hall series (1)
Putnam Hall champions
Winfield, Arthur M
Putnam Hall series (3)
Putnam Hall encampment
Winfield, Arthur M
Putnam Hall series (5)
Putnam Hall mystery
Winfield, Arthur M
Putnam Hall series (6)
Putnam Hall rebellion
Winfield, Arthur M
Putnam Hall series (4)
Putnam Hall rivals
Winfield, Arthur M
Putnam Hall series (2)
Putting the boot in
Kavanagh, Dan
Nick Duffy series (3)
Puzzle
Rathjen, Carl Henry
Waltons series (2)
Thayer, Lee
Peter Clancy series (4)
Puzzle at Pineview School
Keene, Carolyn
Nancy Drew series (90)
Puzzle for fiends
Quentin, Patrick
Peter Duluth series (5)
Puzzle for fools
Quentin, Patrick
Peter Duluth series (1)
Puzzle for inspector West
Creasey, John
Inspector Roger West series (11)
Puzzle for pilgrims
Quentin, Patrick
Peter Duluth series (6)
Puzzle for players
Quentin, Patrick
Peter Duluth series (2)
Puzzle for ponies
Gervaise, Mary
G for Georgia series (9)
Puzzle for puppets
Quentin, Patrick
Peter Duluth series (3)
Puzzle for Sherlock Holmes
Newman, Robert
Sherlock Holmes sequels series (33)
Puzzle for the Secret Seven
Blyton, Enid
Secret Seven series (10)
Puzzle for wantons
Quentin, Patrick
Peter Duluth series (4)
Puzzle in paint
Kootz, Samuel Melvin
Jason Emory series (1)
Puzzle in paisley
Gresham, Elizabeth
Jenny Gilette and Hunter Lewis series (3)
Puzzle in parchment
Gresham, Elizabeth
Jenny Gilette and Hunter Lewis series (6)
Puzzle in parquet
Gresham, Elizabeth
Jenny Gilette and Hunter Lewis series (4)
Puzzle in patchwork
Gresham, Elizabeth
Jenny Gilette and Hunter Lewis series (5)
Puzzle in pearls
Ashe, Gordon
Patrick Dawlish series (20)
Puzzle in petticoats
Kootz, Samuel Melvin
Jason Emory series (2)
Puzzle in pewter
Gresham, Elizabeth
Jenny Gilette and Hunter Lewis series (2)
Puzzle in porcelain
Gresham, Elizabeth
Jenny Gilette and Hunter Lewis series (1)
Puzzle in purple
Allen, Betsy
Connie Blair series (2)
Puzzle in pyrotechnics
Rowland, John
Inspector Shelley series (16)
Puzzle in the pond
Sutton, Margaret
Judy Bolton series (34)
Puzzle lock
Freeman, Richard Austin
Doctor John Evelyn Thorndyke series (13)
Puzzle of the blue banderilla
Palmer, Stuart
Hildegarde Withers series (7)
Puzzle of the briar pipe
Palmer, Stuart
Hildegarde Withers series (6)
Puzzle of the five pistols, and other stories
Carter, Nicholas
Nicholas Carter series (47)
Puzzle of the happy hooligan
Palmer, Stuart
Hildegarde Withers series (8)
Puzzle of the pepper tree
Palmer, Stuart
Hildegarde Withers series (4)
Puzzle of the red stallion
Palmer, Stuart
Hildegarde Withers series (6)
Puzzle of the silver Persian
Palmer, Stuart
Hildegarde Withers series (5)
Puzzle people
Oxenbury, Helen
Seven hundred and twenty nine series (2)
Puzzles at Highcliff
Little, Sylvia
Highcliff series (3)
Puzzles of childhood
Clark, Manning
Historian series (1)
Puzzles of the Black Widowers
Asimov, Isaac
Black Widowers series (5)
Pyms of Yarrambeat
Miller, Rosalind
Pym family series (2)
Pyramid inch
Stewart, Desmond
Sequence of roles trilogy (2)
Pyramid voyagers
Pond, Roy
Archaeology series (1)
Pyramids
Pratchett, Terry
Discworld series (7)
Saberhagen, Fred
Pilgrim series (1)
Pysen
Unnerstad, Edith
Larsson family series (3)
Python
Grant, Maxwell
Shadow series (90)
Python Isle
Robeson, Kenneth
Doc Savage series (183)
Python project
Canning, Victor
Rex Carver series (3)

Q

Q
Grant, Maxwell
Shadow series (188)
Q annual
Milligan, Spike
Q annual series (1)
Q as in quicksand
Treat, Lawrence
Jub Freeman series (3)
Mitch Taylor series (2)
Q.B.I.
Queen, Ellery
Ellery Queen series (32)
Q.E.D.
Brock, Lynn
Colonel Gore series (6)
Queen, Ellery
Ellery Queen series (42)
Thayer, Lee
Peter Clancy series (4)
Q factor
Kirk, Philip
Butler series (11)
Q-in-law
David, Peter
Star trek, the next generation series (18)
Q-man
Carter, Nick
Nick Carter series (145)
Q 33
Goodchild, George
John Trelawney series (1)
Q 33, spycatcher
Goodchild, George
John Trelawney series (3)
Qantas at war
Fysh, Hudson
Qantas series (2)
Qantas rising
Fysh, Hudson
Qantas series (1)
Q's legacy
Hanff, Helene
American in London series (3)
Quadrille
Swinnerton, Frank
Prothero quartet (4)
Quadrophonic homicide
Weisman, John
Headhunters series (4)
Quail message
Ireland, Kenneth
Fogou series (3)
Quaking lands
Vardeman, Robert Edward
Jade demons quartet (1)
Quaking terror
Derrick, Lionel
Penetrator series (45)
Qualified adventurer
Jepson, Selwyn
Ian Macarthur series (1)
Qualinesti
Carter, Tonya R
Elven nations trilogy (3)
Quality Bill's girl
Tyler, Charles Waller
Blue Jean Billy Race series (2)
Quality Chase
Tiltman, Marjorie Hessell
Quality Chase series (1)
Quality Chase's daughter
Tiltman, Marjorie Hessell
Quality Chase series (2)
Quality of hurt
Himes, Chester
Quality of hurt series (1)
Quality of mercy
Howells, William Dean
Annie Kilburn series (2)
Quality of the informant
Petievich, Gerald
Charles Carr and Jack Kelly series (4)
Quallsford inheritance
Biggle, Lloyd
Sherlock Holmes sequels series (87)
Quanah Parker
Dugan, Bill
War chiefs series (4)
Quanah's revenge
Roberts, J R
Gunsmith series (8)
Quantrell's raiders
Gruber, Frank
Historical Western series (8)
William Clarke Quantrell series (2)
Quantum force
Appleton, Victor II
Tom Swift Junior series 3 (13)
Quantum leap
McConnell, Ashley
Quantum leap series (1)
Quantum self
Zohar, Danah
Quantum series (1)
Quantum society
Zohar, Danah
Quantum series (2)
Quarantine child
Symons, Geraldine
Atalanta and Pansy series (2)
Quare women
Furman, Lucy
Quare women trilogy (1)
Quarrel of witches
Storey, Margaret
Timothy, Ellen and Melinda series (2)
Quarreling
Baker, Sharon
Naphar series (1)
Quarry
Collins, Max Allan
Quarry series (1)
Durrenmatt, Friedrich
Kommissar Hans Barlach series (2)
Pike, Robert L
Lieutenant Clancy series (2)
Pronzini, Bill
Private Eye series (20)
Quarry's contract
Hunter, Robin
Simon Quarry series (2)
Quarry's cut
Collins, Max Allan
Quarry series (4)
Quarry's deal
Collins, Max Allan
Quarry series (3)
Quarry's list
Collins, Max Allan
Quarry series (2)
Quarter of eight
Grant, Maxwell
Shadow series (267)
Quarter second draw
Edson, John Thomas
Rockabye County series (5)
Quarterback gamble
Gault, William Campbell
Gridiron series (5)
Quarterback who came to dinner
Johnston, William
Brady Bunch series (4)
Quarterback's pluck
Chadwick, Lester
College sports series (2)
Quartet
Stoddard, William Osborn
Cowboy and college life series (2)
Quartz boyar
Bethancourt, Tomas Ernesto
Doris Fein series (3)
Quatermass
Kneale, Nigel
Quatermass series (3)
Quatermass and the pit
Kneale, Nigel
Quatermass series (3)
Quatermass experiment
Kneale, Nigel
Quatermass series (1)
Quatermass II
Kneale, Nigel
Quatermass series (2)
Quayle of the Yard
Trent, Paul
Peter Quayle series (1)
Quayle's first case
Trent, Paul
Peter Quayle series (2)
Que viva Guevara
De Villiers, Gerard
Malko Linge series (7)
Quebec connection
Derrick, Lionel
Penetrator series (15)
Queen and Lord M
Plaidy, Jean
Queen Victoria series (3)
Queen and the corpse
Murray, Max
Corpse series (3)
Queen Anne Farthings
Dodd, Catherine Isabel
Farthing family series (2)
Queen Calafia
Blasco Ibanez, Vicente
Temptress series (2)
Queen City murder case
Bogart, William
Johnny Saxon series (3)
Queen Cleopatra
Mundy, Talbot
Tros of Samothrace series (2)
Queen Elizabeth family
Blyton, Enid
Mike, Belinda and Ann series (6)
Queen from Provence
Plaidy, Jean
Plantagenet series (6)
Queen, God bless her
Housman, Laurence
Palace plays series (3)
Queen-gold
Wiat, Philippa
Edward III series (1)
Queen' high bid
Sharpe, Jon
Trailsman series (97)
Queen Hildegarde
Richards, Laura Elizabeth
Hildegarde series (1)
Queen in danger
Rattray, Simon
Hugo Bishop series (2)
Queen in waiting
Plaidy, Jean
Caroline of Ansbach series (1)
Georgian series (2)
Queen is dead
Dentinger, Jane
Jocelyn O'Roarke and Phillip Gerard series (5)
Queen Jezebel
Plaidy, Jean
Catherine de Medici trilogy (3)
Queen Lucia
Benson, Edward Frederic
Lucia Billson series (1)
Queen of air and darkness
White, Terence Hanbury
Once and future king series (2)
Queen of Atlantis
Aubrey, Frank
Monella trilogy (2)
Queen of crooks
Dunn, *Detective*
Beautiful devil series (2)
Queen of diamonds
Carter, Nicholas
Nicholas Carter series (162)
Queen of hearts
Dobkin, Kaye
Wonderland series (1)
Queen of Hearts
Martin, Cort
Jared Bolt series (18)
Queen of knaves, and other stories
Carter, Nicholas
Nicholas Carter series (86)
Queen of sorcery
Eddings, David
Belgariad series (2)
Queen of Spades
Bailey, Henry Christopher
Mister Joshua Clunk series (9)
Grover, Marshall
Larry and Stretch series (368)
Queen of springtime
Silverberg, Robert
New springtime series (2)
Queen of the Abbey girls
Oxenham, Elsie J
Abbey girls first generation series (8)
Queen of the black coast
Howard, Robert Ervin
Conan series (27)
Queen of the clouds
Ellis, Edward Sylvester
Paddle your own canoe trilogy (3)
Queen of the damned
Rice, Anne
Vampire chronicles series (3)
Queen of the dawn
Haggard, Henry Rider
Morning Star series (2)
Queen of the Legion
Williamson, Jack
Legion of Space series (4)
Queen of the lightning
Herbert, Kathleen
Cumbrian series (1)

Graves, Richard Latshaw
Hugo Wolfram series (4)
Moore, Amos
Quicksilver series (1)
Pronzini, Bill
Private Eye series (12)
Quicksilver justice
Moore, Amos
Quicksilver series (2)
Quicksilver passion
Gentry, Georgina
Panorama of the old West series (7)
Quicksilver rides
Moore, Amos
Quicksilver series (1)
Quiet as a nun
Fraser, Antonia
Jemima Shore series (1)
Quiet death
Knight, Alanna
Inspector Faro series (5)
Quiet dogs
Gardner, John Edmund
Herbie Kruger series (3)
Quiet earth
Sunley, Margaret
Yorkshire Dales trilogy (1)
Quiet girl
Strange, Nora Kathleen
Kenya series (9)
Quiet hills
Bromige, Iris
Rainwood family series (2)
Quiet life
De Wohl, Louis
Lives of the saints series (5)
Quiet moments with older children
Sorenson, Jane
Quiet moment series (2)
Quiet moments with young children
Sorenson, Jane
Quiet moment series (1)
Quiet murder
Livingston, Nancy
G D H Pringle series (8)
Quiet neighborhood
Macdonald, George
Quiet neighbourhood series (1)
Quiet noisy book
Brown, Margaret Wise
Noisy book series (7)
Quiet of stone
Leigh, Stephen
Neweden trilogy (3)
Quiet ones
Graeme, Bruce
Detective Sergeant Robert Mather series (1)
Quiet revolution
James, Colin
New Zealand revolution series (1)
Quiet road to death
Radley, Sheila
Chief Inspector Douglas Quantrill series (4)
Quiet room in hell
Copper, Basil
Mike Faraday series (27)
Quiet stranger
Hilton, John Buxton
Inspector Thomas Brunt series (5)
Quiet town
Edson, John Thomas
Floating Outfit series (9)
Quiet under the sun
Fitzgerald, Kevin
Bernard Feston series (1)
Quiet violence
Disney, Doris Miles
Jeff Dimarco series (5)
Quiet waits the grave
Janson, Hank
Hank Janson series (99)
Quiet woman
Carmichael, Harry
John Piper and Quinn series (30)
Quiet year
Tangye, Derek
Minack chronicles series (14)
Quietly my captain waits
Eaton, Evelyn
Arcadian trilogy (1)
Quiller
Hall, Adam
Quiller series (12)
Quiller bamboo
Hall, Adam
Quiller series (16)
Quiller barracuda
Hall, Adam
Quiller series (15)
Quiller, KGB
Hall, Adam
Quiller series (14)
Quiller memorandum
Hall, Adam
Quiller series (1)
Quiller meridian
Hall, Adam
Quiller series (18)
Quiller salamander
Hall, Adam
Quiller series (19)
Quiller solitaire
Hall, Adam
Quiller series (17)
Quiller's run
Hall, Adam
Quiller series (13)
Quillian Sector
Tubb, Edwin Charles
Dumarest series (19)
Quincannon
Pronzini, Bill
Quincannon series (1)
Quincy Adams Sawyer and Mason's corner folks
Pidgin, Charles Felton
Quincy Adams Sawyer series (1)
Quinette's crime
Romains, Jules
Men of goodwill series (2)
Quinn
Scanlon, Noel
Quinn series (1)
Quinn and the desert oil
Scanlon, Noel
Quinn series (2)
Quinn at Trafalgar
Styles, Showell
Midshipman Quinn series (4)
Quinn of the Fury
Styles, Showell
Midshipman Quinn series (2)
Quinneys'
Vachell, Horace Annesley
Joe Quinney series (1)
Quinney's adventures
Vachell, Horace Annesley
Joe Quinney series (2)
Quinney's for quality
Vachell, Horace Annesley
Joe Quinney series (4)
Quinn's book
Kennedy, William
Albany series (4)
Quintet
Meynell, Esther
Jakob and Melchior series (2)
Quintilian
Hatfield, John
Quintilian series (1)
Quintilian and the curious weather shop
Hatfield, John
Quintilian series (2)
Quintilian meets Mr Punch
Hatfield, John
Quintilian series (3)
Quintus Oakes
Jackson, Charles Ross
Quintus Oakes series (2)
Quinx
Durrell, Lawrence
Avignon quintet (5)
Quiraing list
Savarin, Julian Jay
Gordon Gallagher series (5)
Quislings over Paris
Cumberland, Marten
Saturnin Dax series (3)
Quit playing dames
Kane, Martin
Martin Kane series (20)
Quite a good address
Hayes, Douglas
History of a selfish man series (6)
Quite unexpected
Thorn, Ismay
Geoff and Jim Harrington series (1)
Quitting time
Conley, Robert Jackson
Oliver Colfax series (3)
Quiver river
Carkeet, David
Ricky and Nate series (2)
Quivering tree
Haymon, Sylvia T
East Anglian childhood series (2)
Quorum
Bentley, Phyllis
West Riding series (12)
Quoth the maven
Safire, William
On language series (7)

R

R.I.S.C.
Frazer, Robert Caine
Mark Kilby series (1)
R in the month
Spain, Nancy
Miriam Birdseye series (4)
R.S.V.P.
Maxwell, Elsa
Celebrity series (1)
Rab Hewison's visit to Edinburgh
Douglas, G A H
Rab Hewison series (1)
Rabbit
Burningham, John
Little book series (1)
Van der Essen, Anne
Yok-yok series (6)
Rabbit and Chicken count eggs
Landa, Norbert
Rabbit and Chicken series (1)
Rabbit and Chicken find the right box
Landa, Norbert
Rabbit and Chicken series (2)
Rabbit and Chicken look at colors
Landa, Norbert
Rabbit and Chicken series (3)
Rabbit and chicken play hide and seek
Landa, Norbert
Rabbit and Chicken series (4)
Rabbit at rest
Updike, John
Rabbit Angstrom series (4)
Rabbit-cadabra!
Howe, James
Bunnicula series (10)
Rabbit finds a way
Delton, Judy
Rabbit series (1)
Rabbit goes to night school
Delton, Judy
Rabbit series (3)
Rabbit Hill
Lawson, Robert
Rabbit Hill series (1)
Rabbit is rich
Updike, John
Rabbit Angstrom series (3)
Rabbit magic
York, Carol Beach
Miss Know It All series (11)
Rabbit redux
Updike, John
Rabbit Angstrom series (2)
Rabbit, run
Updike, John
Rabbit Angstrom series (1)
Rabbit's new run
Delton, Judy
Rabbit series (2)
Rabble in arms
Roberts, Kenneth Lewis
Chronicles of Arundel series (2)
Rabble of rebels
Ashe, Gordon
Patrick Dawlish series (47)
Rabelaisian reprise
Carr, Jayge
Navigator trilogy (3)
Rabid brigadier
Sargent, Craig
Last ranger series (4)
Raccoon twins
Hogan, Inez
Twins series (10)
Tompkins, Jane
Animal twins series (5)
Raccoon's hide and seek
McCue, Dick
Animal shape series (10)
Race
Goscinny, Rene
Twelve tasks of Asterix series (1)
Race across the stars
Cleve, John
Spaceways series (18)
Race against the sun
Rutherford, Douglas
Chequered flag series (4)
Race against time
Baker, Jane
Doctor Who find your fate series (6)
Keene, Carolyn
Nancy Drew series (66)
Race for ten thousand
Carter, Nicholas
Nicholas Carter series (106)
Race forever
Montgomery, Raymond A
Choose your own adventure series (17)
Race into the past
Stine, Megan
Twistaplot series (8)
Race of death
Carter, Nick
Nick Carter series (120)
Race of scorpions
Dunnett, Dorothy
House of Niccolo series (3)
Race of the rails
Bechdolt, Jack
Barrow brothers series (3)
Race the sun
Ward, Lynda
Welles family trilogy (1)
Race to danger
Calmenson, Stephanie
Young Indiana Jones chronicles series (6)
Race toward death
Mackenzie, Nigel
Inspector Charles Tremayne series (2)
Race track gamble
Carter, Nicholas
Nicholas Carter series (138)
Racer boys
Young, Clarence
Racer boys series (1)
Racer boys at boarding school
Young, Clarence
Racer boys series (2)
Racer boys forging ahead
Young, Clarence
Racer boys series (6)
Racer boys on guard
Young, Clarence
Racer boys series (5)
Racer boys on the prairies
Young, Clarence
Racer boys series (4)
Racer boys to the rescue
Young, Clarence
Racer boys series (3)
Racetrack crooks
Ridley, Nat
Nat Ridley series (10)
Rachel
Borntrager, Mary Christner
Ellie's people series (3)
Schurfranz, Vivian
Sunfire series (21)
Rachel and Obadiah
Turkle, Brinton
Obadiah series (4)
Rachel in the Abbey
Oxenham, Elsie J
Abbey girls second generation series (8)
Rachel and Damaris series (6)
Rachel, Rachel
Laurence, Margaret
Manawaka series (2)
Rachel Rosing
Spring, Howard
Manchester series (2)
Rachel, the possessed
Kimbrough, Katheryn
Phenwick women series (5)
Racing around the world
Adams, Eustace Lane
Andy Lane series (3)
Racing cars and cycles
Firmin, Peter
Make it work series (3)
Racing hearts
Pascal, Francine
Sweet Valley High series (9)
Racing with disaster
Dixon, Franklin W
Hardy boys series (126)
Rack
Vance, J Emily
Star trek fan series (18)
Rack of Baal
Smith, Mark
Falcon series (3)
Racket king
Grant, Maxwell
Shadow series (146)
Racket town
Grant, Maxwell
Shadow series (136)
Racketeer's a redhead
Kane, Martin
Martin Kane series (2)
Racketeer's will
Vickery, William
Sexton Blake series (716)
Racoon Lake mystery
Hopkins, Nevil Monroe
Mason Brant series (2)
Radar job
Baddock, James
Cormack and Woodward series (1)
Radcliffe case
Bentley, John
Sir Richard Herrivell series (8)
Radetzky march
Roth, Joseph
Radetzky series (1)
Radford's big race
White, Paul
Ranford series (1)
Radiant dome
Scheer, Karl Herbert
Perry Rhodan series (2)
Radiant warrior
Frankowski, Leo
Adventures of Conrad Stargard series (3)
Radiant way
Drabble, Margaret
Radiant way trilogy (1)
Radiation hit
Derrick, Lionel
Penetrator series (20)
Radical departure
Matera, Lia
Willa Jansson series (2)
Radical moves
Dixon, Franklin W
Hardy boys series (113)
Radical woman
Fraser, Sara
Tildy series (5)
Radio alert
Escott, John
Radio series (1)
Radio beasts
Farley, Ralph Milne
Miles Cabot series (2)
Radio boys aiding the snowbound
Chapman, Allen
Radio boys series (11)
Radio boys at Mountain Pass
Chapman, Allen
Radio boys series (4)
Radio boys at Ocean Point
Chapman, Allen
Radio boys series (2)
Radio boys at the sending station
Chapman, Allen
Radio boys series (3)
Radio boys' first wireless
Chapman, Allen
Radio boys series (1)
Radio boys in Gold Valley
Chapman, Allen
Radio boys series (10)
Radio boys on Secret Service duty
Breckenridge, Gerald
Radio boys series (1)
Radio boys on Signal Island
Chapman, Allen
Radio boys series (9)
Radio boys on the Mexican border
Breckenridge, Gerald
Radio boys series (2)
Radio boys on the Pacific
Chapman, Allen
Radio boys series (12)
Radio boys search for the Incas treasure
Breckenridge, Gerald
Radio boys series (3)
Radio boys seek the lost Atlantis
Breckenridge, Gerald
Radio boys series (5)
Radio boys to the rescue
Chapman, Allen
Radio boys series (13)
Radio boys trailing a voice
Chapman, Allen
Radio boys series (5)
Radio boys with the border patrol
Breckenridge, Gerald
Radio boys series (6)
Radio boys with the flood fighters
Chapman, Allen
Radio boys series (8)
Radio boys with the forest rangers
Chapman, Allen
Radio boys series (6)

Radio boys with the Iceberg Patrol
Chapman, Allen
Radio boys series (7)
Radio boys with the Revenue Guards
Breckenridge, Gerald
Radio boys series (4)
Radio crook
Hardinge, Rex
Sexton Blake series (665)
Radio detective
Escott, John
Radio series (2)
Reeve, Arthur Benjamin
Craig Kennedy series (22)
Radio detectives
Verrill, Alpheus Hyatt
Radio detectives series (1)
Radio detectives in the jungle
Verrill, Alpheus Hyatt
Radio detectives series (4)
Radio detectives southward bound
Verrill, Alpheus Hyatt
Radio detectives series (3)
Radio detectives under the sea
Verrill, Alpheus Hyatt
Radio detectives series (2)
Radio girls at Forest Lodge
Penrose, Margaret
Campfire girls series (4)
Radio girls series (4)
Radio girls of Roselawn
Penrose, Margaret
Campfire girls series (1)
Radio girls series (1)
Radio girls on Station Island
Penrose, Margaret
Campfire girls series (3)
Radio girls series (3)
Radio girls on the program
Penrose, Margaret
Campfire girls series (2)
Radio girls series (2)
Radio man
Farley, Ralph Milne
Miles Cabot series (1)
Radio pals fight the flood
Ludwig, Charles Shelton
Radio pals series (2)
Radio pals in the flaming forest
Ludwig, Charles Shelton
Radio pals series (5)
Radio pals in the hands of the Mau Mau
Ludwig, Charles Shelton
Radio pals series (4)
Radio pals marooned
Ludwig, Charles Shelton
Radio pals series (1)
Radio pals on Bar T Ranch
Ludwig, Charles Shelton
Radio pals series (3)
Radio planet
Farley, Ralph Milne
Miles Cabot series (3)
Radio reporters
Escott, John
Radio series (3)
Radio series (5)
Radio rescue
Escott, John
Radio series (6)
Radio studio murder
Wells, Carolyn
Fleming Stone series (47)
Radio trap
Escott, John
Radio series (4)
Radioactive camel affair
Leslie, Peter
Man from U.N.C.L.E. series (7)
Radish day jubilee
Bruce, Sheilah B
Fraggle Rock series (2)
Radish River caper
Spencer, Ross Harrison
Chance Purdue series (5)
Radium murders
Grant, Maxwell
Shadow series (131)
Radium profiteer
Philips, George Norman
Sexton Blake series (590)
Radius of doubt
Ingrid, Charles
Patterns of chaos series (1)
Radix
Attanasio, A A
Radix Tetrad series (1)
Radkin revenge
Roberts, Willo Davis
Black pearl series (5)
Radney Riding Club
Pullein-Thompson, Josephine
Major Holbrooke series (3)
Rafaella
McNeill, George
Deavors family series (2)
Rafe, the maverick
Hooper, Kay
Shamrock trilogy (3)
Rafferty
Partridge, Jenny
Oakapple Wood series (12)
Rafferty makes a landfall
Woodberry, Joan
Rafferty series (4)
Rafferty rides a winner
Woodberry, Joan
Rafferty series (3)
Rafferty takes to fishing
Woodberry, Joan
Rafferty series (1)
Rafferty's wife
Hooper, Kay
Hagen series (3)
Raffles
Fletcher, David
Raffles series (16)
Raffles after dark
Perowne, Barry
Raffles series (5)
Raffles and the key man
Perowne, Barry
Raffles series (13)
Rick Leroy series (4)
Raffles' crime in Gibraltar
Perowne, Barry
Raffles series (9)
Rick Leroy series (3)
Sexton Blake series (935)
Raffles in pursuit
Perowne, Barry
Raffles series (6)
Raffles of the Albany
Perowne, Barry
Raffles series (15)
Raffles of the M.C.C.
Perowne, Barry
Raffles series (17)
Raffles revisited
Perowne, Barry
Raffles series (14)
Raffles, the Amateur Cracksman
Hornung, Ernest William
Raffles series (1)
Raffles under sentence
Perowne, Barry
Raffles series (7)
Raffles versus Sexton Blake
Perowne, Barry
Raffles series (10)
Sexton Blake series (936)
Rafters were singing
De Lint, Charles
Cerin Songweaver series (7)
Raftmates
Munroe, Kirk
Mates series (4)
Rag Bag Clan
Barth, Richard
Margaret Binton series (1)
Rag doll called Galldora
Sedgwick, Modwena
Galldora series (3)
Rag doll press
Taylor, E J
Biscuits, buttons and pickles series (4)
Rag woman, rich woman
Davis, Margaret Thomson
Rag woman, rich woman series (1)
Raga Six
Lauria, Frank
Doctor Owen Orient series (2)
Ragamuffin mystery
Blyton, Enid
Barney series (6)
Ragdolly Anna
Kenward, Jean
Ragdolly Anna series (2)
Ragdolly Anna and the river picnic
Kenward, Jean
Ragdolly Anna series (4)
Ragdolly Anna goes to the fair
Kenward, Jean
Ragdolly Anna series (3)
Ragdolly Anna stories
Kenward, Jean
Ragdolly Anna series (1)
Ragdolly Anna's circus
Kenward, Jean
Ragdolly Anna series (6)
Ragdolly Anna's treasure hunt
Kenward, Jean
Ragdolly Anna series (7)
Rage
Mazzetti, Lorenza
Penny and Baby series (2)
Moffat, Gwen
Miss Melinda Pink series (11)
Smith, Wilbur Addison
Courtney family series (3)
Rage and desire
Arlen, Leslie
Borodin family series (5)
Rage for revenge
Gerrold, David
War against the Chtorr trilogy (3)
Rage in Babylon
Mitchell, Scott
Brock Devlin series (10)
Rage in Chupadera
Zollinger, Norman
Corey Lane series (2)
Rage in Harlem
Himes, Chester
Grave Digger Jones and Coffin Ed Johnson series (1)
Rage of heaven
Eller, John
Charlie Hope series (2)
Rage of maidens
Douglas, Lauren Wright
Caitlin Reece series (6)
Rage of McAllister
Chisholm, Matt
Rem McAllister series (14)
Rage of the innocent
Smith, Frederick Escreet
Innocent series (1)
Rage to kill
Lovell, B E
Edge Hannegan series (2)
Ragged astronauts
Shaw, Bob
Land and overland trilogy (1)
Ragged Dick
Alger, Horatio
Ragged Dick series (1)
Ragged plot
Barth, Richard
Margaret Binton series (2)
Ragged robin murders
Morton, Guy
Konrad Roque series (3)
Raggedy Andy stories
Gruelle, Johnny
Raggedy Ann series (2)
Raggedy Andy's surprise
Gruelle, Johnny
Raggedy Ann series (32)
Raggedy Ann
Fulton, Janet
Raggedy Ann series (39)
Raggedy Ann and Andy
Daly, Kathleen N
Raggedy Ann series (49)
Gruelle, Johnny
Raggedy Ann series (24)
Raggedy Ann and Andy and the camel with wrinkled knees
Gruelle, Johnny
Raggedy Ann series (3)
Raggedy Ann and Andy and the kindly rag man
Gruelle, Johnny
Raggedy Ann series (45)
Raggedy Ann and Andy and the nice fat policeman
Gruelle, Johnny
Raggedy Ann series (22)
Raggedy Ann and Andy and the rainy day circus
Hazen, Barbara Shook
Raggedy Ann series (43)
Raggedy Ann and Andy and Witchie Kissabye
Gruelle, Johnny
Raggedy Ann series (46)
Raggedy Ann and Andy's animal friends
Gruelle, Johnny
Raggedy Ann series (5)
Raggedy Ann and Andy's cookbook
Hazelton, Nika
Raggedy Ann's household series (1)
Raggedy Ann and Andy's green thumb book
Nelson, Alix R
Raggedy Ann's household series (2)
Raggedy Ann and Andy's merry adventures
Gruelle, Johnny
Raggedy Ann series (6)
Raggedy Ann and Andy's sunny stories
Gruelle, Johnny
Raggedy Ann series (4)
Raggedy Ann and Betsy Bonnet String
Gruelle, Johnny
Raggedy Ann series (23)
Raggedy Ann and Fido
Hazen, Barbara Shook
Raggedy Ann series (38)
Raggedy Ann and Marcella's frist day at school
Gruelle, Johnny
Raggedy Ann series (31)
Raggedy Ann and Raggedy Andy book
Sukus, Jan
Raggedy Ann series (44)
Raggedy Ann and the cookie snatcher
Hazen, Barbara Shook
Raggedy Ann series (42)
Raggedy Ann and the daffy taffy pull
Whalley, Dean
Raggedy Ann series (40)
Raggedy Ann and the golden butterfly
Gruelle, Johnny
Raggedy Ann series (16)
Raggedy Ann and the golden pebble
Gruelle, Johnny
Raggedy Ann series (14)
Raggedy Ann and the golden ring
Gruelle, Johnny
Raggedy Ann series (36)
Raggedy Ann and the happy meadow
Gruelle, Johnny
Raggedy Ann series (35)
Raggedy Ann and the hobby horse
Gruelle, Johnny
Raggedy Ann series (37)
Raggedy Ann and the hoppy toad
Gruelle, Johnny
Raggedy Ann series (17)
Raggedy Ann and the laughing brook
Gruelle, Johnny
Raggedy Ann series (18)
Raggedy Ann and the left-handed safety pin
Gruelle, Johnny
Raggedy Ann series (13)
Raggedy Ann and the paper dragon
Gruelle, Johnny
Raggedy Ann series (8)
Raggedy Ann and the sad and glad days
Carey, Mary Virginia
Raggedy Ann series (41)
Raggedy Ann and the slippery slide
Gruelle, Johnny
Raggedy Ann series (26)
Raggedy Ann and the wonderful witch
Gruelle, Johnny
Raggedy Ann series (34)
Raggedy Ann at the carnival
Thackray, Patricia
Raggedy Ann series (48)
Raggedy Ann at the end of the rainbow
Gruelle, Johnny
Raggedy Ann series (29)
Raggedy Ann goes sailing
Gruelle, Johnny
Raggedy Ann series (21)
Raggedy Ann helps Grandpa Hoppergrass
Gruelle, Johnny
Raggedy Ann series (19)
Raggedy Ann in Cookie Land
Gruelle, Johnny
Raggedy Ann series (11)
Raggedy Ann in the deep, deep woods
Gruelle, Johnny
Raggedy Ann series (10)
Raggedy Ann in the garden
Gruelle, Johnny
Raggedy Ann series (20)
Raggedy Ann in the magic book
Gruelle, Johnny
Raggedy Ann series (15)
Raggedy Ann in the Snow White castle
Gruelle, Johnny
Raggedy Ann series (25)
Raggedy Ann stories
Gruelle, Johnny
Raggedy Ann series (1)
Raggedy Ann's adventure
Gruelle, Johnny
Raggedy Ann series (28)
Raggedy Ann's alphabet book
Daly, Kathleen N
Raggedy Ann series (49)
Raggedy Ann's joyful songs
Gruelle, Johnny
Raggedy Ann's songs series (2)
Raggedy Ann's lucky pennies
Gruelle, Johnny
Raggedy Ann series (12)
Raggedy Ann's magical wishes
Gruelle, Johnny
Raggedy Ann series (9)
Raggedy Ann's merriest Christmas
Gruelle, Johnny
Raggedy Ann series (30)
Raggedy Ann's mystery
Gruelle, Johnny
Raggedy Ann series (27)
Raggedy Ann's number book
Daly, Kathleen N
Raggedy Ann series (49)
Raggedy Ann's sunny songs
Gruelle, Johnny
Raggedy Ann's songs series (1)
Raggedy Ann's sweet and dandy sugar candy fragrance bok
Thackray, Patricia
Raggedy Ann's household series (3)
Raggedy Ann's tea party
Gruelle, Johnny
Raggedy Ann series (33)
Raggedy Ann's wishing pebble
Gruelle, Johnny
Raggedy Ann series (7)
Raging of the deep
Draper, Alfred
Crispin Paton series (3)
Raging peace
Oakgrove, Artemis
Throne trilogy (1)
Raging rivers
Brady, Taylor
Kincaids series (1)
Raging seas, seering skies
Nicole, Christopher
United States Navy series (5)
Raging skies
Leslie, Richard
Victory trilogy (2)
Raging winds of heaven
Shiplett, June Lund
Winds series (1)
Ragman's city
Simon, Boris
Ragpickers series (2)
Rags and Buttons
Dutton, Lewis
Rags series (4)
Rags and Tuppence
Dutton, Lewis
Rags series (5)
Rags, M.D.
Dutton, Lewis
Rags series (1)
Rags, Tatters and Bill
Dutton, Lewis
Rags series (2)
Rags to riches
Pascal, Francine
Sweet Valley High series (16)
Rahab link
Mackenzie, J Alexander
Canaan trilogy (3)
Rahne
Coon, Susan
Living planet series (1)
Raid
Frison-Roche, Roger
Simon Sokki series (1)
Helm, Eric
Super Vietnam series (1)
O'Sullivan, James Brendan
Steve Silk series (11)
Raid a painted wagon
Grover, Marshall
Larry and Stretch series (170)
Raid of the Ottawa
Lange, Dietrich
American Indian series (10)
Raid on Nightmare Castle
McGuire, Catherine
Endless quest series (14)
Raid on Reichswald Fortress
Flynn, J J
Assault series (1)
Raid over England
Leslie, Norman
Jumbo Rutherford series (1)
Raider
Deveraux, Jude
Montgomery annals series (6)
Hardin, J D
Raider series (1)
Williams, Jon
Privateers and gentlemen series (3)
Raiders
Coburn, L J
Caleb Thorn series (2)
Crockett, Samuel Rutherford
Raiders series (1)
Early, Tom
Sons of Texas series (2)

Myers, Barry
Preacher's law series (7)
Robbins, Harold
Jonas Cord series (2)
Willoughby, Lee Davis
Making of America series (52)
Raiders at Medicine Bow
Field, Peter
Powder Valley series (59)
Raider's dawn
Hardy, Adam
Strike Force Falklands series (2)
Raiders from Whiskey Smith
Allen, Eric
Whiskey Smith series (4)
Raider's gold
Hardin, J D
Raider and Doc series (12)
Raider's hell
Hardin, J D
Raider and Doc series (9)
Raiders of Gor
Norman, John
Tarl Cabot series (6)
Raiders of Mars
Moore, Patrick
Maurice Gray series (5)
Raiders of Noomas
Nuetzel, Charles
Noomas series (2)
Raiders of Spanish Creek
Skinner, Mike
Luke Wyatt series (3)
Raiders of Spanish Peaks
Grey, Zane
Laramie Nelson series (1)
Raiders of the Fells
Waterhouse, Arthur
Fellside Farm series (1)
Raiders of the lost ark
Black, Campbell
Indiana Jones series (1)
Martin, Les
Indiana Jones series (1)
Raiders of the lost car park
Rankin, Robert
Ultimate truths trilogy (2)
Raiders of the revolution
Andrews, Keith William
Freedom's Rangers series (2)
Raiders of the Rio Grande
Scott, Bradford
Walt Slade series (66)
Raiders of the valley
Cole, Jackson
Jim Hatfield series (97)
Raiders passed!
Hunter, John
Sexton Blake series (1060)
Raider's revenge
Hardin, J D
Raider and Doc series (10)
Hogan, Ray
John Mosby series (2)
Raiding and trading
Birt, David
Tudors series (14)
Raiding with Morgan
Dunn, Byron Archibald
Young Kentuckians series (5)
Rail warriors
McCarthy, Gary
Derby Man series (9)
Railhead
Shane, Bart
Iron rails trilogy (3)
Railhead roundup
Gentry, Buck
Eli Holten series (22)
Railroad Arthur
Coren, Alan
Arthur series (4)
Railroad engineers and airplane pilots
Greene, Carla
What do they do series (4)
Railroad killers
Ellis, Wesley
Lone Star series (95)
Railroad king
Rothweiler, Paul Roger
Westward rails trilogy (1)
Railroad murder case
Laurenson, Robert Mark
Marc Jordan series (1)
Railroad renegades
Sharpe, Jon
Canyon O'Grady series (12)
Railroad robbers
Rey, Bret
Ned Butler series (3)
Railroad war
Croft, Jesse Taylor
Trainmasters series (2)
Railroads
Fisher, Leonard Everett
Nineteenth century America series (2)
Rails west
Shane, Bart
Iron rails trilogy (2)
Railway Cat
Arkle, Phyllis
Railway Cat series (1)
Railway Cat and Digby
Arkle, Phyllis
Railway Cat series (2)
Railway Cat and the horse
Arkle, Phyllis
Railway Cat series (4)
Railway Cat's secret
Arkle, Phyllis
Railway Cat series (3)
Railway map of the island of Sodor
Awdry, Wilbert
Sodor series (1)
Rain
McDowell, Michael M
Blackwater series (6)
Rain comes to Yamboorah
Ottley, Reginald Leslie
Yamboorah series (3)
Rain forest
Sperry, Armstrong
Chad Powell series (1)
Rain from the west
Ray, Mary
Early Christian series (5)
Rain, hail or shine
Hunt, Nan
Mrs Millie Mack trilogy (2)
Rain in Arnhem Land
Wells, Ann Elizabeth
Arnhem Land series (2)
Rain Island
Wood, James
James Fraser series (2)
Rain of doom
Stivers, Dick
Able Team series (16)
Rain of terror
Murphy, Warren Burton
Destroyer series (75)
Murray, Will
Destroyer series (75)
Rain, rain, go away!
Killingback, Julia
Busy Bears series (6)
Rain rustlers
Roderus, Frank
Carl Heller series (2)
Rain unravelled tales
Heylin, Clinton
Rain unravelled tales series (1)
Rain upon Godshill
Priestley, John Boynton
English journey series (3)
Rain with violence
Shannon, Dell
Lieutenant Luis Mendoza series (14)
Rainbird's revenge
Chesney, Marion
House for the season series (7)
Rainbow
Lawrence, David Herbert
Brangwen family series (1)
Rainbow abyss
Hambly, Barbara
Sun-cross series (1)
Rainbow affair
McDaniel, David
Man from U.N.C.L.E. series (13)
Rainbow after rain
Lambert, Janet
Tippy Parrish series (5)
Rainbow and Speedy
Hamilton, Esme
Speedy series (2)
Rainbow coloured shroud
Hedges, Joseph
John Stark series (5)
Rainbow comes and goes
Cooper, Diana Olivia Winifred Maud
Rainbow series (1)
Rainbow conspiracy
Lees, Dan
Jeff Plummer series (1)
Rainbow fields
Farrington, Liz
Mrs Murgatroyd series (3)
Rainbow Kid
Dexter, Ross
Duke Lawson series (3)
Rainbow promise
Gregory, Lisa
Rainbow season series (2)
Rainbow puzzle
Vivian, Evelyn Charles
Inspector Head series (10)
Rainbow riddle
Sutton, Margaret
Judy Bolton series (17)
Rainbow-seagreen case
Palmer, P K
Jedediah Killinger series (2)
Rainbow season
Gregory, Lisa
Rainbow season series (1)
Rainbow sword
Martine-Barnes, Adrienne
Chronique d'Avebury series (3)
Rainbow Trail
Grey, Zane
Mormon series (2)
Rainbow Valley
Montgomery, Lucy Maud
Avonlea series (8)
Rainbows
Berg, Leila
Small world series (5)
Rainbows are for everyone
Witcomb, Nan
Thoughts of Nanushka series (8)
Rainbow's End
Peters, Ellis
Inspector George Felse series (13)
Rainbow's journey
Abbott, Jacob
Rainbow and Lucky series (2)
Raincrow
Rushing, Jane Gilmore
Walnut Grove series (6)
Rainey Valley
Bosworth, Frank
Earl Morton series (2)
Raining cats and donkeys
Tovey, Doreen
Cats series (5)
Rainy city
Emerson, Earl W
Thomas Black series (1)
Rainy day diversions
Wells, Carolyn
Diversions series (1)
Rainy day Max
Turk, Hanne
Max the Mouse series (4)
Rainy picnic
Rogers, Pamela
Michael series (2)
Raise the roof beam, carpenter and Seymour
Salinger, Jerome David
Glass family series (3)
Raise the Titanic!
Cussler, Clive
Dirk Pitt series (4)
Raising a daughter
Elium, Don
Raising sons and daughters series (2)
Raising a riot
Toombs, Alfred
Raising a riot series (1)
Raising a son
Elium, Don
Raising sons and daughters series (1)
Raising demons
Jackson, Shirley
Savages series (2)
Raising Gordy Gorilla at the San Diego Zoo
Irvine, Georgeanne
Zoo world series (2)
Raising the dead
Simon, Roger Lichtenberg
Moses Wine series (6)
Raj quartet
Scott, Paul
British India quartet (4)
Raja the elephant
Rutley, Cecil Bernard
Wild life story series (8)
Rajah Amar
Myers, Leopold Hamilton
Prince Jali series (3)
Rajah of Ghanapore
Hill, Harry Egbert
Sexton Blake series (231)
Rajah of Monkey Island
Knight, Arthur Lee
Cormorant series (1)
Rajah's revenge
Murray, Andrew
Sexton Blake series (2)
Rajah's ruby
Carter, Nicholas
Nicholas Carter series (354)
Rajan
Lukeman, Tim
Lhas'kar series (1)
Rajbun's story
English, David
Bunburys series (7)
Rajpur
McClung, Robert Marshall
Endangered animals series (7)
Rakehell dynasty
Scott, Michael William
Rakehell dynasty series (1)
Rakehell Mountry
Hammand, Norman Bentley
Sir Nicholas Mountry series (1)
Rakehell's progress
Hammand, Norman Bentley
Sir Nicholas Mountry series (2)
Raker
Scott, Don
Raker series (1)
Rake's progress
Chesney, Marion
House for the season series (4)
Raking leaves with Max
Turk, Hanne
Max the Mouse series (9)
Raking of the embers
Whittaker, June Lovina
Henry and Susannah Kable series (1)
Raleigh's Eden
Fletcher, Inglis
Carolina series (4)
Rally cry
Forstchen, William R
Lost regiment series (1)
Rally to kill
Knox, Bill
Inspector Colin Thane and Phil Moss series (14)
Rally to the death
Rutherford, Douglas
Chequered flag series (3)
Rallying round Gussy
Clifford, Martin
Tom Merry series (3)
Ralph and the missing mail pouch
Chapman, Allen
Ralph Fairbanks of the railroad series (8)
Ralph and the train wreckers
Chapman, Allen
Ralph Fairbanks of the railroad series (10)
Ralph Darnell
Taylor, Philip Meadows
Indian history trilogy (2)
Ralph Fozbek and the amazing black hole patrol
Senn, Steve
Fozbek series (2)
Ralph in the switch tower
Chapman, Allen
Ralph Fairbanks of the railroad series (2)
Ralph of the roundhouse
Chapman, Allen
Ralph Fairbanks of the railroad series (1)
Ralph on the army train
Chapman, Allen
Ralph Fairbanks of the railroad series (6)
Ralph on the engine
Chapman, Allen
Ralph Fairbanks of the railroad series (3)
Ralph on the Midnight Flyer
Chapman, Allen
Ralph Fairbanks of the railroad series (7)
Ralph on the Mountain Division
Chapman, Allen
Ralph Fairbanks of the railroad series (9)
Ralph on the Overland Express
Chapman, Allen
Ralph Fairbanks of the railroad series (4)
Ralph on the railroad
Chapman, Allen
Ralph Fairbanks of the railroad series (4)
Ralph Osborn, midshipman at Annapolis
Beach, Edward Latimer, senior
Ralph Osborn series (1)
Ralph S Mouse
Cleary, Beverly
Ralph S Mouse series (3)
Ralph, the train dispatcher
Chapman, Allen
Ralph Fairbanks of the railroad series (5)
Ralstons
Crawford, Francis Marion
Lauderdale family series (2)
Paul Griggs series (4)
Ram of Sweetriver
Dann, Colin
Farthing Wood series (5)
Ram song
Webb, Sharon
Earth song trilogy (3)
Rama II
Clarke, Arthur Charles
Rama series (2)
Ramage
Pope, Dudley
Lord Nicholas Ramage series (1)
Ramage and the Dido
Pope, Dudley
Lord Nicholas Ramage series (18)
Ramage and the drumbeat
Pope, Dudley
Lord Nicholas Ramage series (2)
Ramage and the freebooters
Pope, Dudley
Lord Nicholas Ramage series (3)
Ramage and the guillotine
Pope, Dudley
Lord Nicholas Ramage series (6)
Ramage and the rebels
Pope, Dudley
Lord Nicholas Ramage series (9)
Ramage and the renegades
Pope, Dudley
Lord Nicholas Ramage series (12)
Ramage and the Saracens
Pope, Dudley
Lord Nicholas Ramage series (17)
Ramage at Trafalgar
Pope, Dudley
Lord Nicholas Ramage series (16)
Ramage touch
Pope, Dudley
Lord Nicholas Ramage series (10)
Ramage's challenge
Pope, Dudley
Lord Nicholas Ramage series (15)
Ramage's devil
Pope, Dudley
Lord Nicholas Ramage series (13)
Ramage's diamond
Pope, Dudley
Lord Nicholas Ramage series (7)
Ramage's mutiny
Pope, Dudley
Lord Nicholas Ramage series (8)
Ramage's prize
Pope, Dudley
Lord Nicholas Ramage series (5)
Ramage's signal
Pope, Dudley
Lord Nicholas Ramage series (11)
Ramage's trial
Pope, Dudley
Lord Nicholas Ramage series (14)
Rambo 3
Morrell, David
John Rambo series (4)
Rameses II and his time
Velikovsky, Immanuel
Ages in chaos series (5)
Ramillies and the union with Scotland
Trevelyan, George Macaulay
Queen Anne's England trilogy (2)
Ramona and her father
Cleary, Beverly
Ramona Quimby series (4)
Ramona and her mother
Cleary, Beverly
Ramona Quimby series (5)
Ramona forever
Cleary, Beverly
Ramona Quimby series (7)
Ramona Quimby, age 8
Cleary, Beverly
Ramona Quimby series (6)
Ramona Quimby diary
Cleary, Beverly
Ramona Quimby series (7)
Ramona the brave
Cleary, Beverly
Ramona Quimby series (3)
Ramona the pest
Cleary, Beverly
Ramona Quimby series (2)
Rampa story
Lobsang Rampa, Tuesday
Third eye series (3)

Rampage
Tralins, Sandor Robert
Black stud trilogy (2)
Black stud trilogy (3)
Rampage at Rico Bend
Grover, Marshall
Larry and Stretch series (118)
Rampage in Rio
Derrick, Lionel
Penetrator series (43)
Rampage in Whiskey Smith
Allen, Eric
Whiskey Smith series (5)
Rampole Place
Holt, Isabella
Rampole family series (1)
Ramsden
Mundy, Talbot
Indian trilogy (3)
Jimgrim series (2)
Ramseys
McLennan, Will
Ramseys series (1)
Ramsey's badge
McLennan, Will
Ramseys series (7)
Ramsey's gold
McLennan, Will
Ramseys series (5)
Ramsey's law
McLennan, Will
Ramseys series (13)
Ramsey's luck
McLennan, Will
Ramseys series (2)
Ramsey's revenge
McLennan, Will
Ramseys series (15)
Ramsgate paradox
Tall, Stephen
Stardust series (2)
Ran away to sea
Reid, Mayne
Ocean waifs series (1)
Ranch at Powder River
Cody, Al
Montana series (6)
Ranch Girls and the mystery of the three roads
Vandercook, Margaret
Ranch Girls series (9)
Ranch Girls and the silver arrow
Vandercook, Margaret
Ranch Girls series (8)
Ranch Girls and their great adventure
Vandercook, Margaret
Ranch Girls series (6)
Ranch Girls and their heart's desire
Vandercook, Margaret
Ranch Girls series (7)
Ranch Girls at boarding school
Vandercook, Margaret
Ranch Girls series (3)
Ranch Girls at home again
Vandercook, Margaret
Ranch Girls series (5)
Ranch Girls at Rainbow Lodge
Vandercook, Margaret
Ranch Girls series (1)
Ranch Girls in Europe
Vandercook, Margaret
Ranch Girls series (4)
Ranch Girls' pot of gold
Vandercook, Margaret
Ranch Girls series (2)
Ranch hands
Bryant, Bonnie
Saddle Club series (29)
Ranch of death
Buckman, Sam
Storm Jackson series (2)
Ranch on the beaver
Adams, Andy
Wells brothers series (2)
Rancher takes a wife
Hobson, Richmond Pearson
Rancher series (3)
Ranchero
Blackburn, Thomas Wakefield
Stanton Empire series (2)
Dawson, Clay
Long Rider series (21)
White, Stewart Edward
Andy Burnett series (2)
Ranchers
Willoughby, Lee Davis
Making of America series (14)
Rancher's blood
Lee, W W
Jefferson Birch series (3)
Rancher's gold
Buckman, Sam
Storm Jackson series (4)
Rand on Shuando
Brogan, Mike
Action Man series (7)
Randolph Cranstone and the glass thimble
Bullock, Michael
Randolph Cranstone series (1)
Randolph Cranstone and the pursuing river
Bullock, Michael
Randolph Cranstone series (1)
Randolph Cranstone and the veil of Maya
Bullock, Michael
Randolph Cranstone series (2)
Randolph Cranstone takes the inward path
Bullock, Michael
Randolph Cranstone series (3)
Random all round
Anderson, Oliver
Guy Random series (6)
Random at random
Anderson, Oliver
Guy Random series (5)
Random commentary
Whipple, Dorothy
Other day series (2)
Random death
Egan, Lesley
Vic Varallo series (12)
Random killer
Pentecost, Hugh
Pierre Chambrun series (14)
Random mating
Anderson, Oliver
Guy Random series (3)
Random rapture
Anderson, Oliver
Guy Random series (4)
Random rendezvous
Anderson, Oliver
Guy Random series (2)
Randy of the river
Alger, Horatio
Rise in life series (9)
Randy Starr above stormy seas
Martin, Eugene
Randy Starr series (2)
Randy Starr after an air prize
Martin, Eugene
Randy Starr series (1)
Randy Starr leading the air circus
Martin, Eugene
Randy Starr series (3)
Randy Starr tracing the air spy
Martin, Eugene
Randy Starr series (4)
Randy Warren, first term missionary
Palmer, Bernard
Career series (8)
Ranford goes fishing
White, Paul
Ranford series (3)
Ranford in flames
White, Paul
Ranford series (4)
Ranford mystery miler
White, Paul
Ranford series (1)
Range and Grange Hustlers at Chicago
Patchin, Frank Gee
Range and Grange Hustlers series (4)
Range and Grange Hustlers' greatest roundup
Patchin, Frank Gee
Range and Grange Hustlers series (2)
Range and Grange Hustlers on the Plains
Patchin, Frank Gee
Range and Grange Hustlers series (3)
Range and Grange Hustlers on the ranch
Patchin, Frank Gee
Range and Grange Hustlers series (1)
Range and trail
Sabin, Edward Legrand
Bar B boys series (2)
Range boss
Young, Gordon Ray
Red Clark series (5)
Range ghost
Scott, Bradford
Walt Slade series (65)
Range guardian
Tuttle, Gene
Silent Slade series (2)
Range justice
Wynne, Brian
Marshal Jeremy Six series (1)
Range killers
Sharpe, Jon
Trailsman series (41)
Range of No Return
Cole, Jackson
Jim Hatfield series (36)
Range rider
Scott, Bradford
Walt Slade series (3)
Range robbers
Strange, Oliver
Sudden series (1)
Range rodeo mystery
Scott, Dan
Bret King series (3)
Range terror
Scott, Bradford
Walt Slade series (25)
Range tramp
Newton, Dwight Bennett
Jim Bannister series (9)
Range war
Mason, Dan
Lex Cranshaw series (4)
McLennan, Will
Ramseys series (17)
Weston, Cole
Andrew Ryder series (9)
Range wolves
Borg, Jack
Hogleg Bailey series (13)
Rangeland guns
Scott, Bradford
Walt Slade series (34)
Rangeland Hercules
Edson, John Thomas
Floating Outfit series (14)
Ranger
Mason, Dan
Lex Cranshaw series (1)
Ranger Boys and the border smugglers
Labelle, Claude A
Ranger Boys series (1)
Ranger Boys and their reward
Labelle, Claude A
Ranger Boys series (2)
Ranger Boys find the hermit
Labelle, Claude A
Ranger Boys series (3)
Ranger Boys outwit the timber thieves
Labelle, Claude A
Ranger Boys series (4)
Ranger Boys to the rescue
Labelle, Claude A
Ranger Boys series (5)
Ranger daring
Scott, Bradford
Walt Slade series (114)
Ranger laughs at death
Scott, Bradford
Walt Slade series (87)
Ranger rides alone
Moore, Amos
Ranger series (1)
Ranger rides to death
Scott, Bradford
Walt Slade series (43)
Ranger, sea dog of the Royal Canadian Mounted Police
Strong, Charles Stanley
Ranger series (1)
Ranger to the rescue
Scott, Bradford
Walt Slade series (104)
Ranger wins
Scott, Bradford
Walt Slade series (115)
Ranger's Arctic patrol
Strong, Charles Stanley
Ranger series (2)
Rangers at bay
Scott, Bradford
Walt Slade series (35)
Ranger's honour
Masterson, Louis
Morgan Kane series (5)
Rangers is powerful hard to kill
Cameron, Caddo
Private Badger Coe and Sergeant Blizzard Wilson series (2)
Rangers of the Universe
Law, Winifred
Ralph Hannon series (2)
Rangers re-united
Miller, Jim
Ex-Rangers series (5)
Rangers' revenge
Miller, Jim
Ex-Rangers series (1)
Ranger's revenge
Scott, Bradford
Walt Slade series (50)
Ranger's round-up
Moore, Amos
Ranger series (2)
Ranger's roundup
Scott, Bradford
Walt Slade series (112)
Rangoon man
Carter, Nick
Nick Carter series (240)
Ranjit and the fire engines
Dhanjal, Beryl
Duets series (2)
Rank and riches
Marshall, Archibald
Clinton series (8)
Rannoch Chase
Vanner, Lyn
Rannoch series (1)
Ransom
Cleary, Jon
Scobie Malone series (3)
Masterson, Louis
Morgan Kane series (20)
Messmann, Jon
Jefferson Boone series (5)
Ransom for a nude
Black, Lionel
Superintendent Francis Foy series (2)
Ransom game
Engel, Howard
Benny Cooperman series (2)
Ransom on a redhead
Grover, Marshall
Nevada Jim series (60)
Ransom racket
Thayer, Lee
Peter Clancy series (25)
Ransom town
Alding, Peter
C.I.D. Room series (11)
Ransom trail
Fuller, Ed
Troubleshooters series (2)
Ransome revisited
Mace, Elisabeth
Swallowdale series (2)
Raoul Wallenberg, missing diplomat
Larsen, Anita
Histories mysteries series (4)
Rape
Trevor, Leslie
Policewoman series (1)
Rape is a no-no
Paul, F W
Man from S.T.U.D. series (6)
Rape of a city
Plievier, Theodor
World War II trilogy (3)
Rape of a quiet town
Lees, Dan
Jeff Plummer series (3)
Rape of a town
Daniels, Norman A
Kelly Carvel series (1)
Rape of Berlin
Baker, William Howard
Richard Quintain series (5)
Rape of Sun Lee Fong
Macao, Marshall
K'ing Kung-Fu series (3)
Rape of Tahiti
Dodd, Edward Howard
Ring of fire series (4)
Rape of the fair country
Cordell, Alexander
Mortymers series (2)
Rape of the rose
Hughes, Glyn
Anne Wylde series (2)
Rape of Venice
Wheatley, Dennis
Roger Brook series (6)
Raphael
Macavoy, Roberta Ann
Lute trilogy (3)
Rapid Robert and Hiss the snake
Reese, Bob
Critterland readers series (3)
Rapid Robert Road-Runner
Reese, Bob
Desert critterland series (3)
Rapido Clint
Edson, John Thomas
Cap Fog series (2)
Rapido Clint strikes back
Edson, John Thomas
Cap Fog series (7)
Rapids of Niagara
Warner, Susan Bagert
Bread and oranges series (2)
Rapist
Kenyon, Michael
Superintendent O'Malley series (5)
Rappaport
Lurie, Morris
Rappaport series (1)
Rappaport's revenge
Lurie, Morris
Rappaport series (2)
Raptor
Van Gieson, Judith
Neil Hamel series (2)
Raptor zone
Moffat, Gwen
Miss Melinda Pink series (12)
Rare coin score
Stark, Richard
Parker series (9)
Rare earth
Owen, Frank
Scobee Trent series (1)
Rascal of quality
Carter, Nicholas
Nicholas Carter series (540)
Rascals and Company
Carter, Nicholas
Nicholas Carter series (571)
Rascals in paradise
Michener, James Albert
South Pacific series (3)
Rasco and the rats of NIMH
Conly, Jane Leslie
NIMH series (2)
Rash reckless love
Sherwood, Valerie
Imogene and Georgiana series (2)
Rashanyn dark
Tedford, William G
Timequest trilogy (1)
Rasmus and the tramp
Lindgren, Astrid
Rasmus series (1)
Rasmus and the vagabond
Lindgren, Astrid
Rasmus series (1)
Rasp
Macdonald, Philip
Colonel Anthony Ruthven Gethryn series (1)
Raspberry jam
Wells, Carolyn
Fleming Stone series (11)
Raspberry tart affair
Halliday, Fred
Stanley Delphond series (2)
Rasselas
Johnson, Samuel
Rasselas series (1)
Rat
Bottome, Phyllis
Rat series (1)
Grass, Gunter
Danzig trilogy (3)
Rat-a-tat mystery
Blyton, Enid
Barney series (5)
Rat began to gnaw the rope
Grafton, Cornelius Warren
Gil Henry series (1)
Rat hunt
Jones, Olive
Barfield series (4)
Rat in a trap
Vinter, Michael
Barry Kegan series (2)
Rat Island
Macdonnell, James Edmond
Dutchy Holland series (18)
Rat on fire
Higgins, George Vincent
Jerry Kennedy series (3)
Rat Patrol
Daniels, Norman A
Rat Patrol series (1)
Rat-pit
Macgill, Patrick
Moleskin Joe series (2)
Rat run
Nolan, Frederick
Garrett dossier series (4)
Rat teeth
Giff, Patricia Reilly
Casey Valentine series (5)
Rat trap
Phillips, Tony
Turbo cowboys series (6)
Ratcatcher
Dunne, Colin
Joe Hussey series (2)

Ratchet hood
Marino, Tony
Widgets series (1)
Ratha and Thistle-Chaser
Bell, Clare
Ratha series (3)
Ratha's creature
Bell, Clare
Ratha series (1)
Rather a common sort of crime
Porter, Joyce
Honourable Constance Ethel Morrison-Burke series (1)
Rather a vicious gentleman
McAuliffe, Frank
Augustus Mandrell series (2)
Ratings are murder
Irvine, Robert Ralstone
Robert Christopher series (4)
Rational option
Wenger, Peter
Logic and order in society series (1)
Ratking
Dibdin, Michael
Aurelio Zen series (1)
Ratlesnake Ranch
Leighton, Robert
Sergeant Silk series (2)
Ratman's notebooks
Gilbert, Stephen
Ben and Willard series (1)
Rats
Herbert, James
Rats trilogy (1)
Rats' Alley
Garner, William
John Morpurgo trilogy (2)
Rats and gargoyles
Gentle, Mary
White crow series (1)
Rat's castle
Severy, Richard
Jinks Gang series (3)
Rats in New Guinea
Glassop, Lawson
Rats series (2)
Rats on the range, and other stories
Marshall, James
Rats series (2)
Rats on the roof, and other stories
Marshall, James
Rats series (1)
Rattle-rat
Van de Wetering, Janwillem
De Gier and Grijpstra series (10)
Rattler
Cassells, John
Superintendent Flagg series (12)
Cleary, Denis
Theodore J Cash series (2)
Rattler Gang
Fieldhouse, William
Klaw series (3)
Rattlesnake bandit
Scott, Bradford
Walt Slade series (51)
Rattlesnake Range
Pearce, Agatha Hunt
Edward, Frank and Gerry series (3)
Rattling of old bones
Ross, Jonathan
Superintendent George Rogers series (8)
Raum
Sherrell, Carl
Raum series (1)
Ravaged range
Field, Peter
Powder Valley series (28)
Ravagers
Hamilton, Donald
Matt Helm series (7)
Rave for a roughneck
Janson, Hank
Hank Janson series (8)
Rave settles a score
Mackenzie, Donald
Johnny Raven series (5)
Ravelston affair
Harrison, Elizabeth
Central London Hospital series (2)
Raven
Carroll, Shana
Paxton women series (2)
Raven after dark
Mackenzie, Donald
Johnny Raven series (6)
Raven and the Kamikaze
Mackenzie, Donald
Johnny Raven series (4)
Raven and the paperhangers
Mackenzie, Donald
Johnny Raven series (7)
Raven and the ratcatcher
Mackenzie, Donald
Johnny Raven series (3)
Raven feathers his nest
Mackenzie, Donald
Johnny Raven series (6)
Raven in flight
Mackenzie, Donald
Johnny Raven series (2)
Raven in the Foregate
Peters, Ellis
Brother Cadfael series (12)
Raven in the wind
Wiat, Philippa
Black Boar series (1)
Raven on the wing
Hooper, Kay
Hagen series (2)
Raven patrol of Bob's Hill
Burton, Charles Pierce
Bob's Hill series (6)
Raven seek thy brother
Maxwell, Gavin
Camusfearna trilogy (3)
Raven, swordsmistress of chaos
Kirk, Richard
Raven series (1)
Raven tree
Knowles, Anne
Matthew Ratton series (2)
Raven's causeway
Hodge, Charles
Jim Raine and Bob Wincourt series (1)
Raven's flight
Boucher, Alan Estcourt
Halli Thordason series (4)
Ravens' gathering
Taylor, Keith
Bard series (4)
Ravens in winter
Sibley, Patricia
Wandlemere series (2)
Raven's longest night
Mackenzie, Donald
Johnny Raven series (9)
Ravens of Blackwater
Marston, Edward
Gervase Bret and Ralph Delchard series (2)
Raven's revenge
Mackenzie, Donald
Johnny Raven series (8)
Ravens roost
Reese, Bob
Grand Canyon series (5)
Raven's shadow
Mackenzie, Donald
Johnny Raven series (10)
Ravensley touch
Heaven, Constance
Oliver Aylsham series (2)
Ravenswyke
White, Alan
Ravenswyke series (1)
Ravi Lancers
Masters, John
Bateman family series (1)
Raviola sneezes
Jellinek, Joanna
Georgina series (2)
Ravished earth
Wilson, Timothy R
Fenland series (2)
Ravishing of Lady Mary Ware
Wheatley, Dennis
Roger Brook series (10)
Raw deal
Janson, Hank
Hank Janson series (159)
Raw Deal
Standiford, Les
John Deal series (2)
Raw gold
Hendryx, James Beardsley
Black John series (1)
Raw Pearl
Bailey, Pearl
Pearl series (1)
Raw Pearl series (1)
Rawhide
Mitchum, Hank
Stage coach station series (30)
Rawhide and justice
Logan, Jake
John Slocum series (96)
Rawhide breed
Logan, Jake
John Slocum series (121)
Rawhide country
Fletcher, Farris
Texans series (1)
Rawhide Jezebel
Martin, Cort
Jared Bolt series (24)
Rawhide Rawlins rides again
Russell, Charles Marion
Rawhide Rawlins series (3)
Rawhide Rawlins stories
Russell, Charles Marion
Rawhide Rawlins series (1)
Rawhide redeemer
Gardner, Jerome
Dripspring series (8)
Rawhide rider
Field, Peter
Powder Valley series (51)
Rawhide River ambush
Grover, Marshall
Larry and Stretch series (7)
Rawhide tenderfoot
Borg, Jack
Hogleg Bailey series (9)
Rawhide woman
Martin, Cort
Jared Bolt series (7)
Rawhider
Shelton, Gene
Texas legends series (3)
Rawhiders
White, James G
Gunslick series (2)
Rawhider's woman
Fletcher, Dirk
Spur McCoy series (16)
Raxl, voodoo princess
Daniels, Dorothy
Strange paradise trilogy (3)
Ray of darkness
Evans, Margiad
Ray of darkness series (2)
Ray of doom
Sykes, William Stanley
Inspector Dennis Drury series (3)
Raymond Chandler omnibus
Chandler, Raymond
Philip Marlowe series (4)
Raymond Chandler's Philip Marlowe
Preiss, Byron
Philip Marlowe series (9)
Ray's daughter
King, Charles
Lieutenant Sandy Ray series (6)
Rays of darkness
Bamburg, Lilian
Septimus March series (2)
Ray's recruit
King, Charles
Lieutenant Sandy Ray series (5)
Razor edge
Blandy, Mary
Youth work series (1)
Razor's edge
Walker, Robert Wayne
Dean Grant series (2)
Re, colonised planet V, Shikasta
Lessing, Doris
Canopus in Argus archives series (1)
Reach for gold
Scott, Bradford
Walt Slade series (113)
Reach to eternity
Cosic, Dobrica
This land, this time series (3)
This land, this time series (4)
Reaching Colorado
Roderus, Frank
Harrison Wilke series (2)
Reaching hand
Mackenzie, Andrew
Nicholas Cornish series (4)
Read one
Burningham, John
Number play series (5)
Reader is warned
Dickson, Carter
Sir Henry Merrivale series (10)
Readiness at dawn
Blake
Fighter Station series (1)
Reading
Allington, Richard L
Beginning to learn series (14)
Ormerod, Jan
Baby books series (2)
Reading is kids' stuff
Baker, Ann
Kids' stuff series (2)
Reading, writing and remembering
Lucas, Edward Verrall
Ancestors series (1)
Ready about
Optic, Oliver
Boat builders series (6)
Ready, aim, die
Buck, Peter
Marc Dean series (6)
Ready for bed
Gretz, Susanna
Teddybear board book series (2)
Ready for blastoff!
North, Rick
Young Astronauts series (2)
Ready for take-off
Hamre, Leif
Peter Hovden series (3)
Ready-made family
Forest, Antonia
Marlow family series (7)
Ready or not
Stolz, Mary
Connor family series (1)
Ready, set, robot!
Hoban, Lillian
Robot series (1)
Ready, steady, go!
Watanabe, Shigeo
I can do it series (4)
Ready, Teddy go!
Ahlberg, Janet
Daisychain series (1)
Ready to burn
Daly, Carroll John
Satan Hall series (2)
Ready to go steady
Johnston, William
Happy days series (1)
Real Boyd
Brown, Carter
Danny Boyd series (32)
Real cool killers
Himes, Chester
Grave Digger Jones and Coffin Ed Johnson series (2)
Real dope
Lardner, Ring
Jack the Kaiser killer series (2)
Real folks
Whitney, Adeline Dutton Train
Girls series (2)
Real gone girls
Mark, Ted
Man from O.R.G.Y. series (4)
Real gone goose
Bagby, George
Inspector Schmidt series (30)
Real gone guy
Kane, Frank
Johnny Liddell series (10)
Real horror
Dixon, Franklin W
Hardy boys case files series (71)
Real serendipitous kill
Stone, Hampton
Jeremiah X Gibson series (13)
Real thing
Barrett, Robert G
Les Norton series (2)
Du Jardin, Rosamond
Tobey and Midge Heydon series (4)
Realist
Broch, Hermann
Sleepwalkers trilogy (3)
Reality barrier
Jadis, Donna
Star trek fan series (31)
Really cute corpse
Hess, Joan
Claire Malloy series (4)
Really, nurse
Brook, Roger
Nursing howlers series (1)
Really useful engines
Awdry, Christopher
Railway series (27)
Realm beneath
Clough, Brenda Wang
Averidan series (3)
Realm of chaos
Brennan, James Herbert
GrailQuest series (6)
Realm of doom
Grant, Maxwell
Shadow series (159)
Realm of the gods
Cooke, Catherine
Winged assassin trilogy (2)
Realm of the tri-planets
Scheer, Karl Herbert
Perry Rhodan series (31)
Realms of day
De Selincourt, Hugh
Constance Howard series (2)
Reap the bitter winds
Shiplett, June Lund
Winds series (2)
Reap the east wind
Cook, Glen
Dread Empire series (6)
Reap the harvest
Briggs, Victor
Way ahead trilogy (2)
Reap the whirlwind
Cherryh, Carolyn Janice
Sword of knowledge series (3)
Sword of knowledge trilogy (3)
Hougron, Jean
Monsieur Lastin series (1)
Reaper man
Pratchett, Terry
Discworld series (11)
Reaping the whirlwind
Carter, Nicholas
Nicholas Carter series (327)
Reardon
Pike, Robert L
Lieutenant Jim Reardon series (1)
Rearguard
Grier, Sydney Carlyon
Island series (1)
Reason for murder
Hocking, Anne
Inspector William Austen series (24)
Reason to kill
Zaremba, Eve
Helen Keremos series (1)
Reasonable man
Busby, Roger
Detective Inspector Leric series (4)
Reasonable world
Knight, Damon
CV trilogy (3)
Reavers of Skaith
Brackett, Leigh
Eric John Stark series (5)
Reawakening
Levi, Primo
Survival in Auschwitz series (2)
Rebecca
Borntrager, Mary Christner
Ellie's people series (2)
Du Maurier, Daphne
Rebecca De Winter series (1)
Francis, Jaye
Hot pursuit series (4)
Rebecca notebook
Du Maurier, Daphne
Rebecca De Winter series (1)
Rebecca of Sunnybrook Farm
Wiggin, Kate Douglas
Rebecca series (1)
Rebecca, the mysterious
Kimbrough, Katheryn
Phenwick women series (7)
Rebecca's brat
Bassett, Ronald
Margaret family series (3)
Rebecca's first year
Digby, Anne
Trebizon series (3)
Rebecca's pride
Douglass, Donald McNutt
Bolivar Manchenil series (1)
Rebel
Burton, Hester
Stephen Parkin series (1)
Myers, Barry
Preacher's law series (6)
Rebel and statesman
Schechtman, Joseph Boris
Vladimir Yabolinsky series (1)
Rebel angels
Davies, Robertson
Francis Cornish trilogy (1)
Rebel at the Chalet School
Brent-Dyer, Elinor Mary
Chalet School series (10)
Rebel attack
Grant, Mark
Mutants amok series (3)
Rebel brumby
Patchett, Mary Elwyn
Joey Meehan series (7)
Rebel dynasty
Busby, Francis Marion
Bran Tregare series (2)
Bran Tregare series (4)
Rebel for good
Kavanagh, Patrick Joseph
Scarf Jack series (2)
Rebel from Alphorion
Tallis, Robyn
Planet builders series (3)

Red desert
Evans, Tabor
Longarm series (137)
Red Devil of the Air Police
Noy, John
Rufus Deville series (1)
Red Diamond, private eye
Schorr, Mark
Red Diamond series (1)
Red dice
Lucas, Norman
Superintendent Bill Rowlands series (2)
Red domino
Sayer, Walter William
Sexton Blake series (257)
Red dragon
Curtis, Wade
Paul Crane series (2)
Rosenberger, Joseph
C.O.B.R.A. series (3)
Red dust
Helm, Eric
Ground Zero series (13)
Houston, David
Tales of tomorrow series (2)
Red dust of Africa
Simpson, Alyse
Rose in the sea series (2)
Red Dwarf
Naylor, Grant
Red Dwarf series (1)
Red dwarf
Symonds, Francis Addington
Sexton Blake series (255)
Red Dwarf omnibus
Naylor, Grant
Red Dwarf series (2)
Red Dwarf scripts
Naylor, Grant
Red Dwarf series (3)
Red Eagle
Ellis, Edward Sylvester
War chief series (3)
Red eagle
Holt, Gavin
Professor Luther Bastion series (8)
Red equinox
Axler, James
Deathlands series (9)
Red-Eye for the Baron
Morton, Anthony
Baron series (30)
Red eye of Betelgeuse
Darlton, Clark
Perry Rhodan series (40)
Red eyes of Kali
Jacobs, Thomas Curtis Hicks
Chief Inspector Barnard series (13)
Temple Fortune series (2)
Red file for Callan
Mitchell, James
David Callan series (1)
Red fire on the lost planet
Macvicar, Angus
Jeremy Grant series (4)
Red fire storm
Schmidt, Dan
Eagle Force series (4)
Red flame burning
Hawkins, Ward
Harry Borg series (1)
Red flame of Erinpura
Mundy, Talbot
Chullunder Ghose series (5)
Red flight two
Dank, Milton
Edward Burton series (2)
Red for adventure
Styles, Showell
Red Six series (1)
Red for murder
Kemp, Harold
Inspector James Brent series (6)
Red fury
Gilman, George G
Edge series (33)
Red gardenias
Latimer, Jonathan
Bill Crane series (5)
Red genesis
Sykes, Sondra Catharine
Next wave series (1)
Red god of tragedy
Carter, Nicholas
Nicholas Carter series (542)
Red grass
Young, Carter Travis
Cullom Blaine series (2)
Red greed
Roberts, Marion
Anne and David Layton series (1)
Red guard
Carter, Nick
Nick Carter series (21)
Red hair
Kyle, Sefton
Inspector J Rason series (6)
Red-haired brat
Dessau, Joanna
Elizabeth I trilogy (1)
Red-haired death
Horler, Sydney
Sir Harker Bellamy series (6)
Red-haired girl
Wells, Carolyn
Fleming Stone series (21)
Red hammer down
Hild, Jack
SOBS series (6)
Red-handed
Thayer, Lee
Peter Clancy series (20)
Red hart magic
Norton, Andre
Magic series (6)
Red harvest
Hammett, Dashiell
Continental Op series (1)
Red Hawk's account of Custer's last battle
Goble, Paul
Red Indian trilogy (1)
Red-headed dames and murder
Daniel, Roland
Michael Grant series (6)
Red-headed woman
Brush, Katharine
Lillian Legendre series (2)
Red heart of the Incas
Lewis, Jack
Sexton Blake series (88)
Red heifer
Davison, Frank Dalby
Man-Shy series (1)
Red heroin
Curtis, Wade
Paul Crane series (1)
Red herring
Lee, Robert
Fishy business series (5)
Tucker, Wilson
Charles Horne series (5)
Red herring murder
Westbrook, Perry Dickie
Doctor Samuel Cutting series (2)
Red herrings
Heald, Tim
Simon Bognor series (8)
Hyne, Charles John Cutcliffe
Captain Owen Kettle series (13)
Morris, Dave
Teenage mutant ninja turtles series (3)
Red hills
Marvin, James W
Crow series (1)
Red holocaust
Axler, James
Deathlands series (2)
Red horse caper
Roper, Lester V
Jerry Roe series (1)
Red Horse Hill
Meader, Stephen Warren
Cedar series (1)
Red horseman
Coonts, Stephen
Jake Grafton series (5)
Red hot and dangerous
Geller, Michael
Bud Dugan series (4)
Red hot and morgue bound
Brody, Marc
Marc Brody series (61)
Red hot ice
Kane, Frank
Johnny Liddell series (9)
Red hot roundup
Hunter, E J
Headhunter series (10)
Red House
Balzac, Honore de
Philosophic studies series (15)
Red house
Lambert, Derek
Angels in the snow series (2)
Red House children at Grafton
Douglas, Amanda Minnie
Little Red House children series (2)
Red House children growing up
Douglas, Amanda Minnie
Little Red House children series (5)
Red House Children's vacation
Douglas, Amanda Minnie
Little Red House children series (3)
Red House Children's year
Douglas, Amanda Minnie
Little Red House children series (4)
Red idol
Greene, L Patrick
Aubrey Saint John Major series (4)
Red in the morning
Yates, Dornford
Jonah Mansel series (11)
Richard Chandos series (8)
Red Inn
Balzac, Honore de
Philosophic studies series (15)
Red iron nights
Cook, Glen
Garrett series (6)
Red is for killing
Bagby, George
Inspector Schmidt series (9)
Red is for murder
Meyers, Martin
Patrick Hardy series (3)
Red is for shrouds
Taylor, Mary Ann
Emil Martin series (1)
Red Jaguar
Manor, Jason
Steve Summers series (2)
Red journey
Cross, John Keir
Albatross series (2)
Red King syndrome
Moore, Alan
Miracleman series (2)
Red kite clue
Jerome, Owen Fox
Philip Maccray series (2)
Red knight
Chance, John Newton
John Newton Chance series (2)
Mister DeHavilland series (4)
Superintendent Black series (4)
Red lady
Wynne, Anthony
Doctor Eustace Hailey series (20)
Red Lawsons and the sons of the desert
Leyland, Eric
Red Lawson series (5)
Red League
Carter, Nicholas
Nicholas Carter series (251)
Red letter holiday
Pye, Virginia
Price family series (1)
Red lilac
Gorell, Ronald Gorell Barnes
Evelyn Temple series (3)
Harry Farrant series (2)
Red limit freeway
De Chancie, John
Skyway trilogy (2)
Red magic
Rabe, Jean
Harpers series (3)
Red mammon
Learmonth, David
Silas Wortenheimer series (2)
Red man contract
McCray, Mike
Black Berets series (7)
Red marauders
Cole, Jackson
Jim Hatfield series (71)
Red Mars
Robinson, Kim Stanley
Mars series (1)
Red mask
Hope, Stanton
Sexton Blake series (658)
Makin, William James
Inspector Evans series (2)
Red masquerade
Vance, Louis Joseph
Michael Lanyard series (4)
Red men of Mars
Fearn, John Russell
Clayton Drew series (3)
Red menace
Grant, Maxwell
Shadow series (4)
Red mirror mystery
Lane, Gret
Inspector Hook series (2)
Red moon
Robeson, Kenneth
Avenger series (26)
Red moon and black mountain
Chant, Joy
Vanderi series (2)
Red mountain
Sayer, Walter William
Sexton Blake series (204)
Red mouse
Osborne, William Hamilton
William Murgatroyd series (1)
Red Muffin book
Hogarth, Ann
Muffin book series (1)
Red Munch Bunch word book
Reed, Giles
Munch Bunch word book series (2)
Red music
Skvorecky, Josef
Danny Smiricky series (4)
Red nails
Howard, Robert Ervin
Conan series (21)
Red net
Jacobs, Thomas Curtis Hicks
Jim Malone series (2)
Red o' the feud
Sutcliffe, Halliwell
Wayne and Ratcliffe series (2)
Red of the Redfields
Richmond, Grace Smith
Red Pepper Burns series (5)
Red on Wight
Winsor, Diana
Tavy Martin series (1)
Red palgue
Carter, Nicholas
Nicholas Carter series (585)
Red Patrol
Leighton, Robert
Red Patrol series (2)
Red pavilion
Gulik, Robert van
Judge Dee series (7)
Red pawns
Griswold, George
Mister Groode series (3)
Wibberley, Leonard
Treegate family trilogy (5)
Red people of the wooded country
Deming, Therese
Indian life series (3)
Red Pepper Burns
Richmond, Grace Smith
Red Pepper Burns series (1)
Red Pepper returns
Richmond, Grace Smith
Red Pepper Burns series (6)
Red Pepper's patients
Richmond, Grace Smith
Red Pepper Burns series (3)
Red plague in Bolivia
Macao, Marshall
K'ing Kung-Fu series (5)
Red planet
Chilton, Charles
Jet Morgan series (2)
Red Plume
Williams, Edward Huntington
Red Plume series (1)
Red Plume returns
Williams, Edward Huntington
Red Plume series (2)
Red Plume with the Royal Northwest Mounted
Williams, Edward Huntington
Red Plume series (3)
Red plush
McCrone, Guy
Moorhouse family trilogy (1)
Red prophet
Card, Orson Scott
Alvin Maker series (2)
Red queen, white queen
Treece, Henry
Early Britain series (3)
Red Rackham's treasure
Herge
Tintin series (12)
Red Radford and Operation Kidnap
Robb, John
Red Radford series (2)
Red Radford and the Black Legion
Robb, John
Red Radford series (1)
Red Radford and the Iron Guard
Robb, John
Red Radford series (3)
Red Randall at Midway
Bowen, Robert Sidney
Red Randall series (1)
Red Randall at Pearl Harbor
Bowen, Robert Sidney
Red Randall series (3)
Red Randall in Burma
Bowen, Robert Sidney
Red Randall series (4)
Red Randall in the Aleutians
Bowen, Robert Sidney
Red Randall series (5)
Red Randall on New Guinea
Bowen, Robert Sidney
Red Randall series (2)
Red Randall's one-man war
Bowen, Robert Sidney
Red Randall series (6)
Red rays
Carter, Nick
Nick Carter series (41)
Red rebellion
Carter, Nick
Nick Carter series (54)
Red Red Baron
Innes, Brian
Red Baron series (2)
Red revenge
Pearce, Charles Edward
Indian mutiny trilogy (2)
Ralston, Gilbert Alexander
Dakota series (2)
Red River
Gilman, George G
Edge series (6)
Red river
Hawkins, Jack
Chopper series (4)
Red River desperadoes
Duncan, Terence
Powell's army series (6)
Red river guns
Hobart, Donald Bayne
Masked Rider and Blue Hawk series (14)
Red River revenge
Boone, James Calder
Ned Remington series (7)
Sharpe, Jon
Trailsman series (33)
Red River showdown
Cole, Jackson
Jim Hatfield series (45)
Red River story
Silver, Alfred
Red River trilogy (1)
Red River to Appomattox
Foote, Shelby
Civil War trilogy (3)
Red road
Harvester, Simon
Asia in turmoil series (14)
Dorian Silk series (4)
Red road to vengeance
Scott, Bradford
Walt Slade series (91)
Red Rock redhead
Fletcher, Dirk
Spur McCoy series (13)
Red room
Mallet-Joris, Francoise
Helene series (2)
Strindberg, Johan August
Soul's development trilogy (3)
Red rope
Gerard, Francis
Sir John Meredith series (5)
Red Rosa
Collins, Michael
Dan Fortune series (13)
Red rose of Anjou
Plaidy, Jean
Plantagenet series (13)
Red roses dying
Maynard, Nan
Frewin family series (2)
Red rosette
Brims, Bernagh
Ballyreagh Jumping Team series (2)
Red runs of the Rio
Cole, Jackson
Jim Hatfield series (70)
Red rust of death
Audemars, Pierre
Monsieur Pinaud series (26)
Red Ryder and the adventure of Chimney Rock
Thomas, H C
Red Ryder series (3)
Red Ryder and the Gun-Smoke gold
McGill, Jerry
Red Ryder series (6)
Red Ryder and the mystery of the whispering walls
Winterbotham, Russell Robert
Red Ryder series (1)
Red Ryder and the riddle of Roaring Range
McGill, Jerry
Red Ryder series (5)

Red Ryder and the secret of the Lucky Mine
Smith, Carl W
Red Ryder series (4)
Red Ryder and the secret of Wolf Canyon
Stevens, S S
Red Ryder series (2)
Red Ryder and the Thunder Trail
McGill, Jerry
Red Ryder series (7)
Red sabbath
Weaver, Graham
Saint series (48)
Red Saunders, his adventures west and east
Phillips, Henry Wallace
Red Saunders series (1)
Red Saunders' pets and other critters
Phillips, Henry Wallace
Red Saunders series (4)
Red Scar
Wynne, Anthony
Doctor Eustace Hailey series (6)
Red Sea patrol
Keddell, Jim
Brockleby series (2)
Red Sea rescue
Catherall, Arthur
Bulldog tugboat series (13)
Red Sea sharks
Herge
Tintin series (19)
Red seal
Lincoln, Natalie Sumner
Detective Ferguson series (1)
Red Shadow
Hogan, Robert Jasper
Secret Six series (1)
Red shadows
Howard, Robert Ervin
Solomon Kane series (1)
Red shift
Nichols, Robert
Daily lives in Nghsi-Altai series (1)
Red signal
Carter, Nicholas
Nicholas Carter series (107)
Red skull
Robeson, Kenneth
Doc Savage series (17)
Red sky
Harper, Theodore Acland
Siberian series (4)
Red snow
Robeson, Kenneth
Doc Savage series (38)
Red snow at Darjeeling
Blochman, Lawrence Goldtree
Inspector Leonidas Prike series (3)
Red spider
Brooks, Edwy Searles
Sexton Blake series (11)
Robeson, Kenneth
Doc Savage series (95)
Red spinner
Snell, Edmund
Reggie Faulkner series (2)
Red Square
Smith, Martin Cruz
Arkady Renko series (3)
Topol, Edward
Shamrayev series (1)
Wood, Andrew
Koregorvsky series (2)
Sasha series (1)
Red squirrel twins
Tompkins, Jane
Animal twins series (6)
Red stain
Abdullah, Achmed
Red stain series (1)
Red star over China
Snow, Edgar
Red China series (1)
Red stilleto
Skene, Anthony
Sexton Blake series (720)
Red stockings
Fry, Pete
Pete Fry series (7)
Red story book
Blyton, Enid
Colour story book series (2)
Red sun of Darkover
Bradley, Marion Zimmer
Darkover anthologies series (4)
Red sun of Nippon
Yardley, Herbert Osborn
Mister Greenleaf series (2)
Red symbol
Ironside, John
Detective Inspector John Freeman series (1)
Red tape murders
Verner, Gerald
Superintendent Robert Budd series (21)
Red tapeworm
Mackenzie, Compton
Oliver Huffam series (1)
Red tassel
Dodge, David
Al Colby series (3)
Red terrors
Robeson, Kenneth
Doc Savage series (83)
Red thirst
Pringle, David
Warhammer series (4)
Red thumb mark
Freeman, Richard Austin
Doctor John Evelyn Thorndyke series (1)
Red top tramp
Hunter, E J
White Squaw series (14)
Red trail of a point forty-one
Tuttle, Wilbur Coleman
Hashknife Hartley and Sleepy Stevens series (32)
Red trance
Zimmerman, R D
Maddy and Alex Phillips series (3)
Red triangle
Carter, Nicholas
Nicholas Carter series (436)
Morrison, Arthur
Martin Hewitt series (4)
Red university
Piccard, Eulalie
Episodes of the great Russian tragedy series (2)
Red van mystery
Chester, Gilbert
Sexton Blake series (1155)
Red vengeance
Hild, Jack
SOBS series (14)
Red, white and blue mystery
Hope, Laura Lee
Bobbsey twins series (64)
Red widow murders
Dickson, Carter
Sir Henry Merrivale series (4)
Red-winged angel
Mackinnon, Allan
Mike Darroch series (1)
Red winter
Cormany, Michael
Dan Kruger series (2)
Redcap
McCutchan, Philip
Commander Esmonde Shaw series (2)
Redcoat spy
Redmayne, John
Peter Maclean series (1)
Reddy Fox leaves in a hurry
Burgess, Thornton Waldo
Animal stories series (4)
Reddy Fox series (1)
Reddy Fox's sudden engagement
Burgess, Thornton Waldo
Animal stories series (4)
Reddy Fox series (1)
Reddy or not
Zacharia, Irwin
Irving Martin Reddy series (3)
Redeemers
Matthews, Clayton
Moraghan family trilogy (3)
Redemption
McGown, Jill
Chief Inspector Lloyd and Sergeant Judy Hill series (2)
Redemption of light
O'Neal, Kathleen M
Powers of light series (3)
Redfields
Richmond, Grace Smith
Red Pepper Burns series (5)
Redgate gold
Slade, Jack
Lassiter series (30)
Redhead
Creasey, John
Department Z series (2)
Redhead for danger
Maclean, Arthur
Sexton Blake series (1452)
Redhead for free
McCall, K T
Johnny Buchanan series (4)
Redhead for Mike Shayne
Halliday, Brett
Michael Shayne series (48)
Redhead of Aztec Wells
Tuttle, Wilbur Coleman
Hashknife Hartley and Sleepy Stevens series (33)
Redheads are poison
Winter, Bevis
Steve Craig series (1)
Redheads at the Chalet School
Brent-Dyer, Elinor Mary
Chalet School series (52)
Redheads cool fast
Winter, Bevis
Steve Craig series (2)
Redheads of Windyridge
Mathews, M E
Cloud family series (1)
Redheap
Lindsay, Norman
Redheap trilogy (1)
Rediscovered!
Coleman, Clay
Lost Island series (4)
Redman Cave murder
Barker, Elsa
Dexter Drake series (3)
Redolmo affair
Carter, Nick
Nick Carter series (126)
Redoubtable Dexter
Hackforth-Jones, Gilbert
Paul Dexter series (6)
Reds and Blues
Hardcastle, Michael
Tony and Jay series (4)
Reds of the Midi
Gras, Felix
French Revolution trilogy (1)
Redshank's warning
Saville, Malcolm
Jillies series (1)
Redskin raiders
Risteen, H L
Red Indian series (5)
Redskin rosebud
Hunter, E J
White Squaw series (16)
Redskin thrust
Gentry, Buck
Eli Holten series (18)
Redskins
Cooper, James Fenimore
Littlepage manuscript trilogy (3)
Redundancy pay
Anderson, John Richard Lane
Major Peter Blair series (6)
Redwall
Jacques, Brian
Redwall series (3)
Redwall trilogy
Jacques, Brian
Redwall series (4)
Redwood raiders
Evans, Tabor
Longarm series (132)
Redwood revenge
Sharpe, Jon
Trailsman series (121)
Reece patrol
Hardy, Adam
Strike Force Falklands series (4)
Reeds and mud
Blasco Ibanez, Vicente
Valencia series (5)
Reeds in the wind
Carthew, Heather Jean
Reeds series (2)
Reedy's mirror
Ford, Webster
Spoon River series (1)
Reef
Stafford-Deitsch, Jeremy
Ocean series (2)
Reefs
O'Donnell, Kevin
Journeys of McGill Feighan series (2)
Reefs of space
Pohl, Frederik
Plan of man trilogy (1)
Reel murder
Babson, Marian
Trixie Dolan and Evangeline Sinclair series (1)
Reel of death
Simons, Roger
Inspector Fadiman Wace series (14)
Reel thrills
Dixon, Franklin W
Hardy boys series (127)
Re-elect Nutty!
Hughes, Dean
Nutty Nutsell series (8)
Reeling earth
Millin, Sarah Gertrude
War diary series (3)
Re-enter Arnholt
Latta, Gordon
Arnholt series (2)
Re-enter Doctor Fu-Manchu
Rohmer, Sax
Fu-Manchu series (13)
Re-enter Fu-Manchu
Rohmer, Sax
Fu-Manchu series (13)
Re-enter Sir John
Dane, Clemence
Sir John Saumerez series (3)
Re-enter the blithe sheriff
Buckley, Frederick Robert
Blithe sheriff series (2)
Refining Felicity
Chesney, Marion
School of manners series (1)
Reflected glory
Cooper, Charles
Russell Cavendish series (1)
Reflections
Roberts, Nora
Flowers series (6)
Reflections on a marine Venus
Durrell, Lawrence
Island series (2)
Reform
Frankland, Edward
Retreat series (2)
Reformation of Royce Remington
Graydon, William Murray
Sexton Blake series (47)
Reforming the Fourth
Chaundler, Christine
Fourth Form series (5)
Refuge
Chilson, Rob
Robot city series (5)
Refugee
Anthony, Piers
Bio of a space tyrant series (1)
Regaining compassion for humanity and nature
Birch, Louis Charles
Science and religion series (2)
Regan
Martin, Ian Kennedy
Sweeney series (1)
Regan and the bent stripper
Balham, Joe
Sweeney series (7)
Regan and the blag
Balham, Joe
Sweeney series (10)
Regan and the deal of the century
Martin, Ian Kennedy
Sweeney series (3)
Regan and the high rollers
Balham, Joe
Sweeney series (9)
Regan and the human pipeline
Balham, Joe
Sweeney series (5)
Regan and the Lebanese shipment
Balham, Joe
Sweeney series (4)
Regan and the Manhattan file
Martin, Ian Kennedy
Sweeney series (2)
Regan and the snout who cried wolf
Balham, Joe
Sweeney series (6)
Regan and the Venetian virgin
Balham, Joe
Sweeney series (8)
Regarding Sherlock Holmes
Derleth, August
Solar Pons series (1)
Regatta mystery
Christie, Agatha
Hercule Poirot series (38)
Miss Jane Marple series (14)
Regency
Harrod-Eagles, Cynthia
Morland family series (13)
Regency buck
Heyer, Georgette
Judith Taverner Worth series (1)
Regency charade
Mansfield, Elizabeth
Regency series (3)
Regency match
Mansfield, Elizabeth
Regency series (2)
Regency rake
Hardwick, Michael
Thomas Rodolfo Rackstraw series (2)
Regency revels
Hardwick, Michael
Thomas Rodolfo Rackstraw series (4)
Regency revenge
Hardwick, Michael
Thomas Rodolfo Rackstraw series (3)
Regency royal
Hardwick, Michael
Thomas Rodolfo Rackstraw series (1)
Regency sting
Mansfield, Elizabeth
Regency series (1)
Regency wager
Mansfield, Elizabeth
Regency series (4)
Regeneration
Barker, Pat
Billy Prior series (1)
Haggard, Henry Rider
Salvation Army series (2)
Svevo, Italo
Zeno series (2)
Regent
Bennett, Arnold
Five towns series (12)
Regent Square
Bramble, Forbes
Kelleway family series (1)
Regent Street raid
Brandon, John Gordon
Arthur Stukeley Pennington series (10)
Inspector Patrick Aloysius McCarthy series (20)
Regent's daughter
Dumas, Alexandre
Regency trilogy (2)
Plaidy, Jean
Georgian series (9)
Reggis Arms caper
Spencer, Ross Harrison
Chance Purdue series (2)
Regiment
Dalmas, John
Regiment series (1)
Skelton, Clement Lister
Maclaren family series (2)
Regimental legends
Winter, John Strange
Bootles series (2)
Regiment's war
Dalmas, John
Regiment series (4)
Regina Blue
Mark, Ted
Man from O.R.G.Y. series (20)
Regina versus Rumpole
Mortimer, John
Horace Rumpole series (4)
Reginald
Saki
Reginald series (1)
Reginald in Russia
Saki
Reginald series (2)
Regina's legacy
Pascal, Francine
Sweet Valley High series (73)
Regretting it
Chapman, Jennifer
Long weekend series (2)
Regulator
Colter, Dale
Regulator series (1)
Rehearsal for murder
Carlson, Patricia McEvoy
Maggie Ryan series (4)
Rehearsal for the funeral
Colter, Eli
Pat Campbell series (3)
Rehearsals for murder
Ferrars, E X
Toby Dyke series (2)
Reich Four
Carter, Nick
Nick Carter series (132)
Reign of fire
Kellogg, Marjorie Bradley
Lear's daughters series (2)
Reign of Queen Bea
Michaels, Angela
Caged women series (5)

Reign of Terror
Dumas, Alexandre
Marie Antoinette series (5)
Reign of terror
Marter, Ian
Doctor Who series (119)
Richmond, Philip
Duke Renny series (2)
Reilly, ace of spies
Lockhart, Robin Bruce
Reilly series (1)
Reilly, the first man
Lockhart, Robin Bruce
Reilly series (2)
Reilly's return
Hoag, Tami
Rainbow chasers series (3)
Reincarnation in Venice
Ehrlich, Max
Peter Proud series (2)
Reincarnation of Peter Proud
Ehrlich, Max
Peter Proud series (1)
Reindeer boy
Braenne, Berit
Torris series (2)
Reindeer girl
Ruthin, Margaret
Elli Sari series (1)
Reindeer moon
Thomas, Elizabeth Marshall
Reindeer moon series (1)
Reindeer people
Lindholm, Megan
Reindeer people series (1)
Reindeer twins
Tompkins, Jane
Animal twins series (10)
Reinhart in love
Berger, Thomas
Carlo Reinhart series (2)
Reinhart's women
Berger, Thomas
Carlo Reinhart series (4)
Rejected bride
Southworth, Emma Dorothy Eliza Nevitte
Gertrude Haddon trilogy (2)
Rejects
Aaseng, Nathan
Inside business series (4)
Relative distance
Lewis, Royston
Inspector John Crow series (12)
Relative murder
Hocking, Anne
Inspector William Austen series (27)
Relative to murder
Warman, Erik
Inspector John Isidore Bloom series (1)
Relative to poison
Lorac, E C R
Inspector Macdonald series (29)
Relatively dangerous
Jeffries, Roderic Graeme
Inspector Enrique Alvarez series (11)
Released for death
Wade, Henry
John Bragg series (2)
Relentless
Garfield, Brian Wynne
Sam Watchman series (1)
Relentless marriage
Lambert, Mortan
Relentless marriage series (1)
Relic of empire
Gear, William Michael
Forbidden borders series (2)
Religion and the sexual life
Pendleton, Don
Sexual life series (2)
Religion in Roman Britain
Birt, David
Roman Britain series (7)
Religious body
Aird, Catherine
Inspector C D Sloan series (1)
Religious conviction
Stockley, Grif
Gideon Page series (3)
Religious difficulties
Housman, Laurence
Palace plays series (3)
Religious life
Hinnebusch, Paul
Religious life series (1)
Reluctant agent
Chance, John Newton
Jonathan Blake series (47)
Reluctant Alice
Naylor, Phyllis Reynolds
Alice series (3)
Reluctant assassin
Dark, James
Mark Kingsley Hood series (15)
Godey, John
Jack Albany series (1)
Reluctant cloak and dagger man
Paul, Ernest
George Barclay series (6)
Reluctant dragon
Grahame, Kenneth
Smith family series (2)
Reluctant executioner
Marsh, John
Simon Luck series (1)
Reluctant ghost
Allen, Sheila Rosalynd
Lovers of Steadford Abbey series (1)
Reluctant gunman
Baker, William Howard
Sexton Blake series (1534)
Reluctant healer
Macmillan, William John
Faith healing series (2)
Reluctant heart
Lambert, Janet
Penny Parrish series (6)
Reluctant heiress
Coxe, George Harmon
Kent Murdock series (20)
Laine, Annabel
Earl of Moriston series (1)
Reluctant hostess
Janson, Hank
Hank Janson series (111)
Reluctant king
De Camp, Lyon Sprague
Jorian series (4)
Reluctant nightingale
Lock, Joan
Lady policeman series (2)
Reluctant nurse
Linton, Cathy
Saint Lawrence's Hospital series (4)
Reluctant odyssey
Pargeter, Edith
Eighth champion of Christendom trilogy (2)
Reluctant rebel
Van de Water, Frederic Franklin
American Revolution series (1)
Reluctant Ronin
Melville, James
Superintendent Tetsuo Otani series (10)
Reluctant spy
Blackburn, John
General Charles Kirk series (1)
Laflin, Jack
Gregory Hiller series (4)
Reluctant swordsman
Duncan, Dave
Seventh sword trilogy (1)
Reluctant vampire
Morecambe, Eric
Reluctant vampire series (1)
Remain to be seen
Cumberland, Marten
Saturnin Dax series (28)
Remains to be seen
Hart, Roy
Detective Superintendent Roper series (4)
Remarkable adventures of Cuthbert the Caterpillar and Wilfred the Wasp
Gilmore, David Hunter
Christopher Cricket series (1)
Rembrandt file
Banks, Oliver
Amos Hatcher series (1)
Rembrandt panel
Banks, Oliver
Amos Hatcher series (1)
Remember and be glad
Asquith, Cynthia
Remember series (2)
Remember Gettysburg!
Randle, Kevin
Remember trilogy (2)
Remember Maybelle?
Brown, Carter
Rick Holman series (33)
Remember me
Stacton, David
Invincible questions trilogy (1)
Stanton, David
Invincible questions series (1)
Remember Mister Bear
Kuratomi, Chizuko
Mister Bear series (1)
Remember Russia, 1915-1925
Fen, Elisaveta
Russia series (3)
Remember that face!
Findley, Ferguson
Johnny Malone series (2)
Remember the Alamo
Fletcher, Farris
Texans series (2)
Randle, Kevin
Remember trilogy (1)
Remember the island
Trent, Trisha
Kylie series (2)
Remember the Little Bighorn!
Randle, Kevin
Remember trilogy (3)
Remember to kill me
Pentecost, Hugh
Pierre Chambrun series (19)
Remember to remember
Miller, Henry
Air-conditioned nightmare series (2)
Remembered death
Christie, Agatha
Colonel Race series (4)
Remembered kiss
Sinclair, Heather
Kiss series (1)
Remembering grandad
Padoan, Gianni
Facing up series (2)
Remembering the bone-house
Mairs, Nancy
Plaintext series (2)
Remembrance day
Aldiss, Brian Wilson
Squire quartet (3)
Remembrance for Kedrigern
Morressy, John
Kedrigern series (5)
Remembrance of Miranda
Ingate, Mary
Ann Fielding series (1)
Remembrance of the Daleks
Aaronovitz, Ben
Doctor Who series (148)
Remi
Malot, Hector
Remi and Perrine series (1)
Remington forty four
Skinner, Mike
Luke Wyatt series (1)
Remington Ridge
Dalton, Kit
Buckskin series (18)
Reminiscences of a vintner
Campbell, Ian Maxwell
Vintner series (2)
Reminiscences of my life and times
Lang, John Dunmore
Life and times series (1)
Reminiscences of Solar Pons
Derleth, August
Solar Pons series (5)
Remittance kid
Edson, John Thomas
Calamity Jane series (10)
Remo
Sapir, Richard
Destroyer series (94)
Remote control
Carmichael, Harry
John Piper and Quinn series (28)
Remove the bodies
Ferrars, Elizabeth
Toby Dyke series (2)
Remover
Daniel, Roland
Bill Saville series (3)
Remover series (1)
Remover returns
Daniel, Roland
Bill Saville series (5)
Remover series (3)
Removers
Hamilton, Donald
Matt Helm series (3)
Rempting fate
Roberts, Nora
Macgregor series (2)
Remscela
Frost, Gregory
Tain series (2)
Renaissance
Coote, Roger
Journey through history series (4)
Rendezvous
Hudson, Alec
Submarine series (3)
Smith, David Alexander
Marathon trilogy (2)
Rendezvous at Skull Mountain
Bagdon, Paul
Scrapper John series (3)
Rendezvous in hell
Druon, Maurice
Curtain falls trilogy (3)
Rendezvous in Rome
Keene, Carolyn
Nancy Drew files series (73)
Passport to romance trilogy (2)
Rendezvous on a lost world
Chandler, Arthur Bertram
John Grimes series (1)
Rim series (15)
Rendezvous on an island
Claymore, Tod
Tod Claymore series (6)
Rendezvous on the South Desert
Slaughter, Jim
Boone Helm series (5)
Rendezvous with death
Bentley, John
Dick Marlow series (4)
Paull, Jessica
Passport to danger series (3)
Rendezvous with destiny
Roosevelt, Elliott
Roosevelt family series (2)
Rendezvous with Rama
Clarke, Arthur Charles
Rama series (1)
Rendezvous with the past
Knight, Kathleen Moore
Margot Blair series (1)
Rene Goscinny and Albert Uderzo present the twelve tasks of Asterix
Goscinny, Rene
Asterix series (24)
Rene Sime
Lichtenberg, Jacqueline
Sime-Gen series (6)
Renee
Schurfranz, Vivian
Sunfire series (30)
Renee Nere
Colette, Sidonie Gabrielle
Renee Nere series (1)
Renegade
Cannon, Mary
O'Hara dynasty trilogy (3)
DeWeese, Gene
Star trek series (55)
Edson, John Thomas
Floating Outfit series (62)
Graham, Winston
Poldark series (1)
Porter, Donald Clayton
White Indian series (2)
Scotten, Cordell
Robots and aliens series (2)
Slade, Jack
Sundance series (12)
Thorne, Ramsay
Captain Gringo series (1)
Renegade agent
Pendleton, Don
Mack Bolan series (47)
Renegade army
Cunningham, Chet
Pony soldiers series (8)
Renegade command
Sharpe, Jon
Trailsman series (42)
Renegade gold
Smith, Russell
Yuma series (2)
Renegade hearts
Chase, Carolyn
Thirteen colonies series (1)
Renegade justice
Cole, Judd
Cheyenne series (3)
Renegade lord
Smith, Mark
Falcon series (1)
Renegade Mi As
Hawkins, Jack
Chopper series (5)
Renegade of Callisto
Carter, Lin
Jandar the Alien series (8)
Renegade rancher
Ellis, Wesley
Lone Star series (92)
Renegade rebellion
Sharpe, Jon
Trailsman series (71)
Renegade riders
Bowden, Jim
Lomax brothers series (1)
Renegade rifles
Sharpe, Jon
Trailsman series (119)
Renegade Steele
Masters, J D
Steele series (5)
Renegade trail
Hart, Matthew S
Cody's law series (6)
Renegade war
McPhee, James
Survival two thousand trilogy (2)
Renegades
Flynn, Jackson
Gunsmoke series (1)
Hunt, Greg
Hartman family trilogy (3)
Renegades of Gor
Norman, John
Tarl Cabot series (23)
Renegades of Kregen
Akers, Alan Burt
Dray Prescot series (13)
Renegades of Luntar
Moore, Roger Elwood
Endless quest crimson crystal adventure series (3)
Renegades of Pern
McCaffrey, Anne
Pern and the Red Planet series (10)
Renegades of the future
Mahr, Kurt
Perry Rhodan series (65)
Renegade's trail
Shirreffs, Gordon Donald
Lee Kershaw series (4)
Renewal
South, Ambrose
Broken house trilogy (3)
Renewal, 1958-62
Gaulle, Charles de
War memoirs series (4)
Renfrew flies again
Erskine, Laurie York
Douglas Renfrew series (9)
Renfrew in the valley of vanished men
Erskine, Laurie York
Douglas Renfrew series (7)
Renfrew of the Royal Mounted
Erskine, Laurie York
Douglas Renfrew series (1)
Renfrew rides again
Erskine, Laurie York
Douglas Renfrew series (2)
Renfrew rides north
Erskine, Laurie York
Douglas Renfrew series (4)
Renfrew rides the range
Erskine, Laurie York
Douglas Renfrew series (6)
Renfrew rides the sky
Erskine, Laurie York
Douglas Renfrew series (3)
Renfrew's long trail
Erskine, Laurie York
Douglas Renfrew series (5)
Renno
Porter, Donald Clayton
White Indian series (5)
Renny's daughter
De la Roche, Mazo
Whiteoak series (14)
Reno rendezvous
Ford, Leslie
Colonel John Primrose series (4)
Grace Latham series (4)
Renown at Stratford
Guthrie, Tyrone
Shakespearean festival in Canada series (1)
Rent-a-robot
Ahlberg, Janet
Daisychain series (8)
Rentaghost enterprises
Morgan, Hugh
Rentaghost trilogy (2)
Rentaghost rules
Morgan, Hugh
Rentaghost trilogy (3)
Rentaghost unlimited
Morgan, Hugh
Rentaghost trilogy (1)
Renunciates of Darkover
Bradley, Marion Zimmer
Darkover anthologies series (7)
Repaid in like coin
Carter, Nicholas
Nicholas Carter series (475)

Repairmen of Cyclops
Brunner, John
Zarathustra trilogy (3)
Repeated doses
Dennys, Joyce
Dose series (2)
Repeater
Mason, Francis Van Wyck
Colonel Hugh North series (10)
Repel boarders
Macdonnell, James Edmond
Captain Peter Bentley series (24)
Repent at leisure
Foley, Rae
Hiram Potter series (7)
Repentance at Boot Hill
Martin, Charles Morris
Gospel Cummings series (2)
Replay, murder
Logue, John
John Moore series (2)
Reply paid
Heard, Henry Fitzgerald
Mister Mycroft series (2)
Report for a corpse
Kane, Henry
Peter Chambers series (4)
Report for murder
McDermid, Val
Lindsay Gordon series (1)
Report from Argyll
Mackinnon, Allan
Donald Kendrick series (1)
Report on the Salvation Army colonies
Haggard, Henry Rider
Salvation Army series (1)
Reprieve
Sartre, Jean Paul
Roads to freedom trilogy (2)
Reprisal
Ahern, Jerry
Survivalist series (11)
Barclay, Ian
Richard Dartley series (2)
Wilson, Francis Paul
Adversary series (3)
Reprisals
Wilson, Francis Paul
Adversary series (3)
Republic and empire
Pournelle, Jerry
Imperial stars series (2)
Reputation dies
Ley, Alice Chetwynd
Justin Rutherford and Anthea series (1)
Reputation of the Upper Fourth
Chaundler, Christine
Fourth Form series (1)
Requiem for a cop
Miller, Victor Brooke
Kojak series (3)
Requiem for a loser
Wainwright, John
Northern Police series (17)
Superintendent Gilliant series (2)
Requiem for a nun
Faulkner, William
Sin and salvation series (8)
Temple Drake series (2)
Requiem for a redhead
Hardy, Lindsay
Gregory Keen series (1)
Requiem for a ruler of worlds
Daley, Brian
Alacrity FitzHugh trilogy (1)
Requiem for a schoolgirl
Ross, Ivan T
Ben Gordon series (2)
Requiem for Anthi
Blakeney, Jay D
Anthi series (2)
Requiem for Charles
Carmichael, Harry
John Piper and Quinn series (17)
Requiem for Pilgrim
Potter, Jay Hill
Pilgrim series (6)
Requiem for redheads
Baker, William Howard
Sexton Blake series (1400)
Requiem for Robert
Fitt, Mary
Superintendent Mallett series (7)
Requiem for rogues
Hume, David
Tony Carter series (3)
Requiem for Sam Wade
Grover, Marshall
Nevada Jim series (48)
Requiem for the conqueror
Gear, William Michael
Forbidden borders series (1)
Requiem for two sisters
Turner, James Ernest
Rampion Savage series (11)
Requiem in Utopia
Starnes, Richard
Maxwell Speed series (1)
Requiem of love
Miller, Calvin
Symphony trilogy (1)
Requiem of sharks
Buchanan, Patrick
Ben Shock and Charity Tucker series (3)
Rescue
Conrad, Joseph
Captain Lingard series (1)
Jones, Nicholas
Wind in the willows series (11)
Mackenzie, Steve
Seals series (3)
Marter, Ian
Doctor Who series (124)
O'Brien, Edna
Dazzle series (3)
Rescue a tall Texan
Grover, Marshall
Larry and Stretch series (420)
Rescue by broomstick
Wood, Lorna
Hag Dowsabel series (2)
Rescue flight
Johns, William Earl
Biggles series (16)
Rescue from The Rose
Hilton, John Buxton
Inspector Thomas Brunt series (2)
Rescue in Mirkwood
Lientz, Gerald
Middle Earth quest series (3)
Rescue in the desert
Dengler, Sandy
Pioneer family series (5)
Rescue mission
Appleton, Victor II
Tom Swift Junior series 2 (6)
Rescue of Athena One
Jahn, Mike
Six Million Dollar Man series (9)
Rescue of Miss Yaskell, and other pipe dreams
Baker, Russell
Good times series (2)
Rescue of Sham
Henry, Marguerite
King of the wind series (3)
Rescue of the red-blooded librarian
Hollands, Judith
Ketchup sisters series (1)
Rescue on skis
Dubrovin, Vivian
Summer fun, winter fun series (4)
Rescue party
Grover, Marshall
Larry and Stretch series (150)
Rescue run
McCaffrey, Anne
Pern and the Red Planet series (12)
Rescued in the clouds
Dixon, Franklin W
Ted Scott flying series (2)
Rescuers
Sharp, Margery
Miss Bianca series (1)
Rescuers downunder
Sharp, Margery
Miss Bianca series (9)
Rescuers rode west
Grover, Marshall
Larry and Stretch series (203)
Reservation for murder
Wright, June
Mother Paul series (1)
Reservations for death
Kendrick, Baynard
Captain Duncan Maclain series (9)
Reservoir ravine
Hood, Hugh
New age series (3)
Resettling
Lingard, Joan
Maggie McKinley quartet (2)
Residency
Bruce, Henry
Eurasian series (2)
Stewart, Cynthia
Victorian India series (1)
Resident
Tute, Warren
George Mado series (4)
Residential quarters
Aragon, Louis
Real world series (2)
Resolved, you're dead
Adams, Nicholas
Horror High series (2)
Resonance of blood
Vardeman, Robert Edward
Peter Thorne series (2)
Resort to murder
Krasner, William
Sam Birge series (6)
Resort to war
Revelli, George
Amanda Nightingale series (2)
Respectability
Blyth, James
Thrift series (2)
Rest Harrow
Hewlett, Maurice
Sanchia and John Maxwell Senhouse series (3)
Rest in pieces
Brown, Rita Mae
Mrs Murphy series (2)
McInerny, Ralph
Father Roger Dowling series (10)
Rest is silence
Barrington, Pamela
Inspector George Marshall series (1)
Rest of the robots
Asimov, Isaac
Robot series (4)
Rest of us
Birmingham, Stephen
American Jewry series (2)
Rest you merry
Macleod, Charlotte
Professor Peter Shandy series (1)
Restaurant at the end of the universe
Adams, Douglas Noel
Arthur Dent series (2)
Restless are the sails
Eaton, Evelyn
Arcadian trilogy (2)
Restless corpse
Pruitt, Alan
Don Carson series (1)
Restless flame
De Wohl, Louis
Lives of the saints series (2)
Restless frontier
Macneil, Duncan
James Ogilvie series (11)
Restless hands
Fischer, Bruno
Ben Helm series (3)
Restless house
Zola, Emile
Rougon Macquart series (10)
Restless is the river
Derleth, August
Sac Prairie series (5)
Restless land
Culp, John Hewett
Martin Cameron series (2)
Restless sea
Thompson, Ernest Victor
Nathan Jago series (1)
Restless waves
Draper, Alfred
Crispin Paton series (2)
Restless wind
Garlock, Dorothy
Colorado trilogy (1)
Restless years
Beaton, Cecil
Years diaries series (5)
Paustovsky, Konstantin Georgievich
Story of a life series (6)
Restoration, abdication and last years, 1914-1920
Fisher, John Arbuthnot
Fear God and dread nought trilogy (3)
Restoration England
Birt, David
Stuarts series (6)
Results of an accident
Jacobs, Thomas Curtis Hicks
Detective Superintendent John Bellamy series (4)
Resume for murder
McCormick, Claire
John Waltz series (1)
Resurgent dust
Garner, Rolf
Kennet trilogy (1)
Resurrection
Barton, James
Wasteworld series (2)
Resurrection day
Pendleton, Don
SuperBolan series (3)
Robeson, Kenneth
Doc Savage series (36)
Resurrection man
Macleod, Charlotte
Sarah Kelling series (10)
Resurrection murder case
Page, Stanley Hart
Christopher Hand series (2)
Resurrection of Candy Sterling
Martin, Russell White
Supernatural series (4)
Resurrection of the gods
Merejkowski, Dmitri Sergeevich
Christ and Antichrist trilogy (2)
Resurrection Row
Perry, Anne
Charlotte Ellison Pitt and Inspector Thomas Pitt series (4)
Retaliators
Hamilton, Donald
Matt Helm series (17)
Retief, ambassador to space
Laumer, Keith
Retief series (5)
Retief and the Pangalactic Pageant of Pulchritude
Laumer, Keith
Retief series (6)
Retief and the warlords
Laumer, Keith
Retief series (4)
Retief at large
Laumer, Keith
Retief series (13)
Retief, diplomat at arms
Laumer, Keith
Retief series (9)
Retief, emissary to the stars
Laumer, Keith
Retief series (8)
Retief, envoy to new worlds
Laumer, Keith
Retief series (1)
Retief in the ruins
Laumer, Keith
Retief series (12)
Retief of the CDT
Laumer, Keith
Retief series (7)
Retief to the rescue
Laumer, Keith
Retief series (10)
Retief unbound
Laumer, Keith
Retief series (6)
Retief's ransom
Laumer, Keith
Retief series (6)
Retief's war
Laumer, Keith
Retief series (3)
Retired from the Yard
Parsons, Anthony
Sexton Blake series (1292)
Retreat
Aminoff, Constance Leonie Caroline
Napoleonic series (10)
Frankland, Edward
Retreat series (1)
Newby, Percy Howard
Hesketh and Jane Oliphant series (2)
Reid, Forrest
Tom Barber trilogy (2)
Retreat Australia fair, and other great Australian legends
Hardy, Frank
Great Australian legends series (2)
Retreat for death
Carter, Nick
Nick Carter series (168)
Retreat from love
Colette, Sidonie Gabrielle
Claudine series (5)
Retreat from Moscow
Delderfield, Ronald Frederick
Napoleon Bonaparte series (3)
Retrieval
Dunne, Colin
Joe Hussey series (1)
Retrospect of flowers
Young, Andrew
Wild flowers series (2)
Return
Gard, Stephen
Sunday the thirteenth series (2)
Gilman, George G
Adam Steele series (46)
Home, Michael
Breckland series (1)
Innes, Evan
American two thousand and forty series (4)
Laymon, Richard Carl
Strange Occurrence Squad series (3)
Return engagement
Murphy, Warren Burton
Destroyer series (71)
Murray, Will
Destroyer series (71)
Return fire
Dalton, Kit
Buckskin series (29)
Ingrid, Charles
Sand wars series (5)
Return for Cormoral
Robeson, Kenneth
Doc Savage series (181)
Return from Omina
Starr, Roland
Omina series (4)
Return from the dead
Burton, Miles
Inspector Arnold and Desmond Merrion series (58)
Jade, Symon
Starship Orpheus trilogy (1)
Return from the inferno
Maloney, Mack
Wingman series (9)
Return from the void
Mahr, Kurt
Perry Rhodan series (51)
Return from Vorkuta
Saint John, David
Peter Ward series (2)
Return from Witch Mountain
Key, Alexander
Witch Mountain series (2)
Return in August
Stong, Philip
State Fair series (2)
Return of A.J.Raffles
Greene, Graham
Raffles series (18)
Return of a man called Horse
Wells, Angus
Man called Horse series (2)
Return of Alexander Graham Wang
Knight, Mallory T
Man from T.O.M.C.A.T. series (9)
Return of Amarillo
Sadler, Jeff
Marshal Andrew Anderson series (9)
Return of Anthony Trent
Martyn, Wyndham
Anthony Trent series (4)
Return of Arsene Lupin
Leblanc, Maurice
Arsene Lupin series (16)
Return of Barmy Jeffers and the Quasimodo walk
Brennan, James Herbert
Barmy Jeffers series (2)
Return of Blackshirt
Graeme, Bruce
Blackshirt series (2)
Return of Blue Mask
Morton, Anthony
Baron series (2)
Return of Blue Pete
Allan, Luke
Blue Pete series (2)
Return of Bulldog Drummond
Sapper
Bulldog Drummond series (7)
Return of Cardannesley
Ellinger, Geoffrey
Roger Hartley series (2)
Return of Cavannagh
Anderson, Ian
Scarlet riders series (2)
Return of Claudia
Franken, Rose
Claudia series (7)
Return of Clubfoot
Williams, Valentine
Clubfoot series (3)
Return of Conan
De Camp, Lyon Sprague
Conan series (7)
Return of Doctor Boris
Cooper, Lisa
Princess Beatrice Hospital series (11)
Return of Doctor Fu-Manchu
Rohmer, Sax
Fu-Manchu series (2)

Return of Doctor O'Grady
Maurois, Andre
Doctor O'Grady series (2)
Return of Doctor Sam, Johnson
De la Torre, Lillian
Doctor Sam, Johnson series (3)
Return of Don Quixote
Chesterton, Gilbert Keith
Don Quixote series (2)
Return of Frank Clamart
Rowland, Henry Cottrell
Frank Clamart series (2)
Return of Frass
Chancellor, John
Captain Frass series (2)
Return of Fursey
Wall, Mervyn
Fursey series (2)
Return of Grey Shadow
Rochester, George Ernest
Grey Shadow series (2)
Return of Gunner Asch
Kirst, Hans Hellmut
Gunner Asch series (3)
Return of Henry Prince
Gregg, Cecil Freeman
Henry Prince series (3)
Return of Hercules
Evans, Gwyn
Bill Kellaway series (4)
Return of Hyman Kaplan
Rosten, Leo
Hyman Kaplan series (2)
Return of Jeeves
Wodehouse, Pelham Grenville
Jeeves and Bertie Wooster series (10)
Return of Jennie Weaver
Turnbull, Margaret
Juliet Jackson series (3)
Return of Jongor
Williams, Robert Moore
Jongor trilogy (2)
Return of Kai Lung
Bramah, Ernest
Kai Lung series (5)
Return of Kavin
Mason, David
Kavin series (2)
Return of Lanny Budd
Sinclair, Upton
World's end series (11)
Return of Long John Silver
Connell, John
Long John Silver series (4)
Return of Mick Cardby
Hume, David
Mick Cardby series (19)
Return of Mister Whisper
Macrow, Brenda Grace
Mister Whisper series (2)
Return of Morgette
Boyer, Glenn G
Dolf Morgette series (4)
Return of Moriarty
Gardner, John Edmund
Professor Moriarty series (1)
Return of Mr Budd
Verner, Gerald
Superintendent Robert Budd series (8)
Return of Nathan Brazil
Chalker, Jack Laurence
Well world series (4)
Return of Nighthawk
Horler, Sydney
Nighthawk series (2)
Return of Picklock Holes
Lehmann, Rudolf Chambers
Picklock Holes series (2)
Return of Raffles
Perowne, Barry
Raffles series (5)
Tremayne, Peter
Raffles series (18)
Return of Rapido Clint and Mister J G Reeder
Edson, John Thomas
Mister J G Reeder series (5)
Return of Rapido Clint and Mr J.G.Reeder
Edson, John Thomas
Cap Fog series (5)
Return of Reginald Perrin
Nobbs, David
Reginald Perrin series (2)
Return of Retief
Laumer, Keith
Retief series (11)
Return of Robinson Crusoe
Treece, Henry
Robinson Crusoe series (2)
Return of Sabata
Fox, Brian
Sabata series (2)
Return of Sanders of the river
Gerard, Francis
Commissioner Sanders series (8)
Return of Sergeant Hawk
Clay, Patrick
Sergeant Hawk series (2)
Return of Sergeant Luck
Bond, Geoffrey
Sergeant Luck series (6)
Return of Sherlock Holmes
Doyle, Arthur Conan
Sherlock Holmes series (6)
Return of Silver Chief
O'Brien, Jack
Silver Chief series (3)
Return of Skull-Face
Howard, Robert Ervin
Skull-Face series (2)
Return of Solar Pons
Derleth, August
Solar Pons series (4)
Return of Sumuru
Rohmer, Sax
Sumuru series (5)
Return of Swamp Thing
David, Peter
Swamp Thing series (2)
Return of Tarzan
Burroughs, Edgar Rice
Tarzan series (2)
Return of Tharn
Browne, Howard
Tharn series (2)
Return of the Antelope Company
Hall, Willis
Antelope Company trilogy (1)
Return of the Black Gang
Fairlie, Gerard
Bulldog Drummond series (17)
Return of the Breakneck Boys
Gravel, Geary
Fading worlds series (2)
Return of the Continental Op
Hammett, Dashiell
Continental Op series (5)
Return of the Eagle
Dorer, Nancy
Eagle series (2)
Return of the emperor
Cole, Allan
Sten series (6)
Return of the Great Bear
Roose-Evans, James
Odd and Elsewhere series (5)
Return of the Great Brain
Fitzgerald, John Dennis
Tom's Great Brain series (6)
Return of the Gumby Gang
Oldfield, Pamela
Gumby Gang series (6)
Return of the gypsy
Carr, Philippa
Daughters of England series (12)
Return of the Home Run Kid
Christopher, Matt
Home Run Kid series (2)
Return of the Howling
Brandner, Gary
Howling series (2)
Return of the Indian
Banks, Lynne Reid
Omri series (2)
Return of the Jedi
Kahn, James
Luke Skywalker series (7)
Vinge, Joan Dennison
Star wars storybook series (3)
Return of the King
Lane, Jane
Stuart series (7)
Tolkien, John Ronald Reuel
Lord of the Rings trilogy (3)
Middle Earth series (5)
Return of the living dead
Russo, John
Living dead series (2)
Return of the lost planet
Macvicar, Angus
Jeremy Grant series (2)
Return of the Mountain Man
Johnstone, William Wallace
Mountain Man series (2)
Return of the Mucker
Burroughs, Edgar Rice
Mucker series (2)
Return of the native
Hardy, Thomas
Novels of character and environment series (4)
Return of the night wind
Vanardy, Varick
Bingham Harvard series (2)
Return of the ninja
Leibold, Jay
Choose your own adventure series (92)
Return of the opium wars
Macao, Marshall
K'ing Kung-Fu series (2)
Return of the Pink Panther
Waldman, Frank
Inspector Clouseau series (3)
Return of the plant that ate dirty socks
McArthur, Nancy
Plant that ate dirty socks series (2)
Return of the Rio Kid
Davis, Don
Rio Kid series (2)
Return of the Seventh Carrier
Albano, Peter
Seventh Carrier series (3)
Return of the Shadow
Grant, Maxwell
Shadow series (281)
Return of the shadow
Tolkien, John Ronald Reuel
History of Middle Earth series (6)
History of the Lord of the Rings series (1)
Return of the sheriff
Bowden, Jim
Dan McCoy series (1)
Return of the Shmoo
Capp, Al
Shmoo series (2)
Return of the Spanish
Coldsmith, Don
Spanish bit series (18)
Return of the Star Man
Byrne, Stuart James
Star Man series (2)
Return of the Tall Man
Fisher, Clay
Ben Allison series (3)
Return of the Texan
Arthur, Burt
Johnny Canavan series (3)
Return of the Thunderbird
Baker, Charlotte
Thunderbird series (2)
Return of the time machine
Friedell, Egon
Time traveller series (2)
Return of the Tuesday dogs
Stoneley, Jack
Tuesday dogs series (2)
Return of the undead
Sharp, Allen
Storytrails series (14)
Return of the werewolf
Smith, Guy Newman
Werewolf trilogy (2)
Return of the white witch
Bell, Rob
Narnia solo games series (5)
Return of the witch
Barry, Margaret Stuart
Simon and the witch series (2)
Return of Wu Fang
Daniel, Roland
Wu Fang series (6)
Return ticket
Delgado, Alan
Mike and Caroline series (3)
Taylor, Geoff
Bomber Command series (2)
Return to action
Masterson, Louis
Morgan Kane series (16)
Return to adventure
Deane, Norman
Liberator series (1)
Return to Ambridge
Gallagher, Jock
Archers of Ambridge series (6)
Return to Anglia
Mays, Spike
Soldering series (6)
Return to Armageddon
Wilson, Gar
Phoenix Force series (11)
Return to Atlantis
Montgomery, Raymond A
Choose your own adventure series (78)
Return to Backsight
Edson, John Thomas
Floating Outfit series (59)
Return to Brookmere
Estes, Rose
Endless quest series (4)
Return to Carnecrane
Williams, Mary
Carnecrane series (2)
Return to Conta Lupe
Jeier, Thomas
Matt Bishop series (1)
Return to Death Valley
Chance, John Newton
Jonathan Blake series (38)
Return to Deathwater
Norris, Curtis
Narnia solo games series (1)
Return to Doomstar
Meyers, Richard S
Doomstar series (2)
Return to Eddarta
Garrett, Randall
Gandalara cycle series (6)
Return to Eden
Harrison, Harry
Eden trilogy (3)
Miles, Rosalind
Eden series (1)
Return to Elysium
Grant, Joan
Far memory series (3)
Return to Fairy Hill
Mitchison, Naomi
Small talk series (4)
Return to Fanglith
Dalmas, John
Fanglith series (2)
Return to Fire Island
Hirschfeld, Burt
Fire Island series (4)
Return to Gone-Away
Enright, Elizabeth
Portia and Julian series (2)
Return to Harrison High
Farris, John
Harrison High series (5)
Return to Howliday Inn
Howe, James
Bunnicula series (9)
Return to Ithaca
Johnson, Eyvind
Olof tetralogy (2)
Return to Jalna
De la Roche, Mazo
Whiteoak series (13)
Return to Kaldak
Lord, Jeffrey
Richard Blade series (36)
Return to Mars
Johns, William Earl
Rex Clinton series (2)
Return to Melnibone
Moorcock, Michael
Elric series (6)
Return to Mottram Park
Chaney, Jill
Mottram Park series (2)
Return to murder
Taylor, Mary Ann
Emil Martin series (2)
Return to Neveryon
Delany, Samuel Ray
Neveryon series (4)
Return to Oz
Vinge, Joan Dennison
Oz series (46)
Return to paradise
Michener, James Albert
South Pacific series (2)
Return to Peyton Place
Metalious, Grace
Peyton Place series (2)
Return to Powder Valley
Field, Peter
Powder Valley series (30)
Return to racing
Butterworth, William Edmund
Tony Fletcher series (2)
Return to Rainton
Craddock, Mary
Rainton series (2)
Return to Rhanna
Fraser, Christine Marion
Rhanna series (4)
Return to South town
Graham, Lorenz
Town series (4)
Return to Sula
Derwent, Lavinia
Magnus series (2)
Return to the Cave of Time
Packard, Edward
Choose your own adventure series (50)
Return to the chateau
Reage, Pauline
O series (2)
Return to the farm
Henrey, Robert
Normandy Farm series (2)
Return to the gate
Corlett, William
Gate of Eden trilogy (3)
Return to the Happy Islands
Kruss, James
Captain Madirankowitch series (2)
Return to the Heron
Treadgold, Mary
Heron series (2)
Return to the islands
Grimble, Arthur
Gilbert and Ellice Islands series (2)
Return to the labyrinth
Scott, Peter Graham
Labyrinth series (2)
Return to the level land
De Jong, Dola
Level land series (2)
Return to the lost world
Nye, Nicholas
Professor Challenger series (5)
Return to the mountains
Frison-Roche, Roger
Zian series (2)
Return to the Reef
Patchett, Mary Elwyn
Ajax series (4)
Return to the Region
Benet, Juan
Region series (2)
Return to the river
Coldsmith, Don
Spanish bit series (11)
Return to the sea
Rasmussen, Albert Henry
Sea fever trilogy (3)
Return to the stars
Daniken, Erich von
Unsolved mysteries series (2)
Hamilton, Edmond
John Gordon series (2)
Return to the Wells
Hill, Lorna
Sadler's Wells series (7)
Return to the Wonderful Farm
Ayme, Marcel
Wonderful Farm series (2)
Return to Thebes
Drury, Allen
Akhenaten series (2)
Return to Thrush Green
Read, *Miss*
Thrush Green series (5)
Return to Tiger Bay
Walsh, James Morgan
Tiger Bay series (2)
Return to Tip Row
Gower, Iris
Catrin series (2)
Return to Treasure Island
Judd, Denis
Long John Silver series (5)
Return to Vietnam
Pendleton, Don
Mack Bolan series (43)
Return to Walden West
Derleth, August
Walden West series (2)
Return to Waminda
Barrett, Helen Elizabeth-Anne
West family series (4)
Return to war
Griffin, Pauline Margaret
Star commandos series (6)
Return to Windhaven
De Jourlet, Marie
Windhaven series (4)
Return to Wuthering Heights
L'Estrange, Anna
Wuthering Heights series (3)
Return to yesterday
Ford, Ford Madox
Memories and impressions series (3)
Shiplett, June Lund
Stacey Gordon series (2)
Returning creation
Morris, Janet Ellen
Silistra series (1)
Returning heart
Charques, Dorothy
Time's harvest trilogy (2)
Reuben
Borntrager, Mary Christner
Ellie's people series (5)
Wideman, John Edgar
Homewood trilogy (3)
Reuben Stone's discovery
Stratemeyer, Edward L
Ship and shore series (2)

Reuben's corner
Mays, Spike
Soldering series (1)
Reunion
Biemiller, Carl Ludwig
Hydronauts series (3)
Friedman, Michael Jan
Star trek, the next generation sequels series (5)
Lingard, Joan
Maggie McKinley quartet (4)
Russell, Richard
Angel Graham series (1)
Reunion for death
Meyers, Martin
Patrick Hardy series (4)
Reunion in Florida
Claymore, Tod
Tod Claymore series (4)
Reunion in San Jose
Grover, Marshall
Larry and Stretch series (316)
Reunion in Slade City
Grover, Marshall
Larry and Stretch series (300)
Reunion with murder
Fuller, Timothy
Jupiter Jones series (3)
Reveille for a Persian village
Najafi, Najmeli
Persia trilogy (2)
Revelation
Bischoff, David
UFO conspiracy series (3)
Cornell, Paul
Timewyrm series (4)
Revelations of a lady detective
Hayward, William Stephens
Lady detective series (2)
Revenelle riddle
Black, Elizabeth Best
Peter Strangely series (1)
Revenge
Blake, Jon
Roboskool series (2)
Coleman, Clay
Lost Island series (5)
Masterson, Louis
Morgan Kane series (11)
Revenge at Black River
Devine, Raynard
Flesh traders series (4)
Revenge at Devil's Tower
Logan, Jake
John Slocum series (175)
Revenge at nightfall
Bailey, Elliot
Inspector Geoffrey Fraser series (3)
Revenge game
Hammond, Gerald
Keith Calder series (3)
Revenge in Red Springs
Bowden, Jim
Dan McCoy series (5)
Revenge in the silent tomb
Fortune, J J
Race against time series (1)
Revenge is the spur
Grover, Marshall
Larry and Stretch series (395)
Revenge of Dracula
Tremayne, Peter
Dracula series (16)
Revenge of Ellis Stack
Fields, Frank
Ellis Stack series (1)
Revenge of Fontomas
Allain, Marcel
Fantomas series (12)
Revenge of Frankenstein
Janes, Henry Hurford
Frankenstein sequels series (2)
Revenge of Increase Sewell
Graat, Heinrich
Ben Camden series (1)
Revenge of Moriarty
Gardner, John Edmund
Professor Moriarty series (2)
Revenge of Taurus
Lory, Robert
Horrorscope series (2)
Revenge of the baby-sat
Watterson, Bill
Calvin and Hobbes series (8)
Revenge of the Brain Sharpeners
Curtis, Philip
Mister Browser series (4)
Revenge of the Buffalo Hunter
Hayes, Ralph Eugene
O'Brien, Buffalo Hunter series (5)
Revenge of the Cybermen
Dicks, Terrance
Doctor Who series (21)
Sarah Jane Smith series (4)
Revenge of the damned
Cole, Allan
Sten series (5)
Revenge of the desert phantom
Dixon, Franklin W
Hardy boys series (84)
Revenge of the Dragonmaster
Brightfield, Richard
Dragonmaster series (2)
Your amazing adventures series (5)
Revenge of the falcon knight
Siegel, Scott
Wizards, warlocks and you series (6)
Revenge of the fluffy bunnies
Gardner, Craig Shaw
Cineverse trilogy (3)
Revenge of the generals
Carter, Nick
Nick Carter series (116)
Revenge of the gunfighter
Logan, Jake
John Slocum series (136)
Revenge of the Hawk
James, Leigh Franklin
John Cooper Baines series (3)
Revenge of the Horseclans
Adams, Robert
Horseclans series (3)
Revenge of the hound
Hardwick, Michael
Sherlock Holmes sequels series (94)
Revenge of the Manitou
Masterton, Graham
Manitou series (2)
Revenge of the master
Ahern, Jerry
Dan Track series (8)
Revenge of the mountain Man
Johnstone, William Wallace
Mountain Man series (4)
Revenge of the rainbow dragons
Estes, Rose
Endless quest series (6)
Revenge of the Raster Gang
McEvoy, Seth
Arcade explorers series (2)
Revenge of the Robins family
Chastain, Thomas
Robins family series (2)
Revenge of the rose
Moorcock, Michael
Elric series (6)
Revenge of the Russian ghost
Leibold, Jay
Choose your own adventure series (99)
Revenge of the Seventh Carrier
Albano, Peter
Seventh Carrier series (7)
Revenge of the Valkyrie
Gunnarsson, Thorarinn
Song series (2)
Revenge of the wizard's ghost
Bellairs, John
Johnny Dixon series (4)
Revenge ride
Gilman, George G
Edge series (49)
Revenger
Messmann, Jon
Revenger series (1)
Revengers
Hamilton, Donald
Matt Helm series (19)
Revenging angels
Masterson, Louis
Morgan Kane series (35)
Reverend Captain Kettle
Hyne, Charles John Cutcliffe
Captain Owen Kettle series (14)
Reverend Randollph and the avenging angel
Smith, Charles Merrill
Reverend Randollph series (2)
Reverend Randollph and the fall from Grace, Inc.
Smith, Charles Merrill
Reverend Randollph series (3)
Reverend Randollph and the holy terror
Smith, Charles Merrill
Reverend Randollph series (4)
Reverend Randollph and the splendid Samaritan
Smith, Charles Merrill
Reverend Randollph series (6)
Reverend Randollph and the unholy Bible
Smith, Charles Merrill
Reverend Randollph series (5)
Reverend Randollph and the wages of sin
Smith, Charles Merrill
Reverend Randollph series (1)
Reversable error
Tanenbaum, Robert K
Assistant District Attorney Butch Karp series (4)
Reverse of the medal
O'Brian, Patrick
Jack Aubrey and Stephen Maturin series (11)
Reverse the charges
Flynn, Brian
Anthony Bathurst series (29)
Reversible giant
Leeson, Robert
Reversible giant series (1)
Revolt
Janson, Hank
Hank Janson series (78)
Rolland, Romain
John Christopher series (2)
Revolt and rebirth
Swycaffer, Jefferson Putnam
Tales of the Concordat trilogy (3)
Revolt in 2100
Heinlein, Robert Anson
Future history series (4)
Revolt of Aphrodite
Durrell, Lawrence
Revolt of Aphrodite series (2)
Revolt of Gunner Asch
Kirst, Hans Hellmut
Gunner Asch series (1)
Revolt of Mamie Stover
Huie, William Bradford
Mamie Stover series (1)
Revolt of the devil men
Steele, Curtis
James Christopher series (4)
Revolt of the dwarves
Estes, Rose
Endless quest series (5)
Revolt of the eaglets
Plaidy, Jean
Plantagenet series (2)
Revolt of the eighth grade
Adorjan, Carol
Junior High series (4)
Kenyon, Kate
Cedar Groves Junior High School series (12)
Revolt of the galaxy
Smith, Edward Elmer
Family d'Alembert series (10)
Revolt of the Micronauts
Williams, Gordon Maclean
Micronauts series (3)
Revolt of the sons
Lindsay, Jack
British way series (5)
Revolt of the Titans
Polch, Boguslaw
Unsolved mysteries series (9)
Revolt of the unemployables
Nelson, Ray Faraday
Timebinders series (2)
Revolt on Majipoor
Costello, Matt
Majipoor trilogy (3)
Revolt on Venus
Rockwell, Carey
Tom Corbett series (5)
Revolting daughter
Housman, Laurence
Palace plays series (1)
Revolution
Aminoff, Constance Leonie Caroline
Napoleonic series (1)
Revolution and roses
Newby, Percy Howard
Eric Blainey series (2)
Revolution and the Napier brothers, 1820-1840
Napier, Priscilla
Napier family trilogy (3)
Revolution besieged
Cliff, Tony
Lenin series (4)
Revolution besieged, 1917-1923
Cliff, Tony
Lenin series (3)
Revolution from Rosinante
Gilliland, Alexis Arnaldus
Rosinante trilogy (1)
Revolutionaries
Harris, John
Martin Falconer series (5)
Revolutionary maid
Blanchard, Amy Ella
Revolutionary War series (2)
Revolutionist
Johnston, William
Matt Lincoln series (1)
Revolution's shore
Rasmussen, Alis A
Highroad trilogy (2)
Revolving lights
Richardson, Dorothy Miller
Pilgrimage series (7)
Reward for Retief
Laumer, Keith
Retief series (13)
Reward for the Baron
Morton, Anthony
Baron series (11)
Reward for treason
Jacobs, Thomas Curtis Hicks
Chief Inspector Barnard series (11)
Reward game
Hammond, Gerald
Keith Calder series (2)
Rewards and fairies
Kipling, Rudyard
Rewards and fairies series (2)
Rewind to yesterday
Pfeffer, Susan Beth
VCR time machine series (1)
Rewolf of Oz
Baum, Roger S
Oz series (50)
Rex Lee, ace of the Air Mail
Burtis, Thomson
Rex Lee series (5)
Rex Lee, aerial acrobat
Burtis, Thomson
Rex Lee series (9)
Rex Lee, flying detective
Burtis, Thomson
Rex Lee series (11)
Rex Lee, gypsy flyer
Burtis, Thomson
Rex Lee series (1)
Rex Lee, night flyer
Burtis, Thomson
Rex Lee series (6)
Rex Lee on the Border Patrol
Burtis, Thomson
Rex Lee series (2)
Rex Lee, ranger of the sky
Burtis, Thomson
Rex Lee series (3)
Rex Lee, rough rider
Burtis, Thomson
Rex Lee series (8)
Rex Lee, sky trailer
Burtis, Thomson
Rex Lee series (4)
Rex Lee, trailing air bandits
Burtis, Thomson
Rex Lee series (10)
Rex Lee's mysterious flight
Burtis, Thomson
Rex Lee series (7)
Rex Milligan holds forth
Buckeridge, Anthony
Rex Milligan series (3)
Rex Milligan raises the roof
Buckeridge, Anthony
Rex Milligan series (2)
Rex Milligan reporting
Buckeridge, Anthony
Rex Milligan series (4)
Rex Milligan's busy term
Buckeridge, Anthony
Rex Milligan series (1)
Rey the fox
Rutley, Cecil Bernard
Wild life story series (13)
Reynard the fox
Masefield, John
Hawbucks series (1)
Rhanna
Fraser, Christine Marion
Rhanna series (1)
Rhanna at war
Fraser, Christine Marion
Rhanna series (2)
Rhapsody in Amber
Zelazny, Roger
Kingdom of Amber series (10)
Rhapsody in black
Stableford, Brian Michael
Star Pilot Grainger series (2)
Rhapsody in red
Gilman, George G
Edge series (21)
Rhea
Hoff, Harry Summerfield
Three marriages series (2)
Rhetoric of motives
Burke, Kenneth
Motives series (2)
Rhialto the marvellous
Vance, Jack
Dying earth series (5)
Rhialto the Marvellous
Vance, Jack
Heroes in hell series (12)
Rhiannon
Gellis, Roberta
Roselynde chronicles series (5)
Rhodesia
Carter, Nick
Nick Carter series (40)
Rhodesian spring
Stonier, George Walter
Rhodesian series (2)
Rhymetime and Baby Jay
VerDorn, Bethea
Baby Jay series (4)
Rhyming Russell
Thomson, Pat
Jets series (2)
Rhythm and movement
Berry, Joy
Can make and do series (6)
Riallaro, the archipelago of exiles
Sweven, Godfrey
Antarctic Utopia series (1)
Ribbon clues
Grant, Maxwell
Shadow series (87)
Ribbon of fire
McLean, Allan Campbell
Alasdair and Lachlann Ban series (1)
Ribbons in her hair
Sanders, Dorothy Lucie
Montgomery family series (4)
Ribsy
Cleary, Beverly
Ribsy series (2)
Rice boy
Mauzey, Merritt
Farm boy series (4)
Riceyman Steps
Bennett, Arnold
Elsie series (1)
Rich and dangerous
Keene, Carolyn
Nancy Drew files series (25)
Rich and famous
Collier, James Lincoln
George Stable series (2)
Rich and famous and bad
Sudbery, Rodie
Polly Devenish series (3)
Rich and humble
Optic, Oliver
Woodville series (1)
Rich and the damned
Himmel, Richard
Johnny Maguire series (5)
Rich are different
Howatch, Susan
Van Zale family series (1)
Rich are with you always
Macdonald, Malcolm
Stevenson family series (2)
Rich die hard
Nichols, Beverley
Mister Horatio Green series (4)
Rich earth
Oldfield, Pamela
Heron saga series (1)
Rich friends
Briskin, Jacqueline
Van Vliet series (2)
Rich inheritance
Nolan, Winefride
Catholic Stuarts series (1)
Rich is the treasure
Procter, Maurice
Chief Inspector Harry Martineau series (5)
Rich man, poor man
Fairbank, Janet Ayer
Rich man, poor man trilogy (3)
Shaw, Irwin
Jordache family series (1)
Rich man's blood
Boland, John C
Donald McCarry series (3)
Rich man's daughter
Mottram, Ralph Hale
Geoffrey Skene series (3)
Spanish Farm series (6)

Rich Mitch
Sharmat, Marjorie Weinman
Rich Mitch series (1)
Rich or dead
Cormany, Michael
Dan Kruger series (3)
Rich pay late
Raven, Simon
Alms for oblivion series (1)
Rich radiant love
Sherwood, Valerie
Imogene and Georgiana series (4)
Rich, radiant slaughter
Papazoglou, Orania
Patience Campbell McKenna series (4)
Rich uncle
Keith, Carlton
Jeff Green series (3)
Richard and Valerie in the garden
Held, Jacqueline
Richard and Valerie series (2)
Richard and Valerie in the mountains
Held, Jacqueline
Richard and Valerie series (3)
Richard and Valerie on the farm
Constant, Anne Marie
Richard and Valerie series (1)
Held, Jacqueline
Richard and Valerie series (1)
Richard Baldock
Marshall, Archibald
Clinton series (2)
Richard Bolitho, midshipman
Kent, Alexander
Captain Richard Bolitho series (1)
Richard Carvel
Churchill, Winston
American national development series (1)
Richard Chatterton, V.C.
Ayres, Ruby Mildred
Richard Chatterton series (1)
Richard Dare's venture
Stratemeyer, Edward L
Bound to succeed series (1)
Working upward series (0)
Richard Furlong
Thurston, Ernest Temple
Richard Furlong series (2)
Richard Halliburton
Halliburton, Richard
Famous adventures series (3)
Richard Halliburton's book of marvels
Halliburton, Richard
Book of marvels series (1)
Richard Halliburton's complete book of marvels
Halliburton, Richard
Book of marvels series (2)
Richard Halliburton's second book of marvels
Halliburton, Richard
Book of marvels series (2)
Richard III
Birt, David
Middle Ages series (20)
Richard Kurt
Hudson, Stephen
Kurt series (1)
Richard, Myrtle and I
Hudson, Stephen
Kurt series (6)
Richard Scarry's Lowly Worm bath book
Scarry, Richard
Lowly Worm series (6)
Richard Scarry's Lowly Worm schoolbag
Scarry, Richard
Lowly Worm series (7)
Richard Scarry's Lowly Worm sniffy book
Scarry, Richard
Lowly Worm series (2)
Richard Scarry's Lowly Worm storybook
Scarry, Richard
Lowly Worm series (1)
Richard Scarry's Lowly Worm word book
Scarry, Richard
Lowly Worm series (3)
Richard Scarry's the cat family takes a trip
Scarry, Richard
Cat family series (1)
Richard Scarry's the cat family's busy day
Scarry, Richard
Cat family series (2)
Richard trilogy
Horgan, Paul
Richard trilogy (3)
Richard's way
Thompson, Kate
Derain family series (4)
Richardson goes abroad
Thomson, Basil
Superintendent Richardson series (4)
Richardson scores again
Thomson, Basil
Superintendent Richardson series (2)
Richardson solves a Dartmoor mystery
Thomson, Basil
Superintendent Richardson series (5)
Richardson's second case
Thomson, Basil
Superintendent Richardson series (2)
Richer dust
Jameson, Storm
Triumph of time trilogy (3)
Richer than a crown
Kamada, Annelise
Love so bold series (2)
Richer than all his tribe
Monsarrat, Nicholas
Pharamaul series (2)
Riches
W, W
Qhe series (3)
Rick afire!
Severn, David
Crusoe series (1)
Rick Dale
Munroe, Kirk
Pacific coast series (3)
Rick goes to Little League
Walker, David Gordon
Rick series (1)
Rick heads for soccer
Walker, David Gordon
Rick series (2)
Rick O'Shay and Hipshot
Lynde, Stan
Rick O'Shay series (1)
Rick O'Shay, Hipshot and me
Lynde, Stan
Rick O'Shay series (3)
Rick tees off
Walker, David Gordon
Rick series (3)
Rickshaw to horror
Quackenbush, Robert Mead
Miss Mallard series (6)
Ricky
Lofgren, Ulf
Ricky series (1)
Ricky and someone
Lofgren, Ulf
Ricky series (2)
Ricky races to the rescue
Palfrey, Heather Mary
Ricky Wilson series (2)
Ricky, Rocky and Ringo count on pizza
Kunnas, Mauri
Ricky, Rocky and Ringo series (1)
Ricky, Rocky and Ringo go to the moon
Kunnas, Mauri
Ricky, Rocky and Ringo series (3)
Ricky, Rocky and Ringo on TV
Kunnas, Mauri
Ricky, Rocky and Ringo series (4)
Ricky, Rocky and Ringo's colorful day
Kunnas, Mauri
Ricky, Rocky and Ringo series (2)
Ricky, Rocky and Ringo's colourful day
Kunnas, Mauri
Ricky, Rocky and Ringo series (2)
Ricochet
Copper, Basil
Mike Faraday series (17)
Riddle and the rune
Chetwin, Grace
Tales of Gom in the Legends of Ulm series (2)
Riddle Club at home
Hardy, Alice Dale
Riddle Club series (1)
Riddle Club at Rocky Falls
Hardy, Alice Dale
Riddle Club series (6)
Riddle Club at Shadowbrook
Hardy, Alice Dale
Riddle Club series (5)
Riddle Club at Sunrise Beach
Hardy, Alice Dale
Riddle Club series (4)
Riddle Club in camp
Hardy, Alice Dale
Riddle Club series (2)
Riddle in red
Allen, Betsy
Connie Blair series (1)
Riddle King's book of jokes, riddles and activities
Thaler, Mike
Riddle King series (4)
Riddle King's camp riddles
Thaler, Mike
Riddle King mini series (2)
Riddle King's food riddles
Thaler, Mike
Riddle King mini series (4)
Riddle King's giant book of jokes, riddles and activities
Thaler, Mike
Riddle King series (1)
Riddle King's jumbo book of jokes, riddles and activities
Thaler, Mike
Riddle King series (2)
Riddle King's pet riddles
Thaler, Mike
Riddle King mini series (1)
Riddle King's school riddles
Thaler, Mike
Riddle King mini series (3)
Riddle King's super book of jokes, riddles and activities
Thaler, Mike
Riddle King series (3)
Riddle-master of Hed
McKillip, Patricia Anne
Morgon trilogy (1)
Riddle me this
Roscoe, Mike
Johnny April series (2)
Riddle of a lady
Gilbert, Anthony
Arthur Crook series (30)
Riddle of Baby Rosalind
Hunt, Angela Elwell
Nicki Holland series (9)
Riddle of Big Ben
Parsons, Anthony
Sexton Blake series (972)
Riddle of Cliff House
Moss, Nancy
Cliff House series (5)
Riddle of Crocodile Creek
Graydon, William Murray
Sexton Blake series (527)
Riddle of Cubicle 7
Parsons, Anthony
Sexton Blake series (1102)
Riddle of Dead Man's Mine
Frazer, Martin
Sexton Blake series (926)
Riddle of Dooley Castle
Hogg, Garry
Jonty series (5)
Riddle of Double Island
Corrigan, Mark
Mark Corrigan and McLean series (28)
Riddle of Five Needle Creek
Blair, Allan
Sexton Blake series (909)
Riddle of identities
Carter, Nicholas
Nicholas Carter series (474)
Riddle of Kittiwake Rock
Westwood, Anne McDougall
Kittiwake Rock series (1)
Riddle of Raggedrock
Ezell, Marilyn
Susan Sand series (4)
Riddle of Ramrod Ridge
Macdonald, William Colt
Nogales Scott and Caliper Maxwell series (2)
Riddle of Riverdale
Bobin, John William
Sexton Blake series (72)
Riddle of stars
McKillip, Patricia Anne
Morgon trilogy (3)
Riddle of the amber room
Hill, Harry Egbert
Sexton Blake series (471)
Riddle of the amber ship
Hanshew, Mary E
Hamilton Cleek series (9)
Riddle of the black racketeers
Hunter, John
Sexton Blake series (1061)
Riddle of the blazing bungalow
Blakesley, Stephen
Sexton Blake series (1274)
Riddle of the bleeding Venus
Richmond, Philip
Duke Renny series (7)
Riddle of the body on the road
Brooks, Edwy Searles
Sexton Blake series (1049)
Riddle of the Burmese curse
Parsons, Anthony
Sexton Blake series (1195)
Riddle of the Cambrian Venus
Hardie, David William Ferguson
Inspector Elwyn Hughes series (2)
Riddle of the captured quisling
Parsons, Anthony
Sexton Blake series (1077)
Riddle of the crooked gambler
Hardinge, Rex
Sexton Blake series (1306)
Riddle of the dead cats
Blackmon, Anita
Adelaide Adams series (2)
Riddle of the dead man's bay
Brandon, John Gordon
Sexton Blake series (1025)
Riddle of the dead man's pit
Armour, R Coutts
Sexton Blake series (553)
Riddle of the disguised crook
Parsons, Anthony
Sexton Blake series (1103)
Riddle of the double ring
Sutton, Margaret
Judy Bolton series (10)
Riddle of the escaped P.O.W.
Parsons, Anthony
Sexton Blake series (1196)
Riddle of the evil eye
Quiroule, Pierre
Sexton Blake series (1006)
Riddle of the film star's jewels
Jackson, Lewis
Sexton Blake series (1190)
Riddle of the Florentine folio
Liddon, Eloise
Peggy Fairfield series (2)
Riddle of the French alibi
Tyrer, Walter
Sexton Blake series (1368)
Riddle of the frozen flame
Hanshew, Mary E
Hamilton Cleek series (6)
Riddle of the frozen mountain
Keene, Carolyn
Dana girls series (26)
Riddle of the gambling den
Parsons, Anthony
Sexton Blake series (1148)
Riddle of the garage
Gibbons, Harry Hornaby Clifford
Sexton Blake series (519)
Riddle of the gas meter
Chester, Gilbert
Sexton Blake series (1031)
Riddle of the golden fingers
Murray, Edgar Joyce
Sexton Blake series (491)
Riddle of the Great Art Exhibition
Armour, R Coutts
Sexton Blake series (554)
Riddle of the Greek financier
Brandon, John Gordon
Sexton Blake series (1026)
Riddle of the green cylinder
Jardine, Warwick
Sexton Blake series (1381)
Riddle of the griffon
Lawson, Susan
Endless quest crimson crystal adventure series (1)
Riddle of the highwayman's stone
Hardinge, Rex
Sexton Blake series (1208)
Riddle of the Indian alibi
Parsons, Anthony
Sexton Blake series (1171)
Riddle of the invisible menace
Hardinge, Rex
Sexton Blake series (1353)
Riddle of the Italian prisoner
Hunter, John
Sexton Blake series (1131)
Riddle of the kidnapped pensioner
Chester, Gilbert
Sexton Blake series (1113)
Riddle of the Lascar's Head
Brooks, Leonard Harold
Sexton Blake series (420)
Riddle of the leather bottle
Drummond, J
Sexton Blake series (1118)
Riddle of the lost emigrant
Armour, R Coutts
Sexton Blake series (411)
Riddle of the lost ship
Hunter, John
Sexton Blake series (1016)
Riddle of the million pound bet
Bayfield, William John
Sexton Blake series (510)
Riddle of the missing fire watcher
Chester, Gilbert
Sexton Blake series (1053)
Riddle of the mummy case
Drummond, J
Sexton Blake series (1138)
Riddle of the murdered fisherman
Chester, Gilbert
Sexton Blake series (1032)
Riddle of the mysterious light
Hanshew, Mary E
Hamilton Cleek series (7)
Riddle of the night
Hanshew, Thomas W
Hamilton Cleek series (3)
Riddle of the night garage
Chester, Gilbert
Sexton Blake series (1229)
Riddle of the painted box
Saville, Malcolm
Michael and Mary series (2)
Riddle of the phantom plague
Verner, Gerald
Sexton Blake series (539)
Riddle of the prince's stooge
Parsons, Anthony
Sexton Blake series (1265)
Riddle of the purple emperor
Hanshew, Thomas W
Hamilton Cleek series (5)
Riddle of the rajah's curios
Parsons, Anthony
Sexton Blake series (1246)
Riddle of the ranch
Jardine, Warwick
Sexton Blake series (1002)
Riddle of the ravens
Gribble, Leonard Reginald
Superintendent Anthony Slade series (8)
Riddle of the receiver's hoard
Drummond, J
Sexton Blake series (1231)
Riddle of the registry office
Gibbons, Harry Hornaby Clifford
Sexton Blake series (379)
Riddle of the roost
Brock, Lynn
Sergeant Venn series (3)
Riddle of the ruins
Jackson, Lewis
Sexton Blake series (1122)
Riddle of the runaway cat
Gibbons, Harry Hornaby Clifford
Sexton Blake series (520)
Riddle of the Russian bride
Parsons, Anthony
Sexton Blake series (1220)
Riddle of the Russian gold
Teed, George Hamilton
Sexton Blake series (454)
Riddle of the Russian princess
Liddon, Eloise
Peggy Fairfield series (1)
Riddle of the sealed room
Hardinge, Rex
Sexton Blake series (1209)
Riddle of the seven realms
Hardy, Lyndon
Arcadia trilogy (3)
Riddle of the smiling man
Hunter, John
Sexton Blake series (1200)
Riddle of the Spanish circus
Corrigan, Mark
Mark Corrigan and McLean series (30)
Riddle of the spinning wheel
Hanshew, Mary E
Hamilton Cleek series (8)
Riddle of the stone elephant
Campbell, Bruce
Ken Holt series (2)
Riddle of the sunken garden
Stuart, Donald
Sexton Blake series (940)
Riddle of the third mile
Dexter, Colin
Inspector Morse series (6)
Riddle of the three marked men
Philips, George Norman
Sexton Blake series (629)
Riddle of the tired pony
Oliver, Marjorie Mary
Alex and Beryl series (2)

Riddle of the Trumpalar
Bernard-Waite, Judy
Trumpalar series (1)
Riddle of the Turkish baths
Evans, Gwyn
Sexton Blake series (662)
Riddle of the ugly face
Quiroule, Pierre
Sexton Blake series (1007)
Riddle of the uncensored letter
Hunter, John
Sexton Blake series (1083)
Riddle of the West End hairdresser
Gibbons, Harry Hornaby Clifford
Sexton Blake series (521)
Riddle of the winged death
Hanshew, Hazel Phillips
Hamilton Cleek series (11)
Riddle of the workman squire
Jackson, Lewis
Sexton Blake series (1143)
Riddle of the Yukon
Douthwaite, Louis Charles
Sexton Blake series (690)
Riddle Vlub through the holidays
Hardy, Alice Dale
Riddle Club series (3)
Riddler
Bamman, Henry A
Checkered flag series (2)
Riddles of Hildegarde Withers
Palmer, Stuart
Hildegarde Withers series (10)
Riddles read
Donovan, Dick
Dick Donovan series (14)
Riddling reaver
Mason, Paul
Fighting fantasy gamebook series (26)
Ride a dark tide
Kenworthy, Christopher
Matthew and Son series (2)
Ride a dead horse
Edmunds, Brent
Pete Marvin series (2)
Ride a high horse
Prather, Richard Scott
Shell Scott series (9)
Ride a paper tiger
Ash, William
Kyle Brandeis series (1)
Ride a tiger
Orgill, Douglas
William Mallett series (2)
Randall, Anthony Asheton
Roger Patten series (1)
Ride a wild pony
Aldridge, James
Kit Quayle series (1)
Ride beyond glory
Randolph, Forrest A
Confederate series (2)
Ride boldly in Dakota
Grover, Marshall
Larry and Stretch series (236)
Ride clear of Daranga
Christian, Frederick H
Frank Angel series (2)
Ride clear, stranger
Tyler, Clarke
Clint Lacey series (1)
Ride for revenge
Logan, Jake
John Slocum series (11)
Roberts, J R
Gunsmith series (100)
Ride for the devil!
Brady, Adam
Buck Halliday series (1)
Ride for Trinidad
Field, Peter
Powder Valley series (47)
Ride for vengeance
Roberts, J R
Gunsmith series (87)
Ride in the sun
Gilman, George G
Edge series (34)
Ride into hell
Skinner, Mike
Luke Wyatt series (2)
Slade, Jack
Lassiter series (17)
Ride like the wind
Leitch, Patricia
Jinny series (8)
Ride of the razorback
Stevens, Carl
Christian Daguerre series (2)
Ride off
Burningham, John
Number play series (6)
Ride on a rainbow
Witcomb, Nan
Thoughts of Nanushka series (16)
Ride on, Tumbleweeds!
Ryan, Tom K
Tumbleweeds series (8)
Ride out of Paradise
Grover, Marshall
Larry and Stretch series (248)
Ride out shooting
Grover, Marshall
Larry and Stretch series (37)
Ride out, Texans
Grover, Marshall
Larry and Stretch series (12)
Ride out the storm
Malcolm, Aleen
Daughters of Cameron series (2)
Ride out to Vengeance
Christian, Frederick H
Frank Angel series (3)
Ride reckless
Grover, Marshall
Larry and Stretch series (15)
Ride, Slocum, ride
Logan, Jake
John Slocum series (1)
Ride slow, ride wary
Grover, Marshall
Larry and Stretch series (52)
Ride tall or hang high
Cunningham, Chet
Outlaws series (1)
Ride the brooding wind
Duke, Madelaine
Sundmans trilogy (2)
Ride the dark trail
L'Amour, Louis
Sackett family series (17)
Ride the free wind
Bittner, F Rosanne
Savage destiny series (2)
Ride the hurricane in
Thompson, Neil
Rand series (2)
Ride the iron horse
Darke, Marjorie
Francis Redmayne series (1)
Ride the lightning
Lutz, John
Alo Nudger series (4)
Ride the man down
Benteen, John
Sundance series (22)
Ride the panther
Newcomb, Kerry
McQueen family series (4)
Ride the river
L'Amour, Louis
Chantry family series (6)
Sackett family series (5)
Ride the roller coaster
Brown, Carter
Rick Holman series (32)
Ride the tiger
Emmett, Robert
American Avenger series (2)
Ride the white stallion
Glynne-Jones, William
Farewell innocence series (2)
Ride the wide country
Harvey, John Barton
Wes Hart series (6)
Ride the wild river
Grover, Marshall
Bleak Creek series (6)
Ride the wild shadow
Sharpe, Jon
Trailsman series (17)
Ride the wind
Gordon, John
Giant under the snow series (2)
Ride to Gold Canyon
Sheldon, Ann
Linda Craig adventures series (6)
Ride to hell
Gruber, Frank
Historical Western series (12)
Ride to the rescue
Pullein-Thompson, Josephine
Moor pony series (3)
Ride to Vengeance
Hunt, Greg
Ridge Parkman series (1)
Ride to vengeance
Logan, Jake
John Slocum series (135)
Ride when you're ready
Bolton, Evelyn
Horse book series (4)
Ride wild to glory
Grover, Marshall
Larry and Stretch series (36)
Ride with me, Mariah Montana
Doig, Ivan
McCaskill family trilogy (3)
Rider of distant trails
Grey, Romer Zane
Buck Duane series (3)
Rider of the Mesquite Trail
Scott, Bradford
Walt Slade series (106)
Riders
Cole, Jackson
Jim Hatfield series (82)
Cooper, Jilly
Rupert Campbell-Black series (1)
Riders and raids
Atkinson, Mary Evelyn
Fricka Hammond series (5)
Riders of death
Floren, Lee
Buckshot McKee and Tortilla Joe series (1)
Riders of judgment
Manfred, Frederick
Buckskin Man tales series (2)
Riders of Lost Creek
L'Amour, Louis
Lance Kilkenny series (2)
Riders of the mesquite trail
Cole, Jackson
Jim Hatfield series (79)
Riders of the night
Cunningham, Eugene
Three Mesquiteers series (1)
Riders of the outlaw trail
Field, Peter
Powder Valley series (40)
Riders of the purple sage
Grey, Zane
Mormon series (1)
Riders of the Renegade
Savage, Buck
Speed Johnson series (2)
Riders of the Rimrock Trail
Cole, Jackson
Jim Hatfield series (7)
Riders of the Ruby Hills
L'Amour, Louis
Lance Kilkenny series (2)
Riders of the sands
Sayer, Walter William
Sexton Blake series (259)
Riders of the shadows
Cole, Jackson
Jim Hatfield series (69)
Riders of the Sidhe
Flint, Kenneth Covey
Sidhe Lugh series (1)
Riders of the storm
Burton, Hester
Stephen Parkin series (2)
Riders of the Whistling Skull
Macdonald, William Colt
Three Mesquiteers series (2)
Riders of the winds
Chalker, Jack Laurence
Changewinds series (2)
Riders to Cibola
Zollinger, Norman
Macandrews Clan series (1)
Riders west
Chisholm, Matt
Storm family series (3)
Ridiculous world records
Scheier, Michael
World records series (1)
Riding camp
Bryant, Bonnie
Saddle Club series (10)
Riding club
Sheldon, Ann
Linda Craig adventures series (9)
Riding for Custer
Curry, Tom
Captain Mesquite series (8)
Riding for justice
Whitehead, David
Judge and Dury series (2)
Riding for ransom
Harris, Catherine
Marsham family series (3)
Riding home
Vail, Virginia
Horse crazy series (5)
Riding lesson
Bryant, Bonnie
Saddle Club series (36)
Riding north one summer
Selby, Bettina
Riding series (4)
Riding, roping and bulldogging, almost
Paulsen, Gary
Sports on the light side series (4)
Riding shotgun
Benteen, John
Sundance series (20)
Miller, Jim
Colt Revolver series (4)
Riding the desert trail
Selby, Bettina
Riding series (3)
Riding the mountains down
Selby, Bettina
Riding series (1)
Riding the storm, 1956-1959
Macmillan, Harold
Winds of change series (4)
Riding to Jerusalem
Selby, Bettina
Riding series (2)
Riding with Marmaduke
Chapman, Elizabeth
Marmaduke series (3)
Ridingdale boys
Bearne, David
Ridingdale series (1)
Ridingdale year
Bearne, David
Ridingdale series (3)
Rififi
Le Breton, Auguste
Rififi series (1)
Rififi in New York
Le Breton, Auguste
Rififi series (2)
Rifka bangs the teakettle
Burstein, Chaya Malamud
Rifka series (1)
Rifka grows up
Burstein, Chaya Malamud
Rifka series (2)
Rifkins
Partridge, Jenny
Oakapple Wood series (10)
Rifle
Gilman, George G
Edge series (61)
Rifle River
LeBeau, Roy
Buckskin series (1)
Rifled gold
Tuttle, Wilbur Coleman
Hashknife Hartley and Sleepy Stevens series (15)
Riflemen of Ohio
Altsheler, Joseph Alexander
Trailers series (4)
Rifles
Vollman, William T
Seven dreams series (6)
Rift
David, Peter
Star trek series (57)
Rig warrior
Johnstone, William Wallace
Rig warrior series (1)
Rigby's romance
Collins, Tom
Such is life series (2)
Rigdale puzzle
Kingston, Charles
Inspector Wake series (4)
Rigged for revenge
Dixon, Franklin W
Hardy boys case files series (70)
Rigging the evidence
Carnac, Carol
Inspector Julian Rivers series (13)
Right for trouble
Easton, Nat
Bill Banning series (6)
Right hand of Dextra
Lake, David John
Breakout series (2)
Dextra series (1)
Right-ho, Jeeves
Wodehouse, Pelham Grenville
Jeeves and Bertie Wooster series (6)
Right honourable corpse
Murray, Max
Corpse series (5)
Right Jack
Maron, Margaret
Lieutenant Sigrid Harald series (4)
Right kind of girl
Francis, Dorothy
Keepsake series (1)
Right line
Macnaghten, Patrick
Jack Heston series (2)
Right line of Cedric
Duggan, Alfred
Saxon trilogy (3)
Right murder
Rice, Craig
John Joseph Malone series (4)
Right on, Relevant
Mark, Ted
Man from C.H.A.R.I.S.M.A. series (2)
Right on Rubens
Cobbett, Pelham
Dog series (5)
Right on the money
Lathen, Emma
John Putnam Thatcher series (22)
Right path
Roberts, Nora
Flowers series (26)
Right royal hassle
Grover, Marshall
Larry and Stretch series (422)
Right royal kidnap
Leeson, Robert
Reversible giant series (2)
Right thing
Stevens, William Oliver
Etiquette series (2)
Right to die
Healy, Jeremiah
John Francis Cuddy series (6)
Stout, Rex
Nero Wolfe and Archie Goodwin series (40)
Right to sing the blues
Lutz, John
Alo Nudger series (3)
Right true end
Barstow, Stan
Vic Brown trilogy (3)
Right where you are sitting now
Wilson, Robert Anton
Illuminatus series (4)
Right you are, Mister Moto
Marquand, John Phillips
Mister Moto series (6)
Righting the wrong
Ellis, Edward Sylvester
Brave and honest trilogy (3)
Riley of the Special Branch
Gribble, Leonard Reginald
Superintendent Anthony Slade series (11)
Rilla of Ingleside
Montgomery, Lucy Maud
Avonlea series (9)
Rilloby Fair mystery
Blyton, Enid
Barney series (2)
Rim-Fire abstains
Ballew, Charles
Rim-Fire series (22)
Rim-Fire and Slats
Ballew, Charles
Rim-Fire series (11)
Rim-Fire and the bear
Ballew, Charles
Rim-Fire series (21)
Rim-Fire, detective
Ballew, Charles
Rim-Fire series (4)
Rim-Fire fights
Ballew, Charles
Rim-Fire series (9)
Rim-Fire gets 'em
Ballew, Charles
Rim-Fire series (16)
Rim-Fire horns in
Ballew, Charles
Rim-Fire series (10)
Rim-Fire in Mexico
Ballew, Charles
Rim-Fire series (15)
Rim-Fire of the Range
Ballew, Charles
Rim-Fire series (5)
Rim-Fire on the desert
Ballew, Charles
Rim-Fire series (12)
Rim-Fire on the prod
Ballew, Charles
Rim-Fire series (19)
Rim-Fire presides
Ballew, Charles
Rim-Fire series (14)
Rim-Fire, ranchero
Ballew, Charles
Rim-Fire series (8)
Rim-Fire returns
Ballew, Charles
Rim-Fire series (18)
Rim-Fire rides
Ballew, Charles
Rim-Fire series (2)

Rim-Fire roams
Ballew, Charles
Rim-Fire series (7)
Rim-Fire runs
Ballew, Charles
Rim-Fire series (17)
Rim-Fire, sheriff
Ballew, Charles
Rim-Fire series (3)
Rim-Fire Six Guns
Ballew, Charles
Rim-Fire series (6)
Rim-Fire skunked
Ballew, Charles
Rim-Fire series (20)
Rim-Fire slips
Ballew, Charles
Rim-Fire series (13)
Rim gods
Chandler, Arthur Bertram
John Grimes series (7)
Rim series (11)
Rim of fire
Wilson, Gar
Phoenix Force series (40)
Rim of fire conspiracy
Rosenberger, Joseph
Death Merchant series (45)
Rim of heaven
Howard, Tom
Sergeant Tom Howard series (5)
Rim of space
Chandler, Arthur Bertram
Rim series (15)
Rim of the pit
Talbot, Hake
Rogan Kincaid series (2)
RIM, the rebel robot
Logan, Nora
Pick-a-path series (14)
Rim-world legacy and beyond
Javor, Frank A
Eli Pike series (1)
Rime isle
Leiber, Fritz
Fafhrd and Gray Mouser series (6)
Rimfire
Slade, Jack
Lassiter series (16)
Rimfire revenge
Dalton, Kit
Buckskin series (30)
Rimrock riders
Field, Peter
Powder Valley series (69)
Rimrocker
Hogan, Ray
Shawn Starbuck series (1)
Rimrunners
Cherryh, Carolyn Janice
Alliance-Union series (6)
Rin-Tin-Tin and the ghost wagon train
Fannin, Cole
Rin-Tin-Tin series (2)
Rin-Tin-Tin and the hidden treasure
Verral, Charles Spain
Rin-Tin-Tin series (3)
Rin-Tin-Tin and the outlaw
Verral, Charles Spain
Rin-Tin-Tin series (1)
Rinehart lifts
Knudson, Rozanne Ruth
Rinehart series (1)
Rinehart shouts
Knudson, Rozanne Ruth
Rinehart series (2)
Ring-a-ding girl
Rico, Don
Casey Grant series (1)
Ring-a-ding UFOs
Tralins, Sandor Robert
Lee Crosley series (3)
Ring-a-ding-ding
Kane, Frank
Johnny Liddell series (21)
Ring around a murder
Bagby, George
Inspector Schmidt series (2)
Ring around Rosa
Gault, William Campbell
Brock Callahan series (1)
Ring for a noose
Gilbert, Anthony
Arthur Crook series (39)
Ring for Jeeves
Wodehouse, Pelham Grenville
Jeeves and Bertie Wooster series (10)
Ring has no end
Armstrong, Thomas
Crowther chronicles series (4)
Ring in the new
Bentley, Phyllis
Oldroyd family series (4)
West Riding series (19)
Ring o' roses
Andrews, Lucilla
Saint Martha's Hospital series (6)
Ring o'Bells mystery
Blyton, Enid
Barney series (3)
Ring of Allaire
Dexter, Susan
Winter King's war trilogy (1)
Ring of bright water
Maxwell, Gavin
Camusfearna trilogy (1)
Ring of dust
Carter, Nicholas
Nicholas Carter series (140)
Ring of endless light
L'Engle, Madeleine
Austin family series (5)
Ring of evil
Dixon, Franklin W
Hardy boys case files series (78)
Ring of fire
Murphy, Shirley Rousseau
Children of Ynell series (1)
Schmidt, Dan
Eagle Force series (5)
Theydon, John
Thunderbirds series (3)
Ring of fortune
Priestley, Margaret
World Dionysus series (1)
Ring of Garamas
Rankine, John
Dag Fletcher series (1)
Ring of Ikribu
Smith, David Claude
Red Sonja series (1)
Ring of Innocent
Flynn, Brian
Anthony Bathurst series (40)
Ring of Kerry
Griffin, John
Richard Raven series (6)
Ring of liars
Chance, John Newton
Jonathan Blake series (19)
Ring of rascals
Carter, Nicholas
Nicholas Carter series (293)
Ring of roses
Blackburn, John
General Charles Kirk series (6)
Brand, Christianna
Inspector Chucky series (3)
Ring of spears
Goodwin, Tim
Ring of spears series (1)
Ring of the red purse
Giff, Patricia Reilly
Polka Dot series (2)
Ring of the ruby dragon
Black, Jeannie
Heartquest series (1)
Ring of truth
Bancroft, John
James Steele series (2)
Ring out, Bow Bells!
Harnett, Cynthia
Fifteenth century London series (1)
Ring the bell at zero
Nelson, Hugh Lawrence
Jim Dunn series (1)
Ring the Judas bell
Forman, James Douglas
Greek Civil War trilogy (2)
Ring, the sword and the unicorn
Ward, James Michael
Fantasy forest series (1)
Ring, the witch and the crystal
Dubowski, Cathy East
Ewok series (3)
Ring twice for murder
Spiller, Andrew
Chief Inspector Duck Mallard series (21)
Ring up Nighthawk
Horler, Sydney
Nighthawk series (5)
Ringed by fire
Everett-Green, Evelyn
Franco-Prussian War series (2)
Ringed castle
Dunnett, Dorothy
Francis Crawford of Lymond series (5)
Ringed horizon
Gilligan, Edmund
Gaunt woman series (2)
Ringer
Shannon, Dell
Lieutenant Luis Mendoza series (20)
Wallace, Edgar
Ringer series (1)
Ringer returns
Wallace, Edgar
Ringer series (2)
Ringing Robinson
Casement, Christina
Robinson series (2)
Ringing up the fire brigade
Carruth, Jean
Trumpton series (6)
Ringmaster of doom
House, Brant
Secret Agent X series (10)
Ringmaster's secret
Keene, Carolyn
Nancy Drew series (31)
Ringnecker
Courtier, Sidney Hobson
Inspector Digger Haig series (4)
Rings of Kether
Chapman, Andrew
Fighting fantasy gamebook series (15)
Rings of Saturn
Asimov, Isaac
David Starr series (6)
Cover, Arthur Byron
Time machine series (6)
Rings of Tantalus
Avery, Richard
Expendables series (2)
Ringside seat
Wilson, Peter
Boxing series (1)
Ringworld
Niven, Larry
Known Space series (5)
Ringworld series (1)
Ringworld engineers
Niven, Larry
Known Space series (12)
Ringworld series (2)
Rinkitink in Oz
Baum, Lyman Frank
Oz series (10)
Rio
Wildey, Doug
Rio series (1)
Rio Casino intrigue
Mason, Francis Van Wyck
Colonel Hugh North series (15)
Rio contract
Newton, William
Joey Binns series (4)
Rio Grande
Masterson, Louis
Morgan Kane series (17)
Porter, Donald Clayton
Winning the West series (1)
Rio Grande ransom
Sharpe, Jon
Canyon O'Grady series (19)
Rio Grande revenge
Cunningham, Chet
Outlaws series (5)
Rio Grande riptide
Richmond, Roe
Lashtrow series (1)
Rio Grande's last race, and other verses
Paterson, Andrew Barton
Man from Snowy River series (3)
Rio guns
Edson, John Thomas
Floating Outfit series (44)
Rio Hondo
Braun, Matt
Brannocks series (3)
Rio Hondo kid
Edson, John Thomas
Floating Outfit series (48)
Rio Hondo war
Edson, John Thomas
Floating Outfit series (54)
Rio Kid
Roan, Tom
Rio Kid series (1)
Rio Kid justice
Davis, Don
Rio Kid series (4)
Rio rampage
Ledd, Paul
Shelter Morgan series (11)
Rio renegades
Duncan, Terence
Powell's army series (8)
Rio rides again
Wildey, Doug
Rio series (2)
Riot
Parker, Roger
Inspector Taff Roberts series (1)
Salkey, Andrew
West Indies series (4)
Riot act
Philmore, R
Swan series (2)
Riot '71
Peters, Ludovic
Ian Firth series (6)
Riotous assembly
Sharpe, Tom
Kommandant Van Heerden series (1)
Rip-off
Brown, Carter
Danny Boyd series (28)
Rip off, Relevant
Mark, Ted
Man from C.H.A.R.I.S.M.A. series (3)
Rip Randall and the pharaoh's tomb
Leyland, Eric
Rip Randall series (5)
Rip-Roaring Russell
Hurwitz, Johanna
Nora and Teddy series (5)
Russell series (1)
Ripe for development
Gloag, John
Lionel Buckby series (1)
Ripe for rapture
Janson, Hank
Hank Janson series (100)
Ripley under ground
Highsmith, Patricia
Tom Ripley series (2)
Ripley's game
Highsmith, Patricia
Tom Ripley series (3)
Ripoff
Maling, Arthur
Brock Potter series (1)
Riposte
Stackpole, Michael
Warrior trilogy (1)
Ripper
Ellis, Wesley
Lone Star series (93)
Newton, Mike
Jon Steel series (1)
Procter, Maurice
Superintendent Philip Hunter series (2)
Ripper file
Jones, Elwyn
Chief Inspector Barlow series (12)
Ripper from Rawhide
Cushman, Dan
Comanche John series (2)
Ripper murders
Procter, Maurice
Superintendent Philip Hunter series (2)
Ripper's apprentice
Thomas, Donald
Inspector Swain series (2)
Ripping yarns
Palin, Michael
Ripping yarns series (1)
Ripple from the storm
Lessing, Doris
Children of violence series (3)
Ripple of murders
Wainwright, John
Northern Police series (39)
Superintendent Gilliant series (3)
Riptide
Daniels, Lee
Surf city series (3)
Rise and fall of Cesar Birotteau
Balzac, Honore de
Scenes of Parisian life series (4)
Rise and reign of His Excellency Eugene Rougon
Zola, Emile
Rougon Macquart series (6)
Rise at dawn
Fisher, Norman
Nigel Morrison series (2)
Rise defiant
Carey, D L
Dorian Trozen series (2)
Rise of Henry Morcar
Bentley, Phyllis
Oldroyd family series (2)
West Riding series (11)
Rise of Ledgar Dunstan
Sheppard, Alfred Tresidder
Ledgar Dunstan series (1)
Rise of Raymond
Moore, Frank Frankfort
Raymond Monk series (1)
Rise of the Spanish-American Empire
Madariaga, Salvador de
Spanish-American empire series (1)
Rise of the Spanish Inquisition
Plaidy, Jean
Spanish Inquisition trilogy (1)
Risen from the ranks
Alger, Horatio
Luck and pluck series (7)
Rishi
Zinkin, Taya
Rishi series (1)
Rishi returns
Zinkin, Taya
Rishi series (2)
Rising of the moon
Mitchell, Gladys
Dame Beatrice Bradley series (18)
Rising star
Bernard, Elizabeth
Satin slippers series (10)
Greene, Yvonne
Kelly Blake series (2)
Rising storm
Allis, Marguerite
Ashbel Field series (4)
Wheatley, Dennis
Roger Brook series (3)
Rising summer
Staples, Mary Jane
South London series (6)
Rising tide
Lindsay, Jack
British way series (2)
Rising Wolf, the white Blackfoot
Schultz, James Willard
Hugh Monroe series (1)
Risk pool
Russo, Richard
Mohawk series (2)
Risking it all
Lowell, Anne Hunter
Sorority girls series (9)
Risky business
Roberts, Nora
Flowers series (41)
Risky way to kill
Lockridge, Richard
Inspector Merton Heimrich series (21)
Rissa and Tregare
Busby, Francis Marion
Rissa Kerguelen series (2)
Rissa Kerguelen
Busby, Francis Marion
Rissa Kerguelen series (1)
Rissa Kerguelen series (2)
Rita
Richards, Laura Elizabeth
Three Margarets series (4)
Rite of spring
Greeley, Andrew Moran
Monsignor John Blackwood Ryan series (4)
Rites for a killer
Fox, James M
John and Suzy Marshall series (13)
Rites of passage
Golding, William
Sea trilogy (1)
Rikhoff, Jean
Timble family trilogy (3)
Ritnym's daughter
Gilluly, Sheila
Greenbriar Queen trilogy (3)
Rittenhouse Square
Solmssen, Arthur Robert George
Conyers and Dean series (1)
Ritual bath
Kellerman, Faye
Sergeant Peter Decker and Rina Lazarus series (1)
Ritual fire dance
Phillips, Leon
Hugh Melling series (3)
Ritual in the dark
Wilson, Colin
Gerard Sorme trilogy (1)
Ritual magic
Butler, Eliza Marian
Faust series (2)
Ritual murder
Haymon, Sylvia T
Inspector Ben Jurnet series (2)

Ritual of blood
Masters, Doug
TNT series (6)
Rival bicyclists
Bonehill, Ralph
Bound to win series (9)
Rival campers
Smith, Ruel Perley
Rival campers series (1)
Rival campers afloat
Smith, Ruel Perley
Rival campers series (2)
Rival campers ashore
Smith, Ruel Perley
Rival campers series (3)
Rival clubs
Russell, Ivy
Princess Susan series (2)
Rival cyclists
Bonehill, Ralph
Bound to win series (9)
Rival detectives
Lynch, Lawrence L
Van Vernet series (1)
Rockwood, Harry
Donald Dyke series (2)
Rival heirs
Crake, Augustus David
Chronicles of Aescendune trilogy (3)
Rival monster
Mackenzie, Compton
Highland series (5)
Rival ocean divers
Rockwood, Roy
Dave Fearless series (1)
Deep sea series (1)
Rival pitchers
Chadwick, Lester
College sports series (1)
Rival Regellians
Reynolds, Mack
Planetary Agent series (4)
Rival riders
Grey, Peter
Kit Hunter series (3)
Rivalries
Balzac, Honore de
Scenes of provincial life series (7)
Rivals
Cooper, Jilly
Rupert Campbell-Black series (2)
Steinke, Anne E
Cheerleaders series (22)
Rivals for the team
Barbour, Ralph Henry
Grafton School trilogy (1)
Rivals of Putnam Hall
Winfield, Arthur M
Putnam Hall series (2)
Rivals of the Chalet School
Brent-Dyer, Elinor Mary
Chalet School series (5)
Rivals to Silver Eagle
Cumming, Primrose
Silver Eagle series (3)
Riven realm
Tranter, Nigel Godwin
James V trilogy (1)
River adventure
Scott, Philip
Algy, Peter and Jeremy series (3)
River and jungle
Ellis, Edward Sylvester
Foreign adventure trilogy (2)
River at Green Knowe
Boston, Lucy Maria
Green Knowe series (3)
River bank
Ommanney, Francis Downes
House in the park series (2)
River boy
Chapman, James
River boy trilogy (1)
River boy at war
Chapman, James
River boy trilogy (3)
River boy returns
Chapman, James
River boy trilogy (2)
River butcher
Sharpe, Jon
Trailsman series (128)
River cats
Pullen, Alan
Sam and Lin series (11)
River detectives
Henson, Jean
Holloway children series (1)
River diary
Eastwood, Dorothea
River diary series (1)
River fugitives
Ellis, Edward Sylvester
River and wilderness trilogy (1)
River full of stars
Hamilton, Elizabeth
Irish childhood series (1)
River gang
Kirk, Thomas Hobson
William and Susan series (2)
River holiday
Young, Emily Hilda
Caravan series (2)
River house mystery
Verner, Gerald
Trevor Lowe series (10)
River kill
Sharpe, Jon
Trailsman series (65)
River kings
Fatchen, Max
Murray River series (1)
River lady
Deveraux, Jude
James River trilogy (3)
River-land
Chambers, Robert William
Land series (3)
River motor-boat boys on the Amazon
Gordon, Harry
River motor-boat boys series (1)
River motor-boat boys on the Colorado
Gordon, Harry
River motor-boat boys series (3)
River motor-boat boys on the Columbia
Gordon, Harry
River motor-boat boys series (2)
River motor-boat boys on the Mississippi
Gordon, Harry
River motor-boat boys series (4)
River motor-boat boys on the Ohio
Gordon, Harry
River motor-boat boys series (6)
River motor-boat boys on the Rio Grande
Gordon, Harry
River motor-boat boys series (8)
River motor-boat boys on the Saint Lawrence
Gordon, Harry
River motor-boat boys series (5)
River motor-boat boys on the Yukon
Gordon, Harry
River motor-boat boys series (7)
River mystery
Rees, Arthur John
Inspector Luckraft series (5)
River of adventure
Blyton, Enid
Adventure series (8)
River of blood
Mackie, John
Rat Bastards series (3)
McLaglen, John J
Herne the Hunter series (2)
River of Dancing Gods
Chalker, Jack Laurence
Dancing Gods series (1)
River of death
Gilman, George G
Adam Steele series (15)
River of decision
Fisher, Clay
Ben Allison series (2)
River of eternity
Farmer, Philip Jose
Riverworld series (5)
River of gold
Ahern, Jerry
Takers series (2)
River of ice
Robeson, Kenneth
Avenger series (11)
River of love
Bittner, F Rosanne
Savage destiny series (3)
River of no return
Ellis, Wesley
Lone Star series (135)
River of Peril
Fannin, Cole
Roy Rogers series (11)
River of revenge
Thorne, Ramsay
Captain Gringo series (21)
River of stars
Wallace, Edgar
Commissioner Sanders series (13)
River of swans
Coldsmith, Don
Spanish bit series (10)
River of tomorrow
Garlock, Dorothy
Wabash trilogy (3)
River people
Willoughby, Lee Davis
Making of America series (12)
River pirates
Ellis, Wesley
Lone Star series (107)
River race verdict
Bishop, Pike
Cord Diamondback series (5)
River raid
Edwards, Hank
Judge Clay Torn series (8)
Helm, Eric
Scorpion Squad series (4)
River raiders
Scott, Bradford
Walt Slade series (89)
Sharpe, Jon
Trailsman series (5)
River rats
Dicks, Terrance
Adventures of Buster and Betty series (3)
River road
Keyes, Frances Parkinson
Fabian and Cresside series (1)
Fabian and Cresside series (2)
River Slea
Ward, Anthony
George trilogy (2)
River song
Lesley, Craig
Danny and Jack Kachiah series (2)
River supreme
Hobart, Alice Tisdale
China series (1)
River to rivet
Messerli, Douglas
River to rivet trilogy (3)
River wall
Garrett, Randall
Gandalara cycle series (7)
Rivera Collection
Adkins, Bill
Dave Hill series (3)
Riverbank rumpus
Joyner, Simon
Tales from the Misty Wood series (3)
Riverbend Bricky
Nesdale, Ira
Bricky series (1)
Riverboat Bill steams again
Green, Cliff
Riverboat Bill series (3)
Riverboat gang
Roberts, J R
Gunsmith series (23)
Riverboat gold
Hardin, J D
Raider series (17)
Sharpe, Jon
Trailsman series (100)
Riverboat queen
Longtree, Warren T
Ruff Justice series (18)
Riverboat rampage
Tanner, Clay
Chance Sharpe series (2)
Riverboat showdown
Masters, Zeke
Faro Blake series (5)
Riverita
Palacio Valdes, Armando
Riverita series (1)
Riverman
White, Stewart Edward
Lumbering trilogy (2)
Orde family series (2)
Riverman's story
Kelsall, Ernest Michael
Riverman series (1)
Rivermist
Harrell, Andrew
Sam Shank series (3)
Rivers and lakes
Hoff, Mary
Our endangered planet series (2)
River's end
Curwood, James Oliver
Three rivers series (1)
Rivers of Babylon
Liddell, Robert
Charles Harbord series (2)
Rivers of flesh
Hild, Jack
SOBS series (7)
Rivers of glory
Mason, Francis Van Wyck
American War of Independence series (3)
Rivers west
L'Amour, Louis
Talon family series (2)
Riverside Club murder
Skene, Anthony
Sexton Blake series (812)
Riverside mystery
Brandon, John Gordon
Arthur Stukeley Pennington series (4)
Inspector Patrick Aloysius McCarthy series (6)
Riverside ninety
Enefer, Douglas
Sam Bawtrey series (3)
Riversong
Kalman, Yvonne
Yardley family trilogy (3)
Riverwind the plainsman
Carter, Tonya R
DragonLance preludes II series (1)
Riverworld war
Farmer, Philip Jose
Riverworld series (5)
Rivet in grandfather's neck
Cabell, James Branch
Dom Manuel and his descendants series (18)
Rivets and Sprockets
Key, Alexander
Sprockets trilogy (2)
Riviera puzzle
McConnor, Vincent
Inspector Damiot series (2)
Riviera showdown
Janson, Hank
Hank Janson series (226)
Rivington Street
Tax, Meredith
Rivington Street series (1)
Road
Chamson, Andre
Roux series (2)
Ehle, John
North Carolina series (4)
Road ahead
Bielenberg, Christabel
Past and future series (2)
Road and the hills
Spedding, Alison
Walk in the dark trilogy (1)
Road back
Remarque, Erich Maria
World War I series (2)
Road between
Farrell, James Thomas
Bernard Clare series (2)
Road block
Waugh, Hillary
Chief Fred Fellows series (2)
Road builders
Campbell, Rod
Little people series (13)
Pocket wheels series (3)
Road fortune
Diack, Hunter
Village series (2)
Road from betrayal
Fackler, Elizabeth
Seth Strummar series (3)
Road from Coorain
Conway, Jill Ker
Coorain series (1)
Road from home
Kherdian, David
Armenian girl series (1)
Road ghost
Drumm, D B
Traveler series (7)
Road home
Rosenberg, Joel
Guardians of the flame series (7)
Road house murder
Skene, Anthony
Sexton Blake series (771)
Road house murders
Koehler, Robert Portner
Avery Gregg and Tony Ellis series (1)
Road leads on
Hamsun, Knut
Edevart and August series (3)
Road of crime
Grant, Maxwell
Shadow series (39)
Road of iron
Saint Germain, Gregory
Resistance series (4)
Road of kings
Wagner, Karl Edward
Conan series (28)
Road of the sea horse
Anderson, Poul
Last Viking trilogy (2)
Road past Mandalay
Masters, John
British India trilogy (2)
Road pirates
Dixon, Franklin W
Hardy boys case files series (74)
Road race
Dean, Anabel
Racing wheels series (5)
Road race of champions
Speed, Eric
Wynn and Lonny racing series (2)
Road returns
Corey, Peter
Three miles square series (2)
Road safety officer
Bentley, Diana
My school series (6)
Road that bends
Ayres, Ruby Mildred
Richard Chatterton series (3)
Road to adventure
Ingram, James Henry
Adventure series (3)
Road to Agra
Sommerfelt, Aimee
Lalu series (1)
Road to anywhere
Pinney, Peter
Dust on my shoes series (4)
Road to Bithynia
Slaughter, Frank Gill
Biblical series (1)
Road to Bordeaux
Saint Albans, Suzanne Marie Adele Beauclerk
Mimosa series (2)
Road to Calvary
Tolstoi, Aleksei Nikolaevich
Ordeal trilogy (3)
Road to Camlann
Sutcliff, Rosemary
Arthurian knights trilogy (3)
Road to Christmas
Park, Ruth
Tales of the south series (3)
Road to Compiegne
Plaidy, Jean
Louis XV trilogy (3)
Road to Corlay
Cowper, Richard
Bird of kinship series (1)
Road to Ehnevor
Rosenberg, Joel
Guardians of the flame series (6)
Road to El Suida
Townend, Peter
McGill series (2)
Road to Falconhurst
Carter, Ashley
Falconhurst series (13)
Road to forever
Rosenberg, Joel
Guardians of the flame series (7)
Road to glory
Austin, Frederick Britten
Napoleon Bonaparte series (1)
Road to Gundagai
McInnes, Graham
Road to Gundagai series (1)
Road to Harley Street
Byam, William
Harley Street series (1)
Road to hell
Groening, Matt
Life in hell series (9)
Road to Laramie
Field, Peter
Powder Valley series (25)
Road to Memphis
Taylor, Mildred Davis
Logan family series (4)
Road to Miklagard
Treece, Henry
Viking trilogy (2)
Road to murder
Gunn, Victor
Chief Inspector Bill Cromwell series (14)
Road to Oz
Baum, Lyman Frank
Oz series (5)
Road to Rhuine
Troy, Simon
Inspector Smith series (1)

Road to Rim
Chandler, Arthur Bertram
Rim series (1)
Road to Testimony
Roberts, J R
Gunsmith series (130)
Road to the Middle Islands
Hancock, Niel
Wilderness of four series (4)
Road to the moon
Tuttle, Wilbur Coleman
Hashknife Hartley and Sleepy Stevens series (27)
Road to the Rim
Chandler, Arthur Bertram
John Grimes series (4)
Road to the stars
Wawn, F T
Masterdillo series (2)
Road to Toytown
Beaman, Sydney George Hulme
Toytown series (1)
Road to Underfall
Jefferies, Mike
Loremasters of Elundium trilogy (1)
Road to Versailles
Golon, Sergeanne
Angelique series (1)
Road to victory, 1941-1945
Gilbert, Martin
Winston S Churchill series (7)
Road to yesterday
Montgomery, Lucy Maud
Avonlea series (11)
Road trip
Morse, Eric
Friday the thirteenth series (4)
Road war
Drumm, D B
Traveler series (5)
Roadhouse girl
Reid, Desmond
Sexton Blake series (1429)
Roadhouse mystery
Brandon, John Gordon
Sexton Blake series (958)
Roads of earth
Drury, Allen
Soviet conquest series (2)
Roads of heaven
Scott, Melissa
Silence Leigh trilogy (3)
Roadshow
Marshall, William Leonard
Yellowthread Street series (10)
Roadtrip
Quin-Harkin, Janet
Sugar and spice series (18)
Roag's Syndicate
Davis, George
Roag's Syndicate series (1)
Roaming round Australia
Clune, Frank
Discovery series (10)
Roaming round the Darling
Clune, Frank
Discovery series (2)
Roan colt of Yamboorah
Ottley, Reginald Leslie
Yamboorah series (2)
Roanoke Hundred
Fletcher, Inglis
Carolina series (1)
Roanoke missing persons case
Larsen, Anita
Histories mysteries series (5)
Roar Devil
Robeson, Kenneth
Doc Savage series (88)
Roar to victory
Hardcastle, Michael
Racing series (1)
Roarin' lead
Macdonald, William Colt
Three Mesquiteers series (5)
Roaring boys
Blishen, Edward
Schoolmaster series (1)
Roaring dragon of Redrose
Slepian, Jan
Listen-hear series (6)
Roaring forty
Chauncy, Nan
Lorenny family series (3)
Roaring guns
Young, Gordon Ray
Red Clark series (1)
Roaring nineties
Prichard, Katharine Susannah
Western Australian Goldfields series (1)
Roaring river mystery
Dixon, Franklin W
Hardy boys series (80)
Roaring Rocketts
Sanders, Charles Wesley
Mournful Martin series (4)
Roaring twenties
Lindsay, Jack
Life rarely tells trilogy (2)
Roaring Valley
Bowden, Jim
Dan McCoy series (4)
Roast beef, medium
Ferber, Edna
Emma McChesney series (1)
Roast eggs
Clark, Douglas
Inspector George Masters series (14)
Rob a bank in Texas
Grover, Marshall
Larry and Stretch series (57)
Rob Ranger, the young ranchman
Lounsberry, Lionel
Rob Ranger series (2)
Rob Ranger's cowboy days
Lounsberry, Lionel
Rob Ranger series (3)
Rob Ranger's mine
Lounsberry, Lionel
Rob Ranger series (1)
Rob Roy
Scott, Walter
Rob Roy Macgregor series (1)
Robak's cross
Hensley, Joe Louis
Donald Robak series (7)
Robak's fire
Hensley, Joe Louis
Donald Robak series (8)
Robak's fun
Hensley, Joe Louis
Donald Robak series (9)
Robak's run
Hensley, Joe Louis
Donald Robak series (10)
Robbed blind
Hart, Roy
Detective Superintendent Roper series (5)
Robber, a robber!
Brandenberg, Franz
Edward and Elizabeth series (3)
Robber barons
Willoughby, Lee Davis
Making of America series (45)
Robber Hotzenplotz
Preussler, Otfried
Robber Hotzenplotz series (1)
Robber meets his match
Burgess, Thornton Waldo
Animal stories series (8)
Robber the rat loses out
Burgess, Thornton Waldo
Animal stories series (8)
Robbers
Whalley, Peter
Harry Sommers and Jill Hanscombe series (1)
Robbers and robots
Carr, Mike
Endless quest series (9)
Robber's roundup
Scott, Bradford
Walt Slade series (97)
Robber's trail
Lee, W W
Jefferson Birch series (4)
Robbery at Foxwood
Paterson, Cynthia
Foxwood series (1)
Robbery at Portage Bend
Lund, Trygve
Dick Weston series (4)
Robbery at the mall
Pascal, Francine
Sweet Valley twins series (81)
Robbery blue
Busby, Roger
Detective Inspector Leric series (1)
Robbery with violence
Rhode, John
Doctor Lancelot Priestley series (64)
Robbie Doo, his reminiscences
Waugh, Joseph Laing
Robbie Doo series (1)
Robe
Douglas, Lloyd Cassel
Apostle Peter series (1)
Robe of honor
Cordell, Alexander
Mortymers series (3)
Robert and Great Granny
Rooke, Anne
Robert James series (3)
Robert and great nanny
Rooke, Anne
Robert series (3)
Robert and Harold
Goulding, Francis Robert
Marooners series (1)
Robert and Harold on the Florida coast
Goulding, Francis Robert
Marooners series (1)
Robert and the pilot
Dupasquier, Philippe
Robert series (3)
Robert and the red balloon
Dupasquier, Philippe
Robert series (2)
Robert Andrew and Skippy
Clark, Leonard
Robert Andrew series (7)
Robert Andrew and the holy family
Clark, Leonard
Robert Andrew series (3)
Robert Andrew and the Red Indian chief
Clark, Leonard
Robert Andrew series (5)
Robert Andrew and Tiffy
Clark, Leonard
Robert Andrew series (2)
Robert Andrew by the sea
Clark, Leonard
Robert Andrew series (4)
Robert Andrew in the country
Clark, Leonard
Robert Andrew series (6)
Robert Andrew tells a story
Clark, Leonard
Robert Andrew series (1)
Robert Elsmore
Ward, Mary Augusta
New Brotherhood series (1)
Robert Graham
Hentz, Caroline Lee Whiting
Belle Creole series (2)
Robert Louis Stevenson's Doctor Jekyll and Mister Hyde
Lee, Samantha
Doctor Jekyll series (1)
Robert, Nana and me
Jacob, Naomi
Me series (9)
Robert Orange
Hobbes, John Oliver
Robert Orange series (2)
Robert the Bruce trilogy
Tranter, Nigel Godwin
Robert the Bruce trilogy (3)
Robert the great
Dupasquier, Philippe
Robert series (1)
Roberta died
Wilson, Gertrude Mary
Inspector Lovick series (8)
Robert's playgroup friends
Rooke, Anne
Robert James series (2)
Robert series (2)
Robert's roost
Duncan, Terence
Powell's army series (4)
Robin
Burnett, Frances Hodgson
House of Coombe series (2)
Robin and Rosie's new room
Trueman, Brian
Stories from Cockleshell Bay series (8)
Robin and the kestrel
Lackey, Mercedes
Bardic voices series (2)
Robin Hood ambush
Wu, William Franking
Time tours series (1)
Robin Hood and his merry men
Serraillier, Ian
Robin Hood series (2)
Robin Hood and Little John
Atterton, Julian
Robin Hood series (1)
Manning-Sanders, Ruth
Robin Hood series (1)
Robin Hood and the gold arrow
Manning-Sanders, Ruth
Robin Hood series (2)
Robin Hood and the miller's son
Atterton, Julian
Robin Hood series (2)
Robin Hood, prince of outlaws
Dumas, Alexandre
Robin Hood series (2)
Robin Hood, prince of thieves
Green, Simon
Robin Hood series (2)
Robin Hood's master stroke
Suddaby, Donald
Robin Hood series (3)
Robin in the greenwood
Serraillier, Ian
Robin Hood series (1)
Robin in the middle
Pascal, Francine
Sweet Valley kids series (40)
Robin of Sherwood and the hounds of Lucifer
May, Robin
Robin of Sherwood series (1)
Robina
Timms, Edward Vivian
Australian saga series (10)
Robins in the Abbey
Oxenham, Elsie J
Abbey girls second generation series (5)
Robin Brent series (3)
Robinson and Slyboots
Casement, Christina
Robinson series (3)
Robinson Crusoe
Defoe, Daniel
Robinson Crusoe series (1)
Robinson Crusoe, junior
Optic, Oliver
Riverdale series (9)
Robinson Max
Turk, Hanne
Max the Mouse series (17)
Robocop
Naha, Ed
Robocop series (1)
Robocop 2
Naha, Ed
Robocop series (2)
Roboskool
Blake, Jon
Roboskool series (1)
Robot
Dicks, Terrance
Doctor Who series (12)
Robot adept
Anthony, Piers
Apprentice adept series (5)
Robot and the flea market
Cook, Ann
Robot series (5)
Robot collection
Asimov, Isaac
Robot series (5)
Robot comes to stay
Cook, Ann
Robot series (1)
Robot commando
Jackson, Steven Gary
Fighting fantasy gamebook series (22)
Robot dreams
Asimov, Isaac
Robot series (7)
Robot goes collecting
Cook, Ann
Robot series (3)
Robot in danger
Cook, Ann
Robot series (2)
Robot invitation
Scheer, Karl Herbert
Perry Rhodan series (136)
Robot master
Grant, Maxwell
Shadow series (240)
Robot novels
Asimov, Isaac
Elijah Baley series (2)
Robot series (3)
Robot series (6)
Robot race
Kraft, David Anthony
Micro adventure series (6)
Robot raiders
Leroe, Ellen Whitney
Bixby Wyler series (2)
Robot rocket
Rockwell, Carey
Tom Corbett series (8)
Robot romance
Leroe, Ellen Whitney
Bixby Wyler series (1)
Robot saves the day
Cook, Ann
Robot series (4)
Robot threat, New York
Shols, W W
Perry Rhodan series (137)
Robot trouble
Coville, Bruce
A.I. Gang series (3)
Robot visions
Asimov, Isaac
Robot series (7)
Robot visits school
Cook, Ann
Robot series (6)
Robots
Skurzynski, Gloria
Your high-tech world series (1)
Robots and empire
Asimov, Isaac
Elijah Baley series (4)
Robots and Empire
Asimov, Isaac
Robot series (7)
Robots, bombs and mutants
Voltz, William
Perry Rhodan series (125)
Robots of dawn
Asimov, Isaac
Elijah Baley series (3)
Robot series (6)
Robots of Saturn
Greene, Joseph
Dig Allen series (5)
Robot's revenge
Dixon, Franklin W
Hardy boys series (123)
Roboworld
Dicks, Terrance
Star quest series (2)
Robthorne mystery
Rhode, John
Doctor Lancelot Priestley series (17)
Robur the conqueror
Verne, Jules
Robur series (2)
Roburta the Conqueress
Allison, Clyde
Agent triple zero eight series (15)
Rocannon's world
Le Guin, Ursula Kroeber
Hain series (4)
Rock and a hard place
David, Peter
Star trek, the next generation series (10)
Sherman, David
Night fighters series (4)
Rock and roll mystery
Wallace, Jim
Choose your own adventure series (69)
Rock baby
Woodhouse, Martin
Giles Yeoman series (2)
Rock City rebels
Stratton, Chris
Bugaloos series (2)
Rock cried out
Douglas, Ellen
Homochito County series (5)
Rock 'n' revenge
Dixon, Franklin W
Hardy boys case files series (48)
Rock 'n' roar
Korman, Justine
Tiny Toon's adventures series (1)
Rock 'n' roll nights
Strasser, Todd
Coming Attractions trilogy (1)
Rock 'n' roll renegades
Dixon, Franklin W
Hardy boys series (116)
Rock of Chikamauga
Altsheler, Joseph Alexander
Civil War series (6)
Rock of diamond
Quartermain, James
Raven series (3)
Rock of three planets
Lightner, Alice Martha
Rock trilogy (1)
Rock sinister
Robeson, Kenneth
Doc Savage series (141)
Rock star's girl
Pascal, Francine
Sweet Valley High series (72)
Rock video strikes again
Adams, Barbara
Kid-TV series (3)
Rockabye contract
Atlee, Philip
Joe Gall series (9)
Rockefeller gift
Winslow, Pauline Glen
Superintendent Merlin Capricorn series (6)

Rocket aircraft, USA
Bergaust, Erik
Rockets series (7)
Rocket divers
Coleman, James Covington
Deep-sea adventure series (8)
Rocket for the Toff
Creasey, John
Toff series (43)
Rocket jumper
Blaine, John
Rick Brant series (21)
Rocket power
Bergaust, Erik
Rockets series (10)
Rocket Riders across the ice
Garis, Howard Roger
Rocket Riders series (1)
Rocket Riders in stormy seas
Garis, Howard Roger
Rocket Riders series (3)
Rocket Riders in the air
Garis, Howard Roger
Rocket Riders series (4)
Rocket Riders over the desert
Garis, Howard Roger
Rocket Riders series (2)
Rocket-ship saboteurs
Townsend, John
Lunar One series (1)
Rocket to earth
Peel, John
Lost in space files series (3)
Rockets
Edmonds, Harry
Hugh Brodie series (2)
Rockets and missiles
Bergaust, Erik
Rockets series (1)
Rockets around the world
Bergaust, Erik
Rockets series (2)
Rockets galore
Mackenzie, Compton
Highland series (7)
Rockets in the dunes
Lamplugh, Lois
Allen family series (4)
Rockets of the Air Force
Bergaust, Erik
Rockets series (4)
Rockets of the armed forces
Bergaust, Erik
Rockets series (11)
Rockets of the Army
Bergaust, Erik
Rockets series (5)
Rockets of the Navy
Bergaust, Erik
Rockets series (3)
Rockets on Moon Island
Seth, Ronald
Brian Grant series (5)
Rocket's red glare
Novak, Kate
Marvel superheroes adventure gamebooks series (2)
Rocket's shadow
Blaine, John
Rick Brant series (1)
Rockets to the moon
Bergaust, Erik
Rockets series (8)
Rockets to the morgue
Holmes, H H
Sister Ursula series (2)
Rockets to the planets
Bergaust, Erik
Rockets series (9)
Rockingdown mystery
Blyton, Enid
Barney series (1)
Rocks in my Scotch
Macvicar, Angus
Confessions series (3)
Rocks remain
Maxwell, Gavin
Camusfearna trilogy (2)
Rocksburg Railroad murders
Constantine, K C
Mario Balzic series (1)
Rockwell
McCurtin, Peter
Sundance series (44)
Rocky
Macdonnell, James Edmond
Captain Peter Bentley series (16)
Rocky and the black eye mystery
Sherry, Sylvia
Rocky O'Rourke series (4)
Rocky and the elephant
Maddock, Reginald Bertram
Jimmy Roxton series (2)
Rocky and the lions
Maddock, Reginald Bertram
Jimmy Roxton series (1)
Rocky and the ratman
Sherry, Sylvia
Rocky O'Rourke series (3)
Rocky mountain
Johnson, Duff
Gutsy Morgan series (1)
Rocky Mountain ball
Gentry, Buck
Eli Holten series (25)
Rocky Mountain boys
Rathborne, Saint George
Canoe and campfire series (6)
Rocky Mountain feud
Sharpe, Jon
Canyon O'Grady series (25)
Rocky Mountain kill
Meek, Joseph
Mountain Jack Pike series (2)
Rocky Mountain vamp
Fletcher, Dirk
Spur McCoy series (4)
Rocky Mountains showdown
Duncan, Terence
Powell's army series (5)
Rod of light
Bayley, Barrington John
Jasperodus series (2)
Rod Serling's The Twilight Zone
Gibson, Walter Brown
Twilight Zone series (4)
Rod Stewart story
Tremlett, George
Rock stars series (13)
Roddy and the miniature railway
Arkle, Phyllis
Roddy series (6)
Roddy and the puma
Arkle, Phyllis
Roddy series (5)
Roddy and the rustlers
Arkle, Phyllis
Roddy series (2)
Roddy on the canal
Arkle, Phyllis
Roddy series (4)
Roddy on the motorway
Arkle, Phyllis
Roddy series (3)
Roddy the roadman
Arkle, Phyllis
Roddy series (1)
Roddy's ideal
Johnson, Helen Kendrick
Roddy series (3)
Roddy's reality
Johnson, Helen Kendrick
Roddy series (2)
Roddy's romance
Johnson, Helen Kendrick
Roddy series (1)
Rodent of doubt
Tapply, William George
Brady Coyne series (4)
Rodeo
Mitchell, Red
Doc McDuff and Popcorn Pruitt series (1)
Rodeo murder
Stout, Rex
Nero Wolfe and Archie Goodwin series (33)
Rodeo murder mystery
Pink, Hal
Inspector Docker series (4)
Rodeo rider
Bryant, Bonnie
Saddle Club series (12)
Roderick
Sladek, John Thomas
Roderick series (1)
Roderick at random
Sladek, John Thomas
Roderick series (2)
Roderick Hudson
James, Henry
Princess Casamassima series (1)
Roderick Random
Smollett, Tobias
Morgan the Welshman series (1)
Rodney Rat and the Sneaky Weasel Gang
Forster, Michelanne
Rodney Rat series (2)
Rodney Rat and the space creatures
Forster, Michelanne
Rodney Rat series (3)
Rodney Rat and the sunken treasure
Forster, Michelanne
Rodney Rat series (1)
Rodolphus
Abbott, Jacob
Franconia series (6)
Roger Bennion's double
Adams, Herbert
Major Roger Bennion series (12)
Roger Paulding, apprentice seaman
Beach, Edward Latimer, senior
Roger Paulding series (1)
Roger Paulding, ensign
Beach, Edward Latimer, senior
Roger Paulding series (4)
Roger Paulding, gunner
Beach, Edward Latimer, senior
Roger Paulding series (3)
Roger Paulding, gunner's mate
Beach, Edward Latimer, senior
Roger Paulding series (2)
Roger Sheringham and the Vane mystery
Berkeley, Anthony
Roger Sheringham series (3)
Roger takes charge
Gretz, Susanna
Roger series (2)
Roger Zelazny's visual guide to Castle Amber
Randall, Neil
Kingdom of Amber series (10)
Rogers' folly
Idell, Albert Edward
Rogers family series (1)
Roger's Rangers
Niven, Larry
Buck Rogers series (10)
Pournelle, Jerry
Buck Rogers series (10)
Rogerson at bay
McInerny, Ralph
Matthew Rogerson series (2)
Rogue Angels
Cave, Peter
Hell's Angels series (5)
Rogue aunt
Chance, John Newton
Jonathan Blake series (10)
Rogue Bolo
Laumer, Keith
Bolo series (2)
Rogue cop
Newman, Gordon F
Inspector Terry Sneed series (1)
Rogue dragon
Davidson, Avram
Kar-Chee series (1)
Rogue emperor
Kilian, Crawford
Chronoplane wars trilogy (3)
Rogue force
Pendleton, Don
SuperBolan series (8)
Rogue Herries
Walpole, Hugh
Herries saga series (1)
Rogue justice
Household, Geoffrey
Raymond Ingelram series (2)
Rogue male
Household, Geoffrey
Raymond Ingelram series (1)
Rogue of Afghanistan
Graydon, William Murray
Sexton Blake series (528)
Rogue of Falconhurst
Carter, Ashley
Falconhurst series (13)
Rogue of Gor
Norman, John
Tarl Cabot series (15)
Rogue of quality
Carter, Nicholas
Nicholas Carter series (490)
Rogue planet
Tubb, Edwin Charles
Space nineteen ninety nine series (9)
Rogue powers
Allen, Roger Macbride
Torch series (2)
Rogue Queen
De Camp, Lyon Sprague
Krishna series (1)
Rogue Ransome, manhunter
Morgan, Dean
Rogue Ransome series (2)
Rogue Ransome, racketbuster
Morgan, Dean
Rogue Ransome series (1)
Rogue Ransome, triggerman
Morgan, Dean
Rogue Ransome series (3)
Rogue registrar
Collins, Lynne
Hartlake Hospital series (2)
Rogue river
Reno, James
Texas Anthem series (4)
Rogue royal
Evans, Gwyn
Quentin Drex series (2)
Rogue running
Procter, Maurice
Chief Inspector Harry Martineau series (21)
Rogue star
Pohl, Frederik
Plan of man trilogy (3)
Rogue trail
Grover, Marshall
Nevada Jim series (54)
Rogue wave
Dunlap, Susan
Kiernan O'Shaughnessy series (2)
Rogue worth trapping
Carter, Nicholas
Nicholas Carter series (544)
Rogues
Smith, George
Glencannon family trilogy (2)
Whalley, Peter
Harry Sommers and Jill Hanscombe series (4)
Rogues and vagabonds
Birt, David
Tudors series (8)
Rogues fall out
Adams, Herbert
Jimmy Haswell series (5)
Major Roger Bennion series (1)
Rogue's gold
Lee, W W
Jefferson Birch series (1)
Rogue's harbor
Fletcher, Inglis
Carolina series (3)
Rogue's harbour
Story, Jack Trevor
Sexton Blake series (1530)
Rogues in the house
Howard, Robert Ervin
Conan series (23)
Rogue's legacy
Foreman, Leonard London
Rogue Bishop series (4)
Rogues' march
Turnbull, Margaret
Juliet Jackson series (2)
Rogue's mistress
Gluyas, Constance
Deep South trilogy (2)
Rogue's murder
Ard, William
Timothy Dane series (4)
Rogues of fortune
Chichester, John Jay
Maxwell Sanderson series (3)
Rogues of ransom
Teed, George Hamilton
Sexton Blake series (779)
Rogues of the desert
Graydon, William Murray
Sexton Blake series (487)
Rogues rampant
Ashe, Gordon
Patrick Dawlish series (12)
Rogue's ransom
Ashe, Gordon
Patrick Dawlish series (38)
Rogue's reach
Carter, Nicholas
Nicholas Carter series (444)
Rogues' republic
Teed, George Hamilton
Sexton Blake series (502)
Roland Blake
Mitchell, Silas Weir
Roland Blake series (1)
Roland montreval
Dumas, Alexandre
Napoleon series (2)
Roland Rat and friends at the seaside
Claridge, David
Roland Rat series (1)
Roland Rat and friends at the shop
Claridge, David
Roland Rat series (4)
Roland Rat and friends in the park
Claridge, David
Roland Rat series (2)
Roland Rat and friends on the farm
Claridge, David
Roland Rat series (3)
Roland Yorke
Wood, Ellen
Channings series (2)
Role of honour
Gardner, John Edmund
James Bond series (21)
Roll call
Bennett, Arnold
Clayhanger series (4)
Five towns series (15)
Roll of thunder, hear my cry
Taylor, Mildred Davis
Logan family series (2)
Roll over and play dead
Hess, Joan
Claire Malloy series (6)
Roll over D.W.
Brown, Marc
D.W. series (1)
Roll-top desk mystery
Wells, Carolyn
Fleming Stone series (33)
Roller coaster
Gilbert, Michael Francis
Patrick Petrella series (5)
Roller coaster ghost
Manushkin, Fran
Pick-a-path series (2)
Roller skates
Sawyer, Ruth
Lucinda Wyman series (1)
Roller skating is for me
Moran, Tom
Sports for me series (1)
Rollerball
McCutchan, Philip
Commander Esmonde Shaw series (17)
Rolling down the Lachlan
Clune, Frank
Discovery series (1)
Rolling down the lea
Gogarty, Oliver St John
Sackville Street series (4)
Rolling heads
Stein, Aaron Marc
Matt Erridge series (16)
Rolling hot
Drake, David
Hammer's Slammers series (5)
Rolling on
Cockett, Mary
Dan and Grum series (1)
Rolling Stones story
Tremlett, George
Rock stars series (4)
Rolling vengeance
Ham, Bob
Overload series (7)
Rollo at play
Abbott, Jacob
Rollo series (4)
Rollo at school
Abbott, Jacob
Rollo series (5)
Rollo at work
Abbott, Jacob
Rollo series (3)
Rollo in Geneva
Abbott, Jacob
Rollo's tour in Europe series (7)
Rollo in Holland
Abbott, Jacob
Rollo's tour in Europe series (8)
Rollo in London
Abbott, Jacob
Rollo's tour in Europe series (4)
Rollo in Naples
Abbott, Jacob
Rollo's tour in Europe series (9)
Rollo in Paris
Abbott, Jacob
Rollo's tour in Europe series (2)
Rollo in Rome
Abbott, Jacob
Rollo's tour in Europe series (10)
Rollo in Sctland
Abbott, Jacob
Rollo's tour in Europe series (6)
Rollo in Switzerland
Abbott, Jacob
Rollo's tour in Europe series (3)
Rollo learning to read
Abbott, Jacob
Rollo series (2)
Rollo learning to talk
Abbott, Jacob
Rollo series (1)
Rollo on the Atlantic
Abbott, Jacob
Rollo's tour in Europe series (1)

Rollo on the Rhine
Abbott, Jacob
Rollo's tour in Europe series (5)
Rollo's code of morals
Abbott, Jacob
Rollo series (14)
Rollo's correspondence
Abbott, Jacob
Rollo series (10)
Rollo's experiments
Abbott, Jacob
Rollo series (7)
Rollo's garden
Abbott, Jacob
Rollo series (14)
Rollo's in the woods
Abbott, Jacob
Rollo series (14)
Rollo's journey to Cambridge
Abbott, Jacob
Rollo's tour in Europe series (10)
Rollo's museum
Abbott, Jacob
Rollo series (8)
Rollo's philosophy, air
Abbott, Jacob
Rollo series (12)
Rollo's philosophy, fire
Abbott, Jacob
Rollo series (13)
Rollo's philosophy, sky
Abbott, Jacob
Rollo series (14)
Rollo's philosophy, water
Abbott, Jacob
Rollo series (11)
Rollo's travels
Abbott, Jacob
Rollo series (9)
Rollo's vacation
Abbott, Jacob
Rollo series (6)
Rolltown
Reynolds, Mack
Bat Hardin series (3)
Roly Poly Bear in the winter
Brook, Sally
Roly Poly series (1)
Roly Poly family
Sherman, Helen
Louie Maude series (2)
Roly Poly Hippo in the bath
Brook, Sally
Roly Poly series (2)
Roly Poly Panda in the sunshine
Brook, Sally
Roly Poly series (3)
Roly Poly Pigs at the party
Brook, Sally
Roly Poly series (4)
Roly-poly pudding
Potter, Beatrix
Peter Rabbit series (13)
Rom-Bom-Bom, and other stories
Ridge, Antonia
Endless and Company series (1)
Roma mater
Anderson, Poul
King of Ys series (1)
Roman
Jones, Douglas Clyde
Hasford family series (5)
Roman army
Birt, David
Roman Britain series (20)
Roman blood
Saylor, Steven
Roma sub rosa series (1)
Roman candle
Chase, Glen
Cherry Delight series (22)
Roman conquest of Britain
Birt, David
Roman Britain series (1)
Roman hat mystery
Queen, Ellery
Ellery Queen series (2)
Roman holiday
Browne, Dik
Hagar the horrible series (34)
Hunter, Joe
Attack force series (3)
Roman mosaics
Birt, David
Roman Britain series (13)
Roman pottery
Birt, David
Roman Britain series (20)
Roman ships
Birt, David
Roman Britain series (16)
Roman soldier in Britain
Birt, David
Roman Britain series (2)
Roman town
Birt, David
Roman Britain series (6)
Roman villa
Birt, David
Roman Britain series (5)
Romance of Alexander and Roxana
Kirkman, Marshall Monroe
Alexander trilogy (3)
Romance of Alexander the king
Kirkman, Marshall Monroe
Alexander trilogy (2)
Romance of Alexander the prince
Kirkman, Marshall Monroe
Alexander trilogy (1)
Romance of Elaine
Reeve, Arthur Benjamin
Craig Kennedy series (8)
Elaine trilogy (2)
Romance of Leonardo da Vinci
Merejkowski, Dmitri Sergeevich
Christ and Antichrist trilogy (2)
Romance of Palombris and Pallogris
Baker, George Philip
Greenwood series (2)
Romance of politics
Upward, Allen
High treason series (2)
Romance of Rosy Ridge
Kantor, Mackinlay
Civil War trilogy (3)
Romance of the nursery
Harker, Lizzie Allen
Fiammetta series (1)
Romance of two worlds
Corelli, Marie
Heliobas series (1)
Two worlds series (1)
Romance to the rescue
Mackail, Denis
David Lawrence series (1)
Romancing the stone
Wilder, Joan
Romancing the stone series (1)
Romanians in America, 1748-1974
Wertsman, Vladimir
Ethnic groups in America series (1)
Romanians in America and Canada
Wertsman, Vladimir
Ethnic groups in America series (4)
Romanoff jewels
Grant, Maxwell
Shadow series (19)
Romans
Cotton, Donald
Doctor Who series (120)
Romans and their world
Burrell, Roy Eric Charles
Romans series (1)
Romans in Britain
Burrell, Roy Eric Charles
Romans series (2)
Romantic
Broch, Hermann
Sleepwalkers trilogy (1)
Romantic tales
Craik, Dinah Maria
Avillion series (1)
Romany and Raq
Evens, George Bramwell
Romany series (2)
Romany Cottage, Silverlake
Hutchings, Monica Mary
Church Farm series (2)
Romany in the country
Evens, George Bramwell
Romany series (3)
Romany in the fields
Evens, George Bramwell
Romany series (1)
Romany, Muriel and Doris
Evens, Glyn Kinnaird
Romany series (14)
Romany of the snows
Parker, Gilbert
Pretty Pierre series (3)
Romany on the farm
Evens, Glyn Kinnaird
Romany series (13)
Romany on the trail
Evens, George Bramwell
Romany series (4)
Romany Rat
Williamson, Roger
Romany Rat trilogy (2)
Romany Rye
Borrow, George
Gypsy series (2)
Romany turns detective
Evens, Glyn Kinnaird
Romany series (12)
Romany's caravan returns
Evens, Glyn Kinnaird
Romany series (14)
Rome
Zola, Emile
Abbe Pierre Fremont trilogy (2)
Rome and the Abbey
Agnew, Emily C
Geraldine series (2)
Rome for sale
Lindsay, Jack
Roman Republic trilogy (1)
Rome haul
Edmonds, Walter Dumaux
Erie Canal series (2)
Romeo and Juliet the lovebirds
Lloyd, David
Great escapes series (6)
Romeo and Juliet, together, and alive, at last
Avi
South Orange River Middle School series (2)
Romeo and Smurfette
Peyo
Smurf series (6)
Romeo becomes a musician
Gree, Alain
Romeo series (5)
Romeo flies a plane
Gree, Alain
Romeo series (3)
Romeo looks for a job
Gree, Alain
Romeo series (1)
Romeo seeks a fortune
Gree, Alain
Romeo series (4)
Romilly Street
Denison, Mary
Romilly Street series (1)
Rommates again
Galbraith, Kathryn O
Roommates series (3)
Rommel, Gunner who?
Milligan, Spike
War memoirs series (2)
Romp in green heat
Sewart, Alan
Detective Sergeant Chamberlayne series (2)
Romula, the dedicated
Kimbrough, Katheryn
Phenwick women series (37)
Romulan way
Duane, Diane
Star trek series (35)
Morwood, Peter
Star trek sequels series (3)
Ronald Morgan goes to bat
Giff, Patricia Reilly
Ronald Morgan series (3)
Ronald Standish
Sapper
Ronald Standish series (3)
Ronicky Doone
Manning, David
Ronicky Doone series (1)
Ronicky Doone's treasure
Manning, David
Ronicky Doone series (2)
Ronnie and the catechism
Hann, Dorothy Owen
Ronnie series (6)
Ronnie and the collects
Hann, Dorothy Owen
Ronnie series (7)
Ronnie and the Commandments
Hann, Dorothy Owen
Ronnie series (3)
Ronnie and the Creed
Hann, Dorothy Owen
Ronnie series (1)
Ronnie and the flying fitted carpet
Antrobus, John
Ronnie series (4)
Ronnie and the great knitted robbery
Antrobus, John
Ronnie series (2)
Ronnie and the haunted Rolls-Royce
Antrobus, John
Ronnie series (1)
Ronnie and the high rise
Antrobus, John
Ronnie series (3)
Ronnie and the Lord's Prayer
Hann, Dorothy Owen
Ronnie series (2)
Ronnie and the parish church
Hann, Dorothy Owen
Ronnie series (5)
Ronnie and the sacraments
Hann, Dorothy Owen
Ronnie series (4)
Ronnie and the saints
Hann, Dorothy Owen
Ronnie series (8)
Ronnie's finest hour
Reeder, Colin
West Meadow series (4)
Roof fall!
Cresswell, Helen
Mike series (2)
Roof over my head
Green, Michael
Coarse series (7)
Roof over your head
Naughton, Bill
Saintly Billy trilogy (2)
Roof-top
Freund, Philip
Volcano god trilogy (2)
Rooftop mystery
Lexau, Joan M
I should have stayed in bed series (2)
Rook-shoot
Duffy, Margaret
Patrick Gillard series (5)
Rook takes knight
Palmer, Stuart
Howie Rook series (2)
Rookie of the year
Tunis, John Roberts
Roy Tucker series (3)
Spike Russell series (2)
Rookie star
Hughes, Dean
Angel Park All-Stars series (5)
Rook's gambit
Rattray, Simon
Hugo Bishop series (5)
Rooksmiths
Truss, Seldon
Inspector Bass series (1)
Room at the bottom
Potter, J L
Jeff Tyler series (1)
Room at the top
Braine, John
Joe Lampton series (1)
Room at the topless
Mark, Ted
Man from O.R.G.Y. series (11)
Room for a body
Bell, Josephine
Claude Warrington-Reeve series (3)
Inspector Steven Mitchell series (12)
Room for Cathy
Woolley, Catherine
Cathy Leonard series (1)
Room for murder
Dewey, Thomas Blanchard
Singer Batts series (1)
Room for one more
Browne, Dik
Hagar the horrible series (22)
Rose, Anna Perrott
Gentle house series (1)
Room fourteen
Annesley, Michael
Lawrence Fenton series (1)
Room in Quiver Court
Cassells, John
Superintendent Flagg series (27)
Room made of windows
Cameron, Eleanor
Julia Redfern series (4)
Room of doom
Grant, Maxwell
Shadow series (221)
Room of mirrors
Carter, Nicholas
Nicholas Carter series (383)
Room thirteen
Wallace, Edgar
Mister J G Reeder series (1)
Room thirty seven
Howard, Hartley
Glenn Bowman series (28)
Room to swing
Lacy, Ed
Toussaint Moore series (1)
Room with a clue
Kingsbury, Kate
Pennyfoot Hotel series (1)
Room with the iron shutters
Wynne, Anthony
Doctor Eustace Hailey series (9)
Room with the tassels
Wells, Carolyn
Alan Ford series (3)
Room within
Church, Richard
John Quickshott series (3)
Roommate
Hoh, Diane
Nightmare Hall series (2)
Roommate and the cowboy
Chase, Emily
Canby Hall series (27)
Roommate returns
Chase, Emily
Canby Hall series (29)
Roommates
Chase, Emily
Canby Hall series (1)
Galbraith, Kathryn O
Roommates series (1)
Roommates and Rachel
Galbraith, Kathryn O
Roommates series (2)
Rooster Cogburn
Julien, Martin
Rooster Cogburn series (2)
Root and the flower
Myers, Leopold Hamilton
Prince Jali series (3)
Prince Jali series (4)
Root of all evil
Ferrars, Elizabeth
Andrew Basnett series (2)
Shannon, Dell
Lieutenant Luis Mendoza series (8)
Root of evil
Goldthwaite, Eaton Kenneth
Lieutenant Joseph Dickerson series (4)
Root of his evil
Ard, William
Timothy Dane series (9)
Rootabaga country
Sandburg, Carl
Rootabaga series (2)
Rootabaga pigeons
Sandburg, Carl
Rootabaga series (2)
Rootabaga stories
Sandburg, Carl
Rootabaga series (1)
Roots
Haley, Alex
Roots series (1)
Jacob, Naomi
Broad acres series (3)
Wesker, Arnold
Chicken soup trilogy (2)
Roots and stars
Vyvyan, Clara Coltman
Roots and stars series (1)
Roots in a parched ground
Foote, Horton
Orphans' home series (1)
Roots of appeasement
Gilbert, Martin
Appeasement series (1)
Roots of bondage
Davis, Margaret Thomson
Scottish historical trilogy (2)
Rooty Tooty Snooty
Cosgrove, Stephen Edward
Snuffin chronicles series (2)
Rope began to hang the butcher
Grafton, Cornelius Warren
Gil Henry series (2)
Rope by arrangement
Clandon, Henrietta
Penny and Vincent Mercer series (1)
William Power series (1)
Rope enough
Strange, John Stephen
Barney Gantt series (3)
Rope for a rustler
Borg, Jack
Hogleg Bailey series (21)
Rope for an ape
Chambers, Dana
Jim Steele series (10)
Rope for General Dietz
Rossiter, John
Roger Tallis series (3)
Rope for the Baron
Morton, Anthony
Baron series (14)
Rope for the hanging
Morland, Nigel
Mrs Palmyra Pym series (7)
Rope for the judge
Hawton, Hector
Asmun Hill series (7)

Rope, in case
Beckwith, Lillian
Hebrides series (5)

Rope law
Victor, Sam
Kilburn series (5)

Rope of gold
Herbst, Josephine
Decay of capitalism trilogy (3)

Rope of sand
Bonnamy, Francis
Peter Shane series (4)
Franklin, Charles
Grant Garfield series (3)
Traill, Peter
Mister Prentice trilogy (3)

Rope of slender threads
Carter, Nicholas
Nicholas Carter series (545)

Rope over Jezebel
Harrison, Richard
Chief Inspector William Bastion series (5)

Rope skips Max
Turk, Hanne
Max the Mouse series (2)

Rope the wild wind
Floren, Lee
Buckshot McKee and Tortilla Joe series (8)

Rope to spare
Macdonald, Philip
Colonel Anthony Ruthven Gethryn series (9)

Roped wolf
Bennet, Robert Ames
Wolf series (2)

Rope's end, rogue's end
Lorac, E C R
Inspector Macdonald series (21)

Rory Rhubarb
Reed, Giles
Munch Bunch character series (19)

Rory Rhubarb and the river monster
Reed, Giles
Munch Bunch story books series (9)

Ros Hackney, halfback
Lawton, Charles
Clarkeville series (2)

Rosa
Hamsun, Knut
Benoni series (2)

Rosalie Dare
Brooks, Amy
Rosalie Dare series (1)

Rosalie Dare's test
Brooks, Amy
Rosalie Dare series (2)

Rosalie's pet
Mathews, Joanna Hooe
Miss Ashton's girls series (3)

Rosalind at Red Gate
Nicholson, Meredith
Rosalind series (2)

Rosamund's castle
Oxenham, Elsie J
Abbey girls first generation series (22)
Tansy series (1)

Rosamund's tuck-shop
Oxenham, Elsie J
Abbey girls first generation series (20)
Rhoda series (1)
Robin Brent series (2)

Rosamund's victory
Oxenham, Elsie J
Abbey girls first generation series (16)

Rosanna joins the Wells
Hill, Lorna
Sadler's Wells series (8)

Rosario murder case
Daniel, Roland
Inspector Neville Langham series (1)
John Hopkins series (1)

Rosary
Barclay, Florence Louisa
Shenstone series (1)

Rosary murders
Kienzle, William Xavier
Father Robert Koesler series (1)

Rosa's dilemma
Underwood, Michael
Rosa Epton series (14)

Rosa's lie
Pascal, Francine
Sweet Valley High series (81)

Roscoe makes good
Cleaver, Hylton
Harley series (4)

Rose
Harrison, Rosina
Rose series (1)
Remick, Grace May
Sheldon Six series (2)

Rose and crown
O'Casey, Sean
I knock at the door series (5)

Rose and her bath
Garland, Sarah
Rose series (1)

Rose and Robbie
Finley, Martha Farquharson
Pewit's nest series (10)

Rose and the thorn
Housman, Laurence
Palace plays series (3)

Rose at harvest end
Fairburn, Eleanor
Wars of the Roses series (3)

Rose bath riddle
Rud, Anthony Melville
J C K Masters series (1)

Rose both red and white
King, Betty
Beaufort family series (5)

Rose Cottage
Allan, Mea
Staveney series (1)

Rose Cottingham married
Syrett, Netta
Rose Cottingham series (2)

Rose dawn
White, Stewart Edward
California trilogy (3)

Rose for Pinkerton
Kellogg, Steven
Pinkerton series (2)

Rose for the surgeon
Cooper, Lisa
Princess Beatrice Hospital series (1)

Rose from the dead
Ernst, Paul
Shirley Leighton and Bill Harper series (2)

Rose-garden husband
Widdemer, Margaret
Rose-garden series (1)

Rose in bloom
Alcott, Louisa May
Rose Campbell series (2)

Rose in darkness
Brand, Christianna
Inspector Charlesworth series (3)

Rose in spring
Fairburn, Eleanor
Wars of the Roses series (1)

Rose o' the sea
Barcynska, Helena Margareta
Honey-pot series (3)

Rose of death
Masterman, Walter Sidney
Sir Arthur Sinclair series (9)

Rose of England
Lewis, Hilda
Mary of England series (1)

Rose of Jericho
Friedman, Rosemary
Shelton family series (2)

Rose of London
Paget, Guy
Rose series (3)

Rose of Raby
Paget, Guy
Rose series (1)

Rose of Rouen
Paget, Guy
Rose series (2)

Rose of Spadgers
Dennis, Clarence James
Sentimental bloke series (6)

Rose petal murders
Givens, Charles Garland
Jimmy Hastings series (1)

Rose rent
Peters, Ellis
Brother Cadfael series (13)

Rose, the bath and the mer boy
Garland, Sarah
Rose series (2)

Rose, the ministering child
Charlesworth, Maria Louisa
Ministering children series (1)

Rose Theatre
Sorrentino, Gilbert
Misterioso trilogy (2)

Rose window
Blanc, Suzanne
Inspector Miguel Menendes series (3)
Symons, Geraldine
Atalanta and Pansy series (1)

Roseanna
Sjowall, Maj
Inspector Martin Beck series (1)

Rosebud Club
Le Baron, Grace
Falcons-Height trilogy (3)

Rosella and the raincloud
Smith, Joan Watson
Jindi series (2)

Roselynde
Gellis, Roberta
Roselynde chronicles series (1)

Rosemary for Chelsea
Bloom, Ursula
Rosemary series (3)

Rosemary for Frinton
Bloom, Ursula
Rosemary series (2)

Rosemary for remembrance
Bax, Clifford
Evenings in Albany series (2)
Sallis, Susan
Rising family series (4)
Thomson, June
Inspector Finch series (14)

Rosemary for Stratford-on-Avon
Bloom, Ursula
Rosemary series (1)

Rosenbergs
Larsen, Anita
Histories mysteries series (1)

Roses are dead
Estleman, Loren D
Peter Macklin series (2)

Roses are pink and yellow
Marzollo, Jean
Thirty nine kids on the block series (3)

Rose's great problem
Hope, Laura Lee
Blythe girls series (3)

Rose's hidden talent
Hope, Laura Lee
Blythe girls series (11)

Roses in December
Fraser, Amy Stewart
Hills of home trilogy (3)
Keyes, Frances Parkinson
Roses series (1)

Rose's odd discovery
Hope, Laura Lee
Blythe girls series (7)

Roses round the door
Fraser, Christine Marion
Blue above the chimneys series (2)
Tovey, Doreen
Cats series (11)

Roses sing on new snow
Yee, Paul
Chinese in the New World series (2)

Rose's story
Brady, Terence
Upstairs, downstairs series (2)

Rose's temptation
Mathews, Joanna Hooe
Flowerets series (3)

Rosettes for Jill
Ferguson, Ruby
Jill series (6)

Rosewood
Leigh, Petra
Garnet series (2)

Rosh Hashanah and Yom Kippur
Drucker, Malka
Jewish holidays series (3)

Rosie and Jim
Cunliffe, John Arthur
Rosie and Jim series (3)

Rosie and Jim and Ragdoll
Cunliffe, John Arthur
Rosie and Jim series (6)

Rosie and Jim and the drink of milk
Cunliffe, John Arthur
Rosie and Jim series (5)

Rosie and Jim and the glassblowers
Cunliffe, John Arthur
Rosie and Jim series (7)

Rosie and Jim and the magic sausages
Cunliffe, John Arthur
Rosie and Jim series (8)

Rosie and Jim and the man in the wind
Cunliffe, John Arthur
Rosie and Jim series (4)

Rosie and Jim and the rainbow
Cunliffe, John Arthur
Rosie and Jim series (2)

Rosie and Jim and the water wizard
Cunliffe, John Arthur
Rosie and Jim series (1)

Rosie and Jim, apple, banana, carrot alphabet book
Cunliffe, John Arthur
Rosie and Jim series (8)

Rosie and Jim special
Cunliffe, John Arthur
Rosie and Jim series (8)

Rosie and Mister Brown
Berg, Leila
Steep Street series (4)

Rosie Darling
Swale, Rosie
Rosie Darling series (1)

Rosie runs away
Macdonald, Maryann
Rosie series (1)

Rosie sips spiders
Lester, Alison
Australian children series (2)

Rosie Swanson, fourth grade geek for president
Park, Barbara
Rosie Swanson series (2)

Rosiebelle Lee Wildcat Tennessee
Andrews, Raymond
Appalachee Red series (2)

Rosie's baby tooth
Macdonald, Maryann
Rosie series (2)

Rosie's double dare
Harris, Robie H
Rosie series (1)

Rosie's razzle dazzle deal
Harris, Robie H
Rosie series (2)

Rosie's rock 'n' roll riot
Harris, Robie H
Rosie series (3)

Rosie's secret spell
Harris, Robie H
Rosie series (4)

Rosie's wonderful dances
Thwaites, Lyndsay
Super Adam and Rosie Wonder series (2)

Rosin the beau
Richards, Laura Elizabeth
Melody trilogy (3)

Rosina and her calf
Farrell, Sally
Rosina series (1)

Rosina and son
Barne, Kitty
Rosina series (2)

Rosina and the show
Farrell, Sally
Rosina series (2)

Rosina Copper, the mystery mare
Barne, Kitty
Rosina series (1)

Ross Grant, gold hunter
Garland, John
Ross Grant series (2)

Ross Grant in Miner's Camp
Garland, John
Ross Grant series (4)

Ross Grant on the trail
Garland, John
Ross Grant series (3)

Ross Grant, tenderfoot
Garland, John
Ross Grant series (1)

Ross Poldark
Graham, Winston
Poldark series (1)

Rossano
Lett, Gordon
Italian Resistance series (1)

Rossetti and the Pre-Raphaelite Brotherhood
Fleming, Gordon Howard
Pre-Raphaelite Brotherhood series (1)

Rostma lure
Dalton, Sean
Operation Star Hawks series (4)

Rostnikov's corpse
Kaminsky, Stuart Melvin
Inspector Porfiry Petrovich Rostnikov series (1)

Rostnikov's vacation
Kaminsky, Stuart Melvin
Inspector Porfiry Petrovich Rostnikov series (7)

Rostron Outfit
Morgan, Dean
Rostron Outfit series (1)

Rostron Outfit in Chicago
Morgan, Dean
Rostron Outfit series (4)

Rostron Outfit in Mexico
Morgan, Dean
Rostron Outfit series (5)

Rostron Outfit in Rio
Morgan, Dean
Rostron Outfit series (2)

Rostron Outfit in Texas
Morgan, Dean
Rostron Outfit series (6)

Rostron Outfit, undercover agents
Morgan, Dean
Rostron Outfit series (3)

Rosy Cole's great American guilt club
Greenwald, Sheila
Rosy Cole series (3)

Rosy noses, freezing toes
Delton, Judy
Pee wee scout series (13)

Rosy pastor
Fitzgerald, Nigel
Alan Russell series (2)
Superintendent Duffy series (2)

Rosy Starling
Garfield, Leon
Apprentices series (8)

Rosy's romance
Greenwald, Sheila
Rosy Cole series (5)

Rotten apples
Green, Edith
Dearborn V Pinch series (1)

Rotten elements
Upward, Edward
Alan Sebrill trilogy (2)
Alan Sebrill trilogy (3)

Rotten Ralph
Gantos, Jack
Rotten Ralph series (1)

Rotten Ralph's rotten Christmas
Gantos, Jack
Rotten Ralph series (3)

Rotten Ralph's show and tell
Gantos, Jack
Rotten Ralph series (5)

Rotten Ralph's trick or treat
Gantos, Jack
Rotten Ralph series (4)

Rotter of Whitelands
Browne, Reginald
Whitelands series (3)

Rouge Calibre
Grover, Marshall
Larry and Stretch series (80)

Rough and Ready
Alger, Horatio
Ragged Dick series (4)

Rough and ready
Hunter, E J
White Squaw series (24)

Rough cut
Cook, Bruce
Antonio Cervantes series (2)
Gorman, Edward
Jack Dwyer series (1)

Rough diamonds
Rodgers, Sherlaw Johnston
Micah Truelove series (3)

Rough edges
Chase, Elaine Raco
Roman Cantrell and Nikki Holden series (3)

Rough-hewn
Canfield, Dorothy
Brimming cup series (2)

Rough justice
Gilman, George G
Adam Steele series (39)
Oster, Jerry
Jake Neuman series (1)

Rough music
Bennett, Barbara
Calladine family series (3)

Rough night for the guilty
Grover, Marshall
Larry and Stretch series (232)

Rough on rats
Francis, William
Anthony Martin series (1)

Rough passage
Douglas, Gavin
Captain Samson series (1)
Hackforth-Jones, Gilbert
Submarine Service series (2)

Rough, ready and Texan
Grover, Marshall
Larry and Stretch series (411)

Rough red
Sylvester, Martin
William Warne series (3)

Rough rider
Logan, Jake
John Slocum series (25)

Rough riders
Willoughby, Lee Davis
Making of America series (53)
Rough riding
Dixon, Franklin W
Hardy boys case files series (68)
Rough road south
Thompson, Valerie
Howell family series (1)
Rough route to Rodd County
Grover, Marshall
Larry and Stretch series (346)
Rough shaft
Hunter, E J
Headhunter series (12)
Rough shoot
Household, Geoffrey
Roger Taine series (1)
Rough time in Dobie
Skinner, Mike
Luke Wyatt series (4)
Rough trade
Meek, Joseph
Mountain Jack Pike series (15)
Rough treatment
Harvey, John Barton
Inspector Charlie Resnick series (2)
Rough water
Pertwee, Roland
Patrick Faraday series (2)
Rough water brown
Garnett, Henry
Benny series (1)
Rough wooing
Tranter, Nigel Godwin
James V trilogy (3)
Roughing it
Twain, Mark
Innocents series (2)
Rougon-Macquart family
Zola, Emile
Rougon Macquart series (1)
Roumanian envoy
Philips, George Norman
Sexton Blake series (201)
Roumeli
Fermor, Patrick Leigh
Greek travels series (2)
Round and round the garden
McGee, Shelagh
Little nursery rhyme series (2)
Round mosaic
Stewart, Desmond
Sequence of roles trilogy (1)
Round River
Leopold, Aldo
Sand County series (2)
Round stories about our world
Haley, Gail Einhart
Round stories series (4)
Round stories about things that grow
Haley, Gail Einhart
Round stories series (3)
Round stories about things that live in water
Haley, Gail Einhart
Round stories series (2)
Round stories about things that live on land
Haley, Gail Einhart
Round stories series (1)
Round table murders
Reynolds, Adrian
Professor Dennis Barrie series (3)
Round-the-clock nurse
Grant, Jane
Nurse series (4)
Round the corner
Cannan, Gilbert
Laurie series (2)
Round the corner trilogy (1)
Round the moon
Verne, Jules
Gun Club series (2)
Round the twist
Jennings, Paul Arthur
Round the twist series (6)
Round the world for a quarter
Carter, Nicholas
Nicholas Carter series (605)
Round the world in eighty days
Verne, Jules
Phileas Fogg series (1)
Round the world with Rosie and Jim
Cunliffe, John Arthur
Rosie and Jim series (8)
Round the year at Blackberry Farm
Pilgrim, Jane
Blackberry Farm series (26)
Round the year with Lady Addle
Dunn, Mary
Lady Addle of Eigg series (4)
Round trip space ship
Slobodkin, Louis
Space ship series (4)
Round trip to nowhere
Maccargo, J T
Mannix series (5)
Round-up
Ellis, Edward Sylvester
Arizona trilogy (3)
Mulford, Clarence Edward
J C series (5)
Round-up on Exmoor
De la Mahotiere, Mary
Newspaper Children series (2)
Roundabout horse
Todd, Herbert Eatton
Bobby Brewster picture book series (3)
Rounders
Evans, Max
Dusty Jones and Wrangler Lewis series (1)
Rounders three
Evans, Max
Dusty Jones and Wrangler Lewis series (2)
Roundhead and Cavalier
Wallace, Edgar
Black Avons series (2)
Roundhead retreat
Sanders, John
Nicholas Pym series (5)
Roundtree women
Lewerth, Margaret
Roundtree women series (1)
Rouse the demon
Weston, Carolyn
Casey Kellog and Al Krug series (3)
Rout of the Ollafubs
Lethbridge, Katharine Greville
Ollafubs series (1)
Route 666
Pringle, David
Dark future series (4)
Routine investigation
Howard, Hartley
Glenn Bowman series (25)
Roux the bandit
Chamson, Andre
Roux series (1)
Rover boys at Big Bear Lake
Winfield, Arthur M
Rover boys series (27)
Rover boys at Big Horn Ranch
Winfield, Arthur M
Rover boys series (26)
Rover boys at Colby Hall
Winfield, Arthur M
Rover boys series (21)
Rover boys at college
Winfield, Arthur M
Rover boys series (14)
Rover boys at school
Winfield, Arthur M
Rover boys series (1)
Rover boys down East
Winfield, Arthur M
Rover boys series (15)
Rover boys in Alaska
Winfield, Arthur M
Rover boys series (18)
Rover boys in business
Winfield, Arthur M
Rover boys series (19)
Rover boys in camp
Winfield, Arthur M
Rover boys series (8)
Rover boys in New York
Winfield, Arthur M
Rover boys series (17)
Rover boys in Southern waters
Winfield, Arthur M
Rover boys series (11)
Rover boys in the air
Winfield, Arthur M
Rover boys series (16)
Rover boys in the jungle
Winfield, Arthur M
Rover boys series (3)
Rover boys in the land of luck
Winfield, Arthur M
Rover boys series (25)
Rover boys in the mountains
Winfield, Arthur M
Rover boys series (6)
Rover boys on a hunt
Winfield, Arthur M
Rover boys series (24)
Rover boys on a tour
Winfield, Arthur M
Rover boys series (20)
Rover boys on land and sea
Winfield, Arthur M
Rover boys series (7)
Rover boys on Snowshoe Island
Winfield, Arthur M
Rover boys series (22)
Rover boys on Sunset Trail
Winfield, Arthur M
Rover boys series (29)
Rover boys on the farm
Winfield, Arthur M
Rover boys series (12)
Rover boys on the Great Lakes
Winfield, Arthur M
Rover boys series (5)
Rover boys on the ocean
Winfield, Arthur M
Rover boys series (2)
Rover boys on the plains
Winfield, Arthur M
Rover boys series (10)
Rover boys on the river
Winfield, Arthur M
Rover boys series (9)
Rover boys on Treasure Isle
Winfield, Arthur M
Rover boys series (13)
Rover boys out West
Winfield, Arthur M
Rover boys series (4)
Rover boys shipwrecked
Winfield, Arthur M
Rover boys series (28)
Rover boys under canvas
Winfield, Arthur M
Rover boys series (23)
Rover boys winning a fortune
Winfield, Arthur M
Rover boys series (30)
Rover's regatta day
Smith, Sam
Crew Cats series (2)
Roving eye
Pakington, Humphrey
Warmstry series (2)
Roving with Nomad
Ellison, Norman
Nomad series (4)
Rowan
McCaffrey, Anne
Rowan series (1)
Rowan Farm
Benary, Margot
Lechow family series (2)
Rowan for a queen
Darby, Catherine
Rowan family series (2)
Rowan Garth
Darby, Catherine
Rowan family series (1)
Rowan maid
Darby, Catherine
Rowan family series (5)
Rowan tree
Sutton, Graham
Fleming family series (1)
Rowan's Raiders
Gentry, Buck
Eli Holten series (1)
Rowena Barnes
O'Riordan, Conal
Stanislaus Priest trilogy (2)
Roweny in Boston
Pool, Maria Louise
Roweny series (1)
Roxana and Alexander
Moray, Helga
Roxana trilogy (2)
Roxanne
Miner, Jane Claypool
Sunfire series (15)
Roxie and Red Rose mystery
Stahl, Hilda
Best friends series (5)
Roxie's mail madness
Stahl, Hilda
Best friends series (15)
Roxy by proxy
Janson, Hank
Hank Janson series (212)
Roy Blakeley
Fitzhugh, Percy Keese
Roy Blakeley series (1)
Roy Blakeley at the haunted camp
Fitzhugh, Percy Keese
Roy Blakeley series (9)
Roy Blakeley, lost, strayed or stolen
Fitzhugh, Percy Keese
Roy Blakeley series (7)
Roy Blakeley on the Mohawk Trail
Fitzhugh, Percy Keese
Roy Blakeley series (12)
Roy Blakeley, pathfinder
Fitzhugh, Percy Keese
Roy Blakeley series (4)
Roy Blakeley up in the air
Fitzhugh, Percy Keese
Roy Blakeley series (18)
Roy Blakeley's adventures in camp
Fitzhugh, Percy Keese
Roy Blakeley series (2)
Roy Blakeley's bee-line hike
Fitzhugh, Percy Keese
Roy Blakeley series (8)
Roy Blakeley's camp on wheels
Fitzhugh, Percy Keese
Roy Blakeley series (3)
Roy Blakeley's elastic hike
Fitzhugh, Percy Keese
Roy Blakeley series (13)
Roy Blakeley's funny bone hike
Fitzhugh, Percy Keese
Roy Blakeley series (10)
Roy Blakeley's go-as-you-please hike
Fitzhugh, Percy Keese
Roy Blakeley series (16)
Roy Blakeley's happy-go-lucky hike
Fitzhugh, Percy Keese
Roy Blakeley series (15)
Roy Blakeley's motor caravan
Fitzhugh, Percy Keese
Roy Blakeley series (6)
Roy Blakeley's roundabout hike
Fitzhugh, Percy Keese
Roy Blakeley series (14)
Roy Blakeley's Silver Fox Patrol
Fitzhugh, Percy Keese
Roy Blakeley series (5)
Roy Blakeley's tangled trail
Fitzhugh, Percy Keese
Roy Blakeley series (11)
Roy Blakeley's wild goose chase
Fitzhugh, Percy Keese
Roy Blakeley series (17)
Roy Rogers and Dale Evans
Fannin, Cole
Dale Evans series (1)
Roy Rogers and the enchanted canyon
Rivers, Jim
Roy Rogers series (7)
Roy Rogers and the ghost of Mystery Rancho
Tompkins, Walker Allison
Roy Rogers series (3)
Roy Rogers and the Gopher Creek gunman
Middleton, Don
Roy Rogers series (1)
Roy Rogers and the new cowboy
Bedford, Annie North
Roy Rogers series (9)
Roy Rogers and the outlaws of Sundown Valley
Miller, Snowden
Roy Rogers series (4)
Roy Rogers and the raiders of Sawtooth Ridge
Miller, Snowden
Roy Rogers series (2)
Roy Rogers and the Rimrock renegades
Miller, Snowden
Roy Rogers series (5)
Roy Rogers and the sure 'nough cowpoke
Beecher, Elizabeth
Roy Rogers series (8)
Roy Rogers, king of the cowboys
Fannin, Cole
Roy Rogers series (10)
Roy Rogers on the Double-R Ranch
Beecher, Elizabeth
Roy Rogers series (6)
Royal adventure of Richard Halliburton
Halliburton, Richard
Royal adventures series (3)
Royal alliance
Dawe, Carlton
Leathermouth series (8)
Royal bed for a corpse
Murray, Max
Corpse series (9)
Royal book of Oz
Thompson, Ruth Plumly
Oz series (15)
Royal Borough
Ferguson, Rachel
Kensington series (2)
Royal box
Keyes, Frances Parkinson
Joe and Judith Racina series (2)
Royal chaos
McGirt, Dan
Jason Cosmo series (2)
Royal chase
Lowndes, Joan Selby
Francis and Anne Woodward series (1)
Royal Coach
Mitchum, Hank
Stage coach station series (31)
Royal command
Grey, Peter
Kit Hunter series (11)
Royal favour
Housman, Laurence
Palace plays series (2)
Royal Flash
Fraser, George Macdonald
Flashman series (2)
Royal flush
Irwin, Margaret
Stuart series (1)
Stivers, Dick
Able Team series (10)
Royal flush murders
Verner, Gerald
Superintendent Robert Budd series (16)
Royal griffin
Dymoke, Juliet
Plantagenets series (2)
Royal intrigue
Anthony, Evelyn
Catherine the Great trilogy (2)
Royal marriage
Grier, Sydney Carlyon
Princess series (1)
Royal murder
Roosevelt, Elliott
Eleanor Roosevelt series (13)
Royal Murdoch
Harlow, Robert
Royal Murdoch series (1)
Royal prisoner
Souvestre, Pierre
Fantomas series (5)
Royal quest
Lide, Mary
Ann of Cambray trilogy (3)
Royal Red
O'Brien, Jack
Silver Chief series (4)
Royal road to Fotheringay
Plaidy, Jean
Mary, Queen of Scots series (1)
Royal road to romance
Halliburton, Richard
Royal adventures series (1)
Royal runaway and Jingalo in revolution
Housman, Laurence
Jingalo series (2)
Royal slave
Fitzgerald, Julia
Slave series (1)
Royal succession
Druon, Maurice
Accursed kings series (4)
Royal suitor
Reeve, Linda Dawn
Anne Boleyn series (2)
Royal table manners
Housman, Laurence
Palace plays series (4)
Royal target
Grover, Marshall
Larry and Stretch series (181)
Royal thief
Carter, Nicholas
Nicholas Carter series (184)
Royal visit
Ashley, Bernard
Clipper Street series (4)
Royal widow
Evans, Jean
Katherine Parr series (1)
Royal Yankee
Suthren, Victor
Paul Gallant series (4)
Roy's dory at the sea-shore
Rand, Edward Augustus
School and camp series (2)
Rozzy Raspberry
Reed, Giles
Munch Bunch character series (27)
Rozzy Raspberry's wallpaper machine
Reed, Giles
Munch Bunch story books series (6)
RT, Margaret and the rats of NIMH
Conly, Jane Leslie
NIMH series (3)

Rub-a-dub-dub
Fish, Robert Lloyd
Murder League series (2)
Rub out the redhead
Brody, Marc
Marc Brody series (82)
Rubadub mystery
Blyton, Enid
Barney series (4)
Rubaiyat of a bridge
Wells, Carolyn
Rubaiyat series (2)
Rubaiyat of a motor car
Wells, Carolyn
Rubaiyat series (1)
Rubber band
Stout, Rex
Nero Wolfe and Archie Goodwin series (3)
Rubber boy
Mauzey, Merritt
Farm boy series (5)
Rubber Rabbit
Ahlberg, Allan
Help your child to read series (6)
Rubber smugglers
Teed, George Hamilton
Sexton Blake series (548)
Rubberband stew
Hodgman, Ann
Lunchroom series (5)
Rubbish dumpers
Fletcher, Audrey
Allsorts series (4)
Ruben and Ivy Sen
Miln, Louise Jordan
Sen family series (2)
Rubicon
McKinney, Jack
Sentinels series (5)
Rubies, emeralds and diamonds
Chetwynd, Bridget
Petunia Best and Max Frend series (2)
Rubout at the Onyx
Jeffers, Harry Paul
Harry Macneil series (1)
Ruby
Aitken, Amy
Ruby series (1)
Guy, Rosa
Edith Jackson series (3)
Ruby and Ruthy
Paull, Minnie E
Ruby and Ruthy series (1)
Ruby at school
Paull, Minnie E
Ruby and Ruthy series (3)
Ruby cup
Vincent, Kitty
Gyp Kidnadze series (2)
Ruby fleet
Moray, Helga
Dean Brothers series (2)
Ruby in the smoke
Pullman, Philip
Sally Lockhart series (1)
Ruby knight
Eddings, David
Elenium trilogy (2)
Ruby of a thousand dreams
Daniel, Roland
Wu Fang series (3)
Ruby pin
Carter, Nicholas
Nicholas Carter series (163)
Ruby ray mystery
Blaine, John
Rick Brant series (19)
Ruby red death
Carter, Nick
Nick Carter series (257)
Ruby, the red knight
Aitken, Amy
Ruby series (2)
Ruby's ups and downs
Paull, Minnie E
Ruby and Ruthy series (2)
Ruby's vacation
Paull, Minnie E
Ruby and Ruthy series (4)
Ruckus at Gila Wells
Grover, Marshall
Larry and Stretch series (415)
Ructions at Ranford
White, Paul
Ranford series (2)
Rudd family
Rudd, Steele
Rudd family series (10)
Rudder Grange
Stockton, Frank Richard
Rudder Grange series (1)
Rudder Grangers abroad, and other stories
Stockton, Frank Richard
Rudder Grange series (2)
Rude awakening
Aldiss, Brian Wilson
Horace Stubbs series (3)
Rudie's goat
Mathews, Joanna Hooe
Kitty and Lulu series (4)
Rudolph Strange
Watson, Edmund Henry Lacon
Strange family trilogy (2)
Rue Plumet
Hugo, Victor Marie
Fate trilogy (1)
Ruey Richardson, Chaletian
Brent-Dyer, Elinor Mary
Chalet School series (44)
Ruffled feathers
Grahame, Iain
Daw's Hall series (2)
Ruffly speaking
Conant, Susan
Dog lover's mystery series (3)
Rufty Tufty and Hattie
Ainsworth, Ruth
Rufty Tufty series (7)
Rufty Tufty at the seaside
Ainsworth, Ruth
Rufty Tufty series (2)
Rufty Tufty flies high
Ainsworth, Ruth
Rufty Tufty series (5)
Rufty Tufty goes camping
Ainsworth, Ruth
Rufty Tufty series (3)
Rufty Tufty makes a house
Ainsworth, Ruth
Rufty Tufty series (8)
Rufty Tufty runs away
Ainsworth, Ruth
Rufty Tufty series (4)
Rufty Tufty the golliwog
Ainsworth, Ruth
Rufty Tufty series (1)
Rufty Tufty's island
Ainsworth, Ruth
Rufty Tufty series (6)
Rufus and Christopher and the box of laughter
Hastings, Ian
Rufus and Christopher series (1)
Rufus and Christopher and the magic bubble
Hastings, Ian
Rufus and Christopher series (3)
Rufus and Christopher in the land of lies
Hastings, Ian
Rufus and Christopher series (2)
Rufus and Rose
Alger, Horatio
Ragged Dick series (6)
Rufus M
Estes, Eleanor
Moffat family series (3)
Rufus rolls on
Herbert, Roy
Rufus series (2)
Rufus to the rescue
Maisner, Heather
Tractors of Thomson's Yard series (4)
Rufus Tractor
Herbert, Roy
Rufus series (1)
Rug and a picnic
Cresswell, Helen
Rug series (4)
Rug is a bear
Cresswell, Helen
Rug series (1)
Rug plays ball
Cresswell, Helen
Rug series (3)
Rug plays tricks
Cresswell, Helen
Rug series (2)
Ruggles of Red Gap
Wilson, Harry Leon
Red Gap series (1)
Ruins of Kaldak
Lord, Jeffrey
Richard Blade series (34)
Ruins of Rangar
Carr, Mike
Fantasy forest series (2)
Ruler of Shahut
Blackburn, Martin
Delgado series (2)
Rulers of Belgian Africa, 1884-1914
Gann, Lewis Henry
Rulers of Africa series (3)
Rulers of British Africa, 1870-1914
Gann, Lewis Henry
Rulers of Africa series (2)
Rulers of German Africa, 1884-1914
Gann, Lewis Henry
Rulers of Africa series (1)
Rulers of the Lakes
Altsheler, Joseph Alexander
French and Indian war series (3)
Rules of engagement
Morwood, Peter
Star trek series (48)
Weber, Joe
Military techno-thrillers series (3)
Rules of prey
Sandford, John
Lucas Davenport series (1)
Rules of the game
Mosley, Nicholas
Sir Oswald Mosley series (1)
Roberts, Nora
Flowers series (18)
White, Stewart Edward
Lumbering trilogy (3)
Orde family series (3)
Ruling passion
Hill, Reginald
Superintendent Andrew Dalziel and Sergeant Pascoe series (5)
Ruling powers
Housman, Laurence
Palace plays series (4)
Ruling the waves
Barker, Dennis
People of the forces trilogy (2)
Rum affair
Dunnett, Dorothy
Johnson and the yacht Dolly series (1)
Rum and Coca-Cola
De Boissiere, Ralph
Trinidad series (2)
Rum and Coca-Cola murders
Brown, Wenzell
Peter Aswell series (2)
Rum, bum and concertina
Melly, George
Owning up series (2)
Rum colony
Bonner, Terry Nelsen
New South Wales series (1)
Rumanian circle
Black, Lionel
Kate Theobald series (7)
Rumanian operation
Rosenberger, Joseph
Death Merchant series (57)
Rumor hath it
Hale, Christopher
Lieutenant Bill French series (9)
Rumor of war
Caputo, Philip
War memoirs series (1)
Rumors
Cooney, Caroline B
Cheerleaders series (3)
Lowell, Anne Hunter
Sorority girls series (10)
Pascal, Francine
Sweet Valley High series (37)
Rumpelstiltskin
McBain, Ed
Matthew Hope series (2)
Rumpole
Mortimer, John
Horace Rumpole series (2)
Rumpole a la carte
Mortimer, John
Horace Rumpole series (8)
Rumpole and the age of miracles
Mortimer, John
Horace Rumpole series (7)
Rumpole and the golden thread
Mortimer, John
Horace Rumpole series (5)
Rumpole for the defence
Mortimer, John
Horace Rumpole series (4)
Rumpole of the Bailey
Mortimer, John
Horace Rumpole series (1)
Rumpole on trial
Mortimer, John
Horace Rumpole series (9)
Rumpole's last case
Mortimer, John
Horace Rumpole series (6)
Rumpole's return
Mortimer, John
Horace Rumpole series (3)
Run
Cave, Peter
Hell's Angels series (3)
Run a golden mile
Joyce, Cyril
Chief Superintendent Pat Stockton series (4)
Run-Abouts' holiday
Blyton, Enid
Caravan family series (2)
Run away!
Danby, Mary
Famous Five and you series (3)
Run away home
Forest, Antonia
Marlow family series (10)
Run away to murder
York, Jeremy
Superintendent Folly series (3)
Run, baby, run
Cruz, Nicky
New York gang series (1)
Run down
Garrett, Robert
Alan Brett series (1)
Run for cover
Benteen, John
Sundance series (16)
Welcome, John
Richard Graham series (1)
Run for lover
Janson, Hank
Hank Janson series (130)
Run for the border
Edson, John Thomas
Rockabye County series (9)
Run for your death
Hossent, Harry
Max Heald series (5)
Run for your life
Foley, Rae
Hiram Potter series (3)
Run fox run
Maile, Ben
Land of tomorrow series (2)
Run from nightmare
O'Callaghan, Maxine
Delilah West series (2)
Run from the buzzards
Grover, Marshall
Larry and Stretch series (211)
Run lethal
Stark, Richard
Alan Grofield series (2)
Parker series (8)
Run, little leather boy
Townsend, Larry
Leather bondage series (1)
Run me a river
Giles, Janice Holt
Fowler family series (9)
Run, mongoose
Wilkinson, Burke
Geoffrey Mildmay series (2)
Run no more
Townsend, Larry
Leather bondage series (2)
Run out the guns
Challoner, Robert
Commander Lord Charles Oakshott series (1)
Run silent, run deep
Beach, Edward Latimer, junior
Rich Richardson series (1)
Run, spy, run
Carter, Nick
Nick Carter series (1)
Run strong, run free
Grover, Marshall
Larry and Stretch series (257)
Run swift, run free
McCaughren, Tom
Foxes of Ireland series (3)
Run-through
Houseman, John
Unfinished business trilogy (1)
Run to Beaver Towers
Hinton, Nigel
Beaver Towers trilogy (3)
Run to Chaos Keep
Chalker, Jack Laurence
Quintara Marathon series (2)
Run to death
Quentin, Patrick
Peter Duluth series (7)
Run to earth
Carter, Nicholas
Nicholas Carter series (108)
McCaughren, Tom
Foxes of Ireland series (2)
Run to evil
Egan, Lesley
Vic Varallo series (3)
Run to ground
Pendleton, Don
Mack Bolan series (106)
Run to the ark
McCaughren, Tom
Foxes of Ireland series (4)
Run wild
McCaughren, Tom
Foxes of Ireland series (5)
Run with the loot
Grover, Marshall
Larry and Stretch series (337)
Run with the wind
McCaughren, Tom
Foxes of Ireland series (1)
Run Zebby run
Schroeder, Binette
Zebby series (5)
Runagates Club
Buchan, John
Richard Hannay series (6)
Sir Edward Leithen series (5)
Runaround
Freemantle, Brian
Charlie Muffin series (9)
Warren, Vernon
Mark Brandon series (7)
Runaway
Clewes, Dorothy
Penny series (1)
Gilman, George G
Adam Steele series (34)
Irvine, Lucy
Runaway series (1)
Morris, Gilbert
Jim Reno series (3)
Pascal, Francine
Sweet Valley High series (21)
Rey, Bret
Will Foreman series (1)
Watson, Clarissa
Persis Willum series (3)
Runaway airship
Adams, Eustace Lane
Andy Lane series (4)
Runaway Bim
Lindsay, Frances
Bim series (3)
Runaway bride
Hodge, Jane Aiken
Purchis family series (3)
Keene, Carolyn
Nancy Drew files series (96)
Runaway caravan
Wirt, Mildred Augustine
Trailer series (1)
Runaway corpse
Warren, James
James Warren series (2)
Runaway giant
Wilhelm, Hans
Merritales series (5)
Runaway hamster
Pascal, Francine
Sweet Valley kids series (2)
Runaway horses
Mishima, Yukio
Sea of fertiligy quartet (2)
Runaway house mystery
Christian, Mary Blount
Goosehill Gang series (7)
Runaway Marie Louise
Carlson, Natalie Savage
Marie Louise series (3)
Runaway marriage brokers
Palmer, Cyril Everard
Beppo Tate series (2)
Runaway mystery at Sugar Creek
Hutchens, Paul
Sugar Creek Gang series (35)
Runaway Ralph
Cleary, Beverly
Ralph S Mouse series (2)
Runaway Ramsey
Grover, Marshall
Larry and Stretch series (392)
Runaway rancher
Hardin, J D
Raider and Doc series (58)
Runaway riders
Brims, Bernagh
Ballyreagh Jumping Team series (1)
Runaway robot
Del Rey, Lester
Ganymede series (2)
Runaway slave
Tralins, Sandor Robert
Black stud trilogy (2)
Runaways
Andom, R
Troddles series (7)

Canning, Victor
Smiler Miles trilogy (1)
Runes
Monaco, Richard
Leitus series (1)
Runes of the lyre
Mayhar, Ardath
House of Enthala trilogy (2)
Runestaff
Moorcock, Michael
History of Runestaff series (4)
Runner Bean
Reed, Giles
Munch Bunch character series (24)
Runner in the street
Grady, James
James Rankin series (1)
Runners of Orford
Whittle, Tyler
Spaniards and Elizabethans series (2)
Running!
Lane, Maxie
Running series (1)
Running back
James, Laurence
American football series (1)
Running bear
Alborough, Jez
Bare bear series (2)
Running blind
Bagley, Desmond
Slade series (1)
Running deep
Petrie, Rhona
Inspector Marcus Maclurg series (3)
Running fight
Osborne, William Hamilton
William Murgatroyd series (2)
Running footman
Owen, John
Edward Bringle series (1)
Running Fox
Gregor, Elmer Russell
Eastern Indians series (1)
Running foxes
Stranger, Joyce
Dai Evans series (1)
Running hot
Pendleton, Don
Mack Bolan series (80)
Running, jumping and throwing, if you can
Paulsen, Gary
Sports on the light side series (5)
Running killer
Elliott, William James
Royston Frere series (2)
Running man
Benson, Ben
Ralph Lindsey series (5)
Running nun
Flynn, Brian
Anthony Bathurst series (42)
Running on empty
Dixon, Franklin W
Hardy boys case files series (36)
Running out of magic, with Houdini
Levy, Elizabeth
Running out series (2)
Running out of time
Levy, Elizabeth
Running out series (1)
Running proud
Monsarrat, Nicholas
Master mariner series (1)
Running scared
Brand, Hilary
Hilary Brand series (7)
Keene, Carolyn
Nancy Drew files series (69)
Running skeletons
Robeson, Kenneth
Doc Savage series (128)
Running spy
Milton, Joseph
Bart Gould series (2)
Running tide
Roberts, Cynthia S
Running tide series (1)
Short, Agnes
Christie family series (2)
Running to paradise
Arnold, Bruce
Coppinger tetralogy (4)
Runs in the sun
Parks, Jim
Runs in the sun series (1)
Runt
Levy, Elizabeth
Fat Albert series (6)
Runway to death
Filgate, Macartney
Charlotte Eliot series (1)
Rupert again
Tourtel, Mary
Rupert Bear series (52)
Rupert and Algernon
Tourtel, Mary
Rupert Bear series (40)
Rupert and Algy at Hawthorne Farm
Tourtel, Mary
Rupert Bear series (25)
Rupert and Bill and the pirates
Tourtel, Mary
Rupert Bear series (44)
Rupert and Bill Badger's Christmas party
Tourtel, Mary
Rupert Bear series (29)
Rupert and Bill keep shop
Tourtel, Mary
Rupert Bear series (39)
Rupert and Bill's aeroplane adventure
Tourtel, Mary
Rupert Bear series (42)
Rupert and Bill's seaside holiday
Tourtel, Mary
Rupert Bear series (49)
Rupert and Bingo
Tourtel, Mary
Rupert Bear series (45)
Rupert and Dapple
Tourtel, Mary
Rupert Bear series (41)
Rupert and Dickory Dock
Bestall, Alfred
Rupert Bear series (86)
Rupert and Edward and the circus
Tourtel, Mary
Rupert Bear series (50)
Rupert and his friend Margot
Tourtel, Mary
Rupert Bear series (11)
Rupert and his pet monkey
Tourtel, Mary
Rupert Bear series (10)
Rupert and his pet monkey again
Tourtel, Mary
Rupert Bear series (30)
Rupert and King Pippin
Tourtel, Mary
Rupert Bear series (19)
Rupert and Neddy
Bestall, Alfred
Rupert Bear series (65)
Rupert and Podgy's picnic day
Chaplain, Frederick
Rupert Bear series (98)
Rupert and Prince Humpty-Dumpty
Tourtel, Mary
Rupert Bear series (32)
Rupert and Raggerty
Bestall, Alfred
Rupert Bear series (89)
Rupert and Reynard Fox
Tourtel, Mary
Rupert Bear series (6)
Rupert and Rollo
Bestall, Alfred
Rupert Bear series (56)
Rupert and the birthday surprise
Bestall, Alfred
Rupert Bear series (77)
Rupert and the bit of magic
Collis, Len
Rupert Bear series (107)
Rupert and the black dwarf
Tourtel, Mary
Rupert Bear series (9)
Rupert and the black moth
Bestall, Alfred
Rupert Bear series (58)
Rupert Bear series (92)
Rupert and the blue mist
Wells, Mick
Rupert TV playbook series (4)
Rupert and the blue mountain
Bestall, Alfred
Rupert Bear series (93)
Rupert and the bottled moonbeams
Bestall, Alfred
Rupert Bear series (81)
Rupert and the boy pirate
Bestall, Alfred
Rupert Bear series (69)
Rupert and the brigands
Tourtel, Mary
Rupert Bear series (6)
Rupert and the carved stick
Bestall, Alfred
Rupert Bear series (91)
Rupert and the Chocolate Buttons Gang
Collis, Len
Rupert Bear series (110)
Rupert and the Christmas crackers
Collis, Len
Rupert Bear series (106)
Rupert and the Christmas tree fairies
Tourtel, Mary
Rupert Bear series (29)
Rupert and the circus clown
Tourtel, Mary
Rupert Bear series (16)
Rupert and the double dream
Bestall, Alfred
Rupert Bear series (70)
Rupert and the dragon
Tourtel, Mary
Rupert Bear series (7)
Rupert and the enchanted princess
Tourtel, Mary
Rupert Bear series (8)
Rupert and the fancy dress party
Tourtel, Mary
Rupert Bear series (22)
Rupert and the flying chariot
Bestall, Alfred
Rupert Bear series (88)
Rupert and the French poodles
Bestall, Alfred
Rupert Bear series (78)
Rupert and the funny joke man
Collis, Len
Rupert Bear series (109)
Rupert and the giant's castle
Bestall, Alfred
Rupert Bear series (82)
Rupert and the greedy princess
Tourtel, Mary
Rupert Bear series (48)
Rupert and the happy wish
Bestall, Alfred
Rupert Bear series (80)
Rupert and the haunted house
Collis, Len
Rupert Bear series (114)
Rupert and the hidden lake
Chaplain, Frederick
Rupert Bear series (99)
Rupert and the holiday ship
Bestall, Alfred
Rupert Bear series (75)
Rupert and the jumping fish
Bestall, Alfred
Rupert Bear series (94)
Rupert and the little plane
Bestall, Alfred
Rupert Bear series (59)
Rupert and the little prince
Tourtel, Mary
Rupert Bear series (18)
Rupert and the little tree
Bestall, Alfred
Rupert Bear series (64)
Rupert and the lonely bird
Chaplain, Frederick
Rupert Bear series (102)
Rupert and the lost railway
Bestall, Alfred
Rupert Bear series (74)
Rupert and the magic hat
Tourtel, Mary
Rupert Bear series (17)
Rupert and the magic key
Tourtel, Mary
Rupert Bear series (6)
Rupert and the magic toy man
Tourtel, Mary
Rupert Bear series (5)
Rupert and the magic whistle
Tourtel, Mary
Rupert Bear series (26)
Rupert and the magician's hat
Wells, Mick
Rupert TV playbook series (3)
Rupert and the magician's umbrella
Tourtel, Mary
Rupert Bear series (43)
Rupert and the miser's hoard
Collis, Len
Rupert Bear series (113)
Rupert and the muddled magic
Chaplain, Frederick
Rupert Bear series (97)
Rupert and the mystery moor
Collis, Len
Rupert Bear series (118)
Rupert and the mystery voice
Bestall, Alfred
Rupert Bear series (96)
Rupert and the new rose
Bestall, Alfred
Rupert Bear series (62)
Rupert and the Nutwood stage
Collis, Len
Rupert Bear series (111)
Rupert and the Nutwood well
Collis, Len
Rupert Bear series (103)
Rupert and the old man of the sea
Tourtel, Mary
Rupert Bear series (24)
Rupert and the old miser
Tourtel, Mary
Rupert Bear series (5)
Rupert and the pink kitten
Bestall, Alfred
Rupert Bear series (87)
Rupert and the pirates
Bestall, Alfred
Rupert Bear series (90)
Rupert and the pirates' den
Collis, Len
Rupert Bear series (115)
Rupert and the postman
Wells, Mick
Rupert TV playbook series (1)
Rupert and the princess
Tourtel, Mary
Rupert Bear series (5)
Rupert and the robber wolf
Tourtel, Mary
Rupert Bear series (7)
Rupert and the rocking horse
Bestall, Alfred
Rupert Bear series (68)
Rupert and the seaside holiday
Bestall, Alfred
Rupert Bear series (71)
Rupert and the seaside mystery
Bestall, Alfred
Rupert Bear series (79)
Rupert and the secret trail
Collis, Len
Rupert Bear series (117)
Rupert and the secret treasure
Collis, Len
Rupert Bear series (119)
Rupert and the seven keys
Collis, Len
Rupert Bear series (116)
Rupert and the smugglers' gold
Collis, Len
Rupert Bear series (112)
Rupert and the snow babe's Christmas
Tourtel, Mary
Rupert Bear series (46)
Rupert and the snow man
Bestall, Alfred
Rupert Bear series (60)
Rupert and the snow pranks
Bestall, Alfred
Rupert Bear series (83)
Rupert and the snow sports
Bestall, Alfred
Rupert Bear series (76)
Rupert and the snowman
Tourtel, Mary
Rupert Bear series (7)
Rupert and the space ship
Bestall, Alfred
Rupert Bear series (72)
Rupert and the stolen apples
Tourtel, Mary
Rupert Bear series (13)
Rupert and the strange kingdom
Chaplain, Frederick
Rupert Bear series (101)
Rupert and the stray puppy
Bestall, Alfred
Rupert Bear series (63)
Rupert and the Swan Lake
Bestall, Alfred
Rupert Bear series (66)
Rupert and the swift journey
Chaplain, Frederick
Rupert Bear series (100)
Rupert and the three robbers
Tourtel, Mary
Rupert Bear series (14)
Rupert and the trouble with Big Ben
Collis, Len
Rupert Bear series (105)
Rupert and the twins' birthday
Tourtel, Mary
Rupert Bear series (49)
Rupert and the white dove
Tourtel, Mary
Rupert Bear series (40)
Rupert and the wicked uncle
Bestall, Alfred
Rupert Bear series (61)
Rupert and the wild goose chase
Bestall, Alfred
Rupert Bear series (73)
Rupert and the wilful princess
Tourtel, Mary
Rupert Bear series (20)
Rupert and the wise goat's Birthday cake
Tourtel, Mary
Rupert Bear series (15)
Rupert and the wobbly witch
Collis, Len
Rupert Bear series (104)
Rupert and the wonderful boots
Tourtel, Mary
Rupert Bear series (28)
Rupert Bear series (54)
Rupert and the wooden soldiers
Tourtel, Mary
Rupert Bear series (23)
Rupert and the wrong presents
Bestall, Alfred
Rupert Bear series (57)
Rupert and the yellow elephant
Collis, Len
Rupert Bear series (108)
Rupert and the young dragon
Bestall, Alfred
Rupert Bear series (95)
Rupert and Uncle Bruno
Bestall, Alfred
Rupert Bear series (55)
Rupert and Wily Wispe
Tourtel, Mary
Rupert Bear series (37)
Rupert at the school
Tourtel, Mary
Rupert Bear series (5)
Rupert at the seaside
Tourtel, Mary
Rupert Bear series (7)
Rupert Bear series (45)
Rupert gets captured
Tourtel, Mary
Rupert Bear series (46)
Rupert gets stolen
Tourtel, Mary
Rupert Bear series (27)
Rupert goes hiking
Tourtel, Mary
Rupert Bear series (36)
Rupert goes to the moon
Wells, Mick
Rupert TV playbook series (2)
Rupert in Dreamland
Tourtel, Mary
Rupert Bear series (6)
Rupert in the tree tops
Bestall, Alfred
Rupert Bear series (67)
Rupert in the wood of mystery
Tourtel, Mary
Rupert Bear series (12)
Rupert in trouble again
Tourtel, Mary
Rupert Bear series (22)
Rupert Little Bear, more stories
Tourtel, Mary
Rupert Bear series (53)
Rupert Little Bear's adventures, volume 1
Tourtel, Mary
Rupert Bear series (5)
Rupert Little Bear's adventures, volume 2
Tourtel, Mary
Rupert Bear series (6)
Rupert Little Bear's adventures, volume 3
Tourtel, Mary
Rupert Bear series (7)
Rupert, Margot and the bandits
Tourtel, Mary
Rupert Bear series (38)
Rupert, Margot and the fairies
Tourtel, Mary
Rupert Bear series (11)
Rupert of Hentzau
Hope, Anthony
Rudolf Rassendyl series (2)
Rupert story book
Tourtel, Mary
Rupert Bear series (51)
Rupert the devil
Hunter, Joan
Rupert of the Rhine series (1)
Rupert, the knight and the lady
Tourtel, Mary
Rupert Bear series (15)
Rupert, the manikin and the black knight
Tourtel, Mary
Rupert Bear series (47)
Rupert, the witch and Tabitha
Tourtel, Mary
Rupert Bear series (35)

Rupert's ambition
Alger, Horatio
How to rise trilogy (2)
Rupert's Christmas adventure
Tourtel, Mary
Rupert Bear series (23)
Rupert's Christmas cards
Wells, Mick
Rupert TV playbook series (5)
Rupert's Christmas thrills
Tourtel, Mary
Rupert Bear series (39)
Rupert's Christmas tree
Tourtel, Mary
Rupert Bear series (34)
Rupert's holiday adventure
Tourtel, Mary
Rupert Bear series (33)
Rupert's latest adventure
Tourtel, Mary
Rupert Bear series (31)
Rupert's message to Father Christmas
Tourtel, Mary
Rupert Bear series (33)
Rupert's mysterious flight
Tourtel, Mary
Rupert Bear series (21)
Rupert's New Year's Eve party
Tourtel, Mary
Rupert Bear series (33)
Rupert's picnic party
Tourtel, Mary
Rupert Bear series (34)
Rupert's summer adventure
Bestall, Alfred
Rupert Bear series (84)
Rupert's winter adventure
Bestall, Alfred
Rupert Bear series (85)
Rural pursuits
Yates, Renate
Inspector Ereache O'Shea series (2)
Rural reflections
Hutchings, Monica Mary
Church Farm series (3)
Rural scene
Gilbert, Bernard
Old England series (4)
Rusalka
Cherryh, Carolyn Janice
Rusalka series (1)
Ruse of the vanished women
Gielgud, Val
Antony Havilland series (1)
Rush for the spoils
Zola, Emile
Rougon Macquart series (2)
Rush hour crime
Skene, Anthony
Sexton Blake series (852)
Rush of golden wings
Baldry, Cherith
Stories of six worlds series (1)
Rush to destiny
Martin, Larry Jay
John Clinton Ryan series (5)
Rushers
Edson, John Thomas
Floating Outfit series (41)
Rushton boys at Rally Hall
Davenport, Spencer
Rushton boys series (1)
Rushton boys at Treasure Cove
Davenport, Spencer
Rushton boys series (2)
Rushton boys in the saddle
Davenport, Spencer
Rushton boys series (3)
Ruskins and the Grays
Lutyens, Mary
Effie Gray series (3)
Ruskin's Berlin
Greatorex, Wilfred
Airline series (2)
Russ Tobin bedside guide to smoother seduction
Morgan, Stanley
Russ Tobin series (15)
Russ Tobin in Hollywood
Morgan, Stanley
Russ Tobin series (15)
Russ Tobin up tight
Morgan, Stanley
Russ Tobin series (14)
Russell and Elisa
Hurwitz, Johanna
Elisa series (1)
Russell series (4)
Russell rides again
Hurwitz, Johanna
Russell series (2)
Russell sprouts
Hurwitz, Johanna
Russell series (3)
Russia, anyone?
Nicol, Eric
Uncalled-for histories series (2)
Russia for beginners
Atkinson, Alex
Rocking-chair series (2)
Russia, what is the Golden Horde?
Packard, Edward
Earth inspectors series (12)
Russian bear
Meek, Joseph
Mountain Jack Pike series (7)
Russian child and Russian wife
Matthews, Tanya
Russian wife series (1)
Russian childhood
Fen, Elisaveta
Russia series (1)
Russian enigma
Egleton, Clive
Charles Winter series (2)
Russian gentleman
Aksakov, Sergei Timofeevich
Russian family chronicle series (3)
Russian history atlas
Gilbert, Martin
History atlas series (6)
Russian intelligence
Moorcock, Michael
Jerry Cornell series (2)
Russian leave
Stuart, Anthony
Vladimir Gull series (6)
Russian lode
Garrett, Charles C
Gunslinger series (9)
Russian River
McCarthy, Gary
Rivers west series (5)
Russian roulette
Mitchell, James
David Callan series (2)
Russian schoolboy
Aksakov, Sergei Timofeevich
Russian family chronicle series (2)
Russian twins
Charnock, Joan
Twin series (35)
Russian wife goes west
Matthews, Tanya
Russian wife series (2)
Russian years
Boyd, Brian
Vladimir Nabokov series (1)
Russians in America, 1727-1970
Wertsman, Vladimir
Ethnic groups in America series (3)
Russka
Rutherford, Edward
Generations series (2)
Rustle of petticoats
McCormick, Renee
Coquette series (2)
Rustler guns
Bexar, Phil
Billy Dupree series (10)
Rustler's empire
Field, Peter
Powder Valley series (77)
Rustler's guns
Scott, Bradford
Walt Slade series (52)
Rustlers of the cattle range
Grey, Romer Zane
Buck Duane series (7)
Rustlers on the High Range
Atwater, Montgomery Meigs
Hank Winton series (4)
Rustlers' Range
Borg, Jack
Hogleg Bailey series (12)
Rustler's Range
Bosworth, Frank
Earl Morton series (7)
Rustler's range
Scott, Bradford
Walt Slade series (8)
Rustler's rock
Field, Peter
Powder Valley series (61)
Rustlers' round-up
Mann, Edward Beverly
Whistler series (1)
Rustlers' trail
Leyland, Eric
Bill, Jake and Ned series (2)
Rustlers' Valley
Mulford, Clarence Edward
Matt Skinner series (1)
Rustler's venom
Lee, W W
Jefferson Birch series (2)
Rustling death
Robeson, Kenneth
Doc Savage series (132)
Rustling end
Browne, Douglas Gordon
Mister Harvey Tuke series (4)
Rustling grass
DeJonge, Joanne E
My Father's world series (1)
Rusty Hines hits the trail
Nickson, Arthur
Rusty Hines series (2)
Rusty Hines, troubleshooter
Nickson, Arthur
Rusty Hines series (3)
Rusty of the high towers
Sterrett, Frances Roberta
Rusty series (2)
Rusty of the meadow lands
Sterrett, Frances Roberta
Rusty series (4)
Rusty of the mountain peaks
Sterrett, Frances Roberta
Rusty series (3)
Rusty of the tall pines
Sterrett, Frances Roberta
Rusty series (1)
Rusty the sheepdog
Pilgrim, Jane
Blackberry Farm series (5)
Ruth and Patience
Charlesworth, Maria Louisa
Ministering children series (1)
Ruth Crane
Morgan, Alison
Llanwern series (3)
Ruth Darrow in the Air Derby
Wirt, Mildred Augustine
Ruth Darrow series (1)
Ruth Darrow in the coast guard
Wirt, Mildred Augustine
Ruth Darrow series (4)
Ruth Darrow in the fire patrol
Wirt, Mildred Augustine
Ruth Darrow series (2)
Ruth Darrow in Yucatan
Wirt, Mildred Augustine
Ruth Darrow series (3)
Ruth Erskine's crosses
Pansy
Ruth Erskine series (1)
Ruth Erskine's son
Pansy
Ruth Erskine series (3)
Ruth Fielding and Baby Jane
Emerson, Alice B
Ruth Fielding series (27)
Ruth Fielding and her crowning victory
Emerson, Alice B
Ruth Fielding series (30)
Ruth Fielding and her double
Emerson, Alice B
Ruth Fielding series (28)
Ruth Fielding and her great scenario
Emerson, Alice B
Ruth Fielding series (23)
Ruth Fielding and her greatest triumph
Emerson, Alice B
Ruth Fielding series (29)
Ruth Fielding and the gypsies
Emerson, Alice B
Ruth Fielding series (8)
Ruth Fielding at Briarwood Hall
Emerson, Alice B
Ruth Fielding series (2)
Ruth Fielding at Cameron Hall
Emerson, Alice B
Ruth Fielding series (24)
Ruth Fielding at college
Emerson, Alice B
Ruth Fielding series (11)
Ruth Fielding at Golden Pass
Emerson, Alice B
Ruth Fielding series (21)
Ruth Fielding at Lighthouse Point
Emerson, Alice B
Ruth Fielding series (4)
Ruth Fielding at Silver Ranch
Emerson, Alice B
Ruth Fielding series (5)
Ruth Fielding at snow camp
Emerson, Alice B
Ruth Fielding series (3)
Ruth Fielding at Sunrise farm
Emerson, Alice B
Ruth Fielding series (7)
Ruth Fielding at the War Front
Emerson, Alice B
Ruth Fielding series (14)
Ruth Fielding clearing her name
Emerson, Alice B
Ruth Fielding series (25)
Ruth Fielding down East
Emerson, Alice B
Ruth Fielding series (16)
Ruth Fielding down in Dixie
Emerson, Alice B
Ruth Fielding series (10)
Ruth Fielding homeward bound
Emerson, Alice B
Ruth Fielding series (15)
Ruth Fielding in Alaska
Emerson, Alice B
Ruth Fielding series (22)
Ruth Fielding in moving pictures
Emerson, Alice B
Ruth Fielding series (9)
Ruth Fielding in talking pictures
Emerson, Alice B
Ruth Fielding series (26)
Ruth Fielding in the Far North
Emerson, Alice B
Ruth Fielding series (20)
Ruth Fielding in the great Northwest
Emerson, Alice B
Ruth Fielding series (17)
Ruth Fielding in the Red Cross
Emerson, Alice B
Ruth Fielding series (13)
Ruth Fielding in the saddle
Emerson, Alice B
Ruth Fielding series (12)
Ruth Fielding of the Red Mill
Emerson, Alice B
Ruth Fielding series (1)
Ruth Fielding on Cliff Island
Emerson, Alice B
Ruth Fielding series (6)
Ruth Fielding on the Saint Lawrwnce
Emerson, Alice B
Ruth Fielding series (18)
Ruth Fielding treasure hunting
Emerson, Alice B
Ruth Fielding series (19)
Ruth Lovell
May, Carrie L
Recovered pearl series (4)
Ruth, the unsuspecting
Kimbrough, Katheryn
Phenwick women series (17)
Ruth, the woman who loved
Newte, Horace Wykeham Can
Ruth series (1)
Ruthless range
Hobart, Donald Bayne
Masked Rider and Blue Hawk series (4)
Ruthless yeoman
Anand, Valerie
Bridges over time series (2)
Rutland mystery
Gregg, Cecil Freeman
Inspector Cuthbert Higgins series (5)
Rutland Place
Perry, Anne
Charlotte Ellison Pitt and Inspector Thomas Pitt series (5)
RV and the haunted garage
Gilden, Mel
Zoomers of Motor City series (2)
Ryan affair
Macdonald, Donald
Tommy Briggs series (4)
Ryan's rules
Leonard, Elmore
Frank Ryan series (1)
Ryder's army
Weston, Cole
Andrew Ryder series (3)
Rye Royal
Saville, Malcolm
Lone Pine Five Club series (17)
Rynosseros
Dowling, Terry
Tom Tyson series (1)

S

S.A.S. versus the C.I.A.
De Villiers, Gerard
Malko Linge series (1)
S.O.R losers
Avi
South Orange River Middle School series (1)
S.O.S. bobomobile
Wahl, Jan
Melvin Spitznagle series (2)
S.O.S. for sheepdog Taff
Berrisford, Judith Mary
Taff series (3)
S O S from Mars
Cross, John Keir
Albatross series (2)
S.O.S. from three worlds
Leinster, Murray
Med Service series (4)
S.O.S. Spaceship Titan
Brand, Kurt
Perry Rhodan series (34)
S.W.F Club
Elliot, Emilia
Joan series (4)
Saba's treasure
Douglass, Donald McNutt
Bolivar Manchenil series (3)
Sabata
Fox, Brian
Sabata series (1)
Sabazel
Carl, Lillian Stewart
Sabazel trilogy (1)
Sabbatical
Barth, John
Fenwick and Susan series (1)
Saber and Shadow
Stirling, Stephen Michael
Fifth millenium series (8)
Saber dance
Glick, Ruth
Charisma Inc. series (1)
Sabine
Freeling, Nicolas
Henri Castang series (3)
Sabine's notebook
Bantock, Nick
Griffin Moss and Sabine Stroheim trilogy (2)
Sable adventure
Rockman, Clint
Sable ivory series (5)
Sable Diana
Rockman, Clint
Sable ivory series (4)
Sable messenger
Vivian, Francis
Inspector Gordon Knollis series (3)
Sable mistress
Rockman, Clint
Sable ivory series (6)
Sable moon
Springer, Nancy
Book of Isle series (3)
Sables spell trouble
Mitchell, Scott
Brock Devlin series (2)
Sabotage
Adams, Cleve Franklin
Rex McBride series (2)
Creasey, John
Department Z series (16)
John, Owen
Haggai Godin series (6)
Leibold, Jay
Choose your own adventure series (38)
Leyland, Eric
Rip Randall series (2)
Macdonnell, James Edmond
Captain Peter Bentley series (32)
Sabotage at sea
Dixon, Franklin W
Hardy boys case files series (92)
Sabotage at Sports City
Dixon, Franklin W
Hardy boys series (115)
Sabotage at Stableways
Berrisford, Judith Mary
Pippa series (2)
Sabotage in space
Rockwell, Carey
Tom Corbett series (7)
Sabotage murder mystery
Allingham, Margery
Albert Campion series (13)
Sabotage unlimited
Groom, Pelham
Peter Mohune series (1)
Saboteurs in A-1
Brand, Kurt
Perry Rhodan series (115)
Saboteurs on the river
Wirt, Mildred Augustine
Penny Parker series (10)

Sabre
Darby, Catherine
Sabre family series (1)
Sabre charge
Randolph, Forrest A
Confederate series (3)
Sabre Squadron
Raven, Simon
Alms for oblivion series (3)
Sabre-Tooth
O'Donnell, Peter
Modesty Blaise series (2)
Sabrehill
Giles, Raymond
Sabrehill series (1)
Sabre's child
Darby, Catherine
Sabre family series (2)
Sabres of the Reich
Kessler, Leo
Black Cossacks series (2)
Sabrina
Ransom, Candice Farris
Sunfire series (17)
Sac Mau, Victor Charlie
Cain, Jonathan
Saigon commandos series (7)
Sac Prairie people
Derleth, August
Sac Prairie series (12)
Sachem
Porter, Donald Clayton
White Indian series (4)
Sachem's daughter
Porter, Donald Clayton
White Indian series (21)
Sachem's son
Porter, Donald Clayton
White Indian series (20)
Sack time
Browne, Dik
Hagar the horrible series (27)
Sackcloth and ashes
Troyat, Henri
Danov family trilogy (2)
Sackett
L'Amour, Louis
Sackett family series (7)
Sackett brand
L'Amour, Louis
Sackett family series (10)
Sacketts
L'Amour, Louis
Sackett family series (8)
Sackett's land
L'Amour, Louis
Sackett family series (1)
Sacking Paris on a budget
Browne, Dik
Hagar the horrible series (12)
Sackside Tumbleweeds
Ryan, Tom K
Tumbleweeds series (10)
Sacred and profane
Kellerman, Faye
Sergeant Peter Decker and Rina Lazarus series (2)
Weiss, David
Wolfgang Amadeus Mozart series (1)
Sacred and profane love
Bennett, Arnold
Five towns series (5)
Sitwell, Sacheverell
Quick and the dead series (2)
Sacred city
Sayer, Walter William
Sexton Blake series (202)
Sacred clowns
Hillerman, Tony
Lieutenant Joe Leaphorn series (8)
Sergeant Jim Chee series (8)
Sacred feather
Judd, Frances K
Kay Tracey series (14)
Sacred giraffe
Madariaga, Salvador de
Julio Arceval series (2)
Sacred ground
Briggs, Victor
Way ahead trilogy (1)
Sacred hills
Coldsmith, Don
Spanish bit series (8)
Sacred journey
Buechner, Frederick
Sacred journey series (1)
Sacred mushroom and the cross
Allegro, John Marco
Christian origins series (1)
Sacred night
Ben Jelloun, Tahar
Sand child series (2)
Sacred science
Schwaller de Lubicz, Isha
Homo sapiens series (2)
Sacred shaft
Weatherhead, John
Professor David Connell series (2)
Sacred stones
Sarabande, William
First Americans series (5)
Sacred symbols of Mu
Churchward, James
Mu series (3)
Sacred tree
Murasaki Shibuku
Genji series (2)
Sacred well of sacrifice
Bamman, Henry A
World of adventure series (7)
Sacrifice for the Quagga god
Edson, John Thomas
Bunduki series (3)
Sacrifice of Ruanon
Dever, Joe
Legends of Lone Wolf series (6)
Sacrificial ground
Cook, Thomas H
Frank Clemons series (1)
Sad and happy summer
Mackenzie, Lee
Emmerdale Farm series (5)
Sad and savage dying
Audemars, Pierre
Monsieur Pinaud series (22)
Sad and tender flesh
Frances, Stephen Daniel
John Gail series (3)
Sad cypress
Christie, Agatha
Hercule Poirot series (20)
Sad-eyed seductress
Brown, Carter
Danny Boyd series (7)
Sad song for singing
Dewey, Thomas Blanchard
Private Eye Mac series (10)
Sad Sontag plays his hunch
Tuttle, Wilbur Coleman
Sad Sontag series (1)
Sad variety
Blake, Nicholas
Nigel Strangeways series (15)
Sadar's keep
Snyder, Midori
Queen's quarter series (2)
Saddle boys at Circle Ranch
Carson, James
Saddle boys series (4)
Saddle boys in the Grand Canyon
Carson, James
Saddle boys series (2)
Saddle boys of the Rockies
Carson, James
Saddle boys series (1)
Saddle boys on Mexican trails
Carson, James
Saddle boys series (5)
Saddle boys on the plains
Carson, James
Saddle boys series (3)
Saddle hawks
Lomax, Bliss
Rainbow Ripley series (1)
Saddle tramp
Borg, Jack
Hogleg Bailey series (14)
Ledd, Paul
Shelter Morgan series (20)
Saddle tramps
Floren, Lee
Buckshot McKee and Tortilla Joe series (6)
Saddle up, Blackbirds
Furminger, Jo
Blackbird series (6)
Saddle up, Tumbleweeds
Ryan, Tom K
Tumbleweeds series (13)
Saddles to Santa Fe!
Field, Peter
Powder Valley series (52)
Saddletramp
Hawkins, Clint
Saddletramp series (1)
Saddletramp justice
Grover, Marshall
Larry and Stretch series (142)
Sadhu of the mountain peak
Macneil, Duncan
James Ogilvie series (3)
Sadie, don't cry now
Janson, Hank
Hank Janson series (44)
Sadie Rose and the champion sharpshooter
Stahl, Hilda
Sadie Rose series (7)
Sadie Rose and the Cottonwood Creek orphan
Stahl, Hilda
Sadie Rose series (2)
Sadie Rose and the dangerous search
Stahl, Hilda
Sadie Rose series (10)
Sadie Rose and the daring escape
Stahl, Hilda
Sadie Rose series (1)
Sadie Rose and the double secret
Stahl, Hilda
Sadie Rose series (4)
Sadie Rose and the impossible birthday wish
Stahl, Hilda
Sadie Rose series (9)
Sadie Rose and the mad fortune hunters
Stahl, Hilda
Sadie Rose series (5)
Sadie Rose and the mysterious stranger
Stahl, Hilda
Sadie Rose series (11)
Sadie Rose and the outlaw rustlers
Stahl, Hilda
Sadie Rose series (3)
Sadie Rose and the phantom warrior
Stahl, Hilda
Sadie Rose series (6)
Sadie Rose and the secret romance
Stahl, Hilda
Sadie Rose series (8)
Sadie Shapiro in Miami
Smith, Robert Kimmel
Sadie Shapiro series (2)
Sadie Shapiro, matchmaker
Smith, Robert Kimmel
Sadie Shapiro series (3)
Sadie Shapiro's knitting book
Smith, Robert Kimmel
Sadie Shapiro series (1)
Sadie Spider
Edwards, Pat
Sadie Spider series (1)
Sadie Spider goes to school
Edwards, Pat
Sadie Spider series (4)
Sadie Spider moves in
Edwards, Pat
Sadie Spider series (3)
Sadie Spider strikes again
Edwards, Pat
Sadie Spider series (2)
Sadie when she died
McBain, Ed
Eighty Seventh Precinct series (26)
Sadist
Hamill, Edson T
Joe Ryker series (7)
SADISTO royale
Allison, Clyde
Agent triple zero eight series (7)
Safari adventure
Price, Willard
Hal and Roger Hunt series (8)
Safari episode
Jennings, D K
Doctor Ralph Conway series (10)
Safari for spies
Carter, Nick
Nick Carter series (4)
Safari in Africa
Bell, Sally
Young Indiana Jones chronicles series (4)
Safari with fear!
Hardinge, Rex
Sexton Blake series (1473)
Safe at first
Hughes, Dean
Angel Park All-Stars series (11)
Safe secret
Carmichael, Harry
John Piper and Quinn series (23)
Safety at home
Higgs, Mike
Learn with Moonbird series (3)
Safety first murders
Radford, Edwin
Doctor Manson series (26)
Safety first with Topsy and Tim
Adamson, Jean
Life with Topsy and Tim series (1)
Safety in the water
Higgs, Mike
Learn with Moonbird series (6)
Safety matches
Sabatier, Robert
Olivier Chateauneuf series (1)
Safety with fire
Higgs, Mike
Learn with Moonbird series (7)
Saffron
Buffery, Judith
Star lords series (2)
Saffron's army
Smith, Frederick Escreet
Saffron series (2)
Saffron's war
Smith, Frederick Escreet
Saffron series (1)
Saga-book of Lunda
Saxby, Jessie Margaret Edmonston
Shetland series (4)
Saga of a wayward sailor
Jones, Tristan
Wayward sailor series (5)
Saga of Andy Burnett
White, Stewart Edward
Andy Burnett series (3)
Saga of Cuckoo
Pohl, Frederik
Cuckoo's saga series (2)
Saga of Halfaday Creek
Hendryx, James Beardsley
Black John series (12)
Saga of lost earths
Petaja, Emil
Kalevala series (1)
Saga of old city
Gygax, Gary
Greyhawk series (1)
Saga of Sam Burdew
Grover, Marshall
Larry and Stretch series (297)
Saga of the reindeer people
Lindholm, Megan
Reindeer people series (2)
Saga of the sea
Sabatini, Rafael
Captain Blood series (3)
Saga of the seas
Grahame, Kenneth
Smith family series (2)
Sage of Sare
Smith, Julie Dean
Caithan Crusade series (3)
Sage River conspiracy
Sharpe, Jon
Trailsman series (133)
Sagebrush sleuth
Edson, John Thomas
Waco series (3)
Sagebrush swindle
Field, Peter
Powder Valley series (62)
Saguaro showdown
Sharpe, Jon
Trailsman series (153)
Sahara
Cussler, Clive
Dirk Pitt series (11)
Sahara boom-de-ay
Baron, Nicole de
Penelope and Guillaume series (1)
Buron, Nicole de
Penelope and Guillaume trilogy (1)
Sahara hostage
Frost, Kelman Dalgety
Captain John Walton series (2)
Sahara road
Harvester, Simon
Asia in turmoil series (23)
Dorian Silk series (11)
Sahara strike
Cleary, Denis
Breakenridge series (2)
Said with flowers
Nash, Anne
Mark Tudor series (1)
Saigon
Carter, Nick
Nick Carter series (6)
Saigon commandos
Cain, Jonathan
Saigon commandos series (1)
Saigon singer
Mason, Francis Van Wyck
Colonel Hugh North series (16)
Saigon slaughter
Buchanan, Jack
M.I.A. Hunter series (7)
Lansing, John
Black Eagles series (5)
Sail ho!
Bisset, James
Years at sea series (1)
Sail with pirates
Gasperini, Jim
Time machine series (4)
Sailing
Gree, Alain
Books and games series (3)
Sailing to Cythera, and other Anatole stories
Willard, Nancy
Anatole series (1)
Sailing to see
Johnson, Irving
Yankee series (2)
Sailor
Bruna, Dick
Toy box tale series (9)
Sailor, beware!
Cary, Falkland
Hornett family series (1)
Duff, Reginald Eustace Bluett
Hornett family series (1)
Sailor boy
Optic, Oliver
Army and navy series (2)
Sailor boy with Dewey
Bonehill, Ralph
Flag and frontier series (8)
Flag of freedom series (2)
Sailor in the East
King, Robin
Merchant Navy trilogy (2)
Sailor Jack
Wassermann, Selma
Sailor Jack series (1)
Sailor Jack and Bluebell
Wassermann, Selma
Sailor Jack series (2)
Sailor Jack and Bluebell's dive
Wassermann, Selma
Sailor Jack series (8)
Sailor Jack and Eddy
Wassermann, Selma
Sailor Jack series (7)
Sailor Jack and Homer Pots
Wassermann, Selma
Sailor Jack series (6)
Sailor Jack and the ball game
Wassermann, Selma
Sailor Jack series (10)
Sailor Jack and the jet plane
Wassermann, Selma
Sailor Jack series (9)
Sailor Jack and the target ship
Wassermann, Selma
Sailor Jack series (4)
Sailor Jack goes north
Wassermann, Selma
Sailor Jack series (5)
Sailor Jack's new friend
Wassermann, Selma
Sailor Jack series (3)
Sailor on the seas of fate
Moorcock, Michael
Elric series (2)
Sailor, take warning!
Roos, Kelley
Jeff and Haila Troy series (4)
Sailor's blood
Hardy, Adam
George Abercrombie Fox series (5)
Sailor's knots
Jacobs, William Wymark
Night-Watchman series (8)
Sailors of fortune
McFee, William
Pilgrims and sailors series (2)
Sailors on horseback
Stuart, Vivian
Captain Alexander Sheridan series (6)
Sailor's rendezvous
Simenon, Georges
Inspector Jules Maigret series (2)
Sailors' wives
Fabian, Warner
Flaming youth series (2)
Sainsbury, V.C.
Macdonnell, James Edmond
Commander Sainsbury series (3)
Saint
Fogazzaro, Antonio
Maironi family trilogy (3)
Saint abroad
Charteris, Leslie
Saint series (41)
Saint and Mister Teal
Charteris, Leslie
Saint series (10)

Saint and the fiction makers
Charteris, Leslie
Saint series (40)
Saint and the Hapsburg necklace
Short, Christopher
Saint series (46)
Saint and the last hero
Charteris, Leslie
Saint series (3)
Saint and the people importers
Charteris, Leslie
Saint series (43)
Saint and the sizzling saboteur
Charteris, Leslie
Saint series (25)
Saint series (26)
Saint and the Templar treasure
Weaver, Graham
Saint series (49)
Saint Angelo
Wright, Sydney Fowler
Siege of Malta series (2)
Saint around the world
Charteris, Leslie
Saint series (31)
Saint at a thieves' picnic
Charteris, Leslie
Saint series (18)
Saint at large
Charteris, Leslie
Saint series (21)
Saint Bernard's
Scalpel, Aesculapius
Saint Bernard's series (1)
Saint bids diamonds
Charteris, Leslie
Saint series (18)
Saint Bride blue
Burr, Sybil
Holly Gordon series (3)
Saint Camber
Kurtz, Katherine
Legends of Camber of Culdi trilogy (2)
Saint Catherine's wheel
Griffin, John
Richard Raven series (7)
Saint cleans up
Bloxsom, Peter
Saint series (51)
Saint closes the case
Charteris, Leslie
Saint series (3)
Saint Cloud affair
Baskerville, Beatrice
Briconi series (2)
Saint Cuthbert's
Copus, John Edwin
Saint Cuthbert's series (1)
Saint Dunstan Boy Scouts
Eldred, Warren L
Saint Dunstan series (4)
Saint Elmo
Wright, Sydney Fowler
Siege of Malta series (1)
Saint errant
Charteris, Leslie
Saint series (28)
Saint-Fiacre affair
Simenon, Georges
Inspector Jules Maigret series (2)
Inspector Jules Maigret series (11)
Saint-Germain chronicles
Yarbro, Chelsea Quinn
Count Ragoczy Saint-Germain series (6)
Saint goes on
Charteris, Leslie
Saint series (14)
Saint goes west
Charteris, Leslie
Saint series (23)
Saint Helena, little island
Aldanov, Mark Aleksandrovich
Thinker series (4)
Saint in action
Charteris, Leslie
Saint series (17)
Saint in England
Charteris, Leslie
Saint series (12)
Saint in Europe
Charteris, Leslie
Saint series (29)
Saint in London
Charteris, Leslie
Saint series (12)
Saint in Miami
Charteris, Leslie
Saint series (22)
Saint in New York
Charteris, Leslie
Saint series (15)
Saint in pursuit
Charteris, Leslie
Saint series (42)
Saint in the sun
Charteris, Leslie
Saint series (36)
Saint in trouble
Weaver, Graham
Saint series (48)
Saint intervenes
Charteris, Leslie
Saint series (13)
Saint Ives
Bleeck, Oliver
Philip Saint Ives series (3)
Saint John and the seven veils
Babula, William
Saint John series (3)
Saint John's
Cabell, James Branch
It happened in Florida trilogy (1)
Saint John's Baptism
Babula, William
Saint John series (1)
Saint John's bestiary
Babula, William
Saint John series (4)
Saint John's Eve
Duhamel, Georges
Pasquier series (4)
Saint Jonathan's in the country
Fidler, Kathleen
Brydon family series (2)
Saint Kelvern's launches out
Pearce, Carol Ann
Saint Kelvern's Bury School series (2)
Saint Lawrence run
Wilcox, Stephen F
T S W Sheridan series (2)
Saint Louis fire
Meek, Joseph
Mountain Jack Pike series (6)
Saint Louis Jezebel
Fletcher, Dirk
Spur McCoy series (3)
Saint Louis showdown
Pendleton, Don
Mack Bolan series (23)
Roberts, J R
Gunsmith series (113)
Saint maker
Holton, Leonard
Father Joseph Bredder series (1)
Saint-Malo mystery
Maske, John
Duncan Cainsforth series (2)
Jeremy Flack series (1)
Saint Martin's Eve
Wood, Ellen
Mildred Arkell series (2)
Saint meets his match
Charteris, Leslie
Saint series (7)
Saint meets the tiger
Charteris, Leslie
Saint series (1)
Saint on guard
Charteris, Leslie
Saint series (25)
Saint on the Spanish Main
Charteris, Leslie
Saint series (30)
Saint on TV
Charteris, Leslie
Saint series (38)
Saint overboard
Charteris, Leslie
Saint series (16)
Saint Patrick's Day magic
Baker, James Webb
Magic series (9)
Saint Peter's fair
Peters, Ellis
Brother Cadfael series (4)
Saint Peter's finger
Mitchell, Gladys
Dame Beatrice Bradley series (9)
Saint plays with fire
Charteris, Leslie
Saint series (19)
Saint Quentin
Dumas, Alexandre
Valois series (3)
Saint returns
Charteris, Leslie
Saint series (39)
Saint sees it through
Charteris, Leslie
Saint series (26)
Saint steps in
Charteris, Leslie
Saint series (24)
Saint Thomas's Eve
Plaidy, Jean
Tudor series (6)
Saint to the rescue
Charteris, Leslie
Saint series (34)
Saint, two in one
Charteris, Leslie
Saint series (21)
Saint Urbain's Horseman
Richler, Mordecai
Saint Urbain's Street series (2)
Saint Valentine's Day murders
Edwards, Ruth Dudley
Robert Amiss series (2)
Saint Valentine's night
Greeley, Andrew Moran
Monsignor John Blackwood Ryan series (6)
Saint versus Scotland Yard
Charteris, Leslie
Saint series (8)
Sainte Monique roundabout
Lister, Stephen
Sainte Monique series (7)
Sainte Monique unlimited
Lister, Stephen
Sainte Monique series (8)
Saintly Billy
Naughton, Bill
Saintly Billy trilogy (1)
Saints alive
Charteris, Leslie
Saint series (44)
Saints and adventurers
Barclay, Vera Charlesworth
Saints series (4)
Saints are sinister
Flynn, Brian
Anthony Bathurst series (53)
Saints by firelight
Barclay, Vera Charlesworth
Saints series (2)
Saints for the harvest
Marbach, Ethel
Saints series (3)
Saints for the journey
Marbach, Ethel
Saints series (2)
Saints for the seasons
Marbach, Ethel
Saints series (4)
Saint's getaway
Charteris, Leslie
Saint series (9)
Saints in waiting
Marbach, Ethel
Saints series (1)
Saints of these islands
Barclay, Vera Charlesworth
Saints series (3)
Saint's progress
Galsworthy, John
Love trilogy (3)
Sakhalin breakout
Hild, Jack
SOBS series (18)
Sal-o-quah
Goulding, Francis Robert
Woodruff trilogy (3)
Salamandastron
Jacques, Brian
Redwall series (6)
Salamander
Janes, Joseph Robert
Jean-Louis Saint-Cyr and Hermann Kohler series (4)
Salamander sword
Wilkinson, Laurence
Mike Daryl series (3)
Salamander war
Carr, Charles
Bel series (2)
Salamanders
Grant, Maxwell
Shadow series (99)
Salavin
Duhamel, Georges
Salavin series (5)
Salavin's journal
Duhamel, Georges
Salavin series (3)
Saleh
Clifford, Hugh
Outskirts series (2)
Salem Chapel
Oliphant, Margaret Oliphant Wilson
Carlingford series (1)
Sales clerk made me buy it
Guisewhite, Cathy
Cathy series (8)
Salesman of death
Leader, Charles
Mike McCall series (3)
Sally again
Bruce, Dorita Fairlie
Sally Scatterbrain series (2)
Sally and billy at the seaside
Gree, Alain
Keith and Sally series (13)
Sally and Billy in the woods
Gree, Alain
Keith and Sally series (4)
Sally and Billy look at the ships
Gree, Alain
Keith and Sally series (7)
Sally and Billy on the farm
Gree, Alain
Keith and Sally series (8)
Sally and her puppy
Carruth, Jean
Fun with Sally series (1)
Sally and Jake and a tortoise
Cosgrove, Brian
Sally and Jake series (1)
Sally and Jake go to the fair
Cosgrove, Brian
Sally and Jake series (2)
Sally and Jake on the farm
Cosgrove, Brian
Sally and Jake series (3)
Sally and Jake play bowls
Cosgrove, Brian
Sally and Jake series (4)
Sally, and other tales of the outskirts
Clifford, Hugh
Outskirts series (1)
Sally and the sixpenny pig
Christian, Catherine Mary
Sally series (1)
Sally and Tom and the digger
Lynam, Terence
Sally and Tom series (2)
Sally and Tom and the helicopter
Lynam, Terence
Sally and Tom series (1)
Sally and Tom and the road roller
Lynam, Terence
Sally and Tom series (4)
Sally and Tom and the tractor
Lynam, Terence
Sally and Tom series (3)
Sally Ann at the ballet
Dicks, Terrance
Sally Ann series (5)
Sally Ann goes to hospital
Dicks, Terrance
Sally Ann series (4)
Sally-Ann in the snow
Breinburg, Petronella
Sally-Ann series (2)
Sally Ann on her own
Dicks, Terrance
Sally Ann series (1)
Sally Ann's experience
Hall, Eliza Calvert
Aunt Jane series (1)
Sally Ann's picnic
Dicks, Terrance
Sally Ann series (3)
Sally Ann's school play
Dicks, Terrance
Sally Ann series (2)
Sally-Ann's skateboard
Breinburg, Petronella
Sally-Ann series (3)
Sally-Ann's umbrella
Breinburg, Petronella
Sally-Ann series (1)
Sally Baxter, girl reporter, and the runaway princess
Edwards, Sylvia
Sally Baxter series (3)
Sally Baxter, girl reporter, and the golden yacht
Edwards, Sylvia
Sally Baxter series (13)
Sally Baxter, girl reporter, and the mystery heiress
Edwards, Sylvia
Sally Baxter series (2)
Sally Baxter, girl reporter, and the underwater adventure
Edwards, Sylvia
Sally Baxter series (8)
Sally Baxter, girl reporter, in Australia
Edwards, Sylvia
Sally Baxter series (7)
Sally Baxter, girl reporter, in Canada
Edwards, Sylvia
Sally Baxter series (1)
Sally Baxter, girl reporter, on location
Edwards, Sylvia
Sally Baxter series (4)
Sally Baxter, girl reporter, on the shamrock mystery
Edwards, Sylvia
Sally Baxter series (15)
Sally Bowles
Isherwood, Christopher
Berlin series (2)
Sally Cinderella
Ashley, Bernard
Clipper Street series (6)
Sally in Rhodesia
Macdonald, Sheila
Rhodesia series (1)
Sally in the jungle
Carruth, Jean
Fun with Sally series (1)
Sally joins the patrol
Christian, Catherine Mary
Sally series (2)
Sally Lunn
Walmsley, Leo
Phantom Lobster series (3)
Sally on holiday
Carruth, Jean
Fun with Sally series (2)
Sally on the farm
Carruth, Jean
Fun with Sally series (3)
Sally Scarth
Jacob, Naomi
Broad acres series (1)
Sally Scatterbrain
Bruce, Dorita Fairlie
Sally Scatterbrain series (1)
Sally Strawberry
Reed, Giles
Munch Bunch character series (5)
Sally Strawberry and the painted snake
Reed, Giles
Munch Bunch story books series (2)
Sally, the screech owl
Darby, Joan
Animal adventure series (5)
Sally's in the alley
Davis, Norbert
Doan and Carstairs series (1)
Sally's story
Morgan, Sally
My place series (1)
Sally's summer term
Bruce, Dorita Fairlie
Sally Scatterbrain series (3)
Sally's sweetheart
Burgin, George Brown
Four Corners series (15)
Salmon in the soup
O'Brien, Meg
Jessica James series (2)
Salome, the wandering Jewess
Viereck, George Sylvester
Wandering Jew trilogy (2)
Saloon girl
Fletcher, Dirk
Spur McCoy series (17)
Sal's book
Liquori, Sal
Psi Patrol trilogy (1)
Salt and spices
Owen, Dilys
Mister Munch series (6)
Salt boy
Mauzey, Merritt
Farm boy series (6)
Salt for the tiger
Tuttle, Wilbur Coleman
Hashknife Hartley and Sleepy Stevens series (20)
Salt in my porridge
Macvicar, Angus
Confessions series (1)
Salt Lake City
Riefe, A R
Fortunes west series (4)
Salt of the earth
Humphreys, Emyr
Amy Parry series (3)
Spencer, Sally
Becky Taylor series (1)
Salt of Vermont
Hard, Walter
Vermont series (2)
Salt water daffy
Wylie, Philip
Crunch and Des series (2)
Salt-water Dick
Mannering, May
Climbing the rope series (5)
Salt-water hero
Rand, Edward Augustus
Fighting the sea series (4)

Salterton trilogy
Davies, Robertson
Salterton trilogy (3)
Saltillo road
Saddler, Jeff
Apache Anderson series (11)
Saltillo Road
Sadler, Jeff
Marshal Andrew Anderson series (11)
Saltmarsh murders
Mitchell, Gladys
Dame Beatrice Bradley series (4)
Saltwater summer
Haig-Brown, Roderic Langmere
Don Morgan series (2)
Salty
Westron, Charles
Salty series (1)
Salty ashore
Westron, Charles
Salty series (3)
Salud!
O'Donnell, Peadar
Another day series (2)
Saludas, Texans
Grover, Marshall
Larry and Stretch series (27)
Salute Blue Mask!
Morton, Anthony
Baron series (4)
Salute for the Baron
Morton, Anthony
Baron series (32)
Salute from a dead man
Mackenzie, Donald
Harry Chalice and Crying Eddie series (1)
Salute Inspector Flagg
Cassells, John
Superintendent Flagg series (13)
Salute Mister Sandyman
Graham, Neill
Mister Sandyman series (7)
Salute the Dreamer
Duncan, William Murdoch
Superintendent Donald Reamer series (7)
Salute the Picaroon
Cassells, John
Ludovic Saxon series (7)
Salute the Toff
Creasey, John
Toff series (6)
Salute to Bazarada, and other stories
Rohmer, Sax
Paul Harley series (2)
Salute to Blackshirt
Graeme, Roderic
Blackshirt series (14)
Salute to Cyrano
Feval, Paul
Years between series (6)
Salute to freedom
Lowe, Eric
Stewart family series (3)
Salute to murder
Graham, Neill
Solo Malcolm series (6)
Salvage for the Saint
Bloxsom, Peter
Saint series (51)
Salvage from Strosa
Pope, Ray
Strosa light series (2)
Salvage job
Macleod, Robert
Andrew Laird series (3)
Salvage of the sea
Graydon, William Murray
Sexton Blake series (63)
Salvation history and the religious life
Hinnebusch, Paul
Religious life series (2)
Salvation, 1944-1946
Gaulle, Charles de
War memoirs series (3)
Salvator
Dumas, Alexandre
Mohicans of Paris series (2)
Salve
Moore, George
Hail and farewell trilogy (2)
Salzburg affair
White, James Dillon
Sebastian Kettle series (2)
Sam
Powell, Jonathan
Sam Wilson series (1)
Sam and Joe
Garland, Sarah
Sam series (4)
Sam and the big machines
Henderson, Kathy
Sam series (1)
Sam and the box
Henderson, Kathy
Sam series (2)
Sam at the seaside
Faulkner, Keith
Sam series (1)
Sam Briggs, his book
Marsh, Richard
Sam Briggs series (1)
Sam Briggs, VC
Marsh, Richard
Sam Briggs series (2)
Sam Delamer
Wisler, Gary Clifton
Willie Delamer series (9)
Sam for sale
Maisner, Heather
Tractors of Thomson's Yard series (2)
Sam goes shopping
Border, Rosemary
Out and about series (3)
Sam helps out
Faulkner, Keith
Sam series (2)
Sam Lawson's Oldtown fireside stories
Stowe, Harriet Beecher
Oldtown series (2)
Sam, Lizzie and the bonfire
Henderson, Kathy
Sam series (3)
Sam Pig and Sally
Uttley, Alison
Sam Pig series (4)
Sam Pig and the singing gate
Uttley, Alison
Sam Pig series (8)
Sam Pig at the circus
Uttley, Alison
Sam Pig series (5)
Sam Pig goes to market
Uttley, Alison
Sam Pig series (2)
Sam Pig goes to the seaside
Uttley, Alison
Sam Pig series (9)
Sam Pig in trouble
Uttley, Alison
Sam Pig series (6)
Sam Pig storybook
Uttley, Alison
Sam Pig series (9)
Sam saves the day
Martin, Charles E
Monhegan Island series (4)
Sam Slick
Haliburton, Thomas Chandler
Sam Slick series (10)
Sam Slick in search of a wife
Haliburton, Thomas Chandler
Sam Slick series (3)
Sam Slick, the clockmaker
Haliburton, Thomas Chandler
Sam Slick series (1)
Sam Slick's wise saws and modern instances
Haliburton, Thomas Chandler
Sam Slick series (8)
Sam Small flies again
Knight, Eric
Sam Small series (2)
Sam Small, the flying Yorkshireman
Knight, Eric
Sam Small series (2)
Sam Sparrow
Pilgrim, Jane
Blackberry Farm series (23)
Sam Steele's adventures in Panama
Fitzgerald, Hugh
Boy fortune hunters series (3)
Sam Steele series (2)
Sam Steele's adventures on land and sea
Fitzgerald, Hugh
Boy fortune hunters series (1)
Sam Steele series (1)
Sam the detective and the Alef Bet mystery
Rosenberg, Amye
Sam series (1)
Sam, the girl detective
Bradman, Tony
Sam, the girl detective series (1)
Sam the referee
Ahlberg, Allan
Brick Street Boys series (3)
Sam the silver bus
Eadington, Joan
Sam series (1)
Samain
Atkins, Meg Elizabeth
Inspector Henry Beaumont series (2)
Samantha
Cunningham, E V
Masao Masuto series (1)
Samantha among the brethren
Holley, Marietta
Samantha and Josiah Allen series (5)
Samantha among the colored folks
Holley, Marietta
Samantha and Josiah Allen series (6)
Samantha at Coney Island and a thousand other islands
Holley, Marietta
Samantha and Josiah Allen series (14)
Samantha at Saratoga
Holley, Marietta
Samantha and Josiah Allen series (4)
Samantha at the Centennial
Holley, Marietta
Samantha and Josiah Allen series (1)
Samantha at the Saint Louis Exposition
Holley, Marietta
Samantha and Josiah Allen series (10)
Samantha at the World's Fair
Holley, Marietta
Samantha and Josiah Allen series (7)
Samantha in Europe
Holley, Marietta
Samantha and Josiah Allen series (9)
Samantha learns a lesson
Tripp, Valerie
Samantha series (2)
Samantha on children's rights
Holley, Marietta
Samantha and Josiah Allen series (13)
Samantha on the race problem
Holley, Marietta
Samantha and Josiah Allen series (6)
Samantha on the woman question
Holley, Marietta
Samantha and Josiah Allen series (15)
Samantha saves the day
Tripp, Valerie
Samantha series (6)
Samantha Slade, monster-sitter
Smith, Susan
Samantha Slade series (1)
Samantha versus Josiah
Holley, Marietta
Samantha and Josiah Allen series (12)
Samantha's hungry day
Miller, Muriel
Woodlanders series (1)
Samantha's surprise
Tripp, Valerie
Samantha series (3)
Samarkand
Diamond, Graham
Samarkand series (1)
Samarkand dawn
Diamond, Graham
Samarkand series (2)
Samax, the gladiator
Faraday, Robert
Adventures in the time machine series (2)
Sambo and the twins
Bannerman, Helen
Little Black series (7)
Same difference
Janson, Hank
Hank Janson series (238)
Same lie twice
Goulart, Ron
John Easy series (3)
Same old Troddles
Andom, R
Troddles series (13)
Same ole Bill, eh, Mable!
Streeter, Edward
Mable series (3)
Same scourge
Goldthorpe, John
Early Christian series (1)
Same sky all over
Smith, David
Sky all over series (2)
Sammy and Mara
Van der Meer, Ron
Sammy and Mara series (2)
Sammy and the cat party
Van der Meer, Ron
Sammy and Mara series (3)
Sammy and the telly
Elliott, Odette
Sammy series (3)
Sammy Brown's treasure hunt
Gordon, Frederick
Fairview boys series (2)
Up and doing series (2)
Sammy goes flying
Elliott, Odette
Sammy series (2)
Sammy's Christmas workshop
Elliott, Odette
Sammy series (4)
Sammy's special day
Szekeres, Cyndy
Sammy day and night series (2)
Sammy's super T-shirt
Robertson, H Macleod
Sammy's super T-shirt series (1)
Sample of French familiar conversation
Balzac, Honore de
Scenes of Parisian life series (11)
Sampson the horse
Kanno, Wendy
Funny Farm series (5)
Sam's ball
Lindgren, Barbro
Sam series (4)
Sam's bath
Lindgren, Barbro
Sam series (6)
Sam's biscuit
Lindgren, Barbro
Sam series (3)
Sam's car
Lindgren, Barbro
Sam series (2)
Sam's cart
Lindgren, Barbro
Sam series (8)
Sam's cat
Garland, Sarah
Sam series (2)
Sam's chance and how he improved it
Alger, Horatio
Tattered Tom series (7)
Sam's cookie
Lindgren, Barbro
Sam series (3)
Sam's lamp
Lindgren, Barbro
Sam series (5)
Sam's potty
Lindgren, Barbro
Sam series (7)
Sam's reading rediness
Rosenberg, Amye
Sam series (2)
Sam's Teddy
Lindgren, Barbro
Sam series (1)
Sam's Teddy bear
Lindgren, Barbro
Sam series (1)
Sam's the name
Garland, Sarah
Sam series (1)
Sam's visit to the zoo
Border, Rosemary
Out and about series (2)
Sam's wagon
Lindgren, Barbro
Sam series (8)
Sam's wonderful week
Eadington, Joan
Sam series (2)
Samson
Daniel, Rebecca
Our greatest heritage series (7)
McClung, Robert Marshall
Endangered animals series (6)
Samson, the strong giant
Blyton, Enid
Bible stories series (5)
Samson's deal
Singer, Shelley
Jake Samson and Rosie Vincente series (1)
Samson's hoard
Verney, John
Callendar family series (5)
Samuel
Ross, Tony
Tales from Mister Toffy's circus series (1)
Samuel Lyle, criminologist
Crabb, Arthur
Samuel Lyle series (1)
Samuel Marchbanks' almanack
Davies, Robertson
Samuel Marchbanks series (3)
Samurai
Macbeth, George
Cadbury series (1)
Sadler, Barry
Casca series (19)
Samurai cat
Roe, JoAnn
Cat series (4)
Samurai Cat in the real world
Rogers, Mark Earl
Samurai Cat series (3)
Samurai combat
Rypel, Thadeus Chester
Gonji series (3)
Samurai contract
McCray, Mike
Black Berets series (11)
Samurai hunt
Roberts, J R
Gunsmith series (140)
Samurai kill
Carter, Nick
Nick Carter series (215)
Samurai steel
Rypel, Thadeus Chester
Gonji series (2)
Samurai wizard
Hawke, Simon
Wizard series (5)
San Angelo shootout
Logan, Jake
John Slocum series (165)
San Angelo showdown
Johnstone, William Wallace
Blood bond series (7)
San Antonio
Mitchum, Hank
Stage coach station series (25)
Orwig, Sara
Danby trilogy (1)
San Diego siege
Pendleton, Don
Mack Bolan series (14)
San Diego sirens
Fletcher, Dirk
Spur McCoy series (23)
San Franciscans
Busch, Niven
San Francisco series (2)
San Francisco
Riefe, A R
Fortunes west series (3)
San Francisco boy
Lenski, Lois
Regional series (11)
San Francisco by night
Spade, Danny
Danny Spade series (9)
San Francisco strumpet
Fletcher, Dirk
Spur McCoy series (7)
San Francisco vendetta
Mallory, Roosevelt
Radcliff series (2)
San Juan inferno
Carter, Nick
Nick Carter series (195)
San Juan shoot-out
Hardin, J D
Raider and Doc series (37)
San Matteo
Duff, Douglas Valder
Adam Macadam series (4)
San Quentin
Lynch, Jack
Peter Bragg series (5)
San Saba blockade
Grover, Marshall
Larry and Stretch series (119)
Sanction to slaughter
Carter, Nick
Nick Carter series (250)
Sanctuary
Asprin, Robert Lynn
Sanctuary series (3)
Faulkner, William
Gavin Stevens trilogy (1)
Narcissa series (2)
Sin and salvation series (4)
Temple Drake series (1)
Kellerman, Faye
Sergeant Peter Decker and Rina Lazarus series (7)
Sanctuary isle
Knox, Bill
Inspector Colin Thane and Phil Moss series (5)

Satan's mistress
Graeme, Bruce
Superintendent William Stevens and Inspector Pierre Allain series (5)
McNaughton, Brian
Mirdath series (2)
Satan's Sabbath
Pendleton, Don
Mack Bolan series (38)
Satan's seductress
McNaughton, Brian
Mirdath series (3)
Satan's seed
Sherman, Jory
Doctor Russell V Chillders series (1)
Satan's sunset
Hufford, Susan
Hilda Hughes tetralogy (4)
Satan's surrogate
McNaughton, Brian
Mirdath series (4)
Satan's swarm
Derrick, Lionel
Penetrator series (49)
Satan's world
Anderson, Poul
Polesotechnic League series (3)
Satanstoe
Cooper, James Fenimore
Littlepage manuscript trilogy (1)
Satchelmouse and the dinosaurs
Barber, Antonia
Satchelmouse series (1)
Satchelmouse and the doll's house
Barber, Antonia
Satchelmouse series (2)
Satchkin Patchkin
Morgan, Helen
Satchkin Patchkin series (1)
Satellite city
Reynolds, Mack
Rex Bader series (2)
Satellite slaughter
Derrick, Lionel
Penetrator series (33)
Satin and steel
Hart, Catherine
Kathleen Hartly Taylor and Reed Taylor series (2)
Satin ice
Johansen, Iris
Delaneys, the untamed years, second trilogy (1)
Satin-wood box
Trowbridge, John Townsend
Tide Mill series (3)
Satori
Schmidt, Dennis
Kensho series (3)
Satori in Paris
Kerouac, Jack
Jack Duluoz series (13)
Saturday adventure
Pudney, John
Fred and I series (1)
Saturday at Blackberry Farm
Pilgrim, Jane
Blackberry Farm series (24)
Saturday at M.I.9
Neave, Airey
Escape series (2)
Saturday city
Webster, Jan
Kate Kilgour trilogy (2)
Saturday horse
Hardcastle, Michael
Horse series (1)
Saturday night
Holmes, Marjorie
Carly and Danny series (1)
Saturday night dead
Rosen, Richard
Harvey Blissberg series (3)
Saturday night fever
Gilmour, H B
Saturday night fever series (1)
Walker, Mort
Hi and Lois series (6)
Saturday night in Candle Rock
Grover, Marshall
Larry and Stretch series (107)
Saturday night stalker
Berry, Joy
Human race club series (8)
Saturday of glory
Serafin, David
Superintendent Luis Bernal series (1)
Saturday the Rabbi went hungry
Kemelman, Harry
Rabbi David Small series (2)
Saturday wild
Grover, Marshall
Nevada Jim series (14)
Saturdays
Enright, Elizabeth
Melendy family series (1)
Saturdee
Lindsay, Norman
Redheap trilogy (2)
Saturn
Simon, Seymour
Space photos series (2)
Saturn, the spectacular planet
Branley, Franklyn Mansfield
Voyage into space series (1)
Saturnalia
Callin, Grant
Saturnalia series (1)
Freund, Philip
Volcano god trilogy (1)
Satying on
Scott, Paul
British India quartet (4)
Sauce for the pigeon
Hammond, Gerald
Keith Calder series (7)
Saucepan journey
Unnerstad, Edith
Larsson family series (1)
Saucers over the moon
Saville, Malcolm
Lone Pine Five Club series (8)
Saucy Jane family
Blyton, Enid
Mike, Belinda and Ann series (2)
Saul Weir
Durrant, Valentine
Saul Weir series (2)
Sauron defeated
Tolkien, John Ronald Reuel
History of Middle Earth series (9)
History of the Lord of the Rings series (4)
Sauron dominion
Pournelle, Jerry
War world series (3)
Sausalito
Lynch, Jack
Peter Bragg series (4)
Sauve qui peut
Durrell, Lawrence
Antrobus series (3)
Savage
McCurtin, Peter
Sundance series (28)
Savage autumn
O'Banyon, Constance
Joanne and Windhawk series (6)
Savage bliss
Edwards, Cassie
Savage series (8)
Savage blood
Cain, Jackson
Torn Slater series (2)
McCoy, Duff
Jeb Cutter series (3)
Savage breast
Long, Manning
Liz Parrott series (7)
Savage conquest
Taylor, Janelle
Sioux series (6)
York, Georgia
Georgia trilogy (3)
Savage dance
Edwards, Cassie
Savage series (10)
Savage dawn
Gilman, George G
Edge series (26)
Savage desire
O'Banyon, Constance
Joanne and Windhawk series (1)
Savage dream
Edwards, Cassie
Savage series (9)
Savage earth
Moray, Helga
Katie and Paul Van Riebeck series (2)
Savage ecstasy
Taylor, Janelle
Sioux series (1)
Savage Eden
Edwards, Cassie
Savage series (5)
Gluyas, Constance
Deep South trilogy (1)
Savage embers
Edwards, Cassie
Savage series (16)
Savage Empire
Lorrah, Jean
Savage Empire series (1)
Savage encounter
Goodchild, George
Inspector McLean series (51)
Savage fire
Pendleton, Don
Mack Bolan series (28)
Savage fury
Bale, Karen A
Sweet Medicine's prophecy series (5)
Savage game
Trevor, James
John Savage series (1)
Savage gunlaw
Scott, Bradford
Walt Slade series (116)
Savage guns
Sharpe, Jon
Trailsman series (150)
Savage heart
Edwards, Cassie
Savage series (1)
Savage height
Trevor, James
John Savage series (2)
Savage hills
Newton, Dwight Bennett
Jim Bannister series (2)
Savage horde
Ahern, Jerry
Survivalist series (6)
Savage horizons
Bittner, F Rosanne
Caleb Sax series (1)
Savage illusion
Edwards, Cassie
Savage series (15)
Savage interlude
Cushman, Dan
Crawford series (2)
Savage key
York, Georgia
Georgia trilogy (1)
Savage land
Ahlswede, Ann
Doctor Cicero Smith series (3)
Gobineau, Marceline
Stephanie series (5)
Savage mists
Edwards, Cassie
Savage series (13)
Savage mountains
Adams, Robert
Horseclans series (5)
Savage night
Ledd, Paul
Shelter Morgan series (15)
Savage obsession
Edwards, Cassie
Savage series (2)
Savage paradise
Edwards, Cassie
Savage series (4)
Savage Paris
Zola, Emile
Rougon Macquart series (3)
Savage Pellucidar
Burroughs, Edgar Rice
Pellucidar series (7)
Savage persuasion
Edwards, Cassie
Savage series (11)
Savage pirates
Chester, Gilbert
Sexton Blake series (798)
Savage place
Parker, Robert Brown
Spenser series (8)
Savage pride
Edwards, Cassie
Savage series (18)
Savage promise
Edwards, Cassie
Savage series (12)
Savage range
Short, Luke
Big Jim Wade series (2)
Savage rendezvous
Thompson, David
Nathaniel King series (3)
Savage revenge
Hardin, J D
Raider and Doc series (70)
Savage rite
Corder, Eric
Shame and glory series (5)
Savage safari
Thorne, Ramsay
Captain Gringo series (27)
Savage Salome
Brown, Carter
Danny Boyd series (6)
Savage Sam
Gipson, Fred
Old Yeller series (2)
Savage Scorpio
Akers, Alan Burt
Dray Prescot series (16)
Savage sequel
Janson, Hank
Hank Janson series (131)
Savage shadow
Sharpe, Jon
Trailsman series (16)
Savage siege
Hardy, Adam
George Abercrombie Fox series (3)
Savage sisters
Brown, Carter
Danny Boyd series (26)
Fletcher, Dirk
Spur McCoy series (14)
Savage slaughter
Rossi, Bruno
Sharpshooter series (13)
Savage spirit
Edwards, Cassie
Savage series (17)
Savage splendor
Edwards, Cassie
Savage series (6)
O'Banyon, Constance
Joanne and Windhawk series (2)
Savage spread
Gentry, Buck
Eli Holten series (33)
Savage spring
O'Banyon, Constance
Joanne and Windhawk series (5)
Savage squeeze
Maclean, Arthur
Sexton Blake series (1570)
Savage stars
Reinsmith, Richard
Bodyguard series (6)
Savage stronghold
Sargent, Craig
Last ranger series (2)
Savage summer
O'Banyon, Constance
Joanne and Windhawk series (4)
Savage Sunday
Grover, Marshall
Nevada Jim series (58)
Savage sunrise
Edwards, Cassie
Savage series (14)
Savage surrender
Edwards, Cassie
Savage series (3)
Savage venture
Ballinger, W A
Sexton Blake series (1537)
Savage warriors
Treece, Henry
Early Britain series (2)
Savage west
Fuller, Ed
Troubleshooters series (3)
Savage whispers
Edwards, Cassie
Savage series (7)
Savage winter
O'Banyon, Constance
Joanne and Windhawk series (3)
Savage world
Wilson, Gar
Phoenix Force series (51)
Savages
Black, Ian Stuart
Doctor Who series (109)
Hill, Peter
Inspector Robert Staunton series (4)
Savages of Gor
Norman, John
Tari Cabot series (17)
Savanna
Giles, Janice Holt
Fowler family series (6)
Savannah
Price, Eugenia
Savannah quartet (1)
Savannah Grey
York, Georgia
Georgia trilogy (2)
Savannah purchase
Hodge, Jane Aiken
Purchis family series (4)
Savannah swingsaw
Pendleton, Don
Mack Bolan series (74)
Savarin's shadow
Goyne, Richard
Padre series (2)
Save a bullet for Kehoe
Grover, Marshall
Larry and Stretch series (303)
Save a rope
Bailey, Henry Christopher
Mister Reggie Fortune series (23)
Save our school
Cross, Gillian
Clipper series (1)
Save the children
Pendleton, Don
Mack Bolan series (94)
Save the Khan
Bartos-Hoppner, Barbara
Mitya series (2)
Save the ponies!
Baxter, Gillian
Angela and Ian Kendall series (2)
Save the Unicorns!
Pascal, Francine
Unicorn Club series (1)
Save the Venturians!
McEvoy, Seth
Arcade explorers series (1)
Saved by a ruse
Carter, Nicholas
Nicholas Carter series (328)
Saved by Jiminy
Daniell, David Scott
Jiminy series (2)
Saved from the street
Samuels, Adelaide Florence
Dick and Daisy Travers series (3)
Saving a rope
Bailey, Henry Christopher
Mister Reggie Fortune series (23)
Saving Grace
Jones, Roger William
Inspector Evans and Sergeant Beddoes series (1)
Saving the Queen
Buckley, William Frank
Blackford Oakes series (1)
Savings and loans
McInerny, Ralph
Andrew Broom series (4)
Savior of the Empire
Scheer, Karl Herbert
Perry Rhodan series (117)
Saviour
Storey, Anthony
Second Coming trilogy (3)
Saviour of the Navy
Bryant, Arthur
Samuel Pepys series (3)
Saviours of society
McKenna, Stephen
Realists trilogy (1)
Savoy book
Britton, David
Savoy series (1)
Savoy dreams
Britton, David
Savoy series (2)
Savta Simcha and the cinnamon tree
Gavta, Yaffa
Savta Simcha series (3)
Savta Simcha and the incredible shabbos bag
Gavta, Yaffa
Savta Simcha series (1)
Savta Simcha and the seven splendid gifts
Gavta, Yaffa
Savta Simcha series (2)
Sawdust angel
Bowman, Gerald
Michael Shannon series (2)
Sawdust trail
Sharpe, Jon
Trailsman series (156)
Saxon Ashe, secret agent
Ashe, Saxon
Saxon Ashe series (2)
Saxon home
Birt, David
Saxons and Vikings series (11)
Saxon invasions
Birt, David
Saxons and Vikings series (1)
Say cheese
Giff, Patricia Reilly
Kids of the Polk Street School series (10)
Walker, Mort
Hi and Lois series (12)
Hi and Lois series (19)

Scent of eucalyptus
Hanrahan, Barbara
Eucalyptus series (1)
Scent of evil
Mayor, Archer Huntington
Lieutenant Joe Gunther series (3)
Scent of fear
Dean, Spencer
Don Cadee series (2)
Scent of mayhem
Bickers, Richard Townshend
Mark Stratton series (2)
Scent of mystery
Howard, Elizabeth Howard
My name is Paris series (3)
Scent of new-mown hay
Blackburn, John
General Charles Kirk series (1)
Scent of Rowan
Darby, Catherine
Rowan family series (3)
Scented flesh
Saber, Robert O
Carl Good series (1)
Sceptre of power
Simon, Morris
Advanced dungeons and dragons adventure gamebook series (4)
Kingdom of sorcery trilogy (1)
Sceptres and crowns
Warner, Susan Bagert
Sceptres and crowns series (1)
Schack job
Kane, Henry
Peter Chambers series (25)
Schemes of dragons
Smeds, Dave
War of the dragons series (2)
Scheming
Norby, Lisa
Cheerleaders series (28)
Cheerleaders series (43)
Schilsinger affair
Temple, Richard
Simon Leigh series (2)
Schimmelhorn file
Bretnor, Reginald
Papa Schimmelhorn series (1)
Schimmelhorn's gold
Bretnor, Reginald
Papa Schimmelhorn series (2)
Schirmer's death legion
Kessler, Leo
Wotan series (18)
Schirmer's headhunters
Kessler, Leo
Wotan series (16)
Schism
Granger, Bill
November Man series (3)
Schloss Fielding
De Born, Edith
De Kailern family series (1)
School
Bruna, Dick
Toy box tale series (10)
Burningham, John
Little book series (2)
School and other problems
Evans, Greg
Luann series (5)
School at Skelton Hall
Brent-Dyer, Elinor Mary
Skelton Hall series (1)
School at the Chalet
Brent-Dyer, Elinor Mary
Chalet School series (1)
School at Thrush Green
Read, *Miss*
Thrush Green series (9)
School bear days
Roy, Anne
Bear for all seasons series (2)
School book fair
Townson, Hazel
Speckled panic series (2)
School bus cat
Sharmat, Marjorie Weinman
Kids on the bus series (1)
School caretaker
Bentley, Diana
My school series (1)
School daze
Kaye, Marilyn
Camp Sunnyside Friends specials series (3)
School dinner disaster
Pinto, Jacqueline
Redwood Primary School series (1)
School donkey disaster
Pinto, Jacqueline
Redwood Primary School series (5)
School fair
Dicks, Terrance
Camden Street kids series (4)
School fete
Bentley, Diana
My school series (9)
School for cats
Averill, Esther
Jenny Linsky series (3)
School for love
Barton, Arthur
Time remembered series (3)
School for murder
Carmichael, Harry
John Piper and Quinn series (4)
School for saints
Hobbes, John Oliver
Robert Orange series (1)
School for slaughter
Buck, Peter
Marc Dean series (5)
Gilman, George G
Edge series (48)
School gala disaster
Pinto, Jacqueline
Redwood Primary School series (2)
School in danger
Allan, Mabel Esther
Harvie family series (2)
School in space
Browne, Reginald
Whitelands series (2)
School in the light-house
Rand, Edward Augustus
Up the Ladder Club series (2)
School is hell
Groening, Matt
Life in hell series (3)
School library disaster
Pinto, Jacqueline
Redwood Primary School series (3)
School mystery
Burgoyne, Peter
Peter Burgoyne series (1)
School nurse
Bentley, Diana
My school series (7)
School of darkness
Wellman, Manly Wade
John Thunstone trilogy (3)
School of wizardry
Doyle, Debra
Circle of magic series (1)
School on the moon
Walters, Hugh
Chris Godfrey series (23)
School on the precipice
Moss, Nancy
Cliff House series (1)
School outing
Bentley, Diana
My school series (8)
School outing disaster
Pinto, Jacqueline
Redwood Primary School series (4)
School secretary
Bentley, Diana
My school series (2)
School spirit
Hurwitz, Johanna
Edison-Armstrong School series (3)
Schooldays at the Abbey
Oxenham, Elsie J
Abbey girls retrospective series (1)
Schooldays of Fred Harley
Winfield, Arthur M
Bound to win series (2)
Bright and bold series (2)
Schooled to kill
Shannon, Dell
Lieutenant Luis Mendoza series (16)
Schoolgirl Jen at the Abbey
Oxenham, Elsie J
Abbey girls retrospective series (4)
Schoolgirl murder case
Wilson, Colin
Chief Inspector Gregory Saltfleet series (1)
Schoolgirls' battlefield
Jacberns, Raymond
Becky Compton series (2)
Schoolhouse in the wind
Treneer, Anne
Schoolhouse trilogy (1)
Schoolhouse in the woods
Caudill, Rebecca
Bonnie series (2)
Schoolhouse mystery
Warner, Gertrude Chandler
Boxcar children series (10)
Schoolma'am Trudy
Faid, Mary Alice
Trudy series (5)
Schoolmaster spy
Burgoyne, Peter
Peter Burgoyne series (3)
Schoolmasters
Fisher, Leonard Everett
Colonial Americans series (11)
Schoolmistress with the golden eyes
Myrivilis, Stratis
Mermaid Madonna series (2)
Schoolroom in the parlor
Caudill, Rebecca
Bonnie series (4)
Schools
Fisher, Leonard Everett
Nineteenth century America series (7)
Schools and education
Birt, David
Saxons and Vikings series (17)
Schools OK if you can stand the food
Evans, Greg
Luann series (13)
School's out
Blake, Susan
Hawthorne College series (6)
Schooner Mary Ann
Abbott, Jacob
August series (3)
Schrodinger's cat trilogy
Wilson, Robert Anton
Schrodinger's cat trilogy (3)
Schroeder's game
Maling, Arthur
Brock Potter series (2)
Schultz
Donleavy, James Patrick
Sigmund Schultz series (1)
Schultz money
Gair, Malcolm
Mark Raeburn series (5)
Sci fi
Marshall, William Leonard
Yellowthread Street series (6)
Science
Allington, Richard L
Beginning to learn series (22)
Science and superstition
Birt, David
Stuarts series (7)
Science experiments you can eat
Cobb, Vicki
You can eat series (1)
Science Metropolis
Statten, Vargo
Liners of time series (2)
Scientific forger
Carter, Nicholas
Nicholas Carter series (161)
Scientific progress goes boink
Watterson, Bill
Calvin and Hobbes series (9)
Scientists
Target, George William
Post-war Britain series (6)
Scions of Shannara
Brooks, Terry
Heritage of Shannara series (1)
Scipio
Gates, Tudor
Vendetta series (1)
Scissors cut paper
Fairlie, Gerard
Victor Caryll series (1)
Scooby Doo and the counterfeit money
Brown, Fern Goldberg
Scooby Doo series (5)
Scooby Doo and the haunted dog house
Lewis, Jean
Scooby Doo series (2)
Scooby Doo and the headless horseman
Brown, Fern Goldberg
Scooby Doo series (4)
Scooby Doo and the mystery monster
Lewis, Jean
Scooby Doo series (3)
Scooby Doo and the pirate treasure
Lewis, Jean
Scooby Doo series (1)
Scooby Doo and the Santa Claus mystery
Brown, Fern Goldberg
Scooby Doo series (6)
Scoop
McClung, Robert Marshall
Endangered animals series (5)
Meynell, Laurence Walter
Robin Weston series (1)
Scoop for Steven Gale
Leyland, Eric
Steven Gale series (3)
Scor-sting
Javor, Frank A
Eli Pike series (2)
Scorched earth
Bainbridge, Chuck
Hard corps series (7)
Stivers, Dick
Able Team series (13)
Scorcher
Lutz, John
Fred Carver series (2)
Scorching wind
Macken, Walter
Macmahon family trilogy (3)
Score
Stark, Richard
Alan Grofield series (1)
Parker series (5)
Score for Superintendent Flagg
Cassells, John
Superintendent Flagg series (20)
Score for the Toff
Creasey, John
Toff series (32)
Score of arms
Meade, Richard
John Allison series (2)
Scorpio
McDonough, Alex
Scorpio series (1)
Scorpio attack
Hoyle, Trevor
Blake's Seven series (3)
Scorpio descending
McDonough, Alex
Scorpio series (3)
Scorpio ghosts and the Black Hole Gang
Tapp, Kathy Kennedy
Moth-kin series (3)
Scorpio rising
McDonough, Alex
Scorpio series (2)
Scorpion
Linaker, Michael R
Scorpion series (1)
McCurtin, Peter
Sundance series (32)
Scorpion in the fire
Davis, Margaret Thomson
Scottish historical trilogy (3)
Scorpion killers
Hogan, Ray
Shawn Starbuck series (17)
Scorpion signal
Hall, Adam
Quiller series (9)
Scorpion swamp
Jackson, Steven Gary
Fighting fantasy gamebook series (8)
Scorpion trail
Sharpe, Jon
Trailsman series (44)
Scorpion's nest
McCutcheon, Hugh
Jimmy Carroll series (3)
Scorpion's tail
Haggard, William
Colonel Charles Russell series (16)
Scorpion's trail
Jacobs, Thomas Curtis Hicks
Chief Inspector Barnard series (1)
Scorpion's treasure
Sernine, Daniel
Grandverger series (1)
Scorpius
Gardner, John Edmund
James Bond series (24)
Scot free
Scott, Alastair
Scot series (1)
Scot goes south
Scott, Alastair
Scot series (2)
Scot returns
Scott, Alastair
Scot series (3)
Scotch and water
Gilpatric, Guy
Mister Colin Andrew Macthrockle Glencannon series (1)
Scotch on the rocks
Hurd, Douglas
Foreign Office trilogy (3)
Scotch twins
Perkins, Lucy Fitch
Twin series (10)
Scotland Yard detective
Reit, Seymour V
Time machine series (17)
Scots quair
Gibbon, Lewis Grassic
Scots Quair trilogy (3)
Scotswoman
Fletcher, Inglis
Carolina series (9)
Scottish adventure
Bayley, Viola
Adventure series (9)
Scottish decision
Hunter, Alan
Inspector George Gently series (27)
Scotty and the hijackers
Swinford, Betty
Scotty series (4)
Scotty and the horse that wouldn't die
Swinford, Betty
Scotty series (1)
Scotty and the lost Dutchman Mine
Swinford, Betty
Scotty series (3)
Scotty and the mysterious message
Swinford, Betty
Scotty series (2)
Scotty and the mysterious Mister J
Swinford, Betty
Scotty series (6)
Scotty and the mystery of the dark angel
Swinford, Betty
Scotty series (7)
Scotty and the phantom monster
Swinford, Betty
Scotty series (5)
Scotty in Gumnut Land
Gibbs, May
Gumnut Land series (15)
Scoundrel time
Hellman, Lillian
Unfinished woman trilogy (3)
Scoundrel's caress
Chase, Carolyn
Thirteen colonies series (2)
Scoundrels rampant
Carter, Nicholas
Nicholas Carter series (575)
Scourge of Scapa Flow
Jones, J Farragut
Silent service series (2)
Scourge of the blood cult
Smith, George Henry
Annwn series (1)
Scourge of the bloody coast
Carpenter, Leonard
Conan series (69)
Scourge of the invisible death
Steele, Curtis
James Christopher series (14)
Scourge of the steel mask
Hogan, Robert Jasper
G-Eight series (9)
Scourge of the wizard
Carter, Nicholas
Nicholas Carter series (355)
Scourged by fear
Carter, Nicholas
Nicholas Carter series (576)
Scouse Mouse
Melly, George
Owning up series (1)
Scout
Idriess, Ion Llewellyn
Australian guerilla series (5)
Simms, William Gilmore
American Revolution series (3)
Scout Grey, detective
Bellamy, Robert Lowe
Scout Grey series (2)
Scout master of Troop Five
Thurston, Ida Treadwell
Troop Five series (1)
Scout of Pea Ridge
Dunn, Byron Archibald
Young Missourians series (2)
Scouting for Light Horse Harry
True, John Preston
Revolution series (4)
Scouting for Sheridan
Dunn, Byron Archibald
Young Virginians series (3)
Scouting for Washington
True, John Preston
Revolution series (1)
Scouting in the desert
Tomlinson, Everett Titsworth
American scouting series (11)

Scouting in the wilderness
Tomlinson, Everett Titsworth
American scouting series (6)
Scouting on Lake Champlain
Tomlinson, Everett Titsworth
American scouting series (8)
Scouting on the border
Tomlinson, Everett Titsworth
American scouting series (2)
Scouting on the Mohawk
Tomlinson, Everett Titsworth
American scouting series (9)
Scouting on the old frontier
Tomlinson, Everett Titsworth
American scouting series (5)
Scouting with Daniel Boone
Tomlinson, Everett Titsworth
American scouting series (13)
Pioneer scout series (1)
Scouting with General Funston
Tomlinson, Everett Titsworth
Pioneer scout series (3)
Scouting with General Pershing
Tomlinson, Everett Titsworth
Pioneer scout series (4)
Scouting with Kit Carson
Tomlinson, Everett Titsworth
American scouting series (14)
Pioneer scout series (2)
Scouting with Mad Anthony
Tomlinson, Everett Titsworth
American scouting series (4)
Scouts of Stonewall
Altsheler, Joseph Alexander
Civil War series (4)
Scouts of the valley
Altsheler, Joseph Alexander
Trailers series (5)
Scraboolee jubilee
Marino, Tony
Widgets series (2)
Scramble
Bamman, Henry A
Checkered flag series (5)
Prince, Alison
Airfield series (3)
Scramble Dieppe
Holden, Matthew
Squadron series (3)
Scrambled egg for Christmas
Anderson, Verily
Anderson family series (7)
Scrambled yeggs
Cohen, Octavus Roy
Jim Hanvey series (5)
Prather, Richard Scott
Shell Scott series (16)
Scrap-metal mystery
Tyrer, Walter
Sexton Blake series (1317)
Scrap of black lace
Carter, Nicholas
Nicholas Carter series (88)
Scratch and Company
Lefebure, Molly
Scratch and Company series (1)
Scratch fever
Collins, Max Allan
Nolan series (6)
Scratch on the dark
Copper, Basil
Mike Faraday series (4)
Scratch on the surface
Harknett, Terry
Stephen Wayne series (2)
Scratchproof
Maguire, Michael
Simon Drake series (3)
Scream
Launay, Droo
Adam Flute series (6)
Scream at midnight
Plummer, Thomas Arthur
Detective Inspector Andrew Frampton series (39)
Scream at the sea
Murphy, Christopher
Sparrow series (1)
Scream bloody murder
Telfair, Richard
Monty Nash series (3)
Scream blue murder
Dacre, Richard
Sam Hoskins series (2)
Scream in Soho
Brandon, John Gordon
Inspector Patrick Aloysius McCarthy series (30)
Scream in the dark
Ridley, Nat
Nat Ridley series (9)
Scream of a Dove
Charles, Robert
Counter-terror series (3)
Scream of murder
Ashe, Gordon
Patrick Dawlish series (45)
Scream of the cat
Beach, Lynn
Phantom Valley series (3)
Scream Street
Brett, Mike
Sam Dakkers series (2)
Scream team
Hoh, Diane
Nightmare Hall series (5)
Screamer
McClung, Robert Marshall
Endangered animals series (2)
Screamers
Dixon, Franklin W
Hardy boys case files series (72)
Screaming dead balloons
McCutchan, Philip
Commander Esmonde Shaw series (9)
Screaming fog
Chance, John Newton
John Newton Chance series (1)
Screaming knife
Vardeman, Robert Edward
Peter Thorne series (1)
Screaming man
Robeson, Kenneth
Doc Savage series (106)
Screaming on the wire
McCurtin, Peter
Carmody series (4)
Screaming orchid
Enefer, Douglas
Dale Shand series (10)
Screaming rabbit
Carmichael, Harry
John Piper and Quinn series (6)
Screaming skull, and other stories
Horler, Sydney
Sebastian Quin series (2)
Sir Harker Bellamy series (9)
Screen for murder
Lorac, E C R
Inspector Macdonald series (30)
Screwball king murder
Platt, Kin
Max Roper series (7)
Screwtape letters
Lewis, Clive Staples
Screwtape series (1)
Screwtape series (2)
Screwtape proposes a toast
Lewis, Clive Staples
Screwtape series (2)
Scribble
Cosgrove, Stephen Edward
Bugg series (23)
Scrimshaw millions
Thayer, Lee
Peter Clancy series (15)
Scroggy, the monster who was scared of the dark
Salmon, Michael
Scaredy monsters series (3)
Scroll of Benevolence
Trenhaile, John
Simon Young series (3)
Scroll of Lucifer
Eshbach, Lloyd Arthur
Gates of Lucifer series (4)
Scrooge
Donaldson, Elaine
Christmas carol series (2)
Scrub-a-dub-dub
Davis, Anne
Pumpkin Hollow series (4)
Scruff Gooseberry
Reed, Giles
Munch Bunch character series (14)
Scruff Gooseberry and the wishing well
Reed, Giles
Munch Bunch story books series (11)
Scruples
Krantz, Judith
Scruples scruples (1)
Scruples two
Krantz, Judith
Scruples scruples (2)
Scully
Bleasdale, Alan
Franny Scully series (1)
Scythe in the apple tree
Warren, Clarence Henry
Happy countryman series (6)
Se-Pah-Poo
Robeson, Kenneth
Doc Savage series (168)
Sea and islands
Innes, Hammond
Sea journeys series (2)
Sea and shore
Optic, Oliver
Onward and upward series (6)
Sea and the sand
Nicole, Christopher
United States Navy series (2)
Sea Angel
Robeson, Kenneth
Doc Savage series (49)
Sea ape
Crisp, Frank
Dirk Rogers series (6)
Sea around us
Carson, Rachel Louise
Sea series (1)
Sea battle
Birmingham, George A
Reverend J J Meldon series (5)
Sea-bed treasure
Duff, Douglas Valder
Adam Macadam series (3)
Sea boots
Du Soe, Robert C
Pedro the fisherman series (2)
Sea City, here we come!
Martin, Ann Matthews
Baby-Sitters Club super specials series (10)
Sea cub
Styles, Showell
Red Six series (3)
Sea Devil
Llewellyn, Sam
George Le Fanu Gurney trilogy (1)
Luckner, Felix von
Sea Devil series (1)
Sea Devil 2
Llewellyn, Sam
George Le Fanu Gurney trilogy (2)
Sea Devil's fo'c'sle
Luckner, Felix von
Sea Devil series (2)
Sea express
Foster, Walter Bertram
Clint Webb series (4)
Sea fairies
Baum, Lyman Frank
Trot and Cap'n Bill series (1)
Sea fever
Rasmussen, Albert Henry
Sea fever trilogy (1)
Sea file
Scott, Jack Denton
Spargo series (2)
Sea flame
Hardy, Adam
George Abercrombie Fox series (13)
Sea for breakfast
Beckwith, Lillian
Hebrides series (3)
Sea Fox
Carter, Nicholas
Nicholas Carter series (627)
Sea gold
Berres, Frances B
Deep-sea adventure series (10)
Blaine, John
Rick Brant series (3)
Sea-green magic
Beresford, Elisabeth
Magic series (3)
Sea horse
Bryant, Bonnie
Saddle Club series (14)
Sea hunt
Berres, Frances B
Deep-sea adventure series (1)
Sea is so wide
Eaton, Evelyn
Arcadian trilogy (3)
Sea island lady
Griswold, Francis
Carolina series (2)
Sea kill
Woodley, Richard
Man from Atlantis series (1)
Sea Lion Island
Edwards, Hugh
Sea Witch series (3)
Sea magician
Robeson, Kenneth
Doc Savage series (44)
Sea mystery
Crofts, Freeman Wills
Inspector Joseph French series (4)
Sea of adventure
Blyton, Enid
Adventure series (4)
Sea of death
Gygax, Gary
Gord the Rogue series (1)
Sea of flames
Greenfield, Irving A
Depth force series (6)
Sea of gold
Hardy, Adam
George Abercrombie Fox series (6)
Sea of savages
Wilson, Gar
Phoenix Force series (19)
Sea of silence
Hancock, Niel
Windameir circle series (3)
Sea of suspicion
Keene, Carolyn
Nancy Drew files series (85)
Sea of troubles
Sea-Lion
John Prentice series (3)
Sea people
Danielson, Peter
Children of the Lion series (11)
Sea Peril
Turner, Philip
Darnley Mills series (3)
Sea piper
Cresswell, Helen
Sea series (3)
Sea priestess
Fortune, Dion
Vivien Le Fay Morgan series (1)
Sea robbers
Crisp, Frank
Dirk Rogers series (1)
Sea routes
Birt, David
Saxons and Vikings series (18)
Sea-running
Lane, Maxie
Running series (2)
Sea Scouts abroad
Westerman, Percy Francis
Sea Scouts series (3)
Sea Scouts alert!
Westerman, Percy Francis
Sea Scouts series (7)
Sea Scouts all
Westerman, Percy Francis
Sea Scouts series (2)
Sea Scouts at Dunkirk
Westerman, Percy Francis
Sea Scouts series (6)
Sea Scouts of the Kestrel
Westerman, Percy Francis
Sea Scouts series (5)
Sea Scouts of the Petrel
Westerman, Percy Francis
Sea Scouts series (1)
Sea Scouts up-channel
Westerman, Percy Francis
Sea Scouts series (4)
Sea scrape
Dark, James
Mark Kingsley Hood series (16)
Sea-Serpent Island
Duff, Douglas Valder
Adam Macadam series (1)
Sea stallion
Dolan, Bill
Afrikorps series (4)
Sea star
Paxson, Diana Lucile
Westria series (5)
Sea Star, orphan of Chincoteague
Henry, Marguerite
Chincoteague series (2)
Chincoteague series (4)
Sea story
Barklem, Jill
Brambly Hedge series (7)
Johnston, Ronald
James Bruce series (3)
Sea stranger
Crossley-Holland, Kevin
Wulf series (1)
Sea sword
Martine-Barnes, Adrienne
Chronique d'Avebury series (4)
Sea tigers
Saxon, Peter
Sexton Blake series (1457)
Sea to Eden
Stanley, Bennett
Alscott experiment series (2)
Sea trap
Carter, Nick
Nick Carter series (44)
Sea urchin
Macpherson, Bruce
Jenny and Sue series (2)
Sea urchins
Jacobs, William Wymark
Night-Watchman series (2)
Sea Urchin's first charter
Stanhope, Douglas
Sea Urchin series (1)
Sea Urchin's last charter
Stanhope, Douglas
Sea Urchin series (4)
Sea Urchin's second charter
Stanhope, Douglas
Sea Urchin series (2)
Sea Urchin's third charter
Stanhope, Douglas
Sea Urchin series (3)
Sea wall
Strong, Leonard Alfred George
Garden series (2)
Sea whispers
Jacobs, William Wymark
Night-Watchman series (12)
Sea Witch comes home
Saville, Malcolm
Lone Pine Five Club series (13)
Sea without a haven
Broster, Dorothy Kathleen
Captain Carew series (1)
Sea-wolf hunter
Collenette, Eric J
Ben Grant series (7)
Sea wolves
Catherall, Arthur
Bulldog tugboat series (5)
Seaboard parish
Macdonald, George
Quiet neighbourhood series (2)
Seacoast of Bohemia
McHugh, Arona
Sally Brimmer series (2)
Seafarers
Long, William Stuart
Australians series (10)
Seafaring stranger
Chase, Carolyn
Thirteen colonies series (6)
Seafire
Gardner, John Edmund
James Bond series (30)
Knox, Bill
Webb Carrick series (6)
Robards, Karen
Lady Catherine Alderly series (2)
Seagold
Johnston, William
Young rebels series (2)
Seagull
Farmer, Penelope
Stephen series (1)
Seagull Crag
Welles, Elizabeth
Janine West series (5)
Seagull said murder
Neville, Margot
Inspector Grogan and Sergeant Manning series (6)
SeaHarp Hotel
Grant, Charles Lewis
Chronicles of Greystone Bay series (3)
Seajet spies
Rich, Nicholas
Adam Hood series (3)
Seal morning
Farre, Rowena
Seal morning series (1)
Seal of death
Carter, Nicholas
Nicholas Carter series (137)
Seal of John Solomon
Bedford-Jones, Henry
John Solomon trilogy (2)
Seal of silence
Carter, Nicholas
Nicholas Carter series (87)
Sealed and despatched
Bream, Freda
Reverend Jabal Jarrett series (4)
Sealed box
Grant, Maxwell
Shadow series (135)
Sealed door
Carter, Nicholas
Nicholas Carter series (601)
Sealed envelope
Howard, Hartley
Glenn Bowman series (38)
Sealed orders
Carter, Nicholas
Nicholas Carter series (46)

Hogg, Garry
Jonty series (1)
Sealed room murder
Penny, Rupert
Chief Inspector Edward Beale series (8)
Sealed with a kiss
Cooper, M E
Couples series (35)
Sealed with a loving kill
Ormerod, Roger
David Mallin and George Coe series (5)
Sealed with blood
Jason, Stuart
Butcher series (9)
Sealer
Wood, James
James Fraser series (3)
Seals
Dickinson, Peter
Superintendent James Pibble series (3)
Seamy side of contemporary history
Balzac, Honore de
Scenes of Parisian life series (13)
Seamy side of history
Balzac, Honore de
Scenes of Parisian life series (13)
Seance
McShane, Mark
Myra Savage series (1)
Seance for a vampire
Saberhagen, Fred
Dracula series (26)
Sherlock Holmes sequels series (101)
Seance for two
McShane, Mark
Myra Savage series (2)
Seance on a wet afternoon
McShane, Mark
Myra Savage series (1)
Sean's red bike
Breinburg, Petronella
Sean series (3)
SeaQuest
Duane, Diane
SeaQuest series (1)
Search
Weverka, Robert
Search series (1)
Search and destroy
Andrews, Keith William
Freedom's Rangers series (3)
Blacker, Irwin Robert
General Le Grande and GENOPS series (3)
Cody, James P
Brian Peterson series (2)
Wilson, Gar
Phoenix Force super series (2)
Search and rescue operations in Southeast Asia, 1961-1975
Tilford, Earl H
USAF in Vietnam series (2)
Search for a missing lady
Graham, Neill
Solo Malcolm series (36)
Search for a scientist
Leonard, Charles L
Paul Kilgerrin series (7)
Search for a soul
Bottome, Phyllis
Search trilogy (1)
Search for a sultan
Coles, Manning
Tommy Hambledon series (25)
Search for Aladdin's lamp
Leibold, Jay
Choose your own adventure series (117)
Search for an island
James, Josephine
Kathy Martin series (7)
Search for Cindy Austin
Keene, Carolyn
Nancy Drew series (88)
Search for dinosaurs
Bischoff, David
Time machine series (2)
Search for Fierra
Lawhead, Stephen
Emphyrion series (1)
Search for Harry Allway
Buzo, Alexander
Prue Foster series (1)
Search for Hissing Sid
Lloyd, Jeremy
Captain Beaky and his band series (5)
Search for home
Brata, Sasthi
Astride two worlds series (2)
Search for justice
Bryant, Arthur
History of Britain and the British people series (3)
Search for Ka
Garrett, Randall
Gandalara cycle series (5)
Search for love
Roberts, Nora
Flowers series (11)
Search for love, 1856-1898
Holroyd, Michael
Bernard Shaw series (1)
Search for Mad Jack's crown
Fortune, J J
Race against time series (4)
Search for Otis Otter
Miller, Muriel
Woodlanders series (2)
Search for Piranha
Bamman, Henry A
World of adventure series (6)
Search for Scorpio
Sheldon, Ann
Linda Craig series (11)
Search for Sergeant Baxter
Cobb, Belton
Bryan Armitage series (2)
Inspector Cheviot Burmann series (26)
Search for smugglers!
Danby, Mary
Famous Five and you series (4)
Search for Spock
McIntyre, Vondra Neil
Star trek series (17)
Roddenberry, Gene
Star trek moving picture series (3)
Search for Spock storybook
Weinberg, Larry
Star trek tie-ins series (6)
Search for the breed
Grove, Frederick Philip
Dude McQuint series (3)
Search for the Dice Man
Rhinehart, Luke
Wim series (3)
Search for the Doctor
Martin, David
Doctor Who find your fate series (1)
Search for the glowing hat
Sutton, Margaret
Judy Bolton series (37)
Search for the golden boomerang
Bingham, Lorna
Golden boomerang series (1)
Search for the little yellow men
Hastings, Macdonald
Eagle Special Investigator series (3)
Search for the lost flyers
Dixon, Franklin W
Ted Scott flying series (5)
Search for the lost mail plane
Theiss, Lewis Edwin
Air mail series (2)
Search for the missing twin
Wells, Helen
Vicki Barr series (10)
Search for the mountain gorillas
Wallace, Jim
Choose your own adventure series (41)
Search for the Nile
Walker, Robert Wayne
Time machine series (12)
Search for the Pegasus
Moore, Roger Elwood
Endless quest crimson crystal adventure series (2)
Search for the silver Persian
Keene, Carolyn
Nancy Drew series (114)
Search for the spy
Kay, Ross
Big war series (1)
Search for the starblade
Taylor, Keith
Danans trilogy (3)
Search for the sun!
Kapp, Colin
Cageworld series (1)
Search for treasure!
Danby, Mary
Famous Five and you series (1)
Search for Zei
De Camp, Lyon Sprague
Krishna series (4)
Search in the dark
Mackenzie, Andrew
Superintendent Brannigan series (2)
Search in the shadows
Warren, Paulette
Caliban series (2)
Search of Mavin Manyshaped
Tepper, Sheri S
Mavin Manyshaped trilogy (3)
Searcher
Edwards, Josh
John Stone series (1)
Searchers
Knott, William Cecil
Golden Hawk series (9)
Searching for dragons
Wrede, Patricia Collins
Enchanted forest series (2)
Searching for Sara
Singer, Shelley
Barrett Lake series (3)
Searching for skylights
Leach, Christopher
Dave Bourne series (3)
Searching spirit
Adamson, Joy
Elsa series (4)
Searching the Hebrides with a camera
Macgregor, Alasdair Alpin
Western Isles trilogy (3)
Searchlight on Hambledon
Dellbridge, John
Rupert Hambledon series (1)
Searchlight on the throne
Peeress
Recollections of royalty series (2)
Sea's in the kitchen
Baker, Denys Val
Cornish series (1)
Seas of blood
Chapman, Andrew
Fighting fantasy gamebook series (16)
Seascape with dead figures
Hart, Roy
Detective Superintendent Roper series (1)
Seashore drama
Balzac, Honore de
Philosophic studies series (13)
Seashore noisy book
Brown, Margaret Wise
Noisy book series (3)
Seaside adventure
McCaughrean, Geraldine
Teddies series (6)
Seaside bunnies
Cartlidge, Michelle
Press and play series (4)
Seaside cafe crime
Jardine, Warwick
Sexton Blake series (894)
Seaside crime
Jardine, Warwick
Sexton Blake series (895)
Seaside donkey
Towers, Joyce
Donkey series (1)
Seaside family
Blyton, Enid
Mike, Belinda and Ann series (4)
Seaside holiday for Jane and Toby
Thwaite, Ann
Jane and Toby series (2)
Seaside mystery
Booth, Christopher B
Jim Bliss series (1)
Hodgman, Ann
Choose your own adventure series (67)
Seaside tragedy
Balzac, Honore de
Philosophic studies series (13)
Season for death
Harrison, Ray
Sergeant Joseph Bragg and Constable James Morton series (6)
Season for murder
Granger, Ann
Meredith Mitchell and Chief Inspector Alan Markby series (2)
Nelson, Hugh Lawrence
Jim Dunn series (4)
Season of adventure
Lamming, George
San Cristobal series (2)
Season of Coole
Stephens, Michael
J Leland Coole series (1)
Season of death
Wren, M K
Conan Flagg series (5)
Season of escape
Ford, James Allan
Hong Kong series (2)
Season of learning
Miller, Connie
Seasons trilogy (2)
Season of mists
Angoff, Charles
Polonsky family series (9)
Gaiman, Neil
Sandman series (4)
Woodhouse, Sarah
Season of mists series (1)
Season of snows and mists
Moyes, Patricia
Henry and Emmy Tibbett series (10)
Season of Swans
De Blasis, Celeste
Wild Swan trilogy (3)
Season of the Falcon
Darby, Catherine
Falcon family series (4)
Season of the skylark
Story, Jack Trevor
Sexton Blake series (1437)
Season of the Spellsing
Foster, Alan Dean
Spellsinger series (3)
Season of the warrior
Thompson, David
Wilderness giants series (1)
Season of the witch
Martin, Jack
Halloween series (3)
Season of weathering
Owen, William A
Stubborn soil series (2)
Season of yellow leaf
Jones, Douglas Clyde
Comanche trilogy (1)
Season-ticket
Haliburton, Thomas Chandler
Sam Slick series (10)
Seasonal and holiday happenings
Berry, Joy
Can make and do series (12)
Seasonal rain, and other stories
Flynn, Robert
Wanderer Springs series (1)
Seasonal tribal feasts
Evans, Stuart
Windmill Hill series (5)
Seasons of my life
Hauxwell, Hannah
Daleswoman series (1)
Seasons of my youth
McIntosh, Dave
Canadian life series (1)
Seat of the scornful
Carr, John Dickson
Doctor Gideon Fell series (14)
Seattle
Lynch, Jack
Peter Bragg series (7)
Mitchum, Hank
Stage coach station series (7)
Seattle run
Robbins, David
Endworld series (14)
Seaways
Bartimeus
Naval occasions series (6)
Sebastian
Durrell, Lawrence
Avignon quintet (4)
Julian-Ottie, Vanessa
Sebastian Kitten series (1)
Sebastian and the space pirates
Plait, Dominique
Sebastian series (2)
Sebastian and the wicked water queen
Plait, Dominique
Sebastian series (1)
Sebastian explores
Julian-Ottie, Vanessa
Sebastian Kitten series (2)
Sebastian Super Sleuth
Christian, Mary Blount
Sebastian Super Sleuth series (1)
Sebastian Super Sleuth and the baffling bigfoot
Christian, Mary Blount
Sebastian Super Sleuth series (12)
Sebastian Super Sleuth and the bone to pick mystery
Christian, Mary Blount
Sebastian Super Sleuth series (4)
Sebastian Super Sleuth and the clumsy cowboy
Christian, Mary Blount
Sebastian Super Sleuth series (7)
Sebastian Super Sleuth and the copycat crime
Christian, Mary Blount
Sebastian Super Sleuth series (15)
Sebastian Super Sleuth and the crummy yummies caper
Christian, Mary Blount
Sebastian Super Sleuth series (3)
Sebastian Super Sleuth and the Egyptian connection
Christian, Mary Blount
Sebastian Super Sleuth series (10)
Sebastian Super Sleuth and the hair of the dog mystery
Christian, Mary Blount
Sebastian Super Sleuth series (2)
Sebastian Super Sleuth and the impossible crime
Christian, Mary Blount
Sebastian Super Sleuth series (14)
Sebastian Super Sleuth and the mystery patient
Christian, Mary Blount
Sebastian Super Sleuth series (13)
Sebastian Super Sleuth and the purloined surloin
Christian, Mary Blount
Sebastian Super Sleuth series (8)
Sebastian Super Sleuth and the Santa Claus caper
Christian, Mary Blount
Sebastian Super Sleuth series (5)
Sebastian Super Sleuth and the secret of the skewered skier
Christian, Mary Blount
Sebastian Super Sleuth series (6)
Sebastian Super Sleuth and the stars-in-his-eyes mystery
Christian, Mary Blount
Sebastian Super Sleuth series (9)
Sebastian Super Sleuth and the time capsule caper
Christian, Mary Blount
Sebastian Super Sleuth series (11)
Secluded garden
Harris, Ruth Elwin
Quantocks quartet (4)
Seclusion room
Neuman, Fredric
Captain Redder series (1)
Second and five
James, Laurence
Gridiron series (2)
Second anti-coloring book
Striker, Susan
Anti-coloring series (2)
Second best
Bernard, Elizabeth
Satin slippers series (5)
Pascal, Francine
Sweet Valley twins series (16)
Second big Monster book
Blance, Ellen
Monster series (9)
Second big Olga da polga book
Bond, Michael
Olga da Polga series (1)
Second big radio Thin King book
Farmer, Derek
Thin King series (2)
Second book of after midnight stories
Myers, Amy
After midnight stories series (2)
Second book of Martha
Dowdall, Mary Frances
Martha series (2)
Second book of naughty children
Blyton, Enid
Naughty children series (2)
Second book of swords
Saberhagen, Fred
Book of swords trilogy (2)
Second book of Tobiah
Silberrad, Una Lucy
Tobiah series (2)
Second bout with the Mildew Gang
Fowler, Sydney
Inspector Cauldron series (2)
Second Brer Rabbit book
Blyton, Enid
Brer Rabbit series (2)
Second bridegroom
Hall, Rodney
Yandilli trilogy (1)
Second browser's dictionary & native guide to the unknown American language
Ciardi, John
Browser's dictionary series (2)
Second bullet
Dutton, Charles Judson
John Bartley series (5)

Secret harbour
Smith, Sam
Crew Cats series (1)
White, Stewart Edward
Skookum Chuck series (2)
Secret harmonies
McAuley, Paul J
Four hundred billion stars series (2)
Secret hideout
Hutchens, Paul
Sugar Creek Gang series (6)
Secret history of today
Upward, Allen
Monsieur V series (1)
Secret house
Wallace, Edgar
Mister T B Smith series (4)
York, Carol Beach
Miss Know It All series (12)
Secret houses
Gardner, John Edmund
Herbie Kruger series (4)
Secret generations trilogy (2)
Secret in the dark
Keene, Carolyn
Nancy Drew series (102)
Secret in the kitchen
Johnson, Lissa Halls
China Tate series (2)
Secret in the old attic
Keene, Carolyn
Nancy Drew series (21)
Secret in the old mansion
Mooser, Stephen
Treasure hound series (4)
Secret in the old place
Keene, Carolyn
Nancy Drew series (59)
Secret in the old well
Keene, Carolyn
Dana girls series (13)
Secret in the pirate's cave
Hope, Laura Lee
Bobbsey twins series (74)
Secret in the Sahara
Hoare, Robert John
Bobby of the Globe series (3)
Secret in the shed
Plain, Neil
Boris Blundle and Gang series (5)
Secret in the sky
Robeson, Kenneth
Doc Savage series (20)
Secret in time
Keene, Carolyn
Nancy Drew series (100)
Secret inquest
Blair, Allan
Sexton Blake series (829)
Secret inquiry
Cobb, Belton
Inspector Cheviot Burmann series (38)
Secret Isaac
Charyn, Jerome
Isaac Sidel series (4)
Secret island
Blyton, Enid
Prince Paul series (1)
Edwards, Sylvia
Sally Baxter series (14)
Secret journey
Hanley, James
Furys chronicle series (2)
Weir, Rosemary
Maybury family series (1)
Secret judges
Grierson, Francis Durham
Inspector Sims and Professor Wells series (2)
Secret kingdom
Richardson, Frank
Sherlock Holmes sequels series (1)
Secret ladder
Harris, Wilson
Guiana series (4)
Secret letters at Trebizon
Digby, Anne
Trebizon series (13)
Secret life of cosmetics
Cobb, Vicki
Secret life series (3)
Secret life of Dagmar Schulz
Hall, Lynn
Dagmar Schultz series (1)
Secret life of hardware
Cobb, Vicki
Secret life series (2)
Secret life of school supplies
Cobb, Vicki
Secret life series (1)
Secret listeners
Goldman, Lawrence Louis
Clinton Judd series (2)
Secret lost at sea
Keene, Carolyn
Nancy Drew series (113)
Secret lovers
McCarry, Charles
Paul Christopher series (3)
Secret magic
Beresford, Elisabeth
Magic series (7)
Secret meeting
Rhode, John
Doctor Lancelot Priestley series (53)
Secret memoirs and manners of several persons of quality
Manley, Mary de la Riviere
New Atalantis series (1)
Secret millionaire
Gibbons, Harry Hornaby Clifford
Sexton Blake series (338)
Secret ministry
Cory, Desmond
Johnny Fedora series (1)
Secret mission
Cook, Canfield
Lucky Terrell series (3)
Secret mission, Angola
Smith, Don
Secret mission series (9)
Secret mission, Athens
Smith, Don
Secret mission series (11)
Secret mission, Cairo
Smith, Don
Secret mission series (7)
Secret mission, Corsica
Smith, Don
Secret mission series (3)
Secret mission, Istanbul
Smith, Don
Secret mission series (5)
Secret mission, Moluk
Voltz, William
Perry Rhodan series (84)
Secret mission, Morocco
Smith, Don
Secret mission series (4)
Secret mission, Munich
Smith, Don
Secret mission series (10)
Secret mission, North Korea
Smith, Don
Secret mission series (8)
Secret mission, Peking
Smith, Don
Secret mission series (1)
Secret mission, Prague
Smith, Don
Secret mission series (2)
Secret mission, the Kremlin plan
Smith, Don
Secret mission series (12)
Secret mission, Tibet
Smith, Don
Secret mission series (6)
Secret mission to Alaska
Barlow, Roger
Sandy Steele series (5)
Secret mission to Bangkok
Mason, Francis Van Wyck
Colonel Hugh North series (21)
Secret mountain
Blyton, Enid
Prince Paul series (3)
Secret murder
Ashe, Gordon
Patrick Dawlish series (5)
Secret notebook
Sharmat, Marjorie Weinman
Kids on the bus series (5)
Secret of Amityville
Holzer, Hans
Amityville horror series (8)
Secret of Annexe 3
Dexter, Colin
Inspector Morse series (7)
Secret of Apache Canyon
Telfair, Richard
Wyoming Jones series (4)
Secret of Barnabas Collins
Ross, Marilyn
Barnabas Collins series (11)
Secret of Baron's Folly
Webster, H M
Shamus Burke series (2)
Secret of Bigfoot Pass
Jahn, Mike
Six Million Dollar Man series (10)
Secret of Black Cat Gulch
Allen, Betsy
Connie Blair series (3)
Secret of Blackoaks
Carter, Ashley
Blackoaks series (2)
Secret of Bogey House
Adams, Herbert
Jimmy Haswell series (1)
Secret of Buzzard Scar
Saville, Malcolm
Nettleford series (4)
Secret of Camp Pioneer
Fairfax, Virginia
Girl Scouts series (2)
Secret of Capri
Jardine, Warwick
Sexton Blake series (1259)
Secret of Cathedral Lake
Torgersen, Don Arthur
Troll series (9)
Secret of Chimneys
Christie, Agatha
Superintendent Battle series (1)
Secret of Clovercrest Castle
Ezell, Marilyn
Susan Sand series (2)
Secret of Cobbet's Farm
Weir, Rosemary
Maybury family series (2)
Secret of Coffin Island
Ellis, Edward Sylvester
True grit trilogy (1)
Secret of Cravenhill Castle
Hunt, Angela Elwell
Nicki Holland series (8)
Secret of Dinosaur Bog
Gilden, Mel
Fifth grade monsters series (15)
Secret of Doctor Kildare
Brand, Max
Doctor Kildare series (1)
Secret of Draker's Folly
Murray, Andrew
Sexton Blake series (44)
Secret of Father Brown
Chesterton, Gilbert Keith
Father Brown series (4)
Secret of Fort Pioneer
Scott, Dan
Bret King series (6)
Secret of Gnome Head
Strong, Ben
Professor Adrian Criddle series (2)
Secret of Grey Walls
Saville, Malcolm
Lone Pine Five Club series (4)
Secret of Greycliffs
Paice, Margaret
Kathy Brown series (2)
Secret of Gumbo Grove
Tate, Eleanora Elaine
Gumbo Grove series (1)
Secret of Halliday House
Fairfax, Virginia
Girl Scouts series (3)
Secret of Hallowdene Farm
Pocock, Doris Alice
Hallowdene Farm series (1)
Secret of Hanging Rock
Lindsay, Joan
Hanging Rock series (2)
Secret of Hangman's Inn
Campbell, Bruce
Ken Holt series (6)
Secret of Hermit's Bay
Lyon, Elinor
Ian and Sovra series (6)
Secret of Hermit's Peak
Scott, Dan
Bret King series (2)
Secret of High Eldersham
Burton, Miles
Inspector Arnold and Desmond Merrion series (1)
Secret of Hollow Hill
Hogg, Garry
Jonty series (2)
Secret of Holm Peel, and other strange stories
Rohmer, Sax
Fu-Manchu series (15)
Secret of Jungle Park
Hope, Laura Lee
New Bobbsey twins series (1)
Secret of Killimooin
Blyton, Enid
Prince Paul series (4)
Secret of Lost Lake
Keene, Carolyn
Dana girls series (24)
Secret of Magnolia Manor
Wells, Helen
Vicki Barr series (4)
Secret of MI6
Smith, Lou
John Spencer series (3)
Secret of Mirror Bay
Keene, Carolyn
Nancy Drew series (49)
Secret of moon Castle
Blyton, Enid
Prince Paul series (5)
Secret of NIMH
O'Brien, Robert C
NIMH series (1)
Secret of Oil Creek
Parsons, Anthony
Sexton Blake series (1042)
Secret of Operation Brain
Carlson, Dale
James Budd series (2)
Secret of Phantom Lake
Arden, William
Three Investigators series (19)
Secret of Pirates' Hill
Dixon, Franklin W
Hardy boys series (36)
Secret of Pony Pass
Gervaise, Mary
G for Georgia series (10)
Secret of Puffin Island
Townsend, John
Lunar One series (3)
Secret of Rainbow Island
Stamper, Judith Bauer
Find your fate: Jem series (3)
Secret of Rancho del Sol
Sheldon, Ann
Linda Craig series (3)
Secret of Red Gate Farm
Keene, Carolyn
Nancy Drew series (6)
Secret of Red Skull
Stahl, Ben
Blackbeard series (2)
Secret of Sam Marlow
Fenady, Andrew J
Sam Marlow series (2)
Secret of San Felipe
Buck, Peter
Marc Dean series (2)
Secret of Sarek
Leblanc, Maurice
Arsene Lupin series (9)
Secret of secrets
Fletcher, Joseph Smith
Inspector Skarratt series (3)
Secret of seven
Stuart, Donald
Sexton Blake series (724)
Secret of Shadow Ranch
Keene, Carolyn
Nancy Drew series (5)
Secret of Shady Glen
Keene, Carolyn
Nancy Drew series (85)
Secret of Shark Reef
Arden, William
Three Investigators series (30)
Secret of Shoreswood Hall
Smith, Dennis O
Sherlock Holmes sequels series (78)
Secret of Sigma Seven
Dixon, Franklin W
Hardy boys series (110)
Secret of Simon Cornell
Howard, Hartley
Glenn Bowman series (26)
Secret of Sinharat
Brackett, Leigh
Eric John Stark series (2)
Secret of sixty-six fathoms
Hope, Stanton
Sexton Blake series (963)
Secret of Skeleton Island
Arthur, Robert
Three Investigators series (6)
Campbell, Bruce
Ken Holt series (1)
Secret of Skull Mountain
Dixon, Franklin W
Hardy boys series (27)
Secret of Spiggy Holes
Blyton, Enid
Prince Paul series (2)
Secret of Spindle Bottom
Allan, Mabel Esther
Spindle Bottom series (1)
Secret of Stillwater Mere
Chester, Gilbert
Sexton Blake series (1091)
Secret of Sulphur Creek
Hayes, Ralph Eugene
O'Brien, Buffalo Hunter series (1)
Secret of Superintendent Manning
Cobb, Belton
Superintendent Manning series (2)
Secret of Tangles
Gribble, Leonard Reginald
Superintendent Anthony Slade series (7)
Secret of Terror Castle
Arthur, Robert
Three Investigators series (1)
Secret of the African settler
Hardinge, Rex
Sexton Blake series (1210)
Secret of the African trader
Hardinge, Rex
Sexton Blake series (709)
Secret of the Alaskan gift
Work, Virginia
Jodi series (5)
Secret of the Ambermere treasure
Saville, Malcolm
Jillies series (6)
Secret of the armaments king
Quiroule, Pierre
Sexton Blake series (851)
Secret of the Balkan heiress
Brisbane, Coutts
Sexton Blake series (876)
Secret of the barred window
Sutton, Margaret
Judy Bolton series (16)
Secret of the Bastille
Feval, Paul
Years between series (3)
Secret of the black hole
Moore, Patrick
Scott Saunders series (6)
Secret of the black wallet
Sayer, Walter William
Sexton Blake series (357)
Secret of the brownstone house
Smaridge, Norah
Robin Miller series (1)
Secret of the bucket shop
Jones, J G
Sexton Blake series (335)
Secret of the bungalow
Casey, Robert J
Jim Sands series (2)
Secret of the buried tomb
Knight, Clayton
Pepe and Ronnie series (2)
Secret of the Burma Road
Parsons, Anthony
Sexton Blake series (1078)
Secret of the Carpathians
Gibbons, Harry Hornaby Clifford
Sexton Blake series (339)
Secret of the cask
Armour, R Coutts
Sexton Blake series (555)
Secret of the castle ruins
Parsons, Anthony
Sexton Blake series (1363)
Secret of the caves
Dixon, Franklin W
Hardy boys series (8)
Milroy, Clarita
Highland quest series (2)
Secret of the cellar
Edwards, Walter
Sexton Blake series (986)
Secret of the chateau
Fearon, Ethelind
Pluckrose series (3)
Secret of the coconut groves
Teed, George Hamilton
Sexton Blake series (405)
Secret of the crooked cat
Arden, William
Three Investigators series (13)
Secret of the dark room
Casey, Robert J
Jim Sands series (3)
Secret of the dead convict
Dix, Maurice Buxton
Sexton Blake series (907)
Secret of the dead man
Urquhart, Paul
Sexton Blake series (979)
Secret of the demolition worker
Hunter, John
Sexton Blake series (1084)
Secret of the dental surgeon
Hardinge, Rex
Sexton Blake series (932)
Secret of the desert
Hardinge, Rex
Sexton Blake series (1284)

Secret of the doubting saint
Holton, Leonard
Father Joseph Bredder series (3)

Secret of the Downs
Masterman, Walter Sidney
Sir Arthur Sinclair series (14)

Secret of the elephant
Scott, Bruce
Superintendent Steve McLaren series (2)

Secret of the evacuee
Urquhart, Paul
Sexton Blake series (1045)

Secret of the farm
Chester, Gilbert
Sexton Blake series (701)

Secret of the fated family
Hardinge, Rex
Sexton Blake series (1329)

Secret of the flames
Graydon, William Murray
Sexton Blake series (575)

Secret of the forgotten city
Keene, Carolyn
Nancy Drew series (52)

Secret of the frozen north
Sayer, Walter William
Sexton Blake series (203)

Secret of the glacier
Jardine, Warwick
Sexton Blake series (849)
Murray, Andrew
Sexton Blake series (144)

Secret of the glen
Brisbane, Coutts
Sexton Blake series (838)

Secret of the gold locket
Quiroule, Peter
Sexton Blake series (315)

Secret of the golden horse
Parsons, Anthony
Sexton Blake series (1011)

Secret of the Golden Path
Gervaise, Mary
Marstons series (2)

Secret of the golden pavilion
Keene, Carolyn
Nancy Drew series (36)

Secret of the gorge
Saville, Malcolm
Lone Pine Five Club series (11)

Secret of the Grange
Cross, Mark
Daphne Wrayne and her Four Adjusters series (23)

Secret of the grave
Hunter, John
Sexton Blake series (1062)

Secret of the green lagoon
Murray, Andrew
Sexton Blake series (532)

Secret of the haunted doghouse
Hollands, Judith
Ketchup sisters series (3)

Secret of the haunted mirror
Carey, Mary Virginia
Three Investigators series (21)

Secret of the hidden pool
Saville, Malcolm
Michael and Mary series (4)

Secret of the hills
Garrett, William
James Drew series (1)

Secret of the hold
Hunter, John
Sexton Blake series (981)

Secret of the Howling Cave
Roddy, Lee
American adventure series (4)

Secret of the hulk
Murray, Andrew
Sexton Blake series (61)
Stuart, Donald
Sexton Blake series (1043)

Secret of the hunger desert
Murray, Andrew
Sexton Blake series (145)

Secret of the identification parade
Edwards, Walter
Sexton Blake series (863)

Secret of the Indian
Banks, Lynne Reid
Omri series (3)

Secret of the Indian lawyer
Parsons, Anthony
Sexton Blake series (1338)

Secret of the invisible city
Carlson, Dale
Jenny Dean series (4)

Secret of the island
Verne, Jules
Captain Grant's children series (2)
Captain Nemo series (2)

Secret of the island treasure
Dixon, Franklin W
Hardy boys series (100)

Secret of the jade pavilion
Sherry, Sylvia
Yusof series (1)

Secret of the jade ring
Keene, Carolyn
Dana girls series (15)

Secret of the jungle
Hardinge, Rex
Sexton Blake series (1183)
Rees, George
Sexton Blake series (1333)

Secret of the Kara Sea
Collenette, Eric J
Ben Grant series (4)

Secret of the kashmir shawl
Garis, Lilian C
Melody Lane series (8)

Secret of the knight's sword
Keene, Carolyn
Nancy Drew and the Hardy boys be a detective mystery series (1)

Secret of the lagoon
Armour, R Coutts
Sexton Blake series (271)

Secret of the living skeleton
Drummond, J
Sexton Blake series (1232)

Secret of the loch
Brisbane, Coutts
Sexton Blake series (750)
Downie, James Millar
Gaunt series (2)

Secret of the long-lost cousin, and other mysteries
Masters, M
Hawkeye Collins and Amy Adams series (1)

Secret of the Loon Lake monster, and other mysteries
Masters, M
Hawkeye Collins and Amy Adams series (10)

Secret of the lost mesa
Striker, Fran
Tom Quest series (4)

Secret of the lost planet
Macvicar, Angus
Jeremy Grant series (3)

Secret of the lost tunnel
Dixon, Franklin W
Hardy boys series (29)

Secret of the man who died
Hardinge, Rex
Sexton Blake series (1380)

Secret of the mansions
Bayfield, William John
Sexton Blake series (367)

Secret of the marble mantle
Carter, Nicholas
Nicholas Carter series (630)

Secret of the mine
Hardy, Arthur Steffens
Sexton Blake series (82)

Secret of the minstrel's guitar
Keene, Carolyn
Dana girls series (29)

Secret of the missing clown
Hunt, Francis
Mary and Jerry Denton series (4)

Secret of the monastery
Shaw, Stanley Gordon
Sexton Blake series (533)

Secret of the Moor House
Stuart, Donald
Sexton Blake series (974)

Secret of the Moroccan bazaar
Parsons, Anthony
Sexton Blake series (1364)

Secret of the musical tree
Sutton, Margaret
Judy Bolton series (19)

Secret of the narrow seas
Robinson, George Bush
James Clifton series (2)

Secret of the night
Leroux, Gaston
Joseph Rouletabille series (3)

Secret of the ninja
Leibold, Jay
Choose your own adventure series (66)

Secret of the oblong chest
Sayer, Walter William
Sexton Blake series (260)

Secret of the old clock
Keene, Carolyn
Nancy Drew series (1)

Secret of the old mill
Dixon, Franklin W
Hardy boys series (3)

Secret of the Old Sleigh
Sheldon, Ann
Linda Craig series (8)

Secret of the past
Graydon, William Murray
Sexton Blake series (39)

Secret of the President's daughter
Teed, George Hamilton
Sexton Blake series (573)

Secret of the Pygmy herd
Marsh, Jean Evelyn
Rick and Pete Clayton series (2)

Secret of the pyramids
Brightfield, Richard
Choose your own adventure series (19)

Secret of the red mountain
Sayer, Walter William
Sexton Blake series (204)

Secret of the red scarf
Judd, Frances K
Kay Tracey series (1)

Secret of the rocks
Garnett, Henry
Benny series (2)

Secret of the Roman temple
Parsons, Anthony
Sexton Blake series (1387)

Secret of the round beast
Forrester, John
Bestiary trilogy (2)

Secret of the royal treasure
Gaskin, Carol
Time machine series (13)

Secret of the Runestaff
Moorcock, Michael
History of Runestaff series (4)

Secret of the Russian refugees
Graydon, William Murray
Sexton Blake series (529)

Secret of the safe
Edgar, Alfred
Sexton Blake series (278)

Secret of the sale room
Hardinge, Rex
Sexton Blake series (892)

Secret of the sanatorium
Brisbane, Coutts
Sexton Blake series (652)

Secret of the sand castle
Hope, Laura Lee
New Bobbsey twins series (4)
Sutton, Margaret
Judy Bolton series (38)

Secret of the sandbanks
Plain, Josephine
Colin Anstruther series (1)

Secret of the sands
Tyrer, Walter
Sexton Blake series (1149)

Secret of the scarlet letter
Conde, Phillip
Dick Pemberty series (8)

Secret of the school
Richards, Frank
Schoolboy series (1)

Secret of the screen
Fowler, Sydney
Professor Blinkwell series (2)

Secret of the sealed room
Stuart, Donald
Sexton Blake series (854)

Secret of the seven bright shiners
Roose-Evans, James
Odd and Elsewhere series (2)

Secret of the seven willows
McKean, Thomas
Doors into time series (1)

Secret of the seventh candle
Bradman, Tony
Sam, the girl detective series (4)

Secret of the shark pit
Roddy, Lee
Ladd family series (1)

Secret of the Siegfried Line
Dix, Maurice Buxton
Sexton Blake series (1020)

Secret of the silver box
Work, Virginia
Jodi series (2)

Secret of the silver car
Martyn, Wyndham
Anthony Trent series (2)

Secret of the silver dolphin
Keene, Carolyn
Dana girls series (27)

Secret of the singing strings
Chambers, Kate
Diana Winthrop series (1)

Secret of the six black dots
Sayer, Walter William
Sexton Blake series (205)

Secret of the sixth magic
Hardy, Lyndon
Arcadia trilogy (2)

Secret of the sixty steps
Drummond, J
Sexton Blake series (1253)

Secret of the smuggler's cove
Hardinge, Rex
Sexton Blake series (848)

Secret of the snows
Gibbons, Harry Hornaby Clifford
Sexton Blake series (478)
Plain, Josephine
Colin Anstruther series (2)
Tyrer, Walter
Sexton Blake series (1342)

Secret of the software spy, and other mysteries
Masters, M
Hawkeye Collins and Amy Adams series (8)

Secret of the spa
Leonard, Charles L
Paul Kilgerrin series (4)

Secret of the stage
Ridley, Nat
Nat Ridley series (7)

Secret of the steps
Chester, Gilbert
Sexton Blake series (881)

Secret of the stolen clue
Hope, Laura Lee
New Bobbsey twins series (15)

Secret of the stolen puppies
Hope, Laura Lee
New Bobbsey twins series (8)

Secret of the Storm Country
White, Grace Miller
Storm country series (2)

Secret of the strong room
Teed, George Hamilton
Sexton Blake series (641)

Secret of the study
Clifford, Martin
Tom Merry series (2)

Secret of the Su
Robeson, Kenneth
Doc Savage series (126)

Secret of the Sudan
Jardine, Warwick
Sexton Blake series (766)

Secret of the Suez Canal
Rees, George
Sexton Blake series (1356)

Secret of the sun god
Packard, Andrea
Choose your own adventure series (68)

Secret of the sundial
Wirt, Ann
Madge Sterling series (3)

Secret of the sunken ships
Chester, Gilbert
Sexton Blake series (961)

Secret of the sunken sub
Roddy, Lee
Ladd family series (5)

Secret of the sunken treasure
Hope, Laura Lee
New Bobbsey twins series (12)

Secret of the surgery
Bobin, John William
Sexton Blake series (565)
Jardine, Warwick
Sexton Blake series (1003)

Secret of the Swiss chalet
Keene, Carolyn
Dana girls series (20)

Secret of the ten bales
Parsons, Anthony
Sexton Blake series (938)

Secret of the thieves' kitchen
Teed, George Hamilton
Sexton Blake series (642)

Secret of the third eye
Carlson, Dale
Jenny Dean series (3)

Secret of the third watch
Fortune, J J
Race against time series (7)

Secret of the Tibetan treasure
Keene, Carolyn
Nancy Drew series (108)

Secret of the time vault
Darlton, Clark
Perry Rhodan series (6)

Secret of the tomb
Bayfield, William John
Sexton Blake series (463)

Secret of the Tong
Gregory, H
Sexton Blake series (221)

Secret of the twin puppets
Keene, Carolyn
Nancy Drew picture books series (2)

Secret of the two blackmailed men
Graydon, William Murray
Sexton Blake series (530)

Secret of the underground room
Bellairs, John
Johnny Dixon series (8)

Secret of the unicorn
Herge
Tintin series (11)

Secret of the vampire actress
Graydon, William Murray
Sexton Blake series (576)

Secret of the vault
Verner, Gerald
Sexton Blake series (627)

Secret of the veld
Hardinge, Rex
Sexton Blake series (1184)

Secret of the video game scorer, and other mysteries
Masters, M
Hawkeye Collins and Amy Adams series (12)

Secret of the white thug
Foster, Reginald Francis
Sexton Blake series (566)

Secret of the windmill
Judd, Frances K
Kay Tracey series (7)

Secret of the witch's stairway
Walker, Holly Beth
Meg Duncan series (2)

Secret of the wooden lady
Keene, Carolyn
Nancy Drew series (27)

Secret of the woods
Quiroule, Pierre
Sexton Blake series (809)

Secret of thirteen
Hiller, Barbara B
Pick-a-path series (13)

Secret of Thirty-Seven Hardy Street
Casey, Robert J
Jim Sands series (1)

Secret of Thunder Mountain
Striker, Fran
Tom Quest series (6)

Secret of Thurlston Towers
Brooks, Leonard Harold
Sexton Blake series (277)

Secret of Tippety-Witchet
Roose-Evans, James
Odd and Elsewhere series (6)

Secret of Torre Island
Armour, R Coutts
Sexton Blake series (412)

Secret of Villa Rosa
Saville, Malcolm
Buckinghams series (5)

Secret of Wildcat Swamp
Dixon, Franklin W
Hardy boys series (31)

Secret pact
Wirt, Mildred Augustine
Penny Parker series (6)

Secret panel
Carter, Nicholas
Nicholas Carter series (160)
Dixon, Franklin W
Hardy boys series (25)

Secret passage
Bawden, Nina
Mallory children series (1)

Secret peace
McCay, William
Young Indiana Jones chronicles series (3)

Secret people
Gibbons, Harry Hornaby Clifford
Sexton Blake series (340)

Secret play
Barbour, Ralph Henry
Purple Pennant trilogy (2)

Secret quest
Sutton, Margaret
Judy Bolton series (33)

Secret range
Sheridan, Matt
David Harcourt series (1)

Secret river
Pinkerton, Kathrene
Baird family series (3)

Secret room
Eames, Marion
Secret room series (1)
Secret Santa
Martin, Ann Matthews
Baby-Sitters Club series (78)
Secret sceptre
Gerard, Francis
Sir John Meredith series (7)
Secret Scorpio
Akers, Alan Burt
Dray Prescot series (15)
Secret search
Punshon, Ernest Robertson
Bobby Owen series (28)
Secret servant
Lyall, Gavin
Major Harry Maxim series (1)
Newman, Bernard
Inspector Marshall series (2)
Secret service
Dale, Norman
Peter and Ginger series (1)
Secret service girl
Walsh, James Morgan
Colonel Ormiston series (2)
Secret service man
Dilnot, George
Jim Strang series (1)
Horler, Sydney
Gerald Lissendale series (1)
Martin Huish series (1)
Secret Service Smith
Scott, Reginald Thomas Maitland
Aurelius Smith series (1)
Secret service woman
De Halsalle, Henry
Olga von Kopf series (1)
Secret session
Janson, Hank
Hank Janson series (39)
Secret seven
Bell, Robert Stanly Warren
Greyhouse series (3)
Secret Seven
Blyton, Enid
Secret Seven series (1)
Secret Seven adventure
Blyton, Enid
Secret Seven series (2)
Secret Seven and the bonfire adventure
Blyton, Enid
Secret Seven series (11)
Secret Seven and the case of the dog lover
Blyton, Enid
Secret Seven series (13)
Secret Seven and the case of the missing medals
Blyton, Enid
Secret Seven series (14)
Secret Seven and the case of the music lover
Blyton, Enid
Secret Seven series (10)
Secret Seven and the case of the old horse
Blyton, Enid
Secret Seven series (15)
Secret Seven and the case of the stolen car
Blyton, Enid
Secret Seven series (6)
Secret Seven and the circus adventure
Blyton, Enid
Secret Seven series (2)
Secret Seven and the grim secret
Blyton, Enid
Secret Seven series (8)
Secret Seven and the hidden cave adventure
Blyton, Enid
Secret Seven series (7)
Secret Seven and the missing girl mystery
Blyton, Enid
Secret Seven series (9)
Secret Seven and the mystery of the empty house
Blyton, Enid
Secret Seven series (1)
Secret Seven and the old fort adventure
Blyton, Enid
Secret Seven series (12)
Secret Seven and the railroad mystery
Blyton, Enid
Secret Seven series (4)
Secret Seven and the tree house adventure
Blyton, Enid
Secret Seven series (3)
Secret Seven fireworks
Blyton, Enid
Secret Seven series (11)
Secret Seven get their man
Blyton, Enid
Secret Seven series (5)
Secret Seven mystery
Blyton, Enid
Secret Seven series (9)
Secret Seven on the trail
Blyton, Enid
Secret Seven series (4)
Secret Seven win through
Blyton, Enid
Secret Seven series (7)
Secret singing
Lewis, Royston
Inspector John Crow series (4)
Secret sisterhood
Rheingold, Howard
Sisterhood trilogy (3)
Secret sixguns
Sharpe, Jon
Trailsman series (103)
Secret sky express
Stone, Richard H
Slim Tyler series (6)
Secret sorcerers
Lowery, Linda
Heartquest series (3)
Secret staircase
Barklem, Jill
Brambly Hedge series (5)
Secret stock
Martin, Toy
Taronga Road Riders series (4)
Secret syndicate
Frazer, Robert Caine
Mark Kilby series (2)
Secret temple
Brisbane, Coutts
Sexton Blake series (795)
Secret trail
Armstrong, Anthony
Jimmie Rezaire series (2)
Secret treasure of Tibet
Brightfield, Richard
Choose your own adventure series (36)
Secret tunnel
Chandler, Edna Walker
Tom Logan series (2)
Secret under Antarctica
Dickson, Gordon Rupert
Robby Hoenig trilogy (2)
Secret under the Caribbean
Dickson, Gordon Rupert
Robby Hoenig trilogy (3)
Secret under the sea
Dickson, Gordon Rupert
Robby Hoenig trilogy (1)
Secret vanguard
Innes, Michael
Sir John Appleby series (6)
Secret victory
McKenna, Stephen
Sensationalists trilogy (3)
Secret warning
Dixon, Franklin W
Hardy boys series (17)
Secret warriors
Baldwin, Alex
Men at war series (2)
Secret water
Ransome, Arthur
Swallows and Amazons series (8)
Secret weapon
Beeding, Francis
Colonel Alastair Granby series (14)
Leyland, Eric
Hunter Hawk series (6)
Macdonnell, James Edmond
Captain Peter Bentley series (8)
Newman, Bernard
Papa Pontivy series (4)
Secret weapons
Walsh, James Morgan
Oliver Keene series (6)
Secret window
Wright, Betty Ren
Secret window series (1)
Secret witch
Willson, Robina Beckles
Witch series (1)
Secret years
Pugh, Edwin
Eyes of a child series (2)
Secretary of state
McKenna, Stephen
Realists trilogy (2)
Secretary of state for death
Carstairs, Henry
Lydford Long series (4)
Secrets
Cooper, M E
Couples series (10)
Pascal, Francine
Sweet Valley High series (2)
Secrets at Black Pony Inn
Pullein-Thompson, Christine
Black Pony Inn series (4)
Secrets at Saxonhill
Duncan, Kathleen Mary
Saxonhill series (1)
Secrets at seventeen
Cole, Jennifer
Cindy and Nicole series (4)
Secrets can kill
Keene, Carolyn
Nancy Drew files series (1)
Secrets can't be kept
Punshon, Ernest Robertson
Bobby Owen series (20)
Secrets d'amour
Villefranche, Anne Marie
Erotic memoirs series (5)
Secrets for sale
Leonard, Charles L
Paul Kilgerrin series (10)
Secrets in the attic
Braga, Meg
William and Wendy series (1)
Secrets man
Holt, Deben
Roger Moore and the Crimefighters series (5)
Secrets of a woman's heart
Spurling, Hilary
Ivy Compton-Burnett series (2)
Secrets of Beacon Hill
Chambers, Kate
Diana Winthrop series (4)
Secrets of Bredon Hill
Archer, Fred
Evesham Vale series (3)
Secrets of Peyton Place
Fuller, Roger
Peyton Place series (6)
Secrets of Stonehenge
Dennison, Milo
Blackstone's magical adventure series (2)
Secrets of the Abbey
Oxenham, Elsie J
Abbey girls retrospective series (2)
Secrets of the deep
Dickson, Gordon Rupert
Robby Hoenig trilogy (3)
Selberg, Ingrid
Nature secrets series (1)
Secrets of the gnomes
Huygen, Willibrord
Gnomes series (2)
Secrets of the knights
Gasperini, Jim
Time machine series (1)
Secrets of the Lake House
Rhode, John
Doctor Lancelot Priestley series (42)
Secrets of the lost island
Beach, Lynn
Twistaplot series (16)
Secrets of the morning
Andrews, Virginia Cleo
Cutler family series (2)
Secrets of the pond
Selberg, Ingrid
Nature secrets series (2)
Secrets of the Princess of Cadignan
Balzac, Honore de
Scenes of Parisian life series (7)
Secrets of the scarry fun
Mooser, Stephen
Creepy Creature Club series (8)
Secrets of Vairy
Oxenham, Elsie J
Patch series (2)
Section five hundred and fifty eight
Hawthorne, Julian
Inspector Byrnes series (5)
Section G, United Planets
Reynolds, Mack
Planetary Agent series (6)
Sector General
White, James
Sector General series (6)
Security secrets sold here
Cobb, Belton
Bryan Armitage series (13)
Inspector Cheviot Burmann series (37)
Kitty Armitage series (10)
Sedan murder mystery
Wallace, John
Conrad Franks series (1)
Detective Sergeant Fuller series (1)
Seduce and destroy
Eastwood, James
Anna Zordan series (2)
Seduction of the minotaur
Nin, Anais
Cities of the interior series (5)
Seductress
Brown, Carter
Danny Boyd series (7)
Sedulous ape
Batchelor, Denzil
Inspector Johnson series (3)
See again, say again
Frasconi, Antonio
See and say series (2)
See and say
Frasconi, Antonio
See and say series (1)
See Charlie run
Freemantle, Brian
Charlie Muffin series (8)
See how they run
Litchfield, Michael
Superintendent Fergus McQueen series (1)
See it again, Sam
Brown, Carter
Rick Holman series (34)
See me dance the polka
Blumenfeld, Josephine
Pin a rose on me series (2)
See no evil
Dixon, Franklin W
Hardy boys case files series (8)
See Rome and die
Revell, Louisa
Julia Tyler series (6)
See Texas and die
Logan, Jake
John Slocum series (14)
See the living crocodiles
Bark, Conrad Voss
Mister William Holmes series (6)
See the red blood run
Peebles, Niles N
Ross McKellar series (1)
See the woman
Barnes, Dallas
Sergeant John Stryker series (1)
See them die
McBain, Ed
Eighty Seventh Precinct series (13)
See who's dying
Courtier, Sidney Hobson
Inspector Digger Haig series (5)
See you later, alligator
Buckley, William Frank
Blackford Oakes series (6)
See you Thursday
Ure, Jean
Thursday trilogy (1)
Seed and the sower
Van der Post, Laurens
Seed and the sower trilogy (2)
Seed beneath the snow
Silone, Ignazio
Pietro Spina series (2)
Seed of doubt
McInerny, Ralph
Father Roger Dowling series (16)
Seed of evil
Plante, Edward
Seed series (1)
Seed of stars
Morgan, Dan
Venturer Twelve series (2)
Seed of the Falcon
Darby, Catherine
Falcon family series (10)
Seed-time and harvest
Arthur, Timothy Shay
Household library series (2)
Seed upon the wind
Douglas, Carole Nelson
Taliswoman trilogy (2)
Seedbearers
Timlett, Peter Valentine
Atlantis trilogy (1)
Seedling
Axler, James
Deathlands series (13)
Seeds of death
Dicks, Terrance
Doctor Who series (112)
Seeds of destruction
Griffin, John
Richard Raven series (4)
Seeds of doom
Hayes, Ralph Eugene
Check Force series (6)
Seeds of evil
Streib, Dan
Michael Hawk series (6)
Seeds of frenzy
Elder, Michael
Barclay series (4)
Seeds of hate
Carmichael, Harry
John Piper and Quinn series (16)
Seeds of Hiroshima
Morris, Edita
Hiroshima series (2)
Seeds of love
Georgeson, Valerie
Shadow of the elephant series (1)
Seeds of murder
Mason, Francis Van Wyck
Colonel Hugh North series (1)
Underwood, Michael
Rosa Epton series (16)
Seeds of mutiny
Trevelyan, Robert
Pendragon series (4)
Seeds of rebellion
Nicole, Christopher
Black majesty series (1)
Seeds of ruin
Voltz, William
Perry Rhodan series (111)
Seeds of time
Kenyon, Frank Wilson
John Churchill, Duke of Marlborough series (1)
Seeds of tomorrow
Sholokhov, Mikhail
Don series (4)
Seeds of war
Randle, Kevin
Seeds of war trilogy (1)
Seeds of yesterday
Andrews, Virginia Cleo
Dollanganger family series (5)
Seeds on the go
Fisher, Aileen
Ways of plants series (4)
Seedtime
Palmer, Vance
Macy Donovan series (2)
Seedtime and harvest
Pearce, Mary Emily
Apple tree series (5)
Seedtime on the Cumberland
Arnow, Harriette
Cumberland series (1)
Seeing
Pluckrose, Henry
Thinking about series (4)
Seeing England with Uncle John
Warner, Anne
Uncle John series (2)
Seeing eye
Bell, Josephine
Doctor David Wintringham series (15)
Inspector Steven Mitchell series (9)
Seeing France with Uncle John
Warner, Anne
Uncle John series (1)
Seeing is believing
Dickson, Carter
Sir Henry Merrivale series (13)
Seeing red
Cooper, Ilene
Hollywood wars series (3)
Du Bois, Theodora
Anne and Jeffrey McNeill series (19)
Seeing the elephant
Roberts, Les
Saxon series (5)
Seek and destroy
Robertson, Manning K
Steve Carradine series (1)
Seek and find
Optic, Oliver
Starry flag series (4)
Seek out and destroy
Evans, Alan
David Cochrane series (4)
Seek, strike and destroy
Stanton, Ken
Aquanauts series (3)
Seek the fair land
Macken, Walter
Macmahon family trilogy (1)
Seeker
Avenell, Donne
Axa series (8)

Seekers
Bonner, Terry Nelsen
New South Wales series (8)
Jakes, John
Kent family series (3)
Lupton, Joyce
Leigh family series (2)
Seekers and the sword
Friedman, Michael Jan
Vidar trilogy (2)
Seekers of Shar-Nuhn
Mayhar, Ardath
Kyrannon series (2)
Seeking sword
Kangilaski, Jaan
Seeking sword series (1)
Seeking the dream brother
Bennett, Marcia Joanne
Ni-lach series (4)
Seeking the mythical future
Hoyle, Trevor
Christian Queghan series (1)
Seems so
Reynolds, Stephen
Nautical series (3)
Seen and the unseen
Marsh, Richard
Augustus Champnell series (2)
Seen any cats?
Modell, Frank B
Milton and Marvin series (1)
Seer
Wisler, Gary Clifton
Antrian series (2)
Seeress of Kell
Eddings, David
Malloreon series (5)
Seesaws, nutcrackers, brooms
Lampton, Christopher
Simple machines series (3)
Seeta
Taylor, Philip Meadows
Indian history trilogy (3)
Seetee
Williamson, Jack
Seetee series (2)
Seetee alert!
Kern, Gregory
Cap Kennedy series (6)
Seetee ship
Williamson, Jack
Seetee series (1)
Seetee shock
Williamson, Jack
Seetee series (2)
Seg the bowman
Prescot, Dray
Dray Prescot series (32)
Segaki
Stacton, David
Invincible questions trilogy (3)
Stanton, David
Invincible questions series (3)
Segelfoss Town
Hamsun, Knut
Segelfoss Town series (2)
Segi finds the radio
Saro-Wiwa, Ken
Mister B series (6)
Segra and Stargull
Downing, Peggy
Exitorn series (2)
Segra and the magician
Downing, Peggy
Exitorn series (5)
Segra in Diamond Castle
Downing, Peggy
Exitorn series (3)
Seidlitz and the super-spy
Brown, Carter
Mavis Seidlitz series (10)
Seidman and Son
Moll, Elick
Morris Seidman series (1)
Seize a passing stranger
Joyce, Cyril
Chief Superintendent Pat Stockton series (5)
Seize the reckless wind
Davis, John Gordon
Hold my hand series (2)
Seize the sky
Johnston, Terry Conrad
General Armstrong Custer series (2)
Seized by love
Johnson, Susan
Kuzan family trilogy (1)
Seizure
Fraser, David
Treason in arms series (4)

Selby screams
Ball, Duncan
Selby series (3)
Selby speaks
Ball, Duncan
Selby series (2)
Selby's secret
Ball, Duncan
Selby series (1)
Self-defense
Kellerman, Jonathan
Alex Delaware series (9)
Self-portrait of murder
Bonnamy, Francis
Peter Shane series (6)
Selfish ones
Best, Rayleigh Breton Amis
Yarrow series (6)
Selicombe murder
Islay, Nicholas
Sydney Vane series (1)
Selina
Kaye-Smith, Sheila
Selina series (2)
Selina crisis
Grover, Marshall
Larry and Stretch series (388)
Selina is older
Kaye-Smith, Sheila
Selina series (2)
Sellers of death
Sayer, Walter William
Barnaby Grayle series (1)
Selling Lucky
Abbott, Jacob
Rainbow and Lucky series (4)
Selling out
Hamovitch, Eric
Brian Mulroney series (2)
Murphy, Rae Allan
Brian Mulroney series (2)
Selling's murder
Tack, Alfred
John Harley series (1)
Sellout
Jewell, Derek
Prospero Group series (2)
Selma at the Abbey
Oxenham, Elsie J
Abbey girls retrospective series (6)
Sembal
Cannan, Gilbert
New time trilogy (2)
Round the corner trilogy (2)
Semi-attached couple
Eden, Emily
Semi series (1)
Semi-detached house
Eden, Emily
Semi series (2)
Seminar for murder
Gill, B M
Inspector Tom Maybridge series (2)
Seminole
Porter, Donald Clayton
White Indian series (12)
Seminole skies
Lederer, Paul Joseph
Indian heritage series (3)
Semi-society
Richardson, Frank
Vincent Skrene series (2)
Semi-tough
Jenkins, Dan
Billy Clyde Puckett series (1)
Semolina Silkpaws comes to Catstown
Williams, Gladys
Semolina Silkpaws series (1)
Semolina Silkpaws' motor-car
Williams, Gladys
Semolina Silkpaws series (3)
Semolina Silkpaws takes a holiday abroad
Williams, Gladys
Semolina Silkpaws series (3)
Semper fi
Griffin, W E B
Corps series (1)
Sempinski affair
Kuniczak, Wieslaw Stanislaw
Polish war trilogy (1)
Semra
Moss, Merrilee
Hot pursuit series (7)
Senator love
Adler, Warren
Fiona Fitzgerald series (4)
Senator Marlowe's daughter
Keyes, Frances Parkinson
Marlowe family series (1)

Senator's plot
Carter, Nicholas
Nicholas Carter series (393)
Send Angel
Christian, Frederick H
Frank Angel series (2)
Send another coffin
Presnell, Frank G
John and Anne Webb series (1)
Send another hearse
Masur, Harold Q
Scott Jordan series (8)
Send Bygraves
Grimes, Martha
Inspector Richard Jury series (11)
Send for Angel
Montrose, Graham
Angel Brown series (8)
Send for Ben
Billam, Rosemary
Ben and Arthur series (1)
Send for Paul Temple
Durbridge, Francis
Paul Temple series (1)
Send for Paul Temple again!
Durbridge, Francis
Paul Temple series (5)
Send for the Saint
Bloxsom, Peter
Saint series (47)
Send him victorious
Hurd, Douglas
Foreign Office trilogy (1)
Send in our shoes
Baker, Margaret Joyce
Ridley family series (3)
Send Inspector West
Creasey, John
Inspector Roger West series (14)
Send no flowers
Brown, Sandra
Alicia series (2)
Holt, Gavin
Inspector Joel Saber series (5)
Send Superintendent West
Creasey, John
Inspector Roger West series (14)
Sendi Lee Mason and the big mistake
Stahl, Hilda
Sendi Lee Mason series (3)
Sendi Lee Mason and the great crusade
Stahl, Hilda
Sendi Lee Mason series (4)
Sendi Lee Mason and the milk carton kids
Stahl, Hilda
Sendi Lee Mason series (1)
Sendi Lee Mason and the stray striped cat
Stahl, Hilda
Sendi Lee Mason series (2)
Sending of dragons
Yolen, Jane
Pit dragons trilogy (3)
Seneca
Porter, Donald Clayton
White Indian series (9)
Seneca patriots
Porter, Donald Clayton
White Indian series (22)
Seneca warriors
Porter, Donald Clayton
White Indian series (17)
Sengler's buys Babette
Brandon, Grania
Sengler's Circus series (5)
Sengler's Circus
Brandon, Grania
Sengler's Circus series (1)
Sengler's comes to town
Brandon, Grania
Sengler's Circus series (4)
Sengler's rising star
Brandon, Grania
Sengler's Circus series (3)
Sengler's sawdust ring
Brandon, Grania
Sengler's Circus series (2)
Senior
Cooney, Linda A
Class of eighty eight series (4)
Class of eighty nine series (4)
Senior co-ed
Lee, Alice Lester
Co-ed series (4)
Senior dreams can come true
Miner, Jane Claypool
Ellynne Aleese series (2)
Senior hostess
Hill, Margaret
Beth Dean series (3)

Senior nurse
James, Josephine
Kathy Martin series (3)
Senior prefect
Bruce, Dorita Fairlie
Dimsie series (1)
Senior prom
Aks, Patricia
Prom series (2)
Du Jardin, Rosamond
Marcy series (4)
Senior sister
Jones, Irene Heywood
Hospital life series (2)
Senior year
Tyler, Vicki
Heart to heart series (8)
Senior year at last
Harrell, Janice
West Mount High trilogy (3)
Senor Baby Elephant
Joslin, Sesyle
Baby Elephant series (3)
Senor Saint
Charteris, Leslie
Saint series (33)
Sensation of Sin Street
Brody, Marc
Marc Brody series (1)
Sensational science activities with Doctor Zed
Penrose, Gordon
Doctor Zed series (4)
Sense and sensibility
Austen, Jane
Brightsea series (1)
Eliza Brandon series (1)
Margaret Dashwood series (1)
Sense of freedom
Boyle, Jimmy
Prison diaries series (1)
Sense of obligation
Harrison, Harry
Brion Brandd series (1)
Sense of place
Mosco, Maisie
Between two worlds trilogy (2)
Sense of responsibility
Mackenzie, Lee
Emmerdale Farm series (6)
Sensitive case
Wright, Eric
Inspector Charlie Salter series (7)
Sensitives
Burkholz, Herbert
Sensitives series (1)
Sensorites
Robinson, Nigel
Doctor Who series (118)
Sensuality
Janson, Hank
Hank Janson series (161)
Sensuous angel
Graham, Heather
Donna Miro and Lorna Doria series (1)
Sent for you yesterday
Wideman, John Edgar
Homewood trilogy (3)
Sent to Coventry
Richards, Frank
Mascot schoolboy series (4)
Sentence deferred
Derleth, August
Judge Ephraim Peck series (5)
Sentence for sin
Janson, Hank
Hank Janson series (17)
Sentence suspended
Joyce, Cyril
Chief Superintendent Pat Stockton series (7)
Sentenced to Prism
Foster, Alan Dean
Thranx series (7)
Sentience
Adams, Terry A
Sentience series (1)
Sentimental kill
Clapperton, Richard
Peter Fleck series (3)
Sentimental smuggler
Douglas, Felicity
Nicholas series (2)
Sentimental Tommy
Barrie, James Matthew
Thrums series (5)
Barrie, James Matthew
Tommy series (1)
Sentimentalists
Benson, Robert Hugh
Supernatural series (1)

Sentinel
Konvitz, Jeffrey
Sentinel series (1)
Sadler, Barry
Casca series (9)
Sentinels of solitude
Darlton, Clark
Perry Rhodan series (127)
Sentry box murder
Gayle, Newton
James Greer series (2)
Separate cases
Randisi, Robert Joseph
Miles Jacoby series (4)
Separate peace
Knowles, John
Devon School series (1)
Separate reality
Castaneda, Carlos
Don Juan series (2)
Separation
Rohmer, Richard
Separation trilogy (2)
Separation two
Rohmer, Richard
Separation trilogy (3)
Sepoy mutiny
Stuart, Vivian
Captain Alexander Sheridan series (3)
September September
Foote, Shelby
Lake Jordan series (5)
September story
Inchbald, Ralph
Colonel Paternoster series (3)
Martin, Robert
Career adventure series (3)
Septimouse, big cheese!
Jungman, Ann
Septimouse series (2)
Septimouse, supermouse
Jungman, Ann
Septimouse series (1)
Septimus and the Danedyke mystery
Chance, Stephen
Septimus Treloar series (1)
Septimus and the minster ghost
Chance, Stephen
Septimus Treloar series (2)
Septimus and the minster ghost mystery
Chance, Stephen
Septimus Treloar series (2)
Septimus and the spy ring
Chance, Stephen
Septimus Treloar series (4)
Septimus and the stone offering
Chance, Stephen
Septimus Treloar series (3)
Sequel to Barrington's Voyage to New South Wales
Barrington, George
Voyage to New South Wales series (2)
Sequel to boldness
Pape, Richard
Boldness series (2)
Sequel to the adventures of Baron Munchausen
Raspe, Rudolf Erich
Baron Munchausen series (2)
Sequel to Tim the scissors grinder
Leslie, Madeline
Tim the scissors grinder series (2)
Sequel to yesterday's crime
Foxall, Peter Augustus
Catford Police series (3)
Sequin syndicate
Hesky, Olga
Inspector Tami Shimoni series (3)
Sequoia scout
Thoeme, Brock
Saga of the Sierras series (3)
Sequoia shootout
Reese, John
Jefferson Hewitt series (8)
Serafina the giraffe
Brunhoff, Laurent de
Serafina series (1)
Serafina's lucky find
Brunhoff, Laurent de
Serafina series (2)
Seraph in a box
Willson, Robina Beckles
Sarah and Alastair series (2)
Seraphita
Balzac, Honore de
Philosophic studies series (20)
Sergeant and the Queen
Crane, Robert
Ben Corbin series (2)

Sergeant Biggleswoth, C.I.D.
Johns, William Earl
Biggles series (31)
Sergeant Cluff and the day of reckoning
North, Gil
Sergeant Caleb Cluff series (8)
Sergeant Cluff and the madmen
North, Gil
Sergeant Caleb Cluff series (5)
Sergeant Cluff and the price of pity
North, Gil
Sergeant Caleb Cluff series (6)
Sergeant Cluff goes fishing
North, Gil
Sergeant Caleb Cluff series (3)
Sergeant Cluff laughs last
North, Gil
Sergeant Caleb Cluff series (5)
Sergeant Cluff rings true
North, Gil
Sergeant Caleb Cluff series (11)
Sergeant Cluff stands firm
North, Gil
Sergeant Caleb Cluff series (1)
Sergeant Corbin's war
Crane, Robert
Ben Corbin series (1)
Sergeant Cork's casebook
Swinson, Arthur
Sergeant Cork series (1)
Sergeant Cork's second casebook
Swinson, Arthur
Sergeant Cork series (2)
Sergeant Death
Browne, Douglas Gordon
Mister Harvey Tuke series (6)
Mayo, James
Charles Hood series (4)
Sergeant Dick
Rowe, John Gabriel
Northwest stories series (7)
Sergeant Dick of the Royal Mounted Police
Rowe, John Gabriel
Sergeant Dick series (1)
Sergeant Gray's victim
Hunter, John
Sexton Blake series (1153)
Sergeant Hawk
Clay, Patrick
Sergeant Hawk series (1)
Sergeant Joe
Staples, Mary Jane
South London series (8)
Sergeant Lamb of the Ninth
Graves, Robert
Sergeant Lamb series (1)
Sergeant Lamb's America
Graves, Robert
Sergeant Lamb series (1)
Sergeant Lancey carries on
Greene, L Patrick
Sergeant Lancey series (2)
Sergeant Lancey reports
Greene, L Patrick
Sergeant Lancey series (1)
Sergeant Lancey tells the tale
Greene, L Patrick
Sergeant Lancey series (4)
Sergeant Luck takes over
Bond, Geoffrey
Sergeant Luck series (2)
Sergeant Luck's secret mission
Bond, Geoffrey
Sergeant Luck series (4)
Sergeant O'Reilly
Anderson, Ian
Scarlet riders series (4)
Sergeant Ritchie's conscience
Branston, Frank
Tommy Tompkins series (2)
Sergeant Robot
Mahr, Kurt
Perry Rhodan series (110)
Sergeant Silk, the prairie scout
Leighton, Robert
Sergeant Silk series (1)
Sergeant Spuds Tamson, V.C.
Campbell, R W
Spud Tamson series (2)
Sergeant Verity and the blood royal
Selwyn, Francis
Sergeant William Verity series (4)
Sergeant Verity and the Cracksman
Selwyn, Francis
Sergeant William Verity series (1)
Sergeant Verity and the imperial diamond
Selwyn, Francis
Sergeant William Verity series (2)
Sergeant Verity and the swell mob
Selwyn, Francis
Sergeant William Verity series (5)
Sergeant Verity presents his compliments
Selwyn, Francis
Sergeant William Verity series (3)
Sergeant's cat, and other stories
Van de Wetering, Janwillem
De Gier and Grijpstra series (12)
Serial adventures of Batman
Van Hise, James
Batman series (10)
Series of murders
Brett, Simon
Charles Paris series (13)
Serious creativity
De Bono, Edward
Lateral thinking series (5)
Serious crimes
Gough, Laurence
Willows and Parker series (5)
Smith, Daniel Wybert
Chief Inspector Harry Fathers series (2)
Serious investigation
Egan, Lesley
Jesse Falkenstein series (5)
Serious reflections during the life & surprising adventures or Robinson Cr
Defoe, Daniel
Robinson Crusoe series (1)
Serious science
Smith, Janice Lea
Adam Joshua series (9)
Serpent
Gaskell, Jane
Atlan saga series (1)
Atlan saga series (1)
Mosley, Nicholas
Catastrophe practice series (3)
Serpent-headed stick
Hawk, John
Mortimer Sark series (2)
Serpent mage
Bear, Greg
Michael Perrin series (2)
Weis, Margaret
Death Gate series (4)
Serpent mound
Saint Alcorn, Lloyd
Dream quest trilogy (3)
Serpent of Senargad
Sampson, Fay
Pangur Ban series (5)
Serpent waltz
Clayton, Jo
Dancer trilogy (2)
Serpentine assassin
Dille, Flint
Agent thirteen series (2)
Serpentine murder
Gribble, Leonard Reginald
Superintendent Anthony Slade series (4)
Serpentor and the mummy warrior
Stine, Robert Lawrence
Find your fate: G.I. Joe series (20)
Serpent's children
Yep, Laurence Michael
Cassia series (1)
Serpent's eye
Barker, Wade
Year of the Ninja Master series (3)
Serpents of Siva
Grant, Maxwell
Shadow series (142)
Serpent's reach
Cherryh, Carolyn Janice
Alliance-Union series (13)
Serpent's silver
Anthony, Piers
Dragon series (2)
Serpent's smile
Hesky, Olga
Inspector Tami Shimoni series (1)
Serpent's tooth
Norton, Andre
Witch World series (18)
Woods, Sara
Sir Nicholas Harding and Antony Maitland series (18)
Serpent's tooth mystery
Dixon, Franklin W
Hardy boys series (93)
Servant of death
Wallis, James Harold
Inspector Wilton Jacks series (2)
Servant of the Empire
Feist, Raymond Elias
Empire series (2)
Servants of the skull
House, Brant
Secret Agent X series (6)
Servants of the Wankh
Vance, Jack
Tschai series (2)
Servant's problem
Johns, Veronica Parker
Webster Flagg series (2)
Service for two
Kingsbury, Kate
Pennyfoot Hotel series (3)
Service of all the dead
Dexter, Colin
Inspector Morse series (4)
Service with a smile
Wodehouse, Pelham Grenville
Blandings Castle series (10)
Uncle Fred, Earl of Ickenham series (4)
Sesame Street book of poetry
Moss, Jeffrey
Sesame Street series (2)
Sesame Street songbook
Moss, Jeffrey
Sesame Street series (3)
Set a thief
Thayer, Lee
Peter Clancy series (13)
Set a-foot
Edson, John Thomas
Floating Outfit series (30)
Set all afire
De Wohl, Louis
Lives of the saints series (8)
Set free
Maclean, Norman
Former days trilogy (2)
Set in a silver sea
Bryant, Arthur
History of Britain and the British people series (1)
Set point
Porter, Mark
Win Hadley series (4)
Set Texas back on her feet
Edson, John Thomas
Floating Outfit series (6)
Set up
Corris, Peter
Luke Dunlop series (1)
Set-up
Miller, Ben E
Cory Barnett series (2)
Moore, Robin
Connection series (5)
Newton, William
Joey Binns series (3)
Set-up for a sinner
Brody, Marc
Marc Brody series (39)
Set-up for murder
Cheyney, Peter
Slim Callaghan series (4)
Set-up for scandal
Brody, Marc
Marc Brody series (28)
Seth and Belle and Mr Quarles and me
Rayner, William
Missouri series (1)
Seth of Colorado
Otis, James
Pioneer series (3)
Seth papers
Lauria, Frank
Doctor Owen Orient series (6)
Seth's brother's wife
Frederic, Harold
New York series (1)
Sets we see from the big red bus
Wood, Leslie
Big red bus series (6)
Setting for murder
Fulton, Eileen
Nina McFall series (5)
Setting out
Breese, Andrea
Setting out series (1)
Setting up shop
Sloan, Carolyn
Mall series (1)
Settled out of court
Cecil, Henry
Mister Tewkesbury series (4)
Knox, Ronald Arbuthnott
Miles Bredon series (3)
Settler or slaver
Murray, Andrew
Sexton Blake series (97)
Settlers
Long, William Stuart
Australians series (2)
Moberg, Vilhelm
Emigrants series (3)
Settlers on a strange shore
McCall, Edith
Frontiers of America series (6)
Settling the score
Lowell, Anne Hunter
Sorority girls series (5)
Setup
Franklin, Max
Starsky and Hutch series (7)
Setup
Tilford, Earl H
USAF in Vietnam series (1)
Seven against Greece
Carter, Nick
Nick Carter series (25)
Seven agate devils
Robeson, Kenneth
Doc Savage series (73)
Seven ages
Dean, Basil
Seven ages series (1)
Seven altars of Dusarra
Watt-Evans, Lawrence
Lords of Dus series (2)
Seven and Father Christmas
Lallemand, Evelyne
Secret Seven series (23)
Seven and the lion hunt
Lallemand, Evelyne
Secret Seven series (16)
Seven and the magician
Lallemand, Evelyne
Secret Seven series (17)
Seven and the racing driver
Lallemand, Evelyne
Secret Seven series (24)
Seven and the UFOs
Lallemand, Evelyne
Secret Seven series (22)
Seven chose murder
Vickers, Roy
Inspector George Rason series (3)
Inspector Peter Curwen and Hugh Stanton series (5)
Seven clues
Verner, Gerald
Michael Dene series (1)
Seven clues in search of a crime
Graeme, Bruce
Theodore I Terhune series (1)
Seven crystal balls
Herge
Tintin series (13)
Seven dawns to death
Gray, Berkeley
Norman Conquest series (22)
Seven-day magic
Eager, Edward
Magic series (7)
Seven days at the Silbersteins
Leroux, Etienne
Welgevonden trilogy (1)
Seven days for hanging
Spender, Jean Maud
Mary Owen series (1)
Seven days to death
Marric, J J
Commander George Gideon series (2)
Seven days to Lomaland
Warner, Esther Sietmann
Liberia series (1)
Seven days with Jan
Cockett, Mary
Jan series (2)
Seven dead
Farjeon, Joseph Jefferson
Inspector Kendall series (2)
Seven Dials
Rayner, Claire
Performers series (12)
Seven Dials mystery
Christie, Agatha
Superintendent Battle series (2)
Seven died
Homes, Geoffrey
Jose Manuel Madero series (1)
Seven drops of blood
Grant, Maxwell
Shadow series (114)
Seven for Banner Pass
Grover, Marshall
Larry and Stretch series (116)
Seven for Cordelia
Maclean, Catherine Macdonald
Tharrus trilogy (1)
Seven for the sea
Cutt, William Towrie
Arkmae series (2)
Seven gates to nowhere
Willis, Ted
Dixon of Dock Green series (2)
Seven go haunting
Lallemand, Evelyne
Secret Seven series (18)
Seven grandmothers
Mirsky, Reba Paeff
Zulu series (2)
Seven graves to Laredo
Logan, Jake
John Slocum series (97)
Seven hills
De Mille, James
Young Dodge Club series (3)
Seven hundred and twenty nine animal allsorts
Oxenbury, Helen
Seven hundred and twenty nine series (1)
Seven hundred and twenty nine curious creatures
Oxenbury, Helen
Seven hundred and twenty nine series (3)
Seven hundred and twenty nine puzzle people
Oxenbury, Helen
Seven hundred and twenty nine series (2)
Seven killers east
Grover, Marshall
Larry and Stretch series (364)
Seven lamps
Verner, Gerald
Superintendent Robert Budd series (15)
Seven-league ballet shoes
Wood, Lorna
Hag Dowsabel series (4)
Seven league boots
Halliburton, Richard
Famous adventures series (2)
Seven little Australians
Turner, Ethel
Woolcot family series (1)
Seven little sisters
Willis, William
Ancient mariner trilogy (1)
Seven little sisters prove their sisterhood
Andrews, Jane
Seven little sisters series (2)
Seven little sisters who live on the round ball that floats in the air
Andrews, Jane
Seven little sisters series (1)
Seven looked on
Malim, Barbara
Simon Chard series (2)
Seven magical jewels of Ireland
Adams, Robert
Castaways in time series (2)
Seven mansions
Cleeve, Brian
Crucifixion trilogy (2)
Seven nights at the resort
Enefer, Douglas
Dale Shand series (12)
Seven no-trump
Randall, Neil
Kingdom of Amber series (10)
Seven o'clock tales
Blyton, Enid
Evening tales series (3)
Seven of hearts
Leblanc, Maurice
Arsene Lupin series (1)
Seven of swords
Douglas, Carole Nelson
Sword and circlet trilogy (3)
Seven on screen
Lallemand, Evelyne
Secret Seven series (21)
Seven or so
Montgomery, Elizabeth
Dick, Jane and Sally series (12)
Seven out of hell
Gilman, George G
Edge series (8)
Seven-per-cent solution
Meyer, Nicholas
Sherlock Holmes sequels series (16)
Seven pilots
Graves, Charles
Royal Air Force series (3)
Seven red herrings
Thorne, Ernest Pollett
Quentin Eady series (1)
Seven sapphires
Kyle, Elisabeth
Furze series (3)

Seven Scamps
Steer, Mary
Seven Scamps series (1)
Seven Scamps solve a mystery
Steer, Mary
Seven Scamps series (2)
Seven schemers
Carter, Nicholas
Nicholas Carter series (439)
Seven screens
Dickson, Grierson
Superintendent Cissie Marlow series (5)
Seven seas murders
Mason, Francis Van Wyck
Colonel Hugh North series (10)
Seven serpents
Jackson, Steve
Sorcery series (3)
Seven sins
Rohmer, Sax
Gaston Max series (4)
Seven sirens
Brown, Carter
Randy Roberts series (3)
Seven sisters
Ballard, Willis Todhunter
Lieutenant Max Hunter series (2)
Seven sleepers
Beeding, Francis
Professor Kreutzemark series (1)
Seven Sleuths' Club
Norton, Carol
Mystery and adventure series (3)
Seven stars for Catfish Bend
Burman, Ben Lucien
Catfish Bend series (2)
Seven steps east
Benson, Ben
Ralph Lindsey series (7)
Seven steps to treason
Hartland, Michael
David Nairn series (2)
Seven-storey mountain
Merton, Thomas
Elected silence series (1)
Seven strange clues
Sutton, Margaret
Judy Bolton series (4)
Seven strike gold
Lallemand, Evelyne
Secret Seven series (19)
Seven summers
Anand, Mulk Raj
Seven ages of man series (1)
Seven sunflower seeds
Verney, John
Callendar family series (4)
Seven suspects
Innes, Michael
Sir John Appleby series (1)
Ryerson, Florence
Jimmy Lane series (1)
Seven thirty Victoria
McGuire, Paul
Chief Inspector Cummings series (5)
Seven thunders
Millin, Sarah Gertrude
War diary series (7)
Seven to die
Long, Harman
Franklyn Keen series (1)
Seven to the rescue
Lallemand, Evelyne
Secret Seven series (20)
Seven wagons west
Sharpe, Jon
Trailsman series (1)
Seven were suspect
Goyne, Richard
Paul Templeton series (7)
Knight, Kathleen Moore
Elisha Macomber series (4)
Seven were veiled
Knight, Kathleen Moore
Elisha Macomber series (4)
Seven westbound
McCoy, Marshall
Nevada Jim series (35)
Seven white gates
Saville, Malcolm
Lone Pine Five Club series (2)
Seven who waited
Derleth, August
Judge Ephraim Peck series (7)
Seven winters
Bowen, Elizabeth
Seven winters series (1)
Seven witches
Macbeth, George
Cadbury series (2)
Seven worlds
Caraker, Mary
Seven worlds series (1)
Seven years dead
Truss, Seldon
Inspector Gidleigh series (16)
Seven years in Tibet
Harrer, Heinrich
Tibet series (1)
Seventeen and in-between
De Clements, Barthe
Elsie Edwards series (4)
Seventeen cards
Vivian, Evelyn Charles
Inspector Head series (3)
Seventeen guns
Grover, Marshall
Larry and Stretch series (11)
Seventeen, part 1
Soya, Carl Erik
Seventeen series (1)
Seventeen, parts 2 and 3
Soya, Carl Erik
Seventeen series (2)
Seventeen thieves of El-Kalil
Mundy, Talbot
Jimgrim series (12)
Seventeen virgins
Vance, Jack
Adventures of Cugel the Clever series (1)
Seventh
Stark, Richard
Parker series (7)
Seventh big Monster book
Blance, Ellen
Monster series (24)
Seventh Brer Rabbit book
Blyton, Enid
Brer Rabbit series (7)
Seventh Carrier
Albano, Peter
Seventh Carrier series (1)
Seventh column
Jones, G Wayman
Black Bat series (16)
Seventh commandment
Sanders, Lawrence
Ten commandments series (2)
Seventh Commandment
Shears, Sarah
Tapioca for tea series (3)
Seventh crossword
Resnicow, Herbert
Crossword series (2)
Seventh enemy
Tapply, William George
Brady Coyne series (13)
Seventh gate
Harris, Geraldine
Seven citadels series (4)
Weis, Margaret
Death Gate series (7)
Seventh grade rumors
Haynes, Betsy
Fabulous Five series (1)
Seventh guilty man
Grover, Marshall
Larry and Stretch series (220)
Seventh Maigret omnibus
Simenon, Georges
Inspector Jules Maigret series (73)
Seventh man
Brand, Max
Dan Barry series (3)
Seventh mourner
Gardiner, Dorothy
Sheriff Moss Magill series (2)
Seventh of October
Romains, Jules
Men of goodwill series (27)
Seventh passenger
Macgowan, Alice
Jerry Boyne series (4)
Seventh sign
Flynn, Brian
Anthony Bathurst series (41)
Seventh sinner
Peters, Elizabeth
Jacqueline Kirby series (1)
Seventh son
Card, Orson Scott
Alvin Maker series (1)
Seventh station
McInerny, Ralph
Father Roger Dowling series (2)
Seventh stone
Murphy, Warren Burton
Destroyer series (62)
Seventy five Brooke Street
Fitzgerald, Percy
Jenny Bell trilogy (3)
Seventy seven Sunset Strip
Huggins, Roy
Stuart Bailey series (2)
Several deaths later
Gorman, Edward
Tobin series (2)
Several minds
Morgan, Dan
Sixth perception series (2)
Severe mercy
Vanauken, Sheldon
Mercy series (1)
Severed hand
Lecale, Errol
Specialist series (3)
Severed key
Nielsen, Helen
Simon Drake series (5)
Severed wasp
L'Engle, Madeleine
Katherine Forrester series (2)
Severn holiday
Nuttall, Nesta
Meri Newman series (1)
Severo siege
Sadler, Jeff
Marshal Andrew Anderson series (4)
Sewing machine man
Morgan, Stanley
Russ Tobin series (1)
Sex angle
Janson, Hank
Hank Janson series (187)
Sex clinic
Brown, Carter
Danny Boyd series (21)
Sex diary of Gerard Sorme
Wilson, Colin
Gerard Sorme trilogy (2)
Sex machine
Conway, Troy
Coxeman series (18)
Geis, Richard Erwin
Sex-ray
Allison, Clyde
Agent triple zero eight series (14)
Roi Kunzer series (1)
Sex trap
Brown, Carter
Randy Roberts series (5)
Turner, Bill
Detective Inspector Manson series (2)
Sexploiters
Christian, Petra
Sally Deenes series (5)
Sexton Blake and the demon god
Garforth, John
Sexton Blake series (1615)
Sexton Blake at the Varsity
Andrews, John
Sexton Blake series (743)
Sexton Blake inb Silesia
Graydon, William Murray
Sexton Blake series (239)
Sexton Blake, special constable
Bobin, John William
Sexton Blake series (27)
Sexton Blake's vow
Hardy, Arthur Steffens
Sexton Blake series (55)
Sexual abuse
Berry, Joy
Danger zones series (3)
Sexual adventures of Sherlock Holmes
Watson, John H
Sherlock Holmes series (10)
Sexus
Miller, Henry
Rosy crucifixion trilogy (1)
Sexy vixen
Janson, Hank
Hank Janson series (188)
Shabbat
Drucker, Malka
Jewish holidays series (5)
Shabby tiger
Spring, Howard
Manchester series (1)
Shabnam's day out
Solomon, Joan
Children's life series (5)
Shackle
Colette, Sidonie Gabrielle
Renee Nere series (2)
Shackles
Pronzini, Bill
Private Eye series (17)
Shade of darkness
Torrie, Malcolm
Timothy Herring series (5)
Shade of difference
Drury, Allen
Washington series (2)
Shades of Dracula
Aldiss, Brian Wilson
Dracula series (26)
Shades of gray
Denning, Mark
John Marshall series (1)
Hooper, Kay
Hagen series (8)
Shades of Hades
Kummer, Frederic Arnold
Hades series (2)
Shades of the wilderness
Altsheler, Joseph Alexander
Civil War series (7)
Shadow
Macdonnell, James Edmond
Dutchy Holland series (42)
Dutchy Holland series (43)
Melville-Ross, Antony
Submarine warfare series (3)
Perez Galdos, Benito
Contemporary novels of Spain series (2)
Van der Essen, Anne
Yok-yok series (7)
Shadow agent
Martyn, Wyndham
Christopher Bond series (7)
Shadow and claw
Wolfe, Gene
Book of the new sun series (2)
Shadow and the golden master
Grant, Maxwell
Shadow series (176)
Shadow and the voice of murder
Grant, Maxwell
Shadow series (270)
Shadow beware
Grant, Maxwell
Shadow series (283)
Shadow catcher
Champlin, Tim
Matt Tierney series (4)
Ellis, Wesley
Lone Star series (88)
Shadow chaser
Cosgrove, Stephen Edward
Barely there series (2)
Shadow climber
Reichert, Mickey Zucker
Bifrost guardians series (2)
Shadow crusade
Mills, Woosnam
Sir John Howden series (1)
Shadow dancers
Carl, Lillian Stewart
Sabazel trilogy (3)
Chalker, Jack Laurence
G.O.D. Inc. series (2)
Curry, Jane Louise
Abaloc series (8)
Lek series (2)
Shadow flight
Weber, Joe
Military techno-thrillers series (2)
Shadow for a lady
Linklater, Joseph Lane
Silas Booth series (1)
Shadow from the Bogue
Wood, Clement
Inspector Colin series (1)
Shadow game
Underwood, Michael
Martin Ainsworth series (2)
Shadow games
Cook, Glen
Chronicles of the Black Company series (4)
Shadow girl
Cummings, Ray
Matter, space and time series (4)
Shadow, go mad!
Grant, Maxwell
Shadow series (287)
Shadow guns
Sharpe, Jon
Canyon O'Grady series (4)
Shadow in red
O'Donnell, Lillian
Detective Norah Mulcahaney series (11)
Shadow in the courtyard
Simenon, Georges
Inspector Jules Maigret series (16)
Shadow in the glass
Derleth, August
Wisconsin series (4)
Shadow in the house
Gluck, Sinclair
Paul Bernard series (2)
Shadow in the north
Pullman, Philip
Sally Lockhart series (2)
Shadow in the plate
Pullman, Philip
Sally Lockhart series (2)
Shadow in the sea
John, Owen
Haggai Godin series (5)
Shadow in the shade
Christian, Mary Blount
Goosehill Gang series (11)
Shadow in the sun
Meynell, Laurence Walter
Robin Weston series (3)
Shadow killers
Dixon, Franklin W
Hardy boys series (92)
Shadow land
Vansittart, Peter
Stories from the past series (2)
Shadow laughs
Grant, Maxwell
Shadow series (3)
Shadow leader
Harper, Tara K
Wolfwalker series (2)
Shadow lord
Yep, Laurence Michael
Star trek series (22)
Shadow magic
Severn, Bill
Magic series (2)
Wrede, Patricia Collins
Lyra trilogy (1)
Shadow man
Goodwin, John
Superintendent Scarfe series (1)
Shadow meets the Mask
Grant, Maxwell
Shadow series (208)
Shadow men
Verner, Gerald
Trevor Lowe series (13)
Shadow of a broken man
Chesbro, George Clark
Mongo series (1)
Shadow of a Colt .45
Grover, Marshall
Nevada Jim series (18)
Shadow of a crime
Rhode, John
Doctor Lancelot Priestley series (41)
Shadow of a dark queen
Feist, Raymond Elias
Riftwar series (6)
Shadow of a doubt
Keene, Carolyn
Nancy Drew files series (40)
Thomson, June
Inspector Finch series (8)
Shadow of a dream
Howells, William Dean
Mister and Mrs March series (4)
Shadow of a god
Buckley, Eunice
Castelferrante series (1)
Shadow of a gun
Spade, Danny
Danny Spade series (17)
Thomas, Martin
Sexton Blake series (1484)
Shadow of a hawk
Bonner, Michael
Roby Maclane trilogy (2)
Carrel, Mark
Andrew McCall series (2)
Shadow of a killer
Mole, William
Casson Duker series (1)
Shadow of a lady
Roth, Holly
Inspector Medford series (1)
Shadow of a spy
Mackenzie, Andrew
Nicholas Cornish series (5)
Shadow of a throne
Hayes, Frederick William
Gwynett trilogy (3)
Shadow of a tiger
Collins, Michael
Dan Fortune series (5)
Shadow of a vendetta
Gunter, Archibald Clavering
Mister Barnes series (2)
Shadow of all night falling
Cook, Glen
Dread Empire series (1)
Shadow of an alibi
Rhode, John
Doctor Lancelot Priestley series (47)

Shadow of Chu-Sheng
Thomas, Eugene
Chu-Sheng series (1)
Shadow of death
Ashe, Gordon
Patrick Dawlish series (44)
Kienzle, William Xavier
Father Robert Koesler series (5)
Shadow of Doctor Ferrari
Thorne, Ernest Pollett
Major Brains Cunningham series (5)
Shadow of Doctor Syn
Thorndike, Russell
Doctor Syn series (7)
Shadow of doom
Creasey, John
Doctor Palfrey series (6)
Shadow of Eagle Rock
Bowden, Jim
Cap Millett series (3)
Shadow of Egypt
Lorimer, Norma
Egypt series (2)
Shadow of evil
Black, Mansell
Richard Vaness series (3)
Dutton, Charles Judson
Harley Manners series (2)
Shadow of fear
Spicer, Bart
Carney Wilde series (5)
Shadow of Fu-Manchu
Rohmer, Sax
Fu-Manchu series (12)
Shadow of God
Crawley, Aileen
Suleiman the Magnificent trilogy (2)
Shadow of guilt
Quentin, Patrick
Lieutenant Timothy Trant series (7)
Shadow of gulls
Finney, Patricia
Lugh the Harper series (1)
Shadow of himself
Delving, Michael
Dave Cannon and Robert Eddison series (4)
Shadow of his crime
Bobin, John William
Sexton Blake series (1)
Shadow of his wings
Fergusson, Bruce
Six kingdoms series (1)
Shadow of Larose
Gask, Arthur
Gilbert Larose series (4)
Shadow of madness
Pentecost, Hugh
Doctor John Smith series (3)
Shadow of murder
Laing, Patrick
Patrick Laing series (6)
Shadow of night
Derleth, August
Sac Prairie series (9)
Shadow of Nordmaar
Despain, Dezra
Advanced dungeons and dragons adventure gamebook series (13)
Shadow of Samain
Wiat, Philippa
Wilmington series (2)
Shadow of the cathedral
Blasco Ibanez, Vicente
Roman Catholic Church in Spain series (1)
Shadow of the Condor
Grady, James
Condor series (2)
Shadow of the Four
Cross, Mark
Daphne Wrayne and her Four Adjusters series (2)
Shadow of the gallows
Gilman, George G
Edge series (50)
Shadow of the grizzly
Martin, Larry Jay
John Clinton Ryan series (6)
Shadow of the Hawk
James, Leigh Franklin
John Cooper Baines series (8)
Shadow of the killer
Chance, John Newton
Jonathan Blake series (32)
Shadow of the leopard
Hartmann, Michael
Ben Dryden series (1)
Shadow of the mutant master
Brand, Kurt
Perry Rhodan series (47)
Shadow of the North
Altsheler, Joseph Alexander
French and Indian war series (2)
Shadow of the palms
Law, Janice
Anna Peters series (4)
Shadow of the pomegranate
Plaidy, Jean
Katharine of Aragon trilogy (2)
Tudor series (2)
Shadow of the Rock
Hackforth-Jones, Gilbert
Paul Dexter series (4)
Shadow of the sun
Pell, Sylvia
Louis XIV series (1)
Shadow of the swan
Wren, M K
Phoenix legacy trilogy (2)
Shadow of the torturer
Wolfe, Gene
Book of the new sun series (1)
Shadow of the vulture
McLaglen, John J
Herne the Hunter series (4)
Shadow of the wolf
Carlsen, Chris
Berserker series (1)
Shadow of the Wolf
Freeman, Richard Austin
Doctor John Evelyn Thorndyke series (12)
Shadow of the wolf
Parker, F M
Luke Coldiron series (2)
Shadow of Tyburn tree
Wheatley, Dennis
Roger Brook series (2)
Shadow of wings
Paice, Margaret
Fletcher family series (2)
Shadow on Harrison High
Farris, John
Harrison High series (4)
Shadow on the cliff
Burton, Miles
Inspector Arnold and Desmond Merrion series (29)
Shadow on the door
Judd, Frances K
Kay Tracey series (4)
Shadow on the Downs
Woodthorpe, Ralph Carter
Matilda Perks series (2)
Shadow on the earth
Dudley, Owen Francis
Problems of human happiness series (2)
Shadow on the glass
Dutton, Charles Judson
John Bartley series (3)
Shadow on the house
Vivian, Evelyn Charles
Inspector Head series (1)
Shadow on the purple
Peeress
Recollections of royalty series (1)
Shadow on the sand
Dever, Joe
Lone Wolf series (5)
Shadow on the sea
Pemberton, Max
Captain Black series (1)
Thompson, Neil
Rand series (1)
Shadow on the stone
Bryant, Marguerite
Stone trilogy (3)
Shadow on the stones
Caldecott, Moyra
Sacred stones series (3)
Shadow on the sun
Harris, Rosemary
Egyptian trilogy (2)
Shadow on the wall
Bailey, Henry Christopher
Mister Reggie Fortune series (9)
Shadow on the window
Bagby, George
Inspector Schmidt series (25)
Shadow over Alcatraz
Grant, Maxwell
Shadow series (156)
Shadow over Mars
Brackett, Leigh
Mars series (1)
Shadow over Mousehaven Manor
Kwitz, Mary DeBall
Mousehaven Manor series (1)
Shadow over the marsh
Sharp, Allen
Storytrails series (15)
Shadow passes
Phillpotts, Eden
Book of Avis series (3)
Shadow patrol
Snell, Leroy
Northwest stories series (2)
Shadow people
Laing, Kenneth
Rolling Stone series (4)
Shadow play
Fyfield, Frances
Sarah Fortune series (3)
Milne, John
James Jenner series (2)
Jimmy Jenner series (2)
Powell, Lester
Philip Odell series (2)
Shadow prey
Sandford, John
Lucas Davenport series (2)
Shadow prince
Wayne, Matt
Nintendo adventure series (10)
Shadow Range
Slaughter, Jim
Boone Helm series (2)
Shadow realm
Alexander, Marc
Wells of Ythan series (3)
Shadow riders
Johnston, Terry Conrad
Plainsmen series (6)
Shane, Steve
Lone Star Kid series (4)
Shadow rising
Jordan, Robert
Wheel of time series (4)
Shadow Shaia
Gilliland, Alexis Arnaldus
Wizenbeak trilogy (2)
Shadow shooter
Tuttle, Wilbur Coleman
Hashknife Hartley and Sleepy Stevens series (22)
Shadow singer
Bennett, Marcia Joanne
Ni-lach series (2)
Shadow steed
Knaak, Richard Allen
Dragonrealm series (4)
Shadow strikes
Grant, Maxwell
Shadow series (282)
Shadow that caught fire
Jobson, Hamilton
Inspector Anders series (6)
Shadow the Baron
Morton, Anthony
Baron series (19)
Shadow, the Hawk and the Skull
Grant, Maxwell
Shadow series (196)
Shadow trade
Furst, Alan
Roger Levin series (4)
Shadow unmasks
Grant, Maxwell
Shadow series (128)
Shadow walker
Reno, James
Texas Anthem series (3)
Shadow war
Dawson, Clay
Long Rider series (6)
Shadow world
Crispin, Ann Carol
StarBridge series (3)
Shadowbreed
Ferring, David
Konrad trilogy (2)
Shadowcastle
Gray, Michael
Fantasy forest series (3)
Shadowdale
Awlinson, Richard
Avatar trilogy (1)
Shadowed by the C.I.D.
Plummer, Thomas Arthur
Detective Inspector Andrew Frampton series (1)
Shadowed by three
Lynch, Lawrence L
Neil Bathurst series (1)
Shadowed lives
Graydon, William Murray
Sexton Blake series (126)
Shadowed millions
Grant, Maxwell
Shadow series (21)
Shadowers
Hamilton, Donald
Matt Helm series (8)
Shadowfane
Wurts, Janny
Cycle of fire trilogy (3)
Shadowfire
Lee, Tanith
Birthgrave trilogy (2)
Shadowkill
Clayton, Jo
Diadem series (12)
Shadith's quest series (3)
Shadowland
Bulis, Christopher
Doctor Who series (157)
Shadowless man
Chamisso, Adalbert von
Peter Schlemihl series (1)
Shadowlight
Jefferies, Mike
Loremasters of Elundium trilogy (3)
Shadowline
Cook, Glen
Starfishers trilogy (1)
Shadowplay
Clayton, Jo
Diadem series (10)
Shadith's quest series (1)
Shadows
Ryerson, Florence
Jimmy Lane series (4)
Scott, Will
Disher series (2)
Sherman, Jory
Doctor Russell V Chillders series (7)
Shadows attack
Darlton, Clark
Perry Rhodan series (118)
Shadows before
Bowers, Dorothy
Inspector Pardoe series (2)
Shadow's bliss
Veryan, Patricia
Tales of the jewelled men series (4)
Shadow's daughter
Stirling, Stephen Michael
Fifth millenium series (5)
Shadows don't bleed
Wright, Wade
Paul Cameron series (1)
Shadow's edge
Murray, Terry
Legends of Larian series (1)
Shadows from the past
Mackenzie, Lee
Emmerdale Farm series (10)
Shadows in a hidden land
Harvester, Simon
Asia in turmoil series (17)
Shadows in bronze
Davis, Lindsey
Marcus Didius Falco series (2)
Shadows in the fire
Dane, Eva
Schroeder family series (1)
Shadows in the water
Lasky, Kathryn
Starbuck family series (2)
Shadow's justice
Grant, Maxwell
Shadow series (28)
Shadows lifted
Copus, John Edwin
Saint Cuthbert's series (2)
Shadows linger
Cook, Glen
Chronicles of the Black Company series (2)
Shadows must talk
Allen, Julia
Mary Livingstone series (2)
Shadows of Alpha
Grant, Charles Lewis
Parric family trilogy (1)
Shadows of death
Saint Germain, Gregory
Resistance series (3)
Shadows of doom
McKiernan, Dennis L
Iron tower trilogy (2)
Shadows of sanctuary
Asprin, Robert Lynn
Sanctuary series (3)
Shadows of the moon
Cameron, Kate
Whispering Hills series (3)
Shadows of the past
Cameron, Kate
Holderly Hall series (2)
Shadows on the grass
Dinesen, Isak
Africa series (2)
Shadows on the landing
Wilson, Gertrude Mary
Inspector Lovick series (4)
Shadows on the mirror
Fyfield, Frances
Sarah Fortune series (1)
Shadows on the mud
Knight, Frank
Chichester Harbour series (4)
Shadows on the river
Mackenzie, Andrew
Superintendent Brannigan series (3)
Shadows on the wall
Naylor, Phyllis Reynolds
York trilogy (1)
Shadows out of hell
Offutt, Andrew Jefferson
War of the gods on earth trilogy (2)
Shadows over Castle Rising
Cradock, Fanny
Lorme family series (2)
Shadow's realm
Reichert, Mickey Zucker
Bifrost guardians series (4)
Shadow's revenge
Grant, Maxwell
Shadow series (285)
Shadow's rival
Grant, Maxwell
Shadow series (125)
Shadow's shadow
Grant, Maxwell
Shadow series (23)
Shadow's son
Stirling, Stephen Michael
Fifth millenium series (4)
Wehrstein, Karen
Fifth millenium series (4)
Shadows tonight
Seifert, Adele
Gregory Trent series (2)
Shadowspan
Offutt, Andrew Jefferson
Sanctuary series (12)
Shadowspeer
Clayton, Jo
Diadem series (11)
Shadith's quest series (2)
Shady deal
Cresswell, Helen
Mike series (8)
Shady doings
Johns, Veronica Parker
Agatha Welch series (2)
Shady lady
Adams, Cleve Franklin
Rex McBride series (6)
Shaft
Tidyman, Ernest
John Shaft series (1)
Shaft among the Jews
Tidyman, Ernest
John Shaft series (2)
Shaft has a ball
Tidyman, Ernest
John Shaft series (4)
Shaftesbury Avenue
Rayner, Claire
Performers series (10)
Shaft's big score
Tidyman, Ernest
John Shaft series (3)
Shaft's carnival of killers
Tidyman, Ernest
John Shaft series (6)
Shag
McClung, Robert Marshall
Endangered animals series (1)
Shag the caribou
Rutley, Cecil Bernard
Wild life story series (4)
Shaggo, the mighty buffalo
Barnum, Richard
Kneetime animal stories series (16)
Shaggy man of Oz
Snow, Jack
Oz series (37)
Shaggy planet
Goulart, Ron
Barnum series (4)
Shags finds a kitten
Fujikawa, Gyo
Shags series (2)
Shags has a dream
Fujikawa, Gyo
Shags series (1)

Shai's destiny
Walther, Daniel
Shai series (2)

Shake a crooked town
Marlowe, Dan James
Johnny Killain series (5)

Shake hands for ever
Rendell, Ruth
Chief Inspector Reginald Wexford series (9)

Shake my sillies out
Raffi
Raffi songs to read series (2)

Shake up
Hughes, Dean
Angel Park Soccer Stars series (7)

Shake-up
James, Breni
Sergeant Gunnar Matson series (2)

Shakedown
Ellington, Richard
Steve Drake series (5)
Nazel, Joseph
Iceman series (7)
Scott, Roney
Joe Puma series (1)

Shakedown kid
Singer, Norman
Robbie Jardino series (1)

Shaken down
Macgowan, Alice
Jerry Boyne series (3)

Shaken leaf
Cory, Desmond
Lindy Grey series (4)

Shakeout
Follett, Ken
Piers Roper series (1)

Shaker home
Bial, Raymond
Home series (3)

Shakespeare and son
Fisher, Edward
Silver falcon trilogy (1)

Shakespeare murders
Gordon, Neil
Peter Kerrigan series (2)
Long, Amelia Reynolds
Edward Trelawny series (1)

Shaking spear
Flynn, Brian
Anthony Bathurst series (46)

Shaking the nickel bush
Moody, Ralph
Ralph series (6)

Shaky relations
Blishen, Edward
Schoolmaster series (7)

Shallow grave
Quinn, Jake
Patrick Shannon series (2)
Scott, Jack S
Detective Inspector Alfred Stanley Rosher series (3)

Shallow graves
Healy, Jeremiah
John Francis Cuddy series (7)

Shallows of night
Lustbader, Eric
Sunset Warrior series (2)

Shalom at last
Dyck, Peter J
Shalom series (2)

Shalom, my love
Janson, Hank
Hank Janson series (244)

Shaman tree
Abshire, Richard
Gants series (2)

Shamballah
Rossmann, John F
Mind Masters series (2)

Shambhala strike
Rosenberger, Joseph
Death Merchant series (30)

Shame of Arizona
Tuttle, Wilbur Coleman
Henry Harrison Conroy and Judge Van Treece series (4)

Shame of man
Anthony, Piers
Geodyssey series (2)

Shame of motley
Sabatini, Rafael
Cesare Borgia series (1)

Shameful
Cleary, Denis
Theodore J Cash series (1)

Shamelady
Mayo, James
Charles Hood series (3)

Shameless Wayne
Sutcliffe, Halliwell
Wayne and Ratcliffe series (1)

Shamrock and thistle
Optic, Oliver
Young America, first series (2)

Shamrock shore
Dengler, Sandy
Heroes of the misty isle series (2)

Shamrock smash
Rosenberger, Joseph
Death Merchant series (41)

Shamutanti Hills
Jackson, Steve
Sorcery series (1)

Shan
Lustbader, Eric
Jake Maroc series (2)

Shane
Nielsen, Susin
Degrassi High School series (2)

Shane McKellar and the face at the window
Burch, T R
Shane McKellar series (1)

Shane McKellar and the treasure hunt
Burch, T R
Shane McKellar series (2)

Shanghai
Marshall, William Leonard
Twentieth century trilogy (3)

Shanghai Bund murders
Mason, Francis Van Wyck
Colonel Hugh North series (6)

Shanghai Jezebel
Corrigan, Mark
Mark Corrigan and McLean series (6)

Shanghai passage
Pease, Howard
Tod Moran series (3)

Shanghai sanctuary
Mason, Francis Van Wyck
Colonel Hugh North series (10)

Shanghaiers
Parker, F M
Luke Coldiron series (3)
Tom Galletin series (2)

Shankill Road contract
Atlee, Philip
Joe Gall series (17)

Shannon
Jenkins, Jerry Bruce
Margo Franklin and Philip Spence series (6)

Shannon's brigade
Stuart, Vivian
Commander Philip Hazard series (8)

Shannon's way
Cronin, Archibald Joseph
Robert Shannon series (2)

Shape
Pluckrose, Henry
Thinking about series (7)

Shape and Barbapapa
Tison, Annette
Barbapapa first book series (4)

Shape changer
Laumer, Keith
Lafayette O'Leary series (3)

Shape I'm in
McKimmie, Christopher
Magic day series (1)

Shape of a stain
Ferrars, E X
Toby Dyke series (4)

Shape of dread
Muller, Marcia
Sharon McCone series (10)

Shape of fear
Pentecost, Hugh
Pierre Chambrun series (2)

Shape of space
Niven, Larry
Known Space series (4)

Shape of terror
Robeson, Kenneth
Doc Savage series (109)

Shape rhymes
Ward, Dorothy Darrell
Teddies series (4)

Shape-shifter, the naming of Pangur Ban
Sampson, Fay
Pangur Ban series (4)

Shape up Monty
West, Colin
Monty series (2)

Shapechanger scenario
Hawke, Simon
Psychodrome series (2)

Shapechangers
Roberson, Jennifer
Chronicles of the Cheysuli series (1)

Shaper's legacy
Finch, Sheila
Shaper exile series (2)

Shapes
Allington, Richard L
Beginning to learn series (1)

Shapes and adventures
Grigson, Geoffrey
Shapes and stories series (2)

Shapes and stories
Grigson, Geoffrey
Shapes and stories series (1)

Shapes we see from the big red bus
Wood, Leslie
Big red bus series (2)

Shaping of a behaviorist
Skinner, Burrhus Frederic
Behaviorist trilogy (2)

Shaping of Middle Earth
Tolkien, John Ronald Reuel
History of Middle Earth series (4)

Shaping the dawn
Finch, Sheila
Shaper exile series (3)

Shapton affairs
Armfelt, Roger
Affairs series (3)

Shard at bay
McCutchan, Philip
Superintendent Simon Shard series (8)

Shard calls the tune
McCutchan, Philip
Superintendent Simon Shard series (6)

Shardik
Adams, Richard
Beklan Empire series (1)

Shards of honor
Bujold, Lois McMaster
Miles Naismith Vorkosigan series (7)

Shards of honour
Bujold, Lois McMaster
Miles Naismith Vorkosigan series (7)

Share in death
Crombie, Deborah
Superintendent Duncan Kincaid and Sergeant Gemma James series (1)

Share of honour
Fullerton, Alexander
Nick Everard series (7)

Share your heart
Quick, Larry
Love trilogy (3)

Sharing story
Erickson, Karen
I can do it series (4)

Shark
Stafford-Deitsch, Jeremy
Ocean series (1)

Shark Africa
Krauss, Bruno
Sea Wolf series (5)

Shark America
Krauss, Bruno
Sea Wolf series (7)

Shark among herrings
Milner, George
Ronald Anglesea series (2)

Shark Bait affair
Arliss, Joen
Kate Graham series (1)

Shark Gotch and Typhoon Bradley
Wetjen, Albert Richard
Shark Gotch series (4)

Shark Gotch of the islands
Wetjen, Albert Richard
Shark Gotch series (1)

Shark Gotch shoots it out
Wetjen, Albert Richard
Shark Gotch series (3)

Shark hunt
Krauss, Bruno
Sea Wolf series (4)

Shark north
Krauss, Bruno
Sea Wolf series (2)

Shark pack
Krauss, Bruno
Sea Wolf series (3)

Shark raid
Krauss, Bruno
Sea Wolf series (6)

Shark trap
Krauss, Bruno
Sea Wolf series (8)

Sharkbait
Geason, Susan
Syd Fish series (3)

Sharp edge
Wright, Wade
Paul Cameron series (2)

Sharp Eyes, the silver fox
Barnum, Richard
Kneetime animal stories series (12)

Sharp quillet
Flynn, Brian
Anthony Bathurst series (33)

Sharp rise in crime
Creasey, John
Inspector Roger West series (43)

Sharp through the hawthorn
Marshall, Sybil
Old Swithinford series (2)

Sharper's downfall
Carter, Nicholas
Nicholas Carter series (139)

Sharpe's company
Cornwell, Bernard
Richard Sharpe series (4)

Sharpe's devil
Cornwell, Bernard
Richard Sharpe series (12)

Sharpe's eagle
Cornwell, Bernard
Richard Sharpe series (2)

Sharpe's enemy
Cornwell, Bernard
Richard Sharpe series (6)

Sharpe's gold
Cornwell, Bernard
Richard Sharpe series (3)

Sharpe's honour
Cornwell, Bernard
Richard Sharpe series (7)

Sharpe's justice
Sharpe, Jon
Trailsman series (34)

Sharpe's regiment
Cornwell, Bernard
Richard Sharpe series (8)

Sharpe's revenge
Cornwell, Bernard
Richard Sharpe series (10)

Sharpe's rifles
Cornwell, Bernard
Richard Sharpe series (1)

Sharpe's siege
Cornwell, Bernard
Richard Sharpe series (9)

Sharpe's sword
Cornwell, Bernard
Richard Sharpe series (5)

Sharpe's Waterloo
Cornwell, Bernard
Richard Sharpe series (11)

Sharpest edge
Stirling, Stephen Michael
Fifth millenium series (2)

Sharpest sight
Owens, Louis
Cole McCurtain series (1)

Sharpshooter
Ladd, Justin
Abilene series (2)
Reese, John
Jefferson Hewitt series (3)

Sharpshooters
Benteen, John
Neal Fargo series (9)

Sharra's exile
Bradley, Marion Zimmer
Darkover series (14)

Shatterbelt
Thiele, Colin
Tracy Chipp series (1)

Shattered chain
Bradley, Marion Zimmer
Darkover series (7)

Shattered eye
Granger, Bill
November Man series (4)

Shattered glass
Bergstrom, Elaine
Shattered glass series (1)

Shattered helmet
Dixon, Franklin W
Hardy boys series (52)

Shattered mask
Devon, D G
Temple Kent series (2)

Shattered moon
Green, Kate
Shattered series (1)
Reaves, Michael
Shattered series (1)

Shattered realm
Smith, Mark
Duelmaster series (4)

Shattered sphere
Asprin, Robert Lynn
Sanctuary series (9)

Shattered stars
McEnroe, Richard S
Far stars and future times series (1)

Shattered steel
Preston, James
Sergeant Bob Christie series (3)

Shattered stone
Newman, Robert
Tertius trilogy (3)

Shattering silence
Dorman, Geoffrey
Carmelo series (2)

Shaved fish
Geason, Susan
Syd Fish series (1)

Shawl of Solomon
Bedford-Jones, Henry
John Solomon trilogy (3)

Shawl-straps
Alcott, Louisa May
Aunt Jo's scrap-bag series (2)

Shawn goes to school
Breinburg, Petronella
Sean series (1)

Shawnee
Mitchum, Hank
Stage coach station series (37)

Shawnee dawn
Lederer, Paul Joseph
Indian heritage series (2)

Shawnee trail
Wisler, Gary Clifton
Willie Delamer series (16)

Shawnee's warning
Lange, Dietrich
American Indian series (8)

Shawn's red bike
Breinburg, Petronella
Sean series (3)

Shay Scally and Manny Wagstaff
Treacy, Sean
Scallywags series (1)

Shayne case
Ferguson, William Blair Morton
Dan Cluer series (2)

Shayne dame
Harragan, Steve
Steve Harragan series (10)

She
Abarbanell, Jacob Ralph
He, she and it trilogy (2)
Haggard, Henry Rider
She series (3)

She ain't got no body
Story, Jack Trevor
Sexton Blake series (1462)

She and Allan
Haggard, Henry Rider
Allan Quatermain series (9)
She series (2)

She and the dubious three
Crayder, Dorothy
She, the adventuress series (2)

She-beast
Adams, Hunter
Man from Planet X trilogy (1)

She came back
Wentworth, Patricia
Miss Maud Silver series (10)

She came in a flash
Wings, Mary
Emma Victor series (2)

She came too late
Wings, Mary
Emma Victor series (1)

She didn't like dying
Morland, Nigel
Chief Inspector Andrew McMurdo series (1)

She died a lady
Dickson, Carter
Sir Henry Merrivale series (15)

She died because
Hopkins, Kenneth
Doctor William Blow and Professor Gideon Manciple series (1)

She died laughing
Gribble, Leonard Reginald
Superintendent Anthony Slade series (23)

She died, of course
Warriner, Thurman
Mister Scotter series (6)

She fell among actors
Warren, James
James Weston series (2)

She fell among thieves
Yates, Dornford
Jonah Mansel series (6)
Richard Chandos series (5)
She had a little knife
Linklater, Joseph Lane
Silas Booth series (4)
She had to have gas
Penny, Rupert
Chief Inspector Edward Beale series (6)
She just wants the hot wax!
Unger, Jim
Herman series (21)
She kept on dying
Wilson, Gertrude Mary
Inspector Lovick series (19)
She married Raffles
Perowne, Barry
Raffles series (8)
She, me and murder
Martin, Robert Lee
Jim Bennett series (12)
She met murder
Desmond, Hugh
Alan Fraser series (12)
She modelled her coffin
Launay, Droo
Adam Flute series (1)
She screamed blue murder
Secrist, Kelliher
Sham Payne series (1)
She sees things
Wilson, Gertrude Mary
Inspector Lovick series (21)
She shall die
Gilbert, Anthony
Arthur Crook series (36)
She shall have murder
Ames, Delano
Dagobert and Jane Brown series (1)
She should have cried on Monday
Russell, Enid Sherry
Ben Louis series (1)
She sleeps to conquer
Janson, Hank
Hank Janson series (113)
She, the adventuress
Crayder, Dorothy
She, the adventuress series (1)
She vanished in the dawn
Gilbert, Anthony
Arthur Crook series (8)
She waif
Janson, Hank
Hank Janson series (132)
She walked in fear
Vickers, Roy
Inspector J Rason series (17)
She walks alone
McCloy, Helen
Miguel Urizar series (2)
She was a lady
Charteris, Leslie
Saint series (7)
She was Carrie Eaton
Corbett, Elizabeth
Mrs Meigs series (1)
She who pays
Henrey, Madeleine
Madeleine series (11)
She who remembers
Shuler, Linda Lay
Time circle series (1)
She woke to darkness
Halliday, Brett
Michael Shayne series (25)
She-wolf
Bennetts, Pamela
Edward I series (2)
She-Wolf of France
Druon, Maurice
Accursed kings series (5)
She-wolves of Machecoul
Dumas, Alexandre
Napoleon series (3)
She wore pink gloves
Dekobra, Maurice
Bradley Adams series (1)
She wouldn't say who
Ames, Delano
Dagobert and Jane Brown series (11)
Shear the black sheep
Dodge, David
Whit Whitney series (2)
Sheba
Rita
Sheba series (1)
Sheba's daughter
Philby, Harry St John Bridger
Arabian travel series (2)
Shed a bitter tear
Moore, Harry F S
Casey Peters series (2)
Shed light on death
Taylor, Laurie Aylma
J J Jamison series (4)
Sheeg
Buffery, Judith
Star lords series (1)
Sheep and the wolves
Afford, Max
Jeffery Blackburn series (5)
Burnett, George
Inspector Gulliver series (2)
Sheep, goats and soap
Malcolm, John
Tim Simpson series (8)
Sheep Grass
Nash, Padder
Grass series (8)
Sheep in a jeep
Shaw, Nancy
Sheep series (1)
Sheep in a shop
Shaw, Nancy
Sheep series (3)
Sheep in wolf's clothing
Graydon, William Murray
Sexton Blake series (66)
Sheep look up
Brunner, John
Zanzibar series (2)
Sheep may safely graze
Harvester, Simon
Roger Fleming series (5)
Sheep on a ship
Shaw, Nancy
Sheep series (2)
Sheep out to eat
Shaw, Nancy
Sheep series (4)
Sheep take a hike
Shaw, Nancy
Sheep series (5)
Sheepdog adventure
Fearon, Ethelind
Pluckrose series (1)
Sheepfarmer's daughter
Moon, Elizabeth
Deed of Paksenarrion series (2)
Sheep's clothing
Lee, Austin
Miss Flora Hogg series (1)
Sheep's eye view
Holgate, John
Farm life series (3)
Sheepskins and grey russet
Thurston, Ernest Temple
Bellwattle and Cruikshank series (4)
Sheer silk
Elliott, William James
Anthony England series (3)
Sheer terror
Dixon, Franklin W
Hardy boys case files series (81)
Sheer torture
Barnard, Robert
Superintendent Perry Trethowan series (1)
Sheik
Hull, Edith Maude
Sheik Ahmed ben Hassan series (1)
Sheikh and the dustbin, and other McAuslan stories
Fraser, George Macdonald
Private McAuslan series (3)
Sheikh's son
Murray, Andrew
Sexton Blake series (146)
Sheiks and adders
Innes, Michael
Sir John Appleby series (32)
Sheila
Vachss, Andrew
Burke series (6)
Sheila at Happy Hills
Pyke, Lillian Maxwell
Sheila Chester series (1)
Sheila in the wind
Hayter, Adrian
Sheila series (1)
Sheila, the prefect
Pyke, Lillian Maxwell
Sheila Chester series (2)
Sheila Vedder
Barr, Amelia Edith
Shetland series (2)
Shelf life
Clark, Douglas
Inspector George Masters series (16)
She'll be dead by morning
Chambers, Dana
Jim Steele series (3)
She'll love you dead
Franklin, Charles
Grant Garfield series (6)
Shell of death
Blake, Nicholas
Nigel Strangeways series (2)
Shell on the beach
Lewin, Hugh
Second chance series (3)
Shell Scott sampler
Prather, Richard Scott
Shell Scott series (40)
Shell Scott's murder mix
Prather, Richard Scott
Shell Scott series (40)
Shell Scott's seven slaughters
Prather, Richard Scott
Shell Scott series (22)
Shelled by an unseen foe
Fiske, James
World's war series (8)
Shelley and the bushfire mystery
Bosworth, Ellen
Shelley Peters series (1)
Shelley and the pony of the year
Bosworth, Ellen
Shelley Peters series (2)
Shelley and the problem pony
Bosworth, Ellen
Shelley Peters series (3)
Shelley Peters and the bushfire mystery
Bosworth, Ellen
Shelley Peters series (1)
Shelley Peters and the pony of the year
Bosworth, Ellen
Shelley Peters series (2)
Shelley Peters and the problem pony
Bosworth, Ellen
Shelley Peters series (3)
Shellfire on the bay
Scofield, Jonathan
Freedom fighters series (9)
Shellshock
Prather, Richard Scott
Shell Scott series (40)
Shelter
Hardcastle, Michael
Tony and Jay series (9)
Sheltered days
Lambert, Derek
Reporter series (1)
Sheltering tree
Bromige, Iris
Rainwood family series (5)
Shenandoah heritage
Reeder, Carolyn
Shenandoah series (1)
Shenandoah secrets
Reeder, Carolyn
Shenandoah series (3)
Shenandoah vestiges
Reeder, Carolyn
Shenandoah series (2)
Shenanigans at Sugar Creek
Hutchens, Paul
Sugar Creek Gang series (11)
Shepherd file
Bark, Conrad Voss
Mister William Holmes series (5)
Shepherd Kings
Danielson, Peter
Children of the Lion series (2)
Shepherd of the hills
Wright, Harold Bell
Dan Matthews series (1)
Shepherd's castle
Macdonald, George
Sir Gibbie series (2)
Shepherd's crook
Chard, Brigid
Hidden journey series (2)
Lorac, E C R
Inspector Macdonald series (38)
Shepherd's gold
Tetlow, L D
Brogan McNally series (7)
Shepherd's pie
Scott, Mary
New Zealand life series (9)
Shepherd's purse
Finlay, Campbell Kirkman
John Macinnes series (2)
Shepherd's warning
Gowans, Elizabeth
Blair family series (2)
Sutton, Graham
Fleming family series (2)
Sherbrooke bride
Coulter, Catherine
Bride trilogy (1)
Sherburne cousins
Douglas, Amanda Minnie
Sherburne series (3)
Sherburne girls
Douglas, Amanda Minnie
Sherburne series (7)
Sherburne House
Douglas, Amanda Minnie
Sherburne series (1)
Sherburne inheritance
Douglas, Amanda Minnie
Sherburne series (9)
Sherburne quest
Douglas, Amanda Minnie
Sherburne series (10)
Sherburne romance
Douglas, Amanda Minnie
Sherburne series (4)
Sheridan Stage
Paine, Lauran
Sheridan Township series (2)
Sheriff and the branding iron murders
Meredith, Doris R
Sheriff Charles Timothy Matthews series (2)
Sheriff and the Folsom man murders
Meredith, Doris R
Sheriff Charles Timothy Matthews series (3)
Sheriff and the Panhandle murders
Meredith, Doris R
Sheriff Charles Timothy Matthews series (1)
Sheriff and the pheasant hunt murders
Meredith, Doris R
Sheriff Charles Timothy Matthews series (4)
Sheriff Jory
Bass, Milton R
Jory series (3)
Sheriff of Bombay
Keating, Henry Reymond Fitzwalter
Inspector Ganesh Ghote series (13)
Sheriff of Clinton
Borg, Jack
Hogleg Bailey series (2)
Sheriff of Fletcher County
Kincaid, J D
Jack Stone series (4)
Sheriff of Painted Post
Gunn, Tom
Sheriff Blue Steele series (2)
Sheriff of Rockabye County
Edson, John Thomas
Rockabye County series (3)
Sheriff of Tonto Town
Tuttle, Wilbur Coleman
Henry Harrison Conroy and Judge Van Treece series (1)
Sheriff on the spot
Field, Peter
Powder Valley series (19)
Sheriff Sally Gopher and the haunted dance hall
Quackenbush, Robert Mead
Sheriff Sally Gopher series (1)
Sheriff Sally Gopher and the Thanksgiving caper
Quackenbush, Robert Mead
Sheriff Sally Gopher series (2)
Sheriff Slocum
Logan, Jake
John Slocum series (168)
Sheriff wanted
Field, Peter
Powder Valley series (32)
Sheriff's deputy
Borg, Jack
Hogleg Bailey series (5)
Sherlock Chick and the giant egg mystery
Quackenbush, Robert Mead
Sherlock Chick series (3)
Sherlock Chick and the noisy shed mystery
Quackenbush, Robert Mead
Sherlock Chick series (4)
Sherlock Chick and the peekaboo mystery
Quackenbush, Robert Mead
Sherlock Chick series (2)
Sherlock Chick's first case
Quackenbush, Robert Mead
Sherlock Chick series (1)
Sherlock Holmes
Gillette, William
Sherlock Holmes drama series (1)
Sherlock Holmes drama series (14)
Hall, Trevor Henry
Sherlock Holmes literary studies series (1)
Kelly, Tim J
Sherlock Holmes drama series (14)
Sherlock Holmes and a theatrical mystery
Andrews, Val
Sherlock Holmes sequels series (45)
Sherlock Holmes and Doctor Watson
Bell, Harold Wilmerding
Sherlock Holmes series (10)
Sherlock Holmes and the arthritic clergyman
Andrews, Val
Sherlock Holmes sequels series (41)
Sherlock Holmes and the curious adventure of the clockwork prince
Haubold, Cleve
Sherlock Holmes drama series (18)
Sherlock Holmes and the curse of the sign of four
Rosa, Dennis
Sherlock Holmes drama series (9)
Sherlock Holmes and the Drood mystery
Pearson, Edmund
Sherlock Holmes sequels series (13)
Sherlock Holmes and the eminent thespian
Andrews, Val
Sherlock Holmes sequels series (93)
Sherlock Holmes and the golden bird
Thomas, Frank
Sherlock Holmes sequels series (43)
Sherlock Holmes and the masquerade murders
Thomas, Frank
Sherlock Holmes sequels series (86)
Sherlock Holmes and the sacred sword
Thomas, Frank
Sherlock Holmes sequels series (44)
Sherlock Holmes and the treasure train
Thomas, Frank
Sherlock Holmes sequels series (81)
Sherlock Holmes and the Wood Green Empire mystery
Lane, W
Sherlock Holmes sequels series (77)
Sherlock Holmes at Elsinore
Muusmann, Carl
Sherlock Holmes sequels series (3)
Sherlock Holmes at Oxford
Utechin, Nicholas
Sherlock Holmes sequels series (25)
Sherlock Holmes at the 1902 Fifth Test
Shaw, Stanley
Sherlock Holmes sequels series (83)
Sherlock Holmes' first case
Kelly, Tim J
Sherlock Holmes drama series (12)
Sherlock Holmes illustrated omnibus
Doyle, Arthur Conan
Sherlock Holmes series (3)
Sherlock Holmes in Australia
Methold, Ken
Sherlock Holmes sequels series (97)
Sherlock Holmes in Dallas
Aubrey, Edmund
Sherlock Holmes sequels series (47)
Sherlock Holmes in modern times
Dworkin, Ira Bernard
Sherlock Holmes sequels series (48)
Sherlock Holmes in New York
Bensen, Donald R
Sherlock Holmes sequels series (22)
Sherlock Holmes in the adventure of the ancient gods
Vaughan, Ralph E
Sherlock Holmes sequels series (96)
Sherlock Holmes in Tibet
Wincor, Richard
Sherlock Holmes sequels series (10)
Sherlock Holmes meets Annie Oakley
Shaw, Stanley
Sherlock Holmes sequels series (85)

Sherlock Holmes meets the Phantom
Kelly, Tim J
Sherlock Holmes drama series (10)
Sherlock Holmes, my life and crimes
Hardwick, Michael
Sherlock Holmes sequels series (71)
Sherlock Holmes on the roof of the world
Miller, Thomas Kent
She series (9)
Sherlock Holmes sequels series (89)
Sherlock Holmes scrapbook
Haining, Peter
Sherlock Holmes series (10)
Sherlock Holmes, the case of the dancing bees
Sharp, Allen
Storytrails series (24)
Sherlock Holmes, the Meyringen papers
Sharp, Allen
Storytrails series (19)
Sherlock Holmes, the published apocrypha
Doyle, Arthur Conan
Sherlock Holmes series (10)
Sherlock Holmes versus Arsene Lupin
Leblanc, Maurice
Arsene Lupin series (2)
Sherlock Holmes versus Dracula
Estleman, Loren D
Dracula series (15)
Sherlock Holmes sequels series (28)
Sherlock Holmes versus Jack the Ripper
Queen, Ellery
Ellery Queen series (39)
Sherlock Holmes versus John Thorndyke and Reginald Fortune
Ward, Alfred C
Sherlock Holmes sequels series (56)
Sherlock Holmes's war of the worlds
Wellman, Manly Wade
Sherlock Holmes sequels series (17)
Sherlock Holmes's War of the worlds
Wellman, Manly Wade
War of the worlds series (3)
Sherston's progress
Sassoon, Siegfried
Sherston trilogy (3)
She's not what she seems
Pascal, Francine
Sweet Valley High series (92)
Shetland ponies
Jones, Olive
Barfield series (11)
Shh, we're writing the Constitution
Fritz, Jean
American Revolution series (6)
Shhh story
Erickson, Karen
I can do it series (2)
Shibo discipline
Barker, Wade
War of the Ninja Master series (2)
Shidt of sands
Robinson, Roland Edward
Drift of things series (2)
Shield of Achilles
Forman, James Douglas
Greek Civil War trilogy (3)
Shield of fear
Dixon, Franklin W
Hardy boys series (91)
Shield of the law
Graydon, William Murray
Sexton Blake series (293)
Shield of the valiant
Derleth, August
Sac Prairie series (10)
Shield of three lions
Kaufman, Pamela
Richard I series (1)
Shield of time
Anderson, Poul
Time Patrol series (4)
Shield Project
Mounce, David R
Paul Fox series (1)
Shift of guilt
Bude, John
Inspector Meredith series (24)
Shifter
Reeves-Stevens, Garfield
Chronicles of Galen Sword series (1)
Shiftinf sands
Bassett, Sara Ware
Cape Cod series (9)
Shifting fires
Helm, Eric
Super Vietnam series (2)
Shifting for himself
Alger, Horatio
Brave and bold series (3)
Shilling a mile
Hardcastle, Michael
Tony and Jay series (2)
Shilling for candles
Tey, Josephine
Inspector Alan Grant series (2)
Shills can't cash chips
Fair, A A
Bertha Cool and Donald Lam series (22)
Shiloh
Walker, Dalton
Shiloh series (1)
Shiner Slattery
Lee, John Alexander
Shiner Slattery series (2)
Shines the name
Acres, Mark
Combat Command series (2)
Starship troopers series (2)
Shining and free
Stern, Gladys Bronwyn
Rakonitz family series (4)
Shining harvest
Timms, Edward Vivian
Australian saga series (9)
Shining headlands
Bassett, Sara Ware
Cape Cod series (13)
Shining morning face
Hanson, Lawrence
Boy and man series (1)
Shining ones
Eddings, David
Tamuli trilogy (2)
Preuss, Paul
Venus prime series (6)
Shining river
Sanders, Dorothy Lucie
Montgomery family series (2)
Shining stars
Vautier, Ghislaine
Greek legends series (1)
Shining with the Shiner
Lee, John Alexander
Shiner Slattery series (1)
Shiny night
Tunstall, Beatrice
West Mercia series (1)
Ship aground
Smith, Cicely Fox
Barty Dale series (1)
Ship ashore
Parkman, Sydney
Captain Bowker series (2)
Ship from Atlantis
Munn, Harold Warner
Gwalchmai trilogy (2)
Ship from outside
Chandler, Arthur Bertram
Rim series (15)
Ship in hiding
Finkel, George
Group Captain Alan Metcalfe series (2)
Ship of adventure
Blyton, Enid
Adventure series (6)
Ship of death
Murphy, Warren Burton
Destroyer series (28)
Ship of dreams
Lumley, Brian
Dreamlands series (2)
Ship of force
Evans, Alan
David Cochrane series (2)
Ship of spies
Sinstadt, Gerald
Geoffrey Landon series (2)
Ship of the line
Forester, Cecil Scott
Horatio Hornblower series (7)
Ship slayers
Duff, Douglas Valder
Jeremy series (1)
Ship that sailed the time stream
Edmondson, Garry Cotton
Alice series (1)
Ship without a crew
Pease, Howard
Tod Moran series (4)
Shipbuilders
Fisher, Leonard Everett
Colonial Americans series (17)
Shipload of rice
Saro-Wiwa, Ken
Mister B series (7)
Shipmaster
Abraham, Cyril
Onedin Line series (1)
Ships afloat in the city
Ledwith, Frank
Ship insurance series (3)
Ships and cranes
Firmin, Peter
Make it work series (2)
Ships and voyages
Birt, David
Middle Ages series (17)
Ship's cat
Park, Ruth
Tales of the south series (1)
Ship's company
Jacobs, William Wymark
Night-Watchman series (9)
Ships in the sky
Gunnarsson, Gunar
Ships in the sky series (1)
Ships of doom
Grant, Maxwell
Shadow series (174)
Ships of Durostorum
Bulmer, Kenneth
Keys to the dimensions series (5)
Ships of Tarshish
Mohoao
Wandering Jew series (2)
Ships of youth
Diver, Maud
Challoners series (4)
Desmond series (6)
Ships that go bump in the night
Ledwith, Frank
Ship insurance series (2)
Shipwrecked detective
Graydon, William Murray
Sexton Blake series (455)
Shipyard menace
Stamper, Joseph
Sexton Blake series (1096)
Shirley Flight, air hostess
Dale, Judith
Shirley Flight series (1)
Shirley Flight, air hostess and the Chinese puzzle
Dale, Judith
Shirley Flight series (13)
Shirley Flight, air hostess and the diamond smugglers
Dale, Judith
Shirley Flight series (2)
Shirley Flight, air hostess and the flying doctor
Dale, Judith
Shirley Flight series (5)
Shirley Flight, air hostess in Canadian capers
Dale, Judith
Shirley Flight series (15)
Shirley Flight, air hostess in Congo rescue
Dale, Judith
Shirley Flight series (7)
Shirley Flight, air hostess in Hollywood
Dale, Judith
Shirley Flight series (4)
Shirley Flight, air hostess in Spain
Arlen, Trudi
Shirley Flight series (12)
Shirley Flight, ait hostess and the rajah's daughter
Dale, Judith
Shirley Flight series (6)
Shirley goes to America
Lewis, Lorna
Shirley series (2)
Shirley goes travelling
Lewis, Lorna
Shirley series (1)
Shirley shops
Ahlberg, Allan
Red nose readers series (12)
Shiva
Brennan, James Herbert
Shiva series (1)
Shiva accused
Brennan, James Herbert
Shiva series (2)
Shivering mountain
Somers, Paul
Hugh Curtis and Mollie Bourne series (3)
Shiwan Khan returns
Grant, Maxwell
Shadow series (176)
Shoal water
Yates, Dornford
Jonah Mansel series (8)
Shock for the Secret Seven
Blyton, Enid
Secret Seven series (13)
Shock tactics
Bruce, Jean
Secret Agent O.S.S.117 series (4)
Shock treatment
Chase, James Hadley
Steve Harmas series (3)
Stillman, Ron
Tracker series (7)
Shock value
Berne, Karin
Ellie Gordon series (2)
Murphy, Warren Burton
Destroyer series (51)
Shock-wave
Copper, Basil
Mike Faraday series (13)
Shock waves
Keene, Carolyn
Nancy Drew and Hardy boys supermystery series (3)
Pendleton, Don
Mack Bolan series (81)
Shocking pink hat
Crane, Frances
Pat and Jean Abbott series (8)
Shocking secret
Roth, Holly
Lieutenant Kelly series (1)
Shocks for the Chalet School
Brent-Dyer, Elinor Mary
Chalet School series (25)
Shockscape
Axler, James
Deathlands series (18)
Shockwave
Cory, Desmond
Feramontov quintet (2)
Johnny Fedora series (13)
Forbes, Colin
Tweed, Grey and Newman series (7)
Siegel, Barbara
Firebrats series (4)
Shod with silence
Ellis, Edward Sylvester
Daniel Boone and Simon Kenton series (1)
Shoddy kingdom
Boothroyd, Derrick
Heavy woollen district series (2)
Shoe fits
Ladline, Robert
J A Remington series (1)
Shoe shop bears
Baker, Margaret Joyce
Three bears series (1)
Shoeless Joe
Kinsella, William Patrick
Shoeless Joe Jackson series (2)
Shoeless Joe Jackson comes to Iowa
Kinsella, William Patrick
Shoeless Joe Jackson series (1)
Shoeless Joe Jackson series (2)
Shoemakers
Fisher, Leonard Everett
Colonial Americans series (10)
Shoes for Tom
Leavy, Una
Tom series (2)
Shoes that had walked twice
Toussant-Samat, Jean
Monsieur Levert series (1)
Shoes were for Sunday
Weir, Molly
Feet series (1)
Shoestring
Ableman, Paul
Eddie Shoestring series (1)
Shoestring's finest hour
Ableman, Paul
Eddie Shoestring series (2)
Shogun
Clavell, James
Asian series (1)
Sholtie burn
Paige, Frances
McGrath family series (1)
Sholtie flyer
Paige, Frances
McGrath family series (5)
Shon'jir
Cherryh, Carolyn Janice
Alliance-Union series (15)
Faded sun trilogy (2)
Shoo-fly girl
Lenski, Lois
Regional series (14)
Shoot a sitting duck
Alexander, David
Bart Hardin series (3)
Lieutenant Romano series (4)
Shoot if you must
Powell, Richard
Arab and Andy Blake series (4)
Shoot McAllister
Chisholm, Matt
Rem McAllister series (23)
Shoot me Dacent
Stein, Aaron Marc
Tim Mulligan and Elsie Mae Hunt series (13)
Shoot on sight
Hardcastle, Michael
Scorton Rovers series (2)
McCann, Sean
Dove's End Football Club series (6)
Shoot-out
Copper, Basil
Mike Faraday series (35)
Enefer, Douglas
Cannon series (6)
Shoot-out at Buffalo Gulch
Palmer, Bernard
Kid Breckinridge series (4)
Shoot out at Cross Fork
Roberts, J R
Gunsmith series (103)
Shoot out at Milk River
Floren, Lee
Buckshot McKee and Tortilla Joe series (2)
Shoot-out at Silver King
Christian, Frederick H
Frank Angel series (5)
Shoot the piper
Hill, Richard
Randall Gatsby Sierra series (2)
Shoot the works
Ellington, Richard
Steve Drake series (1)
Halliday, Brett
Michael Shayne series (30)
Shoot to kill
Bridges, Ben
Carter O'Brien series (8)
Halliday, Brett
Michael Shayne series (49)
Idriess, Ion Llewellyn
Australian guerilla series (1)
Miller, Wade
Lieutenant Austin Clapp series (7)
Max Thursday series (6)
Shoot when ready
Baker, William Howard
Sexton Blake series (1445)
Shootin' man
Scott, Bradford
Walt Slade series (19)
Shootin' sheriff
Colt, Clem
Pony George series (2)
Shooting at loons
Maron, Margaret
Judge Deborah Knott series (3)
Shooting gallery
Rae, Hugh Crauford
Superintendent McCaig series (2)
Shooting it again, Sam
Avallone, Michael
Ed Noon series (23)
Shooting of Dan McGraw
Kenyon, Michael
Superintendent O'Malley series (3)
Shooting of Sergius Leroy
Daniel, Roland
John Hopkins series (2)
Shooting of the green
Poyer, Joe
Cole Brogan series (1)
Shooting schedule
Murphy, Warren Burton
Destroyer series (79)
Murray, Will
Destroyer series (79)
Shooting star
Benary, Margot
Annegret series (2)
Blacker, Terence
Hotshots series (2)
Green, Kate
Theresa Fortunato series (1)
Hardcastle, Michael
Mark Fox series (4)
Herge
Tintin series (10)

Shooting stars
McCann, Sean
Dove's End Football Club series (4)
Shootout!
Brady, William S
Peacemaker series (9)
Shootout
Flynn, Jackson
Gunsmoke series (2)
Shootout at Gold Creek
Johnstone, William Wallace
Blood bond series (6)
Shootout at Las Cruces
Sanders, Brett
Web Steele series (4)
Shootout at Santa Fe
Martin, Cort
Jared Bolt series (5)
Shootout at the Golden Slipper
Mills, Robert E
Davy Watson series (8)
Shootout in Segovia
Thorne, Ramsay
Captain Gringo series (31)
Shootout in Sendero
Miller, Jim
Ex-Rangers series (8)
Shootout trail
Cole, Jackson
Jim Hatfield series (65)
Shop girls of Paris
Zola, Emile
Rougon Macquart series (11)
Shop in the mountain
Styles, Showell
Simon and Mag series (1)
Shop on Coppins Bridge
Daish, Elizabeth
Coppins Bridge trilogy (1)
Shop on the King's Road
Evans, Benjamin Ifor
Bookshop series (1)
Shop stewards
Target, George William
Post-war Britain series (4)
Shopping
Oxenbury, Helen
Baby board books series (2)
Tarsky, Sue
Time to talk series (2)
Wilmer, Diane
Step by step series (4)
Shopping day
Margolin, Harriet
Days series (2)
Shopping with a crocodile
Mahy, Margaret
Crocodile series (4)
Shopping words
Tyler, Jenny
First words series (6)
Shore Road mystery
Dixon, Franklin W
Hardy boys series (4)
Short back and sides
Cresswell, Helen
Mike series (3)
Short bier
Kane, Frank
Johnny Liddell series (15)
Short break in Venice
Inchbald, Peter
Inspector Franco Corti series (3)
Short cases of Inspector Maigret
Simenon, Georges
Inspector Jules Maigret series (78)
Short cruises
Jacobs, William Wymark
Night-Watchman series (7)
Short cut to Santa Fe
Sale, Medora
Inspector John Sanders and Harriet Jeffries series (4)
Short furrows
Hubbard, Kin
Abe Martin series (4)
Short history of American painting
Flexner, James Thomas
History of American painting series (3)
Short leash
Shurtleff, Bertrand Leslie
Awol series (2)
Short list
Lehrer, Jim
One-Eyed Mack series (5)
Philmore, R
Swan series (5)
Walder, David
Charles Lilburne and Rupert Inglis series (2)
Short shrift
Long, Manning
Liz Parrott series (5)
Short sixes
Bunner, Henry Cuyler
Short sixes series (1)
Short stories
Bramah, Ernest
Max Carrados series (5)
Short stories of Saki
Saki
Clovis series (2)
Short-term wife
Janson, Hank
Hank Janson series (114)
Short time to live
Moffat, Gwen
Miss Melinda Pink series (4)
Short wave
Bruce, Jean
Secret Agent O.S.S.117 series (3)
Short-wave mystery
Dixon, Franklin W
Hardy boys series (24)
Shortest way to Hades
Caudwell, Sarah
Professor Hilary Tamar series (2)
Shorthand Tom
Stratemeyer, Edward L
Bound to win series (4)
Shorthand Tom, the reporter
Stratemeyer, Edward L
Working upward series (3)
Shorty activity books
Webster, James
Shorty series (4)
Shorty again
Webster, James
Shorty series (4)
Shorty and the bank robbers
Webster, James
Shorty series (3)
Shorty and Tom Rabbit
Webster, James
Shorty series (2)
Shorty McCabe
Ford, Sewell
Shorty McCabe series (1)
Shorty McCabe gets the hail
Ford, Sewell
Shorty McCabe series (6)
Shorty McCabe looks 'em over
Ford, Sewell
Shorty McCabe series (5)
Shorty McCabe on the job
Ford, Sewell
Shorty McCabe series (4)
Shorty the hero
Webster, James
Shorty series (1)
Shoshone run
Longtree, Warren T
Ruff Justice series (10)
Shoshoni spirits
Sharpe, Jon
Trailsman series (101)
Shot
Hall, Parnell
Stanley Hastings series (7)
Shot at dawn
Rhode, John
Doctor Lancelot Priestley series (19)
Wilson, Gertrude Mary
Inspector Lovick series (11)
Shot at night
Plummer, Thomas Arthur
Detective Inspector Andrew Frampton series (2)
Shot at nothing
Ormerod, Roger
Philipa Lowe series (6)
Shot from midfield
Hallowell, Tommy
Alden All Stars series (3)
Shot from the dark
Chambers, Philip
Sexton Blake series (1512)
Shot from the door
Barry, Charles
Superintendent Lawrence Gilmartin series (11)
Shot in the dark
Fairlie, Gerard
Mister Malcolm series (1)
Usher, Frank
Daye Smith series (9)
Shot in the night
Bolt, Ben
Bob Ponting series (1)
Inspector Godbold series (1)
Shot of murder
Iams, Jack
Rocky Rockwell series (3)
Shot-silk
Elliott, William James
Anthony England series (2)
Shot silk
Maguire, Michael
Simon Drake series (1)
Shot to hell
Stivers, Dick
Able Team series (20)
Shotgun
McBain, Ed
Eighty Seventh Precinct series (23)
Shotgun and sagebrush
Miller, Jim
Long guns series (7)
Shotgun from hell
Logan, Jake
John Slocum series (21)
Shotgun gold
Tuttle, Wilbur Coleman
Hashknife Hartley and Sleepy Stevens series (6)
Shotgun man
Benteen, John
Neal Fargo series (13)
Shotgun rider
Hogan, Ray
Shawn Starbuck series (22)
Shotgun Saturday night
Crider, Bill
Dan Rhodes series (2)
Shotgun Sharkey
Grover, Marshall
Larry and Stretch series (299)
Shotgun Station
Dalton, Kit
Buckskin series (19)
Shotgun Sugar
Ledd, Paul
Shelter Morgan series (21)
Shots at sunrise
Thorne, Ramsay
Captain Gringo series (20)
Shoulder the sky
Stevenson, Dorothy Emily
Drumberley trilogy (3)
Shout against the wind
Ray, Mary
Mycaenean Greece series (2)
Shout for the adder, and other bush yarns
Garvey, Keith
Outback tales series (3)
Show and tell mystery
Hope, Laura Lee
New Bobbsey twins series (19)
Show-and-tell war, and other stories about Adam Joshua
Smith, Janice Lea
Adam Joshua series (3)
Show girl
McEvoy, Joseph Patrick
Show girl series (1)
Show horse
Bryant, Bonnie
Saddle Club series (25)
Show jumper
Peel, Hazel Mary
Ann and Jim Henderson series (4)
Show jumper in the family
Berrisford, Judith Mary
Brooke family series (3)
Show must go on
Meadows, Rose
Hanover succession series (1)
Show no mercy
Hild, Jack
SOBS series (4)
Show of force
Wilson, Gar
Phoenix Force series (37)
Show of violence
Woods, Sara
Sir Nicholas Harding and Antony Maitland series (23)
Show on ice
Verne, Jules
Caesar Cascabel series (2)
Show red for danger
Lockridge, Frances
Inspector Merton Heimrich series (14)
Richards, Francis
Inspector Merton Heimrich series (14)
Show some emotion
Cooper, M E
Couples series (19)
Show stopper
Pulver, Mary Monica
Kori McLeod Price and Peter Brichter series (5)
Show takes off
Peel, John
U.N.C.L.E. files series (6)
Show time at the Polk Street School
Giff, Patricia Reilly
Kids of the Polk Street School series (13)
Showbiz wipeout
Derrick, Lionel
Penetrator series (32)
Showboat summer
Du Jardin, Rosamond
Pam and Penny series (3)
Showboat world
Vance, Jack
Big Planet series (2)
Showdown
Brightfield, Richard
Choose your own adventure series (127)
Reno, Bill
Badge series (6)
Weston, Cole
Andrew Ryder series (7)
Showdown at Black Mesa
Martin, Cort
Jared Bolt series (3)
Showdown at Burnt Rock
Bagdon, Paul
Scrapper John series (2)
Showdown at Comanche Butte
Boone, James Calder
Ned Remington series (3)
Showdown at Emerald Canyon
Clinton, Jeff
Emerald Canyon series (2)
Showdown at Hell's Canyon
Mills, Robert E
Davy Watson series (1)
Showdown at Lone Tree
Grey, Romer Zane
Arizona Ames series (3)
Showdown at Medicine Creek
Kincaid, J D
Jack Stone series (3)
Showdown at Sandy Gulch
Denver, Lee
Deputy Marshal Dave Halloran series (5)
Showdown at Singing Sands
Tyler, Clarke
Clint Lacey series (2)
Showdown at Skull Canyon
Scott, Bradford
Walt Slade series (68)
Showdown at Snakegrass Junction
McCarthy, Gary
Derby Man series (2)
Showdown at the PTA Corral
Johnston, William
Brady Bunch series (2)
Showdown at Trinidad
Christian, Frederick H
Frank Angel series (6)
Showdown in Gunsmoke
Bexar, Phil
Billy Dupree series (1)
Showdown in Raton
Roberts, J R
Gunsmith series (49)
Showdown in Rio Malo
Roberts, J R
Gunsmith series (65)
Showdown in Sonora
Shirreffs, Gordon Donald
Lee Kershaw series (1)
Showdown in Sydney
Reid, Desmond
Sexton Blake series (1476)
Showdown on Front Street
Newman, Paul S
Gunsmoke series (4)
Showing off
Ellis, Carol
Cheerleaders series (31)
Showing up of Larry the lamb
Beaman, Sydney George Hulme
Toytown series (38)
Shown on the screen
Carter, Nicholas
Nicholas Carter series (395)
Shrewbettina goes to work
Goodall, John Strickland
Paddy Pork series (17)
Shrewbettina's birthday
Goodall, John Strickland
Paddy Pork series (3)
Shrieking pit
Rees, Arthur John
David Colwyn series (1)
Shrimp and the anemone
Hartley, Leslie Poles
Eustace and Hilda Cherrington trilogy (1)
Shrine
Faulcon, Robert
Nighthunter series (4)
Shrine of Kali
Hill, Harry Egbert
Sexton Blake series (334)
Shrine of murders
Grace, C L
Kathryn Swinbrooke series (1)
Shrine of the desert mage
Goldin, Stephen
Parsina series (1)
Shrine rites
Pearce, Brian Louis
Thomas Becket series (2)
Shrinking of Treehorn
Heide, Florence Parry
Treehorn series (1)
Shriveling murders
Zorro
Doctor Death series (3)
Shroud for a lady
Daly, Elizabeth
Henry Gamadge series (11)
Shroud for a nightingale
James, Phyllis Dorothy
Commander Adam Dalgliesh series (4)
Shroud for Amos
Hanson, Victor Joseph
Amos Crowle series (14)
Shroud for Aquarius
Collins, Max Allan
Mallory series (4)
Shroud for Delilah
Fraser, Anthea
Inspector David Webb and Sergeant Ken Jackson series (1)
Shroud for her shame
McCall, K T
Johnny Buchanan series (3)
Shroud for Mr Bundy
Fox, James M
John and Suzy Marshall series (11)
Shroud for Rowena
Rath, Virginia
Michael Dundas series (8)
Shroud for Sharon
Kane, Martin
Martin Kane series (14)
Shroud for Unlac
Courtier, Sidney Hobson
Ambrose Mahon series (4)
Shroud of darkness
Lorac, E C R
Inspector Macdonald series (40)
Shroud of vengeance
Bishop, Pike
Cord Diamondback series (6)
Shroud off her back
Ransome, Stephen
Steve Ransome series (2)
Shrouded death
Bailey, Henry Christopher
Mister Joshua Clunk series (11)
Shrouded planet
Randall, Robert
Nidor series (1)
Shrouded realm
Knaak, Richard Allen
Origin of Dragonrealm series (1)
Shrouded walls of Boranga
Sirota, Mike
Ro-Lan series (2)
Shrugg
Cosgrove, Stephen Edward
Bugg series (24)
Shrunken head
Fish, Robert Lloyd
Captain Jose da Silva series (3)
Shrunken heads
Kellerman, Jonathan
Alex Delaware series (1)
Shuck baa
Burningham, John
First words series (5)
Shuddering Mountain game
Blyton, Enid
Famous Five adventure games series (7)
Shudders
Abbot, Anthony
Thatcher Colt series (8)
Shulamite
Askew, Alice
Deborah Krillet series (1)

Shuna and the lost tribe
King, John
Shuna series (2)
Shuna, white queen of the jungle
King, John
Shuna series (1)
Shutterbugg
Cosgrove, Stephen Edward
Bugg series (16)
Shuttered window
Levy, Elizabeth
Fat Albert series (1)
Shutters of silence
Burgin, George Brown
Monastery of Mahota series (1)
Shuttle burn
Bentley, Roy
Spacers series (3)
Shwodown
Pascal, Francine
Sweet Valley High series (19)
Shy girl at Southdown
Moss, Roberta
Jenny series (3)
Shy leopardess
Barringer, Leslie
Neustrian trilogy (3)
Shy stegosaurus of Cricket Creek
Lampman, Evelyn Sibley
Shy stegosaurus series (1)
Shy stegosaurus of Indian Springs
Lampman, Evelyn Sibley
Shy stegosaurus series (2)
Shy young man
Hayes, Douglas
History of a selfish man series (2)
Shyest man in the world
Myers, David
Sebastian, the incredible drawing dog series (3)
Si-Fan mysteries
Rohmer, Sax
Fu-Manchu series (3)
Si le grain ne meurt
Gide, Andre
Journal series (7)
Siamese twin mystery
Queen, Ellery
Ellery Queen series (7)
Siberian alternative
Kilgore, Axel
They call me the Mercenary series (14)
Siberian gold
Harper, Theodore Acland
Siberian series (1)
Siberian road
Harvester, Simon
Asia in turmoil series (26)
Dorian Silk series (13)
Sibling
Hall, Adam
Quiller series (10)
Sibyl
Baldwin, Mary
Sibyl series (2)
Sibyl Sue Blue
Brown, Rosel George
Sibyl Sue Blue series (1)
Sicilain circuit
Cottenham, Mark Pepys
Tom Furness series (2)
Sicilain contract
Sharp, Allen
Storytrails series (11)
Sicilian
Puzo, Mario
Godfather series (2)
Sicilian affair
Mackintosh, May
Laurie Grant and Stewart Noble series (3)
Sicilian carousel
Durrell, Lawrence
Island series (4)
Sicilian slaughter
Peterson, Jim
Mack Bolan series (16)
Sick cow
Todd, Herbert Eatton
Bobby Brewster picture book series (1)
Sick Heart River
Buchan, John
Sir Edward Leithen series (6)
Sick of shadows
McCrumb, Sharon
Elizabeth Macpherson series (1)
Sick to death
Clark, Douglas
Inspector George Masters series (5)
Side-effect
Hawkey, Raymond
Presidential trilogy (2)
Side-show girl
Harragan, Steve
Steve Harragan series (4)
Side-stepping with Shorty
Ford, Sewell
Shorty McCabe series (2)
Sideshow
Resnick, Mike
Tales of the Galactic Midway series (1)
Sideswipe
Willeford, Charles
Hoke Moseley series (3)
Sidewalk Hilton
Cook, Bruce
Antonio Cervantes series (4)
Sidewalk mockers
Graeber, Charlotte Towner
Mister T and me series (7)
Sideways arithmetic from Wayside School
Sachar, Louis
Wayside School series (3)
Sideways stories from Wayside School
Sachar, Louis
Wayside School series (1)
Sidewinder
Edson, John Thomas
Floating Outfit series (13)
Scott, Bradford
Walt Slade series (84)
Slade, Jack
Lassiter series (4)
Walker, Dalton
Shiloh series (6)
Sidney at college
Ray, Anna Chapin
Sidney and Janet series (4)
Sidney, her senior year
Ray, Anna Chapin
Sidney and Janet series (6)
Sidney, her summer on the Saint Lawrence
Ray, Anna Chapin
Sidney and Janet series (1)
Sidney's comet
Herbert, Brian
Sidney series (1)
Sido
Colette, Sidonie Gabrielle
Claudine series (8)
Siege
Adams, Samuel Hopkins
Ruyland family series (1)
Baldwin, Bill
Helmsman series (6)
Daniel, Jack
Desert series (1)
Hardy, Adam
George Abercrombie Fox series (3)
Hulke, Malcolm
Roger Moore and the Crimefighters series (1)
Lodi, Maria
Charlotte Morel series (3)
Miller, Victor Brooke
Kojak series (2)
Siege at Forlorn River
Grey, Romer Zane
Yaqui series (2)
Siege for Panda One
Walker, Peter Norman
Panda One series (4)
Siege in the clouds
Hammel, Eric Maxwell
Khe Sanh series (1)
Siege machines
Birt, David
Roman Britain series (20)
Siege of Arista
Fawcett, Bill
War years series (2)
Siege of Cobb Street School
Towson, Hazel
Lenny and Jake series (2)
Siege of Dome
Lawhead, Stephen
Emphyrion series (2)
Siege of Dragonard Hill
Gilchrist, Rupert
Dragonard series (5)
Siege of earth
Faucette, John Matthew
Peacemakers series (2)
Siege of Jericho
Grover, Marshall
Larry and Stretch series (224)
Siege of Khe Sanh
Hammel, Eric Maxwell
Khe Sanh series (3)
Siege of Krishnapur
Farrell, James Gordon
British Empire trilogy (2)
Siege of London
Henrey, Robert
London in wartime series (3)
Madeleine series (8)
Siege of Norwich Castle
Blake, M M
Norwich series (1)
Siege of pleasure
Hamilton, Patrick
Twenty thousand streets under the sky series (2)
Siege of Serpentor
Stine, Robert Lawrence
G.I.Joe series (1)
Siege of the dragonriders
Affabee, Eric
Wizards, warlocks and you series (2)
Siegfried spy
Newman, Bernard
Papa Pontivy series (3)
Siegfried's journey, 1916-1920
Sassoon, Siegfried
Siegfried series (3)
Sierra adventure
James, Josephine
Kathy Martin series (8)
Sierra death dealers
White, Steve
S-Com series (6)
Sierra gold
Brady, William S
Jared Hawk series (11)
Sierra gold mystery
Keene, Carolyn
Dana girls series (23)
Sierra Madre
Stine, George Harry
Warbots series (4)
Sierra massacre
Reno, Clint
Vigilante series (2)
Sierra sabotage
Ellis, Wesley
Lone Star series (101)
Sierra shootout
Sharpe, Jon
Trailsman series (106)
Sierra showdown
Sadler, Jeff
Marshal Andrew Anderson series (6)
Sierra silver
Hardin, John W
Neal Fargo series (18)
Sierra summer
Schroeder, Doris
Walt Disney's Annette series (1)
Sierra triumph
Ross, Dana Fuller
Holt family series (6)
Sigh for a surgeon
Collins, Lynne
Hartlake Hospital series (7)
Sight of Proteus
Sheffield, Charles
Proteus series (1)
Sight unseen
Latham, Brad
Hook series (2)
Sightblinder's story
Saberhagen, Fred
Book of lost swords series (2)
Sigma curve
Barnwell, William
Blessing trilogy (3)
Sign at Six
White, Stewart Edward
Percy Darrow series (2)
Sign in the sky
Edgar, Alfred
Sexton Blake series (221)
Sign of chaos
Zelazny, Roger
Kingdom of Amber series (8)
Sign of evil
Wynne, Anthony
Doctor Eustace Hailey series (1)
Sign of fear
Derleth, August
Judge Ephraim Peck series (4)
Sign of four
Doyle, Arthur Conan
Sherlock Holmes drama series (16)
Sherlock Holmes series (2)
Sign of Hangletree
Rees, Arthur John
Inspector Luckraft series (2)
Sign of Jonas
Merton, Thomas
Elected silence series (2)
Sign of the alpine rose
Saville, Malcolm
Jillies series (4)
Sign of the black feather
Gregory, Hylton
Sexton Blake series (471)
Sign of the blue triangle
Hope, Stanton
Sexton Blake series (1071)
Sign of the cobra
Carter, Nick
Nick Carter series (89)
Sign of the coin
Carter, Nicholas
Nicholas Carter series (499)
Sign of the crab
Townson, Hazel
Lenny and Jake series (11)
Sign of the crooked arrow
Dixon, Franklin W
Hardy boys series (28)
Sign of the crossed knives
Carter, Nicholas
Nicholas Carter series (48)
Sign of the dagger
Carter, Nicholas
Nicholas Carter series (212)
Sign of the death circle
Snow, Charles Horace
Tommy Thorne series (3)
Sign of the four
Hershey, John
Sherlock Holmes drama series (2)
Sign of the glove
Dawe, Carlton
Leathermouth series (2)
Sign of the moonbow
Offutt, Andrew Jefferson
Cormac Mac Art series (7)
Sign of the mute Medusa
Wallace, Ian
Claudine Saint Cyr series (4)
Sign of the nine
Grierson, Francis Durham
Superintendent Andrew Ash series (12)
Sign of the prayer shawl
Carter, Nick
Nick Carter series (109)
Sign of the raven
Anderson, Poul
Last Viking trilogy (3)
Sign of the scar
Wallace, Robert
Phantom Detective series (7)
Sign of the serpent
Graydon, William Murray
Sexton Blake series (180)
Sign of the seven seas
Dawson, Carley
Mister Wicker series (2)
Sign of the spiral
Striker, Fran
Tom Quest series (1)
Sign of the times
Kee, Robert
Simon Broadstrop series (1)
Sign of the twisted candles
Keene, Carolyn
Nancy Drew series (9)
Sign of the unicorn
Zelazny, Roger
Kingdom of Amber series (3)
Sign of the witch
Clydesdale, Abby
Alys Heavers series (1)
Sign on for Tokyo
Haig, Alec
Alec Haig series (1)
Signal, Blackbird
Tralins, Sandor Robert
Jack Lund series (3)
Signal boys
Eggleston, George Cary
Indian War trilogy (3)
Signal, close action!
Kent, Alexander
Captain Richard Bolitho series (13)
Signal for death
Rhode, John
Doctor Lancelot Priestley series (35)
Signal for invasion
Adams, Herbert
Major Roger Bennion series (14)
Signal in the dark
Wirt, Mildred Augustine
Penny Parker series (14)
Signal, Intruder
Tralins, Sandor Robert
Jack Lund series (2)
Signal victory
Stacton, David
American history trilogy (1)
Signalman's morning
Vaughan, Adrian
Signalman trilogy (1)
Signalman's nightmare
Vaughan, Adrian
Signalman trilogy (3)
Signalman's twilight
Vaughan, Adrian
Signalman trilogy (2)
Significant others
Maupin, Armistead
Tales of the city series (5)
Signs of spring
Lee, Laurel
Godspeed series (3)
Signs of the gods?
Daniken, Erich von
Unsolved mysteries series (7)
Signs of the times and the religious life
Hinnebusch, Paul
Religious life series (3)
Sikanska trail
Gowland, John Stafford
Sikanska series (2)
Silecroft case
Lenehan, John Christopher
Inspector Kilby series (2)
Silence
Kyle, Sefton
Inspector J Rason series (10)
Silence after dinner
Witting, Clifford
Inspector Charlton series (11)
Inspector Peter Bradfield series (6)
Silence for the murderer
Crofts, Freeman Wills
Inspector Joseph French series (28)
Silence in Hanover Close
Perry, Anne
Charlotte Ellison Pitt and Inspector Thomas Pitt series (9)
Silence in solitude
Scott, Melissa
Silence Leigh trilogy (2)
Silence is deadly
Biggle, Lloyd
Jan Darzek series (4)
Silence observed
Innes, Michael
Sir John Appleby series (19)
Silence of a purple shirt
Woodthorpe, Ralph Carter
Nicholas Slade series (1)
Silence of Colonel Bramble
Maurois, Andre
Colonel Bramble series (1)
Silence of Gom
Mahr, Kurt
Perry Rhodan series (39)
Silence of history
Farrell, James Thomas
Universe of time series (1)
Silence of the night
Ormerod, Roger
David Mallin and George Coe series (2)
Silence on the shore
Garner, Hugh
Cabbagetown series (3)
Silence under threat
Cobb, Belton
Bryan Armitage series (15)
Inspector Cheviot Burmann series (39)
Kitty Armitage series (12)
Silencers
Hamilton, Donald
Matt Helm series (5)
Silent accuser
Soutar, Andrew
Phineas Spinnet series (7)
Silent are the dead
Coxe, George Harmon
Flash Casey series (1)
Silent bullet
Reeve, Arthur Benjamin
Craig Kennedy series (1)
Silent call
Royle, Edwin Milton
Squaw Man series (2)
Silent cracksman
Chichester, John Jay
Maxwell Sanderson series (1)

Silent cry
Jobson, Hamilton
Inspector Anders series (4)
Silent dances
Crispin, Ann Carol
StarBridge series (2)
Silent dead
Gask, Arthur
Gilbert Larose series (27)
Silent death
Grant, Maxwell
Shadow series (27)
Silent dreams
Campbell, Drusilla
Hopewell series (2)
Silent drum
Swanson, Neil Harman
American colonial series (4)
Silent dust
Fischer, Bruno
Ben Helm series (5)
Silent enemy
Benteen, John
Sundance series (21)
Netzen, Klaus
Killers series (7)
Silent four
Plummer, Thomas Arthur
Detective Inspector Andrew Frampton series (28)
Silent guardian
Carter, Nicholas
Nicholas Carter series (252)
Silent informer
Foxall, Peter Augustus
Catford Police series (5)
Silent isles
Porteous, Richard Sydney
Tambai series (3)
Silent jury
Evans, Gwyn
Sexton Blake series (618)
Silent kill
Muir, James A
Breed series (2)
Silent killer
Cross, David
Chant series (2)
Silent kind of war
Laflin, Jack
Gregory Hiller series (2)
Silent man
Walsh, James Morgan
Colonel Ormiston series (8)
Silent menace
Skene, Anthony
Sexton Blake series (772)
Silent murder
Cunningham, Chet
Team three series (2)
Silent murders
Paul, Ernest
George Barclay series (5)
Silent night
Stine, Robert Lawrence
Fear Street super chiller series (2)
Silent night 2
Stine, Robert Lawrence
Fear Street super chiller series (5)
Silent ones
Gaunt, Mary
Doctor Craven series (3)
Silent partner
Carter, Nicholas
Nicholas Carter series (292)
Kellerman, Jonathan
Alex Delaware series (4)
McDonnell, Jinny
Kim Aldrich series (2)
Silent passenger
Carter, Nicholas
Nicholas Carter series (71)
Silent people
Macken, Walter
Macmahon family trilogy (2)
Silent places
White, Stewart Edward
Free forest series (2)
Silent pool
Wentworth, Patricia
Miss Maud Silver series (27)
Silent prey
Sandford, John
Lucas Davenport series (4)
Silent salesman
Lewin, Michael Zinn
Albert Samson series (5)
Silent scream
Collins, Michael
Dan Fortune series (6)
Hoh, Diane
Nightmare Hall series (1)
Silent sea
McCaughren, Tom
Irish history series (5)
Silent Seven
Grant, Maxwell
Shadow series (7)
Silent shore
Harris, Ruth Elwin
Quantocks quartet (1)
Silent siren
Sterling, Thomas
Captain Rizzi series (2)
Silent sky
Eckert, Allan Wesley
Extinct birds series (2)
Silent slaughter
Beere, Peter
Trauma 2020 series (3)
Silent slayer
Verner, Gerald
Sexton Blake series (587)
Silent son
Warfield, Gallatin
Gardner Lawson series (2)
Silent song
Andrews, Lucilla
Saint Martha's Hospital series (7)
Silent speaker
Stout, Rex
Nero Wolfe and Archie Goodwin series (11)
Silent spring
Carson, Rachel Louise
Silent spring series (1)
Silent spring revisited
Carson, Rachel Louise
Silent spring series (3)
Silent street
Barnett, Glyn
Inspector Gramport series (5)
Silent suspect
Keene, Carolyn
Nancy Drew series (95)
Silent syndicate
Bidston, Lester
Sexton Blake series (647)
Silent tarn
Closs, Hannah
Albigensian trilogy (3)
Silent tears no more
Baer, Judy
Cedar River daydreams series (7)
Silent terror
Jacobs, Thomas Curtis Hicks
Chief Inspector Barnard series (5)
Silent thunder
Estleman, Loren D
Amos Walker series (10)
Silent tower
Hambly, Barbara
Windrose series (1)
Silent track star
Jenkins, Jerry Bruce
Dallas O'Neil and the Baker Street Sports Club series (8)
Silent treatment
Carkeet, David
Ricky and Nate series (1)
Silent victory
Blair, Clay
Submariners series (2)
Silent warrior
Modesitt, Leland Exton
Forever hero trilogy (2)
Silent warriors
Henrick, Richard P
Sub wars series (1)
Silent watcher
Stevenson, Florence
Kitty Telfair series (6)
Silent witness
Coxe, George Harmon
Jack Fenner series (6)
Kent Murdock series (23)
Desmond, Hugh
Alan Fraser series (22)
Freeman, Richard Austin
Doctor John Evelyn Thorndyke series (6)
Hunter, John
Sexton Blake series (1440)
Wilcox, Collin
Alan Bernhardt series (2)
Yorke, Margaret
Doctor Patrick Grant series (2)
Silent witnesses
Strange, John Stephen
Barney Gantt series (2)
Silent woman
Marston, Edward
Elizabethan whodunits series (6)
Silent women
Hood, Margaret Page
Gil Donan series (1)
Silent wooing
Galsworthy, John
Modern comedy series (3)
Silent world of Nicholas Quinn
Dexter, Colin
Inspector Morse series (3)
Silhouette in scarlet
Peters, Elizabeth
Vicky Bliss series (3)
Silicon mage
Hambly, Barbara
Dragonsbane series (3)
Windrose series (2)
Silicon sabotage
Norton, John
Magic voyage series (2)
Silicon Valley connection
Rosenberger, Joseph
Death Merchant series (58)
Silicon Valley slaughter
Quinn, John
Rod Gavin series (2)
Silinski, master criminal
Wallace, Edgar
Inspector Elk series (1)
Mister T B Smith series (1)
Silk
Elliott, William James
Anthony England series (1)
Silk and cordite
Spade, Danny
Danny Spade series (4)
Silk and steel
Miller, Ron
Bronwyn trilogy (2)
Silk king
Wells, Mary
Expatriates trilogy (2)
Silk maker
Legat, Michael
Silk maker series (1)
Silk road
Harvester, Simon
Asia in turmoil series (12)
Dorian Silk series (3)
Silk stocking murders
Berkeley, Anthony
Roger Sheringham series (4)
Chester, Gilbert
Sexton Blake series (1068)
Silken baroness
Atlee, Philip
Joe Gall series (3)
Silken baroness contract
Atlee, Philip
Joe Gall series (3)
Silken dalliance
Bruce, Henry James
Silken dalliance series (1)
Silken menace
Janson, Hank
Hank Janson series (55)
Silken nightmare
Brown, Carter
Danny Boyd series (12)
Silken sabre
Darby, Catherine
Sabre family series (3)
Silken snare
Janson, Hank
Hank Janson series (55)
Silken thread
Hood, Evelyn
Paisley series (2)
Silken thunder
Preston, Fayrene
Delaneys, the untamed years, second trilogy (2)
Silky!
Rosten, Leo
Silky Pincus series (1)
Silly
Leonard, Marcia
Feelings series (4)
Silly book
Cole, Babette
Hairy book series (4)
Silly games
Lloyd, David
Dinosaur days series (4)
Silly goose
Ormerod, Jan
Little ones series (3)
Silly listening book
Slepian, Jan
Junior listen-hear series (5)
Silly old Uncle Feedle
Postgate, Oliver
Bagpuss beginners series (3)
Silly sailing
Browne, Dik
Hagar the horrible series (41)
Silly Sally and Captain G Rumpy
Tierney, Frank M
Silly Sally series (7)
Silly Sally and the golden pail
Tierney, Frank M
Silly Sally series (3)
Silly Sally and the little pumpkin
Tierney, Frank M
Silly Sally series (4)
Silly Sally and the moon-baker
Tierney, Frank M
Silly Sally series (6)
Silly Sally and the picnic with the porpoises
Tierney, Frank M
Silly Sally series (1)
Silly Sally and the snowman
Tierney, Frank M
Silly Sally series (2)
Silly Sally and the tire and Mrs Corrigan
Tierney, Frank M
Silly Sally series (5)
Silly Sammy
Blyton, Enid
Little bedtime books series (3)
Silly sheep
Ahlberg, Allan
Help your child to read series (2)
Silly Tilly and the Easter bunny
Hoban, Lillian
Silly Tilly series (1)
Silly Tilly's Thanksgiving dinner
Hoban, Lillian
Silly Tilly series (2)
Sillyhen's big surprise
Tripp, Valerie
Just one more stories series (5)
SillyOZbuls of Oz
Baum, Roger S
Oz series (51)
Silmarillion
Tolkien, John Ronald Reuel
Middle Earth series (1)
Silurians
Hulke, Malcolm
Doctor Who series (4)
Silver and death
Simons, Roger
Inspector Fadiman Wace series (7)
Silver and lead
Rodgers, Sherlaw Johnston
Micah Truelove series (1)
Silver arrow
Wynne, Anthony
Doctor Eustace Hailey series (13)
Silver bells and cockle-shells
Jones, Harold
Bunby series (2)
Silver branch
Kennealy, Patricia
Keltiad series (3)
Sutcliff, Rosemary
Roman Britain trilogy (2)
Silver brumbies of the south
Mitchell, Elyne
Silver Brumby series (3)
Silver Brumby
Mitchell, Elyne
Silver Brumby series (1)
Silver Brumby kingdom
Mitchell, Elyne
Silver Brumby series (4)
Silver Brumby whirlwind
Mitchell, Elyne
Silver Brumby series (6)
Silver Brumby's daughter
Mitchell, Elyne
Silver Brumby series (2)
Silver buckshot
Tuttle, Wilbur Coleman
Henry Harrison Conroy and Judge Van Treece series (6)
Silver cache of the Pawnees
Lange, Dietrich
American Indian series (7)
Silver canyon
Winters, Logan
Spectros series (4)
Silver chair
Lewis, Clive Staples
Narnia series (6)
Silver Chief, dog of the north
O'Brien, Jack
Silver Chief series (1)
Silver Chief to the rescue
O'Brien, Jack
Silver Chief series (2)
Silver Chief's big game trail
Miller, Albert Griffith
Silver Chief series (6)
Silver Chief's revenge
O'Brien, Jack
Silver Chief series (5)
Silver Christmas tree
Hutchins, Pat
Surprise party series (2)
Silver citadel
Horowitz, Anthony
Old ones trilogy (3)
Silver City
Norman, David
Frontier rakers series (4)
Scott, Bradford
Walt Slade series (6)
Silver City ambush
Hardin, J D
Raider series (11)
Silver City carbine
Dalton, Kit
Buckskin series (22)
Silver City Rangers
Shappiro, Herbert
Mustang Marshal series (6)
Silver City scandal
Hammond, Gerald
Keith Calder series (9)
Silver City shootout
Logan, Jake
John Slocum series (52)
Silver cobweb
Benson, Ben
Ralph Lindsey series (3)
Keene, Carolyn
Nancy Drew series (71)
Silver cross
Sue, Eugene
Mysteries of the people series (4)
Silver crown
Richards, Laura Elizabeth
Fables for young and old series (2)
Rosenberg, Joel
Guardians of the flame series (3)
Silver Eagle carries on
Cumming, Primrose
Silver Eagle series (2)
Silver Eagle Riding School
Cumming, Primrose
Silver Eagle series (1)
Silver everywhere
Cawley, Winifred
Jinnie Friend series (1)
Silver Eyes
Collins, Laurel
Women of the West series (2)
Silver flame
Foreman, Leonard London
Rogue Bishop series (3)
Johnson, Susan
Blaze Braddock and Jon Hazard Black series (2)
Silver fury
Sharpe, Jon
Trailsman series (138)
Silver ghost
Macleod, Charlotte
Sarah Kelling series (8)
Silver glove
Charnas, Suzy McKee
Sorcery Hall trilogy (2)
Silver goblet
Foxall, Raymond
Harry Adkins series (4)
Silver greyhound
Walsh, James Morgan
Inspector Storm series (1)
Silver guard
Trease, Geoffrey
Stuart kings series (2)
Silver guilt
Meynell, Laurence Walter
Hooky Hefferman series (17)
Silver hair clue
Carter, Nicholas
Nicholas Carter series (435)
Silver hand
Lawhead, Stephen
Song of Albion trilogy (2)
Silver haze
Ruyle, John
Turlock Loams series (10)
Silver highway
Wells, Marian
Amy Randolph trilogy (1)
Silver hoard
Goodwin, Tim
Ring of spears series (2)
Silver horn, and other sporting tales
Grand, Gordon
Colonel John Weatherford series (1)

Silver horseshoe
Verner, Gerald
Superintendent Robert Budd series (7)
Silver in my sporran
Macvicar, Angus
Confessions series (4)
Silver island of the Chippewa
Lange, Dietrich
American Indian series (2)
Silver jackass
Boston, Charles K
Otis Beagle series (1)
Gruber, Frank
Otis Beagle series (1)
Silver king mystery
Greig, Ian
Inspector Swinton series (1)
Silver kingdom
Garnett, Richard
Mark Rutter series (1)
Silver ladies
Erskine, Margaret
Inspector Septimus Finch series (5)
Silver land
Scott, James Maurice
Jeremy Jackson series (2)
Silver leopard
Masterman, Walter Sidney
Sir Arthur Sinclair series (19)
Reilly, Helen
Inspector Christopher McKee series (17)
Silver Ley
Bell, Adrian
Country life series (2)
Silver lie
Harvey, John Barton
Wes Hart series (4)
Silver Maria
Sharpe, Jon
Trailsman series (129)
Silver medal
Trowbridge, John Townsend
Silver medal series (4)
Silver mirror
Gellis, Roberta
Royal dynasty series (4)
Silver mistress
Cunningham, Chet
Agent Brad Spear series (2)
O'Donnell, Peter
Modesty Blaise series (7)
Silver nemesis
Clarke, Kevin
Doctor Who series (143)
Silver new nothing
Marshall, Sybil
Fen family series (1)
Silver nutmeg
Brown, Palmer
Anna Lavinia series (2)
Lofts, Norah
Spice Islands series (1)
Silver on the tree
Cooper, Susan Mary
Dark is rising series (5)
Silver pencil
Dalgliesh, Alice
Silver pencil series (1)
Silver Phantom murder
Stuart, Brian
Knock-Out Kavanagh series (3)
Silver pigs
Davis, Lindsey
Marcus Didius Falco series (1)
Silver princess in Oz
Thompson, Ruth Plumly
Oz series (31)
Silver puma
Riefe, Alan
Huntington Cage series (4)
Silver rages
Allen, Willis Boyd
Pine cone series (2)
Silver ring mystery
Wells, Helen
Vicki Barr series (13)
Silver road
Hamilton, Mary
Robert Erskine series (2)
Silver rose bowl
Linton, Cathy
Saint Lawrence's Hospital series (6)
Silver sandals
Stagg, Clinton Holland
Thornley Colton series (1)
Silver scale mystery
Wynne, Anthony
Doctor Eustace Hailey series (12)
Silver scourge
Grant, Maxwell
Shadow series (34)
Silver secret
Allen, Betsy
Connie Blair series (11)
Silver secrets
Roos, Stephen
Maple Street kids series (3)
Silver shot
McCarthy, Gary
Derby Man series (5)
Silver showdown
Crafton, Dennis
Lobo series (1)
Silver sickle case
Brock, Lynn
Sergeant Venn series (1)
Silver skull
Daniels, Les
Don Sebastien series (2)
Grant, Maxwell
Shadow series (157)
Silver slaughter
Sharpe, Jon
Canyon O'Grady series (2)
Silver spade
Revell, Louisa
Julia Tyler series (3)
Silver spike
Cook, Glen
Chronicles of the Black Company series (6)
Silver spoon
Galsworthy, John
Modern comedy series (2)
Silver squawk box
Graeber, Charlotte Towner
Mister T and me series (8)
Silver stallion
Cabell, James Branch
Dom Manuel and his descendants series (3)
Poictesme trilogy (2)
Sheldon, Ann
Linda Craig adventures series (3)
Silver star
Silliphant, Stirling
John Locke series (4)
Silver Star
Zlotnik, Donald E
Fields of honor series (3)
Silver Street
Johnson, Emil Richard
Tony Lonto series (1)
Silver Street killer
Johnson, Emil Richard
Tony Lonto series (1)
Silver sun
Springer, Nancy
Book of Isle series (1)
Silver swan
Lampitt, Dinah
Sutton Place trilogy (2)
Silver threads
McLaglen, John J
Herne the Hunter series (11)
Silver tombstone
Gruber, Frank
Johnny Fletcher and Sam Cragg series (8)
Silver tombstone mystery
Gruber, Frank
Johnny Fletcher and Sam Cragg series (8)
Silver tombstones
Hardin, J D
Raider and Doc series (13)
Silver Town showdown
Logan, Jake
John Slocum series (162)
Silver trail
Bridges, Ben
Carter O'Brien series (1)
Silver Venus
McElroy, Hugh
Inspector William Brewer series (1)
Silver vortex
Caldecott, Moyra
Sacred stones series (4)
Silver war
Roberts, J R
Gunsmith series (17)
Silver warriors
Moorcock, Michael
Erekose series (2)
Eternal champion trilogy (2)
Silver wings
Montgomery, Raymond A
Choose your own adventure series (123)
Silver wings and leather jackets
Westcott, C T
Eagleheart trilogy (1)
Silver wings for Vicki
Wells, Helen
Vicki Barr series (1)
Silver wish
Scott, Michael
Tales from the Land of Erin trilogy (3)
Silverado
Mitchum, Hank
Stage coach station series (40)
Winters, Logan
Spectros series (1)
Silvered cage
Blayn, Hugo
Inspector Garth series (5)
Silverface
Long, Harman
Silverface series (1)
Silverface surrenders
Long, Harman
Silverface series (2)
Silverfinger
Chase, Glen
Cherry Delight series (3)
Silverglass
Rivkin, J F
Silverglass series (1)
Silverhair the wanderer
Paxson, Diana Lucile
Westria series (3)
Silverlock
Myers, John Myers
Silverlock series (1)
Silver's revenge
Leeson, Robert
Long John Silver series (6)
Silverskull
Edwards, Paul
John Eagle series (14)
Silvertail
Watson, Ina
Australian nature tales series (3)
Silverthorn
Feist, Raymond Elias
Riftwar series (2)
Silvertip
Brand, Max
Silvertip series (3)
Silvertip's chase
Brand, Max
Silvertip series (9)
Silvertip's roundup
Brand, Max
Silvertip series (6)
Silvertip's search
Brand, Max
Silvertip series (10)
Silvertip's strike
Brand, Max
Silvertip series (5)
Silvertip's trap
Brand, Max
Silvertip series (7)
Silvesrsmiths
Fisher, Leonard Everett
Colonial Americans series (2)
Simba
White, Stewart Edward
Simba series (2)
Simisola
Rendell, Ruth
Chief Inspector Reginald Wexford series (17)
Simon
Clouston, Joseph Storer
F T Carrington series (1)
Simon and the boxes
Tibo, Gilles
Simon series (5)
Simon and the chalk drawing army
McLachlan, Edward
Simon series (2)
Simon and the dinosaur
McLachlan, Edward
Simon series (4)
Simon and the land of chalk drawings
McLachlan, Edward
Simon series (1)
Simon and the moon rocket
McLachlan, Edward
Simon series (3)
Simon and the snowflakes
Tibo, Gilles
Simon series (1)
Simon and the wind
Tibo, Gilles
Simon series (2)
Simon and the witch
Barry, Margaret Stuart
Simon and the witch series (1)
Simon and the witch in school
Barry, Margaret Stuart
Simon and the witch series (6)
Simon Black and the spacemen
Southall, Ivan
Simon Black series (6)
Simon Black at sea
Southall, Ivan
Simon Black series (9)
Simon Black in China
Southall, Ivan
Simon Black series (5)
Simon Black in Coastal Command
Southall, Ivan
Simon Black series (4)
Simon Black in peril
Southall, Ivan
Simon Black series (2)
Simon Black in space
Southall, Ivan
Simon Black series (3)
Simon Black in the Antarctic
Southall, Ivan
Simon Black series (7)
Simon Black on Venus
Southall, Ivan
Simon Black series (6)
Simon Black takes over
Southall, Ivan
Simon Black series (8)
Simon Boom gets a letter
Suhl, Yuri
Simon Boom series (2)
Simon Boom gives a wedding
Suhl, Yuri
Simon Boom series (1)
Simon called Peter
Keable, Robert
Peter Graham series (1)
Simon finds a feather
Tibo, Gilles
Simon series (7)
Simon in summer
Tibo, Gilles
Simon series (4)
Simon in the moonlight
Tibo, Gilles
Simon series (6)
Simon Lash, detective
Gruber, Frank
Simon Lash series (1)
Simon Lash, private detective
Gruber, Frank
Simon Lash series (1)
Simon of Hangletree
Rees, Arthur John
Colwin Grey series (2)
Simon on the Tabard
Allison-Williams, Jean
Tabard series (2)
Simon takes the rap
Plummer, Thomas Arthur
Detective Inspector Andrew Frampton series (20)
Simon welcomes spring
Tibo, Gilles
Simon series (3)
Simone
Feuchtwanger, Lion
Waiting-room tetralogy (4)
Simon's quest
Howell, Christopher
Worlds of power series (4)
Simon's rabbits
Jones, Olive
Barfield series (5)
Simpey and his grandmother
Roberts, Elisabeth
Simpey series (1)
Simpey comes to stay
Roberts, Elisabeth
Simpey series (2)
Simpkins plot
Birmingham, George A
Reverend J J Meldon series (2)
Simple art of murder
Chandler, Raymond
Philip Marlowe series (6)
Simple gentleman
Winter, John Strange
Blankhampton series (9)
Simple life
Browne, Dik
Hagar the horrible series (20)
Simple machines that are really pulleys
Lampton, Christopher
Simple machines series (4)
Simple people
Marshall, Archibald
Simple stories series (2)
Simple speaks his mind
Hughes, Langston
Simple series (1)
Simple stakes a claim
Hughes, Langston
Simple series (3)
Simple stories
Marshall, Archibald
Simple stories series (1)
Simple stories from Punch
Marshall, Archibald
Simple stories series (2)
Simple suburban murder
Zubro, Mark Richard
Stonewall Inn series (1)
Simple takes a wife
Hughes, Langston
Simple series (2)
Simple way of poison
Ford, Leslie
Colonel John Primrose series (3)
Grace Latham series (2)
Hocking, Anne
Inspector William Austen series (26)
Simple's Uncle Sam
Hughes, Langston
Simple series (4)
Simply to die for
Christmas, Joyce
Lady Margaret Priam series (2)
Sin and Johnny Inch
Straker, John Foster
Johnny Inch series (1)
Sin city
Hunter, E J
Headhunter series (4)
Sin file
Ransome, Stephen
Lieutenant Lee Barcello series (4)
Sin funnel
Allison, Clyde
Agent triple zero eight series (18)
Sin is a redhead
Harragan, Steve
Steve Harragan series (5)
Sin of angels
Wells, Anna Mary
Doctor Hillis Owen series (3)
Sin of Father Mourot
Zola, Emile
Rougon Macquart series (5)
Sin of Hong Kong
Corrigan, Mark
Mark Corrigan and McLean series (25)
Sin of summer
Carson, Anthony
Soho series (1)
Sin of the Abbe Mouret
Zola, Emile
Rougon Macquart series (5)
Sin sniper
Garner, Hugh
Inspector Walter McDumont series (1)
Sin within her smile
Gash, Jonathan
Lovejoy series (17)
Sinai tapestry
Whittemore, Edward
Jerusalem quartet (1)
Sinbad and me
Platt, Kin
Sinbad trilogy (1)
Sinbad the soldier
Wren, Percival Christopher
Sinbad Dysart series (2)
Sinbad, the thirteenth voyage
Lafferty, Raphael Aloysius
Arabian Nights trilogy (3)
Since fifty
Rothenstein, William
Men and memories series (3)
Since silent spring
Carson, Rachel Louise
Silent spring series (2)
Sincere flattery
Vallins, George Henry
Parodies series (1)
Sinclair in command
Wingate, John
Submariner Sinclair series (3)
Sinclair's luck
Westerman, Percy Francis
Sinclair series (2)
Sine qua nun
Quill, Monica
Sister Mary Teresa series (5)
Sinful priest
Zola, Emile
Rougon Macquart series (5)
Sinful stones
Dickinson, Peter
Superintendent James Pibble series (3)

Sing a song of ambush
Peyton, K M
Mick and Rob series (2)
Sing a song of cyanide
Morland, Nigel
Mrs Palmyra Pym series (17)
Sing a song of homicide
Langham, James R
Samuel G Abbott series (1)
Sing a song of murder
Koehler, Robert Portner
Pecos Appleby series (1)
Langham, James R
Samuel G Abbott series (1)
Michaels, Jan
Darby Castle series (1)
Spiller, Andrew
Chief Inspector Duck Mallard series (26)
Sing and scatter daisies
Laurence, Louise
Wyndcliffe series (2)
Sing baby, Sing Sing
Kane, Martin
Martin Kane series (7)
Sing, clubman, sing
O'Hara, Kevin
Chico Brett series (3)
Sing for a penny
Dowdey, Clifford
Richmond, Virginia series (5)
Sing for your supper
Frankau, Pamela
Clothes of a king's son trilogy (1)
Sing me a moon
Darby, Catherine
Moon series (4)
Sing out, Charley
Hodges, Margaret
Charley series (2)
Sing out Irene
Marshall, James
Four little troubles series (3)
Singapore
Ball, John
Virgil Tibbs series (7)
Singapore downbeat
Corrigan, Mark
Mark Corrigan and McLean series (24)
Singapore exile murders
Mason, Francis Van Wyck
Colonel Hugh North series (13)
Singapore grip
Farrell, James Gordon
British Empire trilogy (3)
Singapore sling
Carter, Nick
Nick Carter series (256)
Singapore to freedom
Gilmour, Oswald Wellington
Singapore series (1)
Singer at the wedding
Arnold, Bruce
Coppinger tetralogy (1)
Singer not the song
Lindop, Audrey Erskine
Father Keogh series (1)
Singer passes
Diver, Maud
Sinclair series (3)
Singermann
Brinig, Myron
Singermann family series (1)
Singin' and swingin' and gettin' merry like Christmas
Angelou, Maya
Heart of a woman series (3)
Singing and the gold
Morrow, Charlotte
Lisa Knighton series (1)
Singing bone
Freeman, Richard Austin
Doctor John Evelyn Thorndyke series (4)
Singing citadel
Moorcock, Michael
Elric series (6)
Singing corpse
Dougall, Bernard
Steve Borden series (2)
Singing diamonds
McCloy, Helen
Basil Willing series (13)
Singing dog
Tripp, Valerie
Just one more stories series (1)
Singing heart
Cadell, Elizabeth
Waynes of Wood Mount trilogy (1)
Singing in the shrouds
Marsh, Ngaio
Inspector Roderick Alleyn series (20)
Singing masons
Vivian, Francis
Inspector Gordon Knollis series (7)
Singing room
Berrow, Norman
Michael Revel series (4)
Singing sands
Finkel, George
Group Captain Alan Metcalfe series (4)
Tey, Josephine
Inspector Alan Grant series (6)
Singing Scorpion
Macdonald, William Colt
Three Mesquiteers series (4)
Singing spears
Thompson, Ernest Victor
Retallick family series (4)
Singing strings
Clewes, Dorothy
Hadley family series (6)
Singing tree
Seredy, Kate
Good master series (2)
Singing Wind Trail
Bosworth, Frank
Earl Morton series (3)
Single clue
Rees, Arthur John
Inspector Luckraft series (8)
Single combat
Ing, Dean
Ted Quantrill trilogy (2)
Single death
Wright, Eric
Inspector Charlie Salter series (4)
Single hair
Adams, Herbert
Major Roger Bennion series (4)
Single-handed passage
Allcard, Edward Cecil
Temptress series (1)
Single in the field
Knowles, Anne
Cotswold vet series (1)
Single man
Miller, Hugh
Eastenders series (10)
Single monstrous act
Benton, Kenneth
Peter Craig series (7)
Single ticket to death
Bellairs, George
Detective Inspector Thomas Littlejohn series (46)
Singletusk
Kurten, Bjorn
Dance series (2)
Singular fury
Oleck, Howard Leoner
Sam Benedict series (2)
Singular spy
Williams, Amanda Kyle
Madison McGuire series (3)
Singularities
Quick, W T
Dreams trilogy (3)
Sinister airfield
Prince, Alison
Airfield series (1)
Sinister alibi
Wallace, Carlton
Superintendent Edmund Bendilow series (2)
Sinister assignment
Fenisong, Ruth
Captain Gridley Nelson series (12)
Sinister cargo
Black, Mansell
Richard Vaness series (2)
Page, Stanley Hart
Christopher Hand series (1)
Sinister Castle
Evans, Gwyn
Sexton Blake series (706)
Sinister craft
Ladline, Robert
J A Remington series (5)
Sinister crag
Gayle, Newton
James Greer series (5)
Sinister errand
Cheyney, Peter
Michael Kells series (1)
Sinister hoard
Hoare, Robert John
Bobby of the Globe series (1)
Sinister house
Verner, Gerald
Superintendent Robert Budd series (1)
Sinister Lake game
Blyton, Enid
Famous Five adventure games series (4)
Sinister light
King, Frank
Dormouse series (11)
Sinister madonna
Jackson, Wallace
Inspector Clancy Martin series (3)
Rohmer, Sax
Sumuru series (6)
Sinister mark
Thayer, Lee
Peter Clancy series (5)
Sinister moonlight
Robertson, Colin
Superintendent Bradley series (6)
Sinister murders
Cheyney, Peter
Michael Kells series (1)
Sinister omen
Keene, Carolyn
Nancy Drew series (67)
Sinister parade
Keene, Carolyn
Nancy Drew files series (23)
Sinister playhouse
Armstrong, Raymond
Inspector Dick Mason series (2)
Sinister power
Brand, Kurt
Perry Rhodan series (124)
Sinister quest
Jacobs, Thomas Curtis Hicks
Chief Inspector Barnard series (3)
Sinister ranch
Hobart, Donald Bayne
Masked Rider and Blue Hawk series (23)
Sinister rapture
Janson, Hank
Hank Janson series (75)
Sinister sanctuary
Thorne, Ernest Pollett
Major Brains Cunningham series (3)
Sinister scourge
House, Brant
Secret Agent X series (7)
Sinister shadow
Holt, Henry
Inspector Silver series (8)
Sinister shelter
Leonard, Charles L
Paul Kilgerrin series (9)
Sinister signpost
Dixon, Franklin W
Hardy boys series (15)
Sinister sister
Brody, Marc
Marc Brody series (32)
Sinister stars
Pattinson, James
Harvey Landon series (4)
Sinister stones
Upfield, Arthur William
Napoleon Bonaparte series (19)
Sinister Street
Burke, Richard
Quinny Hite series (5)
Kelly, Vince
Detective Inspector Price series (2)
Mackenzie, Compton
Sinister Street series (1)
Sinister Street series (1)
Sinister studios KESP-TV
Foley, Louise Munro
Twistaplot series (5)
Sinister talent
Pendower, Jacques
Slade McGinty series (3)
Sinister touch
Castle, Jayne
Guinevere Jones series (3)
Sinister Valley
Cody, Stetson
Cactus Clancy series (6)
Sinister warning
Michel, Milton Scott
Wood Jason series (1)
Sinister Widow
Armstrong, Raymond
Inspector Dick Mason series (3)
Laura Scudamore series (1)
Sinister Widow again
Armstrong, Raymond
Inspector Dick Mason series (4)
Laura Scudamore series (2)
Sinister Widow at sea
Armstrong, Raymond
Inspector Dick Mason series (9)
Laura Scudamore series (7)
Sinister Widow comes back
Armstrong, Raymond
Inspector Dick Mason series (6)
Sinister widow comes back
Armstrong, Raymond
J Rockingham Stone series (4)
Sinister Widow comes back
Armstrong, Raymond
Laura Scudamore series (5)
Sinister Widow down under
Armstrong, Raymond
Inspector Dick Mason series (8)
Laura Scudamore series (6)
Sinister Widow returns
Armstrong, Raymond
Inspector Dick Mason series (5)
Laura Scudamore series (3)
Sink me the ship
Sea-Lion
John Prentice series (2)
Sink or swim
Alger, Horatio
Luck and pluck series (2)
Sink the Ark Royal
Horst, Karl
U-boat series (1)
Sink the armada
Andrews, Keith William
Freedom's Rangers series (5)
Sink the Scharnhorst!
Kessler, Leo
Sea Wolves series (1)
Sinkiang executive
Hall, Adam
Quiller series (8)
Sinking spell
Gorey, Edward
Alphabet series (3)
Sinner
Fogazzaro, Antonio
Maironi family trilogy (2)
Sinner, or later
Brody, Marc
Marc Brody series (15)
Sinner takes all
Corrigan, Mark
Mark Corrigan and McLean series (2)
Sinners
Brown, Carter
Lieutenant Al Wheeler series (29)
Sinners go secretly
Wynne, Anthony
Doctor Eustace Hailey series (5)
Sinners in clover
Toye, Stanley
Anthony Read series (2)
Sinopah, the Indian boy
Schultz, James Willard
Pitamaken series (1)
Sins of Sumuru
Rohmer, Sax
Sumuru series (1)
Sins of surrender
Hart, Alison
Girls in trouble series (5)
Sins of the father
Schmidt, Stanley
Kyyra series (1)
Sins of the fathers
Block, Lawrence
Matthew Scudder series (3)
Howatch, Susan
Van Zale family series (2)
Rendell, Ruth
Chief Inspector Reginald Wexford series (2)
Sins of the gunslinger
Hardin, J D
Raider series (19)
Sins of the wolf
Perry, Anne
Inspector William Monk series (3)
Sion Crossing
Price, Anthony
Doctor David Audley and Jack Butler series (14)
Sioux
Handl, Irene
Benoir family series (1)
Sioux arrow
Robb, John
Shelby series (1)
Sioux captive
Sharpe, Jon
Trailsman series (51)
Sioux City
Downing, John Hyatt
Anthony Trant series (1)
Sioux dawn
Johnston, Terry Conrad
Plainsmen series (1)
Sioux runner
Lange, Dietrich
American Indian series (13)
Sioux showdown
Cunningham, Chet
Pony soldiers series (5)
Sioux slaughter
Cunningham, Chet
Pony soldiers series (6)
Gentry, Buck
Eli Holten series (5)
Sioux slave
Gentry, Georgina
Panorama of the old West series (9)
Sioux swordsman
Gentry, Buck
Eli Holten series (24)
Sioux trail
Hawkins, Clint
Saddletramp series (6)
Sioux uprising
Gilman, George G
Edge series (11)
Sioux wildfire
Hunter, E J
White Squaw series (1)
Sir Bevis
Jefferies, Richard
Bevis series (1)
Sir Charles Danvers
Cholmondeley, Mary
Danvers family series (2)
Sir George Tressady
Ward, Mary Augusta
Marcella Boyce series (2)
Sir Gibbie
Macdonald, George
Sir Gibbie series (1)
Sir Guyon in snowland
Madden, M S
Sir Guyon series (2)
Sir Guyon, the interloper
Madden, M S
Sir Guyon series (1)
Sir Harold and the gnome king
De Camp, Lyon Sprague
Harold Shea series (4)
Sir John Magill's last journey
Crofts, Freeman Wills
Inspector Joseph French series (6)
Sir Joseph's guests
Morrison, Emmeline
Light fingers series (2)
Sir Nigel
Doyle, Arthur Conan
English bowmen series (1)
Sir Oliver Bubb and the Red Knight
Craig, George
Sir Oliver Bubb series (1)
Sir Oliver Bubb and the wolf
Craig, George
Sir Oliver Bubb series (2)
Sir Percy hits back
Orczy, Emmuska
Scarlet Pimpernel series (5)
Sir Percy leads the band
Orczy, Emmuska
Scarlet Pimpernel series (4)
Sir Philip's folly
Chesney, Marion
Poor relation series (4)
Sir Reginald's ward
Everett-Green, Evelyn
Family series (2)
Sir Robert Peel
Gash, Norman
Sir Robert Peel series (2)
Sir Thomas More
Birt, David
Tower prisoners series (1)
Sir Toady Crusoe
Crockett, Samuel Rutherford
Sir Toady series (2)
Sir Tom
Oliphant, Margaret Oliphant Wilson
Greatest heiress series (2)
Sir Walter Raleigh
Birt, David
Tower prisoners series (2)
Sir, you bastard
Newman, Gordon F
Inspector Terry Sneed series (1)
Sire of champions
Henry, Marguerite
King of the wind series (6)
Siren in the night
Ford, Leslie
Colonel John Primrose series (9)
Grace Latham series (9)

Siren on the skids
Brody, Marc
Marc Brody series (69)
Siren song
Gellis, Roberta
Royal dynasty series (1)
Sirens
Achilleos, Chris
Fantasy illustrations series (2)
Sirens song of murder
Caudwell, Sarah
Professor Hilary Tamar series (3)
Siri Ram, revolutionist
Candler, Edmund
Siri Ram series (1)
Siri, the Conquistador
Stolz, Mary
Tales at the Mousehole trilogy (2)
Sirian experiments
Lessing, Doris
Canopus in Argus archives series (3)
Sir's daughter
Ebel, Suzanne
Sir Robert Waring series (2)
Sirs, only seventeen!
Townsend, Virginia Frances
Dorothy Draycott series (1)
Siskiyou
Hoyt, Richard
John Denson series (3)
Siskiyou two-step
Hoyt, Richard
John Denson series (3)
Sister
Jones, Irene Heywood
Hospital life series (1)
Sister at Ryeminster
Ferrari, Ivy
Ryeminster Hospital series (1)
Sister Beatrice and the mission mystery
Anderson, Catherine Corley
Sister Beatrice series (3)
Sister Beatrice goes to bat
Anderson, Catherine Corley
Sister Beatrice series (1)
Sister Beatrice goes west
Anderson, Catherine Corley
Sister Beatrice series (2)
Sister Death
Winslow, Pauline Glen
Superintendent Merlin Capricorn series (5)
Sister, don't hate me
Janson, Hank
Hank Janson series (7)
Sister for Helen
Hogarth, Grace Allen
Helen Hamilton series (2)
Sister in waiting
Linton, Cathy
Saint Lawrence's Hospital series (5)
Sister Jackie
Linton, Cathy
Saint Lawrence's Hospital series (7)
Sister Light, Sister Dark
Yolen, Jane
Great Alta series (1)
Sister of the angels
Goudge, Elizabeth
Torminster series (2)
Sister of the quints
Pevsner, Stella
Quints series (1)
Sister Peters in Amsterdam
Neels, Betty
Adelaide Peters series (1)
Sister Teresa
Moore, George
Evelyn Innes series (2)
Sister to Evangeline
Roberts, Charles George Douglas
Acadia series (2)
Sister trap
Oaks, Tina
Stepsisters series (2)
Sisters
Marvin, James W
Crow series (6)
Tolstoi, Aleksei Nikolaevich
Ordeal trilogy (1)
Sisters and brothers
Glover, Judith
Sussex quartet (2)
Sisters impossible
Landis, James David
Sisters impossible series (1)
Sisters in charge
Oaks, Tina
Stepsisters series (4)
Sisters in crime
Keene, Carolyn
Nancy Drew files series (19)
Sisters in love
Hardwick, Mollie
Atkinson family series (2)
Sister's influence, and other stories
Leslie, Madeline
Play and study series (2)
Sisters of battle
Drury, Rebecca
Women of war series (3)
Sisters of Emergency Ward 10
Falla, Roger
Emergency Ward 10 series (3)
Sisters of Rye
Lindsay, Philip
Sussex series (2)
Sisters of the road
Wilson, Barbara Ellen
Pam Nilsen series (2)
Sisters scheme
Makris, Kathryn
Almost sisters series (1)
Sister's tale
Castle, Frances
Erinn series (1)
Sisters team
Makris, Kathryn
Almost sisters series (3)
Sister's triumph
Boardman, M M
Brown family series (2)
Sisters under their skins
Grant, Jane
Nurse series (3)
Sisters war
Makris, Kathryn
Almost sisters series (2)
Sitting duck
Bagby, George
Inspector Schmidt series (49)
Sitting ducks
Meek, Margaret Reid Duncan
Lennox Kemp series (1)
Sitting target
Henderson, Laurence
Sergeant Arthur Milton series (2)
Sitting up dead
Stein, Aaron Marc
Matt Erridge series (1)
Situation, grave!
Janson, Hank
Hank Janson series (15)
Situation tragedy
Brett, Simon
Charles Paris series (7)
Situation vacant
Burton, Miles
Inspector Arnold and Desmond Merrion series (34)
Situations vacant
Lucas, Norman
Superintendent Bill Rowlands series (4)
Six and a secret
Cuthbert, Derrick
Six series (1)
Six bloody summer days
Carter, Nick
Nick Carter series (97)
Six Bullerby children
Lindgren, Astrid
Bullerby series (1)
Six came to dinner
Vickers, Roy
Inspector Peter Curwen and Hugh Stanton series (1)
Six cousins again
Blyton, Enid
Six cousins series (2)
Six cousins at Mistletoe Farm
Blyton, Enid
Six cousins series (1)
Six curtains for Natasha
Brahms, Caryl
Stroganoff Troupe series (3)
Six curtains for Stroganova
Brahms, Caryl
Stroganoff Troupe series (3)
Six-day week
Gardner, Alan Harold
Davis Troy series (3)
Six days in the life of Cornelius Plum
King, Kay
Cornelius Plum series (2)
Six days of the Condor
Grady, James
Condor series (1)
Six days to death
Alding, Peter
C.I.D. Room series (9)
Six dead men
Steeman, Andre
Wenceslas Vorobeitchik series (1)
Six deadly laws
Nelson, Peter N
Mollie Fox series (6)
Six feet of dynamite
Gray, Berkeley
Norman Conquest series (11)
Six feet under
Simpson, Dorothy
Inspector Luke Thanet series (2)
Six-fingered glove mystery
Judd, Frances K
Kay Tracey series (5)
Six-fingered stud
Horner, Lance
Falconhurst series (9)
Golden stud series (1)
Six for heaven
Sanders, Dorothy Lucie
Montgomery family series (1)
Six for the Toff
Creasey, John
Toff series (32)
Six gils growing older
Taggart, Marion Ames
Six girls series (3)
Six girls and Betty
Taggart, Marion Ames
Six girls series (6)
Six girls and Bob
Taggart, Marion Ames
Six girls series (1)
Six girls and the seventh one
Taggart, Marion Ames
Six girls series (4)
Six girls and the teatoom
Taggart, Marion Ames
Six girls series (2)
Six girls grown up
Taggart, Marion Ames
Six girls series (7)
Six green bottles
Hocking, Anne
Inspector William Austen series (10)
Six guilty men
Grover, Marshall
Larry and Stretch series (347)
Six Gun Angel
Longley, W B
Angel Eyes series (7)
Six-gun bride
Logan, Jake
John Slocum series (84)
Six-gun cavalier
Langley, John
Walt Warren series (10)
Six-gun champion
Langley, John
Walt Warren series (8)
Six-gun citadel
Langley, John
Walt Warren series (9)
Six-gun country
Cole, Jackson
Jim Hatfield series (68)
Six gun drive
Sharpe, Jon
Trailsman series (8)
Six-gun empire
Hobart, Donald Bayne
Masked Rider and Blue Hawk series (8)
Six-gun feud
Langley, John
Walt Warren series (2)
Six-gun fury
Bexar, Phil
Billy Dupree series (3)
Cole, Jackson
Jim Hatfield series (46)
Six-gun gamble
Langley, John
Walt Warren series (7)
Six Gun Gauntlet gets his man
Leyland, Eric
Six Gun Gauntlet series (3)
Six Gun Gauntlet hits back
Leyland, Eric
Six Gun Gauntlet series (4)
Six Gun Gauntlet rides again
Leyland, Eric
Six Gun Gauntlet series (2)
Six Gun Gauntlet strikes the trail
Leyland, Eric
Six Gun Gauntlet series (1)
Six Gun Gauntlet wins through
Leyland, Eric
Six Gun Gauntlet series (5)
Six-gun hills
Cole, Jackson
Jim Hatfield series (58)
Six-gun justice
Langley, John
Walt Warren series (5)
Roberts, J R
Gunsmith series (81)
Six-gun kill
Dalton, Kit
Buckskin series (40)
Six-gun law
Langley, John
Walt Warren series (3)
Six-gun poker
Masters, Zeke
Faro Blake series (11)
Six-gun salute
Langley, John
Walt Warren series (13)
Six-gun salvation
Sharpe, Jon
Trailsman series (47)
Six-Gun Samurai
Lee, Patrick
Six-Gun Samurai series (1)
Six-gun sideshow
Roberts, J R
Gunsmith series (90)
Six-gun smoke
Langley, John
Walt Warren series (11)
Six-gun solution
Hawke, Simon
Timewars series (12)
Six-gun sombreros
Sharpe, Jon
Trailsman series (31)
Six-gun strife
Langley, John
Walt Warren series (6)
Six-gun syndicate
Cole, Jackson
Jim Hatfield series (57)
Six-gun trial
Langley, John
Walt Warren series (1)
Six-gun vengeance
Langley, John
Walt Warren series (12)
Six-gun war
Langley, John
Walt Warren series (4)
Six-gun wedding
Grover, Marshall
Larry and Stretch series (274)
Six guns
Cunningham, Chet
Outlaws series (2)
Six-guns and shurikens
Morris, Dave
Teenage mutant ninja turtles series (5)
Six-guns at Spanish Peak
Boone, James Calder
Ned Remington series (8)
Six-horse hitch
Giles, Janice Holt
Fowler family series (10)
Six-hundred mile stretch
Miller, Jim
Ex-Rangers series (6)
Six hundred pound gorilla
Campbell, Robert Wright
Jimmy Flannery series (2)
Six impossible things
Cadell, Elizabeth
Waynes of Wood Mount trilogy (3)
Six in a castle
Cuthbert, Derrick
Six series (2)
Six iron spiders
Taylor, Phoebe Atwood
Asey Mayo series (18)
Six-letter word for death
Moyes, Patricia
Henry and Emmy Tibbett series (16)
Six little bunkers
Hope, Laura Lee
Six little bunkers series (14)
Six little bunkers at Aunt Jo's
Hope, Laura Lee
Six little bunkers series (2)
Six little bunkers at Captain Ben's
Hope, Laura Lee
Six little bunkers series (6)
Six little bunkers at Cousin Tom's
Hope, Laura Lee
Six little bunkers series (3)
Six little bunkers at Cowboy Jack's
Hope, Laura Lee
Six little bunkers series (7)
Six little bunkers at Farmer Joel's
Hope, Laura Lee
Six little bunkers series (9)
Six little bunkers at Grandma Bell's
Hope, Laura Lee
Six little bunkers series (1)
Six little bunkers at Grandpa Ford's
Hope, Laura Lee
Six little bunkers series (4)
Six little bunkers at Happy Jim's
Hope, Laura Lee
Six little bunkers series (12)
Six little bunkers at Indian John's
Hope, Laura Lee
Six little bunkers series (11)
Six little bunkers at Lighthouse Nell's
Hope, Laura Lee
Six little bunkers series (14)
Six little bunkers at Mammy June's
Hope, Laura Lee
Six little bunkers series (8)
Six little bunkers at Miller Ned's
Hope, Laura Lee
Six little bunkers series (10)
Six little bunkers at Skipper Bob's
Hope, Laura Lee
Six little bunkers series (13)
Six little bunkers at Uncle Fred's
Hope, Laura Lee
Six little bunkers series (5)
Six little Pennypackers
Swett, Sophia Miriam
Pennypackers series (1)
Six little possums
McGill, Marci
Six little possums series (1)
Six little possums and the baby-sitter
McGill, Marci
Six little possums series (4)
Six little possums at home
McGill, Marci
Six little possums series (2)
Six men died
Verner, Gerald
Superintendent Robert Budd series (24)
Six men of evil
Grant, Maxwell
Shadow series (24)
Six minutes past twelve
Holt, Gavin
Professor Luther Bastion series (1)
Six new students
Brandenberg, Franz
Fieldmouse children series (3)
Six nuns and a shotgun
Watson, Colin
Inspector Purbright series (8)
Six o'clock tales
Blyton, Enid
Evening tales series (2)
Six of swords
Douglas, Carole Nelson
Irissa and Kendric trilogy (1)
Six pence for Sam
Tann, Roger
Troopers series (4)
Six ponies
Pullein-Thompson, Josephine
Major Holbrooke series (1)
Six problems for Don Isidro Parodi
Borges, Jorge Luis
Problems and chronicles series (1)
Six proud walkers
Beeding, Francis
Colonel Alastair Granby series (1)
Fraser, Anthea
Inspector David Webb and Sergeant Ken Jackson series (6)
Six rogues riding
Grover, Marshall
Nevada Jim series (29)
Six seconds of darkness
Cohen, Octavus Roy
David Carroll series (3)
Six seconds to kill
Halliday, Brett
Michael Shayne series (62)
Six sign-post murder
Robbins, Clifton
Staveley series (1)
Six silver handles
Homes, Geoffrey
Humphrey Campbell series (5)
Six tales of Brock the Badger
Uttley, Alison
Brock the badger series (3)
Six tales of Sam Pig
Uttley, Alison
Sam Pig series (3)
Six tales of the four pigs
Uttley, Alison
Brock the badger series (2)

Six Three Three Squadron
Smith, Frederick Escreet
Six Three Three Squadron series (1)
Six to kill
Gray, Berkeley
Norman Conquest series (8)
Six were present
Punshon, Ernest Robertson
Bobby Owen series (35)
Six who ran
Chaber, M E
Milo March series (13)
Six years later
Dumas, Alexandre
Marie Antoinette series (3)
Sixgun apostles
Willoughby, Lee Davis
Making of America series (56)
Sixgun cemetery
Logan, Jake
John Slocum series (99)
Sixgun circus
Hardin, J D
Raider series (2)
Sixgun doom
Scott, Bradford
Walt Slade series (107)
Sixgun fury
Scott, Bradford
Walt Slade series (79)
Sixgun law
Logan, Jake
John Slocum series (113)
Sixgun says goodbye
Clay, E Jefferson
Duke Benedict and Hank Brazos series (2)
Sixgun slaughter
McCoy, Duff
Jeb Cutter series (4)
Sixgun talk
Scott, Bradford
Walt Slade series (9)
Sixguns and silk
Martin, Cort
Jared Bolt series (20)
Sixguns at Silverado
Logan, Jake
John Slocum series (107)
Sixguns in a bloody dawn
Scott, Bradford
Walt Slade series (92)
Sixpenny holiday
Mathews, M E
Cloud family series (3)
Sixpenny runner
Lamplugh, Lois
Allen family series (5)
Sixteen and away from home
Richardson, Arleta
Growing up series (1)
Sixteen bells
Hackforth-Jones, Gilbert
Submarine Service series (5)
Sixteen-dollar shooter
Edson, John Thomas
Rockabye County series (1)
Sixteenth stair
Lorac, E C R
Inspector Macdonald series (22)
Sixth anti-coloring book
Striker, Susan
Anti-coloring series (6)
Sixth big Monster book
Blance, Ellen
Monster series (21)
Sixth Brer Rabbit book
Blyton, Enid
Brer Rabbit series (6)
Sixth commandment
Sanders, Lawrence
Ten commandments series (1)
Sixth directorate
Hone, Joseph
Peter Marlow series (2)
Sixth grade can really kill you
De Clements, Barthe
Elsie Edwards series (2)
Sixth heaven
Hartley, Leslie Poles
Eustace and Hilda Cherrington trilogy (2)
Sixth of October
Romains, Jules
Men of goodwill series (1)
Sixth Precinct
Newman, Christopher
Joe Dante series (2)
Sixth raid
Enefer, Douglas
Sam Bawtrey series (10)
Sixth victim
Graydon, William Murray
Sexton Blake series (577)
Sixth wife
Plaidy, Jean
Tudor series (5)
Sixty-four, ninety-four!
Mottram, Ralph Hale
Geoffrey Skene series (2)
Spanish Farm series (2)
Sixty four thousand murder
Gunn, Victor
Chief Inspector Bill Cromwell series (29)
Sixty minutes for Saint George
Fullerton, Alexander
Nick Everard series (2)
Sixty-nine diamonds
Lord, Jeremy
Colonel Winston Creevy series (2)
Sixty-nine pleasures
Gray, Rod
Lady from L.U.S.T. series (3)
Size spies
Needle, Jan
Size spies series (1)
Skate Patrol
Bunting, Eve
Skate Patrol series (1)
Skate Patrol and the mystery writer
Bunting, Eve
Skate Patrol series (3)
Skate Patrol rides again
Bunting, Eve
Skate Patrol series (2)
Skateboard champion
Packard, Edward
Choose your own adventure series (112)
Skateboard dare
Krulick, Nancy E
Lassie series (5)
Skating camp
Lowell, Melissa
Silver blades series (6)
Skating shoes
Streatfeild, Noel
Shoes series (7)
Skeen's leap
Clayton, Jo
Skeen trilogy (1)
Skeen's return
Clayton, Jo
Skeen trilogy (2)
Skeen's search
Clayton, Jo
Skeen trilogy (3)
Skeeter
Cosgrove, Stephen Edward
Bugg series (53)
Skeeter and the computer
Modell, Frank B
Milton and Marvin series (7)
Skeeters Kirby
Masters, Edgar Lee
Mitch Miller series (2)
Skeleton at the feast
Wells, Carolyn
Kenneth Carlisle series (3)
Skeleton closet of Jules de Grandin
Quinn, Seabury
Jules de Grandin series (5)
Skeleton coast contract
Atlee, Philip
Joe Gall series (8)
Skeleton crew
Ahlberg, Allan
Funnybones series (5)
Skeleton in the clock
Dickson, Carter
Sir Henry Merrivale series (19)
Skeleton in the closet
Cunningham, Albert Benjamin
Sheriff Jess Roden series (19)
Southworth, Emma Dorothy Eliza Nevitte
Brandon Coyle series (1)
Skeleton-in-waiting
Dickinson, Peter
King Victor series (2)
Skeleton Island
Dale, Norman
Tim Forest series (3)
Mitchell, Gladys
Dame Beatrice Bradley series (40)
Skeleton key
Charles, Steven
Private school series (4)
Offord, Lenore Glen
Todd McKinnon series (1)
Skeleton lord's key
Moran, Daniel Keys
Keys to paradise trilogy (2)
Skeleton out of the cupboard
Williams, Valentine
Mister Treadgold series (3)
Skeleton riders
Cole, Jackson
Jim Hatfield series (90)
Skeleton trail
Scott, Bradford
Walt Slade series (36)
Skeletons
Sauter, Eric
Robert Lee Hunter series (5)
Skeletons in the closet
Linington, Elizabeth
Sergeant Ivor Maddox series (11)
Skeleton's knee
Mayor, Archer Huntington
Lieutenant Joe Gunther series (4)
Sketching ourdoors in autumn
Arnosky, Jim
Sketching outdoors series (3)
Sketching ourdoors in spring
Arnosky, Jim
Sketching outdoors series (1)
Sketching ourdoors in summer
Arnosky, Jim
Sketching outdoors series (2)
Sketching ourdoors in winter
Arnosky, Jim
Sketching outdoors series (4)
Ski nurse mystery
Wells, Helen
Cherry Ames series (27)
Ski weekend
Stine, Robert Lawrence
Fear Street series (7)
Skid Row
Spade, Danny
Danny Spade series (22)
Skies of Crete
Forman, James Douglas
Greek Civil War trilogy (1)
Skiffy
Mayne, William
Skiffy series (1)
Skiffy and the twin planets
Mayne, William
Skiffy series (2)
Skiing
Paulsen, Gary
Sports on the light side series (7)
Skimpole's sbapshot
Clifford, Martin
Tom Merry series (10)
Skin deep
Dickinson, Peter
Superintendent James Pibble series (1)
Murphy, Warren Burton
Destroyer series (49)
Peters, David
Photon series (6)
Roberts, Nora
O'Hurley trilogy (3)
Skin deep is fatal
Cormany, Michael
Dan Kruger series (5)
Skin game dame
Gray, Rod
Lady from L.U.S.T. series (18)
Skin swindle
Barker, Wade
Ninja Master series (7)
Skin trap
Mole, William
Casson Duker series (3)
Skinflick
Hansen, Joseph
Dave Brandstetter series (5)
Skinhead
Allen, Richard
Joe Hawkins series (1)
Skinner
McEnroe, Richard S
Far stars and future times series (3)
Rae, Hugh Crauford
Glasgow series (1)
Skinner makes it fashionable
Dodge, Henry Irving
Skinner series (4)
Skinner's baby
Dodge, Henry Irving
Skinner series (2)
Skinner's big idea
Dodge, Henry Irving
Skinner series (3)
Skinner's dress suit
Dodge, Henry Irving
Skinner series (1)
Skinning place
Harvey, John Barton
Wes Hart series (10)
Skinny McCord
Fitzhugh, Percy Keese
Buddy series (2)
Skinny on the warpath
Leyland, Eric
Skinny series (2)
Skinny's Christmas Eve
Leyland, Eric
Skinny series (3)
Skinwalkers
Hillerman, Tony
Lieutenant Joe Leaphorn series (4)
Sergeant Jim Chee series (4)
Skip a beat
Kane, Henry
Peter Chambers series (8)
Skip trip
Burningham, John
First words series (2)
Skipper
Dixon, Paige
Skipper series (2)
Skipper and son
Berrisford, Judith Mary
Skipper series (5)
Skipper and the Headland four
Berrisford, Judith Mary
Skipper series (2)
Skipper and the runaway boy
Berrisford, Judith Mary
Skipper series (4)
Skipper of the Cynthia B
Durell, Charles Pendexter
Blue water trilogy (1)
Skipper, the dog from the sea
Berrisford, Judith Mary
Skipper series (1)
Skipper to the rescue
Berrisford, Judith Mary
Skipper series (2)
Skipper Worse
Kielland, Alexander Lange
Garman and Worse series (2)
Skipper's exciting summer
Berrisford, Judith Mary
Skipper series (3)
Skippy and the bird smugglers
Odgers, Sally Farrell
Adventures of Skippy series (1)
Skippy Bedelle
Johnson, Owen McMahon
Lawrenceville series (5)
Skippy goes bush
Boland, Jason
Adventures of Skippy series (2)
Skippy, the skunk
Darby, Joan
Animal adventure series (2)
Skirmish
Michaels, Melisa C
Skyrider series (1)
Skirts bring me sorrow
Janson, Hank
Hank Janson series (35)
Skookum Chuck
White, Stewart Edward
Skookum Chuck series (1)
Skorpion's death
Brierley, David
Cody series (3)
Skraelings
Sherrell, Carl
Raum series (2)
Skryling's blade
Estes, Rose
Runesword series (2)
Skulduggery
Marshall, William Leonard
Yellowthread Street series (5)
Skulduggery on Halfaday Creek
Hendryx, James Beardsley
Black John series (11)
Skull beneath the skin
James, Phyllis Dorothy
Cordelia Gray series (2)
Skull duggery
Murphy, Warren Burton
Destroyer series (83)
Murray, Will
Destroyer series (83)
Skull-Face, and others
Howard, Robert Ervin
Skull-Face series (1)
Skull-Face omnibus
Howard, Robert Ervin
Skull-Face series (1)
Skull Gate
Bailey, Robin Wayne
Frost trilogy (2)
Skull gold
Hogan, Ray
Shawn Starbuck series (14)
Skull Island
Turner, Philip
Darnley Mills series (6)
Skull of Kanaima
Norwood, Victor George Charles
Jacare series (4)
Skull of the waltzing clown
Keeler, Harry Stephen
Vagabond nights series (2)
Skull still bone
Wyllie, John
Doctor Quarshie series (1)
Skulls in the stars
Howard, Robert Ervin
Solomon Kane series (2)
Skunk Ridge papers
Hubbard, Kin
Abe Martin series (18)
Sky attack
Cook, Canfield
Lucky Terrell series (2)
Sky babies
Delton, Judy
Pee wee scout series (15)
Sky blue frame
Dixon, Franklin W
Hardy boys series (89)
Sky cage
Prior, Ann
Felan series (1)
Sky falls
Mazzetti, Lorenza
Penny and Baby series (1)
Sky fire
Teed, Jack Hamilton
Gunships series (4)
Sky fleet of Atlantis
Bloomfield, Frena
Darkworld legends series (2)
Sky high
Johns, William Earl
Steeley Delaroy series (1)
Sky-high
Morris, Dave
Teenage mutant ninja turtles series (2)
Sky-high terror
Trevor, Ralph
Superintendent Curtis Burke series (3)
Sky high to Shanghai
Clune, Frank
Discovery series (4)
Sky is falling
Pearson, Kit
Evacuee trilogy (1)
Sapir, Richard
Destroyer series (63)
Sky Island
Baum, Lyman Frank
Trot and Cap'n Bill series (2)
Sky kill
Da Cruz, Daniel
Jock Sergeant series (3)
Sky-liners
L'Amour, Louis
Sackett family series (15)
Sky lord
Allen, Martin
Fighting fantasy gamebook series (35)
Sky lords
Brosnan, John
Sky lords series (1)
Sky man
Johnson, Stacie
Eighteen Pine Street series (5)
Sky masters
Brown, Dale
Patrick McLanahan series (3)
Sky phantom
Keene, Carolyn
Nancy Drew series (53)
Sky Pilot
Connor, Ralph
Sky Pilot series (1)
Sky Pilot of No Man's Land
Connor, Ralph
Sky Pilot series (3)
Sky pirates of Callisto
Carter, Lin
Jandar the Alien series (3)
Sky riders
Scott, Bradford
Walt Slade series (93)
Sky riders of the Atlantic
Stone, Richard H
Slim Tyler series (1)
Sky rocket
Fitt, Mary
Superintendent Mallett series (2)

Sky sabotage
Dixon, Franklin W
Hardy boys series (79)
Sky strike
Rouch, James
Zone series (4)
Sky walker
Robeson, Kenneth
Avenger series (3)
Sky war
Mackin, Rick
Chopper cops series (4)
Skyborn
Kruchten, Marcia
Omni odysseys trilogy (3)
Skybowl
Rawn, Melanie
Dragon star series (3)
Skybreaker
Halam, Ann
Inland trilogy (3)
Skye O'Malley
Small, Beatrice
Skye O'Malley series (1)
Skyfire
Asch, Frank
Bear series (6)
King, Bernard
Chronicles of the keeper trilogy (3)
Maloney, Mack
Wingman series (8)
Skyfire puzzle
Dixon, Franklin W
Hardy boys series (85)
Skyhigh betrayers
Derrick, Lionel
Penetrator series (28)
Skylark
Hild, Jack
SOBS series (19)
Maclachlan, Patricia
Witting family series (2)
Skylark DuQuesne
Smith, Edward Elmer
Skylark series (4)
Skylark of space
Smith, Edward Elmer
Skylark series (1)
Skylark of Valeron
Smith, Edward Elmer
Skylark series (3)
Skylark Three
Smith, Edward Elmer
Skylark series (2)
Skyline message
Carter, Nicholas
Nicholas Carter series (554)
Skymaze
Rubinstein, Gillian
Space demons trilogy (2)
Skyprobe
McCutchan, Philip
Commander Esmonde Shaw series (8)
Skyrider
Bower, Bertha Muzzy
Skyrider series (1)
Skyriders
Wallace, Trevor
John Tracy series (1)
Skyripper
Drake, David
Kelly series (1)
Skyroad to mystery
Knight, Clayton
Pepe and Ronnie series (3)
Skyrocket Steele
Goulart, Ron
Skyrocket Steele series (1)
Skyrocket Steele conquers the universe, and other media tales
Goulart, Ron
Skyrocket Steele series (2)
Sky's the limit
Ladline, Robert
J A Remington series (3)
Skysweeper
Pendleton, Don
Mack Bolan series (69)
Skytorn
Kruchten, Marcia
Omni odysseys trilogy (3)
Skyway vampire
Conde, Phillip
Irving Todd series (4)
Slab happy
Prather, Richard Scott
Shell Scott series (15)
Slackness
Brooke, Jonathan
Backstreets series (1)
Slade
Deeping, Warwick
James Slade series (1)
Tuttle, Gene
Silent Slade series (1)
Slade of the Yard
Essex, Richard
John Slade series (1)
Lessinger series (1)
Slade, range detective
Tuttle, Gene
Silent Slade series (3)
Slade scores again
Essex, Richard
John Slade series (2)
Lessinger series (2)
Slade story
Tremlett, George
Rock stars series (7)
Slain by the Doones, and other stories
Blackmore, Richard Doddridge
Lorna Doone series (2)
Slam bang!
Burningham, John
First words series (4)
Slam book fever
Pascal, Francine
Sweet Valley High series (48)
Slammers down!
Johnson, Todd
Combat Command series (4)
Slammer's down
Johnson, Todd
Hammer's Slammers series (6)
Slander most savage
Meadows, Rose
Hanover succession series (4)
Slapdash alterations
Barkin, Carol
Slapdash series (3)
Slapdash cooking
Barkin, Carol
Slapdash series (2)
Slapdash decorating
Barkin, Carol
Slapdash series (4)
Slapdash sewing
Barkin, Carol
Slapdash series (1)
Slashback
Levine, Paul
Jake Lassiter series (4)
Slasher
Collins, Max Allan
Quarry series (4)
Collins, Michael
Dan Fortune series (10)
Hamill, Edson T
Joe Ryker series (8)
Slashing blades
Porter, Mark
Win Hadley series (5)
Slate
Aldyne, Nathan
Dan Valentine and Clarissa Lovelace series (3)
Slate landscape
Turner, James Ernest
Rampion Savage series (9)
Slattery
Lawrence, Steven C
Tom Slattery series (1)
Slattery stands alone
Lawrence, Steven C
Tom Slattery series (8)
Slattery's gun says no
Lawrence, Steven C
Tom Slattery series (6)
Slaugher Road
Gilman, George G
Edge series (22)
Slaughter
Clement, Henry
Slaughter series (1)
Kelton, Elmer
Crow Feather series (1)
Slaughter and Son
Majors, E B
Slaughter and Son series (1)
Slaughter at Buffalo Creek
Cunningham, Chet
Pony soldiers series (1)
Slaughter at Paxico
Colter, Dale
Regulator series (12)
Slaughter at Salerno
Kessler, Leo
Wotan series (20)
Slaughter at Ten Sleep
McElwain, Dean L
Preacher's law series (5)
Slaughter City
Davis, Gordon
Sergeant series (6)
Slaughter day
Carter, Nick
Nick Carter series (218)
Slaughter express
Sharpe, Jon
Trailsman series (58)
Slaughter ground
Kessler, Leo
Wotan series (13)
Slaughter horse
Maguire, Michael
Simon Drake series (2)
Slaughter in El Salvador
Rosenberger, Joseph
Death Merchant series (55)
Slaughter in September
Jason, Stuart
Butcher series (29)
Slaughter in Sinaloa
Thorne, Ramsay
Captain Gringo series (17)
Slaughter in the sun
Christie, Stephen
Sexton Blake series (1611)
Slaughter Mountain run
Dever, Joe
Freeway warrior series (2)
Slaughter on Sicily
Bradley, Jack
Battlesquad 1942 series (2)
Slaughter on Sunday
Kane, Henry
Peter Chambers series (8)
Slaughter run
Kilgore, Axel
They call me the Mercenary series (2)
Slaughter summit
Mandell, Mark
Nazi hunter series (2)
Slaughter time
Muir, James A
Breed series (15)
Slaughter zone
Garrett, Frank
Killsquad series (8)
Slaughterday
Gilman, George G
Edge series (24)
Slaughtered lovelies
Stanford, Don
Dallas Webster series (1)
Slaughterhouse
Hutson, Shaun
Sergeant Rolf Kessler series (4)
Scarpetta, Frank
Marksman series (7)
Slaughter's big rip-off
Kane, Abel
Slaughter series (2)
Slave
Corder, Eric
Shame and glory series (1)
Slave bangle
Leroux, Gaston
Joseph Rouletabille series (4)
Slave brain
Reid, Desmond
Sexton Blake series (1602)
Slave girl of Gor
Norman, John
Tarl Cabot series (11)
Slave hunter
Sharpe, Jon
Trailsman series (10)
Slave lady
Fitzgerald, Julia
Slave series (2)
Slave of crime
Carter, Nicholas
Nicholas Carter series (555)
Slave of Frankenstein
Myers, Robert John
Frankenstein sequels series (5)
Slave of Sarma
Lord, Jeffrey
Richard Blade series (4)
Slave of the warmonger
Kilgore, Axel
They call me the Mercenary series (7)
Slave queen
Ledd, Paul
Shelter Morgan series (25)
Slave raiders
Thorne, Ramsay
Captain Gringo series (28)
Slave rebellion
Daniels, Norman A
Jubal trilogy (2)
Slave safari
Murphy, Warren Burton
Destroyer series (12)
Slave ship
Corder, Eric
Shame and glory series (3)
Slave ship from Sergan
Kern, Gregory
Cap Kennedy series (2)
Slave trade
Bainbridge, Chuck
Hard corps series (4)
Slavemaster
Carter, Nick
Nick Carter series (53)
Slavers
McCurtin, Peter
Carmody series (2)
Telfair, Richard
Monty Nash series (5)
Slaver's secret
Quiroule, Pierre
Sexton Blake series (810)
Slaves for seduction
Janson, Hank
Hank Janson series (101)
Slaves of Allah
Burgin, George Brown
Slaves of Allah series (1)
Slaves of Paris
Gaboriau, Emile
Monsieur Lecoq series (4)
Slaves of Reglathium
Sirota, Mike
Dannus series (5)
Slaves of Sabrehill
Giles, Raymond
Sabrehill series (2)
Slaves of space
Verseau, Dominique
Yolanda series (2)
Slaves of Spiegel
Pinkwater, Daniel Manus
Magic Moscow series (3)
Slaves of Sumuru
Rohmer, Sax
Sumuru series (2)
Slaves of the abyss
Mason, Paul
Fighting fantasy gamebook series (33)
Slaves of the lamp
Bronson-Howard, George
Yorke Norroy series (2)
Frankau, Pamela
Clothes of a king's son trilogy (2)
Slaves of the Padishah
Jokai, Mor
Michael Apafi series (2)
Slaves of the scorpion
House, Brant
Secret Agent X series (16)
Slaves of the volcano god
Gardner, Craig Shaw
Cineverse trilogy (1)
Slaves of Venus
Byrne, Stuart James
Star Man series (2)
Slave's revenge
Tralins, Sandor Robert
Black stud trilogy (3)
Slave's tale
Haugaard, Erik Christian
Hakon and Helga series (2)
Slay me a sinner
Audemars, Pierre
Monsieur Pinaud series (23)
Slay ride
Kane, Frank
Johnny Liddell series (3)
Slay-ride for Cutie
Janson, Hank
Hank Janson series (13)
Slay the loose ladies
Quentin, Patrick
Peter Duluth series (4)
Slay the murderer
Holman, Hugh
Sheriff Macready series (2)
Slay time
Muller, Paul
Paul Muller series (7)
Slayboys
Kirk, Philip
Butler series (3)
Slayground
Stark, Richard
Parker series (14)
Slaying in September
Mackintosh, Ian
Tim Blackgrove series (1)
Slaying of Julian Summers
Williams, Richard
Sexton Blake series (1560)
Slaying on the sixteenth floor
Maclean, Arthur
Sexton Blake series (1422)
Slayride
Mitchell, Red
Doc McDuff and Popcorn Pruitt series (2)
Sleaze
Morse, Larry Alan
Sam Hunter series (2)
Sledge hammer crimes
Grant, Maxwell
Shadow series (107)
Sledgehammer
Hutson, Shaun
Sergeant Rolf Kessler series (1)
Sleek the otter
Evens, George Bramwell
Romany readers series (8)
Sleep!
Creasey, John
Doctor Palfrey series (23)
Sleep and his brother
Dickinson, Peter
Superintendent James Pibble series (4)
Sleep for the wicked
Howard, Hartley
Glenn Bowman series (10)
Sleep in a ditch
Birmingham, Maisie
Kate Weatherley series (3)
Sleep in peace
Bentley, Phyllis
West Riding series (10)
Sleep is deep
Nelson, Hugh Lawrence
Jim Dunn series (5)
Sleep is for the rich
Mackenzie, Donald
Harry Chalice and Crying Eddie series (3)
Sleep long, my love
Waugh, Hillary
Chief Fred Fellows series (1)
Sleep long, my lovely
Winter, Bevis
Steve Craig series (8)
Sleep, my love
Martin, Robert Lee
Jim Bennett series (2)
Sleep, my pretty one
Howard, Hartley
Glenn Bowman series (15)
Sleep no more
Erskine, Margaret
Inspector Septimus Finch series (10)
Ryerson, Florence
Jimmy Lane series (3)
Taylor, Sam S
Neal Cotton series (1)
Sleep of death
Morice, Anne
Tessa Crichton Price series (17)
Sleep of reason
Snow, Charles Percy
Strangers and brothers series (10)
Sleep out
Carrick, Carol
Sleep out series (1)
Sleep while I sing
Wright, Laurali R
Sergeant Karl Alberg series (2)
Sleep with nightmares
Cooke, David Coxe
Peter Rourke series (3)
Sleep with slander
Hitchens, Dolores
Jim Sader series (2)
Sleep with strangers
Hitchens, Dolores
Jim Sader series (1)
Sleep with the devil
Keene, Day
Les Ferron series (1)
Sleepbusters
Walker, Mort
Hi and Lois series (11)
Sleepers
Voltz, William
Perry Rhodan series (79)
Sleepers of Erin
Gash, Jonathan
Lovejoy series (7)
Sleeping
Ormerod, Jan
Baby books series (3)

Sleeping beauty
Macdonald, Ross
Lew Archer series (18)

Sleeping Beauty at Sugar Creek
Hutchens, Paul
Sugar Creek Gang series (33)

Sleeping bomb
Moffatt, James
Silas Manners series (1)

Sleeping death
Cole, George Douglas Howard
Everard Blatchington series (4)

Sleeping dog
Lochte, Dick
Leo Bloodworth and Serendipity Dahlquist series (1)

Sleeping dogs
Wells, Carolyn
Kenneth Carlisle series (1)

Sleeping dogs lying
O'Hara, Kenneth
Alun Barry series (2)

Sleeping dragon
Rosenberg, Joel
Guardians of the flame series (1)

Sleeping draught
Adams, Herbert
Major Roger Bennion series (23)

Sleeping in flame
Carroll, Jonathan
Bones series (2)

Sleeping island
Vivian, Francis
Inspector Gordon Knollis series (8)

Sleeping life
Rendell, Ruth
Chief Inspector Reginald Wexford series (10)

Sleeping murder
Christie, Agatha
Miss Jane Marple series (5)

Sleeping policeman
Taylor, Andrew
William Dougal series (7)

Sleeping sorceress
Moorcock, Michael
Elric series (4)

Sleeping sphinx
Carr, John Dickson
Doctor Gideon Fell series (17)

Sleeping spy
Burkholz, Herbert
Eddie Mancuso and Vasily Borgneff series (2)

Sleeping sword
Frye, Pearl
Lord Horatio Nelson series (2)
Jagger, Brenda
Barforth trilogy (3)

Sleeping tiger
Jobson, Hamilton
Inspector Anders series (15)

Sleeping time Bunny
Cosgrove, Stephen Edward
Baby Bunny series (2)

Sleeping warrior
Gowans, Elizabeth
Blair family series (3)

Sleeping witch
Storey, Margaret
Timothy, Ellen and Melinda series (3)

Sleepless man
Evans, Gwyn
Double O'Day series (4)

Sleepless nights
Moberg, Vilhelm
Earth is ours trilogy (2)

Sleepover friends
Saunders, Susan
Sleepover friends series (14)

Sleepwalker
Stine, Robert Lawrence
Fear Street series (12)

Sleepwalkers
Broch, Hermann
Sleepwalkers trilogy (3)

Sleepy death
Ashe, Gordon
Patrick Dawlish series (27)

Sleepy-eyed blonde
Monmouth, Jack
Tom Langley series (3)

Sleepy heads
Fisher, Aileen
Ways of animals series (8)

Sleepy, sleepy
Morris, Ann
Sleepy series (4)

Sleepy time tales of Apricot Farm
Hodgetts, Sheila
Sleepy time tales series (1)

Sleepy time tales of Cherub Village
Hodgetts, Sheila
Sleepy time tales series (2)

Sleepy time tales of Playtime Village
Hodgetts, Sheila
Sleepy time tales series (3)

Sleepy time tales of Playtown
Hodgetts, Sheila
Sleepy time tales series (3)

Sleepy time tales of Puddletown
Hodgetts, Sheila
Sleepy time tales series (4)

Sleepy time tales of the little cherubs
Hodgetts, Sheila
Sleepy time tales series (2)

Sleigh bells for Windy Foot
Frost, Frances Mary
Windy Foot series (2)

Sleight of body
McInerny, Ralph
Father Roger Dowling series (12)

Slender margin
Francis, Basil
Sergeant Paul Dean series (2)

Sleuth hound
Leroux, Gaston
Joseph Rouletabille series (5)

Sleuth of Saint James's Square
Post, Melville Davisson
Sir Henry Marquis series (1)

Sleuth of Study Thirteen
Havilton, Jeffrey
Study Thirteen series (3)

Slice
Miller, Rex
Jack Eichord series (4)

Slice of hell
Roscoe, Mike
Johnny April series (3)

Sliced heather on toast
Johnson, Lissa Halls
China Tate series (1)

Slick and the dead
Cleife, Philip
Martyn Finch series (2)
Hardin, J D
Raider and Doc series (3)

Slick-iron
Scott, Bradford
Walt Slade series (19)

Slick revenge
Nazel, Joseph
Iceman series (3)

Slickensides
Hilton, John Buxton
Inspector Thomas Brunt series (6)

Slicko, the jumping squirrel
Barnum, Richard
Kneetime animal stories series (2)

Slievelea
Lyons, Genevieve
Slievelea series (1)

Slight case of champagne
Halliday, Fred
Stanley Delphond series (3)

Slight case of murder
Desmond, Hugh
Alan Fraser series (23)

Slight mourning
Aird, Catherine
Inspector C D Sloan series (6)

Slightly bitter taste
Carmichael, Harry
John Piper and Quinn series (27)

Slik
Tremlett, George
Rock stars series (11)

Slim Goodbody's health days diary
Burstein, John
Slim Goodbody series (4)

Slime
Halkin, John
Slither trilogy (2)

Slime that at Sweet Valley
Pascal, Francine
Sweet Valley twins series (53)

Slimtails
Chell, Mary
Slimtails series (1)

Slimtails at home
Chell, Mary
Slimtails series (10)

Slimtails' friends
Chell, Mary
Slimtails series (4)

Slimtails' new house
Chell, Mary
Slimtails series (6)

Slimtails' picnic
Chell, Mary
Slimtails series (9)

Slimtails' triplets
Chell, Mary
Slimtails series (5)

Slimy book
Cole, Babette
Hairy book series (2)

Slingshot
Jackman, Stuart
Jesus Davidson series (2)

Slip-carriage mystery
Brock, Lynn
Colonel Gore series (4)

Slip coach
Baines, Cuthbert
Dennis Doyne series (1)

Slip gun
Edson, John Thomas
Waxahachie Smith series (2)

Slipback
Saward, Eric
Doctor Who series (162)

Slippery Ann
Bailey, Henry Christopher
Mister Joshua Clunk series (9)

Slippery as sin
Souvestre, Pierre
Fantomas series (6)

Slippery Dick
Adams, Herbert
Major Roger Bennion series (26)

Slippery staircase
Lorac, E C R
Inspector Macdonald series (15)

Slit my throat
Brett, Michael
Pete McGrath series (9)

Slither
Halkin, John
Slither trilogy (1)

Slitherfoot
Reese, Bob
Grand Canyon series (4)

Slob
Miller, Rex
Jack Eichord series (1)

Slocum and the Abilene swindle
Logan, Jake
John Slocum series (116)

Slocum and the Apache raiders
Logan, Jake
John Slocum series (147)

Slocum and the Arizona cowboys
Logan, Jake
John Slocum series (98)

Slocum and the Arizona kidnappers
Logan, Jake
John Slocum series (114)

Slocum and the avenging gun
Logan, Jake
John Slocum series (79)

Slocum and the blood rage
Logan, Jake
John Slocum series (109)

Slocum and the Bozeman Trail
Logan, Jake
John Slocum series (87)

Slocum and the buffalo hunters
Logan, Jake
John Slocum series (118)

Slocum and the buffalo soldiers
Logan, Jake
John Slocum series (179)

Slocum and the bushwhackers
Logan, Jake
John Slocum series (163)

Slocum and the cattle queen
Logan, Jake
John Slocum series (57)

Slocum and the cattle war
Logan, Jake
John Slocum series (133)

Slocum and the Cherokee manhunt
Logan, Jake
John Slocum series (106)

Slocum and the claim jumpers
Logan, Jake
John Slocum series (105)

Slocum and the cowtown kill
Logan, Jake
John Slocum series (184)

Slocum and the Cracker Creek killers
Logan, Jake
John Slocum series (110)

Slocum and the crooked judge
Logan, Jake
John Slocum series (124)

Slocum and the deadly feud
Logan, Jake
John Slocum series (94)

Slocum and the deadwood treasure
Logan, Jake
John Slocum series (149)

Slocum and the death council
Logan, Jake
John Slocum series (155)

Slocum and the death dealer
Logan, Jake
John Slocum series (145)

Slocum and the forty thieves
Logan, Jake
John Slocum series (170)

Slocum and the gold slaves
Logan, Jake
John Slocum series (187)

Slocum and the gun runners
Logan, Jake
John Slocum series (71)

Slocum and the gunfighter's greed
Logan, Jake
John Slocum series (112)

Slocum and the gunfighter's return
Logan, Jake
John Slocum series (120)

Slocum and the hanging party
Logan, Jake
John Slocum series (152)

Slocum and the hanging tree
Logan, Jake
John Slocum series (115)

Slocum and the hatchet men
Logan, Jake
John Slocum series (64)

Slocum and the horse thieves
Logan, Jake
John Slocum series (88)

Slocum and the Idaho breakout
Logan, Jake
John Slocum series (129)

Slocum and the Indian ghost
Logan, Jake
John Slocum series (95)

Slocum and the invaders
Logan, Jake
John Slocum series (182)

Slocum and the Laredo showdown
Logan, Jake
John Slocum series (104)

Slocum and the law
Logan, Jake
John Slocum series (53)

Slocum and the long wagon train
Logan, Jake
John Slocum series (93)

Slocum and the lost Dutchman mine
Logan, Jake
John Slocum series (61)

Slocum and the mad major
Logan, Jake
John Slocum series (34)

Slocum and the mountain of gold
Logan, Jake
John Slocum series (183)

Slocum and the nightriders
Logan, Jake
John Slocum series (174)

Slocum and the noose of hell
Logan, Jake
John Slocum series (89)

Slocum and the outlaw's trail
Logan, Jake
John Slocum series (126)

Slocum and the phantom gold
Logan, Jake
John Slocum series (180)

Slocum and the Plains massacre
Logan, Jake
John Slocum series (128)

Slocum and the Plains rampage
Logan, Jake
John Slocum series (144)

Slocum and the preacher's daughter
Logan, Jake
John Slocum series (119)

Slocum and the railroad baron
Logan, Jake
John Slocum series (157)

Slocum and the Red River renegade
Logan, Jake
John Slocum series (111)

Slocum and the river chase
Logan, Jake
John Slocum series (158)

Slocum and the sharpshooter
Logan, Jake
John Slocum series (160)

Slocum and the Silver Ranch fight
Logan, Jake
John Slocum series (92)

Slocum and the stagecoach bandits
Logan, Jake
John Slocum series (151)

Slocum and the timber king
Logan, Jake
John Slocum series (156)

Slocum and the tin star swindle
Logan, Jake
John Slocum series (173)

Slocum and the Tong warriors
Logan, Jake
John Slocum series (125)

Slocum and the town tamer
Logan, Jake
John Slocum series (140)

Slocum and the trail of death
Logan, Jake
John Slocum series (150)

Slocum and the widow Kate
Logan, Jake
John Slocum series (3)

Slocum and the wild stallion chase
Logan, Jake
John Slocum series (103)

Slocum and the Wyoming frame-up
Logan, Jake
John Slocum series (164)

Slocum at Outlaw's Haven
Logan, Jake
John Slocum series (176)

Slocum at the El Paso blood feud
Logan, Jake
John Slocum series (108)

Slocum gets even
Logan, Jake
John Slocum series (60)

Slocum in Deadwood
Logan, Jake
John Slocum series (69)

Slocum rides alone
Logan, Jake
John Slocum series (80)

Slocum's blood
Logan, Jake
John Slocum series (16)

Slocum's bust out
Logan, Jake
Slocum giant series (1)

Slocum's code
Logan, Jake
John Slocum series (28)

Slocum's command
Logan, Jake
John Slocum series (59)

Slocum's crime
Logan, Jake
John Slocum series (73)

Slocum's deadly game
Logan, Jake
John Slocum series (100)

Slocum's debt
Logan, Jake
John Slocum series (33)
John Slocum series (132)

Slocum's drive
Logan, Jake
John Slocum series (50)

Slocum's fire
Logan, Jake
John Slocum series (17)

Slocum's flag
Logan, Jake
John Slocum series (30)

Slocum's fortune
Logan, Jake
John Slocum series (148)

Slocum's gamble
Logan, Jake
John Slocum series (32)

Slocum's gold
Logan, Jake
John Slocum series (6)

Slocum's good deed
Logan, Jake
John Slocum series (75)

Slocum's grave
Logan, Jake
John Slocum series (20)

Slocum's hell
Logan, Jake
John Slocum series (19)

Slocum's justice
Logan, Jake
John Slocum series (55)

Slocum's pride
Logan, Jake
John Slocum series (72)

Slocum's rage
Logan, Jake
John Slocum series (26)

Slocum's raid
Logan, Jake
John Slocum series (29)

Slocum's revenge
Logan, Jake
John Slocum series (18)

Slocum's run
Logan, Jake
John Slocum series (31)

Slocum's slaughter
Logan, Jake
John Slocum series (24)
Slocum's stampede
Logan, Jake
John Slocum series (76)
Slocum's standoff
Logan, Jake
John Slocum series (154)
Slocum's war
Logan, Jake
Slocum giant series (2)
Slocum's winning hand
Logan, Jake
John Slocum series (70)
Slocum's woman
Logan, Jake
John Slocum series (9)
Slocum's women
Logan, Jake
John Slocum series (58)
Slogum House
Sandoz, Mari
Nebraska trilogy (1)
Sloop of war
Kent, Alexander
Captain Richard Bolitho series (5)
Slow and sure
Alger, Horatio
Tattered Tom series (4)
Slow approach of thunder
Paustovsky, Konstantin Georgievich
Story of a life series (2)
Slow boats home
Young, Gavin
Slow boats series (2)
Slow boats to China
Young, Gavin
Slow boats series (1)
Slow burn
Bland, Eleanor Taylor
Marti MacAlister series (2)
Ehrlich, Jack
Robert Flick series (2)
Slow burner
Haggard, William
Colonel Charles Russell series (1)
Slow dancing
Cooper, M E
Couples series (22)
Slow death
Logan, Jake
John Slocum series (127)
Wilson, Gar
Phoenix Force series (28)
Slow death at Geneva
Diplomat
Dennis Tyler series (6)
Slow dying
James, William M
Apache series (18)
Slow fall to dawn
Leigh, Stephen
Neweden trilogy (1)
Slow on the feather
Blunt, Wilfrid
Single life series (2)
Slow poison
Barrington, Pamela
Inspector George Marshall series (10)
Rowland, John
Inspector Shelley series (8)
Slow squeeze
Pugh, Dianne G
Iris Thorne series (2)
Slow vengeance
Bude, John
Inspector Meredith series (9)
Slow Wolf and Dan Fox
Grover, Marshall
Larry and Stretch series (398)
Slowly sweats the gun, and other tales of an earlier outback Australia
Garvey, Keith
Outback tales series (5)
Slug it slay
Lanham, Edwin
Lieutenant Madigan series (1)
Slugger
Malloch, Peter
Inspector Dave Norton series (2)
Slugger Mike
Davis, Gibbs
Never sink nine series (3)
Slugs
Hutson, Shaun
Slugs series (1)
Slumber party secret
Keene, Carolyn
Nancy Drew notebooks series (1)
Slump
Kroll, Steven
Hit and Run Gang series (3)
Sly as a serpent
Halliday, Michael
Doctor Emmanuel Cellini series (3)
Sly spy
Sharmat, Marjorie Weinman
Olivia Sharp series (3)
Slype
Thorndike, Russell
Mister Macauley series (1)
Smack man
Demille, Nelson
Joe Keller series (1)
Keller series (1)
Small and deadly
Marsh, John
Ray Felton series (4)
Small boa to Luxembourg
Pilkington, Roger
Small boat series (12)
Small boat in southern France
Pilkington, Roger
Small boat series (9)
Small boat on the Lower Rhine
Pilkington, Roger
Small boat series (16)
Small boat on the Meuse
Pilkington, Roger
Small boat series (11)
Small boat on the Moselle
Pilkington, Roger
Small boat series (13)
Small boat on the Thames
Pilkington, Roger
Small boat series (10)
Small boat on the Upper Rhine
Pilkington, Roger
Small boat series (17)
Small boat through Belgium
Pilkington, Roger
Small boat series (1)
Small boat through France
Pilkington, Roger
Small boat series (8)
Small boat through Germany
Pilkington, Roger
Small boat series (7)
Small boat through Holland
Pilkington, Roger
Small boat series (2)
Small boat through Sweden
Pilkington, Roger
Small boat series (4)
Small boat to Alsace
Pilkington, Roger
Small boat series (5)
Small boat to Bavaria
Pilkington, Roger
Small boat series (6)
Small boat to Elsinore
Pilkington, Roger
Small boat series (14)
Small boat to northern Germany
Pilkington, Roger
Small boat series (15)
Small boat to the Skagerrak
Pilkington, Roger
Small boat series (3)
Small but deadly wars
Heath, Charles
A-Team series (2)
Small change
Philip, Alexander John
James Jameson series (2)
Small general
Standish, Robert
Chinese Civil War series (2)
Small gods
Pratchett, Terry
Discworld series (13)
Small house at Allington
Trollope, Anthony
Chronicles of Barsetshire series (5)
Small masterpiece
Heald, Tim
Simon Bognor series (7)
Small mine
Gallie, Menna
Cilhendre Village series (3)
Small person far away
Kerr, Judith
Anna series (3)
Small piece of paradise
Morgan, Geoffrey
Orphan series (1)
Small poems
Worth, Valerie
Small poems series (1)
Small poems again
Worth, Valerie
Small poems series (4)
Small Potatoes and the birthday party
Ziefert, Harriet
Small Potatoes series (4)
Small Potatoes and the magic show
Ziefert, Harriet
Small Potatoes series (2)
Small Potatoes and the sleep-over
Ziefert, Harriet
Small Potatoes series (3)
Small Potatoes Club
Ziefert, Harriet
Small Potatoes series (1)
Small railway engines
Awdry, Wilbert
Railway series (22)
Small rain
L'Engle, Madeleine
Katherine Forrester series (1)
Small sacrifice
Hart, Ellen
Jane Lawless series (5)
Small slain body
Audemars, Pierre
Monsieur Pinaud series (27)
Small souls
Couperus, Louis
Book of small souls quartet (1)
Small talk
Mitchison, Naomi
Small talk series (1)
Small Texan
Edson, John Thomas
Floating Outfit series (57)
Small venom
Mole, William
Casson Duker series (1)
Small world
King, Tabitha
Nodd's Ridge series (1)
Lodge, David
Rummidge University series (2)
Smallbone deceased
Gilbert, Michael Francis
Inspector Hazelrigg series (4)
Smaller penny
Barry, Charles
Superintendent Lawrence Gilmartin series (1)
Smallest bridesmaid
Storey, Margaret
Molly series (2)
Smallest dinosaur in the world
Salmon, Michael
Dinosaur series (6)
Smallest doll
Storey, Margaret
Molly series (1)
Smart bombs
Kirk, Philip
Butler series (2)
Smart enough to know
Goudge, Eileen
Seniors series (2)
Smart fellow
Walsh, Maurice
Thomasheen James series (2)
Smart girls don't talk
Janson, Hank
Hank Janson series (14)
Smart house
Wilhelm, Kate
Charlie Miklejohn and Constance Leidl series (3)
Smart money doesn't sing or dance
Glazner, Joseph Mark
Billy Nevers series (1)
Smart moves
Kaminsky, Stuart Melvin
Toby Peters series (12)
Smartest grave
White, Reginald James
Inspector David Brock series (1)
Smash and grab
Robbins, Clifton
Clay Harrison series (4)
Smashers at school
Gree, Alain
Smashers series (1)
Smashers by the sea
Gree, Alain
Smashers series (3)
Smashers go to market
Gree, Alain
Smashers series (2)
Smashers in the country
Gree, Alain
Smashers series (4)
Smashing!
Hardcastle, Michael
Tony and Jay series (6)
Smashing the Hindenburg Line
Kay, Ross
Big war series (8)
Smashup
Bamman, Henry A
Checkered flag series (4)
Smear job
Mitchell, James
David Callan series (4)
Smell of brimstone
Lister, Stephen
Sainte Monique series (13)
Smell of burning
Lane, Margaret
Shipwreck series (2)
Smell of fear
Dean, Spencer
Don Cadee series (2)
Smell of hay
Bassani, Giorgio
Ferrara series (6)
Smell of money
Newton, William
Joey Binns series (2)
Smell of murder
Van Dine, S S
Philo Vance series (11)
Smell of peardrops
Carstairs, John Paddy
Garaway Trenton series (6)
Smell of smoke
Burton, Miles
Inspector Arnold and Desmond Merrion series (59)
Smelling
Allington, Richard L
Beginning to learn series (8)
Pluckrose, Henry
Thinking about series (3)
Smelly book
Cole, Babette
Hairy book series (3)
Smile a minute
Witwer, Harry Charles
Baseball series (2)
Smile and be a villain
Jobson, Hamilton
Inspector Anders series (2)
Smile and say murder
Keene, Carolyn
Nancy Drew files series (4)
Smile at me, doctor
Delaney, Joyce
No starch in my coat series (2)
Smile, Ernest and Celestine
Vincent, Gabrielle
Ernest and Celestine series (4)
Smile for the past
Ruck, Berta
Storyteller series (2)
Smile of Cheng Su
Thorne, Ernest Pollett
Major Brains Cunningham series (1)
Smile of the stranger
Aiken, Joan
Petworth series (1)
Smile on the face of the tiger
Hurd, Douglas
Foreign Office trilogy (2)
Smile on the face of the tyger
Riefe, Alan
Tyger Decker series (3)
Smiler Bunn brigade
Atkey, Bertram
Smiler Bunn series (2)
Smiler Bunn, byewayman
Atkey, Bertram
Smiler Bunn series (6)
Smiler Bunn, crook
Atkey, Bertram
Smiler Bunn series (9)
Smiler Bunn, gentleman adventurer
Atkey, Bertram
Smiler Bunn series (3)
Smiler Bunn, gentleman crook
Atkey, Bertram
Smiler Bunn series (3)
Smiler Bunn, manhunter
Atkey, Bertram
Smiler Bunn series (4)
Smiler with the knife
Blake, Nicholas
Nigel Strangeways series (5)
Smiles
Robinson, Eliot Harlow
Smiling pass series (1)
Smiley
Raymond, Moore
Smiley series (1)
Smiley Adams
Burrough, Reath J
Smiley Adams series (1)
Smiley gets a gun
Raymond, Moore
Smiley series (2)
Smiley roams the road
Raymond, Moore
Smiley series (3)
Smiley's people
Le Carre, John
George Smiley series (7)
Smilin' on the vine
Hoult, Norah
Augusta Hortense Carey series (1)
Smiling corpse
Bailey, Hilea
Hilea Bailey and Hilary Dunsany Bailey series (3)
Smiling death
Grierson, Francis Durham
Inspector Sims and Professor Wells series (5)
Smiling dogs
Robeson, Kenneth
Avenger series (10)
Smiling pass
Robinson, Eliot Harlow
Smiling pass series (2)
Smiling Sandy
Dolce, Janet Ellen
Baby doll board books series (1)
Smiling, the boy fell dead
Delving, Michael
Dave Cannon and Robert Eddison series (1)
Smiling tiger
Offord, Lenore Glen
Todd McKinnon series (3)
Smire
Cabell, James Branch
Nightmare trilogy (3)
Smirt
Cabell, James Branch
Nightmare trilogy (1)
Smite the rock!
Davis, Oswald Harcourt
Ardencester series (2)
Smith
Cabell, James Branch
Nightmare trilogy (2)
Christie, Kate
Harold Crane series (1)
Smith and Jones
Monsarrat, Nicholas
Signs of the times series (2)
Smith and the pharaohs, and other tales
Haggard, Henry Rider
Allan Quatermain series (12)
Smith, as hero
Brooks, Jeremy
Bernard Smith series (2)
Smith family at home
Blyton, Enid
Smith family series (1)
Smith family at the circus
Blyton, Enid
Smith family series (3)
Smith family at the zoo
Blyton, Enid
Smith family series (2)
Smith Minor on the moon
Hardy, Philip
Smith Minor series (2)
Smith of the Secret Service
Scott, Reginald Thomas Maitland
Aurelius Smith series (3)
Smith takes a bath
Strong, J J
Smith series (2)
Smithfield slayer
Bruton, Eric
City of London Police series (4)
Smiths
Fairbank, Janet Ayer
Rich man, poor man trilogy (2)
Smiths in war-time
Howard, Keble
Smiths trilogy (3)
Smiths of Surbiton
Howard, Keble
Smiths trilogy (1)
Smiths of Valley View
Howard, Keble
Smiths trilogy (2)
Smith's tail
Strong, J J
Smith series (1)
Smith's week
Bell, Robert Stanly Warren
Greyhouse series (7)
Smithsonian snafu
Conroy, Richard Timothy
Henry Scruggs series (1)
Smithy
Wallace, Edgar
Smithy series (1)

Smithy abroad
Wallace, Edgar
Smithy series (2)
Smithy and the Hun
Wallace, Edgar
Smithy series (4)
Smithy, not to mention Nobby Clark and Spud Murphy
Wallace, Edgar
Smithy series (1)
Smithy's friend Nobby
Wallace, Edgar
Smithy series (3)
Smitty
Gutman, Bill
Smitty series (1)
Smitty does a bunk
Sutton-Smith, Brian
Smitty series (2)
Smocker takes off
Lumbers, Eugene
Smocker series (2)
Smog
Creasey, John
Doctor Palfrey series (28)
Smoke
Barling, Tom
Smoke series (1)
Smoke across the fell
Sutton, Graham
Fleming family series (3)
Smoke against the sky
Cole, Jackson
Jim Hatfield series (7)
Smoke and ashes
Sologub, Fedor
Created legend trilogy (3)
Smoke detector
Wright, Eric
Inspector Charlie Salter series (2)
Smoke dragon
Barling, Tom
Smoke series (2)
Smoke from the ashes
Johnstone, William Wallace
Ashes series (7)
Smoke horse
Faulknor, Cliff
Eagle Child trilogy (3)
Smoke in the lanes
Reeve, Dominic
Gypsy life series (1)
Smoke jumper
Montgomery, Raymond A
Choose your own adventure series (111)
Smoke over Sikanska
Gowland, John Stafford
Sikanska series (1)
Smoke patrol
Atwater, Montgomery Meigs
Hank Winton series (2)
Smoke ring
Niven, Larry
Known Space series (16)
Trees series (2)
Smoke screen
Glick, Ruth
Charisma Inc. series (3)
Hale, Christopher
Lieutenant Bill French series (1)
Smoke screen mystery
Dixon, Franklin W
Hardy boys series (105)
Smoke without fire
Ferrars, Elizabeth
Andrew Basnett series (6)
Seth, Ronald
Brian Grant series (6)
Smoked out
Murphy, Warren Burton
Digger Burroughs series (1)
Smoker's cough
Sewart, Alan
Detective Sergeant Chamberlayne series (3)
Smoking iron
Field, Peter
Powder Valley series (20)
Smoky hell trail
Sharpe, Jon
Trailsman series (79)
Smoky Hill
Coldsmith, Don
Rivers west series (2)
Smoky Joe
Meynell, Laurence Walter
Smoky Joe series (1)
Smoky Joe goes to school
Meynell, Laurence Walter
Smoky Joe series (3)
Smoky Joe in trouble
Meynell, Laurence Walter
Smoky Joe series (2)
Smoky road
Gruber, Frank
Historical Western series (6)
Smoky the bear
Verral, Charles Spain
Smoky the bear series (1)
Smoky the bear and his animal friends
Verral, Charles Spain
Smoky the bear series (2)
Smotherly love
Browne, Dik
Hagar the horrible series (39)
Smouldering fire
Stevenson, Dorothy Emily
Ardfalloch series (1)
Smouldering fuse
French, Fergus
General Ogle-Oxley series (1)
Smudge
Wensell, Ulises
Jackson family series (4)
Smudger's Saturday special
Saddler, Allen
Smudger series (2)
Smudger's seaside spectacular
Saddler, Allen
Smudger series (1)
Smuggled sin
Harragan, Steve
Steve Harragan series (6)
Smugglers
Dicks, Terrance
Doctor Who series (133)
Petersen, Paul
Smugglers series (1)
Willoughby, Lee Davis
Making of America series (34)
Smuggler's brand
Scott, Bradford
Walt Slade series (37)
Smugglers' Castle
Carus, Zena M
Smugglers' Castle series (1)
Smuggler's embrace
Chase, Carolyn
Thirteen colonies series (3)
Smuggler's gap
Atkinson, Mary Evelyn
Lockett family series (4)
Smuggler's gold
Cherryh, Carolyn Janice
Merovingen nights series (4)
Smugglers' moon
Robertson, Colin
Peter Grayleigh series (16)
Smugglers of death
Grant, Maxwell
Shadow series (165)
Smugglers of the skies
Leyland, Eric
Hunter Hawk series (3)
Smuggler's pay for Firebrace
Seafarer
Captain Firebrace series (4)
Smugglers' Reef
Blaine, John
Rick Brant series (7)
Smugglers' secret
Lloyd, Hugh
Hal Keen series (4)
Smurf of one and Smurf a dozen of the other
Peyo
Smurf series (9)
Smurf stories
Peyo
Smurf series (8)
Smurfette
Peyo
Smurf series (2)
Smurfic games
Peyo
Smurf series (9)
Smurfs and the egg
Peyo
Smurf series (4)
Smurfs and the howlibird
Peyo
Smurf series (10)
Smurfs and the magic flute
Peyo
Smurf series (10)
Smurf's apprentice
Peyo
Smurf series (7)
Smurftraps
Peyo
Smurf series (7)
Smurphony in C
Peyo
Smurf series (3)
Smut the hare
Evens, George Bramwell
Romany readers series (2)
Snaggle doodles
Giff, Patricia Reilly
Kids of the Polk Street School series (8)
Snail and caterpillar
Piers, Helen
Little creature series (1)
Snail and the Pennithornes
Willard, Barbara
Snail and Pennithorne series (1)
Snail and the Pennithornes and the princess
Willard, Barbara
Snail and Pennithorne series (3)
Snail and the Pennithornes next time
Willard, Barbara
Snail and Pennithorne series (2)
Snail's tale
Laird, Elizabeth
Toucan Tecs series (12)
Snake
McClure, James
Lieutenant Kramer and Sergeant Zondi series (4)
Spillane, Mickey
Mike Hammer series (9)
Snake boats
Macdonnell, James Edmond
Captain Peter Bentley series (35)
Snake dance
Mariz, Linda
Laura Ireland series (2)
Snake doctor
Garrison, Christian
Ace Chaney series (1)
Snake doctor, and other stories
Cobb, Irwin Shrewsbury
Judge Priest series (4)
Snake eater
Tapply, William George
Brady Coyne series (12)
Snake eyes
Austin, Richard
Guardians series (15)
Snake Eyes
Bishop, Pike
Cord Diamondback series (3)
Snake flag conspiracy
Carter, Nick
Nick Carter series (107)
Snake in the grass
Gilbert, Anthony
Arthur Crook series (27)
Wellard, James
Lucius Hunt series (1)
Snake is living yet
Gilruth, Susan
Inspector Hugh Gordon and Liane Crawford series (7)
Snake oil
Roberts, Les
Saxon series (4)
Snake oil wars
Godwin, Parke
Snake oil wars series (2)
Snake on 99
Farrar, Stewart
Inspector Elwyn Morgan series (1)
Snake pit
Undset, Sigrid
Master of Hestviken series (2)
Snake ring mystery
Wallace, Ivy Lilian
Warrenders series (4)
Snake River
Blevins, Win
Rivers west series (9)
Snake tattoo
Barnes, Linda
Carlotta Carlyle series (3)
Snake, the crocodile and the dog
Peters, Elizabeth
Amelia Peabody Emerson series (7)
Snake who was afraid of people
Polisar, Barry Louis
Snakes series (2)
Snakedance
Dicks, Terrance
Doctor Who series (83)
Snakegod
Goulart, Ron
Vampirella series (6)
Snakes alive!
Davis, Anne
Pumpkin Hill fact series (4)
Snakes and ladders
Bogarde, Dirk
Orderly man series (2)
Broome, Adam
Commissioner Denzil Grigson series (5)
Snakes and the boy who was afraid of them
Polisar, Barry Louis
Snakes series (1)
Snakes in the grass
Hilary, Richard
Ezell Barnes series (1)
Snaketown
Dawson, Clay
Long Rider series (16)
Snap judgment
Stuart, Anthony
Vladimir Gull series (1)
Snapdragon murders
Healey, Ben
Paul Hedley series (7)
Snapper
Doyle, Roddy
Barrytown trilogy (2)
Snappy answers to stupid questions, number five
Jaffee, Al
Snappy answers to stupid questions series (5)
Snappy answers to stupid questions, number seven
Jaffee, Al
Snappy answers to stupid questions series (7)
Snapshot
Barnes, Linda
Carlotta Carlyle series (6)
Taylor, John Robert
Snapshot series (1)
Snapshot Max
Turk, Hanne
Max the Mouse series (12)
Snare
Moffat, Gwen
Miss Melinda Pink series (9)
Snare and the game
Carter, Nicholas
Nicholas Carter series (291)
Snare Andalucian
Stein, Aaron Marc
Matt Erridge series (7)
Snare for Catherine
Benzoni, Juliette
Catherine Legoix series (6)
Snare in the dark
Parrish, Frank
Dan Mallett series (3)
Snares of death
Charles, Kate
David Middleton-Brown series (2)
Snares of ibex
Clayton, Jo
Diadem series (8)
Snark
De Andrea, William Louis
Clifford Driscoll series (2)
Snarkout boys and the avocado of death
Pinkwater, Daniel Manus
Snarkout boys series (1)
Snarkout boys and the Baconbury horror
Pinkwater, Daniel Manus
Snarkout boys series (2)
Snarl of the beast
Daly, Carroll John
Race Williams series (1)
Snarl of the lynx
Charles, Robert
Counter-terror series (6)
Snarled identities
Carter, Nicholas
Nicholas Carter series (621)
Snarly Snuffins
Cosgrove, Stephen Edward
Snuffin chronicles series (1)
Snatch
Ashe, Gordon
Patrick Dawlish series (31)
Goldman, Raymond Leslie
Asaph Clume series (4)
Graeme, Bruce
Detective Sergeant Robert Mather series (4)
Pronzini, Bill
Private Eye series (1)
Snatch an eye
Kane, Henry
Peter Chambers series (22)
Snatch game
Brandon, John Gordon
Arthur Stukeley Pennington series (6)
Inspector Patrick Aloysius McCarthy series (8)
Snatch of music
Peters, Ludovic
Ian Firth series (1)
Snatched dame
Elliott, William James
Ed Gunning series (2)
Sneaking out
Pascal, Francine
Sweet Valley twins series (5)
Sneaks
Green, Edith
Dearborn V Pinch series (2)
Sneaky Sam
Kurland, Michael
Mission series (4)
Sneeze and be slain, and other incredible stories
Hunter, Norman
Kingdom of Incredibilia series (6)
Sneezing spell
Becker, Eve
Abracadabra series (4)
Sniff shout
Burningham, John
First words series (1)
Snipe hunt
Dean, Amber
Albie Harris series (6)
Sniper
Demille, Nelson
Joe Ryker series (1)
Helm, Eric
Super Vietnam series (5)
Mackenzie, Steve
Seals series (10)
Pentecost, Hugh
John Jericho series (1)
Williams, Richard
Sexton Blake series (1576)
Sniping
Idriess, Ion Llewellyn
Australian guerilla series (2)
Snively Snuffin
Cosgrove, Stephen Edward
Snuffin chronicles series (3)
Snobs, beware
Sharmat, Marjorie Weinman
Sorority sisters series (2)
Snook the barn owl
Evens, George Bramwell
Romany readers series (4)
Snopes
Faulkner, William
Snopes family trilogy (3)
Snow
Burningham, John
Little book series (3)
Cooney, Caroline B
Fog series (2)
Porteous, Crichton
Mossdyche series (2)
Van der Essen, Anne
Yok-yok series (10)
Snow along the border
Sawkins, Raymond
Superintendent John Snow series (3)
Snow at Blackberry Farm
Pilgrim, Jane
Blackberry Farm series (21)
Snow bird
Pye, Virginia
Price family series (2)
Snow bowl
Mooser, Stephen
All-Star Meatballs series (5)
Snow Bumble
Eldon, Magdalen
Bumble series (2)
Snow Cubby
Tucker, Jenni
Cubby series (2)
Snow dog
Kjelgaard, Jim
Chiri series (1)
Snow-Eyes
Smith, Stephanie Ann
Snow-Eyes series (1)
Snow Hawk
McFarlane, Leslie
Checkmate series (6)
Snow, ice and bullets
Brogan, Mike
Action Man series (2)

Snow in paradise
Sawkins, Raymond
Superintendent John Snow series (2)
Snow in Venice
Davies, Frederick
Hitman series (2)
Snow-job
Copper, Basil
Mike Faraday series (45)
Snow job
Gair, Malcolm
Mark Raeburn series (6)
Snow kill
Andrews, Keith William
Freedom's Rangers series (6)
Snow lady
Hughes, Shirley
Tale of Trotter Street series (2)
Snow mountain
Gavin, Catherine
Twentieth-century Europe series (2)
Snow on Blueberry Mountain
Meader, Stephen Warren
Blueberry Mountain series (2)
Snow on high ground
Sawkins, Raymond
Superintendent John Snow series (1)
Snow on the high ground
Ward, Ruth Cameron
Swallows eaves series (2)
Snow on the wind
Miller, Hugh
District nurse series (2)
Snow queen
Hamilton, Julia
Habsburg series (4)
Snow Queen
Vinge, Joan Dennison
Snow Queen series (1)
Snow-Queen of the air
Carter, Dorothy
Marise Duncan series (3)
Snow rattlers
Rifkin, Shepard
Damian McQuaid series (2)
Snow ride
Bryant, Bonnie
Saddle Club series (20)
Snow-shoes and sledges
Munroe, Kirk
Pacific coast series (2)
Snow spider
Nimmo, Jenny
Snow spider trilogy (1)
Snow spider trilogy
Nimmo, Jenny
Snow spider trilogy (3)
Snow White and Rose Red
McBain, Ed
Matthew Hope series (5)
Snow-White murder
Ford, Leslie
Colonel John Primrose series (5)
Grace Latham series (5)
Snow Womble
Beresford, Elisabeth
Little Wombles series (1)
Snowball
Allbeury, Ted
Tad Anders series (1)
Snowball in hell
Lassiter, Adam
Dennison's war series (6)
Snowblind moon
Cooke, John Byrne
Snowblind moon trilogy (1)
Snowbound
Martin, Ann Matthews
Baby-Sitters Club super specials series (7)
Snowbound at Forty-Five Acres
Wildsmith, Alan
Forty-Five Acres series (2)
Snowbound bus
Edwin, Maribel
Baird family series (2)
Snowbound in camp
Hope, Laura Lee
Blythe girls series (9)
Snowbound mystery
Warner, Gertrude Chandler
Boxcar children series (13)
Snowbound with Betsy
Haywood, Carolyn
Betsy series (9)
Snowbrother
Stirling, Stephen Michael
Fifth millenium series (1)
Snowcastles
McGeary, Duncan
Greylock of Godshome series (1)
Snowdrift
Hendryx, James Beardsley
Corporal Downey series (2)
Snowdrifts
Postgate, Oliver
Ivor the engine series (2)
Snowdrop story book
Blyton, Enid
Flower story book series (5)
Snowed-in family
Hill, Mabel Betsy
Judy Jo series (6)
Snowey and McGlusky
Hales, Alfred Greenwood
McGlusky series (15)
Snowflake and Shaky
Gould, Chester
Dick Tracy cartoon series (4)
Snowjob
Wood, Ted
Reid Bennett series (9)
Snowline
Brierley, David
Cody series (4)
Mather, Berkely
Idwal Rees series (3)
Snowman
Briggs, Raymond
Snowman series (1)
Haldeman, Charles
Joseph's Landing series (2)
Levy, Muriel
Wonk series (6)
Snowman cometh
Reid, Desmond
Sexton Blake series (1592)
Snowman in flames
Darlton, Clark
Perry Rhodan series (25)
Snows of Jaspre
Caraker, Mary
Seven worlds series (2)
Snows of Sebastopol
Gobineau, Marceline
Stephanie series (2)
Snowshoe twins
Tompkins, Jane
Animal twins series (4)
Snowstone
Scott, James Maurice
Jeremy Jackson series (1)
Snowstorm at Green Valley
Gorelick, Molly Chernow
Rescue series (5)
Snowy day
Keats, Ezra Jack
Peter series (1)
Snowy River brumby
Mitchell, Elyne
Silver Brumby series (9)
Snowy Toes and the magic music box
Matthews, Patrick
Teddy Edward's books for bears series (2)
Snuffy
Bruna, Dick
Snuffy series (1)
Snuffy and the fire
Bruna, Dick
Snuffy series (2)
Snuffy's puppies
Bruna, Dick
Snuffy series (3)
Snug and Serena count twelve
Uttley, Alison
Little Brown Mouse series (13)
Snug and Serena go to town
Uttley, Alison
Little Brown Mouse series (14)
Snug and Serena meet a queen
Uttley, Alison
Little Brown Mouse series (1)
Snug and Serena pick cowslips
Uttley, Alison
Little Brown Mouse series (2)
Snug and the chimney sweeper
Uttley, Alison
Little Brown Mouse series (8)
Snug and the silver spoon
Uttley, Alison
Little Brown Mouse series (12)
Snug harbor
Optic, Oliver
Boat builders series (2)
Snugg
Cosgrove, Stephen Edward
Bugg series (9)
Snugg and shoe fly flue
Cosgrove, Stephen Edward
Bugg series (15)
Snugglepot and Cuddlepie
Gibbs, May
Gumnut Land series (6)
Snugglepot and Cuddlepie find Ragged Blossom
Gibbs, May
Gumnut Land series (6)
Snugglepot and Cuddlepie meet Mister Lizard
Gibbs, May
Gumnut Land series (6)
Snugglepot and Cuddlepie on board the Snag
Gibbs, May
Gumnut Land series (6)
Snuggly
Slater, Jim
A Mazing Monster series (9)
So bad a death
Wright, June
Sergeant Matheson series (2)
So be it
Gide, Andre
Journal series (7)
So blue marble
Hughes, Dorothy Belle
Inspector Tobin series (1)
So brief the spring
Greenwood, Walter
Trelooe series (1)
So can I
Ahlberg, Allan
Red nose readers series (4)
So cold, my bed
Taylor, Sam S
Neal Cotton series (3)
So dead the rose
Chaber, M E
Milo March series (9)
So deadly sinner
Brown, Carter
Danny Boyd series (1)
So deep the river
Spade, Danny
Danny Spade series (11)
So Guy came too
Hill, Lorna
Marjorie series (4)
Patience series (4)
So help me Hannah
Malloy, Lester
Martin Moon series (3)
So Hi and the white horses of Fu
Beaton-Jones, Cynon
So Hi series (2)
So like sleep
Healy, Jeremiah
John Francis Cuddy series (3)
So long, and thanks for all the fish
Adams, Douglas Noel
Arthur Dent series (4)
So long as you both shall live
McBain, Ed
Eighty Seventh Precinct series (31)
So long, senior year
Harrell, Janice
In crowd series (4)
So long to learn
Douie, Charles
Weary road series (3)
So lush, so deadly
Halliday, Brett
Michael Shayne series (59)
So many doors
Hocking, Anne
Inspector William Austen series (3)
Punshon, Ernest Robertson
Bobby Owen series (26)
So many malls
Evans, Greg
Luann series (7)
So Moses was born
Grant, Joan
Far memory series (4)
So move the body
Brown, Carter
Danny Boyd series (24)
So much blood
Brett, Simon
Charles Paris series (2)
So much for Gennaro
Palmer, John
Guy Plante and Freya Matthews series (2)
So much in the dark
Bude, John
Inspector Meredith series (23)
So near, so far
Parkinson, Cyril Northcote
Richard Delancey series (4)
So near the heart
Walden, Amelia
Miranda Welch trilogy (2)
So pretty a problem
Duncan, Francis
Mordecai Euripides Tremaine series (4)
So quiet a death
Morland, Nigel
Mrs Palmyra Pym series (21)
So red the rose
Young, Stark
Feliciana series (1)
So rich, so lovely and so dead
Masur, Harold Q
Scott Jordan series (4)
So sits the turtle
Traill, Peter
Mister Cribbage series (3)
So sweet, so deadly
Rico, Don
Casey Grant series (3)
So the lady died
Hale, Edgar
Inspector Michael Regan series (5)
So thin the line
McLaughlin, William Raffan Davidson
Antarctic series (2)
So this is depravity
Baker, Russell
Good times series (2)
So this is love
Coffman, Elaine
Mackinnon brothers series (7)
So what killed the vampire?
Brown, Carter
Larry Baker series (3)
So who wants to be popular anyway?
Balluck, Georgia Ann
Fifteen series (3)
So wild the sea
Vines, Freda
Western Australian series (2)
So you want to be a wizard?
Duane, Diane
Wizard series (1)
So young, so cold, so fair
Creasey, John
Inspector Roger West series (16)
So young to burn
Creasey, John
Inspector Roger West series (36)
Soap opera slaughters
Kaye, Marvin
Hilary Quayle series (5)
Soap star
Pascal, Francine
Sweet Valley High series (85)
Soaps in the afternoon
Harris, Lavinia
Computer detectives series (2)
Soapy Smith heads north
Strong, Charles Stanley
Soapy Smith series (2)
Sobaka
Duke, Madelaine
Modern youth trilogy (1)
Sober as a judge
Cecil, Henry
Roger Thursby series (3)
Soccer
Gutman, Bill
Go for it series (10)
Soccer at Sandford
Childs, Rob
Sandford series (1)
Soccer for boys and girls
Gutman, Bill
Start right and play well series (5)
Soccer is also a game
Hardcastle, Michael
Scorton Rovers series (1)
Social death
Yates, Renate
Inspector Ereache O'Shea series (1)
Social gangster
Reeve, Arthur Benjamin
Craig Kennedy series (7)
Social order today
Gourley, Frank Alan
Even gods err trilogy (2)
Social storming
Martyn, Wyndham
Anthony Trent series (12)
Society and the sexual life
Pendleton, Don
Sexual life series (3)
Society of fear
Arvay, Harry
Israeli Security Branch series (12)
Triad series (2)
Society of nine
Carter, Nick
Nick Carter series (146)
Society of the dispossessed
Foxall, Raymond
John Crispin series (1)
Society of the Spiders
Daniel, Roland
Bill Saville series (1)
Society of the spiders
Daniel, Roland
Wu Fang series (1)
Sock-it-to-em murders
Deming, Richard
Mod Squad series (3)
Sock it to me
Gray, Rod
Lady from L.U.S.T. series (10)
Sock it to me, zombie!
Paul, F W
Man from S.T.U.D. series (3)
Socorro
Mitchum, Hank
Stage coach station series (44)
Socorro Island treasure
Dengler, Sandy
Daniel Tremain series (1)
Socrates meets Jesus
Kreeft, Peter
Socrates series (2)
Sod house
Coatsworth, Elizabeth
Once-upon-a-time-in-America series (6)
Sod-house days
Hunkins, Ralph Valentine
Tales of the prairies series (3)
Sod-house winter
Judson, Clara Ingram
They came from series (1)
Soeur Angele and the bellringer's niece
Catalan, Henri
Soeur Angele series (6)
Soeur Angele and the embarrassed ladies
Catalan, Henri
Soeur Angele series (1)
Soeur Angele and the ghosts of Chambord
Catalan, Henri
Soeur Angele series (2)
Soft cargo
Janson, Hank
Hank Janson series (189)
Soft centre
Chase, James Hadley
Frank Terrell series (1)
Soft goods
Davis, Oswald Harcourt
Ardencester series (1)
Soft machine
Burroughs, William Seward
Tangier trilogy (1)
Soft sell
Bruce, Jean
Secret Agent O.S.S.117 series (6)
Soft soap
Elsschot, Willem
Laarmans series (1)
Soft target
Nolan, Frederick
Garrett dossier series (6)
Soft whisper of the dead
Grant, Charles Lewis
Oxrun Station series (7)
Soft whisper trilogy (1)
Softball
Gutman, Bill
Go for it series (2)
Softball for boys and girls
Gutman, Bill
Start right and play well series (6)
Softcover kill
Harknett, Terry
Stephen Wayne series (9)
Softener
Bolton, Melvin
Lawson of the Special Branch series (1)
Softly by moonlight
Fane, Bron
La noire series (3)
Softly in the night
Chaber, M E
Milo March series (11)
Softly, softly
Jones, Elwyn
Chief Inspector Barlow series (12)
Softly, softly casebook
Yarrow, Arnold
Chief Inspector Barlow series (6)
Softly, softly murder casebook
Yarrow, Arnold
Chief Inspector Barlow series (7)

Software
Rucker, Rudy
Software series (1)
Software Superslug
Dunbar, Joyce
Software Superslug series (1)
Software Superslug and the great computer stupor
Dunbar, Joyce
Software Superslug series (2)
Software Superslug and the nutty novelty knitting
Dunbar, Joyce
Software Superslug series (3)
Soho Cafe crime
Sayer, Walter William
Sexton Blake series (398)
Soho jungle
Bateson, David
Larry Vernon series (4)
Soho spy
Robertson, Colin
Inspector Robert Strong series (4)
Soho Square
Rayner, Claire
Performers series (4)
Soil
Zola, Emile
Rougon Macquart series (15)
Soil upturned
Sholokhov, Mikhail
Don series (5)
Sojourn
Salvatore, Robert Anthony
Dark elf trilogy (3)
Solal of the Solals
Cohen, Albert
Gallants series (1)
Solander box mystery
Knight, Leonard Alfred
Jerry Scant series (5)
Solar assassins
Mahr, Kurt
Perry Rhodan series (49)
Solar barque
Nin, Anais
Cities of the interior series (5)
Solar invasion
Wellman, Manly Wade
Captain Future series (12)
Solar kill
Ingrid, Charles
Sand wars series (1)
Solar menace
Carter, Nick
Nick Carter series (150)
Solar system
Roop, Peter
Great mysteries series (3)
Sold for slaughter
Pendleton, Don
Mack Bolan series (60)
Soldato!
Conroy, Al
Johnny Morini series (1)
Solden's woman
Turner, Bill
Detective Inspector Manson series (5)
Soldier, ask not
Dickson, Gordon Rupert
Dorsai series (3)
Soldier born
O'Riordan, Conal
Anglo-Irish relations series (1)
Soldier boy
Optic, Oliver
Army and navy series (1)
Soldier erect
Aldiss, Brian Wilson
Horace Stubbs series (2)
Soldier from the wars returning
Carrington, Charles
Subaltern series (2)
Soldier no more
Price, Anthony
Doctor David Audley and Jack Butler series (11)
Soldier of another fortune
Shupp, Mike
Destiny makers series (3)
Soldier of Arete
Wolfe, Gene
Latro series (2)
Soldier of fortune
Palmer, Diana
Mercenary series (1)
Sadler, Barry
Casca series (8)
Soldier of Gideon
Sadler, Barry
Casca series (20)
Soldier of the mist
Wolfe, Gene
Latro series (1)
Soldier of the Queen
Hennessy, Max
Cavalry trilogy (1)
Soldier of the wilderness
Tomlinson, Everett Titsworth
Colonial series (3)
Soldier of Waterloo
O'Riordan, Conal
Anglo-Irish relations series (2)
Soldier returns
Burstall, Terry
Long Tan series (2)
Soldier spies
Baldwin, Alex
Men at war series (3)
Soldier who came back
Chester, Gilbert
Sexton Blake series (1092)
Soldier with the Arabs
Glubb, John Bagot
Desert war series (1)
Soldiering on
Barker, Dennis
People of the forces trilogy (1)
Soldiers and sailors
Greene, Carla
What do they do series (3)
Soldier's art
Powell, Anthony
Dance to the music of time series (8)
Soldier's end
O'Riordan, Conal
Anglo-Irish relations series (4)
Soldier's medal
Helm, Eric
Ground Zero series (5)
Zlotnik, Donald E
Fields of honor series (4)
Soldiers of fortune
Willoughby, Lee Davis
Making of America series (30)
Soldiers of misfortune
Wren, Percival Christopher
Otho Belleme series (1)
Soldiers of paradise
Park, Paul
Starbridge series (1)
Soldiers of the sea
Waite, Jon
Warriors of America trilogy (1)
Soldier's song
Sharpe, Jon
Canyon O'Grady series (11)
Soldier's story
Burstall, Terry
Long Tan series (1)
Soldier's wife
O'Riordan, Conal
Anglo-Irish relations series (3)
Soldiers' wives
Harris, Marion
Soldiers and officers series (1)
Sole agent
Benton, Kenneth
Peter Craig series (2)
Sole survivor
Gee, Maurice
Plumb trilogy (3)
Murphy, Warren Burton
Destroyer series (72)
Murray, Will
Destroyer series (72)
Soledad brother
Jackson, George
Soledad brother series (1)
Solemn high murder
Byfield, Barbara
Simon Bede and Helen Bullock series (1)
Solid as a rock
Hunter, E J
White Squaw series (10)
Solid gold kidnapping
Richards, Evan
Six Million Dollar Man series (7)
Solid gold screw
Paul, F W
Man from S.T.U.D. series (4)
Solid ground
Miller, Hugh
Teen Eastenders series (1)
Solid waste
Snodgrass, Mary Ellen
Environmental awareness series (4)
Solip system
Williams, Walter Jon
Hardwired trilogy (3)
Solitaries of Sambuca
Mauldsley, Daniel
Christopher and Cressida series (1)
Solitary blue
Voigt, Cynthia
Tillermans series (3)
Tillermans series (4)
Solitary summer
Russell, Mary Annette
Elizabeth series (2)
Solitary war
Williamson, Henry
Chronicles of ancient sunlight series (13)
Solo
Mason, Robert Caverly
Weapon series (2)
Solo the dragon learns to fly
Robinson, Mike
Solo the dragon series (1)
Solomon
Daniel, Rebecca
Our greatest heritage series (9)
Solomon builds a temple
Goodman, Montague
Wantoknow series for boys (6)
Solomon goes to school
Goodman, Montague
Wantoknow series for boys (6)
Solomon Kane
Howard, Robert Ervin
Solomon Kane series (1)
Solomon King's mine
Hawkes, Zachary
Fancy Hatch series (3)
Solomon Leviathan's nine hundred and thirty-first trip around the world
Le Guin, Ursula Kroeber
Adventures in Kroy series (2)
Solomon's quest
Bedford-Jones, Henry
John Solomon trilogy (1)
Solstice
Payack, Paul J J
Solstice series (1)
Solstice II
Payack, Paul J J
Solstice series (2)
Solstice III
Payack, Paul J J
Solstice series (3)
Solution, escape
Cooper, Margaret Chilvers
Stefan and Evonn series (1)
Solved in thirty-six hours!
Gibbons, Harry Hornaby Clifford
Sexton Blake series (286)
Solved mysteries
M'Govan, James
James M'Govan series (5)
Soma
Platt, Charles
Aton series (4)
Somali smashout
McCurtin, Peter
Jim Rainey series (17)
Some adventures of the Noah family, including Japhet
Horrabin, James Francis
Noah family series (1)
Some avenger, rise!
Egan, Lesley
Jesse Falkenstein series (4)
Some beasts no more
Giles, Kenneth
Inspector Harry James and Sergeant Honeybody series (1)
Some birds have funny names
Cross, Diana Harding
Funny names series (1)
Some brief folly
Veryan, Patricia
Age of Elegance series (8)
Golden chronicles series (6)
Some buried Caesar
Stout, Rex
Nero Wolfe and Archie Goodwin series (6)
Some can whistle
McMurtry, Larry
Danny Deck series (2)
Some choose hell
Hild, Jack
SOBS series (9)
Some dames are deadly
Latimer, Jonathan
Bill Crane series (5)
Some dames don't
Muller, Paul
Paul Muller series (11)
Some dames play rough
Mitchell, Scott
Brock Devlin series (1)
Some day I'll kill you
Chambers, Dana
Jim Steele series (1)
Some die eloquent
Aird, Catherine
Inspector C D Sloan series (8)
Some die hard
Quarry, Nick
Jake Barrow series (6)
Some die slow
Herber, William
Jimmy Rehm series (1)
Some die young
Duff, James P
Johnny Phelan series (1)
Some died laughing
Dolphin, Rex
Sexton Blake series (1489)
Some distance
Messerli, Douglas
River to rivet trilogy (2)
Some do not
Ford, Ford Madox
Parade's end series (1)
Some ducks have all the luck
Korman, Justine
Donald Duck series (1)
Some experiences of an Irish R.M.
Somerville, Edith Oenone
Irish R.M. series (1)
Some further adventures of Mister P J Davenant
Hamilton, Frederic
P J Davenant series (2)
Some Irish yesterdays
Somerville, Edith Oenone
Irish R.M. series (3)
Some lie and some die
Rendell, Ruth
Chief Inspector Reginald Wexford series (8)
Some like it cool
Kyle, Robert
Ben Gates series (4)
Some look better dead
Janson, Hank
Hank Janson series (18)
Some more memoirs
Burgin, George Brown
Clubman series (4)
Some must watch
Cobb, Belton
Bryan Armitage series (10)
Inspector Cheviot Burmann series (34)
Kitty Armitage series (7)
Some notes on lifemanship
Potter, Stephen
Lifemanship Correspondence College series (2)
Some notes on The flax of dreams, and other essays
Williamson, Henry
Flax of dream series (5)
Some of my best friends are monsters
Coville, Bruce
Camp Haunted Hills series (2)
Some of the days of Everett Anderson
Clifton, Lucille
Everett Anderson series (1)
Some other summer
Adler, Carole Schwerdtfeger
Glits series (2)
Some plants have funny names
Cross, Diana Harding
Funny names series (2)
Some predators are male
Tripp, Miles
John Samson series (8)
Some recollections of my early days written at different periods
Boswell, Annabella
Early day series (1)
Some run crooked
Hilton, John Buxton
Superintendent Simon Kenworthy series (5)
Some slips don't show
Fair, A A
Bertha Cool and Donald Lam series (17)
Some summer lands
Gaskell, Jane
Atlan saga series (4)
Some talk of Alexander
Bridie, James
Mavor series (1)
Some unaccountable exploits of Sherlock Holmes
Fisher, Charles
Sherlock Holmes sequels series (7)
Some unknown hand
Hamilton, Elaine
Inspector Reynolds series (1)
Some Vermonters
Hard, Walter
Vermont series (1)
Some women of the University
Blayre, Christopher
University of Cosmopoli series (3)
Some women won't wait
Fair, A A
Bertha Cool and Donald Lam series (14)
Somebody has to lose
Chambers, Peter
Mark Preston series (18)
Somebody kid
Graeber, Charlotte Towner
Mister T and me series (9)
Somebody killed the messenger
Watson, Clarissa
Persis Willum series (5)
Somebody somewhere
Williams, Donna
Nobody somebody series (2)
Somebody to kill
Reinsmith, Richard
Bodyguard series (7)
Somebody wants me dead
Williams, Richard
Sexton Blake series (1549)
Somebody's awake
Rogers, Paul
Somebody series (2)
Somebody's sleepy
Rogers, Paul
Somebody series (1)
Someday I'll kill you
Desmond, Hugh
Alan Fraser series (26)
Someday soon
Tyler, Vicki
Heart to heart series (1)
Someday the Rabbi will leave
Kemelman, Harry
Rabbi David Small series (8)
Somenody at the door
Postgate, Raymond
Inspector Holly series (1)
Someone else
Stuart, Becky
Kellogg Brown and Carey Ashton series (2)
Someone falling
Ambler, Dail
Danny Spade series (36)
Someone has to take the fall
Newton, William
Joey Binns series (1)
Someone in the attic
Wayne, Jenifer
Winchester family series (5)
Someone in the house
Michaels, Barbara
Greyhaven Manor series (2)
Someone is talking about Hortense
Marshall, James
Four little troubles series (2)
Someone must die
Cumberland, Marten
Saturnin Dax series (1)
Someone to love
Farewell, Nina
Unfair sex series (2)
Someone walked ovr my grave
O'Sullivan, James Brendan
Steve Silk series (8)
Someone's death
Larson, Charles
Nils-Frederick Blixen series (1)
Someone's sleeping in my bed
Gonzales, John
Harry Horne series (2)
Someone's stolen Nellie Grey
Walker, Ira
Steve Rhoden series (1)
Somersaults
Haigh, Sheila
Little gymnast series (2)
Somerset murder case
Flynn, Brian
Anthony Bathurst series (19)
Something about Eve
Cabell, James Branch
Dom Manuel and his descendants series (13)

Something about midnight
Olsen, D B
Professor A Pennyfeather series (4)
Something always happens
Macgregor, Reginald James
Nothing and something series (2)
Something borrowed, something blue
Goudge, Eileen
Super-seniors series (3)
Nordtvedt, Matilda
Bride series (2)
Weber, Lenora Mattingly
Beany Malone series (13)
Something doing
Vanardy, Varick
Crewe series (2)
Something for nothing
Story, Jack Trevor
Albert Argyle series (2)
Something fresh
Wodehouse, Pelham Grenville
Blandings Castle series (1)
Something hidden
Clark, Sheila
Star trek fan series (9)
Something in the air
Lathen, Emma
John Putnam Thatcher series (20)
Something in the barn
Wayne, Jenifer
Winchester family series (6)
Something lost
Clark, Sheila
Star trek fan series (32)
Something more to say
Inchfawn, Fay
Personal recording series (2)
Something nasty in the woodshed
Bonfiglioli, Kyril
Charlie Mortdecai series (2)
Gilbert, Anthony
Arthur Crook series (10)
Something new
Cooper, M E
Couples series (24)
Wodehouse, Pelham Grenville
Blandings Castle series (1)
Something old, something new
Baer, Judy
Cedar River daydreams series (11)
Chase, Emily
Canby Hall series (32)
Hulke, Malcolm
Crossroads series (3)
Nordtvedt, Matilda
Bride series (1)
Something on the stairs
Maddock, Stephen
Timothy Terrel series (16)
Something queer at the ball park
Levy, Elizabeth
Something queer series (2)
Something queer at the birthday party
Levy, Elizabeth
Something queer series (8)
Something queer at the haunted school
Levy, Elizabeth
Something queer series (5)
Something queer at the lemonade stand
Levy, Elizabeth
Something queer series (6)
Something queer at the library
Levy, Elizabeth
Something queer series (3)
Something queer in outer space
Levy, Elizabeth
Something queer series (9)
Something queer in rock 'n roll
Levy, Elizabeth
Something queer series (7)
Something queer is going on
Levy, Elizabeth
Something queer series (1)
Something queer on vacation
Levy, Elizabeth
Something queer series (4)
Something shady
Dreher, Sarah
Stoner McTavish series (2)
Something special for me
Williams, Vera Baker
Something special series (2)
Something the cat dragged in
Macleod, Charlotte
Professor Peter Shandy series (4)
Something to hide
Burton, Miles
Inspector Arnold and Desmond Merrion series (46)
Keene, Carolyn
Nancy Drew files series (41)
Macdonald, Philip
Colonel Anthony Ruthven Gethryn series (11)
Monsarrat, Nicholas
Signs of the times series (4)
Something to hold on to
Cobb, Richard
Still life series (3)
Something to kill about
Reid, Desmond
Sexton Blake series (1593)
Something under the bed is drooling
Watterson, Bill
Calvin and Hobbes series (3)
Something up a sleeve
Lockridge, Richard
Assistant District Attorney Bernie Simmons series (6)
Something very fishy
Tranter, Nigel Godwin
Donald Macdonald series (1)
Something wicked
Ferrars, Elizabeth
Andrew Basnett series (1)
Hart, Carolyn Gimpel
Annie Laurance and Max Darling series (3)
McCutcheon, Hugh
Jimmy Carroll series (5)
Something wrong
Linington, Elizabeth
Sergeant Ivor Maddox series (4)
Something wrong at Chillery
Foster, Reginald Francis
Anthony Ravenhill series (7)
Something's happened to Kate
Holden, Genevieve
Lieutenant Al White series (4)
Sometime never
Pickles, Wilfred
You and me series (2)
Sometime wife
Brown, Carter
Danny Boyd series (14)
Sometimes a great notion
Kesey, Ken
Chief Bromden series (2)
Sometimes a stranger
Weber, Lenora Mattingly
Stacy and Katie Rose Belford series (8)
Sometimes I hate school
Barkin, Carol
Transition series (4)
Sometimes river
Blashki, Pam
Fire, drought and flood trilogy (3)
Sometimes they bite
Block, Lawrence
Bernie Rhodenbarr series (6)
Matthew Scudder series (11)
Sometimes you could die
Mitchell, James
Ron Hogget series (1)
Somewhere a cat is waiting
Tangye, Derek
Minack chronicles series (9)
Somewhere a voice is calling
Lodwick, John
Desmond Thornton series (1)
Somewhere along the way
Coffman, Elaine
Mackinnon brothers series (6)
Somewhere east of life
Aldiss, Brian Wilson
Squire quartet (4)
Somewhere in New Guinea
Clune, Frank
Discovery series (16)
Somewhere in Red Gap
Wilson, Harry Leon
Red Gap series (2)
Somewhere in the house
Daly, Elizabeth
Henry Gamadge series (10)
Somewhere in the night
Barclay, Bill
Jerry Cornell series (1)
Nick Allard series (1)
McMahan, Jeffrey N
Vampires series (1)
Somewhere in this city
Procter, Maurice
Chief Inspector Harry Martineau series (6)
Somewhere in this house
King, Rufus
Lieutenant Valcour series (2)
Somewhere out there
Fane, Bron
La noire series (2)
Somewhere over the orgy
Kaye, Maggie
Oz series (51)
Son
Dixelius, Hildur
Sara Alelia trilogy (2)
Son avenger
Undset, Sigrid
Master of Hestviken series (4)
Son for Roxana
Moray, Helga
Roxana trilogy (3)
Son of a servant
Strindberg, Johan August
Soul's development trilogy (1)
Son of a witch
Conway, Troy
Coxeman series (26)
Son of Billabong
Bruce, Mary Grant
Billabong series (14)
Son of Black Beauty
Briggs, Phyllis
Black Beauty series (2)
Son of Blackshirt
Graeme, Bruce
Lord Blackshirt series (1)
Son of Columbus
Baumann, Hans
America-Africa-Asia trilogy (1)
Son of Dracula
Ambrus, Victor Gyozo
Dracula trilogy (3)
Son of dust
Prescott, Hilda Frances Margaret
Mediaeval France trilogy (3)
Son of Erin
Swan, Annie Shepherd
Son of Erin series (1)
Son of Fletch
McDonald, Gregory
Fletch series (10)
Son of Flynn
Laurie-Long, Ernest
Captain Flynn series (7)
Son of Gun in cheek
Pronzini, Bill
Gun in cheek series (2)
Son of Hylas
Baker, George
Trojan War trilogy (2)
Son of Jesse
Jenkins, Gwyn
Samuel and David series (2)
Son of John Wintringham
Piper, Warrene
Bennet family series (3)
Son of Justin
Vaughan, Richard
Justin Peele series (2)
Son of Kazan
Curwood, James Oliver
Kazan series (2)
Son of liberty
Allen, Willis Boyd
Siege of Boston series (1)
Son of Oscar Wilde
Holland, Vyvyan
Time remembered series (1)
Son of Poop
Locklin, Gerald
Poop series (2)
Son of Porthos
Dumas, Alexandre
Three Musketeers series (3)
Son of Spellsinger
Foster, Alan Dean
Spellsinger series (7)
Son of Taff
Berrisford, Judith Mary
Taff series (2)
Son of Tarzan
Burroughs, Edgar Rice
Tarzan series (4)
Son of the black stallion
Farley, Walter
Black stallion series (3)
Son of the flying tiger
Macao, Marshall
K'ing Kung-Fu series (1)
Son of the hero
Shelley, Rick
Varayan memoir series (1)
Son of the Middle Border
Garland, Hamlin
Middle Border series (1)
Son of the monster
Salmon, Michael
Alexander Bunyip series (2)
Son of the smoky sea
Nutchuk
Smoky sea series (1)
Son of the stars
Jones, Raymond F
Ron Barron series (1)
Son of the werewolf
Smith, Guy Newman
Werewolf trilogy (3)
Son of the whirlwind
Mitchell, Elyne
Silver Brumby series (7)
Son of the White Wolf
Howard, Robert Ervin
El Borak trilogy (2)
Son of the wilderness
Gardner, Maurice Benjamin
Bantan series (2)
Son of Ti-Coyo
Richer, Clement
Ti-Coyo series (2)
Son of Wallingford
Chester, George Randolph
James Rufus Wallingford series (5)
Son of Wu Fang
Daniel, Roland
Wu Fang series (5)
Song dog
McClure, James
Lieutenant Kramer and Sergeant Zondi series (9)
Song for Christina
Saint James, Blakely
Christina Van Bell series (3)
Song for Jess
Cunliffe, John Arthur
Jess the cat series (4)
Song in the green thorn tree
Barke, James
Immortal memory series (2)
Song in their hearts
Lambert, Janet
Jordons series (6)
Tippy Parrish series (7)
Song of a Rowan
Darby, Catherine
Rowan family series (6)
Song of a single note
Barr, Amelia Edith
New York trilogy (3)
Song of corpus juris
Hensley, Joe Louis
Donald Robak series (3)
Song of Erne
Harbinson, Robert
Ulster series (2)
Song of Homana
Roberson, Jennifer
Chronicles of the Cheysuli series (2)
Song of Hugh Glass
Neihardt, John Gneisenau
Cycle of the West series (1)
Song of India
Clune, Frank
Discovery series (9)
Song of Jed Smith
Neihardt, John Gneisenau
Cycle of the West series (5)
Song of Mavin Manyshaped
Tepper, Sheri S
Mavin Manyshaped trilogy (1)
Song of Middle Earth
Harvey, David
Middle Earth series (5)
Song of Orpheus
Hambly, Barbara
Beauty and the Beast trilogy (3)
Song of Pentecost
Corbett, William Jesse
Pentecost trilogy (1)
Song of Phaid the Gambler
Farren, Mick
Song of Phaid the Gambler series (2)
Song of Pongo
Postgate, Oliver
Bagpuss beginners series (2)
Song of Rhanna
Fraser, Christine Marion
Rhanna series (5)
Song of Rhiannon
Walton, Evangeline
Mabinogion series (3)
Song of Ruth
Slaughter, Frank Gill
Biblical series (3)
Song of Salome
Mann, Deborah
Early Christian series (4)
Reign of Herod Antipas trilogy (3)
Song of sixpence
Cronin, Archibald Joseph
Laurence Carroll series (1)
Song of sorcery
Scarborough, Elizabeth Ann
Argonia series (1)
Song of Sula
Derwent, Lavinia
Magnus series (4)
Song of surrender
Bruce, Henry
Eurasian series (3)
Song of the Abbey
Oxenham, Elsie J
Abbey girls second generation series (10)
Patch series (3)
Song of the axe
Williams, Paul Osborne
Pelbar series (6)
Song of the dark druid
Sherman, Josepha
Endless quest series (36)
Song of the dwarves
Gunnarsson, Thorarinn
Song series (1)
Song of the earth
Cordell, Alexander
Mortymers series (4)
Song of the flea
Kersh, Gerald
Harry Fabian series (2)
Song of the Indian wars
Neihardt, John Gneisenau
Cycle of the West series (3)
Song of the messiah
Neihardt, John Gneisenau
Cycle of the West series (4)
Song of the nightingale
Arnold, Bruce
Coppinger tetralogy (2)
Song of the Nile
Roberts, Irene
Ancient Egypt series (4)
Song of the red ruby
Mykle, Agnar
Ash Burlefoot series (2)
Song of the rock
Coldsmith, Don
Spanish bit series (15)
Song of the saurials
Novak, Kate
Finder's stone trilogy (3)
Song of the siren
Carr, Philippa
Daughters of England series (7)
Song of the tide
Raymond, Ernest
London gallery series (11)
Song of the trees
Taylor, Mildred Davis
Logan family series (1)
Song of the unsung
Smith, Vian Crocker
Sappers series (1)
Song of the whip
Evans, Evan
Montana Kid series (3)
Song of the world
Giono, Jean
Song of the world trilogy (1)
Song of three friends
Neihardt, John Gneisenau
Cycle of the West series (2)
Song of Tiadatha
Rutter, Owen
Tiadatha series (1)
Song of war
Braddon, Russell
Hate series (2)
Song of Wirrun
Wrightson, Patricia
Song of Wirrun trilogy (3)
Songs and games of Babyland abroad
Jesse, Louie
Babyland series (2)
Songs for Alex
Duder, Tessa
Alex series (4)
Songs from the drowned lands
Kernaghan, Eileen
Aprilioth trilogy (2)
Songs from the Seashell archives
Scarborough, Elizabeth Ann
Argonia series (2)
Argonia series (4)
Songs my mother taught me
Thomas, Audrey
Isobel Cleary series (1)
Songs of a sentimental bloke
Dennis, Clarence James
Sentimental bloke series (1)
Songs of enchantment
Okri, Ben
Azaro series (2)

Songs of Father Goose for the home, school and nursery
Baum, Lyman Frank
Mother and Father Goose series (2)
Songs of Mister Small
Lenski, Lois
Small family series (10)
Songs of Sesame Street in poems and pictures
Moss, Jeffrey
Sesame Street series (1)
Songs of the Dancing Gods
Chalker, Jack Laurence
Dancing Gods series (4)
Sonia
McKenna, Stephen
Sonia series (1)
Sonia married
McKenna, Stephen
Sonia series (2)
Sonic slave
Kenyon, Paul
Baroness Penelope Saint-John Orsini series (6)
Sonnet for the city
Noonan, Diana
Country and city series (2)
Sonnets from Antan
Cabell, James Branch
Dom Manuel and his descendants series (25)
Sonny
Stuart, Ruth Macenery
Sonny series (1)
Sonny's father
Stuart, Ruth Macenery
Sonny series (2)
Sonny's secret
Delton, Judy
Pee wee scout series (14)
Sonora
Mitchum, Hank
Stage coach station series (9)
Sonora badman
Longtree, Warren T
Ruff Justice series (20)
Sonora lode
Sadler, Jeff
Marshal Andrew Anderson series (2)
Sonora slaughter
James, William M
Apache series (6)
Sonora wildcat
Grover, Marshall
Larry and Stretch series (331)
Sonoran seasons
Jernigan, Gisela
Desert trilogy (3)
Sons
Buck, Pearl Sydenstricker
Wang family series (2)
Sons and daughters
Longstreet, Stephen
Fiore family series (3)
Sons and roses
Morgan, Denise
Ralph de Giret trilogy (3)
Sons and sinners
Hardin, J D
Raider and Doc series (17)
Sons in the saddle
Durack, Mary
Grass castles series (2)
Sons of Eldorado
Cameron, Donald
Eldorado series (2)
Sons of fortune
Macdonald, Malcolm
Stevenson family series (3)
Sons of liberty
Rutledge, Adam
Patriots series (1)
Sons of Satan
Creasey, John
Doctor Palfrey series (8)
Sons of Singermann
Brinig, Myron
Singermann family series (2)
Sons of the Bear-God
Page, Norvell W
Prester John series (2)
Sons of the farm
Porteous, Crichton
Jonas Wishet series (2)
Sons of the forge
Anderson, Helen M
Kelston of Kells series (2)
Sons of the morning
Holden, Matthew
Squadron series (1)
Sons of the others
Gibbs, Philip
Second World War series (1)
Sons of the Sheik
Hull, Edith Maude
Sheik Ahmed ben Hassan series (2)
Sons of the Steppe
Baumann, Hans
America-Africa-Asia trilogy (2)
Sons of the tiger
Case, Patricia
Tiger series (2)
Sons of the titans
Adkins, Patrick H
Titans series (3)
Sons of toil
Sunley, Margaret
Yorkshire Dales trilogy (3)
Sontag of Sundown
Tuttle, Wilbur Coleman
Sad Sontag series (1)
Sad Sontag series (2)
Sonya Begonia and the eleventh birthday blues
Smith, Susan
Best friends series (1)
Sooner or later
Hart, Bruce
Jessie Walters and Michael Skye series (1)
Sooner spy
Lehrer, Jim
One-Eyed Mack series (3)
Sooners
Willoughby, Lee Davis
Making of America series (27)
Soothsayer
Dobson, Margaret
Jane Bailey series (3)
Resnick, Mike
Oracle trilogy (1)
Sooty
Blyton, Enid
Sooty series (2)
Sophie and Gussie
Sharmat, Marjorie Weinman
Sophie and Gussie series (1)
Sophie and Jack
Taylor, Judy
Sophie and Jack series (1)
Sophie and Jack help out
Taylor, Judy
Sophie and Jack series (2)
Sophie and Jack in the rain
Taylor, Judy
Sophie and Jack series (4)
Sophie and Jack in the snow
Taylor, Judy
Sophie and Jack series (3)
Sophie and Nicky and the four seasons
Mangin, Marie France
Suzette and Nicholas series (1)
Willson, Robina Beckles
Suzanne and Nicholas series (3)
Sophie and Nicky go to market
Willson, Robina Beckles
Suzanne and Nicholas series (2)
Sophie and the gipsies
Baker, Harriette Newell Woods
Sophie series (1)
Sophie hits six
King-Smith, Dick
Sophie series (3)
Sophie in the saddle
King-Smith, Dick
Sophie series (4)
Sophie's bucket
Stock, Catherine
Sophie series (1)
Sophie's knapsack
Stock, Catherine
Sophie series (2)
Sophie's letter-book
Baker, Harriette Newell Woods
Sophie series (2)
Sophie's snail
King-Smith, Dick
Sophie series (1)
Sophie's tom
King-Smith, Dick
Sophie series (2)
Sophie's toys
Bruna, Dick
Stories to tell series (3)
Sophomore
Cooney, Linda A
Class of eighty eight series (2)
Class of eighty nine series (2)
Sophomore co-ed
Lee, Alice Lester
Co-ed series (2)
Sophomores of Radcliffe
Kellogg, Elijah
Whispering Pine series (2)
Sophy of Kravonia
Hope, Anthony
Rudolf Rassendyl series (3)
Soppy birthday
Ure, Jean
Woodside School series (3)
Soprano
Barnard, Charles
Soprano series (1)
Crawford, Francis Marion
Paris Opera trilogy (1)
Sorak and the clouded tiger
Richards, Harvey D
Sorak series (2)
Sorak and the sultan's ankus
Richards, Harvey D
Sorak series (3)
Sorak and the tree-men
Richards, Harvey D
Sorak series (4)
Sorak of the Malay jungle
Richards, Harvey D
Sorak series (1)
Sorcerer of the castle
Stevenson, Florence
Kitty Telfair series (5)
Sorcerers
Saint John, David
Peter Ward series (8)
Sorcerer's amulet
Moorcock, Michael
History of Runestaff series (2)
Sorcerer's apprentice
Ewers, Hanns Heinz
Frank Braun series (1)
Rodda, Emily
Teen Power Inc. series (3)
Williams, Michael Leon
From thief to king series (1)
Sorcerer's blood
Coe, Ross Anton
Warrior of vengeance series (1)
Sorcerer's crown
Simon, Morris
Advanced dungeons and dragons adventure gamebook series (6)
Kingdom of sorcery trilogy (2)
Sorcerer's curse
Volsky, Paula
Sorcerer trilogy (3)
Sorcerer's heir
Volsky, Paula
Sorcerer trilogy (2)
Sorcerer's house
Verner, Gerald
Simon Gale series (2)
Sorcerer's lady
Volsky, Paula
Sorcerer trilogy (1)
Sorcerers of Set
Thomas, Martin
Sexton Blake series (1594)
Sorcerers of the frozen isles
Lorrah, Jean
Savage Empire series (5)
Sorcerers' sacred isle
Taylor, Keith
Danans trilogy (1)
Sorcerer's shadow
Smith, David Claude
Oron series (5)
Sorcerer's shaft
Gerard, Francis
Sir John Meredith series (13)
Sorcerer's skull
Vardeman, Robert Edward
Cenotaph Road series (2)
Sorcerer's son
Eisenstein, Phyllis
Sorcerer's son series (1)
Sorcerer's world
Broderick, Damien
Faustus hexagram series (2)
Sorceress
Jakes, John
Brak series (2)
Weinreb, Nathaniel Norsen
Biblical series (2)
Sorceress and the book of spells
Schraff, Anne Elaine
Narnia solo games series (2)
Sorceress and the cygnet
McKillip, Patricia Anne
Cygnet series (1)
Sorceress of Darshiva
Eddings, David
Malloreon series (4)
Sorceress of Qar
White, Ted
Qanar series (2)
Sorceress of Rome
Gallizier, Nathan
Sorceress trilogy (2)
Sorceress of Scath
Eshbach, Lloyd Arthur
Gates of Lucifer series (3)
Sorceress of the Witch World
Norton, Andre
Estcarp series (5)
Witch World series (6)
Sorcery in Shad
Lumley, Brian
Tales of the primal land series (3)
Sorcery spell book
Jackson, Steve
Sorcery series (4)
Sorcery within
Smeds, Dave
War of the dragons series (1)
Sorrowing vengeance
Smith, David Claude
Fall of the first world trilogy (2)
Sorrowing wind
Pearce, Mary Emily
Apple tree series (3)
Sorrows of Priapus
Dahlberg, Edward
Sorrows of Priapus series (1)
Sorrows of Priapus series (2)
Sorrows, passions and alarms
Kirkup, James
Only child series (2)
Sorry, chief
Johnston, William
Maxwell Smart series (2)
Sorry, dad
Blishen, Edward
Schoolmaster series (5)
Sorry I'm late, my hair won't start
Guisewhite, Cathy
Cathy series (7)
Sorry now?
Zubro, Mark Richard
Stonewall Inn series (3)
Sorry state
Kenyon, Michael
Superintendent O'Malley series (4)
Sorry you've been troubled
Cheyney, Peter
Slim Callaghan series (7)
Sort of a cricket person
Swanton, Ernest William
Cricket person series (1)
Sort of introduction
Musil, Robert
Man without qualities series (1)
Sort of madness
Ronald, E B
Rupert Bradley series (3)
Sort of peace
Davis, Margaret Thomson
Glasgow trilogy (3)
Sort of Samurai
Melville, James
Superintendent Tetsuo Otani series (3)
Sort of sisters
Johnson, Stacie
Eighteen Pine Street series (1)
Sort of tragedy
Lauben, Philip
Captain Homer Clay series (3)
Sortie in Cyrenaica
Southall, Ivan
War in the air series (4)
Sos the rope
Anthony, Piers
Battle circle trilogy (1)
Soul brothers and Sister Lou
Hunter, Kristin
Lourette Hawkins series (1)
Soul destroyers
Carter, Nicholas
Nicholas Carter series (579)
Soul drinker
Clayton, Jo
Drinker of souls trilogy (3)
Soul-eater
Brookins, Dana
Bobbie Toppin series (1)
Soul music
Pratchett, Terry
Discworld series (16)
Soul of a child
Bjorkman, Edwin August
Swedish youth series (1)
Soul of Dominic Wildthorne
Hocking, Joseph
Religious questions series (4)
Soul of Lilith
Corelli, Marie
Two worlds series (4)
Soul of London
Ford, Ford Madox
England and the English series (1)
Soul of Melicent
Cabell, James Branch
Dom Manuel and his descendants series (7)
Soul of Susan Yellam
Vachell, Horace Annesley
Fishpingle series (2)
Soul of the bishop
Winter, John Strange
Blankhampton series (7)
Soul of the city
Asprin, Robert Lynn
Sanctuary series (8)
Soul of the robot series
Bayley, Barrington John
Jasperodus series (1)
Soul of the West
Ellison, Suzanne
Living West trilogy (2)
Soul scar
Reeve, Arthur Benjamin
Craig Kennedy series (14)
Soul search project
Rosenberger, Joseph
Death Merchant series (62)
Soul-singer of Tyrnos
Mayhar, Ardath
House of Enthala trilogy (3)
Soul stealers
Huntington, Charles
Space probe six series (1)
Soulforge
Phillips, Terry
Advanced dungeons and dragons adventure gamebook series (1)
DragonLance series (1)
Souls of the poor folk
Irvine, Alexander
Ulster life series (2)
Sound an alarm
Holden, Genevieve
Lieutenant Al White series (2)
Sound and the fury
Faulkner, William
Listener series (1)
Sin and salvation series (2)
Sound evidence
Thomson, June
Inspector Finch series (10)
Sound like laughter
Helwig, David
Kingston tetralogy (3)
Sound now the passing-bell
Wiat, Philippa
Wyatt family series (8)
Sound of chariots
Hunter, Mollie
Bridie McShane series (1)
Sound of crying
Sudbery, Rodie
Polly Devenish series (1)
Sound of midnight
Grant, Charles Lewis
Oxrun Station series (2)
Sound of murder
Bonett, John
Inspector Borges series (4)
Hinxman, Margaret
Detective Inspector Ralph Brand series (4)
Thomas, Martin
Sexton Blake series (1566)
Sound of music
Trapp, Maria Augusta von
Trapp family series (1)
Sound of revelry
Croft-Cooke, Rupert
Sensual life series (10)
Sound of Seeger's guns
Grover, Marshall
Larry and Stretch series (324)
Sound of strings
Keith, Harold
Komantcia series (2)
Sound of the trumpet
Millin, Sarah Gertrude
War diary series (5)
Sound of the weir
Ingate, Mary
Ann Fielding series (1)
Sound of thunder
Smith, Wilbur Addison
Sean Courtney series (2)
Sound of trumpets
McLean, Allan Campbell
Alasdair and Lachlann Ban series (2)
Sound off, Tumbleweeds!
Ryan, Tom K
Tumbleweeds series (14)

Sound the retreat
Raven, Simon
Alms for oblivion series (7)
Sounder
Armstrong, William
Moses Waters series (1)
Sounder of swine
Buchanan, Patrick
Ben Shock and Charity Tucker series (4)
Soundless years
Home, Michael
Breckland series (9)
Sounds
Emberley, Ed
First words series (2)
Soup
Peck, Robert Newton
Soup series (1)
Soup ahoy
Peck, Robert Newton
Soup series (13)
Soup and me
Peck, Robert Newton
Soup series (2)
Soup for president
Peck, Robert Newton
Soup series (3)
Soup in love
Peck, Robert Newton
Soup series (12)
Soup in the saddle
Peck, Robert Newton
Soup series (6)
Soup on fire
Peck, Robert Newton
Soup series (9)
Soup on ice
Peck, Robert Newton
Soup series (8)
Soup on wheels
Peck, Robert Newton
Soup series (5)
Soup's drum
Peck, Robert Newton
Soup series (4)
Soup's goat
Peck, Robert Newton
Soup series (7)
Soup's hoop
Peck, Robert Newton
Soup series (11)
Soup's uncle
Peck, Robert Newton
Soup series (10)
Sour apple tree
Blackburn, John
General Charles Kirk series (2)
Sour cream with everything
Porter, Joyce
Edmund Brown series (1)
Sour lemon score
Stark, Richard
Parker series (12)
Source
Lumley, Brian
Necroscope series (3)
Source of light
Price, Reynolds
Mayfield family series (2)
Source of magic
Anthony, Piers
Xanth series (2)
Sourcery
Pratchett, Terry
Discworld series (5)
Sourdough gold
Hendryx, James Beardsley
Black John series (16)
Corporal Downey series (13)
Sourdough wars
Smith, Julie
Rebecca Schwartz series (2)
Sourland
Armstrong, William
Moses Waters series (2)
South
Toibin, Colm
Enniscorthy series (1)
South African twins
Rooke, Daphne
Twin series (26)
South American mission
Grey, Peter
Kit Hunter series (2)
South Coast mystery
Drummond, J
Sexton Blake series (1233)
Gibbons, Harry Hornaby Clifford
Sexton Blake series (431)
South goes north
Coles, Robert
Children of crisis series (3)
South of the bordello
Gray, Rod
Lady from L.U.S.T. series (8)
South of the border
Brightfield, Richard
Indiana Jones choose your own adventure series (2)
Logan, Jake
John Slocum series (66)
Miller, Jim
Ex-Rangers series (11)
Slade, Jack
Gatling series (4)
South of the Rio Grande
Dixon, Franklin W
Ted Scott flying series (6)
South Pass ambush
Wisler, Gary Clifton
Willie Delamer series (7)
South Pole sabotage
Johnson, Seddon
Choose your own adventure series (89)
South Pole terror
Robeson, Kenneth
Doc Savage series (77)
South Sea adventure
Price, Willard
Hal and Roger Hunt series (2)
South slope
Bosworth, Frank
Earl Morton series (6)
South star
Hearne, Betsy Gould
Megan series (1)
South to destiny
Cosic, Dobrica
This land, this time series (4)
This land, this time series (4)
South to Sabine
Grover, Marshall
Larry and Stretch series (410)
South town
Graham, Lorenz
Town series (1)
South will rise again
Edson, John Thomas
Floating Outfit series (36)
South wind of love
Mackenzie, Compton
Four winds of love series (2)
South with the Kittiwake
Pearson, Parry
Jeremy Barton and Samuel Best series (2)
Southborough fox, and other Colonel Weatherford stories
Grand, Gordon
Colonel John Weatherford series (4)
Southdale mystery
Grant, Maxwell
Shadow series (223)
Southern adventure
Paustovsky, Konstantin Georgievich
Story of a life series (5)
Southern backwash
Thompson, Neil
Rand series (5)
Southern belles
Sharpe, Jon
Trailsman series (113)
Southern Cross
Greenleaf, Stephen
John Marshall Tanner series (9)
McKinney, Jack
Robotech series (7)
Southern discomfort
Maron, Margaret
Judge Deborah Knott series (2)
Southern ghost
Hart, Carolyn Gimpel
Annie Laurance and Max Darling series (8)
Southern showdown
Masterson, Louis
Morgan Kane series (32)
Southern star
Conant, Constance
Star trilogy (1)
Southpaw
Harris, Mark
Henry W Wiggen series (1)
Southpaw's secret
Cooper, John R
Mel Martin series (2)
Southshore
Tepper, Sheri S
Awakeners series (2)
Southward bound
Dempster, Guy
Guy Laurence and Tony Carlisle series (3)
Southward journey
Sutherland, Halliday
Journey series (3)
Souvenir
Carlon, Patricia
Jefferson Shields series (1)
Dell, Floyd
Felix Fay trilogy (3)
Souvenirs
Fuller, Roy
Strange and the good trilogy (1)
Sou'West in Wanderer IV
Hiscock, Eric Charles
Wanderer series (4)
Sovereign lords
Duke, Madelaine
Sundmans trilogy (3)
Soviet history atlas
Gilbert, Martin
History atlas series (8)
Soviet literature in the nineteen eighties
Shneidman, Noah Norman
Soviet literature series (2)
Soviet literature in the nineteen seventies
Shneidman, Noah Norman
Soviet literature series (1)
Soviet sources
Cullen, Robert
Colin Burke series (1)
Sow death, reap death
Pentecost, Hugh
Julian Quist series (11)
Sowboy
Miller, Richard
Squed series (2)
Sowed by the wind
Kellogg, Elijah
Forest Glen series (1)
Sower went forth
Barclay, Tessa
Craigallan family series (1)
Sowing
Woolf, Leonard
Sowing and growing series (1)
Sowing the wind, and other stories
Arthur, Timothy Shay
Home stories series (2)
Sown wind
Duke, Winifred
Harold Fieldend series (3)
Sows ears and silk purses
Drysdale, Ann
Pig farming trilogy (2)
Space age terrors!
Milton, Hilary
Plot your own horror stories series (3)
Space Agent and the ancient peril
Macvicar, Angus
Jeremy Grant series (8)
Space Agent and the Isles of Fire
Macvicar, Angus
Jeremy Grant series (7)
Space agent from the lost planet
Macvicar, Angus
Jeremy Grant series (6)
Space and beyond
Montgomery, Raymond A
Choose your own adventure series (4)
Space Angel
Roberts, John Maddox
Space Angel series (1)
Space ark
Lightner, Alice Martha
Rock trilogy (3)
Space assassin
Chapman, Andrew
Fighting fantasy gamebook series (12)
Space attack
Buckholtz, Eileen
Micro adventure series (1)
Space barbarians
Godwin, Tom
Ragnarok series (2)
Space below my feet
Moffat, Gwen
Mountaineering series (1)
Space blazers
North, Rick
Young Astronauts series (3)
Space brat
Coville, Bruce
Space brat series (1)
Space Cat
Todd, Ruthven
Space Cat series (1)
Space Cat and the kittens
Todd, Ruthven
Space Cat series (4)
Space Cat meets Mars
Todd, Ruthven
Space Cat series (3)
Space Cat visits Venus
Todd, Ruthven
Space Cat series (2)
Space circus
Steffanson, Con
Flash Gordon series (4)
Space crash
Bentley, Roy
Spacers series (4)
Space demons
Rubinstein, Gillian
Space demons trilogy (1)
Space dreadnoughts
Drake, David
Space gladiators trilogy (3)
Space food
Hodgman, Ann
Lunchroom series (8)
Space for hire
Nolan, William Francis
Sam Space series (1)
Space fortress
Packard, Edward
Space hawks series (3)
Space gladiators
Drake, David
Space gladiators trilogy (1)
Space guardians
Ball, Brian Neville
Space nineteen ninety nine series (3)
Space Hawks
Dalton, Sean
Operation Star Hawks series (1)
Space infantry
Drake, David
Space gladiators trilogy (2)
Space intruder
Muirden, James
Eric Kendall series (1)
Space-jackers
Butterworth, Michael
Space nineteen ninety nine series (14)
Space knight and the galactic ice-cream
Gunson, Jonathan
Space knight series (2)
Space knight and the space dragon
Gunson, Jonathan
Space knight series (1)
Space lords
Smith, Cordwainer
Instrumentality series (3)
Space machine
Priest, Christopher
Time traveller series (3)
Space marine
Watson, Ian
Inquisition war series (3)
Space mavericks
Kring, Michael K
Space mavericks series (1)
Space mercenaries
Chandler, Arthur Bertram
Empress of outer space series (2)
Space merchants
Pohl, Frederik
Space merchants series (1)
Space museum
Jones, Glyn
Doctor Who series (117)
Space novels by Jules Verne
Verne, Jules
Hector Servadac series (2)
Space nymph
Lasser, Dustin
Luke Skywalker series (7)
Space out!
Roop, Peter
Make me laugh series (1)
Space patrol
Goodman, Julius
Choose your own adventure series (22)
Space pioneers
North, Rick
Young Astronauts series (5)
Rockwell, Carey
Tom Corbett series (4)
Space pirates
Del Martia, Astron
Space Express Company series (1)
Dicks, Terrance
Doctor Who series (147)
Smith, Edward Elmer
Lord Tedric series (2)
Space platform
Leinster, Murray
Joe Kenmore trilogy (1)
Space police teacher's guide
Kelley, Leo Patrick
Space police series (6)
Space prison
Godwin, Tom
Ragnarok series (1)
Space Puppet
Rackham, John
Space puppet series (1)
Space raiders and the planet of doom
Mooser, Stephen
Which way interactive series (1)
Space ranger
Asimov, Isaac
David Starr series (1)
Space ship in the park
Slobodkin, Louis
Space ship series (5)
Space ship returns to the apple tree
Slobodkin, Louis
Space ship series (2)
Space ship under the apple tree
Slobodkin, Louis
Space ship series (1)
Space spinners
Macdonald, Suse
Discovery series (4)
Space Station ICE-three
Coville, Bruce
Omni odysseys trilogy (2)
Space swimmers
Dickson, Gordon Rupert
Sea people series (2)
Space telescope
Branley, Franklyn Mansfield
Voyage into space series (2)
Space tug
Leinster, Murray
Joe Kenmore trilogy (2)
Space vampire
Packard, Edward
Choose your own adventure series (71)
Space vectors
Vardeman, Robert Edward
Biowarriors trilogy (3)
Space war
Jones, Neil Ronald
Professor Jameson series (3)
Spaceache
Wilson, Snoo
Spaceache series (1)
Spaceboy at Burlap Hall
Ironside, Virginia
Burlap Hall series (2)
Spacebread
Senn, Steve
Spacebread series (1)
Spacehawk, Inc.
Goulart, Ron
Barnum series (9)
Ben Jolson series (4)
Spacejack!
Dicks, Terrance
Star quest series (1)
Spacepaw
Dickson, Gordon Rupert
Dilbia series (2)
Spacer, window of the mind
Roberts, John Maddox
Space Angel series (2)
Spaceship for the king
Pournelle, Jerry
Future history series (5)
Spaceship of ancestors
Darlton, Clark
Perry Rhodan series (73)
Spaceship returns
Lord, Beman
Spaceship series (2)
Spaceship to planet Veta
Goll, Reinhold Weimar
Veta series (2)
Spaceship to Saturn
Walters, Hugh
Chris Godfrey series (10)
Spacial delivery
Dickson, Gordon Rupert
Dilbia series (1)
Spacious adventures of the man in the street
O'Duffy, Eimar
Aloysius Kennedy series (1)

Spade among the rushes
Leigh, Margaret Mary
Highland series (4)
Spades and feathers
Whittle, Tyler
Spaniards and Elizabethans series (1)
Spades are trumps
Spade, Danny
Danny Spade series (12)
Spades at midnight
Maddock, Stephen
Timothy Terrel series (13)
Spain
Maddocks, Peter
Jimbo's journeys series (2)
Spain for the sovereigns
Plaidy, Jean
Ferdinand and Isabella trilogy (2)
Spam tomorrow
Anderson, Verily
Anderson family series (1)
Spandau warrant
Morgan, Allan
Mark Blood series (2)
Spaniard's Gift
Welles, Elizabeth
Janine West series (4)
Spaniards' Isle
Tranter, Nigel Godwin
Ken and Fiona series (1)
Spaniard's thumb
Berrow, Norman
Inspector Lancelot Carolus Smith series (3)
Spanish adventure
Smythe, Pat
Peter and Carol Garret series (2)
Spanish bridegroom
Plaidy, Jean
Tudor series (7)
Spanish cape mystery
Queen, Ellery
Ellery Queen series (10)
Spanish connection
Carter, Nick
Nick Carter series (82)
Spanish duet
Clifford, Francis
Spanish duet series (2)
Spanish Farm
Mottram, Ralph Hale
Geoffrey Skene series (1)
Spanish Farm series (1)
Spanish Farm trilogy
Mottram, Ralph Hale
Spanish Farm series (3)
Spanish general
Bushby, John
Captain James Rollo series (1)
Spanish gold
Birmingham, George A
Reverend J J Meldon series (1)
Muir, James A
Breed series (14)
Spanish gold and Texas guns
Grover, Marshall
Larry and Stretch series (260)
Spanish grant
Foreman, Leonard London
Rogue Bishop series (1)
Spanish holiday
Sutton, Phyllis
Merryl Hastings series (2)
Spanish ingots
Ellsberg, Edward
Sunken treasure series (3)
Spanish Inquisition, its rise, growth and end
Plaidy, Jean
Spanish Inquisition trilogy (3)
Spanish interlude
Jennings, D K
Doctor Ralph Conway series (15)
Spanish journey
Sutherland, Halliday
Journey series (4)
Spanish Maine
Wren, Percival Christopher
Beau Geste series (5)
Spanish Monte Fiasco
Mackenzie, Pierce
T G Horne series (4)
Spanish notebooks
Maisky, Ivan Mikhailovich
Storm series (4)
Spanish peaks
Grey, Zane
Laramie Nelson series (1)
Laramie Nelson series (2)
Spanish roundabout
Daly, Maureen
Roundabout series (2)
Spanish twins
Perkins, Lucy Fitch
Twin series (23)
Spanking girls
Brown, Carter
Lieutenant Al Wheeler series (50)
Spanning the Pacific
Langley, John Prentice
Aviation series (2)
Spare the rod
Levy, Elizabeth
Fat Albert series (4)
Spargo
Scott, Bradford
Walt Slade series (118)
Scott, Jack Denton
Spargo series (1)
Spark
Lutz, John
Fred Carver series (7)
Wharton, Edith
Old New York quartet (3)
Spark fire
Phillips, Tony
Turbo cowboys series (3)
Spark of genius
Kellogg, Elijah
Whispering Pine series (1)
Spark of suspicion
Dixon, Franklin W
Hardy boys series (98)
Sparkling cyanide
Christie, Agatha
Colonel Race series (4)
Sparks
Fritch, Elizabeth
Richmond series (4)
Sparks fly upward
Ronald, James
Quentin Gourlay series (2)
Sparrow falls
Smith, Wilbur Addison
Sean Courtney series (3)
Sparrow falls out of the sky
Fisker, Robert
Sparrow series (1)
Sparrow flies away
Fisker, Robert
Sparrow series (2)
Sparrow gets going
Hadath, John Edward Gunby
Sparrow series (2)
Sparrow in search of expulsion
Hadath, John Edward Gunby
Sparrow series (1)
Sparrow in search of fame
Hadath, John Edward Gunby
Sparrow series (3)
Sparrowhawk
Easton, Thomas Atwood
Sparrowhawk series (1)
Sparrow's flight
Elphinstone, Margaret
Incomer series (2)
Spartan planet
Chandler, Arthur Bertram
John Grimes series (6)
Rim series (4)
Spartan run
Robbins, David
Endworld series (25)
Spartan twins
Perkins, Lucy Fitch
Twin series (8)
Spatchcock plan
McCutchan, Philip
Commander Esmonde Shaw series (20)
Spats' fact'ry
Dyson, Edward
Fact'ry 'ands series (3)
Spawn of dragonspear
Perrin, Steve
Advanced dungeons and dragons adventure gamebook series (14)
Spawn of Laban
Kern, Gregory
Cap Kennedy series (11)
Spawn of space
Harkon, Franz
Space Express Company series (2)
Spawn of the death machine
White, Ted
Android Tanner series (2)
Spawn of the hawk
Conde, Phillip
Dick Pemberty series (4)
Spawn of the winds
Lumley, Brian
Titus Crow series (4)
Spawning
Ravenswood, Fritzen
Kei series (2)
Speak for the dead
Burns, Rex
Gabriel Wager series (3)
Speak ill of the dead
Chambers, Peter
Mark Preston series (16)
Williams, Richard
Sexton Blake series (1561)
Speak justly of the dead
Lorac, E C R
Inspector Macdonald series (37)
Speak no evil
Warner, Mignon
Mrs Edwina Charles series (7)
Speak up
McCord, David
Rhymes of the never was an always is series (6)
Speak up, Christopher
McKissack, Patricia Carwell
Christopher series (2)
Speaker
Ashe, Gordon
Patrick Dawlish series (1)
Speaker for the dead
Card, Orson Scott
Ender Wiggins series (2)
Speaker of Mandarin
Rendell, Ruth
Chief Inspector Reginald Wexford series (14)
Speaking drums of Ashanti
Ballard, Martin
Benjie and Simon series (2)
Speaking eye
Smith, Clark
Nicky Mahoun series (1)
Speaking of Jennings
Buckeridge, Anthony
Jennings series (22)
Speaking of murder
Van Urk, Virginia
Tom Craig series (1)
Speaking stone
Robeson, Kenneth
Doc Savage series (116)
Spear and stockwhip
Graves, Richard Harry
Tidinbilla series (1)
Spear grinner
Barry, Clive
Jamskoni Airline series (1)
Spear gun murders
Kendrick, Baynard
Captain Duncan Maclain series (11)
Spear of Azzura
Stine, Megan
Thundercats series (3)
Spear of fire
Rusoff, Garry
Chariots of fire trilogy (3)
Spear of Mars
Bretnor, Reginald
Future at war series (2)
Spearhead death
Procter, Maurice
Chief Inspector Harry Martineau series (13)
Spears against us
Roberts, Cecil
Pamela series (2)
Special Branch Willie
Clewes, Dorothy
Willie series (2)
Special Christmas
Pascal, Francine
Sweet Valley High super series (2)
Special circumstances
Lysaght, Brian
Ben O'Malley series (1)
Special deception
Fullerton, Alexander
Special Boat Service trilogy (3)
Special deliverance
Fullerton, Alexander
Special Boat Service trilogy (1)
Special delivery
Browne, Dik
Hagar the horrible series (49)
Dixon, Mark
Deadly Force series (2)
Gielgud, Val
Antony Havilland series (4)
Kennealy, Jerry
Nick Polo series (7)
Special detective, Ashton-Kirk
McIntyre, John Thomas
Ashton-Kirk series (3)
Special dynamic
Fullerton, Alexander
Special Boat Service trilogy (2)
Special edition, murder
Kent, Arthur
Sexton Blake series (1420)
Special murders
Douglas, Arthur
Mark Register series (1)
Special occasions
Curzon, Clare
Superintendent Mike Yeadings and Sergeant Angus Mott series (2)
Special operations
Griffin, W E B
Badge of honor series (2)
Special relationship
Clark, William
Patrick Pyrton series (2)
Special relationships
Wheeler-Bennett, John
Special relationships series (2)
Special secret
Mendel, Jo
Tucker family series (2)
Specimen case
Bramah, Ernest
Max Carrados series (3)
Speckled band
Kelly, Tim J
Sherlock Holmes drama series (20)
Speckled panic
Townson, Hazel
Speckled panic series (1)
Speckledy Hen
Uttley, Alison
Little Grey Rabbit series (16)
Specs fortissimo
McNeill, Janet
Specs McCann series (2)
Spectacular stone soup
Giff, Patricia Reilly
New kids at the Polk Street School series (5)
New kids at the Polk Street School series (8)
Specter of death
Wallace, Robert
Phantom Detective series (6)
Specterworld
Haiblum, Isidore
Gunjer series (3)
Spectral stalkers
Darvill-Evans, Peter
Fighting fantasy gamebook series (44)
Spectre
Gorky, Maxim
Life of Klim Samgin series (4)
Spectre in brown
Adams, Herbert
Major Roger Bennion series (25)
Spectre of death
Zeybel, Henry
Gunship series (2)
Spectre Range
Allen, Chester
Justice Colt series (4)
Spectrum of a forgotten sun
Tubb, Edwin Charles
Dumarest series (15)
Speculations about Jakob
Johnson, Uwe
Jakob Abs series (1)
Speed!
Campbell, Rod
Little people series (14)
Pocket wheels series (4)
Speed freaks
Cave, Peter
Hell's Angels series (6)
Speed shift
Phillips, Tony
Turbo cowboys series (8)
Speed six!
Carter, Bruce
Danny Black and Johnny Wild series (2)
Speedwell boys and their ice racer
Rockwood, Roy
Speedwell boys series (5)
Speedwell boys and their power launch
Rockwood, Roy
Speedwell boys series (3)
Speedwell boys and their racing auto
Rockwood, Roy
Speedwell boys series (2)
Speedwell boys in a submarine
Rockwood, Roy
Speedwell boys series (4)
Speedwell boys on motorcycles
Rockwood, Roy
Speedwell boys series (1)
Speedy
Hamilton, Esme
Speedy series (1)
Speedy bears
Cecil, Hugh
Teddy tales series (3)
Speedy death
Mitchell, Gladys
Dame Beatrice Bradley series (1)
Speedy in Oz
Thompson, Ruth Plumly
Oz series (27)
Spell
Beach, Lynn
Phantom Valley series (5)
Spell for Chameleon
Anthony, Piers
Xanth series (1)
Spell for Miss Grimscuttle
Furminger, Jo
Mary, Ben and William series (1)
Spell for my sister
Dicks, Terrance
Macmagics series (3)
Spell of intrigue
Brenner, Mayer Alan
Dance of the gods series (2)
Spell of Siris
Hine, Muriel
Clodagh Laidlaw series (2)
Spell of the black dagger
Watt-Evans, Lawrence
Legend of Ethshar series (6)
Spell of the Northern Lights
Sypher, Lucy Johnstone
Lucy series (3)
Spell of the sorcerer's skull
Bellairs, John
Blue figurine trilogy (3)
Johnny Dixon series (3)
Spell of the winter wizard
Lowery, Linda
Endless quest series (11)
Spell of the Witch World
Norton, Andre
High Hallack series (2)
Witch World series (8)
Spell sword
Bradley, Marion Zimmer
Darkover series (5)
Spellbound
Rabin, Jennifer
Swept away series (5)
Stine, Megan
Micro adventure series (10)
Spellcaster
Brown, Katy
Twistaplot series (15)
Spellcoats
Jones, Diana Wynne
Dalemark series (3)
Spellkey
Downer, Ann
Caitlin series (1)
Spells of binding
Shetterly, Will
Liavek series (4)
Spells of mortal weaving
Friesner, Esther Mona
Chronicles of the twelve kingdoms series (2)
Spellsinger
Foster, Alan Dean
Spellsinger series (1)
Spellsinger at the gate
Foster, Alan Dean
Spellsinger series (2)
Spellsinger's scherzo
Foster, Alan Dean
Spellsinger series (6)
Spence and the holiday makers
Allen, Michael
Superintendent Ben Spence series (1)
Spence at Marlby Manor
Allen, Michael
Superintendent Ben Spence series (3)
Spence at the Blue Bazaar
Allen, Michael
Superintendent Ben Spence series (2)
Spence in Petal Park
Allen, Michael
Superintendent Ben Spence series (1)
Spencer started something
Grover, Marshall
Larry and Stretch series (402)
Spencer's Mountain
Hamner, Earl
Spencer family series (1)
Spencer's revenge
Miller, Jim
Long guns series (4)

Spoilt kill
Kelly, Mary
Nicholson series (1)
Spoke in the wheel
Pullen, Alan
Sam and Lin series (7)
Spoken word
Irvine, Robert Ralstone
Moroni Traveler series (5)
Spongee sponge
Reese, Bob
Ocean critterland series (2)
Spook Hole
Robeson, Kenneth
Doc Savage series (70)
Spook Legion
Robeson, Kenneth
Doc Savage series (16)
Spook of Grandpa Eben
Robeson, Kenneth
Doc Savage series (135)
Spooks sometimes sing
Courage, John
Bill Britain series (1)
Spooky and the bad luck raven
Carlson, Natalie Savage
Spooky series (4)
Spooky and the ghost cat
Carlson, Natalie Savage
Spooky series (2)
Spooky and the witch's goat
Carlson, Natalie Savage
Spooky series (5)
Spooky and the wizard's bats
Carlson, Natalie Savage
Spooky series (3)
Spooky Hollow
Wells, Carolyn
Fleming Stone series (15)
Spooky night
Carlson, Natalie Savage
Spooky series (1)
Spoon River anthology
Masters, Edgar Lee
Spoon River series (1)
Spoon River stud
Sharpe, Jon
Trailsman series (19)
Spoonful of Luger
Ormerod, Roger
David Mallin and George Coe series (4)
Spoor of spooks, and other nonsense
Evans, Bergen Baldwin
Nonsense series (2)
Spoor of the Antis
Voltz, William
Perry Rhodan series (102)
Sport for Inspector West
Creasey, John
Inspector Roger West series (8)
Sport for the Baron
Morton, Anthony
Baron series (38)
Sporting blood
Miall, Robert
UFO series (2)
Sporting proposition
Aldridge, James
Kit Quayle series (1)
Sporting stories and sketches
G, G
Sporting stories series (1)
Sports
Fisher, Leonard Everett
Nineteenth century America series (4)
Sports day at Blackberry Farm
Pilgrim, Jane
Blackberry Farm series (19)
Sports day for Charlie
Allen, Joy
Charlie series (11)
Sports freak
Ocork, Shannon
T T Baldwin series (1)
Sporty witch
Willson, Robina Beckles
Witch series (4)
Spot at home
Hill, Eric
Spot series (38)
Spot at play
Hill, Eric
Spot series (18)
Spot at the fair
Hill, Eric
Spot series (19)
Spot counts from one to ten
Hill, Eric
Spot series (30)
Spot series (39)
Spot goes splash!
Hill, Eric
Spot series (14)
Spot goes to a party
Hill, Eric
Spot series (40)
Spot goes to school
Hill, Eric
Spot series (15)
Spot goes to the beach
Hill, Eric
Spot series (17)
Spot goes to the circus
Hill, Eric
Spot series (20)
Spot goes to the farm
Hill, Eric
Spot series (25)
Spot goes to the park
Hill, Eric
Spot series (35)
Spot in the garden
Hill, Eric
Spot series (36)
Spot learns to count
Hill, Eric
Spot series (7)
Spot looks at colors
Hill, Eric
Spot series (23)
Spot looks at opposites
Hill, Eric
Spot series (31)
Spot looks at shapes
Hill, Eric
Spot series (24)
Spot looks at the weather
Hill, Eric
Spot series (32)
Spot marked X
Gray, Berkeley
Norman Conquest series (19)
Spot of life
Hall, Austin
Blind spot series (2)
Spot on the farm
Hill, Eric
Spot series (16)
Spot sleeps over
Hill, Eric
Spot series (34)
Spot tells the time
Hill, Eric
Spot series (8)
Spot the lady
Powell, Lester
Philip Odell series (3)
Spot visits the hospital
Hill, Eric
Spot series (27)
Spotlight
Wentworth, Patricia
Miss Maud Silver series (13)
Spotlight on a simple case
Morgan, Roberts
Sherlock Holmes sequels series (8)
Spotlight on murder
Symonds, Francis Addington
Superintendent Maxwell Quayne series (3)
Thomas, Martin
Sexton Blake series (1556)
Wellard, James
Lucius Hunt series (2)
Spotlight on Saint Peter's
Andrews, Jane
Saint Peter's Hospital series (3)
Spot's alphabet
Hill, Eric
Spot series (9)
Spot's baby sister
Hill, Eric
Spot series (33)
Spot's big book of words
Hill, Eric
Spot series (28)
Spot's birthday party
Hill, Eric
Spot series (3)
Spot's busy year
Hill, Eric
Spot series (5)
Spot's doghouse
Hill, Eric
Spot series (22)
Spot's dogs and the alley cats
Wild, Robin
Spot's dogs series (1)
Spot's dogs and the kidnappers
Wild, Robin
Spot's dogs series (2)
Spot's first Christmas
Hill, Eric
Spot series (6)
Spot's first Easter
Hill, Eric
Spot series (29)
Spot's first picnic
Hill, Eric
Spot series (26)
Spot's first walk
Hill, Eric
Spot series (2)
Spot's first words
Hill, Eric
Spot series (21)
Spot's friends
Hill, Eric
Spot series (11)
Spots in space
Lavelle, Sheila
Jupiter Jane series (4)
Spots of time, 1897-1920
Willey, Basil
Spots of time series (1)
Spot's toy box
Hill, Eric
Spot series (37)
Spot's toys
Hill, Eric
Spot series (12)
Spotted cats
Tapply, William George
Brady Coyne series (10)
Spotted Deer
Gregor, Elmer Russell
Eastern Indians series (3)
Spotted hemlock
Mitchell, Gladys
Dame Beatrice Bradley series (31)
Spotted men
Robeson, Kenneth
Doc Savage series (87)
Spotted pony
Gregor, Elmer Russell
Eastern Indians series (7)
Western Indian series (6)
Spread Eagle
Feist, Aubrey
Jeremy Shafto series (2)
Spread of sail
White, James Dillon
Roger Kelso series (8)
Spree
Collins, Max Allan
Nolan series (7)
Macgregor, T J
Quin Saint James and Mike McClary series (7)
Sprig of broom
Willard, Barbara
Mantlemass series (3)
Sprig of sea lavender
Anderson, John Richard Lane
Inspector Piet Deventer series (1)
Spring
Allington, Richard L
Beginning to learn series (17)
Best, Jacqueline
Paul and Fritzi's year series (1)
Blyton, Enid
Round the year series (1)
Ehrenburg, Ilya
Dmitry Korotoyev series (2)
Spring adventure
Pudney, John
Fred and I series (8)
Spring and Lent
Haughton, Rosemary
Christian year series (1)
Spring at Brookfield
Hayles, Brian
Archers of Ambridge series (4)
Spring at Cherry-Tree Farm
Kent, Margaret
Four seasons at Cherry-Tree Farm series (1)
Spring at Land's End
Baker, Denys Val
Cornish series (8)
Spring at the Winged Horse
Willis, Ted
Rosie Carr series (1)
Spring break
Grimes, Frances Harley
Sweet savage sophomore year series (2)
Pascal, Francine
Sweet Valley High super series (6)
Sweet Valley twins super special series (3)
Spring cleaning
Browne, Dik
Hagar the horrible series (36)
Spring cleaning, and other stories
Spencer, Thomas Edward
Bridget McSweeney series (2)
Spring comes barefoot
Felicity, *Sister*
Barefoot series (2)
Spring comes to Nettleford
Saville, Malcolm
Nettleford series (3)
Spring comes to World's End
Dickens, Monica
Fielding family series (4)
Spring days
Roth, Harold
Toddler's fun series (3)
Spring dreams
Walker, Mort
Hi and Lois series (2)
Spring fever
Connell, Abby
Heart to heart series (7)
Hoh, Diane
Cheerleaders series (27)
Lambert, Janet
Patty and Ginger series (3)
Pascal, Francine
Sweet Valley High super series (5)
Spring harrowing
Taylor, Phoebe Atwood
Asey Mayo series (14)
Spring house
Tomalin, Ruth
Ralph Oliver series (2)
Spring in a Soho street
Henrey, Madeleine
Madeleine reminiscences series (9)
Spring in Aldgate
Finn, Ralph Leslie
Aldgate series (2)
Spring is here
Lenski, Lois
Seasons series (1)
Spring is not gentle
Kirkbride, Ronald
Gentle series (2)
Spring of the ram
Dunnett, Dorothy
House of Niccolo series (2)
Spring of the year
Vipont, Elfrida
Haverard family series (3)
Spring of violence
Shannon, Dell
Lieutenant Luis Mendoza series (24)
Spring shall plant
Harraden, Beatrice
Patuffa series (1)
Spring snow
Mishima, Yukio
Sea of fertiligy quartet (1)
Spring sowing
Home, Michael
East Anglia seasons series (2)
Spring sprouts
Delton, Judy
Pee wee scout series (9)
Spring story
Barklem, Jill
Brambly Hedge series (3)
Spring-time for Jeanne-Marie
Francoise
Jeanne-Marie series (3)
Spring to remember
Martin, Marcia
Donna Parker series (5)
Springboard
Fores, John
London Airport series (2)
Springboard to summer
Bunting, Eve
High point series (3)
Springboard to Tokyo
Cook, Canfield
Lucky Terrell series (5)
Springers
Mather, Berkely
James Wainwright series (1)
Springfield Armory
Abbott, Jacob
Marco Paul's adventures in pursuit of knowledge series (6)
Springfield sharpshooters
Sharpe, Jon
Trailsman series (149)
Springtime discovery
Jenkins, Jerry Bruce
Tara Chadwick series (1)
Springtime in Noisy Village
Lindgren, Astrid
Bullerby series (8)
Springtime in Paris
Paul, Elliot
Narrow street series (5)
Springtime Mary
Kerouac, Jack
Jack Duluoz series (3)
Springtime of love
Davenat, Colette
Deborah series (1)
Sprint cars
Wilkinson, Sylvia
World of racing series (3)
Sprockets, a little robot
Key, Alexander
Sprockets trilogy (1)
Sprocket's Christmas tale
Gikow, Louise
Fraggle Rock series (7)
Sprout
Wayne, Jenifer
Sprout series (1)
Sprout and the conjuror
Wayne, Jenifer
Sprout series (5)
Sprout and the dogsitter
Wayne, Jenifer
Sprout series (3)
Sprout and the helicopter
Wayne, Jenifer
Sprout series (4)
Sprout and the magician
Wayne, Jenifer
Sprout series (5)
Sprouts of wrath
Rankin, Robert
Brentford series (4)
Sprout's window-cleaner
Wayne, Jenifer
Sprout series (2)
Sprung!
Janson, Hank
Hank Janson series (245)
Spud and the big red balloon
Reed, Giles
Munch Bunch story books series (1)
Spud comes to play
Solomon, Joan
Children's life series (2)
Spud Tamson out west
Campbell, R W
Spud Tamson series (3)
Spud Tamson's pit
Campbell, R W
Spud Tamson series (4)
Spun silk
Elliott, William James
Anthony England series (4)
Spur of pride
Wren, Percival Christopher
Khairastan series (1)
Spur route
Grover, Marshall
Nevada Jim series (46)
Spurs
Holland, Julian
Tottenham Hotspur Football Club series (1)
Spurs of Troodos
Murray, William Hutchinson
John Taunt series (2)
Spurs, the double
Holland, Julian
Tottenham Hotspur Football Club series (2)
Sputnik to space shuttle
Branley, Franklyn Mansfield
Voyage into space series (3)
Spy
Horler, Sydney
Brett Carstairs series (2)
Newman, Bernard
Inspector Marshall series (1)
Spy against the Reich
Annesley, Michael
Lawrence Fenton series (7)
Spy and die
Meyers, Martin
Patrick Hardy series (5)
Spy and the atom-gun
Seth, Ronald
Brian Grant series (4)
Spy and the thief
Hoch, Edward Dentinger
Nick Velvet series (1)
Spy at Angkor Wat
Ballinger, Bill Sanborn
Joaquin Hawks series (4)
Spy at Number Ten
Newman, Bernard
Papa Pontivy series (15)

Stagecoach ransom
Hardin, J D
Raider series (16)
Stagecoach thieves
Roberts, J R
Gunsmith series (94)
Stagecoach to Concho
Borg, Jack
Hogleg Bailey series (22)
Stagecoach to Fort Dodge
Miller, Jim
Ex-Rangers series (7)
Stagecoach to hell
Bridges, Ben
Carter O'Brien series (9)
Sharpe, Jon
Trailsman series (63)
Stagecoach west
Heuman, William
Grady Mulvane series (1)
Stagestruck
Lambert, Janet
Parri Macdonald series (3)
Stagg night
Masters, Zeke
Faro Blake series (24)
Staggering snowman
Townson, Hazel
Lenny and Jake series (6)
Staghorn
Champlin, Tim
Matt Tierney series (3)
Stained glass
Buckley, William Frank
Blackford Oakes series (2)
Stained white radiance
Burke, James Lee
Dave Robicheaux series (5)
Stainless steel rat
Harrison, Harry
Jim Di Griz series (1)
Stainless steel rat for president
Harrison, Harry
Jim Di Griz series (5)
Stainless steel rat gets drafted
Harrison, Harry
Jim Di Griz series (7)
Stainless steel rat is born
Harrison, Harry
Jim Di Griz series (6)
Stainless steel rat saves the world
Harrison, Harry
Jim Di Griz series (3)
Stainless steel rat sings the blues
Harrison, Harry
Jim Di Griz series (9)
Stainless steel rat wants you
Harrison, Harry
Jim Di Griz series (4)
Stainless steel rat's revenge
Harrison, Harry
Jim Di Griz series (2)
Stainless steel visions
Harrison, Harry
Jim Di Griz series (8)
Stainless steel wreath
Hedges, Joseph
John Stark series (9)
Staircase four
Reilly, Helen
Inspector Christopher McKee series (19)
Staircase of the wind
Langley, John Prentice
Aviation series (9)
Stairs lead nowhere
Swiggett, Howard
Garrett Maynard series (1)
Stairs of sand
Grey, Zane
Adam Larey series (2)
Stairstep Farm
Pellowski, Anne
Valley Farm series (3)
Stairway to danger
Blaine, John
Rick Brant series (9)
Stairway to doom
Quackenbush, Robert Mead
Miss Mallard series (5)
Stairway to forever
Adams, Robert
Stairway to forever series (1)
Stairway to murder
Kent, Arthur
Sexton Blake series (1448)
Mills, Osmington
Superintendent William Baker series (5)
Usher, Frank
Daye Smith series (13)
Stake out
Blake, Ken
Professionals series (3)
Staked goat
Healy, Jeremiah
John Francis Cuddy series (2)
Staked plains rendezvous
Richmond, Roe
Lashtrow series (7)
Stakeout at Council Creek
Grover, Marshall
Larry and Stretch series (302)
Stalag sixty nine
Green, Michael
Coarse plays series (3)
Stalingrad
Plievier, Theodor
World War II trilogy (2)
Stalingrad heroes
Eckhardt, Kurt
Heroes series (2)
Stalin's orphans
Appignanesi, Richard
Italia perversa trilogy (1)
Stalk a long shadow
Severn, Richard
Jeff Cass series (1)
Stalker
Cody, Liza
Anna Lee series (3)
Peters, David
Psi-Man series (5)
Stalker from the stars
Silva, Joseph
Incredible Hulk series (1)
Stalkers
Drumm, D B
Traveler series (3)
Johnston, Terry Conrad
Plainsmen series (3)
Stalker's moon
Logan, Jake
John Slocum series (130)
Stalkers of the sea
Stanton, Ken
Aquanauts series (5)
Stalking
Faulcon, Robert
Nighthunter series (1)
Stalking horse
Ash, Constance
Horsegirl series (2)
Gielgud, Val
Antony Havilland series (3)
Sharpe, Jon
Trailsman series (15)
Wilcox, Collin
Lieutenant Frank Hastings series (12)
Stalking man
Tucker, Wilson
Charles Horne series (4)
Stalking stranger
Robertson, Colin
Inspector John Martin series (3)
Peter Grayleigh series (2)
Stalking time
Drumm, D B
Traveler series (9)
Stallion man
Glover, Judith
Sussex quartet (1)
Stallion Valley
McCarthy, Gary
Ballou family series (5)
Stalwart men of early Texas
McCall, Edith
Frontiers of America series (19)
Stamboul intrigue
Charles, Robert
Simon Larren series (8)
Stamp album
Stamp, Terence
Double feature series (1)
Stamped for death
McDowell, Emmett
Jonathan Knox series (1)
Stamped for murder
Benson, Ben
Inspector Wade Paris series (4)
Stampede
Chisholm, Matt
Storm family series (1)
Edwards, Josh
John Stone series (7)
White, Stewart Edward
Andy Burnett series (4)
Stampede Canyon
Hogan, Robert Jasper
Smoke Wade series (2)
Stamping ground
Estleman, Loren D
Page Murdock series (2)
Stand alone
Grover, Marshall
Nevada Jim series (53)
Stand alone Stan
Mann, Phillip
Escape to the wild wood series (2)
Stand and give challenge
Macmanus, Francis
Donnacha Mac Conmara trilogy (1)
Stand by for Mars!
Rockwell, Carey
Tom Corbett series (1)
Stand by, London calling
Keeler, Harry Stephen
Angus Macwhorter series (3)
Stand by the union
Optic, Oliver
Blue and the Gray afloat series (4)
Stand-by to ram!
Macdonnell, James Edmond
Commander Sainsbury series (1)
Stand-in for murder
Gribble, Leonard Reginald
Superintendent Anthony Slade series (27)
Reid, Desmond
Sexton Blake series (1430)
Stand-in for sin
Brody, Marc
Marc Brody series (26)
Stand into danger
Kent, Alexander
Captain Richard Bolitho series (3)
Stand off
Macdonnell, James Edmond
Dutchy Holland series (44)
Stand on me
Norman, Frank
Bang to rights series (3)
Stand on Zanzibar
Brunner, John
Zanzibar series (1)
Stand proud
Kelton, Elmer
Tales of Texas series (14)
Stand tall
Sanders, Bill
Tough issues for teens series (1)
Stand up
Sanders, Bill
Tough issues for teens series (2)
Stand up and die
Lockridge, Frances
Inspector Merton Heimrich series (8)
Stand up Jonny Briggs
Eadington, Joan
Jonny Briggs series (9)
Stand up virgin soldiers
Thomas, Leslie
Virgin soldiers series (3)
Standfast, the Holy Ghost
Grayson, Rupert
Voyage not completed series (2)
Standing alone
Cooney, Linda A
Totally hot series (3)
Standing into danger
Griffin, John
Richard Raven series (2)
Macdonnell, James Edmond
Dutchy Holland series (30)
Standing lions
Ray, Mary
Mycaenean Greece series (1)
Standing out
Pascal, Francine
Sweet Valley twins series (25)
Standish Gaunt case
Patterson, Innis
Sebald Craft series (2)
Standish gets his man
Westerman, Percy Francis
Standish series (2)
Standish holds on
Westerman, Percy Francis
Standish series (5)
Standish loses his man
Westerman, Percy Francis
Standish series (3)
Standish of Standish
Austin, Jane Goodwin
Pilgrims of Plymouth series (1)
Standish of the Air Police
Westerman, Percy Francis
Standish series (1)
Standish pulls it off
Westerman, Percy Francis
Standish series (4)
Standof at Sunrise Creek
Bly, Stephen Arthur
Stuart Brannon series (4)
Standoff in the sky
Thorne, Ramsay
Captain Gringo series (35)
Stands a Calder man
Dailey, Janet
Webb Calder series (3)
Stanley Bagshaw and the fourteen foot wheel
Wilson, Bob
Stanley Bagshaw series (1)
Stanley Bagshaw and the Mafeking Square cheese robbery
Wilson, Bob
Stanley Bagshaw series (3)
Stanley Bagshaw and the rather dangerous miracle cure
Wilson, Bob
Stanley Bagshaw series (5)
Stanley Bagshaw and the short-sighted football trainer
Wilson, Bob
Stanley Bagshaw series (4)
Stanley Bagshaw and the twenty-two ton whale
Wilson, Bob
Stanley Bagshaw series (2)
Stanley goes to school
Edwards, Pat
Stanley series (3)
Stanley, Henry Bear's friend
McPhail, David Michael
Henry Bear series (2)
Stanleys of Alderley
Stanley, Maria Josepha
Alderley series (2)
Stanton's comes of age
Little, Sylvia
Stanton's series (1)
Stanton's pulls it off
Little, Sylvia
Stanton's series (2)
Star anchored, star angered
Elgin, Suzette Haden
Coyote Jones series (4)
Star and the gun
Masterson, Louis
Morgan Kane series (3)
Star baby
Nixon, Joan Lowery
Hollywood daughters trilogy (1)
Star barbarian
Van Arnam, Dave
Jamnar series (1)
Star born
Norton, Andre
Astra series (2)
Star-Born
Williamson, Henry
Flax of dream series (5)
Star bright
Richards, Laura Elizabeth
Captain January series (2)
Star brothers
Bova, Ben
Voyagers series (3)
Star city
Zetford, Tully
Ryder Hook series (3)
Star colony
Laumer, Keith
Star colony series (1)
Star colony series (2)
Star commandos
Griffin, Pauline Margaret
Star commandos series (1)
Star courier
Chandler, Arthur Bertram
John Grimes series (16)
Star crossed
Mead, Matt
Sexton Blake series (1600)
Star-crossed lover
Brown, Carter
Rick Holman series (30)
Star diaries
Lem, Stanislaw
Ijon Tichy series (2)
Star dream
Lambert, Janet
Dria Meredith trilogy (1)
Star explorer
Innes, Evan
American two thousand and forty series (5)
Star fall
Bischoff, David
Star fall series (1)
Star fighters
Mills, Robert E
Fellowship of light trilogy (2)
Star for Christina
Saint James, Blakely
Christina Van Bell series (23)
Star for linda
Sheldon, Ann
Linda Craig adventures series (2)
Star for Starlight
Lister, Gladys
Starlight series (2)
Star force
Mills, Robert E
Fellowship of light trilogy (3)
Star from the east
Housman, Laurence
Palace plays series (4)
Star guard
Norton, Andre
Central Control series (3)
Star guide
Branley, Franklyn Mansfield
Voyage into space series (4)
Star healer
White, James
Sector General series (7)
Star hunters
Clayton, Jo
Diadem series (5)
Star in the saddle
Sheldon, Ann
Linda Craig adventures series (8)
Star Island
Hall, Margery
Star Island trilogy (1)
Star Island again
Hall, Margery
Star Island trilogy (2)
Star Ka'at
Norton, Andre
Star Ka'at series (1)
Star Ka'at world
Norton, Andre
Star Ka'at series (2)
Star Ka'ats and the plant world
Norton, Andre
Star Ka'at series (3)
Star Ka'ats and the winged warriors
Norton, Andre
Star Ka'at series (4)
Star king
Vance, Jack
Kirth Gersen series (1)
Star Kings
Hamilton, Edmond
John Gordon series (1)
Star light
Clement, Hal
Mesklin series (3)
Star light, star bright
Ellin, Stanley
John Milano series (1)
Hunt, Angela Elwell
Cassie Perkins series (7)
Wells, Marian
Starlight trilogy (2)
Star loot
Chandler, Arthur Bertram
John Grimes series (20)
Star maker
Stapledon, Olaf
Last men series (3)
Star Man 1
Byrne, Stuart James
Star Man series (1)
Star Man 2
Byrne, Stuart James
Star Man series (2)
Star man's son, 2250AD
Norton, Andre
Central Control series (1)
Star mill
Petaja, Emil
Kalevala series (2)
Star of danger
Bradley, Marion Zimmer
Darkover series (10)
Star of Delhi
Grant, Maxwell
Shadow series (206)
Star of doom
Smith, David Claude
Red Sonja series (6)
Star of earth
Cohen, Octavus Roy
Jim Hanvey series (4)
Star of Egypt
Sanders, Buck
Ben Slayton series (2)
Star of Gettysburg
Altsheler, Joseph Alexander
Civil War series (5)
Star of Lancaster
Plaidy, Jean
Plantagenet series (11)
Star of Satan
Bernanos, Georges
Spiritual life series (1)

Star of the air
Carter, Dorothy
Marise Duncan series (2)
Star of the East
Pearce, Charles Edward
Indian mutiny trilogy (3)
Star of the goddess
Clare, Marguerite
Merlin Sorrel series (1)
Star of the Orsini
Huna, Ludwig
Borgia trilogy (2)
Star of the parade
Pascal, Francine
Sweet Valley kids series (54)
Star of the West
Conant, Constance
Star trilogy (3)
Star Prince Charlie
Anderson, Poul
Hoka series (2)
Star quality
Cole, Jennifer
Cindy and Nicole series (7)
Star quest
Mills, Robert E
Fellowship of light trilogy (1)
Star rangers
Norton, Andre
Central Control series (2)
Star rangers and the spy
Blashfield, Jean
Fantasy forest series (6)
Star rangers meet the solar robot
Charette, Beverly
Fantasy forest series (8)
Star rebel
Busby, Francis Marion
Bran Tregare series (1)
Star rider
Bryant, Bonnie
Saddle Club series (19)
Star riders of Ren
Miller, Calvin
Singreale trilogy (2)
Star-riders of the moor
Pullein-Thompson, Josephine
Moor pony series (1)
Star rogue
Carter, Lin
History of the Great Imperium trilogy (2)
Star ruby contract
Atlee, Philip
Joe Gall series (7)
Star sapphire
Blunt, Betty
Treacherous moon series (3)
Star scroll
Rawn, Melanie
Dragon prince series (2)
Star-search
Kapp, Colin
Cageworld series (4)
Star shines over Mount Morris Park
Roth, Henry
Mercy of a rude stream series (1)
Star ship
Anderson, Poul
Psychotechnic League series (3)
Star slaver
Cleve, John
Spaceways series (12)
Star-spangled bananas, and other revolutionary riddles
Keller, Charles
Ballpoint bananas series (2)
Star spangled summer
Lambert, Janet
Penny Parrish series (1)
Star spring
Bischoff, David
Star fall series (2)
Star struck
Lantz, Francess Lin
Swept away series (4)
Thornton, Jane Foster
Electric High series (5)
Star surgeon
White, James
Sector General series (2)
Star system Tenopia
Brightfield, Richard
Escape from Tenopia series (4)
Star to steer her by
Jones, Tristan
Wayward sailor series (7)
Star trap
Brett, Simon
Charles Paris series (3)
Darke, Marjorie
Francis Redmayne series (2)
Star trek
Blish, James
Star trek original series (1)
Roddenberry, Gene
Star trek moving picture series (1)
Star trek series (1)
Star trek 1
Blish, James
Star trek original series (1)
Star trek 2
Blish, James
Star trek original series (2)
Star trek 3
Blish, James
Star trek original series (3)
Star trek 4
Blish, James
Star trek original series (4)
Star trek 5
Blish, James
Star trek original series (5)
Star trek 6
Blish, James
Star trek original series (6)
Star trek 7
Blish, James
Star trek original series (7)
Star trek 8
Blish, James
Star trek original series (8)
Star trek 9
Blish, James
Star trek original series (9)
Star trek 10
Blish, James
Star trek original series (10)
Star trek 11
Blish, James
Star trek original series (11)
Star trek 12
Blish, James
Star trek original series (12)
Star trek encyclopaedia
Okuda, Michael
Star trek series (57)
Star trek II biographies
Rotsler, William
Star trek tie-ins series (2)
Star trek II short stories
Rotsler, William
Star trek tie-ins series (4)
Star trek III short stories
Rotsler, William
Star trek tie-ins series (5)
Star trek log
Dillard, Jeanne M
Star trek moving picture series (5)
Star trek reader
Blish, James
Star trek original series (7)
Star trek original series (8)
Star trek original series (9)
Star trek original series (11)
Star trek spaceflight chronology
Goldstein, Stan
Star trek series (57)
Star trek speaks
Goldstein, Fred
Star trek series (57)
Star trek, the classic records
Blish, James
Star trek original series (12)
Star trek, the motion picture make-your-own costume book
Schnurnberger, Lynn Edelman
Star trek tie-ins series (1)
Star trek, the motion picture peel-off graphics book
Cole, Lee
Star trek series (57)
Star trek, the new voyages
Culbreath, Myrna
Star trek originals sequels series (4)
Star trek, the new voyages 2
Culbreath, Myrna
Star trek originals sequels series (7)
Star trek, the next generation officer's manual
Terra, John
Star trek, the next generation sequels series (7)
Star trek, the next generation technical manual
Okuda, Michael
Star trek, the next generation sequels series (7)
Star wars
Lucas, George
Luke Skywalker series (1)
Weinberg, Larry
Star wars storybook series (1)
Star wars storybook
Richelson, Geraldine
Star wars storybook series (1)
Star wars, the first ten years
Vinge, Joan Dennison
Star wars storybook series (3)
Star wars, the roleplaying games
Costikyan, Greg
Luke Skywalker series (7)
Star wars trilogy
Kahn, James
Luke Skywalker series (7)
Star well
Panshin, Alexei
Anthony Villiers series (1)
Star wolf!
White, Ted
Qanar series (3)
Star wreck
Rewolinski, Leah
Luke Skywalker series (7)
Star wreck, the generation gap
Rewolinski, Leah
Star trek series (57)
Starbaby
Asch, Frank
Bear series (2)
Starbloom
Wallis, Redmond
Triangulum trilogy (1)
Starboy
Biemiller, Carl Ludwig
Jonny series (2)
Starbrat
Morressy, John
Del Whitby trilogy (1)
StarBridge
Crispin, Ann Carol
StarBridge series (1)
Starbuck
Selby, John
Trace family trilogy (3)
Starbuck Valley winter
Haig-Brown, Roderic Langmere
Don Morgan series (1)
Starchild
Pohl, Frederik
Plan of man trilogy (2)
Starchild trilogy
Pohl, Frederik
Plan of man trilogy (3)
Starclipper and the galactic final
Earnshaw, Brian
Star Jam Pack trilogy (3)
Starclipper and the snowstone
Earnshaw, Brian
Star Jam Pack trilogy (2)
Starclipper and the song wars
Earnshaw, Brian
Star Jam Pack trilogy (1)
Starcross
James, Laurence
Simon Rack series (2)
Stardance
Robinson, Jeanne
Stardance series (1)
Stardom for Himself
Bird, Kenneth
Himself series (3)
Stardreamer
Smith, Cordwainer
Instrumentality series (7)
Stardrift
Morressy, John
Del Whitby trilogy (2)
Stardust
Parker, Robert Brown
Spenser series (17)
Stardust voyages
Tall, Stephen
Stardust series (1)
Starfarers
McIntyre, Vondra Neil
Starfarers series (1)
Starfire down
McKeone, Lee
Ghoster trilogy (3)
Starfish affair
Chance, John Newton
Jonathan Blake series (30)
Starfishers
Cook, Glen
Starfishers trilogy (2)
Starflight zero
Fickling, David
Fantasy quest book series (2)
Starfollowers of Coramonde
Daley, Brian
Coramonde series (2)
Stargazers and gravediggers
Velikovsky, Immanuel
Worlds in collision series (2)
Starhammer
Rowley, Christopher
Vang trilogy (1)
Starjacked!
Greenleaf, William
Tartarus series (3)
Stark murder
Thayer, Lee
Peter Clancy series (28)
Starkadder
King, Bernard
Starkadder trilogy (1)
Starkahn of Rhada
Gilman, Robert Cham
Rhada series (4)
Starke sisters
Mackenzie, Kathleen
Starke sisters series (1)
Starless night
Lodwick, John
Desmond Thornton series (2)
Starless realm
Darlton, Clark
Perry Rhodan series (87)
Starless world
Eklund, Gordon
Star trek originals sequels series (8)
Starlet for a penny
Ballinger, W A
Sexton Blake series (1584)
Starlight
Hamilton, Esme
Speedy series (3)
Starlight barking
Smith, Dodie
Pongo and Missis series (2)
Starlight belongs to me
Lister, Gladys
Starlight series (1)
Starlight Christmas
Bryant, Bonnie
Saddle Club series (13)
Starlight Motel incident
Weisman, John
Headhunters series (3)
Starlight saves the day
Lewis, Jean
Rainbow Brite series (1)
Starpirate's brain
Goulart, Ron
Exchameleon series (2)
Starquake
Forward, Robert Lull
Dragon's egg series (2)
Starr Bedford dies
Garnett, Roger
John Yardley series (1)
R I Perkins series (1)
Starrigger
De Chancie, John
Skyway trilogy (1)
Starring Jessica
Pascal, Francine
Sweet Valley High series (71)
Starring Miss Seeton
Crane, Hamilton
Miss Emily Seeton series (17)
Starring Punky Brewster
Matthews, Ann
Punky Brewster series (1)
Starring Stephanie
Saunders, Susan
Sleepover friends series (2)
Starring the Baby-Sitters Club
Martin, Ann Matthews
Baby-Sitters Club super specials series (9)
Starring Winston
Pascal, Francine
Sweet Valley kids series (13)
Starr's showdown
Wisler, Gary Clifton
Willie Delamer series (2)
Starry-eyed chipmonk
Schley, Sturges Mason
Doctor Quentin Toby series (3)
Starry flag
Optic, Oliver
Starry flag series (1)
Starry night
Sefton, Catherine
Northern Ireland trilogy (1)
Starry rift
Tiptree, James
Great Central Library series (2)
Stars
Bendick, Jeanne
Early bird astronomy series (4)
Simon, Seymour
Space photos series (4)
Stars above
Newcomb, Ellsworth
Joan and Bill series (3)
Stars and planets
Abetti, Giorgio
Universe series (2)
Stars and swastikas
White, Steve
S-Com series (2)
Stars are dark
Cheyney, Peter
Everard Peter Quayle series (1)
Secret service series (2)
Stars are ours
Norton, Andre
Astra series (1)
Stars at war
Pournelle, Jerry
Imperial stars series (1)
Stars come out within
Little, Jean
Writer's education series (2)
Stars' End
Cook, Glen
Starfishers trilogy (3)
Stars for Cristy
Hunt, Mabel Leigh
Cristy Romano series (1)
Stars for the Toff
Creasey, John
Toff series (51)
Stars grow pale
Bjarnhof, Karl
Blind series (1)
Stars hang high
Lambert, Janet
Jordons series (8)
Stars in her eyes
Bernard, Elizabeth
Satin slippers series (3)
Stars in shroud
Benford, Gregory
Galactic Center series (1)
Ocean series (3)
Stars, like dust
Asimov, Isaac
Trantorian Empire trilogy (2)
Stars must wait
Laumer, Keith
Bolo series (3)
Stars of Beverly Hills 90210
Reisfeld, Randi
Beverly Hills 90210 series (8)
Stars of the South
Green, Julian
Distant lands series (2)
Stars on the sea
Mason, Francis Van Wyck
American War of Independence series (2)
Stars or dust
Rousch, Catherine E
Star trek fan series (42)
Stars promise death
Grant, Maxwell
Shadow series (269)
Stars scream murder
Reeve, Arthur Benjamin
Craig Kennedy series (26)
Stars spell death
Stagge, Jonathan
Doctor Hugh Westlake series (3)
Taylor, Phoebe Atwood
Asey Mayo series (22)
Stars, squares and Busy Bears
Killingback, Julia
Busy Bears series (5)
Stars will speak
Zebrowski, George
Bernal One series (2)
Starseed
Robinson, Jeanne
Stardance series (2)
Starshine connection
Sanders, Buck
Ben Slayton series (4)
Starship Orpheus
Jade, Symon
Starship Orpheus trilogy (1)
Starship Sapphire
Cleve, John
Spaceways series (15)
Starship traveler
Jackson, Steve
Fighting fantasy gamebook series (4)
Starship troopers
Heinlein, Robert Anson
Starship troopers series (1)
Starship troopers series (2)
Starship warrior
Mooser, Stephen
Which way interactive series (2)

Starsilk
Van Scyoc, Sydney Joyce
Sunstone scrolls trilogy (3)
Starsky and Hutch
Franklin, Max
Starsky and Hutch series (1)
Starstone
Chetwin, Grace
Tales of Gom in the Legends of Ulm series (4)
Starstormers
Fisk, Nicholas
Starstormers series (1)
Starstruck
Avenell, Donne
Axa series (9)
Saunders, Susan
Sleepover friends series (21)
Start in life
Balzac, Honore de
Scenes of private life series (6)
Trowbridge, John Townsend
Start in life series (1)
Start screaming
Powell, Talmage
Ed Rivers series (4)
Start shooting, Texans
Grover, Marshall
Larry and Stretch series (22)
Start the invasion without me
Browne, Dik
Hagar the horrible series (42)
Startide rising
Brin, David
Earthclan series (2)
Starting gun
Bagby, George
Inspector Schmidt series (14)
Starting over
Aks, Patricia
Cheerleaders series (20)
Bernard, Elizabeth
Satin slippers series (11)
Lowell, Anne Hunter
Sorority girls series (3)
Pascal, Francine
Sweet Valley High series (33)
Starting school
Heaslip, Peter
Going to school series (2)
Petty, Kate
First timers series (3)
Starting the eighth grade
Kenyon, Kate
Cedar Groves Junior High School series (8)
Starvation island
Hammel, Eric Maxwell
Guadalcanal series (1)
Starvel Hollow tragedy
Crofts, Freeman Wills
Inspector Joseph French series (3)
Starwolf
Hamilton, Edmond
Starwolf trilogy (3)
Starwolves
Gunnarsson, Thorarinn
Starwolves series (1)
Starworld
Harrison, Harry
To the stars trilogy (3)
Stash spots a murder
Peters, Ron
Stash Koval series (2)
State Fair
Stong, Philip
State Fair series (1)
State of corruption
Geddes, Paul
Ludovic Fender series (3)
Paul Venneker series (4)
State of fear
Reid, Desmond
Sexton Blake series (1526)
State of nature
Goodman, Paul
Empire City quartet (1)
Empire city series (1)
State of peace
Elliott, Janice
Wilson family trilogy (1)
State of the art
Banks, Iain Menzies
Culture series (3)
State of Vermont
Abbott, Jacob
Marco Paul's adventures in pursuit of knowledge series (4)
State secrets
Home-Gall, William Benjamin
Sexton Blake series (170)
State Street
Whittingham, Richard
Joe Morrison series (1)
State vs. justice
Warfield, Gallatin
Gardner Lawson series (1)
Stately home murder
Aird, Catherine
Inspector C D Sloan series (3)
Stately homicide
Haymon, Sylvia T
Inspector Ben Jurnet series (3)
Milner, George
Ronald Anglesea series (1)
State's evidence
Greenleaf, Stephen
John Marshall Tanner series (3)
States General
Erckmann, Emile
Story of a peasant series (1)
Statesman
Anthony, Piers
Bio of a space tyrant series (5)
Crozier, Brian
De Gaulle series (2)
Statesman's game
Aldridge, James
Rupert Royce series (2)
Station master's secret
Murray, Andrew
Sexton Blake series (95)
Station of the invisibles
Mahr, Kurt
Perry Rhodan series (133)
Station wagon murder
Propper, Milton
Tommy Rankin series (12)
Station wagon set
Baldwin, Faith
Doctor Bing Irvington series (1)
Little Oxford series (1)
Stationfall
Cover, Arthur Byron
Planetfall series (2)
Statistical history of the Korean War
Clodfelter, Micheal D
Statistical history series (1)
Statistical history of the Vietnam War
Clodfelter, Micheal D
Statistical history series (2)
Statue of Liberty adventure
Kushner, Ellen
Choose your own adventure series (58)
Staunch as a woman
Garvice, Charles
Staunch series (1)
Staveworld
Elliott, Nathan
Hood's Army trilogy (2)
Stay away, Slade!
Grover, Marshall
Larry and Stretch series (322)
Stay of execution
Desmond, Hugh
Alan Fraser series (20)
Stay of execution, and other stories of legal practice
Gilbert, Michael Francis
Inspector Hazelrigg series (7)
Stay on your toes, Maggie Adams
Dean, Karen Strickler
Maggie Adams series (3)
Stay out of the basement
Stine, Robert Lawrence
Goosebumps series (2)
Stay single and live forever
Sands, Leslie
Sam Wilson series (2)
Stay tuned for danger
Keene, Carolyn
Nancy Drew files series (17)
Stay with me till morning
Braine, John
Clive and Robin Lendrick series (1)
Staying alive!
Bailey, Maurice
Small boat series (1)
Staying alive
Fleischer, Leonore
Saturday night fever series (2)
Staying cool
Cooney, Linda A
Totally hot series (5)
Staying overnight
Petty, Kate
First timers series (6)
Staying together
Hoh, Diane
Cheerleaders series (12)
Steady as you go
Bartimeus
Naval occasions series (8)
Steady burns the candle
Ainsworth, Patricia
Burnley series (3)
Steady trade
Jones, Tristan
Wayward sailor series (1)
Steak for breakfast
O'Conner, Elizabeth
Silver Ridge series (1)
Stealer of souls
Martin, Keith
Fighting fantasy gamebook series (36)
Stealer of souls, and other stories
Moorcock, Michael
Elric series (5)
Stealers' sky
Asprin, Robert Lynn
Sanctuary series (12)
Stealing home
Stolz, Mary
Thomas and Grandfather series (3)
Stealing secrets
Steinke, Anne E
Cheerleaders series (25)
Stealing the scene
Zach, Cheryl
Smyth versus Smith series (2)
Steam house
Verne, Jules
Steam house series (2)
Steam on the line
Turner, Philip
Darnley Mills Railway series (1)
Steam pig
McClure, James
Lieutenant Kramer and Sergeant Zondi series (1)
Steamboat Gothic
Keyes, Frances Parkinson
Batchelor series (1)
Batchelor series (2)
Steamboat on the Chesapeke
Holly, David Chauncey
Chesapeke steamboats series (1)
Steamboats to the West
McCall, Edith
Frontiers of America series (2)
Steaming Sam
Dicks, Terrance
Bears series (3)
Steeds of Satan
Leslie, Peter
Father Hayes trilogy (2)
Steel
Drake, David
Generals series (4)
Steel box
Moore, Arthur
Bluestar series (2)
Steel Callaghan
Chesney, Michael
Colonel Steel Callaghan series (2)
Steel casket, and other stories
Carter, Nicholas
Nicholas Carter series (90)
Steel Face
Evans, Gwyn
Sexton Blake series (663)
Steel guitar
Barnes, Linda
Carlotta Carlyle series (5)
Steel hilt
Stark, Richard
Parker series (2)
Steel justice
Edwards, Hank
Judge Clay Torn series (5)
Steel magic
Norton, Andre
Magic series (1)
Steel of Raithskar
Garrett, Randall
Gandalara cycle series (1)
Steel palace
Pentecost, Hugh
Julian Quist series (7)
Steel shark
Krauss, Bruno
Sea Wolf series (1)
Steel shutters
Holt, Gavin
Professor Luther Bastion series (17)
Steel spring
Wahloo, Per
Chief Inspector Peter Jensen series (2)
Steel tiger
Silliphant, Stirling
John Locke series (1)
Steel trap
Sugar, Andrew
Enforcer series (5)
Steel tsar
Moorcock, Michael
Oswald Bastable series (3)
Steel web
Tierney, Ronald
Deets Shanahan series (2)
Steeldust
Brown, Joseph Paul Summers
Steeldust series (1)
Steele
Masters, J D
Steele series (1)
Steeley flies again
Johns, William Earl
Steeley Delaroy series (2)
Steelfingers
Giraud, Jean
Lieutenant Mike S Blueberry series (7)
Steep Atlantick stream
Harling, Robert
Sailor series (2)
Steep Farm stables
Sandler, Mona
Steep Farm series (2)
Steeple folly
Atkinson, Mary Evelyn
Lockett family series (14)
Steeple Thatchby
Thomson, Arthur Alexander
Marigold Cottage trilogy (3)
Steer by the stars
Fitz Roy, Olivia
Stewarts series (2)
Steinway collection
Randisi, Robert Joseph
Miles Jacoby series (2)
Stellar death plan
Vardeman, Robert Edward
Masters of space trilogy (1)
Stem to stern
Optic, Oliver
Boat builders series (4)
Sten
Cole, Allan
Sten series (1)
Stench of poppies
Drummond, Ivor
Lady Jennifer, Sandro and Colly series (8)
Step families
Berry, Joy
Good answers to tough questions series (1)
Step in the dark
Lemarchand, Elizabeth
Superintendent Tom Pollard series (8)
Step into quicksand
Treat, Lawrence
Jub Freeman series (3)
Mitch Taylor series (2)
Step swiftly, sinner
Brody, Marc
Marc Brody series (24)
Step to silence
Newby, Percy Howard
Hesketh and Jane Oliphant series (1)
Step to the stars
Del Rey, Lester
Moon trilogy (1)
Stepdaughter
Bromige, Iris
Rainwood family series (1)
Stephanie
Saunders, Susan
Sleepover friends series (18)
Stephanie and the wedding
Saunders, Susan
Sleepover friends series (25)
Stephanie Kaye
Roberts, Ken
Degrassi High School series (3)
Stephanie strikes back
Saunders, Susan
Sleepover friends series (7)
Stephanie's big story
Saunders, Susan
Sleepover friends series (15)
Stephanie's family secret
Saunders, Susan
Sleepover friends series (11)
Stephen
Kingsley, Florence Morse
Early Christian series (2)
Stephen and Matilda
Birt, David
Middle Ages series (4)
Stepmother for Susan of Saint Bride's
Adam, Ruth
Susan Marsh series (1)
Stepney, the Bluebell engine
Awdry, Wilbert
Railway series (18)
Steppe wolves
Kostov, K N
Punishment battalion series (4)
Stepping into the spotlight
Weir, Molly
Feet series (4)
Stepping out
Bernard, Elizabeth
Satin slippers series (8)
Steps in the dark
Black, Mansell
Richard Vaness series (4)
Cumberland, Marten
Saturnin Dax series (5)
Steps to murder
King, Rufus
Stuff Driscoll series (2)
Koehler, Robert Portner
Al Bronson series (1)
Steps to the empty throne
Tranter, Nigel Godwin
Robert the Bruce trilogy (1)
Steps up the chimney
Corlett, William
Magician's house trilogy (1)
Stepsister
Stine, Robert Lawrence
Fear Street series (6)
Stepsisters
Pascal, Francine
Sweet Valley High series (93)
Stepsisters for Lorna
Brent-Dyer, Elinor Mary
Lorna series (2)
Stepsons
Liddell, Robert
Relations series (2)
Steve Bentley's calypso caper
Dietrich, Robert
Steve Bentley series (7)
Steve Canyon
Caniff, Milton
Steve Canyon series (1)
Steve Carlton, baseball's silent strongman
Aaseng, Nathan
Sports acheivers series (4)
Steven and the zombie
Pascal, Francine
Sweet Valley twins series (78)
Steven's bride
Pascal, Francine
Sweet Valley High series (83)
Steven's enemy
Pascal, Francine
Sweet Valley twins series (82)
Steven's in love
Pascal, Francine
Sweet Valley twins series (57)
Steven's twin
Pascal, Francine
Sweet Valley kids series (50)
Stewardess strangler
Gallagher, Richard
Cannon series (2)
Stewardesses
Sutton, Penny
Stewardesses series (1)
Stewardesses down under
Sutton, Penny
Stewardesses series (2)
Stick-in-the-Mud Turtle
Hoban, Lillian
Stick-in-the-Mud Turtle series (1)
Stick out your tongue!
Roop, Peter
Make me laugh series (4)
Stick to it, Charlie
Allen, Joy
Charlie series (7)
Sticking point
Jackson, Ken
Jud Blade series (2)
Stickit minister, and some common men
Crockett, Samuel Rutherford
Stickit minister series (1)
Stickit minister's wooing, and other Galloway stories
Crockett, Samuel Rutherford
Stickit minister series (2)

Stickman
Fantoni, Barry
Mike Dime series (2)

Sticky beak
Gleitzman, Morris
Rowena Batts series (2)

Stiff as a broad
Fickling, G G
Erik March series (4)
Honey West series (11)

Stiff justice
Gentry, Buck
Eli Holten series (32)

Stiff proposition
Conway, Troy
Coxeman series (28)

Stiff silk
Milne, Shirley
Detective Sergeant Steytler series (1)

Stiff upper lip
Durrell, Lawrence
Antrobus series (2)
Israel, Peter
B F Cage series (3)

Stiff upper lip, Jeeves
Wodehouse, Pelham Grenville
Jeeves and Bertie Wooster series (13)

Stiffs don't vote
Homes, Geoffrey
Humphrey Campbell series (4)

Stiffsons, and other stories
Jenkins, Herbert
Malcolm Sage series (2)

Stiletto
Rossi, Bruno
Sharpshooter series (9)

Stiletto signature
Messmann, Jon
Revenger series (4)

Still among the living
Klein, Zachary
Matthew Jacob series (1)

Still dead
Knox, Ronald Arbuthnott
Miles Bredon series (4)

Still further Northern Territory recollections
Priest, Charles Ashley Vincent
Northern Territory recollections series (4)

Still glides the stream
Thompson, Flora
Lark Rise to Candleford series (4)

Still going bananas
Keller, Charles
Going bananas series (2)

Still I persist in wondering
Pangborn, Edgar
Davy series (4)

Still is the summer night
Derleth, August
Sac Prairie series (2)

Still life
Byatt, Antonia Susan
Virgin in the garden tetralogy (2)
Cobb, Richard
Still life series (1)

Still life with pistol
Ormerod, Roger
Richard Patton series (3)

Still more commonplace
Stocks, Mary
Commonplace series (2)

Still more from Bystander
Bairnsfather, Bruce
Old Bill series (3)

Still more misleading cases
Herbert, Alan Patrick
Misleading cases series (3)

Still more small poems
Worth, Valerie
Small poems series (3)

Still more stories from grandma's attic
Richardson, Arleta
Grandma's attic series (3)

Still more two-minute mysteries
Sobol, Donald J
Two-minute mysteries series (3)

Still Mrs 'Arris
Poultney, Clifford Blake
Mrs 'Arris series (4)

Still no answer
Thayer, Lee
Peter Clancy series (56)

Still of night
Powell, Lester
Philip Odell series (4)

Still small voice of trumpets
Biggle, Lloyd
Cultural survey series (1)

Still the joy of it
Powys, Littleton Charles
Joy series (2)

Still waters
Lorac, E C R
Inspector Macdonald series (32)
Van de Water, Frederic Franklin
John Tarleton series (1)

Still, William
Crompton, Richmal
William series (5)

Stilled life
Dunham, Mikel
Rhea Buerklin series (1)

Stillness at Appomattox
Catton, Bruce
Potomac Army trilogy (3)

Sting of the adder
Carter, Nicholas
Nicholas Carter series (503)

Sting of the honeybee
Parrish, Frank
Dan Mallett series (2)

Sting of the scorpion
Basile, Gloria Vitanza
Global 2000 series (3)
Dixon, Franklin W
Hardy boys series (58)

Stinger
Hornig, Doug
Steven Kirk series (2)

Stingray
Theydon, John
Stingray series (1)

Stingray and the monster
Theydon, John
Stingray series (2)

Stinky Stanley
Hodgman, Ann
Stinky Stanley series (1)

Stinky Stanley stinks again
Hodgman, Ann
Stinky Stanley series (2)

Stir up this stew
Hesling, Bernard
Little and orphan series (3)

Stirrups in the dust
Arthur, Burt
Johnny Canavan series (2)
Texas Rangers series (1)

Stitch in time
Lathen, Emma
John Putnam Thatcher series (7)
Pearson, Ann
Maggie Courtney series (2)

Stitch in time solution
Christian, Mary Blount
Goosehill Gang series (9)

Stitches for Charlie
Allen, Joy
Charlie series (4)

Stoat
Brock, Lynn
Colonel Gore series (7)

Stock car champion
Montgomery, Raymond A
Choose your own adventure series (96)

Stock car race
Dean, Anabel
Racing wheels series (4)

Stock cars
Wilkinson, Sylvia
World of racing series (5)

Stockholders in death
Robeson, Kenneth
Avenger series (7)

Stocking our selection
Rudd, Steele
Rudd family series (1)

Stoic
Dreiser, Theodore
Frank Cowperwood trilogy (3)

Stokesley secret
Yonge, Charlotte Mary
Beechcroft series (3)
Shield series (2)

Stolen aeroplane
Ashton, Lamar
Aeroplane boys series (2)

Stolen aircraft carrier
Duff, Douglas Valder
Adam Macadam series (10)

Stolen brain
Carter, Nicholas
Nicholas Carter series (597)

Stolen continent
Sibson, Francis H
Survivors series (2)

Stolen crown
Bobin, John William
Sexton Blake series (52)

Stolen death
Grex, Leo
Paul Irving series (5)

Stolen diary
Pascal, Francine
Sweet Valley High series (84)

Stolen ecstasy
Taylor, Janelle
Sioux series (7)

Stolen gods
Page, Jake
Mo Bowdre series (1)

Stolen harvest
Williamson, Roger
Romany Rat trilogy (3)

Stolen holiday
Hill, Lorna
Marjorie series (2)

Stolen home secretary
Gribble, Leonard Reginald
Superintendent Anthony Slade series (5)

Stolen horse
Hart, Sharon M
Animal Rescue Farm series (1)

Stolen identity
Carter, Nicholas
Nicholas Carter series (12)

Stolen jewels
Pye, Virginia
Price family series (6)

Stolen kisses
Keene, Carolyn
River Heights series (4)

Stolen lake
Aiken, Joan
Dido Twite series (4)

Stolen law
Mason, Anne
Dancing meteorite series (2)

Stolen Liberty Bonds
Ridley, Nat
Nat Ridley series (11)

Stolen like magic away
Audemars, Pierre
Monsieur Pinaud series (15)

Stolen moments
Preston, John
Mission of Alex Kane series (4)

Stolen name
Carter, Nicholas
Nicholas Carter series (441)

Stolen nugget of gold
Ridley, Nat
Nat Ridley series (6)

Stolen paintings
Ecke, Wolfgang
Super sleuth series (2)

Stolen partnership papers
Bobin, John William
Sexton Blake series (71)

Stolen passions
Campbell, Drusilla
Hopewell series (3)

Stolen past
Knowles, John
Yale University series (3)

Stolen pay train, and other stories
Carter, Nicholas
Nicholas Carter series (52)

Stolen planet
Mastin, John
Regina series (1)

Stolen pony
Rounds, Glen
Blind colt series (2)

Stolen racehorse
Carter, Nicholas
Nicholas Carter series (49)

Stolen seasons
Divine, David
Mig and Peter Manson series (1)

Stolen soprano
Mackenzie, Compton
Highland series (8)

Stolen spacefleet
Darlton, Clark
Perry Rhodan series (109)

Stolen squadron
Leonard, Charles L
Paul Kilgerrin series (2)

Stolen stallion
Brand, Max
Silvertip series (11)

Stolen statesman
Gribble, Leonard Reginald
Superintendent Anthony Slade series (5)

Stolen story, and other newspaper stories
Williams, Jesse Lynch
Stolen story series (1)

Stolen strychnine
Cobb, Belton
Superintendent Manning series (5)

Stolen submarine
Hope, Stanton
Sexton Blake series (928)

Stolen sun
Petaja, Emil
Kalevala series (3)

Stolen test-tube
Jardine, Warwick
Sexton Blake series (850)

Stolen white eagle
Mackenzie, Pierce
T G Horne series (1)

Stone Age Kids discover America
Almqvist, Bertil
Stones series (1)

Stone angel
Albert, Marvin Hubert
Pierre-Ange Sawyer series (1)
Laurence, Margaret
Manawaka series (1)

Stone arrow
Herley, Richard
Pagans trilogy (1)

Stone baby
Healey, Ben
Harcourt d'Espinal series (2)

Stone blunts scissors
Fairlie, Gerard
Victor Caryll series (3)

Stone book
Garner, Alan
Stone book quartet (1)

Stone book quartet
Garner, Alan
Stone book quartet (4)

Stone boy
Levitsky, Ronald
Nate Rosen series (3)

Stone came rolling
Burke, Fielding
Call home series (2)

Stone cold blonde
Knight, Adam
Steve Conacher series (1)

Stone cold dead
Ellington, Richard
Steve Drake series (3)
Garner, Hugh
Inspector Walter McDumont series (1)

Stone-cold dead in the market affair
Oram, John
Man from U.N.C.L.E. series (22)

Stone dead
Ashton, Charles
Jack Atherley series (5)
Laing, Patrick
Patrick Laing series (2)
San Antonio
Berurier series (1)
San Antonio series (1)
Symonds, Francis Addington
Superintendent Maxwell Quayne series (1)

Stone dogs
Stirling, Stephen Michael
Draka trilogy (3)

Stone doll of Sister Brute
Hoban, Russell
Brute family series (2)

Stone dormitory
Turner, James Ernest
Rampion Savage series (12)

Stone for his head
Cobb, Belton
Bryan Armitage series (11)
Inspector Cheviot Burmann series (35)
Kitty Armitage series (8)

Stone giant
Blaylock, James Paul
Jonathan Bing series (3)

Stone hawk
Moffat, Gwen
Miss Melinda Pink series (10)

Stone house at Kilgobbin
Lynch, Patricia
Brogeen the leprechaun series (9)

Stone idol
Dixon, Franklin W
Hardy boys series (65)

Stone in a pool
Softly, Barbara
English Civil War series (3)

Stone in heaven
Anderson, Poul
Sir Dominic Flandry series (9)

Stone in the pool
Tweedsmuir, Susan Buchan
Victorian trilogy (3)

Stone killer
Gardner, John Edmund
Detective Inspector Derek Torry series (1)
Scarpetta, Frank
Marksman series (8)

Stone maiden
Townley, Pamela
Stone maiden series (1)

Stone man
Robeson, Kenneth
Doc Savage series (81)

Stone of Badda
Sharp, Allen
Storytrails series (6)

Stone of farewell
Williams, Tad
Memory, sorrow and thorn series (2)

Stone offering
Chance, Stephen
Septimus Treloar series (3)

Stone shadow
Miller, Rex
Jack Eichord series (3)

Stone sorcerer
Storey, Margaret
Timothy, Ellen and Melinda series (5)

Stone veil
Tierney, Ronald
Deets Shanahan series (1)

Stone warriors
Longtree, Warren T
Ruff Justice series (14)

Stone within
Wingrove, David
Chung Kuo series (4)

Stone wizard
Storey, Margaret
Timothy, Ellen and Melinda series (5)

Stone Wolf's vision
Wisler, Gary Clifton
Medicine Trail series (2)

Stonecroft
Savory, Teo
Stonecroft series (1)

Stonecutter's story
Saberhagen, Fred
Book of lost swords series (3)

Stonefish
West, Charles
Paul Crook series (1)

Stonehenge
Roop, Peter
Great mysteries series (4)

Stoner McTavish
Dreher, Sarah
Stoner McTavish series (1)

Stones discover America
Almqvist, Bertil
Stones series (1)

Stones explore Britain
Almqvist, Bertil
Stones series (2)

Stones of Africa
Muller, Mary
Anna and Johan de Villiers series (3)

Stones of enchantment
Martyn, Wyndham
Anthony Trent series (27)

Stones of Green Knowe
Boston, Lucy Maria
Green Knowe series (7)

Stones of Kiribati
Daniken, Erich von
Unsolved mysteries series (8)

Stones of Satan
Wallace, Robert
Phantom Detective series (34)

Stoneskin's revenge
Deitz, Tom
David Sullivan series (5)

Stonewall Steevens investigates
Kiddy, Maurice George
Stonewall Steevens series (2)

Stoneware monkey
Freeman, Richard Austin
Doctor John Evelyn Thorndyke series (25)

Stony Man doctrine
Pendleton, Don
Stony Man series (1)
SuperBolan series (1)

Stony Man II
Pendleton, Don
Stony Man series (2)

Stony Man III
Pendleton, Don
Stony Man series (3)

Stony Man IV
Pendleton, Don
Stony Man series (4)
Stony Man V
Pendleton, Don
Stony Man series (5)
Stony Man VI
Pendleton, Don
Stony Man series (6)
Stony Man VII
Pendleton, Don
Stony Man series (7)
Stony Man VIII
Pendleton, Don
Stony Man series (8)
Stony places
Barclay, Tessa
Craigallan family series (2)
Stool pigeon
Daniel, Roland
Inspector John Walk series (3)
Stop Angel!
Christian, Frederick H
Frank Angel series (9)
Stop at nothing
Welcome, John
Simon Herald series (1)
Stop at the red light
Fair, A A
Bertha Cool and Donald Lam series (22)
Stop half way and look at the view
Stern, Rhona
South African series (3)
Stop press
Innes, Michael
Sir John Appleby series (4)
Stop press, homicide!
Dolphin, Rex
Sexton Blake series (1468)
Stop press in scarlet
Brody, Marc
Marc Brody series (60)
Stop press standover
Brody, Marc
Marc Brody series (4)
Stop that car!
Hardcastle, Michael
Tony and Jay series (3)
Stop that man
Franklin, Charles
Grant Garfield series (13)
Ladline, Robert
J A Remington series (6)
Stop that witch!
Clark, Mary
Endless quest crimson crystal adventure series (4)
Stop the presses
Saunders, Susan
Bad News Bunny series (3)
Stopgap
Schock, T A
Daniel Keel series (3)
Stopover, Tokyo
Marquand, John Phillips
Mister Moto series (6)
Store
Stribling, Thomas Sigismund
Colonel Miltiades Vaiden trilogy (2)
Store of wrath
Truss, Seldon
Inspector Gidleigh series (11)
Storekeeper
Gilman, George G
Adam Steele series (27)
Steele's war series (3)
Stories
Allington, Richard L
Beginning to learn series (21)
Stories about Henry
Tippett, James Sterling
Henry series (2)
Stories for Monday
Blyton, Enid
Weekday stories series (1)
Stories for telling
Wood, William Hollingsworth
Stories for telling series (1)
Stories for Tuesday
Blyton, Enid
Weekday stories series (2)
Stories for young housekeepers
Arthur, Timothy Shay
Household library series (3)
Stories from Doctor Death
Zorro
Doctor Death series (4)
Stories from my life
Mannin, Ethel
Confessions and impressions series (5)
Stories from my life with the other animals
McConkey, James
Court of memory trilogy (3)
Stories from our house
Tulloch, Richard
Stories series (1)
Stories from our street
Tulloch, Richard
Stories series (2)
Stories from the Bible
De la Mare, Walter
Stories from the Bible series (3)
Stories from the note-book of a detective
Donovan, Dick
Dick Donovan series (4)
Stories from the Peterkin papers
Hale, Lucretia Peabody
Peterkin series (2)
Stories from the Twilight Zone
Serling, Rod
Twilight Zone series (1)
Twilight Zone series (3)
Stories from Toytown
Beaman, Sydney George Hulme
Toytown series (14)
Stories Julian tells
Cameron, Ann
Julian stories series (1)
Stories of Bunny Buffin
Buckels, Alex
Bunny Buffin series (1)
Stories of Mister Bumblemoose
Andreus, Hans
Mister Bumblemoose series (1)
Stories of my home folks
Ober, Frederick Albion
Old farm series (4)
Stories of Professor Branestawm
Hunter, Norman
Professor Branestawm series (3)
Stories of saints by candlelight
Barclay, Vera Charlesworth
Saints series (1)
Stories of the kings, from David to Christ
Evans, Adelaide Bee
Bible pictures and stories series (3)
Stories Polly Pepper told
Sidney, Margaret
Five Little Peppers series (5)
Stories Toto told me
Rolfe, Frederick William
Toto's tales series (1)
Storm
Aminoff, Constance Leonie Caroline
Napoleonic series (9)
Duun, Ole Julius
People of Juvik series (6)
Ehrenburg, Ilya
Wave series (1)
Henry, Marguerite
Chincoteague series (1)
O'Donnell, Peadar
Islanders series (1)
Storm above the Park
Heath-Miller, Mavis
Hardwick family series (2)
Storm across the border
Stevens, Steve
Jack Storm series (2)
Storm ahead
Edwards, Monica
Romney Marsh series (7)
Storm and stress
Rolland, Romain
John Christopher series (2)
Storm at Sandy Point
Gorelick, Molly Chernow
Rescue series (3)
Storm Belgium
Lutz, Gunther
Nazi paratrooper series (1)
Storm Boyd's family
Finlay, Eileen
Boyd family series (2)
Storm breaks
Gask, Arthur
Gilbert Larose series (25)
Storm centre
Clark, Douglas
Inspector George Masters series (24)
Storm child
Netter, Susan
Twilight series (17)
Storm force to Narvik
Fullerton, Alexander
Nick Everard series (4)
Storm from the skies
Jackson, Robert
Bomber Command series (2)
Storm in a teacup
Phillpotts, Eden
Industries of England series (6)
Storm in an inkpot
Franklin, Charles
Grant Garfield series (4)
Storm in Arizona
Stevens, Steve
Jack Storm series (3)
Storm in Montana
Stevens, Steve
Jack Storm series (7)
Storm in the dark
Kenworthy, Christopher
Matthew and Son series (3)
Storm in the mountains
Stevens, Steve
Jack Storm series (4)
Storm in the night
Stolz, Mary
Thomas and Grandfather series (1)
Storm in the south
Scofield, Jonathan
Freedom fighters series (6)
Storm in the village
Read, *Miss*
Fairacre series (3)
Storm in Wyoming
Stevens, Steve
Jack Storm series (6)
Storm island
Berres, Frances B
Deep-sea adventure series (9)
Storm knights
Slavicsek, Bill
Torg series (1)
Storm Lord
Lee, Tanith
Wars of Vis trilogy (1)
Storm Mountain
Ellis, Edward Sylvester
Wyoming Valley trilogy (2)
Storm north
Thompson, Neil
Rand series (3)
Storm of dust
Randall, Neil
Dragon lord series (2)
Storm of fortune
Clarke, Austin Chesterfield
Boysie Cumberbatch trilogy (2)
Storm of steel
Moore, William
Mallandine family trilogy (3)
Storm of time
Dark, Eleanor
Mannion family series (2)
Storm of wings
Harrison, Michael John
Viriconium series (2)
Storm on the sawdust trail
Buckman, Sam
Storm Jackson series (6)
Storm on the trail
Stevens, Steve
Jack Storm series (5)
Storm over Cheviot
Finlay, Winifred
Judith Norton series (3)
Storm over Rhanna
Fraser, Christine Marion
Rhanna series (6)
Storm over Rocktail
Baker, William Howard
Dangerman series (2)
Storm over Sabrehill
Giles, Raymond
Sabrehill series (4)
Storm over Singapore
Draper, Alfred
Crispin Paton series (4)
Storm over Sonora
Masterson, Louis
Morgan Kane series (12)
Storm over Valla
Prescot, Dray
Dray Prescot series (35)
Storm over Warlock
Norton, Andre
Planet Warlock series (1)
Storm over Windhaven
De Jourlet, Marie
Windhaven series (2)
Storm riders
Sanders, Charles Wesley
Mournful Martin series (3)
Storm runner
Harper, Tara K
Wolfwalker series (3)
Storm season
Asprin, Robert Lynn
Sanctuary series (4)
Storm seed
Morris, Janet Ellen
Tempus series (7)
Storm shield
Flint, Kenneth Covey
Finn McCumhal series (2)
Storm testament I
Nelson, Lee
Dan Storm quartet (1)
Storm testament II
Nelson, Lee
Dan Storm quartet (2)
Storm testament III
Nelson, Lee
Dan Storm quartet (3)
Storm testament IV
Nelson, Lee
Dan Storm quartet (4)
Storm the last rampart
Taylor, David
War of Independence trilogy (3)
Storm tide
Ogilvie, Elisabeth May
Bennett Island series (2)
Storm troops of the Baltic skies
Johns, William Earl
Biggles series (20)
Storm warning
Dale, Judith
Shirley Flight series (16)
Roberts, Nora
Flowers series (4)
Storm warnings
Daniels, Lee
Surf city series (2)
Storm warriors
Craig, Brian
Minstrel Orfeo series (3)
Storm water
Ling, Peter
Water series (3)
Stormblade
Berberick, Nancy Varian
DragonLance heroes series (2)
Stormbringer
Moorcock, Michael
Elric series (6)
Stormcock meets trouble
Peyton, K M
Mick and Rob series (1)
Storming Vicksburg
Dunn, Byron Archibald
Young Missourians series (4)
Stormlight
Chance, John Newton
Mister DeHavilland series (12)
Stormqueen!
Bradley, Marion Zimmer
Darkover series (1)
Storm's howling through Tiflis
Oram, Neil
Warp series (1)
Storms of victory
Pournelle, Jerry
Janisseries trilogy (3)
Stormtide
Knox, Bill
Webb Carrick series (7)
Stormtroop
Kessler, Leo
Stormtroop series (1)
Stormwarden
Wurts, Janny
Cycle of fire trilogy (1)
Stormy, Misty's foal
Henry, Marguerite
Chincoteague series (4)
Stormy night
Hale, Christopher
Lieutenant Bill French series (2)
Stormy Petrel
Needham, Violet
Stormy Petrel series (2)
Stormy surrender
Hatcher, Robin Lee
Spring Haven series (1)
Stormy voyage
Barlow, Roger
Sandy Steele series (3)
Story Girl
Montgomery, Lucy Maud
Story Girl series (1)
Story half told
Leslie, Anita
Train to nowhere series (2)
Story like the wind
Van der Post, Laurens
Francois Joubert series (1)
Story of a big ego in a small body
Anand, Mulk Raj
Pilpali Sahab series (2)
Story of a bold tin soldier
Hope, Laura Lee
Make-believe stories series (4)
Story of a calico clown
Hope, Laura Lee
Make-believe stories series (7)
Story of a candy rabbit
Hope, Laura Lee
Make-believe stories series (5)
Story of a car
Gree, Alain
Story series (1)
Story of a castle
Goodall, John Strickland
English village series (2)
Story of a childhood under the Raj
Anand, Mulk Raj
Pilpali Sahab series (1)
Story of a china cat
Hope, Laura Lee
Make-believe stories series (9)
Story of a farm
Goodall, John Strickland
English village series (4)
Story of a fierce bad rabbit
Potter, Beatrix
Peter Rabbit series (9)
Story of a high street
Goodall, John Strickland
English village series (3)
Story of a killer
Spade, Danny
Danny Spade series (31)
Story of a lamb on wheels
Hope, Laura Lee
Make-believe stories series (3)
Story of a little mouse trapped in a book
Felix, Monique
Little mouse trapped in a book series (1)
Story of a monkey on a stick
Hope, Laura Lee
Make-believe stories series (6)
Story of a nodding donkey
Hope, Laura Lee
Make-believe stories series (8)
Story of a Norfolk farm
Williamson, Henry
Shallowford to Norfolk series (3)
Story of a plush bear
Hope, Laura Lee
Make-believe stories series (10)
Story of a puppet
Collodi, Carlo
Pinocchio series (1)
Story of a sailing boat
Gree, Alain
Story series (7)
Story of a sawdust doll
Hope, Laura Lee
Make-believe stories series (1)
Story of a seashore
Goodall, John Strickland
English village series (5)
Story of a ship
Gree, Alain
Story series (2)
Story of a sin
Mathers, Helen
Sin and acquittal series (1)
Story of a space rocket
Gree, Alain
Story series (5)
Story of a stuffed elephant
Hope, Laura Lee
Make-believe stories series (11)
Story of a train
Gree, Alain
Story series (3)
Story of a truck
Gree, Alain
Story series (4)
Story of a white rocking horse
Hope, Laura Lee
Make-believe stories series (2)
Story of a woolly dog
Hope, Laura Lee
Make-believe stories series (12)
Story of Aaron, so called, the son of Ben Ali
Harris, Joel Chandler
Aaron series (1)
Story of an aeroplane
Gree, Alain
Story series (6)
Story of an English village
Goodall, John Strickland
English village series (1)

Story of Anne Beames
Dawson-Scott, Catherine Amy
Some women trilogy (1)
Story of Aroora the red kangaroo
Rees, Leslie
Australian nature tales series (7)
Story of Babar, the little elephant
Brunhoff, Jean de
Babar series (1)
Story of baby Jesus
Davidson, Alice Joyce
Alice in Bibleland series (7)
Story of baby Moses
Davidson, Alice Joyce
Alice in Bibleland series (6)
Story of Benjamin Bee
Wynne-Jones, Pat
Hedgerow tales series (2)
Story of California
White, Stewart Edward
California trilogy (3)
Story of cancer
Bankoff, George Alexis
Conquest of series (5)
Story of Charlotte the Caterpillar
Wynne-Jones, Pat
Hedgerow tales series (1)
Story of Ching-Kwei and the destinies
Bramah, Ernest
Kai Lung series (3)
Story of creation
Davidson, Alice Joyce
Alice in Bibleland series (1)
Story of Daniel and the lions
Davidson, Alice Joyce
Alice in Bibleland series (10)
Story of David and Goliath
Davidson, Alice Joyce
Alice in Bibleland series (5)
Story of David Blythe
Turner, Mary
Blythe family series (1)
Story of Doctor Dolittle
Lofting, Hugh
Doctor Dolittle series (1)
Story of Doctor Esmond Ross
Dwyer-Joyce, Alice
Doctor Esmond Ross series (2)
Story of Dragon seed
Buck, Pearl Sydenstricker
Ling Tan series (2)
Story of Easter
Davidson, Alice Joyce
Alice in Bibleland series (11)
Story of Edward
Dumas, Philippe
Edward series (1)
Story of Esther
Davidson, Alice Joyce
Alice in Bibleland series (16)
Story of Ethan Allen, the Green mountain boy
Fitzhugh, Percy Keese
Young folks colonial series (1)
Story of Exodus
Davidson, Alice Joyce
Alice in Bibleland series (14)
Story of Freginald
Brooks, Walter Rollin
Freddy the pig series (4)
Story of Fuzzypeg, the hedgehog
Uttley, Alison
Fuzzypeg series (1)
Little Grey Rabbit series (4)
Story of General Anthony Wayne, Mad Anthony, the hero of Stony Point
Fitzhugh, Percy Keese
Young folks colonial series (2)
Story of General Francis Marion, the Bayard of the South
Fitzhugh, Percy Keese
Young folks colonial series (6)
Story of General Johann De Kalb
Fitzhugh, Percy Keese
Young folks colonial series (3)
Story of General Richard Montgomery
Fitzhugh, Percy Keese
Young folks colonial series (4)
Story of Hal 5 and the Haywards
Donald, Henry
Linwoodmuir series (2)
Story of Heather
Wynne, May
Heather series (1)
Story of Henri Tod
Buckley, William Frank
Blackford Oakes series (5)
Story of Holly and Ivy
Godden, Rumer
Four dolls series (3)
Story of Isaac's wife
Davidson, Alice Joyce
Alice in Bibleland series (17)
Story of Jeremy Cricket
Wynne-Jones, Pat
Hedgerow tales series (3)
Story of Jesus and his disciples
Davidson, Alice Joyce
Alice in Bibleland series (21)
Story of John Paul Jones
Fitzhugh, Percy Keese
Young folks colonial series (5)
Story of Jonah
Davidson, Alice Joyce
Alice in Bibleland series (3)
Story of Joseph
De la Mare, Walter
Stories from the Bible series (1)
Story of Joshua
Davidson, Alice Joyce
Alice in Bibleland series (15)
Story of Karrawingi the emu
Rees, Leslie
Australian nature tales series (2)
Story of King Arthur and his knights
Pyle, Howard
Arthurian legends series (1)
Story of Koonaworra the black swan
Rees, Leslie
Australian nature tales series (9)
Story of Kurri Kurri the kookaburra
Rees, Leslie
Australian nature tales series (6)
Story of Little Black Bobtail
Bannerman, Helen
Little Black series (6)
Story of Little Black Mingo
Bannerman, Helen
Little Black series (2)
Story of Little Black Quasha
Bannerman, Helen
Little Black series (5)
Story of Little Black Quibba
Bannerman, Helen
Little Black series (3)
Story of Little Black Sambo
Bannerman, Helen
Little Black series (1)
Story of Little Kettle-Head
Bannerman, Helen
Little Black series (4)
Story of Little Knittle and Threadle
Meyer, Renate
Knittle and Threadle series (1)
Story of Little Owl
Boyle, Constance
Little Owl series (1)
Story of Little White Squibba
Bannerman, Helen
Little Black series (8)
Story of Louie
Onions, Oliver
Whom God hath sundered trilogy (3)
Story of Miss Moppet
Potter, Beatrix
Peter Rabbit series (10)
Story of Moses
De la Mare, Walter
Stories from the Bible series (2)
Story of Mrs Tubbs
Lofting, Hugh
Mrs Tubbs series (1)
Story of my days
Raymond, Ernest
My days series (1)
Story of my life
Keller, Helen
My life series (1)
Story of Noah
Davidson, Alice Joyce
Alice in Bibleland series (2)
Story of O
Reage, Pauline
O series (1)
Story of Pat Garrett and Billy the Kid
Everitt, David
Legends series (3)
Story of Paul
Davidson, Alice Joyce
Alice in Bibleland series (18)
Story of Pookie
Wallace, Ivy Lilian
Pookie series (4)
Story of Robin Redbreast
Wynne-Jones, Pat
Hedgerow tales series (4)
Story of Russ the Australian tree kangaroo
Rees, Leslie
Australian nature tales series (12)
Story of Ruth and Naomi
Davidson, Alice Joyce
Alice in Bibleland series (20)
Story of Sambo and the twins
Bannerman, Helen
Little Black series (7)
Story of Samuel and Saul
De la Mare, Walter
Stories from the Bible series (3)
Story of Sarli the Barrier Reef turtle
Rees, Leslie
Australian nature tales series (4)
Story of Shadow the rock wallaby
Rees, Leslie
Australian nature tales series (5)
Story of Shy the platypus
Rees, Leslie
Australian nature tales series (1)
Story of Sir Launcelot and his companions
Pyle, Howard
Arthurian legends series (3)
Story of Strong
Rutley, Cecily Marianne
Children of other days series (3)
Story of Terrible Terry
Fitzhugh, Percy Keese
Buddy series (6)
Story of the amulet
Nesbit, Edith
Five children series (3)
Story of the champions of the Round Table
Pyle, Howard
Arthurian legends series (2)
Story of the good Samaritan
Davidson, Alice Joyce
Alice in Bibleland series (19)
Story of the Grail and the passing of Arthur
Pyle, Howard
Arthurian legends series (4)
Story of the little car
Berg, Leila
Little car series (1)
Story of the little red engine
Ross, Diana
Little red engine series (2)
Story of the loaves and the fishes
Davidson, Alice Joyce
Alice in Bibleland series (8)
Story of the lost sheep
Davidson, Alice Joyce
Alice in Bibleland series (22)
Story of the Phantom
Falk, Lee
Phantom series (1)
Story of the siege of Troy
Blyton, Enid
Stories from world history series (1)
Story of the stone
Hughart, Barry
Master Li Kao and Number Ten Ox series (2)
Story of the Sundance Kid
Everitt, David
Legends series (2)
Story of the Tower of Babel
Davidson, Alice Joyce
Alice in Bibleland series (23)
Story of the Trapp family singers
Trapp, Maria Augusta von
Trapp family series (1)
Story of the Treasure Seekers
Nesbit, Edith
Bastable family series (1)
Story of the unknown
Bankoff, George Alexis
Conquest of series (6)
Story of Two-thumbs the koala
Rees, Leslie
Australian nature tales series (8)
Story of Wan and the remarkable shrub
Bramah, Ernest
Kai Lung series (3)
Story of Widgery Winks
Bennett, Rodney
Widgery Winks series (1)
Story of Wimpy, a wump
Drake, Joan
Wimpy series (1)
Story of Wyatt Earp
Everitt, David
Legends series (1)
Story of Wy-Lah the cockatoo
Rees, Leslie
Australian nature tales series (10)
Story-teller's story
Anderson, Sherwood
Story-teller series (2)
Story the parrot told
Hunt, Francis
Mary and Jerry Denton series (3)
Story to tell
Bruna, Dick
Stories to tell series (1)
Storybook of the green planet
Kotzwinkle, William
E.T. series (2)
Storyteller and the Jann
Goldin, Stephen
Parsina series (2)
Storyteller tells the truth
Ruck, Berta
Storyteller series (1)
Storytrails book of science fiction
Sharp, Allen
Storytrails series (16)
Storytrails book of thrillers
Sharp, Allen
Storytrails series (18)
Stout heart
Kellogg, Elijah
Whispering Pine series (5)
Stover at Yale
Johnson, Owen McMahon
Lawrenceville series (4)
Stowaway of the S.S. Wanderer
Parsons, Anthony
Sexton Blake series (1079)
Stowaway to the mushroom planet
Cameron, Eleanor
Tyco Bass series (2)
Stowaways in the Abbey
Oxenham, Elsie J
Abbey girls retrospective series (3)
Stowmarket mystery
Tracy, Louis
Reginald Brett series (1)
Straf Batalion 999
Konsalik, Heinz Gunther
Stalingrad series (2)
Straight
Knickmeyer, Steve
Steve Cranmer series (1)
Straight ahead for danger
Duncan, William Murdoch
Greensleeves series (2)
Straight man
Simon, Roger Lichtenberg
Moses Wine series (5)
Strand
Rayner, Claire
Performers series (8)
Stranded
Norwood, Warren
Time police series (3)
Stranded duck
Finkel, George
Sabotage series (1)
Strands of red hair!
Glint Green
Inspector Wield series (1)
Strange adventure stories for boys
Thompson, Ames
Jewel series (4)
Strange adventures of Bromley Barnes
Barton, George
Bromley Barnes series (1)
Strange adventures of Jonathan Drew, a rolling stone
Ward, Christopher
Jonathan Drew series (1)
Strange adventures of Mister Collin
Heller, Frank
Mister Collin series (3)
Strange adventures of the spider ship
Nowlan, Philip Francis
Buck Rogers series (5)
Strange affair at Graylands
Cross, Mark
Daphne Wrayne and her Four Adjusters series (24)
Strange affair of Adelaide Harris
Garfield, Leon
Bostock and Harris series (1)
Strange affair of the shot gun sniper
Tyrer, Walter
Sexton Blake series (1392)
Strange affair of the widow's diamonds
Clevely, Hugh
Sexton Blake series (1375)
Strange and the good
Fuller, Roy
Strange and the good trilogy (3)
Strange animals and their stories
Verrill, Alpheus Hyatt
Strange stories from nature series (6)
Strange attractor
Cory, Desmond
John Dobie and Kate Coyle series (1)
Strange bedfellows
Burkholz, Herbert
Sensitives series (2)
Strange birds and their stories
Verrill, Alpheus Hyatt
Strange stories from nature series (4)
Strange capers
Warde, Joan
Forrester family series (3)
Strange case for Archie
Bateman, Robert
Archibald McGillicuddy series (6)
Strange case of Doctor Earle
Crofts, Freeman Wills
Inspector Joseph French series (10)
Strange case of Doctor Jekyll and Mister Hyde
Cameron, Joan
Doctor Jekyll series (1)
Harris, Raymond
Doctor Jekyll series (1)
Stevenson, Robert Louis
Doctor Jekyll series (1)
Strange case of Edgar Heriot
Grierson, Francis Durham
Inspector George Muir series (12)
Strange case of Edgar Herriot
Grierson, Francis Durham
Superintendent Andrew Ash series (5)
Strange case of Habberton's Mile
Bayfield, William John
Sexton Blake series (325)
Strange case of Harriet Hall
Dalton, Moray
Inspector Hugh Collier series (5)
Strange case of Mortimer Fenley
Tracy, Louis
Inspector Furneaux series (3)
Strange case of Pamela Wilson
Cross, Mark
Daphne Wrayne and her Four Adjusters series (33)
Strange case of Peter the Lett
Simenon, Georges
Inspector Jules Maigret series (1)
Strange case of Sir Merton Quest
Soutar, Andrew
Phineas Spinnet series (12)
Strange case of the antlered man
Brooks, Edwy Searles
Inspector William Beeke series (1)
Strange case of the footman's crime
Chester, Gilbert
Sexton Blake series (1114)
Strange case of the Megatherium thefts
Roberts, E C
Sherlock Holmes sequels series (5)
Strange case of William Cook
Keverne, Richard
Franklin Parry and Leonard Harris series (1)
Strange cases of Mason Brent
Hopkins, Nevil Monroe
Mason Brant series (1)
Strange clues
M'Govan, James
James M'Govan series (3)
Strange conflict
Batchelor, John M
Strange conflict series (1)
Wheatley, Dennis
Duc de Richelieu series (5)
Strange corpse on Murder Mile
Boyle, Denis
Commander Moreton Shade series (1)
Strange craft and its wonderful voyage
Ellis, Edward Sylvester
Northwest series (1)
Strange creatures of the sea
Verrill, Alpheus Hyatt
Strange stories from nature series (8)
Strange death of Manny Square
Cunningham, Albert Benjamin
Sheriff Jess Roden series (3)
Strange death of Martin Green
Frome, David
Major Gregory Lewis series (2)
Strange destiny
Janson, Hank
Hank Janson series (73)
Strange disappearance
Green, Anna Katharine
Ebenezer Gryce series (2)
Strange disappearance from Ward 2
Deming, Dorothy
Wendy Brent series (2)
Strange disappearance of Joe Cardona
Grant, Maxwell
Shadow series (113)

Strange disappearance of Mary Young
Propper, Milton
Tommy Rankin series (1)
Strange discovery
Dake, Charles Romyn
Arthur Gordon Pym series (2)
Strange doings on Halfaday Creek
Hendryx, James Beardsley
Black John series (7)
Strange echo
Judd, Frances K
Kay Tracey series (2)
Strange ending
Punshon, Ernest Robertson
Bobby Owen series (31)
Strange eons
Bloch, Robert
Cthulhu Mythos series (7)
Strange face of murder
Ballinger, W A
Sexton Blake series (1568)
Strange family
Watson, Edmund Henry Lacon
Strange family trilogy (1)
Strange felony
Linington, Elizabeth
Sergeant Ivor Maddox series (13)
Strange fish
Robeson, Kenneth
Doc Savage series (138)
Strange fish and their stories
Verrill, Alpheus Hyatt
Strange stories from nature series (5)
Strange fortune
Salt, Jonathan
Jonathan Salt series (1)
Strange hiding place
Beresford, Elisabeth
Gappy, Jim and Jane series (6)
Strange hill
Cockett, Mary
Strange valley trilogy (2)
Strange holiday
Gill, Elizabeth
Benvenuto Brown series (1)
Strange insects and their stories
Verrill, Alpheus Hyatt
Strange stories from nature series (2)
Strange intruder
Catherall, Arthur
Bulldog tugboat series (9)
Strange invader
Catherall, Arthur
Bulldog tugboat series (9)
Strange invasion at Catfish Bend
Burman, Ben Lucien
Catfish Bend series (6)
Strange little snakes
Turner, James Ernest
Rampion Savage series (3)
Strange magic
Beresford, Elisabeth
Magic series (9)
Strange message in the parchment
Keene, Carolyn
Nancy Drew series (54)
Strange motives
Goyne, Richard
Paul Templeton series (1)
Strange ordeal of Sarah Pedlock
Longstreet, Stephen
Pedlock family series (2)
Strange papers of Doctor Blayre
Blayre, Christopher
University of Cosmopoli series (2)
Strange paradise
Daniels, Dorothy
Strange paradise trilogy (1)
Strange people
Batchelor, John M
Strange conflict series (2)
Strange prehistoric animals and their stories
Verrill, Alpheus Hyatt
Strange stories from nature series (7)
Strange prisoner
Home, Michael
John Benham series (1)
Strange quest at Cliff House
Moss, Nancy
Cliff House series (3)
Strange reptiles and their stories
Verrill, Alpheus Hyatt
Strange stories from nature series (3)
Strange return
Cunningham, Albert Benjamin
Sheriff Jess Roden series (21)
Strange riders at Black Pony Inn
Pullein-Thompson, Christine
Black Pony Inn series (1)
Strange ritual
Janson, Hank
Hank Janson series (162)
Strange roads
Diver, Maud
English scene series (2)
Strange schemes of Randolph Mason
Post, Melville Davisson
Randolph Mason series (1)
Strange sea shells and their stories
Verrill, Alpheus Hyatt
Strange stories from nature series (1)
Strange sights abroad
Optic, Oliver
All-over-the-world series (4)
Strange smell of murder
Dundas, Lawrence
Andrew Salmond series (3)
Strange story of Pippin Wood
Byers, Irene
Jeremy and Fenella series (1)
Strange swimming coach
Jenkins, Jerry Bruce
Dallas O'Neil and the Baker Street Sports Club series (7)
Strange times at Fairwood High
Norton, Nancy
Homeroom series (1)
Strange tomorrow
Karl, Jean Edna
Future past series (2)
Strange valley
Cockett, Mary
Strange valley trilogy (1)
Strange woman
Williams, Ben Ames
Thread of scarlet series (3)
Strangely she died
Morland, Nigel
Steven Malone series (1)
Stranger
Gilman, George G
Adam Steele series (28)
Steele's war series (4)
Mottram, Ralph Hale
Spanish Farm series (3)
Reno, Bill
Badge series (8)
Ross, Lillian
Big Sur series (1)
Stranger and afraid
Turner, George Reginald
Treelake series (1)
Stranger at Follyfoot
Dickens, Monica
Follyfoot Farm series (4)
Stranger at Green Knowe
Boston, Lucy Maria
Green Knowe series (4)
Stranger came back
Franklin, Charles
Grant Garfield series (12)
Stranger came to dinner
Soutar, Andrew
Phineas Spinnet series (10)
Stranger city caper
Spencer, Ross Harrison
Chance Purdue series (3)
Stranger danger
Jackson, Ellen B
Safety series (3)
Stranger from nowhere
Miller, Jim
Ex-Rangers series (10)
Stranger from the sea
Graham, Winston
Poldark series (8)
Stranger in a strange town
Gilman, George G
Adam Steele series (35)
Stranger in boots
Scott, Bradford
Walt Slade series (7)
Stranger in Dodge
Bell, Robert Vaughn
McGowan family series (3)
Stranger in Savannah
Price, Eugenia
Savannah quartet (4)
Stranger in the herd
Patchett, Mary Elwyn
Joey Meehan series (4)
Stranger in the Midlands
Treneer, Anne
Schoolhouse trilogy (3)
Stranger in the mirror
Beach, Lynn
Phantom Valley series (4)
Stranger in the shadows
Keene, Carolyn
Nancy Drew series (103)
Stranger in the square
Koestler, Arthur
Arrow in the blue series (3)
Stranger in town
Halliday, Brett
Michael Shayne series (27)
Rey, Bret
Ralph Coates series (2)
Stranger in two worlds
Harris, Jean
Two worlds series (1)
Stranger named O'Shea
Clinton, Jeff
Wildcat O'Shea series (12)
Stranger on Rhanna
Fraser, Christine Marion
Rhanna series (7)
Stranger prince
Irwin, Margaret
Stuart series (3)
Stranger to the town
Hood, Evelyn
Paisley series (1)
Strangers
Memmi, Albert
Tunisian Jew series (2)
Strangers all are gone
Powell, Anthony
To keep the ball rolling series (4)
Strangers among the dead
Bellairs, George
Detective Inspector Thomas Littlejohn series (44)
Strangers and brothers
Snow, Charles Percy
Strangers and brothers series (2)
Strangers at Collins House
Ross, Marilyn
Barnabas Collins series (3)
Strangers at Golden Path
Gervaise, Mary
Marstons series (4)
Strangers at Lisconnel
Barlow, Jane
Lisconnel series (2)
Strangers at the Abbey
Oxenham, Elsie J
Abbey girls retrospective series (5)
Strangers at the door
Lyon, Elinor
Ian and Sovra series (8)
Strangers at the farm
Chambers, Rosamund Mary
Napoleon and Josephine series (3)
Strangers at The Warren
Sindall, Marjorie Aylwynn
Warren series (2)
Strangers at Warrenders' Halt
Wallace, Ivy Lilian
Warrenders series (3)
Strangers at Witchend
Saville, Malcolm
Lone Pine Five Club series (18)
Strangers for tea
Scott, Mary
New Zealand life series (10)
Strangers from the sky
Bonanno, Margaret Wander
Star trek sequels series (4)
Strangers in Carrigmore
Reid, Meta Mayne
Tiffany series (4)
Strangers in Fleet Street
Edwards, Sylvia
Sally Baxter series (16)
Strangers in Florida
Glemser, Bernard
Robert Crane trilogy (2)
Strangers in the land
Troyat, Henri
Danov family trilogy (3)
Strangers of Snowfell
Saville, Malcolm
Jillies series (3)
Strangers on earth
Troyat, Henri
Danov family trilogy (3)
Strangers riding by
Grover, Marshall
Larry and Stretch series (424)
Stranger's son
Keevil, John Joyce
Baldwin Hamey series (2)
Strangers to the Marsh
Edwards, Monica
Romney Marsh series (11)
Stranger's wife
Stahl, Hilda
Prairie series (2)
Strangled prose
Hess, Joan
Claire Malloy series (1)
Strangled queen
Druon, Maurice
Accursed kings series (2)
Strangled witness
Ford, Leslie
Colonel John Primrose series (1)
Stranglehold
Arvay, Harry
Israeli Security Branch series (7)
Carmichael, Harry
John Piper and Quinn series (15)
Conroy, Al
Johnny Morini series (3)
Cory, Desmond
Mister Dee series (1)
Rowe, Jennifer
Verity Birdwood series (5)
Strangler
Hall, Parnell
Stanley Hastings series (4)
Marshall, Lovat
Sugar Kane series (26)
Plummer, Thomas Arthur
Detective Inspector Andrew Frampton series (22)
San Antonio
Berurier series (7)
San Antonio series (6)
Stone, Hampton
Jeremiah X Gibson series (8)
Strangler wwho couldn't let go
Stone, Hampton
Jeremiah X Gibson series (8)
Stranglers
Estleman, Loren D
Page Murdock series (4)
Strangler's holiday
Steel, Kurt
Hank Hyer series (4)
Strangler's moon
Leader, Charles
Paul Mason series (2)
Stranglers' moon
Smith, Edward Elmer
Family d'Alembert series (2)
Stranglers of Paris
Belot, Adolphe
Stranglers series (1)
Strangling man
Hunter, Alan
Inspector George Gently series (35)
Stranleigh's millions
Barr, Robert
Lord Stranleigh series (2)
Strapped for cash
Browne, Dik
Hagar the horrible series (38)
Strasbourg
Margueritte, Paul
Franco-Prussian War series (3)
Strategic moves
Dixon, Franklin W
Hardy boys case files series (43)
Strathmore
Stirling, Jessica
Stalker family trilogy (1)
Stratoship Twenty Two
Herge
Adventures of Jo, Zette and Jocko series (2)
Strausser transfer
Smith, Don
Secret mission series (21)
Stravaigers
Gowans, Elizabeth
Blair family series (1)
Straw donkey case
Fleischman, Sid
Max Brindle series (1)
Straw hats and serge bloomers
Elias, Eileen
Lewisham series (2)
Straw man
Disney, Doris Miles
Jeff Dimarco series (3)
Giono, Jean
Angelo series (3)
Straw without bricks
Delafield, E M
Provincial lady series (4)
Provincial lady series (5)
Strawberries and cream
Levy, Muriel
Wonk series (2)
Strawberry blonde jungle
Brown, Carter
Danny Boyd series (29)
Strawberry girl
Lenski, Lois
Regional series (2)
Strawberry Shortcake and baby needs a name
Elliott, Brian
Strawberry Shortcake series (15)
Strawberry Shortcake and sad Mister Sun
Lexau, Joan M
Strawberry Shortcake series (11)
Strawberry Shortcake and the big balloon race
Winthrop, Elizabeth
Strawberry Shortcake series (9)
Strawberry Shortcake and the birthday surprise
Doyle, Elizabeth
Strawberry Shortcake series (12)
Strawberry Shortcake and the catnabbing
Elliott, Brian
Strawberry Shortcake series (15)
Strawberry Shortcake and the crazy baking contest
Miller, Nell
Strawberry Shortcake series (10)
Strawberry Shortcake and the deep dark woods
Rosenblatt, Arthur
Strawberry Shortcake series (8)
Strawberry Shortcake and the fake cake surprise
Elliott, Brian
Strawberry Shortcake series (15)
Strawberry Shortcake and the picnic plot
Elliott, Brian
Strawberry Shortcake series (15)
Strawberry Shortcake one-two-three
Sustendal, Pat
Strawberry Shortcake series (6)
Strawberry Shortcake pets on parade
Daly, Kathleen
Strawberry Shortcake series (7)
Strawberry Shortcake playhouse
Razzi, Jim
Strawberry Shortcake series (3)
Strawberry Shortcake sunny day poems
Saphore, Athena
Strawberry Shortcake series (5)
Strawberry Shortcake toy book
Razzi, Jim
Strawberry Shortcake series (2)
Strawberry Shortcake's bathtime book
Elliott, Brian
Strawberry Shortcake series (15)
Strawberry Shortcake's cooking fun
Smollin, Michael J
Strawberry Shortcake series (1)
Strawberry Shortcake's favorite Mother Goose rhymes
Llimona, Mercedes
Strawberry Shortcake series (14)
Strawberry Shortcake's make-and-do book
Fahrion, Muriel
Strawberry Shortcake series (4)
Strawberry Shortcake's party fun
Smollin, Michael J
Strawberry Shortcake series (13)
Strawberry Shortcake's year-round coloring book
Shore, Susan
Strawberry Shortcake series (15)
Strawberry summer
Blair, Cynthia
Susan and Christine Pratt series (3)
Strawgirl
Padgett, Abigail
Bo Bradley series (2)
Straws and prayer-books
Cabell, James Branch
Dom Manuel and his descendants series (22)
Stray pearls
Yonge, Charlotte Mary
Rebaumont series (2)
Stray shot
Hammond, Gerald
Keith Calder series (13)
Simon Parbitter series (2)
Strayings of Sandy
Conyers, Dorothea
Sandy series (1)
Streak
Kroll, Steven
Hit and Run Gang series (4)
Streak of light
Lockridge, Richard
Nathan Shapiro series (11)

Streaked-blonde slave
Brown, Carter
Rick Holman series (21)
Streaked peril
Carter, Nicholas
Nicholas Carter series (394)
Streaked with crimson
Dutton, Charles Judson
Harley Manners series (1)
Streaks of life
Smyth, Ethel Mary
Impressions series (2)
Stream in the Wild Wood
Clewes, Dorothy
Wild Wood series (2)
Stream that stood still
Nichols, Beverley
Judy series (2)
Streamlined murder
Macveigh, Sue
Captain Andy and Sue McVeigh series (3)
Streams of silver
Salvatore, Robert Anthony
Icewind Dale trilogy (2)
Street
Richler, Mordecai
Saint Urbain's Street series (1)
Street Hawk
Roberts, Jack
Street Hawk series (1)
Street musician
Berna, Paul
Gaby series (2)
Street of adventure
Gibbs, Philip
Oliver series (1)
Street of grass
Audemars, Pierre
Monsieur Pinaud series (6)
Street of Mars
Jackson, Rosemary Elizabeth
Macgillan family series (4)
Street of the crying woman
Homes, Geoffrey
Jose Manuel Madero series (1)
Street of the five moons
Peters, Elizabeth
Vicky Bliss series (2)
Street of the leopard
Morland, Nigel
Mrs Palmyra Pym series (3)
Street of the small night market
Sherry, Sylvia
Yusof series (1)
Street spies
Dixon, Franklin W
Hardy boys case files series (21)
Street where I live
Kershaw, H V
Coronation Street series (3)
Streetbird
Van de Wetering, Janwillem
De Gier and Grijpstra series (9)
Streets of blood
Rawls, Philip
Richard Bronson series (2)
Streets of death
Shannon, Dell
Lieutenant Luis Mendoza series (27)
Streets of gold
Branson, Karen
Maureen O'Connor series (2)
Streets of Laredo
McMurtry, Larry
Lonesome dove series (2)
Streets of shadow
McFarlane, Leslie
Michael Brent series (1)
Streets of the city
Spedding, Alison
Walk in the dark trilogy (3)
Strega
Vachss, Andrew
Burke series (2)
Strega Nona
De Paola, Tomie
Strega Nona series (1)
Strega Nona's magic lessons
De Paola, Tomie
Strega Nona series (2)
Strelsau dimension
Haythorne, John
Oliver Mandrake series (2)
Strelsen Castle mystery
Pink, Hal
Inspector Docker series (2)
Strenuous years
Beaton, Cecil
Years diaries series (4)
Stressed for success
Guisewhite, Cathy
Cathy series (6)
Stretch-berry smile
Scarborough, Dorothy
Cotton trilogy (3)
Stretching the truth
Pascal, Francine
Sweet Valley twins series (13)
Streuth
Green, Michael
Coarse plays series (1)
Stricken field
Duncan, Dave
Handful of men series (3)
Stricken land
Thompson, Ernest Victor
Retallick family series (5)
Stricken world, 1917-1922
Gilbert, Martin
Winston S Churchill series (4)
Strictly business
Henry, O
Four million series (4)
Strictly corruptible
Brody, Marc
Marc Brody series (19)
Strictly illegal
Bresler, Fenton Shea
British law series (3)
Strictly legal
Bresler, Fenton Shea
British law series (2)
Strictly personal
Horler, Sydney
Strictly personal series (1)
Maugham, William Somerset
Summing up trilogy (2)
Strictly private business
Cronin, Michael
Sam Harris series (8)
Strictly tied up
Hope, Alexander James Beresford
Brandreths series (1)
Strictly wild
Brand, Hilary
Hilary Brand series (6)
Striding folly
Sayers, Dorothy Leigh
Lord Peter Wimsey series (15)
Strife
Tinker, Frances
Old New Orleans quartet (2)
Strike
Hardcastle, Michael
Tony and Jay series (5)
Helm, Eric
Super Vietnam series (3)
Strike at Shane's
Shelton, James S
Black Beauty series (1)
Strike fighters
Willard, Tom
Strike fighters series (1)
Strike for a kingdom
Gallie, Menna
Cilhendre Village series (1)
Strike for death
Creasey, John
Inspector Roger West series (23)
Strike for freedom
Carter, Nicholas
Nicholas Carter series (296)
Strike for Tomahawk
Field, Peter
Powder Valley series (54)
Strike force
Macdonnell, James Edmond
Dutchy Holland series (22)
Strike force terror
Carter, Nick
Nick Carter series (70)
Strike north
Baker, William Howard
Richard Quintain series (3)
Strike of the cobra
Rizzi, Timothy
Major General Duke James series (2)
Strike of the hawk
Carter, Nick
Nick Carter series (134)
Strike out where not applicable
Freeling, Nicolas
Inspector Piet Van der Valk series (7)
Strike terror
Steirman, Hy
Zachary Jones series (1)
Strike the strikers
Target, George William
Post-war Britain series (9)
Strike three!
Bee, Clair
Chip Hilton series (3)
Strike three you're dead
Rosen, Richard
Harvey Blissberg series (1)
Strike Zion!
Stevenson, William Henri
Israeli armed services series (2)
Strike zone
Curtis, Richard
Dave Bolt series (3)
David, Peter
Star trek, the next generation series (5)
Nighbert, David Franklin
Bull Cochran series (1)
Strikefast
Charles, Robert
Simon Larren series (10)
Striker
Cope, Kenneth
Striker series (1)
Striker one down
Pruitt, James H
Soldier of fortune series (8)
Striker portfolio
Hall, Adam
Quiller series (3)
Striker, second leg
Cope, Kenneth
Striker series (2)
String family
Cleveland-Peck, Patricia
String family trilogy (1)
String family at home
Cleveland-Peck, Patricia
String family trilogy (3)
String family in summer
Cleveland-Peck, Patricia
String family trilogy (2)
String family moves house
Cleveland-Peck, Patricia
String family trilogy (3)
String glove mystery
Campbell, Harriette Russell
Simon Brade series (1)
Stringer
Cameron, Lou
Stringer series (1)
Stringer and the border war
Cameron, Lou
Stringer series (11)
Stringer and the deadly flood
Cameron, Lou
Stringer series (8)
Stringer and the hanging judge
Cameron, Lou
Stringer series (6)
Stringer and the hangman's rodeo
Cameron, Lou
Stringer series (4)
Stringer and the hell-bound herd
Cameron, Lou
Stringer series (14)
Stringer and the lost tribe
Cameron, Lou
Stringer series (9)
Stringer and the Mojave
Cameron, Lou
Stringer series (12)
Stringer and the oil well Indians
Cameron, Lou
Stringer series (10)
Stringer and the wild bunch
Cameron, Lou
Stringer series (5)
Stringer in a Texas shoot-out
Cameron, Lou
Stringer series (15)
Stringer in Tombstone
Cameron, Lou
Stringer series (7)
Stringer on Dead Man's Range
Cameron, Lou
Stringer series (2)
Stringer on Pike's Peak
Cameron, Lou
Stringer series (13)
Stringer on the assassin's trail
Cameron, Lou
Stringer series (3)
Strip death naked
Longmate, Norman
Inspector Bradley and Sergeant Raymond series (3)
Strip for murder
Prather, Richard Scott
Shell Scott series (11)
Strip Jack naked
Baron, Alexander
Harryboy Boas series (2)
Strip search
Burns, Rex
Gabriel Wager series (6)
Strip tease
Bruce, Jean
Secret Agent O.S.S.117 series (13)
Strip-tease macabre
Gribble, Leonard Reginald
Superintendent Anthony Slade series (32)
Stripe for a stripe
Sandys, James
James Charlesworth series (1)
Striped holes
Broderick, Damien
Faustus hexagram series (5)
Striped suitcase
Carnac, Carol
Inspector Julian Rivers series (2)
Striplings
Hooke, Nina Warner
Striplings trilogy (1)
Stripped for murder
Fischer, Bruno
Ben Helm series (6)
Stripper
Brown, Carter
Lieutenant Al Wheeler series (21)
Stripper strikes out
McCall, K T
Johnny Buchanan series (22)
Striptease murders
Lee, Gypsy Rose
Gypsy Rose Lee series (1)
Strive and succeed
Alger, Horatio
Luck and pluck series (4)
Striving after wind
Johnston, Norma
Of time series (2)
Stroke of luck
Hughes, Dean
Angel Park All-Stars series (10)
Stroke of one
Walling, Robert Alfred John
Garstang series (1)
Stroke of policy
Carter, Nicholas
Nicholas Carter series (110)
Stroke sinister, and other stories
Horler, Sydney
Martin Huish series (2)
Strong and steady
Alger, Horatio
Luck and pluck series (3)
Strong arm
Barr, Robert
Mediaeval Rhine series (2)
Strong-arm
Copper, Basil
Mike Faraday series (11)
Strong arm
Hardcastle, Michael
Steve and Anna series (2)
Strong arm and a mother's blessing
Kellogg, Elijah
Good old times series (2)
Strong arm stuff
Spade, Danny
Danny Spade series (20)
Strong dose of myself
Abse, Dannie
Poet in the family series (3)
Strong hand
Grier, Sydney Carlyon
Princess series (3)
Strong hours
Diver, Maud
English scene series (3)
Strong medicine
Sutton, Jessica
Bel Air General series (7)
Strong-minded woman
Hammond, William Alexander
Lal series (2)
Strong poison
Sayers, Dorothy Leigh
Harriet Vane series (1)
Lord Peter Wimsey series (6)
Strong wind
Asturias, Miguel Angel
Guatemala trilogy (1)
Strongheld
Mackenzie, Steve
Seals series (12)
Stronghold
Church, Richard
John Quickshott series (2)
Rawn, Melanie
Dragon star series (1)
Strontium code
Carter, Nick
Nick Carter series (151)
Strosa light
Pope, Ray
Strosa light series (1)
Struck down at midnight
Ridley, Nat
Nat Ridley series (16)
Structures of everyday life
Braudel, Fernand
Civilization and capitalism trilogy (1)
Struggle
Ahern, Jerry
Survivalist series (18)
Smith, Lisa J
Vampire diaries series (2)
Struggle at Soltuna
Anckarsvard, Karin
Jon Halvorsson series (2)
Struggle for equality
McPherson, James Munro
Abolitionist series (1)
Struggle with destiny
Carter, Nicholas
Nicholas Carter series (548)
Strychnine for one
Plummer, Thomas Arthur
Detective Inspector Andrew Frampton series (30)
Strychnine stand-off
Tully, Paul
Deputy Marshal Hooky Gibbs series (4)
Stryker
Crawford, William
Colin Stryker series (1)
Stuart fashion
Birt, David
Stuarts series (11)
Stuart legacy
Kerr, Robert
Jamie Stuart series (1)
Stuart navy
Birt, David
Stuarts series (2)
Stuart stain
Roberts, Willo Davis
Black pearl series (3)
Stubborn heart
Slaughter, Frank Gill
American Civil War series (2)
Stucco house
Cannan, Gilbert
Laurie series (4)
Stuck in the middle
McKenna, Colleen O'Shaughnessy
Cousins series (2)
Stud game
Anthony, David
Stanley Bass series (2)
Stud service
Revere, John D
Justin Perry series (5)
Student body
Borthwick, J S
Sarah Deane and Alex Mackenzie series (3)
Fitzgerald, Nigel
Superintendent Duffy series (5)
Student buccaneer
Barbary, James
Adventure in history series (3)
Student fraternity murder
Propper, Milton
Tommy Rankin series (4)
Student nurse
Palmer, Bernard
Career series (1)
Studio crime
Chester, Gilbert
Sexton Blake series (702)
Studio murder mystery
Edingtons
Captain Smith series (1)
Studio mystery
Armour, R Coutts
Sexton Blake series (212)
Studio One murder
Ballinger, W A
Sexton Blake series (1538)
Studmaster of Canning Downs
Nott, Loraine
Ceb Barnes series (2)
Study break
Blake, Susan
Hawthorne College series (15)
Study in courage and fear
Coles, Robert
Children of crisis series (1)
Study in lilac
Oliver, Maria Antonia
Lonia Guiu series (1)

Study in scarlet
Doyle, Arthur Conan
Sherlock Holmes series (1)

Study in sorcery
Kurland, Michael
Lord Darcy series (5)

Study in surmise
Harrison, Michael
Life of Sherlock Holmes series (6)

Study in suspense
Soutar, Andrew
Phineas Spinnet series (14)

Study in terror
Queen, Ellery
Ellery Queen series (39)

Study of death
Leslie, Francis
Jimmy Langry series (1)

Study of woman
Balzac, Honore de
Scenes of private life series (12)

Study Thirteen in a tangle
Havilton, Jeffrey
Study Thirteen series (4)

Study Thirteen to the rescue
Havilton, Jeffrey
Study Thirteen series (2)

Stuffed man
O'Sullivan, James Brendan
Steve Silk series (9)

Stuffed men
Rud, Anthony Melville
J C K Masters series (3)

Stumpfs
Onslow, John
Stumpfs series (1)

Stumpfs and the Cornish witches
Onslow, John
Stumpfs series (2)

Stunning way to die
Christmas, Joyce
Lady Margaret Priam series (4)

Stupids die
Allard, Harry
Stupids series (3)
Marshall, James
Stupids series (3)

Stupids have a ball
Allard, Harry
Stupids series (2)
Marshall, James
Stupids series (2)

Stupids step out
Allard, Harry
Stupids series (1)
Marshall, James
Stupids series (1)

Stupids take off
Allard, Harry
Stupids series (4)
Marshall, James
Stupids series (4)

Stuyvesat
Abbott, Jacob
Franconia series (8)

Sub killers
San Antonio
Berurier series (3)
San Antonio series (3)

Subaltern's choice
Macneil, Duncan
James Ogilvie series (6)

Subaltern's war
Edmonds, Charles
Subaltern series (1)

Subject, murder
Witting, Clifford
Inspector Charlton series (6)
Inspector Peter Bradfield series (2)

Subject of Harry Egypt
Broun, Daniel
Harry Egypt series (1)

Submarine
Wingate, John
Third World War trilogy (3)

Submarine alone
Hackforth-Jones, Gilbert
Submarine Service series (3)

Submarine boys and the middies
Durham, Victor
Submarine boys series (3)

Submarine boys and the smugglers
Durham, Victor
Submarine boys series (7)

Submarine boys and the spies
Durham, Victor
Submarine boys series (4)

Submarine boys for the flag
Durham, Victor
Submarine boys series (6)

Submarine boys' lightning cruise
Durham, Victor
Submarine boys series (5)

Submarine boys on duty
Durham, Victor
Submarine boys series (1)

Submarine boys' secret mission
Durham, Victor
Submarine boys series (8)

Submarine boys' trail trip
Durham, Victor
Submarine boys series (2)

Submarine flotilla
Hackforth-Jones, Gilbert
Submarine Service series (1)

Submarine hunt
Holliday, Joe
Dale of the Mounted series (7)

Submarine island
Gunn, John
Peter Kent series (4)

Submarine mystery
Robeson, Kenneth
Doc Savage series (63)

Submarine rescue
Berres, Frances B
Deep-sea adventure series (3)

Submarine trail
Carter, Nicholas
Nicholas Carter series (392)

Submarine U93
Gilson, Charles
Submarine U93 series (1)

Submariner Sinclair
Wingate, John
Submariner Sinclair series (1)

Subscription to murder
Heberden, Mary Violet
Desmond Shannon series (2)

Subsmash!
Macdonnell, James Edmond
Jim Brady series (3)

Subspace encounter
Smith, Edward Elmer
Subspace explorers series (2)

Subspace explorers
Smith, Edward Elmer
Subspace explorers series (1)

Substance of a dream
Bain, Francis William
Indian mystic love stories series (13)

Substance X
Houston, David
Tales of tomorrow series (3)

Substitute doctor
Seifert, Elizabeth
Bayard series (1)

Substitute general
Redmayne, John
Peter Maclean series (2)

Substitute teacher
Pascal, Francine
Sweet Valley kids series (3)

Substitute victim
Pentecost, Hugh
Julian Quist series (14)

Subterfuge
Maine, Charles Eric
Mike Delaney series (2)

Subterraneans
Kerouac, Jack
Jack Duluoz series (8)

Subtle trail
Gollomb, Joseph
Galt series (2)

Suburban book of the dead
Rankin, Robert
Armageddon trilogy (3)

Suburban girls, and other stories of married life
Cutting, Mary Stewart
Little stories of life series (4)

Sub-zero
Wingate, John
Submariner Sinclair series (5)

Success
Aminoff, Constance Leonie Caroline
Napoleonic series (4)
Feuchtwanger, Lion
Waiting-room tetralogy (1)

Success to the brave
Kent, Alexander
Captain Richard Bolitho series (16)

Succession
Sidgwick, Ethel
Tony Edgwell series (2)

Successors
Irving, Laurence
Irving family trilogy (2)

Succubus
Finch, Matthew
Dick Lingham series (3)

Such bright disguises
Flynn, Brian
Anthony Bathurst series (27)

Such devoted sisters
Linton, Cathy
Saint Lawrence's Hospital series (2)

Such is death
Bruce, Leo
Carolus Deene series (12)

Such is life
Collins, Tom
Such is life series (1)

Such men are dangerous
Thomas, Martin
Sexton Blake series (1582)

Such mighty rage
Clayton, Colin Guy
Blakeney papers series (2)

Such natural deaths
Anson, Lindsay
Peter Allen series (1)

Such pretty toys
Dean, S F X
Professor Neil Kelly series (2)

Such women are dangerous
Webb, Jack
Father Joseph Shanley and Sammy Golden series (2)

Sucker bait
Saber, Robert O
Carl Good series (6)

Sucker bet
Masters, Zeke
Faro Blake series (17)

Sudbury moon chase
Barnes, Michael
Just north series (6)

Sudden
Strange, Oliver
Sudden series (4)

Sudden, apache fighter
Christian, Frederick H
Sudden series (15)

Sudden at bay
Christian, Frederick H
Sudden series (14)

Sudden, dead or alive!
Christian, Frederick H
Sudden series (16)

Sudden death
Adams, Nicholas
Horror High series (6)
Crofts, Freeman Wills
Inspector Joseph French series (8)
Delman, David
Lieutenant Jacob Horowitz series (2)
Kienzle, William Xavier
Father Robert Koesler series (7)
Pendleton, Don
SuperBolan series (7)
Thayer, Lee
Peter Clancy series (20)

Sudden death at Scotland Yard
Begbie, Garstin
Superintendent Samuel Quan series (1)

Sudden death finish
Halleran, Tucker
Cam Maccardle series (2)

Sudden departures
Ross, Jonathan
Superintendent George Rogers series (15)

Sudden, fearful death
Perry, Anne
Inspector William Monk series (1)

Sudden fury
Willard, Tom
Strike fighters series (4)

Sudden glow of gold
Fine, Anne
Genie trilogy (3)

Sudden, gold-seeker
Strange, Oliver
Sudden series (6)

Sudden guns
Brady, William S
Jared Hawk series (1)

Sudden impact
Stinson, Joe
Dirty Harry Callahan series (12)

Sudden makes war
Strange, Oliver
Sudden series (10)

Sudden outlawed
Strange, Oliver
Sudden series (5)

Sudden plays a hand
Strange, Oliver
Sudden series (11)

Sudden puff of glittering smoke
Fine, Anne
Genie trilogy (1)

Sudden rides again
Strange, Oliver
Sudden series (7)

Sudden squall
Nolan, Jeannette Covert
Lace White series (3)

Sudden strikes back
Christian, Frederick H
Sudden series (12)

Sudden swirl of icy wind
Fine, Anne
Genie trilogy (2)

Sudden takes charge
Strange, Oliver
Sudden series (9)

Sudden takes the trail
Strange, Oliver
Sudden series (8)

Sudden thunder
Longtree, Warren T
Ruff Justice series (1)

Sudden, troubleshooter
Christian, Frederick H
Sudden series (13)

Sudden vengeance
Crispin, Edmund
Gervase Fen series (7)

Suddenly a corpse
Masur, Harold Q
Scott Jordan series (2)

Suddenly a hero
Grover, Marshall
Larry and Stretch series (166)

Suddenly at his residence
Brand, Christianna
Inspector Cockrill series (3)

Suddenly, at Singapore
Black, Gavin
Paul Harris series (1)

Suddenly by violence
Brown, Carter
Danny Boyd series (2)

Suddenly in her sorbet
Christmas, Joyce
Lady Margaret Priam series (1)

Suddenly in Vienna
McCutcheon, Hugh
Richard Logan series (2)

Suddenly it's murder
Story, Jack Trevor
Sexton Blake series (1531)

Suddenly it's sin
Janson, Hank
Hank Janson series (20)

Suddenly while gardening
Lemarchand, Elizabeth
Superintendent Tom Pollard series (10)

Suddenly you're dead
Wright, Wade
Bart Condor series (1)

Suds in your eye
Lasswell, Mary
Mrs Feeley series (1)

Sue and the honey machine
Hunt, Peter
Honey machine series (1)

Sue Barton, neighbourhood nurse
Boylston, Helen Dore
Sue Barton series (6)

Sue Barton, rural nurse
Boylston, Helen Dore
Sue Barton series (4)

Sue Barton, senior nurse
Boylston, Helen Dore
Sue Barton series (2)

Sue Barton, staff nurse
Boylston, Helen Dore
Sue Barton series (7)

Sue Barton, student nurse
Boylston, Helen Dore
Sue Barton series (1)

Sue Barton, superintendent nurse
Boylston, Helen Dore
Sue Barton series (5)

Sue Barton, superintendent of nurses
Boylston, Helen Dore
Sue Barton series (5)

Sue Barton, visiting nurse
Boylston, Helen Dore
Sue Barton series (3)

Sue Crowther's marriage
Armstrong, Thomas
Crowther chronicles series (3)

Sue me
Sapir, Richard
Destroyer series (66)

Sue Orcutt
Vaile, Carlotte Marion
Orcutt girls series (2)

Suedehead
Allen, Richard
Joe Hawkins series (2)

Sue's circus horse
Berrisford, Judith Mary
Sue Trent series (1)

Sue's TV pony
Berrisford, Judith Mary
Sue Trent series (3)

Suffer a witch
Fitzgerald, Nigel
Superintendent Duffy series (6)

Sufficient rope
Gregg, Cecil Freeman
Inspector Cuthbert Higgins series (31)

Suffolk childhood
Dewes, Simon
When the world was young trilogy (1)

Sugar
Owen, Dilys
Mister Munch series (3)

Sugar and vice
Janson, Hank
Hank Janson series (84)

Sugar Creek Gang
Hutchens, Paul
Sugar Creek Gang series (1)

Sugar Creek Gang and screams in the night
Hutchens, Paul
Sugar Creek Gang series (12)

Sugar Creek Gang and the battle of the bees
Hutchens, Paul
Sugar Creek Gang series (33)

Sugar Creek Gang and the blue cow
Hutchens, Paul
Sugar Creek Gang series (21)

Sugar Creek Gang and the brown box
Hutchens, Paul
Sugar Creek Gang series (30)

Sugar Creek Gang and the bull fighter
Hutchens, Paul
Sugar Creek Gang series (20)

Sugar Creek Gang and the cemetery vandals
Hutchens, Paul
Sugar Creek Gang series (32)

Sugar Creek Gang and the Chicago adventure
Hutchens, Paul
Sugar Creek Gang series (5)

Sugar Creek Gang and the Colorado kidnapping
Hutchens, Paul
Sugar Creek Gang series (27)

Sugar Creek Gang and the ghost dog
Hutchens, Paul
Sugar Creek Gang series (28)

Sugar Creek Gang and the green tent mystery
Hutchens, Paul
Sugar Creek Gang series (19)

Sugar Creek Gang and the haunted house
Hutchens, Paul
Sugar Creek Gang series (16)

Sugar Creek Gang and the killer bear
Hutchens, Paul
Sugar Creek Gang series (3)

Sugar Creek Gang and the killer cat
Hutchens, Paul
Sugar Creek Gang series (29)

Sugar Creek Gang and the mystery cave
Hutchens, Paul
Sugar Creek Gang series (7)

Sugar Creek Gang and the mystery thief
Hutchens, Paul
Sugar Creek Gang series (9)

Sugar Creek Gang and the palm tree mystery
Hutchens, Paul
Sugar Creek Gang series (8)

Sugar Creek Gang and the runaway rescue
Hutchens, Paul
Sugar Creek Gang series (35)

Sugar Creek Gang and the swamp robber
Hutchens, Paul
Sugar Creek Gang series (1)

Sugar Creek Gang and the teacher trouble
Hutchens, Paul
Sugar Creek Gang series (11)

Sugar Creek Gang and the thousand dollar fish
Hutchens, Paul
Sugar Creek Gang series (15)

Sugar Creek Gang and the timber wolf
Hutchens, Paul
Sugar Creek Gang series (24)
Sugar Creek Gang and the trapline thief
Hutchens, Paul
Sugar Creek Gang series (22)
Sugar Creek Gang and the treasure hunt
Hutchens, Paul
Sugar Creek Gang series (14)
Sugar Creek Gang and the tree house mystery
Hutchens, Paul
Sugar Creek Gang series (26)
Sugar Creek Gang and the watermelon mystery
Hutchens, Paul
Sugar Creek Gang series (23)
Sugar Creek Gang and the Western adventure
Hutchens, Paul
Sugar Creek Gang series (25)
Sugar Creek Gang and the white boat rescue
Hutchens, Paul
Sugar Creek Gang series (31)
Sugar Creek Gang and the winter rescue
Hutchens, Paul
Sugar Creek Gang series (2)
Sugar Creek Gang at Snow Goose Lodge
Hutchens, Paul
Sugar Creek Gang series (24)
Sugar Creek Gang digs for treasure
Hutchens, Paul
Sugar Creek Gang series (14)
Sugar Creek Gang flies to Cuba
Hutchens, Paul
Sugar Creek Gang series (8)
Sugar Creek Gang goes north
Hutchens, Paul
Sugar Creek Gang series (12)
Sugar Creek Gang goes Western
Hutchens, Paul
Sugar Creek Gang series (25)
Sugar Creek Gang in school
Hutchens, Paul
Sugar Creek Gang series (6)
Sugar Creek Gang locked in the attic
Hutchens, Paul
Sugar Creek Gang series (34)
Sugar Creek Gang lost in the blizzard
Hutchens, Paul
Sugar Creek Gang series (17)
Sugar Creek Gang on the Mexican border
Hutchens, Paul
Sugar Creek Gang series (18)
Sugar Creek goes camping
Hutchens, Paul
Sugar Creek Gang series (4)
Sugar Creek in Chicago
Hutchens, Paul
Sugar Creek Gang series (5)
Sugar cuts the corners
Marshall, Lovat
Sugar Kane series (3)
Sugar festival
Park, Paul
Starbridge series (2)
Sugar for the horse
Bates, Herbert Ernest
Uncle Silas series (2)
Sugar for the lady
Marshall, Lovat
Sugar Kane series (1)
Sugar house
White, Antonia
Frost in May series (3)
Sugar in the air
Large, Ernest Charles
Charles Pry series (2)
Sugar-Loaf Mountain
Bancroft, Laura
Twinkle tales series (5)
Sugar on the carpet
Marshall, Lovat
Sugar Kane series (2)
Sugar on the cuff
Marshall, Lovat
Sugar Kane series (5)
Sugar on the kill
Marshall, Lovat
Sugar Kane series (6)
Sugar on the loose
Marshall, Lovat
Sugar Kane series (7)
Sugar on the prowl
Marshall, Lovat
Sugar Kane series (8)
Sugar on the target
Marshall, Lovat
Sugar Kane series (4)
Sugar rain
Park, Paul
Starbridge series (2)
Sugar Street
Mahfouz, Naguib
Cairo trilogy (3)
Sugar sugar
Williams, David
Tank series (3)
Sugar you're a scoop
Brody, Marc
Marc Brody series (71)
Sugarbird
Thompson, Kate
Derain family series (3)
Sugarcane Island
Packard, Edward
Choose your own adventure series (62)
Sugartown
Estleman, Loren D
Amos Walker series (5)
Suicide alibi
Rowland, John
Inspector Shelley series (4)
Suicide attack
Sievert, John
C.A.D.S. series (9)
Suicide clause
Carmichael, Harry
John Piper and Quinn series (25)
Suicide excepted
Hare, Cyril
Inspector Mallett series (3)
Suicide Hill
Ellroy, James
Sergeant Lloyd Hopkins trilogy (3)
Suicide in San Juan
Jason, Stuart
Butcher series (16)
Suicide king
Singer, Shelley
Jake Samson and Rosie Vincente series (5)
Suicide mission
Hawkins, Jack
Chopper series (6)
Suicide most foul
Sturrock, Jeremy
Bow Street Runner series (5)
Suicide murders
Engel, Howard
Benny Cooperman series (1)
Suicide notice
Engel, Howard
Benny Cooperman series (1)
Suicide pact
Desmond, Hugh
Alan Fraser series (1)
Suicide plague
Naha, Ed
Harry Porter series (2)
Suicide River
Mackie, John
Rat Bastards series (14)
Suicide run
Greenfield, Irving A
Depth force series (8)
Suicide season
Burns, Rex
Devlin Kirk series (1)
Suicide seat
Carter, Nick
Nick Carter series (140)
Suicide spies
Annesley, Michael
Lawrence Fenton series (8)
Suicide squad
Cain, Jonathan
Saigon commandos series (12)
Curtis, Richard
Dave Bolt series (4)
Suitable for framing
Buchanan, Edna
Britt Montero series (3)
Suitable vengeance
George, Elizabeth
Inspector Thomas Lynley and Sergeant Barbara Havers series (4)
Sukkot
Drucker, Malka
Jewish holidays series (4)
Sula
Derwent, Lavinia
Magnus series (1)
Sula Sea murders
Mason, Francis Van Wyck
Colonel Hugh North series (7)
Suldrun's garden
Vance, Jack
Lyonesse series (1)
Sullen sky mystery
Bailey, Henry Christopher
Mister Joshua Clunk series (3)
Sullivan's law
Gilman, George G
Edge series (20)
Sullivan's revenge
Cutter, John
Specialist series (3)
Sullivan's woman
Roberts, Nora
Flowers series (22)
Sultan's daughter
Wheatley, Dennis
Roger Brook series (7)
Sultan's gift
Henry, Marguerite
King of the wind series (5)
Sultan's pearls
Carter, Nicholas
Nicholas Carter series (608)
Sultan's renegade
Waltari, Mika
Michael Carvajel series (2)
Sultan's secret
Lerangis, Peter
G.I.Joe series (6)
Sultan's skull
Smith, Willard K
Inspector Dann Carr series (2)
Sultan's turret
Blackburn, Martin
Delgado series (1)
Cullen, Seamus
Noose series (2)
Sultry avenger
Janson, Hank
Hank Janson series (51)
Sum and total of now
Robertson, Don
Morris Bird III series (2)
Sum of things
Green, Roland James
Starcruiser Shenandoah series (3)
Manning, Olivia
Guy and Harriet Pringle series (6)
Sumi and the goat and the Tokyo Express
Uchida, Yoshiko
Sumi series (3)
Sumi's prize
Uchida, Yoshiko
Sumi series (1)
Sumi's special happening
Uchida, Yoshiko
Sumi series (2)
Summer
Allington, Richard L
Beginning to learn series (16)
Best, Jacqueline
Paul and Fritzi's year series (2)
Blyton, Enid
Round the year series (2)
Rolland, Romain
Soul enchanted series (2)
Summer adventure
Pudney, John
Fred and I series (9)
Summer at Cherry-Tree Farm
Kent, Margaret
Four seasons at Cherry-Tree Farm series (2)
Summer at Fairacre
Read, *Miss*
Fairacre series (15)
Summer at Forty-Five Acres
Wildsmith, Alan
Forty-Five Acres series (1)
Summer at Hallowdene Farm
Pocock, Doris Alice
Hallowdene Farm series (2)
Summer at home
Gillespie, Susan
Longdon-Lorristone family series (5)
Summer at Sheepfold Farm
Williams, Susan
Sheepfold Farm series (2)
Summer at the mill
Baker, Denys Val
Cornish series (18)
Summer at World's End
Dickens, Monica
Fielding family series (2)
Summer awakening
Malpass, Eric Lawson
Gaylord series (5)
Summer birds
Farmer, Penelope
Charlotte and Emma Makepeace series (1)
Summer blues
Chase, Emily
Canby Hall series (5)
Summer business
Martin, Charles E
Monhegan Island series (2)
Summer camp at Trebizon
Digby, Anne
Trebizon series (7)
Summer camp creeps
Schoch, Tim
Creeps series (2)
Summer camp mystery
Blake, Nicholas
Nigel Strangeways series (6)
Summer comes to Apple Market Street
Hill, Mabel Betsy
Judy Jo series (2)
Summer dance
Bernard, Elizabeth
Satin slippers series (12)
Summer days
Roth, Harold
Toddler's fun series (4)
Summer days among the Western Isles
Macgregor, Alasdair Alpin
Western Isles trilogy (2)
Summer deserts
Roberts, Nora
Flowers series (23)
Summer dreams
Gutman, Bill
Going for it series (3)
Summer driftwood for the winter fire
Porter, Rose
Winter fire series (1)
Summer for seven
Lambert, Janet
Dria Meredith trilogy (2)
Summer game
Cardus, Neville
Innings series (6)
Summer half
Thirkell, Angela
Barsetshire series (5)
Summer heat
Cooper, M E
Couples series (35)
Summer holiday
Kaye-Smith, Sheila
Selina series (1)
Simenon, Georges
Inspector Jules Maigret series (25)
Inspector Jules Maigret series (30)
Smith, Naomi Royde
Rockmouth and Rockhead township trilogy (2)
Summer-house loon
Fine, Anne
Ione Muffet series (1)
Summer in a canon
Wiggin, Kate Douglas
Polly Oliver series (1)
Summer in Barfield
Jones, Olive
Barfield series (11)
Summer in December
Paul, Elliot
Homer Evans series (5)
Summer in Williamsburg
Fuchs, Daniel
Williamsburg trilogy (1)
Summer kitchen, Mrs Appleyard's of course
Kent, Louise Andrews
Appleyard family series (4)
Summer leaves
Mackail, Denis
Noodles series (2)
Summer lightning
Peach, Bill
Ginger Meggs series (31)
Wodehouse, Pelham Grenville
Blandings Castle series (4)
Summer love
Gilden, Mel
Beverly Hills 90210 series (6)
Summer madness
Lambert, Janet
Patty and Ginger series (4)
Summer 1914
Martin du Gard, Roger
Thibault family series (2)
Summer noisy book
Brown, Margaret Wise
Noisy book series (8)
Summer of decision
Tolliver, Ruby Changes
Decision series (1)
Summer of life
Seymour, Beatrice Kean
Sally Dunn trilogy (3)
Summer of my German soldier
Greene, Bette
Patty Bergen series (1)
Summer of Sir Launcelot
Gordon, Richard
Doctor series (9)
Summer of the Danes
Peters, Ellis
Brother Cadfael series (18)
Summer of the dinosaur
Hall, Willis
Henry Hollins series (1)
Summer of the great secret
Edwards, Monica
Romney Marsh series (2)
Summer of the great-grandmother
L'Engle, Madeleine
Crosswicks journals series (2)
Summer of the osprey
Ogilvie, Elisabeth May
Bennett Island series (6)
Summer of the seventeenth doll
Lawler, Ray
Doll trilogy (3)
Summer of the Sioux
Champlin, Tim
Matt Tierney series (1)
Summer of the wild pig
Dengler, Sandy
Pioneer family series (1)
Summer on Boomerang Ranch
Patchett, Mary Elwyn
Danny and David Delaney series (2)
Summer on the hills
Bullingham, Ann
Penelope series (3)
Summer on Wild Horse Island
Patchett, Mary Elwyn
Danny and David Delaney series (1)
Summer pony
Doty, Jean Slaughter
Pony series (2)
Summer Queen
Vinge, Joan Dennison
Snow Queen series (3)
Summer riders
Leitch, Patricia
Jinny series (3)
Summer rules
Lipsyte, Roger
Summer trilogy (2)
Summer school mystery
Bell, Josephine
Doctor David Wintringham series (10)
Inspector Steven Mitchell series (6)
Summer session
Ripley, Karen
Indiana Jones series (9)
Summer showdown
Delton, Judy
Condo Kids series (2)
Summer snowman
Ahlberg, Janet
Daisychain series (2)
Summer soldier
Guild, Nicholas
Ray Guinness series (1)
Summer song
Oldfield, Pamela
Kent trilogy (2)
Summer storm
Angoff, Charles
Polonsky family series (6)
Marston, Jeffery
Octave trilogy (2)
Summer story
Barklem, Jill
Brambly Hedge series (4)
Summer switch
Rodgers, Mary
Annabel Andrews series (3)
Summer term
Pleydell, Susan
Ledenham School series (1)
Summer term at Highlands
Tarrant, Elizabeth
Highlands series (1)
Summer term at Melling
Biggs, Margaret
Melling School series (7)
Summer term at Saint Clare's
Blyton, Enid
Saint Clare's series (3)
Summer term at the Chalet School
Brent-Dyer, Elinor Mary
Chalet School series (54)

Super Sam
Garland, Sarah
Sam series (3)
Super Sam Snout and the case of the missing marble
Lemieux, Anne
Super Sam Snout series (2)
Super Sam Snout and the case of the stolen snowman
Lemieux, Anne
Super Sam Snout series (1)
Super Sam Snout and the case of the yogurt-poker
Lemieux, Anne
Super Sam Snout series (3)
Super Sleuth
Vivelo, Jacqueline Jones
Super Sleuth series (1)
Super Sleuth and the bare bones
Vivelo, Jacqueline Jones
Super Sleuth series (3)
Super Sweathogs
Johnston, William
Welcome back, Kotter series (3)
Super trail bike
Wenk, Richard
Pick-a-path series (5)
Super Vee
Wilkinson, Sylvia
World of racing series (6)
Super What-a-Mess
Muir, Frank
What-a-Mess series (4)
Superbike
Packard, Edward
Choose your own adventure series (124)
Supercargo
Gibbs, George
Old Philadelphia series (2)
Super-Celeste
Way, Peter
Crispin Bridge series (1)
Supercomputer
Packard, Edward
Choose your own adventure series (39)
Supercooper
Cooper, Jilly
Jolly super series (5)
Superdog
McInerney, Judith Whitelock
Judge Benjamin series (1)
Wilson, David Henry
Superdog series (1)
Superdog gift
McInerney, Judith Whitelock
Judge Benjamin series (5)
Superdog in trouble
Wilson, David Henry
Superdog series (3)
Superdog rescue
McInerney, Judith Whitelock
Judge Benjamin series (3)
Superdog secret
McInerney, Judith Whitelock
Judge Benjamin series (2)
Superdog surprise
McInerney, Judith Whitelock
Judge Benjamin series (4)
Superdog the hero
Wilson, David Henry
Superdog series (2)
Super-duper cookie caper
Hope, Laura Lee
New Bobbsey twins series (22)
Superduper Teddy
Hurwitz, Johanna
Nora and Teddy series (4)
Superfudge
Blume, Judy
Peter Hatcher series (3)
Supergirl, the girl of steel
Helfer, Andrew
Super powers which way series (2)
Supergun mission
Derrick, Lionel
Penetrator series (21)
Superhero
Hodgman, Ann
Stinky Stanley series (3)
Superintendent Slade investigates
Gribble, Leonard Reginald
Superintendent Anthony Slade series (26)
Superintendent Wakely's mistake
Cole, George Douglas Howard
Superintendent Henry Wilson series (11)
Superintendent Wilson's holiday
Cole, George Douglas Howard
Superintendent Henry Wilson series (5)
Superintendent's room
Ashford, Jeffrey
Detective Inspector Don Kerry series (4)
Superior woman
Balzac, Honore de
Scenes of provincial life series (6)
Superjilly
Cooper, Jilly
Jolly super series (4)
Superkill
Tiger, John
I spy series (3)
Superlative relative
Housman, Laurence
Palace plays series (4)
Superlearning
Ostrander, Sheila
Superlearning series (1)
Superlearning 2000
Ostrander, Sheila
Superlearning series (2)
Superman and Spider-Man
Gross, Edward
Superman series (7)
Superman at fifty
Dooley, Dennis
Superman series (7)
Superman files
Van Hise, James
Superman series (7)
Superman II
Fleisher, Michael
Superman series (7)
Superman III
Kotzwinkle, William
Superman series (5)
Superman IV
Hiller, Barbara B
Superman series (6)
Krulik, Nancy E
Superman series (6)
McDonnell, David
Superman series (7)
Superman, last son of Krypton
Maggin, Elliot S
Superman series (1)
Superman of Alpha
Byrne, Stuart James
Star Man series (1)
Superman, serial to cereal
Grossman, Gary Howard
Superman series (7)
Superman, the man of steel
Helfer, Andrew
Super powers which way series (1)
Superman series (4)
Superman, the movie
Libman, Gary
Superman series (7)
Superman's maze challenge
Koziakin, Vladimir
Superman series (7)
Supermanship
Potter, Stephen
Lifemanship Correspondence College series (4)
Supermemory
Ostrander, Sheila
Superlearning series (2)
Supermind
Phillips, Mark
Ken Malone trilogy (3)
Supermouse
Ure, Jean
Nicola Bruce series (1)
Superpowers anti-coloring book
Striker, Susan
Anti-coloring book series (6)
Super-roo of Mungalongaloo
White, Osmar
Doctor McGurk series (1)
Super-spy
Brown, Carter
Mavis Seidlitz series (10)
Superstar
Branley, Franklyn Mansfield
Voyage into space series (6)
Superstar team
Hughes, Dean
Angel Park All-Stars series (9)
Superstars of the sports world
Gutman, Bill
Modern superstars series (9)
Superstars stopped short
Aaseng, Nathan
Sports heroes series (21)
Superstition
Lee, Howard
Kung Fu series (3)
Superstitition Corner
Kaye-Smith, Sheila
Alard family trilogy (1)
Supersub
Clark, Halsey
Periscope series (5)
Supersubs of pro sports
Aaseng, Nathan
Sports heroes series (24)
SuperTed and Bulk's story
Young, Mike
SuperTed series (25)
SuperTed and Mother Nature
Young, Mike
SuperTed series (28)
SuperTed and Tex's magic spell
Young, Mike
SuperTed series (24)
SuperTed and the blue whales
Young, Mike
SuperTed series (22)
SuperTed and the crystal ball
Young, Mike
SuperTed series (17)
SuperTed and the elephant graveyard
Young, Mike
SuperTed series (16)
SuperTed and the giant kites
Young, Mike
SuperTed series (11)
SuperTed and the green planet
Young, Mike
SuperTed series (6)
SuperTed and the gun smugglers
Young, Mike
SuperTed series (20)
SuperTed and the helicopter pirates
Young, Mike
SuperTed series (3)
SuperTed and the hungry monkeys
Young, Mike
SuperTed series (8)
SuperTed and the Inca treasure
Young, Mike
SuperTed series (12)
SuperTed and the lost ponies
Young, Mike
SuperTed series (4)
SuperTed and the lumberjacks
Young, Mike
SuperTed series (27)
SuperTed and the pearl fishers
Young, Mike
SuperTed series (10)
SuperTed and the pothole rescue
Young, Mike
SuperTed series (21)
SuperTed and the stolen rocket ship
Young, Mike
SuperTed series (9)
SuperTed and the train robbers
Young, Mike
SuperTed series (14)
SuperTed at the bottom of the sea
Young, Mike
SuperTed series (7)
SuperTed in Creepy Castle
Young, Mike
SuperTed series (2)
SuperTed in space
Young, Mike
SuperTed series (1)
SuperTed in Spotty and the Indians
Young, Mike
SuperTed series (19)
SuperTed in SuperTed's dream
Young, Mike
SuperTed series (26)
SuperTed in the Arctic
Young, Mike
SuperTed series (18)
SuperTed kicks up the dust
Young, Mike
SuperTed series (23)
SuperTed meets Zappy and Zoppy
Young, Mike
SuperTed series (5)
SuperTed on planet Spot
Young, Mike
SuperTed series (15)
SuperTed returns to Creepy Castle
Young, Mike
SuperTed series (13)
Superworld
Otfinoski, Steven
Magic micro adventure series (2)
Supper at the Maxwell house
Crabb, Alfred Leland
Nashville series (2)
Support Rommel
Lutz, Gunther
Panzer Platoon series (4)
Support yout local wizard
Duane, Diane
Wizard series (3)
Supreme adventures of Inspector Lestrade
Trow, Meirion James
Inspector Sholto Lestrade series (4)
Sure of you
Maupin, Armistead
Tales of the city series (6)
Sure recompense
Bickers, Richard Townshend
Daedalus quartet (4)
Sure thing
Prather, Richard Scott
Shell Scott series (38)
Surefoot
Reese, Bob
Grand Canyon series (6)
Surely not, Doctor
Clifford, Robert
Doctor series (6)
Surf monkeys
Leibold, Jay
Choose your own adventure series (131)
Surface of earth
Price, Reynolds
Mayfield family series (1)
Surfboard to peril
Quackenbush, Robert Mead
Miss Mallard series (10)
Surfeit of alibis
Lauben, Philip
Captain Homer Clay series (2)
Surfeit of lampreys
Marsh, Ngaio
Inspector Roderick Alleyn series (9)
Surfeit of suspects
Bellairs, George
Detective Inspector Thomas Littlejohn series (40)
Surfing country
Bunting, Eve
High point series (2)
Surfing Samurai robots
Gilden, Mel
Zoot Marlowe series (1)
Surf's up
Quin-Harkin, Janet
Sugar and spice series (8)
Surgeon
Macdonnell, James Edmond
Captain Peter Bentley series (9)
Surgeon at arms
Gordon, Richard
Trevose family series (2)
Jennings, D K
Doctor Ralph Conway series (1)
Surgeon at St Mark's
Harrison, Elizabeth
Central London Hospital series (18)
Surgeon called Amanda
Harrison, Elizabeth
Central London Hospital series (14)
Surgeon from Holland
Neels, Betty
Adelaide Peters series (2)
Surgeon in Australia
Bankoff, George Alexis
Surgeon in series (5)
Surgeon in California
Sava, George
Surgeon in series (2)
Surgeon in Cyprus
Bankoff, George Alexis
Surgeon in series (4)
Surgeon in disgrace
Collins, Lynne
Hartlake Hospital series (8)
Surgeon in New Zealand
Bankoff, George Alexis
Surgeon in series (3)
Surgeon in Rome
Sava, George
Surgeon in series (1)
Surgeon of Sedbridge
Emerson, David
George Hanson series (1)
Surgeon on Skora
Collins, Lynne
Hartlake Hospital series (6)
Surgeon she married
Harrison, Elizabeth
Central London Hospital series (19)
Surgeon's affair
Harrison, Elizabeth
Central London Hospital series (17)
Surgeon's call
Harrison, Elizabeth
Central London Hospital series (7)
Surgeon's destiny
Sava, George
Surgeon's destiny series (2)
Surgeon's life
Harrison, Elizabeth
Central London Hospital series (15)
Surgeon's mate
O'Brian, Patrick
Jack Aubrey and Stephen Maturin series (7)
Surgery at Aberffrwd
Smith, Francis Maylett
General practitioner series (1)
Surgery nurse
Deal, Paula
Nurse series (4)
Surgical strike
Ahern, Jerry
Surgical strike series (1)
Surinam affair
Rosenberger, Joseph
Death Merchant series (27)
Surprise!
Chase, Emily
Canby Hall series (30)
Surprise and double surprise
Maguire, Jack
Many lives of Underfoot the cat series (3)
Surprise bear
Cecil, Hugh
Teddy tales series (1)
Surprise fo Oliver
Chappell, Audrey
Oliver series (1)
Surprise for Davy
Lenski, Lois
Davy series (2)
Surprise for Judy Jo
Hill, Mabel Betsy
Judy Jo series (3)
Surprise for Max
Turk, Hanne
Max the Mouse series (1)
Surprise for Mitzi Mouse
Bullock, Kathleen
Mitzi Mouse series (1)
Surprise for Mrs Pinkerton-Trunks
Isherwood, Shirley
Get up and go series (2)
Surprise for the Four
Cross, Mark
Daphne Wrayne and her Four Adjusters series (8)
Surprise island
Warner, Gertrude Chandler
Boxcar children series (2)
Surprise Island
Willard, Barbara
Jill and Limpet series (2)
Surprise paper tearing talks
Westphail, Arnold Carl
Paper tearing series (9)
Surprise party
Hutchins, Pat
Surprise party series (1)
Stine, Robert Lawrence
Fear Street series (5)
Surprise picnic
Goodall, John Strickland
Paddy Pork series (10)
Surprise, surprise
McCloy, Helen
Basil Willing series (13)
Pascal, Francine
Sweet Valley kids series (1)
Zach, Cheryl
Smyth versus Smith series (5)
Surprises at The Warren
Sindall, Marjorie Aylwynn
Warren series (5)
Surprises for the Brydons
Fidler, Kathleen
Brydon family series (8)
Surprises for Topsy and Tim
Adamson, Jean
Topsy and Tim series (98)
Surprising adventures of Mrs Bridget McSweeney
Spencer, Thomas Edward
Bridget McSweeney series (1)
Surprising adventures of Sir Toady Lion
Crockett, Samuel Rutherford
Sir Toady series (1)

Surprising broom
Blyton, Enid
Little bedtime books series (4)
Surprising pets of Billy Brown
Kitt, Tamara
Billy Brown series (4)
Surprising travels and adventures of Baron Munchausen
Raspe, Rudolf Erich
Baron Munchausen series (6)
Surrender none
Moon, Elizabeth
Deed of Paksenarrion series (1)
Surrender the Galactica!
Larson, Glen A
Battlestar Galactica series (14)
Surrender value
Hilton, John Buxton
Superintendent Simon Kenworthy series (8)
Surrogate
Catling, Patrick Skene
Sex research series (2)
Surrounded
Coffey, Brian
Mike Tucker series (2)
Surry of Eagle's Nest
Cooke, John Esten
Southern Army campaign trilogy (1)
Surveillance
May, Julian
Pliocene exile series (1)
Survival
Munro, Rona
Doctor Who series (150)
Survival at sea
Packard, Edward
Choose your own adventure series (16)
Survival count
Moffat, Gwen
Mountaineering series (3)
Survival course
Murphy, Warren Burton
Destroyer series (82)
Survival in Auschwitz
Levi, Primo
Survival in Auschwitz series (1)
Survival in the ashes
Johnstone, William Wallace
Ashes series (12)
Survival run
Dixon, Franklin W
Hardy boys case files series (77)
Survival, zero!
Spillane, Mickey
Mike Hammer series (12)
Surviving fights with your brothers and sisters
Berry, Joy
Ready-set-grow series (5)
Survivor
Butler, Octavia Estelle
Patternists series (3)
Gallacher, Tom
Bill Thompson trilogy (3)
Janifer, Laurence Mark
Gerald Knave trilogy (1)
Q, John
Peter Trees series (2)
Supervielle, Jules
Colonel's children series (2)
Survivor murders
Jones, G Wayman
Black Bat series (26)
Survivors
Behaine, Rene
History of a society series (2)
Bradley, Marion Zimmer
Red moon series (2)
Cannon, Mary
O'Hara dynasty trilogy (2)
Godwin, Tom
Ragnarok series (1)
Lorrah, Jean
Star trek, the next generation series (4)
Nation, Terry
Survivors series (1)
Raven, Simon
Alms for oblivion series (10)
Sandon, J D
Gringos series (10)
Sibson, Francis H
Survivors series (1)
Siegel, Barbara
Firebrats series (2)
Survivors of the Chancellor
Verne, Jules
J R Kazallon series (1)
Survivor's secret
Brandon, John Gordon
Sexton Blake series (744)
Susan
Moore, Melissa
Agency series (1)
Remick, Grace May
Sheldon Six series (4)
Susan and Priscilla
Bond, Freda Constance
Lancasters series (3)
Susan and the wrong baby
Adam, Ruth
Susan Marsh series (2)
Susan at school
Shaw, Jane
Susan series (5)
Susan, Bill and the Bright Star Circus
Saville, Malcolm
Susan and Bill series (7)
Susan, Bill and the dark stranger
Saville, Malcolm
Susan and Bill series (5)
Susan, Bill and the golden clock
Saville, Malcolm
Susan and Bill series (4)
Susan, Bill and the ivy-clad oak
Saville, Malcolm
Susan and Bill series (2)
Susan, Bill and the pirates bold
Saville, Malcolm
Susan and Bill series (8)
Susan, Bill and the Saucy Kate
Saville, Malcolm
Susan and Bill series (6)
Susan, Bill and the vanishing boy
Saville, Malcolm
Susan and Bill series (3)
Susan, Bill and the wolf-dog
Saville, Malcolm
Susan and Bill series (1)
Susan Clegg and a man in the house
Warner, Anne
Susan Clegg series (3)
Susan Clegg and her friend Mrs Lathrop
Warner, Anne
Susan Clegg series (1)
Susan Clegg and her love affairs
Warner, Anne
Susan Clegg series (4)
Susan Clegg and her neighbors' affairs
Warner, Anne
Susan Clegg series (2)
Susan Clegg, her friends and her neighbors
Warner, Anne
Susan Clegg series (2)
Susan Crowther
Jacob, Naomi
Crowther series (1)
Susan grows up
Leonard, Mary Finley
Susan trilogy (3)
Susan in the Sixth
Biggs, Margaret
Melling School series (5)
Susan interferes
Shaw, Jane
Susan series (4)
Susan muddles through
Shaw, Jane
Susan series (6)
Susan Price
Brown, Edith Charlotte
Margaret Dashwood series (3)
Susan pulls the strings
Shaw, Jane
Susan series (1)
Susan rushes in
Shaw, Jane
Susan series (3)
Susan Turnbull
Gunter, Archibald Clavering
Susan Turnbull series (1)
Susannah
Ransom, Candice Farris
Sunfire series (2)
Susannah, a little girl with the Mounties
Denison, Muriel
Susannah series (1)
Susannah adventure
Brent-Dyer, Elinor Mary
Fardingdales series (2)
Susannah and the blue house mystery
Elmore, Patricia
Susannah series (1)
Susannah and the posion green Halloween
Elmore, Patricia
Susannah series (2)
Susannah and the purple mongoose mystery
Elmore, Patricia
Susannah series (3)
Susannah at boarding school
Denison, Muriel
Susannah series (3)
Susannah of the Mounties
Denison, Muriel
Susannah series (1)
Susannah of the Yukon
Denison, Muriel
Susannah series (2)
Susannah rides again
Denison, Muriel
Susannah series (4)
Susannah screaming
Weston, Carolyn
Casey Kellog and Al Krug series (2)
Susannah, the righteous
Kimbrough, Katheryn
Phenwick women series (6)
Susan's helping hand
Shaw, Jane
Susan series (2)
Susan's kind heart
Shaw, Jane
Susan series (9)
Susan's stormy term
Moss, Nancy
Cliff House series (2)
Susan's trying term
Shaw, Jane
Susan series (7)
Susie and Alfred in a busy day in town
Craig, Helen
Susie and Alfred series (4)
Susie and Alfred in a welcome for Annie
Craig, Helen
Susie and Alfred series (3)
Susie and Alfred in the night of the paper bag monster
Craig, Helen
Susie and Alfred series (2)
Suspect
Gill, B M
Inspector Tom Maybridge series (1)
Nelson, Hugh Lawrence
Jim Dunn series (8)
Wright, Laurali R
Sergeant Karl Alberg series (1)
Suspect at Saint Mark's
White, Constance Mary
Saint Mark's Hospital series (5)
Suspect in smoke
Keene, Carolyn
Nancy Drew series (115)
Suspect next door
Keene, Carolyn
Nancy Drew files series (39)
Suspect scientist
Meynell, Laurence Walter
Robin Weston series (2)
Suspected six
Scott, Hedley
Sexton Blake series (970)
Suspects nine
Punshon, Ernest Robertson
Bobby Owen series (12)
Suspense
Janson, Hank
Hank Janson series (45)
Suspension
Fane, Bron
La noire series (6)
Suspicion
McQuay, Mike
Robot city series (2)
Roberts, Lee
Doctor Clinton Shannon series (4)
Suspicion aroused
Donovan, Dick
Dick Donovan series (11)
Suspicion in triplicate
Cobb, Belton
Bryan Armitage series (20)
Inspector Cheviot Burmann series (42)
Kitty Armitage series (17)
Suspicion stalks the moor
Pullein-Thompson, Josephine
Moor pony series (7)
Suspicious characters
Sayers, Dorothy Leigh
Lord Peter Wimsey series (7)
Suspicious death
Simpson, Dorothy
Inspector Luke Thanet series (8)
Sussex cuckoo
Flynn, Brian
Anthony Bathurst series (17)
Sussex Downs murder
Bude, John
Inspector Meredith series (3)
Sussex peep-show
Wilkinson, Walter
Puppets series (4)
Sutburys
Hill, Pamela
Fenfallow series (2)
Sutherland's war
Sutherland, Douglas
English gentleman series (5)
Sutton Place
Lampitt, Dinah
Sutton Place trilogy (1)
Sutton Place murders
Dean, Robert George
Pat Thompson series (1)
Suva Harbour mystery
Arthur, Frank
Inspector Spearpoint series (1)
Suzanne and Joseph Pasquier
Duhamel, Georges
Pasquier series (10)
Suzanne and Nicholas and the four seasons
Mangin, Marie France
Suzette and Nicholas series (1)
Suzanne and Nicholas at the market
Ichikawa, Satomi
Suzanne and Nicholas series (2)
Suzanne and Nicholas in the garden
Ichikawa, Satomi
Suzanne and Nicholas series (1)
Suzanne and the young men
Duhamel, Georges
Pasquier series (9)
Suzanne goes to Brittany
Matchett, Grace
Suzanne series (1)
Suzanne goes to market
Matchett, Grace
Suzanne series (2)
Suzette and Nicholas and the four seasons
Ichikawa, Satomi
Suzanne and Nicholas series (3)
Suzette and Nicholas and the Sunijudi Circus
Lochak, Michelle
Suzette and Nicholas series (2)
Suzettte and Nicholas and the seasons clock
Mangin, Marie France
Suzette and Nicholas series (1)
Suzie Celery
Reed, Giles
Munch Bunch character series (15)
Swag
Leonard, Elmore
Frank Ryan series (1)
Swallow
Thomas, Donald Michael
Russian quartet (2)
Swallowdale
Ransome, Arthur
Swallowdale series (1)
Swallows and Amazons series (2)
Swallows and Amazons
Ransome, Arthur
Swallows and Amazons series (1)
Swallows eaves
Ward, Ruth Cameron
Swallows eaves series (1)
Swami and friends
Narayan, Rasipuram Krishnaswami
Malgudi series (7)
Swami's ring
Keene, Carolyn
Nancy Drew series (61)
Swamp foxes
Logan, Jake
John Slocum series (38)
Swamp Island
Wirt, Mildred Augustine
Penny Parker series (16)
Swamp Master
Spencer, Jake
John Firecloud series (1)
Swamp monster
Dixon, Franklin W
Hardy boys series (83)
Swamp monsters
Christian, Mary Blount
Swamp monsters series (1)
Swamp rats
Falk, Lee
Phantom series (11)
Swamp slayers
Sharpe, Jon
Trailsman series (49)
Swamp Thing
Cannon, Martin
Swamp Thing second series (1)
Wein, Len
Swamp Thing series (1)
Swamp Thing finale
Van Hise, James
Swamp Thing second series (3)
Swamp war
Caillou, Alan
Colonel Matthew Tobin series (5)
Swamp witch
Bridges, Laurie
Dark forces series (6)
Swan-boat plot
Taylor, Phoebe Atwood
Asey Mayo series (19)
Swan dive
Healy, Jeremiah
John Francis Cuddy series (4)
Swan feather
Hill, Lorna
Sadler's Wells series (10)
Swan song
Crispin, Edmund
Gervase Fen series (4)
Galsworthy, John
Modern comedy series (3)
Robertson, Helen
Inspector Lathom Dynes series (3)
Stableford, Brian Michael
Star Pilot Grainger series (6)
Swan song of A.J.Wentworth
Ellis, Humphry Francis
A.J.Wentworth series (3)
Swann's way, part one
Proust, Marcel
Remembrance of things past series (1)
Swann's way, part two
Proust, Marcel
Remembrance of things past series (2)
Swan's chance
De Blasis, Celeste
Wild Swan trilogy (2)
Swan's milk
Marlow, Louis
Swan's milk series (1)
Swansong for a siren
Brown, Carter
Larry Baker series (1)
Swapping partners
Law, Simone
Wife swap series (1)
Swarm
Maeterlinck, Maurice
Insect life series (1)
Swarm in May
Mayne, William
Choir school series (1)
Swarm of bees
Coryn, Marjorie
Napoleonic trilogy (2)
Swastika hunt
Cory, Desmond
Johnny Fedora series (7)
Sway of sin
Carter, Nicholas
Nicholas Carter series (507)
Sweat of fear
Dennis, Robert C
Paul Reeder series (1)
Sweater
Henderson, Kathy
Where does it come from series (3)
Sweathog newshawks
Johnston, William
Welcome back, Kotter series (2)
Sweathog sit-in
Johnston, William
Welcome back, Kotter series (5)
Sweathog trail
Johnston, William
Welcome back, Kotter series (1)
Swedish adventure
Bayley, Viola
Adventure series (6)
Sweeney
Martin, Ian Kennedy
Sweeney series (1)
Sweeper
Paulsen, Gary
Lieutenant Ronnie Gold series (1)
Sweepers
Waine, Charlton
Sweepers series (2)
Sweepstake murders
Connington, John Jervis
Sir Clinton Driffield series (7)

Sweet Adelaide
Symons, Julian
Sheridan Haynes series (3)
Sweet and deadly
Corrigan, Mark
Mark Corrigan and McLean series (11)
Olbrich, Freny
Chief Inspector Frank Desouza series (2)
Sweet and low
Lathen, Emma
John Putnam Thatcher series (15)
Sweet and sour
Cooper, M E
Couples series (27)
Wechsberg, Joseph
Epicure trilogy (2)
Sweet and sour kill
Harknett, Terry
Superintendent John Crown series (1)
Sweet and sour milk
Farah, Nuruddin
African dictatorship trilogy (1)
Sweet but deadly
McCall, K T
Johnny Buchanan series (1)
Sweet but sinful
McCall, K T
Johnny Buchanan series (2)
Sweet Charlie
Kane, Henry
Peter Chambers series (11)
Sweet Cicely
Holley, Marietta
Samantha and Josiah Allen series (3)
Sweet danger
Allingham, Margery
Albert Campion series (5)
Sweet deals
Lysaght, Brian
Ben O'Malley series (2)
Sweet death
Hurt, Freda Mary
Inspector Herbert Broom series (3)
Sweet death, kind death
Cross, Amanda
Professor Kate Fansler series (7)
Sweet dreams
Murphy, Warren Burton
Destroyer series (25)
Preston, John
Mission of Alex Kane series (1)
Sweet dreams, Clown-Arounds
Cole, Joanna
Clown-Arounds series (5)
Sweet dreams, Irene
Burke, Jan
Irene series (2)
Sweet dreams, Spot
Hill, Eric
Spot series (10)
Sweet dreams, sweet princes
Banks, Michael A
Joe Mauser series (3)
Reynolds, Mack
Joe Mauser series (3)
Sweet eyes
Agee, Jonis
Divinity series (2)
Sweet fury
Janson, Hank
Hank Janson series (79)
Sweet Genevieve
Derleth, August
Sac Prairie series (8)
Sweet jeopardy
Jerina, Carol
Jack and Jill series (2)
Sweet justice
Oster, Jerry
Jake Neuman series (1)
Robertson, Colin
Peter Grayleigh series (12)
Sweet La-La Land
Campbell, Robert Wright
Whistler series (3)
Sweet lass of Richmond Hill
Plaidy, Jean
Georgian series (7)
Sweet love, survive
Johnson, Susan
Kuzan family trilogy (3)
Sweet murder
Michel, Milton Scott
Wood Jason series (2)
Sweet Nancy
Taggart, Marion Ames
Doctor's little girl series (2)
Sweet night for murder
Neville, Margot
Inspector Grogan and Sergeant Manning series (12)
Sweet nothings
Cragoe, Elizabeth
Untidy gardener series (4)
Sweet peril
Miles, Patricia Mary
Baines family series (1)
Sweet poison
Clark, Douglas
Inspector George Masters series (4)
Fitt, Mary
Superintendent Mallett series (17)
Jacobs, Thomas Curtis Hicks
Temple Fortune series (16)
Penny, Rupert
Chief Inspector Edward Beale series (7)
Sweet prairie passion
Bittner, F Rosanne
Savage destiny series (1)
Sweet promise
Gray, Juliet
Stephen Power series (1)
Sweet promised land
Laxalt, Robert
Basque trilogy (1)
Sweet rebel
Gray, Juliet
Stephen Power series (2)
Sweet revenge
Gilruth, Susan
Inspector Hugh Gordon and Liane Crawford series (1)
Keene, Carolyn
Nancy Drew files series (61)
Sweet ride
Prather, Richard Scott
Shell Scott series (37)
Sweet running filly
Johnson, Pat
Julie Jefferson series (1)
Sweet, savage death
Papazoglou, Orania
Patience Campbell McKenna series (1)
Sweet savage love
Rogers, Rosemary
Ginny Brandon and Steve Morgan series (1)
Sweet second summer of Kitty Malone
Cohen, Matt
Salem quartet (3)
Sweet seduction
Tetel, Julie
Sweet trilogy (2)
Sweet sensations
Tetel, Julie
Sweet trilogy (3)
Sweet shame of fury
Frances, Stephen Daniel
John Gail series (6)
Sweet sheat gone
Proust, Marcel
Remembrance of things past series (11)
Sweet short grass
Inchbald, Peter
Inspector Franco Corti series (2)
Sweet silver blues
Cook, Glen
Garrett series (1)
Sweet sister death
Nolan, Frederick
Garrett dossier series (1)
Sweet sister seduced
Hough, Stanley Bennett
Inspector Brentford series (3)
Sweet smelling death
Gunn, Victor
Chief Inspector Bill Cromwell series (36)
Sweet-Song the skylark
Rutley, Cecily Marianne
Tales of the wild folk series (3)
Sweet suspicions
Tetel, Julie
Sweet trilogy (1)
Sweet, svelte and sinful
Brody, Marc
Marc Brody series (20)
Sweet, sweet poison
Wilhelm, Kate
Charlie Miklejohn and Constance Leidl series (4)
Sweet talk
Goudge, Eileen
Seniors series (15)
Janson, Hank
Hank Janson series (214)
Sweet talkin' stranger
Copeland, Lori
Passion trilogy (3)
Sweet Texas tart
Sherman, Jory
Gunn series (21)
Sweet Thames run softly
Gibbings, Robert
Sweet Thames series (1)
Sweet Thursday
Salisbury, Ray
Simon series (4)
Steinbeck, John
Cannery Row series (2)
Sweet-tooth Sunil
Solomon, Joan
Children's life series (9)
Sweet Valley clean-up
Pascal, Francine
Sweet Valley kids series (27)
Sweet Valley slumber party
Pascal, Francine
Sweet Valley kids series (22)
Sweet Valley trick or treat
Pascal, Francine
Sweet Valley kids series (12)
Sweet-vendor
Narayan, Rasipuram Krishnaswami
Malgudi series (10)
Sweet water
Cronin, Michael
Richard Maidment series (4)
Sweet wild wench
Gault, William Campbell
Joe Puma series (5)
Sweet Will
Malpass, Eric Lawson
William Shakespeare trilogy (1)
Sweet William
Crompton, Richmal
William series (18)
Sweet women lie
Estleman, Loren D
Amos Walker series (11)
Sweeter for his going
Truss, Seldon
Inspector Gidleigh series (5)
Sweethallow Valley
Trevor, Elleston
Woodlanders series (6)
Sweetheart
Coburn, Andrew
Rita Gardella O'Dea series (1)
Sweetheart, here's your grave!
Janson, Hank
Hank Janson series (15)
Sweetheart travellers
Crockett, Samuel Rutherford
Sweethearts series (1)
Sweetheart, you're a sinner
Brody, Marc
Marc Brody series (46)
Sweethearts
Cooper, M E
Couples series (16)
Sweethearts and wives
Skelton, Clement Lister
Maclaren family series (2)
Sweethearts at home
Crockett, Samuel Rutherford
Sweethearts series (2)
Sweetie hold me tight
Janson, Hank
Hank Janson series (19)
Sweets of life
Romains, Jules
Men of goodwill series (18)
Sweetwater
Faldbakken, Knut
Twilight country series (2)
Rikhoff, Jean
Butte family series (3)
Sweetwater Flats
Wisler, Gary Clifton
Willie Delamer series (8)
Swell night for murder
Brandon, Gordon
Michael and Terry Terence series (1)
Swept away!
Sherman, Josepha
Secret of the Unicorn Queen series (1)
Swept her into space
Macgregor, Ellen
Miss Pickerell series (1)
Swept in the wave of terror
Skurzynski, Gloria
Mountain west series (4)
Swept out to sea
Foster, Walter Bertram
Clint Webb series (1)
Swift to its close
Troy, Simon
Inspector Smith series (11)
Swiftly tilting planet
L'Engle, Madeleine
Meg Murry series (3)
Swiggo
Slater, Jim
A Mazing Monster series (11)
Swimathon!
Cross, Gillian
Clipper series (3)
Swimming
Gutman, Bill
Go for it series (11)
Swimming day
Margolin, Harriet
Days series (3)
Swimming pool
Dowling, Patrick
Amazing adventures of Morph series (1)
Swindler named Zefano
Guenter, C H
Robert Urban series (6)
Swindler's trail
Hardin, J D
Raider and Doc series (68)
Swing away, climber
Carr, Glyn
Sir Abercrombie Lewker series (12)
Swing, brother, swing
Marsh, Ngaio
Inspector Roderick Alleyn series (15)
Swing high, sweet murder
Courtier, Sidney Hobson
Inspector Digger Haig series (3)
Swing in the garden
Hood, Hugh
New age series (1)
Swing in the summerhouse
Langton, Jane
Edward, Eleanor and Georgie Hall series (2)
Swing it, death
Holt, Gavin
Inspector Joel Saber series (3)
Swing low, sweet death
Campbell, R T
Professor John Stubbs series (7)
Swing low, sweet Harriet
Baxt, George
Pharaoh Love series (2)
Swing low, swing dead
Gruber, Frank
Johnny Fletcher and Sam Cragg series (14)
Swing music murder
Reed, Harlan
Dan Jordan series (2)
Swing, swing together
Lovesey, Peter
Sergeant Cribb and Constable Thackeray series (7)
Swinger who swung by the neck
Stone, Hampton
Jeremiah X Gibson series (17)
Swingers
Brown, Carter
Rick Holman series (36)
Swinging death
Flynn, Brian
Anthony Bathurst series (35)
Swinging murder
Black, Lionel
Kate Theobald series (1)
Swinging virgin
Rico, Don
Casey Grant series (2)
Swings and roundabouts
Miller, Hugh
Eastenders series (2)
Ure, Jean
Shrublands Estate series (2)
Swish of the curtain
Brown, Pamela
Blue Door Theatre Company series (1)
Swiss adventure
Smythe, Pat
Peter and Carol Garret series (1)
Swiss deal
Arvay, Harry
Israeli Security Branch series (9)
Swiss family Robinson
Wyss, Johann Rudolf
Swiss family Robinson series (1)
Swiss holiday
Sutton, Phyllis
Merryl Hastings series (4)
Swiss secret
Messmann, Jon
Jefferson Boone series (4)
Swiss secrets
Keene, Carolyn
Nancy Drew files series (72)
Passport to romance trilogy (1)
Swiss shot
Bradley, Michael
Johnny Adrano series (3)
Swiss twins
Perkins, Lucy Fitch
Twin series (13)
Switch around
Lowry, Lois
Caroline Tate series (2)
Switch horse
Hardcastle, Michael
Horse series (2)
Switch off
Optic, Oliver
Lake Shore series (4)
Switchback
Wilcox, Collin
Lieutenant Frank Hastings series (18)
Switchblade
Rawls, Philip
Richard Bronson series (3)
Switherby pilgrims
Spence, Eleanor
Arabella Braithwaite series (1)
Swooning lady
Robeson, Kenneth
Doc Savage series (130)
Swooping vengeance
Dorman, Geoffrey
Carmelo series (1)
Sword and citadel
Wolfe, Gene
Book of the new sun series (4)
Sword and the blossom
Parkin, Ray
Out of the smoke series (3)
Sword and the chain
Rosenberg, Joel
Guardians of the flame series (2)
Sword and the circle
Sutcliff, Rosemary
Arthurian knights trilogy (2)
Sword and the cross
Moore, Arthur
California trilogy (1)
Sword and the dagger
Mayhar, Ardath
BattleTech series (4)
Sword and the distaff
Simms, William Gilmore
American Revolution series (5)
Sword and the doll
Van der Post, Laurens
Seed and the sower trilogy (3)
Sword and the eye
Leiber, Justin Fritz
House of Eigin series (1)
Sword and the flame
Lawhead, Stephen
Dragon King trilogy (3)
Sword and the satchel
Boyer, Elizabeth H
World of the Alfar series (1)
Sword and the sickle
Anand, Mulk Raj
Lal Singh trilogy (3)
Sword and the stallion
Moorcock, Michael
Chronicle of Prince Corum and the silver hand trilogy (3)
Corum series (6)
Sword and the tower
Leiber, Justin Fritz
House of Eigin series (2)
Sword bearer
White, John
Archives of Anthropos series (3)
Sword between
Knight, Brigid
Ardleigh family series (1)
Sword-breaker
Roberson, Jennifer
Tiger and Del series (4)
Sword dance
Napier, Priscilla
Napier family trilogy (1)
Sword-dancer
Roberson, Jennifer
Tiger and Del series (1)
Sword for Kregen
Prescot, Dray
Dray Prescot series (20)

Sword for Mister Fitton
Styles, Showell
Lieutenant Michael Fitton series (1)
Sword for the Baron
Morton, Anthony
Baron series (35)
Sword for the empire
Lancour, Gene
Dirshan series (3)
Sword in sheath
Norton, Andre
Swords trilogy (2)
Sword in the pool
Marfield, Dwight
Dudley Brent series (3)
Gail McGurk series (3)
Inspector Skane series (3)
Sword in the stone
White, Terence Hanbury
Once and future king series (1)
Sword is drawn
Norton, Andre
Swords trilogy (1)
Sword is the king
Ross, Sutherland
Clifton family series (2)
Sword-maker
Roberson, Jennifer
Tiger and Del series (3)
Sword of Aldones
Bradley, Marion Zimmer
Darkover series (15)
Sword of Allah
Elliott, Richard
John Norris series (1)
Olden, Marc
Robert Sand series (7)
Sword of Antietam
Altsheler, Joseph Alexander
Civil War series (3)
Sword of Arhapal
Sernine, Daniel
Grandverger series (2)
Sword of Bheleu
Watt-Evans, Lawrence
Lords of Dus series (3)
Sword of Caesar
Stevenson, Bruce
Time machine series (18)
Sword of Calandra
Dexter, Susan
Winter King's war trilogy (2)
Sword of chaos, and other stories
Bradley, Marion Zimmer
Darkover anthologies series (2)
Sword of Conan
Howard, Robert Ervin
Conan series (2)
Sword of Culann
Levin, Betty
Claudia and Evan trilogy (1)
Sword of death
Vincent, John
James Bond junior series (5)
Sword of fate
Wheatley, Dennis
Julian Day series (2)
Sword of fire
Hawkins, Ward
Harry Borg series (2)
Sword of forbearance
Williams, Paul Osborne
Pelbar series (7)
Sword of Genghis Khan
Dark, James
Mark Kingsley Hood series (8)
Sword of glory
Danielson, Peter
Children of the Lion series (8)
Sword of God
Caillou, Alan
Ian Quayle series (2)
Sword of honor
Sue, Eugene
Mysteries of the people series (18)
Sword of honour
Montague, Jeanne
Loves of Carola Mountjoy series (14)
Waugh, Evelyn
World War II series (3)
Sword of honour trilogy
Waugh, Evelyn
World War II series (3)
Sword of Justice
Duncan, Francis
Peter Justice series (1)
Sword of Monsieur Blackshirt
Graeme, David
Monsieur Blackshirt series (3)
Sword of Morning Star
Meade, Richard
Gray lands series (1)
Sword of Orley
Farrar, Stewart
Bridget and George Blake series (2)
Sword of Poyana
Bailey, Gerald Earl
Nurlingas series (5)
Saga of Thorgrim series (2)
Sword of Rhiannon
Brackett, Leigh
Mars series (2)
Sword of Sagamore
Dalkey, Kara
Sagamore series (2)
Sword of Samurai Cat
Rogers, Mark Earl
Samurai Cat series (4)
Sword of Shannara
Brooks, Terry
Shannara series (1)
Sword of silk
Carrel, Mark
Andrew McCall series (4)
Sword of Skelos
Offutt, Andrew Jefferson
Conan series (30)
Sword of the air
Carter, Dorothy
Marise Duncan series (4)
Sword of the dawn
Moorcock, Michael
History of Runestaff series (3)
Sword of the Gael
Offutt, Andrew Jefferson
Cormac Mac Art series (5)
Sword of the golden stud
Carter, Ashley
Falconhurst series (10)
Golden stud series (2)
Sword of the Lamb
Wren, M K
Phoenix legacy trilogy (1)
Sword of the Lictor
Wolfe, Gene
Book of the new sun series (3)
Sword of the Lord
Hocking, Joseph
Religious movements series (1)
Sword of the Nurlingas
Bailey, Gerald Earl
Nurlingas series (4)
Saga of Thorgrim series (1)
Sword of the raven
Boucher, Alan Estcourt
Halli Thordason series (5)
Sword of the Revolution, 1917-1923
Cliff, Tony
Trotsky series (2)
Sword of the samurai
Perry, Steve
Time machine series (3)
Smith, Mark
Fighting fantasy gamebook series (20)
Sword of the spirits
Christopher, John
Prince trilogy (3)
Sword of the spirits trilogy
Christopher, John
Prince trilogy (3)
Sword of the sun
Dever, Joe
Legends of Lone Wolf series (3)
Legends of Lone Wolf series (3)
Sword of the Templar
Carpenter, Richard
Robin of Sherwood series (3)
Sword of vengeance
Chester, Gilbert
Sexton Blake series (1134)
Newcomb, Kerry
McQueen family series (2)
Sword of Woden
Wiat, Philippa
Black Boar series (3)
Sword-singer
Roberson, Jennifer
Tiger and Del series (2)
Sword sleep
Ray, Mary
Early Christian series (3)
Sword swallower
Goulart, Ron
Ben Jolson series (1)
Sword, the jewel and the mirror
Roberts, John Maddox
Cingulum trilogy (3)
Swordmaker
Barr, Robert
Mediaeval Rhine series (3)
Swordray's first three patrols
Blair, Clay
Submariners series (1)
Swords against death
Leiber, Fritz
Fafhrd and Gray Mouser series (2)
Swords against wizardry
Leiber, Fritz
Fafhrd and Gray Mouser series (4)
Swords and daggers
Fisher, Aileen
Ways of plants series (7)
Swords and deviltry
Leiber, Fritz
Fafhrd and Gray Mouser series (1)
Swords and ice magic
Leiber, Fritz
Fafhrd and Gray Mouser series (6)
Swords from the North
Treece, Henry
Harald Hardrada series (2)
Swords in the mist
Leiber, Fritz
Fafhrd and Gray Mouser series (3)
Swords' masters
Leiber, Fritz
Fafhrd and Gray Mouser series (4)
Swords of Corum omnibus
Moorcock, Michael
Corum series (3)
Swords of Lankhmar
Leiber, Fritz
Fafhrd and Gray Mouser series (5)
Swords of Mars
Burroughs, Edgar Rice
Martian series (8)
Swords of the barbarians
Bulmer, Kenneth
Swords series (1)
Swords of the Horseclans
Adams, Robert
Horseclans series (2)
Swords of the legion
Turtledove, Harry
Videssos series (4)
Swords of Zinjaban
De Camp, Lyon Sprague
Krishna series (10)
Swords trilogy
Moorcock, Michael
Corum series (3)
Corum series (6)
Swordships of Scorpio
Akers, Alan Burt
Dray Prescot series (4)
Swordsman of Mars
Kline, Otis Adelbert
Mars series (1)
Sworn allies
Drake, David
Fleet series (4)
Sworn enemies
Cooper, M E
Couples series (7)
Sybelle
Gellis, Roberta
Roselynde chronicles series (6)
Sybil
Disraeli, Benjamin
Young England trilogy (2)
Lagerkvist, Par
Tobias trilogy (3)
Sybil at sixteen
Pfeffer, Susan Beth
Sebastian sisters quintet (4)
Sybil, the glide of her tongue
Hanscombe, Gillian
Lesbian series (2)
Sydney for sin
Corrigan, Mark
Mark Corrigan and McLean series (18)
Sydney, the temptress
Preston, Fayrene
Delaneys of Killaroo trilogy (3)
Sylvia
Sinclair, Upton
Sylvia series (1)
Sylvia and Arthur
Mackenzie, Compton
Sinister Street series (3)
Sylvia Scarlett series (1)
Sylvia and Michael
Mackenzie, Compton
Sinister Street series (4)
Sylvia Scarlett series (2)
Sylvia Arden decides
Chalmers, Margaret Piper
Sylvia Arden series (3)
Sylvia of the hill top
Chalmers, Margaret Piper
Sylvia Arden series (2)
Sylvia Scarlett
Mackenzie, Compton
Sinister Street series (3)
Sinister Street series (3)
Sylvia Scarlett series (1)
Sylvia Scarlett series (1)
Sylvia Smith-Smith
Nelson, Peter N
Sylvia Smith-Smith series (1)
Sylvia's burden
May, Carrie L
Recovered pearl series (3)
Sylvia's experiment
Chalmers, Margaret Piper
Sylvia Arden series (1)
Sylvia's marriage
Sinclair, Upton
Sylvia series (2)
Sylvie and Bruno
Carroll, Lewis
Sylvie and Bruno series (1)
Sylvie and Bruno, concluded
Carroll, Lewis
Sylvie and Bruno series (2)
Symbol of Terra
Tubb, Edwin Charles
Dumarest series (30)
Symbol of the Cat
Graham, Neill
Mister Sandyman series (1)
Symbols at your door
Fraser, Anthea
Inspector David Webb and Sergeant Ken Jackson series (8)
Symphony in murder
Long, Amelia Reynolds
Edward Trelawny series (5)
Symphony in sand
Miller, Calvin
Symphony trilogy (2)
Symphony in two time
Irving, Alexander
Doctor Anthony Post series (2)
Symphony of light
McKinney, Jack
Robotech series (12)
Symphony of storms
Vardeman, Robert Edward
Demon crown trilogy (3)
Symphony of terror
Sucharitkul, Somtow
V series (14)
Synaptic manhunt
Farren, Mick
Jeb Stuart Ho series (2)
Syndicate for sin
Brody, Marc
Marc Brody series (22)
Syndicate gun
Newton, Dwight Bennett
Jim Bannister series (8)
Syndicate of death
Grant, Maxwell
Shadow series (248)
Syndicate of rascals
Carter, Nicholas
Nicholas Carter series (111)
Synthetic men of Mars
Burroughs, Edgar Rice
Martian series (9)
Syrup of the bees
Bain, Francis William
Indian mystic love stories series (11)
Systemic shock
Ing, Dean
Ted Quantrill trilogy (1)
Syzygy
Coney, Michael Greatrex
Arcadia series (2)

T

T.A.C.K. against time
Miller, Marvin
T.A.C.K. series (3)
T.A.C.K. into danger
Miller, Marvin
T.A.C.K. series (4)
T.A.C.K. secret service
Miller, Marvin
T.A.C.K. series (2)
T.A.C.K. to the rescue
Miller, Marvin
T.A.C.K. series (1)
T as in trapped
Treat, Lawrence
Jub Freeman series (4)
Mitch Taylor series (3)
T-bone's tent
Green, Kate
Fossil family tales series (4)
T-boy and the trial for life
Edler, Timothy J
Tales from the Atchafalaya series (2)
T-boy in Mossland
Edler, Timothy J
Tales from the Atchafalaya series (3)
T-boy, the little Cajun
Edler, Timothy J
Tales from the Atchafalaya series (4)
T F Benson and the dinosaur madness mystery
Adler, David A
T F Benson series (2)
T F Benson and the funny money mystery
Adler, David A
T F Benson series (1)
T F Benson and the Jewelry spy mystery
Adler, David A
T F Benson series (3)
T.G. and Moonie go shopping
Maschler, Fay
T.G. and Moonie series (2)
T.G. and Moonie move out of town
Maschler, Fay
T.G. and Moonie series (1)
T.R. afloat
Dicks, Terrance
T.R.Bear series (4)
T.R. Bear at the zoo
Dicks, Terrance
T.R.Bear series (12)
T.R. down under
Dicks, Terrance
T.R.Bear series (10)
T.R. goes skiing
Dicks, Terrance
T.R.Bear series (9)
T.R. goes to Hollywood
Dicks, Terrance
T.R.Bear series (8)
T.R. goes to school
Dicks, Terrance
T.R.Bear series (2)
T.R. in New York
Dicks, Terrance
T.R.Bear series (11)
T.R.'s big game
Dicks, Terrance
T.R.Bear series (6)
T.R.'s day out
Dicks, Terrance
T.R.Bear series (3)
T.R.'s festival
Dicks, Terrance
T.R.Bear series (7)
T.R.'s Hallowe'en
Dicks, Terrance
T.R.Bear series (5)
T'Zad'U, part 2
Dubois, D
Star trek fan series (28)
T zero
Calvino, Italo
QFWFQ series (2)
Taash and the jesters
McKenzie, Ellen Kindt
Taash series (1)
Tabby magic
De Banke, Cecile
Tabby series (1)
Tabitha at Ivy Hall
Brown, Ruth Alberta
Ivy Hall trilogy (1)
Tabitha's glory
Brown, Ruth Alberta
Ivy Hall trilogy (2)
Tabitha's vacation
Brown, Ruth Alberta
Ivy Hall trilogy (3)
Table and chair
Tarsky, Sue
Look and see series (4)
Table d'hote
Clark, Douglas
Inspector George Masters series (8)
Table talk of Samuel Marchbanks
Davies, Robertson
Samuel Marchbanks series (2)

Tabloid murders
Wood, Clement
Inspector Colin series (2)
Taboo
Fitzgerald, Julia
Desert queen series (1)
Taboo territory
Ledd, Paul
Shelter Morgan series (18)
Tabor and the gunslicks
Evans, Tabor
Longarm series (160)
Tackett
Nofziger, Lyn
Tackett trilogy (1)
Tackett and the saloon keeper
Nofziger, Lyn
Tackett trilogy (3)
Tackett and the teacher
Nofziger, Lyn
Tackett trilogy (2)
Tackle block stop
Graeber, Charlotte Towner
Mister T and me series (10)
Tackling, running and kicking, now and again
Paulsen, Gary
Sports on the light side series (3)
Tac's island
Radin, Ruth Yaffe
Tac series (1)
Tac's turn
Radin, Ruth Yaffe
Tac series (2)
Tactical error
Gunnarsson, Thorarinn
Starwolves series (3)
Tactics of mistake
Dickson, Gordon Rupert
Dorsai series (2)
Tad Sheldon, Boy Scout
Wilson, John Fleming
Tad Sheldon series (1)
Tad Sheldon's Fourth of July
Wilson, John Fleming
Tad Sheldon series (2)
Tadgy on the trail
Davis, Nelson
Tadgy series (3)
Tadgy the mystery boy
Davis, Nelson
Tadgy series (1)
Tadpole Hall
Ashton, Helen
Wilchester chronicles series (1)
Taff and the stolen ponies
Berrisford, Judith Mary
Taff series (4)
Taff the sheepdog
Berrisford, Judith Mary
Taff series (1)
Taffin
Mallet, Lyndon
Taffin series (1)
Taffin's first law
Mallet, Lyndon
Taffin series (2)
Taffy Sinclair and the Melanie makeover
Haynes, Betsy
Taffy Sinclair series (8)
Taffy Sinclair and the romance machine
Haynes, Betsy
Taffy Sinclair series (4)
Taffy Sinclair and the secret admirer epidemic
Haynes, Betsy
Taffy Sinclair series (7)
Taffy Sinclair, Baby Ashley and me
Haynes, Betsy
Taffy Sinclair series (6)
Taffy Sinclair goes to Hollywood
Haynes, Betsy
Taffy Sinclair series (10)
Taffy Sinclair, queen of the soaps
Haynes, Betsy
Taffy Sinclair series (3)
Taffy Sinclair strikes again
Haynes, Betsy
Taffy Sinclair series (2)
Tag murders
Daly, Carroll John
Race Williams series (3)
Tagged for terror
Dixon, Franklin W
Hardy boys case files series (76)
Tago
Harvey, John Barton
Wes Hart series (3)
Tahara among African tribes
Sherman, Harold Morrow
Tahara series (2)
Tahara, boy king of the desert
Sherman, Harold Morrow
Tahara series (1)
Tahara, boy mystic of India
Sherman, Harold Morrow
Tahara series (3)
Tahara in the land of Yucatan
Sherman, Harold Morrow
Tahara series (4)
Tai-Lu flies abroad
Fraser, Shelagh
Tai-Lu series (3)
Tai-Lu talking
Fraser, Shelagh
Tai-Lu series (1)
Tai-Lu's birthday party
Fraser, Shelagh
Tai-Lu series (2)
Tai-pan
Clavell, James
Asian series (2)
Struan family series (1)
Tail dies at Sundown
Cody, Al
Montana series (10)
Tail job
Kane, Henry
Peter Chambers series (29)
Tail of the Arabian, knight
Marsh, Geoffrey
Lincoln Blackthorne series (2)
Tail of two kittens
English, David
Bunburys series (6)
Tail twisters
Fisher, Aileen
Ways of animals series (5)
Tailor of Gloucester
Potter, Beatrix
Peter Rabbit series (2)
Tailsting
Janson, Hank
Hank Janson series (215)
Tailwind to danger
Wallace, C H
Steve Ramsay series (3)
Tain
Frost, Gregory
Tain series (1)
Tainted man
Wainwright, John
Northern Police series (48)
Tainted power
Daly, Carroll John
Race Williams series (4)
Tainted token
Knight, Kathleen Moore
Elisha Macomber series (5)
Tainted turf
Learmonth, David
Silas Wortenheimer series (1)
Taiwan
Wood, Christopher
Taiwan series (1)
Taiwan joss
Grant, Maxwell
Shadow series (266)
Take
James, Bill
Superintendent Colin Harpur series (6)
Take a body
Halliday, Michael
Martin and Richard Fane series (1)
Take a dark journey
Erskine, Margaret
Inspector Septimus Finch series (14)
Take a girl like you
Amis, Kingsley
Patrick Standish series (1)
Take a murder, darling
Prather, Richard Scott
Shell Scott series (17)
Take a nap, Harry
Chalmers, Mary
Harry series (2)
Take a pair of private eyes
McIntosh, J T
Ambrose and Dominique Frayne series (1)
Take all to Nebraska
Winther, Sophus Keith
Grimsen trilogy (1)
Nebraska trilogy (1)
Take Angel
Christian, Frederick H
Frank Angel series (8)
Take care Mick and Mandy
Schmidt, Annie Maria Geertruida
Bob and Jilly series (4)
Take courage
Bentley, Phyllis
West Riding series (2)
Take death for a lover
Baker, William Howard
Richard Quintain series (2)
Take down
Lantz, Francess Lin
Varsity coach series (1)
Take it crooked
Beeding, Francis
Colonel Alastair Granby series (6)
Take it from the top
Lyttleton, Humphrey
As I please series (3)
Take Jennings for instance
Buckeridge, Anthony
Jennings series (9)
Take me back
Cooper, M E
Couples series (29)
Take me to your leader
Peel, John
U.N.C.L.E. files series (8)
Take murder
Wainwright, John
Chief Inspector Lennox series (6)
Northern Police series (43)
Take my word for it
Muir, Frank
My word series (3)
Safire, William
On language series (4)
Take no prisoners
Crosby, John Campbell
Horatio Cassidy series (3)
Take-off
Ash, William
Kyle Brandeis series (2)
Take off
Danby, Mary
Famous Five and you series (5)
Greatorex, Wilfred
Airline series (1)
Take one for murder
Chaber, M E
Milo March series (4)
Fulton, Eileen
Nina McFall series (2)
Take-over
Miller, Victor Brooke
Kojak series (8)
Take-over man
Wainwright, John
Northern Police series (10)
Pewter series (3)
Take sky
McCord, David
Rhymes of the never was an always is series (2)
Take the money and run
Payne, Laurence
Chief Inspector Sam Birkett series (4)
Mark Savage series (1)
Take thee a sharp knife
Campbell, R T
Professor John Stubbs series (3)
Take this, Sweetie
Janson, Hank
Hank Janson series (133)
Take two and rolling
Pfeffer, Susan Beth
Make me a star series (2)
Take two blondes
Janson, Hank
Hank Janson series (239)
Take two, they're small
Levy, Elizabeth
Fat Albert series (3)
Taken at the flood
Christie, Agatha
Hercule Poirot series (26)
Taken by force
Hutson, Shaun
Sergeant Rolf Kessler series (7)
Taken by the enemy
Optic, Oliver
Blue and the Gray afloat series (1)
Takeoff!
Garrett, Randall
Takeoff series (1)
Takeoff too
Garrett, Randall
Takeoff series (2)
Takeover double
Moody, Susan
Cassie Swann series (1)
Takeover time
Solmssen, Arthur Robert George
Conyers and Dean series (4)
Takers
Ahern, Jerry
Takers series (1)
Takersville shoot
Roberts, J R
Gunsmith series (88)
Taking a walk in the countryside
Tarsky, Sue
Taking a walk series (4)
Taking a walk in the park
Tarsky, Sue
Taking a walk series (2)
Taking a walk in the town
Tarsky, Sue
Taking a walk series (1)
Taking a walk on the seashore
Tarsky, Sue
Taking a walk series (3)
Taking care of Carruthers
Marshall, James
Carruthers series (2)
Taking care with strangers
Petty, Kate
First timers series (8)
Taking chances
Miller, Hugh
Eastenders series (11)
Taking charge
Pascal, Francine
Sweet Valley twins series (26)
Taking flight
Watt-Evans, Lawrence
Legend of Ethshar series (5)
Taking life easy
O'Hara, Kevin
Chico Brett series (12)
Taking my cat to the vet
Kuklin, Susan
Taking my pet to the vet series (1)
Taking my dog to the vet
Kuklin, Susan
Taking my pet to the vet series (2)
Taking of Kommand Group 8
Floyd, C J
Assault series (2)
Taking of Monte Carrillo
Brogan, Mike
Action Man series (3)
Taking of Satcon Station
Cohen, Barry
Asher Bockhorn series (1)
Taking of the Bastille
Dumas, Alexandre
Marie Antoinette series (3)
Taking of the Gry
Masefield, John
Sard Harker series (3)
Taking over
Sarasin, Jennifer
Cheerleaders series (26)
Taking risks
Reynolds, Anne
Cheerleaders series (17)
Taking sides
Pascal, Francine
Sweet Valley High series (31)
Taking the biscuit
Addis, Faith
Devon farm series (5)
Taking the Fifth
Jance, Judith A
J P Beaumont series (4)
Taking the Woffle to Pebblecombe-on-Sea
Chaney, Jill
Woffle series (1)
Talbot's secret
Clifford, Martin
Tom Merry series (5)
Tale of Anabelle Hedgehog
Lawhead, Stephen
Riverbank series (3)
Tale of Benjamin Bumble
Gilmore, David Hunter
Christopher Cricket series (6)
Tale of Benjamin Bunny
Potter, Beatrix
Peter Rabbit series (4)
Tale of Captain Brass, the pirate
Beaman, Sydney George Hulme
Toytown series (7)
Tale of Christine Pristine
Beaumont, Laura
Why not series (1)
Tale of Christopher Cricket
Gilmore, David Hunter
Christopher Cricket series (5)
Tale of Doug Smug
Beaumont, Laura
Why not series (2)
Tale of Genji
Murasaki Shibuku
Genji series (1)
Genji series (6)
Tale of Gregory Grasshopper
Gilmore, David Hunter
Christopher Cricket series (3)
Tale of Jemima Puddle-Duck
Potter, Beatrix
Peter Rabbit series (12)
Tale of Jeremy Vole
Lawhead, Stephen
Riverbank series (1)
Tale of Johnny Town-Mouse
Potter, Beatrix
Peter Rabbit series (20)
Tale of little Noddy
Blyton, Enid
Noddy stories series (6)
Tale of Little Pig Robinson
Potter, Beatrix
Peter Rabbit series (21)
Tale of Mister Jeremy Fisher
Potter, Beatrix
Peter Rabbit series (8)
Tale of Mister Tod
Potter, Beatrix
Peter Rabbit series (18)
Tale of Mister Tootleoo
Darwin, Bernard
Mister Tootleoo series (1)
Tale of Mitch Snitch
Beaumont, Laura
Why not series (3)
Tale of Mrs Tiggy-Winkle
Potter, Beatrix
Peter Rabbit series (6)
Tale of Mrs Tittlemouse
Potter, Beatrix
Peter Rabbit series (16)
Tale of Oakapple Wood
Partridge, Jenny
Oakapple Wood series (9)
Tale of Peter Rabbit
Potter, Beatrix
Peter Rabbit series (1)
Tale of Pigling Bland
Potter, Beatrix
Peter Rabbit series (19)
Tale of Samuel Whiskers
Potter, Beatrix
Peter Rabbit series (13)
Tale of Squirrel Nutkin
Potter, Beatrix
Peter Rabbit series (3)
Tale of the flopsy bunnies
Potter, Beatrix
Peter Rabbit series (14)
Tale of the magician
Beaman, Sydney George Hulme
Toytown series (5)
Tale of the pie and the patty-pan
Potter, Beatrix
Peter Rabbit series (7)
Tale of the witch doll
Wirt, Mildred Augustine
Penny Parker series (1)
Tale of three bullets
Tully, Paul
Deputy Marshal Hooky Gibbs series (5)
Tale of three lions
Haggard, Henry Rider
Allan Quatermain series (4)
Allan Quatermain series (6)
Tale of Timmy Tiptoes
Potter, Beatrix
Peter Rabbit series (17)
Tale of Timothy Mallard
Lawhead, Stephen
Riverbank series (2)
Tale of Tom Kitten
Potter, Beatrix
Peter Rabbit series (11)
Tale of Tom Thrush
Rutley, Cecily Marianne
Tales of the wild folk series (2)
Tale of traveling Matt
Muntean, Michaela
Fraggle Rock series (11)
Tale of two bad mice
Potter, Beatrix
Peter Rabbit series (5)
Tale of two clocks
Schmitz, James Henry
Hub series (1)
Telzey Amberdon and Trigger Argee series (1)
Tale of two villages
Sidgwick, Ethel
Sheriff family trilogy (3)

Tallant for trouble
York, Andrew
Colonel Munroe Tallant series (1)
Taller than before
Ashley, Bernard
Clipper Street series (2)
Talleyman
James, John
Talleyman series (1)
Talleyman in the ice
James, John
Talleyman series (2)
Tallyho, Pinkerton!
Kellogg, Steven
Pinkerton series (3)
Tallyman
Knox, Bill
Inspector Colin Thane and Phil Moss series (10)
Tallyman's fate
Jackson, Lewis
Sexton Blake series (1144)
Talon
Melville-Ross, Antony
Submarine warfare series (2)
Talons of Scorpio
Prescot, Dray
Dray Prescot series (30)
Talons of Weng-Chiang
Holmes, Robert
Doctor Who scripts series (3)
Taltos
Brust, Steven
Jhereg series (4)
Rice, Anne
Mayfair witches series (3)
Taltos and the paths of the dead
Brust, Steven
Jhereg series (4)
Taltos the assassin
Brust, Steven
Jhereg series (3)
Tam
Ellis, Edward Sylvester
Bound to win trilogy (3)
Tam Sventon and discovery
Holmberg, Ake
Tam Sventon series (4)
Tam Sventon and the silver-plate gang
Holmberg, Ake
Tam Sventon series (1)
Tam Sventon, desert detective
Holmberg, Ake
Tam Sventon series (3)
Tam Sventon, private detective
Holmberg, Ake
Tam Sventon series (2)
Tam the untamed
Patchett, Mary Elwyn
Ajax series (2)
Tama of the light country
Cummings, Ray
Tama series (1)
Tama, princess of Mercury
Cummings, Ray
Tama series (2)
Tamarind trail
Sharpe, Jon
Trailsman series (114)
Tamarisk
Lorrimer, Claire
Mavreen trilogy (2)
Tamaulipas guns
Sadler, Jeff
Marshal Andrew Anderson series (3)
Tamba, the tame tiger
Barnum, Richard
Kneetime animal stories series (14)
Tambai Island
Porteous, Richard Sydney
Tambai series (1)
Tambai treasure
Porteous, Richard Sydney
Tambai series (2)
Tambari
Saro-Wiwa, Ken
Tambari series (1)
Tambari in Dukana
Saro-Wiwa, Ken
Tambari series (2)
Tame a wild town
Grover, Marshall
Larry and Stretch series (268)
Tame and the wild
Hart, Susanne
African wildlife series (1)
Taming
Malcolm, Aleen
Daughters of Cameron series (1)
Taming a sea-horse
Parker, Robert Brown
Spenser series (13)
Taming of Annabelle
Chesney, Marion
Six sisters series (2)
Taming of Carney Wilde
Spicer, Bart
Carney Wilde series (6)
Taming of Neville Ibbetson
Graydon, William Murray
Sexton Blake series (240)
Taming of Zenas Henry
Bassett, Sara Ware
Cape Cod series (1)
Taming power
W, W
Qhe series (1)
Taming the Forest King
Edwards, Claudia Jane
Forest King trilogy (1)
Taming the furies
Foxall, Peter Augustus
Detective Sergeant Scamp series (6)
Tammy camps in the Rocky Mountains
Baker, Elizabeth
Tammy series (4)
Tammy camps out
Baker, Elizabeth
Tammy series (1)
Tammy climbs Pyramid Mountain
Baker, Elizabeth
Tammy series (2)
Tammy goes canoeing
Baker, Elizabeth
Tammy series (3)
Tammy Troot
Derwent, Lavinia
Tammy Troot series (1)
Tammy Troot's balloon
Derwent, Lavinia
Tammy Troot series (4)
Tammy Troot's capers
Derwent, Lavinia
Tammy Troot series (2)
Tammy Troot's hide-and-seek
Derwent, Lavinia
Tammy Troot series (4)
Tammy Troot's refugee
Derwent, Lavinia
Tammy Troot series (3)
Tammy Troot's telegram
Derwent, Lavinia
Tammy Troot series (3)
Tamworth Pig and the litter
Kemp, Gene
Tamworth Pig series (3)
Tamworth Pig rides again
Kemp, Gene
Tamworth Pig series (5)
Tamworth Pig saves the trees
Kemp, Gene
Tamworth Pig series (2)
Tamworth Pig stories
Kemp, Gene
Tamworth Pig series (4)
Tamzen
Rushing, Jane Gilmore
Walnut Grove series (2)
Tan and sandy silence
Macdonald, John Dann
Travis McGee series (13)
Tan Son Nhut
Helm, Eric
Ground Zero series (20)
Tanar of Pellucidar
Burroughs, Edgar Rice
Pellucidar series (3)
Tancred
Disraeli, Benjamin
Young England trilogy (3)
Tandia
Courtenay, Bryce
Peekay series (2)
Tandy's legacy
Grover, Marshall
Larry and Stretch series (319)
Tangent factor
Sanders, Lawrence
Peter Tangent series (2)
Tangent objective
Sanders, Lawrence
Peter Tangent series (1)
Tangerine house
Croft-Cooke, Rupert
Sensual life series (18)
Tangier assignment
Rougvie, Cameron
Robert Belcourt series (2)
Tangle
Atkins, Meg Elizabeth
Inspector Henry Beaumont series (4)
Wrenn, Harold Albert
William Mitchell series (1)
Tangle box
Brooks, Terry
Magic Kingdom of Landover series (4)
Tangle of terror
Murray, Edgar Joyce
Sexton Blake series (446)
Tangled case
Carter, Nicholas
Nicholas Carter series (189)
Tangled cord
Lockridge, Frances
Bill Wiegand series (22)
Nathan Shapiro series (2)
Tangled Fortunes
Mahy, Margaret
Cousins quartet (4)
Tangled in crime
Carter, Nicholas
Nicholas Carter series (443)
Tangled lands
Shetterly, Will
Kevin Fikkan series (2)
Tangled murders
Stern, Richard Martin
Johnny Ortiz series (5)
Tangled skein
Carter, Nicholas
Nicholas Carter series (551)
Tangled thread
Harrod-Eagles, Cynthia
Morland family series (10)
Tangled threads
Carter, Nicholas
Nicholas Carter series (297)
Tangled up in Beulah Land
Mowbray, Jeanie Pearl
Journey to nature series (2)
Tangled up in blue
Duplechan, Larry
Johnnie Ray Rousseau series (3)
Tangled web
Michael, Judith
Deceptions series (2)
Tangled webs
Mudd, Steve
Tangled webs series (1)
Tangled wood
Bromige, Iris
Rainwood family series (4)
Tanglefoot
Grover, Marshall
Larry and Stretch series (295)
Tanglewood murder
Kallen, Lucille
C.B.Greenfield series (2)
Tanglewood tales for girls and boys
Hawthorne, Nathaniel
Wonder book series (2)
Tango briefing
Hall, Adam
Quiller series (5)
Tango Key
Drake, Alison
Tango Key series (1)
Tanis, the shadow years
Siegel, Barbara
DragonLance preludes II series (3)
Tank
Williams, David
Tank series (1)
Tank-busters!
Kessler, Leo
SS Stuka Squadron series (3)
Tank-engine Thomas again
Awdry, Wilbert
Railway series (4)
Tank commander
Welch, Ronald
Carey family series (10)
Tank of sacred eels
Drummond, Ivor
Lady Jennifer, Sandro and Colly series (6)
Tank ship
Elsschot, Willem
Ship trilogy (3)
Tank war
Kurland, Michael
Mission series (2)
Tanker trap
Catherall, Arthur
Bulldog tugboat series (10)
Tanks are coming
Waite, Jon
Warriors of America trilogy (3)
Tank's choice
Davis, Elizabeth Jane
Jarryn series (3)
Tankwar
Steelbaugh, Larry
Tankwar series (1)
Tannahill tangle
Wells, Carolyn
Fleming Stone series (25)
Tanners
Fisher, Leonard Everett
Colonial Americans series (9)
Tanner's tiger
Block, Lawrence
Evan Tanner series (5)
Tanner's twelve swingers
Block, Lawrence
Evan Tanner series (3)
Tanquillan
Brindley, Louise
Tanquillan series (1)
Tansy
Peters, Maureen
Malone family trilogy (1)
Tantras
Awlinson, Richard
Avatar trilogy (2)
Tao of Pooh
Hoff, Benjamin
Taoist Winnie-the-Pooh series (1)
Taos
Mitchum, Hank
Stage coach station series (32)
Taos terror
Evans, Tabor
Longarm series (170)
Tap roots
Street, James
Dabney family series (2)
Taped
Barnes, Trevor
Blanche Hampton series (3)
Tapestry
Plain, Belva
Anna Friedman series (3)
Tapestry of lions
Roberson, Jennifer
Chronicles of the Cheysuli series (8)
Tapestry of time
Cowper, Richard
Bird of kinship series (3)
Tapestry room murder
Wells, Carolyn
Fleming Stone series (26)
Tapestry warriors
Wilder, Cherry
Torin trilogy (3)
Tapioca for tea
Shears, Sarah
Tapioca for tea series (1)
Tapiola's brave regiment
Nathan, Robert
Tapiola series (2)
Taproots of Falconhurst
Carter, Ashley
Falconhurst series (11)
Taps at Little Big Horn
Benteen, John
Sundance series (9)
Taquisara
Crawford, Francis Marion
Roman society series (5)
Tar
Anderson, Sherwood
Story-teller series (1)
Tar-Aiym Krang
Foster, Alan Dean
Flinx of the Commonwealth series (2)
Tar-Aiym Krang trilogy (1)
Tar-baby, and other rhymes of Uncle Remus
Harris, Joel Chandler
Uncle Remus series (9)
Tara
Taylor, Philip Meadows
Indian history trilogy (1)
Tarakian
Peters, Ludovic
Ian Firth series (2)
Taran Wanderer
Alexander, Lloyd
Prydain series (4)
Tarantula strike
Carter, Nick
Nick Carter series (137)
Tarantulas on the brain
Singer, Marilyn
Lizzie Silver series (1)
Tara's daughter
Castle, Frances
Erinn series (2)
Tara's healing
Giles, Janice Holt
Piney Ridge trilogy (3)
Tardis inside out
Nathan-Turner, John
Doctor Who series (162)
Tares
Thurston, Ernest Temple
Bellwattle and Cruikshank series (3)
Target
Drake, David
Yates series (2)
Helm, Eric
Ground Zero series (24)
Mackenzie, Steve
Seals series (4)
Target, Charity Ross
Bickham, Jack Miles
Charity Ross series (2)
Target Conestoga
Sharpe, Jon
Trailsman series (89)
Target, Doomsday Island
Carter, Nick
Nick Carter series (71)
Target for Conquest
Gray, Berkeley
Norman Conquest series (27)
Target for death
Robeson, Kenneth
Doc Savage series (175)
Target for malice
Cooper, Barbara
Inspector Gibbon series (1)
Target for murder
Giles, Guy Elwyn
Brice Kent series (2)
Target for terror
Jacobs, Thomas Curtis Hicks
Mike Seton series (1)
Temple Fortune series (11)
Target for their dark desire
Brown, Carter
Lieutenant Al Wheeler series (35)
Target for tonight
Gray, Rod
New lady from L.U.S.T. series (3)
King, David
Rat Patrol series (5)
Telfair, Richard
Dangerman series (5)
Target for tragedy
Philips, Judson Pentecost
Peter Styles series (19)
Target in taffeta
Benson, Ben
Inspector Wade Paris series (5)
Target Iran
Adair, James B
World War III series (3)
Target is H
Derrick, Lionel
Penetrator series (1)
Target, Mike Shayne
Halliday, Brett
Michael Shayne series (34)
Target Norway
Cort, Ned
Boxer Unit SS series (4)
Target nuke
Adair, James B
World War III series (2)
Target Rabaul
Darby, John
McLeane's Rangers series (2)
Target red star
Carter, Nick
Nick Carter series (208)
Target Sahara
Saint Germain, Gregory
Resistance series (5)
Target star
Scheer, Karl Herbert
Perry Rhodan series (92)
Target Steele
Masters, J D
Steele series (6)
Target, Terra
Janifer, Laurence Mark
Angelo DiStefano trilogy (1)
Target Texas
Adair, James B
World War III series (1)
Target Tobruk
Jackson, Robert
Flying Officer George Yeoman series (3)
Targets of opportunity
Weber, Joe
Military techno-thrillers series (4)
Tariq
Miles, Keith
Sin bin series (3)
Tarlov cipher
Carter, Nick
Nick Carter series (207)

Tarnham connection
Tute, Warren
George Mado series (3)
Tarnished gold
Mills, Woosnam
Sir John Howden series (4)
Tarnished star
Gilman, George G
Adam Steele series (19)
Tarnished victory
Joyce, Rosemary
Dream girls series (3)
Tarnsman of Gor
Norman, John
Tarl Cabot series (1)
Tarot
Anthony, Piers
Tarot trilogy (3)
Tarot murders
Warner, Mignon
Mrs Edwina Charles series (2)
Tarra Khash, Hrossak!
Lumley, Brian
Tales of the primal land series (2)
Tarradiddle tales
Atkin, Flora Blumenthal
Tarradiddle series (1)
Tarradiddle travels
Atkin, Flora Blumenthal
Tarradiddle series (2)
Tarry and be hanged
Woods, Sara
Sir Nicholas Harding and Antony Maitland series (16)
Tarry awhile
Weber, Lenora Mattingly
Beany Malone series (12)
Tartan ringers
Gash, Jonathan
Lovejoy series (10)
Tartan sell
Gash, Jonathan
Lovejoy series (10)
Tartarin of Tarascon, traveller, Turk and lion-hunter
Daudet, Alphonse
Tartarin series (1)
Tartarin on the Alps
Daudet, Alphonse
Tartarin series (2)
Tartarus incident
Greenleaf, William
Tartarus series (1)
Tarzan alive
Farmer, Philip Jose
Tarzan series (24)
Tarzan and Shane meet the Toad
Locklin, Gerald
Toad series (3)
Stetler, Charles
Toad series (3)
Tarzan and the abominable snowman
Werper, Barton
New Tarzan series (4)
Tarzan and the ant men
Burroughs, Edgar Rice
Tarzan series (10)
Tarzan and the castaways
Burroughs, Edgar Rice
Tarzan series (24)
Tarzan and the cave city
Werper, Barton
New Tarzan series (2)
Tarzan and the City of Gold
Burroughs, Edgar Rice
Tarzan series (16)
Tarzan and the classics
Holtsmark, Erling Bent
Tarzan series (24)
Tarzan and the forbidden city
Burroughs, Edgar Rice
Tarzan series (20)
Tarzan and the Foreign Legion
Burroughs, Edgar Rice
Tarzan series (22)
Tarzan and the golden lion
Burroughs, Edgar Rice
Tarzan series (9)
Tarzan and the jewel of Opar
Burroughs, Edgar Rice
Opar series (2)
Tarzan and the jewels of Opar
Burroughs, Edgar Rice
Tarzan series (5)
Tarzan and the leopard men
Burroughs, Edgar Rice
Tarzan series (18)
Tarzan and the lightning man
Gilmour, William
Tarzan series (24)
Tarzan and the lion man
Burroughs, Edgar Rice
Tarzan series (17)
Tarzan and the lost empire
Burroughs, Edgar Rice
Tarzan series (12)
Tarzan and the lost safari
Burroughs, Edgar Rice
Tarzan series (24)
Tarzan and the madman
Burroughs, Edgar Rice
Tarzan series (23)
Tarzan and the silver globe
Werper, Barton
New Tarzan series (1)
Tarzan and the snake people
Werper, Barton
New Tarzan series (3)
Tarzan and the Tarzan twins
Burroughs, Edgar Rice
Tarzan twins series (2)
Tarzan and the Tarzan twins with Jad-Bal-Ja, the golden lion
Burroughs, Edgar Rice
Tarzan twins series (2)
Tarzan and the tower of diamonds
Reinsmith, Richard
Endless quest series (31)
Tarzan series (24)
Tarzan and the valley of gold
Leiber, Fritz
Tarzan series (24)
Tarzan and the well of slaves
Niles, Douglas
Endless quest series (26)
Tarzan series (24)
Tarzan and the winged invaders
Werper, Barton
New Tarzan series (5)
Tarzan and tradition
Holtsmark, Erling Bent
Tarzan series (24)
Tarzan at Mars' core
Hirschman, Edward
Tarzan series (24)
Tarzan at the earth's core
Burroughs, Edgar Rice
Pellucidar series (4)
Tarzan series (13)
Tarzan encyclopedia
Harwood, John
Tarzan series (24)
Tarzan, king of the apes
Vinge, Joan Dennison
Tarzan series (1)
Tarzan, lord of the jungle
Burroughs, Edgar Rice
Tarzan series (11)
Tarzan of the apes
Burroughs, Edgar Rice
Tarzan series (1)
Tarzan series (15)
Tarzan the invincible
Burroughs, Edgar Rice
Tarzan series (14)
Tarzan the magnificent
Burroughs, Edgar Rice
Tarzan series (21)
Tarzan the terrible
Burroughs, Edgar Rice
Tarzan series (8)
Tarzan the untamed
Burroughs, Edgar Rice
Tarzan series (7)
Tarzan triumphant
Burroughs, Edgar Rice
Tarzan series (15)
Tarzan twins
Burroughs, Edgar Rice
Tarzan twins series (1)
Tarzan's quest
Burroughs, Edgar Rice
Tarzan series (19)
Tas and the postal rocket
Eliott, E C
Tas series (2)
Tas and the space machine
Eliott, E C
Tas series (1)
Tascosa gun
Shelton, Gene
Texas legends series (4)
Task
Martin, David
Sean McCart series (1)
Tasmanian tales
Lyne, Nairda
Powranna series (1)
Taste and smell
Berry, Joy
Can make and do series (10)
Taste for blood
Hayes, Ralph Eugene
John Yard series (3)
West, John B
Rocky Steele series (4)
Taste for death
James, Phyllis Dorothy
Commander Adam Dalgliesh series (8)
O'Donnell, Peter
Modesty Blaise series (4)
Taste for honey
Heard, Henry Fitzgerald
Mister Mycroft series (1)
Taste for murder
Heard, Henry Fitzgerald
Mister Mycroft series (1)
Taste for Noah
Topek, Susan Remick
Noah series (3)
Taste for terror
Dixon, Franklin W
Hardy boys case files series (94)
Taste for violence
Halliday, Brett
Michael Shayne series (19)
Taste of ashes
Browne, Howard
Paul Pine series (4)
Taste of cognac
Halliday, Brett
Michael Shayne series (16)
Taste of death
McGrew, Fenn
Lieutenant Charles Hillary series (1)
Taste of fear
Kruk, Zofia
Taste series (1)
Taste of fears
Millar, Margaret
Inspector Sands series (3)
Woods, Sara
Sir Nicholas Harding and Antony Maitland series (4)
Taste of hope
Kruk, Zofia
Taste series (2)
Taste of murder
Cannan, Joanna
Inspector Ronald Price series (1)
Taste of power
Burley, William John
Doctor Henry Pym series (1)
Taste of proof
Knox, Bill
Inspector Colin Thane and Phil Moss series (7)
Taste of sangria
Keith, Carlton
Jeff Green series (5)
Taste of the hills
Smeeton, Miles
Hills and jungles series (1)
Taste of treason
Maling, Arthur
Brock Potter series (5)
Taste of treasure
Ashe, Gordon
Patrick Dawlish series (42)
Taste of vengeance
Davis, Lavinia Riker
Nora Hughes and Larry Blaine series (2)
Taste of Vengeance
Knott, William Cecil
Vengeance Seeker series (4)
Taste of victory
Dengler, Sandy
Australian destiny series (2)
Tasting
Allington, Richard L
Beginning to learn series (7)
Pluckrose, Henry
Thinking about series (2)
Tasty way to die
Laurence, Janet
Darina Lisle series (2)
Tattered tartan
Cameron, Isabel
Glen folk series (4)
Tattered Tom
Alger, Horatio
Tattered Tom series (1)
Tattle-tail
Ledd, Paul
Shelter Morgan series (32)
Tattletale
Cosgrove, Stephen Edward
Whimsy storybooks series (2)
Tattooed man
Pease, Howard
Tod Moran series (1)
Tattooed triangle
Brandon, John Gordon
Sexton Blake series (917)
Tau Cross mystery
Connington, John Jervis
Sir Clinton Driffield series (10)
Taurus trip
Dewey, Thomas Blanchard
Private Eye Mac series (17)
Tavern
Steen, Marguerite
Spanish trilogy (3)
Tavern talk
Brooks, Collin
Tavern talk series (1)
Tawny talent
Travis, Falcon
Third Bilsley Pack series (2)
Tawny trail
Travis, Falcon
Third Bilsley Pack series (3)
Tax in blood
Schutz, Benjamin Merrill
Leo Haggerty series (3)
Taxed to death
Simons, Roger
Inspector Fadiman Wace series (11)
Taxi
Maestro, Betsy Crippen
Words series (6)
Taxi-cab murder
Brandon, John Gordon
Sexton Blake series (745)
Taxi man's quest
Chester, Gilbert
Sexton Blake series (883)
Taxi to intrigue
Quackenbush, Robert Mead
Miss Mallard series (7)
Taxicab riddle
Carter, Nicholas
Nicholas Carter series (440)
Te of Piglet
Hoff, Benjamin
Taoist Winnie-the-Pooh series (2)
Tea and biscuits
Scott, Mary
New Zealand life series (4)
Tea for two
Beaman, Sydney George Hulme
Toytown series (17)
Tea-on-Friday-Tigger
Huddy, Delia
Tigger series (1)
Tea on Sunday
Cooper, Lettice
Chief Inspector Corby series (1)
Tea-shop in Limehouse
Burke, Thomas
London series (4)
Tea time tragedy
Beckett, Mark
Major Dick Burton series (4)
Tea tray murders
Bush, Christopher
Ludovic Travers series (12)
Tea with the Black Dragon
Macavoy, Roberta Ann
Mayland Long and Martha Macnamara series (1)
Teabag and the bears
Baker, Margaret Joyce
Three bears series (5)
Teach me about bathtime
Berry, Joy
Teach me about series (4)
Teach me about bedtime
Berry, Joy
Teach me about series (5)
Teach me about boredom
Berry, Joy
Teach me about series (6)
Teach me about brothers and sisters
Berry, Joy
Teach me about series (14)
Teach me about crying
Berry, Joy
Teach me about series (7)
Teach me about danger
Berry, Joy
Teach me about series (8)
Teach me about friends
Berry, Joy
Teach me about series (17)
Teach me about getting dressed
Berry, Joy
Teach me about series (2)
Teach me about illness
Berry, Joy
Teach me about series (9)
Teach me about listening
Berry, Joy
Teach me about series (19)
Teach me about looking
Berry, Joy
Teach me about series (20)
Teach me about mealtime
Berry, Joy
Teach me about series (1)
Teach me about mommies and daddies
Berry, Joy
Teach me about series (22)
Teach me about my body
Berry, Joy
Teach me about series (24)
Teach me about pets
Berry, Joy
Teach me about series (13)
Teach me about potty training
Berry, Joy
Teach me about series (3)
Teach me about pretending
Berry, Joy
Teach me about series (15)
Teach me about relatives
Berry, Joy
Teach me about series (16)
Teach me about school
Berry, Joy
Teach me about series (25)
Teach me about security objects
Berry, Joy
Teach me about series (10)
Teach me about separation
Berry, Joy
Teach me about series (11)
Teach me about smelling
Berry, Joy
Teach me about series (26)
Teach me about tasting
Berry, Joy
Teach me about series (27)
Teach me about the baby-sitter
Berry, Joy
Teach me about series (21)
Teach me about the dentist
Berry, Joy
Teach me about series (18)
Teach me about the doctor
Berry, Joy
Teach me about series (23)
Teach me about touching
Berry, Joy
Teach me about series (28)
Teach me about travel
Berry, Joy
Teach me about series (12)
Teach us, Amelia Bedelia
Parish, Peggy
Amelia Bedelia series (7)
Teacher crush
Pascal, Francine
Sweet Valley High series (57)
Teachers
Target, George William
Post-war Britain series (2)
Teacher's hand-Pook
Pook, Peter
Pook series (17)
Teacher's pet
Blake, Susan
Hawthorne College series (5)
Cooper, M E
Couples series (21)
Dicks, Terrance
David and Goliath series (14)
Pascal, Francine
Sweet Valley twins series (2)
Teachers's blood
Ross, Ivan T
Ben Gordon series (5)
Teachings of Don Juan
Castaneda, Carlos
Don Juan series (1)
Team
Peyton, K M
Ruth Hollis series (2)
Team of crooks
Hardy, Arthur Steffens
Sexton Blake series (470)
Team play
Bryant, Bonnie
Saddle Club series (15)
Team that nobody wanted
McCann, Sean
Dove's End Football Club series (7)
Team that wouldn't give in
Hardcastle, Michael
Mascot series (1)
Team trouble
Levy, Elizabeth
Gymnasts series (21)
Team Yankee
Coyle, Harold
World War Three series (3)

Teaming up together
Wilhelm, Hans
Merritales series (6)
Teamsman
Porteous, Crichton
Farmer's creed trilogy (2)
Teamwork
Pascal, Francine
Sweet Valley twins series (27)
Steffanson, Con
Laverne and Shirley series (1)
Teardown
Wuamett, Victor
Chase Randel series (1)
Teardrops of Buddha
Grant, Maxwell
Shadow series (262)
Tears and tenderness
Witcomb, Nan
Thoughts of Nanushka series (12)
Tears before bedtime
Skelton, Barbara
Tears series (1)
Tears for the bride
Martin, Robert Lee
Jim Bennett series (3)
Tears of autumn
McCarry, Charles
Paul Christopher series (2)
Tears of blood
Carrel, Mark
Andrew McCall series (3)
Marvin, James W
Crow series (3)
Tears of the singers
Snodgrass, Melinda Marilyn
Star trek series (19)
Teaser set to kill
Brody, Marc
Marc Brody series (66)
Tech assassins
Sievert, John
C.A.D.S. series (12)
Tech battleground
Sievert, John
C.A.D.S. series (2)
Tech commando
Sievert, John
C.A.D.S. series (3)
Tech inferno
Sievert, John
C.A.D.S. series (6)
Tech Satan
Sievert, John
C.A.D.S. series (5)
Tech strike force
Sievert, John
C.A.D.S. series (4)
Tech war
Stivers, Dick
Able Team series (18)
Technicians of death
Williamson, Tony
Lee Corey series (3)
Technique for treachery
Truss, Seldon
Inspector Gidleigh series (18)
Technos
Tubb, Edwin Charles
Dumarest series (7)
Teckla
Brust, Steven
Jhereg series (3)
Ted and Dolly's fairytale flight
Fowler, Richard
Ted and Dolly series (2)
Ted and Dolly's magic carpet ride
Fowler, Richard
Ted and Dolly series (1)
Ted and Nina go to the grocery store
De Angeli, Marguerite
Ted and Nina series (1)
Ted and Nina have a happy rainy day
De Angeli, Marguerite
Ted and Nina series (2)
Ted and Terri and the broken arrow
Palmer, Bernard
Ted and Terri series (1)
Ted and Terri and the crooked trapper
Palmer, Bernard
Ted and Terri series (2)
Ted and Terri and the secret captive
Palmer, Bernard
Ted and Terri series (5)
Ted and Terri and the stubborn bully
Palmer, Bernard
Ted and Terri series (4)
Ted and Terri and the troubled trumpeter
Palmer, Bernard
Ted and Terri series (3)
Ted and the Chinese princess
Mogenson, Jan
Ted series (2)
Ted Jones at Desperation Island
Patchin, Frank Gee
Ted Jones series (2)
Ted Jones, fortune hunter
Patchin, Frank Gee
Ted Jones series (1)
Ted Jones under sealed orders
Patchin, Frank Gee
Ted Jones series (4)
Ted Jones' weeks of terror
Patchin, Frank Gee
Ted Jones series (3)
Ted runs away from home
Mogenson, Jan
Ted series (6)
Teddy and Towser
Ellis, Edward Sylvester
Strange adventure series (1)
Teddy at the seaside
Davidson, Amanda
Teddy series (2)
Teddy bear baker
Worthington, Phoebe
Teddy bear series (2)
Teddy bear coalman
Worthington, Phoebe
Teddy bear series (1)
Teddy bear farmer
Worthington, Phoebe
Teddy bear series (5)
Teddy bear gardener
Worthington, Phoebe
Teddy bear series (4)
Teddy bear habit
Collier, James Lincoln
George Stable series (1)
Teddy bear postman
Worthington, Phoebe
Teddy bear series (3)
Teddy Bear's bedtime adventure
Slier, Debby
Teddy Bear series (2)
Teddy Bear's bedtime book
Slier, Debby
Teddy Bear series (1)
Teddy Bear's farm
Cradock, Henry Cowper, *Mrs*
Teddy Bear series (5)
Teddy Bear's shop
Cradock, Henry Cowper, *Mrs*
Teddy Bear series (4)
Teddy-boy mystery
Drummond, J
Sexton Blake series (1377)
Teddy boy's picnic
Stucley, Elizabeth
Teddy boy series (1)
Teddy dresses
McCue, Dick
Animal shape series (3)
Teddy Edward and the contraption
Matthews, Patrick
Teddy Edward series (1)
Teddy Edward becomes a Red Indian
Matthews, Patrick
Teddy Edward series (2)
Teddy Edward goes to Mount Everest
Matthews, Patrick
Teddy Edward series (4)
Teddy Edward in Timbuctoo
Matthews, Patrick
Teddy Edward series (3)
Teddy Edward's magic journey
Matthews, Patrick
Teddy Edward's books for bears series (1)
Teddy Edward's magic music box
Matthews, Patrick
Teddy Edward's books for bears series (3)
Teddy, her book
Ray, Anna Chapin
Teddy series (1)
Teddy, her daughter
Ray, Anna Chapin
Teddy series (3)
Teddy in the garden
Davidson, Amanda
Teddy series (8)
Teddy Jo and the abandoned house
Stahl, Hilda
Teddy Jo series (7)
Teddy Jo and the broken locket mystery
Stahl, Hilda
Teddy Jo series (13)
Teddy Jo and the great dive
Stahl, Hilda
Teddy Jo series (10)
Teddy Jo and the kidnapped heir
Stahl, Hilda
Teddy Jo series (9)
Teddy Jo and the magic quill
Stahl, Hilda
Teddy Jo series (11)
Teddy Jo and the missing family
Stahl, Hilda
Teddy Jo series (14)
Teddy Jo and the missing portrait
Stahl, Hilda
Teddy Jo series (12)
Teddy Jo and the ragged beggars
Stahl, Hilda
Teddy Jo series (8)
Teddy Jo and the stolen ring
Stahl, Hilda
Teddy Jo series (3)
Teddy Jo and the strange medallion
Stahl, Hilda
Teddy Jo series (5)
Teddy Jo and the strangers in the pink house
Stahl, Hilda
Teddy Jo series (4)
Teddy Jo and the terrible secret
Stahl, Hilda
Teddy Jo series (1)
Teddy Jo and the wild dog
Stahl, Hilda
Teddy Jo series (6)
Teddy Jo and the yellow room mystery
Stahl, Hilda
Teddy Jo series (2)
Teddy Lester, captain of cricket
Finnemore, John
Teddy Lester series (6)
Teddy Lester in the Fifth
Finnemore, John
Teddy Lester series (5)
Teddy Lester's chums
Finnemore, John
Teddy Lester series (3)
Teddy Lester's schooldays
Finnemore, John
Teddy Lester series (4)
Teddy out-of-doors
Davidson, Amanda
Teddy series (3)
Teddy Robinson
Robinson, Joan Gale
Teddy Robinson series (1)
Teddy Robinson himself
Robinson, Joan Gale
Teddy Robinson series (5)
Teddy Robinson's book
Robinson, Joan Gale
Teddy Robinson series (3)
Teddy Teabury's fabulous fact
Asher, Sandra Fenichel
Teddy Teabury series (1)
Teddy Teabury's peanutty problems
Asher, Sandra Fenichel
Teddy Teabury series (2)
Teddy trucks
Cartlidge, Michelle
Teddy trucks series (1)
Teddybears ABC
Gretz, Susanna
Teddybears series (4)
Teddybears and the cold cure
Gretz, Susanna
Teddybears series (8)
Teddybears cookbook
Gretz, Susanna
Teddybears series (5)
Teddybears go shopping
Gretz, Susanna
Teddybears series (7)
Teddybears moving day
Gretz, Susanna
Teddybears series (6)
Teddybears one to ten
Gretz, Susanna
Teddybears series (1)
Teddy's birthday
Davidson, Amanda
Teddy series (7)
Teddy's ear
Daly, Niki
Storytime series (1)
Teddy's favourite food
Davidson, Amanda
Teddy series (6)
Teddy's first Christmas
Davidson, Amanda
Teddy series (1)
Teddy's new job
Beaman, Sydney George Hulme
Out of the ark series (1)
Teddy's pocket money
Davidson, Amanda
Teddy series (4)
Teddy's wash day
Davidson, Amanda
Teddy series (5)
Ted's seaside adventure
Mogenson, Jan
Ted series (5)
Tee-Bo the incredible talking dog leads the way in the great hort hunt
Whitcomb, Mary Burg
Tee-Bo series (2)
Tee-Bo the talking dog on the trail of the persnickety prowler
Whitcomb, Mary Burg
Tee-Bo series (1)
Teen age adventure stories
Coombs, Charles Ira
Teen age stories series (1)
Teen age champion sports stories
Coombs, Charles Ira
Teen age stories series (3)
Teen-age Mafia
Brown, Wenzell
Teen-age series (2)
Teen-age terror
Brown, Wenzell
Teen-age series (1)
Teen age treasure chest of sports
Coombs, Charles Ira
Teen age stories series (2)
Teenage mutant ninja turtles
Hiller, Barbara B
Teenage mutant ninja turtles series (1)
Teenage mutant ninja turtles knitting book
Gammon, Joy
Teenage mutant ninja turtles series (5)
Teens
Mack, Louise
Lennie Leighton series (1)
Teens triumphant
Mack, Louise
Lennie Leighton series (3)
Teeny the harvest mouse
Rutley, Cecily Marianne
Tales of the wild folk series (6)
Teep and Beep go to sleep
Mayer, Mercer
Tink, tonk tales series (4)
Teeth for Charlie
Allen, Joy
Charlie series (2)
Teeth of the dragon
Grant, Maxwell
Shadow series (134)
Teeth of the gale
Aiken, Joan
Felix Brooke series (3)
Teeth of the tiger
Leblanc, Maurice
Arsene Lupin series (7)
Teething troubles
Finch, Matthew
Dentist series (2)
Teetoncey
Taylor, Theodore
Teetoncey and Ben O'Neal trilogy (1)
Teetoncey and Ben O'Neal
Taylor, Theodore
Teetoncey and Ben O'Neal trilogy (2)
Tehanu
Le Guin, Ursula Kroeber
Earthsea series (4)
Teheran wipeout
Pendleton, Don
Mack Bolan series (76)
TekLab
Shatner, William
TekWar series (3)
TekLords
Shatner, William
TekWar series (2)
TekWar
Shatner, William
TekWar series (1)
Telegram from Le Tourquet
Bude, John
Inspector Meredith series (25)
Telegraph
Stendhal
Lucien Leeuwen series (2)
Telegraph boy
Alger, Horatio
Tattered Tom series (8)
Telephone call
Rhode, John
Doctor Lancelot Priestley series (47)
Telephone never tells
Hinxman, Margaret
Detective Inspector Ralph Brand series (3)
Television adventures of Worzel Gummidge
Waterhouse, Keith
Worzel Gummidge series (11)
Television murders
Ballinger, W A
Sexton Blake series (1509)
Wallace, Robert
Phantom Detective series (27)
Television mystery
Beresford, Elisabeth
Gappy, Jim and Jane series (1)
Telford and the American visitor
Pope, Ray
Telford series (2)
Telford and the Festiniog railway
Pope, Ray
Telford series (5)
Telford and the prairie battle
Pope, Ray
Telford series (10)
Telford goes Dutch
Pope, Ray
Telford series (7)
Telford saves the line
Pope, Ray
Telford series (6)
Telford tells the truth
Pope, Ray
Telford series (8)
Telford's holiday
Pope, Ray
Telford series (4)
Tell a tale of Tuckers
Mendel, Jo
Tucker family series (6)
Tell and draw animal cut-outs
Oldfield, Margaret Jean
Tell and draw series (2)
Tell and draw cut-outs
Oldfield, Margaret Jean
Tell and draw series (6)
Tell and draw paper bag puppet book
Oldfield, Margaret Jean
Tell and draw series (5)
Tell and draw stories
Oldfield, Margaret Jean
Tell and draw series (1)
Tell her it's murder
Reilly, Helen
Inspector Christopher McKee series (24)
Tell it to the birds
Chase, James Hadley
Steve Harmas series (4)
Tell me no lies
Elfman, Blossom
Mike and Ally series (2)
Tell-tale photographs
Carter, Nicholas
Nicholas Carter series (113)
Tell-Tale Tiger
Ahlberg, Allan
Help your child to read series (11)
Tell the time
McCaughrean, Geraldine
Teddies series (5)
Tell us a story
Ahlberg, Allan
Red nose readers series (16)
Tell your fortune
Mitchell Ruth Comfort
Old San Francisco series (4)
Telling each other the truth
Backus, William
Telling the truth series (3)
Telling lies
Hornsby, Wendy
Maggie McGowan series (1)
Norby, Lisa
Cheerleaders series (44)
Telling the time
Higgs, Mike
Learn with Moonbird series (4)
Telling the truth to troubled people
Backus, William
Telling the truth series (2)
Telling yourself the truth
Backus, William
Telling the truth series (1)
Telltale scar
Striker, Fran
Tom Quest series (2)
Telltale telegram
Burnham, Helen
One Week Wimble series (2)

Telsa raiders
Bowen, Robert Sidney
Dusty Ayres and his Battle Birds series (4)
Telzey toy
Schmitz, James Henry
Telzey Amberdon and Trigger Argee series (4)
Telzey toy, and other stories
Schmitz, James Henry
Telzey Amberdon and Trigger Argee series (4)
Tempania mystery
Walsh, James Morgan
Inspector Quaile series (2)
Temperamental Henry
Merwin, Samuel
Henry Calverly series (1)
Tempest
Shakespeare, William
Tempest series (2)
Tempest in a tea-cup
Shand, William
Bill Tempest series (3)
Tempest of Tombstone
Willoughby, Lee Davis
Women who won the West series (1)
Tempest Squadron
Jackson, Robert
Flying Officer George Yeoman series (7)
Tempest-tost
Davies, Robertson
Salterton trilogy (1)
Tempest weaves a shroud
Shand, William
Bill Tempest series (2)
Templar treasure
Kurtz, Katherine
Adept trilogy (3)
Temple at Ilumquh
Laflin, Jack
Adjusters series (5)
Temple falls
Macvicar, Angus
Reverend P J Macfarlane series (1)
Temple girl
Bruce, Henry
Eurasian series (5)
Temple girl series (1)
Temple Kent
Devon, D G
Temple Kent series (1)
Temple of butterflies
Fitzgerald, Julia
Astromance series (8)
Temple of crime
Grant, Maxwell
Shadow series (213)
Temple of dark destiny
Syvertsen, Ryder
Mystic rebel series (4)
Temple of dawn
Mishima, Yukio
Sea of fertiligy quartet (3)
Robertson, Colin
Peter Grayleigh series (1)
Temple of fear
Carter, Nick
Nick Carter series (36)
Temple of flame
Morris, Dave
Golden dragon fantasy gamebooks series (2)
Temple of terror
Livingstone, Ian
Fighting fantasy gamebook series (14)
Temple of the dead
Norwood, Victor George Charles
Jacare series (3)
Temple of the sun
Caldecott, Moyra
Sacred stones series (2)
Temple of topaz
Boreham, Frank William
Texts that made history series (5)
Temple of truth
Tubb, Edwin Charles
Dumarest series (31)
Temple of vice
Carter, Nicholas
Nicholas Carter series (330)
Temple tiger and more man-eaters of Kumaon
Corbett, Jim
Man-eaters series (3)
Temple Tower
Sapper
Bulldog Drummond series (6)
Temples of Ayocan
Lord, Jeffrey
Richard Blade series (14)
Templeton massacre
Carrington, G A
Marcus Cavanaugh series (5)
Temply of Costly Experience
Vare, Daniele
Yen-Ching trilogy (3)
Temporary agency
Pollack, Rachel
Unquenchable fire series (2)
Temporary ghost
Friedman, Mickey
Georgia Lee Maxwell series (2)
Temporary hearths
Evans, Stuart
Windmill Hill series (3)
Temporary kings
Powell, Anthony
Dance to the music of time series (11)
Temporary open air life
Leach, Christopher
Dave Bourne series (2)
Tempt me not
Weymouth, Anthony
Inspector Treadgold series (6)
Temptation
Roberts, Nora
Flowers series (43)
Temptation of Angelique
Golon, Sergeanne
Angelique series (7)
Temptation of Don Volpi
Hayes, Alfred
Love trilogy (3)
Temptations
Bernard, Elizabeth
Satin slippers series (7)
Temptations of Hercule
Audemars, Pierre
Hercule Renard series (2)
Tempted
Avenell, Donne
Axa series (4)
Tempter
Collins, Nancy Averill
Sunglasses series (2)
Tempting fate
Roberts, Nora
Flowers series (13)
Yarbro, Chelsea Quinn
Count Ragoczy Saint-Germain series (5)
Temptress
Blasco Ibanez, Vicente
Temptress series (1)
Brown, Carter
Lieutenant Al Wheeler series (18)
Deveraux, Jude
Montgomery annals series (5)
Temptress returns
Allcard, Edward Cecil
Temptress series (2)
Tempus
Morris, Janet Ellen
Tempus series (4)
Tempus unbound
Morris, Janet Ellen
Tempus series (6)
Ten black pearls
Gregg, Cecil Freeman
Henry Prince series (1)
Inspector Cuthbert Higgins series (12)
Ten boy summer
Quin-Harkin, Janet
Toni Redmond and Jill Gardner series (1)
Ten boys who lived on the road from long ago to now
Andrews, Jane
Seven little sisters series (3)
Ten creeks run
Brent of Bin Bin
Bert Poole series (2)
Ten-day queen
Prole, Lozania
Tudor trilogy (2)
Ten days, Mister Cain?
Freeborn, Brian
Mister Cain series (2)
Ten days to oblivion
Cooney, Michael
Queen's investigator series (2)
Ten days' wonder
Queen, Ellery
Ellery Queen series (25)
Ten degrees backward
Fowler, Ellen Thornycroft
Isabel Carnaby trilogy (3)
Ten doors of doom
Fickling, David
Fantasy quest book series (4)
Ten fast horses
Grover, Marshall
Nevada Jim series (68)
Ten fathoms deep
Catherall, Arthur
Bulldog tugboat series (1)
Ten-gallon tease
Sherman, Jory
Gunn series (20)
Ten grand
Gilman, George G
Edge series (2)
Ten holy terrors
Beeding, Francis
Colonel Alastair Granby series (13)
Ten hours
Keeler, Harry Stephen
Vagabond nights series (2)
Ten jewels
Wynnton, Patrick
Black turret series (2)
Ten kids, no pets
Martin, Ann Matthews
Kids series (1)
Ten little Brownie girls
Hann, Dorothy Owen
Brownie series (4)
Ten little wizards
Kurland, Michael
Lord Darcy series (4)
Ten minute tales
Blyton, Enid
Minute tales series (2)
Ten must die
Hill, Morgan
Dan Colt series (4)
Ten O'Clock Club
York, Carol Beach
Miss Know It All series (5)
Ten percent of trouble
Heath, Charles
A-Team series (5)
Ten Pines killer
Roberts, J R
Gunsmith series (40)
Ten plus one
McBain, Ed
Eighty Seventh Precinct series (17)
Ten ponies and Jackie
Berrisford, Judith Mary
Jackie and Babs series (2)
Ten seconds to play!
Bee, Clair
Chip Hilton series (12)
Ten seconds to zero
Stanton, Ken
Aquanauts series (2)
Ten sixty six and all that
Sellar, Walter Carruthers
All that series (1)
Ten star claws
Punshon, Ernest Robertson
Bobby Owen series (15)
Ten steps to the gallows
Wainwright, John
Northern Police series (2)
Ten tales of Shellover
Ainsworth, Ruth
Shellover series (1)
Ten teacups
Dickson, Carter
Sir Henry Merrivale series (7)
Ten things I know about elephants
Wax, Wendy
Ten things I know series (3)
Ten things I know about kangaroos
Wax, Wendy
Ten things I know series (1)
Ten things I know about penguins
Wax, Wendy
Ten things I know series (2)
Ten things I know about whales
Wax, Wendy
Ten things I know series (4)
Ten thirteen
Edwards, Charman
Percy Aloysius Huff series (3)
Ten-thirty sharp
Gibbs, Henry
Theatre series (2)
Ten thousand dollars, American
Gilman, George G
Edge series (2)
Ten thousand heroes
Barbary, James
Adventure in history series (5)
Ten thousand minutes at Sugar Creek
Hutchens, Paul
Sugar Creek Gang series (20)
Ten thousand shall die
Bourne, Peter
Stewart family series (2)
Ten times dynamite
Carter, Nick
Nick Carter series (138)
Ten to four Sweathogs
Johnston, William
Welcome back, Kotter series (4)
Ten tombstones
Gilman, George G
Edge series (18)
Ten tombstones to Texas
Gilman, George G
Edge series (18)
Ten ton snakes
Robeson, Kenneth
Doc Savage series (114)
Ten trails to Tyburn
Graeme, Bruce
Theodore I Terhune series (5)
Ten were missing
Allingham, Margery
Albert Campion series (18)
Ten words of poison
Perowne, Barry
Raffles series (12)
Ten years after
Bobin, John William
Sexton Blake series (25)
Ten years ago
Mottram, Ralph Hale
Spanish Farm series (4)
Ten years beyond Baker Street
Van Ash, Cay
Fu-Manchu series (16)
Sherlock Holmes sequels series (73)
Ten years later
Dumas, Alexandre
Three Musketeers series (3)
Ten years under the earth
Casteret, Norbert
Under the earth series (1)
Tenant for death
Hare, Cyril
Inspector Mallett series (1)
Tenant for the tomb
Gilbert, Anthony
Arthur Crook series (48)
Tenant of Number Thirteen
Jackson, Lewis
Sexton Blake series (1160)
Tender and violent Elizabeth
Troyat, Henri
Seed and the fruit series (4)
Tender death
Meyers, Annette
Leslie Wetzon series (2)
Tender ecstasy
Taylor, Janelle
Sioux series (5)
Tender expressions
Montgomery, Wendy
Star trek fan series (45)
Tender is the knife
Shepherd, Joan
Inspector Jolivet series (2)
Tender killer
Hough, Stanley Bennett
Inspector Brentford series (1)
Tender leaves of hope
Brindley, Louise
Tanquillan series (2)
Tender loving care
Moura, Joni
Air Force series (1)
Tender promises
Pascal, Francine
Promise trilogy (1)
Tender rebel
Lindsey, Johanna
Anthony Mallory series (2)
Tender stranger
Palmer, Diana
Mercenary series (2)
Tenderfoot
Goscinny, Rene
Lucky Luke series (3)
Thompson, David
Nathaniel King series (14)
Tenderfoot Kid
Field, Peter
Powder Valley series (9)
Tenderfoot veteran
Mack Bride, Johnny
Frank Wady series (1)
Tenko
Masters, Anthony
Tenko series (1)
Tenko reunion
Valery, Anne
Tenko series (3)
Tennant Creek recollections
Priest, Charles Ashley Vincent
Northern Territory recollections series (6)
Tennessee!
Ross, Dana Fuller
Wagons West series (17)
Tennessee bride
Bittner, F Rosanne
Brides series (3)
Caleb Sax series (4)
Tennessee Shad
Johnson, Owen McMahon
Lawrenceville series (3)
Tennessee smash
Pendleton, Don
Mack Bolan series (32)
Tennessee terror
Ham, Bob
Overload series (4)
Tennis
Gutman, Bill
Go for it series (1)
Paulsen, Gary
Sports on the light side series (6)
Tennis for boys and girls
Gutman, Bill
Start right and play well series (7)
Tennis murders
Welch, Timothy L
Dion Quince series (1)
Tennis shoes
Streatfeild, Noel
Shoes series (2)
Tennis term at Trebizon
Digby, Anne
Trebizon series (6)
Tennis trap
Kaye, Marilyn
Camp Sunnyside Friends series (12)
Tenopia Island
Packard, Edward
Escape from Tenopia series (1)
Tension
Janson, Hank
Hank Janson series (46)
Wainwright, John
Northern Police series (41)
Tension at Saint Peter's
Andrews, Jane
Saint Peter's Hospital series (4)
Tent for the sun
Ray, Mary
Early Christian series (1)
Tent of God
Ward, Anthony
George trilogy (1)
Tent on top
Styles, Showell
Ann and John Davies series (2)
Tentacles
Lyon, Dana
Hilda Trenton series (1)
Tenterhooks
Leverson, Ada
Edith Ottley trilogy (2)
Tenth class
Ripley, Karen
Prisoner of dreams series (2)
Tenth commandment
Sanders, Lawrence
Ten commandments series (4)
Tenth leper
Didelot, Francis
Commissaire Orestes Bignon series (2)
Tenth life
Lockridge, Richard
Inspector Merton Heimrich series (25)
Tenth planet
Sterling, Brett
Captain Future series (10)
Tenth victim
Sheckley, Robert
Victim trilogy (1)
Tentmaker
Berstl, Julius
Saint Paul series (1)
Tents of Israel
Stern, Gladys Bronwyn
Rakonitz family series (1)
Tents of wickedness
De Vries, Peter
Chick Swallow series (2)
Teot's war
Gladney, Heather
Song of Naga Teot series (1)
Tepee days
Hunkins, Ralph Valentine
Tales of the prairies series (1)

Terence Duke
Meyerstein, Edward Henry William
Terence Duke series (2)
Terence in love
Meyerstein, Edward Henry William
Terence Duke series (2)
Terence O'Rourke, gentleman adventurer
Vance, Louis Joseph
Terence O'Rourke series (1)
Teresa joins the Red Cross
Martin, Nancy
Red Cross series (1)
Term of terror
Flower, Pat
Inspector Swinton series (6)
Terminal
Forbes, Colin
Tweed, Grey and Newman series (2)
Terminal connection
Moore, Robin
Connection series (6)
Terminal island
Frost, Jason
Warlord series (5)
Terminal road
Drumm, D B
Traveler series (8)
Terminal shock
Dixon, Franklin W
Hardy boys series (102)
Terminal transmission
Murphy, Warren Burton
Destroyer series (93)
Terminal velocity
Pendleton, Don
SuperBolan series (2)
Terminate
Trevor, Dan
Night whistlers series (3)
Night whistlers trilogy (3)
Terminator
Frakes, Randall
Terminator series (1)
Hutson, Shaun
Terminator series (1)
Terminator two
Frakes, Randall
Terminator series (2)
Terminator two, Judgment day
Cameron, James
Terminator series (2)
Terminators
Hamilton, Donald
Matt Helm series (16)
Mather, Berkely
Idwal Rees series (2)
Terminus
Lydecker, John
Doctor Who series (79)
Terms of endearment
McMurtry, Larry
Aurora Greenway series (1)
Urban trilogy (3)
Terms of vengeance
Carter, Nick
Nick Carter series (229)
Tern day's leave
Graydon, William Murray
Sexton Blake series (49)
Teror at Forbidden Falls
Roddy, Lee
Ladd family series (7)
Terra data
Tubb, Edwin Charles
Dumarest series (22)
Terrace suicide mystery
Gribble, Leonard Reginald
Superintendent Anthony Slade series (1)
Terraces of night
Lawrence, Margery
Club of the Round Table series (2)
Terraplane
Womack, Jack
Terraplane trilogy (2)
Terrarium
Head, Lee
Lexey Jane Pelazoni series (1)
Terrible hand
Hay, Lindsay Fitzgerald
Archibald Beldrum and Nigel Blair series (2)
Terrible, horrible Edie
Spykman, Elizabeth Choate
Cares family series (3)
Terrible kidnapping of Cyril Bonhamy
Gathorne-Hardy, Jonathan
Cyril Bonhamy series (1)
Terrible Mister Twitmeyer!
Moore, Lilian
Mister Twitmeyer series (1)
Terrible night
Cheyney, Peter
Everard Peter Quayle series (3)
Secret service series (5)
Shaun O'Mara series (2)
Terrible ones
Carter, Nick
Nick Carter series (13)
Terrible pictures
Healey, Ben
Paul Hedley series (3)
Terrible stork
Robeson, Kenneth
Doc Savage series (154)
Terrible swift sword
Catton, Bruce
Centennial history of the Civil War series (2)
Forstchen, William R
Lost regiment series (3)
Terrible temptation
Arundel, Honor
Janet Meredith series (1)
Terrible ten
Knight, Mallory T
Man from T.O.M.C.A.T. series (3)
Terrible thing
Lloyd, David
Dinosaur days series (3)
Terrible thing has happened to Miss Dupont
Hobson, Polly
Inspector Basil series (2)
Terrible thirteen
Carter, Nicholas
Nicholas Carter series (188)
Terrible threat
Carter, Nicholas
Nicholas Carter series (165)
Terrible tickler
Mooser, Stephen
All-Star Meatballs series (2)
Terrible troll bird
D'Aulaire, Ingri
Ola series (2)
Terrible truth
Roos, Stephen
New Eden series (2)
Terrible Tuesday
Pendleton, Don
Mack Bolan series (34)
Terridae
Tubb, Edwin Charles
Dumarest series (25)
Terror
Ahern, Jerry
Survivalist series (14)
Creasey, John
Doctor Palfrey series (21)
Gras, Felix
French Revolution trilogy (2)
Terror and the lonely widow
Robeson, Kenneth
Doc Savage series (167)
Terror at Boulder Dam
Robinson, Vance
Justice trilogy (2)
Terror at Dark Harbor
Ross, Clarissa
Dark Harbor series (5)
Terror at Morning Cliff
Garis, Lilian C
Melody Lane series (5)
Terror at play
McEvoy, Seth
Not quite human series (5)
Terror at Tree Tops
Parsons, Anthony
Sexton Blake series (1221)
Terror by day
Ashe, Gordon
Patrick Dawlish series (4)
Terror by night
Crosby, Lee
Eric Hazard series (1)
Terror by satellite
Walters, Hugh
Chris Godfrey series (7)
Terror by twilight
Knight, Kathleen Moore
Margot Blair series (3)
Terror code
Carter, Nick
Nick Carter series (224)
Terror comes creeping
Brown, Carter
Danny Boyd series (3)
Lieutenant Al Wheeler series (16)
Terror contract
Kilgore, Axel
They call me the Mercenary series (9)
Terror flight
Jackson, Basil
Air detective series (3)
Southall, Ivan
War in the air series (2)
Terror for sale
Grover, Marshall
Larry and Stretch series (401)
Streib, Dan
Steve Crown series (5)
Terror for the Toff
Creasey, John
Toff series (39)
Terror-go-round
Moffatt, James
Johnny Canuck series (2)
Terror in Australia
Gilligan, Shannon
Choose your own adventure series (81)
Terror in D.C.
Ramm, Carl
James Hawker series (9)
Terror in Guyana
Wilson, Gar
Phoenix Force series (47)
Terror in Rio
Caillou, Alan
Colonel Matthew Tobin series (2)
Terror in Taos
Derrick, Lionel
Penetrator series (11)
Terror in the ashes
Johnstone, William Wallace
Ashes series (15)
Terror in the dark
Wilson, Gar
Phoenix Force series (31)
Terror in the fourth dimension
Sharp, Allen
Storytrails series (4)
Terror in the Navy
Robeson, Kenneth
Doc Savage series (33)
Terror in the night
Blayne, Sebastian
Sebastian Blayne series (2)
Terror in the sky
Roddy, Lee
American adventure series (6)
Terror in the starboard seat
McIntosh, Dave
Canadian life series (2)
Terror in the sun
Avallone, Michael
Hawaii Five-O series (2)
Terror in Turin
White, Steve
S-Com series (1)
Terror in Winnipeg
Wilson, Eric
Canadian trilogy (3)
Terror is my trade
Marlowe, Stephen
Chester Drum series (6)
Terror Island
Armour, R Coutts
Sexton Blake series (159)
Grant, Maxwell
Shadow series (108)
Koltz, Tony
Choose your own adventure series (59)
Terror Keep
Wallace, Edgar
Mister J G Reeder series (3)
Terror Loch
McNeilly, Wilfred
Sexton Blake series (1547)
Terror merchant
Spencer, Rick
Eric Ivorsen series (4)
Terror merchants
Streib, Dan
Michael Hawk series (11)
Terror of Frankenstein
Glut, Donald Frank
Frankenstein sequels series (7)
Terror of Gold-Digger Creek
Teed, George Hamilton
Sexton Blake series (549)
Terror of Lonely Tor
Stuart, Donald
Sexton Blake series (677)
Terror of Tangier
Teed, George Hamilton
Sexton Blake series (503)
Terror of the Pacific
Brandon, John Gordon
Sexton Blake series (1027)
Terror of the tenaments
Skene, Anthony
Sexton Blake series (939)
Terror of the Vervoids
Baker, Pip
Doctor Who series (125)
Trial of the Time Lord series (1)
Terror of the Zygons
Dicks, Terrance
Doctor Who series (18)
Terror of Thunder Creek
Hope, Stanton
Sexton Blake series (886)
Terror of tongues!
Vickers, Roy
Inspector J Rason series (13)
Terror of Tregarwith
Sylvester, John
Sexton Blake series (1097)
Terror on Broadway
Alexander, David
Bart Hardin series (1)
Terror on Compass Lake
Davis, Tech
Aubrey Nash series (1)
Terror on Halfaday Creek
Hendryx, James Beardsley
Black John series (18)
Terror on Kabran
Brightfield, Richard
Escape from Tenopia series (3)
Terror on the docks
Franklin, Max
Starsky and Hutch series (5)
Terror on the moons of Jupiter
Appleton, Victor II
Tom Swift Junior series 2 (2)
Terror on track
Dixon, Franklin W
Hardy boys case files series (57)
Terror over Kansas
Charlier, Jean Michel
Young Blueberry series (5)
Terror ship
Edwards, Charman
Percy Aloysius Huff series (1)
Terror squad
Murphy, Warren Burton
Destroyer series (10)
Terror star
Moore, Patrick
Scott Saunders series (5)
Terror strike
Robbins, David
Blade series (7)
Terror syndicate
Seaman, Donald
Sydenham series (2)
Terror takes seven
Robeson, Kenneth
Doc Savage series (163)
Terror times two
Carter, Nick
Nick Carter series (216)
Terror tower
Verner, Gerald
Trevor Lowe series (5)
Terror town
Gilman, George G
Edge series (59)
Terror trail
Thorne, Ramsay
Captain Gringo series (15)
Terror trail to Tortosa
Grover, Marshall
Larry and Stretch series (306)
Terror trap
Creasey, John
Department Z series (7)
Terror truckers
Jason, Stuart
Butcher series (25)
Terror under the earth
Brightfield, Richard
Your amazing adventures series (3)
Terror under the tent
Anderson, Mary
Mostly ghosts series (3)
Terror Valley
Edson, John Thomas
Floating Outfit series (60)
Terror wears no shoes
Robeson, Kenneth
Doc Savage series (179)
Terrorist summit
Pendleton, Don
Mack Bolan series (44)
Terrorist torment
Derrick, Lionel
Penetrator series (46)
Terrorist trap
Gilligan, Shannon
Choose your own adventure series (119)
Terrorists
Demille, Nelson
Joe Ryker series (3)
Sjowall, Maj
Inspector Martin Beck series (10)
Terrorizers
Hamilton, Donald
Matt Helm series (18)
Terror's long memory
Grover, Marshall
Larry and Stretch series (354)
Terrors of rock and roll
Smith, Susan
Samantha Slade series (4)
Terrorsaur!
Dicks, Terrance
Star quest series (3)
Terry in Australia
Danielsson, Bengt
Terry series (2)
Terry in the South Seas
Danielsson, Bengt
Terry series (1)
Terry Nation's Avon, a terrible aspect
Darrow, Paul
Blake's Seven series (5)
Terry Nation's Blake's Seven
Hoyle, Trevor
Blake's Seven series (1)
Terry's Kon-Tiki adventure
Danielsson, Bengt
Terry series (3)
Tess
Burton, Katherine
Calloway Corners series (3)
Tess of Ithaca
White, Grace Miller
Storm country series (1)
Tess of the D'Urbevilles
Hardy, Thomas
Novels of character and environment series (1)
Tess of the Storm Country
White, Grace Miller
Storm country series (1)
Tessa and some ponies
Ritson, Kitty
Tessa series (1)
Tessa and the Rannoch Dude Ranch
Ritson, Kitty
Tessa series (4)
Tessa in South Africa
Ritson, Kitty
Tessa series (2)
Tessa snaps snakes
Lester, Alison
Australian children series (3)
Tessa to the rescue
Ritson, Kitty
Tessa series (3)
Tessie
Jackson, Jesse
Tessie series (1)
Tessie growing up
Warner, Priscilla Mary
Biddy and Tessie series (2)
Tessie keeps her secret
Jackson, Jesse
Tessie series (2)
Tessie's caravan
Warner, Priscilla Mary
Biddy and Tessie series (2)
Test
Johnson, Stacie
Eighteen Pine Street series (4)
Test match mystery
Pink, Hal
Inspector Docker series (5)
Test of courage
Carter, Nicholas
Nicholas Carter series (573)
Test of the ninja
Smith, Curtis
Advanced dungeons and dragons adventure gamebook series (2)
Test of the twins
Weis, Margaret
DragonLance legends trilogy (3)
Test paper thief
Christian, Mary Blount
Goosehill Gang series (2)
Test time at Tillingfold
Parker, John
Village cricket series (2)
Test to destruction
Williamson, Henry
Chronicles of ancient sunlight series (8)
Testament of Casper Schultz
Fallon, Martin
Paul Chavasse series (1)

Testament of death
Lucas, Norman
Superintendent Bill Rowlands series (3)

Testament of evil
Jones, Bradshaw
Claude Ravel series (7)

Testament of experience
Brittain, Vera
Testament series (3)

Testament of friendship
Brittain, Vera
Testament series (2)

Testament of youth
Brittain, Vera
Testament series (1)

Testimony
Palmer, Frank
Jim Jackson series (1)

Testing
Bolton, Melvin
Lawson of the Special Branch series (2)

Testing of Janice Day
Long, Helen Beecher
Do something series (2)

Testing of Tertius
Newman, Robert
Tertius trilogy (2)

Testing the current
McPherson, William
Sargasso Sea series (1)

Testing year
Clewes, Dorothy
Carrie and Maxwell series (2)

Testkill
Dexter, Ted
Jack Stenton series (1)

Tet
Helm, Eric
Ground Zero series (11)

Tethered goat
Healy, Jeremiah
John Francis Cuddy series (2)

Tether's end
Allingham, Margery
Albert Campion series (18)

Teton gamble
Bishop, Pike
Cord Diamondback series (8)

Teverton Hall
Gillespie, Jane
Teverton Hall series (2)

Tevye's daughters
Aleichem, Sholom
Tevye the milkman series (2)

Tex
Mulford, Clarence Edward
Hopalong Cassidy series (9)

Tex and bad Hank
Garland, Sarah
Tex series (3)

Tex and Gloria
Garland, Sarah
Tex series (2)

Tex of Bar-20
Mulford, Clarence Edward
Hopalong Cassidy series (9)

Tex the cowboy
Garland, Sarah
Tex series (1)

Texan
Arthur, Burt
Johnny Canavan series (1)
Edson, John Thomas
Floating Outfit series (46)

Texan from Montana
Cody, Al
Montana series (2)

Texan in my sights
Grover, Marshall
Larry and Stretch series (51)

Texan killer
Buckman, Sam
Storm Jackson series (3)

Texan scouts
Altsheler, Joseph Alexander
Texas trilogy (2)

Texan star
Altsheler, Joseph Alexander
Texas trilogy (1)

Texan triumph
Altsheler, Joseph Alexander
Texas trilogy (3)

Texans
Bennett, Dwight
Eden Grove series (2)
Toombs, Jane
Making of America series (9)

Texans are trouble
Grover, Marshall
Larry and Stretch series (3)

Texans came shooting
Grover, Marshall
Larry and Stretch series (89)

Texans die hard
Grover, Marshall
Larry and Stretch series (20)

Texans hit hard
Grover, Marshall
Larry and Stretch series (26)

Texan's honor
Harte, Bryce
Slate Creed series (6)

Texans never quit
Grover, Marshall
Larry and Stretch series (24)

Texans ride tall
Grover, Marshall
Larry and Stretch series (30)

Texans walk proud
Grover, Marshall
Larry and Stretch series (38)

Texar the southerner
Verne, Jules
North against South series (2)

Texas!
Ross, Dana Fuller
Wagons West series (5)

Texas Anthem
Reno, James
Texas Anthem series (1)

Texas assassin
Edson, John Thomas
Floating Outfit series (38)

Texas badman
Scott, Bradford
Walt Slade series (22)

Texas Bank Robbing Company
Tippette, Giles
Wilson Young series (8)

Texas blood
Scott, Bradford
Walt Slade series (108)

Texas Blue Bonnet
Jacobs, Caroline Emilia
Blue Bonnet series (1)

Texas born
Reno, James
Texas Anthem series (2)

Texas born, Chicago bound
Grover, Marshall
Larry and Stretch series (298)

Texas bounty
Jeffers, Harry Paul
Morgan trilogy (3)

Texas Brazos
Wisler, Gary Clifton
Texas Brazos series (1)

Texas bride
Bittner, F Rosanne
Brides series (2)

Texas brigade
Hogan, Ray
Shawn Starbuck series (15)

Texas chase!
Brown, Sandra
Texas trilogy (3)

Texas comebacker
McCord, John S
Baynes clan trilogy (2)

Texas crackdown
Roberts, J R
Gunsmith series (63)

Texas death
Scott, Bradford
Walt Slade series (87)

Texas devil
Scott, Bradford
Walt Slade series (45)

Texas drifters
Grover, Marshall
Larry and Stretch series (14)

Texas empire
McCurtin, Peter
Sundance series (43)

Texas feud
Edwards, Hank
Judge Clay Torn series (4)

Texas fury
Cole, Jackson
Jim Hatfield series (10)
Michaels, Fern
Texas series (3)

Texas gold
Hohl, Joan
Sharp family trilogy (1)
Vanzant family trilogy (3)
Reese, John
Jefferson Hewitt series (4)

Texas gun-ghost
Grover, Marshall
Larry and Stretch series (42)

Texas hawk
Scott, Bradford
Walt Slade series (14)

Texas heat
Michaels, Fern
Texas series (2)

Texas hell country
Sharpe, Jon
Trailsman series (86)

Texas killing
James, William M
Apache series (16)

Texas lucky!
Brown, Sandra
Texas trilogy (1)

Texas manhunt
Cole, Jackson
Jim Hatfield series (23)
Dawson, Clay
Long Rider series (18)

Texas massacre
McLaglen, John J
Herne the Hunter series (23)

Texas Mustangers
McCarthy, Gary
Ballou family series (3)

Texas nighthawks
Calhoun, Wes
Chulo trilogy (3)

Texas on the rocks
Da Cruz, Daniel
Forte family trilogy (2)

Texas rampage
Grover, Marshall
Larry and Stretch series (62)

Texas ranch boy
Mauzey, Merritt
Farm boy series (2)

Texas Rangers
Evans, Tabor
Longarm series (139)
Willoughby, Lee Davis
Making of America series (48)

Texas ransom
Roberts, J R
Gunsmith series (83)

Texas rich
Michaels, Fern
Texas series (1)

Texas rider
Scott, Bradford
Walt Slade series (46)

Texas roundup
Chambers, Catherine E
Adventures in frontier America series (9)

Texas run
Proctor, George Wyatt
V series (11)

Texas sage!
Brown, Sandra
Texas trilogy (2)

Texas showdown
Cole, Jackson
Jim Hatfield series (59)
Logan, Jake
John Slocum series (68)
Stivers, Dick
Able Team series (3)

Texas storm
Pendleton, Don
Mack Bolan series (18)

Texas stranger
Dower, Penn
Marshal Bret Malone series (3)

Texas sunrise
Michaels, Fern
Texas series (4)

Texas tart
Fletcher, Dirk
Spur McCoy series (6)

Texas tease
Fletcher, Dirk
Spur McCoy series (21)
Gentry, Buck
Eli Holten series (15)

Texas tenderfoot
Murray, Michael
Timber Trail riders series (2)

Texas terror
Bexar, Phil
Billy Dupree series (8)
Scott, Bradford
Walt Slade series (13)

Texas tomboy
Lenski, Lois
Regional series (7)

Texas tornado
Cole, Jackson
Jim Hatfield series (20)

Texas trail drive
Logan, Jake
John Slocum series (137)

Texas trail to Calamity
Quackenbush, Robert Mead
Miss Mallard series (11)

Texas train
Sharpe, Jon
Trailsman series (93)

Texas tramp
Fletcher, Dirk
Spur McCoy series (40)

Texas treasure
Thompson, Victoria
Kid Collins series (1)

Texas trigger
Cole, Jackson
Jim Hatfield series (37)

Texas triggers
Sharpe, Jon
Trailsman series (136)

Texas trilogy
Brown, Sandra
Texas trilogy (3)
Michaels, Fern
Texas series (3)

Texas trio
Edson, John Thomas
Calamity Jane series (1)

Texas triumph
Thompson, Victoria
Kid Collins series (2)

Texas triumphant
Da Cruz, Daniel
Forte family trilogy (3)

Texas tumble
Hunter, E J
Headhunter series (2)

Texas two-step
Masters, Zeke
Faro Blake series (26)

Texas vengeance
Scott, Bradford
Walt Slade series (23)

Texas wildflower
Lee, Tammie
Leather and lace series (8)

Texas wildflower, Laurian Kane
Brown, Kitt
Frontier women series (3)

Texas wolves
Borg, Jack
Hogleg Bailey series (19)

Texas woman
Johnston, Joan
Sisters of the Lone Star trilogy (3)

Texasville
McMurtry, Larry
Thalia series (2)

Texians
Wyatt, Zach
Texians series (1)

Thaery
Vance, Jack
Gaean series (4)

Thanatos syndrome
Percy, Walker
Doctor Tom More series (2)

Thane Brandon
Bancroft, Francis
South African trilogy (2)

Thank you, Amelia Bedelia
Parish, Peggy
Amelia Bedelia series (2)

Thank you, Doctor Martin Luther King, junior!
Tate, Eleanora Elaine
Gumbo Grove series (2)

Thank you for the tadpole
Thomson, Pat
Share-a-story series (5)

Thank you, Jeeves
Wodehouse, Pelham Grenville
Jeeves and Bertie Wooster series (5)

Thank you, Mister Conquest
Gray, Berkeley
Norman Conquest series (10)

Thank you, Mister Moto
Marquand, John Phillips
Mister Moto series (2)

Thank you, Mister Pendlebury
Webb, Anthony
Mister Pendlebury series (3)

Thank you, Nelson
Spain, Nancy
Thank you series (1)

Thank you, Nicky!
Ziefert, Harriet
Nicky series (9)

Thank you please and I love you book
Smaridge, Nora
Raggedy Ann series (49)

Thanks to Bunter
Richards, Frank
Billy Bunter series (36)

Thanks to Claudius
Leeming, John Fishwick
Claudius the bee series (2)

Thanks to Jennings
Buckeridge, Anthony
Jennings series (8)

Thanks to Miss Winter
Mackenzie, Kathleen
Miss Winter series (1)

Thanks to Mister Jones
Matthewman, Phyllis
Mister Jones series (1)

Thanks to Peculiar
Wallace, Ivy Lilian
Warrenders series (2)

Thanks to the Saint
Charteris, Leslie
Saint series (32)

Thanksgiving Day parade
Markham, Marion M
Dixon twins series (3)

Thanksgiving magic
Baker, James Webb
Magic series (8)

Thanksgiving mystery
Nixon, Joan Lowery
First read-alone mystery series (5)

Thanksgiving treasure
Rock, Gail
Addie series (2)

Thargon menace
Price, Roger
Tomorrow people series (5)

Tharrus three
Maclean, Catherine Macdonald
Tharrus trilogy (2)

That affair at Elizabeth
Stevenson, Burton Egbert
Jim Godfrey series (3)

That affair at the Cedars
Thayer, Lee
Peter Clancy series (3)

That affair next door
Green, Anna Katharine
Ebenezer Gryce series (7)

That Barbara Moore
Adams, Agnes
Shepton children trilogy (2)

That boarding school girl
Bruce, Dorita Fairlie
Nancy series (2)

That brain again
Janson, Hank
Hank Janson series (191)

That Callahan blood!
Ames, Francis Herbert
Callahan series (1)

That Callahan spunk!
Ames, Francis Herbert
Callahan series (1)

That champion chimp
Armstrong, Jennifer
Pets, Inc. series (4)

That charming crook
King, Frank
Dormouse series (20)

That cheating sister
Oaks, Tina
Stepsisters series (5)

That curly headed rogue
Cheesman, Lilian
Peter trilogy (3)

That damn single shot
Miller, Jim
Long guns series (6)

That darn Cat
Gordons
Undercover Cat series (1)

That day alone
Van Paassen, Pierre
Days series (2)

That dreadful day
Stevenson, James
Grandpa series (5)

That droll lady
Spencer, Thomas Edward
Bridget McSweeney series (3)

That early spring
Beckman, Gunnel
Mia series (2)

That Emil
Lindgren, Astrid
Emil series (4)

That fatal feeling
Kennedy, Elliot
Griff Dexter series (3)

That fatal night
Pascal, Francine
Sweet Valley High series (60)

That feeds on men
Wilson, Ivor
Gregory Flamm series (2)

That fellow Macarthur
Jepson, Selwyn
Ian Macarthur series (2)

That fortune
Warner, Charles Dudley
Finance trilogy (3)

That game from outer space
Manes, Stephen
Oscar Noodleman trilogy (1)

That girl from Istanbul
Braun, Maurice-Gilles
Al Glenne series (4)

That great big trenchcoat in the sky
Lovell, Marc
Appleton Porter series (12)

That hideous strength
Lewis, Clive Staples
Space trilogy (3)

That imp Miranda
Gervaise, Mary
Miranda series (1)

That Julia Redfern
Cameron, Eleanor
Julia Redfern series (2)

That man Gull
Stuart, Anthony
Vladimir Gull series (1)

That man on Beta
Steele, Addison E
Buck Rogers teleplay series (2)

That man returns
Fairlie, Gerard
Victor Caryll series (4)

That mushy stuff
Delton, Judy
Pee wee scout series (8)

That near and distant place
Wright, Patrick
Near and distant series (2)

That ne'er shall meet again
Fleming, Gordon Howard
Pre-Raphaelite Brotherhood series (2)

That night it rained
Waugh, Hillary
Chief Fred Fellows series (3)

That old Black magic
Black, Arthur
Basic Black series (3)

That reminds me
Graham, Winifred
That reminds me trilogy (1)

That strange Sylvester affair
Thayer, Lee
Peter Clancy series (26)

That terrible Halloween night
Stevenson, James
Grandpa series (2)

That village on the Don
Diack, Hunter
Village series (2)

That was no lady
Campbell, Keith
Mike Brett series (5)

That was yesterday
Home, Michael
Breckland series (11)
Jameson, Storm
Hervey Russell series (2)

That which hath wings
Dehan, Richard
Dop Doctor series (2)

That wild lie
Jacob, Naomi
Gollantz series (2)

That wilder image
Flexner, James Thomas
History of American painting series (3)

That yew trees shade
Hare, Cyril
Francis Pettigrew series (4)

Thatched roof
Nichols, Beverley
Allways trilogy (2)

That's all I need
Spade, Danny
Danny Spade series (34)

That's me all over, Mable
Streeter, Edward
Mable series (2)

That's me in the middle
Jack, Donald
Journals of Bartholomew Bandy series (2)

That's my baby!
Ahlberg, Janet
Daisychain series (3)

That's my girl
Lambert, Janet
Parri Macdonald series (2)

That's piracy my pet
Brown, Carter
Andy Kane series (2)

That's so funny, I forgot to laugh
Mooser, Stephen
Creepy Creature Club series (6)

That's the spirit
Heberden, Mary Violet
Desmond Shannon series (14)

That's the spirit, Claude
Nixon, Joan Lowery
Claude series (5)

That's where the cat's at, baby
Johnson, B B
Superspade series (3)

Thaw
Ehrenburg, Ilya
Dmitry Korotoyev series (1)

Thaxford's wife
Lambert, Mortan
Relentless marriage series (2)

Thea at sixteen
Pfeffer, Susan Beth
Sebastian sisters quintet (2)

Theater shoes
Streatfeild, Noel
Shoes series (4)

Theatre of war
Richards, Justin
Timewyrm series (10)

Theatre Royal and Punch and Judy
Beaman, Sydney George Hulme
Toytown series (31)

Theatre tapestry
Gibbs, Henry
Theatre series (1)

Theatrical Mister Holmes
Harrison, Michael
Life of Sherlock Holmes series (4)

Theban mysteries
Cross, Amanda
Professor Kate Fansler series (4)

Theft of Magna Carta
Creasey, John
Inspector Roger West series (41)

Theft of the golden cat
Green, Roger Lancelyn
Spearlake children series (3)

Theft of the iron dogs
Lorac, E C R
Inspector Macdonald series (28)

Thefts of Nick Velvet
Hoch, Edward Dentinger
Nick Velvet series (2)

Their chosen people
Nicholson, Celia Anna
Levine family series (1)

Their evil ways
Wainwright, John
Northern Police series (54)

Their father's god
Rolvaag, Ole Edvart
Per Hansa trilogy (3)

Their first ten years
Lochhead, Marion Cleland
Victorian life series (1)

Their great adventure
Graydon, William Murray
Sexton Blake series (16)

Their hearts
Hunt, Violet
Their lives and hearts series (2)

Their island home
Verne, Jules
Swiss family Robinson series (4)

Their kind of town
Whittingham, Richard
Joe Morrison series (2)

Their lawful occasions
Edwards, Herbert Wilson
Under four flags series (2)

Their lives
Hunt, Violet
Their lives and hearts series (1)

Their man in the White House
Ardies, Tom
Charlie Sparrow series (1)

Their own country
Hobart, Alice Tisdale
China series (4)

Their silver wedding journey
Howells, William Dean
Mister and Mrs March series (6)

Their wedding journey
Howells, William Dean
Mister and Mrs March series (1)

Theirs was the kingdom
Delderfield, Ronald Frederick
Adam Swann series (2)

Them
Anonymous
Pronoun series (6)
Oates, Joyce Carol
Jules and Maureen Wendall trilogy (2)

Theme is murder
Holt, Gavin
Inspector Joel Saber series (1)

Themes and episodes
Stravinsky, Igor
Conversations series (5)

Then came Caroline
Richards, Lela Horn
Caroline trilogy (1)

Then came Mulvane
Heuman, William
Grady Mulvane series (3)

Then came the police
Wills, Cecil Melville
Geoffrey Boscobell series (4)

Then came violence
Ball, John
Virgil Tibbs series (6)

Then hang all the liars
Storey, Alice
Samantha Adams series (2)

Then there were five
Enright, Elizabeth
Melendy family series (3)

Then there were three
Homes, Geoffrey
Humphrey Campbell series (1)
Robin Bishop series (5)

Thendara House
Bradley, Marion Zimmer
Darkover series (8)

Theodora and the Chalet School
Brent-Dyer, Elinor Mary
Chalet School series (42)

Theodore
Ingraham, Joseph Holt
Lafitte series (2)

Theory and practice of design
Jackson, Frank George
Decorative design series (2)

Theory and practice of gamesmanship
Potter, Stephen
Lifemanship Correspondence College series (1)

Therapy in dynamite
Miller, Victor Brooke
Kojak series (5)

There and back
Macdonald, George
Thomas Wingfold trilogy (3)

There and back again
Ballinger, W A
Voyageurs series (2)
Jones, Harold
Bunby series (1)

There are dead men in Manhattan
Roeburt, John
Jigger Moran series (2)

There are no spies
Granger, Bill
November Man series (8)

There are thirteen
Beeding, Francis
Colonel Alastair Granby series (17)

There came both mist and snow
Innes, Michael
Sir John Appleby series (5)

There for the picking
Cockett, Mary
Jasper Club series (2)

There goes death
Ashe, Gordon
Patrick Dawlish series (8)

There goes the bride
Maner, William
Parker Rowe series (2)

There hangs the knife
Muller, Marcia
Joanna Stark series (2)

There has been a murder
Holt, Henry
Inspector Silver series (11)

There is a season
Bennett, Barbara
Calladine family series (1)
Colver, Alice Ross
Measure of the years series (2)

There is a tide
Christie, Agatha
Hercule Poirot series (26)

There is another heaven
Nathan, Robert
Barly fields series (5)

There is no justice
Dominic, R B
Congressman Ben Safford series (3)

There is no return
Blackmon, Anita
Adelaide Adams series (2)

There is something about a dame
Avallone, Michael
Ed Noon series (12)

There lies your love
Melville, Jennie
Sergeant Charmian Daniels series (4)

There lived a lady
Morrison, Emmeline
Lovice Clive series (2)

There must be victims
Cumberland, Marten
Saturnin Dax series (29)

There sits death
McGuire, Paul
Superintendent Fillinger series (5)

There was a crooked man
Roos, Kelley
Jeff and Haila Troy series (5)
Witting, Clifford
Inspector Peter Bradfield series (7)

There was a fair maid dwelling
Delderfield, Ronald Frederick
Sennacherib series (1)

There was a king in Egypt
Lorimer, Norma
Egypt series (1)

There was a little girl
Dewhurst, Eileen
Inspector Neil Carter series (4)
McBain, Ed
Matthew Hope series (11)

There was a veil
Morrison, Emmeline
Lovice Clive series (1)

There was a witness
Salter, Elizabeth
Inspector Michael Hornsley series (3)

There was an old man
Phillpotts, Eden
Devonshire village series (2)

There was an old woman
Phillpotts, Eden
Devonshire village series (1)
Queen, Ellery
Ellery Queen series (23)

There were no asper ladies
Ascher, Eugene
Lucian Carolus series (1)

There were two pirates
Cabell, James Branch
It happened in Florida trilogy (2)

There will be another day
O'Donnell, Peadar
Another day series (3)

There will be fighting
O'Donnell, Peadar
Adrigoole series (2)

There will be war
Pournelle, Jerry
There will be war series (1)

There you are, Doctor
Clifford, Robert
Doctor series (7)

Thereby hangs a corpse
Mullen, Clarence
Tony Lantz and Eddie Wright series (1)

Therefore I killed him
Jobson, Hamilton
Inspector Anders series (1)

There's a bat in bunk five
Danziger, Paula
Cat and bat series (2)

There's a batwing in my lunchbox
Hodgman, Ann
Fifth grade monsters series (3)

There's a bear in my bed
Wood, Amanda Jane
Look twice series (1)

There's a dinosaur in the garden
Salmon, Michael
Dinosaur series (1)

There's a dragon in my sleeping bag
Howe, James
Night monsters series (2)

There's a ghost in the coatroom
Smith, Janice Lea
Adam Joshua series (7)

There's a hippie on the highway
Chase, James Hadley
Frank Terrell series (6)

There's a hippopotamus on our roof eating cake
Edwards, Hazel
Hippopotamus series (1)

There's a monster under my bed
Howe, James
Night monsters series (1)

There's a nightmare in my closet
Mayer, Mercer
Fears series (1)

There's a nightmare in my cupboard
Mayer, Mercer
Fears series (1)

There's a panda in the pantry
Wood, Amanda Jane
Look twice series (3)

There's a reason for everything
Punshon, Ernest Robertson
Bobby Owen series (21)

There's a troll in my closet
Ellis, Carol
Troll series (1)

There's a troll in my popcorn
Ellis, Carol
Troll series (2)

There's a troll in my sleeping bag
Ellis, Carol
Troll series (3)

There's a whale in my bath
Wood, Amanda Jane
Look twice series (4)

There's always a price tag
Chase, James Hadley
Steve Harmas series (2)

There's always Danny
Ure, Jean
Vanessa trilogy (2)

There's an alligator under my bed
Mayer, Mercer
Fears series (2)

There's death in the cup
Hocking, Anne
Inspector William Austen series (19)

There's nothing to be afraid of
Muller, Marcia
Sharon McCone series (7)

There's nothing to do
Stevenson, James
Grandfather's problems series (4)

There's nothing worse than first period P.E.
Evans, Greg
Luann series (11)

There's one born every minute
Brindley, Louise
Old peoples' home trilogy (2)

There's only one Harris
Remkiewicz, Frank
Harris series (2)

There's rosemary, there's rue
Fortescue, Winifred
Provence series (3)

There's something in a Sunday
Muller, Marcia
Sharon McCone series (9)

There's trouble brewing
Blake, Nicholas
Nigel Strangeways series (3)

Thermal Thursday
Pendleton, Don
Mack Bolan series (36)

These are they
Duke, Winifred
Harold Fieldend series (5)

These charming people
Arlen, Michael
Charming people series (1)

These days
Hubbard, Kin
Abe Martin series (13)

These girls I knew
Dennison, Dorothy
Wantoknow series for girls (5)

These golden days
Braine, John
Last love series (2)

These green foreign hills
Green, Roland James
Peace Company trilogy (2)

These happy golden years
Wilder, Laura Ingalls
Laura series (7)

These names make clues
Lorac, E C R
Inspector Macdonald series (12)

These old shades
Heyer, Georgette
Avon family series (1)

These, our strangers
Alington, Adrian
Payling Green series (1)

These thousand hills
Guthrie, Alfred Bertram
Settlement of the American West series (4)

These times of travail
Prior, Loveday
Feilmar family series (3)

These twain
Bennett, Arnold
Clayhanger series (3)
Five towns series (14)
They all came back
Courage, John
David Cane series (5)
They also serve
Jennings, D K
Doctor Ralph Conway series (8)
They always call us ladies
Harris, Jean
Two worlds series (2)
They are transformed
Peacey, Seton
William Cargoe series (2)
They burn the thistles
Kemal, Yashar
Slim Memed series (2)
They call it murder
Chambers, Peter
Mark Preston series (17)
They call me Boober Fraggle
Muntean, Michaela
Fraggle Rock series (1)
They called her Patience
Hill, Lorna
Patience series (1)
They called him death
Hume, David
Mick Cardby series (6)
They called him Nighthawk
Horler, Sydney
Nighthawk series (1)
They came and ate us
Rankin, Robert
Armageddon trilogy (2)
They came from France
Judson, Clara Ingram
They came from series (2)
They came from Scotland
Judson, Clara Ingram
They came from series (3)
They came from Sweden
Judson, Clara Ingram
They came from series (1)
They came from the sea
Timms, Edward Vivian
Australian saga series (8)
They came to a river
Mackay, Allis
They came to a river series (1)
They came to camp
Mills, Glynn
Lynton Hall series (1)
They came to Jurado
Grover, Marshall
Larry and Stretch series (219)
They came to kill
Stivers, Dick
Able Team series (15)
They came to plunder
Grover, Marshall
Nevada Jim series (19)
They can only hang you once
Hammett, Dashiell
Sam Spade series (2)
They can't all be guilty
Heberden, Mary Violet
Desmond Shannon series (11)
They can't hang Caroline
Vickers, Roy
Inspector Peter Curwen and Hugh Stanton series (3)
They come to my door
Gee, Herbert Leslie
Friendly series (6)
They die alone
Janson, Hank
Hank Janson series (74)
They die with their boots clean
Kersh, Gerald
Brigade of Guards series (1)
They died in the spring
Pullein-Thompson, Josephine
Inspector James Flecker series (2)
They died twice
Robeson, Kenneth
Doc Savage series (105)
They do it with mirrors
Christie, Agatha
Miss Jane Marple series (7)
Conaway, Jim C
Jana Blake series (2)
They don't make them like that anymore
Leasor, James
Aristo Autos series (1)
They don't shoot cowards
Reese, John
Jefferson Hewitt series (2)
They found a cave
Chauncy, Nan
Tasmania series (1)
They found an elephant
Barclay, Vera Charlesworth
They series (3)
They found him dead
Heyer, Georgette
Inspector Hemingway series (3)
Superintendent Hannasyde series (3)
They hadn't a clue
Downes, Quentin
Detective Inspector Abraham Kozminski series (3)
They hang them in Gibraltar
Perowne, Barry
Raffles series (9)
Rick Leroy series (3)
Sexton Blake series (935)
They have their exits
Neave, Airey
Colditz series (4)
Escape series (1)
They hunted a fox
Campbell, Alice
Alison Young series (2)
Colin Ladbroke series (3)
Inspector Headcorn series (2)
They kidnapped Stanley Matthews
Gribble, Leonard Reginald
Superintendent Anthony Slade series (19)
They liked Entwistle
Walling, Robert Alfred John
Philip Tolefree series (16)
They love not poison
Woods, Sara
Sir Nicholas Harding and Antony Maitland series (1)
They march from yesterday
Surdez, Georges
Foreign Legion series (2)
They met a wizard
Barclay, Vera Charlesworth
They series (2)
They met in heaven
Hepworth, George Hughes
Hiram Golf series (2)
They must have seen me coming
Brindley, Louise
Old peoples' home trilogy (1)
They never came back
Flynn, Brian
Anthony Bathurst series (26)
Hume, David
Mick Cardby series (25)
Thorne, Ernest Pollett
Geoff Fennell series (1)
They never looked inside
Gilbert, Michael Francis
Inspector Hazelrigg series (2)
They never say when
Cheyney, Peter
Slim Callaghan series (9)
They raced for treasure
Serraillier, Ian
David and Uncle Bill series (1)
They rang up the police
Cannan, Joanna
Inspector Guy Northeast series (1)
They rescued a pony
Harris, Catherine
Marsham family series (1)
They seek a country
Young, Francis Brett
Boer War series (1)
They shall have stars
Blish, James
Cities in flight series (1)
They stay for death
Woods, Sara
Sir Nicholas Harding and Antony Maitland series (30)
They talked of poison
Evermay, March
Inspector Glover series (1)
They tell no tales
Coles, Manning
Tommy Hambledon series (3)
Spiller, Andrew
Chief Inspector Duck Mallard series (17)
Thayer, Lee
Peter Clancy series (11)
They that walk in darkness
Zangwill, Israel
Ghetto series (4)
They that walk in the wild
Roberts, Charles George Douglas
Wilderness series (2)
They thought he was dead
Horler, Sydney
Tiger Standish series (11)
They used dark forces
Wheatley, Dennis
Gregory Sallust series (10)
They vanish at night
King, Frank
Dormouse series (7)
They walk in darkness
Verner, Gerald
Peter Chard series (2)
They walk on earth
Buckley, Eunice
Sandor Raimann series (1)
They wanted him dead
Eyles, Leonora
Doctor Joan Marvin series (1)
They wanted to live
Roberts, Cecil
Mrs Brown series (2)
They watched by night
Rhode, John
Doctor Lancelot Priestley series (35)
They went to the sea
Barclay, Vera Charlesworth
They series (1)
They won't forget Sweeney
Grover, Marshall
Larry and Stretch series (112)
They won't lie down
Annesley, Michael
Lawrence Fenton series (12)
They wouldn't be chessmen
Mason, Alfred Edward Woodley
Inspector Hanaud series (4)
They'll hang Billy for sure
Grover, Marshall
Larry and Stretch series (145)
They'll never find out
Duncan, Francis
Mordecai Euripides Tremaine series (1)
They're a weird mob
Culotta, Nino
Weird mob series (1)
They're back
Gross, Edward
V series (16)
They're coming to kill you, Jane!
Carr, Kirby
Hitman series (4)
They're gonna settle out of court, Herman
Unger, Jim
Herman series (19)
They've killed Anna
Olden, Marc
Hawthorne Albert Harker series (3)
Thibaults
Martin du Gard, Roger
Thibault family series (1)
Thick as thieves
Dixon, Franklin W
Hardy boys case files series (29)
Thick blue sweater
Fry, Pete
Pete Fry series (9)
Thicker than blood
Lutz, John
Alo Nudger series (9)
Thicker than water
McInerny, Ralph
Father Roger Dowling series (6)
Sandys, James
Mister Springfield series (1)
Tuttle, Wilbur Coleman
Hashknife Hartley and Sleepy Stevens series (2)
Zimmerman, Bruce
Quinn Parker series (2)
Thief in the night
Carter, Nicholas
Nicholas Carter series (505)
Hornung, Ernest William
Raffles series (3)
Thief of clubs
Johns, Gilbert
Sexton Blake series (1515)
Thief of dreams
Cole, Adrian
Star requiem series (2)
Thief of Llarn
Fox, Gardner Francis
Alan Morgan series (2)
Thief of Thoth
Carter, Lin
Hautley Quicksilver series (1)
Thief of time
Hillerman, Tony
Lieutenant Joe Leaphorn series (5)
Sergeant Jim Chee series (5)
Wainwright, John
Northern Police series (37)
Thief or two
Woods, Sara
Sir Nicholas Harding and Antony Maitland series (26)
Thief River Falls run
Robbins, David
Endworld series (2)
Thief River showdown
Sharpe, Jon
Trailsman series (55)
Thief taker
Sturrock, Jeremy
Bow Street Runner series (1)
Thief who came to dinner
Smith, Terence Lore
Webster Daniels series (1)
Thief who couldn't sleep
Block, Lawrence
Evan Tanner series (1)
Thief who painted sunlight
Bleeck, Oliver
Philip Saint Ives series (3)
Thief who was robbed
Carter, Nicholas
Nicholas Carter series (553)
Thieves of Alexandria
Hunter, John
Sexton Blake series (1344)
Thieves of light
Hudson, Michael
Kar-Chee series (2)
Thieves' picnic
Charteris, Leslie
Saint series (18)
Thieves' world
Asprin, Robert Lynn
Sanctuary series (1)
Thimble Theatre starring Popeye
Segar, Elzie Crisler
Popeye the Sailor series (1)
Thin air
Laymon, Richard Carl
Strange Occurrence Squad series (4)
Marshall, William Leonard
Yellowthread Street series (4)
Thin blue line
Graves, Charles
Royal Air Force series (1)
Thin ghost and others
James, Montague Rhodes
Ghost stories series (3)
Thin ice
Branfield, John
Brown cow series (2)
Raymond, John
Bulman series (3)
Rees, E M
Going for it series (6)
Thin mountain air
Horgan, Paul
Richard trilogy (3)
Thin-spun life
Hocking, Anne
Inspector William Austen series (31)
Thin thighs in thirty years
Guisewhite, Cathy
Cathy series (10)
Thin woman
Cannell, Dorothy
Ellie Simons Haskell series (1)
Thing of the past
Gridban, Volsted
Clifford Brooks series (1)
Thing on the line
Pullen, Alan
Sam and Lin series (2)
Thing, One thing after another
Spector, Warren
Marvel superheroes adventure gamebooks series (5)
Thing that pursued
Robeson, Kenneth
Doc Savage series (134)
Things as they are
Horgan, Paul
Richard trilogy (1)
Things Bunny sees
Szekeres, Cyndy
Bunny series (1)
Things fall apart
Achebe, Chinua
African trilogy (1)
Things hunting men
Drake, David
Starhunters series (2)
Things invisible
Reynolds, William J
Nebraska series (4)
Things near and far
Machen, Arthur
Near and far series (2)
Things that go bark in the park
Gilden, Mel
Fifth grade monsters series (7)
Things that go bump
Browne, Dik
Hagar the horrible series (52)
Things they carried
O'Brien, Tim
Vietnam War series (4)
Things to come
Menville, Douglas
Science fiction film series (1)
Things we do for love
Schutz, Benjamin Merrill
Leo Haggerty series (4)
Things won't be the same
Ewing, Kathryn
Marcy Benson series (2)
Things worthwhile
Cheesman, Evelyn
Time well spent series (1)
Think big, think dirty
Garner, William
John Morpurgo trilogy (1)
Think fast, Mister Moto
Marquand, John Phillips
Mister Moto series (3)
Think fast, Mister Peters
Kaminsky, Stuart Melvin
Toby Peters series (13)
Think Inc.
Diment, Adam
Philip McAlpine series (4)
Think of death
Lockridge, Frances
Inspector Merton Heimrich series (2)
Think on death
McCullough, David Willis
Ziza Todd series (1)
Thinking
Allington, Richard L
Beginning to learn series (11)
Thinking machine
Brierley, John Keith
Human behaviour trilogy (3)
Thinking Machine
Futrelle, Jacques
Professor Augustus S F X Van Dusen series (2)
Thinking machine affair
Bernard, Joel
Man from U.N.C.L.E. series (21)
Thinking Machine on the case
Futrelle, Jacques
Professor Augustus S F X Van Dusen series (3)
Thinking seat
Tate, Peter
Simeon series (1)
Thinner than water
Ferrars, Elizabeth
Virginia and Felix Freer series (3)
Thinning the turkey herd
Campbell, Robert Wright
Jimmy Flannery series (4)
Third and goal
James, Laurence
Gridiron series (3)
Third anti-coloring book
Striker, Susan
Anti-coloring series (3)
Third attempt
Wheeler, H E
Stephen Rant series (2)
Third betrayal
Hartland, Michael
David Nairn series (3)
Third big Monster book
Blance, Ellen
Monster series (12)
Third big radio Thin King book
Farmer, Derek
Thin King series (3)
Third Biggles omnibus
Johns, William Earl
Biggles series (20)
Third book of after midnight stories
Myers, Amy
After midnight stories series (3)
Third book of swords
Saberhagen, Fred
Book of swords trilogy (3)
Third Brer Rabbit book
Blyton, Enid
Brer Rabbit series (3)
Third bullet, and other stories
Carr, John Dickson
Doctor Gideon Fell series (23)
Sir Henry Merrivale series (23)

Third case of Mister Paul Savoy
Gregory, Jackson
Paul Savoy series (3)
Third class genie
Leeson, Robert
Alec Bowden series (1)
Third coarse acting show
Green, Michael
Coarse plays series (3)
Third crime lucky
Gilbert, Anthony
Arthur Crook series (33)
Third deadly sin
Sanders, Lawrence
Edward X Delaney series (3)
Third degree
Barry, Joe
Rush Henry series (1)
Jackson, Charles Ross
Quintus Oakes series (1)
Nelson, Peter N
Mollie Fox series (3)
Third did I ever tell you book
Grender, Iris
Did I ever tell series (3)
Third Doctor Who quiz book
Robinson, Nigel
Doctor Who quiz book series (4)
Third encounter
Woods, Sara
Sir Nicholas Harding and Antony Maitland series (4)
Third Eve book
Fowl
Eve series (3)
Third evil
Stine, Robert Lawrence
Fear Street cheerleaders series (3)
Third eye
Leroux, Etienne
Welgevonden trilogy (3)
Lobsang Rampa, Tuesday
Third eye series (1)
Third figure
Wilcox, Collin
Stephen Drake series (2)
Third flight of the Starfire
Mumford, Edwin Embree
Starfire series (3)
Third force
Kurland, Michael
Mission series (1)
Matheson, Hugh
Gregory Branscombe series (1)
Third Force
Sinclair, Dennis
Greg Ballard series (1)
Third Frank Muir goes into
Muir, Frank
Frank Muir goes into series (3)
Third George
Plaidy, Jean
Georgian series (5)
Third girl
Christie, Agatha
Hercule Poirot series (34)
Mrs Ariadne Oliver series (6)
Third grade stars
Ransom, Candice Farris
Tales of the third grade series (2)
Third horror
Stine, Robert Lawrence
Ninety-nine Fear Street series (3)
Third key
Gibbons, Harry Hornaby Clifford
Sexton Blake series (341)
Third life with Dexter
Fennell, Willie
Dexter Dutton series (3)
Third miracle
Tracy, Louis
Inspector Furneaux series (13)
Third murderer
Daly, Carroll John
Race Williams series (5)
Taylor, Phoebe Atwood
Asey Mayo series (22)
Third on a seesaw
Macneil, Neil
Tony Costaine and Bert McCall series (3)
Third one
Mead, Russell
Doctor Peter Casey series (3)
Third owl
Casey, Robert J
Jim Sands series (5)
Third person rural
Perrin, Noel
Sometime farmer series (3)
Third pilot
Southall, Ivan
War in the air series (1)
Third planet from Altair
Packard, Edward
Choose your own adventure series (7)
Third possibility
Jepson, Selwyn
Eve Gill series (7)
Third-prize surprise
Saunders, Susan
Bad News Bunny series (1)
Third round
Sapper
Bulldog Drummond series (3)
Third shadow
Grant, Maxwell
Shadow series (98)
Third skull
Grant, Maxwell
Shadow series (78)
Third statue
Martin, Shane
Professor Ronald Challis series (4)
Third term at Malory Towers
Blyton, Enid
Malory Towers series (3)
Third term at Rocklands School
Oxenham, Elsie J
Rocklands School trilogy (3)
Third time fatal
Ormerod, Roger
Philipa Lowe series (5)
Third time unlucky
Cross, Mark
Daphne Wrayne and her Four Adjusters series (43)
Third truth
Bar-Zohar, Michael
Jeff Saunders series (1)
Third verdict
Zuk, Beverly C
Star trek fan series (25)
Third victim
Stuart, Donald
Sexton Blake series (1014)
Waltch, Lilla M
Lisa Davis series (1)
Wilcox, Collin
Lieutenant Frank Hastings series (7)
Third world
Daiches, David
Three worlds series (2)
Third World War
Hackett, John
World War Three series (1)
Third world war, the untold story
Hackett, John
World War Three series (2)
Third year in Jerusalem
Finn, Elizabeth Anne MacCaul
Jerusalem series (2)
Thirst
Smith, Guy Newman
Thirst series (1)
Thirst for vengeance
Hardin, J D
Raider series (5)
Thirsty evil
Verner, Gerald
Peter Chard series (1)
Thirteen
Ransom, Candice Farris
Growing up series (3)
Thirteen at dinner
Christie, Agatha
Hercule Poirot series (8)
Thirteen clues for Miss Marple
Christie, Agatha
Miss Jane Marple series (14)
Thirteen days
Jefferies, Ian
Sergeant Craig series (1)
Thirteen for luck
Hurt, Freda Mary
Pinetops series (5)
Thirteen for the kill
Buck, Peter
Marc Dean series (1)
Thirteen guests
Farjeon, Joseph Jefferson
Inspector Kendall series (1)
Thirteen-gun salute
O'Brian, Patrick
Jack Aubrey and Stephen Maturin series (13)
Thirteen means magic
Becker, Eve
Abracadabra series (1)
Thirteen problems
Christie, Agatha
Miss Jane Marple series (2)
Thirteen Stannergate
Wilson, Gertrude Mary
Inspector Lovick series (3)
Thirteen steps to Lime Street
Enefer, Douglas
Sam Bawtrey series (2)
Thirteen trumpeters
Meynell, Laurence Walter
Hooky Hefferman series (6)
Thirteen white tulips
Crane, Frances
Pat and Jean Abbott series (16)
Thirteenth adventure
Atkinson, Mary Evelyn
Lockett family series (13)
Thirteenth chime
Jacobs, Thomas Curtis Hicks
Chief Inspector Barnard series (4)
Thirteenth code
Jardine, Warwick
Sexton Blake series (1004)
Thirteenth lover
Dekobra, Maurice
Lady Diana trilogy (3)
Thirteenth murder
Eberhard, Frederick George
Chief of Police Sutherland series (1)
Thirteenth pearl
Keene, Carolyn
Nancy Drew series (56)
Thirteenth spy
Carter, Nick
Nick Carter series (8)
Thirteenth treasure
Hunt, Charlotte
Doctor Paul Holton series (4)
Thirty days hath September
John, Owen
Haggai Godin series (1)
Thirty days to live
Conway, Peter
Inspector Newton series (2)
Gilbert, Anthony
Arthur Crook series (12)
Thirty dozen moons
Bruce, Henry James
Silken dalliance series (2)
Thirty fathoms deep
Ellsberg, Edward
Sunken treasure series (1)
Thirty-fifth of May
Kastner, Erich
Emil series (3)
Thirty-first floor
Wahloo, Per
Chief Inspector Peter Jensen series (1)
Thirty for a Harry
Hoyt, Richard
John Denson series (2)
Thirty Manhattan East
Waugh, Hillary
Detective Frank Sessions series (1)
Thirty-nine steps
Buchan, John
Richard Hannay series (1)
Thirty-one brothers and sisters
Mirsky, Reba Paeff
Zulu series (1)
Thirty raiders south
Grover, Marshall
Nevada Jim series (23)
Thirty years after
Graydon, William Murray
Sexton Blake series (181)
This animal must die
Scarpetta, Frank
Marksman series (16)
This blessed plot
Meek, Margaret Reid Duncan
Lennox Kemp series (8)
This book is about Aurora
Hester, Randolph Thompson
Aurora series (2)
This bright mantle
Lindsay, Paula
Mark Rendle series (2)
This Calder range
Dailey, Janet
Webb Calder series (2)
This Calder sky
Dailey, Janet
Webb Calder series (1)
This dame dies soon
Janson, Hank
Hank Janson series (30)
This darkening universe
Biggle, Lloyd
Jan Darzek series (3)
This death was murder
Evermay, March
Inspector Glover series (2)
This delicate murder
Clandon, Henrietta
Penny and Vincent Mercer series (2)
William Power series (3)
This doll is dangerous
King, Frank
Dormouse series (6)
This Drakotny
McCutchan, Philip
Commander Esmonde Shaw series (13)
This earth of mankind
Toer, Pramoedya Ananta
All nations series (1)
This fatal writ
Woods, Sara
Sir Nicholas Harding and Antony Maitland series (28)
This girl for hire
Fickling, G G
Honey West series (1)
This great city
Davis, Oswald Harcourt
Ardencester series (4)
This gun for justice
Santiago, V J
Joseph Madden series (6)
This gun is still
Gruber, Frank
Historical Western series (16)
This heart of mine
Small, Beatrice
Skye O'Malley series (3)
This hood for hire
Janson, Hank
Hank Janson series (58)
This I believe
Welk, Laurence
Wunnerful series (4)
This impertinence
Arnott, Peter
Impertinence series (1)
This is Adam
Cheney, Brainard
Adam series (1)
This is Betsy
Wolde, Gunilla
Emma series (2)
This is death calling
Sandys, James
Inspector Millwall series (2)
This is Espie Sanchez
Dunnahoo, Terry
Espie Sanchez series (2)
This is for real
Chase, James Hadley
Herman Radnitz series (1)
Mark Girland series (1)
This is Goggle
Plagemann, Bentz
Wallace family series (1)
This is it, Michael Shayne
Halliday, Brett
Michael Shayne series (20)
This is Jezebel
Cory, Desmond
Lindy Grey series (2)
This is Maggie Muggins
Grannan, Mary
Maggie Muggins series (5)
This is Mister Fortune
Bailey, Henry Christopher
Mister Reggie Fortune series (13)
This is murder
Ard, William
Timothy Dane series (2)
Muller, Paul
Paul Muller series (13)
This is murder, Mr Jones
Fuller, Timothy
Jupiter Jones series (4)
This is my heaven
Macmillan, William John
Faith healing series (2)
This is my life
Bartlett, Vernon
My life series (1)
This is my murder
Dix, Maurice Buxton
Superintendent Simon Bullion series (1)
This is my street
Maynard, Nan
Jubilee is my street (1)
This is the Christmas
Sawyer, Ruth
Christmas stories series (4)
This is the grass
Marshall, Alan
I can jump puddles series (2)
This is the heir
Housman, Laurence
Palace plays series (4)
This is the house
Hill, Deborah
Merrick family series (1)
This is the South Coast news and I'm Paul Murphy
Roland, Betty
Improbable life trilogy (2)
Slaven, Roy
South Coast series (2)
This is Vermont
Hard, Walter
Vermont series (5)
This is what happened
Claymore, Tod
Tod Claymore series (1)
This is your life
Newman, Bernard
Papa Pontivy series (14)
This is your life, Bhodi Li
Peters, David
Photon series (4)
This little measure
Woods, Sara
Sir Nicholas Harding and Antony Maitland series (7)
This little nose
Ormerod, Jan
New baby books series (1)
This little piggy
McGee, Shelagh
Little nursery rhyme series (1)
This magic moment
Roberts, Nora
Flowers series (24)
This man did I kill
Halliday, Michael
Doctor Emmanuel Cellini series (10)
This man is dangerous
Cheyney, Peter
Lemmy Caution series (1)
This man is my brother
Brinig, Myron
Singermann family series (2)
This man must die!
Ballinger, W A
Sexton Blake series (1487)
This man's doom
Thayer, Lee
Peter Clancy series (24)
This moment is forever
Witcomb, Nan
Thoughts of Nanushka series (3)
This murder came to mind
Ormerod, Roger
David Mallin and George Coe series (9)
This nettle, danger
Gibbs, Philip
John Barton trilogy (1)
This nude for hire
Mark, Ted
Man from O.R.G.Y. series (17)
This one's on me
Jack, Donald
Journals of Bartholomew Bandy series (6)
This other Eden
Harris, Marilyn
Eden family series (1)
This passion never dies
Winther, Sophus Keith
Grimsen trilogy (3)
Nebraska trilogy (3)
This place is cold
Cobb, Vicki
Imagine living here series (1)
This place is crowded
Cobb, Vicki
Imagine living here series (6)
This place is dry
Cobb, Vicki
Imagine living here series (2)
This place is high
Cobb, Vicki
Imagine living here series (4)
This place is lonely
Cobb, Vicki
Imagine living here series (5)
This place is wet
Cobb, Vicki
Imagine living here series (3)
This present darkness
Peretti, Frank E
Darkness series (1)
This promised land
Easton, Robert
Saga of California series (1)

This proud and savage land
Cordell, Alexander
Mortymers series (1)

This range is mine!
Grover, Marshall
Larry and Stretch series (60)

This ravaged heart
Riefe, Barbara
Dandridge trilogy (1)

This ravished land
Oldfield, Pamela
Heron saga series (2)

This real night
West, Rebecca
Aubrey family trilogy (2)

This right soft lot
Blishen, Edward
Schoolmaster series (2)

This school is driving me crazy
Hentoff, Nat
This school series (1)

This ship is mine
Macdonnell, James Edmond
Dutchy Holland series (34)

This side murder?
Bonett, John
Inspector Borges series (3)

This side of evil
Keene, Carolyn
Nancy Drew files series (14)

This side of glory
Bristow, Gwen
Louisiana trilogy (3)

This song is for you
Miller, Sandy
Heart to heart series (5)

This splendid earth
Banis, Victor Jerome
Brussac family series (1)

This spy must die
Saxon, Peter
Sexton Blake series (1603)

This star shall abide
Engdahl, Sylvia Louise
Noren series (1)

This string first
Home, Michael
Breckland series (3)

This stubborn soil
Owen, William A
Stubborn soil series (1)

This suitcase is going to explode
Ardies, Tom
Charlie Sparrow series (2)

This sweet and bitter earth
Cordell, Alexander
Merthyr trilogy (2)
Mortymers series (6)

This terrible sword
Cozzens, Peter
American Civil War battles series (2)

This time next week
Thomas, Leslie
Wildest dreams series (1)

This towering passion
Sherwood, Valerie
Geoffrey and Lenore series (1)

This traitor, death
Cory, Desmond
Johnny Fedora series (2)

This turbulent priest
Butler, Margaret
Henry II series (3)

This undesirable residence
Burton, Miles
Inspector Arnold and Desmond Merrion series (26)

This was life
Linn, James Weber
Campus series (1)

This was no accident
Saxon, John A
Sam Welpton series (1)

This was tomorrow
Thane, Elswyth
Williamsburg series (6)

This water laps gently
Ingate, Mary
Ann Fielding series (2)

This way home
Bell, Vicars
Dodo series (2)

This way out
Radley, Sheila
Chief Inspector Douglas Quantrill series (7)

This way, please!
John, Stephen
Albert Divine series (4)

This way to Christmas
Sawyer, Ruth
Christmas stories series (1)

This wicked sex
Janson, Hank
Hank Janson series (102)

This woman is death
Frances, Stephen Daniel
John Gail series (1)
Janson, Hank
Hank Janson series (5)
Storm, Michael
Nick Cranley series (5)

This won't hurt you
Fitzgerald, Nigel
Superintendent Duffy series (7)

This won't kill you
Stout, Rex
Nero Wolfe and Archie Goodwin series (23)

This world is taboo
Leinster, Murray
Med Service series (2)

This'll kill you
Chambers, Peter
Mark Preston series (7)

Thistle and the Rose
Plaidy, Jean
Tudor series (9)

Thistles of Mount Cedar
Tannenforst, Ursula
Mount Cedar series (1)

Thistlewood plot
Sturrock, Jeremy
Bow Street Runner series (8)

Thomas
Creswell, Harry Bulkeley
Thomas series (1)

Thomas' ABC
Awdry, Wilbert
Railway series (37)

Thomas and his cat
Wolde, Gunilla
Thomas series (9)

Thomas and Sarah
Hardwick, Mollie
Upstairs, downstairs series (13)

Thomas and Sarah dress up
Wolde, Gunilla
Thomas series (5)

Thomas and the dinosaur
Awdry, Christopher
Railway series (34)

Thomas and the twins
Awdry, Christopher
Railway series (33)

Thomas bakes a cake
Wolde, Gunilla
Thomas series (8)

Thomas builds a house
Wolde, Gunilla
Thomas series (1)

Thomas cleans his room
Wolde, Gunilla
Thomas series (3)

Thomas comes home
Awdry, Christopher
Railway series (36)

Thomas comes to breakfast
Awdry, Wilbert
Railway series (37)

Thomas' counting book
Awdry, Wilbert
Railway series (37)

Thomas goes out
Wolde, Gunilla
Thomas series (4)

Thomas goes to the doctor
Wolde, Gunilla
Thomas series (6)

Thomas Hardy's later years
Gittings, Robert
Thomas Hardy series (2)

Thomas has a bath
Wolde, Gunilla
Thomas series (2)

Thomas is different
Wolde, Gunilla
Thomas series (10)

Thomas is little
Wolde, Gunilla
Thomas series (7)

Thomas settles down
Creswell, Harry Bulkeley
Thomas series (2)

Thomas, the tank engine
Awdry, Wilbert
Railway series (2)

Thomas Wingfold, curate
Macdonald, George
Thomas Wingfold trilogy (1)

Thomasheen James
Walsh, Maurice
Thomasheen James series (1)

Thomasheen James gets his hair cut
Walsh, Maurice
Thomasheen James series (2)

Thomasina
Gallico, Paul
Jennie series (2)

Thomas's Christmas party
Awdry, Wilbert
Railway series (37)

Thongor against the gods
Carter, Lin
Thongor of Lemuria series (3)

Thongor and the Dragon City
Carter, Lin
Thongor of Lemuria series (2)

Thongor and the pirates of Tarakus
Carter, Lin
Thongor of Lemuria series (6)

Thongor and the wizard of Lemuria
Carter, Lin
Thongor of Lemuria series (1)

Thongor at the end of time
Carter, Lin
Thongor of Lemuria series (5)

Thongor fights the pirates of Tarakus
Carter, Lin
Thongor of Lemuria series (6)

Thongor in the City of Magicians
Carter, Lin
Thongor of Lemuria series (4)

Thongor of Lemuria
Carter, Lin
Thongor of Lemuria series (2)

Thor
McClung, Robert Marshall
Endangered animals series (4)

Thora's sacrifice
Brand, Kurt
Perry Rhodan series (70)

Thorgils of Treadholt
Hewlett, Maurice
Sagas retold series (3)

Thorn
Saberhagen, Fred
Dracula series (20)

Thorn bush
Crompton, Richmal
Wilding family series (3)

Thorn in the dust
Audemars, Pierre
Monsieur Pinaud series (10)

Thorn witch
Taylor, E J
Biscuits, buttons and pickles series (3)

Thornley Colton, blind detective
Stagg, Clinton Holland
Thornley Colton series (2)

Thornley Colton, blind reader of hearts
Stagg, Clinton Holland
Thornley Colton series (1)

Thor's hammer, on or near earth
Bretnor, Reginald
Future at war series (1)

Thorstein of the Mere
Collingwood, William Gershon
Norsemen series (1)

Those craze eighth grade pictures
Adorjan, Carol
Junior High series (2)

Those crazy class pictures
Kenyon, Kate
Cedar Groves Junior High School series (7)

Those fragile years
Franken, Rose
Claudia series (7)

Those kids from town again
Alington, Adrian
Payling Green series (2)

Those Miller girls
Constant, Alberta Wilson
Miller family series (1)

Those of my blood
Lichtenberg, Jacqueline
Luren series (1)

Those on the list
Parsons, Anthony
Sexton Blake series (1266)

Those Plummer children
Govan, Christine Noble
Plummer children series (1)

Those remembered days!
Inchfawn, Fay
Personal recording series (1)

Those Shepton children
Adams, Agnes
Shepton children trilogy (3)

Those were the days
Milne, Alan Alexander
Day's play series (5)

Those who perish
Dahlberg, Edward
Bottom dogs series (3)

Those who pray together slay together
Von Elsner, Don
David Danning series (1)

Those who watch over earth
Semine, Daniel
Argus series (2)

Those without shadows
Sagan, Francoise
Josee and Bernard series (1)

Thou art the man
Poe, Edgar Allan
Monsieur C Auguste Dupin series (1)

Thou shell of death
Blake, Nicholas
Nigel Strangeways series (2)

Though I know she lies
Woods, Sara
Sir Nicholas Harding and Antony Maitland series (9)

Thoughts of Nanushka
Witcomb, Nan
Thoughts of Nanushka series (6)
Thoughts of Nanushka series (12)

Thousand and one nights of Jean Macaque
Cloete, Stuart
Jean Macaque series (1)

Thousand coffins affair
Avallone, Michael
Man from U.N.C.L.E. series (1)

Thousand for Sicily
Trease, Geoffrey
Mark Appleby series (2)

Thousand hands
Norman, Bruce
James Mallaby series (1)

Thousand-headed man
Robeson, Kenneth
Doc Savage series (2)

Thousand hour day
Kuniczak, Wieslaw Stanislaw
Polish war trilogy (1)

Thousand illusions
Tarsis, Valeriy
Black Sea trilogy (3)

Thousand shrine warrior
Salmonson, Jessica Amanda
Tomoe Gozen trilogy (3)

Thousand-year plan
Asimov, Isaac
Foundation series (2)

Thousand years a minute
Claudy, Carl Harry
Adventures in the unknown series (2)

Thousandstar
Anthony, Piers
Cluster series (4)

Thrall and the dragon's heart
Boyer, Elizabeth H
World of the Alfar series (3)

Thrall of Hypno
Darlton, Clark
Perry Rhodan series (20)

Thread of gold
Castle, Frances
Erinn series (3)

Thread of scarlet
Williams, Ben Ames
Thread of scarlet series (1)

Thread that runs so true
Stuart, Jesse
Dark hills trilogy (2)

Threads of light
Kherdian, David
Farm poems series (3)

Threat of Sitting Bull
Lange, Dietrich
American Indian series (9)

Threat of the pirate ship
Chambers, Kate
Diana Winthrop series (6)

Threat to the Barkers
Phipson, Joan
Barker family series (2)

Threateners
Hamilton, Donald
Matt Helm series (26)

Threatening shadows
Robertson, Colin
Vicky McBain series (7)

Three
Hellman, Lillian
Unfinished woman trilogy (3)

Three act tragedy
Christie, Agatha
Hercule Poirot series (10)

Three adventures of Asterix
Goscinny, Rene
Asterix series (25)

Three against the Witch World
Norton, Andre
Estcarp series (3)
Witch World series (3)

Three against the world
Leeson, Robert
Time rope series (2)

Three and one make five
Jeffries, Roderic Graeme
Inspector Enrique Alvarez series (8)

Three at the Angel
Procter, Maurice
Chief Inspector Harry Martineau series (9)

Three at Wolfe's door
Stout, Rex
Nero Wolfe and Archie Goodwin series (33)

Three bad nights
Buckingham, Bruce
Don Pancho series (1)

Three Baers
Moore, Bertha B
Triplets series (2)

Three bamboos
Standish, Robert
Chinese Civil War series (1)

Three beans
Coles, Manning
Tommy Hambledon series (20)

Three bedrooms, one corpse
Harris, Charlaine
Aurora Teagarden series (2)

Three-bladed doom
Howard, Robert Ervin
El Borak trilogy (3)

Three blind mice
Cosgrove, Stephen Edward
DreamMaker series (3)
McBain, Ed
Matthew Hope series (9)
Seifert, Adele
Gregory Trent series (1)
Wood, James
James Fraser series (8)

Three boys and a circus
Pollock, Mary
Dog stories series (1)

Three boys in the wild north land
Young, Egerton Ryerson
Three boys series (1)

Three bright pebbles
Ford, Leslie
Grace Latham series (3)

Three brothers
Grant, Maxwell
Shadow series (164)

Three brothers and a lady
Black, Margaret Katherine
Three brothers series (2)

Three brothers of Ur
Fyson, Jenny Grace
Shamashazir series (1)

Three by Box
Box, Edgar
Peter Cutler Sergeant series (3)

Three by the sea
Marshall, Edward
Fox series (1)

Three came home
Keith, Agnes
Borneo series (2)

Three cases of Shomri Shomar
Klinger, Henry
Lieutenant Shomri Shomar series (3)

Three cheers for Annabelle
O'Farrell, Kathleen
Lattimer children series (1)

Three cheers for me
Jack, Donald
Journals of Bartholomew Bandy series (1)

Three cheers for Noddy
Blyton, Enid
Noddy stories series (13)

Three cheers for Piggy Grunter
Shelley, Noreen
Piggy Grunter series (4)

Three cheers for Ragdolly Anna
Kenward, Jean
Ragdolly Anna series (5)

Three cheers Secret Seven
Blyton, Enid
Secret Seven series (8)

Three cities of bells
Goudge, Elizabeth
Cathedrals series (3)

Three clever mushrooms
Ainsworth, Ruth
Little Mushrooms series (2)

Three coffins
Carr, John Dickson
Doctor Gideon Fell series (6)

Three colonels
Cosgrave, Patrick
Colonel Allen Cheyney series (2)

Three comrades
Remarque, Erich Maria
World War I series (3)

Three-cornered halo
Brand, Christianna
Inspector Cockrill series (7)

Three-cornered murder
Leslie, Jean
Peter Ponsonby series (3)

Three-cornered mystery
Keene, Carolyn
Dana girls series (4)

Three corpse trick
Burton, Miles
Inspector Arnold and Desmond Merrion series (30)

Three corvettes
Monsarrat, Nicholas
Corvette series (3)

Three couriers
Mackenzie, Compton
Commander Roger Waterlow series (2)

Three cousins die
Rhode, John
Doctor Lancelot Priestley series (69)

Three crimes
Burton, Miles
Inspector Arnold and Desmond Merrion series (2)

Three cross
Hogan, Ray
Shawn Starbuck series (3)

Three crowns
Plaidy, Jean
Stuart series (5)
William and Mary trilogy (1)

Three crowns for the queen
Deeley, Roger
Martin Dymoke series (3)

Three-D
Avallone, Michael
Friday the thirteenth series (3)

Three-D traitor
Dank, Milton
Galaxy Gang series (3)

Three daggers
Gregg, Cecil Freeman
Inspector Cuthbert Higgins series (2)

Three dates with death
Gunn, Victor
Chief Inspector Bill Cromwell series (12)

Three days in Davisburg
Grover, Marshall
Larry and Stretch series (185)

Three days in winter
Jenkins, Jerry Bruce
Jennifer Grey series (2)

Three days of the Condor
Grady, James
Condor series (1)

Three dead
Magarshack, David
Superintendent Mooney series (3)

Three dead men
McGuire, Paul
Chief Inspector Cummings series (2)
Superintendent Fillinger series (2)

Three deaths for Buck Duane
Grey, Romer Zane
Buck Duane series (8)

Three detectives and the knight in armour
Brett, Simon
Three detectives series (2)

Three detectives and the missing superstar
Brett, Simon
Three detectives series (1)

Three devils
Robeson, Kenneth
Doc Savage series (137)

Three die at midnight
Hunter, John
Sexton Blake series (821)
Meriton, Peter
Bill Langley series (1)

Three died that night
Lane, Gret
Inspector Hook series (1)

Three died variously
Giles, Guy Elwyn
Brice Kent series (1)

Three doctors
Dicks, Terrance
Doctor Who series (19)

Three domsels
Chapman, Vera
Three damsels trilogy (3)

Three doors to death
Stout, Rex
Nero Wolfe and Archie Goodwin series (16)

Three down vulnerable
Ross, Zola Helen
Beau Smith and Pogy Rogers series (1)

Three Edwards
Costain, Thomas Bertram
History of the Plantagenets tetralogy (3)

Three eyes
Gordon, Stuart
Eyes trilogy (3)

Three faces of death
Weisman, John
Headhunters series (2)

Three faces of time
Merwin, Samuel Kimball
Elspeth Marriner and Mack Fraser series (2)

Three fears
Stagge, Jonathan
Doctor Hugh Westlake series (9)

Three fevers
Walmsley, Leo
Phantom Lobster series (2)

Three fingered death
Wilson, Gertrude Mary
Inspector Lovick series (7)

Three fishers
Beeding, Francis
Ronald Briercliffe series (1)

Three five minute stories
Richards, Laura Elizabeth
Five minute stories series (2)

Three for an orgy
Paul, F W
Man from S.T.U.D. series (1)

Three for Cordelia
Maclean, Catherine Macdonald
Tharrus trilogy (2)

Three for McGee
Macdonald, John Dann
Travis McGee series (21)

Three for pack holiday
Brambleby, Ailsa
Three series (2)

Three for the chair
Stout, Rex
Dol Bonner series (2)
Nero Wolfe and Archie Goodwin series (28)

Three for the gallows
McDowell, Emmett
Jonathan Knox series (3)

Three for the money
Ballard, Willis Todhunter
Lieutenant Max Hunter series (3)

Three for trouble
Brambleby, Ailsa
Three series (1)

Three fountains
Toms, Patricia
Chronicles of Pennycress series (2)

Three friends
Montgomery, Elizabeth
Dick, Jane and Sally series (5)

Three frightened men
Gray, Berkeley
Sexton Blake series (962)

Three from Catfish Bend
Burman, Ben Lucien
Catfish Bend series (3)

Three from the Legion
Williamson, Jack
Legion of Space series (3)

Three Gays
Brown, Ethel C
Three Gays series (1)

Three Gays at Merryton
Brown, Ethel C
Three Gays series (2)

Three Gays at the old farm
Brown, Ethel C
Three Gays series (4)

Three Gays in Maine
Brown, Ethel C
Three Gays series (3)

Three gnomes
Verner, Gerald
Trevor Lowe series (8)

Three goes to Chalet School
Brent-Dyer, Elinor Mary
Chalet School series (20)

Three gold crowns
Robeson, Kenneth
Avenger series (14)

Three Graces
Hobson, Polly
Inspector Basil series (3)
Jackson, Gabrielle Emilie
Three Graces series (1)

Three Graces at college
Jackson, Gabrielle Emilie
Three Graces series (2)

Three graves to a showdown
Gilman, George G
Undertaker series (4)

Three green bottles
De Selincourt, Aubrey
Rutherford series (2)

Three guardsmen
Dumas, Alexandre
Three Musketeers series (1)

Three guns from Colorado
Field, Peter
Powder Valley series (41)

Three guns north
Arthur, Burt
Texas Rangers series (3)

Three guns of glory
Roberts, J R
Gunsmith series (5)

Three happy lions
Fatio, Louise
Happy lion series (4)

Three harbours
Mason, Francis Van Wyck
American War of Independence series (1)

Three hearts and three lions
Anderson, Poul
Alternate world series (1)

Three hostages
Buchan, John
Richard Hannay series (4)

Three hours to hang
Mackenzie, Andrew
Nicholas Cornish series (2)

Three in three
Price, Roger
Tomorrow people series (2)

Three inquisitive people
Wheatley, Dennis
Duc de Richelieu series (1)

Three Jays against the clock
Smythe, Pat
Three Jays series (2)

Three Jays go to Rome
Smythe, Pat
Three Jays series (6)

Three Jays go to town
Smythe, Pat
Three Jays series (4)

Three Jays lend a hand
Smythe, Pat
Three Jays series (7)

Three Jays on holiday
Smythe, Pat
Three Jays series (3)

Three Jays over the border
Smythe, Pat
Three Jays series (5)

Three Just Men
Wallace, Edgar
Just Men series (5)

Three-legged hootch dancer
Resnick, Mike
Tales of the Galactic Midway series (2)

Three legions
Sutcliff, Rosemary
Roman Britain trilogy (3)

Three lepers' heads
Quiroule, Pierre
Sexton Blake series (937)

Three lights went out
Dean, Robert George
Pat Thompson series (3)

Three little bears
Burgess, Thornton Waldo
Animal stories series (2)

Three little funny ones
Hough, Charlotte
Funny ones series (1)

Three little Millers
Pierson, Clara Dillingham
Millers series (1)

Three little Mushrooms
Ainsworth, Ruth
Little Mushrooms series (1)

Three little rabbits go visiting
McCarthy, Ruth
Three little rabbits series (2)

Three little women
Jackson, Gabrielle Emilie
Three little women series (1)

Three little women as wives
Jackson, Gabrielle Emilie
Three little women series (4)

Three little women at work
Jackson, Gabrielle Emilie
Three little women series (2)

Three little women's success
Jackson, Gabrielle Emilie
Three little women series (3)

Three lives for the Czar
Plowman, Stephanie
Alexei Hamilton series (1)
Hamilton family series (1)

Three Margarets
Richards, Laura Elizabeth
Three Margarets series (1)

Three marriages
Hoff, Harry Summerfield
Three marriages series (4)

Three masked men
Pentelow, John Nix
Sexton Blake series (493)

Three masks of death
Chance, John Newton
Jonathan Blake series (20)

Three McMahons
Cody, Al
Montana series (11)

Three men and a girl
Chetham-Strode, Warren
Siamese cats series (1)

Three men and Troddles
Andom, R
Troddles series (12)

Three men for the job
Ambler, Dail
Danny Spade series (40)

Three men in a boat, to say nothing of the dog
Jerome, Jerome Klapka
Three men series (1)

Three men on bicycles
Jerome, Jerome Klapka
Three men series (2)

Three men on the bummel
Jerome, Jerome Klapka
Three men series (2)

Three men out
Stout, Rex
Nero Wolfe and Archie Goodwin series (23)

Three Mesquiteers
Macdonald, William Colt
Three Mesquiteers series (10)

Three miles square
Corey, Peter
Three miles square series (1)

Three million dollar turn-over
Curtis, Richard
Dave Bolt series (1)

Three Milly-Molly-Mandy plays
Brisley, Joyce Lankester
Milly-Molly-Mandy series (6)

Three mint lollipops
Sabatier, Robert
Olivier Chateauneuf series (2)

Three-minute universe
Paul, Barbara
Star trek series (41)

Three missing days
Odgers, Sally Farrell
Bandinangi series (3)

Three motives for murder
Winsor, Roy
Ira Cobb series (3)

Three Musketeers
Dumas, Alexandre
Three Musketeers series (1)

Three names for murder
Campbell, Harriette Russell
Simon Brade series (4)

Three-Notch Cameron
Macdonald, William Colt
Gregory Quist series (3)

Three novels
Beckett, Samuel
Jacques Moran series (3)
Fuchs, Daniel
Williamsburg trilogy (3)

Three of a kind
Chase, Emily
Canby Hall series (16)

Three of Clubs
Williams, Valentine
Clubfoot series (5)

Three of diamonds
Knight, Kathleen Moore
Elisha Macomber series (15)

Three of swords
Leiber, Fritz
Fafhrd and Gray Mouser series (3)

Three on a vacation
Hope, Laura Lee
Blythe girls series (5)

Three on the run
Bawden, Nina
Mallory children series (2)

Three pines
Abbott, Jacob
Rainbow and Lucky series (3)

Three-pipe problem
Symons, Julian
Sheridan Haynes series (1)

Three plays from the Orphans' home cycle
Foote, Horton
Orphans' home series (5)

Three plots for Asey Mayo
Taylor, Phoebe Atwood
Asey Mayo series (19)

Three point murder
Finney, R C
Inspector Bourne series (4)

Three pretty men
Cannan, Gilbert
Laurie series (3)

Three problems for Solar Pons
Derleth, August
Solar Pons series (3)

Three queens
Priestley, Margaret
World Dionysus series (2)

Three quick and five dead
Mitchell, Gladys
Dame Beatrice Bradley series (41)

Three R detectives and the milk bottles mystery
Digby, Anne
Three R detectives series (1)

Three R detectives and the mystery of the missing footprints
Digby, Anne
Three R detectives series (2)

Three railway engines
Awdry, Wilbert
Railway series (1)

Three red flares
Divine, David
Mig and Peter Manson series (3)

Three ride north
Conroy, Al
Clayburn series (3)

Three-ring terror
Dixon, Franklin W
Hardy boys series (111)

Three roses
Blasco Ibanez, Vicente
Valencia series (1)

Three sailors
Blyton, Enid
John and Mary series (5)

Three school chums
Finnemore, John
Teddy Lester series (1)

Three score and ten
Thirkell, Angela
Barsetshire series (29)

Three scouts
Trowbridge, John Townsend
Cudjo's cave series (2)

Three-seated space ship
Slobodkin, Louis
Space ship series (3)

Three sheets in the wind
Gilpatric, Guy
Mister Colin Andrew Macthrockle Glencannon series (4)

Three short biers
Starr, Jimmy
Joe Medford series (1)

Three short men
Vivian, Francis
Inspector Gordon Knollis series (1)

Three Sioux scouts
Gregor, Elmer Russell
Western Indian series (3)

Three slips to a noose
Sinclair, Fiona
Inspector Paul Grainger series (4)

Three slugs for Cheyenne
Denver, Lee
Cheyenne Jones series (3)

Three sons and a mother
Cannan, Gilbert
Laurie series (3)

Three spirits of Vandermeer Manor
Anderson, Mary
Mostly ghosts series (4)

Three stamps of death
Grant, Maxwell
Shadow series (263)
Three stars for Star Island
Hall, Margery
Star Island trilogy (3)
Three strings
Lincoln, Natalie Sumner
Inspector Mitchell series (3)
Three stuffed owls
Robertson, Keith
Neil and Swede trilogy (2)
Three Sundays to live
Daniel, Roland
Buddy Mustard series (9)
Three tales of Basil Brush
Firmin, Peter
Basil Brush series (3)
Basil Brush series (8)
Three taps
Knox, Ronald Arbuthnott
Miles Bredon series (1)
Three, the drive
Mann, Francis Oscar
Albert Grope series (3)
Three thirds of a ghost
Fuller, Timothy
Jupiter Jones series (2)
Three-thirteen murders
Black, Thomas B
Al Delaney series (2)
Three, three the rivals
Fraser, Anthea
Inspector David Webb and Sergeant Ken Jackson series (9)
Three tiers of fantasy
Berrow, Norman
Inspector Lancelot Carolus Smith series (1)
Three-time losers
Bagby, George
Inspector Schmidt series (29)
Three times a corpse
Robeson, Kenneth
Doc Savage series (170)
Three to Dorsai
Dickson, Gordon Rupert
Dorsai series (4)
Three to get Reddy
Zacharia, Irwin
Irving Martin Reddy series (4)
Three to ride
Pullein-Thompson, Christine
David and Pat series (3)
Three-toed pussy
Burley, William John
Superintendent Charles Wycliffe series (1)
Three towers in Tuscany
Saville, Malcolm
Marston Baines series (1)
Simon series (1)
Three toymakers
Williams, Ursula Moray
Toymakers series (1)
Three trails
Graydon, William Murray
Sexton Blake series (30)
Three trails to Modoc
Grover, Marshall
Larry and Stretch series (106)
Three trumps sounding
Schmidt, Dennis
Twilight of the gods trilogy (3)
Three Vassar girls abroad
Champney, Elizabeth Williams
Three Vassar girls series (2)
Three Vassar girls at home
Champney, Elizabeth Williams
Three Vassar girls series (6)
Three Vassar girls in England
Champney, Elizabeth Williams
Three Vassar girls series (3)
Three Vassar girls in France
Champney, Elizabeth Williams
Three Vassar girls series (7)
Three Vassar girls in Italy
Champney, Elizabeth Williams
Three Vassar girls series (5)
Three Vassar girls in Russia and Turkey
Champney, Elizabeth Williams
Three Vassar girls series (8)
Three Vassar girls in South America
Champney, Elizabeth Williams
Three Vassar girls series (4)
Three Vassar girls in Switzerland
Champney, Elizabeth Williams
Three Vassar girls series (9)
Three Vassar girls in the Holy Land
Champney, Elizabeth Williams
Three Vassar girls series (11)
Three Vassar girls in the Tyrol
Champney, Elizabeth Williams
Three Vassar girls series (10)
Three Vassar girls on the Rhine
Champney, Elizabeth Williams
Three Vassar girls series (1)
Three went in
Temple-Ellis, N A
Inspector Wren series (1)
Three who died
Derleth, August
Judge Ephraim Peck series (3)
Three who paid
Stuart, Donald
Sexton Blake series (975)
Three wild men
Robeson, Kenneth
Doc Savage series (121)
Three wilderness scouts
Gregor, Elmer Russell
Jim Mason series (5)
Three with a bullet
Lyons, Arthur
Jacob Asch series (8)
Three, with blood
Stein, Aaron Marc
Tim Mulligan and Elsie Mae Hunt series (11)
Three without fear
Du Soe, Robert C
Pedro the fisherman series (1)
Three witnesses
Stout, Rex
Nero Wolfe and Archie Goodwin series (26)
Three wives
Fraser, Alex
Inspector Noel Tracy series (1)
Seymour, Beatrice Kean
Three wives series (1)
Three women in black
Reilly, Helen
Inspector Christopher McKee series (13)
Three wooden overcoats
Clevely, Hugh
Maxwell Archer series (3)
Three yards of cord
Brooks, Collin
O Swete McTavish series (2)
Threefold cord
Vivian, Francis
Inspector Gordon Knollis series (4)
Threefold disappearance
Carter, Nicholas
Nicholas Carter series (626)
Threepence to Marble Arch
McGuire, Paul
Inspector Wittler series (3)
Threepenny bit
Shaw, Jane
Penny series (3)
Threepersons hunt
Garfield, Brian Wynne
Sam Watchman series (2)
Three's a crew
Pinkerton, Kathrene
Shoestring trilogy (2)
Three's a crowd
Cole, Jennifer
Cindy and Nicole series (1)
James, Dean
Melrose Place series (4)
Pascal, Francine
Sweet Valley twins series (7)
Three's a pack
Stranger, Joyce
German Shepherd series (2)
Three's a shroud
Jason
Jason series (9)
Prather, Richard Scott
Shell Scott series (14)
Threes are wild
Masters, Zeke
Faro Blake series (3)
Threshold
Morris, Janet Ellen
Threshold series (1)
Threshold of fear
Rees, Arthur John
Colwin Grey series (1)
Threshold of the stars
Berna, Paul
Michael Jousse series (1)
Thrice Judas
Grierson, Francis Durham
Inspector George Muir series (6)
Thrice the brinded cat hath mew'd
Davies, Robertson
Shakespearean festival in Canada series (3)
Thrice upon a killing spree
Quinn, Patrick
Pete Riley series (3)
Thrift
Blyth, James
Thrift series (1)
Thrill a minute with Jack Albany
Godey, John
Jack Albany series (1)
Thrill club
Stine, Robert Lawrence
Fear Street series (24)
Thrill killers
Novak, Robert
Joe Blaze series (2)
Thrill machine
Hamilton, Ian Sydney
Pete Heysen series (4)
Thriller
Hart, Ted
Thriller series (1)
Thrilling holiday
Cole, Margaret Alice
Judy Lawler series (2)
Thrilling stories for boys
Moore, Fenworth
Jerry Ford series (4)
Thrilling-sweet and rotten
Stuart, Ian
David Grierson series (4)
Thrilling term at Janeways
Brent-Dyer, Elinor Mary
Janeways series (1)
Thro' a Yorkshire window
Riley, William
Windyridge series (2)
Throbbing dark
Arthur, Frank
Inspector Spearpoint series (4)
Throne of council
Oakgrove, Artemis
Throne trilogy (3)
Throne of fire
Rusoff, Garry
Chariots of fire trilogy (2)
Throne of fools
Cole, Adrian
Omaran series (2)
Throne of madness
Sucharitkul, Somtow
Chronicles of the high inquest series (2)
Throne of peril
Hincks, Cyril Malcolm
Sexton Blake series (616)
Throne of Satan
Dark, James
Mark Kingsley Hood series (9)
Throne of Scone
Kennealy, Patricia
Keltiad series (2)
Throne of Zeus
Goodman, Deborah Lerme
Choose your own adventure series (40)
Throne pharaohs
Roberts, Irene
Ancient Egypt series (1)
Through a glass darkly
Gielgud, Val
Inspector Gregory Pellew and Viscount Clymping series (4)
McCloy, Helen
Basil Willing series (8)
Through Apache land
Jayne, R H
War whoop series (2)
Through by daylight
Optic, Oliver
Lake Shore series (1)
Through darkest America
Barrett, Neal
Darkest America series (1)
Through fire and water
Armour, R Coutts
Sexton Blake series (160)
Through forest and fire
Ellis, Edward Sylvester
Wild woods series (2)
Through midnight streets
Lindsay, Philip
Victorian England series (1)
Through night to light
Spielhagen, Friedrich
Prussian series (2)
Through six dimensions
Varney, Allen
Doctor Strange series (2)
Through sorrow's gates
Sutcliffe, Halliwell
Griff Lomax series (2)
Through space to Mars
Rockwood, Roy
Great marvel series (4)
Through space to the planets
Law, Winifred
Ralph Hannon series (1)
Through Spain with Don Quixote
Croft-Cooke, Rupert
Sensual life series (19)
Through streets broad and narrow
Fielding, Gabriel
Blaydon family trilogy (3)
Through swamp and glade
Munroe, Kirk
White conqueror series (3)
Through the air to Alaska
Dixon, Franklin W
Ted Scott flying series (12)
Through the air to the North Pole
Rockwood, Roy
Great marvel series (1)
Through the Behring Strait
Verne, Jules
Fur country series (2)
Through the black hole
Packard, Edward
Choose your own adventure series (97)
Through the cellar wall
Carter, Nicholas
Nicholas Carter series (217)
Through the dark and hairy wood
Herron, Shaun
Miro series (3)
Through the dark curtain
Saxon, Peter
Guardians series (2)
Through the eye of a needle
Clement, Hal
Needle series (2)
Through the eye of the needle
Howells, William Dean
Altruria series (2)
Through the eye of time
Hoyle, Trevor
Christian Queghan series (2)
Through the lens
Massey, Morrell
Thornton Zane series (2)
Through the looking glass
Hooper, Kay
Once upon a time series (4)
Through the looking glass and what Alice found there
Carroll, Lewis
Alice in Wonderland series (2)
Through the Menin Gate
Mottram, Ralph Hale
Spanish Farm series (5)
Through the mill
Mather, Bertrand
Robinson family series (1)
Through the storm
Gibbs, Philip
Second World War series (5)
Through the sun in an airship
Mastin, John
Regina series (2)
Through the wall
Moffett, Cleveland
Paul Coquenil series (1)
Wentworth, Patricia
Miss Maud Silver series (19)
Through the wheat
Boyd, Thomas Alexander
Wheat series (1)
Through the year with Boris Bear
Bruna, Dick
Boris Bear series (3)
Through the year with Harriet
Maestro, Betsy Crippen
Harriet series (9)
Through the Yellowstone with Paul and Peggy
Scott, Florence E
Paul and Peggy series (3)
Throw a kiss, Harry
Chalmers, Mary
Harry series (1)
Throw of a rope
Sadler, Jeff
Marshal Andrew Anderson series (7)
Thrush Green
Read, *Miss*
Thrush Green series (1)
Thug executive
Chance, John Newton
John Marsh series (3)
Thuggery affair
Forest, Antonia
Marlow family series (6)
Thugs and bottles
San Antonio
Berurier series (4)
San Antonio series (4)
Thunda the buffalo
Rutley, Cecil Bernard
Wild life story series (14)
Thunder at dawn
Evans, Alan
David Cochrane series (1)
Gibbs, Henry
South African history series (3)
Thunder Bay threat
Barnes, Michael
Just north series (3)
Thunder bird
Bower, Bertha Muzzy
Skyrider series (2)
Thunder country
Sperry, Armstrong
Chad Powell series (2)
Thunder Dragon Gate
Mundy, Talbot
Jimgrim series (13)
Thunder in Europe
Creasey, John
Department Z series (6)
Thunder in the bay
Seligman, Adrian
Thunder Reef series (2)
Thunder in the East
Maloney, Mack
Wingman series (4)
Thunder in the west
Chisholm, Matt
Storm family series (7)
Thunder in the wind
Shiplett, June Lund
Winds series (5)
Thunder Island
Johns, Larry
Jacky Ryderbeit series (2)
Thunder king
Grant, Maxwell
Shadow series (205)
Thunder-maker
Creasey, John
Doctor Palfrey series (32)
Thunder Moon's challenge
Brand, Max
Thunder Moon series (1)
Thunder Moon's strike
Brand, Max
Thunder Moon series (2)
Thunder Mountain
Siegel, Barbara
Firebrats series (3)
Thunder Mountain massacre
Hardin, J D
Raider and Doc series (72)
Thunder of hell
Austin, Richard
Guardians series (3)
Thunder of stars
Morgan, Dan
Venturer Twelve series (1)
Thunder over Castle Rising
Cradock, Fanny
Lorme family series (6)
Thunder over Spain
Styles, Showell
Ensign Peter Byrd series (2)
Thunder Point
Higgins, Jack
Sean Dillon series (1)
Thunder Range
Cole, Jackson
Jim Hatfield series (11)
Thunder Reef
Seligman, Adrian
Thunder Reef series (1)
Thunder returning
Mittelholzer, Edgar
Leitmotiv series (2)
Thunder riders
Longtree, Warren T
Ruff Justice series (27)
Thunder trail
Scott, Bradford
Walt Slade series (88)
Thunderball
Fleming, Ian
James Bond series (9)
Thunderbird Trail
Macdonald, William Colt
Gregory Quist series (1)
Thunderbird trail
Macdonald, William Colt
Three Mesquiteers series (11)
Thunderbirds
Theydon, John
Thunderbirds series (1)

Thunderbirds are go
Allan, Angus P
Thunderbirds series (4)
Thunderbolt and the rebel planet
Ohlson, Hereward
Thunderbolt series (2)
Thunderbolt at Catfish Bend
Burman, Ben Lucien
Catfish Bend series (7)
Thunderbolt collects
McCulley, Johnston
Thunderbolt series (1)
Thunderbolt of the spaceways
Ohlson, Hereward
Thunderbolt series (1)
Thunderbolt's jest
McCulley, Johnston
Thunderbolt series (3)
Thundercats and the ghost warrior
Stine, Megan
Thundercats series (1)
Thundercats and the snowmen of Hook Mountain
Stine, Megan
Thundercats series (2)
Thundergate
Adair, Denis
MacLeod family series (3)
Thunderhawk
Sharpe, Jon
Trailsman series (59)
Thunderhead
O'Hara, Mary
Flicka series (2)
Thundering guns
Scott, Bradford
Walt Slade series (76)
Thunderstick
Coldsmith, Don
Spanish bit series (21)
Thunderstrike in Syria
Carter, Nick
Nick Carter series (125)
Thunderworld
Hughes, Zach
Rack the Healer series (2)
Thurb revolution
Panshin, Alexei
Anthony Villiers series (2)
Thursday adventure
Pudney, John
Fred and I series (6)
Thursday ahoy!
Bond, Michael
Thursday series (3)
Thursday in Paris
Bond, Michael
Thursday series (4)
Thursday rides again
Bond, Michael
Thursday series (2)
Thursday the Rabbi walked out
Kemelman, Harry
Rabbi David Small series (7)
Thursday turkey murders
Rice, Craig
Bingo Riggs and Handsome Kusak series (2)
Thursday's blade
Davis, Frederick Clyde
Professor Cyrus Hatch series (7)
Thursday's child
Baldwin, Faith
Little Oxford series (6)
Streatfeild, Noel
Thursday's child series (1)
Thursday's follow
Philips, Judson Pentecost
Peter Styles series (5)
Thus to revisit
Ford, Ford Madox
Memories and impressions series (2)
Thus was Adonis murdered
Caudwell, Sarah
Professor Hilary Tamar series (1)
Thuvia, maid of Mars
Burroughs, Edgar Rice
Martian series (4)
Thy arm alone
Slate, John
Black Maria series (4)
Thy brother's wife
Greeley, Andrew Moran
Passover trilogy (1)
Thy friend, Obadiah
Turkle, Brinton
Obadiah series (2)
Thy guilt is great
Smith, C I D
Inspector Barlowe series (1)
Thy hand, great Anarch!
Chaudhuri, Nirad Chandra
Unknown Indian series (3)
Thy sting, oh death
Drummond, John Keith
Matilda Worthing series (1)
Thyme of death
Albert, Susan Wittig
China Bayles series (1)
Ti-Coyo and his shark
Richer, Clement
Ti-Coyo series (1)
Tibber
Mayne, William
Animal library series (3)
Tiberius
Massie, Allan
Roman emperors quartet (2)
Tibet is my country
Norbu, Thubten Jigme
Tibet series (2)
Tibetan foothold
Murphy, Dervla
Full tilt series (2)
Tibetan journey
Patterson, George Neilson
Asian missionary trilogy (1)
Tic-tac-terror
Dixon, Franklin W
Hardy boys series (74)
Tick of death
Lovesey, Peter
Sergeant Cribb and Constable Thackeray series (5)
Tick of the clock
Asbury, Herbert
Inspector Thomas Conroy series (2)
Tick-tock
Ainsworth, Ruth
Little Mushrooms series (2)
Tickel a bushie's fancy
Thorne, Sandy
Queensland series (2)
Ticker-tape murder
Propper, Milton
Tommy Rankin series (2)
Ticket for a seamstick
Harris, Mark
Henry W Wiggen series (3)
Ticket that exploded
Burroughs, William Seward
Tangier trilogy (2)
Ticket to intrigue
Keene, Carolyn
Nancy Drew and the Hardy boys be a detective mystery series (8)
Ticket to ride
Akrill, Caroline
Eventing trilogy (3)
Perry, Ritchie
Philis series (3)
Ticket to the boneyard
Block, Lawrence
Matthew Scudder series (8)
Tickets for death
Halliday, Brett
Michael Shayne series (5)
Ticking clock
Lockridge, Frances
Bill Wiegand series (27)
Mister and Mrs North series (27)
Ticking heart
Olsen, D B
Lieutenant Stephen Mayhew series (3)
Ticking terrors murders
Teilhet, Darwin Le Ora
Baron Von Kaz series (1)
Tickle
Berg, Leila
Chatterbooks series (1)
Tickle, tickle
Oxenbury, Helen
Big baby series (1)
Tickled to death
Brett, Simon
Charles Paris series (15)
Hess, Joan
Claire Malloy series (9)
Ticktock and Jim
Robertson, Keith
Ticktock and Jim series (1)
Ticktock and Jim, deputy sheriffs
Robertson, Keith
Ticktock and Jim series (2)
Tide for the captain
Cresswell, Helen
Sea series (2)
Tide of desire
Clayton, Sheena
Cthulhu Mythos series (12)
Tides and eddies
Casey, Maie
Australian story series (2)
Tide's ending
B B
Wildfowling series (1)
Tides of fortune, 1945-1955
Macmillan, Harold
Winds of change series (3)
Tides of Kregen
Akers, Alan Burt
Dray Prescot series (12)
Tides of light
Benford, Gregory
Galactic Center series (4)
Tides of Malvern
Griswold, Francis
Carolina series (1)
Tides of treachery
Dever, Joe
Legends of Lone Wolf series (3)
Tides of war
Pearsall, Ronald
Oakwood family series (1)
Tides of youth
Scanlan, Nelle Margaret
Pencarrow family series (2)
Tidewater
Dowdey, Clifford
Richmond, Virginia series (2)
Tidewater by steamboat
Holly, David Chauncey
Chesapeke steamboats series (2)
Tidewater tales
Barth, John
Fenwick and Susan series (2)
Tidinbilla adventure
Graves, Richard Harry
Tidinbilla series (2)
Tidy death
Lombard, Nap
Lord Winterstone series (1)
Tidy-up story
Erickson, Karen
I can do it series (3)
Tiebreaker
Bickham, Jack Miles
Brad Smith series (2)
Tied for murder
Fitzsimmons, Cortland
Percy Peacock series (2)
Tied up in tinsel
Marsh, Ngaio
Inspector Roderick Alleyn series (27)
Ties of blood and silver
Rosenberg, Joel
Metzada series (1)
Ties that bind
Adler, Warren
Fiona Fitzgerald series (6)
Tiffany and the swallow rhyme
Reid, Meta Mayne
Tiffany series (2)
Tiffany Street
Weidman, Jerome
Benny Kramer series (3)
Tiger adventure
Price, Willard
Hal and Roger Hunt series (13)
Tiger and the rose
Scannell, Vernon
Tiger and the rose trilogy (1)
Tiger by the tail
Adams, Hunter
Man from Planet X trilogy (2)
Goldman, Lawrence Louis
Johnny Saturday series (2)
Tiger for Malgudi
Narayan, Rasipuram Krishnaswami
Malgudi series (14)
Tiger from the shadows
Jones, Bradshaw
Claude Ravel series (3)
Tiger Gang and the car thieves
Bidwell, Dafne
Tiger Gang series (2)
Tiger Gang and the hijackers
Bidwell, Dafne
Tiger Gang series (1)
Tiger girl
Casserly, Gordon
Jungle series (4)
Tiger Harry
Ross, Tony
Tales from Mister Toffy's circus series (3)
Tiger in red weather
Wyllie, John
Doctor Quarshie series (7)
Tiger in the bush
Chauncy, Nan
Lorenny family series (1)
Tiger in the dark
Patchett, Mary Elwyn
Jeff James series (4)
Tiger in the north
Harvester, Simon
Asia in turmoil series (2)
Tiger in the smoke
Allingham, Margery
Albert Campion series (16)
Tiger in the snow
Unsworth, Walter
Mountaineering trilogy (2)
Tiger in the well
Pullman, Philip
Sally Lockhart series (3)
Tiger Island
Clay, Patrick
Sergeant Hawk series (4)
Tiger Lily
Dilnot, George
Val Emery series (1)
Tiger of Canton
Teed, George Hamilton
Sexton Blake series (504)
Tiger of gold
Jenkins, Robin
Nuranian series (2)
Tiger of Mayfair
Holt, Henry
Inspector Silver series (10)
Tiger of the night
Walsh, James Morgan
Colonel Ormiston series (7)
Tiger of Tibet
Burrard, Gerald
Tiger of Tibet series (1)
Tiger Patrol
Styles, Showell
Tiger Patrol series (1)
Tiger Patrol at sea
Styles, Showell
Tiger Patrol series (3)
Tiger Patrol presses on
Styles, Showell
Tiger Patrol series (4)
Tiger Patrol wins through
Styles, Showell
Tiger Patrol series (2)
Tiger River
Friel, Arthur Olney
McKay, Knowlton and Ryan series (2)
Tiger rose
Eisenberg, Lisa
Laura Brewster series (4)
Tiger shark
Edwards, Hugh
Sea Witch series (1)
Tiger Standish
Horler, Sydney
Sir Harker Bellamy series (2)
Tiger Standish series (1)
Tiger Standish comes back
Horler, Sydney
Sir Harker Bellamy series (3)
Tiger Standish series (2)
Tiger Standish does his stuff
Horler, Sydney
Tiger Standish series (7)
Tiger Standish has a party
Horler, Sydney
Tiger Standish series (8)
Tiger Standish steps on it
Horler, Sydney
Sir Harker Bellamy series (8)
Tiger Standish series (6)
Tiger Standish takes the field
Horler, Sydney
Sir Harker Bellamy series (7)
Tiger Standish series (5)
Tiger strikes again
Wills, Cecil Melville
Superintendent Roger Ellerdine and Sergeant Cherry Blossom series (9)
Tiger, tiger
Case, Patricia
Tiger series (1)
Goodchild, George
Inspector McLean series (48)
Tiger wants more
Bisset, Donald
Tiger series (2)
Tiger war
Pendleton, Don
Mack Bolan series (61)
Tiger who found the trasure
Spain, Nancy
Tiger series (5)
Tiger who saved the train
Spain, Nancy
Tiger series (4)
Tiger who went to the moon
Spain, Nancy
Tiger series (2)
Tiger who won his star
Spain, Nancy
Tiger series (3)
Tiger who wouldn't eat meat
Spain, Nancy
Tiger series (1)
Tigerman of Terrahpur
Lecale, Errol
Specialist series (1)
Tigers and traitors
Verne, Jules
Steam house series (2)
Tigers burning
Evers, Crabbe
Duffy House series (5)
Tiger's claw
Orde, Lewis
Tiger's heart series (2)
Tiger's claws
Robertson, Colin
Vicky McBain series (1)
Tiger's gold
Gilman, George G
Edge series (14)
Tiger's heart
Douglas, Lauren Wright
Caitlin Reece series (4)
Orde, Lewis
Tiger's heart series (1)
Tigers of justice
Wilson, Gar
Phoenix Force series (4)
Phoenix Force series (34)
Tigers of the sea
Howard, Robert Ervin
Cormac Mac Art series (4)
Tight circle
Straker, John Foster
Johnny Inch series (2)
Tight corner
Copper, Basil
Mike Faraday series (23)
Tight lines
Tapply, William George
Brady Coyne series (11)
Walsh, Bill
Fishing series (3)
Tight little island
Mackenzie, Compton
Highland series (3)
Tight spot
Birch, Claire
Lucy Hill series (1)
Tight squeeze
Fuller, William
Brad Dolan series (7)
Tightening string
Bridge, Ann
Julia Probyn series (4)
Tightrope
Melville-Ross, Antony
Treelake series (3)
White, Teri
Blue Maguire and Spaceman Kowalski series (2)
Tigress
Brown, Carter
Lieutenant Al Wheeler series (22)
Janson, Hank
Hank Janson series (192)
Tigress in Prothero
Swinnerton, Frank
Prothero quartet (2)
Tigress in the village
Swinnerton, Frank
Prothero quartet (2)
Tigris leaps
Brand, Kurt
Perry Rhodan series (63)
Tijuana traffic
Scott, Don
Raker series (2)
Tik Tok
Cosgrove, Stephen Edward
Bugg series (10)
Tik-Tok and the nome King
Baum, Lyman Frank
Little Wizard series (6)
Tik-Tok of Oz
Baum, Lyman Frank
Oz series (8)
Tikal
Peters, Daniel
Pre-Columbian trilogy (2)
'Til death
McBain, Ed
Eighty Seventh Precinct series (9)
Tilda Jane
Saunders, Marshall
Tilda Jane series (1)

Tilda Jane's orphans
Saunders, Marshall
Tilda Jane series (2)
Tildy
Fraser, Sara
Tildy series (1)
Till death
McLaglen, John J
Herne the Hunter series (15)
Till death do us part
Carr, John Dickson
Doctor Gideon Fell series (15)
Keene, Carolyn
Nancy Drew files series (24)
Krich, Rochelle Majer
Jessie Drake series (1)
Till I end my song
Gibbings, Robert
Sweet Thames series (2)
Till it hurts
Quarry, Nick
Jake Barrow series (5)
Till the butchers cut him down
Muller, Marcia
Sharon McCone series (15)
Till the end of time
Appel, Allen
Alex Balfour series (3)
Tillerman saga
Voigt, Cynthia
Tillermans series (3)
Tillingfold's tour
Parker, John
Village cricket series (3)
Tilly
Cookson, Catherine
Tilly Trotter trilogy (1)
Tilly alone
Cookson, Catherine
Tilly Trotter trilogy (3)
Tilly and Tessa
Bruna, Dick
Toy box tale series (3)
Tilly Mint and the dodo
Doherty, Berlie
Tilly Mint series (2)
Tilly Mint tales
Doherty, Berlie
Tilly Mint series (1)
Tilly Trotter
Cookson, Catherine
Tilly Trotter trilogy (1)
Tilly Trotter wed
Cookson, Catherine
Tilly Trotter trilogy (2)
Tilly Trotter widowed
Cookson, Catherine
Tilly Trotter trilogy (3)
Tilly wed
Cookson, Catherine
Tilly Trotter trilogy (2)
Tilly's house
Jaques, Faith
Tilly series (1)
Tilly's rescue
Jaques, Faith
Tilly series (2)
Tim all alone
Ardizzone, Edward
Tim series (6)
Tim and Charlotte
Ardizzone, Edward
Tim series (4)
Tim and Emily meet Nessie
Mosley, Francis
Nessie series (3)
Tim and Ginger
Ardizzone, Edward
Tim series (8)
Tim and Lucy go to sea
Ardizzone, Edward
Tim series (2)
Tim Avery's secret
Stahl, Hilda
Wren House series (3)
Tim Frazer again
Durbridge, Francis
Tim Frazer series (2)
Tim Frazer gets the message
Durbridge, Francis
Tim Frazer series (3)
Tim gets a chance
Blyton, Enid
John and Mary series (8)
Tim Hooley's haunting
Craigie, Dorothy
Tim Hooley series (2)
Tim Hooley's hero
Craigie, Dorothy
Tim Hooley series (1)
Tim in danger
Ardizzone, Edward
Tim series (5)
Tim McCoy and the Sandy Gulch stampede
Du Bois, Gaylord
Tim McCoy series (5)
Tim McCoy fighting the Redskins
Wilson, Buck
Tim McCoy series (4)
Tim McCoy in the Prescott Kid
Packer, Eleanor
Tim McCoy series (1)
Tim McCoy in the Westerner
Packer, Eleanor
Tim McCoy series (2)
Tim McCoy on the Tomahawk Trail
Packer, Eleanor
Tim McCoy series (3)
Tim minds the baby
Monckton, Ella
Tim series (2)
Tim minds the shop
Monckton, Ella
Tim series (1)
Tim Mouse
Brook, Judy
Tim Mouse series (1)
Tim Mouse and Father Christmas
Brook, Judy
Tim Mouse series (6)
Tim Mouse and Helen Mouse
Brook, Judy
Tim Mouse series (5)
Tim Mouse and the major
Brook, Judy
Tim Mouse series (2)
Tim Mouse goes down the stream
Brook, Judy
Tim Mouse series (4)
Tim Mouse visits the farm
Brook, Judy
Tim Mouse series (3)
Tim of Tamberly Forest
Byers, Irene
Tim Digby series (1)
Tim Rabbit and company
Uttley, Alison
Timothy Rabbit series (3)
Tim Rabbit's dozen
Uttley, Alison
Timothy Rabbit series (4)
Tim returns to Tamberly
Byers, Irene
Tim Digby series (2)
Tim the scissors grinder
Leslie, Madeline
Tim the scissors grinder series (1)
Tim thinks of something
Monckton, Ella
Tim series (3)
Tim to the lighthouse
Ardizzone, Edward
Tim series (9)
Tim to the rescue
Ardizzone, Edward
Tim series (3)
Timba
Koenig, Lilli
Kiki series (2)
Timber beasts
Stoddard, Charles
Malloy series (4)
Timber line
Murphy, Warren Burton
Destroyer series (42)
Timber war
Hardin, J D
Raider series (10)
Timbered treasure
Wirt, Mildred Augustine
Trailer series (3)
Timbuktu
Smith, David
Jim Stevens series (2)
Time
Allington, Richard L
Beginning to learn series (23)
Pluckrose, Henry
Knowabouts series (3)
Time after time
Appel, Allen
Alex Balfour series (1)
Time-ago lost
Hamilton, Virginia
Jahdu series (2)
Time-ago tales of Jahdu
Hamilton, Virginia
Jahdu series (1)
Time and a place
Humphrey, William
Red River County trilogy (3)
Time and again
Thomas, Helen
Under storm's wing trilogy (3)
Time and change
Timms, Alma
Australian saga series (12)
Time and eternity
Cannan, Gilbert
Laurie series (5)
Time and Mister Bass
Cameron, Eleanor
Tyco Bass series (5)
Time and space
Le Page, Rand
Terran empire series (2)
Time and space of Uncle Albert
Stannard, Russell
Uncle Albert series (1)
Time and the gods
Dunsany, Edward John Moreton Drax Plunkett
Gods of Pegana series (2)
Time and the hour
Baldwin, Faith
Little Oxford series (4)
Spring, Howard
Dillworth trilogy (3)
Time and the hunter
Calvino, Italo
QFWFQ series (2)
Time and the Rani
Baker, Pip
Doctor Who series (127)
Time and the seasons
Kalman, Bobbie
In my world series (12)
Time at the top
Ormondroyd, Edward
Susan Shaw series (1)
Time before this
Monsarrat, Nicholas
Signs of the times series (1)
Time bender
Laumer, Keith
Lafayette O'Leary series (1)
Time bomb
Howard, Hartley
Glenn Bowman series (21)
Kellerman, Jonathan
Alex Delaware series (5)
Tucker, Wilson
Gilbert Nash series (2)
Wilson, Gar
Phoenix Force series (22)
Time bomb at Brillstone
Heide, Florence Parry
Brillstone Apartments series (6)
Time clock of death
Carter, Nick
Nick Carter series (58)
Time enough for love
Heinlein, Robert Anson
Future history series (7)
Lazarus Long series (2)
Time enough to die
Rabe, Peter
Daniel Port series (5)
Time expired
Dunlap, Susan
Jill Smith series (7)
Time exposure
Lutz, John
Alo Nudger series (6)
Time factor
Starr, Roland
Omina series (3)
Time fighters
Butterworth, Michael
Space nineteen ninety nine series (16)
Time-fighters
King, Bernard
Chronicles of the keeper trilogy (2)
Time flight
Grimwade, Peter
Doctor Who series (74)
Time, flow softly
Cato, Nancy
Australian trilogy (2)
Time for a murder
Warren, John Russell
Inspector M'Guire series (3)
Time for a tiger
Burgess, Anthony
Malayan trilogy (1)
Richard Emmis series (1)
Time for bed, Ned
Zinnemann-Hope, Pam
Ned series (1)
Time for Caution
Cheyney, Peter
Lemmy Caution series (12)
Time for dragons
Gentile, Gary
Dragons series (1)
Time for dying
Ross, Jonathan
Superintendent George Rogers series (16)
Time for giving
Briscoe, Jill
Time for series (1)
Time for haste
Bickers, Richard Townshend
Daedalus quartet (2)
Time for killing
Gilman, George G
Edge series (51)
Rowland, John
Inspector Shelley series (18)
Time for living
Briscoe, Jill
Time for series (2)
Hulke, Malcolm
Crossroads series (4)
Time for murder
Saber, Robert O
Max Keene series (2)
Stagg, James
Sexton Blake series (1475)
Time for payment
Kirst, Hans Hellmut
Munich trilogy (3)
Time for pirates
Black, Gavin
Paul Harris series (8)
Time for scandal
Kirst, Hans Hellmut
Munich trilogy (1)
Time for Sherlock Holmes
Dvorkin, David
Sherlock Holmes sequels series (64)
Time for silence
Heath-Miller, Mavis
Hardwick family series (3)
Time for treason
Hesky, Olga
Inspector Tami Shimoni series (2)
Time for truth
Kirst, Hans Hellmut
Munich trilogy (2)
Time for yesterday
Crispin, Ann Carol
Star trek series (39)
Time from the world
Farre, Rowena
Seal morning series (2)
Time garden
Eager, Edward
Magic series (4)
Time gate
Silverberg, Robert
Time gate series (1)
Time gladiator
Reynolds, Mack
Joe Mauser series (3)
Time in a city
Cooper, Gordon
Kate Bassett series (2)
Time is an ambush
Clifford, Francis
Spanish duet series (2)
Time is ripe
Zweig, Arnold
Werner Bertin and Lenore Wahl series (1)
Time is, time was, time yet to be
Stewart, Janet
Star trek fan series (26)
Time it takes
Stafford, Ann
Victorian and Edwardian London life series (4)
Time keeper
Bartholomew, Barbara
Time keeper trilogy (1)
Time limit
Sheckley, Robert
Stephen Dain series (5)
Time lord
Darvill-Evans, Peter
Doctor Who series (154)
Time machine
Bethancourt, Tomas Ernesto
Time traveller series (6)
Wells, Herbert George
Time traveller series (1)
Time machine to the rescue
Keith, Donald
Time machine series (2)
Time machine 2
Morhaim, Joe
Time traveller series (6)
Grant, Maxwell
Shadow series (201)
Time masters
Tucker, Wilson
Gilbert Nash series (1)
Time meddler
Robinson, Nigel
Doctor Who series (126)
Time monster
Dicks, Terrance
Doctor Who series (102)
Time nomads
Axler, James
Deathlands series (11)
Time of change
Fraser, Mary
Village trilogy (3)
Torr, Iain
Gamboney series (1)
Time of death
Cosic, Dobrica
This land, this time series (2)
This land, this time series (4)
Time of drums
Ehle, John
North Carolina series (3)
Time of dying
Kirk, Richard
Raven series (5)
Time of exile
Kerr, Katharine
Deverry series (5)
Rhodry series (1)
Time of fine weather
Scott, Jack S
Chief Inspector Peter Parsons series (1)
Time of ghosts
Kirk, Richard
Raven series (2)
Time of gifts
Fermor, Patrick Leigh
On foot series (1)
Time of her life, and other stories
Robinson, Maude
Quaker tales series (1)
Time of hope
Kelly, Susan
Alison Hope and Inspector Nick Trevellyan series (2)
Snow, Charles Percy
Strangers and brothers series (1)
Time of justice
Kerr, Katharine
Rhodry series (4)
Time of love
Baker, Carin Greenberg
Last summer, first love series (1)
Pagnol, Marcel
Remembrances of childhood series (3)
Time of omens
Kerr, Katharine
Rhodry series (2)
Time of peace
Williams, Ben Ames
Thread of scarlet series (4)
Time of secrets
Pagnol, Marcel
Remembrances of childhood series (2)
Time of temptation
Audemars, Pierre
Monsieur Pinaud series (9)
Time of terror
Pentecost, Hugh
Pierre Chambrun series (11)
Time of the annihilator
Morressy, John
Iron angel series (4)
Time of the crime
Stuart, Donald
Sexton Blake series (976)
Time of the damned
Pike, Charles R
Jubal Cade series (18)
Time of the dark
Hambly, Barbara
Darwath trilogy (1)
Time of the dragons
Shea, Robert
Shike series (1)
Time of the fox
Costello, Matthew John
Time warrior series (1)
Time of the harvest
Wibberley, Leonard
Man of liberty series (4)
Time of the hawklords
Butterworth, Michael
Hawklords series (1)
Time of the seventh moon
Roberts, Irene
China trilogy (2)

Time of the transference
Foster, Alan Dean
Spellsinger series (6)
Time of the twins
Weis, Margaret
DragonLance legends trilogy (1)
Time of the wolf
Mason, Paul
Robin of Sherwood series (4)
Time of the Wolf
Muir, James A
Breed series (7)
Time of the young soldiers
Richter, Hans Peter
Friedrich trilogy (3)
Time of war
Hocking, Mary
Fleet Air Arm training series (1)
Kerr, Katharine
Rhodry series (3)
Time off for death
Braddon, George
Michael Gaunt series (4)
Time off for murder
Popkin, Zelda
Mary Carner Whittaker series (2)
Time out
Wharton, Joanna
Campus fever series (5)
Time out of mind
Grant, Joan
Far memory series (4)
Time Patrol
Anderson, Poul
Time Patrol series (3)
Time Patrolman
Anderson, Poul
Time Patrol series (2)
Time piece
Jacob, Naomi
Marsden family series (1)
Time piper
Huddy, Delia
Tom Humboldt series (1)
Time pressure
Robinson, Spider
Mindkiller series (2)
Time raider
Stine, Robert Lawrence
Twistaplot series (1)
Time regained
Proust, Marcel
Remembrance of things past series (12)
Time remembered
Finn, Ralph Leslie
Aldgate series (1)
Read, *Miss*
Time remembered series (2)
Time remembered after Pere Lachaise
Holland, Vyvyan
Time remembered series (2)
Time rope
Leeson, Robert
Time rope series (1)
Time running out
Crane, Robert
Ben Corbin series (6)
Time since death
Cornwell, Patricia Daniels
Doctor Kay Scarpetta series (5)
Time terror
Robeson, Kenneth
Doc Savage series (102)
Time to be a friend
Lansing, Karen E
Time series (2)
Time to be born
Lang-Sims, Lois
Time to be born series (1)
Time to betray
Boggis, David
Killer instinct series (2)
Time to change hats
Bennett, Margot
John Davies series (1)
Time to choose
Boissard, Janine
Moreau trilogy (3)
Time to dance, no time to weep
Godden, Rumer
No time to weep series (2)
Time to die
Douglas, George
Inspector Hallam and Sergeant Spratt series (10)
Johns, Larry
Jacky Ryderbeit series (5)
Lawrence, Hilda
Mark East series (2)
Severn, Donald
Garrett dossier series (1)
Time to fly
Lansing, Karen E
Time series (1)
Time to get out of the bath, Shirley
Burningham, John
Shirley series (2)
Time to go on a diet, Fred
Edwards, Pat
Fred series (14)
Time to hate
Truss, Seldon
Inspector Gidleigh series (17)
Time to hit out
Parks, Jim
Runs in the sun series (2)
Time to keep
Sutherland, Halliday
Arches of the years series (2)
Time to kill
Barling, Charles
Inspector George Marshall series (8)
Household, Geoffrey
Roger Taine series (2)
Lynch, Miriam
Nell Willard series (1)
Ormerod, Roger
David Mallin and George Coe series (1)
Pendleton, Don
Mack Bolan series (108)
Reed, Wallace
Sheriff Bill Lloyd series (1)
Robertson, Colin
Superintendent Bradley series (2)
Walsh, James Morgan
Mike Harman series (3)
Time to love
Benary, Margot
Annegret series (3)
Time to murder and create
Block, Lawrence
Matthew Scudder series (4)
Time to prey
Kane, Frank
Johnny Liddell series (14)
Time to reap
Hinkemeyer, Michael Thomas
Sheriff Emil Whippletree series (2)
Time to sleep
Aston, Elizabeth
I am growing up series (3)
Time to tell
Jenkins, Jerry Bruce
Tara Chadwick series (2)
Time to time
Pendleton, Don
Ashton Ford series (6)
Time to weep
Christie, Anne
First act series (3)
Time traders
Norton, Andre
Time war series (1)
Time trap
Byrne, Stuart James
Star Man series (2)
Corris, Peter
Pokerface series (7)
Favors, Jean M
Micro adventure series (4)
Time trap gambit
Maddock, Larry
Hannibal Fortune and Webley series (4)
Time trap of Ming XIII
Steffanson, Con
Flash Gordon series (5)
Time travelers strictly cash
Robinson, Spider
Callahan's Crosstime Saloon series (2)
Time-traveller's guide
Haining, Peter
Doctor Who series (162)
Time trial
Murphy, Warren Burton
Destroyer series (53)
Time trilogy
L'Engle, Madeleine
Meg Murry series (3)
Time tunnel
Leinster, Murray
Time tunnel series (1)
Time twister
Major, H M
Alien trace series (2)
Time wanderers
Strugatsky, Arkady
Maxim trilogy (3)
Time was
Roberts, Nora
Hornblower saga series (1)
Time well spent
Cheesman, Evelyn
Time well spent series (2)
Time when
McCaffrey, Anne
Pern and the Red Planet series (6)
Time window
Byrne, Stuart James
Star Man series (1)
Time windows
Reiss, Kathryn
Time windows series (1)
Time without clocks
Lindsay, Joan
Time without clocks series (1)
Time without end
Jennings, D K
Doctor Ralph Conway series (16)
Timecrime, Inc.
Doyle, Debra
Time tours series (3)
Timefall
Kahn, James
New world trilogy (3)
Timekeeper
Rodda, Emily
Timekeeper series (2)
Timekeeper conspiracy
Hawke, Simon
Timewars series (2)
Timelapse
Nighbert, David Franklin
Anton Stryker series (1)
Timelash
McCoy, Glen
Doctor Who series (105)
Timeless land
Dark, Eleanor
Mannion family series (1)
Timeliner trilogy
Meredith, Richard Carlton
Timeliner trilogy (3)
Timelock
Cory, Desmond
Feramontov quintet (4)
Johnny Fedora series (15)
Timelocke
Barnao, Jack
John Locke series (3)
Timepiece
Ball, Brian Neville
Time series (1)
Timepit
Ball, Brian Neville
Time series (3)
Timepivot
Ball, Brian Neville
Time series (2)
Times change
Roberts, Nora
Hornblower saga series (2)
Time's dark laughter
Kahn, James
New world trilogy (2)
Time's end
Lupoff, Richard Allen
Sun's end series (3)
Time's fool
Veryan, Patricia
Tales of the jewelled men series (1)
Time's harvest
Charques, Dorothy
Time's harvest trilogy (1)
Time's harvest trilogy (3)
Time's last gift
Farmer, Philip Jose
Opar series (3)
Time's lonely one
Scheer, Karl Herbert
Perry Rhodan series (42)
Times of alchemy
Topelius, Zacharias
Surgeon's stories series (6)
Times of battle and of rest
Topelius, Zacharias
Surgeon's stories series (2)
Times of Charles XII
Topelius, Zacharias
Surgeon's stories series (3)
Times of Frederick I
Topelius, Zacharias
Surgeon's stories series (4)
Times of Gustaf Adolf
Topelius, Zacharias
Surgeon's stories series (1)
Times of Linnaeus
Topelius, Zacharias
Surgeon's stories series (5)
Times past
James, William M
Apache series (25)
Times Square connection
Scarpetta, Frank
Marksman series (22)
Time's thievish progress
Rothenstein, John
Summer's lease trilogy (3)
Timeslip!
Leinster, Murray
Time tunnel series (2)
Timetable murder
Denbie, Roger
Doctor Quentin Pace series (1)
Timetrap
Dvorkin, David
Star trek series (40)
Timid tycoon
Frazer, Robert Caine
Mark Kilby series (1)
Timmy and Bingo
Vallance, Rosalind
Timmy series (5)
Timmy and Janet
Vallance, Rosalind
Timmy series (2)
Timmy and Roger
Vallance, Rosalind
Timmy series (3)
Timmy in the country
Vallance, Rosalind
Timmy series (4)
Timmy moves house
Vallance, Rosalind
Timmy series (6)
Timmy Tiger and the butterfly net
Oona, Katherine Deme
Timmy Tiger series (2)
Timmy Tiger and the elephants
Oetting, Ray
Timmy Tiger series (1)
Timmy Tiger and the masked bandit
Oona, Katherine Deme
Timmy Tiger series (1)
Timmy Tiger to the rescue
Oetting, Ray
Timmy Tiger series (2)
Timmy Tiger's new coat
Oetting, Ray
Timmy Tiger series (3)
Timmy Tiger's new friend
Oetting, Ray
Timmy Tiger series (4)
Timmy Turnpenny
Vallance, Rosalind
Timmy series (1)
Timmy Turnpenny's secret
Vallance, Rosalind
Timmy series (7)
Timothy and Tiptoes
Byers, Irene
Tiptoes series (1)
Timothy and two witches
Storey, Margaret
Timothy, Ellen and Melinda series (1)
Timothy Baines
Culp, John Hewett
Five Civilized Tribes series (1)
Timothy Dexter revisited
Marquand, John Phillips
Timothy Dexter series (2)
Timothy files
Sanders, Lawrence
Timothy Cone series (1)
Timothy in the land of storybooks
Smyth, Reitta
Timothy series (2)
Timothy, Minikin and all
Hillyard, Mary Dorothea
Minikin series (4)
Timothy of the Cay
Taylor, Theodore
Cay series (1)
Timothy on tour
Smyth, Reitta
Timothy series (3)
Timothy travels
Storey, Margaret
Timothy, Ellen and Melinda series (5)
Timothy's game
Sanders, Lawrence
Timothy Cone series (2)
Tim's friend Towser
Ardizzone, Edward
Tim series (7)
Tim's last voyage
Ardizzone, Edward
Tim series (10)
Tim's new friends
Ryder, Eileen
Tim series (1)
Tim's rainy day
Ryder, Eileen
Tim series (2)
Timur the tiger
Rutley, Cecil Bernard
Wild life story series (5)
Tin badge
Edwards, Josh
John Stone series (3)
Tin bath murder
Hugi, Maurice G
Martin Speed series (9)
Tin can people
Bond, Edward
War plays series (2)
Tin cravat
Hunter, Jack Dayton
Blue Max series (3)
Tin drum
Grass, Gunter
Danzig trilogy (1)
Tin mine
Eagar, Frances
Laura and Harry series (2)
Tin-plate
Steed, Neville
Peter Marklin series (1)
Tin princess
Pullman, Philip
Sally Lockhart series (4)
Tin star shadow
Grover, Marshall
Larry and Stretch series (253)
Tin-star target
Cole, Jackson
Jim Hatfield series (91)
Tin stars for tall Texans
Grover, Marshall
Larry and Stretch series (144)
Tin toys
Holden, Ursula
Tin toys series (1)
Tin Woodman of Oz
Baum, Lyman Frank
Oz series (12)
Tina and the latchkey child
Oterdahl, Jeanna
Tina series (2)
Tina's dangerous secret
Stahl, Hilda
Tina series (2)
Tina's eighteenth summer
Stahl, Hilda
Tina series (7)
Tina's elusive enemy
Stahl, Hilda
Tina series (3)
Tina's first love
Stahl, Hilda
Tina series (1)
Tina's reluctant friend
Stahl, Hilda
Tina series (4)
Tina's secret rival
Stahl, Hilda
Tina series (6)
Tina's surprise romance
Stahl, Hilda
Tina series (8)
Tina's unwelcome intruder
Stahl, Hilda
Tina series (5)
Tincture of death
Harrison, Ray
Sergeant Joseph Bragg and Constable James Morton series (8)
Tincture of murder
Scott, Sutherland
Doctor Septimus Dodds series (9)
Tincup railroad war
Hardin, J D
Raider and Doc series (55)
Tinfish run
Bassett, Ronald
Lobby Ludd trilogy (1)
Tingalayo
Raffi
Raffi songs to read series (5)
Tinhorn murder case
Grover, Marshall
Larry and Stretch series (307)
Tink goes fishing
Mayer, Mercer
Tink, tonk tales series (3)
Tinka and his friends
Downing, Brownie
Tinka series (1)

Tinka and the bunyip
Downing, Brownie
Tinka series (2)
Tinka bakes a cake
Mayer, Mercer
Tink, tonk tales series (1)
Tinker and Tanker
Scarry, Richard
Tinker and Tanker series (1)
Tinker and Tanker and the pirates
Scarry, Richard
Tinker and Tanker series (4)
Tinker and Tanker and their space ship
Scarry, Richard
Tinker and Tanker series (3)
Tinker and Tanker in Africa
Scarry, Richard
Tinker and Tanker series (6)
Tinker and Tanker, Knights of the Round Table
Scarry, Richard
Tinker and Tanker series (5)
Tinker and Tanker out west
Scarry, Richard
Tinker and Tanker series (2)
Tinker and Tanker tales of pirates and knights
Scarry, Richard
Tinker and Tanker series (6)
Tinker, tailor, soldier, spy
Le Carre, John
George Smiley series (5)
Tinker Tess
Tranter, Nigel Godwin
Tinker Tess series (1)
Tinker's Castle
Mantle, Winifred
Lesters and Westcotts series (2)
Tinker's lone hand
Murray, Andrew
Sexton Blake series (94)
Tinker's summer
Reid, Meta Mayne
Kate and Lynn series (1)
Tinkham Brothers' Tide Mill
Trowbridge, John Townsend
Tide Mill series (1)
Tinkle the trick pony
Barnum, Richard
Kneetime animal stories series (9)
Tinkling symbol
Taylor, Phoebe Atwood
Asey Mayo series (6)
Tinktonks find a home
Mayer, Mercer
Tink, tonk tales series (6)
Tinseltown murders
Blumenthal, John
Mac Slade series (2)
Tintin action play book
Herge
Tintin series (26)
Tintin and the broken ear
Herge
Tintin series (6)
Tintin and the Golden Fleece
Herge
Tintin series (21)
Tintin and the lake of sharks
Herge
Tintin series (25)
Tintin and the Picaros
Herge
Tintin series (26)
Tintin games book
Herge
Tintin series (26)
Tintin in America
Herge
Tintin series (3)
Tintin in Tibet
Herge
Tintin series (20)
Tintin poster book
Herge
Tintin series (26)
Tintin's moon adventure painting book
Herge
Tintin series (26)
Tiny Carteret
Sapper
Ronald Standish series (1)
Tiny diamond
Russell, Charlotte Murray
Jane Amanda Edwards series (3)
Tiny Spook's guessing game
Sandberg, Inger
Little Spook series (3)
Tiny Spook's tugging game
Sandberg, Inger
Little Spook series (6)
Tiny Spook's tumbles
Sandberg, Inger
Little Spook series (4)
Tiny story of Blinky Bill
Wall, Dorothy
Blinky Bill series (4)
Tip on a dead crab
Murray, William Buckley
Lou Anderson series (1)
Tippet shows off Washington
Curtin, Patricia Romero
Show off series (2)
Tipple in the deep
Wood, James
Tipple in the deep series (1)
Tipster
Verner, Gerald
Superintendent Robert Budd series (17)
Tiptilt
Wied, Marie Elisabeth
Tiptilt series (1)
Tiptilt and the pixie
Wied, Marie Elisabeth
Tiptilt series (2)
Tiptilt and the trolls
Wied, Marie Elisabeth
Tiptilt series (3)
Tiptoes wins through
Byers, Irene
Tiptoes series (2)
Tis the season
Gilden, Mel
Beverly Hills 90210 series (4)
'Tis the season to be dying
Drummond, John Keith
Matilda Worthing series (2)
Tish
Rinehart, Mary Roberts
Tish series (2)
Tish marches on
Rinehart, Mary Roberts
Tish series (5)
Tish plays the game
Rinehart, Mary Roberts
Tish series (4)
Tisi and the pageant
Dutton, Geoffrey
Tisi series (2)
Tisi and the yabby
Dutton, Geoffrey
Tisi series (1)
Tisket, a casket
Linklater, Joseph Lane
Silas Booth series (6)
Titan
Dreiser, Theodore
Frank Cowperwood trilogy (2)
Jackson, Steve
Fighting fantasy gamebook series (46)
Varley, John
Gaea trilogy (1)
Titanic Hotel mystery
Hawk, John
Mortimer Sark series (4)
Titans
Jakes, John
Kent family series (5)
Titan's duel
Streib, Dan
Steve Crown series (6)
Titch
Hutchins, Pat
Titch series (1)
Tithe war mystery
Chester, Gilbert
Sexton Blake series (842)
Title is murder
Nelson, Hugh Lawrence
Steve Johnson series (1)
Titled counterfeiter
Carter, Nicholas
Nicholas Carter series (1)
Titty and Tatty by the river
Vallance, Rosalind
Tittymouse and Tattymouse series (2)
Titty and Tatty's housewarming
Vallance, Rosalind
Tittymouse and Tattymouse series (3)
Tittymouse and Tattymouse
Vallance, Rosalind
Tittymouse and Tattymouse series (1)
Titty's dead
Hobson, Polly
Inspector Basil series (2)
Titus
Kingsley, Florence Morse
Early Christian series (1)
Titus alone
Peake, Mervyn
Titus Groan trilogy (3)
Titus Bear goes to school
Kosikowski, Renate
Titus Bear series (1)
Titus Bear goes to the beach
Hall, Mark
Titus Bear series (2)
Kosikowski, Renate
Titus Bear series (2)
Titus Bear's autumn
Kosikowski, Renate
Titus Bear series (5)
Titus Bear's spring
Kosikowski, Renate
Titus Bear series (3)
Titus Bear's summer
Kosikowski, Renate
Titus Bear series (4)
Titus Bear's winter
Kosikowski, Renate
Titus Bear series (6)
Titus books
Peake, Mervyn
Titus Groan trilogy (3)
Titus Groan
Peake, Mervyn
Titus Groan trilogy (1)
Titus unbound
Peake, Mervyn
Titus Groan trilogy (3)
TNT
Masters, Doug
TNT series (1)
To a dubious salvation
Leroux, Etienne
Welgevonden trilogy (3)
To Alaska for gold
Stratemeyer, Edward L
Bound to succeed series (3)
To an unknown shore
Jakes, John
Kent family series (1)
To and again
Brooks, Walter Rollin
Freddy the pig series (1)
To any lengths
Simenon, Georges
Inspector Jules Maigret series (25)
To Arkon!
Darlton, Clark
Perry Rhodan series (30)
To arms, to arms, in Dixie!
Edson, John Thomas
Floating Outfit series (33)
To auntie, with love
De Manio, Jack
Auntie series (1)
To battle the gods
Green, Sharon
Jalav series (5)
To be a country doctor
Duncan, Alex
Country doctor series (1)
To be a dancer
Bernard, Elizabeth
Satin slippers series (1)
To be a farmer's girl
Layberry, Layton George Joseph
Oakleigh Farm series (3)
To be a nurse
Collins, Lynne
Brook's Hospital series (1)
To be an author
Allan, Mabel Esther
Author series (1)
To be pilgrim
Cary, Joyce
Art trilogy (2)
To be the best
Bradford, Barbara Taylor
Emma Harte series (3)
To bed on Thursday
Brode, Anthony
Country vicarage series (2)
To cache a millionaire
Scherf, Margaret
Grace Severance series (3)
To catch a bunyip
Sharp, Allen
Storytrails series (26)
To catch a forger
Wallace, Robert
Essington Holt series (1)
To catch a rat
Harris, Walter
New Avengers series (3)
To catch a spy
Sanders, Bruce
Howard Digburn series (2)
To catch a thief
Burton, Miles
Inspector Arnold and Desmond Merrion series (9)
Thayer, Lee
Peter Clancy series (13)
To catch a viper
Wyllie, John
Doctor Quarshie series (3)
To catch an angel
Russell, Robert William
World I cannot see series (1)
To cease upon the midnight
Hocking, Anne
Inspector William Austen series (29)
To comfort the signora
Cousins, Edmund George
Brigadier Worrall series (1)
Captain Moffat series (2)
To comfort the Signora
Cousins, Edmund George
Larry Grail series (2)
To conquer the throne
Sullivan, Tim
V series (12)
To control the stars
Hoskins, Robert
Master of the stars trilogy (2)
To demons bound
Vardeman, Robert Edward
Swords of Raemllyn series (1)
To die a little
Jobson, Hamilton
Inspector Anders series (12)
To die in Beverly Hills
Petievich, Gerald
Charles Carr and Jack Kelly series (3)
To die in Italbar
Zelazny, Roger
Isle of the dead series (2)
To dream of evil
Comer, Ralph
Robert Lawson series (2)
To dusty death
McCutcheon, Hugh
Richard Logan series (1)
Sperber, Manes
Doino Faber trilogy (2)
To each his own
Brooke, Carol
Marshall family series (5)
To earn a dollar
Tetlow, L D
Brogan McNally series (9)
To end all war
Ahern, Jerry
Survivalist series (21)
To entertain a queen
Birt, David
Tudors series (15)
To escape the stars
Hoskins, Robert
Master of the stars trilogy (3)
To everything a season
Glover, Judith
Sussex quartet (3)
To far horizons
Jennings, D K
Doctor Ralph Conway series (19)
To feed the hungry
Dolci, Danilo
Sicilian inquiry series (2)
To glory we steer
Kent, Alexander
Captain Richard Bolitho series (6)
To guard the right
Zachary, Hugh
Tusk Smith series (1)
To have and to hold
Johnston, Mary
Virginian series (1)
To have and to kill
Martin, Robert Lee
Jim Bennett series (11)
To heal the sick
Rodney, Jonathan
To heal series (1)
To hell in a basket
Blacker, Irwin Robert
General Le Grande and GENOPS series (4)
To his just deserts
Low, Ona
Arvo Laurila series (1)
To horse and away
Harris, Catherine
Marsham family series (4)
To Jess, with love and memories
Johnston, Norma
Carlisle chronicles series (2)
To jump a log
Barrett, Helen Elizabeth-Anne
West family series (3)
To keep or kill
Tucker, Wilson
Charles Horne series (2)
To keep the ball rolling
Powell, Anthony
To keep the ball rolling series (4)
To keep the oath
Bradley, Marion Zimmer
Darkover series (12)
To keep the ship
Chandler, Arthur Bertram
John Grimes series (18)
To keep us free
Allis, Marguerite
Ashbel Field series (2)
To kill a call girl
Foxall, Peter Augustus
Catford Police series (4)
To kill a cat
Burley, William John
Superintendent Charles Wycliffe series (2)
To kill a coconut
Moyes, Patricia
Henry and Emmy Tibbett series (13)
To kill a corpse
Ascher, Eugene
Lucian Carolus series (1)
To kill a judge
Ogan, George
Johnny Bordelon series (1)
To kill a shadow
Drumm, D B
Traveler series (4)
To kill a witch
Knox, Bill
Inspector Colin Thane and Phil Moss series (12)
To kill again
Stout, Rex
Nero Wolfe and Archie Goodwin series (3)
To know is to die
Guenter, C H
Robert Urban series (2)
To let
Galsworthy, John
Forsyte saga trilogy (3)
To live again
Marshall, Catherine
Peter Marshall series (2)
To live and die in Dixie
Trocheck, Kathy Hogan
Callahan Garrity series (2)
To live in peace
Friedman, Rosemary
Shelton family series (3)
To London with love
Barlette, Danielle
Mirrors series (2)
To love and be wise
Tey, Josephine
Inspector Alan Grant series (4)
To love and to dream
Dubus, Elizabeth Nell
Where love rules series (2)
To love and yet to die
Frances, Stephen Daniel
John Gail series (2)
To make a killing
Bedford, Jean
Anna Southwood series (2)
Thomson, June
Inspector Finch series (9)
To make a light
Moray, Helga
Katie and Paul Van Riebeck series (6)
To market, to market!
Spier, Peter
Mother Goose library series (2)
To mend a heart
Harrison, Elizabeth
Central London Hospital series (11)
To outer space
Johns, William Earl
Rex Clinton series (4)
To play the devil
Hall, Angus
Devilday series (2)
To please myself
Starr, Leonard
To please myself series (1)
To please myself again
Starr, Leonard
To please myself series (2)

To pluck a rose
Marten, Jacqueline
Wars of independence trilogy (1)
To prime the pump
Chandler, Arthur Bertram
John Grimes series (8)
Rim series (2)
To raise a rainbow
Savory, Teo
Stonecroft series (3)
To ride Pegasus
McCaffrey, Anne
Pegasus series (1)
To Russia with L.U.S.T.
Gray, Rod
Lady from L.U.S.T. series (6)
To sail beyond the sunset
Heinlein, Robert Anson
Future history series (9)
Lazarus Long series (4)
To sail the century sea
Edmondson, Garry Cotton
Alice series (2)
To sea in a sieve
Bull, Peter
Bulls series (1)
To sea with Sanu
Baker, Denys Val
Cornish series (4)
To see your face again
Price, Eugenia
Savannah quartet (2)
To seek a star
Ebel, Suzanne
Sir Robert Waring series (3)
To serve a queen
Bell, Josephine
English Civil War series (1)
To serve them all my days
Delderfield, Ronald Frederick
To serve them all my days series (2)
To Sir, with love
Braithwaite, Edward Ricardo
Sir series (1)
To sleep, perchance to dream
Sims, L V
Dixie T Struthers series (3)
To speak for the dead
Levine, Paul
Jake Lassiter series (1)
To spite her face
Dolson, Hildegarde
Lucy Ramsdale series (1)
To stalk a specter
Hawke, Simon
Batman series (9)
To study a long silence
Clinton-Baddeley, Victor Clinton
Doctor Davie series (5)
To Sunset and beyond
Lea, Alec
Varden family series (1)
To tame a sister
Avery, Gillian
Julia and Henry Gresham trilogy (1)
Mister Copplestone series (3)
To tell the truth
Chase, Emily
Canby Hall series (15)
To tell you the truth
Merrick, Leonard
Parisian series (5)
To the best of my memory
Terhune, Albert Payson
My memory series (2)
To the castle
Horgan, Paul
Humble powers trilogy (3)
To the coral strand
Masters, John
Savage family series (7)
To the death
Bell, Robert Vaughn
McGowan family series (5)
Macdonnell, James Edmond
Dutchy Holland series (20)
To the death, Senor Kane
Masterson, Louis
Morgan Kane series (24)
To the devil, a daughter
Wheatley, Dennis
Molly Fountain series (1)
To the Eagle's nest
Di Mona, Joseph
George Williams series (3)
To the ends of the earth
Carter, Nicholas
Nicholas Carter series (581)
To the far blue mountains
L'Amour, Louis
Sackett family series (2)
To the front
King, Charles
Cadet series (2)
To the gondolas
Baron, Nicole de
Penelope and Guillaume series (2)
Buron, Nicole de
Penelope and Guillaume trilogy (2)
To the gutter
Romains, Jules
Men of goodwill series (11)
To the harbor light
Hough, Henry Beetle
Martha's Vineyard series (3)
To the haunted mountains
Emerson, Ru
Nedao trilogy (1)
To the hilt
Wren, Percival Christopher
Khairastan series (2)
Major Hazelrigg series (2)
To the is-land
Frame, Janet
Is-land trilogy (1)
To the Isles of Spice
Clune, Frank
Discovery series (5)
To the land of the caribou
Tomlinson, Paul Greene
Four classmates series (1)
To the land of the living
Silverberg, Robert
Gilgamesh series (2)
To the magic born
Stasheff, Christopher
Gramarye series (2)
To the place of shells
Ferguson, Sarah
Guard within series (1)
To the quayside
Golding, Louis
Elsie Silver series (5)
To the rescue
Tranter, Nigel Godwin
Tinker Tess series (2)
To the Sargasso Sea
McPherson, William
Sargasso Sea series (2)
To the stars
Harrison, Harry
To the stars trilogy (3)
Romains, Jules
Men of goodwill series (12)
To the sun?
Verne, Jules
Hector Servadac series (1)
To the turn of the tide
Powell, Jonathan
Ashton family series (2)
To the victor the spoils
Gallagher, Jock
Archers of Ambridge series (5)
To the wild sky
Southall, Ivan
Survival series (1)
To the wood no more
Raymond, Ernest
London gallery series (13)
To this favour
Gilruth, Susan
Inspector Hugh Gordon and Liane Crawford series (5)
To trick a witch
Elliot, Margaret
Witch's gold trilogy (3)
To wake the dead
Carr, John Dickson
Doctor Gideon Fell series (8)
To warm the earth
Belden, David
Galactic connectivity series (2)
To whom be the glory
Mason, Francis Van Wyck
American Civil War, naval series (3)
To whom the glory?
Mackinnon, Charles Roy
Scottish chronicle series (3)
To win and to lose
Netzen, Klaus
Killers series (1)
To worlds unknown
Johns, William Earl
Rex Clinton series (7)
To you, Mister Chips
Hilton, James
Mister Chips series (2)
To your scattered bodies go
Farmer, Philip Jose
Riverworld series (1)
Toad enters a show
Trueman, Brian
Riverbend and Wildwood tales series (2)
Toad for Tuesday
Erickson, Russell Everett
Warton Toad series (1)
Toad of Toad Hall
Milne, Alan Alexander
Toad Hall series (1)
Toad, photographer
Jones, Nicholas
Wind in the willows series (13)
Toad poems
Locklin, Gerald
Toad series (1)
Toad turns fifty
Locklin, Gerald
Toad series (5)
Toad's castle
Uttley, Alison
Little Brown Mouse series (4)
Toad's Europe
Locklin, Gerald
Toad series (2)
Toast for tomorrow
Coles, Manning
Tommy Hambledon series (2)
Toast of the town
Ley, Alice Chetwynd
Eversley Family series (2)
Toast to a corpse
Hume, David
Mick Cardby series (24)
Toba
Mark, Michael
Toba series (1)
Toba at the hands of a thief
Mark, Michael
Toba series (2)
Tobermillin Oracle
Reid, Meta Mayne
Tiffany series (5)
Tobermory's big surprise
Beresford, Elisabeth
Little Wombles series (8)
Tobias
Eldon, Magdalen
Tobias series (1)
Tobias two
Eldon, Magdalen
Tobias series (2)
Tobin down under
Morgan, Stanley
Russ Tobin series (12)
Tobin for hire
Morgan, Stanley
Russ Tobin series (9)
Tobin in Las Vegas
Morgan, Stanley
Russ Tobin series (10)
Tobin in paradise
Morgan, Stanley
Russ Tobin series (7)
Tobin in Tahiti
Morgan, Stanley
Russ Tobin series (11)
Tobin in trouble
Morgan, Stanley
Russ Tobin series (8)
Tobin on safari
Morgan, Stanley
Russ Tobin series (6)
Tobin takes off
Morgan, Stanley
Russ Tobin series (5)
Tobruk to Turkey with the army of the Nile
Clune, Frank
Discovery series (8)
Toby
Weber, Christine
Toby series (1)
Toby alone
Branscum, Robbie
Toby series (2)
Toby and his tail
Weber, Christine
Toby series (2)
Toby and Johnny Joe
Branscum, Robbie
Toby series (3)
Toby Belfer never had a Christmas tree
Pushker, Gloria
Toby Belfer series (1)
Toby Belfer's seder
Pushker, Gloria
Toby Belfer series (2)
Toby, Grannie and George
Branscum, Robbie
Toby series (1)
Toby jug murders
Wrenn, Harold Albert
William Mitchell series (3)
Toby moves house
Thwaite, Ann
Jane and Toby series (3)
Toby stays with Jane
Thwaite, Ann
Jane and Toby series (1)
Toby, the tram engine
Awdry, Wilbert
Railway series (7)
Toby, trucks and trouble
Awdry, Christopher
Railway series (32)
Toby Tucker
Mendel, Jo
Tucker family series (10)
Toby Tyler
Otis, James
Toby Tyler series (1)
Toby's folly
Arnold, Margot
Penelope Spring and Sir Tobias Glendower series (7)
To-day a stranger
Jennings, D K
Doctor Ralph Conway series (22)
Today is mine
Bowen, Marjorie
Exchange royal series (2)
Todd runs away
Pascal, Francine
Sweet Valley twins series (77)
Toddling Terry
Dolce, Janet Ellen
Baby doll board books series (3)
Todd's story
Pascal, Francine
Sweet Valley High super star series (4)
Toddy Nott, schoolboy
Judd, Alfred
Toddy Nott series (1)
Toddy scores again
Judd, Alfred
Toddy Nott series (2)
Todmanhawe Grange
Fletcher, Joseph Smith
Ronald Camberwell series (11)
Toe on the ladder
Weir, Molly
Feet series (3)
Toff
Creasey, John
Toff series (59)
Toff among the millions
Creasey, John
Toff series (11)
Toff and Old Harry
Creasey, John
Toff series (20)
Toff and the crooked copper
Creasey, John
Toff series (58)
Toff and the curate
Creasey, John
Toff series (13)
Toff and the dead man's finger
Creasey, John
Toff series (59)
Toff and the deadly parson
Creasey, John
Toff series (13)
Toff and the deep blue sea
Creasey, John
Toff series (33)
Toff and the fallen angels
Creasey, John
Toff series (53)
Toff and the golden boy
Creasey, John
Toff series (52)
Toff and the great illusion
Creasey, John
Toff series (12)
Toff and the kidnapped girl
Creasey, John
Toff series (42)
Toff and the lady
Creasey, John
Toff series (15)
Toff and the runaway bride
Creasey, John
Toff series (40)
Toff and the sleepy cowboy
Creasey, John
Toff series (57)
Toff and the spider
Creasey, John
Toff series (48)
Toff and the stolen tresses
Creasey, John
Toff series (38)
Toff and the teds
Creasey, John
Toff series (45)
Toff and the terrified taxman
Creasey, John
Toff series (56)
Toff and the toughs
Creasey, John
Toff series (45)
Toff and the trip-trip triplets
Creasey, John
Toff series (55)
Toff at Butlin's
Creasey, John
Toff series (30)
Toff at the fair
Creasey, John
Toff series (31)
Toff breaks in
Creasey, John
Toff series (4)
Toff down under
Creasey, John
Toff series (29)
Toff goes gay
Creasey, John
Toff series (24)
Toff goes on
Creasey, John
Toff series (3)
Toff goes to market
Creasey, John
Toff series (9)
Toff in New York
Creasey, John
Toff series (35)
Toff in town
Creasey, John
Toff series (18)
Toff in wax
Creasey, John
Toff series (49)
Toff is back
Creasey, John
Toff series (8)
Toff on board
Creasey, John
Toff series (21)
Toff on fire
Creasey, John
Toff series (36)
Toff on ice
Creasey, John
Toff series (17)
Toff on the farm
Creasey, John
Toff series (39)
Toff proceeds
Creasey, John
Toff series (7)
Toff steps out
Creasey, John
Toff series (2)
Toff takes shares
Creasey, John
Toff series (19)
Toga war
Shaw, Bob
Warren Peace series (2)
Together again
Sarasin, Jennifer
Cheerleaders series (32)
Together forever
Pascal, Francine
Forever trilogy (3)
Togo commando
Arvay, Harry
Israeli Security Branch series (8)
Toil of the brave
Fletcher, Inglis
Carolina series (10)
Toilers of the sea
Hugo, Victor Marie
Fate trilogy (2)
Toiling, rejoicing, sorrowing
Priest, Charles Ashley Vincent
Nothing to lose series (3)
Token
Tracy, Louis
Inspector Furneaux series (7)
Verner, Gerald
Trevor Lowe series (7)
Tokyo purple
Derrick, Lionel
Penetrator series (6)
Tokyo torpedo
Gray, Edwyn
U-boat series (3)

Told by Peter
Bruce, Mary Grant
Peter series (1)
Told by the Sandman
Walker, Abbie Phillips
Sandman series (1)
Told by Uncle Remus
Harris, Joel Chandler
Uncle Remus series (5)
Toledano
Davis, George
Roag's Syndicate series (2)
Toll call
Greenleaf, Stephen
John Marshall Tanner series (6)
Toll-house murder
Wynne, Anthony
Doctor Eustace Hailey series (19)
Toll of death
Grant, Maxwell
Shadow series (249)
Toll the bell for murder
Bellairs, George
Detective Inspector Thomas Littlejohn series (32)
Tolliver case
Walling, Robert Alfred John
Philip Tolefree series (4)
Tollivers and the mystery of Pirate Island
Stone, Alan
Tollivers series (2)
Tollivers and the mystery of the lost pony
Stone, Alan
Tollivers series (1)
Tollivers and the mystery of the old jalopy
Stone, Alan
Tollivers series (3)
Tom and Jerry scairdy cat
Lewis, Jean
Tom and Jerry series (1)
Tom and Jerry under the big top
Lewis, Jean
Tom and Jerry series (2)
Tom and Pippo and the dog
Oxenbury, Helen
Tom and Pippo series (10)
Tom and Pippo and the washing machine
Oxenbury, Helen
Tom and Pippo series (8)
Tom and Pippo go for a walk
Oxenbury, Helen
Tom and Pippo series (4)
Tom and Pippo go shopping
Oxenbury, Helen
Tom and Pippo series (1)
Tom and Pippo in the garden
Oxenbury, Helen
Tom and Pippo series (3)
Tom and Pippo in the snow
Oxenbury, Helen
Tom and Pippo series (11)
Tom and Pippo make a friend
Oxenbury, Helen
Tom and Pippo series (12)
Tom and Pippo make a mess
Oxenbury, Helen
Tom and Pippo series (5)
Tom and Pippo read a story
Oxenbury, Helen
Tom and Pippo series (6)
Tom and Pippo see the moon
Oxenbury, Helen
Tom and Pippo series (7)
Tom and Pippo's day
Oxenbury, Helen
Tom and Pippo series (2)
Tom and Sam
Hutchins, Pat
Tom and Sam series (1)
Tom Barnes and the blocking back
Runyan, John
Tom Barnes series (2)
Tom Barnes and the substitute second baseman
Runyan, John
Tom Barnes series (1)
Tom Barnes, forward
Runyan, John
Tom Barnes series (3)
Tom Brown at Oxford
Hughes, Thomas
Tom Brown series (2)
Tom Brown's body
Mitchell, Gladys
Dame Beatrice Bradley series (22)
Tom Brown's schooldays
Hughes, Thomas
Flashman series (1)
Tom Brown series (1)
Tom Cook and the German air fleet
Tomlinson, Paul Greene
Tom Cook series (2)
Tom Cook and the German spy
Tomlinson, Paul Greene
Tom Cook series (1)
Tom Cook and the winged messenger
Tomlinson, Paul Greene
Tom Cook series (4)
Tom Cook's brother in the trenches
Tomlinson, Paul Greene
Tom Cook series (3)
Tom, Dick and Harriet
Barbour, Ralph Henry
Hudson River trilogy (2)
Tom Fairfield at sea
Chapman, Allen
Tom Fairfield series (2)
Tom Fairfield in camp
Chapman, Allen
Tom Fairfield series (3)
Tom Fairfield's hunting trip
Chapman, Allen
Tom Fairfield series (5)
Tom Fairfield's pluck and luck
Chapman, Allen
Tom Fairfield series (4)
Tom Fairfield's school days
Chapman, Allen
Tom Fairfield series (1)
Tom Fobble's day
Garner, Alan
Stone book quartet (2)
Tom Fool
Stacton, David
American history trilogy (3)
Tom Jones
Fielding, Henry
Tom Jones series (1)
Tom Kitten's painting book
Potter, Beatrix
Peter Rabbit series (21)
Tom Merry and Company of Saint Jim's
Clifford, Martin
Tom Merry series (1)
Tom Merry's own
Clifford, Martin
Tom Merry series (16)
Tom Merry's rival
Clifford, Martin
Tom Merry series (7)
Tom Merry's secret
Clifford, Martin
Tom Merry series (6)
Tom Paine Maru
Smith, Lester Neil
North American Confederacy trilogy (1)
Tom Sawyer
Twain, Mark
Tom Sawyer series (1)
Tom Sawyer abroad
Twain, Mark
Tom Sawyer series (3)
Tom Sawyer, detective
Twain, Mark
Tom Sawyer series (4)
Tom Sawyer grows up
Wood, Clement
Tom Sawyer series (6)
Tom Slade at Bear Mountain
Fitzhugh, Percy Keese
Tom Slade series (16)
Tom Slade at Black Lake
Fitzhugh, Percy Keese
Tom Slade series (11)
Tom Slade at Shadow Isle
Fitzhugh, Percy Keese
Tom Slade series (19)
Tom Slade at Temple Camp
Fitzhugh, Percy Keese
Tom Slade series (2)
Tom Slade back home
Fitzhugh, Percy Keese
Tom Slade series (9)
Tom Slade, Boy Scout
Fitzhugh, Percy Keese
Tom Slade series (1)
Tom Slade, Forest Ranger
Fitzhugh, Percy Keese
Tom Slade series (17)
Tom Slade in the haunted cavern
Fitzhugh, Percy Keese
Tom Slade series (20)
Tom Slade in the north woods
Fitzhugh, Percy Keese
Tom Slade series (18)
Tom Slade, motorcycle dispatch bearer
Fitzhugh, Percy Keese
Tom Slade series (7)
Tom Slade on a transport
Fitzhugh, Percy Keese
Tom Slade series (5)
Tom Slade on Mystery Trail
Fitzhugh, Percy Keese
Tom Slade series (12)
Tom Slade on Overlook Mountain
Fitzhugh, Percy Keese
Tom Slade series (14)
Tom Slade on the river
Fitzhugh, Percy Keese
Tom Slade series (3)
Tom Slade picks a winner
Fitzhugh, Percy Keese
Tom Slade series (15)
Tom Slade, Scout master
Fitzhugh, Percy Keese
Tom Slade series (10)
Tom Slade with the boys Over There
Fitzhugh, Percy Keese
Tom Slade series (6)
Tom Slade with the colors
Fitzhugh, Percy Keese
Tom Slade series (4)
Tom Slade with the Flying Corps
Fitzhugh, Percy Keese
Tom Slade series (8)
Tom Slade's double dare
Fitzhugh, Percy Keese
Tom Slade series (13)
Tom Swift among the diamond makers
Appleton, Victor
Tom Swift series (7)
Tom Swift among the fire fighters
Appleton, Victor
Tom Swift series (24)
Tom Swift and his aerial warship
Appleton, Victor
Tom Swift series (18)
Tom Swift and his air glider
Appleton, Victor
Tom Swift series (12)
Tom Swift and his air scout
Appleton, Victor
Tom Swift series (22)
Tom Swift and his airline express
Appleton, Victor
Tom Swift series (29)
Tom Swift and his airship
Appleton, Victor
Tom Swift series (3)
Appleton, Victor II
Tom Swift Junior series 3 (13)
Tom Swift and his aquatomic tracker
Appleton, Victor II
Tom Swift Junior series 1 (23)
Tom Swift and his atomic earth blaster
Appleton, Victor II
Tom Swift Junior series 1 (5)
Tom Swift and his big dirigible
Appleton, Victor
Tom Swift series (33)
Tom Swift and his big tunnel
Appleton, Victor
Tom Swift series (19)
Tom Swift and his chest of secrets
Appleton, Victor
Tom Swift series (28)
Tom Swift and his Cosmotron Express
Appleton, Victor II
Tom Swift Junior series 1 (32)
Tom Swift and his deep-sea hydrodome
Appleton, Victor II
Tom Swift Junior series 1 (11)
Tom Swift and his diving seacopter
Appleton, Victor II
Tom Swift Junior series 1 (7)
Tom Swift and his electric locomotive
Appleton, Victor
Tom Swift series (25)
Tom Swift and his electric rifle
Appleton, Victor
Tom Swift series (10)
Tom Swift and his electric runabout
Appleton, Victor
Tom Swift series (5)
Tom Swift and his electronic retroscope
Appleton, Victor II
Tom Swift Junior series 1 (14)
Tom Swift and his flying boat
Appleton, Victor
Tom Swift series (26)
Tom Swift and his flying lab
Appleton, Victor II
Tom Swift Junior series 1 (1)
Tom Swift and his G-force inverter
Appleton, Victor II
Tom Swift Junior series 1 (30)
Tom Swift and his giant cannon
Appleton, Victor
Tom Swift series (16)
Tom Swift and his giant magnet
Appleton, Victor
Tom Swift series (35)
Tom Swift and his giant robot
Appleton, Victor II
Tom Swift Junior series 1 (4)
Tom Swift and his giant telescope
Appleton, Victor
Tom Swift series (39)
Tom Swift and his great oil gusher
Appleton, Victor
Tom Swift series (27)
Tom Swift and his great searchlight
Appleton, Victor
Tom Swift series (15)
Tom Swift and his house on wheels
Appleton, Victor
Tom Swift series (32)
Tom Swift and his jetmarine
Appleton, Victor II
Tom Swift Junior series 1 (2)
Tom Swift and his magnetic silencer
Appleton, Victor
Tom Swift series (40)
Tom Swift and his megascope space prober
Appleton, Victor II
Tom Swift Junior series 1 (20)
Tom Swift and his motor boat
Appleton, Victor
Tom Swift series (2)
Appleton, Victor II
Tom Swift Junior series 3 (13)
Tom Swift and his motor cycle
Appleton, Victor
Tom Swift series (1)
Appleton, Victor II
Tom Swift Junior series 3 (13)
Tom Swift and his ocean airport
Appleton, Victor
Tom Swift series (37)
Tom Swift and his outpost in space
Appleton, Victor II
Tom Swift Junior series 1 (6)
Tom Swift and his photo telephone
Appleton, Victor
Tom Swift series (17)
Tom Swift and his polar-ray dynasphere
Appleton, Victor II
Tom Swift Junior series 1 (25)
Tom Swift and his repelatron skyway
Appleton, Victor II
Tom Swift Junior series 1 (22)
Tom Swift and his rocket ship
Appleton, Victor II
Tom Swift Junior series 1 (3)
Tom Swift and his sky racer
Appleton, Victor
Tom Swift series (9)
Tom Swift and his sky train
Appleton, Victor
Tom Swift series (34)
Tom Swift and his sky wheel
Appleton, Victor II
Tom Swift Junior series 1 (6)
Tom Swift and his sonic boom trap
Appleton, Victor II
Tom Swift Junior series 1 (26)
Tom Swift and his space solartron
Appleton, Victor II
Tom Swift Junior series 1 (13)
Tom Swift and his spectromarine selector
Appleton, Victor II
Tom Swift Junior series 1 (15)
Tom Swift and his submarine boat
Appleton, Victor
Tom Swift series (4)
Tom Swift and his subocean geotron
Appleton, Victor II
Tom Swift Junior series 1 (27)
Tom Swift and his talking pictures
Appleton, Victor
Tom Swift series (31)
Tom Swift and his television detector
Appleton, Victor
Tom Swift series (36)
Tom Swift and his 3-D telejector
Appleton, Victor II
Tom Swift Junior series 1 (24)
Tom Swift and his triphibian atomicar
Appleton, Victor II
Tom Swift Junior series 1 (19)
Tom Swift and his ultrasonic cycloplane
Appleton, Victor II
Tom Swift Junior series 1 (10)
Tom Swift and his undersea search
Appleton, Victor
Tom Swift series (23)
Tom Swift and his war tank
Appleton, Victor
Tom Swift series (21)
Tom Swift and his wireless message
Appleton, Victor
Tom Swift series (6)
Tom Swift and his wizard camera
Appleton, Victor
Tom Swift series (14)
Tom Swift and the asteroid pirates
Appleton, Victor II
Tom Swift Junior series 1 (21)
Tom Swift and the captive planetoid
Appleton, Victor II
Tom Swift Junior series 1 (29)
Tom Swift and the city of gold
Appleton, Victor II
Tom Swift Junior series 1 (15)
Tom Swift and the cosmic astronauts
Appleton, Victor II
Tom Swift Junior series 1 (16)
Tom Swift and the Dyna-4 capsule
Appleton, Victor II
Tom Swift Junior series 1 (31)
Tom Swift and the electric hydrolung
Appleton, Victor II
Tom Swift Junior series 1 (18)
Tom Swift and the galaxy ghosts
Appleton, Victor II
Tom Swift Junior series 1 (33)
Tom Swift and the mystery comet
Appleton, Victor II
Tom Swift Junior series 1 (28)
Tom Swift and the visitor from Planet X
Appleton, Victor II
Tom Swift Junior series 1 (17)
Tom Swift circling the globe
Appleton, Victor
Tom Swift series (30)
Tom Swift in captivity
Appleton, Victor
Tom Swift series (13)
Tom Swift in the caves of ice
Appleton, Victor
Tom Swift series (8)
Tom Swift in the caves of nuclear fire
Appleton, Victor II
Tom Swift Junior series 1 (8)
Tom Swift in the city of gold
Appleton, Victor
Tom Swift series (11)
Tom Swift in the jungle of the Mayas
Appleton, Victor II
Tom Swift Junior series 1 (14)
Tom Swift in the land of wonders
Appleton, Victor
Tom Swift series (20)
Tom Swift in the race to the moon
Appleton, Victor II
Tom Swift Junior series 1 (12)
Tom Swift on the phantom satellite
Appleton, Victor II
Tom Swift Junior series 1 (9)
Tom tackles the Chalet School
Brent-Dyer, Elinor Mary
Chalet School series (32)
Tom Titmarsh's devil
Garfield, Leon
Apprentices series (10)
Tom Tomato
Reed, Giles
Munch Bunch character series (2)
Tom Truxton's ocean liner
Lounsberry, Lionel
Tom Truxton series (2)
Tom Truxton's school days
Lounsberry, Lionel
Tom Truxton series (1)
Tom Tufon's roll
Everett-Green, Evelyn
Tom Tufton series (1)
Tom Tufton's travels
Everett-Green, Evelyn
Tom Tufton series (2)
Tom-walker
Sandoz, Mari
Nebraska trilogy (3)
Tom Ward, policeman
Farmer, Bernard James
Tom Ward series (3)
Tom Willoughby's scouts
Strang, Herbert
Stories of the Great War series (5)
Tomahawk
Leigh, Roberta
Tomahawk series (1)
Porter, Donald Clayton
White Indian series (6)
Tomahawk and long rifles
Scofield, Jonathan
Freedom fighters series (1)

Tomahawk and the animals of the wild
Leigh, Roberta
Tomahawk series (4)
Tomahawk and the river of gold
Leigh, Roberta
Tomahawk series (2)
Tomahawk and the tomb of White Moose
Leigh, Roberta
Tomahawk series (3)
Tomahawk justice
Sharpe, Jon
Trailsman series (141)
Tomahawk revenge
Sharpe, Jon
Trailsman series (39)
Thompson, David
Nathaniel King series (5)
Tomahawk trail
Risteen, H L
Red Indian series (3)
Tomay is loyal
Priestley, Margaret
World Dionysus series (3)
Tomb
Wilson, Francis Paul
Adversary series (4)
Tomb of Amenosis
Sharp, Allen
Storytrails series (8)
Tomb of the Cybermen
Davis, Gerry
Doctor Who scripts series (2)
Tomb of Zwaab
James, Martin
Rick Muldoon series (2)
Tomb travellers
Pond, Roy
Archaeology series (2)
Tomboy
Klein, Norma
Only child series (2)
Tomboy terror in bunk 109
Lewis, Linda
Linda series (10)
Tomboys at the Abbey
Oxenham, Elsie J
Abbey girls retrospective series (7)
Tombs of Atuan
Le Guin, Ursula Kroeber
Earthsea series (2)
Tombs of Kobol
Larson, Glen A
Battlestar Galactica series (3)
Tombstone
Braun, Matt
Luke Starbuck series (3)
Mitchum, Hank
Stage coach station series (4)
Tombstone at Little Horn
Roberts, J R
Gunsmith series (108)
Tombstone courage
Jance, Judith A
Joanna Brady series (2)
Tombstone for a fugitive
Grover, Marshall
Larry and Stretch series (88)
Tombstone for a troubleshooter
Macdonald, William Colt
Gregory Quist series (10)
Tombstone gold
Logan, Jake
John Slocum series (159)
Tombstone honeypot
Martin, Cort
Jared Bolt series (6)
Tombstone in Deadwood
Hardin, J D
Raider and Doc series (42)
Tombstone showdown
Scott, Bradford
Walt Slade series (69)
Tombstone temptress
Hunter, E J
Headhunter series (7)
Tombstone ten gauge
Dalton, Kit
Buckskin series (31)
Tombstone territory
Hardin, J D
Raider series (31)
Tombstone Trail
Cole, Jackson
Jim Hatfield series (28)
Tombstone trail
Hogan, Ray
Shawn Starbuck series (18)
Tomie De Paola's Favourite nursery tales
De Paola, Tomie
Nursery tales series (2)
Tomie De Paola's Mother Goose
De Paola, Tomie
Nursery tales series (1)
Tommie and his mates
Bearne, David
Ridingdale series (4)
Tommy
Hocking, Joseph
Great War, Greek front series (1)
Tommy and Grizel
Barrie, James Matthew
Thrums series (6)
Barrie, James Matthew
Tommy series (2)
Tommy and Sarah dress up
Wolde, Gunilla
Thomas series (5)
Tommy and the island
Thatcher, Dora
Tommy series (12)
Tommy and the lighthouse
Thatcher, Dora
Tommy series (7)
Tommy and the Maid of Athens
Hocking, Joseph
Great War, Greek front series (2)
Tommy and the oil rig
Thatcher, Dora
Tommy series (8)
Tommy and the onion boat
Thatcher, Dora
Tommy series (6)
Tommy and the Spanish galleon
Thatcher, Dora
Tommy series (9)
Tommy and the Wishing Stone
Burgess, Thornton Waldo
Wishing Stone series (1)
Tommy and the yellow submarine
Thatcher, Dora
Tommy series (10)
Tommy-Anne and the three hearts
Wright, Mabel Osgood
Tommy-Anne series (1)
Tommy builds a house
Wolde, Gunilla
Thomas series (1)
Tommy gets a medal
Thatcher, Dora
Tommy series (3)
Tommy goes out
Wolde, Gunilla
Thomas series (4)
Tommy goes to the doctor
Wolde, Gunilla
Thomas series (6)
Tommy has a bath
Wolde, Gunilla
Thomas series (2)
Tommy Hawke at school
Patrick, Michael
Tommy Hawke series (2)
Tommy Hawke, detective
Patrick, Michael
Tommy Hawke series (1)
Tommy Hawke's third case
Patrick, Michael
Tommy Hawke series (3)
Tommy in the Caribbean
Thatcher, Dora
Tommy series (11)
Tommy joins the navy
Thatcher, Dora
Tommy series (2)
Tommy Mac
Barry, Margaret Stuart
Tommy Mac series (1)
Tommy Mac battles on
Barry, Margaret Stuart
Tommy Mac series (2)
Tommy Mac on safari
Barry, Margaret Stuart
Tommy Mac series (3)
Tommy Niner and planet of danger
Bradman, Tony
Tommy Niner series (1)
Tommy Niner and the mystery spaceship
Bradman, Tony
Tommy Niner series (2)
Tommy of the Tanks
Lynn, Escott
British Army trilogy (2)
Tommy the tugboat
Thatcher, Dora
Tommy series (1)
Tommy tidies his room
Wolde, Gunilla
Thomas series (3)
Tommy, Tilly and Mrs Tubbs
Lofting, Hugh
Mrs Tubbs series (2)
Tommy Tiptop and his baseball nine
Stone, Raymond
Tommy Tiptop series (1)
Tommy Tiptop and his boat club
Stone, Raymond
Tommy Tiptop series (4)
Tommy Tiptop and his boy scouts
Stone, Raymond
Tommy Tiptop series (5)
Tommy Tiptop and his football eleven
Stone, Raymond
Tommy Tiptop series (2)
Tommy Tiptop and his great show
Stone, Raymond
Tommy Tiptop series (6)
Tommy Tiptop and his winter sports
Stone, Raymond
Tommy Tiptop series (3)
Tommy Tittlemouse
Judson, Clara Ingram
Tommy Tittlemouse series (1)
Tommy Weston, adventuress
Sheridan, Wilfred
Tommy Weston series (2)
Tommycat comes back at last
Girard, Nicole
Anna, Paul and Tommycat series (5)
Tommycat is gone again
Girard, Nicole
Anna, Paul and Tommycat series (6)
Tommy's change of heart
Burgess, Thornton Waldo
Wishing Stone series (3)
Tommy's new engine
Thatcher, Dora
Tommy series (5)
Tommy's pup, Timothy
Smyth, Reitta
Timothy series (1)
Tommy's wishes come true
Burgess, Thornton Waldo
Wishing Stone series (2)
Tomoe Gozen
Salmonson, Jessica Amanda
Tomoe Gozen trilogy (1)
Tomorrow and today
Janson, Hank
Hank Janson series (64)
To-morrow and to-morrow
McKenna, Stephen
Sonia series (4)
Tomorrow connection
Bethancourt, Tomas Ernesto
Yesterday and tomorrow series (2)
Tomorrow in Atlantis
Leach, Christopher
Dave Bourne series (1)
Tomorrow is also a day
Ure, Jean
Thursday trilogy (3)
Tomorrow is another day
Coles, Lesley
Star trek fan series (10)
Tomorrow is murder
Brown, Carter
Mavis Seidlitz series (6)
Tomorrow plus X
Tucker, Wilson
Gilbert Nash series (2)
Tomorrow testament
Longyear, Barry Brookes
Dracon series (2)
Tomorrow the apricots
Hayes, Douglas
History of a selfish man series (4)
Tomorrow we reap
Street, James
Dabney family series (4)
Tomorrow we'll be sober
Cranston, Maurice
Inspector Mortimer Blunt series (1)
To-morrow will come
Almedingen, Edith Martha
To-morrow will come trilogy (1)
Tomorrow's dawn
Cramer, Helen Catherine
Grief series (1)
Tomorrow's ghost
Price, Anthony
Doctor David Audley and Jack Butler series (9)
Tomorrow's heritage
Coulson, Juanita
Children of the stars series (1)
Tomorrow's journey
Campbell, Drusilla
Hopewell series (4)
Tomorrow's magic
Service, Pamela F
Winter series (2)
Tomorrow's promise
Baer, Judy
Cedar River daydreams series (10)
Tom's amazing machine
Snell, Gordon
Tom's amazing machine trilogy (1)
Tom's amazing machine takes a trip
Snell, Gordon
Tom's amazing machine trilogy (3)
Tom's amazing machine zaps back
Snell, Gordon
Tom's amazing machine trilogy (2)
Tom's garden
Leavy, Una
Tom series (1)
Tom's new shoes
Aston, Elizabeth
I am growing up series (4)
Tomsk and the tired tree
Beresford, Elisabeth
Little Wombles series (3)
Tomten
Lindgren, Astrid
Tomten series (1)
Tondo for short
Inchbald, Peter
Inspector Franco Corti series (1)
Tong in cheek
Chase, Glen
Cherry Delight series (2)
Tong war
Weston, Cole
Andrew Ryder series (4)
Tongue of the ocean
Bunting, Eve
No such things series (4)
Tongue of treason
Crane, Robert
Ben Corbin series (5)
Tongue-tied Texan
Ledd, Paul
Shelter Morgan series (24)
Toni diamonds
Latta, Gordon
Arnholt series (1)
Tonight and tomorrow
Troy, Simon
Inspector Smith series (3)
Tonight they die to Mendelssohn
Gordon, Fritz
Schuyler Townsend series (2)
Tonight we steal the stars
Jakes, John
Dragonard series (3)
Tonk gives a magic show
Mayer, Mercer
Tink, tonk tales series (7)
Tons of fun from A-Z
Mooser, Stephen
Gigglemajig series (4)
Tontine treasure
Webster, H M
Shamus Burke series (3)
Tony
Hudson, Stephen
Kurt series (4)
Tony and Fievel
Teitelbaum, Michael
Fievel series (5)
Tony and the champ
Martin, Robert
Tony series (1)
Tony and the secret money
Martin, Robert
Tony series (2)
Tony beats the band
Lind, Anton
Tony series (2)
Tony Hale, space detective
Walters, Hugh
Chris Godfrey series (15)
Tony hits out
Lind, Anton
Tony series (1)
Tony Rome
Albert, Marvin Henry
Tony Rome series (1)
Tony Swift and his planet stone
Appleton, Victor
Tom Swift series (38)
Tony's book
Hood, Hugh
New age series (7)
Too bed at noon
Gielgud, Val
Inspector Gregory Pellew and Viscount Clymping series (2)
Too big
Keller, Holly
Henry series (1)
Too busy to die
Roden, Henry Wisdom
Sid Ames series (2)
Too clever by half
Jeffries, Roderic Graeme
Inspector Enrique Alvarez series (14)
Meynell, Laurence Walter
Hooky Hefferman series (3)
Too close for comfort
McConnell, Ashley
Quantum leap series (2)
Too close to the edge
Dunlap, Susan
Jill Smith series (4)
Too dangeous to be free
Chase, James Hadley
Vic Malloy series (2)
Too dangerous to live
Hume, David
Mick Cardby series (5)
Too dark!
Gretz, Susanna
Teddybear board book series (4)
Too dead to run
Manor, Jason
Steve Summers series (11)
Too dead to talk
Jones, Arthur E
Felix Holliday series (2)
Too dear for my possessing
Johnson, Pamela Hansford
Helena trilogy (1)
Too French and too deadly
Kane, Henry
Peter Chambers series (10)
Too friendly, too dead
Halliday, Brett
Michael Shayne series (45)
Too good to be true
Halliday, Michael
Doctor Emmanuel Cellini series (5)
Pascal, Francine
Sweet Valley High series (11)
Too hot for Hawaii
Dewey, Thomas Blanchard
Pete Schofield series (3)
Too hot to handle
Davidson, Linda
Endless summer series (2)
Fleming, Ian
James Bond series (3)
Goudge, Eileen
Seniors series (6)
Sterling, Stewart
Ben Pedley series (9)
Fire Marshal Ben Pedley series (9)
Too hot to kill
Sterling, Stewart
Ben Pedley series (6)
Fire Marshal Ben Pedley series (6)
Too innocent to kill
Disney, Doris Miles
Jeff Dimarco series (5)
Too late for love
Cole, Jennifer
Cindy and Nicole series (2)
Too late for morning
Foster, Richard
Pete Draco series (2)
Too late for tears
Carmichael, Harry
John Piper and Quinn series (33)
Henneker, Philip
Susan Campbell and Paul Ross series (3)
Too late for the funeral
Ormerod, Roger
David Mallin and George Coe series (8)
Too late for the tidemill
Rand, Edward Augustus
Look ahead series (3)
Too late the morrow
Bickers, Richard Townshend
Daedalus quartet (3)
Too late to die
Crider, Bill
Dan Rhodes series (1)
Too late to talk
Carter, Nicholas
Nicholas Carter series (568)
Too late to tell
Jenkins, Jerry Bruce
Jennifer Grey series (3)
Too like the dead
Chambers, Dana
Jim Steele series (2)
Too like the lightning
Chambers, Dana
Jim Steele series (2)

Too long endured
Thayer, Lee
Peter Clancy series (47)
Too lovely to live
Fenisong, Ruth
Captain Gridley Nelson series (9)
Too many bottles
Holding, Elisabeth Sanxay
Lieutenant Levy series (2)
Too many boys
Tolles, Martha
Katie series (1)
Too many carrots
Lewis, Jean
Bugs Bunny series (1)
Too many clients
Stout, Rex
Nero Wolfe and Archie Goodwin series (34)
Too many cooks
Cole, Jennifer
Cindy and Nicole series (9)
Too many counselors
Kaye, Marilyn
Camp Sunnyside Friends series (8)
Too many cousins
Browne, Douglas Gordon
Mister Harvey Tuke series (2)
Too many crooks
Prather, Richard Scott
Shell Scott series (9)
Stout, Rex
Nero Wolfe and Archie Goodwin series (5)
Too many crooks spoil the caper
Norman, Frank
Ed Nelson series (2)
Too many detectives
Stout, Rex
Dol Bonner series (2)
Nero Wolfe and Archie Goodwin series (28)
Too many doctors
Linton, Cathy
Saint Lawrence's Hospital series (3)
Roth, Holly
Inspector Medford series (2)
Too many doors
Crosby, Lee
Eric Hazard series (2)
Too many drifters
Miller, Jim
Ex-Rangers series (4)
Too many enemies
Grover, Marshall
Larry and Stretch series (147)
Haggard, William
Colonel Charles Russell series (14)
Too many ghosts
Gallico, Paul
Alexander Hero series (1)
Too many innocents
Beeby, Otto
Tony Spencer series (4)
Too many magicians
Garrett, Randall
Lord Darcy series (1)
Too many murderers
Childerness, George
Chet Phelps series (2)
Too many Murphys
McKenna, Colleen O'Shaughnessy
Murphy family series (1)
Too many pets
Armstrong, Jennifer
Pets, Inc. series (2)
Too many suspects
Rhode, John
Doctor Lancelot Priestley series (40)
Too many Texans
Grover, Marshall
Larry and Stretch series (78)
Too many traitors
Dixon, Franklin W
Hardy boys case files series (14)
Too many women
Ozaki, Milton K
Professor Caldwell and Lieutenant Phelan series (1)
Stout, Rex
Nero Wolfe and Archie Goodwin series (12)
Too mean to die
Mackie, John
Rat Bastards series (7)
Too mini murders
Morgan, Patrick
Operation Hang Ten series (2)
Too much for Mister Jellipot
Fowler, Sydney
Mister Jellipot series (9)
Too much in love
Pascal, Francine
Sweet Valley High series (22)
Too much magic
Becker, Eve
Abracadabra series (6)
Too much poison
Rowe, Anne
Inspector Barry series (1)
Too much too soon
Goudge, Eileen
Seniors series (1)
Too old a cat
Murphy, Warren Burton
Devlin Tracy series (6)
Too rich
Chan, Melissa
Inspector Joe Barnaby and Francesca Miles series (1)
Too rough for San Remo
Grover, Marshall
Larry and Stretch series (91)
Too sane a murder
Martin, Lee
Deb Ralston series (1)
Too short a day
Hart, Susanne
African wildlife series (1)
Too small for his shoes
Payne, Laurence
Chief Inspector Sam Birkett series (2)
Too soon, Mister Bear
Runyon, Catherine
Mister and Mrs Bear series (2)
Too soon to die
Janson, Hank
Hank Janson series (30)
Wade, Henry
Inspector Poole series (7)
Too sweet to die
Goulart, Ron
John Easy series (2)
Too well beloved
Elsna, Hebe
Pleasance series (2)
Too-wise owl
Robeson, Kenneth
Doc Savage series (166)
Too young to die
Saber, Robert O
Carl Good series (5)
Tool of the trade
Paul, F W
Man from S.T.U.D. series (5)
Tooley, Tooley!
Modell, Frank B
Milton and Marvin series (2)
Tools and gadgets
Kalman, Bobbie
Historic communities series (5)
Tools of the trade
Hunter, E J
Headhunter series (9)
Tooner schooner
Lasswell, Mary
Mrs Feeley series (5)
Tooth and claw
Freedman, Russell
Animal behavior series (5)
Silke, James R
Death dealer series (3)
Wilson, Gar
Phoenix Force series (20)
Tooth and nail
Carter, Nicholas
Nicholas Carter series (452)
Tooth day
Margolin, Harriet
Days series (4)
Toothbrush monster
Impey, Rose
Baddies series (6)
Tooting Corner
Bligh, Eric
Tooting Corner series (1)
Tootleoo two
Darwin, Bernard
Mister Tootleoo series (2)
Tootoo, the travelling cat
Chetham-Strode, Warren
Siamese cats series (5)
Tootoo's friends at the farm
Chetham-Strode, Warren
Siamese cats series (4)
Tootsie Tanner, why don't you talk?
Giff, Patricia Reilly
Abby Jones series (2)
Top bloody secret
Hyland, Stanley
Parliament series (3)
Top dog
Sharma, Partap
Ranjha series (2)
Top level death
Zachary, Hugh
Tusk Smith series (2)
Top of the heap
Fair, A A
Bertha Cool and Donald Lam series (13)
Top of the league
Hardcastle, Michael
Kenny Rider series (3)
Top of the world
Ruesch, Hans
Top of the world series (1)
Top off the milk
Chetham-Strode, Warren
Siamese cats series (2)
Top secret
Brent-Dyer, Elinor Mary
Chudleigh Hold series (3)
Bruce, Jean
Secret Agent O.S.S.117 series (2)
Goolden, Barbara
Tabor family series (6)
Top secret kill
Cody, James P
Brian Peterson series (1)
Top secret number one
Jardine, Warwick
Sexton Blake series (1286)
Top storey murder
Berkeley, Anthony
Roger Sheringham series (7)
Top story murder
Berkeley, Anthony
Roger Sheringham series (7)
Top study at Topham
Richards, Frank
Mascot schoolboy series (1)
Top ten
Janson, Hank
Hank Janson series (193)
Toper's end
Cole, George Douglas Howard
Superintendent Henry Wilson series (26)
Topkapi
Ambler, Eric
Arthur Abdel Simpson series (1)
Topless dancer hangup
Morgan, Patrick
Operation Hang Ten series (7)
Topless tulip caper
Harrison, Chip
Leo Haig series (2)
Topper, an improbable adventure
Smith, Thorne
Topper series (1)
Topper takes a trip
Smith, Thorne
Topper series (2)
Toppling terror
Luigi, Belli
Inspector Saint Clair series (2)
Toppling Towers
Willard, Barbara
Tower family series (2)
Topsy
Flack, Marjorie
Angus series (6)
Topsy and Angus and the cat
Flack, Marjorie
Angus series (5)
Topsy and evil
Baxt, George
Pharaoh Love series (3)
Topsy and Tim and the babysitter
Adamson, Jean
Topsy and Tim series (72)
Topsy and Tim and the new baby
Adamson, Jean
Topsy and Tim series (96)
Topsy and Tim at Granny and Grandpa's
Adamson, Jean
Topsy and Tim series (98)
Topsy and Tim at home
Adamson, Jean
Topsy and Tim board book series (4)
Topsy and Tim at school
Adamson, Jean
Topsy and Tim series (20)
Topsy and Tim at the bank
Adamson, Jean
Topsy and Tim series (75)
Topsy and Tim at the biscuit factory
Adamson, Jean
Topsy and Tim series (82)
Topsy and Tim at the circus
Adamson, Jean
Topsy and Tim series (38)
Topsy and Tim at the fairground
Adamson, Jean
Topsy and Tim series (45)
Topsy and Tim at the fire station
Adamson, Jean
Topsy and Tim series (55)
Topsy and Tim at the football match
Adamson, Jean
Topsy and Tim series (69)
Topsy and Tim at the hairdressers
Adamson, Jean
Topsy and Tim series (52)
Topsy and Tim at the jumble sale
Adamson, Jean
Topsy and Tim series (54)
Topsy and Tim at the library
Adamson, Jean
Topsy and Tim series (42)
Topsy and Tim at the pantomime
Adamson, Jean
Topsy and Tim series (56)
Topsy and Tim at the post office
Adamson, Jean
Topsy and Tim series (81)
Topsy and Tim at the safari park
Adamson, Jean
Topsy and Tim series (78)
Topsy and Tim at the school fair
Adamson, Jean
Topsy and Tim series (97)
Topsy and Tim at the seaside
Adamson, Jean
Topsy and Tim series (14)
Topsy and Tim at the TV studio
Adamson, Jean
Topsy and Tim series (83)
Topsy and Tim at the vet
Adamson, Jean
Topsy and Tim series (43)
Topsy and Tim at the wedding
Adamson, Jean
Topsy and Tim series (34)
Topsy and Tim at the zoo
Adamson, Jean
Topsy and Tim series (19)
Topsy and Tim can cook
Adamson, Jean
Topsy and Tim activity series (3)
Topsy and Tim can garden
Adamson, Jean
Topsy and Tim activity series (1)
Topsy and Tim can help birds
Adamson, Jean
Topsy and Tim activity series (8)
Topsy and Tim can look after their pets
Adamson, Jean
Topsy and Tim activity series (5)
Topsy and Tim can make music
Adamson, Jean
Topsy and Tim activity series (7)
Topsy and Tim can play party games
Adamson, Jean
Topsy and Tim activity series (6)
Topsy and Tim can print in colour
Adamson, Jean
Topsy and Tim activity series (2)
Topsy and Tim can sing and play
Adamson, Jean
Topsy and Tim activity series (4)
Topsy and Tim choose a puppy
Adamson, Jean
Topsy and Tim series (44)
Topsy and Tim cross the Channel
Adamson, Jean
Topsy and Tim series (28)
Topsy and Tim dressing-up dolls
Adamson, Jean
Life with Topsy and Tim series (12)
Topsy and Tim go camping
Adamson, Jean
Topsy and Tim series (39)
Topsy and Tim go fishing
Adamson, Jean
Topsy and Tim series (10)
Topsy and Tim go hill walking
Adamson, Jean
Topsy and Tim series (25)
Topsy and Tim go in an aeroplane
Adamson, Jean
Topsy and Tim series (50)
Topsy and Tim go on holiday
Adamson, Jean
Topsy and Tim series (13)
Topsy and Tim go pony-trekkers
Adamson, Jean
Topsy and Tim series (22)
Topsy and Tim go riding
Adamson, Jean
Topsy and Tim series (65)
Topsy and Tim go safely
Adamson, Jean
Topsy and Tim series (21)
Topsy and Tim go sailing
Adamson, Jean
Topsy and Tim series (27)
Topsy and Tim go shopping
Adamson, Jean
Topsy and Tim series (40)
Topsy and Tim go swimming
Adamson, Jean
Topsy and Tim series (86)
Topsy and Tim go to hospital
Adamson, Jean
Topsy and Tim series (18)
Topsy and Tim go to school
Adamson, Jean
Topsy and Tim series (88)
Topsy and Tim go to the dentist
Adamson, Jean
Topsy and Tim series (59)
Topsy and Tim go to the doctor
Adamson, Jean
Topsy and Tim series (58)
Topsy and Tim go to the farm
Adamson, Jean
Topsy and Tim series (87)
Topsy and Tim go to the park
Adamson, Jean
Topsy and Tim series (95)
Topsy and Tim go to the zoo
Adamson, Jean
Topsy and Tim series (19)
Topsy and Tim have a barbecue
Adamson, Jean
Topsy and Tim series (53)
Topsy and Tim have a birthday party
Adamson, Jean
Topsy and Tim series (91)
Topsy and Tim have horse riding lessons
Adamson, Jean
Topsy and Tim series (92)
Topsy and Tim have new shoes
Adamson, Jean
Topsy and Tim series (89)
Topsy and Tim have their eyes tested
Adamson, Jean
Topsy and Tim series (60)
Topsy and Tim have their hair cut
Adamson, Jean
Topsy and Tim series (90)
Topsy and Tim help the dustman
Adamson, Jean
Topsy and Tim series (62)
Topsy and Tim in Belgium
Adamson, Jean
Topsy and Tim series (29)
Topsy and Tim in Europe
Adamson, Jean
Topsy and Tim series (98)
Topsy and Tim in Holland
Adamson, Jean
Topsy and Tim series (30)
Topsy and Tim in the farmyard
Adamson, Jean
Topsy and Tim series (85)
Topsy and Tim in the gym
Adamson, Jean
Topsy and Tim series (76)
Topsy and Tim in the kitchen
Adamson, Jean
Life with Topsy and Tim series (2)
Topsy and Tim learn to dance
Adamson, Jean
Topsy and Tim series (64)
Topsy and Tim learn to horse ride
Adamson, Jean
Topsy and Tim series (80)
Topsy and Tim learn to swim
Adamson, Jean
Topsy and Tim series (26)
Topsy and Tim meet the babysitter
Adamson, Jean
Topsy and Tim series (72)
Topsy and Tim meet the dentist
Adamson, Jean
Topsy and Tim series (31)
Topsy and Tim meet the firefighters
Adamson, Jean
Topsy and Tim series (55)
Topsy and Tim meet the monsters
Adamson, Jean
Topsy and Tim series (49)
Topsy and Tim meet the police
Adamson, Jean
Topsy and Tim series (68)
Topsy and Tim move house
Adamson, Jean
Topsy and Tim series (51)

Topsy and Tim on the farm
Adamson, Jean
Topsy and Tim series (15)

Topsy and Tim on the move
Adamson, Jean
Topsy and Tim board book series (3)

Topsy and Tim out and about
Adamson, Jean
Topsy and Tim series (98)

Topsy and Tim ride their bikes
Adamson, Jean
Topsy and Tim series (77)

Topsy and Tim stay with a friend
Adamson, Jean
Topsy and Tim series (84)

Topsy and Tim take no risks
Adamson, Jean
Topsy and Tim series (23)

Topsy and Tim tell the time
Adamson, Jean
Life with Topsy and Tim series (6)

Topsy and Tim visit the dentist
Adamson, Jean
Topsy and Tim series (31)

Topsy and Tim visit the doctor
Adamson, Jean
Topsy and Tim series (32)

Topsy and Tim visit the police station
Adamson, Jean
Topsy and Tim series (68)

Topsy and Tim visit the supermarket
Adamson, Jean
Topsy and Tim series (67)

Topsy and Tim visit the Tower of London
Adamson, Jean
Topsy and Tim series (35)

Topsy and Tim's ABC
Adamson, Jean
Life with Topsy and Tim series (7)

Topsy and Tim's big fun book
Adamson, Jean
Topsy and Tim series (98)

Topsy and Tim's birthday party
Adamson, Jean
Topsy and Tim series (17)

Topsy and Tim's bonfire night
Adamson, Jean
Topsy and Tim series (11)

Topsy and Tim's caravan holiday
Adamson, Jean
Topsy and Tim series (57)

Topsy and Tim's chocolate cook book
Adamson, Jean
Topsy and Tim activity series (9)

Topsy and Tim's coach journey
Adamson, Jean
Topsy and Tim series (79)

Topsy and Tim's counting book
Adamson, Jean
Life with Topsy and Tim series (8)

Topsy and Tim's eye test
Adamson, Jean
Topsy and Tim series (60)

Topsy and Tim's farm day
Adamson, Jean
Topsy and Tim board book series (1)

Topsy and Tim's foggy day
Adamson, Jean
Topsy and Tim series (8)

Topsy and Tim's football match
Adamson, Jean
Topsy and Tim series (9)

Topsy and Tim's Friday book
Adamson, Jean
Topsy and Tim series (5)

Topsy and Tim's games book
Adamson, Jean
Life with Topsy and Tim series (3)

Topsy and Tim's garden
Adamson, Jean
Topsy and Tim series (71)

Topsy and Tim's Monday book
Adamson, Jean
Topsy and Tim series (1)

Topsy and Tim's motorway games
Adamson, Jean
Topsy and Tim series (73)

Topsy and Tim's music book
Adamson, Jean
Life with Topsy and Tim series (4)

Topsy and Tim's new brother
Adamson, Jean
Topsy and Tim series (33)

Topsy and Tim's new friend
Adamson, Jean
Topsy and Tim series (74)

Topsy and Tim's new playground
Adamson, Jean
Topsy and Tim series (61)

Topsy and Tim's new school
Adamson, Jean
Topsy and Tim series (37)

Topsy and Tim's new shoes
Adamson, Jean
Topsy and Tim series (66)

Topsy and Tim's paddling pool
Adamson, Jean
Topsy and Tim series (16)

Topsy and Tim's pet
Adamson, Jean
Life with Topsy and Tim series (5)

Topsy and Tim's pet show
Adamson, Jean
Topsy and Tim series (36)

Topsy and Tim's picnic
Adamson, Jean
Topsy and Tim series (47)

Topsy and Tim's picture dictionary
Adamson, Jean
Life with Topsy and Tim series (13)

Topsy and Tim's playing rhymes
Adamson, Jean
Topsy and Tim series (70)

Topsy and Tim's safety book
Adamson, Jean
Life with Topsy and Tim series (11)

Topsy and Tim's Saturday book
Adamson, Jean
Topsy and Tim series (6)

Topsy and Tim's school outing
Adamson, Jean
Topsy and Tim series (46)

Topsy and Tim's school play
Adamson, Jean
Topsy and Tim series (63)

Topsy and Tim's small pets
Adamson, Jean
Topsy and Tim series (93)

Topsy and Tim's snowy day
Adamson, Jean
Topsy and Tim series (12)

Topsy and Tim's sports day
Adamson, Jean
Topsy and Tim series (41)

Topsy and Tim's Sunday book
Adamson, Jean
Topsy and Tim series (7)

Topsy and Tim's Thursday book
Adamson, Jean
Topsy and Tim series (4)

Topsy and Tim's toys
Adamson, Jean
Topsy and Tim board book series (2)

Topsy and Tim's train journey
Adamson, Jean
Topsy and Tim series (48)
Topsy and Tim series (94)

Topsy and Tim's Tuesday book
Adamson, Jean
Topsy and Tim series (2)

Topsy and Tim's ups and downs
Adamson, Jean
Topsy and Tim series (24)

Topsy and Tim's Wednesday book
Adamson, Jean
Topsy and Tim series (3)

Topsy and Tim's weekend book
Adamson, Jean
Topsy and Tim series (98)

Topsy and Tim's word book
Adamson, Jean
Life with Topsy and Tim series (9)

Topsy, M.P.
Herbert, Alan Patrick
Topsy series (2)

Topsy-turvies
Anno, Mitsumasa
Pictures to stretch the imagination series (1)

Topsy turvy
Herbert, Alan Patrick
Topsy series (3)

Topsy-turvy teacher
Lavelle, Sheila
Jupiter Jane series (3)

Tor and Azor
Crowley, Maude
Azor series (4)

Torch
Lutz, John
Fred Carver series (8)

Torch bearers
Fullerton, Alexander
Nick Everard series (8)

Torch murder
Jones, Charles Reed
Leighton Swift series (2)

Torch of fear
Hawkins, Ward
Harry Borg series (4)

Torch of honor
Allen, Roger Macbride
Torch series (1)

Torches of desire
Larkin, Rochelle T
Desire trilogy (3)

Torches through the bush
Connor, Ralph
Glengarry series (4)

Torchlight
Aminoff, Constance Leonie Caroline
Napoleonic series (10)

Torchy
Ford, Sewell
Torchy series (1)

Torchy and Bossy Boots
Leigh, Roberta
Torchy series (4)

Torchy and his two best friends
Leigh, Roberta
Torchy series (5)

Torchy and the magic beam
Leigh, Roberta
Torchy series (2)

Torchy and the twinkling star
Leigh, Roberta
Torchy series (3)

Torchy and Vee
Ford, Sewell
Torchy series (7)

Torchy as a pa
Ford, Sewell
Torchy series (8)

Torchy in Topsy Turvy Land
Leigh, Roberta
Torchy series (1)

Torchy, private sec.
Ford, Sewell
Torchy series (4)

Torian pearls
Lord, Jeffrey
Richard Blade series (25)

Torment
Janson, Hank
Hank Janson series (56)
Perez Galdos, Benito
Contemporary novels of Spain series (11)

Torment for Trixy
Janson, Hank
Hank Janson series (20)

Torment was a redhead
Williams, Richard
Sexton Blake series (1550)

Tormentors
Bellairs, George
Detective Inspector Thomas Littlejohn series (38)

Torments
Cantrell, Lisa Wright
Manse series (2)

Tornado alert!
Lampton, Christopher
Alert series (5)

Tornado in town
McCall, K T
Johnny Buchanan series (13)

Tornament and tower
Doyle, Debra
Circle of magic series (2)

Torpedo tomb
Greenfield, Irving A
Depth force series (5)

Torpedo treasure
Greenfield, Irving A
Depth force series (15)

Torpedoes away
Shirreffs, Gordon Donald
Bob Dunbar and Gary Lunt series (5)

Torrek and the elfin girl
Torgersen, Don Arthur
Troll series (10)

Torrent
Blasco Ibanez, Vicente
Valencia series (4)

Torrent of fire
Macdonnell, James Edmond
Dutchy Holland series (27)

Torrid temptress
Janson, Hank
Hank Janson series (91)

Torridons in Spain
Muir, Marie
Torridons series (3)

Torridons in trouble
Muir, Marie
Torridons series (4)

Torridons' surprise
Muir, Marie
Torridons series (2)

Torridons' triumph
Muir, Marie
Torridons series (1)

Torrington Square mystery
Eades, Maud L
Winston Barrows series (2)

Torris, the boy from Broad Valley
Braenne, Berit
Torris series (1)

Torryzany
Nichols, Wallace Bertram
Henry VII series (2)

Tortoise and Turtle
Gendel, Evelyn
Tortoise and Turtle series (1)

Tortoise and Turtle abroad
Gendel, Evelyn
Tortoise and Turtle series (2)

Tortoise for bedtime
East, Helen
Arthur's aunt series (3)

Torture
Darke, James
Witches series (3)

Torture contract
Scarpetta, Frank
Marksman series (18)

Torture in the Tower
Birt, David
Tower topics series (2)

Torture machine
Tabori, Paul
Hunters series (3)

Torture trust
House, Brant
Secret Agent X series (1)

Tortured boy
Davis, Howard Charles
Edward Tope series (2)

Tortured path
Crossen, Kendell Foster
Kim Locke series (1)

Tortured planet
Lewis, Clive Staples
Space trilogy (3)

Torturers of Tet
Cain, Jonathan
Saigon commandos series (10)

Torus
Follett, James
Earthsearch series (3)

Toss of a coin
Carter, Nicholas
Nicholas Carter series (114)

Toss of a penny
Carter, Nicholas
Nicholas Carter series (164)

Tossed and blown
Bannister, S F
Rolling Stone series (1)

Total recall
Murphy, Warren Burton
Destroyer series (58)

Total soccer
Hughes, Dean
Angel Park Soccer Stars series (6)

Total war
Ahern, Jerry
Survivalist series (1)
Drake, David
Fleet series (5)

Totally bored Boris
Wilhelm, Hans
Merritales series (3)

Totem casts a shadow
Bell, Margaret Elizabeth
Florence Monroe series (2)

Toto, the bustling beaver
Barnum, Richard
Kneetime animal stories series (15)

Toto's merry winter
Richards, Laura Elizabeth
Toto series (2)

Tots and the curly-tail piglets
Cunliffe, John Arthur
Tots series (2)

Tots and the hedgehog
Cunliffe, John Arthur
Tots series (3)

Tots and the windy day
Cunliffe, John Arthur
Tots series (1)

Toucans two, and other poems
Prelutsky, Jack
Zoo doings series (2)

Touch
Berry, Joy
Can make and do series (7)
Wilson, Francis Paul
Adversary series (4)

Touch and go
Meek, Margaret Reid Duncan
Lennox Kemp series (9)
Parkinson, Cyril Northcote
Richard Delancey series (3)
Vivian, Evelyn Charles
Inspector Head series (12)

Touch-and-go year
Potter, Margaret Newman
Sinclair family series (1)

Touch gold
Sangster, Jimmy
Katy Touchfeather series (3)

Touch of a French pom-pom
Carstairs, John Paddy
Garaway Trenton series (3)

Touch of Daniel
Tinniswood, Peter
Brandon family series (1)

Touch of darkness
Crowe, John
Buena Costa County series (2)

Touch of death
Creasey, John
Doctor Palfrey series (16)
Sadler, Mark
Paul Shaw series (5)

Touch of earth
David, Janina
Square of sky trilogy (2)

Touch of eternity
Darlton, Clark
Perry Rhodan series (57)

Touch of evil
Tubb, Edwin Charles
Sexton Blake series (1474)

Touch of genius
Gordon, Jeffie Ross
Touch series (1)

Touch of ginger
Goudge, Eileen
Seniors series (9)

Touch of hell
Linaker, Michael R
Scorpion series (1)

Touch of jade
Harrell, Andrew
Sam Shank series (5)

Touch of Jonah
Holton, Leonard
Father Joseph Bredder series (7)

Touch of Judas
Wilkinson, Laurence
Mike Daryl series (2)

Touch of madness
Harris, Lavinia
Computer detectives series (3)

Touch of magic
Gordon, Jeffie Ross
Touch series (2)
Morgan, Geoffrey
Orphan series (2)

Touch of malice
Wainwright, John
Northern Police series (20)
Superintendent Charles Ripley series (4)

Touch of Max
Hooper, Kay
Men of mysteries past series (1)

Touch of myrrh
Hunt, Charlotte
Doctor Paul Holton series (5)

Touch of stagefright
Davey, Jocelyn
Ambrose Usher series (3)

Touch of the memoirs
Sinden, Donald
Touch of laughter series (1)

Touch of the past
Breen, Jon Linn
Rachel Hennings series (2)

Touch of the poet
O'Neill, Eugene
Possessors self-possessed series (1)

Touch of treason
Stein, Sol
George Thomassy series (3)

Touch the devil
Higgins, Jack
Liam Devlin series (2)

Touch the stars
Ward, Lynda
Welles family trilogy (3)

Touchdown!
James, Laurence
Gridiron series (4)

Touchdown pass
Bee, Clair
Chip Hilton series (1)

Touchdown to victory
Lawton, Charles
Clarkeville series (5)

Touchfeather
Sangster, Jimmy
Katy Touchfeather series (1)
Touchfeather, too
Sangster, Jimmy
Katy Touchfeather series (2)
Touching
Allington, Richard L
Beginning to learn series (9)
Pluckrose, Henry
Thinking about series (1)
Touchstone
Armitage, Aileen
Hawksmoor series (3)
Dobson, Margaret
Jane Bailey series (1)
Tough at the top
Levy, Elizabeth
Gymnasts series (19)
Tough bullet
McCurtin, Peter
Carmody series (3)
Tough choices for Roxie
Stahl, Hilda
Best friends series (9)
Tough company
Dawe, Carlton
Leathermouth series (10)
Tough cop
Roeburt, John
Johnny Devereaux series (1)
Tough die hard
Martin, Robert Lee
Jim Bennett series (5)
Tough get going
Bagby, George
Inspector Schmidt series (42)
Tough guys die hard
Mackie, John
Rat Bastards series (13)
Tough Jim
Cohen, Miriam
Best friends series (3)
Tough justice
San Antonio
Berurier series (2)
San Antonio series (2)
Tough-Luck Karen
Hurwitz, Johanna
Aldo Sossi series (4)
Tough luck L.A.
Sinclair, Murray
Ben Crandel series (1)
Tough questions boys ask
Baldwin, Stan
Tough questions series (1)
Tough questions girls ask
Baldwin, Stan
Tough questions series (2)
Tough Teddy
Impey, Rose
Baddies series (3)
Tough Texan
Cook, Will
Guthrie McCabe trilogy (1)
Tough to kill
Chisholm, Matt
Rem McAllister series (7)
Tough way out
Brogan, Mike
Action Man series (6)
Tough winter
Lawson, Robert
Rabbit Hill series (2)
Toughboy and sister
Hill, Kirkpatrick
Toughboy series (1)
Toujours Bernadette
Saint-Laurent, Cecil
Bernadette series (2)
Toujours Diane
Cavanna, Betty
Diane series (3)
Toujours Provence
Mayle, Peter
Provence series (2)
Tour de force
Brand, Christianna
Inspector Cockrill series (6)
Cleife, Philip
Martyn Finch series (1)
Tour of danger
Keene, Carolyn
Nancy Drew and Hardy boys supermystery series (12)
Tour of terror
Bobin, John William
Sexton Blake series (468)
Tour of the world in eighty days
Verne, Jules
Phileas Fogg series (1)
Touring company crime
Hardy, Arthur Steffens
Sexton Blake series (844)
Tourist trap
Smith, Julie
Rebecca Schwartz series (3)
Tourists are for trapping
Babson, Marian
Douglas Perkins and Gerry Tate series (3)
Tournament
Foote, Shelby
Lake Jordan series (1)
Q, John
Peter Trees series (3)
Tournament crisis
Bee, Clair
Chip Hilton series (14)
Tournament for terror
Stine, Harlan William
Wizards, warlocks and you series (10)
Tournament of thorns
Swann, Thomas Burnett
Ancient history series (11)
Tourney
Dumas, Alexandre
Valois series (3)
Touton and pussy
Mathews, Joanna Hooe
Kitty and Lulu series (1)
Tow on a tower
Hardy, Thomas
Romances and fantasies series (3)
Toward love's horizon
Du Barry, Michele
Angela Carlyle series (3)
Toward romance
Brown, Rollo Walter
Emergency series (2)
Toward the horizon
Angoff, Charles
Polonsky family series (11)
Toward the morning
Allen, Hervey
Disinherited series (3)
Towards fidelity
Fausset, Hugh l'Anson
Fidelity series (2)
Towards morning
Wylie, Ida Alexa Ross
Adam Brodie series (1)
Towards October, 1879-1917
Cliff, Tony
Trotsky series (1)
Towards the mountain
Paton, Alan
Mountain journey series (1)
Towards victory
Russell, Ray
Ashton family series (3)
Towards zero
Christie, Agatha
Superintendent Battle series (5)
Tower
Wilson, Colin
Spider world series (1)
Spider world series (1)
Tower Hill mystery
Barrett, Alfred Wilson
Justus Wise series (2)
Tower is everywhere
Jones, Richard
Benson-Williams series (2)
Tower mystery
McGuire, Paul
Superintendent Fillinger series (1)
Tower of blood
Andrews, Spike
C.A.T. series (1)
Tower of darkness
Fultz, Regina Oehler
Endless quest series (29)
Hawton, Hector
Colonel Max Masterson series (1)
Tower of death
Grant, Maxwell
Shadow series (53)
Offutt, Andrew Jefferson
Cormac Mac Art series (2)
Tower of despair
Kelly, David J
Killstar series (2)
Tower of destruction
Martin, Keith
Fighting fantasy gamebook series (46)
Tower of evil
Rhode, John
Doctor Lancelot Priestley series (29)
Tower of Geburah
White, John
Archives of Anthropos series (1)
Tower of strength
Carter, Nicholas
Nicholas Carter series (500)
Tower of terror
Stivers, Dick
Able Team series (1)
Tower of the elephant
Howard, Robert Ervin
Conan series (20)
Tower of the stars
Harris, Rosemary
Orion series (2)
Tower of treason
Hughes, Zach
Hotel Destiny series (4)
Tower of Zanid
De Camp, Lyon Sprague
Krishna series (5)
Tower secret
Garis, Lilian C
Melody Lane series (3)
Tower treasure
Dixon, Franklin W
Hardy boys series (2)
Towering nightmare
Gilman, George G
Edge series (30)
Towers in the mist
Goudge, Elizabeth
Cathedrals series (2)
Towers od pain
Godwin, Felix
Captain John Hunter series (2)
Towers of Melnon
Lord, Jeffrey
Richard Blade series (15)
Towers of silence
Saint John, David
Peter Ward series (3)
Scott, Paul
British India quartet (3)
Towers of Toron
Delany, Samuel Ray
Fall of the towers trilogy (2)
Towers of Utopia
Reynolds, Mack
Bat Hardin series (2)
Town
Faulkner, William
Sin and salvation series (9)
Snopes family trilogy (2)
Lewin, Hugh
Jafta series (6)
Richter, Conrad
American pioneer trilogy (3)
Town and the city
Kerouac, Jack
Jack Duluoz series (4)
Town called Hate
Gilman, George G
Edge series (13)
Town called Yellowdog
Edson, John Thomas
Floating Outfit series (22)
Town hall crime
Blair, Allan
Sexton Blake series (693)
Town house
Lofts, Norah
Suffolk trilogy (1)
Town of blood
Fieldhouse, William
Klaw series (2)
Town of hate
Grant, Maxwell
Shadow series (253)
Town of shadows
Drummond, J
Sexton Blake series (1203)
Town on trial
Gilman, George G
Edge series (36)
Town scold
Sherwin, Judith Johnson
Waste triptych (1)
Town tamer
Dawson, Clay
Long Rider series (17)
Town tamers
Edson, John Thomas
Floating Outfit series (58)
Town that God forgot
Macdonald, William Colt
Three Mesquiteers series (6)
Town that went sick
Truss, Seldon
Inspector Gidleigh series (20)
Town without a prayer
Dana, Mitchell
Dakota Bush series (2)
Townsend of Lichfield
Cabell, James Branch
Dom Manuel and his descendants series (23)
Townsman
Sedges, John
American life series (2)
Towser and Sadie's birthday
Ross, Tony
Towser series (1)
Towser and the funny face
Ross, Tony
Towser series (5)
Towser and the haunted house
Ross, Tony
Towser series (4)
Towser and the magic apple
Ross, Tony
Towser series (6)
Towser and the terrible thing
Ross, Tony
Towser series (2)
Towser and the water rats
Ross, Tony
Towser series (3)
Toxic revenge
Dixon, Franklin W
Hardy boys case files series (83)
Toxic shock
Paretsky, Sara
V I Warshawski series (5)
Toxic waste
Snodgrass, Mary Ellen
Environmental awareness series (5)
Toxin
Swigart, Rob
Vector series (2)
Toy
Clapton, Patricia
Toy series (1)
Toy lamb
Flynn, Brian
Anthony Bathurst series (49)
Toy words
Tyler, Jenny
First words series (1)
Toying with danger
Stevenson, Drew
Sarah Capshaw series (2)
Toying with fate
Carter, Nicholas
Nicholas Carter series (494)
Toymaker's daughter
Williams, Ursula Moray
Toymakers series (3)
Toyman
Tubb, Edwin Charles
Dumarest series (3)
Toyshop bunnies
Cartlidge, Michelle
Press and play series (2)
Toytown and Larry the Lamb
Beaman, Sydney George Hulme
Toytown series (41)
Toytown book
Beaman, Sydney George Hulme
Toytown series (11)
Toytown Christmas party
Beaman, Sydney George Hulme
Toytown series (32)
Toytown goes west
Beaman, Sydney George Hulme
Toytown series (30)
Toytown mystery
Beaman, Sydney George Hulme
Toytown series (12)
Toytown pantomime
Beaman, Sydney George Hulme
Toytown series (39)
Toytown treasure
Beaman, Sydney George Hulme
Toytown series (33)
Trace
Murphy, Warren Burton
Devlin Tracy series (1)
Trace and forty-seven miles of rope
Murphy, Warren Burton
Devlin Tracy series (2)
Traced and tracked
M'Govan, James
James M'Govan series (4)
Traces of Brillhart
Brean, Herbert
William Deacon series (1)
Traces of Merrilee
Brean, Herbert
William Deacon series (2)
Tracing of angels
Minton, Mary
Yesterday's road series (9)
Track
Barea, Arturo
Forging of a rebel trilogy (2)
Bishop, Samuel P
Track series (1)
Track and field
Gutman, Bill
Go for it series (6)
Track down
Mason, Dan
Lex Cranshaw series (5)
Track, enduro and motorcross, unless you fall over
Paulsen, Gary
Sports on the light side series (12)
Track of the bear
Coldsmith, Don
Spanish bit series (22)
Montgomery, Raymond A
Choose your own adventure series (83)
Track of the beast
Hayes, Ralph Eugene
John Yard series (4)
Track of the lawless
Grover, Marshall
Larry and Stretch series (172)
Track of the slayer
Strong, Ben
Professor Adrian Criddle series (1)
Track of the white wolf
Roberson, Jennifer
Chronicles of the Cheysuli series (4)
Track of the zombie
Dixon, Franklin W
Hardy boys series (71)
Track the man down
Grey, Romer Zane
Buck Duane series (9)
Track tramp
Hunter, E J
White Squaw series (13)
Track trophy
Dubrovin, Vivian
Summer fun, winter fun series (3)
Trackdown
Bell, Robert Vaughn
McGowan family series (8)
Hunter, Neil
Bodie the Stalker series (1)
Owen, Dean
Latigo series (1)
Saint James, Daniel
Brothers in blood series (2)
Tracked across the Atlantic
Carter, Nicholas
Nicholas Carter series (18)
Tracked and taken
Donovan, Dick
Dick Donovan series (4)
Tracked to the west
Ridley, Nat
Nat Ridley series (2)
Tracker
Ladd, Justin
Abilene series (9)
Stillman, Ron
Tracker series (1)
Tracking the wolfpack
Jones, J Farragut
Silent service series (5)
Trackless death
Livingston, Armstrong
Peter Creighton series (5)
Tracks
Erdrich, Louise
Argus series (3)
Tracks across Alaska
Scott, Alastair
Scot series (3)
Track's magnificent milers
Aaseng, Nathan
Sports heroes series (11)
Trackwalker
Grant, William
Matthew Faraday series (5)
Tracy's little people
Kirby, Jean
Scott sisters series (5)
Tracy's wartime memories
Collins, Max Allan
Dick Tracy series (8)
Trade and traders
Birt, David
Saxons and Vikings series (14)
Trade off
Miller, Victor Brooke
Kojak series (10)
Trade wind
Kaye, Mary Margaret
Zanzibar series (1)

Trade winds
Abraham, Cyril
Onedin Line series (4)
Trader to the stars
Anderson, Poul
Polesotechnic League series (4)
Trader's daughter
Graydon, William Murray
Sexton Blake series (241)
Trading
Warner, Susan Bagert
Opportunities series (4)
Trading places
Quin-Harkin, Janet
Sugar and spice series (2)
Tradition
Hummel, George Frederick
Heritage series (2)
Tradition of victory
Kent, Alexander
Captain Richard Bolitho series (15)
Traditions
Ebert, Alan
Tiernan family series (1)
Trafalgar
Perez Galdos, Benito
National episodes series, epoch 1 (1)
Trafalgar forty-nine
Seligman, Adrian
Thunder Reef series (4)
Trafalgar Square
Holt, Gavin
Professor Luther Bastion series (14)
Rayner, Claire
Performers series (7)
Trafalgar Square mystery
Brisbane, Coutts
Sexton Blake series (697)
Traffic
Maestro, Betsy Crippen
Words series (3)
Tragedy after tea
Ashton, Charles
Jack Atherley series (2)
Tragedy at Beechcroft
Fielding, A
Inspector Pointer series (17)
Tragedy at Draythorpe
Grex, Leo
Paul Irving series (1)
Tragedy at Freyne
Gilbert, Anthony
Scott Egerton series (1)
Tragedy at law
Hare, Cyril
Francis Pettigrew series (1)
Inspector Mallett series (4)
Tragedy at Ravensthorpe
Connington, John Jervis
Sir Clinton Driffield series (2)
Tragedy at the thirteenth hole
Burton, Miles
Inspector Arnold and Desmond Merrion series (6)
Tragedy at the Unicorn
Rhode, John
Doctor Lancelot Priestley series (5)
Tragedy at Twelvetrees
Rees, Arthur John
Inspector Luckraft series (4)
Tragedy at Wembley
Gregg, Cecil Freeman
Inspector Cuthbert Higgins series (14)
Tragedy business
Timperley, Rosemary
Hospital trilogy (2)
Tragedy day
Roberts, Gareth
Timewyrm series (8)
Tragedy in blue
Bramhall, Marion
Kit Acton series (3)
Tragedy in E flat
Gribble, Leonard Reginald
Superintendent Anthony Slade series (15)
Tragedy in the dark
Hamilton, Elaine
Inspector Reynolds series (6)
Tragedy in the hollow
Crofts, Freeman Wills
Inspector Joseph French series (19)
Tragedy near Tring
Ryland, John Knox
Inspector Rodway series (1)
Tragedy of the Bromleigh's
Hardinge, Rex
Sexton Blake series (1239)
Tragedy of the Chinese mine
Greig, Ian
Inspector Swinton series (2)
Tragedy of the silver moon
Gask, Arthur
Gilbert Larose series (17)
Tragedy of the West End actress
Brandon, John Gordon
Sexton Blake series (746)
Tragedy of Windyridge
Hardinge, Rex
Sexton Blake series (1255)
Tragedy of X
Ross, Barnaby
Drury Lane series (1)
Tragedy of Y
Ross, Barnaby
Drury Lane series (2)
Tragedy of Z
Ross, Barnaby
Drury Lane series (3)
Tragedy on the line
Rhode, John
Doctor Lancelot Priestley series (10)
Tragg's choice
Adams, Clifton
Tragg series (2)
Tragic case of the station master's legacy
Drummond, J
Sexton Blake series (1119)
Tragic curtain
Page, Stanley Hart
Christopher Hand series (5)
Tragic mystery
Hawthorne, Julian
Inspector Byrnes series (3)
Tragic target
Heberden, Mary Violet
Desmond Shannon series (16)
Trail and trading post
Stratemeyer, Edward L
Colonial series (6)
Trail blazers
Willoughby, Lee Davis
Making of America series (43)
Trail blazers of the skies
Langley, John Prentice
Aviation series (1)
Trail boss
Edson, John Thomas
Floating Outfit series (10)
Trail drive
McCurtin, Peter
Sundance series (36)
Trail drive to Montana
Roberts, J R
Gunsmith series (69)
Trail drive war
Roberts, J R
Gunsmith series (59)
Trail dust
Grover, Marshall
Larry and Stretch series (6)
Mulford, Clarence Edward
Hopalong Cassidy series (14)
Trail for the Virginian
Owen, Dean
Virginian series (2)
Trail from Needle Rock
Field, Peter
Powder Valley series (29)
Trail from Taos
Coldsmith, Don
Spanish bit series (14)
Trail heat
Meek, Joseph
Mountain Jack Pike series (14)
Trail herd
Scott, Bradford
Walt Slade series (2)
Trail makers
Burton, Charles Pierce
Bob's Hill series (7)
Trail-makers of the Middle Border
Garland, Hamlin
Middle Border series (3)
Trail mates
Bryant, Bonnie
Saddle Club series (5)
Trail of a tramp
Quarry, Nick
Jake Barrow series (1)
Trail of ashes
Babson, Marian
Family holiday series (2)
Trail of Black Hawk
Tomlinson, Everett Titsworth
American Indian chiefs series (1)
Trail of blood
Langholm, Neil
Vikings series (4)
Rushton, Charles
James O'Hannay and Floyd East series (1)
Trail of blood and bones
Scott, Bradford
Walt Slade series (47)
Trail of Bohu
Saunders, Charles Robert
Imaro trilogy (3)
Trail of Cthulhu
Derleth, August
Cthulhu series (2)
Trail of death
Colter, Dale
Regulator series (11)
Graydon, William Murray
Sexton Blake series (488)
McElwain, Dean L
Preacher's law series (2)
Morgan, G J
Buck Dunne series (1)
Trail of desire
Mills, Robert E
Davy Watson series (7)
Trail of doom
Armour, R Coutts
Sexton Blake series (507)
Trail of empire
Scott, Bradford
Walt Slade series (109)
Trail of fear
Armstrong, Anthony
Jimmie Rezaire series (1)
Trail of Fu-Manchu
Rohmer, Sax
Fu-Manchu series (8)
Trail of lies
Keene, Carolyn
Nancy Drew files series (53)
Trail of McAllister
Chisholm, Matt
Rem McAllister series (24)
Trail of no return
Wrexe, Charles
Bill Mitchum series (1)
Trail of Raider Number One
Blakesley, Stephen
Sexton Blake series (1299)
Trail of revenge
Bowden, Jim
Dan McCoy series (7)
Trail of Soapy Smith
Strong, Charles Stanley
Soapy Smith series (1)
Trail of Tecumseh
Tomlinson, Paul Greene
American Indian chiefs series (3)
Trail of the assassin
Roberts, J R
Gunsmith series (102)
Trail of the bear
Newton, Dwight Bennett
Johnny Logan series (2)
Trail of the black king
Armstrong, Anthony
Jimmie Rezaire series (4)
Trail of the broken snowshoe
Govan, Margaret
Betty Morton series (2)
Trail of the catspaw
Carter, Nicholas
Nicholas Carter series (357)
Trail of the cloven foot
Verrill, Alpheus Hyatt
Trail series (1)
Trail of the dope chief
Hunter, John
Sexton Blake series (901)
Trail of the dragon
Kelly, Susan
Liz Connors and Jack Lingemann series (4)
Trail of the fingerprints
Carter, Nicholas
Nicholas Carter series (552)
Trail of the Gatling
Moore, Arthur
Bluestar series (1)
Trail of the green doll
Sutton, Margaret
Judy Bolton series (27)
Trail of the Gypsy Eight
Fairfax, Virginia
Girl Scouts series (4)
Trail of the human tiger
Carter, Nicholas
Nicholas Carter series (595)
Trail of the iron horse
Cole, Jackson
Jim Hatfield series (99)
Trail of the Lotto
Armstrong, Anthony
Jimmie Rezaire series (3)
Trail of the missing scientist
Parsons, Anthony
Sexton Blake series (1388)
Trail of the Mohawk
Tomlinson, Everett Titsworth
American Indian chiefs series (2)
Trail of the Mountain Man
Johnstone, William Wallace
Mountain Man series (3)
Trail of the old lag
Bayfield, William John
Sexton Blake series (464)
Trail of the ragged robin
Klickmann, Flora
Flower-patch series (3)
Trail of the red canoe
Govan, Margaret
Betty Morton series (1)
Trail of the screaming teenager
Giff, Patricia Reilly
Polka Dot series (7)
Trail of the seahawks
Mayhar, Ardath
Windwalker series (1)
Trail of the Seneca
Braden, James Andrew
John Jerome and Return Kingdom series (4)
Trail of the serpent
Worth, Cedric
Inspector Sevrel series (1)
Trail of the Sioux
Giraud, Jean
Lieutenant Mike S Blueberry series (8)
Trail of the skull
Holt, Gavin
Professor Luther Bastion series (6)
Trail of the Spanish bit
Coldsmith, Don
Spanish bit series (1)
Trail of the squid
Wickham, Harvey
Ferris McClue series (4)
Trail of the Tiger
Armour, R Coutts
Sexton Blake series (319)
Trail of the twisted cross
Sanders, Buck
Ben Slayton series (3)
Trail of the twisted horseshoes
Hobart, Donald Bayne
Masked Rider and Blue Hawk series (3)
Trail of the white Indians
Verrill, Alpheus Hyatt
Trail series (2)
Trail of the white mule
Bower, Bertha Muzzy
Casey Ryan series (2)
Trail of the white turban
Brisbane, Coutts
Sexton Blake series (877)
Trail of the Yoshiga
Carter, Nicholas
Nicholas Carter series (446)
Trail of vengeance
Grant, Maxwell
Shadow series (232)
Trail plowed under
Russell, Charles Marion
Rawhide Rawlins series (3)
Trail sinister
Brumbaugh, James
Advanced dungeons and dragons adventure gamebook series (11)
Delmer, Sefton
Trail sinister series (1)
Trail south from Powder Valley
Field, Peter
Powder Valley series (15)
Trail through Tascosa
Field, Peter
Powder Valley series (76)
Trail to Bear Paw Mountain
Rayner, William
Missouri series (2)
Trail to Boot Hill
Winstan, Matt
Reuben Brown series (9)
Trail to death
Wallace, Robert
Phantom Detective series (29)
Trail to Maverick
Denver, Lee
Deputy Marshal Dave Halloran series (2)
Trail to Slaughter Creek
Bexar, Phil
Billy Dupree series (6)
Trail to Troublesome
Field, Peter
Powder Valley series (65)
Trail to Vengeance
Essex, Saran
Butch Cassidy and the Sundance Kid series (1)
Trail Town guns
Cole, Jackson
Jim Hatfield series (48)
Trail tramp
Sherman, Jory
Gunn series (25)
Trail under the sea
Poole, Reginald Heber
Sexton Blake series (149)
Trail west
James, Cy
Sam Spur series (3)
Trailering troubles
Dubrovin, Vivian
Saddle up series (3)
Trailersnatch
Harrell, Andrew
Sam Shank series (2)
Trailing Geronimo
Ellis, Edward Sylvester
Arizona trilogy (2)
Trailing of the Picaroon
Landon, Herman
Picaroon series (5)
Trailing the air mail bandit
Theiss, Lewis Edwin
Air mail series (3)
Trails can be so tough
Janson, Hank
Hank Janson series (32)
Trails of guns and gold
Scott, Bradford
Walt Slade series (60)
Trails of peril
Coe, Ross Anton
Warrior of vengeance series (2)
Trails of steel
Scott, Bradford
Walt Slade series (70)
Trails of yesteryear
Hutchens, Paul
Sugar Creek Gang series (35)
Train at Bundarbar
Macneil, Duncan
James Ogilvie series (13)
Train of glory
Grant, William
Matthew Faraday series (6)
Train of terror
Foley, Louise Munro
Twistaplot series (2)
Train ride to hell
Hardin, J D
Raider and Doc series (71)
Train to nowhere
Leslie, Anita
Train to nowhere series (1)
Trainer's secret
Hardy, Arthur Steffens
Sexton Blake series (369)
Trainmasters
Croft, Jesse Taylor
Trainmasters series (1)
Traitor
Baker, William Howard
Richard Quintain series (14)
Dixon, Thomas
American Reconstruction series (3)
Fritz, Jean
American Revolution series (6)
Traitor and spy
Hardy, Arthur Steffens
Sexton Blake series (34)
Traitor betrayed
Mills, Osmington
Midset C.I.D. series (22)
Superintendent William Baker series (9)
Traitor spy
Jacobs, Thomas Curtis Hicks
Chief Inspector Barnard series (8)
Traitor to India
Brata, Sasthi
Astride two worlds series (2)
Traitor to the living
Farmer, Philip Jose
Exorcism series (3)
Traitor unmasked
Davison, Gilderoy
Twisted Face series (3)
Traitors
Long, William Stuart
Australians series (3)

Traitor's cross
Grierson, Francis Durham
Inspector George Muir series (14)
Superintendent Andrew Ash series (7)
Traitors' doom
Creasey, John
Doctor Palfrey series (1)
Traitor's end
Hunter, Alan
Inspector George Gently series (36)
Traitor's exit
Gardner, John Edmund
Boysie L Oakes series (6)
Traitors from within
Montgomery, Raymond A
Rebels in the New World series (1)
Traitor's gait
Osborne, Geoffrey
James Dingle and Glyn Jones series (3)
Traitors' gate
Gavin, Catherine
French Resistance series (1)
Traitor's Gate
Wheatley, Dennis
Gregory Sallust series (9)
Traitor's gold
Gentry, Buck
Eli Holten series (10)
Traitors in the Tower
Birt, David
Tower topics series (3)
Traitor's island
Pendower, Jacques
Slade McGinty series (5)
Traitor's market
Dickson, Grierson
Superintendent Cissie Marlow series (1)
Traitor's Mountain
Styles, Showell
Sir Abercrombie Lewker series (1)
Traitor's purse
Allingham, Margery
Albert Campion series (13)
Traitor's son
Fecher, Constance
Ralegh family trilogy (2)
Traitors' territory
Robb, John
Shelby series (2)
Traitor's tide
Goyne, Richard
Padre series (3)
Traitor's wife
Montross, David
Remsen series (1)
Tramontane
Petaja, Emil
Kalevala series (4)
Tramp abroad
Twain, Mark
Tramp series (1)
Tramp-Royal in Spain
Marshall, Matt
Tramp-Royal series (3)
Tramp-Royal on the Toby
Marshall, Matt
Tramp-Royal series (1)
Trampled lilies
Fortescue, Winifred
Provence series (4)
Tramplers
Manor, Jason
Steve Summers series (4)
Tramps and ladies
Bisset, James
Years at sea series (2)
Tramp's evidence
Vivian, Evelyn Charles
Inspector Head series (7)
Tramway engines
Awdry, Wilbert
Railway series (26)
Trans-Am
Wilkinson, Sylvia
World of racing series (9)
Transatlantic ghost
Gardiner, Dorothy
Mister Watson series (1)
Transcendental murder
Langton, Jane
Homer Kelly series (1)
Transfiguration of Miss Philura
Kingsley, Florence Morse
Miss Philura trilogy (1)
Transformation of Miss Mavis Ming
Moorcock, Michael
Dancers at the end of time series (5)
Transformations
Halam, Ann
Inland trilogy (2)
Transformed by the light
Perry, Paul
Near-death series (4)
Transformer
Foster, Michael Anthony
Morphodite trilogy (2)
Transgressor in the tropics
Farson, Negley
Transgressor series (2)
Transgressors
Poyer, Joe
Time of war series (1)
Transistor radio
Saro-Wiwa, Ken
Mister B series (2)
Transit to Scorpio
Akers, Alan Burt
Dray Prescot series (1)
Transition
McIntyre, Vondra Neil
Starfarers series (2)
Welling, Lois
Star trek fan series (27)
Transition of Titus Crow
Lumley, Brian
Titus Crow series (2)
Transmigration of Timothy Archer
Dick, Philip Kindred
VALIS trilogy (3)
Transmitters
Broderick, Damien
Faustus hexagram series (4)
Transmutation of Ling
Bramah, Ernest
Kai Lung series (1)
Transparencies
Sherwin, Judith Johnson
Waste triptych (2)
Transparent traitor
Gerard, Francis
Sir John Meredith series (16)
Transplanted
Atherton, Gertrude Franklin
Wives and husbands series (1)
Niven, Frederick
Flying years trilogy (3)
Transport murders
Brandon, John Gordon
Inspector Patrick Aloysius McCarthy series (35)
Transport of delight
Milligan, Spike
Delight series (1)
Transvection machine
Hoch, Edward Dentinger
Carl Crader and Earl Jazine series (1)
Trap
Cresswell, Helen
Mike series (6)
King, Tabitha
Nodd's Ridge series (3)
Macdonnell, James Edmond
Captain Peter Bentley series (46)
Richardson, Dorothy Miller
Pilgrimage series (8)
Staples, Mary Jane
South London series (10)
Treherne, John
Doctor James Yeo series (1)
Trap Angel
Christian, Frederick H
Frank Angel series (4)
Trap for a redhead
Palmer, Stuart
Hildegarde Withers series (14)
Trap for Buchanan
Ward, Jonas
Tom Buchanan series (10)
Trap for fools
Cross, Amanda
Professor Kate Fansler series (9)
Trap in the tunnel
Ellinger, Geoffrey
Roger Hartley series (1)
Trap number six
Ransome, Stephen
Lieutenant Lee Barcello series (6)
Trap of tangled wire
Carter, Nicholas
Nicholas Carter series (295)
Trap Spider
Royce, Kenneth
Spider Scott series (5)
Trap the Baron
Morton, Anthony
Baron series (18)
Trapline thief at Sugar Creek
Hutchens, Paul
Sugar Creek Gang series (22)
Trapp and World War III
Callison, Brian
Captain Edward Trapp series (3)
Trapp family on wheels
Trapp, Maria Augusta von
Trapp family series (2)
Trapp family singers
Trapp, Maria Augusta von
Trapp family series (1)
Trapped
Bell, Frank
Shen series (3)
Norwood, Warren
Time police series (2)
Trapped at sea
Dixon, Franklin W
Hardy boys series (75)
Trapped by a woman
Carter, Nicholas
Nicholas Carter series (214)
Trapped in his own net
Carter, Nicholas
Nicholas Carter series (187)
Trapped in the ashes
Johnstone, William Wallace
Ashes series (10)
Trapped in the sea kingdom
Brightfield, Richard
Escape from Tenopia series (2)
Trapped in the Slickrock
Skurzynski, Gloria
Mountain west series (2)
Trapped in the U.S.S.R.
Fortune, J J
Race against time series (8)
Trapped on Sugar Loaf Mountain
Palmer, Bernard
Mickey Turner series (2)
Trapper days
Hunkins, Ralph Valentine
Tales of the prairies series (2)
Trapper of Rat River
Stoddard, Charles
Malloy series (1)
Trapper rampage
Sharpe, Jon
Trailsman series (68)
Trapper's blood
Thompson, David
Nathaniel King series (17)
Trappers of Venus
Greene, Joseph
Dig Allen series (4)
Trapper's victim
Brisbane, Coutts
Sexton Blake series (610)
Trapping the Jap
Idriess, Ion Llewellyn
Australian guerilla series (4)
Trapp's peace
Callison, Brian
Captain Edward Trapp series (2)
Trapp's war
Callison, Brian
Captain Edward Trapp series (1)
Traps need fresh bait
Fair, A A
Bertha Cool and Donald Lam series (28)
Trash bash
Delton, Judy
Pee wee scout series (16)
Trask and the fighting Irishman
Heron, Jack
Jason Trask series (2)
Trask the avenger
Heron, Jack
Jason Trask series (1)
Trauma
Barclay, Virginia
Mid-City Hospital series (3)
Travail
Zola, Emile
Four Gospels series (2)
Travails of Jane Saint
Saxton, Josephine
Jane Saint series (1)
Travails of Jane Saint, and other stories
Saxton, Josephine
Jane Saint series (1)
Travel and trade
Birt, David
Roman Britain series (4)
Travel and transport by machine before 1914
Burrell, Roy Eric Charles
Travel and transport series (2)
Travel and transport by muscle power
Burrell, Roy Eric Charles
Travel and transport series (1)
Travel and transport in modern times
Burrell, Roy Eric Charles
Travel and transport series (3)
Travel tales of Mister Joseph Jorkens
Dunsany, Edward John Moreton Drax Plunkett
Jorkens series (1)
Travel with the Tardis
Airey, Jean
Doctor Who series (162)
Traveler
Coldsmith, Don
Spanish bit super series (2)
Traveling corpses
Steel, Kurt
Hank Hyer series (1)
Traveling shoes
Streatfeild, Noel
Shoes series (11)
Traveling with Oma
Kleberger, Ilse
Grandmother Oma series (2)
Traveling with the Innocents abroad
Twain, Mark
Innocents series (2)
Traveller from Altruria
Howells, William Dean
Altruria series (1)
Traveller from Tokyo
Morris, James Humphrey
Japan series (1)
Traveller returns
Wentworth, Patricia
Miss Maud Silver series (10)
Traveller's prelude
Stark, Freya
Traveller series (1)
Travelling circus
Verne, Jules
Caesar Cascabel series (1)
Travelling deadman
Varnam, John
Inspector Semlake series (2)
Travelling magic
Beresford, Elisabeth
Magic series (2)
Travelling man
Mace, Elisabeth
Swallowdale series (3)
Travelling moose
Ahlberg, Allan
Help your child to read series (12)
Travels and adventures of Little Baron Trump and his wonderful dog Bulger
Lockwood, Ingersoll
Baron Trump series (1)
Travels by sea and land of the renowned Baron Munchausen
Raspe, Rudolf Erich
Baron Munchausen series (3)
Travels in a donkey trap
Baker, Daisy
Donkey trap series (1)
Travels into several remote nations of the world
Swift, Jonathan
Lemuel Gulliver series (1)
Lilliput series (1)
Travels into several remote nations of the world, volume III
Gulliver, Lemuel
Lemuel Gulliver series (2)
Travels into several remote nations of the world, volume III, part II
Gulliver, Lemuel
Lemuel Gulliver series (3)
Travels of Babar
Brunhoff, Jean de
Babar series (2)
Travels of Fingerling
Laan, Dick
Fingerling series (5)
Travels of Mister John Gulliver, son to Captain Lemuel Gulliver
Desfontaines, Pierre
Lemuel Gulliver series (4)
Travels of Oggy
Lawrence, Ann
Oggy series (1)
Travels of Tiadatha
Rutter, Owen
Tiadatha series (2)
Travels of Tramp-Royal
Marshall, Matt
Tramp-Royal series (2)
Travels with a donkey
Stevenson, Robert Louis
Inland voyage series (2)
Travels with a donkey in the Cevennes
Stevenson, Robert Louis
Donkey series (1)
Travels with the monster
Salmon, Michael
Alexander Bunyip series (3)
Travesty
Hawkes, John
Blood oranges trilogy (3)
Travis, U.S. Marshal
Jons, Hal
Marshal Carl Travis series (2)
Treacherous gun
Essex, Saran
Butch Cassidy and the Sundance Kid series (2)
Treacherous moon
Blunt, Betty
Treacherous moon series (1)
Treacherous paths
Trevor, Meriol
Luxembourg series (5)
Treacherous road
Harvester, Simon
Asia in turmoil series (18)
Dorian Silk series (6)
Treacherous years, 1895-1901
Edel, Leon
Henry James series (4)
Treachery in outer space
Rockwell, Carey
Tom Corbett series (6)
Treachery in Trieste
Leonard, Charles L
Paul Kilgerrin series (11)
Treachery Pass
Sharpe, Jon
Trailsman series (66)
Tread gently
Koehler, Robert Portner
Al Bronson series (3)
Tread lightly, Angel
Davis, Frederick Clyde
Schyler Cole and Luke Speare series (3)
Tread softly
Flynn, Brian
Anthony Bathurst series (20)
Treading water
Davidson, Linda
Endless summer series (1)
Treason at Helms Deep
Barrett, Kevin
Middle Earth quest series (4)
Treason game
Carter, Nick
Nick Carter series (162)
Treason in my breast
Gilbert, Anthony
Arthur Crook series (4)
Treason in the ashes
Johnstone, William Wallace
Ashes series (19)
Treason in the egg
Strong, Leonard Alfred George
Police diversion series (4)
Treason in time
Andrews, Keith William
Freedom's Rangers series (4)
Treason of Isengard
Tolkien, John Ronald Reuel
History of Middle Earth series (7)
History of the Lord of the Rings series (2)
Treason remembered
Baker, William Howard
Sexton Blake series (1596)
Treason's harbour
O'Brian, Patrick
Jack Aubrey and Stephen Maturin series (9)
Treasure
Cussler, Clive
Dirk Pitt series (9)
Hardy, Adam
George Abercrombie Fox series (4)
Mackenzie, Steve
Seals series (14)
Terhune, Albert Payson
Sunnybank collies series (11)
Treasure at Amorys
Saville, Malcolm
Lone Pine Five Club series (15)
Treasure at Dolphin Bay
Dixon, Franklin W
Hardy boys series (129)
Treasure at Upney Junction
Butterworth, Nick
Upney Junction series (4)
Treasure below
Ellsberg, Edward
Sunken treasure series (4)
Treasure by degrees
Williams, David
Mark Treasure series (2)

Treasure by post
Williams, David
Mark Treasure series (15)
Treasure cave
Lane, Carl Daniel
Altair series (1)
Treasure chest
Chase, Glen
Cherry Delight series (17)
Ledd, Paul
Shelter Morgan series (26)
Treasure code
Dank, Milton
Galaxy Gang series (4)
Treasure diver
Goodman, Julius
Choose your own adventure series (32)
Treasure divers
Streib, Dan
Michael Hawk series (14)
Treasure for three
Severn, David
Warner series (3)
Treasure hunt
Buechner, Frederick
Leo Bebb tetralogy (4)
Pace, Tom
Ben Garden series (1)
Treasure hunters
Baker, William Howard
Richard Quintain series (14)
Curwood, James Oliver
Wolf hunters series (2)
Lloyd, David
Let's pretend series (4)
Wetanson, Burt
Hunters series (2)
Treasure hunters of Bob's Hill
Burton, Charles Pierce
Bob's Hill series (9)
Treasure-hunting trip
Janosch
Little Tiger series (2)
Treasure in Devon
Leyland, Eric
Jack Meredith and Uncle George series (2)
Treasure in Oxford
Williams, David
Mark Treasure series (12)
Treasure in roubles
Williams, David
Mark Treasure series (10)
Treasure in the heart of the maze
Carr, Jayge
Navigator trilogy (2)
Treasure in the Wild Wood
Clewes, Dorothy
Wild Wood series (3)
Treasure Island
Stevenson, Robert Louis
Long John Silver series (1)
Long John Silver series (3)
Treasure Island series (1)
Treasure Island series (2)
Treasure map
Hardy, Adam
George Abercrombie Fox series (4)
Treasure Mountain
L'Amour, Louis
Sackett family series (12)
Treasure mountain
Sabin, Edward Legrand
Bar B boys series (5)
Treasure nobody saw
Walker, Holly Beth
Meg Duncan series (3)
Treasure of Alpheus Winterborn
Bellairs, John
Anthony Monday series (1)
Treasure of Cala Figuera
McCarthy, Maureen
Mission top secret series (4)
Treasure of Ebba
Fidler, Kathleen
Archaeology series (1)
Treasure of Echo Valley
Wees, Frances Shelley
Patterson family series (1)
Treasure of Green Knowe
Boston, Lucy Maria
Green Knowe series (2)
Treasure of Heron's Neck
Ladd, Elizabeth
Meg of Heron's Neck series (6)
Treasure of light
O'Neal, Kathleen M
Powers of light series (2)
Treasure of Nugget Mountain
May, Karl Friedrich
Winnetou trilogy (2)
Treasure of Spanish Bay
Beardmore, George
Lesley Allan series (5)
Treasure of the Cosa Nostra
Ridgway, Jason
Brian Guy series (4)
Treasure of the Johnny Smoker
Comfort, Mildred Houghton
Dustin family series (2)
Treasure of the lake
Haggard, Henry Rider
Allan Quatermain series (10)
Treasure of the Manchus
Armour, R Coutts
Sexton Blake series (413)
Treasure of the Onyx Dragon
Gilligan, Alison
Choose your own adventure series (105)
Treasure of the Reef
Patchett, Mary Elwyn
Ajax series (3)
Treasure of the seas
De Mille, James
Brethren of the White Cross series (6)
Treasure of the stars
Lord, Jeffrey
Richard Blade series (29)
Treasure of the sun
McCutcheon, Hugh
Jimmy Carroll series (1)
Treasure of Tranicos
De Camp, Lyon Sprague
Conan series (33)
Treasure of Westminster
Rae, John
Westminster series (2)
Treasure of Wonders Farm
Williams, Zillah
Wonders Farm series (1)
Treasure of Wonderwhat
Starr, Bill
Farstar and son series (2)
Treasure on the moor
Pullein-Thompson, Josephine
Moor pony series (5)
Treasure planet
Elliott, Nathan
Star pirates trilogy (3)
Treasure preserved
Williams, David
Mark Treasure series (6)
Treasure royal
Garrett, William
James Drew series (1)
Treasure Seekers
Nesbit, Edith
Bastable family series (1)
Treasure seekers of the Andes
Stratemeyer, Edward L
Pan-American series (5)
Treasure sock
Thomson, Pat
Share-a-story series (1)
Treasure trail
Grant, Maxwell
Shadow series (123)
Treasure train
Reeve, Arthur Benjamin
Craig Kennedy series (11)
Treasure trouble
Lambert, Janet
Christie Drayton series (2)
Treasure trove
Dawson-Scott, Catherine Amy
Some women trilogy (3)
Treasure under the sea
Coleman, James Covington
Deep-sea adventure series (2)
Treasure up in smoke
Williams, David
Mark Treasure series (3)
Treasure upstairs
Powell, Margaret
Domestic service series (3)
Treasures
Rathjen, Carl Henry
Waltons series (1)
Treasures from grandma's attic
Richardson, Arleta
Grandma's attic series (4)
Treasures lost, treasures found
Roberts, Nora
Flowers series (40)
Treasures of death
Grant, Maxwell
Shadow series (44)
Treasures of Morrow
Hoover, Helen Mary
Morrow series (2)
Treasures on earth
Stirling, Jessica
Elspeth and Anna Patterson trilogy (1)
Treasury alarm
Davey, Jocelyn
Ambrose Usher series (5)
Treasury of Australian nature stories
Rees, Leslie
Australian nature tales series (8)
Treat 'em rough
Lardner, Ring
Jack the Kaiser killer series (1)
Treat for Minikin
Hillyard, Mary Dorothea
Minikin series (5)
Treat me right
Goudge, Eileen
Seniors series (19)
Treble chance murder
Gunn, Victor
Chief Inspector Bill Cromwell series (30)
Treble cross
Howard, Hartley
Glenn Bowman series (35)
Treble exposure
Morice, Anne
Tessa Crichton Price series (21)
Tree
Glyn, Caroline
Fullie series (3)
Tree Frog
Woodhouse, Martin
Giles Yeoman series (1)
Tree house confessions
McConkey, James
Court of memory trilogy (2)
Tree house mystery
Warner, Gertrude Chandler
Boxcar children series (14)
Tree in your street
Simon, Seymour
Your street series (1)
Tree of Appomattox
Altsheler, Joseph Alexander
Civil War series (8)
Tree of death
Muller, Marcia
Elena Olivirez series (1)
Tree of swords and jewels
Cherryh, Carolyn Janice
Ealdwood series (2)
Tree of the sun
Harris, Wilson
Civilizations quartet (4)
Da Silva series (2)
Tree of Vertigern
Wiat, Philippa
Wyatt family series (5)
Tree of Vortigern
Wiat, Philippa
Black Boar series (4)
Tree on fire
Sillitoe, Alan
Frank Dawley trilogy (2)
Tree Tall and the horse race
Evans, Shirlee
Tree Tall series (2)
Tree Tall and the whiteskins
Evans, Shirlee
Tree Tall series (1)
Tree Tall to the rescue
Evans, Shirlee
Tree Tall series (3)
Tree that sat down
Nichols, Beverley
Judy series (1)
Tree-time Cubby
Tucker, Jenni
Cubby series (3)
Tree with a thousadn uses
Fisher, Aileen
Ways of plants series (9)
Treegate's raiders
Wibberley, Leonard
Treegate family trilogy (3)
Treehorn times three
Heide, Florence Parry
Treehorn series (3)
Treehorn's treasure
Heide, Florence Parry
Treehorn series (2)
Treehorn's wish
Heide, Florence Parry
Treehorn series (3)
Treehouse Gang
Resciniti, Angelo G
Treehouse Gang series (1)
Treehouse Gang's racing revenge
Resciniti, Angelo G
Treehouse Gang series (2)
Trees
Richter, Conrad
American pioneer trilogy (1)
Rippon, Angela
Learn with Victoria Plum series (2)
Trek of doom
Martin, Les
Young Indiana Jones chronicles series (5)
Trek or treat
Saint Clair, Elizabeth
Marilyn Ambers series (3)
Trek to Kraggen-Cor
McKiernan, Dennis L
Silver call series (1)
Trek to madworld
Goldin, Stephen
Star trek originals sequels series (13)
Trekker's trail
Vaughan, Carol
Manorfield Stud series (4)
Trekking on
Reitz, Deneys
Boer War journal trilogy (2)
Trellisane confrontation
Dvorkin, Daniel
Star trek series (14)
Tremaynes and the masterful monk
Dudley, Owen Francis
Problems of human happiness series (6)
Trembling earth
Clifford, Francis
Spanish duet series (1)
Trembling earth contract
Atlee, Philip
Joe Gall series (11)
Trembling heart
Dixon, Dorothy
Leather and lace series (2)
Trena and the old diary
Palmer, Bernard
Bradley series (4)
Trena's rodeo vial
Palmer, Bernard
Bradley series (7)
Trench
Munif, Abdelrahman
Cities of salt trilogy (2)
Trench soldier
Sadler, Barry
Casca series (21)
Trent fights again
Martyn, Wyndham
Anthony Trent series (22)
Trent intervenes
Bentley, Edmund Clerihew
Philip Trent series (3)
Trent of the lone hand
Martyn, Wyndham
Anthony Trent series (6)
Trent trail
Martyn, Wyndham
Anthony Trent series (11)
Trent's last case
Bentley, Edmund Clerihew
Philip Trent series (1)
Trent's own case
Bentley, Edmund Clerihew
Mister Clerihew series (2)
Philip Trent series (2)
Trepidation in Downing Street
Jones, Lawrence Evelyn
Father Lascaut series (1)
Tresillian Court
Lewis, Harriet
Tresillian series (1)
Trespassers at Charlcote
Avery, Gillian
Mister Copplestone series (2)
Smith family series (2)
Trespassers will die
Seuffert, Muir
Mike Hubbard series (2)
Trev the truck falls in love
Negus, George
Trev the truck series (4)
Trev the truck fights fire
Negus, George
Trev the truck series (2)
Trev the truck hits the highway
Negus, George
Trev the truck series (3)
Trev the truck saves the school bus
Negus, George
Trev the truck series (1)
Smith, Craig
Trev the truck series (1)
Treve
Terhune, Albert Payson
Sunnybank collies series (7)
Trey of swords
Norton, Andre
Witch World series (10)
Triad
Rohmer, Richard
Triad series (2)
Triad of darkness
Middleton, Martin
Chronicles of the custodians series (2)
Triad 21
Arvay, Harry
Israeli Security Branch series (11)
Triad series (1)
Trial
Darke, James
Witches series (2)
Kafka, Franz
K series (2)
Pendleton, Don
Mack Bolan series (91)
Yonge, Charlotte Mary
May family series (2)
Pillars of the house series (4)
Trial and error
Berkeley, Anthony
Ambrose Chitterwick series (3)
Trial by fire
Austin, Richard
Guardians series (2)
Keene, Carolyn
Nancy Drew files series (15)
Roberts, J R
Gunsmith series (70)
Trial by fury
Jance, Judith A
J P Beaumont series (3)
Lancer, Jack
Christopher Cool series (6)
Rice, Craig
John Joseph Malone series (5)
Trial by ordeal
Chessman, Caryl
Death row series (2)
Mills, Osmington
Superintendent William Baker series (6)
Trial by sasswood
Warner, Esther Sietmann
Liberia series (1)
Trial by sixgun
Sherman, Jory
Gunn series (11)
Trial by terror
Lockridge, Frances
Inspector Merton Heimrich series (7)
Trial of Billy Jack
Christina, Frank
Billy Jack series (2)
Liebling, Howard
Billy Jack series (2)
Trial of Captain Beaky
Lloyd, Jeremy
Captain Beaky and his band series (2)
Trial of champions
Livingstone, Ian
Fighting fantasy gamebook series (21)
Trial of magic
McGowen, Tom
Age of magic trilogy (2)
Trial of Slow Wolf
Grover, Marshall
Larry and Stretch series (350)
Trial of the golden girl
Dolphin, Rex
Sexton Blake series (1599)
Trial of the King
Lane, Jane
Stuart series (6)
Trial of the Seventh Carrier
Albano, Peter
Seventh Carrier series (6)
Trial of Vincent Doon
Oursler, William
Philip Strong and James Matthews series (1)
Trial valley
Cleaver, Vera
Luther family series (2)
Trials for the Chalet School
Brent-Dyer, Elinor Mary
Chalet School series (41)
Trials of Erica
Carter, Mary
Caged women series (6)

Trials of Rumpole
Mortimer, John
Horace Rumpole series (2)
Trials of the Phidias
Laurie-Long, Ernest
Simpson series (2)
Trials of Topsy
Herbert, Alan Patrick
Topsy series (1)
Trials of Windhaven
De Jourlet, Marie
Windhaven series (6)
Trials of Worzel Gummidge
Waterhouse, Keith
Worzel Gummidge series (14)
Triangle
Asimov, Isaac
Trantorian Empire trilogy (3)
Culbreath, Myrna
Star trek series (9)
Lassiter, Adam
Dennison's war series (5)
Marks, James Macdonald
Jason Wright series (2)
Triangle at Rhodes
Christie, Agatha
Hercule Poirot series (17)
Triangle of death
Hart, Jon
Mercenaries series (3)
Triangle of terror
Evans, Gwyn
Chester Brett series (3)
Tribal war
Garron, Marco
Azan series (5)
Tribe of Gum
Coburn, Anthony
Doctor Who scripts series (1)
Tribe of Jen-Wae
Wright, Meg
Star trek fan series (19)
Tribe that lost its head
Monsarrat, Nicholas
Pharamaul series (1)
Tribesman's plunder
Keddell, Jim
Brockleby series (1)
Tribesmen of Gor
Norman, John
Tarl Cabot series (10)
Tribulations and laughter
Behrman, Samuel Nathaniel
People in a diary series (2)
Tribute to the angels
Doolittle, Hilda
War trilogy (2)
Trick or treat
Disney, Doris Miles
Jeff Dimarco series (4)
Trick or treat, Danny?
Kunhardt, Edith
Danny series (3)
Trick paper tears with Gospel truth
Westphail, Arnold Carl
Paper tearing series (10)
Trick shooter
Dalton, Kit
Buckskin series (34)
Trick shot
Fox, Brian
Alias Smith and Jones series (6)
Trick the tooth fairy
Thaler, Mike
Bully brothers series (1)
Trick top hat
Wilson, Robert Anton
Schrodinger's cat trilogy (2)
Trickle of Welsh blood
Ruck, Berta
Storyteller series (3)
Tricks
McBain, Ed
Eighty Seventh Precinct series (41)
Tricks of the trade
Dixon, Franklin W
Hardy boys series (104)
Fish, Robert Lloyd
Kek Huuygens series (3)
Trickster's touch
Greenhalgh, Zohra
Trickster series (2)
Tricky business
Dixon, Franklin W
Hardy boys series (88)
Tricky tracks
Davis, Anne
Pumpkin Hill fact series (5)
Tricky troggle
Slater, Jim
A Mazing Monster series (3)
Tricolour
Logan, Mark
Nicholas Minnett series (1)
Trident brand
Wisler, Gary Clifton
Willie Delamer series (1)
Trident hijacking
Streib, Dan
Steve Crown series (2)
Trieste
Cory, Desmond
Johnny Fedora series (4)
Trig
Peck, Robert Newton
Trig series (1)
Trig goes ape
Peck, Robert Newton
Trig series (3)
Trig or treat
Peck, Robert Newton
Trig series (4)
Trig sees red
Peck, Robert Newton
Trig series (2)
Trigger
Melville-Ross, Antony
Submarine warfare series (1)
Treelake series (4)
Trigger blazes the trail
Allum, Tom
Captain Michael Triggington series (2)
Trigger fast
Edson, John Thomas
Floating Outfit series (23)
Trigger-fast
Grover, Marshall
Larry and Stretch series (334)
Trigger guard
LeBeau, Roy
Buckskin series (11)
Trigger Kid
Gregory, Lester
Kid Cyclone series (1)
Trigger lady
Swan, Phyllis
Anna J series (2)
Trigger law
Cole, Jackson
Jim Hatfield series (14)
Trigger man
Arthur, Burt
Dan Lovett series (1)
Trigger-man
Copper, Basil
Mike Faraday series (37)
Trigger master
Edson, John Thomas
Floating Outfit series (40)
Trigger mortis
Kane, Frank
Johnny Liddell series (12)
Trigger Spring
LeBeau, Roy
Buckskin series (6)
Trigger talk
Scott, Bradford
Walt Slade series (9)
Trigger trail
Shane, Steve
Lone Star Kid series (2)
Trigger trap
Grover, Marshall
Larry and Stretch series (4)
Triggerman
Rossi, Bruno
Sharpshooter series (11)
Triggers are trumps
Elliott, William James
Ed Gunning series (3)
Trilogy
Bloom, Ursula
No lady series (8)
Castaneda, Carlos
Don Juan series (3)
Doolittle, Hilda
War trilogy (3)
Trilogy in jeopardy
Kane, Henry
Peter Chambers series (8)
Trimmed lamp
Henry, O
Four million series (2)
Trina
Hoff, Harry Summerfield
Three marriages series (1)
Trina finds a brother
Braenne, Berit
Trina series (1)
Trinity
Bridges, Roy
Australian trilogy (3)
Trinity in violence
Kane, Henry
Peter Chambers series (8)
Trio
Bentley, Phyllis
West Riding series (20)
Trio for blunt instruments
Stout, Rex
Nero Wolfe and Archie Goodwin series (39)
Trio for Lute
Macavoy, Roberta Ann
Lute trilogy (3)
Trio in three flats
Dewhurst, Eileen
Inspector Neil Carter series (3)
Trip
Keats, Ezra Jack
Louie series (2)
Trip, and other Sophie and Gussie stories
Sharmat, Marjorie Weinman
Sophie and Gussie series (2)
Trip day
Ziefert, Harriet
Mister Rose's class series (2)
Trip eastwards
Abbott, Edward
Long Look trilogy (3)
Trip on a bus
Greene, Carla
Travel series (10)
Trip on a jet
Greene, Carla
Travel series (8)
Trip on a plane
Greene, Carla
Travel series (5)
Trip on a ship
Greene, Carla
Travel series (6)
Trip on a train
Greene, Carla
Travel series (4)
Trip to Hawaii
Greene, Carla
Travel series (7)
Trip to Jerusalem
Marston, Edward
Elizabethan whodunits series (3)
Trip to Panama
Janosch
Little Tiger series (1)
Trip to Texas
Tippett, James Sterling
Henry series (4)
Trip to the aquarium
Greene, Carla
Travel series (11)
Trip to the moon
Lunatic, Humphry
Noibla series (1)
Trip to the moon, volume II
Lunatic, Humphry
Noibla series (2)
Trip to the zoo
Greene, Carla
Travel series (9)
Trip trap
Rathbone, Julian
Colonel Nur Bey series (3)
Triphammer
McCall, Dan
Trip Bodley series (2)
Triplanetary
Smith, Edward Elmer
Lensman series (1)
Triple bite
Flynn, Brian
Anthony Bathurst series (10)
Triple crime
Carter, Nicholas
Nicholas Carter series (89)
Triple cross
Barry, Joe
Rush Henry series (3)
Carter, Nick
Nick Carter series (113)
Roeburt, John
Jigger Moran series (2)
Triple cross murders
Long, Amelia Reynolds
Edward Trelawny series (4)
Triple crown
Breen, Jon Linn
Jerry Brogan series (3)
Triple death
Carnac, Carol
Inspector Ryvet series (1)
Triple exposure
Townend, Peter
Philip Quest series (4)
Triple hoax
Keene, Carolyn
Nancy Drew series (57)
Triple identity
Carter, Nicholas
Nicholas Carter series (191)
Triple jeopardy
Stout, Rex
Nero Wolfe and Archie Goodwin series (20)
Triple knavery
Carter, Nicholas
Nicholas Carter series (447)
Triple knock
Carter, Nicholas
Nicholas Carter series (397)
Triple murder
Wells, Carolyn
Fleming Stone series (27)
Triple quest
Punshon, Ernest Robertson
Bobby Owen series (34)
Triple slay
Knight, Adam
Steve Conacher series (8)
Triple terror
Kane, Henry
Peter Chambers series (9)
Triple threat
Roos, Kelley
Jeff and Haila Troy series (8)
Triple-threat trouble
Bee, Clair
Chip Hilton series (18)
Triple trail
Grant, Maxwell
Shadow series (76)
Triple trouble
Lambert, Janet
Cinda Hollister series (4)
Thesman, Jean
Whitney cousins series (4)
Triple trouble at Fairwood High
Norton, Nancy
Homeroom series (3)
Triple trouble for Hound Dog Zip
Steele, William Owen
Hound Dog Zip series (2)
Triple zero eight meets Gnatman
Allison, Clyde
Agent triple zero eight series (8)
Triple zero eight meets Modesta Blaze
Allison, Clyde
Agent triple zero eight series (13)
Tripletrap
Hallahan, William Henry
Charley Brewer series (2)
Triplets become good neighbors
Moore, Bertha B
Triplets series (8)
Triplets fly high
Moore, Bertha B
Triplets series (12)
Triplets go places
Moore, Bertha B
Triplets series (6)
Triplets go south
Moore, Bertha B
Triplets series (4)
Triplets go to camp
Moore, Bertha B
Triplets series (13)
Triplets have an adventure
Moore, Bertha B
Triplets series (10)
Triplets in business
Moore, Bertha B
Triplets series (3)
Triplets make a discovery
Moore, Bertha B
Triplets series (11)
Triplets over J.O.Y.
Moore, Bertha B
Triplets series (5)
Triplets receive a reward
Moore, Bertha B
Triplets series (9)
Triplets sign up
Moore, Bertha B
Triplets series (7)
Triplets take over
Moore, Bertha B
Triplets series (14)
Triplets try television
Moore, Bertha B
Triplets series (15)
Tripods trilogy
Christopher, John
Tripods series (4)
Tripoint
Cherryh, Carolyn Janice
Merchanter series (4)
Tripping with the Tucker twins
Sampson, Emma
Tucker twins series (4)
Tristana
Perez Galdos, Benito
Contemporary novels of Spain series (23)
Tristessa
Kerouac, Jack
Jack Duluoz series (9)
Triton brig
Pope, Dudley
Lord Nicholas Ramage series (3)
Triumph
Aminoff, Constance Leonie Caroline
Napoleonic series (6)
Gann, Ernest Kellogg
Triumph series (1)
Payne, Oliver
Northwest Territory series (6)
Triumph and passing of Cuculain
O'Grady, Standish James
Cuculain trilogy (3)
Triumph for Inspector West
Creasey, John
Inspector Roger West series (6)
Triumph in the west, 1943-1946
Bryant, Arthur
Second World War series (2)
Triumph of death
Annunzio, Gabriele d'
Romances of the rose trilogy (1)
Triumph of Elaine
Reeve, Arthur Benjamin
Craig Kennedy series (9)
Elaine trilogy (3)
Triumph of failure
Sheehan, Patrick Augustine
Geoffrey Austin series (2)
Triumph of Inspector Maigret
Simenon, Georges
Inspector Jules Maigret series (3)
Inspector Jules Maigret series (16)
Triumph of McLean
Goodchild, George
Inspector McLean series (6)
Triumph of surgery
Thorwald, Jurgen
Century of the surgeon series (2)
Triumph of the Darksword
Weis, Margaret
Darksword trilogy (3)
Triumph of the Rat
Robins, Denise
Rat series (2)
Triumph of the Scarlet Pimpernel
Orczy, Emmuska
Scarlet Pimpernel series (11)
Triumph of time
Blish, James
Cities in flight series (4)
Jameson, Storm
Triumph of time trilogy (3)
Triumph of Tinker
Jepson, Edgar
Tinker series (2)
Triumphant beast
Bowen, Marjorie
Renaissance trilogy (2)
Triumphant prodigal
Martyn, Wyndham
Anthony Trent series (7)
Triumvirate
Taylor, H Baldwin
David Halliday series (2)
Trivia I
Cranfield, Ingrid
Q challenge quiz series (3)
Trivia II
Cranfield, Ingrid
Q challenge quiz series (4)
Trixie a la mode
Walker, Mort
Hi and Lois series (8)
Trixie Belden and mystery in Arizona
Campbell, Julie
Trixie Belden series (6)
Trixie Belden and the black jacket mystery
Kenny, Kathryn
Trixie Belden series (8)
Trixie Belden and the gatehouse mystery
Campbell, Julie
Trixie Belden series (3)
Trixie Belden and the Happy Valley mystery
Kenny, Kathryn
Trixie Belden series (9)

Trixie Belden and the Hudson River mystery
Kenny, Kathryn
Trixie Belden series (28)
Trixie Belden and the marshland mystery
Kenny, Kathryn
Trixie Belden series (10)
Trixie Belden and the mysterious code
Kenny, Kathryn
Trixie Belden series (7)
Trixie Belden and the mysterious visitor
Campbell, Julie
Trixie Belden series (4)
Trixie Belden and the mystery at Bob-White Cave
Kenny, Kathryn
Trixie Belden series (11)
Trixie Belden and the mystery at Maypenny's
Kenny, Kathryn
Trixie Belden series (31)
Trixie Belden and the mystery at Mead's Mountain
Kenny, Kathryn
Trixie Belden series (22)
Trixie Belden and the mystery at Saratoga
Kenny, Kathryn
Trixie Belden series (24)
Trixie Belden and the mystery of the blinking eye
Kenny, Kathryn
Trixie Belden series (12)
Trixie Belden and the mystery of the castaway children
Kenny, Kathryn
Trixie Belden series (21)
Trixie Belden and the mystery of the emeralds
Kenny, Kathryn
Trixie Belden series (14)
Trixie Belden and the mystery of the ghostly galleon
Kenny, Kathryn
Trixie Belden series (27)
Trixie Belden and the mystery of the headless horseman
Kenny, Kathryn
Trixie Belden series (26)
Trixie Belden and the mystery of the midnight marauder
Kenny, Kathryn
Trixie Belden series (30)
Trixie Belden and the mystery of the missing heiress
Kenny, Kathryn
Trixie Belden series (16)
Trixie Belden and the mystery of the missing millionaire
Kenny, Kathryn
Trixie Belden series (34)
Trixie Belden and the mystery of the phantom grasshopper
Kenny, Kathryn
Trixie Belden series (18)
Trixie Belden and the mystery of the queen's necklace
Kenny, Kathryn
Trixie Belden series (23)
Trixie Belden and the mystery of the uninvited guest
Kenny, Kathryn
Trixie Belden series (17)
Trixie Belden and the mystery of the vanishing victim
Kenny, Kathryn
Trixie Belden series (33)
Trixie Belden and the mystery of the whispering witch
Kenny, Kathryn
Trixie Belden series (32)
Trixie Belden and the mystery off Glen Road
Campbell, Julie
Trixie Belden series (5)
Trixie Belden and the mystery off Old Telegraph Road
Kenny, Kathryn
Trixie Belden series (20)
Trixie Belden and the mystery on Cobbett's Island
Kenny, Kathryn
Trixie Belden series (13)
Trixie Belden and the mystery on the Mississippi
Kenny, Kathryn
Trixie Belden series (15)
Trixie Belden and the red trailer mystery
Campbell, Julie
Trixie Belden series (2)
Trixie Belden and the Sasquatch mystery
Kenny, Kathryn
Trixie Belden series (25)
Trixie Belden and the secret of the mansion
Campbell, Julie
Trixie Belden series (1)
Trixie Belden and the secret of the unseen treasure
Kenny, Kathryn
Trixie Belden series (19)
Trixie Trash, star ascending
Wakefield, Tom
Margaret Davis and Isobel Quirk trilogy (1)
Troddles and us and others
Andom, R
Troddles series (2)
Troddles' farm
Andom, R
Troddles series (11)
Troddles in the trenches
Andom, R
Troddles series (14)
Troddles, not to mention ourselves
Andom, R
Troddles series (10)
Trog
Butterworth, Ben
That boy Trog series (2)
Trog and his axe
Butterworth, Ben
That boy Trog series (1)
Trog and his boat
Butterworth, Ben
That boy Trog series (6)
Trog and the dog
Butterworth, Ben
That boy Trog series (8)
Trog and the fire
Butterworth, Ben
That boy Trog series (2)
Trog and the horse
Butterworth, Ben
That boy Trog series (5)
Trog in trouble
Butterworth, Ben
That boy Trog series (4)
Trog makes a trap
Butterworth, Ben
That boy Trog series (3)
Trog tries again
Butterworth, Ben
That boy Trog series (6)
Trog's grandpa
Butterworth, Ben
That boy Trog series (8)
Troika
Cooper, Louise Antell
Indigo series (5)
Harvester, Simon
Asia in turmoil series (13)
Heron Murmur series (2)
Montross, David
Remsen series (2)
Troika belle
Morris, Ira J
Lavrin family series (2)
Trojan gold
Peters, Elizabeth
Vicky Bliss series (4)
Trojan hearse
Curzon, Clare
Superintendent Mike Yeadings and Sergeant Angus Mott series (5)
Trojan horse
Pendleton, Don
Mack Bolan series (110)
Prather, Richard Scott
Shell Scott series (28)
Trojan horses
Emmett, Robert
American Avenger series (5)
Trojan in Iran
Skimin, Robert
Soldier for hire series (2)
Trojan orbit
Reynolds, Mack
Lagrangia series (4)
Trojan tank
King, David
Rat Patrol series (3)
Troll patrol
Gilden, Mel
Fifth grade monsters series (14)
Troll tales of Tumble Town
Torgersen, Don Arthur
Troll series (1)
Troll who lived in the lake
Torgersen, Don Arthur
Troll series (3)
Troll who went to school
Torgersen, Don Arthur
Troll series (5)
Troll's grindstone
Boyer, Elizabeth H
Wizard's war series (1)
Troll's three Christmas wishes
Torgersen, Don Arthur
Troll series (2)
Trolly to yesterday
Bellairs, John
Johnny Dixon series (6)
Trooper Bluegum at the Dardanelles
Hogue, Oliver
Anzac series (2)
Troops return
Doblin, Alfred
German revolution series (1)
Trophies and dead things
Muller, Marcia
Sharon McCone series (11)
Trophy
Baldwin, Bill
Helmsman series (3)
Tropic days
Banfield, Edmund James
Beachcomber series (3)
Tropic heat
Pendleton, Don
SuperBolan series (9)
Tropic of Cancer
Miller, Henry
Tropics series (1)
Tropic of Capricorn
Miller, Henry
Tropics series (3)
Tropic of fear
Carroll, John Richard
Don Bartholomew series (2)
Tropical deathpact
Carter, Nick
Nick Carter series (128)
Tropical freeze
Hall, James W
Thorn series (2)
Tropical heat
Lutz, John
Fred Carver series (1)
Tropical issue
Dunnett, Dorothy
Johnson and the yacht Dolly series (6)
Tropical rain forests
Hoff, Mary
Our endangered planet series (5)
Tros
Mundy, Talbot
Tros of Samothrace series (1)
Tros of Samothrace series (1)
Tros of Samothrace
Mundy, Talbot
Tros of Samothrace series (1)
Trotsky's run
Hoyt, Richard
James Burlane series (1)
Troubadour
Burns, Richard
Khalindaine series (2)
Troubadours of Provence
Fleming, Arnold
Souvenir de France series (3)
Troubadour's quest
Hunt, Angela Elwell
Theyn chronicles trilogy (2)
Trouble a-brewing
Bude, John
Inspector Meredith series (14)
Trouble among the witches
Cass, Joan Evelyn
Molly Millikens series (4)
Trouble and more trouble
Maguire, Jack
Many lives of Underfoot the cat series (1)
Trouble at Alcott School
Haas, Dorothy
Peanut Butter and Jilly series (4)
Trouble at Aquitaine
Livingston, Nancy
G D H Pringle series (1)
Trouble at Coyote Canyon
Dixon, Franklin W
Hardy boys series (119)
Trouble at Harrison High
Farris, John
Harrison High series (3)
Trouble at Heron's Neck
Ladd, Elizabeth
Meg of Heron's Neck series (5)
Trouble at home
Pascal, Francine
Sweet Valley High series (65)
Trouble at Kittiwake Rock
Westwood, Anne McDougall
Kittiwake Rock series (2)
Trouble at Lake Tahoe
Keene, Carolyn
Nancy Drew series (118)
Trouble at Minimal Farm
Carmichael, Claire
Minimal Farm series (2)
Trouble at Moon Pass
Shappiro, Herbert
Mustang Marshal series (5)
Trouble at Queen's Chantry
Little Sylvia
Queen's Chantry series (1)
Trouble at Saxby's
Creasey, John
Inspector Roger West series (22)
Trouble at Shaplinch
Emerson, David
Parson Carnaby series (2)
Trouble at Skelton Hall
Brent-Dyer, Elinor Mary
Skelton Hall series (2)
Trouble at Tamberly
Byers, Irene
Tim Digby series (3)
Trouble at the Rovers
Kershaw, H V
Coronation Street series (2)
Trouble at Townsend
Saville, Malcolm
Michael and Mary series (1)
Trouble at Tullington Castle
Beresford, Elisabeth
Gappy, Jim and Jane series (3)
Trouble at Turkey Hill
Knight, Kathleen Moore
Elisha Macomber series (8)
Trouble at War Eagle
Tuttle, Wilbur Coleman
Hashknife Hartley and Sleepy Stevens series (33)
Trouble at Wrekin Farm
Bell, Josephine
Doctor David Wintringham series (7)
Trouble busters
Edson, John Thomas
Floating Outfit series (25)
Trouble crossing the Pyrenees
Larsen, Gaylord D
Henry Garrett series (2)
Trouble follows me
Millar, Kenneth
Chet Gordon series (2)
Trouble for Lucia
Benson, Edward Frederic
Lucia Billson series (7)
Trouble for Paddy Joe
Stranger, Joyce
Paddy Joe series (2)
Trouble for Tallon
Ball, John
Jack Tallon series (2)
Trouble for the Tabors
Goolden, Barbara
Tabor family series (5)
Trouble for the twins
Blyton, Enid
Twins series (7)
Trouble for Trimble
Clifford, Martin
Tom Merry series (11)
Trouble for Trumpets
Dallas-Smith, Peter
Trumpets series (1)
Trouble hunters
Atwater, Montgomery Meigs
Hank Winton series (5)
Trouble in Burma
Mason, Francis Van Wyck
Colonel Hugh North series (23)
Trouble in Crumble Lane
Allan, Mabel Esther
Crumble Lane series (2)
Trouble in paradise
Carter, Nick
Nick Carter series (121)
Cooper, Ilene
Hollywood wars series (4)
Trouble in Paradise
Fish, Robert Lloyd
Captain Jose da Silva series (10)
Trouble in paradise
Gilman, George G
Adam Steele series (47)
Trouble in Paradise
Smyth, John George
Ann Sheldon series (2)
Trouble in Tahiti
Keene, Carolyn
Nancy Drew files series (31)
Trouble in the bank
Davis, Howard Charles
Edward Tope series (1)
Trouble in the big top
Mitchell, Lane
Jimmy Grier series (3)
Trouble in the brasses
Craig, Alisa
Inspector Madoc Rhys series (4)
Trouble in the gym
Levy, Elizabeth
Gymnasts series (5)
Trouble in the Jungle
Townsend, John Rowe
Uncle Walter series (1)
Trouble in the mayor's parlour
Carruth, Jean
Trumpton series (5)
Trouble in the pipeline
Dixon, Franklin W
Hardy boys case files series (26)
Trouble in the wind
Leslie, Richard
Heracles trilogy (1)
Trouble in Tinktonk Land
Mayer, Mercer
Tink, tonk tales series (5)
Trouble in Tokyo
Bruce, Jean
Secret Agent O.S.S.117 series (9)
Trouble in Toyland
Beaman, Sydney George Hulme
Toytown series (3)
Hope, Laura Lee
New Bobbsey twins series (7)
Trouble in Transylvania
Wilson, Barbara Ellen
Cassandra Reilly series (2)
Trouble in triplicate
Stout, Rex
Nero Wolfe and Archie Goodwin series (14)
Trouble is my business
Chandler, Raymond
Philip Marlowe series (6)
Trouble is my name
Dolphin, Rex
Sexton Blake series (1514)
Marlowe, Stephen
Chester Drum series (3)
Trouble is our shadow
Grover, Marshall
Larry and Stretch series (65)
Trouble of fools
Barnes, Linda
Carlotta Carlyle series (2)
Trouble on Artule
McGuire, Catherine
Endless quest series (24)
Trouble on Hogback Hill
Summers, James Levingston
Trouble series (4)
Trouble on Janus
Slote, Alfred
Danny One series (5)
Trouble on parade
Robeson, Kenneth
Doc Savage series (159)
Trouble on planet earth
Montgomery, Raymond A
Choose your own adventure series (29)
Trouble on the border
Young, Gordon Ray
Red Clark series (4)
Trouble on the run
Summers, James Levingston
Trouble series (3)
Trouble on the Santa Fe
Striker, Fran
Lone Ranger series (21)
Trouble on Trinity Range
Cole, Jackson
Jim Hatfield series (47)
Trouble on Valley View
Mendel, Jo
Tucker family series (4)
Trouble Range
Cole, Jackson
Jim Hatfield series (66)
Trouble rides a fast horse
Roberts, J R
Gunsmith series (31)
Trouble rides the wind
Bower, Bertha Muzzy
Flying U Ranch series (11)
Trouble shooter
Cody, Stetson
Cactus Clancy series (3)
Cole, Jackson
Jim Hatfield series (25)
Macdonald, William Colt
Gregory Quist series (10)

Trouble town
Arthur, Burt
Texas Rangers series (2)
Trouble trail
Edson, John Thomas
Calamity Jane series (4)
Trouble trail yonder
Grover, Marshall
Larry and Stretch series (84)
Trouble trailer
Tuttle, Wilbur Coleman
Hashknife Hartley and Sleepy Stevens series (19)
Trouble twisters
Anderson, Poul
Future history series (3)
Trouble with a capital T
Baer, Judy
Cedar River daydreams series (2)
Trouble with adventurers
Harris, Christie
Trouble series (2)
Trouble with being in love
Summers, James Levingston
Trouble series (5)
Trouble with crime
Noel, Jeffrey
Johnny Perfect series (2)
Trouble with dad
Cole, Babette
Trouble with series (2)
Trouble with flirting
Haynes, Betsy
Fabulous Five series (2)
Trouble with gran
Cole, Babette
Trouble with series (3)
Trouble with grandad
Cole, Babette
Trouble with series (4)
Trouble with guns
Noel, Jeffrey
Johnny Perfect series (1)
Trouble with Jennings
Buckeridge, Anthony
Jennings series (11)
Trouble with lemons
Hayes, Daniel
Tyler McAllister series (1)
Trouble with love
Keene, Carolyn
River Heights series (8)
Trouble with mom
Cole, Babette
Trouble with series (1)
Trouble with mum
Cole, Babette
Trouble with series (1)
Trouble with murder
Bax, Roger
Inspector James series (1)
Trouble with Patti
Saunders, Susan
Sleepover friends series (22)
Trouble with Penelope
Healey, Ben
Paul Hedley series (5)
Trouble with princesses
Harris, Christie
Trouble series (1)
Trouble with Spider
Kraus, Robert
Spider series (1)
Trouble with the fiend
Lavelle, Sheila
Charlie Ellis and Angela Mitchell series (3)
Trouble with the Johnsons
Teague, Mark
Johnsons trilogy (1)
Trouble with Toni
Quin-Harkin, Janet
Toni Redmond and Jill Gardner series (4)
Trouble with Vanessa
Ure, Jean
Vanessa trilogy (1)
Troublecross
Mann, Jessica
Thea Crawford series (1)
Troubled deaths
Jeffries, Roderic Graeme
Inspector Enrique Alvarez series (3)
Troubled grass
Floren, Lee
Buckshot McKee and Tortilla Joe series (3)
Troubled heritage
Wilson, Jeanne
Island trilogy (2)
Troubled range
Edson, John Thomas
Floating Outfit series (12)
Troubled sleep
Sartre, Jean Paul
Roads to freedom trilogy (3)
Troubled water
Gunning, Sally
Peter Bartholomew series (4)
Troubled waters
Barlow, Roger
Sandy Steele series (6)
Cherryh, Carolyn Janice
Merovingen nights series (3)
Lemarchand, Elizabeth
Superintendent Tom Pollard series (13)
Troublemaker
Chase, Emily
Canby Hall series (22)
Hansen, Joseph
Dave Brandstetter series (3)
Pascal, Francine
Sweet Valley High series (47)
Troubles
Farrell, James Gordon
British Empire trilogy (1)
Troubleshooter
Dodge, David
John Abraham Lincoln series (2)
Troubleshooters
Fuller, Ed
Troubleshooters series (1)
Troubleshooters die hard
Grover, Marshall
Larry and Stretch series (190)
Troublesome engines
Awdry, Wilbert
Railway series (5)
Troubling along the border
Aamodt, Donald
Name to conjure with series (2)
Trough of the wave
Duun, Ole Julius
People of Juvik series (1)
Trout in the milk
Holman, Hugh
Sheriff Macready series (1)
Lewis, Royston
Arnold Landon series (3)
Trout's testament
Fraser, Ronald
Trout series (3)
Troy
Francis, Jaye
Hot pursuit series (5)
Troyana
Meek, Sterner St. Paul
Troyana series (2)
Trozas
Traven, B
Jungle series (4)
Truce
Levi, Primo
Survival in Auschwitz series (2)
Truce, 1921-33
Ehrenburg, Ilya
Men, years and life series (3)
Truck drivers
Greene, Carla
What do they do series (6)
Truckers
Pratchett, Terry
Book of the Nomes trilogy (1)
Truckload of rice
Berna, Paul
Bobby Thiriet series (3)
Trudy and Timothy
Porter, Bertha Currier
Trudy and Timothy series (1)
Trudy and Timothy and the trees
Porter, Bertha Currier
Trudy and Timothy series (3)
Trudy and Timothy, foresters
Porter, Bertha Currier
Trudy and Timothy series (4)
Trudy and Timothy out of doors
Porter, Bertha Currier
Trudy and Timothy series (2)
Trudy in demand
Faid, Mary Alice
Trudy series (9)
Trudy married
Faid, Mary Alice
Trudy series (8)
Trudy on her own
Faid, Mary Alice
Trudy series (6)
Trudy takes charge
Faid, Mary Alice
Trudy series (1)
Trudy's college days
Faid, Mary Alice
Trudy series (4)
Trudy's island holiday
Faid, Mary Alice
Trudy series (2)
Trudy's small corner
Faid, Mary Alice
Trudy series (7)
Trudy's uphill road
Faid, Mary Alice
Trudy series (3)
True adventures of Huckleberry Finn
Seelye, John
Huckleberry Finn series (4)
True confessions of Adrian Albert Mole
Townsend, Sue
Adrian Mole series (3)
True crime
Collins, Max Allan
Nathan Heller series (2)
True detective
Collins, Max Allan
Nathan Heller series (1)
True game
Tepper, Sheri S
True game trilogy (3)
True grit
Portis, Charles
Rooster Cogburn series (1)
True-life adventure
Smith, Julie
Paul McDonald series (1)
True love
Campbell, Joanna
Caitlin trilogy (3)
Pascal, Francine
Love trilogy (3)
True north
Conway, Jill Ker
Coorain series (2)
True son of the Beast!
Brown, Carter
Larry Baker series (5)
True story
Hudson, Stephen
Kurt series (4)
True tales of castles
Fidler, Kathleen
Heritage series (13)
True tales of escapes
Fidler, Kathleen
Heritage series (11)
True tales of mystery
Fidler, Kathleen
Heritage series (12)
True tales of treasure
Fidler, Kathleen
Heritage series (9)
True Thomas
Tranter, Nigel Godwin
Scottish history series (4)
True to himself
Stratemeyer, Edward L
Ship and shore series (3)
Truffles' day in bed
Anholt, Catherine
Truffles series (2)
Truffles for Toy
Clapton, Patricia
Toy series (2)
Truffles in trouble
Anholt, Catherine
Truffles series (1)
Truffles is sick
Anholt, Catherine
Truffles series (2)
Trullion
Vance, Jack
Alastor trilogy (1)
Gaean series (1)
Truly thankful?
Toye, Francis
Truly thankful series (2)
Truman era, 1945-1952
Stone, Isidor Feinstein
Nonconformist history of our times series (2)
Trumpet and the swords
Danielson, Peter
Children of the Lion series (14)
Trumpet Churchdog
Austin, Margot
Church animals series (4)
Trumpet-major
Hardy, Thomas
Romances and fantasies series (2)
Trumpet of terror
Goodman, Deborah Lerme
Choose your own adventure series (55)
Trumpet voluntary
Stern, Gladys Bronwyn
Ragbag chronicles series (3)
Trumpets at Rome
Bowen, Marjorie
Renaissance trilogy (3)
Trumpets from the steep
Cooper, Diana Olivia Winifred Maud
Rainbow series (3)
Trumpets in Grumpetland
Dallas-Smith, Peter
Trumpets series (2)
Trumpets in the West
Trease, Geoffrey
Stuart kings series (4)
Trumpets of war
Adams, Robert
Horseclans series (16)
Trumps of doom
Zelazny, Roger
Kingdom of Amber series (6)
Trumpton story book
Maclean, Moira
Trumpton series (8)
Trunch
Durrant, Digby
Hamish Oath series (2)
Trunk call for murder
Radford, Edwin
Doctor Manson series (27)
Trust Chunky
Berg, Leila
Chunky series (2)
Trust doesn't rust
Larson, Glen A
Knight Rider series (2)
Trust Jennings
Buckeridge, Anthony
Jennings series (19)
Trust McLean
Goodchild, George
Inspector McLean series (41)
Trust me on this
Westlake, Donald Edwin
Sara Joslyn series (1)
Trust territory
Morris, Janet Ellen
Threshold series (2)
Trust the Saint
Charteris, Leslie
Saint series (35)
Trust Tilty
Thomson, Arthur Alexander
Marigold Cottage trilogy (2)
Trusted like the fox
Woods, Sara
Sir Nicholas Harding and Antony Maitland series (6)
Trusted rogue
Carter, Nicholas
Nicholas Carter series (109)
Trusted servant
Macleod, Alison
Tom Vaughan series (1)
Truth
Zola, Emile
Four Gospels series (3)
Truth about Claire Veryan
Truss, Seldon
Inspector Gidleigh series (12)
Truth about Lord Tench
Stuart, Donald
Sexton Blake series (855)
Truth about making out
Lantz, Francess Lin
Making out series (1)
Truth about Mary Rose
Sachs, Marilyn
Veronica Ganz series (4)
Truth about sixth grade
McKenna, Colleen O'Shaughnessy
Murphy family series (6)
Truth about Snake Ridge
Grover, Marshall
Larry and Stretch series (339)
Truth about Stacey
Martin, Ann Matthews
Baby-Sitters Club series (3)
Truth about Taffy Sinclair
Haynes, Betsy
Taffy Sinclair series (9)
Truth came out
Punshon, Ernest Robertson
Carter and Bell series (5)
Truth comes limping
Connington, John Jervis
Sir Clinton Driffield series (12)
Truth shall set you free
Priest, Christopher
Last deadloss vision series (2)
Truthful harp
Alexander, Lloyd
Prydain series (6)
Truthful lady
Clouston, Joseph Storer
Sherlock Holmes sequels series (70)
Truxton King
McCutcheon, George Barr
Graustark series (3)
Try again
Optic, Oliver
Boat Club series (5)
Try again Friday
Webber, Edmund Godfrey
Trout fishing series (2)
Try and trust
Alger, Horatio
Luck and pluck series (5)
Try anything once
Clune, Frank
Try series (1)
Fair, A A
Bertha Cool and Donald Lam series (23)
Try me!
Grover, Marshall
Bleak Creek series (9)
Try nothing twice
Clune, Frank
Try series (2)
Trying out
Cooney, Caroline B
Cheerleaders series (1)
Trying out Torchy
Ford, Sewell
Torchy series (2)
Trying to be useful
Leslie, Madeline
Little Agnes series (1)
Tryst for a tragedy
Lorac, E C R
Inspector Macdonald series (18)
Tsimmis in Tangier
Knight, Mallory T
Man from T.O.M.C.A.T. series (5)
Tsing-boom!
Freeling, Nicolas
Inspector Piet Van der Valk series (8)
Tsing-boum!
Freeling, Nicolas
Inspector Piet Van der Valk series (8)
Tsunami
Kilian, Crawford
Icequake series (2)
Stern, Richard Martin
Johnny Ortiz series (4)
Tub grandfather
Conrad, Pam
Tub People series (2)
Tub People
Conrad, Pam
Tub People series (1)
Tubby and the lantern
Perkins, Al
Tubby series (1)
Tubby and the Poo-Bah
Perkins, Al
Tubby series (2)
Tubby, the little round bear
Lister, Gladys
Leafy series (4)
Round series (5)
Tubular android superheroes
Gilden, Mel
Zoot Marlowe series (3)
Tucker and Co.
Redmond, Phil
Grange Hill series (6)
Tucker in control
Needle, Jan
Tucker series (3)
Tucker's countryside
Selden, George
Chester Cricket series (2)
Tucker's luck
Needle, Jan
Tucker series (2)
Tuckonie on tour
Martin, Marianne
Golden boomerang series (7)
Tuckonie's warrior friend
Bingham, Lorna
Golden boomerang series (5)
Tucson
Mitchum, Hank
Stage coach station series (12)
Riefe, A R
Fortunes west series (1)

Tucson conspiracy
Chisholm, Matt
Joe Blade series (2)

Tucson temptress
Cunningham, Chet
Agent Brad Spear series (3)

Tucson twosome
Sherman, Jory
Gunn series (17)

Tudor agent
Farrington, Robert
Henry Morane series (2)

Tudor garden mystery
Verner, Gerald
Felix Heron series (1)

Tudor Green
Maxwell, William Babington
Men and women trilogy (1)

Tudor London
Birt, David
Tudors series (10)

Tudor maid
Hyde, Eleanor
Tudor series (1)

Tudor malice
Hyde, Eleanor
Tudor series (9)

Tudor mansion
Hyde, Eleanor
Tudor series (8)

Tudor masquerade
Hyde, Eleanor
Tudor series (2)

Tudor mausoleum
Hyde, Eleanor
Tudor series (7)

Tudor mayhem
Hyde, Eleanor
Tudor series (3)

Tudor mystery
Hyde, Eleanor
Tudor series (4)

Tudor myth
Hyde, Eleanor
Tudor series (5)

Tudor Navy
Birt, David
Tudors series (7)

Tudor star
Lowndes, Joan Selby
Francis and Anne Woodward series (2)

Tudort murder
Hyde, Eleanor
Tudor series (6)

Tuesday adventure
Pudney, John
Fred and I series (4)

Tuesday Club murders
Christie, Agatha
Miss Jane Marple series (2)

Tuesday dog
Stoneley, Jack
Tuesday dogs series (1)

Tuesday the Rabbi saw red
Kemelman, Harry
Rabbi David Small series (5)

Tuff stuff
Berry, Joy
Ready-set-grow series (24)

Tuffa and her friends
Schroeder, Binette
Tuffa series (3)

Tuffa and the bone
Schroeder, Binette
Tuffa series (2)

Tuffa and the ducks
Schroeder, Binette
Tuffa series (5)

Tuffa and the picnic
Schroeder, Binette
Tuffa series (1)

Tuffa and the snow
Schroeder, Binette
Tuffa series (4)

Tug of hearts
Winfield, Julia
Private eyes series (2)

Tug of war
Pascal, Francine
Sweet Valley twins series (14)
Quin-Harkin, Janet
Sugar and spice series (7)
Zach, Cheryl
Smyth versus Smith series (3)

Tugboat Annie
Raine, Norman Reilly
Tugboat Annie series (1)
Tugboat Annie series (2)

Tuk takes a trip
Mayer, Mercer
Tink, tonk tales series (2)

Tule Marsh murder
Mavity, Nancy Barr
Peter Piper series (1)

Tulip affair
Carter, Nick
Nick Carter series (42)

Tullington film-makers
Beresford, Elisabeth
Gappy, Jim and Jane series (5)

Tulsa
Mitchum, Hank
Stage coach station series (26)

Tum Tum, the jolly elephant
Barnum, Richard
Kneetime animal stories series (4)

Tumatumari
Harris, Wilson
Agent of personality quartet (3)

Tumbled house
Seymour, Beatrice Kean
Malling-Gaywood family series (2)

Tumbleweed
Sutton, Stack
Marshal Creed Wetherall series (1)
Van de Wetering, Janwillem
De Gier and Grijpstra series (2)

Tumbleweed twosome
Gardner, Jerome
Hanging Judge series (4)

Tumbleweeds
Ryan, Tom K
Tumbleweeds series (2)

Tumbleweeds 3
Ryan, Tom K
Tumbleweeds series (3)

Tumbleweeds 4
Ryan, Tom K
Tumbleweeds series (4)

Tumbleweeds 5
Ryan, Tom K
Tumbleweeds series (5)

Tumbleweeds and Company
Ryan, Tom K
Tumbleweeds series (9)

Tumbleweeds buckaroo
Ryan, Tom K
Tumbleweeds series (17)

Tumbleweeds corral
Ryan, Tom K
Tumbleweeds series (20)

Tumbleweeds country
Ryan, Tom K
Tumbleweeds series (16)

Tumbleweeds express
Ryan, Tom K
Tumbleweeds series (12)

Tumbleweeds revisited
Ryan, Tom K
Tumbleweeds series (15)

Tumbleweeds rodeo!
Ryan, Tom K
Tumbleweeds series (19)

Tumbleweeds roundup!
Ryan, Tom K
Tumbleweeds series (7)

Tumbleweeds wild West
Ryan, Tom K
Tumbleweeds series (18)

Tumbling ghosts
Levy, Elizabeth
Gymnasts series (7)

Tumbling in the hay
Gogarty, Oliver St John
Sackville Street series (2)

Tumbling River Range
Tuttle, Wilbur Coleman
Hashknife Hartley and Sleepy Stevens series (10)

Tumult and the shouting
Gibbs, Henry
South African history series (4)

Tumult at the gate
Grange, Peter
L'Eree family series (3)

Tumult the rabbit
Lloyd, David
Great escapes series (4)

Tuna is not for eating
Kelly, Bill
Pepperoni Hero series (3)

Tunc
Durrell, Lawrence
Revolt of Aphrodite series (1)

Tundra
Mowat, Farley
Top of the world trilogy (3)

Tundra trail
Stoddard, Charles
Malloy series (6)

Tune in yesterday
Bethancourt, Tomas Ernesto
Yesterday and tomorrow series (1)

Tune to a corpse
Drax, Peter
Chief Inspector Thompson series (3)

Tuned for murder
Robeson, Kenneth
Avenger series (9)

Tunes that they play
Clive, William
Joseph Dando series (3)

Tunnel
Richardson, Dorothy Miller
Pilgrimage series (4)
Williams, Eric Ernest
Peter Howard series (1)

Tunnel behind the waterfall
Corlett, William
Magician's house trilogy (3)

Tunnel busters
Channel, A R
Fighting Four series (2)

Tunnel for traitors
Carter, Nick
Nick Carter series (214)

Tunnel mystery
Lenehan, John Christopher
Inspector Kilby series (1)

Tunnel of love
Wolitzer, Hilma
Linda and Robin Reismann series (2)

Tunnel terror
Robeson, Kenneth
Doc Savage series (93)

Tunnel Thirteen
Raison, Milton Michael
Tony Woolrich series (6)

Tunnel vision
Paretsky, Sara
V I Warshawski series (8)

Tunnel warriors
Hawkins, Jack
Chopper series (2)

Tunnelling into Colditz
Rogers, Jim
Colditz series (11)

Turbulence of Tony
Matthewman, Phyllis
Priory series (2)

Turbulent term of Tyke Tiler
Kemp, Gene
Cricklepit School series (1)

Turbulent thirties
Lindop, Edmund
Modern America series (2)

Turbulent years
Macgregor, Alasdair Alpin
Auld Reekie series (4)

Turf-cutter's donkey
Lynch, Patricia
Turf-cutter's donkey series (1)

Turf-cutter's donkey goes visiting
Lynch, Patricia
Turf-cutter's donkey series (2)

Turf-cutter's donkey kicks up his heels
Lynch, Patricia
Turf-cutter's donkey series (3)

Turfs-arenas-fields-pitches
Kostlanetz, Richard
Sports fields series (1)

Turing omnibus
Dewdney, Alexander Keewatin
Turing series (1)

Turkey and Co.
Harris, Ray
Turkey series (3)

Turkey and partners
Harris, Ray
Turkey series (2)

Turkey and the emu
Roughsey, Labamu
Mark and Wendy series (3)

Turkey at twelve
Scott, Mary
New Zealand life series (6)

Turkey's side of it
Smith, Janice Lea
Adam Joshua series (6)

Turkish adventure
Bayley, Viola
Adventure series (5)

Turkish bloodbath
Carter, Nick
Nick Carter series (143)

Turkish mafia conspiracy
Hayes, Ralph Eugene
Agent for Cominsec series (3)

Turkish spy
Cooper, Charles
John Hatherleigh series (1)

Turkish twins
Ucuk, Cahit
Twin series (29)

Turlough and the earthlink dilemma
Attwood, Tony
Companions of Doctor Who series (1)

Turmoil
Tarkington, Booth
Growth trilogy (2)

Turn
Truitt, Anne
Journal of an artist series (2)

Turn-about summer
Mendel, Jo
Tucker family series (8)

Turn and fire
Grover, Marshall
Larry and Stretch series (63)

Turn blue, you murderers
Brett, Michael
Pete McGrath series (5)

Turn down an empty glass
Copper, Basil
Mike Faraday series (49)

Turn for Noah
Topek, Susan Remick
Noah series (2)

Turn for the nurse
Prentis, Evelyn
Nurse series (5)

Turn in, my Lord
Wilkinson, Laurence
Mike Daryl series (1)

Turn it up!
Strasser, Todd
Coming Attractions trilogy (2)

Turn left for danger
Gray, Berkeley
Norman Conquest series (30)

Turn of a card
Carter, Nicholas
Nicholas Carter series (493)

Turn of the screw
James, Henry
Turn of the screw series (2)

Turn of the table
Stagge, Jonathan
Doctor Hugh Westlake series (4)

Turn of the tide
Porter, Eleanor Hodgman
Cross currents series (2)

Turn of the tide, 1939-1943
Bryant, Arthur
Second World War series (1)

Turn of the year
Grove, Frederick Philip
Canadian prairie series (2)

Turn on the heat
Fair, A A
Bertha Cool and Donald Lam series (2)

Turn-out man
Roderus, Frank
Carl Heller series (4)

Turn the key on Emerson
Grover, Marshall
Larry and Stretch series (216)

Turn the other sheik
Conway, Troy
Coxeman series (24)

Turn-up
Sewart, Alan
Detective Chief Superintendent Evans series (1)

Turnabout trick
Corbett, Scott
Kerby Maxwell series (6)

Turnabout year
Sypher, Lucy Johnstone
Lucy series (4)

Turnaround Jack
Abshire, Richard
Jack Kyle series (2)

Turncoat
Carter, Nick
Nick Carter series (108)
Rutledge, Adam
Patriots series (3)

Turned on to L.U.S.T.
Gray, Rod
Lady from L.U.S.T. series (17)

Turning
Norton, Andre
Witch World series (21)

Turning of the tide
Kellogg, Elijah
Whispering Pine series (6)

Scofield, Jonathan
Freedom fighters series (7)

Turning place
Karl, Jean Edna
Future past series (1)

Turning sword
Bayne, Spencer
Hendrik Van Kill series (2)

Turning tide
Bassett, Sara Ware
Cape Cod series (10)

Turning wheels
Cloete, Stuart
Van der Berg family series (1)

Turnip-tops
Boileau, Ethel
Mallory family series (1)

Turns of time
Audemars, Pierre
Monsieur Pinaud series (3)

Turquoise dragon
Wallace, David Rains
Turquoise dragon series (1)

Turquoise hazard
Caldwell, Alfred Betts
Freddy Philpotts series (2)

Turquoise lament
Macdonald, John Dann
Travis McGee series (15)

Turquoise shop
Crane, Frances
Pat and Jean Abbott series (1)

Turquoise spike
Archer, Frank
Inspector Joseph Delaney series (3)

Turquoise toad mystery
McHargue, Georgess
Ben and Frito series (2)

Turquoise-yellow case
Palmer, P K
Jedediah Killinger series (1)

Turret
Sharp, Margery
Miss Bianca series (3)

Turtle baby
Padgett, Abigail
Bo Bradley series (3)

Turtle is born
White, William
Animal is born series (2)

Turtle magic
Young, Ruth
Rhyme-fingerplay-puppet series (1)

Turtle net
Gudmundson, Shirley M
Ebbie series (1)

Turtle spring
Hoban, Lillian
Stick-in-the-Mud Turtle series (2)

Turtles, snakes and alligator jaws
Torgersen, Don Arthur
Animal safari nature series (7)

Tuscan harvest
Bartlett, Vernon
My life series (4)

Tuscan retreat
Bartlett, Vernon
My life series (3)

Tuscany terror
Pendleton, Don
Mack Bolan series (52)

Tuska the boar
Rutley, Cecil Bernard
Wild life story series (12)

Tussock Flat tales
Hayes, Mike
Prickle Farm series (4)

Tut, tut, Mister Tutt!
Train, Arthur
Ephraim Tutt series (4)

Tutt and Mister Tutt
Train, Arthur
Ephraim Tutt series (1)

Tutt for Tutt
Train, Arthur
Ephraim Tutt series (8)

Tuxedo Park
Copper, Basil
Mike Faraday series (43)

TV terror
Butler, Bill
Dean Street detectives series (6)

Twain have met
Chula Chakrabongse
Eastern prince series (1)

Tweak the devil's nose
Deming, Richard
Manville Moon series (2)

Tweedie
Mullins, Iola May
Blossom Shop series (5)
Tweedie-de-dee Tumbleweed
Reese, Bob
Desert critterland series (2)
Twelfth
Stanford, John Keith
Life and death of George Proteron series (1)
Twelfth, an amethyst
Chase, Beatrice
Beatrice Chase series (2)
Twelfth day of July
Lingard, Joan
Sadie and Kevin series (1)
Twelfth man
Marquis, Max
Harry Timberlake series (2)
Twelfth of August
Morris, W R
Sheriff Buford Pusser series (2)
Twelve adventurers, and other stories
Bronte, Charlotte
Angria series (1)
Twelve and a half Plymouth Street
Park, Ruth
Darcy family trilogy (3)
Twelve angels from hell
Wilkerson, David
Cross and the switchblade series (2)
Twelve apostles
Verner, Gerald
Superintendent Robert Budd series (14)
Twelve around the world
Daly, Maureen
Roundabout series (1)
Twelve chairs
Ilf, Ilya Arnoldovich
Chairs series (1)
Twelve Chinamen and a woman
Chase, James Hadley
Carol Blandish series (2)
Twelve Chinks and a woman
Chase, James Hadley
Carol Blandish series (2)
Twelve days in August
Murrow, Liza Ketchum
Fire in the heart series (3)
Twelve disguises
Beeding, Francis
Colonel Alastair Granby series (16)
Twelve fair kingdoms
Elgin, Suzette Haden
Ozark fantasy trilogy (1)
Twelve girls in the garden
Martin, Shane
Professor Ronald Challis series (1)
Twelve horses and the hangman's noose
Mitchell, Gladys
Dame Beatrice Bradley series (29)
Twelve hours to destiny
Robertson, Manning K
Steve Carradine series (4)
Twelve in a grave
Carter, Nicholas
Nicholas Carter series (594)
Twelve maidens
Farrar, Stewart
Bridget and George Blake series (1)
Twelve men
Dreiser, Theodore
Men and women series (1)
Twelve must die
Zorro
Doctor Death series (1)
Twelve tasks of Asterix
Goscinny, Rene
Asterix series (24)
Twelve tasks of Asterix series (12)
Twelve thirty from Croydon
Crofts, Freeman Wills
Inspector Joseph French series (11)
Twelve tin boxes
Carter, Nicholas
Nicholas Carter series (51)
Twelve to dine
Nisot, Elizabeth
Commissaire Payran series (1)
Twelve wise men
Carter, Nicholas
Nicholas Carter series (50)
Twenty-acre plot
Wilcox, Stephen F
Elias Hackshaw series (1)
Twenty-eight Barbary Lane
Maupin, Armistead
Tales of the city series (6)
Twenty eighth day of Elul
Elman, Richard Martin
Yagodah family trilogy (1)
Twenty five
Nichols, Beverley
Candid recollections series (1)
Twenty-five sanitary inspectors
East, Roger
Superintendent Simmonds series (2)
Twenty-five years of the Archers
Gallagher, Jock
Archers of Ambridge series (7)
Twenty four carat assassin
Larson, Glen A
Knight Rider series (4)
Twenty-four days before Christmas
L'Engle, Madeleine
Austin family series (3)
Twenty-four hours at Le Mans
Gregoire, Jean Albert
Auguste Maller series (1)
Twenty fourth horse
Pentecost, Hugh
Luke Bradley series (2)
Twenty-fourth level
Benton, Kenneth
Peter Craig series (1)
Twenty letters to a friend
Alliluyeva, Svetlana
Letters to a friend series (1)
Twenty minute tales
Blyton, Enid
Minute tales series (4)
Twenty minutes to kill
Chase, Arthur Minturn
Lieutenant Dan Durkin series (3)
Twenty-one clues
Connington, John Jervis
Sir Clinton Driffield series (14)
Twenty per cent
Macrae, Travis
Jim and Kate Harris series (2)
Twenty seven ingredient chili con carne murders
Pickard, Nancy
Mrs Eugenia Potter series (3)
Twenty seven rifles
Grover, Marshall
Larry and Stretch series (161)
Twenty-six clues
Ostrander, Isabel
Timothy McCarty series (2)
Twenty-six hours
Hardy, Lindsay
Gregory Keen series (3)
Twenty-six years
Richmond, Arthur Cyril
Years series (1)
Twenty-third man
Mitchell, Gladys
Dame Beatrice Bradley series (30)
Twenty-third Psalm
Davidson, Alice Joyce
Alice in Bibleland series (12)
Twenty thousand leagues under the sea
Verne, Jules
Captain Nemo series (1)
Twenty thousand thieves
Lambert, Eric
Australian Army in World War II series (1)
Twenty two brothers
Sage, Dana
Donald O'Keefe Adams series (2)
Twenty-year man
Grover, Marshall
Larry and Stretch series (242)
Twenty years a Korean missionary
Perry, Jean
News from Korea series (3)
Twenty years after
Dumas, Alexandre
Three Musketeers series (2)
Twenty years before the muse
Kolyer, John
Failure series (2)
Twenty years of hate
Stuart, Donald
Sexton Blake series (1044)
Twentymen
Purser, Philip
Colin Panton series (2)
Twice a victim
Joyce, Cyril
Chief Superintendent Pat Stockton series (3)
Twice as dead
Spade, Danny
Danny Spade series (28)
Twice buried
Havill, Steven F
Bill Gastner series (3)
Twice dead
Bude, John
Inspector Meredith series (22)
Rhode, John
Doctor Lancelot Priestley series (70)
Robertson, Colin
Superintendent Bradley series (9)
Twice have the trumpets sounded
Guthrie, Tyrone
Shakespearean festival in Canada series (2)
Twice in a blue moon
Moyes, Patricia
Henry and Emmy Tibbett series (19)
Twice mice
Smith, Wendy
Only mouse series (2)
Twice retired
Lockridge, Richard
Assistant District Attorney Bernie Simmons series (5)
Twice round the black church
Clarke, Austin
Memories of Ireland and England series (1)
Twice upon a crime
Quinn, Patrick
Pete Riley series (2)
Twice upon a time
Appel, Allen
Alex Balfour series (2)
Twice wronged!
Bobin, John William
Sexton Blake series (121)
Twilight at the Well of Souls
Chalker, Jack Laurence
Well world series (5)
Twilight country
Faldbakken, Knut
Twilight country series (1)
Twilight grey
Vachell, Horace Annesley
Methuselah series (2)
Twilight of death
Langley, Lee
Lieutenant Christopher Jensen series (1)
Twilight of empire
Eckert, Allan Wesley
Winning of America series (6)
Twilight of the serpent
Timlett, Peter Valentine
Atlantis trilogy (3)
Twilight of the Sioux
Neihardt, John Gneisenau
Cycle of the West series (5)
Twilight of the soul
Couperus, Louis
Book of small souls quartet (3)
Twilight on the Floods
Steen, Marguerite
Flood trilogy (2)
Twilight tigress
Janson, Hank
Hank Janson series (255)
Twilight Zone companion
Zicree, Marc Scott
Twilight Zone series (6)
Twilight Zone files
Peel, John
Twilight Zone series (6)
Twilight Zone revisited
Gibson, Walter Brown
Twilight Zone series (5)
Twilight Zone, the movie
Bloch, Roch
Twilight Zone series (6)
Twilight Zone, the original stories
Greenberg, Martin Harry
Twilight Zone series (6)
Twilight's child
Andrews, Virginia Cleo
Cutler family series (3)
Twin babies
Finley, Martha Farquharson
Honest Jim series (4)
Twin bridges murder
Harrell, Andrew
Sam Shank series (1)
Twin cities run
Robbins, David
Endworld series (3)
Twin colts
Hill, Morgan
Dan Colt series (1)
Hogan, Inez
Twins series (9)
Twin deer
Hogan, Inez
Twins series (7)
Twin dilemma
Keene, Carolyn
Nancy Drew series (63)
Saward, Eric
Doctor Who series (103)
Twin engines
Awdry, Wilbert
Railway series (15)
Twin kids
Hogan, Inez
Twins series (3)
Twin killing
Bagby, George
Inspector Schmidt series (13)
Twin kittens
Hogan, Inez
Twins series (14)
Twin lambs
Hogan, Inez
Twins series (12)
Twin lights
Bassett, Sara Ware
Cape Cod series (8)
Twin mystery
Carter, Nicholas
Nicholas Carter series (141)
Twin of fire
Deveraux, Jude
Chandler twins series (2)
Twin of ice
Deveraux, Jude
Chandler twins series (1)
Twin of the Amazon
Fearn, John Russell
Golden Amazon series (6)
Twin otters and the Indians
Hogan, Inez
Twins series (16)
Twin Peaks, or bust
Hunter, E J
White Squaw series (9)
Twin puppies
Hogan, Inez
Twins series (15)
Twin seals
Hogan, Inez
Twins series (6)
Twin soul of O'Take San
Anethan, Eleanora Mary d'
Twin soul series (1)
Twin worlds
Jones, Neil Ronald
Professor Jameson series (4)
Twinkle and Chubbins
Bancroft, Laura
Twinkle tales series (6)
Twinkle, twinkle, little spy
Deighton, Len
Secret file series (7)
Twinkle's enchantment
Bancroft, Laura
Twinkle tales series (6)
Twink's magic carpet ride
Lewis, Jean
Rainbow Brite series (2)
Twins abroad
Whitehill, Dorothy
Janet and Phyllis series (11)
Twins adventuring
Whitehill, Dorothy
Janet and Phyllis series (9)
Twins again
Denton, Phyllis
Twins series (2)
Twins and Felicity
Kent, Margaret
Twins series (4)
Twins and the move
Kent, Margaret
Twins series (5)
Twins and the Wild West
Pascal, Francine
Sweet Valley kids series (10)
Twins and Tim
Whitehill, Dorothy
Janet and Phyllis series (13)
Twins and Tommy junior
Whitehill, Dorothy
Janet and Phyllis series (6)
Twins at camp
Whitehill, Dorothy
Janet and Phyllis series (10)
Twins at Castle School
Little, Sylvia
Castle School series (2)
Twins at Hillside Farm
Kent, Margaret
Twins series (1)
Twins at home
Kent, Margaret
Twins series (3)
Whitehill, Dorothy
Janet and Phyllis series (7)
Twins at Saint Clare's
Blyton, Enid
Saint Clare's series (1)
Twins at the seaside
Kent, Margaret
Twins series (2)
Twins a-visiting
Whitehill, Dorothy
Janet and Phyllis series (12)
Twins big pow-wow
Pascal, Francine
Sweet Valley kids series (44)
Twins from Timber Creek
Clark, Mavis Thorpe
Timber Creek series (1)
Twins get caught
Pascal, Francine
Sweet Valley twins series (41)
Twins go to Nursery Rhyme Land
Blyton, Enid
Nursery Rhyme Land series (1)
Twins series (1)
Twins go to the hospital
Pascal, Francine
Sweet Valley kids series (20)
Twins in Australia
Rooke, Daphne
Twin series (27)
Twins in Ceylon
Woolf, Bella Sidney
Twins in Ceylon series (1)
Twins in South Africa
Rooke, Daphne
Twin series (26)
Twins in the South
Whitehill, Dorothy
Janet and Phyllis series (3)
Twins in the West
Whitehill, Dorothy
Janet and Phyllis series (4)
Twins' little sister
Pascal, Francine
Sweet Valley twins series (49)
Twins of Ceylon
Williams, Harry
Twin series (31)
Twins of crime
Grant, Maxwell
Shadow series (224)
Twins of India
Shaw, Denis
Twin series (32)
Twins of Lapland
Jenkins, Alan Charles
Twin series (33)
Twins summer vacation
Whitehill, Dorothy
Janet and Phyllis series (5)
Twins take charge
Bracken, Anne
Jon and Julie Howard series (1)
Twins to the rescue
Bracken, Anne
Jon and Julie Howard series (2)
Twins' wedding
Whitehill, Dorothy
Janet and Phyllis series (8)
Twist for two
Janson, Hank
Hank Janson series (134)
Twist in the tail
Bayfield, William John
Sexton Blake series (113)
Twist of a stick
Peters, Geoffrey
Inspector Trevor Nichols and Sergeant Tom Burton series (4)
Twist of sand
Jenkins, Geoffrey
Commander Geoffrey Peace series (1)
Twist of the knife
Solomita, Stephen
Stanley Moodrow series (1)
Twist of the rope
Bude, John
Inspector Sherwood series (3)
Twisted arrow
Longtree, Warren T
Ruff Justice series (26)
Twisted claw
Dixon, Franklin W
Hardy boys series (18)
Twisted cross
Maloney, Mack
Wingman series (5)
Wilson, Gar
Phoenix Force series (21)

Twisted evidence
Dix, Maurice Buxton
Tommy Malins, Anthony Mornington and George Hawkins series (1)
Twisted face
Kummer, Frederic Arnold
Judge Henry Tyson series (2)
Twisted Face defends his title
Davison, Gilderoy
Twisted face series (7)
Twisted Face strikes again
Davison, Gilderoy
Twisted Face series (6)
Twisted Face, the avenger
Davison, Gilderoy
Twisted Face series (5)
Twisted noose
Sharpe, Jon
Trailsman series (24)
Twisted people
Philips, Judson Pentecost
Peter Styles series (3)
Twisted reeds
Carthew, Heather Jean
Reeds series (1)
Twisted room
Smith, Janet Patton
Twilight series (12)
Twisted sword
Graham, Winston
Poldark series (11)
Twisted thing
Spillane, Mickey
Mike Hammer series (10)
Twisted trails
Sharpe, Jon
Trailsman series (81)
Tuttle, Wilbur Coleman
Hashknife Hartley and Sleepy Stevens series (14)
Twister
Wallace, Edgar
Inspector Elk series (4)
Twisters
Cate, Dick
Ghost dog series (2)
Twisting the rope
Macavoy, Roberta Ann
Mayland Long and Martha Macnamara series (2)
Twittering bird mystery
Bailey, Henry Christopher
Mister Joshua Clunk series (4)
Twixt north and south
Rutley, Cecily Marianne
Little people in far off lands series (5)
Two
Anonymous
Pronoun series (8)
Two after Malic
Peters, Ludovic
Ian Firth series (5)
Two against Scotland Yard
Frome, David
Evan Pinkerton series (2)
Two American boys aboard a submersible
Crockett, Sherman
Two American boys series (4)
Two American boys in the French war trenches
Crockett, Sherman
Two American boys series (2)
Two American boys with Pershing in France
Crockett, Sherman
Two American boys series (5)
Two American boys with the Allied armies
Crockett, Sherman
Two American boys series (1)
Two American boys with the Dardanelles battle fleet
Crockett, Sherman
Two American boys series (3)
Two and two make five
Graeme, Bruce
Detective Sergeant Robert Mather series (2)
Two-bit heroes
Egan, Doris
Gate of ivory series (2)
Two boy pioneers
Braden, James Andrew
John Jerome and Return Kingdom series (1)
Two boy publishers
Chapman, Allen
Boys of business series (2)
Two-boy weekend
Pascal, Francine
Sweet Valley High series (54)
Two boys in Wyoming
Ellis, Edward Sylvester
Northwest series (3)
Two brothers
Toynbee, Philip
Valediction of Pantaloon series (2)
Two brothers and their animal friends
Lenski, Lois
Two brothers series (1)
Two brothers and their baby sister
Lenski, Lois
Two brothers series (2)
Two bullets for Briggs
Macdonald, Donald
Tommy Briggs series (6)
Two Bunnykins out to tea
Warrener
Bunnykins series (2)
Two by day and one by night
Bell, Vicars
Doctor Douglas Baynes series (2)
Two cadets
Scott, Ian
Naval adventure trilogy (1)
Two cadets with Washington
Stoddard, William Osborn
Revolutionary series (2)
Two careers
Citrine, Walter McLennan
Men and work series (2)
Two children and their jungle zoo
Brown, Rose
Two children series (3)
Two children of Brazil
Brown, Rose
Two children series (1)
Two complete novels
Williamson, Jack
Legion of time series (2)
Two crimes
Ibarguengoitia, Jorge
Dead girls series (2)
Two days of terror
Sheldon, Roy
Magdah series (2)
Two dead charwomen
Morland, Nigel
Chief Inspector Andrew McMurdo series (3)
Two deaths for a penny
Burnaby, Nigel
Chief Inspector Drewry series (2)
Two deaths must die
Himmel, Richard
Johnny Maguire series (4)
Two deputies came riding
Nickson, Arthur
Rusty Hines series (9)
Two Dianas
Dumas, Alexandre
Valois series (2)
Two Dianas in Alaska
Herbert, Agnes
Two Dianas series (2)
Two Dianas in Somaliland
Herbert, Agnes
Two Dianas series (1)
Two died at three
Gregg, Cecil Freeman
Inspector Cuthbert Higgins series (21)
Two died in Singapore
Sherwood, John
Mister Charles Blessington series (4)
Two doctors
Holmes, Robert
Doctor Who series (100)
Two dreams
Balzac, Honore de
Philosophic studies series (16)
Two easy pieces
Sherman, Jory
Gunn series (28)
Two Elsies
Finley, Martha Farquharson
Elsie Dinsmore series (11)
Two ends to my shoestring
Pinkerton, Kathrene
Shoestring trilogy (3)
Two ends to the town
Bude, John
Inspector Sherwood series (1)
Two eyes
Gordon, Stuart
Eyes trilogy (2)
Two-faced
Graeme, Bruce
Detective Sergeant Robert Mather series (5)
Two-faced death
Jeffries, Roderic Graeme
Inspector Enrique Alvarez series (2)
Two-faced enemy
King, David
Rat Patrol series (4)
Two-faced man
Vanardy, Varick
Crewe series (1)
Two faced murder
Leslie, Jean
Peter Ponsonby series (2)
Two faces of Adam
Meyer, Carolyn
Hotline series (4)
Two faces of death
Wright, Wade
Bart Condor series (6)
Two faces of nemesis
Melville-Ross, Antony
Treelake series (2)
Two fair plaits
Saville, Malcolm
Jillies series (2)
Two fiddlers
Brown, George Mackay
Two fiddlers series (1)
Two-five to Mardon
Field, Katherine
Inspector Ross Paterson series (2)
Two flags for France
Dymoke, Juliet
French Revolution series (4)
Two foals for Matilda
Vaughan, Carol
Manorfield Stud series (2)
Two for Inspector West
Creasey, John
Inspector Roger West series (18)
Two for joy
Stranger, Joyce
Dog series (2)
Two for Tanner
Block, Lawrence
Evan Tanner series (4)
Two for the gallows
Grover, Marshall
Larry and Stretch series (104)
Two for the money
Sherman, Jory
Gunn series (27)
Two for three farthings
Staples, Mary Jane
South London series (4)
Two forests
Tabori, Paul
Spider and moonlight trilogy (1)
Two friends
Greenwell, Dora
Two friends series (1)
Two friends too many
Haas, Dorothy
Peanut Butter and Jilly series (8)
Two gentlemen from Texas
Grover, Marshall
Larry and Stretch series (344)
Two giants
Bunting, Eve
Magic circle series (1)
Two girls, one boy
Quin-Harkin, Janet
Sugar and spice series (1)
Two graphs
Rhode, John
Doctor Lancelot Priestley series (50)
Two graves waiting
Grover, Marshall
Larry and Stretch series (355)
Two-gun devil
Cole, Jackson
Jim Hatfield series (27)
Two gun justice
Bowden, Jim
Dan McCoy series (3)
Two-gun man
Young, Gordon Ray
Red Clark series (6)
Two-Gun Rio Kid
Davis, Don
Rio Kid series (5)
Two guns for hire
Macneil, Neil
Tony Costaine and Bert McCall series (2)
Two guns for justice
Roberts, J R
Gunsmith series (133)
Two guns for Texas
Cole, Jackson
Jim Hatfield series (55)
Two guys noticed me, and other miracles
Sharmat, Marjorie Weinman
Notice me series (2)
Two heads are better
Lewis, Elliott
Fred Bennett series (1)
Two hearts
Gilden, Mel
Beverly Hills 90210 series (7)
Two hearts too reckless
Randall, Lindsey
Two hearts series (2)
Two hearts too wild
Randall, Lindsey
Two hearts series (1)
Two Hoots
Cresswell, Helen
Two Hoots series (1)
Two Hoots and the big bad bird
Cresswell, Helen
Two Hoots series (3)
Two Hoots and the king
Cresswell, Helen
Two Hoots series (5)
Two Hoots go to sea
Cresswell, Helen
Two Hoots series (2)
Two Hoots in the snow
Cresswell, Helen
Two Hoots series (4)
Two Hoots play hide and seek
Cresswell, Helen
Two Hoots series (6)
Two hundred and fifty pound marriage case
Brandon, John Gordon
Inspector Patrick Aloysius McCarthy series (23)
Two hundred ghost
Hamilton, Henrietta
Johnny and Sally Heldar series (1)
Two imposters
Audemars, Pierre
Monsieur Pinaud series (1)
Vare, Daniele
Diplomat series (2)
Two in hiding
Emerson, Ru
Night-threads series (2)
Two in the bush
Bagby, George
Inspector Schmidt series (39)
Two in the wilderness
Thompson, Mary Wolfe
Aiken family trilogy (1)
Two is lonely
Banks, Lynne Reid
Jane Graham trilogy (3)
Two Jacks and the Joker
Grover, Marshall
Larry and Stretch series (149)
Two Joans at the Abbey
Oxenham, Elsie J
Abbey girls second generation series (3)
Two kinds of murder
Macdonald, Donald
Tommy Briggs series (5)
Two kingdoms
Saxton, Mark
Islandia series (3)
Two kings
Johnston, Gunnar
Silber series (2)
Two kisses
Onions, Oliver
Taskers series (1)
Two knocks for death
Jackson, Wallace
Inspector Clancy Martin series (1)
Two ladies of Verona
Black, Lionel
Emma Greaves series (3)
Two lamps in our street
Barton, Arthur
Time remembered series (1)
Two lieutenants
Scott, Ian
Naval adventure trilogy (3)
Two little dicky birds
McGee, Shelagh
Little nursery rhyme series (3)
Two little Gumnuts
Gibbs, May
Gumnut Land series (10)
Two little knights of Kentucky
Johnston, Annie Fellows
Little colonel series (4)
Two little women
Wells, Carolyn
Two little women series (1)
Two little women and treasure house
Wells, Carolyn
Two little women series (2)
Two little women on a holiday
Wells, Carolyn
Two little women series (3)
Two LO
Masterman, Walter Sidney
Sir Arthur Sinclair series (3)
Two Medicine Rivers
Wheeler, Richard Seabrook
Rivers west series (9)
Two men
Ollivant, Alfred
Two worlds series (1)
Two men from the east
Plummer, Thomas Arthur
Detective Inspector Andrew Frampton series (10)
Two men in twenty
Procter, Maurice
Chief Inspector Harry Martineau series (18)
Two men missing
Ashe, Gordon
Patrick Dawlish series (11)
Two men o' Mendip
Raymond, Walter
Mendip Hills series (1)
Two mice on holiday
Miller, Margaret Jessy
Willow and Albert series (7)
Two-minute mysteries
Sobol, Donald J
Two-minute mysteries series (1)
Two Mrs Abbotts
Stevenson, Dorothy Emily
Miss Buncle series (3)
Two must die
Robertson, Colin
Peter Grayleigh series (7)
Two mysteries
Teed, George Hamilton
Sexton Blake series (22)
Two of a kind
Gilman, George G
Edge meets Steele series (1)
Two of us
Braine, John
Clive and Robin Lendrick series (2)
Two part invention
L'Engle, Madeleine
Crosswicks journals series (4)
Two pies, one fork
Guisewhite, Cathy
Cathy series (12)
Two plays from the Orphans' home
Foote, Horton
Orphans' home series (9)
Two plus two
Carter, Nicholas
Nicholas Carter series (53)
Two poets
Balzac, Honore de
Scenes of provincial life series (9)
Two points for murder
Keene, Carolyn
Nancy Drew files series (8)
Two queens at the Abbey
Oxenham, Elsie J
Abbey girls second generation series (11)
Two rails west
Tompkins, Walker Allison
Masked Rider and Blue Hawk series (27)
Two rode together
Cook, Will
United States Cavalry trilogy (1)
Two runaways
Jenkins, Jerry Bruce
Bradford family series (6)
Two Salomes
Pool, Maria Louise
Salomes series (1)
Two Sams at the Chalet School
Brent-Dyer, Elinor Mary
Chalet School series (56)
Two selves
Bryher, Winifred
Development series (2)
Two sets to murder
Peters, Ludovic
Ian Firth series (3)
Two shadows for death
Wolf, Jack
Timothy Rourke series (1)
Two shoes, new shoes
Hughes, Shirley
Nursery series (6)

Two sides of the shield
Yonge, Charlotte Mary
Beechcroft series (5)
Shield series (3)
Two smart dames
Ross, Gene
Shaun O'Malley series (1)
Two songs this archangel sings
Chesbro, George Clark
Mongo series (5)
Valhalla trilogy (2)
Two sought adventure
Leiber, Fritz
Fafhrd and Gray Mouser series (8)
Two-star pigeon
Wolfe, Michael
Michael Keefe series (2)
Two-stringed fiddle
Mitton, Geraldine Edith
Diana Forbes series (1)
Two sub-lieutenants
Scott, Ian
Naval adventure trilogy (2)
Two tales of Basil Brush
Firmin, Peter
Basil Brush series (2)
Two tales of Mervyn Mouse
Creche, Sylvia
Mervyn Mouse series (1)
Two tall strangers
Grover, Marshall
Larry and Stretch series (86)
Two-ten conspiracy
Le Grand, Leon
Michael Berresford series (2)
Two thieves and a puma
Reese, John
Jefferson Hewitt series (11)
Two-thirds of a ghost
McCloy, Helen
Basil Willing series (11)
Two thousand and one, a space odyssey
Clarke, Arthur Charles
Space odyssey series (1)
Two thousand and sixty nine
Townsend, Larry
Two thousand and sixty nine trilogy (1)
Two thousand and sixty nine plus one
Townsend, Larry
Two thousand and sixty nine trilogy (2)
Two thousand and sixty nine plus two
Townsend, Larry
Two thousand and sixty nine trilogy (3)
Two thousand and sixty one
Clarke, Arthur Charles
Space odyssey series (3)
Two thousand and ten
Clarke, Arthur Charles
Space odyssey series (2)
Two-thumbs
Rees, Leslie
Australian nature tales series (8)
Two Thyrdes
Denham, Bertie
Derek Thyrde series (2)
Two ticket puzzle
Connington, John Jervis
Superintendent Ross series (2)
Two tickets for Tangier
Mason, Francis Van Wyck
Colonel Hugh North series (19)
Two tickets puzzle
Connington, John Jervis
Superintendent Ross series (2)
Two-time winner
Grover, Marshall
Larry and Stretch series (282)
Two to conquer
Bradley, Marion Zimmer
Darkover series (2)
Two to make friends
Hurt, Freda Mary
Pinetops series (3)
Two to slay
Brinton, Henry
John and Sally Strang series (2)
Two to tangle
Kane, Frank
Johnny Liddell series (28)
Two towers
Tolkien, John Ronald Reuel
Lord of the Rings trilogy (2)
Middle Earth series (4)
Two under the Indian sun
Godden, Rumer
No time to weep series (1)
Two undertakers
Beeding, Francis
Colonel Alastair Granby series (7)
Ronald Briercliffe series (2)
Two Victorian girls
Hall, Emily
Hall sisters series (1)
Sherrard, Owen Aubrey
Victorian girls series (1)
Two Victorian ladies
Hall, Emily
Hall sisters series (3)
Mills, Anthony Reginald
Victorian girls series (3)
Two village dinosaurs
Arkle, Phyllis
Village dinosaur series (2)
Two villains in one
Carter, Nicholas
Nicholas Carter series (112)
Two way cut
Turnbull, Peter
P Division series (5)
Two-way frame
Harknett, Terry
Stephen Wayne series (8)
Two-way mirror
Launay, Droo
Adam Flute series (5)
Two way toll
Klein, Zachary
Matthew Jacob series (2)
Two-way witness
Franklin, Donald
Special Squad series (2)
Two ways to die
Thayer, Lee
Peter Clancy series (57)
Two ways to murder
Radford, Edwin
Doctor Manson series (30)
Two weirdos and a ghost
Windsor, Patricia
Weirdo and ghost series (2)
Two-wheeled terror
Mackenzie, Jake
Secret files of Dakota King series (3)
Two wheels, two heads
Ahlberg, Janet
Two heads series (2)
Two who talked
King, Frank
Dormouse series (19)
Two Wild Cherries
Garis, Howard Roger
Two Wild Cherries series (3)
Two Wild Cherries at the seashore
Garis, Howard Roger
Two Wild Cherries series (4)
Two Wild Cherries in the country
Garis, Howard Roger
Two Wild Cherries series (1)
Two Wild Cherries in the woods
Garis, Howard Roger
Two Wild Cherries series (2)
Two wives
Arthur, Timothy Shay
Household library series (4)
Two women of London
Tennant, Emma
Doctor Jekyll sequels series (3)
Two works in Wyoming
Grover, Marshall
Larry and Stretch series (340)
Two worlds
Daiches, David
Three worlds series (1)
Two X S
Findley, Nigel
Secrets of power series (4)
Two yachts, two voyages
Hiscock, Eric Charles
Wanderer series (5)
Two year's vacation
Verne, Jules
Two years' holiday series (2)
Two young brides
Balzac, Honore de
Scenes of private life series (3)
Two young explorers
Black, Margaret Katherine
Three brothers series (1)
Two young two go four boys
Lewis, Linda
Linda series (4)
Twopence coloured
Shaw, Jane
Penny series (2)
Twopence for a rat's tail
Lott, Stanley Makepeace
Stephen Ringway series (1)
Twopence to cross the Mersey
Forrester, Helen
Mersey series (1)
Two's company
Kaye, Marilyn
Three of a kind series (4)
Stranger, Joyce
Dog series (1)
Twospot
Pronzini, Bill
Private Eye series (5)
Tycoon
Wells, Mary
Expatriates trilogy (3)
Tycoon in Eden
Lister, Stephen
Kilakura series (2)
Sainte Monique series (12)
Tycoon of crime
Wallace, Robert
Phantom Detective series (12)
Tycoon's death bed
Bellairs, George
Detective Inspector Thomas Littlejohn series (49)
Tyger and the lady
Riefe, Alan
Tyger Decker series (4)
Tyger at bay
Riefe, Alan
Tyger Decker series (1)
Tyger by the tail
Riefe, Alan
Tyger Decker series (2)
Tyger, tyger burning bright
Riefe, Alan
Tyger Decker series (6)
Tyler
Palmer, Diana
Long tall Texan series (3)
Tyler cache
Grover, Marshall
Bleak Creek series (4)
Tyler mystery
Durbridge, Francis
Paul Temple series (6)
Temple, Paul
Paul Temple series (6)
Tyler of Barnet
Gilbert, Bernard
Old England series (3)
Tyler twins and the latchkey kids
Stahl, Hilda
Tyler twins series (4)
Tyler twins and the mystery of the missing grandfather
Stahl, Hilda
Tyler twins series (6)
Tyler twins and the pet show adventure
Stahl, Hilda
Tyler twins series (3)
Tyler twins and the surprise at the Big Key Ranch
Stahl, Hilda
Tyler twins series (1)
Tyler twins and the swamp monster
Stahl, Hilda
Tyler twins series (2)
Tyler twins and the tree house hideaway
Stahl, Hilda
Tyler twins series (5)
Tyler's Row
Read, *Miss*
Fairacre series (9)
Tyltyl
Maeterlinck, Maurice
Blue bird series (2)
Tyneside ultimatum
Ross, Angus
Mark Farrow series (18)
Typed for a corpse
Pruitt, Alan
Don Carson series (2)
Typee
Melville, Herman
South Seas series (1)
Typically Jennings
Buckeridge, Anthony
Jennings series (21)
Tyranny of love
Spencer, Colin
Simpson family series (2)
Tyrant
Gaunt, Richard
Borgia series (3)
Veryan, Patricia
Golden chronicles series (3)
Tyrant of Hades
Kapp, Colin
Cageworld series (3)
Tyrolean holiday
Sutton, Phyllis
Merryl Hastings series (3)
Tyrone the double dirty rotten cheater
Wilhelm, Hans
Tyrone series (2)
Tyrone the horrible
Wilhelm, Hans
Tyrone series (1)

U

U-boat
Macdonnell, James Edmond
Commander Sainsbury series (4)
U.N. affair
Jason, Stuart
Butcher series (22)
U.N. sabotage
Skimin, Robert
Soldier for hire series (3)
U.N.C.L.E. technical manual
Magee, Glenn A
Man from U.N.C.L.E. series (24)
U.S.A. for beginners
Atkinson, Alex
Rocking-chair series (1)
U.S.A., what is the great American invention?
Brightfield, Richard
Earth inspectors series (8)
U.S.S.A.
Frey, James
U.S.S.A. series (4)
Madsen, David
U.S.S.A. series (4)
U.S.S.A., book 1
De Haven, Tom
U.S.S.A. series (1)
U.S.S.A., book 2
Lewitt, Shariann N
U.S.S.A. series (2)
U.S.S.A., book 3
Sykes, Sondra Catharine
U.S.S.A. series (3)
U.S.S.A., book 4
Lewitt, Shariann N
U.S.S.A. series (4)
U.S.-Soviet military balance, concepts and capability, 1960-1980
Collins, John Martin
Military balance series (1)
U.S.-Soviet military balance, 1980-1985
Collins, John Martin
Military balance series (2)
UFO
Miall, Robert
UFO series (1)
UFO 1
Miall, Robert
UFO series (1)
UFO 2
Miall, Robert
UFO series (2)
UFO 517
Fane, Bron
La noire series (8)
UFO has landed
Dank, Milton
Galaxy Gang series (2)
UFO mystery
Christian, Mary Blount
Sherlock Street detectives series (3)
UFOs
Christian, Mary Blount
Mystery of series (2)
Ugglians
Fallaw, L M
Ugglians series (1)
Ugglians at large
Fallaw, L M
Ugglians series (2)
Ugly Bugg
Cosgrove, Stephen Edward
Bugg series (21)
Ugly customer
Gregg, Cecil Freeman
Inspector Cuthbert Higgins series (27)
Uhura's song
Kagan, Janet
Star trek series (21)
Ukrainian egg mystery
Stanley, George Edward
Doctor Constance Daniels series (3)
Ukrainians in America and Canada
Wertsman, Vladimir
Ethnic groups in America series (4)
Ukrainians in America, 1608-1975
Wertsman, Vladimir
Ethnic groups in America series (2)
Ukridge
Wodehouse, Pelham Grenville
Ukridge series (2)
Ultima Thule
Richardson, Henry Handel
Fortunes of Richard Mahony trilogy (3)
Ultimate act
Bachmann, Lawrence Paul
Ben Clancy series (2)
Ultimate client
Avallone, Michael
Ed Noon series (22)
Ultimate code
Carter, Nick
Nick Carter series (101)
Ultimate conculsion
Fox-Davies, Arthur Charles
Ashley Tempest series (5)
Ultimate death
Murphy, Warren Burton
Destroyer series (88)
Ultimate deterrent
Janson, Hank
Hank Janson series (256)
Ultimate enemy
Saberhagen, Fred
Berserker series (5)
Ultimate evil
Daly, Wally K
Doctor Who series (162)
Ultimate foe
Baker, Pip
Doctor Who series (131)
Trial of the Time Lord series (2)
Ultimate prize
Mohan, Kim
Cyborg commando trilogy (3)
Ultimate prizes
Howatch, Susan
Church of England series (3)
Ultimate terror
Wilson, Gar
Phoenix Force series (9)
Ultimate weapon
Sloane, Ben
Horn series (4)
Ultimatum
Rohmer, Richard
Ultimatum series (1)
Ultra deadly
Acres, Mark
Sniper series (5)
Ultramarthons
Aaseng, Nathan
Sports talk series (7)
Ultraviolet widow
Crane, Frances
Pat and Jean Abbott series (21)
Ulysses
Joyce, James
Stephen Dedalus series (2)
Umbrella murder
Wells, Carolyn
Fleming Stone series (31)
Umfaan's heroes
Elkon, Jon
Tom Bloch series (1)
Unable by reason of death
Lewis, Catherine
Lisa Thomas series (1)
Unaborted Socrates
Kreeft, Peter
Socrates series (1)
Unaccountable crook
Carter, Nicholas
Nicholas Carter series (213)
Unappointed rounds
Disney, Doris Miles
David Madden series (1)
Unauthorised teenage mutant ninja turtles quiz book
Rovin, Jeff
Teenage mutant ninja turtles series (5)
Unbalanced accounts
Gallison, Kate
Unbalanced accounts series (1)
Unbearable!
Jennings, Paul Arthur
Round the twist series (4)
Unbecoming habits
Heald, Tim
Simon Bognor series (1)

Unbegotten
Creasey, John
Doctor Palfrey series (29)
Unbeheaded king
De Camp, Lyon Sprague
Jorian series (4)
Unbelievable!
Jennings, Paul Arthur
Round the twist series (2)
Unborn
Laurance, Andrew
Nostradamus trilogy (3)
Unborn tomorrow
Goolden, Barbara
Consett trilogy (3)
Unbroken
Mars, Alastair
Royal Navy series (1)
Unc' Billy gets even
Burgess, Thornton Waldo
Wee little books series (3)
Uncanny!
Jennings, Paul Arthur
Round the twist series (3)
Uncanny adventures
Ascher, Eugene
Lucian Carolus series (2)
Uncanny X-men, An X-cellent death
Novak, Kate
Marvel superheroes adventure gamebooks series (6)
Uncensored Adams
Adams, Phillip
Unspeakable series (3)
Uncertain April
Nelson, Betty Palmer
Honest women series (4)
Uncertain death
Gilbert, Anthony
Arthur Crook series (37)
Uncertain joy
Robins, Patricia
Dick and Tamily series (3)
Uncertain sound
Lewis, Royston
Inspector John Crow series (10)
Uncertain trumpet
Macgregor, Bill
Liffey series (2)
Uncertain wings
Saint Albans, Suzanne Marie Adele Beauclerk
Mimosa series (3)
Unchained lightning
Duncan, Terence
Powell's army series (1)
Uncharted stars
Norton, Andre
Murdoc Jern series (2)
Uncivil war
Dixon, Franklin W
Hardy boys case files series (52)
Uncle
Martin, John Percival
Uncle series (1)
Uncle Abner, master of mysteries
Post, Melville Davisson
Uncle Abner series (1)
Uncle Albert and the quantum quest
Stannard, Russell
Uncle Albert series (3)
Uncle and Claudius the camel
Martin, John Percival
Uncle series (5)
Uncle and his detective
Martin, John Percival
Uncle series (3)
Uncle and the battle for Badgertown
Martin, John Percival
Uncle series (6)
Uncle and the treacle trouble
Martin, John Percival
Uncle series (4)
Uncle Anghel
Istrati, Panait
Adrien Zograffi series (2)
Uncle Barney and the shrink-drink
Weir, Rosemary
Uncle Barney series (2)
Uncle Barney and the sleep-destroyer
Weir, Rosemary
Uncle Barney series (1)
Uncle Ben
Optic, Oliver
Flora Lee series (5)
Riverdale series (5)
Uncle Bill
James, Will
Uncle Bill series (1)
Uncle cleans up
Martin, John Percival
Uncle series (2)
Uncle Dynamite
Wodehouse, Pelham Grenville
Uncle Fred, Earl of Ickenham series (2)
Uncle Fred in the springtime
Wodehouse, Pelham Grenville
Blandings Castle series (7)
Uncle Fred, Earl of Ickenham series (1)
Uncle George and aunt Mary
Wensell, Ulises
Jackson family series (8)
Uncle Harry rides again
Garvey, Keith
Outback tales series (4)
Uncle Mac the missionary
Perry, Jean
News from Korea series (3)
Uncle Mary
Mullins, Iola May
Blossom Shop series (6)
Uncle Matt's mountain
Park, Ruth
Tales of the south series (2)
Uncle Mort's North Country
Tinniswood, Peter
Brandon family series (5)
Brigadier series (7)
Uncle Mort's South Country
Tinniswood, Peter
Brandon family series (6)
Uncle Oscar's niece
Goodchild, George
Inspector McLean series (29)
Uncle Remus and Brer Rabbit
Harris, Joel Chandler
Uncle Remus series (6)
Uncle Remus and his friends
Harris, Joel Chandler
Uncle Remus series (4)
Uncle Remus and the little boy
Harris, Joel Chandler
Uncle Remus series (7)
Uncle Remus, his songs and his sayings
Harris, Joel Chandler
Uncle Remus series (1)
Uncle Remus returns
Harris, Joel Chandler
Uncle Remus series (8)
Uncle Rutherford's attic
Mathews, Joanna Hooe
Uncle Rutherford series (1)
Uncle Rutherford's nieces
Mathews, Joanna Hooe
Uncle Rutherford series (2)
Uncle Sam's Army boys in Italy
Burley, Andrew S
Uncle Sam's Army boys series (2)
Uncle Sam's Army boys in khaki under canvas
Burley, Andrew S
Uncle Sam's Army boys series (3)
Uncle Sam's Army boys on the Rhine
Burley, Andrew S
Uncle Sam's Army boys series (1)
Uncle Sam's Army boys with Old Glory in Mexico
Burley, Andrew S
Uncle Sam's Army boys series (4)
Uncle Sam's boys as lieutenants
Hancock, Harrie Irving
Uncle Sam's boys series (6)
Uncle Sam's boys as sergeants
Hancock, Harrie Irving
Uncle Sam's boys series (3)
Uncle Sam's boys in the Philippines
Hancock, Harrie Irving
Uncle Sam's boys series (4)
Uncle Sam's boys in the ranks
Hancock, Harrie Irving
Uncle Sam's boys series (1)
Uncle Sam's boys on field duty
Hancock, Harrie Irving
Uncle Sam's boys series (2)
Uncle Sam's boys on their mettle
Hancock, Harrie Irving
Uncle Sam's boys series (5)
Uncle Sam's boys smash the Germans
Hancock, Harrie Irving
Uncle Sam's boys series (8)
Uncle Sam's boys with Pershing
Hancock, Harrie Irving
Uncle Sam's boys series (7)
Uncle Sam's Navy boys afloat
Jasper, Robert Lee
Uncle Sam's Navy boys series (2)
Uncle Sam's Navy boys in action
Jasper, Robert Lee
Uncle Sam's Navy boys series (3)
Uncle Sam's Navy boys with the Marines
Jasper, Robert Lee
Uncle Sam's Navy boys series (4)
Uncle Sam's Navy boys with the Submarine Chasers
Jasper, Robert Lee
Uncle Sam's Navy boys series (1)
Uncle Sam's outdoor magic
Fitzhugh, Percy Keese
Bobby Cullen series (1)
Uncle Stephen
Reid, Forrest
Tom Barber trilogy (3)
Uncle Target
Lyall, Gavin
Major Harry Maxim series (4)
Uncle Terrible
Willard, Nancy
Anatole series (3)
Uncle Terry
Munn, Charles Clark
Uncle Terry series (1)
Uncle Tom's cabin
Stowe, Harriet Beecher
Uncle Tom series (1)
Uncle Wiggily and his woodland friends
Garis, Howard Roger
Uncle Wiggily series (4)
Uncle Wiggily and the pirates, and other stories
Garis, Howard Roger
Uncle Wiggily series (3)
Uncle Wiggily and the strange notes, and other stories
Garis, M R
Uncle Wiggily series (6)
Uncle Wiggily and the Will-a-wong
Garis, M R
Uncle Wiggily series (5)
Uncle Wiggily book
Garis, Howard Roger
Uncle Wiggily series (1)
Uncle Wiggily stories
Garis, Howard Roger
Uncle Wiggily series (2)
Uncle Will and the Fitzgerald curse
Fitzgerald, John Dennis
Will Fitzgerald trilogy (3)
Uncle William, and other stories
Browne, Douglas Gordon
Major Maurice Hemyock series (1)
Uncle William, the man who was shif'less
Lee, Jennette Barbour Perry
Uncle William series (1)
Uncoffin'd clay
Mitchell, Gladys
Dame Beatrice Bradley series (57)
Uncollected cases of Solar Pons
Copper, Basil
Solar Pons series (16)
Uncomfortable term
Jacberns, Raymond
Becky Compton series (3)
Uncommitted man
Pickering, Robert Easton
Dick Philip series (1)
Uncommon cold
Clements, Eileen Helen
Alister Woodhead series (9)
Uncommon danger
Ambler, Eric
Andreas and Tamara Valeshoff series (1)
Uncommon entrance
Blishen, Edward
Schoolmaster series (4)
Uncommon market
Janson, Hank
Hank Janson series (135)
Uncommon murder
Donald, Anabel
Alex Tanner series (1)
Uncomplaining corpse
Halliday, Brett
Michael Shayne series (3)
Unconditional surrender
Waugh, Evelyn
World War II series (3)
Unconditionally yours
Quick, Larry
Love trilogy (1)
Unconfirmed kill
Helm, Eric
Ground Zero series (3)
Unconquered
Diver, Maud
English scene series (1)
Swanson, Neil Harman
American colonial series (5)
Williams, Ben Ames
Currain family series (2)
Unconscious mummers
Balzac, Honore de
Scenes of Parisian life series (10)
Unconscious witness
Freeman, Richard Austin
Doctor John Evelyn Thorndyke series (27)
Uncover agent
Janson, Hank
Hank Janson series (136)
Uncrowned king
Grier, Sydney Carlyon
Balkan series (1)
Uncrowning a king
Ellis, Edward Sylvester
Colonial trilogy (1)
Uncut jade
Barr, Pat
Alice Greenwood series (2)
Undaunted
Morrison, Margaret
Elizabeth Conway series (4)
Undefeated
Wylie, Ida Alexa Ross
Provencal Hills series (1)
Under a black veil
Carter, Nicholas
Nicholas Carter series (186)
Under a calculating star
Morressy, John
Del Whitby trilogy (3)
Under a cloud
Van Siller, Hilda
Pete Rector series (2)
Under a glass dome
Ross, Jean
Belvie family series (1)
Under a monsoon cloud
Keating, Henry Reymond Fitzwalter
Inspector Ganesh Ghote series (14)
Under a shrieking sky
Leslie, Richard
Heracles trilogy (3)
Under attack
Clay, Patrick
Sergeant Hawk series (3)
Under Black Banner
Trease, Geoffrey
Bannermere series (2)
Under cliff
Leith, Mary Charlotte Julia
Nora's friends series (2)
Under contract
Cody, Liza
Anna Lee series (5)
Under-cover man
Creasey, John
Toff series (27)
Under cover of daylight
Hall, James W
Thorn series (1)
Under Dewey at Manila
Stratemeyer, Edward L
Old Glory series (1)
Under dogs
Footner, Hulbert
Madame Rosika Storey series (1)
Under dragon's wing
Kendall, John
Endless quest series (15)
Under false colors
Carter, Nicholas
Nicholas Carter series (142)
Under false colours
Woodman, Richard
Nathaniel Drinkwater series (11)
Under fire
Housman, Laurence
Palace plays series (3)
Von Gunden, Kenneth
K-Nine series (2)
Under fire for Servia
Fiske, James
World's war series (4)
Under four flags
Edwards, Herbert Wilson
Under four flags series (1)
Under heaven's bridge
Bishop, Michael
Urban nucleus series (3)
Under Macarthur in Luzon
Stratemeyer, Edward L
Old Glory series (6)
Under old earth, and other explorations
Smith, Cordwainer
Instrumentality series (6)
Under orders
Munroe, Kirk
Rail and water series (1)
Under Orion
Law, Janice
Anna Peters series (3)
Under other conditions
Lach-Szyrma, Wladislaw
Somerville
Venus series (2)
Under Otis in the Philippines
Stratemeyer, Edward L
Old Glory series (4)
Under police observation
Chester, Gilbert
Sexton Blake series (1135)
Under police protection
Brandon, John Gordon
Sexton Blake series (794)
Under Sammy's bed
Elliott, Odette
Sammy series (1)
Under Scott in Mexico
Bonehill, Ralph
Mexican war series (3)
Under sealed orders
Bartimeus
Naval occasions series (7)
Macdonnell, James Edmond
Dutchy Holland series (4)
Under secret orders
Brandon, John Gordon
Sexton Blake series (1048)
Under siege
Coonts, Stephen
Jake Grafton series (4)
Under six planets
Brown, Winifred
Duffers of the deep series (3)
Under storm's wing
Thomas, Helen
Under storm's wing trilogy (3)
Under the banyan tree, and other stories
Narayan, Rasipuram Krishnaswami
Malgudi series (15)
Under the black raven
Creswick, Paul
Saga the Dane trilogy (2)
Under the eagle's wing
Teed, George Hamilton
Sexton Blake series (406)
Under the Green Star
Carter, Lin
Green Star series (1)
Under the greenwood tree
Hardy, Thomas
Novels of character and environment series (7)
Under the influence
Travis, Elizabeth
Ben and Carrie Porter series (2)
Under the mercy
Vanauken, Sheldon
Mercy series (2)
Under the Mikado's flag
Stratemeyer, Edward L
Soldiers of fortune series (2)
Under the ocean to the South Pole
Rockwood, Roy
Great marvel series (2)
Under the parish lantern
Archer, Fred
Evesham Vale series (1)
Under the plane trees
Traill, Peter
Mister Cribbage series (2)
Under the sea
Salmon, Michael
Who's behind the door series (10)
Under the shadow
Jones, Henry Llewellyn
Fraser Todd series (1)
Under the shadow of His wings
Rosser, Glenda Dawn
Missionary mum series (1)
Under the stars and bars
Edson, John Thomas
American Civil War series (4)
Under the stars of Druufon
Darlton, Clark
Perry Rhodan series (68)
Under the sun of Satan
Bernanos, Georges
Spiritual life series (1)
Under the tiger's claw
Carter, Nicholas
Nicholas Carter series (215)

Under the Tricolor
Mille, Pierre
Barnavaux series (1)
Under the volcano
Lowry, Malcolm
Voyage that never ends series (1)
Salmon, Michael
Dinosaur swamp series (6)
Under the wall
Carter, Nick
Nick Carter series (117)
Under the wheel
Mitchell, Elizabeth
Alien stars series (3)
Under the yoke
Stirling, Stephen Michael
Draka trilogy (2)
Under their skin
Lindsay, Philip
Victorian England series (2)
Under Togo for Japan
Stratemeyer, Edward L
Soldiers of fortune series (4)
Under twin suns
Cleve, John
Spaceways series (8)
Under water
Gunning, Sally
Peter Bartholomew series (2)
Under Wellington's command
Henty, George Alfred
Peninsular War series (2)
Under world
Hill, Reginald
Superintendent Andrew Dalziel and Sergeant Pascoe series (16)
Undercover
Stahl, Hilda
Amber Ainslie series (3)
Undercover boy
Brown, Roy Frederick
Chips Regan series (1)
Undercover Cat
Gordons
Undercover Cat series (1)
Undercover Cat prowls again
Gordons
Undercover Cat series (2)
Undercover cutie
Brody, Marc
Marc Brody series (58)
Undercurrent
Pronzini, Bill
Private Eye series (3)
Underdog, and other stories
Christie, Agatha
Hercule Poirot series (38)
Underground!
Danby, Mary
Famous Five and you series (6)
Underground cities contract
Atlee, Philip
Joe Gall series (20)
Underground explorers
Fraser, Conon
Underground series (1)
Underground kingdom
Packard, Edward
Choose your own adventure series (18)
Underground man
Macdonald, Ross
Lew Archer series (17)
Underground picnic
Johnston, William
Flying nun series (6)
Underground river
Fraser, Conon
Underground series (2)
Underground spy
Kay, Ross
Big war series (9)
Undergrowth
Young, Francis Brett
Welsh series (1)
Underhand mail
Gardner, Jerome
Dripspring series (3)
Underpeople
Smith, Cordwainer
Instrumentality series (5)
Undersea
Hazel, Paul
Finnbranch trilogy (2)
Undersea city
Pohl, Frederik
Jim Eden series (3)
Undersea fleet
Pohl, Frederik
Jim Eden series (2)
Undersea oiltanker
Duff, Douglas Valder
Adam Macadam series (9)
Undersea quest
Pohl, Frederik
Jim Eden series (1)
Undersea treasure
Garnett, Richard
Mark Rutter series (1)
Undersea treasure hunters
Patchett, Mary Elwyn
Brevitt series (1)
Understanding money
James, Elizabeth
Money series (2)
Understrike
Gardner, John Edmund
Boysie L Oakes series (2)
Understudy magic
Gormley, Beatrice
Fifth grade magic series (1)
Undertaker
Quinn, Jake
Patrick Shannon series (1)
Undertaker dies
Weston, Garnett
Highway series (3)
Undertow
Cory, Desmond
Feramontov quintet (1)
Johnny Fedora series (12)
Underwater adventure
Price, Willard
Hal and Roger Hunt series (3)
Underwater menace
Robinson, Nigel
Doctor Who series (129)
Underwood mystery
Dutton, Charles Judson
John Bartley series (1)
Undignified death
Marquis, Max
Harry Timberlake series (4)
Undiscovered Zane Grey fishing stories
Grey, Zane
Tales of a fisherman series (8)
Undivided union
Optic, Oliver
Blue and the Gray on land series (6)
Undone!
Jennings, Paul Arthur
Round the twist series (6)
Undoubted deed
Davey, Jocelyn
Ambrose Usher series (1)
Undying grass
Kemal, Yashar
Meryemdje series (3)
Undying past
Elsna, Hebe
Pleasance series (3)
Undying wizard
Offutt, Andrew Jefferson
Cormac Mac Art series (6)
Undying world
Lord, Jeffrey
Richard Blade series (8)
Unearthly child
Dicks, Terrance
Doctor Who series (65)
Uneaseful death
Hardwick, Mollie
Doran Fairweather series (3)
Uneasy alliances
Asprin, Robert Lynn
Sanctuary series (11)
Uneasy giant
Tabori, Paul
Spider and moonlight trilogy (2)
Uneasy lies the dead
Chaber, M E
Milo March series (12)
Uneasy lies the head
Plaidy, Jean
Plantagenet series (15)
Tudor series (11)
Uneasy money
Grover, Marshall
Larry and Stretch series (400)
Uneasy peace at Castle Rising
Cradock, Fanny
Lorme family series (5)
Uneasy riders
Gilman, George G
Edge series (55)
Uneasy street
Miller, Wade
Lieutenant Austin Clapp series (4)
Max Thursday series (3)
Uneasy terms
Cheyney, Peter
Slim Callaghan series (10)
Unequal marriage
Tennant, Emma
Pride and prejudice series (3)
Unexpected adventure
Atkinson, Mary Evelyn
Fricka Hammond series (4)
Unexpected corpse
Cushing, E Louise
Inspector Mackay series (3)
Oliphant, B J
Shirley McClintock series (2)
Unexpected death
Shannon, Dell
Lieutenant Luis Mendoza series (18)
Unexpected developments
Dominic, R B
Congressman Ben Safford series (7)
Unexpected legacy
Punshon, Ernest Robertson
Carter and Bell series (1)
Unexpected Mrs Pollifax
Gilman, Dorothy
Mrs Emily Pollifax series (1)
Unexpected night
Daly, Elizabeth
Henry Gamadge series (1)
Unfair fare affair
Leslie, Peter
Man from U.N.C.L.E. series (18)
Unfair sex
Farewell, Nina
Unfair sex series (1)
Unfinished business
Cronin, Michael
Sam Harris series (11)
Houseman, John
Unfinished business trilogy (3)
Unfinished cathedral
Stribling, Thomas Sigismund
Colonel Miltiades Vaiden trilogy (3)
Unfinished funeral
Tucci, Niccolo
Those of the lost continent series (2)
Unfinished house
Sutton, Margaret
Judy Bolton series (11)
Unfinished journey
Jones, Jack
Unfinished journey series (1)
Unfinished letter
Carter, Nicholas
Nicholas Carter series (498)
Unfinished tales of Numenor and Middle Earth
Tolkien, John Ronald Reuel
Middle Earth series (5)
Unfinished woman
Hellman, Lillian
Unfinished woman trilogy (1)
Unfit to plead
Palmer, Frank
Jim Jackson series (2)
Unfolding years
Gask, Arthur
Gilbert Larose series (23)
Unforgiving minute
Nichols, Beverley
Candid recollections series (2)
Unforgiving minutes
Pulver, Mary Monica
Kori McLeod Price and Peter Brichter series (1)
Unforgiving sea
Macdonnell, James Edmond
Captain Peter Bentley series (36)
Dutchy Holland series (11)
Unforgiving years, 1929-1940
Amery, Leopold Stennett
My political life trilogy (3)
Unforsaken Hiero
Lanier, Sterling Edmund
Hiero Desteen series (2)
Unfortunate Fursey
Wall, Mervyn
Fursey series (1)
Unfriendly persuasion
Baker, William Howard
Richard Quintain series (1)
Unfunny money
Alexander, Gary
Superintendent Bamsan Kiet series (2)
Unguarded hours
Wilson, Andrew Norman
Norman Shotover series (1)
Unguarded moment
Wrenn, Harold Albert
William Mitchell series (5)
Unhallowed murder
Nash, Simon
Inspector Montero and Adam Ludlow series (5)
Unhanged man
Hunter, Alan
Inspector George Gently series (31)
Unhappy hooligan
Palmer, Stuart
Howie Rook series (1)
Un-happy New Year, Emma!
Stevenson, James
Emma series (3)
Unhappy returns
Lemarchand, Elizabeth
Superintendent Tom Pollard series (9)
Unhappy ship
Laurie-Long, Ernest
Lizzie Collins series (3)
Unharrying chase
Prescott, Hilda Frances Margaret
Mediaeval France trilogy (1)
Unhatched egghead
Mark, Ted
Man from O.R.G.Y. series (9)
Unheard voices
Baer, Judy
Cedar River daydreams series (16)
Unholy angel
Fox, Brian
Alias Smith and Jones series (2)
Unholy dying
Campbell, R T
Professor John Stubbs series (1)
Unholy grail
Horowitz, Anthony
Groosham Grange series (2)
Unholy terror
Douglas, George
Inspector Bonny Lee series (7)
Unholy trio
Kane, Henry
Peter Chambers series (23)
Unholy writ
Williams, David
Mark Treasure series (1)
Unhung man
Hunter, Alan
Inspector George Gently series (31)
Unicorn
Holzer, Hans
Randy Knowles series (3)
Unicorn and dragon
Abbey, Lynn
Unicorn and dragon series (1)
Unicorn creed
Scarborough, Elizabeth Ann
Argonia series (2)
Unicorn crossing
Luenn, Nancy
Unicorn series (2)
Unicorn dancer
Salsitz, R A V
Alorie series (1)
Unicorn dilemma
Lee, John
Unicorn trilogy (2)
Unicorn gambit
Bischoff, David
Gaming magi series (3)
Unicorn girl
Glyn, Caroline
Fullie series (1)
Kurland, Michael
Greenwich Village trilogy (2)
Unicorn hunt
Dunnett, Dorothy
House of Niccolo series (5)
Unicorn murders
Dickson, Carter
Sir Henry Merrivale series (5)
Unicorn point
Anthony, Piers
Apprentice adept series (6)
Unicorn quest
Lee, John
Unicorn trilogy (1)
Unicorn rampant
Tranter, Nigel Godwin
Stuart series (4)
Unicorn sisters
Holden, Ursula
Tin toys series (2)
Unicorn solution
Lee, John
Unicorn trilogy (3)
Unicorn summer
Martin, Rhona
Black John and Hazel series (2)
Unicorn trap
Severy, Richard
Jinks Gang series (2)
Unicorn U
Friesner, Esther Mona
Gnome series (3)
Unicorns go Hawaiian
Pascal, Francine
Sweet Valley twins series (56)
Unidentified flying riddles
Cohen, Paul S
Unidentified flying riddles series (1)
Unification
Taylor, Jeri
Star trek, the next generation sequels series (7)
Uniformed killers
Wallace, Robert
Phantom Detective series (23)
Unimpeachable source
Wheeler, David
Edwin Mould series (2)
Uninvited
Harold, Clive
Uninvited trilogy (1)
Uninvited corpse
Underwood, Michael
Rosa Epton series (10)
Whelton, Paul
Garry Dean series (4)
Uninvited guests
Gillespie, Jane
Northanger Abbey series (2)
Union
Becker, Jillian
Simon and Josephine Leyton series (2)
Union bust
Murphy, Warren Burton
Destroyer series (7)
Union forever
Forstchen, William R
Lost regiment series (2)
Union Jack
McDermid, Val
Lindsay Gordon series (4)
Union Pacific
Porter, Donald Clayton
Winning the West series (3)
Union Square
Tax, Meredith
Rivington Street series (2)
Unions
Fisher, Leonard Everett
Nineteenth century America series (6)
Unique Hamlet
Starrett, Vincent
Sherlock Holmes sequels series (2)
United!
Hardcastle, Michael
Bank Vale United series (2)
United Chalet School
Brent-Dyer, Elinor Mary
Chalet School series (13)
United States midshipman afloat
Stirling, Yates
United States midshipman series (1)
United States midshipman in China
Stirling, Yates
United States midshipman series (2)
United States midshipman in Japan
Stirling, Yates
United States midshipman series (4)
United States midshipman in the Philippines
Stirling, Yates
United States midshipman series (3)
United States midshipman in the South Seas
Stirling, Yates
United States midshipman series (5)
Unity, 1942-1944
Gaulle, Charles de
War memoirs series (2)
Universal prey
Swycaffer, Jefferson Putnam
Concordat series (3)
Universe
Bendick, Jeanne
Early bird astronomy series (5)
Heinlein, Robert Anson
Future history series (3)
Universe against her
Schmitz, James Henry
Telzey Amberdon and Trigger Argee series (2)

Universe next door
Wilson, Robert Anton
Schrodinger's cat trilogy (1)
Universe one
Silverberg, Robert
Universe series (1)
Universe two
Silverberg, Robert
Universe series (2)
Unjust desserts
Wayne, Matt
Nintendo adventure series (11)
Unjust skies
Delderfield, Ronald Frederick
Sennacherib series (2)
Unjustly branded
Poole, Reginald Heber
Sexton Blake series (107)
Unkindly cup
McElroy, Hugh
Inspector William Brewer series (3)
Unkindness of ravens
Meaney, Dee Morrison
Lady Branwen series (1)
Rendell, Ruth
Chief Inspector Reginald Wexford series (15)
Unknown agent
Annesley, Michael
Lawrence Fenton series (6)
Unknown assailant
Hamilton, Patrick
Ernest Ralph Gorse series (4)
Unknown danger
Leinster, Murray
Land of the giants series (3)
Unknown destiny
Fane, Bron
La noire series (4)
Unknown enemy
Lane, Gret
John Barrin series (3)
Kate Marsh series (4)
Unknown lands
Blasco Ibanez, Vicente
Spanish history series (3)
Unknown man number eighty nine
Leonard, Elmore
Frank Ryan series (2)
Unknown masterpiece
Balzac, Honore de
Philosophic studies series (5)
Unknown menace
Stuart, Donald
Sexton Blake series (941)
Unknown mission
Deane, Norman
Bruce Murdoch series (3)
Unknown Orwell
Stansky, Peter
George Orwell series (1)
Unknown sector, Milky Way
Mahr, Kurt
Perry Rhodan series (45)
Unlatched door
Thayer, Lee
Peter Clancy series (2)
Unleashed powers
Brand, Kurt
Perry Rhodan series (90)
Unleaving
Walsh, Jill Paton
Goldengrove series (2)
Unless she burn
Mezo, Francine
Areia Darenga trilogy (2)
Unloved wife
Southworth, Emma Dorothy Eliza Nevitte
Lilith series (1)
Unlucky break
Mills, Osmington
Superintendent William Baker series (1)
Unlucky dip
Henry, Margaret
Bob and Hilary Dean series (1)
Unmasked
Avenell, Donne
Axa series (7)
Unmasking Kelsey
Hooper, Kay
Hagen series (6)
Unmasking the powers
Wink, Walter Philip
Powers trilogy (2)
Unmcommon law
Herbert, Alan Patrick
Misleading cases series (3)
Unmentionable!
Jennings, Paul Arthur
Round the twist series (5)
Unna you fellas
Ward, Glenyse
Wandering girl series (2)
Unnamable
Beckett, Samuel
Jacques Moran series (3)
Unnatural causes
Hawton, Hector
Asmun Hill series (3)
James, Phyllis Dorothy
Commander Adam Dalgliesh series (3)
Unnatural death
Sayers, Dorothy Leigh
Lord Peter Wimsey series (3)
Unnatural deeds
Nisot, Elizabeth
Commissaire Payran series (4)
Unnatural pursuit
Gray, Simon
Unnatural pursuit series (1)
Unnatural selections
Larson, Gary
Far Side series (12)
Unnatural talent
Logan, Les
Dark forces series (7)
Unneutral murder
Footner, Hulbert
Amos Lee Mappin series (9)
Unorthodox corpse
Brown, Carter
Lieutenant Al Wheeler series (8)
Unorthodox murder of Rabbi Moss
Telushkin, Joseph
Rabbi Daniel Winter series (1)
Unorthodox practices
Piesman, Marissa
Nina Fischman series (1)
Unpleasantness at the Bellona Club
Sayers, Dorothy Leigh
Lord Peter Wimsey series (4)
Unprofessional spy
Underwood, Michael
Martin Ainsworth series (1)
Unquenchable fire
Pollack, Rachel
Unquenchable fire series (1)
Unquenchable flame
Rees, Arthur John
Colwin Grey series (2)
Inspector Luckraft series (2)
Unquiet gods
Padfield, Peter
Guy Grenville series (2)
Unquiet sleep
Haggard, William
Colonel Charles Russell series (4)
Unquote
Lambert, Derek
Quote series (3)
Unravelled knots
Orczy, Emmuska
Old man in the corner series (8)
Unravished bride
Tucker, Terry
King Richard II series (2)
Unreal!
Jennings, Paul Arthur
Round the twist series (1)
Unreal city
Liddell, Robert
Charles Harbord series (1)
Unreality
Bartimeus
Naval occasions series (5)
Unreliable memoirs
James, Clive
Unreliable memoirs series (1)
Unrepentant women
Burnley, Judith
Wife series (2)
Unschooled wizard
Hambly, Barbara
Sun Wolf series (2)
Unscrupulous Mister Callaghan
Cheyney, Peter
Slim Callaghan series (8)
Unseemly end
Jeffries, Roderic Graeme
Inspector Enrique Alvarez series (6)
Unseen assassin
Janson, Hank
Hank Janson series (57)
Unseen ear
Lincoln, Natalie Sumner
Detective Ferguson series (2)
Unseen enemy
Baxter, Betty
Becky Bryan series (2)
Unseen foes
Carter, Nicholas
Nicholas Carter series (550)
Unseen hand
Kellogg, Elijah
Good old times series (3)
Unseen hands
Chipperfield, Robert Orr
Barry O'Dell series (1)
Unseen killer
Grant, Maxwell
Shadow series (67)
Unsleeping eye
Compton, David Guy
Katherine Mortenhoe series (1)
Unsocial socialist
Shaw, George Bernard
Nonage series (1)
Unsolved case of Sherlock Holmes
Sharp, Allen
Storytrails series (13)
Unspeakable Adams
Adams, Phillip
Unspeakable series (1)
Unspeakable Skipton
Johnson, Pamela Hansford
Daniel Skipton trilogy (1)
Unsuitable job for a woman
James, Phyllis Dorothy
Commander Adam Dalgliesh series (5)
Cordelia Gray series (1)
Unsung heroes
Aaseng, Nathan
Inside business series (5)
Unsung road
Harvester, Simon
Asia in turmoil series (10)
Dorian Silk series (2)
Untamed
Avenell, Donne
Axa series (6)
Brand, Max
Dan Barry series (1)
Janson, Hank
Hank Janson series (65)
Killdeer, John
Mountain majesty series (2)
Moray, Helga
Katie and Paul Van Riebeck series (1)
Norwood, Victor George Charles
Jacare series (1)
Peel, Hazel Mary
Ann and Jim Henderson series (9)
Jago series (2)
Roberts, Nora
Flowers series (28)
Untamed breed
Shirreffs, Gordon Donald
Quint Kershaw trilogy (2)
Untamed heart
Lindquiest, Marie
Texas promises trilogy (2)
Untidy gardener
Cragoe, Elizabeth
Untidy gardener series (5)
Untidy murder
Lockridge, Frances
Mister and Mrs North series (12)
Untidy of murder
Lockridge, Frances
Bill Wiegand series (11)
Until forever
Garrett, Sally
Rainbow Hills series (1)
Until proven guilty
Jance, Judith A
J P Beaumont series (1)
Until proven innocent
Kelly, Susan
Liz Connors and Jack Lingemann series (5)
Until she dies
Wright, Wade
Bart Condor series (4)
Until temptation do us part
Brown, Carter
Lieutenant Al Wheeler series (37)
Until the celebration
Snyder, Zilpha Keatley
Green-sky trilogy (3)
Until you are dead
Kane, Henry
Peter Chambers series (6)
Untimely death
Hare, Cyril
Francis Pettigrew series (5)
Inspector Mallett series (6)
Untimely frost
Cousins, Edmund George
Larry Grail series (1)
Unto a good land
Moberg, Vilhelm
Emigrants series (2)
Unto death utterly
Cumberland, Marten
Saturnin Dax series (22)
Unto the altar
Tigges, John
Incubus trilogy (2)
Unto the fourth generation
Street, Pamela
Lodge family series (4)
Unto the grave
Penn, John
Inspector George Thorne and Sergeant Bill Abbot series (6)
Unto Zeor, forever
Lichtenberg, Jacqueline
Sime-Gen series (2)
Untold adventures of Santa Claus
Nash, Ogden
Santa Claus series (1)
Untold Sherlock Holmes
Dudley, William E
Sherlock Holmes sequels series (63)
Untold story
Roosevelt, Elliott
Roosevelt family series (1)
Untold tale
Vincent, Kitty
Gyp Kidnadze series (3)
Untouchable Juli
Aldridge, James
Kit Quayle series (2)
Untouchables
Blake, Ken
Professionals series (14)
Ness, Eliot
Untouchables series (1)
Untried years, 1843-1870
Edel, Leon
Henry James series (1)
Unusual behaviour
Cooper, Lettice
Chief Inspector Corby series (2)
Unvanquished
Bonner, Terry Nelsen
New South Wales series (6)
Fast, Howard
Call of fife and drum trilogy (2)
Unwanted
Benson, Edward Frederic
Old London series (4)
Unwanted corpse
Burton, Miles
Inspector Arnold and Desmond Merrion series (49)
Unwanted witness
Douglas, George
Inspector Hallam and Sergeant Spratt series (2)
Unwelcome presence
Gray, Malcolm
Alan Craig series (3)
Unwilling adventurer
Gloag, John
Lionel Buckby series (2)
Unwilling dictator
Verne, Jules
Survivors of the Jonathan series (2)
Unwilling maid
Lincoln, Jeanie Gould
Wolcott family series (1)
Unwilling smuggler
Catherall, Arthur
Bulldog tugboat series (14)
Unwilling warlord
Watt-Evans, Lawrence
Legend of Ethshar series (3)
Unwillingly to Vegas
Livingston, Nancy
G D H Pringle series (7)
Up and coming
Conway, Troy
Coxeman series (30)
Up and coming man
Branston, Frank
Tommy Tompkins series (1)
Up and down Asia
Patterson, George Neilson
Asian missionary trilogy (3)
Up and down on the farm
Riddell, James
Animal lore and disorder series (3)
Up and down the Nile
Optic, Oliver
All-over-the-world series (7)
Up and down the river
Caudill, Rebecca
Bonnie series (3)
Up for grabs
Fair, A A
Bertha Cool and Donald Lam series (25)
Masters, Zeke
Faro Blake series (31)
Up from Earth's center
Robeson, Kenneth
Doc Savage series (182)
Up from the lizard
Trewin, John Courtenay
Up and down series (1)
Up goes the curtain
Lambert, Janet
Penny Parrish series (4)
Up home
Kelland, Clarence Budington
Peacable kingdom series (2)
Kennelly, Ardyth
Mormon series (2)
Up in the world
Sands, Leslie
Sam Wilson series (3)
Up, into the singing mountain
Llewellyn, Richard
Huw Morgan series (2)
Up jumped the devil
Adams, Cleve Franklin
Rex McBride series (4)
Up, McLean
Goodchild, George
Inspector McLean series (23)
Up Medonte way
Wells, Kenneth McNeil
Owl Pen series (3)
Up north
Lund, Trygve
Dick Weston series (2)
Up north in a whaler
Rand, Edward Augustus
Look ahead series (2)
Up our street
Spencer, Sally
Becky Taylor series (2)
Up Pepper Alley, down Goose Lane
Collin, Paul Ries
Henry and Jane Ellis series (2)
Up spake the cabin boy
Harbinson, Robert
Ulster series (3)
Up the Baltic
Optic, Oliver
Young America, second series (1)
Up the country
Brent of Bin Bin
Bert Poole series (1)
Up the creek
Dover, Harold
Worst day of my life series (1)
Up the faraway tree
Blyton, Enid
Faraway tree series (4)
Up the forked river
Ellis, Edward Sylvester
Strange adventure series (2)
Up the garden path
Burton, Miles
Inspector Arnold and Desmond Merrion series (25)
Rhode, John
Doctor Lancelot Priestley series (49)
Up the north branch
Farrar, Charles Alden John
Lake and forest series (4)
Up the river
Abbott, Jacob
Rainbow and Lucky series (5)
Optic, Oliver
Great Western series (6)
Up the Tapajos
Ellis, Edward Sylvester
Great river series (2)
Up the Town!
Jeffery, Gordon
Milbury series (2)
Up there
Hill, Eric
Baby Bear series (4)
Up this crooked way
Holman, Hugh
Sheriff Macready series (3)
Up-tight blonde
Brown, Carter
Lieutenant Al Wheeler series (39)
Up to bat
Hughes, Dean
Angel Park All-Stars series (12)
Up to Calvin's
Richards, Laura Elizabeth
Calvin Parks series (2)

V

Vasiliko affair
Culpan, Maurice
Inspector Bill Houghton series (4)
Vaster than empires, and more slow
Le Guin, Ursula Kroeber
Hain series (2)
Vatican kill
Revere, John D
Justin Perry series (2)
Vatican rip
Gash, Jonathan
Lovejoy series (5)
Vatican vendetta
Carter, Nick
Nick Carter series (88)
Vault of doom
Skene, Anthony
Sexton Blake series (673)
Vault of horror
Oleck, Jack
Catacombs series (2)
Vaults of Blackarden Castle
Gask, Arthur
Gilbert Larose series (26)
Vautrin's last avatar
Balzac, Honore de
Scenes of Parisian life series (8)
Vazkor, son of Vazkor
Lee, Tanith
Birthgrave trilogy (2)
Vector
Swigart, Rob
Vector series (1)
Vedi
Mehta, Ved
Mehta family series (3)
Vee-Dubb
Cosgrove, Stephen Edward
Bugg series (7)
Veetols
Graham, Anthony
Eric Marsden series (3)
Vega Sector
Scheer, Karl Herbert
Perry Rhodan series (5)
Vegas gamble
Ham, Bob
Overload series (12)
Vegas vampire
Sherman, Jory
Doctor Russell V Childers series (4)
Vegas vendetta
Pendleton, Don
Mack Bolan series (9)
Vegas vengeance
Ramm, Carl
James Hawker series (6)
Vegetable duck
Rhode, John
Doctor Lancelot Priestley series (40)
Veil
Chesbro, George Clark
Veil Kendry series (1)
Veil of death
Simons, Roger
Inspector Fadiman Wace series (10)
Veil of ignorance
Quill, Monica
Sister Mary Teresa series (6)
Veil of shadow
Cooke, Catherine
Mask trilogy (2)
Veiled lady
Falk, Lee
Phantom series (4)
Veiled one
Rendell, Ruth
Chief Inspector Reginald Wexford series (16)
Veiled prisoner
Leroux, Gaston
Carolus Herbert series (2)
Veiled prophet
Grant, Maxwell
Shadow series (183)
Veiled raiders
Blaine, John
Rick Brant series (20)
Veiled threat
Jenkins, Jerry Bruce
Jennifer Grey series (6)
Margo Franklin and Philip Spence series (14)
Veiled world
Lory, Robert
Shamryke Odell series (2)
Veils of fear
Meik, Vivian
Geoffrey Aylett series (2)
Vein of violence
Gault, William Campbell
Brock Callahan series (5)
Veins of compassion
Audemars, Pierre
Monsieur Pinaud series (11)
Veldt dwellers
Bancroft, Francis
South African trilogy (1)
Velocipede handicap
King, Louise Wooster
Miss Moppet series (2)
Velvet and Rough
Black, Margaret Katherine
Honey family trilogy (2)
Velvet angel
Deveraux, Jude
Montgomery annals series (4)
Velvet hammer
Franklin, Donald
Special Squad series (1)
Velvet hand
Footner, Hulbert
Madame Rosika Storey series (3)
Reilly, Helen
Inspector Christopher McKee series (23)
Velvet lightning
Hooper, Kay
Delaneys, the untamed years, second trilogy (3)
Velvet promise
Deveraux, Jude
Montgomery annals series (1)
Velvet song
Deveraux, Jude
Montgomery annals series (3)
Velvet target
Holden, Genevieve
Lieutenant Al White series (3)
Velvet vixen
Brown, Carter
Lieutenant Al Wheeler series (32)
McCall, K T
Johnny Buchanan series (10)
Vendetta
Balzac, Honore de
Scenes of private life series (8)
Carmichael, Harry
John Piper and Quinn series (21)
Corelli, Marie
Two worlds series (2)
Cutter, John
Specialist series (7)
David, Peter
Star trek, the next generation sequels series (6)
Dibdin, Michael
Aurelio Zen series (2)
Gaunt, Richard
Borgia series (2)
McCurtin, Peter
Marksman series (1)
Murdock, Melinda Seabrooke
Vendetta series (1)
Williams, David
Fighter series (2)
Williams, Richard
Sexton Blake series (1519)
Zacharia, Irwin
Vendetta series (1)
Vendetta contract
Messmann, Jon
Revenger series (3)
Vendetta for the Saint
Charteris, Leslie
Saint series (37)
Vendetta in Spain
Wheatley, Dennis
Count de Quesnoy and Condesa Guilia series (2)
Duc de Richelieu series (9)
Vendettists
Haggard, William
Colonel Charles Russell series (26)
Vendor of sweets
Narayan, Rasipuram Krishnaswami
Malgudi series (10)
Veneerings
Johnston, Harry Hamilton
Our mutual friend series (2)
Venetian blind
Haggard, William
Colonel Charles Russell series (2)
Venetian key
Upward, Allen
Doctor Frank Tarleton series (3)
Venetian mask
Robertson, Colin
Vicky McBain series (3)
Venetian spy-glass
Webster, Ernest
Benni Soldano series (4)
Venetian vendetta
Jason, Stuart
Butcher series (24)
Vengeance
Ahern, Jerry
Defender series (7)
Drake, David
Northworld series (2)
Janson, Hank
Hank Janson series (58)
Marquis, Max
Harry Timberlake series (1)
Murray, Andrew
Sexton Blake series (45)
Sloane, Robert C
Marino family series (2)
Vengeance army
Kilgore, Axel
They call me the Mercenary series (6)
Vengeance at Ventura
Gilman, George G
Edge series (37)
Vengeance Bay
Grant, Maxwell
Shadow series (219)
Vengeance business
Ryan, Jim
Igor Kerinsky series (2)
Vengeance day
Austin, Richard
Guardians series (9)
Vengeance due
Sandys, James
Inspector Millwall series (1)
Vengeance game
Carter, Nick
Nick Carter series (200)
Grave, Stephen
Miami Vice series (2)
Vengeance gun
Sanders, Brett
Web Steele series (2)
Vengeance hunt
Pike, Charles R
Jubal Cade series (5)
Vengeance in spades
Grover, Marshall
Larry and Stretch series (234)
Vengeance in the ashes
Johnstone, William Wallace
Ashes series (16)
Vengeance is black
Gilman, George G
Edge series (10)
Vengeance is his
Barker, Wade
Ninja Master series (1)
Vengeance is mine
Grant, Maxwell
Shadow series (116)
Hayes, Ralph Eugene
O'Brien, Buffalo Hunter series (2)
Montague, Jeanne
Loves of Carola Mountjoy series (3)
Spillane, Mickey
Mike Hammer series (2)
Vengeance is ours!
Saxon, Peter
Sexton Blake series (1578)
Vengeance is thine
Crisp, William
Westfall series (2)
Vengeance man
Coles, Manning
Tommy Hambledon series (16)
Vengeance mountain
Cutter, John
Specialist series (9)
Vengeance of Blue Pete
Allan, Luke
Blue Pete series (5)
Vengeance of Chane
Gant, Norman
Chane series (2)
Vengeance of Flynn
Laurie-Long, Ernest
Captain Flynn series (4)
Vengeance of Fortuna West
Hogan, Ray
Fortuna West series (2)
Vengeance of Henry Jerroman
Vickers, Roy
James Segrove series (1)
Vengeance of Larose
Gask, Arthur
Gilbert Larose series (14)
Vengeance of McAllister
Chisholm, Matt
Rem McAllister series (28)
Vengeance of Monsieur Blackshirt
Graeme, David
Monsieur Blackshirt series (2)
Vengeance of Orion
Bova, Ben
Orion series (2)
Vengeance of She
Tremayne, Peter
She series (7)
Vengeance of the Dancing Gods
Chalker, Jack Laurence
Dancing Gods series (3)
Vengeance of the dolphin
Roy, Thomas Albert
Jimmy Brent series (2)
Vengeance of the Golden Hawk
Rosenberger, Joseph
Death Merchant series (14)
Vengeance of the ivory skull
Harvey, Marion
Graydon McKelvie series (2)
Vengeance of the Lion
Danielson, Peter
Children of the Lion series (3)
Vengeance of the Zulu king
Seed, Jenny
Natal series (2)
Vengeance of three
Graydon, William Murray
Sexton Blake series (127)
Vengeance on Varus
Martin, Philip
Doctor Who series (106)
Vengeance pulls the trigger
Schley, Sturges Mason
Doctor Quentin Toby series (1)
Vengeance ride
Hardin, J D
Raider series (7)
Newton, Mike
Bounty Man series (1)
Vengeance rides a black horse
Grover, Marshall
Nevada Jim series (27)
Vengeance road
Kirk, Matthew
Claw series (2)
Logan, Jake
John Slocum series (139)
Vengeance rode west
Winstan, Matt
Reuben Brown series (3)
Vengeance Seeker, number one
Knott, William Cecil
Vengeance Seeker series (1)
Vengeance Seeker, number three
Knott, William Cecil
Vengeance Seeker series (3)
Vengeance Seeker, number two
Knott, William Cecil
Vengeance Seeker series (2)
Vengeance strike
Robbins, David
Blade series (13)
Vengeance town
Dawson, Clay
Long Rider series (13)
Roberts, J R
Gunsmith series (84)
Vengeance trail
Allen, Chester
Justice Colt series (1)
Dancer, J B
Lawmen series (4)
Vengeance Trail
Owen, Dean
Latigo series (2)
Vengeance trail
Roberts, J R
Gunsmith series (120)
Thompson, David
Nathaniel King series (7)
Walker, Dalton
Shiloh series (7)
Vengeance trail of Josey Wales
Carter, Forrest
Josey Wales series (2)
Vengeance Valley
Dawson, Clay
Long Rider series (23)
Gilman, George G
Edge series (17)
Hardin, J D
Raider and Doc series (39)
Venice of the Black Sea
Robertson, Helen
Inspector Lathom Dynes series (1)
Venice, who are the three?
Compton, Sara
Earth inspectors series (5)
Venner crime
Rhode, John
Doctor Lancelot Priestley series (16)
Venom House
Upfield, Arthur William
Napoleon Bonaparte series (16)
Venom in Eden
Boniface, Marjorie
Sheriff Hiram Odom series (2)
Venom of Argus
Avery, Richard
Expendables series (4)
Venom of the cobra
Charles, Robert
Counter-terror series (7)
Venom Squadron
Jackson, Robert
Flying Officer George Yeoman series (11)
Ventura Pass
Grover, Marshall
Larry and Stretch series (304)
Venture of the Thunderbird
Baker, Charlotte
Thunderbird series (1)
Venture once more
Graham, Winston
Poldark series (3)
Venus
Simon, Seymour
Space photos series (10)
Venus belt
Smith, Lester Neil
Win Bear trilogy (2)
Venus deal
Kuhlken, Ken
Tom Hickey trilogy (2)
Venus death
Benson, Ben
Ralph Lindsey series (1)
Venus fly-trap
Wainwright, John
Northern Police series (45)
Venus in copper
Davis, Lindsey
Marcus Didius Falco series (3)
Venus in danger
Mahr, Kurt
Perry Rhodan series (14)
Venus, Inc.
Pohl, Frederik
Space merchants series (2)
Venus makes three
Janson, Hank
Hank Janson series (115)
Venus of dreams
Sargent, Pamela
Venus trilogy (1)
Venus of shadows
Sargent, Pamela
Venus trilogy (2)
Venus of the counting house
Zola, Emile
Rougon Macquart series (2)
Venus probe
Saint John, David
Peter Ward series (5)
Venus project
Patchett, Mary Elwyn
Jeff James series (3)
Venus trap
Mahr, Kurt
Perry Rhodan series (17)
Venus underground
Rainey, Rich
Alex Dartanian series (1)
Verbivor
Brooke-Rose, Christine
Xorandor series (2)
Verdant passage
Denning, Troy
Prism pentad series (1)
Verdict
Knef, Hildegard
Gift horse series (2)
Pascal, Francine
Sweet Valley High series (97)
Verdict in question
Jepson, Selwyn
Eve Gill series (5)
Verdict of you all
Croft-Cooke, Rupert
Sensual life series (17)
Verdict on Doctor Esmond Ross
Dwyer-Joyce, Alice
Doctor Esmond Ross series (3)
Verdict without jury
Webb, Anthony
Mister Pendlebury series (1)
Verdun
Romains, Jules
Men of goodwill series (16)

Verena in the midst
Lucas, Edward Verrall
Richard Haven series (2)
Verge of hell
Macdonnell, James Edmond
Captain Peter Bentley series (44)
Vermilion
Aldyne, Nathan
Dan Valentine and Clarissa Lovelace series (1)
Vermilion boat
Ghose, Sudhindra Nath
Vermilion boat series (1)
Vermilion box
Lucas, Edward Verrall
Richard Haven series (1)
Vermilion parrot
Wallace, David Rains
Turquoise dragon series (2)
Vermont salt and vintage
Hard, Walter
Vermont series (4)
Vermont valley
Hard, Walter
Vermont series (5)
Vermont vintage
Hard, Walter
Vermont series (4)
Vernal equinox
Harrison, Michael
Vernal equinox series (2)
Verney abroad
Verney, John
Going to the wars series (1)
Veron mystery
Bailey, Henry Christopher
Mister Joshua Clunk series (6)
Verona passamezzo
Gollin, James
Antigua Players series (3)
Veronica
Duvoisin, Roger
Veronica series (1)
Miner, Jane Claypool
Sunfire series (18)
Veronica and the birthday present
Duvoisin, Roger
Veronica series (5)
Veronica at Sadler's Wells
Hill, Lorna
Sadler's Wells series (2)
Veronica at the Wells
Hill, Lorna
Sadler's Wells series (2)
Veronica Dean case
Waugh, Hillary
Simon Kaye series (5)
Veronica Ganz
Sachs, Marilyn
Veronica Ganz series (1)
Veronica goes to Petunia's farm
Duvoisin, Roger
Veronica series (2)
Veronica knows best
Robinson, Nancy Konheim
Veronica quartet (2)
Veronica meets her match
Robinson, Nancy Konheim
Veronica quartet (3)
Veronica, the show-off
Robinson, Nancy Konheim
Veronica quartet (1)
Veronica's sisters
Moffat, Gwen
Miss Melinda Pink series (13)
Veronica's smile
Duvoisin, Roger
Veronica series (4)
Veronique
Coffman, Virginia
Napoleonic Europe series (1)
Verratoli inheritance
Webster, Ernest
Benni Soldano series (5)
Versus Inspector Maigret
Simenon, Georges
Inspector Jules Maigret series (54)
Inspector Jules Maigret series (56)
Versus the Baron
Morton, Anthony
Baron series (7)
Versus the Shadow
Leyland, Eric
Red Lawson series (1)
Vertigo
Echlin, Elizabeth Gladys
Chronicles trilogy (3)
Veruchia
Tubb, Edwin Charles
Dumarest series (8)
Very best of Hagar
Browne, Dik
Hagar the horrible series (52)
Very big bang
McCutchan, Philip
Superintendent Simon Shard series (2)
Very Black deed
Manson, Will
Man called Black series (4)
Very breath of hell
Beare, George
Vincent Stallard and Cynthia Godwin series (2)
Very deadly game
Miller, Victor Brooke
Kojak series (7)
Very deadly yours
Keene, Carolyn
Nancy Drew files series (20)
Very good hater
Challis, Mary
Jeremy Locke series (4)
Hill, Reginald
Superintendent Andrew Dalziel and Sergeant Pascoe series (6)
Very good, Jeeves
Wodehouse, Pelham Grenville
Jeeves and Bertie Wooster series (4)
Very hot water-bottle
Delgado, Alan
Mike and Caroline series (1)
Very house
De la Roche, Mazo
Gillian and Diggory series (2)
Very last gambado
Gash, Jonathan
Lovejoy series (13)
Very merry Santa Claus story
Barkan, Joanne
Very merry story series (1)
Very merry snowman story
Barkan, Joanne
Very merry story series (2)
Very old engines
Awdry, Wilbert
Railway series (20)
Very old man with enormous wings
Garcia Marquez, Gabriel
Macondo series (1)
Very ordinary murder
Sewart, Alan
Detective Chief Superintendent Evans series (2)
Very parochial murder
Wainwright, John
Northern Police series (59)
Very particular murder
Haymon, Sylvia T
Inspector Ben Jurnet series (5)
Very quiet war
Arnold, Ralph
Orange Street series (1)
Very scary ghost story
Barkan, Joanne
Very scary story series (3)
Very scary haunted house
Barkan, Joanne
Very scary story series (1)
Very scary Jack o'Lantern
Barkan, Joanne
Very scary story series (2)
Very scary witch story
Barkan, Joanne
Very scary story series (4)
Very wrong number
Douglas, Arthur
Jonathan Craythorne series (3)
Very young actress
Kremenetz, Jill
Very young series (7)
Very young circus flyer
Kremenetz, Jill
Very young series (4)
Very young dancer
Kremenetz, Jill
Very young series (1)
Very young gardener
Kremenetz, Jill
Very young series (8)
Very young gymnast
Kremenetz, Jill
Very young series (3)
Very young musician
Kremenetz, Jill
Very young series (9)
Very young rider
Kremenetz, Jill
Very young series (2)
Very young skater
Kremenetz, Jill
Very young series (5)
Very young skier
Kremenetz, Jill
Very young series (6)
Vesper service murders
Mason, Francis Van Wyck
Colonel Hugh North series (2)
Vespers
McBain, Ed
Eighty Seventh Precinct series (44)
Vespucci papers
Healey, Ben
Harcourt d'Espinal series (1)
Vessel may carry explosives
Harvester, Simon
Roger Fleming series (7)
Vestal fire
Mackenzie, Compton
Capri series (1)
Vestiges of time
Meredith, Richard Carlton
Timeliner trilogy (3)
Vestry murder
Plummer, Thomas Arthur
Detective Inspector Andrew Frampton series (48)
Vet among the pigeons
Duncan, Alex
Vet series (5)
Vet at large!
Straiton, Eddie
Vet series (2)
Vet for all seasons
Lasgarn, Hugh
Vet in green pastures series (2)
Vet has nine lives
Duncan, Alex
Vet series (2)
Vet in a spin
Herriot, James
Vet series (6)
Vet in a state
Duncan, Alex
Vet series (7)
Vet in a storm
Lasgarn, Hugh
Vet in green pastures series (3)
Vet in charge
Straiton, Eddie
Vet series (1)
Vet in downland
Dawson, David
Vet series (1)
Vet in green pastures
Lasgarn, Hugh
Vet in green pastures series (1)
Vet in harness
Herriot, James
Vet series (4)
Vet in the making
Martin, Nancy
Vet series (2)
Vet in the manger
Duncan, Alex
Vet series (6)
Vet in the paddocks
Dawson, David
Vet series (3)
Vet in the vale
Dawson, David
Vet series (2)
Vet in the vestry
Cameron, Alexander
Vet in the vestry series (1)
Vet in the village
Lasgarn, Hugh
Vet in green pastures series (4)
Vet in Tibet
Stevenson, Robert
Highland vet series (4)
Vet it was that died
Silverman, Marguerite Ruth
Inspector Christopher Adrian series (1)
Vet on call
Stranger, Joyce
Timothy Yorke series (1)
Vet on the set!
Straiton, Eddie
Vet series (4)
Vet on the wild side
Taylor, David Conrad
Zoovet series (7)
Vet on vacation
Duncan, Alex
Vet series (8)
Vet riding high
Stranger, Joyce
Timothy Yorke series (3)
Veterans
Lambert, Eric
Australian Army in World War II series (2)
Veteran's Day
Kane, Rod
Veteran's Day series (2)
Vet's family
Robinson, Martha
Vet series (1)
Vet's holiday
Robinson, Martha
Vet series (5)
Vets in congress
Duncan, Alex
Vet series (4)
Vets in the belfry
Duncan, Alex
Vet series (3)
Vets might fly
Herriot, James
Vet series (5)
Vet's nieces
Robinson, Martha
Vet series (3)
Vet's problem
Robinson, Martha
Vet series (4)
Vets rush in
Stevenson, Robert
Highland vet series (2)
Vets rush out
Stevenson, Robert
Highland vet series (3)
Vet's son
Robinson, Martha
Vet series (2)
Vexations of A.J.Wentworth, B.A.
Ellis, Humphry Francis
A.J.Wentworth series (1)
Via Sacra
Rolland, Romain
Soul enchanted series (5)
Vial of death
Carter, Nicholas
Nicholas Carter series (115)
Vibrations in time
Watmough, David
Davey Bryant series (6)
Vicar done it
Bream, Freda
Reverend Jabal Jarrett series (2)
Vicar investigates
Bream, Freda
Reverend Jabal Jarrett series (3)
Vicar of Moura
Coffman, Virginia
Moura series (2)
Vicar of Tours
Balzac, Honore de
Scenes of provincial life series (4)
Vicarage Children
Hill, Lorna
Vicarage Children series (1)
Vicarage Children in Skye
Hill, Lorna
Vicarage Children series (3)
Vicarage family
Streatfeild, Noel
Vicarage series (1)
Vicarious years
Van Druten, John
Vicarious years series (1)
Vicar's daughter
Macdonald, George
Quiet neighbourhood series (3)
Vicar's roses
Breen, Jon Linn
Jerry Brogan series (1)
Vice cop
Deming, Richard
Matt Rudd series (1)
Vice isn't private
Cleeve, Brian
Sean Ryan series (3)
Vice squad
White, Leslie Turner
Captain Barnaby series (1)
Vichy regime, 1940-44
Aron, Robert
Liberation of France series (1)
Vicinity cluster
Anthony, Piers
Cluster series (1)
Vicious circle
Clark, Douglas
Inspector George Masters series (19)
Howe, Imogen
Twilight series (13)
Long, Manning
Liz Parrott series (2)
Vicious circles
Stuart, Anthony
Vladimir Gull series (2)
Vicious pattern
Heberden, Mary Violet
Desmond Shannon series (10)
Vicki finds the answer
Wells, Helen
Vicki Barr series (2)
Vicki in Venice
Hill, Lorna
Sadler's Wells series (13)
Vicky and I
Brindley, Louise
Old peoples' home trilogy (3)
Vicky and the Pentires
Mackenzie, Kathleen
Pentire family series (4)
Vicky Van
Wells, Carolyn
Fleming Stone series (9)
Vicky's victory
Dicks, Terrance
Ask Oliver series (7)
Vicomte de Bragelonne
Dumas, Alexandre
Three Musketeers series (3)
Three Musketeers series (3)
Victim
Annunzio, Gabriele d'
Romances of the rose trilogy (3)
Brown, Carter
Lieutenant Al Wheeler series (6)
Griffin, W E B
Badge of honor series (3)
Victim for hire
Morales, Pablo
Pedro Moreno series (1)
Victim must be found
Engel, Howard
Benny Cooperman series (6)
Hocking, Anne
Inspector William Austen series (28)
Victim of black magic
Teed, George Hamilton
Sexton Blake series (550)
Victim of circumstance
Carter, Nicholas
Nicholas Carter series (6)
Victim of deceit
Carter, Nicholas
Nicholas Carter series (185)
Victim of Devil's Alley
Urquhart, Paul
Sexton Blake series (782)
Victim of the combine
Chester, Gilbert
Sexton Blake series (1069)
Victim of the crooked hypnotist
Hunter, John
Sexton Blake series (1321)
Victim of the cult
Jardine, Warwick
Sexton Blake series (934)
Victim of the Devil's Bowl
Hardinge, Rex
Sexton Blake series (1354)
Victim of the gang
Teed, George Hamilton
Sexton Blake series (643)
Victim of the girl spy
Dix, Maurice Buxton
Sexton Blake series (861)
Victim of the red mask
Hope, Stanton
Sexton Blake series (658)
Victim of the secret service
Brandon, John Gordon
Sexton Blake series (918)
Victim of the thieves' den
Brandon, John Gordon
Sexton Blake series (872)
Victim of the waterway
Philips, George Norman
Sexton Blake series (591)
Victim prime
Sheckley, Robert
Victim trilogy (2)
Victim unknown
Reid, Desmond
Sexton Blake series (1431)
Victim was important
Rayter, Joe
Johnny Powers series (1)
Victims
Gill, B M
Inspector Tom Maybridge series (1)
Wilcox, Collin
Lieutenant Frank Hastings series (13)
Victims of circumstance
Conway, Peter
Inspector Newton series (1)

Victims of love
Spencer, Colin
Simpson family series (4)
Victims of the nova
Brunner, John
Zarathustra trilogy (3)
Victims of villainy
Murray, Andrew
Sexton Blake series (19)
Victims unknown
Clapperton, Richard
Peter Fleck series (2)
Victor
Kirby, Dallas
Victor Garrison series (1)
Nizzi, Guido
Paralyzing ray trilogy (1)
Victor Vane
Alger, Horatio
Victory trilogy (2)
Victor versus Verhasst
Kirby, Dallas
Victor Garrison series (2)
Victoria
Adair, Denis
MacLeod family series (5)
Brady, Terence
Victoria Edgecombe series (1)
Roberts, Willo Davis
Sunfire series (13)
Victoria and Albert
Housman, Laurence
Palace plays series (3)
Victoria and company
Brady, Terence
Victoria Edgecombe series (2)
Victoria and the Parrots Gang
Szudek, Agnes Susan Philomena
Victoria Plumb series (2)
Victoria four-thirty
Roberts, Cecil
Mrs Brown series (1)
Victoria in the wings
Plaidy, Jean
Georgian series (11)
Queen Victoria series (2)
Victoria Line
Binchy, Maeve
London transports series (2)
Victoria Plum and her animal friends
Rippon, Angela
Victoria Plum series (1)
Victoria Plum and her woodland friends
Rippon, Angela
Victoria Plum series (10)
Victoria Plum and the little bird
Rippon, Angela
Victoria Plum series (5)
Victoria Plum and the lost moonbeam
Rippon, Angela
Victoria Plum series (11)
Victoria Plum and the magic spell
Rippon, Angela
Victoria Plum series (7)
Victoria Plum and the squirrels
Rippon, Angela
Victoria Plum series (8)
Victoria Plum at the seaside
Rippon, Angela
Victoria Plum picture book series (3)
Victoria Plum goes for a walk
Rippon, Angela
Victoria Plum series (6)
Victoria Plum goes house hunting
Rippon, Angela
Victoria Plum series (2)
Victoria Plum goes on a picnic
Rippon, Angela
Victoria Plum series (13)
Victoria Plum has a party
Rippon, Angela
Victoria Plum series (3)
Victoria Plum has a surprise party
Rippon, Angela
Victoria Plum series (12)
Victoria Plum has a visitor
Rippon, Angela
Victoria Plum series (14)
Victoria Plum on sports day
Rippon, Angela
Victoria Plum series (9)
Victoria Plum on the farm
Rippon, Angela
Victoria Plum picture book series (4)
Victoria Plum plants a garden
Rippon, Angela
Victoria Plum series (4)
Victoria Plum story book
Rippon, Angela
Victoria Plum series (14)
Victoria Plumb
Szudek, Agnes Susan Philomena
Victoria Plumb series (1)
Victoria Plum's garden
Rippon, Angela
Victoria Plum picture book series (4)
Victoria Plum's one, two, three
Rippon, Angela
Victoria Plum picture book series (1)
Victoria Plum's seaside adventure
Rippon, Angela
Victoria Plum picture book series (4)
Victoria Plum's toys
Rippon, Angela
Victoria Plum picture book series (2)
Victoria Regina
Housman, Laurence
Palace plays series (3)
Victoria victorious
Plaidy, Jean
Queens of England series (3)
Victoria Winters
Ross, Marilyn
Barnabas Collins series (2)
Victorian boyhood
Jones, Lawrence Evelyn
Victorian boyhood series (1)
Victorian household
Lochhead, Marion Cleland
Victorian life series (3)
Victorian Olympus
Gaunt, William
Victorian painting series (4)
Victorian son
Cloete, Stuart
Victorian son series (1)
Victorian vinaigrette
Bloom, Ursula
Elegant Edwardian series (1)
Victorians
Syrett, Netta
Rose Cottingham series (1)
Victorine
Keyes, Frances Parkinson
Winslow family trilogy (3)
Victorious Union
Optic, Oliver
Blue and the Gray afloat series (6)
Victors
Gillespie, Susan
Longdon-Lorristone family series (3)
Harris, John
Martin Falconer series (3)
Victors and lords
Stuart, Vivian
Captain Alexander Sheridan series (1)
Victory
Aminoff, Constance Leonie Caroline
Napoleonic series (5)
Harrod-Eagles, Cynthia
Morland family series (12)
Huch, Ricarda Octavia
Garibaldi and the new Italy series (2)
Victory at Sebastopol
Stuart, Vivian
Commander Philip Hazard series (5)
Victory at the Super Bowl
Resciniti, Angelo G
Super Bowl series (1)
Victory for Kregen
Prescot, Dray
Dray Prescot series (22)
Victory goal
Hughes, Dean
Angel Park Soccer Stars series (3)
Victory on Janus
Norton, Andre
Janus series (2)
Victory song
Adams, Herbert
Major Roger Bennion series (15)
Vida
Delacorta
Serge Gorodish series (5)
Video avenger
Colligan, Douglas
Twistaplot series (7)
Video caper
Waricha, Jean
Find your fate: Jem series (2)
Video vandal
Roderus, Frank
Carl Heller series (3)
Video vengeance
Tripp, Miles
John Samson series (12)
Vienna blood
Payne, Laurence
Mark Savage series (3)
Vienna elephant
Leather, Edwin
Rupert Conway series (1)
Viet rampage
Acres, Mark
Sniper series (1)
Vietnam, reporter's war
Lunn, Hugh
Lunns of Annerley Junction series (4)
Vietnamization
Wright, David K
War in Vietnam series (3)
View-finder
Macgibbon, Jean
Molly and Liz series (1)
View from Deacon Hill
Scott, Jack S
Detective Inspector Alfred Stanley Rosher series (6)
View from Pompey's Head
Basso, Hamilton
Pompey's Head series (2)
View from the pighouse roof
Olsen, Violet
Marie Carlsen series (2)
View from the square
Trenhaile, John
General Povin series (2)
View from the valley
Baker, Denys Val
Cornish series (10)
View from the west
Cockburn, Claud
In time of trouble series (3)
View of vultures
Scholefield, Alan
South African series (1)
View to a death
O'Hara, Kenneth
Alun Barry series (1)
View to a thrill
Vincent, John
James Bond junior series (1)
Views from a lake
Toynbee, Philip
Valediction of Pantaloon series (4)
Vigil on Sundown Ridge
Grover, Marshall
Larry and Stretch series (426)
Vigilante
McLaglen, John J
Herne the Hunter series (10)
Morris, Gilbert
Jim Reno series (4)
Vigilante hunt
Roberts, J R
Gunsmith series (139)
Vigilante justice
Logan, Jake
John Slocum series (82)
Vigilantes
Evans, Tabor
Longarm series (140)
Willoughby, Lee Davis
Making of America series (29)
Viking Bodleys
Scudder, Horace Elisha
Bodley family series (8)
Viking boys
Saxby, Jessie Margaret Edmonston
Shetland series (3)
Viking life
Birt, David
Saxons and Vikings series (9)
Viking raiders
Packard, Edward
Choose your own adventure series (128)
Viking ships
Birt, David
Saxons and Vikings series (5)
Viking slaughter
Frazier, Arthur
Wolfshead series (4)
Viking symbol mystery
Dixon, Franklin W
Hardy boys series (42)
Viking treasure
Bamman, Henry A
World of adventure series (8)
Viking voyages
Birt, David
Saxons and Vikings series (8)
Vikings
O'Donnell, Peter
Modesty Blaise comic strip series (1)
Vikings are fun
Browne, Dik
Hagar the horrible series (10)
Viking's dawn
Treece, Henry
Viking trilogy (1)
Vikings in England
Birt, David
Saxons and Vikings series (6)
Viking's revenge
Neilson, Eric
Haakon series (2)
Viking's sunset
Treece, Henry
Viking trilogy (3)
Viktoria
Glanfield, Jenny
Hotel Quadriga series (2)
Vile village
Sargent, Craig
Last ranger series (7)
Villa Julieta
Sender, Ramon Jose
Before noon trilogy (3)
Villa plot, counterplot
Ross, Cameron
Alistair Duncan series (2)
Village
Anand, Mulk Raj
Lal Singh trilogy (1)
Hinde, Thomas
Henlake series (1)
Shears, Sarah
Franklin family series (1)
Village affairs
Armfelt, Roger
Affairs series (2)
Read, *Miss*
Fairacre series (12)
Village afraid
Burton, Miles
Inspector Arnold and Desmond Merrion series (42)
Village at war
Armstrong, Anthony
Margaret Cottage series (3)
Village centenary
Read, *Miss*
Fairacre series (14)
Village Christmas
Read, *Miss*
Fairacre series (6)
Village contest
Thurston, Ida Treadwell
Bachelor maid series (2)
Village cricket match
Parker, John
Village cricket series (1)
Village cure
Balzac, Honore de
Scenes of country life series (3)
Village daybook
Derleth, August
Sac Prairie series (11)
Village diary
Read, *Miss*
Fairacre series (2)
Village dinosaur
Arkle, Phyllis
Village dinosaur series (1)
Village East
Chambers, Robert
Hank Moody series (1)
Village in a valley
Nichols, Beverley
Allways trilogy (3)
Village in Piccadilly
Henrey, Robert
London in wartime series (1)
Madeleine series (8)
Village in the sun
Chandos, Dane
Mexico series (1)
Village life
Douglas, Peter
Norfolk village series (3)
Village nurse
Deal, Paula
Nurse series (6)
Village of fear
Stuart, Donald
Sexton Blake series (814)
Village of rogues
Sturrock, Jeremy
Bow Street Runner series (1)
Village on the Yarra
Luscombe, Tom
Melbourne series (2)
Village school
Read, *Miss*
Fairacre series (1)
Village year
Derleth, August
Sac Prairie series (7)
Villages under the water
Leyland, Eric
Max and Scrap series (3)
Villain and the virgin
Chase, James Hadley
Carol Blandish series (1)
Villain of the piece
Fisher, Graham
Mike King series (3)
Villainous scheme
Carter, Nicholas
Nicholas Carter series (190)
Villains
Rossiter, John
Criminal Court series (2)
Whalley, Peter
Harry Sommers and Jill Hanscombe series (3)
Villains by necessity
Woods, Sara
Sir Nicholas Harding and Antony Maitland series (35)
Villains of Volturnus
Blashfield, Jean
Endless quest series (8)
Villain's tale
Newman, Gordon F
Law and order trilogy (1)
Villainy at vespers
Cockin, Joan
Inspector Cam and Beaver series (2)
Villainy victorious
Hubbard, Lafayette Ronald
Mission earth series (9)
Ville
Helm, Eric
Ground Zero series (9)
Villette
Bronte, Charlotte
Brussels series (2)
Villon of the piece
Janson, Hank
Hank Janson series (257)
Vindication
Cherryh, Carolyn Janice
Alliance-Union series (11)
Cyteen series (3)
Vindicator
Grant, Maxwell
Shadow series (161)
Vine and olive
Optic, Oliver
Young America, second series (5)
Vinegar and brown paper
Carstairs, John Paddy
Fleur de Lys series (1)
Vinegar Hill
Free, Colin
Pollitt family series (1)
Vines of Ferrara
Coker, Carolyn
Andrea Perkins series (2)
Vineyard of liberty
Burns, James Macgregor
American experiment series (1)
Vintage
Benson, Edward Frederic
Greek War of Independence series (1)
Vintage murder
Marsh, Ngaio
Inspector Roderick Alleyn series (5)
Vintage Polo
Kennealy, Jerry
Nick Polo series (8)
Violence and drugs
Berger, Gilda
Violence series (2)
Violence and the family
Berger, Gilda
Violence series (3)
Violence and the media
Berger, Gilda
Violence series (1)
Violence in quiet places
Story, Jack Trevor
Sexton Blake series (1504)
Violence in sports
Berger, Gilda
Violence series (4)
Violence in the Black Hills
Fuller, Ed
Troubleshooters series (4)

Violence in velvet
Avallone, Michael
Ed Noon series (4)
Violence is golden
Halliday, Brett
Michael Shayne series (58)
Violence is my business
Marlowe, Stephen
Chester Drum series (7)
Violence Trail
Gilman, George G
Edge series (25)
Violence Valley
Heuman, William
Grady Mulvane series (2)
Violent dark
Gribble, Leonard Reginald
Superintendent Anthony Slade series (31)
Violent death of a bitter Englishman
Cleeve, Brian
Sean Ryan series (4)
Violent end
Page, Emma
Inspector Kelsey series (6)
Violent griffin
Sender, Ramon Jose
Before noon trilogy (2)
Violent hills
James, Cy
Rem McAllister series (17)
Violent hours
Saxon, Peter
Sexton Blake series (1435)
Violent keepsake
Grex, Leo
Phil Sanderson series (1)
Violent land
Pike, Charles R
Jubal Cade series (21)
Violent midnight
Gribble, Leonard Reginald
Superintendent Anthony Slade series (43)
Violent ones
Saxon, Peter
Sexton Blake series (1477)
Violent peace
Gilman, George G
Adam Steele series (1)
Violent security
Burnett, George
Inspector Gulliver series (1)
Violent streets
Pendleton, Don
Mack Bolan series (41)
Violent summer
Broome, H B
Tom English series (4)
Violent world of Michael Shayne
Halliday, Brett
Michael Shayne series (53)
Violet's idol
Mathews, Joanna Hooe
Flowerets series (1)
Violin
Van der Essen, Anne
Yok-yok series (11)
Violin lady
Campbell, Daisy Rhodes
Virginia Hammond trilogy (3)
Viper
Footner, Hulbert
Madame Rosika Storey series (3)
Viper and the hawk
Moore, Arthur
California trilogy (3)
Viper factor
Wilson, Gar
Phoenix Force series (15)
Viper in her bosom
Muller, Paul
Paul Muller series (15)
Viper Squad
Hadley, J B
Point Team series (2)
Viper strike
Douglass, Keith
Carrier series (2)
Viperhand
Niles, Douglas
Maztica trilogy (2)
Vipers and Co.
Walker, Frank
Vipers series (1)
Viper's game
Rostand, Robert
Mike Locken series (2)
Viper's sting
Desmond, Hugh
Alan Fraser series (3)
Virgil in Averno
Davidson, Avram
Virgil Magus series (2)
Virgil Nosegay and the cake hunt
Biegel, Paul
Virgil Nosegay series (3)
Virgil Nosegay and the hupmobile
Biegel, Paul
Virgil Nosegay series (4)
Virgil Nosegay and the Wellington boots
Biegel, Paul
Virgil Nosegay series (5)
Virgin
Coon, Susan
Living planet series (3)
Virgin and martyr
Greeley, Andrew Moran
Monsignor John Blackwood Ryan series (1)
Time between the stars (1)
Virgin and the swine
Walton, Evangeline
Mabinogion series (4)
Virgin collector
Ambler, Dail
Danny Spade series (39)
Virgin heiress
Queen, Ellery
Ellery Queen series (15)
Virgin in flames
Rohmer, Sax
Sumuru series (3)
Virgin in the garden
Byatt, Antonia Susan
Virgin in the garden tetralogy (1)
Virgin in the ice
Peters, Ellis
Brother Cadfael series (6)
Virgin of Aldermanbury
Henrey, Madeleine
Madeleine reminiscences series (8)
Virgin of Zesh
De Camp, Lyon Sprague
Krishna series (6)
Virgin outpost
Gentry, Buck
Eli Holten series (16)
Virgin Queen
Peters, Maureen
History's most fascinating women series (2)
Virgin soil
Turgenev, Ivan Sergeevich
Nihilist series (2)
Virgin soil upturned
Sholokhov, Mikhail
Don series (5)
Virgin soldiers
Thomas, Leslie
Virgin soldiers series (1)
Virgin stealers
Streib, Dan
Michael Hawk series (12)
Virgin territory
Hunter, E J
White Squaw series (3)
Virginia
Denuziere, Maurice
Clarence Dandridge series (2)
Virginia and the blue bird
Collonge, Simone
Virginia series (2)
Virginia and the prince of the sea
Collonge, Simone
Virginia series (1)
Virginia at Vine Haven
North, Grace May
Virginia Davis series (2)
Virginia Box and the Unsatisfied
Moffatt, James
Girl from H.A.R.D. series (2)
Virginia City
Mitchum, Hank
Stage coach station series (5)
Virginia City showdown
Logan, Jake
John Slocum series (169)
Virginia City virgin
Martin, Cort
Jared Bolt series (14)
Virginia comedians
Cooke, John Esten
Effingham series (1)
Virginia of Elk Creek Valley
Chase, Mary Ellen
Virginia series (2)
Virginia of V.M. Ranch
North, Grace May
Virginia Davis series (1)
Virginian
Wister, Owen
Virginian series (1)
Western tales series (3)
Virginians
Thackeray, William Makepeace
Virginia series (2)
Virginia's adventure club
North, Grace May
Virginia Davis series (3)
Virginia's ranch neighbors
North, Grace May
Virginia Davis series (4)
Virginia's romance
North, Grace May
Virginia Davis series (5)
Virgins
Rivers, Caryl
Virgins series (1)
Viriconium
Harrison, Michael John
Viriconium series (4)
Viriconium nights
Harrison, Michael John
Viriconium series (4)
Viridian's trail
Edson, John Thomas
Floating Outfit series (6)
Virility gene
Zetford, Tully
Ryder Hook series (4)
Virtual mode
Anthony, Piers
Mode series (1)
Virtual realities
Carmichael, Claire
Virtual realities trilogy (1)
Virtual villainy
Dixon, Franklin W
Hardy boys case files series (86)
Virtuous vamp
Clouston, Joseph Storer
Ursula Dolling series (2)
Virtuous women of Pont Clery
Sandstrom, Flora
Pont Clery series (2)
Virus X
Horler, Sydney
Paul Vivanti series (6)
Visa to limbo
Haggard, William
Colonel Charles Russell series (19)
Viscous circle
Anthony, Piers
Cluster series (5)
Vision is fulfilled
McDonald, Kay L
Ross Chesnut trilogy (3)
Vision of battlements
Burgess, Anthony
Richard Emmis series (5)
Vision of doom
Kirchoff, Mary Lynn
Endless quest series (35)
Vision of light
Riley, Judith Merkle
Margaret of Ashbury series (1)
Vision of Tarot
Anthony, Piers
Tarot trilogy (2)
Vision of the Eagle
McDonald, Kay L
Ross Chesnut trilogy (1)
Vision quest
Cole, Judd
Cheyenne series (4)
Vision sinister
Karta, Nat
Inspector Garth series (5)
Visions
Garrett, Sally
Rainbow Hills series (2)
Visions and jewels
Oyved, Moysheh
Jewels and gems series (1)
Visions from nowhere
Arrow, William
Return to the Planet of the Apes series (1)
Visions from the sea
Tallis, Robyn
Planet builders series (4)
Visions of Cody
Kerouac, Jack
Jack Duluoz series (7)
Visions of Gerard
Kerouac, Jack
Jack Duluoz series (1)
Visions of glory, 1874-1932
Manchester, William
Last lion series (1)
Visions of London
Macinnes, Colin
Visions of London series (3)
Visions of Neal
Kerouac, Jack
Jack Duluoz series (7)
Visit from a broad
Janson, Hank
Hank Janson series (164)
Visit from Raffles
Hornung, Ernest William
Raffles series (18)
Visit of two giant pandas at the San Diego Zoo
Irvine, Georgeanne
Zoo world series (3)
Visit to Birmingham
Housman, Laurence
Palace plays series (4)
Visit to Venus
Fraser, Ronald
Trout series (1)
Visitation
Taylor, Frank
Uninvited trilogy (2)
Visitation of spirits
Kenan, Randall
Tims Creek series (1)
Visiting a village
Kalman, Bobbie
Historic communities series (4)
Visiting the new baby
Graham, Bob
New baby series (2)
Visiting villain
Wells, Carolyn
Fleming Stone series (39)
Visitor
Gilbert, Anthony
Arthur Crook series (44)
Gregory, Julian R
Tomorrow people series (1)
Oxenbury, Helen
First picture books series (9)
Visitor from home
Gilroy, Beryl
Young Roy series (2)
Visitor from the sea
Simpson, Dorothy
Janie Marshal series (6)
Visitors at the flower-patch
Klickmann, Flora
Flower-patch series (5)
Visitors for Edward
Morgan, Michaela
Edward series (2)
Visitors from England
Kyle, Elisabeth
Furze series (1)
Visitors from London
Barne, Kitty
Farrar family series (2)
Visitors from Oz
Baum, Lyman Frank
Oz series (14)
Visitors from planet Veta
Goll, Reinhold Weimar
Veta series (1)
Visits of Elizabeth
Glyn, Elinor
Elizabeth series (1)
Visual evangels
Westphail, Arnold Carl
Gospel magic series (5)
Vital lies
Hart, Ellen
Jane Lawless series (2)
Vital parts
Berger, Thomas
Carlo Reinhart series (3)
Vital signs
Sutton, Jessica
Bel Air General series (4)
Vital statistics
Chastain, Thomas
Inspector Max Kauffman series (3)
J T Spanner series (2)
Vittoria
Meredith, George
Sandra Belloni series (2)
Vittoria Cottage
Stevenson, Dorothy Emily
Drumberley trilogy (1)
Viva McHugh
Flynn, Jay
McHugh series (2)
Vivanti
Horler, Sydney
Paul Vivanti series (2)
Vivanti returns
Horler, Sydney
Paul Vivanti series (4)
Vivian inheritance
Stubbs, Jean
Brief chronicles series (3)
Vivian of Cavendish Square
Douglas, Kathryn
Cavendish series (2)
Vivienne
Hunter, Alan
Inspector George Gently series (19)
Vixen
Brown, Carter
Lieutenant Al Wheeler series (32)
Vixen Zero Three
Cussler, Clive
Dirk Pitt series (5)
Vlad the Drac
Jungman, Ann
Vlad the Drac series (1)
Vlad the Drac down under
Jungman, Ann
Vlad the Drac series (5)
Vlad the Drac returns
Jungman, Ann
Vlad the Drac series (2)
Vlad the Drac, superstar
Jungman, Ann
Vlad the Drac series (3)
Vlad the Drac, vampire
Jungman, Ann
Vlad the Drac series (4)
Voice
Gilbert, Anthony
Arthur Crook series (41)
Grant, Maxwell
Shadow series (154)
Voice for Princess
Morressy, John
Kedrigern series (1)
Voice from another world
Lach-Szyrma, Wladislaw Somerville
Venus series (1)
Voice from nowhere
Butler, Bill
Dean Street detectives series (1)
Voice from the cave
Wirt, Mildred Augustine
Penny Parker series (12)
Voice from the dark
Phillpotts, Eden
John Ringrose series (1)
Voice from the dead
Copper, Basil
Mike Faraday series (15)
Voice from the past
Carter, Nicholas
Nicholas Carter series (216)
Voice in the suitcase
Sutton, Margaret
Judy Bolton series (8)
Voice in the wind
Lasky, Kathryn
Starbuck family series (3)
Voice of Bugle Ann
Kantor, Mackinlay
Bugle Ann series (1)
Civil War trilogy (1)
Voice of death
Grant, Maxwell
Shadow series (181)
Voice of doom
Jones, G Wayman
Black Bat series (14)
Voice of evil
Adams, Nicholas
Horror High series (1)
Voice of murder
Erskine, Margaret
Inspector Septimus Finch series (9)
Voice of the city
Henry, O
Four million series (3)
Voice of the corpse
Murray, Max
Corpse series (1)
Voice of the crowd
Tilsley, Frank
Nap and Ted series (1)
Voice of the eagle
Shuler, Linda Lay
Time circle series (2)
Voice of the great elephant
Seed, Jenny
Natal series (1)
Voice of the house
Erskine, Margaret
Inspector Septimus Finch series (2)
Voice of the mountain
Wellman, Manly Wade
Silver John series (6)
Voice of the past
Leek, Margaret
Stephen Marryat series (3)

Voice of the peacock
Salter, Elizabeth
Inspector Michael Hornsley series (4)
Voice of the whirlwind
Williams, Walter Jon
Hardwired trilogy (2)
Voiceless ones
Creasey, John
Doctor Palfrey series (31)
Voices from the dark
Parrish, Frank
Dan Mallett series (8)
Voices from the haunted house
Smith, Beatrice Schillinger
Kate and Ben King series (6)
Voices in a haunted room
Carr, Philippa
Daughters of England series (11)
Voices in my ear
Stokes, Doris
Voices series (1)
Voices in the dark
Coburn, Andrew
James Morgan series (2)
Haynes, James
Twilight series (6)
Voices in the fog
Cameron, Kate
Holderly Hall series (3)
Voices in the house
Sedges, John
American life series (3)
Voices in the washhouse
Harewood, Jocelyn
Peregrine Merritt series (1)
Voices of love
Stokes, Doris
Voices series (6)
Voices of Mars
Moore, Patrick
Maurice Gray series (3)
Void in hearts
Tapply, William George
Brady Coyne series (7)
Volcano
Fisk, Nicholas
Starstormers series (5)
Roberts, Cecil
Pilgrim Cottage series (3)
Siegman, Meryl
Choose your own adventure series (64)
Volcano adventure
Price, Willard
Hal and Roger Hunt series (4)
Volcano alert!
Lampton, Christopher
Alert series (6)
Volcano of violence
Thorne, Ramsay
Captain Gringo series (23)
Volcano ogre
Carter, Lin
Prince Zarkon series (3)
Volleyball
Gutman, Bill
Go for it series (12)
Start right and play well series (2)
Volleyball for boys and girls
Gutman, Bill
Start right and play well series (2)
Volteface
Adlard, Mark
Jan Caspol trilogy (2)
Volunteer fireman
Elias, Horace J
Flintstones series (10)
Volunteers for Frago
Brand, Kurt
Perry Rhodan series (122)
Volunteers for glory
Scofield, Jonathan
Freedom fighters series (10)
Von Kessel dossier
Le Grand, Leon
Michael Berresford series (1)
Vonnie and Monique
Francis, Dorothy
Keepsake series (2)
Von Ryan's express
Westheimer, David
Von Ryan series (1)
Von Ryan's return
Westheimer, David
Von Ryan series (2)
Voodoo
Esteven, John
Inspector Rae Norse series (2)
Voodoo death
Grant, Maxwell
Shadow series (252)
Voodoo die
Murphy, Warren Burton
Destroyer series (33)
Voodoo drum
Saxon, Peter
Sexton Blake series (1222)
Voodoo game
Niven, Larry
Dream Park series (3)
Voodoo Island
Teed, George Hamilton
Grant Rushton series (5)
Voodoo kill
Gray, Rod
New lady from L.U.S.T. series (5)
Voodoo master
Grant, Maxwell
Shadow series (97)
Voodoo murders
Avallone, Michael
Ed Noon series (8)
Voodoo planet
Norton, Andre
Dane Thorson series (3)
Voodoo plot
Dixon, Franklin W
Hardy boys series (72)
Voodoo slave
Daniels, Norman A
Jubal trilogy (3)
Voodoo trail
Grant, Maxwell
Shadow series (145)
Voodoo violence
Janson, Hank
Hank Janson series (194)
Vor game
Bujold, Lois McMaster
Miles Naismith Vorkosigan series (4)
Vorge against Quinette
Romains, Jules
Men of goodwill series (17)
Vorkosigan's game
Bujold, Lois McMaster
Miles Naismith Vorkosigan series (4)
Vortex blaster
Smith, Edward Elmer
Lensman series (7)
Votan
James, John
Photinus the Greek series (1)
Vote against poison
Sherwood, John
Mister Charles Blessington series (5)
Vote for death
Longmate, Norman
Inspector Bradley and Sergeant Raymond series (4)
Vote for Huggett
Constanduros, Mabel
Huggetts series (2)
Vote for the Toff
Creasey, John
Toff series (54)
Vote for violence
Johns, Gilbert
Sexton Blake series (1516)
Vote X for treason
Cleeve, Brian
Sean Ryan series (1)
Vow of chastity
Black, Veronica
Sister Joan series (2)
Vow of obedience
Black, Veronica
Sister Joan series (4)
Vow of penance
Black, Veronica
Sister Joan series (5)
Vow of sanctity
Black, Veronica
Sister Joan series (3)
Vow of silence
Black, Veronica
Sister Joan series (1)
Vow on the heron
Plaidy, Jean
Plantagenet series (9)
Voyag of life on a paper boat
Westphail, Arnold Carl
Paper tearing series (12)
Voyage home
Church, Richard
Over the bridge series (3)
Jameson, Storm
Triumph of time trilogy (2)
Lerangis, Peter
Star trek moving picture series (4)
McIntyre, Vondra Neil
Star trek moving picture series (4)
Voyage in, voyage out
Rikhoff, Jean
Timble family trilogy (2)
Voyage into violence
Lockridge, Frances
Bill Wiegand series (21)
Mister and Mrs North series (22)
Voyage not completed
Grayson, Rupert
Voyage not completed series (1)
Voyage of consolation
Cotes, Sarah Jeanette
American tourist series (2)
Voyage of death
Cruz, Mark
Kill Squad series (2)
Voyage of fear
Hardinge, Rex
Sexton Blake series (1355)
Voyage of Ormungandr
Taylor, Keith
Bard series (2)
Voyage of terror
Brennan, James Herbert
GrailQuest series (4)
Voyage of the Annie Marble
Forester, Cecil Scott
Annie Marble series (1)
Voyage of the Chianti
Morison, Betty Jane
Elizabeth Lamb Worthington series (4)
Voyage of the Dawn Trader
Lewis, Clive Staples
Narnia series (5)
Voyage of the Girl Pat
Orsborne, Dod
Adventurer in chains series (1)
Voyage of the planetslayer
Swycaffer, Jefferson Putnam
Tales of the Concordat trilogy (2)
Voyage of the Starfire to Atlantis
Mumford, Edwin Embree
Starfire series (5)
Voyage of the Victory
Orsborne, Dod
Adventurer in chains series (3)
Voyage of the Vigilance
Kilworth, Garry
Woodworld series (2)
Voyage of the Vivian to the North Pole and beyond
Knox, Thomas Wallace
Boy travellers series (17)
Voyage of vengeance
Hubbard, Lafayette Ronald
Mission earth series (7)
Voyage out
Woolf, Virginia
Mrs Dalloway series (1)
Voyage round the world in search of castaways
Verne, Jules
Captain Grant's children series (1)
Voyage to adventure
Dodge, Michael J
Star trek tie-ins series (8)
Voyage to Africa
Hoberg, Marielis
Heiner and Elsie series (2)
Voyage to Bengal
Knight, Frank
Clipper ship series (2)
Voyage to Dari
Wallace, Ian
Croyd series (4)
Pan Sagittarius series (3)
Voyage to Inshneefa
Brady, John Paul
Lemuel Gulliver series (11)
Voyage to New South Wales
Barrington, George
Voyage to New South Wales series (1)
Voyage to Santa Fe
Giles, Janice Holt
Fowler family series (5)
Voyage to the bottom of the sea
Jones, Raymond F
Voyage to the bottom of the sea series (2)
Sturgeon, Theodore
Voyage to the bottom of the sea series (1)
Voyage to the city of the dead
Foster, Alan Dean
Thranx series (6)
Voyage to Venus
Lewis, Clive Staples
Space trilogy (2)
Voyage with Columbus
Reit, Seymour V
Time traveler series (1)
Voyager
Gabaldon, Diana
Outlander series (3)
Voyager in bondage
Finch, Simon
Voyager trilogy (3)
Voyagers
Bova, Ben
Voyagers series (1)
Ferra-Mikura, Vera
Stanislaus family series (1)
Voyages of Doctor Dolittle
Lofting, Hugh
Doctor Dolittle series (2)
Voyageurs
Ballinger, W A
Voyageurs series (1)
Willoughby, Lee Davis
Making of America series (35)
Voyaging under sail
Hiscock, Eric Charles
Under sail series (3)
Vulcan!
Sky, Kathleen
Star trek originals sequels series (9)
Vulcan academy murders
Lorrah, Jean
Star trek series (20)
Vulcan disaster
Carter, Nick
Nick Carter series (110)
Vulcan reflections
Langsam, Devra Michele
Vulcan reflections series (1)
Vulcan treasure
Rotsler, William
Star trek tie-ins series (7)
Vulcan's glory
Fontana, Dorothy Catherine
Star trek series (44)
Vulgar boatman
Tapply, William George
Brady Coyne series (6)
Vulture
Reno, Bill
Badge series (17)
Ward, Harold
Vulture series (1)
Vulture in the sun
Bingham, John
Ducane series (2)
Vulture of Sierra Madre
Masterson, Louis
Morgan Kane series (36)
Vulture strikes
Ward, Harold
Vulture series (2)
Vulture Valley
Hobart, Donald Bayne
Masked Rider and Blue Hawk series (10)
Vultures gather
Hocking, Anne
Inspector William Austen series (12)
Vultures in the sky
Downing, Todd
Hugh Rennert series (3)
Vultures in the smoke
Foxall, Peter Augustus
Detective Sergeant Scamp series (1)
Vultures Ltd.
Gray, Berkeley
Norman Conquest series (2)
Vultures of the horn
Hild, Jack
SOBS series (10)
Vultures of the White Death
Hogan, Robert Jasper
G-Eight series (8)
Vulture's vengeance
Pendleton, Don
Mack Bolan series (51)
Vurt
Noon, Jeff
Vurt series (1)
Vye murder
Wray, I
Inspector Digby series (1)
Vygnet and the Firebird
McKillip, Patricia Anne
Cygnet series (2)

W

W.H.O.R.E.
Brown, Carter
Lieutenant Al Wheeler series (42)
W One
McGuire, Paul
Inspector Wittler series (4)
W plan
Seton, Graham
Colonel Duncan Grant series (1)
WAAC demobolized
WAAC
WAAC series (2)
Wabash!
Poole, Helen Lee
Whitewater dynasty series (4)
Wabeno, the magician
Wright, Mabel Osgood
Tommy-Anne series (2)
Wacky Witch and the mystery of the king's gold
Lewis, Jean
Wacky Witch series (2)
Wacky Witch and the royal birthday
Lewis, Jean
Wacky Witch series (1)
Wacky world of Alvin Fernald
Hicks, Clifford Byron
Alvin Fernald series (8)
Waco rides in
Edson, John Thomas
Waco series (5)
Waco's badge
Edson, John Thomas
Waco series (2)
Waco's debt
Edson, John Thomas
Floating Outfit series (50)
Waco series (1)
Wacvie
Bandler, Faith
Wacvie series (1)
Wag-Tail Bess
Flack, Marjorie
Angus series (4)
Wager
Fish, Robert Lloyd
Kek Huuygens series (4)
Woodman, Richard
Nathaniel Drinkwater series (10)
Wagered widow
Veryan, Patricia
Golden chronicles series (6)
Wagered world
Janifer, Laurence Mark
Angelo DiStefano trilogy (3)
Wages of rascality
Carter, Nicholas
Nicholas Carter series (549)
Wages of sin
Braun, Matt
Ash Tallman series (3)
Lord, Tom
Tallman series (3)
Wages of Wayne
McRobbie, David
Wayne Wilson series (3)
Wages of Zen
Melville, James
Superintendent Tetsuo Otani series (1)
Waggon for five
Severn, David
Crusoe series (3)
Waggon Wheelers on tour
Leyland, Eric
Nicky and Simon Carr series (2)
Wagon number three
Grover, Marshall
Larry and Stretch series (290)
Wagon train colt
Stanley, Chuck
Wagon train series (1)
Wagon train hold-up
Stanley, Chuck
Wagon train series (2)
Wagon train to hell
Roberts, J R
Gunsmith series (99)
Wagons east
Gilman, George G
Adam Steele series (21)
Wagons on the Ogden Road
Sheridan, Matt
David Harcourt series (2)

Wagons over the mountains
McCall, Edith
Frontiers of America series (9)

Wagons to Backsight
Edson, John Thomas
Floating Outfit series (11)

Wagons west
Chambers, Catherine E
Adventures in frontier America series (10)

Wagontongue
Kelton, Elmer
Tales of Texas series (8)

Waif of the river
Farnol, Jeffery
Mister Jasper Shrig of Bow Street series (10)

Waikiki widow
Sheridan, Juanita
Lily Wu and Janice Cameron series (4)

Wail for the corpses
Treat, Lawrence
Carl Wayward series (1)

Wailing frail
Prather, Richard Scott
Shell Scott series (12)

Wailing lighthouse game
Blyton, Enid
Famous Five adventure games series (5)

Wailing octopus
Blaine, John
Rick Brant series (11)

Wailing siren mystery
Dixon, Franklin W
Hardy boys series (30)

Wait and hope
Alger, Horatio
Brave and bold series (4)

Wait for a corpse
Murray, Max
Corpse series (11)

Wait for death
Ashe, Gordon
Patrick Dawlish series (33)

Wait for Marcy
Du Jardin, Rosamond
Marcy series (1)

Wait for the judge
Grover, Marshall
Larry and Stretch series (225)

Wait for the wagon
Lasswell, Mary
Mrs Feeley series (4)

Wait for William
Flack, Marjorie
William series (1)

Wait until spring, Bandini
Fante, John
Arturo Bandini series (1)

Waiters on the dance
Savarin, Julian Jay
Lemmus trilogy (1)

Waiting
Theis, Jody Sorenson
Cheerleaders series (15)

Waiting and serving
Butler, Maude Mary
Daffodil series (1)

Waiting for a tiger
Healey, Ben
Paul Hedley series (1)

Waiting for a train
Gilman, George G
Edge series (30)

Waiting for Oliver
Troy, Simon
Inspector Smith series (6)

Waiting for the dark
Berg, Leila
Snaps series (4)

Waiting for the end of the world
Taylor, Andrew
William Dougal series (2)

Waiting for the galactic bus
Godwin, Parke
Snake oil wars series (1)

Waiting for the Mahatma
Narayan, Rasipuram Krishnaswami
Malgudi series (1)

Waiting for the new baby
Graham, Bob
New baby series (1)

Waiting for the night
Hilton, Alec
Doctor Martin Lestrange series (2)

Waiting for Thursday
Jobson, Hamilton
Inspector Anders series (10)

Waiting for Wilkie's wagon
Grover, Marshall
Larry and Stretch series (373)

Waiting game
Mosco, Maisie
Waiting game series (1)
Pike, Charles R
Jubal Cade series (19)
Wayland, Patrick
Lloyd Nicolson series (3)

Waiting games
Hart, Bruce
Jessie Walters and Michael Skye series (2)

Waiting in the night
Millar, George
Maquis series (1)

Waiting in the wings
Norby, Lisa
Heart to heart series (3)
Tovey, Doreen
Cats series (12)

Waiting legacy
Gage, Joy Pennock
Seventh child series (3)

Waiting my turn
Erickson, Karen
I can do it series (12)

Waiting room
Harris, Wilson
Agent of personality quartet (2)
Wright, Terrance Michael
Manhattan series (2)

Waiting room mystery
Blair, Allan
Sexton Blake series (694)

Waiting spirits
Coville, Bruce
Dark forces series (11)

Wake for a lady
Roden, Henry Wisdom
Sid Ames series (4)

Wake for mourning
Martin, Shane
Professor Ronald Challis series (5)

Wake kitten
Schongut, Emanuel
Kitten board book series (2)

Wake me up when I'm a size five
Guisewhite, Cathy
Cathy series (5)

Wake of the werewolf
Caine, Geoffrey
Abraham Stroud series (2)

Wake the dead
Simpson, Dorothy
Inspector Luke Thanet series (11)

Wake up, Busy Bears!
Killingback, Julia
Busy Bears series (7)

Wake up, darlin' Corey
Wren, M K
Conan Flagg series (6)

Wake up, Ginger Meggs
Kemsley, James
Ginger Meggs series (37)

Wake up, nurse
Brook, Roger
Nursing howlers series (2)

Wake up screaming!
Kent, Arthur
Sexton Blake series (1449)

Wake up, stupid!
Harris, Mark
Lee Youngdahl series (1)

Wake up time
Thompson, Carol
Busy baby's day series (1)

Wakefield legacy
Pascal, Francine
Sweet Valley magna series (2)

Wakefield's course
De la Roche, Mazo
Whiteoak series (12)

Wakefields of Sweet Valley
Pascal, Francine
Sweet Valley magna series (1)

Wakeley witch
Smith, Janet
Wakeley witch series (1)

Waking of Orthlund
Taylor, Roger
Hawklan series (3)

Walden
Thoreau, Henry David
Walden series (1)

Walden Pond
Derleth, August
Walden West series (2)

Walden three
Catran, Jack
Walden series (3)

Walden two
Skinner, Burrhus Frederic
Walden series (2)

Walden West
Derleth, August
Walden West series (1)

Waldo and the boattrip
Wilhelm, Hans
Waldo series (4)

Waldo and the Christmas surprise
Wilhelm, Hans
Waldo series (2)

Waldo and the desert island adventure
Wilhelm, Hans
Waldo series (1)

Waldo and the giant splash
Wilhelm, Hans
Waldo series (3)

Waldo and the orchestra
Wilhelm, Hans
Waldo series (5)

Waldo between friends
Wilhelm, Hans
Waldo series (9)

Waldo datebook
Wilhelm, Hans
Waldo series (9)

Waldo Duck
Kanno, Wendy
Funny Farm series (2)

Waldo for old and young
Wilhelm, Hans
Waldo series (9)

Waldo friendship
Wilhelm, Hans
Waldo series (9)

Waldo, tell me about Christ
Wilhelm, Hans
Waldo, tell me series (4)

Waldo, tell me about Christmas
Wilhelm, Hans
Waldo, tell me series (5)

Waldo, tell me about God
Wilhelm, Hans
Waldo, tell me series (3)

Waldo, tell me about guardian angels
Wilhelm, Hans
Waldo, tell me series (1)

Waldo, tell me about me
Wilhelm, Hans
Waldo, tell me series (2)

Waldo the tortoise
Lloyd, David
Great escapes series (5)

Waldo with love
Wilhelm, Hans
Waldo series (9)

Walg
Wongar, B
Nuclear trilogy (1)

Walk a black wind
Collins, Michael
Dan Fortune series (4)

Walk a crooked mile
Philips, Judson Pentecost
Peter Styles series (12)
Truss, Seldon
Inspector Gidleigh series (19)

Walk a narrow trail
Lawrence, Steven C
Tom Slattery series (3)

Walk along the tracks
Davies, Hunter
English walks series (3)

Walk along the Wall
Davies, Hunter
English walks series (1)

Walk around London's parks
Davies, Hunter
English walks series (4)

Walk around the Lakes
Davies, Hunter
English walks series (2)

Walk at a steady pace
Fisher, Norman
Nigel Morrison series (1)

Walk at night
Craig, David
Stephen Bellecroix and Sheila Roath series (2)

Walk for us
Hardcastle, Michael
Tony and Jay series (2)

Walk in darkness
Habe, Hans
Occupied Germany series (2)

Walk in fear
Baker, William Howard
Sexton Blake series (1418)

Walk in the rain
Border, Rosemary
Walk in the woods series (4)

Walk in the shadows
Dolphin, Rex
Sexton Blake series (1469)

Walk in the snow
Border, Rosemary
Walk in the woods series (2)

Walk in the sun
Border, Rosemary
Walk in the woods series (3)

Walk in the wind
Border, Rosemary
Walk in the woods series (1)

Walk into murder
Helm, Peter
Martin Ridgway series (1)

Walk into peril
Kennett, John
Black Circle Gang series (2)

Walk on the blind side
Maccargo, J T
Mannix series (4)

Walk softly, witch
Brown, Carter
Danny Boyd series (1)

Walk softly witch!
Brown, Carter
Lieutenant Al Wheeler series (6)

Walk tall, ride tall
Arthur, Burt
Johnny Canavan series (5)

Walk the bloody boulevard
Marcus, Arthur A
Pete Hunter series (2)

Walk the dark streets
Krasner, William
Sam Birge series (1)

Walk to the end of the world
Charnas, Suzy McKee
Aildera series (1)

Walk, trot, canter and die
Stuart, Donald Robert
Conjuror's years series (2)

Walk with care
Wentworth, Patricia
Benbow Smith and Frank Garratt series (2)

Walker of worlds
De Haven, Tom
Chronicles of the king's tramp series (1)

Walkers of the wind
Sarabande, William
First Americans series (4)

Walkers on the sky
Lake, David John
Breakout series (1)

Walking corpse
Cole, George Douglas Howard
Superintendent Henry Wilson series (9)

Walking dead man
Pentecost, Hugh
Pierre Chambrun series (9)
Roberts, J R
Gunsmith series (56)

Walking fingers
Stanton, Vance
Partridge family series (6)

Walking in the air
Briggs, Raymond
Snowman series (3)

Walking into the Lyons' den
Weir, Molly
Feet series (5)

Walking sands
Shirreffs, Gordon Donald
Dave Hunter series (3)

Walking shadow
Offord, Lenore Glen
Todd McKinnon series (4)
Parker, Robert Brown
Spenser series (21)
Walsh, James Morgan
Mike Harman series (2)

Walking tall
Warren, Doug
Sheriff Buford Pusser series (1)

Walking tall, part 2
Carey, Webster
Sheriff Buford Pusser series (3)

Walking tall, striking fear
Grover, Marshall
Larry and Stretch series (301)

Walking the cat by Tommy Tip Paine
Batchelor, John Calvin
Gordon Liddy is my muse series (2)

Walking the Indian streets
Mehta, Ved
Face to face series (2)

Walking the whirlwind
Knight, Brigid
Ashenden series (1)

Walking through the fire
Lee, Laurel
Godspeed series (2)

Walking wind
Proud, Franklin M
Joe Sanford series (2)

Walking wounded
Murphy, Warren Burton
Destroyer series (74)
Murray, Will
Destroyer series (74)

Walks in the sun
Coldsmith, Don
Spanish bit series (20)

Walks with Romany
Evens, George Bramwell
Romany series (7)

Wall
Cournos, John
John Gombarov trilogy (2)
McConnell, Ashley
Quantum leap series (3)

Wall and three willows
Najafi, Najmeli
Persia trilogy (3)

Wall around star
Pohl, Frederik
Cuckoo's saga series (2)

Wall of eyes
Millar, Margaret
Inspector Sands series (2)

Wall of flame
Wilson, Gar
Phoenix Force super series (4)

Wall of masks
Coffey, Brian
Mike Tucker series (3)

Wall of serpents
De Camp, Lyon Sprague
Harold Shea series (3)

Wall Street haul
Carter, Nicholas
Nicholas Carter series (4)

Wallace
Abbott, Jacob
Franconia series (2)
Tranter, Nigel Godwin
Scottish history series (5)

Wallace at bay
Wilson, Alexander
Sir Leonard Wallace series (7)

Wallace intervenes
Wilson, Alexander
Sir Leonard Wallace series (8)

Wallace of the Secret Service
Wilson, Alexander
Sir Leonard Wallace series (3)

Walled orchard
Holt, Tom
Walled orchard series (2)

Wallet of Kai Lung
Bramah, Ernest
Kai Lung series (1)

Wallingford and Blackie Daw
Chester, George Randolph
James Rufus Wallingford series (4)

Wallingford in his prime
Chester, George Randolph
James Rufus Wallingford series (3)

Wallington case
Jon, Montague
Stephen Kale series (1)

Walls do not fall
Doolittle, Hilda
War trilogy (1)

Walls of air
Hambly, Barbara
Darwath trilogy (2)

Walls of Athens
Walsh, Jill Paton
Children of the fox trilogy (2)

Walls of Jericho
Wellman, Paul Iselin
Jericho series (1)

Wally the kangaroo
Beaman, Sydney George Hulme
Out of the ark series (2)

Wally Walnut
Reed, Giles
Munch Bunch character series (8)

Wallypug birthday book
Farrow, George Edward
Wallypug series (7)

Wallypug book
Farrow, George Edward
Wallypug series (7)

Wallypug in London
Farrow, George Edward
Wallypug series (2)

Wallypug in Pog-Land
Farrow, George Edward
Wallypug series (6)

Wallypug in the moon
Farrow, George Edward
Wallypug series (7)
Wallypug of Why
Farrow, George Edward
Wallypug series (1)
Wallypug tales
Farrow, George Edward
Wallypug series (7)
Walnut Grove
Rushing, Jane Gilmore
Walnut Grove series (3)
Walnut whirl
Townson, Hazel
Lenny and Jake series (8)
Walrus and the warwolf
Cook, Hugh
Chronicles of an age of darkness series (4)
Walt Disney's Andy Burnett
Verral, Charles Spain
Andy Burnett series (4)
Walt Disney's Zorro
Frazee, Steve
Zorro series (7)
Walter
Cook, David
Walter series (1)
Walter and Frank
Leslie, Madeline
Woodbine series (4)
Walter Dragun's town
Sancha, Sheila
Stamford series (1)
Walter Duck and Winifred
Pilgrim, Jane
Blackberry Farm series (16)
Walter Greenway, spy and hero
Holmes, Robert
Walter Greenway series (2)
Walter Greenway, spy and others, sometime criminal
Holmes, Robert
Walter Greenway series (1)
Walter Sherwood's probation
Alger, Horatio
Good fortune trilogy (1)
Walter's friend
Adams, Henry Cadwallader
Nethercourt series (3)
Walter's schooldays series (2)
Walther P.38
Wainwright, John
Lucky Luckhurst series (1)
Northern Police series (29)
Walton boys and gold in the snow
Burton, Hal
Walton boys series (1)
Walton boys in high country
Burton, Hal
Walton boys series (3)
Walton boys in rapids ahead
Burton, Hal
Walton boys series (2)
Waminda
Barrett, Helen Elizabeth-Anne
West family series (1)
Wamphyri!
Lumley, Brian
Necroscope series (2)
Wand
Eckert, Allan Wesley
Mesmerian annals series (2)
Wand from France
Todd, Barbara Euphan
Perdita series (2)
Wander bird plot
Taylor, Phoebe Atwood
Asey Mayo series (19)
Wanderer
Edwards, Monica
Punchbowl Farm series (5)
McQuinn, Donald E
Pacific Northwest trilogy (2)
Schmidt, Dennis
Kensho series (4)
Waltari, Mika
Michael Carvajel series (2)
Wanderer in space
Moore, Patrick
Robin North and Rex Redmayne series (2)
Wanderer of the wasteland
Grey, Zane
Adam Larey series (1)
Wanderer Springs
Flynn, Robert
Wanderer Springs series (2)
Wanderer's return
Hancock, Niel
Windameir circle series (4)
Wandering fire
Kay, Guy Gavriel
Fionavar tapestry trilogy (2)
Wandering girl
Ward, Glenyse
Wandering girl series (1)
Wandering Heath
Quiller-Couch, Arthur
Troy Town series (4)
Wandering Jew
Heym, Stefan
Wandering Jew series (3)
Sue, Eugene
Wandering Jew series (1)
Wandering Jew, an account of his last adventure
Clough, Samuel Dennis Procter
Wandering Jew series (5)
Wandering prince
Plaidy, Jean
Charles II trilogy (1)
Stuart series (2)
Wandering Robinson
Casement, Christina
Robinson series (1)
Wandering star
Fitz Roy, Olivia
Stewarts series (5)
Wandering under sail
Hiscock, Eric Charles
Under sail series (1)
Wandering whale, and other adventures from a zoo vet's casebook
Taylor, David Conrad
Zoovet series (5)
Wandering wind
B B
Bill Badger series (1)
Wandering with Nomad
Ellison, Norman
Nomad series (1)
Wandering Wombles
Beresford, Elisabeth
Wombles series (2)
Wandering years
Beaton, Cecil
Years diaries series (1)
Wanderings of Asaf
Afghan
Asaf Khan series (2)
Wanderings of Mumfie
Tozer, Katharine
Mumfie series (1)
Wanderings of Wuntvor
Gardner, Craig Shaw
Ballad of Wuntvor trilogy (3)
Wanderlust
Kirchoff, Mary Lynn
Meetings series (2)
Manfred, Frederick
World's wanderer trilogy (3)
Wanderlust goes south
Boyd, Edward
Wanderlust Brown series (2)
Wanderlust's third innings
Boyd, Edward
Wanderlust Brown series (3)
Wandl the invader
Cummings, Ray
Gregg Haljan series (2)
Wandor's flight
Green, Roland James
Wandor series (4)
Wandor's journey
Green, Roland James
Wandor series (2)
Wandor's ride
Green, Roland James
Wandor series (1)
Wandor's voyage
Green, Roland James
Wandor series (3)
Wand'ring darling
Rita
Victorian series (2)
Wandy the wild pony
Chaffee, Allen
Wandy series (1)
Wandy wins
Chaffee, Allen
Wandy series (2)
Wang the Ninth
Weale, Putnam
Wang the Ninth trilogy (1)
Wankh
Vance, Jack
Tschai series (2)
Want to trade two brothers for a cat?
Lewis, Linda
Linda series (7)
Wanted
Donovan, Dick
Dick Donovan series (6)
Graydon, William Murray
Sexton Blake series (489)
Harte, Bryce
Slate Creed series (2)
Wanted, a clew
Carter, Nicholas
Nicholas Carter series (546)
Wanted, Belle Starr
Edson, John Thomas
Calamity Jane series (13)
Wanted by two clients
Carter, Nicholas
Nicholas Carter series (54)
Wanted, Dany Fontaine
Ard, William
Danny Fontaine series (1)
Wanted, dead man
Chaber, M E
Milo March series (14)
Wanted, dead or alive
Dawson, Clay
Long Rider series (27)
Wanted for killing
Welcome, John
Richard Graham series (3)
Simon Herald series (2)
Wanted for murder
Charteris, Leslie
Saint series (6)
Gilman, George G
Adam Steele series (20)
Wanted for questioning
Cross, Mark
Daphne Wrayne and her Four Adjusters series (44)
McNeilly, Wilfred
Sexton Blake series (1574)
Wanted gun
Palmer, Bernard
Kid Breckinridge series (2)
Wanted in Texas
Grover, Marshall
Bleak Creek series (7)
Wanted, Mud Blossom
Byars, Betsy
Blossoms series (4)
Wanted, Sammy's super T-shirt!
Robertson, H Macleod
Sammy's super T-shirt series (2)
Wanted, Wildcat O'Shea
Clinton, Jeff
Wildcat O'Shea series (6)
Wanted woman
Ledd, Paul
Shelter Morgan series (23)
Wanting it all
Pfeffer, Susan Beth
Make me a star series (3)
Wanton
Brown, Carter
Lieutenant Al Wheeler series (17)
Wanton chase
Quennell, Peter
Marble foot series (2)
Wanton fires
Trevor, Meriol
Brentland series (3)
Luxembourg series (8)
Wanton for murder
Klinger, Henry
Lieutenant Shomri Shomar series (1)
Wanton princess
Wheatley, Dennis
Roger Brook series (8)
Wantons die hard
Gribble, Leonard Reginald
Superintendent Anthony Slade series (29)
Wapshot chronicle
Cheever, John
Wapshot series (1)
Wapshot scandal
Cheever, John
Wapshot series (2)
War
McDowell, Michael M
Blackwater series (4)
Owen, Harold
Journey from obscurity trilogy (3)
War against the Mafia
Pendleton, Don
Mack Bolan series (1)
War and passion
Arlen, Leslie
Borodin family series (2)
War and peace
Tolstoi, Leo Nikolaevich
War and peace series (1)
War and peace, 1914-1929
Amery, Leopold Stennett
My political life trilogy (2)
War and remembrance
Wouk, Herman
Commander Pug Henry series (2)
War between the sisters
Oaks, Tina
Stepsisters series (1)
War between the twins
Pascal, Francine
Sweet Valley twins series (37)
War birds
McGavock, John
War birds trilogy (1)
War birds and ladybirds
Springs, Elliott White
War birds trilogy (3)
War chariot
Willard, Tom
Strike fighters series (3)
War chest
Hill, Porter
Captain Adam Horne series (2)
War chief
Burroughs, Edgar Rice
Apache series (1)
Gregor, Elmer Russell
Western Indian series (5)
Porter, Donald Clayton
White Indian series (3)
War clouds
Edwards, Hank
Judge Clay Torn series (2)
Miller, Jim
Colt Revolver series (3)
Long guns series (5)
Porter, Donald Clayton
White Indian series (25)
War comes to Castle Rising
Cradock, Fanny
Lorme family series (3)
War comes to Willy
Collier, James Lincoln
Willy Freeman trilogy (2)
War cry
Porter, Donald Clayton
White Indian series (7)
War dance at Red Canyon
Grover, Marshall
Larry and Stretch series (125)
War devils
Wyatt, Zach
Texians series (3)
War dogs
Nik-Uhernik
War dogs series (1)
War drums
Porter, Donald Clayton
White Indian series (13)
War drums of the Blackfoot
Dicks, Terrance
Mounties series (3)
War Eagle
Buntline, Ned
War Eagle series (2)
Gregor, Elmer Russell
Eastern Indians series (4)
War for eternity
Rowley, Christopher
Fenrile trilogy (1)
War from the clouds
Carter, Nick
Nick Carter series (142)
War game
Price, Anthony
Doctor David Audley and Jack Butler series (8)
War-gamer's world
Walker, Hugh
Magira trilogy (1)
War games
Hansen, Karl
Hybrid universe series (1)
War games of Zelos
Avery, Richard
Expendables series (3)
War god
Neilson, Eric
Haakon series (4)
War hound and the world's pain
Moorcock, Michael
Von Bek family trilogy (1)
War in heaven
Williams, Charles Walter Stansby
Sir Giles Tumulty series (1)
War in hell
Morris, Janet Ellen
Heroes in hell series (9)
War in outer space
Appleton, Victor II
Tom Swift Junior series 2 (4)
War in the blood
Madariaga, Salvador de
Conquest of Mexico series (2)
War in the desert
Glubb, John Bagot
Desert war series (2)
War in the painted buttes
Field, Peter
Powder Valley series (48)
War isn't wonderful
Bloom, Ursula
Elegant Edwardian series (5)
War lord
Sadler, Barry
Casca series (3)
War machine
Drake, David
Crisis of empire trilogy (3)
Marshall, William Leonard
Yellowthread Street series (8)
War machines
Black, Ian Stuart
Doctor Who series (136)
War machines of Kalinth
Lancour, Gene
Dirshan series (2)
War minister in the making
Sherrard, Owen Aubrey
Lord Chatham trilogy (1)
War mountain
Ahern, Jerry
Survivalist series (25)
War music
Logue, Christopher
Iliad adaptations series (3)
War, 1941-45
Ehrenburg, Ilya
Men, years and life series (5)
War of brains
Carter, Nicholas
Nicholas Carter series (390)
War of girls
Dwyer, Vera Gladys
Kayle family series (1)
War of nerves
Graham, Robert
Attar the Merman series (2)
War of powers
Vardeman, Robert Edward
War of powers series (3)
War of shadows
Moss, William Stanley
War in Crete series (2)
War of the chariots
Polch, Boguslaw
Unsolved mysteries series (9)
War of the citadels
Hagberg, David
Flash Gordon series (10)
War of the Cybernauts
Bingham, Carson
Flash Gordon series (7)
War of the ghosts
Darlton, Clark
Atlan series (5)
War of the gods
Larson, Glen A
Battlestar Galactica series (7)
War of the gurus
Rheingold, Howard
Savage report series (2)
War of the maelstrom
Chalker, Jack Laurence
Changewinds series (3)
War of the Moonrhymes
Miller, Calvin
Singreale trilogy (3)
War of the Mountain Man
Johnstone, William Wallace
Mountain Man series (8)
War of the Ring
Tolkien, John Ronald Reuel
History of Middle Earth series (8)
History of the Lord of the Rings series (3)
War of the robots
Peel, John
Lost in space files series (1)
War of the sky lords
Brosnan, John
Sky lords series (2)
War of the twins
Weis, Margaret
DragonLance legends trilogy (2)
War of the Wenuses
Graves, Charles Larcom
War of the worlds series (1)
War of the wing-men
Anderson, Poul
Polesotechnic League series (5)
War of the witches
Dicks, Terrance
Horror series (5)
Simon and Sally series (2)

War of the wizards
Gaskin, Carol
Forgotten forest series (1)
Page, Ian
World of Lone Wolf series (4)
War of the worlds
Wells, Herbert George
War of the worlds series (1)
War of thirty nine
Hayes, Douglas
History of a selfish man series (3)
War of wizards
Storey, Margaret
Timothy, Ellen and Melinda series (4)
War on Aleph
James, Laurence
Simon Rack series (2)
War on Charity Ross
Bickham, Jack Miles
Charity Ross series (1)
War on the Darnel
Turner, Philip
Darnley Mills series (4)
War party
Baxter, George Owen
Red Hawk series (1)
Benteen, John
Sundance series (14)
Brady, William S
Peacemaker series (6)
Cole, Judd
Cheyenne series (8)
L'Amour, Louis
Sackett family series (18)
War phases according to Maria
Lane, Anna
Maria trilogy (3)
War plays
Bond, Edward
War plays series (3)
War terror
Reeve, Arthur Benjamin
Craig Kennedy series (4)
War to end wars
Hardwick, Mollie
Upstairs, downstairs series (8)
War trail
Benteen, John
Sundance series (19)
Gregor, Elmer Russell
Western Indian series (2)
War-trail fort
Schultz, James Willard
Pitamaken series (5)
War wagon
Slade, Jack
Gatling series (5)
War weapons
Sargent, Craig
Last ranger series (5)
War wings
Adams, Eustace
Air combat series (7)
Adams, Eustace Lane
Andy Lane series (15)
War with honour
Milne, Alan Alexander
Peace and war series (2)
War with the corsairs
Gaillard, Robert
Marie series (7)
War with the Evil Power Master
Montgomery, Raymond A
Choose your own adventure series (37)
War within and without
Lindbergh, Anne Morrow
Unicorn series (5)
War world
Dietz, William Corey
Sam McCade series (1)
War years, 1939-1945
Stone, Isidor Feinstein
Nonconformist history of our times series (1)
War zone
Austin, Richard
Guardians series (6)
Warbirds
Herman, Richard
Jack Locke series (1)
Warblade
Ferring, David
Konrad trilogy (3)
Warbots
Stine, George Harry
Warbots series (1)
Warbringer!
Smith, Mark
Way of the Tiger series (5)
Warchild
Bowes, Richard
Warchild series (1)
Ward sister
Jennings, D K
Doctor Ralph Conway series (26)
Warden
Trollope, Anthony
Chronicles of Barsetshire series (1)
Warden of Grey's
Emerson, David
George Hanson series (2)
Warden of the Marshes
Grier, Sydney Carlyon
Modern East series (4)
Warden's niece
Avery, Gillian
Maria Henniker-Haddon series (1)
Mister Copplestone series (1)
Smith family series (1)
Wardour Street mystery
Dark, Rex
Bartholomew Dane series (2)
Wards of liberty
Kelly, Myra
School life trilogy (2)
'Ware danger
Ashe, Gordon
Patrick Dawlish series (6)
'Ware Hawk
Norton, Andre
Witch World series (15)
'Ware mines
Hardy, Adam
Strike Force Falklands series (6)
Warfare accomplished
Pargeter, Edith
Eighth champion of Christendom trilogy (3)
Wargamer
Neebel, Richard
Soldier of fortune series (10)
Warhammer forty thousand
Jones, Neal
Inquisition war series (3)
Warhorn
Kramer, Dana
Rifkind series (2)
Warleggan
Graham, Winston
Poldark series (4)
Warlock
Cook, Glen
Darkwar trilogy (2)
Hall, Oakley
Legends west trilogy (1)
Olden, Marc
Robert Sand series (6)
Warlock and son
Stasheff, Christopher
Gramarye series (12)
Warlock enlarged
Stasheff, Christopher
Gramarye series (5)
Warlock heretical
Stasheff, Christopher
Gramarye series (8)
Warlock in spite of himself
Stasheff, Christopher
Gramarye series (2)
Warlock insane
Stasheff, Christopher
Gramarye series (10)
Warlock is missing
Stasheff, Christopher
Gramarye series (7)
Warlock of Firetop Mountain
Jackson, Steve
Fighting fantasy gamebook series (1)
Warlock of Rhada
Gilman, Robert Cham
Rhada series (1)
Warlock of the magic horn
Stasheff, Christopher
Gramarye series (3)
Warlock of the Witch World
Norton, Andre
Estcarp series (4)
Witch World series (5)
Warlock rock
Stasheff, Christopher
Gramarye series (11)
Warlock unlocked
Stasheff, Christopher
Gramarye series (4)
Warlock wandering
Stasheff, Christopher
Gramarye series (6)
Warlock's blade
Perry, Megahn
Gramarye series (12)
Warlock's companion
Stasheff, Christopher
Gramarye series (9)
Warlock's night out
Stasheff, Christopher
Gramarye series (7)
Gramarye series (8)
Warlord
Frost, Jason
Warlord series (1)
Helm, Eric
Ground Zero series (25)
Warlord of Antares
Prescot, Dray
Dray Prescot series (37)
Witch war series (4)
Warlord of Azatlan
Stivers, Dick
Able Team series (6)
Warlord of Heaven
Cole, Adrian
Star requiem series (3)
Warlord of Mars
Burroughs, Edgar Rice
Martian series (3)
Warlord of the air
Moorcock, Michael
Oswald Bastable series (1)
Warlord of Xuma
Lake, David John
Breakout series (5)
Warlord of Zendow
La Plante, Richard
Tegne series (1)
Warlords
Bosse, Malcolm Joseph
Philip Embree series (1)
Warlord's domain
Morwood, Peter
Book of years series (4)
Warlords of Gaikon
Lord, Jeffrey
Richard Blade series (18)
Warlords of Nin
Lawhead, Stephen
Dragon King trilogy (2)
Warlords of Phoenix
O'Donnell, Peter
Modesty Blaise comic strip series (6)
Warlords of Xuma
Lake, David John
Xuma series (2)
Warlord's revenge
Sargent, Craig
Last ranger series (6)
Warm breeze
Hulke, Malcolm
Crossroads series (2)
Warm flesh and hot lead
Mills, Robert E
Davy Watson series (5)
Warmaster
McCutchan, Philip
Commander Esmonde Shaw series (5)
Warmonger
Greenfield, Irving A
Depth force series (13)
Warn Angel
Christian, Frederick H
Frank Angel series (8)
Warn the Baron
Morton, Anthony
Baron series (21)
Warned off!
Hunter, John
Sexton Blake series (1201)
Warning
Byron, Amanda
Twilight series (23)
Warning on the window
Sutton, Margaret
Judy Bolton series (20)
Warning to earth
Townsend, John
Lunar One series (2)
Warning to the curious, and other ghost stories
James, Montague Rhodes
Ghost stories series (4)
Warning voice
Ts'ao, Hsueh-ch'in
Dream of the red chamber series (3)
Warpaint
Wayne, Les
Arvada Jones series (3)
Warpaint rifles
Sharpe, Jon
Trailsman series (26)
Warpath
Edwards, Josh
John Stone series (4)
Ellis, Wesley
Lone Star series (83)
Payne, Oliver
Northwest Territory series (1)
Warrant for arrest
Didelot, Francis
Commissaire Orestes Bignon series (3)
Warrant for X
Macdonald, Philip
Colonel Anthony Ruthven Gethryn series (10)
Warren Peace
Shaw, Bob
Warren Peace series (1)
Warrimoo
Patchett, Mary Elwyn
Jeff James series (1)
Warrior
Crozier, Brian
De Gaulle series (1)
Drake, David
Hammer's Slammers series (6)
Helm, Eric
Ground Zero series (23)
McQuinn, Donald E
Pacific Northwest trilogy (1)
Pournelle, Jerry
There will be war series (5)
Sadler, Barry
Casca series (17)
Warrior and the witch
Miller, Carl
Dragonbound trilogy (2)
Warrior caste
Albany, James
S.A.S. series (1)
Warrior challenged
Green, Sharon
Terrilian series (4)
Warrior enchanted
Green, Sharon
Terrilian series (2)
Warrior lives
Rosenberg, Joel
Guardians of the flame series (5)
Warrior of Llarn
Fox, Gardner Francis
Alan Morgan series (1)
Warrior of Mars
Bradbury, Edward P
Warrior of Mars trilogy (3)
Fearn, John Russell
Clayton Drew series (2)
Warrior of Scorpio
Akers, Alan Burt
Dray Prescot series (3)
Warrior of the dawn
Browne, Howard
Tharn series (1)
Warrior of World's End
Carter, Lin
Gondwane epic series (1)
Warrior queen
Sinclair, James
Boadicea series (1)
Warrior range
Hobart, Donald Bayne
Masked Rider and Blue Hawk series (22)
Warrior rearmed
Green, Sharon
Terrilian series (3)
Warrior shield
Stine, George Harry
Warbots series (11)
Warrior victorious
Green, Sharon
Terrilian series (5)
Warrior witch of Hel
Drake, Asa
Hel trilogy (1)
Warrior within
Green, Sharon
Terrilian series (1)
Warrior women of Weymouth
Siegel, Barbara
Wizards, warlocks and you series (18)
Warriors
Jakes, John
Kent family series (6)
Rosenberg, Joel
Guardians of the flame series (3)
Warrior's apprentice
Bujold, Lois McMaster
Miles Naismith Vorkosigan series (1)
Warriors at ease
Armstrong, Anthony
Warriors series (1)
Warriors at war
Armstrong, Anthony
Warriors series (6)
Warrior's blood
McEnroe, Richard S
Buck Rogers series (8)
Pournelle, Jerry
Buck Rogers series (8)
Warrior's moon
Capon, Paul
Artor series (1)
Warriors of dawn
Foster, Michael Anthony
Ler series (2)
Warriors of Latan
Lord, Jeffrey
Richard Blade series (37)
Warriors of Mars
Bradbury, Edward P
Warrior of Mars trilogy (1)
Warriors of Noomas
Nuetzel, Charles
Noomas series (1)
Warriors of Serpent Land
Connell, Alan
Serpent Land trilogy (3)
Warriors of Spider
Gear, William Michael
Spider series (2)
Warriors of Terra
Faucette, John Matthew
Peacemakers series (1)
Warriors of the code
Willoughby, Lee Davis
Making of America series (54)
Warriors of the deep
Dicks, Terrance
Doctor Who series (87)
Warriors of the night
Newcomb, Kerry
McQueen family series (4)
Warriors of the storm
Chalker, Jack Laurence
Rings of the master series (3)
Warriors of the wasteland
Hill, Douglas
Huntsman trilogy (2)
Warriors of Thlassa Mey
McCarty, Dennis
Thlassa Mey series (2)
Warrior's path
L'Amour, Louis
Sackett family series (3)
Warriors still at ease
Armstrong, Anthony
Warriors series (2)
Warrior's tale
Cole, Allan
Rali series (2)
Warrior's world
McEnroe, Richard S
Buck Rogers series (9)
Pournelle, Jerry
Buck Rogers series (9)
Wars of the Roses
Birt, David
Middle Ages series (19)
Wars of Vis
Lee, Tanith
Wars of Vis trilogy (2)
Warsaw document
Hall, Adam
Quiller series (4)
Warship
Mackintosh, Ian
Warship series (1)
Warton and Morton
Erickson, Russell Everett
Warton Toad series (2)
Warton and the castaways
Erickson, Russell Everett
Warton Toad series (6)
Warton and the contest
Erickson, Russell Everett
Warton Toad series (7)
Warton and the king of the skies
Erickson, Russell Everett
Warton Toad series (4)
Warton and the traders
Erickson, Russell Everett
Warton Toad series (5)
Warton's Christmas Eve adventure
Erickson, Russell Everett
Warton Toad series (3)
Warts and all
Sudbery, Rodie
Polly Devenish series (4)
Warwyck's choice
Laker, Rosalind
Easthampton trilogy (3)
Warwycks of Easthampton
Laker, Rosalind
Easthampton trilogy (3)

Warwyck's wife
Laker, Rosalind
Easthampton trilogy (1)
Warwyck's woman
Laker, Rosalind
Easthampton trilogy (1)
Was it yesterday?
O'Harris, Pixie
Yesterday series (2)
Was the mayor murdered?
Plummer, Thomas Arthur
Detective Inspector Andrew Frampton series (5)
Was there love once
Raymond, Ernest
London gallery series (9)
Washbournes of Otterley
Pakington, Humphrey
Washbourne series (1)
Washerman
Hill, Peter
Commander Allan Dice series (2)
Washers-up
Timperley, Rosemary
Hospital trilogy (1)
Washington!
Ross, Dana Fuller
Wagons West series (9)
Washington crime
Grant, Maxwell
Shadow series (121)
Washington D.C.
Vidal, Gore
Washington series (5)
Washington IOU
Pendleton, Don
Mack Bolan series (13)
Washington legation murders
Mason, Francis Van Wyck
Colonel Hugh North series (9)
Washington, the indispensable man
Flexner, James Thomas
George Washington series (4)
Washington whispers murder
Ford, Leslie
Colonel John Primrose series (15)
Grace Latham series (15)
Washington's young scouts
Tomlinson, Everett Titsworth
American scouting series (10)
Wasp
Grant, Maxwell
Shadow series (193)
Wasp men attack
Shols, W W
Perry Rhodan series (137)
Wasp returns
Grant, Maxwell
Shadow series (198)
Waste
Dolci, Danilo
Sicilian inquiry series (3)
Waste lands
Dawe, Carlton
Leathermouth series (9)
King, Stephen
Dark tower trilogy (3)
Waste no tears
Garner, Hugh
Cabbagetown series (2)
Waste of shame
Turner, George Reginald
Treelake series (3)
Wasted years
Harvey, John Barton
Inspector Charlie Resnick series (5)
Wasteland rider
Scott, Bradford
Walt Slade series (71)
Wastrel goes west
Street, James
Eugene Mulcahy series (3)
Watch and wait
Optic, Oliver
Woodville series (3)
Watch for a pony
Robertson, Keith
Ticktock and Jim series (1)
Watch for danger
Haigh, Sheila
Watch for series (4)
Watch for smoke
Haigh, Sheila
Watch for series (2)
Watch for the champion
Haigh, Sheila
Watch for series (3)
Watch for the dawn
Cloete, Stuart
Van der Berg family series (2)
Watch for the ghost
Haigh, Sheila
Watch for series (1)
Watch for the tide
Haigh, Sheila
Watch for series (5)
Watch it, sailor!
Steen, Shiela
Hornett family series (2)
Watch McLean
Goodchild, George
Inspector McLean series (43)
Watch Mister Moh
Cowdroy, Joan
Li Moh series (1)
Watch of Patterick Fell
Sampson, Fay
Watch and landfall series (1)
Watch out, Busy Bears
Killingback, Julia
Busy Bears series (10)
Watch out for Wildcat
Clinton, Jeff
Wildcat O'Shea series (9)
Watch out, man-eating snake
Giff, Patricia Reilly
New kids at the Polk Street School series (1)
Watch out, Ronald Morgan
Giff, Patricia Reilly
Ronald Morgan series (1)
Watch the tall white sail
Bell, Margaret Elizabeth
Florence Monroe series (1)
Watchdog
Kerrigan, John
SBS series (3)
Watcher
Verner, Gerald
Trevor Lowe series (6)
Wilcox, Collin
Lieutenant Frank Hastings series (9)
Watcher on the cast-iron balcony
Porter, Hal
Watcher series (1)
Watchers
Curry, Jane Louise
Abaloc series (5)
Watchers at the shrine
Ure, Jean
Hal series (4)
Watchers of space
Etchemendy, Nancy
Watchers series (1)
Watchers of the dark
Biggle, Lloyd
Jan Darzek series (2)
Watchers on the shore
Barstow, Stan
Vic Brown trilogy (2)
Watching the detectives
Rathbone, Julian
Jan Argand series (3)
Watchman
Finlay, D G
Watchman chronicles series (1)
Watchstar
Sargent, Pamela
Earthminds trilogy (1)
Watchtower
Lynn, Elizabeth Anne
Chronicles of Tornor trilogy (1)
Water
Coote, Roger
Four elements series (4)
Henderson, Kathy
Where does it come from series (1)
Water house
Olinto, Antonio
Water house series (1)
Water kings' laughter
Friesner, Esther Mona
Chronicles of the twelve kingdoms series (4)
Water on the brain
Mackenzie, Compton
John Touchwood series (4)
Water pollution
Snodgrass, Mary Ellen
Environmental awareness series (6)
Water-Rat's picnic
Uttley, Alison
Little Grey Rabbit series (14)
Water spider
Waterfield, Robin
Fighting fantasy gamebook series (34)
Water tower
Stil, Andre
First clash trilogy (1)
Water watchdog
Krulick, Nancy E
Lassie series (4)
Water widow
Griffiths, Ella
Rudolph and Karsten Nilsen series (2)
Water with berries
Lamming, George
Caribbean series (3)
Waterdeep
Awlinson, Richard
Avatar trilogy (3)
Waterfall
Sanders, Dorothy Lucie
Montgomery family series (3)
Waterfront
Findley, Ferguson
Johnny Malone series (2)
Waterfront rat
Spade, Danny
Danny Spade series (6)
Waterhole
Savarin, Julian Jay
Gordon Gallagher series (1)
Waterloo
Erckmann, Emile
French campaign series (2)
Waterloo legacy
Herring, Christine
Waterloo series (1)
Waterloo's ward
Herring, Christine
Waterloo series (2)
Waterman
Hornig, Doug
Steven Kirk series (1)
Watermelon mystery at Sugar Creek
Hutchens, Paul
Sugar Creek Gang series (23)
Waters dark and deep
Jones, J Farragut
Silent service series (1)
Waters of Centaurus
Brown, Rosel George
Sibyl Sue Blue series (2)
Waters of sadness
Cassells, John
Superintendent Flagg series (7)
Watersmeet
Garden, Nancy
Fours Crossing trilogy (2)
Waterspace
Dunn, Saul
Steeleye series (3)
Watersplash
Wentworth, Patricia
Miss Maud Silver series (22)
Waterview Manor
Welles, Elizabeth
Janine West series (3)
Waterways in Europe
Pilkington, Roger
Small boat series (17)
Waterwheel turns
Baker, Denys Val
Cornish series (19)
Watery grave
Trainor, Joseph
Twilight series (18)
Watsons
Austen, Jane
Watsons series (1)
Coates, John
Watsons series (1)
Watson's choice
Mitchell, Gladys
Dame Beatrice Bradley series (28)
Wattle babies
Gibbs, May
Gumnut Land series (5)
Wave
Scott, Evelyn
American history trilogy (2)
Wave and the flame
Kellogg, Marjorie Bradley
Lear's daughters series (1)
Wave of fatalities
Delving, Michael
Dave Cannon and Robert Eddison series (5)
Wave of terror
Kessler, Leo
Stormtroop series (7)
Wavecrest
Knox, Bill
Webb Carrick series (13)
Waves of death
Robeson, Kenneth
Doc Savage series (165)
Wax apple
Coe, Tucker
Mitchell Tobin series (3)
Wax flowers for Gloria
Flower, Pat
Inspector Swinton series (1)
Wax fruit
McCrone, Guy
Moorhouse family trilogy (1)
Waxing with Wayne
McRobbie, David
Wayne Wilson series (2)
Waxwork
Lovesey, Peter
Sergeant Cribb and Constable Thackeray series (8)
Waxworks murder
Carr, John Dickson
Henri Bencolin series (4)
Waxworks spies
Davis, Howard Charles
Hugh Rudd series (1)
Way back
Chandler, Arthur Bertram
John Grimes series (15)
Way beneath
Wells, Angus
Kingdoms trilogy (3)
Way beyond
Farnol, Jeffery
Vibart series (3)
Way home
Richardson, Henry Handel
Fortunes of Richard Mahony trilogy (2)
Way it happened, 1935-1950
McMillan, James
Way trilogy (3)
Way it was, 1914-1934
McMillan, James
Way trilogy (2)
Way it worked out
Stern, Gladys Bronwyn
Ragbag chronicles series (7)
Way of a dog
Terhune, Albert Payson
Sunnybank collies series (16)
Way of a transgressor
Farson, Negley
Transgressor series (1)
Way of a wanton
Prather, Richard Scott
Shell Scott series (5)
Way of an eagle
Dell, Ethel May
Nick Ratcliffe series (1)
Way of Ecben
Cabell, James Branch
Dom Manuel and his descendants series (5)
Witch woman trilogy (3)
Way of life
Brooke, Carol
Marshall family series (4)
Howard, Tom
Sergeant Tom Howard series (1)
Way of Spider
Gear, William Michael
Spider series (3)
Way of the clans
Thurston, Robert
Legend of the jade phoenix trilogy (1)
Way of the Four
Cross, Mark
Daphne Wrayne and her Four Adjusters series (5)
Way of the north
Hendryx, James Beardsley
Black John series (10)
Way of the phoenix
McKenna, Stephen
Dermott family series (2)
Way of the priests
Conley, Robert Jackson
Real people series (1)
Way of the river
Street, Pamela
Lodge family series (2)
Way of the Scarlet Pimpernel
Orczy, Emmuska
Scarlet Pimpernel series (3)
Way of the spirit
Haggard, Henry Rider
Morning Star series (3)
Way of the stars
Vautier, Ghislaine
Greek legends series (2)
Way of the tiger, the sign of the dragon
Lee, Howard
Kung Fu series (1)
Way of the wicked
Carter, Nicholas
Nicholas Carter series (400)
Way of the wind
Lederer, Paul Joseph
Indian heritage series (5)
Way of wizardry
Morris, Dave
Dragon warriors series (2)
Way out wanton
Janson, Hank
Hank Janson series (138)
Way some people die
Macdonald, Ross
Lew Archer series (3)
Way south
Conley, Robert Jackson
Real people series (4)
Way the ball bounces
Lindsay, Jack
British way series (7)
Way the cookie crumbles
Chase, James Hadley
Frank Terrell series (2)
Way through the woods
Dexter, Colin
Inspector Morse series (10)
Way to Bethlehem
Steuben, Fritz
Bethlehem series (2)
Way to Dawnworld
Starr, Bill
Farstar and son series (1)
Way to do good
Abbott, Jacob
Young Christian series (3)
Way to Minack
Tangye, Derek
Minack chronicles series (6)
Way to nowhere
McShane, Mark
Sergeant Norman Pink series (3)
Way up
Hardwick, Mollie
Duchess of Duke Street series (1)
Way we die now
Lewin, Michael Zinn
Albert Samson series (2)
Way we were, 1900-1914
McMillan, James
Way trilogy (1)
Way west
Guthrie, Alfred Bertram
Settlement of the American West series (2)
Way with widows
Adams, Harold
Carl Wilcox series (11)
Wayfarer
Schmidt, Dennis
Kensho series (1)
Wayfarers at the Angels
Bassett, Sara Ware
Cape Cod series (2)
Waylaid in Boston
Paul, Elliot
Homer Evans series (8)
Waylander
Gemmell, David A
Drenai series (3)
Wayman's Ford
Bowden, Jim
Dan McCoy series (2)
Wayne dynasty
McRobbie, David
Wayne Wilson series (1)
Ways of Miss Barbara
Castle, Agnes
Beau Nash regime romance series (5)
Wayside School is falling down
Sachar, Louis
Wayside School series (2)
Wayward
Brown, Carter
Danny Boyd series (4)
Wayward blonde
Corrigan, Mark
Mark Corrigan and McLean series (4)
Wayward flesh
Maynard, Nan
Katheryn and Gaynor Scarlett series (1)
Wayward heart
Jennings, D K
Doctor Ralph Conway series (3)
Wayward kind
Grover, Marshall
Larry and Stretch series (81)
Wayward lassie
Sharpe, Jon
Trailsman series (60)
Wayward seeds of Grass
Nash, Padder
Grass series (5)

Wayward tendrils on the vine
Campbell, Ian Maxwell
Vintner series (1)
Wayward trail
Wisler, Gary Clifton
Willie Delamer series (6)
Wayward wahine
Brown, Carter
Danny Boyd series (4)
Wayward widow
Gault, William Campbell
Joe Puma series (4)
Wayward wind
Garlock, Dorothy
Colorado trilogy (2)
Wazir and the witch
Cook, Hugh
Chronicles of an age of darkness series (7)
We all went sailing
Dennison, Dorothy
Wantoknow series for girls (6)
We are betrayed
Fisher, Vardis
Tragic life series (3)
We are not amused
Housman, Laurence
Palace plays series (3)
We are not the first
Tomas, Andrew
Ancient science series (1)
We are our neighbors
Stowe, Harriet Beecher
Harry Henderson series (2)
We are the champions
McCann, Sean
Dove's End Football Club series (2)
We bought an island
Atkins, Evelyn Edith
Cornish island series (1)
We bushies
Magoffin, Richard
Bushies series (1)
We call him Tex
Grover, Marshall
Larry and Stretch series (259)
We celebrate Christmas
Kalman, Bobbie
Holidays and festivals series (1)
We celebrate Easter
Kalman, Bobbie
Holidays and festivals series (2)
We celebrate family days
Kalman, Bobbie
Holidays and festivals series (6)
We celebrate Hallowe'en
Kalman, Bobbie
Holidays and festivals series (3)
We celebrate Hanukkah
Kalman, Bobbie
Holidays and festivals series (7)
We celebrate New Year
Kalman, Bobbie
Holidays and festivals series (4)
We celebrate spring
Kalman, Bobbie
Holidays and festivals series (5)
We celebrate Valentine's Day
Kalman, Bobbie
Holidays and festivals series (8)
We celebrate winter
Kalman, Bobbie
Holidays and festivals series (10)
We chose the islands
Grimble, Arthur
Gilbert and Ellice Islands series (1)
We claim these stars!
Anderson, Poul
Sir Dominic Flandry series (1)
Sir Dominic Flandry series (4)
We come and go
Montgomery, Elizabeth
Dick, Jane and Sally series (3)
We cope with the kids
Berkley, Tom
Algernon Alexander Gunning Hendry series (3)
We couldn't leave Dinah
Treadgold, Mary
Mick and Caroline Templeton series (1)
We danced all night
Cartland, Barbara
Years of life series (1)
We daren't go hunting
Lyon, Elinor
Ian and Sovra series (2)
We didn't mean to go to sea
Ransome, Arthur
Swallows and Amazons series (7)
We do love Mary Mouse
Blyton, Enid
Mary Mouse series (9)
We Donkeys on Dartmoor
Gibbons, M S
We Donkeys series (1)
We Donkeys on the coast of Devon
Gibbons, M S
We Donkeys series (2)
We ecelbrate the harvest
Kalman, Bobbie
Holidays and festivals series (9)
We followed our hearts to Hollywood
Kimbrough, Emily
Our hearts series (2)
We four and Sandy
Mackenzie, Kathleen
Pentire family series (2)
We four and the king's treasure
Barr, Nora
We four series (2)
We four on Mouse Island
Barr, Nora
We four series (1)
We girls
Whitney, Adeline Dutton Train
Girls series (1)
We go exploring
Kargaard, Jens
You and me series (3)
We hate everything but boys
Lewis, Linda
Linda series (1)
We have a cat
Campbell, Rod
We have series (1)
We have a dog
Campbell, Rod
We have series (2)
We have a guinea pig
Campbell, Rod
We have series (4)
We have a rabbit
Campbell, Rod
We have series (3)
We hunted hounds
Pullein-Thompson, Christine
Sandy and Lawrence trilogy (1)
We interrupt this semester for an important bulletin
Conford, Ellen
Carrie Wasserman series (2)
We joined the Navy
Winton, John
Navy series (1)
We keep a pub
Berkley, Tom
Algernon Alexander Gunning Hendry series (1)
We keep going
Armstrong, Anthony
Margaret Cottage series (4)
We killed a bear
Hutchens, Paul
Sugar Creek Gang series (3)
We killed a wildcat at Sugar Creek
Hutchens, Paul
Sugar Creek Gang series (29)
We like the country
Armstrong, Anthony
Margaret Cottage series (2)
We live by the river
Lenski, Lois
Roundabout America series (6)
We live in Lemon Yard
Boscawen, Linda
Hollingbury family series (2)
We live in Singapore
Moore, Donald
Eastern nobody series (2)
We live in the city
Lenski, Lois
Roundabout America series (3)
We live in the country
Lenski, Lois
Roundabout America series (7)
We live in the North
Lenski, Lois
Roundabout America series (9)
We live in the South
Lenski, Lois
Roundabout America series (1)
We live in the Southwest
Lenski, Lois
Roundabout America series (8)
We lived in a little cabin in the yard
Hurmence, Belinda
Oral histories of slaves series (3)
We look and see
Montgomery, Elizabeth
Dick, Jane and Sally series (1)
We love only older boys
Lewis, Linda
Linda series (3)
We must have a trial
Leek, Margaret
Stephen Marryat series (2)
We need a bigger zoo
Bunting, Eve
Magic circle series (5)
We never knew Uncle
Boscawen, Linda
Hollingbury family series (1)
We of the Never-Never
Gunn, Jeannie
Never-Never series (2)
We rendezvous at ten
Blake
Fighter Station series (2)
We ride for Circle Six
Grover, Marshall
Larry and Stretch series (245)
We saw the sea
Winton, John
Navy series (2)
We speak no treason
Jarman, Rosemary Hawley
Richard III series (1)
We stood for freedom
Morley, Iris
Monmouth series (2)
We, the accused
Raymond, Ernest
London gallery series (1)
We, the killers
Brett, Michael
Pete McGrath series (6)
We three and Troddles
Andom, R
Troddles series (1)
We three kings from Pepper Street Prime
Smith, Joan Mary
Pepper Street series (1)
We too
Lyall, Edna
Donovan series (2)
We took to the woods
Rich, Louise Dickinson
Woods series (1)
We walk with death
Desmond, Hugh
Alan Fraser series (34)
We were dreamers
Lehrer, Jim
Dreamers series (1)
We were the Rats
Glassop, Lawson
Rats series (1)
We were there on the Oregon Trail
Steele, William Owen
We were there series (1)
We were there with the Pony Express
Steele, William Owen
We were there series (2)
We work and play
Montgomery, Elizabeth
Dick, Jane and Sally series (2)
Weak and the strong
Kent, Arthur
Sexton Blake series (1542)
Weak-eyed bat
Millar, Margaret
Doctor Paul Prye series (2)
Weak-kneed rogue
Carter, Nicholas
Nicholas Carter series (396)
Weald of youth
Sassoon, Siegfried
Siegfried series (2)
Wealth seeker
Grant, Maxwell
Shadow series (46)
Weapon
Mason, Robert Caverly
Weapon series (1)
Weapon from beyond
Hamilton, Edmond
Starwolf trilogy (1)
Weapon heavy
Reese, John
Jefferson Hewitt series (1)
Weapon makers
Van Vogt, Alfred Elton
Isher Empire series (2)
Weapon of night
Carter, Nick
Nick Carter series (19)
Weapon shops of Isher
Van Vogt, Alfred Elton
Isher Empire series (1)
Weapons of chaos
Vardeman, Robert Edward
Weapons of chaos trilogy (3)
Wear a green kirtle
Wiat, Philippa
Howard series (6)
Wear black for Johnny
Grover, Marshall
Nevada Jim series (15)
Weary road
Douie, Charles
Weary road series (1)
Weasel hunt
Macdougall, James K
David Stuart series (1)
Weasel in my meatsafe
Drabble, Phil
Wild animals series (1)
Weasel's luck
Williams, Michael Leon
DragonLance heroes series (3)
Weasel's trap
Jones, Nicholas
Wind in the willows series (4)
Weather
Higgs, Mike
Learn with Moonbird series (8)
Weather in the streets
Lehmann, Rosamond
Olivia, Kate and Reggie series (2)
Weather-smurfing machine
Peyo
Smurf series (8)
Weather tree
Chapman, Maristan
Happy mountain series (3)
Weatherby's innings
Barbour, Ralph Henry
Erskine trilogy (2)
Weathercock
Clements, Eileen Helen
Alister Woodhead series (4)
Weathermonger
Dickinson, Peter
Changes trilogy (3)
Weave a wicked web
Kruger, Paul
Phil Kramer series (2)
Weaver of dreams
Baddeley, Pam
Star trek fan series (20)
Weavers
Fisher, Leonard Everett
Colonial Americans series (7)
Weavers and war
Early, Richard Elliott
Thomas Early series (2)
Weaver's tale
Sedley, Kate
Roger Chapman series (3)
Weaving the web
Carter, Nicholas
Nicholas Carter series (116)
Web
Ahern, Jerry
Survivalist series (5)
Harvey, Andrew
Burning houses series (2)
Wylde, Thomas
Roger Zelazny's Alien speedway series (3)
Web and the rock
Wolfe, Thomas Clayton
George Webber series (1)
Web of Caesar
Jones, Howard
John Haddon series (2)
Web of darkness
Bradley, Marion Zimmer
Atlantean saga series (2)
Web of defeat
Fenn, Lionel
Quest for the white duck trilogy (2)
Web of dreams
Andrews, Virginia Cleo
Casteel-Tatterton family series (5)
Web of hate
Thayer, Lee
Peter Clancy series (56)
Web of horror
Dixon, Franklin W
Hardy boys case files series (53)
Web of light
Bradley, Marion Zimmer
Atlantean saga series (1)
Web of sand
Tubb, Edwin Charles
Dumarest series (20)
Web of Selagor
Mason, Simone
Star trek fan series (11)
Web of shadows
Backhouse, Elizabeth
Inspector Prentis series (1)
Web of silence
Guenter, C H
Robert Urban series (3)
Wainwright, John
Northern Police series (7)
Pewter series (2)
Web of Spider
Gear, William Michael
Spider series (4)
Web of spies
Carter, Nick
Nick Carter series (11)
Web of terror
Cannon, John
Intersect File series (1)
Web of the Romulans
Murdock, Melinda Seabrooke
Star trek series (10)
Web of the spider
Offutt, Andrew Jefferson
War of the wizards trilogy (3)
Web of the Witch World
Norton, Andre
Estcarp series (2)
Witch World series (2)
Web of wind
Rivkin, J F
Silverglass series (2)
Web of wizardry
Coulson, Juanita
Krantin series (1)
Web planet
Strutton, Bill
Doctor Who series (2)
Web to catch a spider
Joyce, Cyril
Chief Superintendent Pat Stockton series (1)
Webfoot
Slater, Jim
A Mazing Monster series (5)
Webster and Arnold and the giant box
Roche, Patricia K
Webster and Arnold series (2)
Webster and Arnold go camping
Roche, Patricia K
Webster and Arnold series (3)
Wedded in prison, and other Quaker stories
Robinson, Maude
Quaker tales series (3)
Wedding
Fletcher, Audrey
Allsorts series (3)
Lewin, Hugh
Jafta series (4)
Pascal, Francine
Sweet Valley High series (98)
Wedding bells
Lambert, Janet
Jordons series (9)
Mackenzie, Lee
Emmerdale Farm series (18)
Wedding chest mystery
Fielding, A
Inspector Pointer series (10)
Wedding-day scramble
Forsyth, Anne
Monster series (2)
Wedding dress
Wells, Marian
Wedding dress series (1)
Wedding in the family
Du Jardin, Rosamond
Tobey and Midge Heydon series (5)
Wedding march murder
Barrett, Monte
Peter Cardigan series (3)
Wedding night murder
Bush, Christopher
Ludovic Travers series (17)
Wedding of cousins
Tennant, Emma
Hospitalities series (2)
Wedding of the jackal
Traill, Peter
Mister Cribbage series (1)
Wedding of the Lady of Lovell, and other matches of Tobiah's making
Silberrad, Una Lucy
Tobiah series (1)
Wedding Treasure
Williams, David
Mark Treasure series (8)
Wedgetail view
Stuart, Donald Robert
Conjuror's years series (4)
Wednesday adventure
Pudney, John
Fred and I series (5)

Wednesday at four
Henrey, Madeleine
Madeleine series (10)
Wednesday the Rabbi got wet
Kemelman, Harry
Rabbi David Small series (6)
Wednesday wizard
Jordan, Sherryl
Denzil series (1)
Wednesday's child
Harper, Stephen
Healers series (2)
Robinson, Peter
Chief Inspector Alan Banks series (6)
Wednesday's wrath
Pendleton, Don
Mack Bolan series (35)
Wee Macgregor
Bell, John Joy
Wee Macgregor series (1)
Wee Macgregor again
Bell, John Joy
Wee Macgregor series (2)
Wee Macgregor enlists
Bell, John Joy
Wee Macgregor series (3)
Wee One, the wren
Rutley, Cecily Marianne
Tales of the wild folk series (181)
Wee ones
Robeson, Kenneth
Doc Savage series (162)
Wee Sir Gibbie of the Highlands
Macdonald, George
Sir Gibbie series (1)
Wee Winkles and her friends
Jackson, Gabrielle Emilie
Wee Winkles series (3)
Wee Winkles and Snowball
Jackson, Gabrielle Emilie
Wee Winkles series (2)
Wee Winkles and Wideawake
Jackson, Gabrielle Emilie
Wee Winkles series (1)
Wee Winkles at the mountains
Jackson, Gabrielle Emilie
Wee Winkles series (4)
Weeding the flower-patch
Klickmann, Flora
Flower-patch series (6)
Weeds
Baroja y Nessi, Pio
Struggle for life trilogy (3)
Imbert-Terry, Henry
Detective Inspector Du Cas series (3)
Weeds grow fast
Zinkin, Taya
Odious child series (2)
Weedy Rough
Jones, Douglas Clyde
Hasford family series (3)
Week by the sea
Ford, Elizabeth
Maplechester series (5)
Week of love
Leasor, James
Doctor Jason Love series (5)
Week one
Miklowitz, Gloria Dubov
After the bomb series (2)
Week to kill
Delman, David
Lieutenant Jacob Horowitz series (1)
Weekend in The Garden
Andrews, Lucilla
Saint Martha's Hospital series (12)
Wally's Ward series (2)
Weekend was murder
Nixon, Joan Lowery
Mary Elizabeth series (2)
Weekend with Captain Jack
Rayner, William
Missouri series (3)
Weekends for us
Makris, Kathryn
Two by two series (9)
Weep for a blonde
Halliday, Brett
Michael Shayne series (29)
Weep for a wanton
Treat, Lawrence
Jub Freeman series (8)
Mitch Taylor series (5)
Weep for her
Woods, Sara
Sir Nicholas Harding and Antony Maitland series (31)
Weep for Willow Green
Kruger, Paul
Phil Kramer series (1)
Weep in the sun
Wilson, Jeanne
Island trilogy (1)
Weep, Moscow, weep
Wilson, Gar
Phoenix Force series (27)
Weep no more
Skelton, Barbara
Tears series (2)
Weep not, my wanton
Maynard, Nan
Frewin family series (1)
Weeping and the laughter
Maass, Joachim
Astride the times series (2)
Weeping ash
Aiken, Joan
Petworth series (2)
Weeping doves
Minton, Mary
Yesterday's road series (3)
Weetzie Bat
Block, Francesca Lia
Weetzie Bat series (1)
Weighed in the balance
Carter, Nicholas
Nicholas Carter series (506)
Weight
Pluckrose, Henry
Knowabouts series (4)
Weight of evidence
Ormerod, Roger
David Mallin and George Coe series (11)
Weight of light
Nelson, Betty Palmer
Honest women series (2)
Weight of the evidence
Innes, Michael
Sir John Appleby series (9)
Weird adventures of the Shadow
Grant, Maxwell
Shadow series (252)
Weird and wacky inventions
Murphy, Jim
Weird and wacky inventions series (1)
Weird heroes
Preiss, Byron
Weird heroes series (1)
Weird heroes, volume 2
Preiss, Byron
Weird heroes series (2)
Weird heroes, volume 6
Preiss, Byron
Weird heroes series (6)
Weird heroes, volume 8
Preiss, Byron
Weird heroes series (8)
Weird moments in sport
Weber, Bruce
Moments in sport series (1)
Weird of the White Wolf
Moorcock, Michael
Elric series (3)
Weird of the white wolf
Moorcock, Michael
Elric series (5)
Weird science mystery
Hope, Laura Lee
New Bobbsey twins series (20)
Weird soccer match
Jenkins, Jerry Bruce
Dallas O'Neil and the Baker Street Sports Club series (6)
Weird treasure
Carter, Nicholas
Nicholas Carter series (580)
Weird valley
Robeson, Kenneth
Doc Savage series (158)
Weird zone
Black, Christopher
Star challenge series (6)
Weirdos from another planet!
Watterson, Bill
Calvin and Hobbes series (7)
Weirdstone
Garner, Alan
Alderley series (1)
Weirdstone of Brisingamen
Garner, Alan
Alderley series (1)
Weirwoods
Swann, Thomas Burnett
Ancient history series (9)
Welcome back, Stacey!
Martin, Ann Matthews
Baby-Sitters Club series (28)
Welcome death
Daniel, Glyn
Sir Richard Cherrington series (2)
Welcome home
Adams, Herbert
Major Roger Bennion series (18)
Welcome home, Jaime
Lottman, Eileen
Bionic woman series (1)
Welcome home, Lily Glow
Henry, Clay
Matt Archer series (1)
Welcome home, Mrs Jordan
Lambert, Janet
Tippy Parrish series (6)
Welcome Josie, Click and Bun
Blyton, Enid
Josie, Click and Bun series (5)
Welcome, Lyle
Waber, Bernard
Lyle series (1)
Welcome Mary Mouse
Blyton, Enid
Mary Mouse series (10)
Welcome stranger
Weber, Lenora Mattingly
Beany Malone series (10)
Welcome strangers
Hocking, Mary
Fairley family trilogy (3)
Welcome to Camp Nightmare
Stine, Robert Lawrence
Goosebumps series (9)
Welcome to Dead House
Stine, Robert Lawrence
Goosebumps series (1)
Welcome to Fraggle Rock
Stevenson, Jocelyn
Fraggle Rock series (5)
Welcome to Mouseville!
Cartlidge, Michelle
Mouse series (2)
Welcome to oblivion
Petersen, Paul
Smugglers series (7)
Welcome to the feast
Wilson, Gar
Phoenix Force series (17)
Welcome twins
Khalsa, Dayal Kaur
Baabee series III (4)
Welcoming
Roberts, Nora
Flowers series (46)
Well
Vassilikos, Vassilis
Modern Greece trilogy (2)
Well-beloved
Hardy, Thomas
Romances and fantasies series (4)
Well caught McLean
Goodchild, George
Inspector McLean series (39)
Well-deserved tea party
Goscinny, Rene
Dogmatix series (2)
Well done, Alison
Stuart, Sheila
Alison series (4)
Well done, Beef Wellington
Davidson, Max
Beef Wellington series (2)
Well done, Jonny Briggs!
Eadington, Joan
Jonny Briggs series (12)
Well done, Noddy
Blyton, Enid
Noddy series (5)
Well done, Secret Seven
Blyton, Enid
Secret Seven series (3)
Well done, Skinny
Leyland, Eric
Skinny series (1)
We'll go round the world tomorrow
Baker, Denys Val
Cornish series (3)
Well, I'll be hanged
O'Hara, Kevin
Chico Brett series (10)
Well in the desert
Lewin, Hugh
Second chance series (4)
Well-known face
Bell, Josephine
Claude Warrington-Reeve series (2)
Inspector Steven Mitchell series (11)
We'll meet again
Miles, Keith
We'll meet again series (1)
Well now, my pretty
Chase, James Hadley
Frank Terrell series (3)
Well of darkness
Garrett, Randall
Gandalara cycle series (4)
Well of Shiuan
Cherryh, Carolyn Janice
Chronicles of Morgaine series (2)
Well of the silent harp
Barke, James
Immortal memory series (5)
Well, really, Mister Twiddle!
Blyton, Enid
Mister Twiddle series (3)
Well-schooled in murder
George, Elizabeth
Inspector Thomas Lynley and Sergeant Barbara Havers series (3)
Well-wisher
Lang, Frances
Gillonne de Beauregard series (1)
Well-wishers
Eager, Edward
Magic series (6)
Wellies drop in
Cinque, Angelo
Wellies series (1)
Reilly, David
Wellies series (1)
Wellies from the Queen
Douglas, Colin
David Campbell series (4)
Wellington and the blue balloon
Beresford, Elisabeth
Little Wombles series (4)
Wellington Pelican
Reese, Bob
Ocean critterland series (5)
Wells Fargo, danger station
Loomis, Noel
Wells Fargo series (2)
Wells Fargo decoys
Grover, Marshall
Larry and Stretch series (389)
Wells Fargo gunguard
Stanley, Chuck
Wells Fargo series (4)
Welly happy Christmas
Reilly, David
Wellies series (4)
Welou, my brother
Bandler, Faith
Wacvie series (2)
Welsh adventure
Bayley, Viola
Adventure series (10)
Wembley Fraggle gets the story
Perlberg, Deborah
Fraggle Rock series (12)
Wench is dead
Dexter, Colin
Inspector Morse series (8)
Fenisong, Ruth
Captain Gridley Nelson series (8)
Wench is wicked
Brown, Carter
Lieutenant Al Wheeler series (1)
Wendigo Mountain
Cole, Judd
Cheyenne series (13)
Wendy and Jinx and the Dutch stamp mystery
Hastings, Valerie
Wendy and Jinx series (1)
Wendy and Jinx and the missing scientist
Hastings, Valerie
Wendy and Jinx series (2)
Wendy and the bullies
Robinson, Nancy Konheim
Wendy series (1)
Wendy at Wembley
Williams, Dorian
Wendy series (3)
Wendy in charge
Potter, Dora Joan
Winterton School series (3)
Wendy moves up
Potter, Dora Joan
Winterton School series (2)
Wendy on the warpath
Robinson, Nancy Konheim
Wendy series (2)
Wendy wins a pony
Williams, Dorian
Wendy series (1)
Wendy wins her spurs
Williams, Dorian
Wendy series (2)
Were death denied
Yates, Dornford
Jonah Mansel series (11)
Richard Chandos series (8)
We're doing lunch
Browne, Dik
Hagar the horrible series (44)
We're from Texas
Grover, Marshall
Larry and Stretch series (32)
We're going steady
Lambert, Janet
Patty and Ginger series (1)
We're in big trouble, Blackboard Bear
Alexander, Martha G
Blackboard Bear series (4)
We're in the sixth!
Pearce, Carol Ann
Saint Kelvern's Bury School series (1)
We're off to see the killer
Murray, William Buckley
Lou Anderson series (4)
Were-wrath
Norton, Andre
Witch World series (16)
Werebeasts of Hel
Drake, Asa
Hel trilogy (3)
Wereblood
Iverson, Eric
Gerin series (1)
Wereboy!
Dicks, Terrance
Horror series (3)
Werenight
Iverson, Eric
Gerin series (2)
Werewolf
McCutchan, Philip
Commander Esmonde Shaw series (16)
Werewolf and the worlord
Cook, Hugh
Chronicles of an age of darkness series (8)
Werewolf by moonlight
Smith, Guy Newman
Werewolf trilogy (1)
Werewolf, come home
Gilden, Mel
Fifth grade monsters series (12)
Werewolf murders
De Andrea, William Louis
Niccolo Benedetti series (1)
Werewolf of Elphinstone
Armour, R Coutts
Sexton Blake series (213)
Werewolf of Fever Swamp
Stine, Robert Lawrence
Goosebumps series (14)
Werewolf of Ponkert
Munn, Harold Warner
Tales of the Werewolf Clan trilogy (1)
Werewolf walks
Avallone, Michael
Satan Sleuth series (2)
Werewolf's revenge
Jaccoma, Richard
Werewolf series (2)
Werewolf's tale
Jaccoma, Richard
Werewolf series (1)
Werewolves of Kregen
Prescot, Dray
Dray Prescot series (33)
Witch war series (1)
Werewolves of London
Stableford, Brian Michael
Werewolves series (1)
Wes Hardin's gun
Reese, John
Jefferson Hewitt series (5)
Wessex tales
Hardy, Thomas
Novels of character and environment series (9)
West African passage
Perham, Margery
African travels series (3)
West against the wind
Murrow, Liza Ketchum
Fire in the heart series (1)
West Coast wildcatting
Cave, Peter
Hell's Angels series (8)
West Country doctor
Lane, Kenneth
Medical nobody series (2)
West End
Brandon, John Gordon
Arthur Stukeley Pennington series (1)
Inspector Patrick Aloysius McCarthy series (3)

West End horror
Meyer, Nicholas
Sherlock Holmes sequels series (18)
West of Eden
Harrison, Harry
Eden trilogy (1)
West of honor
Pournelle, Jerry
Falkenberg's Legion series (2)
Future history series (3)
West of Jerusalem
De Villiers, Gerard
Malko Linge series (3)
West of Laredo
Scott, Bradford
Walt Slade series (72)
West of Omaha
Wayne, Les
Arvada Jones series (1)
West of railhead
Bennett, Dwight
Eden Grove series (1)
West of the Pecos
Boone, James Calder
Ned Remington series (1)
Cole, Jackson
Jim Hatfield series (56)
West Pier
Hamilton, Patrick
Ernest Ralph Gorse series (2)
West Point rivals
Garrison, Frederick
West Point series (5)
West Point treasure
Garrison, Frederick
West Point series (4)
West to north
Mackenzie, Compton
Four winds of love series (3)
West wind
Garstin, Crosbie
Penhales trilogy (3)
Kyle, Elisabeth
Furze series (5)
West wind of love
Mackenzie, Compton
Four winds of love series (3)
West wind of love, book 1
Mackenzie, Compton
Four winds of love series (3)
West wind of love, book 2
Mackenzie, Compton
Four winds of love series (3)
West window
Hartley, Leslie Poles
Eustace and Hilda Cherrington trilogy (1)
West wing
Gorey, Edward
Vinegar works trilogy (3)
Westerbury inheritance
Chesney, Marion
Westerbury series (1)
Westerbury sisters
Chesney, Marion
Westerbury series (2)
Westerfalca
Wiat, Philippa
Black Boar series (6)
Westering sun
Blake, George
Oliphant series (2)
Western boarding school
Specking, Inez
Martha Jane series (1)
Western circus
Goscinny, Rene
Lucky Luke series (5)
Western Express robbery
Ridley, Nat
Nat Ridley series (15)
Western lands
Burroughs, William Seward
Cities of the red night trilogy (3)
Western Trail
Compton, Ralph
Trail drive series (2)
Westlade murders
Plummer, Thomas Arthur
Detective Inspector Andrew Frampton series (37)
Westland case
Latimer, Jonathan
Bill Crane series (2)
Westlin wind
De Lint, Charles
Moonheart series (3)
Westmark
Alexander, Lloyd
Westmark trilogy (1)
Westminster mystery
Hamilton, Elaine
Inspector Reynolds series (1)
Weston of the North-West Mounted Police
Lund, Trygve
Dick Weston series (1)
Weston of the Royal North-West Mounted Police
Lund, Trygve
Dick Weston series (1)
Westward bound in the schooner Yankee
Johnson, Irving
Yankee series (1)
Westward the course of empire
De Voto, Bernard
American West trilogy (3)
Westward winds
Brady, Taylor
Kincaids series (4)
Westways
Mitchell, Silas Weir
Roland Blake series (2)
Westwood mystery
Dutton, Charles Judson
John Bartley series (5)
Fielding, A
Inspector Pointer series (13)
Westy Martin
Fitzhugh, Percy Keese
Westy Martin series (1)
Westy Martin in the land of the purple sage
Fitzhugh, Percy Keese
Westy Martin series (6)
Westy Martin in the Rockies
Fitzhugh, Percy Keese
Westy Martin series (3)
Westy Martin in the Sierras
Fitzhugh, Percy Keese
Westy Martin series (8)
Westy Martin in the Yellowstone
Fitzhugh, Percy Keese
Westy Martin series (2)
Westy Martin on the Mississippi
Fitzhugh, Percy Keese
Westy Martin series (7)
Westy Martin on the Old Indian Trail
Fitzhugh, Percy Keese
Westy Martin series (5)
Westy Martin on the Santa Fe Trail
Fitzhugh, Percy Keese
Westy Martin series (4)
Wet and dry
Laird, Elizabeth
Contrasts series (1)
Simon, Seymour
Let's try it out series (1)
Wet dinner-time
Fletcher, Audrey
Allsorts series (6)
Wet Flanders Plain
Williamson, Henry
Shallowford to Norfolk series (3)
Wet graves
Corris, Peter
Cliff Hardy series (14)
Wet job
Stall, Mike
Daniel Lacey series (2)
Wetherbys
Wisler, Gary Clifton
Willie Delamer series (15)
Wetware
Rucker, Rudy
Software series (2)
Whale adventure
Price, Willard
Hal and Roger Hunt series (5)
Whale hunt
Coleman, James Covington
Deep-sea adventure series (7)
Whalers
Willoughby, Lee Davis
Making of America series (37)
Whale's footprint
Boyer, Richard Lewis
Doctor Charlie Adams series (5)
Wham, bang, thank you ma'am affair
Conway, Troy
Coxeman series (4)
What?
Lionni, Leon
Pictures to talk about (2)
What a catch!
Hughes, Dean
Angel Park All-Stars series (4)
What a gal, Sally the Sleuth!
Barreaux
Sally the Sleuth series (1)
What a heap of cocky chaff
Nelson, Brian
Cocky chaff series (4)
What-a-Mess
Muir, Frank
What-a-Mess series (1)
What-a-Mess and a trip to the vet
Muir, Frank
What-a-Mess series (14)
What-a-Mess and Little Poppet
Muir, Frank
What-a-Mess series (13)
What-a-Mess and the cat next door
Muir, Frank
What-a-Mess series (5)
What-a-Mess and the hairy monster
Muir, Frank
What-a-Mess series (16)
What-a-Mess at the seaside
Muir, Frank
What-a-Mess series (10)
What-a-Mess goes camping
Muir, Frank
What-a-Mess series (12)
What-a-Mess goes to school
Muir, Frank
What-a-Mess series (11)
What-a-Mess goes to town
Muir, Frank
What-a-Mess series (17)
What-a-Mess has a brainwave
Muir, Frank
What-a-Mess series (18)
What-a-Mess has breakfast
Muir, Frank
Four square meals series (1)
What-a-Mess has lunch
Muir, Frank
Four square meals series (2)
What-a-Mess has supper
Muir, Frank
Four square meals series (4)
What-a-Mess has tea
Muir, Frank
Four square meals series (3)
What-a-Mess in autumn
Muir, Frank
What-a-Mess series (6)
What-a-Mess in spring
Muir, Frank
What-a-Mess series (8)
What-a-Mess in summer
Muir, Frank
What-a-Mess series (9)
What-a-Mess in winter
Muir, Frank
What-a-Mess series (7)
What-a-Mess the beautiful
Muir, Frank
What-a-Mess series (15)
What-a-Mess the good
Muir, Frank
What-a-Mess series (2)
What a performance
Tomkinson, Constance
Les Girls series (3)
What a piece of work I am
Kraft, Eric
Peter Leroy series (3)
What a way to go
Chase, Glen
Cherry Delight series (15)
What a way to go!
O'Shea, Sean
Valentine Flynn series (1)
What a week!
Kilroy, Sally
Toddlers' tales series (1)
What Anna saved
Sandberg, Inger
Anna series (3)
What Anna saw
Sandberg, Inger
Anna series (2)
What are the bugles blowing for?
Freeling, Nicolas
Henri Castang series (2)
What are we up to, Herman?
Unger, Jim
Herman series (13)
What are your angels now?
Groom, Pelham
Peter Mohune series (2)
What became of Gunner Asch?
Kirst, Hans Hellmut
Gunner Asch series (4)
What became of Pam
Hutten zum Stolzenberg, Bettina Riddle
Pam series (2)
What beckoning ghost
Browne, Douglas Gordon
Mister Harvey Tuke series (3)
What bloody man is that?
Brett, Simon
Charles Paris series (12)
What bounces?
Duke, Kate
Guinea pig board books series (1)
What Bunny loves
Szekeres, Cyndy
Bunny series (2)
What came afterwards
Arthur, Timothy Shay
Nothing but money series (2)
What can go wrong and how to be strong
Burstein, John
Slim Goodbody series (3)
What can I do?
Wolff, Margaret
Books for me series (11)
What can you make of it?
Brandenberg, Franz
Fieldmouse children series (1)
What crime is it?
Gardiner, Dorothy
Sheriff Moss Magill series (1)
What did it mean?
Thirkell, Angela
Barsetshire series (23)
What do babies do
Slier, Debby
What do series (1)
What do Doozers do?
Muntean, Michaela
Fraggle Rock series (10)
What do Smurfs do all day
Peyo
Smurf series (10)
What do toddlers do
Slier, Debby
What do series (2)
What do we do now, George?
McCann, Helen
George series (1)
What does it matter?
Stuart-Young, John Morag
Johnny Jones series (2)
What dread hand
Brand, Christianna
Inspector Cockrill series (8)
What dread hand?
Gill, Elizabeth
Benvenuto Brown series (2)
Kemp, Sarah
Doctor Tina May series (3)
What dreams may come
Hooper, Kay
Once upon a time series (3)
Wellman, Manly Wade
John Thunstone trilogy (2)
What Eric knew
Howe, James
Sebastian Barth series (1)
What ever happened to the likely lads
Clement, Dick
Likely lads series (2)
What everybody wants
Greenwood, Walter
Trelooe series (2)
What Farmer Brown's boy did
Burgess, Thornton Waldo
Cubby Bear series (3)
What gentleman strangles a lady?
Dean, Robert George
Pat Thompson series (2)
What goes beep?
Tarsky, Sue
Chatterbox series (4)
What grandma says
Haines, Alice Calhoun
According to grandma series (2)
What happened at midnight?
Dixon, Franklin W
Hardy boys series (10)
What happened next
Smyth, Ethel Mary
Impressions series (5)
What happened to A.J.?
Berry, Joy
Human race club series (5)
What happened to Candy Carmichael?
Walden, Amelia
Lisa Clark series (2)
What happened to Hammond?
Blayn, Hugo
Inspector Garth series (4)
What happened to Patrick's dinosaurs?
Carrick, Carol
Patrick's dinosaurs series (2)
What happened to Peg
Hann, Dorothy Owen
Peg series (7)
What hath Nanny wrought?
Johnston, William
Nanny and the professor series (2)
What I wear
Wolff, Margaret
Books for me series (20)
What if they knew?
Hermes, Patricia
Jeremy series (1)
What if they saw me now?
Ure, Jean
Jamie Carr series (1)
What is a monster?
Tester, Sylvia Root
Magic monsters series (1)
What is colour is that?
Campbell, Rod
Little people series (10)
What is Columbus Day?
Parker, Margot
Understanding holidays series (1)
What is love?
Lisle, David
Isola Dering series (2)
What is Martin Luther King, Jr. Day?
Parker, Margot
Understanding holidays series (4)
What is money?
James, Elizabeth
Money series (3)
What is Thanksgiving Day?
Parker, Margot
Understanding holidays series (3)
What is Veteran's Day?
Parker, Margot
Understanding holidays series (2)
What Katy did
Coolidge, Susan
Katy series (1)
What Katy did at home
Coolidge, Susan
Katy series (1)
What Katy did at school
Coolidge, Susan
Katy series (2)
What Katy did next
Coolidge, Susan
Katy series (3)
What Little Anna saved
Sandberg, Inger
Anna series (3)
What love costs an old man
Balzac, Honore de
Scenes of Parisian life series (8)
What, me, Mister Mosley?
Greenwood, John
Inspector Mosley series (6)
What men say
Smith, Joan Mary
Loretta Lawson series (4)
What might have been
Greenberg, Martin Harry
What might have been series (2)
What Mrs McGillicuddy saw!
Christie, Agatha
Miss Jane Marple series (9)
What next, Doctor?
Clifford, Robert
Doctor series (3)
What night will bring
Bailey, Hilea
Hilea Bailey and Hilary Dunsany Bailey series (1)
What price dubloons?
King, Frank
Dormouse series (8)
What really happened
Halliday, Brett
Michael Shayne series (23)
What rhymes with murder?
Iams, Jack
Rocky Rockwell series (2)
What Rosalie Dare won
Brooks, Amy
Rosalie Dare series (3)
What rough beast?
Hill, Richard
Randall Gatsby Sierra series (1)
What rough beast
Trench, John
Martin Cotterell series (3)
What say the jury?
Wills, Cecil Melville
Superintendent Roger Ellerdine and Sergeant Cherry Blossom series (5)
What shall we wear to this party
Wilson, Sloan
Man in the gray flannel suit series (2)
What she could
Warner, Susan Bagert
Opportunities series (1)
What should you know of dying?
Wells, Tobias
Detective Knute Severson series (2)

What size is Andy?
Miller, Moira
Andy series (1)
What the Brownies did
Hann, Dorothy Owen
Brownie series (2)
What the judge saw
Parry, Edward Abbott
Judge trilogy (1)
What the judge thought
Parry, Edward Abbott
Judge trilogy (2)
What they don't teach you in junior high
Blake, Susan
Fifteen series (4)
What time collects
Farrell, James Thomas
Universe of time series (3)
What to do until the undertaker comes
Wells, Tobias
Detective Knute Severson series (8)
What to do when your mom or dad says baby-sit!
Berry, Joy
Survival series (26)
What to do when your mom or dad says be careful!
Berry, Joy
Survival series (14)
What to do when your mom or dad says be good!
Berry, Joy
Survival series (17)
What to do when your mom or dad says be good while you're there!
Berry, Joy
Survival series (8)
What to do when your mom or dad says be kind to your guest!
Berry, Joy
Survival series (6)
What to do when your mom or dad says be prepared!
Berry, Joy
Survival series (3)
What to do when your mom or dad says behave in public!
Berry, Joy
Survival series (29)
What to do when your mom or dad says clean your room!
Berry, Joy
Survival series (1)
What to do when your mom or dad says clean yourself up!
Berry, Joy
Survival series (5)
What to do when your mom or dad says do something besides watch TV!
Berry, Joy
Survival series (11)
What to do when your mom or dad says do the yardwork!
Berry, Joy
Survival series (27)
What to do when your mom or dad says do your homework and schoolwork!
Berry, Joy
Survival series (12)
What to do when your mom or dad says don't hang around with the wrong crowd
Berry, Joy
Survival series (9)
What to do when your mom or dad says don't overdo with video games!
Berry, Joy
Survival series (13)
What to do when your mom or dad says don't slurp your soup!
Berry, Joy
Survival series (21)
What to do when your mom or dad says earn your allowance!
Berry, Joy
Survival series (4)
What to do when your mom or dad says get dressed!
Berry, Joy
Survival series (25)
What to do when your mom or dad says get good grades!
Berry, Joy
Survival series (2)
What to do when your mom or dad says get the phone!
Berry, Joy
Survival series (16)
What to do when your mom or dad says go to bed!
Berry, Joy
Survival series (18)
What to do when your mom or dad says help!
Berry, Joy
Survival series (10)
What to do when your mom or dad says make your breakfast and lunch!
Berry, Joy
Survival series (23)
What to do when your mom or dad says stand up straight!
Berry, Joy
Survival series (20)
What to do when your mom or dad says take care of your clothes!
Berry, Joy
Survival series (7)
What to do when your mom or dad says turn off the water and lights!
Berry, Joy
Survival series (24)
What to do when your mom or dad says we can't afford it!
Berry, Joy
Survival series (15)
What to do when your mom or dad says what should you say dear?
Berry, Joy
Survival series (19)
What to do when your mom or dad says write to grandma!
Berry, Joy
Survival series (22)
What to do when your mom or dad says you want a pet?
Berry, Joy
Survival series (28)
What to expect the first year
Eisenberg, Arlene
What to expect series (2)
What to expect when you're expecting
Eisenberg, Arlene
What to expect series (1)
What we can do about conserving energy
Bailey, Donna
What we can do about series (5)
What we can do about litter
Bailey, Donna
What we can do about series (1)
What we can do about noise and fumes
Bailey, Donna
What we can do about series (3)
What we can do about protecting nature
Bailey, Donna
What we can do about series (6)
What we can do about recycling garbage
Bailey, Donna
What we can do about series (2)
What we can do about wasting water
Bailey, Donna
What we can do about series (4)
What will he do with it?
Lytton, Edward George Earle Lytton Bulwer-Lytton
Real and the ideal trilogy (3)
What would a guinea pig do?
Duke, Kate
Guinea pig series (3)
What would Jesus cook you for breakfast?
Krause, Jonathan
Christian situations series (2)
What would you have done?
Tracy, Louis
Inspector Furneaux series (15)
What your parents don't know
Pascal, Francine
Sweet Valley University series (3)
Whatever became of Johnny Duke?
Grover, Marshall
Larry and Stretch series (404)
Whatever goes up
Conway, Troy
Coxeman series (13)
Whatever happened to Mavis Rooster?
Johnston, William
Room 222 series (1)
Whatever happened to Winklesea?
Cresswell, Helen
Winklesea series (2)
Whatever next
Murphy, Jill
Peace series (2)
Whatever turns you on, Jack
Hackney, Alan
Stanley Windrush series (4)
Whatever's been going on at Mumblesby
Watson, Colin
Inspector Purbright series (12)
What's a Fraggle?
Gikow, Louise
Fraggle Rock series (8)
What's a ghost going to do
Thayer, Jane
Gus series (2)
What's a girl to do?
Chase, Emily
Canby Hall series (14)
What's bred in the bone
Davies, Robertson
Francis Cornish trilogy (2)
What's Claude doing?
Gackenbach, Dick
Claude series (4)
What's cooking, Jenny Archer?
Conford, Ellen
Jenny Archer series (4)
What's for lunch, Charley?
Hodges, Margaret
Charley series (1)
What's French for help, George?
McCann, Helen
George series (2)
What's funny about murder?
Cooper, Craig
Matt Savage series (3)
What's good for a five-year-old?
Cole, William
What's good series (3)
What's good for a four-year-old?
Cole, William
What's good series (2)
What's good for a six-year-old?
Cole, William
What's good series (4)
What's good for a three-year-old?
Cole, William
What's good series (1)
What's in a name?
Spiller, Andrew
Chief Inspector Duck Mallard series (3)
What's in it for me
Weidman, Jerome
Harry Bogen series (2)
What's in the dark?
Queen, Ellery
Tim Corrigan series (6)
What's inside?
Hill, Eric
Peek-a-book series (8)
What's on top, head?
Bentley, Nancy
Busy body series (4)
What's that colour?
Petty, Kate
What's that series (4)
What's that feel?
Petty, Kate
What's that series (7)
What's that noise?
Petty, Kate
What's that series (1)
What's that number?
Petty, Kate
What's that series (6)
What's that shape?
Petty, Kate
What's that series (3)
What's that size?
Petty, Kate
What's that series (8)
What's that smell?
Petty, Kate
What's that series (5)
What's that taste?
Petty, Kate
What's that series (2)
What's the big idea, Ben Franklin?
Fritz, Jean
American Revolution series (6)
What's the good word
Safire, William
On language series (2)
What's the matter with Carruthers?
Marshall, James
Carruthers series (1)
What's the matter with Herbie Jones?
Kline, Suzy
Herbie Jones series (2)
What's the time, Little Bear?
Chapman, Gillian
Little Bear series (7)
What's the time, Mrs Bear?
Killingback, Julia
Busy Bears series (2)
What's under my bed?
Stevenson, James
Grandfather's problems series (2)
Grandpa series (3)
What's with you
Ambler, Dail
Danny Spade series (27)
What's wrong at Pyford?
Fisher, Douglas George
Jeff Tellford series (1)
Wheel in space
Dicks, Terrance
Doctor Who series (130)
Wheel of danger
Leeson, Robert
Demon bike rider series (3)
Wheel of death
Scott, Reginald Thomas Maitland
Richard Wentworth series (2)
Wheel of fate
Clark, Sheila
Star trek fan series (17)
Wheel of fortune
Howatch, Susan
Van Zale family series (3)
Longstreet, Stephen
Dream seekers series (2)
Wheel of Surya
Gavin, Jamila
Surya series (1)
Wheel of the Finfolk
Jackson, Rosemary Elizabeth
Macgillan family series (5)
Wheel that ran away
Blyton, Enid
John and Mary series (4)
Wheel that turned
Knight, Kathleen Moore
Elisha Macomber series (3)
Wheel turns
Lemarchand, Elizabeth
Superintendent Tom Pollard series (14)
Piacentini, Valerie
Star trek fan series (12)
Wheelchair corpse
Levinrew, Will
Professor Herman Brierly series (2)
Wheeler, dealer
Brown, Carter
Lieutenant Al Wheeler series (48)
Wheeler fortune
Brown, Carter
Lieutenant Al Wheeler series (46)
Wheels
Bamman, Henry A
Checkered flag series (1)
Hughes, Shirley
Tale of Trotter Street series (4)
Nielsen, Susin
Degrassi High School series (5)
Wheels in the forest
Chance, John Newton
Mister DeHavilland series (1)
Superintendent Black series (1)
Wheels of commerce
Braudel, Fernand
Civilization and capitalism trilogy (2)
Wheels of death
Johnstone, William Wallace
Rig warrior series (2)
Wheels of fortune
Rayner, William
Devil's picture book series (1)
Walker, Mort
Hi and Lois series (17)
Wheels of thunder
Sandon, J D
Gringos series (8)
Wheels on the bus
Raffi
Raffi songs to read series (4)
Wheels out of Jericho
Grover, Marshall
Larry and Stretch series (98)
Wheels within wheels
Wells, Carolyn
Pennington Wise series (7)
Wilson, Francis Paul
LaNague Federation trilogy (2)
Wheelworld
Harrison, Harry
To the stars trilogy (2)
Wheldon the weed
Jones, Peter
Terry Trotter series (1)
Wheldon the wizard
Jones, Peter
Terry Trotter series (3)
When?
Lionni, Leon
Pictures to talk about (4)
When a man murders
Stout, Rex
Nero Wolfe and Archie Goodwin series (26)
When a man yields
Carter, Nicholas
Nicholas Carter series (399)
When a rogue's in power
Carter, Nicholas
Nicholas Carter series (504)
When Adam was a boy
Archer, Fred
Evesham Vale series (10)
When all is staked
Carter, Nicholas
Nicholas Carter series (502)
When all the world was young
Dewes, Simon
When the world was young trilogy (3)
When Anna had a cold
Sandberg, Inger
Anna series (5)
When blackbirds sing
Boyd, Martin
Langton family series (4)
When brave men tremble
Carter, Nicholas
Nicholas Carter series (578)
When breaks the dawn
Oke, Janette
Elizabeth and Wynn series (3)
When clews are hidden
Carter, Nicholas
Nicholas Carter series (501)
When comes the heart
Oke, Janette
Elizabeth and Wynn series (1)
When comes the spring
Oke, Janette
Elizabeth and Wynn series (2)
When conscience sleeps
Bayfield, William John
Sexton Blake series (24)
When Cornish skies are smiling
Baker, Denys Val
Cornish series (23)
When crook meets crook
Spiller, Andrew
Chief Inspector Duck Mallard series (4)
When dames get tough
Janson, Hank
Hank Janson series (1)
When danger threatens
Cross, Mark
Daphne Wrayne and her Four Adjusters series (41)
Sea-Lion
John Prentice series (5)
When death birds fly
Offutt, Andrew Jefferson
Cormac Mac Art series (3)
When destruction threatens
Carter, Nicholas
Nicholas Carter series (543)
When Dorinda dances
Halliday, Brett
Michael Shayne series (22)
When dreams cease to dream
Bartholomew, Barbara
Time keeper trilogy (3)
When elephants forget
Murphy, Warren Burton
Devlin Tracy series (3)
When Felicity was small
Cockett, Mary
Jonathan and Felicity series (5)
When fell the night?
Queen, Ellery
Tim Corrigan series (6)
When fools endanger us
Ladline, Robert
J A Remington series (4)
When Fred went to school
Edwards, Pat
Fred series (9)
When Gemma's parents got divorced
Gydal, Monica
Olly sees it through series (3)
When grandfather's parrot inherited Kennington Court
Allen, Linda
Parrot in the house series (2)
When grandma was little
Haines, Alice Calhoun
According to grandma series (1)
When gravity fails
Effinger, George Alec
Marid Audran series (1)
When hell laughs
Smith, David Claude
Red Sonja series (3)

When heroes die
Tullock, Joyce
Star trek fan series (33)
When hippo was hairy, and other tales from Africa
Greaves, Nick
African tales series (1)
When Hitler stole Pink Rabbit
Kerr, Judith
Anna series (1)
When honors pall
Carter, Nicholas
Nicholas Carter series (570)
When hope springs new
Oke, Janette
Elizabeth and Wynn series (4)
When humans began
Stidworthy, John
Creatures from the past series (4)
When I grow rich
Fleming, Joan
Nuri Iskirlak series (1)
Sidgwick, Ethel
Sheriff family trilogy (2)
When I see my dentist
Kuklin, Susan
When I see series (2)
When I see my doctor
Kuklin, Susan
When I see series (1)
When I was nine
Stevenson, James
Growing up series (1)
When I was very young
Milne, Alan Alexander
Very young series (1)
When in Greece
Lathen, Emma
John Putnam Thatcher series (9)
When in Rome
Marsh, Ngaio
Inspector Roderick Alleyn series (26)
When iron gates yield
Bull, Geoffrey Taylor
Imprisoned missionary series (1)
When jealousy spurs
Carter, Nicholas
Nicholas Carter series (449)
When Jenny lost her scarf
Averill, Esther
Jenny Linsky series (6)
When Jeremiah found Mrs Ming
Jennings, Sharon
Jeremiah and Mrs Ming series (2)
When Johnny died
Rougvie, Cameron
Robert Belcourt series (4)
When last I died
Mitchell, Gladys
Dame Beatrice Bradley series (13)
When legends die
Hunt, Greg
Ridge Parkman series (3)
Roberts, J R
Gunsmith series (80)
When legends meet
Roberts, J R
Gunsmith series (50)
When life was young at the old farm
Ober, Frederick Albion
Old farm series (1)
When lion could fly, and more tales from Africa
Greaves, Nick
African tales series (2)
When Little Anna had a cold
Sandberg, Inger
Anna series (5)
When love dies
Pascal, Francine
Sweet Valley High series (12)
When love speaks
Walden, Amelia
Miranda Welch trilogy (1)
When men had time to love
Stoeckl, Agnes de
Vanity trilogy (3)
When my naughty little sister was good
Edwards, Dorothy
My naughty little sister series (4)
When necessity drives
Carter, Nicholas
Nicholas Carter series (401)
When no man pursueth
Sharp, David
Professor Henry Arthur Fielding series (1)
When old men die
Crider, Bill
Truman Smith series (2)
When Olly had a little brother
Gydal, Monica
Olly sees it through series (2)
When Olly moved house
Gydal, Monica
Olly sees it through series (6)
When Olly saw an accident
Gydal, Monica
Olly sees it through series (5)
When Olly went to hospital
Gydal, Monica
Olly sees it through series (1)
When Olly's grandad died
Gydal, Monica
Olly sees it through series (4)
When Oriole came to Harbor Light
Marlowe, Amy Bell
Oriole series (1)
When Oriole travelled westward
Marlowe, Amy Bell
Oriole series (2)
When Oriole went to boarding school
Marlowe, Amy Bell
Oriole series (3)
When Patty went to college
Webster, Jean
Patty series (1)
When Peter was lost in the forest
Peterson, Hans
Peter Johnson series (5)
When Polly was eighteen
Dowd, Emma C
Polly series (5)
When Robert went to play group
Rooke, Anne
Robert series (1)
When Robert went to playgroup
Rooke, Anne
Robert James series (1)
When Robert went to stay
Rooke, Anne
Robert James series (4)
Robert series (4)
When rogues conspire
Carter, Nicholas
Nicholas Carter series (593)
When rogues fall out
Freeman, Richard Austin
Doctor John Evelyn Thorndyke series (20)
When Roobarb didn't find treasure
Calveley, Grange
Roobarb series (2)
When Roobarb wasn't as pleased as Punch
Calveley, Grange
Roobarb series (1)
When Santiago fell
Bonehill, Ralph
Flag and frontier series (9)
Flag of freedom series (1)
When Sarah saved the dog
Singmaster, Elsie
Sarah series (1)
When Sarah went to school
Singmaster, Elsie
Sarah series (2)
When scout meets scout
Ashton, Lamar
Aeroplane boys series (7)
When she was bad
Ard, William
Danny Fontaine series (2)
When someone comes along
Winberg, Greta
Maddie series (2)
When someone splits
Winberg, Greta
Maddie series (1)
When summer dies
Jennings, D K
Doctor Ralph Conway series (29)
When the boat comes in
Mitchell, James
When the boat comes in series (1)
When the bough breaks
Kellerman, Jonathan
Alex Delaware series (1)
When the boys came out to play
Salisbury, Ray
Simon series (2)
When the case was opened
Bude, John
Inspector Meredith series (21)
When the cat's away
Friedman, Kinky
Kinky Friedman series (1)
When the changewinds blow
Chalker, Jack Laurence
Changewinds series (1)
When the devil was sick
Carnac, Carol
Inspector Ryvet series (4)
Ross, Charles
Haunted seventh series (2)
When the dolls awoke
Stover, Marjorie Filley
Dolls series (1)
When the dream dies
Chandler, Arthur Bertram
Rim series (15)
When the dust come in between
Shaw, Bruce
East Kimberley series (5)
When the ghost horse returns
Silver, Alfred
Red River trilogy (3)
When the Green Star calls
Carter, Lin
Green Star series (2)
When the green woods laugh
Bates, Herbert Ernest
Larkin family series (3)
When the idols walked
Jakes, John
Brak series (4)
When the jury disagreed
Hunter, John
Sexton Blake series (1272)
When the key turned
Judd, Frances K
Kay Tracey series (11)
When the killing starts
Wood, Ted
Reid Bennett series (6)
When the lion feeds
Smith, Wilbur Addison
Sean Courtney series (1)
When the night crow flies
Elliot, Margaret
Witch's gold trilogy (1)
When the old man died
Ormerod, Roger
Philipa Lowe series (2)
When the sacred gin mill closes
Block, Lawrence
Matthew Scudder series (1)
When the saints slept
Browne, Edith Ophelia
Broken cup series (2)
When the Spirit comes
Urquhart, Colin
Spirit and faith series (1)
When the Star Kings die
Jakes, John
Dragonard series (1)
When the sun shines
Hayden, Karen
Star trek fan series (34)
When the trap was sprung
Carter, Nicholas
Nicholas Carter series (298)
When the tripods came
Christopher, John
Tripods series (1)
When the wicked prosper
Carter, Nicholas
Nicholas Carter series (332)
When the wind blows
Briggs, Raymond
Gentleman Jim series (2)
Hare, Cyril
Francis Pettigrew series (3)
When the winds blow
Tangye, Derek
Minack chronicles series (12)
When the woods became the trees
Brown, Robin
Rhodesian series (1)
When the world screamed, and other stories
Doyle, Arthur Conan
Professor Challenger series (4)
When they kill your wife
Crowe, John
Buena Costa County series (5)
When thief meets thief
Keeler, Harry Stephen
Vagabond nights series (1)
When thieves fall out
Cross, Mark
Daphne Wrayne and her Four Adjusters series (36)
Thomson, Basil
Superintendent Richardson series (8)
When three makes two
Carstairs, Henry
Lydford Long series (11)
When trouble beckons
McQuay, Mike
Mathew Swain series (2)
When Tutt meets Tutt
Train, Arthur
Ephraim Tutt series (6)
When two worlds collide
Pitkethley, Janice
Star trek fan series (35)
When village bells were silent
Archer, Fred
Evesham Vale series (7)
When Voiha wakes
Chant, Joy
Vanderi series (3)
When we first met
Mazer, Norma Fox
Jenny series (2)
When we went to the park
Hughes, Shirley
Nursery series (1)
When we were lovers in Japan
Sladen, Douglas
Japanese marriage series (2)
When we were very young
Milne, Alan Alexander
Christopher Robin series (1)
When Wendy grew up
Barrie, James Matthew
Peter Pan series (3)
When will I read?
Cohen, Miriam
Best friends series (4)
When worlds collide
Balmer, Edwin
Bronson Beta series (1)
When you are only small
Peterson, Hans
Day when series (3)
When you comin' back, Range Rider
Heath, Charles
A-Team series (3)
Where?
Lionni, Leon
Pictures to talk about (3)
Where all the girls are sweeter
Butler, Richard
Max Farne series (1)
Where Angel treads
Montrose, Graham
Angel Brown series (3)
Where are you, Ernest and Celestine?
Vincent, Gabrielle
Ernest and Celestine series (8)
Where are you going, Little Mouse?
Kraus, Robert
Little Mouse series (2)
Where beards wag all
Evans, George Ewart
Farm life series (4)
Where bugles blow no more
Dowdey, Clifford
Richmond, Virginia series (3)
Where danger rides
Grover, Marshall
Larry and Stretch series (23)
Where did Charity go?
Brown, Carter
Rick Holman series (24)
Where do I put my books?
Barkan, Joanne
Where do I put series (1)
Where do I put my clothes?
Barkan, Joanne
Where do I put series (2)
Where do I put my food?
Barkan, Joanne
Where do I put series (3)
Where do I put my toys?
Barkan, Joanne
Where do I put series (4)
Where do you stop?
Kraft, Eric
Peter Leroy series (2)
Where does a letter go?
Greene, Carla
Let's learn about series (1)
Where does go Andy go?
Miller, Moira
Andy series (2)
Where dragons lie
Salsitz, R A V
Dragons trilogy (1)
Where dragons rule
Salsitz, R A V
Dragons trilogy (2)
Where echoes live
Muller, Marcia
Sharon McCone series (12)
Where have all the bullets gone?
Milligan, Spike
War memoirs series (5)
Where is Barbara Prentice?
Burton, Miles
Inspector Arnold and Desmond Merrion series (14)
Where is Batool?
Stone, Susheila
Duets series (3)
Where is Bianca?
Queen, Ellery
Tim Corrigan series (1)
Where is Bill Ojo
Tully, John
Inspector Holt series (3)
Where is Clifford?
Bridwell, Norman
Clifford series (34)
Where is little Anna's dog?
Sandberg, Inger
Anna series (7)
Where is Mary Bostwick?
Foley, Rae
Hiram Potter series (4)
Where is my buggy
Aston, Elizabeth
I am growing up series (1)
Where is Nancy Bostwick?
Foley, Rae
Hiram Potter series (4)
Where is Nicky's Valentine
Ziefert, Harriet
Nicky series (7)
Where is Nicky's Valentine?
Ziefert, Harriet
Where is it series (4)
Where is Sarah?
Graham, Bob
John and friends series (4)
Where is Susan?
Shaw, Jane
Susan series (10)
Where is the Withered Man?
Deane, Norman
Bruce Murdoch series (6)
Where is Tommycat?
Girard, Nicole
Anna, Paul and Tommycat series (3)
Where lawyers fear to tread
Matera, Lia
Willa Jansson series (1)
Where love and friendship dwelt
Lowndes, Marie Belloc
Arcadia series (2)
Where love rules
Dubus, Elizabeth Nell
Where love rules series (1)
Where my love sleeps
Dowdey, Clifford
Richmond, Virginia series (4)
Where no mains flow
Warren, Rebecca
Pet lamb series (1)
Where no stars guide
Kippax, John
Venturer Twelve series (4)
Where no sun shines
Kelley, Leo Patrick
Galaxy Five series (5)
Where nobody dies
Wheat, Carolyn
Cass Jameson series (2)
Where old bones lie
Granger, Ann
Meredith Mitchell and Chief Inspector Alan Markby series (5)
Where peril beckons
Carter, Nicholas
Nicholas Carter series (569)
Where Satan dwells
Stevenson, Florence
Kitty Telfair series (2)
Where should he die?
Woods, Sara
Sir Nicholas Harding and Antony Maitland series (39)
Where the action is
Chase, Glen
Cherry Delight series (28)
Hardcastle, Michael
Kenny Rider series (2)
Where the boys are
Gilden, Mel
Beverly Hills 90210 series (8)
Where the dreams cross
Douglas, Ellen
Homochito County series (3)
Where the heart is
Lambert, Janet
Christie Drayton series (1)
Where the jinn consult
Antonius, Soraya
Lord series (2)
Where the jungle ends
Blake, Ken
Professionals series (1)
Where the lilies bloom
Cleaver, Vera
Luther family series (1)

Where the money's buried
Grover, Marshall
Larry and Stretch series (370)

Where the Ni-lach
Bennett, Marcia Joanne
Ni-lach series (1)

Where the pirates are
Townsend, Tom
Pirates series (1)

Where the rivers meet
Wain, John
Peter and Brian Leonard series (1)

Where the snow was red
Pentecost, Hugh
Doctor John Smith series (2)

Where the spies are
Leasor, James
Doctor Jason Love series (1)

Where the strange roads go down
Page, Gertrude
Joe Lathom series (1)

Where the trail divides
Havard, Aline
Westward series (2)

Where the trail ended
Graydon, William Murray
Sexton Blake series (38)

Where there was smoke
Flynn, Brian
Anthony Bathurst series (38)

Where there's a will
Burton, Anne
Richard Trenton series (2)
Chase, Kip
Justine Carmichael series (1)
Stout, Rex
Nero Wolfe and Archie Goodwin series (8)

Where there's a will, there's a wag
Singer, Marilyn
Samantha Spayed series (3)

Where there's life
Dayus, Kathleen
Birmingham life series (2)

Where there's smoke
Sterling, Stewart
Ben Pedley series (2)
Fire Marshal Ben Pedley series (2)

Where was everyone when Sabrina screamed?
Walden, Amelia
Lisa Clark series (4)

Where was Patrick Henry on the twenty ninth of May?
Fritz, Jean
American Revolution series (4)

Where was Trail murdered?
Plummer, Thomas Arthur
Detective Inspector Andrew Frampton series (43)

Where's Brandy?
Graeme, Roderic
Brandy series (2)

Where's Emily?
Wells, Carolyn
Fleming Stone series (23)

Where's Fred's trumpet
Edwards, Pat
Fred series (12)

Where's my Easter egg?
Ziefert, Harriet
Where is it series (2)

Where's my frog
Mayer, Mercer
Where series (2)

Where's my girl?
Saville, Malcolm
Lone Pine Five Club series (19)

Where's my kitty
Mayer, Mercer
Where series (3)

Where's my sneaker
Mayer, Mercer
Where series (1)

Where's my teddy?
Alborough, Jez
Bear hugs series (1)

Where's Patti?
Saunders, Susan
Sleepover friends series (27)

Where's Spot
Hill, Eric
Spot series (1)

Where's the giraffe?
Benjamin, Floella
Flo and Aston series (1)

Where's the Halloween treat
Ziefert, Harriet
Where is it series (3)

Where's the kids, Herman?
Unger, Jim
Herman series (9)

Where's Waldo?
Handford, Martin
Wally series (1)

Where's Waldo in Hollywood?
Handford, Martin
Wally series (5)

Where's Waldo, the magnificent poster book
Handford, Martin
Wally series (5)

Where's Waldo, the ultimate fun book
Handford, Martin
Wally series (4)

Where's Wally?
Handford, Martin
Wally series (1)

Where's Wally 3, the fantastic journey
Handford, Martin
Wally series (4)

Where's Wally in Hollywood?
Handford, Martin
Wally series (5)

Where's Wally now?
Handford, Martin
Wally series (2)

Where's Wally, the magnificent poster book
Handford, Martin
Wally series (5)

Where's Wumpus?
Trevor, Elleston
Wumpus series (3)

Where's your O.R.G.Y.?
Mark, Ted
Man from O.R.G.Y. series (18)

Whetstone walls
Warren, Lella
Whetstone series (2)

Whetted bronze
Norvil, Manning
Odan the half-god trilogy (2)

Which doctor?
Candy, Edward
Inspector Burnival series (1)

Which I never
Strong, Leonard Alfred George
Police diversion series (3)

Which Mrs Torr?
Parker, Maude
Jim Little series (1)

Which of us is safe?
Cumberland, Marten
Saturnin Dax series (18)

Which one would you choose?
Kunhardt, Edith
Which would you choose series (1)

Which pig would you choose?
Kunhardt, Edith
Which would you choose series (2)

Which side are you on?
Barbary, James
Adventure in history series (7)

Which, then, be fool?
Scott, Barbara Montagu
Grisenbaum family series (1)

Which way are you leading me, Lord?
Aaseng, Nathan
Devotions series (3)

Which way out
Daniel, Mark
Ghostbusters series (2)

Which way to die?
Queen, Ellery
Tim Corrigan series (5)

Which way to the beach?
Gilden, Mel
Beverly Hills 90210 series (3)

Which way to the nearest wilderness?
Springstubb, Tricia
Eunice Gottlieb series (1)

Which witch?
Ahlberg, Janet
Daisychain series (4)

Whiff of burnt boats
Trease, Geoffrey
Burnt boats series (1)

Whiff of madness
Goulart, Ron
Barnum series (5)
Ben Jolson series (5)

Whiff of money
Chase, James Hadley
Herman Radnitz series (3)
Lu Silk series (2)
Mark Girland series (5)

Whiff of sulphur
Linscott, Gillian
Birdie Linnett and Nimue Hawthorne series (4)

While Mrs Coverlet was away
Nash, Mary
Mrs Coverlet series (1)

While murder waits
Cassidy, Bruce
Cash Madigan series (1)
Esteven, John
Miles Le Breton series (2)

While my guitar gently weeps
Breeze, Paul
Billy Dancey series (1)

While Paris laughed
Merrick, Leonard
Parisian series (3)

While the clock ticked
Dixon, Franklin W
Hardy boys series (11)

While the coffin waited
Sheridan, Juanita
Lily Wu and Janice Cameron series (3)

While the fetters were forged
Carter, Nicholas
Nicholas Carter series (496)

While the patient slept
Eberhart, Mignon Good
Sarah Keate and Lance O'Leary series (2)

While the wind howled
Gaines, Audrey
Chauncey O'Day series (2)

While you're here, doctor
Russell, Robert
Doctor Steven Rushton series (2)

Whim of the dragon
Dean, Pamela
Secret country series (3)

Whim to kill
Shannon, Dell
Lieutenant Luis Mendoza series (19)

Whip
Scott, Bradford
Walt Slade series (6)

Whip and the war lance
Edson, John Thomas
Calamity Jane series (11)

Whip hand
Canning, Victor
Rex Carver series (1)
Francis, Dick
Sid Halley series (2)

Whiplash
Brady, William S
Peacemaker series (3)
Janson, Hank
Hank Janson series (47)
Macdonald, William Colt
Gregory Quist series (6)

Whipping-boy
Orum, Poul
Inspector Jonas Morck series (1)

Whipping star
Herbert, Frank
Jorj X McKie series (1)

Whirl of a bird
Peters, Geoffrey
Inspector Trevor Nichols and Sergeant Tom Burton series (3)

Whirligig
Fish, Robert Lloyd
Kek Huuygens series (2)

Whirligig of time
Biggle, Lloyd
Jan Darzek series (5)

Whirling death
Carter, Nicholas
Nicholas Carter series (402)

Whirlpool
Forbes, Colin
Tweed, Grey and Newman series (8)
Henry, Marguerite
Chincoteague series (1)

Whirlpool of stars
Zetford, Tully
Ryder Hook series (1)

Whirlwind
Alexander, David
Phoenix series (5)
Clavell, James
Asian series (5)
Struan family series (3)
Creasey, John
Doctor Palfrey series (33)

Whirlwind at Arromanches
Holden, Matthew
Squadron series (5)

Whirlwind beneath the sea
Stanton, Ken
Aquanauts series (6)

Whisker of Hercules
Robeson, Kenneth
Doc Savage series (103)

Whiskerville Bake Shop
Barkan, Joanne
Whiskerville series (3)

Whiskerville Firehouse
Barkan, Joanne
Whiskerville series (4)

Whiskerville Grocery
Barkan, Joanne
Whiskerville series (8)

Whiskerville Post Office
Barkan, Joanne
Whiskerville series (2)

Whiskerville School
Barkan, Joanne
Whiskerville series (1)

Whiskerville Theater
Barkan, Joanne
Whiskerville series (5)

Whiskerville Toy Shop
Barkan, Joanne
Whiskerville series (7)

Whiskerville Train Station
Barkan, Joanne
Whiskerville series (6)

Whiskey Creek
McCarthy, Gary
Derby Man series (10)

Whiskey Gulch
Grover, Marshall
Larry and Stretch series (342)

Whiskey guns
Sharpe, Jon
Trailsman series (21)

Whiskey River
Estleman, Loren D
Detroit trilogy (1)

Whiskey runners
Ladd, Justin
Abilene series (8)

Whisky galore
Mackenzie, Compton
Highland series (3)

Whisper
Marshall, William Leonard
Battling Mendez series (2)

Whisper down the moon
Darby, Catherine
Moon series (1)

Whisper if you dare!
Mackenzie, Andrew
Superintendent Brannigan series (5)

Whisper in a lonely place
Sinstadt, Gerald
Geoffrey Landon series (2)

Whisper in the gloom
Blake, Nicholas
Nigel Strangeways series (11)

Whisper of Glocken
Kendall, Carol
Minnipins series (2)

Whisper of the wolf
Johnston, Terry Conrad
General Armstrong Custer series (3)

Whisper who dares
Strong, Terence
Special Air Service series (1)

Whispered watchword
Sutton, Margaret
Judy Bolton series (32)

Whisperer
Tufts, Warren
Casey Ruggles series (1)
Walsh, James Morgan
Inspector Storm series (2)

Whispering box mystery
Blaine, John
Rick Brant series (5)

Whispering cat mystery
Kains, Josephine
Terry Spring series (4)

Whispering Cracksman
Perowne, Barry
Raffles series (12)

Whispering death
Macdonnell, James Edmond
Dutchy Holland series (5)

Whispering ear
Clason, Clyde B
Theocritus Lucius Westborough series (6)

Whispering eyes
Grant, Maxwell
Shadow series (280)

Whispering gallery
Lehmann, John
In my own time series (1)

Whispering house
Erskine, Margaret
Inspector Septimus Finch series (2)

Whispering Island game
Blyton, Enid
Famous Five adventure games series (3)

Whispering knights
Mitchell, Gladys
Dame Beatrice Bradley series (58)

Whispering man
Duncan, William Murdoch
Laurie Hume series (2)
Webster, Henry Kitchell
Arthur Jeffrey series (1)

Whispering master
Gruber, Frank
Johnny Fletcher and Sam Cragg series (10)

Whispering mountain
Aiken, Joan
Dido Twite series (7)

Whispering Pine
Kellogg, Elijah
Whispering Pine series (3)

Whispering riders
Bannerman, W B
Domingo Santos series (1)

Whispering roots
Georgeson, Valerie
Shadow of the elephant series (2)

Whispering Sands
Gardner, Erle Stanley
Whispering Sands series (1)

Whispering statue
Keene, Carolyn
Nancy Drew series (14)

Whispering steel
Nicholas, Jerome
Bill Anstruther series (3)

Whispering voices
Stokes, Doris
Voices series (5)

Whispering walls
Wirt, Mildred Augustine
Penny Parker series (15)

Whispering window
Fitzsimmons, Cortland
Ethel Thomas series (1)

Whispering windows
Burke, Thomas
London series (2)

Whispering woman
Verner, Gerald
Superintendent Robert Budd series (18)

Whispers in the dark
Walsh, James Morgan
Oliver Keene series (12)

Whispers of scandal
Mackenzie, Lee
Emmerdale Farm series (9)

Whistle down a dark lane
Jones, Adrienne
Margery Stanfield series (1)

Whistle for Willie
Keats, Ezra Jack
Peter series (2)

Whistle past the graveyard
Deming, Richard
Manville Moon series (3)

Whistle stop party
Hunt, Nan
Mrs Millie Mack trilogy (3)

Whistle up the chimney
Hunt, Nan
Mrs Millie Mack trilogy (1)

Whistler
Aimwell, Walter
Boy series (4)
Mann, Edward Beverly
Whistler series (3)

Whistler in the dark
Malcolm, John
Tim Simpson series (4)

Whistlestop wench
Ledd, Paul
Shelter Morgan series (30)

Whistling hangman
Kendrick, Baynard
Captain Duncan Maclain series (2)

Whistling key
Gunn, Victor
Chief Inspector Bill Cromwell series (21)

Whistling legs
McDougald, Roman
Philip Cabot series (2)

Whistling waddy
Hobart, Donald Bayne
Masked Rider and Blue Hawk series (1)

White alley
Wells, Carolyn
Fleming Stone series (6)

White Apache
Garrett, Charles C
Gunslinger series (3)
White arrow
Sharam, Norman
White dog trilogy (2)
Wynne, Anthony
Doctor Eustace Hailey series (13)
White bell heather
Cameron, Isabel
Glen folk series (2)
White bikini
Brown, Carter
Rick Holman series (7)
White bird flying
Aldrich, Bess Streeter
Abbie Deal series (2)
White blanket
Browne, Belmore
Golden valley series (2)
White Boar
Palmer, Martin
Lovell family series (1)
White boat from England
Millar, George
Boat travel series (2)
White boat rescue at Sugar Creek
Hutchens, Paul
Sugar Creek Gang series (31)
White boots
Streatfeild, Noel
Shoes series (7)
White bungalow
Sommerfelt, Aimee
Lalu series (2)
White butterfly
Mosley, Walter
Ezekiel Rawlins series (3)
White cad cross-up
Nolan, William Francis
Bart Challis series (2)
White calf
Faulknor, Cliff
Eagle Child trilogy (1)
White camellia
Grierson, Francis Durham
Inspector Sims and Professor Wells series (6)
White chalet
Cross, Laurence
Tommy Lumb and Peter Marsham series (2)
White circle
Shrog, J M
Bernard McFoy series (2)
White cockade
Cordell, Alexander
John Regan trilogy (1)
Dymoke, Juliet
French Revolution series (1)
White Company
Doyle, Arthur Conan
English bowmen series (2)
White conquerors
Munroe, Kirk
White conqueror series (1)
White country
Jennings, D K
Doctor Ralph Conway series (14)
White crash helmet
Fry, Pete
Pete Fry series (14)
White crow
Macdonald, Philip
Colonel Anthony Ruthven Gethryn series (2)
White death
Carter, Nick
Nick Carter series (203)
Graydon, William Murray
Sexton Blake series (440)
Macdonnell, James Edmond
Dutchy Holland series (6)
McLaglen, John J
Herne the Hunter series (1)
Sheckley, Robert
Stephen Dain series (4)
White Devil of the Black Sea
Palen, Lewis Stanton
White Devil series (1)
White Devil's mate
Palen, Lewis Stanton
White Devil series (2)
White dragon
Garnett, Richard
Mark Rutter series (2)
McCaffrey, Anne
Pern and the Red Planet series (6)
White dynamite
Donovan, Jean Beradine
Bill Speed series (3)
White earth
Sharam, Norman
White dog trilogy (1)
White elephant mystery
Queen, Ellery, Junior
Djuna and Champ series (6)
White Face
Wallace, Edgar
Inspector Elk series (6)
White-faced man
Holt, Gavin
Professor Luther Bastion series (2)
White fangs
Garron, Marco
Azan series (4)
White fawn
Prouty, Olive Higgins
Vale family series (1)
White feather
Wodehouse, Pelham Grenville
Wrykyn School series (2)
White fire
Saville, Malcolm
Marston Baines series (4)
Simon series (4)
Vardeman, Robert Edward
Jade demons quartet (4)
W, W
Qhe series (2)
White friar
Stuart, Donald
Lionel Crane series (1)
White Fury
Leyland, Eric
Max and Scrap series (6)
White galloper
Hallett, Phyllis
Carlisle family series (1)
White gas
Keverne, Richard
Inspector Mace series (1)
White ghost book
Middleton, Jessie Adelaide
Grey ghost series (3)
White girls eastward
Craig, Thurlow
Lieutenant Bunjy Hearne series (1)
White gold of Texas
Cole, Jackson
Jim Hatfield series (101)
White gold wielder
Donaldson, Stephen Reeder
Second chronicles of Thomas Covenant series (3)
White Hare's horses
Spinka, Penina Keen
Chumash series (2)
White hart
Springer, Nancy
Book of Isle series (2)
White Hart Lane mystery
Hatton, Charles
Dixon of Dock Green series (3)
White harvest
Charbonneau, Louis
Kathy McNeely series (2)
White heat
Bainbridge, Chuck
Hard corps series (3)
White hell
Logan, Jake
John Slocum series (10)
Sharpe, Jon
Trailsman series (74)
Wilson, Gar
Phoenix Force series (6)
White hell trail
Sharpe, Jon
Trailsman series (48)
White horse
Coatsworth, Elizabeth
Sally Smith series (4)
Leeson, Robert
Matthew Morten trilogy (3)
White horse is running
Sampson, Fay
Pangur Ban series (6)
White horse of Morocco
Coatsworth, Elizabeth
Sally Smith series (4)
White horse to Banbury Cross
Llewellyn, Richard
Edmund Trothe series (3)
White House autumn
White, Ellen Emerson
President's daughter series (2)
White House massacre
Victor, Sam
Talbot Lion series (2)
White House pantry murder
Roosevelt, Elliott
Eleanor Roosevelt series (4)
White House years
Kissinger, Henry
White House years series (1)
White Indian
Porter, Donald Clayton
White Indian series (1)
White Indians
Edson, John Thomas
Floating Outfit series (17)
White island
Lister-Kay, John
Camusfearna trilogy (3)
White jazz
Ellroy, James
Los Angeles quartet (4)
White Jenna
Yolen, Jane
Great Alta series (2)
White leaves of death
Audemars, Pierre
Monsieur Pinaud series (12)
White lies
Pascal, Francine
Sweet Valley High series (52)
White light
McQueen, James
Clocks of death trilogy (1)
White line fever
Cave, Peter
Hell's Angels series (7)
White man returns
Keith, Agnes
Borneo series (3)
White man's stride
Greene, L Patrick
Aubrey Saint John Major series (6)
White mask
Walsh, James Morgan
Bromley Kay series (1)
White meat
Corris, Peter
Cliff Hardy series (3)
White menace
Robertson, Colin
Inspector Robert Strong series (3)
White mercenary
Saxon, Peter
Sexton Blake series (1555)
White monkey
Galsworthy, John
Modern comedy series (1)
White mountain
Wingrove, David
Chung Kuo series (3)
White mountains
Christopher, John
Tripods series (2)
White mule
Williams, William Carlos
Stecher trilogy (1)
White mustang
Ellis, Edward Sylvester
Wild adventure series (2)
White Ninja
Lustbader, Eric
Ninja series (3)
White nun's telling
Sampson, Fay
Daughter of Tintagel series (2)
White Otter
Gregor, Elmer Russell
Western Indian series (1)
White Patch
Holden, Philip
Deer trilogy (3)
White path
Conley, Robert Jackson
Real people series (3)
White pawn
Irwin, Frances
Anne Neville series (1)
White peril
Faulknor, Cliff
Eagle Child trilogy (2)
White planet
Main, Carol
Fraser family trilogy (1)
White poppy
Gaan, Margaret
Red barbarian trilogy (2)
Osborne, Helena
White poppy series (1)
White Priory murders
Dickson, Carter
Sir Henry Merrivale series (3)
White python
Channing, Mark
Colin Gray series (2)
White queen
Irwin, Frances
Anne Neville series (2)
White rabbit
Dobkin, Kaye
Wonderland series (2)
Mathews, Joanna Hooe
Kitty and Lulu series (3)
White rage
Sharam, Norman
White dog trilogy (3)
White refugees
Armour, R Coutts
Sexton Blake series (214)
White regiment
Dalmas, John
Regiment series (2)
White rhino
Dolan, Bill
Afrikorps series (3)
White ribbon boys at Long Shore
Sperry, Raymond, junior
White ribbon boys series (2)
White ribbon boys of Chester
Sperry, Raymond, junior
White ribbon boys series (1)
White rider
Charteris, Leslie
Bill Kennedy series (2)
White riders
Edwards, Monica
Romney Marsh series (4)
White robe
Cabell, James Branch
Dom Manuel and his descendants series (6)
Witch woman trilogy (2)
White robin
Read, Miss
Fairacre series (13)
White Rose
Cook, Glen
Chronicles of the Black Company series (3)
White Rose, dark summer
Fairburn, Eleanor
Wars of the Roses series (2)
White Rose dying
Viney, Jayne
Richard III series (2)
White Russian, red face
Danischewsky, Monja
White Russian series (1)
White sail
Bassett, Sara Ware
Cape Cod series (15)
White savage
Sharpe, Jon
Trailsman series (30)
Upfield, Arthur William
Napoleon Bonaparte series (26)
White sea horse
Cresswell, Helen
Sea series (1)
White sea horse, and other stories from the sea
Cresswell, Helen
Sea series (3)
White serpent
Lee, Tanith
Wars of Vis trilogy (3)
White shield
Mitford, Bertram
Untuswa trilogy (2)
White ships
Abraham, Cyril
Onedin Line series (5)
White shoes, white lines and Blackie
Barrett, Robert G
Les Norton series (6)
White siren
Maddock, Stephen
Timothy Terrel series (2)
White sister
Crawford, Francis Marion
Roman society series (6)
White skulls
Grant, Maxwell
Shadow series (268)
White sparrow
Brown, Roy
Sparrows series (2)
White stag adventure
Fraser, Christine Marion
Light on Dumyat series (2)
White stallion, red mare
Edson, John Thomas
Calamity Jane series (9)
White stone
Coccioli, Carlo
Ardito Piccardi series (2)
White stranger
Ainsworth, Ruth
Little Mushrooms series (2)
White Terror
Gras, Felix
French Revolution trilogy (3)
White tiger
Boussenard, Louis
Robinsons of Guiana series (1)
White warlord
Dever, Joe
Combat heroes series (1)
White warlord series (1)
White wash
Ludlow, Ian
Vigilante series (3)
White water
Oldfield, Pamela
Heron saga series (4)
Tanner, Clay
Chance Sharpe series (12)
White water terror
Keene, Carolyn
Nancy Drew files series (6)
White wig
Verner, Gerald
Paul Rivington series (2)
White Wings, a butterfly
Rutley, Cecily Marianne
Tales of the wild folk series (8)
White witch
Jones, G Wayman
Black Bat series (21)
White witch of the South Seas
Wheatley, Dennis
Gregory Sallust series (11)
White Wolf
Gregor, Elmer Russell
Eastern Indians series (2)
White wolf, and other fireside tales
Quiller-Couch, Arthur
Troy Town series (5)
White Wolf's feud
Dunning, Hal
White Wolf series (4)
White Wolf's law
Dunning, Hal
White Wolf series (2)
White Wolf's outlaw legion
Dunning, Hal
White Wolf series (6)
White Wolf's pack
Dunning, Hal
White Wolf series (3)
White wolverine contract
Atlee, Philip
Joe Gall series (14)
White wolves
Bower, Bertha Muzzy
Meadowlark series (2)
Whitebird murders
Black, Thomas B
Al Delaney series (1)
Whitefoot the wood mouse
Burgess, Thornton Waldo
Green forest series (3)
Whitefoot's secret
Burgess, Thornton Waldo
Wee little books series (4)
Whitelands affair
Clarke, Anna
Professor Paula Glenning series (6)
Whiteoak brothers
De la Roche, Mazo
Whiteoak series (6)
Whiteoak harvest
De la Roche, Mazo
Whiteoak series (11)
Whiteoak heritage
De la Roche, Mazo
Whiteoak series (5)
Whiteoaks
De la Roche, Mazo
Whiteoak series (8)
Whiteoaks of Jalna
De la Roche, Mazo
Whiteoak series (8)
Whites and the Blues
Dumas, Alexandre
Napoleon series (1)
Whitewashed uncle
Grahame, Kenneth
Smith family series (1)
Whitewater
Knox, Bill
Webb Carrick series (8)
Whitewater death
Bodine, J D
Quinn's Raiders series (5)
Whitey and Jinglebob
Rounds, Glen
Whitey series (5)
Whitey and the blizzard
Rounds, Glen
Whitey series (7)

Whitey and the colt killer
Rounds, Glen
Whitey series (11)
Whitey and the rustlers
Rounds, Glen
Whitey series (6)
Whitey and the wild horses
Rounds, Glen
Whitey series (10)
Whitey looks for a job
Rounds, Glen
Whitey series (4)
Whitey ropes and rides
Rounds, Glen
Whitey series (9)
Whitey takes a trip
Rounds, Glen
Whitey series (8)
Whitey's first roundup
Rounds, Glen
Whitey series (2)
Whitey's new saddle
Rounds, Glen
Whitey series (7)
Whitey's Sunday horse
Rounds, Glen
Whitey series (3)
Whither Jennifer
Lister, Gladys
Jennifer series (2)
Whither shall I wander?
Lindsay, Philip
Sir John Oldcastle series (2)
Whither thou goest
Foyle, Kathleen
Augherim series (2)
Whitney case
Bentley, John
Sir Richard Herrivell series (7)
Whitney, my love
McNaught, Judith
Westmoreland family series (2)
Whittington pact
Le Grand, Leon
Michael Berresford series (3)
Whizz for atomms
Willans, Geoffrey
Nigel Molesworth series (3)
Who?
Lionni, Leon
Pictures to talk about (1)
Who
Tremlett, George
Rock stars series (6)
Who am I, anyway?
Thesman, Jean
Birthday girls series (3)
Who benefits?
Thayer, Lee
Peter Clancy series (54)
Who called diamonds?
Brodie, Gordon
John Borham series (3)
Who calls from afar?
Brinsmead, Hesba Fay
Clippie Nancarrow series (1)
Who can hop?
Cartwright, Stephen
Boo series (4)
Who cares about Espie Sanchez?
Dunnahoo, Terry
Espie Sanchez series (1)
Who closed the casement?
Cobb, Thomas
Inspector Bedison series (4)
Who closed the door?
Locke, Clinton W
Perry Pierce series (1)
Who dialled 999?
Gregg, Cecil Freeman
Inspector Cuthbert Higgins series (17)
Who did it?
Cartwright, Stephen
Boo series (1)
Who dies next?
Wurr, H J
Inspector Grierson series (2)
Who dies there?
Duff, James P
Johnny Phelan series (2)
Kane, Henry
Peter Chambers series (21)
Who do you love
Sayers, Valerie
Due East series (3)
Who does what?
Hill, Eric
Peek-a-book series (4)
Who fears the devil?
Wellman, Manly Wade
Silver John series (1)
Who fired the factory?
Plummer, Thomas Arthur
Detective Inspector Andrew Frampton series (27)
Who framed Roger Rabbit storybook
Korman, Justine
Roger Rabbit series (2)
Who goes hang?
Hyland, Stanley
Parliament series (1)
Who goes home?
Lemarchand, Elizabeth
Superintendent Tom Pollard series (16)
Who goes moo?
Tarsky, Sue
Chatterbox series (1)
Who goes next?
Wainwright, John
Northern Police series (31)
Who goes splash?
Tarsky, Sue
Chatterbox series (5)
Who goes there?
Benson, Blackwood Ketcham
American Civil War series (1)
Who goes to the park?
Aska, Warabe
Park series (1)
Who helped Hitler?
Maisky, Ivan Mikhailovich
Storm series (3)
Who hid the key?
Locke, Clinton W
Perry Pierce series (3)
Who hides in the park?
Aska, Warabe
Park series (2)
Who invented brothers anyway?
Evans, Greg
Luann series (4)
Who is Bugs Potter?
Korman, Gordon
Bugs Potter series (1)
Who is Carrie?
Collier, James Lincoln
Willy Freeman trilogy (3)
Who is Elissa Sheldon?
Montross, David
Remsen series (2)
Who is my enemy?
Cooper, Barbara
Inspector Gibbon series (3)
Who is number two?
McDaniel, David
Prisoner series (2)
Who is Simon Warwick?
Moyes, Patricia
Henry and Emmy Tibbett series (14)
Who is Teddy Villanova?
Berger, Thomas
Russel Wren series (1)
Who is the tallest?
Cartwright, Stephen
Boo series (5)
Who is this man?
Macgowan, Alice
Jerry Boyne series (5)
Who keeps the keys?
Leslie, Francis
Jimmy Langry series (2)
Who kidnapped Princess Saralinda?
Stine, Harlan William
Wizards, warlocks and you series (3)
Who killed Alfred Crowe?
Fletcher, Joseph Smith
Ronald Camberwell series (5)
Who killed Brother Treasurer?
Wills, Cecil Melville
Superintendent Roger Ellerdine and Sergeant Cherry Blossom series (4)
Who killed Caldwell?
Wells, Carolyn
Fleming Stone series (60)
Who killed Carson?
Gibbons, Harry Hornaby Clifford
Sexton Blake series (479)
Who killed Cavelotti?
Newell, Audrey
Patrick Michael Doyle series (1)
Who killed Charmian Karslake?
Haynes, Annie
Inspector Stoddart series (2)
Who killed Chloe?
Allingham, Margery
Albert Campion series (9)
Who killed Cock Robin?
Duffy, Margaret
Patrick Gillard series (4)
Who killed Coralie?
Aresbys
Parrish Darby series (1)
Who killed daddy?
Woolfolk, Dorothy
Donna Rockford series (1)
Who killed Dick Whittington?
Radford, Edwin
Doctor Manson series (6)
Who killed Doctor Sex?
Brown, Carter
Rick Holman series (11)
Who killed Gatton?
Vivian, Evelyn Charles
Inspector Head series (5)
Who killed Harlowe Thrombey?
Packard, Edward
Choose your own adventure series (9)
Who killed Henry Wickenston?
Cross, Mark
Daphne Wrayne and her Four Adjusters series (28)
Who killed Honey Bee?
Cooper, Craig
Matt Savage series (6)
Who killed me?
Allan, Joan
Valerie Lambert series (1)
Who killed Netta Maul?
Arthur, Frank
Inspector Spearpoint series (1)
Who killed Oliver Cromwell?
Gribble, Leonard Reginald
Superintendent Anthony Slade series (13)
Who killed pretty Becky Low?
Cunningham, Albert Benjamin
Sheriff Jess Roden series (20)
Who killed Robert Prentice?
Wheatley, Dennis
Lieutenant John Milton Schwab series (2)
Who killed Rosie Gray?
Usher, Frank
Daye Smith series (12)
Who killed Stella Pomeroy?
Thomson, Basil
Superintendent Richardson series (6)
Who killed Sweet Sue?
Kane, Henry
Peter Chambers series (11)
Who killed the doctor?
Burton, Miles
Inspector Arnold and Desmond Merrion series (28)
Who killed the husband?
Footner, Hulbert
Amos Lee Mappin series (6)
Who killed the pie man?
Lore, Phillips
Leo Roi series (1)
Who killed the Robins family, & where & when & why did they die?
Chastain, Thomas
Robins family series (1)
Who killed Trainer Lincoln?
Hardy, Arthur Steffens
Sexton Blake series (615)
Who killed you, Candy Castle?
Carr, Kirby
Hitman series (1)
Who killes Rico?
Grover, Marshall
Larry and Stretch series (135)
Who kills my wife
Goyne, Richard
Paul Templeton series (9)
Who lies bleeding?
Carstairs, Henry
Lydford Long series (7)
Who lies here?
Peters, Ellis
Inspector George Felse series (4)
Who likes honey?
Cartwright, Stephen
Boo series (2)
Who lives in alligator swamp
Hirschi, Ron
Where animals live series (2)
Who lives in the forest
Hirschi, Ron
Where animals live series (1)
Who lives in the mountains
Hirschi, Ron
Where animals live series (3)
Who lives on the prairie
Hirschi, Ron
Where animals live series (4)
Who me?
Macdonald, Betty
Who me series (4)
Who murdered Reynard?
Fowler, Sydney
Professor Blinkwell series (3)
Who needs a bratty brother?
Gondosch, Linda
Hopper Street trilogy (1)
Who needs enemies
Foster, Alan Dean
Friends like these series (2)
Who needs Espie Sanchez?
Dunnahoo, Terry
Espie Sanchez series (3)
Who needs third grade?
Ransom, Candice Farris
Tales of the third grade series (1)
Who once eats out of the tin bowl
Fallada, Hans
Germany between the wars series (2)
Who opened the safe?
Locke, Clinton W
Perry Pierce series (2)
Who pays the piper?
Wentworth, Patricia
Inspector Ernest Lamb series (2)
Miss Maud Silver series (4)
Who plays with sin
Spiller, Andrew
Chief Inspector Duck Mallard series (12)
Who poisoned Hetty Duncan, and other detective stories
Donovan, Dick
Dick Donovan series (3)
Who ragged Railton?
Clifford, Martin
Tom Merry series (9)
Who rides a tiger
Robertson, Colin
Vicky McBain series (5)
Who saw her die?
Moyes, Patricia
Henry and Emmy Tibbett series (9)
Who saw him die?
Radley, Sheila
Chief Inspector Douglas Quantrill series (6)
Who saw him die
Stein, Aaron Marc
Tim Mulligan and Elsie Mae Hunt series (6)
Who says a corpse has to be dull
Von Elsner, Don
David Danning series (5)
Who says moo?
Cartwright, Stephen
Boo series (3)
Who shot the bull?
Knox, Bill
Inspector Colin Thane and Phil Moss series (11)
Who should have died
Silverman, Marguerite Ruth
Inspector Christopher Adrian series (2)
Who spies, who kills?
Queen, Ellery
Tim Corrigan series (3)
Who spoke last?
Turner, John Victor
Amos Petrie series (2)
Who steals my name?
Fraser, James
Inspector Bill Aveyard series (8)
Who stole Stonehenge?
Cutter, Leela
Lettie Winterbottom series (2)
Who the heck is Sylvia?
Porter, Joyce
Honourable Constance Ethel Morrison-Burke series (4)
Who told Clutha
Munro, Hugh Macfarlane
Clutha series (1)
Who took the papers?
Locke, Clinton W
Perry Pierce series (4)
Who wanders alone
Pinney, Peter
Dust on my shoes series (2)
Who wants Arthur?
Graham, Amanda
Arthur trilogy (1)
Who was the jester?
Ashe, Gordon
Patrick Dawlish series (3)
Who will comfort Toffle?
Jansson, Tove
Moomin series (10)
Whoa, Matilda!
Lambert, Janet
Candy Kane series (2)
Who'd shoot a genius?
Schley, Sturges Mason
Doctor Quentin Toby series (1)
Who'd want to kill old George?
Upton, Robert
Amos McGuffin series (1)
Whoever I am
Dewhurst, Eileen
Helen Johnson series (1)
Whole armour
Harris, Wilson
Guiana series (3)
Who'll buy my evil?
Caillou, Alan
Mike Benasque series (3)
Who'll save Alfie Atkins?
Bergstrom, Gunilla
Alfie Atkins series (2)
Whom God hath joined
Bennett, Arnold
Five towns series (6)
Whom God hath sundered
Onions, Oliver
Whom God hath sundered trilogy (3)
Whom Kathie married
Douglas, Amanda Minnie
Kathie series (7)
Whom the gods would destroy
Carter, Nicholas
Nicholas Carter series (495)
Whom the sea has taken
Willis, William
Ancient mariner trilogy (2)
Whoop-up Trail
Bower, Bertha Muzzy
Flying U Ranch series (9)
Whores of war
Kessler, Leo
Wotan series (17)
Who's afraid of Haggerty House?
Gondosch, Linda
Hopper Street trilogy (3)
Who's been sleeping in my bed?
Bleasdale, Alan
Franny Scully series (2)
Who's calling
McCloy, Helen
Basil Willing series (4)
Who's for the zoo?
Ure, Jean
Woodside School series (5)
Who's got
Chase, Emily
Canby Hall series (32)
Who's got a secret?
Saunders, Susan
Bad News Bunny series (4)
Who's gunning for Braid?
Grover, Marshall
Larry and Stretch series (335)
Who's haunting the eighth grade?
Kenyon, Kate
Cedar Groves Junior High School series (13)
Who's next
Allan, Joan
Valerie Lambert series (2)
Who's on first?
Allan, Joan
Valerie Lambert series (3)
Buckley, William Frank
Blackford Oakes series (3)
Who's Orp's girlfriend?
Kline, Suzy
Orp series (4)
Who's scaring Alfie Atkins?
Bergstrom, Gunilla
Alfie Atkins series (5)
Who's that laughing in the grave?
Stanton, Vance
Partridge family series (7)
Who's the Junior High hunk?
Kenyon, Kate
Cedar Groves Junior High School series (9)
Who's the new girl
Chase, Emily
Canby Hall series (12)
Who's to blame?
Pascal, Francine
Sweet Valley High series (66)
Who's who
Pascal, Francine
Sweet Valley High series (62)
Whose body?
Sayers, Dorothy Leigh
Lord Peter Wimsey series (1)
Whose dog are you?
Hammond, Gerald
Captain John Cunningham series (3)

Whose furry nose?
Drescher, Henrik
Animals you'd like to meet series (2)
Whose mouse are you?
Kraus, Robert
Little Mouse series (1)
Whose scaly tale?
Drescher, Henrik
Animals you'd like to meet series (1)
Whose town?
Graham, Lorenz
Town series (3)
Whose was the hand?
Bayfield, William John
Sexton Blake series (62)
Why aren't they screaming?
Smith, Joan
Masculine ending series (2)
Why aren't they screaming
Smith, Joan Mary
Loretta Lawson series (2)
Why can't life be a piece of cake?
Springstubb, Tricia
Eunice Gottlieb series (2)
Why can't you unscramble an egg?
Cobb, Vicki
Not such dumb questions series (1)
Why did Trethewy die?
Walling, Robert Alfred John
Philip Tolefree series (17)
Why do all the right words come out of the wrong mouth?
Guisewhite, Cathy
Cathy series (14)
Why do women?
Corrigan, Mark
Mark Corrigan and McLean series (29)
Why doesn't the sun burn out?
Cobb, Vicki
Not such dumb questions series (2)
Why don't you get a horse, Sam Adams?
Fritz, Jean
American Revolution series (3)
Why I'm afraid of Bess
Stine, Robert Lawrence
Goosebumps series (17)
Why I'm not a millionaire
Spain, Nancy
Thank you series (2)
Why kill a butler?
Powell, Percival Henry
Superintendent Gaden series (1)
Why kill Arthur Potter?
Harrison, Ray
Sergeant Joseph Bragg and Constable James Morton series (1)
Why kill Johnnie?
Carmichael, Harry
John Piper and Quinn series (5)
Why me?
Evans, Greg
Luann series (2)
Westlake, Donald Edwin
Dortmunder Gang series (5)
Why murder?
Philips, Judson Pentecost
Peter Styles series (16)
Why murder Mrs Hope?
Courage, John
David Cane series (4)
Why Paul Ferroll killed his wife
Clive, Caroline
Paul Ferroll series (2)
Why pick on me?
Marshall, Raymond
Brick-Top Corridon series (2)
Why pick on me
Muller, Paul
Paul Muller series (9)
Why pick on Pickles?
Durham, Mary
Inspector York series (2)
Why should Sylvia?
Janson, Hank
Hank Janson series (216)
Why slug a postman?
Truss, Seldon
Inspector Gidleigh series (6)
Why so dead?
Queen, Ellery
Tim Corrigan series (2)
Why the hyena does not care for fish, and other tales from the Ashanti
Appiah, Peggy
Ashanti series (3)
Why things go wrong
Peter, Laurence Johnston
Peter series (7)
Why turn a perfectly good toad into a prince?
Locklin, Gerald
Toad series (5)
Why, Virginia!
Griffith, Helen Sherman
Virginia series (4)
Whyte Swan
Wiat, Philippa
Edward III series (3)
Wichita
Mitchum, Hank
Stage coach station series (15)
Wichita gunman
Ledd, Paul
Shelter Morgan series (16)
Wicked and the witless
Cook, Hugh
Chronicles of an age of darkness series (5)
Wicked as the Devil
Halliday, Michael
Doctor Emmanuel Cellini series (2)
Wicked cyborg
Goulart, Ron
Barnum series (6)
Wicked day
Stewart, Mary
Merlin and Arthur series (4)
Wicked designs
O'Donnell, Lillian
Mici Anhalt series (3)
Wicked flea
Hocking, Anne
Inspector William Austen series (5)
Wicked godmother
Chesney, Marion
House for the season series (3)
Wicked lady
Fletcher, Inglis
Carolina series (11)
Carolina series (12)
Wicked, loving murder
Papazoglou, Orania
Patience Campbell McKenna series (2)
Wicked saint
Bruton, Eric
City of London Police series (5)
Wicked uncle
Wentworth, Patricia
Miss Maud Silver series (13)
Wicked uncles
Housman, Laurence
Palace plays series (1)
Wicked way to die
Sturrock, Jeremy
Bow Street Runner series (2)
Wicked widow
Brown, Carter
Lieutenant Al Wheeler series (53)
Wicked Willie's guide to women
Mayle, Peter
Wicked Willie series (2)
Wicked Willie's guide to women II
Mayle, Peter
Wicked Willie series (3)
Wicked witch of the Troll Cave
Torgersen, Don Arthur
Troll series (7)
Wickedest witch in the world
Nichols, Beverley
Judy series (4)
Wicker-work woman
France, Anatole
Contemporary history series (1)
Wicket and the dandelion warriors
Weinberg, Larry
Ewok series (2)
Widdershins Crescent
Townsend, John Rowe
Uncle Walter series (2)
Wide Awake Girls
Ellis, Katherine Ruth
Wide Awake Girls series (1)
Wide Awake Girls at college
Ellis, Katherine Ruth
Wide Awake Girls series (3)
Wide Awake Girls at Winsted
Ellis, Katherine Ruth
Wide Awake Girls series (2)
Wide blue road
Campbell, Marion
Richard De Brun series (1)
Wide horizon
Erdman, Loula Grace
Pierce family series (2)
Macdonald, Peter G
Open road quartet (2)
Wide is the gate
Sinclair, Upton
World's end series (4)
Wide is the water
Hodge, Jane Aiken
Purchis family series (2)
Wide open town
Gardner, Jerome
Dripspring series (10)
Wide Sargasso sea
Rhys, Jean
Rochester series (1)
Wide wide world
Wetherell, Elizabeth
Ellen Montgomery series (1)
Widening circle
Van Druten, John
Vicarious years series (2)
Widening gyre
Parker, Robert Brown
Spenser series (10)
Wider horizons
Morrison, Margaret
Annetze de Steur series (2)
Wider war
Wright, David K
War in Vietnam series (2)
Wideways
Dunn, Saul
Steeleye series (2)
Widgery Winks and his new friends
Bennett, Rodney
Widgery Winks series (3)
Widgery Winks in the wide world
Bennett, Rodney
Widgery Winks series (2)
Widow
Freeling, Nicolas
Arlette Van der Valk series (2)
Widow and the cavalier
Armstrong, Raymond
Inspector Dick Mason series (7)
J Rockingham Stone series (3)
Laura Scudamore series (4)
Widow and the web
Martin, Robert Lee
Jim Bennett series (4)
Widow Barnaby
Trollope, Frances
Widow Barnaby trilogy (1)
Widow Chuan
Lin, Yutang
Chinese village series (2)
Widow Claire
Foote, Horton
Orphans' home series (8)
Widow Creek
Longtree, Warren T
Ruff Justice series (4)
Widow for killing
Halliday, Brett
Mike Shayne stories series (5)
Widow from nowhere
Grover, Marshall
Larry and Stretch series (379)
Widow Gay
Marcus, Arthur A
Pete Hunter series (1)
Widow had a gun
Coxe, George Harmon
Kent Murdock series (13)
Widow Lerouge
Gaboriau, Emile
Monsieur Lecoq series (1)
Widow maker
McElwain, Dean L
Preacher's law series (1)
Widow married
Trollope, Frances
Widow Barnaby trilogy (2)
Widow of Windsor
Plaidy, Jean
Queen Victoria series (5)
Whittle, Tyler
Queen Victoria trilogy (3)
Widow Valley
Reno, Bill
Badge series (20)
Widow watchers
Archer, Frank
Inspector Joseph Delaney series (2)
Widow wedded
Trollope, Frances
Widow Barnaby trilogy (2)
Widow with pink gloves
Dekobra, Maurice
Bradley Adams series (1)
Widow woman
Fraser, Sara
Tildy series (7)
Widowmaker
Brady, William S
Jared Hawk series (9)
Morwood, Peter
Clan wars series (2)
Sherman, Jory
Gunn series (12)
Widows
La Plante, Lynda
Widows series (1)
McBain, Ed
Eighty Seventh Precinct series (45)
Widows' beads
Joyce, Cyril
Chief Superintendent Pat Stockton series (17)
Widows' Club
Cannell, Dorothy
Ellie Simons Haskell series (3)
Widow's cruise
Blake, Nicholas
Nigel Strangeways series (13)
Widow's end
Penn, John
Inspector George Thorne and Sergeant Bill Abbot series (15)
Widows II
La Plante, Lynda
Widows series (2)
Widow's might
Fitzroy, Rosamond
Mallamshire series (2)
Widow's mite
Holding, Elisabeth Sanxay
Lieutenant Levy series (3)
Widows of Broome
Upfield, Arthur William
Napoleon Bonaparte series (13)
Widows only
Tinker, Frances
Old New Orleans quartet (1)
Widow's peak
Nicholas, Jerome
Bill Anstruther series (1)
Widow's son
Wilson, Robert Anton
Historical illuminatus trilogy (2)
Widows wear weeds
Fair, A A
Bertha Cool and Donald Lam series (27)
Wielding a red sword
Anthony, Piers
Incarnations of immortality series (4)
Wiener dog art
Larson, Gary
Far Side series (11)
Wife
Burnley, Judith
Wife series (1)
Wife in Kenya
Strange, Nora Kathleen
Kenya series (1)
Wife of Jean Barnery
Chardonne, Jacques
House of Barnery series (1)
Wife of Ronald Sheldon
Quentin, Patrick
Lieutenant Timothy Trant series (5)
Wife-smuggler
Tripp, Miles
John Samson series (3)
Wife Swap Incorporated
Law, Simone
Wife swap series (2)
Wife who disappeared
Flynn, Brian
Anthony Bathurst series (50)
Wigged and gowned
Draper, Hastings
Wig series (2)
Wiggery pokery
Draper, Hastings
Wig series (1)
Wiggins for president
Brooks, Walter Rollin
Freddy the pig series (6)
Wigmakers
Fisher, Leonard Everett
Colonial Americans series (5)
Wigs at work
Herbert, Alan Patrick
Misleading cases series (5)
Wigwag Weigand
Fitzhugh, Percy Keese
Buddy series (4)
Wilberforce and the blue cave
Coleman, Leslie
Wilberforce series (2)
Wilberforce and the McMonster
Coleman, Leslie
Wilberforce series (5)
Wilberforce, detective
Coleman, Leslie
Wilberforce series (3)
Wilberforce goes on a picnic
Gordon, Margaret
Wilberforce series (1)
Wilberforce goes shopping
Gordon, Margaret
Wilberforce series (2)
Wilberforce goes to a party
Gordon, Margaret
Wilberforce series (3)
Wilberforce goes to playgroup
Gordon, Margaret
Wilberforce series (4)
Wilberforce the whale
Coleman, Leslie
Wilberforce series (1)
Wild adventure
Peel, John
Lost in space files series (4)
Wild adventures round the Pole
Stables, Gordon
Captain McBain series (2)
Wild alien tamer
Resnick, Mike
Tales of the Galactic Midway series (3)
Wild and the wayward
Granger, Georgia
Making of America series (8)
Wild Angel
Christian, Frederick H
Frank Angel series (11)
Wild angel
Spykman, Elizabeth Choate
Cares family series (2)
Wild ass's skin
Balzac, Honore de
Philosophic studies series (1)
Wild baby
Lindgren, Barbro
Wild baby series (1)
Wild baby goes to sea
Lindgren, Barbro
Wild baby series (2)
Wild baby's boat trip
Lindgren, Barbro
Wild baby series (2)
Wild baby's dog
Lindgren, Barbro
Wild baby series (3)
Wild Bill's ghost
Roberts, J R
Gunsmith series (46)
Wild bird
Diver, Maud
Challoners series (3)
Desmond series (5)
Wild blood
McLaglen, John J
Herne the Hunter series (22)
Young, Gordon Ray
Hurricane Williams trilogy (1)
Wild boy in the bush
Dallas, Ruth
Jean, Robbie, Sophie and Helen series (2)
Wild boys
Burroughs, William Seward
Cities of the red night trilogy (3)
Wild card
Hawkey, Raymond
Presidential trilogy (1)
Wild card run
Stamey, Sara
Wild card trilogy (1)
Wild cards
Martin, George Raymond Richard
Wild cards series (1)
Wild Cat Hetty
Kilpatrick, Florence Antoinette
Hetty trilogy (1)
Wild-cat scheme
Keate, Edith Murray
Superintendent Margetson series (1)
Wild cherry
Ross, Diana
Miss Pussy series (2)
Wild country
Ing, Dean
Ted Quantrill trilogy (3)
Killdeer, John
Mountain majesty series (1)
Wild dancer
Calhoun, Chad
Agent Brad Spear series (9)
Wild deer
Baptist, R Hernekin
African negro series (2)
Wild dog
Bell, Frank
Shen series (1)

Wild dog running
Scholefield, Alan
South African series (4)
Wild duck murders
Du Bois, Theodora
Anne and Jeffrey McNeill series (9)
Wild earth's nobility
Waters, Frank
Pike's Peak trilogy (1)
Wild float trip
Palmer, Bernard
Dell Norton series (1)
Wild flower
Harrison, Claire
Tamara series (2)
Wild flowers we know
Burgess, Thornton Waldo
Wild flowers series (1)
Wild flowers we should know
Burgess, Thornton Waldo
Wild flowers series (2)
Wild Geese
Carney, Daniel
Wild Geese series (1)
Wild geese
Dillon, Eilis
Wild geese series (1)
Wild Geese II
Carney, Daniel
Wild Geese series (2)
Wild ghost chase
Enright, Dennis Joseph
Joke shop trilogy (2)
Wild girl
Janson, Hank
Hank Janson series (92)
Wild goose summer
Nortje, Peter Henry
Henk Strydom series (1)
Wild green earth
Fergusson, Bernard
Burma campaign series (2)
Wild harvest
Nicole, Christopher
Black majesty series (2)
Wild heart of youth
Rhodes, Kathlyn
Martin Ryott series (1)
Wild hearts
Bennett, Cherie
Wild hearts series (1)
Wild hearts forever
Bennett, Cherie
Wild hearts series (3)
Wild hearts on fire
Bennett, Cherie
Wild hearts series (2)
Wild hills
Croft-Cooke, Rupert
Sensual life series (8)
Wild Horse Canyon mystery
Hutchens, Paul
Sugar Creek Gang series (27)
Wild horse lightning
Field, Peter
Powder Valley series (55)
Wild Horse Shorty
Nye, Nelson Coral
Wild Horse Shorty series (1)
Wild Horse Valley
Tuttle, Wilbur Coleman
Henry Harrison Conroy and Judge Van Treece series (2)
Sad Sontag series (3)
Wild horses
Bolton, Evelyn
Horse book series (5)
Wild horses of the Red Desert
Rounds, Glen
Whitey series (12)
Wild hunt
Kirk, Matthew
Claw series (4)
Wild Iris blooms
Jukes, Mavis
Maggie and Iris series (2)
Wild is my love
Taylor, Janelle
Princess Alysa series (1)
Wild island
Fraser, Antonia
Jemima Shore series (2)
Wild justice
Grant-Adamson, Lesley
Rain Morgan series (4)
Wild life in Canada
Rutley, Cecil Bernard
Wild life story series (4)
Wild life in the bush and jungle
Rutley, Cecil Bernard
Wild life story series (14)
Wild life in the ice and snow
Rutley, Cecil Bernard
Wild life story series (9)
Wild life in the jungle
Rutley, Cecil Bernard
Wild life story series (8)
Wild Lorings at school
Courtney, Gwendoline
Wild Lorings series (1)
Wild Lorings, detectives!
Courtney, Gwendoline
Wild Lorings series (2)
Wild magic
Clayton, Jo
Wild magic trilogy (1)
Pierce, Tamora
Daine series (1)
Wild man of the woods
Clark, Joan
Barrow family series (1)
Wild midnight falls
Chaber, M E
Milo March series (17)
Wild moves
Wharton, Joanna
Campus fever series (8)
Wild mustang
Hall, Lynn
Dragon series (1)
Wild night
Washburn, Livia Jane
Lucas Hallam series (1)
Wild night in Widow's Peak
Grover, Marshall
Larry and Stretch series (327)
Wild oats
Muspratt, Eric
Fire of youth series (2)
Wild one
Edwards, Monica
Punchbowl Farm series (11)
Wild One
Grey, Peter
Kit Hunter series (1)
Wild ones
Chandler, Arthur Bertram
John Grimes series (24)
Wild orchid
Undset, Sigrid
Modern scene series (1)
Wild ostrich of the Kalahari
Torgersen, Don Arthur
Animal life stories series (10)
Wild pitch
Guthrie, Alfred Bertram
Sheriff Chick Charleston and Jason Beard series (1)
Wild ride
Boyles, William
Bounty Hunter series (3)
Wild rye
Hine, Muriel
Jenny Rorke series (1)
Wild sea
Taylor, Keith
Bard series (3)
Wild seed
Butler, Octavia Estelle
Patternists series (4)
Wild sheep chase
Murakami, Haruki
Wild sheep chase series (1)
Wild shore
Robinson, Kim Stanley
Orange County trilogy (1)
Wild silver
Johansen, Iris
Delaneys, the untamed years trilogy (1)
Wild spell of summer
Ebejer, Francis
Lucija and Rosie series (2)
Wild stallion
Murray, Earl
Dan Sleyter series (4)
Wild stallions
Benteen, John
Sundance series (7)
Wild star
Coulter, Catherine
Star trilogy (2)
Wild storms of heaven
Shiplett, June Lund
Winds series (3)
Wild strawberries
Thirkell, Angela
Barsetshire series (2)
Wild Swan
De Blasis, Celeste
Wild Swan trilogy (1)
Wild sweet promise
Taylor, Janelle
Princess Alysa series (2)
Wild times at West Mount High
Harrell, Janice
West Mount High trilogy (1)
Wild trail to Denver
Grover, Marshall
Larry and Stretch series (79)
Wild trek
Kjelgaard, Jim
Chiri series (2)
Wild turkey
Simon, Roger Lichtenberg
Moses Wine series (2)
Wild turkey run
Reese, Bob
Grand Canyon series (2)
Wild valley
Paul, Charlotte
Snoqualmie Valley series (2)
Wild vines
Leigh, Helena
Vintage years trilogy (2)
Wild warning
Garis, Lilian C
Melody Lane series (4)
Wild week-end
Jacobs, Thomas Curtis Hicks
Tempie Fortune series (18)
Wild West
Mitchum, Hank
Stage coach station series (51)
Wild West rider
Overholser, Stephen
Time machine series (9)
Wild widow of Wolf Creek
Grover, Marshall
Larry and Stretch series (255)
Wild, wild women
Curry, Gene
Jim Saddler series (5)
Wild willful love
Sherwood, Valerie
Imogene and Georgiana series (3)
Wild wind's calling
Shiplett, June Lund
Winds series (6)
Wild wings
Chalmers, Margaret Piper
Sylvia Arden series (4)
Wild Wood
Clewes, Dorothy
Wild Wood series (2)
Wild woods life
Farrar, Charles Alden John
Lake and forest series (2)
Wildcat
Ambler, Dail
Danny Spade series (14)
Brissenden, Robert Francis
Tom Caxton series (2)
Brown, Carter
Lieutenant Al Wheeler series (22)
Wiley, Hugh
Wildcat series (1)
Wildcat against the house
Clinton, Jeff
Wildcat O'Shea series (3)
Wildcat falling
Nyoongah, Mudrooroo
Wildcat trilogy (1)
Wildcat meets Miss Melody
Clinton, Jeff
Wildcat O'Shea series (10)
Wildcat on the loose
Clinton, Jeff
Wildcat O'Shea series (7)
Wildcat roundup
Roberts, J R
Gunsmith series (29)
Wildcat run
Grover, Marshall
Larry and Stretch series (428)
Wildcat screaming
Nyoongah, Mudrooroo
Wildcat trilogy (3)
Wildcat takes his medicine
Clinton, Jeff
Wildcat O'Shea series (5)
Wildcat wagon
Sharpe, Jon
Trailsman series (76)
Wildcat widow
Gentry, Buck
Eli Holten series (21)
Wildcat woman
Curry, Gene
Jim Saddler series (2)
Wildcats
Edson, John Thomas
Floating Outfit series (18)
Wildcat's claim to fame
Clinton, Jeff
Wildcat O'Shea series (13)
Wildcat's rampage
Clinton, Jeff
Wildcat O'Shea series (2)
Wildcat's revenge
Clinton, Jeff
Wildcat O'Shea series (4)
Wildcat's witch hunt
Clinton, Jeff
Wildcat O'Shea series (8)
Wildcatters
Benteen, John
Neal Fargo series (5)
Willoughby, Lee Davis
Making of America series (21)
Wilde boys
Bridges, Ben
Wilde boys series (1)
Wilde fire
Bridges, Ben
Wilde boys series (2)
Wildeblood's empire
Stableford, Brian Michael
Daedalus series (3)
Wilder curse
Robeson, Kenneth
Avenger series (23)
Wilderling
Lorrimer, Claire
Rochford trilogy (2)
Wilderness
Vaughan, Carter A
Lieutenant Gordon Fuller series (2)
Ward, Richard Heron
Neil Falder series (2)
Wilderness blossoms
Green, Russell
Prophet series (2)
Wilderness boy
Harper, Stephen
Healers series (3)
Wilderness empire, 1745
Eckert, Allan Wesley
Winning of America series (2)
Wilderness fugitives
Ellis, Edward Sylvester
River and wilderness trilogy (2)
Wilderness manhunt
Hardin, J D
Raider series (18)
Wilderness of ice
Verne, Jules
Adventures of Captain Hatteras series (2)
Wilderness passage
Blake, Forrester
Johnny Christmas trilogy (2)
Wilderness rendezvous
Killdeer, John
Mountain majesty series (3)
Wilderness renegades
Weddle, Ferris
Clint Wade and Trapper Bill series (3)
Wilderness seekers
Cameron, Lou
Making of America series (1)
Wilderness wanton
Fletcher, Dirk
Spur McCoy giant series (5)
Wilderness war
Eckert, Allan Wesley
Winning of America series (4)
Wilderness wedding
Thompson, Mary Wolfe
Aiken family trilogy (3)
Wilderness wife
Pinkerton, Kathrene
Shoestring trilogy (1)
Wilderness winter
Thompson, Mary Wolfe
Aiken family trilogy (2)
Wilderness years
Townsend, Sue
Adrian Mole series (5)
Wilders walk away
Brean, Herbert
Reynold Frame series (1)
Wilde's law
Bridges, Ben
Wilde boys series (3)
Wildfang
Oldmeadow, Ernest James
Coggin trilogy (3)
Wildfire
Carter, Nicholas
Nicholas Carter series (631)
Clayton, Jo
Wild magic trilogy (2)
Goddard, Kenneth
Prey series (2)
Wildfires
Adair, Denis
MacLeod family series (4)
Wildings
Crompton, Richmal
Wilding family series (1)
Wildings of Westron
Lake, David John
Breakout series (3)
Dextra series (2)
Wildkeeper's guest
Grimshaw, Nigel
Wildkeepers series (2)
Wildlife
Strasser, Todd
Coming Attractions trilogy (3)
Wildlife preserves
Larson, Gary
Far Side series (10)
Wiles of Lim Quong
George, Sidney Charles
Lim Quong series (1)
Wilfred Pickles invits you to have another go
Pickles, Wilfred
You and me series (3)
Wilfred's treasure
Cole, Michael
Edward and friends series (2)
Wilful and premeditated
Crofts, Freeman Wills
Inspector Joseph French series (11)
Wilful lady
Sturrock, Jeremy
Bow Street Runner series (3)
Wilful Walter
Leslie, Madeline
Woodbine series (4)
Wilhelm Meister's apprenticeship
Goethe, Johann Wolfgang von
Wilhelm Meister series (1)
Wilhelm Meister's travels
Goethe, Johann Wolfgang von
Wilhelm Meister series (2)
Wilkes the wizard
Webb, Jackie
Wilkes the wizard series (1)
Wilkes the wizard and the S.P.A.M.
Webb, Jackie
Wilkes the wizard series (2)
Wilkins gets a blanket
Newman, Marjorie
Wilkins series (3)
Wilkins gets a job
Newman, Marjorie
Wilkins series (2)
Wilkins the armchair cat
Newman, Marjorie
Wilkins series (1)
Will and a way
Roberts, Nora
Flowers series (34)
Will anyone who saw the accident
Ashford, Jeffrey
Detective Inspector Don Kerry series (3)
Will in the way
Burton, Miles
Inspector Arnold and Desmond Merrion series (36)
Will men be like gods?
Dudley, Owen Francis
Problems of human happiness series (1)
Will-o'-the-wisp
Elsschot, Willem
Laarmans series (3)
Will-o-the-wisp
Swann, Thomas Burnett
Ancient history series (12)
Will of Dargan
Allcock, Phil
Stories of the realm series (1)
Will of the gods
Green, Sharon
Jalav series (4)
Will of the tribe
Upfield, Arthur William
Napoleon Bonaparte series (27)
Will of the wanderer
Weis, Margaret
Rose of the prophet trilogy (1)
Will-power
Janson, Hank
Hank Janson series (195)
Will the real Becka Morgan stand up?
Kaye, Marilyn
Three of a kind series (3)
Will the real Rod please stand up
Conway, Troy
Coxeman series (21)

Will the real winner please stand?
Groten, Dallas
Winning series (2)
Will to kill
Penn, John
Inspector George Thorne and Sergeant Bill Abbot series (3)
Will to survive
Salter, Elizabeth
Inspector Michael Hornsley series (2)
Will we be tested on this?
Evans, Greg
Luann series (10)
Will you come with me?
Beers, Victor Gilbert
Learning to read from the Bible primer series (4)
Will you love me in September?
Carr, Philippa
Daughters of England series (8)
Will you please feed our cat?
Stevenson, James
Grandfather's problems series (6)
Will you sign here, John Hancock?
Fritz, Jean
American Revolution series (5)
Willard
Gilbert, Stephen
Ben and Willard series (1)
Willerbys and the bank robbers
Oldfield, Pamela
Willerbys series (5)
Willerbys and the burglar
Oldfield, Pamela
Willerbys series (1)
Willerbys and the haunted mill
Oldfield, Pamela
Willerbys series (2)
Willerbys and the mystery man
Oldfield, Pamela
Willerbys series (6)
Willerbys and the old castle
Oldfield, Pamela
Willerbys series (4)
Willerbys and the sad clown
Oldfield, Pamela
Willerbys series (3)
William
Crompton, Richmal
William series (10)
William again
Crompton, Richmal
William series (3)
William and A.R.P.
Crompton, Richmal
William series (21)
William and his kitten
Flack, Marjorie
William series (2)
William and the artist's model
Crompton, Richmal
William series (42)
William and the Brains Trust
Crompton, Richmal
William series (25)
William and the evacuees
Crompton, Richmal
William series (22)
William and the masked ranger
Crompton, Richmal
William series (40)
William and the monster
Crompton, Richmal
William series (35)
William and the moon rocket
Crompton, Richmal
William series (29)
William and the pop singers
Crompton, Richmal
William series (39)
William and the space animal
Crompton, Richmal
William series (30)
William and the tramp
Crompton, Richmal
William series (28)
William and the witch
Crompton, Richmal
William series (34)
William, by the grace of God
Bowen, Marjorie
William the Silent series (2)
William carries on
Crompton, Richmal
William series (24)
William Cook, antique dealer
Keverne, Richard
Franklin Parry and Leonard Harris series (1)
William does his bit
Crompton, Richmal
William series (23)
William in trouble
Crompton, Richmal
William series (7)
William McGonagall meets George Gershwin
Milligan, Spike
William McGonagall series (3)
William McGonagall, the truth at last
Milligan, Spike
William McGonagall series (2)
William Peter Blatty on The exorcist, from novel to film
Blatty, William Peter
Lieutenant Bill Kinderman series (3)
William the ancient Briton
Crompton, Richmal
William series (36)
William the bad
Crompton, Richmal
William series (11)
William the bold
Crompton, Richmal
William series (27)
William the cannibal
Crompton, Richmal
William series (37)
William the conqueror
Crompton, Richmal
William series (6)
William the detective
Crompton, Richmal
William series (17)
William, the dictator
Crompton, Richmal
William series (20)
William, the explorer
Crompton, Richmal
William series (32)
William the film star
Crompton, Richmal
William series (22)
William the fourth
Crompton, Richmal
William series (4)
William the gangster
Crompton, Richmal
William series (16)
William the globetrotter
Crompton, Richmal
William series (38)
William the good
Crompton, Richmal
William series (9)
William the hero
Crompton, Richmal
William series (25)
William the lawless
Crompton, Richmal
William series (42)
William, the outlaw
Crompton, Richmal
William series (8)
William, the pirate
Crompton, Richmal
William series (14)
William, the rebel
Crompton, Richmal
William series (15)
William, the showman
Crompton, Richmal
William series (19)
William the superman
Crompton, Richmal
William series (41)
William the wizard
Cleveland-Peck, Patricia
William the wizard series (1)
William's bad resolution
Crompton, Richmal
William series (21)
William's crowded hours
Crompton, Richmal
William series (13)
William's happy days
Crompton, Richmal
William series (12)
William's television show
Crompton, Richmal
William series (31)
William's treasure trove
Crompton, Richmal
William series (33)
Williamsburg trilogy
Fuchs, Daniel
Williamsburg trilogy (3)
Willie Gavin, crofter man
Cameron, David Kerr
Scottish farm life series (2)
Willing target
Grover, Marshall
Nevada Jim series (52)
Willing witness
Cobb, Belton
Inspector Cheviot Burmann series (17)
Willis the pilot
Paul, Adrien
Swiss family Robinson series (2)
Williver's luck
Hadfield, Alice Mary
Williver family series (1)
Williver's quest
Hadfield, Alice Mary
Williver family series (2)
Williver's return
Hadfield, Alice Mary
Williver family series (3)
Willow
Drew, Wayland
Willow series (1)
Dubowski, Cathy East
Willow series (3)
McDonnell, David
Willow series (3)
Vinge, Joan Dennison
Willow series (2)
Willow and Albert
Miller, Margaret Jessy
Willow and Albert series (2)
Willow and Albert are stowaways
Miller, Margaret Jessy
Willow and Albert series (3)
Willow Brook
Warner, Susan Bagert
Eagle Hill series (2)
Willow Creek home
Shefelman, Janice Jordan
Texas trilogy (2)
Willow garden
Grant, Kathryn
Land of ten thousand willows trilogy (3)
Willow Pattern
Gulik, Robert van
Judge Dee series (13)
Willow Pool
Bradbury, Catherine
Applebury tales series (2)
Willow sourcebook
Costikyan, Greg
Willow series (3)
Willow Wind Farm
Pellowski, Anne
Valley Farm series (4)
Willow Witches Brook
Tempest, Margaret
Potter Pinner series (3)
Willows in winter
Horwood, William
Wind in the willows series (14)
Wills of Jane Kanwhistle
Fowler, Sydney
Mister Jellipot series (7)
Willy the champ
Browne, Anthony
Willy series (2)
Willy the wimp
Browne, Anthony
Willy series (1)
Wilson and some others
Cole, George Douglas Howard
Superintendent Henry Wilson series (22)
Wilson calling
Cole, George Douglas Howard
Superintendent Henry Wilson series (11)
Wilson Young on the run
Tippette, Giles
Wilson Young series (9)
Wilson's choice
Tippette, Giles
Wilson Young series (4)
Wilson's gold
Tippette, Giles
Wilson Young series (2)
Wilson's luck
Tippette, Giles
Wilson Young series (3)
Wilson's revenge
Tippette, Giles
Wilson Young series (5)
Wilson's woman
Tippette, Giles
Wilson Young series (6)
Wilt
Sharpe, Tom
Henry Wilt series (1)
Wilt alternative
Sharpe, Tom
Henry Wilt series (2)
Wilt on high
Sharpe, Tom
Henry Wilt series (3)
Wilt thou Torchy
Ford, Sewell
Torchy series (5)
Wimbledon Common trap
Hunter, John
Sexton Blake series (1177)
Wimpy goes abroad
Drake, Joan
Wimpy series (4)
Wimpy on holiday
Drake, Joan
Wimpy series (3)
Win for Henry Conyers
Vipont, Elfrida
Dowbiggins series (2)
Win, lose, draw
Stamey, Sara
Wild card trilogy (2)
Win, lose or die
Gardner, John Edmund
James Bond series (25)
Win, place or die
Keene, Carolyn
Nancy Drew files series (46)
Win some, lose some
Halliday, Brett
Michael Shayne series (71)
Win with sin
O'Shea, Sean
Valentine Flynn series (3)
Winchester Valley
Dalton, Kit
Buckskin series (16)
Wind and the flame
Sperber, Manes
Doino Faber trilogy (1)
Wind blew west
Lanham, Edwin
Wind in the banner series (1)
Wind blows death
Hare, Cyril
Francis Pettigrew series (3)
Wind blows free
Erdman, Loula Grace
Pierce family series (1)
Wind blows from the west
Baker, Denys Val
Cornish series (12)
Wind child
Meluch, Rebecca M
Wind dancers series (2)
Wind chill factor
Gifford, Thomas
Wind chill series (1)
Wind crystal
Paxson, Diana Lucile
Westria series (6)
Wind dancers
Meluch, Rebecca M
Wind dancers series (1)
Wind for Wing
Burtis, Thomson
Air combat series (3)
Wind force seven
Morrison, J Strang
Monach light series (1)
Wind from Spain
Charlton, Moyra
Treherne family series (2)
Wind from the abyss
Morris, Janet Ellen
Silistra series (3)
Wind from the mountain
Gulbranssen, Trygve
Bjorndal family series (2)
Wind from the mountains
Gulbranssen, Trygve
Bjorndal family series (2)
Wind from the plain
Kemal, Yashar
Meryemdje series (1)
Wind in the ashes
Johnstone, William Wallace
Ashes series (6)
Wind in the ashtree
McMullen, Jeanine
Country living series (2)
Wind in the door
L'Engle, Madeleine
Meg Murry series (2)
Wind in the forest
Fletcher, Inglis
Carolina series (8)
Carolina series (12)
Wind in the rigging
Pease, Howard
Tod Moran series (5)
White, James Dillon
Roger Kelso series (7)
Wind in the willows
Grahame, Kenneth
Riverbend and Wildwood tales series (1)
Toad Hall series (1)
Wind in the willows series (1)
Wind is blowing
Edwards, Monica
Romney Marsh series (16)
Wind is free
Wightman, Frank Armstrong
Wylo series (1)
Wind is rising
Romains, Jules
Men of goodwill series (24)
Wind is silver
Fowler, Thurley
Robinson family series (2)
Wind leans west
Derleth, August
Wisconsin series (6)
Wind of change at Castle Rising
Cradock, Fanny
Lorme family series (4)
Wind of death
Black, Gavin
Paul Harris series (6)
Wind of destiny
Nicole, Christopher
United States Navy series (4)
Wind of promise
Garlock, Dorothy
Colorado trilogy (3)
Wind over Wisconsin
Derleth, August
Sac Prairie series (3)
Wind rises
Danoen, Emile
Jeannot and Lydie series (2)
Wind river
McCarthy, Gary
Wind river series (1)
Wind, sand and stars
Saint-Exupery, Antoine de
Airman's odyssey trilogy (2)
Wind shifts
Sharp, Alan
John Moseby series (2)
Wind that shakes the barley
Barke, James
Immortal memory series (1)
Wind that tramps the world
Owen, Frank
Chinese color series (1)
Wind tunnel
Buckingham, David
Sam Wharton series (1)
Wind up
Steed, Neville
Peter Marklin series (5)
Wind-up doll
Brown, Carter
Rick Holman series (8)
Windfall
Bagley, Desmond
Max Stafford series (2)
Windfall's eve
Lucas, Edward Verrall
Richard series (1)
Windhaven Plantation
De Jourlet, Marie
Windhaven series (1)
Windhaven's bounty
De Jourlet, Marie
Windhaven series (9)
Windhaven's crisis
De Jourlet, Marie
Windhaven series (8)
Windhaven's destiny
De Jourlet, Marie
Windhaven series (12)
Windhaven's fury
De Jourlet, Marie
Windhaven series (11)
Windhaven's hope
De Jourlet, Marie
Windhaven series (13)
Windhaven's peril
De Jourlet, Marie
Windhaven series (5)
Windhaven's triumph
De Jourlet, Marie
Windhaven series (10)
Winding lane
Tangye, Derek
Minack chronicles series (11)
Winding stair
Jones, Douglas Clyde
Hasford family series (2)
Winding stair massacre
Jones, Douglas Clyde
Hasford family series (2)
Winding Valley Farm
Pellowski, Anne
Valley Farm series (2)

Windmaster's bane
Deitz, Tom
David Sullivan series (1)
Windmill Land
Clarke, Allen
Windmill Land series (1)
Windmill Land stories
Clarke, Allen
Windmill Land series (3)
Windmill mystery
Barne, Kitty
Farrar family series (3)
Window box book
Tarsky, Sue
How does your garden grow series (2)
Window for death
Stout, Rex
Nero Wolfe and Archie Goodwin series (28)
Window in the dark
Kilvington, Edwin
Crispin Quane series (2)
Window in Thrums
Barrie, James Matthew
Thrums series (2)
Window of sky
Morgan, Geoffrey
Orphan series (3)
Window on today
Hohl, Joan
Window trilogy (2)
Window on tomorrow
Hohl, Joan
Window trilogy (3)
Window on yesterday
Hohl, Joan
Window trilogy (1)
Window seat
Mottram, Ralph Hale
Life observed series (1)
Window to death
Stout, Rex
Dol Bonner series (2)
Windows
Compton, David Guy
Katherine Mortenhoe series (2)
Windows of the mind
Glaskin, Gerald Marcus
Christos experience trilogy (1)
Windows on the sea
Newcomb, Ellsworth
Joan and Bill series (2)
Winds blow free
Bell, Robert Vaughn
McGowan family series (7)
Winds blow gently
Kirkbride, Ronald
Gentle series (1)
Winds of betrayal
Shiplett, June Lund
Winds series (7)
Winds of blame
Rushing, Jane Gilmore
Walnut Grove series (4)
Winds of change
Lackey, Mercedes
Mage winds series (2)
Pini, Richard
Elfquest series (4)
Winds of change, 1914-1939
Macmillan, Harold
Winds of change series (1)
Winds of Darkover
Bradley, Marion Zimmer
Darkover series (11)
Winds of Deal
Griswold, Latta
Deering series (2)
Winds of evil
Upfield, Arthur William
Napoleon Bonaparte series (5)
Winds of fate
Lackey, Mercedes
Mage winds series (1)
Winds of fury
Lackey, Mercedes
Mage winds series (3)
Winds of Gath
Tubb, Edwin Charles
Dumarest series (1)
Winds of heaven
Scanlan, Nelle Margaret
Pencarrow family series (3)
Winds of limbo
Moorcock, Michael
Dancers at the end of time series (5)
Winds of March
Weber, Lenora Mattingly
Stacy and Katie Rose Belford series (2)
Winds of Sinhala
De Silva, Colin
Sinhala series (1)
Winds of the Heliopolis
Fretland, Donald John
Oleandre series (2)
Winds of the world
Mundy, Talbot
Sikh series (1)
Winds of time
Gibbs, Henry
South African history series (2)
Winds of war
Wouk, Herman
Commander Pug Henry series (1)
Winds over the campus
Linn, James Weber
Campus series (2)
Windshear
Savarin, Julian Jay
Gordon Gallagher series (3)
Windsingers
Lindholm, Megan
Windsingers series (2)
Windsingers series (3)
Windsong
Sherwood, Valerie
Carolina Lightfoot trilogy (2)
Windsor red
Melville, Jennie
Sergeant Charmian Daniels series (9)
Windward west
Braun, Matt
Brannocks series (2)
Windwolf
Longtree, Warren T
Ruff Justice series (9)
Windy day at Upney Junction
Butterworth, Nick
Upney Junction series (3)
Windy Foot at the county fair
Frost, Frances Mary
Windy Foot series (1)
Windy side of the law
Woods, Sara
Sir Nicholas Harding and Antony Maitland series (8)
Windyridge
Riley, William
Windyridge series (1)
Windyridge revisited
Riley, William
Windyridge series (4)
Wine-dark sea
O'Brian, Patrick
Jack Aubrey and Stephen Maturin series (15)
Wine of Calvoro
Piacentini, Valerie
Star trek fan series (13)
Wine of life
Egan, Lesley
Vic Varallo series (14)
Wine of violence
Egan, Lesley
Vic Varallo series (6)
Wine of war
Cousins, Edmund George
Larry Grail series (3)
Wine widow
Barclay, Tessa
Tramont family series (1)
Wine, women and death
Deptula, Walter
Frank Arrow series (2)
Wine, women and murder
Roeburt, John
Jigger Moran series (1)
Wine, women and war
Jahn, Mike
Six Million Dollar Man series (6)
Wineland adventure
Boucher, Alan Estcourt
Halli Thordason series (3)
Winfried
Zweig, Arnold
Werner Bertin and Lenore Wahl series (6)
Wing and a prayer
Kingston, Guy
Royal Air Force trilogy (2)
Winged assassin
Cooke, Catherine
Winged assassin trilogy (1)
Winged Cupid
Matthewman, Phyllis
Cupid trilogy (1)
Winged dagger
Farran, Roy
Special Air Service series (1)
Winged lion
De Mille, James
Young Dodge Club series (4)
Winged mystery
Upfield, Arthur William
Napoleon Bonaparte series (3)
Winged peace
Johns, William Earl
Biggles series (6)
Winged seeds
Prichard, Katharine Susannah
Western Australian Goldfields series (3)
Winged victory
Grand, Sarah
Adnam Pratt series (2)
Wingless eagle
Turnbull, Patrick
Bonaparte series (2)
Wingman
Maloney, Mack
Wingman series (1)
Wingmaster
Houston, David
Gods in a vortex series (2)
Wings
Pratchett, Terry
Book of the Nomes trilogy (3)
Thomas, Barry
Wings series (1)
Wings above Billabong
Bruce, Mary Grant
Billabong series (12)
Wings above the claypan
Upfield, Arthur William
Napoleon Bonaparte series (3)
Wings above the Diamantina
Upfield, Arthur William
Napoleon Bonaparte series (3)
Wings against the sky
Hough, Richard Alexander
World War II trilogy (1)
Wings and winged thoughts
Crowley, Carl Campbell
Nine winds series (2)
Wings of adventure
Adams, Eustace Lane
Andy Lane series (10)
Wings of darkness
Audemars, Pierre
Monsieur Pinaud series (6)
Wings of death
Boniface, Marjorie
Sheriff Hiram Odom series (3)
Wings of desire
Dekobra, Maurice
Lady Diana trilogy (1)
Wings of fear
Keene, Carolyn
Nancy Drew files series (13)
Wings of fire
Zeybel, Henry
Gunship series (3)
Wings of fortune
Johns, William Earl
Biggles series (2)
Wings of madness
Philips, Judson Pentecost
Peter Styles series (4)
Wings of omen
Asprin, Robert Lynn
Sanctuary series (6)
Wings of peace
Creasey, John
Doctor Palfrey series (10)
Wings of Pegasus
McCaffrey, Anne
Pegasus series (2)
Wings of romance
Johns, William Earl
Steeley Delaroy series (5)
Wings of the black death
Stockbridge, Grant
Richard Wentworth series (3)
Wings of the Coast Guard
Theiss, Lewis Edwin
Air mail series (6)
Wings of the Eagle
Dorer, Nancy
Eagle series (3)
Wings of the Hawk
James, Leigh Franklin
John Cooper Baines series (2)
Wings of the morning
Van de Water, Frederic Franklin
American Revolution series (2)
Wings of the navy
Adams, Eustace
Air combat series (6)
Wings of the Navy
Adams, Eustace Lane
Andy Lane series (14)
Wings of to-morrow
Traill, Peter
Mister Prentice trilogy (2)
Wings of victory
Hough, Richard Alexander
World War II trilogy (3)
Wings over enemy lines
Thomas, Barry
Wings series (2)
Wings over Europe
Waite, Jon
Warriors of America trilogy (2)
Wings over Japan
Cook, Canfield
Lucky Terrell series (6)
Wings over Spain
Johns, William Earl
Biggles series (17)
Wings over the outback
Leyland, Eric
Max and Scrap series (8)
Wings over Witchend
Saville, Malcolm
Lone Pine Five Club series (9)
Winifred Bertram and the world she lived in
Charles, Elizabeth
Bertram family series (1)
Winifred's neighbors
Rhoades, Nina
Winifred series (1)
Winkie and Blinkie Bear
Schermele, Willy
Winkie series (3)
Winkie and Brownie Bright-Eyes
Schermele, Willy
Winkie series (12)
Winkie and his magic flute
Schermele, Willy
Winkie series (6)
Winkie and his woodland friends
Schermele, Willy
Winkie series (4)
Winkie and Ruby Robin
Schermele, Willy
Winkie series (2)
Winkie and the secret passage
Schermele, Willy
Winkie series (11)
Winkie and the wily fox
Schermele, Willy
Winkie series (7)
Winkie and Twinkie Twiddle
Schermele, Willy
Winkie series (5)
Winkie and Wobbleena
Schermele, Willy
Winkie series (10)
Winkie and Woolly Wopsie
Schermele, Willy
Winkie series (1)
Winkie in Toadstool Town
Schermele, Willy
Winkie series (9)
Winkie lost in the deep, deep woods
Schermele, Willy
Winkie series (8)
Winkie, the wily woodchuck
Barnum, Richard
Kneetime animal stories series (17)
Winking at the brim
Mitchell, Gladys
Dame Beatrice Bradley series (48)
Winking ruby mystery
Keene, Carolyn
Dana girls series (19)
Winklepicker
Moon, Heather
Winklepicker series (1)
Winklepicker and Paper Dart
Moon, Heather
Winklepicker series (3)
Winklepicker goes south
Moon, Heather
Winklepicker series (2)
Winkybird
Slater, Jim
A Mazing Monster series (7)
Winner
Deal, Borden
Bookman trilogy (3)
Levy, Elizabeth
Gymnasts series (4)
Mottram, Ralph Hale
Spanish Farm series (3)
Winner all the way
Goudge, Eileen
Seniors series (3)
Winner take all
Fairlie, Gerard
Johnny Macall series (1)
Lowell, Anne Hunter
Sorority girls series (6)
Roberts, J R
Gunsmith series (85)
Winner takes all
Dixon, Franklin W
Hardy boys case files series (85)
Green, Simon
Hawk and Fisher series (2)
Winner takes nothing
Mackenzie, Pierce
T G Horne series (3)
Winners and losers
Grover, Marshall
Larry and Stretch series (155)
Pearson, Michael A
Winners and losers series (1)
Winners never quit
Aaseng, Nathan
Sports heroes series (4)
Winnetou, the Apache knight
May, Karl Friedrich
Winnetou trilogy (1)
Winnie O'Wynn and the dark horses
Atkey, Bertram
Winnie O'Wynn series (2)
Winnie O'Wynn and the wolves
Atkey, Bertram
Winnie O'Wynn series (1)
Winnie-the-Pooh
Milne, Alan Alexander
Pooh series (1)
Winnie-the-Pooh and some bees
Milne, Alan Alexander
Piglet series (1)
Winnin men of tennis
Aaseng, Nathan
Sports heroes series (9)
Winnin women of tennis
Aaseng, Nathan
Sports heroes series (10)
Winning
Petersen-Schaefer, Karin
Melody series (2)
Winning forward pass
Lawton, Charles
Clarkeville series (3)
Winning hand
Cutter, Tom
Tracker series (1)
Winning his game
Barbour, Ralph Henry
Grafton School trilogy (2)
Winning his spurs
Kellogg, Elijah
Whispering Pine series (4)
Winning his way
Coffin, Charles Carleton
Civil War trilogy (3)
Winning his Y
Barbour, Ralph Henry
Yardley Hall series (3)
Winning in the air
Cobb, Frank
Stars and Stripes series (1)
Winning is kids' stuff
Baker, Denis
Kids' stuff series (1)
Winning isn't always first place
Groten, Dallas
Winning series (1)
Winning pitcher
Porter, Mark
Win Hadley series (1)
Winning run
Bonehill, Ralph
Lakeport series (2)
Winning streak
Hughes, Dean
Angel Park All-Stars series (3)
Winning the War Cross
Cobb, Frank
Stars and Stripes series (3)
Winning touchdown
Chadwick, Lester
College sports series (4)
Winnowing winds
Bailey, Gerald Earl
Nurlingas series (2)
Winona of Camp Karonya
Widdemer, Margaret
Winona series (2)
Winona of the camp fire
Widdemer, Margaret
Winona series (1)
Winona on her own
Widdemer, Margaret
Winona series (5)
Winona's dreams come true
Widdemer, Margaret
Winona series (6)

Winona's pony cart
Lovelace, Maud Hart
Betsy Ray series (10)

Winona's war farm
Widdemer, Margaret
Winona series (3)

Winona's way
Widdemer, Margaret
Winona series (4)

Winslow's freight
Trimnell, Robert L
Loner series (3)

Winsome for winners
Murphy, David John
Winsome series (1)

Winsome Winnie, and other new nonsense novels
Leacock, Stephen
Nonsense novels series (2)

Winston Churchill, a collection of contemporary documents
Gilbert, Martin
Winston S Churchill series (8)

Winston Churchill murder
Netzen, Klaus
Killers series (2)

Winston Street mystery
Carstairs, Henry
Lydford Long series (13)

Winter
Allington, Richard L
Beginning to learn series (15)
Best, Jacqueline
Paul and Fritzi's year series (4)
Blyton, Enid
Round the year series (4)

Winter adventure
Pudney, John
Fred and I series (11)

Winter adventures of thre boys in Great Lone Land
Young, Egerton Ryerson
Three boys series (2)

Winter and Christmas
Haughton, Rosemary
Christian year series (4)

Winter and rough weather
Stevenson, Dorothy Emily
Drumberley trilogy (3)

Winter and the Wanderer
Gaston, Bill
Lieutenant Jason Winter series (5)

Winter and the widowmakers
Gaston, Bill
Lieutenant Jason Winter series (4)

Winter and the Wild Rover
Gaston, Bill
Lieutenant Jason Winter series (3)

Winter and the Wild Witch
Gaston, Bill
Lieutenant Jason Winter series (2)

Winter at Cherry-Tree Farm
Kent, Margaret
Four seasons at Cherry-Tree Farm series (4)

Winter at Foxendale
Kitchen, Fred
Foxendale series (3)

Winter at Piukey's Steep
Roberts, Constance Evelyn
Pikey's Steep series (4)

Winter at Sheepfold Farm
Williams, Susan
Sheepfold Farm series (3)

Winter bouquet
Tweedsmuir, Susan Buchan
Edwardian lady series (2)

Winter camp
Hill, Kirkpatrick
Toughboy sertties (2)

Winter caravan
Bellhouse, Lucy Wilered
Caravan series (6)

Winter carnival
Pascal, Francine
Sweet Valley High super series (4)
Sweet Valley twins super special series (2)

Winter count
Manfred, Frederick
Winter count series (1)

Winter count II
Manfred, Frederick
Winter count series (2)

Winter danger
Steele, William Owen
Tennessee frontier series (2)

Winter diary of a country rat
Firmin, Peter
Country rat series (1)

Winter donkey
Towers, Joyce
Donkey series (3)

Winter doves
Cook, David
Walter series (2)

Winter drift
Young, Carter Travis
Cullom Blaine series (3)

Winter fire
Porter, Rose
Winter fire series (2)

Winter grass
Owen, Dean
Bonanza series (4)

Winter harvest
Home, Michael
East Anglia seasons series (3)

Winter hawk
Thomas, Craig
Firefox series (3)

Winter hell
Sherman, Jory
Gunn series (5)

Winter holiday
Ransome, Arthur
Swallows and Amazons series (4)

Winter in Eden
Harrison, Harry
Eden trilogy (2)

Winter in France
Masson, Sophie
Seyrac family series (3)

Winter in the morning
Bauman, Janina
Winter in the morning series (1)

Winter in Thrush Green
Read, *Miss*
Thrush Green series (2)

Winter is in July
Napier, Elma
Youth and winter series (2)

Winter journey
Anson, Brian
Gus and Gilly series (2)
Gee, Herbert Leslie
Friendly series (1)

Winter king
Carl, Lillian Stewart
Sabazel trilogy (2)

Winter kitchen, Mrs Appleyard's of course
Kent, Louise Andrews
Appleyard family series (5)

Winter murder case
Van Dine, S S
Philo Vance series (12)

Winter noisy book
Brown, Margaret Wise
Noisy book series (6)

Winter of enchantment
Walker, Victoria
Hadlows series (1)

Winter of madness
Walker, David Harry
Dougal Trocher series (1)

Winter of magic's return
Service, Pamela F
Winter series (1)

Winter of the Wildcat
Gaston, Bill
Lieutenant Jason Winter series (1)

Winter on the Johnny Smoker
Comfort, Mildred Houghton
Dustin family series (1)

Winter people
Ehle, John
North Carolina series (7)

Winter pony
Doty, Jean Slaughter
Pony series (1)

Winter prey
Sandford, John
Lucas Davenport series (5)

Winter sisters
Goodwin, Suzanne
Winter sisters series (2)

Winter song
Gellis, Roberta
Royal dynasty series (2)
Hanley, James
Furys chronicle series (4)

Winter sports
Jones, Nicholas
Wind in the willows series (10)

Winter spring
Goodwin, Suzanne
Winter sisters series (1)

Winter story
Barklem, Jill
Brambly Hedge series (1)

Winter touch
Egleton, Clive
Charles Winter series (1)

Winter twilight
Angoff, Charles
Polonsky family series (8)

Winter wears a shroud
Chapman, Robert
Rex Banner series (3)

Winter wild
Henrey, Madeleine
Madeleine reminiscences series (10)

Winter women murders
Kaufelt, David A
Wyn Lewis series (2)

Winter world
Mills, Carla Johnson
Winter world series (1)

Winter worm business
Giff, Patricia Reilly
Casey Valentine series (4)

Wintercombe
Belle, Pamela
Wintercombe series (1)

Winterkill
Lesley, Craig
Danny and Jack Kachiah series (1)
Thompson, David
Nathaniel King series (15)

Winterking
Hazel, Paul
Finnbranch trilogy (3)

Wintermind
Kaye, Marvin
Solitude trilogy (2)

Winter's end
Silverberg, Robert
New springtime series (1)

Winter's love song
Bale, Karen A
Sweet Medicine's prophecy series (3)

Winters of content
Sitwell, Osbert
Discursions series (2)

Winter's Rose
Fairburn, Eleanor
Wars of the Roses series (4)

Winter's tail
English, David
Bunburys series (4)

Wintersmoke
Davey, Thyrza
Yonderbeyonder series (2)

Wintersmoon
Walpole, Hugh
London Group series (6)

Wintersol
Earnshaw, Anthony
Wintersol series (2)

Winterton holiday cruise
Potter, Dora Joan
Winterton School series (5)

Wintle's Wonders
Streatfeild, Noel
Shoes series (9)

Wintry sea
Croft-Cooke, Rupert
Sensual life series (20)

Wipe-out
Cleary, Denis
Breakenridge series (3)

Wipeout
Daniels, Lee
Surf city series (1)
Dixon, Franklin W
Hardy boys series (96)
Tiger, John
I spy series (6)

Wire tappers
Stringer, Arthur
James Durkin series (1)

Wireless in Toytown
Beaman, Sydney George Hulme
Toytown series (10)

Wisconsin!
Ross, Dana Fuller
Wagons West series (19)

Wisconsin country
Derleth, August
Sac Prairie series (16)

Wisconsin earth
Derleth, August
Sac Prairie series (11)

Wisconsin harvest
Derleth, August
Wisconsin series (5)

Wisconsin in their bones
Derleth, August
Sac Prairie series (14)

Wisdom of Father Brown
Chesterton, Gilbert Keith
Father Brown series (2)

Wisdom of serpents
Levitsky, Ronald
Nate Rosen series (2)

Wisdom of the wilderness
Roberts, Charles George Douglas
Wilderness series (1)

Wisdom's daughter
Haggard, Henry Rider
She series (1)

Wise child
Furlong, Monica
Wise child series (2)

Wise Owl's story
Uttley, Alison
Little Grey Rabbit series (6)

Wise woman's telling
Sampson, Fay
Daughter of Tintagel series (1)

Wish
Hoh, Diane
Nightmare Hall series (4)

Wish again, Big Bear
Margolis, Richard Jules
Big Bear series (1)

Wish and wonder
Redekopp, Elsa
Canadian village life series (1)

Wish for a pony
Edwards, Monica
Romney Marsh series (1)

Wish giver
Brittain, Bill
Coven Tree series (2)

Wish on the moon
Hader, Berta
Willow Hill series (6)

Wish you were dead
Chapman, Robert
Rex Banner series (8)
McCloy, Helen
Miguel Urizar series (2)

Wish you were here
Brown, Rita Mae
Mrs Murphy series (1)

Wishing-chair again
Blyton, Enid
Wishing-chair series (2)

Wishing horse of Oz
Thompson, Ruth Plumly
Oz series (28)

Wishing pear
Coatsworth, Elizabeth
Once-upon-a-time-in-America series (2)

Wishing pool
Lyon, Elinor
Jean and Anna series (2)

Wishing-ring man
Widdemer, Margaret
Rose-garden series (2)

Wishing star
Wells, Marian
Starlight trilogy (1)

Wishing stone stories
Burgess, Thornton Waldo
Wishing Stone series (3)

Wishing well
Wirt, Mildred Augustine
Penny Parker series (8)

Wishsong of Shannara
Brooks, Terry
Shannara series (3)

Wishstone and the wonderworkers
Cook, Hugh
Chronicles of an age of darkness series (6)

Wisp of wool and disk of silver
Upfield, Arthur William
Napoleon Bonaparte series (29)

Wistaria Street will soon be gone
Anthony, Jane
Wistaria Street series (1)

Wistful wanton
Muller, Paul
Paul Muller series (12)

Wit and wisdom of Hagar the horrible
Browne, Dik
Hagar the horrible series (52)

Witch
McQuinn, Donald E
Pacific Northwest trilogy (3)

Witch and the naughty princesses
Cass, Joan Evelyn
Molly Millikens series (2)

Witch baby
Block, Francesca Lia
Weetzie Bat series (2)

Witch family
Estes, Eleanor
Witch family series (1)

Witch finder
Birt, David
Stuarts series (17)

Witch-finder general
Bassett, Ronald
Margaret family series (1)

Witch from the sea
Carr, Philippa
Daughters of England series (3)

Witch goddess
Adams, Robert
Horseclans series (9)

Witch goes for gold
Wright, Ralph
Witch series (3)

Witch goes to school
Bridwell, Norman
Witch series (6)

Witch grows up
Bridwell, Norman
Witch series (5)

Witch herself
Naylor, Phyllis Reynolds
Witch's sister series (3)

Witch hill
Bradley, Marion Zimmer
Leslie Barnes series (3)

Witch Hill murder
Winslow, Pauline Glen
Superintendent Merlin Capricorn series (3)

Witch-hunt!
Reid, Desmond
Sexton Blake series (1500)

Witch in Cabin six
Kaye, Marilyn
Camp Sunnyside Friends series (7)

Witch in the wood
White, Terence Hanbury
Once and future king series (2)

Witch Miss Seeton
Carvic, Heron
Miss Emily Seeton series (3)
Miss Emily Seeton series (6)

Witch next door
Bridwell, Norman
Witch series (1)

Witch of Castlekerry
Jackson, Rosemary Elizabeth
Macgillan family series (3)

Witch of Lagg
Cheetham, Ann
Black harvest series (3)

Witch of Monopoly Manor
Barry, Margaret Stuart
Simon and the witch series (3)

Witch of Redesdale
Finlay, Winifred
Gillian Lindsay series (1)

Witch of Rhostshyl
Rivkin, J F
Silverglass series (3)

Witch of the dark gate
Jakes, John
Gavin Black series (2)

Witch of the Indies
Smith, David Claude
Black Vulmea series (2)

Witch of the low-tide
Carr, John Dickson
Metropolitan Police series (3)

Witch of the North
Jones, Courtway
King Arthur series (2)

Witch of Watergate
Adler, Warren
Fiona Fitzgerald series (5)

Witch of Witchery Wood
Cass, Joan Evelyn
Molly Millikens series (1)

Witch on holiday
Barry, Margaret Stuart
Simon and the witch series (4)

Witch Queen of Lochlann
Smith, George Henry
Annwn series (3)

Witch queen of Lochlann
Smith, George Henry
Duffus January series (2)

Witch Queen of Mongo
Bingham, Carson
Flash Gordon series (6)

Witch returns
Naylor, Phyllis Reynolds
Witch's sister series (6)

Witch shall be born
Howard, Robert Ervin
Conan series (22)

Witch switch
Barnes, Megan
Teen witch series (4)

Witch, the carpet and the boomash
Smith, Janet
Wakeley witch series (2)

Witch tree symbol
Keene, Carolyn
Nancy Drew series (33)
Witch VIP
Barry, Margaret Stuart
Simon and the witch series (5)
Witch water
Naylor, Phyllis Reynolds
Witch's sister series (2)
Witch weed
Naylor, Phyllis Reynolds
Witch's sister series (5)
Witch week
Jones, Diana Wynne
Chrestomanci series (3)
Witch Winnie
Champney, Elizabeth Williams
Witch Winnie series (1)
Witch Winnie at Shinnecock
Champney, Elizabeth Williams
Witch Winnie series (5)
Witch Winnie at Versailles
Champney, Elizabeth Williams
Witch Winnie series (6)
Witch Winnie in Holland
Champney, Elizabeth Williams
Witch Winnie series (7)
Witch Winnie in Paris
Champney, Elizabeth Williams
Witch Winnie series (4)
Witch Winnie in Spain
Champney, Elizabeth Williams
Witch Winnie series (9)
Witch Winnie in Venice
Champney, Elizabeth Williams
Witch Winnie series (8)
Witch Winnie's mystery
Champney, Elizabeth Williams
Witch Winnie series (2)
Witch Winnie's studio
Champney, Elizabeth Williams
Witch Winnie series (3)
Witch Wolf
Harris, Joel Chandler
Uncle Remus series (9)
Witch-woman
Cabell, James Branch
Dom Manuel and his descendants series (6)
Witch woman trilogy (3)
Witch Wood
Hale, Christopher
Lieutenant Bill French series (4)
Witch World
Norton, Andre
Estcarp series (1)
Witch World series (1)
Witchcraft for Panda One
Walker, Peter Norman
Panda One series (3)
Witchdance in Bavaria
Macleod, Robert
Jonathan Gaunt series (4)
Witches
Brown, Carter
Larry Baker series (4)
Witches abroad
Pratchett, Terry
Discworld series (12)
Witches' bane
Albert, Susan Wittig
China Bayles series (2)
Witches' cauldron
Phillpotts, Eden
Book of Avis series (2)
Witches go on a package holiday
Cass, Joan Evelyn
Molly Millikens series (6)
Witches' lost spell book
Cass, Joan Evelyn
Molly Millikens series (3)
Witches' moon
Verner, Gerald
Superintendent Robert Budd series (9)
Witches of Creaky-Cranky Castle
Whitehead, Victoria
Chimney witch series (4)
Witches of Hopper Street
Gondosch, Linda
Hopper Street trilogy (2)
Witches of Kregen
Prescot, Dray
Dray Prescot series (34)
Witch war series (2)
Witches of Notting Hill
Ballinger, W A
Sexton Blake series (1569)
Witches of Wenshar
Hambly, Barbara
Sun Wolf series (2)
Witches' pond
Wells, Susan
Anthony Ware series (4)
Witches' Sabbath
Cordell, Alexander
John Regan trilogy (2)
Sachs, Maurice
Witches' Sabbath series (1)
Witches' school
Cass, Joan Evelyn
Molly Millikens series (5)
Witchfinders
Comer, Ralph
Robert Lawson series (1)
Witchfires of Leth
Greenburg, Dan
Chronicles of Morgaine series (4)
Witching
Ravenswood, Fritzen
Kei series (1)
Witching hour
Krensky, Stephen
Wynd family trilogy (2)
Rice, Anne
Mayfair witches series (1)
Stevenson, Florence
Kitty Telfair series (1)
Witching of Dracula
Lory, Robert
Dracula horror series (6)
Witchline
Macleod, Robert
Andrew Laird series (7)
Witchmaster's key
Dixon, Franklin W
Hardy boys series (55)
Witchrock
Knox, Bill
Webb Carrick series (10)
Witch's big toe
Wright, Ralph
Witch series (1)
Witch's catalog
Bridwell, Norman
Witch series (4)
Witch's Christmas
Bridwell, Norman
Witch series (2)
Witch's curse
Clydesdale, Abby
Alys Heavers series (2)
Witch's eye
Charles, Steven
Private school series (3)
Naylor, Phyllis Reynolds
Witch's sister series (4)
Witch's funny bone
Wright, Ralph
Witch series (2)
Witch's gold
Elliot, Margaret
Witch's gold trilogy (2)
Witch's holiday club
Barry, Margaret Stuart
Simon and the witch series (7)
Witch's moon
Jackson, Giles
Nile Boyd series (1)
Witch's omen
Keene, Carolyn
Dana girls series (34)
Witch's revenge
Hinton, Nigel
Beaver Towers trilogy (2)
Witch's sister
Naylor, Phyllis Reynolds
Witch's sister series (1)
Witch's son
Morris, Ira J
Duke of Burgundy series (2)
Witch's Tower mystery
Kains, Josephine
Terry Spring series (5)
Witch's vacation
Bridwell, Norman
Witch series (3)
Witch's welcome
Skaldaspillir, Sigfriour
Eric Brighteyes series (2)
Witchwater
Wilson, Gertrude Mary
Inspector Lovick series (6)
Witchwood
Lloyd, Alan R
Kine trilogy (2)
Witchwood cradle
Friesner, Esther Mona
Chronicles of the twelve kingdoms series (3)
With a bare bodkin
Hare, Cyril
Francis Pettigrew series (2)
Inspector Mallett series (5)
With a feather on my nose
Burke, Billie
On my nose series (1)
With a madman behind me
Powell, Talmage
Ed Rivers series (3)
With a name like Lulu, who needs more trouble?
Springstubb, Tricia
Lulu series (1)
With a single spell
Watt-Evans, Lawrence
Legend of Ethshar series (2)
With a tangled skein
Anthony, Piers
Incarnations of immortality series (3)
With a vengeance
Shannon, Dell
Lieutenant Luis Mendoza series (12)
With airship and submarine
Collingwood, Harry
Flying Fish trilogy (2)
With all despatch
Kent, Alexander
Captain Richard Bolitho series (9)
With an eye to the future
Lancaster, Osbert
Memory series (2)
With Angus in the forest
Reid, Meta Mayne
Rathcapple series (3)
With bated breath
Campbell, Alice
Inspector Headcorn series (4)
With Boone on the frontier
Bonehill, Ralph
Flag and frontier series (1)
Frontier series (1)
With Carrington on the Bozeman Trail
Hanson, Joseph Mills
Among the Sioux series (2)
With Carson and Fremont
Sabin, Edward Legrand
Trail blazers series (4)
With cause enough
Fowler, Sydney
Mister Jellipot series (10)
With criminal instinct
Hardinge, Rex
Sexton Blake series (1256)
With Crockett and Bowie
Munroe, Kirk
White conqueror series (4)
With Custer in the Black Hills
Bonehill, Ralph
Flag and frontier series (4)
Flag of freedom series (6)
With deadly intent
Hendricksen, Louise
Doctor Amy Prescott series (1)
With extreme prejudice
Mather, Berkely
Peter Feltham series (2)
With fate conspire
Shupp, Mike
Destiny makers series (1)
With fire and sword
Sienkiewicz, Henryk
Polish history trilogy (1)
With flintlock and fife
Tomlinson, Everett Titsworth
Colonial series (1)
With freedom to Singapore
Gilmour, Oswald Wellington
Singapore series (2)
With friends like that
Chase, Emily
Canby Hall series (11)
With friends like these
Foster, Alan Dean
Friends like these series (1)
Kaye, Marilyn
Three of a kind series (1)
Roberts, Gillian
Amanda Pepper series (4)
With George Washington into the West
Sabin, Edward Legrand
Trail blazers series (13)
With Haig on the Somme
Strang, Herbert
Stories of the Great War series (4)
With intent
Henderson, Laurence
Sergeant Arthur Milton series (1)
With intent to deceive
Coles, Manning
Tommy Hambledon series (7)
With intent to kill
Cobb, Belton
Inspector Cheviot Burmann series (23)
Pentecost, Hugh
Pierre Chambrun series (17)
Shannon, Dell
Lieutenant Luis Mendoza series (22)
Vivian, Evelyn Charles
Inspector Head series (6)
With Joffre on the battle line
Kay, Ross
Big war series (4)
With Juliet in England
Richmond, Grace Smith
Juliet Robeson series (2)
With kitchen privileges
Kent, Louise Andrews
Appleyard family series (3)
With links of steel
Carter, Nicholas
Nicholas Carter series (192)
With love
Fitzgibbon, Theodora
With love series (1)
With love from hell
Groening, Matt
Life in hell series (7)
With love from Karen
Killilea, Marie
Karen series (2)
With Lyon in Missouri
Dunn, Byron Archibald
Young Missourians series (1)
With malice toward none
Morrow, Honore Willsie
Great Captain trilogy (2)
With mercy toward none
Cook, Glen
Dread Empire series (5)
With Moore at Corunna
Henty, George Alfred
Peninsular War series (1)
With murder for some
Huston, Howard Chauncey
Detective Charles A Baker series (1)
With murder in mind
Bream, Freda
Reverend Jabal Jarrett series (5)
With my little eye
Durrant, Digby
Hamish Oath series (1)
With one stone
Lockridge, Frances
Inspector Merton Heimrich series (15)
With option to die
Lockridge, Richard
Inspector Merton Heimrich series (20)
With Pershing at the Front
Kay, Ross
Big war series (7)
With Pershing for France
Fiske, James
World's war series (11)
With powder on my nose
Burke, Billie
On my nose series (2)
With Roger's Rangers
Browne, George Waldo
Woodranger series (4)
With Sam Houston in Texas
Sabin, Edward Legrand
Trail blazers series (8)
With shackles of fire
Carter, Nicholas
Nicholas Carter series (539)
With Sully into the Sioux Land
Hanson, Joseph Mills
Among the Sioux series (1)
With swords in their lips
Dyson, Elizabeth
Revill-Gordon series (1)
With Taylor on the Rio Grande
Bonehill, Ralph
Mexican war series (2)
With the army of the Potomac
Dunn, Byron Archibald
Young Virginians series (2)
With the Guards to Mexico, and other excursions
Fleming, Peter
Reflections and excursions series (2)
With the hero of the Marne
Fiske, James
World's war series (10)
With the Indians in the Rockies
Schultz, James Willard
Pitamaken series (2)
With the Red Eagle
Westall, William
Andreas Hofer series (1)
With the revolutionists in Bolivia
Craine, Edith Janice
Airplane Boys series (6)
With this ring
Newcomb, Ellsworth
Joan and Bill series (4)
Wells, Marian
Wedding dress series (2)
With Washington in the West
Stratemeyer, Edward L
Colonial series (1)
With Wendy at Winterton School
Potter, Dora Joan
Winterton School series (1)
With what motive?
Jacobs, Thomas Curtis Hicks
Detective Superintendent John Bellamy series (3)
With wings as eagles
Schulte, Elaine
California pioneer series (4)
Withdrawing room
Macleod, Charlotte
Sarah Kelling series (2)
Withered garland
Gibbs, Henry
Prior Report trilogy (3)
Withered Man
Deane, Norman
Bruce Murdoch series (4)
Within a budding grove, part one
Proust, Marcel
Remembrance of things past series (3)
Within a budding grove, part two
Proust, Marcel
Remembrance of things past series (4)
Within fourteen days
Graydon, William Murray
Sexton Blake series (182)
Within the enemy lines
Optic, Oliver
Blue and the Gray afloat series (2)
Within the gates
Burgin, George Brown
Monastery of Mahota series (2)
Within the harbour
Almedingen, Edith Martha
To-morrow will come trilogy (3)
Within the law?
Bresler, Fenton Shea
British law series (1)
Within the vault
Thayer, Lee
Peter Clancy series (46)
Within these walls
Douglas, Felicity
Faye Boswell series (1)
Without a clue
Carter, Nicholas
Nicholas Carter series (299)
Without a stair
Wallace, Kathleen
I walk alone series (2)
Without a trace
Berlitz, Charles
Bermuda Triangle series (2)
Dixon, Franklin W
Hardy boys case files series (31)
Without blood they die
Jones, G Wayman
Black Bat series (19)
Without due process
Jance, Judith A
J P Beaumont series (10)
Without lawful authority
Coles, Manning
Tommy Hambledon series (4)
Without mercy
Masterson, Louis
Morgan Kane series (1)
Without my cloak
O'Brien, Kate
Considine family series (1)
Without trumpet or drum
Sanders, John
Nicholas Pym series (3)
Without warning
Baker, William Howard
Sexton Blake series (1372)
Witness
Griffin, W E B
Badge of honor series (4)
Roberts, J R
Gunsmith series (131)
Uhnak, Dorothy
Christie Opara series (2)
Witness at the window
Barry, Charles
Superintendent Lawrence Gilmartin series (4)

Witness for the prosecution
Christie, Agatha
Hercule Poirot series (38)
Witness in peril
Marlett, Melba
Sarah O'Brien series (2)
Witness my death
Lewis, Royston
Inspector John Crow series (8)
Witness of bones
Tourney, Leonard
Matthew Stock series (7)
Witness of Canon Welcome
Raymond, Ernest
London gallery series (4)
Witness to murder
Dixon, Franklin W
Hardy boys case files series (20)
Harrison, Edwin
Sexton Blake series (1471)
Witness to the crime
Hunter, John
Sexton Blake series (1273)
Wizard
Varley, John
Gaea trilogy (2)
Wizard and the war machine
Watt-Evans, Lawrence
War surplus series (2)
Wizard and the warlord
Boyer, Elizabeth H
World of the Alfar series (4)
Wizard at large
Brooks, Terry
Magic Kingdom of Landover series (3)
Wizard children of Finn
Tannen, Mary
Finn series (1)
Wizard in waiting
Hughes, Robert Don
Pelmen trilogy (2)
Wizard of Boland
B B
Boland series (2)
Wizard of crime
Grant, Maxwell
Shadow series (169)
Wizard of death
Forrest, Richard
Lyon and Bea Wentworth series (2)
Wizard of Earthsea
Le Guin, Ursula Kroeber
Earthsea series (1)
Wizard of Fourth Street
Hawke, Simon
Wizard series (1)
Wizard of Lemuria
Carter, Lin
Thongor of Lemuria series (1)
Wizard of Linn
Van Vogt, Alfred Elton
Clane series (2)
Wizard of Oz
Baum, Lyman Frank
Oz series (1)
Wizard of Rentoro
Lord, Jeffrey
Richard Blade series (28)
Wizard of Rue Morgue
Hawke, Simon
Wizard series (4)
Wizard of Santa Fe
Hawke, Simon
Wizard series (6)
Wizard of storms
Van Arnam, Dave
Konarr series (2)
Wizard of Sunset Strip
Hawke, Simon
Wizard series (3)
Wizard of the cue
Carter, Nicholas
Nicholas Carter series (166)
Wizard of the wood
Trevor, Elleston
Woodlanders series (2)
Wizard of Tizare
Costello, Matthew John
Guardians of the Three series (3)
Wizard of Venus
Burroughs, Edgar Rice
Venus series (5)
Wizard of Whitechapel
Hawke, Simon
Wizard series (2)
Wizard of Woodworld
Kilworth, Garry
Woodworld series (1)
Wizard of Zao
Carter, Lin
Chronicles of Kylix series (2)
Wizard spawn
Cherryh, Carolyn Janice
Sword of knowledge series (2)
Sword of knowledge trilogy (2)
Wizard war
Cook, Hugh
Chronicles of an age of darkness series (1)
Wizard who was really a nuisance
Blyton, Enid
Little bedtime books series (8)
Wizard Winkle goes abroad
Holland, Muriel
Wizard Winkle series (4)
Wizard Winkle goes north
Holland, Muriel
Wizard Winkle series (2)
Wizard Winkle won't tell
Holland, Muriel
Wizard Winkle series (1)
Wizard Winkle's wishing ring
Holland, Muriel
Wizard Winkle series (3)
Wizard world
Zelazny, Roger
Changeling series (2)
Wizardry compiled
Cook, Rick
Wizard's bane series (2)
Wizardry cursed
Cook, Rick
Wizard's bane series (3)
Wizards and the warriors
Cook, Hugh
Chronicles of an age of darkness series (1)
Wizards and warriors
Miles, Ellen
Worlds of power series (5)
Wizard's bane
Cook, Rick
Wizard's bane series (1)
Wizard's eleven
Tepper, Sheri S
True game trilogy (3)
Wizard's mole
Strickland, Brad
Jeremy Moon series (3)
Wizards of Senchuria
Bulmer, Kenneth
Keys to the dimensions series (4)
Wizards of wonder
Stine, Harlan William
Magic micro adventure series (3)
Wizard's row
Shetterly, Will
Liavek series (3)
Wizenbeak
Gilliland, Alexis Arnaldus
Wizenbeak trilogy (1)
Wobble pop
Burningham, John
First words series (3)
Wobble to death
Lovesey, Peter
Sergeant Cribb and Constable Thackeray series (1)
Woe-begone little bear
Burgess, Thornton Waldo
Cubby Bear series (7)
Woffle, B.A.
Chaney, Jill
Woffle series (2)
Woggle-bug book
Baum, Lyman Frank
Oz series (51)
Wohldorf shipment
O'Hara, Patrick
Yangtse run series (2)
Wolf
Holt, Henry
Inspector Silver series (4)
Mackie, Charles
Stewarts of Badenoch series (1)
Rovin, Jeff
Roger Garrison series (2)
Terhune, Albert Payson
Sunnybank collies series (9)
Wolf and the buffalo
Kelton, Elmer
Tales of Texas series (12)
Wolf and the unicorn
Watson, Julia
Gentian trilogy (3)
Wolf at the door
Shelby, Graham
William Marshal series (2)
Wolf bell
Murphy, Shirley Rousseau
Children of Ynell series (2)
Wolf by the ears
Lewis, Royston
Inspector John Crow series (2)
Wolf country
Sharpe, Jon
Trailsman series (7)
Wolf Creek feud
Hardin, J D
Raider series (14)
Wolf Creek or bust
Grover, Marshall
Larry and Stretch series (390)
Wolf Creek Valley
Tuttle, Wilbur Coleman
Hashknife Hartley and Sleepy Stevens series (18)
Wolf cry
Snell, Leroy
Northwest stories series (3)
Wolf Cub Island
Styles, Showell
Red Six series (2)
Wolf deputy
Dunning, Hal
White Wolf series (5)
Wolf-dreams
Weaver, Michael D
Thyri trilogy (1)
Thyri trilogy (3)
Wolf fangs and fox dns
Torgersen, Don Arthur
Animal safari nature series (6)
Wolf howls murder
Stokes, Manning Lee
Barnabas Jones series (1)
Wolf hunt
Whiting, Charles
Spymaster series (1)
Wolf hunters
Curwood, James Oliver
Wolf hunters series (1)
Wolf in man's clothing
Eberhart, Mignon Good
Sarah Keate and Lance O'Leary series (7)
Wolf in shadow
Gemmell, David A
Sipstrassi tales series (1)
Wolf in sheep's clothing
Riggs, John Raymond
Garth Ryland series (5)
Wolf in the fold
Green, Simon
Hawk and Fisher series (4)
Loder, Vernon
Donald Cairn series (2)
Macneil, Duncan
James Ogilvie series (9)
Wolf in the shadows
Muller, Marcia
Sharon McCone series (14)
Wolf moon
Victor, Sam
Kilburn series (4)
Wolf-net
Graham, Winifred
Miss Woolfe series (3)
Wolf of the evenings
Graham, Winifred
Miss Woolfe series (1)
Wolf pack
Ellis, Wesley
Lone Star series (125)
Kessler, Leo
Submarine series (1)
Newton, Dwight Bennett
Jim Bannister series (6)
Thompson, David
Nathaniel King series (20)
Wolf pack of Lobo Butte
Tuttle, Wilbur Coleman
Hashknife Hartley and Sleepy Stevens series (18)
Wolf Pass
Longley, W B
Angel Eyes series (3)
Wolf path
Van Gieson, Judith
Neil Hamel series (4)
Wolf riders
Pringle, David
Warhammer series (3)
Wolf run
Kellogg, Elijah
Forest Glen series (2)
Wolf song
Fergusson, Harry
Santa Fe Trail trilogy (2)
Fergusson, Harvey
Followers of the sun trilogy (1)
Wolf-speaker
Pierce, Tamora
Daine series (2)
Wolf time
Shipway, George
Walter Tirel series (2)
Wolf to the slaughter
Rendell, Ruth
Chief Inspector Reginald Wexford series (3)
Wolf with no tail
Sharp, Allen
Storytrails series (23)
Wolf within
Carter, Nicholas
Nicholas Carter series (558)
Wolf, wolf!
Bell, Josephine
Amy Tupper series (1)
Wolf worlds
Cole, Allan
Sten series (2)
Wolfhelm
Knaak, Richard Allen
Dragonrealm series (3)
Wolfnight
Freeling, Nicolas
Henri Castang series (6)
Wolfpack trail
Field, Peter
Powder Valley series (70)
Wolfrun
Savarin, Julian Jay
Gordon Gallagher series (2)
Wolf's brother
Lindholm, Megan
Reindeer people series (2)
Wolf's claw
Holt, Henry
Inspector Silver series (4)
Wolf's Crag
Whitelaw, David
Peter Wells series (2)
Wolf's head
Benteen, John
Neal Fargo series (7)
Wolf's Head
Gilliat, Edward
Robin Hood series (2)
Wolfsong
Asprin, Robert Lynn
Elfquest series (3)
Pini, Richard
Elfquest series (3)
Wolfville
Lewis, Alfred Henry
Wolfville series (1)
Wolfville days
Lewis, Alfred Henry
Wolfville series (3)
Wolfville folks
Lewis, Alfred Henry
Wolfville series (6)
Wolfville nights
Lewis, Alfred Henry
Wolfville series (4)
Wolfville yarns
Lewis, Alfred Henry
Wolfville series (7)
Wolfwalker
Harper, Tara K
Wolfwalker series (1)
Wolfwinter
Swann, Thomas Burnett
Ancient history series (8)
Wolverine
Slade, Jack
Lassiter series (25)
Wolves and the lamb
Fletcher, Joseph Smith
Inspector Skarratt series (2)
Soutar, Andrew
Phineas Spinnet series (11)
Wolves and the lambs affair
Holly, Joan Hunter
Man from U.N.C.L.E. series (24)
Wolves of Aam
Curry, Jane Louise
Abaloc series (7)
Lek series (1)
Wolves of chaos
Macgrath, Harold
Cutty Clay series (2)
Wolves of Isle Royale
Torgersen, Don Arthur
Animal life stories series (6)
Wolves of Savernake
Marston, Edward
Gervase Bret and Ralph Delchard series (1)
Wolves of the sea
Leroux, Gaston
Cheri-Bibi series (1)
Wolves of Willoughby Chase
Aiken, Joan
Dido Twite series (1)
Wolves on the border
Charrette, Robert N
BattleTech series (6)
Woman
Anonymous
Pronoun series (9)
Gilman, George G
Adam Steele series (25)
Steele's war series (1)
Woman accused
Vickers, Roy
James Segrove series (2)
Woman at bay
Carter, Nicholas
Nicholas Carter series (333)
Woman at Belguardo
Erskine, Margaret
Inspector Septimus Finch series (12)
Woman at the mill
Davison, Frank Dalby
Man-Shy series (2)
Woman Ayisha
Mundy, Talbot
Jimgrim series (4)
Woman called Mary
Mann, Deborah
Early Christian series (1)
Reign of Herod Antipas trilogy (3)
Woman called Omega
Green, Hilary
Triple S agent series (1)
Woman Deborah
Askew, Alice
Deborah Krillet series (2)
Woman detective
Kerner, Annette
Woman detective series (1)
Woman errant
Wright, Mabel Osgood
Commuter's wife series (3)
Woman from Sarajevo
Andric, Ivo
Bosnian trilogy (3)
Woman from Sicily
Swinnerton, Frank
Prothero quartet (1)
Woman herself
Burnley, Judith
Wife series (3)
Woman hunt
Grover, Marshall
Larry and Stretch series (416)
Roberts, J R
Gunsmith series (3)
Woman in black
Adams, Herbert
Jimmy Haswell series (9)
Bentley, Edmund Clerihew
Philip Trent series (1)
Carter, Nicholas
Nicholas Carter series (454)
Ford, Leslie
Colonel John Primrose series (13)
Grace Latham series (13)
Woman in red
Gilbert, Anthony
Arthur Crook series (9)
Woman in the alcove
Green, Anna Katharine
Caleb Sweetwater series (2)
Woman in the case
Tracy, Louis
Inspector Furneaux series (12)
Woman in the dark
Hammett, Dashiell
Continental Op series (5)
Woman in the wardrobe
Antony, Peter
Mister Verity series (1)
Woman into wolf
Tucker, Terry
King Richard II series (1)
Woman is dead
King, Rufus
Lieutenant Valcour series (2)
Woman of Babylon
Hocking, Joseph
Religious questions series (3)
Woman of Cairo
Flagg, John
Hart Muldoon series (1)
Woman of destiny
Maddock, Stephen
Timothy Terrel series (1)
Woman of evil
Carter, Nicholas
Nicholas Carter series (254)
Woman of flowers
Shwartz, Susan
Heirs to Byzantium trilogy (2)
Woman of mystery
Carter, Nicholas
Nicholas Carter series (448)

Woman of Saigon
Saxon, Peter
Sexton Blake series (1609)
Woman of steel
Carter, Nicholas
Nicholas Carter series (255)
Woman of substance
Bradford, Barbara Taylor
Emma Harte series (1)
Woman of the horizon
Frankau, Gilbert
Peter Jackson series (1)
Woman of the Horseclans
Adams, Robert
Horseclans series (12)
Woman of thirty
Balzac, Honore de
Scenes of private life series (22)
Woman on the spot
Hunter, John
Sexton Blake series (1345)
Woman proposes
Housman, Laurence
Palace plays series (2)
Woman slaughter
Ferrars, Elizabeth
Virginia and Felix Freer series (6)
Woman spy
De Halsalle, Henry
Olga von Kopf series (2)
Woman to be loved
Mitchell, James
Jane Whitcomb series (1)
Woman trap
Janson, Hank
Hank Janson series (59)
Woman who fell from grace
Handler, David
Stewart Hoag series (4)
Woman who rides like a man
Pierce, Tamora
Song of the lioness series (3)
Woman who walked into the sea
Craig, Philip R
Martha's Vineyard series (2)
Woman with a record
Jackson, Lewis
Sexton Blake series (1161)
Woman with the velvet necklace
Dumas, Alexandre
Marie Antoinette series (6)
Woman with two smiles
Leblanc, Maurice
Arsene Lupin series (15)
Woman's estate
Gellis, Roberta
Heiress series (5)
Woman's hand
Carter, Nicholas
Nicholas Carter series (5)
Woman's own mystery
Wakefield, Hannah
Dee Street series (2)
Woman's place
Yorke, Katherine
Woman's place series (1)
Woman's story of the war
WAAC
WAAC series (1)
Woman's tragedy
Lynch, Lawrence L
Carl Masters series (2)
Woman's trials
Arthur, Timothy Shay
Household library series (5)
Wombat and the dingo
Smith, Ivan
Fire, drought and flood trilogy (2)
Wombats don't have Christmas
Dugan, Michael
Wombats series (2)
Wombles
Beresford, Elisabeth
Wombles series (1)
Wombles annual
Beresford, Elisabeth
Wombles series (11)
Wombles at work
Beresford, Elisabeth
Wombles series (5)
Wombles gift book
Beresford, Elisabeth
Wombles series (11)
Wombles go round the world
Beresford, Elisabeth
Wombles series (9)
Wombles go to the seaside
Beresford, Elisabeth
Wombles series (6)
Wombles in danger
Beresford, Elisabeth
Wombles series (4)
Wombles make a clean sweep
Beresford, Elisabeth
Wombles series (7)
Wombles of Wimbledon
Beresford, Elisabeth
Wombles series (8)
Wombles to the rescue
Beresford, Elisabeth
Wombles series (8)
Wombling free
Beresford, Elisabeth
Wombles series (11)
Women
Lundin, John Philip
Erotic autobiography series (1)
Women and super women
Cooper, Jilly
Super men and women series (2)
Women and the warlords
Cook, Hugh
Chronicles of an age of darkness series (3)
Women are like that
Jacobs, Thomas Curtis Hicks
Detective Superintendent John Bellamy series (7)
Temple Fortune series (10)
Women are skin deep
Whelton, Paul
Garry Dean series (4)
Women call, come home
Vesaas, Tarjei
Per Eilevson Bufast series (2)
Women, dope and murder
Daniel, Roland
Michael Grant series (7)
Women from Whitlock
Grover, Marshall
Larry and Stretch series (209)
Women hate till death
Janson, Hank
Hank Janson series (34)
Women in law
Smith, Betsy Covington
Breakthrough series (3)
Women in love
Lawrence, David Herbert
Brangwen family series (2)
Women in mid-life crisis
Conway, Jim
Mid-life crisis series (3)
Women in religion
Smith, Betsy Covington
Breakthrough series (1)
Women in television
Smith, Betsy Covington
Breakthrough series (2)
Women like to know
O'Hara, Kevin
Chico Brett series (8)
Women music makers
Nichols, Janet
Music makers series (2)
Women of Ashdon
Anand, Valerie
Bridges over time series (3)
Women of Dallas
Hirschfeld, Burt
Dallas series (4)
Women of Eden
Harris, Marilyn
Eden family series (4)
Women of no account
Burton, Betty
Nugent family series (3)
Women of Peasenhall
White, Reginald James
Inspector David Brock series (2)
Women of the Old Testament
Daniel, Rebecca
Our greatest heritage series (12)
Women swore revenge
Irwin, Inez Haynes
Patrick O'Brien series (5)
Won by magic
Carter, Nicholas
Nicholas Carter series (610)
Won by the sword
Henty, George Alfred
Thirty Years War series (2)
Wonder book for boys and girls
Hawthorne, Nathaniel
Wonder book series (1)
Wonder city of Oz
Neill, John Rea
Oz series (33)
Wonder for wise men
Nichols, Wallace Bertram
Henry VII series (1)
Wonder Mist
Bruce, Henry
Eurasian series (4)
Wonder of all the gay world
Barke, James
Immortal memory series (3)
Wonder of tomorrow
Witcomb, Nan
Thoughts of Nanushka series (6)
Wonder of war at sea
Rolt-Wheeler, Francis
Wonder of war series (3)
Wonder of war in the air
Rolt-Wheeler, Francis
Wonder of war series (1)
Wonder of war in the holy Land
Rolt-Wheeler, Francis
Wonder of war series (4)
Wonder of war on land
Rolt-Wheeler, Francis
Wonder of war series (2)
Wonder pigs of Jillian Jiggs
Gilman, Phoebe
Jillian Jiggs series (2)
Wonder-worker
Buckley, Eunice
Rex Anderson series (1)
Zero and Rosalind series (3)
Wonderflower of Utik
Mahr, Kurt
Perry Rhodan series (105)
Wonderful adventures of Arthur Gordon Pym
Poe, Edgar Allan
Arthur Gordon Pym series (1)
Wonderful adventures of Nils
Lagerlof, Selma
Nils series (1)
Wonderful birthday
Hurt, Freda Mary
Pinetops series (1)
Wonderful clouds
Sagan, Francoise
Josee and Bernard series (2)
Wonderful day
Coatsworth, Elizabeth
Sally Smith series (5)
Wonderful electric elephant
Montgomery, Frances Trego
Electric elephant series (1)
Wonderful Farm
Ayme, Marcel
Wonderful Farm series (1)
Wonderful flight to the mushroom planet
Cameron, Eleanor
Tyco Bass series (1)
Wonderful house
Mendel, Jo
Tucker family series (1)
Wonderful journey
Brown, Charles
John Bunyan series (1)
Wonderful lamp
Voegeli, Max
Adventures of Ali series (1)
Wonderful land of Up
Barton, Olive Roberts
Nancy and Nick series (1)
Wonderful penny stamp
Boden, Hilda
Anna and James series (1)
Wonderful scheme
Keeler, Harry Stephen
Marceau case trilogy (3)
Wonderful scheme of Mister Christopher Thorne
Keeler, Harry Stephen
Marceau case trilogy (3)
Wonderful stranger
Green, Roger Lancelyn
Spearlake children series (1)
Wonderful wizard of Oz
Baum, Lyman Frank
Oz series (1)
Wonderful world of Barry McKenzie
Humphries, Barry
Barry McKenzie series (1)
Wonderful world of Maggie Muggins
Grannan, Mary
Maggie Muggins series (10)
Wondering heart
Jennings, D K
Doctor Ralph Conway series (25)
Wonderland
Oates, Joyce Carol
Jules and Maureen Wendall trilogy (3)
Wonders Farm Gang
Williams, Zillah
Wonders Farm series (2)
Wonders of animal architecture
Lavine, Sigmund Arnold
Wonders of nature series (7)
Wonders of badgers
Lavine, Sigmund Arnold
Wonders of nature series (32)
Wonders of coyotes
Lavine, Sigmund Arnold
Wonders of nature series (31)
Wonders of draft horses
Lavine, Sigmund Arnold
Wonders of nature series (30)
Wonders of elephants
Lavine, Sigmund Arnold
Wonders of nature series (23)
Wonders of giraffes
Lavine, Sigmund Arnold
Wonders of nature series (33)
Wonders of goats
Lavine, Sigmund Arnold
Wonders of nature series (25)
Wonders of herbs
Lavine, Sigmund Arnold
Wonders of nature series (17)
Wonders of hippos
Lavine, Sigmund Arnold
Wonders of nature series (29)
Wonders of mice
Lavine, Sigmund Arnold
Wonders of nature series (22)
Wonders of peacocks
Lavine, Sigmund Arnold
Wonders of nature series (27)
Wonders of pigs
Lavine, Sigmund Arnold
Wonders of nature series (26)
Wonders of ponies
Lavine, Sigmund Arnold
Wonders of nature series (24)
Wonders of rhinos
Lavine, Sigmund Arnold
Wonders of nature series (28)
Wonders of terrariums
Lavine, Sigmund Arnold
Wonders of nature series (18)
Wonders of the animal disguises
Lavine, Sigmund Arnold
Wonders of nature series (5)
Wonders of the ant hill
Lavine, Sigmund Arnold
Wonders of nature series (3)
Wonders of the aquarium
Lavine, Sigmund Arnold
Wonders of nature series (1)
Wonders of the beetle world
Lavine, Sigmund Arnold
Wonders of nature series (6)
Wonders of the bison world
Lavine, Sigmund Arnold
Wonders of nature series (16)
Wonders of the camel world
Lavine, Sigmund Arnold
Wonders of nature series (21)
Wonders of the donkey world
Lavine, Sigmund Arnold
Wonders of nature series (20)
Wonders of the fly world
Lavine, Sigmund Arnold
Wonders of nature series (10)
Wonders of the hawk world
Lavine, Sigmund Arnold
Wonders of nature series (12)
Wonders of the hive
Lavine, Sigmund Arnold
Wonders of nature series (2)
Wonders of the owl world
Lavine, Sigmund Arnold
Wonders of nature series (11)
Wonders of the spider world
Lavine, Sigmund Arnold
Wonders of nature series (8)
Wonders of the wasps' nest
Lavine, Sigmund Arnold
Wonders of nature series (4)
Wonders of the world of bats
Lavine, Sigmund Arnold
Wonders of nature series (9)
Wonders of the world of cactus
Lavine, Sigmund Arnold
Wonders of nature series (15)
Wonders of the world of eagles
Lavine, Sigmund Arnold
Wonders of nature series (14)
Wonders of the world of horses
Lavine, Sigmund Arnold
Wonders of nature series (13)
Wonders of tigers
Lavine, Sigmund Arnold
Wonders of nature series (34)
Wonderwitch
Muir, Helen
Wonderwitch series (1)
Wonderwitch and the rooftop cats
Muir, Helen
Wonderwitch series (2)
Won't someone help Anna
Pascal, Francine
Sweet Valley twins series (69)
Wood magic
Jefferies, Richard
Bevis series (1)
Wood Street and Mary Ellen
Allan, Mabel Esther
Wood Street series (6)
Wood Street group
Allan, Mabel Esther
Wood Street series (2)
Wood Street helpers
Allan, Mabel Esther
Wood Street series (4)
Wood Street rivals
Allan, Mabel Esther
Wood Street series (3)
Wood Street secret
Allan, Mabel Esther
Wood Street series (1)
Woodbrook
Thomson, David
Highlands youth series (2)
Woodcraft
Simms, William Gilmore
American Revolution series (5)
Woodcraft Girls at Camp Doran
Roy, Lillian Elizabeth
Woodcraft Girls series (1)
Woodcraft Girls camping in Maine
Roy, Lillian Elizabeth
Woodcraft Girls series (3)
Woodcraft Girls in the city
Roy, Lillian Elizabeth
Woodcraft Girls series (2)
Woodcutter operation
Royce, Kenneth
Spider Scott series (6)
Woodcutter's house
Nathan, Robert
Barly fields series (2)
Wooden horse
Williams, Eric Ernest
Peter Howard series (2)
Wooden Indian
Wells, Carolyn
Fleming Stone series (42)
Wooden knight
Beaman, Sydney George Hulme
Toytown series (4)
Wooden shepherdess
Hughes, Richard Arthur Warren
Human predicament series (2)
Wooden spaceships
Shaw, Bob
Land and overland trilogy (2)
Woodentops at the fair
Bird, Maria
Woodentops series (2)
Woodentops washing day
Bird, Maria
Woodentops series (1)
Woodie Thorpe's pilgrimage, and other stories
Trowbridge, John Townsend
Toby Trafford series (2)
Woodland animals
Rippon, Angela
Learn with Victoria Plum series (4)
Woodland gospels according to Captain Beaky and his band
Lloyd, Jeremy
Captain Beaky and his band series (7)
Woodland Pack
Collins, Freda
Woodland Pack series (2)
Woodlanders
Hardy, Thomas
Novels of character and environment series (6)
Woods
Plante, David
Francoeur family series (2)
Woods of Windri
Needham, Violet
Windri series (1)
Woodshed
Heppenstall, Rayner
Harold Atha series (2)
Woodshed mystery
Warner, Gertrude Chandler
Boxcar children series (7)
Woodsmoke
Young, Francis Brett
N'dala series (2)
Woodstock magic
Lantz, Francess Lin
Swept away series (2)
Woofits' day out
Parkinson, Michael
Woofits series (1)
Woofits play cricket
Parkinson, Michael
Woofits series (2)

Woofits play football
Parkinson, Michael
Woofits series (3)
Wooing of Beppo Tate
Palmer, Cyril Everard
Beppo Tate series (1)
Wooing of Calvin Parks
Richards, Laura Elizabeth
Calvin Parks series (1)
Woorroo
Gard, Joyce
Mark Danby series (1)
Woozies go to school
Barry, Margaret Stuart
Woozy series (2)
Woozies go visiting
Barry, Margaret Stuart
Woozy series (5)
Woozies hold a frubard week
Barry, Margaret Stuart
Woozy series (6)
Woozies on television
Barry, Margaret Stuart
Woozy series (3)
Woozy
Barry, Margaret Stuart
Woozy series (1)
Woozy and the Weight Watchers
Barry, Margaret Stuart
Woozy series (4)
Worcester account
Behrman, Samuel Nathaniel
People in a diary series (1)
Word burners
Fletcher, Beryl
Khryse trilogy (1)
Word for world is forest
Le Guin, Ursula Kroeber
Hain series (3)
Word of the sorceress
Mitford, Bertram
Untuswa trilogy (3)
Word wise
Cranfield, Ingrid
Q challenge quiz series (2)
Words
Allington, Richard L
Beginning to learn series (20)
Words and music
Mayne, William
Choir school series (4)
Words can kill
Davis, Kenn
Carver Bascombe series (4)
Words for a murder perhaps
Candy, Edward
Inspector Burnival series (3)
Words for the wise
Arthur, Timothy Shay
Household library series (6)
Words have wings
Berrow, Norman
Michael Revel series (3)
Words to talk about
Lionni, Leon
Colors, letters, numbers and words to talk about series (4)
Words with power
Frye, Northrop
Bible and literature series (2)
Wordsmiths and the warguild
Cook, Hugh
Chronicles of an age of darkness series (2)
Work
Zola, Emile
Four Gospels series (2)
Work and play
Romains, Jules
Men of goodwill series (22)
Work and wedlock
Cooper, Jilly
Work and wedlock series (2)
Work and win
Optic, Oliver
Woodville series (4)
Work for a million
Zaremba, Eve
Helen Keremos series (2)
Work for the hangman
Graeme, Bruce
Theodore I Terhune series (4)
Work is hell
Groening, Matt
Life in hell series (2)
Work of the sun
Edgerton, Teresa
Green lion trilogy (3)
Work of the zoo doctors at the San Diego Zoo
Irvine, Georgeanne
Zoo world series (4)
Work suspended
Waugh, Evelyn
World War II series (4)
Workhouse child
Symons, Geraldine
Atalanta and Pansy series (3)
Working
Oxenbury, Helen
Baby board books series (9)
Working dogs
Goode, Angela
Working dogs series (3)
Working for the man
Dennis, Ralph
Jim Hardman series (7)
Working hard with the busy fire truck
Horowitz, Jordan
Working hard series (2)
Working hard with the mighty dump truck
Korman, Justine
Working hard series (1)
Working hard with the mighty loader
Horowitz, Jordan
Working hard series (3)
Working hard with the mighty mixer
Korman, Justine
Working hard series (3)
Working murder
Boylan, Eleanor
Henry Gamadge series (17)
Workshop of democracy
Burns, James Macgregor
American experiment series (2)
World ablaze
Sellers, Con
Men at arms series (3)
World aflame
Kern, Gregory
Cap Kennedy series (13)
World apart
Joseph, Marie
Daisy Penny series (2)
World asunder
Wallace, Ian
Pan Sagittarius series (4)
World below
Wright, Sydney Fowler
Amphibians series (2)
World bibliography of Sherlock Holmes and Doctor Watson
De Waal, Ronald Burt
Sherlock Holmes series (10)
World blackout
Millin, Sarah Gertrude
War diary series (2)
World called Camelot
Landis, Arthur Harold
Camelot series (1)
World championship mystery
Passingham, William John
Sexton Blake series (1332)
World changer
Byrne, Stuart James
Star Man series (1)
World class gymnast
Levy, Elizabeth
Gymnasts series (14)
World-class marathoners
Aaseng, Nathan
Sports heroes series (18)
World Cup murder
Resnicow, Herbert
Sport series (3)
World enough, and time
Kahn, James
New world trilogy (1)
World from below
Romains, Jules
Men of goodwill series (8)
World from rough stones
Macdonald, Malcolm
Stevenson family series (1)
World gone mad
Darlton, Clark
Perry Rhodan series (29)
World I never made
Farrell, James Thomas
Danny O'Neill series (2)
World in Amber
Orr, Alice
World in Amber series (1)
World in birth
Rolland, Romain
Soul enchanted series (5)
World in eclipse
Dexter, William
Denis Grafton series (1)
World in flames
Slater, Ian
WW III series (2)
World in peril
Chilton, Charles
Jet Morgan series (3)
World in ripeness
Bates, Herbert Ernest
World trilogy (3)
World in the attic
Morris, Wright
Lone Tree series (3)
World is full of divorced women
Collins, Jackie
World of men and women series (2)
World is full of married men
Collins, Jackie
World of men and women series (1)
World is my eggshell
Mulford, Philippa Greene
Abbey series (1)
World is not enough
Oldenbourg, Zoe
Corner-stone series (1)
World is young
Croft-Cooke, Rupert
Sensual life series (25)
World is your adventure
Romains, Jules
Men of goodwill series (20)
World keeps turning
Hardwick, Mollie
Duchess of Duke Street series (3)
World killers
McKinney, Jack
Sentinels series (4)
World menders
Biggle, Lloyd
Cultural survey series (2)
World of A
Van Vogt, Alfred Elton
Null-A series (1)
World of difference
Coles, Lesley
Star trek fan series (36)
Plagemann, Bentz
Wallace family series (4)
Turtledove, Harry
Videssos series (5)
World of God
Sanford, Doris
Advanced theology for very tiny persons series (4)
World of Jennie G
Ogilvie, Elisabeth May
Jennie Hawthorne series (2)
World of Jonny Briggs
Eadington, Joan
Jonny Briggs series (8)
World of Li'l Abner
Capp, Al
Li'l Abner series (1)
World of mazes
Vardeman, Robert Edward
Cenotaph Road series (3)
World of mists
Moore, Patrick
Gregory Quest series (2)
World of Nagaraj
Narayan, Rasipuram Krishnaswami
Malgudi series (17)
World of Null-A
Van Vogt, Alfred Elton
Null-A series (1)
World of promise
Tubb, Edwin Charles
Dumarest series (23)
World of Ptavvs
Niven, Larry
Known Space series (1)
World of Sherlock Holmes
Harrison, Michael
Life of Sherlock Holmes series (3)
World of silence
Coldsmith, Don
Spanish bit super series (3)
World of the sleeper
Wayman, Tony Russell
Dreamhouse series (1)
World of the Starwolves
Hamilton, Edmond
Starwolf trilogy (3)
World of the Wombles
Beresford, Elisabeth
Wombles series (10)
World of Thrush Green
Read, *Miss*
Thrush Green series (10)
World of Tiers
Farmer, Philip Jose
World of Tiers series (3)
World of Tiers series (5)
World of Tim Frazer
Durbridge, Francis
Tim Frazer series (1)
World of upstairs, downstairs
Hardwick, Mollie
Upstairs, downstairs series (13)
World of wonderful reality
Thurston, Ernest Temple
John Grey series (2)
World of wonders
Davies, Robertson
Deptford trilogy (3)
World Series
Tunis, John Roberts
Roy Tucker series (2)
World-shakers
Reid, Desmond
Sexton Blake series (1501)
World shuffler
Laumer, Keith
Lafayette O'Leary series (2)
World to win
Sinclair, Upton
World's end series (7)
World too wide
McDonald, Gregory
Time squared quartet (1)
World War I flying ace
Mueller, Richard
Time machine series (24)
World War II code breaker
Lerangis, Peter
Time machine series (25)
World War III
Harris, Brian
World War Three series (3)
Stanley, John
World War Three series (3)
World War III game
Stivers, Dick
Able Team series (22)
World without end
Haldeman, Joe
Star trek originals sequels series (11)
Thomas, Helen
Under storm's wing trilogy (2)
World without men
Maine, Charles Eric
World without men series (1)
World without mercy
Voltz, William
Perry Rhodan series (131)
World wreckers
Bradley, Marion Zimmer
Darkover series (17)
Worldbreaker
Milton, Joseph
Bart Gould series (3)
Worldover School
Goodman, Montague
Wantoknow series for boys (4)
Worlds
Haldeman, Joe
Marianne O'Hara series (1)
Worlds apart
Chase, Ilka
Travel series (7)
Haldeman, Joe
Marianne O'Hara series (2)
Kelley, Leo Patrick
Space police series (2)
Lach-Szyrma, Wladislaw Somerville
Venus series (3)
World's best party games
Barry, Sheila Anne
World's best games series (2)
World's best travel games
Barry, Sheila Anne
World's best games series (1)
World's end
Sinclair, Upton
World's end series (1)
World's End
Vinge, Joan Dennison
Snow Queen series (2)
Worlds end and after
Karl, Jean Edna
Future past series (1)
World's End in winter
Dickens, Monica
Fielding family series (3)
World's End was home
Chauncy, Nan
Tasmania series (2)
World's Fair
Tedrow, Thomas L
Days of Laura Ingalls Wilder series (5)
World's Fair goblin
Robeson, Kenneth
Doc Savage series (39)
Worlds in collision
Velikovsky, Immanuel
Worlds in collision series (1)
World's my football pitch
Wright, Billy
Football captain series (2)
Worlds of color
Du Bois, William Edward Burghardt
Black flame trilogy (3)
Worlds of the Federation
Johnson, Shane
Star trek, the next generation sequels series (3)
Worlds of the Imperium
Laumer, Keith
Mister Curlon series (1)
Worlds of wonder
Johns, William Earl
Rex Clinton series (9)
Worlds within
Glaskin, Gerald Marcus
Christos experience trilogy (2)
Worldwarp
Carmichael, Claire
Virtual realities trilogy (3)
Worm and the ring
Burgess, Anthony
Richard Emmis series (4)
Worm day
Ziefert, Harriet
Mister Rose's class series (3)
Worm of death
Blake, Nicholas
Nigel Strangeways series (14)
Worm of doubt
Meek, Margaret Reid Duncan
Lennox Kemp series (5)
Worm Ouroboros
Eddison, Eric Rucker
Zimiamvian trilogy (3)
Worm turns
Douglas, Arthur
Jonathan Craythorne series (4)
Worm turns at Sugar Creek
Hutchens, Paul
Sugar Creek Gang series (32)
Wormball
Slater, Jim
A Mazing Monster series (8)
Worms
Berg, Leila
Small world series (3)
Worms must wait
Wainwright, John
Northern Police series (6)
Superintendent Charles Ripley series (2)
Worms of the earth
Howard, Robert Ervin
Bran Mak Morn trilogy (1)
Tales of the Picts series (2)
Worral investigates
Johns, William Earl
Worrals series (11)
Worrals carries on
Johns, William Earl
Worrals series (2)
Worrals down under
Johns, William Earl
Worrals series (8)
Worrals flies again
Johns, William Earl
Worrals series (3)
Worrals goes afoot
Johns, William Earl
Worrals series (9)
Worrals goes east
Johns, William Earl
Worrals series (5)
Worrals in the wastelands
Johns, William Earl
Worrals series (10)
Worrals in the wilds
Johns, William Earl
Worrals series (7)
Worrals of the islands
Johns, William Earl
Worrals series (6)
Worrals of the W.A.A.F.
Johns, William Earl
Worrals series (1)
Worrals on the war-path
Johns, William Earl
Worrals series (4)
Worried widow
Hammond, Gerald
Keith Calder series (11)
Worry warts
Gleitzman, Morris
Misery guts series (2)
Worse than a crime
Burton, Anne
Richard Trenton series (3)
Worse than death
Bedford, Jean
Anna Southwood series (1)
Lamb, Lynton
Superintendent Quill and Inspector Glover series (2)

Marvin, James W
Crow series (2)
Worse than Rotten Ralph
Gantos, Jack
Rotten Ralph series (2)
Worse than wanton
Owen, Roderic
Manahoa series (2)
Worse than Willie
Stevenson, James
Grandfather's problems series (3)
Worse things waiting
Wellman, Manly Wade
Silver John series (6)
Worshipful Lucia
Benson, Edward Frederic
Lucia Billson series (6)
Worst best school year ever
Robinson, Barbara
Herdman family series (2)
Worst case on record
Carter, Nicholas
Nicholas Carter series (253)
Worst day ever
Bradman, Tony
Dilly series (5)
Worst day of your life
Packard, Edward
Choose your own adventure series (100)
Worst enemy
Hackforth-Jones, Gilbert
Submarine Service series (7)
Macdonnell, James Edmond
Captain Peter Bentley series (43)
Worst man in the world
Horler, Sydney
Paul Vivanti series (3)
Worst person in the world
Stevenson, James
Worst person in the world series (1)
Worst person in the world at Crab Beach
Stevenson, James
Worst person in the world series (2)
Worst person's Chrismas
Stevenson, James
Worst person in the world series (3)
Worst way to die
Rossi, Bruno
Sharpshooter series (4)
Worst Witch
Murphy, Jill
Worst Witch series (1)
Worst Witch strikes again
Murphy, Jill
Worst Witch series (2)
Worsted viper
Mitchell, Gladys
Dame Beatrice Bradley series (15)
Worth his while
Blanchard, Amy Ella
Lad and Lassie (3)
Worth wile
Wren, Percival Christopher
Khairastan series (2)
Major Hazelrigg series (2)
Worthing chronicle
Card, Orson Scott
Worthing chronicles series (2)
Worthing saga
Card, Orson Scott
Worthing chronicles series (2)
Worzel Gummidge
Todd, Barbara Euphan
Worzel Gummidge series (1)
Worzel Gummidge again
Todd, Barbara Euphan
Worzel Gummidge series (2)
Worzel Gummidge and Aunt Sally
Waterhouse, Keith
Worzel Gummidge series (17)
Worzel Gummidge and Saucy Nancy
Todd, Barbara Euphan
Worzel Gummidge series (4)
Worzel Gummidge and the railway scarecrows
Todd, Barbara Euphan
Worzel Gummidge series (7)
Worzel Gummidge and the treasure ship
Todd, Barbara Euphan
Worzel Gummidge series (9)
Worzel Gummidge at the circus
Todd, Barbara Euphan
Worzel Gummidge series (8)
Worzel Gummidge at the fair
Waterhouse, Keith
Worzel Gummidge series (13)
Worzel Gummidge down under
Waterhouse, Keith
Worzel Gummidge series (19)
Worzel Gummidge goes to the seaside
Waterhouse, Keith
Worzel Gummidge series (19)
Worzel Gummidge takes a holiday
Todd, Barbara Euphan
Worzel Gummidge series (5)
Worzel Gummidge, the scarecrow of Scatterbrook Farm
Todd, Barbara Euphan
Worzel Gummidge series (2)
Worzel Gummidge's television adventures
Waterhouse, Keith
Worzel Gummidge series (12)
Worzel's birthday
Waterhouse, Keith
Worzel Gummidge series (15)
Wotan's wedge
Gerard, Francis
Sir John Meredith series (10)
Wouldbegoods
Nesbit, Edith
Bastable family series (2)
Wounded buzzard on Christmas eve
Erickson, John R
Hank the cowdog series (13)
Wounded land
Donaldson, Stephen Reeder
Second chronicles of Thomas Covenant series (1)
Wounded sky
Duane, Diane
Star trek series (13)
Woundhealer's story
Saberhagen, Fred
Book of lost swords series (1)
Wounds of treason
Vinter, Michael
Barry Kegan series (3)
Woven web
Audemars, Pierre
Monsieur Pinaud series (8)
Wrack and rune
Macleod, Charlotte
Professor Peter Shandy series (3)
Wrack at Tidesend
Sitwell, Osbert
England reclaimed series (2)
Wraith
Macdonald, Philip
Colonel Anthony Ruthven Gethryn series (7)
Wraith board
Bischoff, David
Gaming magi series (2)
Wraiths and changelings
Mitchell, Gladys
Dame Beatrice Bradley series (53)
Wrangle Creek
Grover, Marshall
Larry and Stretch series (423)
Wranglers
Willoughby, Lee Davis
Making of America series (31)
Wrap it up
Dean, Amber
Albie Harris series (4)
Wrath
Ham, Bob
Overload series (2)
Wrath of Ashar
Wells, Angus
Kingdoms trilogy (1)
Wrath of Fu-Manchu, and other stories
Rohmer, Sax
Fu-Manchu series (15)
Wrath of Garde
La Plante, Jerry
Chameleon series (1)
Wrath of grapes
Wibberley, Leonard
Grand Fenwick series (2)
Wrath of Khan
McIntyre, Vondra Neil
Star trek series (7)
Roddenberry, Gene
Star trek moving picture series (2)
Wrath to come
Mackenzie, Nigel
Professor Christopher Fenton series (2)
Wreath for a redhead
Chambers, Peter
Mark Preston series (2)
Wreath for America
Raine, Richard
David Martini series (1)
Wreath for Miss Wong
Leader, Charles
David Chan series (3)
Wreath for Rivera
Marsh, Ngaio
Inspector Roderick Alleyn series (15)
Wreath for the bride
Lang, Maria
Christer Wick series (3)
Wreath for the innocents
Ebejer, Francis
Lucija and Rosie series (1)
Wreath for the lady
Holt, Henry
Inspector Silver series (15)
Mike Logan series (2)
Wreath for the Maltese innocents
Ebejer, Francis
Lucija and Rosie series (1)
Wreath from Bangkok
Leader, Charles
David Chan series (2)
Wreath of bones
Chance, John Newton
Jonathan Blake series (21)
Wreath of camellias
Mair, George Brown
David Grant series (8)
Wreath of cherry blossom
Leader, Charles
David Chan series (4)
Wreath of cloud
Murasaki Shibuku
Genji series (3)
Wreath of lords and ladies
Fraser, James
Inspector Bill Aveyard series (7)
Wreath of poppies
Leader, Charles
David Chan series (1)
Wreath of roses
Blackburn, John
General Charles Kirk series (6)
Wreath of water-lilies
Flower, Pat
Inspector Swinton series (3)
Wreck
Ethel
Wreck series (1)
Wreck of the Chancellor
Verne, Jules
J R Kazallon series (1)
Wreck of Westminster Abbey
Croft, Herbert
Abbey of Kilkhampton series (3)
Wrecked on a coral island
Houston, Edwin James
Pacific shipwreck series (2)
Wrecked on Cannibal Island
Moore, Fenworth
Jerry Ford series (1)
Wrecked on the Goodwins
Sea-Lion
Tiger Ransome series (2)
Wrecker's Tower game
Blyton, Enid
Famous Five adventure games series (2)
Wrecking crew
Hamilton, Donald
Matt Helm series (2)
Wren Helen
Carter, Dorothy
Wren Helen series (1)
Wren Helen sails north
Carter, Dorothy
Wren Helen series (3)
Wren Helen sails south
Carter, Dorothy
Wren Helen series (2)
Wrens on the trail
Judd, Alfred
Wrens series (2)
Wrens to the rescue
Judd, Alfred
Wrens series (1)
Wrestling
Gutman, Bill
Go for it series (5)
Wrestling with obedience
Gage, Joy Pennock
Obedience series (2)
Wrexham's romance
Ganpat
Harry Lake series (2)
Wrightsville murders
Queen, Ellery
Ellery Queen series (44)
Wrinkle in time
L'Engle, Madeleine
Meg Murry series (1)
Wrinkled people
Balzac, Honore de
Scenes of provincial life series (5)
Writ in water
Grier, Sydney Carlyon
Century series (5)
Write murder down
Lockridge, Richard
Nathan Shapiro series (9)
Write off the redhead
Brody, Marc
Marc Brody series (63)
Write on Rosy
Greenwald, Sheila
Rosy Cole series (4)
Writers in crisis
Geismar, Maxwell
American novel series (3)
Writer's notebook
Maugham, William Somerset
Summing up trilogy (3)
Writing
Allington, Richard L
Beginning to learn series (13)
Writing on the hearth
Harnett, Cynthia
Fifteenth century London series (2)
Writing on the wall
Adams, Herbert
Major Roger Bennion series (17)
Written for Elizabeth
Morrison, Margaret
Elizabeth Conway series (1)
Written in blood
Carter, Nicholas
Nicholas Carter series (450)
Written in dust
Burton, Miles
Inspector Arnold and Desmond Merrion series (21)
Wrong body
Gilbert, Anthony
Arthur Crook series (23)
Wrong case
Crumley, James
Milo Milodragovitch series (1)
Wrong Chalet School
Brent-Dyer, Elinor Mary
Chalet School series (24)
Wrong chemistry
Keene, Carolyn
Nancy Drew files series (42)
Wrong confessed
Bradley, Mary Emily Neely
Proverb trilogy (3)
Wrong house
Gregg, Cecil Freeman
Inspector Cuthbert Higgins series (15)
Wrong impression
Malcolm, John
Tim Simpson series (7)
Wrong kind of girl
Pascal, Francine
Sweet Valley High series (10)
Wrong letter
Masterman, Walter Sidney
Sir Arthur Sinclair series (1)
Wrong man
Bailey, Henry Christopher
Mister Joshua Clunk series (10)
Mister Reggie Fortune series (20)
Gilman, George G
Adam Steele series (32)
Wrong murder
Rice, Craig
John Joseph Malone series (3)
Wrong murder mystery
Barry, Charles
Superintendent Lawrence Gilmartin series (10)
Wrong name for Angela
Fleischer, Leonore
Holly Hills series (3)
Wrong name on a tombstone
Grover, Marshall
Larry and Stretch series (218)
Wrong number
Stine, Robert Lawrence
Fear Street series (2)
Wrong Plantagenet
Palmer, Martin
Lovell family series (2)
Wrong rite
Craig, Alisa
Inspector Madoc Rhys series (5)
Wrong side of Glory Mountain
Grover, Marshall
Larry and Stretch series (291)
Wrong side of love
Hill, Meredith
Chrystal Falls series (1)
Wrong side of the Park
Heath-Miller, Mavis
Hardwick family series (1)
Wrong side of town
Gilchrist, Rupert
Slaves without masters trilogy (3)
Wrong target
Wolfe, John
Johnny McCoy series (1)
Wrong track
Keene, Carolyn
Nancy Drew files series (64)
Wrong verdict
Masterman, Walter Sidney
Sir Arthur Sinclair series (12)
Wrong victim
Grover, Marshall
Larry and Stretch series (417)
Wrong way down
Daly, Elizabeth
Henry Gamadge series (11)
Wu Fang
Daniel, Roland
Bill Saville series (2)
Wu Fang series (2)
Wu Fang's revenge
Daniel, Roland
Wu Fang series (4)
Wulfston's odyssey
Lorrah, Jean
Savage Empire series (6)
Wumpus
Trevor, Elleston
Wumpus series (1)
Wunda the wood ant
Rutley, Cecily Marianne
Tales of the wild folk series (9)
Wunnerful, wunnerful!
Welk, Laurence
Wunnerful series (1)
Wuthering Heights
Bronte, Emily
Heathcliff series (1)
Bronte, Emily Jane
Wuthering Heights series (1)
WW III
Slater, Ian
WW III series (1)
Wyatt
Gethin, David
Wyatt series (1)
Wyatt and the Moresby legacy
Gethin, David
Wyatt series (2)
Wyatt's orphan
Gethin, David
Wyatt series (3)
Wych Hazel
Warner, Susan Bagert
Wych Hazel series (1)
Wycherley woman
Macdonald, Ross
Lew Archer series (10)
Wychford poisoning case
Berkeley, Anthony
Roger Sheringham series (2)
Wychwood
Wiat, Philippa
Charlton Mead series (3)
Wycliffe and death in Stanley Street
Burley, William John
Superintendent Charles Wycliffe series (5)
Wycliffe and how to kill a cat
Burley, William John
Superintendent Charles Wycliffe series (2)
Wycliffe and the Beales
Burley, William John
Superintendent Charles Wycliffe series (11)
Wycliffe and the cycle of death
Burley, William John
Superintendent Charles Wycliffe series (16)
Wycliffe and the dead flautist
Burley, William John
Superintendent Charles Wycliffe series (17)
Wycliffe and the dunes mystery
Burley, William John
Superintendent Charles Wycliffe series (19)
Wycliffe and the four Jacks
Burley, William John
Superintendent Charles Wycliffe series (12)
Wycliffe and the last rites
Burley, William John
Superintendent Charles Wycliffe series (18)
Wycliffe and the pea-green boat
Burley, William John
Superintendent Charles Wycliffe series (6)

Wycliffe and the quiet virgin
Burley, William John
Superintendent Charles Wycliffe series (13)
Wycliffe and the scapegoat
Burley, William John
Superintendent Charles Wycliffe series (8)
Wycliffe and the schoolgirls
Burley, William John
Superintendent Charles Wycliffe series (7)
Wycliffe and the tangled web
Burley, William John
Superintendent Charles Wycliffe series (15)
Wycliffe and the Windsor blue
Burley, William John
Superintendent Charles Wycliffe series (14)
Wycliffe in Paul's Court
Burley, William John
Superintendent Charles Wycliffe series (9)
Wycliffe's wild goose chase
Burley, William John
Superintendent Charles Wycliffe series (10)
Wylo sails again
Wightman, Frank Armstrong
Wylo series (3)
Wyndcliffe
Laurence, Louise
Wyndcliffe series (1)
Wyndham legacy
Coulter, Catherine
Legacy trilogy (1)
Wyndspelle
Vandergriff, Aola
Wyndspelle series (1)
Wyndspelle's child
Vandergriff, Aola
Wyndspelle series (3)
Wyndward forever
Daniels, Norman A
Wyndward series (5)
Wyndward fury
Daniels, Norman A
Wyndward series (3)
Wyndward glory
Daniels, Norman A
Wyndward series (4)
Wyndward passion
Daniels, Norman A
Wyndward series (2)
Wyoming
Ellis, Edward Sylvester
Wyoming Valley trilogy (1)
Ross, Dana Fuller
Wagons West series (3)
Wyoming ambush
Hardin, J D
Raider series (38)
Wyoming blood
Boone, James Calder
Ned Remington series (5)
Wyoming bloodbath
Evans, Tabor
Longarm series (136)
Wyoming cattle kill
Roberts, J R
Gunsmith series (42)
Wyoming cattle war
Logan, Jake
John Slocum series (138)
Wyoming conspiracy
Sharpe, Jon
Canyon O'Grady series (21)
Wyoming giant
McCord, John S
Baynes clan trilogy (3)
Wyoming glory, Eden Richards
Foster, Jeanne
Frontier women series (4)
Wyoming gun war
Floren, Lee
Buckshot McKee and Tortilla Joe series (5)
Wyoming gun-trap
Grover, Marshall
Larry and Stretch series (321)
Wyoming Jones
Telfair, Richard
Wyoming Jones series (1)
Wyoming Jones for hire
Telfair, Richard
Wyoming Jones series (3)
Wyoming justice
Roberts, J R
Gunsmith series (142)
Wyoming longshot
Grover, Marshall
Larry and Stretch series (205)
Wyoming manhunt
Sharpe, Jon
Trailsman series (120)
Wyoming range war
Roberts, J R
Gunsmith series (110)
Wyoming showdown
Floren, Lee
Judge Lemanuel Bates and Tobacco Jones series (10)
Wyoming special
Hardin, J D
Raider and Doc series (35)
Wyoming thunder
Grover, Marshall
Larry and Stretch series (95)
Wyoming wanton
Sherman, Jory
Gunn series (16)
Wyoming war-fever
Grover, Marshall
Larry and Stretch series (371)
Wyoming wench
Fletcher, Dirk
Spur McCoy series (5)
Ledd, Paul
Shelter Morgan series (33)
Wyoming wildcat
Fletcher, Dirk
Spur McCoy series (35)
Wyoming's debt to a dead man
Kidd, Russ
Wyoming series (2)
Wyrd sisters
Pratchett, Terry
Discworld series (6)
Wyss pursuit
Hamilton, Adam
Peacemaker series (4)
Wyst
Vance, Jack
Alastor trilogy (3)
Gaean series (5)
Wyvern spring
Forward, Toby
Wyvern quartet (2)
Wyvern summer
Forward, Toby
Wyvern quartet (3)
Wyvern winter
Forward, Toby
Wyvern quartet (1)
Wyvern's spur
Novak, Kate
Finder's stone trilogy (2)
X Bar X boys and the sagebrush mystery
Ferris, James Cody
X Bar X boys series (18)

XY

X Bar X boys at Copperhead Gulch
Ferris, James Cody
X Bar X boys series (12)
X Bar X boys at Grizzly Pass
Ferris, James Cody
X Bar X boys series (8)
X Bar X boys at Nugget Camp
Ferris, James Cody
X Bar X boys series (6)
X Bar X boys at Rustlers' Gap
Ferris, James Cody
X Bar X boys series (7)
X Bar X boys at the round-up
Ferris, James Cody
X Bar X boys series (5)
X Bar X boys at the strange rodeo
Ferris, James Cody
X Bar X boys series (14)
X Bar X boys at Triangle Mine
Ferris, James Cody
X Bar X boys series (17)
X Bar X boys branding the wild herd
Ferris, James Cody
X Bar X boys series (13)
X Bar X boys following the stampede
Ferris, James Cody
X Bar X boys series (21)
X Bar X boys hunting the prize mustangs
Ferris, James Cody
X Bar X boys series (16)
X Bar X boys in Smoky Valley
Ferris, James Cody
X Bar X boys series (11)
X Bar X boys in the haunted gully
Ferris, James Cody
X Bar X boys series (19)
X Bar X boys in Thunder Canyon
Ferris, James Cody
X Bar X boys series (2)
X Bar X boys lost in the Rockies
Ferris, James Cody
X Bar X boys series (9)
X Bar X boys on Big Bison Trail
Ferris, James Cody
X Bar X boys series (4)
X Bar X boys on the ranch
Ferris, James Cody
X Bar X boys series (1)
X Bar X boys on Whirlpool River
Ferris, James Cody
X Bar X boys series (3)
X Bar X boys riding for life
Ferris, James Cody
X Bar X boys series (10)
X Bar X boys seeking the lost troopers
Ferris, James Cody
X Bar X boys series (20)
X Bar X boys with the secret rangers
Ferris, James Cody
X Bar X boys series (15)
X Bar X Ranch
Ferris, James Cody
X Bar X boys series (21)
X Esquire
Charteris, Leslie
Bill Kennedy series (1)
X in Paris
Brodsky, Michael Mark
Xman series (2)
X Jones
Keeler, Harry Stephen
Marceau case trilogy (2)
X Jones of Scotland Yard
Keeler, Harry Stephen
Marceau case trilogy (2)
X marks the spot
Thayer, Lee
Peter Clancy series (30)
X marks the spy
Lancer, Jack
Christopher Cool series (1)
X-rated corpse
Avallone, Michael
Ed Noon series (29)
X-ray murders
Michel, Milton Scott
Wood Jason series (1)
Xanadu talisman
O'Donnell, Peter
Modesty Blaise series (10)
Xander pursuit
Hamilton, Adam
Peacemaker series (3)
Xavier affair
Fish, Robert Lloyd
Captain Jose da Silva series (8)
Xenocide
Card, Orson Scott
Ender Wiggins series (3)
Xenogenesis
Butler, Octavia Estelle
Xenogenesis trilogy (3)
Xenon file
Hayes, Richard
Secret army series (2)
Xitli, god of fire
Grant, Maxwell
Shadow series (195)
Xman
Brodsky, Michael Mark
Xman series (1)
Xmas gift for Brimhall
Delton, Judy
Brimhall series (4)
Xorandor
Brooke-Rose, Christine
Xorandor series (1)
XYY man
Royce, Kenneth
Spider Scott series (1)
XYZ murders
Ross, Barnaby
Drury Lane series (4)
Y.M.C.A. boys at football
Henderley, Brooks
Y.M.C.A. boys series (3)
Y.M.C.A. boys of Cliffwood
Henderley, Brooks
Y.M.C.A. boys series (1)
Y.M.C.A. boys on Bass Island
Henderley, Brooks
Y.M.C.A. boys series (2)
Y' understand
Glass, Montague
Potash series (4)
Yacht Club
Optic, Oliver
Yacht Club series (2)
Yacht of mystery
Graydon, William Murray
Sexton Blake series (441)
Yage letters
Burroughs, William Seward
Despair trilogy (3)
Yak and the buried treasure
Bisset, Donald
Yak series (4)
Yak and the ice cream
Bisset, Donald
Yak series (3)
Yak and the painted cave
Bisset, Donald
Yak series (2)
Yak and the seashell
Bisset, Donald
Yak series (1)
Yak for Christmas
Hillary, Louise
Himalayan series (1)
Yak goes home
Bisset, Donald
Yak series (5)
Yakari
Derib
Yakari series (1)
Yakari and the white buffalo
Derib
Yakari series (2)
Yan and the battle for Bergania
Paulden, Sydney
Yan series (3)
Yan and the firemonsters
Paulden, Sydney
Yan series (2)
Yan and the golden moutain robbers
Paulden, Sydney
Yan series (1)
Yang and Yin
Hobart, Alice Tisdale
China series (3)
Yang meridian
Leasor, James
Doctor Jason Love series (3)
Yangtse run
O'Hara, Patrick
Yangtse run series (1)
Yankee
Williams, Jon
Privateers and gentlemen series (2)
Yankee Doodle drumsticks
Giff, Patricia Reilly
Lincoln Lions Band series (2)
Yankee flier in Italy
Avery, Al
Yankee flier series (5)
Yankee flier in Normandy
Avery, Al
Yankee flier series (7)
Yankee flier in North Africa
Avery, Al
Yankee flier series (4)
Yankee flier in the Far East
Avery, Al
Yankee flier series (2)
Yankee flier in the South Pacific
Avery, Al
Yankee flier series (3)
Yankee flier on a rescue mission
Avery, Al
Yankee flier series (8)
Yankee flier over Berlin
Avery, Al
Yankee flier series (6)
Yankee flier under secret orders
Avery, Al
Yankee flier series (9)
Yankee flier with the R.A.F.
Avery, Al
Yankee flier series (1)
Yankee girl
Argo, Ellen
Julia Howard trilogy (3)
Yankee girl at Antietam
Curtis, Alice Turner
Yankee girl series (4)
Yankee girl at Bull Horn
Curtis, Alice Turner
Yankee girl series (2)
Yankee girl at Fort Sumter
Curtis, Alice Turner
Yankee girl series (1)
Yankee girl at Gettysburg
Curtis, Alice Turner
Yankee girl series (5)
Yankee Girl at Hampton Roads
Curtis, Alice Turner
Yankee girl series (7)
Yankee girl at Lookout Mountain
Curtis, Alice Turner
Yankee girl series (8)
Yankee girl at Richmond
Curtis, Alice Turner
Yankee girl series (10)
Yankee girl at Shiloh
Curtis, Alice Turner
Yankee girl series (3)
Yankee girl at the Battle of the Wilderness
Curtis, Alice Turner
Yankee girl series (9)
Yankee girl at Vicksburg
Curtis, Alice Turner
Yankee girl series (6)
Yankee in Oz
Thompson, Ruth Plumly
Oz series (40)
Yankee lawyer
Train, Arthur
Ephraim Tutt series (12)
Yankee middy
Optic, Oliver
Army and navy series (4)
Yankee named Blueberry
Charlier, Jean Michel
Young Blueberry series (2)
Yankee rover
Ward, Christopher
Jonathan Drew series (2)
Yankee stories, 1st series
Haliburton, Thomas Chandler
Sam Slick series (1)
Yankee stories, 2nd series
Haliburton, Thomas Chandler
Sam Slick series (2)
Yankee stories 3rd series
Haliburton, Thomas Chandler
Sam Slick series (3)
Yankee stranger
Thane, Elswyth
Williamsburg series (2)
Yankee's people and places
Johnson, Irving
Yankee series (4)
Yankee's wander world
Johnson, Irving
Yankee series (3)
Yanqui
Blackburn, Thomas Wakefield
Stanton Empire series (1)
Yaqui terror
Gentry, Buck
Eli Holten series (11)
Yard-stick and scissors
Rand, Edward Augustus
Up the Ladder Club series (3)
Yardie
Headley, Victor
Yardie series (1)
Yarl's yacht
Saxby, Jessie Margaret Edmonston
Shetland series (2)
Yarns of a shellback
Duff, Douglas Valder
Yarns of a shellback series (1)
Yashar pursuit
Hamilton, Adam
Peacemaker series (2)
Yawning lion
Warwick, Milligan
William Harkness series (1)
Year and a day
Furlong, Monica
Wise child series (1)
Year at Maple Hill Farm
Provensen, Alice
Maple Hill Farm series (2)
Year at Margarets
Armstrong, Anthony
Margaret Cottage series (5)
Year in Provence
Mayle, Peter
Provence series (1)
Year in the life of a badger
Stidworthy, John
Year in the life of an animal series (1)
Year in the life of a chimpanzee
Stidworthy, John
Year in the life of an animal series (6)
Year in the life of a tiger
Stidworthy, John
Year in the life of an animal series (3)
Year in the life of a whale
Stidworthy, John
Year in the life of an animal series (4)

Year in the life of an elephant
Stidworthy, John
Year in the life of an animal series (2)

Year in the life of an owl
Stidworthy, John
Year in the life of an animal series (5)

Year of decision, 1846
De Voto, Bernard
American West trilogy (1)

Year of decision, 1945
Truman, Harry S
Memoirs of the years series (1)

Year of enchantment
Pinkerton, Kathrene
Baird family series (3)

Year of fears
Watmough, David
Davey Bryant series (7)

Year of impossible goodbyes
Choi, Sook Nyul
Sookan series (1)

Year of Jubilo
Sawyer, Ruth
Lucinda Wyman series (2)

Year of my rebirth
Stuart, Jesse
Dark hills trilogy (3)

Year of space
Linklater, Eric
Man on my back series (2)

Year of sweet illusions
Carossa, Hans
Childhood, boyhood and youth trilogy (3)

Year of the ape
Chang, Lee
Kung Fu series (8)

Year of the boat
Chang, Lee
Kung Fu series (6)

Year of the Christmas dragon
Sawyer, Ruth
Christmas stories series (6)

Year of the cock
Fong, C K
Kung Fu series (7)

Year of the cornflake
Addis, Faith
Devon farm series (1)

Year of the dragon
Chang, Lee
Kung Fu series (4)
Copper, Basil
Mike Faraday series (24)

Year of the horse
Chang, Lee
Kung Fu series (5)

Year of the monkey
Berry, Carole
Bonnie Indermill series (2)

Year of the ransom
Anderson, Poul
Time Patrol series (3)

Year of the rat
Chang, Lee
Kung Fu series (3)

Year of the snake
Chang, Lee
Kung Fu series (2)

Year of the tiger
Chang, Lee
Kung Fu series (1)
Fallon, Martin
Paul Chavasse series (2)

Year of the unicorn
Norton, Andre
High Hallack series (3)
Witch World series (4)

Year of winter
Robertson, Denise
Belgate trilogy (2)

Year on Cowleaze Farm
Whitlock, Ralph
Cowleaze Farm series (4)

Year one of the Republic
Erckmann, Emile
Story of a peasant series (3)

Year 2018!
Blish, James
Cities in flight series (1)

Yearbook memories
Haynes, Betsy
Fabulous Five super series (4)

Yearn a little
McGloin, Joseph Thaddeus
Love and life series (2)

Years at Melbury
Darbyshire, Shirley
Melbury trilogy (2)

Years between
Beaton, Cecil
Years diaries series (2)

Years beyond
Mackinnon, Charles Roy
Scottish chronicle series (2)

Years in a mirror
Gielgud, Val
Years series (2)

Years of adventure, 1858-1898
Perham, Margery
Frederick Dealtry Lugard series (1)

Years of authority, 1898-1945
Perham, Margery
Frederick Dealtry Lugard series (2)

Years of awakening
Lutyens, Mary
Krishnamurti series (1)

Years of change
Hardwick, Mollie
Upstairs, downstairs series (7)
White, Alan
Aysgill family trilogy (3)

Years of childhood
Aksakov, Sergei Timofeevich
Russian family chronicle series (1)

Years of combat
Douglas, William Sholto
Years series (1)

Years of command
Douglas, William Sholto
Years series (2)

Years of endurance, 1793-1802
Bryant, Arthur
Napoleonic Wars trilogy (1)

Years of fulfilment
Lutyens, Mary
Krishnamurti series (2)
Maclean, Norman
Former days trilogy (3)

Years of growth, 1861-1893
Sinclair, Harold
American years trilogy (2)

Years of hope
Paustovsky, Konstantin Georgievich
Story of a life series (4)

Years of illusion
Sinclair, Harold
American years trilogy (3)

Years of love
Widdemer, Margaret
Years of love series (1)

Years of opportunity
Cartland, Barbara
Years of life series (3)

Years of peace
Macleod, Le Roy
Years of peace series (1)

Years of peril
Bryant, Arthur
Samuel Pepys series (2)

Years of power, 1904-1914
Fisher, John Arbuthnot
Fear God and dread nought trilogy (2)

Years of promise
Roberts, Cecil
Sunshine and shadow series (2)

Years of promise, 1809-1851
Pope-Hennessy, James
Monckton Milnes series (1)

Years of the forest
Hoover, Helen
Forest trilogy (3)

Years of the locust
Gielgud, Val
Years series (1)

Years of trial and hope, 1946-1953
Truman, Harry S
Memoirs of the years series (2)

Years of upheaval
Kissinger, Henry
White House years series (2)

Years of victory, 1802-1812
Bryant, Arthur
Napoleonic Wars trilogy (2)

Yearwood
Hazel, Paul
Finnbranch trilogy (1)

Yell bloody murder
Shallit, Joseph
Dan Morrison series (3)

Yell ruddy murder
Shallit, Joseph
Dan Morrison series (3)

Yello shadows of death
Wallace, Robert
Phantom Detective series (13)

Yellow arrow murders
Mason, Francis Van Wyck
Colonel Hugh North series (4)

Yellow band
Grant, Maxwell
Shadow series (129)

Yellow bird
Boyer, Richard Lewis
Doctor Charlie Adams series (7)

Yellow bird and me
Hansen, Joyce
Doris series (2)

Yellow book of Hob stories
Mayne, William
Hob stories series (1)

Yellow brand
Carter, Nicholas
Nicholas Carter series (583)

Yellow bungalow mystery
Gribble, Leonard Reginald
Superintendent Anthony Slade series (6)

Yellow cat
Gibbons, Harry Hornaby Clifford
Sexton Blake series (380)

Yellow cat mystery
Queen, Ellery, Junior
Djuna and Champ series (7)

Yellow claw
Rohmer, Sax
Gaston Max series (1)

Yellow cloud
Robeson, Kenneth
Doc Savage series (59)

Yellow crayon
Oppenheim, Edward Phillips
Mister Sabin series (2)

Yellow crystal
Wynne, Anthony
Doctor Eustace Hailey series (10)

Yellow death
Key, Uel
Professor Arnold Rhymer series (2)

Yellow disc murders
Plummer, Thomas Arthur
Detective Inspector Andrew Frampton series (32)

Yellow document
Allain, Marcel
Fantomas series (7)

Yellow dog party
Emerson, Earl W
Thomas Black series (6)

Yellow door
Grant, Maxwell
Shadow series (105)

Yellow face
Graydon, William Murray
Sexton Blake series (183)

Yellow feather mystery
Dixon, Franklin W
Hardy boys series (32)

Yellow fever
Wilson, Trevor Edward
Big Tom Holder trilogy (2)

Yellow fog
Daniels, Les
Don Sebastien series (4)

Yellow gods
Brandon, John Gordon
Inspector Patrick Aloysius McCarthy series (31)

Yellow hen
Baum, Lyman Frank
Snuggle tales series (3)

Yellow hoard
Robeson, Kenneth
Avenger series (2)

Yellow house mystery
Warner, Gertrude Chandler
Boxcar children series (3)

Yellow Jacket
Snell, Edmund
Peter Pennington series (2)

Yellow knight of Oz
Thompson, Ruth Plumly
Oz series (23)

Yellow label
Carter, Nicholas
Nicholas Carter series (622)

Yellow Lotus Tong
Weston, Cole
Andrew Ryder series (11)

Yellow magic
Thomas, Eugene
Chu-Sheng series (2)

Yellow mask
Brandon, John Gordon
Sexton Blake series (835)

Yellow mistletoe
Masterman, Walter Sidney
Sir Arthur Sinclair series (4)

Yellow Munch Bunch word book
Reed, Giles
Munch Bunch word book series (4)

Yellow phantom
Sutton, Margaret
Judy Bolton series (6)

Yellow rain
McCurtin, Peter
Jim Rainey series (10)

Yellow rat
Grierson, Francis Durham
Inspector Sims and Professor Wells series (8)

Yellow rose
Carroll, Shana
Paxton women series (3)
Fletcher, Farris
Texans series (3)

Yellow scourge
Steele, Curtis
James Christopher series (3)

Yellow seven
Snell, Edmund
Peter Pennington series (1)

Yellow shadows
Rohmer, Sax
Red Kerry series (2)

Yellow skull
Teed, George Hamilton
Sexton Blake series (684)

Yellow spider
Beecham, John Charles
Koyola series (2)

Yellow spies
Stewart, William Thomas
Gaff Lee series (2)

Yellow story book
Blyton, Enid
Colour story book series (4)

Yellow streak
Williams, Valentine
Inspector Manderton series (1)

Yellow stripe
Kirk, Matthew
Claw series (3)

Yellow taxi
Stagge, Jonathan
Doctor Hugh Westlake series (5)

Yellow terror
Hardinge, Rex
Sexton Blake series (1185)

Yellow tiger
Teed, George Hamilton
Sexton Blake series (4)

Yellow trousers
Fry, Pete
Pete Fry series (8)

Yellow vengeance
Urquhart, Paul
Sexton Blake series (783)

Yellow villa
Blanc, Suzanne
Inspector Miguel Menendes series (2)

Yellow violet
Crane, Frances
Pat and Jean Abbott series (3)

Yellow warning
Allen, Betsy
Connie Blair series (7)

Yellow wolf
King, T Stanleyan
Dixon Brett series (2)

Yellowstone
Blevins, Winfred
Rivers west series (1)
Wheeler, Richard Seabrook
Skye's West series (4)

Yellowstone jewel
Dixon, Dorothy
Leather and lace series (9)

Yellowstone Kelly
Bowen, Peter
Yellowstone Kelly series (1)

Yellowstone kill
Gentry, Buck
Eli Holten series (12)

Yellowstone run
Robbins, David
Endworld series (23)

Yellowstone thieves
Hardin, J D
Raider series (24)

Yellowthread Street
Marshall, William Leonard
Yellowthread Street series (1)

Yendi
Brust, Steven
Jhereg series (2)

Yensie Walton
Clark, Susanna Rebecca Graham
Yensie Walton series (1)

Yensie Walton's womanhood
Clark, Susanna Rebecca Graham
Yensie Walton series (2)

Yeoman's hospital
Ashton, Helen
Wilchester chronicles series (3)

Yes, Henry
Joynson, Cecile
Henry series (3)

Yes I can
Sanford, Doris
Children of courage series (4)

Yes, Inspector McLean
Goodchild, George
Inspector McLean series (7)

Yes, Virginia!
Griffith, Helen Sherman
Virginia series (5)

Yesterday
Hawker, Ruth Marjorie
Us three series (3)

Yesterday, today and tomorrow
Witcomb, Nan
Thoughts of Nanushka series (1)

Yesterday walkers
Harvester, Simon
Asia in turmoil series (7)

Yesterday's dream
Baer, Judy
Cedar River daydreams series (9)

Yesterday's enemy
Haggard, William
Colonel Charles Russell series (17)

Yesterday's kingdom
Aspinall, Ruth
Malinson brothers trilogy (1)

Yesterday's men
Turner, George Reginald
Ethical culture series (3)

Yesterday's news
Healy, Jeremiah
John Francis Cuddy series (5)

Yesterday's promises
Thorne, Nicola
Askham family series (2)

Yesterday's road
Minton, Mary
Yesterday's road series (1)

Yesterday's son
Crispin, Ann Carol
Star trek series (11)

Yet a lion
Wiat, Philippa
Howard series (5)

Yet do not grieve
O'Riordan, Conal
Anglo-Irish relations series (2)

Yet other waters
Farrell, James Thomas
Bernard Clare series (3)

Yet she must die
Woods, Sara
Sir Nicholas Harding and Antony Maitland series (20)

Ylana of Callisto
Carter, Lin
Jandar the Alien series (7)

Yngling
Dalmas, John
Nils Jarnhan series (1)

Yngling in the circle of power
Dalmas, John
Nils Jarnhan series (3)

Yo Yo and midnight
Jenkins, Jerry Bruce
Bradford family series (9)

Yoke of magic
Vardeman, Robert Edward
Swords of Raemllyn series (2)

Yoke of Shen
Cleve, John
Spaceways series (10)

Yolanda, the girl from the erosphere
Verseau, Dominique
Yolanda series (1)

Yonder comes the other end of time
Elgin, Suzette Haden
Coyote Jones series (5)

Yonderbeyonder
Davey, Thyrza
Yonderbeyonder series (1)

Yorath the wolf
Wilder, Cherry
Rulers of Hylor trilogy (2)

York, the renegade
Johansen, Iris
Shamrock trilogy (1)

Yorks in London
Anderson, Verily
York family series (3)

Yorkshire relish
Cragoe, Elizabeth
Untidy gardener series (3)

Yorkshire suburb
Riley, William
Windyridge series (3)
You
Anonymous
Pronoun series (4)
Montgomery, Elizabeth
Dick, Jane and Sally series (8)
You and your child
Bloom, Ursula
You and yours series (1)
You and your dog
Bloom, Ursula
You and yours series (4)
You and your fun
Bloom, Ursula
You and yours series (7)
You and your holiday
Bloom, Ursula
You and yours series (2)
You and your home
Bloom, Ursula
You and yours series (3)
You and your life
Bloom, Ursula
You and yours series (6)
You and your looks
Bloom, Ursula
You and yours series (5)
You and your needle
Bloom, Ursula
You and yours series (8)
You are a genius
Packard, Edward
Choose your own adventure series (95)
You are a millionaire
Leibold, Jay
Choose your own adventure series (98)
You are a monster
Packard, Edward
Choose your own adventure series (84)
You are a shark
Packard, Edward
Choose your own adventure series (45)
You are a superstar
Packard, Edward
Choose your own adventure series (91)
You are microscopic
Packard, Edward
Choose your own adventure series (130)
You are the manager
Aaseng, Nathan
You are the coach series (1)
You asked for it
Fleming, Ian
James Bond series (1)
You bet your britches, Claude
Nixon, Joan Lowery
Claude series (4)
You bet your life
Kaminsky, Stuart Melvin
Toby Peters series (3)
You can always blame the rain
Fredman, Mike
Willie Halliday series (1)
You can always duck
Cheyney, Peter
Lemmy Caution series (10)
You can be the stainless steel rat
Harrison, Harry
Jim Di Griz series (9)
You can call it a day
Cheyney, Peter
Johnny Vallon series (1)
You can die laughing
Fair, A A
Bertha Cool and Donald Lam series (16)
You can do it
Berry, Joy
Ready-set-grow series (19)
You can get there from here
MacLaine, Shirley
You can get there series (1)
You can help me
Birmingham, Maisie
Kate Weatherley series (1)
You can keep the corpse
Robertson, Colin
Vicky McBain series (2)
You can't call it murder
Graham, Neill
Solo Malcolm series (4)
Ramsay, Diana
Lieutenant Meredith series (4)
You can't die tomorrow
Gribble, Leonard Reginald
Superintendent Anthony Slade series (36)
You can't do business with murder
Von Elsner, Don
David Danning series (4)
You can't gag the dead
Propper, Milton
Tommy Rankin series (13)
You can't get away with murder
Spiller, Andrew
Chief Inspector Duck Maliard series (6)
You can't go home again
Wolfe, Thomas Clayton
George Webber series (2)
You can't have your kayak and heat it
Muir, Frank
My word series (1)
You can't keep the change
Cheyney, Peter
Slim Callaghan series (3)
You can't live forever
Masur, Harold Q
Scott Jordan series (3)
You can't scare me!
Stine, Robert Lawrence
Goosebumps series (15)
You can't stop me
Ard, William
Timothy Dane series (2)
You could look it up
Safire, William
On language series (5)
You did it
Goldthwaite, Eaton Kenneth
Lieutenant Joseph Dickerson series (1)
You die, Du Ma!
Cain, Jonathan
Saigon commandos series (8)
You die next, Jill Baby!
Carr, Kirby
Hitman series (5)
You die today
Kendrick, Baynard
Captain Duncan Maclain series (7)
You don't look like your mother, said the robin to the fawn
Fisher, Aileen
Ways of animals series (9)
You don't need an enemy
Stern, Richard Martin
Johnny Ortiz series (2)
You flash bastard
Newman, Gordon F
Inspector Terry Sneed series (3)
You funny little Noddy!
Blyton, Enid
Noddy series (10)
You get what you pay for
Beinhart, Larry
Tony Cassella series (2)
You have a girl friend, Alfie Atkins?
Bergstrom, Gunilla
Alfie Atkins series (6)
You have yourself a deal
Chase, James Hadley
Mark Girland series (2)
You kill me!
Muller, Paul
Paul Muller series (1)
You know the way it is
Jones, Arthur E
Felix Holliday series (1)
You learn by living
Roosevelt, Eleanor
On my own series (2)
You leave me cold!
Rogers, Samuel
Professor Paul Hatfield series (3)
You may well ask
Mitchison, Naomi
Small talk series (3)
You must die before my eyes as I have before yours
Gibson, Patricia Jeann
Private hells trilogy (1)
You never know till you get there
Longhurst, Henry
Good while it lasted series (3)
You nice bastard
Newman, Gordon F
Inspector Terry Sneed series (2)
You only die once
Copper, Basil
Mike Faraday series (42)
You only hang once
Roden, Henry Wisdom
Sid Ames series (1)
You only live twice
Fleming, Ian
James Bond series (12)
You only live until you die
Weinstein, Sol
Israel Bond series (4)
You pay for pity
Mole, William
Casson Duker series (3)
You remember the case
Claymore, Tod
Tod Claymore series (1)
You should've been here Thursday
Webber, Edmund Godfrey
Trout fishing series (1)
You slay me
Spade, Danny
Danny Spade series (2)
You want to die, Johnny?
Black, Gavin
Paul Harris series (5)
You will never be the same
Smith, Cordwainer
Instrumentality series (1)
You win some, you lose some
Ure, Jean
Jamie Carr series (2)
You wouldn't be dead for quids
Barrett, Robert G
Les Norton series (1)
You'd be surprised
Cheyney, Peter
Lemmy Caution series (6)
You'd better believe it
James, Bill
Superintendent Colin Harpur series (1)
You'll be all right
Blake, Ken
Professionals series (16)
You'll be sorry!
Rogers, Samuel
Professor Paul Hatfield series (2)
You'll be sotty
Mant, Gilbert
War reminiscences series (2)
You'll be the death of me
Lynch, Miriam
Nell Willard series (2)
You'll catch your death
Hume, David
Tony Carter series (1)
You'll die, darling
Grove, Marjorie
Maxine Reynolds series (4)
You'll die in Singapore
McCormac, Charles
War in South-East Asia series (1)
You'll die laughing
Cooper, Craig
Matt Savage series (4)
Grove, Marjorie
Maxine Reynolds series (2)
You'll die today
Grove, Marjorie
Maxine Reynolds series (7)
You'll die tomorrow
Grove, Marjorie
Maxine Reynolds series (3)
You'll die tonight
Grove, Marjorie
Maxine Reynolds series (5)
You'll die when you hear this
Grove, Marjorie
Maxine Reynolds series (1)
You'll die yesterday
Grove, Marjorie
Maxine Reynolds series (6)
You'll fry tomorrow
Heberden, Mary Violet
Desmond Shannon series (15)
You'll never get to heaven
Mitchell, Scott
Brock Devlin series (9)
You'll play this my way
Spade, Danny
Danny Spade series (8)
You'll soon grow into them, Titch
Hutchins, Pat
Titch series (2)
Young adventurer
Alger, Horatio
Pacific series (1)
Young and lonely king
Lane, Jane
Charles I trilogy (1)
Young apprentice
Stevenson, Burton Egbert
Boys' story of the railroad series (4)
Young Art and old Hector
Gunn, Neil Miller
Young Art and old Hector series (1)
Young Astronauts
North, Rick
Young Astronauts series (1)
Young at art
Striker, Susan
Anti-coloring book series (7)
Young atom detective
Coombs, Charles Ira
Young detective series (3)
Young auctioneers
Stratemeyer, Edward L
Bound to win series (7)
Working upward series (1)
Young bandmaster
Bonehill, Ralph
Flag and frontier series (6)
Flag of freedom series (4)
Young bank messenger
Alger, Horatio
Good fortune trilogy (2)
Young Beck
Bodkin, Matthias McDonnell
Dora Myrl series (3)
Paul Beck series (4)
Young Bess
Irwin, Margaret
Elizabeth I series (1)
Young birdmen across the continent
Russell, Keith
Young birdmen series (2)
Young birdmen on the wing
Russell, Keith
Young birdmen series (1)
Young birdmen up the Amazon
Russell, Keith
Young birdmen series (3)
Young Bleys
Dickson, Gordon Rupert
Bleys quartet (1)
Dorsai series (7)
Young blockaders
Tomlinson, Everett Titsworth
War for the Union series (2)
Young book agent
Alger, Horatio
Rise in life series (8)
Young bucks from Texas
Grover, Marshall
Larry and Stretch series (276)
Young Caesar
Warner, Rex
Caesar series (1)
Young can die protesting
Wells, Tobias
Detective Knute Severson series (6)
Young Captain Jack
Alger, Horatio
Rise in life series (3)
Young cattle kings
Adams, Andy
Wells brothers series (1)
Young Christian
Abbott, Jacob
Young Christian series (1)
Young circus detective series
Coombs, Charles Ira
Young detective series (1)
Young circus rider
Alger, Horatio
Atlantic series (1)
Young Claudia
Franken, Rose
Claudia series (4)
Young Clavengers
Stuart, Dorothy Margaret
Clavengers series (2)
Young conductor
Ellis, Edward Sylvester
Through on time series (2)
Young Continentals at Bunker Hill
McIntyre, John Thomas
Young Continentals series (2)
Young Continentals at Lexington
McIntyre, John Thomas
Young Continentals series (1)
Young Continentals at Monmouth
McIntyre, John Thomas
Young Continentals series (4)
Young Continentals at Trenton
McIntyre, John Thomas
Young Continentals series (3)
Young cowboy
James, Will
Cow camps series (2)
Young Crusoes of Pine Island
Gordon, Frederick
Fairview boys series (1)
Up and doing series (1)
Young deliverers of Pleasant Cove
Kellogg, Elijah
Pleasant Cove series (2)
Young detectives
Macgregor, Reginald James
Young detectives series (1)
Young detective's handbook
Butler, William Vivian
Young detective series (1)
Young detectives incorporated
Macgregor, Reginald James
Young detectives series (2)
Young detective's whodunit
Butler, William Vivian
Young detective series (2)
Young Doctor Goddard
Harrison, Elizabeth
Central London Hospital series (12)
Young Doctor Kildare
Brand, Max
Doctor Kildare series (3)
Young doctors downstairs
Andrews, Lucilla
Saint Barnabas' Hospital series (1)
Young Elizabeth
Plowden, Alison
Elizabeth I series (1)
Young Emmanuel
Jacob, Naomi
Gollantz series (3)
Young Emperor
Payne, Robert
Emperor Shah Jahan series (1)
Young enchanted
Walpole, Hugh
London Group series (5)
Peter Westcott series (2)
Trenchard family series (2)
Young engineers in Arizona
Hancock, Harrie Irving
Young engineers series (2)
Young engineers in Colorado
Hancock, Harrie Irving
Young engineers series (1)
Young engineers in Mexico
Hancock, Harrie Irving
Young engineers series (4)
Young engineers in Nevada
Hancock, Harrie Irving
Young engineers series (3)
Young engineers in the Gulf
Hancock, Harrie Irving
Young engineers series (5)
Young experience
Christie, Robert Stuart
Book of Sarah series (1)
Young explorer
Alger, Horatio
Pacific series (3)
Young explorers of the Amazon
Stratemeyer, Edward L
Pan-American series (4)
Young explorers of the Isthmus
Stratemeyer, Edward L
Pan-American series (3)
Young express agent
Chapman, Allen
Boys of business series (1)
Young farmers at Greythorne
Martin, Nancy
Young farmers series (1)
Young farmers in Denmark
Martin, Nancy
Young farmers series (2)
Young farmers in Scotland
Martin, Nancy
Young farmers series (3)
Young Flash, the deer
Burgess, Thornton Waldo
Animal stories series (7)
Young Flynn
Laurie-Long, Ernest
Captain Flynn series (1)
Young forester
Grey, Zane
Ken Ward series (1)
Young fur takers
Rathborne, Saint George
Canoe and campfire series (2)
Young generation
Shears, Sarah
Franklin family series (3)
Young girls
Montherlant, Henry de
Girls series (1)
Young green blade
Gillespie, Susan
Longdon-Lorristone family series (6)
Young gunbearer
Browne, George Waldo
Woodranger series (2)
Young Haggards
Nicole, Christopher
Haggard trilogy (3)

Your future in aviation on the ground
Scribner, Kimball
Your future in aviation series (2)
Your husband's mid-life crisis
Conway, Sally
Mid-life crisis series (2)
Your marriage can survive mid-life crisis
Conway, Jim
Mid-life crisis series (4)
Your money and your wife
Perry, Ritchie
Philis series (5)
Your mother was a neanderthal
Scieszka, Jon
Time warp trio series (4)
Your move, Delaney
Singer, Bant
Denis Delaney series (4)
Your neck in a noose
Ferrars, Elizabeth
Toby Dyke series (5)
Your nine-year-old
Ames, Louise Bates
Your child series (9)
Your obedient servant
Scott, Harold
Obedient servant series (1)
Your old pal, Al
Greene, Constance Clarke
Al series (3)
Your one-year-old
Ames, Louise Bates
Your child series (1)
Haber, Carol Chase
Your child series (1)
Your orders, sir
Du Soe, Robert C
Jonathan Amory series (2)
Your pet bear
Hamsa, Bobbie
Far-fetched pets series (1)
Your pet beaver
Hamsa, Bobbie
Far-fetched pets series (2)
Your pet camel
Hamsa, Bobbie
Far-fetched pets series (4)
Far-fetched pets series (6)
Your pet elephant
Hamsa, Bobbie
Far-fetched pets series (3)
Your pet giraffe
Hamsa, Bobbie
Far-fetched pets series (9)
Your pet gorilla
Hamsa, Bobbie
Far-fetched pets series (7)
Your pet kangaroo
Hamsa, Bobbie
Far-fetched pets series (5)
Your pet lion
Hamsa, Bobbie
Far-fetched pets series (8)
Your pet sea lion
Hamsa, Bobbie
Far-fetched pets series (10)
Your royal hostage
Fraser, Antonia
Jemima Shore series (6)
Your secret friend
Torrie, Malcolm
Timothy Herring series (3)
Your seven-year-old
Ames, Louise Bates
Your child series (7)
Your six-year-old
Ames, Louise Bates
Your child series (6)
Your ten- to fourteen-year-old
Ames, Louise Bates
Your child series (10)
Baker, Sidney M
Your child series (10)
Your three-year-old
Ames, Louise Bates
Your child series (3)
Your turn, Mister Moto
Marquand, John Phillips
Mister Moto series (1)
Your two-year-old
Ames, Louise Bates
Your child series (2)
You're a good friend, Noddy!
Blyton, Enid
Noddy series (16)
You're a long time dead
Clapperton, Richard
Peter Fleck series (1)
You're a sly one, Alfie Atkins!
Bergstrom, Gunilla
Alfie Atkins series (3)
You're a Texas Ranger, Alvin Fog
Edson, John Thomas
Cap Fog series (1)
You're all right
Berry, Joy
Ready-set-grow series (13)
You're better off dead
Chambers, Peter
Mark Preston series (9)
You're dead
Adams, Nicholas
Horror High series (2)
You're dead without money
Chase, James Hadley
Al Barney series (2)
Herman Radnitz series (4)
You're either one or the other
Berry, Joy
Ready-set-grow series (20)
You're fairly welcome
Ditton, James
John Boldre series (2)
You're hired, you're dead
Carr, Kirby
Hitman series (7)
You're in command now, Mr Fog
Edson, John Thomas
American Civil War series (2)
You're lonely when you're dead
Chase, James Hadley
Vic Malloy series (1)
You're never to old to die
Goldstein, Arthur David
Max Guttman series (2)
You're never too young
Welk, Laurence
Wunnerful series (5)
You're no friend of mine
Chase, Emily
Canby Hall series (3)
You're one of a kind
Berry, Joy
Ready-set-grow series (14)
You're out!
Kroll, Steven
Hit and Run Gang series (6)
You're wrong, Delaney
Singer, Bant
Denis Delaney series (1)
Yours affectionately, Peter Rabbit
Emerson, Anne
Peter Rabbit series (21)
Yours ever, Sam Pig
Uttley, Alison
Sam Pig series (7)
Yours for a day
Pascal, Francine
Sweet Valley twins series (76)
Yours is the earth
Briggs, Victor
Way ahead trilogy (3)
Yours till the end
Mann, Jackie
Hostage crisis series (2)
Yours to oblige
Scott, Mary
New Zealand life series (2)
Yourself and the neighbours
Macmanus, Seumas
O'Friel trilogy (3)
Youth
Conrad, Joseph
Lord Jim series (2)
Owen, Harold
Journey from obscurity trilogy (2)
Rolland, Romain
John Christopher series (2)
Tolstoi, Leo Nikolaevich
Nicholas Irtenyev trilogy (3)
Youth at the gate
Bloom, Ursula
Elegant Edwardian series (3)
Youth comes to Kenya
Strange, Nora Kathleen
Kenya series (6)
Youth, 1874-1900
Churchill, Randolph Spencer
Winston S Churchill series (1)
Youth hostel murders
Carr, Glyn
Sir Abercrombie Lewker series (6)
Youth is a blunder
Napier, Elma
Youth and winter series (1)
Youth rides out
Seymour, Beatrice Kean
Three wives series (2)
Youth storms in
Marshall, May
Sister Madge Stillworthy series (2)
Youth's encounter
Mackenzie, Compton
Sinister Street series (1)
You've got him cold
Dewey, Thomas Blanchard
Private Eye Mac series (6)
You've had it girl
Swan, Phyllis
Anna J series (4)
Ysabel Kid
Edson, John Thomas
Floating Outfit series (1)
Yuck!
Stevenson, James
Emma series (1)
Yuckers!
Gilden, Mel
Fifth grade monsters series (8)
Yukon breed
Willoughby, Lee Davis
Making of America series (33)
Yukon ho!
Watterson, Bill
Calvin and Hobbes series (4)
Yukon justice
Ross, Dana Fuller
Holt family series (7)
Yukon kid
Hendryx, James Beardsley
Corporal Cameron Downey series (4)
Yukon Kid
Hendryx, James Beardsley
Corporal Downey series (10)
Yukon ride
Curry, Gene
Jim Saddler series (7)
Yukon target
Carter, Nick
Nick Carter series (178)
Yuma
Smith, Russell
Yuma series (1)
Yuma roundup
Hardin, J D
Raider series (3)
Yuma run
Foley, Craig
Hangman series (4)
Yummers!
Marshall, James
Yummers series (1)
Yummers too
Marshall, James
Yummers series (2)
Yunnan terminus
Neebel, Richard
Erik Chatham series (2)
Yvette in Italy and Titania's Palace
Wilkinson, Nevile
Titania's Palace series (1)
Yvette in Switzerland and Titania's Palace
Wilkinson, Nevile
Titania's Palace series (4)
Yvette in the U.S.A. with Titania's Palace
Wilkinson, Nevile
Titania's Palace series (5)
Yvette in Venice and Titania's Palace
Wilkinson, Nevile
Titania's Palace series (3)
Yvgenie
Cherryh, Carolyn Janice
Rusalka series (3)
Yvonne, the confident
Kimbrough, Katheryn
Phenwick women series (26)

Z

Z car detective
Prendergast, William
Chief Inspector Barlow series (3)
Z car Squad
Prendergast, William
Chief Inspector Barlow series (5)
Z cars
Martin, Troy Kennedy
Chief Inspector Barlow series (1)
Z cars again
Prior, Allan
Chief Inspector Barlow series (2)
Z case
Daniel, Roland
Jim Maitland series (1)
Z document
Carter, Nick
Nick Carter series (99)
Z is for zombie
Gilden, Mel
Fifth grade monsters series (5)
Z-Lensman
Kyle, David Ackerman
Lensman series (11)
Z Marcus
Balzac, Honore de
Scenes of political life series (4)
Z murders
Farjeon, Joseph Jefferson
Z series (2)
Z ray
Snell, Edmund
Reggie Faulkner series (1)
Z-sting
Wallace, Ian
Croyd series (5)
Zach's law
Hooper, Kay
Hagen series (4)
Zadda Street affair
Jackson, Wallace
Archibald Penny series (1)
Zadok's treasure
Arnold, Margot
Penelope Spring and Sir Tobias Glendower series (3)
Zag the Great and Zig the Big
Young, Peter
Zig and Zag series (2)
Zagribud
Statten, Vargo
Liners of time series (2)
Zaharan pursuit
Hamilton, Adam
Peacemaker series (1)
Zaitech sting
Arnett, Jack
Book of justice series (2)
Zakka slaughter
Barker, Wade
War of the Ninja Master series (4)
Zaleski's percentage
Mackenzie, Donald
Johnny Raven series (1)
Zambesi adventure
Macarthur, David Wilson
Larry Pearson series (1)
Zambra the detective, some clues from his notebook
Hill, Headon
Sebastian Zambra series (2)
Zan Hagan's marathon
Knudson, Rozanne Ruth
Zan Hagan series (4)
Zanballer
Knudson, Rozanne Ruth
Zan Hagan series (1)
Zanbanger
Knudson, Rozanne Ruth
Zan Hagan series (2)
Zanboomer
Knudson, Rozanne Ruth
Zan Hagan series (3)
Zane Grey's tales from the fisherman's log
Grey, Zane
Tales of a fisherman series (8)
Zane Grey's Yaqui, and other great Indian stories
Grey, Zane
Yaqui series (1)
Zanek
Stevenson, William Henri
Israeli armed services series (1)
Zanoni
Lytton, Edward George Earle Lytton Bulwer-Lytton
Glyndon series (2)
Zanthar at moon's madness
Williams, Robert Moore
Zanthar series (3)
Zanthar at the edge of never
Williams, Robert Moore
Zanthar series (2)
Zanthar at trip's end
Williams, Robert Moore
Zanthar series (4)
Zanthar of the many worlds
Williams, Robert Moore
Zanthar series (1)
Zanthodon
Carter, Lin
Eric Carstairs series (2)
Zanzibar intrigue
Mason, Francis Van Wyck
Colonel Hugh North series (24)
Zaphod plays it safe
Adams, Douglas Noel
Arthur Dent series (4)
Zaragoz
Craig, Brian
Minstrel Orfeo series (1)
Zarsthor's Bane
Norton, Andre
Witch World series (11)
Zebby gone with the wind
Schroeder, Binette
Zebby series (2)
Zebby shops
Schroeder, Binette
Zebby series (4)
Zebby swims
Schroeder, Binette
Zebby series (1)
Zebby's breakfast
Schroeder, Binette
Zebby series (3)
Zebra-striped hearse
Macdonald, Ross
Lew Archer series (11)
Zeki and the talking cat Shukru
Kubinyi, Laszlo
Shukru series (1)
Zelda
Brown, Carter
Rick Holman series (2)
Zelda strikes again!
Hall, Lynn
Zelda Hammersmith series (2)
Zelerod's doom
Lichtenberg, Jacqueline
Sime-Gen series (8)
Zemba
Grant, Maxwell
Shadow series (91)
Zemlya expedition
Rosenberger, Joseph
Death Merchant series (17)
Zenda vendetta
Hawke, Simon
Timewars series (4)
Zenobia
Ware, William
Zenobia and Aurelian series (1)
Zenya
Tubb, Edwin Charles
Dumarest series (11)
Zephir's holiday
Brunhoff, Jean de
Babar series (5)
Zero clue
Stout, Rex
Nero Wolfe and Archie Goodwin series (23)
Zero eight fifteen
Kirst, Hans Hellmut
Gunner Asch series (1)
Zero eight fifteen, 2
Kirst, Hans Hellmut
Gunner Asch series (2)
Zero hour
Robertson, Colin
Peter Grayleigh series (4)
Zero hour strike force
Carter, Nick
Nick Carter series (186)
Zero in the gate
Farrar, Stewart
Inspector Elwyn Morgan series (2)
Zero minus nine
Thorne, Ernest Pollett
Major Brains Cunningham series (13)
Zero stone
Norton, Andre
Murdoc Jern series (1)
Zero-sum games
Tallis, Robyn
Planet builders series (5)
Zero takes all
Janson, Hank
Hank Janson series (241)
Zero the slaver
Fletcher, Lawrence
Dick Grenville series (2)
Zero with death
Clevely, Hugh
Maxwell Archer series (1)
Zest for life
Zola, Emile
Rougon Macquart series (12)
Zesty
McBratney, Sam
Jimmy Zest series (2)
Zia
O'Dell, Scott
Zia series (2)
Zig and Zag from Planet ZV7
Young, Peter
Zig and Zag series (1)

Ziggy the elephant
Torgersen, Don Arthur
Animal life stories series (1)
Ziggy's working holiday
Redmond, Phil
Grange Hill series (14)
Zigzag
Kenyon, Michael
Inspector Henry Peckover series (2)
Superintendent O'Malley series (6)
Zigzag path
Edwin, Maribel
Curlew Jon series (2)
Zihanne's book
Mills, Carla Johnson
Winter world series (5)
Zion road
Harvester, Simon
Asia in turmoil series (20)
Dorian Silk series (8)
Zip-Zip and his flying saucer
Schealer, John Milton
Zip-Zip series (1)
Zip-Zip and the red planet
Schealer, John Milton
Zip-Zip series (3)
Zip-Zip goes to Venus
Schealer, John Milton
Zip-Zip series (2)
Zodiac
Lees, Dan
Jeff Plummer series (2)
Zola's court of Napoleon III
Zola, Emile
Rougon Macquart series (6)
Zoltan, hound of Dracula
Johnson, Kenneth Rayner
Dracula series (1)
Zombie
Lecale, Errol
Specialist series (5)
Zondra
Rotsler, William
Zandra trilogy (1)
Zone yellow
Laumer, Keith
Mister Curlon series (4)
Zones of silence
Garner, William
John Morpurgo trilogy (3)
Zoo
Ahlberg, Allan
Foldaways series (4)
Zoo doings
Prelutsky, Jack
Zoo doings series (3)
Zoo doings, and other poems
Prelutsky, Jack
Zoo doings series (2)
Zoo for Mister Muster
Lobel, Arnold
Mister Muster series (1)
Zoo in the garden
Taylor, David Conrad
Zoo in series (3)
Zoo in the house
Taylor, David Conrad
Zoo in series (2)
Zoo in town
Taylor, David Conrad
Zoo in series (4)
Zoo in you
Taylor, David Conrad
Zoo in series (1)
Zoo Man again
Gillespie, Thomas Haining
Zoo Man series (4)
Zoo Man stories
Gillespie, Thomas Haining
Zoo Man series (2)
Zoo Man tales
Gillespie, Thomas Haining
Zoo Man series (3)
Zoo Man talks
Gillespie, Thomas Haining
Zoo Man series (1)
Zoo murder
Grierson, Francis Durham
Inspector Sims and Professor Wells series (4)
Zoo quest for a dragon
Attenborough, David
Zoo quest series (2)
Zoo quest for Guyana
Attenborough, David
Zoo quest series (1)
Zoo quest in Madagascar
Attenborough, David
Zoo quest series (5)
Zoo quest in Paraguay
Attenborough, David
Zoo quest series (3)
Zoo tales
Gillespie, Thomas Haining
Zoo ways series (2)
Zoo ways and whys
Gillespie, Thomas Haining
Zoo ways series (1)
Zoom!
Townend, Peter
Philip Quest series (2)
Zoom at sea
Wynne-Jones, Tim
Zoom series (1)
Zoom away
Wynne-Jones, Tim
Zoom series (2)
Zoomer builds a racing car
Mayer, Mercer
Tink, tonk tales series (8)
Zoovet
Taylor, David Conrad
Zoovet series (1)
Zorachus
Rogers, Mark Earl
Zorachus series (1)
Zork chronicles
Effinger, George Alec
Zork series (4)
Zorro
Verral, Charles Spain
Zorro series (3)
Zorro and the pirate raiders
Arneson, Don Jon
Zorro series (6)
Zorro and the secret plan
Verral, Charles Spain
Zorro series (4)
Zorro in old California
Nedaud
Zorro series (7)
Zorro rides again
Arneson, Don Jon
Zorro series (7)
Zorro, the gay blade
Dean, Les
Zorro series (5)
Zozo
Rey, Hans Augusto
Zozo series (1)
Zozo flies a kite
Rey, Margret
Zozo series (5)
Zozo gets a medal
Rey, Hans Augusto
Zozo series (4)
Zozo goes to the hospital
Rey, Margret
Zozo series (7)
Zozo learns the alphabet
Rey, Hans Augusto
Zozo series (6)
Zozo rides a bike
Rey, Hans Augusto
Zozo series (3)
Zozo takes a job
Rey, Hans Augusto
Zozo series (2)
Zuckerman bound
Roth, Philip
Nathan Zuckerman series (3)
Zuckerman unbound
Roth, Philip
Nathan Zuckerman series (2)
Zulu blood
Skimin, Robert
Soldier for hire series (1)
Zulu tak
Cobbett, Pelham
Dog series (3)
Zuni gold
Slade, Jack
Gatling series (1)
Zurich numbers
Granger, Bill
November Man series (6)
Zury
Kirkland, Joseph
McVeys series (1)

AUTHOR INDEX

A

A, A
see **Armstrong, Anthony**
Aamodt, Donald
- Name to conjure with series

Aardema, Verna
- Story hat series

Aaronovitz, Ben
- Doctor Who series

Aarons, Edward Sidney
see also **Ronns, Edward**
- Jerry Benedict series
- Sam Durell series

Aarons, Will B
- Sam Durell series

Aaseng, Nathan
- Devotions series
- Early nature picture book series
- Inside business series
- Nobel Prize winners series
- Sports acheivers series
- Sports heroes series
- Sports talk series
- You are the coach series

Abarbanell, Jacob Ralph
- He, she and it trilogy
- Pa and ma series

Abbey, Edward
- George W Hayduke series
- Jack Burns series

Abbey, Lynn
- Elfquest series
- Rifkind series
- Sanctuary series
- Unicorn and dragon series

Abbey, Marilyn Lorraine
see **Abbey, Lynn**
Abbot, Anthony
see also **Oursler, Fulton**
- Thatcher Colt series

Abbott, Edward
- Long Look trilogy

Abbott, Edwin Abbott
see also **Square**
- Flatland series

Abbott, Jacob
- August series
- Cousin Lucy series
- Florence series
- Franconia series
- Hoaryhead series
- Jonas series
- Juno series
- Marco Paul's adventures in pursuit of knowledge series
- Rainbow and Lucky series
- Rollo series
- Rollo's tour in Europe series
- Young Christian series

Abdullah, Achmed
- Red stain series

Abelson, Danny
- Fraggle Rock series

Abetti, Giorgio
- Universe series

Ableman, Paul
- Eddie Shoestring series
- Porridge series

Abraham, Cyril
- Onedin Line series

Abraham, Suzanne
- Everyperson series

Abrahams, Anthony
- Polonius Penguin series

Abrahams, Doris Caroline
see **Brahms, Caryl**
Abrahams, Robert
- Pete Taylor series

Abrahams, William
- George Orwell series

Abrahamsen, Christine Elizabeth
see **Cristabel**
Abramovitz, Rafael
see **Jordan, Robert**
Abrashkin, Raymond
- Danny Dunn series

Abse, Dannie
- Poet in the family series

Abshire, Richard
- Gants series
- Jack Kyle series

Aburdene, Patricia
- Megatrends series

Achebe, Chinua
- African trilogy

Achilleos, Chris
- Fantasy illustrations series

Ackworth, John
- Clogshop trilogy

Ackworth, Robert Charles
- Doctor Kildare junior series
- Doctor Kildare series

Acres, Mark
Combat Command in the world of Jerry E Pournelle's Janisseries
Janisseries trilogy (3)
- Combat Command series

Lord of the Lances
Janisseries trilogy (3)
- Runesword series
- Sniper series
- Starship troopers series

Acton, Harold
- Aesthete series

Adair, Denis
- MacLeod family series

Adair, Gilbert
- Alice in Wonderland sequels series
- Peter Pan series

Adair, James B
- Deepcore series
- World War III series

Adam, Paul
- Time of life series

Adam, Ronald
see **Blake**
Adam, Ruth
- Susan Marsh series

Adamo, Kara
Baby-Sitters Club trivia and puzzle fun book
Baby-Sitters Club series (78)
Adams, Agnes
- Doddles series
- Shepton children trilogy

Adams, Andy
- Biff Brewster series
- Wells brothers series

Adams, Barbara
- Kid-TV series

Adams, Cleve Franklin
- John J Shannon series
- Rex McBride series

Adams, Clifton
see also **Randall, Clay**
- Desperado series
- Tragg series

Adams, Douglas Noel
- Arthur Dent series
- Dirk Gently series
- Meaning of liff series

Adams, Eustace
- Air combat series

Adams, Eustace Lane
- Andy Lane series

Adams, Georgie
- Great Uncle Prickles series
- Mister Bill series

Adams, Harold
- Carl Wilcox series

Adams, Harrison
see also **Clifton, Oliver Lee; Rathborne, Saint George; Travers, J M**
- Pioneer boys series

Adams, Henry Cadwallader
- Birthday tales series
- Charlton School series
- Nethercourt series
- Walter's schooldays series

Adams, Herbert
- Jimmy Haswell series
- Major Roger Bennion series

Adams, Hunter
see also **Lawrence, Jim**
- Man from Planet X trilogy

Adams, Nicholas
- Horror High series

Adams, Phillip
- Unspeakable series

Adams, Richard
- Beklan Empire series

Adams, Robert
- Barbarians series
- Castaways in time series
- Horseclans series
- Magic in Ithkar series
- Stairway to forever series

Adams Round Table
- Manhattan series

Adams, Samuel Hopkins
see also **Fabian, Warner**
- Percy Darrow series
- Ruyland family series

Adams, Shipley
- Inspector Harrow series

Adams, Terry A
- Sentience series

Adams, William
- Charlton School series

Adams, William Taylor
see **Optic, Oliver**
Adamson, Gareth
- Life with Topsy and Tim series
- Mister Budge series
- Topsy and Tim activity series
- Topsy and Tim board book series
- Topsy and Tim series

Adamson, George
- Elsa series

Adamson, Jean
- Life with Topsy and Tim series
- Topsy and Tim activity series
- Topsy and Tim board book series
- Topsy and Tim series

Adamson, Joy
- Elsa series

Adamson, Lydia
- Alice Nestleton series

Adcock, Thomas
- Neil Hockaday series

Addis, Faith
- Devon farm series

Ade, George
- Fables in slang series

Adelman, Deborah
- Children of Perestroika series

Adelson, Leone
- Mister Twitmeyer series

Adkins, Bill
- Dave Hill series

Adkins, Patrick H
- Titans series

Adlard, Mark
- Jan Caspol trilogy

Adler, Bill
- Robins family series

Adler, Carole Schwerdtfeger
- Footsteps series
- Glits series
- Pink Pig series
- Sisters series

Adler, David A
- Cam Jansen series
- Fourth Floor twins series
- Happy Rebus series
- Jeffrey's ghost series
- My dog series
- Picture book of Jewish holidays series
- T F Benson series

Adler, Mortimer Jerome
- Revolution series

Adler, Warren
- Fiona Fitzgerald series

Adler, William
see **Adler, Bill**
Adorjan, Carol
- Junior High series

Adrian, Jack
- Deathlands series

Adye, John
- Oliver Smaile series

Affabee, Eric
- Find your fate: G.I. Joe series
- Wizards, warlocks and you series

Afford, Max
- Jeffery Blackburn series

Afghan
- Asaf Khan series

Agard, John
- Caribbean series

Agate, James
- Ego series

Agee, Jonis
- Divinity series

Agneau, Marcel d'
see **D'Agneau, Marcel**
Agnew, Emily C
- Geraldine series

Agnus, Orme
- Sarah Tuldon series

Agry, Ed
- O'Reilly series

Aguilar, Grace
- Home influence series

Ahern, Jerry
- Dan Track series
- Defender series
- Surgical strike series
- Survivalist series
- Takers series

Ahern, Sharon
- Takers series

Ahlberg, Allan
- Brick Street Boys series
- Daisychain series
- Foldaways series
- Funnybones series
- Happy family series
- Help your child to read series
- Jolly postman series
- Mrs Butler series
- Red nose readers series
- Two heads series

Ahlberg, Janet
- Brick Street Boys series
- Daisychain series
- Jolly postman series
- Two heads series

Ahlswede, Ann
- Doctor Cicero Smith series

Aicard, Jean
- Maurin series

Aiken, Albert W
- Dick Talbot series
- Fresh series
- Lone Hand series

Aiken, Joan
- Arabel and Mortimer series
- Armitage family series
- Dido Twite series
- Eliza Brandon series
- Felix Brooke series
- Mansfield Park series
- Miss Jane Fairfax series
- Petworth series

Aikman, Anthony
- Boyet Rhodes series

Aimwell, Walter
- Boy series

Ainsworth, Eustace
- Billie Impett series

Ainsworth, Patricia
- Burnley series

Ainsworth, Ruth
- Charles series
- Ghostly tales series
- Little Mushrooms series
- Look about you series
- Lucky dip series
- Rufty Tufty series
- Shellover series

Airault, Dominique
- Little animal series

Aird, Catherine
- Inspector C D Sloan series

Airey, Jean
Travel with the Tardis
Doctor Who series (162)
Airey, John
Doctor and the Enterprise
Star trek series (57)
Aitken, Amy
- Ruby series

Aitken, William Maxwell
see **Beaverbrook, William Maxwell Aitken**
Akers, Alan Burt
see also **Blake, Ken; Bulmer, Kenneth; Frazier, Arthur; Hardy, Adam; Krauss, Bruno; Prescot, Dray; Silver, Richard; Zetford, Tully**
- Dray Prescot series

Akers, Floyd
see also **Bancroft, Laura; Baum, Lyman Frank; Fitzgerald, Hugh**
- Boy fortune hunters series

Akrill, Caroline
- Eventing trilogy

Aks, Patricia
- Cheerleaders series
- Prom series
- Two by two series

Aksakov, Sergei Timofeevich
- Russian family chronicle series

Alais, Ernest W
- Sexton Blake series

Alanbrooke, Alan Francis Brooke
- Second World War series

Albano, Peter
- Seventh Carrier series

Albany, James
see also **Crawford, Robert; Rae, Hugh Crauford**
- S.A.S. series

Albert, Andrew I
- Paul Decker series

Albert, Marvin Henry
Tony Rome
Tony Rome series (1)
Albert, Marvin Hubert
see also **Conroy, Al; Quarry, Nick; Rome, Anthony**
- Clayburn series
- Inspector Clouseau series
- Pierre-Ange Sawyer series

Albert, Susan Wittig
- China Bayles series

Albom, Mitch
- Live Albom series

Alborough, Jez
- Bare bear series
- Bear hugs series

Albrecht, Howard
Exerciser
Lieutenant Bill Kinderman series (1)
Albright, Molly
- Two of a kind series

Alcott, Louisa May
- Aunt Jo's scrap-bag series
- Jo March series
- Rose Campbell series

Aldanov, Mark Aleksandrovich
- Thinker series

Alden, Isabella
see **Pansy**
Alden, William Livingston
- Jimmy Brown series
- Moral Pirates series

Alderman, Gill
- Guna series

Alderson, Sue Ann
- Bonnie McSmithers series

Alding, Peter
see also **Jefferies, Roderic Graeme**
- C.I.D. Room series

Aldiss, Brian Wilson
- Doctor Moreau series
- Dracula series
- Frankenstein series
- Helliconia trilogy
- Horace Stubbs series
- Squire quartet

Aldous, Allan
- McGowan series

Aldrich, Bess Streeter
- Abbie Deal series

Aldridge, Alan
- Butterfly ball series

Aldridge, James
- Kit Quayle series
- Rupert Royce series

Aldridge, Janet
- Meadow-Brook girls series

Aldridge, Ray
- Emancipator series

Aldyne, Nathan
- Dan Valentine and Clarissa Lovelace series

Aleichem, Sholom
- Tevye the milkman series

Alex, Benny
- You and me series

Alex, Marlee
- You and me series

Alexander, David
- Bart Hardin series
- Lieutenant Romano series
- Marty Land series
- Phoenix series
- Tommy Twotoes and Terry Rooke series

Alexander, Gary
- Superintendent Bamsan Kiet series

Alexander, Lloyd
- Prydain series
- Vesper Holly series
- Westmark trilogy

Alexander, Louis George
- Professor Boffin series

Alexander, Marc
- Haunted Britain series
- Legendary castles of Britain series
- Wells of Ythan series

Alexander, Martha G
- Blackboard Bear series

Alexander, Martin
- Alan Kelton series

Alexander, Paul
- Dark forces series

Alexander, Sidney
- Michelangelo Buonarotti trilogy

Alger, Horatio
see also **Bonehill, Ralph; Stratemeyer, Edward L; Winfield, Arthur M**
- Atlantic series
- Brave and bold series
- Campaign trilogy
- Frank and fearless trilogy
- Good fortune trilogy
- How to rise trilogy
- Luck and pluck series
- New world trilogy
- Pacific series
- Ragged Dick series
- Rise in life series
- Tattered Tom series
- Victory trilogy

Algozin, Bruce
- Endless quest series

Aliki
• Dear series
Alington, Adrian
• Inspector Posse series
• Payling Green series
Alington, Cyril Augustine
• Archdeacon series
• Mister Birtley series
Allain, Marcel
• Fantomas series
Allan, Angus P
• Thunderbirds series
Allan, Joan
• Valerie Lambert series
Allan, Lennox
• Living sword series
Allan, Luke
• Blue Pete series
• Tiger Lillie series
Allan, Mabel Esther
see also **Estoril, Jean**
• Author series
• Crumble Lane series
• Garland family series
• Harvie family series
• Pine Street series
• Spindle Bottom series
• Wood Street series
Allan, Mea
• Staveney series
Allard, Harry
• Miss Nelson series
• Stupids series
Allbeury, Ted
see also **Butler, Richard**
• Tad Anders series
Allbury, Albert George
• War in South-East Asia series
Allcard, Edward Cecil
• Temptress series
Allcock, Phil
• Stories of the realm series
Alldritt, Keith
• Black country series
Allee, Marjorie Hill
• Lankester family trilogy
Allegretto, Michael
• Jacob Lomax series
Allegro, John Marco
• Christian origins series
Allen, Alice E
• Martie twins series
Allen, Austen
• Inspector Ord series
Allen, Betsy
see also **Cavanna, Betty**
• Connie Blair series
Allen, Charles Fletcher
• Trail blazers series
Allen, Charlotte Vale
• Hidden meanings series
Allen, Chester
• Justice Colt series
Allen, Edward Heron-
see **Blayre, Christopher**
Allen, Eric
• Pepe Moreno series
• Whiskey Smith series
Allen, Gina
• History of gold series
• Prairie children series
• Tales of the prairies series
Allen, Henry
see **Fisher, Clay**
Allen, Herbert Warner
• Mister Clerihew series
Allen, Hervey
• Disinherited series
Allen, Inglis
• 'Varsity series
Allen, James Lane
• Christmas season series
• Kentucky series
Allen, Jane
• Hello series
Allen, Joy
• Charlie series
• Percy series
Allen, Julia
• Mary Livingstone series
• My first series
Allen, Linda
• Lionel series
• Mrs Simkin series
• Parrot in the house series
Allen, Martin
• Fighting fantasy gamebook series
Allen, Merritt Parmelee
• Mudhen series
Allen, Michael
• Superintendent Ben Spence series
Allen, Pamela
• Mister McGee series
Allen, Quincy
• Outdoor chums series
Allen, Richard
• Joe Hawkins series
Allen, Roger Macbride
• Caliban series
Allen, Roger MacBride
• Crisis of empire trilogy
Allen, Roger Macbride
• Torch series
Allen, Sheila Rosalynd
• Lovers of Steadford Abbey series
Allen, Warner
see **Allen, Herbert Warner**
Allen, Willis Boyd
• Camp and tramp series
• Pine cone series
• Siege of Boston series
Alliluyeva, Svetlana
• Letters to a friend series
Allingham, Margery
• Albert Campion series
Allingham case-book
Albert Campion series (23)
Allingham omnibus
Albert Campion series (23)
Allington, Richard L
• Beginning to learn series
Allis, Marguerite
• Ashbel Field series
Allison, Clyde
• Agent triple zero eight series
Allison, Errol Sampson
• Kiwi series
Allison-Williams, Jean
• Tabard series
Allonby, Edith
• Lucifram series
Allum, Nancy
• Monica series
Allum, Tom
• Captain Michael Triggington series
• Hurricane Harland series
Allyson, Alan
• Martin Ross series
Almedingen, Edith Martha
• Andrew Thornyold series
• To-morrow will come trilogy
Almirall, Roc
• Victor and Maria series
Almqvist, Bertil
• Stones series
Alonso, Alejandro Nunez
see **Nunez Alonso, Alejandro**
Alpers, Mary Rose
see **Campion, Sarah**
Alsop, Mary O'Hara
see **O'Hara, Mary**
Alter, Judy
• Maggie and Devildust series
Althea
• Desmond the dinosaur series
• Gingerbread series
• Jeremy Mouse series
Altsheler, Joseph Alexander
• Civil War series
• French and Indian war series
• Great West series
• Texas trilogy
• Trailers series
• World War trilogy
Alverson, Charles
• Joe Goodey series
Amadieu, Francoise
• Virginia series
Amadio, Nadine
• Alice in Wonderland sequels series
Amberley, Richard
• Inspector Martin series
Ambler, Dail
see also **Spade, Danny**
• Danny Spade series
Ambler, Eric
• Andreas and Tamara Valeshoff series
• Arthur Abdel Simpson series
• Charles Latimer series
Ambrose, Stephen Edward
• Eisenhower series
• Richard Nixon series
Ambrus, Victor Gyozo
• Dracula trilogy
Amery, Leopold Stennett
• My political life trilogy
Ames, Delano
• Dagobert and Jane Brown series
• Juan Llorca series
• Sexton Blake series
Ames, Francis Herbert
• Callahan series
Ames, Franklin T
• Between the lines series
Ames, James Bushnell
• Curly Graham trilogy
Ames, Louise Bates
• Your child series
Ames, Marion
see also **Taggert, Marion Ames**
• Winnetou trilogy
Ames, Sarah Rachel
see **Gainham, Sarah**
Amey, Linda
• Blair Emerson series
Aminoff, Constance Leonie Caroline
• Napoleonic series
Amis, Kingsley
see also **Markham, Robert**
• Patrick Standish series
Ammers-Kuller, Jo van
• Jenny Heysten series
• Leyden trilogy
Amsbury, Mary Anne
see **Littleton, Kay**
Amstutz, Andre
• Funnybones series
Amthor, Terry K
• Middle Earth quest series
Amy, William Lacey
see **Allan, Luke**
Anand, Mulk Raj
• Lal Singh trilogy
• Pilpali Sahab series
• Seven ages of man series
Anand, Valerie
• Bridges over time series
• Norman trilogy
Anckarsvard, Karin
• Bonifacius series
• Jon Halvorsson series
Anderson, Catherine
• Comanche trilogy
Anderson, Catherine Corley
• Sister Beatrice series
Anderson, Chester
• Greenwich Village trilogy
Anderson, Clarence William
• Billy and Blaze series
Anderson, Elaine
• Pleistocene mammals series
Anderson, Frederick Irving
• Deputy Parr series
• Oliver Armiston series
Anderson, Helen M
• Kelston of Kells series
Anderson, Ian
• Scarlet riders series
Anderson, Jack
• Alice in Wonderland parodies series
Anderson, James
• Inspector Wilkins series
• Jessica Fletcher series
• Mikael Petros series
Anderson, John Richard Lane
• Inspector Piet Deventer series
• Major Peter Blair series
Anderson, Karen
• King of Ys series
Anderson, Kevin James
• Gamearth trilogy
Anderson, Margaret Jean
• Time trilogy
Anderson, Mary
• Mostly ghosts series
Anderson, Oliver
• Guy Random series
Anderson, Poul
• Alternate world series
• Conan series
• Future history series
• Hoka series
Inconstant star
Man-Kzin wars series (5)
• King of Ys series
• Known Space series
• Last Viking trilogy
Man-Kzin wars
Man-Kzin wars series (1)
Man-Kzin wars III
Known Space series (19)
• Man-Kzin wars series
• Polesotechnic League series
• Psychotechnic League series
• Sir Dominic Flandry series
• Time Patrol series
• Trygve Yamamura series
Anderson, Sherwood
• Story-teller series
Anderson, Verily
• Anderson family series
• Brownies series
• York family series
Anderson, William Charles
• Penelope series
Andom, R
• Troddles series
Andover, Henry
• Henry Holland series
Andreus, Hans
• Mister Bumblemoose series
Andrew, Christopher
• K.G.B. series
Andrew, Prudence
• Ginger Jenkins series
Andrews, Allen
• Pig Plantagenet series
Andrews, Charlton
• Drexel Ware series
Andrews, Colin
• Crop circles series
Andrews, Jane
• Saint Peter's Hospital series
• Seven little sisters series
Andrews, John
• Sexton Blake series
Andrews, Keith William
• Freedom's Rangers series
Andrews, Lucilla
see also **Marcus, Joanna**
• Saint Barnabas' Hospital series
• Saint Martha's Hospital series
• Wally's Ward series
Andrews, Raymond
• Appalachee Red series
Andrews, Roy Chapman
• Quest series
Andrews, Spike
• C.A.T. series
Andrews, Stephen
• Nobby Clark and Snowy White series
Andrews, Val
• Sherlock Holmes sequels series
Andrews, Virginia Cleo
• Casteel-Tatterton family series
• Cutler family series
• Dollanganger family series
Andrews, Wendy
• Vacation fever series
Andric, Ivo
• Bosnian trilogy
Andriene, Maryat Rollet-
see **Arsan, Emmanuelle**
Anello, Christine
• Farmyard Cat series
Anethan, Eleanora Mary d'
• Twin soul series
Angelou, Maya
• Heart of a woman series
Anglund, Joan Walsh
• Cowboy series
Angoff, Charles
• Polonsky family series
Angus, David
• Grange Hill series
Anholt, Catherine
• Truffles series
Annesley, Michael
• Lawrence Fenton series
Anno, Mitsumasa
• Anno's journey series
• Math games series
• Pictures to stretch the imagination series
Annunzio, Gabriele d'
• Romances of the rose trilogy
Anonymous
• Daniel Deronda series
• Diary series
Indiana Jones, his life and adventure
Indiana Jones series (9)
• Lemuel Gulliver series
• Lilliput series
• Pronoun series
• Star trek fan series
Ansle, Dorothy Phoebe
see **Elsna, Hebe**
Anson, Brian
• Gus and Gilly series
Anson, Jay
• Amityville horror series
Anson, Lindsay
• Peter Allen series
Anstey, Roger
• Congo series
Anstruther, Eileen Harriet
• Farm servant trilogy
Anthony, Barbara
see **Barber, Antonia**
Anthony, David
• Morgan Butler series
• Stanley Bass series
Anthony, Elizabeth
• Pauline Lyons series
Anthony, Evelyn
• Catherine the Great trilogy
• Davina Graham series
Anthony, Frank Sheldon
• Gus Tomlins series
Anthony, Jane
• Wistaria Street series
Anthony, Lotta Rowe
• Anne Thornton series
Anthony, Mark
• Meetings series
Anthony, Piers
• Apprentice adept series
• Aton series
• Battle circle trilogy
• Bio of a space tyrant series
• Cluster series
• Dragon series
• Geodyssey series
• Incarnations of immortality series
• Jason Striker series
• Mode series
• Of man and mantra trilogy
• Tarot trilogy
• Xanth series
Antill, Elizabeth
• Inspector Simon Ashton series
Antonius, Soraya
• Lord series
Antony, Jonquil
• Dale family series
Antony, Peter
• Mister Verity series
Antrobus, John
• Ronnie series
Appel, Allen
• Alex Balfour series
Appiah, Peggy
• Ashanti series
Appignanesi, Richard
• Italia perversa trilogy
Apple, A E
• Mister Chang series
Apple, Margot
• Sheep series
Appleton, Victor
• Don Sturdy series
• Motion picture chums series
• Movie boys series
• Moving picture boys series
• Tom Swift series
Appleton, Victor II
• Tom Swift Junior series 1
• Tom Swift Junior series 2
• Tom Swift Junior series 3
Aragon, Louis
• Real world series
Arbuthnot, John
• Lilliput series
Arceval, Julio
see **Madariaga, Salvador de**
Archer, Frank
see also **Wayland, Patrick**
• Inspector Joseph Delaney series
Archer, Fred
• Evesham Vale series
Archer, Jeffrey
• William Kane and Abel Rosnovski series
Archibald, George, *Mrs*
• Lady Gay trilogy
Architects Adventure
Dzurlord
Jhereg series (5)
Ard, William
see also **Ward, Jonas**
• Danny Fontaine series
• Lou Largo series
• Timothy Dane series
Arden, William
see also **Collins, Michael; Crowe, John; Sadler, Mark**
• Kane Jackson series
• Three Investigators Crimebusters series
• Three Investigators series
Ardies, Tom
• Charlie Sparrow series
Ardizzone, Edward
• Tim series
Ardley, Neil
• Birds series
Arendt, Veronique
• Zoe and George series
Aresbys
• Parrish Darby series
Argo, Ellen
• Julia Howard trilogy
Arkell, Reginald
• Green fingers series

Arkle, Phyllis
- Railway Cat series
- Roddy series
- Village dinosaur series

Arlen, Leslie
see also **Grange, Peter; Logan, Mark; Nicole, Christopher; York, Andrew**
- Borodin family series

Arlen, Michael
- Charming people series

Arlen, Trudi
- Shirley Flight series

Arliss, Joen
- Kate Graham series

Armfelt, Roger
- Affairs series

Armitage, Aileen
- Chapter series
- Hawksmoor series

Armitage, David
- Lighthouse keeper series

Armitage, Ronda
- Lighthouse keeper series

Armitage, Taylor
- Uncle Sam's service series

Armour, R Coutts
- Sexton Blake series

Armour, Richard
- It all started with series

Armstrong, Anthony
- Jimmie Rezaire series
- Margaret Cottage series
- Patrick Kennedy series
- Percival series
- Warriors series

Armstrong, April
- Bible stories series

Armstrong, Campbell
see also **Black, Campbell**
- Detective Frank Pagan series

Armstrong, Carolyn T
- Leather and lace series

Armstrong, Charlotte
- MacDougal Duff series

Armstrong, Evelyn Stewart
- Valdoro series

Armstrong, F W
see also **Wright, Terrance Michael**
- Changing series

Armstrong, Jennifer
see also **Winfield, Julia**
- Pets, Inc. series

Armstrong, Raymond
see also **Corrigan, Mark; Hobart, Robertson**
- Inspector Dick Mason series
- J Rockingham Stone series
- Laura Scudamore series

Armstrong, Richard
- History of seafaring series

Armstrong, Sarah
- Twilight series

Armstrong, Sybil
- Clachan series

Armstrong, Thomas
- Crowther chronicles series

Armstrong, William
- Moses Waters series

Arnam, Dave van
see **Van Arnam, Dave**

Arneson, Don Jon
- Zorro series

Arnett, Jack
- Book of justice series

Arnim, Mary Annette von
see **Russell, Mary Annette**

Arnold, Allan
- Sherlock Holmes sequels series

Arnold, Bruce
- Coppinger tetralogy

Arnold, Emily
- Grandma series

Arnold, Eric H
- Kids talk series

Arnold, Henry
- Bill Bruce series

Arnold, Judith
- Keeping the faith trilogy

Arnold, Margot
- Penelope Spring and Sir Tobias Glendower series

Arnold, Mark Alan
- Borderland series
- Elsewhere trilogy

Arnold, Ralph
- Orange Street series

Arnosky, Jim
- Crinkleroot series
- Mouse series
- Nathaniel series
- Sketching outdoors series

Arnothy, Christine
- Living series

Arnott, Peter
- Impertinence series

Arnott, Tom
see **Stivers, Dick**

Arnow, Harriette
- Cumberland series
- Kentucky trilogy

Aron, Robert
- Liberation of France series

Aronin, Ben
- Raphael Drale series

Arrow, William
- Return to the Planet of the Apes series

Ars, Yvonne de Bremond d'
see **Bremond d'Ars, Yvonne de**

Arsan, Emmanuelle
- Emmanuelle series

Arthur, Budd
- Johnny Canavan series
- Texas Rangers series

Arthur, Burt
see also **Shappiro, Herbert**
- Dan Lovett series
- Johnny Canavan series
- Mustang Marshal series
- Texas Rangers series

Arthur, Frank
- Inspector Spearpoint series

Arthur, Robert
- Three Investigators series

Arthur, Ruth Mabel
- Carolina series
- Crooked brownie series

Arthur, Timothy Shay
- Home stories series
- Household library series
- Nothing but money series

Arthur, William
- Sexton Blake series

Arundel, Honor
- Emma series
- Janet Meredith series

Arundel, Louis
- Motor boat boys series

Arvay, Harry
- Israeli Security Branch series
- Triad series

Asbury, Herbert
- Inspector Thomas Conroy series

Asch, Frank
- Bear series
- I can series
- Pearl series

Asch, Sholem
- Biblical series

Ascher, Eugene
- Lucian Carolus series

Ascott, John
- Sexton Blake series

Ash, Constance
- Horsegirl series

Ash, Russell
Life and times of Paddington Bear
Paddington series (11)

Ash, William
- Kyle Brandeis series

Ashbrook, Harriette
- Philip Tracy series

Ashby, Ruth
- Time machine series

Ashdown, Clifford
- Romney Pringle series

Ashe, Geoffrey
- King Arthur series

Ashe, Gordon
see also **Creasey, John; Deane, Norman; Halliday, Michael; Marric, J J; Morton, Anthony; York, Jeremy**
- Patrick Dawlish series

Ashe, Mary Ann
see also **Brand, Christianna**
- Inspector Chucky series

Ashe, Saxon
- Saxon Ashe series

Asher, Jane
- Moppy series

Asher, Sandra Fenichel
- Ballet One series
- Teddy Teabury series

Ashford, Jeffrey
see also Draper, Hastings; Graeme, Roderic; Jefferies, Roderic Graeme
- Detective Inspector Don Kerry series
- Grand Prix series

Ashley, Bernard
- Clipper Street series

Ashmun, Margaret Eliza
- Isabel Carleton series

Ashton, Charles
- Jack Atherley series

Ashton, Elizabeth
- Renee and Leon Thornton series

Ashton, Helen
- Wilchester chronicles series

Ashton, Lamar
see also **Sayler, Harry Lincoln**
- Aeroplane boys series

Ashton, Winifred
see **Dane, Clemence**

Asimov, Isaac
see also **French, Paul**
Big sun of Mercury
David Starr series (4)
- Black Widowers series
- Caliban series
- Elijah Baley series
- Fantastic voyage series
- Foundation series

Moons of Jupiter
David Starr series (5)
- Norby series

Oceans of Venus
David Starr series (3)
Pirates of the asteroids
David Starr series (2)
Rings of Saturn
David Starr series (6)
- Robot series

Space ranger
David Starr series (1)
- Trantorian Empire trilogy

Asimov, Janet Jeppson
- Norby series

Asire, Nancy
- Sword of knowledge series
- Sword of knowledge trilogy

Aska, Warabe
- Park series

Askew, Alice
- Deborah Krillet series

Askew, Claude
- Deborah Krillet series

Askin, Julian
- Connection series

Aspinall, Ruth
- Malinson brothers trilogy

Asprin, Robert Lynn
Blood of ten chiefs
Elfquest series (2)
- Cold cash war series
- Combat Command series
- Duncan and Mallory series
- Phule series
- Sanctuary series
- Skeeve series

Wolfsong
Elfquest series (3)

Asquith, Cynthia
- Remember series

Assis, Joachim Maria Machado de
see **Machado de Assis, Joachim Maria**

Ast, Janine
- Beebo series

Aston, Elizabeth
- I am growing up series

Astor, Brooke
- Patchwork child series

Astrop, John
- Frog and Dog series
- Peep series

Asturias, Miguel Angel
- Guatemala trilogy

Atherton, Gertrude Franklin
- Wives and husbands series

Atkey, Bertram
- Smiler Bunn series
- Winnie O'Wynn series

Atkey, Philip
see **Perowne, Barry**

Atkin, Flora Blumenthal
- Tarradiddle series

Atkins, Evelyn Edith
- Cornish island series

Atkins, Meg Elizabeth
- Inspector Henry Beaumont series

Atkinson, Alex
- Rocking-chair series

Atkinson, Mary Evelyn
- Fricka Hammond series
- Lockett family series

Atlee, Philip
- Joe Gall series

Attanasio, A A
- Radix Tetrad series

Attenborough, David
- Zoo quest series

Atterton, Julian
- Knights trilogy
- Robin Hood series

Attwood, Tony
- Blake's Seven series
- Companions of Doctor Who series

Atwater, Montgomery Meigs
- Hank Winton series

Atyeo, Don
- Famous last words series

Aubin, Etienne
- Dracula series

Aubrey, Edmund
- Sherlock Holmes sequels series

Aubrey, Frank
- Monella trilogy

Aubrey-Fletcher, Henry Lancelot
see **Wade, Henry**

Audemars, Pierre
- Hercule Renard series
- Monsieur Pinaud series

Audoux, Marguerite
- Marie-Claire series

Auel, Jean Marie
- Earth's children series

Augarde, Steve
- Barnaby Shrew series
- Bertha series

Augustin-Thierry, Gilbert
see **Thierry, Gilbert Augustin**

Aulaire, Edgar Paris d'
see **D'Aulaire, Edgar Parin**

Aulaire, Ingri d'
see **D'Aulaire, Ingri**

Aunt Hattie
see **Hattie, Aunt**

Auntie Muriel
see **Levy, Muriel**

Austen, Jane
- Bennet family series
- Brightsea series
- Eliza Brandon series
- Mansfield Park series
- Margaret Dashwood series
- Miss Jane Fairfax series
- Northanger Abbey series
- Presumption series
- Pride and prejudice series
- Teverton Hall series
- Watsons series

Austen-Leigh, J E
Memoir of Jane Austen
Watsons series (1)

Auster, Paul
- New York trilogy

Austin, Anne
- James F Dundee series

Austin, Brett
see also **Floren, Lee; Smith, Lew**
- Judge Lemanuel Bates and Tobacco Jones series

Austin, Frederick Britten
- Napoleon Bonaparte series

Austin, Hugh
- Peter Quint series
- William Sultan series

Austin, Jane Goodwin
- Dora Darling series
- Nameless nobleman series
- Pilgrims of Plymouth series

Austin, Jim
- John Fury series

Austin, Margot
- Church animals series

Austin, Mary
- Californian Indian series

Austin, Richard
see also **Milan, Victor**
- Guardians series

Austwick, John
see also **Lee, Austin**
- Inspector Parker series

Autry, Gene
- Gene Autry tell-a-tale series

Auty, Phyllis
see **Richards, Phyllis**

Avallone, Michael
see also **Noone, Edwina**
- Charlie Chan series
- Ed Noon series

Friday the thirteenth, part III
Friday the thirteenth series (3)
- Girl from U.N.C.L.E.series
- Hawaii Five-O series
- Man from U.N.C.L.E. series
- Mannix series
- Partridge family series
- Planet of the Apes series
- Satan Sleuth series

Three-D
Friday the thirteenth series (3)

Aveline, Claude
- Suite Policiere series

Avenell, Donne
- Axa series

Averill, Esther
- Jenny Linsky series

Avery, Al
see also **Montgomery, Rutherford George**
- Yankee flier series

Avery, Elizabeth
- Babs series

Avery, Gillian
- Ellen Timms series
- Julia and Henry Gresham trilogy
- Maria Henniker-Haddon series
- Mister Copplestone series
- Onlookers series
- Smith family series

Avery, Richard
- Expendables series

Avery, Robert
- Joe Kelly series

Avery, Valerie
- London trilogy

Avi
- South Orange River Middle School series

Avon, Robert Anthony Eden
see **Eden, Anthony**

Awdry, Christopher
- Railway series

Awdry, Wilbert
- Belinda series
- Railway series
- Sodor series

Thomas' ABC
Railway series (37)
Thomas comes to breakfast
Railway series (37)
Thomas' counting book
Railway series (37)
Thomas's Christmas party
Railway series (37)

Awlinson, Richard
- Avatar trilogy
- Empires trilogy
- Harpers series

Axelrod, David
- Sesame Street series

Axler, James
see also **Darke, James; Fraser, Mary; Haigh, Richard; James, Laurence; Marvin, James W; May, Jonathan; McPhee, James; Netzen, Klaus; Nolan, Christopher; Norman, Mick**
- Deathlands series
- Earthblood series

Axworthy, Anni
- I don't want to series

Ayer, Alfred Jules
- My life series
- Western philosophy series

Aykroyd, Peter
- Gymnast Gilly series

Aylward, Marcus
- Harper series

Ayme, Marcel
- Wonderful Farm series

Ayres, Paul
Dead heat
Flash Casey series (6)

Ayres, Ruby Mildred
- Richard Chatterton series

B

B B
- Bill Badger series
- Boland series
- Monty Woodpig series
- Oak Tree House series
- Wildfowling series

B, H N W
see **Baker, Harriette Newell Woods**

Baantjer, Albert Cornelis
- Inspector De Kok series

Babbin, Jaqueline
- Clovis Kelly series

Babbitt, Lucy Cullyford
- Melde series

Babbitt, Natalie
- Small poems series

Babcock, Dwight Vincent
- Hannah Van Doren series

Baber, Monica
see **Hutchings, Monica Mary**

Babson, Marian
- Douglas Perkins and Gerry Tate series

- Family holiday series
- Trixie Dolan and Evangeline Sinclair series

Babula, William
- Saint John series

Bacchelli, Riccardo
- Mill on the Po series

Bacheller, Irving
- Abraham Lincoln trilogy
- Cheerful Yankee trilogy
- Eben Holden series
- Socrates Potter trilogy

Bachmann, Lawrence Paul
- Ben Clancy series

Backhouse, Elizabeth
- Inspector Christopher Marsden series
- Inspector Prentis series

Backus, Jean Louise
see **Montross, David**

Backus, William
- Telling the truth series

Bacon, Josephine Dodge
- Lowry series

Bacon, Ronald Leonard
- Valley series

Baddeley, Pam
- Star trek fan series

Baddeley, Victor Clinton Clinton-
see **Clinton-Baddeley, Victor Clinton**

Baddock, James
- Cormack and Woodward series

Baen, Jim
- Asher Bockhorn series

Baer, Judy
- Cedar River daydreams series
- Dear Judy series

Baerlein, Henry
- Mariposa series

Bagby, George
see also **Stein, Aaron Marc; Stone, Hampton**
- Inspector Schmidt series

Bagdon, Paul
- Scrapper John series

Bagley, Desmond
- Max Stafford series
- Slade series

Baglio, Ben M
- Choose your own adventure series

Bagnold, Enid
- Girl's journey series
- Velvet series

Bagot, Richard
- Passport series

Bagshaw, Joyce Margaret
- Hobstones series

Bagster, Hubert
- Country doctor series

Bahlke, Valerie Worth
see **Worth, Valerie**

Baigent, Michael
- Order of Sion series

Bailey, Anthony
- America and England series

Bailey, Donna
- Health facts series
- What we can do about series

Bailey, Elliot
- Inspector Geoffrey Fraser series

Bailey, Gerald Earl
- Nurlingas series
- Saga of Thorgrim series

Bailey, Henry Christopher
- Mister Joshua Clunk series
- Mister Reggie Fortune series

Bailey, Hilary
- Polly series
- Sherlock Holmes sequels series

Bailey, Hilea
- Hilea Bailey and Hilary Dunsany Bailey series

Bailey, Jill
- Animals of course series

Bailey, Maralyn
- Small boat series

Bailey, Maurice
- Small boat series

Bailey, Nancy
- Time machine series

Bailey, Pearl
- Pearl series
- Raw Pearl series

Bailey, Robin Wayne
- Dungeon series
- Frost trilogy

Lost city of Zork
Zork series (4)

Bain, Francis William
- Indian mystic love stories series

Bainbridge, Chuck
- Hard corps series

Baines, Cuthbert
- Dennis Doyne series

Baines, Frank
- Sea series

Baines, Lew
- Cimarron series

Baird, Jean Katherine
- Hester trilogy

Bairnsfather, Bruce
- Old Bill series

Baker, Alan
- Benjamin series

Baker, Ann
- Kids' stuff series

Baker, Asa
see also **Blood, Matthew; Davis, Don; Dresser, Davis; Halliday, Brett**
- Jerry Burke series

Baker, Carin Greenberg
- Last summer, first love series

Baker, Charlotte
- Thunderbird series

Baker, Daisy
- Donkey trap series

Baker, Denis
- Kids' stuff series

Baker, Denys Val
- Cornish series

Baker, Donna
- Glassmakers series

Baker, Elizabeth
- Tammy series

Baker, Etta Anthony
- Fairmount girls series

Baker, George
- Trojan War trilogy

Baker, George Philip
- Greenwood series

Baker, Harriette Newell Woods
see also **Hattie, Aunt; Leslie, Madeline**
- Sophie series

Baker, Howard
- Dead and alive series

Baker, Ivon
- David Meynell series

Baker, James
- Cardinal Henry Beaufort series

Baker, James Webb
- Magic series

Baker, Jane
- Doctor Who find your fate series
- Doctor Who series
- Trial of the Time Lord series

Baker, Jeannie
- Grandparents series

Baker, Jennifer
- Last summer, first love series

Baker, Kathleen
- Ashton family series

Baker, Margaret Joyce
- Homer series
- Ridley family series
- Three bears series

Baker, Mary Elizabeth
see **Baker, Elizabeth**

Baker, Mary Gladys Steel
see **Stuart, Sheila**

Baker, Nikki
- Virginia Kelly series

Baker, Penny
see **Anthony, Jane**

Baker, Pip
- Doctor Who find your fate series
- Doctor Who series
- Trial of the Time Lord series

Baker, Ray Stannard
see **Grayson, David**

Baker, Richard Merriam
- Franklin Russell series

Baker, Richard Saint Barbe
- Kabongo series

Baker, Russell
- Good times series

Baker, Samm Sinclair
- Clark Clark Clark series

Baker, Scott
- Ashlu cycle series

Dhampire
Dracula series (26)

Baker, Sharon
- Naphar series

Baker, Sidney M
Your ten- to fourteen-year-old
Your child series (10)

Baker, Stephen
- How to series

Baker, Trudy
- Coffee, tea or me girls series

Baker, Willard F
- Bob Dexter series
- Boy ranchers series

Baker, William Howard
see also **Ballinger, W A; McNeilly, Wilfred; Reid, Desmond**
- Dangerman series
- Guardians series
- Pinkerton series
- Richard Quintain series
- Sexton Blake series

Balaam
- Chalk series

Baldry, Cherith
- Stories of six worlds series

Baldwin, Alex
- Men at war series

Baldwin, Bill
- Helmsman series

Baldwin, Faith
- Condit family series
- Divine corners series
- Doctor Bing Irvington series
- Little Oxford series

Baldwin, James Arthur
- Native son series

Baldwin, Mary
- Fifi series
- Sibyl series

Baldwin, Merl William
see **Baldwin, Bill**

Baldwin, Michael
- Granddad with snails series

Baldwin, Stan
- Tough questions series

Bale, Karen A
- Sweet Medicine's prophecy series

Balfour, Hearnden
- Inspector Jack Strickland series

Balham, Joe
- Sweeney series

Balian, Lorna
- Humbug series

Ball, Brian Neville
- Jackson series
- Keegan series
- Probability series
- Space nineteen ninety nine series
- Time series
- Witchfinder series

Ball, Doris Bell
see **Bell, Josephine**

Ball, Duncan
- Anna and Tim series
- Emily Eyefinger series
- Ghost series
- Selby series

Ball, John
- Jack Tallon series
- Virgil Tibbs series

Ballantyne, Jean
- Maitland series

Ballantyne, Robert Michael
- Coral Island series
- Wandering Will trilogy

Ballard, Charles Martin
see **Ballard, Martin**

Ballard, James Graham
- Urban disaster trilogy

Ballard, Martin
- Benjie and Simon series

Ballard, S M
- Find your fate: G.I. Joe series
- G.I.Joe series

Ballard, Todhunter
see **Ballard, Willis Todhunter**

Ballard, Willis Todhunter
see also **Fox, Brian; Hunter, John; Macneil, Neil; Shepherd, John; Slade, Jack; Turner, Clay**
- Bill Lennox series
- Lieutenant Max Hunter series

Ballenger, Dean
- Mike Gannon series

Ballew, Charles
see also **Snow, Charles Horace**
- Rim-Fire series

Ballinger, Bill Sanborn
- Barr Breed series
- Joaquin Hawks series

Ballinger, W A
see also **Baker, William Howard; McNeilly, Wilfred; Reid, Desmond**
- Dangerman series
- Richard Quintain series
- Sexton Blake series
- Voyageurs series

Ballinger, William Sanborn
see **Ballinger, Bill Sanborn**

Balliol, Anne
- Bed manners series

Ballou, Arthur W
- Marooned in orbit series

Balluck, Georgia Ann
- Fifteen series

Balmer, Edwin
- Bronson Beta series

Balsdon, Dacre
- Oxford life series

Balzac, Honore de
- Marriage series
- Philosophic studies series
- Poor relations series
- Scenes of country life series
- Scenes of military life series
- Scenes of Parisian life series
- Scenes of political life series
- Scenes of private life series
- Scenes of provincial life series

Bamburg, Lilian
- Septimus March series

Bamford, Mary Ellen
- Land and water friends series
- Look-about Club series

Bamman, Henry A
- Checkered flag series
- World of adventure series

Bancks, James Charles
- Ginger Meggs series

Bancroft, Edith
- Jane Allen series

Bancroft, Francis
- Germans in South Africa series
- South African trilogy

Bancroft, John
see also **Jenkins, Alan Charles**
- James Steele series

Bancroft, Laura
see also **Akers, Floyd; Baum, Lyman Frank; Fitzgerald, Hugh; Van Dyne, Edith**
- Birdland series
- Twinkle tales series

Bancroft, Tex
- Angeltown Keeps and Doc Hennessy series

Bandler, Faith
- Wacvie series

Bandy, Franklin
see also **Franklin, Eugene**
- Kevin Macinnes series

Banfield, Edmund James
- Beachcomber series

Bangs, John Kendrick
- Alice in Wonderland parodies series
- Associated shades series
- Baron Munchausen series
- Mollie and the unwisemen series

Banis, Victor Jerome
- Brussac family series

Banke, Cecile de
see **De Banke, Cecile**

Bankoff, George Alexis
see also **Sava, George**
- Conquest of series
- Surgeon in series

Banks, David
Cybermen
Doctor Who series (162)
- Doctor Who series

Banks, Iain Menzies
- Culture series

Banks, Lynne Reid
- Bronte series
- Jane Graham trilogy
- Omri series

Banks, Michael A
Sweet dreams, sweet princes
Joe Mauser series (3)

Banks, Oliver
- Amos Hatcher series

Banks, Raymond E
- Sam King series

Banner, Angela
- Ant and Bee series
- Kind Dog series

Bannerman, David
- Magic Man series

Bannerman, Helen
- Little Black series

Bannerman, W B
- Domingo Santos series

Bannister, Patricia
see **Veryan, Patricia**

Bannister, S F
- Rolling Stone series

Bantock, Nick
- Griffin Moss and Sabine Stroheim trilogy

Banville, John
- Astronomers series

Baptist, R Hernekin
- African negro series

Barbary, James
- Adventure in history series

Barbellion, W N P
- Disappointed man series

Barber, Anne Viccars
- Wickham series

Barber, Antonia
- Satchelmouse series

Barber, Harriet Boomer
see **Templeton, Faith**

Barber, Shirley
- Martha B Rabbit series

Barber, Willetta Ann
- Christopher Storm series

Barbet, Pierre
- Baphomet series
- Eridanus series

Barbette, Jay
see also **Spicer, Bart**
- Harry Butten series

Barbieri, Elaine
- Amber trilogy

Barbour, Ralph Henry
- Big Four trilogy
- Erskine trilogy
- Grafton School trilogy
- Hilton School trilogy
- Hudson River trilogy
- Purple Pennant trilogy
- Yardley Hall series

Barbree, Jay
- Six Million Dollar Man series

Barclay, Bill
see also **Bradbury, Edward P; Moorcock, Michael**
- Nick Allard series

Printer's devil
Jerry Cornell series (2)
Somewhere in the night
Jerry Cornell series (1)

Barclay, Florence Louisa
- Shenstone series

Barclay, Ian
- Richard Dartley series

Barclay, Isabel
- Worlds without end series

Barclay, Tessa
- Craigallan family series
- Tramont family series

Barclay, Vera Charlesworth
see also **Beech, Margaret**
- Danny the detective series
- Jane series
- Joc and Colette series
- Potted stories series
- Saints series
- They series

Barclay, Virginia
- Mid-City Hospital series

Barcynska, Helena Margareta
- Honey-pot series

Bard, Mary
- Best friends series
- Three faces series

Bardin, John Franklin
see **Tree, Gregory**

Bardsley, Michael
- Superintendent Donald Martin series

Barea, Arturo
- Forging of a rebel trilogy

Bark, Conrad Voss
- Mister William Holmes series

Barkan, Joanne
- Circus train come aboard series
- Come aboard series
- Easter series
- My first gardening tools series
- My first kitchen gadgets series
- Very merry story series
- Very scary story series
- Where do I put series
- Whiskerville series

Barke, James
- Immortal memory series

Barker, Albert
- Hawk Macrae series
- Reefe King series

Barker, Cicely Mary
- Flower fairies series

Barker, Clarence Hedley
see **Seafarer**

Barker, Clive
- Books of blood series
- Books of the art series

Barker, Dennis
- People of the forces trilogy

Barker, Dudley
see **Black, Lionel**

Barker, Elsa
• Dexter Drake series
Barker, Kathleen Frances
• Bellman series
Barker, Melvern J
• Henry series
Barker, Muhammad Abd al-Rahman
• Tekumel series
Barker, Pat
• Billy Prior series
Barker, Patrick
• Tac One series
Barker, Ronald Ernest
see **Ronald, E B**
Barker, Squire Omar
see **Scott, Dan**
Barker, Wade
see also **Meyers, Richard S**
• Ninja Master series
• War of the Ninja Master series
• Year of the Ninja Master series
Barkin, Carol
• Money series
• Slapdash series
• Transition series
Barklem, Jill
• Brambly Hedge series
Barlette, Danielle
• Mirrors series
Barling, Charles
see also **Barrington, Pamela**
• Inspector George Marshall series
• Inspector George Travers series
• Inspector Henderson series
Barling, Muriel Vere
see **Barling, Charles**
Barling, Tom
Dracula
Dracula series (1)
Frankenstein
Frankenstein series (1)
• Smoke series
Barlow, Jane
• Fortunes series
• Lisconnel series
Barlow Meyers, Gertrude
see **Meyers, Barlow**
Barlow, Roger
see also **Porter, Mark**
• Sandy Steele series
Barnao, Jack
• John Locke series
Barnard, Charles
• Soprano series
Barnard, Robert
• Charlie Peace series
• Superintendent Perry Trethowan series
Barne, Kitty
• Farrar family series
• Rosina series
Barne, Marion Catherine
see **Barne, Kitty**
Barnes, Dallas
• Sergeant John Stryker series
Barnes, Elmer Tracey
• Motion picture comrades series
Barnes, Hanne
• Ann and Susan series
• John and Hugh series
Barnes, James Strachey
• Half a life series
Barnes, Julian
see **Kavanagh, Dan**
Barnes, Linda
• Carlotta Carlyle series
• Michael Spraggue series
Barnes, Megan
• Teen witch series
Barnes, Michael
• Just north series
• Nelson boys series
Barnes, Ron
• East End series
Barnes, Ronald Gorell
see **Gorell, Ronald Gorell Barnes**
Barnes, Stephen Emory
see **Barnes, Steven**
Barnes, Steven
Dragons of Heorot
Heorot series (2)
• Dream Park series
Legacy of Heorot
Heorot series (1)
Barnes, Trevor
• Blanche Hampton series
Barnett, Glyn
• Inspector Grampport series
Barnett, James
• Superintendent Owen Smith series
Barns, Glenn Miller
• Jonathan Marks series
Barnsley, Alan Gabriel
see **Fielding, Gabriel**
Barnum, Phineas Taylor
• Lion Jack series
Barnum, Richard
• Kneetime animal stories series
Barnum, Vance
see also **Young, Clarence**
Frank and Andy afloat
Racer boys series (1)
Frank and Andy at boarding school
Racer boys series (2)
Frank and Andy in a winter camp
Racer boys series (3)
• Joe Strong series
Barnwell, William
• Blessing trilogy
Baroja y Nessi, Pio
• Struggle for life trilogy
Baron, Alexander
• Harryboy Boas series
Baron, Anthony le
see **Le Baron, Anthony**
Baron, Nick
• Time tours series
Baron, Nicole de
• Penelope and Guillaume series
Barr, Amelia Edith
• New York trilogy
• Shetland series
Barr, Jene
• Little dog series
Barr, Nora
• We four series
Barr, Pat
• Alice Greenwood series
• Westerners in Japan series
Barr, Robert
• Lord Stranleigh series
• Mediaeval Rhine series
• Nick Nicholson series
Barratt, Isabel
• Rosa series
Barreaux
• Sally the Sleuth series
Barren, Charles
• Stemson family series
Barrett, Alfred Walter
see **Andom, R**
Barrett, Alfred Wilson
• Justus Wise series
Barrett, Geoffrey John
see also **Leighton, Edward**
• Inspector Blessingay series
Barrett, Helen Elizabeth-Anne
• West family series
Barrett, Julia
• Presumption series
Barrett, Katherine Ruth
see **Ellis, Katherine Ruth**
Barrett, Kevin
• Middle Earth quest series
Barrett, Monte
• Peter Cardigan series
Barrett, Neal
• Aldair series
• Darkest America series
• Time series
Barrett, Peter
• Sophie, Sarah and Ben series
Barrett, Robert G
• Les Norton series
Barrett, Roger
• Sports on the light side series
Barrett, Susan
• Sophie, Sarah and Ben series
Barrie, Alexander
• Jonathan Kane series
Barrie, James Matthew
• Peter Pan series
• Thrums series
• Tommy series
Barringer, Leslie
• Neustrian trilogy
Barrington, E
• Bennet family series
• Ormond series
Barrington, G W
• Rusty and Peter series
Barrington, George
• Voyage to New South Wales series
Barrington, John
• Ken Williams series
Barrington, Pamela
see also **Barling, Charles**
• Inspector George Marshall series
• Inspector George Travers series
• Inspector Henderson series
Barron, Tom A
• Heartlight series
Barry, Charles
• Superintendent Lawrence Gilmartin series
Barry, Clive
• Jamskoni Airline series
Barry, Jerome
• Chick Varney series
Barry, Joe
• Rush Henry series
Barry, Lynda
• Maybonne series
Barry, Margaret Stuart
• Boffy series
• Maggie Gumption series
• Simon and the witch series
• Tommy Mac series
• Woozy series
Barry, Michele du
see **Du Barry, Michele**
Barry, Mike
see also **Lee, Howard**
• Burton Wulff series
Barry, Sheila Anne
• World's best games series
Barstow, John Montagu Orczy
Gay adventurer
Scarlet Pimpernel series (14)
Barstow, Stan
• Vic Brown trilogy
Bartch, Marian R
• Ernie series
• Malcolm P Muddle series
• Tumtwit series
Barth, John
• Fenwick and Susan series
Barth, Richard
• Margaret Binton series
Bartholomew, Barbara
• Mikrokid mystery series
• Time keeper trilogy
Bartimeus
• Naval occasions series
Bartlett, Anna
• Wych Hazel series
Bartlett, Evelyn
• Dumper series
Bartlett, James Y
• Pete Hacker series
Bartlett, Philip A
• Roy Stover series
Bartlett, Vernon
• My life series
Barton, Arthur
• Time remembered series
Barton, George
• Bromley Barnes series
Barton, James
• Wasteworld series
Barton, Olive Roberts
• Nancy and Nick series
Bartos-Hoppner, Barbara
• Mitya series
Baruch, Bernard Mannes
• My own story series
Bar-Zohar, Michael
• Jeff Saunders series
Basile, Gloria Vitanza
see also **Morgan, Michaela**
• Global 2000 series
Baskerville, Beatrice
• Briconi series
Bass, Milton R
• Jory series
Bass, T J
• Hive series
Bassani, Giorgio
• Ferrara series
Bassett, Lisa
• Beany series
Bassett, Ronald
see also **Clive, William**
• Lobby Ludd trilogy
• Margaret family series
Bassett, Sara Ware
• Cape Cod series
Bassier, Thomas Joseph
see **Bass, T J**
Basso, Hamilton
• Pompey's Head series
Batchelor, Denzil
• Inspector Johnson series
Batchelor, John Calvin
• Gordon Liddy is my muse series
Batchelor, John M
• Strange conflict series
Batchelor, Margaret
• Gwenda series
Batchelor, Mary
• Peg and James series
Batchelor, Reg
• Sergeant Fenwick series
Bate, Lucy
• Baby Rabbit series
Bateman, Robert
• Archibald McGillicuddy series
Bates, Arlo
• Pagans series
Bates, Darrell
• Tanganyika series
Bates, Dianne
• Grandma Cadbury series
Bates, Esther
• Marilda series
Bates, Gordon
see also **Flower, Jessie Graham; Wilkins, Dale**
• Khaki Boys series
Bates, Herbert Ernest
• Achilles series
• Country heart series
• Larkin family series
• Uncle Silas series
• World trilogy
Bateson, David
• Larry Vernon series
Batt, Elisabeth
• Dinah Campion series
Baudino, Gael
• Dragonsword series
Baum, Frank
see **Baum, Lyman Frank**
Baum, Frank Joslyn
Laughing dragon of Oz
Oz series (51)
Baum, Lyman Frank
see also **Akers, Floyd; Bancroft, Laura; Fitzgerald, Hugh**
• Alphabet series
• Daring twins series
• Little Wizard series
Little wizard stories of Oz
Oz series (51)
• Mother and Father Goose series
• Oz series
• Santa Claus series
• Snuggle tales series
• Trot and Cap'n Bill series
Woggle-bug book
Oz series (51)
Baum, Roger S
• Oz series
Bauman, Janina
• Winter in the morning series
Baumann, Amy Brown Beeching
see **Barbary, James**
Baumann, Hans
• America-Africa-Asia trilogy
Baumann, Kurt
• Joachim series
• Piro series
Baume, Eric
• I lived series
Bawden, Juliet
• My Teddy series
Bawden, Nina
• Carrie Willow series
• Mallory children series
Bax, Clifford
• Evenings in Albany series
Bax, Roger
see also **Somers, Paul**
• Inspector James series
Baxt, George
• Pharaoh Love series
• Sylvia Plotkin and Max Van Larsen series
Baxter, Alida
• Flat on my back series
• Frankenstein sequels series
Baxter, Betty
• Becky Bryan series
Baxter, Biddy
• Blue Peter series
Baxter, George Owen
see also **Brand, Max; Evans, Evan; Frost, Frederick; Manning, David**
• Red Hawk series
Baxter, Gillian
• Angela and Ian Kendall series
• Roberta series
Baxter, Gregory
• Superintendent Daniels series
Bay, Sandra du
see **Du Bay, Sandra**
Baybutt, Ron
• Colditz series
Bayer, Oliver Weld
• Paper chase series
Bayer, Sandy
• Crystal series
Bayfield, William John
• Sexton Blake series
Bayley, Barrington John
• Chronos series
• Jasperodus series
Bayley, Nicola
• Copycats series
Patchwork cat
Copycats series (5)
Bayley, Viola
• Adventure series
Bayliss, Clara Kern
• Lolami series
Bayly, Ada Ellen
see **Lyall, Edna**
Bayne, Isabella
• Benedict Breeze series
Bayne, Spencer
• Hendrik Van Kill series
Baynes, Jack
• Morocco Jones series
Baynham, Henry
• Naval life series
Baynton, Martin
• Ponders series
Beach, Charles Amory
• Air service boys series
Beach, Edward Latimer, junior
• Rich Richardson series
Beach, Edward Latimer, senior
• Ralph Osborn series
• Roger Paulding series
Beach, Lynn
see also **Lance, Kathryn**
• Find your fate: G.I. Joe series
• G.I.Joe series
• Junior transformers find your fate series
• Phantom Valley series
• Twistaplot series
• Wizards, warlocks and you series
Beach, Susan Emily Hicks
see **Hicks Beach, Susan Emily**
Beachcomber
see **Morton, John Bingham**
Beaman, Betty Hulme
• Toytown series
Beaman, Sydney George Hulme
• Out of the ark series
• Toytown series
Beamer, Charles
• Legends of Eorthe series
Beamish, Noel de Vic
• Owen Tudor series
Bear, Greg
• Eon series
• Law series
• Michael Perrin series
• Star trek series
Beard, Henry
• Lingua Latina series
Beard, Henry N
Bored of the rings
Middle Earth series (5)
Beardmore, George
• Belle of the ballet series
• Lesley Allan series
Beardsworth, Millicent Monica
• Charles I series
Beare, George
• Vincent Stallard and Cynthia Godwin series
Bearne, David
• Ridingdale series
Bearshaw, Brian
• Superintendent Robert Townley and Sergeant Roger Newman series
Beath, Betty
• Abigail series
Beaton, Cecil
• Years diaries series
Beaton, Clare
• Fingermouse series
Beaton, M C
• Agatha Raisin series
• Hamish Macbeth series
Beaton-Jones, Cynon
• So Hi series
Beatty, Jerome
• Bob Fulton series
• Maria Looney series
• Matthew Looney series
Beatty, Terry
• Ms Tree series
Beaumarchais, Pierre Augustin Caron de
• Figaro series
Beaumont, Laura
• Why not series

Beauvoir, Simone de
- Dutiful daughter series

Beaverbrook, William Maxwell Aitken
- Lloyd George series

Beccaria, Mijo
- Birthday series

Bechdel, Alison
- Dykes series

Bechdolt, Jack
- Barrow brothers series

Beck, Kathrine Kristine
- Iris Cooper and Jack Clancy series
- Jane Da Silva series

Beck, Lily Adams
see **Barrington, E**

Becker, Eve
- Abracadabra series

Becker, Jillian
- Simon and Josephine Leyton series

Becker, Margot
- G.I.Joe series

Becker, Stephen
- Far East trilogy

Becket, Jim
- Choose your own adventure series

Beckett, Mark
- Major Dick Burton series

Beckett, Samuel
- Jacques Moran series

Beckman, Gunnel
- Mia series

Beckwith, Lillian
- Hebrides series

Bedard, Michael
- Emily series

Bede, Cuthbert
- Mister Verdant Green series

Bedford, Annie North
- Roy Rogers series

Bedford, Jean
- Anna Southwood series

Bedford, Sybille
- Constanza and Flavia series

Bedford-Jones, Henry
- John Solomon trilogy

Bee, Clair
- Chip Hilton series

Beebe, Elswyth Thane
see **Thane, Elswyth**

Beebee, Chris
- Cipola series

Beeby, Otto
- Tony Spencer series

Beech, Margaret
see also **Barclay, Vera Charlesworth**
- Peter and Veronica series

Beecham, John Charles
- Koyola series

Beecham, Rose
- Amanda Valentine series

Beecher, Elizabeth
Gene Autry and the red shirt
Gene Autry series (7)
- Gene Autry tell-a-tale series
- Roy Rogers series

Beeching, Amy Brown
see **Barbary, James**

Beeching, Jack
see **Barbary, James**

Beeding, Francis
see also **Pilgrim, David**
- Colonel Alastair Granby series
- Inspector George Martin series
- Inspector Wilkins series
- Professor Kreutzemark series
- Ronald Briercliffe series

Beeler, Cecil Freeman
- Well series

Beere, Peter
- Trauma 2020 series

Beers, Victor Gilbert
- Growing up series
- Learning to read from the Bible primer series
- Learning to read from the Bible series
- Little talks series
- Muffkin series
- Precious moments series

Begbie, Garstin
- Superintendent Samuel Quan series

Begbie, Harold
- Bundy series

Behaine, Rene
- History of a society series

Behan, Brendan
- Borstal boy series

Behrens, Margaret
- Percival Soames series

Behrman, Samuel Nathaniel
- People in a diary series

Beiler, Edna
- Buttonwoods series

Beinhart, Larry
- Tony Cassella series

Beith, John Hay
see **Hay, Ian**

Bekessy, Jean
see **Habe, Hans**

Belden, David
- Galactic connectivity series

Belden, Trixie
see **Bosworth, Ellen**

Belden, Wilanne Schneider
- Mind series

Bell, Adrian
- Country life series
- Roland Pace series

Bell, Anthea
- Asterix push-out series

Bell, Catherine Douglas
- Cousin Kate series

Bell, Clare
- Ratha series

Bell, Frank
- Shen series

Bell, Harold Wilmerding
Sherlock Holmes and Doctor Watson
Sherlock Holmes series (10)

Bell, John Joy
- Christina series
- Mister Craw series
- Wee Macgregor series

Bell, John Keble
see **Howard, Keble**

Bell, Josephine
- Amy Tupper series
- Claude Warrington-Reeve series
- Doctor David Wintringham series
- Doctor Henry Frost series
- English Civil War series
- Inspector Steven Mitchell series
- Jacobean trilogy

Bell, Margaret Elizabeth
- Florence Monroe series

Bell, Rob
- Narnia solo games series

Bell, Robert Stanly Warren
- Greyhouse series

Bell, Robert Vaughn
- McGowan family series

Bell, Sally
- Young Indiana Jones chronicles series

Bell, Vicars
- Doctor Douglas Baynes series
- Dodo series

Bellairs, George
- Detective Inspector Thomas Littlejohn series

Bellairs, John
- Anthony Monday series
- Blue figurine trilogy
- Clock trilogy
- Johnny Dixon series

Bellamann, Henry
- Kings Row series

Bellamann, Katherine
- Kings Row series

Bellamy, Edward
- Julian West series

Looking backward, 2000-1887
Looking backward responses series (1)
Looking backward, 2000-1887
Looking backward sequels series (1)

Bellamy, Frank
Doctor Who timeview
Doctor Who series (162)

Bellamy, Robert Lowe
- Scout Grey series

Belle, Pamela
- Heron family series
- Wintercombe series

Bellem, Robert Leslie
- John J Shannon series
- Sam Welpton series

Bellhouse, Lucy Wilered
- Caravan series
- Helicopter series

Belloc, Hilaire
- Beasts series
- Cautionary tales series
- On series

Belloc, Marie
see **Lowndes, Marie Belloc**

Belloc-Lowndes, Marie
see **Lowndes, Marie Belloc**

Belot, Adolphe
- Stranglers series

Belsy, William
- Arctic world series

Bemelmans, Ludwig
- Hotel series
- Madeline series

Bemelmans, Madeline
- Madeline series

Ben Jelloun, Tahar
- Sand child series

Benary, Margot
- Annegret series
- Lechow family series

Benchley, Peter
- Jaws series

Bendick, Jeanne
- Early bird astronomy series

Benedict, Dorothy
- Pagan series

Benedict, Rex
- Pecos Gang series

Benet, Juan
- Region series

Benford, Gregory
- Fall of night series
- Galactic Center series
- Ocean series
- What might have been series

Benjamin, Floella
- Flo and Aston series

Bennet, Robert Ames
- Primitive series
- Wolf series

Bennett, Arnold
- Clayhanger series
- Elsie series
- Five towns series
- Tales of the Five Towns series

Bennett, Barbara
- Calladine family series

Bennett, Billy L
- Northwest stories series

Bennett, Cherie
- Wild hearts series

Bennett, Dorothy
- Allardyce series
- Dennis Devore series

Bennett, Dwight
see also **Newton, Dwight Bennett**
- Eden Grove series

Bennett, Geoffrey Martin
see **Sea-Lion**

Bennett, John Wheeler-
see **Wheeler-Bennett, John**

Bennett, Marcia Joanne
- Ni-lach series

Bennett, Margot
- John Davies series

Bennett, Rodney
- Little Miss Pink series
- Percy Pig series
- Puffin, Twink and Waggle series
- Widgery Winks series

Bennett, Rolf
- Commander Lawless series

Bennett, William Robert
- Adam Kane series

Bennetts, Pamela
- Cesare Borgia series
- Edward I series

Benney, Mark
- Low company series

Benoit, Hendra
- Psi Patrol trilogy

Bensen, Donald R
see also **Flynn, Jackson**
- Cole Brandon series
- Sherlock Holmes sequels series

Benson, Arthur Christopher
- Molly Davenant series

Benson, Ben
- Inspector Wade Paris series
- Ralph Lindsey series

Benson, Blackwood Ketcham
- American Civil War series

Benson, Edward Frederic
- Colin series
- David Blaize series
- Dodo series
- Greek War of Independence series
- Lucia Billson series
- Old London series

Benson, Irene Elliott
see also **Francis, Stella M**
- Campfire Girls series

Benson, Patrick
- New Baron Munchausen series

Benson, Robert Hugh
- Supernatural series

Bensusan, Samuel Levy
- Joan Winter series

Benteen, John
see also **Douglas, Thorne; Haas, Ben; Meade, Richard**
- Neal Fargo series
- Sundance series

Bentham, Jeremy
Doctor Who, the early years
Doctor Who series (162)

Bentley, Anne
- Groggs series

Bentley, Diana
- Habitats series
- Journey through history series
- Journeys series
- Let's visit a farm series
- My day series
- My family series
- My school series
- My visit series
- My world series
- Outings series

Bentley, Edmund Clerihew
- Clerihews series
- Mister Clerihew series
- Philip Trent series

Bentley, John
- Dick Marlow series
- Glen Gibson series
- Sir Richard Herrivell series

Bentley, Nancy
- Busy body series

Bentley, Phyllis
- Environment series
- Oldroyd family series
- West Riding series

Bentley, Roy
- Spacers series

Benton, John L
- Stephen Duane series

Benton, John W
- Marji Parker series

Benton, Kenneth
- Peter Craig series

Benton, Peggie
- Drylands series

Benton, Will
see also **Batchelor, Reg; Bosworth, Frank; Carrel, Mark; Carter, Nevada; Ingersol, Jared; Paine, Lauran; Slaughter, Jim; Standish, Buck**
- Bushwhacker series

Benzoni, Juliette
- Catherine Legoix series
- Falcon series
- Marianne series

Berberick, Nancy Varian
- DragonLance heroes series

Berdin, Richard
Code name Richard
Connection series (8)

Berdoe, Edward
see **Scalpel, Aesculapius**

Berenstain, Jan
- Berenstain bears series
- Lover boy series

Berenstain, Michael
- Dinosaurs series
- Dwarks series
- Panda series
- Peat Moss and Ivy series

Berenstain, Stan
- Berenstain bears series
- Lover boy series

Berent, Mark
see **Sandberg, Berent**

Beresford, Elisabeth
- Gappy, Jim and Jane series
- Little Wombles series
- Magic series
- Tempest family series
- Wombles series

Beresford, John Davys
- Hillingtons trilogy
- Jacob Stahl series

Beresford, Marcus
see **Brandel, Marc**

Berg, Leila
- Chatterbooks series
- Chunky series
- Little car series
- Small world series
- Snaps series
- Steep Street series
- What-do-you-know series

Bergaust, Erik
- Colonizing series
- Rockets series

Berger, Gilda
- Straight talk about drugs series
- Violence series

Berger, John
- Into their labours trilogy
- Telepathy series

Berger, Phil
- National Football League series

Berger, Thomas
- Carlo Reinhart series
- Russel Wren series

Berglund, Edward Paul
- Cthulhu Mythos series

Bergman, Andrew
- Jack LeVine series

Bergman, Ingmar
- Bergman family series

Bergstrom, Elaine
- Shattered glass series

Bergstrom, Gunilla
- Alfie Atkins series

Bergstrom, Martha Sandwall-
see **Sandwall-Bergstrom, Martha**

Berk, Theodore George
see **George, Theodore**

Berkeley, Anthony
- Ambrose Chitterwick series
- Roger Sheringham series

Berkley, Tom
- Algernon Alexander Gunning Hendry series

Berlin, Sven
- Lazarus series

Berlitz, Charles
- Bermuda Triangle series

Bermingham, Iris
- Hapi series

Berna, Paul
- Bobby Thiriet series
- Gaby series
- Mael family series
- Michael Jousse series

Bernanos, Georges
- Spiritual life series

Bernard, Elizabeth
- Satin slippers series

Bernard, Joel
- Man from U.N.C.L.E. series

Bernard, Rafe
- Invaders series

Bernard, Robert
- Millicent Hetherege series

Bernard-Waite, Judy
- Trumpalar series

Berne, Karin
- Ellie Gordon series

Bernede, Arthur
- Chantecoq series

Bernen, Robert
- Blue Stacks series

Berners, Gerald Hugh Tyrwhitt-Wilson
- Distant prospect series

Bernhardt, William
- Justice series

Bernstein, Abraham Emanuel
see **Rodney, Jonathan**

Bernstein, Alec
see **Baron, Alexander**

Bernstein, Carl
- Watergate series

Berres, Frances B
- Deep-sea adventure series

Berridge, Celia
- Stepping stones 1 2 3 series

Berrigan, Daniel
- Conversations series
- Prison diary series

Berrisford, Judith Mary
- Brooke family series
- Jackie and Babs series
- Pippa series
- Skipper series
- Sue Trent series
- Taff series

Berrow, Norman
- Inspector Courtenay series
- Inspector Lancelot Carolus Smith series
- Michael Revel series

Berry, Adrian
- Koyama series

Berry, Bryan
see **Garner, Rolf**

Berry, Carole
- Bonnie Indermill series

Berry, Joy
- Alerting kids to the danger zones series
- Can make and do series
- Danger zones series
- Good answers to tough questions series
- Human race club series
- Let's talk about series
- Living skills series
- Ready-set-grow series
- Survival series
- Teach me about series

Berry, Liz
- Easy series

Berry, Martha Eugenie
- Crook series

Berry, Stephen Ames
- John Harrison series

Berstl, Julius
- Saint Paul series

Beskow, Elsa
- Peter and Lotta series

Best, Herbert
- Desmond series

Best, Jacqueline
- Paul and Fritzi's year series

Best, Oswald Herbert
see **Best, Herbert**

Best, Rayleigh Breton Amis
- Yarrow series

Bestall, Alfred
- Rupert Bear series

Betancourt, John Gregory
- Doctor Bones series

Bethancort, Tomas Ernesto
Frankenstein
Frankenstein series (1)

Bethancourt, Tomas Ernesto
Doctor Jekyll and Mister Hyde
Doctor Jekyll series (1)
- Doris Fein series
- Odin series

Time machine
Time traveller series (6)
- Yesterday and tomorrow series

Bethke, Bruce
- Robots and aliens series

Bettany, Jeannie Gwynne
see **Kernahan, Jeannie Gwynne**

Betteridge, Don
see also **Newman, Bernard**
- Tiger Lester series

Bevan, Tom
- Dutch in Spain series

Bevir, Harold
- Mrs May series

Bexar, Phil
see also **Borg, Jack**
- Billy Dupree series

Bexell, Eva
- Minister series

Beyle, Marie Henri
see **Stendhal**

Bhatia, Jamunadevi
see **Forrester, Helen**

Bhatia, Margaret Delaney
see **Forrester, Helen**

Bial, Raymond
- Home series

Bialk, Elisa
- Marty Warren series

Bickers, Richard Townshend
see also **Leslie, Richard**
- Daedalus quartet
- Mark Stratton series

Bickham, Jack Miles
see also **Clinton, Jeff**
- Brad Smith series
- Charity Ross series
- John Campbell and Clayton Hartung series

Bicknell, Arthur
- Twilight series

Bidmead, Christopher H
- Doctor Who series

Bidston, Lester
- Sexton Blake series

Bidwell, Dafne
- Tiger Gang series

Bidwell, Margaret
- Mister Hodson series

Bidwell, Marjory Elizabeth Sarah
see **Ford, Elizabeth**

Biegel, Paul
- Little captain series
- Virgil Nosegay series

Bielenberg, Christabel
- Past and future series

Biemiller, Carl Ludwig
- Hydronauts series
- Jonny series

Bierce, Ambrose
- Devil's dictionary series

Bigg, Patricia Nina
see **Ainsworth, Patricia**

Biggers, Earl Derr
- Charlie Chan series

Biggle, Lloyd
- Alien Island series
- Cultural survey series
- Jan Darzek series
- Sherlock Holmes sequels series

Biggs, Margaret
- Melling School series

Bigsby, Christopher
- Hester Prynne series

Biguet, Jacques Napoleon Faure-
see **Decrest, Jacques**

Billam, Rosemary
- Alpaca series
- Ben and Arthur series

Billias, Stephen
Deryni challenge
Chronicles of the Deryni trilogy (3)
- Runesword series

Binchy, Maeve
- London transports series

Binder, Eando
- Adam Link series
- Saucer series

Binder, Otto
see also **Binder, Eando**
- Avengers superheroes series
- Captain America series
- Marvel superheroes series

Binder, Pearl
- Chi Ming series
- Little Lion series

Bingeman, Alison
- Doctor Who series

Bingham, Carson
- Flash Gordon series

Bingham, Charlotte
- Belgravia trilogy
- Coronet series
- Victoria Edgecombe series

Bingham, John
- Ducane series
- Superintendent Badger Brock series

Bingham, Lorna
- Golden boomerang series

Bingham, Roger
- Presidential trilogy

Binstead, Arthur Morris
- Gal's gossip series
- Random reminiscences series

Birch, Claire
- Lucy Hill series

Birch, Louis Charles
- Science and religion series

Bird, Arthur
- Looking backward responses series

Bird, Brandon
- Hampton Hume series

Bird, Kenneth
- Himself series

Bird, Maria
- Andy Pandy series
- Flowerpot Men series
- Woodentops series

Birmingham, George A
- Gorman MP series
- Reverend J J Meldon series

Birmingham, Jamie
- New York gang series

Birmingham, Maisie
- Kate Weatherley series

Birmingham, Stephen
- American Jewry series

Biro, Val
- Bobby Brewster picture book series
- Gumdrop series

Birt, David
- Involvement in history series
- Middle Ages series
- Roman Britain series
- Saxons and Vikings series
- Something to sell series
- Stuarts series
- Tower prisoners series
- Tower topics series
- Tudors series

Bischoff, David
see also **Grant, Mark**
- Bill, the galactic hero series
- Dragonstar trilogy
- Gaming magi series
- Gremlins series
- Nightworld series
- SeaQuest series
- Star fall series
- Star hounds series
- Time machine series
- UFO conspiracy series

Bishop, Gibs
- Captain Comstock series

Bishop, Giles
- United States Marines series

Bishop, Mary
- Vet's wife series

Bishop, Michael
- Urban nucleus series

Bishop, Paul
see **Bishop, Pike**

Bishop, Pike
- Cord Diamondback series

Bishop, Samuel P
see also **Harold, Clive; Hutson, Shaun; Taylor, Frank**
- Track series

Bisset, Donald
- Johnny series
- Paws series
- Tiger series
- Yak series

Bisset, James
- Years at sea series

Bittman, Sam
- Going for it series

Bittner, F Rosanne
- Brides series
- Caleb Sax series
- Montana woman series
- Savage destiny series

Bjarnhof, Karl
- Blind series

Bjork, Christina
- Linnea series

Bjorkman, Edwin August
- Swedish youth series

Bjorn, Thyra Ferre
- Pastor Pontus Franzon series

Black, Arthur
- Basic Black series

Black, Campbell
see also **Armstrong, Campbell**
- Indiana Jones series

Black, Christopher
- Star challenge series

Black, Cindy
- Mojo Swoptops series

Black, Elizabeth Best
- Peter Strangely series

Black, Gavin
- Paul Harris series

Black, Hermina
- Susan Denver trilogy

Black, Ian Stuart
- Doctor Who series
- Peter Munro series

Black, Jeannie
- Heartquest series

Black, Joey
see **Joey**

Black, Ladbroke
- Mister Preed series
- Sexton Blake series

Black, Lionel
see also **Matthews, Anthony**
- Emma Greaves series
- Kate Theobald series
- Superintendent Francis Foy series

Black, Mansell
see also **Dudley-Smith, Trevor; Hall, Adam; Rattray, Simon; Trevor, Elleston**
- Richard Vaness series

Black, Margaret Katherine
- Food and cooking series
- Honey family trilogy
- Three brothers series

Black, Sonia
Baby-Sitters Club notebook
Baby-Sitters Club series (78)

Black, Thomas B
- Al Delaney series

Black, Veronica
see also **Darby, Catherine; Peters, Maureen**
- Sister Joan series

Black, William
- Bella Pivar series
- Hebrides series

Blackbeard, Bill
- Maggie and Jiggs series

Blackburn, Barbara
see **Castle, Frances**

Blackburn, John
- Bill Easter series
- General Charles Kirk series

Blackburn, Martin
- Delgado series

Blackburn, Thomas Wakefield
- Stanton Empire series

Blacker, Irwin Robert
- General Le Grande and GENOPS series

Blacker, Terence
- Hotshots series

Blackmon, Anita
- Adelaide Adams series

Blackmore, Richard Doddridge
- Lorna Doone series

Blackwood, Algernon
- John Silence series
- Maria series
- Reincarnation series
- Uncle Paul series

Blaine, John
- Rick Brant series

Blair, Allan
- Sexton Blake series

Blair, Clay
- Submariners series

Blair, Cynthia
- Susan and Christine Pratt series

Blair, Eric
see **Orwell, George**

Blair, Joan
- Submariners series

Blair, Marcia
- Tory Baxter series

Blair, Tobin
- Belinda series

Blaisdell, Anne
see also **Egan, Lesley; Linington, Elizabeth; Shannon, Dell**
- Sergeant Ivor Maddox series

Blake
- Fighter Station series

Blake, Christina
- Inspector Donald Dobbs series

Blake, Forrester
- Johnny Christmas trilogy

Blake, George
- Oliphant series

Blake, Jon
- Oddly series
- Roboskool series

Blake, Justin
- Garry Halliday series

Blake, Ken
see also **Akers, Alan Burt; Bulmer, Kenneth; Frazier, Arthur; Hardy, Adam; Krauss, Bruno; Silver, Richard; Zetford, Tully**
- Professionals series

Blake, Linda
- Laura series

Blake, M Glaiser
- Ayesthorpe trilogy

Blake, M M
- Norwich series

Blake, Nicholas
- Nigel Strangeways series

Blake, Quentin
- Bear series
- Lester series

Blake, Stacey
- Sexton Blake series

Blake, Susan
- Cheerleaders series
- Fifteen series
- Hawthorne College series
- Twilight series

Blake, Vanessa
- Jenny Winfield series

Blakeney, Jay D
see also **Dalton, Sean**
- Anthi series

Blakeney, John
Gay adventurer
Scarlet Pimpernel series (14)

Blaker, Richard
- Hester Billiter series

Blakesley, Stephen
- Sexton Blake series

Blakeston, Oswell
- Screaming series

Blamires, Harry
- Heaven and Hell trilogy
- Kirkbride series

Blanc, Suzanne
- Inspector Miguel Menendes series

Blance, Ellen
- Monster series

Blanchard, Amy Ella
- Dear little girl series
- Four Corners series
- Lad and Lassie
- Revolutionary War series

Bland, Edith
see **Nesbit, Edith**

Bland, Eleanor Taylor
- Marti MacAlister series

Blandy, Mary
- Youth work series

Blank, Clair
- Adventure girls series
- Beverly Gray series

Blasco Ibanez, Vicente
- Roman Catholic Church in Spain series
- Spanish history series
- Temptress series
- Valencia series

Blashfield, Jean
- Advanced dungeons and dragons adventure gamebook series
- Catacombs series
- Endless quest series
- Fantasy forest series
- Super endless quest adventure gamebook series

Blashki, Pam
- Fire, drought and flood trilogy

Blasis, Celeste de
see **De Blasis, Celeste**

Blathwayt, Jean
- Brownie series

Blatty, William Peter
- Lieutenant Bill Kinderman series

Blau, Diane
- Therapist series

Blaylock, James Paul
- Jonathan Bing series

Blayn, Hugo
see also **Fearn, John Russell; Gridban, Volsted; Slate, John; Statten, Vargo; Titan, Earl**
- Inspector Garth series

Blayne, Sebastian
- Sebastian Blayne series

Blayre, Christopher
- University of Cosmopoli series

Blazer, J S
- Donald Bracken and James Rowland Woodward series

Bleackley, Horace William
- Stumps series

Bleasdale, Alan
- Franny Scully series

Bleeck, Oliver
see also **Thomas, Ross**
- Philip Saint Ives series

Blei, Norbert
- Door County trilogy

Blevins, Win
Snake River
Rivers west series (9)

Blevins, Winfred
- Rivers west series

Bligh, Eric
- Tooting Corner series

Blish, James
- After such knowledge series
- Cities in flight series
- Star trek original series
- Star trek originals sequels series

Blishen, Edward
- Greek mythology series
- Schoolmaster series

Bliss, Adam
- Alice Penny series

Blixen, Karen
see also **Dinesen, Isak**
- Africa series

Blizard, Marie
- Eve Macwilliams series

Bloch, Robert
- Cthulhu Mythos series
- Doctor Jekyll series
- Psycho series

Bloch, Roch
Twilight Zone, the movie
Twilight Zone series (6)

Blochman, Lawrence Goldtree
- Doctor Daniel Webster Coffee series
- Inspector Leonidas Prike series

Block, Francesca Lia
- Weetzie Bat series

Block, Lawrence
- Bernie Rhodenbarr series
- Evan Tanner series

Five little rich girls
Leo Haig series (1)
- Leo Haig series
- Matthew Scudder series

Blomefield, Mathena
- Nessel series

Blood, Matthew
see also **Baker, Asa; Davis, Don; Dresser, Davis; Halliday, Brett**
- Morgan Wayne series

Bloom, Britton
- Inner planets trilogy

Bloom, Ursula
see also **Mann, Deborah; Prole, Lozania**
- Elegant Edwardian series
- Father and mother series
- No lady series
- Rosemary series
- You and yours series

Bloom, William
see **W, W**

Bloomfield, Frena
- Darkworld legends series

Bloxsom, Peter
• Saint series
Blue, Zachary
• Protectors series
Blume, Judy
• Peter Hatcher series
Blumenfeld, Josephine
• Pin a rose on me series
Blumenthal, John
• Mac Slade series
Blundell, Harold
see **Bellairs, George**
Blunt, Betty
• Treacherous moon series
Blunt, Wilfrid
• Single life series
Bly, Janet
• Crystal Blake series
Bly, Stephen Arthur
• Crystal Blake series
• Stuart Brannon series
Blyth, James
• Thrift series
Blythe, Daniel
• Doctor Who series
Blyton, Enid
see also **Pollock, Mary**
• Adventure series
• Adventurous Four series
• Amelia Jane series
• Barney series
• Belinda series
• Bible stories series
• Bimbo series
• Bom series
• Boys' and girls' series
• Brer Rabbit adventures series
• Brer Rabbit series
• Caravan family series
• Chimney corner stories series
• Clicky series
• Colour story book series
Dog stories
Dog stories series (2)
• Evening tales series
• Famous Five adventure games series
• Famous Five series
• Faraway tree series
• Fatty series
Five go adventuring
Famous Five and you series (2)
Five go off in a caravan
Famous Five and you series (5)
Five go to Smuggler's Top
Famous Five and you series (4)
Five on a treasure island
Famous Five and you series (1)
Five on Kirrin Island again
Famous Five and you series (6)
Five run away together
Famous Five and you series (3)
• Flower story book series
• Happy House series
• Holiday stories series
• I'll tell you a story series
• John and Mary series
• John Jolly series
• Josie, Click and Bun series
• Learn with Noddy series
• Little bedtime books series
• Little books series
• Little donkey series
• Malory Towers series
• Mandy, Mops and Cubby series
• Mary Mouse series
• Mike, Belinda and Ann series
• Minute tales series
• Miracles of Jesus series
• Mischief series
• Mister Galliano's circus series
• Mister Meddle series
• Mister Pink-Whistle series
• Mister Tumpy series
• Mister Twiddle series
• Naughtiest girl series
• Naughty children series
• Nighttime tales series
• Noddy picture books series
• Noddy pop-up books series
• Noddy series
• Noddy stories series
• Noddy tall colour series
• Noddy tiny strip books series
• Nursery Rhyme Land series
• Pip series
• Prince Paul series
• Round the year series
• Saint Clare's series
• Scamp series
• Secret Seven series
• Six cousins series
• Smith family series
• Sooty series
• Stories from world history series
• Story book series
• Twins series
• Weekday stories series
• Willow Farm series
• Wishing-chair series
Boaden, Betty
• Blinky Bill adaptations series
Boardman, M M
• Brown family series
• Nellie Gates series
Bobin, John William
• Sexton Blake series
Boden, Hilda
• Anna and James series
• Joanna series
• Marlows series
• Noel series
Bodenham, Hilda Morris
see **Boden, Hilda**
Bodine, J D
see also **Carrington, G A; Cunningham, Chet; Dalton, Kit; Derrick, Lionel; Fletcher, Dirk**
• Pecos Kid series
• Quinn's Raiders series
Bodington, Nancy
see **Smith, Shelley**
Bodkin, Matthias McDonnell
• Dora Myrl series
• Lord Edward Fitzgerald series
• Paul Beck series
Boegehold, Betty
• Pippa Mouse series
Bogarde, Dirk
• Orderly man series
Bogart, William
Crazy Indian
Doc Savage series (183)
• Johnny Saxon series
Bogen, M Arthur
• Burchardt and Decker series
Boggis, David
• Killer instinct series
Boileau, Ethel
• Hippy Buchan series
• Mallory family series
Bois, Theodora du
see **Du Bois, Theodora**
Bois, William Pene du
see **Pene du Bois, William**
Boissard, Janine
• Moreau trilogy
Boissiere, Ralph de
see **De Boissiere, Ralph**
Bojer, Johan
• Peer Holm series
Boland, Jason
• Adventures of Skippy series
Boland, John
• Counterpol series
• John George Norman Hyde series
Boland, John C
• Donald McCarry series
Bolt, Ben
• Bob Ponting series
• Captain Grandison series
• Inspector Godbold series
Bolton, Anne Evelyn
see **Bolton, Evelyn**
Bolton, Evelyn
see also **Bunting, Eve**
• Horse book series
Bolton, Melvin
• Lawson of the Special Branch series
Bonanno, Margaret Wander
• Others trilogy
• Star trek sequels series
• Star trek series
Bond, Edward
• War plays series
Bond, Evelyn
• Ira Yedder series
Bond, Freda Constance
• Lancasters series
Bond, Geoffrey
• Sergeant Luck series
Bond, J Harvey
• Mike Lanson series
Bond, Karen
• Paddington play and learn series
• Paddington slot book series
Bond, Michael
• J D Polson series
• Monsieur Pamplemousse series
• Olga da Polga picture books series
• Olga da Polga series
• Paddington learning and activity series
• Paddington pastime series
• Paddington picture book series
• Paddington play and learn series
• Paddington pop-up series
• Paddington series
• Paddington slot book series
• Paddington's Blue Peter story series
• Parsley series
• Thursday series
Bond, Thomas Michael
see **Bond, Michael**
Bonehill, Ralph
see also **Alger, Horatio; Stratemeyer, Edward L; Winfield, Arthur M**
• Bound to win series
• Boy hunters series
• Flag and frontier series
• Flag of freedom series
• Frontier series
Island camp
Lakeport series (1)
• Mexican war series
Winning run
Lakeport series (2)
Bonett, Emery
• Inspector Borges series
• Professor Mandrake series
Bonett, John
• Inspector Borges series
• Professor Mandrake series
Bonfiglioli, Kyril
• Charlie Mortdecai series
Bonham, Frank
• Dogtown Ghetto series
Boniface, Marjorie
• Sheriff Hiram Odom series
Bonifer, Michael
• Dick Tracy film series
Bonington, Chris
• Climbing series
Bonnamy, Francis
• Peter Shane series
Bonner, Cindy
• Haywood Beatty trilogy
Bonner, Geraldine
• Molly Morganthau series
Bonner, Michael
• Roby Maclane trilogy
Bonner, Richard
• Boy inventors series
Bonner, Terry Nelsen
see also **Yarbro, Chelsea Quinn**
• New South Wales series
Bonney, Joseph L
• Simon Rolfe series
Bonnici, Peter
• Arjuna's family series
Bonsels, Waldemar
• Maya series
Boon, Emilie
• Peterkin series
Boone, James Calder
• Ned Remington series
Boone, Silas K
• Phil Bradley series
Boore, Walter Hugh
• Bryncoed series
Boorstin, Daniel Joseph
• Discoverers and creators series
Booth, Charles Gordon
• Anatole Flique series
Booth, Christopher B
• Amos Clackworthy series
• Jim Bliss series
Booth, Louis F
• Maxwell Fenner series
Boothby, Guy
• Doctor Nikola series
• Jacob Burrell series
Boothroyd, Derrick
• Heavy woollen district series
Borchgrave, Arnaud de
see **De Borchgrave, Arnaud**
Borden, Mary
• Mary of Nazareth series
Border, Rosemary
Caves of steel
Elijah Baley series (4)
Doctor Jekyll and Mister Hyde
Doctor Jekyll series (1)
Dune
Dune series (6)
• Out and about series
• Walk in the woods series
Boreham, Frank William
• Texts that made history series
Boreman, Jean
see **Graeber, Jean Boreman**
Borg, Jack
see also **Bexar, Phil**
• Hogleg Bailey series
• Thady Corey series
Borg, Philip Antony John
see **Borg, Jack**
Borges, Jorge Luis
• Problems and chronicles series
Borie, Lysbeth Boyd
• Poems for Peter series
Born, Edith de
see **De Born, Edith**
Borntrager, Mary Christner
• Ellie's people series
Borrow, George
• Gypsy series
Borthwick, J S
• Sarah Deane and Alex Mackenzie series
Bortner, Norman Stanley
• Professor Clifford Wells series
Boscawen, Linda
• Hollingbury family series
Bosco, Clyde
• Nintendo adventure series
Bosco, Fernand Joseph Marius Henri
see **Bosco, Henri**
Bosco, Henri
• Pascalet and Aunt Martine series
Boshell, Gordon
• Captain Cobwebb series
• Secret Guardians series
Bosher, Kate Lee Langley
• Mary Cary series
Bosse, Malcolm Joseph
• Philip Embree series
Boston, Charles K
see **Gruber, Frank**
Silver jackass
Otis Beagle series (1)
Boston, Lucy Maria
• Green Knowe series
• Memory in a house series
Boswell, Annabella
• Early day series
Boswell, John
• Christopher Kent series
Bosworth, Ellen
• Shelley Peters series
Bosworth, Frank
see also **Batchelor, Reg; Benton, Will; Carrel, Mark; Carter, Nevada; Ingersol, Jared; Paine, Lauran; Slaughter, Jim; Standish, Buck**
• Earl Morton series
Bosworth, Phyllis
• James Montgomerie series
Botsford, Charles Alexander
• Victory series
Bottome, Phyllis
• Rat series
• Search trilogy
Boucher, Alan Estcourt
• Halli Thordason series
Boucher, Anthony
• Fergus O'Breen series
• Sister Ursula series
Boulle, Pierre
• Planet of the Apes series
Bouma, Paddy
• Bertie series
Bouras, Gillian
• Australian wife series
Bourgeau, Art
• Claude Kirlin and F T Zevich series
Bourgeois, Paulette
• Franklin series
Bourne, George
• Frederick Bettesworth series
Bourne, Lawrence R
• Coppernob series
Bourne, Peter
see also **Graeme, Bruce; Graeme, David**
• Henri Christophe series
• Stewart family series
Bourquin, Henry James
see **Amberley, Richard**
Boussenard, Louis
• Robinsons of Guiana series
Bova, Ben
• Chet Kinsman series
• Exiles trilogy
• Orion series
• Voyagers series
Bowden, Jean
see **Curry, Avon**
Bowden, Jim
• Cap Millett series
• Dan McCoy series
• Lomax brothers series
Bowen, Elizabeth
• Seven winters series
Bowen, Marjorie
see also **Preedy, George Runnell**
• Exchange royal series
• French Revolution series
• Renaissance trilogy
• Spiritual history of Great Britain trilogy
• William III trilogy
• William the Silent series
Bowen, Peter
• Yellowstone Kelly series
Bowen, Robert Sidney
• Dave Dawson series
• Dusty Ayres and his Battle Birds series
• Gerry Barnes series
• Hot corner series
• Hot rod series
• Red Randall series
Bowen-Judd, Sara
see **Woods, Sara**
Bower, Bertha Muzzy
• Casey Ryan series
• Flying U Ranch series
• Meadowlark series
• Skyrider series
Bower, Ursula Graham
• Assam series
Bowers, Dorothy
• Inspector Pardoe series
Bowes, Richard
• Warchild series
Bowie, Janetta
• Clydeside series
Bowie, Jim
• Dead Shot Dave series
Bowles, Colin
• Mike Hazzard series
Bowman, Gerald
• Michael Shannon series
• Sexton Blake series
Bowring, Mary
• Animals series
Box, Edgar
see also **Vidal, Gore**
• Peter Cutler Sergeant series
Boyd, Brian
• Vladimir Nabokov series
Boyd, Edward
• Wanderlust Brown series
Boyd, Eunice Mays
• F Millard Smyth series
Boyd, James
• James Fraser series
Boyd, Martin
• Langton family series
Boyd, Neil
• Father Charles Duddleswell series
Boyd, Raymond
• Paul Scarf series
Boyd, Thomas Alexander
• Wheat series
Boyer, Brian
• Headhunters series
Boyer, Elizabeth H
• Wizard's war series
• World of the Alfar series
Boyer, Glenn G
• Dolf Morgette series
Boyer, Richard Lewis
• Doctor Charlie Adams series
• Sherlock Holmes sequels series
Boyington, Gregory
Baa baa Black Sheep
Black Sheep Squadron series (2)
Boylan, Clare
• Nan and Mary Cantwell series
Boylan, Eleanor
• Henry Gamadge series
Boylan, James Finney
• Heavenly bodies series
Boyle, Constance
• Little Owl series
Boyle, Denis
• Commander Moreton Shade series
Boyle, Jimmy
• Prison diaries series
Boyle, Thomas
• Detective Francis De Sales series
Boyles, Tiny
see **Boyles, William**
Boyles, William
• Bounty Hunter series
Boyll, Randall
• Darkman series
Boylston, Helen Dore
• Carol Page series
• Sue Barton series
Boyoi, Waddi
• East Kimberley series
Brace, Timothy
• Anthony Adams series

Bracken, Anne
- Jancy series
- Jon and Julie Howard series
- Patch series
- Penny and Dorabella series

Brackett, Leigh
- Eric John Stark series
- Mars series

Bradburne, Elizabeth Sutton
- Elizabeth Ann series

Bradbury, Bianca
- Brave Fireman series

Bradbury, Catherine
- Applebury tales series

Bradbury, Edward P
see also **Barclay, Bill; Moorcock, Michael**
- Warrior of Mars trilogy

Bradby, Godfrey Fox
- Dick series

Braddon, George
see also **Redwood, Alec; Sava, George**
- Michael Gaunt series

Braddon, Mary Elizabeth
- Valentine Hawkehurst series

Braddon, Russell
- Hate series

Braden, James Andrew
- Auto boys series
- John Jerome and Return Kingdom series

Bradford, Ann
- Maple Street Five series

Bradford, Barbara Taylor
- Emma Harte series
- How to be the perfect wife series

Bradley, Edward
see **Bede, Cuthbert**

Bradley, Helen
- Edwardian Lancashire series

Bradley, Jack
- Battlesquad 1942 series

Bradley, Kenneth
- District officer series

Bradley, Marion Zimmer
- Arwen series
- Atlantean saga series
- Darkover anthologies series
- Darkover series
- Leslie Barnes series

Lythande
Sanctuary series (12)
- Red moon series

Bradley, Mary Emily Neely
- Proverb trilogy

Bradley, Mary Hastings
- Old Chicago series

Bradley, Michael
- Johnny Adrano series

Bradley, Shelland
- A.D.C. series
- American girl series

Bradman, Tony
- Bad babies series
- Ben series
- Bluebeards series
- Daisy series
- Dilly series
- Rhymes with me series
- Sam, the girl detective series
- Tommy Niner series

Bradshaw, Gillian
- Arthur and Gawain trilogy

Bradshaw-Jones, Malcolm Henry
see **Jones, Bradshaw**

Bradwell, James
- Land of the giants series

Brady, Adam
- Buck Halliday series

Brady, Charlotte
see **Bingham, Charlotte**

Brady, Cyrus Townsend
- Bob Dashaway series
- John Paul Jones series
- Lady Susan series

Brady, John Paul
- Lemuel Gulliver series

Brady, Nicholas
see also **Levinson, Leonard**
- Ebenezer Buckle series

Brady, Taylor
- Kincaids series

Brady, Terence
- Upstairs, downstairs series
- Victoria Edgecombe series

Brady, William S
see also **Harvey, John Barton**
- Jared Hawk series
- Peacemaker series

Braenne, Berit
- Torris series
- Trina series

Braga, Meg
- William and Wendy series

Bragg, Melvyn
- Tallentire family series

Brahms, Caryl
- Inspector Adam Quill series
- Stroganoff Troupe series

Braine, John
- Clive and Robin Lendrick series
- Colonel Xavier Flynn series
- Joe Lampton series
- Last love series

Brainerd, Eleanor Hoyt
- Belinda series
- Nancy series

Braithwaite, Edward Ricardo
- Sir series

Braithwaite, Ruth
- Yorkshire trilogy

Bramah, Ernest
- Kai Lung series
- Max Carrados series

Bramble, Forbes
- Kelleway family series

Brambleby, Ailsa
- Three series

Bramhall, Marion
- Kit Acton series

Bramwell Evens, George
see **Evens, George Bramwell**

Brand, Christianna
- Inspector Charlesworth series
- Inspector Chucky series
- Inspector Cockrill series
- Nurse Matilda series

Brand, Hilary
- Hilary Brand series

Brand, Kurt
- Perry Rhodan series

Brand, Max
see also **Baxter, George Owen; Evans, Evan; Frost, Frederick; Manning, David**
- Dan Barry series
- Doctor Kildare series
- Red Hawk series
- Silvertip series
- Thunder Moon series

Brandeis, Julian Walter
- Baron Munchausen series

Brandel, Marc
- Three Investigators Crimebusters series
- Three Investigators series

Brandenberg, Franz
- Aunt Nina series
- Edward and Elizabeth series
- Fieldmouse children series
- Leo and Emily series

Brandewyne, Rebecca
- Chronicles of Tintagel series
- Highclyffe Hall series

Brandner, Gary
- Big Brain series
- Howling series

Brandon, Charles
- John Fortescue series

Brandon, Gordon
- Arthur Stukeley Pennington series
- Inspector Patrick Aloysius McCarthy series
- Michael and Terry Terence series

Brandon, Grania
- Sengler's Circus series

Brandon, John Gordon
- Arthur Stukeley Pennington series
- Inspector Patrick Aloysius McCarthy series
- Sexton Blake series

Brandon, Joyce
- Lady series

Branfield, John
- Brown cow series

Branley, Franklyn Mansfield
- Exploring our universe series
- Mysteries of the universe series
- Voyage into space series

Branscum, Robbie
- Johnny May series
- Toby series

Branson, Henry Clay
- John Bent series

Branson, Karen
- Maureen O'Connor series

Branston, Frank
- Tommy Tompkins series

Brason, John
- Howard's way series
- Secret army series

Brata, Sasthi
- Astride two worlds series

Bratby, John
- Break series
- Peter Carr series

Brathwaite, Errol
- Maori Wars trilogy

Braudel, Fernand
- Civilization and capitalism trilogy
- Identity of France series

Braun, Lilian Jackson
- Jim Qwilleran series

Braun, Matt
- Ash Tallman series
- Brannocks series
- Luke Starbuck series

Braun, Maurice-Gilles
- Al Glenne series

Brawner, Helen
- Inspector Scott Stuart series

Bray, Donald
- Captain Davy series

Bream, Freda
- Reverend Jabal Jarrett series

Brean, Herbert
- Reynold Frame series
- William Deacon series

Brearley, Molly
- Honey family trilogy

Brebner, Percy
- Christopher Quarles series

Breckenridge, Gerald
- Radio boys series

Brede, Arnold
- Bull Rogers series

Breen, Jon Linn
- Jerry Brogan series
- Rachel Hennings series

Breese, Andrea
- Setting out series

Breeze, Paul
- Billy Dancey series

Breinburg, Petronella
- Sally-Ann series
- Sean series

Breitenbach, Louise Marks
- Alma series

Bremond d'Ars, Yvonne de
- Journal of an antique dealer series

Brenan, Gerald
- Life of one's own series

Brenda
- Froggy series

Brennan, Carol
- Liz Wareham series

Brennan, James Herbert
- Barmy Jeffers series

Dracula's castle
Dracula series (26)
- Frankenstein sequels series
- GrailQuest series
- Sagas of the Demonspawn series
- Shiva series

Brennan, John
see **Welcome, John**

Brennan, Joseph Payne
- Lucius Leffing series

Brenner, Barbara
- Lion and Lamb series

Brenner, Mayer Alan
- Dance of the gods series

Brent, Lynton Wright
- Bonnie and Clyde series

Brent, Nigel
- Barney Hyde series

Brent of Bin Bin
see also **Franklin, Miles**
- Bert Poole series

Brent, Peter Ludwig
see **Peters, Ludovic**

Brent, R L
see also **Stivers, Dick**
- Liquidator series

Brent-Dyer, Elinor Mary
- Chalet School series
- Chudleigh Hold series
- Fardingdales series
- Janeways series
- La Rochelle series
- Lorna series
- Skelton Hall series

Bresler, Fenton Shea
- British law series

Bretnor, Reginald
- Future at war series
- Papa Schimmelhorn series

Breton, Thomas le
see **Le Breton, Thomas**

Brett, Jan
- Funny names series

Brett, John Michael
see also **Tripp, Miles**
- Hugo Baron series

Brett, Martin
- Mike Garfin series

Brett, Michael
see also **Brett, John Michael**
- Hugo Baron series
- Pete McGrath series

Brett, Mike
- Sam Dakkers series

Brett, Simon
- Charles Paris series
- Frank Muir goes into series
- Mrs Melita Pargeter series
- Nigel Molesworth series
- Three detectives series

Brett Young, Francis
see **Young, Francis Brett**

Brewer, Gil
- Al Mundy series

Bridge, Ann
- Hetta Atherley series
- Julia Probyn series

Bridges, Ben
- Carter O'Brien series
- Wilde boys series

Bridges, Laurie
- Dark forces series

Bridges, Roy
- Australian trilogy

Bridges, Thomas Charles
- Sexton Blake series

Bridget
see **Pluis, Bridget**

Bridie, James
- Mavor series

Bridwell, Norman
- Clifford series
- Monster series
- Witch series

Brierley, David
- Cody series

Brierley, John Keith
- Human behaviour trilogy

Briffault, Robert
- Europa series

Briggs, Desmond Lawther
see **Fitzroy, Rosamond**

Briggs, Ian
- Doctor Who series

Briggs, Joe Bob
- Joe Bob series

Briggs, Phyllis
- Black Beauty series

Briggs, Raymond
- Father Christmas series
- Fungus the bogeyman series
- Gentleman Jim series
- Snowman series

Briggs, Victor
- Way ahead trilogy

Bright, Pamela
- Nursing trilogy

Bright, Robert
- Georgie series

Bright, Sarah
see also **Harris, Robin; Shine, Deborah; Slier, Debby**
- Hello Kitty series

Brightfield, Richard
- Choose your own adventure series
- Dragonmaster series
- Dragons series
- Earth inspectors series
- Escape from Tenopia series
- Escape from the Kingdom of Frome series
- Indiana Jones choose your own adventure series
- Master series
- Your amazing adventures series

Brims, Bernagh
- Ballyreagh Jumping Team series

Brin, David
- Earthclan series

Brindley, Louise
- Old peoples' home trilogy
- Tanquillan series

Brinig, Myron
- Singermann family series

Brink, Carol Ryrie
- Caddie Woodlawn series

Brinley, Bertrand Russell
- Mad Scientists' Club series

Brinsmead, Hesba Fay
- Clippie Nancarrow series
- Truelance family series

Brinton, Henry
see also **Fraser, Alex**
- John and Sally Strang series

Brisbane, Coutts
- Sexton Blake series

Briscoe, Jill
- Time for series

Briskin, Jacqueline
- Van Vliet series

Brisley, Joyce Lankester
- Bunchy series
- Milly-Molly-Mandy series

Brissenden, Robert Francis
- Tom Caxton series

Brisson, Pat
- Kate series

Bristow, Gwen
- Louisiana trilogy
- Wade series

Brisville, Jean Claude
- Oleg series

Brittain, Bill
- Coven Tree series

Brittain, Harry Ernest
- Pilgrim series

Brittain, Vera
- Testament series

Britten Austin, Frederick
see **Austin, Frederick Britten**

Britton, David
- Savoy series

Broch, Hermann
- Sleepwalkers trilogy

Brochet, Jean Alexandre
see **Bruce, Jean**

Brock, Emma Lillian
- Mary series

Brock, Lynn
- Colonel Gore series
- Sergeant Venn series

Brockway, Fenner
- Left right series

Brode, Anthony
- Country vicarage series

Broderick, Damien
- Faustus hexagram series

Brodie, Gordon
- John Borham series

Brodrick, Alan Hough
- Indo-China series

Brodsky, Michael Mark
- Xman series

Brody, Marc
see also **Hunter, Richard Wilkes**
- Marc Brody series

Brogan, Colm
- Patrick Heron series

Brogan, Mike
- Action Man series

Bromfield, Louis
- Escape series
- Malabar series

Bromige, Iris
- Rainwood family series

Bromley, Gordon
- Inspector Severn series

Bronson-Howard, George
- Yorke Norroy series

Bronte, Charlotte
- Angria series
- Brussels series
- Rochester series

Bronte, Emily
- Heathcliff series

Bronte, Emily Jane
- Wuthering Heights series

Bronte, Louisa
- American dynasty series
- Greystone Tavern series

Brook, Judy
- Belinda series
- Charlie Clown series
- Noah series
- Tim Mouse series

Brook, Roger
- Nursing howlers series

Brook, Sally
- Roly Poly series

Brooke, Carol
- Marshall family series

Brooke, Jocelyn
- Orchid trilogy

Brooke, Jonathan
- Backstreets series

Brooke, Leonard Leslie
- Johnny Crow series

Brooke-Rose, Christine
- Xorandor series

Brookes, Ewart
- Proud waters series

Brookins, Dana
- Bobbie Toppin series

Brooks, Amy
- Dorothy Dainty series
- Princess Polly series
- Prue series
- Rosalie Dare series

Brooks, Bill
- Colour of Canada series

Brooks, Collin
- O Swete McTavish series

• Raeburn Steel series
• Tavern talk series
Brooks, Edna
• Khaki Girls series
Brooks, Edwy Searles
see also **Gray, Berkeley; Gunn, Victor**
• Inspector William Beeke series
• Sexton Blake series
Brooks, Jeremy
• Bernard Smith series
Brooks, Leonard Harold
• Sexton Blake series
Brooks, Terry
• Heritage of Shannara series
• Magic Kingdom of Landover series
• Shannara series
Brooks, Van Wyck
• Scenes and portraits series
Brooks, Vivian Collin
see **Mills, Osmington**
Brooks, Walter Rollin
• Freddy the pig series
Broomall, Robert Walter
see also **Edwards, Hank**
• Jake Moran trilogy
Broome, Adam
• Commissioner Denzil Grigson series
• Inspector Bramley series
Broome, H B
• Tom English series
Brophy, John
• Green series
Brosnan, John
• Sky lords series
Broster, Dorothy Kathleen
• Captain Carew series
• Jacobite trilogy
Broughall, Helen Katherine
• Barbara Winthrop series
Broughton, Josephine Delves-
see **Bryan, John**
Broun, Daniel
• Harry Egypt series
Brown, Alfred John
• High Fell series
Brown, Amy
see **Barbary, James**
Brown, Carter
see also **Brown, Peter Carter**
• Andy Kane series
• Danny Boyd series
• Larry Baker series
• Lieutenant Al Wheeler series
• Mavis Seidlitz series
• Mike Farrel series
• Paul Donavan series
• Randy Roberts series
• Rick Holman series
Brown, Charles
• John Bunyan series
Brown, Christy
• Cerebral palsy series
Brown, Dale
• Patrick McLanahan series
Brown, Deborah
• Little Koala series
Brown, Edith Charlotte
• Margaret Dashwood series
Brown, Edward
• Major Adrian Titterton series
Brown, Eric
• Mountaineering series
Brown, Ethel C
• Three Gays series
Brown, Fern Goldberg
• Scooby Doo series
Brown, Francis, *Mrs*
see **Brown, Edith Charlotte**
Brown, Fredric
• Ed and Am Hunter series
Brown, George Mackay
• Two fiddlers series
Brown, Gerald
• Duke McCale series
Brown, Graham
• My first pop-up series
Brown, Helen Dawes
• Anna Lavinia series
Brown, Hosanna
• Frank Le Roux series
Brown, Jeff
• Stanley Lambchops series
Brown, Joseph Paul Summers
• Arizona saga series
• Steeldust series
Brown, Judith Margaret
• Gandhi series
Brown, Katy
• Twistaplot series
Brown, Kitt
• Frontier women series
Brown, Laurence Krasny
• Dinosaurs series
Brown, Laurene Krasny
• Dinosaurs guide book series
Brown, Marc
• Arthur series
• Dinosaurs guide book series
• Dinosaurs series
• D.W. series
Brown, Margaret Wise
• Noisy book series
Brown, May
see **Blake, Vanessa**
Brown, Mik
• Animal fun series
Brown, Morna Doris
see **Ferrars, Elizabeth**
Brown, Palmer
• Anna Lavinia series
Brown, Pamela
• Blue Door Theatre Company series
Brown, Peter Carter
see also **Brown, Carter**
• Rick Holman series
Brown, Richard
• Nicky series
• Small Potatoes series
• Where is it series
Brown, Rita Mae
• Mrs Murphy series
Brown, Robin
• Rhodesian series
Brown, Roderick Langmere Haig-
see **Haig-Brown, Roderick Langmere**
Brown, Rollo Walter
• Emergency series
Brown, Rose
• Two children series
Brown, Rosel George
• Sibyl Sue Blue series
Brown, Roy
• Sparrows series
Brown, Roy Frederick
• Chips Regan series
• Chubb series
Brown, Ruth
• Our cat and puppy series
Brown, Ruth Alberta
• Ivy Hall trilogy
• Peace Greenfield series
Brown, Sam
• Casey Wills series
Brown, Sandra
see also **Saint Claire, Erin**
• Alicia series
• Coleman family and Jake Langston series
• Texas trilogy
Brown, Sneaky Pie
• Mrs Murphy series
Brown, T Burton
• Peter and Tim series
Brown, Walter C
• Inspector Stephen Harper series
Brown, Wenzell
• Peter Aswell series
• Teen-age series
Brown, Winifred
• Duffers of the deep series
Brown, Zenith
see **Ford, Leslie**
Browne, Anthony
• Bear series
• Willy series
Browne, Belmore
• Golden valley series
Browne, Dik
• Hagar the horrible series
• Hi and Lois series
Browne, Douglas Gordon
• Inspector Thew series
• Major Maurice Hemyock series
• Mister Harvey Tuke series
Browne, Edith Ophelia
• Broken cup series
Browne, Eileen
• Arthur series
• Funny animals series
Browne, George Waldo
• Woodranger series
Browne, Howard
• Paul Pine series
• Tharn series
Browne, Reginald
• Whitelands series
Browne, Richard Arthur Allan
see **Browne, Dik**
Browne, Robert Gore-
see **Gore-Browne, Robert**
Bruce, Dorita Fairlie
• Dimsie series
• Nancy series
• Sally Scatterbrain series
• Springdale series
Bruce, Henry
• Eurasian series
• Temple girl series
Bruce, Henry James
• Silken dalliance series
Bruce, Jean
• Secret Agent O.S.S.117 series
Bruce, Leo
see also **Croft-Cooke, Rupert**
• Carolus Deene series
• Sergeant William Beef series
Bruce, Mary Grant
• Billabong series
• Peter series
Bruce, Sheilah B
• Fraggle Rock series
Bruck, Eva Doman
• Business and legal forms series
Bruller, Jan
see **Vercors**
Bruller, Jean Marcel
see **Vercors**
Brumbaugh, James
• Advanced dungeons and dragons adventure gamebook series
Brun, Vincenz
• Alcibiades series
Bruna, Dick
• Boris Bear series
• I can series
• I know series
• Miffy series
• Poppy Pig series
• Snuffy series
• Stories to tell series
• Toy box tale series
Brunhoff, Jean de
• Babar series
Brunhoff, Laurent de
• Babar series
• Bonhomme series
• Serafina series
Brunn, Robert
• Twilight series
Brunner, Ethel
• Celia series
Brunner, John
• Max Curfew series
• Zanzibar series
• Zarathustra trilogy
Brush, Karen Alexandra
• Pig series
Brush, Katharine
• Lillian Legendre series
Brust, Harold
• Political police officer series
Brust, Steven
• Jhereg series
Bruton, Eric
• City of London Police series
Bryan, John
• Richard Sarel series
Bryant, Arthur
• Historian series
• History of Britain and the British people series
• Napoleonic Wars trilogy
• Samuel Pepys series
• Second World War series
• Story of England series
Bryant, Bonnie
• Saddle Club series
Bryant, Marguerite
• Stone trilogy
Bryce, Charles
• Plando series
Bryce, Charles, *Mrs*
• Mister Gimblet series
Bryce, Iris
• Canals series
Brychta, Jan
• Bunburys series
Bryher, Winifred
• Development series
Bryson, Charles
see **Barry, Charles**
Bryson, Kit
• Naff series
Bubb, Lillian
• Christiansson family trilogy
Bucar, Cary A
Esper
Star wars storybook series (3)
Buchan, Anna
see **Douglas, O**
Buchan, John
• Dickson McCunn series
• Richard Hannay series
• Sir Edward Leithen series
Buchan, Susan
see **Tweedsmuir, Susan Buchan**
Buchanan, Edna
• Britt Montero series
Buchanan, Heather S
• Tales of George and Matilda Mouse series
Buchanan, Jack
• M.I.A. Hunter series
Buchanan, Marie
see **Petrie, Rhona**
Buchanan, Patrick
• Ben Shock and Charity Tucker series
Buchanan, William
• Kelly McCoy series
Buchholtz, Johannes
• Egholm series
Buchholz, Suzanne
Middle Earth quiz book
Middle Earth series (5)
Buchwald, Art
• Caviar series
Buck, Pearl Sydenstricker
see also **Sedges, John**
• Ling Tan series
• Several worlds series
• Spirit and the flesh series
• Wang family series
Buck, Peter
• Marc Dean series
Buck, William Ray
see **Buchanan, William**
Buckels, Alex
• Bunny Buffin series
Buckeridge, Anthony
• Jennings series
• Rex Milligan series
Buckholtz, Eileen
see also **York, Rebecca**
• Charisma Inc. series
• Magic micro adventure series
• Micro adventure series
• Twistaplot series
Buckingham, Bruce
see also **Chandos, Dane**
• Don Pancho series
Buckingham, David
• Sam Wharton series
Buckley, Eunice
• Castelferrante series
• Fiorina series
• Rex Anderson series
• Sandor Raimann series
• Vienna series
• Zero and Rosalind series
Buckley, Frederick Robert
• Blithe sheriff series
Buckley, Helen Elizabeth
• Grandparents series
Buckley, William Frank
• Blackford Oakes series
Buckman, Sam
• Storm Jackson series
Budd, Lillian
• Kristiansson trilogy
Budd, Mavis
• Dust to dust series
Buddee, Paul
• Air Patrol series
• Ann Rankin series
• Peter Devlin series
Bude, John
• Inspector Meredith series
• Inspector Sherwood series
Buechner, Frederick
• Leo Bebb tetralogy
• Sacred journey series
Buffery, Judith
• Star lords series
Bugbee, Emma
• Peggy series
Buhet, Gil
• Boys' Republic series
Bujold, Lois McMaster
• Miles Naismith Vorkosigan series
Bukowski, Charles
• Henry Chinaski series
Bulis, Christopher
• Doctor Who series
Bull, Emma
• Liavek series
Bull, Geoffrey Taylor
• Imprisoned missionary series
Bull, Peter
• Bulls series
Bulla, Clyde Robert
• Squanto series
Bullett, Gerald
see also **Fox, Sebastian**
• History of Pandervil series
• Peacock family series
Bullingham, Ann
• Penelope series
Bullivant, Cecil Henry
• Garnett Bell series
Bullock, Kathleen
• Mitzi Mouse series
Bullock, Michael
• Randolph Cranstone series
Bulluck, Vic
Art of The Empire strikes back
Luke Skywalker series (7)
Bulmer, Henry Kenneth
see **Bulmer, Kenneth**
Bulmer, Kenneth
see also **Akers, Alan Burt; Blake, Ken; Frazier, Arthur; Hardy, Adam; Krauss, Bruno; Pike, Charles R; Silver, Richard; Zetford, Tully**
• Keys to the dimensions series
• Professionals series
• Sea Wolf series
• Swords series
Bulwer-Lytton, Edward George Earle Lytton
see **Lytton, Edward George Earle Lytton Bulwer-Lytton**
Bunch, Chris
• Rali series
• Sten series
Buncher, Walter
• Donald O'Dare series
Bunner, Henry Cuyler
• Short sixes series
Bunting, Anne Evelyn
see **Bunting, Eve**
Bunting, Eve
see also **Bolton, Evelyn**
• Dinosaur machines series
• High point series
• Jane Martin series
• Magic circle series
• No such things series
• Skate Patrol series
Bunting, James
• British International Airways series
Buntline, Ned
• Buffalo Bill series
• War Eagle series
Bunyan, John
Holy war
John Bunyan series (3)
Pilgrim's progress from this world to that which is to come
John Bunyan series (1)
Pilgrim's progress from this world to that which is to come
John Bunyan series (2)
Buranelli, Prosper
• Nick Morro series
Burbridge, Edith Joan
see **Cockin, Joan**
Burch, Robert Joseph
• Ida Early series
Burch, T R
• Shane McKellar series
Burden, Roy
• Big red bus series
Burford, Eleanor
see **Carr, Philippa; Plaidy, Jean**
Burge, Milward Rodon Kennedy
see **Kennedy, Milward**
Burger, Dionys
• Flatland series
Burgess, Anthony
see also **Kell, Joseph**
• Malayan trilogy
• Mister Enderby series
Nineteen eighty five
Big Brother series (2)
• Richard Emmis series
Burgess, Colin
• Colditz series
Burgess, Eric
• Harry Tong series
• Mortorio series
Burgess, Mallory
• Tudor trilogy
Burgess, Mary Alice
Futurevisions
Science fiction film series (2)
Burgess, Thornton Waldo
• Animal stories series
• Bedtime story-books series
• Boy Scouts series
• Cubby Bear series
• Green forest series
• Green Meadow series

• Little color classics series
• Natural history series
• Nature stories series
• Old Mother West Wind series
• Paddy the beaver series
• Peter Rabbit series
• Reddy Fox series
• Smiling Pool series
• Wee little books series
• Wild flowers series
• Wishing Stone series
Burgin, George Brown
• Clubman series
• Four Corners series
• Monastery of Mahota series
• Slaves of Allah series
Burgoyne, Peter
• Peter Burgoyne series
Burian, Zdenek
Jungle scenes of Tarzan
Tarzan series (24)
Burke, Billie
• On my nose series
Burke, Fielding
• Call home series
Burke, Jackson Frederick
• Joe Streeter series
• Samuel Moses Kelly series
Burke, James Lee
• Dave Robicheaux series
Burke, Jan
• Irene series
Burke, John Frederick
see also **Burke, Jonathan; Jones, Joanna; Miall, Robert**
Chitty-Chitty-Bang-Bang
Chitty-Chitty-Bang-Bang series (3)
• Doctor Alexander Caspian series
Dracula, princess of darkness
Dracula series (1)
Burke, Jonathan
see also **Burke, John Frederick; Jones, Joanna; Miall, Robert**
• Mike Merriman series
• Sexton Blake series
Burke, Kenneth
• Attitudes towards history series
• Motives series
Burke, Richard
• Quinny Hite series
Burke, Thomas
• Bill and Beryl series
• London series
Burkett, Molly
• Home for animals series
Burkholz, Herbert
see also **Luckless, John**
• Eddie Mancuso and Vasily Borgneff series
• Sensitives series
Burland, Brian
• James Berkeley series
Burley, Andrew S
• Uncle Sam's Army boys series
Burley, William John
• Doctor Henry Pym series
• Superintendent Charles Wycliffe series
Burman, Ben Lucien
• Catfish Bend series
Burnaby, Nigel
• Chief Inspector Drewry series
Burnand, Francis Cowley
• Happy thoughts series
Burnap, Jennifer
• Cartwright family series
Burne, Alfred Higgins
• Hundred Years' War series
Burnett, Alice Hale
• Merryvale girls series
Burnett, Carolyn Judson
• Blue Grass Seminary girls series
Burnett, Frances Hodgson
• Good wolf series
• House of Coombe series
• Lady of quality series
• Lady Walderhurst series
• Sara Crewe series
Burnett, George
• Inspector Gulliver series
Burnett, William Riley
• Chicago trilogy
• San Miguel series
Burnett-Smith, Annie Shepherd
see **Swan, Annie Shepherd**
Burnham, Clara Louise
• Jewel series
Burnham, Helen
• One Week Wimble series
Burnham, Margaret
• Girl aviators series
Burningham, John
• First words series
• Little book series
• Mister Gumpy series
• Number play series
• Play and learn series
• Shirley series
Burnley, Judith
• Wife series
Burns, James Macgregor
• American experiment series
Burns, Olive Ann
• Tweedy family series
Burns, Patricia
• Kezzy series
Burns, Rex
• Devlin Kirk series
• Gabriel Wager series
Burns, Richard
• Khalindaine series
Burns, Ron
• Harrison Hull series
Burns, Tex
see also **L'Amour, Louis**
• Hopalong Cassidy series
Buron, Nicole de
• Penelope and Guillaume trilogy
Burr, Sybil
• Holly Gordon series
• Lisa Longland series
Burrard, Gerald
• Tiger of Tibet series
Burrell, Jane
• Wombats series
Burrell, Roy Eric Charles
• Romans series
• Travel and transport series
Burress, John
• Singleton family series
Burrough, Reath J
• Smiley Adams series
Burroughs, Edgar Rice
• Apache series
• Barney Custer series
• Bowen Tylor trilogy
• Martian series
• Moon series
• Mucker series
• Opar series
• Pellucidar series
• Tarzan series
• Tarzan twins series
• Venus series
Burroughs, William Seward
• Cities of the red night trilogy
• Despair trilogy
• Tangier trilogy
Burrows, Julie
• Superintendent Bowman and Sergeant Peart series
Burstall, Terry
• Long Tan series
Burstein, Chaya Malamud
• Rifka series
Burstein, John
• Slim Goodbody series
Burt, Michael
• Roger Poynings series
Burtis, Thomson
• Air combat series
• Rex Lee series
Burton, Anne
• Richard Trenton series
Burton, Anthony
• Navigators trilogy
Burton, Betty
• Nugent family series
Burton, Charles Pierce
• Bob's Hill series
Burton, Hal
• Walton boys series
Burton, Hester
• Stephen Parkin series
Burton, Katherine
• Calloway Corners series
Burton, Miles
see also **Rhode, John**
• Inspector Arnold and Desmond Merrion series
Burton, Thomas
• Bloodbird series
Busby, Francis Marion
• Bran Tregare series
• Demu trilogy
• Rissa Kerguelen series
Busby, Roger
• Detective Inspector Leric series
Busch, Niven
• San Francisco series
Bush, Christopher
see also **Home, Michael**
• Ludovic Travers series
Bushby, John
• Captain James Rollo series
Bussell, Jan
• Puppets series
Butler, Bill
see also **Butler, William Vivian**
• Dean Street detectives series
Butler, David
• Edward VII series
• We'll meet again series
Butler, Dorothy
• Barney series
Butler, Eliza Marian
• Faust series
Butler, Guy
• South Africa series
Butler, Gwendoline
see also **Melville, Jennie**
• Inspector John Coffin series
• Inspector William Winter series
Butler, Leslie
• Horton and Jordan series
Butler, Margaret
• Henry II series
Butler, Marion Clifford
see **Dunboyne, Marion Clifford Butler**
Butler, Mark
• Home and away series
Butler, Maude Mary
• Daffodil series
Butler, Octavia Estelle
• Patternists series
• Xenogenesis trilogy
Butler, Peter
• Rounds series
Butler, Ragan
• Captain George Nash series
Butler, Richard
see also **Allbeury, Ted**
• Max Farne series
Butler, Samuel
• Erewhon series
Butler, William Allen
Miss McFlimsey
Miss Flora McFlimsey series (1)
Butler, William Vivian
see also **Butler, Bill**
• Commander George Gideon series
• Old Ireland Yard series
• Toff series
• Young detective series
Butters, Dorothy Gilman
see **Gilman, Dorothy**
Butterworth, Ben
• That boy Trog series
Butterworth, Michael
see also **Salisbury, Carola**
• Hawklords series
• Savoy series
• Space nineteen ninety nine series
Butterworth, Nick
• Upney Junction series
Butterworth, Oliver
• Nate Twitchell series
Butterworth, William Edmund
• M.A.S.H. series
• Tony Fletcher series
Buzo, Alexander
• Prue Foster series
Byam, William
• Harley Street series
Byars, Betsy
• Bingo Brown series
• Blossoms series
Byatt, Antonia Susan
• Virgin in the garden tetralogy
Bye, Beryl
• Cathy, Belinda and Jane series
• People like us series
Byers, Amy Irene
see **Byers, Irene**
Byers, Irene
• Carolyn series
• Foresters series
• Jeremy and Fenella series
• Meredith family series
• Penny and Gillian series
• Tim Digby series
• Tiptoes series
• Tony and Melissa series
Byfield, Barbara
• Simon Bede and Helen Bullock series
Bygraves, Anthony
• Wellies series
Byrd, Max
• Mike Haller series
Byrd, William
• Secret diary series
Byrne, Stuart James
• Star Man series
Byron, Amanda
• Twilight series
Bystander
see **Bairnsfather, Bruce**

C

C, M C
see **Elias, Frank**
Cabell, James Branch
• Conquest series
• Dom Manuel and his descendants series
• It happened in Florida trilogy
• Nightmare trilogy
• Poictesme trilogy
• Witch woman trilogy
Cadell, Elizabeth
• Waynes of Wood Mount trilogy
Cafferty, Jake
• Vic Merritt series
Caggiano, Phyllis
• Rose series
Cagney, Peter
see also **Winter, Bevis**
• Mike Strang series
Caidin, Martin
• Messiah series
• Six Million Dollar Man series
Caillou, Alan
• Cabot Cain series
• Colonel Matthew Tobin series
• Ian Quayle series
• Mike Benasque series
Cain, Jackson
• Torn Slater series
Cain, Jonathan
• Saigon commandos series
Cain, Robert
see also **Keith, William Henry**
• Cybernarc series
Caine, Geoffrey
see also **Robertson, Stephen; Walker, Robert Wayne**
• Abraham Stroud series
Caine, Jeffrey
• Heathcliff series
• Wuthering Heights series
Caine, Oliver Vernon
• Napoleon series
Cake, Patrick
• Dion Quince series
Calahan, Harold Augustin
• Sailing series
• Treasure Island series
Caldecott, Moyra
• Sacred stones series
Calder, Stephen
• Bonanza series
Calderini, Priscilla
• Borderland series
Caldwell, Alfred Betts
• Freddy Philpotts series
Caldwell, Janet Taylor
see **Caldwell, Taylor**
Caldwell, John
• Family voyage series
Caldwell, Patricia Kathleen
• Vivian's series
Caldwell, Taylor
• Bouchard family trilogy
• Listener series
Calhoun, Chad
• Agent Brad Spear series
Calhoun, Mary
• Katie John series
Calhoun, Wes
see also **Sadler, Geoffrey; Sadler, Jeff**
• Chulo trilogy
Calif, Ruth
• Over-the-hill series
Calisher, Hortense
• Ruth series
Callahan, Jay
• Twilight series
Callan, Michael Feeney
• Target series
Callas, Theo
• Kennedys abroad series
Callenbach, Ernest
• Ecotopia series
Callin, Grant
• Saturnalia series
Callison, Brian
• Brevet Cable series
• Captain Edward Trapp series
Callow, Philip
• Colin Patten trilogy
Calmenson, Stephanie
Addams family
Addams family series (3)
• Young Indiana Jones chronicles series
Calveley, Grange
• Roobarb series
Calvert, Mary
see **Danby, Mary**
Calvino, Italo
• QFWFQ series
Cameron, Alexander
• Vet in the vestry series
Cameron, Ann
• Julian stories series
Cameron, Berl
• Terran empire series
Cameron, Caddo
• Private Badger Coe and Sergeant Blizzard Wilson series
Cameron, David Kerr
• Scottish farm life series
Cameron, Donald
• Eldorado series
Cameron, Donald Clough
• Abelard Voss series
Cameron, Eleanor
• Julia Redfern series
• Tyco Bass series
Cameron, Elizabeth Jane
see **Duncan, Jane**
Cameron, Evelyn
• Sheriff Jack Thompson series
Cameron, Ian
• Counter Force series
Cameron, Isabel
• Doctor Lindsay series
• Glen folk series
Cameron, J D
• Omega sub series
Cameron, James
• Point of departure series
Terminator two, Judgment day
Terminator series (2)
Cameron, Joan
Dracula
Dracula series (1)
Strange case of Doctor Jekyll and Mister Hyde
Doctor Jekyll series (1)
Cameron, Kate
• Holderly Hall series
• Whispering Hills series
Cameron, Lou
see also **Dagmar**
• Doc Travis trilogy
• Making of America series
• Stringer series
Cameron, Margaret Locherbie
• Nicolette series
Cameron, Owen
• Deputy Sheriff Jake Brown series
Cammell, Charles Richard
• Continent and Edinburgh series
Camp, John
• Kidd series
Camp, Lyon Sprague de
see **De Camp, Lyon Sprague**
Camp, Wadsworth
• Garth series
Camp, Walter Chauncey
• Danny Fists trilogy
Campbell, Alan
• Bromley Bear series
Campbell, Alice
• Alison Young series
• Colin Ladbroke series
• Geoffrey Macadam and Catherine West series
• Helen Roderick series
• Inspector Headcorn series
• Tommy Rostetter series
Campbell, Bebe Moore
• Blues series
Campbell, Bruce
• Ken Holt series
Campbell, Daisy Rhodes
• Virginia Hammond trilogy
Campbell, Drusilla
• Hopewell series
Campbell, Gabrielle Margaret Vere
see **Bowen, Marjorie; Preedy, George Runnell**
Campbell, Harriette Russell
• Simon Brade series
Campbell, Hubert J
see **Sheldon, Roy**
Campbell, Ian Maxwell
• Vintner series
Campbell, Joanna
• Caitlin trilogy

Campbell, John Wood
- Aarn Munro series
- Arcot, Morey and Wade series

Campbell, Judith
- Ponies series

Campbell, Julie
- Ginny Gordon series
- Trixie Belden series

Campbell, Keith
- Mike Brett series

Campbell, Margaret
see **Bowen, Marjorie; Preedy, George Runnell**

Campbell, Marion
- Richard De Brun series

Campbell, Michael
- Peter Perry series

Campbell, Patricia
- Bromley Bear series

Campbell, Peter
- Amazing Koalas series

Campbell, R T
- Professor John Stubbs series

Campbell, R W
- Spud Tamson series

Campbell, Robert Wright
- Jake Hatch series
- Jimmy Flannery series
- Whistler series

Campbell, Rod
- Buster series
- Little people series
- Pocket wheels series
- We have series

Campbell, Ronald Grayson
see **Morgan, W Ingram**

Campbell, Ross
- Marriage series

Campbell, Roy
- Broken record series

Campbell, Scott
- Felix Boyd series

Campion, Sarah
- Mister Moses Burdekin series

Camps, Luis
- Smashers series

Campton, David
Frankenstein
Frankenstein series (1)

Canaday, John
see **Head, Matthew**

Candaleria, Nash
- Mexican war series

Candler, Edmund
- Siri Ram series

Candy, Edward
- Inspector Burnival series

Canfield, Dorothy
- Brimming cup series

Canfield, Sandra
- Calloway Corners series

Caniff, Milton
- Steve Canyon series

Cannan, Gilbert
- Laurie series
- New time trilogy
- Round the corner trilogy

Cannan, Joanna
- Frank Frobisher series
- Inspector Guy Northeast series
- Inspector Ronald Price series
- Jean series

Cannell, Dorothy
- Ellie Simons Haskell series

Canning, Victor
- Birdcage trilogy
- Crimson chalice trilogy
- Mister Finchley series
- Rex Carver series
- Smiler Miles trilogy

Cannon, Curt
- Curt Cannon series

Cannon, Elliott
see also **Forde, Nicholas**
- Guy Fosse series

Cannon, John
see also **Newton, Mike; Robinson, Vance**
- Intersect File series

Cannon, Martin
- Swamp Thing second series

Cannon, Mary
- O'Hara dynasty trilogy

Cannon, Michael
- Old Melbourne series

Canon, Jack
- Mike Paradise series

Cantone, Vic
- Timmy Tiger series

Cantrell, Lisa Wright
- Manse series

Cantwell, Lois
- Blackstone's magical adventure series

Cao, Xueqin
see **Ts'ao, Hsueh-ch'in**

Capek, Karel
- Truth and democracy trilogy

Capella, Raul Garcia
Leopard of Poitain
Conan series (69)

Capon, Paul
- Antigeos trilogy
- Arnold Wragge series
- Artor series

Capon, Robert
- Parables series

Capp, Al
- Abbie an' Slats series
- Li'l Abner dailies series
- Li'l Abner series
- Shmoo series

Caputo, Philip
- War memoirs series

Caractacus, Uncle
see **Lewis, E W**

Caraker, Mary
- Seven worlds series

Card, Orson Scott
- Alvin Maker series
- Ender Wiggins series
- Worthing chronicles series

Cardus, Neville
- Innings series

Carey, D L
- Dorian Trozen series

Carey, Diane
- Dreadnought series
- Star trek sequels series
- Star trek series
- Star trek, the next generation series

Carey, Ernestine Gilbreth
- Gilbreth family series

Carey, Mary Virginia
- Gnomobile series
Gremlins story book
Gremlins series (2)
- Raggedy Ann series
- Three Investigators series

Carey, Webster
- Sheriff Buford Pusser series

Carey, Wymond
- Monsieur Martin series

Cargill, Leslie
- Major Mosson series
- Morrison Sharpe series

Cargill, Morris
see **Morris, John**

Carkeet, David
- Ricky and Nate series

Carl, Lillian Stewart
- Sabazel trilogy

Carle, Eric
- My very first series

Carleton
see **Coffin, Charles Carleton**

Carlon, Patricia
- Jefferson Shields series

Carlsen, Chris
see also **Faulcon, Robert; Holdstock, Robert; Kirk, Richard**
- Berserker series

Carlson, Dale
Frankenstein
Frankenstein series (1)
- James Budd series
- Jenny Dean series

Carlson, Nancy
- Arnie series
- Bunnies series
- Harriet series
- Louanne Pig series
- Loudmouth George series

Carlson, Natalie Savage
- Luvvy Savage series
- Marie Louise series
- Orphelines series
- Spooky series

Carlson, Patricia McEvoy
- Maggie Ryan series

Carlstrom, Nancy White
- Jesse Bear series

Carlton, Lewis
- Sexton Blake series

Carmichael, Claire
- Minimal Farm series
- Virtual realities trilogy

Carmichael, Fred
- Crane Hammond series

Carmichael, Harry
see also **Howard, Hartley**
- John Piper and Quinn series

Carmichael, Montgomery
- Christopher and Cressida series

Carmody, Isobelle
- Obernewtyn chronicles series

Carnac, Carol
see also **Lorac, E C R**
- Inspector Julian Rivers series
- Inspector Ryvet series
- Inspector Strang series

Carnarvon, Henry
- No regrets series

Carnegie, Sacha
- Destiny of eagles series
- Major Gair Mainwaring series

Carnelle, Inge
- Jane Blonde series

Carney, Daniel
- Wild Geese series

Caro, Robert A
- Years of Lyndon Johnson series

Carossa, Hans
- Childhood, boyhood and youth trilogy

Carpenter, Carleton
- Chester Long series

Carpenter, Humphrey
- Mister Majeika series

Carpenter, Leonard
- Conan series

Carpenter, Richard
- Catweazle series
- Robin of Sherwood series

Carr, Annie Roe
- Nan Sherwood series

Carr, Charles
- Bel series

Carr, Glyn
see also **Styles, Showell**
- Sir Abercrombie Lewker series

Carr, Jayge
- Navigator trilogy

Carr, John Dickson
see also **Dickson, Carter**
- Doctor Gideon Fell series
Door to doom, and other detections
Sherlock Holmes series (10)
- Henri Bencolin series
Men who explained miracles
Sir Henry Merrivale series (23)
- Metropolitan Police series
- Patrick Butler series
Third bullet, and other stories
Sir Henry Merrivale series (23)

Carr, John Francis
- Endless frontier series
- Imperial stars series
- Lord Kalvan series
- Paratime police series
- There will be war series
- War world series

Carr, Joseph Baker
- Oceola Archer series

Carr, Kirby
see also **Platt, Kin**
- Hitman series

Carr, Mike
- Endless quest series
- Fantasy forest series

Carr, Philippa
see also **Kellow, Kathleen; Plaidy, Jean**
- Daughters of England series

Carr, Terry
- Man from U.N.C.L.E. series

Carre, John le
see **Le Carre, John**

Carrel, Mark
see also **Batchelor, Reg; Benton, Will; Bosworth, Frank; Carter, Nevada; Ingersol, Jared; Paine, Lauran; Slaughter, Jim; Standish, Buck**
- Andrew McCall series

Carrick, Carol
- Patrick's dinosaurs series
- Sleep out series

Carrick, Donald
- Harald series

Carrier, Jean Guy
- Family trilogy

Carrington, Charles
- Subaltern series

Carrington, G A
see also **Bodine, J D; Cunningham, Chet; Dalton, Kit; Derrick, Lionel; Fletcher, Dirk**
- Marcus Cavanaugh series

Carr-Martindale, Jesse
- Dempsey and Makepeace series

Carroll, Gladys Hasty
- Shaw family series

Carroll, James
- Doyle brothers series

Carroll, Jim
- New York diaries series

Carroll, John Richard
- Dennis Gatz series
- Don Bartholomew series

Carroll, Jonathan
- Bones series

Carroll, Joy
- Court family series

Carroll, Lewis
- Alice in Wonderland series
- Sylvie and Bruno series

Carroll, Shana
- Paxton women series

Carruth, Jean
- Fun with Sally series
- Trumpton series

Carryl, Charles Edward
- Alice in Wonderland sequels series

Carson, Anthony
- Soho series

Carson, Hilda
- Mary Jane series

Carson, James
- Saddle boys series

Carson, Rachel Louise
- Sea series
- Silent spring series

Carstairs, Henry
- Lydford Long series

Carstairs, John Paddy
- Fleur de Lys series
- Garaway Trenton series

Carter, Alden Richardson
- American Revolution series

Carter, Ashley
see also **Whittington, Harry**
- Blackoaks series
- Falconhurst series
- Golden stud series

Carter, Bruce
- Danny Black and Johnny Wild series
- Nick Bailey series

Carter, Carmen
- Star trek series
- Star trek, the next generation series

Carter, Dorothy
- Jan series
- Marise Duncan series
- Wren Helen series

Carter, Felicity Winifred
see **Bonett, Emery**

Carter, Forrest
- Josey Wales series

Carter, Herbert
- Boy Scout series

Carter, John
- New Avengers series

Carter, John Franklin
see **Diplomat**

Carter, Lin
- Chronicles of Kylix series
Conan
Conan series (8)
Conan of Cimmeria
Conan series (9)
- Conan series
Conan the wanderer
Conan series (11)
- Destiny series
- Eric Carstairs series
- Gondwane epic series
- Green Star series
- Hautley Quicksilver series
- History of the Great Imperium trilogy
- Jandar the Alien series
- Mars series
Middle Earth
Middle Earth series (5)
- Prince Zarkon series
- Tales of the Picts series
- Terra Magica series
- Thongor of Lemuria series

Carter, Margaret Louise
Dracula, the vampire and the critics
Dracula series (26)

Carter, Mary
- Caged women series

Carter, Nevada
see also **Batchelor, Reg; Benton, Will; Bosworth, Frank; Carrel, Mark; Ingersol, Jared; Paine, Lauran; Slaughter, Jim; Standish, Buck**
- Perdition series

Carter, Nicholas
- Doctor Quartz series
- Harrison Keith series
- Nicholas Carter series

Carter, Nick
- Nick Carter series

Carter, Philip Youngman
- Albert Campion series

Carter, Reginald
- Wroth family series

Carter, Robert A
- Nicholas Barlow series

Carter, Tom
- Country music series

Carter, Tonya R
- DragonLance preludes II series
- DragonLance preludes series
- Elven nations trilogy

Carter-Brown, Peter
see **Brown, Carter**

Carthew, Heather Jean
- Reeds series

Cartland, Barbara
- Years of life series

Cartlidge, Michelle
- Little Mouse series
- Mouse series
- Press and play series
- Teddy trucks series

Cartwright, Justin
- New Avengers series

Cartwright, Reg
- My pet series

Cartwright, Stephen
- Boo series
- Roly Poly series

Carus, Zena M
- Smugglers' Castle series

Carver, Jeffrey Allan
- Changeling star series
- Roger Zelazny's Alien speedway series

Carvic, Heron
- Miss Emily Seeton series

Cary, Falkland
Sailor, beware!
Hornett family series (1)

Cary, Joyce
- Art trilogy
- Chester Nimmo trilogy

Cary, Lucian
- Duke series

Casberg, Melvin A
- Captain Prem Narayan series

Case, Frank
- Wayward man series

Case, Jim
- Cody's army series

Case, Patricia
- Tiger series

Casement, Christina
- Robinson series

Casey, Brigid
- Wonders of nature series

Casey, Maie
- Australian story series

Casey, Robert J
- Jim Sands series

Casey, Sara
- Two by two series

Casey, Winifred Rosen
see **Rosen, Winifred**

Caspian, Jonatha Ariadne
- Torg series

Cass, Delysle F
- Airship Boys series

Cass, Joan Evelyn
- Cats series
- Milly Mouse series
- Molly Millikens series

Cass-Beggs, Barbara
- Children need music series

Cassells, John
see also **Duncan, William Murdoch; Graham, Neill; Malloch, Peter; Marshall, Lovat**
- Ludovic Saxon series
- Superintendent Flagg series

Casserley, Anne
- Barney series

Casserly, Gordon
- Jungle series

Cassidy, Bruce
- Cash Madigan series

Castaneda, Carlos
- Don Juan series

Castaneda, Omar S
- Isabel series

Castelhun, Dorothea
- Penelope series

Castellarin, Loretta
- Degrassi High School series

Casteret, Norbert
- Under the earth series

Castle, Agnes
- Beau Nash regime romance series

Castle, Egerton
- Beau Nash regime romance series

Castle, Frances
see also **Grant, Jane**
- Erinn series

Castle, Jayne
see also **Krentz, Jayne Ann**
- Guinevere Jones series

Castle, Peggy Mundy
see **Castle, Frances**
Castle Smith, G, *Mrs*
see **Brenda**
Castronovo, David
- Gentleman series

Caswell, Brian
- Mike and Lisdalia series

Catalan, Henri
- Soeur Angele series

Catalano, Grace
- New kids on the block series

Cate, Dick
- Flying free series
- Ghost dog series

Cate, Richard Edward Nelson
see **Cate, Dick**
Cates, Emily
- Haunting with Louisa series

Catherall, Arthur
see **Hallard, Peter; Ruthin, Margaret**
- Channel, A R
- Bulldog tugboat series

Catlin, Vera
see **Brittain, Vera**
Catling, Gordon
- Gang series
- Mister Puffett series

Catling, Patrick Skene
- Sex research series

Cato, Nancy
- Australian trilogy

Catran, Jack
- Walden series

Catran, Ken
- Deepwater series

Catto, Max
- Limpie series

Catton, Bruce
- Centennial history of the Civil War series
- Potomac Army trilogy

Caudill, Rebecca
- Bonnie series

Caudwell, Sarah
- Professor Hilary Tamar series

Caute, David
- Confrontation trilogy

Cavanna, Betty
see also **Allen, Betsy**
- Diane series

Cave, Peter
see also **Maxwell, Peter**
- Hell's Angels series
- New Avengers series

Caveney, Sylvia
- Little Zip series

Cavoukian, Raffi
see **Raffi**
Cawley, Winifred
- Jinnie Friend series
- Ralph Cole series

Cebulash, Mel
- Herbie series

Cecil, David
- Lord Melbourne series

Cecil, Henry
- Ambrose Low series
- Colonel Brain series
- Mister Tewkesbury series
- Roger Thursby series

Cecil, Hugh
- Teddy tales series

Cecil, Mirabel
- Teddy tales series

Cervantes Saavedra, Miguel de
- Don Quixote series

Chaber, M E
see also **Crossen, Kendell Foster; Monig, Christopher; Richards, Clay**
- Milo March series

Chadwick, Doris
- John series

Chadwick, Lester
- Baseball Joe series
- College sports series

Chaffee, Allen
- Wandy series

Chagnoux, Christine
- Little Hippo series

Chaikin, Miriam
- Molly series

Chakrabongse, Chula
see **Chula Chakrabongse**
Chalk, Gary
- Lone Wolf series
- Prince of shadows series

Chalker, Jack Laurence
- Changewinds series
- Dancing Gods series
- Four Lords of the Diamond series
- G.O.D. Inc. series
- Quintara Marathon series
- Rings of the master series
- Soul rider series
- Well world series

Challans, Mary
see **Renault, Mary**
Challen, John
- Graham's Gang series

Challis, Mary
- Jeremy Locke series

Challoner, Robert
- Commander Lord Charles Oakshott series

Chalmers, Amy D V
- Madge Morton series

Chalmers, Margaret Piper
- Pollyanna series
- Sylvia Arden series

Chalmers, Mary
- Harry series

Chambers, Aidan
- Great ghosts series
- Haunted houses series

Chambers, Catherine E
- Adventures in frontier America series

Chambers, Dana
see also **Jackson, Giles**
Blood on the blonde
Nile Boyd series (1)
- Jim Steele series

Chambers, Kate
- Diana Winthrop series

Chambers, Peter
see also **Chester, Peter**
- Mark Preston series
- Sexton Blake series

Chambers, Philip
- Sexton Blake series

Chambers, Robert
- Hank Moody series

Chambers, Robert William
- American Revolution trilogy
- Athalie series
- Cardigan series
- Franco-Prussian war trilogy
- Land series
- Tales of a naturalist series

Chambers, Rosamund Mary
- Napoleon and Josephine series

Chambers, Rosemary Mary
- Little Creole series

Chamisso, Adalbert von
- Peter Schlemihl series

Champ, Jack
- Colditz series

Champlin, Tim
- Jay McGraw series
- Matt Tierney series

Champney, Elizabeth Williams
- Great-grandmother's girls series
- Three Vassar girls series
- Witch Winnie series

Chamson, Andre
- Roux series

Chan, Melissa
- Inspector Joe Barnaby and Francesca Miles series

Chance, John Newton
see also **Newton, David C**
- Bunst series
- Jason series
- John Marsh series
- John Newton Chance series
- Jonathan Blake series
- Macinnes series
- Mister DeHavilland series
- Superintendent Black series

Chance, Stephen
see also **Turner, Philip**
- Septimus Treloar series

Chancellor, John
- Captain Frass series

Chancie, John de
see **De Chancie, John**
Chandler, A C
- Going for it series

Chandler, Arthur Bertram
- Empress of outer space series
- John Grimes series
- Rim series

Chandler, Edna Walker
- Cowboy Sam series
- Tom Logan series

Chandler, Frank
- Dollar series

Chandler, Raymond
- Big sleep series
- Philip Marlowe series

Chandos, Dane
see also **Buckingham, Bruce**
- Abbie series
- Mexico series

Chaney, Jill
- Christopher series
- Mottram Park series
- Woffle series

Chang, Lee
see also **Levinson, Leonard**
- Kung Fu series

Channel, A R
see also **Catherall, Arthur**
- Fighting Four series

Channing, Mark
- Colin Gray series

Chanslor, Torrey
- Lutie and Amanda Beagle series

Chant, Joy
- Vanderi series

Chaplain, Frederick
- Rupert Bear series

Chapman, Allen
- Boys of business series
- Darewell chums series
- Fred Fenton series
- Radio boys series
- Ralph Fairbanks of the railroad series
- Tom Fairfield series

Chapman, Andrew
- Fighting fantasy gamebook series

Chapman, Eddie
- Free agent series

Chapman, Elizabeth
- Marmaduke series

Chapman, George
- Monsieur d'Olive series

Chapman, George Warren Vernon
see **Warren, Vernon**
Chapman, Gillian
- Little Bear series
- Professor Potts series

Chapman, Graham
see **Monty Python**
Chapman, James
- River boy trilogy

Chapman, Jennifer
- Long weekend series

Chapman, Maristan
- Happy mountain series

Chapman, Raymond
see **Nash, Simon**
Chapman, Robert
- Rex Banner series

Chapman, Vera
- Three damosels trilogy

Chappell, Audrey
- Oliver series

Chappell, Fred
- Cthulhu Mythos series

Chappell, Mollie
- Cressy series
- Tiddy Jeffreys series

Chapple, Joseph Mitchell
- Heart throbs series

Charbonneau, Louis
see also **Young, Carter Travis**
- Kathy McNeely series

Chard, Brigid
- Hidden journey series

Chard, Trevor Edwin Scott-
see **Scott-Chard, Trevor Edwin**
Chardonne, Jacques
- House of Barnery series

Charette, Beverly
- Fantasy forest series

Charles, Elizabeth
- Bertram family series
- Drayton family series

Charles, Eric
- Bertha series

Charles, Ernest F
- Dick Torreyton series

Charles, Hampton
- Miss Emily Seeton series

Charles, Kate
- David Middleton-Brown series

Charles, Robert
see also **Leader, Charles**
- Counter-terror series
- Simon Larren series

Charles, Steven
see also **Fenn, Lionel; Grant, Charles Lewis; Marsh, Geoffrey**
- Private school series

Charles, Theresa
see **Lance, Leslie**
Charles, Wyndham
- Chief Superintendent Sebastian Griffin series

Charlesworth, Maria Louisa
- Ministering children series
- Mrs Dorothy Cope series

Charlier, Jean Michel
- Lieutenant Mike S Blueberry series
- Young Blueberry series

Charlip, Remy
- Handtalk series

Charlton, Moyra
- Treherne family series

Charlwood, Don
- Airman series

Charnas, Suzy McKee
- Alldera series
- Sorcery Hall trilogy

Charnock, Joan
- Twin series

Charques, Dorothy
- Time's harvest trilogy

Charrette, Robert N
- BattleTech series
- Secrets of power series

Charriere, Henri
- Papillon series

Charteris, Leslie
- Bill Kennedy series
- Saint series

Charters, Samuel
- Notebook series

Charyn, Jerome
- Isaac Sidel series

Chase, Arthur Minturn
- Lieutenant Dan Durkin series

Chase, Beatrice
- Beatrice Chase series

Chase, Carolyn
- Thirteen colonies series

Chase, Edna Woolman
- Past imperfect series

Chase, Elaine Raco
- Roman Cantrell and Nikki Holden series

Chase, Emily
- Canby Hall series

Chase, Glen
see also **Levinson, Leonard**
- Cherry Delight series

Chase, Ilka
- Past imperfect series
- Travel series

Chase, James Hadley
see also **Marshall, Raymond**
- Al Barney series
- Carol Blandish series
- Frank Terrell series
- Helga Rolfe series
- Herman Radnitz series
- Lu Silk series
- Mark Girland series
- Steve Harmas series
- Vic Malloy series

Chase, Josephine
see **Bates, Gordon; Flower, Jessie Graham; Wilkins, Dale**
Chase, Kip
- Justine Carmichael series

Chase, Lesley
- Jill Graham series

Chase, Mary Ellen
- Virginia series

Chase, Philip
- Aaron Eisenberg and William Kendall series

Chase, Robert Reynolds
- Game series

Chase, Trevett Coburn
see **Chase, Kip**
Chastain, Madye Lee
- Fripsey series
- Lisa and Emmy and Dodie series

Chastain, Thomas
- Inspector Max Kauffman series
- J T Spanner series
- Perry Mason series
- Robins family series

Chatfield, Keith
- Issi Noho series

Chatrian, Pierre Alexandre
- French campaign series

Chaudhuri, Nirad Chandra
- Unknown Indian series

Chauncy, Nan
- Lorenny family series
- Tasmania series

Chaundler, Christine
- Fourth Form series

Chavannes, Albert
- Socioland series

Chaze, Elliot
- Kiel Saint James and Orson Boles series

Cheesman, Evelyn
- Time well spent series

Cheesman, Lilian
- Peter trilogy

Cheetham, Ann
- Black harvest series

Cheever, John
- Wapshot series

Chell, Mary
- Slimtails series

Cheney, Brainard
- Adam series

Cheney, Ednah Dow
- Nora Helmer series

Chenneviere, Sabine
- Colombine series

Cherryh, Carolyn Janice
- Alliance-Union series
- Chanur series
- Chronicles of Morgaine series
- Cyteen series
- Downbelow Station trilogy
- Ealdwood series
- Faded sun trilogy
- Heroes in hell series
- Merchanter series
- Merovingen nights series
- Rusalka series
- Sword of knowledge series
- Sword of knowledge trilogy

Chesbro, George Clark
- Mongo series
- Valhalla trilogy
- Veil Kendry series

Chesher, Kim
- Cuthbert series
- Inheritance trilogy

Chesney, Marion
- House for the season series
- Poor relation series
- School of manners series
- Six sisters series
- Travelling matchmaker series
- Westerbury series

Chesney, Michael
- Colonel Steel Callaghan series

Chess, Victoria
- Fletcher and Zenobia series

Chesser, Eustace
see **Hilton, Alec**
Chessman, Caryl
- Death row series

Chester, George Randolph
- James Rufus Wallingford series

Chester, Gilbert
- Sexton Blake series

Chester, Lillian Eleanor
- James Rufus Wallingford series

Chester, Peter
see also **Chambers, Peter**
- Johnny Preston series

Chester, William L
- Kioga series

Chesterton, Gilbert Keith
- Don Quixote series
- Father Brown series

Chesterton, Rupert
- Phantom battleship series

Chetham-Strode, Warren
- Siamese cats series

Chetwin, Grace
- Tales of Gom in the Legends of Ulm series

Chetwynd, Bridget
- Petunia Best and Max Frend series

Chetwynd-Hayes, Ronald
- Dracula's children series
- Tales of Clavering Grange series

Chevallier, Gabriel
- Clochemerle series

Cheyne, Irene
- Annette series

Cheyney, Peter
- Alonzo Mactavish series
- Everard Peter Quayle series
- Johnny Vallon series
- Lemmy Caution series
- Michael Kells series
- Secret service series
- Shaun O'Mara series
- Slim Callaghan series

Chica, Marcel
- Celestine series

Chichester, John Jay
- Jimmy Price series
- Maxwell Sanderson series

Child, Nellise
- Jeremiah Irish series

Child, Tim
- Knightmare series

Childerness, George
- Chet Phelps series

Childs, Rob
- Sandford series

Chilson, Rob
- Robot city series

Chilton, Charles
- Jet Morgan series

Chipman, William Pendleton
- Boy spies series

• Firefly series
• Navy boys series
Chipperfield, Robert Orr
see also **Fox, David**
• Barry O'Dell series
• Shadowers Inc. series
Chisholm, Louey
• Fairyland tales series
Chisholm, Matt
see also **James, Cy**
• Joe Blade series
• Rem McAllister series
• Storm family series
Chitty, Thomas Willes
see **Hinde, Thomas**
Chodos, Robert
• Brian Mulroney series
Choi, Sook Nyul
• Sookan series
Cholmondeley, Mary
• Danvers family series
Chorao, Kay
• Ida series
• Kate series
• Molly series
• Oink and Pearl series
Chotzinoff, Samuel
• Lost paradise series
Christian, Catherine Mary
• Sally series
Christian, Frederick H
see also **Nolan, Frederick**
• Frank Angel series
• Sudden series
Christian, John
see also **Dixon, Roger**
• Richard Deutsch series
Christian, Mary Blount
• Determined detectives series
• God's gift to children series
• Goosehill Gang series
• High-low mysteries series
• Mystery of series
• Penrod series
• Sebastian Super Sleuth series
• Sherlock Street detectives series
• Swamp monsters series
Christian, Petra
• Sally Deenes series
Christie, Agatha
• Colonel Race series
• Hercule Poirot series
• Miss Jane Marple series
• Mrs Ariadne Oliver series
• Superintendent Battle series
• Tommy and Tuppence Beresford series
Christie, Anne
• First act series
Christie, Kate
• Harold Crane series
Christie, Robert Stuart
• Book of Sarah series
Christie, Stephen
• Sexton Blake series
Christina, Frank
• Billy Jack series
Christina, Teresa
• Billy Jack series
Christmas, Joyce
• Lady Margaret Priam series
Christopher, John
see also **Ford, Hilary; Godfrey, William**
• Fireball trilogy
• Prince trilogy
• Tripods series
Christopher, Matt
• Dirt bike racer series
• Home Run Kid series
Chrystie, Edward M
• Leathers Auckland series
Chula Chakrabongse
• Eastern prince series
Chun-Chan Yeh
see **Yeh, Chun-Chan**
Church, Leslie Frederic
• Methodist people series
Church, Ralph
• Mork and Mindy series
Church, Richard
• John Quickshott series
• Over the bridge series
• Tomahawk Club series
Churchill, Jill
• Jane Jeffry series
Churchill, Peter
• British spy series
Churchill, Randolph Spencer
• Winston S Churchill series
Churchill, Rosemary
• Mary Tudor series
Churchill, Winston
• American national development series
Churchward, James
• Mu series
Chute, Carolyn
• Egypt, Maine series
Ciardi, John
• Browser's dictionary series
Cinque, Angelo
Wellies drop in
Wellies series (1)
Citrine, Walter McLennan
• Men and work series
• My diary series
Clair, William R
• Gants series
Clancy, Eugene A
• Masked Rider and Blue Hawk series
Clancy, Judith S
Ecotopian sketchbook
Ecotopia series (2)
Clancy, Tom
• Jack Ryan series
Clandon, Henrietta
see also **Loder, Vernon**
• Penny and Vincent Mercer series
• William Power series
Clanmorris, John Bingham
see **Bingham, John**
Clapperton, Richard
• Peter Fleck series
Clapton, Patricia
• Toy series
Clare, Helen
see also **Clarke, Pauline**
• Five dolls series
Clare, Marguerite
• Merlin Sorrel series
Claremont, Chris
• FirstFlight series
Claret, Maria
• Melissa Mouse series
Claridge, David
• Roland Rat series
Clark, Al C
see also **Goines, Donald**
• Kenyatta series
Clark, Alfred Alexander Gordon
see **Hare, Cyril**
Clark, Brenda
• Franklin series
Clark, Charles Manning Hope
see **Clark, Manning**
Clark, Douglas
• Inspector George Masters series
Clark, Frederick Stephen
see **Dalton, Clive**
Clark, Gail
• Dulcie Bligh series
Clark, Halsey
• Periscope series
Clark, Joan
• Barrow family series
• Penny Nichols series
Clark, Kenneth Mackenzie
• Self-portrait series
Clark, Leonard
• Mister Pettigrew series
• Robert Andrew series
Clark, Manning
• Historian series
Clark, Margaret Dianne
• Pugwall series
• Sam and Leanne series
Clark, Mary
• Endless quest crimson crystal adventure series
Clark, Mavis Thorpe
• Timber Creek series
Clark, Patricia Denise
see **Robins, Patricia**
Clark, Sheila
• Star trek fan series
Clark, Susanna Rebecca Graham
• Yensie Walton series
Clark, William
• Patrick Pyrton series
Clarke, Allen
• Windmill Land series
Clarke, Anna
• Professor Paula Glenning series
Clarke, Arthur Charles
Against the fall of night
Fall of night series (2)
• Fall of night series
• Rama series
• Space odyssey series
Clarke, Austin
• Memories of Ireland and England series
Clarke, Austin Chesterfield
• Boysie Cumberbatch trilogy
Clarke, Brenda
see **Honeyman, Brenda**
Clarke, Elf Lewis
• Drowsy Dormouse series
Clarke, Frances Elizabeth Haldane
see **Grand, Sarah**
Clarke, Judith
• Al Capsella series
Clarke, Kevin
• Doctor Who series
Clarke, Mary Stetson
• Ross McCrae series
Clarke, Molly
• Little Bear series
Clarke, Pauline
see also **Clare, Helen**
• James series
Clarke, Roy
• Summer wine series
Claro, Joe
• Herbie series
Clason, Clyde B
• Theocritus Lucius Westborough series
Claudy, Carl Harry
• Adventures in the unknown series
Clavell, James
• Asian series
• Struan family series
Clay, E Jefferson
• Duke Benedict and Hank Brazos series
Clay, John Wood
• Hopalong Cassidy series
Clay, Patrick
• Sergeant Hawk series
Claymore, Tod
see also **Clevely, Hugh**
• Tod Claymore series
Clayton, Colin Guy
• Blakeney papers series
Clayton, Jo
• Dancer trilogy
• Diadem series
• Drinker of souls trilogy
• Duel of sorcery trilogy
• Shadith's quest series
• Skeen trilogy
• Wild magic trilogy
Clayton, John
• Provence trilogy
Clayton, Richard Henry Michael
see **Haggard, William**
Clayton, Sheena
• Cthulhu Mythos series
Cleary, Beverly
• Beezus series
• Henry Huggins series
• Ralph S Mouse series
• Ramona Quimby series
• Ribsy series
Cleary, Denis
• Breakenridge series
• Theodore J Cash series
Cleary, Jon
• Scobie Malone series
Cleaver, Bill
• Ellen Grae series
• Luther family series
Cleaver, Hylton
• Harley series
Cleaver, Vera
• Ellen Grae series
• Luther family series
Cleese, John
see also **Monty Python**
• Survival series
Cleeve, Brian
• Crucifixion trilogy
• Sean Ryan series
Cleeve, Lucas
• Lady Susan series
Cleeves, Ann
• George Palmer-Jones series
• Inspector Stephen Ramsay series
Clegg, Barbara
• Doctor Who series
Cleife, Philip
• Martyn Finch series
Clemens, Samuel Langhorne
see **Twain, Mark**
Clement, Dick
• Likely lads series
Clement, Frank A
• Superintendent Mersey series
Clement, Hal
• Mesklin series
• Needle series
Clement, Henry
• Caged women series
• Columbo series
• Slaughter series
Clements, Barthe de
see **De Clements, Barthe**
Clements, Eileen Helen
• Alister Woodhead series
• Bright intervals series
Cleugh, Sophia
• Matilda series
Cleve, John
see also **Offutt, Andrew Jefferson**
• Spaceways series
Cleveland-Peck, Patricia
• String family trilogy
• William the wizard series
Clevely, Hugh
see also **Claymore, Tod**
• Inspector Williams series
• John Martinson series
• Justin Kelly series
• Maxwell Archer series
• Sexton Blake series
Clevin, Jorgen
• Jacob and Joachim series
Clewes, Dorothy
• Carrie and Maxwell series
• Hadley family series
• Henry Hare series
• Kay and Rory series
• Penny series
• Wild Wood series
• Willie series
Clews, Roy
see also **Fraser, Sara**
• Jethro Stanton series
Cliff, Michelle
• Clare Savage series
Cliff, Tony
• Lenin series
• Trotsky series
Clifford, Elizabeth
see **De la Pasture, Elizabeth**
Clifford, Eth
• Mary Rose Onetree series
Clifford, Francis
• Loyalty trilogy
• Spanish duet series
Clifford, Hugh
• Outskirts series
Clifford, James Lowry
• Samuel Johnson series
Clifford, Martin
see also **Richards, Frank; Richards, Hilda**
• Tom Merry series
Clifford, Robert
• Doctor series
Clift, Charmian
• Greek island series
Clifton, Lucille
• Everett Anderson series
Clifton, Oliver Lee
see also **Adams, Harrison; Rathborne, Saint George; Travers, J M**
• Camp Fire Boys series
Clinton, Jeff
see also **Bickham, Jack Miles**
• Emerald Canyon series
• Wildcat O'Shea series
Clinton-Baddeley, Victor Clinton
• Doctor Davie series
Clive, Archer, *Mrs*
see **Clive, Caroline**
Clive, Caroline
• Paul Ferroll series
Clive, William
see also **Bassett, Ronald**
• Joseph Dando series
Clodfelter, Micheal D
• Statistical history series
Cloete, Stuart
• Jean Macaque series
• Van der Berg family series
• Victorian son series
Closs, Hannah
• Albigensian trilogy
Clough, Brenda Wang
• Averidan series
Clough, Samuel Dennis Procter
• Wandering Jew series
Clouston, Joseph Storer
• F T Carrington series
• Mister Francis Mandell-Essington series
• Sherlock Holmes sequels series
• Ursula Dolling series
Clowes, Carolyn
• Star trek series
Clune, Frank
• Discovery series
• Try series
Clydesdale, Abby
• Alys Heavers series
Coates, Irene
• Claudia series
Coates, John
Watsons
Watsons series (1)
Coatsworth, Elizabeth
• Bob Bodden series
• Once-upon-a-time-in-America series
• Plum Daffy series
• Sally Smith series
Cobb, Belton
• Bryan Armitage series
• Inspector Cheviot Burmann series
• Kitty Armitage series
• Superintendent Manning series
Cobb, Frank
• Aviator series
• Stars and Stripes series
Cobb, Irwin Shrewsbury
• Judge Priest series
Cobb, Ivo Geikie-
see **Weymouth, Anthony**
Cobb, Richard
• Still life series
Cobb, Thomas
• Inspector Bedison series
Cobb, Vicki
• Bet you series
• Imagine living here series
• Not such dumb questions series
• Secret life series
• You can eat series
Cobban, James Maclaren
• Mister Townshend series
Cobbett, Pelham
• Dog series
Cobden, Guy
• John Chadwick series
Coblentz, Catherine
• Beggar's Penny series
Coblentz, Stanton Arthur
• Outlander series
Coburn, Andrew
• James Morgan series
• Rita Gardella O'Dea series
Coburn, Anthony
• Doctor Who scripts series
Coburn, L J
• Caleb Thorn series
Coccioli, Carlo
• Ardito Piccardi series
Cochran, Molly
Balance of power
Destroyer series (44)
Death sentence
Destroyer series (80)
• Destroyer series
Eleventh hour
Destroyer series (70)
• Grandmaster series
Master's challenge
Destroyer series (55)
Cockburn, Claud
• In time of trouble series
Cockburn, Kirsty
• Trev the truck series
Cockcroft, Barry
• Daleswoman series
Cockett, Mary
• Dan and Grum series
• Jan series
• Jasper Club series
• Jonathan and Felicity series
• Strange valley trilogy
Cockin, Joan
• Inspector Cam and Beaver series
Cody, Al
see also **Westland, Lynn**
• Montana series
• Powdersmoke series
Cody, James P
• Brian Peterson series
Cody, Jess
see **Cunningham, Chet**
Cody, Liza
• Anna Lee series
Cody, Stetson
see also **Denver, Lee; Grex, Leo; Gribble, Leonard Reginald; Sanders, Bruce; Shane, Steve**
• Cactus Clancy series
Cody, Stone
• Five Mavericks series
Coe, Ross Anton
• Warrior of vengeance series
Coe, Tucker
see also **Stark, Richard; Westlake, Donald Edwin**
• Mitchell Tobin series

Coffey, Brian
- Mike Tucker series

Coffin, Charles Carleton
- Civil War trilogy

Coffin, Geoffrey
see also **Mason, Francis Van Wyck**
- Inspector Scott Stuart series

Coffman, Elaine
- Mackinnon brothers series

Coffman, Virginia
- Cavalcade series
- Gaynor women series
- Lucifer Cove series
- Moura series
- Napoleonic Europe series

Coghlan, Margaret
see **Stirling, Jessica**

Cogswell, Theodore Rose
- Star trek originals sequels series

Cohen, Albert
- Gallants series

Cohen, Anthea
- Nurse Agnes Carmichael series

Cohen, Barbara
- Animals and their women series

Cohen, Barry
- Asher Bockhorn series

Cohen, Jane
- Cat and Dog series

Cohen, Matt
- Salem quartet

Cohen, Miriam
- Best friends series

Cohen, Octavus Roy
- David Carroll series
- Florian Slappey series
- Jim Hanvey series
- Lieutenant Marty Walsh series
- Max Gold series
- Polished ebony series

Cohen, Paul S
- Unidentified flying riddles series

Cohler, David Keith
- Sam Knight series

Coke, Peter
- Brigadier Rayne series

Coker, Carolyn
- Andrea Perkins series

Colbeck, Maurice
- Queer series

Colbert, Anthony
- Amanda series

Colbron, Grace Isabel
- Joe Muller series

Colburn, Laura
- Carol Gates series

Coldsmith, Don
- Horsin' around series
- Rivers west series
- Spanish bit series
- Spanish bit super series

Cole, Adrian
- Dream Lords trilogy
- Omaran series
- Star requiem series

Cole, Allan
- Rali series
- Sten series

Cole, Babette
- Hairy book series
- Nungu series
- Pingwings series
- Princess Smartypants series
- Promise series
- Trouble with series

Cole, Fannin
- Gene Autry series

Cole, George Douglas Howard
- Doctor Benjamin Tancred series
- Everard Blatchington series
- Mrs Elizabeth Warrender series
- Superintendent Henry Wilson series

Cole, Harry
- Policeman's life series

Cole, Hubert
- Sir John Hawkwood series

Cole, Jackson
see also **Scott, Bradford**
- Jim Hatfield series

Cole, Jennifer
- Cindy and Nicole series

Cole, Joanna
- Clown-Arounds series
- Magic school bus series
- Monster series

Cole, Joanne
- Bod series
- Gran series
- Kate and Sam series

Cole, John Alfred
- Just back series

Cole, Judd
- Cheyenne series

Cole, Lee
Star trek, the motion picture peel-off graphics book
Star trek series (57)

Cole, Margaret Alice
- Jill and Joe series
- Judy Lawler series

Cole, Margaret Isabel
- Doctor Benjamin Tancred series
- Everard Blatchington series
- Mrs Elizabeth Warrender series
- Superintendent Henry Wilson series

Cole, Michael
- Bod series
- Edward and friends series
- Fingermouse series
- Gran series
- Kate and Sam series
- Pigeon Street series

Cole, Royal King
Hopalong Cassidy and the five men of evil
Hopalong Cassidy series (20)

Cole, Tom
- Hunting series

Cole, William
- Knock knocks series
- What's good series

Colegate, Isabel
- King family series

Coleman, Bob
- Tom Jones series

Coleman, Clay
- Lost Island series

Coleman, James Covington
- Deep-sea adventure series

Coleman, Leslie
- Wilberforce series

Coleman, Lonnie
- Beulah Land trilogy

Coleman, Mary
Blinky Bill cookbook
Blinky Bill series (4)

Coleman, Robert William Alfred
see **Insight, James**

Coleman, William Lawrence
see **Coleman, Lonnie**

Coles, Alison
- Michael and Mandy series

Coles, Cyril Henry
see **Coles, Manning; Gaite, Francis**

Coles, Lesley
- Star trek fan series

Coles, Manning
see also **Gaite, Francis**
- Tommy Hambledon series

Coles, P C J
- Champion series

Coles, Robert
- Children of crisis series
- Conversations series
- Life of children series

Colette, Sidonie Gabrielle
- Cheri series
- Claudine series
- Renee Nere series

Colin, Aubrey
- Inspector Bill Murray series

Colin Willcox
- Private Eye series

Collard, Derek
- Dragon series

Collard, Thomas Henry
see **Ross, Sutherland**

Collenette, Eric J
- Ben Grant series

Collier, Christopher
- Willy Freeman trilogy

Collier, James Lincoln
see also **Williams, Charles**
- George Stable series
- Willy Freeman trilogy

Colligan, Douglas
- Twistaplot series

Collin, Paul Ries
- Henry and Jane Ellis series

Collingwood, Harry
- Flying Fish trilogy

Collingwood, William Gershon
- Norsemen series

Collini, Emanuela
- Facing up series

Collins, Alan
- Jacob Kaiser series

Collins, Freda
- Woodland Pack series

Collins, Gilbert
- Hugh Carding series

Collins, Jackie
- Hollywood series
- Santangelo family series
- World of men and women series

Collins, James
- Colt Revolver series

Collins, John Martin
- Military balance series

Collins, Laurel
- Women of the West series

Collins, Lynne
see also **Gray, Juliet**
- Brook's Hospital series
- Hartlake Hospital series

Collins, Max Allan
- Dick Tracy film series
- Dick Tracy series
- Eliot Ness series
- Mallory series
- Ms Tree series
- Nathan Heller series
- Nolan series

One lonely knight
Mike Hammer series (13)
- Quarry series

Collins, Michael
see also **Arden, William; Crowe, John; Sadler, Mark**
- Dan Fortune series

Collins, Michelle
- Megan Marshall series

Collins, Nancy Averill
- Sunglasses series

Collins, Randall
- Sherlock Holmes sequels series

Collins, Tom
- Such is life series

Collins, Warwick
- Challenge series

Collinson, Roger
- Bobby Bax series

Collis, Len
- Rupert Bear series

Collodi, Carlo
Adventures of Pinocchio
Pinocchio series (2)
- Pinocchio series

Collonge, Simone
- Virginia series

Colson, John Henry Charles
- Goose series

Colt, Clem
see also **Nye, Nelson Coral**
- Pony George series

Colter, Dale
- Regulator series

Colter, Eli
- Pat Campbell series

Colter, Frank
- Gang war series

Colver, Alice Ross
- Babs series
- Jeanne series
- Joan Foster series
- Measure of the years series

Colver, Anne
- Barbara Baum series

Colwell, Max
- Mike series

Combe, William
- Devil upon two sticks series

Comber, Elizabeth
see **Han, Suyin**

Comber, Lillian
see **Beckwith, Lillian**

Comer, Ralph
- Robert Lawson series

Comerford, Sherna
- Vulcan reflections series

Comfort, Mildred Houghton
- Dustin family series

Common, Jack
- Newcastle-upon-Tyne series

Compton, David Guy
- Ben Anderson series
- Katherine Mortenhoe series

Compton, Guy
see **Compton, David Guy**

Compton, Ralph
- Trail drive series

Compton, Sara
- Choose your own adventure series
- Earth inspectors series

Compton, Spencer
- Choose your own adventure series

Comstock, Jarrod
- These lawless worlds series

Conan Doyle, Adrian
see **Doyle, Adrian Conan**

Conan Doyle, Arthur
see **Doyle, Arthur Conan**

Conant, Constance
- Star trilogy

Conant, Susan
- Dog lover's mystery series
- Dog trainer mystery series

Conaway, Jim C
- Jana Blake series

Conde, Phillip
- Dick Pemberty series
- Irving Todd series

Condon, Richard
- Captain Colin Huntington series
- Prizzi family series

Cone, Molly
- Mishmash series
- Shema series

Coney, Michael Greatrex
- Arcadia series
- Greataway series

Conford, Ellen
- Carrie Wasserman series
- Jenny Archer series

Conley, Robert Jackson
- Oliver Colfax series
- Real people series

Conlon, Kathleen
- Forgotten season series

Conly, Jane Leslie
- NIMH series

Conly, Robert Leslie
see **O'Brien, Robert C**

Connell, Abby
- Heart to heart series
- Two by two series

Connell, Alan
- Serpent Land trilogy

Connell, Evan Shelby
- Bridge series

Connell, John
- Long John Silver series

Connelly, Michael
- Harry Bosch series

Connington, John Jervis
- Mark Brand series
- Sir Clinton Driffield series
- Superintendent Ross series

Connor, Ralph
- Crow's Nest series
- Glengarry series
- North-West Mounted Police series
- Sky Pilot series

Conquest, Joan
- Jill series

Conrad, Joseph
- Captain Lingard series
- Lord Jim series

Conrad, Pam
- Tub People series

Conrad, Stephen
- Mrs Jim series

Conran, Shirley
- Lace series

Conroy, Al
see also **Albert, Marvin Hubert; Quarry, Nick; Rome, Anthony**
- Clayburn series
- Johnny Morini series

Conroy, Richard Timothy
- Henry Scruggs series

Constable, Trevor James
- Fighter aces series

Constanduros, Denis
- Huggetts series

Constanduros, Mabel
- Huggetts series

Constant, Alberta Wilson
- Miller family series

Constant, Anne Marie
Richard and Valerie on the farm
Richard and Valerie series (1)

Constant, Benjamin
- Adolphe series

Constantine, K C
- Mario Balzic series

Constantine, Storm
- Book of Wraeththu series
- Monstrous regiment series

Conway, Ainslie
- Galapagos series

Conway, Frances
- Galapagos series

Conway, Jill Ker
- Coorain series

Conway, Jim
- Mid-life crisis series

Conway, Laura
see also **Elsna, Hebe**
- Pleasance series

Conway, Norman
- Adam Hunter series

Conway, Peter
see also **Redwood, Alec; Sava, George**
- Inspector Cathy Weston series
- Inspector Newton series
- Lucy Beck series

Conway, Sally
- Mid-life crisis series

Conway, Troy
see also **Avallone, Michael**
- Coxeman series

Conyers, Dorothea
- Meave series
- Peter series
- Sandy series

Cook, Ann
- Monster series
- Robot series

Cook, Bob
- Michael Wyman series

Cook, Bruce
- Antonio Cervantes series

Cook, Canfield
- Lucky Terrell series

Cook, David
- Empires trilogy

Oriental adventures
Advanced dungeons and dragons adventure gamebook series (15)
- Spelljammer series
- Walter series

Cook, Glen
- Chronicles of the Black Company series
- Darkwar trilogy
- Dread Empire series
- Garrett series
- Starfishers trilogy

Cook, Hugh
- Chronicles of an age of darkness series

Cook, Patrick
- Elmer the rat series

Cook, Petronella Marguerite Mary
see **Arnold, Margot**

Cook, Rick
- Wizard's bane series

Cook, Thomas H
- Frank Clemons series

Cook, Will
- Guthrie McCabe trilogy
- United States Cavalry trilogy

Cook, William Wallace
see **Grayson, Donald**

Cooke, Catherine
- Mask trilogy
- Winged assassin trilogy

Cooke, David Coxe
- Peter Rourke series

Cooke, Geoffrey Walter
- Peter Mitchell series

Cooke, John Byrne
- Snowblind moon trilogy

Cooke, John Esten
- Effingham series
- Southern Army campaign trilogy

Cooke, Kaz
- Modern girl series

Cooke, Rupert Croft-
see **Croft-Cooke, Rupert**

Cookson, Catherine
- Bill Bailey series
- Maisie Leviston series
- Mallen family trilogy
- Mary Ann Shaughnessy series
- Matty Doolin and Joe Darling series
- Tilly Trotter trilogy

Coolidge, Susan
- Katy series

Coombes, Marion
- Brenda Bear series

Coombs, Charles Ira
- Be a winner series
- Teen age stories series
- Young detective series
- Young readers series

Coombs, Patricia
- Dorrie series

Coon, Susan
- Living planet series

Cooney, Caroline B
- Cheerleaders series
- Chrystal Falls series
- Fog series
- Vi and Marissa series

Cooney, Kevin
- Totally hot series

Cooney, Linda A
- Class of eighty eight series
- Class of eighty nine series
- Couples series

• Freshman dorm series
• Totally hot series
Cooney, Michael
• Queen's investigator series
Coonts, Stephen
• Jake Grafton series
Cooper, Barbara
• Inspector Gibbon series
Cooper, C Everett
Up your asteroid
Star trek series (57)
Cooper, Charles
• John Hatherleigh series
• Russell Cavendish series
Cooper, Craig
• Matt Savage series
Cooper, Diana Davis
• Animal hotel series
Cooper, Diana Olivia Winifred Maud
• Rainbow series
Cooper, Edmund
see **Avery, Richard**
Cooper, Elizabeth
• Pierre the clown series
Cooper, Gordon
• Kate Bassett series
Cooper, Henry Saint John
• Bulldog series
Cooper, Ilene
• Frances in the fourth grade series
• Hollywood wars series
• Kids from Kennedy Middle School series
Cooper, James Fenimore
• Home series
• Leatherstocking series
• Littlepage manuscript trilogy
• Miles Wallingford series
• Paul Jones series
Cooper, Jeffrey
Nightmare on Elm Street companion
Nightmare on Elm Street series (2)
• Nightmare on Elm Street series
Cooper, Jilly
• Jolly super series
• Little Mabel series
• Rupert Campbell-Black series
• Super men and women series
• Work and wedlock series
Cooper, John C
• Inspector James Dale series
Cooper, John R
• Mel Martin series
• Repositors series
Cooper, Leo
• Far pavilions series
Cooper, Lettice
• Chief Inspector Corby series
Cooper, Lisa
• Princess Beatrice Hospital series
Cooper, Louise Antell
• Chaos gate trilogy
• Indigo series
• Time master trilogy
Cooper, M E
• Couples series
Cooper, Mae Klein
see **Farewell, Nina**
Cooper, Margaret Chilvers
• Stefan and Evonn series
Cooper, Michael
• Pebbles series
Cooper, Morton
• Munsters series
Cooper, Natasha
• Willow King series
Cooper, Sonni
• Star trek series
Cooper, Susan Mary
• Dark is rising series
Cooper, Susan Rogers
• Milton Kovak series
Cooper, Wendy
• Do and Dare Club series
Cooper, William
• Scenes from life series
Coote, Roger
• Four elements series
• Habitats series
• Journey through history series
• Journeys series
• My day series
• My family series
• My world series
• Outings series
Coover, Robert
• Pinocchio series
Cope, Kenneth
• Striker series
Copeland, Lori
• Passion trilogy
• Promise me series
Copeland, Richard
• Doctor Gregor Maclean series
• Doctor Stephen Armitage series
Coppel, Alfred
see **Gilman, Robert Cham**
Copper, Basil
• Mike Faraday series
• Phantom series
• Solar Pons series
Copping, John Edward
• Gotty series
Copplestone, Bennet
• Chief Inspector Dawson series
Copus, John Edwin
• Saint Cuthbert's series
Coram, Christopher
see also **Rhea, Nicholas; Walker, Peter Norman**
• Ross Macallister series
Corbett, Elizabeth
• Faye's folly series
• Graper girls series
• Mount Royal trilogy
• Mrs Meigs series
Corbett, Jim
• Man-eaters series
Corbett, Scott
• Diamonds series
• Doctor Merlin series
• Great McGonnigle series
• Inspector Roger Tearle series
• Kerby Maxwell series
Corbett, William Jesse
• Pentecost trilogy
Corbin, Gary
• Harry Reilly series
Corby, Adam
• Doom-quest of Ara-Karn series
Corby, Michael
Dracula's diary
Dracula series (26)
Corcoran, Barbara
see also **Dixon, Paige**
• Abigail trilogy
Corcoran, Brewer
• Boy Scouts series
Cord, Barry
• Dave Chance series
Cordell, Alexander
• John Regan trilogy
• Merthyr trilogy
• Mortymers series
Corder, Eric
• Shame and glory series
Corelli, Marie
• Heliobas series
• Two worlds series
Coren, Alan
• Arthur series
Cores, Lucy
• Captain Andrew Torrent series
Corey, Peter
• Three miles square series
Corfield, Robin Bell
• Somebody series
Corlett, William
• Gate of Eden trilogy
• Magician's house trilogy
Corley, Edwin
see **Buchanan, Patrick**
Cormany, Michael
• Dan Kruger series
Cormier, Robert
• Chocolate war series
Corne, Molly E
• Mac McIntyre series
Cornell, Louis
• Michael Joyce series
Cornell, Paul
• Timewyrm series
Cornett, Robert
• Remember trilogy
• Seeds of war trilogy
Cornwell, Bernard
• Richard Sharpe series
Cornwell, David John Moore
see **Le Carre, John**
Cornwell, Patricia Daniels
• Doctor Kay Scarpetta series
Correy, Lee
• Star trek series
Corrigan, Mark
see also **Armstrong, Raymond; Hobart, Robertson**
• Mark Corrigan and McLean series
Corris, Peter
• Cliff Hardy series
• Luke Dunlop series
• Pokerface series
• Richard Browning series
Corson, Hazel Wyman
• Peter series
Cort, Ned
• Boxer Unit SS series
Corvo, Frederick
see **Rolfe, Frederick William**
Cory, Desmond
• Feramontov quintet
• John Dobie and Kate Coyle series
• Johnny Fedora series
• Lindy Grey series
• Mister Dee series
• Mister Pilgrim series
Coryell, Jubert V
• Sam Hilton series
Coryn, Marjorie
• Napoleonic trilogy
Cosgrave, Patrick
• Colonel Allen Cheyney series
Cosgrove, Brian
• Sally and Jake series
• Titus Bear series
Cosgrove, Rachel
• Oz series
Cosgrove, Stephen Edward
• Baby Bunny series
• Barely there series
• Bugg series
• Bumble B Bear series
• Buttermilk series
• DreamMaker series
• Leo the Lop series
• Morgan series
• Simple folk series
• Snuffin chronicles series
• Whimsy storybooks series
Cosic, Dobrica
• This land, this time series
Cost, March
• Princess Victoria Babenberg series
Costa, Nicoletta
• Molly and Tom series
Costain, Thomas Bertram
• History of the Plantagenets tetralogy
Costello, Matt
Revolt on Majipoor
Majipoor trilogy (3)
Costello, Matthew John
• Child's play series
• Glory Road series
• Guardians of the Three series
• SeaQuest series
• Time warrior series
Costello, Paul
• Terence O'Hara series
Costello, Peter
• Stephen Dedalus series
Costikyan, Greg
• Dungeon series
Star wars, the roleplaying games
Luke Skywalker series (7)
Willow sourcebook
Willow series (3)
Cotes, Everard, ***Mrs***
see **Cotes, Sarah Jeanette**
Cotes, Sarah Jeanette
• American tourist series
Cottenham, Mark Pepys
• Tom Furness series
Cotton, Donald
• Doctor Who series
Cotton, Gilles
• Gideon series
Couch, Arthur Thomas Quiller-
see **Quiller-Couch, Arthur Thomas**
Coulson, Felicity Winifred Carter
see **Bonett, Emery**
Coulson, John Hubert
see **Bonett, John**
Coulson, Juanita
• Children of the stars series
• Krantin series
Coulson, Robert
• Joe Karns series
Coulter, Catherine
• Bride trilogy
• Legacy trilogy
• Star trilogy
• Victoria Albemarle trilogy
• Viking lords series
Coulter, Stephen
see **Mayo, James**
Coulton, Mary Rose
see **Campion, Sarah**
Counsel, George
• Land in need series
Counsel, June
• Dragon series
Couper, Stephen
• Paradise series
Couperus, Louis
• Book of small souls quartet
Courage, John
see also **Goyne, Richard**
• Bill Britain series
• David Cane series
Cournos, John
• John Gombarov trilogy
Courtenay, Bryce
• Peekay series
Courter, Gay
• Midwife series
Courtier, Sidney Hobson
• Ambrose Mahon series
• Inspector Digger Haig series
Courtney, Edith
• Kit Hemsworthy series
• Swansea series
Courtney, Gwendoline
• Wild Lorings series
Cousins, Edmund George
• Brigadier Worrall series
• Captain Moffat series
• Colonel Richard Barne series
• Larry Grail series
Cove, Joseph Walter
see also **Gibbs, Lewis**
Cover, Arthur Byron
• Autumn angels trilogy
Flash Gordon book
Flash Gordon series (14)
• Flash Gordon series
• Planetfall series
• Robot city series
• Time machine series
Coverack, Gilbert
• Inspector M'Guire series
Coville, Bruce
• A.I. Gang series
• Camp Haunted Hills series
• Dark forces series
• Dungeon series
• Elvie's magic shop series
• Ghost trilogy
• My teacher series
• Omni odysseys trilogy
• Sarah series
• Space brat series
• Twilight series
Cowan, Dale
• Twilight series
Coward, Noel
• Present and future series
Cowdroy, Joan
• Chief Inspector Gorham series
• Li Moh series
Cowen, Frances
see **Hyde, Eleanor**
Cowley, Joy
• Captain Felonius series
Cowper, Richard
• Bird of kinship series
Cox, David
• Abigail series
Cox, Edmund Charles
• John Carruthers series
Cox, Greg
• Time tours series
Cox, John Roberts
• Skipper series
Cox, Josephine
• Her father's sins series
Cox, Stephen
Addams chronicles
Addams family series (3)
Cox, Stephen Angus
• Dare boys series
Cox, Steve
• Roland Rat series
Cox, William Robert
see also **Frederic, Mike; Ward, Jonas**
• Bonanza series
• Cemetery Jones series
• Tom Kincaid series
Coxe, George Harmon
• Flash Casey series
• Jack Fenner series
• Kent Murdock series
• Max Hale series
• Sam Crombie series
Coxhead, Elizabeth
• Alney series
Coxon, Muriel Hine
see **Hine, Muriel**
Coyle, Harold
• World War Three series
Cozzens, Peter
• American Civil War battles series
Crabb, Alfred Leland
• Nashville series
Crabb, Arthur
• Samuel Lyle series
Crabb, Lawrence James
• Captain Al Scabbard series
Crabb, Minnie Rowe
• Gray Bunny series
Craddock, Mary
• Rainton series
Cradock, Fanny
see also **Cradock, Phyllis**
• Lorme family series
Cradock, Henry Cowper, ***Mrs***
• Josephine series
• Teddy Bear series
Cradock, Phyllis
see also **Cradock, Fanny**
• Atlantis series
Craft, Robert
• Conversations series
Crafton, Dennis
• Lobo series
Cragoe, Elizabeth
• Untidy gardener series
Craig, Alisa
see also **Macleod, Charlotte**
• Inspector Madoc Rhys series
• Osbert Monk series
Craig, Brian
• Dark future series
• Minstrel Orfeo series
Craig, Charles William Thurlow
see **Craig, Thurlow**
Craig, Christine
• Emanuel series
Craig, Clifford
• Tasmanian prints series
Craig, David
• Peter Gale series
• Roy Rickman trilogy
• Stephen Bellecroix and Sheila Roath series
Craig, George
• Sir Oliver Bubb series
Craig, Georgiana Ann Randolph
see **Rice, Craig**
Craig, Helen
• Susie and Alfred series
Craig, Jonathan
• Pete Selby series
Craig, Karl
• Emanuel series
Craig, Philip R
• Martha's Vineyard series
Craig, Randolph
• Octopus series
Craig, Thurlow
• Lieutenant Bunjy Hearne series
Craigie, Dorothy
• Captain Flint series
• Nicky and Nigger series
• Tim Hooley series
Craigie, Pearl Mary Teresa
see **Hobbes, John Oliver**
Craik, Dinah Maria
• Avillion series
Craine, Edith Janice
• Airplane Boys series
Crake, Augustus David
• Chronicles of Aescendune trilogy
Cramer, Helen Catherine
• Grief series
Crampton, Patricia
• John and Hugh series
• Patrick series
Crane, Frances
• Pat and Jean Abbott series
Crane, Hamilton
• Miss Emily Seeton series
Crane, Laura Dent
• Automobile girls series
Crane, Robert
• Ben Corbin series
Crane, Stephen
• American Civil War episodes series
Cranfield, Ingrid
• Q challenge quiz series
Cranston, Claudia
• Clarice Claremont series
Cranston, Maurice
• Inspector Mortimer Blunt series
Crauford, William Harold Lane
• Detective Kellerway series
Crawford, Francis Marion
• Lauderdale family series
• Paris Opera trilogy
• Paul Griggs series
• Roman society series
• Saracinesca family series
Crawford, Robert
see also **Albany, James; Rae, Hugh Crauford**
• Arthur Salisbury and Frank Shearer series
Crawford, Tad
• Business and legal forms series

Crawford, William
- Colin Stryker series

Crawley, Aileen
- Suleiman the Magnificent trilogy

Crawley, Rayburn
- Ned Shackleton series

Crayder, Dorothy
- She, the adventuress series

Creasey, John
see also **Ashe, Gordon; Deane, Norman; Frazer, Robert Caine; Halliday, Michael; Marric, J J; Morton, Anthony; York, Jeremy**
- Department Z series
- Doctor Palfrey series
- Inspector Roger West series
- Sexton Blake series
- Toff series

Creaton, David
- Beasts series

Creche, Sylvia
- Mervyn Mouse series

Creighton, Basil
- Amorous cheat series

Cremer, Jan
- Jan Cremer series

Crespi, Francesca
- Little Bear series

Cresswell, Harry Bulkeley
see **Creswell, Harry Bulkeley**

Cresswell, Helen
- Bagthorpes series
- Jumbo Spencer series
- Lizzie Dripping series
- Mike series
- Posy Bates series
- Rug series
- Sea series
- Two Hoots series
- Winklesea series

Creswell, Harry Bulkeley
- Honeywood series
- Marytary series
- Thomas series

Creswick, Paul
- Saga the Dane trilogy

Crews, Lary
- Veronica Slate series

Crick, Michael
- Militant series

Crider, Bill
- Carl Burns series
- Dan Rhodes series
- Truman Smith series

Crippen, Pamela
- Barbarians series

Cripps, Arthur Shearly
- John Kent series

Crisp, Frank
- Dirk Rogers series

Crisp, Jack H
- Special Operations Executive series

Crisp, Norman James
- Inspector Sidney Kenyon series

Crisp, Quentin
- Naked civil servant series

Crisp, William
- Westfall series

Crispin, Ann Carol
- High Hallack series
- Star trek series
- Star trek, the next generation series
- StarBridge series
- V series
- Witch World series

Crispin, Edmund
Best detective stories
Inspector George Rason series (3)
- Gervase Fen series

Cristabel
- Veltakin series

Crocco, Kyle
- Heroes, Inc. series

Crockett, Samuel Rutherford
- Douglas series
- English Revolution series
- Galloway series
- Raiders series
- Red cap series
- Sir Toady series
- Stickit minister series
- Sweethearts series
- Wolfmark series

Crockett, Sherman
- Two American boys series

Croft, Herbert
- Abbey of Kilkhampton series

Croft, Jesse Taylor
- Trainmasters series

Croft-Cooke, Rupert
see also **Bruce, Leo**
- Sensual life series

Crofts, Freeman Wills
- Inspector Joseph French series

Crombie, Deborah
- Superintendent Duncan Kincaid and Sergeant Gemma James series

Crompton, Richmal
- Jimmy series
- Wilding family series
- William series

Cromwell, A G E
- Rodney Wayne series

Cronin, Archibald Joseph
- Doctor Finlay series
- Laurence Carroll series
- Robert Shannon series

Cronin, Bernard
- Coastlanders series

Cronin, Bernard Leo
see **Cronin, Michael**

Cronin, Michael
- James Hellier series
- Richard Maidment series
- Sam Harris series

Crooker, Herbert
- Clay Brooke series

Crosby, John Campbell
- Horatio Cassidy series

Crosby, Lee
- Eric Hazard series

Croson, Bob
- Nick and Company series

Cross, Amanda
- Professor Kate Fansler series

Cross, David
- Chant series

Cross, Diana Harding
- Funny names series

Cross, Gilbert
see **Winters, Jon**

Cross, Gillian
- Clipper series
- Demon headmaster series

Cross, John Keir
- Albatross series

Cross, Laurence
- Tommy Lumb and Peter Marsham series

Cross, Mark
see also **Valentine**
- Daphne Wrayne and her Four Adjusters series

Cross, Peter
- Dinosaur days series
- Dudley Dormouse series
- Trumpets series

Crossen, Kendell Foster
see also **Chaber, M E; Monig, Christopher; Richards, Clay**
- Jason Jones and Necessary Smith series
- Kim Locke series

Crossley, Maude
- Guy Bannister series

Crossley-Holland, Kevin
- Wulf series

Croves, Hal
see **Traven, B**

Crow, Duncan
- Simon Ire series

Crowe, John
see also **Arden, William; Collins, Michael; Sadler, Mark**
- Buena Costa County series

Crowley, Carl Campbell
- Nine winds series

Crowley, Maude
- Azor series

Croy, Catherine
- Julia Arbuthnot series

Crozier, Brian
- De Gaulle series

Crozier, John
- Falcon series

Crume, Vic
- Doctor Syn series

Frankenstein and the whiz kid
Frankenstein series (1)
- Herbie series

Crumley, James
- C W Sughrue series
- Milo Milodragovitch series

Crump, Barry
- Good keen series

Crump, Fred H
- Mouse series

Crump, Irving
see **Crump, James Irving**

Crump, James Irving
- Boys' book series
- Cloud Patrol series
- Jack Straw series
- Og series
- Our services series

Cruz, Mark
- Kill Squad series

Cruz, Nicky
- New York gang series

Cruz, Ray
- Alexander series

Cue, Kerry
- Bloody ratbags series
- Kids' stuff series

Cuffley, Peter
- Australian houses series

Culbertson, Judi
- Guides to the cemeteries of the world's great cities series

Culbreath, Myrna
- Star trek originals sequels series
- Star trek series

Cullen, Robert
- Colin Burke series

Cullen, Seamus
- Noose series

Cullum, Ridgwell
- Inspector Stanley Fyles series

Culotta, Nino
- Weird mob series

Culp, John Hewett
- Five Civilized Tribes series
- Martin Cameron series

Culpan, Maurice
- Inspector Bill Houghton series

Cumberland, Marten
see also **O'Hara, Kevin**
- Saturnin Dax series

Cumming, Primrose
- Silver Eagle series

Cumming, Robert
- Just look series

Cummings, Bruce Frederick
see **Barbellion, W N P**

Cummings, Ray
- Gregg Haljan series
- Incredible adventures series
- Matter, space and time series
- Tama series

Cummins, Jim
- First read-alone mystery series

Cunliffe, John Arthur
- Farmer Barnes series
- Giant series
- Jess the cat series
- Mister Gosling series
- Postman Pat beginners series
- Postman Pat readers series
- Postman Pat series
- Postman Pat's storybook series
- Rosie and Jim series
- Tots series

Cunningham, Albert Benjamin
- Sheriff Jess Roden series

Cunningham, Chet
see also **Bodine, J D; Carrington, G A; Dalton, Kit; Derrick, Lionel; Fletcher, Dirk**
- Agent Brad Spear series
- Jim Steel series
- Matt Hawke series
- Outlaws series
- Pony soldiers series
- Team three series
- Wade Chisholm series

Cunningham, E V
see also **Fast, Howard**
- Harvey Krim series
- John Comaday and Larry Cohen series
- Masao Masuto series

Cunningham, Elaine
- Harpers series

Cunningham, Eugene
Buckaroo
Walt Slade series (1)
Riders of the night
Three Mesquiteers series (1)

Cunningham, Walter
- Australian nature tales series

Curcija-Prodanovic, Nada
- Belgrade Ballet School series

Curlewis, Ethel
see **Turner, Ethel**

Curling, Henry
- Frank Beresford series

Currey, Edward Hamilton
- Ian Hardy series

Currington, Owen Josiah
- Jack Lovel series

Curry, Avon
- Jerome Aylwin series

Curry, Gene
see also **McCurtin, Peter**
- Jim Saddler series

Curry, Graeme
- Doctor Who series

Curry, Jane Louise
- Abaloc series
- Apple Lock series
- California Indian series
- Callie series
- Lek series
- Maccubbin family series
- Prince Lincoas series
- Rosemary series

Curry, Peter
- I like series

Curry, Tom
- Captain Mesquite series
- Masked Rider and Blue Hawk series

Curtin, Marthe Troly-
see **Troly-Curtin, Marthe**

Curtin, Patricia Romero
- Show off series

Curtis, Alice Turner
- Frontier girl series
- Grandpa's little girls series
- Little maid series
- Little runaways series
- Marjorie series
- Yankee girl series

Curtis, Neil
- Bear Dinkum series

Curtis, Philip
- Mister Browser series

Curtis, Richard
- Dave Bolt series

Curtis, Wade
- Paul Crane series

Curtiss, Elizabeth Mangam
- Nathaniel Bunce series

Curwood, James Oliver
- Kazan series
- Quebec series
- Three rivers series
- Wolf hunters series

Curzon, Clare
see also **Petrie, Rhona**
- Superintendent Mike Yeadings and Sergeant Angus Mott series

Curzon, Colin
- Mark Antony series

Cushing, E Louise
- Inspector Mackay series

Cushing, Peter
- Past forgetting series

Cushman, Dan
- Comanche John series
- Crawford series

Cusick, Richie Tankersley
- Twilight series

Cussler, Clive
- Dirk Pitt series

Cutcliffe Hyne, Charles John
see **Hyne, Charles John Cutcliffe**

Cuthbert, Derrick
- Six series

Cuthrell, Faith Baldwin
see **Baldwin, Faith**

Cutler, Ivor
- Herbert series

Cutt, William Towrie
- Arkmae series

Cutter, John
- Specialist series

Cutter, Leela
- Lettie Winterbottom series

Cutter, Tom
see also **Longley, W B; Meek, Joseph; Randall, Joshua; Randisi, Robert Joseph; Roberts, J R; Weston, Cole**
- Tracker series

Cutting, Mary Stewart
- Little stories of life series

Cyon, Francoise Lafitte-
see **Delisle, Francoise**

D

D, H
see **Doolittle, Hilda**

Daalder, Tineke
- Emotions series

Dacey, Philip
- Condom poems series

Dacre, Richard
- Sam Hoskins series

Da Cruz, Daniel
- Ape Swain series
- Forte family trilogy
- Jock Sergeant series

Dagmar
see also **Cameron, Lou**
- Randy Kidd and Regina series

D'Agneau, Marcel
- Sherlock Holmes sequels series

Dahl, Roald
- Charlie Bucket series
- Solo series

Dahlberg, Edward
- Bottom dogs series
- Sorrows of Priapus series

Dahlerup, Rina
- Buffy and Company series

Daiches, David
- Three worlds series

Daiger, Katherine S
- Inspector Everett Anderson series

Dailey, Janet
- Webb Calder series

Daish, Elizabeth
- Coppins Bridge trilogy

Dake, Charles Romyn
Strange discovery
Arthur Gordon Pym series (2)

Dakers, Elaine Kidner
see **Lane, Jane**

Dalby, Richard
Dracula's brood
Dracula series (26)

Dale, Judith
- Shirley Flight series

Dale, Margaret Jessy Miller
see **Miller, Margaret Jessy**

Dale, Norman
- Medenham series
- Peter and Ginger series
- Tim Forest series

Daley, Brian
see also **McKinney, Jack**
- Alacrity FitzHugh trilogy
- Coramonde series
- Luke Skywalker series

Daley, Jim
see **Daly, Jim**

Dalgleish, Joan
- Clarence series

Dalgliesh, Alice
- Davenports series
- Silver pencil series

Dalkey, Kara
- Sagamore series

Dallas, Ruth
- Jean, Robbie, Sophie and Helen series

Dallas-Smith, Peter
- Trumpets series

Dalmas, John
- Fanglith series
- Nils Jarnhan series
- Regiment series

Dalos, Gyorgy
- Big Brother series

Dalrymple, Ian
- Old Bill series

Dalton, Clive
- Malay series

Dalton, Hugh
- Fateful years trilogy

Dalton, Kit
see also **Bodine, J D; Carrington, G A; Cunningham, Chet; Derrick, Lionel; Fletcher, Dirk**
- Buckskin series

Dalton, Moray
- Inspector Hugh Collier series

Dalton, Sean
see also **Blakeney, Jay D**
- Operation Star Hawks series

Daly, Carroll John
- Race Williams series
- Satan Hall series
- Vee Brown series

Daly, Elizabeth
- Henry Gamadge series

Daly, Ita
- Candy series

Daly, Jim
- Gentleman Jack series

Daly, Kathleen
- Strawberry Shortcake series

Daly, Kathleen N
- Raggedy Ann series

Daly, Maureen
- Patrick series
- Roundabout series

Daly, Niki
- Storytime series

Daly, Wally K
Ultimate evil
Doctor Who series (162)

D'Amato, Barbara
- Cat Marsala series
- Doctor Garrett DeGraaf series

Dana, Mitchell
• Dakota Bush series
Danby, Mary
• Famous Five and you series
• Hello series
Dancer, J B
see also **Hart, Jon; Harvey, John Barton**
• Lawmen series
Dane, Christopher
see also **DeBolt, Adriana**
• Myra Morgana series
Dane, Clemence
• Sir John Saumerez series
Dane, Eva
see also **Darrell, Elizabeth**
• Schroeder family series
Dane, Joel Y
• Sergeant Cass Harty series
D'Anethan, Eleanora Mary
see **Anethan, Eleanora Mary d'**
Danheux, Paul
• Anna, Paul and Tommycat series
Daniel, Becky
see **Daniel, Rebecca**
Daniel, Colin
• Twilight series
Daniel, Glyn
• Sir Richard Cherrington series
Daniel, Jack
• Desert series
Daniel, Mark
• Chocky series
Daniel Mark
Movie magic
Ghostbusters series (2)
Daniel, Mark
Which way out
Ghostbusters series (2)
Daniel, Rebecca
• Fun with arithmetic series
• Hooray for arithmetic facts series
• Life of Jesus series
• Mother series
• Our greatest heritage series
Daniel, Roland
• Bill Saville series
• Brian O'Malley series
• Buddy Mustard series
• Gangster series
• Inspector Jack Pearson series
• Inspector John Walk series
• Inspector Neville Langham series
• Jim Maitland series
• John Hopkins series
• John Quicksilver series
• Michael Grant series
• Michael Wallace series
• Remover series
• Wu Fang series
Daniell, David Scott
• Alison and John series
• Drummer Oliver Crowe series
• Jiminy series
Daniels, Dorothy
• Strange paradise trilogy
Daniels, Lee
• Surf city series
Daniels, Les
• Don Sebastien series
Daniels, Norman A
• Arrest and trial series
• Avengers series
• Bruce Baron series
• Doctor Kildare series
• Jubal trilogy
• Kelly Carvel series
• Man from A.P.E. series
• Rat Patrol series
• Wyndward series
Danielson, Peter
• Children of the Lion series
Danielsson, Bengt
• Terry series
Danielsson, Thomas
• Olly sees it through series
Daniken, Erich von
• Unsolved mysteries series
Daninos, Pierre
• Major Thompson series
Danischewsky, Monja
• White Russian series
Dank, Gloria
• Galaxy Gang series
Dank, Milton
• Edward Burton series
• Galaxy Gang series
• Game series
Dann, Colin
• Farthing Wood series
• Vagabonds series
Dannay, Frederic
see **Queen, Ellery; Queen, Ellery, Junior; Ross, Barnaby**
D'Annunzio, Gabriele
see **Annunzio, Gabriele d'**
Danoen, Emile
• Jeannot and Lydie series
Danow, Myron
see **Dana, Mitchell**
Danvers, Milton
• Robert Spicer series
Danzats, Adrien
• Paul Jones series
Danziger, Paula
• Cat and bat series
Darby, Catherine
see also **Black, Veronica; Peters, Maureen**
• Falcon family series
• Moon series
• Rowan family series
• Sabre family series
Darby, Joan
• Animal adventure series
• Jerry series
• Time machine series
Darby, John
• McLeane's Rangers series
Darby, Lyndan
• Eye of time trilogy
Darby, Ruth
• Peter and Janet Barron series
Darbyshire, Shirley
• Melbury trilogy
• Nurse Carter series
Dard, Frederic
see **San Antonio**
Dargan, Olive
see **Burke, Fielding**
Daringer, Helen Fern
• Endicott family trilogy
Dark, Eleanor
• Mannion family series
Dark, James
see also **Macdonnell, James Edmond; Macnell, James**
• Mark Kingsley Hood series
Dark, Rex
• Bartholomew Dane series
Dark, Sidney
• Guide, philosopher and friend trilogy
Darke, James
see also **Axler, James; Fraser, Mary; Haigh, Richard; James, Laurence; Marvin, James W; May, Jonathan; McPhee, James; Netzen, Klaus; Nolan, Christopher; Norman, Mick**
• Witches series
Darke, Marjorie
• Francis Redmayne series
• Kipper series
Darling, David J
• Could you ever series
Darling, Kathy
• Bet you series
Darlington, William Aubrey
• Alf Higgins series
Darlton, Clark
see also **Ernsting, Walter**
• Atlan series
In the center of the galaxy
Perry Rhodan series (137)
• Perry Rhodan series
Darrell, Elizabeth
see also **Dane, Eva**
• Sheridan family series
Darroll, Sally
• Home and away series
Darrow, Paul
• Blake's Seven series
D'Ars, Yvonne de Bremond
see **Bremond d'Ars, Yvonne de**
Dart, Dorothy
• Jo Lacey series
Darvill-Evans, Peter
• Doctor Who series
• Fighting fantasy gamebook series
Darwin, Bernard
• Mister Tootleoo series
Darwin, Elinor
• Mister Tootleoo series
Dashwood, Edmee Elizabeth Monica
see **Delafield, E M**
Dashwood, Rosamond Margaret
Provincial daughter
Provincial lady series (5)
Daudet, Alphonse
• Tartarin series
Dauer, Rosamond
• Bullfrog series
D'Aulaire, Edgar Parin
• Ola series
D'Aulaire, Ingri
• Ola series
Davenat, Colette
• Deborah series
Davenport, Spencer
• Rushton boys series
Davey, Jocelyn
• Ambrose Usher series
Davey, Norman
• Pilgrim series
Davey, Thyrza
• Yonderbeyonder series
David, Jake
• Last rangers series
David, Janina
• Square of sky trilogy
David, Peter
see also **Peters, David**
• Amazing Spiderman series
Doomsday world
Star trek, the next generation series (12)
• Marvel superheroes adventure gamebooks series
• Star trek series
• Star trek, the next generation sequels series
• Star trek, the next generation series
• Swamp Thing series
Davidoff, Leonore
• Victorian day series
Davidson, Alan
• Annabel Fidelity Bunce series
Davidson, Alice Joyce
• Alice in Bibleland series
Davidson, Amanda
• Teddy series
Davidson, Avram
• Kar-Chee series
• Peregrine series
• Virgil Magus series
Davidson, Halsey
• Navy boys of World War I series
Davidson, Helen Beatrice
• Peter Lawson series
Davidson, John
• Fleet Street eclogues series
Davidson, Linda
• Endless summer series
Davidson, Max
• Beef Wellington series
Davies, Andrew
• Marmalade Atkins series
Davies, Ernest
see **Martin, Oliver**
Davies, Evelyn
• Little Bear trilogy
Davies, Frederick
• Hitman series
Davies, Fredric
• Man from U.N.C.L.E. series
Davies, Hunter
• English walks series
• Flossie Teacake series
• Ossie series
Davies, Iris
see **Gower, Iris**
Davies, John Evan Weston
see **Mather, Berkely**
Davies, Peter
• Fighting fantasy gamebook series
Davies, Robertson
• Deptford trilogy
• Francis Cornish trilogy
• Salterton trilogy
• Samuel Marchbanks series
• Shakespearean festival in Canada series
Davies, Sophie
• My visit series
Davies, W X
• Countdown WWIII series
Davies, William Henry
• Super-tramp series
Daviot, Gordon
see also **Tey, Josephine**
• Inspector Alan Grant series
Davis, Albert Belisle
• Mondebon trilogy
Davis, Andrew Jackson
• Spiritualism series
Davis, Anne
• Pumpkin Hill fact series
• Pumpkin Hollow series
Davis, Anne Pence
• Mimi series
Davis, Arthur Hoey
see **Rudd, Steele**
Davis, Don
see also **Baker, Asa; Blood, Matthew; Dresser, Davis; Halliday, Brett**
• Rio Kid series
Davis, Dorothy Salisbury
• Julie Hayes series
• Mrs Norris and Jasper Tully series
Davis, Duff Hart-
see **Hart-Davis, Duff**
Davis, Elizabeth Jane
• Jarryn series
Davis, Franklin Milton
• Quinn Leland series
Davis, Frederick Clyde
see also **Ransome, Stephen; Steele, Curtis**
• Professor Cyrus Hatch series
• Schyler Cole and Luke Speare series
Davis, George
• Roag's Syndicate series
Davis, Gerry
• Doctor Who scripts series
• Doctor Who series
Davis, Gibbs
• Never sink nine series
Davis, Gordon
see also **Hunt, Everette Howard**
• Sergeant series
Davis, Graeme
• Fighting fantasy gamebook series
Davis, Howard Charles
• Edward Tope series
• Hugh Rudd series
Davis, John Gordon
• Hold my hand series
Davis, John H
• Mafia series
Davis, Julia
• Macleods of Virginia series
Davis, Kathryn
• Dakotas series
Davis, Kenn
• Carver Bascombe series
Davis, Lavinia Riker
• Nora Hughes and Larry Blaine series
Davis, Leslie
• Cheerleaders series
Davis, Lindsey
• Marcus Didius Falco series
Davis, Lois Carlile
see **Lamplugh, Lois**
Davis, Margaret Thomson
• Glasgow trilogy
• Rag woman, rich woman series
• Scottish historical trilogy
Davis, Means
• Matthew Higgins series
Davis, Nelson
• Tadgy series
Davis, Norbert
• Doan and Carstairs series
Davis, Oswald Harcourt
• Ardencester series
Davis, Tech
• Aubrey Nash series
Davison, Ann
• Voyages series
Davison, Frank Dalby
• Man-Shy series
Davison, Geoffrey
• Stephen Fletcher series
Davison, Gilderoy
• Mister Brent series
• Peter Castle series
• Twisted Face series
Davy, Colin
• David Sheridan series
Dawe, Carlton
• Leathermouth series
Dawe, William Carlton Lanyon
see **Dawe, Carlton**
Dawes, Edna
see **Dane, Eva; Darrell, Elizabeth**
Dawes, Frank Victor
• Cole family series
Dawlish, Peter
• Captain Peg-Leg series
• Dauntless series
• Sam Macclellan series
Dawson, Alec John
• Finn series
• Joseph Khassan series
Dawson, Carley
• Mister Wicker series
Dawson, Catherine Amy
see **Dawson-Scott, Catherine Amy**
Dawson, Clay
• Long Rider series
Dawson, David
• Vet series
Dawson, Elmer A
• Buck and Larry baseball series
• Garry Grayson football series
Dawson, Helen
• Noreen and Aunt Joan series
Dawson, Suleika
• Modern comedy series
Dawson-Scott, Catherine Amy
• Some women trilogy
Day, Alexandra
• Carl series
• Frank and Ernest series
Day, Arthur Grove
• South Pacific series
Day, Clarence
• Life series
Day, Deforest
• Chase Defoe series
Day, James Wentworth
• Rural rides series
Day, Lillian
• Frederick Hunt series
Day, Marele
• Claudia Valentine series
Day, Will B
• Steven Flagg series
Daykin, Lilian
• Brown Beggarman series
• Fairground family series
Dayus, Kathleen
• Birmingham life series
Deacon, Richard
see also **McCormick, Donald**
• Secret service series
Deal, Borden
• Bookman trilogy
• Olden times series
Deal, Paula
• Nurse series
Dean, Amber
• Albie Harris series
Dean, Anabel
• Racing wheels series
Dean, Basil
• Seven ages series
Dean, Elizabeth
• Emma Marsh and Hank Fairbanks series
Dean, Graham
• Agent Nine series
Dean, Gregory
• Deputy Commissioner Benjamin Simon series
Dean, Karen Strickler
• Maggie Adams series
Dean, Les
• Zorro series
Dean, Pamela
• Secret country series
Dean, Robert George
see also **Griswold, George**
• Pat Thompson series
• Tony Hunter series
Dean, S F X
• Professor Neil Kelly series
Dean, Spencer
see also **Sterling, Stewart**
• Don Cadee series
De Andrea, William Louis
• Clifford Driscoll series
• Matt Cobb series
• Niccolo Benedetti series
Deane, Jim
• Nick Merlotti series
Deane, Norman
see also **Ashe, Gordon; Creasey, John; Frazer, Robert Caine; Halliday, Michael; Marric, J J; Morton, Anthony; York, Jeremy**
• Bruce Murdoch series
• Liberator series
De Angeli, Marguerite
• Ted and Nina series
De Armond, Dale
• Feast of the animals series
Deary, Terry
• Custard Kid series
De Assis, Joachim Maria Machado
see **Machado de Assis, Joachim Maria**
De Balzac, Honore
see **Balzac, Honore de**
De Banke, Cecile
• Hand over hand series
• Tabby series
De Beauvoir, Simone
see **Beauvoir, Simone de**
De Blasis, Celeste
• Wild Swan trilogy
De Boissiere, Ralph
• Trinidad series

DeBolt, Adriana
see also **Dane, Christopher**
- Myra Morgana series

De Bono, Edward
- Lateral thinking series
- Masterthinker series

De Borchgrave, Arnaud
- Robert Hockney series

De Born, Edith
- De Kailern family series
- Jimmy Chester trilogy

De Buron, Nicole
see **Buron, Nicole de**

De Camp, Catherine Crook
- Incorporated knight series
- Krishna series

De Camp, Lyon Sprague
Conan grimoire
Conan series (69)
Conan reader
Conan series (69)
- Conan series

Conan swordbook
Conan series (69)
- Harold Shea series
- Incorporated knight series
- Jorian series
- Krishna series

De Cervantes Saavedra, Miguel
see **Cervantes Saavedra, Miguel de**

De Chair, Somerset
- Golden carpet series

De Chancie, John
- Castle Perilous series
- Skyway trilogy

De Christoforo, Ron
- Grease series

Decker, Jake
- Steve Sinclair series

Decker, Joseph
- Tac One series

De Clements, Barthe
- Elsie Edwards series
- Jerry Johnson trilogy

Decrest, Jacques
- Superintendent Gilles series

Deegan, Jon J
- Dysart trilogy
- Old Growler trilogy

Deeley, Roger
- Martin Dymoke series

Deem, James Morgan
- How to series

Deeping, Warwick
- James Slade series

Deering, Fremont B
see also **Lawton, Wilbur; Payson, Howard; West, Marvin**
- Border Boys series

De Felitta, Frank
- Audrey Rose series

Defoe, Daniel
- Robinson Crusoe series

Deforges, Regine
- Lea Delmas trilogy

De Fossard, Esta
- Koala series

De Fraga, Geoff
- Peter Cardiman and Quong series

De Gaulle, Charles
see **Gaulle, Charles de**

Degras, Henry Ernest
see **Benney, Mark**

De Groot, J Morgan
see **Morgan de Groot, J**

De Haan, Tom
- Brynchmachrye series

De Halsalle, Henry
- Olga von Kopf series

Dehan, Richard
- Dop Doctor series
- Market place series

De Hartog, Jan
- Captain Martinus Harinxma trilogy
- Peaceable kingdom series

De Haven, Tom
- Chronicles of the king's tramp series
- U.S.S.A. series

Dehn, Olive
- Meredith children series

Deighton, Barbara
- Felicity Travers series

Deighton, Len
- Bernard Samson series
- Game, set and match trilogy
- Hook, line and sinker trilogy
- Secret file series

Deitz, Tom
- David Sullivan series

De Jong, Dola
- Level land series

DeJonge, Joanne E
- God's wonderful word series
- My Father's world series

De Jourlet, Marie
- Windhaven series

Dekobra, Maurice
- Bradley Adams series
- Lady Diana trilogy
- Madonna series

Delacorta
- Serge Gorodish series

Delafield, E M
- Provincial lady series

Delahaye, Gilbert
- Debbie learns series
- Mary series

De la Mahotiere, Mary
- Newspaper Children series

De la Mare, Walter
- Stories from the Bible series

Deland, Margaret
- Helen Ritchie series
- If this be I series
- Old Chester series

Delaney, Joyce
- No starch in my coat series

Delannoy, Burford
- Watson Ward series

Delany, Samuel Ray
- Fall of the towers trilogy
- Neveryon series

De la Pasture, Edmee Elizabeth Monica
see **Delafield, E M**

De la Pasture, Elizabeth
- Catherine of Calais series
- Master Christopher series

De la Ramee, Marie Louise
see **Ouida**

De la Roche, Mazo
- Gillian and Diggory series
- Whiteoak series

De Larrabeiti, Michael
- Borribles series

De la Torre, Lillian
- Doctor Sam, Johnson series

Delderfield, Ronald Frederick
- Adam Swann series
- Amusement trilogy
- Avenue series
- Craddocks of Shallowford series
- Long John Silver series
- Napoleon Bonaparte series
- Sennacherib series
- To serve them all my days series

Delessert, Etienne
- Yok-yok series

Delgado, Alan
- Mike and Caroline series

De Lint, Charles
- Cerin Songweaver series
- Dungeon series
- Jack, the giant-killer series
- Moonheart series

Delisle, Francoise
- In love series

Delisle, James
- Gifted kids survival guide series

Dell, Ethel May
- Nick Ratcliffe series

Dell, Floyd
- Felix Fay trilogy

Dellbridge, John
- Rupert Hambledon series

Delman, David
- Lieutenant Jacob Horowitz series

Del Martia, Astron
see also **Fearn, John Russell**
- Space Express Company series

Delmer, Denis Sefton
see **Delmer, Sefton**

Delmer, Sefton
- Trail sinister series

Del Rey, Lester
- Ganymede series
- Moon trilogy

Delton, Judy
- Angel series
- Bear and Duck series
- Brimhall series
- Condo Kids series
- Kitty series
- My mom series
- Pee wee scout series
- Rabbit series

De Lubicz, Isha Schwaller
see **Schwaller de Lubicz, Isha**

Delves-Broughton, Josephine
see **Bryan, John**

Delving, Michael
see also **Williams, Jay**
- Dave Cannon and Robert Eddison series

De Madariaga, Salvador
see **Madariaga, Salvador de**

De Manio, Jack
- Auntie series

De Marco, Gordon
- Riley Kovacks series

De Mille, Agnes
- Ballet memoirs series

De Mille, James
- Brethren of the White Cross series
- Young Dodge Club series

Demille, Nelson
- Joe Keller series
- Joe Ryker series
- Keller series

Deming, Dorothy
- Penny Marsh series
- Wendy Brent series

Deming, Richard
see also **Franklin, Max**
- Dragnet series
- Law at work series
- Manville Moon series
- Matt Rudd series
- Mike Macauley series
- Mod Squad junior series
- Mod Squad series

Deming, Therese
- Indian life series

De Montherlant, Henry
see **Montherlant, Henry de**

Demorest, Stephen
see **Devon, D G**

De Morgan, John
He
She series (3)
It
She series (3)
King Solomon's treasures
Allan Quatermain series (13)
King Solomon's wives
Allan Quatermain series (13)

Dempsey, Al
- Connection series
- Pulsar series

Dempsey, Henry Maxwell
see **Harrison, Harry**

Dempster, Guy
- Guy Laurence and Tony Carlisle series

Den
see **Dennis, Clarence James**

Denbie, Roger
- Doctor Quentin Pace series

Denes, Gee
- John and Jennifer series

Dengler, Sandy
- Australian destiny series
- Daniel Tremain series
- Heroes of the misty isle series
- Jack Prester series
- Mirage mysteries series
- Pioneer family series

Denham, Bertie
- Derek Thyrde series

Denis, Charlotte
- Charles II series

Denis, John
- U.N.A.C.O.series

Denison, Dulcie Winifred Catherine
see **Gray, Dulcie**

Denison, Mary
- Romilly Street series

Denison, Muriel
- Double act series
- Susannah series

Denney, Diana
see **Ross, Diana**

Denning, Mark
- John Marshall series

Denning, Troy
- Combat Command series

Dorsai's command
Dorsai series (11)
- Prism pentad series
- Star colony series

Dennis, Carol Larkey
- Dragon's pawn trilogy

Dennis, Clarence James
- Sentimental bloke series

Dennis, Ian
- Prince of Stars in the Cavern of Time series

Dennis, Patrick
- Auntie Mame series

Dennis, Ralph
- Jim Hardman series

Dennis, Robert C
- Paul Reeder series

Dennis, Wesley
- Flip series

Dennison, Dorothy
- Wantoknow series for girls

Dennison, Milo
- Blackstone's magical adventure series

Denniston, Elinore
see **Foley, Rae**

Denny, Norman George
see **Dale, Norman**

Dennys, Joyce
- Dose series
- Henrietta series
- Puffin, Twink and Waggle series

Dent, Lester
see also **Robeson, Kenneth**
- Chance Malloy series

Incredible radio exploits of Doc Savage
Doc Savage series (183)

Dentinger, Jane
- Jocelyn O'Roarke and Phillip Gerard series

Denton, Derek
- Harry Sellers series

Denton, John
- Jamie series

Denton, Kady Macdonald
- Ned series

Denton, Phyllis
- Twins series

Denuziere, Maurice
- Clarence Dandridge series

Denver, Lee
see also **Cody, Stetson; Grex, Leo; Gribble, Leonard Reginald; Sanders, Bruce; Shane, Steve**
- Cheyenne Jones series
- Deputy Marshal Dave Halloran series

Denver, Paul
- Cannon series

Denver, Rod
see also **Edson, John Thomas**
- Waco series

Denzel, Justin Francis
- Prehistoric adventure series

De Paola, Tomie
- Bill and Pete series
- Funnyman series
- Katie and Kit series
- My first series
- Nursery tales series
- Strega Nona series

De Polnay, Peter
- Death and to-morrow series
- Mario and Giovanna series

Deptula, Walter
- Frank Arrow series

De Puy, Edward Spence
- Sam Houston series

De Regniers, Beatrice Schenk
see **Kitt, Tamara**

De Reneville, Mary Margaret Motley Sheridan
see **Motley, Mary**

Derib
- Yakari series

De Ridder, Alfons
see **Elsschot, Willem**

Derleth, August
- Boy's series
- Cthulhu series
- Judge Ephraim Peck series
- Mill Creek Irregulars series
- Sac Prairie series
- Solar Pons series
- Walden West series
- Wisconsin series

De Rosa, Dee
- Ketchup sisters series
- Two of a kind series

De Rosa, Peter
see **Boyd, Neil**

Derrick, Lionel
see also **Bodine, J D; Carrington, G A; Cunningham, Chet; Dalton, Kit; Fletcher, Dirk**
- Penetrator series

Derwent, Lavinia
- Border series
- Brer Rabbit series
- Huffy Puffy series
- Macpherson series
- Magnus series
- Tammy Troot series

De Saint-Exupery, Antoine
see **Saint-Exupery, Antoine de**

De Saint-Pierre, Michel
see **Saint-Pierre, Michel de**

De Selincourt, Aubrey
- Rutherford series

De Selincourt, Hugh
- Constance Howard series
- Gauvinier series

Desfontaines, Pierre
- Lemuel Gulliver series

De Silva, Colin
- Sinhala series

Desmond, D J
- John and Jennifer series

Desmond, Hugh
- Alan Fraser series

Despain, Dezra
- Advanced dungeons and dragons adventure gamebook series

Dessau, Joanna
- Elizabeth I trilogy

De Stefano, Anthony
- Mondo series

De Stoeckl, Agnes
see **Stoeckl, Agnes de**

Detective Dunn
see **Dunn, *Detective***

De Trevino, Elizabeth Borton
- Pollyanna series

Deutscher, Isaac
- Leon Trotsky trilogy

Deventer, Emma Murdoch van
see **Van Deventer, Emma Murdoch**

Dever, Joe
- Combat heroes series
- Emerald enchanter series
- Freeway warrior series
- Legends of Lone Wolf series
- Lone Wolf series
- White warlord series

Deveraux, Jude
- Chandler twins series
- James River trilogy
- Montgomery annals series

De Vere, V C
- Motto excelsior series

Devi, Maitreyi
- Calcutta series

De Villiers, Gerard
- Malko Linge series

Devine, Raynard
see also **Tresillian, Richard**
- Flesh traders series

Devlin, Harry
- Cranberryport series
- Old Witch series

Devlin, Wende
- Cranberryport series
- Old Witch series

Devon, D G
- Temple Kent series

De Voto, Bernard
- Abbey family series
- American West trilogy

De Vries, Julianne
- Campfire Girls series

De Vries, Peter
- Chick Swallow series

De Waal, Ronald Burt
World bibliography of Sherlock Holmes and Doctor Watson
Sherlock Holmes series (10)

De Water, Frederic Franklin van
see **Van de Water, Frederic Franklin**

Dewdney, Alexander Keewatin
- Turing series

DeWeese, Gene
- Calvin Willeford series
- Joe Karns series
- Star trek series
- Star trek, the next generation series

Deweese, Thomas Eugene
see **Deweese, Gene**

Dewes, Simon
- When the world was young trilogy

De Wetering, Janwillem van
see **Van de Wetering, Janwillem**

Dewey, Thomas Blanchard
- Pete Schofield series
- Private Eye Mac series
- Singer Batts series

Dewhurst, Eileen
- Helen Johnson series
- Inspector Neil Carter series

De Wohl, Louis
- Lives of the saints series

Dexter, Carmen
- Star trek fan series

Dexter, Colin
- Inspector Morse series

Dexter, Ross
- Duke Lawson series

Dexter, Susan
• Winter King's war trilogy
Dexter, Ted
• Jack Stenton series
Dexter, William
• Denis Grafton series
Dhanjal, Beryl
• Duets series
Diack, Hunter
Road fortune
Village series (2)
• Village series
Diamond, Frank
• Ransome Dragoon and Vicky Gaines series
Diamond, Graham
• Haven series
• Marrakesh series
• Samarkand series
• Stacy series
Diaper, John
• Cthulhu Mythos series
Dibdin, Michael
• Aurelio Zen series
• Sherlock Holmes sequels series
Dibell, Ansen
• Kantmorie trilogy
Dick, Alexandra
see also **Erikson, Sibyl**
• Alastair Macalastair series
Dick, Kay
• Robert Stairey series
Dick, Philip Kindred
• VALIS trilogy
Dickens, Charles
Christmas carol
Squanderbug series (1)
• Christmas carol series
• Dombey series
• Magwitch series
• Miss Havisham series
• Our mutual friend series
• Pickwick series
Dickens, Frank
• Albert Henry Hawkins series
• Boffo series
Dickens, Monica
• Fielding family series
• Follyfoot Farm series
• Messenger series
• One pair series
Dickins, Joan
• Jill and Prince series
Dickinson, Anne Hepple
see **Hepple, Anne**
Dickinson, Margaret
• Abbeyford trilogy
Dickinson, Mary
• Alex series
• Jilly series
Dickinson, Mary Anne
• Charm bracelet series
Dickinson, Peter
• Changes trilogy
• King Victor series
• Superintendent James Pibble series
Dickinson, William Croft
• Donald and Jean series
Dicks, Terrance
• Adventures of Buster and Betty series
• Ask Oliver series
• Baker Street Irregulars series
• Bears series
• Camden Street kids series
• Cat called Max series
• David and Goliath series
Doctor Who monster book
Doctor Who series (162)
• Doctor Who series
• Horror series
• Jonathan's ghost series
• Macmagics series
• Mounties series
• Sally Ann series
• Sarah Jane Smith series
• Simon and Sally series
• Star quest series
• Timewyrm series
• T.R.Bear series
Dickson, Carr
• Sir Henry Merrivale series
Dickson, Carter
see also **Carr, John Dickson**
• Sir Henry Merrivale series
Dickson, Gordon Rupert
• Beginnings and ends series
• Bleys quartet
• Combat Command series
• Dilbia series
• Dorsai series
• Dragon series
• Hoka series
Jamie the Red
Sanctuary series (12)
• Robby Hoenig trilogy
• Sea people series
Dickson, Grierson
• Superintendent Cissie Marlow series
Dickson, Helen
• Sunshine Ranch series
Dickson, Lovat
• Ante-room series
Didelot, Francis
• Commissaire Orestes Bignon series
• Inspector Lecain series
Dietrich, Robert
see also **Hunt, Everette Howard; Saint John, David**
• Steve Bentley series
Dietz, William Corey
• Crisis of empire trilogy
• Sam McCade series
Digby, Anne
• Ghostbusters series
Indiana Jones and the last crusade
Indiana Jones series (3)
• Jug Valley Juniors series
• Me and Jill Robinson series
• Three R detectives series
• Trebizon series
D'Ignazio, Fred
• Chip Mitchell computer mystery series
Dillard, Jeanne M
• Star trek moving picture series
• Star trek sequels series
• Star trek series
Dille, Flint
• Agent thirteen series
• Sagard the Barbarian series
Dillon, Deidre
• Trumpton series
Dillon, Eilis
• Bitter sea series
• Inspector Mike Kenny series
• Wild geese series
Dilnot, George
• Horace Augustus Elver series
• Inspector Strickland series
• Jim Strang series
• Sexton Blake series
• Val Emery series
Diment, Adam
• Philip McAlpine series
Dimmock, Frederick Haydon
• Dupree series
Di Mona, Joseph
• George Williams series
Dine, S S van
see **Van Dine, S S**
Dines, Glen
• Jerry and Vic series
Dines, Michael
• Johnny Manning series
Dinesen, Isak
see also **Blixen, Karen**
• Africa series
Dingley, Sally Garrett
see **Garrett, Sally**
Diplomat
• Dennis Tyler series
Dirckx, John H
• Doctor John Evelyn Thorndyke series
Disch, Thomas Michael
• Brave little toaster series
• Prisoner series
Disher, Garry
• Wyatt series
Disney, Doris Miles
• David Madden series
• Jeff Dimarco series
• Jim O'Neill series
Disraeli, Benjamin
• Young England trilogy
Disrobeson, Kin I
Living toilets
Doc Savage series (183)
Ditton, James
• John Boldre series
Ditzen, Rudolf Wilhelm Friedrich
see **Fallada, Hans**
Diver, Maud
• Challoners series
• Desmond series
• Eldred Pottinger series
• English scene series
• Sinclair series
Divine, Arthur Durham
see **Divine, David**
Divine, David
• Mig and Peter Manson series
Dix, Maurice Buxton
• Inspector James Miller series
• Sexton Blake series
• Superintendent Simon Bullion series
• Tommy Malins, Anthony Mornington and George Hawkins series
Dixelius, Hildur
• Sara Alelia trilogy
Dixon, Dorothy
• Leather and lace series
Dixon, Dougal
• Time machine series
Dixon, Franklin W
• Hardy boys case files series
• Hardy boys series
• Nancy Drew and the Hardy boys be a detective mystery series
• Ted Scott flying series
Dixon, James
• It's alive series
Dixon, Mark
• Deadly Force series
Dixon, Paige
see also **Corcoran, Barbara**
• Skipper series
Dixon, Rachel
• Jo and Gemma series
Dixon, Rex
see also **Eliott, E C; Martin, Robert**
• Pete series
• Pocomoto series
Dixon, Roger
see also **Christian, John**
• Jesus Christ series
Dixon, Rosie
• Confessions series
Dixon, Thomas
• American Reconstruction series
• Clansman series
Dobbin, Gertrude Page
see **Page, Gertrude**
Dobkin, Kaye
• Wonderland series
Doblin, Alfred
• German revolution series
Dobson, Margaret
• Jane Bailey series
Dobyns, Stephen
• Charlie Bradshaw series
Doc Smith
see **Smith, Edward Elmer**
Dodd, Catherine Isabel
• Farthing family series
• Red Lattice series
Dodd, Edward Howard
• Ring of fire series
Dodd, Lynley
• Hairy Maclary series
Dodd, Maurice
• Merrymole series
Dodderidge, Esme
• Lemuel Gulliver series
Dodge, David
• Al Colby series
• John Abraham Lincoln series
• Travel diary series
• Whit Whitney series
Dodge, Henry Irving
• Skinner series
Dodge, Louis
• Sandman series
Dodge, Michael J
• Star trek tie-ins series
Dodgson, Charles Lutwidge
see **Carroll, Lewis**
Doeblin, Alfred
see **Doblin, Alfred**
Doell, E W
• Mission doctor trilogy
Doherty, Berlie
• Fingers Finnegan series
• Tilly Mint series
Doherty, Paul C
• Drakulya series
• Hugh Corbett series
Doig, Ivan
• McCaskill family trilogy
Doke, Joseph John
• Karroo series
Dolan, Bill
• Afrikorps series
Dolce, Janet Ellen
• Baby doll board books series
• Daydreamers series
Dolci, Danilo
• Sicilian inquiry series
Dolman, Sue
Brambly Hedge pattern book
Brambly Hedge series (7)
Dolph, Jack
• Doc Connor series
Dolphin, Rex
• Sexton Blake series
Dolson, Hildegarde
• Lucy Ramsdale series
Dombrowski, Katrina
• Abdallah series
Dominic, R B
see also **Lathen, Emma**
• Congressman Ben Safford series
Donahue, Jackson
• Harlan Cole series
Donald, Anabel
• Alex Tanner series
Donald, Henry
• Linwoodmuir series
Donald, Winifred
• Linda Carroll series
Donaldson, Elaine
• Christmas carol series
Donaldson, Frances Annesley
• Farming series
Donaldson, Margaret
• Journey into war series
Donaldson, Norman
• Doctor John Evelyn Thorndyke series
Donaldson, Stephen Reeder
see also **Stephens, Reed**
• First Chronicles of Thomas Covenant series
• Gap series
• Mordant's need series
• Second chronicles of Thomas Covenant series
Donaldson, William
• Ladies and gentlemen series
Donavan, John
• Sergeant Johnny Lamb series
Donleavy, James Patrick
• Darcy Dancer series
• Sigmund Schultz series
Donovan, Dick
• Dick Donovan series
Donovan, Jean Beradine
• Bill Speed series
Donson, Cyril
see **Kidd, Russ**
Dooley, Dennis
Superman at fifty
Superman series (7)
Doolittle, Hilda
• War trilogy
Dorer, Frances
• Eagle series
Dorer, Nancy
• Eagle series
D'Orliac, Jehanne
• Lady Chatterley series
Dorling, Henry Taprell
see **Taffrail**
Dorman, Geoffrey
• Carmelo series
Dornisch, Alcuin C
• Early nature picture book series
Dorrance, Ethel Smith
• Sergeant Alfred Rawson series
Dorrance, James French
• Sergeant Alfred Rawson series
Dorrell, Mike
• Dick Barton series
Dos Passos, John
• Spotswood family series
• U.S.A.trilogy
Dostoevsky, Thedor Mikhailovich
Possessed
Nihilist series (2)
Doty, Jean Slaughter
• Pony series
Dougall, Bernard
• Steve Borden series
Doughty, Sarah
• Let's visit a farm series
Douglas, Amanda Minnie
• Helen Grant series
• Kathie series
• Little girl series
• Little Red House children series
• Sherburne series
Douglas, Arthur
see also **Hammond, Gerald**
• Jonathan Craythorne series
• Mark Register series
Douglas, Carole Nelson
• Irene Adler series
• Irissa and Kendric trilogy
• Midnight Louie series
• Probe series
• Sword and circlet trilogy
• Taliswoman trilogy
Douglas, Colin
• David Campbell series
Douglas, Ellen
• Homochito County series
Douglas, Felicity
• Faye Boswell series
• Nicholas series
Douglas, G A H
• Rab Hewison series
Douglas, Gavin
• Captain Samson series
Douglas, George
see also **Fisher, Douglas George**
• Inspector Bonny Lee series
• Inspector Hallam and Sergeant Spratt series
Douglas, Kathryn
• Cavendish series
Douglas, Lauren Wright
• Caitlin Reece series
Douglas, Lloyd Cassel
• Apostle Peter series
• Doctor Hudson series
• Newell Paige series
Douglas, O
• Priorsford series
Douglas, Peter
• Norfolk village series
Douglas, Sholto
see **Douglas, William Sholto**
Douglas, Thorne
see also **Benteen, John; Haas, Ben; Meade, Richard**
• Rancho Bravo series
Douglas, William Sholto
• Years series
Douglass, Donald McNutt
• Bolivar Manchenil series
Douglass, Keith
see also **Keith, William Henry**
• Carrier series
Douie, Charles
• Weary road series
Douthwaite, Louis Charles
• Sexton Blake series
Dover, Harold
• Worst day of my life series
Dowd, Emma C
• Polly series
Dowdall, Mary Frances
• Martha series
Dowdey, Clifford
• Richmond, Virginia series
Dower, Penn
see also **Jacobs, Thomas Curtis Hicks; Pendower, Jacques**
• Marshal Bret Malone series
Dowling, Patrick
• Amazing adventures of Morph series
Dowling, Terry
• Tom Tyson series
Downe, Patrick
• Doctor series
Downer, Ann
• Caitlin series
Downes, Quentin
see also **Harrison, Michael**
• Detective Inspector Abraham Kozminski series
Downie, Gary
Doctor Who cookbook
Doctor Who series (162)
Downie, James Millar
• Gaunt series
Downing, Brownie
• Tinka series
Downing, John Hyatt
• Anthony Trant series
Downing, Peggy
• Exitorn series
• Help series
Downing, Todd
• Hugh Rennert series
• Peter Bounty series
Downing, Warwick
• Joe Reddman series
Downs, Gerry
• Star trek fan series
Downs, Sarah Elizabeth
see **Sheldon, Georgie**
Doyle, Adrian Conan
• Sherlock Holmes sequels series
Doyle, Arthur Conan
Adventures of Sherlock Holmes
Sherlock Holmes sequels series (97)
• American adventure series
• Brigadier Gerard series
• English bowmen series
• Professor Challenger series
Scandal in Bohemia
Sherlock Holmes sequels series (97)
• Sherlock Holmes series

Sign of four
Sherlock Holmes drama series (16)
Doyle, Brian
- Hubbo O'Driscoll series
- Tommy series

Doyle, Debra
- Circle of magic series
- Time tours series

Doyle, Elizabeth
- Strawberry Shortcake series

Doyle, Lynn
- Ballygullion series

Doyle, Martha
see **James, Martha**
Doyle, Roddy
- Barrytown trilogy

D'Oyley, Elizabeth
- Prince Rupert series

Drabble, Margaret
- Radiant way trilogy

Drabble, Phil
- Wild animals series

Drackett, Phil
- A-American series

Draco, F
- Lord and Lady Tintagel series

Drago, Harry Sinclair
see **Lomax, Bliss**
Dragonwagon, Crescent
- I hate series

Drake, Alison
- Tango Key series

Drake, Asa
- Dracula series
- Hel trilogy

Drake, David
- Crisis of empire trilogy

Dagger
Sanctuary series (12)
- Dragon lord series
- Fleet series
- Generals series
- Hammer's Slammers series
- Heroes in hell series
- Kelly series
- Northworld series
- Space gladiators trilogy
- Starhunters series
- Yates series

Drake, Drexel
- Falcon series

Drake, Joan
- Mister Bubbus series
- Mister Grimpwinkle series
- Wimpy series

Drake, Robert L
see also **Hayes, Clair Wallace**
- Boy allies of the navy series

Drake, Stan
- Juliet Jones series
- Kelly Green series

Draper, Alfred
- Crispin Paton series

Draper, Hastings
see also **Ashford, Jeffrey; Graeme, Roderic; Jefferies, Roderic Graeme**
- Wig series

Drax, Peter
- Chief Inspector Thompson series

Dreadstone, Carl
- Dracula series
- Frankenstein sequels series

Dreher, Sarah
- Stoner McTavish series

Dreiser, Theodore
- Frank Cowperwood trilogy
- Men and women series

Drescher, Henrik
- Animals you'd like to meet series

Dresser, Davis
see also **Baker, Asa; Blood, Matthew; Davis, Don; Halliday, Brett**
- Twister Malone series

Drew, Nicholas
see also **Harling, Robert**
- Sailor series

Drew, Patricia
- Hogglespike series

Drew, Sidney
- Sexton Blake series

Drew, Wayland
- Erthring cycle series
- Willow series

Driscoll, James R
- Brighton Boys series

Drucker, Malka
- Jewish holidays series

Drumm, D B
- Traveler series

Drummond, Charles
see also **Giles, Kenneth; McGirr, Edmund**
- Sergeant Reed series

Drummond, Hamilton
- Religious wars trilogy

Drummond, Ivor
see also **Erskine, Rosalind; Parrish, Frank**
- Lady Jennifer, Sandro and Colly series

Drummond, J
- Sexton Blake series

Drummond, John Keith
- Matilda Worthing series

Drummond, Violet Hilda
- Little Laura series
- Miss Anna Truly series
- Mrs Easter series

Druon, Maurice
- Accursed kings series
- Curtain falls trilogy

Drury, Allen
- Akhenaten series
- Soviet conquest series
- Washington series

Drury, Rebecca
- Women of war series

Drury, William Price
- Flag lieutenant series
- Pagett series

Druten, John van
see **Van Druten, John**
Dryasdust
- Ye Headless Lady Inn series

Drysdale, Ann
- Pig farming trilogy

Drysdale, Margaret
- Robert Dudley series

Drysdale, William
- Brain and brawn series

Duane, Diane
- Epic tales of the five series
- Guardians of the Three series
- SeaQuest series
- Space cops series
- Star trek sequels series
- Star trek series
- Star trek, the next generation series
- Wizard series

Dubanevich, Arlene
- Pigs series

Du Barry, Michele
- Angela Carlyle series

Du Bay, Sandra
- Fidelity series

Dubois, D
- Star trek fan series

Du Bois, Gaylord
- George O'Brien series

Lone Ranger
Lone Ranger series (22)
- Tim McCoy series

Dubois, Ivy Millicent
- Grey mouse series

Du Bois, Mary Constance
- Silver sword series

Du Bois, Theodora
- Anne and Jeffrey McNeill series

Du Bois, William
- Jack Jordan series

Du Bois, William Edward Burghardt
- Black flame trilogy

Du Bois, William Pene
see **Pene du Bois, William**
Du Boisgobey, Fortune
- Monsieur Lecoq series

Dubowski, Cathy East
- Ewok series
- Willow series

Dubrovin, Vivian
- Saddle up series
- Summer fun, winter fun series

Dubus, Elizabeth Nell
- Where love rules series

Duche, Jean
- Juliette series

Duder, Tessa
- Alex series

Dudley, Christine
- Mister Collins and Tony series

Dudley, Ernest
- Doctor Morelle series

Dudley, Nancy
- Linda series

Dudley, Owen Francis
- Problems of human happiness series

Dudley, Terence
- Companions of Doctor Who series
- Doctor Who series

Dudley, William E
- Sherlock Holmes sequels series

Dudley-Smith, Trevor
see also **Black, Mansell; Hall, Adam; Rattray, Simon; Trevor, Elleston**
- Green glade trilogy
- Happy glade series

Duerrenmatt, Friedrich
see **Durrenmatt, Friedrich**
Duff, Douglas Valder
see also **Stanhope, Douglas**
- Adam Macadam series
- Bill Berenger series
- Jack Harding series
- Jeremy series
- Yarns of a shellback series

Duff, James P
- Johnny Phelan series

Duff, Reginald Eustace Bluett
- Hornett family series

Duffield, Elizabeth M
- Lucille series

Duffin, Andrew
- Eddy series

Duffy, Margaret
- Patrick Gillard series

Dugan, Bill
- War chiefs series

Dugan, John K
see **Griffin, W E B**
Dugan, Michael
- Wombats series

Dugdale, Pamela
- Dunkel series

Duggan, Alfred
- Saxon trilogy

Dugon, Nora
- Kelly Ryan series

Duhamel, Georges
- Pasquier series
- Salavin series

Duignan, Peter
- Rulers of Africa series

Du Jardin, Rosamond
- Marcy series
- Pam and Penny series
- Tobey and Midge Heydon series

Duke, Kate
- Guinea pig board books series
- Guinea pig series

Duke, Madelaine
see also **Duncan, Alex**
- Doctor Norah North series
- Modern youth trilogy
- Sundmans trilogy

Duke, Winifred
- Harold Fieldend series

Dulieu, Jean
- Paulus series

Dumas, Alexandre
- Count of Monte Cristo series
- Marie Antoinette series
- Memoirs of a physician series
- Mohicans of Paris series
- Napoleon series
- Nelson in Naples series
- Paul Jones series
- Regency trilogy
- Robin Hood series
- Three Musketeers series
- Valois series

Dumas, Charles Robert
- Second Bureau series

Dumas, Philippe
- Edward series
- Laura series

Du Maurier, Angela
- Sister series

Du Maurier, Daphne
- Rebecca De Winter series

Dumitru, Petru
- Boyars trilogy

Dunbar, Joyce
- Mouse and Mole series
- Software Superslug series

Dunboyne, Marion Clifford Butler
- Little Elsie series

Duncan, Alex
see also **Duke, Madelaine**
- Country doctor series
- Vet series

Duncan, Allan
- Major Charles Douglas Kerrwood series

Duncan, Dave
- Handful of men series
- Man of his word series
- Seventh sword trilogy

Duncan, Francis
- Mordecai Euripides Tremaine series
- Peter Justice series

Duncan, Jane
- Camerons series
- Janet Reachfar series
- Reachfar series

Duncan, Julia K
- Doris Force series

Duncan, Kathleen Mary
- Saxonhill series

Duncan, Norman
- Doctor Luke series
- Down North series

Duncan, Ronald
- All men are islands trilogy
- Don Juan series

Duncan, Terence
- Powell's army series

Duncan, Thomas
- Big river, big man series

Duncan, William Murdoch
see also **Cassells, John; Graham, Neill; Malloch, Peter; Marshall, Lovat**
- Greensleeves series
- Laurie Hume series
- Mister Gilly series
- Superintendent Donald Reamer series
- Superintendent Flagg series
- Superintendent Gaylord series
- Superintendent Leslie series
- Superintendent Macneill series

Dunchock, Arnold C
- Daughter series

Dundas, Lawrence
- Andrew Salmond series

Dunham, Mikel
- Rhea Buerklin series

Dunkerley, Elsie Jeanette
see **Oxenham, Elsie J**
Dunkerley, William Arthur
see **Oxenham, John**
Dunlap, Susan
- Jill Smith series
- Kiernan O'Shaughnessy series
- Vejay Haskell series

Dunlop, Agnes Mary Robertson
see **Kyle, Elisabeth**
Dunn, Byron Archibald
- Young Kentuckians series
- Young Missourians series
- Young Virginians series

Dunn, ***Detective***
see also **Pearce, Charles Edward**
- Beautiful devil series

Dunn, Mary
- Lady Addle of Eigg series

Dunn, Pauline
- Phantoms series

Dunn, Philip
see **Dunn, Saul**
Dunn, Roger
- Matty Trakker series

Dunn, Saul
- Cabal series
- Steeleye series

Dunnahoo, Terry
- Espie Sanchez series

Dunne, Colin
- Joe Hussey series

Dunne, Finley Peter
- Mister Dooley series

Dunne, Jeannette
- Foxes of Ireland series

Dunnett, Dorothy
- Francis Crawford of Lymond series
- House of Niccolo series
- Johnson and the yacht Dolly series

Dunnett, Margaret
- Cobb family series

Dunning, Hal
- White Wolf series

Dunphy, Catherine
- Degrassi High School series

Dunsany, Edward John Moreton Drax Plunkett
- Gods of Pegana series
- Jorkens series

Dunstan, Keith
- Brains series

Dunton, Edith Kellogg
see **Warde, Margaret**
Dunton, Theodore Watts-
see **Watts-Dunton, Theodore**
Dupasquier, Philippe
- Robert series

Duplechan, Larry
- Johnnie Ray Rousseau series

Dupuy, Eliza Ann
- Dethroned heiress series

Dupuy-Mazuel, Henry
see **Catalan, Henri**
Durack, Mary
- Grass castles series

Durbridge, Francis
- Paul Temple series
- Philip Holt series
- Tim Frazer series

Durell, Charles Pendexter
- Blue water trilogy

Durham, David
see also **Kyle, Sefton; Vickers, Roy**
- Inspector George Rason series
- Inspector J Rason series
- James Segrove series

Durham, Mary
- Inspector York series

Durham, Victor
- Submarine boys series

Durrant, Digby
- Hamish Oath series

Durrant, Valentine
- Saul Weir series

Durrell, Gerald
- Corfu series

Durrell, Lawrence
- Alexandria quartet
- Antrobus series
- Avignon quintet
- Island series
- Revolt of Aphrodite series

Durrenmatt, Friedrich
- Kommissar Hans Barlach series

Durst, Paul
- Michael Carmichael series

Du Soe, Robert C
- Jonathan Amory series
- Pedro the fisherman series

Dutton, Charles Judson
- Harley Manners series
- John Bartley series

Dutton, Geoffrey
- Long way series
- Tisi series

Dutton, Kenneth Raymond
- Matrix principle series

Dutton, Lewis
- Rags series

Duun, Ole Julius
- People of Juvik series

Duvaul, Virginia
see **Coffman, Virginia**
Duvoisin, Roger
- Crocus series
- Petunia series
- Veronica series

Dvorkin, Daniel
- Star trek series
- Star trek, the next generation series

Dvorkin, David
- Sherlock Holmes sequels series
- Star trek series
- Star trek, the next generation series

Dwiggins, Clare
Adventures of Huckleberry Finn
Huckleberry Finn series (1)
Adventures of Huckleberry Finn
Tom Sawyer series (2)
Dworkin, Ira Bernard
- Sherlock Holmes sequels series

Dwyer, Vera Gladys
- Kayle family series

Dwyer-Joyce, Alice
- Doctor Catriona Chisholm series
- Doctor Esmond Ross series

Dyce, Gilbert
- Jenny Bell trilogy

Dyck, Peter J
- Shalom series

Dyer, Elinor Mary Brent-
see **Brent-Dyer, Elinor Mary**
Dyer, George
- Catalyst Club series

Dyke, Henry van
see **Van Dyke, Henry**
Dyke, John
- Pigwig series

Dymoke, Juliet
- French Revolution series
- Henry I trilogy
- Plantagenets series

Dyson, Edward
- Fact'ry 'ands series

Dyson, Elizabeth
- Revill-Gordon series

E

E, E
see **Eden, Emily**
E, H F
- Maud Kingslake series

Eade, Charles
see **Prole, Lozania**
Eades, Maud L
• Winston Barrows series
Eadington, Joan
• Jonny Briggs series
• Sam series
Eagar, Frances
• Laura and Harry series
Eager, Edward
• Magic series
Eagle, William
• G-men series
Eames, Marion
• Secret room series
Earle, William
see **Johns, William Earl**
Early, Richard Elliott
• Thomas Early series
Early, Tom
see also **Kelton, Elmer**
• Sons of Texas series
Earnshaw, Anthony
• Wintersol series
Earnshaw, Brian
• Dragonfall 5 series
• Star Jam Pack trilogy
East, Helen
• Arthur's aunt series
East, Roger
• Superintendent Simmonds series
Eastlake, William
• Bowman family trilogy
Easton, Malcolm Coleman
• Kyala series
Easton, Nat
• Bill Banning series
Easton, Robert
• Saga of California series
Easton, Thomas Atwood
• Sparrowhawk series
Eastways, W W
• Greycourt series
Eastwood, Dorothea
• River diary series
Eastwood, James
• Anna Zordan series
Eaton, Evelyn
• Arcadian trilogy
• North star series
Ebdon, John
• Broadcaster's Odyssey trilogy
Ebejer, Francis
• Lucija and Rosie series
Ebel, Suzanne
see also **Goodwin, Suzanne**
• Sir Robert Waring series
Eberhard, Frederick George
• Chief of Police Sutherland series
Eberhart, Mignon Good
• Sarah Keate and Lance O'Leary series
• Susan Dare series
Ebersohn, Wessel
• Yudel Gordon series
Ebert, Alan
• Tiernan family series
Ebert, Arthur Frank
see **Arthur, Frank**
Eccles Williams, Ferelith
see **Williams, Ferelith Eccles**
Echlin, Elizabeth Gladys
• Chronicles trilogy
Ecke, Wolfgang
• Super sleuth series
Eckert, Allan Wesley
• Extinct birds series
• Mesmerian annals series
• Winning of America series
Eckert, Horst
see **Janosch**
Eckhardt, Kurt
• Heroes series
Ecklar, Julia
• Star trek series
Eco, Umberto
• Rose series
Eddings, David
• Belgariad series
• Elenium trilogy
• Malloreon series
• Tamuli trilogy
Eddison, Eric Rucker
• Zimiamvian trilogy
Edel, Leon
• Henry James series
Edelman, Maurice
• Benjamin Disraeli series
• Geoffrey Melville series
Eden, Anthony
• Reckoning series
Eden, Emily
• Semi series
Eden, Matthew
• Marc Savage series
Eden, Robert Anthony
see **Eden, Anthony**
Edgar, Alfred
• Sexton Blake series
Edgar, Josephine
• Viola Corbett series
Edgar, Marriott
• Albert and the lion series
Edgerton, Teresa
• Goblin series
• Green lion trilogy
Edholm, Lizette
• Merriweather girls series
Edington, Arlo Channing
see **Edingtons**
Edingtons
• Captain Smith series
Edler, Timothy J
• Crawfish-Man series
• Tales from the Atchafalaya series
Edmonds, Charles
• Subaltern series
Edmonds, Harry
• Hugh Brodie series
Edmonds, Ivy Gordon
Iron monster raid
Rat Patrol series (6)
Edmonds, Walter Dumaux
• Erie Canal series
Edmondson, Garry Cotton
• Alice series
• Cunningham trilogy
Edmunds, Brent
• Pete Marvin series
Edson, John Thomas
see also **Denver, Rod; Nelson, Chuck**
• American Civil War series
• Bunduki series
• Calamity Jane series
• Cap Fog series
• Floating Outfit series
• J.T.'s ladies series
• Ole Devil Hardin series
Return of Rapido Clint and Mister J G Reeder
Mister J G Reeder series (5)
• Rockabye County series
• Waco series
• Waxahachie Smith series
Edwards, Brian
• Dodo series
Edwards, Cassie
• Savage series
Edwards, Charlotte
• Heaven series
Edwards, Charman
• Percy Aloysius Huff series
Edwards, Claudia Jane
• Forest King trilogy
Edwards, David
• Appleyards series
Edwards, Dorothy
• Joe and Timothy series
• My naughty little sister series
Edwards, Gene
• Chronicles of the door series
Edwards, George
• Golden boomerang series
Edwards, Hank
see also **Broomall, Robert Walter**
• Judge Clay Torn series
Edwards, Hazel
• Hippopotamus series
• O Gang series
Edwards, Herbert Wilson
• Under four flags series
Edwards, Hugh
• Sea Witch series
Edwards, James G
• Inspector Victor Bondurant series
Edwards, Josh
• John Stone series
Edwards, K C
• Find your fate: G.I. Joe series
Edwards, Lynne
• Dodo series
Edwards, Monica
• Punchbowl Farm series
• Romney Marsh series
Edwards, Olwen
see also **Owen, Dilys**
• Devil series
Edwards, Pat
• Fred series
• Ghost series
• Sadie Spider series
• Stanley series
Edwards, Paul
• John Eagle series
Edwards, Rex
Dixon of Dock Green
George Dixon series (2)
Edwards, Ruth Dudley
• Robert Amiss series
Edwards, Sylvia
• Sally Baxter series
Edwards, Walter
• Sexton Blake series
Edwards, Wilfrid S
• Vanity trilogy
Edwards, William Henry
Fenland chronicle
Fen family series (2)
Edwin, Maribel
• Baird family series
• Curlew Jon series
Effinger, George Alec
• Marid Audran series
• Nick of time series
• Planet of the Apes series
Zork chronicles
Zork series (4)
Egan, Doris
• Gate of ivory series
Egan, Lesley
see also **Blaisdell, Anne; Linington, Elizabeth; Shannon, Dell**
• Jesse Falkenstein series
• Vic Varallo series
Egan, Richard Whittington-
see **Whittington-Egan, Richard**
Egan, Ted
• Mark and Wendy series
Eggers, Reinhold
Colditz recaptured
Colditz series (12)
• Colditz series
Escape from Colditz
Colditz series (12)
Eggleston, George Cary
• Indian War trilogy
• Virginia trilogy
Egielski, Richard
• Tub People series
Eginardus
• New Atalantis series
Egleton, Clive
• Charles Winter series
• David Garnett trilogy
• Peter Ashton series
Egremont, Michael
• Frankenstein sequels series
Ehle, John
• North Carolina series
Ehrenburg, Ilya
• Dmitry Korotoyev series
• Men, years and life series
• Wave series
Ehrlich, Amy
• Annie series
• Bunnies series
• Leo, Zack and Emmie series
Ehrlich, Jack
• Robert Flick series
Ehrlich, Jacob Wilburn
• Sam Benedict series
Ehrlich, Max
• Peter Proud series
Eichler, Alfred
• Inspector Knickman series
• Martin Ames series
Eigl, Kurt
• Moro series
Eiloart, Elizabeth
• Ernie Elton series
Einberg, Elizabeth
• Kennedys abroad series
Eisenberg, Arlene
• What to expect series
Eisenberg, Lisa
• Laura Brewster series
• South City cops series
Eisenstein, Phyllis
• Alaric the Minstrel series
• Sorcerer's son series
Eisner, Joel
Official Batman handbook
Batman series (10)
Ekberg, Minna
• You and me series
Eklund, Gordon
• Lord Tedric series
• Star trek originals sequels series
Ekwensi, Cyprian
• Jagua Nana series
Eland, Charles
• Mark Randall series
Elder, Michael
• Barclay series
• Mindslip series
• Oil-seeker series
Eldon, Magdalen
• Bumble series
• Tobias series
Eldred, Warren L
• Saint Dunstan series
Eldredge, Gilbert
• Thibault Parew and Chips Carpenter series
Eldridge, Paul
• Wandering Jew trilogy
Elfman, Blossom
• Mike and Ally series
Elgin, Suzette Haden
• Coyote Jones series
• Native tongue series
• Ozark fantasy trilogy
Eliade, Mircea
• Calcutta series
Elias, David
• Nell Bartlett series
Elias, Eileen
• Lewisham series
Elias, Frank
• Cricket series
Elias, Horace J
• Flintstones series
Eliot, George
• Daniel Deronda series
Eliot, George Fielding
• G-men series
Eliot, Henrietta Robins
• Laura series
Eliot, Thomas Stearns
• Four quartets series
• Old Possum series
• Thomas Becket series
Eliott, E C
see also **Dixon, Rex; Martin, Robert**
• Kemlo series
• Tas series
Elium, Don
• Raising sons and daughters series
Elizabeth
see **Russell, Mary Annette**
Elkins, Aaron J
• Professor Gideon Oliver series
Elkon, Jon
• Tom Bloch series
Elks, Wendy
• Wombats series
Eller, John
• Charlie Hope series
Ellerbeck, Rosemary
see **L'Estrange, Anna; Thorne, Nicola; Yorke, Katherine**
Ellerman, Annie Winifred
see **Bryher, Winifred**
Ellern, William Bert
• Lensman series
Ellery, Jan
• Adrienne Bishop series
Ellin, Stanley
• John Milano series
Ellinger, Geoffrey
• Roger Hartley series
Ellington, Richard
• Steve Drake series
Elliot, Douglass
• American patriot series
Elliot, Emilia
see also **Jacobs, Caroline Emilia**
• Joan series
Elliot, John
• Andromeda series
Elliot, Margaret
• Witch's gold trilogy
Elliott, Brian
• Strawberry Shortcake series
Elliott, George
• Martin Speed series
Elliott, James C
• Private pilot's series
Elliott, Janice
• Alexander Columbus Banyana series
• Sword and the dream series
• Wilson family trilogy
Elliott, Jannean
• StarBridge series
Elliott, Mary
• Clare Carson series
Elliott, Nathan
• Hood's Army trilogy
• Star pirates trilogy
Elliott, Odette
• Sammy series
Elliott, Richard
• John Norris series
Elliott, Robert Cowell
• Sexton Blake series
Elliott, William James
• Anthony England series
• Bren Hardy series
• Ed Gunning series
• Royston Frere series
Elliott-Cannon, Arthur
see **Cannon, Elliott; Forde, Nicholas**
Ellis, Carol
• Cheerleaders series
• Heart to heart series
• Troll series
• Two by two series
Ellis, Edward Sylvester
see also **Jayne, R H**
• Arizona trilogy
• Arthur Helmuth series
• Automobile series
• Bound to win trilogy
• Boy patrol series
• Boy pioneer series
• Brave and honest trilogy
• Catamount Camp series
• Colonial trilogy
• Daniel Boone and Simon Kenton series
• Deerfoot the Showanoe series 4
• Firefly series
• Flying boys series
• Foreign adventure trilogy
• Forest and prairie trilogy
• Great river series
• Launch boys series
• Log cabin series
• New Deerfoot series
• Northwest series
• Overland series
• Paddle your own canoe trilogy
• River and wilderness trilogy
• Strange adventure series
• Through on time series
• True grit trilogy
• War chief series
• Wild adventure series
• Wild woods series
• Wyoming Valley trilogy
Ellis, Havelock
My life
In love series (2)
Ellis, Humphry Francis
• A.J.Wentworth series
Ellis, Julie
• Caroline Hampton series
Ellis, Katherine Ruth
• Wide Awake Girls series
Ellis, Kathryn
• Degrassi High School series
Ellis, Novalyne Price
• Robert Ervin Howard series
Ellis, Odette
• Hampton series
Ellis, Peter Berresford
see **Tremayne, Peter**
Ellis, Terry
• Willow Wood Springs trilogy
Ellis, Vivian
• Hilary series
Ellis, Wesley
• Lone Star series
Longarm and the crooked railman
Longarm series (92)
Longarm and the escape artist
Longarm series (95)
Ellis, William Donohue
• Ohio frontier trilogy
Ellison, Norman
• Nomad series
Ellison, Suzanne
• Living West trilogy
Ellroy, James
• Los Angeles quartet
• Sergeant Lloyd Hopkins trilogy
Ellsberg, Edward
• Sunken treasure series
Elman, Richard Martin
• Professor Robert Harmon series
• Yagodah family trilogy
Elmore, Patricia
• Susannah series
Elphinstone, Margaret
• Incomer series
Elrich, George S
Bubble gum kid
Bonanza series (7)
Elrick, George S
Calcutta affair
Man from U.N.C.L.E. series (24)
Elrod, Patricia Nead
• Vampire files series
Els, Betty Vander
see **Vander Els, Betty**
Elsna, Hebe
see also **Conway, Laura**
• Pleasance series

Elsner, Don von
see **Von Elsner, Don**
Elsschot, Willem
- Laarmans series
- Ship trilogy

Elton, Wallace
- Jud Walton series

Elvestad, Sven
- Osborne Crag series

Elwell, Felicia Rosemary
- Mister Collins and Tony series

Elwood, Roger
- Angelwalk series

Ely, George Herbert
see **Strang, Herbert**
Emberley, Ed
- Ed Emberley's big drawing book series
- Ed Emberley's drawing book series
- Ed Emberley's little drawing books series
- First words series

Emecheta, Buchi
- In the ditch series

Emerson, Alice B
- Betty Gordon series
- Ruth Fielding series

Emerson, Anne
Yours affectionately, Peter Rabbit
Peter Rabbit series (21)
Emerson, David
- George Hanson series
- Parson Carnaby series

Emerson, Earl W
- Thomas Black series

Emerson, Mark
- Two by two series

Emerson, Ru
- Beauty and the Beast trilogy
- Nedao trilogy
- Night-threads series

Emerson, Sally
- Second sight series

Emery, Anne
- Dinny Gordon series
- Spy series

Emery, Clayton
- Amazing stories series
- Runesword series

Tales of Robin Hood
Robin Hood series (2)
Emery, Ralph
- Country music series

Emmett, Robert
- American Avenger series

Emms, William
- Doctor Who find your fate series
- Doctor Who series

Enderle, Judith Ann Ross
see **Gordon, Jeffie Ross**
Endfield, Mercedes
- Ms. Squad series

Endicott, Ruth Belmore
- Carolyn series

Enefer, Douglas
- Cannon series
- Dale Shand series
- Sam Bawtrey series

Engdahl, Sylvia Louise
- Elana series
- Noren series

Engel, Diana
- Josephina series

Engel, Howard
- Benny Cooperman series

England, Edward Oliver
- John Rickshaw series

England, George Allen
- Darkness and dawn series

Engle, Madeleine l'
see **L'Engle, Madeleine**
English, David
- Bunburys series

Enright, Dennis Joseph
- Joke shop trilogy
- Packet series

Enright, Elizabeth
- Melendy family series
- Portia and Julian series

Enriquez, Colin Metcalfe
- Khyberie series

Ensley, Evangeline
see **Walton, Evangeline**
Ephesian
- A B C Hawkes series

Epperson, Jerry
- Marvel superheroes adventure gamebooks series

Epstein, June
- Augustus series

Epstein, Samuel
see **Campbell, Bruce**
Erckmann, Emile
- French campaign series
- Story of a peasant series

Erdman, Loula Grace
- Pierce family series

Erdman, Paul
- Financial series

Erdrich, Louise
- Argus series

Erenburg, Ilya
see **Ehrenburg, Ilya**
Erickson, John R
- Hank the cowdog series

Erickson, Karen
- I can do it series

Erickson, Paul
- Doctor Who series

Erickson, Russell Everett
- Warton Toad series

Ericson, Sibyl
see **Dick, Alexandra**
Erikson, Sibyl
see also **Dick, Alexandra**
- Alastair Macalastair series

Eriksson, Eva
- Wild baby series

Erlbach, Arlene
- Henny series

Ernst, Kathryn Fitzgerald
- ESP McGee series

Ernst, Paul
- Jim Ryan series
- Shirley Leighton and Bill Harper series

Ernsting, Walter
see also **Darlton, Clark**
- Perry Rhodan series

Erskine, George
- Counter Force series

Erskine, Laurie York
- Douglas Renfrew series

Erskine Lindop, Audrey
see **Lindop, Audrey Erskine**
Erskine, Margaret
- Inspector Septimus Finch series

Erskine, Rosalind
see also **Drummond, Ivor**
- Passion Flowers series

Erskine, Thomas
- Armata series

Ervin, Timothy S
- Tumtwit series

Escott, John
- Bells series
- Radio series

Eshbach, Lloyd Arthur
- Gates of Lucifer series
- Subspace explorers series

Eshleman, John Morton
- Lieutenant Larry Koharik series

Esmonde, John
- Good life series

Essex, John Ridgewell
- Doctor Craven series

Essex, Louis
- Sexton Blake series

Essex, Richard
- John Slade series
- Lessinger series

Essex, Saran
- Butch Cassidy and the Sundance Kid series

Estes, Eleanor
- Moffat family series
- Pye family series
- Witch family series

Estes, Rose
- Endless quest series
- Greyhawk series
- Hunter series
- Indiana Jones find your fate series
- Mika trilogy
- Runesword series
- Saga of lost lands trilogy

Esteven, John
- Inspector Rae Norse series
- Miles Le Breton series

Estleman, Loren D
- Amos Walker series
- Detroit trilogy
- Doctor Jekyll sequels series
- Dracula series
- Page Murdock series
- Peter Macklin series
- Sherlock Holmes sequels series

Estoril, Jean
see also **Allan, Mabel Esther**
- Drina series

Estow, Daniel
- William Schaefer series

Estrange, James l'
see **Strang, Herbert**
Etchemendy, Nancy
- Watchers series

Etchison, Dennis
- Masters of darkness series

Ethan, John B
- Victor Grant series

Ethel
- Wreck series

Etra, Jonathan
- Aliens series

Ets, Marie Hall
- Mister Penny series

Eulo, Ken
- Chandal Talon trilogy

Evans, Adelaide Bee
- Bible pictures and stories series

Evans, Alan
- Cragg and Frayne series
- David Cochrane series

Evans, Alwyn
- Pumpkin Hill fact series
- Pumpkin Hollow series

Evans, Benjamin Ifor
- Bookshop series

Evans, Bergen Baldwin
- Nonsense series

Evans, Cherry
- Belinda and Lalage series

Evans, Chris
- Other Edens series

Evans, Edward Everett
- George Hanlon series

Evans, Evan
see also **Baxter, George Owen; Brand, Max; Frost, Frederick; Manning, David**
- Montana Kid series

Evans, George Bird
see **Bird, Brandon**
Evans, George Ewart
- Farm life series

Evans, Greg
- Luann series

Evans, Gwyn
- Bill Kellaway series
- Chester Brett series
- Double O'Day series
- Quentin Drex series
- Sexton Blake series

Evans, Ifor
see **Evans, Benjamin Ifor**
Evans, James Roose-
see **Roose-Evans, James**
Evans, Jean
- Katherine Parr series

Evans, Jean Bell Shaw
see **Gillespie, Jane**
Evans, John
- Habbakuk Parton series
- Paul Pine series

Evans, Julia Rendel
see **Hobson, Polly**
Evans, Kay Harris
see **Bird, Brandon**
Evans, Kenneth
- Crispin Tyler series

Evans, Lawrence Watt-
see **Watt-Evans, Lawrence**
Evans, Margiad
- Ray of darkness series

Evans, Max
- Dusty Jones and Wrangler Lewis series

Evans, Shirlee
- Tree Tall series

Evans, Stuart
- Windmill Hill series

Evans, Tabor
see also **Cameron, Lou**
- Longarm and Lone Star series
- Longarm series

Evarts, Richard Conover
- Alice in Wonderland parodies series

Evelyn, John Michael
see **Underwood, Michael**
Evens, George Bramwell
- Romany readers series
- Romany series

Evens, Glyn Kinnaird
- Romany series

Everett-Green, Evelyn
- Dulcie trilogy
- Family series
- Franco-Prussian War series
- Hallowdene Hall series
- Maud Kingslake series
- Tom Tufton series

Everitt, David
- Legends series

Evermay, March
- Inspector Glover series

Evers, Crabbe
- Duffy House series

Everton, Francis
- Detective Inspector Allport series
- Inspector George Annesley series

Ewers, Hanns Heinz
- Frank Braun series

Ewing, Kathryn
- Marcy Benson series

Exley, Frederick
- Frederick Exley trilogy

Exupery, Antoine de Saint-
see **Saint-Exupery, Antoine de**
Eyers, John
- Survivors series

Eyles, Alfred W
- Paul Chisholm series

Eyles, Leonora
- Doctor Joan Marvin series

Eyre, Donald Cuthbert
- Captain O'Donnell series

Eyton, John
- India series

Ezell, Marilyn
- Susan Sand series

F

F, G
see also **Gordon, Franklin**
- Naval digressions series

Faber, Nancy Weingarten
- Cathy series

Fabian, Warner
see also **Adams, Samuel Hopkins**
- Flaming youth series

Fabricius, Sara
see **Sandel, Cora**
Fackler, Elizabeth
- Seth Strummar series

Faherty, Terence
- Owen Keane series

Fahrion, Muriel
- Strawberry Shortcake series

Faid, Mary Alice
- Trudy series

Fainzilberg, Ilya Arnoldovich
see **Ilf, Ilya Arnoldovich**
Fair, A A
see also **Gardner, Erle Stanley**
- Bertha Cool and Donald Lam series

Fairbank, Janet Ayer
- Rich man, poor man trilogy

Fairbrother, Nan
- Cheerful day series

Fairburn, Edwin
see **Mohoao**
Fairburn, Eleanor
- Wars of the Roses series

Fairclough, Chris
- Knowabouts series
- My class series
- Thinking about series

Fairfax, Virginia
- Girl Scouts series

Fairfield, Cicily Isabel
see **West, Rebecca**
Fairlie, Gerard
- Bulldog Drummond series
- Johnny Macall series
- Mister Malcolm series
- Victor Caryll series

Fairman, Paul Warren
see also **Paul, F W**
- Frankenstein sequels series
- Voyage to the bottom of the sea series

Faldbakken, Knut
- Twilight country series

Falk, Lee
- Phantom series

Falkirk, Richard
see also **Lambert, Derek**
- Edmund Blackstone series

Falkner, Frederick
- Aqualung twins series

Falla, Roger
- Emergency Ward 10 series

Fallada, Hans
- Germany between the wars series

Fallaw, L M
- Ugglians series

Fallon, Martin
see also **Higgins, Jack; Patterson, Henry**
- Paul Chavasse series

Falstaff, Jack
- Jacoby's Corners trilogy

Fane, Bron
- La noire series

Fannin, Cole
- Dale Evans series
- Rin-Tin-Tin series
- Roy Rogers series

Fante, John
- Arturo Bandini series

Fanthorpe, Robert Lionel
see **Fane, Bron**
Fantoni, Barry
- Mike Dime series

Faraday, Robert
- Adventures in the time machine series

Farah, Nuruddin
- African dictatorship trilogy

Faralla, Dana
- Magnificent barb series

Farca, Marie C
- Andrew Ames series

Farely, Alison
- Plantagenet series

Farewell, Nina
- Unfair sex series

Faricy, Robert Leo
- Mary speaks to the world series

Farigoule, Louis
see **Romains, Jules**
Farjeon, Eleanor
- Ameliaranne series
- Martin Pippin series

Farjeon, Joseph Jefferson
- Ben the tramp series
- Inspector Kendall series
- Z series

Farley, Ralph Milne
- Miles Cabot series

Farley, Walter
- Black stallion series

Farmer, Bernard James
- Sergeant Jack Wigan series
- Tom Ward series

Farmer, Derek
- Thin King series

Farmer, Lynne
- My book series

Farmer, Penelope
- Charlotte and Emma Makepeace series
- Stephen series

Farmer, Philip Jose
Adventure of the peerless peer by John H Watson
Tarzan series (24)
- Dayworld series
- Doc Caliban series

Doc Savage, his apocalyptic life
Doc Savage series (183)
Escape from Loki
Doc Savage series (183)
- Exorcism series

Hadon of ancient Opar
Tarzan series (1)
Hadon of ancient Opar
Tarzan series (5)
- Lord Grandith series
- Opar series
- Oz series
- Phileas Fogg series
- Riverworld series

Tarzan alive
Tarzan series (24)
- World of Tiers series

Farmer, Richard Neil
- Islandia series

Farmers, Eileen Elizabeth
see **Lane, Elizabeth**
Farnol, Jeffery
- Jane series
- Martin Conisby series
- Mister Jasper Shrig of Bow Street series
- Oliver Matravers series
- Vibart series

Farquharson, Martha
see **Finley, Martha Farquharson**
Farr, Diana Pullein-Thompson
see **Pullein-Thompson, Diana**
Farran, Roy
- Special Air Service series

Farrar, Charles Alden John
- Lake and forest series

Farrar, Frederic William
- Early Church series

Farrar, Stewart
- Bridget and George Blake series
- Inspector Elwyn Morgan series

Farre, Rowena
- Seal morning series

Farrell, Anne
• Mitchell family series
Farrell, James Gordon
• British Empire trilogy
Farrell, James Thomas
• Bernard Clare series
• Danny O'Neill series
• Studs Lonigan trilogy
• Universe of time series
Farrell, Sally
see also **Odgers, Sally Farrell**
• Rosina series
Farrell, Simon
• City of shadows series
• Glade of dreams series
Farren, Mick
• Jeb Stuart Ho series
• Song of Phaid the Gambler series
Farrer, Katharine
• Inspector Richard Ringwood series
Farrimond, John
• Bob Howarth series
• Graham's Gang series
Farrington, Liz
• Mrs Murgatroyd series
Farrington, Robert
• Henry Morane series
Farris, John
• Harrison High series
Farrow, George Edward
• Panjandrum series
• Wallypug series
Farson, Negley
• Transgressor series
Fast, Howard
see also **Cunningham, E V**
• Call of fife and drum trilogy
• Lavette family series
Fatchen, Max
• Murray River series
Fatio, Louise
• Happy lion series
• Hector Penguin series
Faucette, John Matthew
• Peacemakers series
Faucher, Elizabeth
• Addams family series
Faulcon, Robert
see also **Carlsen, Chris; Holdstock, Robert; Kirk, Richard**
• Nighthunter series
Faulkner, Keith
• Sam series
Faulkner, William
• Gavin Stevens trilogy
• Listener series
• Narcissa series
• Sin and salvation series
• Snopes family trilogy
• Temple Drake series
Faulknor, Cliff
• Eagle Child trilogy
Faure-Biguet, Jacques Napoleon
see **Decrest, Jacques**
Fausset, Hugh I'Anson
• Fidelity series
Faust, Frederick
see **Baxter, George Owen; Brand, Max; Evans, Evan; Frost, Frederick; Manning, David**
Faust, Joe Clifford
• Angel's luck series
Faustus, Johann
• Doctor Johann Faustus series
Faversham, Julie Opp
• Squaw Man series
Favors, Jean M
• James Bond find your fate series
• Micro adventure series
Fawcett, Bill
• Cold cash war series
• Combat Command series
• Fleet series
• Guardians of the Three series
• SwordQuest series
• Time gate series
• War years series
Fawcett, Frank Dubrez
• Sexton Blake series
Fay, Gerard
• Passenger to London series
Fearn, John Russell
see also **Blayn, Hugo; Del Martia, Astron; Gridban, Volsted; Slate, John; Statten, Vargo; Titan, Earl**
• Clayton Drew series
• Golden Amazon series
• Jenkinson Talbot Merridrew series
Fearon, Diana
• Arabella Frant series
Fearon, Ethelind
• Pluckrose series
Fecher, Constance
see also **Heaven, Constance**
• Ralegh family trilogy
Feder, Robert Arthur
see **Arthur, Robert**
Fedorova, Nina
• Klimova family series
Fehler, Johann Heinrich
• German raider series
Feige, Otto
see **Traven, B**
Feikema, Feike
see **Manfred, Frederick**
• Manfred, Frederick
• World's wanderer trilogy
Feist, Aubrey
• Jeremy Shafto series
Feist, Raymond Elias
• Empire series
• Riftwar series
Felicity, *Sister*
• Barefoot series
Felitta, Frank de
see **De Felitta, Frank**
Felix, Monique
• Little mouse trapped in a book series
Felsen, Henry Gregor
• Bertie series
Felton, Ronald Oliver
see **Welch, Ronald**
Fen, Elisaveta
• Russia series
Fenady, Andrew J
• Sam Marlow series
Fenisong, Ruth
• Captain Gridley Nelson series
Fenn, Lionel
see also **Charles, Steven; Grant, Charles Lewis; Marsh, Geoffrey**
• Kent Montana trilogy
• Quest for the white duck trilogy
Fennell, George
• Mike Brent series
Fennell, Willie
• Dexter Dutton series
Fennelly, Tony
• Matty Sinclair series
Fenton, Sylvia
• Beasts in the field series
Fenwick, Jill
• Mister Potter's garden series
Ferber, Edna
• Emma McChesney series
• Peculiar treasure series
Ferguson, Brad
• Star trek series
Ferguson, Donald
• Chums of Scranton High series
Ferguson, James
• Emmerdale Farm series
Ferguson, John
• Francis Macnab series
Ferguson, Rachel
• Kensington series
Ferguson, Ruby
• Jill series
Ferguson, Sarah
• Guard within series
Ferguson, Sarah Margaret
see **Sarah, Duchess of York**
Ferguson, W Humer
Blood-curdling romance
Detective Kilsip and Duncan Calton series (1)
Ferguson, William Blair Morton
see also **Morton, William**
• Dan Cluer series
• Lightnin' Calvert series
Piltditch puzzle
Biff Corrigan series (3)
Fergusson, Bernard
• Burma campaign series
Fergusson, Bruce
• Six kingdoms series
Fergusson, Harry
• Santa Fe Trail trilogy
Fergusson, Harvey
• Followers of the sun trilogy
Fermor, Patrick Leigh
• Greek travels series
• On foot series
Fernandez, Sandra
• Hedgerow tales series
Ferra-Mikura, Vera
• Stanislaus family series
Ferrari, Ivy
• Ryeminster Hospital series
Ferrars, E X
see also **Ferrars, Elizabeth**
Murder of a suicide
Toby Dyke series (3)
Neck in a noose
Toby Dyke series (5)
Rehearsals for murder
Toby Dyke series (2)
Shape of a stain
Toby Dyke series (4)
Ferrars, Elizabeth
see also **Ferrars, E X**
• Andrew Basnett series
• Toby Dyke series
• Virginia and Felix Freer series
Ferring, David
• Konrad trilogy
Ferris, James Cody
• X Bar X boys series
Fert, Valerie
• Colombine series
Fetta, Emma Lou
• Lyle Curtis and Susan Yates series
Fetterless, Arthur
• Officer and gentleman series
Fetzer, Herman
see **Falstaff, Jack**
Feuchtwanger, Lion
• Josephus trilogy
• Waiting-room tetralogy
Feuer, Lewis
• Sherlock Holmes sequels series
Feuvre, Amy le
see **Le Feuvre, Amy**
Feval, Paul
• Years between series
Fickling, David
• Fantasy quest book series
• Rama series
Fickling, G G
• Erik March series
• Honey West series
Fidler, Kathleen
• Archaeology series
• Brydon family series
• Deans series
• Heritage series
• McGills series
Field, Katherine
• Inspector Ross Paterson series
Field, Moira
• Inspector Flower series
Field, Peter
• Powder Valley series
Fieldhouse, W L
see **Fieldhouse, William**
Fieldhouse, William
• Klaw series
• Shaddrock and Cougar series
Fielding, A
• Inspector Pointer series
Fielding, Gabriel
• Blaydon family trilogy
Fielding, Henry
• Tom Jones series
Fields, Frank
• Ellis Stack series
Filgate, Macartney
• Charlotte Eliot series
Filichia, Peter
• Two by two series
Filion, Pierre
• Pikolo series
Finch, John
• Spoils of war series
Finch, Matthew
• Dentist series
• Dick Lingham series
• Stevie O'Dowda series
Finch, Sheila
• Shaper exile series
Finch, Simon
• Voyager trilogy
Findley, Ferguson
• Johnny Malone series
Findley, Nigel
• Secrets of power series
• Spelljammer series
Fine, Anne
• Genie trilogy
• Ione Muffet series
Finkel, George
• Group Captain Alan Metcalfe series
• Sabotage series
Finkell, Max
see **Catto, Max**
Finlay, Campbell Kirkman
• John Macinnes series
Finlay, D G
• Watchman chronicles series
Finlay, Eileen
• Boyd family series
• Caravan series
Finlay, Winifred
• Gillian Lindsay series
• Judith Norton series
• Susan series
Finley, Martha Farquharson
• Elsie Dinsmore series
• Honest Jim series
• Mildred Keith series
• Pewit's nest series
• Roselands series
Finn, Elizabeth Anne MacCaul
• Jerusalem series
Finn, Ralph Leslie
• Aldgate series
Finnegan, Robert
• Dan Banion series
• Dangerous thoughts series
Finnemore, John
• Teddy Lester series
Finney, Patricia
• Lugh the Harper series
Finney, R C
• Inspector Bourne series
Firbank, Thomas
• Mountain series
Firmin, Peter
• Bagpuss beginners series
• Bagpuss series
• Basil Brush series
• Country rat series
• Ivor the engine series
• Make it work series
• Noggin series
• Pinny series
• Saga of Noggin the Nog series
Firth, Barbara
• Great escapes series
Firth, Violet Mary
see **Fortune, Dion**
Fischer, Bruno
• Ben Helm series
• Rick Train series
Fischer, Cindy
• Sherlock Holmes sequels series
Fish, Anne Harriet
• Eve series
Fish, Leslie
• Sword of knowledge series
• Sword of knowledge trilogy
Fish, Robert Lloyd
see also **Pike, Robert L**
• Captain Jose da Silva series
• Kek Huuygens series
• Murder League series
• Schlock Homes series
Fisher, Aileen
• Squanderbug series
• Ways of animals series
• Ways of plants series
Fisher, Charles
• Sherlock Holmes sequels series
Fisher, Clay
• Ben Allison series
• Franciscan prient series
• Nathan Mason Stark series
Fisher, Dave
• Joey series
Fisher, David
• Doctor Who series
Fisher, Dorothy Canfield
see **Canfield, Dorothy**
Fisher, Douglas George
see also **Douglas, George**
• Jeff Tellford series
Fisher, Edward
• Silver falcon trilogy
Fisher, George Louis
see **Lancour, Gene**
Fisher, Graham
• Mike King series
Fisher, John Arbuthnot
• Fear God and dread nought trilogy
Fisher, Leonard Everett
• Colonial Americans series
• Nineteenth century America series
Fisher, Norman
• Nigel Morrison series
Fisher, Paul R
• Ash staff trilogy
Fisher, Steve
• Sheridan Doome series
Fisher, Vardis
• Testament of man series
• Tragic life series
Fisk, Nicholas
• Starstormers series
Fiske, James
• World's war series
Fisker, Robert
• Sparrow series
Fitt, Mary
• Annabella series
• Superintendent Mallett series
Fitzgerald, Hilary
• Alastair, Elizabeth and Peter Robin series
Fitzgerald, Hugh
see also **Akers, Floyd; Bancroft, Laura; Baum, Lyman Frank**
• Sam Steele series
Sam Steele's adventures in Panama
Boy fortune hunters series (3)
Sam Steele's adventures on land and sea
Boy fortune hunters series (1)
Fitzgerald, John Dennis
• Tom's Great Brain series
• Will Fitzgerald trilogy
Fitzgerald, Julia
see also **Hamilton, Julia; Watson, Julia**
• Astromance series
• Desert queen series
• Slave series
Fitzgerald, Kevin
• Bernard Feston series
Fitzgerald, Nigel
• Alan Russell series
• Superintendent Duffy series
Fitzgerald, Percy
• Jenny Bell trilogy
Fitzgerald, Ross
• Grafton Everest series
Fitzgibbon, Theodora
• With love series
Fitzhardinge, Joan
see **Phipson, Joan**
Fitzherbert, Selina
• Naff series
Fitzhugh, Louise
• Harriet M Welsh series
• I am series
Fitzhugh, Percy Kees
• Cloud Patrol series
Fitzhugh, Percy Keese
see also **Lloyd, Hugh**
• Bobby Cullen series
• Boy Scouts series
• Buddy series
• Mark Gilmore series
• Pee-Wee Harris series
• Roy Blakeley series
• Tom Slade series
• Westy Martin series
• Young folks colonial series
Fitz Roy, Olivia
• Jamie and Jean Stewart series
• Stewarts series
Fitzroy, Rosamond
• Mallamshire series
Fitzsimmons, Cortland
• Arthur Martinson series
• Ethel Thomas series
• Percy Peacock series
Fitzwilliam, Jennifer
• Mona series
Fix, Philippe
House that Beebo built
Beebo series (1)
Flack, Marjorie
• Angus series
• William series
Flagg, Edmund
• Count of Monte Cristo series
Flagg, John
• Hart Muldoon series
Flanagan
• Intimate secrets series
Flanders, Jill
• My class series
Flanders, Peter
• Mercenary doctor series
Flanner, Janet
• Paris trilogy
Flannery, Sean
see also **Hagberg, David**
• Wallace and John Mahoney series
Fleetwood, Frances
• Concordia series
Fleischer, Leonore
• Holly Hills series
• Saturday night fever series
Fleischman, Albert Sidney
see **Fleischman, Sid**
Fleischman, Sid
• Bloodhound Gang series
• Ghost series
• Gus series
• Max Brindle series
• McBroom series
• Mister Mysterious series
Fleisher, Michael
Superman II
Superman series (7)
Fleming, Arnold
• Souvenir de France series
Fleming, Gordon Howard
• Pre-Raphaelite Brotherhood series

Fleming, Ian
• Chitty-Chitty-Bang-Bang series
• James Bond series
Fleming, Joan
• Nuri Iskirlak series
Fleming, Peter
• Reflections and excursions series
Fleming, Robert Loren
Back to the future
Back to the future trilogy (1)
• Super powers which way series
Fletcher, Aaron
• Bounty Hunter series
Icepick
Marksman series (19)
• Making of America series
• Marksman series
Fletcher, Audrey
• Allsorts series
Fletcher, Beryl
• Khryse trilogy
Fletcher, David
• Raffles series
Fletcher, Dirk
see also **Bodine, J D; Carrington, G A; Cunningham, Chet; Dalton, Kit; Derrick, Lionel**
• Spur McCoy giant series
• Spur McCoy series
• Spur McCoy special series
Fletcher, Farris
• Texans series
Fletcher, Grace Nies
• Nies family series
Fletcher, Henry Lancelot Aubrey-
see **Wade, Henry**
Fletcher, Inglis
• Carolina series
Fletcher, Joseph Smith
• Inspector Skarratt series
• Mister Poskitt trilogy
• Paul Campenhaye series
• Richard Goulburn series
• Ronald Camberwell series
• Sergeant Charlesworth series
Fletcher, Lawrence
• Dick Grenville series
Fletcher, Robert James
• Gilbert Davison series
Fletcher, Steffi
Lone Ranger
Lone Ranger series (22)
Fletcher, Susan
• Kaeldra series
Flexner, James Thomas
• George Washington series
• History of American painting series
Flint, Elizabeth
• East End series
Flint, Homer Eon
• Blind spot series
Flint, Kenneth Covey
see also **Flynn, Casey**
• Finn McCumhal series
• Sidhe Lugh series
Flora, Fletcher
• Hildegarde Withers series
Floren, Lee
see also **Austin, Brett; Jason, Stuart; Smith, Lew; Wilson, Dave**
• Buckshot McKee and Tortilla Joe series
• Judge Lemanuel Bates and Tobacco Jones series
Florescu, Radu
Dracula, prince of many faces
Dracula series (26)
Flower, Jessie Graham
see also **Bates, Gordon; Wilkins, Dale**
• Grace Harlowe at college series
• Grace Harlowe at high school series
• Grace Harlowe overseas series
• Grace Harlowe's Overland Riders series
Flower, Pat
• Inspector Swinton series
Floyd, C J
• Assault series
Flynn, Brian
• Anthony Bathurst series
Flynn, Casey
see also **Flint, Kenneth Corde**y
• Gods of Ireland series
Flynn, Don
• Ed Fitzgerald series
Flynn, J J
• Assault series
Flynn, J M
see **Flynn, Jay**
Flynn, Jackson
see also **Shirreffs, Gordon Donald**
• Gunsmoke series
Flynn, Jay
• Jim Bannerman series
• McHugh series
Flynn, Mary
• Cornelius Rabbit series
Flynn, Rachel
• Koala Hills Primary Hills series
Flynn, Robert
• Wanderer Springs series
Fogazzaro, Antonio
• Maironi family trilogy
Foley, Craig
• Hangman series
Foley, Louise Munro
• Choose your own adventure series
• Earth inspectors series
• Twistaplot series
Foley, Rae
• Hiram Potter series
• John Harland series
Foley, Winifred
• Forest series
Follett, James
• Earthsearch series
Follett, Ken
• Piers Roper series
Folsom, Franklin
see **Nesbit, Troy**
Fong, C K
• Kung Fu series
Fonstad, Karen Wynn
Atlas of Middle Earth
Middle Earth series (5)
Atlas of Pern
Pern and the Red Planet series (12)
Atlas of the DragonLance world
DragonLance chronicles series (3)
Forgotten Realms atlas
Avatar trilogy (3)
Fontana, Dorothy Catherine
• Star trek series
Fontenot, Mary Alice
• Clovis Crawfish series
Foote, Horton
• Orphans' home series
Foote, John Taintor
• Fatal gesture series
Foote, Shelby
• Civil War trilogy
• Lake Jordan series
Foote-Smith, Elizabeth
• Will Woodfield series
Footman, Robert
• Harry Ryder series
Footner, Hulbert
• Amos Lee Mappin series
• Madame Rosika Storey series
Forbes, Bryan
• Velvet series
Forbes, Colin
see also **Raine, Richard; Sawkins, Raymond**
• Tweed, Grey and Newman series
Forbes, Daniel
see also **Kenyon, Michael**
• Superintendent O'Malley series
Forbes, De Loris Florine Stanton
see **Wells, Tobias**
Forbes, Graham B
• Columbia High School series
• Frank Allen series
Forbes-Lindsey, Charles Harcourt
• Trail blazers series
Ford, Donald
• Child and the community series
• Gwyneth series
Ford, Elizabeth
• Maplechester series
• Tyldens series
Ford, Ford Madox
• England and the English series
• Fifth queen trilogy
• Memories and impressions series
• Parade's end series
• Poems for pictures series
Ford, Hilary
see also **Christopher, John; Godfrey, William**
• Felix series
Ford, James Allan
• Hong Kong series
Ford, John M
• Star trek series
Ford, Leslie
• Colonel John Primrose series
• Grace Latham series
• Lieutenant Joseph Kelly series
Ford, Lillian Cummings
• Arthur Raneleigh series
Ford, Richard
• Faradawn trilogy
Ford, Sewell
• Shorty McCabe series
• Torchy series
Ford, Webster
Reedy's mirror
Spoon River series (1)
Forde, Nicholas
see also **Cannon, Elliott**
• Mark Urgent series
Foreman, Leonard London
• Rogue Bishop series
Foreman, Michael
• Ben series
• Panda series
Foreman, Russell
• Oliver Slater Fijiian series
Fores, John
• London Airport series
Forest, Antonia
• Marlow Ancestors series
• Marlow family series
Forest, Dael
• Roman world series
Forester, Cecil Scott
• Annie Marble series
• Horatio Hornblower cadet series
• Horatio Hornblower series
Forman, James Douglas
• Doomsday series
• Greek Civil War trilogy
Forrest, Anthony
• Captain John Valcourt Justice series
Forrest, Katherine V
• Kate Delafield series
Forrest, Norman
• John Finnegan series
Forrest, Richard
• Lyon and Bea Wentworth series
Forrester, Helen
• Mersey series
Forrester, Izola Louise
• Greenacres series
• Polly Page series
Forrester, John
• Bestiary trilogy
Forsey, Chris
• Look twice series
Forstchen, William R
• Crystal series
• Gamester wars series
• Ice prophet trilogy
• Lost regiment series
Forster, Michelanne
• Rodney Rat series
Forster, Peter
• Alex Smith and Tony Bevan series
Forsyte, Charles
• Inspector Richard Left series
Forsyth, Anne
• Baxter series
• Monster series
Forsythe, Robin
• Anthony Vereker series
Fortescue, Winifred
• Provence series
Fortier, Ron
• Windwalker series
Fortune, Dion
• Vivien Le Fay Morgan series
Fortune, J J
• Race against time series
Forty, George
• Photo history of two world wars series
Forward, Robert Dodson
• Owl series
Forward, Robert Lull
• Dragon's egg series
Forward, Toby
• Wyvern quartet
Fossard, Esta de
see **De Fossard, Esta**
Foster, Alan Dean
see also **Lucas, George**
• Alien series
• Cthulhu Mythos series
• Damned series
• Flinx of the Commonwealth series
• Friends like these series
• Icerigger series
• Luke Skywalker series
• Spellsinger series
• Tar-Aiym Krang trilogy
• Thranx series
Foster, David
• D'Arcy Oliveres series
Foster, Edith Francis
• Marigold series
Foster, Edna Abigail
• Hortense series
Foster, Jeanne
see also **Williams, Jeanne**
• Frontier women series
Foster, Kingsley
• Jonathan Lamb series
Foster, Marian Curtis
see **Mariana**
Foster, Michael Anthony
• Ler series
• Morphodite trilogy
Foster, Reginald Francis
• Anthony Ravenhill series
• Sexton Blake series
Foster, Richard
• Chin Kwang Kham series
• Pete Draco series
Foster, Walter Bertram
• Clint Webb series
Fothergill, John
• Innkeeper series
Foucault, Michel
• History of sexuality series
Foulds, Elfrida Vipont
see **Vipont, Elfrida**
Fountaine, Margaret
• Victorian lady series
Fowkes, Aubrey
• Butterfly days series
Fowl
• Eve series
Fowler, Christopher
• City jitters series
Fowler, Ellen Thornycroft
• Isabel Carnaby trilogy
Fowler, Frank
• Broncho Rider Boys series
Fowler, Richard
• Beans series
• Cat series
• Inspector Smart series
• Let's make it series
• Mister Little series
• Ted and Dolly series
Fowler, Sydney
see also **Wright, Sydney Fowler**
• Inspector Cauldron series
• Inspector Cleveland series
• Mister Jellipot series
• Professor Blinkwell series
Fowler, Thurley
• Robinson family series
Fowler, William Morgan
• American Navy series
Fowles, Anthony
• Richard Powell series
Fox, Brian
see also **Ballard, Willis Todhunter; Hunter, John; Macneil, Neil; Shepherd, John; Slade, Jack; Turner, Clay**
• Alias Smith and Jones series
• Dollar series
• Sabata series
Fox, David
see also **Chipperfield, Robert Orr**
• Shadowers Inc. series
Fox, Gardner Francis
see also **Somers, Bart**
• Alan Morgan series
• Kothar series
• Kyrik series
Fox, Genevieve May
• Mountain girl series
Fox, J N
• Young Indiana Jones series
Fox, James M
• Jerry Long and Chuck Conley series
• John and Suzy Marshall series
• Steve Harvester series
Fox, Sebastian
see also **Bullett, Gerald**
• George Lydney series
Fox-Davies, Arthur Charles
• Ashley Tempest series
Foxall, Peter Augustus
• Catford Police series
• Detective Sergeant Scamp series
• Inspector Frank Derben series
Foxall, Raymond
• Captain James Hind series
• Harry Adkins series
• John Crispin series
Foxell, Nigel
• Emma Hamilton series
Foxx, Jack
see also **Pronzini, Bill**
• Dan Connell series
Foyle, Kathleen
• Augherim series
Fraga, Geoff de
see **De Fraga, Geoff**
Frakes, Randall
• Terminator series
Fraley, Oscar
• Untouchables series
Frame, Janet
• Is-land trilogy
France, Anatole
• Abbe Coignard series
• Contemporary history series
• Pierre Noziere series
France, Victor
• Oliver Galt and Hugo Tower series
Frances, Stephen Daniel
see also **West, Bob**
• Adventures around the compass series
• Hank Janson series
• John Gail series
Francis, Basil
• Inspector Ghent series
• Sergeant Paul Dean series
Francis, Clare
• Voyage series
Francis, Dick
• Kit Fielding series
• Sid Halley series
Francis, Dorothy
• Keepsake series
Francis, Dorothy Brenner
• Twilight series
Francis, Frank
• Grandmother Lucy series
Francis, Jaye
• Hot pursuit series
Francis, Stella M
see also **Benson, Irene Elliott**
• Campfire Girls series
Francis, William
• Anthony Martin series
Francoise
• Jeanne-Marie series
Frank, Lee
• Kane Richards series
Frank, Leonhard
• Carl and Anna series
Frank, Waldo
• David Markand series
Frankau, Gilbert
• One of us series
• Peter Jackson series
Frankau, Mary Evelyn Atkinson
see **Atkinson, Mary Evelyn**
Frankau, Pamela
• Clothes of a king's son trilogy
Frankel, Ellen
• Time traveler series
Franken, Rose
• Claudia series
Frankland, Edward
• Retreat series
Franklin, Charles
see also **Usher, Frank**
• Grant Garfield series
• Inspector Jim Burgess series
• Maxine Dangerfield series
Franklin, Cheryl Jean
• Magical tales of Taormin series
• Network-Consortium series
Franklin, Donald
• Special Squad series
Franklin, Eugene
see also **Bandy, Franklin**
• Berkeley Barnes and Larry Howe series
Franklin, Gordon
see also **F, G**
• Naval digressions series
Franklin, Max
see also **Deming, Richard**
• Charlie's Angels series
• Starsky and Hutch series
Franklin, Miles
see also **Brent of Bin Bin**
• Sybylla Penelope Melvyn series
Frankowski, Leo
• Adventures of Conrad Stargard series
Franzen, Nils Olof
• Agaton Sax series
Franzero, Carlo Maria
• Mrs Caroline series
Frascino, Edward
• Eddie Spaghetti series
• Nanny Noony series
Frasconi, Antonio
• See and say series
Fraser, Alex
see also **Brinton, Henry**
• Inspector Noel Tracy series
Fraser, Amy Stewart
• Hills of home trilogy

Fraser, Anthea
- Inspector David Webb and Sergeant Ken Jackson series

Fraser, Antonia
- Jemima Shore series

Fraser, Christine Marion
- Blue above the chimneys series
- King's series
- Light on Dumyat series
- Rhanna series

Fraser, Conon
- Underground series

Fraser, David
- Treason in arms series

Fraser, Edith
- David John series

Fraser, George Macdonald
- Flashman series
- Private McAuslan series

Fraser, James
see also **White, Alan**
- Inspector Bill Aveyard series

Fraser, Mary
see also **Axler, James; Darke, James; Haigh, Richard; James, Laurence; Marvin, James W; May, Jonathan; McPhee, James; Netzen, Klaus; Nolan, Christopher; Norman, Mick**
- Village trilogy

Fraser, Mary Ann
- Little kids series

Fraser, Ronald
- Trout series

Fraser, Sara
- Tildy series

Fraser, Shelagh
- Tai-Lu series

Frazee, Steve
- High Chaparral series

Killer lion
Bonanza series (7)
Walt Disney's Zorro
Zorro series (7)

Frazer, Andrew
- Duncan Pride series

Frazer, Martin
- Sexton Blake series

Frazer, Robert Caine
see also **Creasey, John; Deane, Norman; Halliday, Michael; Marric, J J; Morton, Anthony; York, Jeremy**
- Mark Kilby series

Frazetta, Frank
- Death dealer series

Frazier, Arthur
see also **Akers, Alan Burt; Blake, Ken; Bulmer, Kenneth; Hardy, Adam; Krauss, Bruno; Prescot, Dray; Silver, Richard; Zetford, Tully**
- Wolfshead series

Frederic, Harold
- New York series

Frederic, Mike
see also **Cox, William Robert; Ward, Jonas**
- Frank Merriwell series

Fredericks, Arnold
- Richard Duvall series

Fredman, John
- Charles Dexter series

Fredman, Mike
- Willie Halliday series

Free, Colin
- Pollitt family series

Freeborn, Brian
- Mister Cain series

Freed, Artelle
- Melanie Gaye series

Freedgood, Morton
see **Godey, John**

Freedman, Russell
- Animal behavior series
- How animals series
- Killer series
- Wild West series

Freeling, Nicolas
- Arlette Van der Valk series
- Henri Castang series
- Inspector Piet Van der Valk series

Freeman, Austin
see **Freeman, Richard Austin**

Freeman, Harold Webber
- Pond Hall series

Freeman, Kathleen
see **Fitt, Mary**

Freeman, Lucy
- Doctor William Ames series

Freeman, Martin Joseph
- Jerry Todd series

Freeman, Richard Austin
- Doctor John Evelyn Thorndyke series

Freemantle, Brian
- Charlie Muffin series

Frees, Harry Whittier
- Four little pets series
- Petland photo tales series
- Sandman series

Freidman, Jerrold David
see **Gerrold, David**

Fremd, Angelika
- Inge Heinrich series

Frenais, Ian la
see **La Frenais, Ian**

French, Anne Warner
see **Warner, Anne**

French, Fergus
- General Ogle-Oxley series

French, Harold
- I swore series

French, Jackie
- Children of the valley trilogy

French, Laura
- Endless quest series

French, Michael
Indiana Jones and the raiders of the lost ark
Indiana Jones series (1)
Indiana Jones and the temple of doom
Indiana Jones series (2)

French, Paul
see also **Asimov, Isaac**
- David Starr series

Frere, Richard
- Highland line series

Freschet, Berniece
- Bernard series

Fretland, Donald John
- Oleandre series

Freund, Philip
- Volcano god trilogy

Frewer, Glyn
- Robertson family series

Frey, Charles Weiser
see **Findley, Ferguson**

Frey, Hildegarde Gertrude
- Winnebagos series

Frey, James
U.S.S.A.
U.S.S.A. series (4)

Friedell, Egon
- Time traveller series

Friedman, Kinky
- Kinky Friedman series

Friedman, Michael Jan
- Star trek series
- Star trek, the next generation sequels series
- Star trek, the next generation series
- Vidar trilogy

Friedman, Mickey
- Georgia Lee Maxwell series

Friedman, Rosemary
see **Tibber, Robert**
- Mistress and wife series
- Shelton family series

Friel, Arthur Olney
- McKay, Knowlton and Ryan series

Friend, Ed
see also **Wormser, Richard**
- Green Hornet series
- High Chaparral series

Friend, Oscar
see also **Smith, Ford**
- Simon Carter series

Friesner, Esther Mona
- Chronicles of the twelve kingdoms series
- Demons trilogy
- Gnome series
- New York trilogy

Friggens, Arthur
- Mortorio series

Frisbie, Carol
- Star trek fan series

Friskey, Margaret
- Indian Two Feet series
- Magic meadow series

Frison-Roche, Roger
- Simon Sokki series
- Zian series

Fritch, Elizabeth
- California trilogy
- Richmond series

Frith, Henry
- Britannia series

Frith, Nigel
- Pangaia trilogy

Fritz, Jean
- American Revolution series

Frome, David
- Evan Pinkerton series
- Major Gregory Lewis series

Frost, Alexandra
- Worlds of power series

Frost, Barbara
- Marka de Lancey series

Frost, C Vernon
- Sexton Blake series

Frost, Frances Mary
- Windy Foot series

Frost, Frederick
see also **Baxter, George Owen; Brand, Max; Evans, Evan; Manning, David**
- Secret service series

Frost, Graham H
- Recon series

Frost, Gregory
- Tain series

Frost, Jason
- Warlord series

Frost, Kelman Dalgety
- Captain John Walton series

Frost, Marie Hibma
- Hattie series

Frow, Gerald
- Young Sherlock Holmes series

Frow, Marion
- Intelligence Corps series

Fry, Pete
- Pete Fry series

Fry, Rosalie Kingsmill
- Lucinda series

Fry, Stephen
- Ted Wallace series

Frye, Northrop
- Bible and literature series

Frye, Pearl
- Lord Horatio Nelson series

Fuchs, Daniel
- Williamsburg trilogy

Fuentes, Roberto
- Jason Striker series

Fujikawa, Gyo
- Jenny series
- Shags series

Fuller, Anna
- Pratt portraits series

Fuller, Ed
- Troubleshooters series

Fuller, Harold Edgar
see **Fulman, Al**

Fuller, Kathleen
- Riverview trilogy

Fuller, Roger
see also **Tracy, Don**
- Peyton Place series

Fuller, Roy
- Joke Shop series
- Oxford lectures on poetry series
- Strange and the good trilogy

Fuller, Timothy
- Jupiter Jones series

Fuller, William
- Brad Dolan series

Fullerton, Alexander
see also **Hilton, Alec**
- Nick Everard series
- Special Boat Service trilogy

Fulman, Al
- Harry Long series

Fulton, Eileen
- Nina McFall series

Fulton, Janet
- Raggedy Ann series

Fultz, Regina Oehler
- Endless quest series

Funnell, Augustine
- Brandyjack series

Furlong, Monica
- Wise child series

Furman, Lucy
- Quare women trilogy

Furminger, Jo
- Blackbird series
- Mary, Ben and William series

Furminger, Justine
- Bobbie series

Furnell, John
- Doctor Furnell series

Furphy, Joseph
see **Collins, Tom**

Furst, Alan
- Roger Levin series

Fussey, Joyce
- Yorkshire farm series

Futrelle, Jacques
- Professor Augustus S F X Van Dusen series

Fyfield, Frances
- Sarah Fortune series

Fynn
- Anna series

Fysh, Hudson
- Qantas series

Fyson, Jenny Grace
- Shamashazir series

G

G, G
- Sporting stories series

G-Man
- F.B.I. series

Gaan, Margaret
- Red barbarian trilogy

Gabaldon, Diana
- Outlander series

Gaboriau, Emile
- Count's secret series
- Dossier series
- Marriage of adventure series
- Monsieur Lecoq series

Gackenbach, Dick
- Claude series
- Hattie Rabbit series
- Hound and Bear series

Gadallah, Leslie
- Cat's pawn series

Gage, Joy Pennock
- Obedience series
- Seventh child series

Gage, Wilson
- Mrs Gaddy series

Gagnon, Maurice
- Deirdre O'Hara trilogy

Gaillard, Robert
- Marie series

Gaiman, Neil
Don't panic
Arthur Dent series (5)
- Miracleman series
- Sandman series

Gaines, Audrey
- Chauncey O'Day series
- Jeff Strange series

Gainham, Sarah
- Viennese trilogy

Gair, Malcolm
- Mark Raeburn series

Gair, Patrick
see **Gurney, David**

Gaite, Francis
see also **Coles, Manning**
- James and Charles Latimer series

Galbraith, Judy
- Gifted kids survival guide series

Galbraith, Kathryn O
- Roommates series

Galdone, Paul
- Grandparents series

Galdos, Benito Perez
see **Perez Galdos, Benito**

Gale, Zora
- Friendship village series

Gall, Edward Reginald Home-
see **Home-Gall, Edward Reginald**

Gallacher, Tom
- Bill Thompson trilogy

Gallagher, Bob
- Cthulhu Mythos series

Gallagher, Gale
see also **Oursler, William**
- Gale Gallagher series

Gallagher, Jock
- Archers of Ambridge series

Gallagher, Patricia
- Castles series

Gallagher, Richard
- Cannon series

Gallagher, Stephen
Last rose of summer
Paradise series (1)

Gallant, Janet
- Everyday parenting series

Gallant, Roy Arthur
- Exploring series

Gallico, Paul
- Alexander Hero series
- Hiram Holliday series
- Jean-Pierre series
- Jennie series
- Mrs Harris series
- Poseidon series

Gallie, Menna
- Cilhendre Village series

Gallison, Kate
- Unbalanced accounts series

Gallizier, Nathan
- Sorceress trilogy

Galsworthy, John
- Country house trilogy
- End of the chapter series
- Forsyte saga trilogy
- Love trilogy
- Modern comedy series

Galt, Katherine Keene
- Rosanna series

Galway, Robert Conington
see also **Macneil, Duncan; McCutchan, Philip; Wigg, T I G**
- James Packard series

Galwey, Geoffrey Valentine
- Inspector Daddy Bourne series

Gammon, Joy
Teenage mutant ninja turtles knitting book
Teenage mutant ninja turtles series (5)

Gamow, George
- Mister Tompkins series

Gandley, Kenneth Royce
see **Royce, Kenneth**

Gann, Ernest Kellogg
- Triumph series

Gann, Lewis Henry
- History of Rhodesia series
- Rulers of Africa series

Gannett, Ruth Stiles
- Dragon series

Ganpat
- Harry Lake series

Gant, Norman
- Chane series

Gantner, Susan
- Sophie and Jack series

Gantos, Jack
- Rotten Ralph series

Garcia Marquez, Gabriel
- Macondo series

Gard, Joyce
- Mark Danby series

Gard, Stephen
- Sunday the thirteenth series

Gardam, Jane
- Kit series

Garden, Nancy
- Dracula series
- Fours Crossing trilogy
- Monster hunters series

Gardener, Jeanne
- Breakthrough series

Gardiner, Dorothy
- Mister Watson series
- Sheriff Moss Magill series

Gardner, Alan Harold
- Davis Troy series

Gardner, Craig Shaw
- Arabian Nights trilogy
- Back to the future trilogy
- Ballad of Wuntvor trilogy
- Batman series
- Cineverse trilogy
- Ebenezum series

Gardner, Elsie Bell
- Maxie series

Gardner, Erle Stanley
see also **Fair, A A**
- Baja California series
- District Attorney series
- Gramps Wiggins series
- Perry Mason series
- Terry Clane series
- Whispering Sands series

Gardner, Hugh
- Marble Mountain series

Gardner, Jerome
see also **Tully, Paul**
- Dripspring series
- Hanging Judge series

Gardner, John Edmund
- Boysie L Oakes series
- Detective Inspector Derek Torry series
- Herbie Kruger series
- James Bond series
- Professor Moriarty series
- Secret generations trilogy

Gardner, Maurice Benjamin
- Bantan series

Gardner, Richard A
Dorothy and the lizard of Oz
Oz series (51)

Garfield, Brian Wynne
see also **Ward, Jonas; Wynne, Brian**
- Paul Benjamin series
- Sam Watchman series

Garfield, Leon
- Apprentices series

• Bostock and Harris series
• Greek mythology series
• Tim and Pistol series
Garforth, John
• Avengers series
• Sexton Blake series
• Victorian day series
Garis, Cleo Fausta
• Arden Blake series
Garis, Howard Roger
see also **Sperry, Raymond**
• Curlytops series
From office boy to reporter
Larry Dexter series (1)
• Great newspaper series
Larry Dexter and the bank mystery
Larry Dexter series (4)
Larry Dexter and the stolen boy
Larry Dexter series (5)
Larry Dexter in Belgium
Larry Dexter series (6)
Larry Dexter, the young reporter
Larry Dexter series (2)
Larry Dexter's great search
Larry Dexter series (3)
• Rocket Riders series
• Two Wild Cherries series
• Uncle Wiggily series
Garis, Lilian C
• Barbara Hale series
• Cleo series
• Girl Scouts series
• Gloria series
• Joan series
• Judy Jordan series
• Melody Lane series
Garis, M R
• Uncle Wiggily series
Garland, Hamlin
• Middle Border series
Garland, John
• Ross Grant series
Garland, Lawrence
• Sherlock Holmes sequels series
Garland, Nicholas
• Barry McKenzie series
Garland, Sarah
• Family life series
Peter Rabbit's gardening book
Peter Rabbit series (4)
• Rose series
• Sam series
• Tex series
Garlock, Dorothy
• Colorado trilogy
• Wabash trilogy
Garner, Alan
• Alderley series
• Stone book quartet
Garner, Hugh
see also **Warwick, Jarvis**
• Cabbagetown series
• Inspector Walter McDumont series
Garner, Rolf
• Kennet trilogy
Garner, William
• John Morpurgo trilogy
• Mike Jagger series
Garnet, A H
• Cyrus Wilson series
Garnett, Catherine Grace
see **Godwin, Catherine Grace**
Garnett, David
• Golden echo trilogy
Garnett, Eve
• Ruggles family series
Garnett, Henry
• Benny series
Garnett, Richard
• Mark Rutter series
Garnett, Roger
see also **Morland, Nigel**
• Chief Inspector Jonathan Black series
• John Yardley series
• R I Perkins series
Garon, Marco
see **Garron, Marco**
Garrard, Phillis
• Hilda series
• Nancy series
Garrett, Charles C
• Gunslinger series
Garrett, Frank
• Killsquad series
Garrett, Randall
see also **Phillips, Mark; Randall, Robert**
• Gandalara cycle series
• Lord Darcy series
• Takeoff series
Garrett, Robert
• Alan Brett series
Garrett, Sally
• Rainbow Hills series
Garrett, William
• James Drew series
Garrido, Mar
• Swept away series
Garrisen, Paul
• Dirk Prine series
Garrison, Christian
• Ace Chaney series
Garrison, Frederick
see also **Sinclair, Upton**
• West Point series
Garrison, Wendell Phillips
• Lemuel Gulliver series
Garron, Marco
• Azan series
Garstin, Crosbie
• Mud larks series
• Penhales trilogy
Garvey, Keith
• Outback tales series
Garvice, Charles
• Staunch series
Gary, Romain
• Genghis Cohn series
Gascoigne, Bamber
• Fearless Freddy series
Gascoigne, Marc
• Fighting fantasy gamebook series
Gash, Joe
• Terry Flynn series
Gash, Jonathan
• Lovejoy series
Gash, Norman
• Sir Robert Peel series
Gask, Arthur
• Gilbert Larose series
Gaskell, Jane
• Atlan saga series
Gaskin, Carol
• Explorer series
• Forgotten forest series
• Time machine series
• Time traveler series
Gasparotti, Elizabeth Seifert
see **Seifert, Elizabeth**
Gasperini, Jim
• Time machine series
Gaston, Bill
• Lieutenant Jason Winter series
• Roy Maclean series
Gaston, William James
see **Gaston, Bill**
Gat, Dimitri
• Yuri Nevsky series
Gater, Dilys
see **Edwards, Olwen; Owen, Dilys**
Gates, Clifford
• Sexton Blake series
Gates, Tudor
• Vendetta series
Gathorne-Hardy, Jonathan
• Cyril Bonhamy series
• Jane Charrington series
Gathorne-Hardy, Robert
• Ottoline series
Gatty, Margaret
Parables of nature
Hedgerow tales series (1)
Gaulle, Charles de
• War memoirs series
Gault, William Campbell
• Brock Callahan series
• Gridiron series
• Joe Puma series
Gaunt, Mary
• Doctor Craven series
Gaunt, Michael
• Belle Isle series
• Brim series
Gaunt, Richard
• Borgia series
• English Civil War series
Gaunt, William
• Victorian painting series
Gautier-Smith, Peter Claudius
see **Conway, Peter**
Gavin, Catherine
• Clyde Valley series
• French Resistance series
• Light woman series
• Second Empire quartet
• Twentieth-century Europe series
Gavin, Jamila
• Surya series
Gavta, Yaffa
• Savta Simcha series
Gay, Michael
• Little vehicle series
Gaye, Carol
• Jane Scott series
Gaye, Phoebe Fenwich
• Vandervoord trilogy
Gayle, Newton
• James Greer series
Gear, Kathleen O'Neal
see also **O'Neal, Kathleen M**
• People series
Gear, William Michael
• Forbidden borders series
• People series
• Spider series
Gearon, John
see **Flagg, John**
Geason, Susan
• Syd Fish series
Geddes, Paul
• Ludovic Fender series
• Paul Venneker series
Geduld, Harry Maurice
Definitive Doctor Jekyll and Mister Hyde companion
Doctor Jekyll series (2)
Girl in the hairy paw
King Kong series (3)
Gee, Herbert Leslie
• Friendly series
• Priory House series
Gee, Howard
• Colditz series
Gee, Joseph
• David Isaacs series
Gee, Maurice
• Plumb trilogy
• World of O trilogy
Geikie-Cobb, Ivo
see **Weymouth, Anthony**
Geis, Richard Erwin
• Roi Kunzer series
Geismar, Maxwell
• American novel series
Geissler, Ludwig A
• Looking backward sequels series
Gelfland, M Howard
E.T., the extraterrestrial
E.T. series (2)
Geller, Michael
• Bud Dugan series
Gellis, Roberta
• Heiress series
• Roselynde chronicles series
• Royal dynasty series
Gemmell, David A
• Drenai series
• Lion of Macedon series
• Sipstrassi tales series
Gendel, Evelyn
• Tortoise and Turtle series
Genet
see **Flanner, Janet**
Gentile, Gary
• Dragons series
Gentle, Mary
• Orthe series
• White crow series
Gentleman, David
• Fenella series
Gentry, Buck
• Eli Holten series
Gentry, Georgina
• Cimarron series
• Panorama of the old West series
George, Charles
Peck's bad boy and his pa
Peck's bad boy series (1)
George, David Lester
• Freddie Freightliner series
George, Elizabeth
• Inspector Thomas Lynley and Sergeant Barbara Havers series
George, Jean Craighead
• All upon series
• How to talk to your animals series
• New York in maps series
• One day series
• Thirteen moons series
George, Peter Bryan
see **Peters, Bryan**
George, Sidney Charles
• Lim Quong series
George, Theodore
• Lieutenant Al Zimmerman series
Georgeson, Valerie
• Angels series
• Shadow of the elephant series
Gerahty, Digby George
see **Standish, Robert**
Gerani, Gary
Batman official souvenir magazine
Batman series (10)
Gerard, Francis
• Commissioner Sanders series
• Marquess de Brussac series
• Sir John Meredith series
Gerberg, Mort
• All-Jewish cartoon series
Gerhardi, William Alexander
• Jazz and Jasper series
Germano, Peter
see **Cord, Barry**
Gerrity, David
• Frank Cardolini series
Gerrold, David
• Dracon series
• Planet of the Apes series
• Star trek originals sequels series
• Star trek, the next generation sequels series
• War against the Chtorr trilogy
Gerry, Margarita Spalding
• Philippa trilogy
Gervaise, Mary
• Belinda Gordon series
• Farthingale series
• G for Georgia series
• Marstons series
• Miranda series
Geston, Mark Symington
• Havengore series
Gethin, David
• Halloran series
• Wyatt series
Gezi, Kal
• Maple Street Five series
Ghose, Sudhindra Nath
• Sister Svenska series
• Vermilion boat series
Ghose, Zulfikar
• Incredible Brazilian trilogy
Gibb, Lee
see also **Waterhouse, Keith**
• Jones series
Gibbings, Robert
• Sweet Thames series
Gibbon, Lewis Grassic
• Scots Quair trilogy
Gibbon, Percival
• Miss Gregory series
Gibbons, Harry Hornaby Clifford
• Sexton Blake series
Gibbons, M S
• We Donkeys series
Gibbons, Stella
• Cold Comfort Farm series
Gibbs, Anthony
• John Archer series
Gibbs, George
• Old Philadelphia series
Gibbs, Henry
see also **Harvester, Simon**
• Prior Report trilogy
• South African history series
• Theatre series
Gibbs, Lewis
• Kitty Villiers series
Gibbs, Mary Ann
see also **Ford, Elizabeth**
Gibbs, May
• Gumnut Land series
Gibbs, Philip
• John Barton trilogy
• Oliver series
• Second World War series
Gibbs-Smith, Charles Harvard
• Paul Harvard series
Gibson, Gloria
• Rachel Payne series
Gibson, Michael
• Motor rally series
Gibson, Morris
• One man series
Gibson, Patricia Jeann
• Private hells trilogy
Gibson, Walter Brown
see also **Grant, Maxwell**
• Norgil series
• Twilight Zone series
Gibson, William
• Neuromancer trilogy
Gibson, William Curtis
• Water Wagon series
Gide, Andre
• Fruits of the earth series
• Journal series
Gielgud, Val
• Antony Havilland series
• Inspector Gregory Pellew and Viscount Clymping series
• Inspector Simon Spears series
• Years series
Giesy, John Ulrich
• Jason Croft trilogy
Giff, Patricia Reilly
• Abby Jones series
• Casey Valentine series
• Kids of the Polk Street School series
• Lincoln Lions Band series
• New kids at the Polk Street School series
• Polka Dot series
• Ronald Morgan series
Gifford, Griselda
• Ben Taylor series
• Jenny and Mirabelle series
Gifford, Thomas
• Wind chill series
Giggal, Kenneth
see **Ross, Angus**
Gikow, Louise
• Fraggle Rock series
Gilbert, Anthony
• Arthur Crook series
• Dupuy series
• Scott Egerton series
Gilbert, Bernard
• Old England series
Gilbert, Edith Laura
• Meenie series
Gilbert, Harry
• Honey the dolphin series
Gilbert, Martin
• Appeasement series
• History atlas series
• Winston S Churchill series
Gilbert, Michael Francis
• Inspector Hazelrigg series
• Patrick Petrella series
Gilbert, Pamela
• Gemma series
Gilbert, Ruth Gallard Ainsworth
see **Ainsworth, Ruth**
Gilbert, Stephen
• Ben and Willard series
Gilbreth, Frank Bunker
• Gilbreth family series
Gilchrist, Beth Bradford
• Helen series
Gilchrist, Ellen
• Anna Hudson series
Gilchrist, Rupert
• Dragonard series
• Slaves without masters trilogy
Gilden, Mel
• Beverly Hills 90210 series
• Fifth grade monsters series
• Star trek, the next generation series
• Zoomers of Motor City series
• Zoot Marlowe series
Giles, Guy Elwyn
• Brice Kent series
Giles, Janice Holt
• Fowler family series
• Piney Ridge trilogy
Giles, Kenneth
see also **Drummond, Charles; McGirr, Edmund**
• Inspector Harry James and Sergeant Honeybody series
Giles, Raymond
• Sabrehill series
Gill, B M
• Inspector Tom Maybridge series
Gill, Bartholomew
• Inspector Peter McGarr series
Gill, Brendan
• New York series
Gill, Elizabeth
• Benvenuto Brown series
Giller, Norman
• Soccer series
Gillespie, Jack
• McGills series
Gillespie, Jane
• Brightsea series
Ladysmead
Mansfield Park series (3)
• Northanger Abbey series
• Teverton Hall series
Gillespie, Robert Byrne
• Ralph Simmons series
Gillespie, Susan
• Longdon-Lorristone family series
Gillespie, Thomas Haining
• Zoo Man series
• Zoo ways series
Gillette, William
Sherlock Holmes
Sherlock Holmes drama series (14)
• Sherlock Holmes drama series
Gillham, Elizabeth Wright Enright
see **Enright, Elizabeth**
Gilliat, Edward
• Robin Hood series
Gilligan, Alison
• Choose your own adventure series

Gilligan, Edmund
- Gaunt woman series

Gilligan, Shannon
- Choose your own adventure series

Gilliland, Alexis Arnaldus
- Rosinante trilogy
- Wizenbeak trilogy

Gillmore, Inez Haynes
see also **Irwin, Inez Haynes**
- Phoebe and Ernest series

Gilluly, Sheila
- Greenbriar Queen trilogy

Gilman, Dorothy
- Mrs Emily Pollifax series

Gilman, George G
see also **Harknett, Terry; Hedges, Joseph; James, William M; Pike, Charles R; Stone, Thomas H**
- Adam Steele series
- Edge meets Steele series
- Edge series
- Steele's war series
- Undertaker series

Gilman, Phoebe
- Jillian Jiggs series

Gilman, Robert Cham
- Rhada series

Gilmore, David Hunter
- Christopher Cricket series

Gilmour, H B
- Saturday night fever series

Gilmour, Margaret
- Ameliaranne series

Gilmour, Oswald Wellington
- Singapore series

Gilmour, William
Lost on Jupiter
Martian series (12)
Tarzan and the lightning man
Tarzan series (24)

Gilpatric, Guy
- Mister Colin Andrew Macthrockle Glencannon series
- Tugboat Annie series

Gilroy, Beryl
- Young Roy series

Gilruth, Susan
- Inspector Hugh Gordon and Liane Crawford series

Gilson, Charles
- Submarine U93 series

Ginsberg, Allen
- Despair trilogy

Ginther, Mary Pemberton
- Beth Anne series
- Betsy Hale series
- Hilda series
- Miss Pat series

Giono, Jean
- Angelo series
- Song of the world trilogy
- Trilogy of earth

Giovanitti, Len
see **Jordan, Robert**

Giovanni, Paul
- Sherlock Holmes drama series

Giovene, Andrea
- Giuliano Sansevero series

Gipe, George
- Back to the future trilogy
- Gremlins series

Gipson, Fred
- Old Yeller series

Girard, Nicole
- Anna, Paul and Tommycat series

Giraud, Jean
- Lieutenant Mike S Blueberry series

Gironella, Jose Maria
- Alvear family trilogy

Giroux, E X
see also **Shannon, Doris**
- Robert Forsythe and Abigail Sanderson series

Girtin, Tom
- Landlord series

Girzone, Joseph Francis
- Joshua series

Gissing, Vera
- Pippins series

Gittings, Robert
- John Keats series
- Thomas Hardy series

Givens, Charles Garland
- Jimmy Hastings series

Glaberson, Cory
Dorsai's command
Combat Command series (8)

Gladney, Heather
- Song of Naga Teot series

Gladstone, Arthur
see **Gladstone, Maggie**

Gladstone, Josephine
see also **Marquand, Josephine**
- Chi Ming series

Gladstone, Maggie
see also **Sebastian, Margaret**
- Lacebridge ladies series

Glanfield, Jenny
- Hotel Quadriga series

Glanville, Alec
- Inspector Dusty Muller and Tiny Meldrum series

Glaskin, Gerald Marcus
- Christos experience trilogy

Glass, Montague
- Potash series

Glasscock, Anne Bonner
see **Bonner, Michael**

Glasser, Ralph
- Gorbals trilogy

Glassop, Lawson
- Rats series

Glatzer, Richard
- Time machine series

Glazer, Mindy
- Star trek fan series

Glazner, Joseph Mark
- Billy Nevers series

Gleitzman, Morris
- Misery guts series
- Rowena Batts series

Glemser, Bernard
- Nicholas Hart series
- Robert Crane trilogy

Glick, Ruth
see also **York, Rebecca**
- Charisma Inc. series
- Magic micro adventure series
- Micro adventure series
- Twistaplot series

Glidden, Frederick Dilley
see **Short, Luke**

Glidden, Minna Wesselhoft
- Carey Brent series

Glint Green
- Inspector Wield series

Gloag, John
- Lionel Buckby series
- Roman Britain series

Glovach, Linda
- Little witch series

Glover, Halcott
- Louise trilogy

Glover, Judith
- Sussex quartet

Glubb, John Bagot
- Arab history series
- Desert war series

Gluck, Sinclair
- Jack Clayton series
- Paul Bernard series
- Ross McCoy series

Glut, Donald Frank
Dracula book
Dracula series (26)
Frankenstein catalog
Frankenstein series (1)
Frankenstein legend
Frankenstein series (1)
- Frankenstein sequels series
- Luke Skywalker series

Gluyas, Constance
- Deep South trilogy

Glyn, Caroline
- Fullie series
- Winston series

Glyn, Elinor
- Elizabeth series

Glynne-Jones, William
- Farewell innocence series

Gober, Don
- James Rhodes series

Gobineau, Marceline
- Stephanie series

Goble, Dorothy
- Red Indian trilogy

Goble, Paul
- Iktomi series
- Red Indian trilogy

Goddard, Kenneth
- Prey series

Goddard, Norman
- Sexton Blake series

Godden, Jon
- No time to weep series

Godden, Rumer
- Four dolls series
- No time to weep series
- Nona Fell series

Godey, John
- Jack Albany series

Godfrey, Jan
- Little Lion series
- Me series

Godfrey, Lionel Robert Holcombe
see **Mitchell, Scott**

Godfrey, William
see also **Christopher, John; Ford, Hilary**
- Test cricket series

Godwin, Catherine Grace
- Cousin Kate series

Godwin, Felix
- Captain John Hunter series

Godwin, John
- Staffordshire characters series

Godwin, Parke
- Arthurian cycle trilogy
- Blue light series
- Snake oil wars series
- Solitude trilogy

Godwin, Tom
- Ragnarok series

Goethe, Johann Wolfgang von
- Wilhelm Meister series

Gogarty, Oliver St John
- Sackville Street series

Gogceli, Kemal Sadik
see **Kemal, Yashar**

Goines, Donald
see also **Clark, Al C**
- Kenyatta series

Gold, Herbert
- Jewish emigrants series

Golden, Christie
- Ravenloft series

Golden Gorse
- Mousie series

Golden Rod
- Bad boy series

Goldfrap, John Henry
see **Deering, Fremont B; Lawton, Wilbur; Payson, Howard; West, Marvin**

Goldie, Kathleen Annie
see **Fidler, Kathleen**

Goldin, Stephen
- Family d'Alembert series
- Honey B series
- Parsina series
- Rehumanization of Jade Darcy series
- Star trek originals sequels series

Golding, Louis
- Elsie Silver series
- Moses series
- Philip Massel series

Golding, William
- Sea trilogy

Goldman, Lawrence Louis
- Clinton Judd series
- Johnny Saturday series

Goldman, Raymond Leslie
- Asaph Clume series

Goldman, William
- Marathon man series

Goldreich, Gloria
- Leah Goldfeder series

Goldring, Douglas
- Love among the artists trilogy

Goldsborough, Robert
- Nero Wolfe and Archie Goodwin series

Goldsmith, John
- It's easy to have series
- Mrs Babcary series

Goldstein, Arthur David
- Max Guttman series

Goldstein, Fred
Star trek speaks
Star trek series (57)

Goldstein, Robin
- Everyday parenting series

Goldstein, Stan
Star trek spaceflight chronology
Star trek series (57)

Goldstein, William
- Doctor Phibes series

Goldstone, Lawrence Arthur
see **Treat, Lawrence**

Goldthorpe, John
- Early Christian series

Goldthwaite, Eaton Kenneth
- Lieutenant Joseph Dickerson series

Goll, Reinhold Weimar
- Veta series

Gollancz, Victor
- Letters to Timothy series

Gollin, James
- Antigua Players series

Gollomb, Joseph
- Galt series

Golon, Sergeanne
- Angelique series

Gompertz, Martin Louis
see **Ganpat**

Gondosch, Linda
- Hopper Street trilogy

Gonzales, John
- Harry Horne series

Gonzalez, Gloria
- Twilight series

Good, Edward
see **Oyved, Moysheh**

Goodall, John Strickland
- Edwardian series
- English village series
- Paddy Pork series

Goodchild, George
- Colorado Jim series
- Inspector McLean series
- John Trelawney series
- Nigel Rix series

Goode, Angela
- Working dogs series

Goode, Evelyn
- Polly-Dear, Rod and Small series

Gooden, Arthur Henry
see **Rider, Brett**

Goodman, Deborah Lerme
- Choose your own adventure series

Goodman, Julius
- Choose your own adventure series

Goodman, Montague
- Wantoknow series for boys

Goodman, Paul
- Empire City quartet
- Empire city series

Goodrum, Charles Alvin
- Edwin George series

Goodwin, Ben
- Rosencrantz family series

Goodwin, Hazel
- Tuddleton Trotter series

Goodwin, John
- Superintendent Scarfe series

Goodwin, Michael
Guide to the Commonwealth
Flinx of the Commonwealth series (6)

Goodwin, Ralph
- Prisoner of war series

Goodwin, Suzanne
see also **Ebel, Suzanne**
- Winter sisters series

Goodwin, Tim
- Ring of spears series

Goolden, Barbara
- Consett trilogy
- Tabor family series

Gordievsky, Oleg
- K.G.B. series

Gordon, Charles William
see **Connor, Ralph**

Gordon, Diana
see also **Andrews, Lucilla; Marcus, Joanna**
- Romney Marsh series

Gordon, Doris
- Backblocks doctor series

Gordon, Elizabeth
- Dolly and Molly series
- Loraine series

Gordon, Frederick
- Fairview boys series
- Up and doing series

Gordon, Fritz
- Schuyler Townsend series

Gordon, Giles
- Edward series

Gordon, Glenda
- Glenda series

Gordon, Gordon
see **Gordons**

Gordon, Grace
- Patsy Carroll series

Gordon, Harry
- River motor-boat boys series

Gordon, Jan
- Inspector Penk series

Gordon, Jeffie Ross
- Sunfire series
- Touch series

Gordon, John
- Giant under the snow series

Gordon, Katharine
- Peacock series

Gordon, Lyndall
- T.S.Eliot series

Gordon, Margaret
- Wilberforce series

Gordon, Mike
- Hello series

Gordon, Mildred
see **Gordons**

Gordon, Neil
- Peter Kerrigan series

Gordon, Peter
- Sexton Blake series

Gordon, Richard
- Doctor series
- Trevose family series

Gordon, Richard Alex Stuart
see **Gordon, Stuart**

Gordon, Stuart
- Eyes trilogy
- Watchers trilogy

Gordon, Victor
- Mansfield Park series

Gordons
- Frank and Gail Mitchell series
- John Ripley series
- Undercover Cat series

Gore, Catherine Grace
- Cecil series

Gore, William
- Inspector Penk series

Gore-Browne, Robert
- Lucien Clay series

Gorelick, Molly Chernow
- Rescue series

Gorell, Ronald Gorell Barnes
- Evelyn Temple series
- Harry Farrant series
- Inspector Gordon Ross series
- Inspector Maurice Hepburn series

Gores, Joe
- DKA file series

Gorey, Edward
- Alphabet series
- Donald series
- Fletcher and Zenobia series
- Vinegar works trilogy

Gorky, Maxim
- Childhood to university trilogy
- Life of Klim Samgin series

Gorman, Edward
- Jack Dwyer series
- Leo Guild series
- Tobin series

Gormley, Beatrice
- Fifth grade magic series
- Focus pocus series

Gorsky, Bernard
- Moana series

Goscinny, Rene
- Asterix series
Asterix, the gladiator
Asterix series (29)
Asterix, the legionary
Asterix series (29)
- Dogmatix series
- Lucky Luke series
- Nicholas series
- Twelve tasks of Asterix series

Gosling, Paula
- Lieutenant Jack Stryker series
- Sheriff Matt Gabriel series

Gotlieb, Phyllis
- Dahlgren series
- Qsaprinel trilogy

Gott, Richard
- Appeasement series

Gottfried, Theodore Mark
see **Mark, Ted**

Gottlieb, Carl
Jaws log
Jaws series (2)

Goudey, Alice Edwards
- Here come series

Goudge, Eileen
- Seniors series
- Super-seniors series
- Swept away series

Goudge, Elizabeth
- Cathedrals series
- Eliot family trilogy
- Torminster series

Gough, Barbara Worsley-
see **Worsley-Gough, Barbara**

Gough, Laurence
- Willows and Parker series

Goulart, Ron
see also **Steffanson, Con**
- Barnum series
- Battlestar Galactica series
- Ben Jolson series
- Cleopatra Jones series
- Exchameleon series
- Gypsy series
- John Easy series
- Odd jobs series
- Skyrocket Steele series
- Star Hawks series
- Troubles with machines series
- Vampirella series
- Weird heroes series
- Wild talents series

Gould, Charles S
- Biff series

Gould, Chester
- Dick Tracy cartoon series
- Dick Tracy series

Gould, Elizabeth
- Green Willow Farm series

Gould, Elizabeth Lincoln
- Admiral's granddaughter series
- Felicia series
- Polly Prentiss series

Gould, Heywood
- Josh Krales series

Gould, Stephen
- Sheridan Doome series

Goulding, Francis Robert
- Boy life among the Indians series
- Marooners series
- Woodruff trilogy

Goullet, Mark
- Doctor Davie series

Gourley, Frank Alan
- Even gods err trilogy

Govan, Christine Noble
- Plummer children series
- Wren twins series

Govan, Margaret
- Betty Morton series

Gover, Robert
- Kitten series

Gowans, Elizabeth
- Blair family series

Gower, Iris
- Catrin series
- Copper kingdom series

Gowing, Sidney Floyd
see **Goodwin, John**

Gowland, John Stafford
- Sikanska series

Goyder, Margot
see **Neville, Margot**

Goyne, Richard
see also **Courage, John**
- Ex-Superintendent Tubby Green series
- Padre series
- Paul Templeton series
- Sexton Blake series

Graaf, Peter
- Joe Dust series

Graat, Heinrich
- Ben Camden series

Graber, George Alexander
see **Cordell, Alexander**

Graber, Richard
- Ray Decker series

Grabowsky, Nicholas
- Halloween series

Grace, C L
- Kathryn Swinbrooke series

Grace, John
- Asterix push-out series

Grady, James
- Condor series
- James Rankin series

Graeber, Charlotte Towner
- Mister T and me series
- Speak for me series

Graeber, Jean Boreman
- Rescue series

Graeme, Bruce
see also **Bourne, Peter; Graeme, David**
- Blackshirt series
- Detective Sergeant Robert Mather series
- Henry Maxwell series
- Inspector Auguste Jantry series
- Lord Blackshirt series
- Superintendent William Stevens and Inspector Pierre Allain series
- Theodore I Terhune series

Graeme, David
see also **Bourne, Peter; Graeme, Bruce**
- Monsieur Blackshirt series

Graeme, Linda
- Helen series

Graeme, Roderic
see also **Ashford, Jeffrey; Draper, Hastings; Jefferies, Roderic Graeme**
- Blackshirt series
- Brandy series

Grafton, Cornelius Warren
- Gil Henry series

Grafton, Sue
- Kinsey Millhone series

Graham, Amanda
- Arthur trilogy

Graham, Anthony
- Eric Marsden series
- Frank Richmond series

Graham, Bob
- John and friends series
- New baby series

Graham, Burton
- Michael Evans series

Graham, Caroline
- BMX series
- Inspector Tom Barnaby series

Graham, Harry
- Reginald Drake Biffin series

Graham, Heather
- Civil War trilogy
- Donna Miro and Lorna Doria series

Graham, Jean
- Dark angel series

Graham, Lorenz
- Momolu series
- Town series

Graham, Margaret Bloy
- Benjy series

Graham, Mark
- Roommates series

Graham, Matilda Winifred
see **Graham, Winifred**

Graham, Neill
see also **Cassells, John; Duncan, William Murdoch; Malloch, Peter; Marshall, Lovat**
- Mister Sandyman series
- Solo Malcolm series

Graham, Paul
- George Dixon series

Graham, Robert
- Attar the Merman series

Graham, Rosemary
- Furry Forest series

Graham Scott, Peter
see **Scott, Peter Graham**

Graham, Winifred
- Miss Woolfe series
- That reminds me trilogy

Graham, Winston
- Poldark series

Grahame, Iain
- Daw's Hall series

Grahame, Kenneth
First whisper of the wind in the willows
Wind in the willows series (1)
- Smith family series
- Toad Hall series

Wind in the willows
Riverbend and Wildwood tales series (1)
- Wind in the willows series

Grainger, Francis Edward
see **Hill, Headon**

Gramatky, Hardie
- Little Toot series

Grambling, Lois Goodwin
- Elephant and mouse series

Grand, Gordon
- Colonel John Weatherford series

Grand, Leon le
see **Le Grand, Leon**

Grand, Sarah
- Adnam Pratt series
- Heavenly twins series

Grange, Peter
see also **Arlen, Leslie; Logan, Mark; Nicole, Christopher; York, Andrew**
- L'Eree family series

Granger, Ann
- Meredith Mitchell and Chief Inspector Alan Markby series

Granger, Bill
- Jimmy Drover series
- November Man series
- Terry Flynn series

Granger, Georgia
- Making of America series

Grannan, Mary
- Just Mary series
- Maggie Muggins series

Grant, Allan
see also **Smith, Arthur Douglas Howden**
- Boys at the Front series

Grant, Charles Lewis
see also **Charles, Steven; Fenn, Lionel; Marsh, Geoffrey**
- Chronicles of Greystone Bay series
- Oxrun Station series
- Parric family trilogy
- Soft whisper trilogy

Grant, Donald M
- Lucius Leffing series

Grant, Gwen
- Private, keep out series

Grant, James
- Mace series

Grant, Jane
see also **Castle, Frances**
- Nurse series

Grant, Joan
- Far memory series
- Ra-ab Hotep series

Grant, John
- Legends of Lone Wolf series
- Littlenose series

Grant, Kathryn
- Land of ten thousand willows trilogy

Grant, Mark
- Mutants amok series

Grant, Maxwell
see also **Gibson, Walter Brown**
- Shadow series

Grant, Pamela
- Fortunes series

Grant, Robert
- Jack Hall series

Grant, William
- Matthew Faraday series

Grant-Adamson, Lesley
- Jim Rush series
- Rain Morgan series

Grape, Oliver
see also **Lea, Timothy; Wood, Christopher**
- Grape family series

Gras, Felix
- French Revolution trilogy

Grass, Gunter
- Danzig trilogy

Grater, Michael
- Alf Gorilla series
- Giant series

Gravatt, Glenn
- Sherlock Holmes sequels series

Grave, Stephen
- Miami Vice series

Gravel, Geary
- Autumn world series
- Fading worlds series

Graver, Fred
- Choose your own adventure series

Graves, Charles
- Royal Air Force series

Graves, Charles Larcom
War of the Wenuses
War of the worlds series (1)

Graves, Clotilde
see **Dehan, Richard**

Graves, John
- Brazos trilogy

Graves, Richard Harry
- Tidinbilla series

Graves, Richard Latshaw
- Hugo Wolfram series

Graves, Robert
- Broken images series
- Claudius series
- Goodbye to all that series
- Love respelt series
- Sergeant Lamb series

Graveson, Caroline Cassandra
- Farthing family series

Gray, Berkeley
see also **Brooks, Edwy Charles; Gunn, Victor**
- Norman Conquest series
- Sexton Blake series

Gray, Dulcie
- Inspector Cardiff series
- Roger Moore and the Crimefighters series

Gray, Edwyn
- U-boat series

Gray, Harold
- Little Orphan Annie series

Gray, Harriet
see also **Robins, Denise**
- Quadroon trilogy

Gray, J M
Hello Kitty's button book
Hello Kitty series (6)

Gray, Juliet
see also **Collins, Lynne**
- Stephen Power series

Gray, Malcolm
- Alan Craig series

Gray, Michael
- Fantasy forest series

Gray, Nicholas Stuart
- Puss in Boots series

Gray, P D
- Three Ds series

Gray, Rod
- Lady from L.U.S.T. series
- New lady from L.U.S.T. series

Gray, Simon
- Unnatural pursuit series

Gray, Walter T
see also **Victor, Metta Victoria**
- Bad boy series

Naughty girl's diary
Bad boy series (4)

Graydon, Robert Murray
- Sexton Blake series

Graydon, William Murray
- Sexton Blake series

Grayland, Valerie Merle
- Hoani Mata series

Graymont, Barbara
- Iroquois series

Grayson, David
- Adventures series

Grayson, Donald
- Bob Steele series

Grayson, Richard
- Inspector Gautier series
- John Bryant series

Grayson, Rupert
- Gun Cotton series
- Voyage not completed series

Graziani, Antoine
- Fanina series

Greatorex, Wilfred
- Airline series

Greaves, Jimmy
- Soccer series

Greaves, Margaret
- Alberic the dragon series
- Little Bear series

Greaves, Nick
- African tales series

Gree, Alain
- Beebo series
- Books and games series
- Find series
- I know series
- Keith and Sally series
- Little Tom series
- Look series
- Romeo series
- Smashers series
- Story series

Gree, Gerard
Little Tom learns about the environment
Little Tom series (1)

Greeley, Andrew Moran
- Cardinal sins and virtues series
- Monsignor John Blackwood Ryan series
- Passover trilogy
- Time between the stars

Green, Anna Katharine
- Amelia Butterworth series
- Caleb Sweetwater series
- Ebenezer Gryce series

Green, Bill
- Mickey McClintock series

Green, Candida Lycett-
see **Lycett-Green, Candida**

Green, Christine
- Kate Kinsella series

Green, Cliff
- Riverboat Bill series

Green, Edith
- Dearborn V Pinch series

Green, Evan
- Kalinda series

Green, Evelyn Everett-
see **Everett-Green, Evelyn**

Green, Glint
see **Glint Green**

Green, Hilary
- Triple S agent series

Green, Jonathon
- Famous last words series

Green, Julian
- Days series
- Distant lands series

Green, Julius Morris
- Colditz series

Green, Kate
- Fossil family tales series
- Shattered series
- Theresa Fortunato series

Green, Michael
- Coarse plays series
- Coarse series

Hobbit's travels
Middle Earth series (2)

Green, Roger James
- Samuel Walton series

Green, Roger Lancelyn
- Spearlake children series

Green, Roland
Burning eye
War world series (1)
- Janisseries trilogy

Green, Roland James
- Conan series
- Lord Kalvan series
- Paratime police series
- Peace Company trilogy
- Starcruiser Shenandoah series
- Wandor series

Green, Russell
- Prophet series

Green, Sharon
- Diana Santee series
- Farside of forever series
- Jalav series
- Terrilian series

Green, Sheila Ellen
see **Greenwald, Sheila**

Green, Simon
- Hawk and Fisher series
- Mistworld series

Robin Hood, prince of thieves
Robin Hood series (2)

Greenaway, Peter van
see **Van Greenaway, Peter**

Greenberg, Dave
- Super Cops series

Greenberg, Martin Harry
Barbarians II
Barbarians series (2)
- Barbarians series
- Batman series

Dick Tracy activity book
Dick Tracy film series (2)
Dick Tracy, the secret files
Dick Tracy film series (2)
Freddy Kreuger's seven sweetest dreams
Nightmare on Elm Street series (2)
- Isaac's universe series

Nightmares on Elm Street
Nightmare on Elm Street series (2)
- Space gladiators trilogy
- Twilight Zone series

Twilight Zone, the original stories
Twilight Zone series (6)
- What might have been series

Greenberger, Robert
Doomsday world
Star trek, the next generation series (12)

Greenburg, Dan
Witchfires of Leth
Chronicles of Morgaine series (4)

Greene, Bette
- Beth Lambert series
- Patty Bergen series

Greene, Carla
- I want to be series
- Let's learn about series
- Science and natural history series
- Travel series
- What do they do series

Greene, Constance Clarke
- Al series
- Isabelle series

Greene, Graham
Return of A.J.Raffles
Raffles series (18)

Greene, Joseph
- Dig Allen series

Greene, L Patrick
- Aubrey Saint John Major series
- Dynamite Drury series
- Sergeant Lancey series

Greene, Yvonne
- Kelly Blake series

Greener, William Oliver
- Jo Salis series

Greenfeld, Josh
- Noah series

Greenfield, Irving A
- Depth force series
- Tom Carey trilogy

Greenhalgh, Zohra
- Trickster series

Greenham, Hazel
- Kennedys abroad series

Greenland, Colin
- Daybreak series

Greenleaf, Stephen
- John Marshall Tanner series

Greenleaf, William
- Tartarus series

Greenwald, Sheila
- Mariah Delany series
- Rosy Cole series

Greenwell, Dora
- Two friends series

Greenwood, Ed
Elminster
Avatar trilogy (3)

Greenwood, John
- Inspector Mosley series

Greenwood, Kerry
- Phryne Fisher series

Greenwood, Robert
- Mister Bunting series
- Rosie Dawes series

Greenwood, Walter
- Trelooe series

Greer, Gery
- Jason series
- Max and me series

Gregg, Cecil Freeman
- Henry Prince series
- Inspector Cuthbert Higgins series

Gregg, Hilda
see **Grier, Sydney Carlyon**

Gregoire, Jean Albert
- Auguste Maller series

Gregor, Elmer Russell
- Eastern Indians series
- Jim Mason series
- Western Indian series

Gregorian, Joyce Ballou
- Tredana trilogy

Gregory, H
Secret of the Tong
Sexton Blake series (221)
- Sexton Blake series

Gregory, Hylton
Curse of the Kali
Sexton Blake series (334)
Mystery of the blackmailed baronet
Sexton Blake series (425)
Sign of the black feather
Sexton Blake series (471)

Gregory, Jackson
- Paul Savoy series

Gregory, Julian R
- Tomorrow people series

Gregory, Lester
- Kid Cyclone series

Gregory, Lisa
- Rainbow season series

Greig, Daisy
- Daisy series

Greig, Ian
- Inspector Swinton series

Grender, Iris
- Did I ever tell series

Grenfell, Joyce
- Pleasant places series

Grenfell, Wilfrid Thomason
- Labrador series

Grenville, Kate
- Lilian Singer series

Gresham, Elizabeth
see also **Grey, Robin**
- Jenny Gilette and Hunter Lewis series

Greth, Roma
- Hana Shaner series

Gretz, Susanna
- Roger series
- Rug series
- Teddybear board book series
- Teddybears series

Greve, Felix Paul Berthold Friedrich
see **Grove, Frederick Philip**

Grex, Leo
see also **Cody, Stetson; Denver, Lee; Gribble, Leonard Reginald; Sanders, Bruce; Shane, Steve**
- Paul Irving series
- Phil Sanderson series

Grey, Charlotte
- Miss Jane Fairfax series

Grey, Estelle
- Julie Gordon series

Grey, Loren Zane
- Lassiter series

Grey, Peter
- Kit Hunter series

Grey, Robin
see also **Gresham, Elizabeth**
- Jenny Gilette and Hunter Lewis series

Grey, Romer Zane
- Arizona Ames series
- Border Legion series
- Buck Duane series
- Laramie Nelson series
- Nevada Jim Lacy series
- Yaqui series

Grey, Zane
- Adam Larey series
- Arizona Ames series
- Border Legion series
- Buck Duane series
- Diamond Outfit series
- Forlorn River Ranch series
- Ken Ward series
- King of the Royal Mounted series
- Laramie Nelson series

Last of the Duanes
Buck Duane series (9)
- Mormon series
- Nevada Jim Lacy series

Spanish peaks
Laramie Nelson series (2)
- Tales of a fisherman series
- Western stars series
- Yaqui series
- Zane family series

Gribble, Leonard Reginald
see also **Cody, Stetson; Denver, Lee; Grex, Leo; Sanders, Bruce; Shane, Steve**
- Paul Irving series
- Superintendent Anthony Slade series

Gribbon, William Lancaster
see **Mundy, Talbot**

Gridban, Volsted
see also **Blayn, Hugo; Fearn, John Russell; Slate, John; Statten, Vargo; Titan, Earl**
- Adam Quirke series
- Clifford Brooks series

Grier, Sydney Carlyon
- Balkan series
- Balkan trilogy
- Century series
- Indian history trilogy
- Island series
- Modern East series
- Princess series

Grierson, Francis Durham
- Commissaire Patras series
- Inspector George Muir series
- Inspector Sims and Professor Wells series
- Richard Furling series
- Superintendent Andrew Ash series

Griffin, John
- Richard Raven series

Griffin, Pauline Margaret
- Star commandos series
- Time war series
- Witch World series

Griffin, Peter
- Ernest Hemingway series

Griffin, Robert J
- Coopersmith series

Griffin, W E B
- Badge of honor series
- Brotherhood of war series
- Corps series

Griffith, George Chetwynd
- Romanoff series

Griffith, Helen Sherman
- Letty series
- Virginia series

Griffith-Jones, George Chetwynd
see **Griffith, George**

Griffiths, Ella
- Rudolph and Karsten Nilsen series

Griffiths, John
- Griff and Tommy series

Griffiths, Vivien
- My class series

Grigson, Geoffrey
- Shapes and stories series

Grigson, Jane
- Shapes and stories series

Grimble, Arthur
- Gilbert and Ellice Islands series

Grimes, Frances Harley
- Sweet savage sophomore year series

Grimes, Martha
- Inspector Richard Jury series

Grimm, Geraldine
- King Goblin series

Grimshaw, Nigel
- Wildkeepers series

Grimwade, Peter
- Doctor Who series

Grindal, Richard
see **Grayson, Richard**

Grinnell, David
see also **Wollheim, Donald Allen**
- Destiny series

Grinnell, George Bird
- Jack Danvers series

Gripe, Maria
- Elvis Karlsson series
- Hugo and Josephine trilogy
- Julia series

Griswold, Francis
- Carolina series

Griswold, George
see also **Dean, Robert George**
- Mister Groode series

Griswold, Latta
- Deering series

Groening, Matt
- Life in hell series

Groner, Augusta
- Joe Muller series

Groom, Arthur John Pelham
see **Groom, Pelham**

Groom, Pelham
- Peter Mohune series

Groot, J Morgan de
see **Morgan de Groot, J**

Gross, Edward
Conclusion
V series (16)
New beginning
V series (16)
Superman and Spider-Man
Superman series (7)
They're back
V series (16)

Gross, Joel
- Rachel series

Gross, Michael
see **Devon, D G**

Grossman, Alfred
- Marie series

Grossman, Gary Howard
Superman, serial to cereal
Superman series (7)

Grossman, Nancy Livright
- Dutch Mill Stable series

Grossmith, George
- Nobody series

Groten, Dallas
- Winning series

Grove, Frederick Philip
- Canadian prairie series
- Dude McQuint series

Grove, Harriet Pyne
- Adventurous Allens series
- Ann Sterling series
- Betty Lee series
- Greycliff girls series
- Merilyn Forrester series

Grove, Marjorie
- Maxine Reynolds series

Grover, Marshall
see also **Malloy, Lester; McCoy, Marshall**
- Bleak Creek series
- Larry and Stretch series
- Nevada Jim series

Groves, Seli
- How in the world series

Grubb, Jeff
- Finder's stone trilogy
- Marvel superheroes adventure gamebooks series

Gruber, Frank
- Historical Western series
- Johnny Fletcher and Sam Cragg series
- Otis Beagle series
- Simon Lash series
- Wells Fargo series
- William Clarke Quantrell series

Gruelle, Johnny
- Mister Twee Deedle series
- Raggedy Ann series
- Raggedy Ann's songs series

Grushkin, Edward
Invincible Doc Savage
Doc Savage series (183)

Guareschi, Giovanni
- Don Camillo series

Gudmundson, Shirley M
- Ebbie series

Guenter, C H
- Robert Urban series

Guerin, Judith
- Lisa Thomas series

Guild, Nicholas
- Ray Guinness series

Guillemin, Anne
- Kennedys abroad series

Guillot, Rene
- Grichka series

Guin, Ursula Kroeber le
see **Le Guin, Ursula Kroeber**

Guinness, Maurice
see **Gayle, Newton**

Guisewhite, Cathy
- Cathy series

Gulbranssen, Trygve
- Bjorndal family series

Gulick, Bill
- Junior Trail Blazers series
- Northwest destiny trilogy

Gulik, Robert van
- Judge Dee series

Gulliver, Captain
- Lilliput series

Gulliver, Lemuel
- Lemuel Gulliver series

Gulliver, Lemuel, junior
- Lilliput series

Gunby Hadath, Florence
see **Hadath, Florence Gunby**

Gunby Hadath, John Edward
see **Hadath, John Edward Gunby**

Gunn, Aeneas, *Mrs*
see **Gunn, Jeannie**

Gunn, Jeannie
- Never-Never series

Gunn, John
- Andrew Blake series
- Peter Kent series

Gunn, Neil Miller
- Young Art and old Hector series

Gunn, Tom
- Sheriff Blue Steele series

Gunn, Victor
see also **Gray, Berkeley**
- Chief Inspector Bill Cromwell series

Gunnarsson, Gunar
- Ships in the sky series

Gunnarsson, Thorarinn
- Dragons series
- Song series
- Starwolves series

Gunning, Sally
- Peter Bartholomew series

Gunson, Jonathan
- Space knight series

Gunter, Archibald Clavering
- Doctor Burton series
- Mister Barnes series
- Princess of Paris series
- Susan Turnbull series

Gunther, Karl H
see **Guenter, C H**

Gurelle, Andrew
- Dick Tracy series

Gurney, Antoinette
see **Chaffee, Allen**

Gurney, David
- Conjurers series

Gurney, Gene
- Kingdoms series
- Private pilot's series

Guth, Paul
- Innocent series

Guthridge, George
- Time machine series

Guthrie, Alfred Bertram
- Settlement of the American West series
- Sheriff Chick Charleston and Jason Beard series

Guthrie, Tyrone
- Shakespearean festival in Canada series

Gutman, Bill
- At bat series
- Go for it series
- Going for it series
- Modern superstars series
- New breed heroes series
- Smitty series
- Start right and play well series

Gutman, Claude
- Empty house trilogy

Gutteridge, Lindsay
- Mathew Dilke series

Guy, Rosa
- Edith Jackson series
- Imamu Jones series

Gydal, Monica
- Olly sees it through series

Gygax, Gary
- Gord the Rogue series
- Greyhawk series
- Sagard the Barbarian series

Gynell, Donna
- Arthur trilogy

H

H, T E
see **Hook, Theodore Edward**

Haar, Jaap ter
- Judy series

Haas, Ben
see also **Benteen, John; Douglas, Thorne; Meade, Richard**
- Chandler family series

Haas, Dorothy
- Peanut Butter and Jilly series

Habberton, John
- Budge and Toddie series

Habe, Hans
- Occupied Germany series

Haber, Carol Chase
- Your child series

Your one-year-old
Your child series (1)

Haber, Karen
- Mutant series
- Universe series

Hackett, John
- World War Three series

Hackforth-Jones, Gilbert
- Commander Wally Phipps-Mangot series
- Green sailors series
- Joe Garton series
- Paul Dexter series
- Submarine Service series

Hackney, Alan
- Stanley Windrush series

Hadath, Florence Gunby
- Pamela series

Hadath, Gunby
see **Hadath, John Edward Gunby**

Hadath, John Edward Gunby
- Sparrow series

Haddad, Carolyn A
- David Haham series

Hader, Berta
- Willow Hill series

Hader, Elmer
- Willow Hill series

Hadfield, Alice Mary
- Williver family series

Hadley, J B
- Point Team series

Hadley, Joan
- Theo Bloomer series

Haedrich, Marcel
- Belle series

Hagan, Chet
- Dewey annals series

Hagan, Patricia
- Coltrane series

Hagberg, David
see also **Flannery, Sean**
- Flash Gordon series

Hagen, Miriam Ann
- Hortense Clinton series

Hager, Jean
- Mitch Bushyhead series

Haggard, Henry Rider
- Allan Quatermain series
- Eric Brighteyes series
- Holy flower trilogy
- King Solomon's mines series
- Morning Star series
- Salvation Army series
- She series
- Umslopogaas series
- Zulu series

Haggard, Lilias Rider
- Norfolk life series

Haggard, Paul
see also **Longstreet, Stephen**
- Mike Warlock series

Haggard, William
- Colonel Charles Russell series
- Paul Martiny series
- William Wilberforce Smith series

Hahn, Emily
- Francie series

Haiblum, Isidore
- Gunjer series
- Mutants series
- Siscoe and Block series

Haig, Alec
- Alec Haig series

Haig-Brown, Roderic Langmere
- Don Morgan series

Haigh, Richard
see also **Axler, James; Darke, James; Fraser, Mary; James, Laurence; Marvin, James W; May, Jonathan; McPhee, James; Netzen, Klaus; Nolan, Christopher; Norman, Mick**
- Farm series

Haigh, Sheila
- Little gymnast series
- Watch for series

Hailey, Arthur
- Airport series

Haines, Alice Calhoun
- According to grandma series
- Dudley Graham series

Haining, Peter
Doctor Who, a celebration
Doctor Who series (162)
Doctor Who file
Doctor Who series (162)
Doctor Who, twenty five glorious years

Doctor Who series (162)
Dracula centneary book
Dracula series (26)
Dracula scrapbook
Dracula series (26)
On call with Doctor Finlay
Doctor Finlay series (2)
Sherlock Holmes scrapbook
Sherlock Holmes series (10)
Time-traveller's guide
Doctor Who series (162)
Haire-Sargeant, Lin
H
Wuthering Heights series (3)
Hakansson, Gunvor
• Pomander series
Halam, Ann
• Inland trilogy
Haldeman, Charles
• Joseph's Landing series
Haldeman, Jack Carroll
• Bill, the galactic hero series
• Star trek originals sequels series
Haldeman, Joe
• Marianne O'Hara series
• Star trek originals sequels series
Hale, Christopher
• Lieutenant Bill French series
Hale, Edgar
• Inspector Michael Regan series
• Montague Migglewade series
Hale, Edward Everett
• Family flight series
Hale, F J
• After the spell wars series
Hale, Helen
• Dale Evans series
Hale, Kathleen
• Henrietta series
• Orlando series
Hale, Lucretia Peabody
• Peterkin series
Hale, Susan
• Family flight series
• Ronnie Smithers series
Hale, Sylvia
• Caroline series
Hales, Alfred Greenwood
• McGlusky series
Haley, Alex
• Roots series
Haley, Gail Einhart
• Jack series
• Round stories series
Haley, George Elvey
• Cormorant series
Haliburton, Thomas Chandler
• Sam Slick series
Halkin, John
• Slither trilogy
Hall, Adam
see also **Black, Mansell; Dudley-Smith, Trevor; Rattray, Simon; Trevor, Elleston**
• Quiller series
Hall, Angus
• Devilday series
• Dracula series
Hall, Austin
• Blind spot series
Hall, Aylmer
• K.F. series
Hall, Dawn Langley
see **Hall, Gordon Langley**
Hall, Eliza Calvert
• Aunt Jane series
Hall, Emily
• Hall sisters series
Hall, Gordon Langley
• Peter Jumping Horse series
Hall, Helen
• Hall sisters series
Hall, James Norman
• Bounty trilogy
Hall, James W
• Thorn series
Hall, Lynn
• Dagmar Schultz series
• Dragon series
• Zelda Hammersmith series
Hall, Malcolm
• Headlines series
Hall, Margaret Helen
see **Mace, Helen**
Hall, Margery
• Star Island trilogy
Hall, Mark
• Sally and Jake series
Titus Bear goes to the beach
Titus Bear series (2)
Hall, Mary Bowen
• Emma Chizzit series
Hall, Oakley
see also **Manor, Jason**
• Legends west trilogy
Hall, Parnell
• Stanley Hastings series
Hall, Patrick
• Harry Thomas trilogy
Hall, Penny
• Miners series
Hall, Richard
• Patrick Costello series
Hall, Robert Lee
• Sherlock Holmes sequels series
Hall, Rodney
• Yandilli trilogy
Hall, Stuart
• Bikie series
Hall, Trevor Henry
• Sherlock Holmes literary studies series
Hall, Willis
• Antelope Company trilogy
• Doctor Jekyll sequels series
• Henry Hollins series
• Megabot series
• Worzel Gummidge series
Hall, Winifred Constance
see **Mallory, Clare**
Hallahan, William Henry
• Charley Brewer series
Hallard, Peter
see also **Catherall, Arthur**
• Con and Ginty series
Halleran, Tucker
• Cam Maccardle series
Hallett, Phyllis
• Carlisle family series
Halliburton, Richard
• Book of marvels series
• Famous adventures series
• Royal adventures series
Halliday, Brett
see also **Baker, Asa; Blood, Matthew; Davis, Don; Dresser, Davis**
• Jerry Burke series
• Michael Shayne series
• Mike Shayne stories series
Halliday, Dorothy
see **Dunnett, Dorothy**
Halliday, Fred
• Stanley Delphond series
Halliday, Michael
see also **Ashe, Gordon; Creasey, John; Deane, Norman; Frazer, Robert Caine; Marric, J J; Morton, Anthony; York, Jeremy**
• Doctor Emmanuel Cellini series
• Martin and Richard Fane series
Halliwell, Leslie
• Sherlock Holmes sequels series
Hallock, Rusty
• Find your fate: Jem series
Hallowell, Tommy
• Alden All Stars series
• Varsity coach series
Halls Johnson, Lissa
see **Johnson, Lissa Halls**
Halsey, Rena Isabelle
• Nathalie Page series
Halstead, John
• Inspector Todd series
Halter, Marek
• Jewish family series
Ham, Bob
• Overload series
Hambledon, Phyllis
• Inspector Tubby Hall series
Hambly, Barbara
• Beauty and the Beast trilogy
• Darwath trilogy
• Dragonsbane series
• Star trek series
• Sun Wolf series
• Sun-cross series
• Windrose series
Hamill, Edson T
• Joe Ryker series
Hamill, Pete
• Sam Briscoe series
Hamilton, Adam
• Peacemaker series
Hamilton, Alexandra
• Nefertiti trilogy
Hamilton, Bob
• Gene Autry series
Hamilton, Charles
see also **Clifford, Martin; Richards, Frank; Richards, Hilda**
Adventures of Herlock Sholmes
Sherlock Holmes series (10)
Hamilton, Cosmo
• Beau Brummell series
• Scandal series
Hamilton, Donald
• Matt Helm series
Hamilton, Edmond
• Captain Future series
• Interstellar Patrol series
• John Gordon series
• Starwolf trilogy
Hamilton, Elaine
• Inspector Reynolds series
Hamilton, Elizabeth
• Irish childhood series
Hamilton, Esme
• Speedy series
Hamilton, Frederic
• P J Davenant series
• Vanished pomps of yesterday series
Hamilton, Henrietta
• Johnny and Sally Heldar series
Hamilton, Ian Sydney
• Pete Heysen series
Hamilton, Julia
see also **Fitzgerald, Julia; Watson, Julia**
• Habsburg series
Hamilton, Mary
• Robert Erskine series
Hamilton, Nigel
• Montgomery of Alamein trilogy
Hamilton, Patrick
• Ernest Ralph Gorse series
• Twenty thousand streets under the sky series
Hamilton, Virginia
• Dies Drear series
• Jahdu series
• Justice trilogy
Hamley, Dennis
• Hare's choice trilogy
Hamlin, Myra Sawyer
• Nan series
Hammand, Norman Bentley
• Sir Nicholas Mountry series
Hammel, Eric Maxwell
• Guadalcanal series
• Khe Sanh series
Hammett, Dashiell
• Continental Op series
• Sam Spade series
• Secret Agent X-9 series
Hammond, Gerald
see also **Douglas, Arthur**
• Beau Pepys series
• Captain John Cunningham series
• Keith Calder series
• Simon Parbitter series
Hammond, Ray
• Bobby series
Hammond, William Alexander
• Lal series
Hammond-Innes, Ralph
see **Innes, Hammond**
Hamner, Earl
• Spencer family series
Hamnett, Nana
• Laughing torso series
Hamovitch, Eric
Selling out
Brian Mulroney series (2)
Hampton, Bill
• Choose your own adventure series
Hampton, Luann
• Choose your own adventure series
Hamre, Leif
• Peter Hovden series
Hamsa, Bobbie
• Far-fetched pets series
Hamsun, Knut
• Benoni series
• Edevart and August series
• Segelfoss Town series
Han, Suyin
• Crippled tree series
Hancock, Harrie Irving
• Conquest of the United States series
• Dave Darrin series
• Motor Boat Club series
• Uncle Sam's boys series
• Young engineers series
Hancock, Niel
• Circle of light series
• Wilderness of four series
• Windameir circle series
Hand, Stephen
• Fighting fantasy gamebook series
Handford, Martin
• Wally series
Handford, Nourma
• Carcoola series
Handl, Irene
• Benoir family series
Handler, David
• Danny Levine series
• Stewart Hoag series
Hands, Hargrave
• Look and see series
Hanff, Helene
• American in London series
Hankins, Robert Maxwell
• Lonesome River series
Hankinson, Charles James
see **Holland, Clive**
Hanley, James
• Furys chronicle series
Hann, Dorothy Owen
• Brownie series
• Peg series
• Ronnie series
Hannah, Barry
• Harry Monroe series
Hannay, James Owen
see **Birmingham, George A**
Hannum, Alberta
• Desert trading post series
Hanrahan, Barbara
• Eucalyptus series
Hanratty, Peter
• Arthur series
Hanscombe, Gillian
• Lesbian series
Hansen, Derek
• Lunch series
Hansen, Gwen
• Secret of the Unicorn Queen series
Hansen, Joseph
• Dave Brandstetter series
Hansen, Joyce
• Doris series
Hansen, Karl
• Hybrid universe series
Hansford Johnson, Pamela
see **Johnson, Pamela Hansford**
Hanshew, Hazel Phillips
• Hamilton Cleek series
Hanshew, Mary E
• Hamilton Cleek series
Hanshew, Thomas W
• Hamilton Cleek series
Hanson, Joseph Mills
• Among the Sioux series
Hanson, Lawrence
• Boy and man series
Hanson, Victor Joseph
see also **Potter, Jay Hill**
• Amos Crowle series
• Sexton Blake series
Hanson, Virginia
• Adam Drew and Katherine Cornish series
Harbage, Alfred
see **Kyd, Thomas**
Harben, William Nathaniel
• Georgians series
Harbinson, Robert
• Ulster series
Harbinson, William Allen
• Projekt Saucer series
Harcourt, Palma
see **Penn, John**
Hard, Walter
• Vermont series
Hardcastle, Michael
• Bank Vale United series
• Horse series
• Kenny Rider series
• Mark Fox series
• Mascot series
• Racing series
• Scorton Rovers series
• Steve and Anna series
• Tony and Jay series
Hardie, David William Ferguson
• Inspector Elwyn Hughes series
Hardin, J D
• Raider and Doc series
• Raider series
Hardin, John W
• Neal Fargo series
Harding, Dolores Charlotte Frederica
• Pendleton series
Harding, Gilbert
• Along my line series
Harding, Ian
• Assault troop series
Harding, Richard
• Outrider series
Hardinge, George
see **Milner, George**
Hardinge, Rex
• Sexton Blake series
Hardison, Osborne Bennett
• Modern culture trilogy
Hardman, Diana
• Windylaw Farm series
Hardwick, John Michael Drinkrow
see **Hardwick, Michael**
Hardwick, Michael
• Bergerac series
• Cedar tree trilogy
• Sherlock Holmes drama series
• Sherlock Holmes sequels series
• Tenko series
• Thomas Rodolfo Rackstraw series
• Upstairs, downstairs series
Hardwick, Mollie
• Atkinson family series
• Doran Fairweather series
• Duchess of Duke Street series
• Juliet Bravo series
• Sherlock Holmes drama series
• Sherlock Holmes sequels series
• Upstairs, downstairs series
Hardy, Adam
see also **Akers, Alan Burt; Blake, Ken; Bulmer, Kenneth; Frazier, Arthur; Krauss, Bruno; Silver, Richard; Zetford, Tully**
• George Abercrombie Fox series
• Strike Force Falklands series
Hardy, Alice Dale
• Flyaways series
• Riddle Club series
Hardy, Arthur Steffens
• Sexton Blake series
Hardy, Dorothy May
• Christabel series
Hardy, Frank
• Great Australian legends series
Hardy, Jonathan Gathorne-
see **Gathorne-Hardy, Jonathan**
Hardy, Lindsay
• Gregory Keen series
Hardy, Lyndon
• Arcadia trilogy
Hardy, Philip
• Smith Minor series
Hardy, Thomas
• Novels of character and environment series
• Novels of ingenuity series
• Romances and fantasies series
Hardy, William George
• Roman trilogy
Hare, Cyril
• Francis Pettigrew series
• Inspector Mallett series
Harewood, Jocelyn
• Peregrine Merritt series
Hargreaves, Eustace Hamilton Ian Stewart-
see **Stewart-Hargreaves, Eustace Hamilton Ian**
Hargreaves, Roger
• Hippo, Potto and Mouse series
Haring, Scott D
• Car wars adventure gamebook series
Harker, Lizzie Allen
• Fiammetta series
• Mister Wycherly series
Harkin, Janet Quin-
see **Quin-Harkin, Janet**
Harkins, Peter
see **Adams, Andy**
Harknett, Terry
see also **Gilman, George G; Hedges, Joseph; James, William M; Pike, Charles R; Stone, Thomas H**
• Stephen Wayne series
• Superintendent John Crown series
Harkon, Franz
• Space Express Company series
Harling, Robert
• Sailor series
Harlow, Robert
• Royal Murdoch series
Harman, Humphrey
• African tales series
Harman, Neal
• Protection Limited series
Harnett, Cynthia
• Fifteenth century London series
Harold, Clive
see also **Bishop, Samuel P; Hutson, Shaun; Taylor, Frank**
• Uninvited trilogy
Harper, Anita
• Daddy and mummy series

Harper, Charles George
• Pickwick series
Harper, Harry
• Dossier series
Harper, Henry George
see **G, G**
Harper, Stephen
• Healers series
Harper, Tara K
• Wolfwalker series
Harper, Theodore Acland
• Siberian series
Harper, Winifred
• Siberian series
Harraden, Beatrice
• Patuffa series
Harragan, Steve
• Steve Harragan series
Harrell, Andrew
• Sam Shank series
Harrell, Janice
• Andie and the boys series
• In crowd series
• Two by two series
• West Mount High trilogy
Harrer, Heinrich
• Tibet series
Harriman, Karl Edwin
• Girl series
Harrington, Emma
• Women of the West series
Harrington, Joseph
• Lieutenant Frank Kerrigan series
Harrington, William
• Columbo series
Harris, Bernice
• Purslane series
Harris, Brian
World War III
World War Three series (3)
Harris, Catherine
• Marsham family series
Harris, Charlaine
• Aurora Teagarden series
Harris, Christie
• Mouse Woman series
• Totem series
• Trouble series
Harris, Colver
• Timothy Fowler series
Harris, Corra
• Circuit rider series
Harris, Deborah Turner
• Adept trilogy
• Mages of Garillon trilogy
Harris, Elsie May
• John and Jennifer series
Harris, Geraldine
• Seven citadels series
Harris, Herbert
• Hawaii Five-O series
Harris, Jean
• Two worlds series
Harris, Joel Chandler
• Aaron series
• Mister Thimblefinger series
• Tales of Uncle Remus series
• Uncle Remus series
Harris, John
see also **Hebden, Mark; Hennessy, Max**
• Ira Penaluna trilogy
• Martin Falconer series
Harris, John Beynon
see **Wyndham, John**
Harris, Larry
• Masked Rider and Blue Hawk series
Harris, Larry Mark
Pickled poodles
John Joseph Malone series (14)
Harris, Laurence Mark
see **Janifer, Laurence Mark**
Harris, Lavinia
• Computer detectives series
Harris, Leon
• Maurice the moose series
Harris, Marilyn
• Eden family series
Harris, Marion
• Soldiers and officers series
Harris, Mark
Doctor Who technical manual
Doctor Who series (162)
• Henry W Wiggen series
• Lee Youngdahl series
Harris, Mollie
• Kind of magic series
Harris, Ray
• Turkey series
Harris, Raymond
Strange case of Doctor Jekyll and Mister Hyde
Doctor Jekyll series (1)
Harris, Robie H
• Rosie series
Harris, Robin
see also **Bright, Sarah; Shine, Deborah; Slier, Debby**
• Hello Kitty series
Harris, Rosemary
• Egyptian trilogy
• Orion series
Harris, Ruth Elwin
• Quantocks quartet
Harris, Timothy Hyde
• Tom Kyd series
Harris, Walter
• New Avengers series
Harris, Wilson
• Agent of personality quartet
• Black Marsden series
• Civilizations quartet
• Da Silva series
• Guiana series
Harrison, C William
• Masked Rider and Blue Hawk series
Harrison, Chip
• Leo Haig series
Harrison, Claire
• Tamara series
Harrison, Edwin
• Sexton Blake series
Harrison, Elizabeth
• Central London Hospital series
Harrison, Harry
• Bill, the galactic hero series
• Brion Brandd series
• Eden trilogy
• Jason Din Alt series
• Jim Di Griz series
• To the stars trilogy
• Tony Hawkin series
Harrison, Mary Saint Leger
see **Malet, Lucas**
Harrison, Michael
see also **Downes, Quentin**
• Life of Sherlock Holmes series
• London archaeology series
• Monsieur C Auguste Dupin series
• Sherlock Holmes sequels series
• Vernal equinox series
Harrison, Michael John
• Viriconium series
Harrison, Ray
• Sergeant Joseph Bragg and Constable James Morton series
Harrison, Richard
• Chief Inspector William Bastion series
Harrison, Rosina
• Rose series
Harrison, Sarah
• Flowers series
• Laura from Lark Rise series
Harrison, Sue
• Mother earth trilogy
Harrod-Eagles, Cynthia
• Morland family series
Harry, Myriam
• Jerusalem series
Hart, Alison
• Girls in trouble series
Hart, Anne
Life and time of Miss Jane Marple
Miss Jane Marple series (14)
Life and times of Hercule Poirot
Hercule Poirot series (38)
Hart, Bruce
• Jessie Walters and Michael Skye series
Hart, Carole
• Jessie Walters and Michael Skye series
Hart, Carolyn Gimpel
• Annie Laurance and Max Darling series
• Henrietta O'Dwyer Collins series
Hart, Catherine
• Kathleen Hartly Taylor and Reed Taylor series
Hart, Ellen
• Jane Lawless series
Hart, John
see also **Dancer, J B**
Hart, Jon
see also **Harvey, John Barton; Ryder, Thom**
• Mercenaries series
Hart, Matthew S
• Cody's law series
Hart, Roy
• Detective Superintendent Roper series
Hart, Sharon M
• Animal Rescue Farm series
Hart, Susanne
• African wildlife series
Hart, Sydney
• British migrant series
Hart, Ted
• Thriller series
Hart, William Surrey
• Injun and Whitey series
Hart-Davis, Duff
• Sam Sholto series
Harte, Bryce
• Slate Creed series
Harthern, Ernest
• Palestine home series
Hartland, Michael
• David Nairn series
Hartley, Leslie Poles
• Eustace and Hilda Cherrington trilogy
• Richard Mardick series
Hartman, Dane
• Dirty Harry Callahan series
Hartmann, Michael
• Ben Dryden series
Hartwell, David Geddes
• Dark descent trilogy
Harvester, Simon
see also **Gibbs, Henry**
• Asia in turmoil series
• Dorian Silk series
• Heron Murmur series
• Malcolm Kenton series
• Roger Fleming series
Harvey, Andrew
• Burning houses series
Harvey, Brett
• My prairie series
Harvey, Caroline
• Legacy of love trilogy
Harvey, David
Song of Middle Earth
Middle Earth series (5)
Harvey, Jack
• Tony Woolrich series
Harvey, James Neal
• Ben Tolliver series
Harvey, John Barton
see also **Dancer, J B; Hart, Jon; James, William M; McLahlen, John J; Ryder, Thom; Sandon, J D**
• Avenging Angel series
• Duty free series
• Inspector Charlie Resnick series
• Scott Mitchell series
• Wes Hart series
Harvey, John Henry
see **Barrington, John**
Harvey, Jon M
• Cthulhu Mythos series
Harvey, Marianne
• Trevarvas family series
Harvey, Marion
• Graydon McKelvie series
Harvey, William Fryer
• Athelstan Digby series
Harwood, John
Tarzan encyclopedia
Tarzan series (24)
Hasek, Jaroslav
• Schweik series
Haskell, Helen Eggleston
• Katrinka series
Haskins, Jim
• Count your way series
Hassett, Margaret
• Miss Dinwiddie series
Hastings, Beverly
• Don't series
Hastings, Eileen
• Rufus and Christopher series
Hastings, Ian
• Rufus and Christopher series
Hastings, Macdonald
• Eagle Special Investigator series
• Montague Cork series
Hastings, Michael
• Turn of the screw series
Hastings, Phyllis
• London quartet
• Sussex trilogy
Hastings, Valerie
• Jill series
• Jo series
• Wendy and Jinx series
Haswell, Peter
• Humbold series
Hatch, Alden
• Smoky sea series
Hatch, Richard Warren
• Bradfords series
• Curious lobster series
Hatcher, Jo
• Gasworks Alley Gang series
Hatcher, Robin Lee
• Spring Haven series
• Women West series
Hatfield, John
• Quintilian series
Hattie, Aunt
see also **Baker, Harriette Newell Baker; Leslie, Madeline**
• Woodlawn series
Hatton, Charles
• Dixon of Dock Green series
• Paul Temple series
Haubold, Cleve
• Sherlock Holmes drama series
Haugaard, Erik Christian
• Hakon and Helga series
• Oliver Cutter series
Haughey, Thomas Brace
• Geoffrey Weston series
Haughton, Rosemary
• Christian year series
• Good news of Jesus series
Hauptman, Laurence Marc
• Iroquois series
Hauptmann, Tatjana
• Petronella and Peregrine Pig series
Hausman, Gerald
• Meditations series
Hautzig, Esther Rudomin
• Four languages series
Hauxwell, Hannah
• Daleswoman series
Havard, Aline
• Lucy Gordon series
• Westward series
Haverfield, Eleanor Luisa
• Our vow series
Havill, Juanita
• Jamaica series
• Leona series
Havill, Steven F
• Bill Gastner series
Havilton, Jeffrey
• George series
• Study Thirteen series
Hawes, Louise
• Nelson Malone series
Hawk, Alex
see also **Garfield, Brian Wynne**
• Elfego O'Reilly series
Hawk, John
• Mortimer Sark series
Hawke, Simon
see also **Masters, J D; Yermakov, Nicholas**
• Batman series
• Friday the thirteenth series
• Predator series
• Psychodrome series
• Timewars series
• Wizard series
Hawker, James Collins
• Early experiences series
Hawker, Ruth Marjorie
• Us three series
Hawkes, Jacquetta
• English journey series
Hawkes, John
• Blood oranges trilogy
Hawkes, Robert
• NARC series
Hawkes, Zachary
see also **Riefe, A R; Riefe, Alan; Riefe, Barbara**
• Fancy Hatch series
Hawkesworth, John
• Upstairs, downstairs series
Hawkey, Raymond
• Presidential trilogy
Hawkins, Anthony Hope
see **Hope, Anthony**
Hawkins, Clint
• Saddletramp series
Hawkins, Jack
• Chopper series
Hawkins, Laura
• Riverview series
Hawkins, Ward
• Harry Borg series
Hawley, Mabel C
• Four Little Blossoms series
Haworth, Betty
see **Haworth, Elizabeth**
Haworth, Elizabeth
• Howton trilogy
Hawthorn, Mike
• Carlotti series
Hawthorne, Julian
• Inspector Byrnes series
Hawthorne, Nathaniel
• Hester Prynne series
• Wonder book series
Hawton, Hector
• Asmun Hill series
• Colonel Max Masterson series
Haxton, Josephine
see **Douglas, Ellen**
Hay, Dean
• Tisi series
Hay, Ian
• First hundred thousand series
Hay, James
• Jefferson Hastings series
Hay, John
• Breadwinners series
Hay, Lindsay Fitzgerald
• Archibald Beldrum and Nigel Blair series
Haycraft, John
• Babel series
Hayden, Karen
• Star trek fan series
Hayes, Alfred
• Love trilogy
Hayes, Barbara
• Town mouse and country mouse series
Hayes, Clair Wallace
see also **Drake, Robert L**
• Boy allies of the army series
• Boy troopers series
Hayes, Daniel
• Tyler McAllister series
Hayes, Douglas
• History of a selfish man series
Hayes, Frederick William
• Gwynett trilogy
Hayes, Mike
• Prickle Farm series
Hayes, Ralph Eugene
• Agent for Cominsec series
• Check Force series
• John Yard series
• Mark Stoner series
• O'Brien, Buffalo Hunter series
Hayes, Richard
• Secret army series
Hayes, Ronald Chetwynd-
see **Chetwynd-Hayes, Ronald**
Hayes, William Edward
• Arthur Halstead series
Hayle, Felicity
• Our brother Nick series
Hayles, Brian
• Archers of Ambridge series
• Doctor Who series
Haymon, Sylvia T
• East Anglian childhood series
• Inspector Ben Jurnet series
Haynes, Ambrose
• Greta series
• Penny series
• Peter series
Haynes, Annie
• Inspector Furnival series
• Inspector Stoddart series
Haynes, Betsy
• Fabulous Five series
• Fabulous Five super series
• Fifteen series
• Taffy Sinclair series
• Twilight series
Haynes, James
• Twilight series
Hays, Lee
• Columbo series
• Harry Orwell series
Hayter, Adrian
• Sheila series
Haythorne, John
• Oliver Mandrake series
Hayward, William Stephens
• Lady detective series
Haywood, Carolyn
• Betsy series
• Eddie Wilson series
• Holiday series
• Penny series
• Santa Claus series
Hazel, Paul
• Finnbranch trilogy
Hazelton, Nika
• Raggedy Ann's household series
Hazen, Barbara Shook
• Raggedy Ann series
Head, Lee
• Lexey Jane Pelazoni series
Head, Matthew
• Doctor Mary Finney series

Hiller, Neil W
- Pick-a-path series

Hillerman, Tony
- Lieutenant Joe Leaphorn series
- Sergeant Jim Chee series

Hillert, Margaret
- Dear Dragon series

Hilliard, Alec Rowley
- Judge Manfred series

Hilliard, Noel
- Netta and Paul tetralogy

Hillier, Fred
- Outhouse series

Hillyard, Mary Dorothea
- Minikin series
- Peggy series

Hilton, Alec
see also **Fullerton, Alexander**
- Doctor Martin Lestrange series

Hilton, Jack
- English ways series

Hilton, James
- Mister Chips series

Hilton, John Buxton
- Inspector Thomas Brunt series
- Superintendent Simon Kenworthy series

Hilton, Joseph
see **Milton, Joseph**
President's agent
Bart Gould series (1)

Him, George
- Giant Alexander series

Himes, Chester
- Grave Digger Jones and Coffin Ed Johnson series
- Quality of hurt series

Himmel, Richard
- Johnny Maguire series

Himmelman, John
- Amanda series

Hinchcliffe, Philip
- Doctor Who series
- Sarah Jane Smith series

Hinckley, Helen
- Persia trilogy

Hincks, Cyril Malcolm
- Sexton Blake series

Hinde, Thomas
- Henlake series

Hindley, Judy
- Best of friends series

Hine, Alfred Blakelee
see also **Kirtland, G B**
- Bewitched series

Hine, Muriel
- April Panhasard series
- Clodagh Laidlaw series
- Jenny Rorke series

Hine, Sesyle Joslin
see **Joslin, Sesyle**

Hines, Anna Grossnickle
- Cassie Bowen series

Hinkemeyer, Michael Thomas
- Sheriff Emil Whippletree series

Hinnebusch, Paul
- In the Lord series
- Religious life series

Hinton, Charles Howard
- Flatland series

Hinton, Nigel
- Beaver Towers trilogy

Hinton, Perry
- Fantasy quest book series

Hinxman, Margaret
- Detective Inspector Ralph Brand series

Hinz, Christopher
- Paratwa trilogy

Hirsch, Gordon
Doctor Jekyll and Mister Hyde after one hundred years
Doctor Jekyll series (2)

Hirschfeld, Burt
- Aspen series
- Bonnie and Clyde series
- Dallas series
- Fire Island series
- General Hospital series

Hirschi, Ron
- Where animals live series

Hirschman, Edward
Tarzan at Mars' core
Tarzan series (24)

Hiscock, Eric Charles
- Under sail series
- Wanderer series

Hiser, Constance
- James and gang series

Hislop, John
- Soldier and gentleman series

Hissey, Jane
- Old Bear series

Hitchcock, Raymond
- Percy series

Hitchens, Bert
- Collins and McKechnie series

Hitchens, Dolores
see also **Olsen, D B**
- Collins and McKechnie series
- Jim Sader series
- John Farrel series

Hite, Shere
- Hite report series

Hitz, Demi
- Demi series

Hoag, Tami
- Rainbow chasers series

Hoare, Bob
see **Hoare, Robert John**

Hoare, Robert John
- Bobby of the Globe series

Hoban, Lillian
- Arthur series
- Best friends series
- Mister Pig series
- Robot series
- Silly Tilly series
- Stick-in-the-Mud Turtle series

Hoban, Phoebe
- Robot series

Hoban, Russell
- Arthur and Emma series
- Brute family series
- Captain Najork series
- Frances series
- Jim Hedgehog series
- Ponders series

Hoban, Tana
- I read series
- Is it series

Hobart, Alice Tisdale
- China series

Hobart, Donald Bayne
- Masked Rider and Blue Hawk series

Hobart, Robertson
see also **Armstrong, Raymond; Corrigan, Mark**
- Grant Vickery series

Hobbes, John Oliver
- Robert Orange series

Hobbs, Jack
- William McGonagall series

Hoberg, Marielis
- Heiner and Elsie series

Hobson, Hank
- Brad Ford series

Hobson, Polly
- Inspector Basil series

Hobson, Richmond Pearson
- Rancher series

Hoch, Edward Dentinger
- Carl Crader and Earl Jazine series
- Nick Velvet series
- Simon Ark series

Hocken, Sheila
- Emma series

Hocking, Anne
- Inspector William Austen series

Hocking, Joseph
- Great War, French Front series
- Great War, Greek front series
- Religious movements series
- Religious questions series

Hocking, Mary
- Fairley family trilogy
- Fleet Air Arm training series

Hodel, Michael P
- Sherlock Holmes sequels series

Hodgart, Matthew
- Lemuel Gulliver series

Hodge, Charles
- Jim Raine and Bob Wincourt series

Hodge, Jane Aiken
- Purchis family series

Hodgell, Patricia Christine
- Kencyrath series

Hodges, Arthur
- Blake family series

Hodges, Cyril Walter
- King Alfred series

Hodges, Doris Marjorie
see **Hunt, Charlotte**

Hodges, Margaret
- Charley series
- Joshua Cobb series

Hodgetts, Sheila
- Sleepy time tales series

Hodgins, Eric
- Blandings series

Hodgman, Ann
- Choose your own adventure series
- Fifth grade monsters series
- Lunchroom series
- Stinky Stanley series

Hodgson, William Hope
- Carnacki series
- Glen Carrig trilogy

Hodson, James Lansdale
- Harvest in the north series

Hoff, Benjamin
- Taoist Winnie-the-Pooh series

Hoff, Carol
- Johnny Texas series

Hoff, Harry Summerfield
see also **Cooper, William**
- Three marriages series

Hoff, Mary
- Our endangered planet series

Hoff, Syd
- Henrietta series

Hoffman, Lee
see **York, Georgia**

Hofmeyer, Hans
- Garibaldi series

Hofrichter, Paul
see also **Stivers, Dick; Winski, Norman**
- Roadblaster trilogy

Hogan, Inez
- Twins series

Hogan, James Patrick
- Minervan experiment series

Hogan, Ray
- Doomsday Marshal series
- Fortuna West series
- John Mosby series
- Shawn Starbuck series

Hogan, Robert Jasper
- G-Eight series
- Secret Six series
- Smoke Wade series

Hogarth, Ann
- Merry Muffin series
- Muffin book series
- Muffin series

Hogarth, Grace Allen
- Helen Hamilton series

Hogg, Garry
- Explorers trilogy
- Jonty series
- Kennedys abroad series
- Nessa and Lance series

Hogstrand, Olle
- Chief Inspector Lars Kollin series

Hogue, Oliver
- Anzac series

Hoh, Diane
- Canby Hall series
- Cheerleaders series
- Chrystal Falls series
- Nightmare Hall series

Hohl, Joan
see also **Lorin, Amii**
- Flint Falcon series
- Sharp family trilogy
- Vanzant family trilogy
- Window trilogy

Holabird, Katharine
- Angelina Ballerina series
- Little mouse series

Holbrook, David
- Flesh wounds trilogy

Holden, Elizabeth Rhoda
see **Lawrence, Louise**

Holden, Genevieve
- Lieutenant Al White series

Holden, J Railton
- Spider Stockwell series

Holden, Matthew
- Squadron series

Holden, Philip
- Deer trilogy

Holden, Ursula
- Tin toys series

Holding, Elisabeth Sanxay
- Lieutenant Levy series

Holding, James
see **Queen, Ellery, Junior**

Holdstock, Robert
see also **Carlsen, Chris; Faulcon, Robert; Kirk, Richard**
- Bulman series
- Mythago series
- Other Edens series

Holgate, John
- Farm life series

Hollan, Linda
- Annie series

Holland, Clive
- Mousme series

Holland, Elizabeth
- House series

Holland, Isabelle
- Claire Aldington series

Holland, Julian
- Tottenham Hotspur Football Club series

Holland, Kevin Crossley-
see **Crossley-Holland, Kevin**

Holland, Marion
- Billy series

Holland, Muriel
- Mister Hare series
- Wizard Winkle series

Holland, Vyvyan
- Time remembered series

Hollands, Judith
- Ketchup sisters series

Holley, Helen
- Tessie Venable series

Holley, Marietta
- Betsey Bobbet series
- Samantha and Josiah Allen series

Holliday, Joe
- Dale of the Mounted series

Hollingsworth, Leonard
- Superintendent Adams series

Hollis, Christopher
- Robert Fossett trilogy

Hollis, Maurice Christopher
see **Hollis, Christopher**

Holloway, Stanley
- Albert and the lion series

Hollowood, Jane
- Maggie series

Holly, David Chauncey
- Chesapeke steamboats series

Holly, Joan Hunter
- Man from U.N.C.L.E. series

Holm, Jens K
- Kim the detective series

Holman, Felice
- Elisabeth series

Holman, Hugh
- Sheriff Macready series

Holmberg, Ake
- Tam Sventon series

Holme, Timothy
- Inspector Achille Peroni series

Holmes, Barbara Ware
- Charlotte Cheetham trilogy

Holmes, Bryan John
- Reaper series

Holmes, Gordon
see also **Tracy, Louis**
- Inspector Furneaux series

Holmes, Grant
see also **Fox, James M**
- Steve Harvester series

Holmes, H H
- Sister Ursula series

Holmes, John Eric
- Buck Rogers series
- Pellucidar series

Holmes, Marjorie
- Carly and Danny series

Holmes, Oliver Wendell
- Breakfast table trilogy
- Heredity series

Holmes, Robert
- Doctor Who scripts series
- Doctor Who series
- Walter Greenway series

Holmes, Wilfred Jay
see **Hudson, Alec**

Holroyd, Michael
- Bernard Shaw series
- Lytton Strachey series

Holt, Deben
- Roger Moore and the Crimefighters series

Holt, Emily Sarah
- Edward II series
- Mistress Margery series

Holt, Gavin
- Inspector Joel Saber series
- Professor Luther Bastion series
- Sherret York series

Holt, Henry
- Inspector Silver series
- Mike Logan series

Holt, Isabella
- Rampole family series

Holt, John Robert
see **Giles, Raymond**

Holt, Michael
- Doctor Who find your fate series

Doctor Who puzzle book
Doctor Who series (162)
- Doctor Who quiz book series

Holt, Tom
- Lucia Billson series
- Walled orchard series

Holt, Victoria
see **Carr, Philippa; Kellow, Kathleen; Plaidy, Jean**

Holt, William
- Unpacked series

Holton, Leonard
see also **Wibberley, Leonard**
- Father Joseph Bredder series

Holtsmark, Erling Bent
Tarzan and the classics
Tarzan series (24)
Tarzan and tradition
Tarzan series (24)

Holzer, Hans
- Amityville horror series
- Randy Knowles series

Home, Michael
see also **Bush, Christopher**
- Breckland series
- East Anglia seasons series
- John Benham series
- Zerzura series

Home-Gall, Edward Reginald
- Human Bat series

Home-Gall, William Benjamin
- Sexton Blake series

Homely Woman
see **Inchfawn, Fay**

Homer
- Trojan War series

Homes, Geoffrey
- Humphrey Campbell series
- Jose Manuel Madero series
- Robin Bishop series

Hone, Joseph
- Collected travels series
- Peter Marlow series

Honeyman, Brenda
- Edward III series

Honeyman, Eileen Elizabeth
see **Lane, Elizabeth**

Hong, James Cooper
Pool of radiance
Avatar trilogy (3)

Honig, Donald
- Jed McLane series

Hoobler, Thomas
- Hunters series

Hood, Evelyn
- Paisley series

Hood, Hugh
- New age series

Hood, Margaret Page
- Gil Donan series

Hood, Stephen
- Sexton Blake series

Hook, Theodore Edward
- Gilbert Gurney series

Hooke, Nina Warner
- Striplings trilogy

Hooker, Richard
- M.A.S.H. series

Hooks, William H
- Lion and Lamb series

Hooper, Kay
- Delaneys of Killaroo trilogy
- Delaneys, the untamed years, second trilogy
- Delaneys, the untamed years trilogy
- Gold class trilogy
- Hagen series
- Men of mysteries past series
- Once upon a time series
- Shamrock trilogy

Hooper, Muriel
- Amelia series

Hoover, Bessie Ray
- Flickinger series

Hoover, Helen
- Forest trilogy

Hoover, Helen Mary
- Morrow series

Hope, Alexander James Beresford
- Brandreths series

Hope, Anthony
- Rudolf Rassendyl series

Hope, Edward
- Alice in Wonderland parodies series

Hope, Jane
- Florence series
- Teaching series

Hope, Laura Lee
- Blythe girls series
- Bobbsey twins series
- Bunny Brown and his sister Sue series
- Make-believe stories series
- Moving picture girls series
- New Bobbsey twins series
- Outdoor girls series
- Six little bunkers series

Hope, Pam Zinnemann-
see **Zinnemann-Hope, Pam**

Hope, Stanton
- Sexton Blake series

Hope-Simpson, Jacynth
- Bishop of Kenelminster series

Hopf, Alice Lightner
see **Lightner, Alice Martha**

Hopgood, Alan
- Sports series

Hopkins, Kenneth
- Doctor William Blow and Professor Gideon Manciple series
- Gerry Lee series

Hopkins, Lee Bennett
- Mama series
- Mother Goose series

Hopkins, Nevil Monroe
- Mason Brant series

Hopkins, Robert Sydney
see **Rostand, Robert**

Hopkins, Stanley
- Peter Marrell series

Hopkins, William John
- Clammer trilogy
- Sandman series

Hoppner, Barbara Bartos-
see **Bartos-Hoppner, Barbara**

Hopson, William L
- Masked Rider and Blue Hawk series

Hopton, Ralph
- Bed manners series

Horgan, Paul
- Clerihews series
- Humble powers trilogy
- Mountain standard time trilogy
- Richard trilogy

Horler, Sydney
- Ace series
- Baron Veseloffsky series
- Brett Carstairs series
- Bunny Chipstead series
- Constable Meatyard series
- Emp series
- Gerald Lissendale series
- Martin Huish series
- Nighthawk series
- Paul Vivanti series
- Peter Scarlett series
- Robert Wynnton series
- Sebastian Quin series
- Sir Brian Fordinghame series
- Sir Charles Knightley series
- Sir Harker Bellamy series
- Strictly personal series
- Tiger Standish series

Hornberger, Richard
see **Hooker, Richard**

Horne, Donald
- Lucky country series
- New boy trilogy

Horne, Geoffrey
see **North, Gil**

Horner, Lance
- Falconhurst series
- Golden stud series

Hornibrook, Isabel
- Campfire Girls series
- Pemrose Lorry series

Hornig, Doug
- Loren Swift series
- Steven Kirk series

Hornsby, Wendy
- Maggie McGowan series

Hornung, Ernest William
- Raffles series

Visit from Raffles
Raffles series (18)

Horowitz, Anthony
- Groosham Grange series
- Nick and Tim Diamond series
- Old ones trilogy
- Robin of Sherwood series

Horowitz, Jordan
- Working hard series

Horrabin, James Francis
- Noah family series

Horseman, Elaine
- Hubbles series

Horst, Karl
see also **Lutz, Gunther; Williams, David**
- U-boat series

Horvat, Dilwyn
- Operation Titan series

Horwood, William
- Duncton chronicles series
- Wind in the willows series

Hosken, Clifford James Wheeler
see **Keverne, Richard**

Hoskins, Robert
- Master of the stars trilogy

Hossent, Harry
- Max Heald series

Hough, Charlotte
- Funny ones series

Hough, Henry Beetle
- Martha's Vineyard series

Hough, Richard Alexander
see also **Carter, Bruce**
- Archy Buller series
- World War II trilogy

Hough, Stanley Bennett
see also **Stanley, Bennett**
- Inspector Brentford series

Hougron, Jean
- Monsieur Lastin series

Hoult, Norah
- Augusta Hortense Carey series
- Holy Ireland series
- Monty Mallory series

Hourihane, Ursula
- Little Blue Engine series

House, Brant
- Secret Agent X series

Household, Geoffrey
- Raymond Ingelram series
- Roger Taine series

Houseman, John
- Unfinished business trilogy

Housman, Laurence
- Jingalo series
- Palace plays series

Houston, David
- Gods in a vortex series
- Swamp Thing series
- Tales of tomorrow series

Houston, Edwin James
- Pacific shipwreck series

How, Ruth W
- Friendly Farm series

Howard, Colin
see **Shaw, Howard**

Howard, Elizabeth Fitzgerald
- Chita series

Howard, Elizabeth Howard
- My name is Paris series

Howard, Francis Morton
- Happy Rascals series

Howard, Hartley
see also **Carmichael, Harry**
- Glenn Bowman series
- Philip Scott series

Howard, James Arch
- Steve Ashe series

Howard, John Wesley
- Easy Company series

Howard, Joseph
- Omen series

Howard, Keble
- Fast Lady and Gentleman series
- Smiths trilogy

Howard, Liz
- Elizabeth Fytton series

Howard, Mary
see **Edgar, Josephine**

Howard, Robert Ervin
- Black Vulmea series
- Bran Mak Morn trilogy
- Breckinridge Elkins series

Conan of Aquilonia
Conan series (17)
- Conan series
- Cormac Mac Art series

Cthulhu, the mythos and kindred horrors
Cthulhu Mythos series (17)
- El Borak trilogy
- Skull-Face series
- Solomon Kane series
- Tales of the Picts series

Howard, Tom
- Jack Reid series
- Sergeant Tom Howard series

Howard, Vechel
- Johnny Church series

Howarth, Trish
- Home and away series

Howatch, Susan
- Church of England series
- Van Zale family series

Howden Smith, Arthur Douglas
see **Smith, Arthur Douglas Howden**

Howe, Bea
- Childhood series

Howe, Deborah
- Bunnicula series

Howe, Doris
- Kootenay series

Howe, Imogen
- Twilight series

Howe, James
- Bunnicula series
- Ewok series
- Night monsters series
- Oz series
- Pinky and Rex series
- Sebastian Barth series

Howell, Christopher
- Worlds of power series

Howells, William Dean
- Altruria series
- Annie Kilburn series
- Mister and Mrs March series

Howes, Royce
- Captain Ben Lucias series

Howlett, Winston A
- Savage Empire series

Howson, John Michael
- Adventure Island story books

Hoyland, Rosemary
- Ethelbert series

Hoyle, Fred
- Andromeda series

Hoyle, Trevor
- Blake's Seven series
- Christian Queghan series

Hoyt, Eleanor
see **Brainerd, Eleanor Hoyt**

Hoyt, Richard
- James Burlane series
- John Denson series

Hubback, Edith Charlotte
see also **Brown, Edith Charlotte**
- Watsons series

Hubbard, Frank McKinney
see **Hubbard, Kin**

Hubbard, Kin
- Abe Martin series

Hubbard, Lafayette Ronald
- Mission earth series

Hubbard, Ron
see **Hubbard, Lafayette Ronald**

Huch, Ricarda Octavia
- Garibaldi and the new Italy series

Huddy, Delia
- Hipster series
- Sandwich Street series
- Tigger series
- Tom Humboldt series

Hudson, Alec
- Submarine series

Hudson, Harry Lindsay
see **Lindsay, Harry**

Hudson, Jay William
- Abbe Pierre series

Hudson, Michael

Thieves of light
Kar-Chee series (2)

Hudson, Stephen
- Kurt series

Hudson, Wade
- Afro-Bets series

Huebner, Frederick D
- Matt Riordan series

Hueffer, Ford Madox
see **Ford, Ford Madox**

Hueston, Ethel
- Ginger Ella trilogy
- Prudence series

Huet, M M
- Jack Rann series

Huff, Tanya
- Wizard crystal series

Huff, Tom E
see **Wilde, Jennifer**

Hufford, Susan
- Hilda Hughes tetralogy

Huggett, Frank Edward
- Victorian day series

Huggins, Roy
- Stuart Bailey series

Hughart, Barry
- Master Li Kao and Number Ten Ox series

Hughes, Dean
- Angel Park All-Stars series
- Angel Park Hoop Stars series
- Angel Park Soccer Stars series
- Haller series
- Lucky Ladd series
- Nutty Nutsell series

Hughes, Dorothy Belle
- Inspector Tobin series

Hughes, Erica
- Here's the church series

Hughes, Fielden
see **Hughes, Gwilym Fielden**

Hughes, Glyn
- Anne Wylde series

Hughes, Gwilym Fielden
- Bill Holmes series
- Roger Moore and the Crimefighters series

Hughes, Jean
- Dooki series

Hughes, Langston
- Simple series

Hughes, Mary Vivian
- London family series

Hughes, Monica
- Arc One series
- Conshelf Ten series
- Isis trilogy
- Sandwriter series

Hughes, Patrick Cairns
see **Hughes, Spike**

Hughes, Richard Arthur Warren
- Gertrude series
- Human predicament series

Hughes, Robert Don
- Pelmen trilogy

Hughes, Rupert
- Lakerim Athletic Club series
- Miss Three Hundred and Eighteen series

Hughes, Sara
- Morgan Swift find your fate series

Hughes, Shirley
- Alfie Rose series
- Charlie Moon series
- Chips series
- Lucy and Tom series
- Nursery series
- Tale of Trotter Street series

Hughes, Spike
- Coarse series
- Opening bars series

Hughes, Thomas
- Tom Brown series

Tom Brown's schooldays
Flashman series (1)

Hughes, Tracy
- Calloway Corners series

Hughes, Virginia
- Peggy Lane series

Hughes, Walter Llewellyn
see **Walters, Hugh**

Hughes, William
- George Willis series

Hughes, Zach
see also **Zachary, Hugh**
- Hotel Destiny series
- Rack the Healer series

Hugi, Maurice G
- Martin Speed series

Hugo, Victor Marie
- Fate trilogy

Huie, William Bradford
- Mamie Stover series

Hulke, Malcolm
- Crossroads series
- Doctor Who series
- Roger Moore and the Crimefighters series
- Sarah Jane Smith series

Hull, Edith Maude
- Sheik Ahmed ben Hassan series

Hull, Katharine
- Oxus series

Hull, Raymond
- Peter series

Hull, Richard
- Inspector Fenby series

Hulme, Joy Nelson
- Disability series

Hulme-Beaman, Emeric
- Ozmar series

Hultman, Helen Joan
- Tim Asher series

Humble, Richard
- High seas fleet series

Hume, David
see also **Turner, John Victor**
- Inspector Sanderson series
- Mick Cardby series
- Tony Carter series

Hume, Fergus
- Detective Kilsip and Duncan Calton series
- Madame Midas series
- Octavius Fanks series

Hummel, George Frederick
- Heritage series

Humphrey, Vernon
- Soldier of fortune series

Humphrey, William
- Red River County trilogy

Humphreys, Eliza
see **Rita**

Humphreys, Emyr
- Amy Parry series

Humphries, Barry
- Barry McKenzie series

Huna, Ludwig
- Borgia trilogy

Hunkins, Ralph Valentine
- Tales of the prairies series

Hunsburger, Ed

Date with death
Destroyer series (57)

Death sentence
Destroyer series (80)
- Destroyer series

Hunt, Angela Elwell
- Asked out series
- Cassie Perkins series
- Nicki Holland series
- Theyn chronicles trilogy

Hunt, Charlotte
- Doctor Paul Holton series

Hunt, Everette Howard
see also **Davis, Gordon; Dietrich, Robert; Saint John, David**
- Jack Novak series
- Peter Ward series
- Steve Bentley series

Hunt, Francis
- Mary and Jerry Denton series

Hunt, Gary
- Asked out series

Hunt, Greg
- Hartman family trilogy
- Ridge Parkman series

Hunt, Howard
see **Hunt, Everette Howard**

Hunt, Isobel Violet
see **Hunt, Violet**

Hunt, John
- Everest series

Hunt, Kyle
see **Halliday, Michael**

Hunt, Mabel Leigh
- Cristy Romano series

Hunt, Nan
- Mrs Millie Mack trilogy

Hunt, Peter
- Alan Miller series
- Honey machine series

Hunt, Richard
- Chief Inspector Walsh and Constable Brenda Phipps series

Hunt, Roderick
- Chutney series

Hunt, Val
- Books for me series

Hunt, Violet
- Their lives and hearts series
- Uneasy series

Hunter, Alan
- Inspector George Gently series

Hunter, Bluebell Matilda
see **Lancing, George**

Hunter, Claire
- Island of stone series

Hunter, E J
- Headhunter series
- White Squaw series

Hunter, Evan
see also **McBain, Ed**
- David, Peter and Sandy series

Hunter, Jack Dayton
- Blue Max series

Hunter, Joan
- Rupert of the Rhine series

Hunter, Joe
- Attack force series

Hunter, John
see also **Ballard, Willis Todhunter; Fox, Brian; Meriton, Peter; Slade, Jack**
- Bill Langley series
- Sexton Blake series

Hunter, Kristin
- Lourette Hawkins series

Hunter, Mollie
- Bridie McShane series

Hunter, Neil
see also **Jordan, Matt; Linaker, Michael R**
- Bodie the Stalker series
- Brand series

Hunter, Norman
- Kingdom of Incredibilia series
- Professor Branestawm series

Hunter, Richard Wilkes
see also **Brody, Marc**
- Congo series

Hunter, Robin
- Simon Quarry series

Hunter, S L
- Steele series

Hunting, Henry Gardner
- Sandsy series

Huntingdon, Margaret Lane
see **Lane, Margaret**

Huntington, Charles
- Space probe six series

Hurd, Douglas
- Foreign Office trilogy

Hurd, Edith Thatcher
- Catfish series
- Johnny Lion series
- Mister Charlie series
- Mother animal series

Hurd, Thacher
• Hobo Dog series
Hurley, Maxwell
• Psi Patrol trilogy
Hurmence, Belinda
• Oral histories of slaves series
Hurt, Freda Mary
• Andy series
• Benny of Crab Island series
• Inspector Herbert Broom series
• Mister Twink series
• Pinetops series
Hurwitz, Johanna
• Aldo Sossi series
• Ali Baba Bernstein series
• Edison-Armstrong School series
• Elisa series
• Nora and Teddy series
• Russell series
Hurwood, Bernhardt Jackson
see also **Knight, Mallory T**
• Invisibles series
Huston, Howard Chauncey
• Detective Charles A Baker series
Hutchens, Paul
• Sugar Creek Gang series
Hutchings, Monica Mary
• Church Farm series
Hutchins, Pat
• House that sailed away trilogy
• Surprise party series
• Titch series
• Tom and Sam series
Hutchinson, William Henry
• Gene Autry series
Hutchison, Graham Seton
see **Seton, Graham**
Hutson, Shaun
see also **Bishop, Samuel P; Harold, Clive; Taylor, Frank**
• Sergeant Rolf Kessler series
• Slugs series
Terminator
Terminator series (1)
Hutten zum Stolzenberg, Bettina Riddle
• Pam series
Huxley, Aldous
• New world series
Huxley, Elspeth
• Kenya childhood series
• Superintendent Vachell series
Huxtable, Marjorie
see **Stewart, Marjorie**
Huyck, Willard
Indiana Jones and the temple of doom
Indiana Jones series (2)
Huygen, Willibrord
• Gnomes series
Huysmans, Joris Karl
• Durtal series
Hyde, D Herbert
• Sexton Blake series
Hyde, Eleanor
• Tudor series
Hyland, Stanley
• Parliament series
Hyman, Inge
• Caspar series
Hyman, Robin
• Caspar series
Hynam, John
see **Kippax, John**
Hyne, Charles John Cutcliffe
• Captain Owen Kettle series

I

Iams, Jack
• Rocky Rockwell series
Ian, Vasilii Grigorievich
see **Yan, Vasily Grigorievich**
Ibanez, Vicente Blasco
see **Blasco Ibanez, Vicente**
Ibarguengoitia, Jorge
• Dead girls series
Ibsen, Henrik
• Nora Helmer series
Icenhower, Joseph Bryan
• Mister Midshipman Murdock series
Ichikawa, Satomi
• Nora series
• Suzanne and Nicholas series
Idell, Albert Edward
• Rogers family series
Idriess, Ion Llewellyn
• Australian guerilla series
Ilf, Ilya Arnoldovich
• Chairs series
Ilg, Frances Lillian
• Your child series
Illingworth, Myra
see **Mills, Glynn**
Imbert-Terry, Henry
• Detective Inspector Du Cas series
Impey, Rose
• Baddies series
• Creepies series
Inchbald, Peter
• Inspector Franco Corti series
Inchbald, Ralph
• Colonel Paternoster series
Inchfawn, Fay
• Personal recording series
Infante, Anne
• Micky Douglas and Inspector Reeves series
Ing, Dean
Cathouse
Man-Kzin wars series (5)
• Lagrangia series
Man-Kzin wars
Known Space series (17)
Man-Kzin wars II
Known Space series (18)
• Man-Kzin wars series
• Ted Quantrill trilogy
Ingalls, Laura
see **Wilder, Laura Ingalls**
Ingate, Mary
• Ann Fielding series
Ingelow, Jean
• Skelligs series
Ingersol, Jared
see also **Batchelor, Reg; Benton, Will; Bosworth, Frank; Carrel, Mark; Carter, Nevada; Paine, Lauran; Slaughter, Jim; Standish, Buck**
• Carl Moore series
Ingleby, Terry
• Messy Malcolm series
Ingraham, Joseph Holt
• Freemantle series
• Lafitte series
Ingram, James Henry
• Adventure series
Ingram, Jim
see **Ingram, James Henry**
Ingrid, Charles
• Marked man series
• Patterns of chaos series
• Sand wars series
Innes, Brian
• Red Baron series
Innes, Evan
• America two thousand and forty series
Innes, Hammond
• Sea journeys series
Innes, Michael
see also **Stewart, John Innes Mackintosh**
• Charles Honeybath series
• Sir John Appleby series
Innes, Ralph Hammond-
see **Innes, Hammond**
Insight, James
• Vicar series
Iraldi, James C
• Sherlock Holmes sequels series
Ireland, Jill
• Life series
Ireland, Kenneth
• Fogou series
Irish, Lola
• Colonial trilogy
Ironside, John
• Detective Inspector John Freeman series
Ironside, Virginia
• Burlap Hall series
Irvine, Alexander
• Ulster life series
Irvine, Georgeanne
• Zoo world series
Irvine, Lucy
• Runaway series
Irvine, Mat
Doctor Who special effects
Doctor Who series (162)
Irvine, Robert Ralstone
• Moroni Traveler series
• Robert Christopher series
Irving, Alexander
• Doctor Anthony Post series
Irving, Clifford
see also **Luckless, John**
• Eddie Mancuso and Vasily Borgneff series
Irving, Laurence
• Irving family trilogy
Irwin, Ann
• Hawkeye series
Irwin, Frances
• Anne Neville series
Irwin, Grace
• Andrew Connington series
Irwin, Inez Haynes
see also **Gillmore, Inez Haynes**
• Maida series
• Patrick O'Brien series
Irwin, Margaret
• Elizabeth I series
• Stuart series
Irwin, Raymond
• English library series
Isadora, Rachel
• Senses series
Iseborg, Harry
• John and Hugh series
• Paul and Sally series
Isherwood, Christopher
• Berlin series
• Christopher series
Isherwood, Shirley
• Get up and go series
Islay, Nicholas
• Sydney Vane series
Ison, Graham
• Superintendent John Gaffney series
Israel, Peter
• B F Cage series
Istrati, Panait
• Adrien Zograffi series
Iverson, Eric
• Gerin series
Iwamura, Kazuo
• Nat series
Iwasaki, Chihiro
• Momoko series

J

Jabavu, Noni
• Bantu series
Jacberns, Raymond
• Becky Compton series
Jaccoma, Richard
• Werewolf series
Jack, Donald
• Journals of Bartholomew Bandy series
Jack Will8amson
• Jim Eden series
Jackman, Stuart
• Jesus Davidson series
Jacks, Jeff
• Shep Stone series
Jacks, Lawrence Pearsall
• Smokeover series
Jacks, T J
• Chaney brothers series
Jackson, Alison
• Leslie Crane series
Jackson, Arthur
• Country practice series
Jackson, Basil
• Air detective series
Jackson, Charles Reginald
• Don Birman series
Jackson, Charles Ross
• Quintus Oakes series
Jackson, Ellen B
• Safety series
Jackson, Frank George
• Decorative design series
Jackson, Gabrielle Emilie
• Captain Polly series
• Denise and Ned Toodles series
• Little Miss Cricket trilogy
• Peggy Stewart series
• Three Graces series
• Three little women series
• Wee Winkles series
Jackson, George
• Soledad brother series
Jackson, Giles
see also **Chambers, Dana**
• Nile Boyd series
Jackson, Jesse
• Charley Moss series
• Tessie series
Jackson, Jon Anthony
• Sergeant Fang Mulheisen series
Jackson, Ken
• Jud Blade series
Jackson, Lewis
• Sexton Blake series
Jackson, Lydia
see **Fen, Elisaveta**
Jackson, Marian J A
• Miss Abigail Patience Danforth series
Jackson, Robert
• Bomber Command series
• Flying Officer George Yeoman series
Jackson, Rosemary Elizabeth
• Macgillan family series
Jackson, Shirley
• Savages series
Jackson, Steve
Fighting fantasy
Fighting fantasy gamebook series (46)
• Fighting fantasy gamebook series
Fighting fantasy poster book
Fighting fantasy gamebook series (46)
• Sorcery series
Titan
Fighting fantasy gamebook series (46)
Jackson, Steven Gary
• Car wars adventure gamebook series
• Fighting fantasy gamebook series
Jackson, Wallace
• Archibald Penny series
• Inspector Clancy Martin series
Jackson, William
Alternative Third World War, 1985-2035
World War Three series (3)
Jacob, Naomi
• Broad acres series
• Crowther series
• Gollantz series
• Marsden family series
• Me series
Jacob, Piers Anthony Dillingham
see **Anthony, Piers**
Jacobs, Barbara
• Fire-proof hero series
Jacobs, Caroline Emilia
see also **Elliot, Emilia**
• Blue Bonnet series
• Joan series
Jacobs, Joseph
• Celtic fairy tales series
• English fairy tales series
Jacobs, Thomas Curtis Hicks
see **Pendower, Jacques**
• Pendower, Jacques
• Chief Inspector Barnard series
• Detective Superintendent John Bellamy series
• Jim Malone series
• Mike Seton series
• Temple Fortune series
Jacobs, William Wymark
• Night-Watchman series
Jacques Bergier
• Dawn of magic series
Jacques, Brian
• Redwall series
Jade, Symon
• Starship Orpheus trilogy
Jadis, Donna
• Star trek fan series
Jaffe, Rona
• Reunion series
Jaffee, Al
• Al Jaffee gags series
• Snappy answers to stupid questions series
Jaffee, Irving
• Sherlock Holmes sequels series
Jaffee, Mary
• Sherlock Holmes sequels series
Jagger, Brenda
• Barforth trilogy
Jahn, Joseph Michael
see **Jahn, Mike**
Jahn, Mike
• Black Sheep Squadron series
• Six Million Dollar Man series
Jahoda, Gloria
• Bickley family series
Jakes, John
see also **Scott, Michael William**
• Brak series
• Dragonard series
• Gavin Black series
• Johnny Havoc series
• Kent family series
• North and South trilogy
• Planet of the Apes series
Jallim, Collins
• Devilgod series
James, Bill
• Superintendent Colin Harpur series
James, Breni
• Sergeant Gunnar Matson series
James, Charles Thomas Clement
• Mrs Grundy series
James, Clive
• Unreliable memoirs series
James, Colin
• New Zealand revolution series
James, Cy
see also **Chisholm, Matt**
My gun is justice
Rem McAllister series (15)
• Sam Spur series
Violent hills
Rem McAllister series (17)
James, Dakota
• Greenhouse series
James, Dean
• Melrose Place series
James, Elizabeth
• Life series
• Money series
• Slapdash series
• Transition series
James, George Payne Rainsford
• Young cavalier series
James, Grace
• John and Mary series
James, Henry
• Princess Casamassima series
• Turn of the screw series
James, Janice
• Brothers series
James, John
• Photinus the Greek series
• Talleyman series
James, Josephine
• Kathy Martin series
James, Judi
• Fashion features series
James, Laurence
see also **Axler, James; Darke, James; Fraser, Mary; Haigh, Richard; James, William M; Marvin, James W; May, Jonathan; McPhee, James; Netzen, Klaus; Nolan, Christopher; Norman, Mick**
• American football series
• Baseball series
• Gridiron series
• Simon Rack series
James, Leigh Franklin
• John Cooper Baines series
James, Martha
• Pigeon Camp series
James, Martin
• Rick Muldoon series
James, Matthew
• American football series
• Baseball series
• Gridiron series
James, Montague Rhodes
• Ghost stories series
James, Peter
• Max Flynn series
James, Phyllis Dorothy
• Commander Adam Dalgliesh series
• Cordelia Gray series
James, Robin
• Baby animal series
James, Stefan
Bitter monsoon
Monsoon trilogy (1)
James, Susan
• Star trek fan series
James, Will
• Cow camps series
• Uncle Bill series
James, William M
see also **Gilman, George G; Harknett, Terry; Harvey, John Barton; Hedges, Joseph; Pike, Charles R; Stone, Thomas H**
• Apache series
James, William Roderick
see **James, Will**
Jameson, E M
• Pendletons trilogy

Jameson, Storm
- Hervey Russell series
- Mirror in darkness trilogy
- Renn series
- Triumph of time trilogy

Jamieson, Leland
- Dan Gregory series

Jance, Judith A
- J P Beaumont series
- Joanna Brady series

Janes, Henry Hurford
- Frankenstein sequels series

Janes, Joseph Robert
- Danger on the river trilogy
- Jean-Louis Saint-Cyr and Hermann Kohler series

Janeshutz, Trish
see **Macgregor, T J**

Janifer, Laurence Mark
see also **Phillips, Mark**
- Angelo DiStefano trilogy
- Gerald Knave trilogy

Janosch
- Little Tiger series

Janovy, John
- Keith County series

Janson, Hank
- Hank Janson series

Jansson, Tove
- Moomin series

Jaques, Faith
- Tilly series

Jardin, Rosamond, du
see **Du Jardin, Rosamond**

Jardine, Warwick
- Sexton Blake series

Jarman, Rosemary Hawley
- Richard III series

Jarvis, Robin
- Deptford histories series
- Deptford mice trilogy

Jason
- Jason series

Jason, Stuart
see also **Avallone, Michael; Floren, Lee; Noone, Edwina**
- Butcher series

Jasper, Robert Lee
- Uncle Sam's Navy boys series

Javor, Frank A
- Eli Pike series

Jay, Ruth Ingrid
see **Johnson, Ruth Ingrid**

Jayne, R H
see also **Ellis, Edward Sylvester**
- War whoop series

Jeffares, Alexander Norman
- Brought up series

Jeffares, Norman
see **Jeffares, Alexander Norman**

Jefferies, Ian
- Sergeant Craig series

Jefferies, Mike
- Heirs to Gnarlsmyre series
- Loremasters of Elundium trilogy

Jefferies, Richard
- Bevis series

Jeffers, Harry Paul
- Harry Macneil series
- Morgan trilogy
- Sherlock Holmes sequels series

Jeffery, Gordon
- Milbury series

Jeffreys, J G
see **Sturrock, Jeremy**

Jeffries, Graham Montague
see **Bourne, Peter; Graeme, Bruce; Graeme, David**

Jeffries, Ira
see **Morris, Ira J**

Jeffries, Roderic Graeme
see also **Alding, Peter; Ashford, Jeffrey; Draper, Hastings; Graeme, Roderic**
- Inspector Enrique Alvarez series
- Police series
- Sunken danger series

Jeier, Thomas
- Matt Bishop series

Jellett, Henry
- Inspector Roderick Alleyn series

Jellinek, Joanna
- Georgina series

Jelloun, Tahar ben
see **Ben Jelloun, Tahar**

Jenkin-Pearce, Susie
- Bad Boris series

Jenkins, Alan Charles
see also **Bancroft, John**
- Twin series

Jenkins, Dan
- Billy Clyde Puckett series

Jenkins, Geoffrey
- Commander Geoffrey Peace series

Jenkins, Gwyn
- Samuel and David series

Jenkins, Herbert
- Bindle series
- Malcolm Sage series

Jenkins, Jerry Bruce
- Bradford family series
- Dallas O'Neil and the Baker Street Sports Club series
- Dallas O'Neil mysteries series
- Jennifer Grey series
- Margo Franklin and Philip Spence series
- Tara Chadwick series

Jenkins, Robin
- Nuranian series

Jenkins, William Fitzgerald
see **Leinster, Murray**

Jennens, Frank
- Mouse series

Jennings, D K
- Doctor Ralph Conway series

Jennings, Gary
- March series

Jennings, Paul Arthur
- Round the twist series

Jennings, Paul Francis
- Oddly series

Jennings, Sharon
- Jeremiah and Mrs Ming series

Jennison, John William
Lost world
Thunderbirds series (5)
Operation Asteroids
Thunderbirds series (5)

Jensen, Johannes Vilhelm
- Long journey trilogy

Jensen, Kris
- Ardel series

Jepson, Edgar
Arsene Lupin
Arsene Lupin series (16)
- Lady Noggs series
- Lord Barradine series
- Memories series
- Passion for romance series
- Pollyooly series
- Tinker series

Jepson, Selwyn
- Eve Gill series
- Ian Macarthur series

Jerina, Carol
- Jack and Jill series

Jernigan, Gisela
- Desert trilogy

Jerome, Jerome Klapka
- Three men series

Jerome, Owen Fox
- Philip Maccray series

Jesse, Louie
- Babyland series

Jessel, Camilla
- Babydays series
- Chatterbooks series

Jessup, Richard
see **Telfair, Richard**

Jeter, Kevin W
- Doctor Adder trilogy
- Time traveller series

Jevons, Marshall
- Henry Spearman series

Jewell, Derek
- Prospero Group series

Jewett, John Howard
- Bunny stories series

Jewett, Sarah Orne
- Betty Leicester series

Jezard, Alison
- Albert series

Joan, Natalie
- Ameliaranne series

Joanny, Andre
- Nim series

Job
- Yakari series

Jobson, Hamilton
- Inspector Anders series

Joensson, Reidar
- Ingemar Johansson series

Joey
- Joey series

Johansen, Iris
- Delaneys of Killaroo trilogy
- Delaneys, the untamed years, second trilogy
- Delaneys, the untamed years trilogy
- Gold class trilogy
- Shamrock trilogy

John, Augustus
- Fragments of autobiography series

John, Eugenie
see **Marlitt, E**

John, Owen
- Haggai Godin series

John, Stephen
- Albert Divine series

Johns, Gilbert
- Sexton Blake series

Johns, Larry
- Jacky Ryderbeit series

Johns, Veronica Parker
- Agatha Welch series
- Webster Flagg series

Johns, William Earl
- Biggles series
- Digger Driscoll series
- Gimlet series
- Rex Clinton series
- Steeley Delaroy series
- Worrals series

Johnson, B B
- Superspade series

Johnson, Barbara Ferry
- Plantation series

Johnson, Colin
see also **Nyoongah, Mudrooroo**
- Wildcat trilogy

Johnson, Crockett
- Barnaby series

Johnson, Donald McIntosh
- Publisher presents himself series

Johnson, Dorothy Marie
- Buffalo Woman series
- Man called Horse series

Johnson, Duff
- Gutsy Morgan series

Johnson, Electa
- Yankee series

Johnson, Emil Richard
- Tony Lonto series

Johnson, Eyvind
- Olof tetralogy

Johnson, George Clayton
- Logan series

Johnson, Helen Kendrick
- Roddy series

Johnson, Irving
- Yankee series

Johnson, James Leonard
- Code name Sebastian series

Johnson, Jane
- Let's pretend series

Johnson, Kenneth Rayner
Dracula's dog
Dracula series (1)
Hounds of Dracula
Dracula series (1)
Zoltan, hound of Dracula
Dracula series (1)

Johnson, Kim Howard
- Monty Python series

Johnson, Lissa Halls
- China Tate series

Johnson, Lonni Sue
- Max and Diana series

Johnson, Martha
- Ann Bartlett series

Johnson, Oliver
- Blood sword series
- Dragon warriors series
- Golden dragon fantasy gamebooks series

Johnson, Owen McMahon
- Lawrenceville series

Johnson, Pamela Hansford
- Daniel Skipton trilogy
- Helena trilogy
- Toby Roberts series

Johnson, Pat
- Julie Jefferson series

Johnson, Patricia Irene
- Moonster series

Johnson, Ruth Ingrid
- Joy Sparton series

Johnson, Samuel
- Rasselas series

Johnson, Seddon
- Choose your own adventure series

Johnson, Shane
- Star trek, the next generation sequels series

Johnson, Stacie
- Eighteen Pine Street series

Johnson, Susan
- Blaze Braddock and Jon Hazard Black series
- Kuzan family trilogy

Johnson, Todd
Combat Command in the world of David Drake's Hammer's Slammers
Hammer's Slammers series (6)
- Combat Command series

Slammer's down
Hammer's Slammers series (6)

Johnson, Uwe
- Jakob Abs series

Johnson, Walter Reed
- Oakhurst series

Johnson, William Henry
- Huguenot series

Johnston, Annie Fellows
- Little colonel series

Johnston, Brian
- Funny game series

Johnston, Dorothy Grunbock
- Ginger series
- Pete and Penny series
- Wagon train series

Johnston, George Henry
see also **Martin, Shane**
- David Meredith trilogy

Johnston, Gunnar
- Silber series

Johnston, Harry Hamilton
- Dombey series
- Mrs Warren series
- Our mutual friend series

Johnston, Joan
- Sisters of the Lone Star trilogy

Johnston, Madeleine
- Noah Bradshaw series

Johnston, Mary
- American Civil War trilogy
- Virginian series

Johnston, Norma
- Carlisle chronicles series
- Of time series
- Sterling family series

Johnston, Ronald
- James Bruce series

Johnston, Terry Conrad
- General Armstrong Custer series
- Plainsmen series
- Titus Bass series

Johnston, Tony
- Mole and Troll series
- Odd jobs series

Johnston, William
see also **Sinclair, Heather**
- Bewitched series
- Brady Bunch series

Dick Tracy
Dick Tracy cartoon series (9)
- Doctor Kildare junior series
- Doctor Kildare series
- Doctor Starr series
- Flying nun series
- Happy days series
- Matt Lincoln series
- Maxwell Smart series
- Mod Squad series
- Munsters series
- Nanny and the professor series
- Room 222 series
- Welcome back, Kotter series
- Young rebels series

Johnstone, Nancy
- Hotel series

Johnstone, William Wallace
- Ashes series
- Beasts series
- Blood bond series
- First Mountain Man trilogy
- Mountain Man Preacher series
- Mountain Man series
- Rig warrior series

Jokai, Mor
- Michael Apafi series

Jolley, Elizabeth
- My father's moon series

Jon, Montague
- Stephen Kale series

Jones, Adrienne
- Margery Stanfield series

Jones, Arthur E
- Felix Holliday series

Jones, Bradshaw
- Claude Ravel series

Jones, Charles Reed
- Leighton Swift series

Jones, Courtway
- King Arthur series

Jones, Cynon Beaton-
see **Beaton-Jones, Cynon**

Jones, Dennis Feltham
- Colossus trilogy

Jones, Diana Wynne
- Chrestomanci series
- Dalemark series
- Howl series

Jones, Douglas Clyde
- Comanche trilogy
- General George Custer trilogy
- Hasford family series

Jones, Edith Constance Turton-
see **Gillespie, Susan**

Jones, Elaine Anthony
see **Jameson, E M**

Jones, Ellen
- Eleanor of Aquitaine series

Jones, Elwyn
- Chief Inspector Barlow series
- Dick Barton series

Jones, G Wayman
- Black Bat series

Jones, Gareth
- Misrule series

Jones, George Chetwynd Griffith-
see **Griffith, George**

Jones, Gilbert Hackforth-
see **Hackforth-Jones, Gilbert**

Jones, Glyn
- Doctor Who series

Jones, Harold
- Bunby series

Jones, Harry Austin
see **Jons, Hal**

Jones, Henry Austin
see **Jons, Hal**

Jones, Henry Llewellyn
- Fraser Todd series

Jones, Howard
- John Haddon series

Jones, Irene Heywood
- Hospital life series

Jones, J Farragut
see also **Levinson, Leonard**
- Silent service series

Jones, J G
- Sexton Blake series

Jones, J Jeff
- Space nineteen ninety nine series

Jones, Jack
- Unfinished journey series

Jones, Jennifer
- Daisy Jane Mott series

Jones, Jenny
- Flight over fire series

Jones, Joan Clement
- James and Susan series

Jones, Joanna
see also **Burke, John Frederick; Burke, Jonathan**
- Artless series
- Nurse Jones series

Jones, John G
- Amityville horror series

Jones, Lawrence Evelyn
- Father Lascaut series
- Victorian boyhood series

Jones, Malcolm Henry Bradshaw-
see **Jones, Bradshaw**

Jones, Neal
- Inquisition war series

Warhammer forty thousand
Inquisition war series (3)

Jones, Neil Ronald
- Professor Jameson series

Jones, Nicholas
- Wind in the willows series

Jones, Olive
- Barfield series

Jones, Pat Wynne-
see **Wynne-Jones, Pat**

Jones, Peter
- Terry Trotter series

Jones, Rachel
- Coffee, tea or me girls series

Jones, Raymond F
- Ron Barron series

Voyage to the bottom of the sea
Voyage to the bottom of the sea series (2)

Jones, Richard
- Benson-Williams series

Jones, Roger William
- Inspector Evans and Sergeant Beddoes series

Jones, Stanley Howard
see **Jones, Howard**

Jones, Terry
- Ripping yarns series

Jones, Tim Wynne-
see **Wynne-Jones, Tim**

Jones, Tristan
- Wayward sailor series

Jones, Valerie
- Miracleman series

Jones, William Glynne
see **Glynne-Jones, William**

Jones, William Llewellyn Lloyd
see **Lloyd-Jones, Buster**

Jong, Erica
- Isadora Wing series

Jons, Hal
- Marshal Carl Travis series

K

- Captain Duncan Maclain series
- Miles Standish Rice series

Kennealy, Jerry
- Nick Polo series

Kennealy, Patricia
- Keltiad series
- Tales of Arthur series

Kennedy, Adam
- Bradshaw trilogy
- Roy Tucker series

Kennedy, Brendan
- Charley Malarkey series

Kennedy, Elliot
- Griff Dexter series

Kennedy, George
- George Kennedy series

Kennedy, Kim
- Two by two series

Kennedy, Margaret
- Sanger family series

Kennedy, Milward
- Inspector Cornford series
- Sir George Bull series

Kennedy, Robert Milward
see **Kennedy, Milward**

Kennedy, William
- Albany series
- Charley Malarkey series
- Phelan family series

Kennelly, Ardyth
- Mormon series

Kenneth, Claire
- Cynthia Doanides series

Kennett, John
- Black Circle Gang series

Kenney, Minnie E
see **Paull, Minnie E**

Kenney, Susan
- Roz Howard series

Kenny, Kathryn
- Trixie Belden series

Kent, Alexander
see also **Reeman, Douglas**
- Captain Richard Bolitho series

Kent, Arthur
- Sexton Blake series

Kent, David
- Jason Burr series

Kent, Louise Andrews
- Appleyard family series

Kent, Margaret
- Four seasons at Cherry-Tree Farm series
- Twins series

Kenward, Jean
- Ragdolly Anna series

Kenworthy, Christopher
- Matthew and Son series

Kenyon, Frank Wilson
- Emperor Napoleon III series
- John Churchill, Duke of Marlborough series

Kenyon, James William
- Peter Trant series

Kenyon, Kate
- Cedar Groves Junior High School series

Kenyon, Michael
- Inspector Henry Peckover series
- Superintendent O'Malley series

Kenyon, Paul
- Baroness Penelope Saint-John Orsini series

Kenyon, Theda
- Staceys of Feathergrant series

Ker Wilson, Barbara
see **Wilson, Barbara Ker**

Kerin, Dorothy
- Faith healing series

Kern, Gregory
see also **Tubb, Edwin Charles**
- Cap Kennedy series

Kernaghan, Eileen
- Aprilioth trilogy

Kernahan, Coulson, *Mrs*
see **Kernahan, Jeannie Gwynne**

Kernahan, Jeannie Gwynne
- Felix series

Kerner, Annette
- Woman detective series

Kerouac, Jack
- Jack Duluoz series

Kerr, James Lennox
see **Dawlish, Peter**

Kerr, Judith
- Anna series
- Mog series

Kerr, Katharine
- Deverry series
- Rhodry series

Kerr, M E
- John Fell series

Kerr, Michael
- Caged women series

Kerr, Philip
- Berlin noir trilogy

Kerr, Robert
- Jamie Stuart series

Kerrigan, David
- Prince of shadows series

Kerrigan, John
- SBS series

Kerry, Lois
- Joyce series

Kersh, Cyril
- Minnie Ashe series

Kersh, Gerald
- Brigade of Guards series
- Harry Fabian series

Kershaw, H V
- Coronation Street series

Kesey, Ken
- Chief Bromden series

Kessel, Maurice
see **Druon, Maurice**

Kessler, Leo
see also **Konrad, Klaus; Whiting, Charles**
- Black Cossacks series
- Otto Stahl series
- Rebel series
- Rommel series
- Sea Wolves series
- SS Stuka Squadron series
- Stormtroop series
- Submarine series
- Wotan series

Kester, Ken
- Steve McCade series

Ketchum, Jack
- Off season series

Ketchum, Philip
- Elijah Cabot Pickering series

Kettle, Jocelyn
- Athelson family series

Keude, Klara
see **Kenneth, Claire**

Keverne, Richard
- Franklin Parry and Leonard Harris series
- Inspector Mace series
- Simon Artifex series

Key, Alexander
- Sprockets trilogy
- Witch Mountain series

Key, Samuel Whittell
see **Key, Uel**

Key, Sean A
- Cain series

Key, Uel
- Professor Arnold Rhymer series

Keyes, Frances Parkinson
- Batchelor series
- Fabian and Cresside series
- Joe and Judith Racina series
- Marlowe family series
- Roses series
- Winslow family trilogy

Keystone, Oliver
- Paul Plush series

Keyte, John Charles
- Minsan series

Khalsa, Dayal Kaur
- Baabee series III

Kherdian, David
- Armenian girl series
- Farm poems series

Kibalchich, Victor Lvovich
see **Serge, Victor**

Kibbe, Pat
- Pinkerton family series

Kibby, Leigh
- Stories for happiness series

Kidd, Ronald
- Littlest angel series

Kidd, Russ
- Wyoming series

Kiddell, John
- Hamish, David and Bottle series

Kiddell-Monroe, Joan
- In his little black waistcoat series

Kiddy, Maurice George
- Stonewall Steevens series

Kidner, John
- Alice in Wonderland parodies series

Kielland, Alexander Lange
- Garman and Worse series

Kienzle, William Xavier
- Father Robert Koesler series

Kilboure, Charles Evans
- Army boy series

Kilbourne, Fannie
- William Horton series

Kile, Joan
- Musty the mustard seed series

Kilgore, Axel
- They call me the Mercenary series

Kilian, Crawford
- Chronoplane wars trilogy
- Icequake series

Killdeer, John
see also **Mayhar, Ardath**
- Mountain majesty series

Killilea, Marie
- Karen series

Killingback, Julia
- Busy Bears series

Killough, Lee
- Blood hunt series
- Brill and Maxwell trilogy

Kilpatrick, Florence Antoinette
- Elizabeth series
- Hetty trilogy

Kilroy, Sally
- Baby series
- Toddlers' tales series

Kilvington, Edwin
- Crispin Quane series

Kilworth, Garry
- Angel series
- Woodworld series

Kim, Richard Eunkook
- Korea series

Kimball, Janus
- Scanners series

Kimberly, Gail
- Dracula series

Kimbriel, Katharine Eliska
- Nuala series

Kimbro, John
see **Kimbrough, Katheryn**

Kimbrough, Emily
- Our hearts series

Kimbrough, Katheryn
- Phenwick women series

Kimenye, Barbara
- Kalasanda series
- Moses series

Kimmel, Edward
- Anti-coloring series

Kimura, Yasuko
- Cuthbert series

Kincade, Wynn
- Vicky Loring series

Kincaid, J D
- Jack Stone series

King, Alexander
- Mine enemy grows older series

King, Anna
- Little Hippo series

King, Bernard
- Chronicles of the keeper trilogy
- Starkadder trilogy

King, Betty
- Beaufort family series
- Tudor series

King, Charles
- Cadet series
- Guy Bannister series
- Lieutenant Sandy Ray series

King, Charles Daly
- Doctor L Rees Pons series
- Michael Lord series

King, Clifford
see **Fry, Pete**

King, David
- Rat Patrol series

King, Frank
- Clarence Knight series
- Doctor Frank King series
- Dormouse series
- Superintendent Gloom series

King, Hilary
- Sexton Blake series

King, John
- Shuna series

King, Kay
- Cornelius Plum series

King, Laurie R
- Sherlock Holmes sequels series

King, Louise Wooster
- Miss Moppet series

King, Lucille Mary
see **Bishop, Mary**

King, Melvin
- Soldier of fortune series

King, Philip
- Hornett family series

King, Robin
- Merchant Navy trilogy

King, Rufus
- Lieutenant Valcour series
- Stuff Driscoll series

King, Stephen
- Dark tower trilogy
- Plant trilogy

King, T Stanleyan
- Dixon Brett series
- Scarsdale Waring series

King, Tabitha
- Nodd's Ridge series

King, Tappan
- Weird heroes series

King-Smith, Dick
- Sophie series

Kingman, Lee
- Peter series

Kingsbury, Kate
- Pennyfoot Hotel series

Kingscote, Georgina
see **Cleeve, Lucas**

Kingsley, Florence Morse
- Early Christian series
- Miss Philura trilogy

Kingston, Charles
- Inspector Wake series

Kingston, Guy
- Royal Air Force trilogy

Kingston, Jeremy
- Time tours series

Kinsella, William Patrick
- Shoeless Joe Jackson series
- Silas Ermineskin series

Kipling, Rudyard
- Jungle book series
- Kim series
- Rewards and fairies series

Kippax, John
- Venturer Twelve series

Kirby, Arthur
- Sexton Blake series

Kirby, Dallas
- Victor Garrison series

Kirby, Jean
- Scott sisters series

Kirby, Joan
see **Dickins, Joan**

Kirchoff, Mary Lynn
- Amazing stories series
- DragonLance preludes II series
- DragonLance preludes series
- Endless quest series
- Meetings series

Kirk, Ellen Olney
- Dorothy Deane series

Kirk, Matthew
see also **Muir, James A; Wells, Angus**
- Claw series

Kirk, Michael
see **Macleod, Robert**

Kirk, Philip
see also **Levinson, Leonard; Rawls, Philip**
- Butler series

Kirk, Richard
see also **Carlsen, Chris; Faulcon, Robert; Holdstock, Robert**
- Raven series

Kirk, Thomas Hobson
- William and Susan series

Kirkbride, Ronald
- Gentle series

Kirkland, Joseph
- McVeys series

Kirkman, Marshall Monroe
- Alexander trilogy

Kirkup, James
- Only child series

Kirst, Hans Hellmut
- Gunner Asch series
- Munich trilogy

Kirsten, Angela
- Ralph Whitgift series

Kirtland, G B
see also **Joslin, Sesyle**
- One day series

Kirwan, Molly Morrow
see **Morrow, Charlotte**

Kissinger, Henry
- White House years series

Kita, Morio
- Kiichiro Nire series

Kitchen, Fred
- Foxendale series

Kitchen, Paddy
- Vanessa Talisend series

Kitchin, Clifford Henry Benn
- Malcolm Warren series

Kitchin, Frederick Harcourt
see **Copplestone, Bennet**

Kitsch, Hieronymous
- Cthulhu Mythos series

Kitt, Tamara
- Billy Brown series

Kittredge, William
see **Rountree, Owen**

Kjelgaard, Jim
- Chiri series
- Red series

Klass, Judy
- Star trek series

Kleberger, Ilse
- Grandmother Oma series

Klein, Dave
- Butch Lewis series

Klein, Grace
see **Farewell, Nina**

Klein, Norma
- Only child series
- Sunshine series

Klein, Robin
- Melling series
- Penny Pollard series

Klein, Zachary
- Matthew Jacob series

Klickmann, Flora
- Flower-patch series

Kline, Bennett
Laura Lee Hope's The Bobbsey twins
Bobbsey twins series (1)

Kline, Otis Adelbert
- Grandon trilogy
- Jan series
- Mars series

Kline, Suzy
- Herbie Jones series
- Horrible Harry series
- Mary Marony series
- Orp series

Klinger, Henry
- Lieutenant Shomri Shomar series

Klip-Klap
see **Rutter, Owen**

Knaak, Richard Allen
- DragonLance heroes series
- Dragonrealm series
- Origin of Dragonrealm series

Kneale, Nigel
- Quatermass series

Knef, Hildegard
- Gift horse series

Kneifel, Hans
- Atlan series

Knickmeyer, Steve
- Steve Cranmer series

Knight, Adam
see also **Lariar, Lawrence**
- Steve Conacher series

Knight, Alanna
Estella
Miss Havisham series (2)
- Inspector Faro series

Knight, Arthur Lee
- Cormorant series

Knight, Brigid
- Ardleigh family series
- Ashenden series
- Christina Brand series
- Van Breda family series

Knight, Clayton
- Pepe and Ronnie series

Knight, Clifford
- Huntoon Rogers series

Knight, Damon
- CV trilogy

Knight, David
see also **Prather, Richard Scott**
- Dragnet series
Pattern for murder
Shell Scott series (16)

Knight, Ellis Cornelia
- Rasselas series

Knight, Eric
- Sam Small series

Knight, Frank
- Chichester Harbour series
- Clipper ship series

Knight, Hilary
- Eloise series

Knight, Kathleen Moore
- Elisha Macomber series
- Margot Blair series

Knight, Leonard Alfred
- Jerry Scant series

Knight, Mallory T
see also **Hurwood, Bernhardt Jackson**
Dracutwig
Dracula series (26)
- Man from T.O.M.C.A.T. series

Knight, Peter
- Anthony Daintrey series
- Roger Vellacott series

Knights, Lionel Charles
- Explorations series

Knipe, Alden Arthur
• Benedict Arnold series
• Denewood series
• Little Miss Fales series
Knipe, Emilie Benson
• Benedict Arnold series
• Denewood series
• Little Miss Fales series
Knipscheer, James
see **Fox, James M**
Knott, Justina Spencer
see **Knott, Tina Spencer**
Knott, Tina Spencer
• Fools series
Knott, William Cecil
see also **Sharpe, Jon**
• Golden Hawk series
• Vengeance Seeker series
Knotts, Raymond
• Jim Hale series
Knowles, Anne
• Cotswold vet series
• Matthew Ratton series
Knowles, Gaye
• Islanders series
Knowles, John
• Devon School series
• Yale University series
Knowles, Mabel Winifred
see **Wynne, May**
Knox, Bill
see also **Macleod, Robert**
Drum of Ungara
Talos Cord series (1)
• Inspector Colin Thane and Phil Moss series
• Webb Carrick series
Knox, Ronald Arbuthnott
• Miles Bredon series
• Oxford conferences series
• Slow motion series
Knox, Thomas Wallace
• Boy travellers series
• Hunting adventures on land and sea series
Knox, William
see **Knox, Bill**
Knudson, Rozanne Ruth
• Rinehart series
• Zan Hagan series
Koehler, Robert Portner
• Al Bronson series
• Avery Gregg and Tony Ellis series
• Pecos Appleby series
Koenig, Lilli
• Kiki series
Koenig, Marion
• Paul and Fritzi's year series
• Richard and Valerie series
Koertge, Ronald
• Toad series
Koestler, Arthur
• Arrow in the blue series
• Ends and means trilogy
Kohill, Malcolm
• Doctor Who series
Koller, Jackie French
• Dragonling series
Koltz, Tony
• Choose your own adventure series
Kolyer, John
• Failure series
Konrad, Klaus
see also **Kessler, Leo; Whiting, Charles**
• Russian series
Konsalik, Heinz Gunther
• Love on the Don series
• Stalingrad series
Konvitz, Jeffrey
• Sentinel series
Kooiker, Leonie
• Chris series
Koontz, Dean Ray
see **Coffey, Brian**
Phantoms
Phantoms series (1)
Koontz, Robin Michal
• Chicago and the cat series
Kootz, Samuel Melvin
• Jason Emory series
Kopper, Lisa
• First timers series
• What's that series
Kopsen, Dorothy Blaxland
• Desert Home series
Korman, Gordon
• Bugs Potter series
Korman, Justine
• Crispy Critter series
• Davy Crockett series
• Donald Duck series
• Oliver and company series
• Peter Pan series
• Pongo and Missis series
• Pound puppies series
• Roger Rabbit series
• Tiny Toon's adventures series
• Working hard series
Kornblatt, Marc
• Time machine series
• Time traveler series
Kornbluth, Cyril M
• Space merchants series
Koscielniak, Bruce
• Hector and Prudence series
Kosikowski, Renate
• Titus Bear series
Koster, Richard Morton
• Tinieblas trilogy
Kostlanetz, Richard
• Constructs series
• Sports fields series
Kostov, K N
• Punishment battalion series
Kotani, Eric
• Act of God trilogy
Kotlan, Charles Michael
• Cunningham trilogy
Kottler, Jeffrey
• Therapist series
Kotzwinkle, William
• E.T. series
• Superman series
Koziakin, Vladimir
Superman's maze challenge
Superman series (7)
Kozlow, Mark J
• Chris Devlin series
Kraft, David Anthony
• Micro adventure series
• Wizards, warlocks and you series
Kraft, Eric
• Peter Leroy series
Kramer, Dana
Combat Command in the world of Piers Anthony's Bio of a space tyrant
Bio of a space tyrant series (5)
• Combat Command series
Cut by emerald
Bio of a space tyrant series (5)
• Star trek series
Warhorn
Rifkind series (2)
Krantz, Judith
• Scruples scruples
Krasner, William
• Sam Birge series
Krasney, Samuel A
• Abe Larson series
• Lieutenant Ben Krahmer series
Kraus, Bruce R
Encyclopedia Galactica
Battlestar Galactica series (14)
Kraus, Robert
• Boogie Woogie Bears series
• Daddy Long Ears series
• Herman the helper series
• Leo the late bloomer series
• Little Mouse series
• Milton series
• Miss Gator series
• Mixed-up Mice series
• Mummy series
• Night light series
• Owliver series
• Pinchpenny Mouse series
• Spider series
Krause, Jonathan
• Christian situations series
Krauss, Bruno
see also **Akers, Alan Burt; Blake, Ken; Bulmer, Kenneth; Frazier, Arthur; Hardy, Adam; Silver, Richard; Zetford, Tully**
• Sea Wolf series
Krautter, Elisa Bialk
see **Bialk, Elisa**
Krauzer, Steven Mark
see **Lassiter, Adam**
Kravchenko, Viktor
• Choice series
Kreeft, Peter
• Socrates series
Kremenetz, Jill
• How it feels series
• Very young series
Krensky, Stephen
• Dinosaurs guide book series
• Lionel series
• Wynd family trilogy
Krentz, Jayne Ann
see also **Castle, Jayne**
• Verity Ames and Jonas Quarrel series
Krich, Rochelle Majer
• Jessie Drake series
Kring, Michael K
• Space mavericks series
Kroeber, Theodora
• Ishi series
Kroll, Steven
• Hit and Run Gang series
• Newsman Ned series
Kronmiller, Hildegarde
see **Lawrence, Hilda**
Kruchten, Marcia
• Omni odysseys trilogy
Kruger, Paul
• Phil Kramer series
Kruimov, Vladimir
see **Krymov, Vladimir**
Kruk, Zofia
• Taste series
Krulick, Nancy E
• Curious George series
• Lassie series
Krulik, Nancy E
Dick Tracy fun book of puzzles and games
Dick Tracy film series (2)
Superman IV
Superman series (6)
Krull, Kathleen
• Beginning to learn series
Kruse, Max
• Lion series
• Urmal series
Kruss, James
• Captain Madirankowitch series
• Florentine series
• Henrietta Chuffertrain series
Krymov, Vladimir
• Imp trilogy
Kubasch, Heike
• Middle Earth quest series
Kubasik, Christopher
• Earthdawn series
Kube-McDowell, Michael Paul
• Robot city series
• Trigon disunity trilogy
Kubinyi, Laszlo
• Shukru series
Kuhlken, Ken
• Tom Hickey trilogy
Kuhn, Dwight
• Hidden life series
Kuklin, Susan
• Going to my class series
• Taking my pet to the vet series
• When I see series
Kuller, Jo van Ammers-
see **Ammers-Kuller, Jo van**
Kumin, Maxine W
• Eggs of things series
Kummer, Frederic Arnold
• Hades series
• Judge Henry Tyson series
Kunhardt, Edith
• Danny series
• Which would you choose series
Kuniczak, Wieslaw Stanislaw
• Polish war trilogy
Kunnas, Mauri
• Ricky, Rocky and Ringo series
Kuntz, Robert
• Advanced dungeons and dragons reference books series
Kupperberg, Paul
• Amazing Spiderman series
• Incredible Hulk series
• Marvel superheroes, new series
Kuratomi, Chizuko
• Mister Bear series
Kurland, Michael
• Greenwich Village trilogy
• Lord Darcy series
• Mission series
• Sherlock Holmes sequels series
Kurten, Bjorn
• Dance series
• Pleistocene mammals series
Kurtz, Katherine
• Adept trilogy
• Chronicles of the Deryni trilogy
• Heirs of Saint Camber trilogy
• Histories of King Kelson trilogy
• Legends of Camber of Culdi trilogy
Kushner, Ellen
• Choose your own adventure series
Kutak, Rosemary
• Doctor Marc Castleman series
Kuttner, Henry
• Doctor Michael Gray series
Kwitz, Mary DeBall
• Little Chick series
• Mousehaven Manor series
Kyd, Thomas
• Sam Phelan series
Kyle, David Ackerman
• Lensman series
Kyle, Elisabeth
• Furze series
Kyle, Robert
• Ben Gates series
Kyle, Sefton
see also **Durham, David; Vickers, Roy**
• Inspector J Rason series
Kyne, Peter Bernard
• Cappy Ricks series

L

Laan, Dick
• Fingerling series
Labelle, Claude A
• Ranger Boys series
Lach-Szyrma, Wladislaw Somerville
• Venus series
Lackey, Mercedes
• Bardic voices series
• Diana Tregarde series
• Heralds of Valdemar trilogy
• Last Herald-Mage trilogy
• Mage winds series
• Sword of knowledge series
• Sword of knowledge trilogy
• Vows and honor series
Lacon Watson, Edmund Henry
see **Watson, Edmund Henry Lacon**
Lacy, Ed
• Lee Hayes series
• Lieutenant Dave Wintino series
• Toussaint Moore series
Ladd, Elizabeth
• Meg of Heron's Neck series
Ladd, Justin
• Abilene series
Ladline, Robert
• J A Remington series
Lafferty, Raphael Aloysius
• Argos mythos series
• Coscuin chronicles series
Sinbad, the thirteenth voyage
Arabian Nights trilogy (3)
Lafitte-Cyon, Francoise
see **Delisle, Francoise**
Laflin, Jack
see also **Winston, Peter**
• Adjusters series
• Gregory Hiller series
La Frenais, Ian
• Likely lads series
Lagerkvist, Par
• Tobias trilogy
Lagerlof, Selma
• Jerusalem series
• Nils series
• Ring of the Lowenskolds trilogy
Laine, Annabel
• Earl of Moriston series
Laing, Alexander
• Doctor Scarlett series
Laing, Kenneth
• Rolling Stone series
Laing, Patrick
• Patrick Laing series
Laird, Elizabeth
• Contrasts series
• Cubby Bears series
• Faces series
• Little red tractor series
• Olaf the Viking series
• Toucan Tecs series
Lait, Jack
• Polack Annie series
Lake, David John
• Breakout series
• Dextra series
• Time traveller series
• Xuma series
Laker, Rosalind
see also **Paul, Barbara**
• Easthampton trilogy
Laklan, Carli
• Nancy Kimball series
Lallemand, Evelyne
• Secret Seven series
La Mahotiere, Mary de
see **De la Mahotiere, Mary**
La Mare, Walter de
see **De la Mare, Walter**
Lamb, Geoffrey Frederick
see **Balaam**
Lamb, Harold
• Crusades series
• Khlit the Cossack series
Lamb, J Dayne
• Teal Stewart series
Lamb, J J
• Zack Rolfe series
Lamb, Lynton
• Superintendent Quill and Inspector Glover series
Lambard, Creede
• Car wars adventure gamebook series
Lambard, Sharleen
• Car wars adventure gamebook series
Fuel's gold
Car wars adventure gamebook series (2)
Lambdin, Dewey
• Alan Lewrie series
Lambert, Derek
see also **Falkirk, Richard**
• Angels in the snow series
• Living and sleeping series
• Quote series
• Reporter series
Lambert, Dudley
• Glyn Morgan series
Lambert, Eric
• Australian Army in World War II series
Lambert, Janet
• Campbells series
• Candy Kane series
• Christie Drayton series
• Cinda Hollister series
• Dria Meredith trilogy
• Jordons series
• Parri Macdonald series
• Patty and Ginger series
• Penny Parrish series
• Tippy Parrish series
Lambert, Mortan
• Relentless marriage series
Lambert, Rosa
• Glyn Morgan series
Lambert, Thelma
• Sam series
Lambert, William J
• Adonis trilogy
• Demon series
• Tlen series
Lambot, Isabel
see **Turner, Mary**
Lambourne, John
• Jim Burnett series
Lamburn, John Battersby Crompton
see **Lambourne, John**
Lamburn, Richmal Crompton
see **Crompton, Richmal**
Lamming, George
• Caribbean series
• San Cristobal series
L'Amour, Louis
see also **Burns, Tex**
• Chantry family series
• Chick Bowdrie series
• Cullen Baker series
• Lance Kilkenny series
• Sackett family series
• Talon family series
Lampitt, Dinah
• Sutton Place trilogy
Lamplugh, Lois
• Allen family series
Lampman, Evelyn Sibley
• Shy stegosaurus series
Lampton, Christopher
• Alert series
• New theories series
• Nintendo series
• Simple machines series
Lan Tso-chi
see **Lancing, George**
Lancaster, Osbert
• Memory series
Lancaster, William Joseph Cosens
see **Collingwood, Harry**
Lance, Kathryn
see also **Beach, Lynn**
• Pandora series

Lance, Leslie
• Nurse Verena Frodesley series
Lancer, Jack
• Christopher Cool series
Lancing, George
• Tzu Hsi series
Lancour, Gene
• Dirshan series
Land, Jon
• Blaine McCracken series
Landa, Norbert
• Rabbit and Chicken series
Landau, Mark Aleksandrovich
see **Aldanov, Mark**
Landis, Arthur Harold
• Camelot series
Landis, James David
• Sisters impossible series
Landon, Herman
• Gray Phantom series
• Picaroon series
Landon, Hilary
• Timothy Drewer series
Landon, Lucinda
• Meg Mackintosh series
Landsborough, Gordon
• Desert commandos series
Lane, Andy
• Timewyrm series
Lane, Anna
• Maria trilogy
Lane, Carl Daniel
• Altair series
Lane Crauford, William Harold
see **Crauford, William Harold Lane**
Lane, Elizabeth
• Uncle Charlie series
Lane, Gret
• Inspector Hook series
• John Barrin series
• Kate Marsh series
Lane, Jane
• Charles I trilogy
• Montague family series
• Stuart series
Lane, Jeremy
• Whitney Wheat series
Lane, John, *Mrs*
see **Lane, Anna**
Lane, Kenneth
• Medical nobody series
Lane, Margaret
• Shipwreck series
Lane, Maxie
• Running series
Lane, W
• Sherlock Holmes sequels series
Lang, Andrew
He
She series (3)
• Pantouflia series
• Pickle series
Lang, Brad
• Fred Crockett series
Lang, Frances
see also **Mantle, Winifred**
• Gillonne de Beauregard series
Lang, John Dunmore
• Life and times series
Lang, Maria
• Christer Wick series
Lang, Simon
• Skipjack series
Lang, Theo
see **Piper, Peter**
Lang-Sims, Lois
• Time to be born series
Lange, Dagmar
see **Lang, Maria**
Lange, Dietrich
• American Indian series
Lange, John Frederick
see **Norman, John**
Langford, George
• Pic series
Langham, James R
• Samuel G Abbott series
Langholm, A D
• Clover Club series
Langholm, Neil
• Vikings series
Langley, John
• Walt Warren series
Langley, John Prentice
• Aviation series
Langley, Lee
• Lieutenant Christopher Jensen series
Langmaid, Kenneth
see **Laing, Kenneth**
Langoulant, Allan
• Captain Ashe series
Langsam, Devra Michele
• Vulcan reflections series
Langton, Jane
• Edward, Eleanor and Georgie Hall series
• Grace Jones series
• Homer Kelly series
Langworthy, John Luther
• Bird Boys series
Lanham, Edwin
• Frank Luther series
• Lieutenant Gray series
• Lieutenant Madigan series
• Wind in the banner series
Lanier, Sterling Edmund
• Brigadier Ffellowes series
• Hiero Desteen series
Lansdale, Joe Richard
• Batman series
• Drive-in series
Lansing, Elizabeth
• Nancy Naylor series
Lansing, John
• Black Eagles series
Lansing, Karen E
• Time series
Lantz, Francess Lin
• Making out series
• Overnight Sensation series
• Swept away series
• Varsity coach series
La Pasture, Elizabeth de
see **De la Pasture, Elizabeth**
Lapierre, Janet
• Meg Halloran series
Lapka, Fay S
• Caro series
La Plante, Jerry
• Chameleon series
La Plante, Lynda
• Widows series
La Plante, Richard
• Josef Tanaka series
• Tegne series
La Prade, Ernest
• Alice in Wonderland sequels series
Laqueur, Walter
• Doctor Richard Lasson series
Larbalestier, Philip George
• Inspector Michael Farrant series
Larbey, Bob
• Good life series
Lardner, Ring
• Jack the Kaiser killer series
Large, Ernest Charles
• Charles Pry series
Large, Jean Henry
• Nancy, Girl Scout series
Lariar, Lawrence
see also **Knight, Adam**
• Ham Macandrew and Homer Bull series
Larkin, Rochelle T
• Desire trilogy
• Donna series
Larminie, Margaret Beda
see **Yorke, Margaret**
La Roche, Mazo de
see **De la Roche, Mazo**
Larom, Henry V
• Mountain pony series
Larrabeiti, Michael de
see **De Larrabeiti, Michael**
Larsen, Anita
• Histories mysteries series
• Lost series
Larsen, Gaylord D
• Henry Garrett series
Larsen, Glen A
Hardy boys and Nancy Drew meet Dracula
Hardy boys series (129)
Hardy boys and Nancy Drew meet Dracula
Nancy Drew series (122)
Larsen, Rebecca
• Going for it series
Larson, Charles
• Nils-Frederick Blixen series
Larson, Gary
• Far Side series
Larson, Glen A
• Battlestar Galactica series
• Knight Rider series
Larson, Majliss
• Star trek series
Larsson, Gosta
• Daily bread series
Larteguy, Jean
• Algerian series
• Central America series
Lascaux, Simon
• Ebony masters series
Lascelles, Walter
see **Downe, Patrick**
Lasgarn, Hugh
• Vet in green pastures series
Lash, Joseph P
• Eleanor Roosevelt series
Lasker, Toy
• New York in maps series
Lasky, Kathryn
• Starbuck family series
Lasser, Dustin
Space nymph
Luke Skywalker series (7)
Lassez, M
• Years between series
Lassiter, Adam
• Dennison's war series
Lasswell, Mary
• Mrs Feeley series
Latham, Albert George, *Mrs*
see **Latham, Katharine Wright**
Latham, Brad
• Hook series
Latham, Katharine Wright
• Christabel series
Latham, Mavis
see **Clark, Mavis Thorpe**
Lathen, Emma
see also **Dominic, R B**
• John Putnam Thatcher series
Latimer, Jim
• James Bear series
Latimer, Jonathan
• Bill Crane series
Latis, Mary J
see **Dominic, R B; Lathen, Emma**
Latta, Gordon
• Arnholt series
Latter, Simon
• Girl from U.N.C.L.E.series
Lattimore, Eleanor Frances
• Little Pear series
Lauben, Philip
• Captain Homer Clay series
Lauber, Patricia
• Clarence series
Laumer, Keith
• Avengers series
• Bolo series
• Invaders series
• Lafayette O'Leary series
• Mister Curlon series
• Retief series
Star colony
Star colony series (2)
• Star colony series
Launay, Andrew Joseph
see **Launay, Droo**
Launay, Droo
• Adam Flute series
Laura, Ronald S
• Matrix principle series
Laurance, Andrew
• Nostradamus trilogy
Laurence, Janet
• Darina Lisle series
Laurence, Louise
• Wyndcliffe series
Laurence, Margaret
• Manawaka series
Laurence, Murray
• Compulsive traveller series
Laurenson, Robert Mark
• Marc Jordan series
Laurent, Cecil Saint-
see **Saint-Laurent, Cecil**
Laurent, Jacques
see **Saint-Laurent, Cecil**
Lauria, Frank
• Doctor Owen Orient series
Laurie-Long, Ernest
• Captain Flynn series
• Lizzie Collins series
• Simpson series
Lavallee, Barbara
• Imagine living here series
Lavell, Edith
• Girl Scouts series
• Linda Carlton series
• Mary Lou series
Lavelle, Sheila
• Charlie Ellis and Angela Mitchell series
• Harry series
• Jupiter Jane series
• Ursula Bear series
Lavender, William
• Hargrave journal series
Laverty, Maura
• Delia Scully series
Lavine, Sigmund Arnold
• Wonders of nature series
Law, Janice
• Anna Peters series
Law, Simone
• Wife swap series
Law, Winifred
• Ralph Hannon series
Lawhead, Stephen
• Brown Ears series
• Dragon King trilogy
• Emphyrion series
• Howard series
• Pendragon trilogy
• Riverbank series
• Song of Albion trilogy
Lawler, Ray
• Doll trilogy
Lawlor, Laurie
• Addie series
Lawrence, Alfred
• Columbo series
Lawrence, Ann
• Oggy series
Lawrence, Cynthia
• Barbie series
Lawrence, David
• Danny Leather series
Lawrence, David Herbert
• Brangwen family series
• Lady Chatterley series
Lawrence, Hilda
• Mark East series
Lawrence, James D
• Angela Harpe series
Lawrence, Jim
see also **Adams, Hunter**
• A.I. Gang series
• ESP McGee series
Lawrence, Josephine
• Brother and sister series
• Elizabeth Ann series
• Linda Lane series
Lawrence, Judith Ann
• Star trek original series
Lawrence, Lars
• Seed series
Lawrence, Margery
• Club of the Round Table series
• Miles Pennoyer series
Lawrence, Michael
• Johnny Amsterdam series
Lawrence, Steven C
• Tom Slattery series
Lawson, Robert
• Rabbit Hill series
Lawson, Robert Neale
• Shipmates series
Lawson, Susan
• Endless quest crimson crystal adventure series
Lawson, W B
• Dalton Boys series
• Jesse James series
Lawton, Charles
• Clarkeville series
Lawton, Wilbur
see also **Deering, Fremont B; West, Marvin**
• Boy aviators series
• Dreadnaught boys series
• Ocean Wireless Boys series
Lax, William Henry
• Poplar series
Laxalt, Robert
• Basque trilogy
Layberry, Layton George Joseph
• Oakleigh Farm series
Laymon, Carl
see **Laymon, Richard Carl**
Laymon, Richard Carl
• Strange Occurrence Squad series
• Twilight series
Lazare, Lewis
• Ernie Astorbilt series
Lea, Alec
• Varden family series
Lea, Fanny Heaslip
• Half-angel series
Lea, Timothy
see also **Grape, Oliver; Wood, Christopher**
• Confessions series
Leach, Christopher
• Dave Bourne series
• Long John Silver series
Leacock, Stephen
• Nonsense novels series
Leader, Charles
see also **Charles, Robert**
• David Chan series
• Mike McCall series
• Paul Mason series
• Rick McAdden series
Leahy, Syrell Rogovin
• Wolfe family series
Learmonth, David
• Silas Wortenheimer series
Learning, Walter
• Sherlock Holmes drama series
Leasor, James
• Aristo Autos series
• Doctor Jason Love series
• Far East series
Leather, Edwin
• Rupert Conway series
Leatherdale, Clive
Dracula, the novel and the legend
Dracula series (26)
Leavy, Una
• Tom series
Le Baron, Anthony
Meteor men
Invaders series (1)
Le Baron, Grace
• Falcons-Height trilogy
• Janet trilogy
LeBeau, Roy
• Buckskin series
Leblanc, Maurice
• Arsene Lupin series
Le Breton, Auguste
• Rififi series
Lebreton, Denise
• Little Tom series
Le Breton Martin, Edward
see **Martin, Edward Le Breton**
Le Breton, Thomas
• Mrs May series
Lebrun, Claude
• Little Brown Bear series
Lecale, Errol
• Specialist series
Le Carre, John
• George Smiley series
Leckie, Robert Hugh
see **Barlow, Roger; Porter, Mark**
Ledd, Paul
• Shelter Morgan series
Lederer, Norbert
• Frederick Hunt series
Lederer, Paul Joseph
see also **Winters, Logan**
• Indian heritage series
Lederer, William Julius
• Mister Roberts series
Leduc, Violette
• Batarde series
Ledwith, Frank
• Ship insurance series
Lee, Alice Lester
• Co-ed series
Lee, Austin
see also **Austwick, John**
• Miss Flora Hogg series
Lee, Babs
• Argus Steele series
Lee, Benjamin
• Mike and Bill Hendry series
Lee, Bernie
• Tony and Pat Pratt series
Lee, Edward
• Red Blake series
Lee, Ella
• Jean Mary series
Lee, Elsie
• Sam Benedict series
Lee, Fleming
• Saint series
Lee, Gentry
• Rama series
Lee, Gypsy Rose
• Gypsy Rose Lee series
Lee, Howard
see also **Barry, Mike; Malzburg, Barry Norman**
• Kung Fu series
Lee, Jennette Barbour Perry
• Millicent Newberry series
• Uncle William series
Lee, John
• Unicorn trilogy
Lee, John Alexander
• Shiner Slattery series
Lee, John Darrell
• Brian Douglas series
Lee, Laurel
• Barnaby Frost series
• Godspeed series
Lee, Laurie
• Cotswolds series
Lee, Leslie
• Furry tales series

Lee, Mabel
• Bloomer girl series
Lee, Manfred Bennington
see **Queen, Ellery; Queen, Ellery, Junior; Ross, Barnaby**
Lee, Marie G
• Ellen series
Lee, Norma
• Beautiful Gunner series
Lee, Norman
see **Armstrong, Raymond; Corrigan, Mark; Hobart, Robertson**
Lee, Patrick
see also **Derrick, Lionel**
• Six-Gun Samurai series
Lee, Robert
• Fishy business series
Lee, Robert Corwin
• Michael Glenn series
Lee, Samantha
• Owen Lightbringer trilogy
Robert Louis Stevenson's Doctor Jekyll and Mister Hyde
Doctor Jekyll series (1)
Lee, Sharon
• Agent series
Lee, Steve
• Kung Fu western series
Lee, Tammie
• Leather and lace series
Lee, Tanith
• Birthgrave trilogy
• Castle of dark series
• Don't bite the sun series
• Secret books of Paradys series
• Tales from the flat earth series
• Wars of Vis trilogy
Lee, Vicki
• My class series
Lee, W W
• Jefferson Birch series
Lee, Wayne
• Bat Masterson series
Leedy, Loreen
• Dragon series
Leek, Margaret
• Stephen Marryat series
Leeming, Jill
see **Chaney, Jill**
Leeming, John Fishwick
• Claudius the bee series
• Fontana d'amore series
Lees, Dan
• Constable Craig series
• Jeff Plummer series
Lees-Milne, James
• Ancestral voices series
Leeson, Muriel
• Promise keeper series
Leeson, Robert
• Alec Bowden series
• Cloud Valley series
• Demon bike rider series
• Frogs series
• Grange Hill series
• Hob Lane series
• Jan series
• Long John Silver series
• Matthew Morten trilogy
• Reversible giant series
• Time rope series
• Tucker series
• Zarnia experiment series
Leeuwen, Jean van
see **Van Leeuwen, Jean**
Lefcourt, Peter
• Hollywood series
Lefebure, Molly
• Scratch and Company series
Le Feuvre, Amy
• Odd series
Leffingwell, Albert
see **Chambers, Dana; Jackson, Giles**
Legat, Michael
• Silk maker series
Le Grand
see **Henderson, Le Grand**
Le Grand, Leon
• Michael Berresford series
Legris, Jean-Luc
Complete Naff guide
Naff series (1)
Naff sex guide
Naff series (2)
Le Guin, Ursula Kroeber
• Adventures in Kroy series
• Catwings series
• Earthsea series
• Hain series
Lehmann, John
• In my own time series
Lehmann, Rosamond
• Olivia, Kate and Reggie series
Lehmann, Rudolf Chambers
• Picklock Holes series
Lehrer, Jim
• Dreamers series
• One-Eyed Mack series
Leib, Franklin Allen
• Vietnam War series
Leiber, Fritz
• Changewar series
• Fafhrd and Gray Mouser series
Tarzan and the valley of gold
Tarzan series (24)
Leiber, Justin Fritz
• Beyond trilogy
• House of Eigin series
Leibold, Jay
• Choose your own adventure series
Leigh, Helena
• Vintage years trilogy
Leigh, J E Austen-
see **Austen-Leigh, J E**
Leigh, Margaret Mary
• Highland series
Leigh, Petra
• Garnet series
Leigh, Richard
• Order of Sion series
Leigh, Robert
• Sam Carroll series
Leigh, Roberta
• Mister Hero series
• Sara and Hoppity series
• Tomahawk series
• Torchy series
Leigh, Stephen
• Doctor Bones series
• Neweden trilogy
• Next wave series
• Robots and aliens series
Leighton, Edward
see also **Barrett, Geoffrey John**
• Muvian series
Leighton, Robert
• Kiddie trilogy
• Red Patrol series
• Sergeant Silk series
Leinster, Murray
• Joe Kenmore trilogy
• Land of the giants series
• Med Service series
• Time tunnel series
Leitch, David
• Family secrets series
Leitch, Patricia
• Jinny series
Leitfred, Robert H
• Simon Crole series
Leith, Disney, ***Mrs***
see **Leith, Mary Charlotte Julia**
Leith, Mary Charlotte Julia
• Lachlan series
• Nora's friends series
Lejeune, Alice
• Barsetshire series
Lejeune, Anthony
• Adam Gifford series
• Glowrey series
Lely, James A
Battlestar Galactica
Battlestar Galactica series (14)
Lem, Stanislaw
• Ijon Tichy series
• Pirx series
Lemarchand, Elizabeth
• Superintendent Tom Pollard series
Lemieux, Anne
• Super Sam Snout series
Lemieux, Kenneth
see **Orvis, Kenneth**
Lenehan, John Christopher
• Charlie Ryan series
• Inspector Kilby series
L'Engle, Madeleine
• Austin family series
• Crosswicks journals series
• Katherine Forrester series
• Meg Murry series
• Poly and Charles O'Keefe series
• Prayers series
Lengstrand, Rof
• Pony Club series
Lenski, Lois
• Davy series
• Debbie series
• Regional series
• Roundabout America series
• Seasons series
• Small family series
• Two brothers series
Lenton, Anthony
• Graham Darren series
Leon, Donna
• Commissario Guido Brunetti series
Leon, Henry Cecil
see **Cecil, Henry**
Leonard, Charles L
• Paul Kilgerrin series
Leonard, Elmore
• Frank Ryan series
Leonard, Marcia
• Feelings series
• Fifteen series
Leonard, Mary Finley
• Susan trilogy
Leopold, Aldo
• Sand County series
Le Page, Rand
• Terran empire series
Leppard, Lois Gladys
• Mandie series
Le Queux, William
• Otto von Heynitz series
Lerangis, Peter
Dick Tracy
Dick Tracy film series (1)
Dick Tracy, a catch-a-crook adventure
Dick Tracy film series (2)
• G.I.Joe series
• Time machine series
• Time traveler series
Voyage home
Star trek moving picture series (4)
Leroe, Ellen Whitney
• Bixby Wyler series
• Cupid Delaney series
• H.O.W.L. High series
Leroux, Etienne
• Welgevonden trilogy
Leroux, Gaston
• Carolus Herbert series
• Cheri-Bibi series
• Joseph Rouletabille series
Leroy, Amelie Claire
see **Stuart, Esme**
Lesage, Alain Rene
• Devil upon two sticks series
Lesley, Craig
• Danny and Jack Kachiah series
Lesley, Martine
• Morgan Swift find your fate series
Leslie, Anita
• Train to nowhere series
Leslie, Colin
• House of Godwin series
Leslie, David Stuart
• Ernie Pratt series
Leslie, Doris
• Follietts and Peverills series
Leslie, Emma
• Leofwine series
Leslie, Francis
• Jimmy Langry series
Leslie, Frederic Andrew
• Sherlock Holmes drama series
Leslie, Henrietta
• Arlington Street trilogy
Leslie, Jean
• Peter Ponsonby series
Leslie, John Randolph Shane
see **Leslie, Shane**
Leslie, Madeline
see also **Baker, Harriette Newell Baker; Hattie, Aunt**
• Little Agnes series
• Little Frankie series
• Little robins series
• Minnie's pets series
• Play and study series
• Tim the scissors grinder series
• Woodbine series
Leslie, Norman
• Jumbo Rutherford series
Leslie, Peter
• Dangerman series
• Father Hayes trilogy
• Girl from U.N.C.L.E.series
• Invaders series
• Man from U.N.C.L.E. series
Leslie, Richard
see also **Bickers, Richard Townshend**
• Heracles trilogy
• Victory trilogy
Leslie, Shane
• Oppidan trilogy
Lesser, Milton
see **Marlowe, Stephen**
Lessing, Doris
see also **Somers, Jane**
• Canopus in Argus archives series
• Children of violence series
Diaries of Jane Somers
Jane Somers series (2)
Lessiter, Mike
• Team names series
Lester, Alison
• Augustus series
• Australian children series
Lester, Edward Castellain
• Nathaniel Moody series
Lester, Frank
• Geoffrey Slade series
Lester, Julius
• Tales of Uncle Remus series
Lester, Pauline
• Marjorie Dean college series
• Marjorie Dean high school series
• Marjorie Dean post-graduate series
Lestienne, Voldemar
• Three Musketeers series
L'Estrange, Anna
see also **Thorne, Nicola; Yorke, Katherine**
• Wuthering Heights series
L'Estrange, James
see **Strang, Herbert**
Lethbridge, Katharine Greville
• Ollafubs series
Lethbridge, Mabel
• Fortune grass series
Lethbridge, Peter
• Jeremy series
Lett, Gordon
• Italian Resistance series
Letts, Barry
• Doctor Who scripts series
• Doctor Who series
Levene, Philip
• Ambrose West series
Lever, Christopher
• Naturalized animals series
Leverich, Kathleen
• Best enemies series
Leverson, Ada
• Edith Ottley trilogy
Levi, Peter
• Ben Jonson series
Levi, Primo
• Survival in Auschwitz series
Levin, Betty
• Claudia and Evan trilogy
Levin, Marcia Lauter Obrasky
see **Martin, Marcia**
Le Vine, Jack
• Jack Le Vine series
Levine, Paul
• Jake Lassiter series
Levinrew, Will
• Professor Herman Brierly series
Levinson, Leonard
see also **Brady, Nicholas; Chang, Lee; Chase, Glen; Jones, J Farragut; Kirk, Philip; Rawls, Philip; Rossi, Bruno**
• Richard Bronson series
Levison, Eric
• Doctor Edward Lester series
Levitsky, Ronald
• Nate Rosen series
Levy, Elizabeth
Dracula is a pain in the neck
Dracula series (26)
• Fat Albert series
• Father John Murphy series
• Gymnasts series
• Jody and Jake series
• Magic mystery series
• Running out series
• Something queer series
Levy, Muriel
• Wonk series
Lewerth, Margaret
• Roundtree women series
Lewi, Charlotte Armstrong
see **Armstrong, Charlotte**
Lewin, Hugh
• Jafta series
• Little Indian series
• Second chance series
Lewin, Michael Zinn
• Albert Samson series
• Lieutenant Leroy Powder series
Lewin, Ted
• World within a world series
Lewis, Alfred Henry
• Wolfville series
Lewis, Caroline
• Alice in Wonderland parodies series
Lewis, Catherine
• Lisa Thomas series
Lewis, Cecil Day
see **Blake, Nicholas**
Lewis, Clive Staples
• Narnia series
• Screwtape series
• Space trilogy
Lewis, Colin
• Howard Hayes trilogy
Lewis, David
• Steve Savage series
Lewis, E W
• Sabo series
Lewis, Elliott
• Fred Bennett series
Lewis, Francine
• Polly French series
Lewis, Harriet
• Edith Trevor series
• Tresillian series
Lewis, Hilda
• Mary of England series
• Mary Tudor trilogy
Lewis, Irwin
• Horace Clarke series
Lewis, Jack
• Sexton Blake series
Lewis, Jean
• Bugs Bunny series
• Flintstones series
• Rainbow Brite series
• Scooby Doo series
• Tom and Jerry series
• Wacky Witch series
Lewis, Judith Mary
see **Berrisford, Judith Mary**
Lewis, Lange
• Lieutenant Richard Tuck series
Lewis, Linda
• Linda series
Lewis, Lorna
• Shirley series
Lewis, Mary Christianna
see **Brand, Christianna**
Lewis, Michael
• Sergeant Hobbs series
Lewis, Norman
• Dragon apparent series
Lewis, Oscar
• Sanchez family series
Lewis, Richard
Lone Ranger adventure stories
Lone Ranger series (22)
Lewis, Roy Harley
• Matthew Coll series
Lewis, Royston
• Arnold Landon series
• Eric Ward series
• Inspector John Crow series
Lewis, Sinclair
• American society series
Lewis, Ted
• Jack Carter series
Lewis, Warren Hamilton
• Louis XIV series
Lewis, Wyndham
• Human age trilogy
Lewitt, Shariann N
• Cyberstealth series
• U.S.S.A. series
Lexau, Joan M
• Benjie series
• I should have stayed in bed series
• Olaf series
• Strawberry Shortcake series
Ley, Alice Chetwynd
• Eversley Family series
• Justin Rutherford and Anthea series
Leyland, Eric
• Abbey series
• Bill, Jake and Ned series
• Captain series
• Flame series
• Hunter Hawk series
• Jack Meredith and Uncle George series
• Jolly Roger series
• Max and Scrap series
• Nicky and Simon Carr series
• Red Lawson series
• Rip Randall series
• Six Gun Gauntlet series
• Skinny series
• Steven Gale series
• Sussex series
Leyland, Mal
• Kerry series
Leyton, E K
• Dracula series
Libenzi, Ermanno
• Ernest series

Libman, Gary
Superman, the movie
Superman series (7)
Lichtenberg, Elisabeth Jacoba
see **Someren, Liesje van**
Lichtenberg, Jacqueline
• Dushau trilogy
• Luren series
• Molt brother series
• Sime-Gen series
Liddell, Robert
• Charles Harbord series
• Relations series
Liddon, Eloise
• Peggy Fairfield series
Lide, Mary
• Ann of Cambray trilogy
Lieberman, Rosalie
• Brother Angelo series
Liebling, Howard
Trial of Billy Jack
Billy Jack series (2)
Lientz, Gerald
• Middle Earth quest series
• Narnia solo games series
Lightner, Alice Martha
• Rock trilogy
Lilar, Francoise
see **Mallet-Joris, Francoise**
Lilius, Irmelin Sandman
see **Sandman Lilius, Irmelin**
Lilley, Peter
see **Buckingham, Bruce; Chandos, Dane**
Lilley, Tom
• Police Special Branch series
Lillie, Lucy Cecil
• Squire's daughter series
Lillington, Kenneth
• Soapy series
Lilly, Jean
• Bruce Perkins series
Lilly, Kenneth
• Animal series
Limonov, Edward
• Eddie Limonov series
Lin, Yutang
• Chinese village series
Linaker, Michael R
see also **Hunter, Neil; Jordan, Matt**
• Scorpion series
Lincoln, Andrew Carey
• Motorcycle chums series
Lincoln, Henry
Holy Blood and the Holy Grail
Order of Sion series (1)
Messianic legacy
Order of Sion series (2)
Lincoln, Jeanie Gould
• Marjorie series
• Wolcott family series
Lincoln, Joseph Crosby
• Captain Eri series
• Mister Pratt series
Lincoln, Maurice
• Reginald Massingham series
Lincoln, Natalie Sumner
• Detective Ferguson series
• Inspector Mitchell series
Lind, Anton
• Tony series
Lind, Jakov
• Steps series
Lindbergh, Anne Morrow
• Pineapple Place series
• Unicorn series
Lindgren, Astrid
• Bill Bergson series
• Bullerby series
• Emil series
• I want series
• Karlsson-on-the-Roof series
• Kati series
• Mardie series
• Marten family series
• Pippi Longstocking series
• Rasmus series
• Tomten series
Lindgren, Barbro
• Sam series
• Wild baby series
Lindholm, Megan
• Reindeer people series
• Windsingers series
Lindop, Audrey Erskine
• Father Keogh series
Lindop, Edmund
• Modern America series
Lindquiest, Marie
• Texas promises trilogy
Lindquist, Jennie Dorothea
• Nancy Bruce series
Lindsay, Barbara
see **James, Josephine**
Lindsay, David T
• Inspector John Jay Jackson series
Lindsay, Elizabeth
• Heggerty Haggerty series
Lindsay, Frances
• Bim series
• Mister Bits and Pieces series
Lindsay, Harry
• Methodist idylls series
Lindsay, Hilarie
• Midget Mouse series
• Mister Poppleberry series
Lindsay, Jack
• British way series
• Life rarely tells trilogy
• Roman Republic trilogy
Lindsay, Joan
• Hanging Rock series
• Time without clocks series
Lindsay, Kathleen
• Cleopatra series
Lindsay, Norman
• Redheap trilogy
Lindsay, Paula
• Mark Rendle series
Lindsay, Philip
• Sir John Oldcastle series
• Sussex series
• Victorian England series
Lindsay, Rose
• Ma and pa series
Lindsey, David L
• Stuart Haydon series
Lindsey, Johanna
• Anthony Mallory series
• Hank Chavez series
• Kristen series
Lindsey, Robert
• Falcon series
Linebarger, Paul
see **Smith, Cordwainer**
Ling, Peter
• Crown series
• Doctor Who series
• Water series
Lingard, Joan
• Maggie McKinley quartet
• Sadie and Kevin series
Lingstrom, Freda
Andy Pandy, the baby clown
Andy Pandy series (42)
Linington, Elizabeth
see also **Blaisdell, Anne; Egan, Lesley; Shannon, Dell**
• Lieutenant Luis Mendoza series
• Sergeant Ivor Maddox series
Linklater, Eric
• Juan series
• Man on my back series
Linklater, Joseph Lane
• Silas Booth series
Links, Joseph Gluckenstein
• Lieutenant John Milton Schwab series
Linn, James Weber
• Campus series
Linscott, Gillian
• Birdie Linnett and Nimue Hawthorne series
Linton, Cathy
• Saint Lawrence's Hospital series
Linzee, David
• Sarah Saber and Chris Rockwell series
Lionni, Leon
• Colors, letters, numbers and words to talk about series
• Frederick series
• Pictures to talk about
Lippmann, Julie Mathilde
• Martha trilogy
Lipsyte, Roger
• Contender trilogy
• Summer trilogy
Liquori, Sal
• Psi Patrol trilogy
Lisle, David
• Isola Dering series
Lister, Gladys
• Jennifer series
• Leafy series
• Round series
• Starlight series
Lister, Stephen
• Kilakura series
• Sainte Monique series
Lister-Kay, John
White island
Camusfearna trilogy (3)
Litchfield, Michael
• Superintendent Fergus McQueen series
Little, Frances
• Lady of the decoration series
Little Georgie
see also **Gray, Walter T**
Bad boy's adventures
Bad boy series (4)
Little, Jean
• Anna series
• Emily Blair and Kate Bloomfield series
• Writer's education series
Little, Sylvia
• Castle School series
• Highcliff series
Little Sylvia
• Queen's Chantry series
Little, Sylvia
• Stanton's series
Littler, Angela
• Jim and Jam series
Littleton, Kay
• Jean Craig series
Litvinoff, Samuel
• Faces of terror series
Litvinoff, Sarah
Allan Quatermain and the lost city of gold
Allan Quatermain series (16)
Allan Quatermain and the lost city of gold
King Solomon's mines series (2)
Allan Quatermain and the lost city of gold
Umslopogaas series (1)
Lively, Penelope
• Fanny series
Livings, Henry
• Ravensgill series
Livingston, Armstrong
• Jimmy Treynor series
• Peter Creighton series
Livingston, Jack
• Joe Birney series
Livingston, Kenneth
• Papers series
Livingston, Marjorie
• Karma series
Livingston, Nancy
• G D H Pringle series
• Mackie family series
Livingstone, Armstrong
see **Livingston, Armstrong**
Livingstone, Ian
• Fighting fantasy gamebook series
Livingstone, Malcolm
• Eric series
Llewellyn, Edward
• Douglas convolution trilogy
Llewellyn Lloyd, Richard David Vivian
see **Llewellyn, Richard**
Llewellyn, Richard
• Edmund Trothe series
• Huw Morgan series
Llewellyn, Sam
• Charlie Agutter series
• George Le Fanu Gurney trilogy
• Treasure Island series
Llewellyn-Jones, Derek
• Everyperson series
Llimona, Mercedes
• Strawberry Shortcake series
Lloyd, Alan R
• Kine trilogy
Lloyd, David
• Dinosaur days series
• Great escapes series
• Let's pretend series
Lloyd, Errol
• Nini series
Lloyd, Hugh
see also **Fitzhugh, Percy Keese**
• Hal Keen series
• Skippy Dare series
Lloyd, Jeremy
• Captain Beaky and his band series
• Captain Gregory Dangerfield series
Lloyd, Joanna
• Catherine series
Lloyd, John
• Meaning of liff series
Lloyd, John William
• Natural man series
Lloyd, Marjorie
• Fell Farm series
Lloyd, Noel
• Sherwood Forest series
Lloyd, Richard David Vivian Llewellyn
see **Llewellyn, Richard**
Lloyd-Jones, Buster
• Vet series
Lloyd-Jones, William Llewellyn
see **Lloyd-Jones, Buster**
Llywelyn, Morgan
• Odyssey of the Irish trilogy
Loates, Glen
• North American wildlife series
Lobe, Mira
• Pig series
Lobel, Arnold
• Frog and Toad series
• Guessing game series
• Mister Muster series
• Mouse series
Lobsang Rampa, Tuesday
• Third eye series
Lochak, Michelle
• Suzette and Nicholas series
Locherbie-Cameron, Margaret
see **Cameron, Margaret Locherbie**
Lochhead, Marion Cleland
• Victorian life series
Lochte, Dick
• Leo Bloodworth and Serendipity Dahlquist series
Lock, Arnold Charles Cooper
see **Cooper, Charles**
Lock, Joan
• Lady policeman series
Locke, Ashley
• Craig Kennedy series
Locke, Clinton W
• Perry Pierce series
Locke, Gladys Edson
• Inspector Burton series
• Mercedes Quero series
Locke, Joseph
• Nightmare on Elm Street series
Lockhart, John Gilbert
• Mrs McNab series
Lockhart, Robin Bruce
• Reilly series
Lockley, Ronald Mathias
• Island farm series
Locklin, Gerald
• Poop series
• Toad series
Lockridge, Frances
see also **Richards, Francis**
• Assistant District Attorney Bernie Simmons series
• Bill Wiegand series
• Cats series
• Inspector Merton Heimrich series
• Mister and Mrs North series
• Nathan Shapiro series
• Paul Lane series
Lockridge, Richard
see also **Richards, Francis**
• Assistant District Attorney Bernie Simmons series
• Bill Wiegand series
• Cats series
• Inspector Merton Heimrich series
• Mister and Mrs North series
• Nathan Shapiro series
• Paul Lane series
Lockwood, Ingersoll
• Baron Trump series
Lockwood, Lee
• Conversations series
Loder, Vernon
see also **Clandon, Henrietta**
• Donald Cairn series
• Inspector Brews series
• Inspector Chace series
Lodge, David
• Rummidge University series
Lodi, Maria
• Charlotte Morel series
Lodwick, John
• Desmond Thornton series
Loeb, Jeffrey
• Kids talk series
Lofgren, Ulf
• Albin series
• Patrick series
• Ricky series
Lofthouse, Jessica
• Countrygoer series
Lofting, Hugh
• Doctor Dolittle series
• Mrs Tubbs series
Lofts, Norah
• Clevely series
• Gad's Hall series
• Sir Godfrey Tallboys series
• Spice Islands series
• Suffolk trilogy
Logan, Jake
• John Slocum series
• Slocum giant series
Logan, Les
• Dark forces series
Logan, Mark
see also **Arlen, Leslie; Grange, Peter; Nicole, Christopher; York, Andrew**
• Nicholas Minnett series
Logan, Nora
• Pick-a-path series
Logue, Christopher
• Iliad adaptations series
Logue, John
• John Moore series
Lomax, Bliss
• Rainbow Ripley series
• Yellowstone series
Lombard, Nap
• Lord Winterstone series
London, Jack
• Jerry series
London, Jonathan
• Froggy series
Long, Amelia Reynolds
• Edward Trelawny series
• Peter Piper series
• Steve Carter series
Long, Derek
• Sexton Blake series
Long, Ernest Laurie-
see **Laurie-Long, Ernest**
Long, Gabrielle Margaret Vere
see **Bowen, Marjorie; Preedy, George Runnell**
Long, Harman
• Franklyn Keen series
• Silverface series
Long, Helen Beecher
• Do something series
Long, Manning
• Liz Parrott series
Long, Martin
• Inspector Keats and Tom Cotter series
Long, Max
• Komako Koa series
Long, Patrick
• Martyn Cale series
Long, William
see **Yates, Peter**
Long, William Stuart
see also **Stuart, Vivian**
• Australians series
Longford, Frank Pakenham
• Born to believe trilogy
Longhurst, Henry
• Good while it lasted series
Longley, W B
see also **Cutter, Tom; Meek, Joseph; Randall, Joshua; Randisi, Robert Joseph; Roberts, J R; Weston, Cole**
• Angel Eyes series
Longmate, Norman
• Inspector Bradley and Sergeant Raymond series
Longrigg, Roger
see **Drummond, Ivor; Erskine, Rosalind; Parrish, Frank**
Longstreet, Stephen
see also **Haggard, Paul**
• Dream seekers series
• Fiore family series
• Pedlock family series
Longstreth, Thomas Morris
• Royal Canadian Mounted Police series
Longtree, Warren T
• Ruff Justice series
Longyear, Barry Brookes
• Circus trilogy
• Dracon series
Lonsdale, Bertha
• Molly Hilton series
Loomis, Noel
• Bonanza series
• Wells Fargo series
Loos, Anita
• Lorelei Lee and Dorothy series
Lopez, Antony
see **Torrio, Vincente**
Lorac, E C R
see also **Carnac, Carol**
• Inspector Macdonald series
Lorbiecki, Marybeth
• Earthwise trilogy
Lord, Beman
• Spaceship series

Lord, Jeffrey
• Richard Blade series
Lord, Jeremy
• Colonel Winston Creevy series
Lord, Tom
• Tallman series
Lore, Phillips
see also **Smith, Terrence Lore**
• Leo Roi series
Lorimer, George Horace
• John Graham series
Lorimer, Graeme
• Street cars trilogy
Lorimer, Norma
• Egypt series
Lorimer, Sarah
• Street cars trilogy
Lorin, Amii
see also **Hohl, Joan**
• Samantha Wade series
Lorrah, Jean
• Savage Empire series
• Sime-Gen series
• Star trek fan series
• Star trek series
• Star trek, the next generation sequels series
• Star trek, the next generation series
Lorrimer, Claire
see also **Robins, Patricia**
• Mavreen trilogy
• Rochford trilogy
Lory, Robert
• Dracula horror series
• Horrorscope series
• Shamryke Odell series
• Trovo series
Lothrop, Harriet Mulford Stone
see **Sidney, Margaret**
Loti, Pierre
• Aziyade series
Lott, Stanley Makepeace
• Stephen Ringway series
Lottman, Eileen
see also **Willis, Maud**
• Bionic woman series
• Chrystal Falls series
Louhi, Kristiina
• Annie series
Lounsberry, Lionel
• Kit Carey series
• Merrill series
• Rob Ranger series
• Tom Truxton series
Lovecraft, Howard Phillips
• Colour out of space and time series
Lovejoy, Jack
• Guardians of the Three series
• Vision of beasts trilogy
Lovelace, Delos
• King Kong series
Lovelace, Maud Hart
• Betsy Ray series
Lovell, B E
• Edge Hannegan series
Lovell, Marc
see also **McShane, Mark**
• Appleton Porter series
• Elsie Vanetti series
Lovesey, Peter
• Bertie series
• Sergeant Cribb and Constable Thackeray series
Low, Ona
• Arvo Laurila series
Lowder, James
• Empires trilogy
• Ravenloft series
Lowe, Eric
• Stewart family series
Lowe, Myra
• Louisiana series
Lowell, Anne Hunter
• Sorority girls series
Lowell, Melissa
• Silver blades series
Lowery, Linda
Earthwise teacher's guide
Earthwise trilogy (3)
• Earthwise trilogy
• Endless quest series
• Heartquest series
Lowndes, Joan Selby
• Francis and Anne Woodward series
Lowndes, Marie Belloc
• Arcadia series
• Duchess Laura series
Lowry, Lois
• Anastasia Krupnik series
• Caroline Tate series
• Sam series
Lowry, Malcolm
• Voyage that never ends series
Lubicz, Isha Schwaller de
see **Schwaller de Lubicz, Isha**
Lucarotti, John
• Doctor Who series
Lucas, Edward Verrall
• Ancestors series
• Richard Haven series
• Richard series
• Winfield series
Lucas, George
see also **Foster, Alan Dean**
• Luke Skywalker series
Lucas, Norman
• Superintendent Bill Rowlands series
Lucas, Saint John
• First round series
Lucia, Rose
• Peter and Polly series
Luckey, William A
• Blue Mitchell series
Luckless, John
see also **Burkholz, Herbert; Irving, Clifford**
• Eddie Mancuso and Vasily Borgneff series
Luckner, Felix von
• Sea Devil series
Ludlow, Ian
• Vigilante series
Ludlum, Robert
• Bourne trilogy
• Tightrope-tense series
Ludwig, Charles Shelton
• Missionary adventure series
• Radio pals series
Luenn, Nancy
• Nessa series
• Unicorn series
Luigi, Belli
• Inspector Saint Clair series
• Vernon Templeton series
Lukeman, Tim
• Lhas'kar series
Lumbers, Eugene
• Smocker series
Lumley, Brian
• Cthulhu Mythos series
• Dreamlands series
• Necroscope series
• Psych trilogy
• Tales of the primal land series
• Titus Crow series
Lunatic, Humphry
• Noibla series
Lund, Helga
Blondie and Dagwood
Blondie and Dagwood series (12)
Lund, Trygve
• Dick Weston series
Lundgren, Ester Ringner-
see **Ringner-Lundgren, Ester**
Lundin, John Philip
• Erotic autobiography series
Lunn, Arnold
• Now I see series
Lunn, Hugh
• Lunns of Annerley Junction series
Lunt, Alice
• Jeanette series
• Redstone Farm series
Lupica, Mike
• Peter Finley series
Lupoff, Richard Allen
• Counterearth series
• Dungeon series
• Skull-Face series
• Sun's end series
Lupton, Joyce
• Leigh family series
Lurie, Morris
• Rappaport series
Luscombe, Tom
• Melbourne series
Lushington, Franklin
• Pigeon Hoo series
Lustbader, Eric
• Jake Maroc series
• Ninja series
• Sunset Warrior series
Luther, Mark Lee
• Arthur Raneleigh series
Lutyens, Emily
• Blessed girl series
Lutyens, Mary
• Effie Gray series
• Krishnamurti series
Lutz, Giles Alfred
see **Thompson, Gene**
Lutz, Gunther
see also **Horst, Karl; Williams, David**
• Nazi paratrooper series
• Panzer Platoon series
Lutz, John
• Alo Nudger series
• Fred Carver series
Luzie, Bernadette Theulet-
see **Theulet-Luzie, Bernadette**
Lyall, Edna
• Donovan series
Lyall, Gavin
• Major Harry Maxim series
Lycett-Green, Candida
• Hadrian series
Lydecker, John
• Doctor Who series
Lyle, Mel
• Power boys series
Lynam, Terence
• BMX Gang series
• Sally and Tom series
Lynch, Jack
• Peter Bragg series
Lynch, Lawrence L
• Carl Masters series
• Madeline Payne series
• Neil Bathurst series
• Van Vernet series
Lynch, Miriam
• Nell Willard series
Lynch, Patricia
• Brogeen the leprechaun series
• Turf-cutter's donkey series
Lynde, Stan
Latigo
Latigo series (4)
• Pardners series
• Rick O'Shay series
Lynds, Dennis
see also **Collins, Michael; Crowe, John; Sadler, Mark**
• Charlie Chan series
Lynds, William
see **Arden, William**
Lyne, Nairda
• Powranna series
Lynn, Elizabeth Anne
• Chronicles of Tornor trilogy
Lynn, Escott
• British Army trilogy
• Great War series
Lyon, Dana
• Hilda Trenton series
Lyon, Elinor
• Ian and Sovra series
• James, Alan and Roslin series
• Jean and Anna series
• Meredith family series
Lyon, Richard Kenneth
• War of the wizards trilogy
Lyon, Winston
• Batman series
Lyons, Arthur
• Jacob Asch series
Lyons, Genevieve
• Slievelea series
Lyons, Steve
• Timewyrm series
Lysaght, Brian
• Ben O'Malley series
Lyttleton, Humphrey
• As I please series
Lytton, Edward George Earle Lytton Bulwer-Lytton
• Eleusinia series
• Glyndon series
• Real and the ideal trilogy
Lytton, Shel
• Mustang Terry Simmons series

M

Maass, Joachim
• Astride the times series
Mabey, Margaret Mary Hamilton
see **Hamilton, Mary**
Maby, Nina Mary
see **Bawden, Nina**
McAdam, Preston
• Shield series
McAllister, Alister
see **Brock, Lynn**
Macao, Marshall
• K'ing Kung-Fu series
Macari, Mario D
• Fantasy forest series
Macarthur, David Wilson
see also **Wilson, David**
• Alec Sinclair series
• Larry Pearson series
McArthur, John
• Jack McBumby series
McArthur, Nancy
• Plant that ate dirty socks series
Macarthur, Ruth Alberta Brown
see **Brown, Ruth Alberta**
Macarthur, Wilson
see **Macarthur, David Wilson**
Macaulay, Fannie Caldwell
see **Little, Frances**
Macaulay, Rose
• Letters to a friend series
McAuley, Paul J
• Four hundred billion stars series
McAuliffe, Frank
• Augustus Mandrell series
Macao, Marshall
• K'ing Kung-Fu series
Macavoy, Roberta Ann
• Lens of the world trilogy
• Lute trilogy
• Mayland Long and Martha Macnamara series
McBain, Ed
see also **Hunter, Evan**
• Bingo Riggs and Handsome Kusak series
• Eighty Seventh Precinct series
• Matthew Hope series
McBain, Gordon
• Exoterra series
McBain, Laurie
• Sabrina Verrick series
Macbeth, George
• Cadbury series
McBratney, Sam
• Jimmy Zest series
• Thorensen Dykes series
McBrier, Michael
• Oliver and company series
McBrier, Page
• Oliver and company series
McCaffrey, Anne
• Damia series
• Ireta adventure series
• Killashandra series
• Pegasus series
• Pern and the Red Planet series
• Planet pirates series
• Rowan series
• Yanaba Maddock series
McCaig, Donald
• Nop series
McCall, Alex
• Soldier of fortune series
McCall, Dan
• Trip Bodley series
McCall, Edith
• Butternut Bill series
• Button family series
• Frontiers of America series
• How series
McCall, K T
• Johnny Buchanan series
McCall Smith, Alexander
• Akimbo series
McCann, Helen
• George series
McCann, Sean
• Dove's End Football Club series
McCardell, Roy Larcom
• Aunt and Uncle series
Maccargo, J T
• Mannix series
McCarry, Charles
• Paul Christopher series
McCarthy, Cormac
• Border trilogy
McCarthy, Gary
• Ballou family series
• Derby Man series
Legend of the Lone Ranger
Lone Ranger series (22)
• Rivers west series
• Wind river series
McCarthy, Justin Huntly
• Francois Villon trilogy
McCarthy, Maureen
• Mission top secret series
McCarthy, Ruth
• Three little rabbits series
McCarthy, Shaun
see **Cory, Desmond**
McCarty, Dennis
• Thlassa Mey series
McCaughrean, Geraldine
• Teddies series
McCaughren, Tom
• Foxes of Ireland series
• Irish history series
McCay, Bill
• Nintendo adventure series
McCay, William
• Young Indiana Jones chronicles series
• Young Indiana Jones series
McClary, Jane Stevenson
see **McIlvaine, Jane**
McCleery, William
Case for Mason
Perry Mason series (84)
McClelland, Diane Margaret
see **Pearson, Diane**
McCloskey, Robert
• Sal series
McCloy, Helen
• Basil Willing series
• Miguel Urizar series
McClung, Robert Marshall
• Endangered animals series
McClure, James
• Lieutenant Kramer and Sergeant Zondi series
Macclure, Victor
• Inspector Archie Burford series
McCollum, Michael
• Antares series
• Makers series
McConkey, James
• Court of memory trilogy
McConnell, Ashley
• Quantum leap series
McConnell, Frank
• Harry Garnish and Bridget O'Toole series
McConnell, James Douglas Rutherford
see **Rutherford, Douglas**
McConnell, Vicki P
• Nyla Wade series
McConnor, Vincent
• Inspector Damiot series
McCord, David
• Rhymes of the never was an always is series
McCord, John S
• Baynes clan trilogy
McCormac, Charles
• War in South-East Asia series
McCormick, Claire
• John Waltz series
McCormick, Dell J
• Paul Bunyan series
McCormick, Donald
see also **Deacon, Richard**
• British Isles series
McCormick, Renee
• Coquette series
McCoy, Duff
• Jeb Cutter series
McCoy, Floyd
• Bytes Brothers series
McCoy, Glen
• Doctor Who series
McCoy, Lois
• Bytes Brothers series
McCoy, Marshall
see also **Grover, Marshall**
Behind a black mask
Nevada Jim series (47)
Bounty on Wes Durand
Nevada Jim series (51)
Bury the guilty
Nevada Jim series (37)
• Larry and Stretch series
• Nevada Jim series
Satan's back-trail
Nevada Jim series (50)
McCray, Mike
• Black Berets series
McCrone, Guy
• Moorhouse family trilogy
McCrum, Robert
• Brontosaurus series
McCrumb, Sharon
• Elizabeth Macpherson series
McCue, Dick
• Animal shape series
McCue, Lisa
• Animal shape series
• Baby animal love series
• Corduroy series
• Fuzzy tales series
• My mom series
• Sebastian Super Sleuth series
McCulley, Johnston
• Avenging Twins series
• Black Star series
• Crimson Clown series

- Spider series
- Thunderbolt series
- Zorro series

McCulloch, Derek
- Cornish series

McCulloch, Sarah
see also **Ure, Jean**
- Georgian series

McCullough, Colleen
- Rome series

McCullough, David Willis
- Ziza Todd series

McCurtin, Peter
see also **Curry, Gene**
- Assassins series
- Carmody series
- Jim Rainey series
- Marksman series
- Sundance series

McCutchan, Philip
see also **Galway, Robert Conington; Macneil, Duncan; Wigg, T I G**
- Commander Esmonde Shaw series
- Convoy series
- Donald Cameron series
- Lieutenant Saint Vincent Halfhyde series
- Superintendent Simon Shard series

McCutcheon, George Barr
- Anderson Crow series
- Graustark series

McCutcheon, Hugh
- Anthony Howard series
- Inspector McKeller series
- Jimmy Carroll series
- Richard Logan series

McDaniel, Becky Bring
- Jewish tales series
- Katie series

McDaniel, David
- Man from U.N.C.L.E. series
- Prisoner series

McDermid, Val
- Kate Brannigan series
- Lindsay Gordon series

McDermott, Gerald
- Brambleberrys series

Macdonald, Amy
- Let's series

Macdonald, Betty
- Mrs Piggle-Wiggle series
- Who me series

Macdonald, Colt
see **Macdonald, William Colt**

Macdonald, Donald
- Tommy Briggs series

Macdonald, Elizabeth
- Magic plant series

Macdonald, Finlay J
- Hebridean boyhood series

Macdonald, George
- Faery trilogy
- Malcolm series
- Quiet neighbourhood series
- Sir Gibbie series
- Thomas Wingfold trilogy

McDonald, Gregory
- Fletch series
- Francis Xavier Flynn series
- Time squared quartet

McDonald, Hugh
- Connection series

Macdonald, Hugh Chisholm
- Paul Williams series

Macdonald, James Douglas
- Circle of magic series
- Time tours series

Macdonald, John
see also **Macdonald, John Ross; Macdonald, Ross**
- Lew Archer series

Macdonald, John Dann
- Travis McGee series

Macdonald, John Ross
see also **Macdonald, John; Macdonald, Ross**
- Lew Archer series

Macdonald, Kate
Anne of Green Gables cookbook
Avonlea series (11)

McDonald, Kay L
- Ross Chesnut trilogy

Macdonald, Malcolm
- Stevenson family series

Macdonald, Maryann
- Little Hippo series
- Rosie series

McDonald, Megan
- Potato man series

Macdonald, Peter G
- Open road quartet

Macdonald, Philip
- Colonel Anthony Ruthven Gethryn series

Macdonald, Ross
see also **Macdonald, John; Macdonald, John Ross; Millar, Kenneth**
- Lew Archer series

Macdonald, Sheila
- Rhodesia series

Macdonald, Shelagh
- Pethi and Tini series

Macdonald, Suse
- Discovery series

Macdonald, Una
- Alys series

Macdonald, William Colt
- Gregory Quist series
- Nogales Scott and Caliper Maxwell series
- Three Mesquiteers series

McDonnell, David
Superman IV
Superman series (7)
Willow
Willow series (3)

Macdonnell, James Edmond
see also **Dark, James; Macnell, James**
- Captain Kenyon series
- Captain Peter Bentley series
- Commander Sainsbury series
- Commander William Mallett series
- Dutchy Holland series
- Eagle series
- Hooky Walker series
- Jim Brady series

McDonnell, Jinny
see also **Barclay, Virginia**
- Kim Aldrich series

McDonnell, Virginia Bleecker
see **McDonnell, Jinny**

McDonough, Alex
- Scorpio series

McDougald, Roman
- Philip Cabot series

Macdougall, James K
- David Stuart series

McDowell, Emmett
- Jonathan Knox series

McDowell, Michael
- Jack Beaumont and Susan Bright series

McDowell, Michael M
- Blackwater series

McDowell, Michael Paul
see **Kube-McDowell, Michael Paul**

Mace, Elisabeth
- Swallowdale series

Mace, Helen
- Noel Vickery series

Mace, Merlda
- Christine Andersen series

McElfresh, Adeline
see also **Wesley, Elizabeth**
- Doctor Jane series
- Jill Nolan series

McElroy, Hugh
- Inspector William Brewer series

McElroy, Lee
- Buckalew tetralogy
- Tales of Texas series

McElwain, Dean L
- Preacher's law series

McEnroe, Richard S
- Buck Rogers series
- Far stars and future times series

McEvoy, Joseph Patrick
- Show girl series

McEvoy, Seth
- Arcade explorers series
- Explorer series
- Not quite human series

McFadyen, Ella
- Pegmen series

McFall, Frances Elizabeth Haldane
see **Grand, Sarah**

McFarlane, Leslie
- Checkmate series
- Michael Brent series

McFee, William
- Pilgrims and sailors series
- Spenlove series

McGann, Michael
see also **Naha, Ed**
- Marauders series

McGarrity, Mark
see **Gill, Bartholomew**

McGarvey, Robert
see **White, Steve**

McGaughey, Dudley Dean
see **Owen, Dean**

McGavock, John
- War birds trilogy

McGeary, Duncan
- Greylock of Godshome series

McGee, Shelagh
- Little activity series
- Little nursery rhyme series

McGeehan, Bernice
- Wunnerful series

McGerr, Patricia
- Selena Mead series

Macgibbon, Jean
- Molly and Liz series
- Sandy, Jane and Stephen series

McGill, Gordon
- Amityville horror series
- Omen series

McGill, Jerry
- Red Ryder series

McGill, Marci
- Six little possums series

Macgill, Patrick
- Moleskin Joe series

McGilvray, Alan
- Cricket series

McGinley, Phyllis
- Joey series

McGirr, Edmund
see also **Drummond, Charles; Giles, Kenneth**
- Jim Piron series

McGirt, Dan
- Jason Cosmo series

McGivern, Maureen Daly
see **Daly, Maureen**

McGloin, Joseph Thaddeus
- Called to love, called to serve series
- Love and life series
- With Him, through Him, to Him series

McGonigle, Thomas
- Patchogue series

M'Govan, James
- Edinburgh detective series
- James M'Govan series

McGovern, Ann
- American history series

Macgowan, Alice
- Jerry Boyne series

McGowen, Tom
- Age of magic trilogy
- Endless quest series
- Magician trilogy

McGown, Jill
- Chief Inspector Lloyd and Sergeant Judy Hill series

Macgrath, Harold
- Cutty Clay series

McGrath, Harold
- Hearts and masks series

McGraw, Eloise Jervis
- Oz series

Macgregor, Alasdair Alpin
- Auld Reekie series
- Golden lamp trilogy
- Western Isles trilogy

Macgregor, Bill
- Liffey series

Macgregor, Ellen
- Miss Pickerell series

Macgregor, James Murdoch
see **McIntosh, J T**

Macgregor, Reginald James
- Chi-Lo series
- Nothing and something series
- Young detectives series

Macgregor, Rob
- Indiana Jones series

Macgregor, T J
- Quin Saint James and Mike McClary series

McGrew, Fenn
- Lieutenant Charles Hillary series

McGuire, Catherine
- Endless quest series

McGuire, Dominic Paul
see **McGuire, Paul**

McGuire, Leslie
- Mrs Murgatroyd series

McGuire, Paul
- Chief Inspector Cummings series
- Inspector Wittler series
- Superintendent Fillinger series

Machado de Assis, Joachim Maria
- Quincas Borba series

McHargue, Georgess
- Ben and Frito series
- Eerie series
- Natural and unnatural history series

Machen, Arthur
- Near and far series

Machetanz, Frederick
- Andy and Panuck series

Machlin, Milt
- Connection series

McHugh, Arona
- Sally Brimmer series

McHugh, Elisabet
- Karen series

McIlvaine, Jane
- Cammie series

McIlvanney, William
- Inspector Jack Laidlaw series

McIlwain, David
see **Maine, Charles Eric**

McIlwraith, Maureen
see **Hunter, Mollie**

McInerney, Judith Whitelock
- Judge Benjamin series

McInerny, Ralph
- Andrew Broom series
- Father Roger Dowling series
- Matthew Rogerson series

Macinnes, Colin
- Visions of London series

McInnes, Graham
- Road to Gundagai series

Macinnes, Helen
- Robert Renwick series

McIntosh, Dave
- Canadian life series

McIntosh, J T
- Ambrose and Dominique Frayne series

Macintyre, Elisabeth
- Ambrose Kangaroo series

McIntosh, Kinn Hamilton
see **Aird, Catherine**

McIntyre, John Thomas
- Ashton-Kirk series
- Buckskin series
- Young Continentals series

Macintyre, Lorn
- Chronicles of Inverness series

McIntyre, Vondra Neil
- Frankenstein sequels series
- Star trek moving picture series
- Star trek sequels series
- Star trek series
- Star wars series
- Starfarers series

Mack, Herb
- Robot series

Mack, Louise
- Lennie Leighton series

Mack Bride, Johnny
- Frank Wady series

Mackail, Denis
- David Lawrence series
- Greenery Street trilogy
- Noodles series

Mackay, Allis
- They came to a river series

Mackay, Amanda
- Hannah Land series

Mackay, Mary
see **Corelli, Marie**

McKean, Thomas
- Doors into time series

McKee, David
- Elmer series
- King Rollo series
- Melric the magician series
- Mister Benn series

McKee, Ruth Eleanor
- Hawaii series

Macken, Walter
- Macmahon family trilogy

McKenna, Colleen O'Shaughnessy
- Cousins series
- Murphy family series

McKenna, Marthe
- Clive Granville series

McKenna, Stephen
- Dermott family series
- Realists trilogy
- Sensationalists trilogy
- Sonia series

McKenney, Kenneth
- Changeling trilogy

Mackenzie, Agnes Mure
- Kinnellan series

Mackenzie, Andrew
- Nicholas Cornish series
- Superintendent Brannigan series

McKenzie, C J
see **Kane, Martin**

Mackenzie, Compton
- Capri series
- Commander Roger Waterlow series
- Faith, hope and charity trilogy
- Four winds of love series
- Highland series
- Jenny Pearl and Maurice Avery series
- John Touchwood series
- Memories series
- Oliver Huffam series
- Sinister Street series
- Sylvia Scarlett series

Mackenzie, Donald
- Fugitives series
- Harry Chalice and Crying Eddie series
- Johnny Raven series

McKenzie, Ellen Kindt
- Taash series

Mackenzie, J Alexander
- Canaan trilogy

Mackenzie, Jake
- Secret files of Dakota King series

Mackenzie, Joan
- Mimosa Winter series

Mackenzie, Kathleen
- Miss Winter series
- Pentire family series
- Starke sisters series

Mackenzie, Lee
- Annie Sugden series
- Beryl Humphries series
- Brothers series
- Emmerdale Farm series

Mackenzie, Nigel
- Inspector Charles Tremayne series
- Professor Christopher Fenton series

Mackenzie, Pierce
- T G Horne series

Mackenzie, Steve
- Seals series

Mackenzie, William Andrew
- Sir Nigel Lacaita series

McKeone, Lee
- Ghoster trilogy

McKeown, Joseph
- Liam series

McKernan, Victoria
- Chicago Nordejoong series

Mackie, Charles
- Stewarts of Badenoch series

Mackie, John
- Rat Bastards series

McKiernan, Dennis L
- Iron tower trilogy
- Silver call series

McKillip, Patricia Anne
- Cygnet series
- Kyreol series
- Morgon trilogy

McKimmie, Christopher
- Magic day series

Mackin, Rick
- Chopper cops series

McKinley, Robin
- Chronicles of Damar series

McKinney, Jack
- Black Hole Travel Agency series
- Robotech series
- Sentinels series

Mackinnon, Allan
- Donald Kendrick series
- Glen Morrock series
- Inspector Duncan Maccallum series
- Mike Darroch series

Mackinnon, Andrew
- Monty Trio series

Mackinnon, Charles Roy
see also **Montrose, Graham; Stuart, Charles; Torr, Iain**
- Scottish chronicle series

Mackintosh, Elizabeth
see **Tey, Josephine**

Mackintosh, Ian
- Tim Blackgrove series
- Warship series

Mackintosh, May
- Laurie Grant and Stewart Noble series

McKissack, Frederick Lemuel
- Big bug series
- Messy Bessey series

McKissack, Patricia Carwell
- Big bug series
- Christopher series
- Messy Bessey series

Mantle, Winifred
see also **Lang, Frances**
- Jonnesty series
- Lesters and Westcotts series

Manuel, Esme
- Trisha Trelawney series

Manushkin, Fran
- Annie series
- Baby Rabbit series
- Pick-a-path series

Marbach, Ethel
see also **Pochocki, Ethel**
- Saints series

Marconi, David
- Agent thirteen series

Marcus, Arthur A
- Pete Hunter series

Marcus, David
- Land of Ireland series

Marcus, Joanna
see also **Andrews, Lucilla**
- Romney Marsh series

Marden, Fay
- Flower fairy series

Mare, Walter de la
see **De la Mare, Walter**

Marenelle
- Midget Mouse series

Marfield, Dwight
- Dudley Brent series
- Gail McGurk series
- Inspector Skane series
- Major Krim series

Marge
see **Henderson, Marge**

Margolin, Harriet
- Busy Bear series
- Days series

Margolis, Richard Jules
- Big Bear series

Margroff, Robert
- Dragon series

Marguerite, Paul
- Franco-Prussian War series

Margueritte, Victor
- Franco-Prussian War series

Mariana
- Miss Flora McFlimsey series

Marianne Helweg
- Ann and Susan series

Marino, Dorothy
- Buzzy Bear series

Marino, Nick
- Mike Macauley series

Marino, Tony
- Widgets series

Mariz, Linda
- Laura Ireland series

Mark, Jan
- Manipulator trilogy

Mark, Michael
- Toba series

Mark, Ted
- Girl from P.U.S.S.Y.C.A.T. series
- Man from C.H.A.R.I.S.M.A. series
- Man from O.R.G.Y. series

Markham, Marion M
- Dixon twins series

Markham, Robert
see also **Amis, Kingsley**
- James Bond series

Markham, Virgil
- Myles Rusby series

Markle, Sandra
- Exploring the seasons series

Marks, James Macdonald
- Jason Wright series

Marks, Laurie J
- Children of Triad trilogy

Markson, David
- Harry Fannin series

Marlett, Melba
- Sarah O'Brien series

Marlitt, E
- Moorland princess series

Marlow, Louis
- Swan's milk series

Marlowe, Amy Bell
- Oriole series

Marlowe, Dan James
- Earl Drake series
- Johnny Killain series

Marlowe, Francis
- Doc Summers series

Marlowe, Greg
- Greg Marlowe series

Marlowe, Piers
- Double Thirteen Club series
- Frank Drury and Inspector Bill Hazard series

Marlowe, Stephen
- Chester Drum series
- Shell Scott series

Marokvia, Artur
- Ann and Paul series

Marokvia, Mireille
- Ann and Paul series

Maron, Margaret
- Judge Deborah Knott series
- Lieutenant Sigrid Harald series

Marquand, John Phillips
- Mister Moto series
- Timothy Dexter series

Marquand, Josephine
see also **Gladstone, Josephine**
- Chi Ming series

Marquez, Gabriel Garcia
see **Garcia Marquez, Gabriel**

Marquis, Don
- Archy and Mehitabel series

Marquis, Max
- General hospital series
- Harry Timberlake series

Marray, Denis
- Duck Street Gang series

Marric, J J
see also **Ashe, Gordon; Creasey, John; Deane, Norman; Frazer, Robert Caine; Halliday, Michael; Morton, Anthony; York, Jeremy**
- Commander George Gideon series

Marriott, Anthony
- Frank Marker series

Mars, Alastair
- Royal Navy series

Marsden, Antony
- Inspector Buck series
- Jim Beverley series

Marsh, Geoffrey
see also **Charles, Steven; Fenn, Lionel; Grant, Charles Lewis**
- Lincoln Blackthorne series

Marsh, Ian
- Doctor Who series

Marsh, Jean Evelyn
- Rick and Pete Clayton series

Marsh, John
see also **Davis, Julia**
- Ray Felton series
- Simon Luck series

Marsh, Kathryn
see **Kathryn**

Marsh, Ngaio
- Inspector Roderick Alleyn series

Marsh, Richard
- Augustus Champnell series
- Judith Lee series
- Sam Briggs series

Marshak, Sondra
- Star trek originals sequels series
- Star trek series

Marshall, Alan
- I can jump puddles series

Marshall, Archibald
- Abington series
- Anthony Dare series
- Clinton series
- Simple stories series

Marshall, Bruce
- Vicar of Christ tetralogy

Marshall, Catherine
- Peter Marshall series

Marshall, Deborah A
- V series

Marshall, Edward
- Fox series

Marshall, Evelyn
see **Marsh, Jean Evelyn**

Marshall, Gene
- Incredible adventures series

Marshall, James
- Carruthers series
- Cut-Ups series
- Four little troubles series
- Fox series
- George and Martha series
- Rats series
- Stupids series
- Yummers series

Marshall, Jonathan
- Porridge series

Marshall, Lovat
see also **Cassells, John; Duncan, William Murdoch; Graham, Neill; Malloch, Peter**
- Sugar Kane series

Marshall, Matt
- Tramp-Royal series

Marshall, May
- Sister Madge Stillworthy series

Marshall, Mel
see **Tyler, Zack**

Marshall, Raymond
see also **Chase, James Hadley**
- Brick-Top Corridon series
- Don Micklem series

Marshall, Sidney John
- She series

Marshall, Sybil
- Fen family series
- Old Swithinford series

Marshall, William Leonard
- Battling Mendez series
- Tillman and Muldoon series
- Twentieth century trilogy
- Yellowthread Street series

Marston, Edward
- Elizabethan whodunits series
- Gervase Bret and Ralph Delchard series

Marston, Jeffery
- Octave trilogy

Marston, John
- Antonio series

Marten, Jacqueline
- Wars of independence trilogy

Marter, Ian
- Companions of Doctor Who series
- Doctor Who series
- Sarah Jane Smith series

Martia, Astron del
see **Del Martia, Astron**

Martin, A Richard
- Branders Noble series

Martin, Ann Matthews
- Baby-Sitters Club mystery series
- Baby-Sitters Club readers special request series
- Baby-Sitters Club series
- Baby-Sitters Club super specials series
- Baby-Sitters little sister series
- Baby-Sitters little sister super specials series
- Feather Town series
- Kids series

Martin, Archibald Edward
- Pel Pelham and Detective Linley series

Martin, Aylwin Lee
- Matt Hughes series

Martin, Basil Kingsley
see **Martin, Kingsley**

Martin, Betty
- Miracle series

Martin, Bill
- Freedom series

Martin, Charles E
- Monhegan Island series

Martin, Charles Morris
- Alamo Bowie series
- Gospel Cummings series
- Roaming Reynolds and Texas Joe series

Martin, Chuck
see **Martin, Charles Morris**

Martin, Cort
see also **Sherman, Jory**
- Jared Bolt series

Martin, David
- Doctor Who find your fate series
- Sean McCart series

Martin du Gard, Roger
- Thibault family series

Martin, Ed
Frankenstein sixty nine
Frankenstein series (1)

Martin, Edward Le Breton
- Otter Patrol series

Martin, Eugene
- Randy Starr series

Martin, George Madden
- Emmy Lou series

Martin, George Raymond Richard
- Wild cards series

Martin, Graham
- Giftwish series

Martin, Ian Kennedy
- Sweeney series

Martin, Jack
- Halloween series

Martin, James E
- Gil Disbro series

Martin, John Percival
- Uncle series

Martin, Keith
- Fighting fantasy gamebook series

Martin, Killer
see **Martin, Jack**

Martin, Kingsley
- Father figures series

Martin, Larry Jay
- John Clinton Ryan series

Martin, Lee
- Deb Ralston series

Martin, Les
- Frankenstein sequels series
Indiana Jones and the last crusade
Indiana Jones series (3)
Indiana Jones and the temple of doom
Indiana Jones series (2)
Raiders of the lost ark
Indiana Jones series (1)
- Thundercats series
- Young Indiana Jones chronicles series
- Young Indiana Jones series

Martin, Marcia
- Donna Parker series
- Merry mailman series

Martin, Marianne
- Golden boomerang series

Martin, Martha
- Alaska series

Martin, Nancy
- Anne Clarke series
- Jean Thomas series
- Kennedys abroad series
- Red Cross series
- Vet series
- Young farmers series

Martin, Oliver
- Timothy Cullinan series

Martin, Philip
- Doctor Who find your fate series
- Doctor Who series
- John Kline series
Mission to Magnus
Doctor Who series (162)
- Trial of the Time Lord series

Martin, Reginald Alec
see **Dixon, Rex; Eliott, E C; Martin, Robert**

Martin, Rhona
- Black John and Hazel series

Martin, Richard E
Alphie and the dream machine
Listen-hear series (1)
- Junior listen-hear series

Martin, Robert
see also **Dixon, Rex; Eliott, E C**
- Career adventure series
- Dance and Company series
- Ginger Pennylove series
- Joey series
- Tony series
- Trew twins series

Martin, Robert Bernard
see **Bernard, Robert**

Martin, Robert Lee
see also **Roberts, Lee**
- Doctor Clinton Shannon series
- Jim Bennett series

Martin, Roy Peter
see **Melville, James**

Martin, Russell White
- Supernatural series

Martin, Shane
see also **Johnston, George Henry**
- Professor Ronald Challis series

Martin, Toy
- Taronga Road Riders series

Martin, Troy Kennedy
- Chief Inspector Barlow series

Martin, Violet Florence
see **Ross, Martin**

Martin, William Leon
see **Martin, Bill**

Martindale, Cyril Charlie
- Mister Francis Newnes series

Martindale, T Chris
- Advanced dungeons and dragons adventure gamebook series
- Endless quest series

Martine-Barnes, Adrienne
- Chronique d'Avebury series

Martinek, Frank V
- Don Winslow series

Marton, Francesca
- Jordan family series

Martyn, Harriet
- Balcombe Hall series

Martyn, Wyndham
- Anthony Trent series
- Christopher Bond series

Marut, Ret
see **Traven, B**

Marvell, Holt
- Inspector Simon Spears series

Marvin, James W
see also **Axler, James; Darke, James; Fraser, Mary; Haigh, Richard; James, Laurence; May, Jonathan; McPhee, James; Netzen, Klaus; Nolan, Christopher; Norman, Mick**
- Crow series

Marzollo, Claudio
- Jed series

Marzollo, Jean
- Baby unicorn series
- I spy series
- Jed series
- Thirty nine kids on the block series

Maschler, Fay
- T.G. and Moonie series

Maschwitz, Eric
see **Marvell, Holt**

Masefield, John
- Autobiography of a corpse series
- Byzantium series
- Hawbucks series
- In the mill series
- Kay Harker series
- Sard Harker series

Maske, John
- Clarence E Hemingway series
- Duncan Cainsforth series
- Jeremy Flack series

Mason, Alfred Edward Woodley
- Inspector Hanaud series

Mason, Anne
- Dancing meteorite series

Mason, Chuck
see also **Morgan, G J; Shane, Bart; Starr, Roland**
- Lee Caton series

Mason, Connie
- Women West series

Mason, Dan
- Lex Cranshaw series

Mason, David
- Kavin series

Mason, Douglas Rankine
see **Rankine, John**

Mason, Francis Van Wyck
see also **Coffin, Geoffrey**
- American Civil War, naval series
- American War of Independence series
- Colonel Hugh North series
Murder in the Senate
Inspector Scott Stuart series (1)

Mason, Henrietta
- Spencer family series

Mason, Lucy Mansfield
- Joan series

Mason, Mary
- Rehumanization of Jade Darcy series

Mason, Miriam Evangeline
- Caroline series
- Lightning series

Mason, Paul
- Fighting fantasy gamebook series
- Robin of Sherwood series

Mason, Peter
- Private education series

Mason, Philip
see **Woodruff, Philip**

Mason, Robert
- Captain James Donald Macgregor series

Mason, Robert Caverly
- Chickenhawk series
- Weapon series

Mason, Roger
see also **De Vere, V C**
Idea
Motto excelsior series (3)

Mason, S C
- Derek Glover series

Mason, Sara Elizabeth
- Sheriff Bill Davies series

Mason, Simone
- Star trek fan series

Mason, Stanley Weston
- Kestrels series

Mason, Van Wyck
see **Mason, Francis Van Wyck**

Massey, Craig
- Captain Daley's crew series

Massey, Morrell
- Thornton Zane series

Massie, Allan
- Roman emperors quartet

Masson, Sophie
- Seyrac family series

Masterman, John Cecil
- Ernst Brendel series

Masterman, Walter Sidney
- Dick Seldon series
- Sir Arthur Sinclair series

Masters, Anthony
see also **Tate, Richard**
- Murphy's mob series
- Tenko series

Masters, Christopher
- Miss Priscilla series

Masters, Doug
- TNT series

Masters, Edgar Lee
- Domesday Book series
- Mitch Miller series
- Spoon River series

Masters, J D
see also **Hawke, Simon; Yermakov, Nicholas**
- Steele series

Masters, John
- Bateman family series
- British India trilogy
- Indian trilogy
- Loss of Eden trilogy
- Savage family series

Masters, M
- Hawkeye Collins and Amy Adams series

Masters, Simon
- Target series

Masters, Zeke
- Faro Blake series

Masterson, Louis
- Morgan Kane series

Masterton, Graham
- Manitou series
- Night warriors series

Mastin, John
- Regina series

Masur, Harold Q
- Scott Jordan series

Matchett, Grace
- Suzanne series

Matera, Lia
- Willa Jansson series

Mather, Berkely
- Idwal Rees series
- James Wainwright series
- Peter Feltham series
- Stafford family trilogy

Mather, Bertrand
- Robinson family series

Mather, James Marshall
- Lancashire idylls series

Mathers, Helen
- Sin and acquittal series

Matheson, Hugh
- Gregory Branscombe series

Matheson, Sylvia
see **Mundy, Max**

Mathew, David
- Post-war trilogy

Mathew, Theobald
see **O**

Mathews, Joanna Hooe
- Bessie Bradford series
- Bradford family series
- Flowerets series
- Haps and mishaps series
- Kitty and Lulu series
- Little sunbeams series
- Maggie Bradford series
- Miss Ashton's girls series
- Uncle Rutherford series

Mathews, M E
- Cloud family series

Mathewson, Joseph
- Alicia von Helsing series

Mati, Robert
see **Hoberg, Marielis**

Matranga, Frances Carfi
- Nina Cristina series

Matschat, Cecile Hulse
- Andrea Reid and David Ramsay series

Matson, Norman
- Jennifer series

Matterson, Neil
- Baby series
- Cliff series

Matteson, Stefanie
- Charlotte Graham series

Matthew, Christopher
- Simon Crisp series

Matthewman, Phyllis
- Cupid trilogy
- Daneswood series
- Mister Jones series
- Priory series

Matthews, Andrew
- Human relations series

Matthews, Ann
- Junior transformers find your fate series

Mad Max beyond the Thunderdome
Mad Max series (3)
- Punky Brewster series

Matthews, Anthony
see also **Black, Lionel**
- Kate Theobald series

Matthews, Clayton
- Moraghan family trilogy

Matthews, Greg
- Burris Weems series
- Huckleberry Finn series

Matthews, Mollie
- Teddy Edward series
- Teddy Edward's books for bears series

Matthews, Patrick
- Teddy Edward series
- Teddy Edward's books for bears series

Matthews, Stanley
- Feet first series

Matthews, Tanya
- Russian wife series

Matthias, Lee A
- Sherlock Holmes sequels series

Mattson, Olle
- Mickel Mickelson series

Maud, Constance Elisabeth
- English girl series

Maugham, William Somerset
- Summing up trilogy

Maughan, Anne Margery
- Young Pitt series

Maul, Norman
- Our services series

Mauldsley, Daniel
- Christopher and Cressida series

Maupin, Armistead
- Tales of the city series

Maur, Nick auf der
Brian Mulroney, the boy from Baie Comeau
Brian Mulroney series (1)

Mauriac, Claude
- Interior dialogue series

Mauriac, Francois
- Leper series

Maurice, Michael
- Not in our stars series

Maurois, Andre
- Colonel Bramble series
- Doctor O'Grady series

Mauzey, Merritt
- Farm boy series

Mavity, Nancy Barr
- Peter Piper series

Mavor, Osborne Henry
see **Bridie, James**

Maxim, John R
- Bannerman series

Maxwell, Allan
- Sexton Blake series

Maxwell, Ann
- Dancer trilogy

Maxwell, Elsa
- Celebrity series

Maxwell, Gavin
- Camusfearna trilogy

Maxwell, Peter
see also **Cave, Peter**
- Ralph Ledermann series

Maxwell, William Babington
- Men and women trilogy

May, Carrie L
- Recovered pearl series

May, Charles
see **May, Karl Friedrich**

May, F Stocks
- Blackberry Farm series

May, Jonathan
see also **Axler, James; Darke, James; Fraser, Mary; Haigh, Richard; James, Laurence; Marvin, James W; McPhee, James; Netzen, Klaus; Nolan, Christopher; Norman, Mick**
- Confessions series

May, Julian
- Jack the bodiless series
- Pliocene exile series

May, Karl Friedrich
- Winnetou trilogy

May, Robin
- Robin of Sherwood series

May, Stephen
- Planet of the monsters series

Maybee, Bette Lou
- Barbie series

Mayer, Marianna
- Brambleberrys series

Mayer, Mercer
- Ah-choo series
- Fears series
- Frog series
- I am series
- Little monster series
- Professor Wormbog series
- Tink, tonk tales series
- Where series

Mayhar, Ardath
see also **Killdeer, John**
- Amerindian prehistory series
- BattleTech series
- Fuzzy series
- House of Enthala trilogy
- Kyrannon series
- Windwalker series

Mayle, Peter
- Provence series
- Wicked Willie series

Maymaru, Narritjan
- Mark and Wendy series

Maynard, Kenneth
- Lieutenant Lamb series

Maynard, Nan
- Frewin family series
- Jubilee is my street
- Katheryn and Gaynor Scarlett series

Mayne, William
- Animal library series
- Choir school series
- Hob stories series
- Islands series
- Skiffy series

Mayo, James
- Charles Hood series

Mayor, Archer Huntington
- Lieutenant Joe Gunther series

Mayor, Flora Macdonald
- Daughter series

Mays, Cedric Wesley
see **Mays, Spike**

Mays, Spike
- Soldering series

Maze, Deborah
- Elephant and mouse series

Mazer, Norma Fox
- Jenny series
- My name series

Mazuel, Henry Dupuy-
see **Catalan, Henri**

Mazzaro, Ed
- Undercover series

Mazzetti, Lorenza
- Penny and Baby series

Meacham, Beth
- Weird heroes series

Meacham, Ellis Kirby
- Captain Percival Merewether series

Mead, Matt
- Sexton Blake series

Mead, Russell
- Doctor Peter Casey series

Meade, Elizabeth Thomasina
see **Meade, Lillie Thomas**

Meade, Lillie Thomas
- Betty Vivian series

Meade, Richard
see also **Benteen, John; Douglas, Thorne; Haas, Ben**
- Gray lands series
- John Allison series

Meader, Jay
Dick Tracy, the official biography
Dick Tracy series (8)

Meader, Stephen Warren
- Blueberry Mountain series
- Cedar series

Meadows, Rose
- Hanover succession series

Meaker, Marijane
see **Kerr, M E**

Meaney, Dee Morrison
- Lady Branwen series

Means, Eldred Kurtz
- Is this a title, it is not series

Means, Mary
see **Scott, Denis**

Mears, Leonard
see **Grover, Marshall; McCoy, Marshall**

Meddaugh, Susan
- Martha series

Meehan, Jeannette Porter
see **Porter, Jeannette Stratton**

Meek, Joseph
see also **Cutter, Tom; Longley, W B; Randall, Joshua; Randisi, Robert Joseph; Roberts, J R; Weston, Cole**
- Mountain Jack Pike series

Meek, Margaret Reid Duncan
- Lennox Kemp series

Meek, Sterner St. Paul
- Troyana series

Meek, Victor
- Coppering series

Meer, Atie van der
see **Van der Meer, Atie**

Meer, Ron van der
see **Van der Meer, Ron**

Mehdevi, Anne Sinclair
- Pillar to post series

Mehta, Ved
- Face to face series
- Mehta family series

Meier, Shirley
- Fifth millenium series

Meik, Vivian
- Geoffrey Aylett series

Melinsky, Renate
- Crescent children series

Melly, George
- Owning up series

Meltzer, David
- Agency trilogy
- Brain plant series

Meluch, Rebecca M
- Wind dancers series

Melville, Anne
see also **Potter, Margaret Newman**
- Hardie family series
- Lorimer family series

Melville, Herman
- South Seas series

Melville, James
- Superintendent Tetsuo Otani series

Melville, Jennie
see also **Butler, Gwendoline**
- Sergeant Charmian Daniels series

Melville-Ross, Antony
- Submarine warfare series
- Treelake series

Memmi, Albert
- Jewish colonist series
- Tunisian Jew series

Mendel, Jo
- Tucker family series

Menville, Douglas
- Science fiction film series

Menzies, Robert Gordon
- Afternoon light series

Mercer, Cecil William
see **Yates, Dornford**

Mercer, Charles Edward
Battlestar Galactica storybook
Battlestar Galactica series (14)

Meredith, Doris R
- John Lloyd Branson series
- Sheriff Charles Timothy Matthews series

Meredith, George
- Sandra Belloni series

Meredith, Gwen
- Blue Hills series

Meredith, Louisa Anne
- Notes and sketches series

Meredith, Nicolete
see **Kenny, Kathryn**

Meredith, Richard Carlton
- Timeliner trilogy

Merejkowski, Dmitri Sergeevich
- Christ and Antichrist trilogy
- Dio series

Meretzky, S Eric
- Zork series

Merezhkovski, Dmitri Sergeevich
see **Merejkowski, Smitri Sergeevich**

Merino, Jose Maria
- Miguel series

Meriton, Peter
see also **Hunter, John**
- Bill Langley series
- Captain Dack series
- Sexton Blake series

Merland, Oliver
- Sexton Blake series

Merriam, Frank
- Mommies and daddies at work series

Merriam, Lillie Fuller
- Jenny series

Merrick, Leonard
- Parisian series

Merrick, Mollie
- Red Hanlon series

Merriman, Effie Woodward
- Millers series

Merritt, Abraham
- Doctor Goodwin series
- Doctor Lowell series

Merritt, Don
- Captain Franklin Hatcher series

Mersey, Charles Clive
- Picture of life series

Merton, Thomas
- Elected silence series

Mertz, Barbara Gross
see **Peters, Elizabeth**

Merwin, Samuel
- Henry Calverly series

Merwin, Samuel Kimball
- Amy Brewster series
- Elspeth Marriner and Mack Fraser series

Messerli, Douglas
- River to rivet trilogy

Messman, Jon
see **Sharpe, Jon**

Messmann, Jon
- Jefferson Boone series
- Revenger series

Messmann, Richard R
Lost in space technical manual
Lost in space files series (4)

Messner-Loebs, William
- Wolverine MacAlistaire series

Metalious, Grace
- Peyton Place series

Metcalfe, Penny
- Baby's day series

Metcalfe, Thomas Washington
- Santa Anna trilogy

Methold, Ken
- Sherlock Holmes sequels series

Meyer, Carolyn
- Earth inspectors series
- Hotline series

Meyer, Nicholas
- Sherlock Holmes sequels series

Meyer, Renate
- Knittle and Threadle series

Meyers, Annette
- Leslie Wetzon series

Meyers, Barlow
- Janet Lennon series
- Walt Disney's Annette series

Meyers, Gertrude Barlow
see **Meyers, Barlow**

Meyers, Maan
- Pieter Tonneman series

Meyers, Martin
- Patrick Hardy series

Meyers, Richard S
see also **Barker, Wade**
- Book of the undead series
- Destroyer series
- Doomstar series

Final death
Destroyer series (29)
- Incredible Hulk series
- Marvel superheroes, new series

Meyers, Roy
- Dolphins trilogy

Meyerstein, Edward Henry William
- Terence Duke series

Meyler, Eileen
- Elwood family series
- Jocelyn series

Meynell, Esther
- Jakob and Melchior series

Meynell, Laurence Walter
see also **Tring, A Stephen**
- Bluefeather series
- Hooky Hefferman series
- Nurse Carter series
- Nurse Ross series
- Robin Weston series
- Smoky Joe series

Meynell, Shirley Ruth
see **Darbyshire, Shirley**

Meyrick, Bette
- Morgan family series

Mezo, Francine
- Areia Darenga trilogy

Miall, Robert
see also **Burke, John Frederick; Burke, Jonathan**
- Jason King series
- UFO series

Michael, John
- Chokra series

Michael, Judith
- Deceptions series

Michaelis, Karin
- Bibi series
- Elsie Lindtner series

Michaelis, Richard
- Looking backward sequels series

Michaels, Angela
- Caged women series

Michaels, Barbara
see also **Peters, Elizabeth**
- Greyhaven Manor series

Michaels, Fern
- Captive series
- Texas series

Michaels, Jan
- Darby Castle series

Michaels, Melisa C
- Skyrider series

Michel, Milton Scott
- Doctor Alexander Cornell series
- Wood Jason series

Michel, Scott
see **Michel, Milton Scott**

Michelet, Claude
- Wood trilogy

Michelinie, David
- Avengers superheroes series
- Marvel superheroes, new series

Michener, James Albert
- South Pacific series

Mickle, Alan Durward
Execution of Newcome Bowles
Sherlock Holmes series (10)

Middlebrook, Roger
- Cubby series

Middleton, Don
- Roy Rogers series

Middleton, Elizabeth
see **Antill, Elizabeth**

Middleton, Haydn
- People in the picture series

Middleton, Ivy Florence Emily
- Poppies series

Middleton, Jessie Adelaide
- Grey ghost series

Middleton, Martin
- Chronicles of the custodians series

Middleton-Murry, John
see **Cowper, Richard**

Miklowitz, Gloria Dubov
- After the bomb series

Miksch, William
- Addams family series

Mikura, Vera Ferra-
see **Ferra-Mikura, Vera**

Milan, Victor
- Cybernetic shogun series
- War of powers series

Miles, Betty
- Day of the seasons series

Miles, David
see also **Cronin, Michael**

Miles, Ellen
- Worlds of power series

Miles, Keith
- Alan Saxton series
- Archers of Ambridge series
- Crossroads series
- Sin bin series
- Spoils of war series
- We'll meet again series

Miles, Patricia Mary
- Baines family series

Miles, Rosalind
- Eden series

Milkomane, George Alexis Milkomanovich
see **Braddon, George; Redwood, Alec; Sava, George**

Millar, Florence N
- Chief Inspector Douglas Grant series

Millar, George
- Boat travel series
- Maquis series

Millar, Kenneth
see also **Macdonald, Ross**
- Chet Gordon series

Millar, Margaret
- Doctor Paul Prye series
- Inspector Sands series
- Tom Aragon series

Millard, Joe
- Hec Ramsey series

Millard, Joseph John
- Dollar series

Mille, Pierre
- Barnavaux series

Miller, Agnes
- Linger-Nots series

Miller, Albert Griffith
- Fury series
- Silver Chief series

Miller, Basil
- Ken series
- Patty Lou series

Miller, Ben E
- Cory Barnett series

Miller, Bill
see **Miller, Wade**

Miller, Blaine
- Bob Wakefield series

Miller, Calvin
- Singreale trilogy
- Symphony trilogy

Miller, Carl
- Dragonbound trilogy

Miller, Connie
- Seasons trilogy

Miller, Dupont
- Bob Wakefield series

Miller, Edna
- Mousekin series

Miller, Elizabeth
- Cat and Dog series

Miller, Frances Abbott
- Losers and winners series

Miller, Henry
- Air-conditioned nightmare series
- Rosy crucifixion trilogy
- Tropics series

Miller, Henry Russell
- Life and love series

Miller, Hugh
- District nurse series
- Eastenders series
- McBain family series
- Teen Eastenders series

Miller, Jane
- Birth series

Miller, Jim
- Colt Revolver series
- Ex-Rangers series
- Long guns series
- Old-timers series

Miller, John Joseph
- Inner planets trilogy
- Wild cards series

Miller, Leo Edward
- Hidden people series

Miller, Marcia
- Private Eye series

Miller, Margaret Jessy
- Fearsome series
- Kingdom of Caledon series
- Willow and Albert series

Miller, Marvin
- T.A.C.K. series

Miller, Mavis Heath-
see **Heath-Miller, Mavis**

Miller, Moira
- Abigail series
- Andy series

Miller, Muriel
- Woodlanders series

Miller, Nell
- Strawberry Shortcake series

Miller, Olive Thorne
- Kristy series

Miller, Orlo
- Donnellys series

Miller, Peter Schuyler
Alicia in Blunderland
Alice in Wonderland parodies series (9)

Miller, Rex
- Jack Eichord series

Miller, Richard
- Squed series

Miller, Ron
- Bronwyn trilogy

Miller, Rosalind
- Pym family series

Miller, Sandy
- Heart to heart series

Miller, Snowden
- Gene Autry series
- Roy Rogers series

Miller, Steve
- Agent series

Miller, Thomas Kent
- She series
- Sherlock Holmes sequels series

Miller, Victor Brooke
- Kojak series

Miller, Wade
- Lieutenant Austin Clapp series
- Max Thursday series

Miller, Warren
see **Vail, Amanda**

Miller, Warren Hastings
- Boy explorers series

Miller, William
see **Miller, Wade**

Millett, Nigel Stansbury-
see **Chandos, Dane**

Milligan, Elsie
- Penny Dawson series

Milligan, Spike
- Delight series
- Goon cartoons series
- Milligan letters series
- Q annual series
- War memoirs series
- William McGonagall series

Milligan, Terence Alan
see **Milligan, Spike**

Millin, Sarah Gertrude
- Dark river series
- War diary series

Mills, Anita
- Lady of fire series

Mills, Annette
- Merry Muffin series
- Muffin series

Mills, Anthony Reginald
- Victorian girls series

Mills, Bart
- Melrose Place series

Mills, Carla Johnson
- Winter world series

Mills, Craig
- Caladon series

Mills, Frederick John
- Dinkum oil series

Mills, Glynn
- Lynton Hall series

Mills, Hugh Travers
see **Travers, Hugh**

Mills, Martin
see **Boyd, Martin**

Mills, Osmington
- Midset C.I.D. series
- Sergeant Patrick Shirley and Inspector Rip Irving series
- Superintendent William Baker series

Mills, Robert E
- Davy Watson series
- Fellowship of light trilogy

Mills, Woosnam
- John Melrose series
- Sir John Howden series

Millward, Edward J
- Inspector Gil Flicker series

Miln, H Crichton
- Sexton Blake series

Miln, Louise Jordan
- Sen family series

Milne, Alan Alexander
- Christopher Robin series
- Day's play series
- Peace and war series
- Piglet series
- Pooh series

Toad of Toad Hall
Toad Hall series (1)
- Very young series

Milne, Christopher
- Enchanted places series
- Naughty stories series

Milne, James Lees-
see **Lees-Milne, James**

Milne, John
- James Jenner series
- Jimmy Jenner series

Milne, Paula
- Angels series

Milne, Shirley
- Detective Sergeant Steytler series

Milner, George
- Ronald Anglesea series

Milroy, Clarita
- Highland quest series

Milton, Hilary
- Plot your own horror stories series

Milton, Joseph
- Bart Gould series

Milton, Joyce
- Pick-a-path series

Minahan, John
- Little John Rawlings series

Minarik, Else Holmelund
- Little Bear series

Miner, Jane Claypool
- Ellynne Aleese series
- Sunfire series

Minton, Mary
- Yesterday's road series

Miranda, Anne
- Baby series

Mirsky, Reba Paeff
- Zulu series

Mishima, Yukio
- Sea of fertiligy quartet

Miss Read
see **Read,** ***Miss***

Mitcham, Gilroy
- Nick Marshall series

Mitchell Ruth Comfort
- Old San Francisco series

Mitchell, Adrian
- New Baron Munchausen series

Mitchell, Alan Williams
- Harley Street series

Mitchell, Elizabeth
- Alien stars series

Mitchell, Elyne
- Man from Snowy River series
- Silver Brumby series

Mitchell, Gladys
see also **Torrie, Malcolm**
- Dame Beatrice Bradley series

Mitchell, James
see also **Munro, James**
- David Callan series
- Jane Whitcomb series
- Ron Hogget series
- When the boat comes in series

Mitchell, James Leslie
see **Gibbon, Lewis Grassic**

Mitchell, John Hanson
- Scratch Flat series

Mitchell, Kirk
- Procurator trilogy

Mitchell, Lane
- Jimmy Grier series

Mitchell, Margaret
- Scarlett O'Hara series

Mitchell, Mary
see **Plain, Josephine**

Mitchell, Red
- Doc McDuff and Popcorn Pruitt series

Mitchell, Scott
- Brock Devlin series

Mitchell, Silas Weir
- Doctor North series
- Roland Blake series
- War of Independence series

Mitchell, Victoria Estelle
- Star trek series

Mitchell, William Ormond
- Jake and the Kid series

Mitchell, Yvonne
- Cathy series

Mitchelson, Austin
- Sherlock Holmes sequels series

Mitchison, Naomi
- Small talk series

Mitchum, Hank
- Stage coach station series

Mitford, Bertram
- Untuswa trilogy

Mitford, Nancy
Ladies of Alderley
Alderley series (1)
- Love trilogy

Mitgang, Herbert
- Sam Linkum series

Mitgutsch, Ali
- Start to finish series

Mitson, Angela
- Munch Bunch series

Mittelholzer, Edgar
- Kaywana series
- Leitmotiv series

Mitton, Geraldine Edith
- Diana Forbes series

Mixon, Laura J
- Omni odysseys trilogy

Moberg, Vilhelm
- Earth is ours trilogy
- Emigrants series

Modell, Frank B
- Milton and Marvin series

Modesitt, Leland Exton
- Ecolitan trilogy
- Forever hero trilogy

Moffat, Bill
- Press Gang series

Moffat, Gwen
- Miss Melinda Pink series
- Mountaineering series

Moffatt, Frank
- Farmer Beans series

Moffatt, James
see **Allen, Richard**
- Girl from H.A.R.D. series
- Johnny Canuck series
- Silas Manners series

Moffett, Cleveland
- Paul Coquenil series

Moffitt, Donald
- Genesis quest series
- Mechanical sky series

Moffitt, Virginia May
- Pollyanna series

Mogenson, Jan
- Ted series

Mogridge, Stephen
- Barry Parker series
- New Forest series
- Peter series

Mohan, Kim
- Cyborg commando trilogy

Mohoao
- Wandering Jew series

Mohotiere, Mary de la
see **De la Mahotiere, Mary**

Mohr, Nicholasa
- Felita series

Mohr, Ulrich
- German raider series

Moldoff, Sheldon
- Marco Polo Junior series

Mole, William
- Casson Duker series

Molesworth, Mary Louisa
- Boys and girls and I series
- Fairies series
- Grandmother series

Moll, Elick
- Morris Seidman series

Mollin, Alexander
- Doctor Zhivago series

Molnar, Agnes
- Georgina series

Moloney, James
- Dougy and Gracey series

Mona, Joseph di
see **Di Mona, Joseph**

Monaco, Richard
- Leitus series
- Parsival series
- She series

Monckton, Ella
- Tim series

Monette, Paul
- Predator series

Monig, Christopher
see also **Chaber, M E; Crossen, Kendell Foster; Richards, Clay**
- Brian Brett series

Monk, Elliot
- Briconi series

Monkhouse, Allan
- Helen and Marmaduke series

Monmouth, Jack
- Tom Langley series

Monroe, Donald
see **Keith, Donald**

Monroe, Joan Kiddell-
see **Kiddell-Monroe, Joan**

Monsarrat, Nicholas
- Corvette series
- Life is a four letter word series
- Master mariner series
- Pharamaul series
- Signs of the times series

Montagu Scott, Barbara
see **Scott, Barbara Montagu**

Montague, J J
- Black Swan series

Montague, Jeanne
- Loves of Carola Mountjoy series

Montague, Jeffrey
- John Jeremy series

Monteleone, Thomas Francis
- Dragonstar trilogy

Montfort, Auguste
see **Le Breton, Auguste**

Montfort, Grace May North
see **Norton, Carol**

Montgomery, Elizabeth
- Dick, Jane and Sally series

Montgomery, Frances Trego
- Electric elephant series

Montgomery, Ione
- Christopher Gibson series

Montgomery, John
- Foxy series

Montgomery, Leslie Alexander
see **Doyle, Lynn**

Montgomery, Lucy Maud
- Avonlea series
- Emily Starr trilogy
- Silver Bush series
- Story Girl series

Montgomery, Ramsey
- Choose your own adventure series

Montgomery, Raymond A
- Choose your own adventure series
- Choose your own adventure super series
- Rebels in the New World series

Montgomery, Robert Bruce
see **Crispin, Edmund**

Montgomery, Rutherford George
see also **Avery, Al**
- Golden stallion series
- Kent Barstow series

Montgomery, Wendy
- Star trek fan series

Montherlant, Henry de
- Alban de Bricoule trilogy
- Girls series

Montrose, David
- Russell Teed series

Montrose, Graham
see also **Mackinnon, Charles Roy**
- Angel Brown series

Montross, David
- Remsen series

Monty Python
- Monty Python series

Moody, Laurence
• Tudor trilogy
Moody, Ralph
• Ralph series
Moody, Raymond
• Near-death series
Moody, Susan
• Cassie Swann series
• Penny Wanawake series
Moon, Elizabeth
• Deed of Paksenarrion series
• Planet pirates series
Moon, Heather
• Winklepicker series
Moon, Sheila
• Maris series
Mooney, Brian
• Cthulhu Mythos series
Moorcock, Michael
see also **Barclay, Bill; Bradbury, Edward P**
• Catherine Cornelius series
• Chronicle of Prince Corum and the Silver Hand trilogy
• Chronicle of Prince Corum and the silver hand trilogy
• Chronicles of Castle Brass series
City of the beast
Warrior of Mars trilogy (1)
• Colonel Pyat series
• Corum series
• Dancers at the end of time series
• Elric series
• Erekose series
• Eternal champion trilogy
• Hawklords series
• History of Runestaff series
• Jerry Cornelius series
• Jerry Cornell series
• Jherek Carnelian and Amelia Underwood series
• Karl Glogauer series
Lord of the Spiders
Warrior of Mars trilogy (2)
Masters of the pit
Warrior of Mars trilogy (3)
• Oswald Bastable series
• Una Persson series
• Von Bek family trilogy
Moore, Alan
• Miracleman series
Moore, Amos
• Quicksilver series
• Ranger series
Moore, Arthur
• Alamo series
• Bluestar series
• California trilogy
• River of fortune trilogy
Moore, Bertha B
• Triplets series
Moore, Donald
• Eastern nobody series
Moore, Fenworth
• Jerry Ford series
Moore, Frank Frankfort
• Cromwellian Ireland series
• Doctor Samuel Johnson series
• Raymond Monk series
Moore, George
• Evelyn Innes series
• Hail and farewell trilogy
Moore, Gerald
• Memoirs of an accompanist series
Moore, Harry F S
• Casey Peters series
Moore, John
• Dick Tracy cartoon series
Moore, John Cecil
• Brensham trilogy
Moore, Lilian
• Cucumbers trilogy
• Little raccoon series
• Mister Twitmeyer series
Moore, Melissa
• Agency series
Moore, Patrick
• Gregory Quest series
• Grenfell and Wright series
• Maurice Gray series
• Robin North and Rex Redmayne series
• Scott Saunders series
Moore, Paula
• Making of America series
Moore, Richard A
• Bob Whitfield series
Moore, Robert Lowell
see **Moore, Robin**
Moore, Robin
• Connection series
French connection
Connection series (8)
• Pat Kenney series
• Pulsar series
Moore, Roger Elwood
• Advanced dungeons and dragons adventure gamebook series
• Conan series
• Endless quest crimson crystal adventure series
• Endless quest series
• Fantasy forest series
Moore, Wallace
• Balzan of the cat people trilogy
Moore, William
• Mallandine family trilogy
Moorhouse, Hopkins
• Addison Kent series
Moorman, Frederic William
• Tales of the Ridings series
Mooser, Stephen
• All-Star Meatballs series
• Creepy Creature Club series
• Funnyman series
• Gigglemajig series
• Treasure hound series
• Which way interactive series
Morales, Pablo
• Pedro Moreno series
Moran, Daniel Keys
• Keys to paradise trilogy
• Tales of the continuing time series
Moran, Tom
• Sports for me series
Moray, Helga
• Dean Brothers series
• Katie and Paul Van Riebeck series
• Roxana trilogy
Moray Williams, Ursula
see **Williams, Ursula Moray**
Morecambe, Eric
• Reluctant vampire series
Morecamp, Arthur
• Live boys series
Morell, William
• Damyo series
Moreton, Douglas Arthur
see **Douglas, Arthur**
Morgan, Alison
• Llanwern series
Morgan, Allan
• Mark Blood series
Morgan, Bill
• Morgan family series
Morgan, Damian
• Andrea Quill series
Morgan, Dan
• Sixth perception series
• Venturer Twelve series
Morgan de Groot, J
• Lotus flower series
Morgan, Dean
• Rogue Ransome series
• Rostron Outfit series
Morgan, Denise
• Ralph de Giret trilogy
Morgan, G J
see also **Mason, Chuck; Shane, Bart; Starr, Roland**
• Buck Dunne series
Morgan, Geoffrey
• Conways series
• Orphan series
• Ricky Straight series
Morgan, Helen
• Mary Kate series
• Mrs Pinny series
• Satchkin Patchkin series
Morgan, Hugh
• Rentaghost trilogy
Morgan, Jill Meredith
• Eden trilogy
Morgan, John de
see **De Morgan, John**
Morgan, Mary
• Hugs and kisses series
Morgan, Michael
• Bill Ryan series
Morgan, Michaela
see also **Basile, Gloria Vitanza**
• Edward series
Morgan, Patrick
• Operation Hang Ten series
Morgan, Roberts
• Sherlock Holmes sequels series
Morgan, Sally
• My place series
Morgan, Stanley
• Fly boys series
• Russ Tobin series
Morgan, W Ingram
• Colossal Corcoran series
Morgan, Win
• Kippy Koala series
Morhaim, Joe
• Time traveller series
Morice, Anne
• Tessa Crichton Price series
Morier, James
• Hajji Baba series
Morison, Betty Jane
• Elizabeth Lamb Worthington series
Morlan, A R
• Ewerton series
Morland, Nigel
see also **Garnett, Roger**
• Chief Inspector Andrew McMurdo series
• Detective Inspector Rory Luccan series
• Mrs Palmyra Pym series
• Steven Malone series
Morley, Christopher
• Roger and Helen Mifflin series
Morley, Iris
• Monmouth series
Moroso, John Antonio
• James Tierney series
Morrell, David
• Chris Kilmoonie and Saul Grisman series
• John Rambo series
Morrell, Ottoline
• Ottoline series
Morressy, John
• Del Whitby trilogy
• Iron angel series
• Kedrigern series
• Ziax II series
Morris
• Lucky Luke series
Morris, Alfred
• Looking backward responses series
Morris, Ann
• Eleanora Mousie series
• Sleepy series
Morris, Anthony Paschel
• Mark Magic series
Morris, Chris
• Heroes in hell series
• Tempus series
• Threshold series
Morris, Dave
• Blood sword series
• Dragon warriors series
• Golden dragon fantasy gamebooks series
• Knightmare series
• Teenage mutant ninja turtles series
• Transformers series
Morris, David Henry Saint Lawrence
see **Lawrence, David**
Morris, Desmond
• Men and animals series
• Watching series
Morris, Edita
• Hiroshima series
Morris, Ethelberta
• Ameliaranne series
Morris, Gilbert
• Jim Reno series
Morris, Ira J
• Duke of Burgundy series
• Lavrin family series
Morris, Irene Dagny
• Ann and Susan series
• Paul and Sally series
Morris, James Humphrey
• British Empire trilogy
• Japan series
Morris, Jan
see **Morris, James Humphrey**
Morris, Janet Ellen
Basileus
Heroes in hell series (12)
Beyond sanctuary
Sanctuary series (12)
• Heroes in hell series
• Kerrion Empire series
• Silistra series
• Tempus series
• Threshold series
• Yates series
Morris, Jean
see **O'Hara, Kenneth**
Morris, John
• Commissioner Robin McKay series
Morris, Michael
• Paws series
Morris, Neil
• My life series
Morris, Ramona
• Men and animals series
Morris, Thomas Baden
• Inspector Headley series
Morris, Ting
• My life series
Morris, W R
• Sheriff Buford Pusser series
Morris, Wright
• Floyd Warner series
• Lone Tree series
Morrison, Arthur
• Martin Hewitt series
Morrison, Emmeline
• Light fingers series
• Lovells trilogy
• Lovice Clive series
Morrison, Gertrude W
• Girls of Central High series
Morrison, Greg
• Crystal series
Morrison, J Strang
• Monach light series
Morrison, Margaret
• Annetze de Steur series
• Elizabeth Conway series
Morrison, Margaret Mackie
see **Cost, March**
Morrison, Peggy
see **Cost, March**
Morrison, Strang
see **Morrison, J Strang**
Morriss, James E
• Animal behavior series
• How animals series
Morrissey, Di
• Heart of the dreaming series
Morrow, Anne
see **Lindbergh, Anne Morrow**
Morrow, Charlotte
• Lisa Knighton series
Morrow, Honore Willsie
• Abraham Lincoln series
• Great Captain trilogy
Morrow, Molly
see **Morrow, Charlotte**
Morse, Eric
• Friday the thirteenth series
Morse, Larry Alan
• Sam Hunter series
Morse, Melvin
• Near-death series
Mortimer, Chapman
• Father Goose series
Mortimer, Derek
• Tom Holiday series
Mortimer, John
• Horace Rumpole series
Morton, Anthony
see also **Ashe, Gordon; Creasey, John; Deane, Norman; Frazer, Robert Caine; Halliday, Michael; Marric, J J; York, Jeremy**
• Baron series
Morton, Guy
see also **Traill, Peter**
• Konrad Roque series
Morton, James
• Lowspeak series
Morton, John
• Jimmy series
Morton, John Bingham
• Enchanter's nightshade series
• Mister Thake trilogy
Morton, William
see also **Ferguson, William Blair Morton**
• Biff Corrigan series
Morton Howard, Francis
see **Howard, Francis Morton**
Morwood, Peter
• Book of years series
• Clan wars series
• Guardians of the Three series
• SeaQuest series
• Space cops series
• Star trek sequels series
• Star trek series
Mosco, Maisie
• Almonds and raisins trilogy
• Between two worlds trilogy
• Waiting game series
Mosley, Francis
• Nessie series
Mosley, Nicholas
• Catastrophe practice series
• Sir Oswald Mosley series
Mosley, Walter
• Ezekiel Rawlins series
Moss, Elaine
• Peter Pipers series
Moss, Jeffrey
• Sesame Street people series
• Sesame Street series
Moss, Merrilee
• Hot pursuit series
Moss, Nancy
• Cliff House series
Moss, Robert Alfred
see also **Moss, Roberta**
• Brownie stories series
Moss, Robert John
• Robert Hockney series
Moss, Roberta
see also **Moss, Robert Alfred**
• Jenny series
Moss, William Stanley
• War in Crete series
Mostyn, David
• BMX Gang series
Motley, Mary
• Morning glory series
Motley, Willard
• Romano series
Mottram, Ralph Hale
• Captain Dormer series
• Geoffrey Skene series
• Life observed series
• Spanish Farm series
Mounce, David R
• Paul Fox series
Mount, Thomas Ernest
see **Cody, Stone**
Mountain, Robert
• Choose your own adventure series
Mountford, Charles Pearcy
• Dreamtime series
Mountjoy, Roberta Jean
• Night wind series
Moura, Joni
• Air Force series
Mowat, Farley
• Canada north series
• Canadian North series
• Top of the world trilogy
Mowbray, Jeanie Pearl
• Journey to nature series
Moxon, Oliver
• Monsoon trilogy
Moyes, Patricia
• Henry and Emmy Tibbett series
Mudd, Steve
• Tangled webs series
Muddock, Joyce Emerson
see **Donovan, Dick**
Mueller, Richard
• Time machine series
Muggeridge, Malcolm
• Chronicles of wasted time series
Muir, Augustus
• Blue bonnet series
Muir, Dorothy Erskine
• Inspector Woods series
Muir, Frank
• Four square meals series
• Frank Muir goes into series
• My word series
• What-a-Mess series
Muir, Helen
• Wonderwitch series
Muir, James A
see also **Kirk, Matthew; Wells, Angus**
• Breed series
Muir, Marie
• Kettle series
• Torridons series
Muir, Thomas
• Roger Crammond series
Muirden, James
• Eric Kendall series
Mulford, Clarence Edward
• Dave Sanders series
• Hopalong Cassidy series
• J C series
• Johnny Nelson series
• Matt Skinner series
• Mesquite Jenkins series
• Wyatt Duncan series
Mulford, Philippa Greene
• Abbey series
Mulkeen, Thomas Patrick
• Clem Talbot series
Mullally, Frederic
• Bob Sullivan series
Mullen, Clarence
• Tony Lantz and Eddie Wright series
Muller, Ernst
see **West, Julian**

Muller, Jorg
• Changing environment series
Muller, Marcia
• Elena Olivirez series
• Joanna Stark series
• Quincannon series
• Sharon McCone series
Muller, Mary
• Anna and Johan de Villiers series
Muller, Paul
• Paul Muller series
Muller, Richard
Ghostbusters
Ghostbusters series (2)
Mullins, Iola May
• Blossom Shop series
Mumford, Edwin Embree
• Starfire series
Mumford, Ruth
see **Dallas, Ruth**
Mundis, Jerrold
see **Corder, Eric**
Mundy, Max
• Russell Jones series
Mundy, Talbot
• Athelstan King series
• Chullunder Ghose series
• Cotswold Ommony series
• Indian trilogy
• Ivory trail series
• Jimgrim series
• Sikh series
• Tros of Samothrace series
Munif, Abdelrahman
• Cities of salt trilogy
Munn, Charles Clark
• Uncle Terry series
Munn, Harold Warner
• Gwalchmai trilogy
• Tales of the Werewolf Clan trilogy
Munnings, Alfred
• Artist's life trilogy
Munro, Donald Jacques
• Man in China series
Munro, Hector Hugh
see **Saki**
Munro, Hugh
see **Jason**
Munro, Hugh Macfarlane
• Clutha series
Munro, James
see also **Mitchell, James**
• John Craig series
Munro, Rona
• Doctor Who series
Munro, Roxie
• Inside-outside series
Munroe, Kirk
• Mates series
• Pacific coast series
• Rail and water series
• White conqueror series
Muntean, Michaela
• Fraggle Rock series
Murakami, Haruki
• Wild sheep chase series
Murari, Timeri
• Kim series
Murasaki Shibuku
• Genji series
Murdoch, Nina
• Miss Emily trilogy
Murdoch, Ruth Templeton
• Trapp family series
Murdoch van Deventer, Emma
see **Van Deventer, Emma Murdoch**
Murdock, Melinda Seabrooke
• Inner planets trilogy
• Martian wars trilogy
• Star trek series
• Vendetta series
Mure, David
• Deception series
Mure, Geoffrey
• Josephine series
Muriel, Auntie
see **Levy, Muriel**
Muriel, John Saint Clair
see **Dewes, Simon**
Murphy, Christopher
• Sparrow series
Murphy, David John
• Winsome series
Murphy, Dervla
• Full tilt series
Murphy, Jill
• Larges family trilogy
• Peace series
• Worst Witch series
Murphy, Jim
• Last dinosaur series
• Weird and wacky inventions series
Murphy, Lawrence
see **Lawrence, Steven C**
Murphy, Marguerite
• Patricia trilogy
Murphy, Rae Allan
• Brian Mulroney series
Murphy, Robert Franklin
• Girl factory series
Murphy, Shirley Rousseau
• Children of Ynell series
• Dragonbards trilogy
Murphy, Warren Burton
• Destroyer series
• Devlin Tracy series
• Digger Burroughs series
• Edward Razoni and William Jackson series
• Grandmaster series
Murray, Andrew
• Sexton Blake series
Murray, Earl
• Dan Sleyter series
Murray, Edgar Joyce
• Sexton Blake series
Murray, Lillian
• Virginia Nixon series
Murray, Mary
• Freedom series
Murray, Max
• Corpse series
Murray, Michael
• Timber Trail riders series
Murray, Terry
• Legends of Larian series
Murray, Will
Arabian nightmare
Destroyer series (86)
Assassin's handbook
Destroyer series (94)
Blood lust
Destroyer series (85)
Blood ties
Destroyer series (69)
Blue smoke and mirrors
Destroyer series (78)
Coin of the realm
Destroyer series (77)
• Destroyer series
Final crusade
Destroyer series (76)
Ground zero
Destroyer series (84)
Hostile takeover
Destroyer series (81)
Inside Sinanju
Destroyer series (94)
Line of succession
Destroyer series (73)
Rain of terror
Destroyer series (75)
Return engagement
Destroyer series (71)
Shooting schedule
Destroyer series (79)
Skull duggery
Destroyer series (83)
Sole survivor
Destroyer series (72)
Walking wounded
Destroyer series (74)
Murray, William
Eleventh hour
Destroyer series (70)
Murray, William Buckley
• Lou Anderson series
Murray, William Hutchinson
• John Taunt series
Murrow, Liza Ketchum
• Fire in the heart series
Musil, Robert
• Man without qualities series
Muskett, Netta
• Blaike family series
Muspratt, Eric
• Fire of youth series
Musselman, Morris McNeil
• Marriage series
Musson, Margaret
• Mister Popplecorn series
Muusmann, Carl
• Sherlock Holmes sequels series
Myers, Amy
• After midnight stories series
• Auguste Didier series
Myers, Barry
• Making of America series
• Preacher's law series
Myers, David
• Sebastian, the incredible drawing dog series
Myers, Isabel Briggs
• Peter Jerningham series
Myers, John Myers
• Silverlock series
Myers, Leopold Hamilton
• Prince Jali series
Myers, Paul
• Mark Holland series
Myers, Robert John
• Frankenstein sequels series
Myers, Walter Dean
• Arrow series
• Mop and Moondance series
Mykle, Agnar
• Ash Burlefoot series
Myles da Gopaleen
see **O'Brien, Flann**
Myles, Simon
• Apples Carstairs series
Myrdal, Jan
• Another world series
Myrivilis, Stratis
• Mermaid Madonna series

N

Nabb, Magdalen
• Josie Smith series
• Marshal Guarnaccia series
Naglerowa, Herminia
• Krauzes and others trilogy
Naha, Ed
see also **Drumm, D B; McGann, Michael**
• Ghostbusters series
• Harry Porter series
• Robocop series
Naillen, Albert van der
see **Van der Naillen, Albert**
Naisbitt, John
• Megatrends series
Naismith, Robert Stevenson
see **Stevenson, Robert**
Najafi, Najmeli
• Persia trilogy
Nakatani, Chiyoko
• My series
Nanogak, Agnes
• Tales from the igloo series
Nanovic, John Leonard
Doc Savage, the supreme adventurer
Doc Savage series (183)
Nanus, Susan
• Time machine series
Napier, Elma
• Youth and winter series
Napier, Priscilla
• Napier family trilogy
Narasaka, Tomoko
• Peter Pig series
Narayan, Rasipuram Krishnaswami
• Malgudi series
Nash, Anne
• Mark Tudor series
Nash, Frances Olivia Hartopp
• Audrey series
Nash, Jay Robert
• Jack Journey series
Nash, Mary
• Mrs Coverlet series
Nash, Ogden
• Custard series
• Santa Claus series
Nash, Padder
• Grass series
Nash, Simon
• Inspector Montero and Adam Ludlow series
Nassivera, John
• Sherlock Holmes drama series
Nathan, Paul
• Bert Swain series
Nathan, Robert
• Barly fields series
• Tapiola series
Nathan-Turner, John
Companions
Doctor Who series (162)
Tardis inside out
Doctor Who series (162)
Nathanson, E M
• John Reisman series
Nation, Terry
• Doctor Who scripts series
Official Doctor Who and the Daleks book
Doctor Who series (162)
• Survivors series
Naughton, Bill
• Alfie series
• Saintly Billy trilogy
Naylor, Grant
• Red Dwarf series
Naylor, Phyllis Reynolds
• Alice series
• Bessledorf series
• Witch's sister series
• York trilogy
Nazel, Joseph
• Black series
• Iceman series
Neale, John Ernest
• Elizabethan England trilogy
Neame, Alan
• Maud Noakes series
Neave, Airey
• Colditz series
• Escape series
Nedaud
Zorro in old California
Zorro series (7)
Neebel, Richard
• Erik Chatham series
• Soldier of fortune series
Needham, Violet
• Stormy Petrel series
• Windri series
Needle, Jan
• Grange Hill series
• Size spies series
• Tucker series
Neels, Betty
• Adelaide Peters series
Negus, George
• Trev the truck series
Neihardt, John Gneisenau
• All is but a beginning series
• Cycle of the West series
Neil
see **Matterson, Neil**
Neill, Alexander Sutherland
• Dominie series
Neill, John Rea
• Oz series
Neill, Robert
• Sir Harry Barnaby series
Neilson, Eric
• Haakon series
Neitzel, Shirley
• My clothes series
Nelson, Al P
• Badwater series
Nelson, Alix R
• Raggedy Ann's household series
Nelson, Betty Palmer
• Honest women series
Nelson, Brian
• Cocky chaff series
Nelson, Chuck
see also **Edson, John Thomas**
• Floating Outfit series
Nelson, Hugh Lawrence
• Jim Dunn series
• Steve Johnson series
Nelson, Lee
• Dan Storm quartet
Nelson, Michael
• Captain Blossom series
Nelson, Peter N
• Melrose Place series
• Mollie Fox series
• Sylvia Smith-Smith series
Nelson, Ray Faraday
• Timebinders series
Nelson, Richard King
• Eskimos series
Nepean, Evelyn Maud
• Charles II trilogy
Nesbit, Edith
• Arden series
• Bastable family series
• Five children series
Nesbit, Troy
• Wilderness mystery series
Nesdale, Ira
• Bricky series
Nesmith, Bruce
Lankhmar, city of adventure
Fafhrd and Gray Mouser series (8)
Ness, Eliot
• Untouchables series
Nethercot, Arthur Hobart
• Annie Besant series
Netter, Susan
• Twilight series
Netton, Budleigh
• Derek Carrington series
Nettson, Klaus
see **Netzen, Klaus**
Netzen, Klaus
see also **Axler, James; Darke, James; Fraser, Mary; Haigh, Richard; James, Laurence; Marvin, James W; May, Jonathan; McPhee, James; Nolan, Christopher; Norman, Mick**
• Killers series
Neuman, Berman Paul
• Paths of the blind trilogy
Neuman, Fredric
• Captain Redder series
Neumann, Alfred
• Carbonari revolt series
• Napoleon III trilogy
Neumeyer, Peter F
• Donald series
Neville, Alison
see **Candy, Edward**
Neville, Malcolm
• Sandmen series
Neville, Margot
• Inspector Grogan and Sergeant Manning series
Nevins, Francis Michael
• Loren Mensing series
Nevinson, Henry Woodd
• Changes and chances series
Newberry, Perry
• Jerry Boyne series
Newbery, Esylt
• Parson's daughter series
Newby, Percy Howard
• Eric Blainey series
• Hesketh and Jane Oliphant series
Newcomb, Ellsworth
• Joan and Bill series
Newcomb, Kerry
• McQueen family series
Newell, Audrey
• Patrick Michael Doyle series
Newell, Hope
• Mary Ellis series
Newman, Andrea
• Bouquet series
Newman, Bernard
see also **Betteridge, Don**
• Inspector Marshall series
• Papa Pontivy series
Newman, Christopher
• Joe Dante series
Newman, Gordon F
• Inspector Terry Sneed series
• Law and order trilogy
Newman, Marc
• Choose your own adventure series
Newman, Margaret
see **Potter, Margaret Newman**
Newman, Marjorie
• Wilkins series
Newman, Paul S
• Invaders series
Showdown on Front Street
Gunsmoke series (4)
Newman, Robert
• Sherlock Holmes sequels series
• Tertius trilogy
Newman, Sharan
• Guinevere trilogy
Newnham, Yve
• Golden dragon fantasy gamebooks series
Newsham, Ian
• Dynamite twins series
Newsham, Wendy
• Dynamite twins series
Newsom, Ed
• Chagro Brannigan series
Newte, Horace Wykeham Can
• Calico Jack series
• Ruth series
Newton, David C
see also **Chance, John Newton**
• Bunst series
Newton, Dwight Bennett
see also **Bennett, Dwight**
• Jim Bannister series
• Johnny Logan series
Newton, John W
• Our services series
Newton, Michael
see **Kozlow, Mark J**
Newton, Mike
see also **Cannon, John; Robinson, Vance**
• Bounty Man series
• Jon Steel series
• Lawman series

Newton, Suzanne
• Arden Gifford series
Newton, William
• Joey Binns series
Newton, William Simpson
see **Mitcham, Gilroy**
Nexo, Martin Andersen
• Ditte trilogy
• Pelle the conqueror series
Neznansky, Fridrikh
• Shamrayev series
Ngabidj, Grant
• East Kimberley series
Niall, Ian
• Billy Boyo and Albert Finn series
• Galloway series
Nicholas, Jerome
• Bill Anstruther series
Nichols, Beverley
• Allways trilogy
• Candid recollections series
• Cat series
• Judy series
• Merry Hall trilogy
• Mister Horatio Green series
• Open garden series
Nichols, Janet
• Music makers series
Nichols, John
• New Mexico trilogy
Nichols, Robert
• Daily lives in Nghsi-Altai series
Nichols, Wallace Bertram
• Henry VII series
Nicholson, Celia Anna
• Duchess series
• Levine family series
Nicholson, Joyce
• Gulls' Point series
Nicholson, Margaret Beda
see **Yorke, Margaret**
Nicholson, Meredith
• Rosalind series
Nickerson, Sheila Bunker
• Feast of the animals series
Nicklaus, Carol
• Busy Bear series
• Days series
Nickless, Will
• Rotherside series
Nickson, Arthur
see also **Winstan, Matt**
• Rusty Hines series
Nicol, Eric
• Uncalled-for histories series
Nicol, Jean
• Hotel series
Nicolai, Charles
• John Nolan series
Nicole, Christopher
see also **Arlen, Leslie; Grange, Peter; Logan, Mark; York, Andrew**
• Amyot family series
• Black majesty series
• China trilogy
• Haggard trilogy
• Japan trilogy
• Jonathan Anders series
• Kenya trilogy
• New Americans series
• United States Navy series
• West Indies series
Nicoll, Helen
• Meg and Mog series
Nicolson, Robert
• Mrs Ross series
Nielsen, Helen
• Simon Drake series
Nielsen, Susin
• Degrassi High School series
Nighbert, David Franklin
• Anton Stryker series
• Bull Cochran series
Nik-Uhernik
• War dogs series
Niland, Deborah
• Hippopotamus series
Niles, Douglas
• Advanced dungeons and dragons adventure gamebook series
• DragonLance preludes II series
• DragonLance series
• Elven nations trilogy
• Endless quest series
• Maztica trilogy
• Moonshae trilogy
• Super endless quest adventure gamebook series
Tarzan and the well of slaves
Tarzan series (24)
Nilsson, Eleanor Ann
• Heffalump series
Nimmo, Jenny
• Snow spider trilogy
Nin, Anais
• Cities of the interior series
Nisot, Elizabeth
• Commissaire Payran series
Niven, David
• Moon's a ballon series
Niven, Frederick
• Flying years trilogy
• Lost Cabin Mine series
Niven, Larry
• Buck Rogers series
• Dream Park series
• Future history series
• Gil Hamilton series
• Heorot series
• Known Space series
• Magic trilogy
• Man-Kzin wars series
• Ringworld series
• Trees series
Nixon, Alan
• Larry Maver series
Nixon, Allan
• Tony Garrity series
Nixon, Joan Lowery
• Claude series
• Deadly promise series
• Ellis Island series
• First read-alone mystery series
• Hollywood daughters trilogy
• Honeycutt Street series
• Huricane Castle series
• Kleep, space detective series
• Maggie series
• Mary Elizabeth series
• Orphan train quintet
• Shirley and Claude series
Nizzi, Guido
• Paralyzing ray trilogy
Nizzi, Skipper
see **Nizzi, Guido**
Nobbs, David
• Henry Pratt series
• Reginald Perrin series
Noble, Trinka Hakes
• Jimmy's boa series
Noel, Jeffrey
• Johnny Perfect series
Nofziger, Lyn
• Tackett trilogy
Nokes, Ethel
• Billy Bunker series
Nolan, Brian
see **O'Brien, Flann**
Nolan, Christopher
see also **Axler, James; Darke, James; Fraser, Mary; Haigh, Richard; James, Laurence; Marvin, James W; May, Jonathan; McPhee, James; Netzen, Klaus; Norman, Mick**
• Journals of Tom Goane series
Nolan, Frederick
see also **Christian, Frederick H**
• Davy Strong series
• Garrett dossier series
• Lieutenant Joe Petrosino series
Nolan, Jeannette Covert
• Lace White series
Nolan, Keith William
• Vietnam War series
Nolan, William Francis
• Bart Challis series
• Logan series
• Sam Space series
Nolan, Winefride
• Catholic Stuarts series
Noon, Jeff
• Vurt series
Noonan, Diana
• Country and city series
Noonan, Michael
• Choker series
• Flying Doctor series
• Magwitch series
Noone, Edwina
see also **Avallone, Michael**
• Craghold series
Norbu, Thubten Jigme
• Tibet series
Norby, Lisa
• Cheerleaders series
• Heart to heart series
• Two by two series
Norden, Denis
• My word series
Nordhoff, Charles
• Bounty trilogy
Nordtvedt, Matilda
• Bride series
Norman, Barry
• Paul Baker series
Norman, Bruce
• James Mallaby series
Norman, David
• Frontier rakers series
Norman, Diana
• Henry II trilogy
Norman, Earl
• Burns Bannion series
Norman, Frank
• Bang to rights series
• Ed Nelson series
Norman, James
• Gimiendo Hernandez Quinto series
Norman, John
• Martin Speed series
• Tarl Cabot series
• Telnarian histories series
Norman, Mick
see also **Axler, James; Darke, James; Fraser, Mary; Haigh, Richard; James, Laurence; Marvin, James W; May, Jonathan; McPhee, James; Netzen, Klaus; Nolan, Christopher**
• Gerry Vinson series
Norris, Benjamin Franklin
see **Norris, Frank**
Norris, Curtis
• Narnia solo games series
Norris, Frank
• Epic of wheat series
Norris, Kathleen
• Crabtree family series
• Rachel Fairfax series
Norris, Stanley
• Phil, the showman series
Norsworthy, George
• Martin Crow series
North, Andrew
see also **Norton, Andre**
• Dane Thorson series
North, David
• Time warriors series
North, Gerry
• Gerry North series
North, Gil
• Sergeant Caleb Cluff series
North, Grace May
see **Norton, Carol**
• Adele Doring series
• Virginia Davis series
North, Joe
see also **Frances, Stephen Daniel**
• Adventures around the compass series
North, Rick
• Young Astronauts series
North, Sterling
• Plowing series
Nortje, Peter Henry
• Henk Strydom series
Norton, Alice Mary
see **North, Andrew; Norton, Andre**
Norton, Andre
see also **North, Andrew**
• Arvon series
• Arzor series
• Astra series
• Blake Walker series
• Central Control series
• Dane Thorson series
• Dipple trilogy
• Doctor Jekyll series
• Estcarp series
• High Hallack series
• Janus series
• Krip Vorland series
• Magic in Ithkar series
• Magic series
• Murdoc Jern series
• Planet Warlock series
• Star Ka'at series
• Swords trilogy
• Time war series
• Witch World series
Norton, Carol
• Mystery and adventure series
Norton, John
• Magic voyage series
Norton, Mary
• Bed-knob and broomstick series
• Borrowers series
Norton, Nancy
• Homeroom series
Norvil, Manning
see also **Prescot, Dray**
• Odan the half-god trilogy
Norwich, Diana Cooper
see **Cooper, Diana Olivia Winifred Maud**
Norwood, Victor George Charles
• Jacare series
• Man alone series
Norwood, Warren
• Double-spiral war series
• Time police series
• Windhover tapes series
Nott, Loraine
• Ceb Barnes series
Nourse, S Waukley Roy
• Little Washingtons series
Novak, Kate
• Finder's stone trilogy
• Heartquest series
• Marvel superheroes adventure gamebooks series
Novak, Robert
• Joe Blaze series
Nowlan, Alden
• Sherlock Holmes drama series
Nowlan, Philip Francis
• Buck Rogers series
Noy, John
• Rufus Deville series
Nuetzel, Charles
• Noomas series
Nugent, Jean
• Twistaplot series
Null, Gary
• Secret circle series
Nunez Alonso, Alejandro
• Early Christianity series
Nunn, Judy
• Eye series
Nusbaum, Deric
• Deric series
Nussbaum, Hedda
see **Scott, R C**
Nutchuk
• Smoky sea series
Nuttall, Nesta
• Meri Newman series
Nuwer, Hank
• Bounty Hunter series
Nyberg, Bjorn
• Conan series
Conan the avenger
Conan series (16)
Conan the swordman
Conan series (26)
Nye, Jody Lynn
Dragonfire
Pern and the Red Planet series (12)
Dragonharper
Pern and the Red Planet series (12)
Dragonlover's guide to Pern
Pern and the Red Planet series (12)
Encyclopedia of Xanth
Xanth series (16)
Ghost of a chance
Xanth series (16)
• Mythology series
• Planet pirates series
• World of Pern series
Nye, Nelson Coral
see also **Colt, Clem**
• Pony George series
• Wild Horse Shorty series
Nye, Nicholas
• Professor Challenger series
Nyoongah, Mudrooroo
• Wildcat trilogy

O

O
• Forensic fables series
Oakden, David
• Buttercup Willie series
Oakes, Bill
• Discovery series
Oakes, Philip
• Middle England trilogy
Oakeshott, Ewart
see **Oakeshott, Ronald Ewart**
Oakeshott, Ronald Ewart
• Knight series
Oakgrove, Artemis
• Throne trilogy
Oakley, Graham
• Church mice series
Oaks, Tina
• Stepsisters series
Oates, Joyce Carol
• Bellefleur series
• Jules and Maureen Wendall trilogy
O'Banyon, Constance
• Joanne and Windhawk series
Obenchain, Eliza Calvert
see **Hall, Eliza Calvert**
Ober, Frederick Albion
• Knockabout Club series
• Navy boys series
• Old farm series
O'Brian, Patrick
• Jack Aubrey and Stephen Maturin series
O'Brien, Anne Sibley
• Jamaica series
O'Brien, Edna
• Caithleen series
• Dazzle series
O'Brien, Flann
• Cruiskeen Lawn series
O'Brien, George
• George O'Brien series
O'Brien, Jack
• Silver Chief series
O'Brien, Kate
• Considine family series
O'Brien, Meg
• Jessica James series
O'Brien, Patrick
• Captain Jack Aubrey series
O'Brien, Robert C
• NIMH series
O'Brien, Tim
• Vietnam War series
O'Brine, Manning
• Michael O'Kelly series
• Mills series
Obstfeld, Raymond
• Harry Gould series
O'Callaghan, Maxine
• Delilah West series
O'Casey, Sean
• I knock at the door series
O'Conner, Elizabeth
• Silver Ridge series
O'Connor, Frank
• Only child series
O'Connor, Jane
• Lulu series
• Pick-a-path series
O'Connor, Jim
• Pick-a-path series
O'Connor, Patrick
see also **Wibberley, Leonard**
• Black Tiger series
• Glasgow series
O'Connor, Philip
• Lower view series
O'Connor, Richard
see also **Archer, Frank; Wayland, Patrick**
• Bat Masterson series
Ocork, Shannon
• T T Baldwin series
Odaga, Asenath
• Kip series
• Munde series
Odell, Carol
• Blinky Bill adaptations series
O'Dell, Scott
• Julian Escobar trilogy
• Zia series
Odgers, Sally Farrell
see also **Farrell, Sally**
• Adventures of Skippy series
• Bandinangi series
• Helen and Dominic series
• Rosina series
Odom, Mel
• Time police series
O'Donnell, Kevin
• Journeys of McGill Feighan series
O'Donnell, Lillian
• Detective Norah Mulcahaney series
• Mici Anhalt series
O'Donnell, Peadar
• Adrigoole series
• Another day series
• Islanders series
O'Donnell, Peter
• Modesty Blaise comic strip series
• Modesty Blaise series
O'Donoghue, John
• In a quiet land series
• Irish labourer trilogy
O'Donovan, Michael
see **O'Connor, Frank**

O'Duffy, Eimar
- Aloysius Kennedy series
- King Goshawk series

Oellrichs, Inez
- Matt Winters series

Oetting, Ray
- Timmy Tiger series

O'Farrell, Kathleen
- Lattimer children series

Offord, Lenore Glen
- Bill and Coco Hastings series
- Todd McKinnon series

Offutt, Andrew Jefferson
see also **Cleve, John**
Black sorcerer of the Black Castle
Conan series (69)
- Conan series
- Cormac Mac Art series

Shadowspan
Sanctuary series (12)
- War of the gods on earth trilogy
- War of the wizards trilogy

Ogan, George
- Johnny Bordelon series

Ogden, Angela
- Mrs Fluster series

Ogilvie, Elisabeth May
- Bennett Island series
- Jennie Hawthorne series

Ognall, Leopold Horace
see **Carmichael, Harry; Howard, Hartley**

O'Grady, John
see **Culotta, Nino**

O'Grady, Standish James
- Cuculain trilogy

O'Hanlon, James
- Jason Cordrey series

O'Hara, John
- Dallas series

O'Hara, Kenneth
- Alun Barry series

O'Hara, Kevin
see also **Cumberland, Marten**
- Chico Brett series

O'Hara, Mary
- Flicka series

O'Hara, Patrick
- Yangtse run series

O'Harris, Pixie
- Loveleaves series
- Marmaduke series
- Poppy Treloar series
- Yesterday series

Ohlson, Edith Emilie
- Pippa series

Ohlson, Hereward
- Thunderbolt series

Ohtomo, Yasuo
- I can do it series

Oke, Janette
- Davis family series
- Elizabeth and Wynn series

Okrand, Mark
Klingon dictionary
Star trek series (57)

Okri, Ben
- Azaro series

Okuda, Michael
Encyclopedia of Star trek
Star trek, the next generation sequels series (7)
Star trek encyclopaedia
Star trek series (57)
Star trek, the next generation technical manual
Star trek, the next generation sequels series (7)

Olbrich, Freny
- Chief Inspector Frank Desouza series

Olcott, Anthony
- Ivan Kovakin series

Olden, Marc
- Hawthorne Albert Harker series
- Robert Sand series

Oldenbourg, Zoe
- Corner-stone series
- Paris series

Older, Jules
- Hank Prank series

Oldfield, Margaret Jean
- Tell and draw series

Oldfield, Pamela
- Barnaby and Bell series
- Gumby Gang series
- Heron saga series
- Katy and Dom series
- Kent trilogy
- Melanie Brown series
- Willerbys series

Oldmeadow, Ernest James
- Coggin trilogy

Oldmeadow, Katharine Louise
- Princess series

Oleck, Howard Leoner
- Sam Benedict series

Oleck, Jack
- Catacombs series

Oleksiw, Susan
- Joe Silva series

Olinto, Antonio
- Water house series

Oliphant, B J
see also **Tepper, Sheri S**
- Shirley McClintock series

Oliphant, Margaret Oliphant Wilson
- Carlingford series
- Greatest heiress series
- Lady Car series
- Mrs Margaret Maitland series
- Stories of the seen and the unseen series

Oliver, Anthony
- Lizzie Thomas and Inspector John Webber series

Oliver, Frederick Spencer
see **Phylos the Thibetan**

Oliver, George
see **Onions, Oliver**

Oliver, Maria Antonia
- Lonia Guiu series

Oliver, Marjorie Mary
- Alex and Beryl series

Oliver, Simeon
see **Nutchuk**

Ollivant, Alfred
- Two worlds series

Olsen, D B
see also **Hitchens, Dolores**
- Lieutenant Stephen Mayhew series
- Professor A Pennyfeather series
- Rachel and Jennifer Murdock series

Olsen, Violet
- Marie Carlsen series

Oltion, Jerry
- Robots and aliens series

O'Malley, Kathleen
- StarBridge series

O'Malley, Mary Dolling
see **Bridge, Ann**

O'Malley, Patrick
- Harrigan and Hoeffler series

Oman, Carola
- Johel series

O'Marie, Carol Anne
- Sister Mary Helen series

Ommanney, Francis Downes
- House in the park series

One of Them
see **Bacon, Josephine Daskam**

O'Neal, Kathleen M
see also **Gear, Kathleen O'Neal**
- Powers of light series

O'Neal, Reagan
- Fallon trilogy

O'Neil, Harry F
- Broncho Bill series

O'Neil, Kerry
- Jerry Mooney series

O'Neill, Archie
- Jeff Pride series

O'Neill, Donal
- Brian series

O'Neill, Eugene
- Possessors self-possessed series

O'Neill, Pamela
- Cyborg commando trilogy

Onions, Oliver
- Gandelyn the Jester trilogy
- Taskers series
- Whom God hath sundered trilogy

O'Nolan, Brian
see **O'Brien, Flann**

Onslow, John
- Stumpfs series

Onstott, Kyle
- Falconhurst series

Oona, Katherine Deme
- Bobbie Bear series
- Timmy Tiger series

Oort, Jan van
see **Dulieu, Jean**

Oppenheim, Edward Phillips
- General Besserley series
- Major Charles Lyson series
- Mister Sabin series
- Peter Ruff series

Optic, Oliver
- All-over-the-world series
- Army and navy series
- Blue and the Gray afloat series
- Blue and the Gray on land series
- Boat builders series
- Boat Club series
- Flora Lee series
- Great Western series
- Lake Shore series
- Onward and upward series
- Riverdale series
- Starry flag series
- Woodville series
- Yacht Club series
- Young America, first series
- Young America, second series

Oram, John
- Man from U.N.C.L.E. series

Oram, Neil
- Warp series

Orczy, Emmuska
- Dutch War of Independence series
- Old man in the corner series
- Scarlet Pimpernel series

Orde, A J
- Jason Lynx series

Orde, Lewis
- Daniel Kerr series
- Tiger's heart series

Orde-Powlett, Nigel
- Anthony Rillington series

Ore, Rebecca
- Tom Red Clay trilogy

Orenburgsky, Sergei Gussiev
- Russian history series

Orenstein, Frank
- Ev Franklin series

Orgel, Doris
- Cindy series

Orgill, Douglas
- William Mallett series

O'Riordan, Conal
- Anglo-Irish relations series
- Stanislaus Priest trilogy

O'Riordan, Robert
- Cadre trilogy

Orlovitz, Gil
- Emanuel family series

Orman, Kate
- Doctor Who series

Ormerod, Jan
- Baby books series
- Little ones series
- New baby books series
- Sun and moon series

Ormerod, Roger
- David Mallin and George Coe series
- Philipa Lowe series
- Richard Patton series

Ormondroyd, Edward
- Susan Shaw series

O'Rourke, Frank
see **O'Malley, Patrick**

Orr, Alice
- World in Amber series

Orsborne, Dod
- Adventurer in chains series

Orsborne, George Black
see **Orsborne, Dod**

Orum, Poul
- Inspector Jonas Morck series

Orvis, Kenneth
- Adam Breck series

Orwell, George
- Big Brother series

Orwig, Sara
- Danby trilogy

Osborne, Eileen
- Ameliaranne series

Osborne, Geoffrey
- James Dingle and Glyn Jones series

Osborne, Helena
- White poppy series

Osborne, Mark
- Sexton Blake series

Osborne, Maureen
- Horribilly series

Osborne, William Hamilton
- William Murgatroyd series

Osbourne, Ivor
- Mango season series

Osgood, Mary A
- Little Canary series

O'Shea, Sean
see also **Tralins, Sandor Robert**
- Valentine Flynn series

O'Shell, Maggie
- Caged women series

Osman, Karen
Knight of the shadows
Star wars storybook series (3)

Osmond, Andrew
- Foreign Office trilogy

Oster, Jerry
- Jake Neuman series

Ostlere, Gordon
see **Gordon, Richard**

Ostrander, Isabel
see also **Chipperfield, Robert Orr**
- Timothy McCarty series

Ostrander, Sheila
- Superlearning series

Ostrove, Karen
- Jewish tales series

O'Sullivan, James Brendan
- Steve Silk series

Oterdahl, Jeanna
- Tina series

Otfinoski, Steven
- James Bond find your fate series
- Magic micro adventure series
- Twistaplot series

Otis, James
- Boy spies series
- Minute boys series
- Navy boys series
- Pioneer series
- Toby Tyler series

Otterbourg, Edwin Max
- Alice in Wonderland parodies series

Ottie, Vanessa Julian-
see **Julian-Ottie, Vanessa**

Ottley, Reginald Leslie
- Yamboorah series

Ottolengui, Rodrigues
- John Barnes series
- Robert Leroy Mitchell series

Ouida
- Princess Napraxine series

Oursler, Fulton
see also **Abbot, Anthony**
- Bible stories series

Oursler, William
see also **Gallagher, Gale**
- Philip Strong and James Matthews series

Overgard, William
- Hero Haggity series

Overholser, Stephen
- Molly Owens series
- Time machine series

Overton, Jenny
- Creed series

Ovstedal, Barbara
see **Paul, Barbara**

Owen, Dean
- Bonanza series
- Dracula series
- Hec Ramsey series
- Latigo series
- Virginian series

Owen, Dilys
see also **Edwards, Olwen**
- Mister Munch series

Owen, Frank
- Chinese color series
- Free agent series
- Scobee Trent series

Owen, Guy
- Flim-flam man series

Owen, Harold
- Journey from obscurity trilogy

Owen, John
- Edward Bringle series

Owen, Richard
- David Morgan series

Owen, Roderic
- Manahoa series

Owen, William A
- Stubborn soil series

Owens, Agnes
- Gentlemen of the west series

Owens, Louis
- Cole McCurtain series

Oxenbury, Helen
- Baby board books series
- Big baby series
- First picture books series
- Seven hundred and twenty nine series
- Tom and Pippo series

Oxenham, Elsie J
- Abbey girls first generation series
- Abbey girls retrospective series
- Abbey girls second generation series
- Patch series
- Rachel and Damaris series
- Rhoda series
- Robin Brent series
- Rocklands School trilogy
- Tansy series

Oxenham, John
- Beatrice Chase series
- Jesus Christ series

Oyved, Moysheh
- Jewels and gems series

Ozaki, Milton K
- Professor Caldwell and Lieutenant Phelan series

P

Paassen, Pierre van
see **Van Paassen, Pierre**

Pace, Tom
- Ben Garden series

Packard, Andrea
- Choose your own adventure series

Packard, Edward
- Choose your own adventure series
- Choose your own adventure super series
- Earth inspectors series
- Escape from Tenopia series
- Escape from the Kingdom of Frome series
- ESP McGee series
- Space hawks series

Packard, Frank Lucius
- Jimmie Dale series

Packer, Eleanor
- George O'Brien series
- Tim McCoy series

Packer, Jo
- Pepper series

Packer, Joy
- Pack and follow series

Padfield, Peter
- Guy Grenville series

Padgett, Abigail
- Bo Bradley series

Padoan, Gianni
- Facing up series

Page, Emma
- Inspector Kelsey series

Page, Gertrude
- Jill series
- Joe Lathom series

Page, Ian
- World of Lone Wolf series

Page, Jake
- Mo Bowdre series

Page, Norvell W
- Prester John series

Page, Stanley Hart
- Christopher Hand series

Paget, Guy
- Rose series

Pagnol, Marcel
- Remembrances of childhood series

Paice, Margaret
- Fletcher family series
- Kathy Brown series

Paige, Frances
- McGrath family series

Pain, Barry
- Eliza series

Paine, Lauran
see also **Batchelor, Reg; Benton, Will; Bosworth, Frank; Carrel, Mark; Carter, Nevada; Ingersol, Jared; Ketchum, Jack; Slaughter, Jim; Standish, Buck**
- Sheridan Township series

Pairo, Preston
- Dallas Henry series

Paisley, Thomas
see **Bethancourt, Tomas Ernesto**

Pakenham, Antonia
see **Fraser, Antonia**

Pakenham, Frank
see **Longford, Frank Pakenham**

Pakington, Humphrey
- Warmstry series
- Washbourne series

Pal, George
- Time traveller series

Palacio Valdes, Armando
- Riverita series

Palen, Lewis Stanton
- White Devil series

Paley, Grace
- Little disturbances series

Palfrey, Heather Mary
- Norah the snorer series
- Ricky Wilson series

Palin, Michael
- Cyril series
- Ripping yarns series

Palmer, Anna Campbell
see **Archibald, George, Mrs**

Palmer, Bernard
see also **Runyan, John**
- Bradley series
- Brigade Boys series
- Career series
- Danny Orlis series
- Dell Norton series
- Felicia Cartwright series
- Golden Boy series
- Halliwell boys series
- Jim Dunlap series
- Kid Breckinridge series
- Little Feather series
- Lori Adams series
- Mel Webb series
- Mickey Turner series
- Orlis twins series
- Pat Collins series
- Pioneer girls series
- Powell family series
- Ted and Terri series

Palmer, Cyril Everard
- Beppo Tate series

Palmer, Diana
- Long tall Texan series
- Mercenary series
- Most wanted trilogy

Palmer, Don
see also **Wirt, Mildred Augustine**
- Boy Scout Explorers series

Palmer, Frank
- Jim Jackson series

Palmer, Geoffrey
- Sherwood Forest series

Palmer, Jane
- Planet dweller series

Palmer, John
- Guy Plante and Freya Matthews series

Palmer, John Leslie
see **Beeding, Francis; Pilgrim, David**

Palmer, Juliette
- Barley series

Palmer, Marjorie
- Career series
- Pioneer girls series

Palmer, Martin
- Lovell family series

Palmer, P K
- Jedediah Killinger series

Palmer, Stuart
- Hildegarde Withers series
- Howie Rook series
- John Joseph Malone series
- Sherlock Holmes sequels series

Palmer, Vance
- Macy Donovan series

Pangborn, Edgar
- Davy series

Panshin, Alexei
- Anthony Villiers series

Pansy
- Chautauqua series
- Ester Ried series
- Ruth Erskine series

Pantell, Dora
- Miss Pickerell series

Papazoglou, Orania
- Patience Campbell McKenna series

Pape, Richard
- Boldness series

Paradis, Vincent A
- Tut Claw series

Pardoe, Margot
- Boat series
- Bunkle series
- Macalister children series
- Western Highlands series

Paretsky, Sara
- V I Warshawski series

Pargeter, Edith
see also **Peters, Ellis**
- Brothers of Gwynedd tetralogy
- Eighth champion of Christendom trilogy
- Inspector George Felse series
- Mediaeval Wales trilogy

Parish, Peggy
- Amelia Bedelia series
- Granny series
- Liza, Bill and Jed series

Park, Barbara
- Janie B Jones series
- Rosie Swanson series

Park, Paul
- Starbridge series

Park, Ruth
- Callie series
- Cuckoo series
- Darcy family trilogy
- Muddle-headed wombat series
- Tales of the south series

Park, William Bryan
- Off the leash series

Parker, F M
- Luke Coldiron series
- Tom Galletin series

Parker, Gilbert
- Pretty Pierre series

Parker, John
- Village cricket series

Parker, Lee
- Donovan's Devils series

Parker, Margot
- Understanding holidays series

Parker, Maude
- Jim Little series

Parker, Nancy Winslow
- My clothes series

Parker, Richard
- Pipers series

Parker, Robert Brown
- Big sleep series
- Philip Marlowe series
- Spenser series

Parker, Roger
- Inspector Taff Roberts series

Parkin, Ray
- Out of the smoke series

Parkinson, Cyril Northcote
Jeeves, a gentleman's personal gentleman
Jeeves and Bertie Wooster series (15)
Life and times of Horatio Hornblower
Horatio Hornblower series (11)
- Richard Delancey series

Parkinson, Dan
- DragonLance heroes series
- Fox trilogy

Parkinson, Michael
- Daft series
- Woofits series

Parkinson, Roger
see also **Holden, Matthew**
- War Cabinet trilogy

Parkman, Sydney
- Captain Bowker series

Parks, Jim
- Runs in the sun series

Parrish, Frank
see also **Drummond, Ivor; Erskine, Rosalind**
- Dan Mallett series

Parry, Anne Spencer
- Bara quartet

Parry, Edward Abbott
- Judge trilogy
- Krab series

Parry, Michel
- Dracula series

Parsons, Anthony
- Sexton Blake series

Parsons, Virginia
- Pinocchio series

Partridge, Frances
- Pacifist series

Partridge, Jenny
- Oakapple Wood series

Pascal, Francine
- Forever trilogy
- Love series
- Love trilogy
- Promise trilogy
- Sweet Valley High series
- Sweet Valley High super series
- Sweet Valley High super star series
- Sweet Valley High super thriller series
- Sweet Valley kids magna series
- Sweet Valley kids series
- Sweet Valley kids super snooper series
- Sweet Valley magna series
- Sweet Valley twins magna series
- Sweet Valley twins series
- Sweet Valley twins super chiller series
- Sweet Valley twins super series
- Sweet Valley twins super special series
- Sweet Valley University series
- Unicorn Club series
- Victoria Martin trilogy

Pascal, Jamie
- Pick-a-path series

Pascal, Laurie
- Pick-a-path series

Pascall, Jeremy
- King Kong series

Passailaigue, Thomas Ernesto
see **Bethancourt, Tomas Ernesto**

Passingham, William John
- Sexton Blake series

Passmore, Richard
- Blenheim boy series

Passos, John dos
see **Dos Passos, John**

Pasternak, Boris
- Doctor Zhivago series

Pasture, Elizabeth de la
see **De la Pasture, Elizabeth**

Patchett, Mary Elwyn
- Ajax series
- Brevitt series
- Danny and David Delaney series
- Jeff James series
- Joey Meehan series

Patchin, Frank Gee
- Battleship boys series
- Pony Rider Boys series
- Range and Grange Hustlers series
- Ted Jones series

Paternoster, George Sidney
- Randolph Mannering series

Paterson, Andrew Barton
- Man from Snowy River series

Paterson, Banjo
see **Paterson, Andrew Barton**

Paterson, Bettina
- Bun series

Paterson, Brian
- Foxwood series

Paterson, Cynthia
- Foxwood series

Paton, Alan
- Mountain journey series

Paton Walsh, Jill
see **Walsh, Jill Paton**

Patrick, Michael
- Tommy Hawke series

Patrick, Q
see also **Quentin, Patrick; Stagge, Jonathan**
- Lieutenant Timothy Trant series

Patten, Gilbert
- Don Kirk series

Patterson, George Neilson
- Asian missionary trilogy

Patterson, Harry
see **Patterson, Henry**

Patterson, Henry
see also **Fallon, Martin; Higgins, Jack**
- Nick Miller series

Patterson, Innis
- Sebald Craft series

Patterson, John
- Johnson and friends series

Pattinson, James
- Harvey Landon series

Paul, Adrien
- Swiss family Robinson series

Paul, Barbara
- Enrico Caruso series
- Star trek series

Paul, Charlotte
- Snoqualmie Valley series

Paul, Elliot
- Homer Evans series
- Narrow street series

Paul, Ernest
- George Barclay series

Paul, F W
see also **Fairman, Paul Warren**
- Man from S.T.U.D. series

Paul, Leslie
- Angry young man series

Paulden, Sydney
- Yan series

Paull, George A., *Mrs*
see **Paull, Minnie E**

Paull, Jessica
- Passport to danger series

Paull, Minnie E
- Christie series
- Marjorie series
- Mother's bedtime tales series
- Prince Dimple trilogy
- Ruby and Ruthy series

Paulsen, Gary
- Al Murphy series
- Lieutenant Ronnie Gold series
- Sports on the light side series

Paustovsky, Konstantin Georgievich
- Story of a life series

Pauwels, Louis
- Dawn of magic series

Paxson, Diana Lucile
- Westria series

Paxton, Tom
- Aesop in verse series

Payack, Paul J J
- Solstice series

Payes, Rachel
- Forsythia Brown series

Payne, Donald Gordon
see **Cameron, Ian**

Payne, L R
see **Stivers, Dick**

Payne, Laurence
- Chief Inspector Sam Birkett series
- John Tibbet series
- Mark Savage series

Payne, Oliver
- Northwest Territory series

Payne, Robert
- Chinese diaries series
- Emperor Shah Jahan series
- Lifeng, Shaofeng and Rose series

Payson, Howard
see also **Deering, Fremont B; Lawton, Wilbur; West, Marvin**
- Motor cycle chums series

Peacey, Seton
- William Cargoe series

Peach, Bill
- Ginger Meggs series

Peacock, Max
- Colonel Blood series

Peake, Mervyn
- Titus Groan trilogy

Pearce, Agatha Hunt
- Edward, Frank and Gerry series

Pearce, Ann Philippa
see **Warrener**

Pearce, Brian Louis
- Thomas Becket series

Pearce, Carol Ann
- Saint Kelvern's Bury School series

Pearce, Charles Edward
see also **Dunn, *Detective***
- Indian mutiny trilogy

Pearce, Colin
- Fax Pack series

Pearce, Margaret
- Home and away series

Pearce, Mary Emily
- Apple tree series

Pearce, Michael
- Mamur Zapt series

Pearce, Philippa
see also **Warrener**
- Obedient servant series

Pearl, Irene
- Janey series

Pearl, Jack
Dam of death
Invaders series (6)
- Derek Flint series
- Garrison's Gorillas series
- Space Eagle series

Pearlman, Gilbert
- Sherlock Holmes sequels series

Pearsall, Ronald
- Oakwood family series

Pearson, Ann
- Maggie Courtney series

Pearson, Diane
- Whitman series

Pearson, Edmund
- Sherlock Holmes sequels series

Pearson, John
James Bond
James Bond series (30)
- Upstairs, downstairs series

Pearson, Kit
- Evacuee trilogy

Pearson, Michael A
- Winners and losers series

Pearson, Parry
- Jeremy Barton and Samuel Best series

Pearson, Violet T
- Benjie series

Pease, Howard
- Border trilogy
- Tod Moran series

Pechey, Archibald Thomas
see **Cross, Mark; Valentine**

Peck, George Wilbur
- Peck's bad boy series

Peck, Patricia Cleveland-
see **Cleveland-Peck, Patricia**

Peck, Richard
- Blossom Culp series

Peck, Robert Newton
- Arly series
- Little Soup series
- Soup series
- Trig series
- Vermont farm series

Peck, Winifred
- Childhood series

Pedersen, Knut
see **Hamsun, Knut**

Pediment, George Augustus
see **Alington, Cyril Augustine**

Pedler, Ann
see **Stafford, Ann**

Pedler, Kit
- Doctor Who scripts series

Pedneau, Dave
- Whit Pynchon and Annie Tyson-Tyree series

Peebles, Niles N
- Ross McKellar series

Peel, Hazel Mary
- Ann and Jim Henderson series
- Jago series
- Pilot series

Peel, John
- Doctor Who series
Gallifrey chronicles
Doctor Who series (162)
Gerry Anderson's Stingray files
Stingray series (2)
- Lost in space files series
- Timewyrm series
Twilight Zone files
Twilight Zone series (6)
- U.N.C.L.E. files series

Peeress
- Recollections of royalty series

Pegram, Lorna
- Blood and fire series

Peguero, Leone
- Mervyn series

Pele
- Sport series

Pelham Groom, Arthur John
see **Groom, Pelham**

Pell, Sylvia
- Louis XIV series

Pellow, John
- Village parson trilogy

Pellowski, Anne
- Valley Farm series

Pemberton, Max
- Captain Black series

Pemberton, Victor
- Doctor Who series

Pender, Lydia
- Barnaby series

Pendleton, Don
- Ashton Ford series
- Joe Copp series
- Mack Bolan series
- Phoenix Force series
- Sexual life series
- Stony Man series
- SuperBolan series

Pendower, Jacques
see also **Jacobs, Thomas Curtis Hicks**
- Slade McGinty series

Pendower, Thomas Curtis Hicks
see **Dower, Penn; Jacobs, Thomas Curtis Hicks**

Pene du Bois, William
- Alligator case series
- Otto series

Penman, Sharon Kay
- Princes of Gwynedd trilogy

Penn, H
- Sherlock Holmes sequels series

Penn, John
- Inspector George Thorne and Sergeant Bill Abbot series

Penn, Margaret
- Hilda Winstanley trilogy

Pennington, Link
- Frank Slade series

Penny, Rupert
- Chief Inspector Edward Beale series

Penrose, Gordon
- Doctor Zed series

Penrose, Margaret
- Campfire girls series
- Dorothy Dale series
- Motor girls series
- Radio girls series

Pentecost, Hugh
see also **Philips, Judson Pentecost**
- Doctor John Smith series
- George Crowder series
- Grant Simon series
- John Jericho series
- Julian Quist series
- Lieutenant Pascal series
- Luke Bradley series
- Pierre Chambrun series

Pentelow, John Nix
- Sexton Blake series

Penton, Brian
- Derek Cabell series

Peppe, Rodney
- Henry series
- Huxley Pig series
- Little toy board books series
- Mice series

Pepys, Mark
see **Cottenham, Mark Pepys**

Pepys, Samuel, junior
- Great Warr trilogy

Perce, Elbert
- Lemuel Gulliver series

Percy, Walker
- Doctor Tom More series
- Will Barrett series

Perdue, Tito
- Leland and Judy Pefley series

Perdue, Virginia
- Eleanora Burke series

Peretti, Frank E
- Darkness series

Perez Galdos, Benito
- Contemporary novels of Spain series
- National episodes series, epoch 1

Perham, Margery
- African travels series
- Frederick Dealtry Lugard series

Perkins, Al
- Tubby series

Perkins, D M
- Linda Lovelace series

Perkins, Eleanor Ellis
- Dutch twins series

Perkins, Janet
- Haffertee Hamster series

Perkins, John
- Haffertee Hamster series

Perkins, Lucy Fitch
- Dutch twins series
- Twin series

Perlberg, Deborah
- Fraggle Rock series

Perle, Lila
- Fat Glenda series

Perlman, Dory
- Secret of the Unicorn Queen series

Perowne, Barry
- Raffles series
- Rick Leroy series
- Sexton Blake series

Perowne, Stewart
- Herod family series

Perrault-Harry, Myriam
see **Harry, Myriam**

Perrin, Noel
- Sometime farmer series

Perrin, Steve
- Advanced dungeons and dragons adventure gamebook series

Perry, Anne
- Charlotte Ellison Pitt and Inspector Thomas Pitt series
- Inspector William Monk series

Perry, Jean
- News from Korea series

Perry, Lawrence
- Football series

Perry, Mark Christopher
- Morigu series

Perry, Megahn
Warlock's blade
Gramarye series (12)

Perry, Michel
- Chariots of fire trilogy

Perry, Paul
- Near-death series

Perry, Ritchie
- Fenella Fang series
- George H Ghastly series
- Macallister series
- Philis series

Perry, Stephani
- Aliens series

Perry, Steve
- Aliens series
- Conan series
- Khadaji series
- Stellar rangers series
- Time machine series

Pertwee, Roland
- Patrick Faraday series

Peshkov, Maxim
see **Gorky, Maxim**

Petaja, Emil
- Green Planet series
- Kalevala series

Peter, Laurence Johnston
- Peter series

Peters, Bryan
- Brandon and Lundstrom series

Peters, Daniel
- Pre-Columbian trilogy

Peters, David
see also **David, Peter**
- Photon series
- Psi-Man series

Peters, Elizabeth
- Amelia Peabody Emerson series
- Jacqueline Kirby series
- Vicky Bliss series

Peters, Ellis
see also **Pargeter, Edith**
- Brother Cadfael series
- Inspector George Felse series

Peters, Geoffrey
- Inspector Trevor Nichols and Sergeant Tom Burton series

Peters, Lance
- Detective Sergeant Joe Church trilogy

Peters, Ludovic
- Ian Firth series

Peters, Maureen
see also **Black, Veronica; Darby, Catherine**
- History's most fascinating women series
- Malone family trilogy

Peters, Ron
- Stash Koval series

Peters, Saul
- Middle Earth quest series

Petersen, Herman
- Doc Miller series

Petersen, Paul
- Smugglers series

Petersen-Schaefer, Karin
- Melody series

Peterson, Audrey
- Jane Winfield and Andrew Quentin series

Peterson, Hans
- Day when series
- Lisa series
- Magnus series
- New series
- Pelle Jansson series
- Peter Johnson series
- Sara series

Peterson, Jim
- Mack Bolan series

Peterson, Richard Hermann
- Western mining series

Petievich, Gerald
- Charles Carr and Jack Kelly series

Petrie, Rhona
- Doctor Nassim Pride series
- Inspector Marcus Maclurg series

Petrocelli, Orlando Ralph
- Giacomo Carlona series

Petrou, David Michael
Making of Superman, the movie
Superman series (7)

Petrov, Eugene
- Chairs series

Pettersson, Allan Rune
- Frankenstein's aunt series

Petty, Kate
- First timers series
- What's that series

Pevsner, Stella
- Quints series

Peyo
- Smurf series

Peyrefitte, Roger
- Diplomatic series

Peyton, K M
- Flambards series
- Hero series
- Mick and Rob series
- Patrick Pennington series
- Ruth Hollis series

Peyton, Kathleen Wendy
see **Peyton, K M**

Peyton, Michael
see **Peyton, K M**

Pfanner, Louise
- Louise series

Pfeffer, Susan Beth
- Kid power series
- Make me a star series
- Sebastian sisters quintet
- VCR time machine series

Pfister, Marcus
- Hopper series
- Penguin Pete series

Phelan, Jim
- Real life criminals series

Phelps, Elizabeth Stuart Ward
- Gypsy Breynton series

Phelps, Humphrey
- Just trilogy

Philburn, Dennis K
- Soldier of fortune series

Philby, Harry St John Bridger
- Arabian travel series

Philip, Alexander John
- James Jameson series

Philips, George Norman
- Sexton Blake series

Philips, Judson Pentecost
see also **Pentecost, Hugh**
- Carole Trevor and Max Blythe series
- Coyle and Donovan series
- Peter Styles series

Phillifent, John Thomas
see also **Rackham, John**
- Man from U.N.C.L.E. series

Phillips, Dennis John Andrew
see **Chambers, Peter; Chester, Peter**

Phillips, Henry Wallace
- Red Saunders series

Phillips, James Atlee
- Joe Gall series

Phillips, Leon
- Hugh Melling series

Phillips, Mark
see also **Garrett, Randall; Janifer, Laurence Mark; Randall, Robert**
- Ken Malone trilogy

Phillips, Stella
- Inspector Matthew Furnival series

Phillips, Terry
- Advanced dungeons and dragons adventure gamebook series
- DragonLance series

Phillips, Tony
- Turbo cowboys series

Phillpotts, Beatrice
- Clem series
- Rainy day playbooks series

Phillpotts, Eden
- Book of Avis series
- Dartmoor series
- Devonshire village series
- Human boy series
- Industries of England series
- John Ringrose series

Philmore, R
- Inspector Garnett series
- Swan series

Phipson, Joan
- Barker family series

Phylos the Thibetan
- Zailm series

Piacentini, Valerie
- Star trek fan series

Picard, Sam
- John Scott series

Piccard, Eulalie
- Episodes of the great Russian tragedy series

Pickard, Nancy
- Jenny Cain series
Twenty seven ingredient chili con carne murders
Mrs Eugenia Potter series (3)

Pickering, Robert Easton
- Dick Philip series

Pickford, Ted
- Scared to death trilogy

Pickles, Wilfred
- You and me series

Pidgin, Charles Felton
- Quincy Adams Sawyer series

Pienkowski, Jan
- Meg and Mog series

Pier, Arthur Stanwood
- Saint Timothy's School series

Pierce, Meredith Ann
- Aeriel trilogy
- Firebringer trilogy

Pierce, Tamora
- Daine series
- Song of the lioness series

Piercy, Rohase
- Sherlock Holmes sequels series

Piers, Helen
- Little creature series
- Two hungry mice trilogy

Pierson, Clara Dillingham
- Among the animals series
- Millers series

Piesman, Marissa
- Nina Fischman series

Pike, Charles R
see also **Bulmer, Kenneth; Gilman, George G; Harknett, Terry; Hedges, Joseph; James, William M; Stone, Thomas H**
- Jubal Cade series

Pike, Christopher
- Cheerleaders series
- Final friends series

Pike, Geoffrey
- Henry Golightly series

Pike, Robert L
see **Fish, Robert Lloyd**
- Lieutenant Clancy series
- Lieutenant Jim Reardon series

Pilgrim, David
see also **Beeding, Francis**
- James De la Cloche series

Pilgrim, Jane
- Blackberry Farm series

Pilgrim, Thomas
see **Morecamp, Arthur**

Pilkey, Dav
- Dragon series

Pilkington, Roger
- Branxome family series
- Small boat series

Pini, Richard
- Elfquest series

Pini, Wendy
- Elfquest series

Pink, Hal
- Inspector Docker series

Pinkerton, Kathrene
- Ann Jackman series
- Baird family series
- Shoestring trilogy

Pinkney, Gloria Jean
- Ernestine series

Pinkwater, Daniel Manus
- Magic Moscow series
- Snarkout boys series

Pinney, Peter
- Australian soldier series
- Dust on my shoes series

Pinto, Jacqueline
- Redwood Primary School series

Piper, Horace Beam
- Fuzzy series
- Lord Kalvan series
- Paratime police series

Piper, Peter
- Inspector Gray series

Piper, Warrene
- Bennet family series

Pirincci, Akif
- Felidae series

Pitchford, Denys James Watkins-
see **B B**

Pitkethley, Janice
- Star trek fan series

Pizer, Abigail
- Henrietta and Nosey series

Plagemann, Bentz
- Wallace family series

Plaidy, Jean
see also **Carr, Philippa; Kellow, Kathleen**
- Caroline of Ansbach series
- Catherine de Medici trilogy
- Charles II trilogy
- Ferdinand and Isabella trilogy
- Georgian series
- Katharine of Aragon trilogy
- Louis XV trilogy
- Lucrezia Borgia series
- Mary, Queen of Scots series
- Norman trilogy
- Plantagenet series
- Queen Victoria series
- Queens of England series
- Spanish Inquisition trilogy
- Stuart series
- Tudor series
- Victorian England series
- William and Mary trilogy

Plain, Belva
- Anna Friedman series

Plain, Josephine
- Colin Anstruther series

Plain, Neil
- Boris Blundle and Gang series

Plaisted, Eleanor
- My prairie series

Plait, Dominique
- Sebastian series

Plant, Jack
- Rusty Mason series

Plante, David
- Francoeur family series

Plante, Edward
- Seed series

Plater, Alan
- Beiderbecke series

Platt, Charles
- Aton series

Platt, Jock Ellison
- Colditz series

Platt, Kin
see also **Carr, Kirby**
- Big Max series
- Chloris series
Dracula go home
Dracula series (26)
- Max Roper series
- Sinbad trilogy

Platt, Marc
- Doctor Who scripts series
- Doctor Who series

Pleydell, Susan
- Ledenham School series

Plievier, Theodor
- World War II trilogy

Plomer, William
- Double lives series

Plowden, Alison
- Elizabeth I series

Plowman, Stephanie
- Alexei Hamilton series
- Hamilton family series

Pluckrose, Henry
- Knowabouts series
- Thinking about series

Pluis, Bridget
- Psychic series

Plum, Mary
- John Smith series

Plumb, John Harold
- Sir Robert Walpole series

Plummer, Thomas Arthur
- Detective Inspector Andrew Frampton series

Plunkett, Edward John Moreton Drax
see **Dunsany, Edward John Moreton Drax Plunkett**

Poate, Ernest M
- Doctor Bentiron series

Pochocki, Ethel
see also **Marbach, Ethel**
- Grandma Bagley series

Pocock, Doris Alice
- Hallowdene Farm series

Pocock, Roger
- Frontiersman series

Poe, Edgar Allan
- Arthur Gordon Pym series
- Monsieur C Auguste Dupin series

Pohl, Frederik
- Cuckoo's saga series
- Heechee series
- Jim Eden series
- Plan of man trilogy
- Space merchants series

Pohlmann, Lillian
- Myrtle Albertina series

Poidevin, Leslie
- Country practice series

Polacco, Patricia
- Babushka series

Polch, Boguslaw
Atlantis, men and monsters
Unsolved mysteries series (9)
Revolt of the Titans
Unsolved mysteries series (9)
War of the chariots
Unsolved mysteries series (9)

Polcovar, Jane
- Dark forces series

Polisar, Barry Louis
- Snakes series

Pollack, Rachel
- Unquenchable fire series

Pollard, Alfred Oliver
- David Wilshaw series

Pollock, Edith Caroline
see **Thorn, Ismay**

Pollock, Mary
see also **Blyton, Enid**
- Dog stories series

Pollotta, Nick
- Bureau thirteen series

Polnay, Peter de
see **De Polnay, Peter**

Polsky, Thomas
- L F Griddle series

Pond, Roy
- Archaeology series
- Mummy series

Ponsonby, Doris Almon
- Jaspard family series

Pontoppidan, Henrik
- Emmanuel trilogy

Pook, Peter
- Pook series

Pool, Maria Louise
- Roweny series
- Salomes series

Q

• Piet Potter series
• Sheriff Sally Gopher series
• Sherlock Chick series
Quantrill, Malcolm
• Gotobed trilogy
Quarry, Nick
see also **Albert, Marvin Hubert; Conroy, Al; Rome, Anthony**
• Jake Barrow series
Quartermain, James
• Raven series
Queen, Ellery
see also **Ross, Barnaby**
• Ellery Queen series
• Mike McCall series
Misadventures of Sherlock Holmes
Sherlock Holmes series (10)
• Tim Corrigan series
Queen, Ellery, Junior
• Djuna and Champ series
• Gulliver Queen series
Quennell, Peter
• Lord Byron series
• Marble foot series
Quentin, Patrick
see also **Patrick, Q; Stagge, Jonathan**
• Lieutenant Timothy Trant series
• Peter Duluth series
Quest, Rodney
• Peter Quentin series
Quick, Dorothy
• Lieutenant Peter Donnegan series
Quick, Herbert
• Iowa pioneer life series
Quick, Larry
• Love trilogy
Quick, W T
• Dreams trilogy
Quigley, John
• King family series
Quill, Monica
• Sister Mary Teresa series
Quiller-Couch, Arthur
• Troy Town series
Quin, Basil Godfrey
• James Clarkson-Parry series
Quinain, Louis
• Country beat series
Quin-Harkin, Janet
• Sugar and spice series
• Toni Redmond and Jill Gardner series
Quinn, Eleanor Baker
• James Strange series
Quinn, Jake
• Patrick Shannon series
Quinn, John
• Rod Gavin series
Quinn, Olga
• Marieanne Payne series
Quinn, Patrick
• Pete Riley series
Quinn, Seabury
• Jules de Grandin series
Quinn, Simon
see also **Smith, Martin Cruz**
• Inquisitor series
Quinn, Tim
Doctor Who fun book
Doctor Who series (162)
Quinnell, A J
• Creasy series
Quirk, John Edward
see **Q, John**
Quiroule, Peter
Secret of the gold locket
Sexton Blake series (315)
Quiroule, Pierre
see also **Sayer, Walter William**
• Sexton Blake series
Quoirez, Francoise
see **Sagan, Francoise**

R

Rabe, Jean
• Harpers series
Rabe, Peter
• Daniel Port series
• Manny De Witt series
Rabier, Benjamin
• Gideon series
Rabin, Jennifer
• Swept away series
Rabinowitz, Sandy
• Mischief series
Rabinowitz, Shalom
see **Aleichem, Sholom**
Rackham, John
see also **Phillifent, John Thomas**
• Space puppet series
Radau, Hans
• Little Fox series
Radford, Edwin
• Doctor Manson series
• Superintendent Carmichael series
Radford, John P
• Illusionist series
Radford, Mona Augusta
• Doctor Manson series
• Superintendent Carmichael series
Radin, Ruth Yaffe
• Tac series
Radley, Sheila
• Chief Inspector Douglas Quantrill series
Radnor, Alan
• Dick Barton series
Rae, Gwynedd
• Mary Plain series
Rae, Hugh Crauford
see also **Albany, James; Crawford, Robert; Stirling, Jessica**
• Arthur Salisbury and Frank Shearer series
• Glasgow series
• Superintendent McCaig series
Rae, John
• Westminster series
Raffi
• Raffi songs to read series
Ragged, Hyder
King Solomon's wives
Allan Quatermain series (13)
Raine, Kathleen
• Happy fields trilogy
Raine, Norman Reilly
• Tugboat Annie series
Raine, Richard
see also **Forbes, Colin; Sawkins, Raymond**
• David Martini series
Rainey, Rich
• Alex Dartanian series
Raintree, Lee
• Dallas series
Raison, Milton Michael
• Tony Woolrich series
Raj Anand, Mulk
see **Anand, Mulk Raj**
Raleigh, Michael
• Paul Whelan series
Ralston, Gilbert Alexander
• Ben and Willard series
• Dakota series
Rambeau, John
• Morgan Bay series
Rambeau, Nancy
• Morgan Bay series
Ramm, Carl
• James Hawker series
Ramos, Manuel
• Luis Montez series
Rampa, Tuesday Lobsang
see **Lobsang Rampa, Tuesday**
Rampersad, Arnold
• Life of Langston Hughes series
Ramsay, Diana
• Lieutenant Meredith series
Ramsay, Jay
• Great return series
Ramsay, Mark
• Falcon trilogy
Ramskill, Valerie Patricia Roskams
see **Brooke, Carol**
Ramstedt, Viveka
• Penny series
Rand, Edward Augustus
• All aboard series
• Fighting the sea series
• Look ahead series
• Margie series
• School and camp series
• Up the Ladder Club series
Rand, Suzanne
• Winners series
Randall, Anthony Asheton
• Roger Patten series
Randall, Clay
see also **Adams, Clifton**
• Amos Flagg series
• Tragg series
Randall, Homer
• Army boys series
Randall, Joshua
see also **Cutter, Tom; Longley, W B; Meek, Joseph; Randisi, Robert Joseph; Roberts, J R; Weston, Cole**
• Bounty Hunter series
Randall, Lindsey
• Two hearts series
Randall, Marta
• Newhome series
Randall, Neil
Black Road war
Kingdom of Amber series (1)
Combat Command in the world of Roger Zelazny's Nine princes in Amber
Kingdom of Amber series (1)
• Combat Command series
• Dragon lord series
• Guardians of the Three series
Roger Zelazny's visual guide to Castle Amber
Kingdom of Amber series (10)
Seven no-trump
Kingdom of Amber series (10)
Randall, Robert
see also **Garrett, Randall; Phillips, Mark; Silverberg, Robert**
• Nidor series
Randall, Rona
• Drayton series
Randall, Tom
• Guides to the cemeteries of the world's great cities series
Randisi, Robert Joseph
see also **Cutter, Tom; Longley, W B; Meek, Joseph; Randall, Joshua; Roberts, J R; Weston, Cole**
• Destroyer series
• Digger Burroughs series
• Miles Jacoby series
Randle, Kevin
• Global war series
• Jefferson's war series
• Remember trilogy
• Seeds of war trilogy
Randolph, Forrest A
• Confederate series
Rankin, Carroll Watson
• Dandelion Cottage series
Rankin, Robert
• Armageddon trilogy
• Brentford series
• Ultimate truths trilogy
Rankine, John
• Dag Fletcher series
• Space corporation series
• Space nineteen ninety nine series
Ransom, Bill
• Pandora series
Ransom, Candice Farris
• Chrystal Falls series
• Growing up series
• My sister series
• Sunfire series
• Tales of the third grade series
Ransome, Arthur
• Swallowdale series
• Swallows and Amazons series
Ransome, Stephen
see also **Davis, Frederick Clyde; Steele, Curtis**
• Lieutenant Lee Barcello series
Murder doesn't always out
Professor Cyrus Hatch series (3)
One murder too many
Professor Cyrus Hatch series (1)
• Professor Cyrus Hatch series
• Schyler Cole and Luke Speare series
• Steve Ransome series
Raq
see **Evens, Glyn Kinnaird**
Rasmussen, Albert Henry
• Sea fever trilogy
Rasmussen, Alis A
• Highroad trilogy
Raspe, Rudolf Erich
• Baron Munchausen series
Ratel, Simonne
• Isabelle Comtat series
Rath, Virginia
• Michael Dundas series
• Rocky Allan series
Rathbone, Julian
• Colonel Nur Bey series
• Jan Argand series
Rathborne, Saint George
see also **Adams, Harrison; Clifton, Oliver Lee; Travers, J M**
• Canoe and campfire series
• Doctor Jack series
• Lend-a-hand boys series
• Ranch and range series
Rathjen, Carl Henry
• Land of the giants series
• Waltons series
Rattenburg, Peter Burgoyne
see **Burgoyne, Peter**
Rattray, Simon
see also **Black, Mansell; Dudley-Smith, Trevor; Hall, Adam; Trevor, Elleston**
• Hugo Bishop series
Ratye, Helene
• Gideon series
Rau, Pearl Frye
see **Frye, Pearl**
Raven, Simon
• Alms for oblivion series
Ravenswood, Fritzen
• Kei series
Rawls, Philip
see also **Kirk, Philip; Levinson, Leonard**
• Richard Bronson series
Rawn, Melanie
• Dragon prince series
• Dragon star series
Rawson, Clayton
• Great Merlini series
Rawson, Maud Stepney
• Rye Town series
Ray, Anna Chapin
• Sidney and Janet series
• Teddy series
Ray, Delia
• American Civil War series
Ray, Mary
• Early Christian series
• Mycaenean Greece series
Raymond, Alex
• Flash Gordon series
Raymond, Derek
• Factory series
Raymond, Ernest
• Daphne Bruno series
• London gallery series
• My days series
• Once in England trilogy
Raymond, Evelyn Hunt
• Dorothy Chester series
• Jessica Trent series
Raymond, John
• Bulman series
• Dempsey and Makepeace series
• Prospects series
Raymond, Moore
• Smiley series
Raymond, Rene
see **Chase, James Hadley; Marshall, Raymond**
Raymond, Walter
• Mendip Hills series
Rayner, Claire
• Performers series
• Poppy series
Rayner, Mary
• Mister and Mrs Pig series
Rayner, William
• Devil's picture book series
• Missouri series
Rayter, Joe
• Johnny Powers series
Razzi, Jim
• Dick Tracy series
• Junior transformers find your fate series
• Strawberry Shortcake series
Rea, Margaret Lucile Paine
• Lieutenant Powledge series
Reach, James
• Wing series
Read, Conyers
• William Cecil series
Read, Edyth Ellerbeck
• Blue Bonnet series
Read, Mark Brandon
• Chopper series
Read, *Miss*
• Caxley series
• Fairacre series
• Hobby Horse Cottage series
• Thrush Green series
• Time remembered series
Reade, Charles
• David Dodd and Lucy Fountain series
Reage, Pauline
• O series
Reasoner, James Morris
see **Ladd, Justin**
Reaves, Michael
• Darkworld detective series
• Khadaji series
• Shattered series
• Time machine series
Redekopp, Elsa
• Canadian village life series
Redgrove, Peter
• Beekeepers series
• Geoffrey Glass series
Redmayne, John
• Peter Maclean series
Redmond, Anton Edward
• Bill Slaker series
Redmond, Phil
• Grange Hill series
Redwood, Alec
see also **Braddon, George; Sava, George**
• Michael Grant series
Reed, Douglas
• Insanity fair trilogy
Reed, Giles
• Learn with the Munch Bunch series
• Munch Bunch character series
• Munch Bunch series
• Munch Bunch story books series
• Munch Bunch stretch series
• Munch Bunch word book series
Reed, Harlan
• Dan Jordan series
Reed, Helen Leah
• Brenda series
Reed, Ishmael
• Papa LaBas series
Reed, Maud Dorothy
• Candy series
Reed, Wallace
• Sheriff Bill Lloyd series
Reeder, Carolyn
• Shenandoah series
Reeder, Colin
• Adventures of Dunlop series
• Little red tractor series
• West Meadow series
Reeder, Jack
• Shenandoah series
Reeman, Douglas
see also **Kent, Alexander**
• Blackwood family series
Rees, Arthur John
• Colwin Grey series
• Crewe series
• David Colwyn series
• Inspector Luckraft series
Rees, Dilwyn
see also **Daniel, Glyn**
• Sir Richard Cherrington series
Rees, E M
• Going for it series
Rees, George
• Sexton Blake series
Rees, Goronwy
• Sensations and accidents series
Rees, Leslie
• Australian nature tales series
• Digit Dick series
Rees, Rod
• Worst day of my life series
Reese, Bob
• Critterland readers series
• Desert critterland series
• Freddie Freightliner series
• Going ape series
• Grand Canyon series
• Ocean critterland series
• Yellowstone critter series
Reese, John
• Jefferson Hewitt series
• Jesus on horseback trilogy
Reeve, Arthur Benjamin
• Craig Kennedy series
• Elaine trilogy
Reeve, Dominic
• Gypsy life series
Reeve, Linda Dawn
• Anne Boleyn series
Reeves, James
• Animiles series
Reeves, James R
• Navy Seals series
Reeves, Joyce
see **Gard, Joyce**
Reeves, Robert
• Cellini Smith series
Reeves-Stevens, Garfield
• Chronicles of Galen Sword series
• Star trek sequels series
• Star trek series
Reeves-Stevens, Judith
• Chronicles of Galen Sword series
• Star trek sequels series
• Star trek series
Regan, Jackie
• Star trek fan series

Reginald, Robert
• Science fiction film series
Regis, Julius
• Maurice Wallion series
Reibel, Paula
see **Mansfield, Elizabeth**
Reichert, Mickey Zucker
• Bifrost guardians series
• Disasters series
Reid, Desmond
see also **Baker, William Howard; Ballinger, W A; McNeilly, Wilfred**
• Pinkerton series
• Sexton Blake series
Reid, Forrest
• Tom Barber trilogy
Reid, John Thomas Howard
see **Howard, Tom**
Reid, Mayne
• Boy hunters series
• Bush boys series
• Himalayas series
• Ocean waifs series
Reid, Meta Mayne
• Kate and Lynn series
• Peyton children series
• Rathcapple series
• Tiffany series
Reid, Patrick Robert
• Colditz series
Reid, William Scott Hill-
see **Hill-Reid, William Scott**
Reid Banks, Lynne
see **Banks, Lynne Reid**
Reid, Colin
Reida, Bernice
• Hawkeye series
Reilly, Bernard F
• Kingdom of Leon-Castilla series
Reilly, David
• Wellies series
Reilly, Helen
• Inspector Christopher McKee series
Reinius, Trish
• White Wolf series
Reinsmith, Richard
• Bodyguard series
• Endless quest series
Tarzan and the tower of diamonds
Tarzan series (24)
Reisfeld, Randi
Melrose Place
Melrose Place series (4)
Stars of Beverly Hills 90210
Beverly Hills 90210 series (8)
Reiss, Johanna
• Upstairs room series
Reiss, Kathryn
• Time windows series
Reit, Seymour V
• Time machine series
• Time traveler series
Reitz, Deneys
• Boer War journal trilogy
Remarque, Erich Maria
• World War I series
Remenham, John
• Inspector Bliss series
Remi, Georges
see **Herge**
Remick, Grace May
• Glenloch girls series
• Jane Stuart series
• Sheldon Six series
Remkiewicz, Frank
• Froggy series
• Harris series
Remy
• Silent company trilogy
Renauld, Ron
see also **Heath, Charles**
• A-Team series
Renault, Mary
• Alexander the Great series
• Theseus series
Renault-Roulier, Gilbert Leon Etienne Theodore
see **Remy**
Rendel, Alexander Meadows
Appointment in Crete
War in Crete series (1)
Rendell, Ruth
• Chief Inspector Reginald Wexford series
Reneville, Mary Margaret Motley Sheridan de
see **Motley, Mary**
Renfroe, Martha Kay
see **Wren, M K**
Rennert, Maggie
• Guy Silvestri series
Reno, Bill
• Badge series
Reno, Clint
• Vigilante series
Reno, James
• Texas Anthem series
Renwick, Peter
• Leatherface Lonergan series
Repp, Ed Earl
• Jim Hayfield series
Resciniti, Angelo G
• C J Watson series
• Liz and Will series
• Super Bowl series
• Treehouse Gang series
Resnick, Mike
• Battlestar Galactica series
• Ganymede series
• Martian series
• Oracle trilogy
• Tales of the Galactic Midway series
• Tales of the velvet comet series
Resnick, Sylvia
• Debbie Preston, teenage reporter series
Resnicow, Herbert
• Alexander Magnus and Norma Gold series
• Crossword series
• Ed and Warren Baer series
• Sport series
Revell, Louisa
• Julia Tyler series
Revelli, George
• Amanda Nightingale series
Revere, John D
• Justin Perry series
Rewolinski, Leah
Star wreck
Luke Skywalker series (7)
Star wreck, the generation gap
Star trek series (57)
Rey, Bret
• Ned Butler series
• Ralph Coates series
• Will Foreman series
Rey, Hans Augusto
• Curious George series
• Pretzel series
• Zozo series
Rey, Lester del
see **Del Rey, Lester**
Rey, Margret
• Curious George series
• Pretzel series
• Zozo series
Reymond, Henry
• Bulldog Drummond series
Reynolds, Adrian
• Professor Dennis Barrie series
Reynolds, Anne
• Cheerleaders series
Reynolds, Dallas McCord
see **Reynolds, Mack**
Reynolds, Ethel
see **Mannin, Ethel**
Reynolds, George Macarthur
• Pickwick series
Reynolds, Kay
• Fortune's Friends series
Reynolds, Mack
• Bat Hardin series
• Homer Crawford trilogy
• Joe Mauser series
• Julian West series
• Lagrangia series
• Planetary Agent series
• Rex Bader series
• Star trek originals sequels series
Reynolds, Mike
• Fortune's Friends series
Reynolds, Stephen
• Nautical series
Reynolds, Warwick
• Sexton Blake series
Reynolds, William J
• Nebraska series
Rhea, Nicholas
see also **Walker, Peter Norman**
• Aidensfield series
Rheingold, Howard
• Savage report series
• Sisterhood trilogy
Rhinehart, Luke
• Wim series
Rhoades, Nina
• Miss Rosamund series
• Winifred series
Rhode, John
see also **Burton, Miles**
• Doctor Lancelot Priestley series
Rhodes, Daniel
• Guilhelm de Courdeval series
Rhodes, Evan Harold
• American palace series
Rhodes, John
• Tim and Betsy series
Rhodes, Kathlyn
• Martin Ryott series
Rhodes, Susan
• Bad girls series
Rhyne, Nancy
• Murder in the Carolinas series
• Tales of South Carolina series
Rhys, Jean
• Rochester series
Riasonovsky, Antonina Fedorovna Podgozinova
see **Fedorova, Nina**
Ricci, Lewis Anselm da Costa
see **Bartimeus**
Rice, Alice Hegan
• Mrs Wiggs series
Rice, Anne
see also **Roquelaure, A N**
• Mayfair witches series
• Vampire chronicles series
Rice, Craig
• Bingo Riggs and Handsome Kusak series
• Gypsy Rose Lee series
• Hildegarde Withers series
• John Joseph Malone series
Rice, Jeff
• Carl Kolchak series
Rice, Peter
• Renegade legion series
Rice, William
• Doctor James Wiscock series
Rich, Louise Dickinson
• Woods series
Rich, Nicholas
• Adam Hood series
Rich, Virginia
• Mrs Eugenia Potter series
Richards, Alun
• Ennal's Point series
Richards, Anna Matlock
• Alice in Wonderland sequels series
Richards, Clay
see also **Chaber, M E; Crossen, Kendell Foster; Monig, Christopher**
• Grant Kirby series
• Kim Locke series
Richards, Curtis
• Halloween series
Richards, Evan
• Six Million Dollar Man series
Richards, Francis
see also **Lockridge, Frances; Lockridge, Richard**
Accent on murder
Inspector Merton Heimrich series (13)
• Assistant District Attorney Bernie Simmons series
Burnt offering
Inspector Merton Heimrich series (10)
Case of the murdered redhead
Nathan Shapiro series (3)
Distant clue
Inspector Merton Heimrich series (17)
Drill is death
Nathan Shapiro series (4)
First come, first kill
Inspector Merton Heimrich series (16)
Four hours to fear
Assistant District Attorney Bernie Simmons series (2)
• Inspector Merton Heimrich series
Let dead enough alone
Inspector Merton Heimrich series (11)
• Nathan Shapiro series
Night of shadows
Paul Lane series (1)
No dignity in death
Inspector Merton Heimrich series (15)
Practise to deceive
Inspector Merton Heimrich series (12)
Show red for danger
Inspector Merton Heimrich series (14)
Richards, Frank
see also **Clifford, Martin; Richards, Hilda**
• Billy Bunter series
• Mascot schoolboy series
• Schoolboy series
Richards, Harvey D
• Sorak series
Richards, Hilda
see also **Clifford, Martin; Richards, Frank**
• Bessie Bunter series
Richards, J T
• Whitmarsh chronicles series
Richards, James
• Donkey series
Richards, Justin
• Timewyrm series
Richards, Kel
• Ben Bartholomew series
• Father Koala series
Richards, Laura Elizabeth
• Calvin Parks series
• Captain January series
• Fables for young and old series
• Five minute stories series
• Hildegarde series
• Honor Bright series
• Melody trilogy
• Mrs Tree series
• Three Margarets series
• Toto series
Richards, Lela Horn
• Blue Bonnet series
• Caroline trilogy
Richards, Milton
• Dick Kent series
Richards, Paul
• Grant Fowler series
Richards, Penny
• Calloway Corners series
Richards, Phyllis
• Kennedys abroad series
Richards, Ronald Charles William
see **Saddler, Allen**
Richards, Ross
• Sexton Blake series
Richards, Vicki
• Star trek fan series
Richardson, Arleta
• Grandma's attic series
• Growing up series
Richardson, Dorothy
• Brownies series
Richardson, Dorothy Miller
• Pilgrimage series
Richardson, Frank
• Sherlock Holmes sequels series
• Vincent Skrene series
Richardson, Henry Handel
• Fortunes of Richard Mahony trilogy
Richardson, Jean
• Moth Graham series
Richardson, Judith Benet
• Maushope's Landing series
Richardson, Pat
• Belle the bushie series
Richardson, Robert
• Augustus Maltravers series
Richelson, Geraldine
• Star wars storybook series
Richer, Clement
• Ti-Coyo series
Richler, Mordecai
• Jacob Two-Two series
• Saint Urbain's Street series
Richmond, Arthur Cyril
• Years series
Richmond, Grace Smith
• Juliet Robeson series
• Red Pepper Burns series
Richmond, Philip
• Duke Renny series
Richmond, Robin
• Story in a picture series
Richmond, Roe
• Lashtrow series
Richter, Conrad
• American pioneer trilogy
• Pioneer children series
Richter, Hans Peter
• Friedrich trilogy
Rico, Don
• Burgess Cardigan series
• Casey Grant series
Riddell, Chris
• Humphrey the Hippo series
Riddell, James
• Animal lore and disorder series
Ridder, Alfons de
see **Elsschot, Willem**
Rider, Brett
• Circle C series
Rider Haggard, Henry
see **Haggard, Henry Rider**
Rider Haggard, Lilias
see **Haggard, Lilias Rider**
Ridge, Antonia
• Endless and Company series
Ridgway, Bill
• Lucky Harry series
Ridgway, Jason
• Brian Guy series
Ridley, Nat
• Nat Ridley series
Ridley, Sheila
• Nurse Jane Taylor series
Riefe, A R
see also **Hardin, J D; Hawkes, Zachary; Riefe, Alan; Riefe, Barbara**
• Fortunes west series
Riefe, Alan
see also **Hardin, J D; Hawkes, Zachary; Riefe, A R; Riefe, Barbara**
• Huntington Cage series
• Tyger Decker series
Riefe, Barbara
see also **Hardin, J D; Hawkes, Zachary; Riefe, A R; Riefe, Alan**
• Dandridge trilogy
• Shackleford legacy trilogy
Rienow, Leona Train
• Dark pool series
Rifkin, Shepard
• Damian McQuaid series
Rigby, Ray
• Hill series
• Private Johnny Jackson series
Riggs, John Raymond
• Garth Ryland series
Riggs, Kate Douglas
see **Wiggin, Kate Douglas**
Rigsby, Howard
see **Howard, Vechel**
Rikhoff, Jean
• Butte family series
• Timble family trilogy
Riley, Frank
• Father Anton Dymek series
Riley, Judith Merkle
• Margaret of Ashbury series
Riley, William
• Windyridge series
Rimmer, Robert Henry
• Harrad College series
Rinehart, Mary Roberts
• Nurse Hilda Adams series
• Tish series
Ringner-Lundgren, Ester
• Little Trulsa series
Rios, Marie Teresa
see **Rios, Tere**
Rios, Tere
• Flying nun series
Ripley, Alexandra
• Charleston series
• Scarlett O'Hara series
Ripley, Jack
see also **Wainwright, John**
• John George Davis series
Ripley, Karen
Gross purposes
Indiana Jones series (9)
• Prisoner of dreams series
Summer session
Indiana Jones series (9)
Tales for the telling
Indiana Jones series (9)
Ripperger, Henrietta
• Elm Street series
Rippon, Angela
• Learn with Victoria Plum series
• Victoria Plum picture book series
• Victoria Plum series
Rippon, Marion
• Inspector Maurice Ygrec series
Risteen, H L
• Red Indian series
Rita
• Sheba series
• Victorian series
Ritchie, Lewis Anselm
see **Bartimeus**
Ritchie, Lily Munsel
• Chicken Little Jane series
Ritson, Kitty
see also **Vincent, Kitty**
• John and Jennifer series
• Tessa series
Ritthaler, Shelly
• Dinosaurs series
Rivers, Caryl
• Virgins series
Rivers, Jim
• Roy Rogers series

Riverton, Stein
- Osborne Crag series

Rives, Amelie
- Barbara Dering series

Rivett, Edith Caroline
see **Carnac, Carol; Lorac, E C R**

Rivkin, J F
- Runesword series
- Silverglass series

Rizzi, Timothy
- Major General Duke James series

Road, Alan
Doctor Who, the making of a television series
Doctor Who series (162)

Roan, Tom
- Rio Kid series

Robards, Karen
- Lady Catherine Alderly series

Robb, John
- Catsfoot series
- Red Radford series
- Shelby series

Robbins, Clifton
- Clay Harrison series
- Staveley series

Robbins, David
- Blade series
- Endworld series

Robbins, Harold
- Hollywood trilogy
- Jonas Cord series

Robbins, Orison
- French and Indian war series

Roberson, Jennifer
- Chronicles of the Cheysuli series
- Tiger and Del series

Roberts, Ainslie
- Dreamtime series

Roberts, Ann Victoria
- Louisa Elliot series

Roberts, Beth
- Drenee series

Roberts, Carl Eric Bechhofer
see **Ephesian**

Roberts, Cecil
- And so series
- Half way series
- Mrs Brown series
- Pamela series
- Pilgrim Cottage series
- Rustic series
- Sunshine and shadow series

Roberts, Charles George Douglas
- Acadia series
- Wilderness series

Roberts, Constance Evelyn
- Pikey's Steep series

Roberts, Cynthia S
- Running tide series

Roberts, Doreen
- Joe series

Roberts, Dorothy James
- Arthurian series

Roberts, E C
- Sherlock Holmes sequels series

Roberts, Elisabeth
- Simpey series

Roberts, Gareth
- Timewyrm series

Roberts, Gillian
- Amanda Pepper series

Roberts, Gruffydd Dewi
- Pikey's Steep series

Roberts, I M
see **Roberts, Irene**

Roberts, Irene
- Ancient Egypt series
- China trilogy

Roberts, J R
see also **Cutter, Tom; Longley, W B; Meek, Joseph; Randall, Joshua; Randisi, Robert Joseph; Weston, Cole**
- Gunsmith series

Roberts, J W
- Looking backward responses series

Roberts, Jack
- Street Hawk series

Roberts, Jane
- Oversoul Seven series

Roberts, Janet Louise
see **Bronte, Louisa**

Roberts, John Maddox
- Act of God trilogy
- Cingulum trilogy
- Conan series
- Space Angel series
- Stromlands series

Roberts, K H
- Bingo Bones and the Boggart series

Roberts, Keith
- Kaeti series

Roberts, Ken
- Degrassi High School series

Roberts, Kenneth
- Black fire series

Roberts, Kenneth Lewis
- Chronicles of Arundel series

Roberts, Lee
see also **Martin, Robert Lee**
- Doctor Clinton Shannon series

Roberts, Les
- Milan Jacovich series
- Saxon series

Roberts, Marion
- Anne and David Layton series

Roberts, Mark Kelly
- Liberty Corps series
- Soldier for hire series

Roberts, Melva Jean
- Dreamtime series

Roberts, Nora
- Cordina series
- Flowers series
- Hornblower saga series
- Macgregor series
- O'Hurley trilogy

Roberts, Sidney Castle
- Sherlock Holmes sequels series

Roberts, Willo Davis
- Black pearl series
- Minden curse series
- Sunfire series

Robertshaw, James Denis
see **Gaunt, Michael**

Robertson, Alexander
- Irish Monte Cristo series

Robertson, Colin
- Alan Steel series
- Edward North series
- Inspector John Martin series
- Inspector Robert Strong series
- Peter Grayleigh series
- Superintendent Bradley series
- Vicky McBain series

Robertson, Denise
- Belgate trilogy

Robertson, Don
- Morris Bird III series

Robertson, Ethel Florence Lindesay
see **Richardson, Henry Handel**

Robertson, H Macleod
- Sammy's super T-shirt series

Robertson, Helen
- Inspector Lathom Dynes series

Robertson, Jean
- Little Black Nickum series

Robertson, Jenny
- Circle series

Robertson, Kate
- Dilbert series

Robertson, Keith
see also **Keith, Carleton**
- Henry Reed series
- Neil and Swede trilogy
- Ticktock and Jim series

Robertson, Manning K
- Steve Carradine series

Robertson, Stephen
see also **Walker, Robert Wayne**
- Ryne Lanark series

Robeson, Kenneth
see also **Goulart, Ron**
- Avenger series
- Doc Savage series

Robins, Denise
see also **Gray, Harriet**
Fauna
Quadroon trilogy (3)
- Rat series

Robins, Patricia
see also **Lorrimer, Claire**
- Dick and Tamily series
- Lady Chatterley series

Robinson, Barbara
- Herdman family series

Robinson, Chaille Howard Payne
see **Kirby, Jean**

Robinson, Edith
- Little Puritan series

Robinson, Eliot Harlow
- Smiling pass series

Robinson, George Bush
- James Clifton series

Robinson, Jeanne
- Stardance series

Robinson, Joan Gale
- Mary-Mary series
- Teddy Robinson series

Robinson, Kim Stanley
- Mars series
- Orange County trilogy

Robinson, Lynda S
- Lord Meren series

Robinson, Mabel Louise
- Little Lucia series

Robinson, Martha
- Matty series
- Vet series

Robinson, Maude
- Quaker tales series

Robinson, Mike
- Solo the dragon series

Robinson, Nancy Konheim
- Angela trilogy
- Tripper and Sam series
- Veronica quartet
- Wendy series

Robinson, Nigel
Doctor Who crossword book
Doctor Who series (162)
Doctor Who quiz book
Doctor Who quiz book series (4)
- Doctor Who series

Second Doctor Who quiz book
Doctor Who quiz book series (4)
Third Doctor Who quiz book
Doctor Who quiz book series (4)
- Timewyrm series

Robinson, Peter
- Chief Inspector Alan Banks series

Robinson, Roland Edward
- Drift of things series

Robinson, Sheila Mary
see also **Radley, Sheila Mary**

Robinson, Spider
- Callahan's Crosstime Saloon series
- Mindkiller series
- Stardance series

Robinson, Vance
see also **Cannon, John; Newton, Mike**
- Justice trilogy

Robinson, Warren F
- G-man's son series

Robitaille, Julie
- Quantum leap series

Robsky, Paul
- Untouchables series

Robson, Norman
see **Robb, John**

Roc, Margaret
- Little Koala series

Roche, Eliane
- Fortune and power series

Roche, Mazo de la
see **De la Roche, Mazo**

Roche, Patricia K
- Webster and Arnold series

Roche, Roger Frison-
see **Frison-Roche, Roger**

Rochester, George Ernest
- Grey Shadow series

Rock, Gail
- Addie series

Rock, Nova
- Bobo series

Rock, Philip
Dirty Harry
Dirty Harry Callahan series (12)

Rock, Phillip
- Greville family trilogy

Rockman, Clint
- Sable ivory series

Rockwell, Anne
- Our life series

Rockwell, Anne Foote
- Bear child series
- Gogo series
- Paul and Arthur series

Rockwell, Carey
- Tom Corbett series

Rockwell, Thomas
- Billy Forrester series

Rockwood, Harry
- Donald Dyke series

Rockwood, Roy
- Bomba series
- Dave Dashaway series
- Dave Fearless series
- Deep sea series
- Great marvel series
- Speedwell boys series

Rodda, Charles
see **Holt, Gavin**

Rodda, Emily
- Teen Power Inc. series
- Timekeeper series

Roddenberry, Gene
- Star trek moving picture series
- Star trek series

Roddy, Lee
- American adventure series
- Davey Dillon series
- Ladd family series

Roden, Henry Wisdom
- Sid Ames series

Roderus, Frank
- Billy Ray series
- Carl Heller series
- Harrison Wilke series
- J Aubrey Whitford series

Rodgers, Frank
- Intergalactic kitchen series

Rodgers, Jesse
- ESP McGee series

Rodgers, Mary
- Annabel Andrews series

Rodgers, Mary Madeline
- Our endangered planet series

Rodgers, Sherlaw Johnston
- Micah Truelove series

Rodney, Bryan
- Francis Villiers series

Rodney, Jonathan
- To heal series

Roe, Harry Mason
- Lanky Lawson series

Roe, JoAnn
- Cat series

Roe, Sue
- Miss Havisham series

Roeburt, John
- Jigger Moran series
- Johnny Devereaux series

Roffey, Maureen
- I can do it series
- Sleepy series

Roffman, Jan
- Sergeant Ratlin series

Rofheart, Martha
- Henry V series

Rogers, Alan
- Clever Trevor series
- Pigeon Street series

Rogers, Chuck
see **Stivers, Dick**

Rogers, Jim
- Colditz series

Rogers, Mark Earl
- Blood of the lamb series
- Samurai Cat series
- Zorachus series

Rogers, Pamela
- Michael series

Rogers, Paul
- Boneshaker series
- Me and Alice series
- Somebody series

Rogers, Rosemary
- Ginny Brandon and Steve Morgan series

Rogers, Samuel
- Professor Paul Hatfield series

Rogerson, James
- King Wilbur series

Roggeveen, Leonard
- Jan series
- Okkie series

Rohan, Michael Scott
- Winter of the world trilogy

Rohmer, Richard
- Separation trilogy
- Triad series
- Ultimatum series

Rohmer, Sax
- Anthony Ferrara series
- Fu-Manchu series
- Gaston Max series
- Paul Harley series
- Red Kerry series
- Sumuru series

Rohrbach, Peter Thomas
see **Cody, James P**

Roland, Betty
- Improbable life trilogy
- Jamie series

Rolen, Pierre Louis
- Pony Club series

Rolfe, Frederick William
- Toto's tales series

Rolland, Romain
- John Christopher series
- Soul enchanted series

Rollet-Andriene, Maryat
see **Arsan, Emmanuelle**

Rolph, C H
- Particulars series

Rolt-Wheeler, Francis
- Wonder of war series

Rolvaag, Ole Edvart
- Per Hansa trilogy

Romains, Jules
- Men of goodwill series

Romano, Don
- Mafia series

Romanoff, Alexander Nicholayevitch
see **Abdullah, Achmed**

Romany
see **Evens, George Bramwell**

Rome, Anthony
see also **Albert, Marvin Hubert; Conroy, Al; Quarry, Nick**
- Tony Rome series

Romero, Enrique
- Axa series

Romero, George Andrew
- Living dead series

Romilly, Giles
- Colditz series

Ronald, E B
- Rupert Bradley series

Ronald, James
- Julian Mendoza series
- Quentin Gourlay series

Ronan, Tom
- Deep of the sky series

Ronns, Edward
see also **Aarons, Edward Sidney**
- Jerry Benedict series

Rooke, Anne
- Robert James series
- Robert series

Rooke, Daphne
- Herman Jozef series
- Twin series

Rooney, Lucy
- Mary speaks to the world series

Roop, Connie
- Great mysteries series
- Make me laugh series

Roop, Peter
- Great mysteries series
- Make me laugh series

Roos, Audrey
see **Roos, Kelley**

Roos, Kelley
- Jeff and Haila Troy series

Roos, Stephen
- Maple Street kids series
- New Eden series
- Pet Lovers Club series

Roos, William
see **Roos, Kelley**

Roose-Evans, James
- Odd and Elsewhere series

Roosevelt, Eleanor
- On my own series

Roosevelt, Elliott
- Blackjack Endicott series
- Eleanor Roosevelt series
- Roosevelt family series

Roosevelt, Wyn
- Frontier Boys series

Roper, Lester V
- Jerry Roe series

Roquelaure, A N
see also **Rice, Anne**
- Sleeping Beauty series

Rorem, Ned
- Musical diaries series

Rosa, Dennis
- Sherlock Holmes drama series

Rosa, Peter de
see **Boyd, Neil**

Roscoe, Mike
- Johnny April series

Rose, Anna Perrott
- Gentle house series

Rose, Christine Brooke-
see **Brooke-Rose, Christine**

Rose, Gerald
- PB series

Rose, Mitchell
- Rhyme-fingerplay-puppet series

Rose, Pamela
- Star trek fan series

Rosen, Richard
- Harvey Blissberg series

Rosen, Winifred
- Henrietta series

Rosenbaum, Ray
- Army Air Corps series

Rosenberg, Amye
- Animals series
- Sam series

Rosenberg, Joel
- Guardians of the flame series
- Metzada series

Rosenberger, Joseph
- C.O.B.R.A. series
- Death Merchant series
- Murder Master series

Rosenblatt, Arthur
- Strawberry Shortcake series

Rosenbloom, Joseph
- Deputy Dan series

Rosenblum, Lawrence
see **Lariar, Lawrence**
Rosenhayn, Paul
• Joe Jenkins series
Rosenstock, Janet
• MacLeod family series
Rosenthal, Lesley Sharon
• Esmeralda Bloom series
Ross, Angus
• Mark Farrow series
Ross, Antony Melville-
see **Melville-Ross, Antony**
Ross, Barnaby
see also **Queen, Ellery**
• Drury Lane series
Ross, Cameron
• Alistair Duncan series
Ross, Charles
• Haunted seventh series
Ross, Clarissa
see also **Ross, Marilyn**
• Dark Harbor series
Ross, Dana Fuller
• Holt family series
• Wagons West series
Ross, David D
• Dreamers of the day series
Ross, Diana
• Little red engine series
• Miss Pussy series
Ross, Gene
• Shaun O'Malley series
Ross, Ian
• Mind Masters series
Ross, Ivan T
• Ben Gordon series
Ross, James Davidson
• Ross family series
Ross, Jean
• Belvie family series
Ross, John
• Major Hutton Seary series
Ross, Jonathan
see also **Rossiter, John**
• Superintendent George Rogers series
Ross, Katharine
• Fuzzy tales series
Ross, Leonard Q
see also **Rosten, Leo**
• Hyman Kaplan series
Ross, Lillian
• Big Sur series
Ross, Malcolm
see **Macdonald, Malcolm**
Ross, Marilyn
see also **Ross, Clarissa**
• Barnabas Collins series
• Fog Island series
• Phantoms series
Ross, Martin
• Irish R.M. series
Ross, Melville
see **Melville-Ross, Antony**
Ross, Pat
• M and M series
Ross, Paul
• Chopper Cop series
Ross, Robert
• Medici series
Ross, Sutherland
• Clifton family series
Ross, Tony
• Hugo series
• Tales from Mister Toffy's circus series
• Towser series
Ross, William Edward Daniel
see **Ross, Clarissa; Ross, Marilyn**
Ross Williamson, Hugh
see **Williamson, Hugh Ross**
Ross, Zola Helen
• Beau Smith and Pogy Rogers series
Ross-Macdonald, Malcolm
see **Macdonald, Malcolm**
Rosser, Glenda Dawn
• Missionary mum series
Rossi, Bruno
see also **Levinson, Leonard**
• Sharpshooter series
Rossiter, John
see also **Ross, Jonathan**
• Criminal Court series
• Roger Tallis series
Rossmann, John F
• Mind Masters series
Rossner, Robert
see **Ross, Ivan T**
Rossow, William Brigance
• Lear's daughters series

Rostand, Robert
• Mike Locken series
Rosten, Leo
see also **Ross, Leonard Q**
• Hyman Kaplan series
• Silky Pincus series
Rotchstein, Janice
• Tiernan family series
Roth, Arthur
• Twistaplot series
Roth, Harold
• Toddler's fun series
Roth, Henry
• Mercy of a rude stream series
Roth, Holly
• Inspector Medford series
• Lieutenant Kelly series
Roth, Joseph
• Radetzky series
Roth, Lillian
• I'll cry tomorrow series
Roth, Philip
• Nathan Zuckerman series
Rothenstein, John
• Summer's lease trilogy
Rothenstein, William
• Men and memories series
Rothrock, Thomas
• Junior Trail Blazers series
Rothweiler, Paul Roger
• Westward rails trilogy
Rothwell, Henry Talbot
• Michael Brooks series
Rotsler, William
• Doctor Strange series
• Goonies series
• Grease series
• Marvel superheroes, new series
• Mister Merlin series
• Star trek tie-ins series
• Zandra trilogy
Rottman, Gordon
• World War III series
Rouaud, Jean
• Fields of glory series
Rouch, James
• Zone series
Roughsey, Labamu
• Mark and Wendy series
Rougvie, Cameron
• Robert Belcourt series
Rounds, Glen
• Blind colt series
• Mister Yowder series
• Whitey series
Rountree, Owen
• Jim Cord series
Rousch, Catherine E
• Star trek fan series
Routh, Jonathan
• Nuns series
Rovin, Jeff
• Roger Garrison series
Unauthorised teenage mutant ninja turtles quiz book
Teenage mutant ninja turtles series (5)
Rowe, Anne
• Inspector Barry series
• Inspector Pettengill series
Rowe, Jennifer
• Verity Birdwood series
Rowe, John Gabriel
• Northwest stories series
• Sergeant Dick series
Rowland, Donald Sydney
see **Mason, Chuck; Morgan, G J; Shane, Bart; Starr, Roland**
Rowland, Henry Cottrell
• Frank Clamart series
Rowland, John
• Inspector Shelley series
Rowlands, Avril
• God's wonderful railway series
• Little red metro series
Rowlands, Betty
• Melissa Craig series
Rowley, Christopher
• Fenrile trilogy
• Vang trilogy
Rowley, Phillis Garrard
see **Garrard, Phillis**
Rowse, Alfred Leslie
• Churchill family series
• Cornishman series
• Elizabethan age series
Roy, Anne
• Bear for all seasons series
Roy, Lillian Elizabeth
• Blue Birds series
• Girl Scouts series
• Girl Scouts trilogy

• Little Washingtons series
• Polly Brewster series
• Woodcraft Girls series
Roy, Thomas Albert
• Jimmy Brent series
Royce, Kenneth
• Spider Scott series
Royle, Edwin Milton
• Squaw Man series
Ruark, Robert
• Grenadine Etching series
• Old man series
Rubel, James Lyon
• Medico series
Rubin, Harold
see **Robbins, Harold**
Rubin, Susan G
• Mrs Murgatroyd series
Rubinstein, Arthur
• Many years series
Rubinstein, Gillian
• Space demons trilogy
Ruck, Berta
• Storyteller series
Ruck, Ruth Janette
• Hill Farm trilogy
Rucker, Rudy
• Software series
Rud, Anthony Melville
• J C K Masters series
Rudd, Steele
• Dashwood family series
• Duncan McClure series
• Rudd family series
Ruddick, Bob
• Jason series
• Max and me series
Ruddy, Jon
• Dracula series
Rudorff, Raymond
Dracula archives
Dracula series (26)
Rudowsky, Colby
• Slug series
Ruegg, Alfred Henry
• Rosie Bright series
Ruemmler, John David
• Middle Earth quest series
Ruesch, Hans
• Top of the world series
Ruff, Agnes
• Pinkie series
Ruffell, Ann
• Gribble the dragon series
Ruggero, Ed
• Mark Isen series
Ruhen, Carl
• Mad Max series
Runbeck, Margaret Lee
• Miss Boo series
Rundle, Anne
see also **Manners, Alexandra**
• Amberwood series
Runyan, John
see also **Palmer, Bernard**
• Biff Norris series
• Tom Barnes series
Runyon, Catherine
• Mister and Mrs Bear series
Rush, Caroline
• Mister Pengachoosa series
Rush, Robert
• Birthday series
Rushing, Jane Gilmore
• Walnut Grove series
Rushton, Charles
• Inspector Cadman series
• James O'Hannay and Floyd East series
Rusoff, Garry
• Chariots of fire trilogy
Russ, Joanna
• Adventures of Alyx series
Russell, Bertrand
• Western philosophy series
Russell, Charles Marion
• Rawhide Rawlins series
Russell, Charlotte Murray
• Homer Fitzgerald series
• Jane Amanda Edwards series
Russell, Dora
• Tamarisk tree series
Russell, Enid Sherry
• Ben Louis series
Russell, Gary
• Timewyrm series
Russell, Ivy
• Princess Susan series
Russell, Keith
• Young birdmen series

Russell, Martin
• Jim Larkin series
Russell, Mary Annette
• Elizabeth series
Russell, Paul
• Beauty of Canada series
Russell, Ray
• Ashton family series
Russell, Richard
• Angel Graham series
Russell, Robert
• Doctor Steven Rushton series
Russell, Robert William
• World I cannot see series
Russell, Steven
• Bulldozer Brown series
Russo, John
• Living dead series
Russo, Richard
• Mohawk series
Rutherford, Douglas
• Chequered flag series
• Paul Temple series
Rutherford, Edward
• Generations series
Rutherford, Mark
see **White, William Hale**
Rutherford, Meg
• Bluff and Bran series
• Foggy series
Ruthin, Margaret
see also **Catherall, Arthur**
• Elli Sari series
Rutland, Harriet
• Mister Winkley series
Rutledge, Adam
• Patriots series
Rutley, Cecil Bernard
• Colin and Patricia series
• Tales of stirring times series
• Wild life story series
Rutley, Cecily Marianne
• Children of other days series
• Little people in far off lands series
• Tales of the wild folk series
Rutter, Eileen Joyce
see **Chant, Joy**
Rutter, Owen
• Tiadatha series
Rutzebeck, Hjalmar
• Frozen north series
Ruyle, John
• Turlock Loams series
Ryan, Cornelius
• Normandy Campaign trilogy
Ryan, Gavin
• Mister Poppleberry series
Ryan, Isobel
• Black man trilogy
Ryan, Jessica
• Gregory Pavlov and O'Shaughnessey series
Ryan, Jim
• Igor Kerinsky series
Ryan, John
• Captain Pugwash series
• Doodle series
• Flying sorcerer series
Ryan, Mary Elizabeth
• Katie Kusik series
Ryan, Tom
• Brannigan series
Ryan, Tom K
• Tumbleweeds series
Rybakov, Anatoli
• Arbat trilogy
• Dirk series
Ryder, Eileen
• Tim series
Ryder, Thom
see also **Hart, Jon; Harvey, John Barton**
• Avenging Angel series
Ryerson, Florence
• Jimmy Lane series
Ryland, Clive
• Chief Inspector George Bassett series
• Inspector Beck series
• Superintendent Shannon series
Ryland, John Knox
• Inspector Rodway series
Rylant, Cynthia
• Best wishes series
• Everyday series
• Henry and Mudge series
• Mister Putter and Tabby series
Rynd, Evelyne Elise
• Mrs Green series
Rypel, Thadeus Chester
• Gonji series

S

S, K O
see **Dombrowski, Katrina**
S, W S L
see **Lach-Szyrma, Wladislaw Somerville**
Sabatier, Robert
• Olivier Chateauneuf series
Sabatini, Rafael
• Captain Blood series
• Cesare Borgia series
• Scaramouche series
Sabbagh, Pierre
• Fanina series
Saber, Robert O
• Carl Good series
• Max Keene series
Saberhagen, Fred
• Berserker series
• Book of lost swords series
• Book of swords trilogy
• Chup trilogy
• Dracula series
• Frankenstein sequels series
• Pilgrim series
Seance for a vampire
Dracula series (26)
• Sherlock Holmes sequels series
Sabey, Ian
• Melodie series
Sabin, Edward Legrand
• Bar B boys series
• Great West series
• Trail blazers series
Sachar, Louis
• Wayside School series
Sachs, Marilyn
• Amy and Laura series
• Veronica Ganz series
Sachs, Maurice
• Witches' Sabbath series
Saddler, Allen
• Dave Stevens series
• Jerry series
• King and queen series
• Smudger series
Saddler, K Allen
see **Saddler, Allen**
Sadiq, Nazneen
• Degrassi High School series
Sadler, Barry
• Casca series
Sadler, Geoffrey
see also **Calhoun, Wes; Sadler, Jeff**
• Justus trilogy
Sadler, Jeff
see also **Calhoun, Wes; Sadler, Geoffrey**
• Marshal Andrew Anderson series
Sadler, Mark
see also **Arden, William; Collins, Michael; Crowe, John**
• Paul Shaw series
Safire, William
• On language series
Sagan, Francoise
• Josee and Bernard series
• Sweden series
Sagara, Michele M
• Sundered series
Sage, Dana
• Donald O'Keefe Adams series
Sahgal, Nayantara
• Prison series
Sainsbury, Noel
• Bill Bolton series
• Billy Smith series
Saint Albans, Suzanne Marie Adele Beauclerk
• Mimosa series
Saint Alcorn, Lloyd
• Dream quest trilogy
Saint Antoine, Sara
• Green musketeers series
Saint Barbe Baker, Richard
see **Baker, Richard Saint Barbe**
Saint Clair, Elizabeth
• Marilyn Ambers series
Saint Claire, Erin
see also **Brown, Sandra**
• Jennifer and Cage series
Saint Dennis, Madelon
• Sydney Treherne series
Saint, Dora Jessie
see **Read, *Miss***
Saint-Exupery, Antoine de
• Airman's odyssey trilogy

Saint Germain, Gregory
- Resistance series

Saint James, Blakely
- Christina Van Bell series

Saint James, Daniel
- Brothers in blood series

Saint John, David
see also **Dietrich, Robert; Hunt, Everette Howard**
- Peter Ward series

Saint John, Mabel
- Daisy Peach series
- Gipsy trilogy
- Pollie Green series

Saint-Laurent, Cecil
- Bernadette series
- Cherie series
- Clotilde series

Saint Meyer, Ned
- Match series

Saint-Pierre, Michel de
- Aristocrats series

Saki
- Clovis series
- Reginald series

Sale, Medora
- Inspector John Sanders and Harriet Jeffries series

Sale, Richard
- Daniel Webster series

Salinger, Jerome David
- Glass family series

Salisbury, Carola
see also **Butterworth, Michael**
- War and peace series

Salisbury Davis, Dorothy
see **Davis, Dorothy Salisbury**

Salisbury, Ray
- Simon series

Salkey, Andrew
- West Indies series

Sallis, James
- Lew Griffin series

Sallis, Susan
- Rising family series

Salmon, Annie Elizabeth
see **Martin, Nancy**

Salmon, Jan
Little monster cook book
Alexander Bunyip series (12)

Salmon, Michael
- Alexander Bunyip series
- Animal antics series
- Dinosaur series
- Dinosaur swamp series
- Scaredy monsters series
- Who did it series
- Who's behind the door series

Salmon, Ross
- Payo series

Salmonson, Jessica Amanda
- Amazons series
- Tomoe Gozen trilogy

Salsitz, R A V
- Alorie series
- Dragons trilogy

Salt, Jonathan
- Jonathan Salt series

Salten, Felix
- Bambi series

Salter, Elizabeth
- Inspector Michael Hornsley series

Saltmarsh, Max
- Archie Lumsden series

Salvatore, Robert Anthony
- Cleric quintet
- Dark elf trilogy
- Icewind Dale trilogy

Salzmann, Sigmund
see **Salten, Felix**

Sampson, Derek
- Grump series

Sampson, Emma
see also **Sanderson, Margaret Love; Speed, Nell; Van Dyne, Edith**
- Mary Louise and Josie O'Gorman series
- Miss Minerva series
- Priscilla Payson series
- Tucker twins series

Sampson, Fay
- Daughter of Tintagel series
- Pangur Ban series
- Watch and landfall series

Sampson, George
- Paola and George series

Sampson, Richard Henry
see **Hull, Richard**

Sampson, Victor
- Inspector Downes and Sergeant Hopkins series

Samuels, Adelaide Florence
- Dick and Daisy Travers series
- Dick Travers series

Samuels, Ernest
- Henry Adams trilogy

Samuels, Victor
- Dracula series

San Antonio
- Berurier series
- San Antonio series

Sanborn, Katherine Abbott
- Abandoned farm series

Sanborn, Ruth Burr
- Angeline Tredennick series

Sancha, Sheila
- Stamford series

Sanchez-Silva, Jose Maria
- Ladis series

Sand, George
- Consuelo series
- Socialist trilogy

Sandberg, Berent
- Matt Eberhart series

Sandberg, Inger
- Anna series
- Boy's possessions series
- Daniel series
- Dusty series
- Johan series
- Kate series
- Little Spook series
- Nicholas series

Sandberg, Lasse
- Anna series
- Boy's possessions series
- Daniel series
- Dusty series
- Johan series
- Kate series
- Little Spook series
- Nicholas series

Sandberg, Peter Lars
see **Sandberg, Berent**

Sandbrook, Richard
- African politics series

Sandburg, Carl
- Rootabaga series

Sandel, Cora
- Alberta series

Sanders, Beryl
- Allsorts series

Sanders, Bill
- Goalposts series
- Outtakes series
- Tough issues for teens series

Sanders, Brett
see also **Barrett, Geoffrey John**
- Web Steele series

Sanders, Bruce
see also **Cody, Stetson; Denver, Lee; Grex, Leo; Gribble, Leonard Reginald; Shane, Steve**
- Howard Digburn series

Sanders, Buck
- Ben Slayton series

Sanders, Charles Wesley
- Mournful Martin series

Sanders, Dorothy Lucie
see also **Walker, Lucy**
- Montgomery family series

Sanders, J R
- Container series

Sanders, John
- Nicholas Pym series

Sanders, Lawrence
- Archy McNally series
- Edward X Delaney series
- Peter Tangent series
- Ten commandments series
- Timothy Cone series

Sanders, Leonard
- Clay Loomis series

Sanders, Ruth Manning-
see **Manning-Sanders, Ruth**

Sanderson, Douglas
see **Brett, Martin**

Sanderson, Margaret Love
see also **Sampson, Emma**
- Campfire Girls series

Sandford, John
- Lucas Davenport series

Sandford, Ken
- Max Hale series

Sandison, Janet
see also **Duncan, Jane**
- Apology for the life of Jean Robertson series

Sandler, Mona
- Steep Farm series

Sandman Lilius, Irmelin
- Sola trilogy

Sandon, J D
see also **Harvey, John Barton**
- Gringos series

Sandoz, Mari
- Nebraska trilogy

Sandring, Lesley
Doctor Who illustrated A-Z
Doctor Who series (162)

Sands, Leslie
- Sam Wilson series

Sandstrom, Eve K
- Down home series

Sandstrom, Flora
- Pont Clery series

Sandwall-Bergstrom, Martha
- Anna series

Sandys, James
- Inspector Millwall series
- James Charlesworth series
- Mister Springfield series

Sandys, Oliver
see also **Barcynska, Helene**
- Pleasure garden series

Sanford, Doris
- Advanced theology for very tiny persons series
- Children of courage series
- Hurts of childhood series
- In our neighborhood series
- You'll never guess what series

Sangster, Jimmy
- John Smith series
- Katy Touchfeather series

Santayana, George
- Persons and places trilogy

Santiago, V J
- Joseph Madden series

Saperstein, David
- Cocoon series

Saphore, Athena
- Strawberry Shortcake series

Sapir, Richard
- Destroyer series

Remo
Destroyer series (94)

Sapper
- Bulldog Drummond series
- Jim Maitland series
- John Walters series
- Ronald Standish series

Sarabande, William
- First Americans series

Sarah, Duchess of York
- Budgie series

Sarasin, Jennifer
- Cheerleaders series

Sargent, Craig
- Last ranger series

Sargent, Pamela
- Earthminds trilogy
- Venus trilogy

Sargeson, Frank
- Enough series

Saro-Wiwa, Ken
- Mister B series
- Tambari series

Saroyan, William
- Mama and papa series

Sarsfield, Maureen
- Inspector Lane Parry series

Sarto, Ben
- Miss Otis series

Sartre, Jean Paul
- Roads to freedom trilogy

Sassoon, Siegfried
- Sherston trilogy
- Siegfried series

Sasthi Brata
see **Brata, Sasthi**

Saum, Karen
- Brigid Donovan series

Saunders, Charles Robert
- Imaro trilogy

Saunders, Clare Castler
- Argus Steele series

Saunders, David
Encyclopaedia of the worlds of Doctor Who
Doctor Who series (162)

Saunders, Hilary Saint George
see **Beeding, Francis; Pilgrim, David**

Saunders, Lawrence
- Wylie King and Nels Lundberg series

Saunders, Marjorie
- Madge series

Saunders, Marshall
- Beautiful Joe series
- Tilda Jane series

Saunders, Michael
see also **Simpson, Margaret**
- Murphy's mob series

Saunders, Susan
- Bad News Bunny series
- Morgan Swift find your fate series
- Mystery cat series
- Oz series
- Sleepover friends series

Saunders, Theodore
see **Scott, Denis**

Sauter, Eric
- Robert Lee Hunter series

Sava, George
see also **Braddon, George; Redwood, Alec**
- Peter Slavine series
- Surgeon in series
- Surgeon's destiny series

Savage, Buck
- Speed Johnson series

Savage, Deborah
- Peregrine Piecrust series

Savage, Jack
- Dempsey and Makepeace series

Savage, Richard
- Doctor Ferenc series

Savarin, Julian Jay
- Gordon Gallagher series
- Lemmus trilogy

Saville, Andrew
- Bergerac series

Saville, Malcolm
- Buckinghams series
- Jillies series
- Lone Pine Five Club series
- Marston Baines series
- Michael and Mary series
- Nettleford series
- Simon series
- Susan and Bill series

Savory, Gerald
- Dracula series

Savory, Teo
- Stonecroft series

Saward, Eric
- Doctor Who series

Slipback
Doctor Who series (162)

Sawkins, Raymond
see also **Forbes, Colin; Raine, Richard**
- Superintendent John Snow series

Sawyer, Corinne Holt
- Senior citizens series

Sawyer, Ruth
- Christmas stories series
- Lucinda Wyman series

Sawyer, Walter Leon
see **Standish, Winn**

Saxby, Jessie Margaret Edmonston
- Shetland series

Saxe, R B
- John Dobbs series

Saxon, John A
- Sam Welpton series

Saxon, Nancy
- Panky series

Saxon, Peter
- Guardians series
- Sexton Blake series

Saxton, Josephine
- Jane Saint series

Saxton, Judith
- Neyler family series

Saxton, Mark
- Islandia series

Sayer, Mandy
- Rose trilogy

Sayer, Walter William
see also **Quiroule, Pierre**
- Barnaby Grayle series
- Sexton Blake series

Sayers, Dorothy Leigh
- Harriet Vane series
- Lord Peter Wimsey series

Sayers, Valerie
- Due East series
- Mary Faith Rapple series

Sayler, Harry Lincoln
see also **Ashton, Lamar**
- Airship Boys series

Saylor, Steven
- Roma sub rosa series

Scalpel, Aesculapius
- Saint Bernard's series

Scanlan, Nelle Margaret
- Pencarrow family series

Scanlon, Noel
- Quinn series

Scannell, Dorothy
- Bright series
- Dolly trilogy

Scannell, Florence
- Cinderella series

Scannell, Vernon
- Tiger and the rose trilogy

Scarborough, Dorothy
- Cotton trilogy

Scarborough, Elizabeth Ann
- Argonia series
- Songkiller series
- Yanaba Maddock series

Scarlett, Roger
- Inspector Kane series

Scarpetta, Frank
- Marksman series

Scarry, Richard
- Cat family series
- Going places series
- Lowly Worm series
- Smallest pop-up book ever series
- Tinker and Tanker series

Schabelitz, Rudolph Frederick
- Christopher Storm series

Schealer, John Milton
- Zip-Zip series

Schechtman, Joseph Boris
- Vladimir Yabolinsky series

Scheer, Karl Herbert
- Atlan series
- Perry Rhodan series

Scheier, Michael
- World records series

Schenk, Craig
- Columbo series

Scherf, Margaret
- Emily and Henry Bryce series
- Grace Severance series
- Lieutenant Ryan series
- Reverend Martin Buell series

Schermele, Willy
- Deedle Dumpy series
- Peter series
- Winkie series

Schertle, Alice
- Cathy and Company series

Schickele, Rene
- Rhineland heritage series

Schiddel, Edmund
- Bucks County trilogy

Schier, Norma
- Kay Barth series

Schiff, Sydney Alfred
see **Hudson, Stephen**

Schildt, Goran
- Wake series

Schlesinger, Arthur Meier
- Age of Roosevelt series

Schley, Sturges Mason
- Doctor Quentin Toby series

Schmidt, Annie Maria Geertruida
- Bob and Jilly series
- Dusty and Smudge series

Schmidt, Dan
- Eagle Force series

Schmidt, Dennis
- Kensho series
- Questioner trilogy
- Twilight of the gods trilogy

Schmidt, James Norman
see **Norman, James**

Schmidt, Stanley
- Kyyra series

Schmitz, Ettore
see **Svevo, Italo**

Schmitz, James Henry
- Hub series
- Telzey Amberdon and Trigger Argee series

Schneck, Paul D
Mork and Mindy
Mork and Mindy series (2)

Schneour, Salman
- Noah Pandre series

Schnitzler, Arthur
- Three women trilogy

Schnurnberger, Lynn Edelman
- Star trek tie-ins series

Schoch, Tim
- Creeps series

Schock, T A
- Daniel Keel series

Schoenstedt, Walter
- Cradle builder series

Scholefield, Alan
- South African series

Schongut, Emanuel
- Kitten board book series

Schorr, Mark
- Red Diamond series

Schraff, Anne Elaine
- Narnia solo games series

Schreiner, Samuel Agnew
- Van Alen family series

Schroeder, Binette
- Tuffa series
- Zebby series

Schroeder, Doris
- Annie Oakley series
- Lassie series
- Walt Disney's Annette series

Schroeder, Lynn
- Superlearning series

Schuller, Gary
- Bouncing series

Schulman, Lester Martin
see **Martin, Les**

Schulte, Elaine
- California pioneer series

Schultz, James Willard
- Blackfoot series
- Hugh Monroe series
- Pitamaken series

Schulze, Doris
- Star trek fan series

Schumacher, Heinrich
- Lady Hamilton series

Schumann, Peter
- Daily lives in Nghsi-Altai series

Schurfranz, Vivian
- Cheerleaders series
- Sunfire series

Schuster, Hal
Batman
Batman series (10)

Schutz, Benjamin Merrill
- Leo Haggerty series

Schwaller de Lubicz, Isha
- Homo sapiens series

Schwartz, David Martin
- Hidden life series
- Million series

Schwartz, Joel L
- Best friends series

Schweitzer, Albert
- Primeval forest series

Scieszka, Jon
- Time warp trio series

Scofield, Jonathan
- Freedom fighters series

Scoggins, Charles Elbert
- Colin O'Leary series

Scoppettone, Sandra
- Lauren Laurano series

Scott, Alastair
- Scot series

Scott, Barbara Montagu
- Grisenbaum family series

Scott, Bill
- Boori series

Scott, Bradford
see also **Cole, Jackson**
- Walt Slade series

Scott, Bruce
- Superintendent Steve McLaren series

Scott, Carol Wensby-
see **Wensby-Scott, Carol**

Scott, Catherine Amy Dawson-
see **Dawson-Scott, Catherine Amy**

Scott, Dan
- Bret King series

Scott, Denis
- Mike James series

Scott, Dixon
- Toad Hall series

Scott, Don
- Raker series

Scott, Evelyn
- American history trilogy

Scott, Florence E
- Paul and Peggy series

Scott, Geraldine Edith Mitton
see **Mitton, Geraldine Edith**

Scott, Gertrude Fisher
- Jean Cabot series

Scott, Harold
- Obedient servant series

Scott, Hedley
- Sexton Blake series

Scott, Ian
- Naval adventure trilogy

Scott, Jack Denton
- Spargo series

Scott, Jack S
- Chief Inspector Peter Parsons series
- Detective Inspector Alfred Stanley Rosher series

Scott, James George
- Diana Forbes series

Scott, James Maurice
- Jeremy Jackson series

Scott, Jeremy
see **Dick, Kay**

Scott, Jody
- Sterling O'Blivion series

Scott, John Reed
- Red Hussars series

Scott, Jonathan
see **Scott, Jack S**

Scott, Justin
see **Blazer, J S**

Scott, Leroy
- Bob Clifford series

Scott, Leslie
see **Cole, Jackson**

Scott, Mansfield
- Inspector Malcome Steele series

Scott, Mary
- Freddie series
- Inspector Wright series
- New Zealand life series

Scott, Melissa
- Silence Leigh trilogy

Scott, Michael
- Tales from the Land of Erin trilogy
- Tales of the bard trilogy

Scott, Michael William
see also **Jakes, John**
- Rakehell dynasty series

Scott, Milton
- Doctor Alexander Cornell series

Scott, Paul
- British India quartet

Scott, Peter Graham
- Dragonfire series
- Labyrinth series

Scott, Philip
- Algy, Peter and Jeremy series

Scott, R C
- Dark forces series

Scott, Reginald Thomas Maitland
- Aurelius Smith series
- Richard Wentworth series

Scott, Roney
- Joe Puma series

Scott, Sheila
- Air pilot series

Scott, Sutherland
- Doctor Septimus Dodds series

Scott, Walter
- Mary, Queen of Scots series
- Rob Roy Macgregor series
- Tales of my landlord series
- Tales of the Crusaders series

Scott, Will
- Cherrys series
- Disher series

Scott, William Neville
see **Scott, Bill**

Scott Card, Orson
see **Card, Orson Scott**

Scott-Chard, Trevor Edwin
- Hunter Hawk series

Scotten, Cordell
- Robots and aliens series

Scribner, Kimball
- Your future in aviation series

Scudder, Horace Elisha
- Bodley family series

Scuro, Vincent
- Wonders of nature series

Scyoc, Sydney Joyce van
see **Van Scyoc, Sydney Joyce**

Sea-Lion
- Desmond Drake series
- John Prentice series
- Tiger Ransome series

Seafarer
- Captain Firebrace series

Seagrave, Gordon Stifler
- Burma surgeon trilogy

Seaman, Donald
- Sydenham series

Searle, Ronald
- Nigel Molesworth series
- Rocking-chair series

Searls, Hank
- Jaws series

Seaton, Stuart
- Inspector Martin Laidman series

Seaver, Tom
- Sport series

Sebastian, Margaret
see also **Gladstone, Maggie**
- Bow Street series

Secrist, Kelliher
- Sham Payne series

Sedges, John
see also **Buck, Pearl Sydenstricker**
- American life series

Sedgwick, Modwena
- Galldora series
- Jan Perry series

Sedley, Kate
- Roger Chapman series

Seed, Jenny
- Natal series

Seelye, John
True adventures of Huckleberry Finn
Huckleberry Finn series (4)

Seferiadis, George
see **Seferis, George**

Seferis, George
- Log book series

Sefton, Catherine
see also **Waddell, Martin**
- Northern Ireland trilogy

Segal, Erich
- Oliver and Jenny series

Segar, Elzie Crisler
- Popeye the Sailor series

Seger, Maura
- Callahan and Gargano families trilogy
- Calvert trilogy

Seide, Diane
- Medical power series

Seidler, Ann
- Junior listen-hear series
- Listen-hear series

Seifert, Adele
- Gregory Trent series

Seifert, Elizabeth
- Bayard series

Seignobosc, Francoise
see **Francoise**

Sela, Owen
- Nicholas Maasten series

Selberg, Ingrid
- Nature secrets series

Selby, Bettina
- Riding series

Selby, John
- Trace family trilogy

Selden, George
- Chester Cricket series

Selden, Neil
- Twilight series

Seldon Truss, Leslie
see **Truss, Seldon**

Selig, Sylvie
- T.G. and Moonie series

Seligman, Adrian
- Thunder Reef series

Selincourt, Aubrey de
see **De Selincourt, Aubrey**

Selincourt, Hugh de
see **De Selincourt, Hugh**

Sellar, Walter Carruthers
- All that series

Sellers, Con
- Men at arms series

Sellers, Connie Leslie
see **Raintree, Lee**

Sellers, Michael
- Calouste Fisher series

Sellwood, Arthur Victor
- German raider series

Selmark, George
see also **Truss, Seldon**
- Inspector Bass series

Seltzer, David
- Omen series

Selvon, Samuel
Calypsonian
Peter Aswell series (2)
- Lonely Londoners trilogy

Selway, Martina
- Dear Grandad series
- Grunts series

Selwyn, Francis
- Sergeant William Verity series

Sempe, Jean Jacques
- Nicholas series

Sender, Ramon Jose
- Before noon trilogy

Senior, Margaret
- Australian nature tales series

Senn, Steve
- Fozbek series
- Spacebread series

Sennocke, T J R
- Sergeant Mallory series

Serafin, David
- Superintendent Luis Bernal series

Seredy, Kate
- Good master series

Serge, Victor
- Resistance trilogy
- Revolution trilogy

Serling, Robert
- Jeremy Haines series

Serling, Rod
- Twilight Zone series

Sernine, Daniel
- Argus series
- Grandverger series

Serraillier, Ian
- David and Uncle Bill series
- Robin Hood series

Service, Pamela F
- Winter series

Service, Robert William
- Adventures in memory series
- Ploughman of heaven series

Serviss, Garrett Putnam
- War of the worlds series

Seth, Ronald
- Brian Grant series

Seton, Graham
- Colonel Duncan Grant series

Seton, Hilary
- Minty Humble series

Setoun, Gabriel
- Barncraig series

Settle, Mary Lee
- Beulah series

Seuffert, Muir
- Mike Hubbard series

Seuss, *Doctor*
- Cat in the hat series

Severn, Bill
- Magic series

Severn, David
- Crusoe series
- Warner series

Severn, Donald
- Garrett dossier series
Time to die
Garrett dossier series (1)

Severn, June
- Cathedral cat series

Severn, Richard
- Jeff Cass series

Severy, Martin
- George Maitland series

Severy, Richard
- Jinks Gang series

Seward, Jack
- Curt Stone series

Sewart, Alan
- Detective Chief Superintendent Evans series
- Detective Sergeant Chamberlayne series

Sewell, Anna
- Black Beauty series

Sewell, Elizabeth Missings
- Home and after life series

Sewell, Helen
- Peggy series

Sexton, Anne
- Eggs of things series

Seymour, Arabella
- Jane Beaufort series

Seymour, Aubrey
- Fertile earth series

Seymour, Beatrice Kean
- Malling-Gaywood family series
- Sally Dunn trilogy
- Three wives series

Seymour, Harold
- Baseball history series

Seymour, Janette
- Purity series

Seymour, John
- Fat of the land series

Shadwell, Thomas
- Time tours series

Shafer, Sara Andrew
- Day before yesterday series

Shaffer, Anthony
see also **Antony, Peter**
- Mister Verity series

Shaffer, Peter
see also **Antony, Peter**
How doth the little crocodile
Mister Verity series (2)

Shaio, C J
see **Stivers, Dick**

Shakespeare, Brian
- Fox series

Shakespeare, William
- Tempest series

Shalleck, Allen J
- Curious George series

Shallit, Joseph
- Dan Morrison series

Shalom Aleichem
see **Aleichem, Sholom**

Shanahan, Warren
- Phantom series

Shand, William
- Bill Tempest series

Shane, Bart
see also **Mason, Chuck; Morgan, G J; Starr, Roland**
- Iron rails trilogy

Shane, Steve
see also **Cody, Stetson; Denver, Lee; Grex, Leo; Gribble, Leonard Reginald; Sanders, Bruce**
- Lone Star Kid series

Shane, Susannah
- Christopher Saxe series

Shann, Renee
see **Gaye, Carol**

Shannon, Brad
- Lefty O'Connor series

Shannon, Dell
see also **Blaisdell, Anne; Egan, Lesley; Linington, Elizabeth**
- Lieutenant Luis Mendoza series

Shannon, Doris
see also **Giroux, E X**
- Robert Forsythe and Abigail Sanderson series

Shappiro, Herbert
see also **Arthur, Burt**
- Johnny Canavan series
- Mustang Marshal series

Sharam, Norman
- White dog trilogy

Sharber, Kate Trimble
- Ann and Eve series

Sharee, Keith
- Star trek, the next generation series

Sharkey, Jack
- Addams family series
- George Herbert Henry series

Sharma, Partap
- Ranjha series

Sharmat, Andrew
- Kids on the bus series

Sharmat, Craig
- Nate the great series

Sharmat, Marjorie Weinman
- Gorgeous guys and girls series
- Kids on the bus series
- Maggie Marmelstein series
- Mooch series
- Morris Brookside series
- Mother's and Father's Day series
- Nate the great series
- Notice me series
- Olivia Sharp series
- Rich Mitch series
- Sophie and Gussie series
- Sorority sisters series
- Vacation fever series

Sharmat, Mitchell
- Olivia Sharp series

Sharp, Alan
- John Moseby series

Sharp, Alastair
- Worst day of my life series

Sharp, Allen
- Storytrails series

Sharp, David
- Professor Henry Arthur Fielding series

Sharp, Luke
- Fighting fantasy gamebook series

Sharp, Margery
- Martha Diver series
- Miss Bianca series

Sharp, Marilyn
- Richard Owen series

Sharpe, Jon
- Canyon O'Grady series
- Trailsman series

Sharpe, Tom
- Henry Wilt series
- Kommandant Van Heerden series

Shatner, William
- TekWar series

Shaw, Bob
- Land and overland trilogy
- Orbitsville trilogy
- Warren Peace series

Shaw, Bruce
- East Kimberley series

Shaw, Charles
see also **Singer, Bant**
- Denis Delaney series

Shaw, Denis
- Twin series

Shaw, Felicity
see **Morice, Anne**

Shaw, George Bernard
- Mrs Warren series
- Nonage series

Shaw, Howard
- Inspector Barnaby series

Shaw, Irwin
- Jordache family series

Shaw, Jane
- Ali and Dizzy series
- Caroline and Sara series
- Moochers series

Sitwell, Sacheverell
• Quick and the dead series
Sivers, Brenda
• Sherlock Hound series
Sjowall, Maj
• Inspector Martin Beck series
Skaldaspillir, Sigfriour
• Eric Brighteyes series
Skelton, Barbara
• Tears series
Skelton, Clement Lister
• Hardacre series
• Maclaren family series
Skelton, Peter
• Edwin series
Skene, Anthony
• Sexton Blake series
Skidelsky, Simon Jasha
see **Simon, S J**
Skidmore, Hubert
• My salvation series
Skidmore, Ian
• Welsh island series
Skiera, Joseph A
• Private pilot's series
Skimin, Robert
• Soldier for hire series
Skinner, Burrhus Frederic
• Behaviorist trilogy
• Walden series
Skinner, Cornelia Otis
• Our hearts series
Skinner, Mike
• Luke Wyatt series
Skinner, Stephanie
Dracula
Dracula series (1)
• Superman series
Skirrow, Desmond
• John Brock series
Skoglund, Elizabeth
• Coping series
Skurzynski, Gloria
• Mountain west series
• Your high-tech world series
Skvorecky, Josef
• Danny Smiricky series
Sky, Kathleen
• Star trek originals sequels series
Skynner, Robin
• Survival series
Slade, Jack
see also **Ballard, Willis Todhunter; Fox, Brian; Hunter, John; Macneil, Neil**
• Gatling series
• Lassiter series
• Sundance series
Slade, Ruth
• Congo series
Sladek, John Thomas
• Roderick series
• Thackeray Phin series
Sladen, Douglas
• Japanese marriage series
Slate, John
see also **Blayn, Hugo; Fearn, John Russell; Gridban, Volsted; Statten, Vargo; Titan, Earl**
• Black Maria series
Slater, Catherine Ponton
• Marget Pow trilogy
Slater, Ian
• WW III series
Slater, Jim
• A Mazing Monster series
• Goldenrod series
• Grasshopper series
Slaughter, Frank Gill
• American Civil War series
• Biblical series
Slaughter, Jim
see also **Batchelor, Reg; Benton, Will; Bosworth, Frank; Carrel, Mark; Carter, Nevada; Ingersol, Jared; Paine, Lauran; Standish, Buck**
• Boone Helm series
Slaven, Roy
• South Coast series
Slavicsek, Bill
• Torg series
Sleigh, Barbara
• Carbonel series
Slepian, Jan
• Alfred and Lester series
• Junior listen-hear series
• Listen-hear series
Slick, Sam
see **Haliburton, Thomas Chandler**
Slier, Debby
see also **Bright, Sarah; Harris, Robin; Shine, Deborah**
• Potato Head series
• Teddy Bear series
• What do series
Sloan, Carolyn
• Mall series
• Mister Cogg series
Sloane, Ben
• Horn series
Sloane, Robert C
• Marino family series
Slobodkin, Louis
• Space ship series
Sloman, Robert
• Doctor Who scripts series
Slote, Alfred
• Danny One series
Slovo, Gillian
• Kate Baeier series
Slyke, Helen van
see **Van Slyke, Helen**
Small, Beatrice
• Skye O'Malley series
Smaridge, Nora
I can do it, you can do it
Raggedy Ann series (49)
Thank you please and I love you book
Raggedy Ann series (49)
Smaridge, Norah
• Robin Miller series
Smedley, Elisabeth
• Jays series
Smeds, Dave
• War of the dragons series
Smee, Donald
• Jeremy Smith series
Smee, Nicola
• Benny series
Smeeton, Miles
• Chronicles of Tzu Hang series
• Hills and jungles series
Smile, R Elton
• Manatitlans series
Smilie, Elton R
see **Smile, R Elton**
Smith, Alexander
• Alfred Hagart series
Smith, Alexander McCall
see **McCall Smith, Alexander**
Smith, Amanda Joan Mackay
see **Mackay, Amanda**
Smith, Andrew
• Doctor Who series
Smith, Annie Shepherd Burnett-
see **Swan, Annie Shepherd**
Smith, Arthur Douglas Howden
see also **Grant, Allan**
• David Balfour series
• Doom trail series
• Treasure Island series
Smith, Beatrice Schillinger
• Kate and Ben King series
Smith, Betsy Covington
• Breakthrough series
Smith, Brian Sutton-
see **Sutton-Smith, Brian**
Smith, C I D
• Inspector Barlowe series
Smith, Carl W
• Red Ryder series
Smith, Chard Powers
• Lathrop family series
Smith, Charles Harvard Gibbs-
see **Gibbs-Smith, Charles Harvard**
Smith, Charles Merrill
• Reverend Randollph series
Smith, Cicely Fox
• Barty Dale series
Smith, Clark
• Nicky Mahoun series
Smith, Cordwainer
• Instrumentality series
Smith, Craig
• Koala Hills Primary Hills series
• Mrs Millie Mack trilogy
Trev the truck saves the school bus
Trev the truck series (1)
Smith, Curtis
• Advanced dungeons and dragons adventure gamebook series
Smith, Daniel Wybert
• Chief Inspector Harry Fathers series
Smith, David
• Jim Stevens series
• Sky all over series
Smith, David Alexander
• Marathon trilogy
Smith, David Claude
• Black Vulmea series
• Bran Mak Morn trilogy
• Fair rules series
• Fall of the first world trilogy
• Oron series
• Red Sonja series
Smith, Dennis O
• Sherlock Holmes sequels series
Smith, Doc
see **Smith, Edward Elmer**
Smith, Dodie
• Look back series
• Pongo and Missis series
Smith, Don
• Secret mission series
• Tim Parnell series
Smith, Doris Buchanan
• Lloyd Albert and Ancil Witherspoon series
Smith, Dorothy Gladys
see **Smith, Dodie**
Smith, Dorothy Stafford
see **Smith, Sarah Stafford**
Smith, Edward Elmer
• Family d'Alembert series
Imperial stars
Family d'Alembert series (1)
• Lensman series
• Lord Tedric series
• Skylark series
• Subspace explorers series
Smith, Elizabeth Thomasina
see **Meade, Lillie Thomas**
Smith, Emma
• Emily series
Smith, Ernest Bramah
see **Bramah, Ernest**
Smith, Eunice Young
• Jennifer Hill series
Smith, Evelyn E
• Miss Susan Melville series
Smith, Ford
• Dark Knight series
Smith, Francis Hopkinson
• Civil War society series
• Colonel Carter series
Smith, Francis Maylett
• General practitioner series
Smith, Frank Allan
• Superintendent Pepper series
Smith, Frederick Escreet
• Innocent series
• Persuaders series
• Saffron series
• Six Three Three Squadron series
• Stars series
Smith, Frederick R
see **Ackworth, John**
Smith, G Castle, ***Mrs***
see **Brenda**
Smith, George
• Glencannon family trilogy
Smith, George Henry
• Annwn series
• Duffus January series
• Sherlock Holmes sequels series
Smith, Gregory Jon
• StarQuest series
Smith, Guy Newman
• Crabs series
• Deathbell series
• Sabat series
• Thirst series
• Truckers series
• Werewolf trilogy
Smith, Hannah
see **Stretton, Hesba**
Smith, Harriet Lummis
• Friendly Terrace series
• Pollyanna series
Smith, Helen Zenna
see also **Price, Evadne**
• Skinny series
Smith, Hendy
• Johnny Black series
Smith, Herbert Maynard
• Inspector Frost series
Smith, Ivan
• Fire, drought and flood trilogy
Smith, J C S
• Quentin Jacoby series
Smith, James V
• Beast series
Smith, Janet
• Wakeley witch series
Smith, Janet Patton
• Twilight series
Smith, Janice Lea
• Adam Joshua series
Smith, Jim
• Frog band series
• Nimbus series
Smith, Joan
• Masculine ending series
Smith, Joan Mary
• Loretta Lawson series
• Pepper Street series
Smith, Joan Watson
• Jindi series
Smith, Julie
• Paul McDonald series
• Rebecca Schwartz series
• Skip Langdon series
Smith, Julie Dean
• Caithan Crusade series
Smith, Keith
• Supernatural series
Smith, Lane
• Time warp trio series
Smith, Laure
• Arcade explorers series
Smith, Laurence Dwight
• Dick Whelan series
Smith, Lawrence Dwight
• G-men series
Smith, Lester Neil
• Contact and commune series
• Lando Calrissian trilogy
• North American Confederacy trilogy
• Win Bear trilogy
Smith, Lew
see also **Austin, Brett; Floren, Lee**
• Judge Lemanuel Bates and Tobacco Jones series
Smith, Lisa J
• Forbidden game trilogy
• Secret circle series
• Solstice series
• Vampire diaries series
Smith, Lou
• John Spencer series
Smith, Mabell Shipple Clarke
• Ethel Morton series
Smith, Mark
• Duelmaster series
• Falcon series
• Fighting fantasy gamebook series
• Way of the Tiger series
Smith, Martin Cruz
see also **Quinn, Simon**
• Arkady Renko series
• Roman Grey series
Smith, Mavis
• Jessie series
Smith, Naomi Royde
• Richard Lingard series
• Rockmouth and Rockhead township trilogy
Smith, Pauline
• Karoo series
Smith, Peter Charles
• Cname Sname series
Smith, Peter Claudius Gautier-
see **Conway, Peter**
Smith, Richard Rein
see **Reinsmith, Richard**
Smith, Robert Charles
see **Charles, Robert; Leader, Charles**
Smith, Robert Kimmel
• Sadie Shapiro series
Smith, Ruel Perley
• Rival campers series
Smith, Russell
• Yuma series
Smith, Sam
• Crew Cats series
Smith, Sarah
see **Stretton, Hesba**
Smith, Sarah Stafford
• Ink-Bottle Club series
Smith, Sheila Kaye-
see **Kaye-Smith, Sheila**
Smith, Shelley
• Jacob Chaos series
Smith, Stephanie Ann
• Snow-Eyes series
Smith, Susan
• Best friends series
• Samantha Slade series
Smith, Terence Lore
• Webster Daniels series
Smith, Terrence Lore
see also **Lore, Phillips**
• Reverend Randollph series
Smith, Thorne
• Jennifer series
• Topper series
Smith, Trevor Dudley
see **Dudley-Smith, Trevor**
Smith, Vian Crocker
• Sappers series
Smith, Wendy
• My first day series
• Only mouse series
Smith, Wilbur Addison
• Courtney family series
• Sean Courtney series
• Zouga Ballantyne series
Smith, Willard K
• Inspector Dann Carr series
Smith, William Dale
see **Anthony, David**
Smith, William Jay
• Laughing time series
Smithers, Jack
• Berry series
• Bulldog Drummond series
• Richard Hannay series
Smithies, Richard Hugo Ripman
• Inspector William McAlpin series
Smollett, Tobias
• Morgan the Welshman series
Smollin, Michael J
• Strawberry Shortcake series
Smyth, Ethel Mary
• Impressions series
Smyth, Gwenda
• Mrs Arbuckle series
Smyth, John George
• Ann Sheldon series
• Beloved cats series
Smyth, Reitta
• Timothy series
Smyth, Robin
• Roger Moore and the Crimefighters series
Smythe, Pat
• Peter and Carol Garret series
• Show jumping series
• Three Jays series
Smythe, R John
• Conception series
Snaith, John Collis
• Love Lane series
Snedeker, Caroline Dale
• Dencey Coffyn series
Snell, Edmund
• Peter Pennington series
• Reggie Faulkner series
Snell, Gordon
• Tom's amazing machine trilogy
Snell, Leroy
• Northwest stories series
Sno, William
• Find your fate: G.I. Joe series
• Wizards, warlocks and you series
Snodgrass, Mary Ellen
• Environmental awareness series
Snodgrass, Melinda Marilyn
• Circuit trilogy
Dead man's hand
Wild cards series (7)
• Star trek series
• Wild cards series
Snow, Charles Horace
see also **Ballew, Charles**
• Tommy Thorne series
Snow, Charles Percy
• Strangers and brothers series
Snow, Dorothea Johnston
• Lassie series
Snow, Edgar
• Red China series
Snow, Jack
• Oz series
Snow, Pamela Hansford
see **Johnson, Pamela Hansford**
Snowden, James Keighley
• King Jack series
Snyder, Carol
• Ike and Mama series
Snyder, Midori
• Queen's quarter series
Snyder, Zilpha Keatley
• Green-sky trilogy
• Stanley family series
Sobol, Donald J
• Encyclopedia Brown series
• Encyclopedia Brown's wacky series
• Two-minute mysteries series
Soderback, Marianne
• Middles series
Softly, Barbara
• English Civil War series
• Magic people series
• Ponder and William series
Sohl, Jerry
see **Mountjoy, Roberta Jean**
Solmssen, Arthur Robert George
• Conyers and Dean series
Sologub, Fedor
• Created legend trilogy
Solomita, Stephen
• Stanley Moodrow series
Solomon, Helen
• Ollie series

Steiner, Charlotte
- Karoleena series
- Kiki series

Steiner, Merrilee
- Going for it series
- Swept away series

Steiner, Paul
- Useless information series

Steinke, Anne E
- Cheerleaders series

Steinkuehler, Pearl
- Bride series

Steirman, Hy
- Zachary Jones series

Stendhal
- Lucien Leeuwen series

Steneman, Shep
- Star wars storybook series

Stephens, Charles Asbury
- Camping out series
- Knockabout Club series

Stephens, Eve
see **Anthony, Evelyn**

Stephens, Michael
- J Leland Coole series

Stephens, Reed
see also **Donaldson, Stephen Reed**
- Mick Axbrewder series

Stephenson, Percival Reginald
- Years at sea series

Sterling, Brett
- Captain Future series

Sterling, Peter
see also **Stern, David**
- Francis trilogy

Sterling, Stewart
see also **Dean, Spencer**
- Ben Pedley series
- Fire Marshal Ben Pedley series
- Gil Vine series

Sterling, Thomas
- Captain Rizzi series

Stern, David
see also **Sterling, Peter**
- Doctor Bones series
- Francis trilogy

Stern, Gladys Bronwyn
- Ragbag chronicles series
- Rakonitz family series

Stern, Rhona
- South African series

Stern, Richard Martin
- Johnny Ortiz series

Stern, Roger
- Superman series

Stern, Simon
- Astonishing adventures of Captain Ketchup series

Stern, Sonia
- Little Zip series

Sterne, Emma Gelders
see **James, Josephine**

Sterrett, Frances Roberta
- Rusty series

Stetler, Charles
Tarzan and Shane meet the Toad
Toad series (3)

Steuben, Fritz
- Bethlehem series

Steussy, Marti
- Forest series

Stevens, Arthur Joseph
see **Stevens, Steve**

Stevens, Carl
- Christian Daguerre series

Stevens, Clive
- Boris Blundle and Gang series

Stevens, David
- Roots series

Stevens, Fae Hewston
- Koronglea series

Stevens, Kathleen
- Beast series

Stevens, S S
- Red Ryder series

Stevens, Steve
- Jack Storm series

Stevens, William Oliver
- Annapolis alphabet series
- Etiquette series
- Peewee Clinton series

Stevenson, Bruce
- Time machine series

Stevenson, Burton Egbert
- Boys' story of the railroad series
- Jim Godfrey series

Stevenson, Dorothy Emily
- Ardfalloch series
- Ayrton family series
- Barbie France series
- Drumberley trilogy
- Gerald Burleigh Brown series
- Katherine Wentworth series
- Miss Buncle series
- Mrs Tim series
- Ryddelton series
- Sarah Morris series

Stevenson, Drew
- J Huntley English series
- Sarah Capshaw series

Stevenson, Edward
- Twilight series

Stevenson, Florence
- Kitty Telfair series

Stevenson, James
- Emma series
- Grandfather's problems series
- Grandpa series
- Growing up series
- Worst person in the world series

Stevenson, Jane
see **McIlvaine, Jane**

Stevenson, Jocelyn
- Fraggle Rock series

Stevenson, Richard
- Donald Strachey series

Stevenson, Robert
- Highland vet series

Stevenson, Robert Louis
- David Balfour series
- Doctor Jekyll series
- Inland voyage series
- Long John Silver series

Travels with a donkey in the Cevennes
Donkey series (1)
Treasure Island
Long John Silver series (1)
Treasure Island
Treasure Island series (1)
- Treasure Island series

Stevenson, Robin
- Time machine series

Stevenson, William Henri
- Israeli armed services series
- William Stephenson series

Steward, Barbara
- Edgar Allan Poe series

Steward, Dwight
- Edgar Allan Poe series

Steward, Paull
- Donald Everhard series

Stewart, Alfred Walter
see **Connington, John Jervis**

Stewart, Averil
- Stewart family series

Stewart, Cynthia
- Victorian India series

Stewart, Desmond
- Sequence of roles trilogy

Stewart, Diana
Frankenstein
Frankenstein series (1)

Stewart, Flora
- Flora and Dickie series
- Inspector Newsom series

Stewart, Jane L
- Camp Fire Girls series

Stewart, Janet
- Star trek fan series

Stewart, John Innes Mackintosh
see also **Innes, Michael**
- Duncan Pattullo series

Stewart, Kerry
- Airport series

Stewart, Marjorie
- Adam Square series

Stewart, Mary
- Merlin and Arthur series

Stewart, Maureen
- Emily series
- Henry and Voula series
- Maria series

Stewart, William Thomas
- Gaff Lee series

Stewart-Hargreaves, Eustace Hamilton Ian
- Cotswold Cider Company series

Stidworthy, John
- Creatures from the past series
- Year in the life of an animal series

Stiessel, Lena
- Mick and Muff series

Stil, Andre
- First clash trilogy

Stillman, Norman Arthur
- Jews in Arab lands series

Stillman, Ron
- Tracker series

Stilson, Charles Billings
- Polaris trilogy

Stinde, Julius
- Buchholz family series

Stine, George Harry
- Warbots series

Stine, Hank
- Prisoner series

Stine, Harlan William
- Find your fate: G.I. Joe series
- Find your fate: Jem series
- Indiana Jones find your fate series
- Jeffrey and the fourth grade ghost series
- Jeffrey and the third grade ghost series
- Magic micro adventure series
- Micro adventure series
- Thundercats series
- Twistaplot series
- Wizards, warlocks and you series

Stine, Jane
- Everything you need to survive series

Stine, Jovial Bob
see **Stine, Robert Lawrence**

Stine, Megan
- Find your fate: G.I. Joe series
- Find your fate: Jem series
- Indiana Jones find your fate series
- Jeffrey and the fourth grade ghost series
- Jeffrey and the third grade ghost series
- Magic micro adventure series
- Micro adventure series
- Thundercats series
- Twistaplot series
- Wizards, warlocks and you series
- Young Indiana Jones chronicles series
- Young Indiana Jones series

Stine, Robert Lawrence
- Baby-sitter series
- Dynamite series
- Everything you need to survive series
- Fear Street cheerleaders series
- Fear Street saga series
- Fear Street series
- Fear Street super chiller series
- Find your fate: G.I. Joe series

Ghostbusters 2
Ghostbusters series (2)
- G.I.Joe series
- Golden Girl and the Guardians of the Gemstones trilogy
- Goosebumps series
- Hark series
- Indiana Jones find your fate series
- James Bond find your fate series
- Ninety-nine Fear Street series
- Space cadets series
- Twistaplot series
- Wizards, warlocks and you series

Stine, William
- Young Indiana Jones chronicles series
- Young Indiana Jones series

Stinson, Joe
Sudden impact
Dirty Harry Callahan series (12)

Stirling, Jessica
see also **Rae, Hugh Crauford**
- Beckman family trilogy
- Elspeth and Anna Patterson trilogy
- Stalker family trilogy

Stirling, Stephen Michael
- Draka trilogy
- Falkenberg's Legion series
- Fifth millenium series
- Future history series
- Generals series

Man-Kzin wars II
Known Space series (18)
Man-Kzin wars II
Man-Kzin wars series (2)
Man-Kzin wars III
Known Space series (19)
Man-Kzin wars III
Man-Kzin wars series (3)
- Spartan series

Stirling, Yates
- United States midshipman series

Stivens, Dal
- Ironbark Bill series

Stivers, Dick
see also **Brent, R L; Hofrichter, Paul; Winski, Norman**
- Able Team series

Stobbs, William
- Gregory series

Stock, Catherine
- Sophie series

Stockbridge, Grant
- Richard Wentworth series

Stockley, Cynthia
- Dalla series

Stockley, Grif
- Gideon Page series

Stocks, Mary
- Commonplace series

Stockton, Frank Richard
- Captain Horn series
- Mrs Lecks and Mrs Aleshine series
- Rolling stones series
- Rudder Grange series

Stockum, Hilda van
see **Van Stockum, Hilda**

Stockwell, Gail
- Kingsley Toplitt series

Stoddard, Charles
see also **Stanley, Chuck; Strong, Charles Stanley**
- Malloy series

Stoddard, William Osborn
- Cowboy and college life series
- Revolutionary series

Stoeckl, Agnes de
- Vanity trilogy

Stoff, Joshua
- Long Island aerospace series

Stoker, Alan
see **Evans, Alan**

Stoker, Bram
- Dracula series

Stokes, Arthur M
- Sherlock Holmes drama series

Stokes, Doris
- Voices series

Stokes, Francis William
see **Everton, Francis**

Stokes, Katherine
- Motor Maids series

Stokes, Manning Lee
- Barnabas Jones series
- Christopher Fenn series

Stokes, Roy Eliot
- University series

Stolz, Mary
- Barkham Street trilogy
- Connor family series
- Emmett series
- Polly Lewis series
- Tales at the Mousehole trilogy
- Thomas and Grandfather series

Stone, Alan
- Tollivers series

Stone, C H
- Looking backward sequels series

Stone, Elizabet M
- Maggie Slone series

Stone, Gene
- Jane series

Stone, Hampton
see also **Bagby, George; Stein, Aaron Marc**
- Jeremiah X Gibson series

Stone, Isidor Feinstein
- Nonconformist history of our times series

Stone, Ned
- Other Day Logan series

Stone, Nick
- Ben Kane series

Stone, Raymond
- Tommy Tiptop series

Stone, Richard H
- Slim Tyler series

Stone, Simon
- Sir Brian Dinsmore Conway series

Stone, Susheila
- Duets series

Stone, Thomas H
see also **Gilman, George G; Harknett, Terry; Hedges, Joseph; James, William M; Pike, Charles R**
- Chester Fortune series

Stoneham, Charles Thurley
- Kaspa series

Stonehouse, Bernard
- Closer look at series
- Just look at series

Stoneley, Jack
- Tuesday dogs series

Stones, Anthony
- Bill of Grimley Grange series

Stong, Philip
- Ivanhoe Keeler series
- State Fair series

Stonier, George Walter
- Rhodesian series

Storer Clouston, Joseph
see **Clouston, Joseph Storer**

Storey, Alice
- Golden Girl and the Guardians of the Gemstones trilogy
- Samantha Adams series

Storey, Anthony
- Platinum series
- Second Coming trilogy

Storey, Margaret
- Molly series
- Superintendent Bone series
- Timothy, Ellen and Melinda series

Storm, Joan
- Sarah Vanessa series

Storm, Michael
- Baby don't series
- Nick Cranley series

Storr, Catherine
- Grandparents series
- Lucy series
- Marianne series
- Polly and the wolf series

Story, Jack Trevor
- Albert Argyle series
- Horace Spurgeon Fenton series
- Sexton Blake series

Stott, Dorothy
- Baby series

Stott, Mary
- Forgetting series

Stout, Rex
- Dol Bonner series
- Nero Wolfe and Archie Goodwin series

Nero Wolfe cook book
Nero Wolfe and Archie Goodwin series (52)
- Tecumseh Fox series

Stover, Marjorie Filley
- Dolls series

Stowe, Harriet Beecher
- Harry Henderson series
- Oldtown series
- Uncle Tom series

Strahan, Kay Cleaver
- Lynn Macdonald series

Straiton, Eddie
- Vet series

Straker, John Foster
- David Wright series
- Inspector Pitt series
- Johnny Inch series

Straker, Philip
- Night series

Strang, Herbert
- Russo-Japanese War series
- Stories of the Great War series

Strange, John Stephen
- Barney Gantt series
- Captain George Honegger series
- Van Dusen Ormsberry series

Strange, Nora Kathleen
- Kenya series

Strange, Oliver
- Sudden series

Stranger, Joyce
- Dai Evans series
- Dog series
- German Shepherd series
- Paddy Joe series
- Timothy Yorke series

Strasser, Todd
- Coming Attractions trilogy

Stratemeyer, Edward L
see also **Alger, Horatio; Bonehill, Ralph; Winfield, Arthur M**
- Bound to succeed series
- Bound to win series
- Colonial series
- Dave Porter series
- Frontier series
- Lakeport series
- Minute boys series
- Old Glory series
- Pan-American series
- Ship and shore series
- Soldiers of fortune series
- Working upward series

Stratford, Esme Wingfield-
see **Wingfield-Stratford, Esme**

Stratton, Alan
- Gina series

Stratton, Chris
- Bugaloos series

Gunsmoke
Gunsmoke series (4)

Stratton, Roy
- Scott Gregory and Justin Bassett series

Stratton, Thomas
- Man from U.N.C.L.E. series

Stratton-Porter, Gene
see **Porter, Gene Stratton**

Stratton-Porter, Jeannette
see **Porter, Jeannette Stratton**

Stravinsky, Igor
- Conversations series

Taylor, Elizabeth Atwood
• Maggie Elliott series
Taylor, Frank
see also **Bishop, Samuel P; Harold, Clive; Hutson, Shaun**
• Uninvited trilogy
Taylor, Geoff
• Bomber Command series
Taylor, H Baldwin
see also **Waugh, Hillary**
• David Halliday series
Taylor, James C
• Navy Seals series
Taylor, Janelle
• Cordell series
• Princess Alysa series
• Sioux series
Taylor, Jenny
• Messy Malcolm series
Taylor, Jeri
• Star trek, the next generation sequels series
Taylor, John Robert
see also **Taylor, Andrew**
• Snapshot series
Taylor, Judy
• Dudley Dormouse series
• My pet series
• Sophie and Jack series
Taylor, Keith
• Bard series
• Cormac Mac Art series
• Danans trilogy
Taylor, Laurie Aylma
• J J Jamison series
Taylor, Louise
• Animals and their women series
Taylor, Mark
• Henry series
Taylor, Mary Ann
• Emil Martin series
Taylor, Mildred Davis
• Logan family series
Taylor, Peter
• Memphis series
Taylor, Philip Meadows
• Indian history trilogy
Taylor, Philip Neville Walker
• Commander Wraithlea series
Taylor, Philip Walker
see **Taylor, Philip Neville Walker**
Taylor, Phoebe Atwood
see also **Tilton, Alice**
• Asey Mayo series
Taylor, Reginald
• Andy series
Taylor, Roger
• Hawklan series
Taylor, Sam S
• Neal Cotton series
Taylor, Selman
• Inspector May series
Taylor, Sydney
• All-of-a-kind family series
Taylor, Talus
• Barbapapa first book series
• Barbapapa series
Taylor, Theodore
• Cay series
• Teetoncey and Ben O'Neal trilogy
Taylor, Walker
see **Taylor, Philip Neville Walker**
Tazewell, Charles
• Littlest series
Tea, Traves
Orgy in orbit
Luke Skywalker series (7)
Teague, Kati
My week
My life series (1)
Teague, Mark
• Johnsons trilogy
Tedeschi, Frank L
• Simon Bede and Helen Bullock series
Tedford, William G
• Timequest trilogy
Tedrow, Thomas L
• Days of Laura Ingalls Wilder series
Teed, George Hamilton
• Grant Rushton series
• Sexton Blake series
Teed, Jack Hamilton
• Dracula series
• Gunships series
Teilhet, Darwin Le Ora
• Baron Von Kaz series
• Jean Henri Saint Amand series
• Sam Hook series
Teilhet, Hildegarde Tolman
• Baron Von Kaz series
• Sam Hook series
Teitelbaum, Michael
• Blinkins series
• Fievel series
• Photon series
Telfair, Richard
• Monty Nash series
Sundance
Sundance series (44)
Target for tonight
Dangerman series (5)
• Wyoming Jones series
Telscombe, Anne
• Miss Bagshot series
Telushkin, Joseph
• Rabbi Daniel Winter series
Tempest, Margaret
• Potter Pinner series
Temple, Paul
see **Durbridge, Francis; Rutherford, Douglas**
East of Algiers
Paul Temple series (7)
Tyler mystery
Paul Temple series (6)
Temple, Richard
• Simon Leigh series
Temple Thurston, Ernest
see **Thurston, Ernest Temple**
Temple, William Frederick
• Martin Magnus trilogy
Temple-Ellis, N A
• Inspector Wren series
• Montrose Arbuthnot series
Templeton, Faith
• Breadwinners series
Tempski, Armine von
• Paradise series
Tennant, Emma
• Doctor Jekyll sequels series
• Hospitalities series
• Pride and prejudice series
Tepper, Sheri S
see also **Oliphant, B J**
• Awakeners series
• Blood heritage series
• Jinian trilogy
• Marianne trilogy
• Mavin Manyshaped trilogy
• True game trilogy
Ter Haar, Jaap
see **Haar, Jaap ter**
Terhune, Albert Payson
• My memory series
• Sunnybank collies series
Terman, Douglas
• Choose your own adventure series
Terra, John
Star trek, the next generation officer's manual
Star trek, the next generation sequels series (7)
Terry, Carolyn
• King of diamonds series
Tessier, Ernest Maurice
see **Dekobra, Maurice**
Tessler, Stephanie Gordon
see **Gordon, Jeffie Ross**
Tester, Sylvia Root
• Magic monsters series
Tetel, Julie
• Sweet trilogy
Teternikov, Fyodor Kuzmich
see **Sologub, Fyodor**
Tetlow, L D
• Brogan McNally series
Tevis, Walter Stone
• Hustler series
Tey, Josephine
see also **Daviot, Gordon**
• Inspector Alan Grant series
Thacker, Eric
• Wintersol series
Thackeray, William Makepeace
• Arthur Pendennis series
• Barry Lyndon series
• Virginia series
Thackray, Patricia
• Raggedy Ann series
• Raggedy Ann's household series
Thaler, Mike
• Bully brothers series
• Hippo series
• Knock knocks series
• Riddle King mini series
• Riddle King series
Thane, Elswyth
• Williamsburg series
Thatcher, Billy
• Tai-Lu series
Thatcher, Dora
• Henry series
• Tommy series
Thayer, Charles Wheeler
• Caviar series
Thayer, Jane
• Gus series
Thayer, Lee
• Peter Clancy series
Theis, Jody Sorenson
• Cheerleaders series
Theiss, Lewis Edwin
• Air mail series
Theroux, Paul
• Spencer Monroe Savage series
Thesman, Jean
• Birthday girls series
• Whitney cousins series
Theulet-Luzie, Bernadette
• Jeremy series
Thewes, John
• Paul Temple series
Theydon, John
• Captain Scarlet series
• Stingray series
• Thunderbirds series
Thibault, Jacques Anatole Francois
see **France, Anatole**
Thiele, Colin
• Gloop series
• Tracy Chipp series
Thierry, Gilbert Augustin
• Conspirators and police under Napoleon series
Thiess, Frank
• Centaur trilogy
Thirkell, Angela
• Barsetshire series
Thoeme, Bodie
• Saga of the Sierras series
Thoeme, Brock
• Saga of the Sierras series
Thom, James Alexander
• George Rogers Clark series
Thomas, Alan
• Inspector Widgeon series
Thomas, Audrey
• Isobel Cleary series
Thomas, Barry
• Wings series
Thomas, Craig
• Firefox series
• Kenneth Aubrey series
Thomas, D
• Gulf Coast series
Thomas, Donald
• Inspector Swain series
Thomas, Donald Michael
• Russian quartet
Thomas, Elizabeth Marshall
• Reindeer moon series
Thomas, Ernest Lewys
see **Vaughan, Richard**
Thomas, Eugene
• Chu-Sheng series
• Mrs Caywood Weston series
Thomas, Frank
• Sherlock Holmes sequels series
Thomas, Gordon
• David Morton series
Thomas, H C
• Red Ryder series
Thomas, Helen
see also **T, H**
• Under storm's wing trilogy
Thomas, Iolette
• Janine series
Thomas, Joan Gale
see **Robinson, Joan Gale**
Thomas, Joyce Bissell
• Dragon Green series
Thomas, Joyce Carol
• Abyssinia Jackson series
Thomas, Leslie
• Dangerous Davies series
• Virgin soldiers series
• Wildest dreams series
Thomas, Lowell
• Sea Devil series
Thomas, Martin
• Sexton Blake series
Thomas, Millicent Inglis
• Ken, Candy and Co series
Thomas, Murray
• Inspector Wilkins series
Thomas, Ross
see also **Bleeck, Oliver**
• Artie Wu and Quincy Durant series
• McCorkle and Padillo series
Thomas, Thomas Thurston
• Crisis of empire trilogy
Thompson, Ames
• Jewel series
Thompson, Arthur Leonard Bell
see **Clifford, Francis**
Thompson, Carol
• Busy baby's day series
Thompson, Christine Pullein-
see **Pullein-Thompson, Christine**
Thompson, David
• Nathaniel King series
• Wilderness giants series
Thompson, Diana Pullein-
see **Pullein-Thompson, Diana**
Thompson, Edward
• Arnison series
• Indian trilogy
• Warren Remfrey series
Thompson, Edward Anthony
see **Lejeune, Anthony**
Thompson, Eric
• Dougal series
Thompson, Ernest Victor
• Nathan Jago series
• Retallick family series
Thompson, Flora
• Lark Rise to Candleford series
Thompson, Gene
• Dade Cooley series
Thompson, George Selden
see **Selden, George**
Thompson, James Matthew
• French history trilogy
Thompson, Joanna Pullein-
see **Cannan, Joanna**
Thompson, Josephine Pullein-
see **Pullein-Thompson, Josephine**
Thompson, K L
• Ameliaranne series
Thompson, Kate
• Derain family series
Thompson, Kay
• Eloise series
Thompson, Lloyd S
• Shimoru Kyota series
Thompson, Mark
• Gay spirit and soul series
Thompson, Mary Wolfe
• Aiken family trilogy
Thompson, Nancy
• Departing and return series
Thompson, Neil
• Rand series
Thompson, Paul B
• DragonLance preludes II series
• DragonLance preludes series
• Elven nations trilogy
Thompson, Robert
• Vietnam War series
Thompson, Ruth Plumly
• Oz series
Thompson, Sharon
• Farmyard Cat series
Thompson, Steven Lynn
• Max Moss series
Thompson, Thomas
• Bonanza series
Thompson, Valerie
• Howell family series
Thompson, Vance
• Mister Guelpa series
Thompson, Victoria
• Kid Collins series
Thomson, Arthur Alexander
• Marigold Cottage trilogy
Thomson, Basil
• Peter Graham series
• Superintendent Richardson series
Thomson, David
• Highlands youth series
Thomson, David Robert Alexander
• Daniel Cullen series
• Danny Fox series
Thomson, Jamie
• Duelmaster series
• Falcon series
• Fighting fantasy gamebook series
• Way of the Tiger series
Thomson, June
• Inspector Finch series
Thomson, Pat
• Jets series
• Share-a-story series
Thomson, Ruth
• Detective Peabody series
• My class series
Thoreau, Henry David
• Walden series
Thorn, Ismay
• Geoff and Jim Harrington series
Thorndike, Russell
• Doctor Syn series
• Mister Macauley series
Thorndyke, Helen Louise
• Honey Bunch series
Thorne, Ernest Pollett
• Geoff Fennell series
• Major Brains Cunningham series
• Quentin Eady series
Thorne, Ian
Dracula
Dracula series (1)
King Kong
King Kong series (3)
Thorne, Nicola
see also **L'Estrange, Anna; Yorke, Katherine**
• Askham family series
Enchantress saga
Enchantress trilogy (3)
Thorne, Ramsay
• Captain Gringo series
Thorne, Sandy
• Queensland series
Thornton, Jane Foster
• Electric High series
Thorp, Roderick
• Joe Leland series
Thorwald, Jurgen
• Century of the detective series
• Century of the surgeon series
Threadgall, Colin
• Find my series
Thubten Jigme Norbu
see **Norbu, Thorbten Jigme**
Thurlow, David
• East country crimes series
Thurman, Mark
• Elephant series
Thurston, Ernest Temple
• Bellwattle and Cruikshank series
• John Grey series
• Richard Furlong series
Thurston, Ida Treadwell
• Bachelor maid series
• Theodore Bryan series
• Troop Five series
Thurston, Robert
• Battlestar Galactica series
• Legend of the jade phoenix trilogy
• Robots and aliens series
• Rugger series
Thurston, Temple
see **Thurston, Ernest Temple**
Thwaite, Ann
• Jane and Toby series
Thwaites, Frederick Joseph
• Doctor Joszef Venesz series
• Husky series
• Mad doctor series
• Melody series
Thwaites, Lyndsay
• Super Adam and Rosie Wonder series
Thynne, Molly
• Doctor Constantine series
Tibber, Robert
• General practice series
• General practitioner series
Tibber, Rosemary
see **Tibber, Robert**
Tibble, Anne
• Greenhorn trilogy
Tibo, Gilles
• Pikolo series
• Simon series
Tidyman, Ernest
• John Shaft series
Tiegreen, Alan
• Condo Kids series
• Pee wee scout series
Tierney, Frank M
• Silly Sally series
Tierney, Richard Louis
• Bran Mak Morn trilogy
• Red Sonja series
Tierney, Ronald
• Deets Shanahan series
Tiger, John
• I spy series
• Mission impossible series
Tigges, John
• Incubus trilogy
Tilford, Earl H
• USAF in Vietnam series
Tillett, Dorothy
see **Strange, John Stephen**
Tilley, Patrick
• Amtrak wars series
Tilman, Harold William
• Mischief series
Tilsley, Frank
• Nap and Ted series
Tiltman, Marjorie Hessell
• Country life trilogy
• Quality Chase series
Tilton, Alice
see also **Taylor, Phoebe Atwood**
• Leonidas Witherall series

Timlett, Peter Valentine
• Atlantis trilogy
Timlow, Elizabeth Weston
• Cricket series
• Dorothy Dot series
Timms, Alma
• Australian saga series
Timms, Edward Vivian
• Australian saga series
Timperley, Rosemary
• Hospital trilogy
Tindall, Gillian
• Twin series
Tinker, Edward Larocque
• Old New Orleans quartet
Tinker, Frances
• Old New Orleans quartet
Tinniswood, Peter
• Brandon family series
• Brigadier series
Tippett, James Sterling
• Henry series
Tippette, Giles
• Justa Williams series
• Wilson Young series
Tiptree, James
• Great Central Library series
Tirbutt, Honoria
see **Page, Emma**
Tison, Annette
• Barbapapa first book series
• Barbapapa series
Titan, Earl
see also **Blayn, Hugo; Fearn, John Russell; Gridban, Volsted; Slate, John; Statten, Vargo**
• Anjani series
Titus, Eve
• Anatole series
• Basil of Baker Street series
T'Lan, K S
• Star trek fan series
Todd, Barbara Euphan
• Perdita series
• Worzel Gummidge series
Todd, Burbank L
• Back to the soil series
Todd, Casey
• Junior transformers find your fate series
Todd, Herbert Eatton
• Bobby Brewster picture book series
• Bobby Brewster series
Todd, Laura
• Lavarni family series
Todd, Ruthven
• Space Cat series
Toer, Pramoedya Ananta
• All nations series
Toibin, Colm
• Enniscorthy series
Tokson, Elliot
• Alec Cavender series
Tolan, Stephanie Stein
• Great Skinner series
Toland, John
• McGlynn and Toda families series
Toliver, Raymond F
• Fighter aces series
Tolkien, John Ronald Reuel
• History of Middle Earth series
• History of the Lord of the Rings series
• Lord of the Rings trilogy
• Middle Earth series
Tolles, Martha
• Darci Daniels series
• Katie series
Tolliver, Ruby Changes
• Decision series
Tolman, Hildegarde
see **Teilhet, Hildegarde Tolman**
Tolstoi, Aleksei Nikolaevich
• Ordeal trilogy
Tolstoi, Leo Nikolaevich
• Nicholas Irtenyev trilogy
• War and peace series
Tolstoy, Alexei
see **Tolstoi, Aleksei Nikolaevich**
Tolstoy, Leo Nikolaevich
see **Tolstoi, Leo Nikolaevich**
Tomalin, Ruth
• Ralph Oliver series
Tomas, Andrew
• Ancient science series
Tomino, Yoshiyuki
• Gundam mobile suit trilogy
Tomkinson, Constance
• Les Girls series
Tomlinson, Everett Titsworth
• American Indian chiefs series
• American scouting series
• Colonial series
• Pioneer scout series
• War for the Union series
Tomlinson, Paul Greene
• American Indian chiefs series
• Four classmates series
• Princeton boy series
• Tom Cook series
Tompkins, Jane
• Animal twins series
Tompkins, Walker Allison
• Masked Rider and Blue Hawk series
• Roy Rogers series
Toms, Patricia
• Chronicles of Pennycress series
Tone, Teona
• Kyra Keaton series
Tong, Gary
• Crazy cut-outs series
Toombs, Alfred
• Raising a riot series
Toombs, Jane
• Making of America series
Topek, Susan Remick
• Noah series
Topelius, Zacharias
• Surgeon's stories series
Topham, Anne
• Daphne series
Topol, Edward
• Shamrayev series
Topor, Tom
• Kevin Fitzgerald series
Torgersen, Don Arthur
• Animal life stories series
• Animal safari nature series
• Troll series
Torgerson, Edwin Dial
• Pierre Montigny series
Torquemada
• Ronald Camberwell series
Torr, Iain
see also **Mackinnon, Charles Roy; Stuart, Charles**
• Gamboney series
Torres, Edwin
• Carlito series
Torrie, Malcolm
see also **Mitchell, Gladys**
• Timothy Herring series
Torrio, Vincente
• Hoods series
Torsvan, Traven
see **Traven, B**
Totleben, John
• Miracleman series
Tourgee, Albion Winegar
• Comfort Servosse series
Tourneur, Dina Kathelyn
• Caspar series
Tourney, Leonard
• Matthew Stock series
Tourtel, Mary
• Rupert Bear series
Toussant-Samat, Jean
• Monsieur Levert series
Tovey, Doreen
• Cats series
Towers, Joyce
• Donkey series
Townend, Peter
• McGill series
• Philip Quest series
Townley, Houghton
• Sexton Blake series
Townley, Pamela
• Stone maiden series
Townsend, Edward Waterman
• Chimmie Fadden series
Townsend, John
• Lunar One series
Townsend, John Rowe
• Hallersage series
• Uncle Walter series
Townsend, Larry
• Leather bondage series
• Mind master series
• Sado-masochism series
• Two thousand and sixty nine trilogy
Townsend, Peter
• Duels in the air series
Townsend, Sue
• Adrian Mole series
Townsend, Tom
• Pirates series
Townsend, Virginia Frances
• Dorothy Draycott series
Townson, Hazel
• Lenny and Jake series
• Speckled panic series
Toy, Barbara
• Fool trilogy
Toye, Francis
• Truly thankful series
Toye, Stanley
• Anthony Read series
Toynbee, Arnold Joseph
• Acquaintances series
• German terror series
Toynbee, Philip
• Valediction of Pantaloon series
Tozer, Katharine
• Mumfie series
Tozer, Mary
• Queen Yesno series
Tracy, Don
see also **Fuller, Roger**
• Giff Speer series
Tracy, Louis
see also **Holmes, Gordon**
• Inspector Furneaux series
• Reginald Brett series
• Vansittart series
Traill, Peter
• Mister Cribbage series
• Mister Prentice trilogy
Train, Arthur
• Benjamin Hooker series
• Ephraim Tutt series
Trainor, Joseph
• Twilight series
Tralins, Robert
see **Tralins, Sandor Robert**
Tralins, Sandor Robert
see also **O'Shea, Sean**
• Black stud trilogy
• Dragnet series
• Jack Lund series
• Lee Crosley series
Tramontana, C J
• Torg series
Tranquilli, Secondo
see **Silone, Ignazio**
Tranter, Nigel Godwin
• Donald Macdonald series
• Hawick series
• James Graham, Earl of Montrose series
• James V trilogy
• Ken and Fiona series
• Patrick Gray series
• Rob Roy Macgregor series
• Robert the Bruce trilogy
• Scottish history series
• Stuart series
• Tinker Tess series
Trapp, Maria Augusta von
• Trapp family series
Traven, B
• Gerard Gales series
• Jungle series
Travers, Ben
• Vale of laughter series
Travers, Hugh
• Madame Dominique Aubry series
Travers, J M
see also **Adams, Harrison; Clifton, Oliver Lee; Rathborne, Saint George**
• Jack Anderson series
• Jack Sharp series
Travers, Pamela Lyndon
• Mary Poppins series
Travis, Elizabeth
• Ben and Carrie Porter series
Travis, Falcon
• Third Bilsley Pack series
Treacy, Sean
• Scallywags series
Treadgold, Mary
• Heron series
• Mick and Caroline Templeton series
• Patty series
Trease, Geoffrey
• Bannermere series
• Burnt boats series
• Mandeville trilogy
• Mark Appleby series
• Mike and Sandra series
• Stuart kings series
Treat, Lawrence
• Bill Decker series
• Carl Wayward series
• Crime and puzzlement series
• Jub Freeman series
• Mitch Taylor series
Trecker, Janice Law
see **Law, Janice**
Tree, Gregory
• Bill Bradley and Noel Mayberry series
Treece, Henry
• Early Britain series
• Gordon Stewart series
• Greek trilogy
• Harald Hardrada series
• Robinson Crusoe series
• Roman Britain series
• Viking trilogy
Treger, Anne
• Nurse series
Treherne, John
• Doctor James Yeo series
Treibich, Stephen John
• Angelo DiStefano trilogy
Treloar, Bruce
• Baggable tales series
• Bumble series
Tremayne, Peter
• Dracula series
• Frankenstein sequels series
• Lan-Kern trilogy
• Raffles series
• She series
Tremlett, George
• Rock stars series
Trench, John
• Martin Cotterell series
Treneer, Anne
• Schoolhouse trilogy
Trenhaile, John
• General Povin series
• Simon Young series
Trent, Paul
• Peter Quayle series
Trent, Trisha
• Kylie series
Tresillian, Richard
see also **Devine, Raynard**
• Bloodheart series
• Bondmaster series
• Flesh traders series
Trevanian
• Jonathan Hemlock series
Trevelyan, George Macaulay
• Giuseppe Garibaldi trilogy
• Queen Anne's England trilogy
Trevelyan, Robert
• Pendragon series
Trevena, John
• Dartmoor trilogy
Trevor, Dan
• Night whistlers series
• Night whistlers trilogy
Trevor, Elleston
see also **Black, Mansell; Dudley-Smith, Trevor; Hall, Adam; Rattray, Simon**
• Green glade trilogy
• Quiller series
• Richard Vaness series
• Squirrel's Island series
• Woodlanders series
• Wumpus series
Trevor, James
• John Savage series
Trevor, Leslie
• Policewoman series
Trevor, Meriol
• Brentland series
• Luxembourg series
• World Dionysus trilogy
Trevor, Ralph
• Superintendent Curtis Burke series
Trewin, John Courtenay
• Up and down series
Trezise, Percy
• Ngali and Mayli series
Trick, Edgar Harold
• Tommy Tad and Polly Wog series
Trimble, Louis
• Anthropol Detective Agency series
• Martin Zane series
Trimby, Elisa
• Mister Plum series
Trimnell, Robert L
• Loner series
Tring, A Stephen
see also **Meynell, Laurence Walter**
• Barry series
• Penny series
Tripp, Miles
see also **Brett, John Michael**
• John Samson series
Tripp, Valerie
• Felicity series
• Just one more stories series
• Molly series
• Samantha series
Trippe, Peter
see **Peters, Geoffrey**
Tritten, Charles
• Heidi series
Trocheck, Kathy Hogan
• Callahan Garrity series
Trollope, Anthony
• Chronicles of Barsetshire series
• Palliser novels series
Trollope, Frances
• Widow Barnaby trilogy
Trollope, Joanna
see **Harvey, Caroline**
Troly-Curtin, Marthe
• Phrynette series
Trotman, Jack Harry
see **Penn, John**
Troubetzkoy, Amelie
see **Rives, Amelie**
Trow, Meirion James
• Inspector Sholto Lestrade series
Trowbridge, John Townsend
• Brighthope series
• Cudjo's cave series
• Jack Hazard series
• Silver medal series
• Start in life series
• Tide Mill series
• Toby Trafford series
Troy, Simon
see also **Warriner, Thurman**
• Inspector Smith series
Troyat, Henri
• Danov family trilogy
• Light of the just series
• Seed and the fruit series
True, John Preston
• Revolution series
Trueman, Brian
• Riverbend and Wildwood tales series
• Stories from Cockleshell Bay series
Truitt, Anne
• Journal of an artist series
Truman, Harry S
• Memoirs of the years series
Truman, Margaret
• Capital crime series
Truman, Timothy
• Emanuel Santana series
• Simon Girty series
Trumper, Hubert Bagster
see **Bagster, Hubert**
Truss, Seldon
see also **Selmark, George**
• Inspector Bass series
• Inspector Gidleigh series
Ts'ao, Hsueh-ch'in
• Dream of the red chamber series
Tubb, Edwin Charles
see also **Kern, Gregory**
• Dumarest series
• Sexton Blake series
• Space nineteen ninety nine series
Tubby, I M
• I'm a little series
Tucci, Niccolo
• Those of the lost continent series
Tucker, Audrie Manley-
see **Manley-Tucker, Audrie**
Tucker, Augusta
• Miss Susie Slagle series
Tucker, James
see **Craig, David**
Tucker, Jenni
• Cubby series
Tucker, Terry
• King Richard II series
Tucker, Wilson
• Charles Horne series
• Gilbert Nash series
Tudor, Tasha
• Becky series
Tufts, Warren
• Casey Ruggles series
Tuite, Hugh
• Helpless Annie series
• Pottleton series
Tuleja, Thaddeus Francis
see **Macao, Marshall**
Tulloch, John
Doctor Who, the unfolding text
Doctor Who series (162)
Tulloch, Richard
• Stories series
Tullock, Joyce
• Star trek fan series
Tully, John
• Inspector Holt series
• Johnny Goodlooks series
Tully, Paul
see also **Gardner, Jerome**
• Deputy Marshal Hooky Gibbs series

Tully, Tom
• Little Ed series
Tuning, William
• Fuzzy series
Tunis, John Roberts
• Iron Duke series
• Roy Tucker series
• Spike Russell series
Tunstall, Beatrice
• West Mercia series
Turgenev, Ivan Sergeevich
• Nihilist series
Turk, Hanne
• Max the Mouse series
• Rabbit and Chicken series
Turkle, Brinton
• Obadiah series
Turley, Charles
• Godfrey Marten series
Turnbull, Dora Amy
see **Wentworth, Patricia**
Turnbull, Margaret
• Juliet Jackson series
Turnbull, Patrick
• Bonaparte series
Turnbull, Peter
• P Division series
Turner, Bill
• Detective Inspector Manson series
Turner, Clay
see also **Ballard, Willis Todhunter; Fox, Brian; Macneil, Neil; Shepherd, John**
• Ben Gold series
Turner, Ethel
• Cub series
• Woolcot family series
Turner, George Reginald
• Ethical culture series
• Nugan series
• Treelake series
Turner, James Ernest
• Nicholas de la Haye series
• Rampion Savage series
Turner, John Nathan-
see **Nathan-Turner, John**
Turner, John Victor
see also **Hume, David**
• Amos Petrie series
Turner, Judy
• Sir Francis Drake series
Turner, Lilian
• Perry family series
Turner, Mary
• Blythe family series
Turner, Philip
see also **Chance, Stephen**
• Darnley Mills Railway series
• Darnley Mills series
Turner, Sheila
• Mary Carrick series
Turow, Scott
• Sandy Stern series
Turpin, Allan
• Geoffrey Gillard series
Turtledove, Harry
• Tale of Krispos series
• Videssos series
Turton, David
• Captain Ashe series
Turton-Jones, Edith Constance
see **Gillespie, Susan**
Tute, Warren
• Felthams series
• George Mado series
Tuttle, Gene
• Silent Slade series
Tuttle, Wilbur Coleman
• Hashknife Hartley and Sleepy Stevens series
• Henry Harrison Conroy and Judge Van Treece series
• Sad Sontag series
Tuyl, Barbara van
see **Van Tuyl, Barbara**
Twain, Mark
• Colonel Sellers series
• Diaries of Adam and Eve series
• Huckleberry Finn series
• Innocents series
• Sellers series
• Tom Sawyer series
• Tramp series
Tweedsmuir, John Buchan
see **Buchan, John**
Tweedsmuir, Susan Buchan
• Edwardian lady series
• Victorian trilogy
Tyers, Kathy
• Firebird series
Tyler, Alison
• Jennifer Heath series
Tyler, Charles Waller
• Blue Jean Billy Race series
Tyler, Clarke
• Clint Lacey series
Tyler, Jenny
• Duck series
• First words series
Tyler, Vicki
• Heart to heart series
Tyler, Zack
• Foxx series
Tyler-Whittle, Michael Sidney
see **Whittle, Tyler**
Tyndall, John
• Roger Turnbull series
Tyrer, Walter
• Sexton Blake series
Tytler, Ann Fraser
• Leila trilogy
• Mary and Florence series

U

Uchida, Yoshiko
• Japanese-American evacuation series
• Rinko trilogy
• Sumi series
Ucuk, Cahit
• Twin series
Uderzo, Albert
• Asterix series
• Dogmatix series
• Twelve tasks of Asterix series
Uhernik, Nik
see **Nik-Uhernik**
Uhnak, Dorothy
• Christie Opara series
Ulasi, Adaora Lily
• Nigerian series
Ulyatt, Kenneth
• Portugee Philips trilogy
Uncle Caractacus
see **Lewis, E W**
Underhill, Charles
see also **Hill, Reginald**
• Captain Fantom series
Underwood, Michael
• Martin Ainsworth series
• Richard Monk series
• Rosa Epton series
• Sergeant Nick Attwell series
• Superintendent Simon Manton series
Undset, Sigrid
• Kristin Lavransdatter trilogy
• Master of Hestviken series
• Modern scene series
Unger, Jim
• Herman series
• Herman treasury series
Unnerstad, Edith
• Anders series
• Larsson family series
Unsworth, Walter
• Mountaineering trilogy
Unwin, David Storr
see **Severn, David**
Updike, John
• Bech series
• Rabbit Angstrom series
Upfield, Arthur William
• Napoleon Bonaparte series
Upham, Grace Le Baron
see **Le Baron, Grace**
Upson, William Hazlett
• Alexander Botts series
Upton, Bertha
• Golliwogg series
Upton, Robert
• Amos McGuffin series
Upward, Allen
• Doctor Frank Tarleton series
• High treason series
• Monsieur V series
Upward, Edward
• Alan Sebrill trilogy
Ure, Jean
see also **McCulloch, Sarah**
• Hal series
• Jamie Carr series
• Nicola Bruce series
• Riverside Theatre series
• Shrublands Estate series
• Thursday trilogy
• Vanessa trilogy
• Woodside School series
Urquhart, Colin
• Spirit and faith series
Urquhart, Fred
• Bessie Hipkiss series
Urquhart, Macgregor
• Chief Inspector Joshua Smarles series
Urquhart, Paul
• Sexton Blake series
Usher, Frank
see also **Franklin, Charles**
• Amanda Curzon and Oscar Sallis series
• Daye Smith series
Usher, Gray
• Superintendent Michael Drexel series
Utechin, Nicholas
• Sherlock Holmes sequels series
Uttley, Alison
• Brock the badger series
• Country child series
• Fuzzypeg series
• Little Brown Mouse series
• Little Grey Rabbit series
• Little Red Fox series
• Sam Pig series
• Timothy Rabbit series

V

Vachell, Horace Annesley
• Fishpingle series
• Harrow School series
• Joe Quinney series
• Methuselah series
Vachss, Andrew
• Burke series
Vahey, John Haslette
see **Clandon, Henrietta**
Vail, Amanda
• Emily and Amy series
Vail, Virginia
• Animal Inn series
• Horse crazy series
Vaile, Carlotte Marion
• Orcutt girls series
Vaizey, George de Horne, ***Mrs***
see **Vaizey, Jessie Bell**
Vaizey, Jessie Bell
• Peggy Saville series
• Pixie O'Shaughnessy series
Val Baker, Denys
see **Baker, Denys Val**
Valdes, Armando Palacio
see **Palacio Valdes, Armando**
Valentine
see also **Cross, Mark**
• Daphne Wrayne and her Four Adjusters series
Valentine, Douglas
see also **Williams, Valentine**
• Clubfoot series
Valentine, Joseph Manson
• Bermuda Triangle series
Valery, Anne
• Tenko series
Valin, Jonathan
• Harry Stoner series
Vallance, Rosalind
• Timmy series
• Tittymouse and Tattymouse series
Valley, Mel
Enforcer
Dirty Harry Callahan series (12)
Vallins, George Henry
• Parodies series
Van Ammers-Kuller, Jo
see **Ammers-Kuller, Jo van**
Vanardy, Varick
• Bingham Harvard series
• Crewe series
Van Arnam, Dave
• Jamnar series
• Konarr series
Van Ash, Cay
• Fu-Manchu series
• Sherlock Holmes sequels series
Van Asten, Gail
• Charlemagne's champion series
Vanauken, Sheldon
• Mercy series
Van Buren, Raeburn
• Abbie an' Slats series
Vance, J Emily
• Star trek fan series
Vance, Jack
see also **Vance, John Holbrook**
• Adventures of Cugel the Clever series
• Alastor trilogy
• Big Planet series
• Cadwal chronicles series
• Durdane trilogy
• Dying earth series
• Gaean series
• Kirth Gersen series
• Lyonesse series
Rhialto the Marvellous
Heroes in hell series (12)
• Tschai series
Vance, John Holbrook
see also **Vance, Jack**
• Sheriff Joe Bain series
Vance, Louis Joseph
• Michael Lanyard series
• Terence O'Rourke series
Van Clief, Sylvia Worth
• Spotlight Detective Club series
Van de Plas, Rob
• Mountain bike series
Vandercook, John Womack
• Bertram Lynch and Robert Deane series
Vandercook, Margaret
• Camp Fire girls series
• Girl Scouts series
• Ranch Girls series
• Red Cross girls series
Vander Els, Betty
• Ruth series
Van der Essen, Anne
• Yok-yok series
Vandergriff, Aola
• Daughters series
• Wyndspelle series
Van der Meer, Atie
• Sammy and Mara series
Van der Meer, Ron
• Sammy and Mara series
Van der Meersch, Maxence
• Poor girl series
Van der Naillen, Albert
• Magi trilogy
Van der Post, Laurens
• Francois Joubert series
• Kalahari series
• Seed and the sower trilogy
Van der Voo, Jan
• Moonster series
Van der Zant, Johan Willem
see **Andreus, Hans**
Van Deventer, Emma Murdoch
• Carl Masters series
• Madeline Payne series
Van de Water, Frederic Franklin
• American Revolution series
• John Tarleton series
Van de Wetering, Janwillem
• De Gier and Grijpstra series
• Hugh Pine trilogy
• Zen series
Van Dine, S S
• Philo Vance series
Van Druten, John
I am a camera
Berlin series (3)
• Vicarious years series
Van Dyke, Henry
• Oliver series
Van Dyne, Edith
see also **Sampson, Emma**
• Aunt Jane's nieces series
• Flying girl series
• Mary Louise and Josie O'Gorman series
Van Epps, Margaret T
• Nancy Pembroke series
Van Gieson, Judith
• Neil Hamel series
Van Greenaway, Peter
• Inspector Cherry and Sergeant Duff series
Van Gulik, Robert
see **Gulik, Robert van**
Van Hise, Della
• Star trek series
Van Hise, James
Addams family revealed
Addams family series (3)
Arrival
V series (16)
Batmania
Batman series (10)
Comics file magazine spotlight on The Fantastic Four files
Marvel superheroes, new series (11)
It's a bird, it's a plane, no, it's the television adventures of Superman
Superman series (7)
Lost in space tribute book
Lost in space files series (4)
Lost in space twenty fifth anniversary tribute book
Lost in space files series (4)
Serial adventures of Batman
Batman series (10)
Superman files
Superman series (7)
• Swamp Thing second series
Van Leeuwen, Jean
• Oliver Pig series
Van Lustbader, Eric
see **Lustbader, Eric**
Vanner, Lyn
• Rannoch series
Van Oort, Jan
see **Dulieu, Jean**
Van Paassen, Pierre
• Days series
Van Scyoc, Sydney Joyce
• Sunstone scrolls trilogy
Van Siller, Hilda
• Allan Stewart series
• Pete Rector series
• Richard Massey series
Vansittart, Peter
• Stories from the past series
Van Slyke, Helen
see also **Ashton, Helen**
• Elizabeth Quigly series
Van Someren, Liesje
see **Someren, Liesje van**
Van Stockum, Hilda
• Jeremy Bear series
Van Tuyl, Barbara
• Julie Jefferson series
Van Urk, Virginia
• Tom Craig series
Van Vogt, Alfred Elton
• Clane series
• Isher Empire series
• Null-A series
Van Woerkom, Dorothy
• Abu Ali series
Vardeman, Robert Edward
• Biowarriors trilogy
• Cenotaph Road series
• Demon crown trilogy
• Jade demons quartet
• Masters of space trilogy
• Peter Thorne series
• Star trek series
• Swords of Raemllyn series
• War of powers series
• Weapons of chaos trilogy
Vare, Daniele
• Diplomat series
• Yen-Ching trilogy
Varley, John
• Gaea trilogy
Varnam, John
• Inspector Semlake series
Varney, Allen
• Advanced dungeons and dragons adventure gamebook series
• Doctor Strange series
• Marvel superheroes adventure gamebooks series
Vasa, Mary O'Hara Sture-
see **O'Hara, Mary**
Vasilikos, Vasilis
see **Vassilikos, Vassilis**
Vassilikos, Vassilis
• Modern Greece trilogy
Vaughan, Adrian
• Signalman trilogy
Vaughan, Carol
• Kennedys abroad series
• Manorfield Stud series
Vaughan, Carter A
• Lieutenant Gordon Fuller series
Vaughan, Marcia
• Dangerous and deadly series
Vaughan, Ralph E
• Sherlock Holmes sequels series
Vaughan, Richard
• Justin Peele series
Vautier, Ghislaine
• Greek legends series
Vaz, Mark
Tales of the dark knight
Batman series (10)
Vedral, Joyce Lauretta
• Driving me crazy series
Veley, Charles
• Twilight series
Velikovsky, Immanuel
• Ages in chaos series
• Worlds in collision series

Velthuijs, Max
- Little man series

Venables, Hubert
- Frankenstein sequels series

Vendrell, Carme Sole
- Victor and Maria series

Venning, Michael
- Melville Fairr series

Venters, Archie
- Gil Kennedy series

Vercors
- On the shore trilogy

VerDorn, Bethea
- Baby Jay series
- Moon glows series

Vereker, Barbara
- Caroline series

Verga, Giovanni
- Vinti family series

Verne, Henry
- Bob Moran series

Verne, Jules
- Adventures of Captain Hatteras series
- Arthur Gordon Pym series
- Barsac mission series
- Caesar Cascabel series
- Captain Grant's children series
- Captain Nemo series
- Family without a name series
- Floating city series
- Fur country series
- Giant raft series
- Golden volcano series
- Gun Club series
- Hector Servadac series
- J R Kazallon series
- Kereban the Inflexible series
- North against South series
- Phileas Fogg series
- Robur series
- Steam house series
- Survivors of the Jonathan series
- Swiss family Robinson series
- Thompson Travel Agency series
- Two years' holiday series

Verner, Christopher Stuart
see **Chase, Lesley**

Verner, Gerald
see also **Stuart, Donald**
- Felix Heron series
- Michael Dene series
- Paul Rivington series
- Peter Chard series
- Sexton Blake series
- Simon Gale series
- Superintendent Robert Budd series
- Trevor Lowe series

Verney, John
- Callendar family series
- Going to the wars series

Vernon, Barbara
- Bellbird series

Vernon, Edward
- Practice trilogy

Vernon, Frances
- Edwardian trilogy

Vernon, Rosemary
- Frannie Bronson series

Verral, Charles Spain
- Brains Benton series
- Lassie series
- Popeye series
- Rin-Tin-Tin series
- Smoky the bear series

Walt Disney's Andy Burnett
Andy Burnett series (4)
- Zorro series

Verrill, Alpheus Hyatt
- Boy adventurers series
- Cormorant series
- Cuba series
- Deep sea hunters series
- Panama series
- Radio detectives series
- Strange stories from nature series
- Trail series

Versace, Marie Teresa Rios
see **Rios, Tere**

Verseau, Dominique
- Yolanda series

Veryan, Patricia
- Age of Elegance series
- Golden chronicles series
- Sanguinet series
- Tales of the jewelled men series

Vesaas, Tarjei
- Per Eilevson Bufast series

Vesey, Christopher
- Iroquois series

Vestly, Anna Catharina
- Aurora series
- Eight children series

Viaud, Louis Marie Julien
see **Loti, Pierre**

Vickers, Bette
- Bridlington series

Vickers, Roy
see also **Durham, David; Kyle, Sefton**
- Department of Dead Ends series
- Inspector George Rason series
- Inspector J Rason series
- Inspector Peter Curwen and Hugh Stanton series
- James Segrove series

Vickery, William
- Sexton Blake series

Victor, Metta Victoria
see also **Gray, Walter T**
- Miss Slimmens series

Victor, Paul
- Porridge series

Victor, Roger
- Soldier of fortune series

Victor, Sam
- Kilburn series
- Talbot Lion series

Vidal, Gore
see also **Box, Edgar**
- Myra, Myron series
- Washington series

Viereck, George Sylvester
- Wandering Jew trilogy

Vigilant
- Barry Link series

Vigliante, Mary
- Aftermath series

Villefranche, Anne Marie
- Erotic memoirs series

Villiers, David Hugh
see **Buckingham, David**

Vincent, Gabrielle
- Ernest and Celestine series

Vincent, John
- James Bond junior series

Vincent, Kitty
- Gyp Kidnadze series

Vines, Freda
- Western Australian series

Viney, Jayne
- Richard III series

Vinge, Joan Dennison
Dune storybook
Dune series (6)
- Heaven chronicles series
- Mad Max series
- Oz series
- Psion series
- Snow Queen series
- Star wars storybook series

Tarzan, king of the apes
Tarzan series (1)
- Willow series

Vinge, Vernor
- Realtime series

Vinter, Michael
- Barry Kegan series

Vinton, Arthur Dudley
- Looking backward sequels series

Viorst, Judith
- Alexander series

Vipont, Elfrida
- Dowbiggins series
- Haverard family series

Virin, Anna
- Elsa series

Viscott, David Steven
- Portrait of a psychiatrist series

Vivelo, Jacqueline Jones
- Super Sleuth series

Vivian, Evelyn Charles
see also **Mann, Jack**
- Aia series
- Inspector Byrne series
- Inspector Head series

Vivian, Francis
- Inspector Gordon Knollis series
- Inspector John Burnell series
- Sergeant Ronnie Drew series

Vivian, Ron
Ginger Meggs annual
Ginger Meggs series (37)

Viviers, Lyn
- Star trek fan series

Vixen, Richard M
- Deep foot series

Vlasto, John Alexander
see **Remenham, John**

Vlcek, Ernst
- Atlan series

Voegeli, Max
- Adventures of Ali series

Vogt, Alfred Elton van
see **Van Vogt, Alfred Elton**

Voigt, Cynthia
- Tillermans series

Voilier, Charles
- Famous Five television series

Voinovich, Vladimir Nikolaevich
- Private Ivan Chonkin series

Volk, Gordon
- Jim Hale series

Vollman, William T
- Seven dreams series

Volsky, Paula
- Sorcerer trilogy

Voltz, William
- Perry Rhodan series

Von Arnim, Mary Annette
see **Russell, Mary Annette**

Von Chamisso, Adalbert
see **Chamisso, Adalbert von**

Von Daniken, Erich
see **Daniken, Erich von**

Von Elsner, Don
- David Danning series
- Jake Winkman series

Von Gunden, Kenneth
- K-Nine series

Von Heidenstam, Verner
see **Heidenstam, Verner von**

Von Hutten zum Stolzenberg, Bettina Riddle
see **Hutten zum Stolzenberg, Bettina Riddle**

Von Luckner, Felix
see **Luckner, Felix von**

Von Tempski, Armine
see **Tempski, Armine von**

Von Trapp, Maria Augusta
see **Trapp, Maria Augusta von**

Von Wacker, Alexander
see **Masters, M**

Von Wohl, Ludwig
see **De Wohl, Louis**

Vornholt, John
- Star trek, the next generation series

Voss Bark, Conrad
see **Bark, Conrad Voss**

Vowell, David
- Dragnet series

Voynich, Ethel Lillian
- Gadfly series

Vries, Julianne de
see **De Vries, Julianne**

Vries, Peter de
see **De Vries, Peter**

Vyvyan, Clara Coltman
- Roots and stars series

W

W, W
- Qhe series

WAAC
- WAAC series

Waal, Ronald Burt de
see **De Waal, Ronald Burt**

Wabbes, Marie
- Little Rabbit series

Waber, Bernard
- Ira series
- Lyle series

Wacker, Alexander von
see **Masters, M**

Wada, Yoshiomi
- Peter Pig series

Waddell, Martin
see also **Sefton, Catherine**
- Ernie series
- Gerald Otley quartet
- Great Gran Gorilla series
- Harriet the Troublemaker series
- Little Dracula series
- Mystery Squad series
- Napper series
- Owl and Billy series

Waddell, Sid
- Jossy's Giants series

Wade, Graham
- Kippy Koala series

Wade, Henry
- Inspector Lott series
- Inspector Poole series
- John Bragg series
- Major Faide series

Wade, Robert
see **Miller, Wade**

Waedt, Carl F
- Incredible adventures series

Wager, Walter
- Alison Gordon series
- King Kong series

Wagner, Karl Edward
- Bran Mak Morn trilogy
- Conan series
- Kane series

Wagner, Lauren McGraw
- Oz series

Wagner, Robin S
- Mork and Mindy series

Wagner, Sharon
- Gypsy series

Wahl, Jan
- Doctor Rabbit series
- Melvin Spitznagle series
- Muffletump series
- Pipkins series
- Pleasant Fieldmouse series

Wahloo, Per
- Chief Inspector Peter Jensen series
- Inspector Martin Beck series

Wahlstedt, Viola
- Ann and Susan series

Wain, John
- Peter and Brian Leonard series

Waine, Charlton
- Sweepers series

Wainwright, Francis
- Freddie series

Wainwright, John
see also **Ripley, Jack**
- Chief Inspector Lennox series
- Inspector Lyle series
- John George Davis series
- Lucky Luckhurst series
- Northern Police series
- Pewter series
- Superintendent Blayde series
- Superintendent Charles Ripley series
- Superintendent Gilliant series

Wainwright, Sheila
- Freddie series

Waite, Jon
- Warriors of America trilogy

Waite, Judy Bernard-
see **Bernard-Waite, Judy**

Wajenberg, Earl
- Amazing stories series

Wakefield, Hannah
- Dee Street series

Wakefield, Sydney Alexander
- Gumbles series

Wakefield, Tom
- Margaret Davis and Isobel Quirk trilogy

Walden, Amelia
- Lisa Clark series
- Miranda Welch trilogy

Walder, David
- Charles Lilburne and Rupert Inglis series

Waldman, Emerson
- Land and the way series

Waldman, Frank
- Inspector Clouseau series

Waldo, Dale
- Johnny Ross series

Waldo, Edward Hamilton
see **Sturgeon, Theodore**

Waldron, Simon
- Steve Essex series

Waldy, Frances Helen
- Scarsborough series

Wales, Mike
- Leatherhand series

Walker, Abbie Phillips
- Sandman series

Walker, Dalton
- Shiloh series

Walker, David Esdaile
- Pimpernel series

Walker, David Gordon
- Rick series

Walker, David Harry
- Dougal Trocher series
- Geordie Mactaggart series

Walker, Elizabeth
- Gingerbread Man series

Walker, Frank
- Vipers series

Walker, Holly Beth
- Meg Duncan series

Walker, Hugh
- Magira trilogy

Walker, Ira
see also **Walker, Irma**
- Steve Rhoden series

Walker, Irma
see also **Walker, Ira**
- Steve Rhoden series

Walker, Jerry
- Lawrence Marley series

Walker, Lucy
see also **Sanders, Dorothy Lucie**
Bell branch
Montgomery family series (3)
- Montgomery family series

Walker, Martin
- Maddox series

Walker, Max
- Cricketer series
- Mission impossible series

Walker, Mort
- Hi and Lois series

Walker, Peter Norman
see also **Coram, Christopher; Rhea, Nicholas**
- Detective Sergeant Carnaby-King series
- Panda One series

Walker, Robert Wayne
see also **Caine, Geoffrey; Robertson, Stephen**
- Dean Grant series
- Time machine series

Walker, Roger Wade
- Eric series

Walker, Rowland
- Captain Deville McKeene series
- Fifth Form series

Walker, Victoria
- Hadlows series

Walker-Taylor, Philip Neville
see **Taylor, Philip Neville Walker**

Wall, Adrian
- Cardles Farm series

Wall, Anthony
- Roger Moore and the Crimefighters series

Wall, Dorothy
- Blinky Bill adaptations series
- Blinky Bill series

Wall, Mervyn
- Fursey series

Wall, Robert Emmet
- Nowell family series

Wallace, Barbara Brooks
- Claudia series
- Hawkins series

Wallace, Bryan Edgar
- Bill Tern series

Wallace, C H
- Steve Ramsay series

Wallace, Carlton
- Superintendent Edmund Bendilow series

Wallace, David Rains
- Turquoise dragon series

Wallace, Edgar
- Black Avons series
- Commissioner Sanders series
- Educated Evans series
- Inspector Elk series
- Just Men series
- Mister J G Reeder series
- Mister T B Smith series
- Ringer series
- Smithy series
- Superintendent Minter series

Wallace, Ian
- Claudine Saint Cyr series
- Croyd series
- Pan Sagittarius series

Wallace, Ivy Lilian
- Pookie series
- Warrenders series

Wallace, Jim
- Choose your own adventure series

Wallace, John
- Conrad Franks series
- Detective Sergeant Fuller series
- Millionaire gangster series

Wallace, Kathleen
- I walk alone series
- Veronica Ramsay series

Wallace, Marilyn
- Jay Goldstein and Carlos Cruz series

Wallace, Robert
- Essington Holt series
- Phantom Detective series

Wallace, Trevor
- John Tracy series

Waller, Leslie
- Woods Palmer series

Walling, Robert Alfred John
- Garstang series
- Philip Tolefree series

Wallingford, Lee
- Frank Carver and Ginny Trask series

Wallis, James Harold
• Inspector Wilton Jacks series
Wallis, Redmond
• Triangulum trilogy
Wallis, Ruth Sawtell
• Eric Lund series
Wallman, Jeffrey
• Matt Bishop series
Walmsley, Leo
• Phantom Lobster series
Walpole, Hugh
• Herries ancestors series
• Herries saga series
• Jeremy trilogy
• London Group series
• Maradick series
• Mister Durward series
• Peter Westcott series
• Provincial group series
• Trenchard family series
Walsh, Bill
• Fishing series
Walsh, Gillian Paton
see **Walsh, Jill Paton**
Walsh, James Morgan
see also **Maddock, Stephen**
• Bromley Kay series
• Colonel Ormiston series
• Inspector Quaile series
• Inspector Storm series
• Mike Harman series
• Oliver Keene series
• Tiger Bay series
Walsh, Jill Paton
• Children of the fox trilogy
• Goldengrove series
Walsh, Maurice
• Thomasheen James series
Walsh, Ray
• Sherlock Holmes sequels series
Waltari, Mika
• Michael Carvajel series
Waltch, Lilla M
• Lisa Davis series
Walter, Alexia E
• Sir Edgar Ewart series
Walter, Francis V
• Benjie series
Walter, Hubert Conrad
• Sir Edgar Ewart series
Walter, Mildred Pitts
• Lillie of Watts series
Walter, William Wilfred
• Pastor's son trilogy
Walters, Hugh
• Chris Godfrey series
• Peter Hill series
Walther, Daniel
• Shai series
Walton, Catherine Augusta
• Christie series
Walton, Evangeline
• Mabinogion series
Walton, Marion
• Inspector James Cardinal series
Walton, Oriel Farnell, ***Mrs***
see **Walton, Catherine Augusta**
Wambaugh, Joseph
• Bumper Morgan series
Wangerin, Walter
• Coop series
Warburg, Fredric
• Publishing series
Ward, Alfred C
• Sherlock Holmes sequels series
Ward, Anthony
• George trilogy
Ward, Arthur Sarsfield
see **Rohmer, Sax**
Ward, Christopher
• Jonathan Drew series
Ward, Dorothy Darrell
• Teddies series
Ward, Edward
• Number one boy series
Ward, Elizabeth Rebecca
see **Inchfawn, Fay**
Ward, Elizabeth Stuart Phelps
see **Phelps, Elizabeth Stuart**
Ward, Glenyse
• Wandering girl series
Ward, Harold
see also **Zorro**
• Vulture series
Ward, Humphry, ***Mrs***
see **Ward, Mary Augusta**
Ward, James Michael
• Advanced dungeons and dragons reference books series
• Catacombs series
• Conan series
Dragonsword of Lankhmar
Fafhrd and Gray Mouser series (8)
• Endless quest series
• Fantasy forest series
• Find your fate: G.I. Joe series
Greyhawk adventures
Advanced dungeons and dragons adventure gamebook series (15)
Greyhawk adventures
Greyhawk series (7)
• Marvel superheroes adventure gamebooks series
Ward, Jonas
see also **Ard, William; Cox, William Robert; Frederic, Mike**
• Tom Buchanan series
Ward, Kenneth
• Boy volunteers series
Ward, Lynda
• Welles family trilogy
Ward, Mary Augusta
• Marcella Boyce series
• New Brotherhood series
Ward, Richard Heron
• Neil Falder series
Ward, Ruth Cameron
• Swallows eaves series
Warde, Joan
• Forrester family series
Warde, Margaret
• Betty Wales series
• Nancy Lee series
Warden, Mike
• Hank Bradford series
Ware, William
• Zenobia and Aurelian series
Warfield, Catherine Ann
• Ferne Fleming series
Warfield, Gallatin
• Gardner Lawson series
Waricha, Jean
• Find your fate: Jem series
Warman, Erik
• Inspector John Isidore Bloom series
Warner, Anne
• Susan Clegg series
• Uncle John series
Warner, Charles Dudley
• Colonel Sellers series
• Finance trilogy
• Sellers series
Warner, Esther Sietmann
• Liberia series
Warner, Frank A
• Bob Chase series
• Bobby Blake series
Warner, Gertrude Chandler
• Boxcar children series
• Boxcar children special series
Warner, Mignon
• Mrs Edwina Charles series
Warner, Priscilla Mary
• Biddy and Tessie series
• Frances series
Warner, Rex
• Caesar series
Warner, Susan Bagert
see also **Wetherell, Elizabeth**
• Bread and oranges series
• Daisy trilogy
• Eagle Hill series
• Mister Rutherford series
• Opportunities series
• Sceptres and crowns series
• Wych Hazel series
Warren, Clarence Henry
• Happy countryman series
Warren, Doug
• Sheriff Buford Pusser series
Warren, George A
• Musket boys series
Warren, James
• James Warren series
• James Weston series
Warren, Joanna
• Conrad chronicles series
Warren, John Russell
• Inspector M'Guire series
Warren, Lella
• Whetstone series
Warren, Paulette
• Caliban series
Warren, Rebecca
• Pet lamb series
Warren, Vernon
• Mark Brandon series
Warrener
see also **Pearce, Philippa**
• Bunnykins series
Warriner, Thurman
see also **Troy, Simon**
• Mister Scotter series
Warrington, Freda
• Quest of the serpent series
Warwick, Audrey
• Carroll family series
Warwick, Jarvis
see also **Garner, Hugh**
• Cabbagetown series
Warwick, Milligan
• William Harkness series
Washburn, Livia Jane
• Lucas Hallam series
Washburn, Mark
• Sam Boggs series
Wassermann, Jack
• Sailor Jack series
Wassermann, Jakob
• Doctor Joseph Kerkhoven trilogy
Wassermann, Selma
• Sailor Jack series
Wasson, Mildred
• Nancy Prentiss series
Watanabe, Shigeo
• I can do it series
Water, Frederic Franklin van de
see **Van de Water, Frederic Franklin**
Waterfield, Robin
• Fighting fantasy gamebook series
Waterhouse, Arthur
• Fellside Farm series
Waterhouse, Keith
see also **Gibb, Lee**
• Billy Liar series
• Nobody series
• Worzel Gummidge series
Waterman, Jill
• Harry series
Waters, Frank
• Pike's Peak trilogy
Waters, Thomas Allen
• Greenwich Village trilogy
Watkins, Alex
see **Linklater, Joseph Lane**
Watkins, Peter
• Here's the church series
Watkins, Ron
• Thomas Tilling series
Watkins, William John
• Legrange League series
Watkins-Pitchford, Denys James
see **B B**
Watmough, David
• Davey Bryant series
Watson, Charles Wauchope
see **Chrystie, Edward M**
Watson, Clarissa
• Persis Willum series
Watson, Clyde
• Father Fox series
Watson, Colin
• Inspector Purbright series
Watson, Edmund Henry Lacon
• Bohemia series
• Strange family trilogy
Watson, Henry Brereton Marriott
• Dick Ryder series
Watson, Ian
• Black Current trilogy
• Inquisition war series
• Urban nucleus series
Watson, Ina
• Australian nature tales series
Watson, Jean
• Alot series
• I wonder about series
• In times of series
• Meet the Samuel family series
Watson, John
see **Maclaren, Ian**
Watson, John H
Sexual adventures of Sherlock Holmes
Sherlock Holmes series (10)
Watson, John Reay
• Crewe series
Watson, Julia
see also **Fitzgerald, Julia; Hamilton, Julia**
• Gentian trilogy
Watson, Julian
• Hoggie series
Watson, Kathleen
• Litanies series
Watson, Keith Campbell West-
see **Campbell, Keith**
Watson, Sydney
• Second Coming series
Watson, Wendy
• Feelings series
Watson, Will
see also **Austin, Brett; Floren, Lee; Smith, Lew**
• Judge Lemanuel Bates and Tobacco Jones series
Watt-Evans, Lawrence
• Legend of Ethshar series
• Lords of Dus series
• War surplus series
Watterson, Bill
• Calvin and Hobbes series
Watts, Edgar John Palmer
see **Palmer, John**
Watts, Isaac
• Catechisms and prayers series
• Logick series
Watts, Marjorie Ann
• Crocodile series
Watts, Peter Christopher
see **Chisholm, Matt; James, Cy**
Watts, Walter Theodore
see **Watts-Dunton, Theodore**
Watts-Dunton, Theodore
• Aylwin series
Waugh, Charles Gordon
Barbarians
Barbarians series (1)
Waugh, Evelyn
• Basil Seal series
• World War II series
Waugh, Hillary
see also **Taylor, H Baldwin**
• Chief Fred Fellows series
• Detective Frank Sessions series
• Sheridan Wesley series
• Simon Kaye series
Waugh, Joseph Laing
• Robbie Doo series
Wawn, F T
• Masterdillo series
Wax, Wendy
• Ten things I know series
Way, Peter
• Crispin Bridge series
Waye, Cecil
• Christopher Perrin series
Wayland, Patrick
see also **Archer, Frank**
• Lloyd Nicolson series
Wayman, Tony Russell
• Dreamhouse series
Wayne, Dorothy
• Dorothy Dixon series
Wayne, Jenifer
• Purple dress series
• Sprout series
• Winchester family series
Wayne, Les
• Arvada Jones series
Wayne, Matt
• Nintendo adventure series
Weale, Putnam
• Wang the Ninth trilogy
Weatherhead, John
• Professor David Connell series
Weaver, Graham
• Saint series
Weaver, Michael D
• Thyri trilogy
Weaver, Nicky
• Nicky Weaver series
Weaver, Rix
• New Holland series
Webb, Alex
• Josh Dekker series
Webb, Anthony
• Mister Pendlebury series
Webb, Beatrice
• Partnership series
Webb, Diana
• Lily series
Webb, Geoffrey
• Archers of Ambridge series
Webb, Henry Bertram Law
see **Clayton, John**
Webb, Jack
• Father Joseph Shanley and Sammy Golden series
Webb, Jackie
• Wilkes the wizard series
Webb, Jean Francis
see **Willoughby, Lee Davis**
King Solomon's mines
Allan Quatermain series (13)
Webb, Kaye
• Nat series
Webb, Margot
• Coping series
Webb, Martha
see **Martin, Lee**
Webb, Michael
• Giants in the earth trilogy
Webb, Richard Wilson
see **Patrick, Q; Quentin, Patrick; Stagge, Jonathan**
Webb, Sharon
• Earth song trilogy
Webber, Edmund Godfrey
• Trout fishing series
Weber, Bruce
• Moments in sport series
Weber, Christine
• Toby series
Weber, Joe
• Military techno-thrillers series
Weber, Judith
• Cheerleaders series
Weber, Ken
• Five minute mysteries series
Weber, Lenora Mattingly
• Beany Malone series
• Stacy and Katie Rose Belford series
Webster, Ernest
• Benni Soldano series
Webster, Frederick Annesley Michael
• Ebbie Entwhistle series
Webster, H M
• Shamus Burke series
Webster, Henry Kitchell
• Arthur Jeffrey series
Webster, Jack
• Grain of truth series
Webster, James
• Shorty series
Webster, Jan
• Kate Kilgour trilogy
Webster, Jean
• Judy Abbott series
• Patty series
Webster, Joanne
• Marigold series
• Nobody's horse trilogy
Webster, Noah
see **Macleod, Robert**
Wechsberg, Joseph
• Epicure trilogy
Weddle, Ferris
• Clint Wade and Trapper Bill series
Wees, Frances Shelley
• Michael Forrester series
• Patterson family series
Weese, Gene de
see **Deweese, Gene**
Wegner, Fritz
• Mrs Butler series
Wehrstein, Karen
• Fifth millenium series
Shadow's son
Fifth millenium series (4)
Weidman, Jerome
• Benny Kramer series
• Harry Bogen series
Weikel, Anna Hamline
• Betty Baird trilogy
Weil, Jennifer C
• Mrs Murgatroyd series
Wein, Len
• Amazing Spiderman series
• Marvel superheroes, new series
• Swamp Thing series
Weinberg, Larry
see also **Scott, R C**
• Chuck Norris and the Karate Kommandos series
• Dark forces series
Empire strikes back
Star wars storybook series (2)
• Ewok series
• Father John Murphy series
• Star trek tie-ins series
Star wars
Star wars storybook series (1)
Weinberg, Robert
• Alex Werner series
Weinreb, Nathaniel Norsen
• Biblical series
Weinstein, Howard
• Star trek series
• Star trek, the next generation series
• V series
Weinstein, Sol
• Israel Bond series
Weir, Molly
• Feet series
Weir, Rosemary
• Albert the dragon series
• Green Street series
• Maybury family series
• Tempest family series
• Uncle Barney series
Weis, Margaret
• Darksword trilogy
• Death Gate series
• DragonLance chronicles series
• DragonLance legends trilogy

- DragonLance series
- DragonLance tales trilogy
- Endless quest series
- Rose of the prophet trilogy
- Star of the guardians series

Weiser, Francis Xavier
- Christian festivals trilogy

Weisman, John
- Headhunters series

Weiss, David
- Wolfgang Amadeus Mozart series

Weiss, Ellen
- Indiana Jones find your fate series

Weiss, Mike
- Ben Henry series

Weiss, Peter
- Exile series

Welch, Amanda
- Sammy series

Welch, Ronald
- Carey family series

Welch, Timothy L
- Dion Quince series

Welcome, John
- Bellary Bay series
- Mister Merston series
- Richard Graham series
- Simon Herald series

Welk, Laurence
- Wunnerful series

Wellard, James
- Lucius Hunt series

Welles, Elizabeth
- Janine West series

Welling, Lois
- Star trek fan series

Wellman, Manly Wade
- Captain Future series
- John Thunstone trilogy
- Sherlock Holmes sequels series
- Silver John series
- War of the worlds series

Wellman, Paul Iselin
- Death on horseback series
- Jericho series

Wellman, Wade
- Sherlock Holmes sequels series
- War of the worlds series

Wells, Angus
see also **Dancer, J B; Kirk, Matthew; Muir, James A; Sandon, J D**
- Kingdoms trilogy
- Man called Horse series

Wells, Ann Elizabeth
- Arnhem Land series

Wells, Anna Mary
- Doctor Hillis Owen series

Wells, Carolyn
- Alan Ford series
- Dick and Dolly series
- Diversions series
- Dorrance series
- Fleming Stone series
- Folly series
- Kenneth Carlisle series
- Lorimer Lane series
- Marjorie Maynard series
- Patty Fairfield series
- Pennington Wise series
- Rubaiyat series
- Two little women series

Wells, Chrissie
- Teddies series

Wells, David Dwight
- Ladyship and lordship series

Wells, Evelyn
- Miracle series

Wells, Helen
- Cherry Ames series
- Vicki Barr series

Wells, Herbert George
- Doctor Moreau series
- Time traveller series
- War of the worlds series

Wells, Kenneth McNeil
- Owl Pen series

Wells, Marian
- Amy Randolph trilogy
- Starlight trilogy
- Wedding dress series

Wells, Mary
- Expatriates trilogy

Wells, Mick
- Rupert TV playbook series

Wells, Rosemary
- Max series

Wells, Susan
- Anthony Ware series

Wells, Tobias
- Detective Knute Severson series

Welsh, Ken
- Hero series

Wendorf, Patricia
- Patteran trilogy

Wenger, Peter
- Logic and order in society series

Wenk, Richard
- Batman series
- Indiana Jones find your fate series
- Pick-a-path series
- Super powers which way series

Wensby-Scott, Carol
- Percy trilogy

Wensell, Ulises
- Jackson family series

Wentworth, Patricia
- Benbow Smith and Frank Garratt series
- Inspector Ernest Lamb series
- Miss Maud Silver series
- Waveneys series

Werner, Ellis
National Lampoon's Doon
Dune series (6)

Wernher, Hilda
- Indian family series

Werper, Barton
- New Tarzan series

Werstein, Irving
Danger at Dry Creek
Wells Fargo series (4)

Wertsman, Vladimir
- Ethnic groups in America series

Wesker, Arnold
- Chicken soup trilogy

Wesley, Elizabeth
see also **McElfresh, Adeline**
- Doctor Dorothy Dee series

Wesley, Valerie Wilson
- Afro-Bets series

West, Annie
- Brinkworth Bear series

West, Bob
see also **Frances, Stephen Daniel**
- Adventures around the compass series

West, Charles
- Paul Crook series

West, Chassie L
- Micro adventure series

West, Colin
- King of Kenilwick Castle series
- Monty series

West, Donald James
- Homosexuality series

West, Dorothy
- Dot and Dash series

West, Elizabeth
- Hafod Garden series

West, Jerry
- Happy Hollisters series

West, Jessamyn
- Jess and Eliza Birdwell series

West, John B
- Rocky Steele series

West, Joyce
- Gabrielle Allan series
- Inspector Wright series

West, Julian
- Looking backward responses series

West, Marvin
see also **Deering, Fremont B; Lawton, Wilbur; Payson, Howard**
- Motor Rangers series

West, Morris Langlo
- George Harlequin series

West, Nick
- Three Investigators series

West, Paul
- Jaggers family series

West, Rebecca
- Aubrey family trilogy

West-Watson, Keith Campbell
see **Campbell, Keith**

Westall, Robert
- Machine gunners trilogy

Westall, William
- Andreas Hofer series

Westbrook, Perry Dickie
- Doctor Samuel Cutting series

Westcott, C T
- Eagleheart trilogy

Westendorp, Fiep
- Dusty and Smudge series

Westerman, John Francis Cyril
- John Wentley series

Westerman, Percy Francis
- Alan Carr series
- Captain Cain series
- Sea Scouts series
- Sinclair series
- Standish series

Westermann, John
- Orin Boyd series

Westheimer, David
- Von Ryan series

Westlake, Donald Edwin
see also **Coe, Tucker; Stark, Richard**
- Dortmunder Gang series
- Sara Joslyn series

Westland, Lynn
see also **Cody, Al**
- Powdersmoke series

Weston, Carolyn
- Casey Kellog and Al Krug series

Weston, Cole
see also **Cutter, Tom; Longley, W B; Meek, Joseph; Randall, Joshua; Randisi, Robert Joseph; Roberts, J R**
- Andrew Ryder series

Weston, Garnett
- Highway series

Weston, Matt
- Drifter Morgan series

Westphail, Arnold Carl
- Gospel magic series
- Paper tearing series

Westron, Charles
- Salty series

Westrup, Margaret
- Elizabeth series

Westwood, Anne McDougall
- Kittiwake Rock series

Wetanson, Burt
- Hunters series

Wetering, Janwillem van de
see **Van de Wetering, Janwillem**

Wetherell, Elizabeth
see also **Warner, Susan Bagert**
- Ellen Montgomery series

Wetjen, Albert Richard
- Shark Gotch series

Weverka, Robert
- Search series
- Sherlock Holmes sequels series

Wevill, Lilian F
- Betty series

Weymouth, Anthony
- Inspector Treadgold series

Weyn, Suzanne
- Secret of the Unicorn Queen series

Whalley, Dean
- Raggedy Ann series

Whalley, Peter
- Harry Sommers and Jill Hanscombe series
- Uncalled-for histories series

Wham, Tom
Prospero's island
Harold Shea series (4)
- Runesword series

Wharton, Edith
- Old New York quartet
- Vance Weston series

Wharton, Joanna
- Campus fever series

Wheat, Carolyn
- Cass Jameson series

Wheatley, Dennis
- Count de Quesnoy and Condesa Guilia series
- Duc de Richelieu series
- Gregory Sallust series
- Julian Day series
- Lieutenant John Milton Schwab series
- Molly Fountain series
- Roger Brook series
- Time has come series
- War game series

Wheelahan, Paul
see **Clay, E Jefferson**

Wheeler, Anthony George
- Captain Jonas series

Wheeler, Cindy
- Little Mouse series
- Marmalade series

Wheeler, David
- Edwin Mould series

Wheeler, Francis Rolt-
see **Rolt-Wheeler, Francis**

Wheeler, H E
- Kendal Graydon series
- Stephen Rant series

Wheeler, Hugh
see **Patrick, Q; Quentin, Patrick**

Wheeler, Janet D
- Billie Bradley series

Wheeler, Richard Seabrook
- Rivers west series
- Rocky Mountain Company series
- Sheriff Santiago Toole series
- Skye's West series

Wheeler-Bennett, John
- Special relationships series

Whelpton, Eric
- Making series

Whelton, Paul
- Garry Dean series

Whipple, Dorothy
- Other day series

Whitaker, Beryl
- John Abbot series

Whitaker, David
- Doctor Who series

Whitaker, Evelyn
- Honor Bright series
- Miss Toosie series

Whitaker, Rodney
see **Trevanian**

Whitbread, Elizabeth
- Georgie Pony Club series

Whitby, Beatrice
- Mary Fenwick series

Whitcomb, Mary Burg
- Tee-Bo series

White, Alan
see also **Fraser, James; Whitney, Alec**
- Aysgill family trilogy
- Commando series
- Inspector Armstrong series
- Ravenswyke series

White, Antonia
- Frost in May series
- Minka and Curdy series

White, Ared
- Captain Fox Elton series

White, Constance Mary
- Ballet school series
- Saint Mark's Hospital series
- Westways series

White, Edmund
- Beautiful room series

White, Edmund Valentine
- Indian romance series

White, Ellen Emerson
- President's daughter series

White, Frank James
see **Stewart-Hargreaves, Eustace Hamilton Ian**

White, Grace Miller
- Storm country series

White, James
- Sector General series

White, James Dillon
- Roger Kelso series
- Sebastian Kettle series

White, James G
- Gunslick series

White, John
- Archives of Anthropos series

White, Jon Manchip
- Colonel Rickman trilogy

White, Jude
see **Deveraux, Jude**

White, Leslie Turner
- Captain Barnaby series

White, Mel
- Duncan and Mallory series

White, Myrtle Rose
- White family series

White, Osmar
- Doctor McGurk series

White, Palmer
- Mystery Island series

White, Paul
- Doctor of Tanganyika series
- Jungle Doctor series
- Jungle Doctor's fables series
- Ranford series

White, Percy
- Countess series
- Mister Bailey-Martin series

White, Ramy Allison
- Sunny Boy series

White, Reginald James
- Inspector David Brock series

White, Robb
- Midshipman Lee series

White, Simon
- Penhaligon trilogy

White, Stanley
see **White, James Dillon**

White, Steve
- S-Com series

White, Stewart Edward
- Andy Burnett series
- California trilogy
- Free forest series
- Lumbering trilogy
- Orde family series
- Percy Darrow series

- Simba series
- Skookum Chuck series

White, Ted
- Android Tanner series
- Captain America series
- Marvel superheroes series
- Qanar series
- Weird heroes series

White, Terence Hanbury
- Lilliput series
- Mister Marx series
- Once and future king series
- Scandal series

White, Teri
- Blue Maguire and Spaceman Kowalski series

White, Theodore Edwin
see **White, Ted**

White, Valerie
- John Case series

White, William
- Animal is born series

White, William Anthony Parker
see **Boucher, Anthony**

White, William Hale
- Mark Rutherford series

White, William Patterson
- Lazy River series

Whited, Charles
- Spirit of America series

Whitehead, David
see also **Bridges, Ben**
- Heller series
- Judge and Dury series

Whitehead, Robert John
- Checkered flag series
- World of adventure series

Whitehead, Victoria
- Chimney witch series

Whitehill, Dorothy
- Janet and Phyllis series
- Joy Payton series
- Polly series

Whitehouse, Arch
- Air war series

Whiteing, Richard
- Rich and poor series

Whitelaw, David
- Peter Wells series

Whiteson, Leon
- Scanners series

Whiting, Charles
- Destroyer series
- Spymaster series
- T-Force series

Whitlock, Judith
- Bunyip series

Whitlock, Pamela
- Oxus series

Whitlock, Ralph
- Cowleaze Farm series

Whitman, Charles
- Inspector Lindon and Sergeant Gray series

Whitman, Sidney Edgerton
- Captain Cullah Burnett series

Whitmore, Adam
- Max the cat series

Whitney, Adeline Dutton Train
- Girls series

Whitney, Alec
see also **Fraser, James; White, Alan**
- Inspector Armstrong series

Whittaker, June Lovina
- Henry and Susannah Kable series

Whittemore, Edward
- Jerusalem quartet

Whittemore, Louis Henry
- Super Cops series

Whittingham, Richard
- Joe Morrison series

Whittington, Harry
see also **Carter, Ashley**
- Man from U.N.C.L.E. series

Whittington-Egan, Richard
- Liverpool series

Whittle, Michael Sidney Tyler-
see **Whittle, Tyler**

Whittle, Tyler
- Edward VII series
- Queen Victoria trilogy
- Spaniards and Elizabethans series

Wiat, Philippa
- Allington trilogy
- Black Boar series
- Charlton Mead series
- Edward III series
- Grey family series
- Howard series
- Wilmington series
- Wyatt family series

Wiater, Stanley
Official teenage mutant ninja turtles treasury
Teenage mutant ninja turtles series (5)
Wibberley, Leonard
see also **Holton, Leonard; O'Connor, Patrick**
• Grand Fenwick series
• Man of liberty series
• Treasure Island series
• Treegate family series
• Treegate family trilogy
• Uncle Bill series
Wickham, Harvey
• Ferris McClue series
Wicking, George Walter
• Inspector Greenwood series
Widdemer, Margaret
• Rose-garden series
• Winona series
• Years of love series
Wideman, John Edgar
• Homewood trilogy
Wied, Marie Elisabeth
• Tiptilt series
Wienecke, Otto
see **Traven, B**
Wiesel, Elie
• Night trilogy
Wiewandt, Thomas
• Hidden life series
Wigg, T I G
see also **Galway, Robert Conington; Macneil, Duncan; McCutchan, Philip**
• Teaching series
Wiggin, Bernard
see **Cornwell, Bernard**
Wiggin, Kate Douglas
• Penelope Hamilton series
• Polly Oliver series
• Rebecca series
Wight, James Alfred
see **Herriot, James**
Wightman, Frank Armstrong
• Wylo series
Wignall, Trevor C
• Sexton Blake series
Wilcox, Barbara
• Bunty Brown series
Wilcox, Collin
• Alan Bernhardt series
• Lieutenant Frank Hastings series
• Marshal Sam McCloud series
• Stephen Drake series
Wilcox, James
• Tula Springs trilogy
Wilcox, Stephen F
• Elias Hackshaw series
• T S W Sheridan series
Wild, Jocelyn
• Bears series
• Spot's dogs series
Wild, Robin
• Bears series
• Spot's dogs series
Wilde, Jennifer
• Marietta Danvers series
Wilde, Vyvyan
see **Holland, Vyvyan**
Wilder, Cherry
• Rulers of Hylor trilogy
• Torin trilogy
Wilder, Joan
• Romancing the stone series
Wilder, Laura Ingalls
• Laura series
Wildey, Doug
• Rio series
Wildsmith, Alan
• Forty-Five Acres series
Wiles, John
• Grand Trunk Road series
Wiley, Hugh
• Wildcat series
Wilhelm, Hans
• Bunny trouble series
• Elfie series
• Merritales series
• Tyrone series
• Waldo series
• Waldo, tell me series
Wilhelm, Kate
• Barbara Holloway series
• Charlie Miklejohn and Constance Leidl series
Wilkerson, David
• Cross and the switchblade series
Wilkes, Marilyn Z
• C.L.U.T.Z. series
Wilkes Hunter, Richard
see **Hunter, Richard Wilkes**
Wilkins, Dale
see also **Bates, Gordon; Flower, Jessie Graham**
• Long Trail Boys series
Wilkins, Vaughan
• Victoria series
Wilkinson, Brenda
• Ludell Wilson trilogy
Wilkinson, Burke
• Geoffrey Mildmay series
Wilkinson, Laurence
• Mike Daryl series
Wilkinson, Nevile
• Titania's Palace series
Wilkinson, Sylvia
• World of racing series
Wilkinson, Walter
• Puppets series
Will, George Frederick
• Pursuit series
Willans, Geoffrey
• Nigel Molesworth series
Willard, Barbara
• Dippers series
• Jill and Limpet series
• Mantlemass series
• Proposed series
• Snail and Pennithorne series
• Tower family series
Willard, Nancy
• Anatole series
• John to James series
Willard, Tom
• Strike fighters series
Willcox, Kathleen Mary
• Kennedys abroad series
Willeford, Charles
• Hoke Moseley series
Willey, Basil
• Spots of time series
Williams, Alan
• Beria papers series
• Rupert Quinn series
Williams, Alexander
• Detective Sergeant Pietro Tonelli series
Williams, Amanda Kyle
• Madison McGuire series
Williams, Barbara
• Mirage mysteries series
• Mitzi series
Williams, Ben Ames
• Currain family series
• Inspector Tope series
• Thread of scarlet series
Williams, Bill
see **Brody, Marc**
Williams, Brad
• Sam Benedict series
Williams, Charles
see also **Collier, James Lincoln**
• John Ingram series
Williams, Charles Walter Stansby
• Sir Giles Tumulty series
Williams, David
see also **Horst, Karl; Lutz, Gunther**
• Fighter series
• Mark Treasure series
• Tank series
Williams, Donna
• Nobody somebody series
Williams, Dorian
• Wendy series
Williams, Edward Huntington
• Red Plume series
Williams, Elma Mary
• Wildlife series
Williams, Emlyn
• George Emlyn series
Williams, Eric Ernest
• Peter Howard series
• Roger and Kate Starte series
Williams, Ferelith Eccles
• Oxford Ox trilogy
Williams, Gladys
• Semolina Silkpaws series
Williams, Gordon Maclean
• Micronauts series
• Pomeroy series
Williams, Graham
Nightmare fair
Doctor Who series (162)
Williams, Guy Richard
• Use your series
Williams, Harry
• Twin series
Williams, J X
Her
She series (3)
Williams, Jay
• Danny Dunn series
Williams, Jeanne
see also **Foster, Jeanne**
• Arizona trilogy
• Clanna series
Williams, Jesse Lynch
• Princeton series
• Stolen story series
Williams, Jon
• Privateers and gentlemen series
Williams, Jude
• McLaffertys series
Williams, Lawrence
• Lgendary murders series
Williams, Leigh Anne
• Taylor House trilogy
Williams, Mary
• Carnecrane series
Williams, Michael
• Soldier of fortune series
Williams, Michael Leon
• DragonLance heroes series
• From thief to king series
Williams, Michael Lindsay
• Martian series
Williams, Octavia
• Applebury tales series
Williams, Patry
• Canute series
Williams, Paul Osborne
• Pelbar series
Williams, Philip Claxton
• Mister Hoyland series
Williams, Raymond
• Glynmawr series
Williams, Richard
• Sexton Blake series
Williams, Robert Moore
• Jongor trilogy
• Zanthar series
Williams, Sidney
• Jabez Twombley series
Williams, Steve
• Fighting fantasy gamebook series
Williams, Susan
• Sheepfold Farm series
Williams, Tad
• Memory, sorrow and thorn series
• Tempest series
Williams, Tennessee
• Baby doll series
Williams, Timothy
• Commissario Trotti series
Williams, Ursula Moray
• Binklebys series
• Brownies series
• Gobbolino series
• Toymakers series
Williams, Valentine
see also **Valentine, Douglas**
• Clubfoot series
• Inspector Manderton series
• Mister Treadgold series
• Sergeant Trevor Dene series
Williams, Vera Baker
• Something special series
Williams, Walter Jon
• Crown jewels series
• Hardwired trilogy
Williams, Wetherby
see **Erskine, Margaret**
Williams, William Carlos
• Stecher trilogy
Williams, William H
see **Brody, Marc**
Williams, Zillah
• Wonders Farm series
Williamson, Alice Muriel
• Lord and Lady Loveland series
• Motoring series
Williamson, Anthony George
see **Williamson, Tony**
Williamson, Audrey
• Superintendent Richard York series
Williamson, Charles Norris
• Lord and Lady Loveland series
• Motoring series
Williamson, Geoffrey
• Silva d'Croy series
Williamson, Henry
• Chronicles of ancient sunlight series
• Devon village series
• Flax of dream series
• Norfolk life series
• Shallowford to Norfolk series
Williamson, Hugh Ross
• Catherine de Valois trilogy
• Passing of the Plantagenets series
Williamson, Jack
• Cuckoo's saga series
• Humanoids series
• Legion of Space series
• Legion of time series
• Plan of man trilogy
• Seetee series
Williamson, Jerry Neal
• Devil's dictionary series
• Lamia Zacharias series
• Minnifield series
Williamson, Margaret
• John and Betty series
Williamson, Philip G
• Firstworld chronicles series
Williamson, Roger
• Romany Rat trilogy
Williamson, Thames
• Hunky series
Williamson, Tony
• Lee Corey series
Willis, Anne Marie
• Blinky Bill adaptations series
Willis, Edward Henry Willis
see **Willis, Ted**
Willis, Frederick
• Edwardian London trilogy
Willis, George Anthony Armstrong
see **Armstrong, Anthony**
Willis, Jeanne
• Doctor Xargle series
Willis, Maud
see also **Lottman, Eileen**
Double identity
Bionic woman series (1)
Question of life
Bionic woman series (2)
Willis, Ted
• Dixon of Dock Green series
• George Dixon series
• Rosie Carr series
Willis, William
• Ancient mariner trilogy
Willock, Colin Dennistoun
• Nathaniel Ironsides Goss series
Willoughby, Lee Davis
see also **Jahn, Mike**
• Americana series
• Making of America series
• Women who won the West series
Wills, Cecil Melville
• Geoffrey Boscobell series
• Superintendent Roger Ellerdine and Sergeant Cherry Blossom series
• Sylvester Horatio Pinkney series
Willsie, Honore
see **Morrow, Honore Willsie**
Willson, Robina Beckles
• Sarah and Alastair series
Sophie and Nicky and the four seasons
Suzanne and Nicholas series (3)
Sophie and Nicky go to market
Suzanne and Nicholas series (2)
• Witch series
Wilmer, Diane
• Benny series
• Step by step series
Wilmot, Robert Patrick
• Steve Considine series
Wilmott, Phyllis
• Green girl series
Wilson, Alexander
• Sir Leonard Wallace series
Wilson, Andrew Norman
• Norman Shotover series
Wilson, Anthony Clifford
• Norman and Henry Bones series
Wilson, Barbara Ellen
• Cassandra Reilly series
• Pam Nilsen series
Wilson, Barbara Ker
• Kennedys abroad series
• My place series
Wilson, Bob
• Stanley Bagshaw series
Wilson, Buck
• Tim McCoy series
Wilson, Budge
• Blue Harbour series
Wilson, Colin
• Chief Inspector Gregory Saltfleet series
• Gerard Sorme trilogy
• Murder series
• Outsider series
• Spider world series
Wilson, Dave
see also **Floren, Lee**
• Judge Lemanuel Bates and Tobacco Jones series
Wilson, David
see also **Macarthur, David Wilson**
• Marshal Sam McCloud series
Wilson, David Alec
• Lilliput series
Wilson, David Henry
• Jeremy James series
• Superdog series
Wilson, Derek
• Robert Dudley series
Wilson, Eric
• Canadian trilogy
Wilson, Forrest
• Super Gran series
Wilson, Francis Paul
• Adversary series
• LaNague Federation trilogy
Wilson, Gar
• Phoenix Force series
• Phoenix Force super series
Wilson, Gertrude Mary
• Inspector Lovick series
Wilson, Harry Leon
• Red Gap series
Wilson, Hazel
• Herbert series
Wilson, Ivor
• Gregory Flamm series
Wilson, Jacqueline
• Is there anybody there series
Wilson, Jeanne
• Island trilogy
Wilson, John Anthony Burgess
see **Burgess, Anthony**
Wilson, John Fleming
• Tad Sheldon series
Wilson, Joyce Muriel Judson
see **Stranger, Joyce**
Wilson, Keane
• Pip and Andrew series
Wilson, Margaret
• Kenworthys series
• McLaughlin family series
Wilson, Marjorie
see **Wilson, Budge**
Wilson, Peter
• Boxing series
Wilson, Philip Whitwell
• Sir Julian Morthoe series
Wilson, Phillip
• Roberts family series
Wilson, Robert Anton
• Historical illuminatus trilogy
• Illuminatus series
• Schrodinger's cat trilogy
Wilson, Sandra
• Lady Cicely Plantagenet trilogy
Wilson, Sloan
• Man in the gray flannel suit series
Wilson, Snoo
• Spaceache series
Wilson, Steve
• Dealer series
Wilson, Timothy R
• Fenland series
Wilson, Trevor Edward
• Big Tom Holder trilogy
Wilson, Yates
• Alice in Wonderland sequels series
Wiltz, Chris
• Neal Rafferty series
Wimble, Edward
• Cthulhu Mythos series
Wimhurst, Cecil Gordon Eugene
see **Brent, Nigel**
Winberg, Greta
• Maddie series
Winchell, Prentice
see **Dean, Spencer; Sterling, Stewart**
Wincor, Richard
• Sherlock Holmes sequels series
Windling, Terri
• Borderland series
• Elsewhere trilogy
Windsor, Patricia
• Weirdo and ghost series
Winfield, Arthur M
see also **Alger, Horatio; Bonehill, Ralph; Stratemeyer, Edward L**
• Bound to win series
• Bright and bold series
• Putnam Hall series
• Rover boys series
Winfield, Julia
see also **Armstrong, Jennifer**
• Private eyes series
Wingate, John
• Submariner Sinclair series
• Third World War trilogy

Wingfield-Stratford, Esme
- Charles I trilogy

Wingrove, David
- Chung Kuo series

Wings, Mary
- Emma Victor series

Wink, Walter Philip
- Powers trilogy

Winn, Alison
- Emma series
- Thomas series

Winn, Godfrey
- Dreams of youth series
- Infirm glory series

Winn, Patrick
- Inspector Lyon series

Winski, Norman
see also **Hofrichter, Paul; Stivers, Dick**
- Dirk Spencer series

Winslow, Pauline Glen
- Superintendent Merlin Capricorn series

Winsor, Diana
- Tavy Martin series

Winsor, Roy
- Ira Cobb series

Winstan, Matt
see also **Nickson, Arthur**
- Reuben Brown series

Winston, Peter
see also **Laflin, Jack**
- Adjusters series

Winter, Bevis
see also **Cagney, Peter**
- Steve Craig series

Winter, John Strange
- Binks family series
- Blankhampton series
- Bootles series

Winter, Steve
- Meetings series

Winterbotham, Russell Robert
- Red Ryder series

Winterfeld, Henry
- Lilliput series

Winters, Jon
- Anton Drakov series

Winters, Logan
see also **Lederer, Paul Joseph**
- Spectros series

Winterton, Paul
see **Bax, Roger; Somers, Paul**

Winther, Sophus Keith
- Grimsen trilogy
- Nebraska trilogy

Winthrop, Elizabeth
- Lizzie and Harold series
- Miranda series
- Strawberry Shortcake series
- William series

Winton, John
- Navy series

Winton, Tim
- Lockie Leonard series

Winward, Walter
- Canaris series

Wirries, Mary Mabel
- Mary Rose series

Wirt, Ann
- Madge Sterling series

Wirt, Mildred Augustine
see also **Palmer, Don**
- Brownie Scout series
- Dan Carter series
- Girl Scout series
- Penny Parker series
- Ruth Darrow series
- Trailer series

Wise, Arthur
see also **McArthur, John**
- Mac Wingate series

Wisher, William H
- Terminator series

Wisler, Gary Clifton
see also **McLennan, Will**
- Antrian series
- Darby Prescott series
- Medicine Trail series
- Texas Brazos series
- Willie Delamer series

Wister, Owen
- Swiss family Robinson series
- Virginian series
- Western tales series

Witcomb, Nan
- Thoughts of Nanushka series

Witting, Clifford
- Inspector Charlton series
- Inspector Peter Bradfield series

Witwer, Harry Charles
- Baseball series

Wodehouse, Pelham Grenville
- Blandings Castle series
- Drones Club series
- Ivor Llewellyn series
- Jeeves and Bertie Wooster series
- Mister Mulliner series
- Monty Bodkin series
- Oldest member series
- Performing flea series
- Psmith series
- Ukridge series
- Uncle Fred, Earl of Ickenham series
- Wrykyn School series

Woerkom, Dorothy van
see **Van Woerkom, Dorothy**

Wogan, Charles
- Sebastian Stole series

Wohl, James Paul
- Sam Gross series

Wohl, Louis de
see **De Wohl, Louis**

Wohlfahrt, Irene
- Star trek fan series

Woiwode, Larry
- Neumiller family series

Wold, Allen
- V series

Wolde, Gunilla
- Emma series
- Thomas series

Wolf, Jack
- Timothy Rourke series

Wolfe, Gene
- Book of the new sun series
- Latro series

Wolfe, Humbert
- Anguish series

Wolfe, John
- Johnny McCoy series

Wolfe, Michael
- Michael Keefe series

Wolfe, Thomas Clayton
- Eugene Gant series
- George Webber series

Wolff, Benjamin
- John Byron Hyde series

Wolff, Margaret
- Books for me series

Wolff, William Almon
- Lieutenant Charley Mitchell series

Wolffe, Katherine
- Captain Courtney Brade series

Wolfman, Marv
- Amazing Spiderman series
- Marvel superheroes, new series
- Weird heroes series

Wolfson, Evelyn
- American Indian series

Wolitzer, Hilma
- Linda and Robin Reismann series

Wolk, George
see **Graat, Heinrich**

Wollheim, Donald Allen
see also **Grinnell, David**
- Mike Mars series

Wolverton, Dave
- Star wars series

Womack, Jack
- Terraplane trilogy

Wongar, B
- Dingo series
- Nuclear trilogy

Wood, Amanda Jane
- Look twice series

Wood, Andrew
- Bunch and Alexander series
- Koregorvsky series
- Magnus Keeble series
- Sasha series

Wood, Barry
- Questions series

Wood, Bridget
- Lute series

Wood, Christopher
see also **Grape, Oliver; Lea, Timothy**
- Barry Lyndon series
- James Bond series
- John Adam series
- Taiwan series

Wood, Clement
- Huckleberry Finn series
- Inspector Colin series
- Lal Reed series
- Skelton Keyne series
- Tom Sawyer series

Wood, Ellen
- Channings series
- Mildred Arkell series

Wood, Eric
- Arnold Keene and Bernard Young series

Wood, George
- Peter Schlemihl series

Wood, Henry, *Mrs*
see **Wood, Ellen**

Wood, James
- Ian Ross series
- James Fraser series
- Jumbo Collins series
- Tipple in the deep series

Wood, Joyce
- Grandmother Lucy series

Wood, Kenneth
- Gulls series

Wood, Leslie
- Barfield series
- Big red bus series

Wood, Lorna
- Ameliaranne series
- Hag Dowsabel series
- Pangers series

Wood, Robert Williams
- Benjamin Hooker series

Wood, Ted
- Reid Bennett series

Wood, William Hollingsworth
- Stories for telling series

Woodard, Christopher Roy
- Faith healing trilogy

Woodberry, Joan
- Rafferty series

Woodbury, David Oakes
- George Riam series

Woodhouse, Martin
- Giles Yeoman series
- Medici series

Woodhouse, Sarah
- Season of mists series

Woodiwiss, John Cecil
- Inspector Hopton series

Woodley, Richard
- It's alive series
- Man from Atlantis series

Woodman, Michael
- Paul Gane series

Woodman, Richard
- Nathaniel Drinkwater series

Woodrooffe, Anne
- Michael Kemp series

Woodruff, Philip
- Men who ruled India series

Woods, Sara
- Sir Nicholas Harding and Antony Maitland series

Woodthorpe, Ralph Carter
- Matilda Perks series
- Nicholas Slade series

Woodward, Bob
- Watergate series

Woolf, Bella Sidney
- Twins in Ceylon series

Woolf, Leonard
- Sowing and growing series

Woolf, Virginia
- Mrs Dalloway series

Woolfolk, Dorothy
- Donna Rockford series

Woolley, Catherine
- Cathy Leonard series
- Ginnie Fellows series
- Libby series

Woolley, Lazelle Thayer
- Faith Palmer series

Woolley, Persia
- Guinevere trilogy

Woolsey, Sarah Chauncey
see **Coolidge, Susan**

Worboise, Emma Jane
- Grace Hamilton series
- Mister Montmorency series

Worby, John
- Spiv series

Worcester, Donald Emmet
- Lone Hunter series

Worfel, W G
- Baron Munchausen series

Work, Virginia
- Jodi series

Wormser, Richard
see also **Friend, Ed**
- Lieutenant Andy Bastian series
- Sergeant Joe Dixon series

Worsley, Thomas Cuthbert
- Flannelled fool series

Worsley-Gough, Barbara
- Aloysius Kelly series

Worth, Cedric
- Inspector Sevrel series

Worth, Maurice
- Derek Harding series

Worth, Valerie
- Small poems series

Worthington, Phoebe
- Teddy bear series

Worthington, Selby
- Teddy bear series

Wortis, Avi
see **Avi**

Wortley, Violet Stuart-
see **Stuart-Wortley, Violet**

Wouk, Herman
- Commander Pug Henry series
- Hope series

Wray, I
- Inspector Digby series

Wrede, Patricia Collins
- Enchanted forest series
- Lyra trilogy

Wren, M K
- Conan Flagg series
- Phoenix legacy trilogy

Wren, Percival Christopher
- Beau Geste series
- Karabad series
- Khairastan series
- Major Hazelrigg series
- Otho Belleme series
- Sinbad Dysart series

Wrenn, Harold Albert
- William Mitchell series

Wrexe, Charles
- Bill Mitchum series

Wright, Austin Tappan
- Islandia series

Wright, Betty Ren
- Secret window series

Wright, Billy
- Football captain series

Wright, David K
- War in Vietnam series

Wright, Eric
- Inspector Charlie Salter series

Wright, Harold Bell
- Dan Matthews series

Wright, Harry Norman
- Answer series

Wright, John
see **Wright, Wade**

Wright, June
- Inspector Savage series
- Mother Paul series
- Sergeant Matheson series

Wright, Kit
see also **Spence, Peter**
- Arthur series

Wright, Laurali R
- Sergeant Karl Alberg series

Wright, Mabel Osgood
- Commuter's wife series
- Tommy-Anne series

Wright, Meg
- Star trek fan series

Wright, Norman
see **Wright, Harry Norman**

Wright, Patrick
- Near and distant series

Wright, Philip Lee
- Air pilot series

Wright, Ralph
- Witch series

Wright, Richard Nathaniel
- Horror and the glory series

Wright, Sean M
- Sherlock Holmes sequels series

Wright, Steve
- Barry Donovan series

Wright, Sydney Fowler
see also **Fowler, Sydney**
- Amphibians series
- Marguerite Cranleigh series
- Martin Webster series
- Siege of Malta series
- War of 1938 trilogy

Wright, Terrance Michael
see also **Armstrong, F W**
- Manhattan series

Wright, Wade
- Bart Condor series
- Paul Cameron series

Wright, Willard Huntingdon
see **Van Dine, S S**

Wrightson, Patricia
- Society of the Crooked Snake series
- Song of Wirrun trilogy

Wu, William Franking
- Doctor Bones series
- Robot city series
- Time tours series

Wuamett, Victor
- Chase Randel series

Wulffson, Don L
- Incredible true adventures series

Wuorio, Eva Lis
- Jersey series
- Twin series

Wurr, H J
- Inspector Grierson series

Wurts, Janny
- Cycle of fire trilogy
- Empire series

Wyatt, George
- Brains Benton series

Wyatt, Horace
- Alice in Wonderland parodies series

Wyatt, Stephen
- Doctor Who series

Wyatt, Woodrow Lyle
- Mister Saucy Squirrel series

Wyatt, Zach
- Texians series

Wylde, Thomas
- Doctor Bones series
- Roger Zelazny's Alien speedway series

Wylie, Ida Alexa Ross
- Adam Brodie series
- Provencal Hills series

Wylie, Jonathan
- Servants of Ark trilogy
- Unbalanced earth trilogy

Wylie, Philip
- Bronson Beta series
- Crunch and Des series

Wyllie, John
- Doctor Quarshie series

Wyman, Levi Parker
- Hunniwell boys series

Wynd, Oswald
see **Black, Gavin**

Wyndham, Joan
- Love diary series

Wyndham, John
- Chocky series

Wynne, Anthony
- Doctor Eustace Hailey series

Wynne, Brian
see also **Garfield, Brian Wynne**
- Marshal Jeremy Six series

Wynne Jones, Diana
see **Jones, Diana Wynne**

Wynne, May
- Comrades from Canada series
- Heather series
- Jean series
- Tala series

Wynne-Jones, Pat
- Hedgerow tales series

Wynne-Jones, Tim
- Zoom series

Wynnton, Patrick
- Black turret series

Wyss, Johann Rudolf
- Swiss family Robinson series

Y

Yaeger, Carl H
- Soldier of fortune series

Yan, Vasiliy Grigorievich
- Mongol series

Yanchevetsky, Vasily Grigorievich
see **Yan, Vasily Grigorievich**

Yarbro, Chelsea Quinn
see also **Bonner, Terry Nelson**
- Atta Olivia Clemens trilogy
- Charlie Spotted Moon series
- Count Ragoczy Saint-Germain series
- Messages from Michael series
- Sheriff Jason Russell series

Yardley, Herbert Osborn
- Mister Greenleaf series

Yardley, James
- Kiss Darling and Angus Fane series

Yarrow, Arnold
- Chief Inspector Barlow series

Yates, Alan Geoffrey
see **Brown, Carter**

Yates, Dornford
- Anthony Lyveden series
- Berry series
- Jonah Mansel series
- Richard Chandos series
- Superintendent Richard Falcon series

Yates, Elizabeth
- Journeyman series
- Mountain born series
- One writer's trilogy

Yates, George Worthing
- Hazlitt Woar series

Yates, Margaret Tayler
- Anne Davenport McLean series

Yates, Peter
- Sandy Blunt series
- Thatcher family series

Yates, Renate
- Inspector Ereache O'Shea series

Ycas, Martynas
- Mister Tompkins series

Yeager, Dorian
- Victoria Bowering series

Yeatman, Robert Julian
- All that series

Yee, Paul
- Chinese in the New World series

Yeh, Chun-Chan
- Quiet are the mountains series

Yeoman, John
- Bear series

Yeovil, Jack
- Dark future series
- Warhammer series

Yep, Laurence Michael
- Cassia series
- Shimmer and Thorn series
- Star trek series

Yerby, Frank
- Costa Verde series
- Hwesu series

Yerex, Cuthbert
- Looking backward responses series

Yermakov, Nicholas

see also **Hawke, Simon; Masters, J D**
- Battlestar Galactica series
- Last communion trilogy

Yin, Leslie Charles Bowyer

see **Charteris, Leslie**

Yolen, Jane
- Commander Toad series
- Great Alta series
- Piggins series
- Pit dragons trilogy

Yonge, Charlotte Mary
- Beechcroft series
- Honor Charlecote series
- Lady Herbert Somerville series
- Long vacation series
- May family series
- Morville family series
- Pillars of the house series
- Rebaumont series
- Shield series

York, Andrew

see also **Arlen, Leslie; Grange, Peter; Logan, Mark; Nicole, Christopher**
- Colonel Munroe Tallant series
- Jonas Wilde series
- Jonathan Anders series

York, Carol Beach
- Heart to heart series
- Miss Know It All series

York, Georgia
- Georgia trilogy

York, Jeremy

see also **Ashe, Gordon; Creasey, John; Deane, Norman; Frazer, Robert Caine; Halliday, Michael; Marric, J J; Morton, Anthony**
- Superintendent Folly series

York, Rebecca

see also **Buckholtz, Eileen; Glick, Ruth**
- Peregrine connection trilogy

Yorke, Katherine

see also **L'Estrange, Anna; Thorne, Nicola**
- Enchantress trilogy
- Woman's place series

Yorke, Margaret
- Doctor Patrick Grant series

Youd, Samuel

see **Christopher, John; Ford, Hilary; Godfrey, William; Graaf, Peter**

Young, Andrew
- Wild flowers series

Young, Carter Travis

see also **Charbonneau, Louis**
- Cullom Blaine series

Young, Chic
- Blondie and Dagwood series

Young, Clarence

see also **Barnum, Vance**
- Jack Ranger series
- Motor boys series
- Racer boys series

Young, David
- Fraggle Rock series

Young, Egerton Ryerson
- Three boys series

Young, Emily Hilda
- Caravan series
- Jenny Wren series

Young, Eric Brett
- Welsh series

Young, Ernest A
- Dossier series

Young, Francis Brett
- Boer War series
- N'dala series
- Welsh series

Young, Gavin
- Slow boats series

Young, Gordon Ray
- Hurricane Williams trilogy
- Red Clark series

Young, Mike
- SuperTed series

Young, Murat Bernard

see **Young, Chic**

Young, Peter
- Zig and Zag series

Young, Ruth
- Eleanora Mousie series
- My series
- Rhyme-fingerplay-puppet series

Young, Stark
- Feliciana series

Young, William Arthur

Kipling dictionary

Rewards and fairies series (2)

Youngson, Jeanne

Count Dracula book of classic vampire stories

Dracula series (26)

Count Dracula cookbook

Dracula series (26)

Count Dracula Fan Club book of vampire stories

Dracula series (26)

Count Dracula's favorite Christmas cookie recipes

Dracula series (26)
- Dracula series

Yuill, P B
- James Hazell series

Yutang, Lin

see **Lin, Yutang**

Z

Zabel, Jennifer
- Miss Priscilla series

Zach, Cheryl
- Benny series
- Smyth versus Smith series

Zacharia, Irwin
- Irving Martin Reddy series
- Landshark series
- Vendetta series

Zachary, Elizabeth
- Making of America series

Zachary, Hugh

see also **Hughes, Zach**
- Sheriff Jug Watson series
- Tusk Smith series

Zackel, Fred
- Michael Brennan series

Zahn, Timothy
- Blackcollar series
- Cobra trilogy
- Star wars series

Zangwill, Israel
- Celibates' Club series
- Ghetto series

Zaremba, Eve
- Helen Keremos series

Zebrowski, George
- Bernal One series
- Omega Point trilogy

Zelazny, Roger
- Changeling series
- Dilvish the Damned trilogy
- Isle of the dead series
- Kingdom of Amber series

Zenowich, Christopher
- Bob Bodewicz series

Zetford, Tully

see also **Akers, Alan Burt; Blake, Ken; Bulmer, Kenneth; Frazier, Arthur; Hardy, Adam; Krauss, Bruno; Prescot, Dray; Silver, Richard**
- Ryder Hook series

Zeybel, Henry
- Gunship series

Zicree, Marc Scott

Twilight Zone companion

Twilight Zone series (6)

Ziefert, Harriet
- Guessing game series
- Jessie series
- Lewis series
- Max and Diana series
- Mister Rose's class series
- Nicky series
- On our way series
- Small Potatoes series
- Where is it series

Ziefert, Jon
- Small Potatoes series

Zilahy, Lajos
- Dukay family series

Zimmer, Paul Edwin
- Dark border series
- Red moon series

Zimmerman, Bruce
- Quinn Parker series

Zimmerman, R D
- Maddy and Alex Phillips series

Zinberg, Leonard

see **Lacy, Ed**

Zindel, Paul
- Pigman series
- Wacky facts lunch bunch series

Zinkin, Taya
- Odious child series
- Rishi series

Zinnemann-Hope, Pam
- Ned series

Zion, Gene
- Harry the dirty dog series

Zlotnik, Donald E
- Fields of honor series
- Survivors of Nam series

Zochert, Donald
- Nick Caine series

Zohar, Danah
- Quantum series

Zola, Emile
- Abbe Pierre Fremont trilogy
- Four Gospels series
- Rougon Macquart series

Zollinger, Norman
- Corey Lane series
- Macandrews Clan series

Zorro

see also **Ward, Harold**
- Doctor Death series

Zubro, Mark Richard
- Stonewall Inn series

Zuk, Beverly C
- Star trek fan series

Zukofsky, Louis
- A series
- I's series

Zweig, Arnold
- Werner Bertin and Lenore Wahl series

Also available from D W Thorpe ...

Australian Books in Print 1996

This is the 34th edition of *Australian Books in Print.*

Published annually, this title is used every day by libraries and booksellers to identify titles for clients, information on new titles, locating overseas distributors and in tracking down series and imprint information.

More than 5000 national and international subscribers throughout the book trade and library communities rely on this title as the most comprehensive bibliographic tool for ordering new and backlist titles.

It includes over 60,000 titles and over 5000 publishers, with 5000 out-of-print titles since 1995.

ISBN 1875589676
RRP AUD$120

Periodicals in Print: Australia, New Zealand & the South Pacific 1996

This completely updated 13th edition of *Periodicals in Print* lists over 12,000 significant regional periodicals, ranging from mass-market newspapers and magazines to esoteric yet important special interest serials.

Periodicals in Print is based on the definitive in-print periodicals database available in Australia, and is the result of an ongoing cooperative venture between D W Thorpe and ISA Australia.

Published May 1996
ISBN 1875589899
ISSN 1322-3895
RRP AUD$85

Australian Men and Women of Science, Engineering and Technology

This work is a significant step in the drive to forge closer links between science, engineering and technological disciplines with industry, while also contributing to a greater public awareness of its practitioners.

The directory includes 3500 scientists and engineers from all areas in Australia – academia, media, industry, medicine, research, government departments and professional societies and associations. It has two indexes which enable access to data by more than 400 areas of specialisation, and a unique method of accessing scientists through geographical location.

This work has been published in association with the Australian Academy of Science and the Australian Academy of Technological Sciences and Engineering.

ISBN 1875589643

RRP AUD$110

Who's Who of Australian Writers
Second Edition

With more than 5400 living Australian writers included, this second edition of Thorpe's *Who's Who of Australian Writers* continues to be an invaluable reference work.

This completely revised and updated edition incorporates more than 16,000 changes. Hundreds of new writers have been added to ensure this edition is as comprehensive as ever.
Published in association with the National Centre for Australian Studies, Monash University.

'a much needed reference'
The Australian

'a gold mine'
Canberra Times

'far more comprehensive than any other guide … a very valuable reference'
The Age

ISBN 1875589201
RRP AUD$75

Also available: *Who's Who of Australian Children's Writers* second edition

Out of the Closet and Into the Classroom

Second Edition

Laurel A Clyde & Marjorie Lobban

Many young people on reaching adolescence will become aware that they or perhaps members of their family are homosexual. Recognition of this fact in novels or stories for young people is the main area of exploration for this bibliography.

This completely updated second edition has 74 additional titles, bringing a total of 194 books discussed in some detail.

Out of the Closet and Into the Classroom also includes 28 picture books for younger readers, with many of the titles aimed at children growing up as part of lesbian or gay families.

Published March 1996
ISBN 1875589864
RRP AUD$39

Contemporary Australian Women 1996/97

This book focuses on over 2000 women currently making the news in Australia.

Contains information on lobbyists, ethnic and Aboriginal community leaders, figures from business, sport, the arts, the media, science, medicine, religion and politics.

Contemporary Australian Women includes:

- first job after leaving school
- most formative influences
- major achievements (including films, plays, buildings, patents, inventions, sporting records, musical compositions)
- recreations/interests/obsessions

Published May 1996
ISBN 1875589929
RRP AUD$39.95

Also available: *Contemporary Australians 1995/96*